BECKETT®
THE #1 AUTHORITY ON COLLECTIBLES

HOCKEY CARD PRICE GUIDE

35TH EDITION 2026

THE HOBBY'S MOST RELIABLE AND RELIED UPON SOURCE™

Founder: Dr. James Beckett III • Edited by the staff of Beckett Hockey

Prices in this guide reflect current retail rates determined just prior to printing. They do not reflect for-sale prices by the author, publisher, distributors, advertisers, or any card dealers associated with this guide. Every effort has been made to eliminate errors. Readers are invited to write us noting any errors which may be researched and corrected in subsequent printings. The publisher will not be held responsible for losses which may occur in the sale or purchase of cards because of information contained herein.

BECKETT is a registered trademark of BECKETT COLLECTIBLES LLC, PLANO, TEXAS
Manufactured in the United States of America | Published by Beckett Collectibles LLC

BECKETT®
Beckett Collectibles LLC
2700 Summit Ave, Ste 100, Plano, TX 75074
1 (866) 287-9383 • beckett.com

First Printing ISBN: 978-1-953801-82-1

Front Cover: Getty Images

CONTENTS

HOW TO USE AND CONDITION GUIDE

Every year, this book gets bigger and better. This edition has been enhanced and expanded from the previous volume with the addition of new releases, updated prices and changes to older listings. The Beckett Hockey Card Price Guide has been successful where other attempts have failed because it is complete, current, and valid. The prices were added to the card lists just prior to printing and reflect not the author's opinions or desires, but the going retail prices for each card, based on the marketplace - sports memorabilia conventions and shows, sports card shops, online trading, auction results and other firsthand reports of realized sales.

What is the best price guide available on the market today? Of course, sellers will prefer the price guide with the highest prices, while buyers will naturally prefer the one with the lowest prices. Accuracy, however, is the true test. The Beckett Hockey Card Price Guide may not always have the highest or lowest values, but the accuracy of both our checklists and pricing - produced with the utmost integrity - has made it the most widely used reference book in the industry.

To facilitate your use of this book, please read the complete introductory section before going on to the pricing pages, paying special attention to the section on grading and card conditions, as the condition of the card greatly affects its value. We hope you find the book both interesting and useful in your collecting pursuits.

ADVERTISING

Within this Price Guide you will find advertisements for sports memorabilia material, mail order, and retail sports collectibles establishments. All advertisements were accepted in good faith based on the reputation of the advertiser. However, neither the author, publisher, the distributors, nor the other advertisers in this Price Guide accept any responsibility for any advertiser not complying with the terms of his or her ad.

HOW TO COLLECT

Each collection is personal and reflects the individuality of its owner. There are no set rules on how to collect cards. Since card collecting is a hobby or leisure pastime, what you collect, how much you collect, and how much time and money you spend collecting are entirely up to you. The funds you have available for collecting and your own personal taste should determine how you collect. It is impossible to collect every card ever produced. Therefore, beginners as well as intermediate and advanced collectors usually specialize in some way. One of the reasons this hobby is popular is that individual collectors can define and tailor their collecting methods to match their own tastes. Many collectors select complete sets from particular years, acquire only certain players, some collectors are only interested in the first cards or Rookie Cards of certain players, and others collect cards by team. Remember, this is a hobby, so pick a style of collecting that appeals to you.

UNDERSTANDING CARD VALUES

Why are some cards more valuable than others? Obviously, the economic laws of supply and demand are applicable to card collecting just as they are to any other field where a commodity is bought, sold or traded in a free, unregulated market. Supply (the number of cards available on the market) is less than the total number of cards originally produced since attrition diminishes that original quantity. Each year a percentage of cards is typically thrown away, destroyed or otherwise lost to collectors. This percentage is much, much smaller today than it was in the past because more and more people have become increasingly aware of the value of their cards. For those who collect only Mint condition cards, the supply of older cards can be quite small indeed. Until recently, collectors were not so conscious of the need to preserve the condition of their cards. For this reason, it is difficult to know exactly how many 1958-59 Topps are currently available, Mint or otherwise. It is generally accepted that there are fewer 1958-59 Topps available than 1963-64, 1973-74 or 1986-87 Topps cards. If demand were equal for each of these sets, the law of supply and demand would increase the price for the least available sets. Demand, however, is never equal for all sets, so price correlations can be complicated. The demand for a card is influenced by many factors. These include the age of the card, the number of cards printed, the player(s) portrayed on the card, the attractiveness and popularity of the set and the physical condition of the card. In general, the older the card, the fewer the number of cards printed, the more famous, popular and talented the player, the more attractive and popular the set, and the better the condition of the card, the higher the value of the card will be. There are exceptions to all but one of these factors: the condition of the card. Given two cards similar in all respects except condition, the one in the best condition will always be valued higher. While those guidelines help to establish the value of a card, the countless exceptions and peculiarities make any simple, direct mathematical formula to determine card values impossible.

HOW THE PRICE GUIDE IS ORGANIZED

The Beckett Hockey Card Price Guide is listed alphabetically, followed by chronological order. Please note that for some brands, as a reflection of the secondary market, the manufacturer has been stripped from the set name. This includes, but is not limited to, the brands Exquisite Collection, Finest, SPx, SP Authentic, Stadium Club, Ultra, and Ultimate Collection. In other cases, "Upper Deck" has been shortened to "UD", as in UD Black, UD Masterpieces, UD Choice, or UD Top Shelf.

WHAT THE COLUMNS MEAN

The LO and HI columns reflect a range of current retail selling prices and are listed in U.S. dollars. The HI column represents the typical full retail selling price while the LO column represents the lowest price one could expect to find through extensive shopping. Both columns represent the same condition for the card listed. Keep in mind that market conditions can change quickly up and down based on extreme levels of demand.

PRICING PREMIUMS

Some cards can trade at premium price levels compared to values listed in this issue. Those include but are not limited to cards of players who became hot since this book went to press, regional stars or fan favorites in high demand locally and memorabilia cards with unusually dramatic swatches or patches.

SET PRICES

A somewhat paradoxical situation exists in the price of a complete set vs. the combined cost of the individual cards in the set. In nearly every case, the sum of the prices for the individual cards is higher than the cost for the complete set. This is prevalent especially in the cards of the last few years. The reasons for this apparent anomaly stem from the habits of collectors and from the carrying costs to dealers. Today, each card in a set normally is produced in the same quantity as all other cards in its set. Many collectors collect only stars, superstars and particular teams. As a result, the dealer is left with a shortage of certain player cards and an abundance of others. He therefore incurs an expense in simply "carrying" these less-desirable cards in stock. On the other hand, if he sells a complete set, he gets rid of large numbers of cards at one time. For this reason, he generally is willing to receive less money for a complete set. By doing this, he recovers all his costs and makes a profit. The disparity between the price of the complete set and the sum of the individual cards also has been influenced by the fact that some of the major manufacturers now are pre-collating card sets. Since "pulling" individual cards from the sets involves a specific type of labor (and cost), the singles or star card market is not affected significantly by pre-collation. Set prices also do not include rare card varieties, unless specifically stated. Of course, the prices for sets do include one example of each type for the given set, but this is the least expensive variety.

MULTIPLIERS

Some parallel sets and lightly traded insert sets are listed with multipliers to provide values of unlisted cards. Multiplier ranges (i.e. 10X to 20X HI) apply only to the HI column. Example: If basic-issue card A or the insert card in question lists for 20 to 50 cents, and the multiplier is "20X to 40X HI", then the parallel version of card A or the insert card in question is valued at $10 to $20. Please note that the term "basic card" used in the Price Guide refers to a player's standard regular issue card. A "basic card" cannot be an insert or parallel card.

STATED ODDS AND PRINT RUNS

Odds of pulling insert cards are often listed as a ratio (1:12 - one in 12 packs). If the odds vary by pack type, they are generally listed separately. Stated print runs are also included in the set header lines or after the player's name for many serial numbered cards or for sets which the manufacturer has chosen to announce print runs. Stated odds and print runs are provided by the manufacturer based on the entire print run and should be considered very close estimates and not exact figures. The data provided in this book has been verified by Beckett to the best of our ability. Neither the stated odds nor print runs should be viewed as a guarantee by either Beckett or the manufacturer.

ONLY A REFERENCE

The data and pricing information contained within this publication is intended for reference only and is not to be used as an endorsement of any specific product(s) or as a recommendation to buy or sell any product(s). Beckett's goal is to provide the most accurate and verifiable information in the industry. However, Beckett cannot guarantee the accuracy of all data published. Typographical errors occasionally occur, and unverifiable information may reach print from time to time. Buyers and sellers of sports collectibles should be aware of this and handle their personal transactions at their own risk. If you discover an error or misprint in this book, please notify us via email at customerservice@beckett.com.

CONDITION GUIDE

Much of the value of your card is dependent on the condition or "grade" of your card. Prices in this issue reflect the highest raw condition (i.e. not professionally graded by a third party) of the card most found at shows, shops, on the internet and right out of the pack for brand new releases. This generally means Near Mint-Mint condition for modern era cards. Use the chart below as a guide to estimate the value of your card in a variety of conditions using the prices found in this Price Guide. A complete condition guide follows, and the most widely used grades are defined below. Obviously, many cards will not perfectly fit one of the definitions. Therefore, categories between the major grades known as in-between grades are used, such as Good to Very Good (G-Vg), Very Good to Excellent (VgEx), and Excellent-Mint to Near Mint (ExMt-NrMt). Such grades indicate a card with all qualities of the lower category but with at least a few qualities of the higher category. Unopened packs, boxes and factory-collated sets are considered Mint in their unknown state. Once opened, however, each card can be graded (and valued) by considering any defects that may be present although the card has never been handled.

Price Guide Percentage by Grade

	1933/34-1940/41	1951/52-1967/68	1968/69-1979/80	1980/81-1989/90	1990/91-Present
MT	300%+	300%+	250%+	125-150%	100-125%
NrMt-Mt	150-300%	150-250%	200%+	100%	100%
NrMt	100-150%	100%	100%	40-60%	30-50%
Ex-Mt	100%	50-75%	40-60%	25-40%	20-30%
Ex	50-75%	30-50%	20-40%	15-25%	10-20%
VG	30-50%	15-30%	10-20%	5-15%	5-10%
G/F/P	15-30%	5-15%	5-10%	5%	5%

GENERAL CARD FLAWS

CENTERING

Current centering terminology uses numbers representing the percentage of border on either side of the main design. Obviously, centering is diminished in importance for borderless cards.

SLIGHTLY OFF-CENTER (60/40)

A slightly off-center card is one that upon close inspection is found to have one border bigger than the opposite border. This degree once was offensive to only purists, but now some hobbyists try to avoid cards that are anything other than perfectly centered.

OFF-CENTER (70/30)

An off-center card has one border that is noticeably more than twice as wide as the opposite border.

BADLY OFF-CENTER (80/20 OR WORSE)

A badly off-center card has virtually no border on one side of the card.

MISCUT

A miscut card actually shows part of the adjacent card in its larger border and consequently a corresponding amount of its card is cut off.

CORNER WEAR

Corner wear is the most scrutinized grading criteria in the hobby.

CORNER WITH A SLIGHT TOUCH OF WEAR

The corner still is sharp, but there is a slight touch of wear showing. On a dark-bordered card, this shows as a dot of white.

FUZZY CORNER

The corner still comes to a point, but the point has just begun to fray. A slightly "dinged" corner is considered the same as a fuzzy corner.

SLIGHTLY ROUNDED CORNER

The fraying of the corner has increased to where there is only a hint of a point. Mild layering may be evident. A "dinged" corner is considered the same as a slightly rounded corner.

ROUNDED CORNER

The point is completely gone. Some layering is noticeable.

BADLY ROUNDED CORNER

The corner is completely round and rough. Severe layering is evident.

CREASES

A third common defect is the crease. The degree of creasing in a card is difficult to show in a drawing or picture. On giving the specific condition of an expensive card for sale, the seller should note any creases additionally. Creases can be categorized as to severity according to the following scale.

LIGHT CREASE

A light crease is a crease that is barely noticeable upon close inspection. In fact, when cards are in plastic sheets or holders, a light crease may not be seen (until the card is taken out of the holder). A light crease on the front is much more serious than a light crease on the card back only.

MEDIUM CREASE

A medium crease is noticeable when held and studied at arm's length by the naked eye, but does not overly detract from the appearance of the card. It is an obvious crease, but not one that breaks the picture surface of the card.

HEAVY CREASE

A heavy crease is one that has torn or broken through the card's picture surface, e.g., puts a tear in the photo surface.

ALTERATIONS

DECEPTIVE TRIMMING

This occurs when someone alters the card in order (1) to shave off edge wear, (2) to improve the sharpness of the corners, or (3) to improve centering— obviously their objective is to falsely increase the perceived value of the card to an unsuspecting buyer. The shrinkage usually is evident only if the trimmed card is compared to an adjacent full-sized card or if the trimmed card is itself measured.

OBVIOUS TRIMMING

Obvious trimming is noticeable and unfortunate. It is usually performed by non-collectors who give no thought to the present or future value of their cards.

DECEPTIVELY RETOUCHED BORDERS

This occurs when the borders (especially on those cards with dark borders) are touched up on the edges and corners with magic marker or crayons of appropriate color in order to make the card appear to be Mint.

Miscellaneous Card Flaws

The following are common minor flaws that, depending on severity, lower a card's condition by one to four grades and often render it no better than Excellent-Mint: bubbles (lumps in surface), gum and wax stains, diamond cutting (slanted borders), notching, off-centered backs, paper wrinkles, scratched-off cartoons or puzzles on back, rubber band marks, scratches, surface impressions and warping. The following are common serious flaws that, depending on severity, lower a card's condition at least four grades and often render it no better than Good: chemical or sun fading, erasure marks, mildew, miscutting (severe off-centering), holes, bleached or retouched borders, tape marks, tears, trimming, water or coffee stains and writing.

GRADES

MINT (MT)

A card with no flaws or wear. The card has four perfect corners, 55/45 or better centering from top to bottom and from left to right, original gloss, smooth edges and original color borders. A Mint card does not have print spots, color or focus imperfections.

NEAR MINT-MINT (NRMT-MT)

A card with one minor flaw. Any one of the following would lower a Mint card to Near Mint-Mint: one corner with a slight touch of wear, barely noticeable print spots, color or focus imperfections. The card must have 60/40 or better centering in both directions, original gloss, smooth edges and original color border.

NEAR MINT (NRMT)

A card with one minor flaw. Any one of the following would lower a Mint card to Near Mint: one fuzzy corner or two to four corners with slight touches of wear, 70/30 to 60/40 centering, slightly rough edges, minor print spots, color or focus imperfections. The card must have original gloss and original color borders.

EXCELLENT-MINT (EXMT)

A card with two or three fuzzy, but not rounded, corners and centering no worse than 80/20. The card may have no more than two of the following: slightly rough edges, very slightly discolored borders, minor print spots, color or focus imperfections. The card must have original gloss.

EXCELLENT (EX)

A card with four fuzzy but definitely not rounded corners and centering no worse than 70/30. The card may have a small amount of original gloss lost, rough edges, slightly discolored borders and minor print spots, color or focus imperfections.

VERY GOOD (VG)

A card that has been handled but not abused: slightly rounded corners with slight layering, slight notching on edges, a significant amount of gloss lost from the surface but no scuffing and moderate discoloration of borders. The card may have a few light creases.

GOOD (G), FAIR (F), POOR (P)

A well-worn, mishandled or abused card: badly rounded and layered corners, scuffing, most or all original gloss missing, seriously discolored borders, moderate or heavy creases, and one or more serious flaws. The grade of Good, Fair or Poor depends on the severity of wear and flaws. Good, Fair and Poor cards generally are used only as fillers.

NHL

2013-14 Absolute
1 Sidney Crosby 1.25 3.00
2 Sven Baertschi .25 .60
3 Patrick Kane .60 1.50
4 Gabriel Landeskog .40 1.00
5 Tyler Seguin .40 1.00
6 Pavel Datsyuk .50 1.25
7 Ryan Nugent-Hopkins .40 1.00
8 P.K. Subban .40 1.00
9 John Tavares .50 1.25
10 Rick Nash .30 .75
11 Bobby Ryan .25 .60
12 Claude Giroux .30 .75
13 Dustin Brown .30 .75
14 Joe Thornton .50 1.25
15 Steven Stamkos .60 1.50
16 Nazem Kadri .40 1.00
17 D.Sedin/H.Sedin .40 1.00
18 Alex Ovechkin 1.25 3.00
19 Andrew Ladd .20 .50
20 Zdeno Chara .30 .75
21 Filip Forsberg 1.00 2.50
22 Tomas Hertl .60 1.50
23 Damien Brunner .25 .60
24 Brendan Gallagher .75 2.00
25 Mikhail Grigorenko .20 .50
26 Sean Monahan .50 1.25
27 Valeri Nichushkin .60 1.50
28 Jacob Trouba .50 1.25
29 Aleksander Barkov 1.00 2.50
30 Seth Jones .60 1.50
31 Danny Dekeyser .40 1.00
32 Ryan Murray .50 1.25
33 Boone Jenner .60 1.50
34 Morgan Rielly .75 2.00
35 Mathew Dumba .20 .50
36 Nail Yakupov JSY 6.00 15.00
37 Nathan MacKinnon JSY 15.00 40.00
38 Jonathan Huberdeau JSY 3.00 8.00
39 Alex Galchenyuk JSY 10.00 25.00
40 Anthony Bennett BK JSY 3.00 8.00

2013-14 Absolute Holo Lava Flow
VETS/25: 1X TO 2.5X BASIC CARDS
ROOKIES/25: 1X TO 2.5X BASIC CARDS

2013-14 Absolute Absolute Goalies
*LAVA FLOW/25: .6X TO 1.5X BASIC INSERTS
1 Carey Price 2.00 5.00
2 Corey Crawford 1.25 3.00
3 Craig Anderson 1.00 2.50
4 Sergei Bobrovsky 1.50 4.00
5 Henrik Lundqvist 2.50 6.00
6 Marc-Andre Fleury 2.00 5.00
7 Pekka Rinne 1.00 2.50
8 Jonathan Quick 1.25 3.00
9 Jonathan Bernier .75 2.00
10 Martin Brodeur 2.50 6.00
11 Ondrejo Pavelec 1.00 2.50
12 Tuukka Rask 1.25 3.00
13 Roberto Luongo 1.50 4.00
14 Cory Schneider 1.00 2.50
15 Jimmy Howard 1.25 3.00
16 Felix Potvin 1.50 4.00
17 Patrick Roy 2.50 6.00

2013-14 Absolute Draft Day Materials
*LAVA FLOW/25: .5X TO 1.2X BASIC JSY
1 Nathan MacKinnon 8.00 20.00
2 Jacob Trouba 2.50 6.00
3 Aleksander Barkov 5.00 12.00
4 Seth Jones 3.00 8.00
5 Sean Monahan 2.50 6.00
6 Ryan Murray 2.50 6.00
7 Valeri Nichushkin 3.00 8.00

2013-14 Absolute Happy Holidays Materials
*LAVA FLOW/25: .5X TO 1.2X BASIC JSY
NM Nathan MacKinnon 12.00 30.00

2013-14 Absolute Ink
CK Carl Klingberg 2.50 6.00
JF Justin Faulk 2.50 6.00
JM John Moore 2.00 5.00
RE Ryan Ellis 2.50 6.00
SD Simon Despres 2.50 6.00
TE Tim Erixon 2.00 5.00
OEL Oliver Ekman-Larsson 3.00 8.00

2013-14 Absolute Logo Patch Autographs
CP Chet Pickard 2.50 6.00
DH Dougie Hamilton 12.00 30.00
JA Jake Allen 6.00 15.00
JS Jaden Schwartz 5.00 12.00
JS Jordan Schroeder 4.00 10.00
JT Jarred Tinordi 8.00 20.00
MR Morgan Rielly 10.00 25.00
NB Nathan Beaulieu 8.00 20.00
NY Nail Yakupov 15.00 40.00
RM Ryan Murray 15.00 40.00
TB Tyson Barrie 2.50 6.00

2013-14 Absolute NHL Icons
*LAVA FLOW/25: X TO X BASIC INSERTS
1 Jaromir Jagr 5.00 12.00
2 Jarome Iginla 2.00 5.00
3 Teemu Selanne 3.00 8.00
4 Martin Brodeur 4.00 10.00
5 Daniel Alfredsson 1.50 4.00

2013-14 Absolute Retired
*LAVA FLOW/25: .5X TO 1.2X BASIC INSERTS
1 Gordie Howe 5.00 12.00
2 Mario Lemieux 6.00 15.00
3 Ray Bourque 2.50 6.00
4 Chris Chelios 1.50 4.00
5 Eric Lindros 2.50 6.00
6 Steve Yzerman 4.00 10.00
7 Mark Messier 3.00 8.00
8 Brendan Shanahan 1.50 4.00

2013-14 Absolute Rookie Roundup Materials
*LAVA FLOW/25: .5X TO 1.2X BASIC JSY
1 Justin Schultz 3.00 8.00
2 Tom Wilson 6.00 15.00
3 Petr Mrazek 6.00 15.00
4 Charlie Coyle 5.00 12.00
5 Jarred Tinordi 3.00 8.00
6 Cory Conacher 2.00 5.00
7 Nicklas Jensen 2.50 6.00
8 Morgan Rielly 8.00 20.00
9 Beau Bennett 4.00 10.00
10 Ryan Murray 5.00 12.00

2013-14 Absolute Rookie Showcase Materials
*LAVA FLOW/25: .5X TO 1.2X BASIC JSY
1 Chris Kreider 3.00 8.00
2 Tyson Barrie 1.50 4.00
3 Jake Allen 2.50 6.00
4 Jussi Rynnas 1.50 4.00
5 Jaden Schwartz 3.00 8.00
6 Ryan Nugent-Hopkins 3.00 8.00
7 Gabriel Landeskog 6.00 15.00
8 Adam Henrique 2.00 5.00

2013-14 Absolute Rookie Tool of the Trade
*LAVA FLOW/25: .5X TO 1.2X BASIC JSY
1 Jonathan Toews 8.00 20.00
2 Steven Stamkos 10.00 25.00
3 Alex Ovechkin 12.00 30.00
4 Sidney Crosby 20.00 50.00

1989-90 Action Packed Prototypes
COMPLETE SET (4) 125.00 300.00
1 Wayne Gretzky 50.00 100.00
2 Mario Lemieux 30.00 75.00
3 Mario Lemieux White border 30.00 75.00
4 Steve Yzerman 50.00 100.00

1990 Action Packed Promos Gold
COMPLETE SET (4) 100.00 200.00
*SILVER: .4X TO 1X GOLD
5 Mario Lemieux 15.00 40.00
6 Wayne Gretzky 25.00 60.00

1993 Action Packed HOF Induction
COMPLETE SET (10) 8.00 20.00
1 Edgar Laprade .75 2.00
2 Guy Lapointe 2.00 5.00
3 Billy Smith 3.00 8.00
4 Steve Shutt 2.00 5.00
5 John D'Amico .40 1.00
6 Al Shaver .20 .50
7 Seymour Knox III .20 .50
8 Frank Griffiths .20 .50
9 Fred Page .20 .50
10 Al Strachan .20 .50

1993 Action Packed Prototypes
COMPLETE SET (2) 3.00 8.00
1 Bobby Hull (Color) 1.50 4.00
2 Bobby Hull (Gold) 2.00 5.00

1994 Action Packed Badge of Honor Promos
COMPLETE SET (4) 10.00 25.00
1 Sergei Fedorov 4.00 10.00
2 Doug Gilmour 2.00 5.00
3 Mike Modano 3.00 8.00
4 Patrick Roy 5.00 12.00

1994-95 Action Packed Big Picture Promos
COMPLETE SET (4) 8.00 20.00
BP1 Jeremy Roenick 1.25 3.00
BP2 John Vanbiesbrouck 1.25 3.00
BP3 Jaromir Jagr 4.00 10.00
BP4 Steve Yzerman 4.00 10.00

1994-95 Action Packed Mammoth
COMPLETE SET (16) 10.00 25.00
MM1 Pavel Bure 1.25 3.00
MM2 Chris Chelios 1.00 2.50
MM3 Sergei Fedorov 1.25 3.00
MM4 Doug Gilmour .75 2.00
MM5 Wayne Gretzky 2.50 6.00
MM6 Brett Hull 1.25 3.00
MM7 Jaromir Jagr 1.00 2.50
MM8 Eric Lindros 1.25 3.00
MM9 Mark Messier 1.00 2.50
MM9 Felix Potvin 1.25 3.00
MM10 Alexander Mogilny 1.00 2.50
MM11 Adam Oates 1.00 2.50
MM13 Jeremy Roenick 1.25 3.00
MM14 Patrick Roy 1.50 4.00
MM15 John Vanbiesbrouck 1.00 2.50
MM16 Alexei Yashin .75 2.00

2010-11 Adrenalyn XL
1 Ilya Kovalchuk .10 .25
2 Zach Parise .10 .25
3 Travis Zajac .05 .15
4 Patrik Elias .10 .25
5 Dainius Zubrus .05 .15
6 Jason Arnott .07 .20
7 Colin White .05 .15
8 Anton Volchenkov .05 .15
9 Andy Greene .05 .15
10 Martin Brodeur .25 .60
11 John Tavares .15 .40
12 Matt Moulson .07 .20
13 Rob Schremp .05 .15
14 Trent Hunter .05 .15
15 Josh Bailey .07 .20
16 Kyle Okposo .05 .15
17 Mark Streit .05 .15
18 Bruno Gervais .05 .15
19 Jack Hillen .05 .15
20 Dwayne Roloson .07 .20
21 Marian Gaborik .10 .25
22 Chris Drury .07 .20
23 Ryan Callahan .05 .15
24 Brandon Dubinsky .05 .15
25 Vinny Prospal .05 .15
26 Alexander Frolov .05 .15
27 Michael Del Zotto .07 .20
28 Daniel Girardi .05 .15
29 Marc Staal .05 .15
30 Henrik Lundqvist .25 .60
31 Mike Richards .07 .20
32 Jeff Carter .07 .20
33 Nikolai Zherdev .05 .15
34 Daniel Briere .10 .25
35 Claude Giroux .10 .25
36 Ville Leino .07 .20
37 Matt Carle .07 .20
38 Kimmo Timonen .05 .15
39 Chris Pronger .10 .25
40 Michael Leighton .07 .20
41 Evgeni Malkin .20 .50
42 Sidney Crosby .40 1.00
43 Jordan Staal .07 .20
44 Chris Kunitz .10 .25
45 Pascal Dupuis .05 .15
46 Max Talbot .05 .15
47 Paul Martin .05 .15
48 Zbynek Michalek .05 .15
49 Kristopher Letang .12 .30
50 Marc-Andre Fleury .20 .50
51 Marc Savard .05 .15
52 Nathan Horton .07 .20
53 Milan Lucic .10 .25
54 Patrice Bergeron .12 .30
55 David Krejci .10 .25
56 Tyler Seguin RC .25 .60
57 Zdeno Chara .10 .25
58 Dennis Seidenberg .05 .15
59 Johnny Boychuk .07 .20
60 Tuukka Rask .12 .30
61 Thomas Vanek .07 .20
62 Jason Pominville .05 .15
63 Tim Connolly .05 .15
64 Derek Roy .05 .15
65 Jochen Hecht .05 .15
66 Nathan Gerbe .05 .15
67 Craig Rivet .05 .15
68 Tyler Myers .05 .15
69 Jordan Leopold .05 .15
70 Ryan Miller .10 .25
71 Scott Gomez .07 .20
72 Michael Cammalleri .10 .25
73 Brian Gionta .05 .15
74 Benoit Pouliot .05 .15
75 Andrei Kostitsyn .07 .20
76 Tomas Plekanec .05 .15
77 Josh Gorges .05 .15
78 P.K. Subban RC .25 .60
79 Andrei Markov .10 .25
80 Carey Price .20 .50
81 Jason Spezza .10 .25
82 Daniel Alfredsson .10 .25
83 Milan Michalek .05 .15
84 Mike Fisher .05 .15
85 Alex Kovalev .07 .20
86 Peter Regin .07 .20
87 Sergei Gonchar .05 .15
88 Chris Phillips .05 .15
89 Erik Karlsson .12 .30
90 Brian Elliott .07 .20
91 Phil Kessel .10 .25
92 Tyler Bozak .05 .15
93 Mikhail Grabovski .05 .15
94 Kris Versteeg .05 .15
95 Colby Armstrong .05 .15
96 Nikolai Kulemin .05 .15
97 Tomas Kaberle .05 .15
98 Dion Phaneuf .07 .20
99 Luke Schenn .10 .25
100 Jonas Gustavsson .12 .30
101 Evander Kane .10 .25
102 Dustin Byfuglien .10 .25
103 Nik Antropov .07 .20
104 Rich Peverley .10 .25
105 Bryan Little .10 .25
106 Nicklas Bergfors .07 .20
107 Andrew Ladd .05 .15
108 Zach Bogosian .07 .20
109 Tobias Enstrom .05 .15
110 Ondrej Pavelec .10 .25
111 Eric Staal .12 .30
112 Tuomo Ruutu .07 .20
113 Erik Cole .05 .15
114 Chad LaRose .05 .15
115 Brandon Sutter .05 .15
116 Zach Boychuk .07 .20
117 Joni Pitkanen .07 .20
118 Jamie McBain RC .07 .20
119 Joe Corvo .05 .15
120 Cam Ward .10 .25
121 Stephen Weiss .07 .20
122 David Booth .05 .15
123 Cory Stillman .05 .15
124 Rostislav Olesz .05 .15
125 Michael Frolik .05 .15
126 Steve Reinprecht .05 .15
127 Dmitry Kulikov .07 .20
128 Bryan McCabe .05 .15
129 Dennis Wideman .05 .15
130 Tomas Vokoun .07 .20
131 Vincent Lecavalier .10 .25
132 Steven Stamkos .20 .50
133 Martin St. Louis .10 .25
134 Ryan Malone .05 .15
135 Steve Downie .05 .15
136 Simon Gagne .10 .25
137 Mattias Ohlund .05 .15
138 Victor Hedman .12 .30
139 Pavel Kubina .05 .15
140 Mike Smith .10 .25
141 Alex Ovechkin .40 1.00
142 Alexander Semin .10 .25
143 Nicklas Backstrom .10 .25
144 Mike Knuble .05 .15
145 Eric Fehr .05 .15
146 Marcus Johansson RC .12 .30
147 Mike Green .07 .20
148 Jeff Schultz .05 .15
149 John Carlson .10 .25
150 Semyon Varlamov .10 .25
151 Marian Hossa .10 .25
152 Patrick Sharp .10 .25
153 Patrick Kane .20 .50
154 Jonathan Toews .15 .40
155 Dave Bolland .07 .20
156 Troy Brouwer .05 .15
157 Brent Seabrook .05 .15
158 Duncan Keith .07 .20
159 Brian Campbell .05 .15
160 Marty Turco .10 .25
161 Rick Nash .10 .25
162 Kristian Huselius .05 .15
163 R.J. Umberger .05 .15
164 Antoine Vermette .05 .15
165 Jakub Voracek .07 .20
166 Derick Brassard .05 .15
167 Mike Commodore .05 .15
168 Kris Russell .05 .15
169 Jan Hejda .05 .15
170 Steve Mason .07 .20
171 Pavel Datsyuk .15 .40
172 Henrik Zetterberg .12 .30
173 Tomas Holmstrom .05 .15
174 Johan Franzen .07 .20
175 Valtteri Filppula .05 .15
176 Mike Modano .15 .40
177 Nicklas Lidstrom .10 .25
178 Brian Rafalski .05 .15
179 Niklas Kronwall .07 .20
180 Jimmy Howard .12 .30
181 Martin Erat .05 .15
182 Patric Hornqvist .05 .15
183 Matthew Lombardi .05 .15
184 J.P. Dumont .05 .15
185 Steve Sullivan .05 .15
186 David Legwand .07 .20
187 Shea Weber .07 .20
188 Ryan Suter .07 .20
189 Kevin Klein .05 .15
190 Pekka Rinne .10 .25
191 T.J. Oshie .10 .25
192 Andy McDonald .07 .20
193 Brad Boyes .05 .15
194 David Backes .05 .15
195 Alex Steen .05 .15
196 David Perron .07 .20
197 Erik Johnson .05 .15
198 Barret Jackman .05 .15
199 Carlo Colaiacovo .05 .15
200 Jaroslav Halak .10 .25
201 Jarome Iginla .12 .30
202 Daymond Langkow .05 .15
203 Rene Bourque .05 .15
204 Olli Jokinen .07 .20
205 Matt Stajan .05 .15
206 Mikael Backlund .07 .20
207 Jay Bouwmeester .05 .15
208 Robyn Regehr .05 .15
209 Mark Giordano .10 .25
210 Miikka Kiprusoff .10 .25
211 Paul Stastny .07 .20
212 Milan Hejduk .07 .20
213 Matt Duchene .10 .25
214 Peter Mueller .07 .20
215 Chris Stewart .07 .20
216 Brandon Yip RC .07 .20
217 Adam Foote .05 .15
218 John-Michael Liles .05 .15
219 Kyle Cumiskey .05 .15
220 Craig Anderson .10 .25
221 Dustin Penner .05 .15
222 Sam Gagner .05 .15
223 Ales Hemsky .07 .20
224 Taylor Hall RC .20 .50
225 Jordan Eberle RC .20 .50
226 Gilbert Brule .10 .25
227 Kurtis Foster .05 .15
228 Tom Gilbert .05 .15
229 Ryan Whitney .05 .15
230 Jeff Deslauriers .05 .15
231 Mikko Koivu .10 .25
232 Martin Havlat .07 .20
233 Andrew Brunette .05 .15
234 Matt Cullen .05 .15
235 Chuck Kobasew .05 .15
236 Guillaume Latendresse .07 .20
237 Brent Burns .10 .25
238 Greg Zanon .05 .15
239 Cam Barker .05 .15
240 Niklas Backstrom .10 .25
241 Henrik Sedin .12 .30
242 Daniel Sedin .12 .30
243 Alexandre Burrows .05 .15
244 Mason Raymond .05 .15
245 Ryan Kesler .10 .25
246 Mikael Samuelsson .05 .15
247 Christian Ehrhoff .05 .15
248 Dan Hamhuis .07 .20
249 Keith Ballard .05 .15
250 Roberto Luongo .15 .40
251 Nick Bonino RC .10 .25
252 Saku Koivu .10 .25
253 Ryan Getzlaf .10 .25
254 Corey Perry .15 .40
255 Bobby Ryan .07 .20
256 Teemu Selanne .20 .50
257 Luca Sbisa .07 .20
258 Toni Lydman .05 .15
259 Lubomir Visnovsky .05 .15
260 Jonas Hiller .07 .20
261 Brad Richards .10 .25
262 Brenden Morrow .07 .20
263 Loui Eriksson .05 .15
264 Steve Ott .05 .15
265 Jamie Benn .12 .30
266 James Neal .05 .15
267 Trevor Daley .05 .15
268 Stephane Robidas .05 .15
269 Nicklas Grossman .05 .15
270 Kari Lehtonen .07 .20
271 Anze Kopitar .15 .40
272 Ryan Smyth .07 .20
273 Dustin Brown .10 .25
274 Alexei Ponikarovsky .05 .15
275 Justin Williams .07 .20
276 Wayne Simmonds .12 .30
277 Drew Doughty .12 .30
278 Rob Scuderi .05 .15
279 Jack Johnson .05 .15
280 Jonathan Quick .12 .30
281 Wojtek Wolski .05 .15
282 Shane Doan .07 .20
283 Ray Whitney .07 .20
284 Radim Vrbata .05 .15
285 Scottie Upshall .05 .15
286 Martin Hanzal .05 .15
287 Adrian Aucoin .05 .15
288 Keith Yandle .05 .15
289 Ed Jovanovski .05 .15
290 Ilya Bryzgalov .07 .20
291 Joe Thornton .15 .40
292 Joe Pavelski .12 .30
293 Patrick Marleau .10 .25
294 Dany Heatley .07 .20
295 Devin Setoguchi .07 .20
296 Logan Couture .12 .30
297 Marc-Edouard Vlasic .05 .15
298 Dan Boyle .05 .15
299 Jason Demers .05 .15
300 Antti Niemi .07 .20

2010-11 Adrenalyn XL Extra
E1 Zach Parise .60 1.50
E2 Dwayne Roloson .50 1.25
E3 Marc Staal .40 1.00
E4 Jeff Carter .50 1.25
E5 Jordan Staal .50 1.25
E6 Nathan Horton .50 1.25
E7 Derek Roy .40 1.00
E8 Brian Gionta .40 1.00
E9 Sergei Gonchar .40 1.00
E10 Phil Kessel .60 1.50
E11 Rich Peverley .60 1.50
E12 Brandon Sutter .40 1.00
E13 Cory Stillman .40 1.00
E14 Vincent Lecavalier .60 1.50
E15 Mike Green .50 1.25
E16 Patrick Kane 1.25 3.00
E17 R.J. Umberger .40 1.00
E18 Nicklas Lidstrom .60 1.50
E19 Patric Hornqvist .40 1.00
E20 Andy McDonald .50 1.25
E21 Jay Bouwmeester .40 1.00
E22 Matt Duchene .60 1.50
E23 Ales Hemsky .50 1.25
E24 Andrew Brunette .40 1.00
E25 Roberto Luongo 1.00 2.50
E26 Bobby Ryan .50 1.25
E27 James Neal .40 1.00
E28 Jonathan Quick .75 2.00
E29 Ray Whitney .50 1.25
E30 Patrick Marleau .60 1.50

2010-11 Adrenalyn XL Extra Signature
ES1 Martin Brodeur 3.00 8.00
ES2 John Tavares 2.00 5.00
ES3 Henrik Lundqvist 3.00 8.00
ES4 Mike Richards 1.00 2.50
ES5 Evgeni Malkin 2.50 6.00
ES6 Zdeno Chara 1.25 3.00
ES7 Tyler Myers .75 2.00
ES8 Michael Cammalleri 1.25 3.00
ES9 Jason Spezza 1.25 3.00
ES10 Tomas Kaberle .75 2.00
ES11 Niclas Bergfors 1.00 2.50
ES12 Cam Ward 1.25 3.00
ES13 Stephen Weiss 1.00 2.50
ES14 Martin St. Louis 1.25 3.00
ES15 Nicklas Backstrom 1.25 3.00
ES16 Duncan Keith 1.00 2.50
ES17 Antoine Vermette .75 2.00
ES18 Henrik Zetterberg 1.50 4.00
ES19 Pekka Rinne 1.25 3.00
ES20 Erik Johnson .75 2.00
ES21 Miikka Kiprusoff 1.25 3.00
ES22 Craig Anderson 1.25 3.00
ES23 Jordan Eberle 2.50 6.00
ES24 Niklas Backstrom 1.25 3.00
ES25 Daniel Sedin 1.50 4.00
ES26 Teemu Selanne 2.50 6.00
ES27 Loui Eriksson .75 2.00
ES28 Anze Kopitar 2.00 5.00
ES29 Shane Doan 1.00 2.50
ES30 Dany Heatley 1.00 2.50

2010-11 Adrenalyn XL Special
S1 Andy Greene .50 1.25
S2 Patrik Elias .75 2.00
S3 Kyle Okposo .50 1.25
S4 Matt Moulson .60 1.50
S5 Brandon Dubinsky .50 1.25
S6 Vinny Prospal .50 1.25
S7 Claude Giroux .75 2.00
S8 Kimmo Timonen .50 1.25
S9 Marc-Andre Fleury 1.50 4.00
S10 Zbynek Michalek .50 1.25
S11 Marc Savard .50 1.25
S12 Patrice Bergeron 1.00 2.50
S13 Tim Connolly .50 1.25
S14 Thomas Vanek .60 1.50
S15 Carey Price 1.50 4.00
S16 P.K. Subban 2.00 5.00
S17 Alex Kovalev .60 1.50
S18 Milan Michalek .50 1.25
S19 Kris Versteeg .50 1.25
S20 Jonas Gustavsson 1.00 2.50
S21 Ondrej Pavelec .75 2.00
S22 Dustin Byfuglien .75 2.00
S23 Jamie McBain .60 1.50
S24 Joe Corvo .50 1.25
S25 David Booth .50 1.25
S26 Bryan McCabe .50 1.25
S27 Ryan Malone .50 1.25
S28 Simon Gagne .75 2.00
S29 Semyon Varlamov .75 2.00
S30 Alexander Semin .75 2.00
S31 Marian Hossa .75 2.00
S32 Brent Seabrook .50 1.25
S33 Steve Mason .60 1.50
S34 Jakub Voracek .60 1.50
S35 Johan Franzen .60 1.50
S36 Jimmy Howard 1.00 2.50
S37 David Legwand .60 1.50
S38 Ryan Suter .60 1.50
S39 Alex Steen .50 1.25
S40 T.J. Oshie .75 2.00
S41 Olli Jokinen .60 1.50
S42 Robyn Regehr .50 1.25
S43 Chris Stewart .60 1.50
S44 Milan Hejduk .60 1.50
S45 Sam Gagner .50 1.25
S46 Dustin Penner .50 1.25
S47 Martin Havlat .60 1.50
S48 Brent Burns .75 2.00
S49 Alexandre Burrows .50 1.25
S50 Keith Ballard .50 1.25
S51 Saku Koivu .75 2.00
S52 Corey Perry 1.25 3.00
S53 Stephane Robidas .50 1.25
S54 Steve Ott .50 1.25
S55 Dustin Brown .75 2.00
S56 Ryan Smyth .60 1.50
S57 Keith Yandle .50 1.25
S58 Ed Jovanovski .50 1.25
S59 Joe Pavelski 1.00 2.50
S60 Dan Boyle .50 1.25

2010-11 Adrenalyn XL Ultimate Signature
U1 Ilya Kovalchuk 4.00 10.00
U2 Mark Streit 2.50 6.00
U3 Marian Gaborik 4.00 10.00
U4 Chris Pronger 4.00 10.00
U5 Sidney Crosby 12.00 30.00
U6 Tuukka Rask 5.00 12.00
U7 Ryan Miller 4.00 10.00
U8 Andrei Markov 4.00 10.00
U9 Daniel Alfredsson 4.00 10.00
U10 Dion Phaneuf 3.00 8.00
U11 Zach Bogosian 3.00 8.00
U12 Eric Staal 5.00 12.00
U13 Tomas Vokoun 3.00 8.00
U14 Steven Stamkos 8.00 20.00
U15 Alex Ovechkin 15.00 40.00
U16 Jonathan Toews 6.00 15.00
U17 Rick Nash 6.00 15.00
U18 Pavel Datsyuk 6.00 15.00
U19 Shea Weber 3.00 8.00
U20 Jaroslav Halak 4.00 10.00
U21 Jarome Iginla 5.00 12.00
U22 Paul Stastny 3.00 8.00
U23 Taylor Hall 8.00 20.00
U24 Mikko Koivu 4.00 10.00
U25 Henrik Sedin 5.00 12.00
U26 Ryan Getzlaf 4.00 10.00
U27 Brad Richards 4.00 10.00
U28 Drew Doughty 5.00 12.00
U29 Ilya Bryzgalov 3.00 8.00
U30 Joe Thornton 6.00 15.00

1990-91 Alberta International Team Canada
COMPLETE SET (24) 6.00 15.00
1 Craig Billington .40 1.00
2 Doug Dadswell .40 1.00
3 Greg Andrusak .25 .60
4 Karl Dykhuis .25 .60
5 Gord Hynes .25 .60
6 Ken MacArthur .25 .60
7 Jim Paek .25 .60
8 Brad Schlegel .25 .60
9 Dave Archibald .25 .60
10 Stu Barnes .40 1.00
11 Brad Bennett .25 .60
12 Todd Brost .25 .60
13 Jose Charbonneau .25 .60
14 Jason Lafreniere .25 .60
15 Chris Lindberg .25 .60
16 Ken Priestlay .25 .60
17 Stephane Roy .25 .60
18 Randy Smith .25 .60
19 Todd Strueby .25 .60
20 Vladislav Tretiak 1.50 4.00
21 Dave King CO .25 .60
23 Checklist Card .04 .10
NNO Title Card .04 .10

1991-92 Alberta International Team Canada
COMPLETE SET (24) 4.80 12.00
1 Dave Archibald .20 .50
2 Todd Brost .20 .50
3 Sean Burke .75 2.00
4 Terry Crisp ACO .20 .50
5 Kevin Dahl .20 .50
6 Karl Dykhuis .20 .50
7 Wayne Fleming AGM/ACO .02 .10
8 Curt Giles .20 .50
9 Gord Hynes .20 .50
10 Fabian Joseph .20 .50
11 Joe Juneau .40 1.00
12 Trevor Kidd .40 1.00
13 Dave King GM/CO .20 .50
14 Chris Kontos .20 .50
15 Chris Lindberg .20 .50
16 Kent Manderville .20 .50
17 Adrien Plavsic .20 .50
18 Dan Ratushny .20 .50
19 Stephane Roy .20 .50
20 Brad Schlegel .20 .50
21 Scott Scissons .20 .50
22 Randy Smith .20 .50
23 Jason Woolley .30 .75
24 Title Card .02 .10

1992-93 Alberta International Team Canada
COMPLETE SET (22) 8.00 20.00
1 Dominic Amodeo .20 .50
2 Mark Astley .20 .50
3 Adrian Aucoin .40 1.00
4 Mark Bassen .20 .50
5 Eric Bellerose .20 .50
6 Mike Brewer .20 .50
7 Dany Dube CO .02 .10
8 Mike Fountain .30 .75
9 Todd Hlushko .20 .50
10 Hank Lammens .20 .50
11 Derek Laxdal .20 .50
12 Derek Mayer .20 .50
13 Keith Morris .20 .50
14 Mike Myers SNL 4.00 10.00
15 Jackson Penney .20 .50
16 Garth Premak .20 .50
17 Tom Renney CO .20 .50
18 Allain Roy .30 .75
19 Stephane Roy .20 .50
20 Trevor Sim .20 .50
21 Vladislav Tretiak 1.25 3.00
22 Title Card .02 .10

1993-94 Alberta International Team Canada
COMPLETE SET (23) 12.00 30.00
1 Adrian Aucoin .30 .75
2 Todd Brost .20 .50
3 Dany Dube .02 .10
4 David Harlock .20 .50
5 Corey Hirsch .30 .75
6 Todd Hlushko .20 .50
7 Fabian Joseph .20 .50
8 Paul Kariya 6.00 15.00
9 Chris Kontos .20 .50
10 Manny Legace 2.00 5.00
11 Brett Lindros .20 .50
12 Ken Lovsin .20 .50
13 Jason Marshall .20 .50

14 Derek Mayer .20 .50
15 Dwayne Norris .20 .50
16 Tom Renney CO .20 .50
17 Russ Romaniuk .20 .50
18 Brian Savage .60 1.50
19 Trevor Sim .20 .50
20 Chris Therien .30 .75
21 Todd Warriner .20 .50
22 Craig Woodcroft .20 .50
23 Title Card .02 .10

2008 All-Star Collection Series 1

COMPLETE SET (7) 10.00 20.00
1 Bobby Hull 2.50 6.00
2 Johnny Bower 1.50 4.00
3 Dick Duff 1.25 3.00
4 Dennis Hull 1.50 4.00
5 Pierre Pilote 1.50 4.00
6 Tony Esposito 1.50 4.00
7 Bobby Hull HOF 2.50 6.00

2008 All-Star Collection Series 1 Autographs

AUBH1 Bobby Hull 30.00 60.00
AUDD3 Dick Duff 10.00 20.00
AUDH4 Dennis Hull 12.50 25.00
AUJB2 Johnny Bower 15.00 30.00
AUPP5 Pierre Pilote 20.00 40.00
AUTE6 Tony Esposito 20.00 40.00

1992-93 All World Mario Lemieux Promos

COMPLETE SET (6) 10.00 25.00
COMMON CARD (1A-1F) 2.00 5.00

1993 American Licorice Sour Punch Caps

COMPLETE SET (8) 4.80 12.00
1 Theo Fleury .50 1.25
2 Guy Lafleur
Blue Raspbe 1.00 2.50
3 Chris Chelios
Strawberr .50 1.25
4 Stan Mikita
Sour Apple Cap .50 1.25
5 Rocket Richard
Strawber 1.00 2.50
6 Steve Thomas
Blue Raspberry Cap .20 .50
7 Checklist 1
Sour Punch Cap Logo .08 .25
8 Checklist 2
Sour Punch Cap Logo .08 .25
P Bobby Hull
Sour Punch C 1.00 2.50

2007 Americana Sports Legends

6 Tony Esposito 1.50 4.00
9 Patrick Roy 4.00 10.00

2007 Americana Sports Legends Material

6 Tony Esposito Jsy/500 4.00 10.00

2007 Americana Sports Legends Signature

6 Tony Esposito/25 15.00 40.00
9 Patrick Roy/25 50.00 100.00

2007 Americana Sports Legends Signature Material

*MTL: .5X TO 1.2X BASIC SIG

2005-06 Artifacts

COMP.SET w/o SPs (100) 15.00 30.00
1 Jean-Sebastien Giguere .30 .75
2 Sergei Fedorov .50 1.25
3 Joffrey Lupul .20 .50
4 Dany Heatley .25 .60
5 Ilya Kovalchuk .30 .75
6 Kari Lehtonen .25 .60
7 Andrew Raycroft .25 .60
8 Joe Thornton .50 1.25
9 Glen Murray .25 .60
10 Sergei Samsonov .25 .60
11 Patrice Bergeron .40 1.00
12 Martin Biron .25 .60
13 Maxim Afinogenov .20 .50
14 Chris Drury .25 .60
15 Jarome Iginla .40 1.00
16 Miikka Kiprusoff .30 .75
17 Jordan Leopold .20 .50
18 Eric Staal .40 1.00
19 Justin Williams .25 .60
20 Erik Cole .20 .50
21 Tuomo Ruutu .30 .75
22 Eric Daze .25 .60
23 Tyler Arnason .20 .50
24 Joe Sakic .60 1.50
25 Rob Blake .30 .75
26 David Aebischer .25 .60
27 Milan Hejduk .25 .60
28 Alex Tanguay .30 .75
29 Geoff Sanderson .20 .50
30 Rick Nash .30 .75
31 Nikolai Zherdev .20 .50
32 Mike Modano .50 1.25
33 Bill Guerin .30 .75
34 Brenden Morrow .25 .60
35 Marty Turco .30 .75
36 Manny Legace .30 .75
37 Pavel Datsyuk .50 1.25
38 Brendan Shanahan .30 .75
39 Steve Yzerman .75 2.00
40 Henrik Zetterberg .40 1.00
41 Ty Conklin .25 .60
42 Ryan Smyth .25 .60
43 Stephen Weiss .20 .50
44 Roberto Luongo .50 1.25
45 Olli Jokinen .30 .75
46 Alexander Frolov .20 .50
47 Dustin Brown .30 .75
48 Luc Robitaille .30 .75
49 Dwayne Roloson .25 .60
50 Marian Gaborik .30 .75
51 Mike Ribeiro .20 .50
52 Michael Ryder .25 .60
53 Jose Theodore .30 .75
54 Saku Koivu .30 .75
55 Steve Sullivan .20 .50
56 Jordin Tootoo .30 .75
57 Tomas Vokoun .25 .60
58 Martin Brodeur .75 2.00
59 Scott Gomez .25 .60
60 Jeff Friesen .20 .50
61 Patrik Elias .30 .75
62 Tom Poti .20 .50
63 Mark Messier .60 1.50
64 Jaromir Jagr 1.00 2.50
65 Mark Parrish .20 .50
66 Rick DiPietro .25 .60
67 Alexei Yashin .25 .60
68 Daniel Alfredsson .30 .75
69 Dominik Hasek .50 1.25
70 Marian Hossa .30 .75
71 Jason Spezza .30 .75
72 Martin Havlat .30 .75
73 Robert Esche .25 .60
74 Keith Primeau .25 .60
75 Simon Gagne .30 .75
76 Michal Handzus .25 .60
77 Brett Hull .60 1.50
78 Mike Comrie .25 .60
79 Shane Doan .25 .60
80 Marc-Andre Fleury .60 1.50
81 Mario Lemieux 1.25 3.00
82 Mark Recchi .40 1.00
83 Evgeni Nabokov .25 .60
84 Patrick Marleau .30 .75
85 Jonathan Cheechoo .25 .60
86 Mike Sillinger .20 .50
87 Doug Weight .30 .75
88 Keith Tkachuk .30 .75
89 Brad Richards .30 .75
90 Fredrik Modin .20 .50
91 Martin St. Louis .30 .75
92 Vincent Lecavalier .30 .75
93 Ed Belfour .30 .75
94 Owen Nolan .30 .75
95 Mats Sundin .30 .75
96 Nik Antropov .25 .60
97 Ed Jovanovski .25 .60
98 Markus Naslund .30 .75
99 Trevor Linden .30 .75
100 Olaf Kolzig .30 .75
101 Glenn Anderson AL .75 2.00
102 Bill Barber AL .75 2.00
103 Jean Beliveau AL 1.00 2.50
104 Mike Bossy AL 1.00 2.50
105 Johnny Bower AL 1.00 2.50
106 Scotty Bowman AL 1.00 2.50
107 Johnny Bucyk AL 1.00 2.50
108 Wayne Cashman AL .60 1.50
109 Gerry Cheevers AL 1.00 2.50
110 Don Cherry AL 1.00 2.50
111 Bobby Clarke AL 1.50 4.00
112 Gordie Howe AL 3.00 8.00
113 Wayne Gretzky AL 6.00 15.00
114 Marcel Dionne AL 1.25 3.00
115 Phil Esposito AL 1.50 4.00
116 Tony Esposito AL 1.00 2.50
117 Grant Fuhr AL 1.50 4.00
118 Bernie Geoffrion AL .75 2.00
119 Clark Gillies AL 1.00 2.50
120 Butch Goring AL .60 1.50
121 Glenn Hall AL 1.00 2.50
122 Paul Henderson AL .75 2.00
123 Ron Hextall AL 1.00 2.50
124 Al Iafrate AL .75 2.00
125 Red Kelly AL 1.00 2.50
126 Jari Kurri AL 1.00 2.50
127 Guy LaFleur AL 1.25 3.00
128 Igor Larionov AL 1.00 2.50
129 Reggie Leach AL .60 1.50
130 Hakan Loob AL .60 1.50
131 Frank Mahovlich AL 1.00 2.50
132 Rick Martin AL .60 1.50
133 Lanny McDonald AL 1.00 2.50
134 Stan Mikita AL 1.25 3.00
135 Dickie Moore AL .60 1.50
136 Ken Morrow AL .60 1.50
137 Larry Murphy AL .75 2.00
138 Cam Neely AL 1.00 2.50
139 Mats Naslund AL .60 1.50
140 Bob Nystrom AL .60 1.50
141 Terry O'Reilly AL .75 2.00
142 Brad Park AL .75 2.00
143 Gilbert Perreault AL 1.00 2.50
144 Rene Robert AL .60 1.50
145 Derek Sanderson AL 1.00 2.50
146 Denis Savard AL 1.00 2.50
147 Peter Stastny AL .75 2.00
148 Thomas Steen AL .60 1.50
149 Dave Taylor AL .75 2.00
150 Bryan Trottier AL 1.00 2.50
151 Sergei Fedorov AS 1.50 4.00
152 Ilya Kovalchuk AS 1.00 2.50
153 Dany Heatley AS .75 2.00
154 Joe Thornton AS 1.50 4.00
155 Glen Murray AS .75 2.00
156 Jarome Iginla AS 1.25 3.00
157 Eric Daze AS .75 2.00
158 Joe Sakic AS 2.00 5.00
159 Rob Blake AS 1.00 2.50
160 Milan Hejduk AS .75 2.00
161 Alex Tanguay AS 1.00 2.50
162 Rick Nash AS 1.00 2.50
163 Mike Modano AS 1.50 4.00
164 Bill Guerin AS 1.00 2.50
165 Marty Turco AS 1.00 2.50
166 Brendan Shanahan AS 1.00 2.50
167 Steve Yzerman AS 2.50 6.00
168 Pavel Datsyuk AS 1.50 4.00
169 Roberto Luongo AS 1.50 4.00
170 Luc Robitaille AS 1.00 2.50
171 Marian Gaborik AS 1.00 2.50
172 Jose Theodore AS 1.00 2.50
173 Saku Koivu AS 1.00 2.50
174 Tomas Vokoun AS .75 2.00
175 Martin Brodeur AS 2.50 6.00
176 Scott Gomez AS .75 2.00
177 Patrik Elias AS 1.00 2.50
178 Mark Messier AS 2.00 5.00
179 Jaromir Jagr AS 3.00 8.00
180 Alexei Yashin AS .75 2.00
181 Mark Parrish AS .60 1.50
182 Dominik Hasek AS 1.50 4.00
183 Marian Hossa AS 1.00 2.50
184 Daniel Alfredsson AS 1.00 2.50
185 Keith Primeau AS .75 2.00
186 Simon Gagne AS 1.00 2.50
187 Brett Hull AS 2.00 5.00
188 Shane Doan AS .75 2.00
189 Mario Lemieux AS 4.00 10.00
190 Mark Recchi AS 1.25 3.00
191 Evgeni Nabokov AS .75 2.00
192 Keith Tkachuk AS 1.00 2.50
193 Martin St. Louis AS 1.00 2.50
194 Vincent Lecavalier AS 1.00 2.50
195 Ed Belfour AS 1.00 2.50
196 Mats Sundin AS 1.00 2.50
197 Owen Nolan AS 1.00 2.50
198 Markus Naslund AS 1.00 2.50
199 Ed Jovanovski AS .75 2.00
200 Olaf Kolzig AS 1.00 2.50
201 Corey Perry RC 6.00 15.00
202 Braydon Coburn RC 3.00 8.00
203 Hannu Toivonen RC 3.00 8.00
204 Thomas Vanek RC 6.00 15.00
205 Dion Phaneuf RC 5.00 12.00
206 Cam Ward RC 5.00 12.00
207 Brent Seabrook RC 6.00 15.00
208 Wojtek Wolski RC 2.50 6.00
209 Gilbert Brule RC 3.00 8.00
210 Jussi Jokinen RC 3.00 8.00
211 Jim Howard RC 8.00 20.00
212 Brad Winchester RC 3.00 8.00
213 Rostislav Olesz RC 2.50 6.00
214 George Parros RC 2.00 5.00
215 Matt Foy RC 2.00 5.00
216 Alexander Perezhogin RC 2.50 6.00
217 Ryan Suter RC 4.00 10.00
218 Zach Parise RC 8.00 20.00
219 Henrik Lundqvist RC 15.00 40.00
220 Robert Nilsson RC 3.00 8.00
221 Andrej Meszaros RC 2.50 6.00
222 Jeff Carter RC 5.00 12.00
223 David Leneveu RC 2.50 6.00
224 Sidney Crosby RC 150.00 300.00
225 Ryane Clowe RC 4.00 10.00
226 Jeff Woywitka RC 2.00 5.00
227 Evgeny Artykuhin RC 2.50 6.00
228 Alexander Steen RC 5.00 12.00
229 Rob McVicar RC 2.50 6.00
230 Alexander Ovechkin RC 150.00 400.00
231 Peter Budaj RC 4.00 10.00
232 Rene Bourque RC 3.00 8.00
233 Yann Danis RC 2.50 6.00
234 Eric Nystrom RC 2.50 6.00
235 Mike Richards RC 6.00 15.00
236 Kevin Nastiuk RC 2.00 5.00
237 Petteri Nokelainen RC 2.00 5.00
238 Ryan Getzlaf RC 8.00 20.00
239 Johan Franzen RC 5.00 12.00
240 Brandon Bochenski RC 3.00 8.00
241 Patrick Eaves RC 3.00 8.00
242 Jim Slater RC 2.50 6.00
243 Dustin Penner RC 3.00 8.00
244 Zenon Konopka RC 2.00 5.00
245 Michael Wall RC 2.50 6.00
246 Adam Berkhoel RC 2.50 6.00
247 Andrew Alberts RC 2.00 5.00
248 Milan Jurcina RC 2.50 6.00
249 Ben Walter RC 2.00 5.00
250 Jordan Sigalet RC 2.00 5.00
251 Nathan Paetsch RC 2.50 6.00
252 Chris Thorburn RC 2.50 6.00
253 Daniel Paille RC 3.00 8.00
254 Mark Giordano RC 4.00 10.00
255 Niklas Nordgren RC 3.00 8.00
256 Andrew Ladd RC 4.00 10.00
257 Chad Larose RC 2.00 5.00
258 Danny Richmond RC 2.00 5.00
259 Duncan Keith RC 6.00 15.00
260 Cam Barker RC 2.50 6.00
261 Martin St. Pierre RC 2.00 5.00
262 Corey Crawford RC 8.00 20.00
263 James Wisniewski RC 2.50 6.00
264 Brad Richardson RC 3.00 8.00
265 Vitaly Kolesnik RC 2.50 6.00
266 Alexandre Picard RC 2.00 5.00
267 Ole-Kristian Tollefsen RC 2.50 6.00
268 Steven Goertzen RC 2.00 5.00
269 Geoff Platt RC 2.50 6.00
270 Joakim Lindstrom RC 2.00 5.00
271 Junior Lessard RC 2.00 5.00
272 Vojtech Polak RC 2.00 5.00
273 Brett Lebda RC 2.00 5.00
274 Kyle Quincey RC 2.50 6.00
275 Valtteri Filppula RC 4.00 10.00
276 Danny Syvret RC 2.00 5.00
277 Kyle Brodziak RC 2.00 5.00
278 J-F Jacques RC 2.00 5.00
279 Matt Greene RC 2.00 5.00
280 Anthony Stewart RC 2.50 6.00
281 Greg Jacina RC 2.00 5.00
282 Petr Taticek RC 2.50 6.00
283 Yanick Lehoux RC 3.00 8.00
284 Jeff Tambellini RC 2.00 5.00
285 Petr Kanko RC 2.50 6.00
286 Richard Petiot RC 2.50 6.00
287 Mikko Koivu RC 4.00 10.00
288 Derek Boogaard RC 5.00 12.00
289 Jonathan Ferland RC 2.50 6.00
290 Maxim Lapierre RC 3.00 8.00
291 Jean-Philippe Cote RC 2.00 5.00
292 Andrei Kostitsyn RC 4.00 10.00
293 Greg Zanon RC 2.50 6.00
294 Kevin Klein RC 2.00 5.00
295 Pekka Rinne RC 5.00 12.00
296 Barry Tallackson RC 2.50 6.00
297 Cam Janssen RC 2.50 6.00
298 Jason Ryznar RC 2.00 5.00
299 Jeremy Colliton RC 2.00 5.00
300 Chris Campoli RC 2.00 5.00
301 Bruno Gervais RC 2.00 5.00
302 Petr Prucha RC 3.00 8.00
303 Ryan Hollweg RC 2.00 5.00
304 Al Montoya RC 3.00 8.00
305 Brian McGrattan RC 2.00 5.00
306 Christoph Schubert RC 2.00 5.00
307 R.J. Umberger RC 3.00 8.00
308 Stefan Ruzicka RC 2.00 5.00
309 Ben Eager RC 2.50 6.00
310 Alexandre Picard RC 2.00 5.00
311 Keith Ballard RC 2.50 6.00
312 Matt Jones RC 2.00 5.00
313 Maxime Talbot RC 3.00 8.00
314 Erik Christensen RC 2.00 5.00
315 Ryan Whitney RC 3.00 8.00
316 Colby Armstrong RC 3.00 8.00
317 Josh Gorges RC 2.50 6.00
318 Dimitri Patzold RC 2.00 5.00
319 Steve Bernier RC 3.00 8.00
320 Grant Stevenson RC 2.00 5.00
321 Doug Murray RC 2.00 5.00
322 Jay McClement RC 2.00 5.00
323 Jeff Hoggan RC 2.00 5.00
324 Colin Hemingway RC 2.00 5.00
325 Dennis Wideman RC 2.00 5.00
326 Lee Stempniak RC 3.00 8.00
327 Chris Beckford-Tseu RC 2.50 6.00
328 Gerald Coleman RC 2.00 5.00
329 Nick Tarnasky RC 2.00 5.00
330 Paul Ranger RC 2.00 5.00
331 Darren Reid RC 2.00 5.00
332 Ryan Craig RC 2.00 5.00
333 Andrew Wozniewski RC 2.50 6.00
334 Staffan Kronwall RC 2.00 5.00
335 Jay Harrison RC 2.50 6.00
336 Kevin Bieksa RC 5.00 12.00
337 Rick Rypien RC 6.00 15.00
338 Rob McVicar 2.50 6.00
339 Tomas Mojzis RC 2.00 5.00
340 Tomas Fleischmann RC 3.00 8.00
341 Jakub Klepis RC 2.00 5.00
342 Mike Green RC 4.00 10.00

2005-06 Artifacts Blue

*1-100 VETS/75: 2.5X TO 6X BASIC CARDS
*101-200 AL/AS/75: .8X TO 2X AL/AS/899
63 Mark Messier 5.00 12.00
178 Mark Messier 5.00 12.00

2005-06 Artifacts Green

*1-100 VETS/25: 4X TO 10X BASIC CARDS
*101-200 AL/AS/25: 1.2X TO 3X AL/AS/899
63 Mark Messier 8.00 20.00
178 Mark Messier 8.00 20.00

2005-06 Artifacts Pewter

*1-100 VETS/100: 2X TO 5X BASIC CARDS
*101-200 AL/AS/100: 6X TO 1.5X AL/AS/899
63 Mark Messier 4.00 10.00
178 Mark Messier 4.00 10.00

2005-06 Artifacts Red

*1-100 VETS/50: 3X TO 8X BASIC CARDS
*101-200 AL/AS/50: 1X TO 3X AL/AS/899
63 Mark Messier 6.00 15.00
178 Mark Messier 8.00 20.00

2005-06 Artifacts Autofacts

AFAF Alexander Frolov 6.00 15.00
AFAH Ales Hemsky 6.00 15.00
AFAM Antti Miettinen 4.00 10.00
AFAR Andrew Raycroft 6.00 15.00
AFAT Alex Tanguay 6.00 15.00
AFBB Brad Boyes 4.00 10.00
AFBC Bobby Clarke 10.00 25.00
AFBI Martin Biron 6.00 15.00
AFBL Brian Leetch 8.00 20.00
AFBM Bryan McCabe 4.00 10.00
AFBO Mike Bossy 10.00 25.00
AFBR Brad Richards 6.00 15.00
AFCD Chris Drury 6.00 15.00
AFCE Christian Ehrhoff 4.00 10.00
AFCN Cam Neely 8.00 20.00
AFCO Bob Cole 4.00 10.00
AFCP Chris Pronger 6.00 15.00
AFDA David Aebischer 6.00 15.00
AFDC Don Cherry 15.00 40.00
AFDL David Legwand 4.00 10.00
AFDM Darren McCarty 8.00 20.00
AFDS Denis Savard 6.00 15.00
AFDU Dustin Brown 5.00 12.00
AFEC Erik Cole 4.00 10.00
AFES Eric Staal 10.00 25.00
AFGF Grant Fuhr 10.00 25.00
AFGL Georges Laraque 4.00 10.00
AFGW Gump Worsley 8.00 20.00
AFHE Milan Hejduk 8.00 20.00
AFHO Marcel Hossa 4.00 10.00
AFHS Marian Hossa 8.00 20.00
AFHZ Henrik Zetterberg 10.00 25.00
AFIK Ilya Kovalchuk 10.00 25.00
AFJB Jay Bouwmeester 4.00 10.00
AFJC Jonathan Cheechoo 10.00 25.00
AFJG Jean-Sebastien Giguere 6.00 15.00
AFJI Jarome Iginla 12.00 30.00
AFJK Jari Kurri 8.00 20.00
AFJL Joffrey Lupul 6.00 15.00
AFJR Jeremy Roenick 8.00 20.00
AFJS Jason Spezza 8.00 20.00
AFJT Joe Thornton 12.00 30.00
AFJW Justin Williams 4.00 10.00
AFKD Kris Draper 4.00 10.00
AFKH Ken Hodge 4.00 10.00
AFKL Kari Lehtonen 8.00 20.00
AFLN Ladislav Nagy 4.00 10.00
AFLR Luc Robitaille 6.00 15.00
AFMA Maxim Afinogenov 6.00 15.00
AFMC Mike Cammalleri 6.00 15.00
AFMF Marc-Andre Fleury 12.00 30.00
AFMG Marian Gaborik 10.00 25.00
AFMH Martin Havlat 8.00 20.00
AFML Manny Legace 6.00 15.00
AFMM Mike Modano 10.00 25.00
AFMN Markus Naslund 6.00 15.00
AFMO Brendan Morrison 4.00 10.00
AFMP Mark Popovic 4.00 10.00
AFMR Mike Ribeiro 4.00 10.00
AFMT Marty Turco 6.00 15.00
AFNA Nikolai Antropov 4.00 10.00
AFNH Nathan Horton 5.00 12.00
AFNO Mika Noronen 4.00 10.00
AFNY Bob Nystrom 4.00 10.00
AFNZ Nikolai Zherdev 4.00 10.00
AFOK Dave Taylor 4.00 10.00
AFPB Patrice Bergeron 8.00 20.00
AFPS Philippe Sauve 4.00 10.00
AFPW Peter Worrell 4.00 10.00
AFRB Rob Blake 4.00 10.00
AFRE Robert Esche 8.00 20.00
AFRF Ruslan Fedotenko 4.00 10.00
AFRH Ron Hextall 15.00 40.00
AFRK Ryan Kesler 12.00 30.00
AFRL Roberto Luongo 8.00 20.00
AFRM Ryan Miller 6.00 15.00
AFRN Rick Nash 10.00 25.00
AFRS Ryan Smyth 6.00 15.00
AFRY Michael Ryder 8.00 20.00
AFRZ Richard Zednik 4.00 10.00
AFSC Dave Schultz 6.00 15.00
AFSG Simon Gagne 8.00 20.00
AFSK Saku Koivu 8.00 20.00
AFSL Martin St. Louis 6.00 15.00
AFSS Steve Sullivan 4.00 10.00
AFST Matt Stajan 6.00 15.00
AFSU Mats Sundin 10.00 25.00
AFSW Stephen Weiss 4.00 10.00
AFTC Ty Conklin 4.00 10.00
AFTH Trent Hunter 4.00 10.00
AFTL Trevor Linden 10.00 25.00
AFTR Tuomo Ruutu 6.00 15.00
AFTS Tony Salmelainen 4.00 10.00
AFVL Vincent Lecavalier 8.00 20.00
AFWC Wayne Cashman 4.00 10.00
AFZC Zdeno Chara 6.00 15.00

2005-06 Artifacts Autofacts Copper

*COPPER/75: .5X TO 1.2X BASIC AUTO
AFDH Dominik Hasek 10.00 25.00
AFGH Gordie Howe 60.00 120.00
AFMB Martin Brodeur 40.00 100.00
AFWG Wayne Gretzky 125.00 300.00

2005-06 Artifacts Autofacts Silver

*SILVER/50: .6X TO 1.5X BASIC AUTO
AFDH Dominik Hasek 12.00 30.00
AFGH Gordie Howe 50.00 100.00
AFMB Martin Brodeur 40.00 100.00
AFWG Wayne Gretzky 200.00 500.00

2005-06 Artifacts Frozen Artifacts

*COPPER/125: .5X TO 1.2X JSY/275
*SILVER/50: .6X TO 1.5X JSY/275
*MAROON/25: .8X TO 2X JSY/275
*DUAL SWATCH/65: .8X TO 2X JSY/275
*DUAL COPPER/50: .8X TO 2X JSY/275
*DUAL MAROON/15: 1.2X TO 3X JSY/275
*DUAL SILVER/25: 1X TO 2.5X JSY/275
*PATCH/50: 1X TO 2.5X JSY/275
*DUAL PATCH/15: 1.5X TO 4X JSY/275
FAAF Alexander Frolov 2.50 6.00
FAAM Al MacInnis 5.00 12.00
FABC Bobby Clarke 6.00 15.00
FABG Bernie Geoffrion 2.50 6.00
FABH Brett Hull 8.00 20.00
FABM Brendan Morrison 2.50 6.00
FABO Jay Bouwmeester 2.50 6.00
FABR Brad Richards 4.00 10.00
FABS Borje Salming 4.00 10.00
FABT Bryan Trottier 4.00 10.00
FACO Chris Osgood 4.00 10.00
FADC Dan Cloutier 3.00 8.00
FADH Dominik Hasek 6.00 15.00
FADR Derek Roy 2.50 6.00
FADS Darryl Sittler 5.00 12.00
FADU Dustin Brown 4.00 10.00
FADW Doug Weight 4.00 10.00
FAEB Ed Belfour 4.00 10.00
FAEL Eric Lindros 6.00 15.00
FAGR Gary Roberts 2.50 6.00
FAGU Bill Guerin 4.00 10.00
FAHO Marcel Hossa 2.50 6.00
FAHZ Henrik Zetterberg 5.00 12.00
FAJB Jean Beliveau 4.00 10.00
FAJK Jari Kurri 4.00 10.00
FAJL Joffrey Lupul 2.50 6.00
FAJO Jose Theodore 4.00 10.00
FAJT Jocelyn Thibault 3.00 8.00
FAJW Justin Williams 3.00 8.00
FAKD Kris Draper 5.00 12.00
FAMG Marian Gaborik 4.00 10.00
FAMH Martin Havlat 4.00 10.00
FAML Mario Lemieux 15.00 40.00
FAMO Alexander Mogilny 3.00 8.00
FAMR Mike Ribeiro 2.50 6.00
FAMT Marty Turco 4.00 10.00
FANH Nathan Horton 4.00 10.00
FAON Owen Nolan 4.00 10.00
FAPK Paul Kariya 4.00 10.00
FARA Bill Ranford 4.00 10.00
FARB Ray Bourque 4.00 10.00
FARD Rick DiPietro 3.00 8.00
FARE Mark Recchi 5.00 12.00
FARH Ron Hextall 4.00 10.00
FARL Roberto Luongo 6.00 15.00
FASA Denis Savard 4.00 10.00
FASL Martin St. Louis 4.00 10.00
FATE Tony Esposito 4.00 10.00
FAWG Wayne Gretzky 25.00 60.00

2005-06 Artifacts Goalie Gear

*DUAL PATCH/15: 1X TO 2.5X JSY/50
FGCO Chris Osgood 6.00 15.00
FGDH Dominik Hasek 10.00 25.00
FGEB Ed Belfour 6.00 15.00
FGGC Gerry Cheevers 6.00 15.00
FGJO Jose Theodore 6.00 15.00
FGJT Jocelyn Thibault 5.00 12.00
FGMT Marty Turco 6.00 15.00
FGRA Bill Ranford 6.00 15.00
FGRD Rick DiPietro 5.00 12.00
FGRL Roberto Luongo 10.00 25.00
FGTE Tony Esposito 6.00 15.00

2005-06 Artifacts Treasured Patches

TPAT Alex Tanguay 6.00 15.00
TPBL Brian Leetch 5.00 12.00
TPBS Brendan Shanahan 6.00 15.00
TPCJ Curtis Joseph 8.00 20.00
TPCP Chris Pronger 6.00 15.00
TPDA Daniel Alfredsson 6.00 15.00
TPDH Dany Heatley 5.00 12.00
TPEB Ed Belfour 6.00 15.00
TPHA Dominik Hasek 10.00 25.00
TPHO Marian Hossa 6.00 15.00
TPIK Ilya Kovalchuk 6.00 15.00
TPJG Jean-Sebastien Giguere 6.00 15.00
TPJI Jarome Iginla 8.00 20.00
TPJJ Jaromir Jagr 20.00 50.00
TPJO Jose Theodore 6.00 15.00
TPJR Jeremy Roenick 10.00 25.00
TPJS Joe Sakic 12.00 30.00
TPJT Joe Thornton 10.00 25.00
TPKP Keith Primeau 5.00 12.00
TPMB Martin Brodeur 15.00 40.00
TPMD Marc Denis 5.00 12.00
TPMG Marian Gaborik 6.00 15.00
TPMH Milan Hejduk 5.00 12.00
TPML Mario Lemieux 25.00 60.00
TPMM Mike Modano 10.00 25.00
TPMN Markus Naslund 6.00 15.00
TPMS Mark Messier 12.00 30.00
TPNK Nikolai Khabibulin 6.00 15.00
TPPD Pavel Datsyuk 10.00 25.00
TPPE Patrik Elias 6.00 15.00
TPPF Peter Forsberg 12.00 30.00
TPRN Rick Nash 6.00 15.00
TPSD Shane Doan 5.00 12.00
TPSF Sergei Fedorov 10.00 25.00
TPSK Saku Koivu 6.00 15.00
TPSL Martin St. Louis 6.00 15.00
TPSP Jason Spezza 6.00 15.00
TPSS Scott Stevens 6.00 15.00
TPSU Mats Sundin 6.00 15.00
TPSY Steve Yzerman 15.00 40.00
TPTB Todd Bertuzzi 6.00 15.00
TPTR Tuomo Ruutu 6.00 15.00
TPTS Teemu Selanne 12.00 30.00
TPWG Wayne Gretzky 40.00 100.00
TPZP Zigmund Palffy 6.00 15.00

2005-06 Artifacts Treasured Swatches

*COPPER/125: .5X TO 1.2X BASIC JSY/275
*SILVER/50: .6X TO 1.5X BASIC JSY/275
*MAROON/25: .8X TO 2X BASIC JSY/275
*DUAL PATCH/15: 1.5X TO 4X BASIC JSY/275
*DUAL SWATCH/65: .8X TO 2X JSY/275
*DUAL COPPER/50: .8X TO 2X JSY/275
*DUAL MAROON/15: 1.2X TO 3X JSY/275
*DUAL SILVER/25: 1X TO 2.5X JSY/275
*PATCH/50: 1X TO 2.5X BASIC JSY/275
TSAT Alex Tanguay 2.50 6.00
TSBL Brian Leetch 2.00 5.00
TSBS Brendan Shanahan 2.50 6.00
TSCJ Curtis Joseph 3.00 8.00
TSCP Chris Pronger 2.50 6.00
TSDA Daniel Alfredsson 2.50 6.00
TSDH Dany Heatley 2.00 5.00
TSEB Ed Belfour 2.50 6.00
TSHA Dominik Hasek 4.00 10.00
TSHO Marian Hossa 2.50 6.00
TSIK Ilya Kovalchuk 2.50 6.00
TSJG Jean-Sebastien Giguere 2.50 6.00
TSJI Jarome Iginla 3.00 8.00
TSJJ Jaromir Jagr 8.00 20.00
TSJO Jose Theodore 2.50 6.00
TSJR Jeremy Roenick 4.00 10.00
TSJS Joe Sakic 5.00 12.00
TSJT Joe Thornton 4.00 10.00
TSKP Keith Primeau 2.00 5.00
TSMB Martin Brodeur 6.00 15.00
TSMD Marc Denis 2.00 5.00
TSMG Marian Gaborik 2.50 6.00
TSMH Milan Hejduk 2.00 5.00
TSML Mario Lemieux 10.00 25.00
TSMM Mike Modano 4.00 10.00
TSMN Markus Naslund 2.50 6.00
TSMP Michael Peca 2.00 5.00
TSMS Mark Messier 5.00 12.00
TSNK Nikolai Khabibulin 2.50 6.00
TSPD Pavel Datsyuk 4.00 10.00
TSPE Patrik Elias 2.50 6.00
TSPF Peter Forsberg 5.00 12.00
TSRN Rick Nash 2.50 6.00
TSRS Ryan Smyth 2.00 5.00
TSSD Shane Doan 2.00 5.00
TSSF Sergei Fedorov 4.00 10.00
TSSK Saku Koivu 2.50 6.00
TSSL Martin St. Louis 2.50 6.00
TSSP Jason Spezza 2.50 6.00
TSSS Scott Stevens 2.50 6.00
TSST Matt Stajan 1.50 4.00
TSSU Mats Sundin 2.50 6.00
TSSY Steve Yzerman 6.00 15.00
TSTB Todd Bertuzzi 2.50 6.00
TSTR Tuomo Ruutu 2.50 6.00
TSTS Teemu Selanne 5.00 12.00
TSVL Vincent Lecavalier 2.50 6.00
TSWG Wayne Gretzky 15.00 40.00
TSZP Zigmund Palffy 2.50 6.00

2006-07 Artifacts

1 Alexander Ovechkin 1.50 4.00
2 Olaf Kolzig .40 1.00
3 Roberto Luongo .60 1.50
4 Markus Naslund .40 1.00
5 Brendan Morrison .20 .50
6 Mats Sundin .40 1.00
7 Darcy Tucker .30 .75
8 Alexander Steen .20 .50
9 Andrew Raycroft .30 .75
10 Michael Peca .30 .75
11 Brad Richards .40 1.00
12 Vincent Lecavalier .40 1.00
13 Martin St. Louis .40 1.00
14 Keith Tkachuk .40 1.00
15 Doug Weight .40 1.00
16 Patrick Marleau .40 1.00
17 Joe Thornton .60 1.50
18 Jonathan Cheechoo .30 .75
19 Vesa Toskala .30 .75
20 Mark Recchi .40 1.00
21 Sidney Crosby 1.50 4.00
22 Marc-Andre Fleury .75 2.00
23 Colby Armstrong .30 .75
24 Shane Doan .30 .75
25 Curtis Joseph .40 1.00
26 Jeremy Roenick .60 1.50
27 Mike Richards .30 .75
28 Peter Forsberg .75 2.00
29 Simon Gagne .40 1.00
30 Jeff Carter .30 .75
31 Jason Spezza .40 1.00
32 Dany Heatley .30 .75
33 Daniel Alfredsson .40 1.00
34 Martin Gerber .30 .75
35 Brendan Shanahan .40 1.00
36 Jaromir Jagr 1.00 3.00
37 Henrik Lundqvist .75 2.00
38 Petr Prucha .30 .75
39 Miroslav Satan .30 .75
40 Rick DiPietro .30 .75
41 Alexei Yashin .30 .75
42 Patrik Elias .40 1.00
43 Martin Brodeur .75 2.00
44 Brian Gionta .20 .50
45 Paul Kariya .40 1.00
46 Tomas Vokoun .30 .75
47 Saku Koivu .40 1.00
48 Cristobal Huet .30 .75
49 Michael Ryder .20 .50
50 Alex Kovalev .30 .75
51 Pavol Demitra .40 1.00
52 Marian Gaborik .40 1.00
53 Manny Fernandez .20 .50
54 Alexander Frolov .20 .50
55 Rob Blake .40 1.00
56 Nathan Horton .40 1.00
57 Olli Jokinen .40 1.00
58 Todd Bertuzzi .40 1.00
59 Ed Belfour .40 1.00
60 Ales Hemsky .30 .75
61 Joffrey Lupul .20 .50
62 Ryan Smyth .30 .75
63 Henrik Zetterberg .40 1.00
64 Pavel Datsyuk .60 1.50
65 Nicklas Lidstrom .40 1.00
66 Dominik Hasek .60 1.50
67 Mike Modano .60 1.50
68 Marty Turco .40 1.00
69 Brenden Morrow .30 .75
70 Eric Lindros .60 1.50
71 Fredrik Modin .20 .50
72 Rick Nash .40 1.00
73 Sergei Fedorov .60 1.50
74 Joe Sakic .75 2.00
75 Milan Hejduk .30 .75
76 Jose Theodore .40 1.00
77 Marek Svatos .20 .50
78 Martin Havlat .20 .50
79 Nikolai Khabibulin .40 1.00
80 Tuomo Ruutu .40 1.00
81 Eric Staal .40 1.00
82 Cam Ward .40 1.00
83 Rod Brind'Amour .40 1.00
84 Jarome Iginla .40 1.00
85 Miikka Kiprusoff .40 1.00
86 Dion Phaneuf .30 .75
87 Alex Tanguay .20 .50
88 Ryan Miller .40 1.00
89 Chris Drury .30 .75
90 Daniel Briere .40 1.00
91 Brad Boyes .20 .50
92 Patrice Bergeron .40 1.00
93 Zdeno Chara .40 1.00
94 Marc Savard .20 .50
95 Ilya Kovalchuk .40 1.00
96 Marian Hossa .40 1.00
97 Kari Lehtonen .30 .75
98 Teemu Selanne .75 2.00
99 Jean-Sebastien Giguere .40 1.00
100 Chris Pronger .40 1.00
101 Glenn Anderson .75 2.00
102 Jean Beliveau 1.00 2.50
103 Bob Bourne .60 1.50
104 Mike Bossy 1.00 2.50
105 Richard Brodeur .75 2.00
106 Johnny Bucyk 1.00 2.50
107 Gerry Cheevers 1.00 2.50
108 Don Cherry 1.50 4.00
109 Wendel Clark 1.50 4.00
110 Bobby Clarke 1.50 4.00
111 Phil Esposito 1.50 4.00
112 Tony Esposito 1.00 2.50
113 Grant Fuhr 1.50 4.00
114 Doug Gilmour 1.25 3.00
115 Peter Stastny .75 2.00
116 Glenn Hall 1.00 2.50
117 Ron Hextall 1.00 2.50
118 Guy Lafleur 1.25 3.00
119 Guy Lapointe .75 2.00
120 Reggie Leach .60 1.50
121 Ted Lindsay 1.00 2.50
122 Lanny McDonald 1.00 2.50
123 Joe Mullen .75 2.00
124 Kirk Muller .60 1.50
125 Cam Neely 1.00 2.50
126 Bob Nystrom .60 1.50
127 Terry O'Reilly .60 1.50
128 Bernie Parent 1.25 3.00
129 Gilbert Perreault 1.00 2.50
130 Denis Potvin 1.00 2.50
131 Bill Ranford 1.00 2.50
132 Derek Sanderson 1.00 2.50
133 Denis Savard 1.00 2.50
134 Steve Shutt 1.00 2.50
135 Darryl Sittler 1.25 3.00
136 Billy Smith 1.00 2.50
137 Thomas Steen .60 1.50
138 Rick Vaive 1.00 2.50
139 Ron Ellis .60 1.50
140 Doug Wilson .75 2.00
141 Wayne Gretzky 6.00 15.00
142 Patrick Roy 2.50 6.00
143 Gordie Howe 3.00 8.00
144 Ray Bourque 1.50 4.00
145 Al MacInnis 1.25 3.00
146 Mike Krushelnyski .60 1.50
147 Mario Lemieux 4.00 10.00
148 Bob Probert 1.00 2.50
149 Tiger Williams .60 1.50
150 Clark Gillies 1.00 2.50
151 Teemu Selanne 2.00 5.00
152 Ilya Kovalchuk 1.00 2.50
153 Marian Hossa 1.00 2.50
154 Patrice Bergeron 1.25 3.00
155 Cristobal Huet .75 2.00
156 Ryan Miller 1.00 2.50
157 Miikka Kiprusoff 1.00 2.50
158 Jarome Iginla 1.25 3.00

159 Eric Staal 1.25 3.00
160 Nikolai Khabibulin 1.00 2.50
161 Joe Sakic 2.00 5.00
162 Alex Tanguay .60 1.50
163 Rick Nash 1.00 2.50
164 Mike Modano 1.50 4.00
165 Marty Turco 1.00 2.50
166 Henrik Zetterberg 1.25 3.00
167 Pavel Datsyuk 1.50 4.00
168 Brendan Shanahan 1.00 2.50
169 Ales Hemsky .75 2.00
170 Chris Pronger 1.00 2.50
171 Roberto Luongo 1.50 4.00
172 Olli Jokinen 1.00 2.50
173 Alexander Frolov .60 1.50
174 Marian Gaborik 1.00 2.50
175 Saku Koivu 1.00 2.50
176 Michael Ryder .60 1.50
177 Paul Kariya 1.00 2.50
178 Tomas Vokoun .75 2.00
179 Martin Brodeur 2.50 6.00
180 Patrik Elias 1.00 2.50
181 Brian Gionta .60 1.50
182 Miroslav Satan .75 2.00
183 Jaromir Jagr 3.00 8.00
184 Henrik Lundqvist 2.50 6.00
185 Dany Heatley .75 2.00
186 Ed Belfour 1.00 2.50
187 Jason Spezza 1.00 2.50
188 Peter Forsberg 2.00 5.00
189 Simon Gagne 1.00 2.50
190 Shane Doan .75 2.00
191 Sidney Crosby 4.00 10.00
192 Marc-Andre Fleury 2.00 5.00
193 Joe Thornton 1.50 4.00
194 Patrick Marleau 1.00 2.50
195 Jonathan Cheechoo .75 2.00
196 Martin St. Louis 1.00 2.50
197 Vincent Lecavalier 1.00 2.50
198 Brad Richards 1.00 2.50
199 Mats Sundin 1.00 2.50
200 Markus Naslund 1.00 2.50
201 Dustin Byfuglien RC 5.00 12.00
202 Yan Stastny RC 2.00 5.00
203 Mark Stuart RC 2.00 5.00
204 Eric Fehr RC 3.00 8.00
205 Bill Thomas RC 2.00 5.00
206 Joel Perrault RC 2.00 5.00
207 Carsen Germyn RC 2.00 5.00
208 Ryan Potulny RC 2.00 5.00
209 David Printz RC 2.00 5.00
210 Rob Collins RC 2.00 5.00
211 Steve Regier RC 2.00 5.00
212 Matt Koalska RC 2.00 5.00
213 Masi Marjamaki RC 2.00 5.00
214 Konstantin Pushkarev RC 2.50 6.00
215 Ben Ondrus RC 2.00 5.00
216 Brendan Bell RC 2.00 5.00
217 Ian White RC 2.50 6.00
218 Jeremy Williams RC 2.00 5.00
219 Marc-Antoine Pouliot RC 2.00 5.00
220 Noah Welch RC 2.00 5.00
221 Michel Ouellet RC 2.50 6.00
222 Shea Weber RC 5.00 12.00
223 Jarkko Immonen RC 2.50 6.00
224 David Liffiton RC 2.00 5.00
225 Tomas Kopecky RC 2.50 6.00
226 Billy Thompson RC 2.00 5.00
227 Filip Novak RC 2.00 5.00
228 Matt Carle RC 2.00 5.00
229 Erik Reitz RC 2.00 5.00
230 Miroslav Kopriva RC 2.00 5.00
231 Ryan Shannon RC 2.50 6.00
232 Benoit Pouliot RC 3.00 8.00
233 Phil Kessel RC 8.00 20.00
234 Drew Stafford RC 4.00 10.00
235 Dustin Boyd RC 2.50 6.00
236 Josh Hennessey RC 2.50 6.00
237 Dave Bolland RC 4.00 10.00
238 Paul Stastny RC 6.00 15.00
239 Fredrik Norrena RC 2.50 6.00
240 Loui Eriksson RC 5.00 12.00
241 Derek Meech RC 2.50 6.00
242 Ladislav Smid RC 2.50 6.00
243 Janis Sprukts RC 2.50 6.00
244 Anze Kopitar RC 12.00 30.00
245 Niklas Backstrom RC 5.00 12.00
246 G. Latendresse RC 4.00 10.00
247 Alexander Radulov RC 5.00 12.00
248 Travis Zajac RC 5.00 12.00
249 Blake Comeau RC 4.00 10.00
250 Nigel Dawes RC 2.50 6.00
251 Alexei Kaigorodov RC 2.50 6.00
252 Martin Houle RC 3.00 8.00
253 Enver Lisin RC 2.50 6.00
254 Evgeni Malkin RC 15.00 40.00
255 M-E Vlasic RC 4.00 10.00
256 Marek Schwarz RC 4.00 10.00
257 Karri Ramo RC 2.50 6.00
258 Kris Newbury RC 2.50 6.00
259 Luc Bourdon RC 4.00 10.00
260 Darren Machesney RC 2.50 6.00
261 Jordan Staal RC 6.00 15.00
262 Patrick O'Sullivan RC 4.00 10.00
263 Patrik Thoresen RC 2.50 6.00
264 Mikhail Grabovski RC 5.00 12.00
265 Jesse Schultz RC 2.50 6.00
266 Michael Blunden RC 2.50 6.00
267 David Booth RC 3.00 8.00
268 Brandon Prust RC 2.50 6.00
269 Matt Lashoff RC 2.50 6.00
270 Niklas Grossman RC 4.00 10.00
271 Joe Pavelski RC 12.00 30.00
272 Clarke MacArthur RC 3.00 8.00

2006-07 Artifacts Gold

*1-100 VETS/50: 3X TO 8X BASIC CARDS
*101-200 L/S/50: 1X TO 2.5X L/S/999
*201-230 ROOKIES/50: .6X TO 1.5X RC/999

2006-07 Artifacts Bronze

*1-100 VETS/25: 4X TO 10X BASIC CARDS
*101-200 L/S/25: 1.2X TO 3X L/S/999
*201-230 ROOKIES/25: 1.2X TO 3X RC/999

2006-07 Artifacts Silver

*1-100 VETS/100: 2X TO 5X BASIC CARDS
*101-200 L/S/100: .6X TO 1.5X L/S/999
*201-230 ROOKIES/100: .5X TO 1.2X RC/999

2006-07 Artifacts Autofacts

AFAA Adrian Aucoin 3.00 8.00
AFAH Ales Hemsky 6.00 15.00
AFAK Andrei Kostitsyn 8.00 20.00
AFAO Alexander Ovechkin SP 200.00 500.00
AFAP Alexandre Picard 3.00 8.00
AFBB Bob Bourne 3.00 8.00
AFBC Bobby Clarke 10.00 25.00
AFBE Jean Beliveau SP 50.00 100.00
AFBI Martin Biron 3.00 8.00
AFBL Brett Lebda 3.00 8.00
AFBN Bob Nystrom 5.00 12.00
AFBO Jay Bouwmeester 10.00 25.00
AFBP Bob Probert 15.00 40.00
AFBR Brad Boyes 3.00 8.00
AFBS Billy Smith UER
(Chico Resch pictured) 8.00 20.00
AFBU Johnny Bucyk SP 6.00 15.00
AFBW Ben Walter 3.00 8.00
AFBY Mike Bossy 6.00 15.00
AFCA Jeff Carter 6.00 15.00
AFCD Chris Drury 5.00 12.00
AFCG Clark Gillies 5.00 12.00
AFCK Chuck Kobasew 3.00 8.00
AFCN Cam Neely 10.00 25.00
AFCP Corey Perry 6.00 15.00
AFDA David Aebischer 5.00 12.00
AFDB Doug Bodger 3.00 8.00
AFDE Derek Boogaard 20.00 40.00
AFDP Dion Phaneuf 12.00 30.00
AFDR Dwayne Roloson 5.00 12.00
AFDS Denis Savard 5.00 12.00
AFDW Doug Wilson 3.00 8.00
AFFP Fernando Pisani 3.00 8.00
AFGA Glenn Anderson SP 6.00 15.00
AFGF Grant Fuhr SP 15.00 40.00
AFGL Guy Lafleur SP 20.00 50.00
AFHO Gordie Howe 40.00 80.00
AFHR Ryan Hollweg 3.00 8.00
AFHZ Henrik Zetterberg SP 15.00 40.00
AFIK Ilya Kovalchuk SP 15.00 40.00
AFJB Jaroslav Balastik 3.00 8.00
AFJC Jonathan Cheechoo 8.00 20.00
AFJH Jeff Halpern 3.00 8.00
AFJI Jarome Iginla SP 15.00 40.00
AFJL Joffrey Lupul SP 8.00 20.00
AFJM Joe Mullen 4.00 10.00
AFJT Jose Theodore SP 12.00 30.00
AFKD Kris Draper 3.00 8.00
AFKM Kirk Muller 5.00 12.00
AFLE Reggie Leach 8.00 20.00
AFLN Ladislav Nagy 3.00 8.00
AFLS Lee Stempniak 3.00 8.00
AFMA Marian Gaborik SP 15.00 40.00
AFMB Martin Brodeur SP 50.00 125.00
AFMC Mike Cammalleri 4.00 10.00
AFMG Martin Gerber 5.00 12.00
AFMI Mike Richards 8.00 20.00
AFMK Miikka Kiprusoff SP 15.00 40.00
AFML Mario Lemieux SP 150.00 300.00
AFMR Michael Ryder 5.00 12.00
AFMS Marek Svatos 5.00 12.00
AFMT Mikael Tellqvist 5.00 12.00
AFNH Nathan Horton 5.00 12.00
AFOJ Olli Jokinen 4.00 10.00
AFPB Pierre-Marc Bouchard SP 25.00 50.00
AFPE Phil Esposito SP 40.00 100.00
AFPM Patrick Marleau 8.00 20.00
AFRA Ray Bourque SP 25.00 60.00
AFRB Rob Blake SP 12.00 30.00
AFRE Ron Ellis 5.00 12.00
AFRF Ruslan Fedotenko 3.00 8.00
AFRG Ryan Getzlaf 6.00 15.00
AFRH Ron Hextall SP 20.00 50.00
AFRI Richard Brodeur 5.00 12.00
AFRK Rostislav Klesla 3.00 8.00
AFRL Rod Langway 4.00 10.00
AFRM Ryan Malone SP 12.00 30.00
AFRO Mike Ribeiro 4.00 10.00
AFRS Ryan Smyth EXCH 12.00 30.00
AFRY Ryan Miller 15.00 30.00
AFSC Sidney Crosby 90.00 200.00
AFSG Scott Gomez 4.00 10.00
AFSH Scott Hartnell 5.00 12.00
AFSS Steve Shutt 4.00 10.00
AFSW Stephen Weiss 3.00 8.00
AFTE Tony Esposito SP 20.00 50.00
AFTH Joe Thornton SP 10.00 25.00
AFTL Ted Lindsay 8.00 20.00
AFTS Thomas Steen 3.00 8.00
AFTV Thomas Vanek 10.00 25.00
AFVO Tomas Vokoun 5.00 12.00
AFWC Wendel Clark 20.00 50.00
AFWG Wayne Gretzky SP 150.00 400.00
AFWI Tiger Williams 5.00 12.00
AFWR Wade Redden SP 15.00 40.00
AFZC Zdeno Chara 8.00 20.00

2006-07 Artifacts Frozen Artifacts

*BLUE/50 .6X TO 1.5X BASIC JSY
*GOLD/25 .8X TO 2X BASIC JSY
*RED/100 .5X TO 1.2X BASIC JSY
*PATCH BLUE/25: 1.2X TO 3X BASIC JSY
*PATCH RED/35: 1.2X TO 3X BASIC JSY
FAAO Adam Oates 3.00 8.00
FAAT Alex Tanguay 2.00 5.00
FABG Brian Gionta 2.00 5.00
FABM Brenden Morrow 2.50 6.00
FABP Brad Park 2.50 6.00
FABR Bill Ranford 3.00 8.00
FABS Brad Stuart 2.00 5.00
FACC Chris Chelios 3.00 8.00
FACD Chris Drury 2.50 6.00
FACK Chuck Kobasew 2.00 5.00
FACP Chris Pronger 3.00 8.00
FACW Cam Ward 3.00 8.00
FADA Daniel Alfredsson 3.00 8.00
FADS Darryl Sittler 4.00 10.00
FAES Eric Staal 4.00 10.00
FAGA Glenn Anderson 2.50 6.00
FAHZ Henrik Zetterberg 4.00 10.00
FAJB Jay Bouwmeester 2.00 5.00
FAJC Jeff Carter 2.50 6.00
FAJI Jarome Iginla 4.00 10.00
FAJL Joffrey Lupul 2.00 5.00
FAJO Jonathan Cheechoo 2.50 6.00
FAJS Joe Sakic 6.00 15.00
FALM Lanny McDonald 3.00 8.00
FAMC Bryan McCabe 2.00 5.00
FAMH Milan Hejduk 2.50 6.00
FAMK Miikka Kiprusoff 3.00 8.00
FAMM Mike Modano 5.00 12.00
FAMO Brendan Morrison 2.00 5.00
FAMR Mark Recchi 4.00 10.00
FANL Nicklas Lidstrom 3.00 8.00
FAPB Patrice Bergeron 4.00 10.00
FAPD Pavol Demitra 4.00 10.00
FAPE Patrik Elias 3.00 8.00
FAPM Patrick Marleau 3.00 8.00
FAPR Patrick Roy 8.00 20.00
FAPS Peter Stastny 2.50 6.00
FARB Rod Brind'Amour 3.00 8.00
FARL Roberto Luongo 5.00 12.00
FARM Ryan Miller 3.00 8.00
FARS Ryan Smyth 2.50 6.00
FASG Simon Gagne 3.00 8.00
FASK Saku Koivu 3.00 8.00
FASP Jason Spezza 3.00 8.00
FASS Steve Shutt 3.00 8.00
FASU Steve Sullivan 2.00 5.00
FASW Stephen Weiss 2.00 5.00
FATS Teemu Selanne 6.00 15.00
FATV Tomas Vokoun 2.50 6.00
FAWC Wendel Clark 5.00 12.00

2006-07 Artifacts Treasured Swatches

*GOLD/25: 1X TO 2.5X BASIC JSY
*RED/100: .5X TO 1.2X BASIC JSY
*SILVER/50: .6X TO 1.5X BASIC JSY
*PATCH BLUE/25: 1.2X TO 3X BASIC JSY
*PATCH RED/35: 1.2X TO 3X BASIC JSY
TSAF Alexander Frolov 2.00 5.00
TSAH Ales Hemsky 2.50 6.00
TSAK Alex Kovalev 2.50 6.00
TSAM Al MacInnis 4.00 10.00
TSAO Alexander Ovechkin 8.00 20.00
TSAR Jason Arnott 2.50 6.00
TSBB Bob Bourne 2.00 5.00
TSBC Bobby Clarke 5.00 12.00
TSBG Bill Guerin 3.00 8.00
TSBL Rob Blake 3.00 8.00
TSBN Bob Nystrom 2.00 5.00
TSBP Bob Probert 5.00 12.00
TSBS Borje Salming 3.00 8.00
TSCJ Curtis Joseph 4.00 10.00
TSCN Cam Neely 3.00 8.00
TSDG Doug Gilmour 4.00 10.00
TSDW Tiger Williams 2.00 5.00
TSEB Ed Belfour 3.00 8.00
TSEL Eric Lindros 5.00 12.00
TSGF Grant Fuhr 5.00 12.00
TSIK Ilya Kovalchuk 3.00 8.00
TSJA Jason Allison 2.50 6.00
TSJG Jean-Sebastien Giguere 3.00 8.00
TSJJ Jaromir Jagr 10.00 25.00
TSJN Joe Nieuwendyk 2.50 6.00
TSJT Joe Thornton 5.00 12.00
TSKP Keith Primeau 2.50 6.00
TSKT Keith Tkachuk 3.00 8.00
TSMB Martin Brodeur 8.00 20.00
TSMF Manny Fernandez 2.00 5.00
TSMH Marian Hossa 3.00 8.00
TSML Mario Lemieux 12.00 30.00
TSMM Mike Modano 4.00 10.00
TSMN Markus Naslund 3.00 8.00
TSMR Mark Recchi 4.00 10.00
TSMT Marty Turco 3.00 8.00
TSNK Nikolai Khabibulin 3.00 8.00
TSOK Olaf Kolzig 3.00 8.00
TSPF Peter Forsberg 6.00 15.00
TSPK Paul Kariya 3.00 8.00
TSRB Ray Bourque 5.00 12.00
TSRN Rick Nash 3.00 8.00
TSRV Rick Vaive 3.00 8.00
TSRY Michael Ryder 2.00 5.00
TSSC Sidney Crosby 12.00 30.00
TSSF Sergei Fedorov 5.00 12.00
TSSG Scott Gomez 2.50 6.00
TSSK Saku Koivu 3.00 8.00
TSSN Scott Niedermayer 3.00 8.00
TSWE Doug Weight 3.00 8.00

2006-07 Artifacts Tundra Tandems

*BLUE/25: .6X TO 1.5X BASIC TANDEM/125
*BLUE/25: .5X TO 1.2X BASIC TANDEM/50
*PATCH RED/25: 1X TO 2.5X TANDEM/125
*PATCH RED/25: .8X TO 2X TANDEM/50
*RED/50: .5X TO 1.2X BASIC TANDEM/125
*RED/50: .4X TO 1X BASIC TANDEM/50
TTAB A.Raycroft/B.McCabe 3.00 8.00
TTAD M.Afinogenov/C.Drury 3.00 8.00
TTAG Anderson/Gretzky/50 25.00 60.00
TTAK G.Anderson/M.Krushelnyski 3.00 8.00
TTAM M.Stajan/A.Steen 2.50 6.00
TTAS S.Samsonov/A.Kovalev 3.00 8.00
TTBB Boyes/Bergeron 5.00 12.00
TTBE M.Brodeur/P.Elias 10.00 25.00
TTBJ Shanahan/Jagr 12.00 30.00
TTBN B.Nystrom/B.Bourne 2.50 6.00
TTBO Bucyk/Bourque 6.00 15.00
TTBR B.Rolston/P.Bouchard 4.00 10.00
TTCA C.Neely/A.Oates 4.00 10.00
TTCE C.Joseph/E.Jovo 5.00 12.00
TTCG W.Clark/D.Gilmour 6.00 15.00
TTCL D.Ciccarelli/R.Langway 4.00 10.00
TTCN M.Comrie/L.Nagy 3.00 8.00
TTCR C.Neely/R.Bourque 6.00 15.00
TTDB D.Sittler/B.Salming 6.00 15.00
TTDD Alfredsson/Heatley 4.00 10.00
TTDH T.Holmstrom/P.Datsyuk 6.00 15.00
TTDO T.Daley/S.Ott 2.50 6.00
TTDR R.Brodeur/T.Williams 3.00 8.00
TTDW K.Draper/J.Williams 2.50 6.00
TTEJ E.Belfour/J.Bouwmeester 4.00 10.00
TTFB R.Blake/A.Frolov 4.00 10.00
TTFG P.Forsberg/S.Gagne 8.00 20.00
TTFP M.Fernandez/M.Parrish 2.50 6.00
TTFR G.Fuhr/B.Ranford 6.00 15.00
TTGC S.Gagne/J.Carter 4.00 10.00
TTGD M.Gaborik/P.Demitra 5.00 12.00
TTGG S.Gomez/B.Gionta 3.00 8.00
TTGP G.Lafleur/P.Stastny 5.00 12.00
TTHD H.Sedin/D.Sedin 5.00 12.00
TTHK Hossa/Kovalchuk 4.00 10.00
TTHO D.Hasek/C.Osgood 6.00 15.00
TTHP M.Hossa/P.Prucha 3.00 8.00
TTHS M.Hejduk/M.Svatos 3.00 8.00
TTHU S.Harnell/S.Upshall 2.50 6.00
TTIT J.Iginla/A.Tanguay 5.00 12.00
TTJA J.Mullen/A.MacInnis 5.00 12.00
TTJH J.Spezza/D.Heatley 4.00 10.00
TTJJ J.Lupul/J.Stoll 3.00 8.00
TTKA P.Kariya/J.Arnott 4.00 10.00
TTKH N.Khabibulin/M.Havlat 4.00 10.00
TTKK S.Koivu/A.Kovalev 4.00 10.00
TTKL I.Kovalchuk/K.Lehtonen 4.00 10.00
TTKO O.Kolzig/A.Ovechkin 15.00 40.00
TTKP Kiprusoff/Phaneuf 6.00 15.00
TTLB Lafleur/Beliveau 15.00 40.00
TTLC M.Lemieux/S.Crosby 40.00 80.00
TTLM J.LeClair/M.Recchi 5.00 12.00
TTLN M.Naslund/R.Luongo 6.00 15.00
TTLR V.Lecavalier/B.Richards 4.00 10.00
TTLS G.Lafleur/S.Shutt 5.00 12.00
TTLZ L.Robitaille/Z.Palffy 4.00 10.00
TTMB R.Miller/M.Biron 4.00 10.00
TTMC L.Murphy/C.Chelios 4.00 10.00
TTME L.McDonald/R.Ellis 4.00 10.00
TTML M.Modano/E.Lindros 6.00 15.00
TTMM L.McDonald/A.MacInnis 5.00 12.00
TTMR M.Satan/R.DiPietro 3.00 8.00
TTMS G.Murray/M.Savard 3.00 8.00
TTMT B.McCabe/D.Tucker 3.00 8.00
TTNF R.Nash/S.Federov 6.00 15.00
TTNG S.Niedermayer/J.Giguere 4.00 10.00
TTNH N.Lidstrom/H.Zetter 5.00 12.00
TTNO M.Naslund/M.Ohlund 4.00 10.00
TTNP C.Pronger/S.Niedermayer 4.00 10.00
TTNR J.Nieuwendyk/G.Roberts 3.00 8.00
TTNY M.York/T.Hunter 2.50 6.00
TTOT O.Jokinen/T.Bertuzzi 4.00 10.00
TTPJ P.Roy/J.Sakic 10.00 25.00
TTPK P.Roy/K.Muller 10.00 25.00
TTPM P.Marleau/M.Bell 4.00 10.00
TTPT P.Leclaire/T.Conklin 3.00 8.00
TTRB P.Roy/R.Bourque 10.00 25.00
TTRD S.Doan/J.Roenick 6.00 15.00
TTRK T.Ruutu/N.Khabibulin 4.00 10.00
TTRM M.Recchi/R.Malone 5.00 12.00
TTRR M.Ribeiro/M.Ryder 2.50 6.00
TTRS R.Smyth/S.Horcoff 3.00 8.00
TTSF M.St.Louis/R.Fedotenko 4.00 10.00
TTSJ S.Kapanen/J.Pitkanen 2.50 6.00
TTSM M.Denis/S.Burke 3.00 8.00
TTSP T.Selanne/C.Perry 8.00 20.00
TTST Sakic/Theodore 8.00 20.00
TTSV D.Sittler/R.Vaive 5.00 12.00
TTSW E.Staal/C.Ward 5.00 12.00
TTTC J.Thornton/J.Cheechoo 6.00 15.00
TTTG K.Tkachuk/B.Guerin 4.00 10.00
TTTM M.Turco/B.Morrow 4.00 10.00
TTTO M.Sundin/M.Peca 4.00 10.00
TTTW D.Weight/K.Tkachuk 4.00 10.00
TTVE T.Vokoun/M.Erat 3.00 8.00
TTWA W.Redden/A.Meszaros 2.50 6.00
TTWB J.Williams/R.Brind'Amour 4.00 10.00
TTWG D.Weight/B.Guerin 4.00 10.00
TTWS D.Savard/D.Wilson 4.00 10.00
TTZM Z.Chara/M.Jurcina 4.00 10.00

2007-08 Artifacts

COMP.SET w/o SPs (100) 12.00 30.00
1 Ryan Miller .40 1.00
2 Thomas Vanek .30 .75
3 Chris Drury .30 .75
4 Daniel Briere .40 1.00
5 Zach Parise .40 1.00
6 Patrik Elias .40 1.00
7 Martin Brodeur 1.00 2.50
8 Marian Hossa .40 1.00
9 Ilya Kovalchuk .40 1.00
10 Kari Lehtonen .30 .75
11 Dany Heatley .30 .75
12 Ray Emery .30 .75
13 Jason Spezza .40 1.00
14 Daniel Alfredsson .40 1.00
15 Sidney Crosby 1.50 4.00
16 Evgeni Malkin .75 2.00
17 Marc-Andre Fleury .75 2.00
18 Jordan Staal .30 .75
19 Jaromir Jagr 1.25 3.00
20 Henrik Lundqvist 1.00 2.50
21 Martin Straka .25 .60
22 Vincent Lecavalier .40 1.00
23 Brad Richards .40 1.00
24 Martin St. Louis .40 1.00
25 Alexei Yashin .30 .75
26 Rick DiPietro .30 .75
27 Miroslav Satan .30 .75
28 Mats Sundin .40 1.00
29 Andrew Raycroft .30 .75
30 Darcy Tucker .30 .75
31 Alexander Steen .25 .60
32 Saku Koivu .40 1.00
33 Guillaume Latendresse .30 .75
34 Cristobal Huet .30 .75
35 Michael Ryder .25 .60
36 Eric Staal .50 1.25
37 Cam Ward .40 1.00
38 Ray Whitney .30 .75
39 Nathan Horton .40 1.00
40 Olli Jokinen .30 .75
41 Tomas Vokoun .30 .75
42 Patrice Bergeron .50 1.25
43 Marc Savard .25 .60
44 Tim Thomas .40 1.00
45 Alexander Ovechkin 1.50 4.00
46 Olaf Kolzig .40 1.00
47 Alexander Semin .40 1.00
48 Simon Gagne .40 1.00
49 Martin Biron .30 .75
50 Jeff Carter .30 .75
51 Henrik Zetterberg .50 1.25
52 Pavel Datsyuk .60 1.50
53 Nicklas Lidstrom .40 1.00
54 Tomas Holmstrom .30 .75
55 Jean-Sebastien Giguere .40 1.00
56 Chris Pronger .40 1.00
57 Ryan Getzlaf .40 1.00
58 Teemu Selanne .75 2.00
59 Markus Naslund .40 1.00
60 Roberto Luongo .60 1.50
61 Henrik Sedin .50 1.25
62 Daniel Sedin .50 1.25
63 Chris Mason .30 .75
64 Alexander Radulov .40 1.00
65 Paul Kariya .40 1.00
66 Peter Forsberg .75 2.00
67 Jonathan Cheechoo .30 .75
68 Joe Thornton .60 1.50
69 Evgeni Nabokov .30 .75
70 Mike Modano .60 1.50
71 Marty Turco .40 1.00
72 Mike Ribeiro .25 .60
73 Marian Gaborik .40 1.00
74 Pavol Demitra .50 1.25
75 Pierre-Marc Bouchard .40 1.00
76 Jarome Iginla .50 1.25
77 Dion Phaneuf .30 .75
78 Miikka Kiprusoff .40 1.00
79 Alex Tanguay .30 .75
80 Joe Sakic .75 2.00
81 Milan Hejduk .30 .75
82 Paul Stastny .30 .75
83 Brad Boyes .25 .60
84 Manny Legace .30 .75
85 Doug Weight .40 1.00
86 Rick Nash .40 1.00
87 Pascal Leclaire .30 .75
88 Sergei Fedorov .60 1.50
89 Ales Hemsky .30 .75
90 Dwayne Roloson .30 .75
91 Shawn Horcoff .25 .60
92 Martin Havlat .40 1.00
93 Nikolai Khabibulin .40 1.00
94 Tuomo Ruutu .40 1.00
95 Anze Kopitar .60 1.50
96 Alexander Frolov .25 .60
97 Mike Cammalleri .30 .75
98 Shane Doan .30 .75
99 Mikael Tellqvist .30 .75
100 Zbynek Michalek .25 .60
101 Wayne Gretzky L 8.00 20.00
102 Mario Lemieux L 5.00 12.00
103 Gordie Howe L 4.00 10.00
104 Bobby Orr L 5.00 12.00
105 Mark Messier L 2.50 6.00
106 Patrick Roy L 3.00 8.00
107 Ray Bourque L 2.00 5.00
108 Gilbert Perreault L 1.25 3.00
109 Bobby Clarke L 2.00 5.00
110 Guy Lafleur L 1.50 4.00
111 Don Cherry L 1.50 4.00
112 Ron Hextall L 1.25 3.00
113 Grant Fuhr L 2.00 5.00
114 Larry Robinson L 1.25 3.00
115 Cam Neely L 1.25 3.00
116 Bernie Parent L 1.50 4.00
117 Frank Mahovlich L 1.25 3.00
118 Tony Esposito L 1.25 3.00
119 Phil Esposito L 2.00 5.00
120 Stan Mikita L 1.50 4.00
121A Sidney Crosby S 5.00 12.00
121B Joe Sakic S 2.50 6.00
123 Martin Brodeur S 3.00 8.00
124 Dany Heatley S 1.00 2.50
125 Joe Thornton S 2.00 5.00
126 Henrik Zetterberg S 1.50 4.00
127 Jaromir Jagr S 4.00 10.00
128 Simon Gagne S 1.25 3.00
129 Jarome Iginla S 1.50 4.00
130 Roberto Luongo S 2.00 5.00
131 Alexander Ovechkin S 5.00 12.00
132 Ilya Kovalchuk S 1.25 3.00
133 Mats Sundin S 1.25 3.00
134 Rick Nash S 1.25 3.00
135 Patrice Bergeron S 1.50 4.00
136 Saku Koivu S 1.25 3.00
137 Henrik Lundqvist S 3.00 8.00
138 Evgeni Malkin S 2.50 6.00
139 Vincent Lecavalier S 1.25 3.00
140 Ryan Miller S 1.25 3.00
141 Jeff Finger RC 2.00 5.00
142 Colin Fraser RC 2.00 5.00
143 Pierre Parenteau RC 2.50 6.00
144 David Koci RC 2.00 5.00
145 Bryan Bickell RC 4.00 10.00
146 Jonas Nordqvist RC 2.00 5.00
147 Tomas Popperle RC 2.00 5.00
148 Curtis Glencross RC 3.00 8.00
149 Marc Methot RC 2.00 5.00
150 David Krejci RC 8.00 20.00
151 Jonathan Sigalet RC 2.00 5.00
152 Petr Kalus RC 2.00 5.00
153 Jaroslav Halak RC 6.00 15.00
154 Duncan Milroy RC 2.00 5.00
155 Jannik Hansen RC 2.50 6.00
156 Jeff Schultz RC 2.50 6.00
157 Jamie Hunt RC 2.00 5.00
158 Daniel Carcillo RC 2.50 6.00
159 Andy Greene RC 2.50 6.00
160 Mark Fraser RC 2.00 5.00
161 Rod Pelley RC 2.00 5.00
162 David Clarkson RC 2.00 5.00
163 Aaron Rome RC 2.50 6.00
164 Kent Huskins RC 2.00 5.00
165 Bjorn Melin RC 2.00 5.00
166 Drew Miller RC 2.50 6.00
167 David Moss RC 3.00 8.00
168 Tomi Maki RC 2.00 5.00
169 Scott Munroe RC 2.00 5.00
170 Nathan Guenin RC 2.50 6.00
171 Ryan Parent RC 2.00 5.00
172 Frans Nielsen RC 3.00 8.00
173 Lauri Tukonen RC 2.00 5.00
174 Yutaka Fukufuji RC 2.50 6.00
175 John Zeiler RC 2.00 5.00
176 Gabe Gauthier RC 2.00 5.00
177 Shay Stephenson RC 2.00 5.00
178 Joe Piskula RC 2.00 5.00
179 Jack Johnson RC 2.50 6.00
180 Tom Gilbert RC 2.50 6.00
181 Mathieu Roy RC 2.00 5.00
182 Zack Stortini RC 2.00 5.00
183 Bryan Young RC 2.00 5.00
184 Sebastien Bisaillon RC 2.00 5.00
185 Rob Schremp RC 2.50 6.00
186 Martin Lojek RC 2.00 5.00
187 Rich Peverley RC 2.00 5.00
188 Ryan Callahan RC 4.00 10.00
189 Daniel Girardi RC 2.50 6.00
190 Brandon Dubinsky RC 4.00 10.00
191 Matt Ellis RC 2.50 6.00
192 Patrick Kaleta RC 2.00 5.00
193 Mark Mancari RC 2.00 5.00
194 Danny Bois RC 2.00 5.00
195 Thomas Plihal RC 2.00 5.00
196 Tobias Stephan RC 2.50 6.00
197 Joel Lundqvist RC 2.00 5.00
198 Chris Conner RC 2.00 5.00
199 Krys Barch RC 2.50 6.00
200 Joel Ward RC 3.00 8.00
201 T.J. Hensick RC 4.00 10.00
202 Jonathan Toews RC 25.00 50.00
203 Kris Russell RC 5.00 12.00
204 Tuukka Rask RC 12.00 30.00
205 Carey Price RC 25.00 50.00
206 Mason Raymond RC 5.00 12.00
207 Nicklas Backstrom RC 10.00 25.00
208 Peter Mueller RC 4.00 10.00
209 Nicklas Bergfors RC 3.00 8.00
210 Bobby Ryan RC 8.00 20.00
211 Curtis McElhinney RC 5.00 12.00
212 Steve Downie RC 4.00 10.00
213 Casey Borer RC 3.00 8.00
214 Martin Hanzal RC 4.00 10.00
215 Jonathan Bernier RC 6.00 15.00
216 Matt Smaby RC 3.00 8.00
217 Sam Gagner RC 6.00 15.00
218 Stefan Meyer RC 4.00 10.00
219 Ville Koistinen RC 3.00 8.00
220 Marc Staal RC 5.00 12.00
221 Kyle Chipchura RC 5.00 12.00
222 Mike Weber RC 3.00 8.00
223 Nick Foligno RC 6.00 15.00
224 Devin Setoguchi RC 5.00 12.00
225 Matt Niskanen RC 5.00 12.00
226 James Sheppard RC 3.00 8.00
227 Bryan Little RC 5.00 12.00
228 Tyler Kennedy RC 3.00 8.00
229 Erik Johnson RC 5.00 12.00
230 Jiri Tlusty RC 5.00 12.00
231 Patrick Kane RC 25.00 60.00
232 Andrew Cogliano RC 4.00 10.00
233 David Jones RC 3.00 8.00
234 Anton Stralman RC 3.00 8.00
235 Brian Elliott RC 6.00 15.00
236 Tobias Enstrom RC 5.00 12.00
237 David Perron RC 6.00 15.00
238 Chris Bourque RC 4.00 10.00
239 Ondrej Pavelec RC 6.00 15.00
240 Milan Lucic RC 12.00 30.00
241 Jack Skille RC 4.00 10.00
242 Sergei Kostitsyn RC 4.00 10.00

2007-08 Artifacts Blue

*1-100 VETS/25: 5X TO 12X BASIC CARDS
*101-140 S/L/25: 1.5X TO 4X S/L/1499
*141-200 ROOKIES/25: 1.2X TO 3X RC/999
*201-242 ROOKIES/25: .8X TO 2X RC/599

2007-08 Artifacts Gold

*1-100 VETS/50: 4X TO 10X BASIC CARDS
*101-140 S/L/50: 1.2X TO 3X S/L/1499
*141-200 ROOKIES/50: 1X TO 2.5X RC/999
*201-242 ROOKIES/50: .6X TO 1.5X RC/599

2007-08 Artifacts Silver

*1-100 VETS/100: 2.5X TO 6X BASIC CARDS
*101-140 S/L/100: .8X TO 2X S/L/1499
*141-200 ROOKIES/100: .8X TO 2X RC/999
*201-242 ROOKIES/100: .5X TO 1.2X RC/599

2007-08 Artifacts Autofacts

AFAF Alexander Frolov 4.00 10.00
AFAK Andrei Kostitsyn 5.00 12.00
AFAL Andrew Ladd 4.00 10.00
AFAM Al MacInnis 8.00 20.00
AFAN Andrew Raycroft 5.00 12.00
AFAO Alex Ovechkin SP 50.00 125.00
AFAT Alex Tanguay 5.00 12.00
AFBC Bobby Clarke 10.00 25.00
AFBG Butch Goring 4.00 10.00
AFBI Martin Biron 5.00 12.00
AFBM Brendan Morrison 4.00 10.00
AFBO Ray Bourque SP 10.00 25.00
AFBP Bernie Parent SP 8.00 20.00
AFBR Brad Richardson 4.00 10.00
AFBS Borje Salming SP 6.00 15.00
AFBY Brad Boyes 4.00 10.00
AFCH Erik Christensen 4.00 10.00
AFCM Clarke MacArthur 4.00 10.00
AFCP Chris Pronger 6.00 15.00
AFDB Daniel Briere 6.00 15.00
AFDE Denis Potvin 6.00 15.00
AFDL David Leneveu 5.00 12.00
AFDP Dion Phaneuf 5.00 12.00
AFDS Drew Stafford 4.00 10.00
AFDT Darcy Tucker SP 5.00 12.00
AFDU Dustin Brown 6.00 15.00
AFEC Erik Cole 4.00 10.00
AFEM Evgeni Malkin 12.00 30.00
AFES Eric Staal 8.00 20.00
AFGA Glenn Anderson 5.00 12.00
AFGB Gilbert Brule SP 5.00 12.00
AFGC Gerry Cheevers 6.00 15.00
AFGH Gordie Howe SP 30.00 80.00
AFGL Guillaume Latendresse 5.00 12.00
AFGP Gilbert Perreault 6.00 15.00
AFHA Dale Hawerchuk 8.00 20.00
AFHE Milan Hejduk 5.00 12.00
AFHL Henrik Lundqvist 15.00 40.00
AFHZ Henrik Zetterberg 8.00 20.00
AFIK Ilya Kovalchuk 6.00 15.00
AFJA Jason Arnott 5.00 12.00
AFJB Johnny Bucyk 6.00 15.00
AFJC Jeff Carter 5.00 12.00
AFJK Jari Kurri SP 6.00 15.00
AFJR Jeremy Roenick 10.00 25.00
AFJS Jarret Stoll 5.00 12.00
AFKL Kari Lehtonen 5.00 12.00
AFKM Kirk Muller 4.00 10.00
AFLA Guy Lafleur 8.00 20.00
AFLM Lanny McDonald SP 6.00 15.00
AFLR Luc Robitaille 6.00 15.00
AFMB Martin Brodeur SP 15.00 40.00
AFMC Mike Cammalleri 5.00 12.00
AFMG Marian Gaborik 6.00 15.00
AFMH Martin Havlat 6.00 15.00
AFMI Mike Bossy 6.00 15.00
AFMK Miikka Kiprusoff 6.00 15.00
AFML Mario Lemieux SP 30.00 80.00
AFMM Mark Messier SP 30.00 80.00
AFMR Mike Richards 5.00 12.00
AFNB Niklas Backstrom 6.00 15.00
AFNZ Nikolai Zherdev 4.00 10.00
AFOR Bobby Orr SP 30.00 80.00
AFPE Corey Perry 10.00 25.00
AFPK Phil Kessel 6.00 15.00
AFPO Patrick O'Sullivan 5.00 12.00
AFPR Patrick Roy SP 30.00 80.00
AFPS Paul Stastny 5.00 12.00
AFRA Bill Ranford 6.00 15.00
AFRB Richard Brodeur 5.00 12.00
AFRE Ron Ellis 4.00 10.00
AFRH Ron Hextall 6.00 15.00
AFRM Ryan Malone 4.00 10.00
AFRN Rick Nash 6.00 15.00
AFSC Sidney Crosby 60.00 150.00
AFSG Scott Gomez 5.00 12.00
AFST Peter Stastny 5.00 12.00
AFTL Ted Lindsay SP 6.00 15.00
AFTV Tomas Vokoun 5.00 12.00
AFTW Tiger Williams 4.00 10.00
AFWC Wayne Cashman 4.00 10.00
AFWG Wayne Gretzky SP 200.00 500.00
AFZC Zdeno Chara 6.00 15.00

2007-08 Artifacts Frozen Artifacts

FAAK Alex Kovalev 3.00 8.00
FAAO Alexander Ovechkin 15.00 40.00
FAAR Andrew Raycroft 3.00 8.00
FAAS Alexander Steen 2.50 6.00
FAAT Alex Tanguay 3.00 8.00
FAAY Alexei Yashin 3.00 8.00
FABB Brad Boyes 2.50 6.00
FABF Bernie Federko 3.00 8.00
FABG Brian Gionta 2.50 6.00
FABM Brendan Morrison 2.50 6.00
FABR Bill Ranford 4.00 10.00
FABS Billy Smith 4.00 10.00
FACC Chris Chelios 4.00 10.00
FACD Chris Drury 3.00 8.00
FACI Dino Ciccarelli 4.00 10.00
FACJ Curtis Joseph 5.00 12.00
FACN Cam Neely 4.00 10.00
FACP Chris Pronger 4.00 10.00
FACW Cam Ward 4.00 10.00
FADA Daniel Alfredsson 4.00 10.00
FADC Dan Cloutier 3.00 8.00
FADH Dale Hawerchuk 5.00 12.00
FADL David Legwand 3.00 8.00
FADP Rick DiPietro 3.00 8.00
FADS Darryl Sittler 5.00 12.00
FADW Doug Weight 4.00 10.00
FAEB Ed Belfour 4.00 10.00
FAEM Evgeni Malkin 8.00 20.00
FAES Eric Staal 5.00 12.00
FAGA Glenn Anderson 3.00 8.00
FAGL Guy Lafleur 5.00 12.00
FAHA Dominik Hasek 6.00 15.00
FAHZ Henrik Zetterberg 5.00 12.00
FAIK Ilya Kovalchuk 4.00 10.00
FAJB Jay Bouwmeester 2.50 6.00
FAJC Jonathan Cheechoo 3.00 8.00
FAJI Jarome Iginla 5.00 12.00
FAJL Jere Lehtinen 2.50 6.00
FAJO Joe Sakic 8.00 20.00
FAJS Jason Spezza 4.00 10.00
FAKL Kari Lehtonen 3.00 8.00
FAKT Keith Tkachuk 4.00 10.00
FALM Lanny McDonald 4.00 10.00
FALR Larry Robinson 4.00 10.00
FAMC Bryan McCabe 2.50 6.00
FAMH Marian Hossa 4.00 10.00
FAML Mario Lemieux 15.00 40.00
FAMO Brenden Morrow 3.00 8.00
FARI Brad Richards 4.00 10.00
FASA Borje Salming 4.00 10.00
FASH Brendan Shanahan 4.00 10.00

2007-08 Artifacts Frozen Artifacts Gold

*GOLD: .6X TO 1.5X BASE

2007-08 Artifacts Frozen Artifacts Icy Blue

*ICY BLUE: .8X TO 2X BASE

2007-08 Artifacts Frozen Artifacts Silver

*SILVER: .5X TO 1.2X BASE

2007-08 Artifacts Frozen Artifacts Patches Bronze

FAAK Alex Kovalev 8.00 20.00
FAAO Alexander Ovechkin 40.00 100.00
FAAR Andrew Raycroft 8.00 20.00
FAAS Alexander Steen 6.00 15.00
FAAT Alex Tanguay 8.00 20.00
FABB Brad Boyes 6.00 15.00
FABF Bernie Federko 8.00 20.00
FABG Brian Gionta 6.00 15.00
FABM Brendan Morrison 6.00 15.00
FABR Bill Ranford 10.00 25.00
FABS Billy Smith 10.00 25.00
FACC Chris Chelios 10.00 25.00
FACD Chris Drury 8.00 20.00
FACI Dino Ciccarelli 10.00 25.00
FACJ Curtis Joseph 12.00 30.00
FACN Cam Neely 10.00 25.00
FACP Chris Pronger 10.00 25.00
FACW Cam Ward 10.00 25.00
FADA Daniel Alfredsson 10.00 25.00
FADC Dan Cloutier 8.00 20.00
FADH Dale Hawerchuk 12.00 30.00
FADL David Legwand 8.00 20.00
FADP Rick DiPietro 8.00 20.00
FADW Doug Weight 10.00 25.00
FAEB Ed Belfour 10.00 25.00
FAEM Evgeni Malkin 20.00 50.00
FAES Eric Staal 12.00 30.00
FAGA Glenn Anderson 8.00 20.00
FAHA Dominik Hasek 15.00 40.00

FAHZ Henrik Zetterberg 12.00 30.00
FAIK Ilya Kovalchuk 10.00 25.00
FAJB Jay Bouwmeester 6.00 15.00
FAJC Jonathan Cheechoo 8.00 20.00
FAJI Jarome Iginla 12.00 30.00
FAJL Jere Lehtinen 6.00 15.00
FAJO Joe Sakic 20.00 50.00
FAJS Jason Spezza 10.00 25.00
FAKL Kari Lehtonen 8.00 20.00
FAKT Keith Tkachuk 10.00 25.00
FALM Lanny McDonald 10.00 25.00
FALR Larry Robinson 10.00 25.00
FAMC Bryan McCabe 6.00 15.00
FAMH Marian Hossa 10.00 25.00
FAML Mario Lemieux 40.00 100.00
FAMO Brenden Morrow 8.00 20.00
FARI Brad Richards 10.00 25.00
FASA Borje Salming 10.00 25.00
FASH Brendan Shanahan 10.00 25.00

2007-08 Artifacts Frozen Artifacts Patches Gold

*GOLD: .5X TO 1.2X BASE

2007-08 Artifacts Treasured Patches Bronze

*PATCHES BRONZE: .8X TO 2X SWATCHES

2007-08 Artifacts Treasured Patches Gold

*PATCHES GOLD: 1.5X TO 4X SWATCHES

2007-08 Artifacts Treasured Swatches

TSAF Alexander Frolov 3.00 8.00
TSAH Ales Hemsky 4.00 10.00
TSAK Alex Kovalev 4.00 10.00
TSAM Al MacInnis 6.00 15.00
TSAO Alexander Ovechkin 20.00 50.00
TSBB Bob Bourne 3.00 8.00
TSBG Bill Guerin 5.00 12.00
TSBL Rob Blake 5.00 12.00
TSBN Bob Nystrom 3.00 8.00
TSBR Brad Richards 5.00 12.00
TSBS Borje Salming 5.00 12.00
TSCJ Curtis Joseph 6.00 15.00
TSCN Cam Neely 5.00 12.00
TSDB Daniel Briere 5.00 12.00
TSDG Doug Gilmour 6.00 15.00
TSDH Dany Heatley 4.00 10.00
TSDW Doug Weight 5.00 12.00
TSEB Ed Belfour 5.00 12.00
TSEL Eric Lindros 8.00 20.00
TSGO Scott Gomez 4.00 10.00
TSIK Ilya Kovalchuk 5.00 12.00
TSJG Jean-Sebastien Giguere 5.00 12.00
TSJJ Jaromir Jagr 15.00 40.00
TSJT Joe Thornton 8.00 20.00
TSKT Keith Tkachuk 5.00 12.00
TSMB Martin Brodeur 12.00 30.00
TSMF Manny Fernandez 3.00 8.00
TSMH Marian Hossa 5.00 12.00
TSMM Mike Modano 8.00 20.00
TSMN Markus Naslund 5.00 12.00
TSMR Mark Recchi 6.00 15.00
TSMT Marty Turco 5.00 12.00
TSNK Nikolai Khabibulin 5.00 12.00
TSOK Olaf Kolzig 5.00 12.00
TSPF Peter Forsberg 10.00 25.00
TSPK Paul Kariya 5.00 12.00
TSRB Ray Bourque 8.00 20.00
TSRN Rick Nash 5.00 12.00
TSRY Michael Ryder 3.00 8.00
TSSC Sidney Crosby 12.00 30.00
TSSF Sergei Fedorov 8.00 20.00
TSSG Simon Gagne 5.00 12.00
TSSK Saku Koivu 5.00 12.00
TSSN Scott Niedermayer 5.00 12.00
TSSS Steve Shutt 4.00 10.00
TSTH Tomas Holmstrom 4.00 10.00
TSTS Teemu Selanne 10.00 25.00
TSTW Tiger Williams 3.00 8.00
TSVL Vincent Lecavalier 5.00 12.00
TSWG Wayne Gretzky 30.00 80.00

2007-08 Artifacts Treasured Swatches Gold

*GOLD: .6X TO 1.5X BASE

2007-08 Artifacts Treasured Swatches Icy Blue

*ICY BLUE: .8X TO 2X BASE

2007-08 Artifacts Treasured Swatches Silver

*SILVER: .5X TO 1.2X BASE

2007-08 Artifacts Tundra Tandems

TTAL A.MacInnis/L.McDonald 8.00 20.00
TTAM A.Steen/M.Stajan 4.00 10.00
TTBB Belfour/Bouwmeester 6.00 15.00
TTBC S.Bernier/M.Carle 4.00 10.00
TTBE M.Biron/R.Esche 5.00 12.00
TTBK P.Bergeron/P.Kessel 8.00 20.00
TTBM R.Bourque/A.MacInnis 10.00 25.00
TTBO K.Bieksa/M.Ohlund 5.00 12.00
TTBP B.Salming/P.Forsberg 12.00 30.00
TTBS M.Brodeur/S.Stevens 15.00 40.00
TTBT P.Budaj/J.Theodore 6.00 15.00
TTCF S.Crosby/M.Fleury 15.00 40.00
TTCG J.Cheechoo/B.Guerin 6.00 15.00
TTCM S.Crosby/E.Malkin 25.00 60.00
TTCR C.Perry/R.Getzlaf 10.00 25.00
TTDG C.Drury/S.Gomez 5.00 12.00
TTDH D.Sedin/H.Sedin 8.00 20.00
TTDJ S.Doan/E.Jovanovski 5.00 12.00
TTDL P.Datsyuk/N.Lidstrom 10.00 25.00
TTDR P.Demitra/B.Rolston 8.00 20.00
TTER E.Staal/R.Brind'Amour 8.00 20.00
TTFM B.Federko/J.Mullen 5.00 12.00
TTFT M.Fernandez/T.Thomas 6.00 15.00
TTFV P.Forsberg/T.Vokoun 12.00 30.00
TTGC S.Gagne/J.Carter 6.00 15.00
TTGE B.Gionta/P.Elias 6.00 15.00
TTGK M.Gaborik/M.Koivu 6.00 15.00
TTGL W.Gretzky/M.Lemieux 40.00 100.00
TTGS J.Giguere/T.Selanne 12.00 30.00
TTHA D.Heatley/D.Alfredsson 6.00 15.00
TTHB M.Havlat/P.Bondra 6.00 15.00
TTHC Hawerchuk/Ciccarelli 8.00 20.00
TTHL G.Howe/M.Lemieux 25.00 60.00
TTHO D.Hasek/C.Osgood 10.00 25.00
TTHR A.Hemsky/D.Roloson 5.00 12.00
TTHS M.Hejduk/M.Svatos 5.00 12.00
TTHW N.Horton/S.Weiss 6.00 15.00
TTIH I.Kovalchuk/M.Hossa 6.00 15.00
TTIT J.Iginla/A.Tanguay 8.00 20.00
TTJJ C.Joseph/E.Jovanovski 8.00 20.00
TTJL J.Jokinen/J.Lehtinen 4.00 10.00
TTJM J.Sakic/M.Hejduk 12.00 30.00
TTJP J.Sakic/P.Roy 15.00 40.00
TTJS J.Jagr/M.Straka 20.00 50.00
TTKA J.Kurri/G.Anderson 6.00 15.00
TTKF A.Kopitar/A.Frolov 10.00 25.00
TTKK A.Kovalev/A.Kostitsyn 5.00 12.00
TTKP M.Kiprusoff/D.Phaneuf 6.00 15.00
TTKR S.Koivu/M.Ryder 6.00 15.00
TTKT P.Kariya/K.Tkachuk 6.00 15.00
TTLA D.Legwand/J.Arnott 5.00 12.00
TTLC N.Lidstrom/C.Chelios 6.00 15.00
TTLH K.Lehtonen/M.Hossa 6.00 15.00
TTLN R.Luongo/M.Naslund 10.00 25.00
TTLR V.Lecavalier/B.Richards 6.00 15.00
TTLS M.Legace/C.Sanford 5.00 12.00
TTLV P.Leclaire/D.Vyborny 5.00 12.00
TTMB M.Sundin/B.Salming 6.00 15.00
TTML B.Morrison/T.Linden 6.00 15.00
TTMM M.Modano/J.Mullen 10.00 25.00
TTMO G.Lafleur/L.Robinson 8.00 20.00
TTMP M.Brodeur/P.Elias 10.00 25.00
TTMR M.Modano/M.Ribeiro 10.00 25.00
TTMS G.Murray/M.Savard 5.00 12.00
TTMW B.McCabe/I.White 4.00 10.00
TTNF R.Nash/S.Fedorov 10.00 25.00
TTNT E.Nabokov/V.Toskala 5.00 12.00
TTNY B.Witt/T.Hunter 4.00 10.00
TTOK A.Ovechkin/O.Kolzig 25.00 60.00
TTOM A.Ovechkin/E.Malkin 25.00 60.00
TTPA P.Stastny/A.Stastny 5.00 12.00
TTPB G.Perreault/D.Briere 6.00 15.00
TTPG Z.Parise/B.Gionta 6.00 15.00
TTPN C.Pronger/S.Niedermayer 6.00 15.00
TTPP F.Pisani/M.Pouliot 4.00 10.00
TTRB P.Roy/R.Bourque 15.00 40.00
TTRG W.Redden/M.Gerber 5.00 12.00
TTRH M.Ryder/C.Higgins 4.00 10.00
TTRJ R.Bourque/J.Bucyk 10.00 25.00
TTSB B.Smith/B.Bourne 6.00 15.00
TTSD M.St. Louis/M.Denis 6.00 15.00
TTSE J.Spezza/P.Eaves 6.00 15.00
TTSF M.Sundin/P.Forsberg 12.00 30.00
TTSG M.Satan/B.Guerin 6.00 15.00
TTSH J.Stoll/S.Horcoff 5.00 12.00
TTSK B.Seabrook/D.Keith 5.00 12.00
TTSL Shanahan/Lundqvist 15.00 40.00
TTSR M.Sundin/A.Raycroft 6.00 15.00
TTSS D.Sittler/B.Salming 8.00 20.00
TTST J.Sakic/P.Turgeon 12.00 30.00
TTSW D.Savard/D.Wilson 6.00 15.00
TTTM J.Thornton/P.Marleau 10.00 25.00
TTTS R.Smyth/J.Theodore 6.00 15.00
TTTZ M.Turco/S.Zubov 6.00 15.00
TTWB D.Weight/B.Boyes 6.00 15.00
TTWP T.Williams/B.Probert 4.00 10.00
TTWW C.Ward/J.Williams 6.00 15.00
TTYS A.Yashin/M.Satan 5.00 12.00
TTZH H.Zetterberg/T.Holmstrom 8.00 20.00

2007-08 Artifacts Tundra Tandems Icy Blue

*ICY BLUE: .5X TO 1.2X BASE

2007-08 Artifacts Tundra Tandems Metallic Purple

*SINGLES: .4X TO 1X BASIC CARDS

2007-08 Artifacts Tundra Tandems Red

*RED: .6X TO 1.5X BASE

2007-08 Artifacts Tundra Tandems Patches Icy Blue

*SILVER: 1X TO 2.5X BASIC TANDEMS

2007-08 Artifacts Tundra Tandems Patches Silver

*SILVER: .8X TO 2 X BASIC TANDEMS

2007-08 Artifacts Tundra Trios Blue

T3AMV Vanek/Afino/Miller 10.00 25.00
T3ASD Arnott/Sulli/Dumont 8.00 20.00
T3ASH Heat/Spezza/Alfred 10.00 25.00
T3BLK Brod/Luongo/Kipr 15.00 40.00
T3BWH Horton/Bouw/Weiss 10.00 25.00
T3CHD Hasek/Dats/Chelios 15.00 40.00
T3CMS Crosby/Staal/Malkin 40.00 100.00
T3DGK Gab/Koivu/Demitra 12.00 30.00
T3FCK Frolov/Kopitar/Camm 15.00 40.00
T3GEP Gionta/Elias/Parise 10.00 25.00
T3GRC Gagne/Cart/Richards 10.00 25.00
T3GYS Guerin/Satan/Yashin 10.00 25.00
T3HRK Havlat/Khabi/Ruutu 10.00 25.00
T3ITK Iginla/Kipr/Tanguay 12.00 30.00
T3JJD Doan/Joseph/Jovo 12.00 30.00
T3KHL Kovy/Hossa/Lehton 10.00 25.00
T3KPK Kovalev/Kostit/Perez 8.00 20.00
T3KRH Koivu/Ryder/Higgins 10.00 25.00
T3LBS Laraque/Shell/Brash 8.00 20.00
T3LGH Gretz/Howe/Lemieux 60.00 150.00
T3LHZ Zett/Lidstrom/Holms 12.00 30.00
T3LMK Linden/Morr/Kesler 10.00 25.00
T3LRC Lem/Crosby/Recchi 40.00 100.00
T3LRS Lecav/St. Lou/Rich 10.00 25.00
T3LTC Crosby/Thorn/Lecav 30.00 80.00
T3LZB Leclair/Brule/Zherd 8.00 20.00
T3MCB Marleau/Carle/Bernier 10.00 25.00
T3MCT Murray/Chara/Thomas 10.00 25.00
T3MGM McD/Gilmour/MacIn 12.00 30.00
T3MLR Modano/Lindros/Rib 15.00 40.00
T3MRM Mo/Mullen/Roenick 15.00 40.00
T3MSW Salming/McD/Williams 10.00 25.00
T3NBO Bourque/Neely/Oates 15.00 40.00
T3NPG Getzlaf/Nied/Perry 15.00 40.00
T3NSS Nasl/Sedin/Sedin 12.00 30.00
T3OGF Ovech/Green/Fehr 40.00 100.00
T3PRB Bouch/Rolston/Parrish 10.00 25.00
T3PSB Smith/Potvin/Bourne 25.00 60.00
T3RBB Roy/Belfour/Brodeur 20.00 50.00
T3REE Emery/Redden/Eaves 8.00 20.00
T3RLR Roy/Lafleur/Robinson 25.00 60.00
T3RSS Raycroft/Steen/Stajan 8.00 20.00
T3SBK Berg/Kessel/Savard 12.00 30.00
T3SDG Straka/Drury/Gomez 8.00 20.00
T3SHB Sakic/Hejduk/Budaj 20.00 50.00
T3SJL Shan/Jagr/Lundqvist 30.00 80.00
T3SNF Sundin/Forsberg/Nasl 20.00 50.00
T3SPG Selanne/Gig/Pronger 20.00 50.00
T3SRH Hem/Roloson/Stoll 8.00 20.00
T3STM Sundin/Tuck/McCabe 10.00 25.00
T3TCM Thorn/Cheech/Michal 15.00 40.00
T3TKL Kipr/Leht/Toskala 10.00 25.00
T3TKS Tkach/Kariya/Stemp 10.00 25.00
T3VHB Hasek/Vok/Budaj 15.00 40.00
T3VNF Nash/Fed/Vyborny 15.00 40.00
T3WLB Weight/Legace/Boyes 10.00 25.00
T3WPP Williams/Probert/Plett 6.00 15.00
T3WSW Staal/Ward/Williams 12.00 30.00
T3ZLT Turco/Zubov/Leht 10.00 25.00

2008-09 Artifacts

1 Alexander Ovechkin 1.50 4.00
2 Nicklas Backstrom .40 1.00
3 Markus Naslund .40 1.00
4 Roberto Luongo .60 1.50
5 Daniel Sedin .50 1.25
6 Henrik Sedin .50 1.25
7 Mats Sundin .40 1.00
8 Vesa Toskala .50 1.25
9 Alexander Steen .25 .60
10 Vincent Lecavalier .40 1.00
11 Martin St. Louis .40 1.00
12 Paul Kariya .40 1.00
13 Manny Legace .40 1.00
14 Brad Boyes .25 .60
15 Joe Thornton .60 1.50
16 Patrick Marleau .40 1.00
17 Evgeni Nabokov .30 .75
18 Jonathan Cheechoo .30 .75
19 Peter Stastny .30 .75
20 Mario Lemieux 1.50 4.00
21 Sidney Crosby 1.50 4.00
22 Marc-Andre Fleury .75 2.00
23 Evgeni Malkin .75 2.00
24 Jordan Staal .30 .75
25 Peter Mueller .30 .75
26 Shane Doan .30 .75
27 Daniel Briere .40 1.00
28 Simon Gagne .40 1.00
29 Mike Richards .30 .75
30 Jason Spezza .40 1.00
31 Dany Heatley .30 .75
32 Daniel Alfredsson .40 1.00
33 Mark Messier .75 2.00
34 Marian Hossa .40 1.00
35 Henrik Lundqvist 1.00 2.50
36 Brendan Shanahan .40 1.00
37 Brian Leetch .30 .75
38 Rick DiPietro .30 .75
39 Bill Guerin .40 1.00
40 Mike Bossy .40 1.00
41 Zach Parise .40 1.00
42 Martin Brodeur 1.00 2.50
43 Jason Arnott .30 .75
44 J.P. Dumont .25 .60
45 Patrick Roy 1.00 2.50
46 Carey Price .75 2.00
47 Saku Koivu .40 1.00
48 Alex Tanguay .25 .60
49 Alex Kovalev .30 .75
50 Larry Robinson .40 1.00
51 Marian Gaborik .40 1.00
52 Josh Harding .30 .75
53 Anze Kopitar .60 1.50
54 Jack Johnson .25 .60
55 Tomas Vokoun .30 .75
56 Nathan Horton .40 1.00
57 Wayne Gretzky 2.50 6.00
58 Andrew Cogliano .25 .60
59 Sam Gagner .25 .60
60 Ales Hemsky .30 .75
61 Dustin Penner .30 .75
62 Jari Kurri .40 1.00
63 Gordie Howe 1.25 3.00
64 Nicklas Lidstrom .40 1.00
65 Henrik Zetterberg .50 1.25
66 Pavel Datsyuk .60 1.50
67 Dominik Hasek .60 1.50
68 Mike Modano .60 1.50
69 Brad Richards .40 1.00
70 Marty Turco .40 1.00
71 Rick Nash .40 1.00
72 Nikolai Zherdev .25 .60
73 Paul Stastny .30 .75
74 Joe Sakic .75 2.00
75 Peter Forsberg .75 2.00
76 Ryan Smyth .30 .75
77 Patrick Kane .75 2.00
78 Jonathan Toews .60 1.50
79 Patrick Sharp .30 .75
80 Bobby Hull .75 2.00
81 Eric Staal .50 1.25
82 Cam Ward .40 1.00
83 Miikka Kiprusoff .40 1.00
84 Jarome Iginla .50 1.25
85 Dion Phaneuf .30 .75
86 Mike Cammalleri .30 .75
87 Thomas Vanek .30 .75
88 Ryan Miller .40 1.00
89 Drew Stafford .25 .60
90 Gilbert Perreault .40 1.00
91 Bobby Orr 1.50 4.00
92 Tim Thomas .40 1.00
93 Phil Kessel .40 1.00
94 Marc Savard .25 .60
95 Ilya Kovalchuk .40 1.00
96 Kari Lehtonen .50 1.25
97 Teemu Selanne .75 2.00
98 Jean-Sebastien Giguere .40 1.00
99 Scott Niedermayer .40 1.00
100 Ryan Getzlaf .40 1.00
101 Dale Hawerchuk LEG 1.50 4.00
102 Rod Langway LEG 1.00 2.50
103 Johnny Bower LEG 1.25 3.00
104 Borje Salming LEG 1.25 3.00
105 Frank Mahovlich LEG 1.25 3.00
106 Bernie Federko LEG 1.00 2.50
107 Al MacInnis LEG 1.50 4.00
108 Peter Stastny LEG 1.00 2.50
109 Mario Lemieux LEG 5.00 12.00
110 Joe Mullen LEG 1.00 2.50
111 Bobby Clarke LEG 2.00 5.00
112 Ron Hextall LEG 1.25 3.00
113 Andy Bathgate LEG 1.25 3.00
114 Brian Leetch LEG 1.00 2.50
115 Walt Tkaczuk LEG .75 2.00
116 Mike Bossy LEG 1.25 3.00
117 Bob Bourne LEG .75 2.00
118 Clark Gillies LEG 1.25 3.00
119 Jean Beliveau LEG 1.25 3.00
120 Scotty Bowman LEG 1.25 3.00
121 Guy Lafleur LEG 1.50 4.00
122 Steve Shutt LEG 1.25 3.00
123 Larry Robinson LEG 1.25 3.00
124 Patrick Roy LEG 3.00 8.00
125 Dino Ciccarelli LEG 1.25 3.00
126 Marcel Dionne LEG 1.50 4.00
127 Bernie Nicholls LEG 1.00 2.50
128 Luc Robitaille LEG 1.25 3.00
129 Grant Fuhr LEG 2.00 5.00
130 Wayne Gretzky LEG 8.00 20.00
131 Jari Kurri LEG 1.25 3.00
132 Alex Delvecchio LEG 1.25 3.00
133 Gordie Howe LEG 4.00 10.00
134 Red Kelly LEG 1.25 3.00
135 Ted Lindsay LEG 1.25 3.00
136 Doug Wilson LEG 1.00 2.50
137 Tony Esposito LEG 1.25 3.00
138 Bobby Hull LEG 2.50 6.00
139 Denis Savard LEG 1.25 3.00
140 Stan Mikita LEG 1.50 4.00
141 Lanny McDonald LEG 1.25 3.00
142 Gilbert Perreault LEG 1.25 3.00
143 Ray Bourque LEG 2.00 5.00
144 Johnny Bucyk LEG 1.25 3.00
145 Don Cherry LEG 3.00 8.00
146 Phil Esposito LEG 2.00 5.00
147 Cam Neely LEG 1.25 3.00
148 Willie O'Ree LEG 1.50 4.00
149 Bobby Orr LEG 5.00 12.00
150 Terry O'Reilly LEG 1.00 2.50
151 Alexander Ovechkin S 5.00 12.00
152 Roberto Luongo S 2.00 5.00
153 Henrik Sedin S 1.50 4.00
154 Mats Sundin S 1.25 3.00
155 Vincent Lecavalier S 1.25 3.00
156 Martin St. Louis S 1.25 3.00
157 Paul Kariya S 1.25 3.00
158 Joe Thornton S 2.00 5.00
159 Patrick Marleau S 1.25 3.00
160 Sidney Crosby S 5.00 12.00
161 Evgeni Malkin S 2.50 6.00
162 Marc-Andre Fleury S 2.50 6.00
163 Simon Gagne S 1.25 3.00
164 Daniel Briere S 1.25 3.00
165 Dany Heatley S 1.00 2.50
166 Jason Spezza S 1.25 3.00
167 Daniel Alfredsson S 1.25 3.00
168 Markus Naslund S 1.25 3.00
169 Brendan Shanahan S 1.25 3.00
170 Martin Brodeur S 3.00 8.00
171 Zach Parise S 1.25 3.00
172 Carey Price S 2.50 6.00
173 Saku Koivu S 1.25 3.00
174 Marian Gaborik S 1.25 3.00
175 Josh Harding S 1.25 3.00
176 Anze Kopitar S 2.00 5.00
177 Sam Gagner S .75 2.00
178 Andrew Cogliano S .75 2.00
179 Henrik Zetterberg S 1.50 4.00
180 Chris Osgood S 1.25 3.00
181 Pavel Datsyuk S 2.00 5.00
182 Mike Modano S 2.00 5.00
183 Marty Turco S 1.25 3.00
184 Rick Nash S 1.25 3.00
185 Joe Sakic S 2.50 6.00
186 Peter Forsberg S 2.50 6.00
187 Paul Stastny S 1.00 2.50
188 Patrick Kane S 2.50 6.00
189 Jonathan Toews S 2.00 5.00
190 Eric Staal S 1.50 4.00
191 Jarome Iginla S 1.50 4.00
192 Miikka Kiprusoff S 1.25 3.00
193 Ryan Miller S 1.25 3.00
194 Thomas Vanek S 1.25 3.00
195 Patrice Bergeron S 1.50 4.00
196 Ilya Kovalchuk S 1.25 3.00
197 Teemu Selanne S 2.50 6.00
198 Jean-Sebastien Giguere S 1.25 3.00
199 Ryan Getzlaf S 1.25 3.00
200 Scott Niedermayer S 1.25 3.00
201 Derick Brassard RC 3.00 8.00
202 Mark Fistric RC 2.50 6.00
203 Alex Goligoski RC 4.00 10.00
204 Claude Giroux RC 6.00 15.00
205 Jon Filewich RC 2.50 6.00
206 Robbie Earl RC 2.00 5.00
207 Ilya Zubov RC 2.50 6.00
208 Steve Mason RC 5.00 12.00
209 Brian Boyle RC 2.50 6.00
210 Shawn Matthias RC 3.00 8.00
211 Ryan Stone RC 2.00 5.00
212 Teddy Purcell RC 2.50 6.00
213 Mike Iggulden RC 2.50 6.00
214 Tim Ramholt RC 2.50 6.00
215 Kyle Okposo RC 4.00 10.00
216 Sami Lepisto RC 2.50 6.00
217 Colin Stuart RC 2.50 6.00
218 Brandon Nolan RC 2.50 6.00
219 Andrew Murray RC 2.50 6.00
220 Kevin Doell RC 2.50 6.00
221 Tim Conboy RC 2.00 5.00
222 Pascal Pelletier RC 2.50 6.00
223 Chris Minard RC 3.00 8.00
224 Joey Mormina RC 2.50 6.00
225 Peter Vandermeer RC 2.50 6.00
226 Darryl Boyce RC 2.50 6.00
227 Cody McLeod RC 2.50 6.00
228 Corey Locke RC 2.50 6.00
229 Jordan Hendry RC 2.50 6.00
230 Mike Brown RC 3.00 8.00
231 B.J. Crombeen RC 2.50 6.00
232 David Brine RC 2.00 5.00
233 Joe Jensen RC 3.00 8.00
234 Kyle Greentree RC 3.00 8.00
235 Zach Fitzgerald RC 3.00 8.00
236 Marc-Andre Gragnani RC 2.50 6.00
237 Andrew Ebbett RC 2.00 5.00
238 Erik Ersberg RC 2.50 6.00
239 Jonathan Ericsson RC 3.00 8.00
240 Theo Peckham RC 2.50 6.00
241 Tyler Plante RC 2.50 6.00
242 Niklas Hjalmarsson RC 3.00 8.00
243 Tom Sestito RC 3.00 8.00
244 Tom Cavanagh RC 2.50 6.00
245 Alex Foster RC 2.50 6.00
246 Kyle Turris RC 5.00 12.00
247 Brian Lee RC 2.50 6.00
248 Justin Abdelkader RC 5.00 12.00
249 Adam Pineault RC 2.50 6.00
250 Boris Valabik RC 3.00 8.00
251 Darren Helm RC 3.00 8.00
252 Matt D'Agostini RC 2.50 6.00
253 Mattias Ritola RC 2.50 6.00
254 Dan LaCosta RC 3.00 8.00
255 Danny Taylor RC 2.50 6.00
256 Clay Wilson RC 2.00 5.00
257 Jordan LaVallee RC 2.00 5.00
258 Mike Mole RC 2.50 6.00
259 Jack Hillen RC 2.50 6.00
260 Garrett Stafford RC 3.00 8.00
271 Karl Alzner RC 3.00 8.00
272 Cory Schneider RC 8.00 20.00
273 Luke Schenn RC 4.00 10.00
274 Steven Stamkos RC 8.00 20.00
275 Alex Pietrangelo RC 5.00 12.00
276 Jamie McGinn RC 3.00 8.00
277 Dustin Jeffery RC 3.00 8.00
278 Mikkel Boedker RC 4.00 10.00
279 Luca Sbisa RC 2.00 5.00
280 Zach Smith RC 2.50 6.00
281 Corey Potter RC 5.00 12.00
282 Josh Bailey RC 4.00 10.00
283 Petr Vrana RC 2.00 5.00
284 Patric Hornqvist RC 3.00 8.00
285 Max Pacioretty RC 6.00 15.00
286 Colton Gillies RC 2.50 6.00
287 Drew Doughty RC 8.00 20.00
288 Michael Frolik RC 3.00 8.00
289 Tim Sestito RC 2.50 6.00
290 Patrik Berglund RC 2.50 6.00
291 Fabian Brunnstrom RC 2.50 6.00
292 Jakub Voracek RC 6.00 15.00
293 Chris Stewart RC 3.00 8.00
294 Viktor Tikhonov RC 2.50 6.00
295 Brandon Sutter RC 3.00 8.00
296 Brett Sutter RC 3.00 8.00
297 Tim Kennedy RC 3.00 8.00
298 Blake Wheeler RC 8.00 20.00
299 Zach Bogosian RC 4.00 10.00
300 Brendan Mikkelson RC 2.00 5.00
301 Justin Pogge RC 2.50 6.00
302 Zach Boychuk RC 3.00 8.00
303 Nathan Gerbe RC 3.00 8.00
304 Nikita Filatov RC 3.00 8.00
305 James Neal RC 6.00 15.00
306 Kenndal McArdle RC 2.50 6.00
307 Ben Maxwell RC 3.00 8.00
308 T.J. Oshie RC 6.00 15.00
309 Ty Wishart RC 2.50 6.00
310 Nikolai Kulemin RC 3.00 8.00
311 Simeon Varlamov RC 6.00 15.00
312 Michal Repik RC 3.00 8.00
P1 Cover Card Promo .75 2.00

2008-09 Artifacts Blue

*1-100 VETS/50: 3X TO 8X BASIC CARDS
*101-200 L/S/50: 1X TO 2.5X L/S/999
*201-260 ROOKIES/50: .8X TO 2X RC/999
2 Nicklas Backstrom 3.00 8.00

2008-09 Artifacts Copper Spectrum

*1-100 VETS/25: 4X TO 10X BASIC CARDS
*101-200 L/S/25: 1.2X TO 3X L/S/999
*201-260 ROOKIES/25: 1X TO 2.5X RC/999
2 Nicklas Backstrom 4.00 10.00

2008-09 Artifacts Gold

*1-100 VETS/75: 2.5X TO 6X BASIC CARDS
*101-200 L/S/75: .8X TO 2X L/S/999
*201-260 ROOKIES/75: .6X TO 1.5X RC/999
2 Nicklas Backstrom 2.50 6.00

2008-09 Artifacts Silver

*1-100 VETS/100: 2X TO 5X BASIC CARDS
*101-200 L/S/100: .6X TO 1.5X L/S/999
*201-260 ROOKIES/100: .5X TO 1.2X RC/999
2 Nicklas Backstrom 2.00 5.00

2008-09 Artifacts Autofacts

AFAK Anze Kopitar 12.00 30.00
AFAO Alexander Ovechkin 50.00 100.00
AFAP Alexandre Picard 4.00 10.00
AFAR Andrew Raycroft 5.00 12.00
AFBB Brian Boyle 4.00 10.00
AFBC Chris Bourque 5.00 12.00
AFBJ Johnny Bower 6.00 15.00
AFBL Michael Blunden 4.00 10.00
AFBN Bob Nystrom 4.00 10.00
AFBO Bobby Orr 100.00 200.00
AFBR Bobby Ryan 5.00 12.00
AFCA Daniel Carcillo 4.00 10.00
AFCB Casey Borer 6.00 15.00
AFCD Chris Drury 12.00 30.00
AFCG Claude Giroux 20.00 50.00
AFCH Kyle Chipchura 5.00 12.00
AFCK Chris Kunitz 6.00 15.00
AFCM Clarke MacArthur 4.00 10.00
AFCN Cam Neely 15.00 40.00
AFCP Corey Perry 10.00 25.00
AFCW Cam Ward 10.00 25.00
AFDA David Perron 5.00 12.00
AFDB Dan Boyle 4.00 10.00
AFDC Dan Cleary 5.00 12.00
AFDE Derick Brassard 5.00 12.00
AFDH Dany Heatley 5.00 12.00
AFDP Dustin Penner 5.00 12.00
AFDR Drew Stafford 5.00 12.00
AFDS Daniel Sedin 8.00 20.00
AFEJ Erik Johnson 4.00 10.00
AFEM Evgeni Malkin 25.00 50.00
AFEN Eric Nystrom 4.00 10.00
AFES Tony Esposito 10.00 25.00
AFGH Gordie Howe 60.00 120.00
AFGL Guillaume Latendresse 4.00 10.00
AFGP Gilbert Perreault 6.00 15.00
AFHA Dominik Hasek 12.00 30.00
AFHS Henrik Sedin 8.00 20.00
AFHZ Henrik Zetterberg 20.00 40.00
AFIK Ilya Kovalchuk 12.00 30.00
AFIZ Ilya Zubov 4.00 10.00
AFJA Jared Boll 4.00 10.00
AFJB Johnny Bucyk 6.00 15.00
AFJC Jeff Carter 5.00 12.00
AFJF Jon Filewich 4.00 10.00
AFJH Josh Harding 6.00 15.00
AFJI Jarome Iginla SP 25.00 60.00
AFJJ Jack Johnson 4.00 10.00
AFJL Joffrey Lupul 4.00 10.00
AFJO Johnny Boychuk 6.00 15.00
AFJP Jason Pominville 4.00 10.00
AFJS Jack Skille 5.00 12.00
AFJT Jonathan Toews 25.00 50.00
AFKA Patrick Kane 20.00 50.00
AFKC Kyle Calder 4.00 10.00
AFLE Mario Lemieux 75.00 150.00
AFLK Lukas Kaspar 4.00 10.00
AFMA Martin Brodeur 60.00 120.00
AFMB Mike Bossy 6.00 15.00
AFME Mark Messier 40.00 80.00
AFMH Marian Hossa 6.00 15.00
AFML Matt Lashoff 4.00 10.00
AFMM Mike Modano 10.00 25.00
AFMR Mike Ribeiro 4.00 10.00
AFMT Maxime Talbot 4.00 10.00
AFNA Evgeni Nabokov 5.00 12.00
AFNF Nick Foligno 6.00 15.00
AFNH Nathan Horton 5.00 12.00
AFNK Niklas Kronwall 5.00 12.00
AFOP Ondrej Pavelec 8.00 20.00
AFPB Peter Budaj 5.00 12.00
AFPE Patrik Elias 6.00 15.00
AFPK Phil Kessel 6.00 15.00
AFPR Carey Price 12.00 30.00
AFPS Paul Stastny 6.00 15.00
AFRB Ray Bourque 20.00 50.00
AFRE Robbie Earl 3.00 8.00
AFRG Ryan Getzlaf 6.00 15.00
AFRL Rod Langway 5.00 12.00
AFRN Rick Nash 12.00 30.00
AFRO Dwayne Roloson 5.00 12.00
AFRS Ryan Smyth 5.00 12.00
AFSC Sidney Crosby 75.00 150.00
AFSD Steve Downie 6.00 15.00
AFSE Devin Setoguchi 5.00 12.00
AFSG Sam Gagner 4.00 10.00
AFSH James Sheppard 4.00 10.00
AFSK Sergei Kostitsyn 4.00 10.00
AFSM Steve Mason 10.00 25.00
AFST Jordan Staal 10.00 25.00
AFTE Tobias Enstrom 4.00 10.00
AFTH T.J. Hensick 5.00 12.00
AFTJ Joe Thornton 15.00 40.00
AFTK Tyler Kennedy 5.00 12.00
AFTL Jiri Tlusty 4.00 10.00
AFTO Tomas Kaberle 4.00 10.00
AFTR Tuukka Rask 15.00 30.00
AFTV Tomas Vokoun 5.00 12.00
AFVL Vincent Lecavalier 10.00 25.00
AFWG Wayne Gretzky 200.00 500.00

2008-09 Artifacts Frozen Artifacts Retail

*SINGLES: .4X TO 1X BASIC INSERTS

2008-09 Artifacts Frozen Artifacts Dual

FADAK Anze Kopitar 6.00 15.00
FADAM Al MacInnis 5.00 12.00
FADAO Adam Oates 4.00 10.00
FADAS Alexander Semin 4.00 10.00
FADAT Alex Tanguay 2.50 6.00
FADBB Brad Boyes 2.50 6.00
FADBG Bill Guerin 4.00 10.00
FADBS Brendan Shanahan 4.00 10.00
FADCC Chris Chelios 4.00 10.00
FADCN Cam Neely 4.00 10.00
FADCW Cam Ward 4.00 10.00
FADDA Daniel Alfredsson 4.00 10.00
FADDB Daniel Briere 4.00 10.00
FADDC Dino Ciccarelli 4.00 10.00
FADDH Dominik Hasek 6.00 15.00
FADDP Dion Phaneuf 3.00 8.00
FADDS Daniel Sedin 5.00 12.00
FADDT Darcy Tucker 3.00 8.00
FADEM Evgeni Malkin 8.00 20.00
FADEN Evgeni Nabokov 3.00 8.00
FADES Eric Staal 5.00 12.00
FADHA Dale Hawerchuk 5.00 12.00
FADHE Dany Heatley 3.00 8.00
FADHL Henrik Lundqvist 10.00 25.00
FADHS Henrik Sedin 5.00 12.00
FADIK Ilya Kovalchuk 4.00 10.00
FADJC Jonathan Cheechoo 3.00 8.00
FADJG Jean-Sebastien Giguere 4.00 10.00
FADJS Joe Sakic 8.00 20.00
FADJT Joe Thornton 6.00 15.00
FADKO Alex Kovalev 3.00 8.00
FADMB Martin Brodeur 10.00 25.00
FADMF Manny Fernandez 2.50 6.00
FADMG Marian Gaborik 4.00 10.00
FADMK Miikka Kiprusoff 4.00 10.00
FADMM Mark Messier 8.00 20.00
FADMN Markus Naslund 4.00 10.00
FADMO Mike Modano 6.00 15.00
FADMS Marc Savard 2.50 6.00
FADOV Alexander Ovechkin 15.00 40.00
FADPF Peter Forsberg 8.00 20.00
FADPR Patrick Roy 8.00 20.00
FADRB Ray Bourque 6.00 15.00
FADSA Borje Salming 4.00 10.00
FADSC Sidney Crosby 10.00 25.00
FADSP Jason Spezza 5.00 12.00
FADSU Mats Sundin 4.00 10.00
FADTV Thomas Vanek 5.00 12.00

2008-09 Artifacts Frozen Artifacts Dual Blue

*BLUE: .8X TO 2X BASE

2008-09 Artifacts Frozen Artifacts Jersey Patch Combo

*GOLD/25: .6X TO 1.5X BASE COMBO/50
*SILVER/35: .5X TO 1.2X BASE COMBO/50
FADAK Anze Kopitar 10.00 25.00
FADAM Al MacInnis 8.00 20.00
FADAO Adam Oates 6.00 15.00
FADAS Alexander Semin 6.00 15.00
FADAT Alex Tanguay 4.00 10.00
FADBB Brad Boyes 4.00 10.00
FADBG Bill Guerin 6.00 15.00
FADBS Brendan Shanahan 6.00 15.00
FADCC Chris Chelios 6.00 15.00
FADCN Cam Neely 6.00 15.00
FADCW Cam Ward 6.00 15.00
FADDA Daniel Alfredsson 6.00 15.00
FADDB Daniel Briere 6.00 15.00
FADDC Dino Ciccarelli 6.00 15.00
FADDH Dominik Hasek 10.00 25.00
FADDP Dion Phaneuf 5.00 12.00
FADDS Daniel Sedin 8.00 20.00
FADDT Darcy Tucker 5.00 12.00
FADEM Evgeni Malkin 12.00 30.00
FADEN Evgeni Nabokov 5.00 12.00
FADES Eric Staal 8.00 20.00
FADHA Dale Hawerchuk 8.00 20.00
FADHE Dany Heatley 5.00 12.00
FADHL Henrik Lundqvist 15.00 40.00
FADHS Henrik Sedin 8.00 20.00
FADIK Ilya Kovalchuk 6.00 15.00
FADJC Jonathan Cheechoo 5.00 12.00
FADJG Jean-Sebastien Giguere 6.00 15.00
FADJS Joe Sakic 12.00 30.00
FADJT Joe Thornton 10.00 25.00
FADKO Alex Kovalev 5.00 12.00
FADMB Martin Brodeur 15.00 40.00
FADMF Manny Fernandez 4.00 10.00
FADMG Marian Gaborik 6.00 15.00
FADMK Miikka Kiprusoff 6.00 15.00
FADMM Mark Messier 12.00 30.00
FADMN Markus Naslund 6.00 15.00
FADMO Mike Modano 10.00 25.00
FADMS Marc Savard 4.00 10.00
FADOV Alexander Ovechkin 25.00 60.00
FADPF Peter Forsberg 12.00 30.00
FADPR Patrick Roy 15.00 40.00
FADRB Ray Bourque 10.00 25.00
FADSA Borje Salming 6.00 15.00
FADSC Sidney Crosby 25.00 60.00
FADSP Jason Spezza 6.00 15.00
FADSU Mats Sundin 6.00 15.00
FADTV Thomas Vanek 5.00 12.00

2008-09 Artifacts Treasured Swatches Retail

TSAK Alex Kovalev 3.00 8.00
TSAM Andrej Meszaros 2.50 6.00
TSAO Adam Oates 4.00 10.00
TSAS Alexander Steen 2.50 6.00
TSBS Borje Salming 4.00 10.00
TSCW Cam Ward 4.00 10.00
TSDP David Perron 3.00 8.00
TSDT Darcy Tucker 3.00 8.00
TSEM Evgeni Malkin 8.00 20.00
TSES Eric Staal 5.00 12.00
TSGA Glenn Anderson 3.00 8.00
TSGE Martin Gerber 3.00 8.00
TSGH Gordie Howe SP 15.00 30.00
TSIK Ilya Kovalchuk 4.00 10.00
TSJG Jean-Sebastien Giguere 4.00 10.00
TSJL Jere Lehtinen 2.50 6.00
TSJM Joe Mullen 3.00 8.00
TSJO Jussi Jokinen 2.50 6.00
TSJP Joni Pitkanen 2.50 6.00
TSJW Justin Williams 3.00 8.00
TSKC Kyle Calder 2.50 6.00
TSKL Kari Lehtonen 5.00 12.00
TSKO Anze Kopitar 6.00 15.00
TSKT Keith Tkachuk 4.00 10.00
TSLI John-Michael Liles 2.50 6.00
TSLM Lanny McDonald 4.00 10.00
TSLR Larry Robinson 4.00 10.00
TSLS Lee Stempniak 2.50 6.00
TSLU Joffrey Lupul 2.50 6.00
TSMG Marian Gaborik 4.00 10.00
TSMK Mikko Koivu 3.00 8.00
TSMN Markus Naslund 4.00 10.00
TSMR Mark Recchi 5.00 12.00
TSMS Marc Savard 2.50 6.00
TSMT Marty Turco 4.00 10.00
TSNL Nicklas Lidstrom 4.00 10.00
TSOV Alexander Ovechkin 15.00 40.00
TSPB Patrice Bergeron 5.00 12.00
TSPF Peter Forsberg 8.00 20.00
TSPH Dion Phaneuf 3.00 8.00
TSPK Paul Kariya 4.00 10.00
TSPM Patrick Marleau 4.00 10.00
TSPS Peter Stastny 3.00 8.00
TSRA Andrew Raycroft 3.00 8.00
TSRI Mike Richards 3.00 8.00
TSSU Mats Sundin 4.00 10.00
TSWG Wayne Gretzky SP 20.00 40.00

2008-09 Artifacts Treasured Swatches Dual

*BLUE/50: .8X TO 2X BASIC JSY/199
*GOLD/75: .6X TO 1.5X BASIC JSY/199
*SILVER/100: .5X TO 1.2X BASIC JSY/199
TSDAH Ales Hemsky 3.00 8.00
TSDAO Alexander Ovechkin 15.00 40.00
TSDAS Alexander Steen 2.50 6.00
TSDBB Bob Bourne 2.50 6.00
TSDBL Brian Leetch 3.00 8.00
TSDBM Brendan Morrison 2.50 6.00
TSDBR Brad Richards 4.00 10.00
TSDBS Brendan Shanahan 4.00 10.00
TSDCD Chris Drury 3.00 8.00
TSDCP Chris Pronger 4.00 10.00
TSDCW Cam Ward 4.00 10.00
TSDDH Dany Heatley 3.00 8.00
TSDDS Daniel Sedin 5.00 12.00
TSDES Eric Staal 5.00 12.00
TSDGA Glenn Anderson 3.00 8.00
TSDGP Gilbert Perreault 3.00 8.00
TSDHS Henrik Sedin 5.00 12.00
TSDJC Jonathan Cheechoo 3.00 8.00
TSDJI Jarome Iginla 5.00 12.00
TSDJM Joe Mullen 3.00 8.00

Card	Low	High
TSDJR Jeremy Roenick	6.00	15.00
TSDJS Jordan Staal	3.00	8.00
TSDJT Jonathan Toews	8.00	20.00
TSDKA Paul Kariya	4.00	10.00
TSDKL Kari Lehtonen	5.00	12.00
TSDKT Keith Tkachuk	4.00	10.00
TSDLM Lanny McDonald	4.00	10.00
TSDLR Luc Robitaille	4.00	10.00
TSDLU Roberto Luongo	6.00	15.00
TSDMB Martin Brodeur	10.00	25.00
TSDMO Brenden Morrow	3.00	8.00
TSDMS Mats Sundin	4.00	10.00
TSDMT Marty Turco	4.00	10.00
TSDNB Nicklas Backstrom	4.00	10.00
TSDPB Pierre-Marc Bouchard	4.00	10.00
TSDPD Pavol Demitra	5.00	12.00
TSDPE Patrik Elias	4.00	10.00
TSDPK Patrick Kane	8.00	20.00
TSDPL Pascal Leclaire	3.00	8.00
TSDPM Patrick Marleau	4.00	10.00
TSDPS Paul Stastny	3.00	8.00
TSDRD Rick DiPietro	3.00	8.00
TSDRG Ryan Getzlaf	4.00	10.00
TSDRN Rick Nash	4.00	10.00
TSDSA Miroslav Satan	4.00	10.00
TSDSD Shane Doan	3.00	8.00
TSDST Peter Stastny	3.00	8.00
TSDTS Teemu Selanne	8.00	20.00

2008-09 Artifacts Treasured Swatches Jersey Patch Combo

*GOLD/25: .8X TO 2X BASE COMBO/50
*SILVER/35: .6X TO 1.5X BASE COMBO/50

Card	Low	High
TSDAH Ales Hemsky	5.00	12.00
TSDAO Alexander Ovechkin	25.00	60.00
TSDAS Alexander Steen	4.00	10.00
TSDBB Bob Bourne	4.00	10.00
TSDBL Brian Leetch	5.00	12.00
TSDBM Brendan Morrison	4.00	10.00
TSDBR Brad Richards	6.00	15.00
TSDBS Brendan Shanahan	6.00	15.00
TSDCD Chris Drury	5.00	12.00
TSDCP Chris Pronger	6.00	15.00
TSDCW Cam Ward	6.00	15.00
TSDDH Dany Heatley	5.00	12.00
TSDDS Daniel Sedin	8.00	20.00
TSDES Eric Staal	8.00	20.00
TSDGA Glenn Anderson	5.00	12.00
TSDGP Gilbert Perreault	6.00	15.00
TSDHS Henrik Sedin	8.00	20.00
TSDJC Jonathan Cheechoo	5.00	12.00
TSDJI Jarome Iginla	8.00	20.00
TSDJM Joe Mullen	5.00	12.00
TSDJR Jeremy Roenick	10.00	25.00
TSDJS Jordan Staal	5.00	12.00
TSDJT Jonathan Toews	12.00	30.00
TSDKA Paul Kariya	6.00	15.00
TSDKL Kari Lehtonen	8.00	20.00
TSDKT Keith Tkachuk	6.00	15.00
TSDLM Lanny McDonald	6.00	15.00
TSDLR Luc Robitaille	6.00	15.00
TSDLU Roberto Luongo	10.00	25.00
TSDMB Martin Brodeur	15.00	40.00
TSDMO Brenden Morrow	5.00	12.00
TSDMS Mats Sundin	6.00	15.00
TSDMT Marty Turco	6.00	15.00
TSDNB Nicklas Backstrom	6.00	15.00
TSDPB Pierre-Marc Bouchard	6.00	15.00
TSDPD Pavol Demitra	8.00	20.00
TSDPE Patrik Elias	6.00	15.00
TSDPK Patrick Kane	12.00	30.00
TSDPL Pascal Leclaire	5.00	12.00
TSDPM Patrick Marleau	6.00	15.00
TSDPS Paul Stastny	5.00	12.00
TSDRD Rick DiPietro	5.00	12.00
TSDRG Ryan Getzlaf	6.00	15.00
TSDRN Rick Nash	6.00	15.00
TSDSA Miroslav Satan	6.00	15.00
TSDSD Shane Doan	5.00	12.00
TSDST Peter Stastny	5.00	12.00
TSDTS Teemu Selanne	12.00	30.00

2008-09 Artifacts Tundra Tandems

*BRONZE/75: .4X TO 1X BASE
*GOLD/25: .6X TO 1.5X BASE
*SILVER/50: .5X TO 1.2X BASE

Card	Low	High
TTAR S.Weber/J.Arnott	5.00	12.00
TTAS D.Alfredsson/J.Spezza	6.00	15.00
TTBD B.Seabrook/D.Keith	6.00	15.00
TTBJ J.Johnson/R.Blake	6.00	15.00
TTBL M.Brodeur/R.Luongo	15.00	40.00
TTBN M.Biron/A.Niittymaki	5.00	12.00
TTBR M.Richards/D.Briere	6.00	15.00
TTBS D.Stafford/S.Bernier	4.00	10.00
TTBT D.Tucker/J.Blake	5.00	12.00
TTCL N.Lidstrom/C.Chelios	6.00	15.00
TTCM S.Crosby/E.Malkin	15.00	40.00
TTCR J.Cheechoo/M.Ryder	5.00	12.00
TTDF P.Datsyuk/S.Fedorov	10.00	25.00
TTDG M.Gaborik/P.Demitra	8.00	20.00
TTDM S.Doan/P.Mueller	5.00	12.00
TTDS M.Modano/D.Weight	10.00	25.00
TTDZ P.Datsyuk/H.Zetterberg	10.00	25.00
TTEC E.Staal/C.Ward	8.00	20.00
TTEM E.Staal/M.Staal	8.00	20.00
TTEP P.Elias/Z.Parise	6.00	15.00
TTFB P.Forsberg/N.Backstrom	12.00	30.00
TTFM M.Fleury/E.Malkin	12.00	30.00
TTFS P.Forsberg/B.Salming	12.00	30.00
TTGB S.Gagne/D.Briere	6.00	15.00
TTGD S.Gomez/C.Drury	5.00	12.00
TTGH S.Gagne/D.Heatley	6.00	15.00
TTGK M.Gaborik/M.Koivu	6.00	15.00
TTGL W.Gretzky/M.Lemieux	20.00	50.00
TTGM W.Gretzky/M.Messier	40.00	100.00
TTGS M.Satan/B.Guerin	6.00	15.00
TTHG A.Hemsky/S.Gagner	5.00	12.00
TTHM G.Howe/M.Messier	20.00	50.00
TTHO D.Hasek/C.Osgood	10.00	25.00
TTHV N.Horton/T.Vokoun	5.00	12.00
TTIK J.Iginla/M.Kiprusoff	8.00	20.00
TTJJ E.Johnson/B.Jackman	4.00	10.00
TTJL H.Lundqvist/V.Toskala	15.00	40.00
TTJR J.Staal/R.Malone	5.00	12.00
TTJS O.Jokinen/S.Koivu	6.00	15.00
TTKB P.Kariya/B.Boyes	6.00	15.00
TTKF S.Fedorov/V.Kozlov	8.00	20.00
TTKJ A.Kopitar/J.Johnson	10.00	25.00
TTKK A.Kovalev/A.Kostitsyn	5.00	12.00
TTKL I.Kovalchuk/K.Lehtonen	8.00	20.00
TTKP S.Koivu/C.Price	12.00	30.00
TTKT M.Kiprusoff/V.Toskala	8.00	20.00
TTLG R.Langway/M.Green	5.00	12.00
TTLH N.Lidstrom/T.Holmstrom	6.00	15.00
TTLM M.Lemieux/E.Malkin	25.00	60.00
TTLN R.Nash/P.Leclaire	6.00	15.00
TTLS S.Shutt/L.Robinson	6.00	15.00
TTLT J.Thornton/V.Lecavalier	10.00	25.00
TTMC P.Marleau/J.Cheechoo	6.00	15.00
TTMK R.Kesler/B.Morrison	6.00	15.00
TTMP M.Modano/Z.Parise	10.00	25.00
TTMR M.Modano/B.Richards	10.00	25.00
TTMS L.McDonald/B.Salming	6.00	15.00
TTMT J.Thornton/P.Marleau	10.00	25.00
TTMV R.Miller/T.Vanek	6.00	15.00
TTMW M.Gaborik/P.Bouchard	6.00	15.00
TTNK C.Neely/P.Kessel	6.00	15.00
TTNL R.Luongo/M.Naslund	10.00	25.00
TTNY R.DiPietro/B.Guerin	6.00	15.00
TTOE A.Edler/M.Ohlund	4.00	10.00
TTOM A.Ovechkin/E.Malkin	25.00	60.00
TTOS A.Oates/M.Savard	6.00	15.00
TTPF S.Gagne/M.Biron	6.00	15.00
TTPN S.Niedermayer/C.Pronger	6.00	15.00
TTPP P.Stastny/P.Stastny	5.00	12.00
TTPR P.Stastny/R.Smyth	5.00	12.00
TTPS D.Stafford/D.Paille	4.00	10.00
TTRC W.Redden/M.Commodore	4.00	10.00
TTRD M.Dionne/L.Robitaille	8.00	20.00
TTRL M.Ryder/G.Latendresse	4.00	10.00
TTRM M.Ribeiro/B.Morrow	5.00	12.00
TTRP P.Roy/C.Price	15.00	40.00
TTRS L.Robitaille/S.Shutt	6.00	15.00
TTSA S.Sullivan/J.Arnott	5.00	12.00
TTSB P.Bergeron/M.Savard	8.00	20.00
TTSF J.Sakic/P.Forsberg	12.00	30.00
TTSG T.Selanne/J.Giguere	12.00	30.00
TTSH S.Horcoff/J.Stoll	5.00	12.00
TTSJ J.Cheechoo/M.Michalek	5.00	12.00
TTSK J.Kurri/T.Selanne	12.00	30.00
TTSM S.Koivu/M.Koivu	6.00	15.00
TTSO A.Ovechkin/A.Semin	25.00	60.00
TTSR J.Sakic/P.Roy	12.00	30.00
TTSS H.Sedin/D.Sedin	8.00	20.00
TTSW M.Svatos/W.Wolski	5.00	12.00
TTTB P.Budaj/J.Theodore	6.00	15.00
TTTK P.Kane/J.Toews	12.00	30.00
TTTL M.Legace/K.Tkachuk	6.00	15.00
TTTM M.Sundin/A.Steen	6.00	15.00
TTTT J.Thornton/J.Toews	10.00	25.00
TTVB T.Vokoun/J.Bouwmeester	5.00	12.00
TTVP V.Lecavalier/P.Ranger	6.00	15.00
TTWB R.Brind'Amour/J.Williams	6.00	15.00
TTWH S.Weiss/N.Horton	5.00	12.00
TTWL R.Whitney/K.Letang	8.00	20.00
TTZG S.Gonchar/S.Zubov	5.00	12.00

2008-09 Artifacts Tundra Tandems Bronze

*BRONZE/75: .4X TO 1X BASE

Card	Low	High
TTFB P.Forsberg/N.Backstrom	12.00	30.00

2008-09 Artifacts Tundra Tandems Gold

*GOLD/25: .6X TO 1.5X BASE

Card	Low	High
TTFB P.Forsberg/N.Backstrom	20.00	50.00

2008-09 Artifacts Tundra Trios Gold

Card	Low	High
T3ASE Spezza/Alfredsson/Redden	10.00	25.00
T3ASR Weber/Arnott/Sullivan	8.00	20.00
T3BEP Elias/Parise/Brodeur	25.00	60.00
T3BKJ Kopitar/Brown/Johnson	15.00	40.00
T3BSW Staal/Brind'Amour/Ward	12.00	30.00
T3CLO Ciccarelli/Oates/Lngwy	10.00	25.00
T3FCM Crosby/Malkin/Fleury	40.00	100.00
T3FKM Messier/Kurri/Fuhr	10.00	25.00
T3GBK Gabrk/Koiv/Bouchrd	10.00	25.00
T3GBR Gagne/Richards/Biron	10.00	25.00
T3GSD Satan/Guerin/DiPietro	10.00	25.00
T3HKL Koval/Holik/Leht	12.00	30.00
T3HLD Datsyuk/Lidstrom/Hasek	15.00	40.00
T3ICK Iginla/Cammllr/Kiprsff	12.00	30.00
T3JDM Doan/Mueller/Jovanovski	8.00	20.00
T3KKP Koivu/Kovalev/Price	20.00	50.00
T3KLB Kariya/Boyes/Legace	10.00	25.00
T3KOM Ovech/Malkin/Koval	15.00	40.00
T3KTK Kane/Toews/Khabibulin	20.00	50.00
T3LAM Messier/Leetch/Anderson	20.00	50.00
T3LBR Bourq/Robnsn/Lngwy	15.00	40.00
T3LGM Gretz/Mario/Mess	60.00	150.00
T3LNB Nash/Brule/Leclaire	10.00	25.00
T3LSD Lecavlr/St.Louis/Denis	10.00	25.00
T3MMM McDon/MacInn/Mulln	12.00	30.00
T3MRM Modano/Roenick/Mullen	15.00	40.00
T3MRT Modano/Richards/Turco	15.00	40.00
T3MVS Vanek/Stafford/Miller	10.00	25.00
T3NBO Neely/Oates/Bourque	15.00	40.00
T3NLS Naslund/Sedin/Bourque	15.00	40.00
T3RBL Roy/Brodeur/Luongo	25.00	60.00
T3RHG Hemsky/Gagner/Roloson	8.00	20.00
T3SBS Sakic/Stastny/Budaj	20.00	50.00
T3SBT Bergern/Savrd/Thoms	12.00	30.00
T3SJL Shanh/Staal/Lundqvst	25.00	60.00
T3SNG Selanne/Nieder/Giguere	20.00	50.00
T3STS Sundin/Steen/Toskala	12.00	30.00
T3STT Thornton/Sakic/Toews	20.00	50.00
T3SWV Savard/Vaive/Wilson	10.00	25.00
T3TNC Thornton/Chee/Nabok	15.00	40.00
T3TSB Trottier/Smith/Bourne	10.00	25.00
T3VWH Weiss/Horton/Vokoun	8.00	20.00

2009-10 Artifacts

Card	Low	High
1 Henrik Lundqvist	.75	2.00
2 Chris Osgood	.30	.75
3 Jason Spezza	.30	.75
4 Brian Campbell	.25	.60
5 Kris Versteeg	.20	.50
6 Wojtek Wolski	.20	.50
7 Simon Gagne	.30	.75
8 Phil Kessel	.30	.75
9 Eric Staal	.40	1.00
10 Doug Weight	.30	.75
11 Pavel Datsyuk	.50	1.25
12 Niklas Backstrom	.30	.75
13 Zach Parise	.30	.75
14 Steven Stamkos	.60	1.50
15 Olli Jokinen	.25	.60
16 Jonas Hiller	.25	.60
17 Cam Ward	.30	.75
18 Henrik Zetterberg	.40	1.00
19 Miikka Kiprusoff	.30	.75
20 Roberto Luongo	.50	1.25
21 Andrei Kostitsyn	.25	.60
22 Patrice Bergeron	.40	1.00
23 Jeff Carter	.25	.60
24 Carey Price	.60	1.50
25 Teemu Selanne	.60	1.50
26 Chris Drury	.25	.60
27 Thomas Vanek	.25	.60
28 Patrick Kane	.60	1.50
29 Peter Budaj	.25	.60
30 Daniel Alfredsson	.30	.75
31 Joe Thornton	.50	1.25
32 Patrick Marleau	.30	.75
33 Tim Thomas	.30	.75
34 Blake Wheeler	.30	.75
35 Jason Arnott	.25	.60
36 Shane Doan	.25	.60
37 Nathan Horton	.30	.75
38 Jonathan Toews	.50	1.25
39 Ryan Kesler	.30	.75
40 Patrick O'Sullivan	.25	.60
41 Tomas Kaberle	.20	.50
42 Jordan Staal	.25	.60
43 Tomas Vokoun	.25	.60
44 Dany Heatley	.25	.60
45 Patrik Berglund	.20	.50
46 Vincent Lecavalier	.30	.75
47 David Backes	.20	.50
48 Derick Brassard	.20	.50
49 Patrik Elias	.30	.75
50 Martin St. Louis	.30	.75
51 Ray Whitney	.25	.60
52 Evgeni Nabokov	.25	.60
53 Martin Brodeur	.75	2.00
54 Evgeni Malkin	.60	1.50
55 Pierre-Marc Bouchard	.30	.75
56 Nicklas Backstrom	.30	.75
57 Shea Weber	.25	.60
58 Bobby Ryan	.25	.60
59 Mikhail Grabovski	.20	.50
60 Sidney Crosby	1.25	3.00
61 Nicklas Lidstrom	.20	.50
62 Brad Richards	.30	.75
63 Jason Pominville	.20	.50
64 Rick DiPietro	.25	.60
65 Ales Hemsky	.25	.60
66 Marty Turco	.30	.75
67 Mason Raymond	.20	.50
68 Ilya Kovalchuk	.30	.75
69 Mike Modano	.50	1.25
70 Ryan Getzlaf	.30	.75
71 Alexander Frolov	.25	.60
72 Steve Mason	.25	.60
73 Zach Bogosian	.25	.60
74 Bryan Little	.30	.75
75 David Booth	.20	.50
76 Nikolai Zherdev	.20	.50
77 Alexander Ovechkin	1.25	3.00
78 Mike Richards	.25	.60
79 Ryan Miller	.30	.75
80 J.P. Dumont	.20	.50
81 Jarome Iginla	.40	1.00
82 Sam Gagner	.20	.50
83 Anze Kopitar	.50	1.25
84 Milan Hejduk	.25	.60
85 Drew Doughty	.40	1.00
86 Peter Mueller	.25	.60
87 Marc Staal	.20	.50
88 Andrei Markov	.30	.75
89 Simeon Varlamov	.30	.75
90 Rick Nash	.30	.75
91 Marc-Andre Fleury	.60	1.50
92 Dion Phaneuf	.25	.60
93 Paul Stastny	.25	.60
94 Tomas Plekanec	.20	.50
95 Andrew Cogliano	.20	.50
96 Mikko Koivu	.30	.75
97 Jakub Voracek	.25	.60
98 Luke Schenn	.30	.75
99 Devin Setoguchi	.25	.60
100 Paul Kariya	.30	.75
101 Denis Potvin L	1.00	2.50
102 Steve Shutt L	1.00	2.50
103 Dale Hawerchuk L	1.25	3.00
104 Stan Mikita L	1.25	3.00
105 Mario Lemieux L	4.00	10.00
106 Denis Savard L	1.00	2.50
107 Alex Delvecchio L	1.00	2.50
108 Johnny Bucyk L	1.00	2.50
109 Ted Lindsay L	.75	2.00
110 Clark Gillies L	1.00	2.50
111 Red Kelly L	1.00	2.50
112 Gilbert Perreault L	1.00	2.50
113 Jean Beliveau L	1.00	2.50
114 Mark Messier L	2.00	5.00
115 Guy Carbonneau L	1.50	4.00
116 Steve Yzerman L	2.50	6.00
117 Frank Mahovlich L	1.00	2.50
118 Lanny McDonald L	1.00	2.50
119 Peter Stastny L	.75	2.00
120 Larry Robinson L	1.00	2.50
121 Bobby Orr L	4.00	10.00
122 Cam Neely L	1.00	2.50
123 Rogie Vachon L	1.25	3.00
124 Phil Esposito L	1.50	4.00
125 Johnny Bower L	1.00	2.50
126 Luc Robitaille L	1.00	2.50
127 Patrick Roy L	2.50	6.00
128 Doug Gilmour L	1.25	3.00
129 Mike Bossy L	1.00	2.50
130 Bobby Clarke L	1.50	4.00
131 Ray Bourque L	1.50	4.00
132 Al MacInnis L	1.25	3.00
133 Bobby Hull L	2.00	5.00
134 Gordie Howe L	3.00	8.00
135 Wayne Gretzky L	6.00	15.00
136 Alexander Ovechkin S	4.00	10.00
137 Jonathan Toews S	1.50	4.00
138 Henrik Zetterberg S	1.25	3.00
139 Joe Thornton S	1.50	4.00
140 Evgeni Malkin S	2.00	5.00
141 Henrik Lundqvist S	2.50	6.00
142 Pavel Datsyuk S	1.50	4.00
143 Martin Brodeur S	2.50	6.00
144 Ilya Kovalchuk S	1.00	2.50
145 Patrick Kane S	2.00	5.00
146 Carey Price S	2.00	5.00
147 Jeff Carter S	.75	2.00
148 Vincent Lecavalier S	1.00	2.50
149 Jarome Iginla S	1.25	3.00
150 Sidney Crosby S	4.00	10.00
151 Chris Durno RC	1.50	4.00
152 Peter Regin RC	1.50	4.00
153 Kevin Quick RC	1.25	3.00
154 Kurtis McLean RC	1.50	4.00
155 Mike Santorelli RC	2.00	5.00
156 Alexander Sulzer RC	1.25	3.00
157 Troy Bodie RC	1.50	4.00
158 Matt Beleskey RC	1.50	4.00
159 Kevin Westgarth RC	1.50	4.00
160 John Scott RC	2.00	5.00
161 Mikael Backlund RC	3.00	8.00
162 Byron Bitz RC	1.50	4.00
163 Bryan Rodney RC	1.50	4.00
164 Tim Wallace RC	1.25	3.00
165 Ben Lovejoy RC	2.00	5.00
166 Riley Armstrong RC	1.50	4.00
167 Jaime Sifers RC	1.50	4.00
168 Sean Collins RC	1.50	4.00
169 Riku Helenius RC	2.00	5.00
170 Ville Leino RC	1.50	4.00
171 Michal Neuvirth RC	3.00	8.00
172 Artem Anisimov RC	1.25	3.00
173 Davis Drewiske RC	2.00	5.00
174 David Schlemko RC	1.50	4.00
175 Luca Caputi RC	2.00	5.00
176 Jakub Petruzalek RC	2.00	5.00
177 Ryan Vesce RC	1.50	4.00
178 Jay Beagle RC	2.50	6.00
179 Jhonas Enroth RC	2.50	6.00
180 Brandon Segal RC	1.50	4.00
181 Tim Stapleton RC	2.00	5.00
182 Jesse Joensuu RC	1.50	4.00
183 David Van Der Gulik RC	1.50	4.00
184 Antti Niemi RC	3.00	8.00
185 Grant Lewis RC	1.50	4.00
186 Cal O'Reilly RC	1.50	4.00
187 Brian Salcido RC	1.25	3.00
188 Phil Oreskovic RC	2.00	5.00
189 Kris Chucko RC	1.25	3.00
190 Joel Rechlicz RC	1.25	3.00
191 Andrew MacDonald RC	1.25	3.00
192 Spencer Machacek RC	2.00	5.00
193 T.J. Galiardi RC	2.00	5.00
194 Michael Sauer RC	1.50	4.00
195 Yannick Weber RC	2.00	5.00
196 Christian Hanson RC	2.00	5.00
197 Ivan Vishnevskiy RC	1.25	3.00
198 Taylor Chorney RC	2.00	5.00
199 John Negrin RC	2.00	5.00
200 Matt Pelech RC	2.00	5.00
201 John Carlson RC	4.00	10.00
202 Michael Grabner RC	2.00	5.00
203 Jonas Gustavsson RC	2.50	6.00
204 Victor Hedman RC	5.00	12.00
205 Lars Eller RC	2.00	5.00
206 Logan Couture RC	4.00	10.00
207 Mark Letestu RC	2.00	5.00
208 Shawn Heshka RC	2.00	5.00
209 James van Riemsdyk RC	4.00	10.00
210 Erik Karlsson RC	6.00	15.00
211 Michael Del Zotto RC	2.00	5.00
212 John Tavares RC	8.00	20.00
213 Matthew Corrente RC	1.50	4.00
214 Colin Wilson RC	2.00	5.00
215 Mathieu Carle RC	2.00	5.00
216 Danny Irmen RC	1.25	3.00
217 Andrei Loktionov RC	2.50	6.00
218 Dmitry Kulikov RC	2.00	5.00
219 Devan Dubnyk RC	3.00	8.00
220 Jakub Kindl RC	2.00	5.00
221 Jamie Benn RC	6.00	15.00
222 Ryan Stoa RC	1.50	4.00
223 Matt Duchene RC	4.00	10.00
224 Matt Gilroy RC	2.00	5.00
225 Viktor Stalberg RC	2.00	5.00
226 Sergei Shirokov RC	1.25	3.00
227 Tyler Myers RC	3.00	8.00
228 Brad Marchand RC	8.00	20.00
229 Evander Kane RC	4.00	10.00
230 MacGregor Sharp RC	2.00	5.00
231 Ryan Oâ•™Reilly RC	4.00	10.00
232 Daniel Larsson RC	1.50	4.00
233 Ryan O'Marra RC	1.25	3.00
234 Bobby Sanguinetti RC	1.25	3.00
235 Jason Demers RC	3.00	8.00
236 Tyler Ennis RC	2.50	6.00
237 Tyler Bozak RC	3.00	8.00
238 Benn Ferriero RC	2.00	5.00
239 Mikko Lehtonen RC	3.00	8.00
240 Anton Khudobin RC	3.00	8.00
241 Tyler Eckford RC	1.50	4.00
242 James Reimer RC	5.00	12.00

2009-10 Artifacts Gold

*1-100 VETS/75: 3X TO 8X BASIC CARDS
*101-150 L/S/75: 1X TO 2.5X L/S/999
*151-200 ROOKIES/75: .8X TO 2X RC/999

2009-10 Artifacts Silver

*1-100 VETS/75: 2.5X TO 6X BASIC CARDS
*101-150 L/S/75: .8X TO 2X L/S/999
*151-200 ROOKIES/75: .6X TO 1.5X RC/999

2009-10 Artifacts Silver Spectrum

*1-100 VETS/25: 4X TO 10X BASIC CARDS
*101-150 L/S/25: 1.2X TO 3X L/S/999
*151-200 ROOKIES/25: 1X TO 2.5X RC/999

2009-10 Artifacts Autofacts

Card	Low	High
AFAC Andrew Cogliano	4.00	10.00
AFAE Andrew Ebbett	4.00	10.00
AFAM Al MacInnis	8.00	20.00
AFAO Adam Oates	6.00	15.00
AFAT Alex Tanguay	4.00	10.00
AFBB Bob Bourne	4.00	10.00
AFBG Brian Gionta	4.00	10.00
AFBL Brian Lee	6.00	15.00
AFBM Brenden Morrow	5.00	12.00
AFBO Brian Boyle	4.00	10.00
AFBP Pierre-Marc Bouchard	6.00	15.00
AFCA Mike Cammalleri	5.00	12.00
AFCG Clark Gillies	6.00	15.00
AFCH Don Cherry	6.00	15.00
AFCR Sidney Crosby	60.00	150.00
AFCS Cory Stillman	5.00	12.00
AFDA Matt D'Agostini	5.00	12.00
AFDB David Booth	4.00	10.00
AFDC David Clarkson	5.00	12.00
AFDD Drew Doughty	8.00	20.00
AFDG Daniel Girardi	4.00	10.00
AFDH Dale Hawerchuk	8.00	20.00
AFDJ David Jones	4.00	10.00
AFDL Dan LaCosta	5.00	12.00
AFDP David Perron	5.00	12.00
AFDS Darryl Sittler	8.00	20.00
AFDU Dustin Boyd	4.00	10.00
AFDW Doug Weight	6.00	15.00
AFEL Patrik Elias	6.00	15.00
AFEM Evgeni Malkin	12.00	30.00
AFEN Evgeni Nabokov	5.00	12.00
AFES Phil Esposito	10.00	25.00
AFFB Fabian Brunnstrom	5.00	12.00
AFFI Mark Fistric	4.00	10.00
AFFM Frank Mahovlich	6.00	15.00
AFGA Glenn Anderson	5.00	12.00
AFGH Gordie Howe	50.00	125.00
AFHE Dany Heatley	5.00	12.00
AFHM Milan Hejduk	5.00	12.00
AFJB Jean Beliveau	6.00	15.00
AFJD Jeff Drouin-Deslauriers	4.00	10.00
AFJE Jonathan Ericsson	4.00	10.00
AFJG Jean-Sebastien Giguere	6.00	15.00
AFJJ Jack Johnson	4.00	10.00
AFJK Jari Kurri	6.00	15.00
AFJM Joe Mullen	5.00	12.00
AFJP Jason Pominville	4.00	10.00
AFJS Jack Skille	4.00	10.00
AFJT Joe Thornton	10.00	25.00
AFKC Kyle Chipchura	5.00	12.00
AFKD Kris Draper	4.00	10.00
AFKL Kari Lehtonen	5.00	12.00
AFKT Kyle Turris	6.00	15.00
AFLI Bryan Little	6.00	15.00
AFLR Larry Robinson	6.00	15.00
AFLS Luke Schenn	6.00	15.00
AFMB Mike Bossy	6.00	15.00
AFMC Bryan McCabe	5.00	12.00
AFMD Marcel Dionne	8.00	20.00
AFMF Marc-Andre Fleury	12.00	30.00
AFMH Martin Havlat	5.00	12.00
AFMI Mike Iggulden	4.00	10.00
AFMK Miikka Kiprusoff	6.00	15.00
AFML Milan Lucic	5.00	12.00
AFMM Milan Michalek	4.00	10.00
AFMO Mike Modano	10.00	25.00
AFMP Michael Peca	5.00	12.00
AFMR Mason Raymond	4.00	10.00
AFNK Nikolai Khabibulin	6.00	15.00
AFNZ Nikolai Zherdev	4.00	10.00
AFPB Peter Budaj	5.00	12.00
AFPE Dustin Penner	4.00	10.00
AFPI Alex Pietrangelo	5.00	12.00
AFPK Phil Kessel	6.00	15.00
AFPM Patrick Marleau	6.00	15.00
AFPO Denis Potvin	6.00	15.00
AFPR Patrick Roy	50.00	125.00
AFRB Rob Blake	6.00	15.00
AFRC Ryane Clowe	4.00	10.00
AFRH Ron Hextall	6.00	15.00
AFRI Mattias Ritola	5.00	12.00
AFRK Rostislav Klesla	6.00	15.00
AFRM Mike Ribeiro	4.00	10.00
AFRV Rogie Vachon	8.00	20.00
AFRY Ryan Miller	6.00	15.00
AFSA Derek Sanderson	6.00	15.00
AFSC Marek Schwarz	4.00	10.00
AFSE Devin Setoguchi	5.00	12.00
AFSH James Sheppard	4.00	10.00
AFSS Steven Stamkos	12.00	30.00
AFTG Tom Gilbert	4.00	10.00
AFTS Tom Sestito	4.00	10.00
AFTV Thomas Vanek	5.00	12.00
AFTW Ty Wishart	5.00	12.00
AFVF Valtteri Filppula	4.00	10.00
AFWI Doug Wilson	5.00	12.00
AFZB Zach Boychuk	5.00	12.00

2009-10 Artifacts Frozen Artifacts

*BLUE/25: .6X TO 1.5X BASIC JSY
*COPPER/50: .6X TO 1.5X BASIC JSY
*JSY-PATCH/35: .8X TO 2X BASIC JSY
*BLU JSY-PTCH/25: 1X TO 2.5X BASIC JSY
*RETAIL JSY: .4X TO 1X BASIC JSY

Card	Low	High
FAAM Al MacInnis	4.00	10.00
FABC Bobby Clarke	5.00	12.00
FABL Brian Leetch	2.50	6.00
FABN Bernie Nicholls	2.50	6.00
FABO Mike Bossy	3.00	8.00
FABR Rob Blake	3.00	8.00
FABS Borje Salming	3.00	8.00
FABU Johnny Bucyk	3.00	8.00
FACJ Curtis Joseph	4.00	10.00
FACN Cam Neely	3.00	8.00
FADC Dino Ciccarelli	3.00	8.00
FADG Doug Gilmour	4.00	10.00
FADH Dale Hawerchuk	4.00	10.00
FADW Doug Weight	3.00	8.00
FAFM Frank Mahovlich	3.00	8.00
FAGA Glenn Anderson	2.50	6.00
FAGC Guy Carbonneau	5.00	12.00
FAGF Grant Fuhr	5.00	12.00
FAGH Gordie Howe	10.00	25.00
FAGP Gilbert Perreault	3.00	8.00
FAJK Jari Kurri	3.00	8.00
FAJS Joe Sakic	6.00	15.00
FALM Lanny McDonald	3.00	8.00
FALR Larry Robinson	3.00	8.00
FAMB Martin Brodeur	8.00	20.00
FAML Mario Lemieux	12.00	30.00
FAMM Mark Messier	6.00	15.00
FAMO Mike Modano	5.00	12.00
FAMS Mats Sundin	3.00	8.00
FANI Scott Niedermayer	3.00	8.00
FANL Nicklas Lidstrom	2.00	5.00
FAPE Phil Esposito	5.00	12.00
FAPK Paul Kariya	3.00	8.00
FAPR Patrick Roy	8.00	20.00
FAPS Peter Stastny	2.50	6.00
FARB Ray Bourque	5.00	12.00
FARH Ron Hextall	3.00	8.00
FARL Rod Langway	2.50	6.00
FARO Luc Robitaille	3.00	8.00
FASF Sergei Fedorov	5.00	12.00
FASH Brendan Shanahan	3.00	8.00
FASK Saku Koivu	3.00	8.00
FASS Steve Shutt	3.00	8.00
FATE Tony Esposito	3.00	8.00
FATS Teemu Selanne	6.00	15.00
FAWG Wayne Gretzky	20.00	50.00
FAWI Doug Wilson	2.50	6.00

2009-10 Artifacts Treasured Swatches

*BLUE/25: .6X TO 1.5X BASIC JSY
*COPPER/50: .5X TO 1.2X BASIC JSY
*JSY-PATCH/35: .8X TO 2X BASIC JSY
*BLU JSY-PTCH/25: 1X TO 2.5X BASIC JSY

Card	Low	High
TSAK Alex Kovalev	2.50	6.00
TSAO Alexander Ovechkin	12.00	30.00
TSBR Brad Richards	3.00	8.00
TSBW Blake Wheeler	3.00	8.00
TSCD Chris Drury	2.50	6.00
TSCP Carey Price	6.00	15.00
TSDD Drew Doughty	4.00	10.00
TSDH Dany Heatley	2.50	6.00
TSDP Dion Phaneuf	2.50	6.00
TSDS Daniel Sedin	4.00	10.00
TSEM Evgeni Malkin	6.00	15.00
TSEN Evgeni Nabokov	2.50	6.00
TSES Eric Staal	4.00	10.00
TSGA Marian Gaborik	3.00	8.00
TSHL Henrik Lundqvist	8.00	20.00
TSIK Ilya Kovalchuk	3.00	8.00
TSJB Jay Bouwmeester	2.00	5.00
TSJC Duncan Keith	2.50	6.00
TSJI Jarome Iginla	4.00	10.00
TSJP Jason Pominville	2.00	5.00
TSJS Jason Spezza	3.00	8.00
TSJT Jonathan Toews	5.00	12.00
TSKO Anze Kopitar	5.00	12.00
TSLS Luke Schenn	3.00	8.00
TSMA Patrick Marleau	3.00	8.00
TSMF Marc-Andre Fleury	6.00	15.00
TSMG Mike Green	2.50	6.00
TSMH Marian Hossa	3.00	8.00
TSMK Miikka Kiprusoff	3.00	8.00
TSMN Markus Naslund	3.00	8.00
TSMR Mike Richards	2.50	6.00
TSMS Marc Savard	2.00	5.00
TSMT Marty Turco	3.00	8.00
TSNB Nicklas Backstrom	3.00	8.00
TSOJ Olli Jokinen	2.50	6.00
TSPD Pavel Datsyuk	5.00	12.00
TSPL Pascal Leclaire	3.00	8.00
TSPM Peter Mueller	2.50	6.00
TSPS Paul Stastny	2.50	6.00
TSRD Rick DiPietro	2.50	6.00
TSRG Ryan Getzlaf	3.00	8.00
TSRL Roberto Luongo	5.00	12.00
TSRM Ryan Miller	3.00	8.00
TSRN Rick Nash	3.00	8.00
TSSC Sidney Crosby	12.00	30.00
TSSE Devin Setoguchi	2.50	6.00
TSSM Martin St. Louis	3.00	8.00
TSST Jordan Staal	2.50	6.00
TSSV Marek Svatos	2.00	5.00
TSWR Wade Redden	2.00	5.00

2009-10 Artifacts Treasured Swatches Retail

Card	Low	High
TSRAH Adam Hall	2.00	5.00
TSRAK Alex Kovalev	2.50	6.00
TSRAN Antero Niittymaki	3.00	8.00
TSRAO Alexander Ovechkin	12.00	30.00
TSRAW Andy Wozniewski	2.00	5.00
TSRBO Pierre-Marc Bouchard	3.00	8.00
TSRBS Brent Seabrook	2.00	5.00
TSRCC Chris Campoli	2.00	5.00
TSRCP Carey Price	6.00	15.00
TSRDH Dany Heatley	2.50	6.00
TSRDT Darcy Tucker	2.50	6.00
TSRES Eric Staal	4.00	10.00
TSRFB Francis Bouillon	2.00	5.00
TSRGO Scott Gomez	2.50	6.00
TSRHL Henrik Lundqvist	8.00	20.00
TSRIK Ilya Kovalchuk	3.00	8.00
TSRJC Jonathan Cheechoo	2.50	6.00
TSRJS Jordan Staal	2.50	6.00
TSRKA Anze Kopitar	5.00	12.00
TSRKL Kari Lehtonen	2.50	6.00
TSRKO Andrei Kostitsyn	2.50	6.00
TSRMC Matt Carle	2.50	6.00
TSRMF Manny Fernandez	2.00	5.00
TSRMG Marian Gaborik	3.00	8.00
TSRMJ Milan Jurcina	2.00	5.00
TSRMK Mike Komisarek	2.50	6.00
TSRMP Marc-Antoine Pouliot	2.50	6.00
TSRMR Mike Richards	2.50	6.00
TSRMS Marc Savard	2.00	5.00
TSRMT Marty Turco	3.00	8.00
TSRMU Peter Mueller	2.50	6.00
TSRNL Nicklas Lidstrom	2.00	5.00
TSRPB Patrice Brisebois	2.00	5.00
TSRPM Patrick Marleau	3.00	8.00
TSRPP Petr Prucha	2.00	5.00
TSRRD Rick DiPietro	2.50	6.00
TSRRM Ryan Miller	3.00	8.00
TSRSB Steve Bernier	2.00	5.00
TSRSC Sidney Crosby	12.00	30.00
TSRSD Shane Doan	2.50	6.00
TSRSE Sergei Gonchar	2.00	5.00
TSRSG Sam Gagner	2.00	5.00
TSRSW Shea Weber	2.50	6.00
TSRTB Todd Bertuzzi	3.00	8.00
TSRTH Tomas Holmstrom	2.50	6.00
TSRTP Tomas Plekanec	2.00	5.00
TSRTV Thomas Vanek	2.50	6.00
TSRVK Viktor Kozlov	2.00	5.00
TSRWE Stephen Weiss	2.00	5.00
TSRZP Zach Parise	3.00	8.00

2009-10 Artifacts Tundra Tandems

*RED/50: .4X TO 1X BASIC DUAL
*SILVER/25: .6X TO 1.5X BASIC DUAL
*PATCH/35: .8X TO 2X BASIC DUAL

Card	Low	High
TTBE Brodeur/Elias	8.00	20.00
TTBK Kopitar/Brown	5.00	12.00
TTCM Malkin/Crosby	12.00	30.00
TTCR Chelios/Rafalski	3.00	8.00
TTDM Mueller/Doan	2.50	6.00
TTDT Selanne/Hawerchuk	6.00	15.00
TTED Perron/Johnson	2.50	6.00
TTFM Federko/Mullen	2.50	6.00
TTFS Fleury/Staal	6.00	15.00
TTFT Thomas/Fernandez	3.00	8.00
TTGA Zherdev/Gaborik	3.00	8.00
TTGF Gilmour/Fleury	5.00	12.00
TTGR Richards/Gagne	3.00	8.00
TTGS Selanne/Getzlaf	6.00	15.00
TTHB Booth/Horton	3.00	8.00
TTHH Hextall/Howe	3.00	8.00
TTHZ Zetterberg/Holmstrom	4.00	10.00
TTIB Bouwmeester/Iginla	4.00	10.00
TTJD Doughty/Johnson	4.00	10.00
TTJK Jokinen/Kiprusoff	3.00	8.00
TTJP Leclaire/Spezza	3.00	8.00
TTKL Kovalchuk/Little	3.00	8.00
TTKT Kariya/Tkachuk	3.00	8.00
TTKW Kessel/Wheeler	3.00	8.00
TTLC Crosby/Lemieux	12.00	30.00
TTLD Datsyuk/Lidstrom	5.00	12.00
TTLM Messier/Leetch	6.00	15.00
TTLS Stamkos/Lecavalier	6.00	15.00
TTMF Fuhr/Messier	6.00	15.00
TTMS Marleau/Setoguchi	3.00	8.00
TTMT Modano/Turco	5.00	12.00
TTNB Bourque/Neely	5.00	12.00
TTNK Kurri/Nicholls	3.00	8.00
TTNL Naslund/Lundqvist	8.00	20.00
TTNU Nash/Umberger	3.00	8.00
TTOB Backstrom/Ovechkin	12.00	30.00
TTOD Draper/Osgood	3.00	8.00
TTOG Gagner/O'Sullivan	2.50	6.00
TTPB Seabrook/Sharp	3.00	8.00
TTPC Clarkson/Parise	3.00	8.00
TTPS Stafford/Pominville	2.00	5.00
TTPW Stastny/Wolski	2.50	6.00
TTRG Robitaille/Gretzky	20.00	50.00
TTRS Savard/Roy	8.00	20.00
TTRV Roy/Vanek	2.50	6.00
TTSB Sakic/Bourque	6.00	15.00
TTSG Gilmour/Sundin	4.00	10.00
TTSH Spezza/Heatley	3.00	8.00
TTSL Sundin/Luongo	5.00	12.00
TTSS Sundin/Salming	3.00	8.00
TTSW Ward/Staal	4.00	10.00
TTTG Theodore/Green	3.00	8.00
TTTK Kane/Toews	6.00	15.00
TTWD DiPietro/Weight	3.00	8.00
TTWS Weber/Sullivan	2.50	6.00

2009-10 Artifacts Tundra Trios

Card	Low	High
TRIASW Arnott/Sullivan/Weber	4.00	10.00
TRIBEP Parise/Elias/Brodeur	12.00	30.00
TRIBHS Weiss/Horton/Booth	5.00	12.00
TRIBKP Phaneuf/Kiprsf/Bouwm	5.00	12.00
TRIBSW Staal/Brind`Amour/Ward	6.00	15.00
TRICGM Crosby/Mess/Gretzky	30.00	80.00
TRICMS Crosby/Staal/Malkin	20.00	50.00
TRIDMB Mueller/Doan/Boedker	4.00	10.00
TRIEJM Staal/Staal/Staal	6.00	15.00
TRIFCT Ferrndz/Thomas/Chara	5.00	12.00
TRIFKD Frolov/Doughty/Kopitar	8.00	20.00
TRIGCK Gomez/Kostits/Cammall	4.00	10.00
TRIGFL Letang/Fleury/Gonchar	10.00	25.00
TRIGOB Green/Bckstrm/Ovech	20.00	50.00
TRIGRC Richards/Gagne/Carter	5.00	12.00
TRIHOD Holmstrm/Datsyk/Osgd	8.00	20.00
TRIJIB Bouwmstr/Jokin/Iginla	6.00	15.00
TRIKGG Giguere/Koivu/Getzlaf	5.00	12.00
TRIKLL Little/Kovalchk/Lehtnen	5.00	12.00
TRIKTP Tkachuk/Kariya/Perron	5.00	12.00
TRILBE Edler/Bieksa/Luongo	8.00	20.00
TRILGH Howe/Gretzky/Lemieux	30.00	80.00
TRILHZ Holmstrm/Zetter/Lidstrm	6.00	15.00
TRILSS Stamkos/Lecav/St.L	10.00	25.00
TRIMGP Price/Markov/Gionta	10.00	25.00
TRIMNC Cheech/Nabkv/Marleau	5.00	12.00
TRIMRT Turco/Richards/Modano	8.00	20.00
TRINLZ Naslund/Lundq/Zhrdev	12.00	30.00
TRINSS Sundin/Sakic/Nolan	10.00	25.00
TRIOCG O'Sulli/Cogliano/Gagner	4.00	10.00
TRIPMV Vanek/Pominville/Miller	5.00	12.00
TRIPRS Pominville/Roy/Stafford	3.00	8.00
TRISHS Stastny/Hejduk/Sakic	10.00	25.00
TRISJK Jokinen/Selanne/Kurri	10.00	25.00
TRISLH Spezza/Leclaire/Heatley	5.00	12.00
TRISTK Kane/Toews/Sharp	10.00	25.00
TRITSS Toskala/Stajan/Schenn	5.00	12.00
TRIWDT Weight/DiPietro/Tambllni	5.00	12.00

2010-11 Artifacts

Card	Low	High
COMP.SET w/o SPs (100)	12.00	30.00
1 Brad Richards	.40	1.00
2 Henrik Lundqvist	1.00	2.50
3 Jonathan Toews	.60	1.50
4 Thomas Vanek	.30	.75
5 Andrew Cogliano	.25	.60
6 Patrick Kane	.75	2.00
7 Carey Price	.75	2.00
8 Miikka Kiprusoff	.40	1.00
9 John Tavares	.60	1.50
10 Jimmy Howard	.50	1.25
11 Ryan Miller	.40	1.00
12 Ilya Kovalchuk	.40	1.00
13 Vincent Lecavalier	.40	1.00
14 Pascal Leclaire	.30	.75
15 Kyle Okposo	.25	.60
16 Matt Duchene	.40	1.00
17 Nicklas Backstrom	.40	1.00
18 Shane Doan	.30	.75
19 Tomas Vokoun	.30	.75
20 Patrik Elias	.40	1.00
21 Patrick Marleau	.40	1.00
22 Marc-Andre Fleury	.75	2.00
23 Alexander Ovechkin	1.50	4.00
24 Mike Cammalleri	.40	1.00
25 Dustin Penner	.25	.60

26 Marc Savard .25 .60
27 Cam Ward .40 1.00
28 Martin St. Louis .40 1.00
29 Patrik Berglund .25 .60
30 Evander Kane .40 1.00
31 Andrei Markov .40 1.00
32 Mike Green .30 .75
33 Brandon Sutter .25 .60
34 Derick Brassard .25 .60
35 Claude Giroux .40 1.00
36 Phil Kessel .40 1.00
37 Chris Stewart .30 .75
38 Joe Pavelski .50 1.25
39 Jonas Gustavsson .50 1.25
40 Ryan Kesler .40 1.00
41 Daniel Briere .40 1.00
42 Brandon Dubinsky .25 .60
43 Jeff Carter .30 .75
44 Anze Kopitar .60 1.50
45 Milan Lucic .40 1.00
46 Bobby Ryan .30 .75
47 Dion Phaneuf .30 .75
48 Steven Stamkos .75 2.00
49 Rene Bourque .25 .60
50 Jason Spezza .40 1.00
51 James Neal .25 .60
52 Tuukka Rask .50 1.25
53 Eric Staal .50 1.25
54 Evgeni Malkin .75 2.00
55 Stephen Weiss .30 .75
56 Tyler Myers .25 .60
57 Rich Peverley .40 1.00
58 Henrik Sedin .50 1.25
59 Mikko Koivu .40 1.00
60 Ilya Bryzgalov .30 .75
61 Roberto Luongo .60 1.50
62 Sidney Crosby 1.50 4.00
63 Zach Parise .40 1.00
64 Joe Thornton .60 1.50
65 J.P. Dumont .25 .60
66 Paul Stastny .30 .75
67 Ryan Getzlaf .40 1.00
68 David Perron .30 .75
69 Rick Nash .40 1.00
70 Michael Frolik .25 .60
71 Zach Bogosian .30 .75
72 Dany Heatley .30 .75
73 Jamie Benn .50 1.25
74 David Backes .25 .60
75 Antti Niemi .30 .75
76 Sam Gagner .25 .60
77 Daniel Alfredsson .40 1.00
78 Jack Johnson .25 .60
79 Scottie Upshall .25 .60
80 Patric Hornqvist .25 .60
81 Jordan Staal .30 .75
82 Corey Perry .60 1.50
83 Mike Richards .30 .75
84 Jarome Iginla .50 1.25
85 Shea Weber .30 .75
86 Tyler Bozak .25 .60
87 Niklas Backstrom .40 1.00
88 Drew Doughty .50 1.25
89 Daniel Sedin .50 1.25
90 Pavel Datsyuk .60 1.50
91 Derek Roy .25 .60
92 Duncan Keith .30 .75
93 Martin Brodeur 1.00 2.50
94 Josh Bailey .30 .75
95 Nicklas Lidstrom .40 1.00
96 Jakub Voracek .30 .75
97 Zdeno Chara .40 1.00
98 Marian Gaborik .40 1.00
99 Henrik Zetterberg .50 1.25
100 Guillaume Latendresse .30 .75
101 Nick Palmieri RC 2.00 5.00
102 Zach Hamill RC 2.00 5.00
103 Jamie McBain RC 2.00 5.00
104 Nick Johnson RC 1.50 4.00
105 Dean Arsene RC 2.00 5.00
106 P.K. Subban RC 12.00 30.00
107 Jared Cowen RC 2.00 5.00
108 Justin Mercier RC 2.00 5.00
109 Grant Clitsome RC 2.00 5.00
110 Kaspars Daugavins RC 2.50 6.00
111 Kyle Wilson RC 2.50 6.00
112 Alex Plante RC 2.00 5.00
113 Nate Prosser RC 2.00 5.00
114 Dylan Reese RC 2.00 5.00
115 Brock Trotter RC 4.00 10.00
116 Raymond Sawada RC 1.50 4.00
117 Arturs Kulda RC 2.00 5.00
118 Tomas Kana RC 2.00 5.00
119 Jerome Samson RC 2.00 5.00
120 Chad Kolarik RC 2.00 5.00
121 Corey Elkins RC 1.50 4.00
122 Derek Smith RC 2.00 5.00
123 Brayden Irwin RC 2.00 5.00
124 Charles Linglet RC 2.00 5.00
125 Matt Zaba RC 2.50 6.00
126 Bobby Butler RC 2.00 5.00
127 Cody Almond RC 2.00 5.00
128 Dustin Tokarski RC 2.00 5.00
129 Casey Wellman RC 2.00 5.00
130 Alexander Pechurski RC 2.50 6.00
131 Francis Wathier 2.00 5.00
132 Matt Martin RC 3.00 8.00
133 Ilkka Heikkinen RC 3.00 8.00
134 Maxim Noreau RC 1.50 4.00
135 Jeff Penner RC 3.00 8.00
136 Adam McQuaid RC 2.50 6.00
137 Nick Bonino RC 2.50 6.00
138 Dustin Kohn RC 2.00 5.00
139 Eric Tangradi RC 2.00 5.00
140 Andrew Bodnarchuk RC 2.00 5.00
141 Brandon Yip RC 2.00 5.00
142 Evgeny Dadonov RC 2.50 6.00
143 Justin Falk RC 1.50 4.00
144 J.T. Wyman RC 2.00 5.00
145 Richard Clune RC 2.50 6.00
146 Johan Motin RC 1.50 4.00
147 Nick Spaling RC 2.00 5.00
148 Nazem Kadri RC 6.00 15.00
149 Philip Larsen RC 2.00 5.00
150 Maxime Fortunus RC 1.50 4.00
151 Patrick Kane S 2.50 6.00
152 Jaroslav Halak S 1.25 3.00
153 Sidney Crosby S 5.00 12.00
154 Nicklas Backstrom S 1.25 3.00
155 Joe Thornton S 2.00 5.00
156 Eric Staal S 1.50 4.00
157 Matt Duchene S 1.25 3.00
158 Jonathan Toews S 2.00 5.00
159 Ilya Kovalchuk S 1.25 3.00
160 Evgeni Malkin S 2.50 6.00
161 Marian Gaborik S 1.25 3.00
162 Martin Brodeur S 3.00 8.00
163 Drew Doughty S 1.50 4.00
164 Daniel Sedin S 1.50 4.00
165 Jeff Carter S 1.00 2.50
166 Ryan Miller S 1.25 3.00
167 Marc-Andre Fleury S 2.50 6.00
168 Thomas Vanek S 1.00 2.50
169 Henrik Lundqvist S 3.00 8.00
170 Steven Stamkos S 2.50 6.00
171 Mike Richards S 1.00 2.50
172 Henrik Zetterberg S 1.50 4.00
173 Jonas Gustavsson S 1.50 4.00
174 Vincent Lecavalier S 1.25 3.00
175 Pavel Datsyuk S 2.00 5.00
176 Antti Niemi S 1.00 2.50
177 John Tavares S 2.00 5.00
178 Alexander Ovechkin S 5.00 12.00
179 Jarome Iginla S 1.50 4.00
180 Anze Kopitar S 2.00 5.00
181 Jean Beliveau L 1.25 3.00
182 Luc Robitaille L 1.25 3.00
183 Cam Neely L 1.25 3.00
184 Mike Modano L 2.00 5.00
185 Jari Kurri L 1.25 3.00
186 Bobby Clarke L 2.00 5.00
187 Gordie Howe L 4.00 10.00
188 Mark Messier L 2.50 6.00
189 Gilbert Perreault L 1.25 3.00
190 Ron Hextall L 1.25 3.00
191 Bobby Hull L 2.50 6.00
192 Steve Yzerman L 3.00 8.00
193 Denis Potvin L 1.25 3.00
194 Dale Hawerchuk L 1.50 4.00
195 Bobby Orr L 5.00 12.00
196 Mario Lemieux L 5.00 12.00
197 Patrick Roy L 3.00 8.00
198 Phil Esposito L 2.00 5.00
199 Brian Leetch L 1.00 2.50
200 Wayne Gretzky L 8.00 20.00
201 Cam Fowler RC 8.00 20.00
202 Alexander Burmistrov RC 3.00 8.00
203 Tyler Seguin RC 15.00 30.00
204 Luke Adam RC 3.00 8.00
205 Henrik Karlsson RC 3.00 8.00
206 Jeff Skinner RC 8.00 20.00
207 Nick Leddy RC 4.00 10.00
208 Kevin Shattenkirk RC 6.00 15.00
209 Nick Holden RC 3.00 8.00
210 Philip Larsen RC 3.00 8.00
211 Alexander Vasyunov RC 3.00 8.00
212 Taylor Hall RC 12.00 30.00
213 Jamie Arniel RC 3.00 8.00
214 Brayden Schenn RC 8.00 20.00
215 Marco Scandella RC 3.00 8.00
216 Stefan Della Rovere RC 8.00 20.00
217 Anders Lindback RC 3.00 8.00
218 Jacob Josefson RC 3.00 8.00
219 Nino Niederreiter RC 5.00 12.00
220 Derek Stepan RC 4.00 10.00
221 Robin Lehner RC 6.00 15.00
222 Sergei Bobrovsky RC 12.00 30.00
223 Oliver Ekman-Larsson RC 5.00 12.00
224 Kyle Palmieri RC 6.00 15.00
225 Justin Braun RC 3.00 8.00
226 Ian Cole RC 3.00 8.00
227 Dana Tyrell RC 3.00 8.00
228 Keith Aulie RC 3.00 8.00
229 Matt Kassian RC 3.00 8.00
230 Marcus Johansson RC 5.00 12.00
231 Jordan Eberle RC 8.00 20.00
232 Magnus Paajarvi RC 4.00 10.00
233 Jordan Caron RC 4.00 10.00
234 Brandon Pirri RC 3.00 8.00
235 Jeremy Morin RC 5.00 12.00
236 Evgeny Grachev RC 3.00 8.00
237 Mattias Tedenby RC 3.00 8.00
238 Mark Olver RC 3.00 8.00
239 Eric Wellwood RC 4.00 10.00
240 Kyle Clifford RC 4.00 10.00
241 Zac Dalpe RC 4.00 10.00
242 Travis Hamonic RC 4.00 10.00

2010-11 Artifacts Emerald

*1-100 VETS/50: 3X TO 8X BASIC CARDS
*101-150 ROOKIES/50: .8X TO 2X RC/999
*151-200 L/S/50: 1X TO 2.5X L/S/999
106 P.K. Subban 20.00 50.00

2010-11 Artifacts Gold

*1-100 VETS/35: 3X TO 8X BASIC CARDS
*101-150 ROOKIES/35: .8X TO 2X RC/999
*151-200 L/S/35: 1X TO 2.5X L/S/999
106 P.K. Subban 40.00 80.00

2010-11 Artifacts Silver

*1-100 VETS/25: 4X TO 10X BASIC CARDS
*101-150 ROOKIES: 1X TO 2.5X RC/999
*151-200 L/S/25: 1.2X TO 3X L/S/999
106 P.K. Subban 50.00 100.00
148 Nazem Kadri 20.00 50.00

2010-11 Artifacts Autofacts

AFAE Andrew Ebbett 2.50 6.00
AFAG Alex Goligoski 5.00 12.00
AFAK Anze Kopitar 8.00 20.00
AFAM Al MacInnis 5.00 12.00
AFAN Andrei Markov 4.00 10.00
AFAO Alexander Ovechkin 40.00 80.00
AFAP Alex Pietrangelo 6.00 15.00
AFAT Alex Tanguay 5.00 12.00
AFBA Mikael Backlund 3.00 8.00
AFBD Brandon Dubinsky 5.00 12.00
AFBF Benn Ferriero 2.50 6.00
AFBH Bobby Hull 30.00 60.00
AFBM Brad Marchand 8.00 20.00
AFBO Bobby Orr 50.00 100.00
AFBR Bobby Ryan 6.00 15.00
AFBS Billy Smith 4.00 10.00
AFBW Blake Wheeler 6.00 15.00
AFCA Luca Caputi 3.00 8.00
AFCG Claude Giroux 12.50 30.00
AFCH Don Cherry 15.00 40.00
AFCO Cal O'Reilly 3.00 8.00
AFCS Cory Schneider 4.00 10.00
AFDA Darren Helm 2.50 6.00
AFDB David Backes 2.50 6.00
AFDC Daniel Carcillo 5.00 12.00
AFDD Drew Doughty 5.00 12.00
AFDH Dale Hawerchuk 6.00 15.00
AFDP Denis Potvin 5.00 12.00
AFDS Denis Savard 4.00 10.00
AFEK Evander Kane 4.00 10.00
AFEM Evgeni Malkin 15.00 40.00
AFER Jonathan Ericsson 2.50 6.00
AFES Eric Staal 10.00 25.00
AFET Eric Tangradi 3.00 8.00
AFFE Bernie Federko 8.00 20.00
AFGB Gilbert Brule 4.00 10.00
AFGH Gordie Howe 50.00 100.00
AFHE Dany Heatley 8.00 20.00
AFIK Ilya Kovalchuk 6.00 15.00
AFJC Jared Cowen 3.00 8.00
AFJD J.P. Dumont 2.50 6.00
AFJE Jhonas Enroth 4.00 10.00
AFJG Jonas Gustavsson 5.00 12.00
AFJI Jarome Iginla 15.00 40.00
AFJS Jordan Staal 6.00 15.00
AFJT Joe Thornton 6.00 15.00
AFJV Jakub Voracek 3.00 8.00
AFKC Kris Chucko 2.50 6.00
AFKE Phil Kessel 6.00 15.00
AFLC Logan Couture 5.00 12.00
AFMA Alec Martinez 5.00 12.00
AFMB Martin Brodeur 40.00 80.00
AFMD Matt Duchene 4.00 10.00
AFME Matt Ellis 2.50 6.00
AFMF Mark Fraser 2.50 6.00
AFMI Mike Bossy 10.00 25.00
AFML Mario Lemieux 50.00 100.00
AFMM Mark Messier 20.00 50.00
AFMN Michal Neuvirth 8.00 20.00
AFMP Matt Pelech 2.50 6.00
AFMR Mike Ribeiro 2.50 6.00
AFMS Marek Svatos 2.50 6.00
AFNG Nathan Gerbe 2.50 6.00
AFNH Nathan Horton 3.00 8.00
AFNI Antti Niemi 3.00 8.00
AFNK Nazem Kadri 10.00 25.00
AFPE Phil Esposito 10.00 25.00
AFPK Patrick Kane 15.00 40.00
AFPO Patrick O'Sullivan 2.50 6.00
AFPS P.K. Subban 15.00 40.00
AFRH Ron Hextall 10.00 25.00
AFRM Ryan Miller 8.00 20.00
AFRN Rick Nash 20.00 50.00
AFRV Rogie Vachon 5.00 12.00
AFSA Bobby Sanguinetti 2.50 6.00
AFSC Sidney Crosby 75.00 150.00
AFSE Devin Setoguchi 3.00 8.00
AFSG Simon Gagne 4.00 10.00
AFSH Steve Shutt 6.00 15.00
AFSM Steve Mason 6.00 15.00
AFSP Spencer Machacek 2.50 6.00
AFSS Steven Stamkos 20.00 50.00
AFSU Brandon Sutter 2.50 6.00
AFSV Sergei Shirokov 3.00 8.00
AFSY Steve Yzerman 100.00 175.00
AFTA John Tavares 20.00 50.00
AFTE Tyler Ennis 6.00 15.00
AFTG T.J. Galiardi 3.00 8.00
AFTM Tyler Myers 4.00 10.00
AFTO Jonathan Toews 20.00 40.00
AFVA James van Riemsdyk 3.00 8.00
AFVH Victor Hedman 5.00 12.00
AFWG Wayne Gretzky 150.00 400.00
AFYW Yannick Weber 2.50 6.00
AFZA Zach Boychuk 3.00 8.00
AFZB Zach Bogosian 3.00 8.00

2010-11 Artifacts Frozen Artifacts

*BLUE/35:.8X TO 2X BASIC JSY
FAAF Alexander Frolov 2.00 5.00
FAAK Anze Kopitar 3.00 8.00
FAAM Andrei Markov 2.00 5.00
FABB Bob Bourne 1.25 3.00
FABG Brian Gionta 1.25 3.00
FABR Derick Brassard 1.25 3.00
FACG Claude Giroux 2.00 5.00
FACO Chris Osgood 2.00 5.00
FACP Carey Price 4.00 10.00
FACW Cam Ward 2.00 5.00
FADB David Backes 1.25 3.00
FADD Drew Doughty 2.50 6.00
FADH Dany Heatley 1.50 4.00
FADR Derek Roy 1.25 3.00
FADS Devin Setoguchi 1.50 4.00
FAEL Patrik Elias 2.00 5.00
FAES Eric Staal 2.50 6.00
FAGL Guillaume Latendresse 1.50 4.00
FAHS Henrik Sedin 2.50 6.00
FAJC Jeff Carter 1.50 4.00
FAJJ Jack Johnson 1.25 3.00
FAJO Jordan Staal 1.50 4.00
FAJP Jason Pominville 1.25 3.00
FAJS Jason Spezza 2.00 5.00
FAJT Joe Thornton 3.00 8.00
FAJV Jakub Voracek 1.50 4.00
FALR Luc Robitaille 2.00 5.00
FAMF Marc-Andre Fleury 4.00 10.00
FAMG Mike Green 1.50 4.00
FAMK Miikka Kiprusoff 2.00 5.00
FAMR Mike Richards 1.50 4.00
FAMS Martin St. Louis 2.00 5.00
FAMT Marty Turco 2.00 5.00
FAMU Peter Mueller 1.50 4.00
FAPE Corey Perry 3.00 8.00
FAPM Patrick Marleau 2.00 5.00
FAPS Paul Stastny 1.50 4.00
FARL Roberto Luongo 3.00 8.00
FARM Ryan Miller 2.00 5.00
FARN Rick Nash 2.00 5.00
FASC Sidney Crosby 8.00 20.00
FASG Scott Gomez 1.50 4.00
FASM Steve Mason 1.50 4.00
FAST Drew Stafford 1.25 3.00
FASW Shea Weber 1.50 4.00
FATP Tomas Plekanec 1.25 3.00
FATV Thomas Vanek 1.50 4.00
FAVL Vincent Lecavalier 2.00 5.00
FAWG Wayne Gretzky 12.00 30.00
FAZP Zach Parise 2.00 5.00

2010-11 Artifacts Frozen Artifacts Silver

*SILVER: .5X TO 1.2X BASIC INSERTS

2010-11 Artifacts Jerseys Bronze

1 Brad Richards 4.00 10.00
2 Henrik Lundqvist 10.00 25.00
3 Jonathan Toews 6.00 15.00
4 Thomas Vanek 3.00 8.00
6 Patrick Kane 8.00 20.00
7 Carey Price 8.00 20.00
8 Miikka Kiprusoff 4.00 10.00
9 John Tavares 6.00 15.00
11 Ryan Miller 4.00 10.00
12 Ilya Kovalchuk 4.00 10.00
13 Vincent Lecavalier 4.00 10.00
14 Pascal Leclaire 3.00 8.00
15 Kyle Okposo 2.50 6.00
16 Matt Duchene 4.00 10.00
17 Nicklas Backstrom 4.00 10.00
18 Shane Doan 3.00 8.00
19 Tomas Vokoun 3.00 8.00
20 Patrik Elias 4.00 10.00
21 Patrick Marleau 4.00 10.00
22 Marc-Andre Fleury 6.00 15.00
23 Alexander Ovechkin 15.00 40.00
24 Mike Cammalleri 8.00 20.00
27 Cam Ward 4.00 10.00
28 Martin St. Louis 4.00 10.00
29 Patrik Berglund 3.00 8.00
30 Evander Kane 4.00 10.00
31 Andrei Markov 4.00 10.00
32 Mike Green 3.00 8.00
34 Derick Brassard 2.50 6.00
35 Claude Giroux 4.00 10.00
36 Phil Kessel 4.00 10.00
38 Joe Pavelski 5.00 12.00
40 Ryan Kesler 12.00 30.00
41 Daniel Briere 4.00 10.00
43 Jeff Carter 3.00 8.00
44 Anze Kopitar 6.00 15.00
45 Milan Lucic 4.00 10.00
46 Bobby Ryan 3.00 8.00
47 Dion Phaneuf 3.00 8.00
48 Steven Stamkos 8.00 20.00
49 Rene Bourque 2.50 6.00
50 Jason Spezza 4.00 10.00
51 James Neal 2.50 6.00
53 Eric Staal 5.00 12.00
54 Evgeni Malkin 8.00 20.00
55 Stephen Weiss 3.00 8.00
58 Henrik Sedin 5.00 12.00
59 Mikko Koivu 4.00 10.00
60 Ilya Bryzgalov 3.00 8.00
61 Roberto Luongo 6.00 15.00
62 Sidney Crosby 15.00 40.00
63 Zach Parise 4.00 10.00
64 Joe Thornton 6.00 15.00
65 J.P. Dumont 2.50 6.00
66 Paul Stastny 3.00 8.00
67 Ryan Getzlaf 4.00 10.00
69 Rick Nash 4.00 10.00
70 Michael Frolik 2.50 6.00
71 Zach Bogosian 3.00 8.00
72 Dany Heatley 3.00 8.00
74 David Backes 2.50 6.00
75 Antti Niemi 3.00 8.00
76 Sam Gagner 2.50 6.00
77 Daniel Alfredsson 4.00 10.00
78 Jack Johnson 2.50 6.00
81 Jordan Staal 3.00 8.00
82 Corey Perry 6.00 15.00
83 Mike Richards 3.00 8.00
84 Jarome Iginla 5.00 12.00
85 Shea Weber 3.00 8.00
87 Niklas Backstrom 4.00 10.00
88 Drew Doughty 5.00 12.00
89 Daniel Sedin 5.00 12.00
90 Pavel Datsyuk 6.00 15.00
91 Derek Roy 2.50 6.00
92 Duncan Keith 3.00 8.00
93 Martin Brodeur 10.00 25.00
94 Josh Bailey 3.00 8.00
95 Nicklas Lidstrom 4.00 10.00
96 Jakub Voracek 3.00 8.00
98 Marian Gaborik 4.00 10.00
99 Henrik Zetterberg 5.00 12.00
100 Guillaume Latendresse 3.00 8.00

2010-11 Artifacts Jerseys Patches Emerald

*EMER.PATCH/50: .8X TO 2X BASIC JSY
22 Marc-Andre Fleury 10.00 25.00
40 Ryan Kesler 15.00 40.00

2010-11 Artifacts Jerseys Patches Gold

*GOLD PATCH/15: 1.2X TO 3X BASIC JSY
5 Andrew Cogliano 8.00 20.00
25 Dustin Penner 8.00 20.00
26 Marc Savard 8.00 20.00
42 Brandon Dubinsky 8.00 20.00
52 Tuukka Rask 15.00 40.00
68 David Perron 10.00 25.00
79 Scottie Upshall 8.00 20.00
97 Zdeno Chara 12.00 30.00

2010-11 Artifacts Treasured Swatches

*BLUE/35: .6X TO 1.5X BASIC JSY
*EMERALD/15: 1X TO 2.5X BASIC JSY
*RETAIL: .4X TO 1X BASIC JSY
*SILVER/50: .5X TO 1.2X BASIC JSY
*BLUE PATCH/50: .8X TO 2X BASIC JSY
*EMER.PATCH/25: 1X TO 2.5X BASIC JSY
*GOLD PATCH/15: 1.2X TO 3X BASIC JSY
TSAF Alexander Frolov 2.50 6.00
TSAK Anze Kopitar 6.00 15.00
TSAO Alexander Ovechkin 8.00 20.00
TSBG Brian Gionta 2.50 6.00
TSCG Claude Giroux 4.00 10.00
TSCO Chris Osgood 4.00 10.00
TSCP Corey Perry 6.00 15.00
TSDB Derick Brassard 2.50 6.00
TSDD Drew Doughty 5.00 12.00
TSDR Derek Roy 2.50 6.00
TSDS Drew Stafford 2.50 6.00
TSEM Evgeni Malkin 8.00 20.00
TSES Eric Staal 5.00 12.00
TSGL Guillaume Latendresse 3.00 8.00
TSHS Henrik Sedin 5.00 12.00
TSHZ Henrik Zetterberg 5.00 12.00
TSJA Jason Arnott 3.00 8.00
TSJC Jeff Carter 3.00 8.00
TSJI Jarome Iginla 5.00 12.00
TSJJ Jack Johnson 2.50 6.00
TSJP Jason Pominville 2.50 6.00
TSJS Jason Spezza 4.00 10.00
TSJT Jonathan Toews 6.00 15.00
TSJV Jakub Voracek 3.00 8.00
TSMD Matt Duchene 4.00 10.00
TSMG Mike Green 3.00 8.00
TSMK Miikka Kiprusoff 4.00 10.00
TSMM Mark Messier 8.00 20.00
TSMR Mike Richards 3.00 8.00
TSMT Marty Turco 4.00 10.00
TSPD Pavel Datsyuk 6.00 15.00
TSPE Patrik Elias 4.00 10.00
TSPK Patrick Kane 8.00 20.00
TSPS Paul Stastny 3.00 8.00
TSRG Ryan Getzlaf 4.00 10.00
TSRL Roberto Luongo 6.00 15.00
TSRM Ryan Miller 4.00 10.00
TSRN Rick Nash 4.00 10.00
TSSC Sidney Crosby 15.00 40.00
TSSE Daniel Sedin 5.00 12.00
TSSG Scott Gomez 3.00 8.00
TSSM Steve Mason 3.00 8.00
TSSS Steven Stamkos 8.00 20.00
TSST Jordan Staal 3.00 8.00
TSSW Shea Weber 3.00 8.00
TSTA John Tavares 6.00 15.00
TSTP Tomas Plekanec 4.00 10.00
TSTV Thomas Vanek 3.00 8.00
TSZP Zach Parise 4.00 10.00

2010-11 Artifacts Tundra Tandems Bronze

*EMERALD/35: .6X TO 1.5X BASIC JSY
*SILVER/75: .5X TO 1.2X BASIC JSY
*EMER.PATCH/40: .8X TO 2X BASIC JSY
*GOLD PATCH/15: 1.2X TO 3X BASIC JSY
TT2ANA R.Getzlaf/C.Perry 6.00 15.00
TT2ATL Z.Bogosian/E.Kane 4.00 10.00
TT2AVS P.Stastny/M.Duchene 4.00 10.00
TT2BOS M.Lucic/M.Ryder 4.00 10.00
TT2CBJ J.Voracek/S.Mason 3.00 8.00
TT2CHI J.Toews/P.Kane 8.00 20.00
TT2CZE T.Vokoun/J.Voracek 3.00 8.00
TT2DET Datsyuk/H.Zetterberg 6.00 15.00
TT2EDM B.Ranford/B.Nicholls 4.00 10.00
TT2FLA D.Booth/S.Weiss 3.00 8.00
TT2FLY Briere/van Riemsdyk 4.00 10.00
TT2NJD Z.Parise/M.Brodeur 10.00 25.00
TT2OTT Alfredsson/J.Spezza 4.00 10.00
TT2SJS D.Heatley/R.Blake 4.00 10.00
TT2SVK M.Hossa/M.Gaborik 4.00 10.00
TT2SWE Lundqvist/Zetterberg 10.00 25.00
TT2TBL S.Yzerman/S.Stamkos 10.00 25.00
TT22004 A.Ovechkin/E.Malkin 15.00 40.00
TT22005 S.Crosby/B.Ryan 10.00 25.00
TT22007 P.Kane/van Riemsdyk 6.00 15.00
TT22008 S.Stamkos/D.Doughty 8.00 20.00
TT22009 J.Tavares/V.Hedman 6.00 15.00
TT2BUFF D.Stafford/T.Vanek 3.00 8.00
TT2CALG R.Bourque/J.Iginla 5.00 12.00
TT2CALI J.Thornton/R.Getzlaf 6.00 15.00
TT2CAPS Backstrom/Ovechkin 6.00 15.00
TT2CNAO A.Oates/C.Neely 4.00 10.00
TT2COLO D.Tucker/A.Foote 3.00 8.00
TT2DEER D.Phaneuf/C.Ward 4.00 10.00
TT2DRUM Briere/G.Latendresse 4.00 10.00
TT2FLAM J.Iginla/Bouwmeester 5.00 12.00
TT2FLYR D.Briere/C.Giroux 4.00 10.00
TT2NEWJ van Riemsdyk/B.Ryan 3.00 8.00
TT2PENS S.Crosby/M.Fleury 10.00 25.00
TT2PORT M.Hossa/C.Neely 4.00 10.00
TT2RMDR R.Miller/D.Roy 4.00 10.00
TT2RUSD S.Gonchar/A.Markov 4.00 10.00
TT2RUSG Bryzgalov/E.Nabokov 3.00 8.00
TT2SCAO S.Crosby/A.Ovechkin 10.00 25.00
TT2SSMA Thornton/W.Gretzky 25.00 60.00
TT2WILD Backstrom/M.Koivu 6.00 15.00
TT2BLUES D.Backes/P.Kariya 4.00 10.00
TT2CANES T.Ruutu/E.Staal 5.00 12.00
TT2FNGOL M.Kiprusoff/A.Niemi 4.00 10.00
TT2GIANT E.Kane/M.Lucic 4.00 10.00
TT2HAWKD B.Campbell/D.Keith 3.00 8.00
TT2KINGD J.Johnson/D.Doughty 5.00 12.00
TT2KOIVU S.Koivu/M.Koivu 8.00 20.00
TT2LEAFS J.Giguere/P.Kessel 8.00 20.00
TT2PREDS S.Sullivan/S.Weber 3.00 8.00
TT2STAAL J.Staal/E.Staal 5.00 12.00
TT2SWEDE Backstrom/J.Franzen 4.00 10.00
TT2TWINS D.Sedin/H.Sedin 5.00 12.00
TT2VALDOR J.Dumont/R.Luongo 6.00 15.00

2010-11 Artifacts Tundra Trios Bronze

*EMERALD/15: .8X TO 2X BASIC TRIO
*SILVER/50: .5X TO 1.2X BASIC TRIO
*GOLD PATCH/15: 1X TO 2.5X BASIC TRIO
*EMER.PATCH/40: .8X TO 2X BASIC TRIO
TT3CBJ Nash/Mason/Voracek 5.00 12.00
TT3DEF Bouwme/Phanf/Hedmn 6.00 15.00
TT3FLA Vokoun/Weiss/Frolik 4.00 10.00
TT3NO1 Crosby/Tavres/Stmkos 12.00 30.00
TT3OSH Horton/Arnott/Tavares 8.00 20.00
TT3TRI Tavres/Brodr/Gaborik 12.00 30.00
TT3BRAM Spezza/Wolski/Duch 5.00 12.00
TT3BRNS Thomas/Ryder/Whler 5.00 12.00
TT3BUDS Kessel/Kulemin/Schenn 5.00 12.00
TT3BUFF Roy/Vanek/Miller 5.00 12.00
TT3CALG Bourque/Igla/Kiprsoff 6.00 15.00
TT3CAPS Ovechkin/Semin/Green 10.00 25.00
TT3DEVS Parise/Brodeur/Elias 12.00 30.00
TT3DUCK Koivu/Perry/Lupul 8.00 20.00
TT3FLYS Richards/Carter/Giroux 10.00 25.00
TT3HABS Cammi/Markov/Gionta 10.00 25.00
TT3HAWK Kane/Hossa/Toews 10.00 25.00
TT3HERO Howe/Lemieux/Gretzky 40.00 80.00
TT3JCKT Mason/Voracek/Brass 4.00 10.00
TT3KING Brown/Doughty/Kopitar 8.00 20.00
TT3LEAF Kaberle/Giguere/Kessel 8.00 20.00
TT3LOND Nash/Kane/Perry 6.00 15.00
TT3MICH Camm/Johnson/Turco 5.00 12.00
TT3PENS Fleury/Staal/Malkin 10.00 25.00
TT3PNTH Vokoun/Booth/Frolik 4.00 10.00
TT3SABS Miller/Stafford/Pomin 5.00 12.00
TT3SBRS Roy/Pominville/Vanek 4.00 10.00
TT3SENS Kovalev/Alfred/Foligno 5.00 12.00
TT3SSMA Thornt/P.Espo/Carter 8.00 20.00
TT3VANC Luongo/Sedin/Sedin 8.00 20.00
TT3WILD Koivu/Backstr/Latend 5.00 12.00
TT3WING Datsyuk/Zetter/Osgood 8.00 20.00
TT3WISC Heatley/Pavelski/Brque 6.00 15.00
TT3LOOPS Tucker/Doan/Iginla 6.00 15.00
TT3NODAK Stafford/Parise/Toews 8.00 20.00
TT3PETES Pronger/Yzerman/Staal 10.00 25.00
TT3RMSKI Crosby/Lecav/Richards 12.00 30.00
TT3SHARK Heatley/Thorn/Marleau 8.00 20.00

2011-12 Artifacts

*VETS/99: 2.5X TO 6X BASIC CARDS
*LEGS/99: 1.25X TO 3X BASIC CARDS
*RC/99: .50X TO 1.25X BASIC CARDS
*VETS/25: 3X TO 8X BASIC CARDS
*LEGS/25: 1.5X TO 4X BASIC CARDS
*RC/25: .50X TO 1.25X BASIC CARDS
1 Roberto Luongo .60 1.50
2 Matt Stajan .25 .60
3 Marian Hossa .40 1.00
4 Taylor Hall .40 1.00
5 Nicklas Lidstrom .25 .60
6 Shea Weber .30 .75
7 Tim Thomas .40 1.00
8 Alexander Ovechkin 1.50 4.00
9 Zach Parise .40 1.00
10 Marian Gaborik .40 1.00
11 Mark Messier .75 2.00
12 Patrick Marleau .40 1.00
13 Pavel Datsyuk .60 1.50
14 Jordan Eberle .40 1.00
15 Paul Coffey .40 1.00
16 Evander Kane .40 1.00
17 Ryan Kesler .40 1.00
18 Nathan Horton .40 1.00
19 Jonathan Toews .60 1.50
20 Luc Robitaille .40 1.00
21 Derek Stepan .25 .60
22 Brian Boyle .25 .60
23 Milan Hejduk .30 .75
24 Jonas Hiller .30 .75
25 Chris Stewart .30 .75
26 Thomas Vanek .30 .75
27 Scott Niedermayer .40 1.00
28 Claude Giroux .40 1.00
29 Tomas Vokoun .30 .75
30 Ryan Miller .40 1.00
31 Carey Price .75 2.00
32 Kris Versteeg .25 .60
33 Patrick Roy 1.00 2.50
34 Patrick Kane .75 2.00
35 Brad Richards .40 1.00
36 Lars Eller .25 .60
37 Patrice Bergeron .50 1.25
38 Chris Drury .30 .75
39 Derek Roy .25 .60
40 Tuukka Rask .50 1.25
41 Jaroslav Halak .40 1.00
42 David Backes .25 .60
43 Drew Stafford .25 .60
44 Jay Bouwmeester .25 .60
45 Jonathan Bernier .30 .75
46 Anze Kopitar .60 1.50
47 Henrik Lundqvist 1.00 2.50
48 Guillaume Latendresse .30 .75
49 Dustin Byfuglien .40 1.00
50 Tyler Ennis .25 .60
51 Brendan Shanahan .40 1.00
52 Mike Green .30 .75
53 Ales Hemsky .30 .75
54 Jean-Sebastien Giguere .40 1.00
55 Maxime Talbot .25 .60
56 Stephen Weiss .30 .75
57 Tyler Myers .25 .60
58 Cam Ward .40 1.00
59 Martin Brodeur 1.00 2.50
60 Logan Couture .50 1.25
61 Jakub Voracek .30 .75
62 Brandon Dubinsky .25 .60
63 Nikita Filatov .25 .60
64 Alex Tanguay .25 .60
65 Erik Karlsson .50 1.25
66 Mario Lemieux 1.50 4.00
67 Alex Pietrangelo .30 .75
68 Jeff Carter .30 .75
69 Vincent Lecavalier .40 1.00
70 Tyler Seguin .50 1.25
71 Evgeni Malkin .75 2.00
72 Marc-Andre Fleury .75 2.00
73 Marc Staal .25 .60
74 Jamie Benn .40 1.00
75 Jarome Iginla .50 1.25
76 P.K. Subban .50 1.25
77 Victor Hedman .50 1.25
78 Ilya Kovalchuk .40 1.00
79 Andrei Markov .25 .60
80 Paul Stastny .30 .75
81 Phil Kessel .40 1.00
82 Mike Richards .30 .75
83 Kyle Okposo .25 .60
84 Drew Doughty .50 1.25
85 Matt Duchene .40 1.00
86 Ondrej Pavelec .40 1.00
87 Sidney Crosby 1.50 4.00
88 Eric Lindros .60 1.50
89 Sam Gagner .25 .60
90 Mike Modano .60 1.50
91 Steven Stamkos .75 2.00
92 Joe Thornton .60 1.50
93 Bill Ranford .40 1.00
94 Daniel Carcillo .25 .60
95 Jason Spezza .40 1.00
96 Ryan Getzlaf .40 1.00
97 Robin Lehner .30 .75
98 Pekka Rinne .40 1.00
99 Wayne Gretzky 2.50 6.00
100 Joe Sakic .75 2.00
101 Bobby Orr L 3.00 8.00
102 Gilbert Perreault L .75 2.00
103 Bobby Hull L 1.50 4.00
104 Wayne Gretzky L 5.00 12.00
105 Igor Larionov L .75 2.00
106 Mario Lemieux L 3.00 8.00
107 Gordie Howe L 2.50 6.00
108 Grant Fuhr L 1.25 3.00
109 Jari Kurri L .75 2.00
110 Ron Francis L 1.00 2.50
111 Marcel Dionne L 1.00 2.50
112 Luc Robitaille L .75 2.00
113 Larry Robinson L .75 2.00
114 Guy Lafleur L 1.00 2.50
115 Clark Gillies L .75 2.00
116 Mike Bossy L .75 2.00
117 Denis Potvin L .75 2.00
118 Brian Leetch L .60 1.50
119 Bobby Clarke L 1.25 3.00
120 Markus Naslund L .75 2.00
121 Alexander Ovechkin S 3.00 8.00
122 Nicklas Backstrom S .75 2.00
123 Ryan Kesler S .75 2.00
124 Henrik Sedin S 1.00 2.50
125 Jaroslav Halak S .75 2.00
126 Patrick Marleau S .75 2.00
127 Dany Heatley S .60 1.50
128 Evgeni Malkin S 1.50 4.00
129 Sidney Crosby S 3.00 8.00
130 Mike Richards S .60 1.50
131 Jeff Carter S .60 1.50
132 Erik Karlsson S 1.00 2.50
133 Marian Gaborik S .75 2.00
134 Henrik Lundqvist S 2.00 5.00
135 John Tavares S 1.25 3.00
136 Ryan Getzlaf S .75 2.00
137 Dustin Byfuglien S .75 2.00
138 Martin Brodeur S 2.00 5.00
139 Carey Price S 1.50 4.00
140 P.K. Subban S 1.00 2.50
141 Anze Kopitar S 1.25 3.00
142 Drew Doughty S 1.00 2.50
143 Nicklas Lidstrom S .50 1.25
144 Brad Richards S .75 2.00
145 Rick Nash S .75 2.00
146 Matt Duchene S .75 2.00
147 Jonathan Toews S 1.25 3.00
148 Patrick Kane S 1.50 4.00
149 Eric Staal S 1.00 2.50
150 Jarome Iginla S 1.00 2.50
151 Tim Thomas S .75 2.00
152 Timo Pielmeier 2.50 6.00
153 Jean-Philippe Levasseur 2.00 5.00
154 Greg Nemisz RC 2.00 5.00
155 Lance Bouma RC 2.00 5.00
156 Marcus Kruger RC 3.00 8.00
157 Hugh Jessiman RC 2.00 5.00
158 Cameron Gaunce RC 1.50 4.00
159 John Moore RC 2.00 5.00
160 Tomas Kubalik RC 2.00 5.00
161 Tomas Vincour RC 2.00 5.00
162 Colton Sceviour RC 2.00 5.00
163 Teemu Hartikainen RC 2.00 5.00
164 Chris Vande Velde RC 3.00 8.00
165 Scott Timmins RC 2.00 5.00
166 Drew Bagnall RC 2.00 5.00
167 Carson McMillan RC 2.50 6.00
168 Aaron Palushaj RC 2.00 5.00
169 Brendon Nash RC 2.00 5.00
170 Jonathon Blum RC 2.00 5.00
171 Blake Geoffrion RC 2.00 5.00
172 Adam Henrique RC 5.00 12.00
173 Matt Campanale RC 2.00 5.00
174 Shane Sims RC 2.00 5.00
175 Mikko Koskinen RC 2.50 6.00
176 Jamie Doornbosch RC 2.00 5.00
177 Mark Katic RC 2.00 5.00
178 Justin DiBenedetto RC 1.50 4.00
179 Cam Talbot RC 5.00 12.00
180 Patrick Wiercioch RC 2.00 5.00
181 Erik Condra RC 2.00 5.00
182 Roman Wick RC 2.50 6.00
183 Colin Greening RC 2.00 5.00
184 Andre Benoit RC 2.50 6.00
185 Stephane Da Costa RC 2.00 5.00
186 Erik Gustafsson RC 2.50 6.00
187 Ben Holmstrom RC 2.00 5.00
188 Zac Rinaldo RC 2.00 5.00
189 Joe Vitale RC 2.00 5.00
190 Brian Strait RC 2.50 6.00
191 Alex Stalock 1.50 4.00
192 Joe Colborne RC 2.00 5.00
193 Ben Scrivens RC 2.00 5.00
194 Matt Frattin RC 2.00 5.00
195 Cody Hodgson RC 3.00 8.00
196 Yann Sauve RC 2.00 5.00
197 Todd Ford RC 2.50 6.00
198 Paul Postma RC 2.00 5.00
199 Andrei Zubarev RC 2.50 6.00
200 Carl Klingberg RC 2.00 5.00
201 Devante Smith-Pelly RC 2.50 6.00
202 Mark Scheifele RC 8.00 20.00
203 Anton Lander RC 2.00 5.00
204 Zack Kassian RC 2.50 6.00
205 Roman Horak RC 2.00 5.00
206 Justin Faulk RC 3.00 8.00
207 Brandon Saad RC 4.00 10.00
208 Gabriel Landeskog RC 6.00 15.00
209 Ryan Johansen RC 6.00 15.00
210 Kevin Marshall RC 2.00 5.00
211 Brendan Smith RC 2.00 5.00
212 Ryan Nugent-Hopkins RC 8.00 20.00
213 Erik Gudbranson RC 2.50 6.00
214 Viatcheslav Voynov RC 2.00 5.00
215 Brett Bulmer RC 2.00 5.00
216 Louis Leblanc RC 2.00 5.00
217 Craig Smith RC 2.50 6.00
218 Adam Larsson RC 2.50 6.00
219 David Ullstrom RC 2.00 5.00
220 Tim Erixon RC 2.00 5.00
221 Sean Couturier RC 4.00 10.00
222 David Rundblad RC 2.00 5.00
223 Andy Miele RC 2.00 5.00
224 Robert Bortuzzo RC 2.00 5.00
225 Harri Sateri RC 2.00 5.00
226 Cade Fairchild RC 1.50 4.00
227 Brett Connolly RC 2.00 5.00

228 Jake Gardiner RC 3.00 8.00
229 Eddie Lack RC 2.00 5.00
230 Cody Eakin RC 3.00 8.00
231 Matt Read RC 2.50 6.00
232 Mika Zibanejad RC 6.00 15.00
233 Gustav Nyquist RC 5.00 12.00
234 Lennart Petrell RC 2.50 6.00
235 Dmitry Orlov RC 5.00 12.00
236 Raphael Diaz RC 2.00 5.00
237 Alexei Emelin RC 2.00 5.00
238 Peter Holland RC 2.00 5.00
239 Colten Teubert RC 2.00 5.00
240 Corey Tropp RC 2.00 5.00
241 Stefan Elliott RC 2.00 5.00
242 David Savard RC 2.00 5.00

2011-12 Artifacts Autofacts

AAB Andrew Bodnarchuk F 3.00 8.00
AAD Luke Adam E 4.00 10.00
AAH Ales Hemsky B 12.00 30.00
AAK Arturs Kulda F 3.00 8.00
AAL Karl Alzner F 3.00 8.00
AAO Alexander Ovechkin B 40.00 100.00
AAP Alex Pietrangelo C 5.00 12.00
ABA Andy Bathgate E 5.00 12.00
ABB Brian Boyle F 3.00 8.00
ABI Brayden Irwin F 3.00 8.00
ABM Brett MacLean F 3.00 8.00
ABN Brent Burns F 5.00 12.00
ABO Butch Bouchard C 12.00 30.00
ABR Derick Brassard E 3.00 8.00
ABS Brandon Sutter F 3.00 8.00
ABU Bobby Butler F 4.00 10.00
ACA Cal O'Reilly F 3.00 8.00
ACE Corey Elkins F 3.00 8.00
ACG Colton Gillies E 3.00 8.00
ACL Dan Cleary D 5.00 12.00
ACM Clarke MacArthur F 3.00 8.00
ACO Chris Osgood D 5.00 12.00
ACS Chris Stewart D 4.00 10.00
ADA David Backes F 3.00 8.00
ADB Dan Boyle F 4.00 10.00
ADC Daniel Carcillo F 3.00 8.00
ADE Michael Del Zotto F 3.00 8.00
ADS Duane Sutter E 3.00 8.00
AEB Jordan Eberle D 15.00 40.00
AEK Evander Kane C 20.00 40.00
AEM Evgeni Malkin B 40.00 80.00
AEN Eric Nystrom F 3.00 8.00
AEW Eric Wellwood D 3.00 8.00
AFW Francis Wathier D 6.00 15.00
AGH Gordie Howe A 125.00 200.00
AIL Igor Larionov B 8.00 20.00
AJB Jamie Benn F 5.00 12.00
AJC Jared Cowen D 5.00 12.00
AJD J.P. Dumont D 3.00 8.00
AJE Jhonas Enroth E 5.00 12.00
AJF Justin Falk F 3.00 8.00
AJG Jonas Gustavsson C 6.00 15.00
AJM Jacob Markstrom F 5.00 12.00
AJO Jim O'Brien F 3.00 8.00
AJP Jeff Penner E 4.00 10.00
AJS James Sheppard F 3.00 8.00
AJT Joe Thornton B 12.00 30.00
AJV Jakub Voracek D 4.00 10.00
AJW J.T. Wyman D 3.00 8.00
AKA Keith Aulie F 4.00 10.00
AKD Kaspars Daugavins F 3.00 8.00
AKT Kyle Turris E 3.00 8.00
AKU Nikolai Kulemin D 3.00 8.00
ALA Andrew Ladd F 3.00 8.00
ALE Lars Eller F 3.00 8.00
ALS Luke Schenn C 6.00 15.00
AMA Rick MacLeish B 25.00 50.00
AMB Matt Beleskey F 3.00 8.00
AMC Thomas McCollum F 4.00 10.00
AMD Matt Duchene C 10.00 25.00
AME Barry Melrose E 4.00 10.00
AMG Matt Gilroy F 3.00 8.00
AMM Mark Messier A 40.00 80.00
AMN Michal Neuvirth E 4.00 10.00
AMS Marco Scandella F 3.00 0.00
AMT Mattias Tedenby E 3.00 8.00
AMZ Mats Zuccarello-Aasen E 5.00 12.00
ANA Markus Naslund C 12.00 30.00
ANH Nathan Horton C 6.00 15.00
ANK Nazem Kadri C 10.00 25.00
ANZ Nikolay Zherdev D 5.00 12.00
AOR Bobby Orr B 90.00 150.00
APA Patrick Marleau B 10.00 25.00
APB Patrice Bergeron B 60.00 120.00
APC Patrice Cormier F 3.00 8.00
APH Patric Hornqvist F 3.00 8.00
APJ Joe Pavelski C 8.00 20.00
APL Perttu Lindgren E 3.00 8.00
APM Peter Mueller C 5.00 12.00
ARB Richard Bachman F 4.00 10.00
ARE Ray Emery D 4.00 10.00
ARM Ryan McDonagh F 8.00 20.00
ARY Bobby Ryan E 4.00 10.00
ASA Jerome Samson F 3.00 8.00
ASC Brayden Schenn D 5.00 12.00
ASD Stefan Della Rovere F 3.00 8.00
ASM Stefan Meyer F 3.00 8.00
ASR Michael Sauer F 3.00 8.00
ASS Steve Shutt D 10.00 25.00
AST Marc Staal C 10.00 25.00
ASW Shea Weber C 8.00 20.00
ATA Maxime Talbot D 3.00 8.00
ATE Tyler Ennis F 3.00 8.00
ATL Jiri Tlusty F 3.00 8.00
ATM Tyler Myers D 3.00 8.00
ATT Tomas Tatar F 3.00 8.00
AVS Viktor Stalberg D 3.00 8.00
AWC Wendel Clark B 15.00 40.00
AWG Wayne Gretzky A 200.00 500.00
AZA Matt Zaba D 3.00 8.00

2011-12 Artifacts Frozen Artifacts Jerseys Blue

*EMERALD/35: 1X TO 2.5X BLUE/135
*PURPLE RETAIL: .6X TO 1.5X BLUE/135
FAAK Anze Kopitar 4.00 10.00
FAAS Alexander Semin 2.50 6.00
FABR Daniel Briere 2.50 6.00
FABY Dustin Byfuglien 2.50 6.00
FACA Craig Anderson 2.50 6.00
FACN Cam Neely 2.50 6.00
FACP Carey Price 5.00 12.00
FADB David Backes 1.50 4.00
FADC Dino Ciccarelli 2.50 6.00
FADD Drew Doughty 3.00 8.00
FADP Dion Phaneuf 2.00 5.00
FADR Derek Roy 1.50 4.00
FADS Drew Stafford 1.50 4.00
FADU Dustin Brown 2.50 6.00
FAEM Evgeni Malkin 5.00 12.00
FAHL Henrik Lundqvist 6.00 15.00
FAHZ Henrik Zetterberg 3.00 8.00
FAIK Ilya Kovalchuk 2.50 6.00
FAJB Jay Bouwmeester 1.50 4.00
FAJC Jeff Carter 2.00 5.00
FAJE Jonathan Ericsson 1.50 4.00
FAJG Jean-Sebastien Giguere 2.50 6.00
FAJI Jarome Iginla 3.00 8.00
FAJS Jordan Staal 2.00 5.00
FAJV James van Riemsdyk 2.00 5.00
FAKL Kristopher Letang 3.00 8.00
FAKR David Krejci 2.50 6.00
FALE Lars Eller 1.50 4.00
FAMB Martin Brodeur 6.00 15.00
FAMG Mike Green 2.00 5.00
FAML Mario Lemieux 10.00 25.00
FAMR Mike Richards 2.00 5.00
FANH Nathan Horton 2.50 6.00
FANK Nikolai Kulemin 1.50 4.00
FAPE Corey Perry 4.00 10.00
FAPK Phil Kessel 2.50 6.00
FAPS Paul Stastny 2.00 5.00
FARB Rene Bourque 1.50 4.00
FARH Ron Hextall 2.50 6.00
FARI Brad Richards 2.50 6.00
FARL Roberto Luongo 4.00 10.00
FARY Bobby Ryan 2.00 5.00
FASB Sergei Bobrovsky 4.00 10.00
FASC Sidney Crosby 10.00 25.00
FATE Tyler Ennis 1.50 4.00
FATH Taylor Hall 2.50 6.00
FATP Tomas Plekanec 1.50 4.00
FATS Tyler Seguin 3.00 8.00
FATV Thomas Vanek 2.00 5.00
FAZC Zdeno Chara 2.50 6.00

2011-12 Artifacts Horizontal Jerseys

*EMERALD/35: .8X TO 2X BASIC JSY/50
1 Roberto Luongo 5.00 12.00
2 Matt Stajan 2.00 5.00
3 Marian Hossa 3.00 8.00
4 Taylor Hall 3.00 8.00
5 Nicklas Lidstrom 2.00 5.00
6 Shea Weber 2.50 6.00
7 Tim Thomas 3.00 8.00
8 Alexander Ovechkin 12.00 30.00
9 Zach Parise 3.00 8.00
10 Marian Gaborik 3.00 8.00
11 Mark Messier 6.00 15.00
12 Patrick Marleau 3.00 8.00
13 Pavel Datsyuk 5.00 12.00
14 Jordan Eberle 3.00 8.00
15 Paul Coffey 3.00 8.00
16 Evander Kane 3.00 8.00
17 Ryan Kesler 3.00 8.00
18 Nathan Horton 3.00 8.00
19 Jonathan Toews 5.00 12.00
20 Luc Robitaille 3.00 8.00
21 Derek Stepan 2.00 5.00
22 Brian Boyle 2.00 5.00
23 Milan Hejduk 2.50 6.00
24 Jonas Hiller 2.50 6.00
25 Chris Stewart 2.50 6.00
26 Thomas Vanek 2.50 6.00
27 Scott Niedermayer 3.00 8.00
28 Claude Giroux 3.00 8.00
29 Tomas Vokoun 2.50 6.00
30 Ryan Miller 3.00 8.00
31 Carey Price 6.00 15.00
32 Kris Versteeg 2.00 5.00
33 Patrick Roy 8.00 20.00
34 Patrick Kane 6.00 15.00
35 Brad Richards 3.00 8.00
36 Lars Eller 2.00 5.00
37 Patrice Bergeron 4.00 10.00
38 Chris Drury 2.50 6.00
39 Derek Roy 2.00 5.00
40 Tuukka Rask 4.00 10.00
41 Jaroslav Halak 3.00 8.00
42 David Backes 2.00 5.00
43 Drew Stafford 2.00 5.00
44 Jay Bouwmeester 2.00 5.00
45 Jonathan Bernier 2.50 6.00
46 Anze Kopitar 5.00 12.00
47 Henrik Lundqvist 8.00 20.00
48 Guillaume Latendresse 2.50 6.00
49 Dustin Byfuglien 3.00 8.00
50 Tyler Ennis 2.00 5.00
52 Mike Green 2.50 6.00
53 Ales Hemsky 2.50 6.00
54 Jean-Sebastien Giguere 3.00 8.00
55 Maxime Talbot 2.00 5.00
56 Stephen Weiss 2.50 6.00
57 Tyler Myers 2.00 5.00
58 Cam Ward 3.00 8.00
59 Martin Brodeur 8.00 20.00
60 Logan Couture 4.00 10.00
61 Jakub Voracek 2.50 6.00
62 Brandon Dubinsky 2.00 5.00
63 Nikita Filatov 2.00 5.00
64 Alex Tanguay 2.00 5.00
65 Erik Karlsson 4.00 10.00
66 Mario Lemieux 12.00 30.00
67 Alex Pietrangelo 2.50 6.00
68 Jeff Carter 2.50 6.00
69 Vincent Lecavalier 3.00 8.00
70 Tyler Seguin 4.00 10.00
71 Evgeni Malkin 6.00 15.00
72 Marc-Andre Fleury 6.00 15.00
73 Marc Staal 2.00 5.00
74 Jamie Benn 3.00 8.00
75 Jarome Iginla 4.00 10.00
76 P.K. Subban 4.00 10.00
77 Victor Hedman 4.00 10.00
78 Ilya Kovalchuk 3.00 8.00
79 Andrei Markov 2.00 5.00
80 Paul Stastny 2.50 6.00
81 Phil Kessel 3.00 8.00
82 Mike Richards 2.50 6.00
83 Kyle Okposo 2.00 5.00
84 Drew Doughty 4.00 10.00
85 Matt Duchene 3.00 8.00
86 Ondrej Pavelec 3.00 8.00
87 Sidney Crosby 12.00 30.00
88 Eric Lindros 5.00 12.00
89 Sam Gagner 2.00 5.00
90 Mike Modano 5.00 12.00
91 Steven Stamkos 6.00 15.00
92 Joe Thornton 5.00 12.00
93 Bill Ranford 3.00 8.00
94 Daniel Carcillo 2.00 5.00
95 Jason Spezza 3.00 8.00
96 Ryan Getzlaf 3.00 8.00
97 Robin Lehner 2.50 6.00
98 Pekka Rinne 3.00 8.00
100 Joe Sakic 6.00 15.00

2011-12 Artifacts Jerseys

*EMERALD/65: .8X TO 2X JERSEY/125
1 Roberto Luongo 5.00 12.00
2 Matt Stajan 2.00 5.00
3 Marian Hossa 3.00 8.00
4 Taylor Hall 3.00 8.00
5 Nicklas Lidstrom 2.00 5.00
6 Shea Weber 2.50 6.00
7 Tim Thomas 3.00 8.00
8 Alexander Ovechkin 12.00 30.00
9 Zach Parise 3.00 8.00
10 Marian Gaborik 3.00 8.00
11 Mark Messier 6.00 15.00
12 Patrick Marleau 3.00 8.00
13 Pavel Datsyuk 5.00 12.00
14 Jordan Eberle 3.00 8.00
15 Paul Coffey 3.00 8.00
16 Evander Kane 3.00 8.00
17 Ryan Kesler 3.00 8.00
18 Nathan Horton 3.00 8.00
19 Jonathan Toews 5.00 12.00
20 Luc Robitaille 3.00 8.00
21 Derek Stepan 2.00 5.00
22 Brian Boyle 2.00 5.00
23 Milan Hejduk 2.50 6.00
24 Jonas Hiller 2.50 6.00
25 Chris Stewart 2.50 6.00
26 Thomas Vanek 2.50 6.00
27 Scott Niedermayer 3.00 8.00
28 Claude Giroux 3.00 8.00
29 Tomas Vokoun 2.50 6.00
30 Ryan Miller 3.00 8.00
31 Carey Price 6.00 15.00
32 Kris Versteeg 2.00 5.00
33 Patrick Roy 8.00 20.00
34 Patrick Kane 6.00 15.00
35 Brad Richards 3.00 8.00
36 Lars Eller 2.00 5.00
37 Patrice Bergeron 4.00 10.00
38 Chris Drury 2.50 6.00
39 Derek Roy 2.00 5.00
40 Tuukka Rask 4.00 10.00
41 Jaroslav Halak 3.00 8.00
42 David Backes 2.00 5.00
43 Drew Stafford 2.00 5.00
44 Jay Bouwmeester 2.00 5.00
45 Jonathan Bernier 2.50 6.00
46 Anze Kopitar 5.00 12.00
47 Henrik Lundqvist 8.00 20.00
48 Guillaume Latendresse 2.50 6.00
49 Dustin Byfuglien 3.00 8.00
50 Tyler Ennis 2.00 5.00
52 Mike Green 2.50 6.00
53 Ales Hemsky 2.50 6.00
54 Jean-Sebastien Giguere 3.00 8.00
55 Maxime Talbot 2.00 5.00
56 Stephen Weiss 2.50 6.00
57 Tyler Myers 2.00 5.00
59 Martin Brodeur 8.00 20.00
60 Logan Couture 4.00 10.00
61 Jakub Voracek 2.50 6.00
62 Brandon Dubinsky 2.00 5.00
63 Nikita Filatov 2.00 5.00
64 Alex Tanguay 2.00 5.00
65 Erik Karlsson 4.00 10.00
66 Mario Lemieux 12.00 30.00
67 Alex Pietrangelo 2.50 6.00
68 Jeff Carter 2.50 6.00
69 Vincent Lecavalier 3.00 8.00
70 Tyler Seguin 4.00 10.00
71 Evgeni Malkin 6.00 15.00
72 Marc-Andre Fleury 6.00 15.00
73 Marc Staal 2.00 5.00
74 Jamie Benn 3.00 8.00
75 Jarome Iginla 4.00 10.00
76 P.K. Subban 4.00 10.00
77 Victor Hedman 4.00 10.00
78 Ilya Kovalchuk 3.00 8.00
79 Andrei Markov 2.00 5.00
80 Paul Stastny 2.50 6.00
81 Phil Kessel 3.00 8.00
82 Mike Richards 2.50 6.00
83 Kyle Okposo 2.00 5.00
84 Drew Doughty 4.00 10.00
85 Matt Duchene 3.00 8.00
86 Ondrej Pavelec 3.00 8.00
87 Sidney Crosby 12.00 30.00
88 Eric Lindros 5.00 12.00
89 Sam Gagner 2.00 5.00
90 Mike Modano 5.00 12.00
91 Steven Stamkos 6.00 15.00
92 Joe Thornton 5.00 12.00
93 Bill Ranford 3.00 8.00
94 Daniel Carcillo 2.00 5.00
95 Jason Spezza 3.00 8.00
96 Ryan Getzlaf 3.00 8.00
97 Robin Lehner 2.50 6.00
98 Pekka Rinne 3.00 8.00
100 Joe Sakic 6.00 15.00

2011-12 Artifacts Rookie Autographs Redemptions

REDA1 Ryan Nugent-Hopkins 25.00 60.00
REDA2 Gabriel Landeskog 25.00 60.00
REDA3 Cody Hodgson 10.00 25.00
REDA4 Sean Couturier 12.00 30.00
REDA5 Brett Connolly 6.00 15.00
REDA6 Mark Scheifele 25.00 60.00
REDA7 Ryan Johansen 20.00 50.00
REDA8 Adam Larsson 8.00 20.00
REDA9 Mika Zibanejad 20.00 50.00
REDA10 Jake Gardiner 10.00 25.00
REDA11 Erik Gudbranson 8.00 20.00
REDA12 Matt Read 8.00 20.00
REDA13 Teemu Hartikainen 6.00 15.00
REDA14 Joe Colborne 6.00 15.00
REDA15 Matt Frattin 6.00 15.00
REDA16 Craig Smith 8.00 20.00

2011-12 Artifacts Treasured Swatches Blue

*EMERALD/35: 1X TO 2.5X BLUE/135
*PURPLE RETAIL: .4X TO 1X BLUE/135
TSAB Alexandre Burrows 1.50 4.00
TSAO Alexander Ovechkin 10.00 25.00
TSCG Claude Giroux 2.50 6.00
TSCM Clarke MacArthur 1.50 4.00
TSCO Chris Osgood 2.50 6.00
TSCP Chris Pronger 2.50 6.00
TSDG Doug Gilmour 3.00 8.00
TSDS Daniel Sedin 3.00 8.00
TSEK Evander Kane 2.50 6.00
TSHO Marian Hossa 2.50 6.00
TSHS Henrik Sedin 3.00 8.00
TSIB Ilya Bryzgalov 2.50 6.00
TSIL Igor Larionov 2.50 6.00
TSJB Jamie Benn 2.50 6.00
TSJC John Carlson 2.50 6.00
TSJE Jordan Eberle 2.50 6.00
TSJH Jonas Hiller 2.00 5.00
TSJJ Jack Johnson 1.50 4.00
TSJN James Neal 1.50 4.00
TSJQ Jonathan Quick 3.00 8.00
TSJT Jonathan Toews 4.00 10.00
TSKO Kyle Okposo 1.50 4.00
TSKS Kevin Shattenkirk 1.50 4.00
TSMB Mike Bossy 2.50 6.00
TSMD Matt Duchene 2.50 6.00
TSMF Marc-Andre Fleury 5.00 12.00
TSMG Marian Gaborik 2.50 6.00
TSMH Milan Hejduk 2.00 5.00
TSMI Ryan Miller 2.50 6.00
TSMK Miikka Kiprusoff 2.50 6.00
TSMM Mark Messier 5.00 12.00
TSMS Martin St. Louis 2.50 6.00
TSNL Nicklas Lidstrom 1.50 4.00
TSOP Ondrej Pavelec 2.50 6.00
TSPB Patrik Berglund 1.50 4.00
TSPK Patrick Kane 5.00 12.00
TSPS P.K. Subban 3.00 8.00
TSRB Ray Bourque 4.00 10.00
TSRG Ryan Getzlaf 2.50 6.00
TSRK Ryan Kesler 2.50 6.00
TSRS Ryan Smyth 2.00 5.00
TSSH Scott Hartnell 1.50 4.00
TSSS Steven Stamkos 5.00 12.00
TSTT Tim Thomas 2.50 6.00
TSTV Thomas Vanek 2.00 5.00
TSTZ Travis Zajac 1.50 4.00
TSVL Vincent Lecavalier 2.50 6.00
TSZP Zach Parise 2.50 6.00

2011-12 Artifacts Tundra Tandems Jerseys Blue

*EMERALD/50: .8X TO 2X BLUE/225
TT2AS J.Spezza/D.Alfredsson 5.00 12.00
TT2BB D.Backes/P.Berglund 3.00 8.00
TT2BP P.Berglund/A.Pietrangelo 4.00 10.00
TT2BQ J.Quick/J.Bernier 6.00 15.00
TT2CD P.Datsyuk/D.Cleary 8.00 20.00
TT2CM S.Crosby/E.Malkin 20.00 50.00
TT2CP C.Price/P.Subban 10.00 25.00
TT2CR C.Anderson/R.Lehner 5.00 12.00
TT2DD D.Stafford/D.Roy 3.00 8.00
TT2DE D.Byfuglien/E.Kane 5.00 12.00
TT2DS M.Staal/B.Dubinsky 3.00 8.00
TT2EH T.Hall/J.Eberle 5.00 12.00
TT2EZ T.Zajac/P.Elias 5.00 12.00
TT2FH C.Fowler/J.Hiller 5.00 12.00
TT2FL M.Fleury/K.Letang 10.00 25.00
TT2GD M.Gaborik/B.Dubinsky 5.00 12.00
TT2GS N.Gerbe/D.Stafford 3.00 0.00
TT2HC J.Carter/S.Hartnell 4.00 10.00
TT2HK N.Horton/D.Krejci 5.00 12.00
TT2IB J.Iginla/R.Bourque 6.00 15.00
TT2JM J.Staal/M.Staal 4.00 10.00
TT2KD D.Doughty/A.Kopitar 8.00 20.00
TT2KJ K.Letang/J.Neal 6.00 15.00
TT2KK P.Kessel/N.Kulemin 5.00 12.00
TT2LE N.Lidstrom/J.Ericsson 3.00 8.00
TT2LG V.Lecavalier/S.Gagne 5.00 12.00
TT2LK R.Luongo/R.Kesler 8.00 20.00
TT2LM M.Lemieux/M.Messier 20.00 50.00
TT2MB J.Bailey/M.Moulson 4.00 10.00
TT2MH M.Modano/B.Hull 10.00 25.00
TT2MJ Kiprusoff/Bouwmeester 5.00 12.00
TT2MK A.Markov/A.Kostitsyn 4.00 10.00
TT2MM R.Miller/T.Myers 5.00 12.00
TT2MS D.Setoguchi/P.Marleau 5.00 12.00
TT2M7 M.Brodeur/Z.Parise 12.00 30.00
TT2OB Ovechkin/Backstrom 20.00 50.00
TT2OH J.Howard/C.Osgood 6.00 15.00
TT2PE T.Plekanec/L.Eller 3.00 8.00
TT2PG R.Getzlaf/C.Perry 8.00 20.00
TT2PS D.Phaneuf/L.Schenn 5.00 12.00
TT2RB B.Richards/J.Benn 5.00 12.00
TT2RG M.Richards/C.Giroux 5.00 12.00
TT2RH P.Rinne/P.Hornqvist 5.00 12.00
TT2RJ R.Smyth/J.Williams 4.00 10.00
TT2RO M.Ribeiro/S.Ott 3.00 8.00
TT2SB E.Staal/P.Bergeron 6.00 15.00
TT2SD M.Duchene/P.Stastny 5.00 12.00
TT2SG W.Gretzky/J.Sakic 30.00 80.00
TT2SM S.Stamkos/M.St. Louis 10.00 25.00
TT2SS H.Sedin/D.Sedin 6.00 15.00
TT2SV S.Varlamov/A.Semin 5.00 12.00
TT2SW S.Weber/R.Suter 4.00 10.00
TT2TK J.Toews/P.Kane 10.00 25.00
TT2TR T.Thomas/T.Rask 6.00 15.00
TT2UF R.Umberger/N.Filatov 3.00 8.00
TT2VE T.Ennis/T.Vanek 4.00 10.00
TT2WB D.Booth/S.Weiss 4.00 10.00
TT2ZH Zetterberg/Holmstrom 6.00 15.00

2011-12 Artifacts Tundra Trios Jerseys Blue

TT3ANA Perry/Getzlaf/Fowler 10.00 25.00
TT3AVS Sakic/Roy/Bourque 15.00 40.00
TT3BOS Rask/Thomas/Chara 8.00 20.00
TT3BUF Ennis/Vanek/Gerbe 5.00 12.00
TT3CAN Thornton/Staal/Berg 10.00 25.00
TT3CBJ Vorack/Filatv/Brassard 5.00 12.00
TT3CGY Iginla/Kipru/Bouwmstr 8.00 20.00
TT3CHI Kane/Toews/Hossa 12.00 30.00
TT3COL Duchene/Stastny/Liles 6.00 15.00
TT3DAL Richards/Benn/Eriksson 6.00 15.00
TT3DET Zetter/Lidstrm/Franzn 8.00 20.00
TT3DRW Datsyk/Cleary/Osgd 10.00 25.00
TT3EDM Hall/Eberle/Paajarvi 6.00 15.00
TT3LAK Dghty/Kopitar/Quick 10.00 25.00
TT3NJD Parise/Zajac/Elias 6.00 15.00
TT3NSH Weber/Suter/Rinne 6.00 15.00
TT3NYI Mlson/Okposo/Bailey 5.00 12.00
TT3NYR Staal/Dubinsky/Gaborik 6.00 15.00
TT3OTT Spezza/Alfred/Foligno 6.00 15.00
TT3PHI Giroux/Richrds/Bobrov 10.00 25.00
TT3SJS Marleau/Setog/Thrntn 10.00 25.00
TT3VAN Kesler/Sedin/Sedin 8.00 20.00
TT3WPG Byfuglien/Kane/Pavelec 6.00 15.00
TT3BEES Chara/Thomas/Seguin 8.00 20.00
TT3BOLT Stamk/St. Louis/Lecav 12.00 30.00
TT3BUFF Pomin/Vanek/Stafford 5.00 12.00
TT3CAPS Bckstrm/Ovech/Semin 25.00 60.00
TT3FLYR Carter/Hartnell/Briere 6.00 15.00
TT3LBBR Subban/Price/Plekanec 12.00 30.00
TT3PENS Fleury/Letang/Neal 12.00 30.00
TT3PITT Malkin/Crosby/Staal 25.00 60.00
TT3SABR Myers/Miller/Stafford 6.00 15.00
TT3STAR Ribeiro/Lehtn/Goligoski 5.00 12.00
TT3WILD Gonchar/Spez/Andersn 6.00 15.00
TT3BLUES Back/Halak/Berglund 6.00 15.00
TT3KINGS Williams/Smyth/Bernier 5.00 12.00
TT3LEAFS Kulemin/Kessel/Phanf 6.00 15.00
TT3NUCKS Luongo/Kesler/Edler 10.00 25.00

2012-13 Artifacts

*EMERALD.VET/99: 3X TO 8X BASIC CARDS
*EMERALD.TC/99: 1.25X TO 3X BASIC CARDS
*EMERALD.RC/99: .5X TO 1.25X BASIC CARDS
*SAPPHIRE.VET/85: 3X TO 8X BASIC CARDS
*SAPPHIRE.TC/85: 1.25X TO 3X BASIC CARDS
*SAPPHIRE.RC/85: .5X TO 1.25X BASIC CARDS
*SPECT.VET/25: 4X TO 10X BASIC CARDS
*SPECT.TC/25: 1.5X TO 4X BASIC CARDS
*SPECT.RC/25: .6X TO 1.5X BASIC CARDS
1 Alex Tanguay .30 .75
2 Alexander Ovechkin 1.50 4.00
3 Anze Kopitar .60 1.50
4 Bobby Orr 1.50 4.00
5 Bobby Ryan .30 .75
6 Brandon Dubinsky .25 .60
7 Brendan Shanahan .40 1.00
8 Brett Hull .75 2.00
9 Cam Neely .40 1.00
10 Chris Drury .30 .75
11 Claude Giroux .40 1.00
12 Colton Orr .40 1.00
13 Cam Fowler .40 1.00
14 Dale Hawerchuk .50 1.25
15 Daniel Alfredsson .40 1.00
16 Daniel Sedin .50 1.25
17 Denis Savard .40 1.00
18 Derek Roy .25 .60
19 Derek Stepan .25 .60
20 Dino Ciccarelli .40 1.00
21 Doug Wilson .30 .75
22 Drew Doughty .50 1.25
23 Drew Stafford .25 .60
24 Duncan Keith .30 .75
25 Eric Lindros .60 1.50
26 Eric Staal .50 1.25
27 Erik Karlsson .50 1.25
28 Evgeni Malkin .75 2.00
29 George Parros .30 .75
30 Henrik Sedin .50 1.25
31 Henrik Zetterberg .50 1.25
32 Ilya Kovalchuk .40 1.00
33 Jari Kurri .40 1.00
34 Jarome Iginla .50 1.25
35 Jaromir Jagr 1.25 3.00
36 Jason Spezza .40 1.00
37 Jean Beliveau .40 1.00
38 Jeff Carter .30 .75
39 Joe Sakic .75 2.00
40 Joe Thornton .60 1.50
41 Johan Franzen .30 .75
42 John Tavares .60 1.50
43 Dustin Brown .40 1.00
44 Jonathan Toews .60 1.50
45 Jordan Eberle .40 1.00
46 Jordan Staal .30 .75
47 Keith Yandle .25 .60
48 Kristopher Letang .50 1.25
49 Larry Robinson .40 1.00
50 Logan Couture .50 1.25
51 Luc Robitaille .40 1.00
52 Kevin Shattenkirk .25 .60
53 Marian Gaborik .40 1.00
54 Marian Hossa .40 1.00
55 Sam Gagner .25 .60
56 Mario Lemieux 1.50 4.00
57 Mark Messier .75 2.00
58 Markus Naslund .40 1.00
59 Matt Duchene .40 1.00
60 Matt Moulson .25 .60
61 Maxime Talbot .25 .60
62 Mike Green .30 .75
63 Mike Modano .60 1.50
64 Mike Richards .30 .75
65 Milan Lucic .40 1.00
66 Nathan Horton .40 1.00
67 Nicklas Backstrom .40 1.00
68 Nicklas Lidstrom .40 1.00
69 P.K. Subban .50 1.25
70 Patrice Bergeron .50 1.25
71 Patrick Kane .75 2.00
72 Patrick Sharp .40 1.00
73 Paul Coffey .40 1.00
74 Paul Stastny .30 .75
75 Pavel Datsyuk .60 1.50
76 Rene Bourque .25 .60
77 Ray Bourque .60 1.50
78 Nikolai Kulemin .25 .60
79 Rick Nash .40 1.00
80 Ron Francis .50 1.25
81 Ryan Callahan .25 .60
82 Ryan Getzlaf .40 1.00
83 Ryan Kesler .40 1.00
84 Ryan Nugent-Hopkins .50 1.25
85 Shane Doan .30 .75
86 Sidney Crosby 1.50 4.00
87 Stephen Weiss .30 .75
88 Steve Ott .25 .60
89 Steven Stamkos .75 2.00
90 Taylor Hall .40 1.00
91 Teemu Selanne .75 2.00
92 Tony Twist .25 .60
93 Trevor Linden .40 1.00
94 Tyler Ennis .25 .60
95 Tyler Myers .25 .60
96 Tyler Seguin .50 1.25
97 Vincent Lecavalier .40 1.00
98 Wayne Gretzky 2.50 6.00
99 Zach Parise .40 1.00
100 Zdeno Chara .40 1.00
101 Antti Niemi .75 2.00
102 Carey Price 2.00 5.00
103 Cory Schneider 1.00 2.50
104 Corey Crawford 1.25 3.00
105 Curtis Joseph 1.25 3.00
106 Dominik Hasek 1.50 4.00
107 Ed Belfour 1.00 2.50
108 Pekka Rinne 1.00 2.50
109 Jean-Sebastien Giguere 1.00 2.50
110 Jim Howard 1.25 3.00
111 Johnny Bower 1.00 2.50
112 Ondrej Pavelec 1.00 2.50
113 Jonathan Quick 1.25 3.00
114 Kari Lehtonen .75 2.00
115 Marc-Andre Fleury 2.00 5.00
116 Martin Brodeur 2.50 6.00
117 Miikka Kiprusoff 1.00 2.50
118 Patrick Roy 2.50 6.00
119 Semyon Varlamov 1.00 2.50
120 Ryan Miller 1.00 2.50
121 Steve Mason .75 2.00
122 Tim Thomas 1.00 2.50
123 Tomas Vokoun .75 2.00
124 Tony Esposito 1.00 2.50
125 Tuukka Rask 1.25 3.00
126 Alex Pietrangelo TC .75 2.00
127 Brayden Schenn TC 1.00 2.50
128 Brenden Morrow TC .75 2.00
129 Brent Seabrook TC .60 1.50
130 Calvin de Haan TC .60 1.50
131 Chris Pronger TC 1.00 2.50
132 Cody Eakin TC .60 1.50
133 Corey Perry TC 1.50 4.00
134 Dale Hawerchuk TC 1.25 3.00
135 Dan Boyle TC .60 1.50
136 Drew Doughty TC 1.25 3.00
137 Duncan Keith TC .75 2.00
138 Erik Gudbranson TC .60 1.50
139 Dustin Tokarski TC .75 2.00
140 Jarome Iginla TC 1.25 3.00
141 Louis Leblanc TC .60 1.50
142 Marcus Foligno TC .75 2.00
143 Patrice Bergeron TC 1.25 3.00
144 Roberto Luongo TC 1.50 4.00
145 Ryan Ellis TC .60 1.50
146 Ryan Getzlaf TC 1.00 2.50
147 Shea Weber TC .75 2.00
148 Simon Despres TC .75 2.00
149 Wayne Gretzky TC 6.00 15.00
150 Zack Kassian TC .60 1.50
151 Mat Clark RC 2.00 5.00
152 Carter Camper RC 1.50 4.00
153 Maxime Sauve RC 1.50 4.00
154 Lane MacDermid RC 2.00 5.00
155 Torey Krug RC 5.00 12.00
156 Michael Hutchinson RC 2.50 6.00
157 Travis Turnbull RC 1.50 4.00
158 Sven Baertschi RC 2.50 6.00
159 Akim Aliu RC 2.00 5.00
160 Jeremy Welsh RC 2.00 5.00
161 Brandon Bollig RC 1.50 4.00
162 Tyson Barrie RC 5.00 12.00
163 Mike Connolly RC 2.00 5.00
164 Dalton Prout RC 1.50 4.00
165 Cody Goloubef RC 1.50 4.00
166 Shawn Hunwick RC 1.50 4.00
167 Andrew Joudrey RC 2.00 5.00
168 Ryan Garbutt RC 1.50 4.00
169 Reilly Smith RC 5.00 12.00
170 Brenden Dillon RC 2.00 5.00
171 Scott Glennie RC 2.00 5.00
172 Riley Sheahan RC 2.50 6.00
173 Philippe Cornet RC 2.00 5.00
174 Colby Robak RC 1.50 4.00
175 Jordan Nolan RC 1.50 4.00
176 Kristopher Foucault RC 1.50 4.00
177 Jason Zucker RC 4.00 10.00
178 Tyler Cuma RC 1.50 4.00
179 Chay Genoway RC 1.50 4.00
180 Gabriel Dumont RC 2.00 5.00
181 Robert Mayer RC 2.50 6.00
182 Chet Pickard RC 2.00 5.00
183 Aaron Ness RC 1.50 4.00
184 Casey Cizikas RC 2.00 5.00
185 Matt Donovan RC 2.00 5.00
186 Chris Kreider RC 6.00 15.00
187 Jakob Silfverberg RC 3.00 8.00
188 Mark Stone RC 6.00 15.00
189 Brandon Manning RC 2.00 5.00
190 Michael Stone RC 2.00 5.00
191 Matt Watkins RC 1.50 4.00
192 Tyson Sexsmith RC 1.50 4.00
193 Jake Allen RC 5.00 12.00
194 Jaden Schwartz RC 5.00 12.00
195 J.T. Brown RC 2.00 5.00
196 Carter Ashton RC 1.50 4.00
197 Ryan Hamilton RC 1.50 4.00
198 Jussi Rynnas RC 1.50 4.00
RED199 Viktor Fasth XRC 2.50 6.00
RED200 Dougie Hamilton XRC 5.00 12.00
RED201 Mikhail Grigorenko XRC 5.00 12.00
RED202 Max Reinhart XRC 2.50 6.00
RED203 Ryan Murphy XRC 2.50 6.00
RED204 Drew LeBlanc XRC 2.00 5.00
RED205 Michael Sgarbossa XRC 2.00 5.00
RED206 J.Audy-Marchessault XRC 5.00 12.00
RED207 Jack Campbell XRC 2.50 6.00
RED208 Damien Brunner XRC 2.50 6.00
RED209 Nail Yakupov XRC 8.00 20.00
RED210 Jonathan Huberdeau XRC 6.00 15.00
RED211 Tyler Toffoli XRC 5.00 12.00
RED212 Mikael Granlund XRC 5.00 12.00
RED213 Alex Galchenyuk XRC 8.00 20.00
RED214 Filip Forsberg XRC 6.00 15.00
RED215 Stefan Matteau XRC 2.50 6.00
RED216 Brock Nelson XRC 4.00 10.00
RED217 J.T. Miller XRC 2.50 6.00
RED218 Cory Conacher XRC 2.50 6.00
RED219 Scott Laughton XRC 2.50 6.00
RED220 Chris Brown XRC 2.00 5.00
RED221 Beau Bennett XRC 4.00 10.00
RED222 Matthew Irwin XRC 2.50 6.00
RED223 Vladimir Tarasenko XRC 6.00 15.00
RED224 Richard Panik XRC 3.00 8.00
RED225 Mike Kostka XRC 2.50 6.00
RED226 Jordan Schroeder XRC 2.50 6.00
RED227 Tom Wilson XRC 5.00 12.00
RED228 Zach Redmond XRC 2.50 6.00
RED229 Brendan Gallagher XRC 8.00 20.00
RED230 Justin Schultz XRC 4.00 10.00
RED231 Charlie Coyle XRC 3.00 8.00
RED232 Nathan Beaulieu XRC 1.50 4.00
RED233 Emerson Etem XRC 3.00 8.00
RED234 Ryan Spooner XRC 4.00 10.00
RED235 Petr Mrazek XRC 5.00 12.00
RED236 Jonas Brodin XRC 2.50 6.00
RED237 Jarred Tinordi XRC 2.50 6.00
RED238 Jean-Gabriel Pageau XRC 2.50 6.00
RED239 Nicklas Jensen XRC 2.50 6.00
RED240 Nick Bjugstad XRC 2.50 6.00

2012-13 Artifacts Autofacts

AAG Aaron Gagnon E 4.00 10.00
AAM Adam McQuaid E 5.00 12.00
AAO Alexander Ovechkin C 25.00 60.00
AAS Anthony Stewart D 3.00 8.00
ABH Bobby Hull A 25.00 60.00
ABL Brian Lee E 4.00 10.00
ABM Brendan Mikkelson E 3.00 8.00
ABO Bobby Orr C 40.00 100.00
ABT Bryan Trottier B 5.00 12.00
ACE Cody Eakin TC E 3.00 8.00
ACF Cam Fowler E 5.00 12.00
ACH Cody Hodgson E 3.00 8.00
ACJ Curtis Joseph A 6.00 15.00
ACK Chris Kunitz B 5.00 12.00
ADB Drayson Bowman E 3.00 8.00
ADG Daniel Girardi E 3.00 8.00
ADP David Perron B 4.00 10.00
ADU Dustin Brown C 5.00 12.00
AEL Eric Lindros A 30.00 80.00
AEN Evgeni Nabokov D 4.00 10.00
AFW Francis Wathier E 4.00 10.00
AGL Gabriel Landeskog B 6.00 15.00
AJB Jamie Benn B 5.00 12.00
AJD Jason Demers E 4.00 10.00
AJE Jordan Eberle B 5.00 12.00
AJJ Jaromir Jagr A 30.00 80.00
AJM John Moore E 3.00 8.00
AJN James Neal D 3.00 8.00
AJO Johan Motin E 4.00 10.00
AKC Kyle Clifford E 3.00 8.00
AKT Kimmo Timonen E 3.00 8.00
ALA Guillaume Latendresse B 4.00 10.00
ALE Mario Lemieux A 30.00 80.00
AMB Mike Bossy B 5.00 12.00
AML Maxim Lapierre E 3.00 8.00
AMM Mark Messier A 25.00 60.00
AMN Michal Neuvirth E 4.00 10.00
AMS Matt Stajan E 3.00 8.00
ANF Nick Foligno E 4.00 10.00
ANG Nicklas Grossman E 3.00 8.00
APC Paul Coffey A 5.00 12.00
APL Pascal Leclaire TC E 4.00 10.00
APR Patrick Roy A 50.00 125.00
ARA Tuukka Rask B 6.00 15.00
ARJ Ryan Jones E 4.00 10.00
ARL Robin Lehner C 4.00 10.00
ARN Ryan Nugent-Hopkins A 6.00 15.00
ARO Ryan O'Reilly E 5.00 12.00
ASC Sidney Crosby A 60.00 150.00
ASG Sam Gagner D 3.00 8.00
ASS Steven Stamkos C 15.00 40.00
AST Marco Sturm E 3.00 8.00
ASW Stephen Weiss B 4.00 10.00
ATL Trevor Lewis E 3.00 8.00
ATR Tuomo Ruutu B 4.00 10.00
ATS Tim Stapleton E 3.00 8.00
ATW Tom Wandell E 3.00 8.00
AVF Valtteri Filppula E 3.00 8.00
AWG Wayne Gretzky A 200.00 500.00
AZK Zack Kassian E 3.00 8.00

2012-13 Artifacts Frozen Artifacts Jerseys Blue

*EMERALD/36: .6X TO 1.5X BASIC INSERTS
FAAK Anze Kopitar C 5.00 12.00
FAAO Alexander Ovechkin C 12.00 30.00
FAAS Alexander Semin C 3.00 8.00
FAAT Alex Tanguay B 2.50 6.00
FABD Brandon Dubinsky A 2.00 5.00
FABH Brett Hull C 6.00 15.00
FABS Brendan Shanahan C 3.00 8.00
FACD Chris Drury C 2.50 6.00
FACF Cam Fowler C 3.00 8.00
FACG Claude Giroux C 3.00 8.00
FADA Daniel Alfredsson C 3.00 8.00
FADD Drew Doughty C 4.00 10.00
FADP David Perron C 2.50 6.00
FADR Derek Roy C 2.00 5.00
FADS Daniel Sedin C 4.00 10.00
FAGR Mike Green C 2.50 6.00
FAJC Jeff Carter C 2.50 6.00
FAJG Jean-Sebastien Giguere C 3.00 8.00
FAJI Jarome Iginla C 4.00 10.00
FAJQ Jonathan Quick C 4.00 10.00
FAJS Jason Spezza C 3.00 8.00
FALC Logan Couture C 4.00 10.00
FALO Linus Omark C 2.50 6.00
FALR Larry Robinson AS C 3.00 8.00
FAMG Michael Grabner C 2.50 6.00
FAMN Markus Naslund C 3.00 8.00
FAMS Marc Staal C 2.00 5.00
FAST Derek Stepan C 2.00 5.00
FATS Tyler Seguin C 4.00 10.00

2012-13 Artifacts Horizontal Jerseys

*EMERALD/24: .5X TO 1.25X HORIZONTAL JSY/36
2 Alexander Ovechkin 12.00 30.00
3 Anze Kopitar 5.00 12.00
5 Bobby Ryan 2.50 6.00
6 Brandon Dubinsky 2.00 5.00
7 Brendan Shanahan 3.00 8.00
8 Brett Hull 6.00 15.00
11 Claude Giroux 3.00 8.00
12 Colton Orr 3.00 8.00
13 Cam Fowler 3.00 8.00
15 Daniel Alfredsson 3.00 8.00
16 Daniel Sedin 4.00 10.00
17 Denis Savard 3.00 8.00
18 Derek Roy 2.00 5.00
19 Derek Stepan 2.00 5.00
20 Dino Ciccarelli 3.00 8.00
21 Doug Wilson 2.50 6.00
22 Drew Doughty 4.00 10.00
23 Drew Stafford 2.00 5.00
24 Duncan Keith AS 2.50 6.00
25 Eric Lindros AS 5.00 12.00
27 Erik Karlsson 4.00 10.00
28 Evgeni Malkin 6.00 15.00
31 Henrik Zetterberg 4.00 10.00
32 Ilya Kovalchuk 3.00 8.00
34 Jarome Iginla 4.00 10.00
35 Jaromir Jagr AS 10.00 25.00
36 Jason Spezza 3.00 8.00
38 Jeff Carter 2.50 6.00
41 Johan Franzen 2.50 6.00
42 John Tavares 5.00 12.00
45 Jordan Eberle 3.00 8.00
46 Jordan Staal 2.50 6.00
47 Keith Yandle 2.00 5.00
48 Kristopher Letang 4.00 10.00
49 Larry Robinson AS 3.00 8.00
50 Logan Couture 4.00 10.00
51 Luc Robitaille 3.00 8.00
52 Kevin Shattenkirk 2.00 5.00
53 Marian Gaborik 3.00 8.00
54 Marian Hossa AS 3.00 8.00
55 Sam Gagner 2.00 5.00
56 Mario Lemieux AS 12.00 30.00
58 Markus Naslund AS 3.00 8.00
59 Matt Duchene 3.00 8.00
60 Matt Moulson 2.00 5.00
61 Maxime Talbot 2.00 5.00
62 Mike Green 2.50 6.00
63 Mike Modano 5.00 12.00
64 Mike Richards 2.50 6.00
65 Milan Lucic 3.00 8.00
66 Nathan Horton 3.00 8.00
67 Nicklas Backstrom 3.00 8.00
69 P.K. Subban 4.00 10.00
70 Patrice Bergeron 4.00 10.00
72 Patrick Sharp 3.00 8.00
74 Paul Stastny 2.50 6.00
75 Pavel Datsyuk 5.00 12.00
77 Ray Bourque 5.00 12.00
78 Nikolai Kulemin 2.00 5.00
79 Rick Nash AS 3.00 8.00
80 Ron Francis 4.00 10.00
81 Ryan Callahan 2.00 5.00
82 Ryan Getzlaf 3.00 8.00
83 Ryan Kesler 3.00 8.00
85 Shane Doan 2.50 6.00
86 Sidney Crosby 12.00 30.00
87 Stephen Weiss 2.50 6.00
94 Tyler Ennis 2.00 5.00
95 Tyler Myers 2.00 5.00
96 Tyler Seguin 4.00 10.00
97 Vincent Lecavalier 3.00 8.00
98 Wayne Gretzky AS 20.00 50.00
99 Zach Parise 3.00 8.00
100 Zdeno Chara 3.00 8.00
105 Curtis Joseph 4.00 10.00
107 Ed Belfour 3.00 8.00
109 Jean-Sebastien Giguere 3.00 8.00
110 Jim Howard 4.00 10.00
113 Jonathan Quick 4.00 10.00
115 Marc-Andre Fleury 6.00 15.00
116 Martin Brodeur 8.00 20.00
117 Miikka Kiprusoff 3.00 8.00
118 Patrick Roy 8.00 20.00
119 Semyon Varlamov 3.00 8.00
122 Tim Thomas 3.00 8.00
123 Tomas Vokoun 2.50 6.00
126 Alex Pietrangelo TC 2.50 6.00
127 Brayden Schenn TC 3.00 8.00
133 Corey Perry TC 5.00 12.00
134 Dale Hawerchuk TC 4.00 10.00
136 Drew Doughty TC 4.00 10.00
137 Duncan Keith TC 2.50 6.00
140 Jarome Iginla TC 4.00 10.00
141 Louis Leblanc TC 2.00 5.00
143 Patrice Bergeron TC 4.00 10.00
145 Ryan Ellis TC 2.00 5.00
146 Ryan Getzlaf TC 3.00 8.00
150 Zack Kassian TC 2.00 5.00

2012-13 Artifacts Jerseys

*EMERALD/75: .8X TO 2X BASIC JSY/125
*EMERALD/75: .4X TO 1X BASIC JSY/35
*EMERALD/50: .5X TO 1.2X BASIC JSY/25
*GOLD/15: 1.2X TO 3X BASIC JSY/125
*GOLD/15: .8X TO 2X BASIC JSY/35
*GOLD/15: .8X TO 2X BASIC JSY/25
1 Alex Tanguay AS/125 3.00 8.00
2 Alexander Ovechkin/125 15.00 40.00
3 Anze Kopitar/125 6.00 15.00
5 Bobby Ryan/125 3.00 8.00
6 Brandon Dubinsky/125 2.50 6.00
7 Brendan Shanahan/125 4.00 10.00
8 Brett Hull/125 5.00 12.00
9 Cam Neely/125 4.00 10.00
10 Chris Drury/125 3.00 8.00
11 Claude Giroux/125 4.00 10.00
12 Colton Orr/125 4.00 10.00
13 Cam Fowler/125 4.00 10.00
14 Dale Hawerchuk/125 5.00 12.00
15 Daniel Alfredsson/125 4.00 10.00
16 Daniel Sedin/125 5.00 12.00
17 Denis Savard/125 4.00 10.00
18 Derek Roy/125 2.50 6.00
19 Derek Stepan/125 2.50 6.00
20 Dino Ciccarelli/125 4.00 10.00
21 Doug Wilson/125 3.00 8.00
22 Drew Doughty/125 5.00 12.00
23 Drew Stafford/125 2.50 6.00
24 Duncan Keith AS/125 3.00 8.00
25 Eric Lindros AS/125 5.00 12.00
26 Eric Staal/125 5.00 12.00
27 Erik Karlsson/125 5.00 12.00
28 Evgeni Malkin/125 8.00 20.00
29 George Parros/125 3.00 8.00
30 Henrik Sedin/125 5.00 12.00
31 Henrik Zetterberg/125 5.00 12.00
32 Ilya Kovalchuk/125 4.00 10.00
33 Jari Kurri/125 4.00 10.00
34 Jarome Iginla/125 5.00 12.00
35 Jaromir Jagr AS/125 6.00 15.00
36 Jason Spezza/125 4.00 10.00
37 Jean Beliveau AS/65 20.00 50.00
38 Jeff Carter/125 3.00 8.00
40 Joe Thornton/125 6.00 15.00
41 Johan Franzen/125 3.00 8.00
42 John Tavares/25 15.00 40.00
43 Dustin Brown/125 4.00 10.00
44 Jonathan Toews/125 6.00 15.00
45 Jordan Eberle/125 4.00 10.00
46 Jordan Staal/125 3.00 8.00
47 Keith Yandle/125 2.50 6.00
48 Kristopher Letang/125 5.00 12.00
49 Larry Robinson AS/125 4.00 10.00
50 Logan Couture/125 5.00 12.00
51 Luc Robitaille/125 4.00 10.00
52 Kevin Shattenkirk/125 6.00 15.00
53 Marian Gaborik/125 4.00 10.00
54 Marian Hossa AS/125 4.00 10.00
55 Sam Gagner/125 2.50 6.00
56 Mario Lemieux AS/125 15.00 40.00
57 Mark Messier/125 8.00 20.00
58 Markus Naslund AS/125 4.00 10.00
59 Matt Duchene/125 4.00 10.00
60 Matt Moulson/125 2.50 6.00
61 Maxime Talbot/125 2.50 6.00
62 Mike Green/125 4.00 10.00
63 Mike Modano/125 6.00 15.00
64 Mike Richards/125 3.00 8.00
65 Milan Lucic/125 5.00 12.00
66 Nathan Horton/125 4.00 10.00
67 Nicklas Backstrom/125 4.00 10.00
68 Nicklas Lidstrom/125 4.00 10.00
69 P.K. Subban/125 5.00 12.00
70 Patrice Bergeron/125 5.00 12.00
71 Patrick Kane/125 8.00 20.00
72 Patrick Sharp/125 4.00 10.00
73 Paul Coffey/125 4.00 10.00
74 Paul Stastny/125 3.00 8.00
75 Pavel Datsyuk/125 5.00 12.00
76 Rene Bourque/125 3.00 8.00
77 Ray Bourque/125 6.00 15.00
78 Nikolai Kulemin/125 6.00 15.00
79 Rick Nash AS/125 4.00 10.00
80 Ron Francis/125 5.00 12.00
81 Ryan Callahan/125 3.00 8.00
82 Ryan Getzlaf/125 4.00 10.00
83 Ryan Kesler/125 4.00 10.00
85 Shane Doan/125 3.00 8.00
86 Sidney Crosby/125 15.00 40.00
87 Stephen Weiss/125 3.00 8.00
88 Steve Ott/125 2.50 6.00
89 Steven Stamkos/125 8.00 20.00
90 Taylor Hall/125 4.00 10.00
91 Teemu Selanne AS/35 8.00 20.00
92 Tony Twist/125 4.00 10.00
93 Trevor Linden/125 5.00 12.00
94 Tyler Ennis/125 2.50 6.00
95 Tyler Myers/125 2.50 6.00
96 Tyler Seguin/125 5.00 12.00
97 Vincent Lecavalier/125 4.00 10.00
98 Wayne Gretzky AS/125 20.00 50.00
99 Zach Parise/125 4.00 10.00
100 Zdeno Chara/125 4.00 10.00
101 Antti Niemi/125 3.00 8.00
102 Carey Price/125 8.00 20.00
103 Cory Schneider/125 4.00 10.00
104 Corey Crawford/125 5.00 12.00
105 Curtis Joseph/125 5.00 12.00
106 Dominik Hasek/125 6.00 15.00
107 Ed Belfour/125 4.00 10.00
108 Pekka Rinne/125 4.00 10.00
109 Jean-Sebastien Giguere/125 4.00 10.00
110 Jim Howard/125 5.00 12.00
111 Johnny Bower/125 10.00 25.00
112 Ondrej Pavelec/125 4.00 10.00
113 Jonathan Quick/125 10.00 25.00
114 Kari Lehtonen/125 3.00 8.00
115 Marc-Andre Fleury/125 8.00 20.00
116 Martin Brodeur/125 10.00 25.00
117 Miikka Kiprusoff/125 4.00 10.00
118 Patrick Roy/125 10.00 25.00
119 Semyon Varlamov/125 4.00 10.00
120 Ryan Miller/125 4.00 10.00
121 Steve Mason/125 3.00 8.00
122 Tim Thomas/125 6.00 15.00
123 Tomas Vokoun/125 8.00 20.00
124 Tony Esposito/125 5.00 12.00
125 Tuukka Rask/125 5.00 12.00
126 Alex Pietrangelo TC/125 4.00 10.00
127 Brayden Schenn TC/125 5.00 12.00
128 Brenden Morrow TC/125 4.00 10.00
129 Brent Seabrook TC/125 3.00 8.00
130 Calvin de Haan TC/125 3.00 8.00
131 Chris Pronger TC/125 5.00 12.00
132 Cody Eakin TC/125 3.00 8.00
133 Corey Perry TC/125 8.00 20.00
134 Dale Hawerchuk TC/125 6.00 15.00
135 Dan Boyle TC/125 3.00 8.00
136 Drew Doughty TC/125 6.00 15.00
137 Duncan Keith TC/125 4.00 10.00
138 Erik Gudbranson TC/125 3.00 8.00
139 Dustin Tokarski TC/125 4.00 10.00
140 Jarome Iginla TC/125 6.00 15.00
141 Louis Leblanc TC/125 3.00 8.00
142 Marcus Foligno TC/125 4.00 10.00
143 Patrice Bergeron TC/125 6.00 15.00
144 Roberto Luongo TC/125 4.00 10.00
145 Ryan Ellis TC/125 3.00 8.00
146 Ryan Getzlaf TC/125 5.00 12.00
147 Shea Weber TC/125 4.00 10.00
148 Simon Despres TC/125 4.00 10.00
149 Wayne Gretzky TC/125 30.00 80.00
150 Zack Kassian TC/125 3.00 8.00

2012-13 Artifacts Rookie Autographs Redemptions

I Alex Galchenyuk 60.00 120.00
II Beau Bennett 15.00 40.00
III Brendan Gallagher 20.00 50.00
IV Charlie Coyle 12.00 30.00
V Cory Conacher 12.00 30.00
VI Damien Brunner 30.00 80.00
VII Dougie Hamilton 20.00 50.00
VIII Vladimir Tarasenko 60.00 120.00
IX Filip Forsberg 25.00 50.00
X Mikhail Grigorenko 15.00 40.00
XI Jonathan Huberdeau 20.00 50.00
XII Justin Schultz 15.00 40.00
XIII Mikael Granlund 20.00 50.00
XIV J.T. Miller 15.00 40.00
XV Nail Yakupov 60.00 120.00
XVI Nathan Beaulieu 15.00 40.00
XVII Tyler Toffoli 15.00 40.00
XVIII Emerson Etem 12.00 30.00

2012-13 Artifacts Treasured Swatches Jerseys Blue

*EMERALD/36: .8X TO 2X BLUE GRP B-C
TSBE Patrice Bergeron C 5.00 12.00
TSEK Evander Kane C 4.00 10.00
TSEL Eric Lindros C 6.00 15.00
TSGA Sam Gagner C 2.50 6.00
TSIK Ilya Kovalchuk C 4.00 10.00
TSJF Johan Franzen C 3.00 8.00
TSJV James van Riemsdyk C 3.00 8.00
TSMH Milan Hejduk C 3.00 8.00
TSML Mario Lemieux AS C 15.00 40.00
TSMM Mike Modano C 6.00 15.00
TSMR Mike Richards C 3.00 8.00
TSNB Nicklas Backstrom C 4.00 10.00
TSNK Nikolai Kulemin C 2.50 6.00
TSPB Patrik Berglund C 2.50 6.00
TSPD Pavel Datsyuk C 6.00 15.00
TSRB Ray Bourque C 6.00 15.00
TSRG Ryan Getzlaf C 4.00 10.00
TSSC Sidney Crosby C 15.00 40.00
TSSD Shane Doan C 3.00 8.00
TSSG Simon Gagne C 4.00 10.00
TSST Jordan Staal C 3.00 8.00
TSTE Tyler Ennis C 2.50 6.00
TSTM Tyler Myers C 2.50 6.00
TSTV Tomas Vokoun C 3.00 8.00
TSVA Thomas Vanek C 3.00 8.00
TSVL Vincent Lecavalier C 4.00 10.00
TSZC Zdeno Chara C 4.00 10.00
TSZP Zach Parise B 4.00 10.00

2012-13 Artifacts Tundra Tandems Jerseys Blue

*EMERALD/36: 1X TO 2.5X BASIC TANDEM
*EMERALD/20: 1.2X TO 3X BASIC TANDEM
TTBE B.Shanahan/E.Lindros 5.00 12.00
TTBH P.Bergeron/N.Horton 5.00 12.00
TTBK E.Kane/D.Byfuglien 4.00 10.00
TTBL M.Brodeur/R.Luongo 10.00 25.00
TTBQ J.Bernier/J.Quick 10.00 25.00
TTBS D.Backes/C.Stewart 3.00 8.00
TTCD B.Dubinsky/R.Callahan 2.50 6.00
TTDD D.Wilson/D.Savard 4.00 10.00
TTDY S.Doan/K.Yandle 3.00 8.00
TTEB J.Benn/L.Eriksson 4.00 10.00
TTEH J.Eberle/T.Hall 4.00 10.00
TTEJ E.Staal/J.Staal 5.00 12.00
TTEL C.Eakin/L.Leblanc TC 8.00 20.00
TTFK Kassian/M.Foligno TC 6.00 15.00
TTFS M.Fleury/J.Staal 8.00 20.00
TTGB M.Green/N.Backstrom 4.00 10.00
TTGF R.Getzlaf/C.Fowler 4.00 10.00
TTGR R.Getzlaf/B.Ryan 4.00 10.00
TTGS M.Gaborik/D.Stepan 4.00 10.00
TTHB B.Hull/E.Belfour 6.00 15.00
TTHG S.Hartnell/C.Giroux 4.00 10.00
TTHH D.Hasek/J.Howard 6.00 15.00
TTJP Thornton/P.Marleau TC 6.00 15.00
TTKB Kiprusoff/Bouwmeester 4.00 10.00
TTKC K.Shattenkirk/C.Stewart 3.00 8.00
TTKD A.Kopitar/D.Doughty 8.00 20.00
TTKE N.Kronwall/J.Ericsson 3.00 8.00
TTKP I.Kovalchuk/Z.Parise 4.00 10.00
TTLD N.Lidstrom/P.Datsyuk 6.00 15.00
TTLH N.Lidstrom/J.Howard 5.00 12.00
TTLJ M.Lemieux/J.Jagr 10.00 25.00
TTLK R.Luongo/R.Kesler 6.00 15.00
TTMB Bergeron/B.Morrow TC 5.00 12.00
TTME T.Myers/T.Ennis 2.50 6.00
TTMG M.Messier/M.Gartner 5.00 12.00
TTMJ Bouwmeester/Kiprusoff 4.00 10.00
TTMV R.Miller/T.Vanek 4.00 10.00
TTNF M.Naslund/R.Francis 5.00 12.00
TTNM R.Nash/S.Mason 4.00 10.00
TTPB C.Pronger/I.Bryzgalov 4.00 10.00
TTPD P.Sharp/D.Keith 4.00 10.00
TTPE T.Plekanec/L.Eller 2.50 6.00
TTPO M.Paajarvi/L.Omark 3.00 8.00
TTRC M.Richards/J.Carter 3.00 8.00
TTRO M.Ribeiro/S.Ott 2.50 6.00
TTRS L.Robinson/P.Subban 5.00 12.00
TTSA C.Anderson/J.Spezza 4.00 10.00
TTSC Shanahan/Ciccarelli 4.00 10.00
TTSD P.Stastny/M.Duchene 4.00 10.00
TTSL J.Staal/K.Letang 5.00 12.00
TTSO A.Semin/A.Ovechkin 15.00 40.00
TTSS H.Sedin/D.Sedin 5.00 12.00
TTSW S.Weber/R.Suter 3.00 8.00
TTTR T.Rask/T.Thomas 5.00 12.00
TTVN T.Vokoun/M.Neuvirth 5.00 12.00
TTWK Khabibulin/R.Whitney 4.00 10.00
TTWV S.Weiss/K.Versteeg 3.00 8.00
TTYE Yandle/Ekman-Larsson 4.00 10.00
TTZF H.Zetterberg/J.Franzen 5.00 12.00

2012-13 Artifacts Tundra Trios Jerseys Blue

*EMERALD/18: 1X TO 2.5X BLUE GRP B
TT3ASA Alfrdsn/Spezza/Andrsn B 5.00 12.00
TT3BHP Backs/Halk/Pietran B 6.00 15.00
TT3BJB Brodr/Belfr/Josph B 12.00 30.00
TT3BKM Bergrn/Mrchnd/Krejci B 6.00 15.00
TT3BMH Belfour/Hull/Modano A 6.00 15.00
TT3BPK Pavelc/Kane/Byfug B 8.00 20.00
TT3BQD Quick/Dghty/Bernr B 6.00 15.00
TT3BSS Backes/Stwart/Shatt B 4.00 10.00
TT3CBP Bourque/Park/Chara B 8.00 20.00
TT3CTR Thomas/Rask/Chara B 8.00 20.00
TT3DYE Doan/Yndle/Ek-Lars B 5.00 12.00
TT3DZF Franzn/Datsyk/Zettr B 8.00 20.00
TT3EGO Ellis/Gdbrnsn/Olsn TC B 5.00 12.00
TT3FMS Staal/Fleury/Malkin B 10.00 25.00
TT3GRF Getzlaf/Ryan/Fowler B 5.00 12.00
TT3GSD Giguere/Ststny/Duch B 6.00 15.00
TT3GSS Staal/Stepan/Boyle B 3.00 8.00
TT3GSV Gigre/Varlmv/Ststny B 8.00 20.00
TT3HVV van Rms/Hrtnll/Vrack B 4.00 10.00
TT3IKC Kiprsff/Iginla/Camml B 6.00 15.00
TT3KMK Kessel/Kulmin/McArt B 5.00 12.00
TT3KPC Koval/Parise/Clarksn B 5.00 12.00
TT3LJG Gretzky/Jagr/Lindros B 12.00 30.00
TT3LSS Lecav/StLoui/Stamk B 10.00 25.00
TT3MOT Mlsn/Okpso/Tavres B 8.00 20.00
TT3NBM Brassard/Mason/Nash B 5.00 12.00
TT3OPC Orr/Parros/Carkner B 5.00 12.00
TT3PBG Pronger/Giroux/Bryz B 5.00 12.00
TT3PPS Price/Subban/Plek B 10.00 25.00
TT3PSK Seabrk/Keith/Prngr TC B 6.00 15.00
TT3RCK Kopitr/Richrds/Cartr B 8.00 20.00
TT3RMV Miller/Vanek/Roy B 10.00 25.00
TT3SLJ Jagr/Lindros/Shanhn B 10.00 25.00
TT3SOB Semn/Ovech/Bckstrm B 8.00 20.00
TT3SSK Sedin/Sedin/Kesler B 6.00 15.00
TT3SSS Staal/Staal/Staal B 6.00 15.00
TT3TMB Mrrw/Thrntn/Berg TC B 6.00 15.00
TT3VME Vanek/Myers/Ennis B 4.00 10.00

2013-14 Artifacts

COMP.SET w/o SP's (100) 12.00 30.00
*ROOK.EXCH: .3X TO .8X ROOKIE/899
1 Adam Henrique .30 .75
2 Adam Larsson .40 1.00
3 Alex Tanguay .25 .60
4 Alexander Ovechkin 1.50 4.00
5 Alexandre Burrows .25 .60
6 Andrei Markov .25 .60
7 Blake Wheeler .40 1.00
8 Bob Nystrom .25 .60
9 Bobby Ryan .30 .75
10 Brad Marchand .75 2.00
11 Brayden Schenn .40 1.00
12 Bryan Little .40 1.00
13 Bryan Trottier .40 1.00
14 Claude Lemieux .30 .75
15 Colin Greening .25 .60
16 Corey Perry .60 1.50
17 Dale Hawerchuk .50 1.25
18 Daniel Briere .40 1.00
19 David Perron .30 .75
20 Dion Phaneuf .30 .75
21 Doug Gilmour .50 1.25
22 Drew Doughty .50 1.25
23 Drew Stafford .25 .60
24 Duncan Keith .30 .75
25 Dustin Brown .40 1.00
26 Eric Lindros .60 1.50
27 Evgeni Malkin .75 2.00
28 Gabriel Landeskog .50 1.25
29 Harold Snepsts .25 .60
30 Henrik Zetterberg .50 1.25
31 Ilya Kovalchuk .40 1.00
32 Jacques Lemaire .30 .75
33 James Neal .25 .60
34 Jamie McBain .25 .60
35 Jaromir Jagr 1.25 3.00
36 Jason Pominville .25 .60
37 Jason Spezza .40 1.00
38 Jay Bouwmeester .25 .60
39 Jeff Carter .30 .75
40 Jeff Skinner .50 1.25
41 Joe Sakic .75 2.00
42 Jonathan Toews .60 1.50
43 Jordan Eberle .40 1.00
44 Justin Williams .30 .75
45 Keith Yandle .25 .60
46 Kevin Shattenkirk .25 .60
47 Kris Letang .50 1.25
48 Larry Murphy .30 .75
49 Lars Eller .25 .60
50 Luke Adam .30 .75
51 Luke Schenn .40 1.00
52 Marc Staal .25 .60
53 Marian Gaborik .40 1.00
54 Mario Lemieux 1.50 4.00
55 Markus Naslund .40 1.00
56 Mats Sundin .40 1.00
57 Matt Duchene .40 1.00
58 Matt Read .25 .60
59 Matt Stajan .25 .60
60 Maxime Talbot .25 .60
61 Michael Cammalleri .30 .75
62 Michael Frolik .25 .60
63 Michel Goulet .30 .75
64 Mike Gartner .50 1.25
65 Mike Green .30 .75
66 Mike Modano .60 1.50
67 Mike Ribeiro .25 .60
68 Mike Richards .30 .75
69 Milan Hejduk .30 .75
70 Milan Lucic .40 1.00
71 Nathan Horton .40 1.00
72 Nick Foligno .30 .75
73 Nicklas Lidstrom .40 1.00
74 Slava Voynov .30 .75
75 Niklas Kronwall .30 .75
76 Oliver Ekman-Larsson .40 1.00
77 P.K. Subban .50 1.25
78 Patric Hornqvist .25 .60
79 Patrice Bergeron .50 1.25
80 Patrick Marleau .40 1.00
81 Patrik Elias .40 1.00
82 Paul Coffey .40 1.00
83 Paul Stastny .30 .75
84 Pavel Bure .40 1.00
85 Peter Mueller .25 .60
86 Ron Francis .50 1.25
87 Ryan Getzlaf .40 1.00
88 Ryan Nugent-Hopkins .50 1.25
89 Scott Hartnell .25 .60
90 Scott Niedermayer .40 1.00
91 Shea Weber .30 .75
92 Sidney Crosby 1.50 4.00
93 Taylor Hall .40 1.00
94 Theoren Fleury .50 1.25
95 Tomas Plekanec .25 .60
96 Tyler Seguin .50 1.25
97 Valtteri Filppula .25 .60
98 Wayne Gretzky 2.50 6.00
99 Zach Parise .40 1.00
100 Zdeno Chara .40 1.00
101 Bernie Parent G 2.00 5.00
102 Bill Ranford G 1.50 4.00
103 Braden Holtby G 2.00 5.00
104 Carey Price G 3.00 8.00
105 Chris Osgood G 1.50 4.00
106 Corey Crawford G 2.00 5.00
107 Cory Schneider G 1.50 4.00
108 Craig Anderson G 1.50 4.00
109 Curtis Joseph G 2.00 5.00
110 Dominik Hasek G 2.50 6.00
111 Ed Belfour G 1.50 4.00
112 Ilya Bryzgalov G 1.50 4.00
113 Jean-Sebastien Giguere G 1.50 4.00
114 Jim Howard G 2.00 5.00
115 Jonathan Quick G 2.00 5.00
116 Kari Lehtonen G 1.25 3.00
117 Marc-Andre Fleury G 3.00 8.00
118 Martin Brodeur G 4.00 10.00
119 Miikka Kiprusoff G 1.50 4.00
120 Ondrej Pavelec G 1.50 4.00
121 Patrick Roy G 4.00 10.00
122 Pekka Rinne G 1.50 4.00
123 Roberto Luongo G 2.50 6.00
124 Robin Lehner G 1.25 3.00
125 Tuukka Rask G 2.00 5.00
126 Brett Connolly TC 1.00 2.50
127 Bryan Trottier TC 1.50 4.00
128 Carter Ashton TC 1.00 2.50
129 Chet Pickard TC 1.00 2.50
130 Cody Goloubef TC 1.00 2.50
131 Colten Teubert TC 1.00 2.50
132 Corey Perry TC 2.50 6.00
133 Dany Heatley TC 1.25 3.00
134 Devante Smith-Pelly TC 1.25 3.00
135 Duncan Keith TC 1.25 3.00
136 Evander Kane TC 1.50 4.00
137 Jaden Schwartz TC 2.00 5.00
138 Jamie Benn TC 1.50 4.00
139 Jared Cowen TC 1.00 2.50
140 Joe Sakic TC 3.00 8.00
141 Joe Thornton TC 2.50 6.00
142 Keith Aulie TC 1.00 2.50
143 Mark Stone TC 2.00 5.00
144 Patrice Cormier TC 1.00 2.50
145 Ryan Johansen TC 1.25 3.00
146 Stefan Della Rovere TC 1.00 2.50
147 Steve Shutt TC 1.25 3.00
148 Tyler Ennis TC 1.00 2.50
149 Wayne Gretzky TC 10.00 25.00
150 Zach Boychuk TC 1.00 2.50
151 Alex Chiasson RC 2.00 5.00
152 Alex Galchenyuk RC 6.00 15.00
153 Austin Watson RC 1.50 4.00
154 Beau Bennett RC 2.50 6.00
155 Brendan Gallagher RC 6.00 15.00
156 Calvin Pickard RC 2.50 6.00
157 Charlie Coyle RC 3.00 8.00
158 Chris Brown RC 1.25 3.00
159 Christian Thomas RC 1.50 4.00
160 Cory Conacher RC 1.25 3.00
161 Cristopher Nilstorp RC 1.50 4.00
162 Damien Brunner RC 1.50 4.00
163 Dougie Hamilton RC 3.00 8.00
164 Drew Shore RC 1.50 4.00
165 Emerson Etem RC 2.00 5.00
166 Filip Forsberg RC 6.00 15.00
167 Jack Campbell RC 5.00 12.00
168 Jamie Oleksiak RC 1.50 4.00
169 Jared Staal RC 1.50 4.00
170 Jarred Tinordi RC 2.00 5.00
171 Johan Larsson RC 2.50 6.00
172 Jonas Brodin RC 2.50 6.00
173 Jonathan Huberdeau RC 5.00 12.00
174 Jordan Schroeder RC 2.00 5.00
175 Justin Schultz RC 2.00 5.00
176 Leo Komarov RC 2.00 5.00
177 Mark Pysyk RC 2.00 5.00
178 Max Reinhart RC 2.00 5.00
179 Mikael Granlund RC 3.00 8.00
180 Mikhail Grigorenko RC 1.25 3.00
181 Nail Yakupov RC 6.00 15.00
182 Nathan Beaulieu RC 1.25 3.00
183 Nick Bjugstad RC 2.50 6.00
184 Nick Petrecki RC 1.25 3.00
185 Nicklas Jensen RC 1.50 4.00
186 Petr Mrazek RC 4.00 10.00
187 Quinton Howden RC 1.50 4.00
188 Richard Panik RC 2.00 5.00
189 Rickard Rakell RC 2.00 5.00
190 Roman Cervenka RC 1.50 4.00
191 Ryan Murphy RC 2.00 5.00
192 Ryan Spooner RC 2.00 5.00
193 Scott Laughton RC 2.50 6.00
194 Stefan Matteau RC 1.50 4.00
195 Thomas Hickey RC 1.50 4.00
196 Tye McGinn RC 2.00 5.00
197 Tyler Toffoli RC 4.00 10.00
198 Viktor Fasth RC 2.00 5.00
199 Vladimir Tarasenko RC 5.00 12.00
200 Zach Redmond RC 1.50 4.00
RED201 Hampus Lindholm RC 3.00 8.00
RED202 Carl Soderberg RC 2.00 5.00
RED203 Zemgus Girgensons RC 3.00 8.00
RED204 Sean Monahan RC 3.00 8.00
RED205 Elias Lindholm RC 5.00 12.00
RED206 Antti Raanta RC 4.00 10.00
RED207 Nathan MacKinnon RC 15.00 40.00
RED208 Ryan Murray RC 3.00 8.00
RED209 Valeri Nichushkin RC 4.00 10.00
RED210 Danny DeKeyser RC 2.50 6.00
RED211 Mark Arcobello RC 2.00 5.00
RED212 Aleksander Barkov RC 6.00 15.00
RED213 Linden Vey RC 1.25 3.00
RED214 Mathew Dumba RC 1.25 3.00
RED215 Michael Bournival RC 2.00 5.00
RED216 Seth Jones RC 4.00 10.00
RED217 Reid Boucher RC 2.00 5.00
RED218 Ryan Strome RC 3.00 8.00
RED219 Dylan McIlrath RC 1.25 3.00
RED220 Cody Ceci RC 1.50 4.00
RED221 Michael Raffl RC 1.50 4.00
RED222 Lucas Lessio RC 1.25 3.00
RED223 Olli Maatta RC 3.00 8.00
RED224 Tomas Hertl RC 4.00 10.00
RED225 Dmitrij Jaskin RC 2.00 5.00
RED226 Nikita Kucherov RC 12.00 30.00
RED227 Morgan Rielly RC 5.00 12.00
RED228 Joacim Eriksson RC 2.00 5.00
RED229 Philipp Grubauer RC 5.00 12.00
RED230 Jacob Trouba RC 3.00 8.00
RED231 Josh Leivo RC 1.50 4.00
RED232 Boone Jenner RC 4.00 10.00
RED233 Tyler Johnson RC 4.00 10.00
RED234 Frederik Andersen RC 5.00 12.00
RED235 Jon Merrill RC 2.00 5.00
RED236 Marek Mazanec RC 2.00 5.00
RED237 Freddie Hamilton RC 2.00 5.00
RED238 Rasmus Ristolainen RC 3.00 8.00
RED239 Martin Jones RC 3.00 8.00
RED240 Justin Fontaine RC 2.00 5.00
RED241 John Gibson RC 5.00 12.00
RED242 Tomas Jurco RC 2.50 6.00

2013-14 Artifacts Emerald

*1-100 VETS/99: 3X TO 8X BASIC CARDS
*101-150 G/TC/99: 1X TO 2.5X BASIC G/TC
*151-200 ROOKIES/99: .6X TO 1.5X BASIC RC
152 Alex Galchenyuk 12.00 30.00
181 Nail Yakupov 20.00 50.00

2013-14 Artifacts Ruby

*1-100 VETS/399: 2X TO 5X BASIC CARDS
*101-150 G/TC/299: .6X TO 1.5X BASIC G/TC
*151-200 ROOKIES/299: .5X TO 1.2X BASIC RC

2013-14 Artifacts Sapphire

*1-100 VETS/85: 3X TO 8X BASIC CARDS
*101-150 G/TC/85: 1X TO 2.5X BASIC G/TC
*151-200 ROOKIES/85: .8X TO 2X BASIC RC
152 Alex Galchenyuk 15.00 40.00

2013-14 Artifacts Spectrum

*1-100 VETS/25: 6X TO 15X BASIC CARDS
*101-150 G/TC/25: 1.5X TO 4X BASIC G/TC
*151-200 ROOKIES/25: 1.2X TO 3X BASIC RC
152 Alex Galchenyuk 60.00 120.00
155 Brendan Gallagher 40.00 80.00
181 Nail Yakupov 40.00 100.00

2013-14 Artifacts Autofacts

AAG Alex Goligoski E 3.00 8.00
ABB Brett Bulmer D 3.00 8.00
ABL Brian Lee F 3.00 8.00
ABM Brendan Mikkelson F 3.00 8.00
ABN Brendon Nash D 3.00 8.00
ABO Bobby Orr B 50.00 120.00
ABS Brayden Schenn D 5.00 12.00
ACG Cameron Gaunce D 3.00 8.00
ACO Cal O'Reilly F 3.00 8.00
ACP Corey Perry C 8.00 20.00
ACW Colin Wilson E 4.00 10.00
ADA Stephane Da Costa E 3.00 8.00
ADB Drayson Bowman E 3.00 8.00
ADS David Savard F 3.00 8.00
AEN Evgeni Nabokov E 5.00 12.00
AET Eric Tangradi D 3.00 8.00
AGR Andy Greene D 3.00 8.00
AJB Josh Bailey E 4.00 10.00
AJC Jared Cowen F 3.00 8.00
AJE Jonathan Ericsson F 3.00 8.00
AJF Justin Falk D 3.00 8.00
AJG Jake Gardiner D 3.00 8.00
AJH Josh Harding E 5.00 12.00
AJR Jay Rosehill F 3.00 8.00
ALI Leland Irving F 4.00 10.00
AMA Shawn Matthias D 3.00 8.00
AMH Matthew Halischuk F 3.00 8.00
AML Mario Lemieux B 30.00 80.00
AMM Matt Martin D 3.00 8.00
AMS Marco Sturm E 3.00 8.00
ANG Nicklas Grossman E 3.00 8.00
APB Pavel Bure B 25.00 60.00
APE Patrik Elias C 5.00 12.00
APO Patrick O'Sullivan F 3.00 8.00
ARO Ryan O'Marra D 3.00 8.00
ASD Simon Despres F 4.00 10.00
ASM Brendan Smith E 3.00 8.00
ASS Steven Stamkos B 25.00 60.00
AST Mark Streit F 3.00 8.00
ASU Mats Sundin B 20.00 50.00
ATE Tim Erixon E 3.00 8.00
ATL Trevor Lewis F 3.00 8.00
ATR Tuomo Ruutu E 4.00 10.00
ATS Tim Stapleton E 3.00 8.00
ATV Tomas Vincour E 3.00 8.00
ATW Tommy Wingels D 3.00 8.00
AVS Viktor Stalberg E 3.00 8.00
AWG Wayne Gretzky A 200.00 500.00

2013-14 Artifacts Buyback Autographs

1 S.Crosby/40 '09-10ART 75.00 125.00
3 S.Stamkos/25 '10-11ART 30.00 80.00
4 J.Tavares/18 '09-10ART 50.00 100.00

2013-14 Artifacts Frozen Artifacts Jerseys Blue

*GREEN PATCH/36: ..6X TO 1.5X BLUE JSY
FAAL Adam Larsson B 2.50 6.00
FABE Patrik Berglund A 1.50 4.00
FABO Pierre-Marc Bouchard A 2.50 6.00
FABS Brayden Schenn B 2.50 6.00
FACG Colin Greening A 1.50 4.00
FADD David Desharnais B 1.50 4.00
FAGA Simon Gagne B 2.50 6.00
FAGO Michel Goulet B 2.00 5.00
FAGR Mike Green B 2.00 5.00
FAJS Joe Sakic A 5.00 12.00
FALE Lars Eller A 1.50 4.00
FALS Luke Schenn B 2.50 6.00
FAMG Marian Gaborik B 2.50 6.00
FAMR Mike Richards B 2.00 5.00
FAMR Matt Duchene B 2.50 6.00
FANG Nathan Gerbe B 1.50 4.00
FANK Nikolai Khabibulin B 2.50 6.00
FAOE Oliver Ekman-Larsson B 2.50 6.00
FAPB Patrice Bergeron B 3.00 8.00
FAPE Patrik Elias B 2.50 6.00
FAPM Peter Mueller B 1.50 4.00
FAPR Pekka Rinne B 2.50 6.00
FAPS P.K. Subban B 3.00 8.00
FAPS Paul Stastny B 2.00 5.00
FARD Raphael Diaz A 1.50 4.00
FASG Sam Gagner B 1.50 4.00
FASW Shea Weber B 2.00 5.00
FAWE Stephen Weiss A 2.00 5.00

2013-14 Artifacts Jerseys

*EMERALD/75: .8X TO 2X BASIC JSY/125
*SPECTRUM/15: 1.2X TO 3X BASIC JSY/125
*HORIZNTL/36: 1X TO 2.5X BASIC JSY/125
*HRZN EMERALD/24: 1X TO 2.5X JSY/125
1 Adam Henrique 2.00 5.00
2 Adam Larsson 2.50 6.00
4 Alexander Ovechkin 10.00 25.00
5 Alexandre Burrows 1.50 4.00
6 Andrei Markov 1.50 4.00
8 Bob Nystrom 1.50 4.00
9 Bobby Ryan 2.00 5.00
10 Brad Marchand 5.00 12.00
11 Brayden Schenn 2.50 6.00
13 Bryan Trottier 2.50 6.00
14 Claude Lemieux 2.00 5.00
15 Colin Greening 1.50 4.00
16 Corey Perry 4.00 10.00
17 Dale Hawerchuk 3.00 8.00
18 Daniel Briere 2.50 6.00
19 David Perron 2.00 5.00
20 Dion Phaneuf 2.00 5.00
21 Doug Gilmour 3.00 8.00
22 Drew Doughty 3.00 8.00
23 Drew Stafford 1.50 4.00
24 Duncan Keith 2.00 5.00
25 Dustin Brown 2.50 6.00
26 Eric Lindros 4.00 10.00
27 Evgeni Malkin 5.00 12.00
28 Gabriel Landeskog 3.00 8.00
29 Harold Snepsts 1.50 4.00
30 Henrik Zetterberg 3.00 8.00
31 Ilya Kovalchuk 2.50 6.00
32 Jacques Lemaire 2.00 5.00
34 Jamie McBain 1.50 4.00
35 Jaromir Jagr 8.00 20.00
36 Jason Pominville 1.50 4.00
37 Jason Spezza 2.50 6.00
38 Jay Bouwmeester 1.50 4.00
39 Jeff Carter 2.00 5.00
40 Jeff Skinner 3.00 8.00
41 Joe Sakic 5.00 12.00
42 Jonathan Toews 4.00 10.00
43 Jordan Eberle 2.50 6.00
44 Justin Williams 2.00 5.00
45 Keith Yandle 1.50 4.00
46 Kevin Shattenkirk 1.50 4.00
47 Kris Letang 3.00 8.00
48 Larry Murphy 2.00 5.00
49 Lars Eller 1.50 4.00
50 Luke Adam 2.00 5.00
51 Luke Schenn 2.50 6.00
53 Marian Gaborik 2.50 6.00
54 Mario Lemieux 10.00 25.00
55 Markus Naslund 2.50 6.00
56 Mats Sundin 2.50 6.00
57 Matt Duchene 2.50 6.00
58 Matt Read 1.50 4.00
59 Matt Stajan 1.50 4.00
60 Maxime Talbot 1.50 4.00
61 Michael Cammalleri 2.00 5.00
62 Michael Frolik 1.50 4.00
63 Michel Goulet 2.00 5.00
64 Mike Gartner 3.00 8.00
65 Mike Green 2.00 5.00
66 Mike Modano 4.00 10.00
67 Mike Ribeiro 1.50 4.00
68 Mike Richards 2.00 5.00
69 Milan Hejduk 2.00 5.00
70 Milan Lucic 2.50 6.00
71 Nathan Horton 2.50 6.00
72 Nick Foligno 2.00 5.00
73 Nicklas Lidstrom 2.50 6.00
74 Slava Voynov 2.00 5.00
75 Niklas Kronwall 2.00 5.00
76 Oliver Ekman-Larsson 2.50 6.00
77 P.K. Subban 3.00 8.00
78 Patric Hornqvist 1.50 4.00
79 Patrice Bergeron 3.00 8.00
80 Patrick Marleau 2.50 6.00
81 Patrik Elias 2.50 6.00
82 Paul Coffey 2.50 6.00
83 Paul Stastny 2.00 5.00
84 Pavel Bure 2.50 6.00
85 Peter Mueller 1.50 4.00
86 Ron Francis 3.00 8.00
87 Ryan Getzlaf 2.50 6.00
88 Ryan Nugent-Hopkins 3.00 8.00
90 Scott Niedermayer 2.50 6.00
91 Shea Weber 2.00 5.00
92 Sidney Crosby 10.00 25.00
93 Taylor Hall 2.50 6.00
94 Theoren Fleury 3.00 8.00
95 Tomas Plekanec 1.50 4.00
96 Tyler Seguin 3.00 8.00
97 Valtteri Filppula 1.50 4.00
98 Wayne Gretzky 15.00 40.00
99 Zach Parise 2.50 6.00
100 Zdeno Chara 2.50 6.00
101 Bernie Parent G 3.00 8.00
102 Bill Ranford G 2.50 6.00
103 Braden Holtby G 3.00 8.00
104 Carey Price G 5.00 12.00
106 Corey Crawford G 3.00 8.00
107 Cory Schneider G 2.50 6.00
108 Craig Anderson G 2.50 6.00
109 Curtis Joseph G 3.00 8.00
110 Dominik Hasek G 4.00 10.00
111 Ed Belfour G 2.50 6.00
112 Ilya Bryzgalov G 2.50 6.00
113 Jean-Sebastien Giguere G 2.50 6.00
114 Jim Howard G 3.00 8.00
115 Jonathan Quick G 3.00 8.00
116 Kari Lehtonen G 2.00 5.00
117 Marc-Andre Fleury G 5.00 12.00
118 Martin Brodeur G 6.00 15.00
119 Miikka Kiprusoff G 2.50 6.00
120 Ondrej Pavelec G 2.50 6.00
121 Patrick Roy G 6.00 15.00
122 Pekka Rinne G 2.50 6.00

123 Roberto Luongo G 4.00 10.00
124 Robin Lehner G 2.00 5.00
125 Tuukka Rask G 3.00 8.00
126 Brett Connolly TC 1.50 4.00
127 Bryan Trottier TC 2.50 6.00
129 Chet Pickard TC 1.50 4.00
130 Cody Goloubef TC 1.50 4.00
131 Colten Teubert TC 1.50 4.00
132 Corey Perry TC 4.00 10.00
133 Dany Heatley TC 2.00 5.00
134 Devante Smith-Pelly TC 2.00 5.00
135 Duncan Keith TC 2.00 5.00
136 Evander Kane TC 2.50 6.00
137 Jaden Schwartz TC 3.00 8.00
138 Jamie Benn TC 2.50 6.00
139 Jared Cowen TC 1.50 4.00
140 Joe Sakic TC 5.00 12.00
141 Joe Thornton TC 4.00 10.00
142 Keith Aulie TC 1.50 4.00
144 Patrice Cormier TC 1.50 4.00
145 Ryan Johansen TC 2.00 5.00
146 Stefan Della Rovere TC 1.50 4.00
147 Steve Shutt TC 2.00 5.00
148 Tyler Ennis TC 1.50 4.00
149 Wayne Gretzky TC 15.00 40.00
150 Zach Boychuk TC 1.50 4.00
152 Alex Galchenyuk 6.00 15.00
153 Austin Watson 2.00 5.00
154 Beau Bennett 3.00 8.00
155 Brendan Gallagher 6.00 15.00
156 Calvin Pickard 3.00 8.00
157 Charlie Coyle 4.00 10.00
158 Chris Brown 1.50 4.00
159 Christian Thomas 2.00 5.00
160 Cory Conacher 1.50 4.00
161 Cristopher Nilstorp 2.00 5.00
162 Damien Brunner 2.00 5.00
163 Dougie Hamilton 4.00 10.00
164 Drew Shore 2.00 5.00
165 Emerson Etem 2.50 6.00
167 Jack Campbell 6.00 15.00
168 Jamie Oleksiak 2.00 5.00
169 Jared Staal 2.00 5.00
170 Jarred Tinordi 2.50 6.00
172 Jonas Brodin 3.00 8.00
173 Jonathan Huberdeau 6.00 15.00
174 Jordan Schroeder 2.50 6.00
175 Justin Schultz 2.50 6.00
177 Mark Pysyk 2.50 6.00
180 Mikhail Grigorenko 1.50 4.00
181 Nail Yakupov 5.00 12.00
182 Nathan Beaulieu 1.50 4.00
184 Nick Petrecki 1.50 4.00
185 Nicklas Jensen 2.00 5.00
186 Petr Mrazek 5.00 12.00
187 Quinton Howden 2.00 5.00
189 Rickard Rakell 2.50 6.00
190 Roman Cervenka 2.00 5.00
191 Ryan Murphy 2.50 6.00
192 Ryan Spooner 2.50 6.00
193 Scott Laughton 3.00 8.00
194 Stefan Matteau 2.00 5.00
195 Thomas Hickey 2.00 5.00
197 Tyler Toffoli 5.00 12.00
198 Viktor Fasth 2.50 6.00
199 Vladimir Tarasenko 6.00 15.00
200 Zach Redmond 2.00 5.00

2013-14 Artifacts Rookie Autographs Redemptions

I Nathan MacKinnon 100.00 200.00
II Tomas Hertl 30.00 60.00
III Sean Monahan 30.00 80.00
IV Seth Jones 40.00 80.00
V Valeri Nichushkin 25.00 50.00
VI Morgan Rielly 25.00 50.00
VII Aleksander Barkov 20.00 50.00
VIII Jacob Trouba 25.00 50.00
IX Elias Lindholm 12.00 30.00
X Ryan Murray 12.00 30.00
XI Rasmus Ristolainen 15.00 40.00
XII Boone Jenner 15.00 40.00
XIII Olli Maatta 15.00 40.00
XIV Matt Nieto 10.00 25.00
XV Freddie Hamilton 12.00 30.00
XVI Mathew Dumba 10.00 25.00
XVII Michael Bournival 15.00 40.00
XVIII Nikita Zadorov 12.00 30.00
XIX Zemgus Girgensons 15.00 40.00
XX Danny DeKeyser 12.00 30.00
XXI Mark Arcobello 10.00 25.00
XXII Sami Vatanen 12.00 30.00
XXIII Joakim Nordstrom 10.00 25.00
XXIV Hampus Lindholm 10.00 25.00

2013-14 Artifacts Top 12 Rookie Signatures

RSAG Alex Galchenyuk EXCH 10.00 25.00
RSBB Beau Bennett 10.00 25.00
RSBG Brendan Gallagher 20.00 50.00
RSCC Charlie Coyle 12.00 30.00
RSCO Cory Conacher 5.00 12.00
RSDH Dougie Hamilton 10.00 25.00
RSEE Emerson Etem 8.00 20.00
RSJH Jonathan Huberdeau 6.00 15.00
RSJS Justin Schultz 8.00 20.00
RSNY Nail Yakupov EXCH 15.00 40.00
RSTT Tyler Toffoli 15.00 40.00
RSVT Vladimir Tarasenko 20.00 50.00

2013-14 Artifacts Treasured Swatches Jerseys Blue

*EMERALD/36: .8X TO 2X BASIC JSY
TSAH Ales Hemsky B 2.50 6.00
TSBO Ray Bourque C 6.00 15.00
TSCS Craig Smith B 2.50 6.00
TSEB Ed Belfour C 4.00 10.00
TSGA Sam Gagner C 2.50 6.00
TSJC Jeff Carter C 3.00 8.00
TSJH Jim Howard C 5.00 12.00
TSMB Martin Brodeur C 10.00 25.00
TSMK Miikka Kiprusoff C 4.00 10.00
TSMR Mike Richards B 3.00 8.00
TSMS Matt Stajan B 2.50 6.00
TSPR Pekka Rinne C 4.00 10.00
TSPS Paul Stastny B 3.00 8.00
TSRB Rene Bourque B 3.00 8.00
TSRD Raphael Diaz B 2.50 6.00
TSRG Ryan Getzlaf B 4.00 10.00
TSRJ Ryan Johansen A 5.00 12.00
TSRL Roberto Luongo C 6.00 15.00
TSSC Sean Couturier C 3.00 8.00
TSSG Simon Gagne B 4.00 10.00
TSSH Scott Hartnell C 2.50 6.00
TSSO Steve Ott B 2.50 6.00
TSSV Semyon Varlamov B 4.00 10.00
TSSW Stephen Weiss B 3.00 8.00
TSTR Tuukka Rask C 5.00 12.00
TSTV Thomas Vanek C 3.00 8.00
TSZC Zdeno Chara B 4.00 10.00
TSZP Zach Parise C 4.00 10.00

2013-14 Artifacts Tundra Sixes Jerseys Blue

T6AVS Colorado Avalanche 12.00 30.00
T6BOS Boston Bruins 12.00 30.00
T6HOF 1990s Stars 30.00 80.00
T62010 Young Stars 15.00 40.00
T62011 Young Stars 12.00 30.00
T6BEES Boston Bruins 15.00 40.00
T6LBBR Montreal Canadiens 20.00 50.00
T6ASTAR All Star Greats 15.00 40.00
T6LEAFS Toronto Maple Leafs 15.00 40.00
T6WINGS Detroit Red Wings 15.00 40.00
T6CHAMPS Los Angeles Kings 12.00 30.00
T6FLYERS Philadelphia Flyers 12.00 30.00
T6OILERS Edmonton Oilers 12.00 30.00

2013-14 Artifacts Tundra Tandems Jerseys Blue

*EMERALD/36: 1X TO 2.5X BLUE TANDEM
TTAG A.Hemsky/S.Gagner B 2.50 6.00
TTBL P.Bergeron/M.Lucic B 5.00 12.00
TTBM E.Belfour/M.Modano B 6.00 15.00
TTBP R.Bourque/B.Park C 6.00 15.00
TTCD D.Alfredsson/C.Greening B 4.00 10.00
TTCR T.Rask/Z.Chara B 5.00 12.00
TTDZ P.Datsyuk/H.Zetterberg B 6.00 15.00
TTEH T.Hall/J.Eberle B 4.00 10.00
TTEK P.Elias/I.Kovalchuk A 5.00 12.00
TTFL K.Letang/M.Fleury B 8.00 20.00
TTGB M.Green/N.Backstrom C 4.00 10.00
TTGC R.Callahan/M.Gartner C 5.00 12.00
TTGH M.Green/B.Holtby B 5.00 12.00
TTHB S.Hartnell/D.Briere B 5.00 12.00
TTHG S.Hartnell/C.Giroux B 4.00 10.00
TTHM N.Horton/B.Marchand B 8.00 20.00
TTHS P.Hornqvist/C.Smith B 2.50 6.00
TTJD J.Carter/D.Doughty B 5.00 12.00
TTKC D.Keith/C.Crawford B 5.00 12.00
TTKO A.Ovechkin/I.Kovalchuk B 15.00 40.00
TTLG E.Lindros/C.Giroux B 6.00 15.00
TTLJ M.Lemieux/J.Jagr B 15.00 40.00
TTLK R.Luongo/R.Kesler B 6.00 15.00
TTLS R.Luongo/C.Schneider C 6.00 15.00
TTMA R.Miller/L.Adam B 4.00 10.00
TTMC P.Marleau/L.Couture B 5.00 12.00
TTNH M.Neuvirth/B.Holtby B 5.00 12.00
TTNK E.Nabokov/N.Khabibulin B 4.00 10.00
TTPE T.Plekanec/L.Eller B 2.50 6.00
TTPK O.Pavelec/E.Kane C 4.00 10.00
TTPO M.Paajarvi/L.Omark B 3.00 8.00
TTPS P.Subban/T.Plekanec B 5.00 12.00
TTRB R.Getzlaf/B.Ryan B 4.00 10.00
TTRC J.Carter/M.Richards B 3.00 8.00
TTRD M.Richards/D.Doughty B 5.00 12.00
TTRW P.Rinne/S.Weber B 4.00 10.00
TTSA C.Anderson/J.Spezza B 4.00 10.00
TTSD M.Duchene/P.Stastny C 4.00 10.00
TTSG M.Sundin/D.Gilmour C 5.00 12.00
TTSH J.Sakic/M.Hejduk A 8.00 20.00
TTSS C.Stewart/K.Shattenkirk B 4.00 10.00
TTVS T.Vanek/D.Stafford C 3.00 8.00
TTWM S.Weiss/P.Mueller C 3.00 8.00
TTWP J.Williams/D.Penner C 3.00 8.00
TTWS S.Weber/C.Smith B 3.00 8.00

2013-14 Artifacts Tundra Trios Jerseys Blue

*EMERALD/18: 1X TO 2.5X BLUE GRP C-D
*EMERALD/18: .8X TO 2X BLUE GRP D
*EMERALD/18: .6X TO 1.5X BLUE GRP A
T3ASK Spezza/Karlsson/Alfredsson C 5.00 12.00
T3BEK Brodeur/Elias/Kovlchk C 10.00 25.00
T3BJB Brodeur/Belfour/Josph D 10.00 25.00
T3BLM Marchand/Bergeron/Lucic C 8.00 20.00
T3BPK Pavelec/Kane/Byfuglien C 4.00 10.00
T3CBP Chara/Bourque/Park C 6.00 15.00
T3CHR Rask/Chara/Horton C 5.00 12.00
T3EHN Eberle/Hall/RNH C 5.00 12.00
T3GRH Ryan/Hiller/Getzlaf B 5.00 12.00
T3GSD Duchene/Giguere/Stastny D 4.00 10.00
T3GSV Giguere/Varlamov/Stastny D 4.00 10.00
T3HBB Hartnell/Briere/Bryzgalov C 4.00 10.00
T3HSS Hartnell/Schenn/Schenn C 4.00 10.00
T3HVG Hartnell/Voracek/Gagne C 4.00 10.00
T3IKS Kiprusoff/Stajan/Iginla B 6.00 15.00
T3LJG Lindros/Jagr/Gartner A 12.00 30.00
T3LLJ Lemieux/Lindros/Jagr C 15.00 40.00
T3LSG Gretzky/Lemieux/Sakic B 20.00 50.00
T3OGH Holtby/Green/Ovchkn D 15.00 40.00
T3PED Plekanec/Eller/Desharnais C 2.50 6.00
T3RCD Richards/Carter/Doughty C 5.00 12.00
T3RCP Carter/Penner/Richards D 3.00 8.00
T3RWH Rinne/Weber/Hornqvist C 4.00 10.00
T3SDG Gilmour/Sundin/Domi D 6.00 15.00
T3SGT Sundin/Twist/Goulet C 6.00 15.00
T3SHS Sakic/Hull/Sundin C 8.00 20.00
T3TMB Thorntn/Morrw/Bergrn C 6.00 15.00
T3VEA Ennis/Adam/Vanek C 3.00 8.00
T3VYE Yandle/Ekman-Lar/Vermte C 4.00 10.00

2014-15 Artifacts

COMP.SET w/o SP's (100) 12.00 30.00
1 Ryan McDonagh .25 .60
2 Brendan Gallagher .40 1.00
3 Jason Spezza .40 1.00
4 Kyle Turris .40 1.00
5 Peter Forsberg .75 2.00
6 Cody Hodgson .25 .60
7 Larry Murphy .30 .75
8 Cody Eakin .25 .60
9 Henrik Zetterberg .50 1.25
10 Jaromir Jagr 1.25 3.00
11 Hampus Lindholm .25 .60
12 Georges Laraque .30 .75
13 Slava Voynov .40 1.00
14 Sam Gagner .25 .60
15 Sean Couturier .30 .75
16 Joe Thornton .60 1.50
17 Chris Pronger .40 1.00
18 Dustin Byfuglien .40 1.00
19 Mike Green .30 .75
20 Eric Lindros .60 1.50
21 Luc Robitaille .40 1.00
22 Max Pacioretty .40 1.00
23 Mats Sundin .40 1.00
24 Paul Coffey .40 1.00
25 Markus Naslund .40 1.00
26 Josh Gorges .25 .60
27 Doug Harvey .40 1.00
28 Brett Hull .75 2.00
29 Cam Fowler .40 1.00
30 Eddie Shack .40 1.00
31 Trevor Linden .40 1.00
32 Rob Brown .30 .75
33 Jeremy Roenick .60 1.50
34 Alex Chiasson .30 .75
35 Nicklas Backstrom .40 1.00
36 Brad Park .30 .75
37 Jakub Voracek .30 .75
38 Rick Nash .40 1.00
39 Tyler Seguin .50 1.25
40 Paul Stastny .30 .75
41 Wayne Gretzky 2.50 6.00
42 Wayne Simmonds .50 1.25
43 Olli Maatta .25 .60
44 Simon Despres .40 1.00
45 Anze Kopitar .60 1.50
46 Jonathan Toews .60 1.50
47 Travis Zajac .25 .60
48 Brian Campbell .25 .60
49 Ron Francis .50 1.25
50 Eric Lindros .60 1.50
51 Mike Richards .30 .75
52 Dustin Brown .40 1.00
53 Patrice Bergeron .50 1.25
54 Adam Oates .40 1.00
55 John Tavares .60 1.50
56 Jordan Eberle .40 1.00
57 Brian Bellows .30 .75
58 Larry Robinson .40 1.00
59 Chris Kreider .50 1.25
60 Brent Seabrook .25 .60
61 John Carlson .40 1.00
62 Corey Perry .60 1.50
63 Matt Read .25 .60
64 Shea Weber .30 .75
65 Alexander Ovechkin 1.50 4.00
66 John LeClair .40 1.00
67 Marcel Dionne .50 1.25
68 Milan Lucic .40 1.00
69 Victor Hedman .50 1.25
70 Vincent Damphousse .30 .75
71 Kyle Okposo .25 .60
72 Bill Guerin .40 1.00
73 Rob Blake .40 1.00
74 Steve Yzerman 1.00 2.50
75 Ryan Nugent-Hopkins .50 1.25
76 Teemu Selanne .75 2.00
77 Duncan Keith .30 .75
78 Erik Karlsson .50 1.25
79 Niklas Kronwall .30 .75
80 Ryan Kesler .40 1.00
81 Pierre Turgeon .30 .75
82 Dan Boyle .25 .60
83 Brad Richards .40 1.00
84 Scott Hartnell .25 .60
85 Alexander Edler .25 .60
86 Alex Tanguay .25 .60
87 Drew Doughty .50 1.25
88 Michel Goulet .30 .75
89 Cody Eakin .25 .60
90 Sidney Crosby 1.50 4.00
91 Ryan Getzlaf .40 1.00
92 Logan Couture .50 1.25
93 Brian Gionta .25 .60
94 Jeff Carter .30 .75
95 Drew Stafford .25 .00
96 Josh Bailey .30 .75
97 Cam Neely .40 1.00
98 Bryan Bickell .25 .60
99 Andrew Ladd .25 .60
100 Nikolai Kulemin .25 .60
101 Henrik Lundqvist G 4.00 10.00
102 Marc-Andre Fleury G 3.00 8.00
103 Antti Niemi G 1.25 3.00
104 Dominik Hasek G 2.50 6.00
105 Bill Ranford G 1.50 4.00
106 Marty Turco G 1.50 4.00
107 Jonathan Quick G 2.00 5.00
108 Olaf Kolzig G 1.50 4.00
109 Carey Price G 3.00 8.00
110 Cory Schneider G 1.50 4.00
111 Semyon Varlamov G 1.50 4.00
112 Cam Ward G 1.50 4.00
113 Ed Belfour G 1.50 4.00
114 Tony Esposito G 1.50 4.00
115 Pekka Rinne G 1.50 4.00
116 Jonas Hiller G 1.25 3.00
117 Ondrej Pavelec G 1.50 4.00
118 Grant Fuhr G 2.50 6.00
119 Pelle Lindbergh G 1.25 3.00
120 Richard Brodeur G 1.50 4.00
121 Evgeny Kuznetsov RC 4.00 10.00
122 Mark Visentin RC 1.50 4.00
123 Greg McKegg RC 1.25 3.00
124 Matt Lindblad RC 1.25 3.00
125 Teuvo Teravainen RC 2.50 6.00
126 Colton Sissons RC 1.50 4.00
127 Ty Rattie RC 1.50 4.00
128 Andrey Makarov RC 1.50 4.00
129 Calle Jarnkrok RC 1.50 4.00
130 Jake McCabe RC 1.50 4.00
131 Brandon Gormley RC 1.50 4.00
132 Bill Arnold RC 1.25 3.00
133 Alexander Khokhlachev RC 1.50 4.00
134 Jonathan Racine RC 1.50 4.00
135 Patrik Nemeth RC 1.50 4.00
136 Corban Knight RC 1.50 4.00
137 Laurent Brossoit RC 1.50 4.00
138 Joey Hishon RC 2.00 5.00
139 Teemu Pulkkinen RC 2.00 5.00
140 Scott Mayfield RC 1.25 3.00
141 Joni Ortio RC 2.00 5.00
142 Vladislav Namestnikov RC 2.50 6.00
143 Markus Granlund RC 2.50 6.00
144 Cedric Paquette RC 1.50 4.00
145 Oscar Klefbom RC 3.00 8.00
146 Johnny Gaudreau RC 8.00 20.00
147 Simon Moser RC 1.00 2.50
148 Ryan Sproul RC 1.50 4.00
149 Tyler Wotherspoon RC 1.50 4.00
150 Vincent Trocheck RC 3.00 8.00
151 William Karlsson RC 4.00 10.00
152 Seth Griffith RC 3.00 8.00
153 Sam Reinhart RC 10.00 25.00
154 Josh Jooris RC 4.00 10.00
155 Victor Rask RC 2.50 6.00
156 Adam Clendening RC 2.50 6.00
157 Dennis Everberg RC 4.00 10.00
158 Alexander Wennberg RC 4.00 10.00
159 Curtis McKenzie RC 2.00 5.00
160 Landon Ferraro RC 1.50 4.00
161 Leon Draisaitl RC 12.00 30.00
162 Aaron Ekblad RC 6.00 15.00
163 Andy Andreoff RC 2.50 6.00
164 Christian Folin RC 2.50 6.00
165 Jiri Sekac RC 2.00 5.00
166 Mark Van Guilder RC 2.50 6.00
167 Damon Severson RC 2.50 6.00
168 Griffin Reinhart RC 2.50 6.00
169 Anthony Duclair RC 4.00 10.00
170 Curtis Lazar RC 2.50 6.00
171 Shayne Gostisbehere RC 5.00 12.00
172 Tobias Rieder RC 2.50 6.00
173 Adam Payerl RC 2.00 5.00
174 Chris Tierney RC 2.50 6.00
175 Jori Lehtera RC 3.00 8.00
176 Jonathan Drouin RC 8.00 20.00
177 Stuart Percy RC 2.50 6.00
178 Bo Horvat RC 6.00 15.00
179 Andre Burakovsky RC 4.00 10.00
180 Adam Lowry RC 3.00 8.00
181 Darnell Nurse RC 5.00 12.00
182 Kerby Rychel RC 2.00 5.00
183 Kevin Hayes RC 8.00 20.00
184 Marko Dano RC 2.50 6.00
185 Brandon Kozun RC 4.00 10.00
186 Mirco Mueller RC 2.50 6.00
187 Phillip Danault RC 5.00 12.00
188 Joe Morrow RC 4.00 10.00
189 Seth Helgeson RC 2.00 5.00
190 Rocco Grimaldi RC 4.00 10.00
191 Justin Hodgman RC 3.00 8.00
192 Barclay Goodrow RC 2.50 6.00

2014-15 Artifacts Emerald

*1-100 VETS/99: 3X TO 8X BASIC CARDS
*101-120 G/99: 1X TO 2.5X BASIC G
*121-150 ROOKIES/99: .8X TO 2X BASIC RC

2014-15 Artifacts Ruby

*1-100 VETS/399: 2X TO 5X BASIC CARDS
*101-120 G/299: .6X TO 1.5X BASIC G
*121-150 ROOKIES/299: .6X TO 1.5X BASIC RC

2014-15 Artifacts Sapphire

*1-100 VETS/85: 3X TO 8X BASIC CARDS
*101-120 G/85: 1X TO 2.5X BASIC G
*121-150 ROOKIES/85: 1X TO 2.5X BASIC RC

2014-15 Artifacts Spectrum

*1-100 VETS/25: 6X TO 15X BASIC CARDS
*101-120 G/25: 1.5X TO 4X BASIC G
*121-150 ROOKIES/25: 1.5X TO 4X BASIC RC
125 Teuvo Teravainen 30.00 60.00

2014-15 Artifacts Autofacts

AAL Anders Lindback F 2.50 6.00
AAR Antti Raanta G 6.00 15.00
ABD Brenden Dillon G 2.50 6.00
ABH Braden Holtby D 15.00 40.00
ABO Bobby Orr B 75.00 150.00
ABR Mike Brown H 3.00 8.00
ACC Casey Cizikas H 2.50 6.00
ACF Cam Fowler F 4.00 10.00
ACG Cody Goloubef F 2.50 6.00
ACK Chris Kreider C 6.00 15.00
ADL Drew LeBlanc H 2.50 6.00
ADM Dylan McIlrath H 3.00 8.00
AFM Frazer McLaren G 2.50 6.00
AJA Jake Allen G 4.00 10.00
AJB J.T. Brown H 2.50 6.00
AJH Josh Harding E 3.00 8.00
AJJ Jaromir Jagr A 50.00 100.00
AJL Johan Larsson H 3.00 8.00
AJS Jeff Skinner D 5.00 12.00
AJT John Tavares D 15.00 40.00
ALA Luke Adam F 3.00 8.00
AMB Mike Bossy B 10.00 25.00
AMC Ryan McDonagh H 2.50 6.00
AMF Marc-Andre Fleury C 6.00 15.00
AMG Michel Goulet C 4.00 10.00
AMH Milan Hejduk C 4.00 10.00
AML Mario Lemieux A 40.00 80.00
ANF Nick Foligno F 3.00 8.00
APD Pavel Datsyuk D 10.00 25.00
APK Patrick Kane B 20.00 40.00
ARP Richard Panik G 2.50 6.00
ARS Riley Sheahan E 2.50 6.00
ASA Brandon Saad H 6.00 15.00
ASB Sergei Bobrovsky D 6.00 15.00
ASC Scotty Bowman C 8.00 20.00
ATB Tyler Bozak E 2.50 6.00
ATJ Tomas Jurco H 2.50 6.00
ATK Tim Kennedy F 2.50 6.00
ATM Tye McGinn D 2.50 6.00
ATT Tomas Tatar H 6.00 15.00
ATW Tom Wilson H 4.00 10.00
AWG Wayne Gretzky B 125.00 300.00

2014-15 Artifacts Frozen Artifacts Jerseys Blue

*EMERALD PATCH/36: .75X TO 2X BASIC JSY
FAAM Andrei Markov 2.50 6.00
FAAO Adam Oates 4.00 10.00
FABB Brian Bellows 3.00 8.00
FABH Brett Hull 5.00 12.00
FABM Brad Marchand 8.00 20.00
FABO Brooks Orpik 2.50 6.00
FABR Richard Brodeur 4.00 10.00
FABS Brandon Saad 3.00 8.00
FACO Colton Orr 2.50 6.00
FADB Dave Bolland 2.50 6.00
FADC David Clarkson 2.50 6.00
FADD David Desharnais 2.50 6.00
FADP David Perron 3.00 8.00
FADS Denis Savard 4.00 10.00
FAJL John LeClair 4.00 10.00
FAMG Michael Grabner 3.00 8.00
FAMK Marcus Kruger 2.50 6.00
FAMN Matt Niskanen 3.00 8.00
FAOK Olaf Kolzig 4.00 10.00
FAPC Paul Coffey 4.00 10.00
FAPF Peter Forsberg 8.00 20.00
FAPS P.K. Subban 5.00 12.00
FAPT Pierre Turgeon 3.00 8.00
FARB Ray Bourque 6.00 15.00
FASC Sean Couturier 3.00 8.00
FATR Tuukka Rask 5.00 12.00
FATS Tyler Seguin 5.00 12.00
FAVH Victor Hedman 5.00 12.00

2014-15 Artifacts Jerseys

*EMERALD/75: .8X TO 2X BASIC JSY/125
*EMERALD/25: 1X TO 2.5X BASIC JSY/125
*EMRLD ROOK/75: 1X TO 2.5X ROOK JSY/399
1 Ryan McDonagh 2.50 6.00
2 Brendan Gallagher 4.00 10.00
4 Kyle Turris 4.00 10.00
5 Peter Forsberg 8.00 20.00
6 Cody Hodgson 2.50 6.00
7 Larry Murphy 3.00 8.00
8 Cody Eakin 2.50 6.00
9 Henrik Zetterberg 5.00 12.00
11 Hampus Lindholm 2.50 6.00
12 Georges Laraque 3.00 8.00
13 Slava Voynov 4.00 10.00
14 Sam Gagner 2.50 6.00
15 Sean Couturier 3.00 8.00
16 Joe Thornton 6.00 15.00
17 Chris Pronger 4.00 10.00
19 Mike Green 3.00 8.00
21 Luc Robitaille 4.00 10.00
22 Max Pacioretty 4.00 10.00
23 Mats Sundin 4.00 10.00
25 Markus Naslund 4.00 10.00
26 Josh Gorges 2.50 6.00
28 Brett Hull 8.00 20.00
29 Cam Fowler 4.00 10.00
30 Eddie Shack 4.00 10.00
31 Trevor Linden 4.00 10.00
32 Rob Brown 3.00 8.00
33 Jeremy Roenick 6.00 15.00
34 Alex Chiasson 3.00 8.00
35 Nicklas Backstrom 4.00 10.00
37 Jakub Voracek 3.00 8.00
38 Rick Nash 4.00 10.00
39 Tyler Seguin 5.00 12.00
41 Wayne Gretzky 20.00 40.00
42 Wayne Simmonds 5.00 12.00
43 Olli Maatta 2.50 6.00
44 Simon Despres 4.00 10.00
45 Anze Kopitar 6.00 15.00
46 Jonathan Toews 6.00 15.00
47 Travis Zajac 2.50 6.00
49 Ron Francis 5.00 12.00
50 Eric Lindros 6.00 15.00
51 Mike Richards 3.00 8.00
52 Dustin Brown 4.00 10.00
53 Patrice Bergeron 5.00 12.00
54 Adam Oates 4.00 10.00
55 John Tavares 6.00 15.00
56 Jordan Eberle 4.00 10.00
57 Brian Bellows 3.00 8.00
58 Larry Robinson 2.50 6.00
59 Chris Kreider 5.00 12.00
60 Brent Seabrook 2.50 6.00
62 Corey Perry 6.00 15.00
63 Matt Read 2.50 6.00
64 Shea Weber 3.00 8.00
65 Alexander Ovechkin 5.00 12.00
66 John LeClair 4.00 10.00
67 Marcel Dionne 5.00 12.00
68 Milan Lucic 6.00 15.00
69 Victor Hedman 5.00 12.00
70 Vincent Damphousse 3.00 8.00
73 Rob Blake 4.00 10.00
74 Steve Yzerman 6.00 15.00
75 Ryan Nugent-Hopkins 5.00 12.00
77 Duncan Keith 3.00 8.00
78 Erik Karlsson 5.00 12.00
79 Niklas Kronwall 3.00 8.00
80 Ryan Kesler 4.00 10.00
81 Pierre Turgeon 3.00 8.00
82 Dan Boyle 2.50 6.00
83 Brad Richards 4.00 10.00
85 Alexander Edler 2.50 6.00
87 Drew Doughty 5.00 12.00
88 Michel Goulet 3.00 8.00
89 Cody Eakin 2.50 6.00
90 Sidney Crosby 15.00 40.00
91 Ryan Getzlaf 4.00 10.00
92 Logan Couture 5.00 12.00
93 Brian Gionta 2.50 6.00
94 Jeff Carter 3.00 8.00
95 Drew Stafford 2.50 6.00
97 Cam Neely 4.00 10.00
98 Bryan Bickell 2.50 6.00
99 Andrew Ladd 2.50 6.00
100 Nikolai Kulemin 2.50 6.00
101 Henrik Lundqvist 10.00 25.00
102 Marc-Andre Fleury 6.00 15.00
103 Antti Niemi 3.00 8.00
104 Dominik Hasek 6.00 15.00
105 Bill Ranford 4.00 10.00
106 Marty Turco 4.00 10.00
107 Jonathan Quick 5.00 12.00
108 Olaf Kolzig 4.00 10.00
109 Carey Price 10.00 25.00
110 Cory Schneider 4.00 10.00
111 Semyon Varlamov 4.00 10.00
112 Cam Ward 4.00 10.00
113 Ed Belfour 4.00 10.00
114 Tony Esposito 4.00 10.00
115 Pekka Rinne 4.00 10.00
116 Jonas Hiller 3.00 8.00
117 Ondrej Pavelec 4.00 10.00
118 Grant Fuhr 10.00 25.00
120 Richard Brodeur 4.00 10.00
121 Evgeny Kuznetsov 8.00 20.00
122 Mark Visentin 3.00 8.00
123 Greg McKegg 2.50 6.00
125 Teuvo Teravainen 5.00 12.00
126 Colton Sissons 3.00 8.00
127 Ty Rattie 3.00 8.00
130 Jake McCabe 3.00 8.00
131 Brandon Gormley 3.00 8.00
136 Corban Knight 4.00 10.00
138 Joey Hishon 4.00 10.00
140 Scott Mayfield 2.50 6.00
142 Vladislav Namestnikov 5.00 12.00
143 Markus Granlund 5.00 12.00
145 Oscar Klefbom 6.00 15.00
146 Johnny Gaudreau 25.00 60.00
148 Ryan Sproul 3.00 8.00
149 Tyler Wotherspoon 3.00 8.00
150 Vincent Trocheck 6.00 15.00

2014-15 Artifacts Stick to Stick Duos

SSCB Z.Chara/P.Bergeron 15.00 40.00
SSDJ D.Hasek/J.Howard 20.00 50.00
SSFC P.Coffey/G.Fuhr 20.00 50.00
SSFM G.Fuhr/A.Moog 25.00 50.00
SSGG D.Gilmour/M.Gartner 15.00 40.00
SSHH D.Hasek/D.Hasek 20.00 50.00
SSKC A.Kopitar/J.Carter 20.00 50.00
SSLC M.Lemieux/P.Coffey 50.00 125.00
SSLN R.Nash/H.Lundqvist 25.00 50.00
SSME T.Ennis/T.Myers 8.00 20.00
SSOB A.Ovechkin/N.Backstrom 40.00 100.00
SSSS H.Sedin/D.Sedin 15.00 40.00
SSYH S.Yzerman/B.Hull 30.00 80.00
SSZF J.Franzen/H.Zetterberg 20.00 50.00

2014-15 Artifacts Stick to Stick Trios

STGK Fhr/Moog/Brdr 20.00 50.00
STTC Nsh/St.Ls/Dghty 10.00 25.00
STAVS Roy/Frsbrg/Skc 20.00 50.00
STBUF Hwrchk/Hsk/Fhr 12.00 30.00
STCAN Lmx/Rbtlle/Mssr 30.00 80.00
STDET Frnzn/Zttrbrg/Hwrd 10.00 25.00
STDRW Yzrmn/Hll/Zttrbrg 20.00 50.00
STLAK Krri/Grtzky/Rbtlle 50.00 125.00
STMON Blveau/Glmr/Bllws 10.00 25.00
STMTL Bllws/Dmphse/LClr 8.00 20.00
STNET Prce/Qck/Hwrd 15.00 40.00
STPHI Lndrs/Hwrchk/LClr 12.00 30.00
STRAN Lflr/Lndrs/Mssr 15.00 40.00
STTOR Mrphy/Grtnr/Glmr 10.00 25.00
STUSA Kssl/Kne/Qck 15.00 40.00
STKING Dghty/Rchrds/Crtr 10.00 25.00
STLBBR Crbneau/Dmphse/Svrd 8.00 20.00
STKINGS Qck/Kptr/Dghty 12.00 30.00
STWINGS Rbtlle/Hll/Yzrmn 20.00 50.00
STNETUSA Qck/Mllr/Hwrd 10.00 25.00

2014-15 Artifacts Top 12 Rookie Signatures

RSCK Corban Knight 8.00 20.00
RSEK Evgeny Kuznetsov 60.00 120.00
RSGM Greg McKegg 6.00 15.00
RSTR Ty Rattie 8.00 20.00
RSTT Teuvo Teravainen 12.00 30.00
RSVN Vladislav Namestnikov 12.00 30.00

2014-15 Artifacts Treasured Swatches Jerseys Blue

*PATCH EMERALD/36: .8X TO 2X BASIC JSY
TSAK Anze Kopitar C 6.00 15.00
TSAN Antti Niemi C 3.00 8.00
TSCF Cody Franson C 2.50 6.00
TSCH Carl Hagelin B 2.50 6.00
TSCK Chris Kreider C 5.00 12.00
TSCN Cam Neely C 4.00 10.00
TSCS Cory Schneider C 4.00 10.00
TSDB Daniel Briere C 3.00 8.00
TSJH Jonas Hiller C 3.00 8.00
TSKL Kari Lehtonen C 3.00 8.00
TSMG Mike Green C 3.00 8.00
TSNB Nicklas Backstrom C 4.00 10.00
TSNL Nicklas Lidstrom B 4.00 10.00
TSPB Patrik Berglund B 2.50 6.00
TSPF Peter Forsberg C 8.00 20.00
TSRF Ron Francis C 5.00 12.00
TSRG Ryan Getzlaf C 4.00 10.00
TSRM Ryan McDonagh B 2.50 6.00
TSRN Ryan Nugent-Hopkins A 8.00 20.00
TSSG Sam Gagner B 2.50 6.00
TSSK Saku Koivu C 4.00 10.00
TSSM Steve Mason C 3.00 8.00
TSSV Slava Voynov C 4.00 10.00
TSTL Trevor Linden C 4.00 10.00
TSTP Tomas Plekanec A 4.00 10.00
TSVA Semyon Varlamov C 4.00 10.00
TSZB Zach Bogosian C 3.00 8.00

2014-15 Artifacts Tundra Sixes Jerseys Blue

T6AS All Stars A 15.00 40.00
T6TC Team Canada B 25.00 60.00
T6LAK LA Kings Stars B 12.00 30.00
T6MON Canadiens Stars B 20.00 50.00
T6LOSANA Ducks/Kings Stars B 15.00 40.00
T6NJDNYR Devils/Rangers Stars A 25.00 60.00
T6NYINJD Devils/Islanders Stars A 25.00 60.00
T6NYRNYI Rangers/Islanders Stars A 12.00 30.00
T6OTTBUF Senators/Sabres Stars B 10.00 25.00
T6STLCHI Blackhawks/Blues Stars B 12.00 30.00

2014-15 Artifacts Tundra Tandems Jerseys Blue

*EMERALD/36: .75X TO 2X BASIC INSERTS
TTAT C.Anderson/K.Turris C 3.00 8.00
TTBD D.Briere/D.Desharnais C 2.50 6.00
TTBH D.Brunner/A.Henrique C 2.50 6.00
TTBN D.Brown/J.Nolan C 3.00 8.00
TTBV Bobrovsky/Varlamov C 5.00 12.00
TTCD J.Carter/D.Doughty C 4.00 10.00
TTCE G.Cheevers/P.Esposito C 5.00 12.00
TTEC C.Eakin/A.Chiasson C 2.50 6.00
TTEH J.Eberle/RNH B 4.00 10.00
TTFB C.Fowler/N.Bonino C 3.00 8.00
TTGD J.Gorges/Desharnais C 2.00 5.00
TTGG Galchenyuk/Gallagher C 3.00 8.00
TTGR M.Greene/M.Richards C 2.50 6.00
TTGS B.Gallagher/P.Subban C 4.00 10.00
TTHG T.Hall/S.Gagner C 3.00 8.00
TTKB Kronwall/Backstrom C 3.00 8.00
TTKL Karlsson/Landeskog B 4.00 10.00
TTKN D.Keith/R.Nash C 3.00 8.00
TTKS E.Karlsson/J.Spezza C 4.00 10.00
TTLC Lehtonen/A.Chiasson C 2.50 6.00
TTLM M.Naslund/L.Murphy B 3.00 8.00
TTMH T.Myers/C.Hodgson C 2.00 5.00
TTMN M.Green/N.Backstrom B 3.00 8.00
TTOM A.Ovechkin/E.Malkin C 12.00 30.00
TTQM R.Miller/J.Quick C 4.00 10.00
TTQP J.Quick/C.Price C 6.00 15.00
TTRR Robitaille/L.Robinson A 3.00 8.00
TTSB C.Schneider/M.Brodeur C 8.00 20.00
TTSH Schneider/A.Henrique C 3.00 8.00
TTSL M.Sundin/E.Lindros C 5.00 12.00
TTSP P.Subban/M.Pacioretty C 4.00 10.00
TTSZ Stepan/Zuccarello C 3.00 8.00
TTVK J.Voracek/D.Krejci C 3.00 8.00
TTVR J.Voracek/M.Read C 2.50 6.00
TTWR S.Weber/P.Rinne C 4.00 10.00

2014-15 Artifacts Tundra Trios Patches Emerald

*BLUE TRIO: .15X TO .4X PATCH/18
T3MC Markov/Price/Subban 20.00 50.00
T3ANA Fowler/Lindholm/Perry 15.00 40.00
T3BOS Bergeron/Lucic/Rask 25.00 60.00
T3BUF Hodgson/Stafford/Myers 6.00 15.00
T3CAN Brodeur/Weber/Richards 25.00 60.00
T3CBJ Bobrvsky/Hortn/Schultz 15.00 40.00
T3CZE Voracek/Krejci/Elias 10.00 25.00
T3EDM Gagner/Eberle/Hall 10.00 25.00
T3FIN Koivu/Rask/Selanne 20.00 50.00
T3LAK Richards/Brown/Carter 12.00 30.00
T3MON Subban/Pacrty/Dshrns 12.00 30.00
T3MTL Desharn/Briere/Gionta 12.00 30.00
T3NET Quick/Niemi/Hiller 12.00 30.00
T3NYI Okposo/Bailey/Nielsen 12.00 30.00
T3NYR McDonagh/Staal/Hagelin 6.00 15.00
T3PHI Hartnell/Voracek/Read 8.00 20.00
T3RUS Markov/Voynov/Semin 25.00 50.00
T3STL Elliott/Berglund/Jackman 8.00 20.00
T3SVK Palffy/Handzus/Chara 40.00 80.00
T3USA Kesler/Stepan/McDonagh 10.00 25.00
T3VAN Kesler/Edler/Sedin 20.00 40.00
T3WAS Green/Carlson/Ovechkin 40.00 100.00
T3GOALIE Schneider/Howard/Rinne 12.00 30.00

2014-15 Artifacts Upper Deck Ice Previews

P1 Sidney Crosby 6.00 15.00
P2 Henrik Lundqvist 4.00 10.00
P3 P.K. Subban 2.00 5.00
P4 Jonathan Bernier 1.25 3.00
P5 Jonathan Toews 2.50 6.00
P6 Tuukka Rask 2.00 5.00

2014-15 Artifacts Rookie Autographs Redemptions

I Jonathon Drouin 40.00 80.00
II Aaron Ekblad 30.00 60.00
III Sam Reinhart 30.00 60.00
IV Leon Draisaitl 30.00 80.00
V Bo Horvat 25.00 50.00
VI Andre Burakovsky 15.00 40.00
VII Curtis Lazar 15.00 40.00
VIII Alexander Wennberg 15.00 40.00
IX Anthony Duclair 15.00 40.00
X Seth Griffith 12.00 30.00
XI Jiri Sekac 8.00 20.00
XII Griffin Reinhart 10.00 25.00
XIII David Pastrnak 150.00 400.00
XIV Damon Severson 10.00 25.00
XV Adam Clendening 10.00 25.00
XVI Shayne Gostisbehere 40.00 80.00
XVII Stuart Percy 10.00 25.00
XVIII Kerby Rychel 8.00 20.00

2015-16 Artifacts

1 Gabriel Landeskog .50 1.25
2 Brandon Dubinsky .25 .60
3 Marian Gaborik .40 1.00
4 Sam Gagner .25 .60
5 John Gibson .40 1.00
6 Alex Galchenyuk .25 .60
7 Jakub Voracek .30 .75
8 Cam Ward .40 1.00
9 P.K. Subban .50 1.25
10 Calle Jarnkrok .30 .75
11 Tomas Hertl .40 1.00
12 Jeff Carter .30 .75
13 Jason Pominville .25 .60
14 Ondrej Pavelec .40 1.00
15 Semyon Varlamov .40 1.00
16 Mike Smith .40 1.00
17 Kari Lehtonen .30 .75
18 Morgan Rielly .40 1.00
19 Tanner Pearson .25 .60
20 Alexandre Burrows .25 .60
21 Ondrej Palat .30 .75
22 Wayne Simmonds .50 1.25
23 Chris Kunitz .40 1.00
24 Scott Hartnell .25 .60
25 Corey Perry .60 1.50
26 Craig Anderson .40 1.00
27 David Backes .25 .60
28 Nick Bjugstad .25 .60
29 Bobby Ryan .30 .75
30 Frederik Andersen .50 1.25
31 Charlie Coyle .40 1.00
32 Elias Lindholm .40 1.00
33 Gustav Nyquist .25 .60
34 Paul Stastny .30 .75
35 Jori Lehtera .25 .60
36 Jonathan Drouin .30 .75
37 Sam Reinhart .75 2.00
38 Daniel Sedin .50 1.25
39 Tomas Jurco .25 .60
40 John Carlson .40 1.00
41 James Neal .25 .60
42 Roberto Luongo .60 1.50
43 Sean Monahan .25 .60
44 Duncan Keith .30 .75
45 Victor Hedman .50 1.25
46 Nicklas Backstrom .40 1.00
47 Corey Crawford .50 1.25
48 Henrik Lundqvist 1.00 2.50
49 Olli Maatta .25 .60
50 Erik Karlsson .50 1.25
51 Henrik Zetterberg .50 1.25

52 Thomas Vanek .30 .75
53 Marian Hossa .40 1.00
54 Darcy Kuemper .40 1.00
55 Patrick Kane .75 2.00
56 Mats Zuccarello .40 1.00
57 Ryan Kesler .40 1.00
58 Patrik Elias .40 1.00
59 Jamie Benn .40 1.00
60 Brayden Schenn .40 1.00
61 Ryan Strome .40 1.00
62 Nazem Kadri .50 1.25
63 Leon Draisaitl 1.25 3.00
64 Johan Franzen .30 .75
65 Brendan Gallagher .40 1.00
66 Dustin Brown .40 1.00
67 Griffin Reinhart .25 .60
68 Adam Henrique .30 .75
69 Michael Cammalleri .30 .75
70 Patrick Marleau .40 1.00
71 Tyler Johnson .25 .60
72 Brian Elliott .30 .75
73 Pekka Rinne .40 1.00
74 Kyle Okposo .25 .60
75 Ryan McDonagh .25 .60
76 Zdeno Chara .40 1.00
77 Jeff Skinner .50 1.25
78 David Krejci .40 1.00
79 Nail Yakupov .25 .60
80 Cody Hodgson .25 .60
81 Ryan Murray .25 .60
82 Henrik Sedin .50 1.25
83 Sean Couturier .30 .75
84 Jacob Trouba .30 .75
85 Phil Kessel .40 1.00
86 Chris Kreider .50 1.25
87 Matt Moulson .25 .60
88 Evgeni Malkin .75 2.00
89 Joe Pavelski .50 1.25
90 Jason Spezza .40 1.00
91 Jonathan Huberdeau .50 1.25
92 Oliver Ekman-Larsson .40 1.00
93 Evgeny Kuznetsov .50 1.25
94 Jarome Iginla .50 1.25
95 Ryan Johansen .30 .75
96 Mark Scheifele .60 1.50
97 Ryan Nugent-Hopkins .50 1.25
98 Jiri Hudler .30 .75
99 Milan Lucic .30 .75
100 Jonas Hiller .30 .75
101 Pavel Datsyuk S 2.50 6.00
102 Logan Couture S 2.00 5.00
103 Anze Kopitar S 2.50 6.00
104 Jonathan Bernier S 1.25 3.00
105 Johnny Gaudreau S 2.50 6.00
106 Ryan Miller S 1.50 4.00
107 Tyler Seguin S 2.00 5.00
108 Ryan Getzlaf S 1.50 4.00
109 Zemgus Girgensons S 1.25 3.00
110 Blake Wheeler S 1.50 4.00
111 Sergei Bobrovsky S 2.50 6.00
112 Eric Staal S 2.00 5.00
113 John Tavares S 2.50 6.00
114 Alexander Ovechkin S 6.00 15.00
115 Jonathan Toews S 2.50 6.00
116 Zach Parise S 1.50 4.00
117 Shane Doan S 1.25 3.00
118 Sidney Crosby S 6.00 15.00
119 Nathan MacKinnon S 6.00 15.00
120 Shea Weber S 1.25 3.00
121 Tuukka Rask S 2.00 5.00
122 Cory Schneider S 1.50 4.00
123 Carey Price S 3.00 8.00
124 Aaron Ekblad S 2.00 5.00
125 Taylor Hall S 1.50 4.00
126 Vladimir Tarasenko S 2.00 5.00
127 Kyle Turris S 1.25 3.00
128 Steven Stamkos S 3.00 8.00
129 Claude Giroux S 1.50 4.00
130 Rick Nash S 1.50 4.00
131 Mats Sundin LEG 2.00 5.00
132 Mike Gartner LEG 2.50 6.00
133 Pierre Turgeon LEG 1.50 4.00
134 Marty Turco LEG 2.00 5.00
135 Wendel Clark LEG 3.00 8.00
136 Rod Brind'Amour LEG 1.50 4.00
137 Mario Lemieux LEG 8.00 20.00
138 Dale Hawerchuk LEG 2.50 6.00
139 Tony Esposito LEG 2.00 5.00
140 Jari Kurri LEG 2.00 5.00
141 Lanny McDonald LEG 2.00 5.00
142 Martin Brodeur LEG 5.00 12.00
143 Mike Keane LEG 1.50 4.00
144 Tom Barrasso LEG 2.00 5.00
145 John Vanbiesbrouck LEG 2.00 5.00
146 Patrick Roy LEG 5.00 12.00
147 Joe Sakic LEG 4.00 10.00
148 Owen Nolan LEG 2.00 5.00
149 Glen Murray LEG 1.50 4.00
150 Theoren Fleury LEG 2.50 6.00
151 Glenn Hall LEG 2.00 5.00
152 Pelle Lindbergh LEG 1.50 4.00
153 Marcel Dionne LEG 2.50 6.00
154 Wayne Gretzky LEG 12.00 30.00
155 Doug Weight LEG 2.00 5.00
156 Ron Francis LEG 2.50 6.00
157 Steve Larmer LEG 1.50 4.00
158 Steve Yzerman LEG 5.00 12.00
159 Gerry Cheevers LEG 2.00 5.00
160 Rob Blake LEG 2.00 5.00
161 Henrik Samuelsson RC 1.00 2.50
162 Antoine Bibeau RC 1.50 4.00
163 Slater Koekkoek RC 1.00 2.50
164 Ryan Hartman RC 2.00 5.00
165 Shane Prince RC 1.00 2.50
166 Nick Shore RC 1.00 2.50
167 Stefan Noesen RC 1.00 2.50
168 Emile Poirier RC 1.25 3.00
169 Anthony Stolarz RC 4.00 10.00
170 Josh Anderson RC 3.00 8.00
171 Nick Cousins RC 1.50 4.00
172 Matt Puempel RC 1.25 3.00
173 Kevin Fiala RC 2.00 5.00
174 Brendan Ranford RC 1.25 3.00
175 Kyle Baun RC 1.50 4.00
176 Jacob de la Rose RC 1.50 4.00
177 Connor Hellebuyck RC 6.00 15.00
178 Ronalds Kenins RC 1.00 2.50
179 Sam Bennett RC 5.00 12.00
180 Malcolm Subban RC 2.50 6.00
181 Canadiens/Fucale EXCH 1.25 3.00
182 Blues/Fabbri EXCH 2.00 5.00
183 Rangers/Lindberg EXCH 1.50 4.00
184 Ducks/Ritchie EXCH 1.50 4.00
185 Lightning/Vermin EXCH 1.25 3.00
186 Predators/Saros EXCH 4.00 10.00
187 Capitals/Stephenson EXCH 2.00 5.00
188 Canucks/Virtanen EXCH 2.00 5.00
189 Red Wings/Larkin EXCH 5.00 12.00
190 Blackhawks/Panarin EXCH 6.00 15.00
191 Islanders/Pelech EXCH 1.25 3.00
192 Flames/Kulak EXCH 1.25 3.00
193 Senators/Wideman EXCH 1.50 4.00
194 Wild/Olofsson EXCH 1.50 4.00
195 Penguins/Sprong EXCH 2.00 5.00
196 Kings/Mersch EXCH 1.50 4.00
197 Bruins/Miller EXCH 1.25 3.00
198 Jets/Ehlers EXCH 3.00 8.00
199 Blue Jackets EXCH 8.00 20.00
200 Sharks/Goldobin EXCH 1.50 4.00
201 Stars/Janmark EXCH 1.50 4.00
202 Maple Leafs/Sparks EXCH 1.50 4.00
203 Avalanche/Rantanen EXCH 8.00 20.00
204 Flyers/Leier EXCH 1.50 4.00
205 Connor McDavid RC 150.00 400.00
206 Sabres/Eichel EXCH 6.00 15.00
207 Coyotes/Domi EXCH 3.00 8.00
208 Devils/Kalinin EXCH 1.00 2.50
209 Panthers/Brickley EXCH 1.25 3.00
210 Hurricanes/Hanifin EXCH 2.50 6.00
211 Wild Card/McCann EXCH 2.00 5.00
212 Wild Card/Ullmark EXCH 3.00 8.00
213 Wild Card/Shinkaruk EXCH 1.50 4.00
214 Wild Card/Parayko EXCH 2.50 6.00
215 Wild Card/Petan EXCH 1.50 4.00
216 Wild Card/Condon EXCH 1.50 4.00
217 Wild Card/Hudon EXCH 1.50 4.00
218 Wild Card/McCarron EXCH 2.00 5.00
219 Wild Card/Murray EXCH 6.00 15.00
220 Wild Card/Hutton EXCH 1.50 4.00

2015-16 Artifacts Emerald

*1-100 VETS/99: 2.5X TO 6X BASIC CARDS
*101-130 S/99: .6X TO 1.5X BASIC S/999
*131-160 LEG/99: .6X TO 1.5X BASIC LEG/499
*161-180 ROOKIES/99: .6X TO 1.5X BASIC RC/999
205 Connor McDavid 500.00 1200.00

2015-16 Artifacts Ruby

*1-100 VETS/399: 2X TO 5X BASIC
*101-130 S/399: .5X TO 1.2X BASIC S/999
*131-160 LEG/399: .4X TO 1X BASIC LEG/499
*161-180 ROOKIES/399: .5X TO 1.2X BASIC RC/999
205 Connor McDavid 300.00 800.00

2015-16 Artifacts Sapphire

*1-100 VETS/85: 2.5X TO 6X BASIC CARDS
*101-130 S/85: .6X TO 1.5X BASIC S/999
*131-160 LEG/85: .6X TO 1.5X BASIC LEG/499
*161-180 ROOKIES/85: .6X TO 1.5X BASIC RC/999
205 Connor McDavid 500.00 1200.00
206 Jack Eichel
Issued in SPx 20.00 50.00

2015-16 Artifacts Spectrum

*1-100 VETS/25: 5X TO 12X BASIC CARDS
*101-130 S/25: 1.2X TO 3X BASIC S/999
*131-160 LEG/25: 1.2X TO 3X BASIC LEG/499
*161-180 ROOKIES/25: 1.2X TO 3X BASIC RC/999
205 Connor McDavid 600.00 1500.00

2015-16 Artifacts Autofacts

AAG Alex Goligoski E 4.00 10.00
AAN Andrej Nestrasil E 4.00 10.00
AAP Alex Pietrangelo B 5.00 12.00
ABR Brett Ritchie D 4.00 10.00
ABS Brendan Smith E 4.00 10.00
ACJ Calle Jarnkrok E 5.00 12.00
ACN Cam Neely A 6.00 15.00
ADH Dougie Hamilton C 5.00 12.00
AEL Elias Lindholm C 6.00 15.00
AJB Jonathan Bernier B 5.00 12.00
AJM Jon Merrill E 4.00 10.00
AJO Joni Ortio E 6.00 15.00
AML Michael Latta E 4.00 10.00
AMM Mirco Mueller D 4.00 10.00
AMP Mark Pysyk E 4.00 10.00
ANY Nail Yakupov B 4.00 10.00
APB Pierre-Edouard Bellemare E 4.00 10.00
APN Patrik Nemeth E 4.00 10.00
ARJ Ryan Johansen B 5.00 12.00
ARN Ryan Nugent-Hopkins B 8.00 20.00
ARS Reilly Smith D 6.00 15.00
ASB Sven Baertschi D 4.00 10.00
ASC Brayden Schenn C 6.00 15.00
ASG Shayne Gostisbehere E 6.00 15.00
AST Ryan Strome C 6.00 15.00
ATB Tyson Barrie E 4.00 10.00
ATT Tomas Tatar C 4.00 10.00
AVR Victor Rask E 4.00 10.00
AWC Wendel Clark A 10.00 25.00
AWG Wayne Gretzky A 200.00 500.00
AWK William Karlsson E 8.00 20.00
AZG Zemgus Girgensons D 5.00 12.00

2015-16 Artifacts Frozen Artifacts Jerseys Blue

FAAB Aleksander Barkov B 5.00 12.00
FAAG Alex Galchenyuk C 2.00 5.00
FABD Brandon Dubinsky B 2.00 5.00
FABE Brian Elliott B 2.50 6.00
FABR Bobby Ryan C 2.50 6.00
FABS Brandon Saad C 2.50 6.00
FABU Alexandre Burrows B 2.00 5.00
FACC Charlie Coyle B 3.00 8.00
FACK Chris Kunitz C 3.00 8.00
FAEK Evgeny Kuznetsov C 4.00 10.00
FAGI John Gibson B 3.00 8.00
FAJC Jeff Carter B 2.50 6.00
FAJD Jonathan Drouin A 3.00 8.00
FAJG Johnny Gaudreau A 6.00 15.00
FAJI Jarome Iginla C 4.00 10.00
FAJN James Neal B 2.00 5.00
FAKL Kari Lehtonen C 2.50 6.00
FAML Milan Lucic C 2.50 6.00
FAMS Martin St. Louis A 4.00 10.00
FANY Nail Yakupov B 2.00 5.00
FAPK Phil Kessel C 3.00 8.00
FAPM Patrick Marleau C 3.00 8.00
FARS Ryan Strome C 3.00 8.00
FASC Sean Couturier B 2.50 6.00
FASM Mike Smith A 4.00 10.00
FASR Sam Reinhart A 8.00 20.00
FATJ Tomas Jurco A 2.50 6.00

2015-16 Artifacts Honoured Members Relics

HMRAO Adam Oates Stick 20.00 50.00
HMRBC Bobby Clarke Stick 30.00 80.00
HMRBH Brett Hull Patch 40.00 100.00
HMRBL Brian Leetch Stick 15.00 40.00
HMRBO Ray Bourque GLV-STK 30.00 80.00
HMRBP Brad Park PTCH-STK 15.00 40.00
HMRCC Chris Chelios Patch 20.00 50.00
HMRCN Cam Neely Stick 20.00 50.00
HMRDG Doug Gilmour Stick 25.00 60.00
HMRDP Denis Potvin Stick 20.00 50.00
HMREB Ed Belfour Patch 20.00 50.00
HMRGA Glenn Anderson Stick 15.00 40.00
HMRGF Grant Fuhr PTCH-STK 30.00 80.00
HMRHU Bobby Hull Stick 40.00 100.00
HMRJB Jean Beliveau GLV-STK 20.00 50.00
HMRJS Joe Sakic Patch 40.00 100.00
HMRMD Marcel Dionne Stick 25.00 60.00
HMRME Mark Messier PTCH-STK 40.00 100.00
HMRML Mario Lemieux PTCH-GLV 80.00 200.00
HMRMM Mike Modano Patch 30.00 80.00
HMRMS Mats Sundin PTCH-STK 20.00 50.00
HMRPC Paul Coffey Stick 20.00 50.00
HMRPE Phil Esposito Stick 30.00 80.00
HMRRB Rob Blake Pants-STK 20.00 50.00
HMRSI Darryl Sittler Stick 25.00 60.00
HMRSY Steve Yzerman PTCH-STK 50.00 125.00
HMRTS Terry Sawchuk Stick 20.00 50.00

2015-16 Artifacts Honoured Members Signatures

HMSBH Brett Hull 40.00 100.00
HMSBO Bobby Orr 80.00 200.00
HMSGF Grant Fuhr 30.00 80.00
HMSMB Mike Bossy 20.00 50.00
HMSPR Patrick Roy 50.00 125.00

2015-16 Artifacts Jerseys

*1-100 EMERALD/75: .6X TO 1.5X JSY/125
*101-130 EMERALD/49: .5X TO 1.2X JSY/125
*131-160 EMERALD/25: .6X TO 1.5X JSY/99
*161-179 EMERALD/199: .6X TO 1.5X JSY/399
1 Gabriel Landeskog 4.00 10.00
2 Brandon Dubinsky 2.00 5.00
3 Marian Gaborik 3.00 8.00
4 Sam Gagner 2.00 5.00
5 John Gibson 3.00 8.00
6 Alex Galchenyuk 2.00 5.00
7 Jakub Voracek 2.50 6.00
8 Cam Ward 3.00 8.00
9 P.K. Subban 4.00 10.00
10 Calle Jarnkrok 2.50 6.00
11 Tomas Hertl 3.00 8.00
12 Jeff Carter 2.50 6.00
13 Jason Pominville 2.00 5.00
14 Ondrej Pavelec 3.00 8.00
15 Semyon Varlamov 3.00 8.00
16 Mike Smith 3.00 8.00
17 Kari Lehtonen 2.50 6.00
18 Morgan Rielly 3.00 8.00
19 Tanner Pearson 2.00 5.00
20 Alexandre Burrows 2.00 5.00
21 Ondrej Palat 2.50 6.00
23 Chris Kunitz 3.00 8.00
24 Scott Hartnell 2.00 5.00
25 Corey Perry 5.00 12.00
26 Craig Anderson 3.00 8.00
27 David Backes 2.00 5.00
28 Nick Bjugstad 2.00 5.00
29 Bobby Ryan 2.50 6.00
30 Frederik Andersen 4.00 10.00
31 Charlie Coyle 3.00 8.00
32 Elias Lindholm 3.00 8.00
33 Gustav Nyquist 2.00 5.00
34 Paul Stastny 2.50 6.00
36 Jonathan Drouin 2.50 6.00
37 Sam Reinhart 6.00 15.00
38 Daniel Sedin 4.00 10.00
39 Tomas Jurco 2.00 5.00
40 John Carlson 3.00 8.00
41 James Neal 2.00 5.00
42 Roberto Luongo 5.00 12.00
43 Sean Monahan 2.00 5.00
44 Duncan Keith 2.50 6.00
45 Victor Hedman 4.00 10.00
46 Nicklas Backstrom 3.00 8.00
47 Corey Crawford 4.00 10.00
48 Henrik Lundqvist 8.00 20.00
49 Olli Maatta 2.00 5.00
50 Erik Karlsson 4.00 10.00
51 Henrik Zetterberg 4.00 10.00
52 Thomas Vanek 2.50 6.00
53 Marian Hossa 3.00 8.00
54 Darcy Kuemper 3.00 8.00
55 Patrick Kane 6.00 15.00
56 Mats Zuccarello 3.00 8.00
57 Ryan Kesler 3.00 8.00
58 Patrik Elias 3.00 8.00
59 Jamie Benn 3.00 8.00
60 Brayden Schenn 3.00 8.00
61 Ryan Strome 3.00 8.00
62 Nazem Kadri 4.00 10.00
63 Leon Draisaitl 10.00 25.00
64 Johan Franzen 2.50 6.00
65 Brendan Gallagher 3.00 8.00
66 Dustin Brown 3.00 8.00
70 Patrick Marleau 3.00 8.00
72 Brian Elliott 2.50 6.00
73 Pekka Rinne 3.00 8.00
74 Kyle Okposo 2.00 5.00
75 Ryan McDonagh 2.00 5.00
76 Zdeno Chara 3.00 8.00
77 Jeff Skinner 4.00 10.00
78 David Krejci 3.00 8.00
79 Nail Yakupov 2.00 5.00
80 Cody Hodgson 2.00 5.00
82 Henrik Sedin 4.00 10.00
83 Sean Couturier 2.50 6.00
84 Jacob Trouba 2.50 6.00
85 Phil Kessel 3.00 8.00
86 Chris Kreider 4.00 10.00
87 Matt Moulson 2.00 5.00
88 Evgeni Malkin 6.00 15.00
89 Joe Pavelski 4.00 10.00
90 Jason Spezza 3.00 8.00
91 Jonathan Huberdeau 4.00 10.00
92 Oliver Ekman-Larsson 3.00 8.00
93 Evgeny Kuznetsov 4.00 10.00
94 Jarome Iginla 4.00 10.00
95 Ryan Johansen 2.50 6.00
96 Mark Scheifele 5.00 12.00
97 Ryan Nugent-Hopkins 4.00 10.00
98 Jiri Hudler 2.50 6.00
99 Milan Lucic 2.50 6.00
100 Jonas Hiller 2.50 6.00
101 Pavel Datsyuk S 5.00 12.00
102 Logan Couture S 4.00 10.00
103 Anze Kopitar S 5.00 12.00
104 Jonathan Bernier S 2.50 6.00
105 Johnny Gaudreau S 5.00 12.00
106 Ryan Miller S 3.00 8.00
107 Tyler Seguin S 4.00 10.00
108 Ryan Getzlaf S 3.00 8.00
109 Zemgus Girgensons S 2.50 6.00
110 Blake Wheeler S 3.00 8.00
111 Sergei Bobrovsky S 5.00 12.00
112 Eric Staal S 4.00 10.00
113 John Tavares S 5.00 12.00
114 Alexander Ovechkin S 12.00 30.00
115 Jonathan Toews S 5.00 12.00
116 Zach Parise S 3.00 8.00
117 Shane Doan S 2.50 6.00
118 Sidney Crosby S 12.00 30.00
119 Nathan MacKinnon S 12.00 30.00
120 Shea Weber S 2.50 6.00
121 Tuukka Rask S 4.00 10.00
123 Carey Price S 6.00 15.00
124 Aaron Ekblad S 4.00 10.00
125 Taylor Hall S 3.00 8.00
126 Vladimir Tarasenko S 4.00 10.00
127 Kyle Turris S 2.50 6.00
128 Steven Stamkos S 6.00 15.00
129 Claude Giroux S 3.00 8.00
130 Rick Nash S 3.00 8.00
131 Mats Sundin LEG 3.00 8.00
132 Mike Gartner LEG 4.00 10.00
134 Marty Turco LEG 3.00 8.00
135 Wendel Clark LEG 5.00 12.00
136 Rod Brind'Amour LEG 2.50 6.00
137 Mario Lemieux LEG 12.00 30.00
138 Dale Hawerchuk LEG 4.00 10.00
139 Tony Esposito LEG 3.00 8.00
140 Jari Kurri LEG 3.00 8.00
141 Lanny McDonald LEG 3.00 8.00
142 Martin Brodeur LEG 8.00 20.00
143 Mike Keane LEG 2.50 6.00
146 Patrick Roy LEG 8.00 20.00
148 Owen Nolan LEG 3.00 8.00
149 Glen Murray LEG 2.50 6.00
150 Theoren Fleury LEG 4.00 10.00
151 Glenn Hall LEG 3.00 8.00
152 Pelle Lindbergh LEG 2.50 6.00
153 Marcel Dionne LEG 4.00 10.00
154 Wayne Gretzky LEG 20.00 50.00
156 Ron Francis LEG 4.00 10.00
158 Steve Yzerman LEG 8.00 20.00
159 Gerry Cheevers LEG 3.00 8.00
160 Rob Blake LEG 3.00 8.00
161 Henrik Samuelsson 2.00 5.00
162 Antoine Bibeau 3.00 8.00
163 Slater Koekkoek 2.00 5.00
165 Shane Prince 2.00 5.00
168 Emile Poirier 2.50 6.00
170 Josh Anderson 6.00 15.00
171 Nick Cousins 3.00 8.00
172 Matt Puempel 2.50 6.00
173 Kevin Fiala 4.00 10.00
176 Jacob de la Rose 3.00 8.00
177 Connor Hellebuyck 12.00 30.00
178 Ronalds Kenins 2.00 5.00
179 Sam Bennett 10.00 25.00
180 Malcolm Subban 5.00 12.00
182 Robby Fabbri
Issued in SPx 4.00 10.00
188 Jake Virtanen
Issued in SPx 4.00 10.00
189 Dylan Larkin 10.00 25.00
190 Artemi Panarin 12.00 30.00
205 Connor McDavid 200.00 500.00
206 Jack Eichel
Issued in SPx 12.00 30.00
210 Noah Hanifin
Issued in SPx 5.00 12.00

2015-16 Artifacts Jerseys Patch Spectrum

*161-179 SPECT/99: .8X TO 2X BASIC JSY/399
205 Connor McDavid 300.00 800.00

2015-16 Artifacts Jerseys Autographs

*161-179 EMER/49: .6X TO 1.5X AU/125
1 Gabriel Landeskog/49 10.00 25.00
2 Brandon Dubinsky/49 5.00 12.00
3 Marian Gaborik/49 8.00 20.00
4 Sam Gagner/49 5.00 12.00
5 John Gibson/49 8.00 20.00
6 Alex Galchenyuk/49 5.00 12.00
8 Cam Ward/49 8.00 20.00
9 P.K. Subban/49 10.00 25.00
10 Calle Jarnkrok/49 6.00 15.00
11 Tomas Hertl/49 8.00 20.00
13 Jason Pominville/49 5.00 12.00
15 Semyon Varlamov/49 8.00 20.00
17 Kari Lehtonen/49 6.00 15.00
18 Morgan Rielly/49 8.00 20.00
19 Tanner Pearson/49 5.00 12.00
20 Alexandre Burrows/49 5.00 12.00
23 Chris Kunitz/49 8.00 20.00
24 Scott Hartnell/49 5.00 12.00
25 Corey Perry/49 12.00 30.00
27 David Backes/49 5.00 12.00
29 Bobby Ryan/49 6.00 15.00
30 Frederik Andersen/49 10.00 25.00
31 Charlie Coyle/49 8.00 20.00
32 Elias Lindholm/49 8.00 20.00
33 Gustav Nyquist/49 5.00 12.00
34 Paul Stastny/49 6.00 15.00
37 Sam Reinhart/49 15.00 40.00
39 Tomas Jurco/49 5.00 12.00
43 Sean Monahan/49 5.00 12.00
49 Olli Maatta/49 5.00 12.00
56 Mats Zuccarello/49 8.00 20.00
57 Ryan Kesler/49 8.00 20.00
58 Patrik Elias/49 8.00 20.00
59 Jamie Benn/49 8.00 20.00
60 Brayden Schenn/49 8.00 20.00
61 Ryan Strome/49 8.00 20.00
63 Leon Draisaitl/49 25.00 60.00
64 Johan Franzen/49 6.00 15.00
65 Brendan Gallagher/49 8.00 20.00
70 Patrick Marleau/49 8.00 20.00
73 Pekka Rinne/49 8.00 20.00
74 Kyle Okposo/49 5.00 12.00
75 Ryan McDonagh/49 5.00 12.00
77 Jeff Skinner/49 10.00 25.00
78 David Krejci/49 8.00 20.00
79 Nail Yakupov/49 5.00 12.00
80 Cody Hodgson/49 5.00 12.00
83 Sean Couturier/49 6.00 15.00
84 Jacob Trouba/49 6.00 15.00
86 Chris Kreider/49 10.00 25.00
87 Matt Moulson/49 5.00 12.00
88 Evgeni Malkin/49 15.00 40.00
89 Joe Pavelski/49 10.00 25.00
90 Jason Spezza/49 8.00 20.00
91 Jonathan Huberdeau/49 10.00 25.00
93 Evgeny Kuznetsov/49 10.00 25.00
94 Jarome Iginla/49 10.00 25.00
95 Ryan Johansen/49 6.00 15.00
96 Mark Scheifele/49 12.00 30.00
97 Ryan Nugent-Hopkins/49 10.00 25.00
100 Jonas Hiller/49 6.00 15.00
102 Logan Couture/25 15.00 40.00
103 Anze Kopitar/25 20.00 50.00
104 Jonathan Bernier/25 10.00 25.00
105 Johnny Gaudreau/25 20.00 50.00
106 Ryan Miller/25 12.00 30.00
109 Zemgus Girgensons/25 10.00 25.00
111 Sergei Bobrovsky/25 20.00 50.00
112 Eric Staal/25 15.00 40.00
113 John Tavares/25 20.00 50.00
114 Alexander Ovechkin/25 50.00 120.00
115 Jonathan Toews/25 20.00 50.00
116 Zach Parise/25 12.00 30.00
120 Shea Weber/25 10.00 25.00
121 Tuukka Rask/25 15.00 40.00
123 Carey Price/25 25.00 60.00
124 Aaron Ekblad/25 15.00 40.00
127 Kyle Turris/25 10.00 25.00
129 Claude Giroux/25 12.00 30.00
130 Rick Nash/25 12.00 30.00
132 Mike Gartner/25 20.00 50.00
133 Pierre Turgeon/25 12.00 30.00
134 Marty Turco/25 15.00 40.00
135 Wendel Clark/25 25.00 60.00
136 Rod Brind'Amour/25 12.00 30.00
137 Mario Lemieux/25 60.00 150.00
138 Dale Hawerchuk/25 20.00 50.00
139 Tony Esposito/25 15.00 40.00
140 Jari Kurri/25 15.00 40.00
141 Lanny McDonald/25 15.00 40.00
142 Martin Brodeur/25 40.00 100.00
143 Mike Keane/25 12.00 30.00
146 Patrick Roy/25 40.00 100.00
148 Owen Nolan/25 15.00 40.00
149 Glen Murray/25 12.00 30.00
150 Theoren Fleury/25 20.00 50.00
153 Marcel Dionne/25 20.00 50.00
154 Wayne Gretzky/25 200.00 500.00
158 Steve Yzerman/25 40.00 100.00
160 Rob Blake/25 15.00 40.00
161 Henrik Samuelsson/125 4.00 10.00
162 Antoine Bibeau/125 6.00 15.00
163 Slater Koekkoek/125 4.00 10.00
165 Shane Prince/125 4.00 10.00
168 Emile Poirier/125 5.00 12.00
170 Josh Anderson/125 12.00 30.00
171 Nick Cousins/125 6.00 15.00
172 Matt Puempel/125 5.00 12.00
176 Jacob de la Rose/125 6.00 15.00
177 Connor Hellebuyck/125 25.00 60.00
179 Sam Bennett/125 20.00 50.00
180 Malcolm Subban/125 10.00 25.00
182 Robby Fabbri/125
Issued in SPx 8.00 20.00
188 Jake Virtanen/125
Issued in SPx 8.00 20.00
205 Connor McDavid/125 800.00 2000.00
210 Noah Hanifin/125
Issued in SPx 10.00 25.00
211 Jared McCann/125
Issued in SPx 8.00 20.00

2015-16 Artifacts Lord Stanley's Legacy Relics

LSLRAK Anze Kopitar D 6.00 15.00
LSLRBH Brett Hull A 8.00 20.00
LSLRCC Corey Crawford D 5.00 12.00
LSLRCH Chris Chelios D 4.00 10.00
LSLRCP Corey Perry C 6.00 15.00
LSLRDD Drew Doughty D 5.00 12.00
LSLREM Evgeni Malkin C 8.00 20.00
LSLREP Patrik Elias D 4.00 10.00
LSLRES Eric Staal D 5.00 12.00
LSLRGC Gerry Cheevers A 4.00 10.00
LSLRGF Grant Fuhr B 6.00 15.00
LSLRJQ Jonathan Quick C 5.00 12.00
LSLRJT Jonathan Toews B 6.00 15.00
LSLRLM Lanny McDonald B 4.00 10.00
LSLRMH Marian Hossa D 4.00 10.00
LSLRML Mario Lemieux A 15.00 40.00
LSLRMM Mark Messier A 8.00 20.00
LSLRPB Patrice Bergeron D 5.00 12.00
LSLRPC Paul Coffey C 4.00 10.00
LSLRPD Pavel Datsyuk C 6.00 15.00
LSLRPF Peter Forsberg B 8.00 20.00
LSLRPK Patrick Kane D 8.00 20.00
LSLRPR Patrick Roy B 10.00 25.00
LSLRRF Ron Francis C 5.00 12.00
LSLRRG Ryan Getzlaf D 4.00 10.00
LSLRSC Sidney Crosby B 15.00 40.00
LSLRSY Steve Yzerman B 10.00 25.00
LSLRZC Zdeno Chara D 4.00 10.00

2015-16 Artifacts Lord Stanley's Legacy Signatures

LSAK Anze Kopitar C 15.00 40.00
LSBO Bobby Orr B 40.00 100.00
LSBS Brandon Saad D 8.00 20.00
LSCC Chris Chelios C 10.00 25.00
LSDS Dave Schultz D 10.00 25.00
LSJS Joe Sakic B 20.00 50.00
LSMB Mike Bossy B 10.00 25.00
LSMM Mark Messier A 20.00 50.00
LSMS Martin St. Louis C 10.00 25.00
LSNL Nicklas Lidstrom B 10.00 25.00
LSTS Teemu Selanne B 20.00 50.00
LSTT Tyler Toffoli C 10.00 25.00
LSWG Wayne Gretzky C 250.00 600.00

2015-16 Artifacts Rookie Autographs Redemptions

I Auto EXCH I/McDavid 400.00 1000.00
II Auto EXCH II/Larkin 90.00 150.00
III Auto EXCH III/Domi 60.00 100.00
IV Auto EXCH IV/Ehlers 25.00 50.00
V Auto EXCH V/Panarin 75.00 125.00
VI Auto EXCH VI/Virtanen 12.00 30.00
VII Auto EXCH VII/Fabbri 12.00 30.00
VIII Auto EXCH VIII/Hanifin 15.00 40.00
IX Auto EXCH IX/McCann 12.00 30.00
X Auto EXCH X/Lindberg 10.00 25.00
XI Auto EXCH XI/Fucale 25.00 50.00
XII Auto EXCH XII/Rantanen 80.00 200.00
XIII Auto EXCH XIII/Ritchie 12.00 30.00
XIV Auto EXCH XIV/Condon 25.00 50.00
XV Auto EXCH XV/Miller 12.00 30.00
XVI Auto EXCH XVI/Sparks 10.00 25.00
XVII Auto EXCH XVII/Parayko 15.00 40.00
XVIII Auto EXCH XVIII/Hutton 20.00 40.00
XIX Auto EXCH XIX/Ullmark 20.00 50.00
XX Auto EXCH XX/Petan 12.00 30.00

2015-16 Artifacts Rookie Jersey Autographs Redemptions

*EMERALD: .6X TO 1.5X BASIC JSY AU EXCH
I Rdmpt I/McDavid EXCH 800.00 2000.00
II Rdmpt II/Larkin EXCH 50.00 125.00
III Rdmpt III/Domi EXCH 30.00 80.00
IV Rdmpt IV/Ehlers EXCH 30.00 80.00
V Rdmpt V/Panarin EXCH 60.00 150.00

2015-16 Artifacts Rookie Jersey Redemptions

*EMERALD: .5X TO 1.2X BASIC JSY EXCH
*SPECTRUM: .6X TO 1.5X BASIC JSY EXCH
I Rdmpt I/McDavid EXCH 60.00 150.00
II Rdmpt II/Larkin EXCH 40.00 80.00
III Rdmpt III/Domi EXCH 20.00 50.00
IV Rdmpt IV/Ehlers EXCH 10.00 25.00
V Rdmpt V/Panarin EXCH 15.00 40.00

2015-16 Artifacts Rookie Redemption Ruby

*EMERALD: .5X TO 1.2X BASIC JSY EXCH
*SAPPHIRE: .6X TO 1.5X RUBY
*SPECTRUM: .8X TO 2X BASIC JSY EXCH
I Rdmpt I/McDavid EXCH 200.00 500.00
II Rdmpt II/Larkin EXCH 30.00 60.00
III Rdmpt III/Domi EXCH 20.00 50.00
IV Rdmpt IV/Ehlers EXCH 10.00 25.00
V Rdmpt V/Panarin EXCH 15.00 40.00

2015-16 Artifacts Stick to Stick Green

STSBC Bobby Clarke 10.00 25.00
STSCP Carey Price 12.00 30.00
STSDD Drew Doughty 8.00 20.00
STSDG Doug Gilmour 8.00 20.00
STSGL Guy Lafleur 8.00 20.00
STSJB Jean Beliveau 6.00 15.00
STSML Milan Lucic 5.00 12.00
STSRM Ryan McDonagh 4.00 10.00
STSTB Tom Barrasso 6.00 15.00
STSVD Vincent Damphousse 5.00 12.00

2015-16 Artifacts Stick to Stick Duos Green

STS2CP F.Potvin/W.Clark 25.00 50.00
STS2GC J.Carlson/M.Green 10.00 25.00
STS2GL D.Gilmour/M.Liut 12.00 30.00
STS2LR M.Richter/G.Lafleur 12.00 30.00
STS2SF P.Forsberg/J.Sakic 12.00 30.00
STS2SS H.Sedin/D.Sedin 12.00 30.00
STS2YL S.Yzerman/N.Lidstrom 25.00 60.00
STS2YZ H.Zetterberg/S.Yzerman 25.00 60.00

2015-16 Artifacts Stick to Stick Trios Green

STS3LAK Carter/Pearson/Toffoli 12.00 30.00
STS3LOS Blake/Gretzky/Kurri 40.00 80.00
STS3NYR Richter/Vanbiesbrouck/Park 12.0030.00
STS3TML Bernier/Kessel
van Riemsdyk 12.00 30.00
STS3WAS Backstrom
Ovechkin/Green 50.00 125.00
STS3BLUES Joseph/Hull/Oates 25.00 50.00
STS3KINGS Gaborik/Williams/Quick 25.00 50.00

2015-16 Artifacts Top 12 Rookie Signatures

RSCM Conner McDavid A 300.00 800.00
RSDL Dylan Larkin B 40.00 100.00
RSEP Emile Poirier 6.00 15.00
RSHS Henrik Samuelsson 5.00 12.00
RSJR Jacob de la Rose 8.00 20.00
RSMS Malcolm Subban 12.00 30.00
RSNE Nikolaj Ehlers C 15.00 40.00
RSRF Robby Fabbri C 10.00 25.00
RSRH Ryan Hartman 10.00 25.00
RSSB Sam Bennett 25.00 60.00
RSSR Sam Reinhart 15.00 40.00

2015-16 Artifacts Treasured Swatches Jerseys Blue

TSAS Alexander Semin B 3.00 8.00
TSBG Brendan Gallagher A 3.00 8.00
TSBH Braden Holtby B 4.00 10.00
TSBS Brayden Schenn B 3.00 8.00
TSCJ Calle Jarnkrok B 2.50 6.00
TSCK Chris Kreider B 4.00 10.00
TSDK David Krejci A 3.00 8.00
TSFA Frederik Andersen B 4.00 10.00
TSJH Jiri Hudler A 2.50 6.00
TSKA Nazem Kadri B 4.00 10.00
TSKU Darcy Kuemper B 3.00 8.00
TSLD Leon Draisaitl B 10.00 25.00
TSMM Matt Moulson A 2.00 5.00
TSMS Mark Scheifele B 5.00 12.00
TSMZ Mika Zibanejad B 4.00 10.00
TSNB Nick Bjugstad B 2.00 5.00
TSOE Oliver Ekman-Larsson B 3.00 8.00
TSOM Olli Maatta A 2.00 5.00
TSPE Patrik Elias B 3.00 8.00
TSPS Paul Stastny A 2.50 6.00
TSSE Brent Seabrook B 2.00 5.00
TSSV Semyon Varlamov B 3.00 8.00
TSTH Tomas Hertl A 3.00 8.00
TSTT Tyler Toffoli B 3.00 8.00
TSVH Victor Hedman B 4.00 10.00
TSZK Zack Kassian B 2.00 5.00

2015-16 Artifacts Tundra Sixes Jerseys Blue

T6TC Ptr/Cnly/Sch/Myr/Schf/Hck 12.00 30.00
T6CAR Stl/Stl/Sknr/Wrd/Lnd/Smn 10.00 25.00
T6CHI Sbrk/Kth/Crwf/Hsa/Shp/Sd 10.00 25.00
T6LAK Crtr/Tfli/Prs/Brw/Kptr/Wlms 12.00 30.00
T6RC1 Bnt/Pr/Ros/Csn/Sms/Fla 15.00 40.00
T6RC2 Pm/M.Sb/Hlk/Kn/Bu/An 30.00 80.00
T6VAN Mlr/Sdn/Brw/Sdn/Edlr/Ksn 10.00 25.00
T6BLUES Bck/Trs/Elt/Osh/Stst/Aln 10.00 25.00

2015-16 Artifacts Tundra Tandems Jerseys Blue

*EMERALD/15: 1.2X TO 3X BLUE/399
TTBB N.Bjugstad/A.Barkov 5.00 12.00
TTBH B.Bishop/V.Hedman 4.00 10.00
TTBK N.Backstrom/E.Kuznetsov 4.00 10.00
TTBL P.Bergeron/M.Lucic 4.00 10.00
TTBS T.Seguin/J.Benn 4.00 10.00
TTCT J.Carter/T.Toffoli 3.00 8.00
TTDP J.Drouin/O.Palat 2.50 6.00
TTGA F.Andersen/J.Gibson 4.00 10.00
TTGR Z.Girgensons/S.Reinhart 6.00 15.00
TTHN T.Hall/R.Nugent-Hopkins 4.00 10.00
TTMG S.Monahan/J.Gaudreau 5.00 12.00
TTNJ T.Jurco/G.Nyquist 2.00 5.00
TTPC L.Couture/J.Pavelski 4.00 10.00
TTPG M.Pacioretty/A.Galchenyuk 3.00 8.00
TTSB D.Backes/P.Stastny 2.50 6.00
TTSS D.Sedin/H.Sedin 4.00 10.00
TTTK K.Turris/E.Karlsson 4.00 10.00
TTVC S.Couturier/J.Voracek 2.50 6.00
TTVK J.van Riemsdyk/N.Kadri 4.00 10.00
TTWJ S.Weber/S.Jones 3.00 8.00
TTWS B.Wheeler/M.Scheifele 5.00 12.00
TTYD N.Yakupov/L.Draisaitl 10.00 25.00

2015-16 Artifacts Tundra Trios Jerseys Blue

T3AZ Gagner/Boedker/Ekmn-Lrsn 4.00 10.00
T3ANA Gibson/Kesler/Andersen 5.00 12.00
T3BUF Hodgson/Girgensons/Reinhart 8.00 20.00
T3CAN Sedin/Miller/Sedin 5.00 12.00
T3CBJ Hartnell/Dubinsky/Johansen 3.00 8.00
T3FLA Ekblad/Huberdeau/Barkov 6.00 15.00
T3LAK Quick/Kopitar/Doughty 6.00 15.00
T3NYI Okposo/Tavares/Strome 6.00 15.00
T3NYR Nash/Kreider/St. Louis 5.00 12.00
T3OIL RNH/Eberle/Draisaitl 12.00 30.00
T3TBL Drouin/Palat/Hedman 5.00 12.00
T3TOR Kessel/Rielly/Kadri 5.00 12.00
T3CAPS Ovchkn/Bckstrm/Kzntsv 15.00 40.00
T3JETS Wheeler/Pavelec/Scheifele 6.00 15.00
T3NASH Jones/Neal/Jarnkrok 4.00 10.00
T3WILD Coyle/Pominville/Kuemper 4.00 10.00
T3BLUES Backes/Stastny/Oshie 4.00 10.00

2015-16 Artifacts Year One Rookie Sweaters

RGAE Aaron Ekblad 5.00 12.00
RGBR Brett Ritchie 2.50 6.00
RGCJ Calle Jarnkrok 3.00 8.00
RGEK Evgeny Kuznetsov 5.00 12.00
RGJD Jonathan Drouin 3.00 8.00
RGJG Johnny Gaudreau 6.00 15.00
RGKL Kari Lehtonen 3.00 8.00
RGLD Leon Draisaitl 12.00 30.00
RGSR Sam Reinhart 8.00 20.00

2016-17 Artifacts

*VETS/25: 2X TO 5X BASIC CARDS
*S/25: .8X TO 2X BASIC S/499
*LEG/25: .8X TO 2X BASIC LEG/499
*RC/25: .8X TO 2X BASIC RC/999
1 Evgeni Malkin .75 2.00
2 Evgeny Kuznetsov .50 1.25
3 Sam Reinhart .75 2.00
4 Sergei Bobrovsky .60 1.50
5 Jonathan Toews .60 1.50
6 Ryan Strome .40 1.00
7 Victor Hedman .50 1.25
8 Matt Beleskey .30 .75
9 Marian Gaborik .40 1.00
10 Johnny Gaudreau .60 1.50
11 Derek Stepan .25 .60
12 Patrick Marleau .40 1.00
13 Michael Raffl .25 .60
14 Shea Weber .30 .75
15 Tyler Seguin .50 1.25
16 Frederik Andersen .50 1.25
17 Gustav Nyquist .25 .60
18 Nazem Kadri .50 1.25
19 Gabriel Landeskog .50 1.25
20 Vladimir Tarasenko .50 1.25
21 Kyle Turris .30 .75
22 Zach Parise .40 1.00
23 Alex Galchenyuk .25 .60
24 Cam Ward .40 1.00
25 Taylor Hall .40 1.00
26 Michael Cammalleri .30 .75
27 Dustin Byfuglien .40 1.00
28 Matt Murray .60 1.50
29 Mike Smith .40 1.00
30 Aaron Ekblad .50 1.25
31 Kyle Palmieri .30 .75
32 Evander Kane .40 1.00
33 Nicklas Backstrom .40 1.00
34 Sam Bennett .60 1.50
35 Anders Lee .40 1.00
36 Ryan Miller .40 1.00
37 Tomas Hertl .40 1.00

38 Roberto Luongo .60 1.50
39 T.J. Oshie .40 1.00
40 Drew Doughty .50 1.25
41 Duncan Keith .30 .75
42 Kevin Shattenkirk .25 .60
43 Kevin Hayes .30 .75
44 Steven Stamkos .75 2.00
45 Jonathan Huberdeau .50 1.25
46 Scott Hartnell .25 .60
47 Justin Faulk .30 .75
48 Mike Hoffman .25 .60
49 James van Riemsdyk .30 .75
50 Ryan Kesler .40 1.00
51 Tomas Tatar .25 .60
52 David Krejci .40 1.00
53 Phil Kessel .40 1.00
54 Pekka Rinne .40 1.00
55 Max Domi .40 1.00
56 Brendan Gallagher .40 1.00
57 Claude Giroux .40 1.00
58 Cory Schneider .40 1.00
59 Nathan MacKinnon 1.50 4.00
60 Jason Spezza .40 1.00
61 Brent Burns .40 1.00
62 Kris Letang .50 1.25
63 Devan Dubnyk .30 .75
64 Anze Kopitar .60 1.50
65 Jarome Iginla .50 1.25
66 Tyler Johnson .25 .60
67 Mark Stone .50 1.25
68 Nikolaj Ehlers .40 1.00
69 Corey Crawford .50 1.25
70 Jake Allen .40 1.00
71 Jaroslav Halak .40 1.00
72 Rick Nash .40 1.00
73 Carey Price .75 2.00
74 John Klingberg .40 1.00
75 Jordan Eberle .40 1.00
76 Wayne Simmonds .50 1.25
77 Tyler Toffoli .40 1.00
78 Cam Talbot .40 1.00
79 Dougie Hamilton .30 .75
80 Henrik Zetterberg .50 1.25
81 Artemi Panarin .75 2.00
82 Nino Niederreiter .25 .60
83 Nick Foligno .30 .75
84 Roman Josi .40 1.00
85 Ryan O'Reilly .40 1.00
86 Noah Hanifin .40 1.00
87 Henrik Lundqvist 1.00 2.50
88 Anthony Duclair .30 .75
89 Bobby Ryan .30 .75
90 Patrick Sharp .30 .75
91 Joe Thornton .60 1.50
92 Petr Mrazek .40 1.00
93 Aleksander Barkov .60 1.50
94 Loui Eriksson .25 .60
95 Bo Horvat .50 1.25
96 Braden Holtby .50 1.25
97 Leon Draisaitl 1.25 3.00
98 Tomas Plekanec .25 .60
99 Ryan Getzlaf .40 1.00
100 Blake Wheeler .40 1.00
101 Patrick Kane S 2.00 5.00
102 Jonathan Quick S 1.25 3.00
103 Mats Zuccarello S 1.00 2.50
104 Mikael Granlund S .75 2.00
105 Alexander Ovechkin S 4.00 10.00
106 Corey Perry S 1.50 4.00
107 Patrice Bergeron S 1.25 3.00
108 Sean Monahan S .60 1.50
109 Matt Duchene S 1.00 2.50
110 Connor McDavid S 5.00 12.00
111 Jaromir Jagr S 3.00 8.00
112 P.K. Subban S 1.25 3.00
113 Jeff Skinner S 1.25 3.00
114 Nikita Kucherov S 2.00 5.00
115 John Tavares S 1.50 4.00
116 Jakub Voracek S .75 2.00
117 Erik Karlsson S 1.25 3.00
118 Adam Henrique S .75 2.00
119 Filip Forsberg S 1.50 4.00
120 Jack Eichel S 1.50 4.00
121 Oliver Ekman-Larsson S 1.00 2.50
122 Mark Scheifele S 1.50 4.00
123 Morgan Rielly S 1.00 2.50
124 Joe Pavelski S 1.25 3.00
125 Sidney Crosby S 4.00 10.00
126 Brandon Saad S .75 2.00
127 Alexander Steen S .60 1.50
128 Jamie Benn S 1.00 2.50
129 Daniel Sedin S 1.25 3.00
130 Dylan Larkin S 1.25 3.00
131 Steve Yzerman LEG 2.50 6.00
132 Pavel Bure LEG 1.00 2.50
133 Larry Murphy LEG .75 2.00
134 Jeremy Roenick LEG 1.50 4.00
135 Paul Coffey LEG 1.00 2.50
136 John LeClair LEG 1.00 2.50
137 Bob Bourne LEG .60 1.50
138 Trevor Linden LEG 1.00 2.50
139 Mike Bossy LEG 1.00 2.50
140 Ron Hextall LEG 1.00 2.50
141 Chris Chelios LEG 1.00 2.50
142 Denis Savard LEG 1.00 2.50
143 Grant Fuhr LEG 1.50 4.00
144 Larry Robinson LEG 1.00 2.50
145 Wayne Gretzky LEG 6.00 15.00
146 Johnny Bucyk LEG 1.00 2.50
147 Kirk McLean LEG 1.00 2.50
148 Borje Salming LEG 1.00 2.50
149 Martin Brodeur LEG 2.50 6.00
150 Mark Messier LEG 2.00 5.00
151 Dominik Hasek LEG 1.50 4.00
152 Patrick Roy LEG 2.50 6.00
153 Peter Forsberg LEG 2.00 5.00
154 Pierre Turgeon LEG .75 2.00
155 Joe Sakic LEG 2.00 5.00
156 Mike Richter LEG 1.00 2.50
157 Brett Hull LEG 2.00 5.00
158 Mario Lemieux LEG 4.00 10.00
159 Teemu Selanne LEG 2.00 5.00
160 Guy Lafleur LEG 1.25 3.00
161 William Nylander RC 4.00 10.00
162 Sonny Milano RC 1.25 3.00
163 Kasperi Kapanen RC 1.50 4.00
164 Josh Morrissey RC 2.50 6.00
165 Trevor Carrick RC 1.00 2.50
166 Anthony Mantha RC 2.00 5.00
167 Michael Matheson RC 1.00 2.50
168 Hudson Fasching RC 1.00 2.50
169 Oliver Bjorkstrand RC 1.25 3.00
170 Brendan Leipsic RC .75 2.00
171 Pavel Zacha RC 1.50 4.00
172 Justin Bailey RC 1.00 2.50
173 Esa Lindell RC 1.00 2.50
174 Steven Santini RC .75 2.00
175 Nikita Soshnikov RC .60 1.50
176 Sergey Tolchinsky RC .75 2.00
177 Ryan Pulock RC 1.00 2.50
178 Jason Dickinson RC .75 2.00
179 Connor Brown RC 1.50 4.00
180 Charlie Lindgren RC 1.50 4.00
181 Nick Sorensen RC 2.50 6.00
182 Dylan Strome RC 6.00 15.00
183 Brandon Carlo RC 4.00 10.00
184 Nick Baptiste RC 2.50 6.00
185 Matthew Tkachuk RC 10.00 25.00
186 Sebastian Aho RC 8.00 20.00
187 Tyler Motte RC 2.50 6.00
188 A.J. Greer RC 2.50 6.00
189 Zach Werenski RC 8.00 20.00
190 Gemel Smith RC 2.50 6.00
191 Tyler Bertuzzi RC 4.00 10.00
192 Jesse Puljujarvi RC 5.00 12.00
193 Denis Malgin RC 2.00 5.00
194 Nic Dowd RC 2.00 5.00
195 Joel Eriksson Ek RC 4.00 10.00
196 Mikhail Sergachev RC 4.00 10.00
197 Pontus Aberg RC 3.00 8.00
198 Nick Lappin RC 2.50 6.00
199 Anthony Beauvillier RC 2.50 6.00
200 Jimmy Vesey RC 4.00 10.00
201 Thomas Chabot RC 5.00 12.00
202 Travis Konecny RC 5.00 12.00
203 Tristan Jarry RC 5.00 12.00
204 Kevin Labanc RC 2.50 6.00
205 Alex Friesen RC 3.00 8.00
206 Brayden Point RC 6.00 15.00
207 Auston Matthews RC 40.00 100.00
208 Troy Stecher RC 2.50 6.00
209 Zach Sanford RC 2.50 6.00
210 Patrik Laine RC 6.00 15.00
211 Mitch Marner RC 8.00 20.00
212 Ivan Provorov RC 4.00 10.00
213 Kyle Connor RC 8.00 20.00
214 Christian Dvorak RC 3.00 8.00
215 Pavel Buchnevich RC 4.00 10.00
216 Jakub Vrana RC 3.00 8.00
217 Brendan Perlini RC 2.50 6.00
218 Drake Caggiula RC 2.50 6.00
219 Julius Honka RC 2.50 6.00
220 Mathew Barzal RC 8.00 20.00

2016-17 Artifacts Emerald

*1-100 VETS/99: 21X TO 2.5X BASIC CARDS
*101-130 S/99: .6X TO 1.5X BASIC S/499
*131-160 LEG/99: .6X TO 1.5X BASIC LEG/499
*161-180 ROOKIES/99: 1.25X TO 3X BASIC RC/999
207 Auston Matthews 60.00 150.00

2016-17 Artifacts Aurum

*GOLD: .6X TO 1.5X BASIC INSERTS
A1 Alexander Ovechkin 6.00 15.00
A2 Oliver Ekman-Larsson 1.50 4.00
A3 Jamie Benn 1.50 4.00
A4 Vladimir Tarasenko 2.00 5.00
A5 Derick Brassard 1.00 2.50
A6 Jussi Jokinen 1.50 4.00
A7 Anze Kopitar 2.50 6.00
A8 Ryan Getzlaf 1.50 4.00
A9 Brad Marchand 3.00 8.00
A10 Connor McDavid 8.00 20.00
A11 Victor Rask 1.00 2.50
A12 John Tavares 2.50 6.00
A13 Logan Couture 2.00 5.00
A14 Cam Atkinson 1.50 4.00
A15 Sidney Crosby 6.00 15.00
A16 Filip Forsberg 2.50 6.00
A17 Braden Holtby 2.00 5.00
A18 Patrick Kane 3.00 8.00
A19 Matt Murray 2.50 6.00
A20 Max Domi 1.50 4.00
A21 Erik Karlsson 2.00 5.00
A22 Carey Price 3.00 8.00
A23 Henrik Zetterberg 2.00 5.00
A24 Daniel Sedin 2.00 5.00
A25 Kyle Palmieri 1.25 3.00
A26 Joe Thornton 2.50 6.00
A27 Johnny Gaudreau 2.50 6.00
A28 Mikko Koivu 1.25 3.00
A29 Steven Stamkos 3.00 8.00
A30 Artemi Panarin 3.00 8.00
A31 Matt Duchene 1.50 4.00
A32 Shayne Gostisbehere 1.50 4.00
A33 Patric Hornqvist 1.00 2.50
A34 Jaromir Jagr 5.00 12.00
A35 Jack Eichel 2.50 6.00
A36 William Nylander 6.00 15.00
A37 Anthony Mantha 3.00 8.00
A38 Kasperi Kapanen 2.50 6.00
A39 Pavel Zacha 2.50 6.00
A40 Hudson Fasching 1.50 4.00
A41 Wayne Gretzky 10.00 25.00
A42 Mark Messier 3.00 8.00
A43 Steve Yzerman 4.00 10.00
A44 Doug Harvey 1.25 3.00
A45 Mario Lemieux 6.00 15.00
A46 Luc Robitaille 1.50 4.00
A47 Kirk McLean 1.50 4.00
A48 Curtis Joseph 2.00 5.00
A49 Patrick Roy 4.00 10.00
A50 Bobby Orr 6.00 15.00

2016-17 Artifacts Autofacts

AAE Aaron Ekblad A 10.00 25.00
AAK Anze Kopitar A 12.00 30.00
AAL Anders Lee C 8.00 20.00
AAW Alexander Wennberg C 5.00 12.00
ABJ Boone Jenner C 8.00 20.00
ACO Chris Osgood B 8.00 20.00
AEP Emile Poirier D 5.00 12.00
AJG John Gibson D 8.00 20.00
AJH Jiri Hudler B 6.00 15.00
AJW Jordan Weal D 5.00 12.00
AJZ Jason Zucker B 8.00 20.00
AMG Mikhail Grigorenko D 5.00 12.00
AMM Mike McCarron D 8.00 20.00
ANB Nick Bjugstad C 5.00 12.00
ANS Nick Shore D 5.00 12.00
ARB Rod Brind'Amour C 8.00 20.00
ARS Ryan Spooner D 6.00 15.00
ATL Trevor Linden A 8.00 20.00
AVN Vladislav Namestnikov D 5.00 12.00
AWG Wayne Gretzky A 100.00 250.00

2016-17 Artifacts Autograph Materials Silver

1 Evgeni Malkin/25 15.00 40.00
3 Sam Reinhart/49 15.00 40.00
4 Sergei Bobrovsky/25 12.00 30.00
6 Ryan Strome/75 8.00 20.00
8 Matt Beleskey/75 6.00 15.00
9 Marian Gaborik/25 8.00 20.00
11 Derek Stepan/25 5.00 12.00
12 Patrick Marleau/25 8.00 20.00
16 Frederik Andersen/75 10.00 25.00
19 Gabriel Landeskog/25 10.00 25.00
21 Kyle Turris/49 6.00 15.00
22 Zach Parise/25 8.00 20.00
23 Alex Galchenyuk/25 5.00 12.00
24 Cam Ward/49 8.00 20.00
25 Taylor Hall/25 8.00 20.00
30 Aaron Ekblad/25 10.00 25.00
34 Sam Bennett/49 12.00 30.00
35 Anders Lee/75 8.00 20.00
36 Ryan Miller/25 8.00 20.00
37 Tomas Hertl/25 8.00 20.00
43 Kevin Hayes/75 6.00 15.00
45 Jonathan Huberdeau/49 10.00 25.00
48 Mike Hoffman/75 5.00 12.00
49 James van Riemsdyk/49 6.00 15.00
51 Tomas Tatar/49 5.00 12.00
52 David Krejci/25 8.00 20.00
54 Pekka Rinne/49 8.00 20.00
56 Brendan Gallagher/25 8.00 20.00
57 Claude Giroux/25 8.00 20.00
58 Cory Schneider/49 8.00 20.00
60 Jason Spezza/25 8.00 20.00
64 Anze Kopitar/25 12.00 30.00
65 Jarome Iginla/25 10.00 25.00
66 Tyler Johnson/49 5.00 12.00
67 Mark Stone/75 10.00 25.00
68 Nikolaj Ehlers/49 8.00 20.00
70 Jake Allen/75 8.00 20.00
71 Jaroslav Halak/75 8.00 20.00
72 Rick Nash/25 8.00 20.00
73 Carey Price/25 30.00 80.00
74 John Klingberg/49 8.00 20.00
77 Tyler Toffoli/25 8.00 20.00
84 Roman Josi/49 8.00 20.00
86 Noah Hanifin/49 8.00 20.00
87 Henrik Lundqvist/25 20.00 50.00
88 Anthony Duclair/75 6.00 15.00
89 Bobby Ryan/25 6.00 15.00
93 Aleksander Barkov/49 12.00 30.00
94 Loui Eriksson/25 5.00 12.00
95 Bo Horvat/75 10.00 25.00
102 Jonathan Quick 10.00 25.00
105 Alexander Ovechkin 30.00 80.00
106 Corey Perry 12.00 30.00
108 Sean Monahan 5.00 12.00
109 Matt Duchene 8.00 20.00
110 Connor McDavid 150.00 250.00
111 Jaromir Jagr 25.00 60.00
112 P.K. Subban 10.00 25.00
113 Jeff Skinner 10.00 25.00
115 John Tavares 12.00 30.00
116 Jakub Voracek 6.00 15.00
118 Adam Henrique 6.00 15.00
122 Mark Scheifele 12.00 30.00
123 Morgan Rielly 8.00 20.00
124 Joe Pavelski 10.00 25.00
128 Jamie Benn 8.00 20.00
131 Steve Yzerman 30.00 80.00
132 Pavel Bure 8.00 20.00
134 Jeremy Roenick 12.00 30.00
135 Paul Coffey 8.00 20.00
136 John LeClair 8.00 20.00
137 Bob Bourne 5.00 12.00
138 Trevor Linden 8.00 20.00
139 Mike Bossy 8.00 20.00
140 Ron Hextall 8.00 20.00
141 Chris Chelios 8.00 20.00
142 Denis Savard 8.00 20.00
143 Grant Fuhr 12.00 30.00
144 Larry Robinson 8.00 20.00
145 Wayne Gretzky 200.00 500.00
146 Johnny Bucyk 15.00 40.00
147 Kirk McLean 8.00 20.00
149 Martin Brodeur 20.00 50.00
152 Patrick Roy 40.00 100.00
154 Pierre Turgeon 6.00 15.00
157 Brett Hull 15.00 40.00
158 Mario Lemieux 40.00 100.00
162 Sonny Milano 10.00 25.00
163 Kasperi Kapanen 12.00 30.00
164 Josh Morrissey 20.00 50.00
165 Trevor Carrick 8.00 20.00
166 Anthony Mantha 15.00 40.00
167 Michael Matheson 8.00 20.00
168 Hudson Fasching 8.00 20.00
169 Oliver Bjorkstrand 10.00 25.00
170 Brendan Leipsic 6.00 15.00
171 Pavel Zacha 12.00 30.00
172 Justin Bailey 8.00 20.00
173 Esa Lindell 8.00 20.00
174 Steven Santini 6.00 15.00
175 Nikita Soshnikov 5.00 12.00
177 Ryan Pulock 8.00 20.00
178 Jason Dickinson 6.00 15.00
179 Connor Brown 12.00 30.00
180 Charlie Lindgren 12.00 30.00

2016-17 Artifacts Frozen Artifacts

FAAH Andrew Hammond C 2.50 6.00
FABB Bob Bourne A 2.00 5.00
FACA Jeff Carter B 2.50 6.00
FACK Chris Kreider C 4.00 10.00
FAHS Henrik Sedin C 4.00 10.00
FAJC John Carlson C 3.00 8.00
FAJJ Jack Johnson C 2.00 5.00
FAJS Jakob Silfverberg B 2.00 5.00
FAJT Jacob Trouba C 2.50 6.00
FAJZ Jason Zucker C 3.00 8.00
FAKL Kris Letang B 4.00 10.00
FAMH Martin Hanzal C 2.50 6.00
FAMJ Martin Jones C 2.50 6.00
FAMP Max Pacioretty B 3.00 8.00
FANL Nick Leddy C 2.00 5.00
FAOP Ondrej Palat C 2.50 6.00
FAPE Patrik Elias C 3.00 8.00
FAPT Pierre Turgeon A 2.50 6.00
FARH Ron Hextall A 3.00 8.00
FARL Roberto Luongo B 5.00 12.00
FARR Rasmus Ristolainen C 2.00 5.00
FASM Steve Mason C 2.50 6.00
FASV Semyon Varlamov C 3.00 8.00
FAZC Zdeno Chara C 3.00 8.00

2016-17 Artifacts Honoured Members Relics

HMRBH Brett Hull 40.00 100.00
HMRBO Johnny Bower 20.00 50.00
HMRBS Borje Salming 20.00 50.00
HMRDH Doug Harvey 15.00 40.00
HMRDS Denis Savard UER 20.00 50.00
HMRGL Guy Lafleur 25.00 60.00
HMRJB Johnny Bucyk 20.00 50.00
HMRLM Lanny McDonald 20.00 50.00
HMRLR Luc Robitaille 20.00 50.00
HMRMU Larry Murphy 15.00 40.00
HMRPF Peter Forsberg 40.00 100.00
HMRPR Patrick Roy 50.00 125.00
HMRRB Rob Blake 20.00 50.00
HMRTE Tony Esposito 20.00 50.00
HMRWG Wayne Gretzky 125.00 300.00

2016-17 Artifacts Honoured Members Signatures

HMSAM Al MacInnis 60.00 150.00
HMSBS Billy Smith 50.00 125.00
HMSCG Clark Gillies 50.00 125.00
HMSDG Doug Gilmour 60.00 150.00
HMSDH Dominik Hasek 80.00 200.00
HMSGP Gilbert Perreault 50.00 125.00
HMSJK Jari Kurri 50.00 125.00
HMSPC Paul Coffey 50.00 125.00
HMSSY Steve Yzerman 125.00 300.00

2016-17 Artifacts Lord Stanley's Legacy Relics

LSLRCW Cam Ward C 3.00 8.00
LSLRDK Duncan Keith B 2.50 6.00
LSLRHZ Henrik Zetterberg A 4.00 10.00
LSLRJC Jeff Carter B 2.50 6.00
LSLRLR Larry Robinson A 3.00 8.00
LSLRMB Martin Brodeur A 8.00 20.00
LSLRMF Marc-Andre Fleury C 6.00 15.00
LSLRPB Patrice Bergeron B 4.00 10.00

2016-17 Artifacts Lord Stanley's Legacy Signatures

LSLSCP Corey Perry D 15.00 40.00
LSLSJK Jari Kurri D 10.00 25.00
LSLSML Mario Lemieux B 40.00 100.00
LSLSPE Phil Esposito C 15.00 40.00
LSLSPR Patrick Roy B 25.00 60.00
LSLSRB Ray Bourque C 15.00 40.00
LSLSSY Steve Yzerman B 25.00 60.00
LSLSWY Wayne Gretzky A 200.00 500.00

2016-17 Artifacts Piece de Resistance

*SPECTRUM/25: .6X TO 1.5X BASIC INSERTS
PRCM Connor McDavid B 15.00 40.00
PRCP Corey Perry C 5.00 12.00
PRDS Daniel Sedin C 4.00 10.00
PRGF Grant Fuhr A 5.00 12.00
PRJJ Jaromir Jagr C 10.00 25.00
PRJQ Jonathan Quick C 4.00 10.00
PRJS Jason Spezza C 3.00 8.00
PRLM Larry Murphy A 2.50 6.00
PRMD Max Domi C 3.00 8.00
PRMH Marian Hossa C 3.00 8.00
PRML Mario Lemieux A 12.00 30.00
PROV Alexander Ovechkin A 12.00 30.00
PRPC Paul Coffey A 3.00 8.00
PRPK Patrick Kane B 6.00 15.00
PRSC Sidney Crosby A 12.00 30.00
PRSS Steven Stamkos C 6.00 15.00
PRVN Valeri Nichushkin C 3.00 8.00

2016-17 Artifacts Rookie Autograph Relics Redemptions Emerald

I Auston Matthews 400.00 800.00
II Patrik Laine 60.00 150.00
III Jesse Puljujarvi 40.00 100.00
IV Jimmy Vesey 20.00 50.00
V Zach Werenski 25.00 60.00

2016-17 Artifacts Rookie Autograph Relics Redemptions Silver

I Auston Matthews 300.00 600.00
II Patrik Laine 80.00 150.00
III Jesse Puljujarvi 20.00 50.00
IV Jimmy Vesey 12.00 30.00
V Zach Werenski 25.00 60.00

2016-17 Artifacts Rookie Autographs Redemptions

X Mikhail Sergachev 15.00 40.00
I Auston Matthews 250.00 500.00
II Patrik Laine 25.00 60.00
III Jesse Puljujarvi 20.00 50.00
IV Jimmy Vesey 15.00 40.00
V Zach Werenski 30.00 80.00
VI Travis Konecny 20.00 50.00
VII Ivan Provorov 15.00 40.00
VIII Kyle Connor 30.00 80.00
XI Dylan Strome 25.00 60.00
IX Matthew Tkachuk 40.00 100.00
XV Jakub Vrana 12.00 30.00
XX Anthony DeAngelo 8.00 20.00
XII Sebastian Aho 30.00 80.00
XIV Tyler Motte 10.00 25.00
XIX John Quenneville 10.00 25.00
XVI Joel Eriksson Ek 15.00 40.00
XIII Christian Dvorak 12.00 30.00
XVII Brendan Perlini 10.00 25.00
XVIII Julius Honka 10.00 25.00

2016-17 Artifacts Rookie Relics Redemptions Emerald

I Auston Matthews 90.00 150.00
II Patrik Laine 25.00 60.00
III Jesse Puljujarvi 20.00 50.00
IV Jimmy Vesey 10.00 25.00
V Zach Werenski 20.00 50.00

2016-17 Artifacts Rookie Relics Redemptions Silver

I Auston Matthews 50.00 125.00
II Patrik Laine 20.00 50.00
III Jesse Puljujarvi 15.00 40.00
IV Jimmy Vesey 12.00 30.00
V Zach Werenski 25.00 60.00

2016-17 Artifacts Top 12 Rookie Signatures

RSAM Anthony Mantha A 12.00 30.00
RSHF Hudson Fasching B 6.00 15.00
RSKK Kasperi Kapanen B 10.00 25.00
RSPZ Pavel Zacha B 10.00 25.00
RSSM Sonny Milano B 8.00 20.00

2016-17 Artifacts Tundra Teammates Duos Materials

T2BOS T.Rask/Z.Chara 4.00 10.00
T2BUF R.Ristolainen/E.Kane 3.00 8.00
T2COY J.Roenick/S.Doan 5.00 12.00
T2EDM R.Nugent-Hopkins/N.Yakupov 4.00 10.00
T2MTL L.Robinson/G.Carbonneau 3.00 8.00
T2NYI N.Leddy/A.Lee 3.00 8.00
T2NYR C.Kreider/K.Hayes 4.00 10.00
T2CALG J.Gaudreau/S.Monahan 5.00 12.00
T2HABS A.Galchenyuk/B.Gallagher 3.00 8.00
T2NASH P.Rinne/J.Neal 3.00 8.00
T2PENG E.Malkin/P.Kessel 6.00 15.00
T2WILD N.Niederreiter/J.Pominville 2.00 5.00
T2BLUES K.Shattenkirk/J.Allen 3.00 8.00
T2KINGS D.Doughty/D.Brown 4.00 10.00

2016-17 Artifacts Tundra Teammates Quads Materials

T4ANA Perry/Kesler Silfverberg/Gibson 6.00 15.00
T4CHB Kane/Keith/Toews/Hossa 8.00 20.00
T4EDM McDavid Draisaitl/Eberle/Talbot 20.00 50.00
T4FLA Jagr/Barkov/Ekblad/Luongo 12.00 30.00
T4OTT Karlsson/Stone Hoffman/Anderson 4.00 10.00
T4SJS Pavelski/Burns/Thornton/Jones 6.00 15.00
T4VAN Linden/Sedin/Bure/Sedin 5.00 12.00
T4CAPS Ovechkin/Backstrom Kuznetsov/Holtby 15.00 40.00
T4STAR Benn/Seguin Spezza/Klingberg 5.00 12.00
T4WINGS Chelios/Coffey Yzerman/Zetterberg 10.00 25.00

2016-17 Artifacts Year One Rookie Sweaters

RSCM Connor McDavid B 20.00 50.00
RSJE Jack Eichel B 6.00 15.00
RSJV Jake Virtanen B 5.00 12.00
RSMC Mike Condon B 4.00 10.00
RSMD Max Domi B 4.00 10.00
RSNE Nikolaj Ehlers B 4.00 10.00
RSPB Pavel Bure A 10.00 25.00
RSSB Sam Bennett B 6.00 15.00

2017-18 Artifacts

1 Adam Henrique .30 .75
2 Steven Stamkos .75 2.00
3 Eric Staal .50 1.25
4 Braden Holtby .50 1.25
5 Johnny Gaudreau .60 1.50
6 Aaron Ekblad .50 1.25
7 Charlie Coyle .40 1.00
8 Patrice Bergeron .50 1.25
9 Sebastian Aho .60 1.50
10 Drew Doughty .50 1.25
11 Filip Forsberg .60 1.50
12 Nino Niederreiter .25 .60
13 Victor Rask .25 .60
14 Dylan Larkin .50 1.25
15 Daniel Sedin .50 1.25
16 Morgan Rielly .40 1.00
17 Frans Nielsen .25 .60
18 James Neal .25 .60
19 Cory Schneider .40 1.00
20 Jordan Eberle .40 1.00
21 Andrew Ladd .25 .60
22 Zach Werenski .60 1.50
23 John Carlson .40 1.00
24 Ivan Provorov .30 .75
25 Derek Stepan .25 .60
26 Brayden Schenn .40 1.00
27 Nick Leddy .25 .60
28 Robby Fabbri .25 .60
29 Shea Weber .30 .75
30 Oliver Ekman-Larsson .40 1.00
31 Mark Stone .50 1.25
32 Max Pacioretty .40 1.00
33 Nikita Kucherov .75 2.00
34 Brad Marchand .75 2.00
35 Jamie Benn .40 1.00
36 Pavel Zacha .30 .75
37 Ryan O'Reilly .40 1.00
38 Brandon Saad .30 .75
39 Nazem Kadri .50 1.25
40 Tyler Seguin .50 1.25
41 Mark Scheifele .60 1.50
42 Evgeni Malkin .75 2.00
43 Jason Spezza .40 1.00
44 Leon Draisaitl 1.25 3.00
45 Jonathan Toews .60 1.50
46 Rickard Rakell .30 .75
47 Andreas Athanasiou .40 1.00
48 Alexander Wennberg .25 .60
49 Erik Karlsson .50 1.25
50 Frederik Andersen .50 1.25
51 Tuukka Rask .50 1.25
52 Mats Zuccarello .40 1.00
53 Claude Giroux .40 1.00
54 Blake Wheeler .40 1.00
55 Jaromir Jagr 1.25 3.00
56 Gustav Nyquist .25 .60
57 Gabriel Landeskog .50 1.25
58 Bo Horvat .50 1.25
59 Jonathan Drouin .30 .75
60 Nathan MacKinnon 1.50 4.00
61 Jack Eichel .60 1.50
62 Milan Lucic .40 1.00
63 Mike Smith .40 1.00
64 Joe Thornton .60 1.50
65 T.J. Oshie .40 1.00
66 Joe Pavelski .50 1.25
67 Patrick Kane .75 2.00
68 Jake Allen .40 1.00
69 Ryan Spooner .30 .75
70 Roberto Luongo .60 1.50
71 Alex Pietrangelo .30 .75
72 Carey Price .75 2.00
73 Jake Muzzin .40 1.00
74 Logan Couture .50 1.25
75 John Gibson .40 1.00
76 Kyle Palmieri .30 .75
77 Jimmy Vesey .30 .75
78 David Pastrnak 1.00 2.50
79 Teuvo Teravainen .40 1.00
80 Cam Atkinson .40 1.00
81 Artemi Panarin .75 2.00
82 Ryan Getzlaf .40 1.00
83 Jaden Schwartz .50 1.25
84 Christian Dvorak .30 .75
85 Sean Monahan .25 .60
86 Anze Kopitar .60 1.50
87 Nicklas Backstrom .40 1.00
88 Matt Murray .60 1.50
89 Nick Bjugstad .25 .60
90 Ryan Johansen .30 .75
91 Matt Duchene .40 1.00
92 Vincent Trocheck .40 1.00
93 Matthew Tkachuk .75 2.00
94 Kyle Okposo .25 .60
95 Kris Letang .50 1.25
96 Loui Eriksson .25 .60
97 Nikolaj Ehlers .40 1.00
98 Anders Lee .40 1.00
99 Tyler Toffoli .40 1.00
100 Derick Brassard .25 .60
101 P.K. Subban S 1.50 4.00
102 Ryan Kesler S 1.25 3.00
103 Henrik Zetterberg S 1.50 4.00
104 Taylor Hall S 1.25 3.00
105 Mike Hoffman S .75 2.00
106 Alex Galchenyuk S .75 2.00
107 Wayne Simmonds S 1.50 4.00
108 Aleksander Barkov S 2.00 5.00
109 Devan Dubnyk S 1.00 2.50
110 Auston Matthews S 5.00 12.00
111 John Klingberg S 1.25 3.00
112 Max Domi S 1.25 3.00
113 Corey Crawford S 1.50 4.00
114 Jeff Carter S 1.00 2.50
115 Sidney Crosby S 5.00 12.00
116 Tyson Barrie S .75 2.00
117 Justin Faulk S 1.00 2.50
118 Mark Giordano S 1.25 3.00
119 Henrik Lundqvist S 3.00 8.00
120 Henrik Sedin S 1.50 4.00
121 David Krejci S 1.25 3.00
122 Alexander Ovechkin S 5.00 12.00
123 Brent Burns S 1.25 3.00
124 John Tavares S 2.00 5.00
125 Connor McDavid S 8.00 20.00
126 Sam Reinhart S 2.50 6.00
127 Patrik Laine S 1.50 4.00
128 Sergei Bobrovsky S 2.00 5.00
129 Victor Hedman S 1.50 4.00
130 Vladimir Tarasenko S 1.50 4.00
131 Mario Lemieux LEG 5.00 12.00
132 Dave Taylor LEG 1.00 2.50
133 Martin Brodeur LEG 3.00 8.00
134 Owen Nolan LEG 1.25 3.00
135 Ed Belfour LEG 1.50 4.00
136 Larry Murphy LEG 1.00 2.50
137 Mark Recchi LEG 1.50 4.00
138 Tom Barrasso LEG 1.00 2.50
139 Vincent Damphousse LEG 1.00 2.50
140 Felix Potvin LEG 2.00 5.00
141 Lanny McDonald LEG 1.25 3.00
142 Nicklas Lidstrom LEG 1.25 3.00
143 Teemu Selanne LEG 2.50 6.00
144 Marcel Dionne LEG 1.50 4.00
145 Bob Probert LEG 1.25 3.00
146 Igor Larionov LEG 1.25 3.00
147 Guy Lafleur LEG 1.50 4.00
148 Pelle Lindbergh LEG 1.00 2.50
149 Theoren Fleury LEG 1.25 3.00
150 Rod Brind'Amour LEG 1.25 3.00
151 Dale Hawerchuk LEG 1.50 4.00
152 Patrick Roy LEG 3.00 8.00
153 Doug Gilmour LEG 1.50 4.00
154 Brett Hull LEG 2.50 6.00
155 Paul Coffey LEG 1.25 3.00
156 Dominik Hasek LEG 2.00 5.00
157 Wayne Gretzky LEG 8.00 20.00
158 Joe Sakic LEG 2.50 6.00
159 Mike Gartner LEG 1.50 4.00
160 Ray Bourque LEG 2.00 5.00
161 Ivan Barbashev RC 2.00 5.00
162 Vladislav Kamenev RC 1.50 4.00
163 Jonny Brodzinski RC 1.50 4.00
164 Tyson Jost RC 3.00 8.00
165 Evgeny Svechnikov RC 3.00 8.00
166 J.T. Compher RC 1.50 4.00
167 Jon Gillies RC 1.50 4.00
168 Adrian Kempe RC 3.00 8.00
169 Lucas Wallmark RC 1.50 4.00
170 Alexander Nylander RC 2.50 6.00
171 Brock Boeser RC 10.00 25.00
172 Nikita Scherbak RC 2.00 5.00
173 Christian Fischer RC 2.00 5.00
174 Colin White RC 2.00 5.00
175 Charlie McAvoy RC 8.00 20.00
176 Josh Ho-Sang RC 2.00 5.00
177 Samuel Morin RC 1.00 2.50
178 Jack Roslovic RC 2.00 5.00
179 Clayton Keller RC 4.00 10.00
180 Alex Tuch RC 4.00 10.00
181 Jaycob Megna RC 1.50 4.00
182 Nick Merkley RC 1.50 4.00
183 Anders Bjork RC 2.00 5.00
184 C.J. Smith RC 1.25 3.00
185 Rasmus Andersson RC 1.50 4.00
186 Haydn Fleury RC 1.50 4.00
187 Alex DeBrincat RC 4.00 10.00
188 Alex Kerfoot RC 3.00 8.00
189 Pierre-Luc Dubious RC 2.50 6.00
190 Denis Gurianov RC 4.00 10.00
191 Robbie Russo RC 1.50 4.00
192 Kailer Yamamoto RC 4.00 10.00
193 Owen Tippett RC 3.00 8.00
194 Michael Amadio RC 1.50 4.00
195 Luke Kunin RC 1.50 4.00
196 Victor Mete RC 1.50 4.00
197 Alexandre Carrier RC 1.25 3.00
198 Nico Hischier RC 5.00 12.00
199 Connor Jones RC 1.25 3.00
200 Filip Chytil RC 1.50 4.00
201 Logan Brown RC 1.50 4.00
202 Nolan Patrick RC 3.00 8.00
203 Casey DeSmith RC 2.50 6.00
204 Joakim Ryan RC 1.50 4.00
205 Tage Thompson RC 4.00 10.00
206 Jake Dotchin RC 1.25 3.00
207 Calle Rosen RC 1.50 4.00
208 Griffen Molino RC 1.25 3.00
209 Madison Bowey RC 1.00 2.50
210 Eric Comrie RC 1.25 3.00
211 Maxime Lagace RC 1.50 4.00
212 Will Butcher RC 2.00 5.00
213 Jake DeBrusk RC 4.00 10.00
214 Filip Chlapik RC 1.25 3.00
215 Henrik Haapala RC 1.50 4.00
216 Robert Hagg RC 1.50 4.00
217 Jesper Bratt RC 3.00 8.00
218 Janne Kuokkanen RC 1.50 4.00
219 Brendan Lemieux RC 1.50 4.00
220 Alex Tuch RC 4.00 10.00

2017-18 Artifacts Emerald

*VETS/99: 2.5X TO 6X BASIC INSERTS
*RC/99: 1X TO 2.5X BASIC INSERTS
175 Charlie McAvoy 25.00 60.00
176 Josh Ho-Sang 8.00 20.00
179 Clayton Keller 12.00 30.00

2017-18 Artifacts Orange

*VETS/55: 4X TO 10X BASIC CARDS
*S.LEG/55: .75X TO 2X BASIC CARDS
*ROOKIES: 1X TO 2.5X BASIC CARDS
171 Brock Boeser 30.00 80.00
175 Charlie McAvoy 30.00 80.00
176 Josh Ho-Sang 5.00 12.00
179 Clayton Keller 15.00 40.00

2017-18 Artifacts Purple

*VETS/55: 6X TO 15X BASIC CARDS
*S.LEG/55: 1.25X TO 3X BASIC CARDS
*ROOKIES: 2X TO 5X BASIC CARDS
171 Brock Boeser 90.00 150.00
175 Charlie McAvoy 60.00 150.00
179 Clayton Keller 50.00 125.00

2017-18 Artifacts Aurum

A1 Ace Bailey 8.00 20.00
A2 Frank Mahovlich 2.50 6.00
A3 Darryl Sittler 3.00 8.00
A4 Charlie Conacher 2.00 5.00
A5 Doug Gilmour 3.00 8.00
A6 Wendel Clark 4.00 10.00
A7 Alexander Ovechkin 10.00 25.00
A8 Aleksander Barkov 4.00 10.00
A9 Alex Pietrangelo 2.00 5.00
A10 John Tavares 4.00 10.00
A11 Leon Draisaitl 8.00 20.00
A12 Alexander Wennberg 1.50 4.00
A13 Sean Monahan 1.50 4.00
A14 Connor McDavid 12.00 30.00
A15 Brent Burns 2.50 6.00
A16 Rickard Rakell 2.00 5.00
A17 Cam Atkinson 2.50 6.00
A18 Claude Giroux 2.50 6.00
A19 Sidney Crosby 10.00 25.00
A20 Tyler Seguin 3.00 8.00
A21 Jeff Carter 2.00 5.00
A22 Mats Zuccarello 2.50 6.00
A23 Tuukka Rask 3.00 8.00
A24 P.K. Subban 3.00 8.00
A25 Henrik Sedin 3.00 8.00
A26 Auston Matthews 15.00 40.00
A27 Mike Hoffman 1.50 4.00
A28 Corey Crawford 3.00 8.00
A29 Ryan O'Reilly 2.50 6.00
A30 Marc-Andre Fleury 5.00 12.00
A31 Jeff Skinner 3.00 8.00
A32 Mike Green 2.00 5.00
A33 Devan Dubnyk 2.00 5.00
A34 Victor Hedman 3.00 8.00
A35 Carey Price 5.00 12.00
A36 Nicklas Backstrom 2.50 6.00
A37 Taylor Hall 2.50 6.00
A38 Jonathan Drouin 2.00 5.00
A39 Jake Guentzel 4.00 10.00
A40 Craig Anderson 2.50 6.00
A41 Mark Scheifele 4.00 10.00
A42 Pekka Rinne 2.50 6.00
A43 Ryan Getzlaf 2.50 6.00
A44 Nikita Kucherov 5.00 12.00
A45 Tyson Jost 5.00 12.00
A46 Charlie McAvoy 15.00 40.00
A47 Brock Boeser 15.00 40.00
A48 Alexander Nylander 10.00 25.00
A49 Clayton Keller 15.00 40.00
A50 Josh Ho-Sang 8.00 20.00

2017-18 Artifacts Autofacts

AAL Artturi Lehkonen D 4.00 10.00
ABR Bobby Ryan A 12.00 30.00
ADF Derek Forbort D 3.00 8.00
ADS Derek Sanderson A 8.00 20.00
AEK Evander Kane C 5.00 12.00
AFA Radek Faksa B 4.00 10.00
AJE Joel Edmundson D 3.00 8.00
AJF Justin Falk D 4.00 10.00
AJN Joakim Nordstrom D 3.00 8.00
AJS Jason Spezza A 8.00 20.00
AON Owen Nolan C 6.00 15.00
APH Phil Housley C 4.00 10.00
ARU Bryan Rust C 40.00 100.00
ASA Sebastian Aho B 8.00 20.00

ATW Tom Wilson C 5.00 12.00
AVA Viktor Arvidsson D 3.00 8.00
AVH Victor Hedman C 6.00 15.00
AWK William Karlsson D 6.00 15.00
AZP Zach Parise A 8.00 20.00

2017-18 Artifacts Autograph Materials Emerald

*VETS/25: 12X TO 30X BASIC CARDS
*ROOKIES: 3X TO 10X BASIC CARDS
44 Leon Draisaitl/25 30.00 80.00
50 Frederik Andersen/25 30.00 80.00
58 Bo Horvat/25 30.00 80.00
164 Tyson Jost/35 40.00 100.00
166 J.T. Compher/35 20.00 50.00
167 Jon Gillies/35 25.00 60.00
168 Adrian Kempe/35 40.00 100.00
170 Alexander Nylander/35 30.00 80.00
171 Brock Boeser/35 50.00 125.00
172 Nikita Scherbak/35 25.00 60.00
175 Charlie McAvoy/35 150.00 250.00
176 Josh Ho-Sang/35 80.00 150.00
177 Samuel Morin/35 25.00 60.00
179 Clayton Keller/35 80.00 150.00

2017-18 Artifacts Autograph Materials Silver

*VETS/25: 12X TO 30X BASIC CARDS
*VETS/35: 10X TO 25X BASIC CARDS
*ROOKIES: 2.5X TO 6X BASIC CARDS
164 Tyson Jost/99 30.00 80.00
165 Evgeny Svechnikov/99 30.00 80.00
168 Adrian Kempe/99 20.00 50.00
170 Alexander Nylander/99 20.00 50.00
171 Brock Boeser/99 40.00 100.00
176 Josh Ho-Sang/99 50.00 125.00
179 Clayton Keller/99 50.00 125.00

2017-18 Artifacts Centennial Remnants

CRAM Auston Matthews C 20.00 50.00
CRCM Connor McDavid B 30.00 80.00
CREK Erik Karlsson C 6.00 15.00
CRJJ Jaromir Jagr C 15.00 40.00
CRJT Joe Thornton C 8.00 20.00
CRMB Martin Brodeur B 12.00 30.00
CRMD Marcel Dionne A 12.00 30.00
CRML Mario Lemieux A 20.00 50.00
CRPK Patrick Kane C 10.00 25.00
CRPR Patrick Roy A 15.00 40.00
CRRB Ray Bourque B 12.00 30.00
CRSC Sidney Crosby B 15.00 40.00
CRSY Steve Yzerman B 25.00 60.00
CRWG Wayne Gretzky A 30.00 80.00

2017-18 Artifacts Frozen Artifacts

FAAA Andreas Athanasiou C 4.00 10.00
FAAS Andrew Shaw C 2.50 6.00
FAAW Alexander Wennberg B 2.50 6.00
FABH Braden Holtby A 5.00 12.00
FACP Colton Parayko B 3.00 8.00
FADB Dustin Byfuglien A 4.00 10.00
FADD Devan Dubnyk B 3.00 8.00
FADH Dale Hawerchuk A 5.00 12.00
FADP David Pastrnak D 10.00 25.00
FAEK Erik Karlsson A 5.00 12.00
FAJN James Neal B 2.50 6.00
FAJP Joe Pavelski A 5.00 12.00
FAKO Kyle Okposo C 2.50 6.00
FAKP Kyle Palmieri C 3.00 8.00
FAML Milan Lucic B 4.00 10.00
FAMZ Mats Zuccarello B 4.00 10.00
FANB Nicklas Backstrom A 4.00 10.00
FANK Nikita Kucherov A 8.00 20.00
FANL Nick Leddy C 2.50 6.00
FAPR Pekka Rinne B 4.00 10.00
FARI Mike Richter A 4.00 10.00
FARK Ryan Kesler B 4.00 10.00
FARR Rickard Rakell C 3.00 8.00
FASG Shayne Gostisbehere C 4.00 10.00
FASR Sam Reinhart C 8.00 20.00
FAVR Victor Rask C 2.50 6.00
FAVT Vincent Trocheck C 4.00 10.00

2017-18 Artifacts Honoured Hopefuls Relics

HHDS Daniel Sedin 30.00 80.00
HHHL Henrik Lundqvist 80.00 150.00
HHHS Henrik Sedin 60.00 150.00
HHJJ Jaromir Jagr 150.00 250.00
HHJT Joe Thornton 40.00 100.00
HHMH Marian Hossa 80.00 150.00

2017-18 Artifacts Honoured Hopefuls Signatures

HHSCP Carey Price 100.00 250.00
HHS-RL Roberto Luongo 100.00 200.00

2017-18 Artifacts Honoured Members Relics

HMRBL Brian Leetch 60.00 150.00
HMRHA Dale Hawerchuk 40.00 100.00
HMRIL Igor Larionov 80.00 150.00
HMRJB Johnny Bower 80.00 150.00
HMRPL Pat LaFontaine 40.00 100.00

2017-18 Artifacts Honoured Members Signatures

HMSEB Ed Belfour 80.00 150.00
HMSGA Glenn Anderson 30.00 80.00
HMSMG Mike Gartner 25.00 60.00
HMSRV Rogie Vachon 40.00 100.00

2017-18 Artifacts Lord Stanley's Legacy Relics

LSLRBM Brad Marchand C 15.00 40.00
LSLRBM Vincent Damphousse B 6.00 15.00
LSLRDD Drew Doughty C 10.00 25.00
LSLREB Ed Belfour B 10.00 25.00
LSLRKL Kris Letang C 10.00 25.00
LSLRLM Lanny McDonald A 8.00 20.00
LSLRPR Patrick Kane B 15.00 40.00
LSLRRG Patrick Roy A 20.00 50.00
LSLRSY Ryan Getzlaf C 8.00 20.00
LSLRVD Steve Yzerman A 20.00 50.00

2017-18 Artifacts Materials Emerald

*VETS/65: 8X TO 20X BASIC INSERTS
*VETS/25: 2X TO 5X BASIC INSERTS
*RC/99: 2X TO 5X BASIC INSERTS
165 Evgeny Svechnikov 20.00 50.00
171 Brock Boeser 25.00 60.00
176 Josh Ho-Sang 20.00 50.00
179 Clayton Keller 20.00 50.00

2017-18 Artifacts Materials Purple

*RC/49: 3X TO 8X BASIC CARDS
171 Brock Boeser 50.00 125.00

2017-18 Artifacts Rookie Autograph Redemptions

III Alex DeBrincat 20.00 50.00
IV Kailer Yamamoto 20.00 50.00
V Will Butcher 20.00 50.00
VI Luke Kunin 20.00 50.00
VII Pierre-Luc Dubois 15.00 40.00
VIII Anders Bjork 15.00 40.00
IX Owen Tippett 12.00 30.00
X Logan Brown 12.00 30.00
XI Jesper Bratt 25.00 60.00
XII Haydn Fleury 12.00 30.00
XIII Filip Chlapik 10.00 25.00
XIV Denis Gurianov 10.00 25.00
XIX Victor Mete 15.00 40.00
XV Tage Thompson 80.00 200.00
XVI Calle Rosen 8.00 20.00
XVII Alex Tuch 12.00 30.00
XVIII Madison Bowey 15.00 40.00
XX Janne Kuokkanen 10.00 25.00

2017-18 Artifacts Rookie Autograph Relic Redemptions Silver

III Alex DeBrincat 15.00 40.00
IV Kailer Yamamoto 8.00 20.00
V Will Butcher 12.00 30.00
VI Luke Kunin 8.00 20.00
VII Pierre-Luc Dubois 8.00 20.00

2017-18 Artifacts Top 12 Rookie Signatures

RSAN Alexander Nylander B 8.00 20.00
RSBB Brock Boeser A 40.00 100.00
RSCW Colin White B 8.00 20.00
RSNS Nikita Scherbak B 8.00 20.00
RSTJ Tyson Jost A 20.00 50.00

2017-18 Artifacts Tundra Teammates Duo Materials

T2ANA R.Rakell/J.Gibson 4.00 10.00
T2CBJ A.Wennberg/S.Jones 4.00 10.00
T2CHI B.Seabrook/C.Crawford 5.00 12.00
T2DET D.Larkin/A.Athanasiou 5.00 12.00
T2FLA A.Ekblad/V.Trocheck 5.00 12.00
T2MIN E.Staal/N.Niederreiter 5.00 12.00
T2NJD T.Hall/C.Schneider 4.00 10.00
T2NYI J.Tavares/B.Nelson 6.00 15.00
T2OTT E.Karlsson/M.Hoffman 5.00 12.00
T2PHI S.Gostisbehere/B.Schenn 4.00 10.00
T2PIT K.Letang/P.Kessel 5.00 12.00
T2SAN B.Burns/L.Couture 5.00 12.00
T2TBL V.Hedman/N.Kucherov 8.00 20.00
T2WAS E.Kuznetsov/A.Burakovsky 5.00 12.00

2017-18 Artifacts Tundra Teammates Quad Materials

T4BOS Bergeron/Pastrnak Marchand/Spooner 12.00 30.00
T4BUF Eichel/Reinhart O'Reilly/Ristolainen 10.00 25.00
T4CAR Staal/Teravainen Lindholm/Rask 5.00 12.00
T4DAS Benn/Klingberg/Seguin/Spezza 6.00 15.00
T4MON Price/Weber Pacioretty/Galchenyuk 20.00 50.00
T4NAS Subban/Forsberg Johansen/Josi 8.00 20.00
T4STL Tarasenko/Pietrangelo Fabbri/Parayko 6.00 15.00
T4WIN Scheifele/Byfuglien Wheeler/Laine 8.00 20.00

2017-18 Artifacts Year One Rookie Sweaters

RSAM Auston Matthews A 30.00 80.00
RSCD Christian Dvorak C 6.00 15.00
RSIP Ivan Provorov C 6.00 15.00
RSJG Jake Guentzel A 25.00 60.00
RSJV Jimmy Vesey C 6.00 15.00
RSMM Mitch Marner B 12.00 30.00
RSPL Patrik Laine A 10.00 25.00
RSPZ Pavel Zacha C 6.00 15.00
RSWN William Nylander B 15.00 40.00
RSZW Zach Werenski B 12.00 30.00

2017-18 Artifacts Year One Rookie Sweaters Red

*RED/25: .5X TO 1.25X BASIC INSERTS
RSAM Auston Matthews 80.00 150.00

2018-19 Artifacts

*AQUA.VETS/45: 3X TO 8X BASIC CARDS
*AQUA.S.LEG/45: .8X TO 2X BASIC CARDS
*AQUA.RC/45: .6X TO 1.25X BASIC CARDS
*EMERALD.VETS/99: 2.5X TO 6X BASIC CARDS
*EMERALD.RC/99: .5X TO 1.25X BASIC CARDS
1 William Karlsson .40 1.00
2 P.K. Subban .40 1.00
3 Jonathan Quick .40 1.00
4 Evgeni Malkin .75 2.00
5 Braden Holtby .40 1.00
6 Jonathan Drouin .30 .75
7 Nico Hischier .60 1.50
8 Drew Doughty .40 1.00
9 Patrik Laine .40 1.00
10 Anthony Mantha .30 .75
11 Pekka Rinne .40 1.00
12 Nazem Kadri .40 1.00
13 Blake Wheeler .40 1.00
14 Reilly Smith .40 1.00
15 Jake Virtanen .30 .75
16 Mitch Marner .60 1.50
17 Sean Couturier .30 .75
18 Mark Stone .40 1.00
19 Chris Kreider .40 1.00
20 Dylan Larkin .40 1.00
21 Nolan Patrick .40 1.00
22 Max Pacioretty .40 1.00
23 Nino Niederreiter .20 .50
24 Ryan Johansen .30 .75
25 Charlie McAvoy .40 1.00
26 Patrick Marleau .40 1.00
27 Ben Bishop .30 .75
28 Matt Duchene .40 1.00
29 J.T. Miller .40 1.00
30 Shea Weber .40 1.00
31 Ryan Suter .30 .75
32 Phil Kessel .40 1.00
33 Jonathan Huberdeau .40 1.00
34 Brad Marchand .75 2.00
35 Leon Draisaitl 1.00 3.00
36 Jonathan Toews .60 1.50
37 Kyle Okposo .20 .50
38 Corey Crawford .30 .75
39 Jamie Benn .40 1.00
40 Sean Monahan .20 .50
41 Jonathan Marchessault .40 1.00
42 Mike Smith .30 .75
43 Nikolaj Ehlers .40 1.00
44 Evgeny Kuznetsov .40 1.00
45 Seth Jones .40 1.00
46 David Pastrnak .75 2.00
47 William Nylander .75 2.00
48 Jakub Voracek .30 .75
49 Roman Josi .40 1.00
50 Ondrej Palat .30 .75
51 Dustin Brown .40 1.00
52 Kevin Shattenkirk .20 .50
53 Devan Dubnyk .30 .75
54 Aleksander Barkov .60 1.50
55 Jesse Puljujarvi .40 1.00
56 Brandon Saad .30 .75
57 Matthew Tkachuk .75 2.00
58 Martin Jones .30 .75
59 Matt Murray .40 1.00
60 Jordan Eberle .40 1.00
61 Bo Horvat .40 1.00
62 Cory Schneider .40 1.00
63 T.J. Oshie .40 1.00
64 Joe Pavelski .40 1.00
65 Tyler Toffoli .40 1.00
66 John Klingberg .40 1.00
67 Andreas Athanasiou .30 .75
68 Gabriel Landeskog .40 1.00
69 Brayden Schenn .40 1.00
70 Jeff Skinner .40 1.00
71 Rasmus Ristolainen .20 .50
72 Brent Burns .40 1.00
73 Derek Stepan .20 .50
74 Corey Perry .60 1.50
75 Jaden Schwartz .40 1.00
76 Tuukka Rask .40 1.00
77 Cam Fowler .40 1.00
78 Vincent Trocheck .40 1.00
79 Ryan Nugent-Hopkins .40 1.00
80 Anders Lee .30 .75
81 Kyle Palmieri .30 .75
82 Tyson Barrie .20 .50
83 Jordan Staal .30 .75
84 Sam Reinhart .75 2.00
85 Alex Pietrangelo .30 .75
86 Victor Hedman .40 1.00
87 Mark Scheifele .60 1.50
88 Pierre-Luc Dubois .30 .75
89 Mikko Rantanen .75 2.00
90 Andrei Vasilevskiy .60 1.50
91 Brock Nelson .40 1.00
92 Teuvo Teravainen .40 1.00
93 Christian Dvorak .30 .75
94 Steven Stamkos .75 2.00
95 Artemi Panarin .75 2.00
96 Rickard Rakell .30 .75
97 Oliver Ekman-Larsson .40 1.00
98 Alexander Wennberg .20 .50
99 Mark Giordano .40 1.00
100 Nicklas Backstrom .40 1.00
101 Connor McDavid S 6.00 15.00
102 Anze Kopitar S 2.00 5.00
103 Erik Karlsson S 1.50 4.00
104 Filip Forsberg S 2.00 5.00
105 Sidney Crosby S 5.00 12.00
106 Mikael Granlund S 1.00 2.50
107 Marc-Andre Fleury S 2.50 6.00
108 Vladimir Tarasenko S 1.50 4.00
109 Johnny Gaudreau S 2.00 5.00
110 Brock Boeser S 1.50 4.00
111 Patrice Bergeron S 1.50 4.00
112 Mathew Barzal S 1.50 4.00
113 Clayton Keller S 1.50 4.00
114 Taylor Hall S 1.25 3.00
115 Jack Eichel S 2.00 5.00
116 Aaron Ekblad S 1.50 4.00
117 Sergei Bobrovsky S 2.00 5.00
118 Auston Matthews S 5.00 12.00
119 Patrick Kane S 2.50 6.00
120 Nathan MacKinnon S 5.00 12.00
121 Sebastian Aho S 2.00 5.00
122 Henrik Zetterberg S 1.50 4.00
123 Nikita Kucherov S 2.50 6.00
124 Claude Giroux S 1.25 3.00
125 Connor Hellebuyck S 2.50 6.00
126 Alexander Ovechkin S 5.00 12.00
127 Henrik Lundqvist S 3.00 8.00
128 Tyler Seguin S 1.50 4.00
129 Carey Price S 2.50 6.00
130 Logan Couture S 1.50 4.00
131 Wilf Paiement LEG 1.00 2.50
132 Willie O'Ree LEG 1.50 4.00
133 Pavel Bure LEG 1.25 3.00
134 Mario Lemieux LEG 5.00 12.00
135 Brian Propp LEG 1.00 2.50
136 Wendel Clark LEG 2.00 5.00
137 Wayne Gretzky LEG 8.00 20.00
138 Pat LaFontaine LEG 1.25 3.00
139 Chris Chelios LEG 1.25 3.00
140 Larry Robinson LEG 1.25 3.00
141 Ron Hextall LEG 1.25 3.00
142 Paul Coffey LEG 1.25 3.00
143 Charlie Simmer LEG .75 2.00
144 Gerry Cheevers LEG 1.25 3.00
145 Steve Yzerman LEG 3.00 8.00
146 Grant Fuhr LEG 2.00 5.00
147 Peter Forsberg LEG 2.50 6.00
148 Dominik Hasek LEG 2.00 5.00
149 Tony Amonte LEG 1.00 2.50
150 Shayne Corson LEG 1.00 2.50
151 Patrick Roy LEG 3.00 8.00
152 Mark Messier LEG 2.50 6.00
153 Doug Gilmour LEG 1.50 4.00
154 Martin Brodeur LEG 3.00 8.00
155 Rod Langway LEG 1.00 2.50
156 Brett Hull LEG 2.50 6.00
157 Teemu Selanne LEG 2.50 6.00
158 Dale Hawerchuk LEG 1.50 4.00
159 Jaromir Jagr LEG 4.00 10.00
160 Pavel Datsyuk LEG 2.00 5.00
161 Noah Juulsen RC 2.00 5.00
162 Ethan Bear RC 3.00 8.00
163 Dylan Sikura RC 2.50 6.00
164 Ryan Donato RC 3.00 8.00
165 Tomas Hyka RC 2.00 5.00
166 Dominic Turgeon RC 2.00 5.00
167 Eeli Tolvanen RC 4.00 10.00
168 Jordan Greenway RC 2.00 5.00
169 Dylan Gambrell RC 2.00 5.00
170 Henrik Borgstrom RC 3.00 8.00
171 Zach Aston-Reese RC 3.00 8.00
172 Michael Dal Colle RC 2.00 5.00
173 Travis Dermott RC 3.00 8.00
174 Anthony Cirelli RC 3.00 8.00
175 Sami Niku RC 1.50 4.00
176 Casey Mittelstadt RC 4.00 10.00
177 Lias Andersson RC 3.00 8.00
178 Adam Gaudette RC 3.00 8.00
179 Andreas Johnsson RC 2.50 6.00
180 Troy Terry RC 3.00 8.00
SP1 Rasmus Dahlin 25.00 60.00
SP2 Andrei Svechnikov 25.00 60.00
RED181 Maxime Comtois 3.00 8.00
RED182 Trevor Murphy 2.50 6.00
RED183 Urho Vaakanainen 6.00 15.00
RED184 Rasmus Dahlin 8.00 20.00
RED185 Juuso Valimaki 3.00 8.00
RED186 Andrei Svechnikov 8.00 20.00
RED187 Henri Jokiharju 2.50 6.00
RED188 Sheldon Dries 2.50 6.00
RED189 Eric Robinson 2.50 6.00
RED190 Miro Heiskanen 8.00 20.00
RED191 Michael Rasmussen 4.00 10.00
RED192 Evan Bouchard 8.00 20.00
RED193 Maxim Mamin 3.00 8.00
RED194 Jaret Anderson-Dolan 2.50 6.00
RED195 Nick Seeler 2.50 6.00
RED196 Jesperi Kotkaniemi 6.00 15.00
RED197 Eeli Tolvanen 6.00 15.00
RED198 Joey Anderson 3.00 8.00
RED199 Michael Dal Colle 3.00 8.00
RED200 Brett Howden 4.00 10.00
RED201 Brady Tkachuk 10.00 25.00
RED202 Oskar Lindblom 5.00 12.00
RED203 Juuso Riikola 2.50 6.00
RED204 Antti Suomela 2.50 6.00
RED205 Jordan Kyrou 6.00 15.00
RED206 Mathieu Joseph 4.00 10.00
RED207 Par Lindholm 3.00 8.00
RED208 Elias Pettersson 10.00 25.00
RED209 Zach Whitecloud 2.50 6.00
RED210 Ilya Samsonov 6.00 15.00
RED211 Kristian Vesalainen 4.00 10.00
RED212 Robert Thomas 6.00 15.00
RED213 Maxime Lajoie 5.00 12.00
RED214 Dominik Kahun 3.00 8.00
RED215 Warren Foegele 3.00 8.00
RED216 Dillon Dube 4.00 10.00
RED217 Isac Lundestrom 2.50 6.00
RED218 Dennis Cholowski 3.00 8.00
RED219 Drake Batherson 6.00 15.00
RED220 Sam Steel 3.00 8.00

2018-19 Artifacts Purple

*VETS/20: 6X TO 15X BASIC CARDS
*S.LEG/20: 2X TO 5X BASIC CARDS
*RC/20: 1.25X TO 3X BASIC CARDS
162 Ethan Bear 20.00 50.00
164 Ryan Donato 30.00 80.00
176 Casey Mittelstadt 15.00 40.00
178 Adam Gaudette 20.00 50.00

2018-19 Artifacts Ruby

*VETS/299: 2.5X TO 6X BASIC CARDS
*S.LEG/349: .75X TO 2X BASIC CARDS
*RC/399: 1.25X TO 3X BASIC CARDS
164 Ryan Donato 15.00 40.00

2018-19 Artifacts Arena Artifacts

FRDM Dickie Moore 40.00 100.00
FRFM Frank Mahovlich 40.00 100.00
FRGL Guy Lafleur 50.00 120.00
FRJB Jean Beliveau 40.00 100.00
FRLR Larry Robinson 40.00 100.00
FRMR Maurice Richard 80.00 200.00
FRPR Patrick Roy 100.00 250.00
FRSB Scotty Bowman 40.00 100.00
FRVD Vincent Damphousse 40.00 100.00

2018-19 Artifacts Aurum

A1 Mathew Barzal 2.00 5.00
A2 Connor McDavid 8.00 20.00
A3 John Klingberg 1.50 4.00
A4 Andrei Vasilevskiy 2.50 6.00
A5 Roman Josi 1.50 4.00
A6 Brock Boeser 2.00 5.00
A7 Jonathan Huberdeau 2.00 5.00
A8 Alexander Ovechkin 6.00 15.00
A9 Taylor Hall 1.50 4.00
A10 Jonathan Marchessault 2.00 5.00
A11 Anze Kopitar 2.50 6.00
A12 William Karlsson 2.00 5.00
A13 Johnny Gaudreau 2.50 6.00
A14 Clayton Keller 2.00 5.00
A15 Jack Eichel 2.50 6.00
A16 Vladimir Tarasenko 2.00 5.00
A17 Dylan Larkin 2.00 5.00
A18 Drew Doughty 2.00 5.00
A19 Jonathan Toews 2.50 6.00
A20 Sebastian Aho 2.50 6.00
A21 Sergei Bobrovsky 2.50 6.00
A22 Eric Staal 1.50 4.00
A23 Nico Hischier 2.50 6.00
A24 Pekka Rinne 1.50 4.00
A25 Ryan Getzlaf 1.50 4.00
A26 Blake Wheeler 1.50 4.00
A27 Evgeny Kuznetsov 2.00 5.00
A28 Claude Giroux 1.50 4.00
A29 Nathan MacKinnon 6.00 15.00
A30 Henrik Lundqvist 4.00 10.00
A31 Carey Price 3.00 8.00
A32 Jakub Voracek 1.25 3.00
A33 Connor Hellebuyck 3.00 8.00
A34 Auston Matthews 6.00 15.00
A35 Erik Karlsson 2.00 5.00
A36 Steven Stamkos 3.00 8.00
A37 David Pastrnak 4.00 10.00
A38 Patrick Kane 3.00 8.00
A39 Logan Couture 2.00 5.00
A40 Sidney Crosby 6.00 15.00
A41 John Tavares SP 30.00 80.00
A42 Auston Matthews SP 20.00 50.00
A43 Sidney Crosby SP 20.00 50.00
A44 Connor McDavid SP 80.00 150.00
A45 Lias Andersson SP 40.00 100.00
A46 Casey Mittelstadt SP 40.00 100.00
A47 Ryan Donato SP 30.00 80.00
A48 Adam Gaudette SP 15.00 40.00
A49 Andrei Svechnikov Bounty Exclusive 20.00 50.00
A50 Rasmus Dahlin Bounty Exclusive 20.00 50.00

2018-19 Artifacts Autofacts

AAD Anthony Duclair B 6.00 15.00
ABR Bobby Ryan B 6.00 15.00
ACH Connor Hellebuyck A 15.00 40.00
ACS Chandler Stephenson D 6.00 15.00
ADH Danton Heinen C 6.00 15.00
ADP Derrick Pouliot C 5.00 12.00
AJA Josh Anderson B 6.00 15.00
AJM Jared McCann C 6.00 15.00
AJW Jordan Weal C 5.00 12.00
AMG Mark Giordano B 8.00 20.00
AMR Mike Reilly D 5.00 12.00
ANB Nick Bjugstad B 5.00 12.00
ANC Nick Cousins C 5.00 12.00
AOK Oscar Klefbom D 6.00 15.00
AOP Ondrej Palat B 6.00 15.00
APB Pavel Buchnevich B 6.00 15.00
APE Pierre-Edouard Bellemare C 5.00 12.00
APM Petr Mrazek B 8.00 20.00
ARF Radek Faksa C 6.00 15.00
ARM Ryan Murray B 6.00 15.00
ARS Ryan Spooner C 6.00 15.00
ASN Stefan Noesen D 5.00 12.00
ATL Taylor Leier D 6.00 15.00
AVN Vladislav Namestnikov C 5.00 12.00

2018-19 Artifacts Autograph Materials Silver

102 Anze Kopitar/45 12.00 30.00
106 Mikael Granlund/45 6.00 15.00
107 Marc-Andre Fleury/45 15.00 40.00
108 Vladimir Tarasenko/45 10.00 25.00
109 Johnny Gaudreau/45 12.00 30.00
110 Brock Boeser/45 10.00 25.00
112 Mathew Barzal/45 10.00 25.00
113 Clayton Keller/45 10.00 25.00
114 Taylor Hall/45 8.00 20.00
116 Aaron Ekblad/45 10.00 25.00
117 Sergei Bobrovsky/45 12.00 30.00
121 Sebastian Aho/45 12.00 30.00
122 Henrik Zetterberg/45 10.00 25.00
123 Nikita Kucherov/45 15.00 40.00
125 Connor Hellebuyck/45 15.00 40.00
127 Henrik Lundqvist/45 20.00 50.00
130 Logan Couture/45 10.00 25.00
131 Wilf Paiement/45 6.00 15.00
135 Brian Propp/45 6.00 15.00
139 Chris Chelios/45 8.00 20.00
140 Larry Robinson/45 8.00 20.00
143 Charlie Simmer/45 5.00 12.00
144 Gerry Cheevers/45 8.00 20.00
146 Grant Fuhr/45 12.00 30.00
148 Dominik Hasek/45 12.00 30.00
149 Tony Amonte/45 6.00 15.00
150 Shayne Corson/45 6.00 15.00
152 Mark Messier/45 15.00 40.00
155 Rod Langway/45 6.00 15.00
156 Brett Hull/45 15.00 40.00
157 Teemu Selanne/45 15.00 40.00
158 Dale Hawerchuk/45 10.00 25.00
160 Pavel Datsyuk/45 12.00 30.00
161 Noah Juulsen/99 8.00 20.00
162 Ethan Bear/99 12.00 30.00
163 Dylan Sikura/99 10.00 25.00
164 Ryan Donato/99 12.00 30.00
166 Dominic Turgeon/99 8.00 20.00
167 Eeli Tolvanen/99 15.00 40.00
168 Jordan Greenway/99 8.00 20.00
169 Dylan Gambrell/99 8.00 20.00
170 Henrik Borgstrom/99 12.00 30.00
171 Zach Aston-Reese/99 12.00 30.00
172 Michael Dal Colle/99 8.00 20.00
173 Travis Dermott/99 12.00 30.00
174 Anthony Cirelli/99 12.00 30.00
175 Sami Niku/99 6.00 15.00
176 Casey Mittelstadt/99 15.00 40.00
178 Adam Gaudette/99 20.00 50.00

2018-19 Artifacts Divisional Artifacts

DAAB Aleksander Barkov C 4.00 10.00
DAAM Auston Matthews A 10.00 25.00
DAAO Alexander Ovechkin A 10.00 25.00
DAAP Artemi Panarin B 5.00 12.00
DABO Brock Boeser B 8.00 20.00
DABW Blake Wheeler B 2.50 6.00
DACC Corey Crawford C 2.00 5.00
DACG Claude Giroux B 2.50 6.00
DACK Clayton Keller C 3.00 8.00
DACM Connor McDavid A 15.00 40.00
DADD Drew Doughty A 3.00 8.00
DAEK Erik Karlsson A 3.00 8.00
DAEM Evgeni Malkin A 5.00 12.00
DAHL Henrik Lundqvist B 6.00 15.00
DAJB Jamie Benn B 2.50 6.00
DAJD Jonathan Drouin C 2.00 5.00
DAJM Jonathan Marchessault B 8.00 20.00
DAMA Anthony Mantha C 2.00 5.00
DAMB Mathew Barzal A 3.00 8.00
DAMR Mikko Rantanen C 6.00 15.00
DANK Nikita Kucherov B 5.00 12.00
DANN Nino Niederreiter C 1.50 4.00
DAPS P.K. Subban B 3.00 8.00
DARR Rickard Rakell C 2.00 5.00
DASC Sidney Crosby A 10.00 25.00
DASM Sean Monahan C 1.50 4.00
DASS Steven Stamkos A 5.00 12.00
DATH Taylor Hall A 2.50 6.00
DATR Tuukka Rask C 3.00 8.00
DAVT Vladimir Tarasenko B 3.00 8.00

2018-19 Artifacts Esteemed Endorsements

EEAD Alex Delvecchio 15.00 40.00
EEBB Bill Barber 15.00 40.00
EEBO Bobby Orr 150.00 250.00
EEJK Jari Kurri 15.00 40.00
EELR Larry Robinson 15.00 40.00
EEMB Martin Brodeur 40.00 100.00
EEMD Marcel Dionne 20.00 50.00
EEMM Mark Messier 30.00 80.00
EESB Scotty Bowman 15.00 40.00
EEWO Willie O'Ree 20.00 50.00

2018-19 Artifacts Honoured Hopefuls Relics

HHAK Anze Kopitar 30.00 80.00
HHAO Alexander Ovechkin 80.00 200.00
HHDD Drew Doughty 50.00 125.00
HHEM Evgeni Malkin 40.00 100.00
HHNB Nicklas Backstrom 20.00 50.00
HHPB Patrice Bergeron 60.00 150.00
HHPM Patrick Marleau 20.00 50.00
HHRG Ryan Getzlaf 20.00 50.00
HHRL Roberto Luongo 50.00 125.00
HHSS Steven Stamkos 40.00 100.00
HHZC Zdeno Chara 60.00 150.00

2018-19 Artifacts Honoured Hopefuls Signatures

HHSMF Marc-Andre Fleury 80.00 200.00
HHSSC Sidney Crosby 200.00 500.00
HHSSS Steven Stamkos 80.00 200.00

2018-19 Artifacts Lord Stanley's Legacy Relics

LSLRAM Alec Martinez C 2.00 5.00
LSLRBS Brandon Saad C 2.00 5.00
LSLRDB Dustin Brown C 2.50 6.00
LSLRDK David Krejci B 2.50 6.00
LSLREK Evgeny Kuznetsov C 3.00 8.00
LSLRGL Guy Lafleur A 3.00 8.00
LSLRMM Mark Messier A 5.00 12.00
LSLRMU Matt Murray B 2.50 6.00
LSLRPK Phil Kessel B 2.50 6.00
LSLRPS Patrick Sharp A 2.00 5.00

2018-19 Artifacts Lord Stanley's Legacy Signatures

LSLSAD Alex Delvecchio C 6.00 15.00
LSLSAO Alexander Ovechkin A 25.00 60.00
LSLSBH Brett Hull A 12.00 30.00
LSLSDK Duncan Keith B 5.00 12.00
LSLSGL Guy Lafleur B 8.00 20.00
LSLSJC Jeff Carter C 5.00 12.00
LSLSMB Martin Brodeur A 15.00 40.00
LSLSPD Pavel Datsyuk B 10.00 25.00
LSLSPR Patrick Roy A 15.00 40.00
LSLSTB Tom Barrasso C 6.00 15.00

2018-19 Artifacts Materials Silver

*EMERALD/25-99: .8X TO 2X BASIC INSERTS
*PURPLE/49: 1.5X TO 4X BASIC INSERTS
1 William Karlsson 4.00 10.00
2 P.K. Subban 4.00 10.00
3 Jonathan Quick 4.00 10.00
4 Evgeni Malkin 6.00 15.00
5 Braden Holtby 4.00 10.00
6 Jonathan Drouin 2.50 6.00
7 Nico Hischier 5.00 12.00
8 Drew Doughty 4.00 10.00
9 Patrik Laine 4.00 10.00
10 Anthony Mantha 2.50 6.00
11 Pekka Rinne 3.00 8.00
12 Nazem Kadri 4.00 10.00
13 Blake Wheeler 3.00 8.00
15 Jake Virtanen 2.50 6.00
16 Mitch Marner 5.00 12.00
17 Sean Couturier 2.50 6.00
18 Mark Stone 4.00 10.00
19 Chris Kreider 4.00 10.00
20 Dylan Larkin 4.00 10.00
21 Nolan Patrick 3.00 8.00
22 Max Pacioretty 3.00 8.00
23 Nino Niederreiter 2.00 5.00
24 Ryan Johansen 2.50 6.00
25 Charlie McAvoy 4.00 10.00
26 Patrick Marleau 3.00 8.00
27 Ben Bishop 2.50 6.00
28 Matt Duchene 3.00 8.00
29 J.T. Miller 4.00 10.00
30 Shea Weber 3.00 8.00
31 Ryan Suter 2.50 6.00
32 Phil Kessel 3.00 8.00
33 Jonathan Huberdeau 4.00 10.00
34 Brad Marchand 6.00 15.00
35 Leon Draisaitl 10.00 25.00
36 Jonathan Toews 5.00 12.00
37 Kyle Okposo 2.00 5.00
38 Corey Crawford 2.50 6.00
39 Jamie Benn 3.00 8.00
40 Sean Monahan 2.00 5.00
41 Jonathan Marchessault 4.00 10.00
42 Mike Smith 2.50 6.00
43 Nikolaj Ehlers 3.00 8.00
44 Evgeny Kuznetsov 4.00 10.00
45 Seth Jones 3.00 8.00
46 David Pastrnak 8.00 20.00
47 William Nylander 6.00 15.00
48 Jakub Voracek 2.50 6.00
49 Roman Josi 3.00 8.00
50 Ondrej Palat 2.50 6.00
51 Dustin Brown 3.00 8.00
52 Kevin Shattenkirk 2.00 5.00
53 Devan Dubnyk 2.50 6.00
54 Aleksander Barkov 5.00 12.00
55 Jesse Puljujarvi 3.00 8.00
56 Brandon Saad 2.50 6.00
57 Matthew Tkachuk 6.00 15.00
58 Martin Jones 2.50 6.00
59 Matt Murray 3.00 8.00
60 Jordan Eberle 3.00 8.00
61 Bo Horvat 4.00 10.00
62 Cory Schneider 3.00 8.00
63 T.J. Oshie 3.00 8.00
64 Joe Pavelski 4.00 10.00
65 Tyler Toffoli 3.00 8.00
66 John Klingberg 3.00 8.00
67 Andreas Athanasiou 2.50 6.00
68 Gabriel Landeskog 4.00 10.00
69 Brayden Schenn 3.00 8.00
70 Jeff Skinner 4.00 10.00
71 Rasmus Ristolainen 2.00 5.00
72 Brent Burns 3.00 8.00
73 Derek Stepan 2.00 5.00
74 Corey Perry 5.00 12.00
75 Jaden Schwartz 4.00 10.00
76 Tuukka Rask 4.00 10.00
77 Cam Fowler 3.00 8.00
78 Vincent Trocheck 3.00 8.00
79 Ryan Nugent-Hopkins 4.00 10.00
80 Anders Lee 2.50 6.00
81 Kyle Palmieri 2.50 6.00
82 Tyson Barrie 2.00 5.00
83 Jordan Staal 2.50 6.00
84 Sam Reinhart 6.00 15.00
85 Alex Pietrangelo 2.50 6.00
86 Victor Hedman 4.00 10.00
87 Mark Scheifele 5.00 12.00
88 Pierre-Luc Dubois 2.50 6.00
89 Mikko Rantanen 8.00 20.00
90 Andrei Vasilevskiy 5.00 12.00
91 Brock Nelson 3.00 8.00
92 Teuvo Teravainen 3.00 8.00
93 Christian Dvorak 2.50 6.00
94 Steven Stamkos 6.00 15.00
95 Artemi Panarin 6.00 15.00
96 Rickard Rakell 2.50 6.00
97 Oliver Ekman-Larsson 3.00 8.00
98 Alexander Wennberg 2.00 5.00
99 Mark Giordano 3.00 8.00
100 Nicklas Backstrom 3.00 8.00
101 Connor McDavid 15.00 40.00
102 Anze Kopitar 5.00 12.00
103 Erik Karlsson 4.00 10.00
104 Filip Forsberg 5.00 12.00
105 Sidney Crosby 12.00 30.00
106 Mikael Granlund 2.50 6.00
107 Marc-Andre Fleury 6.00 15.00
108 Vladimir Tarasenko 4.00 10.00
109 Johnny Gaudreau 5.00 12.00
110 Brock Boeser 4.00 10.00
111 Patrice Bergeron 4.00 10.00
112 Mathew Barzal 4.00 10.00
113 Clayton Keller 4.00 10.00
114 Taylor Hall 3.00 8.00
115 Jack Eichel 5.00 12.00
116 Aaron Ekblad 4.00 10.00
117 Sergei Bobrovsky 5.00 12.00
118 Auston Matthews 12.00 30.00
119 Patrick Kane 6.00 15.00
120 Nathan MacKinnon 12.00 30.00
121 Sebastian Aho 5.00 12.00
122 Henrik Zetterberg 4.00 10.00
123 Nikita Kucherov 6.00 15.00
124 Claude Giroux 3.00 8.00
125 Connor Hellebuyck 6.00 15.00
126 Alexander Ovechkin 12.00 30.00
127 Henrik Lundqvist 8.00 20.00
128 Tyler Seguin 4.00 10.00
129 Carey Price 6.00 15.00
130 Logan Couture 4.00 10.00
131 Wilf Paiement 2.50 6.00
133 Pavel Bure 3.00 8.00
135 Brian Propp 2.50 6.00
137 Wayne Gretzky 20.00 50.00
138 Pat LaFontaine 3.00 8.00
139 Chris Chelios 3.00 8.00
140 Larry Robinson 3.00 8.00
142 Paul Coffey 3.00 8.00
143 Charlie Simmer 2.00 5.00
144 Gerry Cheevers 3.00 8.00
145 Steve Yzerman 8.00 20.00
146 Grant Fuhr 5.00 12.00
147 Peter Forsberg 6.00 15.00
148 Dominik Hasek 5.00 12.00
149 Tony Amonte 2.50 6.00
150 Shayne Corson 2.50 6.00
151 Patrick Roy 8.00 20.00
152 Mark Messier 6.00 15.00
154 Martin Brodeur 8.00 20.00
155 Rod Langway 2.50 6.00
156 Brett Hull 6.00 15.00
157 Teemu Selanne 6.00 15.00
160 Pavel Datsyuk 5.00 12.00
161 Noah Juulsen 3.00 8.00
162 Ethan Bear 5.00 12.00
163 Dylan Sikura 4.00 10.00
164 Ryan Donato 5.00 12.00
166 Dominic Turgeon 3.00 8.00
167 Eeli Tolvanen 6.00 15.00
168 Jordan Greenway 3.00 8.00
169 Dylan Gambrell 3.00 8.00
170 Henrik Borgstrom 5.00 12.00
171 Zach Aston-Reese 5.00 12.00
172 Michael Dal Colle 3.00 8.00
173 Travis Dermott 5.00 12.00
174 Anthony Cirelli 5.00 12.00
175 Sami Niku 2.50 6.00
176 Casey Mittelstadt 6.00 15.00
178 Adam Gaudette 5.00 12.00
180 Troy Terry 5.00 12.00

2018-19 Artifacts Rookie Autograph Redemptions

I Elias Pettersson 30.00 80.00
II Andrei Svechnikov 25.00 60.00
III Jesperi Kotkaniemi 20.00 50.00
IV Brady Tkachuk 30.00 80.00
V Evan Bouchard 25.00 60.00
VI Miro Heiskanen 25.00 60.00
VII Drake Batherson 20.00 50.00
VIII Robert Thomas 20.00 50.00
IX Ilya Samsonov 20.00 50.00
X Michael Rasmussen 12.00 30.00
XI Maxime Comtois 10.00 25.00
XII Henri Jokiharju 8.00 20.00
XIII Brett Howden 12.00 30.00
XIV Juuso Valimaki 10.00 25.00
XV Kristian Vesalainen 12.00 30.00
XVI Maxime Lajoie 15.00 40.00

XVII Jordan Kyrou 20.00 50.00
XVIII Sam Steel 10.00 25.00

2018-19 Artifacts Threads of Time

TTBH Brett Hull A 6.00 15.00
TTDG Doug Gilmour A 4.00 10.00
TTDH Dominik Hasek A 5.00 12.00
TTEB Ed Belfour B 3.00 8.00
TTEK Evander Kane C 3.00 8.00
TTJC Jeff Carter C 2.50 6.00
TTJK Jari Kurri A 3.00 8.00
TTJS Jordan Staal C 2.50 6.00
TTJT Joe Thornton B 5.00 12.00
TTKS Kevin Shattenkirk C 2.00 5.00
TTMB Martin Brodeur A 8.00 20.00
TTMG Marian Gaborik C 3.00 8.00
TTPF Peter Forsberg B 6.00 15.00
TTTA Tony Amonte C 2.50 6.00

2018-19 Artifacts Threads of Time Premium

*PREMIUM/25: 1.25X TO 3X BASIC INSERTS
TTWG Wayne Gretzky 200.00 300.00

2018-19 Artifacts Top 12 Rookies Signatures

RSAG Adam Gaudette 12.00 30.00
RSAS Andrei Svechnikov B 20.00 50.00
RSBT Brady Tkachuk B 25.00 60.00
RSCH Carter Hart B 15.00 40.00
RSEP Elias Pettersson A 25.00 60.00
RSET Eeli Tolvanen 15.00 40.00
RSJG Jordan Greenway 8.00 20.00
RSJK Jesperi Kotkaniemi B 15.00 40.00
RSMH Miro Heiskanen B 20.00 50.00
RSMI Casey Mittelstadt 15.00 40.00
RSRD Ryan Donato 12.00 30.00

2018-19 Artifacts Tundra Teammates Duo Materials

T2BOS D.Krejci/T.Rask 5.00 12.00
T2BUF J.Eichel/R.O'Reilly 6.00 15.00
T2CAL J.Gaudreau/S.Monahan 6.00 15.00
T2CAR S.Aho/J.Skinner 6.00 15.00
T2COL N.MacKinnon/M.Rantanen 15.00 40.00
T2DAL T.Seguin/A.Radulov 5.00 12.00
T2MON J.Drouin/C.Price 8.00 20.00
T2NAS P.Subban/F.Forsberg 6.00 15.00
T2NJD K.Palmieri/M.Johansson 3.00 8.00
T2NYR H.Lundqvist/C.Kreider 10.00 25.00
T2STL V.Tarasenko/J.Schwartz 5.00 12.00
T2TOR P.Marleau/M.Marner 4.00 10.00
T2VAN B.Horvat/B.Boeser 5.00 12.00
T2VEG J.Marchessault/M.Fleury 8.00 20.00
T2WIN M.Scheifele/B.Wheeler 6.00 15.00

2018-19 Artifacts Year One Rookie Sweaters

*PREMIUM/25: 1.25X TO 3X BASIC INSERTS
RSBB Brock Boeser A 4.00 10.00
RSCK Clayton Keller A 4.00 10.00
RSCM Charlie McAvoy A 4.00 10.00
RSJH Josh Ho-Sang C 2.50 6.00
RSJP Jesse Puljujarvi C 3.00 8.00
RSMB Mathew Barzal C 4.00 10.00
RSNH Nico Hischier B 5.00 12.00
RSNP Nolan Patrick B 3.00 8.00
RSPL Pierre-Luc Dubois B 2.50 6.00
RSTJ Tyson Jost C 2.50 6.00

2019-20 Artifacts

1 Mitch Marner .60 1.50
2 Ryan O'Reilly .40 1.00
3 Nolan Patrick .40 1.00
4 Thomas Chabot .40 1.00
5 Mark Giordano .40 1.00
6 Ben Bishop .30 .75
7 Filip Forsberg .60 1.50
8 Victor Rask .20 .50
9 Tomas Hertl .40 1.00
10 Ryan Nugent-Hopkins .40 1.00
11 Andrew Ladd .20 .50
12 Adam Henrique .30 .75
13 Matthew Tkachuk .75 2.00
14 Dougie Hamilton .30 .75
15 Andrei Vasilevskiy .60 1.50
16 Alex Kerfoot .30 .75
17 Pierre-Luc Dubois .30 .75
18 Anthony Mantha .30 .75
19 Patrice Bergeron .40 1.00
20 Alex Galchenyuk .20 .50
21 Aleksander Barkov .60 1.50
22 Darnell Nurse .30 .75
23 Mika Zibanejad .40 1.00
24 Kyle Palmieri .30 .75
25 Rasmus Dahlin .40 1.00
26 Ilya Kovalchuk .40 1.00
27 Alex DeBrincat .40 1.00
28 Bo Horvat .40 1.00
29 Mark Stone .40 1.00
30 Tom Wilson .40 1.00
31 Nikolaj Ehlers .40 1.00
32 Claude Giroux .40 1.00
33 Frederik Andersen .40 1.00
34 Evander Kane .40 1.00
35 Brayden Schenn .40 1.00
36 Sean Monahan .20 .50
37 Craig Anderson .30 .75
38 Jake Guentzel .60 1.50
39 Alexander Radulov .40 1.00
40 Gabriel Landeskog .40 1.00
41 Ryan Strome .40 1.00
42 Alex Tuch .40 1.00
43 Nick Leddy .20 .50
44 Duncan Keith .30 .75
45 Jonathan Drouin .30 .75
46 Casey Mittelstadt .40 1.00
47 Kyle Turris .30 .75
48 Jason Zucker .40 1.00
49 Nino Niederreiter .20 .50
50 Evgeny Kuznetsov .40 1.00
51 Torey Krug .30 .75
52 Elias Lindholm .40 1.00
53 Jakob Silfverberg .20 .50
54 Teuvo Teravainen .40 1.00
55 John Carlson .40 1.00
56 Jesper Bratt .40 1.00
57 Jonathan Huberdeau .40 1.00
58 Jaden Schwartz .40 1.00
59 Andreas Athanasiou .30 .75
60 Patrik Laine .40 1.00
61 Loui Eriksson .20 .50
62 Ryan McDonagh .20 .50
63 Jeff Skinner .40 1.00
64 Derek Stepan .20 .50
65 William Karlsson .40 1.00
66 Kris Letang .40 1.00
67 Sean Couturier .30 .75
68 Andrei Svechnikov .40 1.00
69 Nicklas Backstrom .40 1.00
70 Pekka Rinne .40 1.00
71 Mikkel Boedker .20 .50
72 Mike Hoffman .20 .50
73 Tomas Tatar .20 .50
74 Tyler Bozak .20 .50
75 Max Pacioretty .40 1.00
76 Brayden Point .40 1.00
77 John Gibson .40 1.00
78 Tyler Seguin .40 1.00
79 Tyson Jost .30 .75
80 Drew Doughty .40 1.00
81 Kyle Okposo .20 .50
82 Taylor Hall .40 1.00
83 Jimmy Vesey .30 .75
84 Patric Hornqvist .20 .50
85 Brendan Gallagher .40 1.00
86 Jake DeBrusk .40 1.00
87 Artem Anisimov .20 .50
88 William Nylander .75 2.00
89 Logan Couture .40 1.00
90 Seth Jones .40 1.00
91 Devan Dubnyk .30 .75
92 Vincent Hinostroza .20 .50
93 Blake Wheeler .40 1.00
94 Frans Nielsen .20 .50
95 Milan Lucic .30 .75
96 Josh Bailey .30 .75
97 James Neal .20 .50
98 Tanner Pearson .40 1.00
99 Tyler Johnson .20 .50
100 Roman Josi .40 1.00
101 Connor McDavid S 6.00 15.00
102 Anze Kopitar S 2.00 5.00
103 Patrick Kane S 2.50 6.00
104 Nikita Kucherov S 2.50 6.00
105 John Tavares S 2.00 5.00
106 Brock Boeser S 1.50 4.00
107 Marc-Andre Fleury S 2.50 6.00
108 David Pastrnak S 3.00 8.00
109 Mark Scheifele S 2.00 5.00
110 Sidney Crosby S 5.00 12.00
111 Miro Heiskanen S 1.50 4.00
112 Mikko Rantanen S 3.00 8.00
113 Ryan Johansen S 1.00 2.50
114 Sebastian Aho S 2.00 5.00
115 Johnny Gaudreau S 2.00 5.00
116 Brad Marchand S 2.50 6.00
117 Clayton Keller S 1.50 4.00
118 Ryan Getzlaf S 1.25 3.00
119 Jack Eichel S 2.00 5.00
120 Carey Price S 2.50 6.00
121 Dylan Larkin S 1.50 4.00
122 Roberto Luongo S 2.00 5.00
123 Zach Parise S 1.25 3.00
124 Cam Atkinson S 1.25 3.00
125 Nico Hischier S 2.00 5.00
126 Mathew Barzal S 1.50 4.00
127 Brent Burns S 1.25 3.00
128 Bobby Ryan S 1.00 2.50
129 Carter Hart S 1.25 3.00
130 Henrik Lundqvist S 3.00 8.00
131 Vladimir Tarasenko S 1.50 4.00
132 Jonathan Toews S 2.00 5.00
133 Nathan MacKinnon S 5.00 12.00
134 Jamie Benn S 1.25 3.00
135 Evgeni Malkin S 2.50 6.00
136 Connor Hellebuyck S 2.50 6.00
137 Jordan Binnington S 2.00 5.00
138 Steven Stamkos S 2.50 6.00
139 Max Domi S 1.25 3.00
140 Auston Matthews S 5.00 12.00
141 Jonathan Marchessault S 1.50 4.00
142 Jonathan Quick S 1.50 4.00
143 Elias Pettersson S 2.00 5.00
144 Leon Draisaitl S 4.00 10.00
145 Alexander Ovechkin S 5.00 12.00
146 Guy Lafleur LEG 1.50 4.00
147 Nicklas Lidstrom LEG 1.25 3.00
148 Ray Bourque LEG 2.00 5.00
149 Mike Liut LEG .75 2.00
150 Joe Sakic LEG 2.50 6.00
151 Yvan Cournoyer LEG 1.25 3.00
152 Bernie Nicholls LEG 1.00 2.50
153 Kirk McLean LEG 1.00 2.50
154 Henrik Sedin LEG 1.50 4.00
155 Mike Modano LEG 2.00 5.00
156 Mario Lemieux LEG 5.00 12.00
157 Bill Ranford LEG 1.00 2.50
158 Doug Gilmour LEG 1.50 4.00
159 Curtis Joseph LEG 1.50 4.00
160 Wayne Gretzky LEG 8.00 20.00
161 Cale Makar RC 12.00 30.00
162 Rudolfs Balcers RC 2.50 6.00
163 Philippe Myers RC 2.00 5.00
164 Max Jones RC 2.50 6.00
165 Filip Zadina RC 4.00 10.00
166 Dante Fabbro RC 2.50 6.00
167 Nathan Bastian RC 2.50 6.00
168 Trent Frederic RC 2.50 6.00
169 Erik Brannstrom RC 2.50 6.00
170 Ryan Poehling RC 4.00 10.00
171 Alexandre Texier RC 2.50 6.00
172 Zack MacEwen RC 2.00 5.00
173 Libor Hajek RC 2.00 5.00
174 Taro Hirose RC 2.50 6.00
175 Vitaly Abramov RC 2.50 6.00
176 Carl Grundstrom RC 2.50 6.00
177 Brady Keeper RC 2.50 6.00
178 Zach Senyshyn RC 2.50 6.00
179 Teddy Blueger RC 2.50 6.00
180 Quinn Hughes RC 12.00 30.00
RED181 Kevin Boyle RC 2.50 6.00
RED182 Barrett Hayton RC 5.00 12.00
RED183 Connor Clifton RC 2.50 6.00
RED184 Victor Olofsson RC 5.00 12.00
RED185 Dillon Dube RC 1.50 4.00
RED186 Julien Gauthier RC 2.50 6.00
RED187 Kirby Dach RC 5.00 12.00
RED188 Conor Timmins RC 2.50 6.00
RED189 Emil Bemstrom RC 2.50 6.00
RED190 Rhett Gardner RC 2.00 5.00
RED191 Givani Smith RC 2.00 5.00
RED192 Joakim Nygard RC 2.00 5.00
RED193 Riley Stillman RC 2.50 6.00
RED194 Tobias Bjornfot RC 2.50 6.00
RED195 Gerald Mayhew RC 2.00 5.00
RED196 Nick Suzuki RC 10.00 25.00
RED197 Rem Pitlick RC 2.50 6.00
RED198 Jack Hughes RC 12.00 30.00
RED199 Noah Dobson RC 6.00 15.00
RED200 Kaapo Kakko RC 4.00 10.00
RED201 Scott Sabourin RC 2.00 5.00
RED202 Joel Farabee RC 4.00 10.00
RED203 Sam Lafferty RC 2.00 5.00
RED204 Mario Ferraro RC 2.00 5.00
RED205 Mackenzie MacEachern RC 2.50 6.00
RED206 Carter Verhaeghe RC 4.00 10.00
RED207 Ilya Mikheyev RC 4.00 10.00
RED208 Guillaume Brisebois RC 2.50 6.00
RED209 Cody Glass RC 4.00 10.00
RED210 Martin Fehervary RC 2.00 5.00
RED211 Ville Heinola RC 3.00 8.00
RED212 Adam Fox RC 6.00 15.00
RED213 Cale Fleury RC 3.00 8.00
RED214 Nicolas Hague RC 2.50 6.00
RED215 Dominik Kubalik RC 5.00 12.00
RED216 Jesper Boqvist RC 2.00 5.00
RED217 Oliver Wahlstrom RC 4.00 10.00
RED218 Rasmus Sandin RC 4.00 10.00
RED219 Adam Boqvist RC 2.50 6.00
RED220 Nikita Gusev RC 4.00 10.00

2019-20 Artifacts Aqua

*AQUA.VETS/45: 3X TO 8X BASIC
*AQUA.S.LEG/45: 1.5X TO 4X BASIC
*AQUA.RC/45: 1X TO 2.5X BASIC

2019-20 Artifacts Copper

*COPPER.VETS/299: 1.5X TO 4X BASIC
*COPPER.S.LEG/299: .5X TO 1.25X BASIC
*COPPER.RC/299: .5X TO 1.25X BASIC

2019-20 Artifacts Emerald

*EMERALD.VETS/99: 3X TO 8X BASIC
*EMERALD.S.LEG/99: .75X TO 2X BASIC
*EMERALD.RC/99: .75X TO 2X BASIC

2019-20 Artifacts Pink

*PINK.VETS/85: 3X TO 8X BASIC CARDS

2019-20 Artifacts Purple

*PURPLE.VETS/20: 6X TO 15X BASIC
*PURPLE.S.LEG/20: 2X TO 5X BASIC
*PURPLE.RC/20: 1.5X TO 4X BASIC

2019-20 Artifacts Ruby

*RUBY.S.LEG/399: .5X TO 1.25X BASIC
*RUBY.RC/399: .5X TO 1.25X BASIC

2019-20 Artifacts Admirable Impressions Autographs

AIBB Brent Burns 40.00 100.00
AIBO Brock Boeser 50.00 125.00
AIJE Jack Eichel 60.00 150.00
AIJS Joe Sakic 80.00 200.00
AIJT John Tavares 60.00 150.00
AIMF Marc-Andre Fleury 80.00 200.00
AIMM Mike Modano 60.00 150.00
AISC Sidney Crosby 150.00 400.00
AISS Steven Stamkos 80.00 200.00
AIWG Wayne Gretzky 500.00 1200.00

2019-20 Artifacts Arena Artifacts

CSBH Bobby Hull 40.00 100.00
CSCC Chris Chelios 15.00 40.00
CSDS Denis Savard 15.00 40.00
CSEB Ed Belfour 15.00 40.00
CSGH Glenn Hall 15.00 40.00
CSJR Jeremy Roenick 25.00 60.00
CSPP Pierre Pilote 15.00 40.00
CSSM Stan Mikita 15.00 40.00
CSTE Tony Esposito 15.00 40.00

2019-20 Artifacts Aurum

A1 Alexander Ovechkin 6.00 15.00
A2 Max Pacioretty 1.50 4.00
A3 Steven Stamkos 3.00 8.00
A4 Mikko Rantanen 4.00 10.00
A5 Auston Matthews 6.00 15.00
A6 Tyler Seguin 2.00 5.00
A7 Roberto Luongo 2.50 6.00
A8 Anze Kopitar 2.50 6.00
A9 Nico Hischier 2.50 6.00
A10 Sidney Crosby 6.00 15.00
A11 Brady Tkachuk 2.50 6.00
A12 Evander Kane 1.50 4.00
A13 Ryan O'Reilly 1.50 4.00
A14 Elias Pettersson 2.50 6.00
A15 Henrik Lundqvist 4.00 10.00
A16 Patrik Laine 2.00 5.00
A17 Carter Hart 1.50 4.00
A18 Mathew Barzal 2.00 5.00
A19 Max Domi 1.50 4.00
A20 Connor McDavid 8.00 20.00
A21 Derek Stepan 1.00 2.50
A22 Brad Marchand 3.00 8.00
A23 Sean Monahan 1.00 2.50
A24 Teuvo Teravainen 1.50 4.00
A25 Patrick Kane 3.00 8.00
A26 John Gibson 1.50 4.00
A27 Filip Forsberg 2.50 6.00
A28 Dylan Larkin 2.00 5.00
A29 Cam Atkinson 1.50 4.00
A30 Jack Eichel 2.50 6.00
A31 Evgeni Malkin 3.00 8.00
A32 Victor Rask 1.00 2.50
A33 Nikita Kucherov 3.00 8.00
A34 Marc-Andre Fleury 3.00 8.00
A35 John Tavares 2.50 6.00
A36 Leon Draisaitl 5.00 12.00

2019-20 Artifacts Aurum Red

*RED/25-99: .5X TO 1.25X BASIC INSERTS
A48 Quinn Hughes 60.00 150.00

2019-20 Artifacts Autofacts

AAS Anthony Stolarz B 10.00 25.00
ABR Brett Ritchie C 6.00 15.00
ABS Brady Skjei C 6.00 15.00
ACH Charles Hudon C 6.00 15.00
ADD Dillon Dube B 5.00 12.00
ADH Danton Heinen B 6.00 15.00
AEB Ethan Bear C 5.00 12.00
AJH Jaroslav Halak B 8.00 20.00
AJL JC Lipon C 6.00 15.00
AJM Jake McCabe B 6.00 15.00
AJO Jamie Oleksiak C 6.00 15.00
AJV Jimmy Vesey B 6.00 15.00
AJW Jordan Weal C 5.00 12.00
AKF Kevin Fiala B 6.00 15.00
ALA Johan Larsson C 6.00 15.00
ALD Louis Domingue C 6.00 15.00
AMB Madison Bowey C 5.00 12.00
AMJ Mark Jankowski B 5.00 12.00
AMP Mark Pysyk C 5.00 12.00
ANG Nikolay Goldobin B 6.00 15.00
ANH Noah Hanifin B 8.00 20.00
AOK Ondrej Kase A 5.00 12.00
AOL Oscar Lindberg A 6.00 15.00
ARD Ryan Dzingel C 6.00 15.00
ARF Radek Faksa C 6.00 15.00
ARP Ryan Pulock B 6.00 15.00
ASL Scott Laughton C 5.00 12.00
ATB Tyler Bertuzzi A 6.00 15.00
ATM Tyler Motte A 5.00 12.00
ATP Tanner Pearson A 8.00 20.00
ATR Tobias Rieder B 5.00 12.00
ATT Tage Thompson A 10.00 25.00
AVH Vincent Hinostroza A 5.00 12.00
AVL Vinni Lettieri C 6.00 15.00

2019-20 Artifacts Autograph Materials Horizontal Gold

103 Patrick Kane/25 50.00 125.00
105 John Tavares/25 40.00 100.00
106 Brock Boeser/25 30.00 80.00
111 Miro Heiskanen/25 30.00 80.00
114 Sebastian Aho/25 40.00 100.00
116 Brad Marchand/25 50.00 125.00
119 Jack Eichel/25 40.00 100.00
124 Cam Atkinson/25 25.00 60.00
125 Nico Hischier/25 40.00 100.00
127 Brent Burns/25 25.00 60.00
135 Evgeni Malkin/25 50.00 125.00
139 Max Domi/25 25.00 60.00
144 Leon Draisaitl/25 80.00 200.00
161 Cale Makar/49 125.00 300.00
163 Philippe Myers/49 20.00 50.00
164 Max Jones/49 25.00 60.00
165 Filip Zadina/49 40.00 100.00
166 Dante Fabbro/49 25.00 60.00
169 Erik Brannstrom/49 25.00 60.00
170 Ryan Poehling/49 40.00 100.00
173 Libor Hajek/49 20.00 50.00
175 Vitaly Abramov/49 25.00 60.00
176 Carl Grundstrom/49 25.00 60.00
177 Brady Keeper/49 25.00 60.00
180 Quinn Hughes/49 125.00 300.00

2019-20 Artifacts Esteemed Endorsements

EEBH Brett Hull 60.00 150.00
EECM Connor McDavid 200.00 500.00
EEEM Evgeni Malkin 125.00 300.00
EEGL Guy Lafleur 40.00 100.00
EEHL Henrik Lundqvist 80.00 200.00
EEJE Jack Eichel 60.00 150.00
EEJT Joe Thornton 50.00 125.00
EEML Mario Lemieux 125.00 300.00
EEPC Paul Coffey 30.00 80.00
EEPL Pat Lafontaine 60.00 150.00
EEPR Patrick Roy 125.00 300.00
EESY Steve Yzerman 125.00 300.00

2019-20 Artifacts Honoured Hopefuls Signatures

HH3AM Auston Matthews 125.00 300.00
HHSBM Brad Marchand 60.00 150.00
HHSCM Connor McDavid 150.00 400.00
HHSHL Henrik Lundqvist 80.00 200.00
HHSHZ Henrik Zetterberg 40.00 100.00
HHSPD Pavel Datsyuk 50.00 125.00

2019-20 Artifacts Lord Stanley's Legacy Relics

*PREMIUM/25: 1.25X TO 3X BASIC INSERTS
LSLRAO Alexander Ovechkin B 8.00 20.00
LSLRBS Brendan Shanahan A 2.00 5.00
LSLRJT Jonathan Toews A 3.00 8.00
LSLRKL Kris Letang B 2.50 6.00
LSLRRG Ryan Getzlaf B 2.00 5.00
LSLRSE Brent Seabrook B 1.25 3.00
LSLRTF Theoren Fleury B 2.00 5.00
LSLRTR Tuukka Rask B 2.50 6.00
LSLRVT Vladimir Tarasenko A 2.50 6.00

2019-20 Artifacts Lord Stanley's Legacy Signatures

LSLSBM Brad Marchand B 30.00 80.00
LSLSBR Bill Ranford D 5.00 12.00
LSLSEK Evgeny Kuznetsov C 8.00 20.00
LSLSEM Evgeni Malkin B 12.00 30.00
LSLSJB Jordan Binnington A 30.00 80.00
LSLSJJ Jaromir Jagr A 50.00 125.00
LSLSMM Matt Murray D 6.00 15.00
LSLSPF Peter Forsberg A 50.00 125.00
LSLSRA Rod Brind'Amour C 6.00 15.00
LSLSSS Steve Shutt D 5.00 12.00

2019-20 Artifacts Materials Gold

*PURPLE.VETS/25: 1X TO 2.5X BASIC INSERTS
*PURPLE.RC/49: 1.5X TO 4X BASIC INSERTS
*EMERALD/25-99: .8X TO 2X BASIC INSERTS
1 Mitch Marner 5.00 12.00
2 Ryan O'Reilly 3.00 8.00
3 Nolan Patrick 3.00 8.00
4 Thomas Chabot 3.00 8.00
6 Ben Bishop 2.50 6.00
7 Filip Forsberg 5.00 12.00
8 Victor Rask 2.00 5.00
9 Tomas Hertl 3.00 8.00
10 Ryan Nugent-Hopkins 4.00 10.00
11 Andrew Ladd 2.00 5.00
12 Adam Henrique 2.50 6.00
13 Matthew Tkachuk 6.00 15.00
14 Dougie Hamilton 2.50 6.00
15 Andrei Vasilevskiy 5.00 12.00
16 Alex Kerfoot 2.50 6.00
17 Pierre-Luc Dubois 2.50 6.00
18 Anthony Mantha 2.50 6.00
19 Patrice Bergeron 4.00 10.00
20 Alex Galchenyuk 2.00 5.00
21 Aleksander Barkov 5.00 12.00
22 Darnell Nurse 2.50 6.00
23 Mika Zibanejad 4.00 10.00
24 Kyle Palmieri 2.50 6.00
25 Rasmus Dahlin 4.00 10.00
26 Ilya Kovalchuk 3.00 8.00
27 Alex DeBrincat 4.00 10.00
28 Bo Horvat 4.00 10.00
29 Mark Stone 4.00 10.00
30 Tom Wilson 3.00 8.00
31 Nikolaj Ehlers 3.00 8.00
32 Claude Giroux 3.00 8.00
33 Frederik Andersen 4.00 10.00
34 Evander Kane 3.00 8.00
35 Brayden Schenn 3.00 8.00
36 Sean Monahan 2.00 5.00
37 Craig Anderson 2.50 6.00
38 Jake Guentzel 5.00 12.00
39 Alexander Radulov 3.00 8.00
40 Gabriel Landeskog 4.00 10.00
41 Ryan Strome 3.00 8.00
42 Alex Tuch 3.00 8.00
43 Nick Leddy 2.00 5.00
44 Duncan Keith 2.50 6.00
45 Jonathan Drouin 2.50 6.00
46 Casey Mittelstadt 3.00 8.00
47 Kyle Turris 2.50 6.00
48 Jason Zucker 3.00 8.00
49 Nino Niederreiter 2.00 5.00
50 Evgeny Kuznetsov 4.00 10.00
52 Elias Lindholm 3.00 8.00
53 Jakob Silfverberg 2.00 5.00
54 Teuvo Teravainen 3.00 8.00
55 John Carlson 3.00 8.00
56 Jesper Bratt 3.00 8.00
57 Jonathan Huberdeau 4.00 10.00
58 Jaden Schwartz 4.00 10.00
59 Andreas Athanasiou 2.50 6.00
60 Patrik Laine 4.00 10.00
61 Loui Eriksson 2.00 5.00
63 Jeff Skinner 3.00 8.00
64 Derek Stepan 2.00 5.00
65 William Karlsson 4.00 10.00
66 Kris Letang 4.00 10.00
67 Sean Couturier 2.50 6.00
68 Andrei Svechnikov 4.00 10.00
69 Nicklas Backstrom 3.00 8.00
70 Pekka Rinne 3.00 8.00
71 Mikkel Boedker 2.00 5.00
72 Mike Hoffman 2.00 5.00
73 Tomas Tatar 2.00 5.00
74 Tyler Bozak 2.00 5.00
75 Max Pacioretty 3.00 8.00
76 Brayden Point 4.00 10.00
77 John Gibson 3.00 8.00
78 Tyler Seguin 4.00 10.00
79 Tyson Jost 2.50 6.00
80 Drew Doughty 4.00 10.00
81 Kyle Okposo 2.00 5.00
82 Taylor Hall 3.00 8.00
83 Jimmy Vesey 2.50 6.00
84 Patric Hornqvist 2.00 5.00
85 Brendan Gallagher 3.00 8.00
86 Jake DeBrusk 3.00 8.00
87 Artem Anisimov 2.00 5.00
88 William Nylander 6.00 15.00
89 Logan Couture 4.00 10.00
90 Seth Jones 3.00 8.00
91 Devan Dubnyk 2.50 6.00
92 Vincent Hinostroza 2.00 5.00
93 Blake Wheeler 3.00 8.00
94 Frans Nielsen 2.00 5.00
95 Milan Lucic 2.50 6.00
96 Josh Bailey 2.50 6.00
97 James Neal 2.00 5.00
98 Tanner Pearson 3.00 8.00
99 Tyler Johnson 2.00 5.00
100 Roman Josi 3.00 8.00
101 Connor McDavid 15.00 40.00
102 Anze Kopitar 5.00 12.00
103 Patrick Kane 6.00 15.00
104 Nikita Kucherov 6.00 15.00
105 John Tavares 5.00 12.00
106 Brock Boeser 4.00 10.00
107 Marc-Andre Fleury 6.00 15.00
108 David Pastrnak 8.00 20.00
109 Mark Scheifele 5.00 12.00
110 Sidney Crosby 12.00 30.00
111 Miro Heiskanen 4.00 10.00
112 Mikko Rantanen 8.00 20.00
113 Ryan Johansen 2.50 6.00
114 Sebastian Aho 5.00 12.00
115 Johnny Gaudreau 5.00 12.00
116 Brad Marchand 6.00 15.00
117 Clayton Keller 4.00 10.00
118 Ryan Getzlaf 3.00 8.00
119 Jack Eichel 5.00 12.00
120 Carey Price 6.00 15.00
121 Dylan Larkin 4.00 10.00
122 Roberto Luongo 5.00 12.00
123 Zach Parise 3.00 8.00
124 Cam Atkinson 3.00 8.00
125 Nico Hischier 5.00 12.00
126 Mathew Barzal 4.00 10.00
127 Brent Burns 3.00 8.00
128 Bobby Ryan 2.50 6.00
130 Henrik Lundqvist 8.00 20.00
131 Vladimir Tarasenko 4.00 10.00
132 Jonathan Toews 5.00 12.00
133 Nathan MacKinnon 12.00 30.00
134 Jamie Benn 3.00 8.00
135 Evgeni Malkin 6.00 15.00
136 Connor Hellebuyck 6.00 15.00
138 Steven Stamkos 6.00 15.00
139 Max Domi 3.00 8.00
140 Auston Matthews 12.00 30.00
141 Jonathan Marchessault 4.00 10.00
142 Jonathan Quick 4.00 10.00
143 Elias Pettersson 5.00 12.00
144 Leon Draisaitl 10.00 25.00
145 Alexander Ovechkin 12.00 30.00
146 Guy Lafleur 4.00 10.00
148 Ray Bourque 5.00 12.00
150 Joe Sakic 6.00 15.00
153 Kirk McLean 2.50 6.00
154 Henrik Sedin 4.00 10.00
156 Mario Lemieux 12.00 30.00
157 Bill Ranford 2.50 6.00
158 Doug Gilmour 4.00 10.00
160 Wayne Gretzky 20.00 50.00
161 Cale Makar 15.00 40.00
162 Rudolfs Balcers 3.00 8.00
163 Philippe Myers 2.50 6.00
164 Max Jones 3.00 8.00
165 Filip Zadina 5.00 12.00
166 Dante Fabbro 3.00 8.00
167 Nathan Bastian 3.00 8.00
168 Trent Frederic 3.00 8.00
169 Erik Brannstrom 3.00 8.00
170 Ryan Poehling 5.00 12.00
171 Alexandre Texier 3.00 8.00
172 Zack MacEwen 2.50 6.00
173 Libor Hajek 2.50 6.00
174 Taro Hirose 3.00 8.00
175 Vitaly Abramov 3.00 8.00
176 Carl Grundstrom 3.00 8.00
177 Brady Keeper 3.00 8.00
178 Zach Senyshyn 3.00 8.00
179 Teddy Blueger 3.00 8.00
180 Quinn Hughes 15.00 40.00
I Jack Hughes 15.00 40.00
II Kirby Dach 6.00 15.00
III Cody Glass 5.00 12.00
IV Nick Suzuki 12.00 30.00
V Victor Olofsson 6.00 15.00

2019-20 Artifacts Materials Horizontal Gold

*EMERALD/25: .6X TO 1.5X BASIC INSERTS
101 Connor McDavid 25.00 60.00
103 Patrick Kane 10.00 25.00
105 John Tavares 8.00 20.00
106 Brock Boeser 6.00 15.00
107 Marc-Andre Fleury 10.00 25.00
110 Sidney Crosby 20.00 50.00
111 Miro Heiskanen 6.00 15.00
114 Sebastian Aho 8.00 20.00
116 Brad Marchand 10.00 25.00
119 Jack Eichel 8.00 20.00
124 Cam Atkinson 5.00 12.00
125 Nico Hischier 8.00 20.00
127 Brent Burns 5.00 12.00
135 Evgeni Malkin 10.00 25.00
139 Max Domi 5.00 12.00
140 Auston Matthews 20.00 50.00
143 Elias Pettersson 8.00 20.00
144 Leon Draisaitl 15.00 40.00
161 Cale Makar 25.00 60.00
163 Philippe Myers 4.00 10.00
164 Max Jones 5.00 12.00
165 Filip Zadina 8.00 20.00
166 Dante Fabbro 5.00 12.00
169 Erik Brannstrom 5.00 12.00
170 Ryan Poehling 8.00 20.00
173 Libor Hajek 4.00 10.00
175 Vitaly Abramov 5.00 12.00
176 Carl Grundstrom 5.00 12.00
177 Brady Keeper 5.00 12.00
180 Quinn Hughes 25.00 60.00

2019-20 Artifacts NHL Remnants

*PREMIUM/25: 1.25X TO 3X BASIC INSERTS
NRAA Andreas Athanasiou B 2.00 5.00
NRAE Aaron Ekblad B 3.00 8.00
NRAG Alex Galchenyuk B 1.50 4.00
NRAO Alexander Ovechkin A 10.00 25.00
NRBA Sven Baertschi B 1.50 4.00
NRBB Brock Boeser A 3.00 8.00
NRCG Claude Giroux B 2.50 6.00
NRCM Connor McDavid A 12.00 30.00
NRCP Carey Price A 5.00 12.00
NRCW Colin White D 1.50 4.00
NRDP David Perron B 2.00 5.00
NREM Evgeni Malkin A 5.00 12.00
NRFF Filip Forsberg B 4.00 10.00
NRJR James van Riemsdyk B 2.00 5.00
NRJS Jordan Staal B 2.00 5.00
NRJT Jonathan Toews A 4.00 10.00
NRJV Jakub Vrana B 2.50 6.00
NRMB Mathew Barzal B 3.00 8.00
NRMR Morgan Rielly B 2.50 6.00
NRMS Mark Scheifele B 4.00 10.00
NRPB Pavel Buchnevich B 2.00 5.00
NRPD Pierre-Luc Dubois B 2.00 5.00
NRSB Sergei Bobrovsky B 4.00 10.00
NRST Shea Theodore B 3.00 8.00
NRTH Tomas Hertl B 2.50 6.00
NRTR Tuukka Rask B 3.00 8.00
NRTS Tyler Seguin A 3.00 8.00
NRVH Victor Hedman B 3.00 8.00
NRWB Will Butcher B 2.00 5.00

2019-20 Artifacts Threads of Time

*PREMIUM/25: 1X TO 2.5X BASIC INSERTS
TTAL Andrew Ladd 1.50 4.00
TTAR Alexander Radulov 2.50 6.00
TTEK Evander Kane 2.50 6.00
TTFA Frederik Andersen 3.00 8.00
TTJV Jakub Voracek 2.00 5.00
TTJW Justin Williams 2.00 5.00
TTKO Kyle Okposo 1.50 4.00
TTLE Loui Eriksson 1.50 4.00
TTMD Matt Duchene 2.50 6.00
TTMJ Martin Jones 2.00 5.00
TTPK Phil Kessel 2.50 6.00
TTPS P.K. Subban 3.00 8.00
TTSW Shea Weber 2.50 6.00
TTTS Tyler Seguin 3.00 8.00

2019-20 Artifacts Top 12 Rookie Signatures

RSAF Adam Fox 10.00 25.00
RSAT Alexandre Texier 12.00 30.00
RSCM Cale Makar 80.00 200.00
RSDK Dominik Kubalik 20.00 50.00
RSEB Erik Brannstrom 12.00 30.00
RSEM Elvis Merzlikins 25.00 60.00
RSFZ Filip Zadina 20.00 50.00
RSJM John Marino 15.00 40.00
RSNS Nick Suzuki 50.00 125.00
RSQH Quinn Hughes 80.00 200.00
RSRP Ryan Poehling 20.00 50.00
RSVO Victor Olofsson 8.00 20.00

2019-20 Artifacts Tundra Teammates Duo Materials

T2BUF J.Eichel/R.Dahlin 6.00 15.00
T2CAL J.Gaudreau/E.Lindholm 6.00 15.00
T2CBJ C.Atkinson/P.Dubois 4.00 10.00
T2CHI P.Kane/A.DeBrincat 8.00 20.00
T2DET D.Larkin/T.Bertuzzi 5.00 12.00
T2EDM R.Nugent-Hopkins/D.Nurse 5.00 12.00
T2FLO A.Barkov/A.Ekblad 6.00 15.00
T2LAK A.Kopitar/I.Kovalchuk 6.00 15.00
T2MIN Z.Parise/M.Granlund 4.00 10.00
T2NYI M.Barzal/A.Lee 5.00 12.00
T2OTT B.Tkachuk/T.Chabot 6.00 15.00
T2PIT E.Malkin/J.Guentzel 8.00 20.00
T2SJS T.Hertl/L.Couture 5.00 12.00
T2TBL S.Stamkos/N.Kucherov 8.00 20.00
T2WAS A.Ovechkin/B.Holtby 15.00 40.00

2019-20 Artifacts Tundra Teammates Quad Materials

T4BOS Rask/Marchand Pastrnak/DeBrusk 12.00 30.00
T4CAR Aho/Teravainen Hamilton/Svechnikov 8.00 20.00
T4DAL Benn/Seguin Klingberg/Heiskanen 6.00 15.00
T4MTL Price/Drouin/Domi/Gallagher 10.00 25.00
T4NAS Rinne/Subban/Josi/Ellis 6.00 15.00
T4STL Tarasenko/Schwartz Schenn/O'Reilly 6.00 15.00
T4TOR Tavares/Marleau Nylander/Marner 10.00 25.00
T4VAN Pettersson/Boeser Horvat/Eriksson 8.00 20.00
T4VEG Fleury/Tuch Marchessault/Stone 10.00 25.00
T4WIN Scheifele/Laine/Ehlers/Connor 8.00 20.00

2019-20 Artifacts Year One Rookie Sweaters

*PATCH/25: .8X TO 2X BASIC INSERTS
RSAS Andrei Svechnikov 5.00 12.00
RSBT Brady Tkachuk 6.00 15.00
RSCM Casey Mittelstadt 4.00 10.00
RSEP Elias Pettersson 6.00 15.00
RSJG Jordan Greenway 2.50 6.00
RSMH Miro Heiskanen 5.00 12.00
RSRD Rasmus Dahlin 5.00 12.00
RSTT Tage Thompson 5.00 12.00

2019-20 Artifacts Year One Rookie Sweaters Photo Variations

RSAS Andrei Svechnikov 8.00 20.00
RSBT Brady Tkachuk 10.00 25.00
RSCM Casey Mittelstadt 6.00 15.00
RSEP Elias Pettersson 10.00 25.00
RSJG Jordan Greenway 4.00 10.00
RSMH Miro Heiskanen 8.00 20.00
RSRD Rasmus Dahlin 8.00 20.00
RSTT Tage Thompson 8.00 20.00

2020-21 Artifacts

1 Anders Lee .30 .75
2 Tomas Tatar .25 .60
3 Kyle Palmieri .30 .75
4 Mikko Koskinen .25 .60
5 Ryan Getzlaf .40 1.00
6 Ryan Ellis .30 .75
7 Carter Hart .40 1.00
8 Timo Meier .40 1.00
9 Phil Kessel .40 1.00
10 Tony DeAngelo .25 .60
11 Evander Kane .40 1.00
12 Bo Horvat .50 1.25
13 Zach Parise .40 1.00
14 Petr Mrazek .40 1.00
15 Kris Letang .50 1.25
16 Jack Hughes 1.00 2.50
17 Victor Hedman .50 1.25
18 Brock Boeser .50 1.25
19 Pekka Rinne .40 1.00
20 Shea Theodore .50 1.25
21 Logan Couture .50 1.25
22 Filip Forsberg .60 1.50
23 Jonathan Quick .50 1.25
24 Ben Bishop .30 .75
25 Matt Murray .40 1.00
26 Sean Monahan .25 .60
27 Max Domi .40 1.00
28 Sean Couturier .30 .75
29 Mika Zibanejad .50 1.25
30 Mark Stone .50 1.25
31 Nikita Gusev .30 .75
32 Roope Hintz .50 1.25
33 Brady Tkachuk .60 1.50
34 Andrei Svechnikov .50 1.25
35 Seth Jones .40 1.00
36 Tomas Hertl .40 1.00
37 Tyler Bertuzzi .30 .75
38 Pierre-Luc Dubois .30 .75
39 Ryan Nugent-Hopkins .50 1.25
40 Jacob Markstrom .40 1.00
41 Dominik Kubalik .40 1.00
42 Tuukka Rask .50 1.25
43 Drew Doughty .50 1.25
44 Brayden Point .50 1.25
45 Frederik Andersen .50 1.25
46 Brent Burns .40 1.00
47 Evgeni Malkin .75 2.00
48 Tyler Toffoli .40 1.00
49 Brendan Gallagher .40 1.00
50 David Perron .30 .75
51 Ryan Suter .30 .75
52 Gustav Nyquist .25 .60
53 Connor Hellebuyck .75 2.00
54 Keith Yandle .25 .60
55 Evgeny Kuznetsov .50 1.25
56 Cam Atkinson .40 1.00
57 Mats Zuccarello .40 1.00
58 Rickard Rakell .30 .75
59 Mark Giordano .40 1.00
60 Nazem Kadri .50 1.25
61 Andrei Vasilevskiy .60 1.50
62 Darcy Kuemper .40 1.00
63 Joe Pavelski .50 1.25

64 Dougie Hamilton .30 .75
65 Joe Thornton .60 1.50
66 Jakob Silfverberg .25 .60
67 Tristan Jarry .40 1.00
68 Andreas Athanasiou .30 .75
69 Miro Heiskanen .50 1.25
70 Shea Weber .40 1.00
71 Tom Wilson .40 1.00
72 David Krejci .40 1.00
73 Oliver Ekman-Larsson .40 1.00
74 Travis Konecny .40 1.00
75 Brock Nelson .40 1.00
76 Anthony Mantha .30 .75
77 Sergei Bobrovsky .60 1.50
78 Victor Olofsson .40 1.00
79 William Nylander .75 2.00
80 Anthony Duclair .30 .75
81 Braden Holtby .50 1.25
82 Matt Duchene .40 1.00
83 Alex Pietrangelo .30 .75
84 Jonathan Huberdeau .50 1.25
85 Rasmus Dahlin .50 1.25
86 Jake Guentzel .60 1.50
87 Sam Reinhart .75 2.00
88 Teuvo Teravainen .40 1.00
89 Alex DeBrincat .50 1.25
90 Kyle Connor .60 1.50
91 Brayden Schenn .40 1.00
92 Jakub Voracek .30 .75
93 Nick Schmaltz .30 .75
94 Jean-Gabriel Pageau .25 .60
95 Jonathan Toews .60 1.50
96 Matthew Tkachuk .75 2.00
97 James van Riemsdyk .30 .75
98 Igor Shesterkin .75 2.00
99 Philipp Grubauer .40 1.00
100 Semyon Varlamov .40 1.00
101 Leon Draisaitl 4.00 10.00
102 Eric Staal 1.25 3.00
103 Quinn Hughes 3.00 8.00
104 Roman Josi 1.25 3.00
105 Marc-Andre Fleury 2.50 6.00
106 John Carlson 1.25 3.00
107 Nikita Kucherov 2.50 6.00
108 Sebastian Aho 2.00 5.00
109 Patrick Kane 2.50 6.00
110 John Gibson 1.25 3.00
111 Alex Ovechkin 5.00 12.00
112 Patrice Bergeron 1.50 4.00
113 Johnny Gaudreau 2.00 5.00
114 Nico Hischier 2.00 5.00
115 Aleksander Barkov 2.00 5.00
116 Cale Makar 3.00 8.00
117 Dylan Larkin 1.50 4.00
118 John Tavares 2.00 5.00
119 Thomas Chabot 1.25 3.00
120 Brad Marchand 2.50 6.00
121 Ryan O'Reilly 1.25 3.00
122 Connor McDavid 6.00 15.00
123 Auston Matthews 5.00 12.00
124 Carey Price 2.50 6.00
125 Anze Kopitar 2.00 5.00
126 Steven Stamkos 2.50 6.00
127 Mitch Marner 2.00 5.00
128 Erik Karlsson 1.50 4.00
129 Nathan MacKinnon 5.00 12.00
130 Elias Pettersson 2.00 5.00
131 Claude Giroux 1.25 3.00
132 David Pastrnak 3.00 8.00
133 Tyler Seguin 1.50 4.00
134 Artemi Panarin 2.50 6.00
135 Zach Werenski 2.00 5.00
136 Taylor Hall 1.25 3.00
137 Mark Scheifele 2.00 5.00
138 Jack Eichel 2.00 5.00
139 Mathew Barzal 1.50 4.00
140 Mikko Rantanen 3.00 8.00
141 Henrik Lundqvist 3.00 8.00
142 Jordan Binnington 2.00 5.00
143 Max Pacioretty 1.25 3.00
144 Blake Wheeler 1.25 3.00
145 Sidney Crosby 5.00 12.00
146 Dominik Hasek 2.00 5.00
147 Cam Ward 1.25 3.00
148 Henrik Zetterberg 1.50 4.00
149 Ken Morrow .75 2.00
150 Shayne Corson 1.00 2.50
151 Felix Potvin 2.00 5.00
152 Guy Lafleur 1.50 4.00
153 Chris Chelios 1.25 3.00
154 Saku Koivu 1.25 3.00
155 Daniel Sedin 1.50 4.00
156 Scott Gomez 1.00 2.50
157 John LeClair 1.25 3.00
158 Pat LaFontaine 1.25 3.00
159 Martin St. Louis 1.25 3.00
160 Jaromir Jagr 4.00 10.00
161 Martin Kaut RC 2.50 6.00
162 Liam Foudy RC 2.50 6.00
163 Kieffer Bellows RC 2.00 5.00
164 Nicolas Beaudin RC 2.50 6.00
165 Maxim Letunov RC 2.00 5.00
166 Morgan Geekie RC 2.50 6.00
167 Jake Evans RC 2.50 6.00
168 Egor Korshkov RC 1.50 4.00
169 Gabe Vilardi RC 4.00 10.00
170 Jason Robertson RC 6.00 15.00
171 Nick Robertson RC 4.00 10.00
172 Tyler Benson RC 2.50 6.00
173 Gustav Lindstrom RC 2.00 5.00
174 Josh Norris RC 4.00 10.00
175 Peyton Krebs RC 4.00 10.00
176 Timothy Liljegren RC 2.50 6.00
177 Lucas Carlsson RC 2.00 5.00
178 Mikey Anderson RC 2.50 6.00
179 Bowen Byram RC 5.00 12.00
180 Alexis Lafreniere RC 8.00 20.00

2020-21 Artifacts Aqua

*AQUA.VETS: 3X TO 8X BASIC
*AQUA.S/L: 1X TO 2.5X BASIC
*AQUA.RC: 1X TO 2.5X BASIC
180 Alexis Lafreniere 20.00 50.00

2020-21 Artifacts Autumn

*AUTUMN.VETS: 2.5X TO 6X BASIC
*AUTUMN.S/L: .75X TO 2X BASIC
*AUTUMN.RC: .75X TO 2X BASIC

2020-21 Artifacts Blue Sapphire

*BLUE: 1.25X TO 3X BASIC

2020-21 Artifacts Copper

*BLUE.VETS: 1.5X TO 4X BASIC
*BLUE.S/L: .5X TO 1.25X BASIC
*BLUE.RC: .5X TO 1.25X BASIC
180 Alexis Lafreniere 10.00 25.00

2020-21 Artifacts Emerald

*EMRLD.VETS: 2X TO 5X BASIC
*EMRLD.S/L: .6X TO 1.5X BASIC
*EMRLD.RC: .6X TO 1.5X BASIC
180 Alexis Lafreniere 12.00 30.00

2020-21 Artifacts Pink

*PINK.VETS: 4X TO 10X BASIC
*PINK.S/L: 1.25X TO 3X BASIC
*PINK.RC: 1.25X TO 3X BASIC
180 Alexis Lafreniere 60.00 150.00

2020-21 Artifacts Purple

*PURPLE.VETS: 6X TO 15X BASIC
*PURPLE.S/L: 2X TO 5X BASIC
*PURPLE.RC: 1.5X TO 4X BASIC
180 Alexis Lafreniere 125.00 300.00

2020-21 Artifacts Ruby

*RUBY: .5X TO 1.25X BASIC
180 Alexis Lafreniere 10.00 25.00

2020-21 Artifacts '10-11 10th Anniversary Retro Autofacts

RAFAT Alex Tuch/49 10.00 25.00
RAFBG Brendan Gallagher/49 10.00 25.00
RAFCH Carter Hart/49 30.00 80.00
RAFHE Connor Hellebuyck/49 20.00 50.00
RAFIS Igor Shesterkin/49 20.00 50.00
RAFNH Nico Hischier/49 15.00 40.00
RAFPR Pekka Rinne/49 10.00 25.00
RAFSA Sebastian Aho/49 15.00 40.00
RAFTC Thomas Chabot/49 10.00 25.00
RAFTS Tyler Seguin/49 12.00 30.00
RAFZP Zach Parise/49 10.00 25.00

2020-21 Artifacts Admirable Impressions Patch Autographs

AICH Carter Hart 50.00 125.00
AICM Connor McDavid 300.00 800.00
AICP Carey Price 80.00 200.00
AINH Nico Hischier 80.00 200.00

2020-21 Artifacts Arena Artifacts

MLGBB Bob Baun 40.00 100.00
MLGBS Borje Salming 50.00 125.00
MLGDG Doug Gilmour 50.00 125.00
MLGDS Darryl Sittler 50.00 125.00
MLGFM Frank Mahovlich 40.00 100.00
MLGJB Johnny Bower 80.00 200.00
MLGKC King Clancy 80.00 200.00
MLGTH Tim Horton 60.00 150.00
MLGWC Wendel Clark 60.00 150.00

2020-21 Artifacts Aurum

A1 Sidney Crosby 8.00 20.00
A2 Connor McDavid 10.00 25.00
A3 Jordan Binnington 3.00 8.00
A4 Matthew Tkachuk 4.00 10.00
A5 Matt Duchene 2.00 5.00
A6 Carter Hart 2.00 5.00
A7 Alex Ovechkin 8.00 20.00
A8 Steven Stamkos 4.00 10.00
A9 Nathan MacKinnon 8.00 20.00
A10 Tyler Bertuzzi 1.50 4.00
A11 Anze Kopitar 3.00 8.00
A12 Phil Kessel 2.00 5.00
A13 Kyle Palmieri 1.50 4.00
A14 Brady Tkachuk 3.00 8.00
A15 Patrick Kane 4.00 10.00
A16 Mark Stone 2.50 6.00
A17 Shea Weber 2.00 5.00
A18 Elias Pettersson 3.00 8.00
A19 David Pastrnak 5.00 12.00
A20 Tyler Seguin 2.50 6.00
A21 Auston Matthews 8.00 20.00
A22 John Gibson 2.00 5.00
A23 Artemi Panarin 4.00 10.00
A24 Ryan Suter 1.50 4.00
A25 Jack Eichel 3.00 8.00
A26 Tomas Hertl 2.00 5.00
A27 Seth Jones 2.00 5.00
A28 Mark Scheifele 3.00 8.00
A29 Sebastian Aho 3.00 8.00
A30 Jonathan Huberdeau 2.50 6.00
A31 Jason Robertson 3.00 8.00
A32 Michael DiPietro 8.00 20.00
A33 Timothy Liljegren 4.00 10.00
A34 Jake Evans 4.00 10.00
A35 Morgan Geekie 2.50 6.00
A36 Liam Foudy 2.50 6.00
A37 Nick Robertson 15.00 40.00
A38 Bowen Byram 10.00 25.00
A39 Josh Norris 4.00 10.00
A40 Gabe Vilardi 8.00 20.00
A41 David Pastrnak AS 15.00 40.00
A42 Patrick Kane AS 15.00 40.00
A43 Connor McDavid AS 30.00 80.00
A44 Leon Draisaitl AS 15.00 40.00
A45 Steve Yzerman 25.00 60.00
A46 Jaromir Jagr 80.00 200.00
A47 Teemu Selanne 40.00 100.00
A48 Wayne Gretzky 60.00 150.00

2020-21 Artifacts Autofacts

AAB Adam Boqvist C 5.00 12.00
AAL Artturi Lehkonen B 5.00 12.00
AAM Andrew Mangiapane C 6.00 15.00
ABH Brett Howden F 4.00 10.00
ABM Brock McGinn B 4.00 10.00
ACD Chris Driedger E 4.00 10.00
ACH Carl Hagelin B 4.00 10.00
ACM Cale Makar A 80.00 200.00
ACS Carl Soderberg C 4.00 10.00
AFC Filip Chytil D 5.00 12.00
AGM Greg McKegg E 4.00 10.00
AGU Radko Gudas B 5.00 12.00
AHF Haydn Fleury D 4.00 10.00
AJA Mattias Janmark D 4.00 10.00
AJC Jack Campbell D 6.00 15.00
AJG Jordan Greenway B 5.00 12.00
AJL Johan Larsson F 5.00 12.00
AJW Jordan Weal F 4.00 10.00
ALB Laurent Brossoit E 4.00 10.00
ALW Lucas Wallmark D 4.00 10.00
AMD Michael Dal Colle E 4.00 10.00
AMJ Mathieu Joseph D 4.00 10.00
AMR Mike Reilly C 4.00 10.00
AND Nicolas Deslauriers D 4.00 10.00
AOK Oliver Kylington D 4.00 10.00
APM Petr Mrazek D 6.00 15.00
ARA Rasmus Asplund F 4.00 10.00
ARG Rocco Grimaldi E 4.00 10.00
ASK Slater Koekkoek C 4.00 10.00
AST Chandler Stephenson E 5.00 12.00
ATR Tobias Rieder E 4.00 10.00
AVA Viktor Arvidsson F 4.00 10.00
AVK Vladislav Kamenev C 4.00 10.00
AVN Valeri Nichushkin E 6.00 15.00
AVO Victor Olofsson F 6.00 15.00
AYW Yannick Weber C 4.00 10.00

2020-21 Artifacts Esteemed Endorsements

EEBH Bobby Hull 150.00 400.00
EEBS Billy Smith 60.00 150.00
EEDS Darryl Sittler 80.00 200.00
EEGF Grant Fuhr 80.00 200.00
EEGH Glenn Hall 60.00 150.00
EEJJ Jaromir Jagr 200.00 500.00
EENL Nicklas Lidstrom 60.00 150.00
EENU Norm Ullman 25.00 60.00
EEPL Pat LaFontaine 60.00 150.00
EEYC Yvan Cournoyer 60.00 150.00

2020-21 Artifacts Honoured Hopefuls Signatures

HHSDS Daniel Sedin 80.00 200.00
HHSHS Henrik Sedin 40.00 100.00
HHSJI Jarome Iginla 80.00 200.00

2020-21 Artifacts Honoured Members Signatures

HMSBB Bill Barber 80.00 200.00

2020-21 Artifacts Lord Stanley's Legacy Relics

*PREMIUM: 1.5X TO 4X BASIC
LSLRAP Alex Pietrangelo 2.50 6.00
LSLRBH Braden Holtby 3.00 8.00
LSLRDH Dominik Hasek 10.00 25.00
LSLRJG Jake Guentzel 6.00 15.00
LSLRJS Joe Sakic 6.00 15.00
LSLRMS Martin St. Louis 3.00 8.00
LSLRRO Ryan O'Reilly 4.00 10.00
LSLRSG Scott Gomez 5.00 12.00
LSLRTO T.J. Oshie 3.00 8.00
LSLRTS Teemu Selanne 6.00 15.00

2020-21 Artifacts Lord Stanley's Legacy Signatures

LSLSBK Bob Kelly B 6.00 15.00
LSLSDB Dustin Brown B 10.00 25.00
LSLSDD Dick Duff B 8.00 20.00
LSLSDG Doug Gilmour A 12.00 30.00
LSLSKM Ken Morrow B 6.00 15.00
LSLSMN Mats Naslund B 20.00 50.00
LSLSNL Nicklas Lidstrom A 10.00 25.00
LSLSOR Brooks Orpik B 10.00 25.00

2020-21 Artifacts Material Autographs Gold

*HOR.GOLD: .6X TO 1.5X BASIC
*EMERALD: .6X TO 1.5X BASIC
102 Eric Staal/65 15.00 40.00
103 Quinn Hughes/45 40.00 100.00
104 Roman Josi/65 20.00 50.00
105 Marc-Andre Fleury/45 30.00 80.00
108 Sebastian Aho/45 25.00 60.00
110 John Gibson/65 15.00 40.00
114 Nico Hischier/65 25.00 60.00
115 Aleksander Barkov/65 25.00 60.00
116 Cale Makar/45 40.00 100.00
118 John Tavares/45 25.00 60.00
119 Thomas Chabot/65 15.00 40.00
120 Brad Marchand/45 30.00 80.00
121 Ryan O'Reilly/45 15.00 40.00
123 Auston Matthews/25 100.00 250.00
124 Carey Price/45 30.00 80.00
126 Steven Stamkos/45 30.00 80.00
127 Mitch Marner/45 25.00 60.00
133 Tyler Seguin/65 20.00 50.00
137 Mark Scheifele/65 25.00 60.00
141 Henrik Lundqvist/65 40.00 100.00
145 Sidney Crosby/25 125.00 300.00
147 Cam Ward/65 15.00 40.00
150 Shayne Corson/45 12.00 30.00
151 Felix Potvin/45 25.00 60.00
153 Chris Chelios/45 15.00 40.00
154 Saku Koivu/45 15.00 40.00
155 Daniel Sedin/45 20.00 50.00
156 Scott Gomez/65 12.00 30.00
157 John LeClair/45 12.00 30.00
159 Martin St. Louis/45 15.00 40.00
160 Jaromir Jagr/25 125.00 300.00
161 Martin Kaut/149 20.00 50.00
162 Liam Foudy/99 20.00 50.00
163 Kieffer Bellows/99 15.00 40.00
164 Nicolas Beaudin/149 20.00 50.00
165 Maxim Letunov/99 15.00 40.00
166 Morgan Geekie/99 20.00 50.00
167 Jake Evans/149 20.00 50.00
168 Egor Korshkov/149 12.00 30.00
169 Gabe Vilardi/99 30.00 80.00
170 Jason Robertson/99 50.00 125.00
171 Nick Robertson/99 30.00 80.00
172 Tyler Benson/149 20.00 50.00
174 Josh Norris/99 30.00 80.00
175 Peyton Krebs/99 30.00 80.00
176 Timothy Liljegren/149 20.00 50.00
177 Lucas Carlsson/149 20.00 50.00
178 Mikey Anderson/149 20.00 50.00
179 Bowen Byram/99 40.00 100.00
180 Alexis Lafreniere/25 300.00 800.00

2020-21 Artifacts Materials Gold

*HOR.GOLD: .6X TO 1.5X BASIC
*HOR.EMRLD: 1.5X TO 4X BASIC
1 Anders Lee 2.50 6.00
2 Tomas Tatar 2.00 5.00
3 Kyle Palmieri 2.50 6.00
4 Mikko Koskinen 2.00 5.00
5 Ryan Getzlaf 3.00 8.00
6 Ryan Ellis 2.50 6.00
7 Carter Hart 3.00 8.00
8 Timo Meier 3.00 8.00
9 Phil Kessel 3.00 8.00
11 Evander Kane 3.00 8.00
12 Bo Horvat 4.00 10.00
13 Zach Parise 3.00 8.00
15 Kris Letang 4.00 10.00
16 Jack Hughes 8.00 20.00
17 Victor Hedman 4.00 10.00
18 Brock Boeser 4.00 10.00
19 Pekka Rinne 3.00 8.00
20 Shea Theodore 4.00 10.00
21 Logan Couture 4.00 10.00
22 Filip Forsberg 5.00 12.00
23 Jonathan Quick 4.00 10.00
24 Ben Bishop 2.50 6.00
25 Matt Murray 3.00 8.00
26 Sean Monahan 2.00 5.00
27 Max Domi 3.00 8.00
28 Sean Couturier 2.50 6.00
29 Mika Zibanejad 4.00 10.00
30 Mark Stone 4.00 10.00
31 Nikita Gusev 2.50 6.00
33 Brady Tkachuk 5.00 12.00
34 Andrei Svechnikov 4.00 10.00
35 Seth Jones 3.00 8.00
36 Tomas Hertl 3.00 8.00
37 Tyler Bertuzzi 2.50 6.00
38 Pierre-Luc Dubois 2.50 6.00
39 Ryan Nugent-Hopkins 3.00 8.00
42 Tuukka Rask 4.00 10.00
43 Drew Doughty 4.00 10.00
44 Brayden Point 4.00 10.00
45 Frederik Andersen 4.00 10.00
46 Brent Burns 3.00 8.00
47 Evgeni Malkin 6.00 15.00
48 Tyler Toffoli 3.00 8.00
49 Brendan Gallagher 3.00 8.00
51 Ryan Suter 2.50 6.00
52 Gustav Nyquist 2.00 5.00
53 Connor Hellebuyck 6.00 15.00
54 Keith Yandle 2.00 5.00
55 Evgeny Kuznetsov 4.00 10.00
56 Cam Atkinson 3.00 8.00
57 Mats Zuccarello 3.00 8.00
58 Rickard Rakell 2.50 6.00
59 Mark Giordano 3.00 8.00
60 Nazem Kadri 4.00 10.00
61 Andrei Vasilevskiy 5.00 12.00
63 Joe Pavelski 4.00 10.00
64 Dougie Hamilton 2.50 6.00
65 Joe Thornton 5.00 12.00
66 Jakob Silfverberg 2.50 6.00
68 Andreas Athanasiou 2.50 6.00
69 Miro Heiskanen 4.00 10.00
70 Shea Weber 3.00 8.00
71 Tom Wilson 3.00 8.00
72 David Krejci 3.00 8.00
73 Oliver Ekman-Larsson 3.00 8.00
74 Travis Konecny 3.00 8.00
75 Brock Nelson 3.00 8.00
76 Anthony Mantha 2.50 6.00
77 Sergei Bobrovsky 5.00 12.00
78 Victor Olofsson 3.00 8.00
79 William Nylander 6.00 15.00
81 Braden Holtby 4.00 10.00
82 Matt Duchene 3.00 8.00
83 Alex Pietrangelo 2.50 6.00
84 Jonathan Huberdeau 4.00 10.00
85 Rasmus Dahlin 4.00 10.00
86 Jake Guentzel 5.00 12.00
87 Sam Reinhart 6.00 15.00
88 Teuvo Teravainen 3.00 8.00
89 Alex DeBrincat 4.00 10.00
90 Kyle Connor 5.00 12.00
91 Brayden Schenn 3.00 8.00
92 Jakub Voracek 2.50 6.00
93 Nick Schmaltz 2.50 6.00
95 Jonathan Toews 5.00 12.00
96 Matthew Tkachuk 6.00 15.00
97 James van Riemsdyk 2.50 6.00
99 Philipp Grubauer 3.00 8.00
100 Semyon Varlamov 3.00 8.00
101 Leon Draisaitl 10.00 25.00
102 Eric Staal 2.00 5.00
103 Quinn Hughes 8.00 20.00
104 Roman Josi 3.00 8.00
105 Marc-Andre Fleury 6.00 15.00
106 John Carlson 3.00 8.00
107 Nikita Kucherov 6.00 15.00
108 Sebastian Aho 5.00 12.00
109 Patrick Kane 6.00 15.00
110 John Gibson 3.00 8.00
111 Alex Ovechkin 12.00 30.00
112 Patrice Bergeron 4.00 10.00
113 Johnny Gaudreau 5.00 12.00
114 Nico Hischier 5.00 12.00
115 Aleksander Barkov 5.00 12.00
116 Cale Makar 8.00 20.00
117 Dylan Larkin 4.00 10.00
118 John Tavares 5.00 12.00
119 Thomas Chabot 3.00 8.00
120 Brad Marchand 6.00 15.00
121 Ryan O'Reilly 3.00 8.00
122 Connor McDavid 15.00 40.00
123 Auston Matthews 12.00 30.00
124 Carey Price 6.00 15.00
125 Anze Kopitar 5.00 12.00
126 Steven Stamkos 6.00 15.00
127 Mitch Marner 5.00 12.00
128 Erik Karlsson 4.00 10.00
129 Nathan MacKinnon 12.00 30.00
130 Elias Pettersson 5.00 12.00
131 Claude Giroux 3.00 8.00
132 David Pastrnak 8.00 20.00
133 Tyler Seguin 4.00 10.00
134 Artemi Panarin 6.00 15.00
135 Zach Werenski 6.00 15.00
137 Mark Scheifele 5.00 12.00
138 Jack Eichel 5.00 12.00
139 Mathew Barzal 4.00 10.00
140 Mikko Rantanen 8.00 20.00
141 Henrik Lundqvist 8.00 20.00
142 Jordan Binnington 5.00 12.00
143 Max Pacioretty 3.00 8.00
144 Blake Wheeler 3.00 8.00
145 Sidney Crosby 12.00 30.00
147 Cam Ward 3.00 8.00
148 Henrik Zetterberg 4.00 10.00
150 Shayne Corson 2.50 6.00
151 Felix Potvin 5.00 12.00
152 Guy Lafleur 4.00 10.00
153 Chris Chelios 3.00 8.00
154 Saku Koivu 3.00 8.00
155 Daniel Sedin 4.00 10.00
157 John LeClair 3.00 8.00
158 Pat LaFontaine 3.00 8.00
160 Jaromir Jagr 10.00 25.00
161 Martin Kaut 3.00 8.00
162 Liam Foudy 4.00 10.00
163 Kieffer Bellows 3.00 8.00
164 Nicolas Beaudin 3.00 8.00
165 Maxim Letunov 3.00 8.00
166 Morgan Geekie 4.00 10.00
167 Jake Evans 4.00 10.00
168 Egor Korshkov 2.50 6.00
169 Gabe Vilardi 6.00 15.00
170 Jason Robertson 10.00 25.00
171 Nick Robertson 6.00 15.00
172 Tyler Benson 4.00 10.00
174 Josh Norris 6.00 15.00
175 Peyton Krebs 6.00 15.00
176 Timothy Liljegren 4.00 10.00
177 Lucas Carlsson 3.00 8.00
178 Mikey Anderson 4.00 10.00
179 Bowen Byram 8.00 20.00
180 Alexis Lafreniere 20.00 50.00

2020-21 Artifacts Materials Emerald

*EMERALD: .75X TO 2X BASIC
105 Marc-Andre Fleury 40.00 100.00
109 Patrick Kane 25.00 60.00
114 Nico Hischier 20.00 50.00
116 Cale Makar 30.00 80.00
122 Connor McDavid 125.00 300.00
123 Auston Matthews 40.00 100.00
132 David Pastrnak 25.00 60.00
145 Sidney Crosby 50.00 125.00
152 Guy Lafleur 12.00 30.00
155 Daniel Sedin 8.00 20.00
157 John LeClair 15.00 40.00
160 Jaromir Jagr 100.00 250.00
180 Alexis Lafreniere/25 80.00 200.00

2020-21 Artifacts Materials Purple

*PURPLE: 1.5X TO 4X BASIC
89 Alex DeBrincat 25.00 60.00
177 Lucas Carlsson/49 20.00 50.00

2020-21 Artifacts NHL Remnants

NRAK Anze Kopitar 4.00 10.00
NRAP Alex Pietrangelo 2.00 5.00
NRBH Bo Horvat 3.00 8.00
NRBN Brock Nelson 2.50 6.00
NRCM Connor McDavid 12.00 30.00
NRDK Duncan Keith 2.00 5.00
NREK Erik Karlsson 3.00 8.00
NRGN Gustav Nyquist 1.50 4.00
NRHO Braden Holtby 3.00 8.00
NRJB Jordan Binnington 4.00 10.00
NRJG Johnny Gaudreau 4.00 10.00
NRJH Jonathan Huberdeau 3.00 8.00
NRKC Kyle Connor 4.00 10.00
NRKH Kevin Hayes 2.00 5.00
NRKY Keith Yandle 1.50 4.00
NRMD Max Domi 2.50 6.00
NRMR Morgan Rielly 2.50 6.00
NRMZ Mika Zibanejad 3.00 8.00
NRNB Nicklas Backstrom 2.50 6.00
NRNM Nathan MacKinnon 5.00 12.00
NROE Oliver Ekman-Larsson 2.50 6.00
NRPB Patrice Bergeron 3.00 8.00
NRRD Rasmus Dahlin 3.00 8.00
NRRR Rickard Rakell 2.00 5.00
NRRS Ryan Suter 2.00 5.00
NRSS Steven Stamkos 5.00 12.00
NRST Shea Theodore 5.00 12.00
NRTB Tyler Bertuzzi 2.00 5.00
NRTC Thomas Chabot 2.50 6.00
NRTS Tyler Seguin 3.00 8.00

2020-21 Artifacts NHL Remnants Premium

*PREMIUM: 1X TO 2.5X BASIC
NRBN Brock Nelson 8.00 20.00
NRCM Connor McDavid 50.00 125.00
NRDK Duncan Keith 10.00 25.00
NRKY Keith Yandle 8.00 20.00
NRNB Nicklas Backstrom 10.00 25.00
NRRR Rickard Rakell 8.00 20.00
NRST Shea Theodore 15.00 40.00

2020-21 Artifacts Signature Apparel

SABM Brad Marchand/36 30.00 80.00
SACJ Curtis Joseph/36 60.00 150.00
SACM Cale Makar/36 200.00 500.00
SAQH Quinn Hughes/36 60.00 150.00

2020-21 Artifacts Threads of Time

TTAP Artemi Panarin 4.00 10.00
TTJI Jarome Iginla 2.50 6.00
TTJJ Jaromir Jagr 15.00 40.00
TTJN James Neal 1.25 3.00
TTMD Max Domi 2.00 5.00
TTPK Phil Kessel 2.00 5.00
TTRM Ryan Miller 2.00 5.00
TTRO Robin Lehner 1.50 4.00
TTRY Ryan O'Reilly 2.00 5.00
TTSB Sergei Bobrovsky 3.00 8.00
TTSV Semyon Varlamov 2.00 5.00

2020-21 Artifacts Threads of Time Premium

*PREMIUM: 1.25X TO 3X BASIC
TTCJ Curtis Joseph 40.00 100.00
TTJI Jarome Iginla 12.00 30.00
TTRM Ryan Miller 10.00 25.00
TTRO Robin Lehner 8.00 20.00
TTSB Sergei Bobrovsky 10.00 25.00

2020-21 Artifacts Top 12 Rookie Signatures

RSBO Bowen Byram A 20.00 50.00
RSGV Gabe Vilardi B 20.00 50.00
RSJN Josh Norris A 15.00 40.00
RSJR Jason Robertson B 25.00 60.00
RSLF Liam Foudy B 12.00 30.00
RSNR Nick Robertson A 15.00 40.00

2020-21 Artifacts Treasured Swatches

TSAP Artemi Panarin 4.00 10.00
TSAV Andrei Vasilevskiy 3.00 8.00
TSBB Ben Bishop 1.50 4.00
TSBG Brendan Gallagher 2.00 5.00
TSBM Brad Marchand 4.00 10.00
TSCH Carter Hart 3.00 8.00
TSCM Connor McDavid 10.00 25.00
TSKY Keith Yandle 1.25 3.00
TSMG Mark Giordano 2.00 5.00
TSMK Mikko Koivu 1.50 4.00
TSMM Mitch Marner 3.00 8.00
TSNH Nico Hischier 3.00 8.00
TSPD Pierre-Luc Dubois 1.50 4.00
TSPR Pekka Rinne 2.00 5.00
TSTC Thomas Chabot 2.00 5.00
TSTT Teuvo Teravainen 2.00 5.00

2020-21 Artifacts Treasured Swatches Autographs

TSAV Andrei Vasilevskiy 12.00 30.00
TSBG Brendan Gallagher 8.00 20.00
TSKY Keith Yandle 5.00 12.00
TSMG Mark Giordano 8.00 20.00
TSMK Mikko Koivu 6.00 15.00
TSPR Pekka Rinne 8.00 20.00
TSTC Thomas Chabot 8.00 20.00

2020-21 Artifacts Tundra Teammates Duos

T2ANA R.Rakell/S.Steel 2.00 5.00
T2ARZ P.Kessel/O.Ekman-Larsson 2.50 6.00
T2BOS P.Bergeron/T.Krug 3.00 8.00
T2CBJ C.Atkinson/G.Nyquist 2.50 6.00
T2CHI A.DeBrincat/D.Strome 3.00 8.00
T2DAL J.Pavelski/T.Seguin 3.00 8.00
T2EDM L.Draisaitl/O.Klefbom 8.00 20.00
T2NAS M.Duchene/V.Arvidsson 2.50 6.00
T2NJD P.Subban/K.Palmieri 3.00 8.00
T2NYR A.Panarin/J.Trouba 5.00 12.00
T2OTT A.Anisimov/C.White 1.50 4.00
T2TOR K.Kapanen/W.Nylander 4.00 10.00
T2VAN B.Horvat/J.Miller 8.00 20.00
T2VGK M.Stone/M.Fleury 15.00 40.00
T2WIN M.Scheifele/C.Hellebuyck 5.00 12.00

2020-21 Artifacts Tundra Teammates Quads

T4BUF Hut/Eic/Dah/Rei 10.00 25.00
T4CAL Lin/Gau/Tka/Mon 10.00 25.00
T4FLA Ekb/Bob/Hub/Bar 8.00 20.00
T4FLY Har/Gir/Cou/Vor 12.00 30.00
T4LAK Kop/Dou/Qui/Car 10.00 25.00
T4NYI Var/Bar/Nel/Ebe 6.00 15.00
T4PIT Mal/Mur/Gue/Let 10.00 25.00
T4RED Zad/Man/Lar/Ber 12.00 30.00
T4SJS Mei/Vla/Kan/Jon 5.00 12.00
T4WAS Hol/Wil/Kuz/Car 6.00 15.00

2020-21 Artifacts Year One Rookie Sweaters

*PATCH/25: 1.5X TO 4X BASIC
RSCM Cale Makar 5.00 12.00
RSFZ Filip Zadina 1.50 4.00
RSJH Jack Hughes 5.00 12.00
RSKD Kirby Dach 2.00 5.00
RSKK Kaapo Kakko 1.50 4.00
RSNG Nikita Gusev 1.50 4.00
RSNP Nikolai Prokhorkin 1.25 3.00
RSQH Quinn Hughes 5.00 12.00
RSVO Victor Olofsson 2.00 5.00

2021-22 Artifacts

1 Bo Horvat .50 1.25
2 Alex Tuch .40 1.00
3 Igor Shesterkin .75 2.00
4 Zach Parise .40 1.00
5 Pius Suter .30 .75
6 Jakob Chychrun .40 1.00
7 Tyson Barrie .25 .60
8 Gabriel Landeskog .50 1.25
9 Carter Hart .40 1.00
10 Jakub Vrana .30 .75
11 Ondrej Palat .30 .75
12 William Nylander .75 2.00
13 Semyon Varlamov .40 1.00
14 Jonathan Marchessault .50 1.25
15 Dominik Kubalik .40 1.00
16 John Klingberg .40 1.00
17 Nick Suzuki .75 2.00
18 Adrian Kempe .40 1.00
19 Kris Letang .50 1.25
20 John Gibson .40 1.00
21 Dougie Hamilton .30 .75
22 Jakub Voracek .30 .75
23 John Tavares .60 1.50
24 Yanni Gourde .30 .75
25 Adam Fox .50 1.25
26 Jason Robertson .60 1.50
27 Drake Batherson .40 1.00
28 Charlie McAvoy .50 1.25
29 Tim Stutzle .50 1.25
30 Drew Doughty .50 1.25
31 Taylor Hall .40 1.00
32 Vincent Trocheck .40 1.00
33 Jordan Binnington .60 1.50
34 Ilya Sorokin .60 1.50
35 Tomas Hertl .40 1.00
36 Sam Reinhart .75 2.00
37 Andrei Svechnikov .50 1.25
38 Maxime Comtois .30 .75
39 Jake Muzzin .40 1.00
40 Patrice Bergeron .50 1.25
41 Anthony Mantha .30 .75
42 Rasmus Dahlin .50 1.25
43 Thomas Greiss .30 .75
44 Cam Atkinson .40 1.00
45 Blake Wheeler .40 1.00
46 Jacob Markstrom .40 1.00
47 Shea Theodore .50 1.25
48 Keith Yandle .25 .60
49 Joe Pavelski .50 1.25
50 Josh Bailey .30 .75
51 Thatcher Demko .50 1.25
52 Jeff Petry .40 1.00
53 Martin Jones .30 .75
54 Kevin Fiala .30 .75
55 Pierre-Luc Dubois .30 .75
56 Elias Lindholm .40 1.00
57 Seth Jones .40 1.00
58 Dustin Brown .40 1.00
59 Nicklas Backstrom .40 1.00
60 Jason Zucker .40 1.00
61 Ty Smith .40 1.00
62 James van Riemsdyk .30 .75
63 Mark Giordano .40 1.00
64 Brendan Gallagher .40 1.00
65 Sergei Bobrovsky .60 1.50
66 Tuukka Rask .50 1.25
67 Ryan Nugent-Hopkins .50 1.25
68 J.T. Miller .50 1.25
69 Mika Zibanejad .50 1.25
70 Filip Hronek .25 .60
71 Carter Verhaeghe .40 1.00
72 Kevin Lankinen .40 1.00
73 Nico Hischier .60 1.50
74 Oliver Bjorkstrand .40 1.00
75 Darnell Nurse .30 .75
76 Martin Necas .60 1.50
77 Conor Garland .40 1.00
78 Logan Couture .50 1.25
79 Tyler Bertuzzi .30 .75
80 Ryan Suter .30 .75
81 Brayden Schenn .40 1.00
82 Eeli Tolvanen .40 1.00
83 Victor Olofsson .40 1.00
84 Roope Hintz .50 1.25
85 Mikko Rantanen 1.00 2.50
86 Brayden Point .50 1.25
87 Roman Josi .40 1.00
88 Clayton Keller .50 1.25
89 Joel Farabee .40 1.00
90 Tyler Toffoli .40 1.00
91 Mackenzie Blackwood .40 1.00
92 John Carlson .40 1.00
93 Philipp Grubauer .40 1.00
94 Nikolaj Ehlers .40 1.00
95 Rickard Rakell .40 1.00
96 Bryan Rust .30 .75
97 David Perron .30 .75
98 Thomas Chabot .40 1.00
99 Filip Forsberg .60 1.50
100 Morgan Rielly .40 1.00
101 Connor McDavid 6.00 15.00
102 Brady Tkachuk 2.00 5.00
103 Patrick Kane 2.50 6.00
104 Alex Ovechkin 5.00 12.00
105 Auston Matthews 5.00 12.00
106 Alexis Lafreniere 2.00 5.00
107 David Pastrnak 3.00 8.00
108 Jonathan Huberdeau 2.00 5.00
109 Kirill Kaprizov 4.00 10.00
110 Andrei Vasilevskiy 2.00 5.00
111 Matthew Tkachuk 2.50 6.00
112 Connor Hellebuyck 2.50 6.00
113 Miro Heiskanen 1.50 4.00
114 Mark Stone 1.50 4.00
115 Steven Stamkos 2.50 6.00
116 Sidney Crosby 5.00 12.00
117 Johnny Gaudreau 2.00 5.00
118 Cale Makar 3.00 8.00
119 Quinn Hughes 3.00 8.00
120 Aleksander Barkov 2.00 5.00
121 Jack Hughes 3.00 8.00
122 Brent Burns 1.25 3.00
123 Phil Kessel 1.25 3.00
124 Artemi Panarin 2.50 6.00
125 Sebastian Aho 2.00 5.00
126 Kyle Connor 2.00 5.00
127 Dylan Larkin 1.50 4.00
128 Jake Guentzel 2.00 5.00
129 Alex DeBrincat 1.50 4.00
130 Carey Price 2.50 6.00
131 Max Pacioretty 1.25 3.00
132 Mathew Barzal 1.50 4.00
133 Mark Scheifele 2.00 5.00
134 Brad Marchand 2.50 6.00
135 Evgeni Malkin 2.50 6.00
136 Elias Pettersson 2.00 5.00
137 Leon Draisaitl 4.00 10.00
138 Anze Kopitar 2.00 5.00
139 Jack Eichel 2.00 5.00
140 Marc-Andre Fleury 2.50 6.00
141 Mitch Marner 2.00 5.00
142 Ryan O'Reilly 1.25 3.00
143 Victor Hedman 2.00 5.00
144 Brock Boeser 1.50 4.00
145 Nathan MacKinnon 5.00 12.00
146 Theoren Fleury 1.25 3.00
147 Teemu Selanne 2.50 6.00
148 Mike Modano 2.00 5.00
149 Doug Gilmour 1.50 4.00
150 Gerry Cheevers 1.25 3.00
151 John LeClair 1.25 3.00
152 Peter Forsberg 2.50 6.00
153 Bernie Nicholls 1.00 2.50
154 Mike Gartner 1.50 4.00
155 Brett Hull 2.00 5.00
156 Mike Richter 1.25 3.00
157 Joe Sakic 2.50 6.00
158 Eric Lindros 2.00 5.00
159 Martin Brodeur 3.00 8.00
160 Paul Coffey 1.50 4.00
161 Quinton Byfield RC 5.00 12.00
162 Joseph Veleno RC 3.00 8.00
163 Jeremy Swayman RC 6.00 15.00
164 Rasmus Kupari RC 2.00 5.00
165 Grigori Denisenko RC 2.00 5.00
166 Trevor Zegras RC 4.00 10.00
167 Cam York RC 2.50 6.00
168 Ross Colton RC 2.50 6.00
169 Alex Newhook RC 3.00 8.00
170 Jacob Bernard-Docker RC 2.00 5.00
171 Alex Barre-Boulet RC 2.00 5.00
172 Wyatt Kalynuk RC 2.00 5.00
173 Ukko-Pekka Luukkonen RC 3.00 8.00

174 Spencer Knight RC 4.00 10.00
175 Jamie Drysdale RC 3.00 8.00
176 Shane Pinto RC 3.00 8.00
177 Wade Allison RC 2.00 5.00
178 Calen Addison RC 2.00 5.00
179 Zac Jones RC 2.50 6.00
180 Cole Caufield RC 20.00 50.00
RED181 Mason McTavish RC 4.00 10.00
RED182 Karel Vejmelka RC 2.50 6.00
RED183 Oskar Steen RC 2.50 6.00
RED184 John-Jason Peterka RC 4.00 10.00
RED185 Adam Ruzicka RC 2.00 5.00
RED186 Seth Jarvis RC 5.00 12.00
RED187 Mike Hardman RC 2.00 5.00
RED188 Sampo Ranta RC 2.00 5.00
RED189 Cole Sillinger RC 3.00 8.00
RED190 Riley Tufte RC 2.00 5.00
RED191 Lucas Raymond RC 6.00 15.00
RED192 Markus Niemelainen RC 2.00 5.00
RED193 Anton Lundell RC 4.00 10.00
RED194 Alex Turcotte RC 2.50 6.00
RED195 Brandon Duhaime RC 2.00 5.00
RED196 Jesse Ylonen RC 2.00 5.00
RED197 Philip Tomasino RC 2.50 6.00
RED198 Dawson Mercer RC 5.00 12.00
RED199 Robin Salo RC 2.00 5.00
RED200 Nils Lundkvist RC 2.00 5.00
RED201 Lassi Thomson RC 2.00 5.00
RED202 Maxwell Willman RC 2.00 5.00
RED203 Radim Zohorna RC 2.00 5.00
RED204 William Eklund RC 5.00 12.00
RED205 Kole Lind RC 2.50 6.00
RED206 Scott Perunovich RC 2.00 5.00
RED207 Taylor Raddysh RC 3.00 8.00
RED208 Michael Bunting RC 2.00 5.00
RED209 Vasily Podkolzin RC 2.50 6.00
RED210 Jake Leschyshyn RC 2.00 5.00
RED211 Hendrix Lapierre RC 2.00 5.00
RED212 Cole Perfetti RC 4.00 10.00
RED213 Moritz Seider RC 5.00 12.00
RED214 Alexander Holtz RC 3.00 8.00
RED215 Tanner Jeannot RC 2.00 5.00
RED216 Jonathan Dahlen RC 2.00 5.00
RED217 Jake Neighbours RC 4.00 10.00
RED218 Yegor Chinakhov RC 3.00 8.00
RED219 Adam Beckman RC 2.00 5.00
RED220 Egor Sokolov RC 2.00 5.00
RED221 Justus Annunen RC 2.50 6.00
RED222 David Farrance RC 2.00 5.00
RED223 Ryan Merkley RC 2.50 6.00
RED224 Daniil Tarasov RC 2.00 5.00
RED225 Benoit-Olivier Groulx RC 2.00 5.00
RED226 Aliaksei Protas RC 2.00 5.00
RED227 Jan Jenik RC 2.50 6.00
RED228 Boris Katchouk RC 1.50 4.00
RED229 Nico Daws RC 3.00 8.00
RED230 Pavel Dorofeyev RC 2.50 6.00

2021-22 Artifacts Autumn
*AUTUMN VETS: 2.5X TO 6X BASIC
*AUTUMN S/L: .75X TO 2X BASIC
*AUTUMN RC: .75X TO 2X BASIC
180 Cole Caufield 50.00 125.00

2021-22 Artifacts Clear Cut
161 Quinton Byfield 25.00 60.00
162 Joseph Veleno 10.00 25.00
163 Jeremy Swayman 60.00 150.00
164 Rasmus Kupari 10.00 25.00
165 Grigori Denisenko 12.00 30.00
166 Trevor Zegras 60.00 150.00
167 Cam York 10.00 25.00
168 Ross Colton 12.00 30.00
169 Alex Newhook 15.00 40.00
170 Jacob Bernard-Docker 10.00 25.00
171 Alex Barre-Boulet 10.00 25.00
172 Wyatt Kalynuk 10.00 25.00
173 Ukko-Pekka Luukkonen 15.00 40.00
174 Spencer Knight 60.00 150.00
175 Jamie Drysdale 15.00 40.00
176 Shane Pinto 15.00 40.00
177 Wade Allison 10.00 25.00
178 Calen Addison 10.00 25.00
179 Zac Jones 12.00 30.00
180 Cole Caufield 80.00 200.00

2021-22 Artifacts Emerald
*EMERALD VETS: 2X TO 5X BASIC
*EMERALD S/L: .6X TO 1.5X BASIC
*EMERALD RC: .6X TO 1.5X BASIC
180 Cole Caufield 40.00 100.00

2021-22 Artifacts Light Blue Steel
*LIGHT BLUE VETS: 2.5X TO 6X BASIC
*LIGHT BLUE S/L: .75X TO 2X BASIC
*LIGHT BLUE RC: .75X TO 2X BASIC
180 Cole Caufield 50.00 125.00

2021-22 Artifacts Neon Green
*NEON GREEN VETS: .5X TO 1.25X BASIC
*NEON GREEN S/L: .5X TO 1.25X BASIC
*NEON GREEN RC: .3X TO .75X BASIC

2021-22 Artifacts Pink
*PINK VETS: 4X TO 10X BASIC
*PINK S/L: 1.25X TO 3X BASIC
*PINK RC: 1.25X TO 3X BASIC
180 Cole Caufield 80.00 200.00

2021-22 Artifacts Purple
*PURPLE VETS: 5X TO 12X BASIC
*PURPLE S/L: 1.5X TO 4X BASIC
*PURPLE RC: 1.5X TO 4X BASIC
180 Cole Caufield 100.00 250.00

2021-22 Artifacts Rose
*ROSE VETS: 3X TO 8X BASIC
*ROSE S/L: 1X TO 2.5X BASIC
*ROSE RC: 1X TO 2.5X BASIC
180 Cole Caufield 60.00 150.00

2021-22 Artifacts Rose Gold
*ROSE GOLD VETS: .5X TO 1.25X BASIC
*ROSE GOLD S/L: .5X TO 1.25X BASIC
*ROSE GOLD RC: .3X TO .75X BASIC

2021-22 Artifacts Royal Blue
*ROYAL BLUE VETS: 1.5X TO 4X BASIC
*ROYAL BLUE S/L: .5X TO 1.25X BASIC
*ROYAL BLUE RC: .6X TO 1.5X BASIC
180 Cole Caufield 40.00 100.00

2021-22 Artifacts Ruby
*RUBY VETS: 1.25X TO 3X BASIC
*RUBY S/L: .4X TO 1X BASIC
*RUBY RC: .5X TO 1.25X BASIC

2021-22 Artifacts Silver Spectrum
*SILVER VETS: 1.5X TO 4X BASIC
*SILVER S/L: .5X TO 1.25X BASIC
*SILVER RC: .6X TO 1.5X BASIC

2021-22 Artifacts Turquoise
*TURQUOISE VETS: .5X TO 1.25X BASIC
*TURQUOISE S/L: .5X TO 1.25X BASIC
*TURQUOISE RC: .3X TO .75X BASIC

2021-22 Artifacts Yellow
*YELLOW VETS: 3X TO 8X BASIC
*YELLOW S/L: 1X TO 2.5X BASIC
*YELLOW RC: 1X TO 2.5X BASIC
180 Cole Caufield 60.00 150.00

2021-22 Artifacts '05-06 Clear Cut Retro Rookies
CC051 Auston Matthews 80.00 200.00
CC052 Kirill Kaprizov 40.00 100.00
CC053 Andrei Vasilevskiy 20.00 50.00
CC054 Patrick Kane 25.00 60.00
CC055 Cale Makar 30.00 80.00
CC056 Brad Marchand 25.00 60.00
CC057 Carey Price 25.00 60.00
CC058 David Pastrnak 30.00 80.00
CC059 Artemi Panarin 25.00 60.00
CC0510 Leon Draisaitl 40.00 100.00
CC0511 Cole Caufield 125.00 300.00
CC0512 Shane Pinto 20.00 50.00
CC0513 Jamie Drysdale 20.00 50.00
CC0514 Spencer Knight 25.00 60.00
CC0515 Alex Newhook 20.00 50.00
CC0516 Quinton Byfield 30.00 80.00
CC0517 Joseph Veleno 12.00 30.00
CC0518 Cam York 12.00 30.00
CC0519 Trevor Zegras 80.00 200.00
CC0520 Jeremy Swayman 40.00 100.00

2021-22 Artifacts '05-06 Retro Autofacts
RAFAS Andrei Svechnikov D 12.00 30.00
RAFAT Alex Tuch C 10.00 25.00
RAFAV Andrei Vasilevskiy D 15.00 40.00
RAFBB Brent Burns D 10.00 25.00
RAFBT Brady Tkachuk D 15.00 40.00
RAFDP David Perron D 8.00 20.00
RAFEL Elias Lindholm F 10.00 25.00
RAFES Eric Staal E 10.00 25.00
RAFJB Jamie Benn C 10.00 25.00
RAFJL Jacques Lemaire E 8.00 20.00
RAFJP Joe Pavelski D 12.00 30.00
RAFJV James van Riemsdyk F 8.00 20.00
RAFJZ Jason Zucker F 10.00 25.00
RAFKF Kevin Fiala F 8.00 20.00
RAFKY Keith Yandle E 6.00 15.00
RAFMA Cale Makar C 80.00 200.00
RAFMD Max Domi D 10.00 25.00
RAFMM Mitch Marner B 15.00 40.00
RAFMO Mike Modano B 15.00 40.00
RAFMP Max Pacioretty E 10.00 25.00
RAFMS Mark Stone C 12.00 30.00
RAFNE Nikolaj Ehlers E 10.00 25.00
RAFRH Ron Hextall D 10.00 25.00
RAFSC Mark Scheifele D 15.00 40.00
RAFSK Saku Koivu D 10.00 25.00
RAFTH Tomas Hertl E 10.00 25.00
RAFTL Trevor Linden E 10.00 25.00
RAFWC Wendel Clark D 15.00 40.00

2021-22 Artifacts '05-06 Retro Rookies
1 Lucas Raymond 6.00 15.00
2 Cole Caufield 25.00 60.00
3 Mason McTavish 4.00 10.00
4 Alexander Holtz 3.00 8.00
5 William Eklund 5.00 12.00
6 Anton Lundell 4.00 10.00
7 Cole Perfetti 4.00 10.00
8 Dawson Mercer 5.00 12.00
9 Trevor Zegras 4.00 10.00
10 Moritz Seider 15.00 40.00

2021-22 Artifacts Admirable Impressions
AIAM Auston Matthews 150.00 400.00
AIAV Andrei Vasilevskiy 60.00 150.00
AIML Mario Lemieux 150.00 400.00
AIPK Patrick Kane 80.00 200.00
AISK Saku Koivu 40.00 100.00

2021-22 Artifacts Arena Artifacts
JLABP Bob Probert 40.00 100.00
JLABS Brendan Shanahan 60.00 150.00
JLACC Chris Chelios 40.00 100.00
JLADH Dominik Hasek 80.00 200.00
JLAHZ Henrik Zetterberg 50.00 120.00
JLAIL Igor Larionov 40.00 100.00
JLAMV Mike Vernon 40.00 100.00
JLANL Nicklas Lidstrom 40.00 100.00
JLASY Steve Yzerman 100.00 250.00

2021-22 Artifacts Aurum
A1 Leon Draisaitl 6.00 15.00
A2 Cam Atkinson 2.00 5.00
A3 Brad Marchand 4.00 10.00
A4 Andrei Vasilevskiy 3.00 8.00
A5 Jack Hughes 5.00 12.00
A6 Connor Hellebuyck 4.00 10.00
A7 Sidney Crosby 8.00 20.00
A8 Ilya Sorokin 3.00 8.00
A9 Alex DeBrincat 2.50 6.00
A10 Roman Josi 2.00 5.00
A11 Clayton Keller 2.50 6.00
A12 Shea Theodore 2.50 6.00
A13 Alexis Lafreniere 3.00 8.00
A14 Jakub Vrana 1.50 4.00
A15 Rasmus Dahlin 2.50 6.00
A16 Elias Lindholm 2.00 5.00
A17 Logan Couture 2.50 6.00
A18 Alex Ovechkin 8.00 20.00
A19 Tyler Toffoli 2.00 5.00
A20 Drew Doughty 2.50 6.00
A21 Cale Makar 5.00 12.00
A22 Andrei Svechnikov 2.50 6.00
A23 Josh Norris 2.00 5.00
A24 Kirill Kaprizov 6.00 15.00
A25 Claude Giroux 2.00 5.00
A26 Auston Matthews 8.00 20.00
A27 Bo Horvat 2.50 6.00
A28 Joe Pavelski 2.50 6.00
A29 Ryan O'Reilly 2.00 5.00
A30 Aleksander Barkov 3.00 8.00
A31 Jamie Drysdale 3.00 8.00
A32 Grigori Denisenko 5.00 12.00
A33 Joseph Veleno 4.00 10.00
A34 Ukko-Pekka Luukkonen 4.00 10.00
A35 Shane Pinto 3.00 8.00
A36 Cam York 8.00 20.00
A37 Alex Newhook 10.00 25.00
A38 Spencer Knight 10.00 25.00
A39 Trevor Zegras 12.00 30.00
A40 Jeremy Swayman 12.00 30.00
A41 Eric Lindros AS 20.00 50.00
A42 Wayne Gretzky AS 60.00 150.00
A43 Mario Lemieux AS 25.00 60.00
A44 Bobby Hull AS 20.00 50.00
A45 Marcel Dionne 12.00 30.00
A46 Cam Neely 25.00 60.00
A47 Martin Brodeur 20.00 50.00
A48 Mike Modano 30.00 80.00

2021-22 Artifacts Aurum Signatures
ASAV Andrei Vasilevskiy 30.00 80.00
ASBM Brad Marchand 40.00 100.00
ASBT Brady Tkachuk 30.00 80.00
ASCM Cale Makar 50.00 125.00
ASCN Cam Neely 15.00 40.00
ASDG Doug Gilmour 25.00 60.00
ASEP Elias Pettersson 30.00 80.00
ASJD Jamie Drysdale 30.00 80.00
ASMD Marcel Dionne 25.00 60.00
ASMM Mike Modano 30.00 80.00
ASMR Mike Richter 20.00 50.00
ASMS Mark Scheifele 30.00 80.00
ASMT Matthew Tkachuk 40.00 100.00
ASNL Nicklas Lidstrom 20.00 50.00
ASPC Paul Coffey 25.00 60.00
ASPF Peter Forsberg 40.00 100.00
ASPK Patrick Kane 40.00 100.00
ASQB Quinton Byfield 30.00 80.00
ASRO Ryan O'Reilly 20.00 50.00
ASST Mark Stone 25.00 60.00
ASUL Ukko-Pekka Luukkonen 30.00 80.00

2021-22 Artifacts Autofacts
AFAN Craig Anderson C 4.00 10.00
AFAT Alex Tuch F 6.00 15.00
AFBB Brock Boeser B 8.00 20.00
AFBH Brett Howden F 4.00 10.00
AFBN Bernie Nicholls G 5.00 12.00
AFBR Brett Ritchie E 4.00 10.00
AFCA Cam Atkinson E 6.00 15.00
AFCP Colton Parayko F 5.00 12.00
AFCT Cam Talbot H 6.00 15.00
AFDF Derek Forbort H 4.00 10.00
AFDH Dougie Hamilton F 5.00 12.00
AFDI Phil Di Giuseppe F 4.00 10.00
AFDO Ryan Donato D 5.00 12.00
AFDR David Rittich G 4.00 10.00
AFDT Devon Toews H 5.00 12.00
AFDU Pierre-Luc Dubois E 5.00 12.00
AFDW Doug Weight E 6.00 15.00
AFEB Evan Bouchard H 8.00 20.00
AFEL Eetu Luostarinen G 4.00 10.00
AFEM Elvis Merzlikins F 6.00 15.00
AFES Evgeny Svechnikov G 4.00 10.00
AFET Eeli Tolvanen F 6.00 15.00
AFGE Morgan Geekie H 4.00 10.00
AFGL Guy Lafleur A 8.00 20.00
AFHA Brandon Hagel H 5.00 12.00
AFJA Josh Anderson E 5.00 12.00
AFJB Jake Bean H 4.00 10.00
AFJD Jason Dickinson E 5.00 12.00
AFJK Jordan Kyrou D 6.00 15.00
AFJM Jacob Markstrom F 6.00 15.00
AFJO Jonathan Marchessault F 8.00 20.00
AFJP Jean-Gabriel Pageau F 4.00 10.00
AFJS Justin Schultz F 5.00 12.00
AFJZ Jakub Zboril H 4.00 10.00
AFKF Kevin Fiala F 5.00 12.00
AFKI Joel Kiviranta H 4.00 10.00
AFKK Karson Kuhlman E 4.00 10.00
AFKP Kyle Palmieri F 5.00 12.00
AFKT Keith Tkachuk D 6.00 15.00
AFKU Janne Kuokkanen G 4.00 10.00
AFKY Keith Yandle E 4.00 10.00
AFLH Libor Hajek E 4.00 10.00
AFMC Maxime Comtois G 5.00 12.00
AFMF Mario Ferraro G 4.00 10.00
AFMG Marian Gaborik D 6.00 15.00
AFMI J.T. Miller D 8.00 20.00
AFMJ Max Jones B 4.00 10.00
AFMM Mitch Marner B 30.00 80.00
AFMO Josh Morrissey F 8.00 20.00
AFMS Marc Staal G 4.00 10.00
AFMZ Mats Zuccarello C 6.00 15.00
AFNO Noah Hanifin H 6.00 15.00
AFOT Owen Tippett G 4.00 10.00
AFPD Phillip Danault E 6.00 15.00
AFPF Pavel Francouz G 5.00 12.00
AFPG Philipp Grubauer D 6.00 15.00
AFRB Rod Brind'Amour D 6.00 15.00
AFRD Ryan Dzingel G 5.00 12.00
AFRG Rhett Gardner F 4.00 10.00
AFRL Ryan Lindgren G 4.00 10.00
AFRN Ryan Nugent-Hopkins E 8.00 20.00
AFRT Robert Thomas G 6.00 15.00
AFSC Sasha Chmelevski H 4.00 10.00
AFSG Simon Gagne F 6.00 15.00
AFSK Slater Koekkoek F 4.00 10.00
AFSR Sam Reinhart F 12.00 30.00
AFST Jordan Staal F 5.00 12.00
AFSU Malcolm Subban G 5.00 12.00
AFTE Alexandre Texier H 4.00 10.00
AFTF Trent Frederic G 4.00 10.00
AFTH Tomas Hertl F 6.00 15.00
AFTJ Tristan Jarry G 6.00 15.00
AFTK Tanner Kero F 4.00 10.00
AFTL Trevor Linden E 6.00 15.00
AFTS Travis Sanheim F 4.00 10.00
AFTW Tom Wilson F 6.00 15.00
AFVH Ville Husso F 4.00 10.00
AFVN Vladislav Namestnikov F 4.00 10.00
AFWC Wendel Clark E 10.00 25.00
AFYG Yanni Gourde E 5.00 12.00
AFYS Yegor Sharangovich G 6.00 15.00
AFZH Zach Hyman G 10.00 25.00

2021-22 Artifacts Esteemed Endorsements
EEBB Brent Burns 60.00 150.00
EEBM Brad Marchand 125.00 300.00
EEDG Doug Gilmour 80.00 200.00
EEJI Jarome Iginla 80.00 200.00
EELD Leon Draisaitl 200.00 500.00
EELM Lanny McDonald 60.00 150.00
EEMG Mike Gartner 100.00 250.00
EEMR Mike Richter 100.00 250.00
EERO Ryan O'Reilly 60.00 150.00

2021-22 Artifacts Honoured Members Signatures
HMSDW Doug Wilson 125.00 300.00
HMSHU Bobby Hull 200.00 500.00
HMSPE Phil Esposito 125.00 300.00

2021-22 Artifacts Horizontal Rookie Autographs
SP3 Cole Caufield 125.00 300.00

2021-22 Artifacts Horizontal Rookies
SP1 Lucas Raymond 5.00 12.00
SP2 Trevor Zegras 3.00 8.00
SP3 Cole Caufield 15.00 40.00
SP4 Moritz Seider 4.00 10.00
SP5 Quinton Byfield 4.00 10.00

2021-22 Artifacts Material Autographs Gold
*HOR.GOLD: .5X TO 1.25X BASIC
V Seth Jarvis/35 125.00 300.00
II Moritz Seider/35 125.00 300.00
IV Anton Lundell/35 30.00 80.00
VI Scott Perunovich/35 15.00 40.00
101 Connor McDavid/25 250.00 600.00
102 Brady Tkachuk/65 25.00 60.00
103 Patrick Kane/25 50.00 125.00
105 Auston Matthews/25 200.00 500.00
106 Alexis Lafreniere/25 80.00 200.00
110 Andrei Vasilevskiy/45 25.00 60.00
111 Matthew Tkachuk/45 30.00 80.00
112 Connor Hellebuyck/65 30.00 80.00
113 Miro Heiskanen/65 20.00 50.00
114 Mark Stone/65 20.00 50.00
118 Cale Makar/45 80.00 200.00
120 Aleksander Barkov/65 25.00 60.00
121 Jack Hughes/45 40.00 100.00
122 Brent Burns/45 15.00 40.00
128 Jake Guentzel/65 25.00 60.00
130 Carey Price/25 30.00 80.00
131 Max Pacioretty/65 15.00 40.00
133 Mark Scheifele/45 25.00 60.00
134 Brad Marchand/45 30.00 80.00
136 Elias Pettersson/45 25.00 60.00
138 Anze Kopitar/45 25.00 60.00
141 Mitch Marner/45 25.00 60.00
142 Ryan O'Reilly/45 15.00 40.00
144 Brock Boeser/45 20.00 50.00
149 Doug Gilmour/45 20.00 50.00
153 Bernie Nicholls/65 12.00 30.00
154 Mike Gartner/65 20.00 50.00
155 Brett Hull/25 40.00 100.00
156 Mike Richter/45 15.00 40.00
161 Quinton Byfield/99 40.00 100.00
162 Joseph Veleno/149 15.00 40.00
163 Jeremy Swayman/99 60.00 150.00
164 Rasmus Kupari/149 15.00 40.00
165 Grigori Denisenko/149 20.00 50.00
168 Ross Colton/149 20.00 50.00
169 Alex Newhook/99 25.00 60.00
170 Jacob Bernard-Docker/149 15.00 40.00
172 Wyatt Kalynuk/149 15.00 40.00
173 Ukko-Pekka Luukkonen/149 25.00 60.00
174 Spencer Knight/99 30.00 80.00
175 Jamie Drysdale/99 25.00 60.00
177 Wade Allison/149 15.00 40.00
178 Calen Addison/149 15.00 40.00
179 Zac Jones/149 20.00 50.00
III Dawson Mercer/35 60.00 150.00

2021-22 Artifacts Material Autographs Emerald
*EMERALD/45: .5X TO 1.25X BASIC
174 Spencer Knight/45 80.00 200.00

2021-22 Artifacts Materials Gold
*HORIZONTAL: .5X TO 1.25X BASIC
*HOR.EMRLD: 1.2X TO 3X BASIC
1 Bo Horvat 4.00 10.00
2 Alex Tuch 3.00 8.00
3 Igor Shesterkin 6.00 15.00
4 Zach Parise 3.00 8.00
6 Jakob Chychrun 3.00 8.00
7 Tyson Barrie 2.00 5.00
8 Gabriel Landeskog 4.00 10.00
9 Carter Hart 3.00 8.00
I Lucas Raymond 20.00 50.00
V Seth Jarvis 8.00 20.00
10 Jakub Vrana 2.50 6.00
11 Ondrej Palat 2.50 6.00
12 William Nylander 6.00 15.00
13 Semyon Varlamov 3.00 8.00
14 Jonathan Marchessault 4.00 10.00
15 Dominik Kubalik 3.00 8.00
16 John Klingberg 3.00 8.00
17 Nick Suzuki 6.00 15.00
18 Adrian Kempe 3.00 8.00
19 Kris Letang 4.00 10.00
20 John Gibson 3.00 8.00
21 Dougie Hamilton 2.50 6.00
22 Jakub Voracek 2.50 6.00
23 John Tavares 5.00 12.00
24 Yanni Gourde 2.50 6.00
28 Charlie McAvoy 4.00 10.00
29 Tim Stutzle 4.00 10.00
30 Drew Doughty 4.00 10.00
31 Taylor Hall 3.00 8.00
32 Vincent Trocheck 3.00 8.00
33 Jordan Binnington 5.00 12.00
34 Ilya Sorokin 5.00 12.00
35 Tomas Hertl 3.00 8.00
36 Sam Reinhart 6.00 15.00
37 Andrei Svechnikov 4.00 10.00
39 Jake Muzzin 3.00 8.00
40 Patrice Bergeron 4.00 10.00
41 Anthony Mantha 2.50 6.00
42 Rasmus Dahlin 4.00 10.00
43 Thomas Greiss 2.50 6.00
44 Cam Atkinson 3.00 8.00
45 Blake Wheeler 3.00 8.00
46 Jacob Markstrom 3.00 8.00
47 Shea Theodore 4.00 10.00
48 Keith Yandle 2.00 5.00
49 Joe Pavelski 4.00 10.00
50 Josh Bailey 2.50 6.00
51 Thatcher Demko 4.00 10.00
53 Martin Jones 2.50 6.00
54 Kevin Fiala 2.50 6.00
55 Pierre-Luc Dubois 2.50 6.00
56 Elias Lindholm 3.00 8.00
57 Seth Jones 3.00 8.00
58 Dustin Brown 3.00 8.00
59 Nicklas Backstrom 3.00 8.00
60 Jason Zucker 3.00 8.00
61 Ty Smith 3.00 8.00
62 James van Riemsdyk 2.50 6.00
63 Mark Giordano 3.00 8.00
64 Brendan Gallagher 3.00 8.00
65 Sergei Bobrovsky 5.00 12.00
66 Tuukka Rask 4.00 10.00
67 Ryan Nugent-Hopkins 4.00 10.00
68 J.T. Miller 4.00 10.00
69 Mika Zibanejad 4.00 10.00
71 Carter Verhaeghe 3.00 8.00
73 Nico Hischier 5.00 12.00
74 Oliver Bjorkstrand 2.50 6.00
75 Darnell Nurse 2.50 6.00
76 Martin Necas 5.00 12.00
77 Conor Garland 2.50 6.00
78 Logan Couture 4.00 10.00
79 Tyler Bertuzzi 2.50 6.00
80 Ryan Suter 2.50 6.00
81 Brayden Schenn 3.00 8.00
83 Victor Olofsson 3.00 8.00
84 Roope Hintz 4.00 10.00
85 Mikko Rantanen 8.00 20.00
86 Brayden Point 4.00 10.00
87 Roman Josi 3.00 8.00
88 Clayton Keller 4.00 10.00
89 Joel Farabee 3.00 8.00
90 Tyler Toffoli 3.00 8.00
91 Mackenzie Blackwood 3.00 8.00
92 John Carlson 3.00 8.00
93 Philipp Grubauer 3.00 8.00
94 Nikolaj Ehlers 3.00 8.00
95 Rickard Rakell 2.50 6.00
97 David Perron 2.50 6.00
98 Thomas Chabot 3.00 8.00
99 Filip Forsberg 5.00 12.00
II Moritz Seider 20.00 50.00
IV Anton Lundell 6.00 15.00
VI Scott Perunovich 3.00 8.00
100 Morgan Rielly 3.00 8.00
101 Connor McDavid 15.00 40.00
102 Brady Tkachuk 5.00 12.00
103 Patrick Kane 6.00 15.00
104 Alex Ovechkin 12.00 30.00
105 Auston Matthews 12.00 30.00
106 Alexis Lafreniere 5.00 12.00
107 David Pastrnak 8.00 20.00
108 Jonathan Huberdeau 4.00 10.00
109 Kirill Kaprizov 10.00 25.00
110 Andrei Vasilevskiy 5.00 12.00
111 Matthew Tkachuk 6.00 15.00
112 Connor Hellebuyck 6.00 15.00
113 Miro Heiskanen 4.00 10.00
114 Mark Stone 4.00 10.00
115 Steven Stamkos 6.00 15.00
116 Sidney Crosby 12.00 30.00
117 Johnny Gaudreau 5.00 12.00
118 Cale Makar 8.00 20.00
119 Quinn Hughes 8.00 20.00
120 Aleksander Barkov 5.00 12.00
121 Jack Hughes 8.00 20.00
122 Brent Burns 3.00 8.00
123 Phil Kessel 3.00 8.00
124 Artemi Panarin 6.00 15.00
125 Sebastian Aho 5.00 12.00
126 Kyle Connor 5.00 12.00
127 Dylan Larkin 4.00 10.00
128 Jake Guentzel 5.00 12.00
129 Alex DeBrincat 4.00 10.00
130 Carey Price 6.00 15.00
131 Max Pacioretty 3.00 8.00
132 Mathew Barzal 4.00 10.00
133 Mark Scheifele 5.00 12.00
134 Brad Marchand 6.00 15.00
135 Evgeni Malkin 6.00 15.00
136 Elias Pettersson 5.00 12.00
137 Leon Draisaitl 10.00 25.00
138 Anze Kopitar 5.00 12.00
139 Jack Eichel 5.00 12.00
140 Marc-Andre Fleury 6.00 15.00
141 Mitch Marner 5.00 12.00
142 Ryan O'Reilly 3.00 8.00
143 Victor Hedman 4.00 10.00
144 Brock Boeser 4.00 10.00
145 Nathan MacKinnon 12.00 30.00
146 Theoren Fleury 3.00 8.00
147 Teemu Selanne 6.00 15.00
149 Doug Gilmour 4.00 10.00
152 Peter Forsberg 6.00 15.00
153 Bernie Nicholls 2.50 6.00
154 Mike Gartner 4.00 10.00
155 Brett Hull 5.00 12.00
156 Mike Richter 3.00 8.00
157 Joe Sakic 6.00 15.00
158 Eric Lindros 5.00 12.00
159 Martin Brodeur 8.00 20.00
161 Quinton Byfield 8.00 20.00
162 Joseph Veleno 3.00 8.00
163 Jeremy Swayman 10.00 25.00
164 Rasmus Kupari 3.00 8.00
165 Grigori Denisenko 4.00 10.00
166 Trevor Zegras 6.00 15.00
167 Cam York 3.00 8.00
168 Ross Colton 4.00 10.00
169 Alex Newhook 5.00 12.00
170 Jacob Bernard-Docker 3.00 8.00
172 Wyatt Kalynuk 3.00 8.00
173 Ukko-Pekka Luukkonen 5.00 12.00
174 Spencer Knight 6.00 15.00
175 Jamie Drysdale 5.00 12.00
177 Wade Allison 3.00 8.00
178 Calen Addison 3.00 8.00
179 Zac Jones 4.00 10.00
180 Cole Caufield 30.00 80.00
III Dawson Mercer 8.00 20.00

2021-22 Artifacts Materials Emerald
*EMERALD: .75X TO 2X BASIC
I Lucas Raymond 60.00 150.00
II Moritz Seider 50.00 125.00
166 Trevor Zegras 60.00 150.00
180 Cole Caufield 80.00 200.00

2021-22 Artifacts Materials Purple
*PURPLE: 1.25X TO 3X BASIC
I Lucas Raymond 80.00 200.00
II Moritz Seider 100.00 250.00
166 Trevor Zegras 80.00 200.00
180 Cole Caufield 100.00 250.00

2021-22 Artifacts Net Gear
NGAV Andrei Vasilevskiy C 3.00 8.00
NGCH Carter Hart C 2.00 5.00
NGCP Carey Price C 4.00 10.00
NGHE Connor Hellebuyck C 4.00 10.00
NGIS Ilya Sorokin C 3.00 8.00
NGJG John Gibson C 2.00 5.00
NGJM Jacob Markstrom C 2.00 5.00
NGMB Martin Brodeur B 5.00 12.00
NGMF Marc-Andre Fleury B 4.00 10.00
NGPR Pekka Rinne C 2.00 5.00
NGRO Patrick Roy A 5.00 12.00
NGSB Sergei Bobrovsky C 3.00 8.00
NGSV Semyon Varlamov C 2.00 5.00
NGTR Tuukka Rask C 2.50 6.00

2021-22 Artifacts Net Gear Autographs
NGAV Andrei Vasilevskiy 50.00 125.00
NGCH Carter Hart 40.00 100.00
NGHE Connor Hellebuyck 80.00 200.00
NGIS Ilya Sorokin 125.00 300.00
NGJG John Gibson 40.00 100.00
NGJM Jacob Markstrom 40.00 100.00
NGMB Martin Brodeur 80.00 200.00
NGMF Marc-Andre Fleury 40.00 100.00
NGPR Pekka Rinne 40.00 100.00
NGSB Sergei Bobrovsky 60.00 150.00

2021-22 Artifacts NHL Remnants
*PREMIUM/25: 1X TO 2.5X BASIC
NRAB Aleksander Barkov 4.00 10.00
NRAD Alex DeBrincat 3.00 8.00
NRAP Alex Pietrangelo 2.00 5.00
NRBB Brent Burns 2.50 6.00
NRBP Brayden Point 3.00 8.00
NRCG Claude Giroux 2.50 6.00
NRCK Clayton Keller 3.00 8.00
NRCM Connor McDavid 12.00 30.00
NRDD Drew Doughty 3.00 8.00
NRDL Dylan Larkin 3.00 8.00
NRDP David Pastrnak 6.00 15.00
NREP Elias Pettersson 4.00 10.00
NRJB Jamie Benn 2.50 6.00
NRJC John Carlson 2.50 6.00
NRJE Jack Eichel 4.00 10.00
NRJG Johnny Gaudreau 4.00 10.00
NRKF Kevin Fiala 2.00 5.00
NRKL Kris Letang 3.00 8.00
NRMB Mathew Barzal 3.00 8.00
NRMM Mitch Marner 4.00 10.00
NRMR Mikko Rantanen 6.00 15.00
NRMZ Mika Zibanejad 3.00 8.00
NRNE Nikolaj Ehlers 2.50 6.00
NRPS P.K. Subban 3.00 8.00
NRRG Ryan Getzlaf 2.50 6.00
NRRJ Roman Josi 2.50 6.00
NRRO Ryan O'Reilly 2.50 6.00
NRSA Sebastian Aho 4.00 10.00
NRTT Tyler Toffoli 2.50 6.00
NRZW Zach Werenski 4.00 10.00

2021-22 Artifacts Signature Apparel
SAMT Matthew Tkachuk/36 25.00 60.00

2021-22 Artifacts Signs of Success
SOSBT Brady Tkachuk/49 20.00 50.00
SOSES Eric Staal/49 10.00 25.00
SOSJB Jamie Benn/49 10.00 25.00
SOSMP Max Pacioretty/49 10.00 25.00
SOSRN Ryan Nugent-Hopkins/49 12.00 30.00
SOSTS Ty Smith/49 10.00 25.00

2021-22 Artifacts Storied Scripts
SSBO Bobby Orr 200.00 500.00
SSWG Wayne Gretzky 300.00 800.00

2021-22 Artifacts Top 12 Rookie Signatures
RSAN Alex Newhook B 25.00 60.00
RSJS Jeremy Swayman C 25.00 60.00
RSQB Quinton Byfield A 20.00 50.00
RSSK Spencer Knight B 15.00 40.00
RSSP Shane Pinto C 20.00 50.00
RSTZ Trevor Zegras A 400.00 1000.00

2021-22 Artifacts Treasured Swatches
TSAM Auston Matthews 8.00 20.00
TSAS Andrei Svechnikov 2.50 6.00
TSBB Brock Boeser 2.50 6.00
TSDC Dylan Cozens 2.00 5.00
TSJB Jordan Binnington 3.00 8.00
TSJG Jake Guentzel 3.00 8.00
TSJH Jonathan Huberdeau 2.50 6.00
TSLD Leon Draisaitl 6.00 15.00
TSMH Miro Heiskanen 2.50 6.00
TSMS Mark Stone 2.50 6.00
TSMT Matthew Tkachuk 4.00 10.00
TSNM Nathan MacKinnon 8.00 20.00
TSPK Patrick Kane 4.00 10.00
TSSM Ty Smith 2.00 5.00
TSTS Tim Stutzle 2.50 6.00

2021-22 Artifacts Tundra Teammates Duos
T2ARI C.Garland/J.Chychrun 2.50 6.00
T2BUF J.Eichel/R.Dahlin 4.00 10.00
T2CAL E.Lindholm/J.Markstrom 2.50 6.00
T2CBJ P.Laine/M.Domi 3.00 8.00
T2DAL M.Heiskanen/R.Hintz 3.00 8.00
T2EDM D.Nurse/R.Nugent-Hopkins 3.00 8.00
T2FLA C.Verhaeghe/O.Tippett 2.50 6.00
T2NAS R.Ellis/M.Ekholm 2.00 5.00
T2NYI M.Barzal/S.Varlamov 3.00 8.00
T2OTT M.Murray/T.Chabot 2.50 6.00
T2PHI J.Farabee/J.Voracek 2.50 6.00
T2PIT S.Crosby/E.Malkin 10.00 25.00
T2STL R.O'Reilly/B.Schenn 2.50 6.00
T2TBL S.Stamkos/A.Vasilevskiy 5.00 12.00
T2WAS A.Ovechkin/J.Carlson 10.00 25.00

2021-22 Artifacts Tundra Teammates Quads
T4ANA Gibson/Steel/Terry/Fowler 5.00 12.00
T4AVS Makar/MacKinnon Grubauer/Rantanen 20.00 50.00
T4BOS Pastrnak/Marchand McAvoy/Bergeron 12.00 30.00
T4CHI Kane/DeBrincat/Kubalik/Dach 10.00 25.00
T4MON Price/Toffoli/Suzuki/Weber 10.00 25.00
T4NYR Lafreniere/Panarin Fox/Shesterkin 10.00 25.00
T4TOR Matthews/Marner Tavares/Rielly 20.00 50.00
T4VAN Horvat/Pettersson Boeser/Hughes 12.00 30.00
T4VGK Fleury/Pacioretty Stone/Theodore 10.00 25.00
T4WPG Hellebuyck/Ehlers Connor/Scheifele 10.00 25.00

2021-22 Artifacts Year One Rookie Sweaters
*PATCH/25: 1.5X TO 4X BASIC
RSAL Alexis Lafreniere 3.00 8.00
RSBB Bowen Byram 2.50 6.00
RSDC Dylan Cozens 2.00 5.00
RSIS Ilya Sorokin 3.00 8.00
RSKK Kirill Kaprizov 6.00 15.00
RSNR Nick Robertson 2.00 5.00
RSSM Ty Smith 2.00 5.00
RSTS Tim Stutzle 2.50 6.00
RSTZ Trevor Zegras 4.00 10.00

2022-23 Artifacts
1 Tim Stutzle .50 1.25
2 Jaccob Slavin .30 .75
3 Nikita Kucherov .75 2.00
4 Cole Perfetti .40 1.00
5 Ryan Nugent-Hopkins .50 1.25
6 Mats Zuccarello .40 1.00
7 Spencer Knight .40 1.00
8 Blake Coleman .30 .75
9 Jordan Eberle .40 1.00
10 Ryan O'Reilly .40 1.00
11 Joel Farabee .40 1.00
12 Philip Tomasino .25 .60
13 Rasmus Dahlin .50 1.25
14 Jake Oettinger .60 1.50
15 William Karlsson .50 1.25
16 Karel Vejmelka .25 .60
17 Kyle Connor .60 1.50
18 Evgeni Malkin .75 2.00
19 Nick Suzuki .75 2.00
20 Joe Pavelski .50 1.25
21 Alexis Lafreniere .60 1.50
22 Clayton Keller .50 1.25
23 Ryan Pulock .30 .75
24 David Farrance .25 .60
25 Jamie Drysdale .30 .75
26 Jesper Bratt .40 1.00
27 Jonathan Toews .60 1.50
28 Maxime Comtois .30 .75
29 Jack Roslovic .25 .60
30 Jaden Schwartz .30 .75
31 Connor McMichael .40 1.00
32 Brock Nelson .40 1.00
33 Mitch Marner .60 1.50
34 Tyler Bertuzzi .30 .75
35 Carter Verhaeghe .40 1.00
36 Darnell Nurse .30 .75
37 Quinn Hughes 1.00 2.50
38 Anders Lee .30 .75
39 Logan Couture .50 1.25
40 Shane Pinto .30 .75
41 Martin Necas .60 1.50
42 Alex Killorn .25 .60
43 John Carlson .40 1.00
44 Erik Karlsson .50 1.25
45 Jeremy Swayman .60 1.50
46 Jakub Voracek .30 .75
47 Henri Jokiharju .25 .60
48 Seth Jones .40 1.00
49 Yanni Gourde .30 .75
50 Jasper Weatherby .25 .60
51 Nathan MacKinnon 1.50 4.00
52 Cal Petersen .25 .60
53 Drake Batherson .40 1.00
54 Dawson Mercer .50 1.25
55 Cale Makar 1.00 2.50
56 Dylan Cozens .40 1.00
57 John Marino .40 1.00
58 Jesse Puljujarvi .40 1.00
59 Trevor Zegras .40 1.00
60 Jordan Binnington .60 1.50
61 Patrick Kane .75 2.00
62 Moritz Seider .50 1.25
63 Sean Monahan .25 .60
64 Alex Newhook .30 .75
65 Mark Stone .50 1.25
66 Taylor Hall .40 1.00
67 Shayne Gostisbehere .40 1.00
68 Alex Iafallo .25 .60
69 John Tavares .60 1.50
70 Yegor Sharangovich .40 1.00
71 Carter Hart .40 1.00
72 Cam Fowler .40 1.00

73 Nicklas Backstrom .40 1.00
74 Jason Robertson .60 1.50
75 Pavel Buchnevich .30 .75
76 Kris Letang .50 1.25
77 Jeff Petry .40 1.00
78 Cam Atkinson .40 1.00
79 Nikolaj Ehlers .40 1.00
80 Charlie McAvoy .50 1.25
81 Matt Duchene .40 1.00
82 Jonathan Marchessault .50 1.25
83 Mika Zibanejad .50 1.25
84 Sam Reinhart .75 2.00
85 Marcus Foligno .30 .75
86 Teuvo Teravainen .40 1.00
87 David Pastrnak 1.00 2.50
88 Matthew Tkachuk .75 2.00
89 William Nylander .75 2.00
90 Eeli Tolvanen .40 1.00
91 Drew Doughty .50 1.25
92 Josh Morrissey .50 1.25
93 Filip Hronek .25 .60
94 Conor Garland .30 .75
95 Cole Sillinger .30 .75
96 Adam Fox .50 1.25
97 Elias Pettersson .60 1.50
98 Jake Guentzel .60 1.50
99 Josh Anderson .30 .75
100 Steven Stamkos .75 2.00
101 Artemi Panarin 2.50 6.00
102 Carey Price 2.50 6.00
103 Brock Boeser 1.50 4.00
104 Jack Eichel 2.00 5.00
105 Alex Tuch 1.25 3.00
106 James van Riemsdyk 1.00 2.50
107 Jared McCann 1.00 2.50
108 Alex Ovechkin 5.00 12.00
109 Brad Marchand 2.50 6.00
110 Dylan Larkin 1.50 4.00
111 Troy Terry 1.00 2.50
112 Brady Tkachuk 2.00 5.00
113 Jordan Kyrou 1.25 3.00
114 Victor Hedman 1.50 4.00
115 Johnny Gaudreau 2.00 5.00
116 Timo Meier 1.25 3.00
117 Jack Hughes 3.00 8.00
118 Connor McDavid 6.00 15.00
119 Mathew Barzal 1.50 4.00
120 Aleksander Barkov 2.00 5.00
121 Nazem Kadri 1.50 4.00
122 Chris Kreider 1.50 4.00
123 Boone Jenner 1.25 3.00
124 Andrei Svechnikov 1.50 4.00
125 Alex DeBrincat 1.50 4.00
126 Sidney Crosby 5.00 12.00
127 Auston Matthews 5.00 12.00
128 Roope Hintz 1.50 4.00
129 Kirill Kaprizov 4.00 10.00
130 Roman Josi 1.25 3.00
131 Shayne Gostisbehere 1.25 3.00
132 Leon Draisaitl 4.00 10.00
133 Alexander Wennberg .75 2.00
134 Anze Kopitar 2.00 5.00
135 Brayden Point 1.50 4.00
136 Igor Shesterkin 2.50 6.00
137 Alex Nedeljkovic 1.00 2.50
138 Linus Ullmark 1.25 3.00
139 John Gibson 1.25 3.00
140 Cam Talbot 1.25 3.00
141 Connor Hellebuyck 2.50 6.00
142 Philipp Grubauer 1.25 3.00
143 Tristan Jarry 1.25 3.00
144 Robin Lehner 1.00 2.50
145 Sergei Bobrovsky 2.00 5.00
146 Jack Campbell 1.25 3.00
147 Ilya Sorokin 2.00 5.00
148 Thatcher Demko 1.50 4.00
149 Juuse Saros 1.50 4.00
150 Jonathan Quick 1.50 4.00
151 Andrei Vasilevskiy 2.00 5.00
152 Frederik Andersen 1.50 4.00
153 Marc-Andre Fleury 2.50 6.00
154 Jacob Markstrom 1.25 3.00
155 Darcy Kuemper 1.25 3.00
156 Peter Forsberg 2.50 6.00
157 Pekka Rinne 1.25 3.00
158 Scott Gomez 1.00 2.50
159 Doug Weight 1.25 3.00
160 Bernie Nicholls 1.00 2.50
161 Mattias Ohlund .75 2.00
162 Teemu Selanne 2.50 6.00
163 Vincent Lecavalier 1.25 3.00
164 Ron Hextall 1.25 3.00
165 Dave Taylor 1.00 2.50
166 Ed Belfour 1.25 3.00
167 Keith Tkachuk 1.25 3.00
168 Martin Brodeur 3.00 8.00
169 Mats Sundin 1.25 3.00
170 Wayne Gretzky 8.00 20.00
171 Owen Power RC 4.00 10.00
172 Matias Maccelli RC 3.00 8.00
173 Nicholas Abruzzese RC 2.00 5.00
174 Lukas Dostal RC 4.00 10.00
175 Samuel Fagemo RC 1.50 4.00
176 Matt Boldy RC 6.00 15.00
177 Mads Sogaard RC 2.50 6.00
178 Thomas Bordeleau RC 2.00 5.00
179 Bobby Brink RC 2.00 5.00
180 Matty Beniers RC 25.00 60.00
181 Jack Quinn RC 3.00 8.00
182 Brayden Tracey RC 1.50 4.00
183 Lukas Reichel RC 4.00 10.00
184 Nathan Smith RC 1.50 4.00
185 Braden Schneider RC 3.00 8.00
186 Marco Rossi RC 5.00 12.00
187 Dylan Samberg RC 2.00 5.00
188 Trey Fix-Wolansky RC 2.00 5.00
189 Jack LaFontaine RC 2.00 5.00
190 Noah Cates RC 2.00 5.00
191 Erik Kallgren RC 2.00 5.00
192 Marc McLaughlin RC 2.00 5.00
193 Brandon Biro RC 3.00 8.00
194 Jacob Perreault RC 2.00 5.00
195 Jordan Spence RC 2.00 5.00
196 Isaac Ratcliffe RC 2.00 5.00
197 Kaedan Korczak RC 1.50 4.00
198 Jakub Galvas RC 2.00 5.00
199 Jack McBain RC 2.00 5.00
200 Kent Johnson RC 4.00 10.00

2022-23 Artifacts Autumn
*AUTUMN VETS: 2.5X TO 6X BASIC
*AUTUMN S/L: .75X TO 2X BASIC
*AUTUMN RC: .75X TO 2X BASIC
180 Matty Beniers 60.00 150.00

2022-23 Artifacts Copper
*COPPER VETS: 1.5X TO 4X BASIC
*COPPER S/L: .5X TO 1.25X BASIC
*COPPER RC: .6X TO 1.5X BASIC

2022-23 Artifacts Emerald
*EMERALD VETS: 2X TO 5X BASIC
*EMERALD S/L: .6X TO 1.5X BASIC
*EMERALD RC: .6X TO 1.5X BASIC
180 Matty Beniers 60.00 150.00

2022-23 Artifacts Leather
*LEATHER S/L: .6X TO 1.5X BASIC
*LEATHER RC: .75X TO 2X BASIC
180 Matty Beniers 80.00 200.00

2022-23 Artifacts Light Blue Steel
*LIGHT BLUE VETS: 2.5X TO 6X BASIC
*LIGHT BLUE S/L: .75X TO 2X BASIC
*LIGHT BLUE RC: .75X TO 2X BASIC
180 Matty Beniers 60.00 150.00

2022-23 Artifacts Pink
*PINK VETS: 4X TO 10X BASIC
*PINK S/L: 1.25X TO 3X BASIC
*PINK RC: 1.25X TO 3X BASIC
180 Matty Beniers 80.00 200.00

2022-23 Artifacts Plexi
*PLEXI: 1.5X TO 4X BASIC
180 Matty Beniers 100.00 250.00

2022-23 Artifacts Purple
*PURPLE VETS: 5X TO 12X BASIC
*PURPLE S/L: 1.5X TO 4X BASIC
*PURPLE RC: 1.5X TO 4X BASIC

2022-23 Artifacts Rose
*ROSE VETS: 3X TO 8X BASIC
*ROSE S/L: 1X TO 2.5X BASIC
*ROSE RC: 1X TO 2.5X BASIC

2022-23 Artifacts Royal Blue
*ROYAL BLUE VETS: 1.5X TO 4X BASIC
*ROYAL BLUE S/L: .5X TO 1.25X BASIC
*ROYAL BLUE RC: .6X TO 1.5X BASIC

2022-23 Artifacts Ruby
*RUBY VETS: 1.25X TO 3X BASIC
*RUBY S/L: .4X TO 1X BASIC
*RUBY RC: .5X TO 1.25X BASIC

2022-23 Artifacts Turquoise
*TURQUOISE VETS: .5X TO 1.25X BASIC
*TURQUOISE S/L: .5X TO 1.25X BASIC
*TURQUOISE RC: .3X TO .75X BASIC

2022-23 Artifacts Wood
*WOOD: .5X TO 1.25X BASIC
180 Matty Beniers 40.00 100.00

2022-23 Artifacts Yellow
*YELLOW VETS: 3X TO 8X BASIC
*YELLOW S/L: 1X TO 2.5X BASIC
*YELLOW RC: 1X TO 2.5X BASIC
180 Matty Beniers 80.00 200.00

2022-23 Artifacts '05-06 Clear Cut Retro Rookies
CCRR1 Aleksander Barkov 8.00 20.00
CCRR2 Lukas Reichel 10.00 25.00
CCRR3 Evgeni Malkin 10.00 25.00
CCRR4 Bobby Brink 5.00 12.00
CCRR5 John Gibson 5.00 12.00
CCRR6 Marco Rossi 12.00 30.00
CCRR7 Nikita Kucherov 10.00 25.00
CCRR8 Samuel Fagemo 4.00 10.00
CCRR9 Alex Ovechkin 80.00 200.00
CCRR10 Matty Beniers 50.00 125.00
CCRR11 Kyle Connor 8.00 20.00
CCRR12 Ben Meyers 5.00 12.00
CCRR13 Logan Couture 6.00 15.00
CCRR14 Jordan Spence 5.00 12.00
CCRR15 Dylan Larkin 6.00 15.00
CCRR16 Marc McLaughlin 5.00 12.00
CCRR17 Elias Pettersson 8.00 20.00
CCRR18 Matt Boldy 15.00 40.00
CCRR19 Owen Power 10.00 25.00
CCRR20 Anze Kopitar 8.00 20.00
CCRR21 Erik Kallgren 5.00 12.00
CCRR22 Sebastian Aho 8.00 20.00
CCRR23 Kent Johnson 10.00 25.00
CCRR24 Nazem Kadri 6.00 15.00
CCRR25 Jack Quinn 8.00 20.00
CCRR26 Miro Heiskanen 6.00 15.00
CCRR27 Matias Maccelli 8.00 20.00
CCRR28 Juuse Saros 6.00 15.00
CCRR29 Nick Blankenburg 4.00 10.00
CCRR30 Connor McDavid 60.00 150.00

2022-23 Artifacts '05-06 Retro Autofacts
RAFAB Aleksander Barkov A 15.00 40.00
RAFAH Alexander Holtz C 10.00 25.00
RAFAK Arthur Kaliyev D 10.00 25.00
RAFAN Alex Newhook C 8.00 20.00
RAFAR Arttu Ruotsalainen D 6.00 15.00
RAFBB Brent Burns A 10.00 25.00
RAFBG Benoit-Olivier Groulx C 6.00 15.00
RAFBJ Boone Jenner D 10.00 25.00
RAFBM Brad Marchand A 20.00 50.00
RAFBN Brock Nelson A 10.00 25.00
RAFBS Billy Smith A 10.00 25.00
RAFCP Carey Price A 20.00 50.00
RAFDH Dominik Hasek A 15.00 40.00
RAFDM Dawson Mercer D 12.00 30.00
RAFDS Daniel Sedin A 12.00 30.00
RAFDW Doug Wilson B 8.00 20.00
RAFFG Filip Gustavsson D 10.00 25.00
RAFJH Jonathan Huberdeau A 12.00 30.00
RAFJI Jarome Iginla A 12.00 30.00
RAFJL John LeClair A 10.00 25.00
RAFJS Jeremy Swayman D 15.00 40.00
RAFJW Jasper Weatherby D 6.00 15.00
RAFKT Keith Tkachuk A 10.00 25.00
RAFLT Logan Thompson D 12.00 30.00
RAFMA Mason Appleton D 6.00 15.00
RAFMB Michael Bunting B 10.00 25.00
RAFMG Matt Grzelcyk C 8.00 20.00
RAFMO Brenden Morrow A 8.00 20.00
RAFMS Moritz Seider A 60.00 150.00
RAFNI Bernie Nicholls A 8.00 20.00
RAFNR Nick Robertson B 10.00 25.00
RAFPA Colton Parayko C 8.00 20.00
RAFPS Pius Suter D 8.00 20.00
RAFPT Philip Tomasino C 6.00 15.00
RAFQB Quinton Byfield A 12.00 30.00
RAFRH Roope Hintz A 12.00 30.00
RAFSP Scott Perunovich C 6.00 15.00
RAFTJ Tanner Jeannot D 6.00 15.00
RAFTK Torey Krug D 8.00 20.00
RAFWG Wayne Gretzky A 150.00 400.00
RAFZP Zach Parise A 10.00 25.00

2022-23 Artifacts Arena Artifacts
AABP Brad Park 20.00 50.00
AACN Cam Neely 25.00 60.00
AAGC Gerry Cheevers 25.00 60.00
AAJB Johnny Bucyk 25.00 60.00
AAPE Phil Esposito 40.00 100.00
AARB Ray Bourque 25.00 60.00
AATO Terry O'Reilly 25.00 60.00
AATS Terry Sawchuk 30.00 80.00
AAWC Wayne Cashman 15.00 40.00
AAWO Willie O'Ree 30.00 80.00

2022-23 Artifacts Aurum
*GREEN/25: 1X TO 2.5X BASIC
AAM Auston Matthews 15.00 40.00
AAW Alexander Wennberg 1.25 3.00
ABB Bobby Brink 2.00 5.00
ABH Brandon Hagel 1.50 4.00
ABO Bobby Orr 20.00 50.00
ABS Brayden Schenn 2.00 5.00
ABY Matt Boldy 10.00 25.00
ACK Chris Kreider 2.50 6.00
ACM Charlie McAvoy 2.50 6.00
ACV Carter Verhaeghe 2.00 5.00
ADL Dylan Larkin 2.50 6.00
ADS Dylan Strome 2.50 6.00
AEB Evan Bouchard 2.50 6.00
AEK Evgeny Kuznetsov 2.50 6.00
AGN Gustav Nyquist 1.25 3.00
AJE Jack Eichel 3.00 8.00
AJM J.T. Miller 2.50 6.00
AJO Jake Oettinger 3.00 8.00
AJS Jaccob Slavin 1.50 4.00
AKJ Kent Johnson 12.00 30.00
ALD Leon Draisaitl 15.00 40.00
ALR Lukas Reichel 4.00 10.00
AMB Matty Beniers 30.00 80.00
AMM Marc McLaughlin 2.00 5.00
AMR Mikko Rantanen 5.00 12.00
AMZ Mika Zibanejad 2.50 6.00
ANC Noah Cates 2.00 5.00
ANE Nikolaj Ehlers 2.00 5.00
ANS Nick Schmaltz 1.50 4.00
AOP Owen Power 12.00 30.00
APD Phillip Danault 2.00 5.00
APF Peter Forsberg 20.00 50.00
APR Patrick Roy 30.00 80.00
ARA Rasmus Andersson 1.50 4.00
ARH Ryan Hartman 1.25 3.00
ARI Marco Rossi 12.00 30.00
ARJ Roman Josi 8.00 20.00
ASA Juuse Saros 2.50 6.00
ASE Jordan Spence 2.00 5.00
AST Steven Stamkos 8.00 20.00
ATC Thomas Chabot 2.00 5.00
ATH Tage Thompson 2.50 6.00
ATJ Tristan Jarry 2.00 5.00
ATK Travis Konecny 2.00 5.00
ATM Timo Meier 2.00 5.00
ATT Troy Terry 1.50 4.00
AWG Wayne Gretzky 60.00 150.00
AWN William Nylander 4.00 10.00

2022-23 Artifacts Aurum Signatures
ASAM Auston Matthews 100.00 250.00
ASBB Bob Bourne 12.00 30.00
ASBK Bobby Brink 20.00 50.00
ASBO Matt Boldy 125.00 300.00
ASCN Cam Neely 20.00 50.00
ASJP Joe Pavelski 25.00 60.00
ASKJ Kent Johnson 40.00 100.00
ASKL Kris Letang 25.00 60.00
ASLD Leon Draisaitl 60.00 150.00
ASMB Matty Beniers 250.00 600.00
ASMR Marco Rossi 50.00 125.00
ASMS Mark Scheifele 30.00 80.00
ASMT Matthew Tkachuk 40.00 100.00
ASOP Owen Power 125.00 300.00
ASRH Roope Hintz 25.00 60.00
ASSK Spencer Knight 20.00 50.00
ASSZ Sergei Zubov 15.00 40.00
ASTH Tomas Hertl 20.00 50.00
ASTJ Tanner Jeannot 12.00 30.00
ASTK Tim Kerr 12.00 30.00
ASTL Trevor Linden 20.00 50.00
ASWC Wendel Clark 30.00 80.00

2022-23 Artifacts Autofacts
AFAB Adam Beckman F 4.00 10.00
AFAL Alexis Lafreniere D 30.00 80.00
AFAN Alex Newhook E 5.00 12.00
AFAP Aliaksei Protas F 4.00 10.00
AFAR Alec Regula F 4.00 10.00
AFBA Alexander Barabanov F 4.00 10.00
AFBB Bowen Byram D 8.00 20.00
AFBD Brandon Duhaime F 4.00 10.00
AFBM Barry Melrose C 5.00 12.00
AFBO Bob Bourne D 4.00 10.00
AFBR Brock Boeser C 8.00 20.00
AFBT Alex Barre-Boulet F 4.00 10.00
AFCA Calen Addison B 4.00 10.00
AFCC Charlie Coyle D 6.00 15.00
AFCD Connor Dewar E 4.00 10.00
AFCF Cal Foote F 5.00 12.00
AFCH Cameron Hillis F 4.00 10.00
AFCM Connor McMichael F 6.00 15.00
AFCR Cliff Ronning C 4.00 10.00
AFCS Cole Schwindt F 4.00 10.00
AFDC Dylan Cozens F 6.00 15.00
AFDF David Farrance F 4.00 10.00
AFDG Dirk Graham B 5.00 12.00
AFDM Dawson Mercer F 8.00 20.00
AFDO Drew O'Connor F 4.00 10.00
AFDT Dave Taylor B 5.00 12.00
AFDW Doug Weight B 6.00 15.00
AFES Egor Sokolov F 4.00 10.00
AFFZ Fabian Zetterlund F 4.00 10.00
AFGF Gabriel Fortier E 4.00 10.00
AFGS Gary Suter B 4.00 10.00
AFHJ Henri Jokiharju E 4.00 10.00
AFIL Isac Lundestrom F 4.00 10.00
AFIM Ilya Mikheyev F 5.00 12.00
AFJA Jack Ahcan F 4.00 10.00
AFJB Jacob Bernard-Docker F 4.00 10.00
AFJC Jonathan Cheechoo B 5.00 12.00
AFJE Jordan Eberle B 6.00 15.00
AFJJ Jan Jenik E 5.00 12.00
AFJN Jake Neighbours F 6.00 15.00
AFJP Jesse Puljujarvi B 6.00 15.00
AFJW Jasper Weatherby F 4.00 10.00
AFKK Keegan Kolesar D 4.00 10.00
AFKL Kris Letang B 8.00 20.00
AFKP Kyle Palmieri C 5.00 12.00
AFLO Logan Stanley F 4.00 10.00
AFLP Lane Pederson F 4.00 10.00
AFLR Lucas Raymond A 10.00 25.00
AFMA Mikey Anderson F 5.00 12.00
AFMD Marcel Dionne B 8.00 20.00
AFMM Mason McTavish B 6.00 15.00
AFMN Martin Necas C 10.00 25.00
AFMO Mike Modano B 25.00 60.00
AFMS Martin St. Louis B 6.00 15.00
AFNR Nick Robertson D 6.00 15.00
AFPB Paul Bissonnette D 4.00 10.00
AFPC Paul Coffey B 6.00 15.00
AFPE Phil Esposito A 10.00 25.00
AFPG Philipp Grubauer B 6.00 15.00
AFPK Peyton Krebs F 5.00 12.00
AFQB Quinton Byfield D 8.00 20.00
AFRB Ray Bourque B 10.00 25.00
AFRD Ryan Dzingel F 5.00 12.00
AFRM Ryan Merkley E 5.00 12.00
AFRR Rob Ray E 4.00 10.00
AFSB Sam Bennett D 10.00 25.00
AFSC Shayne Corson B 5.00 12.00
AFSE Teemu Selanne B 50.00 125.00
AFSG Scott Gomez A 5.00 12.00
AFSH Mike Smith C 4.00 10.00
AFSK Spencer Knight D 6.00 15.00
AFSR Sampo Ranta F 4.00 10.00
AFSZ Sergei Zubov B 5.00 12.00
AFTF Theoren Fleury B 6.00 15.00
AFTJ Tanner Jeannot F 4.00 10.00
AFTL Trevor Linden B 6.00 15.00
AFTS Tim Stutzle B 20.00 50.00
AFTT Troy Terry B 5.00 12.00
AFTW Tony Twist A 4.00 10.00
AFWO Willie O'Ree B 8.00 20.00
AFYS Yegor Sharangovich F 6.00 15.00

2022-23 Artifacts Clear Cut Rookies
CCR1 Matty Beniers 60.00 150.00
CCR2 Michael Eyssimont 8.00 20.00
CCR3 Ronnie Attard 8.00 20.00
CCR4 Jack Quinn 12.00 30.00
CCR5 Jack McBain 8.00 20.00
CCR6 Kent Johnson 15.00 40.00
CCR7 Mads Sogaard 10.00 25.00
CCR8 Marc McLaughlin 8.00 20.00
CCR9 Braden Schneider 12.00 30.00
CCR10 Samuel Fagemo 6.00 15.00
CCR11 Dylan Samberg 8.00 20.00
CCR12 Nick Blankenburg 6.00 15.00
CCR13 Kaedan Korczak 6.00 15.00
CCR14 Lukas Dostal 15.00 40.00
CCR15 Thomas Bordeleau 8.00 20.00
CCR16 Marco Rossi 20.00 50.00
CCR17 Noah Cates 8.00 20.00
CCR18 Erik Kallgren 8.00 20.00
CCR19 Carson Meyer 6.00 15.00
CCR20 Nicholas Abruzzese 8.00 20.00
CCR21 Bobby Brink 8.00 20.00
CCR22 Jordan Spence 8.00 20.00
CCR23 Lukas Reichel 15.00 40.00
CCR24 Matias Maccelli 12.00 30.00
CCR25 Matt Boldy 25.00 60.00
CCR26 Brayden Tracey 6.00 15.00
CCR27 Ben Meyers 8.00 20.00
CCR28 Nathan Smith 6.00 15.00
CCR29 Jacob Perreault 8.00 20.00
CCR30 Owen Power 15.00 40.00

2022-23 Artifacts Esteemed Endorsements
EEAO Alex Ovechkin 400.00 1000.00
EEJV John Vanbiesbrouck 80.00 200.00
EEQH Quinn Hughes 80.00 200.00
EERB Ray Bourque 125.00 300.00

2022-23 Artifacts Game Ticket Artifacts
GTAAO Alex Ovechkin/60 300.00 800.00
GTABB Brock Boeser/16 60.00 150.00
GTACM Connor McDavid/16 250.00 600.00
GTAJT Jonathan Toews/16 80.00 200.00
GTAMZ Mats Zuccarello/16 50.00 125.00
GTAPF Peter Forsberg/40 100.00 250.00

2022-23 Artifacts Material Autographs Gold
*HOR.GOLD: .5X TO 1.25X BASIC
102 Carey Price/45 30.00 80.00
103 Brock Boeser/65 20.00 50.00
104 Jack Eichel/45 25.00 60.00
105 Alex Tuch/65 15.00 40.00
107 Jared McCann/65 12.00 30.00
108 Alex Ovechkin/25 200.00 500.00
109 Brad Marchand/45 30.00 80.00
110 Dylan Larkin/45 20.00 50.00
111 Troy Terry/45 12.00 30.00
112 Brady Tkachuk/45 25.00 60.00
118 Connor McDavid/25 250.00 600.00
120 Aleksander Barkov/45 25.00 60.00
124 Andrei Svechnikov/45 20.00 50.00
126 Sidney Crosby/25 150.00 400.00
127 Auston Matthews/25 125.00 300.00
128 Roope Hintz/45 20.00 50.00
130 Roman Josi/45 15.00 40.00
132 Leon Draisaitl/45 50.00 125.00
134 Anze Kopitar/45 25.00 60.00
136 Igor Shesterkin/25 30.00 80.00
137 Alex Nedeljkovic/65 12.00 30.00
139 John Gibson/65 15.00 40.00
140 Cam Talbot/65 15.00 40.00
141 Connor Hellebuyck/45 30.00 80.00
142 Philipp Grubauer/65 15.00 40.00
145 Sergei Bobrovsky/45 25.00 60.00
147 Ilya Sorokin/65 25.00 60.00
151 Andrei Vasilevskiy/45 25.00 60.00
153 Marc-Andre Fleury/45 30.00 80.00
154 Jacob Markstrom/45 15.00 40.00
155 Darcy Kuemper/65 15.00 40.00
156 Peter Forsberg/25 30.00 80.00
159 Doug Weight/45 15.00 40.00
162 Teemu Selanne/45 30.00 80.00
168 Martin Brodeur/25 40.00 100.00
170 Wayne Gretzky/25 300.00 800.00
171 Owen Power/25 125.00 300.00
174 Lukas Dostal/149 30.00 80.00
175 Samuel Fagemo/149 12.00 30.00
176 Matt Boldy/25 125.00 300.00
178 Thomas Bordeleau/149 15.00 40.00
180 Matty Beniers/25 250.00 600.00
181 Jack Quinn/149 25.00 60.00
183 Lukas Reichel/99 30.00 80.00
185 Braden Schneider/149 25.00 60.00
186 Marco Rossi/99 40.00 100.00
187 Dylan Samberg/149 15.00 40.00
197 Kaedan Korczak/149 12.00 30.00
200 Kent Johnson/99 30.00 80.00

2022-23 Artifacts Material Autographs Emerald
*EMERALD/45: .5X TO 1.25X BASIC
174 Lukas Dostal/45 40.00 100.00

2022-23 Artifacts Materials Gold
*HORIZONTAL: .5X TO 1.25X BASIC
*HOR.EMRLD/25: 1.2X TO 3X BASIC
1 Tim Stutzle 4.00 10.00
2 Jaccob Slavin 2.50 6.00
3 Nikita Kucherov 6.00 15.00
5 Ryan Nugent-Hopkins 4.00 10.00
6 Mats Zuccarello 3.00 8.00
7 Spencer Knight 3.00 8.00
8 Blake Coleman 2.50 6.00
9 Jordan Eberle 3.00 8.00
10 Ryan O'Reilly 3.00 8.00
11 Joel Farabee 3.00 8.00
12 Philip Tomasino 2.00 5.00
13 Rasmus Dahlin 4.00 10.00
14 Jake Oettinger 5.00 12.00
15 William Karlsson 4.00 10.00
17 Kyle Connor 5.00 12.00
18 Evgeni Malkin 6.00 15.00
19 Nick Suzuki 6.00 15.00
20 Joe Pavelski 4.00 10.00
21 Alexis Lafreniere 5.00 12.00
22 Clayton Keller 4.00 10.00
23 Ryan Pulock 2.50 6.00
25 Jamie Drysdale 2.50 6.00
26 Jesper Bratt 3.00 8.00
27 Jonathan Toews 5.00 12.00
28 Maxime Comtois 2.50 6.00
29 Jack Roslovic 2.00 5.00
30 Jaden Schwartz 2.50 6.00
31 Connor McMichael 3.00 8.00
32 Brock Nelson 3.00 8.00
34 Tyler Bertuzzi 2.50 6.00
35 Carter Verhaeghe 3.00 8.00
36 Darnell Nurse 2.50 6.00
37 Quinn Hughes 8.00 20.00
38 Anders Lee 2.50 6.00
39 Logan Couture 4.00 10.00
41 Martin Necas 5.00 12.00
42 Alex Killorn 2.00 5.00
43 John Carlson 3.00 8.00
44 Erik Karlsson 4.00 10.00
45 Jeremy Swayman 5.00 12.00
46 Jakub Voracek 2.50 6.00
47 Henri Jokiharju 2.00 5.00
48 Seth Jones 3.00 8.00
49 Yanni Gourde 2.50 6.00
51 Nathan MacKinnon 12.00 30.00
53 Drake Batherson 3.00 8.00
54 Dawson Mercer 4.00 10.00
55 Cale Makar 8.00 20.00
56 Dylan Cozens 3.00 8.00
57 John Marino 3.00 8.00
58 Jesse Puljujarvi 3.00 8.00
59 Trevor Zegras 3.00 8.00
60 Jordan Binnington 5.00 12.00
61 Patrick Kane 6.00 15.00
62 Moritz Seider 4.00 10.00
63 Sean Monahan 2.00 5.00
64 Alex Newhook 2.50 6.00
65 Mark Stone 4.00 10.00
67 Shayne Gostisbehere 3.00 8.00
69 John Tavares 5.00 12.00
70 Yegor Sharangovich 3.00 8.00
71 Carter Hart 3.00 8.00
72 Cam Fowler 3.00 8.00
73 Nicklas Backstrom 3.00 8.00
74 Jason Robertson 5.00 12.00
75 Pavel Buchnevich 2.50 6.00
76 Kris Letang 4.00 10.00
77 Jeff Petry 3.00 8.00
78 Cam Atkinson 3.00 8.00
79 Nikolaj Ehlers 3.00 8.00
80 Charlie McAvoy 4.00 10.00
81 Matt Duchene 3.00 8.00
82 Jonathan Marchessault 4.00 10.00
83 Mika Zibanejad 4.00 10.00
84 Sam Reinhart 6.00 15.00
86 Teuvo Teravainen 3.00 8.00
87 David Pastrnak 8.00 20.00
88 Matthew Tkachuk 6.00 15.00
89 William Nylander 6.00 15.00
90 Eeli Tolvanen 3.00 8.00
91 Drew Doughty 4.00 10.00
92 Josh Morrissey 4.00 10.00
95 Cole Sillinger 2.50 6.00
96 Adam Fox 4.00 10.00
97 Elias Pettersson 5.00 12.00
98 Jake Guentzel 5.00 12.00
99 Josh Anderson 2.50 6.00
100 Steven Stamkos 6.00 15.00
101 Artemi Panarin 6.00 15.00
102 Carey Price 6.00 15.00
103 Brock Boeser 4.00 10.00
104 Jack Eichel 5.00 12.00
106 James van Riemsdyk 2.50 6.00
107 Jared McCann 2.50 6.00
108 Alex Ovechkin 12.00 30.00
109 Brad Marchand 6.00 15.00
110 Dylan Larkin 4.00 10.00
111 Troy Terry 2.50 6.00
112 Brady Tkachuk 5.00 12.00
114 Victor Hedman 4.00 10.00
115 Johnny Gaudreau 5.00 12.00
116 Timo Meier 3.00 8.00
117 Jack Hughes 8.00 20.00
118 Connor McDavid 15.00 40.00
119 Mathew Barzal 4.00 10.00
120 Aleksander Barkov 5.00 12.00
121 Nazem Kadri 4.00 10.00
122 Chris Kreider 4.00 10.00
124 Andrei Svechnikov 4.00 10.00
125 Alex DeBrincat 4.00 10.00
126 Sidney Crosby 12.00 30.00
127 Auston Matthews 12.00 30.00
128 Roope Hintz 4.00 10.00
129 Kirill Kaprizov 10.00 25.00
130 Roman Josi 3.00 8.00
131 Shayne Gostisbehere 3.00 8.00
132 Leon Draisaitl 10.00 25.00
134 Anze Kopitar 5.00 12.00
135 Brayden Point 4.00 10.00
136 Igor Shesterkin 6.00 15.00
137 Alex Nedeljkovic 2.50 6.00
139 John Gibson 3.00 8.00
140 Cam Talbot 3.00 8.00
141 Connor Hellebuyck 6.00 15.00
142 Philipp Grubauer 3.00 8.00
143 Tristan Jarry 3.00 8.00
144 Robin Lehner 2.50 6.00
145 Sergei Bobrovsky 5.00 12.00
147 Ilya Sorokin 5.00 12.00
148 Thatcher Demko 4.00 10.00
149 Juuse Saros 4.00 10.00
150 Jonathan Quick 4.00 10.00
151 Andrei Vasilevskiy 5.00 12.00
152 Frederik Andersen 4.00 10.00
153 Marc-Andre Fleury 6.00 15.00
154 Jacob Markstrom 3.00 8.00
155 Darcy Kuemper 3.00 8.00
156 Peter Forsberg 6.00 15.00
157 Pekka Rinne 3.00 8.00
159 Doug Weight 3.00 8.00
162 Teemu Selanne 6.00 15.00
168 Martin Brodeur 8.00 20.00
169 Mats Sundin 3.00 8.00
170 Wayne Gretzky 20.00 50.00
171 Owen Power 6.00 15.00
172 Matias Maccelli 5.00 12.00
174 Lukas Dostal 6.00 15.00
175 Samuel Fagemo 2.50 6.00
176 Matt Boldy 10.00 25.00
178 Thomas Bordeleau 3.00 8.00
180 Matty Beniers 60.00 150.00
181 Jack Quinn 5.00 12.00
183 Lukas Reichel 6.00 15.00
185 Braden Schneider 5.00 12.00
186 Marco Rossi 8.00 20.00
187 Dylan Samberg 3.00 8.00
197 Kaedan Korczak 2.50 6.00
200 Kent Johnson 6.00 15.00

2022-23 Artifacts Materials Emerald
*EMERALD: .75X TO 2X BASIC
180 Matty Beniers 80.00 200.00

2022-23 Artifacts Materials Purple
*PURPLE: 1.25X TO 3X BASIC
171 Owen Power 40.00 100.00
176 Matt Boldy 60.00 150.00
180 Matty Beniers 125.00 300.00

2022-23 Artifacts Net Gear
NGCH Connor Hellebuyck 6.00 15.00
NGCP Cal Petersen 2.00 5.00
NGGC Gerry Cheevers 3.00 8.00
NGGH Glenn Hall 3.00 8.00
NGIS Igor Shesterkin 6.00 15.00
NGJS Jeremy Swayman 5.00 12.00
NGMB Martin Brodeur 8.00 20.00
NGMF Marc-Andre Fleury 6.00 15.00
NGPG Philipp Grubauer 3.00 8.00
NGPR Patrick Roy 8.00 20.00
NGRI Pekka Rinne 3.00 8.00
NGSK Spencer Knight 3.00 8.00
NGTD Thatcher Demko 4.00 10.00

2022-23 Artifacts Net Gear Autographs
NGCH Connor Hellebuyck 40.00 100.00
NGCP Cal Petersen 12.00 30.00
NGGC Gerry Cheevers 20.00 50.00
NGGH Glenn Hall 20.00 50.00
NGJS Jeremy Swayman 30.00 80.00
NGMB Martin Brodeur 50.00 125.00
NGMF Marc-Andre Fleury 40.00 100.00
NGPG Philipp Grubauer 20.00 50.00
NGPR Patrick Roy 50.00 125.00
NGSK Spencer Knight 20.00 50.00

2022-23 Artifacts NHL Remnants
*PREMIUM/25: 1.2X TO 3X BASIC
NRBB Brent Burns 2.00 5.00
NRBG Brendan Gallagher 2.00 5.00
NRBH Bo Horvat 2.50 6.00
NRBW Blake Wheeler 2.00 5.00
NRCC Charlie Coyle 2.00 5.00
NRCF Cam Fowler 2.00 5.00
NRCK Clayton Keller 2.50 6.00
NRCP Colton Parayko 1.50 4.00
NRDD Drew Doughty 2.50 6.00
NRDL Dylan Larkin 2.50 6.00
NRDS Dylan Strome 2.50 6.00
NREK Evgeny Kuznetsov 2.50 6.00
NRJB Jamie Benn 2.00 5.00
NRJC John Carlson 2.00 5.00
NRJG Jordan Greenway 1.25 3.00
NRJP Joe Pavelski 2.50 6.00
NRJS Jeff Skinner 2.00 5.00
NRJT Jacob Trouba 1.50 4.00
NRKL Kris Letang 2.50 6.00
NRKY Kailer Yamamoto 2.00 5.00
NRMB Mathew Barzal 2.50 6.00
NRMR Morgan Rielly 2.00 5.00
NRMS Mark Stone 2.50 6.00
NRNH Noah Hanifin 2.00 5.00
NRNM Nathan MacKinnon 8.00 20.00
NROB Oliver Bjorkstrand 1.50 4.00
NRPU Jesse Puljujarvi 2.00 5.00
NRRA Rasmus Andersson 1.50 4.00
NRRG Ryan Getzlaf 2.00 5.00
NRRT Robert Thomas 2.00 5.00
NRSC Sean Couturier 1.50 4.00
NRTO Jonathan Toews 3.00 8.00
NRTT Teuvo Teravainen 2.00 5.00
NRYG Yanni Gourde 1.50 4.00

2022-23 Artifacts Signature Apparel
SAAL Alexis Lafreniere 50.00 125.00
SATZ Trevor Zegras 60.00 150.00

2022-23 Artifacts Signs of Success
SOSAS Andrei Svechnikov/49 12.00 30.00
SOSAV Andrei Vasilevskiy/49 15.00 40.00
SOSBE Matty Beniers/49 200.00 500.00
SOSBT Brady Tkachuk/49 15.00 40.00
SOSCG Conor Garland/49 8.00 20.00
SOSCS Cole Sillinger/49 8.00 20.00
SOSDT Devon Toews/49 8.00 20.00
SOSGD Grigori Denisenko/49 6.00 15.00
SOSJA Jake Allen/49 10.00 25.00
SOSJB Jesper Bratt/49 10.00 25.00
SOSJP Joe Pavelski/49 12.00 30.00
SOSJR Jack Roslovic/49 6.00 15.00
SOSKJ Kent Johnson/49 20.00 50.00
SOSLR Lukas Reichel/49 20.00 50.00
SOSMB Matt Boldy/49 80.00 200.00
SOSMF Marc-Andre Fleury/49 20.00 50.00
SOSMP Max Pacioretty/49 10.00 25.00
SOSMS Moritz Seider/49 12.00 30.00
SOSMT Matthew Tkachuk/49 20.00 50.00
SOSOP Owen Power/49 80.00 200.00
SOSPA Jean-Gabriel Pageau/49 6.00 15.00
SOSSR Sam Reinhart/49 20.00 50.00
SOSTJ Tanner Jeannot/49 6.00 15.00
SOSTZ Trevor Zegras/49 125.00 300.00

2022-23 Artifacts Storied Scripts
SSAO Alex Ovechkin 400.00 1000.00
SSCM Connor McDavid 300.00 800.00

2022-23 Artifacts Threads of Time
*PREMIUM/25: 1.25X TO 3X BASIC
TTCP Chris Pronger 2.00 5.00
TTMS Martin St. Louis 2.00 5.00
TTNK Nazem Kadri 2.50 6.00
TTRB Rob Blake 2.00 5.00
TTRN Rick Nash 2.00 5.00
TTSG Shayne Gostisbehere 2.00 5.00
TTTF Theoren Fleury 2.00 5.00
TTTH Taylor Hall 2.00 5.00
TTTO T.J. Oshie 2.00 5.00
TTTT Tyler Toffoli 2.00 5.00
TTVD Vincent Damphousse 1.50 4.00
TTWS Wayne Simmonds 2.00 5.00
TTYG Yanni Gourde 1.50 4.00
TTZC Zdeno Chara 2.00 5.00

2022-23 Artifacts Top Tier Rookie Signatures
TTRBO Matt Boldy 60.00 150.00
TTRJQ Jack Quinn 20.00 50.00
TTRJS Jordan Spence 12.00 30.00
TTRKJ Kent Johnson 25.00 60.00
TTRLR Lukas Reichel 25.00 60.00
TTRMB Matty Beniers 250.00 600.00
TTRMR Marco Rossi 30.00 80.00
TTROP Owen Power 80.00 200.00

2022-23 Artifacts Treasured Swatches
TSAO Alex Ovechkin 8.00 20.00
TSAS Andrei Svechnikov 2.50 6.00
TSBT Brady Tkachuk 3.00 8.00
TSCM Connor McDavid 10.00 25.00
TSIS Igor Shesterkin 4.00 10.00
TSJG Jake Guentzel 3.00 8.00
TSJH Jonathan Huberdeau 2.50 6.00
TSJQ Jack Quinn 3.00 8.00
TSJR Jason Robertson 3.00 8.00
TSKK Kirill Kaprizov 6.00 15.00
TSLR Lukas Reichel 4.00 10.00
TSMB Matt Boldy 6.00 15.00
TSMR Marco Rossi 5.00 12.00
TSQH Quinn Hughes 5.00 12.00
TSTH Taylor Hall 2.00 5.00

2022-23 Artifacts Treasured Swatches Autographs Gold
TSAS Andrei Svechnikov/25 20.00 50.00
TSBT Brady Tkachuk/25 25.00 60.00
TSJG Jake Guentzel/25 25.00 60.00
TSJQ Jack Quinn/25 25.00 60.00
TSLR Lukas Reichel/25 30.00 80.00
TSMB Matt Boldy/25 125.00 300.00
TSMR Marco Rossi/25 40.00 100.00
TSQH Quinn Hughes/25 40.00 100.00

2022-23 Artifacts Tundra Teammates Duos
T2BOS C.McAvoy/J.DeBrusk 3.00 8.00
T2CAR M.Necas/S.Aho 4.00 10.00
T2CGY J.Gaudreau/M.Tkachuk 5.00 12.00
T2CHI A.DeBrincat/P.Kane 5.00 12.00
T2EDM C.McDavid/L.Draisaitl 12.00 30.00
T2FLA J.Huberdeau/A.Ekblad 3.00 8.00
T2MTL B.Gallagher/C.Price 5.00 12.00
T2NJD B.Nicholls/M.Brodeur 6.00 15.00
T2NYI P.LaFontaine/B.Trottier 2.50 6.00
T2PIT S.Gonchar/E.Malkin 5.00 12.00
T2TOR A.Matthews/W.Nylander 10.00 25.00
T2VAN D.Sedin/H.Sedin 3.00 8.00

2022-23 Artifacts Tundra Teammates Quads

T4COL Makar/Landeskog MacKinnon/Rantanen 20.00 50.00
T4DAL Heiskanen/Klingberg Benn/Pavelski 6.00 15.00
T4DET Shanahan/Lidstrom Zetterberg/Larionov 6.00 15.00
T4LAK Kempe/Kopitar/Quick/Doughty 8.00 20.00
T4MIN Spurgeon/Greenway Kaprizov/Zuccarello 15.00 40.00
T4MTL Roy/Damphousse Koivu/Recchi 12.00 30.00
T4SEA Grubauer/Eberle Schwartz/Gourde 5.00 12.00
T4SJS Cheechoo/Toskala Nolan/Nabokov 4.00 10.00
T4VAN Horvat/Boeser/Miller/Hughes 12.00 30.00
T4WPG Wheeler/Hellebuyck Scheifele/Ehlers 10.00 25.00

2022-23 Artifacts Year One Rookie Sweaters

*PATCH/25: 1.5X TO 4X BASIC
RSAN Alex Newhook 1.50 4.00
RSCC Cole Caufield 4.00 10.00
RSDM Dawson Mercer 2.50 6.00
RSJD Jamie Drysdale 1.50 4.00
RSJS Jeremy Swayman 3.00 8.00
RSMS Moritz Seider 2.50 6.00
RSPT Philip Tomasino 1.25 3.00
RSQB Quinton Byfield 2.50 6.00
RSSK Spencer Knight 2.00 5.00
RSVP Vasily Podkolzin 1.25 3.00

2023-24 Artifacts

1 Mika Zibanejad .50 1.25
2 Artturi Lehkonen .30 .75
3 Bryan Rust .40 1.00
4 Philipp Kurashev .30 .75
5 Miro Heiskanen .50 1.25
6 Mitch Marner .60 1.50
7 Mathew Barzal .50 1.25
8 Dawson Mercer .50 1.25
9 David Perron .30 .75
10 Nathan MacKinnon 1.50 4.00
11 Brandon Saad .30 .75
12 Andrei Svechnikov .50 1.25
13 Juraj Slafkovsky .75 2.00
14 Sam Reinhart .75 2.00
15 Brady Tkachuk .60 1.50
16 Troy Terry .30 .75
17 Cale Makar 1.00 2.50
18 Seth Jarvis .50 1.25
19 Jordan Kyrou .40 1.00
20 Sonny Milano .30 .75
21 Seth Jones .40 1.00
22 Brad Marchand .75 2.00
23 Leon Draisaitl 1.25 3.00
24 Matias Maccelli .30 .75
25 Pavel Buchnevich .30 .75
26 Rasmus Dahlin .50 1.25
27 Jack Eichel .60 1.50
28 Drake Batherson .40 1.00
29 Patrik Laine .50 1.25
30 Moritz Seider .50 1.25
31 Steven Stamkos .75 2.00
32 Frank Vatrano .30 .75
33 Brent Burns .40 1.00
34 Ryan Nugent-Hopkins .50 1.25
35 J.T. Miller .50 1.25
36 Phillip Danault .40 1.00
37 Neal Pionk .25 .60
38 Johnny Gaudreau .60 1.50
39 Mats Zuccarello .40 1.00
40 Carter Verhaeghe .40 1.00
41 Michael Bunting .40 1.00
42 Dylan Larkin .50 1.25
43 Brock Boeser .50 1.25
44 Charlie McAvoy .50 1.25
45 Michael Matheson .25 .60
46 Matt Boldy .60 1.50
47 Aleksander Barkov .60 1.50
48 Chandler Stephenson .30 .75
49 Nikolaj Ehlers .40 1.00
50 Tyson Barrie .25 .60
51 William Nylander .75 2.00
52 K'Andre Miller .30 .75
53 Evgeni Malkin .75 2.00
54 Torey Krug .30 .75
55 Matt Duchene .40 1.00
56 Jeff Skinner .40 1.00
57 Noah Dobson .50 1.25
58 Josh Morrissey .50 1.25
59 Mason McTavish .60 1.50
60 Joel Farabee .40 1.00
61 Anze Kopitar .60 1.50
62 Joel Eriksson Ek .30 .75
63 Nico Hischier .60 1.50
64 Jamie Benn .40 1.00
65 Charlie Coyle .40 1.00
66 Jonathan Marchessault .50 1.25
67 Brandon Hagel .30 .75
68 Zach Werenski .60 1.50
69 Andre Burakovsky .25 .60
70 Bo Horvat .50 1.25
71 Jesper Bratt .40 1.00
72 Peyton Krebs .30 .75
73 Erik Karlsson .50 1.25
74 Noah Cates .25 .60
75 Jared McCann .30 .75
76 Tyler Toffoli .40 1.00
77 Braden Schneider .30 .75
78 Patrice Bergeron .50 1.25
79 Jake Sanderson .50 1.25
80 Andrei Kuzmenko .40 1.00
81 Dylan Guenther .50 1.25
82 Mario Ferraro .25 .60
83 Filip Forsberg .60 1.50
84 Zach Hyman .60 1.50
85 Tanner Jeannot .25 .60
86 Gabe Vilardi .40 1.00
87 Logan Couture .50 1.25
88 Nick Schmaltz .30 .75
89 Elias Lindholm .40 1.00
90 Alex DeBrincat .40 1.00
91 Brayden Point .50 1.25
92 Nick Suzuki .75 2.00
93 Dylan Strome .50 1.25
94 Lukas Reichel .40 1.00
95 Kevin Hayes .30 .75
96 Jordan Eberle .40 1.00
97 Chris Kreider .50 1.25
98 Jacob Markstrom .40 1.00
99 Roope Hintz .50 1.25
100 Sebastian Aho .60 1.50
101 Connor McDavid 6.00 15.00
102 Tage Thompson 1.50 4.00
103 Kirill Kaprizov 4.00 10.00
104 Matty Beniers 1.50 4.00
105 Clayton Keller 1.50 4.00
106 Travis Konecny 1.25 3.00
107 Matthew Tkachuk 2.50 6.00
108 Martin Necas 2.00 5.00
109 Elias Pettersson 2.00 5.00
110 Kent Johnson 1.25 3.00
111 Owen Power 1.25 3.00
112 Kevin Fiala 1.00 2.50
113 Mark Stone 1.50 4.00
114 Mikko Rantanen 3.00 8.00
115 Kyle Connor 2.00 5.00
116 Trevor Zegras 1.25 3.00
117 David Pastrnak 3.00 8.00
118 Roman Josi 1.25 3.00
119 Robert Thomas 1.25 3.00
120 Lucas Raymond 2.00 5.00
121 Jonathan Huberdeau 1.50 4.00
122 Taylor Raddysh 1.00 2.50
123 Jack Hughes 3.00 8.00
124 Alex Ovechkin 5.00 12.00
125 Nikita Kucherov 2.50 6.00
126 Tomas Hertl 1.25 3.00
127 Artemi Panarin 2.50 6.00
128 Sidney Crosby 5.00 12.00
129 Quinn Hughes 3.00 8.00
130 Jason Robertson 2.00 5.00
131 Brock Nelson 1.25 3.00
132 Tim Stutzle 1.50 4.00
133 Cole Caufield 2.50 6.00
134 Adam Fox 1.50 4.00
135 Auston Matthews 5.00 12.00
136 Ilya Sorokin 2.00 5.00
137 Frederik Andersen 1.50 4.00
138 Carter Hart 1.25 3.00
139 Linus Ullmark 1.25 3.00
140 Tristan Jarry 1.25 3.00
141 Philipp Grubauer 1.25 3.00
142 Alexandar Georgiev 1.25 3.00
143 Vitek Vanecek 1.25 3.00
144 Andrei Vasilevskiy 2.00 5.00
145 Darcy Kuemper 1.25 3.00
146 Karel Vejmelka .75 2.00
147 Stuart Skinner 1.50 4.00
148 Igor Shesterkin 2.50 6.00
149 Logan Thompson 1.50 4.00
150 Ukko-Pekka Luukkonen 1.00 2.50
151 Jake Oettinger 2.00 5.00
152 Sergei Bobrovsky 2.00 5.00
153 Juuse Saros 1.50 4.00
154 Connor Hellebuyck 2.50 6.00
155 Marc-Andre Fleury 2.50 6.00
156 Pat LaFontaine 1.25 3.00
157 Martin St. Louis 1.25 3.00
158 Jaromir Jagr 4.00 10.00
159 Chris Chelios 1.25 3.00
160 Dany Heatley 1.00 2.50
161 Brett Hull 2.50 6.00
162 Denis Potvin 1.25 3.00
163 Cam Neely 1.25 3.00
164 Eric Lindros 2.00 5.00
165 Luc Robitaille 1.25 3.00
166 Wayne Gretzky 8.00 20.00
167 John LeClair 1.25 3.00
168 Larry Robinson 1.25 3.00
169 Jarome Iginla 1.50 4.00
170 Nicklas Lidstrom 1.25 3.00
171 Matthew Coronato RC 3.00 8.00
172 Nikita Nesterenko RC 2.00 5.00
173 Marco Kasper RC 5.00 12.00
174 Henry Thrun RC 2.00 5.00
175 Adam Ginning RC 2.00 5.00
176 Leevi Merilainen RC 2.00 5.00
177 Arnaud Durandeau RC 2.00 5.00
178 Hunter McKown RC 2.00 5.00
179 Aidan McDonough RC 1.50 4.00
180 Lukas Rousek RC 1.50 4.00
181 Akito Hirose RC 1.50 4.00
182 Dustin Wolf RC 6.00 15.00
183 Yaroslav Askarov RC 8.00 20.00
184 Matthew Kessel RC 1.50 4.00
185 Jackson LaCombe RC 2.00 5.00
186 Sean Farrell RC 2.00 5.00
187 Simon Edvinsson RC 4.00 10.00
188 Cole Guttman RC 2.00 5.00
189 Brock Faber RC 5.00 12.00
190 Ridly Greig RC 3.00 8.00
191 Tristen Robins RC 2.00 5.00
192 Luke Hughes RC 6.00 15.00
193 Devon Levi RC 5.00 12.00
194 Tyson Foerster RC 4.00 10.00
195 Luke Evangelista RC 3.00 8.00
196 Drew Helleson RC 2.00 5.00
197 Jakob Pelletier RC 2.50 6.00
198 Owen Beck RC 3.00 8.00
199 Danil Gushchin RC 2.00 5.00
200 Matthew Knies RC 8.00 20.00

2023-24 Artifacts Autumn

*AUTUMN VETS: 2.5X TO 6X BASIC
*AUTUMN S/L: .75X TO 2X BASIC
*AUTUMN RC: .75X TO 2X BASIC
192 Luke Hughes 20.00 50.00

2023-24 Artifacts Copper

*COPPER VETS: 1.5X TO 4X BASIC
*COPPER S/L: .5X TO 1.2X BASIC
*COPPER RC: .6X TO 1.5X BASIC

2023-24 Artifacts Emerald

*EMERALD VETS: 2X TO 5X BASIC
*EMERALD S/L: .6X TO 1.5X BASIC
*EMERALD RC: .6X TO 1.5X BASIC
192 Luke Hughes 15.00 40.00

2023-24 Artifacts Leather

*LEATHER S/L: .6X TO 1.5X BASIC
*LEATHER RC: .75X TO 2X BASIC
192 Luke Hughes 15.00 40.00

2023-24 Artifacts Light Blue Steel

*LIGHT BLUE VETS: 2.5X TO 6X BASIC
*LIGHT BLUE S/L: .75X TO 2X BASIC
*LIGHT BLUE RC: .75X TO 2X BASIC
192 Luke Hughes 15.00 40.00

2023-24 Artifacts Pink

*PINK VETS: 4X TO 10X BASIC
*PINK S/L: 1.25X TO 3X BASIC
*PINK RC: 1.25X TO 3X BASIC
192 Luke Hughes 30.00 80.00

2023-24 Artifacts Plexi

*PLEXI: 1.5X TO 4X BASIC

2023-24 Artifacts Polychrome

*POLYCHROME VETS: 3X TO 8X BASIC
*POLYCHROME S/L: 1X TO 2.5X BASIC
*POLYCHROME RC: 1X TO 2.5X BASIC
192 Luke Hughes 20.00 50.00

2023-24 Artifacts Purple

*PURPLE VETS: 5X TO 12X BASIC
*PURPLE S/L: 1.5X TO 4X BASIC
*PURPLE RC: 1.5X TO 4X BASIC
192 Luke Hughes 40.00 100.00

2023-24 Artifacts Royal Blue

*ROYAL BLUE VETS: 1.5X TO 4X BASIC
*ROYAL BLUE S/L: .5X TO 1.2X BASIC
*ROYAL BLUE RC: .6X TO 1.5X BASIC
192 Luke Hughes 15.00 40.00

2023-24 Artifacts Ruby

*RUBY VETS: 1.2X TO 3X BASIC
*RUBY S/L: .4X TO 1X BASIC
*RUBY RC: .5X TO 1.2X BASIC

2023-24 Artifacts Turquoise

*TURQUOISE VETS: .5X TO 1.2X BASIC
*TURQUOISE S/L: .5X TO 1.2X BASIC
*TURQUOISE RC: .3X TO .75X BASIC

2023-24 Artifacts Wood

*WOOD: .5X TO 1.2X BASIC
192 Luke Hughes 12.00 30.00

2023-24 Artifacts Yellow

*YELLOW VETS: 3X TO 8X BASIC
*YELLOW S/L: 1X TO 2.5X BASIC
*YELLOW RC: 1X TO 2.5X BASIC

2023-24 Artifacts '05-06 Clear Cut Retro Rookies

CCRR1 Connor Bedard 200.00 500.00
CCRR2 Adam Fantilli 25.00 60.00
CCRR3 Dylan Guenther 6.00 15.00
CCRR4 Shane Wright 6.00 15.00
CCRR5 Brandt Clarke 5.00 12.00
CCRR6 Wyatt Johnston 10.00 25.00
CCRR7 Juraj Slafkovsky 10.00 25.00
CCRR8 Jake Sanderson 6.00 15.00
CCRR9 Andrei Kuzmenko 5.00 12.00
CCRR10 Kirill Marchenko 6.00 15.00
CCRR11 Luke Hughes 20.00 50.00
CCRR12 Nathan MacKinnon 20.00 50.00
CCRR13 Devon Levi 12.00 30.00
CCRR14 Patrice Bergeron 6.00 15.00
CCRR15 Jakob Pelletier 6.00 15.00
CCRR16 Steven Stamkos 10.00 25.00
CCRR17 Luke Evangelista 8.00 20.00
CCRR18 Igor Shesterkin 10.00 25.00
CCRR19 Yaroslav Askarov 12.00 30.00
CCRR20 Sidney Crosby 30.00 80.00
CCRR21 Tyson Foerster 10.00 25.00
CCRR22 Erik Karlsson 6.00 15.00
CCRR23 Brock Faber 12.00 30.00
CCRR24 Jason Robertson 8.00 20.00
CCRR25 Matthew Knies 20.00 50.00
CCRR26 Connor Hellebuyck 10.00 25.00
CCRR27 Simon Edvinsson 10.00 25.00
CCRR28 Mitch Marner 8.00 20.00
CCRR29 Dustin Wolf 15.00 40.00
CCRR30 Jack Hughes 12.00 30.00

2023-24 Artifacts '05-06 Retro Autofacts

RAFAC Andrew Copp C 6.00 15.00
RAFAG Adam Graves D 8.00 20.00
RAFAL Anders Lee D 8.00 20.00
RAFAX Arber Xhekaj E 10.00 25.00
RAFBR Bill Ranford C 8.00 20.00
RAFCC Chris Chelios D 10.00 25.00
RAFCM Connor McDavid A 150.00 400.00
RAFCP Cole Perfetti C 10.00 25.00
RAFDP Denis Potvin C 10.00 25.00
RAFJO Jake Oettinger A 15.00 40.00
RAFJQ Jack Quinn E 8.00 20.00
RAFKJ Kent Johnson E 10.00 25.00
RAFKV Karel Vejmelka D 6.00 15.00
RAFLD Lukas Dostal D 10.00 25.00
RAFLR Lukas Reichel E 10.00 25.00
RAFMD Matt Duchene C 10.00 25.00
RAFMI Sonny Milano E 8.00 20.00
RAFMM Matias Maccelli D 8.00 20.00
RAFMO Mike Modano B 15.00 40.00
RAFMS Marco Sturm D 6.00 15.00
RAFNC Noah Cates D 6.00 15.00
RAFNP Neal Pionk C 6.00 15.00
RAFPE Nick Perbix E 6.00 15.00
RAFPG Philipp Grubauer C 10.00 25.00
RAFPL Pat LaFontaine C 10.00 25.00
RAFRL Robin Lehner D 8.00 20.00
RAFRO Ryan O'Reilly C 10.00 25.00
RAFRS Ryan Strome E 10.00 25.00
RAFSM Mike Smith D 6.00 15.00
RAFST Mark Stone D 12.00 30.00
RAFSZ Sergei Zubov D 8.00 20.00
RAFTC Thomas Chabot C 10.00 25.00
RAFTF Theoren Fleury B 10.00 25.00
RAFTJ Tanner Jeannot E 6.00 15.00
RAFTK Torey Krug E 8.00 20.00
RAFTM Timo Meier E 10.00 25.00
RAFTS Tim Stutzle B 12.00 30.00
RAFTT Tage Thompson E 12.00 30.00
RAFVV Vitek Vanecek D 10.00 25.00
RAFWC Wendel Clark B 15.00 40.00
RAFZH Zach Hyman D 15.00 40.00
RAFZW Zach Werenski C 15.00 40.00

2023-24 Artifacts Admirable Impressions

AIAO Alex Ovechkin 250.00 600.00
AIMB Matty Beniers 60.00 150.00
AIMS Mark Stone 150.00 400.00
AITS Tim Stutzle 40.00 100.00
AITT Tage Thompson 100.00 250.00

2023-24 Artifacts All Star Tickets

ASABH Brett Hull/26 50.00 125.00
ASADL Dylan Larkin/32 80.00 200.00
ASAGF Grant Fuhr/34 80.00 200.00
ASAJJ Jaromir Jagr/32 100.00 250.00
ASAJT John Tavares/32 50.00 125.00
ASALR Luc Robitaille/24 50.00 125.00
ASAML Mario Lemieux/24 150.00 400.00
ASAMR Mike Richter/30 80.00 200.00

2023-24 Artifacts Arena Artifacts

AABT Bryan Trottier 30.00 80.00
AAEM Evgeni Malkin 60.00 150.00
AAJJ Jaromir Jagr 60.00 150.00
AAJM Joe Mullen 30.00 80.00
AALM Larry Murphy 30.00 80.00
AAMF Marc-Andre Fleury 60.00 150.00
AAML Mario Lemieux 60.00 150.00
AAMR Mark Recchi 30.00 80.00
AAPC Paul Coffey 25.00 60.00
AASC Sidney Crosby 80.00 200.00

2023-24 Artifacts Aurum

A1 Matt Boldy 3.00 8.00
A2 Auston Matthews 8.00 20.00
A3 David Pastrnak 5.00 12.00
A4 Jordan Kyrou 2.00 5.00
A5 Connor McDavid 10.00 25.00
A6 Sidney Crosby 8.00 20.00
A7 Brayden Point 2.50 6.00
A8 Nathan MacKinnon 8.00 20.00
A9 Artemi Panarin 4.00 10.00
A10 Linus Ullmark 2.00 5.00
A11 Johnny Gaudreau 3.00 8.00
A12 Matty Beniers 2.50 6.00
A13 Clayton Keller 2.50 6.00
A14 Erik Karlsson 2.50 6.00
A15 Tim Stutzle 2.50 6.00
A16 Jason Robertson 3.00 8.00
A17 Jack Hughes 5.00 12.00
A18 Alex Ovechkin 8.00 20.00
A19 Trevor Zegras 2.00 5.00
A20 Mitch Marner 3.00 8.00
A21 Matthew Tkachuk 4.00 10.00
A22 Igor Shesterkin 4.00 10.00
A23 Cale Makar 5.00 12.00
A24 Jack Eichel 3.00 8.00
A25 Elias Pettersson 3.00 8.00
A26 Kevin Fiala 1.50 4.00
A27 Cole Caufield 4.00 10.00
A28 Kirill Kaprizov 6.00 15.00
A29 Dylan Larkin 2.50 6.00
A30 Tage Thompson 2.50 6.00
A31 Brock Faber 5.00 12.00
A32 Devon Levi 10.00 25.00
A33 Dustin Wolf 6.00 15.00
A34 Jakob Pelletier 2.50 6.00
A35 Luke Evangelista 3.00 8.00
A36 Simon Edvinsson 4.00 10.00
A37 Luke Hughes 15.00 40.00
A38 Tyson Foerster 12.00 30.00
A39 Yaroslav Askarov 5.00 12.00
A40 Matthew Knies 8.00 20.00
A41 Steve Yzerman 25.00 60.00
A42 Bobby Orr 30.00 80.00
A43 Dominik Hasek 30.00 80.00
A44 Eric Lindros 25.00 60.00
A45 Mario Lemieux 30.00 80.00
A46 Terry Sawchuk 25.00 60.00
A47 Maurice Richard 30.00 80.00
A48 Joe Sakic 30.00 80.00

2023-24 Artifacts Aurum Signatures

ASAM Aidan McDonough 12.00 30.00
ASBF Brock Faber 80.00 200.00
ASGC Gerry Cheevers 25.00 60.00
ASJE Jordan Eberle 15.00 40.00
ASJP Jakob Pelletier 20.00 50.00
ASJV John Vanbiesbrouck 15.00 40.00
ASKT Keith Tkachuk 15.00 40.00
ASLE Luke Evangelista 25.00 60.00
ASLH Luke Hughes 50.00 125.00
ASMB Michael Bunting 15.00 40.00
ASMD Matt Duchene 15.00 40.00
ASMH Miro Heiskanen 20.00 50.00
ASRG Ryan Getzlaf 15.00 40.00
ASRH Ron Hextall 15.00 40.00
ASRO Ryan O'Reilly 15.00 40.00
ASSC Shayne Corson 12.00 30.00
ASSD Shane Doan 12.00 30.00
ASSE Simon Edvinsson 30.00 80.00
ASSR Sam Reinhart 30.00 80.00
ASSZ Sergei Zubov 12.00 30.00
ASTT Tyler Toffoli 15.00 40.00
ASTZ Roope Hintz 20.00 50.00
ASVH Victor Hedman 20.00 50.00

2023-24 Artifacts Autofacts

AFAB Adam Beckman E 4.00 10.00
AFAK Arthur Kaliyev E 6.00 15.00
AFAL Jake Allen D 6.00 15.00
AFAM Andy Moog D 6.00 15.00
AFAN Alex Nedeljkovic E 5.00 12.00
AFAR Aatu Raty E 4.00 10.00
AFBA Aleksander Barkov C 10.00 25.00
AFBC Blake Coleman D 5.00 12.00
AFBG Brendan Gallagher C 6.00 15.00
AFBH Brandon Hagel D 5.00 12.00
AFBJ Josh Bailey E 5.00 12.00
AFBM Ben Meyers E 4.00 10.00
AFBP Brad Park B 5.00 12.00
AFBR Bryan Rust D 6.00 15.00
AFCA Cam Atkinson E 6.00 15.00
AFCC Charlie Coyle E 6.00 15.00
AFCH Carter Hart C 6.00 15.00
AFCJ Calle Jarnkrok C 4.00 10.00
AFCM Maxime Comtois E 5.00 12.00
AFCP Cal Petersen E 4.00 10.00
AFCW Chris Wideman E 4.00 10.00
AFDB Drake Batherson E 6.00 15.00
AFDG Dennis Gilbert E 5.00 12.00
AFDH Dany Heatley C 5.00 12.00
AFDK Darcy Kuemper E 6.00 15.00
AFDO Shane Doan D 5.00 12.00
AFDT Dave Taylor B 5.00 12.00
AFEB Evan Bouchard D 8.00 20.00
AFED Evgenii Dadonov C 4.00 10.00
AFEK Evgeny Kuznetsov D 8.00 20.00
AFET Eeli Tolvanen E 6.00 15.00
AFFE Mario Ferraro D 4.00 10.00
AFFG Filip Gustavsson D 6.00 15.00
AFGC Gerry Cheevers E 6.00 15.00
AFGF Grant Fuhr B 12.00 30.00
AFGU Dylan Guenther D 8.00 20.00
AFGV Gabe Vilardi C 6.00 15.00
AFIS Ilya Sorokin D 12.00 30.00
AFJA Craig Janney D 5.00 12.00
AFJB Jonatan Berggren E 5.00 12.00
AFJH Jordan Harris E 4.00 10.00
AFJO Jonathan Marchessault C 8.00 20.00
AFJP Jeff Petry D 6.00 15.00
AFJS Jaccob Slavin E 5.00 12.00
AFJU Justin Barron E 5.00 12.00
AFJV James van Riemsdyk E 5.00 12.00
AFKD Kirby Dach E 6.00 15.00
AFKG Kaiden Guhle E 6.00 15.00
AFKM K'Andre Miller E 5.00 12.00
AFKT Keith Tkachuk B 5.00 12.00
AFLJ Lucas Johansen E 4.00 10.00
AFMA John Marino D 6.00 15.00
AFMB Michael Bunting D 6.00 15.00
AFMC Jack McBain E 4.00 10.00
AFMD Marcel Dionne C 8.00 20.00
AFMF Marcus Foligno E 5.00 12.00
AFMG Matt Grzelcyk E 5.00 12.00
AFMI Jacob Middleton E 4.00 10.00
AFMS Martin St. Louis B 6.00 15.00
AFPA Juuso Parssinen E 6.00 15.00
AFPG Philipp Grubauer E 6.00 15.00
AFPK Peyton Krebs E 5.00 12.00
AFPR Brian Propp E 5.00 12.00
AFPU Jesse Puljujarvi E 6.00 15.00
AFRB Rod Brind'Amour A 6.00 15.00
AFRF Robby Fabbri E 4.00 10.00
AFRH Roope Hintz C 8.00 20.00
AFRK Rick Middleton D 6.00 15.00
AFSA Juuse Saros D 8.00 20.00
AFSC Shayne Corson D 5.00 12.00
AFSD Sean Durzi E 4.00 10.00
AFSI Charlie Simmer D 4.00 10.00
AFSJ Seth Jarvis E 8.00 20.00
AFSM Sonny Milano E 5.00 12.00
AFSR Sam Reinhart D 12.00 30.00
AFSS Sergei Samsonov E 5.00 12.00
AFSW Jeremy Swayman D 20.00 50.00
AFSZ Sergei Zubov E 5.00 12.00
AFTJ Tanner Jeannot E 5.00 12.00
AFTM Timo Meier E 6.00 15.00
AFTT Tony Twist D 4.00 10.00
AFUL Ukko-Pekka Luukkonen D 5.00 12.00
AFWE William Eklund E 8.00 20.00
AFYS Yegor Sharangovich D 6.00 15.00
AFZH Zach Hyman D 10.00 25.00

2023-24 Artifacts Award Winners Autographs

AWAAE Aaron Ekblad 30.00 80.00
AWACC Chris Chelios 25.00 60.00
AWACJ Curtis Joseph 60.00 150.00
AWADG Doug Gilmour 30.00 80.00
AWADP Denis Potvin 25.00 60.00
AWAJK Jari Kurri 25.00 60.00
AWAJS Jaccob Slavin 40.00 100.00
AWAMD Marcel Dionne 30.00 80.00
AWARB Rod Brind'Amour 25.00 60.00
AWARF Ron Francis 30.00 80.00
AWARJ Roman Josi 25.00 60.00
AWARM Rick Middleton 25.00 60.00
AWASD Shane Doan 20.00 50.00
AWAWG Wayne Gretzky 400.00 1000.00

2023-24 Artifacts Clear Cut Rookies

CCR1 Nikita Nesterenko 4.00 10.00
CCR2 Owen Beck 6.00 15.00
CCR3 Leevi Merilainen 4.00 10.00
CCR4 Adam Ginning 4.00 10.00
CCR5 Aidan McDonough 3.00 8.00
CCR6 Tristen Robins 4.00 10.00
CCR7 Jakob Pelletier 5.00 12.00
CCR8 Devon Levi 10.00 25.00
CCR9 Luke Hughes 25.00 60.00
CCR10 Sean Farrell 4.00 10.00
CCR11 Cole Guttman 4.00 10.00
CCR12 Akito Hirose 3.00 8.00
CCR13 Matthew Knies 15.00 40.00
CCR14 Hunter McKown 4.00 10.00
CCR15 Drew Helleson 4.00 10.00
CCR16 Arnaud Durandeau 4.00 10.00
CCR17 Luke Evangelista 6.00 15.00
CCR18 Matthew Coronato 6.00 15.00
CCR19 Yaroslav Askarov 10.00 25.00
CCR20 Tyson Foerster 8.00 20.00
CCR21 Dustin Wolf 12.00 30.00
CCR22 Brock Faber 10.00 25.00
CCR23 Matthew Kessel 3.00 8.00
CCR24 Jackson LaCombe 3.00 8.00
CCR25 Lukas Rousek 3.00 8.00
CCR26 Danil Gushchin 4.00 10.00
CCR27 Marco Kasper 10.00 25.00
CCR28 Henry Thrun 4.00 10.00
CCR29 Ridly Greig 6.00 15.00
CCR30 Simon Edvinsson 8.00 20.00

2023-24 Artifacts Esteemed Endorsements

EEAB Aleksander Barkov 25.00 60.00
EEAG Adam Graves 40.00 100.00
EECJ Curtis Joseph 80.00 200.00
EEKP Keith Primeau 40.00 100.00
EERB Rob Blake 80.00 200.00
EERJ Roman Josi 80.00 200.00
EESD Shane Doan 60.00 150.00
EETS Tim Stutzle 50.00 125.00

2023-24 Artifacts Material Autographs Gold

*EMERALD/45: .5X TO 1.2X GOLD
101 Connor McDavid/25 250.00 600.00
102 Tage Thompson/45 20.00 50.00
104 Matty Beniers/45 20.00 50.00
107 Matthew Tkachuk/45 30.00 80.00
110 Kent Johnson/65 15.00 40.00
111 Owen Power/65 15.00 40.00
112 Kevin Fiala/65 12.00 30.00
113 Mark Stone/65 20.00 50.00
119 Robert Thomas/65 15.00 40.00
121 Jonathan Huberdeau/65 20.00 50.00
122 Taylor Raddysh/65 12.00 30.00
124 Alex Ovechkin/25 200.00 500.00
126 Tomas Hertl/65 15.00 40.00
128 Sidney Crosby/25 150.00 400.00
129 Quinn Hughes/65 40.00 100.00
132 Tim Stutzle/45 20.00 50.00
135 Auston Matthews/25 125.00 300.00
136 Ilya Sorokin/45 25.00 60.00
138 Carter Hart/45 15.00 40.00
140 Tristan Jarry/65 15.00 40.00
141 Philipp Grubauer/65 15.00 40.00
143 Vitek Vanecek/65 15.00 40.00
144 Andrei Vasilevskiy/45 25.00 60.00
145 Darcy Kuemper/65 15.00 40.00
146 Karel Vejmelka/65 10.00 25.00
150 Ukko-Pekka Luukkonen/65 12.00 30.00
151 Jake Oettinger/45 25.00 60.00
153 Juuse Saros/65 20.00 50.00
154 Connor Hellebuyck/65 30.00 80.00
155 Marc-Andre Fleury/45 30.00 80.00
156 Pat LaFontaine/45 15.00 40.00
157 Martin St. Louis/45 15.00 40.00
159 Chris Chelios/45 15.00 40.00
160 Dany Heatley/45 12.00 30.00
161 Brett Hull/45 30.00 80.00
162 Denis Potvin/45 15.00 40.00
164 Eric Lindros/45 25.00 60.00
165 Luc Robitaille/45 15.00 40.00
166 Wayne Gretzky/25 300.00 800.00
168 Larry Robinson/45 15.00 40.00
169 Jarome Iginla/45 20.00 50.00
170 Nicklas Lidstrom/45 15.00 40.00
171 Matthew Coronato/149 25.00 60.00
173 Marco Kasper/149 40.00 100.00
176 Leevi Merilainen/149 15.00 40.00
177 Arnaud Durandeau/149 15.00 40.00
178 Hunter McKown/149 15.00 40.00
179 Aidan McDonough/149 12.00 30.00
181 Akito Hirose/149 12.00 30.00
183 Yaroslav Askarov/99 40.00 100.00
184 Matthew Kessel/149 12.00 30.00
186 Sean Farrell/149 15.00 40.00
187 Simon Edvinsson/99 30.00 80.00
189 Brock Faber/99 40.00 100.00
190 Ridly Greig/149 25.00 60.00
191 Tristen Robins/149 15.00 40.00
194 Tyson Foerster/99 30.00 80.00
195 Luke Evangelista/25 25.00 60.00
197 Jakob Pelletier/99 20.00 50.00
198 Owen Beck/149 25.00 60.00
200 Matthew Knies/25 125.00 300.00

2023-24 Artifacts Material Autographs Horizontal Gold

*HOR GOLD: .5X TO 1.2X GOLD
132 Tim Stutzle/25 60.00 150.00
136 Ilya Sorokin/25 60.00 150.00

2023-24 Artifacts Materials Gold

*EMERALD: .75X TO 2X BASIC
*PURPLE: 1.2X TO 3X BASIC
*HORIZONTAL: .5X TO 1.2X BASIC
*HOR EMRLD: 1.2X TO 3X BASIC
1 Mika Zibanejad/249 4.00 10.00
3 Bryan Rust/249 3.00 8.00
4 Philipp Kurashev/249 2.50 6.00
5 Miro Heiskanen/249 4.00 10.00
6 Mitch Marner/249 5.00 12.00
7 Mathew Barzal/249 4.00 10.00
8 Dawson Mercer/249 4.00 10.00
9 David Perron/249 2.50 6.00
10 Nathan MacKinnon/249 12.00 30.00
11 Brandon Saad/249 2.50 6.00
12 Andrei Svechnikov/249 4.00 10.00
13 Juraj Slafkovsky/249 6.00 15.00
14 Sam Reinhart/249 6.00 15.00
15 Brady Tkachuk/249 5.00 12.00
16 Troy Terry/249 2.50 6.00
17 Cale Makar/249 8.00 20.00
18 Seth Jarvis/249 4.00 10.00
19 Jordan Kyrou/249 3.00 8.00
20 Sonny Milano/249 2.50 6.00
21 Seth Jones/249 3.00 8.00
22 Brad Marchand/249 6.00 15.00
23 Leon Draisaitl/249 10.00 25.00
24 Matias Maccelli/249 2.50 6.00
25 Pavel Buchnevich/249 2.50 6.00
26 Rasmus Dahlin/249 4.00 10.00
27 Jack Eichel/249 5.00 12.00
28 Drake Batherson/249 3.00 8.00
29 Patrik Laine/249 4.00 10.00
30 Moritz Seider/249 4.00 10.00
31 Steven Stamkos/249 6.00 15.00
33 Brent Burns/249 3.00 8.00
34 Ryan Nugent-Hopkins/249 4.00 10.00
35 J.T. Miller/249 4.00 10.00
36 Phillip Danault/249 3.00 8.00
38 Johnny Gaudreau/249 5.00 12.00
39 Mats Zuccarello/249 3.00 8.00
40 Carter Verhaeghe/249 3.00 8.00
41 Michael Bunting/249 3.00 8.00
42 Dylan Larkin/249 4.00 10.00
43 Brock Boeser/249 4.00 10.00
44 Charlie McAvoy/249 4.00 10.00
46 Matt Boldy/249 5.00 12.00
47 Aleksander Barkov/249 5.00 12.00
48 Chandler Stephenson/249 2.50 6.00
49 Nikolaj Ehlers/249 3.00 8.00
50 Tyson Barrie/249 2.00 5.00
51 William Nylander/249 6.00 15.00
52 K'Andre Miller/249 2.50 6.00
53 Evgeni Malkin/249 6.00 15.00
54 Torey Krug/249 2.50 6.00
55 Matt Duchene/249 3.00 8.00
56 Jeff Skinner/249 3.00 8.00
58 Josh Morrissey/249 4.00 10.00
59 Mason McTavish/249 3.00 8.00
60 Joel Farabee/249 3.00 8.00
61 Anze Kopitar/249 5.00 12.00
62 Joel Eriksson Ek/249 2.50 6.00
63 Nico Hischier/249 5.00 12.00
64 Jamie Benn/249 3.00 8.00
65 Charlie Coyle/249 3.00 8.00
66 Jonathan Marchessault/249 4.00 10.00
67 Brandon Hagel/249 2.50 6.00
68 Zach Werenski/249 5.00 12.00
69 Andre Burakovsky/249 2.00 5.00
70 Bo Horvat/249 4.00 10.00
71 Jesper Bratt/249 3.00 8.00
72 Peyton Krebs/249 2.50 6.00
73 Erik Karlsson/249 4.00 10.00
75 Jared McCann/249 2.50 6.00
76 Tyler Toffoli/249 3.00 8.00
77 Braden Schneider/249 2.50 6.00
78 Patrice Bergeron/249 4.00 10.00
79 Jake Sanderson/249 4.00 10.00
81 Dylan Guenther/249 4.00 10.00
82 Mario Ferraro/249 2.00 5.00
83 Filip Forsberg/249 5.00 12.00
84 Zach Hyman/249 5.00 12.00
85 Tanner Jeannot/249 2.00 5.00
86 Gabe Vilardi/249 3.00 8.00
87 Logan Couture/249 4.00 10.00
88 Nick Schmaltz/249 2.50 6.00
89 Elias Lindholm/249 3.00 8.00
90 Alex DeBrincat/249 4.00 10.00
91 Brayden Point/249 4.00 10.00
92 Nick Suzuki/249 6.00 15.00
93 Dylan Strome/249 4.00 10.00
95 Kevin Hayes/249 2.50 6.00
96 Jordan Eberle/249 3.00 8.00
97 Chris Kreider/249 4.00 10.00
98 Jacob Markstrom/249 3.00 8.00
99 Roope Hintz/249 4.00 10.00
100 Sebastian Aho/249 5.00 12.00
101 Connor McDavid/199 15.00 40.00
102 Tage Thompson/199 4.00 10.00
103 Kirill Kaprizov/199 10.00 25.00
104 Matty Beniers/199 4.00 10.00
105 Clayton Keller/199 4.00 10.00
106 Travis Konecny/199 3.00 8.00
107 Matthew Tkachuk/199 6.00 15.00
108 Martin Necas/199 5.00 12.00
109 Elias Pettersson/199 5.00 12.00
110 Kent Johnson/199 3.00 8.00
111 Owen Power/199 3.00 8.00
112 Kevin Fiala/199 2.50 6.00
113 Mark Stone/199 4.00 10.00
114 Mikko Rantanen/199 8.00 20.00
115 Kyle Connor/199 5.00 12.00
116 Trevor Zegras/199 3.00 8.00
117 David Pastrnak/199 8.00 20.00
118 Roman Josi/199 3.00 8.00
119 Robert Thomas/199 3.00 8.00
120 Lucas Raymond/199 5.00 12.00
121 Jonathan Huberdeau/199 4.00 10.00
122 Taylor Raddysh/199 2.50 6.00
123 Jack Hughes/199 8.00 20.00
124 Alex Ovechkin/199 12.00 30.00
125 Nikita Kucherov/199 6.00 15.00
126 Tomas Hertl/199 3.00 8.00
127 Artemi Panarin/199 6.00 15.00
128 Sidney Crosby/199 12.00 30.00
129 Quinn Hughes/199 8.00 20.00
130 Jason Robertson/199 5.00 12.00
131 Brock Nelson/199 3.00 8.00
132 Tim Stutzle/199 4.00 10.00
133 Cole Caufield/199 6.00 15.00
134 Adam Fox/199 4.00 10.00
135 Auston Matthews/199 12.00 30.00
136 Ilya Sorokin/199 5.00 12.00
137 Frederik Andersen/199 4.00 10.00
138 Carter Hart/199 3.00 8.00
140 Tristan Jarry/199 3.00 8.00
141 Philipp Grubauer/199 3.00 8.00
142 Alexandar Georgiev/199 3.00 8.00
143 Vitek Vanecek/199 3.00 8.00
144 Andrei Vasilevskiy/199 5.00 12.00
145 Darcy Kuemper/199 3.00 8.00
146 Karel Vejmelka/199 2.00 5.00
148 Igor Shesterkin/199 6.00 15.00
150 Ukko-Pekka Luukkonen/199 2.50 6.00
151 Jake Oettinger/199 5.00 12.00
152 Sergei Bobrovsky/199 5.00 12.00
153 Juuse Saros/199 4.00 10.00
154 Connor Hellebuyck/199 6.00 15.00
155 Marc-Andre Fleury/199 6.00 15.00
156 Pat LaFontaine/149 3.00 8.00
157 Martin St. Louis/149 3.00 8.00
158 Jaromir Jagr/149 10.00 25.00
159 Chris Chelios/149 3.00 8.00
161 Brett Hull/149 6.00 15.00
162 Denis Potvin/149 3.00 8.00
164 Eric Lindros/149 5.00 12.00
165 Luc Robitaille/149 3.00 8.00
166 Wayne Gretzky/149 20.00 50.00
168 Larry Robinson/149 3.00 8.00
169 Jarome Iginla/149 4.00 10.00
170 Nicklas Lidstrom/149 3.00 8.00
171 Matthew Coronato/599 5.00 12.00
173 Marco Kasper/599 8.00 20.00
175 Adam Ginning/599 3.00 8.00
176 Leevi Merilainen/599 3.00 8.00
177 Arnaud Durandeau/599 3.00 8.00
178 Hunter McKown/599 3.00 8.00
179 Aidan McDonough/599 2.50 6.00
181 Akito Hirose/599 2.50 6.00
182 Dustin Wolf/599 10.00 25.00
183 Yaroslav Askarov/599 8.00 20.00
184 Matthew Kessel/599 2.50 6.00
186 Sean Farrell/599 3.00 8.00
187 Simon Edvinsson/599 6.00 15.00
189 Brock Faber/599 8.00 20.00
190 Ridly Greig/599 5.00 12.00
191 Tristen Robins/599 3.00 8.00
194 Tyson Foerster/599 6.00 15.00
195 Luke Evangelista/599 5.00 12.00
197 Jakob Pelletier/599 4.00 10.00
198 Owen Beck/599 5.00 12.00
200 Matthew Knies/599 12.00 30.00

2023-24 Artifacts NHL Remnants
NRAM Auston Matthews C 8.00 20.00
NRAO Alex Ovechkin C 8.00 20.00
NRAP Artemi Panarin D 4.00 10.00
NRBP Brayden Point C 2.50 6.00
NRBT Brady Tkachuk D 3.00 8.00
NRCC Cole Caufield C 4.00 10.00
NRCH Connor Hellebuyck D 4.00 10.00
NRCM Cale Makar D 5.00 12.00
NRDP David Pastrnak D 5.00 12.00
NREK Erik Karlsson D 2.50 6.00
NREM Evgeni Malkin D 4.00 10.00
NRHL Henrik Lundqvist B 5.00 12.00
NRHZ Henrik Zetterberg B 2.50 6.00
NRJG Johnny Gaudreau C 3.00 8.00
NRJH Jack Hughes C 5.00 12.00
NRJR Jason Robertson A 3.00 8.00
NRKK Kirill Kaprizov C 6.00 15.00
NRLD Leon Draisaitl D 6.00 15.00
NRMC Connor McDavid C 10.00 25.00
NRMM Mitch Marner C 3.00 8.00
NRMT Matthew Tkachuk C 4.00 10.00
NRNM Nathan MacKinnon C 8.00 20.00
NRPB Patrice Bergeron C 2.50 6.00
NRQH Quinn Hughes D 5.00 12.00
NRRB Ray Bourque A 3.00 8.00
NRRG Ryan Getzlaf B 2.00 5.00
NRSC Sidney Crosby B 8.00 20.00
NRSS Steven Stamkos D 4.00 10.00
NRTZ Trevor Zegras D 2.00 5.00
NRWN William Nylander D 4.00 10.00

2023-24 Artifacts NHL Remnants Premium
*PREMIUM/25: 1.2X TO 3X BASIC
NRMC Connor McDavid 50.00 125.00

2023-24 Artifacts Selection Souvenirs
*PREMIUM/25: 1X TO 2.5X BASIC
SSAM Auston Matthews A 10.00 25.00
SSCC Cole Caufield B 5.00 12.00
SSCM Cale Makar B 6.00 15.00
SSEP Elias Pettersson B 4.00 10.00
SSJH Jack Hughes A 6.00 15.00
SSJR Jason Robertson B 4.00 10.00
SSMC Connor McDavid A 12.00 30.00
SSMM Mitch Marner B 4.00 10.00
SSQH Quinn Hughes B 6.00 15.00
SSTZ Trevor Zegras B 2.50 6.00

2023-24 Artifacts Signature Apparel
SACB Connor Bedard/36 1500.00 4000.00
SALR Luc Robitaille/36 60.00 150.00
SASR Sam Reinhart/36 40.00 100.00
SAYA Yaroslav Askarov/36 80.00 200.00

2023-24 Artifacts Signs of Success
SOSAK Andrei Kuzmenko/49 10.00 25.00
SOSBE Matty Beniers/49 12.00 30.00
SOSJE Jack Eichel/49 15.00 40.00
SOSJH Jonathan Huberdeau/49 12.00 30.00
SOSJP Joe Pavelski/49 12.00 30.00
SOSJQ Jonathan Quick/49 12.00 30.00
SOSJS Jake Sanderson/49 12.00 30.00
SOSKF Kevin Fiala/49 8.00 20.00
SOSKM Kirill Marchenko/49 12.00 30.00
SOSLD Leon Draisaitl/49 30.00 80.00
SOSLH Luke Hughes/49 60.00 150.00
SOSMB Matt Boldy/49 15.00 40.00
SOSMF Marc-Andre Fleury/49 20.00 50.00
SOSMH Miro Heiskanen/49 12.00 30.00
SOSMZ Mats Zuccarello/49 10.00 25.00
SOSNS Nick Suzuki/49 20.00 50.00
SOSSW Shane Wright/49 12.00 30.00
SOSTT Tyler Toffoli/49 10.00 25.00
SOSVH Victor Hedman/49 12.00 30.00
SOSWJ Wyatt Johnston/49 20.00 50.00

2023-24 Artifacts Silky Mits
SMAK Anze Kopitar 8.00 20.00
SMAM Auston Matthews 20.00 50.00
SMAO Alex Ovechkin 20.00 50.00
SMBH Brett Hull 10.00 25.00
SMCM Connor McDavid 25.00 60.00
SMEB Jordan Eberle 5.00 12.00
SMEI Jack Eichel 8.00 20.00
SMGL Gabriel Landeskog 6.00 15.00
SMHZ Henrik Zetterberg 6.00 15.00
SMJE Joel Eriksson Ek 4.00 10.00
SMJM Jared McCann 4.00 10.00
SMKP Keith Primeau 4.00 10.00
SMKT Keith Tkachuk 5.00 12.00
SMMS Mark Stone 6.00 15.00
SMRB Ray Bourque 8.00 20.00

2023-24 Artifacts Silky Mits Autographs
SMAM Auston Matthews/25 150.00 400.00
SMAO Alex Ovechkin/25 250.00 600.00
SMCM Connor McDavid/25 300.00 800.00
SMEI Jack Eichel/25 80.00 200.00

2023-24 Artifacts Storied Scripts
SSAG Adam Graves 12.00 30.00
SSCC Chris Chelios 30.00 80.00
SSTE Teuvo Teravainen 15.00 40.00
SSTH Tage Thompson 20.00 50.00
SSTM Timo Meier 15.00 40.00
SSTT Tyler Toffoli 15.00 40.00
SSYC Yvan Cournoyer 50.00 125.00

2023-24 Artifacts Threads of Time
*PREMIUM/25: 1.2X TO 3X BASIC
TTAB Andre Burakovsky B 1.25 3.00
TTAP Artemi Panarin C 4.00 10.00
TTBS Brandon Saad C 1.50 4.00
TTCT Cam Talbot C 2.00 5.00
TTDP David Perron C 1.50 4.00
TTEK Evander Kane C 2.00 5.00
TTEL Eric Lindros A 3.00 8.00
TTFA Frederik Andersen C 2.50 6.00
TTJI Jarome Iginla A 2.50 6.00
TTJJ Jaromir Jagr A 6.00 15.00
TTSE Tyler Seguin C 2.50 6.00
TTTO Tyler Toffoli C 2.00 5.00
TTTS Teemu Selanne A 4.00 10.00
TTTT Tage Thompson C 2.50 6.00

2023-24 Artifacts Top Tier Rookie Signatures
TTRBF Brock Faber 60.00 150.00
TTRCG Cole Guttman 12.00 30.00
TTRJP Jakob Pelletier 15.00 40.00
TTRKA Marco Kasper 30.00 80.00
TTRLE Luke Evangelista 20.00 50.00
TTRLH Luke Hughes 80.00 200.00
TTRMK Matthew Knies 80.00 200.00
TTRSE Simon Edvinsson 25.00 60.00
TTRTF Tyson Foerster 25.00 60.00
TTRYA Yaroslav Askarov 30.00 80.00

2023-24 Artifacts Treasured Swatches
TSAB Aleksander Barkov B 4.00 10.00
TSAM Auston Matthews A 10.00 25.00
TSCH Carter Hart B 2.50 6.00
TSCM Cale Makar A 6.00 15.00
TSCS Chandler Stephenson B 2.00 5.00
TSDM Dawson Mercer A 3.00 8.00
TSIS Ilya Sorokin A 4.00 10.00
TSJP Jakob Pelletier C 3.00 8.00
TSNS Nick Suzuki B 5.00 12.00
TSRG Ridly Greig C 4.00 10.00
TSRH Roope Hintz B 3.00 8.00
TSRJ Roman Josi B 2.50 6.00
TSRN Ryan Nugent-Hopkins A 3.00 8.00
TSRS Ryan Strome C 2.50 6.00
TSTT Tage Thompson A 3.00 8.00
TSYA Yaroslav Askarov C 6.00 15.00

2023-24 Artifacts Treasured Swatches Autographs
TSCH Carter Hart/25 15.00 40.00
TSJP Jakob Pelletier/25 20.00 50.00
TSRG Ridly Greig/25 25.00 60.00
TSRH Roope Hintz/25 20.00 50.00
TSRS Ryan Strome/25 15.00 40.00
TSYA Yaroslav Askarov/25 40.00 100.00

2023-24 Artifacts Tundra Tandems
TTANA J.Gibson/L.Dostal 2.50 6.00
TTCAR F.Andersen/P.Kochetkov 3.00 8.00
TTFLA S.Bobrovsky/S.Knight 4.00 10.00
TTLAK J.Quick/C.Petersen 3.00 8.00
TTNJD V.Vanecek/M.Blackwood 2.50 6.00
TTNSH J.Saros/Y.Askarov 6.00 15.00
TTNYI I.Sorokin/S.Varlamov 4.00 10.00
TTNYR H.Lundqvist/I.Shesterkin 6.00 15.00
TTPHI C.Hart/B.Elliott 2.50 6.00
TTVGK R.Lehner/M.Fleury 5.00 12.00

2023-24 Artifacts Tundra Teammates Duos
T2BOS D.Pastrnak/P.Bergeron/249 6.00 15.00
T2COL N.MacKinnon/C.Makar/249 10.00 25.00
T2DAL J.Robertson/R.Hintz/249 4.00 10.00
T2EDM C.McDavid/L.Draisaitl/249 12.00 30.00
T2FLA A.Barkov/M.Tkachuk/249 5.00 12.00
T2MIN K.Kaprizov/M.Zuccarello/249 8.00 20.00
T2NYR A.Panarin/A.Fox/249 5.00 12.00
T2OTT T.Stutzle/B.Tkachuk/249 4.00 10.00
T2TOR A.Matthews/M.Marner/249 10.00 25.00
T2PPWC S.Crosby/A.Ovechkin/35 30.00 80.00

2023-24 Artifacts Tundra Teammates Quads
T4ANA Zegras/McTavish/Terry/Gibson 5.00 12.00
T4BOS Pastrnak/Marchand Bergeron/McAvoy 12.00 30.00
T4COL Rantanen/Makar MacKinnon/Girard 20.00 50.00
T4EDM Draisaitl/Nugent-Hopkins/Hyman/Nurse 15.00 40.00
T4MIN Kaprizov/Fleury Zuccarello/Eriksson Ek 15.00 40.00
T4NJD Hughes/Mercer/Tatar/Bratt 12.00 30.00
T4NYR Shesterkin Panarin/Fox/Kreider 10.00 25.00
T4TOR Matthews/Marner Nylander/Tavares 20.00 50.00
T4VAN Hughes/Boeser Garland/Pettersson 12.00 30.00
T4WPG Connor/Scheifele Ehlers/Wheeler 8.00 20.00

2024-25 Artifacts
1 Quinton Byfield .50 1.25
2 Carter Verhaeghe .40 1.00
3 Ryan Strome .40 1.00
4 Victor Hedman .50 1.25
5 Moritz Seider .50 1.25
6 Brandon Saad .30 .75
7 Linus Ullmark .30 .75
8 William Nylander .75 2.00
9 Mitch Marner .60 1.50
10 Tyler Seguin .50 1.25
11 Mario Ferraro .25 .60
12 Jaden Schwartz .30 .75
13 Nathan MacKinnon 1.50 4.00
14 Teuvo Teravainen .40 1.00
15 Dawson Mercer .50 1.25
16 Mark Scheifele .60 1.50
17 Troy Terry .30 .75
18 Chandler Stephenson .30 .75
19 Jason Robertson .60 1.50
20 Zach Hyman .60 1.50
21 Jaccob Slavin .30 .75
22 Matty Beniers .50 1.25
23 Kirill Marchenko .50 1.25
24 Drew Doughty .40 1.00
25 Josh Morrissey .50 1.25
26 Robert Thomas .40 1.00
27 Adrian Kempe .40 1.00
28 Steven Stamkos .75 2.00
29 Thatcher Demko .50 1.25
30 Blake Coleman .30 .75
31 Tom Wilson .40 1.00
32 Brock Nelson .40 1.00
33 Conor Garland .30 .75
34 Devon Toews .30 .75
35 Lucas Raymond .60 1.50
36 Luke Hughes .60 1.50
37 Owen Power .40 1.00
38 Anze Kopitar .60 1.50
39 Adam Fantilli .60 1.50
40 Yanni Gourde .30 .75
41 Mika Zibanejad .50 1.25
42 Clayton Keller .50 1.25
43 Mark Stone .50 1.25
44 Yegor Sharangovich .40 1.00
45 Artemi Panarin .75 2.00
46 Evander Kane .40 1.00
47 Rasmus Dahlin .50 1.25
48 Alex Pietrangelo .30 .75
49 Roman Josi .40 1.00
50 Cam Fowler .40 1.00
51 Philipp Kurashev .30 .75
52 Ryan O'Reilly .40 1.00
53 Charlie McAvoy .50 1.25
54 Mikael Granlund .30 .75
55 Kris Letang .50 1.25
56 Adam Fox .50 1.25
57 J.T. Miller .50 1.25
58 Morgan Rielly .40 1.00
59 Nick Schmaltz .30 .75
60 Henri Jokiharju .25 .60
61 Claude Giroux .40 1.00
62 Taylor Raddysh .30 .75
63 Colton Parayko .30 .75
64 Cole Caufield .75 2.00
65 Sean Couturier .30 .75
66 Gabe Vilardi .40 1.00
67 Tyson Foerster .40 1.00
68 Erik Karlsson .50 1.25
69 Evgeni Malkin .75 2.00
70 Brendan Gallagher .40 1.00
71 Matias Maccelli .30 .75
72 Alex DeBrincat .50 1.25
73 Seth Jones .40 1.00
74 Jake Sanderson .50 1.25
75 Kaiden Guhle .40 1.00
76 John Carlson .40 1.00
77 Nico Hischier .60 1.50
78 Noah Dobson .50 1.25
79 Dylan Strome .50 1.25
80 Mikko Rantanen 1.00 2.50
81 David Pastrnak 1.00 2.50
82 Kyle Connor .60 1.50
83 Aaron Ekblad .50 1.25
84 Filip Forsberg .60 1.50
85 Sergei Bobrovsky .60 1.50
86 Josh Norris .40 1.00
87 Jonathan Huberdeau .50 1.25
88 Zach Werenski .60 1.50
89 Jake Neighbours .40 1.00
90 Sam Reinhart .75 2.00
91 Joel Farabee .40 1.00
92 Joe Pavelski .50 1.25
93 Anders Lee .30 .75
94 Ivan Barbashev .30 .75
95 Patrick Kane .75 2.00
96 Patrik Laine .50 1.25
97 Brent Burns .40 1.00
98 Ryan Nugent-Hopkins .50 1.25
99 Nazem Kadri .50 1.25
100 Owen Tippett .25 .60
101 Devon Levi/699 1.50 4.00
102 Samuel Montembeault/699 1.25 3.00
103 Juuse Saros/699 1.50 4.00
104 Petr Mrazek/699 1.00 2.50
105 Stuart Skinner/699 1.50 4.00
106 Tristan Jarry/699 1.25 3.00
107 Logan Thompson/699 1.50 4.00
108 Philipp Grubauer/699 1.25 3.00
109 Jordan Binnington/699 2.00 5.00
110 Filip Gustavsson/699 1.25 3.00
111 Jacob Markstrom/699 1.25 3.00
112 Joseph Woll/699 1.50 4.00
113 Darcy Kuemper/699 1.25 3.00
114 Igor Shesterkin/699 2.50 6.00
115 Yaroslav Askarov/699 1.50 4.00
116 Ilya Sorokin/699 2.00 5.00
117 Jake Oettinger/699 2.00 5.00
118 Jeremy Swayman/699 2.00 5.00
119 Andrei Vasilevskiy/699 2.00 5.00
120 Marc-Andre Fleury/699 2.50 6.00
121 Logan Cooley/699 2.50 6.00
122 Leo Carlsson/699 2.00 5.00
123 Tage Thompson/699 1.50 4.00
124 Brad Marchand/699 2.50 6.00
125 Wyatt Johnston/699 2.50 6.00
126 Matthew Tkachuk/699 2.50 6.00
127 Brady Tkachuk/699 2.00 5.00
128 Elias Pettersson/699 2.00 5.00
129 Mason McTavish/699 1.25 3.00
130 Luke Evangelista/699 1.00 2.50
131 Sebastian Aho/699 2.00 5.00
132 William Eklund/699 1.50 4.00
133 Seth Jarvis/699 1.50 4.00
134 Jordan Kyrou/699 1.25 3.00
135 Marco Rossi/699 1.50 4.00
136 Dylan Larkin/699 1.50 4.00
137 Tim Stutzle/699 1.50 4.00
138 Johnny Gaudreau/699 2.00 5.00
139 Shane Wright/699 1.50 4.00
140 Alexis Lafreniere/699 2.00 5.00
141 Quinn Hughes/699 3.00 8.00
142 Dylan Cozens/699 1.25 3.00
143 Aleksander Barkov/699 2.00 5.00
144 Timo Meier/699 1.25 3.00
145 Travis Konecny/699 1.25 3.00
146 Mathew Barzal/699 1.50 4.00
147 Kirill Kaprizov/699 4.00 10.00
148 Cale Makar/699 3.00 8.00
149 Jack Hughes/699 3.00 8.00
150 Sidney Crosby/699 5.00 12.00
151 Connor Bedard/699 12.00 30.00
152 Connor McDavid/699 6.00 15.00
153 Auston Matthews/699 5.00 12.00
154 Leon Draisaitl/699 4.00 10.00
155 Alex Ovechkin/699 5.00 12.00
156 Tony Twist/599 .75 2.00
157 Bill Ranford/599 1.00 2.50
158 Rick Nash/599 1.25 3.00
159 Rod Brind'Amour/599 1.25 3.00
160 Keith Primeau/599 1.00 2.50
161 Derek Sanderson/599 1.25 3.00
162 Mike Gartner/599 1.50 4.00
163 Paul Coffey/599 1.25 3.00
164 Ray Bourque/599 2.00 5.00
165 Teemu Selanne/599 2.50 6.00
166 Ron Francis/599 1.50 4.00
167 Trevor Linden/599 1.25 3.00
168 Jarome Iginla/599 1.50 4.00
169 Martin Brodeur/599 3.00 8.00
170 Wayne Gretzky/599 8.00 20.00
171 Brennan Othmann/999 RC 4.00 10.00
172 Jesper Wallstedt/999 RC 5.00 12.00
173 Brendan Brisson/999 RC 2.50 6.00
174 Josh Doan/999 RC 4.00 10.00
175 Logan Stankoven/999 RC 5.00 12.00
176 Joshua Roy/999 RC 3.00 8.00
177 Lukas Cormier/999 RC 2.00 5.00
178 Zach Dean/999 RC 2.00 5.00
179 Shakir Mukhamadullin/999 RC 2.50 6.00
180 Olen Zellweger/999 RC 5.00 12.00
181 Arshdeep Bains/999 RC 2.50 6.00
182 Zachary Bolduc/999 RC 4.00 10.00
183 Mason Morelli/999 RC 2.00 5.00
184 Vasily Ponomarev/999 RC 2.00 5.00
185 Zack Ostapchuk/999 RC 2.00 5.00
186 Devin Cooley/999 RC 2.00 5.00
187 Landon Slaggert/999 RC 2.00 5.00
188 Emil Lilleberg/999 RC 2.00 5.00
189 Marshall Rifai/999 RC 2.00 5.00
190 Jason Polin/999 RC 2.00 5.00
191 Marat Khusnutdinov/999 RC 2.00 5.00
192 Brian Halonen/999 RC 2.00 5.00
193 Maxwell Crozier/999 RC 2.00 5.00
194 Liam Ohgren/999 RC 4.00 10.00
195 Gage Goncalves/999 RC 2.50 6.00
196 Akil Thomas/999 RC 2.00 5.00
197 Logan Morrison/999 RC 2.00 5.00
198 Graeme Clarke/999 RC 2.00 5.00
199 Cutter Gauthier/999 RC 5.00 12.00
200 Frank Nazar/999 RC 6.00 15.00

2024-25 Artifacts Copper
*COPPER: 2.5X TO 6X BASIC
*COPPER G/S/L: .6X TO 1.5X BASIC
*COPPER RC: .6X TO 1.5X BASIC

2024-25 Artifacts Emerald
*EMERALD: 2X TO 5X BASIC
*EMERALD G/S/L: .6X TO 1.5X BASIC
*EMERALD RC: .6X TO 1.5X BASIC

2024-25 Artifacts Foilboard
*FOILBOARD: .5X TO 1.2X BASIC

2024-25 Artifacts Foilboard Gold
*FOIL GOLD: .8X TO 2X BASIC

2024-25 Artifacts Neon Green
*NEON GREEN: 1X TO 2.5X BASIC
*NEON GRN G/S/L: .5X TO 1.2X BASIC
*NEON GRN RC: .5X TO 1.2X BASIC
151 Connor Bedard 10.00 25.00

2024-25 Artifacts Orange
*ORANGE: 3X TO 8X BASIC
*ORANGE G/S/L: .8X TO 2X BASIC
*ORANGE RC: .8X TO 2X BASIC

2024-25 Artifacts Pink
*PINK: 4X TO 10X BASIC
*PINK G/S/L: 1.2X TO 3X BASIC
*PINK RC: 1X TO 2.5X BASIC

2024-25 Artifacts Plexi
*PLEXI G/S/L: 1.5X TO 4X BASIC
*PLEXI RC: 1X TO 2.5X BASIC

2024-25 Artifacts Purple
*PURPLE: 5X TO 12X BASIC
*PURPLE G/S/L: 1.5X TO 4X BASIC
*PURPLE RC: 1.5X TO 4X BASIC

2024-25 Artifacts Ruby
*RUBY: 1.2X TO 3X BASIC
*RUBY G/S/L: .4X TO 1X BASIC
*RUBY RC: .5X TO 1.2X BASIC

2024-25 Artifacts Yellow
*YELLOW: 3X TO 8X BASIC
*YELLOW G/SL: 1X TO 2.5X BASIC
*YELLOW RC: 1X TO 2.5X BASIC

2024-25 Artifacts Antiquity
AT1 Connor McDavid 40.00 100.00
AT2 Auston Matthews 30.00 80.00
AT3 Sidney Crosby 30.00 80.00
AT4 Alex Ovechkin 30.00 80.00
AT5 Nikita Kucherov 15.00 40.00
AT6 Jack Hughes 20.00 50.00
AT7 Leon Draisaitl 25.00 60.00
AT8 Connor Bedard 25.00 60.00
AT9 Marc-Andre Fleury 15.00 40.00
AT10 Nathan MacKinnon 30.00 80.00
AT11 Kirill Kaprizov 25.00 60.00
AT12 Quinn Hughes 20.00 50.00
AT13 Mitch Marner 12.00 30.00
AT14 Brad Marchand 15.00 40.00
AT15 Cale Makar 20.00 50.00
AT16 Nick Suzuki 15.00 40.00
AT17 Jason Robertson 12.00 30.00
AT18 Andrei Vasilevskiy 12.00 30.00
AT19 Igor Shesterkin 15.00 40.00
AT20 Elias Pettersson 12.00 30.00

2024-25 Artifacts Antiquity Rookies
ATR1 Brendan Brisson 10.00 25.00
ATR2 Brennan Othmann 15.00 40.00
ATR3 Olen Zellweger 20.00 50.00
ATR4 Logan Stankoven 20.00 50.00
ATR5 Zach Dean 8.00 20.00
ATR6 Macklin Celebrini 40.00 100.00
ATR7 Jesper Wallstedt 20.00 50.00
ATR8 Frank Nazar 25.00 60.00
ATR9 Joshua Roy 15.00 40.00
ATR10 Cutter Gauthier 20.00 50.00

2024-25 Artifacts Arena Artifacts
AAAD Andre Dupont 30.00 80.00
AABB Bill Barber 50.00 125.00
AABC Bobby Clarke 80.00 200.00
AABP Bernie Parent 60.00 150.00
AADS Dave Schultz 40.00 100.00
AAGD Gary Dornhoefer 30.00 80.00
AALE Reggie Leach 50.00 125.00
AAOK Orest Kindrachuk 30.00 80.00
AAPH Paul Holmgren 40.00 100.00
AARL Ross Lonsberry 30.00 80.00

2024-25 Artifacts Aurum
*PURPLE: .6X TO 1.5X BASIC
AAF Adam Fantilli 5.00 12.00
AAM Auston Matthews 12.00 30.00
ABF Brock Faber 4.00 10.00
ABM Brad Marchand 6.00 15.00
ACB Connor Bedard 10.00 25.00
ACC Cole Caufield 6.00 15.00
ACG Cutter Gauthier 8.00 20.00
ACM Connor McDavid 15.00 40.00
ADP David Pastrnak 8.00 20.00
AEP Elias Pettersson 5.00 12.00
AGH Gordie Howe 15.00 40.00
AIS Igor Shesterkin 6.00 15.00
AJD Josh Doan 8.00 20.00
AJE Jack Eichel 5.00 12.00
AJH Jack Hughes 8.00 20.00
AJO Joshua Roy 6.00 15.00
AJR Jason Robertson 5.00 12.00
AJW Jesper Wallstedt 8.00 20.00
AKK Kirill Kaprizov 10.00 25.00
ALC Leo Carlsson 5.00 12.00
ALD Leon Draisaitl 10.00 25.00
ALE Mario Lemieux AS 60.00 150.00
ALH Luke Hughes 5.00 12.00
ALS Logan Stankoven 8.00 20.00
AMA Cale Makar 8.00 20.00
AMB Matty Beniers 4.00 10.00
AMC Macklin Celebrini 80.00 200.00
AMF Marc-Andre Fleury 6.00 15.00
AMI Mitch Marner 5.00 12.00
AML Mario Lemieux 60.00 150.00
AMM Mark Messier AS 50.00 125.00
ANK Nikita Kucherov 6.00 15.00
ANM Nathan MacKinnon 12.00 30.00
AOZ Olen Zellweger 8.00 20.00
APC Paul Coffey AS 40.00 100.00
APK Patrick Kane 6.00 15.00
APR Patrick Roy 60.00 150.00
AQH Quinn Hughes 8.00 20.00
ARD Rasmus Dahlin 4.00 10.00
ASC Sidney Crosby 12.00 30.00
ASK Steven Stamkos 6.00 15.00
ASM Frank Nazar 10.00 25.00
ASY Steve Yzerman AS 40.00 100.00
ATS Tim Stutzle 4.00 10.00
AWG Wayne Gretzky 50.00 125.00
AWJ Wyatt Johnston 6.00 15.00
AZB Zachary Bolduc 6.00 15.00
AZD Zach Dean 3.00 8.00

2024-25 Artifacts Aurum Signatures
ASAL Alexis Lafreniere 25.00 60.00
ASBO Brennan Othmann 30.00 80.00
ASCE Macklin Celebrini 1000.00 2500.00
ASCG Cutter Gauthier 40.00 100.00
ASDH Dominik Hasek 25.00 60.00
ASEP Elias Pettersson 25.00 60.00
ASFN Frank Nazar 50.00 125.00
ASJS Juraj Slafkovsky 30.00 80.00
ASKK Kirill Kaprizov 50.00 125.00
ASLC Leo Carlsson 25.00 60.00
ASLD Leon Draisaitl 50.00 125.00
ASLS Logan Stankoven 40.00 100.00
ASMA Cale Makar 60.00 150.00
ASMB Martin Brodeur 40.00 100.00
ASML Mario Lemieux 150.00 400.00
ASMM Mark Messier 30.00 80.00
ASNK Nikita Kucherov 30.00 80.00
ASNL Nicklas Lidstrom 15.00 40.00
ASOZ Olen Zellweger 40.00 100.00
ASQH Quinn Hughes 40.00 100.00
ASSY Steve Yzerman 60.00 150.00

2024-25 Artifacts Autofacts
AFAR Alexander Romanov 5.00 12.00
AFAX Arber Xhekaj 6.00 15.00
AFBB Bobby Brink 4.00 10.00
AFCC Connor Clifton 4.00 10.00
AFCI Connor Ingram 4.00 10.00
AFCT Calvin Thurkauf 4.00 10.00
AFDB Drake Batherson 6.00 15.00
AFDG Dennis Gilbert 5.00 12.00
AFDH Dylan Holloway 6.00 15.00
AFDS Dylan Samberg 4.00 10.00
AFED Evgenii Dadonov 4.00 10.00
AFES Elmer Soderblom 6.00 15.00
AFIL Isac Lundestrom 4.00 10.00
AFIR Isak Rosen 4.00 10.00
AFJE Joel Eriksson Ek 5.00 12.00
AFJM Jack McBain 4.00 10.00
AFJU Juuso Parssinen 4.00 10.00
AFJW Jake Walman 4.00 10.00
AFKK Kasperi Kapanen 5.00 12.00
AFLU Tristan Luneau 4.00 10.00
AFMI Jacob Middleton 4.00 10.00
AFMP Matthew Phillips 4.00 10.00
AFMS Matt Savoie SP 6.00 15.00
AFNA Nils Aman 4.00 10.00
AFNH Nils Hoglander 5.00 12.00
AFNL Nils Lundkvist 4.00 10.00
AFNP Nick Perbix 4.00 10.00
AFOL Oskar Lindblom 5.00 12.00
AFPA Jean-Gabriel Pageau 4.00 10.00
AFPO Martin Pospisil 4.00 10.00
AFRE Ryker Evans 4.00 10.00
AFRS Ryan Strome 6.00 15.00
AFSH Simon Holmstrom 4.00 10.00
AFSW Shane Wright 8.00 20.00
AFTK Torey Krug 5.00 12.00
AFTL Timothy Liljegren 4.00 10.00
AFTR Taylor Raddysh 5.00 12.00
AFTT Teuvo Teravainen 6.00 15.00

2024-25 Artifacts Clear Cut
171 Brennan Othmann 6.00 15.00
172 Jesper Wallstedt 10.00 25.00
173 Brendan Brisson 5.00 12.00
174 Josh Doan 6.00 15.00
175 Logan Stankoven 10.00 25.00
176 Joshua Roy 6.00 15.00
177 Lukas Cormier 4.00 10.00
178 Zach Dean 4.00 10.00
179 Shakir Mukhamadullin 5.00 12.00
180 Olen Zellweger 8.00 20.00
181 Arshdeep Bains 5.00 12.00
182 Zachary Bolduc 8.00 20.00
183 Mason Morelli 4.00 10.00
184 Vasily Ponomarev 4.00 10.00
185 Zack Ostapchuk 4.00 10.00
186 Devin Cooley 4.00 10.00
187 Landon Slaggert 4.00 10.00
188 Emil Lilleberg 4.00 10.00
189 Marshall Rifai 4.00 10.00
190 Jason Polin 4.00 10.00
191 Marat Khusnutdinov 4.00 10.00
192 Brian Halonen 4.00 10.00
193 Maxwell Crozier 4.00 10.00
194 Ivan Fedotov 8.00 20.00
195 Gage Goncalves 5.00 12.00
196 Akil Thomas 4.00 10.00
197 Logan Morrison 4.00 10.00
198 Graeme Clarke 4.00 10.00
199 Frank Nazar 12.00 30.00
200 Cutter Gauthier 10.00 25.00

2024-25 Artifacts Esteemed Endorsements
EEDS Darryl Sittler 60.00 150.00
EEDT Devon Toews 20.00 50.00
EEJC John Carlson 40.00 100.00
EETW Tiger Williams 20.00 50.00

2024-25 Artifacts Fresco Signatures
FSAB Aleksander Barkov 12.00 30.00
FSBN Brock Nelson 8.00 20.00
FSCM Connor McDavid SP 40.00 100.00
FSCS Cole Sillinger 6.00 15.00
FSJC John Carlson 8.00 20.00
FSJQ Jack Quinn 6.00 15.00
FSKH Kevin Hayes 6.00 15.00
FSKM Kirill Marchenko 10.00 25.00
FSSG Samuel Girard 5.00 12.00
FSTM Trevor Moore 5.00 12.00
FSTN Thomas Novak 5.00 12.00
FSVD Vince Dunn 6.00 15.00
FSWJ Wyatt Johnston 15.00 40.00

2024-25 Artifacts Inaugural Access Tickets
IAGH Guy Hebert/49 50.00 125.00
IAGV Garry Valk/48 25.00 60.00
IAMM Mike Modano/18 80.00 200.00
IASG Stu Grimson/49 40.00 100.00

2024-25 Artifacts Material Autographs Gold
*EMERALD/45: .5X TO 1.2X BASIC
101 Devon Levi/65 20.00 50.00
103 Juuse Saros/65 20.00 50.00
104 Petr Mrazek/65 12.00 30.00
105 Stuart Skinner/65 20.00 50.00
107 Logan Thompson/65 20.00 50.00
108 Philipp Grubauer/65 15.00 40.00
109 Jordan Binnington/65 25.00 60.00
110 Filip Gustavsson/65 15.00 40.00
111 Jacob Markstrom/65 15.00 40.00
114 Igor Shesterkin/65 30.00 80.00
116 Ilya Sorokin/65 25.00 60.00
117 Jake Oettinger/45 25.00 60.00
118 Jeremy Swayman/45 25.00 60.00
119 Andrei Vasilevskiy/25 25.00 60.00
120 Marc-Andre Fleury/25 30.00 80.00
121 Logan Cooley/65 30.00 80.00
122 Leo Carlsson/65 25.00 60.00
123 Tage Thompson/45 20.00 50.00
124 Brad Marchand/45 30.00 80.00
125 Wyatt Johnston/65 30.00 80.00
126 Matthew Tkachuk/45 30.00 80.00
127 Brady Tkachuk/45 25.00 60.00
128 Elias Pettersson/45 25.00 60.00
129 Mason McTavish/45 15.00 40.00
130 Luke Evangelista/65 12.00 30.00
132 William Eklund/65 20.00 50.00
133 Seth Jarvis/65 20.00 50.00
134 Jordan Kyrou/45 15.00 40.00
135 Marco Rossi/65 20.00 50.00
137 Tim Stutzle/45 20.00 50.00
139 Shane Wright/65 20.00 50.00
140 Alexis Lafreniere/45 25.00 60.00
141 Quinn Hughes/45 40.00 100.00
142 Dylan Cozens/45 15.00 40.00
143 Aleksander Barkov/45 25.00 60.00
144 Timo Meier/45 15.00 40.00
145 Travis Konecny/45 15.00 40.00
147 Kirill Kaprizov/45 50.00 125.00
148 Cale Makar/45 40.00 100.00
150 Sidney Crosby/25 125.00 300.00
153 Auston Matthews/25 100.00 250.00
154 Leon Draisaitl/25 60.00 150.00
155 Alex Ovechkin/25 125.00 300.00
156 Tony Twist/65 10.00 25.00
157 Bill Ranford/65 12.00 30.00
158 Rick Nash/65 15.00 40.00
159 Rod Brind'Amour/65 15.00 40.00
160 Keith Primeau/65 12.00 30.00
161 Derek Sanderson/65 15.00 40.00
162 Mike Gartner/45 20.00 50.00
163 Paul Coffey/45 15.00 40.00
164 Ray Bourque/45 25.00 60.00
165 Teemu Selanne/45 30.00 80.00
166 Ron Francis/45 20.00 50.00
167 Trevor Linden/45 15.00 40.00
168 Jarome Iginla/45 20.00 50.00
169 Martin Brodeur/25 40.00 100.00
171 Brennan Othmann/99 25.00 60.00
172 Jesper Wallstedt/99 30.00 80.00
173 Brendan Brisson/99 15.00 40.00
174 Josh Doan/99 25.00 60.00
176 Joshua Roy/99 20.00 50.00
177 Lukas Cormier/199 12.00 30.00
178 Zach Dean/99 12.00 30.00
179 Shakir Mukhamadullin/199 15.00 40.00
180 Olen Zellweger/99 30.00 80.00
181 Arshdeep Bains/199 15.00 40.00
182 Zachary Bolduc/199 25.00 60.00
183 Mason Morelli/199 12.00 30.00
184 Vasily Ponomarev/199 12.00 30.00
185 Zack Ostapchuk/199 12.00 30.00
186 Devin Cooley/199 12.00 30.00
188 Emil Lilleberg/199 12.00 30.00
189 Marshall Rifai/199 12.00 30.00
190 Jason Polin/199 12.00 30.00
192 Brian Halonen/199 12.00 30.00
193 Maxwell Crozier/199 12.00 30.00
194 Liam Ohgren/199 25.00 60.00
195 Gage Goncalves/199 15.00 40.00
196 Akil Thomas/199 12.00 30.00
197 Logan Morrison/199 12.00 30.00
198 Graeme Clarke/199 12.00 30.00
199 Cutter Gauthier/25 80.00 200.00
200 Frank Nazar/25 40.00 100.00

2024-25 Artifacts Materials Gold
*EMERALD: .8X TO 2X GOLD
*PURPLE: 1.2X TO 3X GOLD
1 Quinton Byfield/299 4.00 10.00
2 Carter Verhaeghe/299 3.00 8.00
3 Ryan Strome/299 3.00 8.00
4 Victor Hedman/299 4.00 10.00
5 Moritz Seider/299 4.00 10.00
6 Brandon Saad/299 2.50 6.00
7 Linus Ullmark/299 2.50 6.00
8 William Nylander/299 6.00 15.00
9 Mitch Marner/299 5.00 12.00
10 Tyler Seguin/299 4.00 10.00
11 Mario Ferraro/299 2.00 5.00
12 Jaden Schwartz/299 2.50 6.00
13 Nathan MacKinnon/299 12.00 30.00
14 Teuvo Teravainen/299 3.00 8.00
15 Dawson Mercer/299 4.00 10.00
16 Mark Scheifele/299 5.00 12.00
17 Troy Terry/299 2.50 6.00
18 Chandler Stephenson/299 2.50 6.00
19 Jason Robertson/299 5.00 12.00
20 Zach Hyman/299 5.00 12.00
21 Jaccob Slavin/299 2.50 6.00
22 Matty Beniers/299 4.00 10.00
23 Kirill Marchenko/299 4.00 10.00
24 Drew Doughty/299 3.00 8.00
25 Josh Morrissey/299 4.00 10.00
26 Robert Thomas/299 3.00 8.00
27 Adrian Kempe/299 3.00 8.00
28 Steven Stamkos/299 6.00 15.00
29 Thatcher Demko/299 4.00 10.00
30 Blake Coleman/299 2.50 6.00
31 Tom Wilson/299 3.00 8.00
32 Brock Nelson/299 3.00 8.00
33 Conor Garland/299 2.50 6.00
34 Devon Toews/299 2.50 6.00
35 Lucas Raymond/299 5.00 12.00
36 Luke Hughes/299 5.00 12.00
37 Owen Power/299 3.00 8.00
38 Anze Kopitar/299 5.00 12.00
39 Adam Fantilli/299 5.00 12.00
40 Yanni Gourde/299 2.50 6.00
41 Mika Zibanejad/299 4.00 10.00
42 Clayton Keller/299 4.00 10.00
43 Mark Stone/299 4.00 10.00
44 Yegor Sharangovich/299 3.00 8.00
45 Artemi Panarin/299 6.00 15.00
46 Evander Kane/299 3.00 8.00
47 Rasmus Dahlin/299 4.00 10.00
48 Alex Pietrangelo/299 2.50 6.00
49 Roman Josi/299 3.00 8.00
50 Cam Fowler/299 3.00 8.00
51 Philipp Kurashev/299 2.50 6.00
52 Ryan O'Reilly/299 3.00 8.00
53 Charlie McAvoy/299 4.00 10.00
54 Mikael Granlund/299 2.50 6.00
55 Kris Letang/299 4.00 10.00
56 Adam Fox/299 4.00 10.00
57 J.T. Miller/299 4.00 10.00
58 Morgan Rielly/299 3.00 8.00
59 Nick Schmaltz/299 2.50 6.00
60 Henri Jokiharju/299 2.00 5.00
61 Claude Giroux/299 3.00 8.00
62 Taylor Raddysh/299 2.50 6.00
63 Colton Parayko/299 2.50 6.00
64 Cole Caufield/299 6.00 15.00
65 Sean Couturier/299 2.50 6.00
66 Gabe Vilardi/299 3.00 8.00
67 Tyson Foerster/299 3.00 8.00
68 Erik Karlsson/299 4.00 10.00
69 Evgeni Malkin/299 6.00 15.00
70 Brendan Gallagher/299 3.00 8.00
71 Matias Maccelli/299 2.50 6.00
72 Alex DeBrincat/299 4.00 10.00
73 Seth Jones/299 3.00 8.00
74 Jake Sanderson/299 4.00 10.00
75 Kaiden Guhle/299 3.00 8.00
76 John Carlson/299 3.00 8.00
77 Nico Hischier/299 5.00 12.00
78 Noah Dobson/299 4.00 10.00
79 Dylan Strome/299 4.00 10.00
80 Mikko Rantanen/299 8.00 20.00
81 David Pastrnak/299 8.00 20.00
82 Kyle Connor/299 5.00 12.00
83 Aaron Ekblad/299 4.00 10.00
84 Filip Forsberg/299 5.00 12.00
85 Sergei Bobrovsky/299 5.00 12.00
86 Josh Norris/299 3.00 8.00
87 Jonathan Huberdeau/299 4.00 10.00
88 Zach Werenski/299 5.00 12.00
89 Jake Neighbours/299 3.00 8.00
90 Sam Reinhart/299 6.00 15.00
91 Joel Farabee/299 3.00 8.00
92 Joe Pavelski/299 4.00 10.00
93 Anders Lee/299 2.50 6.00
94 Ivan Barbashev/299 2.50 6.00
95 Patrick Kane/299 6.00 15.00
96 Patrik Laine/299 4.00 10.00
97 Brent Burns/299 3.00 8.00
98 Ryan Nugent-Hopkins/299 4.00 10.00
99 Nazem Kadri/299 4.00 10.00
100 Owen Tippett/299 2.00 5.00
101 Devon Levi/199 4.00 10.00
102 Samuel Montembeault/199 3.00 8.00
103 Juuse Saros/199 4.00 10.00
104 Petr Mrazek/199 2.50 6.00
105 Stuart Skinner/199 4.00 10.00
106 Tristan Jarry/199 3.00 8.00
107 Logan Thompson/199 4.00 10.00
108 Philipp Grubauer/199 3.00 8.00
109 Jordan Binnington/199 5.00 12.00
110 Filip Gustavsson/199 3.00 8.00
111 Jacob Markstrom/199 3.00 8.00
113 Darcy Kuemper/199 3.00 8.00
114 Igor Shesterkin/199 6.00 15.00
116 Ilya Sorokin/199 5.00 12.00
117 Jake Oettinger/199 5.00 12.00
118 Jeremy Swayman/199 5.00 12.00
119 Andrei Vasilevskiy/199 5.00 12.00

120 Marc-Andre Fleury/199 6.00 15.00
121 Logan Cooley/199 6.00 15.00
122 Leo Carlsson/199 5.00 12.00
123 Tage Thompson/199 4.00 10.00
124 Brad Marchand/199 6.00 15.00
125 Wyatt Johnston/199 6.00 15.00
126 Matthew Tkachuk/199 6.00 15.00
127 Brady Tkachuk/199 5.00 12.00
128 Elias Pettersson/199 5.00 12.00
129 Mason McTavish/199 3.00 8.00
130 Luke Evangelista/199 2.50 6.00
131 Sebastian Aho/199 5.00 12.00
132 William Eklund/199 4.00 10.00
133 Seth Jarvis/199 4.00 10.00
134 Jordan Kyrou/199 3.00 8.00
135 Marco Rossi/199 4.00 10.00
136 Dylan Larkin/199 4.00 10.00
137 Tim Stutzle/199 4.00 10.00
139 Shane Wright/199 4.00 10.00
140 Alexis Lafreniere/199 5.00 12.00
141 Quinn Hughes/199 8.00 20.00
142 Dylan Cozens/199 3.00 8.00
143 Aleksander Barkov/199 5.00 12.00
144 Timo Meier/199 3.00 8.00
145 Travis Konecny/199 3.00 8.00
146 Mathew Barzal/199 4.00 10.00
147 Kirill Kaprizov/199 10.00 25.00
148 Cale Makar/199 8.00 20.00
149 Jack Hughes/199 8.00 20.00
150 Sidney Crosby/199 12.00 30.00
151 Connor Bedard/199 30.00 80.00
152 Connor McDavid/199 15.00 40.00
153 Auston Matthews/199 12.00 30.00
154 Leon Draisaitl/199 10.00 25.00
155 Alex Ovechkin/199 12.00 30.00
158 Rick Nash/99 3.00 8.00
159 Rod Brind'Amour/99 3.00 8.00
160 Keith Primeau/99 2.50 6.00
161 Derek Sanderson/99 3.00 8.00
162 Mike Gartner/99 4.00 10.00
163 Paul Coffey/99 3.00 8.00
164 Ray Bourque/99 5.00 12.00
165 Teemu Selanne/99 6.00 15.00
166 Ron Francis/99 4.00 10.00
168 Jarome Iginla/99 4.00 10.00
169 Martin Brodeur/99 8.00 20.00
170 Wayne Gretzky/99 20.00 50.00
171 Brennan Othmann/499 6.00 15.00
172 Jesper Wallstedt/499 8.00 20.00
173 Brendan Brisson/499 4.00 10.00
174 Josh Doan/499 6.00 15.00
175 Logan Stankoven/499 8.00 20.00
176 Joshua Roy/499 5.00 12.00
177 Lukas Cormier/499 3.00 8.00
178 Zach Dean/499 3.00 8.00
179 Shakir Mukhamadullin/499 4.00 10.00
180 Olen Zellweger/499 8.00 20.00
181 Arshdeep Bains/499 4.00 10.00
182 Zachary Bolduc/499 6.00 15.00
183 Mason Morelli/499 3.00 8.00
184 Vasily Ponomarev/499 3.00 8.00
185 Zack Ostapchuk/499 3.00 8.00
186 Devin Cooley/499 3.00 8.00
188 Emil Lilleberg/499 3.00 8.00
189 Marshall Rifai/499 3.00 8.00
190 Jason Polin/499 3.00 8.00
192 Brian Halonen/499 3.00 8.00
193 Maxwell Crozier/499 3.00 8.00
194 Liam Ohgren/499 6.00 15.00
195 Gage Goncalves/499 4.00 10.00
196 Akil Thomas/499 3.00 8.00
197 Logan Morrison/499 3.00 8.00
198 Graeme Clarke/499 3.00 8.00
199 Cutter Gauthier/499 8.00 20.00
200 Frank Nazar/499 10.00 25.00

2024-25 Artifacts NHL Remnants

*PREMIUM/25: 1.2X TO 3X BASIC
NR1 Trevor Zegras 2.00 5.00
NR2 Clayton Keller 2.00 5.00
NR3 David Pastrnak 5.00 12.00
NR4 Rasmus Dahlin 2.50 6.00
NR5 Nazem Kadri 2.50 6.00
NR6 Andrei Svechnikov 2.50 6.00
NR7 Kevin Korchinski 1.50 4.00
NR8 Nathan MacKinnon 8.00 20.00
NR10 Wyatt Johnston 4.00 10.00
NR11 Alex DeBrincat 2.50 6.00
NR12 Connor McDavid 10.00 25.00
NR13 Aleksander Barkov 3.00 8.00
NR14 Adrian Kempe 2.00 5.00
NR15 Kirill Kaprizov 6.00 15.00
NR16 Cole Caufield 4.00 10.00
NR17 Roman Josi 2.00 5.00
NR18 Jack Hughes 5.00 12.00
NR19 Ilya Sorokin 3.00 8.00
NR20 Artemi Panarin 4.00 10.00
NR21 Claude Giroux 2.00 5.00
NR22 Travis Konecny 2.00 5.00
NR23 Evgeni Malkin 4.00 10.00
NR24 Mikael Granlund 1.50 4.00
NR25 Jaden Schwartz 1.50 4.00
NR26 Robert Thomas 2.00 5.00
NR27 Steven Stamkos 4.00 10.00
NR28 William Nylander 4.00 10.00
NR29 Thatcher Demko 2.50 6.00
NR30 Alex Pietrangelo 1.50 4.00
NR31 Darcy Kuemper 2.00 5.00
NR32 Mark Scheifele 3.00 8.00

2024-25 Artifacts Orchestrators Signatures

OBB Brock Boeser 40.00 100.00
OCB Connor Bedard 800.00 2000.00
OGU Jake Guentzel 40.00 100.00
OMM Mitch Marner 50.00 125.00
OMN Martin Necas 50.00 120.00
ORH Roope Hintz 40.00 100.00
ORN Ryan Nugent-Hopkins 40.00 100.00
OTT Tage Thompson 40.00 100.00

2024-25 Artifacts Signature Apparel

SABM Brad Marchand/36 60.00 150.00
SACG Cutter Gauthier/36 80.00 200.00
SALS Logan Stankoven/36 100.00 250.00
SATS Tim Stutzle/36 50.00 125.00

2024-25 Artifacts Signs of Success

SOSAB Aleksander Barkov/49 15.00 40.00
SOSCZ Connor Zary/49 15.00 40.00
SOSIS Ilya Sorokin/49 15.00 40.00
SOSLC Leo Carlsson/49 30.00 80.00
SOSMK Matthew Knies/49 25.00 60.00
SOSMR Mikko Rantanen/49 25.00 60.00
SOSPM Pavel Mintyukov/49 8.00 20.00

2024-25 Artifacts Silky Mitts

SMAF Adam Fantilli 20.00 50.00
SMAK Anze Kopitar 12.00 30.00
SMBT Bryan Trottier 8.00 20.00
SMDD Drew Doughty 8.00 20.00
SMDH Dale Hawerchuk 10.00 25.00
SMGL Guy Lafleur 10.00 25.00
SMJQ Jonathan Quick 20.00 50.00
SMJT John Tavares 12.00 30.00
SMNK Nikita Kucherov 15.00 40.00
SMSW Shane Wright 10.00 25.00
SMTS Teemu Selanne 15.00 40.00
SMZH Zach Hyman 12.00 30.00

2024-25 Artifacts Silky Mitts Autographs

SMAK Anze Kopitar 30.00 80.00
SMBT Bryan Trottier 50.00 125.00
SMGL Guy Lafleur 25.00 60.00
SMJQ Jonathan Quick 40.00 100.00
SMNK Nikita Kucherov 40.00 100.00
SMSW Shane Wright 25.00 60.00

2024-25 Artifacts Stanley Cup Showdowns Jerseys

*PATCH/25: 1X TO 2.5X BASIC
SD14A Anze Kopitar 5.00 12.00
SD14B Mats Zuccarello 3.00 8.00
SD14C Drew Doughty 3.00 8.00
SD14D Cam Talbot 3.00 8.00
SD15A Patrick Kane 6.00 15.00
SD15B Victor Hedman 4.00 10.00
SD15C Corey Crawford 3.00 8.00
SD15D Tyler Johnson 2.00 5.00
SD16A Sidney Crosby 12.00 30.00
SD16B Joe Thornton 5.00 12.00
SD16C Evgeni Malkin 6.00 15.00
SD16D Joe Pavelski 4.00 10.00
SD18A Marc-Andre Fleury 6.00 15.00
SD18B Alex Ovechkin 12.00 30.00
SD18C William Karlsson 4.00 10.00
SD18D Evgeny Kuznetsov 4.00 10.00
SD19A Ryan O'Reilly 3.00 8.00
SD19B David Pastrnak 8.00 20.00
SD19C Vladimir Tarasenko 4.00 10.00
SD19D Brad Marchand 6.00 15.00
SD22A Nathan MacKinnon 12.00 30.00
SD22B Nikita Kucherov 6.00 15.00
SD22C Cale Makar 8.00 20.00
SD22D Steven Stamkos 6.00 15.00

2024-25 Artifacts Storied Scripts

SSAK Andrei Kuzmenko 40.00 100.00
SSCS Chandler Stephenson 30.00 80.00
SSDS Darryl Sittler 40.00 100.00
SSGF Grant Fuhr 60.00 150.00
SSLR Larry Robinson 40.00 100.00
SSNH Nico Hischier 60.00 150.00
SSSB Scotty Bowman 40.00 100.00
SSTT Tage Thompson 50.00 125.00

2024-25 Artifacts Top Tier Rookie Signatures

TTRBO Brennan Othmann 25.00 60.00
TTRCG Cutter Gauthier SP 30.00 80.00
TTRDC Devin Cooley 12.00 30.00
TTRFN Frank Nazar 40.00 100.00
TTRJD Josh Doan 25.00 60.00
TTRJR Joshua Roy 25.00 60.00
TTRJW Jesper Wallstedt SP 30.00 80.00
TTRLH Lane Hutson 150.00 400.00
TTRLS Logan Stankoven 30.00 80.00
TTRMR Matt Rempe 50.00 125.00
TTROZ Olen Zellweger 30.00 80.00
TTRSM Shakir Mukhamadullin SP 15.00 40.00

2024-25 Artifacts Tundra Teammates Duos

T2ANA M.McTavish/T.Zegras 3.00 8.00
T2BOS D.Pastrnak/B.Marchand 8.00 20.00
T2BRU J.Swayman/C.McAvoy 5.00 12.00
T2COL N.MacKinnon/C.Makar 12.00 30.00
T2DET L.Raymond/D.Larkin 5.00 12.00
T2DEV J.Hughes/L.Hughes 8.00 20.00
T2EDM Z.Hyman/R.Nugent-Hopkins 5.00 12.00
T2FLA S.Reinhart/M.Tkachuk 6.00 15.00
T2LAK A.Kopitar/D.Doughty 5.00 12.00
T2MTL C.Caufield/J.Slafkovsky 6.00 15.00
T2NJD D.Mercer/T.Meier 4.00 10.00
T2NYI M.Barzal/B.Nelson 4.00 10.00
T2NYR A.Panarin/A.Lafreniere 6.00 15.00
T2OIL C.McDavid/L.Draisaitl 15.00 40.00
T2RGR I.Shesterkin/J.Quick 6.00 15.00
T2SEA J.Schwartz/Y.Gourde 2.50 6.00
T2TOR A.Matthews/M.Marner 12.00 30.00
T2PITT E.Karlsson/K.Letang 4.00 10.00

2024-25 Artifacts Tundra Teammates Quads

T4BASJ Aho/Svechnikov/Burns/Jarvis 12.00 30.00
T4ESBT Eichel/Stone Barbashev/Theodore 12.00 30.00
T4FPLS Panarin/Lafreniere Fox/Shesterkin 15.00 40.00
T4KDFB Kopitar/Fiala Byfield/Doughty 12.00 30.00
T4LDSR Seider/Raymond Larkin/DeBrincat 12.00 30.00
T4MBPH Hughes/Pettersson Boeser/Miller 20.00 50.00
T4MRMG MacKinnon/Makar Rantanen/Georgiev 30.00 80.00
T4PHKV Kucherov/Vasilevskiy Hedman/Point 15.00 40.00
T4RBKF Boldy/Kaprizov/Faber/Rossi 25.00 60.00
T4RHOJ Robertson/Johnston Oettinger/Hintz 15.00 40.00
T4RNMM Matthews/Marner Nylander/Rielly 30.00 80.00
T4SHCP Connor/Scheifele Perfetti/Hellebuyck 15.00 40.00

2001-02 Atomic

*1-100 GOLD/200: 4X TO 10X BASIC CARDS
*1-100 RED/290: 3X TO 8X BASIC CARDS
*1-100 BLUE: 5X TO 12X BASIC CARDS
*1-100 VETS/90: 6X TO 15X BASIC CARDS
1 Paul Kariya .30 .75
2 Steve Shields .25 .60
3 Milan Hnilicka .25 .60
4 Patrick Stefan .25 .60
5 Jason Allison .25 .60
6 Byron Dafoe .25 .60
7 Bill Guerin .30 .75
8 Sergei Samsonov .25 .60
9 Joe Thornton .50 1.25
10 Martin Biron .25 .60
11 Tim Connolly .20 .50
12 J-P Dumont .20 .50
13 Jarome Iginla .40 1.00
14 Marc Savard .20 .50
15 Roman Turek .25 .60
16 Ron Francis .40 1.00
17 Arturs Irbe .25 .60
18 Jeff O'Neill .25 .60
19 Tony Amonte .25 .60
20 Steve Sullivan .20 .50
21 Jocelyn Thibault .25 .60
22 Rob Blake .30 .75
23 Chris Drury .25 .60
24 Peter Forsberg .60 1.50
25 Milan Hejduk .25 .60
26 Patrick Roy .75 2.00
27 Joe Sakic .60 1.50
28 Alex Tanguay .25 .60
29 Marc Denis .25 .60
30 Geoff Sanderson .20 .50
31 Ed Belfour .30 .75
32 Mike Modano .50 1.25
33 Joe Nieuwendyk .25 .60
34 Pierre Turgeon .25 .60
35 Sergei Fedorov .50 1.25
36 Dominik Hasek .50 1.25
37 Brett Hull .60 1.50
38 Luc Robitaille .30 .75
39 Brendan Shanahan .30 .75
40 Steve Yzerman .75 2.00
41 Mike Comrie .25 .60
42 Tommy Salo .25 .60
43 Ryan Smyth .25 .60
44 Pavel Bure .30 .75
45 Valeri Bure .20 .50
46 Roberto Luongo .50 1.25
47 Zigmund Palffy .30 .75
48 Felix Potvin .50 1.25
49 Manny Fernandez .20 .50
50 Marian Gaborik .30 .75
51 Saku Koivu .30 .75
52 Yanic Perreault .20 .50
53 Jose Theodore .30 .75
54 Mike Dunham .25 .60
55 David Legwand .25 .60
56 Jason Arnott .25 .60
57 Martin Brodeur .75 2.00
58 Patrik Elias .30 .75
59 Mariusz Czerkawski .20 .50
60 Rick DiPietro .25 .60
61 Michael Peca .25 .60
62 Alexei Yashin .25 .60
63 Theo Fleury .40 1.00
64 Brian Leetch .25 .60
65 Eric Lindros .50 1.25
66 Mark Messier .60 1.50
67 Daniel Alfredsson .30 .75
68 Martin Havlat .25 .60
69 Marian Hossa .25 .60
70 Patrick Lalime .25 .60
71 Roman Cechmanek .25 .60
72 John LeClair .30 .75
73 Mark Recchi .40 1.00
74 Jeremy Roenick .50 1.25
75 Sean Burke .20 .50
76 Daymond Langkow .25 .60
77 Johan Hedberg .25 .60
78 Alexei Kovalev .25 .60
79 Mario Lemieux 1.25 3.00
80 Martin Straka .20 .50
81 Brent Johnson .25 .60
82 Chris Pronger .30 .75
83 Keith Tkachuk .30 .75
84 Doug Weight .30 .75
85 Evgeni Nabokov .25 .60
86 Owen Nolan .30 .75
87 Teemu Selanne .60 1.50
88 Nikolai Khabibulin .30 .75
89 Vincent Lecavalier .30 .75
90 Brad Richards .30 .75
91 Curtis Joseph .40 1.00
92 Alexander Mogilny .25 .60
93 Mats Sundin .30 .75
94 Markus Naslund .30 .75
95 Daniel Sedin .30 .75
96 Henrik Sedin .40 1.00
97 Peter Bondra .30 .75
98 Jaromir Jagr 1.00 2.50
99 Olaf Kolzig .30 .75
100 Adam Oates .30 .75
101 Ilja Bryzgalov RC 8.00 20.00
102 Timo Parssinen RC 4.00 10.00
103 Dany Heatley 4.00 10.00
104 Ilya Kovalchuk RC 15.00 40.00
105 Kamil Piros RC 3.00 8.00
106 Erik Cole RC 6.00 15.00
107 Vaclav Nedorost RC 3.00 8.00
108 Pavel Datsyuk RC 25.00 60.00
109 Niklas Hagman RC 4.00 10.00
110 Kristian Huselius RC 5.00 12.00
111 Jaroslav Bednar RC 3.00 8.00
112 Pascal Dupuis RC 5.00 12.00
113 Martin Erat RC 4.00 10.00
114 Scott Clemmensen RC 3.00 8.00
115 Radek Martinek RC 3.00 8.00
116 Dan Blackburn RC 3.00 8.00
117 Ivan Ciernik RC 3.00 8.00
118 Chris Neil RC 4.00 10.00
119 Pavel Brendl 3.00 8.00
120 Jiri Dopita RC 3.00 8.00
121 Krystofer Kolanos RC 3.00 8.00
122 Mark Rycroft RC 4.00 10.00
123 Jeff Jillson RC 3.00 8.00
124 Nikita Alexeev RC 3.00 8.00
125 Brian Sutherby RC 3.00 8.00
NNO Johan Hedberg Promo .50 1.25
NNO Mats Sundin Promo .50 1.25
NNO Keith Tkachuk Promo .50 1.25

2001-02 Atomic Red

66 Mark Messier 4.00 10.00

2001-02 Atomic Blast

1 Paul Kariya 5.00 12.00
2 Peter Forsberg 10.00 25.00
3 Joe Sakic 10.00 25.00
4 Steve Yzerman 12.00 30.00
5 Mike Comrie 4.00 10.00
6 Pavel Bure 5.00 12.00
7 Alexei Yashin 4.00 10.00
8 Eric Lindros 8.00 20.00
9 Mario Lemieux 20.00 50.00
10 Jaromir Jagr 15.00 40.00

2001-02 Atomic Core Players

1 Paul Kariya 1.50 4.00
2 Joe Thornton 2.50 6.00
3 Patrick Roy 4.00 10.00
4 Mike Modano 2.50 6.00
5 Steve Yzerman 4.00 10.00
6 Pavel Bure 1.50 4.00
7 Zigmund Palffy 1.50 4.00
8 Marian Gaborik 1.50 4.00
9 Saku Koivu 1.50 4.00
10 Martin Brodeur 4.00 10.00
11 Alexei Yashin 1.25 3.00
12 Mark Messier 3.00 8.00
13 Marian Hossa 1.50 4.00
14 John LeClair 1.50 4.00
15 Mario Lemieux 6.00 15.00
16 Chris Pronger 1.50 4.00
17 Teemu Selanne 3.00 8.00
18 Vincent Lecavalier 1.50 4.00
19 Curtis Joseph 2.00 5.00
20 Jaromir Jagr 5.00 12.00

2001-02 Atomic Jerseys

1 Jean-Sebastien Giguere 3.00 8.00
2 Steve Rucchin 2.00 5.00
3 Byron Dafoe 2.50 6.00
4 Erik Rasmussen 2.00 5.00
5 Phil Housley 2.50 6.00
6 Marc Savard 2.00 5.00
7 Jeff Shantz 2.00 5.00
8 Tony Amonte 2.50 6.00
9 Eric Daze 2.50 6.00
10 Jocelyn Thibault 2.50 6.00
11 Peter Forsberg 6.00 15.00
12 Dave Reid 2.50 6.00
13 Patrick Roy 8.00 20.00
14 Joe Sakic 6.00 15.00
15 Lyle Odelein 2.00 5.00
16 Ed Belfour 3.00 8.00
17 Benoit Hogue 2.00 5.00
18 Jyrki Lumme 2.00 5.00
19 Mike Modano 5.00 12.00
20 Sergei Zubov 2.50 6.00
21 Mathieu Dandenault 2.00 5.00
22 Dominik Hasek 5.00 12.00
23 Darren McCarty 2.00 5.00
24 Chris Osgood 3.00 8.00
25 Brendan Shanahan 3.00 8.00
26 Steve Yzerman 8.00 20.00
27 Valeri Bure 2.00 5.00
28 Wade Flaherty 2.00 5.00
29 Felix Potvin 5.00 12.00
30 Sergei Zholtok 2.00 5.00
31 Benoit Brunet 2.00 5.00
32 Jeff Hackett 2.50 6.00
33 Saku Koivu 3.00 8.00
34 Mike Dunham 2.50 6.00
35 Tom Fitzgerald 2.00 5.00
36 Scott Walker 2.00 5.00
37 Scott Niedermayer 3.00 8.00
38 Mariusz Czerkawski 2.00 5.00
39 Chris Terreri 2.50 6.00
40 Guy Hebert 3.00 8.00
41 Mike York 2.00 5.00
42 Mika Alatalo 2.00 5.00
43 Rene Corbet 2.00 5.00
44 Jan Hrdina 2.00 5.00
45 Mario Lemieux 12.00 30.00
47 Teemu Selanne 6.00 15.00
48 Mats Sundin 3.00 8.00
49 Dimitri Yushkevich 2.00 5.00
50 Jaromir Jagr 10.00 25.00

2001-02 Atomic Patches

1 Jean-Sebastien Giguere/403 5.00 12.00
2 Steve Rucchin/303 3.00 8.00
3 Byron Dafoe/128 4.00 10.00
4 Erik Rasmussen/153 3.00 8.00
5 Phil Housley/106 4.00 10.00
6 Marc Savard/403 3.00 8.00
7 Jeff Shantz/203 3.00 8.00
8 Tony Amonte/403 4.00 10.00
9 Eric Daze/328 4.00 10.00
10 Jocelyn Thibault/328 4.00 10.00
12 Dave Reid/328 4.00 10.00
13 Patrick Roy/53 40.00 100.00
14 Joe Sakic/303 10.00 25.00
15 Lyle Odelein/153 3.00 8.00
16 Ed Belfour/153 4.00 10.00
17 Benoit Hogue/123 3.00 8.00
18 Jyrki Lumme/303 3.00 8.00
19 Mike Modano/128 8.00 20.00
20 Sergei Zubov/268 4.00 10.00
21 Mathieu Dandenault/178 3.00 8.00
22 Dominik Hasek/283 8.00 20.00
23 Darren McCarty/16 25.00 60.00
24 Chris Osgood/203 5.00 12.00
25 Brendan Shanahan/203 6.00 15.00
26 Steve Yzerman/53 25.00 60.00
27 Valeri Bure/428 3.00 8.00
28 Wade Flaherty/302 3.00 8.00
29 Felix Potvin/103 20.00 50.00
30 Sergei Zholtok/138 3.00 8.00
33 Saku Koivu/53 5.00 12.00
34 Mike Dunham/193 4.00 10.00
35 Tom Fitzgerald/378 3.00 8.00
36 Scott Walker/428 3.00 8.00
37 Scott Niedermayer/478 5.00 12.00
38 Mariusz Czerkawski/503 3.00 8.00
39 Chris Terreri/153 4.00 10.00
40 Guy Hebert/115 5.00 12.00
41 Mike York/403 3.00 8.00
42 Mika Alatalo/283 3.00 8.00
43 Rene Corbet/53 3.00 8.00
44 Jan Hrdina/353 3.00 8.00
46 Kevin Stevens/353 4.00 10.00
47 Teemu Selanne/153 15.00 40.00
48 Mats Sundin/203 5.00 12.00
49 Dimitri Yushkevich/128 3.00 8.00
50 Jaromir Jagr/78 15.00 40.00

2001-02 Atomic Power Play

1 Paul Kariya .30 .75
2 Patrik Stefan .25 .60
3 Sergei Samsonov .25 .60
4 Joe Thornton .50 1.25
5 Jarome Iginla .40 1.00
6 Jeff O'Neill .25 .60
7 Tony Amonte .25 .60
8 Peter Forsberg .60 1.50
9 Milan Hejduk .25 .60
10 Joe Sakic .60 1.50
11 Mike Modano .50 1.25
12 Sergei Fedorov .50 1.25
13 Brendan Shanahan .30 .75
14 Steve Yzerman .75 2.00
15 Mike Comrie .25 .60
16 Pavel Bure .30 .75
17 Zigmund Palffy .30 .75
18 Marian Gaborik .30 .75
19 Saku Koivu .30 .75
20 Jason Arnott .25 .60
21 Alexei Yashin .25 .60
22 Theo Fleury .40 1.00
23 Eric Lindros .50 1.25
24 Mark Messier .60 1.50
25 Marian Hossa .30 .75
26 John LeClair .30 .75
27 Mario Lemieux 1.25 3.00
28 Chris Pronger .30 .75
29 Keith Tkachuk .30 .75
30 Teemu Selanne .60 1.50
31 Vincent Lecavalier .30 .75
32 Mats Sundin .30 .75
33 Daniel Sedin .40 1.00
34 Henrik Sedin .40 1.00
35 Peter Bondra .30 .75
36 Jaromir Jagr 1.00 2.50

2001-02 Atomic Rookie Reaction

1 Dany Heatley 1.25 3.00
2 Ilya Kovalchuk 5.00 12.00
3 Vaclav Nedorost 1.00 2.50
4 Rostislav Klesla 1.00 2.50
5 Rick DiPietro 1.25 3.00
6 Pavel Brendl 1.00 2.50
7 Jiri Dopita 1.00 2.50
8 Kris Beech 1.00 2.50
9 Johan Hedberg 1.25 3.00
10 Nikita Alexeev 1.00 2.50

2001-02 Atomic Statosphere

1 Patrick Roy 2.00 5.00
2 Ed Belfour .75 2.00
3 Dominik Hasek 1.25 3.00
4 Martin Brodeur 2.00 5.00
5 Rick DiPietro .60 1.50
6 Mike Richter .75 2.00
7 Roman Cechmanek .60 1.50
8 Johan Hedberg .60 1.50
9 Evgeni Nabokov .60 1.50
10 Curtis Joseph 1.00 2.50
11 Peter Forsberg 1.50 4.00
12 Joe Sakic 1.50 4.00
13 Brett Hull 1.50 4.00
14 Pavel Bure .75 2.00
15 Zigmund Palffy .75 2.00
16 Alexei Yashin .60 1.50
17 Alexei Kovalev .60 1.50
18 Mario Lemieux 3.00 8.00
19 Martin Straka .60 1.50
20 Jaromir Jagr 2.50 6.00

2001-02 Atomic Team Nucleus

1 Boston Bruins 1.25 3.00
2 Calgary Flames 1.00 2.50
3 Carolina Hurricanes 1.00 2.50
4 Colorado Avalanche 2.00 5.00
5 Dallas Stars 1.25 3.00
6 Detroit Red Wings 2.00 5.00
7 Edmonton Oilers .60 1.50
8 New Jersey Devils 2.00 5.00
9 New York Islanders .60 1.50
10 New York Rangers 1.50 4.00
11 Pittsburgh Penguins 3.00 8.00
12 San Jose Sharks 1.50 4.00
13 Toronto Maple Leafs 1.00 2.50
14 Vancouver Canucks 1.00 2.50
15 Washington Capitals 2.50 6.00

2001-02 Atomic Toronto Fall Expo

101 Ilja Bryzgalov 4.00 10.00
102 Timo Parssinen 2.00 5.00
103 Dany Heatley 2.00 5.00
104 Ilya Kovalchuk 8.00 20.00
105 Kamil Piros 1.50 4.00
106 Erik Cole 3.00 8.00
107 Vaclav Nedorost 1.50 4.00
108 Pavel Datsyuk 25.00 60.00
109 Niklas Hagman 2.00 5.00
110 Kristian Huselius 2.50 6.00
111 Jaroslav Bednar 1.50 4.00
112 Pascal Dupuis 2.50 6.00
113 Martin Erat 2.00 5.00
114 Scott Clemmensen 1.50 4.00
115 Radek Martinek 1.50 4.00
116 Dan Blackburn 2.00 5.00
117 Ivan Ciernik 1.50 4.00
118 Chris Neil 2.00 5.00
119 Pavel Brendl 1.50 4.00
120 Jiri Dopita 1.50 4.00
121 Krystofer Kolanos 1.50 4.00
122 Mark Rycroft 1.50 4.00
123 Jeff Jillson 1.50 4.00
124 Nikita Alexeev 1.50 4.00
125 Brian Sutherby 1.50 4.00

2002-03 Atomic

1 Jean-Sebastien Giguere .25 .60
2 Paul Kariya .25 .60
3 Adam Oates .25 .60
4 Dany Heatley .20 .50
5 Ilya Kovalchuk .30 .75
6 Glen Murray .20 .50
7 Sergei Samsonov .20 .50
8 Joe Thornton .40 1.00
9 Martin Biron .20 .50
10 J-P Dumont .15 .40
11 Miroslav Satan .25 .60
12 Craig Conroy .15 .40
13 Jarome Iginla .30 .75
14 Roman Turek .25 .60
15 Erik Cole .15 .40
16 Ron Francis .30 .75
17 Arturs Irbe .20 .50
18 Jeff O'Neill .15 .40
19 Mark Bell .15 .40
20 Eric Daze .15 .40
21 Jocelyn Thibault .20 .50
22 Rob Blake .25 .60
23 Chris Drury .25 .60
24 Peter Forsberg .50 1.25
25 Steven Reinprecht .15 .40
26 Patrick Roy .60 1.50
27 Joe Sakic .50 1.25
28 Marc Denis .20 .50
29 Espen Knutsen .15 .40
30 Ray Whitney .20 .50
31 Jason Arnott .20 .50
32 Bill Guerin .25 .60
33 Mike Modano .40 1.00
34 Marty Turco .25 .60
35 Pavel Datsyuk .40 1.00
36 Sergei Fedorov .40 1.00
37 Brett Hull .50 1.25
38 Curtis Joseph .30 .75
39 Nicklas Lidstrom .25 .60
40 Brendan Shanahan .25 .60
41 Steve Yzerman .60 1.50
42 Mike Comrie .20 .50
43 Tommy Salo .20 .50
44 Ryan Smyth .15 .40
45 Kristian Huselius .15 .40
46 Roberto Luongo .40 1.00
47 Stephen Weiss .20 .50
48 Jason Allison .20 .50
49 Zigmund Palffy .20 .50
50 Felix Potvin .40 1.00
51 Andrew Brunette .15 .40
52 Manny Fernandez .15 .40
53 Marian Gaborik .25 .60
54 Doug Gilmour .30 .75
55 Saku Koivu .25 .60
56 Yanic Perreault .15 .40
57 Jose Theodore .25 .60
58 Denis Arkhipov .15 .40
59 Mike Dunham .15 .40
60 Martin Brodeur .60 1.50
61 Patrik Elias .25 .60
62 Joe Nieuwendyk .20 .50
63 Chris Osgood .25 .60
64 Michael Peca .20 .50
65 Alexei Yashin .20 .50
66 Dan Blackburn .20 .50
67 Pavel Bure .25 .60
68 Eric Lindros .40 1.00
69 Mike Richter .25 .60
70 Daniel Alfredsson .25 .60
71 Marian Hossa .25 .60
72 Patrick Lalime .20 .50
73 Roman Cechmanek .20 .50
74 Simon Gagne .25 .60
75 Jeremy Roenick .40 1.00
76 Tony Amonte .25 .60
77 Daniel Briere .20 .50
78 Sean Burke .15 .40
79 Johan Hedberg .20 .50
80 Mario Lemieux 1.00 2.50
81 Alexei Morozov .15 .40
82 Brent Johnson .20 .50
83 Chris Pronger .25 .60
84 Keith Tkachuk .25 .60
85 Patrick Marleau .25 .60
86 Evgeni Nabokov .25 .60
87 Owen Nolan .25 .60
88 Teemu Selanne .50 1.25
89 Nikolai Khabibulin .25 .60
90 Vincent Lecavalier .25 .60
91 Ed Belfour .25 .60
92 Alexander Mogilny .20 .50
93 Gary Roberts .15 .40
94 Mats Sundin .25 .60
95 Todd Bertuzzi .25 .60
96 Dan Cloutier .20 .50
97 Markus Naslund .25 .60
98 Peter Bondra .25 .60
99 Jaromir Jagr .75 2.00
100 Olaf Kolzig .25 .60
101 Stanislav Chistov RC .75 2.00
102 Martin Gerber RC 1.25 3.00
103 Alexei Smirnov RC 1.00 2.50
104 Chuck Kobasew RC 1.00 2.50
105 Rick Nash RC 5.00 12.00
106 Dmitri Bykov RC .75 2.00
107 Henrik Zetterberg RC 8.00 20.00
108 Kari Haakana RC .75 2.00
109 Ales Hemsky RC 3.00 8.00
110 Alex Henry RC 1.00 2.50
111 Jay Bouwmeester RC 2.50 6.00
112 Alexander Frolov RC 2.00 5.00
113 P-M Bouchard RC 1.25 3.00
114 Sylvain Blouin RC .75 2.00
115 Ron Hainsey RC .75 2.00
116 Adam Hall RC .75 2.00
117 Scottie Upshall RC 1.00 2.50
118 Mike Danton .75 2.00
119 Ray Schultz RC .75 2.00
120 Anton Volchenkov RC .75 2.00
121 Dennis Seidenberg RC 1.25 3.00
122 Patrick Sharp RC 2.50 6.00
123 Dick Tarnstrom RC .75 2.00
124 Alexander Svitov RC .75 2.00
125 Steve Eminger RC .75 2.00
126 Jordan Leopold RC 1.25 3.00
127 Stephane Veilleux RC .75 2.00
128 Jason Spezza RC 5.00 12.00
129 Radovan Somik RC .75 2.00
130 Jeff Taffe RC .75 2.00
131 Tom Koivisto RC .75 2.00

2002-03 Atomic Blue

*1-100 VETS/175: 2X TO 5X BASIC CARDS
*101-125 ROOKIES/175: .5X TO 1.2X

2002-03 Atomic Gold

*1-100 VETS/99: 2.5X TO 6X BASIC CARDS
*101-125 ROOKIES/99: .6X TO 1.5X

2002-03 Atomic Red

*1-100 VETS/125: 2.5X TO 6X BASIC CARDS
*101-125 ROOKIES/25: .6X TO 1.5X

2002-03 Atomic Cold Fusion

COMPLETE SET (24) 30.00 60.00
1 Paul Kariya .75 2.00
2 Dany Heatley 1.00 2.50
3 Ilya Kovalchuk 1.00 2.50
4 Joe Thornton 1.25 3.00
5 Jarome Iginla 1.00 2.50
6 Jeff O'Neill .60 1.50
7 Eric Daze .60 1.50
8 Peter Forsberg 2.00 5.00
9 Joe Sakic 1.50 4.00
10 Pavel Datsyuk .75 2.00
11 Brendan Shanahan 1.25 3.00
12 Steve Yzerman 3.00 8.00
13 Mike Comrie .60 1.50
14 Kristian Huselius .60 1.50
15 Saku Koivu .75 2.00
16 Pavel Bure 1.00 2.50
17 Eric Lindros .75 2.00
18 Daniel Alfredsson .60 1.50
19 Simon Gagne .75 2.00
20 Mario Lemieux 5.00 12.00
21 Teemu Selanne .75 2.00
22 Mats Sundin .75 2.00
23 Markus Naslund .75 2.00
24 Jaromir Jagr 1.25 3.00

2002-03 Atomic Denied

COMPLETE SET (20) 15.00 40.00
1 Jean-Sebastien Giguere .75 2.00
2 Roman Turek .75 2.00
3 Arturs Irbe .75 2.00
4 Jocelyn Thibault .75 2.00
5 Patrick Roy 5.00 12.00
6 Marty Turco .75 2.00
7 Curtis Joseph 1.00 2.50
8 Roberto Luongo 1.50 4.00
9 Felix Potvin 1.00 2.50
10 Jose Theodore 1.00 2.50
11 Martin Brodeur 2.50 6.00
12 Chris Osgood .75 2.00
13 Mike Richter .75 2.00
14 Patrick Lalime .75 2.00
15 Roman Cechmanek .75 2.00
16 Sean Burke .75 2.00
17 Brent Johnson .75 2.00
18 Evgeni Nabokov .75 2.00
19 Nikolai Khabibulin 1.00 2.50
20 Ed Belfour 1.00 2.50

2002-03 Atomic Hobby Parallel

*1-100 VETS/775: 1.2X TO 3X BASIC CARDS
*101-125 ROOKIES/775: .4X TO 1X

2002-03 Atomic Jerseys

*GOLD/25: .6X TO 1.5X BASIC JSY
*PATCH/164-339: .75X TO 2X BASIC JSY
*PATCH/61-70: 1X TO 2.5X BASIC JSY
1 Adam Oates 3.00 8.00
2 Roman Turek 3.00 8.00
3 Jason Arnott 2.50 6.00
4 Bill Guerin 3.00 8.00
5 Scott Young 2.00 5.00
6 Dominik Hasek 5.00 12.00
7 Brett Hull 6.00 15.00
8 Curtis Joseph 4.00 10.00
9 Luc Robitaille 3.00 8.00
10 Ryan Smyth 2.50 6.00
11 Jose Theodore 3.00 8.00
12 Jeff Friesen 2.00 5.00
13 Oleg Tverdovsky 2.00 5.00
14 Alexei Yashin 2.50 6.00
15 Pavel Bure 3.00 8.00
16 Mark Messier 6.00 15.00
17 John LeClair 3.00 8.00
18 Daymond Langkow 2.50 6.00
19 Mario Lemieux 12.00 30.00
20 Pavol Demitra 4.00 10.00
21 Ray Ferraro 2.50 6.00
22 Tom Barrasso 2.50 6.00
23 Darcy Tucker 2.00 5.00
24 Jaromir Jagr 10.00 25.00
25 Robert Lang 2.00 5.00

2002-03 Atomic National Pride

C1 Paul Kariya 1.00 2.50
C2 Jarome Iginla 1.25 3.00
C3 Rob Blake 1.00 2.50
C4 Joe Sakic 2.00 5.00
C5 Curtis Joseph 1.25 3.00
C6 Brendan Shanahan 1.00 2.50
C7 Steve Yzerman 2.50 6.00
C8 Martin Brodeur 2.50 6.00
C9 Mario Lemieux 4.00 10.00
C10 Chris Pronger 1.00 2.50
U1 Bill Guerin 1.00 2.50
U2 Mike Modano 1.50 4.00
U3 Chris Chelios 1.00 2.50
U4 Brett Hull 2.00 5.00
U5 Brian Leetch .75 2.00
U6 Mike Richter .75 2.00
U7 Jeremy Roenick 1.50 4.00
U8 Tony Amonte .75 2.00
U9 Keith Tkachuk 1.00 2.50
U10 Tom Barrasso .75 2.00

2002-03 Atomic Power Converters

1 Dany Heatley .75 2.00
2 Ilya Kovalchuk 1.25 3.00
3 Miroslav Satan 1.00 2.50
4 Jarome Iginla 1.25 3.00

5 Ron Francis 1.25 3.00
6 Sami Kapanen .60 1.50
7 Nicklas Lidstrom 1.00 2.50
8 Luc Robitaille 1.00 2.50
9 Jason Allison .75 2.00
10 Zigmund Palffy 1.00 2.50
11 Andrew Brunette .60 1.50
12 Alexei Yashin .75 2.00
13 Pavel Bure 1.00 2.50
14 Eric Lindros 1.50 4.00
15 Daniel Briere .75 2.00
16 Pavol Demitra 1.25 3.00
17 Keith Tkachuk 1.00 2.50
18 Todd Bertuzzi 1.00 2.50
19 Markus Naslund 1.00 2.50
20 Peter Bondra 1.00 2.50

2002-03 Atomic Super Colliders

1 Ilya Kovalchuk 1.25 3.00
2 Joe Thornton 1.50 4.00
3 Jarome Iginla 1.25 3.00
4 Erik Cole .60 1.50
5 Jason Arnott .75 2.00
6 Brendan Shanahan 1.00 2.50
7 Ryan Smyth .75 2.00
8 Jason Allison .75 2.00
9 Michael Peca .75 2.00
10 Eric Lindros 1.50 4.00
11 Jeremy Roenick 1.50 4.00
12 Chris Pronger 1.00 2.50
13 Keith Tkachuk 1.00 2.50
14 Owen Nolan 1.00 2.50
15 Gary Roberts .60 1.50
16 Todd Bertuzzi 1.00 2.50

1998-99 Aurora

1 Travis Green .15 .40
2 Guy Hebert .20 .50
3 Paul Kariya .25 .60
4 Steve Rucchin .15 .40
5 Tomas Sandstrom .15 .40
6 Teemu Selanne .50 1.25
7 Jason Allison .20 .50
8 Ray Bourque .40 1.00
9 Anson Carter .20 .50
10 Byron Dafoe .20 .50
11 Ted Donato .15 .40
12 Dave Ellett .20 .50
13 Dimitri Khristich .15 .40
14 Sergei Samsonov .20 .50
15 Matthew Barnaby .15 .40
16 Michal Grosek .15 .40
17 Dominik Hasek .40 1.00
18 Brian Holzinger .15 .40
19 Michael Peca .15 .40
20 Miroslav Satan .20 .50
21 Dixon Ward .20 .50
22 Alexei Zhitnik .15 .40
23 Andrew Cassels .15 .40
24 Theo Fleury .30 .75
25 Jarome Iginla .30 .75
26 Marty McInnis .15 .40
27 Derek Morris .15 .40
28 Michael Nylander .20 .50
29 Cory Stillman .15 .40
30 Kevin Dineen .15 .40
31 Nelson Emerson .15 .40
32 Martin Gelinas .15 .40
33 Sami Kapanen .15 .40
34 Trevor Kidd .15 .40
35 Robert Kron .15 .40
36 Jeff O'Neill .15 .40
37 Keith Primeau .20 .50
38 Tony Amonte .20 .50
39 Chris Chelios .25 .60
40 Eric Daze .20 .50
41 Jeff Hackett .15 .40
42 Jean-Yves Leroux .20 .50
43 Jeff Shantz .15 .40
44 Alexei Zhamnov .15 .40
45 Adam Deadmarsh .15 .40
46 Peter Forsberg 1.00 2.50
47 Valeri Kamensky .15 .40
48 Claude Lemieux .20 .50
49 Eric Messier .15 .40
50 Sandis Ozolinsh .15 .40
51 Patrick Roy 1.00 2.50
52 Joe Sakic .50 1.25
53 Ed Belfour .25 .60
54 Derian Hatcher .15 .40
55 Brett Hull .50 1.25
56 Jamie Langenbrunner .15 .40
57 Jere Lehtinen .20 .50
58 Mike Modano .40 1.00
59 Joe Nieuwendyk .20 .50
60 Darryl Sydor .15 .40
61 Sergei Zubov .20 .50
62 Sergei Fedorov .40 1.00
63 Vyacheslav Kozlov .20 .50
64 Igor Larionov .25 .60
65 Nicklas Lidstrom .30 .75
66 Darren McCarty .15 .40
67 Chris Osgood .25 .60
68 Brendan Shanahan .25 .60
69 Steve Yzerman .60 1.50
70 Kelly Buchberger .15 .40
71 Mike Grier .15 .40
72 Bill Guerin .25 .60
73 Roman Hamrlik .15 .40
74 Boris Mironov .15 .40
75 Janne Niinimaa .15 .40
76 Ryan Smyth .20 .50
77 Doug Weight .25 .60
78 Dino Ciccarelli .25 .60
79 Dave Gagner .15 .40
80 Ed Jovanovski .20 .50
81 Viktor Kozlov .20 .50
82 Paul Laus .20 .50
83 Scott Mellanby .15 .40
84 Ray Whitney .15 .40
85 Rob Blake .25 .60
86 Stephane Fiset .20 .50
87 Yanic Perreault .15 .40
88 Luc Robitaille .25 .60
89 Jamie Storr .20 .50
90 Jozef Stumpel .15 .40
91 Vladimir Tsyplakov .15 .40
92 Shayne Corson .20 .50
93 Vincent Damphousse .20 .50
94 Saku Koivu .25 .60
95 Mark Recchi .30 .75
96 Martin Rucinsky .15 .40
97 Brian Savage .15 .40
98 Jocelyn Thibault .20 .50
99 Andrew Brunette .20 .50
100 Mike Dunham .20 .50
101 Tom Fitzgerald .20 .50
102 Sergei Krivokrasov .15 .40
103 Denny Lambert .20 .50
104 Mikhail Shtalenkov .15 .40
105 Darren Turcotte .20 .50
106 Dave Andreychuk .25 .60
107 Jason Arnott .20 .50
108 Martin Brodeur .60 1.50
109 Patrik Elias .25 .60
110 Bobby Holik .15 .40
111 Randy McKay .20 .50
112 Scott Niedermayer .25 .60
113 Scott Stevens .25 .60
114 Bryan Berard .20 .50
115 Jason Dawe .15 .40
116 Trevor Linden .25 .60
117 Zigmund Palffy .25 .60
118 Robert Reichel .15 .40
119 Tommy Salo .20 .50
120 Bryan Smolinski .15 .40
121 Adam Graves .15 .40
122 Wayne Gretzky 1.50 4.00
123 Alexei Kovalev .20 .50
124 Brian Leetch .20 .50
125 Mike Richter .25 .60
126 Ulf Samuelsson .20 .50
127 Kevin Stevens .20 .50
128 Daniel Alfredsson .25 .60
129 Andreas Dackell .15 .40
130 Igor Kravchuk .15 .40
131 Shawn McEachern .15 .40
132 Chris Phillips .15 .40
133 Damian Rhodes .25 .60
134 Alexei Yashin .20 .50
135 Rod Brind'Amour .25 .60
136 Alexandre Daigle .15 .40
137 Eric Desjardins .20 .50
138 Chris Gratton .20 .50
139 Ron Hextall .25 .60
140 John LeClair .25 .60
141 Eric Lindros .40 1.00
142 John Vanbiesbrouck .25 .60
143 Dainius Zubrus .15 .40
144 Brad Isbister .15 .40
145 Nikolai Khabibulin .25 .60
146 Jeremy Roenick .40 1.00
147 Cliff Ronning .15 .40
148 Keith Tkachuk .25 .60
149 Rick Tocchet .20 .50
150 Oleg Tverdovsky .25 .60
151 Stu Barnes .15 .40
152 Tom Barrasso .20 .50
153 Kevin Hatcher .15 .40
154 Jaromir Jagr .75 2.00
155 Darius Kasparaitis .15 .40
156 Alexei Morozov .15 .40
157 Martin Straka .15 .40
158 Jim Campbell .15 .40
159 Geoff Courtnall .20 .50
160 Grant Fuhr .40 1.00
161 Al MacInnis .30 .75
162 Jamie McLennan .20 .50
163 Chris Pronger .25 .60
164 Pierre Turgeon .20 .50
165 Tony Twist .15 .40
166 Jeff Friesen .15 .40
167 Tony Granato .15 .40
168 Patrick Marleau .25 .60
169 Marty McSorley .20 .50
170 Owen Nolan .25 .60
171 Marco Sturm .15 .40
172 Mike Vernon .20 .50
173 Karl Dykhuis .15 .40
174 Mikael Renberg .20 .50
175 Stephane Richer .15 .40
176 Alexander Selivanov .15 .40
177 Paul Ysebaert .15 .40
178 Rob Zamuner .15 .40
179 Sergei Berezin .20 .50
180 Tie Domi .20 .50
181 Mike Johnson .15 .40
182 Curtis Joseph .30 .75
183 Igor Korolev .15 .40
184 Mathieu Schneider .15 .40
185 Mats Sundin .25 .60
186 Todd Bertuzzi .25 .60
187 Donald Brashear .15 .40
188 Pavel Bure .25 .60
189 Mark Messier .50 1.25
190 Alexander Mogilny .20 .50
191 Mattias Ohlund .15 .40
192 Garth Snow .20 .50
193 Brian Bellows .20 .50
194 Peter Bondra .25 .60
195 Sergei Gonchar .15 .40
196 Calle Johansson .15 .40
197 Joe Juneau .15 .40
198 Olaf Kolzig .25 .60
199 Adam Oates .25 .60
200 Richard Zednik .15 .40
S108 Martin Brodeur SAMPLE .60 1.50

1998-99 Aurora Atomic Laser Cuts

1 Paul Kariya .75 2.00
2 Teemu Selanne 1.50 4.00
3 Sergei Samsonov .60 1.50
4 Dominik Hasek 1.25 3.00
5 Peter Forsberg 1.50 4.00
6 Patrick Roy 2.00 5.00
7 Joe Sakic 1.50 4.00
8 Mike Modano 1.25 3.00
9 Sergei Fedorov 1.25 3.00
10 Brendan Shanahan .75 2.00
11 Steve Yzerman 2.00 5.00
12 Martin Brodeur 2.00 5.00
13 Wayne Gretzky 5.00 12.00
14 John LeClair .75 2.00
15 Eric Lindros 1.25 3.00
16 Jaromir Jagr 2.50 6.00
17 Mats Sundin .75 2.00
18 Pavel Bure .75 2.00
19 Mark Messier 1.50 4.00
20 Peter Bondra .75 2.00

1998-99 Aurora Championship Fever

*COPPER/20: 10X TO 25X BASIC INSERTS
*ICE BLUE/100: 5X TO 12X BASIC INSERTS
*RED: .8X TO 2X BASIC INSERTS
*SILVER/250: 2X TO 5X BASIC INSERTS
1 Paul Kariya .40 1.00
2 Teemu Selanne .75 2.00
3 Ray Bourque .60 1.50
4 Byron Dafoe .30 .75
5 Sergei Samsonov .30 .75
6 Dominik Hasek .60 1.50
7 Michael Peca .25 .60
8 Theo Fleury .50 1.25
9 Keith Primeau .30 .75
10 Chris Chelios .40 1.00
11 Peter Forsberg .75 2.00
12 Patrick Roy 1.00 2.50
13 Joe Sakic .75 2.00
14 Ed Belfour .40 1.00
15 Mike Modano .60 1.50
16 Sergei Fedorov .60 1.50
17 Nicklas Lidstrom .50 1.25
18 Chris Osgood .40 1.00
19 Brendan Shanahan .40 1.00
20 Steve Yzerman 1.00 2.50
21 Doug Weight .40 1.00
22 Dino Ciccarelli .40 1.00
23 Rob Blake .40 1.00
24 Saku Koivu .40 1.00
25 Mark Recchi .50 1.25
26 Martin Brodeur 1.00 2.50
27 Patrik Elias .40 1.00
28 Trevor Linden .40 1.00
29 Zigmund Palffy .40 1.00
30 Wayne Gretzky 2.50 6.00
31 Mike Richter .40 1.00
32 Daniel Alfredsson .40 1.00
33 Damian Rhodes .40 1.00
34 Alexei Yashin .30 .75
35 John LeClair .40 1.00
36 Eric Lindros .60 1.50
37 Dainius Zubrus .25 .60
38 Keith Tkachuk .40 1.00
39 Tom Barrasso .30 .75
40 Jaromir Jagr 1.25 3.00
41 Grant Fuhr .60 1.50
42 Pierre Turgeon .30 .75
43 Patrick Marleau .40 1.00
44 Mike Vernon .30 .75
45 Rob Zamuner .25 .60
46 Mats Sundin .40 1.00
47 Pavel Bure .40 1.00
48 Mark Messier .75 2.00
49 Peter Bondra .40 1.00
50 Olaf Kolzig .40 1.00
NNO M.Brodeur Gold AU/97 50.00 125.00

1998-99 Aurora Cubes

1 Paul Kariya 1.50 4.00
2 Teemu Selanne 3.00 8.00
3 Dominik Hasek 2.50 6.00
4 Peter Forsberg 3.00 8.00
5 Patrick Roy 4.00 10.00
6 Joe Sakic 3.00 8.00
7 Mike Modano 2.50 6.00
8 Sergei Fedorov 2.50 6.00
9 Brendan Shanahan 1.50 4.00
10 Steve Yzerman 4.00 10.00
11 Martin Brodeur 4.00 10.00
12 Wayne Gretzky 10.00 25.00
13 John LeClair 1.50 4.00
14 Eric Lindros 2.50 6.00
15 Jaromir Jagr 5.00 12.00
16 Mats Sundin 1.50 4.00
17 Pavel Bure 1.50 4.00
18 Mark Messier 3.00 8.00
19 Peter Bondra 1.50 4.00
20 Olaf Kolzig 1.50 4.00

1998-99 Aurora Front Line Copper

*ICE BLUE/15: .8X TO 2X COPPER/80
1 Dominik Hasek 10.00 25.00
2 Peter Forsberg 12.00 30.00
3 Patrick Roy 15.00 40.00
4 Joe Sakic 12.00 30.00
5 Steve Yzerman 15.00 40.00
6 Daniel Alfredsson 6.00 15.00
7 Eric Lindros 10.00 25.00
8 Jaromir Jagr 20.00 50.00
9 Wayne Gretzky 40.00 100.00
10 Tie Domi 5.00 12.00

1998-99 Aurora Man Advantage

1 Paul Kariya 1.25 3.00
2 Teemu Selanne 2.50 6.00
3 Ray Bourque 2.00 5.00
4 Michael Peca .75 2.00
5 Peter Forsberg 2.50 6.00
6 Joe Sakic 2.50 6.00
7 Mike Modano 2.00 5.00
8 Joe Nieuwendyk 1.00 2.50
9 Brendan Shanahan 1.25 3.00
10 Steve Yzerman 3.00 8.00
11 Shayne Corson 1.00 2.50
12 Zigmund Palffy 1.25 3.00
13 Wayne Gretzky 8.00 20.00
14 John LeClair 1.25 3.00
15 Eric Lindros 2.00 5.00
16 Jaromir Jagr 4.00 10.00
17 Mats Sundin 1.25 3.00
18 Pavel Bure 1.25 3.00
19 Mark Messier 2.50 6.00
20 Peter Bondra 1.25 3.00

1998-99 Aurora NHL Command

1 Teemu Selanne 2.50 6.00
2 Dominik Hasek 2.00 5.00
3 Peter Forsberg 2.50 6.00
4 Patrick Roy 3.00 8.00
5 Mike Modano 2.00 5.00
6 Steve Yzerman 3.00 8.00
7 Martin Brodeur 3.00 8.00
8 Wayne Gretzky 8.00 20.00
9 Eric Lindros 2.00 5.00
10 Jaromir Jagr 4.00 10.00

1999-00 Aurora

*STRIPED: .4X TO 1X BASIC CARDS
1 Guy Hebert .20 .50
2 Paul Kariya .20 .50
3 Marty McInnis .12 .30
4 Steve Rucchin .12 .30
5 Teemu Selanne .40 1.00
6 Andrew Brunette .12 .30
7 Kelly Buchberger .12 .30
8 Damian Rhodes .12 .30
9 Jason Allison .15 .40
10 Ray Bourque .30 .75
11 Anson Carter .15 .40
12 Byron Dafoe .15 .40
13 Sergei Samsonov .15 .40
14 Joe Thornton .30 .75
15 Curtis Brown .12 .30
16 Dominik Hasek .30 .75
17 Joe Juneau .12 .30
18 Michael Peca .15 .40
19 Miroslav Satan .15 .40
20 Valeri Bure .12 .30
21 Jean-Sebastien Giguere .20 .50
22 Phil Housley .15 .40
23 Jarome Iginla .25 .60
24 Cory Stillman .12 .30
25 Ron Francis .25 .60
26 Arturs Irbe .15 .40
27 Sami Kapanen .12 .30
28 Keith Primeau .15 .40
29 Ray Sheppard .12 .30
30 Tony Amonte .15 .40
31 J-P Dumont .15 .40
32 Doug Gilmour .25 .60
33 Jocelyn Thibault .15 .40
34 Alexei Zhamnov .12 .30
35 Adam Deadmarsh .12 .30
36 Chris Drury .15 .40
37 Theo Fleury .25 .60
38 Peter Forsberg .40 1.00
39 Milan Hejduk .15 .40
40 Claude Lemieux .15 .40
41 Patrick Roy .50 1.25
42 Joe Sakic .40 1.00
43 Ed Belfour .20 .50
44 Brett Hull .40 1.00
45 Jamie Langenbrunner .12 .30
46 Jere Lehtinen .15 .40
47 Mike Modano .30 .75
48 Joe Nieuwendyk .15 .40
49 Chris Chelios .20 .50
50 Sergei Fedorov .30 .75
51 Nicklas Lidstrom .20 .50
52 Darren McCarty .12 .30
53 Chris Osgood .20 .50
54 Brendan Shanahan .20 .50
55 Steve Yzerman .50 1.25
56 Bill Guerin .20 .50
57 Mike Grier .12 .30
58 Tommy Salo .15 .40
59 Ryan Smyth .15 .40
60 Doug Weight .20 .50
61 Pavel Bure .20 .50
62 Sean Burke .12 .30
63 Viktor Kozlov .12 .30
64 Rob Niedermayer .12 .30
65 Mark Parrish .12 .30
66 Ray Whitney .15 .40
67 Donald Audette .12 .30
68 Rob Blake .20 .50
69 Zigmund Palffy .20 .50
70 Luc Robitaille .20 .50
71 Jamie Storr .12 .30
72 Jozef Stumpel .12 .30
73 Shayne Corson .15 .40
74 Jeff Hackett .12 .30
75 Saku Koivu .20 .50
76 Martin Rucinsky .12 .30
77 Brian Savage .12 .30
78 Mike Dunham .12 .30
79 Sergei Krivokrasov .12 .30
80 David Legwand .12 .30
81 Cliff Ronning .12 .30
82 Scott Walker .12 .30
83 Jason Arnott .15 .40
84 Martin Brodeur .50 1.25
85 Patrik Elias .20 .50
86 Bobby Holik .12 .30
87 Brendan Morrison .15 .40
88 Petr Sykora .15 .40
89 Mariusz Czerkawski .12 .30
90 Kenny Jonsson .12 .30
91 Felix Potvin .30 .75
92 Mike Watt .12 .30
93 Adam Graves .15 .40
94 Brian Leetch .15 .40
95 John MacLean .15 .40
96 Petr Nedved .12 .30
97 Mike Richter .20 .50
98 Magnus Arvedson .12 .30
99 Marian Hossa .20 .50
100 Shawn McEachern .12 .30
101 Ron Tugnutt .15 .40
102 Alexei Yashin .15 .40
103 Rod Brind'Amour .20 .50
104 Eric Desjardins .15 .40
105 John LeClair .20 .50
106 Eric Lindros .30 .75
107 Mark Recchi .25 .60
108 John Vanbiesbrouck .20 .50
109 Nikolai Khabibulin .15 .40
110 Teppo Numminen .12 .30
111 Jeremy Roenick .30 .75
112 Rick Tocchet .15 .40
113 Keith Tkachuk .20 .50
114 Matthew Barnaby .12 .30
115 Tom Barrasso .20 .50
116 Jaromir Jagr .60 1.50
117 Alexei Kovalev .15 .40
118 Martin Straka .12 .30
119 Vincent Damphousse .15 .40
120 Jeff Friesen .15 .40
121 Patrick Marleau .20 .50
122 Steve Shields .15 .40
123 Mike Vernon .15 .40
124 Pavol Demitra .25 .60
125 Grant Fuhr .30 .75
126 Al MacInnis .25 .60
127 Chris Pronger .20 .50
128 Pierre Turgeon .15 .40
129 Chris Gratton .12 .30
130 Kevin Hodson .12 .30
131 Vincent Lecavalier .20 .50
132 Paul Mara .12 .30
133 Darcy Tucker .12 .30
134 Sergei Berezin .12 .30
135 Mike Johnson .15 .40
136 Curtis Joseph .25 .60
137 Yanic Perreault .12 .30
138 Mats Sundin .20 .50
139 Steve Thomas .12 .30
140 Mark Messier .40 1.00
141 Bill Muckalt .12 .30
142 Alexander Mogilny .15 .40
143 Markus Naslund .20 .50
144 Mattias Ohlund .12 .30
145 Garth Snow .15 .40
146 Peter Bondra .20 .50
147 Sergei Gonchar .12 .30
148 Benoit Gratton RC .12 .30
149 Olaf Kolzig .20 .50
150 Adam Oates .20 .50

1999-00 Aurora Premiere Date

*PREMIERE DATE/60: 15X TO 40X BASIC CARDS
*STRIPED/60: .4X TO 1X BASIC PD/60

1999-00 Aurora Canvas Creations

1 Paul Kariya 2.00 5.00
2 Teemu Selanne 4.00 10.00
3 Dominik Hasek 3.00 8.00
4 Peter Forsberg 4.00 10.00
5 Patrick Roy 5.00 12.00
6 Steve Yzerman 5.00 12.00
7 Pavel Bure 2.00 5.00
8 John LeClair 2.00 5.00
9 Eric Lindros 3.00 8.00
10 Jaromir Jagr 6.00 15.00

1999-00 Aurora Championship Fever

*SILVER/250: .6X TO 1.5X BASIC INSERTS
*ICE BLUE/100: 2.5X TO 6X BASIC INSERTS
*COPPER/20: 5X TO 12X BASIC INSERTS
1 Paul Kariya .75 2.00
2 Teemu Selanne 1.50 4.00
3 Ray Bourque 1.25 3.00
4 Dominik Hasek 1.25 3.00
5 Michael Peca .60 1.50
6 Theo Fleury 1.00 2.50
7 Peter Forsberg 1.50 4.00
8 Patrick Roy 2.00 5.00
9 Joe Sakic 1.50 4.00
10 Ed Belfour .75 2.00
11 Mike Modano 1.25 3.00
12 Brendan Shanahan .75 2.00
13 Steve Yzerman 2.00 5.00
14 Pavel Bure .75 2.00
15 Martin Brodeur 2.00 5.00
16 John LeClair .75 2.00
17 Eric Lindros 1.25 3.00
18 Jaromir Jagr 2.50 6.00
19 Curtis Joseph 1.00 2.50
20 Mats Sundin .75 2.00
NNO Martin Brodeur AU/197 30.00 80.00

1999-00 Aurora Complete Players

1 Paul Kariya 2.50 6.00
2 Teemu Selanne 5.00 12.00
3 Dominik Hasek 4.00 10.00
4 Peter Forsberg 5.00 12.00
5 Patrick Roy 6.00 15.00
6 Mike Modano 4.00 10.00
7 Steve Yzerman 6.00 15.00
8 John LeClair 2.50 6.00
9 Eric Lindros 4.00 10.00
10 Jaromir Jagr 8.00 20.00

1999-00 Aurora Glove Unlimited

COMPLETE SET (20) 50.00 100.00
1 Guy Hebert 1.50 4.00
2 Byron Dafoe 1.50 4.00
3 Dominik Hasek 4.00 10.00
4 Arturs Irbe 1.50 4.00
5 Jocelyn Thibault 1.50 4.00
6 Patrick Roy 12.50 25.00
7 Ed Belfour 2.00 5.00
8 Chris Osgood 1.50 4.00
9 Tommy Salo 1.50 4.00
10 Jeff Hackett 1.50 4.00
11 Martin Brodeur 6.00 12.00
12 Felix Potvin 2.00 5.00
13 Mike Richter 2.00 5.00
14 Ron Tugnutt 1.50 4.00
15 John Vanbiesbrouck 1.50 4.00
16 Nikolai Khabibulin 1.50 4.00
17 Grant Fuhr 1.50 4.00
18 Steve Shields 1.50 4.00
19 Curtis Joseph 2.00 5.00
20 Olaf Kolzig 1.50 4.00

1999-00 Aurora Styrotechs

1 Paul Kariya 1.00 2.50
2 Teemu Selanne 2.00 5.00
3 Dominik Hasek 1.50 4.00
4 Theo Fleury 1.25 3.00
5 Peter Forsberg 2.00 5.00
6 Patrick Roy 2.50 6.00
7 Ed Belfour 1.00 2.50
8 Mike Modano 1.50 4.00
9 Brendan Shanahan 1.00 2.50
10 Steve Yzerman 2.50 6.00
11 Pavel Bure 1.00 2.50
12 Martin Brodeur 2.50 6.00
13 Alexei Yashin .75 2.00
14 John LeClair 1.00 2.50
15 Eric Lindros 1.50 4.00
16 Keith Tkachuk 1.00 2.50
17 Jaromir Jagr 3.00 8.00
18 Curtis Joseph 1.25 3.00
19 Mats Sundin 1.00 2.50
20 Mark Messier 2.00 5.00

2000-01 Aurora

*PINSTRIPE: .8X TO 2X BASIC CARDS
1 Guy Hebert .25 .60
2 Paul Kariya .30 .75
3 Steve Rucchin .20 .50
4 Teemu Selanne .60 1.50
5 Andrew Brunette .20 .50
6 Scott Fankhouser .20 .50
7 Damian Rhodes .20 .50
8 Patrik Stefan .25 .60
9 Jason Allison .25 .60
10 Anson Carter .25 .60
11 Paul Coffey .30 .75
12 Byron Dafoe .25 .60
13 John Grahame .20 .50
14 Sergei Samsonov .25 .60
15 Joe Thornton .50 1.25
16 Maxim Afinogenov .20 .50
17 Martin Biron .25 .60
18 Doug Gilmour .40 1.00
19 Dominik Hasek .50 1.25
20 Michael Peca .25 .60
21 Miroslav Satan .20 .50
22 Fred Brathwaite .25 .60
23 Valeri Bure .25 .60
24 Jarome Iginla .40 1.00
25 Derek Morris .20 .50
26 Marc Savard .20 .50
27 Rod Brind'Amour .30 .75
28 Ron Francis .40 1.00
29 Arturs Irbe .25 .60
30 Sami Kapanen .20 .50
31 Tony Amonte .25 .60
32 Eric Daze .25 .60
33 Steve Sullivan .20 .50
34 Jocelyn Thibault .25 .60
35 Alexei Zhamnov .25 .60
36 Ray Bourque .50 1.25
37 Chris Drury .25 .60
38 Peter Forsberg .60 1.50
39 Milan Hejduk .25 .60
40 Patrick Roy .75 2.00
41 Joe Sakic .60 1.50
42 Alex Tanguay .25 .60
43 Ed Belfour .30 .75
44 Brett Hull .60 1.50
45 Mike Modano .50 1.25
46 Brenden Morrow .25 .60
47 Joe Nieuwendyk .25 .60
48 Chris Chelios .30 .75
49 Sergei Fedorov .50 1.25
50 Nicklas Lidstrom .30 .75
51 Chris Osgood .30 .75
52 Brendan Shanahan .30 .75
53 Pat Verbeek .25 .60
54 Steve Yzerman .75 2.00
55 Mike Grier .20 .50
56 Bill Guerin .30 .75
57 Tommy Salo .25 .60
58 Ryan Smyth .25 .60
59 Doug Weight .30 .75
60 Pavel Bure .30 .75
61 Trevor Kidd .20 .50
62 Viktor Kozlov .25 .60
63 Roberto Luongo .50 1.25
64 Ray Whitney .25 .60
65 Rob Blake .30 .75
66 Stephane Fiset .20 .50
67 Zigmund Palffy .30 .75
68 Luc Robitaille .30 .75
69 Jamie Storr .25 .60
70 Jozef Stumpel .20 .50
71 Jeff Hackett .20 .50
72 Saku Koivu .30 .75
73 Trevor Linden .30 .75
74 Martin Rucinsky .20 .50
75 Jose Theodore .30 .75
76 Mike Dunham .20 .50
77 Patric Kjellberg .20 .50
78 David Legwand .30 .75
79 Cliff Ronning .20 .50
80 Jason Arnott .25 .60
81 Martin Brodeur .75 2.00
82 Patrik Elias .30 .75
83 Scott Gomez .25 .60
84 John Madden .25 .60
85 Scott Stevens .30 .75
86 Petr Sykora .25 .60
87 Tim Connolly .20 .50
88 Mariusz Czerkawski .20 .50
89 Brad Isbister .20 .50
90 Mark Parrish .20 .50
91 John Vanbiesbrouck .30 .75
92 Theo Fleury .40 1.00
93 Adam Graves .25 .60
94 Jan Hlavac .20 .50
95 Brian Leetch .25 .60
96 Mark Messier .60 1.50
97 Petr Nedved .25 .60
98 Mike Richter .30 .75
99 Daniel Alfredsson .30 .75
100 Radek Bonk .25 .60
101 Marian Hossa .30 .75
102 Shawn McEachern .20 .50
103 Vaclav Prospal .20 .50
104 Brian Boucher .25 .60
105 Eric Desjardins .25 .60
106 Simon Gagne .30 .75
107 John LeClair .30 .75
108 Eric Lindros .50 1.25
109 Mark Recchi .40 1.00
110 Shane Doan .25 .60
111 Joe Juneau .20 .50
112 Jeremy Roenick .50 1.25
113 Keith Tkachuk .30 .75
114 Jean-Sebastien Aubin .25 .60
115 Jan Hrdina .20 .50
116 Jaromir Jagr 1.00 2.50
117 Alexei Kovalev .25 .60
118 Martin Straka .25 .60
119 Pavol Demitra .40 1.00
120 Dallas Drake .20 .50
121 Michal Handzus .20 .50
122 Al MacInnis .40 1.00
123 Chris Pronger .30 .75
124 Roman Turek .25 .60
125 Pierre Turgeon .25 .60
126 Vincent Damphousse .25 .60
127 Jeff Friesen .20 .50
128 Patrick Marleau .30 .75
129 Owen Nolan .30 .75
130 Steve Shields .20 .50
131 Dan Cloutier .25 .60
132 Matt Elich RC .25 .60
133 Mike Johnson .20 .50
134 Vincent Lecavalier .30 .75
135 Kevin Weekes .20 .50
136 Nikolai Antropov .25 .60
137 Tie Domi .25 .60
138 Jeff Farkas .20 .50
139 Curtis Joseph .40 1.00
140 Mats Sundin .30 .75
141 Steve Thomas .20 .50
142 Andrew Cassels .20 .50
143 Steve Kariya .20 .50
144 Markus Naslund .30 .75
145 Felix Potvin .50 1.25
146 Peter Bondra .30 .75
147 Jeff Halpern .20 .50
148 Olaf Kolzig .30 .75
149 Adam Oates .30 .75
150 Chris Simon .20 .50

2000-01 Aurora Premiere Date

*PREM.DATE/50: 12X TO 30X BASIC CARDS
*PINSTRIPES: .4X TO 1X BASIC INSERTS
96 Mark Messier 15.00 40.00

2000-01 Aurora Autographs

23 Valeri Bure/300 6.00 15.00
37 Chris Drury/250 6.00 15.00
42 Alex Tanguay/500 6.00 15.00
46 Brenden Morrow/500 6.00 15.00
55 Mike Grier/500 5.00 12.00
75 Jose Theodore/500 8.00 20.00
78 David Legwand/500 8.00 20.00
81 Martin Brodeur/197 40.00 100.00
115 Jean-Sebastien Aubin/500 6.00 15.00
135 Nikolai Antropov/500 6.00 15.00
148 Olaf Kolzig/250 8.00 20.00

2000-01 Aurora Canvas Creations

1 Paul Kariya 2.00 5.00
2 Peter Forsberg 4.00 10.00
3 Patrick Roy 5.00 12.00
4 Mike Modano 3.00 8.00
5 Steve Yzerman 5.00 12.00
6 Pavel Bure 2.00 5.00
7 Martin Brodeur 5.00 12.00
8 John LeClair 2.00 5.00
9 Jaromir Jagr 6.00 15.00
10 Curtis Joseph 2.50 6.00

2000-01 Aurora Championship Fever

*COPPER/90: 10X TO 25X BASIC INSERT
*BLUE/92: 10X TO 25X BASIC INSERT
*SILVER/221: 6X TO 15X BASIC INSERT
1 Paul Kariya .60 1.50
2 Teemu Selanne 1.25 3.00
3 Dominik Hasek 1.00 2.50
4 Ray Bourque 1.00 2.50
5 Peter Forsberg 1.25 3.00
6 Patrick Roy 1.50 4.00
7 Ed Belfour .60 1.50
8 Brett Hull 1.25 3.00
9 Mike Modano 1.00 2.50
10 Sergei Fedorov 1.00 2.50
11 Brendan Shanahan .60 1.50
12 Steve Yzerman 1.50 4.00
13 Pavel Bure .60 1.50
14 Martin Brodeur 1.50 4.00
15 Scott Gomez .50 1.25
16 Mark Messier 1.25 3.00
17 Brian Boucher .50 1.25
18 John LeClair .60 1.50
19 Jaromir Jagr 2.00 5.00
20 Curtis Joseph .75 2.00
NNO John LeClair AU/197 8.00 20.00

2000-01 Aurora Dual Game-Worn Jerseys

1 P.Sykora/S.Koivu 6.00 15.00
2 J.Vanbiesbrouck/R.Luongo 6.00 15.00
3 S.Yzerman/B.Shanahan 8.00 20.00
4 J.Jagr/P.Bondra 12.00 30.00

2000-01 Aurora Game Worn Jerseys

1 Paul Coffey 5.00 12.00
2 Brendan Shanahan 5.00 12.00
3 Steve Yzerman 8.00 20.00
4 Steve Yzerman 12.00 30.00
5 Saku Koivu 5.00 12.00
6 John Vanbiesbrouck 5.00 12.00
7 Mark Messier 10.00 25.00
8 Petr Sykora 4.00 10.00
9 Eric Lindros 8.00 20.00
10 Peter Bondra 5.00 12.00

2000-01 Aurora Scouting Reports

1 Paul Kariya 1.50 4.00
2 Teemu Selanne 3.00 8.00
3 Patrik Stefan 1.25 3.00
4 Joe Thornton 2.50 6.00
5 Peter Forsberg 3.00 8.00
6 Milan Hejduk 1.25 3.00
7 Brett Hull 3.00 8.00
8 Ed Belfour 1.50 4.00
9 Sergei Fedorov 2.50 6.00
10 Brendan Shanahan 1.50 4.00
11 Pavel Bure 1.50 4.00
12 Roberto Luongo 2.50 6.00
13 Martin Brodeur 4.00 10.00
14 Scott Gomez 1.25 3.00
15 Marian Hossa 1.50 4.00
16 Brian Boucher 1.25 3.00
17 John LeClair 1.50 4.00
18 Vincent Lecavalier 1.50 4.00
19 Curtis Joseph 2.00 5.00
20 Mats Sundin 1.50 4.00

2000-01 Aurora Styrotechs

1A Paul Kariya .75 2.00
1B Teemu Selanne 1.50 4.00
2A Doug Gilmour 1.00 2.50

2B Dominik Hasek 1.25 3.00
3A Peter Forsberg 1.50 4.00
3B Patrick Roy 2.00 5.00
4A Joe Sakic 1.50 4.00
4B Ray Bourque 1.25 3.00
5A Brett Hull 1.50 4.00
5B Mike Modano 1.25 3.00
6A Brendan Shanahan .75 2.00
6B Steve Yzerman 2.00 5.00
7A Scott Gomez .60 1.50
7B Martin Brodeur 2.00 5.00
8A John LeClair .75 2.00
8B Brian Boucher .60 1.50
9A Jaromir Jagr 2.50 6.00
9B Jean-Sebastien Aubin .60 1.50
10A Curtis Joseph 1.00 2.50
10B Mats Sundin .75 2.00

1996 Avalanche Photo Pucks

COMPLETE SET (5) 6.00 15.00
1 Claude Lemieux
Peter Forsberg 2.00 5.00
2 Joe Sakic
Adam Deadmarsh 1.50 4.00
3 Patrick Roy
Adam Foote 2.00 5.00
4 Valeri Kamensky
Mike Ricci 1.25 3.00
5 Colorado Avalanche 1.25 3.00

1997 Avalanche Pins

1 Team Logo .40 1.00
2 Joe Sakic 1.50 4.00
3 Patrick Roy 2.50 6.00
4 Marc Crawford CO .40 1.00
5 Peter Forsberg 1.50 4.00
6 Claude Lemieux .40 1.00
7 Olympic Break .40 1.00
8 Sandiz Ozolinsh .40 1.00
9 Adam Foote .75 2.00

1999-00 Avalanche Pins

COMPLETE SET (8)
1 Joe Sakic 1.50 4.00
2 Adam Foote 1.25 3.00
3 Adam Deadmarsh .40 1.00
4 Patrick Roy 2.50 6.00
5 Peter Forsberg 2.00 5.00
6 Sandis Ozolinsh .40 1.00
7 Chris Drury .40 1.00
8 Milan Hejduk 1.25 3.00

1999-00 Avalanche Team Issue

COMPLETE SET (24) 8.00 20.00
1 Greg DeVries .08 .25
2 Adam Deadmarsh .20 .50
3 Marc Denis .40 1.00
4 Chris Dingman .08 .25
5 Chris Drury .40 1.00
6 Adam Foote .20 .50
7 Peter Forsberg 1.25 3.00
8 Alexei Gusarov .08 .25
9 Milan Hejduk .60 1.50
10 Sami Helenius .08 .25
11 Dan Hinote .30 .75
12 Jon Klemm .15 .40
13 Eric Messier .08 .25
14 Aaron Miller .08 .25
15 Jeff Odgers .08 .25
16 Sandis Ozolinsh .20 .50
17 Shjon Podein .08 .25
18 Dave Reid .08 .25
19 Brian Rolston .20 .50
20 Patrik Roy 2.00 5.00
21 Joe Sakic .75 2.00
22 Martin Skoula .20 .50
23 Alex Tanguay .60 1.50
24 Stephane Yelle .15 .40

2001-02 Avalanche Team Issue

COMPLETE SET (22) 15.00 30.00
1 David Aebischer .75 2.00
2 Stephane Yelle .40 1.00
3 Rob Blake .75 2.00
4 Shjon Podein .40 1.00
5 Scott Parker .40 1.00
6 Brian Willsie .40 1.00
7 Brad Larsen .40 1.00
8 Radim Vrbata .40 1.00
9 Rick Berry .40 1.00
10 Adam Foote .40 1.00
11 Chris Drury .40 1.00
12 Alex Tanguay .75 2.00
13 Dan Hinote .40 1.00
14 Eric Messier .40 1.00
15 Joe Sakic 1.25 3.00
16 Pascal Trepanier .40 1.00
17 Martin Skoula .40 1.00
18 Steven Reinprecht .40 1.00
19 Patrick Roy 2.00 5.00
20 Milan Hejduk .75 2.00
21 Todd Gill .40 1.00
22 Greg DeVries .40 1.00
23 Peter Forsberg 1.50 4.00

2002-03 Avalanche Postcards

COMPLETE SET (18) 10.00 25.00
1 Mike Keane .40 1.00
2 Riku Hahl .60 1.50
3 Scott Parker .60 1.50
4 David Aebischer .60 1.50
5 Steven Reinprecht .40 1.00
6 Greg deVries .40 1.00
7 Eric Messier .40 1.00
8 Peter Forsberg 2.00 5.00
9 Joe Sakic 2.00 5.00
10 Martin Skoula .40 1.00
11 Adam Foote .40 1.00
12 Derek Morris .40 1.00
13 Brian Willsie .40 1.00
14 Jeff Shantz .40 1.00
15 Milan Hejduk .60 1.50
16 Rob Blake .60 1.50
17 Dan Hinote .40 1.00
18 Bryan Muir .40 1.00

2003-04 Avalanche Team Issue

COMPLETE SET (20) 10.00 25.00
1 David Aebischer .40 1.00
2 Rob Blake .75 2.00
3 Jim Cummins .40 1.00
4 Adam Foote .40 1.00
5 Peter Forsberg 1.25 3.00
6 Chris Gratton .40 1.00
7 Riku Hahl .40 1.00
8 Milan Hejduk .75 2.00
9 Dan Hinote .40 1.00
10 Paul Kariya .75 2.00
11 Steve Konowalchuk .40 1.00
12 John-Michael Liles .40 1.00
13 Andrei Nikolishin .40 1.00
14 Joe Sakic 1.25 3.00
15 Phil Sauve .40 1.00
16 Teemu Selanne .75 2.00
17 Karlis Skrastins .40 1.00
18 Marek Svatos .75 2.00
19 Alex Tanguay .75 2.00
20 Peter Worrell .40 1.00

2006-07 Avalanche Postcards

COMPLETE SET (21) 15.00 30.00
1 Tyler Arnason .40 1.00
2 Patrice Brisebois .40 1.00
3 Andrew Brunette .40 1.00
4 Peter Budaj .75 2.00
5 Brett Clark .40 1.00
6 Milan Hejduk .75 2.00
7 Ken Klee .40 1.00
8 Ian Laperriere .40 1.00
9 Jordan Leopold .40 1.00
10 Brett McLean .40 1.00
11 Brad Richardson .40 1.00
12 Mark Rycroft .40 1.00
13 Joe Sakic 2.00 5.00
14 Kurt Sauer .40 1.00
15 Karlis Skrastins .40 1.00
16 Paul Stastny 2.00 5.00
17 Marek Svatos .75 2.00
18 Jose Theodore .75 2.00
19 Pierre Turgeon .40 1.00
20 Ossi Vaananen .40 1.00
21 Wojtek Wolski .75 2.00
22 Ken Klee .40 1.00
23 Paul Stastny 2.00 5.00
24 Antii Laaksonen .75 2.00
25 Brett Clark .75 2.00
26 Brad May .40 1.00
27 Pierre Lacroix .75 2.00
28 Jeff Hackett .75 2.00
29 Tony Granato .75 2.00
30 Jacques Cloutier .75 2.00
31 Francois Giguere .75 2.00
32 Joel Quenneville .40 1.00

2003-04 Backcheck: A Hockey Retrospective

COMPLETE SET (20) 8.00 20.00
1 Choosing Sides .20 .50
2 Outdoor Game .20 .50
3 Early Skating .20 .50
4 Ottawa Rebels .40 1.00
5 Renfrew hockey team .40 1.00
6 Oxford Canadian Hockey Club .40 1.00
7 Gore Bay Hockey Club .40 1.00
8 Ottawa Silver Seven .75 2.00
9 Maurice Richard 2.00 5.00
10 Clarence Campbell .40 1.00
11 Bodychecking .20 .50
12 Asahi Athletic Club .40 1.00
13 Lester B. Pearson
Swiss game .20 .50
14 Prisoners' hockey team .40 1.00
15 Sydney Millionaires .40 1.00
16 Jacques Plante
Quebec Citadelles 2.00 5.00
17 Shinny .20 .50
18 Montreal Canadiens 1942 .75 2.00
19 Eva Ault .20 .50
20 Orillia Hockey Club .40 1.00

1995-96 Bashan Imperial Super Stickers

COMPLETE SET (136) 15.00 30.00
1 Ducks Logo .08 .25
2 Paul Kariya .60 1.50
3 Chad Kilger .08 .25
4 Oleg Tverdovsky .08 .25
5 Bruins Logo .08 .25
6 Ray Bourque .60 1.50
7 Cam Neely .60 1.50
8 Adam Oates .20 .50
9 Kevin Stevens .20 .50
10 Sabres Logo .08 .25
11 Pat LaFontaine .20 .50
12 Dominik Hasek .75 2.00
13 Alexei Zhitnik .08 .25
14 Flames Logo .08 .25
15 Theo Fleury .40 1.00
16 Phil Housley .08 .25
17 Trevor Kidd .20 .50
18 Joe Nieuwendyk .20 .50
19 Zarley Zalapski .08 .25
20 Blackhawks Logo .08 .25
21 Jeremy Roenick .60 1.50
22 Chris Chelios .40 1.00
23 Ed Belfour .60 1.50
24 Joe Murphy .08 .25
25 Patrick Poulin .08 .25
26 Avalanche Logo .08 .25
27 Joe Sakic .75 2.00
28 Peter Forsberg 1.00 2.50
29 Sandis Ozolinsh .08 .25
30 Mike Ricci .08 .25
31 Valeri Kamensky .08 .25
32 Stars Logo .08 .25
33 Mike Modano .60 1.50
34 Kevin Hatcher .08 .25
35 Andy Moog .20 .50
36 Red Wings Logo .08 .25
37 Steve Yzerman 1.25 3.00
38 Sergei Fedorov .60 1.50
39 Paul Coffey .40 1.00
40 Keith Primeau .08 .25
41 Nicklas Lidstrom .40 1.00
42 Oilers Logo .08 .25
43 Doug Weight .08 .25
44 Jason Arnott .08 .25
45 Bill Ranford .20 .50
46 Panthers Logo .08 .25
47 John Vanbiesbrouck .40 1.00
48 Stu Barnes .08 .25
49 Scott Mellanby .08 .25
50 Rob Niedermayer .08 .25
51 Whalers Logo .08 .25
52 Brendan Shanahan .40 1.00
53 Geoff Sanderson .08 .25
54 Sean Burke .20 .50
55 Jeff O'Neill .08 .25
56 Kings Logo .08 .25
57 Wayne Gretzky 2.00 5.00
58 Rob Blake .20 .50
59 Rick Tocchet .20 .50
60 Dimitri Khristich .08 .25
61 Kelly Hrudey .20 .50
62 Canadiens Logo .08 .25
63 Pierre Turgeon .08 .25
64 Mark Recchi .20 .50
65 Saku Koivu .40 1.00
66 Patrick Roy 1.50 4.00
67 Vincent Damphousse .08 .25
68 Devils Logo .08 .25
69 Stephane Richer .08 .25
70 Martin Brodeur 1.25 3.00
71 Scott Niedermayer .08 .25
72 Scott Stevens .08 .25
73 Islander Logo .08 .25
74 Kirk Muller .08 .25
75 Mathieu Schneider .08 .25
76 Derek King .08 .25
77 Wendel Clark .20 .50
78 Ranger Logo .08 .25
79 Brian Leetch .40 1.00
80 Mark Messier .60 1.50
81 Alexei Kovalev .08 .25
82 Luc Robitaille .40 1.00
83 Mike Richter .40 1.00
84 Senators Logo .08 .25
85 Dan Quinn .08 .25
86 Alexandre Daigle .08 .25
87 Steve Duchesne .08 .25
88 Radek Bonk .08 .25
89 Flyers Logo .08 .25
90 Eric Lindros .60 1.50
91 Mikael Renberg .08 .25
92 John LeClair .20 .50
93 Eric Desjardins .08 .25
94 Rod Brind'Amour .08 .25
95 Penguins Logo .08 .25
96 Jaromir Jagr .75 2.00
97 Mario Lemieux 1.50 4.00
98 Ron Francis .20 .50
99 Sergei Zubov .08 .25
100 Blues Logo .08 .25
101 Brett Hull .60 1.50
102 Al MacInnis .20 .50
103 Dale Hawerchuk .20 .50
104 Chris Pronger .40 1.00
105 Sharks Logo .08 .25
106 Craig Janney .08 .25
107 Pat Falloon .08 .25
108 Arturs Irbe .40 1.00
109 Ulf Dahlen .08 .25
110 Owen Nolan .20 .50
111 Lightning Logo .08 .25
112 Roman Hamrlik .08 .25
113 Brian Bradley .08 .25
114 Chris Gratton .08 .25
115 Brian Bellows .08 .25
116 Maple Leafs Logo .08 .25
117 Doug Gilmour .40 1.00
118 Mats Sundin .60 1.50
119 Dave Andreychuk .08 .25
120 Felix Potvin .40 1.00
121 Larry Murphy .08 .25
122 Canucks Logo .08 .25
123 Pavel Bure .40 1.00
124 Alexander Mogilny .20 .50
125 Trevor Linden .20 .50
126 Jeff Brown .08 .25
127 Kirk McLean .20 .50
128 Capitals Logo .08 .25
129 Joe Juneau .08 .25
130 Peter Bondra .20 .50
131 Jim Carey .20 .50
132 Calle Johansson .08 .25
133 Jets Logo .08 .25
134 Teemu Selanne .60 1.50
135 Alexei Zhamnov .08 .25
136 Keith Tkachuk .40 1.00

1995-96 Bashan Imperial Super Stickers Die Cut

COMPLETE SET (25) 8.00 20.00
1 Pierre Turgeon .08 .25
2 Patrick Roy 1.50 4.00
3 Pat LaFontaine .20 .50
4 Joe Sakic 1.00 2.50
5 Paul Coffey .40 1.00
6 Ray Bourque .60 1.50
7 Brian Leetch .40 1.00
8 Joe Juneau .08 .25
9 Jeremy Roenick .60 1.50
10 Chris Chelios .40 1.00
11 Brett Hull .60 1.50
12 Paul Kariya .40 1.00
13 Jason Arnott .08 .25
14 Pavel Bure .40 1.00
15 Steve Duchesne .08 .25
16 Martin Brodeur 1.25 3.00
17 Eric Lindros .60 1.50
18 Mikael Renberg .08 .25
19 Felix Potvin .40 1.00
20 Roman Hamrlik .08 .25
21 Wayne Gretzky 2.00 5.00
22 Brendan Shanahan .60 1.50
23 Jaromir Jagr .75 2.00
24 Mario Lemieux 1.50 4.00
25 Steve Yzerman 1.25 3.00

1968 Bauer Ads

COMPLETE SET (21) 300.00 600.00
1 Andy Bathgate 12.50 25.00
2 Gary Bergman 12.50 25.00
3 Charlie Burns 12.50 25.00
4 Ray Cullen 12.50 25.00
5 Gary Dornhoeffer 12.50 25.00
6 Kent Douglas 12.50 25.00
7 Tim Ecclestone 12.50 25.00
8 Bill Flett 12.50 25.00
9 Ed Giacomin 20.00 40.00
10 Ted Harris 12.50 25.00
11 Paul Henderson 20.00 40.00
12 Ken Hodge 12.50 25.00
13 Harry Howell 12.50 25.00
14 Earl Ingarfield 12.50 25.00
15 Gilles Marotte 12.50 25.00
16 Doug Mohns 12.50 25.00
17 Bobby Orr 75.00 150.00
18 Claude Provost 12.50 25.00
19 Gary Sabourin 12.50 25.00
20 Brian Smith 12.50 25.00
21 Bob Woytowich 12.50 25.00

1991-92 BayBank Bobby Orr

COMPLETE SET (4) 12.00 30.00
1 Bobby Orr
(Skating with Flyer
in pursuit) 3.00 8.00
2 Bobby Orr
(Skating alone
with puck) 3.00 8.00
3 Bobby Orr
(Skating behind the net) 3.00 8.00
NNO Bobby Orr 8 1/2 x 11 4.00 10.00

1995 BayBank Bobby Orr

COMPLETE SET (2) 6.00 15.00
1 Bobby Orr
(Oversized card) 4.00 10.00
2 Bobby Orr
(Regular size card) 2.00 5.00

1971-72 Bazooka

COMPLETE SET (36) 4500.00 9000.00
1 Phil Esposito 375.00 750.00
2 Frank Mahovlich 200.00 400.00
3 Ed Van Impe 25.00 50.00
4 Bobby Hull 500.00 1000.00
5 Henri Richard 150.00 300.00
6 Gilbert Perreault 375.00 750.00
7 Alex Delvecchio 125.00 250.00
8 Denis DeJordy 75.00 150.00
9 Ted Harris 30.00 60.00
10 Gilles Villemure 75.00 150.00
11 Dave Keon 150.00 300.00
12 Derek Sanderson 150.00 300.00
13 Orland Kurtenbach 30.00 60.00
14 Bob Nevin 30.00 60.00
15 Yvan Cournoyer 100.00 200.00
16 Andre Boudrias 25.00 50.00
17 Frank St.Marseille 25.00 50.00
18 Norm Ullman 100.00 200.00
19 Garry Unger 40.00 80.00
20 Pierre Bouchard 25.00 50.00
21 Roy Edwards 75.00 150.00
22 Ralph Backstrom 30.00 60.00
23 Guy Trottier 25.00 50.00
24 Serge Bernier 25.00 50.00
25 Bert Marshall 25.00 50.00
26 Wayne Hillman 25.00 50.00
27 Tim Ecclestone 25.00 50.00
28 Walt McKechnie 25.00 50.00
29 Tony Esposito 375.00 750.00
30 Rod Gilbert 100.00 200.00
31 Walt Tkaczuk 30.00 60.00
32 Roger Crozier 75.00 150.00
33 Ken Schinkel 25.00 50.00
34 Ron Ellis 25.00 50.00
35 Stan Mikita 300.00 600.00
36 Bobby Orr 1800.00 3000.00

1994 Be A Player Magazine

COMPLETE SET (4) 4.00 10.00
1 Paul Kariya 2.00 5.00
2 Felix Potvin .60 1.50
3 Joe Sakic 1.25 3.00
4 Toomu Selanne .75 2.00

1994-95 Be A Player

R1 Doug Gilmour .20 .50
R2 Joel Otto .10 .25
R3 Kirk Muller .10 .26
R4 Marty McInnis .10 .25
R5 Dave Gagner .12 .30
R6 Geoff Courtnall .10 .25
R7 Dale Hawerchuk .20 .50
R8 Mike Modano .25 .60
R9 Roman Hamrlik .10 .25
R10 Marty McSorley .12 .30
R11 Teemu Selanne .30 .75
R12 Jeremy Roenick .25 .60
R13 Glenn Healy .12 .30
R14 Darren Turcotte .10 .25
R15 Derian Hatcher .10 .25
R16 Enrico Ciccone .10 .25
R17 Tony Amonte .12 .30
R18 Mark Recchi .20 .50
R19 Eric Weinrich .10 .25
R20 John Vanbiesbrouck .15 .40
R21 Nick Kypreos .10 .25
R22 Gilbert Dionne .10 .25
R23 Theo Fleury .15 .40
R24 Todd Gill .15 .40
R25 Jari Kurri .12 .30
R26 Brad May .10 .25
R27 Russ Courtnall .10 .25
R28 Bill Ranford .12 .30
R29 Steve Yzerman .40 1.00
R30 Alexandre Daigle .10 .25
R31 Mike Hudson .10 .25
R32 Ray Bourque .25 .60
R33 Dave Andreychuk .15 .40
R34 Jason Arnott .12 .30
R35 Pavel Bure .15 .40
R36 Keith Tkachuk .15 .40
R37 Scott Niedermayer .15 .40
R38 Johan Garpenlov .10 .25
R39 Dino Ciccarelli .12 .30
R40 Rob Blake .15 .40
R41 Dave Manson .10 .25
R42 Adam Foote .10 .25
R43 Chris Pronger .15 .40
R44 Scott Lachance .10 .25
R45 Adam Oates .15 .40
R46 Brian Leetch .12 .30
R47 Guy Hebert .12 .30
R48 Brett Hull .30 .75
R49 Mike Ricci .10 .25
R50 Dave Ellett .10 .25
R51 Owen Nolan .15 .40
R52 Craig Janney .12 .30
R53 Trevor Linden .15 .40
R54 Ray Sheppard .12 .30
R55 Rob Niedermayer .12 .30
R56 Kevin Haller .10 .25
R57 Jeff Norton .10 .25
R58 Martin Brodeur .40 1.00
R59 Robb Stauber .10 .25
R60 Sylvain Turgeon .10 .25
R61 Pat Verbeek .12 .30
R62 Steve Smith .10 .25
R63 Jaromir Jagr .50 1.25
R64 Steve Duchesne .10 .25
R65 Tie Domi .12 .30
R66 Sylvain Lefebvre .10 .25
R67 Guy Carbonneau .10 .25
R68 Alexander Mogilny .12 .30
R69 Mario Lemieux .60 1.50
R70 Neil Wilkinson .10 .25
R71 Curtis Joseph .20 .50
R72 Wendel Clark .25 .60
R73 Kirk McLean .12 .30
R74 Mikael Renberg .12 .30
R75 Shawn McEachern .10 .25
R76 Mats Sundin .15 .40
R77 Craig Simpson .10 .25
R78 Phil Housley .12 .30
R79 Pat LaFontaine .15 .40
R80 Pierre Turgeon .12 .30
R81 Felix Potvin .25 .60
R82 Kevin Stevens .12 .30
R83 Steve Chiasson .10 .25
R84 Robert Petrovicky .10 .25
R85 Joe Juneau .10 .25
R86 Brendan Shanahan .15 .40
R87 Joe Sacco .10 .25
R88 David Reid .10 .25
R89 Louie DeBrusk .10 .25
R90 Darryl Sydor .10 .25
R91 Paul Coffey .15 .40
R92 Alexei Yashin .15 .40
R93 Jason Arnott .12 .30
R94 Gary Suter TT .10 .25
R95 Luc Robitaille TT .15 .40
R96 Joe Sakic .30 .75
R97 Chris Chelios .15 .40
R98 Tony Granato TT .10 .25
R99 Wayne Gretzky 1.00 2.50
R100 Joe Juneau .10 .25
R101 Curtis Joseph .20 .50
R102 Vincent Damphousse TT .12 .30
R103 Paul Kariya .15 .40
R104 Brendan Shanahan .15 .40
R105 Eric Desjardins TT .12 .30
R106 Eric Lindros .25 .60
R107 Kirk McLean SS .12 .30
R108 Mike Ricci SS .10 .25
R109 Chris Chelios .15 .40
R110 Chris Gratton SS .10 .25
R111 Doug Gilmour .20 .50
R112 Vincent Damphousse SS .12 .30
R113 Mark Osborne SS .10 .25
R114 Mike Modano .25 .60
R115 Steve Yzerman .40 1.00
R116 Garry Valk SS .10 .25
R117 Adam Graves SS .10 .25
R118 Doug Weight SS .12 .30
R119 Rob Niedermayer SS .12 .30
R120 Craig Simpson SS .10 .25
R121 Patrick Roy .40 1.00
R122 Ronnie Stern SS .10 .25
R123 Jiri Slegr SS .10 .25
R124 Darren Turcotte SS .10 .25
R125 Vladimir Malakhov SS .15 .40
R126 Paul Kariya TN .15 .40
R127 Mike Gartner TN .20 .50
R128 Scott Niedermayer TN .15 .40
R129 Dino Ciccarelli TN .15 .40
R130 Martin Brodeur TN .40 1.00
R131 Kevin Hatcher TN .10 .25
R132 Pat LaFontaine TN .15 .40
R133 Joel Otto TN .10 .25
R134 Jason Arnott .12 .30
R135 John Vanbiesbrouck TN .15 .40
R136 Derian Hatcher TN .10 .25
R137 Brendan Shanahan TN .15 .40
R138 Felix Potvin .25 .60
R139 Trevor Linden TN .15 .40
R140 Ken Baumgartner TN .10 .25
R141 Denis Leary .10 .25
R142 Wendel Clark DLO .25 .60
R143 Cam Neely .15 .40
R144 Jeremy Roenick .25 .60
R145 Sergei Fedorov .25 .60
R146 Scott Stevens DLO .15 .40
R147 Wayne Gretzky 1.00 2.50
R148 Darius Kasparaitis DLO .10 .25
R149 Brian Leetch DLO .12 .30
R150 Marty McSorley DLO .12 .30
R151 Paul Kariya .15 .40
R152 Peter Forsberg .30 .75
R153 Brett Lindros .10 .25
R154 Kenny Jonsson .10 .25
R155 Jason Allison .12 .30
R156 Aaron Gavey .10 .25
R157 Jamie Storr .10 .25
R158 Viktor Kozlov .10 .25
R159 Valeri Bure .10 .25
R160 Oleg Tverdovsky .12 .30
R161 Brent Gretzky RH .10 .25
R162 Todd Harvey .10 .25
R163 Todd Warriner RH .10 .25
R164 Jeff Friesen .10 .25
R165 Adam Deadmarsh .10 .25
R166 Ken Baumgartner NHLPA .10 .25
R167 Terry Carkner NHLPA .10 .25
R168 Tie Domi NHLPA .12 .30
R169 Steve Larmer NHLPA .12 .30
R170 Larry Murphy NHLPA .12 .30
R171 Steve Thomas NHLPA .10 .25
R172 Alexei Yashin .15 .40
R173 Felix Potvin .25 .60
R174 Curtis Joseph .20 .50
R175 Rob Zamuner NHLPA .10 .25
R176 Wayne Gretzky FAN 1.00 2.50
R177 Pavel Bure FAN .15 .40
R178 Eric Lindros FAN .25 .60
R179 Patrick Roy FAN .40 1.00
R180 Doug Gilmour FAN .20 .50
NNO Wayne Gretzky PROMO 4.00 10.00

1994-95 Be A Player 99 All-Stars

COMPLETE SET (19) 30.00 80.00
G1 Wayne Gretzky 10.00 25.00
G2 Paul Coffey 2.00 5.00
G3 Rob Blake 2.00 5.00
G4 Pat Conacher 1.00 2.50
G5 Russ Courtnall 1.00 2.50
G6 Sergei Fedorov 2.00 5.00
G7 Grant Fuhr 2.00 5.00
G8 Todd Gill 1.00 2.50
G9 Tony Granato 1.00 2.50
G10 Brett Hull 3.00 8.00
G11 Charlie Huddy 1.00 2.50
G12 Steve Larmer 2.00 5.00
G13 Kelly Hrudey 2.00 5.00
G14 Al MacInnis 2.00 5.00
G15 Marty McSorley 2.00 5.00
G16 Jari Kurri 2.00 5.00
G17 Kirk Muller 1.00 2.50
G18 Rick Tocchet 2.00 5.00
G19 Steve Yzerman 3.00 8.00

1994-95 Be A Player Autographs

1 Doug Gilmour/1250* 8.00 20.00
2 Adam Foote 2.00 5.00
3 Martin Brodeur 25.00 60.00
4 Alexander Semak 2.00 5.00
5 Dale Hawerchuk 4.00 10.00
6 Derek King 2.00 5.00
7 Mark Recchi 4.00 10.00
8 Fredrik Olausson 2.00 5.00
9 Dave McLlwain 2.00 5.00
10 Marc Bergevin 2.00 5.00
11 Teemu Selanne/600* 40.00 100.00
12 Jeremy Roenick/600* 15.00 40.00
13 Eric Lacroix 3.00 8.00
14 Marty McInnis 2.00 5.00
15 Kris King 2.00 5.00
16 Bill Ranford 2.50 6.00
17 Gary Roberts 2.00 5.00
18 Mark Osborne 2.00 5.00
19 Dmitri Mironov 2.00 5.00
20 John Vanbiesbrouck/600* 25.00 60.00
21 Alexei Zhamnov 2.50 6.00
22 Brad May 2.00 5.00
23 Doug Lidster 2.00 5.00
24 Mikael Renberg 2.50 6.00
25 Kris Draper 2.00 5.00
26 Darryl Sydor 2.00 5.00
27 Claude Lemieux 3.00 8.00
28 Doug Brown 2.00 5.00
29 Louie DeBrusk 2.00 5.00
30 Andy Moog 5.00 12.00
31 Donald Audette 2.00 5.00
32 Ray Bourque/600* 25.00 60.00
33 Brian Rolston 2.50 6.00
34 Ted Drury 2.00 5.00
35 Darren Turcotte 2.00 5.00
36 Gary Shuchuk 2.50 6.00
37 Mike Ricci 2.00 5.00
38 Kirk Maltby 2.00 5.00
39 Doug Bodger 2.00 5.00
40 Kirk Muller 2.00 5.00
41 Sylvain Lefebvre 2.00 5.00
42 Brent Grieve 2.00 5.00
43 Bill Houlder 2.00 5.00
44 Neil Wilkinson 2.00 5.00
45 Donald Dufresne 2.00 5.00
46 Brian Leetch/600* 25.00 60.00
47 Bryan Smolinski 2.00 5.00
48 Kevin Hatcher 2.00 5.00
49 Steven Rice 2.00 5.00
50 Bill Guerin 3.00 8.00
51 Grant Jennings 2.00 5.00
52 Dave Andreychuk 3.00 8.00
53 Sean Burke 2.50 6.00
54 Nick Kypreos 2.00 5.00
55 Drake Berehowsky 2.00 5.00
56 Kevin Haller 2.00 5.00
57 Bill Berg 2.00 5.00
58 Chris Simon 2.00 5.00
59 Owen Nolan UER 3.00 8.00
60 Don Sweeney 2.00 5.00
61 Johan Garpenlov 2.00 5.00
62 Gary Galley 2.00 5.00
63 Pat LaFontaine 5.00 12.00
64 Craig Berube 2.00 5.00
65 Dave Ellett 2.00 5.00
66 Robert Kron 2.00 5.00
67 Alexander Godynyuk 2.00 5.00
68 Markus Naslund 3.00 8.00
69 Joel Otto 2.00 5.00
70 Igor Ulanov 2.00 5.00
71 Pat Verbeek 2.50 6.00
72 Craig MacTavish 2.00 5.00
73 Gary Leeman 2.00 5.00
74 Kevin Todd 2.00 5.00
75 Mike Sullivan 2.00 5.00
76 Rob Pearson 2.00 5.00
77 Dave Gagner 2.50 6.00
78 Dirk Graham 2.00 5.00
79 Joe Sacco 2.00 5.00
80 Jassen Cullimore 2.00 5.00
81 Glen Featherstone 2.00 5.00
82 Scott Lachance 2.00 5.00
83 Kerry Huffman 2.00 5.00
84 Troy Loney 2.00 5.00
85 Rob Gaudreau 2.00 5.00
86 Brendan Shanahan/600* 20.00 50.00
87 Joe Murphy 2.00 5.00
88 Scott Niedermayer 3.00 8.00
89 Dan Quinn 2.50 6.00
90 Jeff Norton 2.00 5.00
91 Jim Dowd 2.00 5.00
92 Ray Ferraro 2.00 5.00
93 Shawn Burr 2.00 5.00
94 Denis Savard 3.00 8.00
95 Dave Manson 2.00 5.00
96 Joe Nieuwendyk 4.00 10.00
97 Tony Amonte 2.50 6.00
98 James Patrick 2.00 5.00
99 Guy Hebert 2.50 6.00
100 Peter Zezel 2.00 5.00
101 Shawn McEachern 2.00 5.00
102 Dave Lowry 2.00 5.00
103 David Reid 2.00 5.00
104 Todd Gill 2.00 5.00
105 John Cullen 2.00 5.00
106 Guy Carbonneau 2.00 5.00
107 Jeff Beukeboom 2.00 5.00
108 Wayne Gretzky/300* 600.00 1500.00
109 Curtis Joseph 4.00 10.00
110 Jason Arnott 2.50 6.00
111 Eric DeSjardins 2.50 6.00
112 Gary Suter 2.00 5.00
113 Luc Robitaille 6.00 15.00
114 Tony Granato 2.00 5.00
115 Steve Yzerman/600* 50.00 125.00
116 Chris Gratton 2.00 5.00
117 Doug Weight 2.50 6.00
118 Garry Valk 2.00 5.00
119 Jiri Slegr 4.00 10.00
120 Vincent Damphousse 2.50 6.00
121 Vladimir Malakhov 2.00 5.00
122 Craig Simpson 2.00 5.00
123 Theo Fleury 6.00 15.00
124 Dave Poulin 2.00 5.00
125 Derian Hatcher 2.00 5.00
126 Jimmy Waite 2.00 5.00
127 Norm Maciver 2.00 5.00
128 Glenn Healy 2.50 6.00
129 Jocelyn Lemieux 2.00 5.00
130 Steve Chiasson 2.00 5.00
131 Keith Jones 2.00 5.00
132 Enrico Ciccone 2.00 5.00
133 Martin Lapointe 2.00 5.00
134 John MacLean 2.50 6.00
135 Geoff Courtnall 2.00 5.00
136 David Shaw 2.00 5.00
137 Steve Duchesne 2.00 5.00
138 Dean Evason 2.00 5.00
139 Eric Weinrich 2.00 5.00
140 Kelly Hrudey 2.50 6.00
141 Ted Donato 2.00 5.00
142 Darius Kasparaitis 2.00 5.00
143 Tie Domi 2.50 6.00
144 Terry Carkner 2.00 5.00
145 Steve Thomas 2.00 5.00
146 Steve Larmer 2.50 6.00
147 Rob Zamuner 2.00 5.00
148 Larry Murphy 2.50 6.00
149 Ken Baumgartner 2.00 5.00
150 Alexei Yashin/600* 3.00 8.00
151 Paul Kariya/600* 60.00 150.00
152 Todd Harvey 2.00 5.00
153A V.Kozlov VK 4.00 10.00
153B V.Kozlov full auto 20.00 50.00
154 Brent Gretzky 2.00 5.00
155 Petr Klima 2.00 5.00
156 Kent Manderville 2.00 5.00
157 Mike Eagles 2.00 5.00
158 Valeri Kamensky 2.50 6.00
159 Thomas Steen 2.00 5.00
160 Michal Pivonka 2.00 5.00
161 Steve Heinze 2.00 5.00
162 Nicklas Lidstrom 20.00 50.00
163 Uwe Krupp 2.00 5.00
164 Pat Elynuik 2.00 5.00
165 Mike Peca 2.50 6.00
166 Sylvain Cote 2.00 5.00
167 Trevor Kidd 2.50 6.00
168 Patrick Poulin 2.00 5.00
169 Shane Churla 2.00 5.00
170 Scott Mellanby 2.50 6.00
171 Mike Sillinger 2.00 5.00
172 Shayne Corson 2.50 6.00
173 Micah Aivazoff 2.00 5.00
174 Robert Lang 2.00 5.00
175 Rod Brind'Amour 2.50 6.00
176 Troy Murray 2.00 5.00
177 Mike Krushelnyski 2.00 5.00
178 Sergio Momesso 3.00 8.00

1994-95 Be A Player Up Close and Personal

COMPLETE SET (10) 20.00 50.00
UC1 Wayne Gretzky 6.00 15.00
UC2 Eric Lindros 1.00 2.50
UC3 Pavel Bure 1.00 2.50
UC4 Teemu Selanne 1.00 2.50
UC5 Steve Yzerman 4.00 10.00
UC6 Jeremy Roenick 1.25 3.00
UC7 Sergei Fedorov 1.50 4.00
UC8 Patrick Roy 6.00 15.00
UC9 Paul Kariya 1.00 2.50
UC10 Doug Gilmour .50 1.25

1995-96 Be A Player

1 Brett Hull .20 .50
2 Jyrki Lumme .05 .15
3 Shean Donovan .05 .15
4 Yuri Khmylev .05 .15
5 Stephane Matteau .05 .15
6 Basil McRae .05 .15
7 Dimitri Yushkevich .05 .15
8 Ron Francis .12 .30
9 Keith Carney .05 .15
10 Brad Dalgarno .05 .15
11 Bob Carpenter .07 .20
12 Kevin Stevens .07 .20
13 Patrick Flatley .05 .15
14 Craig Muni .05 .15
15 Travis Green .07 .20
16 Derek Plante .05 .15
17 Mike Craig .05 .15
18 Chris Pronger .10 .25
19 Bret Hedican .05 .15
20 Mathieu Schneider .05 .15
21 Chris Therien .05 .15
22 Greg Adams .05 .15
23 Arturs Irbe .07 .20
24 Zigmund Palffy .10 .25
25 Peter Douris .05 .15
26 Bob Sweeney .05 .15
27 Chris Terreri .07 .20
28 Alexei Zhitnik .05 .15
29 Jay Wells .05 .15
30 Andrew Cassels .05 .15
31 Radek Bonk .05 .15
32 Brian Bellows .07 .20

33 Frantisek Kucera .05 .15
34 Valeri Bure .05 .15
35 Randy Wood .05 .15
36 Dimitri Khristich .05 .15
37 Randy Ladouceur .05 .15
38 Nelson Emerson .05 .15
39 Bryan Marchment .05 .15
40 Kevin Lowe .07 .20
41 Trevor Linden .10 .25
42 Neal Broten .07 .20
43 Tom Chorske .05 .15
44 Patrice Brisebois .05 .15
45 Wayne Presley .05 .15
46 Murray Craven .05 .15
47 Craig Janney .05 .15
48 Ken Daneyko .05 .15
49 Dino Ciccarelli .07 .20
50 Jason Dawe .05 .15
51 Brad McCrimmon .05 .15
52 Randy McKay .05 .15
53 Rudy Poeschek .05 .15
54 Calle Johansson .05 .15
55 Wendel Clark .15 .40
56 Rob Ray .05 .15
57 Garth Snow .07 .20
58 Joe Juneau .05 .15
59 Craig Wolanin .05 .15
60 Ray Sheppard .07 .20
61 Oleg Tverdovsky .10 .25
62 Geoff Sanderson .05 .15
63 Mike Ridley .05 .15
64 David Oliver .05 .15
65 Russ Courtnall .05 .15
66 Joe Reekie .05 .15
67 Ken Wregget .07 .20
68 Teppo Numminen .05 .15
69 Mikhail Shtalenkov .05 .15
70 Luke Richardson .05 .15
71 Brent Gilchrist .05 .15
72 Phil Housley .07 .20
73 Greg Johnson .05 .15
74 Sean Hill .05 .15
75 Karl Dykhuis .05 .15
76 Tim Cheveldae .07 .20
77 Shjon Podein .05 .15
78 Rene Corbet .05 .15
79 Ronnie Stern .05 .15
80 Mike Donnelly .05 .15
81 Randy Cunneyworth .05 .15
82 Rick Tocchet .07 .20
83 Dallas Drake .05 .15
84 Cam Russell .05 .15
85 Daren Puppa .07 .20
86 Benoit Brunet .05 .15
87 Paul Ranheim .05 .15
88 Bob Rouse .05 .15
89 Todd Elik .05 .15
90 Darcy Wakaluk .05 .15
91 Cliff Ronning .05 .15
92 Pat Conacher .05 .15
93 Todd Krygier .05 .15
94 Dave Babych .05 .15
95 Pat Falloon .05 .15
96 Don Beaupre .07 .20
97 Wayne Gretzky .60 1.50
98 Chris Joseph .05 .15
99 Vyacheslav Kozlov .07 .20
100 Brent Fedyk .05 .15
101 Tim Taylor .05 .15
102 Mike Eastwood .05 .15
103 Mike Keane .05 .15
104 Grant Ledyard .05 .15
105 Rob Dimaio .05 .15
106 Martin Straka .05 .15
107 Scott Young .05 .15
108 Zarley Zalapski .05 .15
109 Steve Leach .05 .15
110 Jody Hull .05 .15
111 Lyle Odelein .05 .15
112 Bob Corkum .05 .15
113 Rob Blake .07 .20
114 Randy Burridge .05 .15
115 Keith Primeau .07 .20
116 Glen Wesley .05 .15
117 Brian Bradley .07 .20
118 Andrei Kovalenko .05 .15
119 Patrik Juhlin .05 .15
120 John Tucker .05 .15
121 Stephane Fiset .07 .20
122 Mike Hough .05 .15
123 Steve Smith .05 .15
124 Tom Barrasso .07 .20
125 Ray Whitney .07 .20
126 Benoit Hogue .05 .15
127 Stu Barnes .05 .15
128 Craig Ludwig .05 .15
129 Curtis Leschyshyn .05 .15
130 John LeClair .10 .25
131 Dennis Vial .05 .15
132 Cory Stillman .05 .15
133 Roman Hamrlik .05 .15
134 Al MacInnis .12 .30
135 Igor Korolev .05 .15
136 Rick Zombo .05 .15
137 Zdeno Ciger .07 .20
138 Brian Savage .05 .15
139 Paul Ysebaert .05 .15
140 Brent Sutter .05 .15
141 Ed Olczyk .05 .15
142 Adam Creighton .05 .15
143 Jesse Belanger .05 .15
144 Glen Murray .07 .20
145 Alexander Selivanov .07 .20
146 Trent Yawney .05 .15
147 Bruce Driver .05 .15
148 Michael Nylander .05 .15
149 Martin Gelinas .05 .15
150 Yanic Perreault .05 .15
151 Craig Billington .07 .20
152 Pierre Turgeon .07 .20
153 Mike Modano .15 .40
154 Joe Mullen .07 .20
155 Todd Ewen .05 .15
156 Petr Nedved .07 .20
157 Dominic Roussel .05 .15
158 Murray Baron .05 .15
159 Robert Dirk .05 .15
160 Tomas Sandstrom .07 .20
161 Brian Holzinger RC .20 .50
162 Ken Klee RC .05 .15
163 Radek Dvorak RC .12 .30
164 Marcus Ragnarsson RC .12 .30
165 Aaron Gavey .05 .15
166 Jeff O'Neill .10 .25
167 Chad Kilger RC .10 .25
168 Todd Bertuzzi RC .12 .30
169 Robert Svehla .05 .15
170 Eric Daze .20 .50
171 Daniel Alfredsson RC .50 1.25
172 Shane Doan RC .30 .75
173 Kyle McLaren .05 .15
174 Saku Koivu .10 .25
175 Jere Lehtinen .07 .20
176 Nikolai Khabibulin .07 .20
177 Niklas Sundstrom .05 .15
178 Ed Jovanovski .10 .25
179 Jason Bonsignore .05 .15
180 Kenny Jonsson .10 .25
181 Vitali Yachmenev .10 .25
182 Alexei Kovalev .07 .20
183 Sandis Ozolinsh .05 .15
184 Rob Niedermayer .07 .20
185 Richard Park .10 .25
186 Adam Deadmarsh .05 .15
187 Sergei Krivokrasov .05 .15
188 Alexandre Daigle .05 .15
189 Jim Carey .07 .20
190 Todd Marchant .05 .15
191 Mike Richter .10 .25
192 Dominik Hasek .15 .40
193 Chris Osgood .10 .25
194 Ed Belfour .07 .20
195 Felix Potvin .15 .40
196 Grant Fuhr .15 .40
197 Patrick Roy .25 .60
198 Ron Hextall .10 .25
199 Jocelyn Thibault .07 .20
200 Kirk McLean .07 .20
201 Jari Kurri .10 .25
202 Bobby Holik .10 .25
203 Mats Sundin .10 .25
204 Alexander Mogilny .07 .20
205 Valeri Karpov .05 .15
206 Igor Larionov .05 .15
207 Valeri Zelepukin .05 .15
208 Jozef Stumpel .05 .15
209 Sergei Nemchinov .05 .15
210 Peter Bondra .10 .25
211 Chris Chelios .10 .25
212 Adam Graves .07 .20
213 Dale Hunter .07 .20
214 Tony Twist .05 .15
215 Keith Tkachuk .10 .25
216 Vladimir Konstantinov .07 .20
217 Sandy McCarthy .05 .15
218 Jamie Macoun .05 .15
219 Scott Stevens .10 .25
220 Mark Tinordi .05 .15
221 Bob Probert .10 .25
222 Gino Odjick .05 .15
223 Ulf Samuelsson .05 .15
224 Stu Grimson .05 .15
225 Marty McSorley .07 .20

1995-96 Be A Player Autographs

S1 Brett Hull 6.00 15.00
S2 Jyrki Lumme 2.50 6.00
S3 Shean Donovan 2.50 6.00
S4 Yuri Khmylev 2.50 6.00
S5 Stephane Matteau 2.50 6.00
S6 Basil McRae 2.50 6.00
S7 Dimitri Yushkevich 2.50 6.00
S8 Ron Francis 6.00 15.00
S9 Keith Carney 2.50 6.00
S10 Brad Dalgarno 2.50 6.00
S11 Bob Carpenter 2.50 6.00
S12 Kevin Stevens 2.50 6.00
S13 Pat Flatley 2.50 6.00
S14 Craig Muni 2.50 6.00
S15 Travis Green 2.50 6.00
S16 Derek Plante 2.50 6.00
S17 Mike Craig 2.50 6.00
S18 Chris Pronger 6.00 15.00
S19 Bret Hedican 2.50 6.00
S20 Mathieu Schneider 2.50 6.00
S21 Chris Therien 2.50 6.00
S22 Greg Adams 2.50 6.00
S23 Arturs Irbe 4.00 10.00
S24 Zigmund Palffy 4.00 10.00
S25 Peter Douris 2.50 6.00
S26 Bob Sweeney 2.50 6.00
S27 Chris Terreri 2.50 6.00
S28 Alexei Zhitnik 2.50 6.00
S29 Jay Wells 2.50 6.00
S30 Andrew Cassels 2.50 6.00
S31 Radek Bonk 4.00 10.00
S32 Brian Bellows 2.50 6.00
S33 Frantisek Kucera 2.50 6.00
S34 Valeri Bure 4.00 10.00
S35 Randy Wood 2.50 6.00
S36 Dimitri Khristich 2.50 6.00
S37 Randy Ladouceur 2.50 6.00
S38 Nelson Emerson 2.50 6.00
S39 Bryan Marchment 4.00 10.00
S40 Kevin Lowe 4.00 10.00
S41 Trevor Linden 6.00 15.00
S42 Neal Broten 4.00 10.00
S43 Tom Chorske 2.50 6.00
S44 Patrice Brisebois 2.50 6.00
S45 Wayne Presley 2.50 6.00
S46 Murray Craven 2.50 6.00
S47 Craig Janney 2.50 6.00
S48 Ken Daneyko 2.50 6.00
S49 Dino Ciccarelli 4.00 10.00
S50 Jason Dawe 2.50 6.00
S51 Brad McCrimmon 8.00 20.00
S52 Randy McKay 2.50 6.00
S53 Rudy Poeschek 2.50 6.00
S54 Calle Johansson 2.50 6.00
S55 Wendel Clark 6.00 15.00
S56 Rob Ray 4.00 10.00
S57 Garth Snow 4.00 10.00
S58 Joe Juneau 4.00 10.00
S59 Craig Wolanin 2.50 6.00
S60 Ray Sheppard 2.50 6.00
S61 Oleg Tverdovsky 2.50 6.00
S62 Geoff Sanderson 2.50 6.00
S63 Mike Ridley 2.50 6.00
S64 David Oliver 2.50 6.00
S65 Russ Courtnall 2.50 6.00
S66 Joe Reekie 2.50 6.00
S67 Ken Wregget 5.00 12.00
S68 Teppo Numminen 2.50 6.00
S69 Mikhail Shtalenkov 2.50 6.00
S70 Luke Richardson 2.50 6.00
S71 Brent Gilchrist 2.50 6.00
S72 Phil Housley 2.50 6.00
S73 Greg Johnson 2.50 6.00
S74 Sean Hill 2.50 6.00
S75 Karl Dykhuis 2.50 6.00
S76 Tim Cheveldae 2.50 6.00
S77 Shjon Podein 2.50 6.00
S78 Rene Corbet 2.50 6.00
S79 Ron Stern 2.50 6.00
S80 Mike Donnelly 2.50 6.00
S81 Randy Cunneyworth 2.50 6.00
S82 Rick Tocchet 4.00 10.00
S83 Dallas Drake 2.50 6.00
S84 Cam Russell 2.50 6.00
S85 Daren Puppa 2.50 6.00
S86 Benoit Brunet 2.50 6.00
S87 Paul Ranheim 2.50 6.00
S88 Bob Rouse 2.50 6.00
S89 Todd Elik 2.50 6.00
S90 Darcy Wakaluk 2.50 6.00
S91 Cliff Ronning 2.50 6.00
S92 Pat Conacher 2.50 6.00
S93 Todd Krygier 2.50 6.00
S94 Dave Babych 2.50 6.00
S95 Pat Falloon 2.50 6.00
S96 Don Beaupre 4.00 10.00
S97 Wayne Gretzky/648* 200.00 500.00
S98 Chris Joseph 2.50 6.00
S99 Vyacheslav Kozlov 4.00 10.00
S100 Brent Fedyk 2.50 6.00
S101 Tim Taylor 2.50 6.00
S102 Mike Eastwood 2.50 6.00
S103 Mike Keane 2.50 6.00
S104 Grant Ledyard 2.50 6.00
S105 Rob Dimaio 2.50 6.00
S106 Martin Straka 2.50 6.00
S107 Scott Young 2.50 6.00
S108 Zarley Zalapski 3.00 8.00
S109 Steve Leach 2.50 6.00
S110 Jody Hull 2.50 6.00
S111 Lyle Odelein 2.50 6.00
S112 Bob Corkum 2.50 6.00
S113 Rob Blake 4.00 10.00
S114 Randy Burridge 2.50 6.00
S115 Keith Primeau 4.00 10.00
S116 Glen Wesley 2.50 6.00
S117 Brian Bradley 2.50 6.00
S118 Andrei Kovalenko 2.50 6.00
S119 Patrik Juhlin 2.50 6.00
S120 John Tucker 2.50 6.00
S121 Stephane Fiset 4.00 10.00
S122 Mike Hough 2.50 6.00
S123 Steve Smith 2.50 6.00
S124 Tom Barrasso 4.00 10.00
S125 Ray Whitney 2.50 6.00
S126 Benoit Hogue 2.50 6.00
S127 Stu Barnes 2.50 6.00
S128 Craig Ludwig 4.00 10.00
S129 Curtis Leschyshyn 2.50 6.00
S130 John LeClair 6.00 15.00
S131 Dennis Vial 2.50 6.00
S132 Cory Stillman 2.50 6.00
S133 Roman Hamrlik 2.50 6.00
S134 Al MacInnis 6.00 15.00
S135 Igor Korolev 2.50 6.00
S136 Rick Zombo 2.50 6.00
S137 Zdeno Ciger 2.50 6.00
S138 Brian Savage 2.50 6.00
S139 Paul Ysebaert 2.50 6.00
S140 Brent Sutter 4.00 10.00
S141 Ed Olczyk 2.50 6.00
S142 Adam Creighton 2.50 6.00
S143 Jesse Belanger 2.50 6.00
S144 Glen Murray 2.50 6.00
S145 Alexander Selivanov 2.50 6.00
S146 Trent Yawney 2.50 6.00
S147 Bruce Driver 2.50 6.00
S148 Michael Nylander 2.50 6.00
S149 Martin Gelinas 3.00 8.00
S150 Yanic Perreault 2.50 6.00
S151 Craig Billington 4.00 10.00
S152 Pierre Turgeon 4.00 10.00
S153 Mike Modano 10.00 25.00
S154 Joe Mullen 4.00 10.00
S155 Todd Ewen 2.50 6.00
S156 Petr Nedved 2.50 6.00
S157 Dominic Roussel 2.50 6.00
S158 Murray Baron 2.50 6.00
S159 Robert Dirk 2.50 6.00
S160 Tomas Sandstrom 2.50 6.00
S161 Brian Holzinger 2.50 6.00
S162 Ken Klee 2.50 6.00
S163 Radek Dvorak 2.50 6.00
S164 Marcus Ragnarsson 2.50 6.00
S165 Aaron Gavey 2.50 6.00
S166 Jeff O'Neill 2.50 6.00
S167 Chad Kilger 2.50 6.00
S168 Todd Bertuzzi 6.00 15.00
S169 Robert Svehla 2.50 6.00
S170 Eric Daze 2.50 6.00
S171 Daniel Alfredsson 6.00 15.00
S172 Shane Doan 4.00 10.00
S173 Kyle McLaren 2.50 6.00
S174 Saku Koivu 6.00 15.00
S175 Jere Lehtinen 4.00 10.00
S176 Nikolai Khabibulin 4.00 10.00
S177 Niklas Sundstrom 2.50 6.00
S178 Ed Jovanovski 4.00 10.00
S179 Jason Bonsignore 2.50 6.00
S180 Kenny Jonsson 2.50 6.00
S181 Vitali Yachmenev 2.50 6.00
S182 Alexei Kovalev 4.00 10.00
S183 Sandis Ozolinsh 2.50 6.00
S184 Rob Niedermayer 6.00 15.00
S185 Richard Park 2.50 6.00
S186 Adam Deadmarsh 2.50 6.00
S187 Sergei Krivokrasov 2.50 6.00
S188 Alexandre Daigle 4.00 10.00
S189 Jim Carey 4.00 10.00
S190 Todd Marchant 4.00 10.00
S191 Mike Richter Mail In 60.00 120.00
S192 Dominik Hasek 10.00 25.00
S193 Chris Osgood 6.00 15.00
S194 Ed Belfour 6.00 15.00
S195 Felix Potvin 8.00 20.00
S196 Grant Fuhr 6.00 15.00
S197 Patrick Roy 20.00 50.00
S198 Ron Hextall 6.00 15.00
S199 Jocelyn Thibault 4.00 10.00
S200 Kirk McLean 4.00 10.00
S201 Jari Kurri 6.00 15.00
S202 Bobby Holik 4.00 10.00
S203 Mats Sundin 8.00 20.00
S204 Alexander Mogilny 5.00 12.00
S205 Valeri Karpov 2.50 6.00
S206 Igor Larionov 4.00 10.00
S207 Valeri Zelepukin 2.50 6.00
S208 Jozef Stumpel 2.50 6.00
S209 Sergei Nemchinov 2.50 6.00
S210 Peter Bondra 4.00 10.00
S211 Chris Chelios 6.00 15.00
S212 Adam Graves 2.50 6.00
S213 Dale Hunter 4.00 10.00
S214 Tony Twist 5.00 12.00
S215 Keith Tkachuk 4.00 10.00
S216 Vladimir Konstantinov 25.00 60.00
S217 Sandy McCarthy 2.50 6.00
S218 Jamie Macoun 2.50 6.00
S219 Scott Stevens 6.00 15.00
S220 Mark Tinordi 2.50 6.00
S221 Bob Probert 8.00 20.00
S222 Gino Odjick 2.50 6.00
S223 Ulf Samuelsson 2.50 6.00
S224 Stu Grimson 4.00 10.00
S225 Marty McSorley 2.50 6.00

1995-96 Be A Player Autographs Die Cut

*DIE CUT: .6X TO 1.5X BASE AU/3000
S97 Wayne Gretzky/234* 400.00 1000.00

1995-96 Be A Player Gretzky's Great Memories

COMPLETE SET (10) 40.00 80.00
COMMON GRETZKY (GM1-GM10) 4.00 10.00

1995-96 Be A Player Lethal Lines

COMPLETE SET (15) 20.00 50.00
LL1 Keith Tkachuk 1.50 4.00
LL2 Wayne Gretzky 5.00 12.00
LL3 Brett Hull 2.00 5.00
LL4 Eric Daze 1.50 4.00
LL5 Saku Koivu 1.50 4.00
LL6 Daniel Alfredsson 1.50 4.00
LL7 Pavel Bure 1.50 4.00
LL8 Sergei Fedorov 1.50 4.00
LL9 Alexander Mogilny 1.50 4.00
LL10 Paul Kariya 1.50 4.00
LL11 Mario Lemieux 3.00 8.00
LL12 Jaromir Jagr 2.00 5.00
LL13 Brendan Shanahan 1.50 4.00
LL14 Eric Lindros 1.50 4.00
LL15 Alexei Kovalev 1.25 3.00

1996-97 Be A Player

1 Todd Gill .15 .40
2 Dave Andreychuk .20 .50
3 Igor Kravchuk .12 .30
4 Tom Fitzgerald .12 .30
5 Jeremy Roenick .40 1.00
6 Peter Popovic .12 .30
7 Andy Moog .20 .50
8 Steven Rice .12 .30
9 Darren Langdon .12 .30
10 Mark Fitzpatrick .12 .30
11 Alexei Zhamnov .15 .40
12 Luc Robitaille .20 .50
13 Michal Pivonka .12 .30
14 Kevin Hatcher .12 .30
15 Stephane Yelle .12 .30
16 Bill Ranford .15 .40
17 Jamie Baker .12 .30
18 Sean Burke .12 .30
19 Al Iafrate .12 .30
20 Mark Recchi .25 .60
21 Rod Brind'Amour .20 .50
22 Doug Gilmour .25 .60
23 Mike Wilson .12 .30
24 Barry Potomski RC .12 .30
25 Mike Gartner .25 .60
26 Jason Wiemer .12 .30
27 Scott Lachance .12 .30
28 Joe Murphy .12 .30
29 Bill Guerin .20 .50
30 Byron Dafoe .15 .40
31 Esa Tikkanen .12 .30
32 Ken Baumgartner .12 .30
33 Valeri Kamensky .15 .40
34 J.J. Daigneault .12 .30
35 Ulf Dahlen .12 .30
36 Jason Allison .15 .40
37 Ted Donato .12 .30
38 Pat Verbeek .12 .30
39 Miroslav Satan .15 .40
40 Eric Desjardins .15 .40
41 Dave Karpa .12 .30
42 Jeff Hackett .15 .40
43 Doug Brown .12 .30
44 Gord Murphy .12 .30
45 Kelly Hrudey .15 .40
46 Kelly Miller .12 .30
47 Tie Domi .15 .40
48 Alexei Yashin .15 .40
49 German Titov .12 .30
50 Stephane Richer .15 .40
51 Corey Hirsch .15 .40
52 Brad May .12 .30
53 Joe Nieuwendyk .15 .40
54 Sylvain Lefebvre .12 .30
55 Brian Leetch .30 .75
56 Petr Svoboda .12 .30
57 Dave Manson .12 .30
58 Jason Woolley .12 .30
59 Scott Niedermayer .20 .50
60 Kelly Chase .12 .30
61 Guy Hebert .15 .40
62 Shayne Corson .15 .40
63 Jon Casey .15 .40
64 Rob Zettler .12 .30
65 Mikael Andersson .12 .30
66 Tony Amonte .15 .40
67 Johan Garpenlov .12 .30
68 Denny Lambert .12 .30
69 Jim McKenzie .12 .30
70 Darren Turcotte .12 .30
71 Eric Weinrich .12 .30
72 Troy Mallette .12 .30
73 Donald Audette .12 .30
74 Philippe Boucher .12 .30
75 Shawn Chambers .12 .30
76 Joel Otto .12 .30
77 Tommy Salo .15 .40
78 Olaf Kolzig .30 .75
79 Adrian Aucoin .12 .30
80 Alek Stojanov .12 .30
81 Robert Reichel .12 .30
82 Marc Bureau .12 .30
83 Alexander Godynyuk .12 .30
84 Bill Berg .12 .30
85 Marc Bergevin .12 .30
86 Kevin Kaminski .12 .30
87 Uwe Krupp .12 .30
88 Boris Mironov .12 .30
89 Bob Bassen .12 .30
90 Darryl Shannon .12 .30
91 Mikael Renberg .15 .40
92 Mike Stapleton .12 .30
93 David Roberts .12 .30
94 Peter Zezel .12 .30
95 Mathieu Dandenault .12 .30
96 Bobby Dollas .12 .30
97 Don Sweeney .12 .30
98 Niklas Andersson .12 .30
99 Pat Jablonski .15 .40
100 John Slaney .12 .30
101 Kevin Todd .12 .30
102 Jamie Pushor .12 .30
103 Andreas Johansson RC .12 .30
104 Corey Schwab .15 .40
105 Todd Simpson RC .12 .30
106 Landon Wilson .12 .30
107 Daniel Goneau RC .20 .50
108 David Wilkie .12 .30
109 Andreas Dackell RC .20 .50
110 Marek Malik .12 .30
111 Mark Messier .30 .75
112 Francois Leroux .12 .30
113 Michal Sykora .12 .30
114 Rob Zamuner .12 .30
115 Craig Berube .12 .30
116 Mike Ricci .12 .30
117 Adam Burt .12 .30
118 Alexander Karpovtsev .12 .30
119 Shawn McEachern .12 .30
120 Shawn Antoski .12 .30
121 Dave Reid .12 .30
122 Todd Warriner .12 .30
123 Markus Naslund .20 .50
124 Martin Rucinsky .12 .30
125 Bob Carpenter .15 .40
126 Dean McAmmond .12 .30
127 Trevor Kidd .12 .30
128 Martin Lapointe .12 .30
129 Enrico Ciccone .12 .30
130 Dixon Ward .12 .30
131 Jason Muzzatti .15 .40
132 Bryan Smolinski .12 .30
133 Norm Maciver .12 .30
134 Fredrik Olausson .12 .30
135 Daniel Lacroix .12 .30
136 Mike Peluso .12 .30
137 Andrei Nikolishin .12 .30
138 Rhett Warrener .12 .30
139 Ray Ferraro .12 .30
140 Glenn Healy .15 .40
141 Steve Duchesne .12 .30
142 Tony Granato .12 .30
143 Cory Cross .12 .30
144 Jon Klemm .12 .30
145 Sami Kapanen .12 .30
146 Grant Marshall .12 .30
147 Matthew Barnaby .12 .30
148 Lyle Odelein .12 .30
149 Joe Dziedzic .12 .30
150 Sergei Gonchar .12 .30
151 Doug Zmolek .12 .30
152 Sean O'Donnell RC .12 .30
153 Scott Thornton .12 .30
154 Steve Heinze .12 .30
155 Garry Valk .12 .30
156 Jeff Finley .12 .30
157 Trent Klatt .12 .30
158 Jeff Beukeboom .12 .30
159 Theo Fleury .40 1.00
160 Dana Murzyn .12 .30
161 Tommy Albelin .15 .40
162 Bryan McCabe .12 .30
163 Shaun Van Allen .12 .30
164 Rick Tabaracci .15 .40
165 Kevin Miller .12 .30
166 Mariusz Czerkawski .12 .30
167 Gerald Diduck .12 .30
168 Brad McCrimmon .12 .30
169 Stephane Matteau .12 .30
170 Scott Daniels .12 .30
171 Scott Mellanby .15 .40
172 Sandy Moger .12 .30
173 Steve Konowalchuk .12 .30
174 Doug Weight .20 .50
175 Darren McCarty .15 .40
176 Darryl Sydor .12 .30
177 Dave Ellett .12 .30
178 Bob Boughner RC .12 .30
179 Derek Armstrong .12 .30
180 Gary Suter .12 .30
181 Donald Brashear .12 .30
182 Chris Tamer .12 .30
183 Darrin Shannon .12 .30
184 Stanislav Neckar .12 .30
185 Brent Severyn .12 .30
186 Steve Rucchin .12 .30
187 Jeff Norton .15 .40
188 Steven Finn .12 .30
189 Kjell Samuelsson .12 .30
190 Jeff Friesen .12 .30
191 Shawn Burr .12 .30
192 Paul Laus .12 .30
193 Jeff Odgers .12 .30
194 Keith Jones .12 .30
195 Richard Matvichuk .12 .30
196 Adam Foote .12 .30
197 Bob Errey .12 .30
198 Ryan Smyth .15 .40
199 Mark Janssens .12 .30
200 Claude Lapointe .12 .30
201 Brian Noonan .12 .30
202 Damian Rhodes .15 .40
203 Dale Hawerchuk .25 .60
204 Bill Lindsay .12 .30
205 Brian Skrudland .12 .30
206 Curtis Joseph .30 .75
207 Jon Rohloff .12 .30
208 Doug Bodger .12 .30
209 Steve Sullivan RC .15 .40
210 Ricard Persson .12 .30
211 Dwayne Roloson RC 2.00 5.00
212 Mike Dunham .12 .30
213 Marcel Cousineau RC .12 .30
214 Eric Fichaud .15 .40
215 Matt Johnson .12 .30
216 Fredrik Modin RC .20 .50
217 Denis Pederson .12 .30
218 Kevin Hodson RC .20 .50
219 Drew Bannister .12 .30
220 Mike Grier RC .50 1.25
P44 Gord Murphy PROMO .12 .30
P52 Brad May PROMO .12 .30
P55 Brian Leetch PROMO .15 .40
P67 Johan Garpenlov PROMO .12 .30
P89 Bob Bassen PROMO .12 .30
P91 Mikael Renberg PROMO .15 .40
P119 Shawn MacEachern PROMO .12 .30
P176 Darryl Sydor PROMO .12 .30
P181 Donald Brashear PROMO .12 .30
P217 Denis Pederson PROMO .12 .30
P218 Kevin Hodson PROMO .20 .50
P219 Drew Bannister PROMO .12 .30

1996-97 Be A Player Autographs

*SILVER AUTO: .6X TO 1.5X BASIC AU
1 Todd Gill 2.00 5.00
2 Dave Andreychuk 2.50 6.00
3 Igor Kravchuk 1.50 4.00
4 Tom Fitzgerald 1.50 4.00
5 Jeremy Roenick 4.00 10.00
6 Peter Popovic 1.50 4.00
7 Andy Moog 2.50 6.00
8 Steven Rice 1.50 4.00
9 Darren Langdon 1.50 4.00
10 Mark Fitzpatrick 1.50 4.00
11 Alexei Zhamnov 1.50 4.00
12 Luc Robitaille 2.50 6.00
13 Michal Pivonka 1.50 4.00
14 Kevin Hatcher 1.50 4.00
15 Stephane Yelle 1.50 4.00
16 Bill Ranford 2.00 5.00
17 Jamie Baker 1.50 4.00
18 Sean Burke 1.50 4.00
19 Al Iafrate 1.50 4.00
20 Mark Recchi 3.00 8.00
21 Rod Brind'Amour 2.50 6.00
22 Doug Gilmour 3.00 8.00
23 Mike Wilson 1.50 4.00
24 Barry Potomski 1.50 4.00
25 Mike Gartner 3.00 8.00
26 Jason Wiemer 1.50 4.00
27 Scott Lachance 1.50 4.00
28 Joe Murphy 1.50 4.00
29 Bill Guerin 2.50 6.00
30 Byron Dafoe 2.00 5.00
31 Esa Tikkanen 1.50 4.00
32 Ken Baumgartner 1.50 4.00
33 Valeri Kamensky 2.00 5.00
34 J.J. Daigneault 1.50 4.00
35 Ulf Dahlen 1.50 4.00
36 Jason Allison 2.00 5.00
37 Ted Donato 1.50 4.00
38 Pat Verbeek 1.50 4.00
39 Miroslav Satan 1.50 4.00
40 Eric Desjardins 2.00 5.00
41 Dave Karpa 1.50 4.00
42 Jeff Hackett 2.00 5.00
43 Doug Brown 1.50 4.00
44 Gord Murphy 1.50 4.00
45 Kelly Hrudey 2.00 5.00
46 Kelly Miller 1.50 4.00
47 Tie Domi 2.00 5.00
48 Alexei Yashin 2.00 5.00
49 German Titov 1.50 4.00
50 Stephane Richer 2.00 5.00
51 Corey Hirsch 2.00 5.00
52 Brad May 1.50 4.00
53 Joe Nieuwendyk 2.00 5.00
54 Sylvain Lefebvre 1.50 4.00
55 Brian Leetch 2.00 5.00
56 Petr Svoboda 1.50 4.00
57 Dave Manson 1.50 4.00
58 Jason Woolley 1.50 4.00
59 Scott Niedermayer 2.50 6.00
60 Kelly Chase 1.50 4.00
61 Guy Hebert 2.00 5.00
62 Shayne Corson 2.00 5.00
63 Jon Casey 2.00 5.00
64 Rob Zettler 1.50 4.00
65 Mikael Andersson 1.50 4.00
66 Tony Amonte 2.00 5.00
67 Johan Garpenlov 1.50 4.00
68 Denny Lambert 1.50 4.00
69 Jim McKenzie 1.50 4.00
70 Darren Turcotte 1.50 4.00
71 Eric Weinrich 1.50 4.00
72 Troy Mallette 1.50 4.00
73 Donald Audette 1.50 4.00
74 Philippe Boucher 1.50 4.00
75 Shawn Chambers 1.50 4.00
76 Joel Otto 1.50 4.00
77 Tommy Salo 2.00 5.00
78 Olaf Kolzig 2.50 6.00
79 Adrian Aucoin 1.50 4.00
80 Alek Stojanov 1.50 4.00
81 Robert Reichel 1.50 4.00
82 Marc Bureau 1.50 4.00
83 Alexander Godynyuk 1.50 4.00
84 Bill Berg 1.50 4.00
85 Marc Bergevin 1.50 4.00
86 Kevin Kaminski 1.50 4.00
87 Uwe Krupp 1.50 4.00
88 Boris Mironov 1.50 4.00
89 Bob Bassen 1.50 4.00
90 Darryl Shannon 1.50 4.00
91 Mikael Renberg 2.00 5.00
92 Mike Stapleton 1.50 4.00
93 David Roberts 1.50 4.00
94 Peter Zezel 1.50 4.00
95 Mathieu Dandenault 1.50 4.00
96 Bobby Dollas 1.50 4.00
97 Don Sweeney 1.50 4.00
98 Niklas Andersson 1.50 4.00
99 Pat Jablonski 2.00 5.00
100 John Slaney 1.50 4.00
101 Kevin Todd 1.50 4.00
102 Jamie Pushor 1.50 4.00
103 Andreas Johansson 1.50 4.00
104 Corey Schwab 2.00 5.00
105 Todd Simpson 1.50 4.00
106 Landon Wilson 1.50 4.00
107 Daniel Goneau 2.50 6.00
108 David Wilkie 1.50 4.00
109 Andreas Dackell 2.50 6.00
110 Marek Malik 1.50 4.00
111 Mark Messier 12.00 30.00
112 Francois Leroux 1.50 4.00
113 Michal Sykora 1.50 4.00
114 Rob Zamuner 1.50 4.00
115 Craig Berube 1.50 4.00
116 Mike Ricci 1.50 4.00
117 Adam Burt 1.50 4.00
118 Alexander Karpovtsev 1.50 4.00
119 Shawn McEachern 1.50 4.00
120 Shawn Antoski 1.50 4.00
121 Dave Reid 1.50 4.00
122 Todd Warriner 1.50 4.00
123 Markus Naslund 2.50 6.00
124 Martin Rucinsky 1.50 4.00
125 Bob Carpenter 2.00 5.00
126 Dean McAmmond 1.50 4.00
127 Trevor Kidd 1.50 4.00
128 Martin Lapointe 1.50 4.00
129 Enrico Ciccone 1.50 4.00
130 Dixon Ward 1.50 4.00
131 Jason Muzzatti 2.00 5.00
132 Bryan Smolinski 1.50 4.00
133 Norm Maciver 1.50 4.00
134 Fredrik Olausson 1.50 4.00
135 Daniel Lacroix 1.50 4.00
136 Mike Peluso 1.50 4.00
137 Andrei Nikolishin 1.50 4.00
138 Rhett Warrener 1.50 4.00
139 Ray Ferraro 1.50 4.00
140 Glenn Healy 2.00 5.00
141 Steve Duchesne 1.50 4.00
142 Tony Granato 1.50 4.00
143 Cory Cross 1.50 4.00
144 Jon Klemm 1.50 4.00
145 Sami Kapanen 1.50 4.00
146 Grant Marshall 1.50 4.00
147 Matthew Barnaby 1.50 4.00
148 Lyle Odelein 1.50 4.00
149 Joe Dziedzic 1.50 4.00
150 Sergei Gonchar 1.50 4.00
151 Doug Zmolek 1.50 4.00
152 Sean O'Donnell 1.50 4.00
153 Scott Thornton 1.50 4.00
154 Steve Heinze 1.50 4.00
155 Garry Valk 1.50 4.00
156 Jeff Finley 1.50 4.00
157 Trent Klatt 1.50 4.00
158 Jeff Beukeboom 1.50 4.00
159 Theo Fleury 5.00 12.00
160 Dana Murzyn 1.50 4.00
161 Tommy Albelin 2.00 5.00
162 Bryan McCabe 1.50 4.00
163 Shaun Van Allen 1.50 4.00
164 Rick Tabaracci 2.00 5.00
165 Kevin Miller 1.50 4.00
166 Mariusz Czerkawski 1.50 4.00
167 Gerald Diduck 1.50 4.00
168 Brad McCrimmon 1.50 4.00
169 Stephane Matteau 1.50 4.00
170 Scott Daniels 1.50 4.00
171 Scott Mellanby 2.00 5.00
172 Sandy Moger 1.50 4.00
173 Steve Konowalchuk 1.50 4.00
174 Doug Weight 2.50 6.00
175 Darren McCarty 1.50 4.00
176 Darryl Sydor 1.50 4.00
177 Dave Ellett 1.50 4.00
178 Bob Boughner 1.50 4.00
179 Derek Armstrong 1.50 4.00
180 Gary Suter 1.50 4.00
181 Donald Brashear 1.50 4.00
182 Chris Tamer 1.50 4.00
183 Darrin Shannon 1.50 4.00
184 Stanislav Neckar 1.50 4.00
185 Brent Severyn 1.50 4.00
186 Steve Rucchin 1.50 4.00
187 Jeff Norton 2.00 5.00
188 Steven Finn 1.50 4.00
189 Kjell Samuelsson 1.50 4.00
190 Jeff Friesen 1.50 4.00
191 Shawn Burr 1.50 4.00
192 Paul Laus 1.50 4.00
193 Jeff Odgers 1.50 4.00
194 Keith Jones 1.50 4.00
195 Richard Matvichuk 1.50 4.00
196 Adam Foote 1.50 4.00
197 Bob Errey 1.50 4.00
198 Ryan Smyth 2.00 5.00
199 Mark Janssens 1.50 4.00
200 Claude Lapointe 1.50 4.00
201 Brian Noonan 1.50 4.00
202 Damian Rhodes 2.00 5.00
203 Dale Hawerchuk 3.00 8.00
204 Bill Lindsay 1.50 4.00
205 Brian Skrudland 1.50 4.00
206 Curtis Joseph 5.00 12.00
207 Jon Rohloff 1.50 4.00
208 Doug Bodger 1.50 4.00

209 Steve Sullivan 2.00 5.00
210 Ricard Persson 1.50 4.00
211 Dwayne Roloson 1.50 4.00
212 Mike Dunham 1.50 4.00
213 Marcel Cousineau 1.50 4.00
214 Eric Fichaud 2.00 5.00
215 Matt Johnson 1.50 4.00
216 Fredrik Modin 2.50 6.00
217 Denis Pederson 1.50 4.00
218 Kevin Hodson 2.50 6.00
219 Drew Bannister 1.50 4.00
220 Mike Grier 3.00 8.00

1996-97 Be A Player Biscuit In The Basket

COMPLETE SET (25) 25.00 60.00
1 Wayne Gretzky 8.00 20.00
2 Mario Lemieux 5.00 12.00
3 Eric Lindros 2.00 5.00
4 Theo Fleury 2.50 6.00
5 Peter Forsberg 2.50 6.00
6 Keith Tkachuk 1.25 3.00
7 Sergei Fedorov 2.00 5.00
8 Mike Modano 2.00 5.00
9 Jaromir Jagr 4.00 10.00
10 Brendan Shanahan 1.25 3.00
11 Teemu Selanne 2.50 6.00
12 Mats Sundin 1.25 3.00
13 Steve Yzerman 3.00 8.00
14 Brett Hull 2.50 6.00
15 Zigmund Palffy 1.25 3.00
16 Joe Sakic 2.50 6.00
17 John LeClair 1.25 3.00
18 Pavel Bure 1.25 3.00
19 Mark Messier 2.50 6.00
20 Paul Kariya 1.25 3.00
21 Jason Arnott 1.00 2.50
22 Saku Koivu 1.25 3.00
23 Daniel Alfredsson 1.25 3.00
24 Alexander Mogilny 1.00 2.50
25 Owen Nolan 1.25 3.00

1996-97 Be A Player Lemieux Die Cut

1 Mario Lemieux 100.00 200.00
2 Mario Lemieux 100.00 200.00

1996-97 Be A Player Lindros Die Cut

1 Eric Lindros AU 60.00 150.00
2 Eric Lindros AU 60.00 150.00

1996-97 Be A Player Link to History

COMPLETE SET (20) 8.00 20.00
COMP.SERIES 1 (10) 4.00 10.00
COMP.SERIES 2 (10) 4.00 10.00
1A Jarome Iginla .75 2.00
1B Teemu Selanne 1.25 3.00
2A Harry York .60 1.50
2B Peter Forsberg 1.25 3.00
3A Sergei Berezin 1.00 2.50
3B Brendan Shanahan .60 1.50
4A Ethan Moreau .60 1.50
4B Pavel Bure .60 1.50
5A Rem Murray .60 1.50
5B Jason Arnott .50 1.25
6A Jamie Langenbrunner .40 1.00
6B Paul Kariya .60 1.50
7A Jim Campbell .40 1.00
7B Eric Lindros 1.00 2.50
8A Jonas Hoglund .40 1.00
8B Pat LaFontaine .60 1.50
9A Wade Redden .40 1.00
9B Steve Yzerman 1.50 4.00
10A Patrick Lalime .75 2.00
10B John Vanbiesbrouck .60 1.50
2B Peter Forsberg PROMO 1.25 3.00

1996-97 Be A Player Link to History Autographs

*SILVER AUTO: .8X TO 2X BASIC AU
1A Jarome Iginla 6.00 15.00
1B Teemu Selanne 10.00 25.00
2A Harry York 5.00 12.00
2B Peter Forsberg 12.00 30.00
3A Sergei Berezin 8.00 20.00
3B Brendan Shanahan 5.00 12.00
4A Ethan Moreau 5.00 12.00
4B Pavel Bure 10.00 25.00
5A Rem Murray 5.00 12.00
5B Jason Arnott 4.00 10.00
6A Jamie Langenbrunner 3.00 8.00
6B Paul Kariya 12.00 30.00
7A Jim Campbell 3.00 8.00
7B Eric Lindros 15.00 40.00
8A Jonas Hoglund 3.00 8.00
8B Pat LaFontaine 5.00 12.00
9A Wade Redden 3.00 8.00
9B Steve Yzerman 15.00 40.00
10A Patrick Lalime 6.00 15.00
10B John Vanbiesbrouck 5.00 12.00

1996-97 Be A Player Stacking the Pads

COMPLETE SET (15) 12.00 30.00
1 Patrick Lalime .75 2.00
2 Chris Osgood .60 1.50
3 Ron Hextall .60 1.50
4 John Vanbiesbrouck .60 1.50
5 Martin Brodeur 4.00 10.00
6 Felix Potvin 1.50 4.00
7 Nikolai Khabibulin .50 1.25
8 Jim Carey .60 1.50
9 Grant Fuhr 1.00 2.50
10 Mike Richter .60 1.50
11 Dominik Hasek 1.25 3.00
12 Andy Moog .60 1.50
13 Patrick Roy 4.00 10.00
14 Curtis Joseph .75 2.00
15 Jocelyn Thibault .50 1.25

1997-98 Be A Player

COMPLETE SET (250) 6.00 15.00
1 Eric Lindros .50 1.25
2 Martin Brodeur .75 2.00
3 Saku Koivu .30 .75
4 Felix Potvin .50 1.25
5 Adam Oates .30 .75
6 Rob DiMaio .20 .50
7 Jari Kurri .30 .75
8 Andrew Cassels .20 .50
9 Trevor Linden .30 .75
10 Jocelyn Thibault .25 .60
11 Chris Chelios .30 .75
12 Paul Coffey .30 .75
13 Nikolai Khabibulin .30 .75
14 Robert Lang .20 .50
15 Brett Hull .60 1.50
16 Mike Sillinger .20 .50
17 Lyle Odelein .20 .50
18 Bryan Berard .20 .50
19 Craig Muni .20 .50
20 Kris Draper .20 .50
21 Ed Jovanovski .20 .50
22 Keith Tkachuk .30 .75
23 Dean Malkoc .25 .60
24 Cory Stillman .25 .60
25 Chris Osgood .30 .75
26 Dainius Zubrus .25 .60
27 Yves Racine .25 .60
28 Eric Cairns RC .30 .75
29 Dan Bylsma .25 .60
30 Chris Terreri .20 .50
31 Bill Huard .25 .60
32 Warren Rychel .25 .60
33 Scott Walker .25 .60
34 Brian Holzinger .25 .60
35 Roman Turek .25 .60
36 Ron Tugnutt .30 .75
37 Mike Richter .30 .75
38 Mattias Norstrom .25 .60
39 Joe Sacco .25 .60
40 Derek King .25 .60
41 Brad Werenka .20 .50
42 Paul Kruse .25 .60
43 Mike Knuble RC .30 .75
44 Mike Peca .25 .60
45 Jean-Yves Leroux RC .30 .75
46 Ray Sheppard .25 .60
47 Reid Simpson .25 .60
48 Rob Brown .25 .60
49 Dave Babych .20 .50
50 Scott Pellerin .20 .50
51 Bruce Gardiner RC .25 .60
52 Adam Deadmarsh .20 .50
53 Curtis Brown .20 .50
54 Jason Marshall .20 .50
55 Gerald Diduck .20 .50
56 Mick Vukota .20 .50
57 Kevin Dean .20 .50
58 Adam Graves .20 .50
59 Craig Conroy .20 .50
60 Cale Hulse .25 .60
61 Dimitri Khristich .25 .60
62 Chris Wells .25 .60
63 Travis Green .25 .60
64 Tyler Wright .25 .60
65 Chris Simon .25 .60
66 Mikhail Shtalenkov .25 .60
67 Anson Carter .20 .50
68 Zarley Zalapski .20 .50
69 Per Gustafsson .25 .60
70 Jayson More .25 .60
71 Steve Thomas .25 .60
72 Todd Marchant .25 .60
73 Gary Roberts .25 .60
74 Richard Smehlik .20 .50
75 Aaron Miller .20 .50
76 Daren Puppa .25 .60
77 Garth Snow .25 .60
78 Greg DeVries .25 .60
79 Randy Burridge .20 .50
80 Jim Cummins .25 .60
81 Rich Pilon .25 .60
82 Chris McAlpine .20 .50
83 Joe Sakic .60 1.50
84 Ted Drury .25 .60
85 Brent Gilchrist .30 .75
86 Dallas Eakins RC .30 .75
87 Bruce Driver .25 .60
88 Jamie Huscroft .25 .60
89 Jeff Brown .25 .60
90 Janne Laukkanen .25 .60
91 Ken Klee .25 .60
92 Peter Bondra .30 .75
93 Ian Moran .25 .60
94 Stephane Quintal .25 .60
95 Jason York .25 .60
96 Todd Harvey .25 .60
97 Slava Kozlov .25 .60
98 Kevin Haller .25 .60
99 Alexei Zhamnov .20 .50
100 Craig Johnson .20 .50
101 Mike Keane .20 .50
102 Craig Rivet .25 .60
103 Roman Vopat .25 .60
104 Jim Johnson .25 .60
105 Ray Whitney .25 .60
106 Ron Sutter .25 .60
107 Jamie McLennan .20 .50
108 Kris King .20 .50
109 Lance Pitlick RC .30 .75
110 Mike Dunham .25 .60
111 Jim Dowd .25 .60
112 Geoff Sanderson .25 .60
113 Vladimir Vujtek .25 .60
114 Tim Taylor .25 .60
115 Sandis Ozolinsh .20 .50
116 Scott Daniels .25 .60
117 Bob Corkum .25 .60
118 Kirk McLean .25 .60
119 Darcy Tucker .30 .75
120 Dennis Vaske .25 .60
121 Kirk Muller .20 .50
122 Jay McKee .20 .50
123 Jere Lehtinen .25 .60
124 Ruslan Salei .25 .60
125 Al MacInnis .40 1.00
126 Ulf Samuelsson .30 .75
127 Rick Tocchet .20 .50
128 Nick Kypreos .20 .50
129 Joel Bouchard .20 .50
130 Jeff O'Neill .25 .60
131 Daniel McGillis RC .25 .60
132 Sean Pronger .20 .50
133 Vladimir Malakhov .20 .50
134 Petr Sykora .20 .50
135 Zigmund Palffy .30 .75
136 Joe Reekie .20 .50
137 Chris Gratton .20 .50
138 Craig Billington .20 .50
139 Steve Washburn .20 .50
140 Robert Kron .20 .50
141 Larry Murphy .25 .60
142 Shean Donovan .25 .60
143 Scott Young .25 .60
144 Janne Niinimaa .25 .60
145 Ken Belanger RC .30 .75
146 Pavol Demitra .40 1.00
147 Roman Hamrlik .20 .50
148 Lonny Bohonos .25 .60
149 Mike Eagles .25 .60
150 Kelly Buchberger .25 .60
151 Mattias Timander .25 .60
152 Benoit Hogue .25 .60
153 Joey Kocur .20 .50
154 Mats Lindgren .20 .50
155 Aki Berg .20 .50
156 Tim Sweeney .20 .50
157 Vincent Damphousse .25 .60
158 Dan Kordic .25 .60
159 Darius Kasparaitis .25 .60
160 Randy McKay .25 .60
161 Steve Staios .25 .60
162 Brendan Witt .25 .60
163 Paul Ysebaert .25 .60
164 Greg Adams .25 .60
165 Kent Manderville .20 .50
166 Steve Dubinsky .20 .50
167 David Nemirovsky .20 .50
168 Todd Bertuzzi .30 .75
169 Frederic Chabot RC .25 .60
170 Dmitri Mironov .25 .60
171 Pat Peake .25 .60
172 Ed Ward .25 .60
173 Jeff Shantz .25 .60
174 Dave Gagner .20 .50
175 Randy Cunneyworth .20 .50
176 Daymond Langkow .20 .50
177 Alex Hicks .20 .50
178 Darby Hendrickson .20 .50
179 Mike Sullivan .20 .50
180 Anders Eriksson .25 .60
181 Turner Stevenson .25 .60
182 Shane Churla .25 .60
183 Dave Lowry .20 .50
184 Joe Juneau .20 .50
185 Bob Essensa .25 .60
186 James Black .20 .50
187 Michal Grosek .20 .50
188 Tomas Holmstrom .20 .50
189 Ian Laperriere .20 .50
190 Terry Yake .20 .50
191 Jason Smith .20 .50
192 Sergei Zholtok .25 .60
193 Doug Houda .25 .60
194 Guy Carbonneau .30 .75
195 Terry Carkner .25 .60
196 Alexei Gusarov .25 .60
197 Vladimir Tsyplakov .25 .60
198 Jarrod Skalde .25 .60
199 Marty Murray .25 .60
200 Aaron Ward .20 .50
201 Bobby Holik .20 .50
202 Steve Chiasson .20 .50
203 Brantt Myhres .20 .50
204 Eric Messier RC .30 .75
205 Rene Corbet .25 .60
206 Mathieu Schneider .25 .60
207 Tom Chorske .25 .60
208 Doug Lidster .25 .60
209 Igor Ulanov .25 .60
210 Blair Atcheynum RC .30 .75
211 Sebastien Bordeleau .25 .60
212 Alexei Morozov .25 .60
213 Vaclav Prospal RC .25 .60
214 Brad Bombardir RC .25 .60
215 Mattias Ohlund .25 .60
216 Chris Dingman RC .30 .75
217 Erik Rasmussen .25 .60
218 Mike Johnson RC .25 .60
219 Chris Phillips .25 .60
220 Sergei Samsonov .25 .60
221 Patrick Marleau .30 .75
222 Alyn McCauley .25 .60
223 Ryan Vandenbussche RC .25 .60
224 Daniel Cleary .25 .60
225 Magnus Arvedson RC .30 .75
226 Brad Isbister .25 .60
227 Pascal Rheaume RC .25 .60
228 Patrik Elias RC .50 1.25
229 Krzysztof Oliwa RC .30 .75
230 Tyler Moss RC .25 .60
231 Jamie Rivers .25 .60
232 Joe Thornton .50 1.25
233 Steve Shields RC .30 .75
234 Dave Scatchard RC .25 .60
235 Patrick Cote RC .25 .60
236 Rich Brennan RC .25 .60
237 Boyd Devereaux .25 .60
238 Per Johan Axelsson RC .30 .75
239 Craig Millar RC .25 .60
240 Juha Ylonen .25 .60
241 Donald MacLean RC .30 .75
242 Jaroslav Svejkovsky .25 .60
243 Marco Sturm RC .30 .75
244 Steve McKenna RC .40 1.00
245 Derek Morris RC .30 .75
246 Dean Chynoweth .25 .60
247 Alexander Mogilny .25 .60
248 Ray Bourque .50 1.25
249 Ed Belfour .30 .75
250 John LeClair .30 .75
P3 Saku Koivu PROMO .30 .75

1997-98 Be A Player Autographs

*DIE CUT: .8X TO 2X BASIC AUTO
*DIE CUT: .5X TO 1.2X BASIC AU SP
*PRISM/100: 1.2X TO 3X BASIC AUTO
*PRISM/100: .6X TO 1.5X BASIC AU SP
1 Eric Lindros SP 5.00 12.00
2 Martin Brodeur SP 20.00 50.00
3 Saku Koivu 3.00 8.00
4 Felix Potvin 5.00 12.00
5 Adam Oates 3.00 8.00
6 Rob DiMaio 2.00 5.00
7 Jari Kurri 3.00 8.00
8 Andrew Cassels 2.00 5.00
9 Trevor Linden 3.00 8.00
10 Jocelyn Thibault 2.50 6.00
11 Chris Chelios 3.00 8.00
12 Paul Coffey 3.00 8.00
13 Nikolai Khabibulin 3.00 8.00
14 Robert Lang 2.00 5.00
15 Brett Hull SP 15.00 40.00
16 Mike Sillinger 2.00 5.00
17 Lyle Odelein 2.00 5.00
19 Craig Muni 2.00 5.00
20 Kris Draper 2.00 5.00
21 Ed Jovanovski 2.00 5.00
22 Keith Tkachuk 3.00 8.00
23 Dean Malkoc 2.50 6.00
24 Cory Stillman 2.50 6.00
25 Chris Osgood 3.00 8.00
26 Dainius Zubrus 2.50 6.00
27 Yves Racine 2.50 6.00
28 Eric Cairns 3.00 8.00
29 Dan Bylsma 2.50 6.00
30 Chris Terreri 2.00 5.00
31 Bill Huard 2.50 6.00
32 Warren Rychel 2.50 6.00
33 Scott Walker 2.50 6.00
34 Brian Holzinger 2.50 6.00
35 Roman Turek 2.50 6.00
36 Ron Tugnutt 3.00 8.00
37 Mike Richter 5.00 12.00
38 Mattias Norstrom 2.50 6.00
39 Joe Sacco 2.50 6.00
40 Derek King 2.50 6.00
41 Brad Werenka 2.00 5.00
42 Paul Kruse 2.50 6.00
43 Mike Knuble 3.00 8.00
44 Mike Peca 2.50 6.00
45 Jean-Yves Leroux 3.00 8.00
46 Ray Sheppard 2.50 6.00
47 Reid Simpson 2.50 6.00
48 Rob Brown 2.50 6.00
49 Dave Babych 2.00 5.00
50 Scott Pellerin 2.00 5.00
51 Bruce Gardiner 2.50 6.00
52 Adam Deadmarsh 2.00 5.00
53 Curtis Brown 2.00 5.00
54 Jason Marshall 2.00 5.00
55 Gerald Diduck 2.00 5.00
56 Mick Vukota 2.00 5.00
57 Kevin Dean 2.00 5.00
58 Adam Graves 2.00 5.00
59 Craig Conroy 2.00 5.00
60 Cale Hulse 2.50 6.00
61 Dimitri Khristich 2.50 6.00
62 Chris Wells 2.50 6.00
63 Travis Green 2.50 6.00
64 Tyler Wright 2.50 6.00
65 Chris Simon 2.50 6.00
66 Mikhail Shtalenkov 2.50 6.00
67 Anson Carter 2.00 5.00
68 Zarley Zalapski 2.00 5.00
69 Per Gustafsson 2.50 6.00
70 Jayson More 2.50 6.00
71 Steve Thomas 2.50 6.00
72 Todd Marchant 2.50 6.00
73 Gary Roberts 2.50 6.00
74 Richard Smehlik 2.00 5.00
75 Aaron Miller 2.00 5.00
76 Daren Puppa 2.50 6.00
77 Garth Snow 2.50 6.00
78 Greg DeVries 2.50 6.00
79 Randy Burridge 2.00 5.00
80 Jim Cummins 2.50 6.00
81 Rich Pilon 2.50 6.00
82 Chris McAlpine 2.00 5.00
83 Joe Sakic SP 25.00 60.00
84 Ted Drury 2.50 6.00
85 Brent Gilchrist 3.00 8.00
86 Dallas Eakins 3.00 8.00
87 Bruce Driver 2.50 6.00
88 Jamie Huscroft 2.50 6.00
89 Jeff Brown 2.50 6.00
90 Janne Laukkanen 2.50 6.00
91 Ken Klee 2.50 6.00
92 Peter Bondra 3.00 8.00
93 Ian Moran 2.50 6.00
94 Stephane Quintal 2.50 6.00
95 Jason York 2.50 6.00
96 Todd Harvey 2.50 6.00
97 Slava Kozlov 2.50 6.00
98 Kevin Haller 2.50 6.00
99 Alexei Zhamnov 2.00 5.00
100 Craig Johnson 2.00 5.00
101 Mike Keane 2.00 5.00
102 Craig Rivet 2.50 6.00
103 Roman Vopat 2.50 6.00
104 Jim Johnson 2.50 6.00
105 Ray Whitney 2.50 6.00
106 Ron Sutter 2.50 6.00
107 Jamie McLennan 2.00 5.00
108 Kris King 2.00 5.00
109 Lance Pitlick 3.00 8.00
110 Mike Dunham 2.50 6.00
111 Jim Dowd 2.50 6.00
112 Geoff Sanderson 2.50 6.00
113 Vladimir Vujtek 2.50 6.00
114 Tim Taylor 2.50 6.00
115 Sandis Ozolinsh 2.00 5.00
116 Scott Daniels 2.50 6.00
117 Bob Corkum 2.50 6.00
118 Kirk McLean 2.50 6.00
119 Darcy Tucker 3.00 8.00
120 Dennis Vaske 2.50 6.00
121 Kirk Muller 2.00 5.00
122 Jay McKee 2.00 5.00
123 Jere Lehtinen 2.50 6.00
124 Ruslan Salei 2.50 6.00
125 Al MacInnis SP 8.00 20.00
126 Ulf Samuelsson 3.00 8.00
127 Rick Tocchet 2.00 5.00
128 Nick Kypreos 2.00 5.00
129 Joel Bouchard 2.00 5.00
130 Jeff O'Neill 2.50 6.00
131 Daniel McGillis 2.50 6.00
132 Sean Pronger 2.00 5.00
133 Vladimir Malakhov 2.00 5.00
134 Petr Sykora 2.00 5.00
135 Zigmund Palffy 3.00 8.00
136 Joe Reekie 2.00 5.00
137 Chris Gratton 2.00 5.00
138 Craig Billington 2.00 5.00
139 Steve Washburn 2.00 5.00
140 Robert Kron 2.00 5.00
141 Larry Murphy 2.50 6.00
142 Shean Donovan 2.50 6.00
143 Scott Young 2.50 6.00
144 Janne Niinimaa 2.50 6.00
145 Ken Belanger 3.00 8.00
146 Pavol Demitra 4.00 10.00
147 Roman Hamrlik 2.00 5.00
148 Lonny Bohonos 2.50 6.00
149 Mike Eagles 2.50 6.00
150 Kelly Buchberger 2.50 6.00
151 Mattias Timander 2.50 6.00
152 Benoit Hogue 2.50 6.00
153 Joey Kocur 2.00 5.00
154 Mats Lindgren 2.00 5.00
155 Aki Berg 2.00 5.00
156 Tim Sweeney 2.00 5.00
157 Vincent Damphousse 2.50 6.00
158 Dan Kordic 2.50 6.00
159 Darius Kasparaitis 2.50 6.00
160 Randy McKay 2.50 6.00
161 Steve Staios 2.50 6.00
162 Brendan Witt 2.50 6.00
163 Paul Ysebaert 2.50 6.00
164 Greg Adams 2.50 6.00
165 Kent Manderville 2.00 5.00
166 Steve Dubinsky 2.00 5.00
167 David Nemirovsky 2.00 5.00
168 Todd Bertuzzi 3.00 8.00
169 Frederic Chabot 2.50 6.00
170 Dmitri Mironov 2.50 6.00
171 Pat Peake 2.50 6.00
172 Ed Ward 2.50 6.00
173 Jeff Shantz 2.50 6.00
174 Dave Gagner 2.00 5.00
175 Randy Cunneyworth 2.00 5.00
176 Daymond Langkow 2.00 5.00
177 Alex Hicks 2.00 5.00
178 Darby Hendrickson 2.00 5.00
179 Mike Sullivan 2.00 5.00
180 Anders Eriksson 2.50 6.00
181 Turner Stevenson 2.50 6.00
182 Shane Churla 2.50 6.00
183 Dave Lowry 2.00 5.00
184 Joe Juneau 2.00 5.00
185 Bob Essensa 2.50 6.00
186 James Black 2.00 5.00
187 Michal Grosek 2.00 5.00
188 Tomas Holmstrom 2.00 5.00
189 Ian Laperriere 2.00 5.00
190 Terry Yake 2.00 5.00
191 Jason Smith 2.00 5.00
192 Sergei Zholtok 2.50 6.00
193 Doug Houda 2.50 6.00
194 Guy Carbonneau 3.00 8.00
195 Terry Carkner 2.50 6.00
196 Alexei Gusarov 2.50 6.00
197 Vladimir Tsyplakov 2.50 6.00
198 Jarrod Skalde 2.50 6.00
199 Marty Murray 2.50 6.00
200 Aaron Ward 2.00 5.00
201 Bobby Holik 2.00 5.00
202 Steve Chiasson 2.00 5.00
203 Brantt Myhres 2.00 5.00
204 Eric Messier 3.00 8.00
205 Rene Corbet 2.50 6.00
206 Mathieu Schneider 2.50 6.00
207 Tom Chorske 2.50 6.00
208 Doug Lidster 2.50 6.00
209 Igor Ulanov 2.50 6.00
210 Blair Atcheynum 3.00 8.00
211 Sebastien Bordeleau 2.50 6.00
212 Alexei Morozov 2.50 6.00
213 Vaclav Prospal 2.50 6.00
214 Brad Bombardir 2.50 6.00
215 Mattias Ohlund 2.50 6.00
216 Chris Dingman 3.00 8.00
217 Erik Rasmussen 2.50 6.00
218 Mike Johnson 2.50 6.00
219 Chris Phillips 2.50 6.00
220 Sergei Samsonov 2.50 6.00
221 Patrick Marleau 3.00 8.00
222 Alyn McCauley 2.50 6.00
223 Ryan Vandenbussche 2.50 6.00
224 Daniel Cleary 2.50 6.00
225 Magnus Arvedson 3.00 8.00
226 Brad Isbister 2.50 6.00
227 Pascal Rheaume 2.50 6.00
228 Patrik Elias 5.00 12.00
229 Krzysztof Oliwa 3.00 8.00
230 Tyler Moss 2.50 6.00
231 Jamie Rivers 2.50 6.00
232 Joe Thornton 5.00 12.00
233 Steve Shields 3.00 8.00
234 Dave Scatchard 2.50 6.00
235 Patrick Cote 2.50 6.00
236 Rich Brennan 2.50 6.00
237 Boyd Devereaux 2.50 6.00
238 Per Johan Axelsson 3.00 8.00
239 Craig Millar 2.50 6.00
240 Juha Ylonen 2.50 6.00
241 Donald MacLean 3.00 8.00
242 Jaroslav Svejkovsky 2.50 6.00
243 Marco Sturm 3.00 8.00
244 Steve McKenna 4.00 10.00
245 Derek Morris 3.00 8.00
246 Dean Chynoweth 2.50 6.00
247 Alexander Mogilny SP 12.00 30.00
248 Ray Bourque SP 25.00 60.00
249 Ed Belfour SP 15.00 40.00
250 John LeClair SP 12.00 30.00

1997-98 Be A Player One Timers

COMPLETE SET (20) 12.50 30.00
1 Wayne Gretzky 4.00 10.00
2 Keith Tkachuk .60 1.50
3 Eric Lindros 1.00 2.50
4 Brendan Shanahan .60 1.50
5 Paul Kariya .60 1.50
6 Brett Hull 1.25 3.00
7 Jaromir Jagr 2.00 5.00
8 Teemu Selanne 1.25 3.00
9 John LeClair .60 1.50
10 Mike Modano 1.00 2.50
11 Peter Forsberg 1.25 3.00
12 Pavel Bure .60 1.50
13 Peter Bondra .60 1.50
14 Saku Koivu .60 1.50
15 Pat LaFontaine .60 1.50
16 Patrik Elias 1.00 2.50
17 Richard Zednik .50 1.25
18 Mike Johnson .50 1.25
19 Marco Sturm .60 1.50
20 Joe Thornton 1.00 2.50

1997-98 Be A Player Stacking the Pads

COMPLETE SET (15) 12.00 30.00
1 Guy Hebert .50 1.25
2 Dominik Hasek 3.00 8.00
3 Felix Potvin 1.00 2.50
4 Patrick Roy 3.00 8.00
5 Ed Belfour .60 1.50
6 Chris Osgood .60 1.50
7 Curtis Joseph .75 2.00
8 John Vanbiesbrouck .60 1.50
9 Jocelyn Thibault .50 1.25
10 Mike Richter .60 1.50
11 Martin Brodeur 3.00 8.00
12 Garth Snow .50 1.25
13 Nikolai Khabibulin .60 1.50
14 Tommy Salo .40 1.00
15 Byron Dafoe .50 1.25

1997-98 Be A Player Take A Number

COMPLETE SET (20) 30.00 60.00
TN1 Ray Bourque 2.00 5.00
TN2 Eric Daze .75 2.00
TN3 Ed Belfour 1.00 2.50
TN4 Patrick Roy 5.00 12.00
TN5 Sergei Fedorov 1.25 3.00
TN6 John Vanbiesbrouck .75 2.00
TN7 Doug Gilmour .75 2.00
TN8 Wayne Gretzky 6.00 15.00
TN9 Bryan Berard .75 2.00
TN10 Eric Lindros 1.00 2.50
TN11 Paul Coffey 1.00 2.50
TN12 Jeremy Roenick 1.25 3.00
TN13 Brett Hull 1.25 3.00
TN14 Pierre Turgeon .75 2.00
TN15 Keith Primeau .75 2.00
TN16 Daren Puppa .75 2.00
TN17 Mark Messier 1.00 2.50
TN18 Alexander Mogilny .75 2.00
TN19 Joe Sakic 2.00 5.00
TN20 Jaromir Jagr 1.50 4.00

1998-99 Be A Player

1 Jason Marshall .20 .50
2 Paul Kariya .30 .75
3 Teemu Selanne .60 1.50
4 Guy Hebert .25 .60
5 Ted Drury .20 .50
6 Byron Dafoe .25 .60
7 Rob Dimaio .20 .50
8 Ray Bourque .50 1.25
9 Joe Thornton .50 1.25
10 Sergei Samsonov .25 .60
11 Dimitri Khristich .20 .50
12 Michael Peca .20 .50
13 Jason Woolley .20 .50
14 Matthew Barnaby .20 .50
15 Brian Holzinger .20 .50
16 Dixon Ward .25 .60
17 Tyler Moss .20 .50
18 Jarome Iginla .40 1.00
19 Marty McInnis .20 .50
20 Andrew Cassels .20 .50
21 Jason Wiemer .20 .50
22 Trevor Kidd .20 .50
23 Keith Primeau .25 .60
24 Sami Kapanen .20 .50
25 Robert Kron .20 .50
26 Glen Wesley .20 .50
27 Jeff Hackett .20 .50
28 Tony Amonte .25 .60
29 Alexei Zhamnov .20 .50
30 Eric Weinrich .20 .50
31 Jeff Shantz .20 .50
32 Christian Laflamme .20 .50
33 Adam Foote .20 .50
34 Patrick Roy .75 2.00
35 Peter Forsberg .60 1.50
36 Adam Deadmarsh .20 .50
37 Joe Sakic .60 1.50
38 Eric Lacroix .20 .50
39 Guy Carbonneau .20 .50
40 Mike Modano .50 1.25
41 Roman Turek .20 .50
42 Mike Keane .20 .50
43 Sergei Zubov .25 .60
44 Jere Lehtinen .25 .60
45 Sergei Fedorov .50 1.25
46 Steve Yzerman .75 2.00
47 Chris Osgood .30 .75
48 Larry Murphy .25 .60
49 Vyacheslav Kozlov .20 .50
50 Darren McCarty .20 .50
51 Boris Mironov .20 .50
52 Roman Hamrlik .20 .50
53 Bill Guerin .30 .75
54 Mike Grier .20 .50
55 Todd Marchant .20 .50
56 Ray Whitney .20 .50
57 Dave Gagner .20 .50
58 Scott Mellanby .20 .50
59 Robert Svehla .20 .50
60 Viktor Kozlov .25 .60
61 Luc Robitaille .30 .75
62 Yanic Perreault .20 .50
63 Jozef Stumpel .20 .50
64 Sandy Moger .20 .50
65 Ian Laperriere .20 .50
66 Jocelyn Thibault .25 .60
67 Dave Manson .20 .50
68 Mark Recchi .40 1.00
69 Patrick Poulin .20 .50
70 Benoit Brunet .20 .50
71 Turner Stevenson .20 .50
72 Mike Dunham .25 .60
73 Tom Fitzgerald .25 .60
74 Darren Turcotte .25 .60
75 Brad Smyth .20 .50
76 J.J. Daigneault .20 .50
77 Dave Andreychuk .30 .75
78 Jason Arnott .25 .60
79 Martin Brodeur .75 2.00
80 Randy McKay .25 .60
81 Patrik Elias .30 .75
82 Kevin Dean .20 .50
83 Tommy Salo .25 .60
84 Scott Lachance .20 .50
85 Bryan Berard .25 .60
86 Robert Reichel .20 .50
87 Kenny Jonsson .20 .50
88 Kevin Stevens .25 .60
89 Mike Richter .30 .75
90 Wayne Gretzky 2.00 5.00
91 Adam Graves .20 .50
92 Alexei Kovalev .25 .60
93 Ulf Samuelsson .25 .60
94 Radek Bonk .20 .50
95 Wade Redden .20 .50
96 Damian Rhodes .30 .75
97 Bruce Gardiner .20 .50
98 Daniel Alfredsson .30 .75
99 Ron Hextall .30 .75
100 Eric Lindros .50 1.25
101 Chris Gratton .25 .60
102 Dainius Zubrus .20 .50
103 Luke Richardson .20 .50
104 Petr Svoboda .20 .50
105 Rick Tocchet .25 .60
106 Teppo Numminen .20 .50
107 Jeremy Roenick .50 1.25
108 Nikolai Khabibulin .30 .75
109 Brad Isbister .20 .50
110 Peter Skudra .20 .50
111 Alexei Morozov .20 .50
112 Kevin Hatcher .20 .50
113 Darius Kasparaitis .20 .50
114 Stu Barnes .20 .50
115 Martin Straka .20 .50
116 Andrei Zyuzin .20 .50
117 Marcus Ragnarsson .20 .50
118 Murray Craven .20 .50
119 Marco Sturm .20 .50
120 Patrick Marleau .30 .75
121 Shawn Burr .20 .50
122 Grant Fuhr .50 1.25
123 Chris Pronger .30 .75
124 Geoff Courtnall .25 .60
125 Jim Campbell .20 .50
126 Pavol Demitra .40 1.00
127 Todd Gill .20 .50
128 Cory Cross .20 .50
129 Daymond Langkow .20 .50
130 Alexander Selivanov .20 .50
131 Mikael Renberg .25 .60
132 Rob Zamuner .20 .50
133 Stephane Richer .20 .50
134 Fredrik Modin .20 .50
135 Derek King .20 .50
136 Mats Sundin .30 .75
137 Mike Johnson .20 .50
138 Alyn McCauley .20 .50
139 Jason Smith .20 .50
140 Markus Naslund .30 .75
141 Alexander Mogilny .25 .60
142 Mattias Ohlund .20 .50
143 Donald Brashear .20 .50
144 Garth Snow .25 .60
145 Brian Bellows .25 .60
146 Peter Bondra .30 .75
147 Joe Juneau .20 .50
148 Steve Konowalchuk .20 .50
149 Ken Klee .20 .50
150 Michal Pivonka .20 .50
151 Steve Rucchin .20 .50
152 Stu Grimson .20 .50
153 Tomas Sandstrom .20 .50
154 Fredrik Olausson .20 .50
155 Travis Green .20 .50
156 Jason Allison .25 .60
157 Steve Heinze .20 .50
158 Rob Tallas .20 .50
159 Darren Van Impe .20 .50
160 Ken Baumgartner .20 .50
161 Peter Ferraro .20 .50
162 Dominik Hasek .50 1.25
163 Geoff Sanderson .20 .50
164 Miroslav Satan .25 .60
165 Rob Ray .20 .50
166 Alexei Zhitnik .20 .50
167 Phil Housley .25 .60
168 Theo Fleury .40 1.00
169 Ken Wregget .25 .60
170 Valeri Bure .20 .50
171 Rico Fata .25 .60
172 Arturs Irbe .25 .60
173 Sean Hill .20 .50
174 Ron Francis .40 1.00
175 Jeff O'Neill .20 .50
176 Paul Ranheim .20 .50
177 Paul Coffey .30 .75
178 Doug Gilmour .40 1.00
179 Eric Daze .25 .60
180 Chris Chelios .30 .75
181 Bob Probert .30 .75
182 Mark Fitzpatrick .20 .50
183 Alexei Gusarov .20 .50
184 Sylvain Lefebvre .20 .50
185 Craig Billington .20 .50
186 Valeri Kamensky .20 .50
187 Milan Hejduk RC .50 1.25
188 Sandis Ozolinsh .20 .50
189 Brett Hull .60 1.50
190 Ed Belfour .30 .75
191 Darryl Sydor .20 .50
192 Sergei Gusev RC .20 .50
193 Joe Nieuwendyk .25 .60
194 Derian Hatcher .20 .50
195 Brendan Shanahan .30 .75
196 Tomas Holmstrom .20 .50
197 Nicklas Lidstrom .40 1.00
198 Martin Lapointe .20 .50

Card	Low	High
199 Igor Larionov	.30	.75
200 Kris Draper	.20	.50
201 Kelly Buchberger	.20	.50
202 Andrei Kovalenko	.20	.50
203 Josef Beranek	.20	.50
204 Mikhail Shtalenkov	.20	.50
205 Pat Falloon	.20	.50
206 Mark Parrish RC	.50	1.25
207 Terry Carkner	.20	.50
208 Rob Niedermayer	.20	.50
209 Sean Burke	.20	.50
210 Oleg Kvasha RC	.30	.75
211 Pavel Bure	.30	.75
212 Rob Blake	.30	.75
213 Vladimir Tsyplakov	.20	.50
214 Stephane Fiset	.25	.60
215 Steve Duchesne	.25	.60
216 Patrice Brisebois	.20	.50
217 Vincent Damphousse	.25	.60
218 Saku Koivu	.30	.75
219 Jose Theodore	.30	.75
220 Brett Clark RC	.20	.50
221 Martin Rucinsky	.20	.50
222 Vladimir Malakhov	.20	.50
223 Sergei Krivokrasov	.20	.50
224 Scott Walker	.25	.60
225 Greg Johnson	.20	.50
226 Cliff Ronning	.20	.50
227 Eric Fichaud	.20	.50
228 Bob Carpenter	.25	.60
229 Scott Daniels	.20	.50
230 Brian Rolston	.25	.60
231 Sergei Brylin	.20	.50
232 Scott Niedermayer	.30	.75
233 Bryan Smolinski	.20	.50
234 Trevor Linden	.30	.75
235 Eric Brewer	.30	.75
236 Zigmund Palffy	.30	.75
237 Sergei Nemchinov	.20	.50
238 Brian Leetch	.25	.60
239 Mathieu Schneider	.20	.50
240 Niklas Sundstrom	.20	.50
241 Manny Malhotra	.30	.75
242 Jeff Beukeboom	.20	.50
243 Petr Nedved	.20	.50
244 Ron Tugnutt	.20	.50
245 Shaun Van Allen	.20	.50
246 Alexei Yashin	.25	.60
247 Jason York	.20	.50
248 Shawn McEachern	.20	.50
249 Marian Hossa	.30	.75
250 John LeClair	.30	.75
251 Rod Brind'Amour	.30	.75
252 John Vanbiesbrouck	.30	.75
253 Eric Desjardins	.25	.60
254 Valeri Zelepukin	.20	.50
255 Karl Dykhuis	.20	.50
256 Keith Tkachuk	.30	.75
257 Dallas Drake	.20	.50
258 Oleg Tverdovsky	.30	.75
259 Jyrki Lumme	.20	.50
260 Jimmy Waite	.20	.50
261 Jaromir Jagr	1.00	2.50
262 German Titov	.20	.50
263 Robert Lang	.20	.50
264 Brad Werenka	.20	.50
265 Rob Brown	.20	.50
266 Bobby Dollas	.20	.50
267 Jeff Friesen	.20	.50
268 Andy Sutton RC	.20	.50
269 Steve Shields	.20	.50
270 Mike Ricci	.20	.50
271 Joe Murphy	.20	.50
272 Tony Granato	.20	.50
273 Jamie McLennan	.25	.60
274 Al MacInnis	.40	1.00
275 Pierre Turgeon	.25	.60
276 Kelly Chase	.20	.50
277 Craig Conroy	.20	.50
278 Scott Young	.20	.50
279 Vincent Lecavalier	.60	1.50
280 Wendel Clark	.50	1.25
281 Daren Puppa	.25	.60
282 Sandy McCarthy	.20	.50
283 Daniil Markov	.25	.60
284 Curtis Joseph	.40	1.00
285 Sergei Berezin	.25	.60
286 Steve Sullivan	.20	.50
287 Tomas Kaberle RC	.40	1.00
288 Kris King	.20	.50
289 Igor Korolev	.20	.50
290 Mark Messier	.60	1.50
291 Bill Muckalt RC	.20	.50
292 Todd Bertuzzi	.30	.75
293 Brad May	.20	.50
294 Peter Zezel	.20	.50
295 Dmitri Mironov	.20	.50
296 Adam Oates	.30	.75
297 Calle Johansson	.20	.50
298 Craig Berube	.20	.50
299 Sergei Gonchar	.20	.50
300 Andrei Nikolishin	.20	.50

1998-99 Be A Player Press Release

*SINGLES: 12X TO 30X BASIC CARDS

1998-99 Be A Player Gold

*VETERANS: 2X TO 5X BASIC CARDS
*ROOKIES: 1.2X TO 3X BASIC CARDS

1998-99 Be A Player Autographs

Card	Low	High
1 Jason Marshall	2.50	6.00
2 Paul Kariya SP	10.00	25.00
3 Teemu Selanne SP	15.00	40.00
4 Guy Hebert	4.00	10.00
5 Ted Drury	2.50	6.00
6 Byron Dafoe	2.50	6.00
7 Rob Dimaio	2.50	6.00
8 Ray Bourque SP	15.00	40.00
9 Joe Thornton	10.00	25.00
10 Sergei Samsonov	4.00	10.00
11 Dimitri Khristich	2.50	6.00
12 Michael Peca	2.50	6.00
13 Jason Woolley	2.50	6.00
14 Matthew Barnaby	2.50	6.00
15 Brian Holzinger	2.50	6.00
16 Dixon Ward	2.50	6.00
17 Tyler Moss	2.50	6.00
18 Jarome Iginla	8.00	20.00
19 Marty McInnis	2.50	6.00
20 Andrew Cassels	2.50	6.00
21 Jason Wiemer	2.50	6.00
22 Trevor Kidd	4.00	10.00
23 Keith Primeau	2.50	6.00
24 Sami Kapanen	2.50	6.00
25 Robert Kron	2.50	6.00
26 Glen Wesley	2.50	6.00
27 Jeff Hackett	4.00	10.00
28 Tony Amonte SP	6.00	15.00
29 Alexei Zhamnov	2.50	6.00
30 Eric Weinrich	2.50	6.00
31 Jeff Shantz	2.50	6.00
32 Christian Laflamme	2.50	6.00
33 Adam Foote	2.50	6.00
34 Patrick Roy SP	30.00	80.00
35 Peter Forsberg SP	20.00	40.00
36 Adam Deadmarsh	3.00	8.00
37 Joe Sakic SP	20.00	50.00
38 Eric Lacroix	2.50	6.00
39 Guy Carbonneau	3.00	8.00
40 Mike Modano SP	12.00	30.00
41 Roman Turek	2.50	6.00
42 Mike Keane	2.50	6.00
43 Sergei Zubov	3.00	8.00
44 Jere Lehtinen	4.00	10.00
45 Sergei Fedorov SP	10.00	25.00
46 Steve Yzerman SP	40.00	100.00
47 Chris Osgood	5.00	12.00
48 Larry Murphy	2.50	6.00
49 Vyacheslav Kozlov	4.00	10.00
50 Darren McCarty	4.00	10.00
51 Boris Mironov	2.50	6.00
52 Roman Hamrlik	2.50	6.00
53 Bill Guerin	2.50	6.00
54 Mike Grier	2.50	6.00
55 Todd Marchant	2.50	6.00
56 Ray Whitney	2.50	6.00
57 Dave Gagner	2.50	6.00
58 Scott Mellanby	2.50	6.00
59 Robert Svehla	2.50	6.00
60 Viktor Kozlov	2.50	6.00
61 Luc Robitaille	8.00	20.00
62 Yanic Perreault	2.50	6.00
63 Jozef Stumpel	2.50	6.00
64 Sandy Moger	2.50	6.00
65 Ian Laperriere	2.50	6.00
66 Jocelyn Thibault	4.00	10.00
67 Dave Manson	2.50	6.00
68 Mark Recchi SP	6.00	15.00
69 Patrick Poulin	2.50	6.00
70 Benoit Brunet	2.50	6.00
71 Turner Stevenson	2.50	6.00
72 Mike Dunham	4.00	10.00
73 Tom Fitzgerald	2.50	6.00
74 Darren Turcotte	2.50	6.00
75 Brad Smyth	2.50	6.00
76 J.J. Daigneault	2.50	6.00
77 Dave Andreychuk	4.00	10.00
78 Jason Arnott	3.00	8.00
79 Martin Brodeur SP	25.00	60.00
80 Randy McKay	2.50	6.00
81 Patrik Elias	4.00	10.00
82 Kevin Dean	2.50	6.00
83 Tommy Salo	4.00	10.00
84 Scott Lachance	2.50	6.00
85 Bryan Berard	2.50	6.00
86 Robert Reichel	2.50	6.00
87 Kenny Jonsson	2.50	6.00
88 Kevin Stevens	2.50	6.00
89 Mike Richter SP	10.00	25.00
90 Wayne Gretzky/90*	300.00	800.00
91 Adam Graves	4.00	10.00
92 Alexei Kovalev	4.00	10.00
93 Ulf Samuelsson	2.50	6.00
94 Radek Bonk	2.50	6.00
95 Wade Redden	2.50	6.00
96 Damian Rhodes	2.50	6.00
97 Bruce Gardiner	2.50	6.00
98 Daniel Alfredsson	6.00	15.00
99 Ron Hextall	6.00	15.00
100 Eric Lindros SP	15.00	30.00
101 Chris Gratton	2.50	6.00
102 Dainius Zubrus	2.50	6.00
103 Luke Richardson	2.50	6.00
104 Petr Svoboda	2.50	6.00
105 Rick Tocchet	4.00	10.00
106 Teppo Numminen	2.50	6.00
107 Jeremy Roenick SP	12.00	30.00
108 Nikolai Khabibulin	4.00	10.00
109 Brad Isbister	2.50	6.00
110 Peter Skudra	2.50	6.00
111 Alexei Morozov	2.50	6.00
112 Kevin Hatcher	2.50	6.00
113 Darius Kasparaitis	4.00	10.00
114 Stu Barnes	2.50	6.00
115 Martin Straka	2.50	6.00
116 Andrei Zyuzin	2.50	6.00
117 Marcus Ragnarsson	2.50	6.00
118 Murray Craven	2.50	6.00
119 Marco Sturm	2.50	6.00
120 Patrick Marleau	4.00	10.00
121 Shawn Burr	2.50	6.00
122 Grant Fuhr	5.00	12.00
123 Chris Pronger	4.00	10.00
124 Geoff Courtnall	2.50	6.00
125 Jim Campbell	2.50	6.00
126 Pavol Demitra	6.00	15.00
127 Todd Gill	2.50	6.00
128 Cory Cross	2.50	6.00
129 Daymond Langkow	2.50	6.00
130 Alexander Selivanov	2.50	6.00
131 Mikael Renberg	2.50	6.00
132 Rob Zamuner	2.50	6.00
133 Stephane Richer	2.50	6.00
134 Fredrik Modin	2.50	6.00
135 Derek King	2.50	6.00
136 Mats Sundin SP	15.00	40.00
137 Mike Johnson	2.50	6.00
138 Alyn McCauley	2.50	6.00
139 Jason Smith	2.50	6.00
140 Markus Naslund	6.00	15.00
141 Alexander Mogilny SP	10.00	25.00
142 Mattias Ohlund	2.50	6.00
143 Donald Brashear	2.50	6.00
144 Garth Snow	3.00	8.00
145 Brian Bellows	2.50	6.00
146 Peter Bondra SP	6.00	15.00
147 Joe Juneau	2.50	6.00
148 Steve Konowalchuk	2.50	6.00
149 Ken Klee	2.50	6.00
150 Michal Pivonka	2.50	6.00
151 Steve Rucchin	2.50	6.00
152 Stu Grimson	2.50	6.00
153 Tomas Sandstrom	2.50	6.00
154 Fredrik Olausson	2.50	6.00
155 Travis Green	2.50	6.00
156 Jason Allison	2.50	6.00
157 Steve Heinze	2.50	6.00
158 Rob Tallas	2.50	6.00
159 Darren Van Impe	2.50	6.00
160 Ken Baumgartner	2.50	6.00
161 Peter Ferraro	2.50	6.00
162 Dominik Hasek SP	25.00	60.00
163 Geoff Sanderson	2.50	6.00
164 Miroslav Satan	4.00	10.00
165 Rob Ray	4.00	10.00
166 Alexei Zhitnik	2.50	6.00
167 Phil Housley	2.50	6.00
168 Theo Fleury SP	10.00	25.00
169 Ken Wregget	2.50	6.00
170 Valeri Bure	2.50	6.00
171 Rico Fata	2.50	6.00
172 Arturs Irbe	4.00	10.00
173 Sean Hill	2.50	6.00
174 Ron Francis SP	10.00	25.00
175 Jeff O'Neill	2.50	6.00
176 Paul Ranheim	2.50	6.00
177 Paul Coffey SP	12.00	30.00
178 Doug Gilmour SP	12.00	30.00
179 Eric Daze	2.50	6.00
180 Chris Chelios SP	10.00	25.00
181 Bob Probert	10.00	20.00
182 Mark Fitzpatrick	2.50	6.00
183 Alexei Gusarov	2.50	6.00
184 Sylvain Lefebvre	2.50	6.00
185 Craig Billington	2.50	6.00
186 Valeri Kamensky	2.50	6.00
187 Milan Hejduk	6.00	15.00
188 Sandis Ozolinsh	2.50	6.00
189 Brett Hull SP	15.00	40.00
190 Ed Belfour SP	12.00	30.00
191 Darryl Sydor	2.50	6.00
192 Sergei Gusev	2.50	6.00
193 Joe Nieuwendyk SP	6.00	15.00
194 Derian Hatcher	2.50	6.00
195 Brendan Shanahan SP	8.00	20.00
196 Tomas Holmstrom	5.00	12.00
197 Nicklas Lidstrom	5.00	12.00
198 Martin Lapointe	4.00	10.00
199 Igor Larionov	5.00	12.00
200 Kris Draper	3.00	8.00
201 Kelly Buchberger	2.50	6.00
202 Andrei Kovalenko	2.50	6.00
203 Josef Beranek	2.50	6.00
204 Mikhail Shtalenkov	2.50	6.00
205 Pat Falloon	2.50	6.00
206 Mark Parrish	2.50	6.00
207 Terry Carkner	2.50	6.00
208 Rob Niedermayer	4.00	10.00
209 Sean Burke	4.00	10.00
210 Oleg Kvasha	2.50	6.00
211 Pavel Bure SP	15.00	40.00
212 Rob Blake	4.00	10.00
213 Vladimir Tsyplakov	2.50	6.00
214 Stephane Fiset	2.50	6.00
215 Steve Duchesne	2.50	6.00
216 Patrice Brisebois	2.50	6.00
217 Vincent Damphousse	2.50	6.00
218 Saku Koivu	6.00	15.00
219 Jose Theodore	8.00	20.00
220 Brett Clark	2.50	6.00
221 Martin Rucinsky	2.50	6.00
222 Vladimir Malakhov	2.50	6.00
223 Sergei Krivokrasov	2.50	6.00
224 Scott Walker	2.50	6.00
225 Greg Johnson	2.50	6.00
226 Cliff Ronning	2.50	6.00
227 Eric Fichaud	2.50	6.00
228 Bob Carpenter	2.50	6.00
229 Scott Daniels	2.50	6.00
230 Brian Rolston	2.50	6.00
231 Sergei Brylin	2.50	6.00
232 Scott Niedermayer	5.00	12.00
233 Bryan Smolinski	2.50	6.00
234 Trevor Linden	4.00	10.00
235 Eric Brewer	2.50	6.00
236 Zigmund Palffy SP	6.00	15.00
237 Sergei Nemchinov	2.50	6.00
238 Brian Leetch SP	8.00	20.00
239 Mathieu Schneider	2.50	6.00
240 Niklas Sundstrom	2.50	6.00
241 Manny Malhotra	2.50	6.00
242 Jeff Beukeboom	2.50	6.00
243 Petr Nedved	2.50	6.00
244 Ron Tugnutt	3.00	8.00
245 Shawn Van Allen	2.50	6.00
246 Alexei Yashin	3.00	8.00
247 Jason York	2.50	6.00
248 Shawn McEachern	2.50	6.00
249 Marian Hossa	6.00	15.00
250 John LeClair SP	8.00	20.00
251 Rod Brind'Amour	4.00	10.00
252 John Vanbiesbrouck	4.00	10.00
253 Eric Desjardins	3.00	8.00
254 Valeri Zelepukin	2.50	6.00
255 Karl Dykhuis	2.50	6.00
256 Keith Tkachuk	5.00	12.00
257 Dallas Drake	2.50	6.00
258 Oleg Tverdovsky	2.50	6.00
259 Jyrki Lumme	2.50	6.00
260 Jimmy Waite	2.50	6.00
261 Jaromir Jagr SP	20.00	50.00
262 German Titov	2.50	6.00
263 Robert Lang	2.50	6.00
264 Brad Werenka	2.50	6.00
265 Rob Brown	2.50	6.00
266 Bobby Dollas	2.50	6.00
267 Jeff Friesen	2.50	6.00
268 Andy Sutton	2.50	6.00
269 Steve Shields	4.00	10.00
270 Mike Ricci	2.50	6.00
271 Joe Murphy	2.50	6.00
272 Tony Granato	2.50	6.00
273 Jamie McLennan	2.50	6.00
274 Al MacInnis SP	8.00	20.00
275 Pierre Turgeon	3.00	8.00
276 Kelly Chase	2.50	6.00
277 Craig Conroy	2.50	6.00
278 Scott Young	2.50	6.00
279 Vincent Lecavalier	8.00	20.00
280 Wendel Clark	4.00	10.00
281 Daren Puppa	2.50	6.00
282 Sandy McCarthy	2.50	6.00
283 Daniil Markov	2.50	6.00
284 Curtis Joseph SP	15.00	30.00
285 Sergei Berezin	2.50	6.00
286 Steve Sullivan	2.50	6.00
287 Tomas Kaberle	2.50	6.00
288 Kris King	2.50	6.00
289 Igor Korolev	2.50	6.00
290 Mark Messier SP	20.00	50.00
291 Bill Muckalt	2.50	6.00
292 Todd Bertuzzi	6.00	15.00
293 Brad May	3.00	8.00
294 Peter Zezel	2.50	6.00
295 Dmitri Mironov	2.50	6.00
296 Adam Oates SP	10.00	25.00
297 Calle Johansson	2.50	6.00
298 Craig Berube	2.50	6.00
299 Sergei Gonchar	2.50	6.00
300 Andrei Nikolishin	2.50	6.00

1998-99 Be A Player Autographs Gold

*GOLD: .8X TO 2X SILVER AU
*GOLD: .6X TO 1.5X SILVER AU SP

1998-99 Be A Player All-Star Game Used Sticks

Card	Low	High
S1 Eric Lindros	10.00	25.00
S2 Peter Forsberg	12.00	30.00
S3 Teemu Selanne	12.00	30.00
S4 Mike Modano	10.00	25.00
S5 Mats Sundin	6.00	15.00
S6 Patrick Roy	15.00	40.00
S7 Paul Kariya	6.00	15.00
S8 Martin Brodeur	15.00	40.00
S9 Steve Yzerman	15.00	40.00
S10 Mark Messier	12.00	30.00
S11 Brett Hull	12.00	30.00
S12 Joe Sakic	12.00	30.00
S13 Alexander Mogilny	5.00	12.00
S14 Sergei Fedorov	10.00	25.00
S15 Ray Bourque	10.00	25.00
S16 Jeremy Roenick	10.00	25.00
S17 Jaromir Jagr	20.00	50.00
S18 Dominik Hasek	10.00	25.00
S19 Chris Chelios	6.00	15.00
S20 John LeClair	6.00	15.00
S21 Brendan Shanahan	6.00	15.00
S22 Ed Belfour	6.00	15.00
S23 Wayne Gretzky	40.00	100.00

1998-99 Be A Player All-Star Game Used Jerseys

Card	Low	High
AS1 Eric Lindros	8.00	20.00
AS2 Peter Forsberg	10.00	25.00
AS3 Teemu Selanne	10.00	25.00
AS4 Mike Modano	8.00	20.00
AS5 Mats Sundin	5.00	12.00
AS6 Patrick Roy	12.00	30.00
AS7 Paul Kariya	5.00	12.00
AS8 Martin Brodeur	12.00	30.00
AS9 Steve Yzerman	12.00	30.00
AS10 Mark Messier	10.00	25.00
AS11 Paul Coffey	5.00	12.00
AS12 Brett Hull	10.00	25.00
AS13 Joe Sakic	10.00	25.00
AS14 Alexander Mogilny	4.00	10.00
AS15 Sergei Fedorov	8.00	20.00
AS16 Ray Bourque	8.00	20.00
AS17 Jeremy Roenick	8.00	20.00
AS18 Jaromir Jagr	15.00	40.00
AS19 Pavel Bure	5.00	12.00
AS20 Dominik Hasek	8.00	20.00
AS21 Chris Chelios	5.00	12.00
AS22 John LeClair	5.00	12.00
AS23 Brendan Shanahan	5.00	12.00
AS24 Ed Belfour	5.00	12.00
AS25 Wayne Gretzky	30.00	80.00

1998-99 Be A Player All-Star Legend Gordie Howe

Card	Low	High
GH1 G.Howe GJ AU	125.00	250.00
GH2 Gordie Howe AU	100.00	200.00

1998-99 Be A Player All-Star Milestones

Card	Low	High
M1 Wayne Gretzky	5.00	12.00
M2 Mark Messier	1.50	4.00
M3 Dino Ciccarelli	.75	2.00
M4 Steve Yzerman	2.00	5.00
M5 Dave Andreychuk	.75	2.00
M6 Brett Hull	1.50	4.00
M7 Wayne Gretzky	5.00	12.00
M8 Mark Messier	1.50	4.00
M9 Dino Ciccarelli	.75	2.00
M10 Steve Yzerman	2.00	5.00
M11 Bernie Nicholls	.60	1.50
M12 Ron Francis	1.00	2.50
M13 Ray Bourque	1.25	3.00
M14 Paul Coffey	.75	2.00
M15 Adam Oates	.75	2.00
M16 Phil Housley	.60	1.50
M17 Dale Hunter	.60	1.50
M18 Luc Robitaille	.75	2.00
M19 Doug Gilmour	1.00	2.50
M20 Larry Murphy	.60	1.50
M21 Dave Andreychuk	.75	2.00
M22 Al MacInnis	1.00	2.50

1998-99 Be A Player Playoff Game Used Jerseys

Card	Low	High
G1 Wayne Gretzky	50.00	100.00
G2 Mats Sundin	12.50	30.00
G3 Jeremy Roenick	12.50	30.00
G4 Eric Lindros	12.50	30.00
G5 John LeClair	12.50	30.00
G6 Joe Sakic	25.00	50.00
G7 Peter Forsberg	12.00	30.00
G8 Patrick Roy	30.00	80.00
G9 Martin Brodeur	25.00	60.00
G10 Pavel Bure	12.50	30.00
G11 Teemu Selanne	12.50	30.00
G12 Paul Kariya	12.50	30.00
G13 Ray Bourque	20.00	50.00
G14 Brendan Shanahan	12.50	30.00
G15 Steve Yzerman	30.00	80.00
G16 Sergei Fedorov	15.00	40.00
G17 Mike Modano	12.50	30.00
G18 Brett Hull	12.50	30.00
G19 Ed Belfour	12.50	30.00
G20 Mark Messier	15.00	40.00
G21 Alexander Mogilny	8.00	20.00
G22 Tony Amonte	8.00	20.00
G23 Jaromir Jagr	20.00	50.00
G24 Alexei Yashin	8.00	20.00

1998-99 Be A Player Playoff Highlights

Card	Low	High
COMPLETE SET (18)	40.00	100.00
H1 Mark Messier	2.00	5.00
H2 Peter Forsberg	5.00	12.00
H3 Wayne Gretzky	12.50	30.00
H4 Martin Brodeur	5.00	12.00
H5 Jaromir Jagr	3.00	8.00
H6 Mike Richter	2.00	5.00
H7 Steve Yzerman	10.00	25.00
H8 Patrick Roy	8.00	20.00
H9 Paul Coffey	2.00	5.00
H10 Joe Sakic	4.00	10.00
H11 John Vanbiesbrouck	2.00	5.00
H12 Pavel Bure	2.00	5.00
H13 Chris Osgood	2.00	5.00
H14 Chris Chelios	2.00	5.00
H15 Curtis Joseph	2.00	5.00
H16 Brian Leetch	2.00	5.00
H17 Sergei Fedorov	3.00	8.00
H18 Doug Gilmour	2.00	5.00

1998-99 Be A Player Playoff Legend Mario Lemieux

Card	Low	High
L1 All-Star Jersey AU	150.00	300.00
L2 Penguins Jersey AU	150.00	300.00
L3 All-Star Jsy/Stick AU	200.00	400.00
L4 Penguins Jsy/Stick AU	200.00	400.00

1998-99 Be A Player Playoff Practice Used Jerseys

Card	Low	High
P1 Brett Hull	8.00	20.00
P2 Alexander Mogilny	6.00	15.00
P3 Ray Bourque	15.00	40.00
P4 Pavel Bure	10.00	25.00
P5 Steve Yzerman	25.00	60.00
P6 Ed Belfour	10.00	25.00
P7 Jaromir Jagr	12.50	30.00
P8 Sergei Fedorov	12.50	30.00
P9 Teemu Selanne	10.00	25.00
P10 Eric Lindros	10.00	25.00
P11 Tony Amonte	8.00	20.00
P12 Jeremy Roenick	10.00	25.00
P13 John LeClair	10.00	25.00
P14 Mike Modano	10.00	25.00
P15 Joe Sakic	12.50	30.00
P16 Patrick Roy	30.00	80.00
P17 Mark Messier	10.00	25.00
P18 Paul Kariya	10.00	25.00
P19 Martin Brodeur	20.00	50.00
P20 Mats Sundin	25.00	60.00
P21 Brendan Shanahan	10.00	25.00
P22 Peter Forsberg	15.00	40.00
P23 Alexei Yashin	6.00	15.00
P24 Wayne Gretzky	100.00	150.00

1998-99 Be A Player Atlanta National

*SINGLES: 1.2X TO 3X BASIC CARDS

1998-99 Be A Player Toronto Spring Expo

*SINGLES: 15X TO 40X BASIC CARDS

1998-99 Be A Player Tampa Bay All-Star Game

*SINGLES: 10X TO 25X BASIC CARDS

2005-06 Be A Player

Card	Low	High
COMPLETE SET (90)	15.00	40.00
1 Jean-Sebastien Giguere	.50	1.25
2 Joffrey Lupul	.30	.75
3 Ilya Kovalchuk	.50	1.25
4 Dany Heatley	.40	1.00
5 Kari Lehtonen	.40	1.00
6 Glen Murray	.40	1.00
7 Joe Thornton	.75	2.00
8 Andrew Raycroft	.40	1.00
9 Miroslav Satan	.40	1.00
10 Chris Drury	.40	1.00
11 Daniel Briere	.50	1.25
12 Jarome Iginla	.60	1.50
13 Miikka Kiprusoff	.50	1.25
14 Martin Gelinas	.30	.75
15 Erik Cole	.30	.75
16 Eric Staal	.60	1.50
17 Tuomo Ruutu	.50	1.25
18 Eric Daze	.40	1.00
19 Joe Sakic	1.00	2.50
20 Peter Forsberg	1.00	2.50
21 Milan Hejduk	.40	1.00
22 Rob Blake	.50	1.25
23 Alex Tanguay	.50	1.25
24 Rick Nash	.50	1.25
25 Nikolai Zherdev	.30	.75
26 Todd Marchant	.30	.75
27 Marty Turco	.50	1.25
28 Brenden Morrow	.40	1.00
29 Mike Modano	.75	2.00
30 Brendan Shanahan	.50	1.25
31 Nicklas Lidstrom	.50	1.25
32 Pavel Datsyuk	.75	2.00
33 Steve Yzerman	1.25	3.00
34 Curtis Joseph	.60	1.50
35 Ryan Smyth	.40	1.00
36 Jason Smith	.30	.75
37 Ty Conklin	.40	1.00
38 Olli Jokinen	.50	1.25
39 Roberto Luongo	.75	2.00
40 Jay Bouwmeester	.30	.75
41 Zigmund Palffy	.50	1.25
42 Luc Robitaille	.50	1.25
43 Alexander Frolov	.30	.75
44 Marian Gaborik	.50	1.25
45 Dwayne Roloson	.40	1.00
46 Saku Koivu	.50	1.25
47 Jose Theodore	.50	1.25
48 Michael Ryder	.40	1.00
49 Tomas Vokoun	.40	1.00
50 Steve Sullivan	.30	.75
51 Jordin Tootoo	.50	1.25
52 Martin Brodeur	1.25	3.00
53 Patrik Elias	.50	1.25
54 Scott Gomez	.40	1.00
55 Rick DiPietro	.40	1.00
56 Mike Peca	.40	1.00
57 Trent Hunter	.30	.75
58 Jaromir Jagr	1.50	4.00
59 Bobby Holik	.30	.75
60 Dan Blackburn	.25	.60
61 Marian Hossa	.50	1.25
62 Jason Spezza	.50	1.25
63 Daniel Alfredsson	.50	1.25
64 Keith Primeau	.40	1.00
65 Simon Gagne	.50	1.25
66 Robert Esche	.40	1.00
67 Brett Hull	1.00	2.50
68 Shane Doan	.40	1.00
69 Mike Comrie	.40	1.00
70 Marc-Andre Fleury	1.00	2.50
71 Mark Recchi	.60	1.50
72 Mario Lemieux	2.00	5.00
73 Patrick Marleau	.50	1.25
74 Jonathan Cheechoo	.40	1.00
75 Evgeni Nabokov	.40	1.00
76 Chris Pronger	.50	1.25
77 Doug Weight	.50	1.25
78 Keith Tkachuk	.50	1.25
79 Martin St. Louis	.50	1.25
80 Vincent Lecavalier	.50	1.25
81 Nikolai Khabibulin	.50	1.25
82 Brad Richards	.50	1.25
83 Dave Andreychuk	.50	1.25
84 Gary Roberts	.30	.75
85 Mats Sundin	.50	1.25
86 Joe Nieuwendyk	.40	1.00
87 Markus Naslund	.50	1.25
88 Brendan Morrison	.30	.75
89 Ed Jovanovski	.40	1.00
90 Olaf Kolzig	.50	1.25

2005-06 Be A Player First Period

*STARS: 2X TO 5X

2005-06 Be A Player Second Period

*STARS: 5X TO 12X

2005-06 Be A Player Class Action

Card	Low	High
CA1 Keith Tkachuk	3.00	8.00
CA2 Dany Heatley	2.50	6.00
CA3 Ilya Kovalchuk	3.00	8.00
CA4 Joe Thornton	5.00	12.00
CA5 Jarome Iginla	4.00	10.00
CA6 Peter Forsberg	6.00	15.00
CA7 Joe Sakic	6.00	15.00
CA8 Rick Nash	3.00	8.00
CA9 Mike Modano	5.00	12.00
CA10 Steve Yzerman	8.00	20.00
CA11 Mats Sundin	3.00	8.00
CA12 Martin St. Louis	3.00	8.00
CA13 Jose Theodore	3.00	8.00
CA14 Miikka Kiprusoff	3.00	8.00
CA15 Martin Brodeur	8.00	20.00
CA16 Mark Messier	6.00	15.00
CA17 Markus Naslund	3.00	8.00
CA18 Jeremy Roenick	5.00	12.00
CA19 Brett Hull	6.00	15.00
CA20 Mario Lemieux	12.00	30.00

2005-06 Be A Player Dual Signatures

Card	Low	High
AR D.Andreychuk/L.Robitaille	8.00	20.00
BD D.Briere/C.Drury	8.00	20.00
BF M. Brodeur/M.Fleury	40.00	80.00
BS B.Rafalski/S.Niedermayer	5.00	12.00
DK D.Heatley/K.Lehtonen	10.00	25.00
DL K.Draper/N.Lidstrom SP	20.00	50.00
DR M.Denis/D.Roloson	8.00	20.00
DT E.Daze/J.Thibault	5.00	12.00
FL M.Fleury/R.Luongo	15.00	40.00
GB B.Guerin/B.Morrow	5.00	12.00
GD B.Guerin/C.Drury	5.00	12.00
HH M.Hossa/D.Hasek	12.00	30.00
HR M.Hossa/W.Redden	8.00	20.00
HT G.Howe/J.Thornton SP	75.00	150.00
IM J.Iginla/P.Marleau	10.00	25.00
JE J.Spezza/E.Staal	12.00	30.00
KC K.Tkachuk/C.Pronger	10.00	25.00
LI M.St. Louis/J.Iginla	12.00	30.00
LL M.St.Louis/V.Lecavalier	12.00	30.00
LP N.Lidstrom/C.Pronger	20.00	50.00
LW R.Luongo/S.Weiss	8.00	20.00
MA M.Peca/A.Aucoin	5.00	12.00
MC P.Marleau/J.Cheechoo	8.00	20.00
ND R.Nash/M.Denis	12.00	30.00
NL M.Naslund/T.Linden	12.00	30.00
NT R.Nash/J.Thornton	15.00	40.00
PA P.Kariya/A.Tanguay	12.00	30.00
PE K.Primeau/R.Esche	5.00	12.00
PP M.Peca/M.Parrish	5.00	12.00
RB L.Robitaille/D.Brown	10.00	25.00
RJ R.Blake/J.Bouwmeester	5.00	12.00
RL R.Luongo/K.Lehtonen	15.00	40.00
RR M.Ryder/M.Ribeiro	6.00	15.00
RT M.Ryder/J.Theodore	8.00	20.00
SB J.Sakic/R.Blake SP	20.00	50.00
SR J.Spezza/M.Ryder	12.00	30.00
SS R.Smyth/J.Smith	8.00	20.00
ST M.Sillinger/K.Tkachuk	5.00	12.00
TL M.Turco/R.Luongo	10.00	25.00
TM J.Thornton/G.Murray	10.00	25.00
TP J.Thornton/K.Primeau	10.00	25.00
TR J.Theodore/M.Ribeiro	8.00	20.00
VR V.Lecavalier/R.Fedotenko	10.00	25.00

2005-06 Be A Player Ice Icons

Card	Low	High
ICE1 Martin Brodeur	12.00	30.00
ICE2 Mario Lemieux	20.00	50.00
ICE3 Joe Sakic	10.00	25.00
ICE4 Peter Forsberg	10.00	25.00
ICE5 Steve Yzerman	12.00	30.00

2005-06 Be A Player Outtakes

Card	Low	High
OT1 Jean-Sebastien Giguere	6.00	15.00
OT2 Sergei Fedorov	10.00	25.00
OT3 Dany Heatley	5.00	12.00
OT4 Ilya Kovalchuk	6.00	15.00
OT5 Andrew Raycroft	5.00	12.00
OT6 Joe Thornton	10.00	25.00
OT7 Chris Drury	5.00	12.00
OT8 Jarome Iginla	8.00	20.00
OT9 Miikka Kiprusoff	6.00	15.00
OT10 Eric Staal	8.00	20.00
OT11 Tuomo Ruutu	6.00	15.00
OT12 Peter Forsberg	12.00	30.00
OT13 Rob Blake	6.00	15.00
OT14 Alex Tanguay	6.00	15.00
OT15 Joe Sakic	12.00	30.00
OT16 Nikolai Zherdev	4.00	10.00
OT17 Rick Nash	6.00	15.00
OT18 Mike Modano	10.00	25.00
OT19 Marty Turco	6.00	15.00
OT20 Pavel Datsyuk	10.00	25.00
OT21 Brendan Shanahan	6.00	15.00
OT22 Steve Yzerman	15.00	40.00
OT23 Ryan Smyth	5.00	12.00
OT24 Roberto Luongo	10.00	25.00
OT25 Luc Robitaille	6.00	15.00
OT26 Marian Gaborik	6.00	15.00
OT27 Saku Koivu	6.00	15.00
OT28 Jose Theodore	6.00	15.00
OT29 Tomas Vokoun	5.00	12.00
OT30 Steve Sullivan	4.00	10.00
OT31 Martin Brodeur	15.00	40.00
OT32 Jaromir Jagr	20.00	50.00
OT33 Mark Messier	12.00	30.00
OT34 Michael Peca	5.00	12.00
OT35 Daniel Alfredsson	6.00	15.00
OT36 Jason Spezza	6.00	15.00
OT37 Jeremy Roenick	10.00	25.00
OT38 Simon Gagne	6.00	15.00
OT39 Shane Doan	5.00	12.00
OT40 Mario Lemieux	25.00	60.00
OT41 Patrick Marleau	6.00	15.00
OT42 Keith Tkachuk	6.00	15.00
OT43 Chris Pronger	6.00	15.00
OT44 Vincent Lecavalier	6.00	15.00
OT45 Martin St. Louis	6.00	15.00
OT46 Mats Sundin	6.00	15.00
OT47 Ed Belfour	6.00	15.00
OT48 Markus Naslund	6.00	15.00
OT49 Ed Jovanovski	5.00	12.00
OT50 Olaf Kolzig	6.00	15.00

2005-06 Be A Player Quad Signatures

Card	Low	High
BLTG Brodr/Lngo/Theo/Ggy	250.00	500.00
BLUE Prng/Tkchk/Wnrch/Silln	30.00	80.00
BOST Thorn/Ray/Murry/Berg	60.00	150.00
COLO Tangy/Sakc/Absh/Dmph	75.00	150.00
GDEF Prongr/Ldstrm/Blke/J-Bo	100.00	200.00
GOAL Brodr/Theo/Giggy/Flry	150.00	300.00
HAWK Rutu/Dze/Thiblt/Berard	30.00	80.00
IMPL Iginla/Marl/Prmeau/St.Ls	50.00	100.00
ITLB Iginla/Tangy/St.Lu/Bergr	50.00	125.00
MAPL Sundn/Stjn/McCbe/Rbrts	40.00	100.00
MONT Theo/Ryder/Ribro/Sray	125.00	250.00
OTWA Hossa/Rddn/Bndr/Hask	100.00	200.00
RBSS Rutu/Brgrn/Staal/Stjan	60.00	125.00
SCCH Andry/St.Lu/Rchr/Stllm	60.00	100.00
SDPH Smyth/Dze/Prmu/Hlik	30.00	80.00
SHSL Sakc/Htly/Sndn/St.Lu	60.00	125.00
SSIR Smyth/Smth/Ignla/Rghr	100.00	200.00
TLAL Trco/Lngo/Absch/Lhtnn	60.00	150.00

2005-06 Be A Player Signatures

Card	Low	High
AA Adrian Aucoin	2.50	6.00
AB Andrew Brunette	2.50	6.00
AC Andrew Cassels	2.50	6.00
AE David Aebischer	3.00	8.00
AH Adam Hall	2.50	6.00
AL Andreas Lilja	2.50	6.00
AM Alyn McCauley	2.50	6.00
AN Dave Andreychuk	4.00	10.00
AR Andrew Raycroft	5.00	12.00
AT Alex Tanguay	4.00	10.00
AV Sean Avery	2.50	6.00
BA Matthew Barnaby	3.00	8.00
BB Bryan Berard	2.50	6.00
BD Boyd Devereaux	2.50	6.00
BE Brenden Morrow	4.00	10.00
BG Bill Guerin SP	8.00	20.00
BH Bobby Holik	2.50	6.00
BI Martin Biron	3.00	8.00
BJ Barret Jackman	2.50	6.00
BM Brendan Morrison	4.00	10.00
BN Brian Boucher	3.00	8.00
BO Bob Boughner	2.50	6.00
BR Brian Rolston	2.50	6.00
BS Brendan Shanahan	10.00	25.00
BT Brent Sopel	2.50	6.00
BW Brendan Witt	2.50	6.00
BY Bryan McCabe	2.50	6.00
CC Carlo Colaiacovo	2.50	6.00
CD Chris Drury SP	30.00	80.00
CO Craig Conroy	2.50	6.00
CP Chris Pronger	4.00	10.00
CR Craig Rivet	2.50	6.00
CS Cory Stillman	2.50	6.00
DB Daniel Briere	6.00	15.00
DC Daniel Cleary	3.00	8.00
DD Dallas Drake	2.50	6.00
DE Derian Hatcher	3.00	8.00
DI Daniel Alfredsson	5.00	12.00
DL David Legwand	3.00	8.00
DN Dan Cloutier	3.00	8.00
DO Shean Donovan	2.50	6.00
DR Dwayne Roloson	4.00	10.00
DT Mathieu Schneider	2.50	6.00
DU Dustin Brown	6.00	15.00
DY Darryl Sydor	2.50	6.00
EB Eric Brewer	2.50	6.00
EC Erik Cole	4.00	10.00
EI Eric Staal	8.00	20.00
EL Eric Lindros	8.00	20.00
ER Eric Belanger	2.50	6.00
ES Robert Esche	3.00	8.00
EW Eric Weinrich	2.50	6.00
FA Brian Rafalski	2.50	6.00
FE Ruslan Fedotenko	2.50	6.00

GI Brian Gionta 2.50 6.00
GL Martin Gelinas 2.50 6.00
GM Glen Murray 2.50 6.00
GS Garth Snow 2.50 6.00
HA Dominik Hasek 15.00 40.00
HE Bret Hedican 2.50 6.00
HF Shawn Horcoff 2.50 6.00
HO Gordie Howe SP 250.00 400.00
HT Dany Heatley 8.00 20.00
HZ Henrik Zetterberg 10.00 25.00
IG Jarome Iginla 12.00 30.00
IL Ian Laperriere 2.50 6.00
JA Jason Arnott 2.50 6.00
JB Jay Bouwmeester 5.00 12.00
JC Jonathan Cheechoo 4.00 10.00
JD Jody Shelley 2.50 6.00
JG Jean-Sebastien Giguere 4.00 10.00
JI Jim Dowd 2.50 6.00
JL Joffrey Lupul 3.00 8.00
JM John-Michael Liles 2.50 6.00
JO Jeff O'Neill 2.50 6.00
JP J-P Dumont 2.50 6.00
JS Jason Smith 2.50 6.00
JT Jocelyn Thibault 4.00 10.00
JW Justin Williams 2.50 6.00
KA Trent Klatt 2.50 6.00
KD Kris Draper 4.00 10.00
KE Kevyn Adams 2.50 6.00
KL Kari Lehtonen 12.00 30.00
KP Keith Primeau SP 8.00 20.00
KT Keith Tkachuk SP 20.00 50.00
KW Kevin Weekes 3.00 8.00
LA Robert Lang 2.50 6.00
LE Jordan Leopold 2.50 6.00
LU Luc Robitaille SP 20.00 50.00
LW Daymond Langkow 2.50 6.00
MA Brad May 3.00 8.00
MD Mathieu Dandenault 2.50 6.00
ME Mike Knuble 2.50 6.00
MF Marc-Andre Fleury 8.00 20.00
MH Marian Hossa 8.00 20.00
MI Mike Comrie 4.00 10.00
ML Martin Lapointe 2.50 6.00
MO Mattias Ohlund 2.50 6.00
MP Mark Parrish 2.50 6.00
MR Marc Denis 4.00 10.00
MS Matt Stajan 3.00 8.00
MT Martin Brodeur SP 150.00 250.00
MU Bryan Muir 2.50 6.00
MW Mattias Weinhandl 2.50 6.00
NA Markus Naslund SP 12.00 30.00
NB Nick Boynton 2.50 6.00
ND Niko Dimitrakos 2.50 6.00
NH Nathan Horton 5.00 12.00
NI Rob Niedermayer 3.00 8.00
NL Nicklas Lidstrom SP 25.00 60.00
OK Olaf Kolzig 5.00 12.00
OR Brooks Orpik 4.00 10.00
OT Steve Ott 3.00 8.00
PA Paul Martin 2.50 6.00
PB Peter Bondra 4.00 10.00
PC Patrice Bergeron 20.00 50.00
PD Pascal Dupuis 2.50 6.00
PE Mike Peca 4.00 10.00
PK Paul Kariya 12.00 30.00
PM Patrick Marleau SP 25.00 60.00
PT Pierre Turgeon 3.00 8.00
RA Rod Brind'Amour 4.00 10.00
RB Rob Blake 4.00 10.00
RC Brad Richards 5.00 12.00
RD Rick DiPietro 5.00 12.00
RF Rico Fata 2.50 6.00
RI Mike Ribeiro 3.00 8.00
RK Ryan Kesler 6.00 15.00
RL Roberto Luongo SP 25.00 60.00
RN Rick Nash 10.00 25.00
RO Gary Roberts 2.50 6.00
RR Robyn Regehr 2.50 6.00
RS Ryan Smyth 3.00 8.00
RU Tuomo Ruutu 3.00 8.00
RW Ray Whitney 2.50 6.00
RY Michael Ryder SP 8.00 20.00
SA Joe Sakic 25.00 60.00
SB Sean Burke 4.00 10.00
SC Scott Niedermayer 4.00 10.00
SD Shane Doan 2.50 6.00
SE Steve Sullivan 2.50 6.00
SG Mike Sillinger 2.50 6.00
SH Shawn McEachern 2.50 6.00
SI Steve Shields 3.00 8.00
SJ Joe Thornton 15.00 40.00
SL Martin St. Louis 4.00 10.00
SM Scott Mellanby 2.50 6.00
SN Geoff Sanderson 3.00 8.00
SO Steve Staios 2.50 6.00
SP Jason Spezza 12.00 30.00
SQ Stephane Quintal 2.50 6.00
SR Steve Rucchin 2.50 6.00
SS Sheldon Souray 2.50 6.00
SU Mats Sundin 25.00 60.00
TE Mikael Tellqvist 3.00 8.00
TH Jose Theodore 5.00 12.00
TI Mattias Timander 2.50 6.00
TL Trevor Linden 6.00 15.00
TM Todd Marchant 2.50 6.00
TN Tyson Nash 2.50 6.00
TO Steve Thomas 2.50 6.00
TP Tom Poti 2.50 6.00
TR Trent Hunter 2.50 6.00
TT Tim Taylor 2.50 6.00
TU Marty Turco 4.00 10.00
TW Todd White 2.50 6.00
VD Vincent Damphousse 3.00 8.00
VL Vincent Lecavalier 20.00 50.00
WA Scott Walker 2.50 6.00
WE Stephen Weiss 2.50 6.00
WR Wade Redden 2.50 6.00
YO Scott Young 2.50 6.00
ZE Eric Daze 2.50 6.00

2005-06 Be A Player Triple Signatures

AVS Sakic/Tanguay/Kariya SP 30.00 80.00
BSH Bondra/Spezza/Hossa SP 40.00 100.00
BUF Drury/Briere/Biron 20.00 50.00
DAL Turco/Morrow/Guerin SP 20.00 50.00
DEV Brodeur/Niedrmyr/Rafalski SP 125.00250.00
DRL Dipietro/Raycroft/Luongo SP 30.00 80.00
FGR Fleury/Giguere/Raycroft SP 30.00 80.00
HGT Howe/Guerin/Tkachuk SP 100.00 200.00
HSN Hossa/Sundin/Naslund SP 40.00 100.00
IBM Iginla/Bergeron/Marleau SP 20.00 50.00
LBP Lidstrom/Blake/Pronger SP 30.00 80.00
LLA Luongo/Lehtnen/Aebischr SP 30.00 80.00
MTL Theodore/Ryder/Ribeiro SP 30.00 80.00
NKI Naslund/Kariya/Iginla SP 50.00 100.00
NMS Naslund/Morrison/Sopel 20.00 50.00
PAN Weiss/Horton/Bouwmeester 20.00 50.00
PDL Primeau/Daze/Lindros SP 20.00 50.00
PTS Primeau/Thornton/Sundin SP 30.00 80.00
SIS Sakic/Iginla/Sundin SP 75.00 150.00
SNL Sundin/Naslund/Lidstrom SP 20.00 50.00
STL Tkachuk/Pronger/Drake SP 20.00 50.00
STS Sakic/Thornton/Spezza SP 100.00 200.00
TBL St.Louis/Richards/Lecavlr SP 60.00 120.00
TGR Turco/Giguere/Raycroft 25.00 60.00
TLP Thorntn/Lecavalr/Primeau SP 25.00 60.00

2005-06 Be A Player World Cup Salute

WCS1 Fredrik Modin 2.50 6.00
WCS2 Vincent Lecavalier 4.00 10.00
WCS3 Keith Tkachuk 4.00 10.00
WCS4 Joe Sakic 8.00 20.00
WCS5 Martin Havlat 4.00 10.00
WCS6 Kimmo Timonen 10.00 25.00
WCS7 Joe Thornton 6.00 15.00
WCS8 Mike Modano 6.00 15.00
WCS9 Daniel Alfredsson 4.00 10.00
WCS10 Patrik Elias 4.00 10.00
WCS11 Martin Brodeur 10.00 25.00
WCS12 Tomas Vokoun 3.00 8.00
WCS13 Miikka Kiprusoff 4.00 10.00
WCS14 Robert Esche 3.00 8.00
WCS15 Bill Guerin 4.00 10.00

2006-07 Be A Player

COMP.SET w/o SPs (170) 20.00 50.00
1 Dainius Zubrus .15 .40
2 Nikolai Zherdev .15 .40
3 Alexei Yashin .20 .50
4 Curtis Joseph .30 .75
5 Justin Williams .20 .50
6 Todd White .15 .40
7 Kyle Wellwood .20 .50
8 Doug Weight .25 .60
9 Cam Ward .25 .60
10 Aaron Ward .15 .40
11 Scott Walker .15 .40
12 David Vyborny .15 .40
13 Radim Vrbata .15 .40
14 Antoine Vermette .20 .50
15 Stephane Veilleux .15 .40
16 Thomas Vanek .20 .50
17 Mike Van Ryn .15 .40
18 R.J. Umberger .15 .40
19 Marty Turco .25 .60
20 Darcy Tucker .20 .50
21 Vesa Toskala .20 .50
22 Kimmo Timonen .15 .40
23 Joe Thornton .40 1.00
24 Jose Theodore .25 .60
25 Tim Taylor .15 .40
26 Alex Tanguay .15 .40
27 Steve Sullivan .15 .40
28 Brad Stuart .15 .40
29 Martin Straka .15 .40
30 Jarret Stoll .20 .50
31 Lee Stempniak .15 .40
32 Matt Stajan .15 .40
33 Eric Staal .30 .75
34 Martin St. Louis .25 .60
35 Jason Spezza .25 .60
36 Sheldon Souray .15 .40
37 Ryan Smyth .20 .50
38 Jason Smith .15 .40
39 Chris Simon .15 .40
40 Mike Sillinger .15 .40
41 Jody Shelley .15 .40
42 Teemu Selanne .50 1.25
43 Henrik Sedin .30 .75
44 Brent Seabrook .15 .40
45 Nick Schultz .15 .40
46 Marc Savard .15 .40
47 Sergei Samsonov .20 .50
48 Sami Salo .15 .40
49 Joe Sakic .50 1.25
50 Michael Ryder .15 .40
51 Tuomo Ruutu .25 .60
52 Derek Roy .15 .40
53 Dwayne Roloson .20 .50
54 Mike Richards .20 .50
55 Brad Richards .25 .60
56 Robyn Regehr .15 .40
57 Wade Redden .15 .40
58 Andrew Raycroft .20 .50
59 Brian Rafalski .20 .50
60 Petr Prucha .20 .50
61 Wayne Primeau .15 .40
62 Tom Poti .15 .40
63 Joni Pitkanen .15 .40
64 Dion Phaneuf .20 .50
65 Andrew Peters .15 .40
66 Yanic Perreault .15 .40
67 Dustin Penner .20 .50
68 Michael Peca .20 .50
69 Mark Parrish .15 .40
70 Alexander Ovechkin 1.00 2.50
71 Steve Ott .15 .40
72 Michael Nylander .15 .40
73 Mattias Norstrom .15 .40
74 Antero Niittymaki .20 .50
75 Scott Niedermayer .25 .60
76 Markus Naslund .25 .60
77 Glen Murray .20 .50
78 Bryan Muir .15 .40
79 Brendan Morrison .15 .40
80 Steve Montador .15 .40
81 Ryan Miller .25 .60
82 Milan Michalek .15 .40
83 Andrej Meszaros .15 .40
84 Andy McDonald .20 .50
85 Jamal Mayers .15 .40
86 Patrick Marleau .25 .60
87 Andrei Markov .25 .60
88 Ryan Malone .15 .40
89 Manny Malhotra .15 .40
90 Roberto Luongo .40 1.00
91 Henrik Lundqvist .60 1.50
92 John-Michael Liles .15 .40
93 Nicklas Lidstrom .25 .60
94 Jordan Leopold .15 .40
95 Jere Lehtinen .15 .40
96 David Legwand .20 .50
97 Vincent Lecavalier .25 .60
98 Georges Laraque .20 .50
99 Andrew Ladd .15 .40
100 Chris Kunitz .25 .60
101 Slava Kozlov .15 .40
102 Alexei Kovalev .20 .50
103 Olaf Kolzig .25 .60
104 Saku Koivu .25 .60
105 Chuck Kobasew .15 .40
106 Mike Knuble .15 .40
107 Nikolai Khabibulin .25 .60
108 Duncan Keith .20 .50
109 Olli Jokinen .25 .60
110 Jarome Iginla .30 .75
111 Trent Hunter .15 .40
112 Cristobal Huet .20 .50
113 Marian Hossa .25 .60
114 Shawn Horcoff .15 .40
115 Bobby Holik .15 .40
116 Chris Higgins .15 .40
117 Dany Heatley .20 .50
118 Martin Havlat .15 .40
119 Dan Hamhuis .20 .50
120 Bill Guerin .25 .60
121 Mike Green .20 .50
122 Hal Gill .15 .40
123 Martin Gerber .20 .50
124 Simon Gagne .25 .60
125 Alexander Frolov .15 .40
126 Kurtis Foster .15 .40
127 Peter Forsberg .50 1.25
128 Marc-Andre Fleury .50 1.25
129 Ruslan Fedotenko .15 .40
130 Sergei Federov .40 1.00
131 Garnet Exelby .15 .40
132 Robert Esche .20 .50
133 Steve Eminger .15 .40
134 Patrik Elias .25 .60
135 Patrick Eaves .15 .40
136 J.P. Dumont .15 .40
137 Chris Drury .20 .50
138 Shane Doan .20 .50
139 Marc Denis .20 .50
140 Craig Conroy .15 .40
141 Erik Cole .15 .40
142 Chris Clark .15 .40
143 Jonathan Cheechoo .20 .50
144 Zdeno Chara .25 .60
145 Jeff Carter .20 .50
146 Brian Campbell .20 .50
147 Mike Cammalleri .15 .40
148 Kyle Calder .15 .40
149 Brent Burns .25 .60
150 Gilbert Brule .20 .50
151 Dustin Brown .25 .60
152 Curtis Brown .15 .40
153 Rod Brind`Amour .25 .60
154 Daniel Briere .25 .60
155 Eric Brewer .15 .40
156 Dan Boyle .15 .40
157 Brad Boyes .15 .40
158 Jay Bouwmeester .15 .40
159 Pierre-Marc Bouchard .25 .60
160 Rob Blake .25 .60
161 Steve Bernier .15 .40
162 Patrice Bergeron .30 .75
163 Mark Bell .15 .40
164 Keith Ballard .15 .40
165 Sean Avery .15 .40
166 Adrian Aucoin .15 .40
167 Daniel Alfredsson .25 .60
168 Maxim Afinogenov .15 .40
169 Kevyn Adams .15 .40
170 Shawn Bates .15 .40
201 Evgeni Malkin RC 10.00 25.00
202 Phil Kessel RC 5.00 12.00
203 Luc Bourdon RC 2.50 6.00
204 Dustin Boyd RC 1.50 4.00
205 Patrick O'Sullivan RC 2.50 6.00
206 Blake Comeau RC 2.50 6.00
207 Shea Weber RC 4.00 10.00
208 Matt Carle RC 1.50 4.00
209 Loui Eriksson RC 3.00 8.00
210 Mark Stuart RC 1.50 4.00
211 Eric Fehr RC 2.50 6.00
212 Travis Zajac RC 3.00 8.00
213 Anze Kopitar RC 8.00 20.00
214 Ladislav Smid RC 1.50 4.00
215 Noah Welch RC 1.50 4.00
216 Jordan Staal RC 4.00 10.00
217 Alexander Radulov RC 3.00 8.00
218 Drew Stafford RC 2.50 6.00
219 Paul Stastny RC 4.00 10.00
220 Dave Bolland RC 2.50 6.00
221 Marek Schwarz RC 2.50 6.00
222 Ryan Potulny RC 1.50 4.00
223 Marc-Antoine Pouliot RC 1.50 4.00
224 Jarkko Immonen RC 2.00 5.00
225 Josh Hennessy RC 1.50 4.00
226 Benoit Pouliot RC 2.00 5.00
227 Nigel Dawes RC 1.50 4.00
228 Matt Lashoff RC 1.50 4.00
229 Keith Yandle RC 4.00 10.00
230 Karri Ramo RC 1.50 4.00
231 Guillaume Latendresse RC 2.50 6.00
232 Marc-Edouard Vlasic RC 2.50 6.00
233 Patrick Thoresen RC 1.50 4.00
234 Niklas Grossman RC 2.50 6.00
235 Ian White RC 2.00 5.00
236 Clarke MacArthur RC 2.00 5.00
237 Jesse Schultz RC 1.50 4.00
238 David Booth RC 2.00 5.00
239 Joe Pavelski RC 8.00 20.00
240 Martin Houle RC 2.00 5.00
241 Mikhail Grabovski RC 3.00 8.00
242 David McKee RC 1.50 4.00
243 Brandon Prust RC 1.50 4.00
244 Kristopher Letang RC 6.00 15.00
245 Shawn Belle RC 1.50 4.00

2006-07 Be A Player Autographs

202 Phil Kessel 10.00 25.00
203 Luc Bourdon 15.00 30.00
205 Patrick O'Sullivan 5.00 12.00
207 Shea Weber 8.00 20.00
208 Matt Carle 3.00 8.00
216 Jordan Staal 8.00 20.00
219 Paul Stastny 10.00 25.00
227 Nigel Dawes 3.00 8.00
231 Guillaume Latendresse 5.00 12.00
233 Patrick Thoresen 3.00 8.00

2006-07 Be A Player Profiles

COMPLETE SET (30) 50.00 100.00
PP1 Vincent Lecavalier 1.50 4.00
PP2 Thomas Vanek 1.25 3.00
PP3 Teemu Selanne 3.00 8.00
PP4 Simon Gagne 1.50 4.00
PP5 Sergei Federov 2.50 6.00
PP6 Scott Niedermayer 1.50 4.00
PP7 Saku Koivu 1.50 4.00
PP8 Ryan Smyth 1.25 3.00
PP9 Pierre-Marc Bouchard 1.50 4.00
PP10 Phil Kessel 3.00 8.00
PP11 Peter Forsberg 3.00 8.00
PP12 Paul Stastny 2.50 6.00
PP13 Patrice Bergeron 2.00 5.00
PP14 Nicklas Lidstrom 1.50 4.00
PP15 Markus Naslund 1.50 4.00
PP16 Marian Hossa 1.50 4.00
PP17 Marc-Andre Fleury 3.00 8.00
PP18 Jordan Staal 2.00 5.00
PP19 Jonathan Cheechoo 1.25 3.00
PP20 Joe Thornton 2.50 6.00
PP21 Joe Sakic 3.00 8.00
PP22 Jay Bouwmeester 1.00 2.50
PP23 Jarome Iginla 2.00 5.00
PP24 Guillaume Latendresse 1.25 3.00
PP25 Eric Staal 2.00 5.00
PP26 Dion Phaneuf 1.25 3.00
PP27 Dany Heatley 1.25 3.00
PP28 Daniel Alfredsson 1.50 4.00
PP29 Alexander Ovechkin 5.00 12.00
PP30 Alexander Frolov 1.00 2.50

2006-07 Be A Player Signatures

AA Adrian Aucoin 4.00 10.00
AD Daniel Alfredsson 6.00 15.00
AF Alexander Frolov 4.00 10.00
AK Alexei Kovalev 5.00 12.00
AL Andrew Ladd 4.00 10.00
AM Andrei Markov 6.00 15.00
AN Antero Niittymaki 5.00 12.00
AO Alexander Ovechkin 150.00 400.00
AP Andrew Peters 4.00 10.00
AR Andrew Raycroft 5.00 12.00
AS Sean Avery 4.00 10.00
AT Alex Tanguay 4.00 10.00
AV Antoine Vermette 5.00 12.00
AW Aaron Ward 4.00 10.00
AY Alexei Yashin 5.00 12.00
BA Shawn Bates 4.00 10.00
BB Brad Boyes 4.00 10.00
BC Brian Campbell 5.00 12.00
BD Daniel Briere 6.00 15.00
BE Patrice Bergeron 8.00 20.00
BG Bill Guerin 6.00 15.00
BH Bobby Holik 4.00 10.00
BL Rob Blake 6.00 15.00
BM Bryan Muir 4.00 10.00
BO Dan Boyle 4.00 10.00
BR Brad Richards 6.00 15.00
BS Brad Stuart 4.00 10.00
BU Brent Burns 6.00 15.00
CA Jeff Carter 5.00 12.00
CB Curtis Brown 4.00 10.00
CC Craig Conroy 4.00 10.00
CD Chris Drury 5.00 12.00
CH Chuck Kobasew 4.00 10.00
CJ Curtis Joseph 8.00 20.00
CK Chris Kunitz 6.00 15.00
CL Chris Clark 4.00 10.00
CM Mike Cammalleri 4.00 10.00
CR Cristobal Huet 5.00 12.00
CS Chris Simon 4.00 10.00
CW Cam Ward 6.00 15.00
DA Dan Hamhuis 5.00 12.00
DB Dustin Brown 6.00 15.00
DH Dany Heatley 5.00 12.00
DK Duncan Keith 5.00 12.00
DL David Legwand 5.00 12.00
DP Dion Phaneuf 5.00 12.00
DR Derek Roy 4.00 10.00
DT Darcy Tucker 5.00 12.00
DV David Vyborny 4.00 10.00
DW Doug Weight 6.00 15.00
DZ Dainius Zubrus 4.00 10.00
EA Patrick Eaves 4.00 10.00
EB Eric Brewer 4.00 10.00
EC Erik Cole 4.00 10.00
FI Patrik Elias 6.00 15.00
EM Steve Eminger 4.00 10.00
ES Eric Staal 8.00 20.00
EX Garnet Exelby 4.00 10.00
GA Simon Gagne 6.00 15.00
GB Gilbert Brule 5.00 12.00
GE Martin Gerber 5.00 12.00
GL Georges Laraque 5.00 12.00
GM Glen Murray 5.00 12.00
HA Martin Havlat 4.00 10.00
HG Hal Gill 4.00 10.00
HI Chris Higgins 4.00 10.00
HL Henrik Lundqvist 15.00 40.00
HO Shawn Horcoff 4.00 10.00
HS Henrik Sedin 8.00 20.00
HU Trent Hunter 4.00 10.00
JA Jason Smith 4.00 10.00
JB Jay Bouwmeester 4.00 10.00
JC Jonathan Cheechoo 5.00 12.00
JD J.P. Dumont 4.00 10.00
JE Jere Lehtinen 4.00 10.00
JI Jarome Iginla 8.00 20.00
JL John-Michael Liles 4.00 10.00
JM Jamal Mayers 4.00 10.00
JO Joe Sakic 12.00 30.00
JP Joni Pitkanen 4.00 10.00
JS Jarret Stoll 5.00 12.00
JT Joe Thornton SP 100.00 200.00
JW Justin Williams 5.00 12.00
KA Kevyn Adams 4.00 10.00
KB Keith Ballard 4.00 10.00
KC Kyle Calder 4.00 10.00
KF Kurtis Foster 4.00 10.00
KN Mike Knuble 4.00 10.00
KO Saku Koivu 6.00 15.00
KT Kimmo Timonen 4.00 10.00
KW Kyle Wellwood 5.00 12.00
KZ Slava Kozlov 4.00 10.00
LE Jordan Leopold 4.00 10.00
LS Lee Stempniak 4.00 10.00
MA Manny Malhotra 4.00 10.00
MB Mark Bell 4.00 10.00
MC Andy McDonald 5.00 12.00
MD Marc Denis 5.00 12.00
MF Marc-Andre Fleury 12.00 30.00
MG Mike Green 5.00 12.00
MH Marian Hossa 6.00 15.00
MI Milan Michalek 4.00 10.00
MN Michael Nylander 4.00 10.00
MO Brendan Morrison 4.00 10.00
MP Michael Peca 5.00 12.00
MS Marc Savard 4.00 10.00
MT Marty Turco 6.00 15.00
MV Mike Van Ryn 4.00 10.00
MX Maxim Afinogenov 4.00 10.00
MZ Andrej Meszaros 4.00 10.00
NA Markus Naslund 6.00 15.00
NK Nikolai Khabibulin 6.00 15.00
NL Nicklas Lidstrom 8.00 20.00
NO Mattias Norstrom 4.00 10.00
NS Nick Schultz 4.00 10.00
NZ Nikolai Zherdev 4.00 10.00
OJ Olli Jokinen 6.00 15.00
OK Olaf Kolzig 6.00 15.00
OT Steve Ott 4.00 10.00
PA Mark Parrish 4.00 10.00
PB Pierre-Marc Bouchard 6.00 15.00
PE Dustin Penner 5.00 12.00
PF Peter Forsberg 30.00 60.00
PM Patrick Marleau 6.00 15.00
PP Petr Prucha 5.00 12.00
RA Brian Rafalski 5.00 12.00
RB Rod Brind`Amour 6.00 15.00
RD Michael Ryder 4.00 10.00
RE Robert Esche 5.00 12.00
RF Ruslan Fedotenko 4.00 10.00
RI Mike Richards 5.00 12.00
RL Roberto Luongo 20.00 50.00
RM Ryan Malone 4.00 10.00
RO Dwayne Roloson 5.00 12.00
RR Robyn Regehr 4.00 10.00
RS Ryan Smyth 5.00 12.00
RU R.J. Umberger 4.00 10.00
RV Radim Vrbata 4.00 10.00
RY Ryan Miller 6.00 15.00
SB Steve Bernier 4.00 10.00
SD Shane Doan 5.00 12.00
SE Sergei Samsonov 5.00 12.00
SF Sergei Federov 8.00 20.00
SH Jody Shelley 4.00 10.00
SI Mike Sillinger 4.00 10.00
SJ Matt Stajan 4.00 10.00
SK Brent Seabrook 4.00 10.00
SL Martin St. Louis 6.00 15.00
SM Steve Montador 4.00 10.00
SN Scott Niedermayer 6.00 15.00
SO Sheldon Souray 4.00 10.00
SP Jason Spezza 6.00 15.00
SS Sami Salo 4.00 10.00
ST Martin Straka 4.00 10.00
SU Steve Sullivan 4.00 10.00
TH Jose Theodore 6.00 15.00
TP Tom Poti 4.00 10.00
TR Tuomo Ruutu 6.00 15.00
TS Teemu Selanne 15.00 40.00
TT Tim Taylor 4.00 10.00
TV Thomas Vanek 5.00 12.00
TW Todd White 4.00 10.00
VE Stephane Veilleux 4.00 10.00
VL Vincent Lecavalier 0.00 15.00
VT Vesa Toskala 5.00 12.00
WA Scott Walker 4.00 10.00
WP Wayne Primeau 4.00 10.00
WR Wade Redden 4.00 10.00
YP Yanic Perreault 4.00 10.00
ZC Zdeno Chara 6.00 15.00

2006-07 Be A Player Signatures 25

AL Andrew Ladd 10.00 25.00
AM Andy McDonald 12.00 30.00
AO Alexander Ovechkin 250.00 600.00
AP Andrew Peters 10.00 25.00
AR Andrew Raycroft 12.00 30.00
AT Alex Tanguay 10.00 25.00
AY Alexei Yashin 12.00 30.00
BC Brian Campbell 12.00 30.00
BG Bill Guerin 15.00 40.00
BH Bobby Holik 10.00 25.00
BR Brad Richards 15.00 40.00
BS Brad Stuart 10.00 25.00
CC Craig Conroy 10.00 25.00
CD Chris Drury 12.00 30.00
CH Chuck Kobasew 10.00 25.00
CK Chris Kunitz 15.00 40.00
CL Chris Clark 10.00 25.00
CR Cristobal Huet 12.00 30.00
DA Daniel Alfredsson 15.00 40.00
DB Dustin Brown 15.00 40.00
DH Dany Heatley 12.00 30.00
DK Duncan Keith 12.00 30.00
DP Dion Phaneuf 12.00 30.00
DR Derek Roy 10.00 25.00
DT Darcy Tucker 12.00 30.00
DV David Vyborny 10.00 25.00
DW Doug Weight 15.00 40.00
EA Patrik Elias 15.00 40.00
EB Eric Brewer 10.00 25.00
ES Eric Staal 20.00 50.00
GL Guillaume Latendresse 15.00 40.00
GM Glen Murray 12.00 30.00
HI Chris Higgins 10.00 25.00
HL Henrik Lundqvist 40.00 100.00
HO Shawn Horcoff 10.00 25.00
JA Jason Smith 10.00 25.00
JC Jonathan Cheechoo 12.00 30.00
JI Jarome Iginla 20.00 50.00
JL John-Michael Liles 10.00 25.00
JO Joe Sakic 30.00 80.00
JS Jarret Stoll 12.00 30.00
JW Justin Williams 12.00 30.00
KC Kyle Calder 10.00 25.00
KO Saku Koivu 15.00 40.00
KT Kimmo Timonen 10.00 25.00
KW Kyle Wellwood 12.00 30.00
KZ Slava Kozlov 10.00 25.00
LE Jordan Leopold 10.00 25.00
MA Maxim Afinogenov 10.00 25.00
MF Marc-Andre Fleury 30.00 80.00
MH Marian Hossa 15.00 40.00
MK Mike Knuble 10.00 25.00
MN Michael Nylander 10.00 25.00
MP Michael Peca 12.00 30.00
MS Martin St. Louis 15.00 40.00
MT Marty Turco 15.00 40.00
MV Mike Van Ryn 10.00 25.00
NA Markus Naslund 15.00 40.00
ND Nigel Dawes 10.00 25.00
NL Nicklas Lidstrom 15.00 40.00
OJ Olli Jokinen 15.00 40.00
PB Patrice Bergeron 20.00 50.00
PE Dustin Penner 12.00 30.00
PF Peter Forsberg 75.00 150.00
PK Phil Kessel 30.00 80.00
PM Patrick Marleau 15.00 40.00
PS Paul Stastny 25.00 60.00
PT Patrick Thoresen 10.00 25.00
RB Rob Blake 15.00 40.00
RD Michael Ryder 10.00 25.00
RF Ruslan Fedotenko 10.00 25.00
RL Roberto Luongo 50.00 120.00
RM Ryan Miller 15.00 40.00
RO Dwayne Roloson 12.00 30.00
RS Ryan Smyth 12.00 30.00
RU R.J. Umberger 10.00 25.00
SE Sergei Samsonov 12.00 30.00
SF Sergei Federov 25.00 60.00
SG Simon Gagne 15.00 40.00
SH Jody Shelley 10.00 25.00
SK Brent Seabrook 10.00 25.00
SN Scott Niedermayer 15.00 40.00
SP Jason Spezza 15.00 40.00
SS Sami Salo 10.00 25.00
ST Jordan Staal 25.00 60.00
SU Steve Sullivan 10.00 25.00
SW Shea Weber 25.00 60.00
TH Trent Hunter 10.00 25.00
TP Tom Poti 10.00 25.00
TS Teemu Selanne 40.00 100.00
VL Vincent Lecavalier 15.00 40.00
WA Scott Walker 10.00 25.00

2006-07 Be A Player Signatures Duals

DAS C.Simon/S.Avery 4.00 10.00
DBC R.Blake/M.Cammalleri 6.00 15.00
DBK P.Bergeron/P.Kessel 15.00 40.00
DBO M.Savard/G.Murray 5.00 12.00
DBP M.Parrish/P.Bouchard 6.00 15.00
DBU D.Briere/T.Vanek 6.00 15.00
DBV D.Vyborny/G.Brule 5.00 12.00
DCA C.Conroy/A.Tanguay 4.00 10.00
DCB S.Bernier/M.Carle 4.00 10.00
DCH B.Seabrook/D.Keith 15.00 30.00
DCW A.Ward/Z.Chara 6.00 15.00
DDR C.Drury/D.Roy 5.00 12.00
DED J.Smith/D.Roloson 5.00 12.00
DER B.Rafalski/P.Elias 6.00 15.00
DEV A.Vermette/P.Eaves 5.00 12.00
DFL N.Lidstrom/P.Forsberg 15.00 40.00
DFS M.Fleury/J.Staal 10.00 25.00
DFZ N.Zherdev/S.Federov 10.00 25.00
DGC S.Gagne/J.Carter 6.00 15.00
DGE S.Eminger/M.Green 5.00 12.00
DHK S.Koivu/C.Huet 6.00 15.00
DHM M.Straka/H.Lundqvist 15.00 40.00
DHS J.Spezza/D.Heatley 6.00 15.00
DIH J.Iginla/D.Heatley 0.00 20.00
DIP J.Iginla/D.Phaneuf 8.00 20.00
DJS J.Stoll/S.Horcoff 5.00 12.00
DKH M.Hossa/S.Kozlov 6.00 15.00
DKR T.Ruutu/N.Khabibulin 6.00 15.00
DKS S.Samsonov/A.Kovalev 5.00 12.00
DLN M.Naslund/R.Luongo 10.00 25.00
DLS V.Lecavalier/M.St. Louis 8.00 20.00
DMB B.Morrison/L.Bourdon(((((6.00 15.00
DMC B.Campbell/R.Miller 6.00 15.00
DMG P.Marleau/B.Guerin 6.00 15.00
DMK A.McDonald/C.Kunitz 6.00 15.00
DMS M.Malhotra/J.Shelley 4.00 10.00
DNA D.Legwand/S.Sullivan 5.00 12.00
DNE R.Esche/A.Niittymaki 5.00 12.00
DOC A.Ovechkin/C.Clark 60.00 150.00
DPL G.Laraque/A.Peters 5.00 12.00
DRF B.Richards/R.Fedotenko 6.00 15.00
DRH M.Ryder/C.Higgins 4.00 10.00
DRM W.Redden/A.Meszaros 4.00 10.00
DRS R.Regehr/B.Stuart 4.00 10.00
DRT D.Tucker/A.Raycroft 5.00 12.00
DRU M.Richards/R.Umberger 5.00 12.00
DSA D.Alfredsson/J.Spezza 12.00 30.00
DSB R.Brind'Amour/E.Staal 8.00 20.00
DSH M.Sillinger/T.Hunter 4.00 10.00
DSK T.Selanne/S.Koivu 12.00 30.00
DSM A.Markov/S.Souray 6.00 15.00
DSN T.Selanne/S.Niedermayer 12.00 30.00
DSO J.Shelley/S.Ott 4.00 10.00
DSS J.Sakic/P.Stastny 12.00 30.00
DSY A.Yashin/R.Smyth 5.00 12.00
DTL J.Lehtinen/M.Turco 6.00 15.00
DVB M.Van Ryn/J.Bouwmeester 4.00 10.00
DWB D.Weight/B.Boyes 6.00 15.00
DWS K.Wellwood/M.Stajan 5.00 12.00

2006-07 Be A Player Signatures Trios

TBKS Savard/Bergeron/Kessel 50.00 125.00
TCWB Weber/Carle/Bourdon 40.00 100.00
TDBV Drury/Briere/Vanek 25.00 60.00
TFCO Frolov/Cam/O'Sully 25.00 60.00
TFLS Sully/Leg/Forsberg 50.00 125.00
TFSM Malone/Fleury/Staal 50.00 125.00
TGCR Gagne/Richards/Carter 25.00 60.00
THHK Huet/Higgins/Kovalev 20.00 50.00
THKH Hossa/Holik/Kozlov 25.00 60.00
TIPT Iginla/Tanguay/Phaneuf 30.00 80.00
TKRL Koivu/Ryder/Laten 25.00 60.00
TLNM Naslund/Luongo/Morris 40.00 100.00
TLRS Lecav/Richards/St. Lou 40.00 100.00
TMAR Afinogenov/Roy/Miller 25.00 60.00
TOKC Kolzig/Ovechkin/Clark 250.00 600.00
TRKS Ruutu/Seabrook/Khabi 25.00 60.00
TRPP Peca/Perr/Raycroft 20.00 50.00
TRSH Stoll/Horcoff/Roloson 20.00 50.00
TSBC Cole/Brind'Amour/Staal 30.00 80.00
TSNP Straka/Nylander/Prucha 20.00 50.00
TSTS Sakic/Theodore/Stastny 50.00 125.00
TTBM Toskala/Michal/Bernier 20.00 50.00
TTCM Marleau/Thorn/Cheech 40.00 100.00
TTLO Lehtinen/Turco/Ott 25.00 60.00
TTWS Tucker/Wellw/Stajan 20.00 50.00
TWBS Weight/Boyes/Stemp 25.00 60.00
TYSS Yashin/Smyth/Sillinger 20.00 50.00

2006-07 Be A Player Unmasked Warriors

UM1 Ryan Miller 6.00 15.00
UM2 Jose Theodore 6.00 15.00
UM3 Marty Turco 6.00 15.00
UM4 Dwayne Roloson 5.00 12.00
UM5 Cristobal Huet 5.00 12.00
UM6 Henrik Lundqvist 15.00 40.00
UM7 Cam Ward 6.00 15.00
UM8 Marc-Andre Fleury 12.00 30.00
UM9 Andrew Raycroft 5.00 12.00
UM10 Roberto Luongo 10.00 25.00

2006-07 Be A Player Up Close and Personal

UC1 Alex Tanguay .60 1.50
UC2 Justin Williams .75 2.00
UC3 Alexander Ovechkin 4.00 10.00
UC4 Alexei Yashin .75 2.00
UC5 Andrew Raycroft .75 2.00
UC6 Andy McDonald .75 2.00
UC7 Bill Guerin 1.00 2.50
UC8 Brad Richards 1.00 2.50
UC9 Brian Campbell .75 2.00
UC10 Chris Drury .75 2.00
UC11 Cristobal Huet .75 2.00
UC12 Dany Heatley .75 2.00
UC13 Darcy Tucker .75 2.00
UC14 Ryan Miller 1.00 2.50
UC15 Dion Phaneuf .75 2.00
UC16 Doug Weight 1.00 2.50
UC17 Dwayne Roloson .75 2.00
UC18 Eric Staal 1.25 3.00
UC19 Henrik Lundqvist 2.50 6.00
UC20 Henrik Sedin 1.25 3.00
UC21 Jarome Iginla 1.25 3.00
UC22 Jason Spezza 1.00 2.50
UC23 Jonathan Cheechoo .75 2.00
UC24 Daniel Briere 1.00 2.50
UC25 Joe Sakic 2.00 5.00
UC26 Joe Thornton 1.50 4.00
UC27 Lee Stempniak .60 1.50
UC28 Marc Savard .60 1.50
UC29 Marc-Andre Fleury 2.00 5.00
UC30 Marian Hossa 1.00 2.50
UC31 Mark Parrish .60 1.50
UC32 Markus Naslund 1.00 2.50
UC33 Martin St. Louis 1.00 2.50
UC34 Martin Straka .60 1.50
UC35 Marty Turco 1.00 2.50
UC36 Michael Peca .75 2.00
UC37 Michael Ryder .60 1.50
UC38 Nicklas Lidstrom 1.00 2.50
UC39 Nikolai Khabibulin 1.00 2.50
UC40 Olaf Kolzig 1.00 2.50
UC41 Martin Havlat .60 1.50
UC42 Patrice Bergeron 1.25 3.00
UC43 Patrick Marleau 1.00 2.50
UC44 Patrik Elias 1.00 2.50
UC45 Paul Stastny 1.50 4.00
UC46 Peter Forsberg 2.00 5.00
UC47 Rob Blake 1.00 2.50
UC48 Roberto Luongo 1.50 4.00
UC49 Rod Brind`Amour 1.00 2.50
UC50 Ryan Smyth .75 2.00
UC51 Saku Koivu 1.00 2.50
UC52 Scott Niedermayer 1.00 2.50
UC53 Sergei Federov 1.50 4.00
UC54 Simon Gagne 1.00 2.50
UC55 Kimmo Timonen .60 1.50
UC56 Teemu Selanne 2.00 5.00
UC57 Jordan Staal 1.50 4.00
UC58 Vincent Lecavalier 1.00 2.50
UC59 Wade Redden .60 1.50
UC60 Zdeno Chara 1.00 2.50

2007-08 Be A Player

COMP.SET w/o SPs (200) 20.00 50.00
1 Ryan Getzlaf .30 .75
2 Jean-Sebastien Giguere .30 .75
3 Corey Perry .50 1.25
4 Teemu Selanne .60 1.50
5 Chris Pronger .30 .75
6 Chris Kunitz .30 .75
7 Scott Niedermayer .30 .75
8 Ilya Kovalchuk .30 .75
9 Eric Perrin .20 .50
10 Colby Armstrong .20 .50
11 Kari Lehtonen .25 .60
12 Mark Recchi .40 1.00
13 Slava Kozlov .20 .50
14 Patrice Bergeron .40 1.00
15 Marc Savard .20 .50
16 Tim Thomas .30 .75
17 Zdeno Chara .30 .75
18 Marco Sturm .20 .50
19 Phil Kessel .30 .75
20 Glen Murray .25 .60
21 Thomas Vanek .25 .60
22 Ryan Miller .30 .75
23 Derek Roy .20 .50
24 Jason Pominville .20 .50
25 Drew Stafford .20 .50
26 Steve Bernier .20 .50
27 Miikka Kiprusoff .30 .75
28 Jarome Iginla .40 1.00
29 Daymond Langkow .20 .50
30 Dion Phaneuf .25 .60
31 Alex Tanguay .25 .60

32 Kristian Huselius .20 .50
33 Matthew Lombardi .20 .50
34 Curtis Joseph .40 1.00
35 Eric Staal .40 1.00
36 Rod Brind'Amour .30 .75
37 Cam Ward .30 .75
38 Justin Williams .25 .60
39 Ray Whitney .25 .60
40 Erik Cole .20 .50
41 Jason Williams .20 .50
42 Nikolai Khabibulin .30 .75
43 Patrick Sharp .30 .75
44 Brent Seabrook .20 .50
45 Robert Lang .20 .50
46 Martin Havlat .30 .75
47 Duncan Keith .25 .60
48 Joe Sakic .60 1.50
49 Jose Theodore .30 .75
50 Ryan Smyth .25 .60
51 Milan Hejduk .25 .60
52 Marek Svatos .20 .50
53 Paul Stastny .25 .60
54 Wojtek Wolski .25 .60
55 Rick Nash .30 .75
56 Gilbert Brule .25 .60
57 Pascal Leclaire .25 .60
58 Nikolai Zherdev .20 .50
59 Rostislav Klesla .20 .50
60 Michael Peca .25 .60
61 Mike Modano .50 1.25
62 Brad Richards .30 .75
63 Marty Turco .30 .75
64 Mike Ribeiro .20 .50
65 Brenden Morrow .25 .60
66 Jere Lehtinen .20 .50
67 Dominik Hasek .50 1.25
68 Nicklas Lidstrom .30 .75
69 Pavel Datsyuk .50 1.25
70 Chris Osgood .30 .75
71 Henrik Zetterberg .40 1.00
72 Dan Cleary .25 .60
73 Tomas Holmstrom .25 .60
74 Valtteri Filppula .20 .50
75 Jarret Stoll .25 .60
76 Ales Hemsky .25 .60
77 Mathieu Garon .25 .60
78 Shawn Horcoff .20 .50
79 Dustin Penner .25 .60
80 Joni Pitkanen .20 .50
81 Dwayne Roloson .25 .60
82 Olli Jokinen .25 .60
83 Tomas Vokoun .25 .60
84 Nathan Horton .30 .75
85 David Booth .20 .50
86 Stephen Weiss .20 .50
87 Jay Bouwmeester .20 .50
88 Anze Kopitar .50 1.25
89 Rob Blake .30 .75
90 Alexander Frolov .20 .50
91 Dustin Brown .30 .75
92 Mike Cammalleri .25 .60
93 Patrick O'Sullivan .25 .60
94 Marian Gaborik .30 .75
95 Niklas Backstrom .30 .75
96 Pierre-Marc Bouchard .30 .75
97 Brian Rolston .25 .60
98 Josh Harding .30 .75
99 Mikko Koivu .25 .60
100 Saku Koivu .30 .75
101 Mark Streit .20 .50
102 Tomas Plekanec .20 .50
103 Michael Ryder .20 .50
104 Alex Kovalev .25 .60
105 Chris Higgins .20 .50
106 Andrei Markov .30 .75
107 Guillaume Latendresse .25 .60
108 Alexander Radulov .30 .75
109 Jason Arnott .25 .60
110 Chris Mason .25 .60
111 Martin Erat .20 .50
112 J.P. Dumont .20 .50
113 David Legwand .25 .60
114 Martin Brodeur .75 2.00
115 Zach Parise .30 .75
116 Patrik Elias .30 .75
117 Brian Gionta .20 .50
118 John Madden .20 .50
119 Travis Zajac .20 .50
120 Rick DiPietro .25 .60
121 Mike Comrie .25 .60
122 Bill Guerin .30 .75
123 Miroslav Satan .25 .60
124 Trent Hunter .20 .50
125 Ruslan Fedotenko .20 .50
126 Jaromir Jagr 1.00 2.50
127 Henrik Lundqvist .75 2.00
128 Chris Drury .25 .60
129 Scott Gomez .25 .60
130 Brendan Shanahan .30 .75
131 Michal Rozsival .20 .50
132 Sean Avery .20 .50
133 Jason Spezza .30 .75
134 Dany Heatley .25 .60
135 Ray Emery .25 .60
136 Antoine Vermette .20 .50
137 Mike Fisher .20 .50
138 Daniel Alfredsson .30 .75
139 Wade Redden .20 .50
140 Martin Gerber .25 .60
141 Mike Richards .25 .60
142 Martin Biron .25 .60
143 Daniel Briere .30 .75
144 Simon Gagne .30 .75
145 Mike Knuble .20 .50
146 Jeff Carter .25 .60
147 R.J. Umberger .20 .50
148 Steven Reinprecht .20 .50
149 Shane Doan .25 .60
150 Ilya Bryzgalov .30 .75
151 Ed Jovanovski .25 .60
152 Radim Vrbata .20 .50
153 Keith Ballard .20 .50
154 Petr Sykora .25 .60
155 Marc-Andre Fleury .60 1.50
156 Marian Hossa .30 .75
157 Evgeni Malkin .60 1.50
158 Sergei Gonchar .20 .50
159 Ryan Malone .20 .50
160 Jordan Staal .25 .60
161 Ryan Whitney .25 .60
162 Joe Thornton .50 1.25
163 Evgeni Nabokov .25 .60
164 Jonathan Cheechoo .25 .60
165 Milan Michalek .20 .50
166 Brian Campbell .25 .60
167 Patrick Marleau .30 .75
168 Paul Kariya .30 .75
169 Manny Legace .25 .60
170 Andy McDonald .25 .60
171 Brad Boyes .20 .50
172 Lee Stempniak .20 .50
173 Keith Tkachuk .30 .75
174 Vincent Lecavalier .30 .75
175 Mike Smith .30 .75
176 Jussi Jokinen .20 .50
177 Martin St. Louis .30 .75
178 Paul Ranger .20 .50
179 Karri Ramo .30 .75
180 Mats Sundin .30 .75
181 Vesa Toskala .25 .60
182 Alexander Steen .20 .50
183 Darcy Tucker .25 .60
184 Tomas Kaberle .20 .50
185 Nikolai Antropov .25 .60
186 Matt Stajan .20 .50
187 Jason Blake .20 .50
188 Roberto Luongo .50 1.25
189 Daniel Sedin .40 1.00
190 Markus Naslund .30 .75
191 Ryan Kesler .30 .75
192 Alexander Edler .20 .50
193 Brendan Morrison .20 .50
194 Henrik Sedin .40 1.00
195 Alexander Ovechkin 1.25 3.00
196 Olaf Kolzig .30 .75
197 Michael Nylander .20 .50
198 Sergei Fedorov .50 1.25
199 Mike Green .25 .60
200 Alexander Semin .30 .75
201 Bobby Ryan RC 12.00 30.00
202 Drew Miller RC 6.00 15.00
203 Ryan Carter RC 5.00 12.00
204 Kent Huskins RC 5.00 12.00
205 Petteri Wirtanen RC 5.00 12.00
206 Ondrej Pavelec RC 10.00 25.00
207 Bryan Little RC 8.00 20.00
208 Brett Sterling RC 5.00 12.00
209 Tobias Enstrom RC 8.00 20.00
210 Tuukka Rask RC 20.00 50.00
211 David Krejci RC 15.00 40.00
212 Vladimir Sobotka RC 6.00 15.00
213 Milan Lucic RC 20.00 50.00
214 Matt Hunwick RC 5.00 12.00
215 Mike Weber RC 5.00 12.00
216 Patrick Kaleta RC 5.00 12.00
217 Curtis McElhinney RC 8.00 20.00
218 Matt Keetley RC 5.00 12.00
219 Casey Borer RC 5.00 12.00
220 Patrick Kane RC 40.00 100.00
221 Jack Skille RC 6.00 15.00
222 Jonathan Toews RC 80.00 150.00
223 Kris Versteeg RC 15.00 40.00
224 Petri Kontiola RC 5.00 12.00
225 Jake Dowell RC 5.00 12.00
226 David Koci RC 5.00 12.00
227 T.J. Hensick RC 6.00 15.00
228 Tyler Weiman RC 6.00 15.00
229 David Jones RC 5.00 12.00
230 Jaroslav Hlinka RC 6.00 15.00
231 Johnny Boychuk RC 8.00 20.00
232 Jared Boll RC 6.00 15.00
233 Kris Russell RC 8.00 20.00
234 Matt Niskanen RC 8.00 20.00
235 Tobias Stephan RC 6.00 15.00
236 Sam Gagner RC 10.00 25.00
237 Andrew Cogliano RC 6.00 15.00
238 Tom Gilbert RC 6.00 15.00
239 Rob Schremp RC 6.00 15.00
240 Liam Reddox RC 5.00 12.00
241 Cory Murphy RC 5.00 12.00
242 Stefan Meyer RC 6.00 15.00
243 Tanner Glass RC 5.00 12.00
244 Jack Johnson RC 6.00 15.00
245 Jonathan Bernier RC 10.00 25.00
246 Lauri Tukonen RC 5.00 12.00
247 Jonathan Quick RC 150.00 300.00
248 Matt Moulson RC 8.00 20.00
249 Brady Murray RC 5.00 12.00
250 James Sheppard RC 5.00 12.00
251 Aaron Voros RC 5.00 12.00
252 Cal Clutterbuck RC 8.00 20.00
253 Carey Price RC 50.00 125.00
254 Jaroslav Halak RC 15.00 40.00
255 Kyle Chipchura RC 8.00 20.00
256 Sergei Kostitsyn RC 6.00 15.00
257 Ryan O'Byrne RC 8.00 20.00
258 Ville Koistinen RC 5.00 12.00
259 Antti Pihlstrom RC 6.00 15.00
260 Nicklas Bergfors RC 5.00 12.00
261 David Clarkson RC 5.00 12.00
262 Andy Greene RC 6.00 15.00
263 Olli Malmivaara RC 5.00 12.00
264 Frans Nielsen RC 8.00 20.00
265 Marc Staal RC 8.00 20.00
266 Brandon Dubinsky RC 10.00 25.00
267 Ryan Callahan RC 10.00 25.00
268 Ivan Baranka RC 6.00 15.00
269 Greg Moore RC 5.00 12.00
270 Daniel Girardi RC 6.00 15.00
271 Nick Foligno RC 10.00 25.00
272 Brian Elliott RC 10.00 25.00
273 Alexander Nikulin RC 5.00 12.00
274 Steve Downie RC 6.00 15.00
275 Riley Cote RC 6.00 15.00
276 Ryan Parent RC 5.00 12.00
277 Denis Tolpeko RC 5.00 12.00
278 Peter Mueller RC 6.00 15.00
279 Martin Hanzal RC 6.00 15.00
280 Daniel Carcillo RC 6.00 15.00
281 Daniel Winnik RC 6.00 15.00
282 Craig Weller RC 5.00 12.00
283 Tyler Kennedy RC 5.00 12.00
284 Devin Setoguchi RC 8.00 20.00
285 Thomas Greiss RC 10.00 25.00
286 Torrey Mitchell RC 6.00 15.00
287 Lukas Kaspar RC 5.00 12.00
288 Tomas Plihal RC 5.00 12.00
289 Erik Johnson RC 8.00 20.00
290 David Perron RC 10.00 25.00
291 Steve Wagner RC 5.00 12.00
292 Matt Smaby RC 5.00 12.00
293 Mike Lundin RC 5.00 12.00
294 Jiri Tlusty RC 8.00 20.00
295 Anton Stralman RC 5.00 12.00
296 Mason Raymond RC 8.00 20.00
297 Jannik Hansen RC 6.00 15.00
298 Drew MacIntyre RC 5.00 12.00
299 Nicklas Backstrom RC 20.00 50.00
300 Chris Bourque RC 6.00 15.00
301 Steven Stamkos XRC 40.00 100.00
302 Michael Frolik XRC 8.00 20.00
303 Alex Pietrangelo XRC 15.00 40.00
304 Zach Bogosian XRC 15.00 40.00
305 Oscar Moller XRC 8.00 20.00
306 Colton Gillies XRC 10.00 25.00
307 Viktor Tikhonov XRC 10.00 25.00
308 Luke Schenn XRC 12.00 30.00
309 Andreas Nodl XRC 8.00 20.00
310 Blake Wheeler XRC 20.00 40.00
311 Fabian Brunnstrom XRC 12.00 30.00
312 Drew Doughty XRC 25.00 50.00
313 Kyle Okposo XRC 15.00 40.00
314 Kyle Turris XRC 30.00 60.00
315 Zach Boychuk XRC 10.00 25.00
316 Nikita Filatov XRC 8.00 20.00
317 Petr Vrana XRC 8.00 20.00
318 Luca Sbisa XRC 6.00 15.00
319 Mikkel Boedker XRC 12.00 30.00
320 Patric Hornqvist XRC 6.00 15.00
321 T.J. Oshie XRC 20.00 50.00
322 Nikolai Kulemin XRC 6.00 15.00
323 Brandon Sutter XRC 10.00 25.00
324 Derick Brassard XRC 6.00 15.00
325 James Neal XRC 15.00 40.00
326 Claude Giroux XRC 30.00 60.00
327 Vladimir Mihalik XRC 6.00 15.00
328 Patrik Berglund XRC 15.00 40.00
329 Adam Pardy XRC 6.00 15.00
330 Jonas Frogren XRC 8.00 20.00
331 Jakub Voracek XRC 10.00 25.00
332 Mark Fistric XRC 8.00 20.00
333 Marc-Andre Gragnani XRC 8.00 20.00
334 Justin Abdelkader XRC 12.00 30.00
335 Brian Boyle XRC 12.00 30.00
336 Shawn Matthias XRC 6.00 15.00
337 Lauri Korpikoski XRC 6.00 15.00
338 Robbie Earl XRC 6.00 15.00
339 Steve Mason XRC 25.00 60.00
340 Brian Lee XRC 12.00 30.00
341 Kevin Porter XRC 6.00 15.00
342 Alex Goligoski XRC 12.00 30.00
343 Ryan Jones XRC 10.00 25.00
344 Boris Valabik XRC 8.00 20.00
345 Darren Helm XRC 10.00 25.00
346 Derek Dorsett XRC 6.00 15.00
347 Wayne Simmonds XRC 10.00 25.00
348 Ben Bishop XRC 15.00 40.00
349 John Mitchell XRC 6.00 15.00
350 Jonathan Ericsson XRC 8.00 20.00
351 Tyler Plante XRC 8.00 20.00
352 Andrew Ebbett XRC 6.00 15.00
353 Tom Sestito XRC 8.00 20.00
354 Jonathan Filewich XRC 6.00 15.00
355 Ilya Zubov XRC 8.00 20.00
356 Anssi Salmela XRC 8.00 20.00
357 Dane Byers XRC 6.00 15.00
358 Adam Pineault XRC 6.00 15.00
359 Mike Iggulden XRC 8.00 20.00
360 Matt D'Agostini XRC 6.00 15.00

2007-08 Be A Player Player's Club

*PLAYER'S CLUB: 2.5X TO 6X BASE

2007-08 Be A Player Player's Club Platinum

*PLATINUM: 10X TO 25X BASE

2007-08 Be A Player Signatures

SAA Adrian Aucoin 4.00 10.00
SAF Andrew Ference 4.00 10.00
SAK Anze Kopitar 8.00 20.00
SAM Andrei Markov 6.00 15.00
SAO Alexander Ovechkin 125.00 300.00
SAP Andrew Peters 4.00 10.00
SAR Jason Arnott 5.00 12.00
SAS Alexander Semin 6.00 15.00
SAT Alex Tanguay 5.00 12.00
SAV Aaron Voros 4.00 10.00
SBA Nicklas Backstrom 8.00 20.00
SBB Brad Boyes 4.00 10.00
SBC Brian Campbell 5.00 12.00
SBD Daniel Briere 6.00 15.00
SBM Brendan Morrison 4.00 10.00
SBO Dan Boyle 4.00 10.00
SBP Brian Pothier 4.00 10.00
SBR Brian Rafalski 5.00 12.00
SBS Brent Seabrook 8.00 20.00
SBW Brendan Witt 4.00 10.00
SCA Mike Cammalleri 5.00 12.00
SCC Chris Clark 4.00 10.00
SCH Chris Higgins 4.00 10.00
SCI Chris Campoli 4.00 10.00
SCK Chuck Kobasew 4.00 10.00
SCL David Clarkson 4.00 10.00
SCM Chris Mason 5.00 12.00
SCN Chris Neil 4.00 10.00
SCO Mike Commodore 4.00 10.00
SCP Carey Price 30.00 80.00
SCR Chris Conner 4.00 10.00
SCS Cory Stillman 4.00 10.00
SCW Cam Ward 6.00 15.00
SCY Dan Cleary 5.00 12.00
SDA Dan Hamhuis 5.00 12.00
SDB Dustin Brown 6.00 15.00
SDC Daniel Carcillo 5.00 12.00
SDE Derian Hatcher 5.00 12.00
SDH Dominik Hasek 12.00 30.00
SDK Duncan Keith 5.00 12.00
SDM David Moss 6.00 15.00
SDO Donald Brashear 4.00 10.00
SDP Dion Phaneuf 5.00 12.00
SDR Derek Roy 4.00 10.00
SDS Daniel Sedin 8.00 20.00
SDT Darcy Tucker 5.00 12.00
SDV David Vyborny 4.00 10.00
SEC Erik Cole 4.00 10.00
SES Eric Staal 8.00 20.00
SFI Mike Fisher 4.00 10.00
SFR Alexander Frolov 4.00 10.00
SGA Simon Gagne 6.00 15.00
SGC Gregory Campbell 4.00 10.00
SGE Garnet Exelby 4.00 10.00
SHA Josh Harding 6.00 15.00
SHE Dany Heatley 5.00 12.00
SHM Martin Hanzal 5.00 12.00
SHO Marian Hossa 6.00 15.00
SHS Henrik Sedin 8.00 20.00
SHU Cristobal Huet 5.00 12.00
SIB Ilya Bryzgalov 6.00 15.00
SJB Jay Bouwmeester 4.00 10.00
SJC Jonathan Cheechoo 5.00 12.00
SJE Jeff Carter 5.00 12.00
SJH Johan Hedberg 5.00 12.00
SJI Jarome Iginla 8.00 20.00
SJJ Jack Johnson 5.00 12.00
SJL Jamie Langenbrunner 4.00 10.00
SJM Jamal Mayers 4.00 10.00
SJO Joe Thornton 12.00 30.00
SJP Jason Pominville 4.00 10.00
SJR Jarkko Ruutu 4.00 10.00
SJS Joe Sakic 25.00 50.00
SJT Jonathan Toews 25.00 60.00
SJW Jason Williams 4.00 10.00
SKB Keith Ballard 4.00 10.00
SKC Kyle Chipchura 6.00 15.00
SKD Kris Draper 4.00 10.00
SKE Tyler Kennedy 4.00 10.00
SKI Miikka Kiprusoff 6.00 15.00
SKM Kimmo Timonen 4.00 10.00
SKN Mike Knuble 4.00 10.00
SKO Saku Koivu 6.00 15.00
SKQ Kyle Quincey 4.00 10.00
SKR Kris Russell 6.00 15.00
SKS Phil Kessel 8.00 20.00
SLE Jere Lehtinen 4.00 10.00
SLJ Andreas Lilja 4.00 10.00
SLS Lee Stempniak 4.00 10.00
SLU Milan Lucic 15.00 40.00
SMA Manny Malhotra 4.00 10.00
SMC Matt Carle 4.00 10.00
SMF Marc-Andre Fleury 12.00 30.00
SMI Milan Michalek 4.00 10.00
SMK Mike Komisarek 4.00 10.00
SML Mike Lundin 4.00 10.00
SMN Markus Naslund 6.00 15.00
SMP Michael Peca 5.00 12.00
SMU Peter Mueller 5.00 12.00
SMY Cory Murphy 4.00 10.00
SNA Nikolai Antropov 5.00 12.00
SNB Niklas Backstrom 6.00 15.00
SNI Matt Niskanen 6.00 15.00
SNL Nicklas Lidstrom 8.00 20.00
SNS Nick Schultz 4.00 10.00
SOJ Olli Jokinen 5.00 12.00
SOK Olaf Kolzig 6.00 15.00
SOS Chris Osgood 6.00 15.00
SPA Mark Parrish 4.00 10.00
SPD David Perron 8.00 20.00
SPH Chris Phillips 4.00 10.00
SPI Pierre-Marc Bouchard 6.00 15.00
SPK Patrick Kane 30.00 60.00
SPM Patrick Marleau 6.00 15.00
SPN Paul Martin 4.00 10.00
SPR Paul Ranger 4.00 10.00
SPS Paul Stastny 5.00 12.00
SRB Rod Brind'Amour 6.00 15.00
SRD Rob Davison 4.00 10.00
SRI Mike Richards 5.00 12.00
SRK Ryan Kesler 6.00 15.00
SRL Roberto Luongo 12.00 30.00
SRN Rick Nash 6.00 15.00
SRO Rostislav Olesz 4.00 10.00
SRR Robyn Regehr 4.00 10.00
SRS Ryan Smyth 5.00 12.00
SRW Ryan Whitney 5.00 12.00
SSA Marc Savard 4.00 10.00
SSF Sergei Fedorov 10.00 25.00
SSG Sergei Gonchar 4.00 10.00
SSH James Sheppard 4.00 10.00
SSI Mike Sillinger 4.00 10.00
SSJ Matt Stajan 4.00 10.00
SSK Slava Kozlov 4.00 10.00
SSM Martin St. Louis 6.00 15.00
SSO Steve Ott 4.00 10.00
SSP Jason Spezza 6.00 15.00
SSR Steven Reinprecht 4.00 10.00
SST Jordan Staal 5.00 12.00
SSW Stephen Weiss 4.00 10.00
SSY Petr Sykora 5.00 12.00
STC Tim Connolly 4.00 10.00
STE Tobias Enstrom 6.00 15.00
STI Tim Thomas 6.00 15.00
STL Trevor Linden 6.00 15.00
STM Torrey Mitchell 5.00 12.00
STO Jordin Tootoo 6.00 15.00
STP Tomas Plekanec 4.00 10.00
STR Tuomo Ruutu 6.00 15.00
STT Tim Taylor 4.00 10.00
STV Thomas Vanek 5.00 12.00
STW Todd White 4.00 10.00
STZ Travis Zajac 4.00 10.00
SVL Vincent Lecavalier 6.00 15.00
SWA Scott Walker 4.00 10.00
SWE Shea Weber 5.00 12.00
SWH Ray Whitney 5.00 12.00
SWI Justin Williams 5.00 12.00
SWR Wade Redden 4.00 10.00
SWW Wojtek Wolski 5.00 12.00
SZP Zach Parise 6.00 15.00

2007-08 Be A Player Signatures Duals

2SAM J.Arnott/C.Mason 6.00 15.00
2SBD B.Seabrook/D.Keith 15.00 30.00
2SBH J.Harding/N.Backstrom 8.00 20.00
2SBL D.Boyle/M.Lundin 5.00 12.00
2SBS E.Staal/R.Brind'Amour 10.00 25.00
2SCB J.Carter/D.Briere 8.00 20.00
2SCK A.Kopitar/M.Cammalleri 12.00 30.00
2SCR D.Roy/T.Connolly 5.00 12.00
2SCV D.Carcillo/A.Voros 6.00 15.00
2SCW E.Cole/R.Whitney 6.00 15.00
2SDC D.Cleary/K.Draper 8.00 20.00
2SEJ E.Staal/J.Staal 12.00 30.00
2SEN T.Enstrom/M.Miskanen 8.00 20.00
2SFS M.Fleury/J.Staal 10.00 25.00
2SGW S.Gonchar/R.Whitney 6.00 15.00
2SHO D.Hasek/C.Osgood 15.00 40.00
2SHS M.Hossa/P.Sykora 8.00 20.00
2SIM J.Iginla/D.Moss 12.00 30.00
2SJB Jokinen/Bouwmeester 6.00 15.00
2SJP J.Sakic/P.Stastny 20.00 50.00
2SJR J.Johnson/K.Russell 8.00 20.00
2SJT J.Sheppard/T.Kennedy 5.00 12.00
2SKL M.Kiprusoff/R.Luongo 12.00 30.00
2SKR M.Richards/M.Knuble 6.00 15.00
2SLH M.Lucic/M.Hanzal 8.00 20.00
2SLS Lecavalier/M.St. Louis 8.00 20.00
2SMC P.Marleau/J.Cheechoo 8.00 20.00
2SMK A.Markov/M.Komisarek 8.00 20.00
2SMT T.Thomas/G.Murray 8.00 20.00
2SNL M.Naslund/R.Luongo 12.00 30.00
2SNV R.Nash/D.Vyborny 8.00 20.00
2SOT J.Spezza/M.Fisher 8.00 20.00
2SPP C.Price/T.Plekanec 25.00 60.00
2SPV T.Vanek/J.Pominville 6.00 15.00
2SRA R.Regehr/A.Aucoin 5.00 12.00
2SRC W.Radden/M.Commodore 5.00 12.00
2SRQ B.Rafalski/K.Quincey 6.00 15.00
2SSB L.Stempniak/B.Boyes 5.00 12.00
2SSH S.Fedorov/C.Huet 12.00 30.00
2SSK M.Savard/P.Kessel 8.00 20.00
2SSS H.Sedin/D.Sedin 10.00 25.00
2STC J.Thornton/B.Campbell 12.00 30.00
2STK J.Toews/P.Kane 75.00 150.00
2STM J.Toews/P.Mueller 20.00 50.00
2SWC B.Witt/C.Campoli 5.00 12.00

2007-08 Be A Player Signatures Trios

3SASF Heatley/Spezza/Fisher 20.00 50.00
3SBTP Toews/Mueller/Price 100.00 200.00
3SCAP Carcillo/Peters/Neil 15.00 40.00
3SCPV Vanek/Connolly/Pominville 15.00 40.00
3SCWS Williams/Staal/Cole 25.00 60.00
3SHKS Kennedy/Hossa/Staal 20.00 50.00
3SHPK Plekanec/Higgins/Koivu 20.00 50.00
3SIKT Tanguay/Kiprusoff/Iginla 25.00 60.00
3SKBR Knuble/Richards/Briere 20.00 50.00
3SKPL Kiprusoff/Price/Luongo 100.00 200.00
3SKSM Kane/Mitchell/Sheppard 30.00 80.00
3SLMH Michalek/Hanzal/Lucic 50.00 125.00
3SMBS Mayers/Boyes/Stempniak 12.00 30.00
3SMHF Fleury/Mason/Huet 15.00 40.00
3SNSS Naslund/Sedin/Sedin 25.00 60.00
3SPDB Brind'Amour/Draper/Peca 30.00 60.00
3SPRC Redden/Phillips/Commodore 12.00 30.00
3SSBH Sheppard/Bouchard/Harding 20.00 50.00
3SSHN St. Louis/Nash/Heatley 20.00 50.00
3SSMK Savard/Murray/Kessel 30.00 60.00
3SSSS Sakic/Stastny/Smyth 30.00 60.00
3SSTT Sakic/Thornton/Toews 100.00 200.00
3STCM Thornton/Cheech/Michalek 30.00 80.00

2008-09 Be A Player

1 Ryan Getzlaf .30 .75
2 Corey Perry .50 1.25
3 Chris Pronger .30 .75
4 Teemu Selanne .60 1.50
5 Bobby Ryan .25 .60
6 Scott Niedermayer .30 .75
7 Jean-Sebastien Giguere .30 .75
8 Ilya Kovalchuk .30 .75
9 Bryan Little .25 .60
10 Kari Lehtonen .40 1.00
11 Slava Kozlov .20 .50
12 Todd White .20 .50
13 Patrice Bergeron .40 1.00
14 Marc Savard .20 .50
15 David Krejci .30 .75
16 Phil Kessel .30 .75
17 Zdeno Chara .30 .75
18 Tim Thomas .30 .75
19 Michael Ryder .20 .50
20 Derek Roy .20 .50
21 Thomas Vanek .25 .60
22 Jason Pominville .20 .50
23 Ryan Miller .30 .75
24 Drew Stafford .20 .50
25 Jarome Iginla .40 1.00
26 Mike Cammalleri .25 .60
27 Daymond Langkow .20 .50
28 Todd Bertuzzi .30 .75
29 Dion Phaneuf .25 .60
30 Miikka Kiprusoff .30 .75
31 Rene Bourque .20 .50
32 Ray Whitney .25 .60
33 Cam Ward .30 .75
34 Eric Staal .40 1.00
35 Tuomo Ruutu .30 .75
36 Rod Brind`Amour .30 .75
37 Sergei Samsonov .25 .60
38 Patrick Kane .60 1.50
39 Jonathan Toews .50 1.25
40 Kris Versteeg .20 .50
41 Patrick Sharp .30 .75
42 Brian Campbell .25 .60
43 Nikolai Khabibulin .30 .75
44 Cristobal Huet .25 .60
45 Paul Stastny .25 .60
46 Milan Hejduk .25 .60
47 Ryan Smyth .25 .60
48 Wojtek Wolski .25 .60
49 Joe Sakic .60 1.50
50 Peter Budaj .25 .60
51 Rick Nash .30 .75
52 Kristian Huselius .20 .50
53 R.J. Umberger .20 .50
54 Mike Commodore .20 .50
55 Fredrik Modin .20 .50
56 Brenden Morrow .25 .60
57 Brad Richards .30 .75
58 Mike Ribeiro .20 .50
59 Loui Eriksson .20 .50
60 Mike Modano .50 1.25
61 Marty Turco .30 .75
62 Pavel Datsyuk .50 1.25
63 Marian Hossa .30 .75
64 Henrik Zetterberg .40 1.00
65 Nicklas Lidstrom .30 .75
66 Tomas Holmstrom .25 .60
67 Johan Franzen .25 .60
68 Chris Osgood .30 .75
69 Sam Gagner .20 .50
70 Ales Hemsky .25 .60
71 Sheldon Souray .20 .50
72 Andrew Cogliano .20 .50
73 Shawn Horcoff .20 .50
74 Dwayne Roloson .25 .60
75 Stephen Weiss .20 .50
76 David Booth .20 .50
77 Jay Bouwmeester .20 .50
78 Nathan Horton .25 .60
79 Tomas Vokoun .25 .60
80 Anze Kopitar .50 1.25
81 Dustin Brown .30 .75
82 Alexander Frolov .20 .50
83 Patrick O'Sullivan .25 .60
84 Jarret Stoll .25 .60
85 Marek Zidlicky .20 .50
86 Mikko Koivu .25 .60
87 Antti Miettinen .20 .50
88 Andrew Brunette .20 .50
89 Pierre-Marc Bouchard .30 .75
90 Niklas Backstrom .30 .75
91 Robert Lang .20 .50
92 Alex Kovalev .25 .60
93 Andrei Markov .30 .75
94 Alex Tanguay .20 .50
95 Carey Price .60 1.50
96 Andrei Kostitsyn .25 .60
97 Saku Koivu .30 .75
98 J.P. Dumont .20 .50
99 Shea Weber .25 .60
100 Martin Erat .20 .50
101 Jason Arnott .25 .60
102 Dan Ellis .20 .50
103 Martin Brodeur .75 2.00
104 Patrik Elias .30 .75
105 Zach Parise .30 .75
106 Brian Gionta .20 .50
107 Travis Zajac .20 .50
108 Scott Clemmensen .20 .50
109 Mark Streit .20 .50
110 Doug Weight .30 .75
111 Bill Guerin .30 .75
112 Trent Hunter .20 .50
113 Joey MacDonald .30 .75
114 Rick DiPietro .25 .60
115 Nikolai Zherdev .20 .50
116 Scott Gomez .25 .60
117 Markus Naslund .30 .75
118 Chris Drury .25 .60
119 Brandon Dubinsky .20 .50
120 Henrik Lundqvist .75 2.00
121 Wade Redden .20 .50
122 Dany Heatley .25 .60
123 Daniel Alfredsson .30 .75
124 Jason Spezza .30 .75
125 Nick Foligno .30 .75
126 Antoine Vermette .20 .50
127 Alex Auld .20 .50
128 Jeff Carter .25 .60
129 Mike Richards .25 .60
130 Simon Gagne .30 .75
131 Scott Hartnell .20 .50
132 Mike Knuble .20 .50
133 Martin Biron .25 .60
134 Peter Mueller .25 .60
135 Shane Doan .25 .60
136 Olli Jokinen .25 .60
137 Ed Jovanovski .25 .60
138 Martin Hanzal .25 .60
139 Ilya Bryzgalov .25 .60
140 Sidney Crosby 1.25 3.00
141 Jordan Staal .25 .60
142 Evgeni Malkin .60 1.50
143 Petr Sykora .25 .60
144 Miroslav Satan .30 .75
145 Marc-Andre Fleury .60 1.50
146 Ruslan Fedotenko .20 .50
147 Joe Thornton .50 1.25
148 Devin Setoguchi .25 .60
149 Patrick Marleau .30 .75
150 Milan Michalek .20 .50
151 Dan Boyle .20 .50
152 Jonathan Cheechoo .25 .60
153 Evgeni Nabokov .25 .60
154 David Backes .20 .50
155 Brad Boyes .20 .50
156 Keith Tkachuk .30 .75
157 David Perron .25 .60
158 Paul Kariya .30 .75
159 Manny Legace .30 .75
160 Martin St. Louis .30 .75
161 Vincent Lecavalier .30 .75
162 Vaclav Prospal .20 .50
163 Mark Recchi .40 1.00
164 Mike Smith .30 .75
165 Nik Antropov .25 .60
166 Matt Stajan .20 .50
167 Alexei Ponikarovsky .20 .50
168 Tomas Kaberle .20 .50
169 Lee Stempniak .20 .50
170 Vesa Toskala .40 1.00
171 Daniel Sedin .40 1.00
172 Henrik Sedin .40 1.00
173 Pavol Demitra .40 1.00
174 Kyle Wellwood .25 .60
175 Roberto Luongo .50 1.25
176 Alexander Ovechkin 1.25 3.00
177 Nicklas Backstrom .30 .75
178 Alexander Semin .30 .75
179 Mike Green .25 .60
180 Jose Theodore .30 .75
181 Zach Bogosian RC 5.00 12.00
182 Brandon Sutter RC 4.00 10.00
183 Jakub Voracek RC 8.00 20.00
184 Fabian Brunnstrom RC 3.00 8.00
185 Drew Doughty RC 10.00 25.00
186 Colton Gillies RC 3.00 8.00
187 Josh Bailey RC 5.00 12.00
188 Kyle Okposo RC 5.00 12.00
189 Kyle Turris RC 6.00 15.00
190 Patrik Berglund RC 3.00 8.00
191 Steven Stamkos RC 40.00 100.00
192 Luke Schenn RC 5.00 12.00
193 Cory Schneider RC 10.00 25.00
194 Karl Alzner RC 2.50 6.00
195 Blake Wheeler RC 10.00 25.00
196 Zach Boychuk RC 4.00 10.00
197 Derick Brassard RC 4.00 10.00
198 James Neal RC 8.00 20.00
199 Max Pacioretty RC 8.00 20.00
200 Patric Hornqvist RC 4.00 10.00
201 Mikkel Boedker RC 5.00 12.00
202 T.J. Oshie RC 8.00 20.00
203 Nikolai Kulemin RC 4.00 10.00
204 Tim Kennedy RC 4.00 10.00
205 Nikita Filatov RC 4.00 10.00
206 Mark Fistric RC 3.00 8.00
207 Michael Frolik RC 4.00 10.00
208 Oscar Moller RC 3.00 8.00
209 Brian Lee RC 3.00 8.00
210 Claude Giroux RC 8.00 20.00
211 Alex Goligoski RC 5.00 12.00
212 Jamie McGinn RC 4.00 10.00
213 Alex Pietrangelo RC 6.00 15.00
214 Justin Pogge RC 3.00 8.00
215 Simeon Varlamov RC 12.00 30.00
216 Chris Stewart RC 4.00 10.00
217 Michal Repik RC 4.00 10.00
218 Jon Filewich RC 3.00 8.00
219 Dustin Jeffrey RC 4.00 10.00
220 Robbie Earl RC 2.50 6.00
221 Tom Cavanagh RC 3.00 8.00
222 Nathan Gerbe RC 4.00 10.00
223 Steve Mason RC 6.00 15.00
224 Brian Boyle RC 3.00 8.00
225 Ben Maxwell RC 4.00 10.00
226 Ilya Zubov RC 3.00 8.00
227 Brendan Mikkelson RC 2.50 6.00
228 Justin Abdelkader RC 6.00 15.00
229 Trevor Smith RC 3.00 8.00
230 Ty Wishart RC 3.00 8.00
231 Oskar Osala RC 4.00 10.00
232 Theo Peckham RC 3.00 8.00
233 Shawn Matthias RC 4.00 10.00
234 Tyler Plante RC 3.00 8.00
235 Kenndal McArdle RC 3.00 8.00
236 Derek Joslin RC 3.00 8.00
237 Ben Bishop RC 6.00 15.00
238 Adam Pineault RC 3.00 8.00
239 Brett Carson RC 5.00 12.00
240 Jonathan Ericsson RC 4.00 10.00
241 Trevor Lewis RC 4.00 10.00
242 Lauri Korpikoski RC 2.50 6.00
243 Ryan Stone RC 2.50 6.00
244 Boris Valabik RC 4.00 10.00
245 John Curry RC 4.00 10.00
246 Niklas Hjalmarsson RC 4.00 10.00
247 Darren Helm RC 4.00 10.00
248 Teddy Purcell RC 3.00 8.00
249 Radek Smolenak RC 5.00 12.00
250 Andrew Gordon RC 6.00 15.00
251 Josh Tordjman RC 8.00 20.00
252 Justin Peters RC 4.00 10.00
253 Tom Sestito RC 4.00 10.00
254 Matt D'Agostini RC 3.00 8.00
255 Martins Karsums RC 8.00 20.00
256 Paul Szczechura RC 4.00 10.00
257 Andrew Ebbett RC 2.50 6.00
258 Dan LaCosta RC 4.00 10.00
259 Jonas Junland RC 6.00 15.00
260 Maxsim Mayorov RC 4.00 10.00
261 Mattias Ritola RC 3.00 8.00
262 Corey Potter RC 6.00 15.00
263 Sami Lepisto RC 3.00 8.00
264 Danny Taylor RC 3.00 8.00
265 Brett Sutter RC 4.00 10.00
266 Derek Dorsett RC 5.00 12.00
267 Tim Sestito RC 3.00 8.00
268 Wayne Simmonds RC 6.00 15.00
269 Ryan Jones RC 4.00 10.00
270 Zack Smith RC 3.00 8.00
271 Luca Sbisa RC 2.50 6.00
272 Jonathon Kalinski RC 4.00 10.00
273 Viktor Tikhonov RC 3.00 8.00
274 Kevin Porter RC 3.00 8.00
275 Chris Porter RC 4.00 10.00
276 Vladimir Mihalik RC 2.50 6.00
277 Jonas Frogren RC 2.50 6.00
278 John Mitchell RC 3.00 8.00
279 Andreas Nodl RC 2.50 6.00
280 Janne Pesonen RC 3.00 8.00
RR281 John Tavares XRC 15.00 40.00
RR282 Victor Hedman XRC 12.00 30.00
RR283 Matt Duchene XRC 10.00 25.00
RR284 Jonas Gustavsson XRC 10.00 25.00
RR285 Oskars Bartulis XRC 5.00 12.00
RR286 Daniel Larsson XRC 8.00 20.00
RR287 Ryan O'Marra XRC 5.00 12.00
RR288 Mathieu Perreault XRC 6.00 15.00
RR289 Lars Eller XRC 5.00 12.00
RR290 Mathieu Carle XRC 5.00 12.00
RR291 Brad Marchand XRC 15.00 40.00
RR292 Logan Couture XRC 10.00 25.00
RR293 Perttu Lindgren XRC 4.00 10.00
RR294 Braden Holtby XRC 12.00 30.00
RR295 Michael Grabner XRC 5.00 12.00
RR296 Cody Franson XRC 4.00 10.00
RR297 James Reimer XRC 10.00 25.00
RR298 Jason Demers XRC 5.00 12.00
RR299 Sergei Shirokov XRC 5.00 12.00
RR300 Viktor Stalberg XRC 5.00 12.00
RR301 Benn Ferriero XRC 5.00 12.00
RR302 Tyler Bozak XRC 8.00 20.00
RR303 James van Riemsdyk XRC 8.00 20.00
RR304 Erik Karlsson XRC 10.00 25.00
RR305 Matt Gilroy XRC 5.00 12.00
RR306 Colin Wilson XRC 5.00 12.00
RR307 Alec Martinez XRC 6.00 15.00
RR308 Dmitry Kulikov XRC 5.00 12.00
RR309 Jamie Benn XRC 10.00 25.00
RR310 Ryan O'Reilly XRC 6.00 15.00
RR311 Tyler Myers XRC 5.00 12.00
RR312 Evander Kane XRC 10.00 25.00
RR313 Antti Niemi XRC 12.00 30.00
RR314 Frazer McLaren XRC 3.00 8.00
RR315 Michael Del Zotto XRC 4.00 10.00
RR316 Ville Leino XRC 6.00 15.00
RR317 Michal Neuvirth XRC 6.00 15.00

RR318 Matt Pelech XRC 6.00 15.00
RR319 Riku Helenius XRC 4.00 10.00
RR320 Ivan Vishnevskiy XRC 4.00 10.00
RR321 Jhonas Enroth XRC 4.00 10.00
RR322 Artem Anisimov XRC 3.00 8.00
RR323 Mikael Backlund XRC 5.00 12.00
RR324 Christian Hanson XRC 5.00 12.00
RR325 Yannick Weber XRC 5.00 12.00
RR326 T.J. Galiardi XRC 4.00 10.00
RR327 Spencer Machacek XRC 3.00 8.00
RR328 Luca Caputi XRC 5.00 12.00
RR329 Brian Salcido XRC 6.00 15.00
RR330 Tyler Ennis XRC 3.00 8.00
RR331 Carl Gunnarsson XRC 3.00 8.00
RR332 Alexander Salak XRC 5.00 12.00
RR333 Scott Parse XRC 3.00 8.00
RR334 Matt Beleskey XRC 6.00 15.00
RR335 Cal O'Reilly XRC 4.00 10.00
RR336 Taylor Chorney XRC 4.00 10.00
RR337 Mike Santorelli XRC 4.00 10.00
RR338 Peter Regin XRC 5.00 12.00
RR339 Kris Chucko XRC 4.00 10.00
RR340 John Scott XRC 3.00 8.00

2008-09 Be A Player Rookie Jerseys

RJAP Alex Pietrangelo 4.00 10.00
RJBM Ben Maxwell 2.50 6.00
RJBS Brandon Sutter 2.50 6.00
RJBW Blake Wheeler 6.00 15.00
RJCG Colton Gillies 2.00 5.00
RJCS Cory Schneider 6.00 15.00
RJDB Derick Brassard 2.50 6.00
RJDD Drew Doughty 6.00 15.00
RJFB Fabian Brunnstrom 2.00 5.00
RJGI Claude Giroux 5.00 12.00
RJJB Josh Bailey 3.00 8.00
RJJN James Neal 5.00 12.00
RJJP Justin Pogge 2.00 5.00
RJJV Jakub Voracek 5.00 12.00
RJKA Karl Alzner 1.50 4.00
RJKO Kyle Okposo 3.00 8.00
RJKT Kyle Turris 4.00 10.00
RJLS Luke Schenn 3.00 8.00
RJMB Mikkel Boedker 3.00 8.00
RJMF Michael Frolik 2.50 6.00
RJMP Max Pacioretty 5.00 12.00
RJNF Nikita Filatov 2.50 6.00
RJNK Nikolai Kulemin 2.50 6.00
RJPB Patrik Berglund 2.00 5.00
RJSB Luca Sbisa 1.50 4.00
RJSM Steve Mason 6.00 15.00
RJSS Steven Stamkos 8.00 20.00
RJST Chris Stewart 2.50 6.00
RJTO T.J. Oshie 5.00 12.00
RJVT Viktor Tikhonov 2.00 5.00
RJZB Zach Bogosian 3.00 8.00

2008-09 Be A Player Rookie Redemption Bonus

RR281 John Tavares 25.00 60.00
RR282 Victor Hedman 15.00 40.00
RR283 Matt Duchene 12.00 30.00
RR284 Jonas Gustavsson 12.00 30.00
RR285 Oskars Bartulis 6.00 15.00
RR286 Daniel Larsson 6.00 15.00
RR287 Ryan O'Marra 6.00 15.00
RR288 Mathieu Perreault 5.00 12.00
RR289 Lars Eller 6.00 15.00
RR290 Mathieu Carle 4.00 10.00
RR291 Brad Marchand 20.00 50.00
RR292 Logan Couture 12.00 30.00
RR293 Perttu Lindgren 5.00 12.00
RR294 Braden Holtby 20.00 40.00
RR295 Michael Grabner 6.00 15.00
RR296 Cody Franson 5.00 12.00
RR297 James Reimer 30.00 60.00
RR298 Jason Demers 6.00 15.00
RR299 Sergei Shirokov 6.00 15.00
RR300 Viktor Stalberg 6.00 15.00
RR301 Benn Ferriero 6.00 15.00
RR302 Tyler Bozak 10.00 25.00
RR303 James van Riemsdyk 10.00 25.00
RR304 Erik Karlsson 12.00 30.00
RR305 Matt Gilroy 6.00 15.00
RR306 Colin Wilson 6.00 15.00
RR307 Alec Martinez 8.00 20.00
RR308 Dmitry Kulikov 6.00 15.00
RR309 Jamie Benn 12.00 30.00
RR310 Ryan O'Reilly 8.00 20.00
RR311 Tyler Myers 6.00 15.00
RR312 Evander Kane 12.00 30.00
RR313 Antti Niemi 15.00 40.00
RR314 Frazer McLaren 4.00 10.00
RR315 Michael Del Zotto 5.00 12.00
RR316 Ville Leino 8.00 20.00
RR317 Michal Neuvirth 8.00 20.00
RR318 Matt Pelech 8.00 20.00
RR319 Riku Helenius 5.00 12.00
RR320 Ivan Vishnevskiy 5.00 12.00
RR321 Jhonas Enroth 6.00 15.00
RR322 Artem Anisimov 4.00 10.00
RR323 Mikael Backlund 6.00 15.00
RR324 Christian Hanson 6.00 15.00
RR325 Yannick Weber 6.00 15.00
RR326 T.J. Galiardi 5.00 12.00
RR327 Spencer Machacek 4.00 10.00
RR328 Luca Caputi 6.00 15.00
RR329 Brian Salcido 8.00 20.00
RR330 Tyler Ennis 4.00 10.00
RR331 Carl Gunnarsson 2.50 6.00
RR332 Alexander Salak 4.00 10.00
RR333 Scott Parse 4.00 10.00
RR334 Matt Beleskey 8.00 20.00
RR335 Cal O'Reilly 5.00 12.00
RR336 Taylor Chorney 5.00 12.00
RR337 Mike Santorelli 5.00 12.00
RR338 Peter Regin 6.00 15.00
RR339 Kris Chucko 5.00 12.00
RR340 John Scott 8.00 20.00

2008-09 Be A Player Signatures

SAA Adrian Aucoin 3.00 8.00
SAB Adam Burish 4.00 10.00
SAE Alexander Edler 3.00 8.00
SAF Andrew Ference 3.00 8.00
SAK Anze Kopitar 8.00 20.00
SAL Andreas Lilja 3.00 8.00
SAM Andy McDonald 4.00 10.00
SAP Andrew Peters 3.00 8.00
SBA Bryan Allen 3.00 8.00
SBB Brad Boyes 3.00 8.00
SBC Brian Campbell 4.00 10.00
SBE Patrik Berglund 3.00 8.00
SBG Ben Guite 3.00 8.00
SBI Kevin Bieksa 4.00 10.00
SBJ Josh Bailey 5.00 12.00
SBK Rob Blake 5.00 12.00
SBL Brian Lee 3.00 8.00
SBO David Booth 3.00 8.00
SBR Derick Brassard 4.00 10.00
SBRI Daniel Briere 5.00 12.00
SBS Brian Sutherby 3.00 8.00
SBU Alexandre Burrows 3.00 8.00
SBUR Brent Burns 5.00 12.00
SBY Dan Boyle 3.00 8.00
SCD Chris Drury 4.00 10.00
SCG Colton Gillies 3.00 8.00
SCH Cristobal Huet 4.00 10.00
SCL David Clarkson 4.00 10.00
SCO Chris Osgood 5.00 12.00
SCP Corey Perry 8.00 20.00
SCS Cory Stillman 3.00 8.00
SDA Daniel Sedin 6.00 15.00
SDB Dustin Boyd 3.00 8.00
SDC Dan Cleary 4.00 10.00
SDE Dan Ellis 3.00 8.00
SDH Dan Hamhuis 4.00 10.00
SDK Duncan Keith 8.00 20.00
SDM Darren McCarty 5.00 12.00
SDO Dominic Moore 3.00 8.00
SDP Daniel Paille 3.00 8.00
SDR Derek Roy 3.00 8.00
SDU Dustin Brown 5.00 12.00
SDV Devin Setoguchi 4.00 10.00
SDW Doug Weight 5.00 12.00
SEB Eric Brewer 3.00 8.00
SEM Evgeni Malkin 25.00 60.00
SEN Evgeni Nabokov 4.00 10.00
SES Eric Staal 8.00 20.00
SFL Marc-Andre Fleury 10.00 25.00
SFM Fredrik Modin 3.00 8.00
SFR Alexander Frolov 3.00 8.00
SGA Simon Gagne 5.00 12.00
SGI Brian Gionta 3.00 8.00
SGP George Parros 3.00 8.00
SGU Bill Guerin 5.00 12.00
SHA Scott Hartnell 3.00 8.00
SHE Dany Heatley 4.00 10.00
SHO Patric Hornqvist 4.00 10.00
SHS Henrik Sedin 6.00 15.00
SIB Ilya Bryzgalov 4.00 10.00
SJA Jason Arnott 4.00 10.00
SJB Jay Bouwmeester 3.00 8.00
SJC Jeff Carter 4.00 10.00
SJD J.P. Dumont 3.00 8.00
SJF Johan Franzen 6.00 15.00
SJH Josh Harding 10.00 25.00
SJO John Oduya 4.00 10.00
SJP Jason Pominville 3.00 8.00
SJS Joe Sakic 15.00 40.00
SJV Jakub Voracek 8.00 20.00
SJW James Wisniewski 3.00 8.00
SKB Keith Ballard 3.00 8.00
SKE Ryan Kesler 5.00 12.00
SKT Kyle Turris 6.00 15.00
SLA Brooks Laich 3.00 8.00
SLO Matthew Lombardi 3.00 8.00
SLS Luca Sbisa 2.50 6.00
SLU Brad Lukowich 3.00 8.00
SMA Paul Martin 3.00 8.00
SMAR Andrei Markov 5.00 12.00
SMB Martin Biron 4.00 10.00
SMC Mike Commodore 3.00 8.00
SMF Mike Fisher 3.00 8.00
SMH Marian Hossa 5.00 12.00
SMI Mikkel Boedker 5.00 12.00
SMK Mike Komisarek 3.00 8.00
SMM Milan Michalek 3.00 8.00
SMN Markus Naslund 6.00 12.00
SMO Derek Morris 3.00 8.00
SMR Mason Raymond 3.00 8.00
SMT Maxime Talbot 3.00 8.00
SMU Peter Mueller 4.00 10.00
SMV Marc-Edouard Vlasic 3.00 8.00
SMY Manny Malhotra 3.00 8.00
SNA Nik Antropov 4.00 10.00
SNB Niklas Backstrom 5.00 12.00
SNF Nick Foligno 5.00 12.00
SNH Nathan Horton 4.00 10.00
SNK Nikolai Kulemin 4.00 10.00
SNL Nicklas Lidstrom 15.00 30.00
SNS Nick Schultz 3.00 8.00
SOJ Olli Jokinen 4.00 10.00
SOK Kyle Okposo 5.00 12.00
SOM Oscar Moller 3.00 8.00
SPA Paul Kariya 8.00 20.00
SPC Chris Phillips 3.00 8.00
SPD David Perron 4.00 10.00
SPE Patrik Elias 5.00 12.00
SPH Dion Phaneuf 4.00 10.00
SPM Patrick Marleau 5.00 12.00
SPO Patrick O'Sullivan 4.00 10.00
SPS Paul Stastny 4.00 10.00
SRA Brian Rafalski 4.00 10.00
SRB Rod Brind`Amour 5.00 12.00
SRG Ryan Getzlaf 5.00 12.00
SRI Mike Richards SP 50.00 120.00
SRK Rostislav Klesla 3.00 8.00
SRO Rostislav Olesz 3.00 8.00
SRR Robyn Regehr 3.00 8.00
SRS Ryan Smyth 4.00 10.00
SRT Raffi Torres 3.00 8.00
SRU R.J. Umberger 3.00 8.00
SRW Ray Whitney 4.00 10.00
SSC Sidney Crosby 60.00 120.00
SSD Shane Doan 4.00 10.00
SSE Brent Seabrook 3.00 8.00
SSF Sergei Fedorov 10.00 25.00
SSG Scott Gomez 4.00 10.00
SSH James Sheppard 3.00 8.00
SSI Mike Sillinger 3.00 8.00
SSJ Jordan Staal 4.00 10.00
SSL Luke Schenn 5.00 12.00
SSN Scott Niedermayer 5.00 12.00
SSP Jason Spezza 5.00 12.00
SST Matt Stajan 3.00 8.00
SSTA Marc Staal 3.00 8.00
SSU Ryan Suter 4.00 10.00
SSW Scott Walker 3.00 8.00
STA Jeff Tambellini 3.00 8.00
STG Tim Gleason 3.00 8.00
STH Jose Theodore 5.00 12.00
STM Travis Moen 3.00 8.00
STN Teppo Numminen 3.00 8.00
STO T.J. Oshie 4.00 10.00
STP Tom Preissing 3.00 8.00
STR Tuomo Ruutu 5.00 12.00
STT Tim Thomas 10.00 25.00
STV Thomas Vanek 4.00 10.00
STZ Travis Zajac 3.00 8.00
SVO Tomas Vokoun 4.00 10.00
SWE Stephen Weiss 3.00 8.00
SWM Willie Mitchell 3.00 8.00
SWS Shea Weber 4.00 10.00
SWW Wojtek Wolski 4.00 10.00
SZP Zach Parise 5.00 12.00

2008-09 Be A Player Signatures Dual

S2AD Dumont/Arnott 6.00 15.00
S2AK Kulemin/Antropov 8.00 20.00
S2BB Blake/Boyle 8.00 20.00
S2BH Harding/Backstrom 8.00 20.00
S2BS Brind`Amour/Staal 10.00 25.00
S2BV Voracek/Brassard 10.00 25.00
S2CH Huet/Campbell 6.00 15.00
S2FM M-A Fleury/Malkin 15.00 40.00
S2GB Briere/Gagne 6.00 15.00
S2GP Gionta/Parise 8.00 20.00
S2HB Horton/Booth 6.00 15.00
S2HC Cleary/Hossa 15.00 40.00
S2JK Bouwmeester/Ballard 5.00 12.00
S2JP Stastny/Sakic 20.00 50.00
S2KB Kariya/Boyes 12.00 30.00
S2KJ Okposo/Bailey 10.00 25.00
S2LB Boyd/Lombardi 5.00 12.00
S2ME Edler/Mitchell 5.00 12.00
S2MK Markov/Komisarek 8.00 20.00
S2MS Setoguchi/Marleau 8.00 20.00
S2MT Mueller/Turris 12.00 30.00
S2NG Getzlaf/Niedermayer 8.00 20.00
S2OK Kopitar/O'Sullivan 12.00 30.00
S2PV Vanek/Pominville 6.00 15.00
S2RC Carter/Richards 25.00 60.00
S2SG Sheppard/Gillies 6.00 15.00
S2SH Heatley/Spezza 8.00 20.00
S2SK Seabrook/Keith 25.00 50.00
S2SS Sedin/Sedin 15.00 30.00
S2SW Weber/Suter 6.00 15.00
S2TP Berglund/Oshie 8.00 20.00
S2WG Guerin/Weight 8.00 20.00

2008-09 Be A Player Signatures Trios

S3AWE Arnott/Weber/Ellis 15.00 40.00
S3BRC Briere/Richrds/Carter 100.00 175.00
S3BSG Bckstm/Shpprd/Gillis 20.00 50.00
S3EGP Elias/Gionta/Parise 20.00 50.00
S3FMS Fleury/Malkin/Staal 30.00 80.00
S3FSH Fisher/Spezza/Heatley 20.00 50.00
S3HOF Hossa/Osgood/Franzen 20.00 50.00
S3JDM Jokinen/Doan/Mueller 15.00 40.00
S3KBM Kariya/Boyes/McDonald 20.00 50.00
S3MNB Marleau/Nabokov/Boyle 20.00 50.00
S3SSE Sedin/Sedin/Edler 25.00 60.00
S3SSS Sakic/Smyth/Stastny 40.00 100.00
S3TOB Tambellini/Okposo/Bailey 30.00 80.00
S3VBH Vokoun/Bouwm/Horton 15.00 40.00
S3WBS Whitney/Brind/Staal 25.00 60.00

2009-10 Be A Player

*VETS/25: 3X TO 8X BASIC CARDS
1 Sidney Crosby 1.25 3.00
2 Joe Thornton .50 1.25
3 Jamal Mayers .20 .50
4 Ryan Getzlaf .30 .75
5 Pierre-Marc Bouchard .30 .75
6 Eric Staal .40 1.00
7 Mikkel Boedker .20 .50
8 Daniel Sedin .40 1.00
9 Patric Hornqvist .20 .50
10 Zdeno Chara .30 .75
11 Mike Richards .25 .60
12 Nicklas Lidstrom .20 .50
13 Patrick Kane .60 1.50
14 Mark Stuart .20 .50
15 Oscar Moller .20 .50
16 Josh Bailey .25 .60
17 Luca Sbisa .30 .75
18 Ethan Moreau .20 .50
19 Phil Kessel .30 .75
20 Ondrej Pavelec .40 1.00
21 Mike Sillinger .20 .50
22 Boyd Gordon .20 .50
23 Kristopher Letang .40 1.00
24 Brad Richards .30 .75
25 Nathan McIver .20 .50
26 Martin Brodeur .75 2.00
27 Zach Parise .30 .75
28 Dany Heatley .25 .60
29 Mike Cammalleri .25 .60
30 Tomas Vokoun .25 .60
31 Scott Hartnell .20 .50
32 Roberto Luongo .50 1.25
33 Wojtek Wolski .20 .50
34 Ryan Callahan .20 .50
35 Aaron Voros .20 .50
36 Bobby Ryan .25 .60
37 Nick Schultz .20 .50
38 Henrik Zetterberg .40 1.00
39 Nick Foligno .25 .60
40 Patrick O'Sullivan .25 .60
41 Dan Hamhuis .25 .60
42 Scott Walker .20 .50
43 Eric Brewer .20 .50
44 Simon Gagne .30 .75
45 Paul Martin .20 .50
46 Milan Lucic .25 .60
47 Rostislav Klesla .30 .75
48 Adrian Aucoin .20 .50
49 Ryan Kesler .30 .75
50 Brad Boyes .20 .50
51 Ryan Suter .25 .60
52 Mike Komisarek .25 .60
53 Tim Gleason .20 .50
54 Brooks Laich .20 .50
55 Dustin Brown .30 .75
56 Blake Wheeler .30 .75
57 Ilya Bryzgalov .25 .60
58 Manny Malhotra .20 .50
59 Jason Spezza .30 .75
60 Rich Peverley .25 .60
61 Paul Stastny .25 .60
62 Tim Connolly .20 .50
63 Jeff Halpern .20 .50
64 Nathan Horton .30 .75
65 Kris Versteeg .20 .50
66 Andrew Cogliano .20 .50
67 Jonathan Quick .40 1.00
68 Nik Antropov .25 .60
69 David Perron .25 .60
70 Krys Barch .20 .50
71 Derek Roy .20 .50
72 Jordan Staal .25 .60
73 Evgeni Malkin .60 1.50
74 Mark Streit .20 .50
75 Carey Price .60 1.50
76 Jean-Sebastien Giguere .30 .75
77 Cal Clutterbuck .20 .50
78 Mike Modano .50 1.25
79 Jay Bouwmeester .20 .50
80 Pavel Datsyuk .50 1.25
81 Jeff Carter .25 .60
82 Marc Savard .20 .50
83 Luke Schenn .30 .75
84 Patrick Marleau .30 .75
85 R.J. Umberger .25 .60
86 Marc Staal .20 .50
87 Drew Doughty .40 1.00
88 Erik Johnson .20 .50
89 Patrik Elias .30 .75
90 Alexandre Burrows .20 .50
91 Niklas Backstrom .30 .75
92 David Krejci .30 .75
93 Ryan Malone .20 .50
94 J.P. Dumont .20 .50
95 Mike Commodore .20 .50
96 Daniel Alfredsson .30 .75
97 Johan Franzen .25 .60
98 Erik Cole .20 .50
99 Peter Budaj .25 .60
100 Bryan McCabe .25 .60
101 Jonathan Toews .50 1.25
102 Nikolai Kulemin .20 .50
103 Mikko Koivu .30 .75
104 Robert Lang .20 .50
105 Tomas Plekanec .20 .50
106 Marty Turco .30 .75
107 Chris Campoli .20 .50
108 Mike Knuble .20 .50
109 Vincent Lecavalier .30 .75
110 Jussi Jokinen .20 .50
111 Matt Greene .20 .50
112 Willie Mitchell .20 .50
113 Thomas Vanek .25 .60
114 Scott Niedermayer .30 .75
115 Shea Weber .25 .60
116 Bryan Little .30 .75
117 Pascal Leclaire .30 .75
118 Brian Rafalski .20 .50
119 Olli Jokinen .25 .60
120 Shawn Horcoff .20 .50
121 Rene Bourque .20 .50
122 Joni Pitkanen .25 .60
123 Matt Bradley .20 .50
124 Matt Moulson .25 .60
125 Raffi Torres .20 .50
126 Miikka Kiprusoff .30 .75
127 Shane Doan .25 .60
128 Patrice Bergeron .40 1.00
129 Scott Hannan .20 .50
130 Evgeni Nabokov .25 .60
131 Steven Stamkos .60 1.50
132 Corey Perry .50 1.25
133 T.J. Oshie .30 .75
134 Mikael Samuelsson .20 .50
135 Steve Mason .25 .60
136 Drew Stafford .20 .50
137 Chris Pronger .30 .75
138 Jonas Hiller .25 .60
139 Robyn Regehr .25 .60
140 Bryan Allen .20 .50
141 Andrei Markov .30 .75
142 David Backes .20 .50
143 Derick Brassard .20 .50
144 Tuukka Rask .40 1.00
145 Martin Havlat .25 .60
146 Mike Grier .20 .50
147 Dan Boyle .20 .50
148 Shawn Thornton .20 .50
149 Marc-Andre Fleury .60 1.50
150 Matt Stajan .20 .50
151 Daniel Briere .30 .75
152 Maxim Afinogenov .20 .50
153 Duncan Keith .25 .60
154 Dan Cleary .30 .75
155 Anze Kopitar .50 1.25
156 Kyle Okposo .20 .50
157 Brent Burns .30 .75
158 Brenden Morrow .25 .60
159 Ryan Miller .30 .75
160 Henrik Sedin .40 1.00
161 Darcy Tucker .25 .60
162 Ray Whitney .25 .60
163 Jakub Voracek .25 .60
164 Tomas Fleischmann .20 .50
165 Braydon Coburn .20 .50
166 Saku Koivu .30 .75
167 Adam Burish .40 1.00
168 George Parros .20 .50
169 Jarome Iginla .40 1.00
170 Brandon Sutter .20 .50
171 Pekka Rinne .30 .75
172 Sam Gagner .20 .50
173 Chris Drury .25 .60
174 Niklas Kronwall .25 .60
175 Dion Phaneuf .25 .60
176 Zach Bogosian .25 .60
177 Maxime Talbot .20 .50
178 Daniel Winnik .20 .50
179 Scott Gomez .25 .60
180 Cam Ward .30 .75
181 Ilya Kovalchuk .30 .75
182 Devin Setoguchi .25 .60
183 Mike Fisher .20 .50
184 James Neal .20 .50
185 Ryan Smyth .25 .60
186 Loui Eriksson .20 .50
187 Stephen Weiss .20 .50
188 Mason Raymond .20 .50
189 Jason Pominville .20 .50
190 Teemu Selanne .60 1.50
191 Martin St. Louis .30 .75
192 Rod Brind`Amour .30 .75
193 Brent Seabrook .20 .50
194 Ron Hainsey .20 .50
195 Milan Hejduk .25 .60
196 Tim Thomas .30 .75
197 David Legwand .25 .60
198 Jeff Tambellini .20 .50
199 Georges Laraque .25 .60
200 Alexander Ovechkin 1.25 3.00
201 John Tavares RC 15.00 40.00
202 Devan Dubnyk RC 6.00 15.00
203 Andrei Loktionov RC 5.00 12.00
204 Lars Eller RC 4.00 10.00
205 Tyler Eckford RC 3.00 8.00
206 Drayson Bowman RC 4.00 10.00
207 Artem Anisimov RC 2.50 6.00
208 Mikko Lehtonen RC 6.00 15.00
209 Dan Sexton RC 3.00 8.00
210 Ryan O'Reilly RC 8.00 20.00
211 Kris Chucko RC 2.50 6.00
212 Cal O'Reilly RC 3.00 8.00
213 Victor Hedman RC 10.00 25.00
214 Mike Brodeur RC 3.00 8.00
215 Carl Gunnarsson RC 2.50 6.00
216 Luca Caputi RC 4.00 10.00
217 Danny Irmen RC 2.50 6.00
218 Antti Niemi RC 6.00 15.00
219 Benn Ferriero RC 4.00 10.00
220 Jhonas Enroth RC 5.00 12.00
221 Keaton Ellerby RC 3.00 8.00
222 James Wright RC 4.00 10.00
223 Michael Del Zotto RC 4.00 10.00
224 Alexander Salak RC 3.00 8.00
225 Jonas Gustavsson RC 5.00 12.00
226 David Desharnais RC 8.00 20.00
227 Ville Leino RC 3.00 8.00
228 Riku Helenius RC 4.00 10.00
229 Braden Holtby RC 10.00 25.00
230 Joel Rechlicz RC 2.50 6.00
231 Ivan Vishnevskiy RC 2.50 6.00
232 Peter Regin RC 3.00 8.00
233 MacGregor Sharp RC 4.00 10.00
234 Michael Grabner RC 4.00 10.00
235 Alexander Sulzer RC 2.50 6.00
236 David Laliberte RC 3.00 8.00
237 Logan Couture RC 8.00 20.00
238 Vladimir Zharkov RC 4.00 10.00
239 Colin McDonald RC 3.00 8.00
240 Matt Hendricks RC 3.00 8.00
241 Brad Marchand RC 15.00 40.00
242 Taylor Chorney RC 4.00 10.00
243 T.J. Galiardi RC 4.00 10.00
244 Erik Karlsson RC 12.00 30.00
245 Perttu Lindgren RC 3.00 8.00
246 Ryan Keller RC 4.00 10.00
247 Tyler Ennis RC 5.00 12.00
248 Michael Sauer RC 3.00 8.00
249 Teemu Laakso RC 2.50 6.00
250 James van Riemsdyk RC 8.00 20.00
251 John Negrin RC 4.00 10.00
252 Ryan Stoa RC 3.00 8.00
253 Tom Wandell RC 4.00 10.00
254 Michal Neuvirth RC 6.00 15.00
255 John Carlson RC 8.00 20.00
256 Mike Santorelli RC 4.00 10.00
257 Anton Khudobin RC 6.00 15.00
258 Brian Salcido RC 2.50 6.00
259 James Reimer RC 10.00 25.00
260 Colin Wilson RC 4.00 10.00
261 Deryk Engelland RC 5.00 12.00
262 Scott Parse RC 4.00 10.00
263 Tyler Bozak RC 6.00 15.00
264 Yannick Weber RC 4.00 10.00
265 Andrew MacDonald RC 2.50 6.00
266 Matthew Corrente RC 3.00 8.00
267 Shaun Heshka RC 4.00 10.00
268 Jakub Kindl RC 4.00 10.00
269 Mark Letestu RC 4.00 10.00
270 Oskars Bartulis RC 4.00 10.00
271 Viktor Stalberg RC 4.00 10.00
272 Frazer McLaren RC 3.00 8.00
273 Jason Demers RC 6.00 15.00
274 Ryan Wilson RC 4.00 10.00
275 Evander Kane RC 8.00 20.00
276 Sergei Shirokov RC 2.50 6.00
277 Aaron Gagnon RC 2.50 6.00
278 Cody Franson RC 4.00 10.00
279 Ryan O'Marra RC 2.50 6.00
280 Mikael Backlund RC 6.00 15.00
281 Jamie Benn RC 12.00 30.00
282 Andreas Thuresson RC 3.00 8.00
283 Christian Hanson RC 4.00 10.00
284 Mathieu Carle RC 4.00 10.00
285 Phil Oreskovic RC 4.00 10.00
286 Matt Beleskey RC 3.00 8.00
287 Tyler Myers RC 6.00 15.00
288 Ryan Vesce RC 3.00 8.00
289 Bobby Sanguinetti RC 2.50 6.00
290 Mario Bliznak RC 4.00 10.00
291 Spencer Machacek RC 4.00 10.00
292 Tom Pyatt RC 4.00 10.00
293 Byron Bitz RC 3.00 8.00
294 Dmitry Kulikov RC 4.00 10.00
295 Mathieu Perreault RC 5.00 12.00
296 Chad Johnson RC 4.00 10.00
297 Daniel Larsson RC 3.00 8.00
298 Matt Pelech RC 4.00 10.00
299 Matt Gilroy RC 4.00 10.00
300 Matt Duchene RC 8.00 20.00
301 Taylor Hall XRC 12.00 30.00
302 Jordan Caron XRC 4.00 10.00
303 Nino Niederreiter XRC 4.00 10.00
304 Cody Almond XRC 4.00 10.00
305 Nick Leddy XRC 4.00 10.00
306 J.T. Wyman XRC 4.00 10.00
307 Alexander Burmistrov XRC 4.00 10.00
308 Jeff Penner XRC 4.00 10.00
309 Brandon Yip XRC 4.00 10.00
310 Anders Lindback XRC 4.00 10.00
311 Bryan Pitton XRC 4.00 10.00
312 Magnus Paajarvi XRC 4.00 10.00
313 Maxime Fortunus XRC 4.00 10.00
314 Philip Larsen XRC 4.00 10.00
315 Tommy Wingels XRC 4.00 10.00
316 Tyler Seguin XRC 12.00 30.00
317 Brayden Schenn XRC 8.00 20.00
318 Arturs Kulda XRC 4.00 10.00
319 Mark Olver XRC 4.00 10.00
320 Eric Tangradi XRC 4.00 10.00
321 Brayden Irwin XRC 4.00 10.00
322 Derek Stepan XRC 6.00 15.00
323 Zach Hamill XRC 4.00 10.00
324 Alex Plante XRC 4.00 10.00
325 Henrik Karlsson XRC 4.00 10.00
326 Clayton Stoner XRC 4.00 10.00
327 Kyle Clifford XRC 4.00 10.00
328 Oliver Ekman-Larsson XRC 5.00 12.00
329 Matt Martin XRC 5.00 12.00
330 Andrew Bodnarchuk XRC 4.00 10.00
331 Evan Oberg XRC 4.00 10.00
332 Dustin Kohn XRC 4.00 10.00
333 Jordan Eberle XRC 8.00 20.00
334 Dana Tyrell XRC 4.00 10.00
335 Jake Muzzin XRC 4.00 10.00
336 Justin Falk XRC 4.00 10.00
337 Jared Cowen XRC 4.00 10.00
338 Nazem Kadri XRC 8.00 20.00
339 Dean Arsene XRC 4.00 10.00
340 Justin Mercier XRC 4.00 10.00
341 Sergei Bobrovsky XRC 12.00 30.00
342 Casey Wellman XRC 4.00 10.00
343 Derek Smith XRC 4.00 10.00
344 Jeff Skinner XRC 6.00 15.00
345 Nick Bonino XRC 3.00 8.00
346 Alexander Pechurski XRC 4.00 10.00
347 Cam Fowler XRC 5.00 12.00
348 Dustin Tokarski XRC 4.00 10.00
349 Alexander Urbom XRC 4.00 10.00
350 Nick Palmieri XRC 4.00 10.00
351 Kevin Shattenkirk XRC 4.00 10.00
352 Zac Dalpe XRC 4.00 10.00
353 Brandon Pirri XRC 4.00 10.00
354 Jacob Josefson XRC 3.00 8.00
355 Nick Holden XRC 3.00 8.00
356 Jamie McBain XRC 4.00 10.00
357 Evgeny Dadonov XRC 4.00 10.00
358 Matt Taormina XRC 4.00 10.00
359 Marcus Johansson XRC 5.00 12.00
360 P.K. Subban XRC 12.00 30.00

2009-10 Be A Player Goalies Unmasked

GU1 Martin Brodeur 4.00 10.00
GU2 Ryan Miller 1.50 4.00
GU3 Marc-Andre Fleury 3.00 8.00
GU4 Carey Price 3.00 8.00
GU5 Jose Theodore 1.50 4.00
GU6 Brian Elliott 1.25 3.00
GU7 Antero Niittymaki 1.50 4.00
GU8 Ray Emery 1.25 3.00
GU9 Tim Thomas 1.50 4.00
GU10 Henrik Lundqvist 4.00 10.00
GU11 Ondrej Pavelec 2.00 5.00
GU12 Tomas Vokoun 1.25 3.00
GU13 Dwayne Roloson 1.25 3.00
GU14 Cam Ward 1.50 4.00
GU15 Jean-Sebastien Giguere 1.50 4.00
GU16 Evgeni Nabokov 1.25 3.00
GU17 Cristobal Huet 1.50 4.00
GU18 Roberto Luongo 2.50 6.00
GU19 Jonathan Quick 2.00 5.00
GU20 Ilya Bryzgalov 1.25 3.00
GU21 Craig Anderson 1.50 4.00
GU22 Miikka Kiprusoff 1.50 4.00
GU23 Pekka Rinne 1.50 4.00
GU24 Chris Osgood 1.50 4.00
GU25 Marty Turco 1.50 4.00
GU26 Niklas Backstrom 1.50 4.00
GU27 Jonas Hiller 1.25 3.00
GU28 Chris Mason 1.25 3.00
GU29 Steve Mason 1.25 3.00
GU30 Nikolai Khabibulin 1.50 4.00

2009-10 Be A Player Meet The Rookies

MR1 John Tavares 6.00 15.00
MR2 Victor Hedman 4.00 10.00
MR3 Matt Duchene 3.00 8.00
MR4 James van Riemsdyk 3.00 8.00
MR5 Mikael Backlund 2.50 6.00
MR6 Jonas Gustavsson 2.00 5.00
MR7 Colin Wilson 1.50 4.00
MR8 Logan Couture 3.00 8.00
MR9 Bobby Sanguinetti 1.00 2.50
MR10 Tyler Bozak 2.50 6.00

2009-10 Be A Player Rookie Jerseys

RJAA Artem Anisimov 1.50 4.00
RJAM Andrew MacDonald 1.50 4.00
RJAN Antti Niemi 4.00 10.00
RJBA Mikael Backlund 4.00 10.00
RJBB Byron Bitz 2.00 5.00
RJBF Benn Ferriero 2.50 6.00
RJBM Brad Marchand 10.00 25.00
RJBO Tyler Bozak 4.00 10.00
RJBS Brian Salcido 1.50 4.00
RJCF Cody Franson 2.50 6.00
RJCH Christian Hanson 2.50 6.00
RJCM Colin McDonald 2.00 5.00
RJCO Cal O'Reilly 2.00 5.00
RJCW Colin Wilson 2.50 6.00
RJDD Devan Dubnyk 4.00 10.00
RJDE Michael Del Zotto 2.50 6.00
RJDI Danny Irmen 1.50 4.00
RJDK Dmitry Kulikov 2.50 6.00
RJEK Evander Kane 5.00 12.00
RJFM Frazer McLaren 2.00 5.00
RJGR Michael Grabner 2.50 6.00
RJIV Ivan Vishnevskiy 1.50 4.00
RJJB Jamie Benn 8.00 20.00
RJJD Jason Demers 4.00 10.00
RJJE Jhonas Enroth 3.00 8.00
RJJG Jonas Gustavsson 3.00 8.00
RJJK Jakub Kindl 2.50 6.00
RJJT John Tavares 10.00 25.00
RJJV James van Riemsdyk 5.00 12.00
RJKA Erik Karlsson 8.00 20.00
RJKE Keaton Ellerby 2.00 5.00
RJLC Luca Caputi 2.50 6.00
RJLE Lars Eller 2.50 6.00
RJLO Logan Couture 5.00 12.00
RJMB Matt Beleskey 2.00 5.00
RJMC Matthew Corrente 2.00 5.00
RJMD Matt Duchene 5.00 12.00
RJMG Matt Gilroy 2.50 6.00
RJMN Michal Neuvirth 4.00 10.00
RJMP Matt Pelech 2.50 6.00
RJMS Mike Santorelli 2.50 6.00
RJOB Oskars Bartulis 2.50 6.00
RJOM Ryan O'Marra 1.50 4.00
RJPL Perttu Lindgren 2.00 5.00
RJPR Peter Regin 2.00 5.00
RJRH Riku Helenius 2.50 6.00
RJRS Ryan Stoa 2.00 5.00
RJSA Bobby Sanguinetti 1.50 4.00
RJSM Spencer Machacek 2.50 6.00
RJSS Sergei Shirokov 1.50 4.00
RJTC Taylor Chorney 2.50 6.00
RJTG T.J. Galiardi 2.50 6.00
RJTM Tyler Myers 4.00 10.00
RJVH Victor Hedman 6.00 15.00
RJVL Ville Leino 2.00 5.00
RJVS Viktor Stalberg 2.50 6.00
RJYW Yannick Weber 2.50 6.00

2009-10 Be A Player Rookie Jerseys Autographs

RJAA Artem Anisimov 4.00 10.00
RJCF Cody Franson 6.00 15.00
RJEK Evander Kane 12.00 30.00
RJJB Jamie Benn 20.00 50.00
RJJV James van Riemsdyk 12.00 30.00
RJKA Erik Karlsson 20.00 50.00
RJMD Matt Duchene 12.00 30.00
RJMG Matt Gilroy 6.00 15.00
RJVH Victor Hedman 15.00 40.00

2009-10 Be A Player Sidelines

S1 Alexander Ovechkin 2.50 6.00
S2 Anze Kopitar 1.00 2.50
S3 Brad Richards .60 1.50
S4 Cam Ward .60 1.50
S5 Carey Price 1.25 3.00
S6 Daniel Alfredsson .60 1.50
S7 Dany Heatley .50 1.25
S8 Dion Phaneuf .50 1.25
S9 Drew Doughty .75 2.00
S10 Dustin Penner .40 1.00
S11 Eric Staal .75 2.00
S12 Evander Kane 1.25 3.00
S13 Evgeni Malkin 1.25 3.00
S14 Henrik Lundqvist 1.50 4.00
S15 Henrik Sedin .75 2.00
S16 Henrik Zetterberg .75 2.00
S17 Ilya Kovalchuk .60 1.50
S18 Jarome Iginla .75 2.00
S19 Jason Spezza .60 1.50
S20 Jay Bouwmeester .40 1.00
S21 Jean-Sebastien Giguere .60 1.50
S22 Jeff Carter .50 1.25
S23 Joe Thornton 1.00 2.50
S24 John Tavares 2.50 6.00
S25 Jonathan Toews 1.00 2.50
S26 Marc-Andre Fleury 1.25 3.00
S27 Marian Gaborik .60 1.50
S28 Martin Brodeur 1.50 4.00
S29 Marty Turco .60 1.50
S30 Matt Duchene 1.25 3.00
S31 Miikka Kiprusoff .60 1.50
S32 Mike Cammalleri .50 1.25
S33 Mike Green .50 1.25
S34 Mike Modano 1.00 2.50
S35 Mike Richards .50 1.25
S36 Mikko Koivu .60 1.50
S37 Nicklas Backstrom .60 1.50
S38 Nicklas Lidstrom .40 1.00
S39 Patrick Kane 1.25 3.00
S40 Patrick Marleau .60 1.50
S41 Paul Kariya .60 1.50
S42 Paul Stastny .50 1.25
S43 Pavel Datsyuk 1.00 2.50
S44 Phil Kessel .60 1.50
S45 Rick DiPietro .50 1.25
S46 Rick Nash .60 1.50
S47 Roberto Luongo 1.00 2.50
S48 Ryan Getzlaf .60 1.50
S49 Ryan Miller .60 1.50
S50 Sam Gagner .40 1.00
S51 Scott Niedermayer .60 1.50
S52 Shane Doan .50 1.25
S53 Shea Weber .50 1.25
S54 Sidney Crosby 2.50 6.00
S55 Steve Mason .50 1.25
S56 Steven Stamkos 1.25 3.00
S57 Thomas Vanek .50 1.25
S58 Vincent Lecavalier .60 1.50
S59 Zach Parise .60 1.50
S60 Zdeno Chara .60 1.50

2009-10 Be A Player Signatures

SAA Adrian Aucoin 3.00 8.00
SAB Adam Burish 6.00 15.00
SAK Anze Kopitar 8.00 20.00
SAL Bryan Allen 3.00 8.00
SAM Andrei Markov 5.00 12.00
SAN Artem Anisimov 3.00 8.00
SAV Aaron Voros 3.00 8.00
SAX Alexandre Burrows 3.00 8.00
SBB Brent Burns 5.00 12.00
SBE Jamie Benn 15.00 40.00
SBG Boyd Gordon 3.00 8.00
SBK David Backes 3.00 8.00
SBL Brooks Laich 3.00 8.00
SBM Brenden Morrow 4.00 10.00
SBO Bobby Ryan 4.00 10.00
SBR Derick Brassard 3.00 8.00
SBS Brent Seabrook 3.00 8.00
SBU Peter Budaj 4.00 10.00
SBY Brad Boyes 3.00 8.00
SCA Chris Campoli 3.00 8.00
SCD Chris Drury 4.00 10.00

SCF Cody Franson 5.00 12.00
SCK David Clarkson 4.00 10.00
SCL Ryan Callahan 3.00 8.00
SCO Mike Commodore 3.00 8.00
SCP Carey Price 10.00 25.00
SCY Corey Perry 8.00 20.00
SDA Daniel Briere 5.00 12.00
SDB Dustin Brown 5.00 12.00
SDC Dan Cleary 5.00 12.00
SDH Dan Hamhuis 4.00 10.00
SDN Dan Boyle 3.00 8.00
SDP Dion Phaneuf 4.00 10.00
SDR Derek Roy SP 3.00 8.00
SDS Daniel Sedin 6.00 15.00
SDT Darcy Tucker 4.00 10.00
SDV David Perron 4.00 10.00
SDW Daniel Winnik 3.00 8.00
SEB Eric Brewer 3.00 8.00
SEC Erik Cole 3.00 8.00
SEK Erik Karlsson 15.00 40.00
SFI Mike Fisher 3.00 8.00
SGI Matt Gilroy 5.00 12.00
SGL Georges Laraque 4.00 10.00
SGP George Parros 3.00 8.00
SHA Scott Hannan 3.00 8.00
SHE Milan Hejduk 4.00 10.00
SHI Jonas Hiller 4.00 10.00
SHS Henrik Sedin 6.00 15.00
SHT Dany Heatley 4.00 10.00
SHZ Henrik Zetterberg SP 20.00 50.00
SIB Ilya Bryzgalov SP 20.00 50.00
SJB Jay Bouwmeester 3.00 8.00
SJC Jeff Carter SP 4.00 10.00
SJF Johan Franzen SP 4.00 10.00
SJH Jeff Halpern 3.00 8.00
SJI Jarome Iginla 15.00 40.00
SJM Jamal Mayers 3.00 8.00
SJN James Neal 3.00 8.00
SJO Joe Thornton 8.00 20.00
SJP Joni Pitkanen 4.00 10.00
SPO Jason Pominville 3.00 8.00
SJS Jason Spezza 5.00 12.00
SJT Jeff Tambellini 3.00 8.00
SJV Jakub Voracek 4.00 10.00
SKA Evander Kane 10.00 25.00
SKB Krys Barch 3.00 8.00
SKE Ryan Kesler 5.00 12.00
SKL Kristopher Letang 6.00 15.00
SKN Mike Knuble 3.00 8.00
SKU Nikolai Kulemin 3.00 8.00
SLS Luca Sbisa 5.00 12.00
SLU Roberto Luongo 8.00 20.00
SMB Mikkel Boedker 3.00 8.00
SMC Mike Cammalleri 4.00 10.00
SMD Matt Duchene 10.00 25.00
SMF Marc-Andre Fleury 15.00 40.00
SMM Manny Malhotra 3.00 8.00
SMN Matt Moulson 4.00 10.00
SMR Mike Richards SP 4.00 10.00
SMS Mike Sillinger 3.00 8.00
SMT Maxime Talbot 3.00 8.00
SMY Matt Bradley 3.00 8.00
SNB Niklas Backstrom 5.00 12.00
SNF Nick Foligno 4.00 10.00
SNK Niklas Kronwall 4.00 10.00
SNL Nicklas Lidstrom 3.00 8.00
SNM Nathan McIver 3.00 8.00
SNS Nick Schultz 3.00 8.00
SOJ Olli Jokinen 4.00 10.00
SOK Kyle Okposo 3.00 8.00
SOM Oscar Moller 3.00 8.00
SOP Ondrej Pavelec 6.00 15.00
SOS Patrick O'Sullivan 4.00 10.00
SPB Patrice Bergeron 25.00 60.00
SPB Pierre-Marc Bouchard 5.00 12.00
SPD Pavel Datsyuk 8.00 20.00
SPE Patrik Elias 5.00 12.00
SPH Patric Hornqvist 3.00 8.00
SPK Patrick Kane 20.00 50.00
SPL Pascal Leclaire 5.00 12.00
SPM Paul Martin 3.00 8.00
SPR Chris Pronger 5.00 12.00
SPS Paul Stastny SP 4.00 10.00
SPT Patrick Marleau 5.00 12.00
SPV Rich Peverley 4.00 10.00
SRA Mason Raymond 3.00 8.00
SRB Rene Bourque 3.00 8.00
SRC Brad Richards 5.00 12.00
SRE Peter Regin 4.00 10.00
SRF Brian Rafalski 3.00 8.00
SRG Ryan Getzlaf 5.00 12.00
SRH Ron Hainsey 3.00 8.00
SRI Pekka Rinne 5.00 12.00
SRK Rostislav Klesla 5.00 12.00
SRO Ryan O'Reilly 10.00 25.00
SRR Robyn Regehr 4.00 10.00
SRS Ryan Suter SP 4.00 10.00
SRT Raffi Torres 3.00 8.00
SRU R.J. Umberger 4.00 10.00
SRY Ryan Smyth 4.00 10.00
SSA Marc Staal 3.00 8.00
SSC Luke Schenn 5.00 12.00
SSD Shane Doan 4.00 10.00
SSE Devin Setoguchi 4.00 10.00
SSG Scott Gomez 4.00 10.00
SSH Scott Hartnell 3.00 8.00
SSI Sidney Crosby 80.00 150.00
SSK Saku Koivu 5.00 12.00
SSM Steve Mason 4.00 10.00
SSR Mark Stuart 3.00 8.00
SST Martin St. Louis 5.00 12.00
SSU Brandon Sutter 3.00 8.00
SSW Shea Weber 4.00 10.00
STF Tomas Fleischmann 3.00 8.00
STG Tim Gleason 3.00 8.00
STH Shawn Thornton 3.00 8.00
STJ T.J. Oshie SP 5.00 12.00
STM Tyler Myers 8.00 20.00
STP Tomas Plekanec 3.00 8.00
STT Tim Thomas 5.00 12.00
STU Marty Turco 5.00 12.00
STV Thomas Vanek 4.00 10.00
STZ Travis Zajac 3.00 8.00
SVA James van Riemsdyk 10.00 25.00
SVH Victor Hedman 12.00 30.00
SVL Vincent Lecavalier 5.00 12.00
SVO Tomas Vokoun 4.00 10.00
SWE Stephen Weiss 3.00 8.00
SWK Scott Walker 3.00 8.00
SWM Willie Mitchell 3.00 8.00
SWW Wojtek Wolski 3.00 8.00
SZB Zach Bogosian 4.00 10.00
SZC Zdeno Chara SP 5.00 12.00
SZP Zach Parise 5.00 12.00

2009-10 Be A Player Signatures Duals

S2BB Boedker/Bryzgalov 4.00 10.00
S2BC Briere/Carter 5.00 12.00
S2BK Kane/Bogosian 10.00 25.00
S2BM Mason/Brassard 4.00 10.00
S2CP Price/Cammalleri 10.00 25.00
S2CS Staal/Cole 6.00 15.00
S2DJ Drury/Jokinen 4.00 10.00
S2DO O'Reilly/Duchene 10.00 25.00
S2DZ Datsyuk/Zetterberg 8.00 20.00
S2GP Gomez/Plekanec 4.00 10.00
S2GR Getzlaf/Ryan 5.00 12.00
S2HM Hedman/Myers 12.00 30.00
S2HR Richards/Hartnell 4.00 10.00
S2HS Hejduk/Stastny 4.00 10.00
S2IB Bourque/Iginla 6.00 15.00
S2KV Kane/van Riemsdyk 10.00 25.00
S2LK Kronwall/Lidstrom 4.00 10.00
S2MH Marleau/Heatley 5.00 12.00
S2MT Marleau/Thornton 8.00 20.00
S2NB Neal/Benn 15.00 40.00
S2PO Oshie/Perron 5.00 12.00
S2RB Regehr/Bouwmeester 4.00 10.00
S2RM Morrow/Richards 5.00 12.00
S2RV Roy/Vanek 4.00 10.00
S2SF Spezza/Foligno 5.00 12.00
S2SG Staal/Gilroy 5.00 12.00
S2SS Sedin/Sedin 6.00 15.00
S2SW Weber/Suter 4.00 10.00

2009-10 Be A Player Signatures Foursomes

S4SWE2 Hornqvst/Franz/Kron/Lids 30.00 80.00

2009-10 Be A Player Signatures Trios

S3BPO Boyes/Perron/Oshie 6.00 15.00
S3CSS Staal/Sutter/Cole 8.00 20.00
S3DZF Datsyk/Zetter/Franzn 10.00 25.00
S3GCP Plekan/Gomz/Camm 5.00 12.00
S3HWS Stastny/Wolski/Hejduk 5.00 12.00
S3IMB Bourge/Mayers/Igin 8.00 20.00
S3MKH Hedmn/Karlssn/Myers 20.00 50.00
S3MTH Thorntn/Heatly/Marleu 10.00 25.00
S3PRV Vanek/Pominville/Roy 5.00 12.00
S3RCV Richrds/Carter/Riemsdyk 12.00 30.00
S3RMB Richrds/Morrw/Benn 20.00 50.00
S3SBK Kopitar/Smyth/Brown 10.00 25.00
S3SSK Kesler/Sedin/Sedin 8.00 20.00
S3UBV Brassard/Voracek/Umberger 5.00 12.00

2002-03 BAP All-Star Edition

1 Daniel Alfredsson .25 .60
2 Tony Amonte .20 .50
3 Ed Belfour .25 .60
4 Rob Blake .25 .60
5 Peter Bondra .25 .60
6 Radek Bonk .20 .50
7 Martin Brodeur .60 1.50
8 Martin Brodeur .60 1.50
9 Martin Brodeur .60 1.50
10 Valeri Bure .20 .50
11 Pavel Bure .25 .60
12 Pavel Bure .25 .60
13 Sean Burke .15 .40
14 Roman Cechmanek .20 .50
15 Chris Chelios .25 .60
16 Vincent Damphousse .20 .50
17 Eric Daze .15 .40
18 Pavol Demitra .30 .75
19 Patrik Elias .25 .60
20 Sergei Fedorov .40 1.00
21 Sergei Fedorov .40 1.00
22 Theo Fleury .30 .75
23 Peter Forsberg .50 1.25
24 Peter Forsberg .50 1.25
25 Peter Forsberg .50 1.25
26 Simon Gagne .25 .60
27 Scott Gomez .20 .50
28 Bill Guerin .25 .60
29 Milan Hejduk .20 .50
30 Phil Housley .20 .50
31 Brett Hull .50 1.25
32 Jarome Iginla .30 .75
33 Arturs Irbe .20 .50
34 Jaromir Jagr .75 2.00
35 Jaromir Jagr .75 2.00
36 Jaromir Jagr .75 2.00
37 Curtis Joseph .30 .75
38 Ed Jovanovski .20 .50
39 Tomas Kaberle .15 .40
40 Sami Kapanen .15 .40
41 Paul Kariya .25 .60
42 Paul Kariya .25 .60
43 Paul Kariya .25 .60
44 Nikolai Khabibulin .25 .60
45 Saku Koivu .25 .60
46 Olaf Kolzig .25 .60
47 Alexei Kovalev .20 .50
48 John LeClair .25 .60
49 Brian Leetch .20 .50
50 Brian Leetch .20 .50
51 Mario Lemieux 1.00 2.50
52 Mario Lemieux 1.00 2.50
53 Mario Lemieux 1.00 2.50
54 Nicklas Lidstrom .25 .60
55 Nicklas Lidstrom .25 .60
56 Eric Lindros .40 1.00
57 Al MacInnis .30 .75
58 Mark Messier .50 1.25
59 Mark Messier .50 1.25
60 Mike Modano .40 1.00
61 Mike Modano .40 1.00
62 Alexander Mogilny .20 .50
63 Evgeni Nabokov .20 .50
64 Markus Naslund .25 .60
65 Scott Niedermayer .25 .60
66 Owen Nolan .25 .60
67 Teppo Numminen .15 .40
68 Chris Osgood .25 .60
69 Sandis Ozolinsh .15 .40
70 Zigmund Palffy .25 .60
71 Felix Potvin .40 1.00
72 Chris Pronger .25 .60
73 Mark Recchi .30 .75
74 Mike Richter .25 .60
75 Luc Robitaille .25 .60
76 Jeremy Roenick .40 1.00
77 Patrick Roy .60 1.50
78 Patrick Roy .60 1.50
79 Patrick Roy .60 1.50
80 Joe Sakic .50 1.25
81 Joe Sakic .50 1.25
82 Tommy Salo .20 .50
83 Teemu Selanne .50 1.25
84 Brendan Shanahan .25 .60
85 Brendan Shanahan .25 .60
86 Brendan Shanahan .25 .60
87 Scott Stevens .25 .60
88 Mats Sundin .25 .60
89 Mats Sundin .25 .60
90 Darryl Sydor .15 .40
91 Jose Theodore .25 .60
92 Joe Thornton .40 1.00
93 Keith Tkachuk .25 .60
94 Ron Tugnutt .20 .50
95 Roman Turek .25 .60
96 Doug Weight .25 .60
97 Alexei Yashin .20 .50
98 Steve Yzerman .60 1.50
99 Steve Yzerman .60 1.50
100 Alexei Zhamnov .20 .50
101 Dany Heatley SP 2.50 6.00
102 Ilya Kovalchuk SP 4.00 10.00
103 Marian Gaborik SP 3.00 8.00
104 Marty Turco SP 3.00 8.00
105 Mike Comrie SP 3.00 8.00
106 Cody Rudkowsky RC 2.00 5.00
107 Levente Szuper RC 3.00 8.00
108 Alex Henry RC 2.50 6.00
109 Lynn Loyns RC 2.00 5.00
110 Tomi Pettinen RC 2.00 5.00
111 Micki Dupont RC 2.00 5.00
112 Shaone Morrisonn RC 2.00 5.00
113 Ryan Miller RC 20.00 50.00
114 Mikael Tellqvist RC 2.00 5.00
115 Dany Sabourin RC 2.00 5.00
116 Tim Thomas RC 12.00 30.00
117 Kurt Sauer RC 2.00 5.00
118 Kari Haakana RC 2.00 5.00
119 Lasse Pirjeta RC 2.00 5.00
120 Shawn Thornton RC 2.50 6.00
121 Curtis Sanford RC 3.00 8.00
122 Dick Tarnstrom RC 2.00 5.00
123 Radovan Somik RC 2.00 5.00
124 Martin Gerber RC 3.00 8.00
125 Dennis Seidenberg RC 3.00 8.00
126 P-M Bouchard RC 3.00 8.00
127 Alexei Smirnov RC 2.50 6.00
128 Ales Hemsky RC 8.00 20.00
129 Stephane Veilleux RC 2.00 5.00
130 Tom Koivisto RC 2.00 5.00
131 Jeff Taffe RC 2.00 5.00
132 Jordan Leopold RC 3.00 8.00
133 Stanislav Chistov RC 2.00 5.00
134 Rick Nash RC 25.00 60.00
135 Chuck Kobasew RC 2.50 6.00
136 Alexander Svitov RC 2.00 5.00
137 Carlo Colaiacovo RC 3.00 8.00
138 Jason Spezza RC 20.00 50.00
139 Henrik Zetterberg RC 30.00 80.00
140 Anton Volchenkov RC 2.00 5.00
141 Ron Hainsey RC 2.00 5.00
142 Jay Bouwmeester RC 6.00 15.00
143 Adam Hall RC 2.00 5.00
144 Steve Eminger RC 2.00 5.00
145 Mike Cammalleri RC 6.00 15.00
146 Dmitri Bykov RC 2.00 5.00
147 Ivan Majesky RC 2.00 5.00
148 Alexander Frolov RC 5.00 12.00
149 Scottie Upshall RC 2.50 6.00
150 Patrick Sharp RC 6.00 15.00

2002-03 BAP All-Star Edition Silver

*101-105 SILVER/20: .8X TO 2X BASIC SP
*106-150 SILVER/20: .8X TO 2X BASIC ROOKIE

2002-03 BAP All-Star Edition Bobble Heads

1 Mario Lemieux/1066 20.00 50.00
2 Jose Theodore/1560 10.00 25.00
3 Pavel Bure/2010 10.00 25.00
4 Curtis Joseph/1031 10.00 25.00
5 Martin Brodeur/1530 12.50 30.00
6 Peter Forsberg/2031 12.50 30.00
7 Steve Yzerman/2019 12.50 30.00
8 Jaromir Jagr/2068 10.00 25.00
9 Joe Sakic/1519 10.00 25.00
10 Patrick Roy/1033 20.00 50.00

2002-03 BAP All-Star Edition He Shoots He Score Prizes

1 Brian Leetch 1 pt. .12 .30
2 Eric Lindros 1 pt. .25 .60
3 Mark Messier 1 pt. .30 .75
4 Owen Nolan 1 pt. .15 .40
5 Teemu Selanne 1 pt. .30 .75
6 Brendan Shanahan 1 pt. .15 .40
7 Mats Sundin 1 pt. .15 .40
8 Alexei Yashin 1 pt. .12 .30
9 Martin Brodeur 2 pt. .50 1.25
10 Pavel Bure 2 pt. .20 .50
11 Sergei Fedorov 2 pt. .30 .75
12 Jaromir Jagr 2 pt. .60 1.50
13 Curtis Joseph 2 pt. .25 .60
14 Nicklas Lidstrom 2 pt. .20 .50
15 Mike Modano 2 pt. .30 .75
16 Patrick Roy 2 pt. .50 1.25
17 Joe Sakic 2 pt. .40 1.00
18 Peter Forsberg 3 pt. .40 1.00
19 Mario Lemieux 3 pt. .75 2.00
20 Steve Yzerman 3 pt. .50 1.25

2002-03 BAP All-Star Edition He Shoots He Scores Prizes

1 Tony Amonte 8.00 20.00
2 Ed Belfour 10.00 25.00
3 Martin Brodeur 25.00 60.00
4 Pavel Bure 10.00 25.00
5 Chris Chelios 10.00 25.00
6 Sergei Fedorov 15.00 40.00
7 Peter Forsberg 20.00 50.00
8 Jaromir Jagr 30.00 80.00
9 Curtis Joseph 12.00 30.00
10 Paul Kariya 10.00 25.00
11 Nikolai Khabibulin 10.00 25.00
12 John LeClair 10.00 25.00
13 Brian Leetch 8.00 20.00
14 Mario Lemieux 40.00 100.00
15 Nicklas Lidstrom 10.00 25.00
16 Eric Lindros 15.00 40.00
17 Al MacInnis 12.00 30.00
18 Mark Messier 20.00 50.00
19 Mike Modano 30.00 60.00
20 Markus Naslund 10.00 25.00
21 Owen Nolan 10.00 25.00
22 Chris Pronger 10.00 25.00
23 Mark Recchi 12.00 30.00
24 Patrick Roy 25.00 60.00
25 Joe Sakic 20.00 50.00
26 Teemu Selanne 20.00 50.00
27 Brendan Shanahan 10.00 25.00
28 Mats Sundin 10.00 25.00
29 Alexei Yashin 8.00 20.00
30 Steve Yzerman 25.00 60.00

2002-03 BAP All-Star Edition Jerseys

*SILVER/30: .6X TO 1.5X BASE HI
1 Daniel Alfredsson 5.00 12.00
2 Tony Amonte 4.00 10.00
3 Ed Belfour 5.00 12.00
4 Rob Blake 5.00 12.00
5 Peter Bondra 5.00 12.00
6 Radek Bonk 4.00 10.00
7 Martin Brodeur 12.00 30.00
8 Martin Brodeur 12.00 30.00
9 Martin Brodeur 12.00 30.00
10 Valeri Bure 4.00 10.00
11 Pavel Bure 5.00 12.00
12 Pavel Bure 5.00 12.00
13 Sean Burke 3.00 8.00
14 Roman Cechmanek 4.00 10.00
15 Chris Chelios 5.00 12.00
16 Vincent Damphousse 4.00 10.00
17 Eric Daze 3.00 8.00
18 Pavol Demitra 6.00 15.00
19 Patrik Elias 5.00 12.00
20 Sergei Fedorov 8.00 20.00
21 Sergei Fedorov 8.00 20.00
22 Theo Fleury 6.00 15.00
23 Peter Forsberg 10.00 25.00
24 Peter Forsberg 10.00 25.00
25 Peter Forsberg 10.00 25.00
26 Simon Gagne 5.00 12.00
27 Scott Gomez 4.00 10.00
28 Bill Guerin 5.00 12.00
29 Milan Hejduk 4.00 10.00
30 Phil Housley 4.00 10.00
31 Brett Hull 10.00 25.00
32 Jarome Iginla 6.00 15.00
33 Arturs Irbe 4.00 10.00
34 Jaromir Jagr 15.00 40.00
35 Jaromir Jagr 15.00 40.00
36 Jaromir Jagr 15.00 40.00
37 Curtis Joseph 6.00 15.00
38 Ed Jovanovski 4.00 10.00
39 Tomas Kaberle 3.00 8.00
40 Sami Kapanen 3.00 8.00
41 Paul Kariya 5.00 12.00
42 Paul Kariya 5.00 12.00
43 Paul Kariya 5.00 12.00
44 Nikolai Khabibulin 5.00 12.00
45 Saku Koivu 5.00 12.00
46 Olaf Kolzig 5.00 12.00
47 Alexei Kovalev 4.00 10.00
48 John LeClair 5.00 12.00
49 Brian Leetch 4.00 10.00
50 Brian Leetch 4.00 10.00
51 Mario Lemieux 20.00 50.00
52 Mario Lemieux 20.00 50.00
53 Mario Lemieux 20.00 50.00
54 Nicklas Lidstrom 5.00 12.00
55 Nicklas Lidstrom 5.00 12.00
56 Eric Lindros 8.00 20.00
57 Al MacInnis 6.00 15.00
58 Mark Messier 10.00 25.00
59 Mark Messier 10.00 25.00
60 Mike Modano 8.00 20.00
61 Mike Modano 8.00 20.00
62 Alexander Mogilny 4.00 10.00
63 Evgeni Nabokov 4.00 10.00
64 Markus Naslund 5.00 12.00
65 Scott Niedermayer 5.00 12.00
66 Owen Nolan 5.00 12.00
67 Teppo Numminen 3.00 8.00
68 Chris Osgood 5.00 12.00
69 Sandis Ozolinsh 3.00 8.00
70 Zigmund Palffy 5.00 12.00
71 Felix Potvin 8.00 20.00
72 Chris Pronger 5.00 12.00
73 Mark Recchi 6.00 15.00
74 Mike Richter 5.00 12.00
75 Luc Robitaille 5.00 12.00
76 Jeremy Roenick 8.00 20.00
77 Patrick Roy 12.00 30.00
78 Patrick Roy 12.00 30.00
79 Patrick Roy 12.00 30.00
80 Joe Sakic 10.00 25.00
81 Joe Sakic 10.00 25.00
82 Tommy Salo 4.00 10.00
83 Teemu Selanne 10.00 25.00
84 Brendan Shanahan 5.00 12.00
85 Brendan Shanahan 5.00 12.00
86 Brendan Shanahan 5.00 12.00
87 Scott Stevens 5.00 12.00
88 Mats Sundin 5.00 12.00
89 Mats Sundin 5.00 12.00
90 Darryl Sydor 3.00 8.00
91 Jose Theodore 5.00 12.00
92 Joe Thornton 8.00 20.00
93 Keith Tkachuk 5.00 12.00
94 Ron Tugnutt 4.00 10.00
95 Roman Turek 5.00 12.00
96 Doug Weight 5.00 12.00
97 Alexei Yashin 4.00 10.00
98 Steve Yzerman 12.00 30.00
99 Steve Yzerman 12.00 30.00
100 Alexei Zhamnov 4.00 10.00

2002-03 BAP First Edition

1 Mario Lemieux 1.00 2.50
2 Sergei Gonchar .20 .50
3 Brian Leetch .20 .50
4 Felix Potvin .40 1.00
5 Sandis Ozolinsh .15 .40
6 Steven Reinprecht .15 .40
7 Byron Dafoe .20 .50
8 Mark Bell .15 .40
9 Jeff O'Neill .15 .40
10 Sean Burke .15 .40
11 Darcy Tucker .15 .40
12 Scott Stevens .25 .60
13 David Aebischer .20 .50
14 Jocelyn Thibault .20 .50
15 Radek Bonk .20 .50
16 Milan Hejduk .20 .50
17 Zigmund Palffy .25 .60
18 Luc Robitaille .25 .60
19 Tomas Kaberle .15 .40
20 Rostislav Klesla .15 .40
21 Alexei Zhamnov .20 .50
22 Ron Francis .30 .75
23 Mike Fisher .15 .40
24 Dany Heatley .20 .50
25 Kyle McLaren .15 .40
26 Doug Weight .25 .60
27 Henrik Sedin .30 .75
28 Roman Turek .25 .60
29 Adam Deadmarsh .15 .40
30 Sami Kapanen .15 .40
31 Sergei Samsonov .20 .50
32 Kristian Huselius .15 .40
33 Dimitri Yushkevich .15 .40
34 Patrik Elias .25 .60
35 Nick Boynton .15 .40
36 Martin Biron .20 .50
37 Brad Richards .25 .60
38 Alyn McCauley .15 .40
39 Daniel Sedin .30 .75
40 Teppo Numminen .15 .40
41 Luke Richardson .15 .40
42 Manny Fernandez .15 .40
43 Vincent Lecavalier .25 .60
44 Mattias Ohlund .15 .40
45 Milan Kraft .15 .40
46 Mike Dunham .20 .50
47 Derian Hatcher .20 .50
48 Oleg Tverdovsky .15 .40
49 Shane Doan .20 .50
50 Martin Skoula .15 .40
51 John LeClair .25 .60
52 Tommy Salo .20 .50
53 Miroslav Satan .25 .60
54 Bryan Berard .15 .40
55 Roman Cechmanek .20 .50
56 Alexei Morozov .15 .40
57 Jean-Sebastien Giguere .25 .60
58 Pierre Turgeon .20 .50
59 Martin Straka .20 .50
60 Stephane Yelle .15 .40
61 Marc Savard .15 .40
62 Sergei Zubov .20 .50
63 Jeff Friesen .15 .40
64 Daniel Briere .20 .50
65 Patrik Stefan .20 .50
66 Pavol Demitra .30 .75
67 Radek Dvorak .20 .50
68 Marty Turco .25 .60
69 Keith Tkachuk .25 .60
70 Maxim Afinogenov .15 .40
71 Mika Noronen .20 .50
72 Evgeni Nabokov .20 .50
73 Todd Bertuzzi .25 .60
74 Valeri Bure .20 .50
75 Marian Hossa .25 .60
76 J-P Dumont .15 .40
77 Niklas Sundstrom .15 .40
78 Eric Daze .15 .40
79 Brian Boucher .20 .50
80 Nikolai Khabibulin .25 .60
81 Darren McCarty .20 .50
82 Pavel Brendl .15 .40
83 Mark Recchi .30 .75
84 Dan Cloutier .20 .50
85 Manny Legace .25 .60
86 Keith Primeau .20 .50
87 Alex Tanguay .20 .50
88 Ed Jovanovski .20 .50
89 Roberto Luongo .40 1.00
90 Andreas Johansson .15 .40
91 Steve Shields .20 .50
92 Saku Koivu .25 .60
93 Chris Drury .25 .60
94 Olaf Kolzig .25 .60
95 Jan Hrdina .15 .40
96 Ivan Novoseltsev .15 .40
97 Kenny Jonsson .15 .40
98 Martin Havlat .20 .50
99 Scott Niedermayer .25 .60
100 Chris Phillips .15 .40
101 Tony Amonte .20 .50
102 Alexander Mogilny .20 .50
103 Chris Pronger .25 .60
104 Chris Gratton .15 .40
105 Sergei Fedorov .40 1.00
106 David Legwand .20 .50
107 Ron Tugnutt .20 .50
108 Steven McCarthy .15 .40
109 Brian Rolston .20 .50
110 Bobby Holik .15 .40
111 Darryl Sydor .15 .40
112 Steve Sullivan .15 .40
113 Toby Petersen .15 .40
114 Scott Gomez .20 .50
115 Adam Foote .15 .40
116 Rob Niedermayer .20 .50
117 Arturs Irbe .20 .50
118 Al MacInnis .30 .75
119 Jeff Hackett .20 .50
120 Pavel Bure .25 .60
121 Patrick Lalime .20 .50
122 Vincent Damphousse .20 .50
123 Steve Passmore .15 .40
124 Simon Gagne .25 .60
125 Shawn McEachern .15 .40
126 Bryan McCabe .15 .40
127 Jamie Storr .20 .50
128 Mike Richter .25 .60
129 Petr Sykora .20 .50
130 Trevor Kidd .15 .40
131 Jaromir Jagr .75 2.00
132 Bill Guerin .25 .60
133 Mark Messier .50 1.25
134 Ilya Kovalchuk .30 .75
135 Teemu Selanne .50 1.25
136 Dominik Hasek .40 1.00
137 Mats Sundin .25 .60
138 Jose Theodore .25 .60
139 Brendan Shanahan .25 .60
140 Daniel Alfredsson .25 .60
141 Martin Brodeur .60 1.50
142 Jarome Iginla .30 .75
143 Peter Bondra .25 .60
144 Peter Forsberg .50 1.25
145 Curtis Joseph .30 .75
146 Alexei Yashin .20 .50
147 Patrick Roy .60 1.50
148 Markus Naslund .25 .60
149 Jeremy Roenick .40 1.00
150 Eric Lindros .40 1.00
151 Steve Yzerman .60 1.50
152 Marian Gaborik .25 .60
153 Mike Modano .40 1.00
154 Joe Sakic .50 1.25
155 Paul Kariya .25 .60
156 Owen Nolan .25 .60
157 Rob Blake .25 .60
158 Nicklas Lidstrom .25 .60
159 Joe Thornton .40 1.00
160 Mario Lemieux 1.00 2.50
161 Magnus Arvedson .15 .40
162 Chris Clark .15 .40
163 Don Sweeney .15 .40
164 Fredrik Modin .15 .40
165 Matt Cooke .15 .40
166 Rhett Warrener .15 .40
167 Tim Taylor .15 .40
168 Viktor Kozlov .15 .40
169 Michal Rozsival .20 .50
170 Mathieu Schneider .15 .40
171 Matt Cullen .15 .40
172 Vladimir Malakhov .15 .40
173 Mattias Norstrom .15 .40
174 Greg Johnson .15 .40
175 Eric Desjardins .15 .40
176 Damian Rhodes .15 .40
177 Stephane Quintal .15 .40
178 Sami Salo .15 .40
179 Craig Rivet .15 .40
180 Oleg Saprykin .15 .40
181 Chris Therien .15 .40
182 Robyn Regehr .15 .40
183 Erik Cole .15 .40
184 Ed Belfour .25 .60
185 Chris Chelios .25 .60
186 Pavel Datsyuk .40 1.00
187 Mike Comrie .25 .60
188 Doug Gilmour .30 .75
189 Johan Hedberg .25 .60
190 Brett Hull .50 1.25
191 Theo Fleury .30 .75
192 Rick DiPietro .20 .50
193 Marcus Ragnarsson .15 .40
194 Mike Peca .20 .50
195 Ryan Smyth .20 .50
196 Ruslan Salei .15 .40
197 Anson Carter .20 .50
198 Eric Brewer .15 .40
199 Alexei Kovalev .20 .50
200 Gary Roberts .15 .40
201 Micki Dupont RC .15 .40
202 Pat Verbeek .15 .40
203 Dmitri Kalinin .15 .40
204 Brad Stuart .15 .40
205 Brent Johnson .20 .50
206 Todd White .15 .40
207 Andy McDonald .25 .60
208 Glen Murray .20 .50
209 Chris Osgood .25 .60
210 Tim Connolly .15 .40
211 Scott Hartnell .15 .40
212 Radim Vrbata .15 .40
213 Dimitri Khristich .15 .40
214 Brendan Morrison .20 .50
215 Matt Henderson RC .15 .40
216 Jason Allison .20 .50
217 Ray Whitney .20 .50
218 Niklas Hagman .15 .40
219 Andrew Brunette .15 .40
220 Brian Rafalski .15 .40
221 Mark Parrish .15 .40
222 Dave Andreychuk .25 .60
223 Dainius Zubrus .15 .40
224 P.J. Stock .15 .40
225 Espen Knutsen .15 .40
226 Jiri Dopita .15 .40
227 Jeff Jillson .15 .40
228 Tie Domi .20 .50
229 Milan Hnilicka .20 .50
230 Martin Lapointe .20 .50
231 Taylor Pyatt .15 .40
232 Kyle Calder .15 .40
233 Marc Denis .20 .50
234 Brenden Morrow .20 .50
235 Cliff Ronning .15 .40
236 Wade Redden .15 .40
237 Kris Beech .15 .40
238 Patrick Marleau .25 .60
239 Corey Schwab .20 .50
240 Nikita Alexeev .15 .40
241 Miikka Kiprusoff .25 .60
242 Jason Arnott .20 .50
243 Joe Nieuwendyk .20 .50
244 Adam Oates .25 .60
245 Darius Kasparaitis .15 .40
246 Mike York .15 .40
247 Donald Brashear .15 .40
248 Kevin Weekes .20 .50
249 Jaroslav Spacek .15 .40
250 Alex Auld .15 .40
251 Denis Arkhipov .15 .40
252 Cory Stillman .15 .40
253 Craig Conroy .15 .40
254 Dan Blackburn .20 .50
255 Vaclav Nedorost .15 .40
256 Ladislav Nagy .15 .40
257 Lukas Krajicek .20 .50
258 Raffi Torres .15 .40
259 Richard Zednik .15 .40
260 Brad Bombardir .15 .40
261 Ilja Bryzgalov .20 .50
262 Frederic Cassivi .15 .40
263 Geoff Sanderson .20 .50
264 Dwayne Roloson .15 .40
265 Jani Hurme .20 .50
266 Sebastien Centomo .15 .40
267 Jeff Halpern .15 .40
268 Mikael Renberg .15 .40
269 Vaclav Prospal .15 .40
270 Sylvain Blouin RC .15 .40
271 Olivier Michaud .15 .40
272 Pascal Dupuis .15 .40
273 Michael Nylander .15 .40
274 Daymond Langkow .20 .50
275 Mike Sillinger .15 .40
276 Yanic Perreault .15 .40
277 Oleg Petrov .15 .40
278 Rod Brind'Amour .25 .60
279 Scott Clemmensen .15 .40
280 Jason Smith .15 .40
281 Vladimir Orszagh .15 .40
282 Stephen Weiss .25 .60
283 Tony Hrkac .15 .40
284 Ty Conklin .20 .50
285 Ulf Dahlen .15 .40
286 Karel Pilar .15 .40
287 Krys Kolanos .15 .40
288 Marcel Hossa .15 .40
289 Martin Prusek .15 .40
290 Robert Svehla .15 .40
291 Radoslav Suchy .15 .40
292 Alexander Khavanov .15 .40
293 Andy Delmore .15 .40
294 Adrian Aucoin .15 .40
295 Bates Battaglia .15 .40
296 Jussi Markkanen .15 .40
297 Martin Erat .15 .40
298 Jim Dowd .15 .40
299 Mark Hartigan .15 .40
300 Neil Little .15 .40
301 Markus Naslund UC .30 .75
302 Bill Guerin UC .30 .75
303 Nicklas Lidstrom UC .30 .75
304 Sergei Fedorov UC .50 1.25
305 Mats Sundin UC .30 .75
306 Teemu Selanne UC .60 1.50
307 Sergei Gonchar UC .25 .60
308 Brian Leetch UC .25 .60
309 Jeremy Roenick UC .50 1.25
310 Jaromir Jagr UC 1.00 2.50
311 Mark Recchi UC .40 1.00
312 Sandis Ozolinsh UC .20 .50
313 Jarome Iginla UC .40 1.00
314 Jose Theodore UC .30 .75
315 Steve Yzerman UC .75 2.00
316 Paul Kariya UC .30 .75
317 Eric Daze UC .20 .50
318 Ilya Kovalchuk UC .40 1.00
319 Brendan Shanahan UC .30 .75
320 Marian Gaborik UC .30 .75
321 Joe Sakic UC .60 1.50
322 Peter Forsberg UC .60 1.50
323 Mario Lemieux UC 1.25 3.00
324 Luc Robitaille UC .30 .75
325 Eric Lindros UC .50 1.25
326 Mike Modano UC .50 1.25
327 Patrick Roy UC .75 2.00
328 Dominik Hasek UC .50 1.25
329 Scott Stevens UC .30 .75
330 Martin Brodeur UC .75 2.00
331 Keith Tkachuk UC .30 .75
332 Rostislav Klesla UC .20 .50
333 Joe Thornton UC .50 1.25
334 Alexei Yashin UC .25 .60
335 Brett Hull UC .60 1.50
336 Olaf Kolzig UC .30 .75
337 Roberto Luongo UC .50 1.25
338 Pavel Bure UC .30 .75
339 Chris Chelios UC .30 .75
340 Owen Nolan UC .30 .75
341 Paul Kariya FP .30 .75
342 Ilya Kovalchuk FP .40 1.00
343 Joe Thornton FP .50 1.25
344 Miroslav Satan FP .30 .75
345 Jarome Iginla FP .40 1.00
346 Jeff O'Neill FP .20 .50
347 Eric Daze FP .20 .50
348 Patrick Roy FP .75 2.00
349 Rostislav Klesla FP .20 .50
350 Mike Modano FP .50 1.25
351 Steve Yzerman FP .75 2.00
352 Mike Comrie FP .30 .75
353 Roberto Luongo FP .50 1.25
354 Zigmund Palffy FP .30 .75
355 Marian Gaborik FP .30 .75
356 Jose Theodore FP .30 .75
357 Scott Hartnell FP .20 .50
358 Martin Brodeur FP .75 2.00
359 Alexei Yashin FP .25 .60
360 Pavel Bure FP .30 .75
361 Marian Hossa FP .30 .75
362 Simon Gagne FP .30 .75
363 Daniel Briere FP .25 .60
364 Mario Lemieux FP 1.25 3.00
365 Chris Pronger FP .30 .75
366 Owen Nolan FP .30 .75
367 Nikolai Khabibulin FP .30 .75
368 Mats Sundin FP .30 .75
369 Markus Naslund FP .30 .75
370 Jaromir Jagr FP 1.00 2.50
371 Iginla/Naslund/Bertuzzi SL .40 1.00
372 Iginla/Sundin/Mury/Grin SL .40 1.00
373 Oates/Allison/Sakic SL .30 .75
374 Chel/Rnick/Mury/Ggne SL .50 1.25
375 Worrell/Ference/Neil SL .20 .50
376 Roy/Cechmanek/Turco SL .75 2.00
377 Theo/Roy/Cech./Turco SL .75 2.00

378 Demitra/Murray/Sundin SL .40 1.00
379 Rolston/Peca/Satan SL .30 .75
380 Hasek/Brodeur/Nabokv SL .75 2.00
381 Svehla/Kaspar/Hatcher SL .25 .60
382 Lidstrom/Gonchar SL .30 .75
383 Htley/Kovalchuk/Huslius SL .40 1.00
384 Koval/Heatley/Huselius SL .40 1.00
385 Aucoin/Pronger/Lidstrom SL .30 .75
386 Perreault/Brind/Francis SL .40 1.00
387 Bondra/Iginla SL .40 1.00
388 Briere/Ddmrsh/Hrdina SL .25 .60
389 Patrick Roy AS .75 2.00
390 Chris Pronger AS .30 .75
391 Rob Blake AS .30 .75
392 Vincent Damphousse AS .25 .60
393 Owen Nolan AS .30 .75
394 Brendan Shanahan AS .30 .75
395 Dominik Hasek AS .50 1.25
396 Nicklas Lidstrom AS .30 .75
397 Sandis Ozolinsh AS .20 .50
398 Sergei Fedorov AS .50 1.25
399 Jaromir Jagr AS 1.00 2.50
400 Teemu Selanne AS .60 1.50
401H Mike Modano Draft .50 1.25
401R Trevor Linden Draft .30 .75
402H Jeremy Roenick Draft .50 1.25
402R Mats Sundin Draft .30 .75
403H Bill Guerin Draft .30 .75
403R Olaf Kolzig Draft .30 .75
404H Owen Nolan Draft .30 .75
404R Jaromir Jagr Draft 1.00 2.50
405H Martin Brodeur Draft .75 2.00
405R Eric Lindros Draft .50 1.25
406H Scott Niedermayer Draft .30 .75
406R Peter Forsberg Draft .60 1.50
407H Markus Naslund Draft .30 .75
407R Alexei Yashin Draft .25 .60
408H Chris Pronger Draft .30 .75
408R Paul Kariya Draft .30 .75
409H Jason Arnott Draft .25 .60
409R Jocelyn Thibault Draft .25 .60
410H Adam Deadmarsh Draft .20 .50
410R Jason Allison Draft .25 .60
411H Todd Bertuzzi Draft .30 .75
411R Ed Jovanovski Draft .25 .60
412H Jeff O'Neill Draft .20 .50
412R Ryan Smyth Draft .25 .60
413H Dan Cloutier Draft .25 .60
413R Jarome Iginla Draft .40 1.00
414H Jean-Sebastien Giguere Draft .30 .75
414R Martin Biron Draft .25 .60
415H Petr Sykora Draft .25 .60
415R Brian Boucher Draft .25 .60
416H Marc Denis Draft .25 .60
416R Joe Thornton Draft .50 1.25
417H Roberto Luongo Draft .50 1.25
417R Eric Brewer Draft .20 .50
418H Sergei Samsonov Draft .25 .60
418R Marian Hossa Draft .30 .75
419H Vincent Lecavalier Draft .30 .75
419R Mark Bell Draft .20 .50
420H Alex Tanguay Draft .25 .60
420R Simon Gagne Draft .30 .75
421H Martin Havlat Draft .25 .60
421R Rick DiPietro Draft .25 .60
422H Dany Heatley Draft .25 .60
422R Marian Gaborik Draft .30 .75
423H Rostislav Klesla Draft .20 .50
423R Scott Hartnell Draft .20 .50
424H Ilya Kovalchuk Draft .40 1.00
424R Stephen Weiss Draft .30 .75
425H Dan Blackburn Draft .25 .60
425R Lukas Krajicek Draft .25 .60
426H Steve Yzerman Draft 5.00 12.00
426R Mario Lemieux Draft 5.00 12.00
427H Gary Roberts Draft .20 .50
427R Brian Leetch Draft .25 .60
428H Brendan Shanahan Draft .30 .75
428R Pierre Turgeon Draft .25 .60
429H Joe Sakic Draft 1.50 4.00
429R Teemu Selanne Draft .60 1.50
430H Keith Tkachuk Draft .30 .75
430R Sedin/Sedin Draft .40 1.00
431H Steve Ott Draft RC .75 2.00
431R Brooks Orpik Draft RC .75 2.00
432H Pascal Leclaire Draft RC 1.00 2.50
432R Shaone Morrisonn Draft RC .75 2.00
433H Alexei Smirnov Draft RC 1.00 2.50
433R Ron Hainsey Draft RC .75 2.00
434H Alexander Frolov Draft RC 2.00 5.00
434R Anton Volchenkov Draft RC .75 2.00
435H Jeff Taffe Draft RC .75 2.00
435R Jason Spezza Draft RC 5.00 12.00
436H Alexander Svitov Draft RC .75 2.00
436R Stanislav Chistov Draft RC .75 2.00
437H Chuck Kobasew Draft RC 1.00 2.50
437R Ales Hemsky Draft RC 3.00 8.00
438H Carlo Colaiacovo Draft RC 1.25 3.00
438R Jay Bouwmeester Draft RC 2.50 6.00
439H Rick Nash Draft RC 5.00 12.00
439R Scottie Upshall Draft RC 1.00 2.50
440H P-M Bouchard Draft RC 1.25 3.00
440R Steve Eminger Draft RC .75 2.00

2002-03 BAP First Edition Debut Jerseys

1 Pavel Bure 15.00 40.00
2 Patrick Roy 20.00 50.00
3 Curtis Joseph 15.00 40.00
4 Mats Sundin 12.00 30.00
5 Ed Belfour 15.00 40.00
6 Teemu Selanne 20.00 50.00
7 Martin Brodeur 25.00 60.00
8 Owen Nolan 10.00 25.00
9 Jarome Iginla 20.00 50.00
10 Steve Yzerman 25.00 60.00
11 Marian Gaborik 20.00 50.00
12 Jaromir Jagr 12.00 30.00
13 Eric Lindros 12.00 30.00
14 Ilya Kovalchuk 15.00 40.00
15 Nicklas Lidstrom 12.00 30.00
16 Paul Kariya 15.00 40.00
17 Joe Thornton 20.00 50.00
18 Mark Messier 20.00 50.00
19 Keith Tkachuk 10.00 25.00
20 Joe Sakic 15.00 40.00

2002-03 BAP First Edition He Shoots He Scores Points

2 Sergei Fedorov 1 pt. .25 .60
3 Milan Hejduk 1 pt. .12 .30
3 Saku Koivu 1 pt. .15 .40
4 Dany Heatley 1 pt. .12 .30
5 Ilya Kovalchuk 1 pt. .20 .50
7 Teemu Selanne 1 pt. .30 .75
8 Eric Lindros 1 pt. .25 .60
9 Mark Messier 1 pt. .30 .75
10 Owen Nolan 1 pt.. .15 .40
11 Joe Thornton 1 pt. .25 .60
12 Pavel Bure 2 pts. .20 .50
13 Jarome Iginla 2 pts. .25 .60
14 Paul Kariya 2 pts. .20 .50
15 Joe Sakic 2 pts. .40 1.00
16 Steve Yzerman 2 pts. .50 1.25
17 Mike Modano 2 pts. .30 .75
18 Peter Forsberg 3 pts. .40 1.00
19 Mats Sundin 3 pts. .20 .50
20 Mario Lemieux 3 pts. .75 2.00

2002-03 BAP First Edition He Shoots He Scores Prizes

1 Peter Forsberg 20.00 50.00
2 Mario Lemieux 40.00 100.00
3 Mats Sundin 10.00 25.00
4 Jarome Iginla 12.00 30.00
5 Pavel Bure 10.00 25.00
6 Joe Sakic 20.00 50.00
7 Steve Yzerman 25.00 60.00
8 Paul Kariya 10.00 25.00
9 Mike Modano 15.00 40.00
10 Mark Messier 20.00 50.00
11 Milan Hejduk 8.00 20.00
12 Ron Francis 12.00 30.00
13 Saku Koivu 10.00 25.00
14 Owen Nolan 10.00 25.00
15 Joe Thornton 15.00 40.00
16 Ilya Kovalchuk 12.00 30.00
17 Dany Heatley 8.00 20.00
18 Eric Lindros 15.00 40.00
19 Teemu Selanne 20.00 50.00
20 Sergei Fedorov 15.00 40.00
21 Brendan Shanahan 10.00 25.00
22 Marian Gaborik 10.00 25.00
23 Patrick Roy 25.00 60.00
24 Martin Brodeur 25.00 60.00
25 Jose Theodore 10.00 25.00
26 Dominik Hasek 15.00 40.00
27 Jeremy Roenick 15.00 40.00
28 Jaromir Jagr 30.00 80.00
29 Keith Tkachuk 10.00 25.00
30 Markus Naslund 10.00 25.00

2002-03 BAP First Edition Jerseys

1 Mario Lemieux 15.00 40.00
2 Sergei Gonchar 5.00 12.00
3 Brian Leetch 5.00 12.00
4 Felix Potvin 8.00 20.00
5 Sandis Ozolinsh 5.00 12.00
6 Steven Reinprecht 5.00 12.00
7 Byron Dafoe 5.00 12.00
8 Mark Bell 5.00 12.00
9 Jeff O'Neill 5.00 12.00
10 Sean Burke 5.00 12.00
11 Darcy Tucker 5.00 12.00
12 Scott Stevens 5.00 12.00
13 David Aebischer 5.00 12.00
14 Jocelyn Thibault 5.00 12.00
15 Radek Bonk 5.00 12.00
16 Milan Hejduk 6.00 15.00
17 Zigmund Palffy 5.00 12.00
18 Luc Robitaille 5.00 12.00
19 Tomas Kaberle 5.00 12.00
20 Rostislav Klesla 5.00 12.00
21 Alexei Zhamnov 5.00 12.00
22 Ron Francis 5.00 12.00
23 Mike Fisher 5.00 12.00
24 Dany Heatley 8.00 20.00
25 Kyle McLaren 5.00 12.00
26 Doug Weight 5.00 12.00
27 Henrik Sedin 5.00 12.00
28 Roman Turek 5.00 12.00
29 Adam Deadmarsh 5.00 12.00
30 Sami Kapanen 5.00 12.00
31 Sergei Samsonov 5.00 12.00
32 Kristian Huselius 5.00 12.00
33 Dimitri Yushkevich 5.00 12.00
34 Patrik Elias 5.00 12.00
35 Nick Boynton 5.00 12.00
36 Martin Biron 5.00 12.00
37 Brad Richards 5.00 12.00
38 Alyn McCauley 5.00 12.00
39 Daniel Sedin 5.00 12.00
40 Teppo Numminen 5.00 12.00
41 Luke Richardson 5.00 12.00
42 Manny Fernandez 5.00 12.00
43 Vincent Lecavalier 6.00 15.00
44 Mattias Ohlund 5.00 12.00
45 Milan Kraft 5.00 12.00
46 Mike Dunham 5.00 12.00
47 Derian Hatcher 5.00 12.00
48 Oleg Tverdovsky 5.00 12.00
49 Shane Doan 5.00 12.00
50 Martin Skoula 5.00 12.00
51 John LeClair 6.00 15.00
52 Tommy Salo 5.00 12.00
53 Miroslav Satan 5.00 12.00
54 Bryan Berard 5.00 12.00
55 Roman Cechmanek 5.00 12.00
56 Alexei Morozov 5.00 12.00
57 Jean-Sebastien Giguere 5.00 12.00
58 Pierre Turgeon 5.00 12.00
59 Martin Straka 5.00 12.00
60 Stephane Yelle 5.00 12.00
61 Marc Savard 5.00 12.00
62 Sergei Zubov 5.00 12.00
63 Jeff Friesen 5.00 12.00
64 Daniel Briere 5.00 12.00
65 Patrik Stefan 5.00 12.00
66 Pavol Demitra 5.00 12.00
67 Radek Dvorak 5.00 12.00
68 Marty Turco 5.00 12.00
69 Keith Tkachuk 6.00 15.00
70 Maxim Afinogenov 5.00 12.00
71 Mika Noronen 5.00 12.00
72 Evgeni Nabokov 5.00 12.00
73 Todd Bertuzzi 6.00 15.00
74 Valeri Bure 5.00 12.00
75 Marian Hossa 6.00 15.00
76 J-P Dumont 5.00 12.00
77 Niklas Sundstrom 5.00 12.00
78 Eric Daze 5.00 12.00
79 Brian Boucher 5.00 12.00
80 Nikolai Khabibulin 6.00 15.00
81 Darren McCarty 5.00 12.00
82 Pavel Brendl 5.00 12.00
83 Mark Recchi 5.00 12.00
84 Dan Cloutier 5.00 12.00
85 Manny Legace 5.00 12.00
86 Keith Primeau 5.00 12.00
87 Alex Tanguay 5.00 12.00
88 Ed Jovanovski 5.00 12.00
89 Roberto Luongo 10.00 25.00
90 Andreas Johansson 5.00 12.00
91 Steve Shields 5.00 12.00
92 Saku Koivu 6.00 15.00
93 Chris Drury 5.00 12.00
94 Olaf Kolzig 5.00 12.00
95 Jan Hrdina 5.00 12.00
96 Ivan Novoseltsev 5.00 12.00
97 Kenny Jonsson 5.00 12.00
98 Martin Havlat 5.00 12.00
99 Scott Niedermayer 5.00 12.00
100 Chris Phillips 5.00 12.00
101 Tony Amonte 5.00 12.00
102 Alexander Mogilny 5.00 12.00
103 Chris Pronger 5.00 12.00
104 Chris Gratton 5.00 12.00
105 Sergei Fedorov 8.00 20.00
106 David Legwand 5.00 12.00
107 Ron Tugnutt 5.00 12.00
108 Steven McCarthy 5.00 12.00
109 Brian Rolston 5.00 12.00
110 Bobby Holik 5.00 12.00
111 Darryl Sydor 5.00 12.00
112 Steve Sullivan 5.00 12.00
113 Toby Petersen 5.00 12.00
114 Scott Gomez 5.00 12.00
115 Adam Foote 5.00 12.00
116 Rob Niedermayer 5.00 12.00
117 Arturs Irbe 5.00 12.00
118 Al MacInnis 5.00 12.00
119 Jeff Hackett 5.00 12.00
120 Pavel Bure 6.00 15.00
121 Patrick Lalime 5.00 12.00
122 Vincent Damphousse 5.00 12.00
123 Steve Passmore 5.00 12.00
124 Simon Gagne 6.00 15.00
125 Shawn McEachern 5.00 12.00
126 Bryan McCabe 5.00 12.00
127 Jamie Storr 5.00 12.00
128 Mike Richter 6.00 15.00
129 Petr Sykora 5.00 12.00
130 Trevor Kidd 5.00 12.00
131 Jaromir Jagr 10.00 25.00
132 Bill Guerin 5.00 12.00
133 Mark Messier 6.00 15.00
134 Ilya Kovalchuk 10.00 25.00
135 Teemu Selanne 6.00 15.00
136 Dominik Hasek 15.00 40.00
137 Mats Sundin 6.00 15.00
138 Jose Theodore 10.00 25.00
139 Brendan Shanahan 6.00 15.00
140 Daniel Alfredsson 5.00 12.00
141 Martin Brodeur 12.00 30.00
142 Jarome Iginla 10.00 25.00
143 Peter Bondra 6.00 15.00
144 Peter Forsberg 15.00 40.00
145 Curtis Joseph 6.00 15.00
146 Alexei Yashin 5.00 12.00
147 Patrick Roy 20.00 50.00
148 Markus Naslund 6.00 16.00
149 Jeremy Roenick 10.00 25.00
150 Eric Lindros 6.00 15.00
151 Steve Yzerman 10.00 25.00
152 Marian Gaborik 12.50 30.00
153 Mike Modano 8.00 20.00
154 Joe Sakic 12.50 30.00
155 Paul Kariya 6.00 15.00
156 Owen Nolan 5.00 12.00
157 Rob Blake 5.00 12.00
158 Nicklas Lidstrom 6.00 15.00
159 Joe Thornton 10.00 25.00
160 Mario Lemieux 15.00 40.00

2002-03 BAP First Edition Magnificent Inserts

MI1 2000-01 Jersey 30.00 80.00
MI2 1985-86 Jersey 30.00 80.00
MI3 2002 All-Star Jersey 30.00 80.00
MI4 1987 Canada Cup Jersey 30.00 80.00
MI5 Dual Jersey 50.00 125.00

2002-03 BAP First Edition Scoring Leaders

1 Paul Kariya 12.50 30.00
2 Dany Heatley 20.00 50.00
3 Sergei Samsonov 12.50 30.00
4 Jarome Iginla 15.00 40.00
5 Ron Francis 12.50 30.00
6 Eric Daze 12.50 30.00
7 Joe Sakic 20.00 50.00
8 Mike Modano 15.00 40.00
9 Brendan Shanahan 12.50 30.00
10 Patrik Elias 12.50 30.00
11 Alexei Yashin 12.50 30.00
12 Eric Lindros 12.50 30.00
13 Daniel Alfredsson 12.50 30.00
14 Jeremy Roenick 15.00 40.00
15 Alexei Kovalev 12.50 30.00
16 Owen Nolan 12.50 30.00
17 Brad Richards 12.50 30.00
18 Mats Sundin 12.50 30.00
19 Markus Naslund 12.50 30.00
20 Jaromir Jagr 15.00 40.00

1999-00 BAP Memorabilia

*SILVER/1000: .75X TO 2X BASE CARDS
*GOLD: 5X TO 12X BASE
1 Patrik Stefan RC .20 .50
2 Glen Murray .15 .40
3 Nicklas Lidstrom .20 .50
4 Arturs Irbe .15 .40
5 Viktor Kozlov .12 .30
6 Dimitri Yushkevich .12 .30
7 Byron Ritchie RC .12 .30
8 Robert Svehla .12 .30
9 Jeremy Roenick .30 .75
10 Ron Francis .25 .60
11 Oleg Kvasha .12 .30
12 Marian Hossa .20 .50
13 Mark Recchi .25 .60
14 Scott Mellanby .12 .30
15 Adam Graves .15 .40
16 Boris Mironov .12 .30
17 Derian Hatcher .15 .40
18 Brian Leetch .15 .40
19 Mattias Ohlund .12 .30
20 Ray Whitney .15 .40
21 Mike Richter .20 .50
22 Paul Mara .12 .30
23 Todd Bertuzzi .15 .40
24 Sergei Zubov .15 .40
25 Cliff Ronning .12 .30
26 Anson Carter .15 .40
27 Dmitri Mironov .12 .30
28 Shane Willis .12 .30
29 Shayne Corson .15 .40
30 Chris Chelios .20 .50
31 Pavel Kubina .12 .30
32 Michal Grosek .12 .30
33 Gary Suter .12 .30
34 Greg Adams .12 .30
35 Joe Thornton .30 .75
36 Matt Higgins .12 .30
37 Chris Gratton .12 .30
38 Ray Bourque .30 .75
39 Tommy Salo .15 .40
40 Igor Kravchuk .12 .30
41 Byron Dafoe .15 .40
42 Larry Murphy .15 .40
43 Bryan McCabe .15 .40
44 John Vanbiesbrouck .20 .50
45 Brett Hull .40 1.00
46 Christian Dube .12 .30
47 Kyle McLaren .12 .30
48 Jere Lehtinen .15 .40
49 Petr Nedved .12 .30
50 Jason Allison .15 .40
51 Brad Lukowich RC .15 .40
52 Scott Stevens .20 .50
53 Sergei Krivokrasov .12 .30
54 Olaf Kolzig .20 .50
55 Sami Kapanen .12 .30
56 Sami Salo .15 .40
57 Cory Stillman .12 .30
58 Darcy Tucker .12 .30
59 Rod Brind'Amour .20 .50
60 John Jakopin RC .12 .30
61 Martin Brodeur .50 1.25
62 Jiri Slegr .12 .30
63 Rem Murray .12 .30
64 Jason Arnott .15 .40
65 Jon Sim RC .20 .50
66 Cory Sarich .12 .30
67 Brian Rafalski RC .20 .50
68 Kevin Hatcher .12 .30
69 Ted Donato .12 .30
70 Dan LaCouture .12 .30
71 Alexei Kovalev .15 .40
72 Peter Bondra .20 .50
73 John LeClair .20 .50
74 Matthew Barnaby .12 .30
75 Adam Oates .20 .50
76 Janne Niinimaa .12 .30
77 Tom Barrasso .20 .50
78 Sergei Gonchar .12 .30
79 Alex Tanguay .15 .40
80 Jean-Luc Grand-Pierre RC .12 .30
81 Alexei Tezikov RC .20 .50
82 Doug Gilmour .25 .60
83 Sergei Brylin .12 .30
84 Ron Tugnutt .15 .40
85 Stephane Richer .15 .40
86 Marc Denis .15 .40
87 Sergei Fedorov .30 .75
88 Brian Rolston .15 .40
89 Chris Pronger .20 .50
90 Dan Cloutier .12 .30
91 Anders Eriksson .12 .30
92 Donald Audette .12 .30
93 Ed Jovanovski .15 .40
94 Tony Amonte .15 .40
95 Jamie Storr .12 .30
96 German Titov .12 .30
97 Eric Daze .15 .40
98 Zigmund Palffy .20 .50
99 Dan McGillis .12 .30
100 Nikolai Khabibulin .15 .40
101 Mathieu Schneider .12 .30
102 Magnus Arvedson .12 .30
103 Joe Sakic .40 1.00
104 Brian Campbell RC .20 .50
105 Wade Redden .12 .30
106 Andrei Nikolishin .12 .30
107 Steve Rucchin .12 .30
108 Shawn McEachern .12 .30
109 Alexander Karpovtsev .12 .30
110 Miroslav Satan .15 .40
111 Andreas Dackell .12 .30
112 Niklas Sundstrom .12 .30
113 Scott Niedermayer .20 .50
114 Ken Wregget .12 .30
115 Olli Jokinen .15 .40
116 Vincent Lecavalier .20 .50
117 Paul Kariya .20 .50
118 Alexei Zhamnov .12 .30
119 Martin Rucinsky .12 .30
120 Daniel Cleary .12 .30
121 Yanic Perreault .12 .30
122 Alexei Zhitnik .12 .30
123 Vadim Sharifijanov .12 .30
124 Derek King .12 .30
125 Jason Woolley .12 .30
126 Pavel Bure .20 .50
127 Darius Kasparaitis .15 .40
128 Stu Barnes .15 .40
129 Josef Beranek .12 .30
130 Milan Hejduk .15 .40
131 Michael Peca .15 .40
132 Tomas Holmstrom .12 .30
133 Patrick Marleau .20 .50
134 Dominik Hasek .30 .75
135 Chris Osgood .20 .50
136 Radek Bonk .12 .30
137 Martin Biron .15 .40
138 Igor Larionov .20 .50
139 Felix Potvin .30 .75
140 Oleg Tverdovsky .12 .30
141 Steve Yzerman .50 1.25
142 Bobby Holik .12 .30
143 Landon Wilson .12 .30
144 Marty McInnis .12 .30
145 Remi Royer .12 .30
146 Brendan Morrison .15 .40
147 Jaromir Jagr .60 1.50
148 Steve Thomas .12 .30
149 Rico Fata .12 .30
150 John Madden RC .20 .50
151 Miroslav Guren .12 .30
152 Jochen Hecht RC .30 .75
153 Gary Roberts .12 .30
154 Patrik Elias .20 .50
155 Al MacInnis .25 .60
156 Jonathan Girard .12 .30
157 Jan Hlavac .12 .30
158 Pierre Turgeon .15 .40
159 Matt Cullen .12 .30
160 Trevor Letowski .12 .30
161 Roman Turek .15 .40
162 Luc Robitaille .20 .50
163 Marcus Nilsson .12 .30
164 Pavol Demitra .25 .60
165 Fredrik Olausson .12 .30
166 Blake Sloan .15 .40
167 Eric Lindros .30 .75
168 Guy Hebert .20 .50
169 Adam Deadmarsh .12 .30
170 Mike Leclerc .12 .30
171 Teemu Selanne .40 1.00
172 Ty Jones .12 .30
173 Calle Johansson .12 .30
174 Ed Belfour .20 .50
175 Craig MacDonald RC .20 .50
176 Todd Harvey .12 .30
177 Martin Straka .12 .30
178 Mariusz Czerkawski .12 .30
179 Grant Fuhr .30 .75
180 Mark Parrish .12 .30
181 Sandis Ozolinsh .12 .30
182 Patrice Brisebois .12 .30
183 Geoff Courtnall .15 .40
184 Chris Drury .15 .40
185 Saku Koivu .20 .50
186 Teppo Numminen .12 .30
187 Alexei Morozov .15 .40
188 Stephane Quintal .12 .30
189 Eric Desjardins .15 .40
190 Pavel Patera RC .12 .30
191 Vladimir Malakhov .12 .30
192 Jean-Sebastien Giguere .20 .50
193 Niclas Havelid RC .20 .50
194 Trevor Linden .20 .50
195 Simon Gagne .20 .50
196 Kevin Weekes .12 .30
197 Joe Nieuwendyk .15 .40
198 Cameron Mann .12 .30
199 Adam Mair RC .12 .30
200 Kim Johnsson RC .12 .30
201 Mikael Renberg .12 .30
202 Curtis Joseph .25 .60
203 Juha Lind .12 .30
204 Doug Weight .20 .50
205 Mats Lindgren .12 .30
206 Marcus Ragnarsson .12 .30
207 Igor Korolev .12 .30
208 Claude Lemieux .15 .40
209 Jeff Hackett .12 .30
210 Brendan Witt .12 .30
211 Steve Kariya RC .20 .50
212 Jarome Iginla .25 .60
213 Pavol Roca .12 .30
214 Andrei Zyuzin .12 .30
215 Oleg Saprykin RC .20 .50
216 Sean Burke .12 .30
217 Mike Modano .30 .75
218 Phil Housley .15 .40
219 Ryan Smyth .15 .40
220 Daren Puppa .12 .30
221 Aki Berg .12 .30
222 Mike Grier .12 .30
223 Keith Jones .12 .30
224 Marc Savard .12 .30
225 Bill Guerin .20 .50
226 Theo Fleury .25 .60
227 Shawn Heins RC .12 .30
228 Tom Poti .12 .30
229 Tim Connolly .12 .30
230 Glen Wesley .12 .30
231 Brendan Shanahan .20 .50
232 Kenny Jonsson .12 .30
233 Mats Sundin .20 .50
234 Damian Rhodes .12 .30
235 Martin Lapointe .15 .40
236 David Legwand .12 .30
237 Rob Niedermayer .12 .30
238 Bill Muckalt .12 .30
239 Valeri Bure .12 .30
240 Manny Malhotra .15 .40
241 Jozef Stumpel .12 .30
242 Brad Stuart .15 .40
243 Curtis Brown .12 .30
244 Alexei Yashin .15 .40
245 Owen Nolan .20 .50
246 Shawn Bates .12 .30
247 Jan Hrdina .12 .30
248 Marco Sturm .12 .30
249 Nelson Emerson .12 .30
250 Stephane Fiset .15 .40
251 Mike Vernon .15 .40
252 Jason Botterill .12 .30
253 Marty Reasoner .12 .30
254 Roman Hamrlik .12 .30
255 Ray Ferraro .12 .30
256 Jamie Langenbrunner .12 .30
257 Brian Holzinger .12 .30
258 Andrew Brunette .12 .30
259 Peter Forsberg .40 1.00
260 Jyrki Lumme .12 .30
261 Keith Primeau .15 .40
262 Patrick Roy .50 1.25
263 Dmitri Nabokov .12 .30
264 Darryl Laplante .12 .30
265 Mark Messier .40 1.00
266 Benoit Gratton RC .12 .30
267 Bryan Berard .12 .30
268 Wendel Clark .30 .75
269 Vincent Damphousse .15 .40
270 J-P Dumont .15 .40
271 Darryl Sydor .15 .40
272 Darren Turcotte .12 .30
273 Sergei Berezin .12 .30
274 Jeff Friesen .15 .40
275 Ville Peltonen .12 .30
276 Rick Tocchet .15 .40
277 Darren McCarty .12 .30
278 Greg Johnson .12 .30
279 Dan Smith RC .12 .30
280 Sergei Samsonov .15 .40
281 Petr Sykora .15 .40
282 Dallas Drake .12 .30
283 Steve Konowalchuk .12 .30
284 Yan Golubovsky .12 .30
285 Dan Boyle RC .15 .40
286 Alexander Mogilny .15 .40
287 Daniel Alfredsson .20 .50
288 Steve Shields .15 .40
289 Markus Naslund .20 .50
290 Vyacheslav Kozlov .12 .30
291 Keith Tkachuk .20 .50
292 Adrian Aucoin .12 .30
293 Jocelyn Thibault .15 .40
294 Kevin Stevens .15 .40
295 John MacLean .15 .40
296 Mike Ricci .12 .30
297 Rob Blake .20 .50
298 Radek Dvorak .12 .30
299 Mike Dunham .12 .30
300 Richard Matvichuk .12 .30
301 Scott Gomez .15 .40
302 Nikolai Antropov RC .50 1.25
303 Glen Metropolit RC .12 .30
304 Robyn Regehr .12 .30
305 Mathieu Biron .12 .30
306 Nathan Dempsey RC .12 .30
307 Roberto Luongo .30 .75
308 Andreas Karlsson RC .12 .30
309 Ray Bourque .30 .75
310 Artem Chubarov .12 .30
311 Mike Fisher RC .20 .50
312 Andrew Ference .12 .30
313 Todd Reirden RC .12 .30
314 Martin Skoula RC .12 .30
315 Radislav Suchy RC .12 .30
316 Joel Prpic RC .12 .30
317 Yuri Butsayev RC .12 .30
318 Andy Delmore RC .12 .30
319 Steve McCarthy .12 .30
320 Brian Rolston .15 .40
321 Dimitri Kalinin RC .12 .30
322 Brenden Morrow .20 .50
323 Mike Vernon .15 .40
324 Nils Ekman RC .12 .30
325 Felix Potvin .30 .75
326 Jan Nemecek RC .12 .30
327 Michael York .12 .30
328 Evgeni Nabokov RC .75 2.00
329 Rick Tocchet .15 .40
330 Vitali Vishnevsky .15 .40
331 Francis Bouillon RC .20 .50
332 Robert Esche RC .20 .50
333 Ray Giroux RC .12 .30
334 Per Svartvadet RC .12 .30
335 Kyle Calder RC .15 .40
336 Brian Boucher .20 .50
337 Dan Hinote RC .15 .40
338 Darrel Scoville RC .12 .30
339 Ivan Novoseltsev RC .25 .60
340 Petr Schastlivy RC .12 .30
341 Andre Savage RC .12 .30
342 Michal Grosek .12 .30
343 Richard Lintner RC .12 .30
344 Tyson Nash RC .12 .30
345 Tommy Westlund RC .12 .30
346 Jason Krog RC .12 .30
347 Jarkko Ruutu RC .12 .30
348 Mike Ribeiro .12 .30
349 Alexander Mogilny .15 .40
350 Maxim Afinogenov .12 .30
351 Ron Tugnutt .15 .40
352 Jaroslav Spacek .12 .30
353 Petr Buzek .12 .30
354 Sami Helenius RC .15 .40
355 Peter Schaefer .12 .30
356 Alan Letang RC .20 .50
357 Keith Primeau .15 .40
358 Jay Henderson RC .12 .30
359 Dave Tanabe .12 .30
360 Fred Brathwaite .12 .30
361 Chris Gratton .12 .30
362 Maxim Balmochnyk .12 .30
363 John Emmons .12 .30
364 Mark Eaton RC .12 .30
365 Kevyn Adams .12 .30
366 Alfie Michaud RC .12 .30
367 Chris Herperger RC .12 .30
368 Scott Langkow .12 .30
369 Marquis Mathieu RC .12 .30
370 Milan Hnilicka RC .12 .30
371 Michal Rozsival RC .12 .30
372 Sergei Krivokrasov .12 .30
373 Brad Chartrand RC .12 .30
374 Ryan Bonni RC .12 .30
375 Roman Lyashenko .12 .30
376 Denis Hamel RC .12 .30
377 Stephane Robidas RC .12 .30
378 Jeff Halpern RC .12 .30
379 Karlis Skrastins RC .12 .30
380 Jeff Zehr RC .12 .30
381 Brian Holzinger .12 .30
382 Josef Beranek .12 .30
383 Harold Druken .12 .30
384 Doug Gilmour .25 .60
385 Ladislav Nagy RC .12 .30
386 Bert Robertsson RC .12 .30
387 Scott Fankhouser RC .12 .30
388 Brian Willsie .12 .30
389 Eric Boguniecki RC .12 .30
390 Dmitri Yakushin RC .12 .30
391 Chris Clark RC .12 .30
392 Paul Comrie RC .30 .75
393 John Grahame RC .15 .40
394 Rod Brind'Amour .20 .50
395 Vladimir Malakhov .12 .30
396 Jiri Fischer .12 .30
397 Kimmo Timonen .12 .30
398 Brad Ference .12 .30
399 Marc Lamothe RC .12 .30
400 Radek Dvorak .12 .30
DT5 Dimitri Tertyshny TRIB .12 .30
SC3 Steve Chiasson TRIB .12 .30

1999-00 BAP Memorabilia Gold

*VETERANS: 12X TO 30X BASIC CARDS
*TRIBUTE: 4X TO 10X BASIC TRIB
*ROOKIES: 8X TO 20X BASIC RC

1999-00 BAP Memorabilia Jersey

*JSY AND STICK: .6X TO 1.5X BASIC JSY
*JSY EMBLEMS: .8X TO 2X BASIC JSY
*JSY NUMBERS: .8X TO 2X BASIC JSY
J1 Eric Lindros 10.00 25.00
J2 Peter Forsberg 8.00 20.00
J3 Teemu Selanne 10.00 25.00
J4 Mike Modano 8.00 20.00
J5 Mats Sundin 10.00 25.00
J6 Patrick Roy 15.00 40.00
J7 Paul Kariya 8.00 20.00
J8 Martin Brodeur 10.00 25.00
J9 Ray Bourque 15.00 40.00
J10 Mark Messier 10.00 25.00
J11 Curtis Joseph 8.00 20.00
J12 Brett Hull 8.00 20.00
J13 Al MacInnis 6.00 15.00
J14 Theo Fleury 8.00 20.00
J15 Sergei Fedorov 8.00 20.00
J16 Brian Leetch 6.00 15.00
J17 Alexei Yashin 6.00 15.00
J18 Jaromir Jagr 10.00 25.00
J19 Pavel Bure 8.00 20.00
J20 Dominik Hasek 6.00 15.00
J21 Chris Chelios 6.00 15.00
J22 John LeClair 6.00 15.00
J23 Brendan Shanahan 8.00 20.00
J24 Ed Belfour 8.00 20.00
J25 Wayne Gretzky 30.00 80.00
J26 Saku Koivu 6.00 15.00
J27 Tony Amonte 6.00 15.00
J28 Peter Bondra 6.00 15.00

1999-00 BAP Memorabilia All-Star Selects Silver

COMPLETE SET (24) 20.00 40.00
*GOLD: 2X TO 5X SILVER
SL1 Peter Forsberg 2.50 6.00
SL2 Pavol Demitra .75 2.00
SL3 Jaromir Jagr 1.50 4.00
SL4 Sandis Ozolinsh .50 1.25
SL5 Nicklas Lidstrom 1.00 2.50
SL6 Dominik Hasek 2.00 5.00
SL7 Eric Lindros 1.00 2.50
SL8 Paul Kariya 1.00 2.50
SL9 Tony Amonte .75 2.00
SL10 Brian Leetch 1.00 2.50
SL11 Al MacInnis 1.00 2.50
SL12 Martin Brodeur 2.50 6.00
SL13 Petr Sykora .50 1.25
SL14 Sergei Samsonov .75 2.00
SL15 Marian Hossa 1.00 2.50
SL16 Andrei Zyuzin .50 1.25
SL17 Sami Salo .50 1.25
SL18 Roman Turek 1.00 2.50
SL19 Chris Drury .75 2.00
SL20 Vincent Lecavalier 1.00 2.50
SL21 J-P Dumont .75 2.00
SL22 Kyle McLaren .50 1.25
SL23 Adrian Aucoin .50 1.25
SL24 Marc Denis 1.00 2.50

1999-00 BAP Memorabilia AS American Hobby

AH1 Ken Hodge .75 2.00
AH2 Cam Neely .75 2.00
AH3 Derek Sanderson .75 2.00
AH4 Gerry Cheevers .75 2.00
AH5 Johnny Bucyk .75 2.00
AH6 Wayne Cashman .75 2.00
AH7 Vic Hadfield .75 2.00
AH8 Andy Bathgate .75 2.00
AH9 Brad Park .75 2.00
AH10 Ed Giacomin .75 2.00
AH11 John Davidson .75 2.00
AH12 Rod Gilbert .75 2.00

1999-00 BAP Memorabilia AS American Hobby Autographs

AH1 Ken Hodge 8.00 20.00
AH2 Cam Neely 8.00 20.00
AH3 Derek Sanderson 8.00 20.00
AH4 Gerry Cheevers 8.00 20.00
AH5 Johnny Bucyk 8.00 20.00
AH6 Wayne Cashman 8.00 20.00
AH7 Vic Hadfield 8.00 20.00
AH8 Andy Bathgate 8.00 20.00
AH9 Brad Park 8.00 20.00
AH10 Ed Giacomin 8.00 20.00
AH11 John Davidson 8.00 20.00
AH12 Rod Gilbert 8.00 20.00

1999-00 BAP Memorabilia AS Canadian Hobby

COMPLETE SET (12) 15.00 30.00
CH1 Borje Salming 1.50 4.00
CH2 Dave Keon 2.00 5.00
CH3 Darryl Sittler 2.00 5.00
CH4 Frank Mahovlich 2.00 5.00
CH5 Johnny Bower 2.00 5.00
CH6 Lanny McDonald 1.25 3.00
CH7 Peter Mahovlich 1.25 3.00
CH8 Dickie Moore 1.25 3.00
CH9 John Ferguson 1.25 3.00
CH10 Larry Robinson 1.25 3.00
CH11 Yvan Cournoyer 1.25 3.00
CH12 Serge Savard 1.25 3.00

1999-00 BAP Memorabilia AS Canadian Hobby Autographs

CH1 Borje Salming 20.00 50.00
CH2 Dave Keon 25.00 60.00
CH3 Darryl Sittler 25.00 60.00
CH4 Frank Mahovlich 25.00 60.00
CH5 Johnny Bower 25.00 60.00
CH6 Lanny McDonald 15.00 40.00
CH7 Peter Mahovlich 15.00 40.00
CH8 Dickie Moore 15.00 40.00
CH9 John Ferguson 15.00 40.00
CH10 Larry Robinson 15.00 40.00
CH11 Yvan Cournoyer 15.00 40.00
CH12 Serge Savard 15.00 40.00

1999-00 BAP Memorabilia AS Retail

COMPLETE SET (12) 20.00 40.00
R1 Bobby Hull 4.00 10.00
R2 Dennis Hull 1.25 3.00
R3 Denis Savard 1.25 3.00
R4 Pierre Pilote 1.25 3.00
R5 Stan Mikita 2.50 6.00
R6 Tony Esposito 2.00 5.00
R7 Alex Delvecchio 1.50 4.00
R8 Bill Gadsby 1.25 3.00
R9 Mickey Redmond 2.00 5.00
R10 Norm Ullman 1.25 3.00
R11 Red Kelly 1.50 4.00
R12 Ted Lindsay 1.50 4.00

1999-00 BAP Memorabilia AS Retail Autographs

R1 Bobby Hull 30.00 80.00
R2 Dennis Hull 20.00 40.00
R3 Denis Savard 20.00 40.00
R4 Pierre Pilote 20.00 40.00
R5 Stan Mikita 30.00 80.00
R6 Tony Esposito 30.00 80.00
R7 Alex Delvecchio 20.00 40.00
R8 Bill Gadsby 20.00 40.00
R9 Mickey Redmond 25.00 60.00
R10 Norm Ullman 20.00 40.00
R11 Red Kelly 20.00 40.00
R12 Ted Lindsay 25.00 50.00

1999-00 BAP Memorabilia AS Heritage Ruby

COMPLETE SET (24) 60.00 125.00
*SAPPHIRE/100: 3X TO 8X RUBY/1000
H1 Brendan Shanahan 2.00 5.00
H2 John LeClair 2.00 5.00
H3 Jeremy Roenick 2.00 5.00
H4 John Vanbiesbrouck 1.50 4.00
H5 Dominik Hasek 4.00 10.00
H6 Adam Oates 1.50 4.00
H7 Teemu Selanne 2.00 5.00
H8 Ron Francis 1.50 4.00
H9 Al MacInnis 1.50 4.00
H10 Patrick Roy 8.00 20.00
H11 Doug Gilmour 1.50 4.00
H12 Brett Hull 2.50 6.00
H13 Curtis Joseph 2.00 5.00
H14 Mark Messier 2.00 5.00
H15 Paul Coffey 2.00 5.00
H16 Byron Dafoe 1.50 4.00
H17 Ed Belfour 2.00 5.00
H18 Wayne Gretzky 10.00 25.00
H19 Pavel Bure 2.00 5.00
H20 Chris Chelios 2.00 5.00
H21 Mats Sundin 2.00 5.00
H22 Joe Nieuwendyk 1.50 4.00
H23 Pavol Demitra 1.50 4.00
H24 Grant Fuhr 2.00 5.00

1999-00 BAP Update Double All Star Jerseys

D1 Jaromir Jagr 15.00 40.00
D2 Eric Lindros 15.00 40.00
D3 Peter Forsberg 20.00 50.00
D4 Patrick Roy 20.00 50.00
D5 Paul Kariya 15.00 40.00
D6 Mats Sundin 15.00 40.00
D7 Ray Bourque 20.00 50.00
D8 Ed Belfour 12.00 30.00
D9 Wayne Gretzky 75.00 200.00
D10 Teemu Selanne 15.00 40.00
D11 Brendan Shanahan 15.00 40.00
D12 Dominik Hasek 25.00 60.00
D13 Pavel Bure 15.00 40.00
D14 John LeClair 15.00 40.00
D15 Al MacInnis 10.00 25.00
D16 Brett Hull 12.00 30.00
D17 Brian Leetch 15.00 40.00
D18 Mark Messier 15.00 40.00
D19 Martin Brodeur 20.00 50.00
D20 Sergei Fedorov 20.00 50.00

1999-00 BAP Update Teammates Jerseys

TM1 C.Joseph/J.Roenick 12.50 30.00
TM2 W.Gretzky/R.Blake 25.00 60.00
TM3 P.Roy/M.Messier 15.00 40.00
TM4 T.Selanne/B.Hull 12.50 30.00
TM5 B.Shanahan/S.Fedorov 15.00 40.00
TM6 R.Bourque/B.Leetch 15.00 40.00
TM7 E.Lindros/J.LeClair 12.50 30.00
TM8 J.Jagr/M.Messier 15.00 40.00
TM9 M.Brodeur/B.Shanahan 15.00 40.00
TM10 P.Forsberg/P.Kariya 15.00 40.00
TM11 E.Belfour/C.Chelios 12.50 30.00
TM12 T.Selanne/P.Kariya 12.50 30.00
TM13 D.Hasek/P.Bondra 15.00 40.00
TM14 S.Yzerman/P.Bure 15.00 40.00
TM15 J.LeClair/R.Bourque 20.00 50.00
TM16 T.Fleury/O.Nolan 12.50 30.00
TM17 M.Brodeur/P.Coffey 20.00 50.00
TM18 J.LeClair/E.Lindros 12.50 30.00
TM19 J.Jagr/P.Bure 20.00 50.00
TM20 D.Hasek/N.Khabibulin 15.00 40.00
TM21 P.Roy/B.Leetch 20.00 50.00
TM22 W.Gretzky/M.Modano 30.00 80.00
TM23 P.Forsberg/S.Ozolinsh 15.00 40.00
TM24 C.Chelios/R.Bourque 15.00 40.00
TM25 M.Sundin/N.Lidstrom 12.50 30.00
TM26 P.Kariya/M.Modano 12.50 30.00
TM27 T.Fleury/T.Amonte 12.50 30.00
TM28 P.Forsberg/T.Selanne 12.00 30.00
TM29 E.Lindros
D.Sydor 12.50 30.00
TM30 P.Bure/M.Sundin 12.50 30.00
TM31 J.Roenick/S.Stevens 12.50 30.00
TM32 J.Jagr/O.Kolzig 15.00 40.00
TM33 M.Richter/T.Amonte 12.50 30.00
TM34 C.Pronger/A.MacInnis 12.50 30.00
TM35 B.Shanahan/M.Brodeur 15.00 40.00
TM36 A.Mogilny/M.Messier 12.50 30.00
TM37 S.Yzerman/S.Fedorov 25.00 60.00
TM38 B.Shanahan/S.Fedorov 15.00 40.00
TM39 S.Yzerman/C.Chelios 20.00 50.00
TM40 S.Yzerman/B.Shanahan 15.00 40.00
TM41 M.Sundin/C.Joseph 12.50 30.00
TM42 P.Forsberg/P.Roy 20.00 50.00
TM43 P.Forsberg/J.Sakic 15.00 40.00
TM44 J.Sakic/P.Roy 20.00 50.00
TM45 T.Selanne/P.Kariya 12.50 30.00
TM46 B.Hull/M.Modano 15.00 40.00
TM47 B.Hull/E.Belfour 12.50 30.00
TM48 E.Belfour/M.Modano 12.00 30.00
TM49 E.Lindros/J.LeClair 12.50 30.00
TM50 B.Leetch/T.Fleury 15.00 40.00

2000-01 BAP Memorabilia

1 Jaromir Jagr .75 2.00
2 Scott Mellanby .15 .40
3 Mike Fisher .15 .40
4 Slava Kozlov .20 .50
5 Steve Valiquette RC .20 .50
6 Simon Gagne .25 .60
7 Alexei Morozov .15 .40
8 Alexei Zhitnik .20 .50
9 Jochen Hecht .15 .40
10 Jamie Allison .15 .40
11 Olli Jokinen .20 .50
12 Bobby Holik .15 .40
13 Keith Primeau .20 .50
14 Bryan McCabe .15 .40
15 Tim Connolly .15 .40
16 Marco Sturm .15 .40
17 Craig Darby .15 .40
18 Jeff Cowan RC .15 .40
19 Brad Stuart .20 .50
20 Sean O'Donnell .15 .40
21 Mike Minard RC .25 .60
22 Rob Blake .25 .60
23 Marek Malik .15 .40
24 Marek Posmyk .15 .40
25 Alex Tanguay .20 .50
26 Steven McCarthy .15 .40
27 Bill Guerin .25 .60
28 Ed Jovanovski .20 .50
29 Martin Skoula .20 .50
30 Jeff Hackett .15 .40
31 Vladimir Tsyplakov .15 .40
32 Sergei Zubov .20 .50
33 Damian Rhodes .15 .40
34 Brent Sopel RC .25 .60
35 Frantisek Kaberle .15 .40
36 Michael Peca .20 .50
37 Steve Kelly .15 .40
38 Geoff Sanderson .20 .50
39 Petr Svoboda .15 .40
40 Martin Brodeur .60 1.50
41 Markus Naslund .25 .60
42 Steve Thomas .15 .40
43 Anson Carter .20 .50
44 Theo Fleury .30 .75
45 Felix Potvin .40 1.00
46 Adam Deadmarsh .15 .40
47 Dave Tanabe .15 .40
48 Trevor Kidd .15 .40
49 Jeff Friesen .15 .40
50 Marc Moro RC .15 .40
51 Luc Robitaille .25 .60
52 Mike Richter .25 .60
53 Eric Desjardins .20 .50
54 Jean-Sebastien Aubin .20 .50
55 Paul Laus .15 .40
56 Kimmo Timonen .15 .40
57 Steve Sullivan .15 .40
58 Eric Cairns .15 .40
59 Scott Stevens .25 .60
60 Andy Delmore .15 .40
61 Jeff Nielsen .15 .40
62 Mathieu Biron .15 .40
63 Juha Lind .15 .40
64 Maxim Afinogenov .15 .40
65 Guy Hebert .20 .50
66 Sergei Brylin .15 .40
67 Mike Modano .40 1.00
68 Tommy Salo .20 .50
69 Bryan Smolinski .20 .50
70 Sergei Varlamov .15 .40
71 Paul Mara .15 .40
72 Peter Forsberg .50 1.25
73 Doug Weight .25 .60
74 Peter Bondra .25 .60
75 Marc Denis .20 .50
76 Jamie Storr .20 .50
77 Alexei Kovalev .20 .50
78 Dainius Zubrus .15 .40
79 Mike Grier .15 .40
80 Olaf Kolzig .25 .60
81 Bryan Adams RC .15 .40
82 Scott Niedermayer .25 .60
83 David Gosselin RC .20 .50
84 Boris Mironov .15 .40
85 Kyle McLaren .15 .40
86 Steve Kariya .15 .40
87 Dimitri Yushkevich .15 .40
88 Paul Kariya .25 .60
89 Brian Leetch .20 .50
90 Jeff Daniels .15 .40
91 Brendan Morrison .25 .60
92 Brian Campbell .15 .40
93 Ray Whitney .20 .50
94 Marian Hossa .25 .60
95 Sergei Samsonov .20 .50
96 Mike York .15 .40
97 Mark Eaton .15 .40
98 Ryan VandenBussche .15 .40
99 Vladimir Malakhov .15 .40
100 Jeff Finley .15 .40
101 John Vanbiesbrouck .25 .60
102 Brad Isbister .15 .40
103 John Madden .20 .50
104 Patrick Roy .60 1.50
105 Radek Bonk .20 .50
106 Brett Hull .50 1.25
107 Andreas Dackell .15 .40
108 Pierre Turgeon .20 .50
109 Jason Woolley .15 .40
110 Jeff O'Neill .20 .50
111 John LeClair .25 .60
112 Darryl Sydor .20 .50
113 Ryan Smyth .20 .50
114 Curtis Joseph .30 .75
115 Gary Roberts .15 .40
116 Pavel Kubina .15 .40
117 Roman Hamrlik .15 .40
118 Sandis Ozolinsh .15 .40
119 Manny Fernandez .15 .40
120 Adam Oates .25 .60
121 Darby Hendrickson .15 .40
122 Glen Murray .20 .50
123 Jiri Slegr .15 .40
124 Steve Yzerman .60 1.50
125 Mats Lindgren .15 .40
126 Sergei Gonchar .15 .40
127 Joe Thornton .40 1.00
128 Petr Sykora .20 .50
129 Pavol Demitra .30 .75
130 Tyler Wright .15 .40
131 Johan Davidsson .15 .40
132 Brian Rolston .20 .50
133 Mark Messier .50 1.25
134 Darcy Tucker .15 .40
135 Oleg Tverdovsky .15 .40
136 Petr Nedved .20 .50
137 Harold Druken .15 .40
138 Valeri Bure .20 .50
139 Mikael Andersson .15 .40
140 Evgeni Nabokov .20 .50
141 Janne Laukkanen .15 .40
142 Radek Dvorak .20 .50
143 Brian Boucher .20 .50
144 Eric Daze .20 .50
145 Dan Cloutier .20 .50
146 Scott Gomez .20 .50
147 Dallas Drake .15 .40
148 Shawn McEachern .15 .40
149 Joe Nieuwendyk .20 .50
150 Kenny Jonsson .15 .40
151 Saku Koivu .25 .60
152 Roman Turek .20 .50
153 Chris Gratton .15 .40
154 Steve Rucchin .15 .40
155 Teppo Numminen .15 .40
156 Jamie Langenbrunner .20 .50
157 Johnathan Aitken RC .15 .40
158 Nikolai Antropov .20 .50
159 Stephane Fiset .15 .40
160 Manny Malhotra .15 .40
161 Pavel Bure .25 .60
162 Chris Drury .20 .50
163 Roberto Luongo .40 1.00
164 Norm Maracle .15 .40
165 Brendan Shanahan .25 .60
166 Calle Johansson .15 .40
167 Cory Stillman .15 .40
168 Jozef Stumpel .15 .40
169 Ron Tugnutt .20 .50
170 Brian Savage .15 .40
171 Viktor Kozlov .20 .50
172 Chris Simon .15 .40
173 Chris Joseph .15 .40
174 Willie Mitchell RC .25 .60
175 Randy Robitaille .15 .40
176 Sami Kapanen .15 .40
177 Jonathan Girard .15 .40
178 Andrew Cassels .15 .40
179 Jani Hurme RC .15 .40
180 Maxim Balmochnyk .15 .40
181 Adam Graves .20 .50
182 Steve Shields .15 .40
183 Marc Savard .15 .40
184 Zigmund Palffy .25 .60
185 Magnus Arvedson .15 .40
186 Byron Dafoe .20 .50
187 Jan Hlavac .15 .40
188 Len Barrie .15 .40
189 Jocelyn Thibault .20 .50
190 Fred Brathwaite .20 .50
191 Fredrik Modin .15 .40
192 Shane Doan .20 .50
193 Petr Mika RC .15 .40
194 Larry Murphy .20 .50
195 Daniel Alfredsson .25 .60
196 Brenden Morrow .20 .50
197 Martin Rucinsky .15 .40
198 Michal Handzus .15 .40
199 Dominik Hasek .40 1.00
200 Rod Brind'Amour .25 .60
201 Trevor Letowski .15 .40
202 Derian Hatcher .20 .50
203 Phil Housley .20 .50
204 Martin Biron .20 .50
205 Sergei Berezin .15 .40
206 Ron Francis .30 .75
207 Cliff Ronning .15 .40
208 Robert Svehla .15 .40
209 Vincent Lecavalier .25 .60
210 Kent Manderville .15 .40
211 Andrew Brunette .15 .40
212 Chris Chelios .25 .60
213 Alexander Karpovtsev .15 .40
214 Robyn Regehr .15 .40
215 Mika Alatalo .15 .40
216 Jan Hrdina .15 .40
217 Nicklas Lidstrom .25 .60
218 Ivan Novoseltsev .15 .40
219 Alexander Mogilny .20 .50
220 Chris Pronger .25 .60
221 Paul Coffey .25 .60
222 John Grahame .15 .40
223 Jeff Farkas .15 .40
224 Eric Lindros .40 1.00
225 Jorgen Jonsson .15 .40
226 Jean-Francois Labbe RC .15 .40
227 Owen Nolan .25 .60
228 Oleg Saprykin .15 .40
229 Patrick Marleau .25 .60
230 Aaron Downey RC .15 .40
231 Chris Osgood .25 .60
232 Mike Wilson .15 .40
233 Joe Sakic .50 1.25
234 Dieter Kochan RC .15 .40
235 Jeremy Roenick .40 1.00
236 Alexei Zhamnov .20 .50
237 Sergei Fedorov .40 1.00
238 Petr Schastlivy .15 .40
239 Milan Hejduk .20 .50
240 Patrice Brisebois .15 .40
241 Marty Reasoner .15 .40
242 Ed Belfour .25 .60
243 Vitali Vishnevsky .15 .40
244 Keith Tkachuk .25 .60
245 Petr Buzek .15 .40
246 Miroslav Satan .15 .40
247 Adam Mair .15 .40
248 Jere Karalahti .15 .40
249 Mike Dunham .15 .40
250 Mike Sillinger .15 .40
251 Andrei Skopintsev RC .15 .40
252 S.Vyshedkevich RC .15 .40
253 Steve Duchesne .15 .40
254 Tomas Kaberle .15 .40
255 Arturs Irbe .20 .50
256 Niklas Sundstrom .15 .40
257 Al MacInnis .30 .75
258 Mike Ribeiro .15 .40
259 Rob Niedermayer .20 .50
260 Jean-Guy Trudel RC .15 .40
261 Martin Straka .20 .50
262 Jason Arnott .20 .50
263 David Legwand .25 .60
264 Tony Amonte .20 .50
265 Jason Allison .20 .50
266 Patrik Elias .25 .60
267 Mark Recchi .30 .75
268 Patrik Stefan .20 .50
269 Mariusz Czerkawski .15 .40
270 Vincent Damphousse .20 .50
271 Sergei Krivokrasov .15 .40
272 Teemu Selanne .50 1.25
273 Patrick Lalime .20 .50
274 Nick Boynton .15 .40
275 Darren McCarty .15 .40
276 Jaroslav Spacek .15 .40
277 Chris Dingman .15 .40
278 Jarome Iginla .30 .75
279 Andrei Zyuzin .15 .40
280 Jyrki Lumme .15 .40
281 Michal Grosek .15 .40
282 Janne Niinimaa .15 .40
283 Wade Redden .15 .40
284 Ray Bourque .40 1.00
285 Trevor Linden .25 .60
286 Ladislav Nagy .15 .40
287 Jose Theodore .25 .60
288 Bates Battaglia .15 .40
289 Mikael Renberg .15 .40
290 Donald Audette .20 .50
291 Doug Gilmour .30 .75
292 Yanic Perreault .15 .40
293 Anders Eriksson .15 .40
294 Gary Suter .15 .40
295 Brad Ference .15 .40
296 Mats Sundin .25 .60
297 Ray Ferraro .15 .40
298 Jiri Fischer .15 .40
299 Todd Bertuzzi .20 .50
300 Derek Morris .15 .40
301 Patric Kjellberg .15 .40
302 Pat Verbeek .20 .50
303 Kip Miller .15 .40
304 Alexei Vasilyev .15 .40
305 Marcus Ragnarsson .15 .40
306 Arron Asham .15 .40
307 Sylvain Cote .15 .40
308 Vaclav Prospal .15 .40
309 Aki Berg .15 .40
310 Alexander Selivanov .15 .40
311 Wayne Primeau .15 .40
312 Brian Rafalski .15 .40
313 Jonas Hoglund .15 .40
314 Adam Foote .20 .50
315 Steve Konowalchuk .15 .40
316 Robert Dome .15 .40
317 Antti Laaksonen .15 .40
318 Mike Ricci .15 .40
319 Gino Odjick .15 .40
320 Eric Weinrich .15 .40
321 Jason Strudwick .15 .40
322 Kim Johnsson .15 .40
323 Dimitri Kalinin .15 .40
324 Daymond Langkow .15 .40
325 Todd Marchant .15 .40
326 Richard Matvichuk .15 .40
327 Travis Green .15 .40
328 Igor Larionov .25 .60
329 Mattias Ohlund .15 .40
330 Igor Kravchuk .15 .40
331 Richard Zednik .15 .40
332 Curtis Brown .15 .40
333 Krzysztof Oliwa .15 .40
334 Darius Kasparaitis .20 .50
335 Michael Nylander .15 .40
336 Stan Drulia .15 .40
337 Nelson Emerson .15 .40
338 Greg Johnson .15 .40
339 Sean Hill .15 .40
340 Keith Jones .15 .40
341 Bill Muckalt .15 .40
342 Randy McKay .15 .40
343 Stu Grimson .15 .40
344 Tyson Nash .15 .40
345 Dan Hinote .15 .40
346 Mike Rathje .15 .40
347 Brian Holzinger .15 .40
348 Eric Nickulas RC .15 .40
349 Alexandre Daigle .20 .50
350 Jan Bulis .15 .40
351 Tom Poti .15 .40
352 Kevyn Adams .15 .40
353 Scott Thornton .20 .50
354 Sean Burke .15 .40
355 Peter Worrell .15 .40
356 Josef Beranek .15 .40
357 Matt Cullen .15 .40
358 Sandy McCarthy .15 .40
359 Sergei Zholtok .15 .40
360 Darren Langdon .15 .40
361 Martin Lapointe .20 .50
362 Adrian Aucoin .15 .40
363 Dmitri Nabokov .15 .40
364 Jason Blake .15 .40
365 Jeff Halpern .15 .40
366 Rico Fata .15 .40
367 Dave Reid .15 .40
368 Vitali Yachmenev .15 .40
369 Hnat Domenichelli .15 .40
370 Rick Tocchet .20 .50
371 Tommy Westlund .15 .40
372 Chris Phillips .15 .40
373 Claude Lemieux .20 .50
374 Greg Adams .15 .40
375 Todd Simpson .15 .40
376 Ken Klee .15 .40
377 Andre Savage .15 .40
378 Bryan Marchment .20 .50
379 Dean McAmmond .15 .40
380 Mike Johnson .15 .40
381 Tomas Holmstrom .20 .50
382 Robert Lang .15 .40
383 Dan McGillis .15 .40
384 Jamie Rivers .15 .40
385 Dave Andreychuk .25 .60
386 Marty McInnis .20 .50
387 Sami Salo .15 .40
388 Daniel Cleary .20 .50
389 Robert Esche .15 .40
390 Aaron Gavey .15 .40
391 Andrei Nikolishin .15 .40
392 Jason Krog .15 .40
393 Stu Barnes .20 .50
394 Tomas Vokoun .20 .50
395 Peter Schaefer .15 .40
396 Daniil Markov .15 .40
397 Daniel Sedin .30 .75
398 Kris Beech .15 .40
399 Samuel Pahlsson .15 .40
400 Gary Roberts .15 .40
401 Marian Gaborik RC .50 1.25
402 Oleg Kvasha .15 .40
403 Martin Havlat RC .50 1.25
404 Roman Simicek RC .15 .40
405 Dallas Drake .15 .40
406 Jakub Cutta RC .15 .40
407 German Titov .15 .40
408 Jarno Kultanen RC .15 .40
409 Sandis Ozolinsh .15 .40
410 David Vyborny .15 .40
411 Olli Jokinen .20 .50
412 Maxim Sushinski .15 .40
413 John Vanbiesbrouck .25 .60
414 Shane Hnidy RC .15 .40
415 Milan Kraft .15 .40
416 Alexander Kharitonov RC .15 .40
417 Andrei Nazarov .15 .40
418 Dave Andreychuk .25 .60
419 Niclas Wallin RC .20 .50
420 Rostislav Klesla RC .40 1.00
421 Denis Shvidki .15 .40
422 Mathieu Garon .15 .40
423 Taylor Pyatt .15 .40
424 Roman Cechmanek RC .20 .50
425 Mark Smith RC .15 .40
426 Shayne Corson .20 .50
427 Jonas Ronnqvist RC .15 .40
428 J-P Dumont .15 .40
429 Josef Vasicek RC .40 1.00
430 Tyler Bouck RC .15 .40
431 Matt Schneider .15 .40
432 Andrei Markov .30 .75
433 Vladimir Malakhov .15 .40
434 Maxime Ouellet .25 .60
435 Matt Bradley .15 .40
436 Dave Manson .15 .40
437 Brad Tapper RC .15 .40
438 Eric Boulton RC .15 .40
439 Brent Johnson .20 .50
440 Marty Turco RC .30 .75
441 Tomas Vlasak .15 .40
442 Greg Classen RC .15 .40
443 Mark Messier .50 1.25
444 Justin Williams RC .40 1.00
445 Sean Hill .15 .40
446 Bryan McCabe .15 .40
447 Andreas Karlsson .15 .40
448 Mika Noronen .15 .40
449 Alexander Karpovtsev .15 .40
450 Boyd Devereaux .15 .40
451 Lubomir Visnovsky RC .30 .75
452 Scott Hartnell RC .40 1.00
453 Jason Labarbera RC .20 .50
454 Petr Hubacek RC .15 .40
455 Alexander Khavanov RC .15 .40
456 Petr Svoboda RC .20 .50
457 Tomi Kallio .15 .40
458 Mike Vernon .20 .50
459 Reto Von Arx RC .20 .50
460 Maxim Kuznetsov .20 .50
461 Steven Reinprecht RC .25 .60
462 Turner Stevenson .15 .40
463 Roberto Luongo .40 1.00
464 Brad Richards .25 .60
465 Bryce Salvador RC .20 .50
466 Kevin Hatcher .15 .40
467 Paul Coffey .25 .60
468 Marty Murray .15 .40
469 Todd Fedoruk RC .15 .40
470 Brian Swanson RC .15 .40
471 Christian Matte .15 .40
472 Sascha Goc RC .15 .40
473 Dale Purinton RC .15 .40
474 Brad May .15 .40
475 Brad Brown .20 .50
476 Petteri Nummelin RC .15 .40
477 Ruslan Fedotenko RC .15 .40
478 Ronald Petrovicky RC .15 .40
479 David Aebischer RC .30 .75
480 Michel Riesen RC .20 .50
481 Ladislav Benysek RC .15 .40
482 Mark Parrish .15 .40
483 Mike Mottau .15 .40
484 Ossi Vaananen RC .20 .50
485 Andrew Raycroft RC .40 1.00
486 Sylvain Cote .15 .40
487 Richard Jackman .15 .40
488 Toni Lydman .15 .40
489 Ron Tugnutt .20 .50
490 Igor Larionov .25 .60
491 Lubomir Sekeras RC .15 .40
492 Roman Hamrlik .15 .40
493 Johan Holmqvist RC .15 .40
494 Josef Melichar RC .15 .40
495 Sheldon Keefe .15 .40
496 Henrik Sedin .30 .75
497 Rick DiPietro RC .30 .75
498 Teemu Selanne .50 1.25
499 Keith Tkachuk .25 .60
500 Rob Blake .25 .60
501 Mario Lemieux 1.00 2.50
502 Johan Hedberg RC .20 .50
503 Felix Potvin .40 1.00
504 Branislav Mezei .15 .40
505 Mike Comrie RC .40 1.00
506 Miikka Kiprusoff .25 .60
507 Petr Tenkrat RC .15 .40
508 Mark Bell .15 .40
509 Steve Gainey RC .15 .40
510 Jason Williams RC .25 .60
511 Shawn Horcoff RC .30 .75
512 Eric Chouinard .15 .40
513 Derek Gustafson RC .15 .40
514 Bryan Allen .15 .40
515 Kristian Kudroc .15 .40
516 Gregg Naumenko RC .15 .40
517 Pierre Dagenais .15 .40
518 Juraj Kolnik RC .15 .40
519 Tomas Kloucek RC .15 .40
520 Andreas Lilja RC .15 .40
521 Alexei Ponikarovsky RC .25 .60
NNO Trevor Linden AU 15.00 25.00

2000-01 BAP Memorabilia Ruby

*RUBY/200: 2.5X TO 6X BASIC CARDS

2000-01 BAP Memorabilia Sapphire

*SAPPHIRE/100: 4X TO 10X BASIC CARDS

2000-01 BAP Memorabilia All-Star Tickets

COMPLETE SET (10) 150.00 300.00
AST1 1990 All-Star Game 12.50 30.00
AST2 1991 All-Star Game 12.50 30.00
AST3 1992 All-Star Game 12.50 30.00
AST4 1993 All-Star Game 12.50 30.00
AST5 1994 All-Star Game 12.50 30.00
AST6 1996 All-Star Game 12.50 30.00
AST7 1997 All-Star Game 12.50 30.00
AST8 1998 All-Star Game 12.50 30.00
AST9 1999 All-Star Game 12.50 30.00
AST10 2000 All-Star Game 12.50 30.00

2000-01 BAP Memorabilia Georges Vezina

V1 Olaf Kolzig 200.00 500.00
V2 Dominik Hasek 250.00 600.00
V3 Dominik Hasek 250.00 600.00
V4 Dominik Hasek 250.00 600.00
V5 Jim Carey 150.00 400.00
V6 Dominik Hasek 250.00 600.00
V7 Dominik Hasek 250.00 600.00
V8 Ed Belfour 200.00 500.00
V9 Patrick Roy 250.00 600.00
V10 Ed Belfour 250.00 600.00
V11 Patrick Roy 250.00 600.00
V12 Patrick Roy 250.00 600.00
V13 Grant Fuhr 250.00 600.00
V14 John Vanbiesbrouck 200.00 500.00
V15 Tom Barrasso 150.00 400.00
V16 Georges Vezina 500.00 800.00

2000-01 BAP Memorabilia Goalie Memorabilia

G1 Mike Richter J/S 20.00 50.00
G2 Patrick Roy G/S 100.00 200.00
G3 Dominik Hasek G/S 75.00 150.00
G4 Ed Belfour J/S 20.00 50.00
G5 Curtis Joseph G/S 25.00 60.00
G6 Terry Sawchuk G/S 75.00 150.00
G7 Vladislav Tretiak J/G 100.00 200.00
G8 Gerry Cheevers S/P 20.00 50.00
G9 Felix Potvin G/J 25.00 60.00
G10 Frank Brimsek G/J 20.00 50.00
G11 Bernie Parent P/J 20.00 50.00
G12 B.Parent/T.Esposito J/J 40.00 100.00
G13 J.Bower/C.Joseph S/S 75.00 150.00
G14 Brimsek/Cheevers G/S 40.00 100.00
G15 P.Roy/J.Plante S/G 75.00 150.00
G16 V.Tretiak/T.Esposito J/J 75.00 150.00
G17 Sawchuk/C.Joseph S/J 75.00 150.00
G18 T.Broda/C.Joseph G/J 40.00 100.00
G19 J.Bower/T.Broda S/G 40.00 100.00
G20 F.Potvin/C.Joseph G/S 75.00 150.00
G21 E.Belfour/P.Roy J/J 40.00 100.00
G22 E.Belfour/V.Tretiak J/J 40.00 100.00
G23 Sawchuk/J.Plante S/G 100.00 200.00
G24 J.Bower/T.Sawchuk S/S 75.00 150.00
G25 T.Esposito/Cheevers S/S 25.00 60.00
G26 F.Brimsek/Cheevers G/P 30.00 80.00
G27 C.Joseph/T.Broda G/G 40.00 100.00
G28 P.Roy/T.Sawchuk G/G 100.00 200.00
G29 Joseph/Bower/Sawch S 75.00 150.00
G30 Cheev/Parent/Espo S 75.00 150.00

2000-01 BAP Memorabilia Jersey

*NUMBERS: .6X TO 1.5X JERSEY CARDS
*JSY/STICK: .5X TO 1.2X BASIC JSY
*EMBLEMS: .8X TO 2X BASIC JSY
J1 Jeremy Roenick 12.00 30.00
J2 Mats Sundin 8.00 20.00
J3 Pavel Bure 8.00 20.00
J4 Martin Brodeur 20.00 50.00
J5 Mike Richter 8.00 20.00
J6 Brendan Shanahan 8.00 20.00
J7 Chris Pronger 8.00 20.00
J8 Al MacInnis 10.00 25.00
J9 Jaromir Jagr 25.00 60.00
J10 Olaf Kolzig 8.00 20.00
J11 Tony Amonte 6.00 15.00
J12 Scott Stevens 8.00 20.00
J13 Dominik Hasek 12.00 30.00
J14 Peter Forsberg 15.00 40.00
J15 Teemu Selanne 15.00 40.00
J16 Eric Lindros 12.00 30.00
J17 Nicklas Lidstrom 8.00 20.00
J18 Theo Fleury 10.00 25.00
J19 Darryl Sydor 6.00 15.00
J20 Mike Modano 12.00 30.00
J21 Nikolai Khabibulin 12.00 30.00
J22 Sandis Ozolinsh 5.00 12.00
J23 Mark Messier 15.00 40.00
J24 Joe Sakic 15.00 40.00
J25 Wayne Gretzky 50.00 125.00
J26 Owen Nolan 8.00 20.00
J27 Daniel Alfredsson 8.00 20.00
J28 Paul Coffey 8.00 20.00
J29 Steve Yzerman 20.00 50.00
J30 Brett Hull 15.00 40.00
J31 Paul Kariya 8.00 20.00
J32 John LeClair 8.00 20.00
J33 Ed Belfour 8.00 20.00
J34 Patrick Roy 20.00 50.00
J35 Sergei Fedorov 12.00 30.00
J36 Mark Recchi 10.00 25.00
J37 Ray Bourque 12.00 30.00
J38 Brian Leetch 6.00 15.00
J39 Rob Blake 8.00 20.00
J40 Curtis Joseph 10.00 25.00

2000-01 BAP Memorabilia Mario Lemieux Legends

L1 1987-88 Jsy 60.00 150.00
L2 1991-92 Jsy 60.00 150.00
L3 1987 Jsy 1991 Glove 60.00 150.00
L4 1991-92 Jsy-Glove 60.00 150.00
L5 1991-92 Jsy Emblem 90.00 150.00
L6 1991-92 Jsy Number 60.00 150.00
L7 1991-92 Glove 60.00 150.00
L8 1996 AS Jsy 60.00 150.00
L9 1987 Jsy/1996 AS Jsy 60.00 150.00
L10 1991 Jsy/1996 Jsy 90.00 150.00

2000-01 BAP Memorabilia Patent Power Jerseys

PP1 M.Lemieux/W.Gretzky 80.00 200.00
PP2 P.Kariya/S.Yzerman 30.00 80.00
PP3 P.Bure/J.Jagr 25.00 60.00
PP4 M.Sundin/P.Forsberg 15.00 40.00
PP5 T.Selanne/B.Hull 20.00 50.00
PP6 B.Shanahan/J.LeClair 15.00 40.00

2000-01 BAP Memorabilia Update Heritage Jerseys

H1 Mark Messier 12.00 30.00
H2 Pavel Bure 15.00 40.00
H3 Paul Coffey 15.00 40.00
H4 Mats Sundin 15.00 40.00
H5 Curtis Joseph 15.00 40.00
H6 Ed Belfour 15.00 40.00
H7 Mike Modano 20.00 50.00
H8 Brett Hull 15.00 40.00
H9 Teemu Selanne 20.00 50.00
H10 Keith Tkachuk 10.00 25.00
H11 Patrick Roy 30.00 80.00
H12 Chris Chelios 10.00 25.00
H13 Al MacInnis 10.00 25.00
H14 Theo Fleury 10.00 25.00
H15 Keith Primeau 10.00 25.00
H16 Ray Bourque 20.00 50.00
H17 Brendan Shanahan 20.00 50.00
H18 Owen Nolan 10.00 25.00
H19 Felix Potvin 20.00 50.00
H20 Trevor Linden 15.00 40.00
H21 Scott Stevens 10.00 25.00
H22 Adam Oates 10.00 25.00

2000-01 BAP Memorabilia Update Record Breakers

BB1 P.Bure/V.Bure 25.00 60.00
RB1 P.Roy/T.Sawchuk/33 100.00 250.00

2000-01 BAP Memorabilia Update Teammates

TM1 P.Sykora/M.Brodeur 15.00 40.00
TM2 S.Gonchar/A.Oates 10.00 25.00
TM3 J.Jagr/M.Lemieux 40.00 100.00
TM4 T.Amonte/B.Probert 12.50 30.00
TM5 J.Roenick/K.Tkachuk 10.00 25.00
TM6 M.Peca/D.Hasek 10.00 25.00
TM7 M.Messier/B.Leetch 20.00 50.00
TM8 P.Bure/P.Laus 10.00 25.00
TM9 T.Domi/M.Sundin 10.00 25.00
TM10 M.Brodeur/S.Niedermayer 20.00 50.00
TM11 K.McLaren/B.Dafoe 10.00 25.00
TM12 N.Lidstrom/C.Chelios 20.00 50.00
TM13 D.McCarty/S.Yzerman 20.00 50.00
TM14 D.Sydor/E.Belfour 10.00 25.00
TM15 B.Hull/M.Modano 12.00 30.00
TM16 B.Shanahan/S.Fedorov 20.00 50.00
TM17 N.Lidstrom/S.Kozlov 10.00 25.00
TM18 P.Roy/P.Forsberg 40.00 100.00
TM19 M.Richter/T.Fleury 10.00 25.00
TM20 M.Straka/J.Jagr 10.00 25.00
TM21 J.Arnott/S.Stevens 10.00 25.00
TM22 B.Shanahan/C.Osgood 10.00 25.00
TM23 P.Kariya/G.Hebert 10.00 25.00
TM24 C.Joseph/M.Sundin 10.00 25.00
TM25 T.Amonte/E.Daze 10.00 25.00
TM26 T.Selanne/P.Kariya 10.00 25.00
TM27 P.Sykora/J.Arnott 10.00 25.00
TM28 P.Roy/J.Sakic 30.00 80.00
TM29 S.Yzerman/S.Fedorov 20.00 50.00
TM30 K.Tkachuk/T.Numminen 10.00 25.00
TM31 S.Niedermayer/S.Stevens 10.00 25.00
TM32 M.Messier/M.Richter 10.00 25.00
TM33 T.Numminen/N.Khabibulin 10.00 25.00
TM34 P.Forsberg/J.Sakic 20.00 50.00
TM35 C.Osgood/S.Kozlov 10.00 25.00
TM36 E.Belfour/M.Modano 12.50 30.00
TM37 T.Domi/C.Joseph 10.00 25.00
TM38 J.Roenick/N.Khabibulin 10.00 25.00
TM39 G.Hebert/T.Selanne 10.00 25.00
TM40 T.Fleury/B.Leetch 10.00 25.00

2000-01 BAP Memorabilia Update Tough Materials

T1 Bob Probert 20.00 50.00
T2 Tie Domi 30.00 80.00
T3 Stu Grimson 25.00 60.00
T4 Eric Cairns 8.00 20.00
T5 Paul Laus 8.00 20.00
T6 Donald Brashear 15.00 40.00

T7 Rob Ray 15.00 40.00
T8 Wade Belak 8.00 20.00
T9 Kelly Chase 8.00 20.00
T10 Peter Worrell 8.00 20.00
T11 Darren McCarty 20.00 50.00
T12 Todd Simpson 8.00 20.00
T13 Krzysztof Oliwa 12.00 30.00
T14 Sandy McCarthy 8.00 20.00
T15 Brad Brown 8.00 20.00
T16 Luke Richardson 8.00 20.00
T17 Jeff Odgers 8.00 20.00
T18 Chris Dingman 8.00 20.00
T19 Enrico Ciccone 8.00 20.00
T20 Ryan VandenBussche 12.00 30.00
T21 Bob Boughner 8.00 20.00
T22 Gino Odjick 8.00 20.00
T23 Matt Johnson 8.00 20.00
T24 Jean-Luc Grand-Pierre 8.00 20.00
T25 Craig Berube 15.00 40.00
T26 Ian Laperriere 8.00 20.00

2001-02 BAP Memorabilia

1 Rick DiPietro .15 .40
2 Radek Dvorak .15 .40
3 Radek Bonk .12 .30
4 Evgeni Nabokov .15 .40
5 Roman Turek .15 .40
6 Daniel Sedin .25 .60
7 Jeff Halpern .12 .30
8 Joe Thornton .30 .75
9 Maxim Afinogenov .12 .30
10 Oleg Saprykin .12 .30
11 Shane Willis .12 .30
12 Jocelyn Thibault .15 .40
13 Alex Tanguay .15 .40
14 Brenden Morrow .15 .40
15 Steve Yzerman .50 1.25
16 Anson Carter .15 .40
17 Brad Richards .20 .50
18 Mike York .12 .30
19 Brian Rafalski .12 .30
20 Maxime Ouellet .20 .50
21 Ruslan Fedotenko .12 .30
22 Brad Stuart .12 .30
23 Daniel Corso .12 .30
24 Mika Noronen .12 .30
25 Jason Williams .12 .30
26 Scott Stevens .20 .50
27 Patrick Lalime .15 .40
28 Johan Hedberg .15 .40
29 Vincent Damphousse .15 .40
30 Jochen Hecht .12 .30
31 Ed Jovanovski .15 .40
32 Jean-Sebastien Giguere .20 .50
33 Fred Brathwaite .15 .40
34 Arturs Irbe .15 .40
35 Ron Tugnutt .15 .40
36 Ed Belfour .20 .50
37 Chris Osgood .20 .50
38 Mike Comrie .15 .40
39 Aaron Miller .12 .30
40 Martin Brodeur .50 1.25
41 Martin Havlat .15 .40
42 Roman Cechmanek .15 .40
43 Teppo Numminen .12 .30
44 Milan Kraft .12 .30
45 Pavol Demitra .25 .60
46 Henrik Sedin .25 .60
47 Byron Dafoe .15 .40
48 Dave Tanabe .12 .30
49 Chris Drury .15 .40
50 Tommy Salo .15 .40
51 Lubomir Visnovsky .12 .30
52 Andrei Markov .20 .50
53 Jason Arnott .15 .40
54 Adam Foote .15 .40
55 Vitali Vishnevski .12 .30
56 Ville Nieminen .12 .30
57 Mike Mottau .12 .30
58 Brendan Morrison .15 .40
59 Lee Goren .12 .30
60 Scott Gomez .15 .40
61 Tim Connolly .12 .30
62 Daniel Alfredsson .20 .50
63 Owen Nolan .20 .50
64 Chris Pronger .20 .50
65 Fredrik Modin .12 .30
66 Mario Lemieux .75 2.00
67 Olaf Kolzig .20 .50
68 Jeff Friesen .12 .30
69 Patrik Stefan .15 .40
70 Sergei Samsonov .15 .40
71 J-P Dumont .12 .30
72 Sandis Ozolinsh .12 .30
73 Milan Hejduk .15 .40
74 Sergei Zubov .15 .40
75 Sergei Fedorov .30 .75
76 Janne Niinimaa .12 .30
77 Roberto Luongo .30 .75
78 Felix Potvin .30 .75
79 Petr Sykora .12 .30
80 Petr Nedved .15 .40
81 Shawn McEachern .12 .30
82 Simon Gagne .20 .50
83 Sean Burke .12 .30
84 Al MacInnis .25 .60
85 Vincent Lecavalier .20 .50
86 Sergei Gonchar .12 .30
87 Oleg Tverdovsky .12 .30
88 Bill Guerin .20 .50
89 Miroslav Satan .15 .40
90 Marc Savard .12 .30
91 Peter Forsberg .40 1.00
92 Brett Hull .40 1.00
93 Nicklas Lidstrom .20 .50
94 Ryan Smyth .15 .40
95 Luc Robitaille .20 .50
96 Alexander Mogilny .15 .40
97 Mark Messier .40 1.00
98 Marian Hossa .20 .50
99 Keith Primeau .15 .40
100 Todd Bertuzzi .20 .50
101 Justin Williams .15 .40
102 Ossi Vaananen .12 .30
103 Robert Lang .12 .30
104 Pavel Bure .20 .50
105 Tomas Kaberle .12 .30
106 Nikolai Antropov .12 .30
107 Tomi Kallio .12 .30
108 David Vyborny .12 .30
109 Denis Shvidki .12 .30
110 Jozef Stumpel .12 .30
111 Dimitri Kalinin .12 .30
112 Stephane Robidas .12 .30
113 Scott Walker .12 .30
114 Jamie Langenbrunner .12 .30
115 Maxim Kuznetsov .12 .30
116 Mike Grier .12 .30
117 Michael Nylander .12 .30
118 Derian Hatcher .12 .30
119 Scott Niedermayer .20 .50
120 Petr Schastlivy .12 .30
121 Tomas Divisek RC .30 .75
122 Toby Petersen .12 .30
123 Jarkko Ruutu .12 .30
124 Chris Chelios .20 .50
125 Andrew Raycroft .15 .40
126 Jason Woolley .12 .30
127 Derek Morris .12 .30
128 David Legwand .15 .40
129 Jaromir Jagr .60 1.50
130 Serge Aubin .12 .30
131 Jere Lehtinen .15 .40
132 Manny Legace .15 .40
133 Patrick Roy .50 1.25
134 Glen Murray .15 .40
135 Jan Bulis .12 .30
136 Mike Dunham .15 .40
137 Jan Hlavac .12 .30
138 Wade Redden .12 .30
139 Jan Hrdina .12 .30
140 Keith Tkachuk .20 .50
141 Yanic Perreault .12 .30
142 Jonas Ronnqvist .12 .30
143 John Madden .15 .40
144 Jani Hurme .15 .40
145 Chris Gratton .12 .30
146 Toni Lydman .12 .30
147 Mike Modano .30 .75
148 Boris Mironov .12 .30
149 Joe Sakic .40 1.00
150 Chris Nielsen .12 .30
151 Marty Turco .20 .50
152 Bryan Smolinski .12 .30
153 Daniel Cleary .15 .40
154 Anders Eriksson .12 .30
155 Pierre Dagenais .12 .30
156 Wes Walz .12 .30
157 Brian Savage .12 .30
158 Stu Barnes .15 .40
159 Eric Desjardins .15 .40
160 Juraj Kolnik .12 .30
161 Brendan Shanahan .20 .50
162 Karel Rachunek .12 .30
163 Marc Denis .15 .40
164 Martin Straka .12 .30
165 Alexander Kharitonov .12 .30
166 Sergei Brylin .12 .30
167 Eric Daze .15 .40
168 Alexei Kovalev .15 .40
169 Jiri Slegr .12 .30
170 Brian Rolston .15 .40
171 Phil Housley .15 .40
172 Josef Vasicek .12 .30
173 Patrick Marleau .20 .50
174 Steven Reinprecht .12 .30
175 Gary Roberts .12 .30
176 Darryl Sydor .12 .30
177 Michel Riesen .12 .30
178 Kevyn Adams .12 .30
179 Andreas Lilja .12 .30
180 Roman Hamrlik .12 .30
181 Mathieu Garon .15 .40
182 Scott Hartnell .12 .30
183 Kenny Jonsson .12 .30
184 Jeff Ulmer .12 .30
185 Petr Hubacek .12 .30
186 Jeremy Roenick .30 .75
187 Scott Young .12 .30
188 Sergei Berezin .12 .30
189 Steve Konowalchuk .12 .30
190 Curtis Joseph .25 .60
191 Jonathan Girard .12 .30
192 Brian Campbell .12 .30
193 Markus Naslund .20 .50
194 David Aebischer .15 .40
195 Peter Bondra .20 .50
196 Paul Kariya .20 .50
197 Jason Allison .15 .40
198 Dominik Hasek .30 .75
199 Branislav Mezei .12 .30
200 Peter Smrek RC .20 .50
201 Miikka Kiprusoff .20 .50
202 Kristian Kudroc .12 .30
203 Kyle McLaren .12 .30
204 Calle Johansson .15 .40
205 Gregg Naumenko .12 .30
206 Damian Rhodes .15 .40
207 Willie Mitchell .12 .30
208 Daniel Tkaczuk .12 .30
209 Mike Ribeiro .12 .30
210 Rostislav Klesla .12 .30
211 Denis Arkhipov .12 .30
212 Andy McDonald .12 .30
213 Ivan Novoseltsev .12 .30
214 Manny Fernandez .12 .30
215 Reto Von Arx .12 .30
216 Ray Bourque .30 .75
217 Mike Jefferson RC .20 .50
218 Jason Chimera RC .20 .50
219 Mattias Ohlund .12 .30
220 Rico Fata .12 .30
221 Brad Tapper .12 .30
222 Mike Richter .20 .50
223 Nick Boynton .12 .30
224 Harold Druken .12 .30
225 Chris Clark .12 .30
226 Colin White .12 .30
227 Tyler Bouck .12 .30
228 Jesse Wallin .12 .30
229 Jeff Hackett .15 .40
230 Greg Classen .12 .30
231 Adam Mair .12 .30
232 Ivan Ciernik RC .20 .50
233 Marc Chouinard .12 .30
234 Chris Mason .12 .30
235 Ronald Petrovicky .12 .30
236 Kyle Calder .12 .30
237 Rick Berry .12 .30
238 Mathieu Darche RC .40 1.00
239 Theo Fleury .25 .60
240 Mike Commodore .12 .30
241 Michal Handzus .12 .30
242 Bill Tibbetts RC .20 .50
243 Cory Stillman .12 .30
244 Valeri Bure .12 .30
245 Matt Pettinger .12 .30
246 Rod Brind'Amour .20 .50
247 Pascal Dupuis RC .40 1.00
248 Martin Rucinsky .12 .30
249 Cliff Ronning .12 .30
250 Brad Isbister .12 .30
251 Antti-Jussi Niemi .12 .30
252 Mark Bell .12 .30
253 Martin Spanhel RC .20 .50
254 Andrew Cassels .12 .30
255 Andrew Brunette .12 .30
256 Ron Francis .25 .60
257 Tony Amonte .15 .40
258 Espen Knutsen .12 .30
259 Viktor Kozlov .12 .30
260 Sergei Krivokrasov .12 .30
261 Richard Zednik .15 .40
262 Bubba Berenzweig .12 .30
263 Pavel Patera .12 .30
264 Mike Johnson .12 .30
265 Teemu Selanne .40 1.00
266 John LeClair .20 .50
267 Adam Deadmarsh .12 .30
268 Herbert Vasilijevs .12 .30
269 Steven McCarthy .12 .30
270 Mathieu Schneider .12 .30
271 Peter Bartos .12 .30
272 Ray Ferraro .12 .30
273 Eric Chouinard .12 .30
274 Marian Cisar .12 .30
275 Jarome Iginla .25 .60
276 Jeff O'Neill .15 .40
277 Steve Sullivan .12 .30
278 Rob Blake .20 .50
279 Geoff Sanderson .12 .30
280 Niclas Wallin .12 .30
281 Vitali Yeremeyev .12 .30
282 Doug Weight .20 .50
283 Martin Skoula .15 .40
284 Zigmund Palffy .20 .50
285 Marian Gaborik .20 .50
286 Saku Koivu .20 .50
287 Joe Nieuwendyk .15 .40
288 Patrik Elias .20 .50
289 Mariusz Czerkawski .12 .30
290 Brian Leetch .15 .40
291 Alexei Yashin .15 .40
292 Mark Recchi .25 .60
293 Shane Doan .15 .40
294 Brian Holzinger .12 .30
295 Mikael Samuelsson RC .30 .75
296 Pierre Turgeon .15 .40
297 Sheldon Keefe .12 .30
298 Mats Sundin .20 .50
299 Bryan Allen .12 .30
300 Adam Oates .20 .50
301 Ilja Bryzgalov RC .60 1.50
302 Erik Cole RC .40 1.00
303 Pavel Datsyuk RC 4.00 10.00
304 Nikolai Khabibulin .20 .50
305 Dan Blackburn RC .30 .75
306 Jeff Jillson RC .20 .50
307 Brian Sutherby RC .20 .50
308 Vaclav Nedorost RC .20 .50
309 Byron Ritchie .12 .30
310 Martin Erat RC .30 .75
311 Vaclav Pletka RC .20 .50
312 Karel Pilar RC .20 .50
313 Jaroslav Obsut RC .20 .50
314 Jason Allison .15 .40
315 Eric Lindros .30 .75
316 Mike Farrell RC .20 .50
317 Doug Gilmour .25 .60
318 Bruno St. Jacques RC .20 .50
319 Martin Lapointe .12 .30
320 Dan Focht RC .20 .50
321 Ben Simon RC .30 .75
322 Mike Peluso RC .20 .50
323 Martin Cibak RC .20 .50
324 Marcel Hossa RC .40 1.00
325 Chris Neil .15 .40
326 Mark Rycroft RC .30 .75
327 Timo Parssinen RC .30 .75
328 Sebastien Charpentier RC .20 .50
329 Kip Brennan RC .20 .50
330 Christian Berglund RC .30 .75
331 Tom Kostopoulos RC .20 .50
332 Pat Kavanagh RC .30 .75
333 Sebastien Centomo RC .20 .50
334 Andrew Brunette .12 .30
335 Toni Dahlman RC .20 .50
336 Kamil Piros RC .20 .50
337 Robert Schnabel RC .20 .50
338 Radim Vrbata .12 .30
339 Chris Osgood .20 .50
340 Steve Montador RC .20 .50
341 Reinhard Divis RC .20 .50
342 Steve Moore RC .40 1.00
343 Branko Radivojevic RC .20 .50
344 Zdenek Kutlak RC .20 .50
345 Jiri Dopita RC .20 .50
346 Josef Boumedienne RC .20 .50
347 Phil Housley .15 .40
348 Niko Kapanen RC .40 1.00
349 Travis Roche RC .20 .50
350 Raffi Torres RC .40 1.00
351 Randy Robitaille .12 .30
352 Chris Corrinet RC .20 .50
353 Pierre Turgeon .15 .40
354 Pavel Skrbek RC .20 .50
355 Jeremy Roenick .30 .75
356 Riku Hahl RC .20 .50
357 Stanislav Gron RC .20 .50
358 Pasi Nurminen RC .20 .50
359 Nick Smith RC .20 .50
360 Shane Endicott RC .20 .50
361 Ales Kotalik RC .40 1.00
362 Blake Bellefeuille RC .20 .50
363 Jaroslav Bednar RC .20 .50
364 Andreas Salomonsson RC .20 .50
365 Krystofer Kolanos RC .20 .50
366 Tim Connolly .12 .30
367 Ivan Huml RC .20 .50
368 Sean Avery RC .20 .50
369 Trent Hunter RC .40 1.00
370 Richard Scott RC .20 .50
371 Doug Weight .20 .50
372 Ilya Kovalchuk RC 1.00 3.00
373 Dominik Hasek .30 .75
374 Scott Clemmensen RC .20 .50
375 Nikita Alexeev RC .20 .50
376 Luc Robitaille .20 .50
377 Mike Peca .15 .40
378 Brett Hull .40 1.00
379 Valeri Bure .12 .30
380 Pavel Brendl .12 .30
381 Jukka Hentunen RC .20 .50
382 John Erskine RC .20 .50
383 Nick Schultz RC .20 .50
384 Radek Martinek RC .20 .50
385 Dany Heatley .15 .40
386 Alex Auld .12 .30
387 Tyler Arnason RC .30 .75
388 Ty Conklin RC .40 1.00
389 Olivier Michaud RC .40 1.00
390 Sandis Ozolinsh .12 .30
391 Evgeny Konstantinov RC .20 .50
392 Roman Turek .15 .40
393 Kristian Huselius RC .40 1.00
394 Alexei Yashin .15 .40
395 Alexander Mogilny .15 .40
396 Eric Meloche RC .20 .50
397 Andy McDonald .12 .30
398 Niklas Hagman RC .30 .75
399 Ryan Flinn RC .20 .50
400 Mike Weaver RC .20 .50
401 Nolan Yonkman .12 .30
402 Ryan Jardine .12 .30
403 Andrej Nedorost RC .20 .50
404 Andrej Podkonicky RC .20 .50
405 Hnat Domenichelli .12 .30
406 Bob Wren RC .20 .50
407 Brad Norton RC .20 .50
408 Brian Pothier RC .20 .50
409 Trevor Letowski .12 .30
410 Chris Bala RC .20 .50
411 Tom Fitzgerald .12 .30
412 Petr Tenkrat .12 .30
413 Dan Snyder RC .30 .75
414 David Cullen RC .20 .50
415 David Ling RC .20 .50
416 Dean Melanson RC .20 .50
417 Duvie Westcott RC .20 .50
418 Eric Beaudoin RC .20 .50
419 Marty McInnis .15 .40
420 Francis Lessard RC .20 .50
421 Frederic Cassivi RC .20 .50
422 Bill Lindsay .12 .30
423 Kim Johnsson .12 .30
424 Daniil Markov .12 .30
425 Guillaume Lefebvre RC .20 .50
426 Hannes Hyvonen RC .20 .50
427 Jeff Daw RC .20 .50
428 Jody Shelley RC .30 .75
429 Joel Kwiatkowski RC .20 .50
430 Josh Langfeld RC .20 .50
431 Kelly Fairchild RC .20 .50
432 Kevin Sawyer RC .20 .50
433 Kriby Law RC .20 .50
434 Kyle Rossiter RC .20 .50
435 Lukas Krajicek RC .20 .50
436 Mark Hartigan RC .20 .50
437 Martin Prusek RC .20 .60
438 Matt Davidson RC .20 .50
439 Andre Roy .12 .30
440 Chris Kelleher RC .20 .50
441 Mike Matteucci RC .20 .50
442 Nathan Perrott RC .20 .50
443 Neil Little RC .20 .50
444 Rocky Thompson RC .20 .50
445 Ryan Tobler RC .30 .75
446 Scott Nichol RC .20 .50
447 Jiri Slegr .12 .30
448 Stephen Weiss RC .60 1.50
449 Jeff Cowan .12 .30
450 Thomas Ziegler RC .30 .75
451 Todd Rohloff RC .20 .50
452 Blake Sloan .12 .30
453 Tony Tuzzolino RC .20 .50
454 Tony Virta RC .20 .50
455 Adam Oates .20 .50
456 Benoit Brunet .12 .30
457 Benoit Hogue .12 .30
458 Brian Savage .12 .30
459 Cliff Ronning .12 .30
460 Darius Kasparaitis .12 .30
461 Dean McAmmond .12 .30
462 Donald Brashear .12 .30
463 Glen Murray .15 .40
464 Jamie Allison .12 .30
465 Jamie Langenbrunner .12 .30
466 Jan Hlavac .12 .30
467 Jason Arnott .15 .40
468 Joe Nieuwendyk .15 .40
469 Jozef Stumpel .12 .30
470 Juha Ylonen .12 .30
471 Kevin Weekes .15 .40
472 Kirill Safronov .12 .30
473 Manny Malhotra .15 .40
474 Martin Rucinsky .12 .30
475 Matthew Barnaby .12 .30
476 Mike Keane .15 .40
477 Mike York .12 .30
478 Mikko Eloranta .12 .30
479 Pascal Rheaume .12 .30
480 Pavel Bure .20 .50
481 Pierre Dagenais .12 .30
482 Randy McKay .12 .30
483 Ray Ferraro .12 .30
484 Rem Murray .15 .40
485 Rick Berry .12 .30
486 Sean Brown .12 .30
487 Sean Hill .12 .30
488 Sergei Berezin .12 .30
489 Shane Willis .12 .30
490 Stephane Fiset .15 .40
491 Stephane Richer .12 .30
492 Steve Thomas .12 .30
493 Tom Barrasso .15 .40
494 Tom Poti .12 .30
495 Trevor Linden .20 .50
496 Valeri Kamensky .12 .30
497 Ville Nieminen .12 .30
498 Zdeno Chara .20 .50
499 Shjon Podein .12 .30
500 Shaun Van Allen .12 .30

2001-02 BAP Memorabilia Ruby

*VETS/200: 3X TO 8X BASIC CARDS
*ROOKIES/200: 2X TO 5X BASIC RC
97 Mark Messier 5.00 12.00

2001-02 BAP Memorabilia Sapphire

*VETS/100: 5X TO 12X BASIC CARDS
*ROOKIES/100: 3X TO 8X BASIC RC
6 Daniel Sedin 5.00 12.00
97 Mark Messier 8.00 20.00

2001-02 BAP Memorabilia All-Star Jerseys

ASJ1 Evgeni Nabokov 4.00 10.00
ASJ2 Paul Kariya 5.00 12.00
ASJ3 Zigmund Palffy 5.00 12.00
ASJ4 Milan Hejduk 4.00 10.00
ASJ5 Patrick Roy 12.00 30.00
ASJ6 Rob Blake 5.00 12.00
ASJ7 Nicklas Lidstrom 5.00 12.00
ASJ8 Martin Brodeur 12.00 30.00
ASJ9 Doug Weight 5.00 12.00
ASJ10 Bill Guerin 5.00 12.00
ASJ11 Dominik Hasek 8.00 20.00
ASJ12 Joe Sakic 10.00 25.00
ASJ13 Alexei Kovalev 4.00 10.00
ASJ14 Roman Cechmanek 4.00 10.00
ASJ15 Pavel Bure 5.00 12.00
ASJ16 Mario Lemieux 20.00 50.00
ASJ17 Ray Bourque 8.00 20.00
ASJ18 Teppo Numminen 3.00 8.00
ASJ19 Sandis Ozolinsh 3.00 8.00
ASJ20 Tony Amonte 4.00 10.00
ASJ21 Peter Forsberg 10.00 25.00
ASJ22 Brian Leetch 4.00 10.00
ASJ23 Radek Bonk 3.00 8.00
ASJ24 Theo Fleury 6.00 15.00
ASJ25 Simon Gagne 5.00 12.00
ASJ26 Valeri Bure 3.00 8.00
ASJ27 Pavol Demitra 6.00 15.00
ASJ28 Scott Gomez 4.00 10.00
ASJ29 Curtis Joseph 6.00 15.00
ASJ30 Viktor Kozlov 3.00 8.00
ASJ31 Mark Messier 10.00 25.00
ASJ32 Mike Modano 8.00 20.00
ASJ33 Owen Nolan 5.00 12.00
ASJ34 Tommy Salo 4.00 10.00
ASJ35 Roman Turek 4.00 10.00
ASJ36 Steve Yzerman 12.00 30.00
ASJ37 Jaromir Jagr 15.00 40.00
ASJ38 Mats Sundin 5.00 12.00
ASJ39 Nikolai Khabibulin 5.00 12.00
ASJ40 Markus Naslund 5.00 12.00
ASJ41 Keith Tkachuk 5.00 12.00
ASJ42 Alexei Yashin 4.00 10.00
ASJ43 Chris Pronger 5.00 12.00
ASJ44 Al MacInnis 6.00 15.00
ASJ45 Peter Bondra 5.00 12.00
ASJ46 Arturs Irbe 4.00 10.00
ASJ47 Eric Lindros 8.00 20.00
ASJ48 Teemu Selanne 10.00 25.00
ASJ49 Daniel Alfredsson 5.00 12.00
ASJ50 Brett Hull 10.00 25.00

2001-02 BAP Memorabilia All-Star Jersey Doubles

DASJ1 Paul Kariya 6.00 15.00
DASJ2 Patrick Roy 15.00 40.00
DASJ3 Rob Blake 6.00 15.00
DASJ4 Nicklas Lidstrom 6.00 15.00
DASJ5 Martin Brodeur 15.00 40.00
DASJ6 Dominik Hasek 10.00 25.00
DASJ7 Joe Sakic 12.00 30.00
DASJ8 Ray Bourque 10.00 25.00
DASJ9 Tony Amonte 5.00 12.00
DASJ10 Peter Forsberg 12.00 30.00
DASJ11 Brian Leetch 5.00 12.00
DASJ12 Theo Fleury 8.00 20.00
DASJ13 Mats Sundin 6.00 15.00
DASJ14 Pavel Bure 6.00 15.00
DASJ15 Steve Yzerman 15.00 40.00
DASJ16 Mike Modano 10.00 25.00
DASJ17 Mark Messier 12.00 30.00
DASJ18 Curtis Joseph 8.00 20.00
DASJ19 Brendan Shanahan 6.00 15.00
DASJ20 Jaromir Jagr 20.00 50.00
DASJ21 Eric Lindros 10.00 25.00
DASJ22 Mario Lemieux 25.00 60.00
DASJ23 Al MacInnis 8.00 20.00
DASJ24 John LeClair 6.00 15.00
DASJ25 Chris Pronger 6.00 15.00
DASJ26 Wayne Gretzky 40.00 100.00
DASJ27 Teemu Selanne 12.00 30.00
DASJ28 Owen Nolan 6.00 15.00
DASJ29 Alexei Yashin 5.00 12.00
DASJ30 Jeremy Roenick 10.00 25.00

2001-02 BAP Memorabilia All-Star Starting Lineup

S1 Dominik Hasek 8.00 20.00
S2 Nicklas Lidstrom 5.00 12.00
S3 Sandis Ozolinsh 3.00 8.00
S4 Milan Hejduk 4.00 10.00
S5 Peter Forsberg 10.00 25.00
S6 Pavel Bure 5.00 12.00
S7 Patrick Roy 12.00 30.00
S8 Ray Bourque 8.00 20.00
S9 Rob Blake 5.00 12.00
S10 Paul Kariya 5.00 12.00
S11 Theo Fleury 6.00 15.00
S12 Joe Sakic 10.00 25.00

2001-02 BAP Memorabilia All-Star Teammates

AST1 Nabokov/Hejduk/Palffy 5.00 12.00
AST2 Kariya/Lemieux/Gagne 20.00 50.00
AST3 Blake/Roy/Sakic 12.00 30.00
AST4 Brodeur/Weight/Leetch 12.00 30.00
AST5 Cechmanek/Bure/Forsberg 10.00 25.00
AST6 Nabokov/Hejduk/Palffy 8.00 20.00
AST7 Bourque/Leetch/Fleury 8.00 20.00
AST8 Amonte/Guerin/Weight 5.00 12.00
AST9 Nabokov/Cech/Hasek 8.00 20.00
AST10 Kariya/Sakic/Fleury 10.00 25.00
AST11 P.Forsberg/M.Hejduk 10.00 25.00
AST12 P.Roy/M.Lemieux 20.00 50.00
AST13 R.Bourque/R.Blake 8.00 20.00
AST14 P.Bure/V.Bure/Kozlov 5.00 12.00
AST15 Brodeur/Gomez/Stevens 12.00 30.00
AST16 C.Pronger/A.MacInnis 6.00 15.00
AST17 Amnte/Modno/Roenck 8.00 20.00
AST18 Kolzig/Salo/Turek 5.00 12.00
AST19 B.Shanahan/S.Yzerman 12.00 30.00
AST20 M.Sundin/T.Salo 5.00 12.00
AST21 J.Jagr/P.Bure 15.00 40.00
AST22 Modno/Joseph/Yzrmn 12.00 30.00
AST23 P.Bure/V.Bure 5.00 12.00
AST24 Yzerman/Messier/Gomez 12.00 30.00
AST25 M.Modano/E.Lindros 8.00 20.00
AST26 P.Forsberg/T.Selanne 10.00 25.00
AST27 Naslund/Yashin/Bondra 5.00 12.00
AST28 Hasek/Irbe/Khab 8.00 20.00
AST29 Sundin/Lidstrom/Naslund 5.00 12.00
AST30 C.Pronger/A.MacInnis 6.00 15.00
AST31 P.Kariya/T.Amonte 5.00 12.00
AST32 P.Forsberg/J.Jagr 15.00 40.00
AST33 M.Modano/J.LeClair 8.00 20.00
AST34 Grtzky/Modno/Lndros 30.00 80.00
AST35 P.Roy/J.Sakic 12.00 30.00
AST36 Jagr/Forsberg/Bure 15.00 40.00
AST37 W.Gretzky/P.Roy 30.00 80.00
AST38 Bourque/Chelios/Leetch 8.00 20.00
AST39 E.Lindros/M.Messier 10.00 25.00
AST40 D.Hasek/N.Khabibulin 8.00 20.00
AST41 J.Sakic/M.Modano 10.00 25.00
AST42 D.Hasek/R.Bourque 8.00 20.00
AST43 S.Yzerman/M.Sundin 12.00 30.00
AST44 P.Kariya/P.Bure 5.00 12.00
AST45 M.Sundin/T.Selanne 10.00 25.00
AST46 B.Hull/E.Belfour 10.00 25.00
AST47 J.Jagr/E.Lindros 15.00 40.00
AST48 P.Forsberg/P.Kariya 10.00 25.00
AST49 W.Gretzky/C.Joseph 30.00 80.00
AST50 P.Roy/R.Bourque 12.00 30.00

2001-02 BAP Memorabilia Draft Redemptions

1 Ilya Kovalchuk/74* 60.00 150.00
2 Jason Spezza/55* 125.00 250.00
3 Alexander Svitov/52* 20.00 50.00
4 Stephen Weiss/55* 40.00 80.00
5 Stanislav Chistov/53* 15.00 40.00
6 Mikko Koivu/56* 10.00 25.00
7 Mike Komisarek/47* 25.00 60.00
8 Pascal LeClaire/49* 30.00 60.00
9 Tuomo Ruutu/64* 30.00 60.00
10 Dan Blackburn/67* 15.00 40.00
11 Fredrik Sjostrom/100 10.00 25.00
12 Dan Hamhuis/63* 25.00 60.00
13 Ales Hemsky/52* 40.00 100.00
14 Chuck Kobasew/50* 25.00 50.00
16 R.J. Umberger/58* 10.00 25.00
17 Carlo Colaiacovo/50* 25.00 60.00
19 Shaone Morrisonn/48* 20.00 50.00
20 Marcel Goc/57* 10.00 25.00
21 Colby Armstrong/45* 10.00 25.00
23 Tim Gleason/61* 15.00 40.00
24 Lukas Krajicek/31* 25.00 60.00
25 Alexander Perezhogin/47* 10.00 25.00
26 Jason Bacashihua/46* 25.00 60.00
27 Jeff Woywitka/48* 8.00 20.00
29 Adam Munro/100 8.00 20.00
30 Dave Steckel/35* 8.00 20.00

2001-02 BAP Memorabilia 500 Goal Scorers

GS1 Wayne Gretzky/20 100.00 250.00
GS2 Gordie Howe/20 60.00 150.00
GS3 Marcel Dionne/50 12.00 30.00
GS4 Phil Esposito/40 15.00 40.00
GS5 Mike Gartner/99 12.00 30.00
GS6 Mark Messier/99 20.00 50.00
GS7 Steve Yzerman/99 25.00 60.00
GS8 Brett Hull/99 20.00 50.00
GS9 Mario Lemieux/20 60.00 150.00
GS10 Dino Ciccarelli/99 10.00 25.00
GS11 Jari Kurri/99 10.00 25.00
GS12 Luc Robitaille/99 10.00 25.00
GS13 Mike Bossy/50 10.00 25.00
GS14 Dave Andreychuk/99 10.00 25.00
GS15 Guy Lafleur/50 12.00 30.00
GS16 John Bucyk/99 10.00 25.00
GS17 Maurice Richard/20 60.00 150.00
GS18 Stan Mikita/40 15.00 40.00
GS19 Frank Mahovlich/40 10.00 25.00
GS20 Bryan Trottler/99 10.00 25.00
GS21 Dale Hawerchuk/99 12.00 30.00
GS22 Gilbert Perreault/99 10.00 25.00
GS23 Jean Beliveau/20 40.00 100.00
GS24 Pat Verbeek/99 8.00 20.00
GS25 Michel Goulet/99 8.00 20.00
GS26 Joe Mullen/99 8.00 20.00
GS27 Lanny McDonald/99 8.00 20.00
GS28 Bobby Hull/40 20.00 50.00
NNO Brendan Shanahan/25 10.00 25.00
NNO Ron Francis/25 12.00 30.00

2001-02 BAP Memorabilia Goalies Jerseys

GJ1 Byron Dafoe 4.00 10.00
GJ2 Dominik Hasek 8.00 20.00
GJ3 Mike Vernon 4.00 10.00
GJ4 Arturs Irbe 4.00 10.00
GJ5 Jocelyn Thibault 4.00 10.00
GJ6 Patrick Roy 12.00 30.00
GJ7 Ed Belfour 5.00 12.00
GJ8 Chris Osgood 5.00 12.00
GJ9 Johan Hedberg 4.00 10.00
GJ10 R.Luongo/T.Kid 8.00 20.00
GJ11 J.Theodore/J.Hackett 5.00 12.00
GJ12 Mike Dunham 4.00 10.00
GJ13 Martin Brodeur 12.00 30.00
GJ14 Mike Richter 5.00 12.00
GJ15 R.Cechmanek/B.Boucher 4.00 10.00
GJ16 Jean-Sebastien Aubin 4.00 10.00
GJ17 Roman Turek 4.00 10.00
GJ18 Curtis Joseph 6.00 15.00
GJ19 Olaf Kolzig 5.00 12.00
GJ20 Felix Potvin 8.00 20.00

2001-02 BAP Memorabilia Goalie Traditions

GT1 Curtis Joseph 6.00 15.00
GT2 Johnny Bower 5.00 12.00
GT3 Turk Broda 4.00 10.00
GT4 Patrick Roy 12.00 30.00
GT5 Jacques Plante 8.00 20.00
GT6 Jose Theodore 5.00 12.00
GT7 Glenn Hall 5.00 12.00
GT8 Tony Esposito 8.00 20.00
GT9 Jocelyn Thibault 4.00 10.00
GT10 Chuck Rayner 3.00 8.00
GT11 Ed Giacomin 5.00 12.00
GT12 Mike Richter 5.00 12.00
GT13 Frank Brimsek 4.00 10.00
GT14 Gerry Cheevers 5.00 12.00
GT15 Byron Dafoe 4.00 10.00
GT16 Terry Sawchuk 8.00 20.00
GT17 Glenn Hall 5.00 12.00
GT18 Chris Osgood 5.00 12.00
GT19 C.Joseph/T.Broda 10.00 25.00
GT20 C.Joseph/J.Bower 10.00 25.00
GT21 J.Bower/T.Broda 8.00 20.00
GT22 T.Sawchuk/G.Hall 12.00 30.00
GT23 G.Hall/C.Osgood 8.00 20.00
GT24 T.Sawchuck/C.Osgood 12.00 30.00
GT25 G.Hall/J.Thibault 8.00 20.00
GT26 G.Hall/T.Esposito 12.00 30.00
GT27 T.Esposito/J.Thibault 12.00 30.00
GT28 J.Plante/P.Roy 20.00 50.00
GT29 J.Plante/J.Theodore 12.00 30.00
GT30 P.Roy/J.Theodore 20.00 50.00
GT31 F.Brimsek/B.Dafoe 6.00 15.00
GT32 F.Brimsek/G.Cheevers 8.00 20.00
GT33 G.Cheevers/B.Dafoe 8.00 20.00
GT34 C.Rayner/E.Giacomin 8.00 20.00
GT35 C.Rayner/M.Richter 8.00 20.00
GT36 E.Giacomin/M.Richter 8.00 20.00
GT37 Joseph/Bower/Broda 12.00 30.00
GT38 Sawchuk/Hall/Osgood 15.00 40.00
GT39 Esposito/Hall/Thibault 15.00 40.00
GT40 Plante/Roy/Theodore 25.00 60.00
GT41 Brimsek/Cheevers/Dafoe 5.00 12.00
GT42 Richter/Rayner/Giacomin 10.00 25.00

2001-02 BAP Memorabilia He Shoots He Scores Points

1 Roman Cechmanek 1 pt. .25 .60
2 Martin Havlat 1 pt. .25 .60
3 Milan Hejduk 1 pt. .30 .75
4 Curtis Joseph 1 pt. .30 .75
5 Saku Koivu 1 pt. .30 .75
6 Mark Messier 1 pt. .30 .75
7 Mike Modano 1 pt. .50 1.25
8 Evgeni Nabokov 1 pt. .25 .60
9 Chris Pronger 1 pt. .25 .60
10 Mats Sundin 1 pt. .30 .75
11 Martin Brodeur 2 pts. .75 2.00
12 Peter Forsberg 2 pts. .60 1.50
13 Paul Kariya 2 pts. .30 .75
14 Vincent Lecavalier 2 pts. .30 .75
15 Patrick Roy 2 pts. 1.50 4.00
16 Joe Sakic 2 pts. .60 1.50
17 Steve Yzerman 2 pts. 1.50 4.00
18 Pavel Bure 3 pts. .30 .75
19 Mario Lemieux 3 pts. 2.00 5.00
20 Teemu Selanne 3 pts. .30 .75

2001-02 BAP Memorabilia Patented Power

PP1 J.Jagr/M.Sundin 15.00 40.00
PP2 M.Lemieux/W.Gretzky 50.00 125.00
PP3 P.Bure/M.Hejduk 5.00 12.00
PP4 M.Modano/C.Pronger 8.00 20.00
PP5 P.Kariya/J.Sakic 10.00 25.00
PP6 P.Forsberg/S.Yzerman 12.00 30.00

2001-02 BAP Memorabilia Rocket's Mates

RM1 Jacques Plante 50.00 125.00
RM2 Doug Harvey 25.00 60.00
RM3 Jean Beliveau 30.00 80.00
RM4 Henri Richard 25.00 60.00
RM5 Bernie Geoffrion 30.00 80.00
RM6 Dollard St. Laurent 25.00 60.00
RM7 Elmer Lach 25.00 60.00
RM8 Dickie Moore 25.00 60.00
RM9 Butch Bouchard 25.00 60.00
RM10 Jean-Guy Talbot 25.00 60.00

2001-02 BAP Memorabilia Stanley Cup Champions

CA1 Patrick Roy 75.00 150.00
CA2 Adam Foote 12.00 30.00
CA3 Ray Bourque 60.00 120.00
CA4 Martin Skoula 15.00 40.00
CA5 Shjon Podein 15.00 40.00
CA6 Alex Tanguay 15.00 40.00
CA7 Chris Dingman 15.00 40.00
CA8 Milan Hejduk 15.00 40.00
CA9 Peter Forsberg 20.00 50.00
CA10 Joe Sakic 30.00 80.00
CA11 Eric Messier 15.00 40.00
CA12 Jon Klemm 15.00 40.00
CA13 Dave Reid 15.00 40.00
CA14 Chris Drury 15.00 40.00

2001-02 BAP Memorabilia Stanley Cup Playoffs

SC1 Mats Sundin/95 10.00 25.00
SC2 Daniel Alfredsson/95 10.00 25.00
SC3 Scott Stevens/95 10.00 25.00
SC4 Arturs Irbe/95 6.00 15.00
SC5 Martin Straka/95 10.00 25.00
SC6 Olaf Kolzig/95 10.00 25.00
SC7 Doug Gilmour/95 10.00 25.00
SC8 Roman Cechmanek/95 10.00 25.00
SC9 Joe Sakic/95 15.00 40.00
SC10 Daniel Sedin/95 10.00 25.00
SC11 Zigmund Palffy/95 10.00 25.00
SC12 Sergei Fedorov/95 10.00 25.00
SC13 Ed Belfour/95 10.00 25.00
SC14 Tommy Salo/95 10.00 25.00

SC15 Roman Turek/95 10.00 25.00
SC16 Owen Nolan/95 10.00 25.00
SC17 Patrick Roy/80 20.00 50.00
SC18 Luc Robitaille/80 10.00 25.00
SC19 Chris Pronger/80 10.00 25.00
SC20 Mike Modano/80 12.50 30.00
SC21 Martin Brodeur/80 20.00 50.00
SC22 Curtis Joseph/80 10.00 25.00
SC23 Dominik Hasek/80 12.50 30.00
SC24 Mario Lemieux/80 30.00 80.00
SC25 Jason Arnott/60 10.00 25.00
SC26 Johan Hedberg/60 10.00 25.00
SC27 Ray Bourque/60 15.00 40.00
SC28 Al MacInnis/60 10.00 25.00
SC29 Scott Gomez/40 10.00 25.00
SC30 Chris Drury/40 10.00 25.00

2002-03 BAP Memorabilia

1 Steve Yzerman .60 1.50
2 Steve Reinprecht .15 .40
3 Jean-Sebastien Giguere .25 .60
4 Chris Simon .15 .40
5 Dany Heatley .20 .50
6 Brendan Morrison .20 .50
7 Bill Guerin .25 .60
8 Alexander Mogilny .20 .50
9 Martin Biron .20 .50
10 Brad Richards .25 .60
11 Craig Conroy .15 .40
12 Al MacInnis .30 .75
13 Arturs Irbe .20 .50
14 Evgeni Nabokov .20 .50
15 Alexei Zhamnov .20 .50
16 Daniel Briere .20 .50
17 Alex Tanguay .20 .50
18 Milan Kraft .15 .40
19 Marc Denis .20 .50
20 Adam Oates .25 .60
21 Darryl Sydor .15 .40
22 Daniel Alfredsson .25 .60
23 Brendan Shanahan .25 .60
24 Brian Leetch .20 .50
25 Anson Carter .20 .50
26 Adrian Aucoin .15 .40
27 Kristian Huselius .15 .40
28 Jamie Langenbrunner .20 .50
29 Adam Deadmarsh .15 .40
30 Denis Arkhipov .15 .40
31 Andrew Brunette .15 .40
32 Donald Audette .15 .40
33 Rob Blake .25 .60
34 Jaromir Jagr .75 2.00
35 Felix Potvin .40 1.00
36 Dan Cloutier .20 .50
37 Niklas Hagman .15 .40
38 Alyn McCauley .15 .40
39 Eric Brewer .15 .40
40 Nikolai Khabibulin .25 .60
41 Brett Hull .50 1.25
42 Brent Johnson .20 .50
43 Brenden Morrow .20 .50
44 Mike Ricci .15 .40
45 Ray Whitney .20 .50
46 Alexei Kovalev .20 .50
47 Chris Drury .25 .60
48 Daymond Langkow .20 .50
49 Eric Daze .15 .40
50 Pavel Brendl .15 .40
51 Bates Battaglia .15 .40
52 Jani Hurme .20 .50
53 Dean McAmmond .15 .40
54 Dan Blackburn .20 .50
55 Maxim Afinogenov .15 .40
56 Alexei Yashin .20 .50
57 Steve Shields .20 .50
58 Joe Nieuwendyk .20 .50
59 Frantisek Kaberle .15 .40
60 Jan Lasak .20 .50
61 Ron Francis .30 .75
62 Jeff Friesen .15 .40
63 Doug Gilmour .30 .75
64 Jeff Halpern .15 .40
65 Ilya Kovalchuk .30 .75
66 Daniel Sedin .30 .75
67 Glen Murray .20 .50
68 Bryan McCabe .15 .40
69 Miroslav Satan .25 .60
70 Pavel Kubina .15 .40
71 Derek Morris .15 .40
72 Chris Pronger .25 .60
73 Erik Cole .15 .40
74 Owen Nolan .25 .60
75 Jocelyn Thibault .20 .50
76 Jan Hrdina .15 .40
77 Greg DeVries .15 .40
78 Krystofer Kolanos .15 .40
79 David Vyborny .15 .40
80 Jeremy Roenick .40 1.00
81 Jason Arnott .20 .50
82 Mike Leclerc .15 .40
83 Marian Hossa .25 .60
84 Chris Chelios .25 .60
85 Eric Lindros .40 1.00
86 Jochen Hecht .15 .40
87 Chris Osgood .25 .60
88 Roberto Luongo .40 1.00
89 Martin Brodeur .60 1.50
90 Jaroslav Modry .15 .40
91 Martin Erat .15 .40
92 Manny Fernandez .15 .40
93 Jose Theodore .25 .60
94 Olaf Kolzig .25 .60
95 Ed Jovanovski .20 .50
96 Sandis Ozolinsh .15 .40
97 Corey Schwab .20 .50
98 Sami Kapanen .15 .40
99 Mike Comrie .25 .60
100 Shane Willis .15 .40
101 Dominik Hasek .40 1.00
102 Jason Allison .20 .50
103 Doug Weight .25 .60
104 Marty Turco .25 .60
105 Patrick Marleau .25 .60
106 Rostislav Klesla .15 .40
107 Johan Hedberg .25 .60
108 Joe Sakic .50 1.25
109 Marian Gaborik .25 .60
110 Sean Burke .15 .40
111 Mark Bell .15 .40
112 John LeClair .25 .60
113 Jaroslav Svoboda .15 .40
114 Todd Bertuzzi .25 .60
115 Martin Havlat .20 .50
116 Pavel Datsyuk .40 1.00
117 Jarome Iginla .30 .75
118 Mark Messier .50 1.25
119 Stu Barnes .15 .40
120 Shayne Corson .20 .50
121 Mark Parrish .15 .40
122 Joe Thornton .40 1.00
123 Patrik Elias .25 .60
124 Milan Hnilicka .20 .50
125 Mike Dunham .20 .50
126 Oleg Tverdovsky .15 .40
127 Richard Zednik .15 .40
128 Peter Forsberg .50 1.25
129 Mikko Eloranta .15 .40
130 Zdeno Chara .25 .60
131 Curtis Joseph .30 .75
132 Steve Rucchin .15 .40
133 Sergei Fedorov .40 1.00
134 Josef Vasicek .15 .40
135 Ryan Smyth .20 .50
136 Scott Niedermayer .25 .60
137 Shane Doan .20 .50
138 Steve Sullivan .15 .40
139 Stephen Weiss .25 .60
140 Alexander Daigle .15 .40
141 Fred Brathwaite .20 .50
142 Peter Bondra .25 .60
143 Patrik Stefan .20 .50
144 Tony Amonte .20 .50
145 Valeri Bure .20 .50
146 Rick DiPietro .20 .50
147 Martin Straka .20 .50
148 Jeff O'Neill .15 .40
149 Milan Hejduk .20 .50
150 Kirk Maltby .15 .40
151 Mike York .15 .40
152 Scott Gomez .20 .50
153 Mike Peca .20 .50
154 Mike Richter .25 .60
155 Patrick Lalime .20 .50
156 Justin Williams .20 .50
157 Mario Lemieux 1.00 2.50
158 Kevin Weekes .20 .50
159 Scott Young .15 .40
160 Tommy Salo .20 .50
161 Steve Webb .15 .40
162 Teemu Selanne .50 1.25
163 Jozef Stumpel .15 .40
164 Patrick Roy .60 1.50
165 Zigmund Palffy .25 .60
166 Pavel Bure .25 .60
167 Vincent Damphousse .20 .50
168 Sergei Gonchar .20 .50
169 Sergei Samsonov .20 .50
170 Luc Robitaille .25 .60
171 Scott Stevens .25 .60
172 Robert Lang .15 .40
173 Henrik Sedin .30 .75
174 Tim Connolly .15 .40
175 Pierre Turgeon .20 .50
176 Yanic Perreault .15 .40
177 Radek Bonk .20 .50
178 Keith Tkachuk .25 .60
179 Paul Kariya .25 .60
180 Mike Modano .40 1.00
181 Saku Koivu .25 .60
182 Mark Recchi .30 .75
183 Roman Turek .25 .60
184 Kris Draper .15 .40
185 Scott Hartnell .15 .40
186 Keith Primeau .20 .50
187 Vincent Lecavalier .25 .60
188 Darcy Tucker .15 .40
189 Markus Naslund .25 .60
190 Pavol Demitra .30 .75
191 Gary Roberts .15 .40
192 Rod Brind'Amour .25 .60
193 Radim Vrbata .15 .40
194 Nicklas Lidstrom .25 .60
195 Tom Poti .15 .40
196 Roman Cechmanek .20 .50
197 Scott Mellanby .15 .40
198 Mats Sundin .25 .60
199 Filip Kuba .15 .40
200 Simon Gagne .25 .60
201 Paul Kariya FP .40 1.00
202 Ilya Kovalchuk FP .50 1.25
203 Joe Thornton FP .60 1.50
204 Miroslav Satan FP .40 1.00
205 Jarome Iginla FP .50 1.25
206 Ron Francis FP .50 1.25
207 Eric Daze FP .25 .60
208 Patrick Roy FP 1.00 2.50
209 Rostislav Klesla FP .25 .60
210 Mike Modano FP .60 1.50
211 Steve Yzerman FP 1.00 2.50
212 Mike Comrie FP .40 1.00
213 Roberto Luongo FP .60 1.50
214 Zigmund Palffy FP .40 1.00
215 Marian Gaborik FP .40 1.00
216 Jose Theodore FP .40 1.00
217 Scott Hartnell FP .25 .60
218 Martin Brodeur FP 1.00 2.50
219 Alexei Yashin FP .30 .75
220 Pavel Bure FP .40 1.00
221 Marian Hossa FP .40 1.00
222 Simon Gagne FP .40 1.00
223 Daniel Briere FP .30 .75
224 Mario Lemieux FP 1.50 4.00
225 Chris Pronger FP .40 1.00
226 Owen Nolan FP .40 1.00
227 Nikolai Khabibulin FP .40 1.00
228 Mats Sundin FP .40 1.00
229 Markus Naslund FP .40 1.00
230 Jaromir Jagr FP 1.25 3.00
231 P.Forsberg/E.Lindros .75 2.00
232 P.Roy/J.Thibault 1.00 2.50
233 T.Sawchuk/J.Bucyk .75 2.00
234 J.Plante/G.Worsley .50 1.25
235 C.Pronger/B.Shanahan .40 1.00
236 E.Lindros/P.Brendl .60 1.50
237 K.Beech/J.Jagr 1.25 3.00
238 E.Jovanovski/P.Bure .40 1.00
239 J.Iginla/J.Nieuwendyk .50 1.25
240 D.Hasek/E.Daze .60 1.50
241 D.Savard/C.Chelios .40 1.00
242 A.Oates/J.Allison .40 1.00
243 D.Hasek/S.Kozlov .60 1.50
244 R.Svehla/D.Yushkevich .25 .60
245 T.Linden/T.Bertuzzi .40 1.00
246 G.Lafleur/S.Zubov .50 1.25
247 J.Arnott/B.Guerin .40 1.00
248 A.Mogilny/M.Peca .30 .75
249 B.Shanahan/K.Primeau .40 1.00
250 J.LeClair/M.Recchi .50 1.25
251 R.Blake/A.Deadmarsh .40 1.00
252 J.Roenick/A.Zhamnov .60 1.50
253 M.Peca/T.Connolly .30 .75
254 S.Ozolinsh/O.Nolan .40 1.00
255 C.Drury/M.Fernandez .40 1.00
256 R.Turek/F.Braithwaite .40 1.00
257 J.Arnott/J.Nieuwendyk .30 .75
258 D.Andreychuk/B.Rolston .40 1.00
259 B.Berard/F.Potvin .60 1.50
260 V.Bure/R.Niedermayer .30 .75
261 B.Boucher/M.Handzus .30 .75
262 Adam Oates .40 1.00
263 Bobby Holik .25 .60
264 Robert Lang .25 .60
265 Curtis Joseph .50 1.25
266 Ed Belfour .40 1.00
267 Darius Kasparaitis .25 .60
268 Bill Guerin .40 1.00
269 Petr Sykora
Oleg Tverdovsky .30 .75
270 Tony Amonte .30 .75
271 P-M Bouchard RC .75 2.00
272 Rick Nash RC 4.00 10.00
273 Dennis Seidenberg RC .75 2.00
274 Jay Bouwmeester RC 2.50 6.00
275 Stanislav Chistov RC .50 1.25
276 Kurt Sauer RC .50 1.25
277 Ivan Majesky RC .50 1.25
278 Chuck Kobasew RC .60 1.50
279 Jeff Taffe RC .50 1.25
280 Mikael Tellqvist RC .50 1.25
281 Ales Hemsky RC 2.00 5.00
282 Patrick Sharp RC 1.50 4.00
283 Jordan Leopold RC .75 2.00
284 Dmitri Bykov RC .50 1.25
285 Alex Henry RC .60 1.50
286 Henrik Zetterberg RC 5.00 12.00
287 Alexander Frolov RC 1.25 3.00
288 Steve Eminger RC .50 1.25
289 Carlo Colaiacovo RC .75 2.00
290 Tom Koivisto RC .50 1.25
291 Shawn Thornton RC .60 1.50
292 Ron Hainsey RC .50 1.25
293 Martin Gerber RC .75 2.00
294 Adam Hall RC .50 1.25
295 Jason Spezza RC 3.00 8.00
296 Anton Volchenkov RC .50 1.25
297 Jeff Paul RC .50 1.25
298 Scottie Upshall RC .60 1.50
299 Alexander Svitov RC .50 1.25
300 Alexei Smirnov RC .60 1.50
301 Ed Belfour .75 2.00
302 Ryan Bayda RC .50 1.25
303 Jerred Smithson RC .50 1.25
304 Mike Komisarek RC .75 2.00
305 Jarret Stoll RC 2.00 5.00
306 Radovan Somik RC .50 1.25
307 Rob Davison RC .50 1.25
308 Jason King RC .75 2.00
309 Tony Amonte .20 .50
310 Cam Severson RC .50 1.25
311 Matt Walker RC .50 1.25
312 Jesse Fibiger RC .50 1.25
313 Ray Emery RC 1.50 4.00
314 Vernon Fiddler RC .60 1.50
315 Alex Kovalev .20 .50
316 Marc-Andre Bergeron RC .60 1.50
317 Jason Elliott RC .50 1.25
318 Craig Andersson RC 2.50 6.00
319 Sandis Ozolinsh .15 .40
320 Ryan Miller RC 3.00 8.00
321 Chris Osgood .25 .60
322 Michael Garnett RC .50 1.25
323 Bobby Allen RC .50 1.25
324 Cristobal Huet RC 1.00 2.50
325 Curtis Murphy RC .50 1.25
326 Darren Haydar RC .50 1.25
327 Mathieu Schneider .15 .40
328 Ray Schultz RC .50 1.25
329 Jim Vandermeer RC .50 1.25
330 Miroslav Zalesak RC .50 1.25
331 Christian Backman RC .50 1.25
332 John Craighead RC .50 1.25
333 Doug Gilmour .30 .75
334 Dick Tarnstrom RC .50 1.25
335 Chad Wiseman RC .50 1.25
336 John Tripp RC .50 1.25
337 Ari Ahonen RC .50 1.25
338 Rickard Wallin RC .50 1.25
339 Jonathan Hedstrom RC .50 1.25
340 Daniel Briere .20 .50
341 Paul Manning RC .50 1.25
342 Igor Radulov RC .50 1.25
343 Tomas Malec RC .50 1.25
344 Sean McMorrow RC .50 1.25
345 Dany Sabourin RC .50 1.25
346 Steve Thomas .15 .40
347 Shaone Morrisonn RC .50 1.25
348 Brad Defauw RC .50 1.25
349 Michael Leighton RC .75 2.00
350 Pascal Leclaire RC .60 1.50
351 Chris Schmidt RC .50 1.25
352 Stephane Veilleux RC .50 1.25
353 Jim Fahey RC .50 1.25
354 Konstantin Koltsov RC .60 1.50
355 Cody Rudkowsky RC .60 1.50
356 Anson Carter .20 .50
357 Francois Beauchemin RC .75 2.00
358 Patrick Boileau RC .50 1.25
359 Sylvain Blouin RC .50 1.25
360 Eric Bertrand RC .50 1.25
361 Jamie Hodson RC .50 1.25
362 Curtis Sanford RC .75 2.00
363 Ryan Kraft RC .50 1.25
364 Owen Nolan .25 .60
365 Niko Dimitrakos RC .50 1.25
366 Simon Gamache RC .50 1.25
367 Doug Janik RC .50 1.25
368 Tomas Kurka UER RC .50 1.25
369 Josh Harding RC 6.00 15.00
370 Radoslav Hecl RC .50 1.25
371 Kris Vernarsky RC .50 1.25
372 Steve Ott RC .50 1.25
373 Frederic Cloutier RC .50 1.25
374 Eric Godard RC .50 1.25
375 Kari Haakana RC .50 1.25
376 Tomi Pettinen RC .50 1.25
377 Brooks Orpik RC .50 1.25
378 Lynn Loyns RC .50 1.25
379 Radim Vrbata .15 .40
380 Fernando Pisani RC .60 1.50
381 Alexei Semenov RC .50 1.25
382 Burke Henry RC .50 1.25
383 Tim Thomas RC 2.50 6.00
384 Mike Siklenka RC 1.25 3.00
385 Lasse Pirjeta RC .50 1.25
386 Tomas Zizka RC .50 1.25
387 Tomas Surovy RC .50 1.25
388 Paul Gaustad RC .50 1.25
389 Martin Samuelsson RC .50 1.25
390 Matt Henderson RC .50 1.25
391 Mike Dunham .20 .50
392 Levente Szuper RC .75 2.00
393 Jared Aulin RC .50 1.25
394 Brandon Reid RC .50 1.25
395 Mike Cammalleri RC 1.50 4.00
396 Ian MacNeil RC .50 1.25
397 Brad Isbister .15 .40
398 Garnet Exelby RC .50 1.25
399 Jason Bacashihua RC .60 1.50
400 Sami Kapanen .15 .40

2002-03 BAP Memorabilia Ruby

*1-200 VETS: 2X TO 5X BASE HI
*201-270 VETS: 1X TO 2.5X BASE SP
*271-300 ROOKIES: .6X TO 1.5X

2002-03 BAP Memorabilia Sapphire

*1-200 VETS: 4X TO 10X BASE HI
*201-270 VETS: 5X TO 5X BASE SP
*271-300 ROOKIES: 1.2X TO 3X

2002-03 BAP Memorabilia All-Star Jerseys

ASJ1 Daniel Alfredsson 6.00 15.00
ASJ2 Tony Amonte 6.00 15.00
ASJ3 Ed Belfour 6.00 15.00
ASJ4 Rob Blake 6.00 15.00
ASJ5 Peter Bondra 6.00 15.00
ASJ6 Martin Brodeur 12.50 30.00
ASJ7 Pavel Bure 6.00 15.00
ASJ8 Chris Chelios 6.00 15.00
ASJ9 Eric Daze 6.00 15.00
ASJ10 Pavol Demitra 6.00 15.00
ASJ11 Patrik Elias 6.00 15.00
ASJ12 Sergei Fedorov 10.00 25.00
ASJ13 Theo Fleury 6.00 15.00
ASJ14 Peter Forsberg 12.50 30.00
ASJ15 Simon Gagne 6.00 15.00
ASJ16 Bill Guerin 6.00 15.00
ASJ17 Dominik Hasek 12.50 30.00
ASJ18 Milan Hejduk 6.00 15.00
ASJ19 Brett Hull 12.50 30.00
ASJ20 Jarome Iginla 8.00 20.00
ASJ21 Arturs Irbe 8.00 20.00
ASJ22 Jaromir Jagr 12.50 30.00
ASJ23 Curtis Joseph 6.00 15.00
ASJ24 Ed Jovanovski 6.00 15.00
ASJ25 Paul Kariya 6.00 15.00
ASJ26 Nikolai Khabibulin 6.00 15.00
ASJ27 Saku Koivu 6.00 15.00
ASJ28 Alexei Kovalev 6.00 15.00
ASJ29 John LeClair 6.00 15.00
ASJ30 Brian Leetch 6.00 15.00
ASJ31 Mario Lemieux 15.00 40.00
ASJ32 Nicklas Lidstrom 6.00 15.00
ASJ33 Eric Lindros 6.00 15.00
ASJ34 Al MacInnis 6.00 15.00
ASJ35 Mark Messier 6.00 15.00
ASJ36 Mike Modano 8.00 20.00
ASJ37 Alexander Mogilny 6.00 15.00
ASJ38 Evgeni Nabokov 6.00 15.00
ASJ39 Markus Naslund 6.00 15.00
ASJ40 Scott Niedermayer 6.00 15.00
ASJ41 Owen Nolan 6.00 15.00
ASJ42 Felix Potvin 8.00 20.00
ASJ43 Sandis Ozolinsh 6.00 15.00
ASJ44 Zigmund Palffy 6.00 15.00
ASJ45 Chris Pronger 6.00 15.00
ASJ46 Mark Recchi 6.00 15.00
ASJ47 Mike Richter 6.00 15.00
ASJ48 Luc Robitaille 6.00 15.00
ASJ49 Jeremy Roenick 8.00 20.00
ASJ50 Patrick Roy 20.00 50.00
ASJ51 Joe Sakic 12.50 30.00
ASJ52 Teemu Selanne 6.00 15.00
ASJ53 Brendan Shanahan 6.00 15.00
ASJ54 Mats Sundin 6.00 15.00
ASJ55 Jose Theodore 8.00 20.00
ASJ56 Joe Thornton 8.00 20.00
ASJ57 Keith Tkachuk 6.00 15.00
ASJ58 Doug Weight 6.00 15.00
ASJ59 Alexei Yashin 6.00 15.00
ASJ60 Steve Yzerman 15.00 40.00

2002-03 BAP Memorabilia All-Star Starting Lineup

AS1 Patrick Roy 60.00 125.00
AS2 Chris Pronger 20.00 50.00
AS3 Rob Blake 20.00 50.00
AS4 Vincent Damphousse 20.00 50.00
AS5 Owen Nolan 20.00 50.00
AS6 Brendan Shanahan 20.00 50.00
AS7 Dominik Hasek 30.00 80.00
AS8 Nicklas Lidstrom 20.00 50.00
AS9 Sandis Ozolinsh 20.00 50.00
AS10 Sergei Fedorov 20.00 50.00
AS11 Jaromir Jagr 25.00 60.00
AS12 Teemu Selanne 20.00 50.00

2002-03 BAP Memorabilia All-Star Teammmates

AST1 S.Fedorov/T.Selanne 12.50 30.00
AST2 C.Joseph/J.Roenick 12.50 30.00
AST3 P.Roy/M.Messier 20.00 50.00
AST4 M.Lemieux/M.Messier 25.00 60.00
AST5 B.Shanahan/J.Jagr 12.50 30.00
AST6 A.Mogilny/P.Kariya 12.50 30.00
AST7 S.Yzerman/O.Nolan 25.00 60.00
AST8 T.Fleury/M.Sundin 12.50 30.00
AST9 M.Brodeur/D.Hasek 25.00 60.00
AST10 P.Bure/P.Forsberg 12.50 30.00
AST11 J.Jagr/D.Hasek 12.50 30.00
AST12 E.Lindros/M.Modano 12.50 30.00
AST13 E.Lindros/K.Tkachuk 12.50 30.00
AST14 P.Forsberg/D.Hasek 15.00 40.00
AST15 A.Yashin/T.Selanne 12.50 30.00
AST16 J.Jagr/M.Sundin 12.50 30.00
AST17 S.Yzerman/J.Roenick 20.00 50.00
AST18 M.Brodeur/C.Joseph 20.00 50.00
AST19 C.Pronger/T.Amonte 12.50 30.00
AST20 E.Lindros/M.Messier 15.00 40.00
AST21 J.Sakic/B.Guerin 12.50 30.00
AST22 M.Lemieux/P.Roy 30.00 80.00
AST23 E.Nabokov/D.Hasek 12.50 30.00
AST24 P.Forsberg/P.Bure 20.00 50.00
AST25 P.Kariya/M.Brodeur 20.00 50.00
AST26 J.Theodore/P.Roy 30.00 80.00
AST27 B.Shanahan/O.Nolan 12.50 30.00
AST28 J.Iginla/M.Lemieux 25.00 60.00
AST29 J.Jagr/N.Lidstrom 12.50 30.00
AST30 T.Selanne/S.Fedorov 12.50 30.00

2002-03 BAP Memorabilia All-Star Triple Jerseys

ASTJ1 Rob Blake 12.50 30.00
ASTJ2 Martin Brodeur 30.00 80.00
ASTJ3 Pavel Bure 12.50 30.00
ASTJ4 Peter Forsberg 25.00 60.00
ASTJ5 Dominik Hasek 15.00 40.00
ASTJ6 Jaromir Jagr 15.00 40.00
ASTJ7 Paul Kariya 12.50 30.00
ASTJ8 John LeClair 12.50 30.00
ASTJ9 Brian Leetch 12.50 30.00
ASTJ10 Mario Lemieux 40.00 100.00
ASTJ11 Nicklas Lidstrom 12.50 30.00
ASTJ12 Eric Lindros 12.50 30.00
ASTJ13 Al MacInnis 12.50 30.00
ASTJ14 Mark Messier 25.00 60.00
ASTJ15 Mike Modano 15.00 40.00
ASTJ16 Owen Nolan 12.50 30.00
ASTJ17 Patrick Roy 50.00 100.00
ASTJ18 Teemu Selanne 12.50 30.00
ASTJ19 Brendan Shanahan 12.50 30.00
ASTJ20 Mats Sundin 12.50 30.00

2002-03 BAP Memorabilia Draft Redemptions

1 Rick Nash/67* 60.00 120.00
2 Kari Lehtonen/64* 40.00 80.00
3 Jay Bouwmeester/63* 25.00 60.00
4 Joni Pitkanen/100 20.00 50.00
5 Ryan Whitney/63* 15.00 40.00
6 Scottie Upshall/52* 12.00 30.00
7 Joffrey Lupul/56* 20.00 50.00
8 P-M Bouchard/50* 25.00 60.00
9 Petr Taticek/40* 8.00 20.00
10 Eric Nystrom/54* 6.00 15.00
11 Keith Ballard/45* 6.00 15.00
12 Steve Eminger/51* 12.00 30.00
13 Alexander Semin/45* 25.00 60.00
14 Chris Higgins/61* 15.00 40.00
16 Jakub Klepis/38* 8.00 20.00
17 Boyd Gordon/54* 10.00 25.00
18 Denis Grebeshkov/44* 10.00 25.00
20 Daniel Paille/46* 20.00 50.00
21 Anton Babchuk/38* 10.00 25.00
22 Sean Bergenheim/45* 12.50 30.00
23 Ben Eager/44* 10.00 25.00
24 Alexander Steen/49* 20.00 40.00
25 Cam Ward/57* 15.00 40.00
28 Jones Johansson/36* 8.00 20.00
29 Hannu Toivonen/59* 12.00 30.00
30 Jim Slater/48* 6.00 15.00

2002-03 BAP Memorabilia Franchise Players

FP1 Paul Kariya 8.00 20.00
FP2 Ilya Kovalchuk 12.00 30.00
FP3 Joe Thornton 12.00 30.00
FP4 Miroslav Satan 8.00 20.00
FP5 Jarome Iginla 10.00 25.00
FP6 Ron Francis 8.00 20.00
FP7 Eric Daze 8.00 20.00
FP8 Patrick Roy 12.00 30.00
FP9 Rostislav Klesla 8.00 20.00
FP10 Mike Modano 10.00 25.00
FP11 Steve Yzerman 15.00 40.00
FP12 Mike Comrie 8.00 20.00
FP13 Roberto Luongo 10.00 25.00
FP14 Zigmund Palffy 8.00 20.00
FP15 Marian Gaborik 12.00 30.00
FP16 Jose Theodore 10.00 25.00
FP17 Scott Hartnell 10.00 25.00
FP18 Martin Brodeur 12.00 30.00
FP19 Alexei Yashin 8.00 20.00
FP20 Pavel Bure 8.00 20.00
FP21 Marian Hossa 8.00 20.00
FP22 Simon Gagne 10.00 25.00
FP23 Daniel Briere 8.00 20.00
FP24 Mario Lemieux 20.00 50.00
FP25 Chris Pronger 8.00 20.00
FP26 Owen Nolan 8.00 20.00
FP27 Nikolai Khabibulin 8.00 20.00
FP28 Mats Sundin 8.00 20.00
FP29 Markus Naslund 8.00 20.00
FP30 Jaromir Jagr 10.00 25.00

2002-03 BAP Memorabilia Future of the Game

FG1 Pavel Datsyuk 15.00 40.00
FG2 Dan Blackburn 12.50 30.00
FG3 Ilya Kovalchuk 20.00 50.00
FG4 Roberto Luongo 20.00 50.00
FG5 Dany Heatley 20.00 50.00
FG6 Jose Theodore 15.00 40.00
FG7 Mike Comrie 12.50 30.00
FG8 Marian Gaborik 25.00 60.00
FG9 Simon Gagne 15.00 40.00
FG10 Joe Thornton 25.00 60.00
FG11 Trent Hunter 12.50 30.00
FG12 Martin Havlat 12.50 30.00
FG13 Scott Hartnell 15.00 40.00
FG14 Kristian Huselius 12.50 30.00
FG15 Rick DiPietro 12.50 30.00
FG16 Kyle Calder 12.50 30.00
FG17 Alex Tanguay 12.50 30.00
FG18 Brad Richards 12.50 30.00
FG19 Rostislav Klesla 12.50 30.00
FG20 Justin Williams 12.50 30.00
FG21 Jason Spezza 30.00 80.00
FG22 Jay Bouwmeester 12.50 30.00

2002-03 BAP Memorabilia He Shoots He Scores Points

1 Mike Modano 1 pt. .25 .60
2 Jeremy Roenick 1 pt. .25 .60
3 Owen Nolan 1 pt. .15 .40
4 Chris Pronger 1 pt. .15 .40
6 Jose Theodore 1 pt. .15 .40
7 Brendan Shanahan 1 pt. .15 .40
8 Dany Heatley 1 pt. .12 .30
9 Paul Kariya 2 pts. .20 .50
10 Pavel Bure 2 pts. .20 .50
11 Peter Forsberg 2 pts. .40 1.00
12 Joe Sakic 2 pts. .40 1.00
13 Dominik Hasek 2 pts. .30 .75
14 Martin Brodeur 2 pts. .50 1.25
15 Eric Lindros 2 pts. .30 .75
16 Ilya Kovalchuk 2 pts. .25 .60
17 Jaromir Jagr 2 pts. .60 1.50
18 Patrick Roy 3 pts. .50 1.25
19 Mario Lemieux 3 pts. .75 2.00
20 Steve Yzerman 3 pts. .50 1.25

2002-03 BAP Memorabilia He Shoots He Scores Prizes

1 Steve Yzerman 25.00 60.00
2 Mario Lemieux 40.00 100.00
3 Patrick Roy 25.00 60.00
4 Jaromir Jagr 30.00 80.00
5 Ilya Kovalchuk 12.00 30.00
6 Eric Lindros 15.00 40.00
7 Martin Brodeur 25.00 60.00
8 Dominik Hasek 15.00 40.00
9 Joe Sakic 20.00 50.00
10 Peter Forsberg 20.00 50.00
11 Pavel Bure 10.00 25.00
12 Paul Kariya 10.00 25.00
13 Dany Heatley 8.00 20.00
14 Brendan Shanahan 10.00 25.00
15 Jose Theodore 10.00 25.00
16 Ron Francis 12.00 30.00
17 Chris Pronger 10.00 25.00
18 Owen Nolan 10.00 25.00
19 Jeremy Roenick 15.00 40.00
20 Mike Modano 15.00 40.00
21 Roberto Luongo 15.00 40.00
22 Marian Gaborik 10.00 25.00
23 Todd Bertuzzi 10.00 25.00
24 Pavel Datsyuk 15.00 40.00
25 Jarome Iginla 12.00 30.00
26 Mats Sundin 10.00 25.00
27 Mark Messier 20.00 50.00
28 Sergei Fedorov 15.00 40.00
29 Nicklas Lidstrom 10.00 25.00
30 Teemu Selanne 20.00 50.00

2002-03 BAP Memorabilia Magnificent Inserts

MI1 2000-01 Jersey 30.00 80.00
MI2 1985-86 Jersey 30.00 80.00
MI3 2002 All-Star Jersey 30.00 80.00
MI4 1987 Canada Cup Jersey 30.00 80.00
MI5 Dual Jersey 50.00 125.00

2002-03 BAP Memorabilia Magnificent Inserts Autographs

MI1 Mario Lemieux 75.00 150.00
MI2 Mario Lemieux 75.00 150.00
MI3 Mario Lemieux 75.00 150.00
MI4 Mario Lemieux 75.00 150.00
MI5 Mario Lemieux Dual 100.00 200.00

2002-03 BAP Memorabilia Mini Stanley Cups

1 Johnny Bower 8.00 20.00
2 Tim Horton 12.00 30.00
3 Jean Beliveau 15.00 40.00
4 Lorne Worsley 8.00 20.00
5 Terry Sawchuk 12.00 30.00
6 Serge Savard 8.00 20.00
7 Henri Richard 8.00 20.00
8 Phil Esposito 8.00 20.00
9 Frank Mahovlich 8.00 20.00
10 Gerry Cheevers 8.00 20.00
11 Yvan Cournoyer 8.00 20.00
12 Bobby Clarke 8.00 20.00
13 Bernie Parent 8.00 20.00
14 Steve Shutt 8.00 20.00
15 Larry Robinson 8.00 20.00
16 Guy Lafleur 15.00 40.00
17 Guy Lapointe 8.00 20.00
18 Bryan Trottier 8.00 20.00
19 Mike Bossy 10.00 25.00
20 Denis Potvin 8.00 20.00
21 Bob Nystrom 8.00 20.00
22 Mark Messier 8.00 20.00
23 Andy Moog 8.00 20.00
24 Patrick Roy 20.00 50.00
25 Jari Kurri 10.00 25.00
26 Grant Fuhr 8.00 20.00
27 Doug Gilmour 8.00 20.00
28 Adam Graves 8.00 20.00
29 Mario Lemieux 20.00 50.00
30 Jaromir Jagr 15.00 40.00
31 John LeClair 8.00 20.00
32 Brian Leetch 8.00 20.00
33 Martin Brodeur 15.00 40.00
34 Peter Forsberg 12.00 30.00
35 Steve Yzerman 15.00 40.00
36 Nicklas Lidstrom 12.00 30.00
37 Mike Modano 12.00 30.00
38 Scott Stevens 8.00 20.00
39 Joe Sakic 12.00 30.00
40 Dominik Hasek 12.00 30.00

2002-03 BAP Memorabilia Stanley Cup Champions

SCC1 Jiri Fischer 15.00 40.00
SCC2 Mathieu Dandenault 15.00 40.00
SCC3 Chris Chelios 15.00 40.00
SCC4 Dominik Hasek 25.00 50.00
SCC5 Steve Yzerman 20.00 50.00
SCC6 Brendan Shanahan 15.00 40.00
SCC7 Luc Robitaille 15.00 40.00
SCC8 Nicklas Lidstrom 15.00 40.00
SCC9 Manny Legace 20.00 40.00
SCC10 Sergei Fedorov 30.00 60.00
SCC11 Darren McCarty 15.00 40.00
SCC12 Jason Williams 15.00 40.00
SCC13 Pavel Datsyuk 15.00 40.00
SCC14 Tomas Holmstrom 15.00 40.00
SCC15 Brett Hull 12.00 30.00

2002-03 BAP Memorabilia Stanley Cup Playoffs

SC1 Roman Cechmanek/90 8.00 20.00
SC2 Patrick Lalime/90 8.00 20.00
SC3 Gary Roberts/90 8.00 20.00
SC4 Alexei Yashin/90 8.00 20.00
SC5 Joe Thornton/90 12.00 30.00
SC6 Jose Theodore/90 15.00 40.00
SC7 Ron Francis/90 12.00 30.00
SC8 Martin Brodeur/90 20.00 50.00
SC9 Owen Nolan/90 8.00 20.00
SC10 Sean Burke/90 8.00 20.00
SC11 Felix Potvin/90 15.00 40.00
SC12 Peter Forsberg/90 15.00 40.00
SC13 Todd Bertuzzi/90 8.00 20.00
SC14 Steve Yzerman/90 20.00 50.00
SC15 Eric Daze/90 8.00 20.00
SC16 Brent Johnson/90 8.00 20.00
SC17 Teemu Selanne/60 8.00 20.00
SC18 Chris Drury/60 8.00 20.00
SC19 Alexander Mogilny/60 8.00 20.00
SC20 Daniel Alfredsson/60 8.00 20.00
SC21 Sergei Fedorov/60 15.00 40.00
SC22 Keith Tkachuk/60 12.00 30.00
SC23 Saku Koivu/60 8.00 20.00
SC24 Jeff O'Neill/60 8.00 20.00
SC25 Curtis Joseph/40 15.00 40.00
SC26 Arturs Irbe/40 15.00 40.00
SC27 Dominik Hasek/40 30.00 80.00
SC28 Patrick Roy/40 30.00 80.00
SC29 Ron Francis/30 25.00 60.00
SC30 Dominik Hasek/30 20.00 50.00

2002-03 BAP Memorabilia Teammates

TM1 D.Hasek/S.Yzerman 25.00 60.00
TM2 S.Fedorov/B.Shanahan 15.00 40.00
TM3 L.Robitaille/B.Hull 15.00 40.00
TM4 J.Sakic/P.Forsberg 25.00 60.00
TM5 R.Blake/P.Roy 15.00 40.00
TM6 P.Bure/E.Lindros 12.50 30.00
TM7 B.Leetch/M.Messier 15.00 40.00
TM8 M.Sundin/C.Joseph 12.50 30.00
TM9 J.Roenick/R.Cechmanek 12.50 30.00
TM10 M.Recchi/S.Gagne 12.50 30.00
TM11 J.Jagr/P.Bondra 12.50 30.00
TM12 J.Theodore/S.Koivu 12.50 30.00
TM13 Z.Palffy/F.Potvin 12.50 30.00
TM14 M.Brodeur/P.Elias 20.00 50.00
TM15 M.Lemieux/A.Kovalev 25.00 60.00
TM16 C.Pronger/A.MacInnis 12.50 30.00
TM17 D.Weight/K.Tkachuk 12.50 30.00
TM18 T.Selanne/O.Nolan 12.50 30.00
TM19 E.Jovanovski/M.Naslund 12.50 30.00
TM20 J.Iginla/R.Turek 15.00 40.00

2003-04 BAP Memorabilia

COMP. SET w/o UPDATE (200) 20.00 50.00
COMP.SET w/o SP's (170) 10.00 25.00
1 Al MacInnis .40 1.00
2 Alexei Morozov .20 .50
3 Ales Hemsky .30 .75
4 Ales Kotalik .20 .50
5 Alex Kovalev .25 .60
6 Alexander Frolov .25 .60
7 Alexander Mogilny .25 .60
8 Alexei Yashin .25 .60
9 Alexei Zhamnov .25 .60
10 Anson Carter .25 .60
11 Barret Jackman .20 .50
12 Bill Guerin .30 .75
13 Brad Richards .30 .75
14 Brad Stuart .20 .50
15 Brendan Shanahan .30 .75
16 Chris Drury .25 .60
17 Brett Hull .60 1.50
18 Daniel Alfredsson .30 .75
19 Daniel Briere .30 .75
20 Dany Heatley .25 .60
21 David Legwand .25 .60
22 Daymond Langkow .20 .50
23 Derian Hatcher .20 .50
24 Doug Weight .30 .75
25 Ed Jovanovski .25 .60
26 Eric Daze .25 .60
27 Eric Lindros .50 1.25
28 Geoff Sanderson .20 .50
29 Glen Murray .25 .60
30 Henrik Zetterberg .40 1.00
31 Ilya Kovalchuk .30 .75
32 Jamie Langenbrunner .25 .60
33 Jarome Iginla .40 1.00
34 Jaromir Jagr 1.00 2.50
35 Jason Allison .25 .60
36 Jason Spezza .30 .75
37 Jay Bouwmeester .20 .50
38 Jeff O'Neill .20 .50
39 Jere Lehtinen .25 .60
40 Jeremy Roenick .50 1.25
41 Joe Sakic .60 1.50
42 Joe Thornton .50 1.25
43 John LeClair .30 .75
44 Keith Tkachuk .30 .75
45 Kristian Huselius .20 .50
46 Marian Gaborik .30 .75
47 Marian Hossa .30 .75
48 Mario Lemieux 1.25 3.00
49 Mark Messier .60 1.50
50 Markus Naslund .30 .75
51 Martin Havlat .30 .75

52 Martin St. Louis .30 .75
53 Mats Sundin .30 .75
54 Michael Peca .25 .60
55 Mike Comrie .25 .60
56 Mike Johnson .20 .50
57 Mike Komisarek .20 .50
58 Mike Modano .50 1.25
59 Milan Hejduk .25 .60
60 Miroslav Satan .25 .60
61 Nicklas Lidstrom .30 .75
62 Olli Jokinen .30 .75
63 Owen Nolan .30 .75
64 Pascal Dupuis .20 .50
65 Patrick Marleau .30 .75
66 Patrik Elias .30 .75
67 Patrik Stefan .20 .50
68 Paul Kariya .30 .75
69 Pavel Bure .30 .75
70 Pavol Demitra .40 1.00
71 Peter Bondra .30 .75
72 Peter Forsberg .60 1.50
73 Petr Sykora .25 .60
74 Ray Whitney .25 .60
75 Richard Zednik .20 .50
76 Rick Nash .30 .75
77 Rob Blake .30 .75
78 Ron Francis .40 1.00
79 Ryan Smyth .25 .60
80 Saku Koivu .30 .75
81 Sandis Ozolinsh .20 .50
82 Scott Hartnell .20 .50
83 Scott Niedermayer .30 .75
84 Scottie Upshall .25 .60
85 Sergei Fedorov .50 1.25
86 Sergei Gonchar .20 .50
87 Sergei Samsonov .25 .60
88 Sergei Zubov .25 .60
89 Simon Gagne .30 .75
90 Zdeno Chara .30 .75
91 Chuck Kobasew .20 .50
92 Steve Yzerman .75 2.00
93 Teemu Selanne .60 1.50
94 Todd Bertuzzi .30 .75
95 Tony Amonte .25 .60
96 Vaclav Prospal .20 .50
97 Vincent Lecavalier .30 .75
98 Slava Kozlov .25 .60
99 Sylvester Flis .50 1.25
100 Zigmund Palffy .30 .75
101 Alex Auld .20 .50
102 Andrew Raycroft .25 .60
103 Ari Ahonen .20 .50
104 Brent Johnson .20 .50
105 Brian Boucher .25 .60
106 Brian Finley .20 .50
107 Byron Dafoe .25 .60
108 Chris Osgood .30 .75
109 Cristobal Huet .25 .60
110 Corey Schwab .25 .60
111 Curtis Joseph .40 1.00
112 Curtis Sanford .20 .50
113 Dan Blackburn .20 .50
114 Dan Cloutier .20 .50
115 David Aebischer .25 .60
116 Dwayne Roloson .25 .60
117 Ed Belfour .30 .75
118 Evgeni Nabokov .25 .60
119 Felix Potvin .50 1.25
120 Fred Brathwaite .25 .60
121 Garth Snow .25 .60
122 Jani Hurme .20 .50
123 Jason Bacashihua .20 .50
124 Jean-Sebastien Giguere .30 .75
125 Jeff Hackett .25 .60
126 Jocelyn Thibault .25 .60
127 Johan Hedberg .25 .60
128 John Grahame .20 .50
129 Jose Theodore .30 .75
130 Josh Harding .25 .60
131 Jussi Markkanen .20 .50
132 Kevin Weekes .20 .50
133 Manny Fernandez .20 .50
134 Manny Legace .20 .50
135 Marc Denis .25 .60
136 Martin Biron .25 .60
137 Martin Brodeur .75 2.00
138 Martin Gerber .20 .50
139 Martin Prusek .20 .50
140 Marty Turco .30 .75
141 Mathieu Garon .20 .50
142 Maxime Ouellet .25 .60
143 Michael Leighton .20 .50
144 Miikka Kiprusoff .25 .60
145 Mika Noronen .20 .50
146 Mikael Tellqvist .25 .60
147 Mike Dunham .25 .60
148 Nikolai Khabibulin .30 .75
149 Olaf Kolzig .30 .75
150 Pascal Leclaire .20 .50
151 Pasi Nurminen .25 .60
152 Patrick Lalime .25 .60
153 Patrick Roy .75 2.00
154 Ray Emery .25 .60
155 Rick DiPietro .25 .60
156 Robert Esche .20 .50
157 Roberto Luongo .50 1.25
158 Roman Cechmanek .25 .60
159 Roman Turek .25 .60
160 Ron Tugnutt .25 .60
161 Ryan Miller .30 .75
162 Sean Burke .20 .50
163 Sebastien Caron .25 .60
164 Sebastien Charpentier .20 .50
165 Steve Shields .20 .50
166 Tomas Vokoun .20 .50
167 Tommy Salo .25 .60
168 Trevor Kidd .20 .50
169 Vesa Toskala .20 .50
170 Zac Bierk .20 .50
171 Tuomo Ruutu RC .75 2.00
172 Jordin Tootoo RC 1.00 2.50
173 Joni Pitkanen RC .75 2.00
174 Peter Sejna RC .60 1.50
175 Dan Hamhuis RC .60 1.50
176 Eric Staal RC 2.50 6.00
177 Dan Fritsche RC .50 1.25
178 Dustin Brown RC 1.25 3.00
179 Christopher Higgins RC 1.00 2.50
180 Nathan Horton RC 1.25 3.00
181 Milan Michalek RC 1.00 2.50
182 Boyd Gordon RC .60 1.50
183 Marc-Andre Fleury RC 3.00 8.00
184 Joffrey Lupul RC 1.25 3.00
185 David Hale RC .50 1.25
186 Sean Bergenheim RC .60 1.50
187 Tim Gleason RC .60 1.50
188 Pavel Vorobiev RC .60 1.50
189 Paul Martin RC .60 1.50
190 Marek Svatos RC 1.00 2.50
191 Antoine Vermette RC 1.00 2.50
192 Matt Stajan RC .75 2.00
193 Alexander Semin RC 1.50 4.00
194 Brent Burns RC 1.50 4.00
195 Jiri Hudler RC 1.25 3.00
196 Matthew Lombardi RC .60 1.50
197 Maxim Kondratiev RC .50 1.25
198 Brent Krahn RC .50 1.25
199 Antti Miettinen RC .75 2.00
200 Patrice Bergeron RC 2.50 6.00
201 Cover Card Checklist .20 .50
202 Marek Zidlicky XRC .30 .75
203 John-Michael Liles XRC .40 1.00
204 Ryan Malone XRC .60 1.50
205 Tom Preissing XRC .40 1.00
206 Rastislav Stana XRC .30 .75
207 Mike Commodore .20 .50
208 Jaromir Jagr 1.00 2.50
209 Fredrik Sjostrom XRC .50 1.25
210 Nikolai Zherdev XRC .60 1.50
211 Derek Roy XRC .50 1.25
212 Marcus Nilsson .20 .50
213 Milan Michalek XRC .60 1.50
214 Tomas Plekanec XRC 1.00 2.50
215 Mark Popovic XRC .40 1.00
216 Frederic Henry XRC .40 1.00
217 Nolan Schaefer XRC .30 .75
218 Colton Orr XRC .40 1.00
219 Mike Smith XRC 1.00 2.50
220 Cory Stillman .20 .50
221 Carl Corazzini XRC .30 .75
222 Eric Heffler XRC .40 1.00
223 Dimitri Afanasenkov .25 .60
224 Garth Murray .25 .60
225 Matt Ellison XRC .30 .75
226 Ville Nieminen .20 .50
227 Brooks Laich XRC .50 1.25
228 Sergei Gonchar .20 .50
229 Fedor Tyutin XRC .30 .75
230 Ron Francis .40 1.00
231 Phil Osaer XRC .30 .75
232 Miikka Kiprusoff .30 .75
233 Michal Barinka XRC .30 .75
234 Brad Boyes XRC .50 1.25
235 Erik Westrum XRC .30 .75
236 Kari Lehtonen XRC 1.25 3.00
237 Chad Alban XRC .50 1.25
238 Thomas Pock XRC .40 1.00
239 Darryl Sydor .20 .50
240 Greg Mauldin XRC .40 1.00
241 Eric Perrin XRC .30 .75
242 Michael Ryder .25 .60
243 Esa Pirnes XRC .30 .75
244 Matt Murley XRC .40 1.00
245 Trevor Daley XRC .50 1.25
246 Libor Pivko XRC .30 .75
247 John Pohl XRC .30 .75
248 Seamus Kotyk XRC .30 .75
249 Sergei Zinovjev XRC .30 .75
250 Joe Nieuwendyk .25 .60

2003-04 BAP Memorabilia Ruby

*1-170 VETS/200: 2X TO 5X BASIC CARDS
*171-200 ROOKIES/200: .8X TO 2X

2003-04 BAP Memorabilia Sapphire

*1-170 VETS/100: 3X TO 8X BASIC CARDS
*171-200 ROOKIE/100: 1.2X TO 3X

2003-04 BAP Memorabilia All-Star Jerseys

SEMISTARS 6.00 15.00
UNLISTED STARS 8.00 20.00
ASJ1 Peter Forsberg 10.00 25.00
ASJ2 Jaromir Jagr 10.00 25.00
ASJ3 Mike Modano 8.00 20.00
ASJ4 Bill Guerin 6.00 15.00
ASJ5 Paul Kariya 6.00 15.00
ASJ6 Nicklas Lidstrom 6.00 15.00
ASJ7 Teemu Selanne 6.00 15.00
ASJ8 Patrick Roy 15.00 40.00
ASJ9 Alex Kovalev 6.00 15.00
ASJ11 Sergei Fedorov 10.00 25.00
ASJ12 Jaromir Jagr 10.00 25.00
ASJ13 Brian Leetch 6.00 15.00
ASJ14 Joe Thornton 8.00 20.00
ASJ15 Jose Theodore 8.00 20.00
ASJ16 Brendan Shanahan 6.00 15.00
ASJ17 Patrick Roy 15.00 40.00
ASJ18 Chris Pronger 6.00 15.00
ASJ19 Nicklas Lidstrom 6.00 15.00
ASJ21 Martin Brodeur 15.00 40.00
ASJ22 Pavel Bure 6.00 15.00
ASJ23 Peter Forsberg 12.50 30.00
ASJ24 Paul Kariya 6.00 15.00
ASJ25 Brian Leetch 6.00 15.00
ASJ26 Nicklas Lidstrom 6.00 15.00
ASJ27 Markus Naslund 6.00 15.00
ASJ28 Patrick Roy 15.00 40.00
ASJ29 Joe Sakic 10.00 25.00
ASJ31 Al MacInnis 6.00 15.00
ASJ32 Jaromir Jagr 10.00 25.00
ASJ33 John LeClair 6.00 15.00
ASJ34 Martin Brodeur 15.00 40.00
ASJ35 Mike Modano 8.00 20.00
ASJ36 Jeremy Roenick 8.00 20.00
ASJ37 Brendan Shanahan 6.00 15.00
ASJ38 Mats Sundin 6.00 15.00
ASJ39 Steve Yzerman 12.50 30.00

2003-04 BAP Memorabilia All-Star Staring Lineup

1 Nikolai Khabibulin 8.00 20.00
2 Brian Leetch 8.00 20.00
3 Sandis Ozolinsh 8.00 20.00
4 Mario Lemieux 15.00 40.00
5 Jaromir Jagr 10.00 25.00
6 Alex Kovalev 8.00 20.00
7 Patrick Roy 15.00 40.00
8 Nicklas Lidstrom 8.00 20.00
9 Rob Blake 8.00 20.00
10 Mike Modano 10.00 25.00
11 Bill Guerin 8.00 20.00
12 Teemu Selanne 8.00 20.00

2003-04 BAP Memorabilia All-Star Teammates

AST1 P.Forsberg/P.Roy 30.00 80.00
AST2 D.Heatley/J.Jagr 20.00 50.00
AST3 M.Modano/B.Guerin 20.00 50.00
AST4 N.Lidstrom/P.Kariya 20.00 50.00
AST5 B.Leetch/J.Thornton 25.00 60.00
AST6 J.Theodore/P.Roy 40.00 100.00
AST7 B.Shanahan/B.Leetch 20.00 50.00
AST8 M.Brodeur/P.Roy 40.00 100.00
AST9 P.Forsberg/N.Lidstrom 25.00 60.00
AST10 J.Sakic/B.Leetch 30.00 80.00

2003-04 BAP Memorabilia Brush with Greatness

COMMON CONTEST CARD .60 1.50
1 Mario Lemieux 6.00 15.00
2 Martin Brodeur 5.00 12.00
3 Marian Gaborik 3.00 8.00
4 Paul Kariya 2.00 5.00
5 Peter Forsberg 5.00 12.00
6 Jason Spezza 3.00 6.00
7 Maurice Richard 4.00 10.00
8 Jacques Plante 3.00 8.00
9 Henrik Zetterberg 3.00 6.00
10 Ed Belfour 2.00 5.00
11 Nicklas Lidstrom 2.00 5.00
12 Rick Nash 2.50 6.00
13 Bill Barilko 2.00 5.00
14 Jean-Sebastien Giguere 2.00 5.00
15 Jose Theodore 2.00 5.00
16 Pavel Bure 2.00 5.00
17 Ilya Kovalchuk 2.50 6.00
18 Mats Sundin 2.00 5.00
19 Terry Sawchuk 3.00 8.00
20 Joe Thornton 3.00 8.00
21 Dominik Hasek 4.00 10.00
22 Joe Sakic 4.00 10.00
23 Dany Heatley 2.50 6.00
24 Steve Yzerman 5.00 12.00
25 Patrick Roy 6.00 15.00

2003-04 BAP Memorabilia Deep in the Crease

COMPLETE SET (15) 12.00 30.00
D1 Atlanta Thrashers .75 2.00
D2 Chicago Blackhawks .75 2.00
D3 Montreal Canadiens .75 2.00
D4 New Jersey Devils .75 2.00
D5 New York Rangers .75 2.00
D6 Nashville Predators .75 2.00
D7 Anaheim Mighty Ducks .75 2.00
D8 Detroit Red Wings 2.50 6.00
D9 Toronto Maple Leafs 1.25 3.00
D10 Vancouver Canucks .75 2.00
D11 Minnesota Wild .75 2.00
D12 St.Louis Blues .75 2.00
D13 Buffalo Sabres 1.25 3.00
D14 Florida Panthers 1.25 3.00
D15 Pittsburgh Penguins 2.00 5.00

2003-04 BAP Memorabilia Draft Redemptions

1 Marc-Andre Fleury/56* 40.00 100.00
2 Eric Staal/51* 40.00 100.00
3 Nathan Horton/48* 25.00 60.00
4 Nikolai Zherdev/52* 25.00 60.00
5 Thomas Vanek/66* 20.00 50.00
6 Milan Michalek/41* 25.00 60.00
7 Ryan Suter/46* 15.00 40.00
8 Braydon Coburn/56* 15.00 40.00
9 Dion Phaneuf/65* 25.00 60.00
10 Andrei Kostitsyn/55* 12.00 30.00
11 Jeff Carter/52* 30.00 60.00
13 Dustin Brown/43* 20.00 50.00
14 Brent Seabrook/46* 12.50 30.00
15 Robert Nilsson/49* 12.50 30.00
16 Steve Bernier/56* 12.50 30.00
17 Zach Parise/57* 25.00 60.00
18 Eric Fehr/43* 12.50 30.00
19 Ryan Getzlaf/59* 40.00 80.00
20 Brent Burns/46* 15.00 40.00
21 Mark Stuart/36* 8.00 20.00
22 Marc-Antoine Pouliot/35* 8.00 20.00
23 Ryan Kesler/40* 20.00 50.00
24 Mike Richards/60* 20.00 50.00
25 Anthony Stewart/51* 12.50 30.00
27 Jeff Tambellini/50* 8.00 20.00
28 Corey Perry/57* 25.00 60.00
29 Patrick Eaves/52* 12.50 30.00
30 Shawn Belle/27* 8.00 20.00

2003-04 BAP Memorabilia Future of the Game

FG1 Scottie Upshall 10.00 25.00
FG2 Ray Emery 10.00 25.00
FG3 Rick Nash 25.00 60.00
FG4 Stanislav Chistov 8.00 20.00
FG5 Ryan Miller 15.00 40.00
FG6 Henrik Zetterberg 20.00 50.00
FG7 Alexander Frolov 8.00 20.00
FG8 Barret Jackman 8.00 20.00
FG9 Brandon Reid 8.00 20.00
FG10 Mike Komisarek 8.00 20.00
FG11 Alexei Smirnov 8.00 20.00
FG12 Steve Ott 10.00 25.00
FG13 Mike Cammalleri 10.00 25.00
FG14 Jason Spezza 25.00 60.00
FG15 Carlo Colaiacovo 8.00 20.00
FG16 Jared Aulin 8.00 20.00
FG17 Ales Hemsky 12.00 30.00
FG18 Marc-Andre Fleury 20.00 50.00
FG19 Eric Staal 20.00 50.00
FG20 Dustin Brown 12.00 30.00

2003-04 BAP Memorabilia Future Wave

FW1 Marc-Andre Fleury 25.00 60.00
FW2 Ray Emery 12.00 30.00
FW3 David Aebischer 12.00 30.00
FW4 Rick DiPietro 12.00 30.00
FW5 Dan Blackburn 8.00 20.00
FW6 Mathieu Garon 8.00 20.00
FW7 Ryan Miller 15.00 40.00
FW8 Brian Finley 8.00 20.00
FW9 Alex Auld 8.00 20.00
FW10 Mika Noronen 8.00 20.00
FW11 Mikael Tellqvist 12.00 30.00
FW12 Andrew Raycroft 12.00 30.00

2003-04 BAP Memorabilia Gloves

GUG1 Jean-Sebastien Giguere 15.00 40.00
GUG2 Patrick Roy 30.00 60.00
GUG3 Marty Turco 15.00 40.00
GUG4 Olaf Kolzig 12.00 30.00
GUG5 Patrick Lalime 15.00 40.00
GUG6 Jacques Plante 30.00 80.00
GUG7 Bill Durnan 15.00 40.00
GUG8 Bernie Parent 15.00 40.00
GUG9 Vladislav Tretiak 25.00 60.00
GUG10 Charlie Hodge 15.00 40.00
GUG11 Keith Tkachuk 15.00 40.00
GUG12 Mario Lemieux 30.00 60.00
GUG13 Eric Lindros 15.00 40.00
GUG14 Sergei Samsonov 15.00 40.00
GUG15 Jarome Iginla 15.00 40.00
GUG16 Wendel Clark 15.00 40.00
GUG17 Dickie Moore 15.00 40.00
GUG18 Bill Gadsby 30.00 60.00
GUG19 Bernie Geoffrion 15.00 40.00
GUG20 Eddie Shore 30.00 60.00

2003-04 BAP Memorabilia He Shoots He Scores Points

1 Jose Theodore 1 Pt. .40 1.00
2 Jeremy Roenick 1 Pt. .40 1.00
3 Chris Pronger 1 Pt. .40 1.00
4 Markus Naslund 1 Pt. .40 1.00
5 Nicklas Lidstrom 1 Pt. .40 1.00
6 Dany Heatley 1 Pt. .40 1.00
7 Bill Guerin 1 Pt. .40 1.00
8 Pavel Bure 1 Pt. .40 1.00
9 Steve Yzerman 2 Pts. .40 1.00
10 Joe Thornton 2 Pts. .40 1.00
11 Mats Sundin 2 Pts. .40 1.00
12 Brendan Shanahan 2 Pts. .40 1.00
13 Teemu Selanne 2 Pts. .40 1.00
14 Joe Sakic 2 Pts. .40 1.00
15 Mike Modano 2 Pts. .40 1.00
16 Paul Kariya 2 Pts. .40 1.00
17 Sergei Fedorov 2 Pts. .40 1.00
18 Patrick Roy 3 Pts. .40 1.00
19 Peter Forsberg 3 Pts. .40 1.00
20 Martin Brodeur 3 Pts. .40 1.00

2003-04 BAP Memorabilia Jersey and Stick

SJ1 Joe Thornton 12.00 30.00
SJ2 Sergei Samsonov 8.00 20.00
SJ3 Jarome Iginla 10.00 25.00
SJ4 Ron Francis 8.00 20.00
SJ5 Jocelyn Thibault 8.00 20.00
SJ6 Mats Sundin 8.00 20.00
SJ7 Rob Blake 8.00 20.00
SJ8 Al MacInnis 8.00 20.00
SJ9 Rick Nash 15.00 40.00
SJ10 Marty Turco 8.00 20.00
SJ11 Bill Guerin 8.00 20.00
SJ12 Chris Chelios 8.00 20.00
SJ13 Luc Robitaille 8.00 20.00
SJ14 Mike Comrie 8.00 20.00
SJ15 Markus Naslund 8.00 20.00
SJ16 Roberto Luongo 10.00 25.00
SJ17 Peter Bondra 8.00 20.00
SJ18 John LeClair 8.00 20.00
SJ19 Rick DiPietro 8.00 20.00
SJ20 Tony Amonte 8.00 20.00
SJ21 Eric Lindros 8.00 20.00
SJ22 Jeremy Roenick 10.00 25.00
SJ23 Ilya Kovalchuk 12.50 30.00
SJ24 Dany Heatley 12.50 30.00
SJ25 Patrick Roy 12.00 30.00
SJ26 Joe Sakic 15.00 40.00
SJ27 Peter Forsberg 12.50 30.00
SJ28 Mike Modano 10.00 25.00
SJ29 Steve Yzerman 20.00 50.00
SJ30 Nicklas Lidstrom 8.00 20.00
SJ31 Brett Hull 12.50 30.00
SJ32 Jose Theodore 10.00 25.00
SJ33 Martin Brodeur 15.00 40.00
SJ34 Pavel Bure 10.00 25.00
SJ35 Mario Lemieux 20.00 50.00
SJ36 Jaromir Jagr 12.50 30.00
SJ37 Marian Gaborik 20.00 50.00
SJ38 Brendan Shanahan 8.00 20.00
SJ39 Dominik Hasek 12.50 30.00
SJ40 Todd Bertuzzi 8.00 20.00

2003-04 BAP Memorabilia Jerseys

GJ1 Joe Thornton 10.00 25.00
GJ2 Dominik Hasek 10.00 25.00
GJ3 Jarome Iginla 10.00 25.00
GJ4 Ron Francis 6.00 15.00
GJ5 Henrik Zetterberg 8.00 20.00
GJ6 Mats Sundin 6.00 15.00
GJ7 Rob Blake 6.00 15.00
GJ8 Al MacInnis 6.00 15.00
GJ9 Milan Hejduk 6.00 15.00
GJ10 Rick Nash 10.00 25.00
GJ11 Marty Turco 6.00 15.00
GJ12 Jean-Sebastien Giguere 6.00 15.00
GJ13 Jason Spezza 8.00 20.00
GJ14 Luc Robitaille 6.00 15.00
GJ15 Alexander Mogilny 6.00 15.00
GJ16 Mike Comrie 6.00 15.00
GJ17 Markus Naslund 6.00 15.00
GJ18 Roberto Luongo 10.00 25.00
GJ19 Jay Bouwmeester 6.00 15.00
GJ20 Marian Hossa 6.00 15.00
GJ21 Todd Bertuzzi 6.00 15.00
GJ22 Saku Koivu 6.00 15.00
GJ23 Curtis Joseph 6.00 15.00
GJ24 Rick DiPietro 6.00 15.00
GJ25 Ed Belfour 6.00 15.00
GJ26 Eric Lindros 6.00 15.00
GJ27 Jeremy Roenick 6.00 15.00
GJ28 Brian Leetch 6.00 15.00
GJ29 Owen Nolan 6.00 15.00
GJ30 Simon Gagne 6.00 15.00
GJ31 Brendan Shanahan 6.00 15.00
GJ32 Ilya Kovalchuk 10.00 25.00
GJ33 Dany Heatley 10.00 25.00
GJ34 Patrick Roy 15.00 40.00
GJ35 Joe Sakic 12.00 30.00
GJ36 Peter Forsberg 8.00 20.00
GJ37 Mike Modano 8.00 20.00
GJ38 Steve Yzerman 15.00 40.00
GJ39 Nicklas Lidstrom 6.00 15.00
GJ40 Brett Hull 8.00 20.00
GJ41 Jose Theodore 8.00 20.00
GJ42 Martin Brodeur 12.00 30.00
GJ43 Pavel Bure 6.00 15.00
GJ44 Mark Messier 6.00 15.00
GJ45 Mario Lemieux 20.00 50.00
GJ46 Jaromir Jagr 10.00 25.00
GJ47 Marian Gaborik 12.00 30.00
GJ48 Teemu Selanne 6.00 15.00
GJ49 Paul Kariya 6.00 15.00
GJ50 Sergei Fedorov 8.00 20.00

2003-04 BAP Memorabilia Masks III

COMPLETE SET (20) 15.00 40.00
1 Jean-Sebastien Giguere 4.00 10.00
2 Roman Cechmanek 3.00 8.00
3 Dominik Hasek 5.00 12.00
4 Roberto Luongo 5.00 12.00
5 Ryan Miller 6.00 15.00
6 Sean Burke 3.00 8.00
7 Kevin Weekes 3.00 8.00
8 Mike Dunham 3.00 8.00
9 Jeff Hackett 3.00 8.00
10 Martin Prusek 3.00 8.00
11 Olaf Kolzig 3.00 8.00
12 Nikolai Khabibulin 3.00 8.00
13 Pasi Nurminen 3.00 8.00
14 Johan Hedberg 3.00 8.00
15 Marty Turco 3.00 8.00
16 Felix Potvin 3.00 8.00
17 Marc Denis 3.00 8.00
18 Marc-Andre Fleury 8.00 20.00
19 David Aebischer 3.00 8.00
20 Jocelyn Thibault 3.00 8.00

2003-04 BAP Memorabilia Masks III Gold

*GOLD: 2.5X TO 6X BASIC MASKS

2003-04 BAP Memorabilia Masks III Silver

*SILVER: 1X TO 2.5X BASIC MASKS

2003-04 BAP Memorabilia Practice Jerseys

PMP1 Curtis Joseph 10.00 25.00
PMP2 Martin Brodeur 15.00 40.00
PMP3 Ed Jovanovski 10.00 25.00
PMP4 Scott Neidermayer 10.00 25.00
PMP5 Al MacInnis 10.00 25.00
PMP6 Rob Blake 10.00 25.00
PMP7 Chris Pronger 10.00 25.00
PMP8 Owen Nolan 10.00 25.00
PMP9 Eric Lindros 10.00 25.00
PMP10 Paul Kariya 10.00 25.00
PMP11 Steve Yzerman 15.00 40.00
PMP12 Brendan Shanahan 10.00 25.00
PMP13 Theo Fleury 10.00 25.00
PMP14 Ryan Smyth 10.00 25.00
PMP15 Joe Nieuwendyk 10.00 25.00
PMP16 Jarome Iginla 12.50 30.00

2003-04 BAP Memorabilia Stanley Cup Champions

SCC1 Martin Brodeur 40.00 100.00
SCC2 Jamie Langenbrunner 12.50 30.00
SCC3 Scott Gomez 12.50 30.00
SCC4 Joe Nieuwendyk 12.50 30.00
SCC5 John Madden 12.50 30.00
SCC6 Scott Niedermayer 12.50 30.00
SCC7 Jeff Friesen 12.50 30.00
SCC8 Scott Stevens 25.00 60.00
SCC9 Patrik Elias 12.50 30.00
SCC10 Corey Schwab 12.50 30.00

2003-04 BAP Memorabilia Stanley Cup Playoffs

SCP1 Steve Yzerman 15.00 40.00
SCP2 Jean-Sebastien Giguere 6.00 15.00
SCP3 Doug Weight 6.00 15.00
SCP4 Ed Jovanovski 6.00 15.00
SCP5 Joe Sakic 12.00 30.00
SCP6 Marian Gaborik 10.00 25.00
SCP7 Mike Modano 10.00 25.00
SCP8 Georges Laraque 6.00 15.00
SCP9 Marian Hossa 8.00 20.00
SCP10 Alexei Yashin 6.00 15.00
SCP11 Scott Niedermayer 6.00 15.00
SCP12 Jeff Hackett 6.00 15.00
SCP13 Martin St.Louis 6.00 15.00
SCP14 Jaromir Jagr 10.00 25.00
SCP15 Mark Recchi 6.00 15.00
SCP16 Alex Mogilny 6.00 15.00
SCP17 Paul Kariya 8.00 20.00
SCP18 Marty Turco 6.00 15.00
SCP19 Dwayne Roloson 6.00 15.00
SCP20 Markus Naslund 8.00 20.00
SCP21 Daniel Alfredsson 6.00 15.00
SCP22 Jeremy Roenick 8.00 20.00
SCP23 Vincent Lecavalier 8.00 20.00
SCP24 Jamie Langenbrunner 6.00 15.00
SCP25 Jean-Sebastien Giguere 6.00 15.00
SCP26 Manny Fernandez 6.00 15.00
SCP27 Jason Spezza 12.50 30.00
SCP28 John Madden 6.00 15.00

2003-04 BAP Memorabilia Super Rookies

COMPLETE SET (12) 20.00 50.00
*SILVER: .75X TO 2X BASE HI
SR1 Tuomo Ruutu 4.00 10.00
SR2 Joffrey Lupul 4.00 10.00
SR3 Brent Burns 2.00 5.00
SR4 David Hale 2.00 5.00
SR5 Patrice Bergeron 5.00 12.00
SR6 Joni Pitkanen 2.50 6.00
SR7 Sean Bergenheim 2.50 6.00
SR8 Boyd Gordon 2.00 5.00
SR9 Eric Staal 4.00 10.00
SR10 Nathan Horton 4.00 10.00
SR11 Dustin Brown 3.00 8.00
SR12 Tim Gleason 2.00 5.00
SR13 Dan Hamhuis 2.00 5.00
SR14 Jordin Tootoo 4.00 10.00
SR15 Jiri Hudler 4.00 10.00
SR16 Marc-Andre Fleury 8.00 20.00
SR17 Christopher Higgins 2.00 5.00
SR18 Pavel Vorobiev 2.00 5.00
SR19 Alexander Semin 2.50 6.00
SR20 Brent Krahn 2.00 5.00

2003-04 BAP Memorabilia Tandems

T1 D.Roloson/M.Fernandez 10.00 25.00
T2 P.Lalime/M.Prusek 12.50 30.00
T3 D.Hasek/M.Legace 25.00 60.00
T4 M.Biron/R.Miller 12.50 30.00
T5 M.Brodeur/C.Schwab 15.00 40.00
T6 M.Turco/R.Tugnutt 10.00 25.00
T7 J.Giguere/M.Gerber 10.00 25.00
T8 J.Theodore/M.Garon 12.50 30.00
T9 R.Luongo/J.Hurme 12.50 30.00
T10 E.Belfour/T.Kidd 12.50 30.00

1999-00 BAP Millennium Prototypes

COMPLETE SET (8) 4.80 12.00
1 Teemu Selanne 1.25 3.00
2 Sergei Samsonov .60 1.50
3 Mike Modano .75 2.00
4 Sergei Fedorov 1.25 3.00
5 Saku Koivu .60 1.50
6 John Vanbiesbrouck .60 1.50
7 Sergei Berezin .20 .50
8 Olaf Kolzig .60 1.50

1999-00 BAP Millennium

1 Paul Kariya .20 .50
2 Teemu Selanne .40 1.00
3 Oleg Tverdovsky .12 .30
4 Niclas Havelid RC .20 .50
5 Guy Hebert .20 .50
6 Stu Grimson .15 .40
7 Pavel Trnka .12 .30
8 Ladislav Kohn .12 .30
9 Matt Cullen .12 .30
10 Steve Rucchin .12 .30
11 Dominic Roussel .12 .30
12 Patrik Stefan RC .20 .50
13 Damian Rhodes .12 .30
14 Ray Ferraro .12 .30
15 Andrew Brunette .12 .30
16 Johan Garpenlov .12 .30
17 Nelson Emerson .12 .30
18 Jason Botterill .12 .30
19 Kelly Buchberger .12 .30
20 Ray Bourque .30 .75
21 Ken Belanger .12 .30
22 Sergei Samsonov .15 .40
23 Byron Dafoe .15 .40
24 Joe Thornton .30 .75
25 Kyle McLaren .12 .30
26 Cameron Mann .12 .30
27 Mikko Eloranta RC .15 .40
28 Jonathan Girard .12 .30
29 Dominik Hasek .30 .75
30 Michael Peca .15 .40
31 Erik Rasmussen .12 .30
32 Brian Campbell RC .20 .50
33 Miroslav Satan .15 .40
34 Vaclav Varada .12 .30
35 Martin Biron .15 .40
36 Dixon Ward .12 .30
37 Cory Sarich .12 .30
38 Grant Fuhr .30 .75
39 Jarome Iginla .25 .60
40 Valeri Bure .12 .30
41 Oleg Saprykin RC .20 .50
42 Rene Corbet .12 .30
43 Cory Stillman .12 .30
44 Denis Gauthier .12 .30
45 Steve Dubinsky .12 .30
46 Rico Fata .12 .30
47 Steve Halko RC .15 .40
48 Keith Primeau .15 .40
49 Sami Kapanen .12 .30
50 Arturs Irbe .15 .40
51 Jeff O'Neill .12 .30
52 Kent Manderville .12 .30
53 Gary Roberts .12 .30
54 Nolan Pratt .12 .30
55 Brad Brown .12 .30
56 Tony Amonte .15 .40
57 J-P Dumont .15 .40
58 Anders Eriksson .12 .30
59 Bryan Muir .12 .30
60 Dean McAmmond .12 .30
61 Jocelyn Thibault .15 .40
62 Eric Daze .15 .40
63 Shean Donovan .12 .30
64 Scott Parker .12 .30
65 Peter Forsberg .40 1.00
66 Patrick Roy .50 1.25
67 Joe Sakic .40 1.00
68 Sandis Ozolinsh .12 .30
69 Chris Drury .15 .40
70 Milan Hejduk .15 .40
71 Shjon Podein .12 .30
72 Marc Denis .15 .40
73 Alex Tanguay .15 .40
74 Blake Sloan .12 .30
75 Jamie Langenbrunner .12 .30
76 Mike Modano .30 .75
77 Derian Hatcher .12 .30
78 Joe Nieuwendyk .15 .40
79 Ed Belfour .20 .50
80 Brad Lukowich RC .15 .40
81 Jere Lehtinen .15 .40
82 Brett Hull .40 1.00
83 Shawn Chambers .12 .30
84 Pavel Patera RC .12 .30
85 Darryl Sydor .15 .40
86 Jiri Fischer .12 .30
87 Nicklas Lidstrom .20 .50
88 Steve Yzerman .50 1.25
89 Sergei Fedorov .30 .75
90 Brendan Shanahan .20 .50
91 Chris Chelios .20 .50
92 Aaron Ward .12 .30
93 Kirk Maltby .12 .30
94 Yuri Butsayev RC .12 .30
95 Mathieu Dandenault .12 .30
96 Doug Weight .20 .50
97 Bill Guerin .20 .50
98 Tom Poti .12 .30
99 Wayne Gretzky 1.25 3.00
100 Georges Laraque RC .40 1.00
101 Sean Brown .12 .30
102 Mike Grier .12 .30
103 Tommy Salo .15 .40
104 Rem Murray .12 .30
105 Paul Comrie RC .30 .75
106 Pavel Bure .20 .50
107 Rob Niedermayer .12 .30
108 Oleg Kvasha .12 .30
109 Filip Kuba RC .12 .30
110 Viktor Kozlov .12 .30
111 Radek Dvorak .12 .30
112 Ray Whitney .15 .40
113 Mark Parrish .12 .30
114 Dan Boyle RC .15 .40
115 Marcus Nilsson .12 .30
116 Lance Pitlick .12 .30
117 Paul Laus .12 .30
118 Rob Blake .20 .50
119 Stephane Fiset .12 .30
120 Zigmund Palffy .20 .50
121 Donald Audette .12 .30
122 Luc Robitaille .15 .40
123 Jamie Storr .12 .30
124 Dan Bylsma .12 .30
125 Pavel Rosa .12 .30
126 Jason Blake RC .15 .40
127 Mattias Norstrom .12 .30
128 Saku Koivu .20 .50
129 Trevor Linden .20 .50
130 Arron Asham .12 .30
131 Matt Higgins .12 .30
132 Martin Rucinsky .12 .30
133 Brian Savage .12 .30
134 Jeff Hackett .15 .40
135 Scott Thornton .12 .30
136 David Legwand .12 .30
137 Cliff Ronning .12 .30
138 Ville Peltonen .12 .30
139 Tomas Vokoun .20 .50
140 Sergei Krivokrasov .12 .30
141 Greg Johnson .12 .30
142 Mike Dunham .15 .40
143 Martin Brodeur .50 1.25
144 Scott Niedermayer .12 .30
145 Petr Sykora .15 .40
146 Vadim Sharifijanov .12 .30
147 Denis Pederson .12 .30
148 Jason Arnott .15 .40
149 Brendan Morrison .15 .40
150 Bobby Holik .12 .30
151 Brian Rafalski RC .20 .50
152 Olli Jokinen .15 .40
153 Tim Connolly .12 .30
154 Gino Odjick .12 .30
155 Zdeno Chara .20 .50
156 Kenny Jonsson .12 .30
157 Mariusz Czerkawski .12 .30
158 Kim Johnsson RC .12 .30
159 Brian Leetch .15 .40
160 Theo Fleury .25 .60
161 Petr Nedved .12 .30
162 John MacLean .15 .40
163 Manny Malhotra .15 .40
164 Jan Hlavac .12 .30
165 Valeri Kamensky .12 .30
166 Adam Graves .15 .40
167 Michael York .12 .30
168 Mike Richter .20 .50
169 Chris Phillips .12 .30
170 Marian Hossa .20 .50
171 Magnus Arvedson .12 .30
172 Ron Tugnutt .15 .40
173 Vaclav Prospal .12 .30
174 Sami Salo .12 .30
175 Jason York .12 .30
176 Shawn McEachern .12 .30
177 Rob Zamuner .12 .30
178 Eric Lindros .30 .75
179 John LeClair .15 .40
180 Eric Desjardins .15 .40
181 Rod Brind'Amour .20 .50
182 Mark Recchi .25 .60
183 Simon Gagne .20 .50
184 Sandy McCarthy .12 .30
185 John Vanbiesbrouck .15 .40
186 Dan McGillis .12 .30
187 Keith Jones .12 .30
188 Keith Tkachuk .20 .50
189 Teppo Numminen .12 .30
190 Jeremy Roenick .30 .75
191 Nikolai Khabibulin .15 .40
192 Deron Quint .12 .30
193 Trevor Letowski .12 .30
194 Jaromir Jagr .60 1.50
195 Jan Hrdina .12 .30
196 Andrew Ference .12 .30
197 Alexei Kovalev .15 .40
198 Martin Straka .12 .30
199 Kip Miller .12 .30
200 Martin Sonnenberg RC .12 .30
201 Alexei Morozov .15 .40
202 Chris Pronger .20 .50
203 Al MacInnis .25 .60
204 Pavol Demitra .25 .60
205 Pierre Turgeon .15 .40
206 Jamal Mayers .12 .30
207 Chris McAlpine .12 .30
208 Ron Sutter .12 .30
209 Mike Rathje .12 .30
210 Patrick Marleau .20 .50
211 Jeff Friesen .15 .40
212 Niklas Sundstrom .12 .30
213 Steve Shields .15 .40
214 Brad Stuart .15 .40
215 Alexander Korolyuk .12 .30
216 Mike Ricci .12 .30
217 Paul Mara .12 .30

218 Fredrik Modin .12 .30
219 Dan Cloutier .12 .30
220 Vincent Lecavalier .20 .50
221 Pavel Kubina .12 .30
222 Chris Gratton .12 .30
223 Mike Sillinger .12 .30
224 Nikolai Antropov RC .50 1.25
225 Todd Warriner .12 .30
226 Mats Sundin .20 .50
227 Curtis Joseph .25 .60
228 Chris McAllister RC .12 .30
229 Bryan Berard .12 .30
230 Tomas Kaberle .12 .30
231 Igor Korolev .12 .30
232 Sergei Berezin .12 .30
233 Artem Chubarov .12 .30
234 Ed Jovanovski .15 .40
235 Mark Messier .40 1.00
236 Bill Muckalt .12 .30
237 Brad May .12 .30
238 Adrian Aucoin .12 .30
239 Mattias Ohlund .12 .30
240 Greg Hawgood .12 .30
241 Steve Kariya RC .20 .50
242 Markus Naslund .20 .50
243 Alexander Mogilny .15 .40
244 Jamie Huscroft .12 .30
245 Peter Bondra .20 .50
246 Olaf Kolzig .20 .50
247 Brendan Witt .12 .30
248 Adam Oates .20 .50
249 Sergei Gonchar .12 .30
250 Jan Bulis .12 .30
NNO J.Jagr GJ Special 30.00 80.00

1999-00 BAP Millennium Ruby

*VETERANS: 1.5X TO 4X BASIC CARDS
*ROOKIES: 1.2X TO 3X BASIC CARDS

1999-00 BAP Millennium Sapphire

*VETERANS: 10X TO 25X BASIC CARDS
*ROOKIES: 8X TO 20X BASIC CARD

1999-00 BAP Millennium Autographs

1 Paul Kariya SP 20.00 50.00
2 Teemu Selanne SP 15.00 40.00
3 Oleg Tverdovsky 2.50 6.00
4 Niclas Havelid 4.00 10.00
5 Guy Hebert 4.00 10.00
6 Stu Grimson 3.00 8.00
7 Pavel Trnka 2.50 6.00
8 Ladislav Kohn 2.50 6.00
9 Matt Cullen 2.50 6.00
10 Steve Rucchin 2.50 6.00
11 Dominic Roussel 2.50 6.00
12 Patrik Stefan 4.00 10.00
13 Damian Rhodes 2.50 6.00
14 Ray Ferraro 2.50 6.00
15 Andrew Brunette 2.50 6.00
16 Johan Garpenlov 2.50 6.00
17 Nelson Emerson 2.50 6.00
18 Jason Botterill 2.50 6.00
19 Kelly Buchberger 2.50 6.00
20 Ray Bourque SP 15.00 40.00
21 Ken Belanger 2.50 6.00
22 Sergei Samsonov SP 3.00 8.00
23 Byron Dafoe SP 6.00 15.00
24 Joe Thornton 6.00 15.00
25 Kyle McLaren 2.50 6.00
26 Cameron Mann 2.50 6.00
27 Mikko Eloranta 3.00 8.00
28 Jonathan Girard 2.50 6.00
29 Dominik Hasek SP 150.00 250.00
30 Michael Peca SP 5.00 12.00
31 Erik Rasmussen 2.50 6.00
32 Brian Campbell 4.00 10.00
33 Miroslav Satan 3.00 8.00
34 Vaclav Varada 2.50 6.00
35 Martin Biron 3.00 8.00
36 Dixon Ward 2.50 6.00
37 Cory Sarich 2.50 6.00
38 Grant Fuhr SP 8.00 20.00
39 Jarome Iginla 8.00 20.00
40 Valeri Bure 2.50 6.00
41 Oleg Saprykin 4.00 10.00
42 Rene Corbet 2.50 6.00
43 Cory Stillman 2.50 6.00
44 Denis Gauthier 2.50 6.00
45 Steve Dubinsky 2.50 6.00
46 Rico Fata 2.50 6.00
47 Steve Halko 2.50 6.00
48 Keith Primeau SP 3.00 8.00
49 Sami Kapanen 2.50 6.00
50 Arturs Irbe 3.00 8.00
51 Jeff O'Neill 2.50 6.00
52 Kent Manderville 2.50 6.00
53 Gary Roberts 2.50 6.00
54 Nolan Pratt 2.50 6.00
55 Brad Brown 2.50 6.00
56 Tony Amonte SP 3.00 8.00
57 J-P Dumont 3.00 8.00
58 Anders Eriksson 2.50 6.00
59 Bryan Muir 2.50 6.00
60 Dean McAmmond 2.50 6.00
61 Jocelyn Thibault 3.00 8.00
62 Eric Daze 3.00 8.00
63 Shean Donovan 2.50 6.00
64 Scott Parker 2.50 6.00
65 Peter Forsberg SP 20.00 50.00
66 Patrick Roy SP 10.00 25.00
67 Joe Sakic SP 15.00 40.00
68 Sandis Ozolinsh 2.50 6.00
69 Chris Drury 3.00 8.00
70 Milan Hejduk 3.00 8.00
71 Shjon Podein 2.50 6.00
72 Marc Denis 3.00 8.00
73 Alex Tanguay 3.00 8.00
74 Blake Sloan 3.00 8.00
75 Jamie Langenbrunner 2.50 6.00
76 Mike Modano SP 12.00 30.00
77 Derian Hatcher 3.00 8.00
78 Joe Nieuwendyk SP 3.00 8.00
79 Ed Belfour SP 12.00 30.00
80 Brad Lukowich 3.00 8.00
81 Jere Lehtinen 3.00 8.00
82 Brett Hull SP 12.00 30.00
83 Shawn Chambers 2.50 6.00
84 Pavel Patera 2.50 6.00
85 Darryl Sydor 3.00 8.00
86 Jiri Fischer 2.50 6.00
87 Nicklas Lidstrom 8.00 20.00
88 Steve Yzerman SP 30.00 80.00
89 Sergei Fedorov SP 10.00 25.00
90 Brendan Shanahan SP 8.00 20.00
91 Chris Chelios SP 8.00 20.00
92 Aaron Ward 2.50 6.00
93 Kirk Maltby 2.50 6.00
94 Yuri Butsayev 2.50 6.00
95 Mathieu Dandenault 2.50 6.00
96 Doug Weight SP 4.00 10.00
97 Bill Guerin 4.00 10.00
98 Tom Poti 2.50 6.00
99 Wayne Gretzky SP 300.00 800.00
100 Georges Laraque 8.00 20.00
101 Sean Brown 2.50 6.00
102 Mike Grier 2.50 6.00
103 Tommy Salo 3.00 8.00
104 Rem Murray 2.50 6.00
105 Paul Comrie 6.00 15.00
106 Pavel Bure SP 8.00 20.00
107 Rob Niedermayer 2.50 6.00
108 Oleg Kvasha 2.50 6.00
109 Filip Kuba 2.50 6.00
110 Viktor Kozlov 2.50 6.00
111 Radek Dvorak 2.50 6.00
112 Ray Whitney 3.00 8.00
113 Mark Parrish 2.50 6.00
114 Dan Boyle 3.00 8.00
115 Marcus Nilsson 2.50 6.00
116 Lance Pitlick 2.50 6.00
117 Paul Laus 2.50 6.00
118 Rob Blake 4.00 10.00
119 Stephane Fiset 3.00 8.00
120 Zigmund Palffy SP 4.00 10.00
121 Donald Audette 2.50 6.00
122 Luc Robitaille 4.00 10.00
123 Jamie Storr 2.50 6.00
124 Dan Bylsma 2.50 6.00
125 Pavel Rosa 2.50 6.00
126 Jason Blake 3.00 8.00
127 Mattias Norstrom 2.50 6.00
128 Saku Koivu SP 6.00 15.00
129 Trevor Linden 4.00 10.00
130 Arron Asham 2.50 6.00
131 Matt Higgins 2.50 6.00
132 Martin Rucinsky 2.50 6.00
133 Brian Savage 2.50 6.00
134 Jeff Hackett 2.50 6.00
135 Scott Thornton 2.50 6.00
136 David Legwand 2.50 6.00
137 Cliff Ronning 2.50 6.00
138 Ville Peltonen 2.50 6.00
139 Tomas Vokoun 4.00 10.00
140 Sergei Krivokrasov 2.50 6.00
141 Greg Johnson 2.50 6.00
142 Mike Dunham 2.50 6.00
143 Martin Brodeur SP 15.00 40.00
144 Scott Niedermayer SP 6.00 15.00
145 Petr Sykora 3.00 8.00
146 Vadim Sharifijanov 2.50 6.00
147 Denis Pederson 2.50 6.00
148 Jason Arnott SP 3.00 8.00
149 Brendan Morrison 3.00 8.00
150 Bobby Holik 2.50 6.00
151 Brian Rafalski 4.00 10.00
152 Olli Jokinen 3.00 8.00
153 Tim Connolly 2.50 6.00
154 Gino Odjick 2.50 6.00
155 Zdeno Chara 4.00 10.00
156 Kenny Jonsson 2.50 6.00
157 Mariusz Czerkawski 2.50 6.00
158 Kim Johnsson 2.50 6.00
159 Brian Leetch SP 3.00 8.00
160 Theo Fleury SP 8.00 20.00
161 Petr Nedved 2.50 6.00
162 John MacLean 3.00 8.00
163 Manny Malhotra 3.00 8.00
164 Jan Hlavac 2.50 6.00
165 Valeri Kamensky 2.50 6.00
166 Adam Graves 3.00 8.00
167 Michael York 2.50 6.00
168 Mike Richter SP 4.00 10.00
169 Chris Phillips 2.50 6.00
170 Marian Hossa 4.00 10.00
171 Magnus Arvedson 2.50 6.00
172 Ron Tugnutt 3.00 8.00
173 Vaclav Prospal 2.50 6.00
174 Sami Salo 3.00 8.00
175 Jason York 2.50 6.00
176 Shawn McEachern 2.50 6.00
177 Rob Zamuner 2.50 6.00
178 Eric Lindros SP 10.00 25.00
179 John LeClair SP 4.00 10.00
180 Eric Desjardins 3.00 8.00
181 Rod Brind'Amour 4.00 10.00
182 Mark Recchi 5.00 12.00
183 Simon Gagne 4.00 10.00
184 Sandy McCarthy 2.50 6.00
185 John Vanbiesbrouck SP 6.00 15.00
186 Dan McGillis 2.50 6.00
187 Keith Jones 2.50 6.00
188 Keith Tkachuk SP 6.00 15.00
189 Teppo Numminen 2.50 6.00
190 Jeremy Roenick SP 8.00 20.00
191 Nikolai Khabibulin 3.00 8.00
192 Deron Quint 2.50 6.00
193 Trevor Letowski 2.50 6.00
194 Jaromir Jagr SP 30.00 80.00
195 Jan Hrdina 2.50 6.00
196 Andrew Ference 2.50 6.00
197 Alexei Kovalev 3.00 8.00
198 Martin Straka 2.50 6.00
199 Kip Miller 2.50 6.00
200 Martin Sonnenberg 2.50 6.00
201 Alexei Morozov 3.00 8.00
202 Chris Pronger SP 4.00 10.00
203 Al MacInnis SP 5.00 12.00
204 Pavol Demitra 5.00 12.00
205 Pierre Turgeon 3.00 8.00
206 Jamal Mayers 2.50 6.00
207 Chris McAlpine 2.50 6.00
208 Ron Sutter 2.50 6.00
209 Mike Rathje 2.50 6.00
210 Patrick Marleau 4.00 10.00
211 Jeff Friesen SP 6.00 15.00
212 Niklas Sundstrom 2.50 6.00
213 Steve Shields 3.00 8.00
214 Brad Stuart 3.00 8.00
215 Alexander Korolyuk 2.50 6.00
216 Mike Ricci 2.50 6.00
217 Paul Mara 2.50 6.00
218 Fredrik Modin 2.50 6.00
219 Dan Cloutier 2.50 6.00
220 Vincent Lecavalier 4.00 10.00
221 Pavel Kubina 2.50 6.00
222 Chris Gratton SP 6.00 15.00
223 Mike Sillinger 2.50 6.00
224 Nikolai Antropov 10.00 25.00
225 Todd Warriner 2.50 6.00
226 Mats Sundin SP 6.00 15.00
227 Curtis Joseph SP 6.00 15.00
228 Chris McAllister 2.50 6.00
229 Bryan Berard SP 5.00 12.00
230 Tomas Kaberle 2.50 6.00
231 Igor Korolev 2.50 6.00
232 Sergei Berezin 2.50 6.00
233 Artem Chubarov 2.50 6.00
234 Ed Jovanovski 3.00 8.00
235 Mark Messier SP 12.00 30.00
236 Bill Muckalt 2.50 6.00
237 Brad May 2.50 6.00
238 Adrian Aucoin 2.50 6.00
239 Mattias Ohlund 2.50 6.00
240 Greg Hawgood 2.50 6.00
241 Steve Kariya 4.00 10.00
242 Markus Naslund 4.00 10.00
243 Alexander Mogilny SP 3.00 8.00
244 Jamie Huscroft 2.50 6.00
245 Peter Bondra SP 6.00 15.00
246 Olaf Kolzig SP 6.00 15.00
247 Brendan Witt 2.50 6.00
248 Adam Oates SP 6.00 15.00
249 Sergei Gonchar 2.50 6.00
250 Jan Bulis 2.50 6.00

1999-00 BAP Millennium Autographs Gold

*GOLD: 1X TO 2.5X BASIC AU
GOLD/50: .8X TO 2X BASIC AU
29 Dominik Hasek/50* 200.00 350.00
99 Wayne Gretzky/50* 600.00 1500.00

1999-00 BAP Millennium Calder Candidates Ruby

COMPLETE SET (50) 100.00 200.00
*SAPPHIRE/100: 1.5X TO 4X RUBY/1000
*EMERALD/10: 4X TO 10X RUBY/1000
C1 Alex Tanguay 2.50 6.00
C2 Simon Gagne 3.00 8.00
C3 Kyle Calder 2.00 5.00
C4 Ryan Johnson 2.00 5.00
C5 Dave Tanabe 2.00 5.00
C6 Scott Gomez 2.00 5.00
C7 Patrik Stefan 2.00 5.00
C8 Jiri Fischer 2.00 5.00
C9 Blake Sloan 2.00 5.00
C10 Trevor Letowski 2.00 5.00
C11 Michael York 2.00 5.00
C12 Mike Ribeiro 2.00 5.00
C13 Ladislav Kohn 2.00 5.00
C14 Martin Skoula 2.00 5.00
C15 Steve Kariya 2.00 5.00
C16 Nikolai Antropov 2.00 5.00
C17 David Legwand 2.50 6.00
C18 J-P Dumont 2.00 5.00
C19 Filip Kuba 2.00 5.00
C20 Mike Fisher 2.00 5.00
C21 Tim Connolly 2.00 5.00
C22 Martin Biron 2.50 6.00
C23 Oleg Saprykin 2.00 5.00
C24 Maxim Afinogenov 2.00 5.00
C25 Petr Buzek 2.00 5.00
C26 Paul Comrie 2.00 5.00
C27 Brian Boucher 2.50 6.00
C28 Peter Schaefer 2.00 5.00
C29 Alex Tezikov 2.00 5.00
C30 Milan Hnilicka 2.50 6.00
C31 Brian Rafalski 2.00 5.00
C32 Sami Helenius 2.00 5.00
C33 Frantisek Kaberle 2.00 5.00
C34 Jochen Hecht 2.00 5.00
C35 Mathieu Biron 2.00 5.00
C36 Randy Robitaille 2.00 5.00
C37 Roberto Luongo 4.00 10.00
C38 Steve McCarthy 2.00 5.00
C39 Brad Lukowich 2.00 5.00
C40 Kim Johnsson 2.00 5.00
C41 Brad Stuart 2.00 5.00
C42 Glen Metropolit 2.00 5.00
C43 Marc Denis 2.50 6.00
C44 Robyn Regehr 2.00 5.00
C45 Per Svartvadet 2.00 5.00
C46 Jonathan Girard 2.00 5.00
C47 Mark Eaton 2.00 5.00
C48 Ivan Novoseltsev 2.00 5.00
C49 Jan Hlavac 2.00 5.00
C50 Richard Jackman 2.00 5.00

1999-00 BAP Millennium Goalie Memorabilia

G1 Curtis Joseph 75.00 200.00
G2 Patrick Roy 60.00 150.00
G3 Grant Fuhr 60.00 150.00
G4 Garth Snow 40.00 100.00
G5 Jeff Hackett 30.00 80.00
G6 Chris Osgood 25.00 60.00
G7 Dominik Hasek 40.00 100.00
G8 Arturs Irbe 30.00 80.00

1999-00 BAP Millennium Jerseys

*JSY NUMBER: .6X TO 1.5X BASIC JSY
*JSY EMBLEMS: .8X TO 2X BASIC JSY
*JSY AND STICK: .5X TO 1.2X BASIC JSY
J1 Theo Fleury 8.00 20.00
J2 Brendan Shanahan 12.00 30.00
J3 Curtis Joseph 12.00 30.00
J4 Saku Koivu 12.00 30.00
J5 Dominik Hasek 25.00 60.00
J6 Al MacInnis 8.00 20.00
J7 John LeClair 12.00 30.00
J8 Teemu Selanne 15.00 40.00
J9 Wayne Gretzky 40.00 100.00
J10 Pavel Bure 12.00 30.00
J11 Mark Messier 12.00 30.00
J12 Jaromir Jagr 15.00 40.00
J13 Ray Bourque 20.00 50.00
J14 Chris Chelios 12.00 30.00
J15 Mats Sundin 12.00 30.00
J16 Paul Kariya 12.00 30.00
J17 Peter Bondra 8.00 20.00
J18 Eric Lindros 12.00 30.00
J19 Sergei Fedorov 15.00 40.00
J20 Peter Forsberg 20.00 50.00
J21 Brett Hull 12.00 30.00
J22 Tony Amonte 8.00 20.00
J23 Patrick Roy 30.00 80.00
J24 Ed Belfour 12.00 30.00
J25 Martin Brodeur 25.00 60.00
J26 Brian Leetch 8.00 20.00
J27 Mike Modano 12.00 30.00
J28 Joe Sakic 15.00 40.00
J29 Jeremy Roenick 15.00 40.00
J30 Steve Yzerman 25.00 60.00
J31 Alexander Mogilny 8.00 20.00
J32 Paul Coffey 12.00 30.00

1999-00 BAP Millennium Pearson

COMPLETE SET (16) 125.00 250.00
P1 Jaromir Jagr 10.00 25.00
P2 Dominik Hasek 10.00 25.00
P3 Mario Lemieux 20.00 50.00
P4 Eric Lindros 2.50 6.00
P5 Sergei Fedorov 8.00 20.00
P6 Mark Messier 2.50 6.00
P7 Brett Hull 6.00 15.00
P8 Steve Yzerman 15.00 40.00
P9 Wayne Gretzky 25.00 60.00
P10 Mike Liut 2.50 6.00
P11 Marcel Dionne 4.00 10.00
P12 Guy Lafleur 5.00 12.00
P13 Bobby Orr 25.00 60.00
P14 Phil Esposito 6.00 15.00
P15 Bobby Clarke 6.00 15.00
P16 Jean Ratelle 2.50 6.00

1999-00 BAP Millennium Pearson Autographs

P1 Jaromir Jagr 75.00 200.00
P2 Dominik Hasek 75.00 200.00
P3 Mario Lemieux 125.00 250.00
P4 Eric Lindros 40.00 80.00
P5 Sergei Fedorov 40.00 100.00
P6 Mark Messier 75.00 200.00
P7 Brett Hull 40.00 100.00
P8 Steve Yzerman 75.00 200.00
P9 Wayne Gretzky 500.00 1200.00
P10 Mike Liut 30.00 60.00
P11 Marcel Dionne 40.00 80.00
P12 Guy Lafleur 60.00 150.00
P13 Bobby Orr 250.00 500.00
P14 Phil Esposito 40.00 80.00
P15 Bobby Clarke 40.00 100.00
P16 Jean Ratelle 30.00 60.00

1999-00 BAP Millennium Players of the Decade

COMPLETE SET (10) 60.00 120.00
D1 Wayne Gretzky 15.00 40.00
D2 Mark Messier 3.00 8.00
D3 Patrick Roy 12.50 30.00
D4 Dominik Hasek 5.00 12.00
D5 Jaromir Jagr 4.00 10.00
D6 Eric Lindros 5.00 10.00
D7 Sergei Fedorov 5.00 12.00
D8 Brett Hull 3.00 8.00
D9 Ray Bourque 4.00 10.00
D10 Steve Yzerman 15.00 40.00

1999-00 BAP Millennium Players of the Decade Autographs

D1 Wayne Gretzky 250.00 600.00
D2 Mark Messier 40.00 100.00
D3 Patrick Roy 75.00 200.00
D4 Dominik Hasek 60.00 150.00
D5 Jaromir Jagr 60.00 150.00
D6 Eric Lindros 25.00 60.00
D7 Sergei Fedorov 40.00 100.00
D8 Brett Hull 30.00 80.00
D9 Ray Bourque 40.00 100.00
D10 Steve Yzerman 75.00 200.00

2000-01 BAP Parkhurst 2000

COMPLETE SET (250) 50.00 125.00
COMP.SERIES 1 (100) 20.00 50.00
COMP.UPDATE SET (50) 10.00 25.00
COMP.SIG.SERIES SET (100) 20.00 50.00
P1 Pavel Bure .40 1.00
P2 Tony Amonte .30 .75
P3 Chris Pronger .40 1.00
P4 John Madden .30 .75
P5 Kimmo Timonen .25 .60
P6 Marc Savard .25 .60
P7 Peter Forsberg .75 2.00
P8 Arturs Irbe .30 .75
P9 Mike York .25 .60
P10 Brendan Shanahan .40 1.00
P11 Simon Gagne .40 1.00
P12 Maxim Afinogenov .25 .60
P13 Joe Sakic .75 2.00
P14 Curtis Joseph .50 1.25
P15 Jozef Stumpel .25 .60
P16 Vitali Vishnevsky .25 .60
P17 Owen Nolan .40 1.00
P18 Jan Hrdina .25 .60
P19 Brenden Morrow .30 .75
P20 Todd Bertuzzi .30 .75
P21 Vincent Lecavalier .40 1.00
P22 Andrew Brunette .25 .60
P23 Brendan Morrison .40 1.00
P24 Rod Brind'Amour .40 1.00
P25 Patrik Elias .40 1.00
P26 Joe Thornton .60 1.50
P27 Roman Turek .30 .75
P28 Fred Brathwaite .30 .75
P29 Brian Leetch .30 .75
P30 Trevor Linden .40 1.00
P31 Janne Niinimaa .25 .60
P32 Nikolai Antropov .30 .75
P33 Teemu Selanne .75 2.00
P34 Calle Johansson .25 .60
P35 Boris Mironov .25 .60
P36 Eric Desjardins .30 .75
P37 Mark Parrish .25 .60
P38 Alex Tanguay .30 .75
P39 Jason Arnott .30 .75
P40 Vincent Damphousse .30 .75
P41 Dominik Hasek .60 1.50
P42 Teppo Numminen .25 .60
P43 Patrick Lalime .30 .75
P44 Valeri Bure .30 .75
P45 Adam Oates .40 1.00
P46 Sergei Zubov .30 .75
P47 Tim Connolly .25 .60
P48 Pavel Kubina .25 .60
P49 Nicklas Lidstrom .40 1.00
P50 Mark Recchi .50 1.25
P51 Chris Drury .30 .75
P52 Kyle McLaren .25 .60
P53 Steve Kariya .25 .60
P54 Scott Gomez .30 .75
P55 Rob Blake .40 1.00
P56 Miroslav Satan .25 .60
P57 Cliff Ronning .25 .60
P58 Radek Dvorak .30 .75
P59 Jeff O'Neill .30 .75
P60 Dainius Zubrus .25 .60
P61 Brad Ference .25 .60
P62 Jarome Iginla .50 1.25
P63 Chris Simon .25 .60
P64 Darryl Sydor .30 .75
P65 Daniel Alfredsson .40 1.00
P66 Sandis Ozolinsh .25 .60
P67 Brian Rafalski .25 .60
P68 Ryan Smyth .30 .75
P69 John LeClair .40 1.00
P70 Patrik Stefan .30 .75
P71 Patrick Marleau .40 1.00
P72 Roberto Luongo .60 1.50
P73 Chris Osgood .40 1.00
P74 Pierre Turgeon .30 .75
P75 Zigmund Palffy .40 1.00
P76 Jeff Farkas .25 .60
P77 Milan Hejduk .30 .75
P78 Ray Whitney .30 .75
P79 Felix Potvin .60 1.50
P80 Chris Gratton .25 .60
P81 Brad Stuart .30 .75
P82 Ron Francis .50 1.25
P83 Oleg Tverdovsky .25 .60
P84 Alexei Kovalev .30 .75
P85 Sergei Fedorov .60 1.50
P86 Nick Boynton .25 .60
P87 David Legwand .40 1.00
P88 Robyn Regehr .25 .60
P89 Brian Boucher .30 .75
P90 Roman Hamrlik .25 .60
P91 Jochen Hecht .25 .60
P92 Alexei Zhamnov .30 .75
P93 Olaf Kolzig .40 1.00
P94 Jose Theodore .40 1.00
P95 Jeremy Roenick .60 1.50
P96 Theo Fleury .50 1.25
P97 Patrick Roy 1.00 2.50
P98 Marian Hossa .40 1.00
P99 Martin Brodeur 1.00 2.50
P100 Brett Hull .75 2.00
P101 Daniel Sedin .50 1.25
P102 Paul Coffey .40 1.00
P103 Ray Bourque .60 1.50
P104 Glen Murray .30 .75
P105 Mariusz Czerkawski .25 .60
P106 Jeff Friesen .25 .60
P107 Sergei Samsonov .30 .75
P108 Tyler Wright .25 .60
P109 Manny Fernandez .25 .60
P110 Mike Richter .40 1.00
P111 Pavol Demitra .50 1.25
P112 Brian Rolston .30 .75
P113 Ron Tugnutt .30 .75
P114 Alexander Mogilny .30 .75
P115 Radek Bonk .30 .75
P116 Al MacInnis .50 1.25
P117 J-P Dumont .25 .60
P118 Ed Belfour .40 1.00
P119 Jeff Hackett .25 .60
P120 Shawn McEachern .25 .60
P121 Dan Cloutier .30 .75
P122 Mika Noronen .25 .60
P123 Derian Hatcher .30 .75
P124 Saku Koivu .40 1.00
P125 Keith Primeau .30 .75
P126 Mats Sundin .40 1.00
P127 Damian Rhodes .25 .60
P128 Chris Chelios .40 1.00
P129 Mike Dunham .25 .60
P130 Keith Tkachuk .40 1.00
P131 Steve Thomas .25 .60
P132 Phil Housley .30 .75
P133 Doug Weight .40 1.00
P134 Kris Beech .25 .60
P135 Jyrki Lumme .25 .60
P136 Guy Hebert .30 .75
P137 Sami Kapanen .25 .60
P138 Trevor Kidd .25 .60
P139 Marian Gaborik .75 2.00
P140 Martin Straka .30 .75
P141 Ed Jovanovski .30 .75
P142 Jean-Sebastien Aubin .30 .75
P143 Viktor Kozlov .30 .75
P144 Scott Stevens .40 1.00
P145 Jiri Slegr .25 .60
P146 Steve Yzerman 1.00 2.50
P147 Jocelyn Thibault .30 .75
P148 Stephane Fiset .25 .60
P149 Kenny Jonsson .25 .60
P150 Steve Shields .25 .60
P151 Paul Kariya .40 1.00
P152 Shane Willis .25 .60
P153 Martin Lapointe .30 .75
P154 Brian Savage .25 .60
P155 Alexei Yashin .30 .75
P156 Marcus Ragnarsson .25 .60
P157 Petr Tenkrat .25 .60
P158 Sandis Ozolinsh .25 .60
P159 Anson Carter .30 .75
P160 Scott Hartnell .60 1.50
P161 Rick Tocchet .30 .75
P162 Brad Richards .40 1.00
P163 Byron Dafoe .30 .75
P164 Marc Denis .30 .75
P165 Steve Reinprecht .40 1.00
P166 Mario Lemieux 1.50 4.00
P167 Taylor Pyatt .25 .60
P168 Mike Vernon .30 .75
P169 Scott Niedermayer .40 1.00
P170 Milan Kraft .25 .60
P171 Donald Audette .30 .75
P172 Steve Sullivan .25 .60
P173 Todd Marchant .25 .60
P174 Scott Walker .25 .60
P175 Daymond Langkow .25 .60
P176 Fredrik Modin .25 .60
P177 Ray Ferraro .25 .60
P178 Michael Nylander .25 .60
P179 Robert Svehla .25 .60
P180 Petr Sykora .30 .75
P181 Claude Lemieux .30 .75
P182 Sergei Berezin .25 .60
P183 Doug Gilmour .50 1.25
P184 Jere Lehtinen .30 .75
P185 Maxim Sushinski .25 .60
P186 Jan Hlavac .25 .60
P187 Michal Handzus .25 .60
P188 Jamie Langenbrunner .30 .75
P189 John Vanbiesbrouck .40 1.00
P190 Brent Johnson .30 .75
P191 Jason Allison .30 .75
P192 Adam Deadmarsh .25 .60
P193 Scott Mellanby .25 .60
P194 Sergei Brylin .25 .60
P195 Shane Doan .30 .75
P196 Jonas Hoglund .25 .60
P197 Bill Guerin .40 1.00
P198 Espen Knutsen .25 .60
P199 Bryan Smolinski .30 .75
P200 Brad Isbister .25 .60
P201 Robert Lang .25 .60
P202 Andrew Cassels .25 .60
P203 Daniel Tkaczuk .30 .75
P204 Igor Larionov .40 1.00
P205 Andrei Markov .50 1.25
P206 Magnus Arvedson .25 .60
P207 Henrik Sedin .50 1.25
P208 Manny Legace .25 .60
P209 Adam Graves .30 .75
P210 Marty Turco .50 1.25
P211 Stu Barnes .30 .75
P212 Geoff Sanderson .30 .75
P213 Luc Robitaille .40 1.00
P214 Roman Hamrlik .25 .60
P215 Jaromir Jagr 1.25 3.00
P216 Markus Naslund .40 1.00
P217 Alexei Zhitnik .30 .75
P218 Joe Nieuwendyk .30 .75
P219 Lubomir Sekeras .25 .60
P220 Petr Nedved .30 .75
P221 Dallas Drake .25 .60
P222 Sergei Gonchar .25 .60
P223 Dave Tanabe .25 .60
P224 Tommy Salo .30 .75
P225 Rick DiPietro .50 1.25
P226 Justin Williams .60 1.50
P227 Dimitri Khristich .25 .60
P228 Lubomir Visnovsky .50 1.25
P229 Jani Hurme .25 .60
P230 Roman Cechmanek .30 .75
P231 Cory Stillman .25 .60
P232 Mike Modano .60 1.50
P233 Scott Pellerin .25 .60
P234 Mark Messier .75 2.00
P235 Scott Young .25 .60
P236 Peter Bondra .40 1.00
P237 Oleg Saprykin .25 .60
P238 Pat Verbeek .30 .75
P239 Martin Rucinsky .25 .60
P240 Martin Havlat .75 2.00
P241 Evgeni Nabokov .30 .75
P242 Tomi Kallio .25 .60
P243 Eric Daze .30 .75
P244 Roberto Luongo .60 1.50
P245 Bobby Holik .25 .60
P246 Sean Burke .25 .60
P247 Martin Biron .30 .75
P248 Mathieu Garon .25 .60
P249 Jamie Storr .30 .75
P250 Maxime Ouellet .40 1.00

2006-07 Be A Player Portraits

COMP.SET w/o SPs (100) 12.00 30.00
1 Jean-Sebastien Giguere .30 .75
2 Chris Pronger .30 .75
3 Teemu Selanne .60 1.50
4 Scott Niedermayer .30 .75
5 Ilya Kovalchuk .30 .75
6 Kari Lehtonen .25 .60
7 Marian Hossa .30 .75
8 Marc Savard .20 .50
9 Brad Boyes .20 .50
10 Patrice Bergeron .40 1.00
11 Hannu Toivonen .25 .60
12 Zdeno Chara .30 .75
13 Daniel Briere .30 .75
14 Chris Drury .25 .60
15 Ryan Miller .30 .75
16 Jarome Iginla .40 1.00
17 Miikka Kiprusoff .30 .75
18 Dion Phaneuf .25 .60
19 Alex Tanguay .20 .50
20 Rod Brind`Amour .30 .75
21 Erik Cole .20 .50
22 Eric Staal .40 1.00
23 Cam Ward .30 .75
24 Nikolai Khabibulin .30 .75
25 Martin Havlat .20 .50
26 Tuomo Ruutu .30 .75
27 Marek Svatos .20 .50
28 Joe Sakic .60 1.50
29 Jose Theodore .30 .75
30 Milan Hejduk .25 .60
31 Rick Nash .30 .75
32 Nikolai Zherdev .20 .50
33 Sergei Federov .50 1.25
34 Gilbert Brule .25 .60
35 Mike Modano .50 1.25
36 Marty Turco .30 .75
37 Brenden Morrow .25 .60
38 Eric Lindros .50 1.25
39 Dominik Hasek .50 1.25
40 Pavel Datsyuk .50 1.25
41 Nicklas Lidstrom .30 .75
42 Henrik Zetterberg .40 1.00
43 Ales Hemsky .25 .60
44 Ryan Smyth .25 .60
45 Joffrey Lupul .20 .50
46 Shawn Horcoff .20 .50
47 Ed Belfour .30 .75
48 Olli Jokinen .30 .75
49 Nathan Horton .30 .75
50 Todd Bertuzzi .30 .75
51 Rob Blake .30 .75
52 Alexander Frolov .20 .50
53 Pavol Demitra .40 1.00
54 Manny Fernandez .20 .50
55 Marian Gaborik .30 .75
56 Cristobal Huet .25 .60
57 Sergei Samsonov .25 .60
58 Saku Koivu .30 .75
59 Michael Ryder .20 .50
60 Paul Kariya .30 .75
61 Tomas Vokoun .25 .60
62 Martin Brodeur .75 2.00
63 Patrik Elias .30 .75
64 Brian Gionta .20 .50
65 Alexei Yashin .25 .60
66 Miroslav Satan .25 .60
67 Rick DiPietro .25 .60
68 Jaromir Jagr 1.00 2.50
69 Henrik Lundqvist .75 2.00
70 Brendan Shanahan .30 .75
71 Dany Heatley .25 .60
72 Jason Spezza .30 .75
73 Wade Redden .20 .50
74 Daniel Alfredsson .30 .75
75 Peter Forsberg .60 1.50
76 Antero Niittymaki .25 .60
77 Jeff Carter .25 .60
78 Simon Gagne .30 .75
79 Curtis Joseph .40 1.00
80 Jeremy Roenick .50 1.25
81 Shane Doan .25 .60
82 Marc-Andre Fleury .60 1.50
83 Sidney Crosby 1.25 3.00
84 Joe Thornton .50 1.25
85 Patrick Marleau .30 .75
86 Jonathan Cheechoo .25 .60
87 Keith Tkachuk .30 .75
88 Doug Weight .30 .75
89 Brad Richards .30 .75
90 Vincent Lecavalier .30 .75
91 Martin St. Louis .30 .75
92 Mats Sundin .30 .75
93 Alexander Steen .20 .50
94 Michael Peca .25 .60
95 Andrew Raycroft .25 .60
96 Markus Naslund .30 .75
97 Brendan Morrison .20 .50
98 Roberto Luongo .50 1.25
99 Alexander Ovechkin 1.25 3.00
100 Olaf Kolzig .30 .75
101 Yan Stastny RC 1.25 3.00
102 Mark Stuart RC 1.25 3.00
103 Evgeni Malkin RC 8.00 20.00
104 Patrick Thoresen RC 1.25 3.00
105 Patrick O'Sullivan RC 2.00 5.00
106 Tomas Kopecky RC 1.50 4.00
107 M-A Pouliot RC 1.25 3.00
108 Konstantin Pushkarev RC 1.50 4.00
109 Phil Kessel RC 4.00 10.00
110 Luc Bourdon RC 2.00 5.00
111 Shea Weber RC 3.00 8.00
112 G. Latendresse RC 2.00 5.00
113 Jordan Staal RC 3.00 8.00
114 Paul Stastny RC 3.00 8.00
115 Anze Kopitar RC 6.00 15.00
116 Jarkko Immonen RC 1.50 4.00
117 Travis Zajac RC 2.50 6.00
118 Nigel Dawes RC 1.25 3.00
119 Kristopher Letang RC 5.00 12.00
120 Ryan Potulny RC 1.25 3.00
121 Ryan Shannon RC 1.25 3.00
122 Marc-Edouard Vlasic RC 2.00 5.00
123 Noah Welch RC 1.25 3.00
124 Ladislav Smid RC 1.25 3.00
125 Matt Carle RC 1.25 3.00
126 Loui Eriksson RC 2.50 6.00
127 Brendan Bell RC 1.25 3.00
128 Ian White RC 1.50 4.00
129 Jeremy Williams RC 1.25 3.00
130 Eric Fehr RC 2.00 5.00

2006-07 Be A Player Portraits First Exposures

FEAK Andrei Kostitsyn 3.00 8.00
FEAL Andrew Ladd 2.50 6.00
FEAM Andrej Meszaros 2.50 6.00
FEAO Alexander Ovechkin 10.00 25.00
FEAP Alexander Perezhogin 2.50 6.00
FEAS Alexander Steen 2.50 6.00
FEBB Brandon Bochenski 2.50 6.00
FEBW Brad Winchester 2.50 6.00
FECB Cam Barker 2.50 6.00
FECP Corey Perry 6.00 15.00
FECW Cam Ward 4.00 10.00
FEDB Derek Boogaard 6.00 15.00
FEDP Daniel Paille 3.00 8.00
FEDP Dion Phaneuf 3.00 8.00
FEEN Eric Nystrom 2.50 6.00
FEGB Gilbert Brule 3.00 8.00
FEHL Henrik Lundqvist 10.00 25.00
FEHT Hannu Toivonen 3.00 8.00
FEJC Jeff Carter 3.00 8.00
FEJF Johan Franzen 3.00 8.00
FEJG Josh Gorges 2.50 6.00
FEJH Jim Howard 6.00 15.00
FEJJ Jussi Jokinen 3.00 8.00
FEJK Jakub Klepis 2.50 6.00
FEJT Jeff Tambellini 2.50 6.00
FEMJ Milan Jurcina 2.50 6.00
FEMK Mikko Koivu 3.00 8.00
FEMR Mike Richards 3.00 8.00
FEPB Peter Budaj 3.00 8.00
FEPN Petteri Nokelainen 2.50 6.00
FEPP Petr Prucha 3.00 8.00
FERG Ryan Getzlaf 4.00 10.00

FERO Rostislav Olesz 2.50 6.00
FERS Ryan Suter 3.00 8.00
FERU R.J. Umberger 2.50 6.00
FERW Ryan Whitney 3.00 8.00
FESC Sidney Crosby 15.00 40.00
FETV Thomas Vanek 3.00 8.00
FEVF Valtteri Filppula 2.50 6.00
FEWW Wojtek Wolski 3.00 8.00
FEYD Yann Danis 3.00 8.00
FEZP Zach Parise 4.00 10.00

2006-07 Be A Player Portraits Signature Portraits

SPAL Andrew Ladd 8.00 20.00
SPAO Alexander Ovechkin 80.00 200.00
SPAT Alex Tanguay 8.00 20.00
SPBB Brad Boyes 8.00 20.00
SPBG Bill Guerin 12.00 30.00
SPBH Bobby Holik 8.00 20.00
SPBL Brian Leetch 10.00 25.00
SPBM Brenden Morrow 10.00 25.00
SPBR Brian Rolston 10.00 25.00
SPBS Brent Seabrook 8.00 20.00
SPBW Brad Winchester 8.00 20.00
SPCA Colby Armstrong 10.00 25.00
SPCB Cam Barker 8.00 20.00
SPCD Chris Drury SP 15.00 40.00
SPCH Jonathan Cheechoo 10.00 25.00
SPCW Cam Ward 12.00 30.00
SPDB Daniel Briere SP 20.00 50.00
SPDH Dany Heatley 10.00 25.00
SPDP Daniel Paille 10.00 25.00
SPDR Dwayne Roloson 10.00 25.00
SPDW Doug Weight SP 20.00 50.00
SPEJ Ed Jovanovski 10.00 25.00
SPEM Evgeni Malkin 30.00 80.00
SPEN Evgeni Nabokov 10.00 25.00
SPES Robert Esche 10.00 25.00
SPGM Glen Murray 10.00 25.00
SPHA Jeff Halpern 8.00 20.00
SPHE Milan Hejduk 10.00 25.00
SPHK Dominik Hasek 20.00 50.00
SPHL Henrik Lundqvist 30.00 80.00
SPHT Hannu Toivonen 10.00 25.00
SPJB Jay Bouwmeester SP 12.00 30.00
SPJC Jeff Carter 10.00 25.00
SPJG Jean-Sebastien Giguere SP 20.00 50.00
SPJI Jarome Iginla 15.00 40.00
SPJJ Jussi Jokinen 10.00 25.00
SPJO Joe Thornton 20.00 50.00
SPJP Joni Pitkanen 8.00 20.00
SPJS Joe Sakic 25.00 60.00
SPKB Keith Ballard 8.00 20.00
SPKL Kari Lehtonen 10.00 25.00
SPKO Mikko Koivu 10.00 25.00
SPKP Keith Primeau 10.00 25.00
SPLE John LeClair 12.00 30.00
SPLS Lee Stempniak 8.00 20.00
SPMA Marc-Andre Fleury 25.00 60.00
SPMB Mark Bell 8.00 20.00
SPMG Martin Gerber 10.00 25.00
SPMH Marian Hossa 12.00 30.00
SPMJ Milan Jurcina 8.00 20.00
SPMK Miikka Kiprusoff 12.00 30.00
SPMM Mike Modano SP 30.00 80.00
SPMN Markus Naslund 12.00 30.00
SPMO Brendan Morrison 8.00 20.00
SPMS Marek Svatos 8.00 20.00
SPMT Marty Turco 12.00 30.00
SPNH Nathan Horton 12.00 30.00
SPNK Nikolai Khabibulin SP 20.00 50.00
SPNL Nicklas Lidstrom 12.00 30.00
SPNZ Nikolai Zherdev 8.00 20.00
SPOJ Olli Jokinen SP 20.00 50.00
SPOK Olaf Kolzig 12.00 30.00
SPPB Patrice Bergeron 30.00 80.00
SPPK Paul Kariya 12.00 30.00
SPPM Patrick Marleau 12.00 30.00
SPPP Petr Prucha 10.00 25.00
SPRB Rob Blake 12.00 30.00
SPRD Mike Richards 10.00 25.00
SPRJ R.J. Umberger 8.00 20.00
SPRL Roberto Luongo 20.00 50.00
SPRM Ryan Miller 12.00 30.00
SPRN Rick Nash 12.00 30.00
SPRO Rostislav Olesz 8.00 20.00
SPRW Ryan Whitney 10.00 25.00
SPSB Steve Bernier 8.00 20.00
SPSC Sidney Crosby SP 200.00 500.00
SPSD Shane Doan 10.00 25.00
SPSF Sergei Fedorov SP 30.00 80.00
SPSG Simon Gagne SP 20.00 50.00
SPSJ Matt Stajan 8.00 20.00
SPSK Saku Koivu 12.00 30.00
SPSM Mats Sundin 12.00 30.00
SPSN Scott Niedermayer 12.00 30.00
SPSP Jason Spezza 12.00 30.00
SPSR Ryan Suter 10.00 25.00
SPSS Steve Sullivan 8.00 20.00
SPST Eric Staal 15.00 40.00
SPTP Tom Poti 8.00 20.00
SPTR Tuomo Ruutu 12.00 30.00
SPTV Thomas Vanek 10.00 25.00
SPVO Tomas Vokoun 10.00 25.00
SPWR Wade Redden 8.00 20.00
SPWW Wojtek Wolski 10.00 25.00
SPZC Zdeno Chara 12.00 30.00

2006-07 Be A Player Portraits Dual Signature Portraits

DSBB B.Boyes/P.Bergeron 12.00 30.00
DSCJ Z.Chara/M.Jurcina 10.00 25.00
DSCT J.Thornton/J.Cheech SP 40.00 80.00
DSDB C.Drury/D.Briere 10.00 25.00
DSDJ J.Spezza/D.Heatley 10.00 25.00
DSFN R.Nash/S.Fedorov 15.00 40.00
DSFW M.Fleury/R.Whitney 20.00 50.00
DSGC S.Gagne/J.Carter 10.00 25.00
DSGN S.Nieder/J.Giguere 10.00 25.00
DSHL D.Hasek/N.Lidstrom 15.00 40.00
DSHS M.Hejduk/M.Svatos 8.00 20.00
DSIT J.Iginla/A.Tanguay 12.00 30.00
DSJB O.Jokinen/J.Bouwmeester 10.00 25.00
DSKK S.Koivu/M.Koivu 10.00 25.00
DSKV P.Kariya/T.Vokoun 10.00 25.00
DSLN M.Naslund/R.Luongo 15.00 40.00
DSLP H.Lundqvist/P.Prucha 25.00 60.00
DSMT M.Modano/M.Turco 15.00 40.00
DSNT T.Ruutu/N.Khabibulin 10.00 25.00
DSOK O.Kolzig/A.Ovechkin 80.00 200.00
DSRU M.Richards/R.Umberger 8.00 20.00
DSSM J.Sakic/M.Modano SP 50.00 100.00
DSWG D.Weight/B.Guerin 10.00 25.00
DSWS E.Staal/C.Ward 12.00 30.00

2006-07 Be A Player Portraits Triple Signature Portraits

TBOS Murray/Boyes/Berg 50.00 125.00
TBUF Drury/Briere/Miller 40.00 100.00
TCLB Nash/Zherd/Fed 60.00 150.00
TCOL Sakic/Hejd/Svat 80.00 200.00
TLWF Luongo/Fleury/Ward 80.00 200.00
TNSS Spezza/Nash/Staal 50.00 125.00
TOTT Heat/Redd/Spezza 40.00 100.00
TSJS Thorn/Bell/Cheech 60.00 150.00
TSSM Sakic/Mo/Sundin 80.00 200.00

2000-01 BAP Signature Series

COMP.SET w/o SP's (250) 50.00 100.00
1 Doug Gilmour .75 2.00
2 Todd Reirden .40 1.00
3 Mike Johnson .40 1.00
4 Scott Walker .40 1.00
5 Mike York .40 1.00
6 Roman Turek .50 1.25
7 Sergei Zubov .50 1.25
8 Brad Stuart .50 1.25
9 Michael Peca .50 1.25
10 Jyrki Lumme .40 1.00
11 Steve Yzerman 1.50 4.00
12 Olaf Kolzig .60 1.50
13 Ray Bourque 1.00 2.50
14 Clarke Wilm .40 1.00
15 Eric Desjardins .50 1.25
16 Rod Brind'Amour .60 1.50
17 Marc Savard .40 1.00
18 Jarome Iginla .75 2.00
19 Daniel Alfredsson .60 1.50
20 Alexei Yashin .50 1.25
21 Keith Tkachuk .60 1.50
22 Jaromir Jagr 2.00 5.00
23 Trevor Kidd .40 1.00
24 Alexei Kovalev .50 1.25
25 Jan Hrdina .40 1.00
26 Tom Poti .40 1.00
27 Jere Karalahti .40 1.00
28 Janne Niinimaa .40 1.00
29 Ray Whitney .50 1.25
30 Nicklas Lidstrom .60 1.50
31 Martin Lapointe .50 1.25
32 Matt Cullen .40 1.00
33 Theo Fleury .75 2.00
34 Mats Sundin .60 1.50
35 Kimmo Timonen .40 1.00
36 Joe Thornton 1.00 2.50
37 Adam Graves .50 1.25
38 Andrei Zyuzin .40 1.00
39 Michal Handzus .40 1.00
40 Jamie Storr .50 1.25
41 Teemu Selanne 1.25 3.00
42 Brian Rafalski .40 1.00
43 Aaron Gavey .40 1.00
44 Jose Theodore .60 1.50
45 Tyler Wright .40 1.00
46 Alexander Mogilny .50 1.25
47 Brad Isbister .40 1.00
48 Guy Hebert .50 1.25
49 Chris Simon .40 1.00
50 Dominik Hasek 1.00 2.50
51 Dan Cloutier .50 1.25
52 Brian Holzinger .40 1.00
53 Dimitri Khristich .40 1.00
54 Tyson Nash .40 1.00
55 Patrick Marleau .60 1.50
56 Marty Reasoner .40 1.00
57 Manny Fernandez .40 1.00
58 Brenden Morrow .50 1.25
59 Darren McCarty .40 1.00
60 Milan Hejduk .50 1.25
61 Darius Kasparaitis .50 1.25
62 Jere Lehtinen .50 1.25
63 Andrew Brunette .40 1.00
64 Wayne Gretzky 4.00 10.00
65 Robyn Regehr .40 1.00
66 Travis Green .40 1.00
67 John Grahame .40 1.00
68 Mike Fisher .40 1.00
69 Josef Marha .40 1.00
70 Randy McKay .40 1.00
71 Brett Hull 1.25 3.00
72 Anson Carter .50 1.25
73 Owen Nolan .60 1.50
74 Sean Burke .40 1.00
75 Mario Lemieux 2.50 6.00
76 Brian Savage .40 1.00
77 Jason Ward .40 1.00
78 Patrick Lalime .50 1.25
79 Glen Murray .50 1.25
80 Mathieu Biron .40 1.00
81 Todd Bertuzzi .50 1.25
82 Chris Drury .50 1.25
83 Maxim Afinogenov .40 1.00
84 Michal Rozsival .40 1.00
85 Glen Metropolit .40 1.00
86 Mariusz Czerkawski .40 1.00
87 Byron Dafoe .50 1.25
88 Mark Recchi .75 2.00
89 Mike Modano 1.00 2.50
90 Felix Potvin 1.00 2.50
91 Saku Koivu .60 1.50
92 Jay Pandolfo .40 1.00
93 Todd Simpson .40 1.00
94 Calle Johansson .40 1.00
95 Bill Guerin .60 1.50
96 Oleg Tverdovsky .40 1.00
97 Kyle McLaren .40 1.00
98 Mark Messier 1.25 3.00
99 Chris Gratton .40 1.00
100 Sergei Brylin .40 1.00
101 David Legwand .60 1.50
102 Jason Allison .50 1.25
103 Daniel Cleary .50 1.25
104 Curtis Joseph .75 2.00
105 Sergei Fedorov 1.00 2.50
106 Jeremy Roenick 1.00 2.50
107 Frantisek Kaberle .40 1.00
108 Chris Pronger .60 1.50
109 Martin Skoula .50 1.25
110 Jiri Slegr .40 1.00
111 Trevor Letowski .40 1.00
112 Colin Forbes .40 1.00
113 Sergei Zholtok .40 1.00
114 David Harlock .40 1.00
115 Scott Stevens .60 1.50
116 Dave Tanabe .40 1.00
117 Mattias Timander .40 1.00
118 Stu Barnes .50 1.25
119 Simon Gagne .60 1.50
120 Paul Coffey .60 1.50
121 Peter Bondra .60 1.50
122 Ed Jovanovski .50 1.25
123 J-P Dumont .40 1.00
124 Pavol Demitra .75 2.00
125 Mike Vernon .50 1.25
126 Brendan Morrison .60 1.50
127 Dainius Zubrus .40 1.00
128 Al MacInnis .75 2.00
129 Kevyn Adams .40 1.00
130 Petr Buzek .40 1.00
131 Steve Kariya .40 1.00
132 Keith Primeau .50 1.25
133 Kenny Jonsson .40 1.00
134 Lance Pitlick .40 1.00
135 Randy Robitaille .40 1.00
136 Brian Rolston .50 1.25
137 Alex Tanguay .50 1.25
138 Alexei Zhamnov .50 1.25
139 Peter Forsberg 1.25 3.00
140 Cam Stewart .40 1.00
141 Vitali Vishnevsky .40 1.00
142 Tim Connolly .40 1.00
143 Tie Domi .50 1.25
144 Jaroslav Modry .40 1.00
145 Jarno Kultanen RC .40 1.00
146 Igor Larionov .60 1.50
147 Derian Hatcher .50 1.25
148 Scott Niedermayer .60 1.50
149 Shawn McEachern .40 1.00
150 Sergei Berezin .40 1.00
151 Rob Blake .60 1.50
152 Steve Thomas .40 1.00
153 Ryan Smyth .50 1.25
154 Petr Nedved .50 1.25
155 Jochen Hecht .40 1.00
156 Richard Zednik .50 1.25
157 Tommy Salo .50 1.25
158 Ed Belfour .60 1.50
159 Lyle Odelein .40 1.00
160 Steve Sullivan .40 1.00
161 Vincent Damphousse .50 1.25
162 Andy Delmore .40 1.00
163 Harold Druken .40 1.00
164 Martin Brodeur 1.50 4.00
165 Mike Richter .60 1.50
166 Radek Bonk .50 1.25
167 Joe Sakic 1.25 3.00
168 John Vanbiesbrouck .60 1.50
169 Jeff Shantz .40 1.00
170 Jean-Sebastien Aubin .50 1.25
171 Shayne Corson .50 1.25
172 Jeff Friesen .40 1.00
173 Jeff Hackett .40 1.00
174 Jozef Stumpel .40 1.00
175 Daymond Langkow .40 1.00
176 Nikolai Antropov .50 1.25
177 Ron Tugnutt .50 1.25
178 Viktor Kozlov .50 1.25
179 Adam Oates .60 1.50
180 Steve Webb .40 1.00
181 Pierre Turgeon .50 1.25
182 Fred Brathwaite .50 1.25
183 Martin Biron .50 1.25
184 John LeClair .60 1.50
185 Steve Rucchin .40 1.00
186 Patrik Elias .60 1.50
187 Boris Mironov .40 1.00
188 Mika Alatalo .40 1.00
189 Jocelyn Thibault .50 1.25
190 Jason York .40 1.00
191 Zigmund Palffy .60 1.50
192 Paul Kariya .60 1.50
193 Stu Grimson .40 1.00
194 Jeff Halpern .40 1.00
195 Scott Gomez .50 1.25
196 Tomas Vlasak .40 1.00
197 Roman Hamrlik .40 1.00
198 Radek Dvorak .50 1.25
199 Martin Straka .50 1.25
200 Martin Rucinsky .40 1.00
201 Valeri Bure .50 1.25
202 Scott Mellanby .40 1.00
203 Steve McKenna .40 1.00
204 Luc Robitaille .60 1.50
205 Joe Nieuwendyk .50 1.25
206 Brendan Shanahan .60 1.50
207 Robert Lang .40 1.00
208 Todd Marchant .40 1.00
209 Doug Weight .60 1.50
210 Andre Roy .40 1.00
211 Patrick Roy 1.50 4.00
212 Vincent Lecavalier .60 1.50
213 Trevor Linden .60 1.50
214 Patrik Stefan .50 1.25
215 Jan Hlavac .40 1.00
216 Ron Francis .75 2.00
217 Brian Boucher .50 1.25
218 Tony Hrkac .40 1.00
219 Brian Leetch .50 1.25
220 Tony Amonte .50 1.25
221 Nikolai Khabibulin 1.00 2.50
222 Sandis Ozolinsh .40 1.00
223 Darryl Sydor .50 1.25
224 Bobby Holik .40 1.00
225 Sami Kapanen .40 1.00
226 Pavel Bure .60 1.50
227 Steve Konowalchuk .40 1.00
228 Brent Gilchrist .40 1.00
229 Jeff O'Neill .50 1.25
230 Andre Savage .40 1.00
231 Pavel Kubina .40 1.00
232 Jason Arnott .50 1.25
233 Petr Sykora .50 1.25
234 Miroslav Satan .40 1.00
235 Chris Osgood .60 1.50
236 Sergei Samsonov .50 1.25
237 Marian Hossa .60 1.50
238 Arturs Irbe .50 1.25
239 Josh Holden .40 1.00
240 Phil Housley .50 1.25
241 Dimitri Yushkevich .40 1.00
242 Cliff Ronning .40 1.00
243 John Madden .50 1.25
244 Jaroslav Spacek .40 1.00
245 Craig Darby .40 1.00
246 Eric Lindros 1.00 2.50
247 Markus Naslund .60 1.50
248 Sergei Gonchar .40 1.00
249 Gary Roberts .40 1.00
250 Steve Shields .40 1.00
251 Petteri Nummelin RC 1.00 2.50
252 Mika Noronen SP 1.00 2.50
253 Andrew Raycroft RC 2.50 6.00
254 Taylor Pyatt SP 1.00 2.50
255 Toni Lydman SP 1.00 2.50
256 Matt Bradley SP 1.00 2.50
257 Petr Hubacek RC 1.00 2.50
258 Ossi Vaananen RC 1.25 3.00
259 Dimitri Kalinin SP 1.00 2.50
260 Justin Williams RC 2.50 6.00
261 Jeff Farkas SP 1.00 2.50
262 Brent Sopel RC 1.50 4.00
263 Samuel Pahlsson SP 1.00 2.50
264 Josef Vasicek RC 2.50 6.00
265 Shane Willis SP 1.00 2.50
266 Petr Svoboda RC 1.25 3.00
267 Petr Schastlivy SP 1.00 2.50
268 Roman Simicek RC 1.00 2.50
269 Reto Von Arx RC 1.25 3.00
270 Colin White RC 1.00 2.50
271 Lubomir Sekeras RC 1.00 2.50
272 Alexander Kharitonov RC 1.00 2.50
273 Maxim Sushinski SP 1.00 2.50
274 Sergei Vyshedkevich RC 1.00 2.50
275 Brad Ference SP 1.00 2.50
276 Martin Havlat RC 5.00 12.00
277 Maxime Ouellet SP 2.50 6.00
278 Roberto Luongo SP 4.00 10.00
279 Marian Gaborik RC 8.00 20.00
280 Daniel Sedin SP 3.00 8.00
281 Henrik Sedin SP 3.00 8.00
282 Milan Kraft SP 1.50 4.00
283 Denis Shvidki SP 1.50 4.00
284 Kris Beech SP 1.50 4.00
285 Rostislav Klesla RC 4.00 10.00
286 Jani Hurme RC 1.50 4.00
287 Oleg Saprykin SP 1.50 4.00
288 Marty Turco RC 3.00 8.00
289 Brad Richards SP 2.50 6.00
290 Steve McCarthy SP 1.50 4.00
291 Tomi Kallio SP 1.50 4.00
292 Evgeni Nabokov SP 2.00 5.00
293 Steven Reinprecht RC 2.50 6.00
294 Andrei Markov SP 3.00 8.00
295 Brent Johnson SP 2.00 5.00
296 Rick DiPietro RC 3.00 8.00
297 Roman Cechmanek RC 2.00 5.00
298 Daniel Tkaczuk SP 2.00 5.00
299 Mathieu Garon SP 1.50 4.00
300 Scott Hartnell RC 4.00 10.00

2000-01 BAP Signature Series Ruby

*1-250 VETS/200: 1.5X TO 4X BASIC CARDS
*251-275 SP/200: .5X TO 1.5X BASIC SP/1000
*276-230 SP/200: .5X TO 1X BASIC SP/500
98 Mark Messier 5.00 12.00

2000-01 BAP Signature Series Sapphire

*STARS: 2X TO 6X BASIC CARDS
*SP's 251-275: .4X TO 1X
*SP's 276-300: .3X TO .8X

2000-01 BAP Signature Series Autographs

*GOLD: .6X TO 1.2X SILVER AU
*GOLD: .4X TO 1X SILVER AU SP
1 Pavel Bure SP 12.00 30.00
2 Valeri Bure SP 8.00 20.00
3 Mike Johnson 2.50 6.00
4 Rob Blake 4.00 10.00
5 Brendan Morrison 4.00 10.00
6 David Legwand 4.00 10.00
7 Dimitri Kalinin 2.50 6.00
8 Jeff Farkas 2.50 6.00
9 Brian Savage 2.50 6.00
10 Dan Cloutier 3.00 8.00
11 Tom Poti 2.50 6.00
12 Doug Gilmour SP 12.00 30.00
13 Steve Konowalchuk 2.50 6.00
14 Scott Mellanby 2.50 6.00
15 Brent Sopel 4.00 10.00
16 Ron Tugnutt SP 8.00 20.00
17 Steve Thomas 2.50 6.00
18 Dainius Zubrus 2.50 6.00
19 Jason Allison SP 8.00 20.00
20 Jason Ward 2.50 6.00
21 Brian Holzinger 2.50 6.00
22 Jere Karalahti 2.50 6.00
23 Todd Reirden 2.50 6.00
24 Brent Gilchrist 2.50 6.00
25 Steve McKenna 2.50 6.00
26 Viktor Kozlov 3.00 8.00
27 Ryan Smyth 3.00 8.00
28 Al MacInnis SP 12.00 30.00
29 Daniel Cleary 3.00 8.00
30 Patrick Lalime 3.00 8.00
31 Dimitri Khristich 2.50 6.00
32 Janne Niinimaa 2.50 6.00
33 Mike Johnson 2.50 6.00
34 Jeff O'Neill SP 8.00 20.00
35 Luc Robitaille SP 10.00 25.00
36 Adam Oates SP 10.00 25.00
37 Petr Nedved 3.00 8.00
38 Kevyn Adams 2.50 6.00
39 Curtis Joseph SP 12.00 30.00
40 Glen Murray 3.00 8.00
41 Tyson Nash 2.50 6.00
42 Ray Whitney 3.00 8.00
43 Scott Walker 2.50 6.00
44 Andre Savage 2.50 6.00
45 Joe Nieuwendyk SP 8.00 20.00
46 Steve Webb 2.50 6.00
47 Jochen Hecht 2.50 6.00
48 Petr Buzek 2.50 6.00
49 Sergei Fedorov SP 25.00 60.00
50 Mathieu Biron 2.50 6.00
51 Patrick Marleau 4.00 10.00
52 Nicklas Lidstrom SP 10.00 25.00
53 Mike York 2.50 6.00
54 Pavel Kubina 2.50 6.00
55 Brendan Shanahan SP 20.00 50.00
56 Pierre Turgeon SP 8.00 20.00
57 Richard Zednik 2.50 6.00
58 Steve Kariya 2.50 6.00
59 Jeremy Roenick SP 15.00 40.00
60 Todd Bertuzzi 3.00 8.00
61 Marty Reasoner 2.50 6.00
62 Martin Lapointe 3.00 8.00
63 Roman Turek 3.00 8.00
64 Jason Arnott SP 8.00 20.00
65 Robert Lang 2.50 6.00
66 Fred Brathwaite 3.00 8.00
67 Tommy Salo 3.00 8.00
68 Keith Primeau SP 8.00 20.00
69 Frantisek Kaberle 2.50 6.00
70 Chris Drury 3.00 8.00
71 Manny Fernandez 2.50 6.00
72 Shane Willis 2.50 6.00
73 Matt Cullen 2.50 6.00
74 Sergei Zubov 3.00 8.00
75 Petr Sykora 3.00 8.00
76 Todd Marchant 2.50 6.00
77 Martin Biron 3.00 8.00
78 Ed Belfour SP 20.00 50.00
79 Kenny Jonsson SP 6.00 15.00
80 Chris Pronger SP 10.00 25.00
81 Maxim Afinogenov 2.50 6.00
82 Brenden Morrow 3.00 8.00
83 Theo Fleury SP 12.00 30.00
84 Brad Stuart 3.00 8.00
85 Miroslav Satan 2.50 6.00
86 Doug Weight SP 10.00 25.00
87 John LeClair SP 10.00 25.00
88 Lyle Odelein 2.50 6.00
89 Lance Pitlick 2.50 6.00
90 Martin Skoula 3.00 8.00
91 Michal Rozsival 2.50 6.00
92 Darren McCarty 2.50 6.00
93 Mats Sundin SP 10.00 25.00
94 Michael Peca 3.00 8.00
95 Chris Osgood SP 15.00 40.00
96 Andre Roy 2.50 6.00
97 Steve Rucchin 2.50 6.00
98 Steve Sullivan 2.50 6.00
99 Randy Robitaille 2.50 6.00
100 Jiri Slegr 2.50 6.00
101 Glen Metropolit 2.50 6.00
102 Milan Hejduk 3.00 8.00
103 Kimmo Timonen 2.50 6.00
104 Jyrki Lumme 2.50 6.00
105 Sergei Samsonov SP 8.00 20.00
106 Patrick Roy SP 25.00 60.00
107 Patrik Elias 4.00 10.00
108 Vincent Damphousse 3.00 8.00
109 Brian Rolston 3.00 8.00
110 Peter Forsberg SP 20.00 50.00
111 Mariusz Czerkawski 2.50 6.00
112 Darius Kasparaitis 3.00 8.00
113 Joe Thornton 6.00 15.00
114 Steve Yzerman SP 25.00 60.00
115 Marian Hossa 4.00 10.00
116 Vincent Lecavalier 4.00 10.00
117 Colin White 2.50 6.00
118 Boris Mironov 2.50 6.00
119 Andy Delmore 2.50 6.00
120 Alex Tanguay 3.00 8.00
121 Colin Forbes 2.50 6.00
122 Byron Dafoe 3.00 8.00
123 Jere Lehtinen 3.00 8.00
124 Adam Graves 3.00 8.00
125 Olaf Kolzig SP 10.00 25.00
126 Arturs Irbe 3.00 8.00
127 Trevor Linden 4.00 10.00
128 Mika Alatalo 2.50 6.00
129 Harold Druken 2.50 6.00
130 Alexei Zhamnov 3.00 8.00
131 Sergei Zholtok 2.50 6.00
132 Mark Recchi SP 12.00 30.00
133 Andrew Brunette 2.50 6.00
134 Andrei Zyuzin 2.50 6.00
135 Ray Bourque SP 15.00 40.00
136 Josh Holden 2.50 6.00
137 Patrik Stefan 3.00 8.00
138 Jocelyn Thibault 3.00 8.00
139 Martin Brodeur SP 25.00 60.00
140 Trevor Letowski 2.50 6.00
141 David Harlock 2.50 6.00
142 Mike Modano SP 15.00 40.00
143 Wayne Gretzky SP 500.00 1200.00
144 Michal Handzus 2.50 6.00
145 Clarke Wilm 2.50 6.00
146 Phil Housley 3.00 8.00
147 Jan Hlavac 2.50 6.00
148 Jason York 2.50 6.00
149 Mike Richter SP 10.00 25.00
150 Sergei Vyshedkevich 2.50 6.00
151 Cam Stewart 2.50 6.00
152 Scott Stevens SP 10.00 25.00
153 Felix Potvin 6.00 15.00
154 Robyn Regehr 3.00 8.00
155 Jamie Storr 3.00 8.00
156 Eric Desjardins 3.00 8.00
157 Dimitri Yushkevich 2.50 6.00
158 Ron Francis SP 12.00 30.00
159 Zigmund Palffy SP 10.00 25.00
160 Radek Bonk 3.00 8.00
161 Vitali Vishnevsky 2.50 6.00
162 Dave Tanabe 2.50 6.00
163 Saku Koivu 4.00 10.00
164 Travis Green 2.50 6.00
165 Teemu Selanne SP 20.00 50.00
166 Rod Brind'Amour 4.00 10.00
167 Cliff Ronning 2.50 6.00
168 Brian Boucher 3.00 8.00
169 Paul Kariya SP 10.00 25.00
170 Joe Sakic SP 20.00 50.00
171 Tim Connolly 2.50 6.00
172 Mattias Timander 2.50 6.00
173 Jay Pandolfo 2.50 6.00
174 John Grahame 2.50 6.00
175 Brian Rafalski 2.50 6.00
176 Marc Savard 2.50 6.00
177 John Madden 3.00 8.00
178 Tony Hrkac 2.50 6.00
179 Stu Grimson 2.50 6.00
180 John Vanbiesbrouck SP 10.00 25.00
181 Tie Domi 3.00 8.00
182 Stu Barnes 3.00 8.00
183 Todd Simpson 2.50 6.00
184 Mike Fisher 2.50 6.00
185 Aaron Gavey 2.50 6.00
186 Jarome Iginla 5.00 12.00
187 Jaroslav Spacek 2.50 6.00
188 Brian Leetch SP 8.00 20.00
189 Jeff Halpern 2.50 6.00
190 Jeff Shantz 2.50 6.00
191 Jaroslav Modry 2.50 6.00
192 Simon Gagne 4.00 10.00
193 Calle Johansson 2.50 6.00
194 Josef Marha 2.50 6.00
195 Jose Theodore 4.00 10.00
196 Daniel Alfredsson 4.00 10.00
197 Craig Darby 2.50 6.00
198 Tony Amonte SP 8.00 20.00
199 Scott Gomez 3.00 8.00
200 Jean-Sebastien Aubin 3.00 8.00
201 Jarno Kultanen 2.50 6.00
202 Paul Coffey SP 10.00 25.00
203 Bill Guerin SP 10.00 25.00
204 Roberto Luongo 6.00 15.00
205 Randy McKay 2.50 6.00
206 Tyler Wright 2.50 6.00
207 Alexei Yashin 3.00 8.00
208 Eric Lindros SP 25.00 60.00
209 Nikolai Khabibulin 6.00 15.00
210 Tomas Vlasak 2.50 6.00
211 Shayne Corson 3.00 8.00
212 Igor Larionov SP 10.00 25.00
213 Peter Bondra SP 10.00 25.00
214 Mika Noronen 2.50 6.00
215 Andrew Raycroft 6.00 15.00
216 Taylor Pyatt 2.50 6.00
217 Toni Lydman 2.50 6.00
218 Matt Bradley 2.50 6.00
219 Brad Richards 4.00 10.00
220 Steve McCarthy 2.50 6.00
221 Tomi Kallio 2.50 6.00
222 Justin Williams 6.00 15.00
223 Brad Ference 2.50 6.00
224 Steven Reinprecht 4.00 10.00
225 Samuel Pahlsson 2.50 6.00
226 Josef Vasicek 6.00 15.00
227 Jani Hurme 2.50 6.00
228 Petr Svoboda 3.00 8.00
229 Petr Schastlivy 2.50 6.00
230 Roman Simicek 2.50 6.00
231 Reto Von Arx 3.00 8.00
232 Oleg Saprykin 2.50 6.00
233 Lubomir Sekeras 2.50 6.00
234 Alexander Kharitonov 2.50 6.00
235 Maxim Sushinski 2.50 6.00
236 Andrei Markov 5.00 12.00
237 Scott Hartnell 6.00 15.00
238 Martin Havlat 8.00 20.00
239 Maxime Ouellet 4.00 10.00
240 Petteri Nummelin 2.50 6.00
241 Marian Gaborik 8.00 20.00
242 Daniel Sedin 5.00 12.00
243 Henrik Sedin 5.00 12.00
244 Milan Kraft 2.50 6.00
245 Denis Shvidki 2.50 6.00
246 Kris Beech 2.50 6.00
247 Rostislav Klesla 6.00 15.00
248 Petr Hubacek 2.50 6.00
249 Ussi Vaananen 3.00 8.00
250 Marty Turco 5.00 12.00

2000-01 BAP Signature Series Department of Defense

DD1 Brian Leetch 10.00 25.00
DD2 Ray Bourque 20.00 50.00
DD3 Chris Chelios 12.50 30.00
DD4 Nicklas Lidstrom 20.00 50.00
DD5 Sandis Ozolinsh 8.00 20.00
DD6 Scott Stevens 10.00 25.00
DD7 Al MacInnis 10.00 25.00
DD8 Kyle McLaren 8.00 20.00
DD9 Kenny Jonsson 8.00 20.00
DD10 Teppo Numminen 8.00 20.00
DD11 Sergei Zubov 8.00 20.00
DD12 Scott Niedermayer 8.00 20.00
DD13 Paul Coffey 15.00 40.00
DD14 Adam Foote 8.00 20.00
DD15 Sergei Gonchar 8.00 20.00
DD16 Phil Housley 8.00 20.00
DD17 Eric Desjardins 8.00 20.00
DD18 Dimitri Yushkevich 8.00 20.00
DD19 Chris Pronger 10.00 25.00
DD20 Rob Blake 10.00 25.00

2000-01 BAP Signature Series Franchise Players

F1 Paul Kariya 5.00 12.00
F2 Patrik Stefan 4.00 10.00
F3 Joe Thornton 8.00 20.00
F4 Dominik Hasek 12.00 30.00
F5 Jarome Iginla 6.00 15.00
F6 Jeff O'Neill 4.00 10.00
F7 Tony Amonte 4.00 10.00
F8 Peter Forsberg 10.00 25.00
F9 Ron Tugnutt 4.00 10.00
F10 Mike Modano 8.00 20.00
F11 Steve Yzerman 12.00 30.00
F12 Doug Weight 5.00 12.00
F13 Pavel Bure 5.00 12.00
F14 Rob Blake 5.00 12.00
F15 Marian Gaborik 10.00 25.00
F16 Saku Koivu 5.00 12.00
F17 David Legwand 5.00 12.00
F18 Martin Brodeur 12.00 30.00
F19 Mariusz Czerkawski 3.00 8.00
F20 Brian Leetch 4.00 10.00
F21 Marian Hossa 5.00 12.00
F22 John LeClair 5.00 12.00
F23 Keith Tkachuk 5.00 12.00
F24 Jaromir Jagr 15.00 40.00
F25 Chris Pronger 5.00 12.00
F26 Owen Nolan 5.00 12.00
F27 Vincent Lecavalier 5.00 12.00
F28 Curtis Joseph 6.00 15.00
F29 Daniel Sedin 6.00 15.00
F30 Olaf Kolzig 5.00 12.00

2000-01 BAP Signature Series Goalie Memorabilia Autographs

GLS1 Gerry Cheevers 50.00 125.00
GLS2 Vladislav Tretiak 90.00 150.00
GLS3 Tony Esposito 40.00 100.00
GLS4 Johnny Bower 40.00 100.00
GLS5 Bernie Parent 50.00 125.00

2000-01 BAP Signature Series He Shoots He Scores Points

1 P.Bure 3pts. .40 1.00
2 M.Brodeur 1pts. 1.00 2.50
3 T.Fleury 3pts. .50 1.25
4 P.Forsberg 1pts. .75 2.00
5 P.Forsberg 3pts. .75 2.00
6 D.Hasek 2pts. .60 1.50
7 B.Hull 2pts. .75 2.00
8 J.Jagr 3pts 1.25 3.00
9 C.Joseph 1pts. .50 1.25
10 P.Kariya 2pts. .40 1.00
11 M.Lemieux 3pts. 1.50 4.00
12 M.Messier 2pts. .75 2.00
13 M.Modano 2pts. .60 1.50
14 Z.Palffy 1pts. .40 1.00
15 L.Robitaille 2pts. .40 1.00
16 P.Roy 2pts. 1.00 2.50
17 J.Sakic 2pts. .75 2.00
18 B.Shanahan 1pts. .40 1.00
19 M.Sundin 1pts. .40 1.00
20 S.Yzerman 3pts. 1.00 2.50

2000-01 BAP Signature Series Jersey

*JSY/STICK/100: .5X TO 1.2X BASIC JSY
J1 Theo Fleury 10.00 25.00
J2 Brendan Shanahan 10.00 25.00
J3 Curtis Joseph 10.00 25.00
J4 Saku Koivu 10.00 25.00
J5 Dominik Hasek 20.00 50.00
J6 Al MacInnis 10.00 25.00
J7 John LeClair 10.00 25.00
J8 Teemu Selanne 10.00 25.00
J9 Scott Niedermayer 10.00 25.00
J10 Pavel Bure 10.00 25.00
J11 Mark Messier 10.00 25.00
J12 Jaromir Jagr 12.00 30.00
J13 Chris Pronger 10.00 25.00
J14 Chris Osgood 10.00 25.00
J15 Mats Sundin 10.00 25.00
J16 Paul Kariya 10.00 25.00
J17 Scott Stevens 10.00 25.00
J18 Kenny Jonsson 10.00 25.00
J19 Sergei Fedorov 12.50 30.00
J20 Peter Forsberg 15.00 40.00
J21 Brett Hull 12.50 30.00
J22 Tony Amonte 10.00 25.00
J23 Patrick Roy 12.00 30.00
J24 Ed Belfour 10.00 25.00
J25 Martin Brodeur 25.00 60.00
J26 Brian Leetch 10.00 25.00
J27 Mike Modano 12.50 30.00
J28 Jeff Friesen 10.00 25.00
J29 Jeremy Roenick 12.50 30.00
J30 Steve Yzerman 30.00 80.00
J31 Joe Sakic 20.00 50.00
J32 Mike Peca 10.00 25.00
J33 Luc Robitaille 10.00 25.00
J34 Adam Oates 10.00 25.00
J35 Valeri Bure 10.00 25.00
J36 Kyle McLaren 10.00 25.00
J37 Nicklas Lidstrom 10.00 25.00
J38 Jason Arnott 10.00 25.00
J39 Mike Richter 10.00 25.00
J40 Keith Tkachuk 10.00 25.00

2000-01 BAP Signature Series Mario Lemieux Legend

LM1 Mario Lemieux EMB 80.00 200.00
LM2 Mario Lemieux Jsy/Glv 100.00 250.00
LM3 Mario Lemieux Jsy/Glv 100.00 250.00
LM4 Mario Lemieux Jsy/Jsy 100.00 250.00
LM5 Mario Lemieux Jsy/Jsy/Jsy 250.00 500.00

2000-01 BAP Signature Series Mario Lemieux Retrospective

COMPLETE SET (20) 30.00 80.00
R1 M.Lemieux-Laval Juniors 2.00 5.00
R2 M.Lemieux-NHL Draft 2.00 5.00
R3 M.Lemieux-1st NHL Game 2.00 5.00
R4 M.Lemieux-1st NHL Season 2.00 5.00
R5 M.Lemieux-'85-'86 Season HL 2.00 5.00
R6 M.Lemieux-'86-'87 Season HL 2.00 5.00
R7 M.Lemieux-'87 Canada Cup 2.00 5.00
R8 M.Lemieux-'87-'88 Season HL 2.00 5.00
R9 M.Lemieux-'88-'89 Season HL 2.00 5.00
R10 M.Lemieux-'90-'91 Season HL 2.00 5.00
R11 M.Lemieux-'91-'92 Season HL 2.00 5.00
R12 M.Lemieux-'92-'93 Season HL 2.00 5.00
R13 M.Lemieux-'93-'94 Season HL 2.00 5.00
R14 M.Lemieux-'95-'96 Season HL 2.00 5.00
R15 M.Lemieux-'96 All-Star Game 2.00 5.00
R16 M.Lemieux-Final NHL Game 2.00 5.00
R17 M.Lemieux-Pitts.retires 66 2.00 5.00
R18 M.Lemieux-HOF induction 2.00 5.00
R19 M.Lemieux-Mario Returns 2.00 5.00
R20 M.Lemieux-1500th Point 2.00 5.00

2001-02 BAP Signature Series

COMP.SER. 1 SET (225) 100.00 200.00
1 Rick DiPietro .30 .75
2 Patrik Stefan .30 .75
3 Hal Gill .25 .60
4 J-P Dumont .25 .60
5 Jarome Iginla .50 1.25
6 Shane Willis .25 .60
7 Chris Phillips .25 .60
8 Rostislav Klesla .25 .60
9 Brenden Morrow .30 .75
10 Manny Legace .30 .75
11 Anson Carter .30 .75
12 Roberto Luongo .60 1.50
13 Aaron Miller .25 .60

14 Wayne Primeau .25 .60
15 Brian Savage .25 .60
16 John Jakopin .25 .60
17 Greg Johnson .25 .60
18 Marc Chouinard .25 .60
19 Steve Martins .25 .60
20 Marian Hossa .40 1.00
21 Brent Johnson .30 .75
22 Sean Burke .25 .60
23 Jan Hrdina .25 .60
24 Evgeni Nabokov .30 .75
25 Adam Deadmarsh .25 .60
26 Brad Richards .40 1.00
27 Wade Redden .25 .60
28 David Legwand .30 .75
29 Jean-Sebastien Giguere .40 1.00
30 Ray Ferraro .25 .60
31 Denis Hamel .25 .60
32 Marc Savard .25 .60
33 Craig Adams .25 .60
34 Landon Wilson .25 .60
35 Marc Denis .30 .75
36 Roman Lyashenko .25 .60
37 Tomas Holmstrom .25 .60
38 Mike Comrie .30 .75
39 Scott Hartnell .25 .60
40 Sergei Krivokrasov .25 .60
41 Mathieu Garon .30 .75
42 Denis Arkhipov .25 .60
43 Roman Hamrlik .25 .60
44 Mike Mottau .25 .60
45 Shawn McEachern .25 .60
46 Peter White .25 .60
47 Shane Doan .30 .75
48 Janne Laukkanen .25 .60
49 Martin St. Louis .40 1.00
50 Tomas Kaberle .25 .60
51 Daniel Sedin .50 1.25
52 Jonas Ronnqvist .25 .60
53 Damian Rhodes .30 .75
54 Vaclav Varada .25 .60
55 Ronald Petrovicky .25 .60
56 Tommy Westlund .25 .60
57 Michael Nylander .25 .60
58 Serge Aubin .25 .60
59 Jiri Fischer .30 .75
60 Shawn Horcoff .30 .75
61 Peter Worrell .25 .60
62 Willie Mitchell .25 .60
63 Oleg Petrov .25 .60
64 Scott Walker .25 .60
65 Tomi Kallio .25 .60
66 Jason Strudwick .25 .60
67 Magnus Arvedson .25 .60
68 Eric Daze .30 .75
69 Johan Hedberg .30 .75
70 Fredrik Modin .25 .60
71 Nathan Dempsey .25 .60
72 Henrik Sedin .50 1.25
73 Mike LeClerc .25 .60
74 Hnat Domenichelli .25 .60
75 Jeff Cowan .25 .60
76 Brad Stuart .25 .60
77 Bryan Allen .25 .60
78 Wes Walz .25 .60
79 Patrick Traverse .25 .60
80 Markus Naslund .40 1.00
81 Brad Isbister .25 .60
82 Jan Hlavac .25 .60
83 Steve Sullivan .25 .60
84 Marian Gaborik .40 1.00
85 Kristian Kudroc .25 .60
86 Peter Schaefer .25 .60
87 Pascal Trepanier .25 .60
88 Milan Hnilicka .30 .75
89 Dave Lowry .25 .60
90 Jamie Allison .25 .60
91 Jeff Nielsen .25 .60
92 Sheldon Souray .25 .60
93 Mike Dunham .30 .75
94 Branislav Mezei .25 .60
95 Dale Purinton .25 .60
96 Cory Sarich .25 .60
97 Jarkko Ruutu .25 .60
98 Kyle Calder .25 .60
99 Frantisek Musil .25 .60
100 Tomas Kloucek .25 .60
101 Karel Rachunek .25 .60
102 Darcy Tucker .25 .60
103 Alex Tanguay .30 .75
104 Patrick Lalime .30 .75
105 Ossi Vaananen .25 .60
106 Martin Skoula .30 .75
107 Lubomir Visnovsky .25 .60
108 Richard Zednik .30 .75
109 Jani Hurme .30 .75
110 Teppo Numminen .25 .60
111 Scott Young .25 .60
112 Robert Reichel .25 .60
113 Dave Tanabe .25 .60
114 Steven Reinprecht .25 .60
115 Ryan Smyth .30 .75
116 Jozef Stumpel .25 .60
117 Martin Rucinsky .25 .60
118 Radek Dvorak .30 .75
119 Chris Herperger .25 .60
120 Eric Weinrich .25 .60
121 Claude Lemieux .30 .75
122 Mike Ricci .25 .60
123 Cory Stillman .25 .60
124 Alyn McCauley .25 .60
125 Trevor Linden .40 1.00
126 Vitali Vishnevsky .25 .60
127 Tim Connolly .25 .60
128 Oleg Saprykin .25 .60
129 Arturs Irbe .30 .75
130 Ville Nieminen .25 .60
131 David Vyborny .25 .60
132 Janne Niinimaa .25 .60
133 Joey Tetarenko .25 .60
134 Bryan Smolinski .25 .60
135 Stacy Roest .25 .60
136 Mikael Renberg .25 .60
137 Gino Odjick .25 .60
138 Petr Sykora .25 .60
139 Alexei Yashin .30 .75
140 Martin Havlat .30 .75
141 Rick Tocchet .25 .60
142 Daymond Langkow .30 .75
143 Kevin Stevens .30 .75
144 Patrick Marleau .40 1.00
145 Reed Low .25 .60
146 Bryan McCabe .30 .75
147 Dimitri Khristich .25 .60
148 Oleg Tverdovsky .25 .60
149 Yannick Tremblay .25 .60
150 Martin Biron .30 .75
151 Rob Niedermayer .30 .75
152 Rod Brind'Amour .40 1.00
153 Adam Foote .30 .75
154 Geoff Sanderson .25 .60
155 Pat Verbeek .30 .75
156 Nicklas Lidstrom .40 1.00
157 Jochen Hecht .25 .60
158 Robert Svehla .25 .60
159 Mathieu Schneider .25 .60
160 Antti Laaksonen .25 .60
161 Jeff Hackett .30 .75
162 Scott Niedermayer .40 1.00
163 Sandis Ozolinsh .25 .60
164 Radek Bonk .25 .60
165 Roman Cechmanek .30 .75
166 Mike Johnson .25 .60
167 Milan Kraft .25 .60
168 Adam Graves .30 .75
169 Pavol Demitra .50 1.25
170 Kevin Weekes .30 .75
171 Travis Green .25 .60
172 Jeff Halpern .25 .60
173 Steve Shields .30 .75
174 Lubos Bartecko .25 .60
175 P.J. Stock .25 .60
176 Maxim Afinogenov .25 .60
177 Derek Morris .25 .60
178 Bates Battaglia .25 .60
179 Boris Mironov .25 .60
180 David Aebischer .30 .75
181 Espen Knutsen .25 .60
182 Darryl Sydor .25 .60
183 Igor Larionov .40 1.00
184 Eric Brewer .25 .60
185 Trevor Kidd .25 .60
186 Eric Belanger .25 .60
187 Manny Fernandez .25 .60
188 Francois Bouillon .25 .60
189 Patrik Elias .40 1.00
190 Mariusz Czerkawski .25 .60
191 Daniel Alfredsson .40 1.00
192 Brian Boucher .30 .75
193 Sergei Berezin .25 .60
194 Kris Beech .25 .60
195 Vincent Damphousse .30 .75
196 Fred Brathwaite .30 .75
197 Ben Clymer .25 .60
198 Wade Belak .30 .75
199 Ed Jovanovski .30 .75
200 Sergei Gonchar .25 .60
201 Dan Blackburn RC .60 1.50
202 Daniel Tjarnqvist .50 1.25
203 Andreas Salomonsson RC .50 1.25
204 Vaclav Nedorost RC .50 1.25
205 Justin Kurtz RC .75 2.00
206 Jiri Dopita RC .50 1.25
207 Ilya Kovalchuk RC 4.00 10.00
208 Richard Jackman .60 1.50
209 Scott Nichol RC .50 1.25
210 Brad Larsen .50 1.25
211 Jason Williams .50 1.25
212 Kristian Huselius RC .75 2.00
213 Andreas Lilja .50 1.25
214 Nick Schultz RC .50 1.25
215 Marc Moro .50 1.25
216 Scott Clemmensen RC .50 1.25
217 Brad Tapper .50 1.25
218 Barrett Heisten .50 1.25
219 Chris Neil RC .60 1.50
220 Pavel Brendl .50 1.25
221 Miikka Kiprusoff .75 2.00
222 Jimmie Olvestad .50 1.25
223 Brian Sutherby RC .50 1.25
224 Timo Parssinen RC .60 1.50
225 Sascha Goc .50 1.25
226 Dany Heatley .60 1.50
227 Nick Boynton .50 1.25
228 Steve Begin .50 1.25
229 Erik Cole RC 1.00 2.50
230 Mark Bell .50 1.25
231 Rick Berry .50 1.25
232 Niko Kapanen RC .75 2.00
233 Pavel Datsyuk RC 5.00 12.00
234 Niklas Hagman RC .60 1.50
235 Jaroslav Bednar RC .50 1.25
236 Pascal Dupuis RC .75 2.00
237 Mike Ribeiro .50 1.25
238 Martin Erat RC .60 1.50
239 Jiri Bicek .50 1.25
240 Radek Martinek RC .50 1.25
241 Ivan Ciernik RC .50 1.25
242 Jesse Boulerice .50 1.25
243 Krys Kolanos RC .50 1.25
244 Toby Petersen .50 1.25
245 Jeff Jillson RC .50 1.25
246 Mark Rycroft RC .60 1.50
247 Kamil Piros RC .50 1.25
248 Nikita Alexeev RC .50 1.25
249 Stephen Peat .50 1.25
250 Pierre Dagenais .50 1.25

2001-02 BAP Signature Series Certified 100

*CERTIFIED 50: .8X TO 2X CERT/100
C1 Al MacInnis 4.00 10.00
C2 Adam Oates 4.00 10.00
C3 Byron Dafoe 4.00 10.00
C4 Bill Guerin 4.00 10.00
C5 Brian Leetch 4.00 10.00
C6 Brendan Shanahan 3.00 8.00
C7 Chris Drury 4.00 10.00
C8 Chris Gratton 2.50 6.00
C9 Curtis Joseph 3.00 8.00
C10 Chris Pronger 2.50 6.00
C11 Donald Audette 2.50 6.00
C12 Doug Weight 2.50 6.00
C13 Ed Belfour 3.00 8.00
C14 Eric Lindros 3.00 8.00
C15 Jason Allison 2.50 6.00
C16 Jason Arnott 2.50 6.00
C17 John LeClair 3.00 8.00
C18 Jeff O'Neill 2.50 6.00
C19 Jeremy Roenick 3.00 8.00
C20 Joe Sakic 5.00 12.00
C21 Joe Thornton 4.00 10.00
C22 Kyle McLaren 2.50 6.00
C23 Luc Robitaille 4.00 10.00
C24 Martin Brodeur 8.00 20.00
C25 Milan Hejduk 3.00 8.00
C26 Martin Lapointe 2.50 6.00
C27 Mike Modano 4.00 10.00
C28 Mark Recchi 2.50 6.00
C29 Mats Sundin 3.00 8.00
C30 Olaf Kolzig 2.50 6.00
C31 Peter Bondra 3.00 8.00
C32 Pavel Bure 3.00 8.00
C33 Paul Kariya 3.00 8.00
C34 Pierre Turgeon 2.50 6.00
C35 Rob Blake 2.50 6.00
C36 Ron Francis 2.50 6.00
C37 Roman Turek 2.50 6.00
C38 Sergei Fedorov 4.00 10.00
C39 Scott Gomez 2.50 6.00
C40 Sami Kapanen 2.50 6.00
C41 Saku Koivu 3.00 8.00
C42 Sergei Samsonov 2.50 6.00
C43 Scott Stevens 2.50 6.00
C44 Steve Yzerman 8.00 20.00
C45 Tony Amonte 4.00 10.00
C46 Theo Fleury 2.50 6.00
C47 Teemu Selanne 3.00 8.00
C48 Tommy Salo 2.50 6.00
C49 Vincent Lecavalier 3.00 8.00
C50 Zigmund Palffy 4.00 10.00
C51 Brett Hull 3.00 8.00
C52 Dominik Hasek 5.00 12.00
C53 Jaromir Jagr 4.00 10.00
C54 Mario Lemieux 12.50 30.00
C55 Mark Messier 3.00 8.00
C56 Mike Vernon 2.50 6.00
C57 Owen Nolan 2.50 6.00
C58 Peter Forsberg 8.00 20.00
C59 Patrick Roy 8.00 20.00
C60 Wayne Gretzky 12.50 30.00

2001-02 BAP Signature Series Autographs

1 Rick DiPietro 6.00 15.00
2 Patrik Stefan 3.00 8.00
3 Hal Gill 3.00 8.00
4 J-P Dumont 3.00 8.00
5 Jarome Iginla 10.00 25.00
6 Shane Willis 3.00 8.00
7 Chris Phillips 3.00 8.00
8 Rostislav Klesla 3.00 8.00
9 Brenden Morrow 4.00 10.00
10 Manny Legace 4.00 10.00
11 Anson Carter SP 12.50 30.00
12 Roberto Luongo 8.00 20.00
13 Aaron Miller 3.00 8.00
14 Wayne Primeau 3.00 8.00
15 Brian Savage 3.00 8.00
16 John Jakopin 3.00 8.00
17 Greg Johnson 3.00 8.00
18 Marc Chouinard 3.00 8.00
19 Steve Martins 3.00 8.00
20 Marian Hossa 6.00 15.00
21 Brent Johnson SP 40.00 100.00
22 Sean Burke 4.00 10.00
23 Jan Hrdina 3.00 8.00
24 Evgeni Nabokov 4.00 10.00
25 Adam Deadmarsh 3.00 8.00
26 Brad Richards 3.00 8.00
27 Wade Redden 3.00 8.00
28 David Legwand 3.00 8.00
29 Jean-Sebastien Giguere 4.00 10.00
30 Ray Ferraro 3.00 8.00
31 Denis Hamel 3.00 8.00
32 Marc Savard 3.00 8.00
33 Craig Adams 3.00 8.00
34 Landon Wilson 3.00 8.00
35 Marc Denis 4.00 10.00
36 Roman Lyashenko 3.00 8.00
37 Tomas Holmstrom 3.00 8.00
38 Mike Comrie 3.00 8.00
39 Scott Hartnell 3.00 8.00
40 Sergei Krivokrasov 3.00 8.00
41 Mathieu Garon 4.00 10.00
42 Denis Arkhipov 3.00 8.00
43 Roman Hamrlik 3.00 8.00
44 Mike Mottau 3.00 8.00
45 Shawn McEachern 3.00 8.00
46 Peter White SP 50.00 100.00
47 Shane Doan 3.00 8.00
48 Janne Laukkanen 3.00 8.00
49 Martin St. Louis 10.00 25.00
50 Tomas Kaberle 3.00 8.00
51 Daniel Sedin 8.00 20.00
52 Jonas Ronnqvist 3.00 8.00
53 Damian Rhodes 4.00 10.00
54 Vaclav Varada 3.00 8.00
55 Ronald Petrovicky 3.00 8.00
56 Tommy Westlund 3.00 8.00
57 Michael Nylander 3.00 8.00
58 Serge Aubin 3.00 8.00
59 Jiri Fischer SP 25.00 60.00
60 Shawn Horcoff 3.00 8.00
61 Peter Worrell 3.00 8.00
62 Willie Mitchell 3.00 8.00
63 Oleg Petrov 3.00 8.00
64 Scott Walker 3.00 8.00
65 Tomi Kallio 3.00 8.00
66 Jason Strudwick 3.00 8.00
67 Magnus Arvedson 3.00 8.00
68 Eric Daze 4.00 10.00
69 Johan Hedberg 4.00 10.00
70 Fredrik Modin 3.00 8.00
71 Nathan Dempsey 3.00 8.00
72 Henrik Sedin 8.00 20.00
73 Mike LeClerc 3.00 8.00
74 Hnat Domenichelli 3.00 8.00
75 Jeff Cowan 3.00 8.00
76 Brad Stuart 3.00 8.00
77 Bryan Allen 3.00 8.00
78 Wes Walz 3.00 8.00
79 Patrick Traverse 3.00 8.00
80 Markus Naslund 4.00 10.00
81 Brad Isbister 3.00 8.00
82 Jan Hlavac SP 30.00 80.00
83 Steve Sullivan 3.00 8.00
84 Marian Gaborik 12.50 30.00
85 Kristian Kudroc 3.00 8.00
86 Peter Schaefer 3.00 8.00
87 Pascal Trepanier 3.00 8.00
88 Milan Hnilicka 4.00 10.00
89 Dave Lowry 3.00 8.00
90 Jamie Allison 3.00 8.00
91 Jeff Nielsen 3.00 8.00
92 Sheldon Souray 3.00 8.00
93 Mike Dunham 4.00 10.00
94 Branislav Mezei 3.00 8.00
95 Dale Purinton 3.00 8.00
96 Cory Sarich 3.00 8.00
97 Jarkko Ruutu 3.00 8.00
98 Kyle Calder 3.00 8.00
99 Frantisek Musil 3.00 8.00
100 Tomas Kloucek 3.00 8.00
101 Karel Rachunek 3.00 8.00
102 Darcy Tucker 3.00 8.00
103 Alex Tanguay 4.00 10.00
104 Patrick Lalime 4.00 10.00
105 Ossi Vaananen 3.00 8.00
106 Martin Skoula 3.00 8.00
107 Lubomir Visnovsky 3.00 8.00
108 Richard Zednik 3.00 8.00
109 Jani Hurme 4.00 10.00
110 Teppo Numminen 3.00 8.00
111 Scott Young 3.00 8.00
112 Robert Reichel 4.00 10.00
113 Dave Tanabe 3.00 8.00
114 Steven Reinprecht 3.00 8.00
115 Ryan Smyth 3.00 8.00
116 Jozef Stumpel 3.00 8.00
117 Martin Rucinsky 3.00 8.00
118 Radek Dvorak 3.00 8.00
119 Chris Herperger 3.00 8.00
120 Eric Weinrich 3.00 8.00
121 Claude Lemieux 4.00 10.00
122 Mike Ricci 4.00 10.00
123 Cory Stillman 3.00 8.00
124 Alyn McCauley 3.00 8.00
125 Trevor Linden 4.00 10.00
126 Vitaly Vishnevsky 3.00 8.00
127 Tim Connolly 3.00 8.00
128 Oleg Saprykin 3.00 8.00
129 Arturs Irbe 6.00 15.00
130 Ville Nieminen 3.00 8.00
131 David Vyborny 3.00 8.00
132 Janne Niinimaa 3.00 8.00
133 Joey Tetarenko 3.00 8.00
134 Bryan Smolinski 3.00 8.00
135 Stacy Roest 3.00 8.00
136 Mikael Renberg 3.00 8.00
137 Gino Odjick 3.00 8.00
138 Petr Sykora 3.00 8.00
139 Alexei Yashin 4.00 10.00
140 Martin Havlat 4.00 10.00
141 Rick Tocchet 3.00 8.00
142 Daymond Langkow 3.00 8.00
143 Kevin Stevens 3.00 8.00
144 Patrick Marleau 4.00 10.00
145 Reed Low 3.00 8.00
146 Bryan McCabe 3.00 8.00
147 Dimitri Khristich 3.00 8.00
148 Oleg Tverdovsky 3.00 8.00
149 Yannick Tremblay 3.00 8.00
150 Martin Biron 4.00 10.00
151 Rob Niedermayer 3.00 8.00
152 Rod Brind'Amour 4.00 10.00
153 Adam Foote 3.00 8.00
154 Geoff Sanderson 3.00 8.00
155 Pat Verbeek 3.00 8.00
156 Nicklas Lidstrom 10.00 25.00
157 Jochen Hecht 3.00 8.00
158 Robert Svehla 3.00 8.00
159 Mathieu Schneider 3.00 8.00
160 Antti Laaksonen 3.00 8.00
161 Jeff Hackett 4.00 10.00
162 Scott Niedermayer 3.00 8.00
163 Sandis Ozolinsh 3.00 8.00
164 Radek Bonk 3.00 8.00
165 Roman Cechmanek 4.00 10.00
166 Mike Johnson 3.00 8.00
167 Milan Kraft 3.00 8.00
168 Adam Graves 3.00 8.00
169 Pavol Demitra 8.00 20.00
170 Kevin Weekes 4.00 10.00
171 Travis Green 3.00 8.00
172 Jeff Halpern 3.00 8.00
173 Steve Shields 4.00 10.00
174 Lubos Bartecko 3.00 8.00
175 P.J. Stock 4.00 10.00
176 Maxim Afinogenov 3.00 8.00
177 Derek Morris 3.00 8.00
178 Bates Battaglia 4.00 10.00
179 Boris Mironov 3.00 8.00
180 David Aebischer 8.00 20.00
181 Espen Knutsen 3.00 8.00
182 Darryl Sydor 3.00 8.00
183 Igor Larionov 12.00 30.00
184 Eric Brewer 3.00 8.00
185 Trevor Kidd 4.00 10.00
186 Eric Belanger 3.00 8.00
187 Manny Fernandez 15.00 40.00
188 Francois Bouillon 3.00 8.00
189 Patrik Elias 4.00 10.00
190 Mariusz Czerkawski 3.00 8.00
191 Daniel Alfredsson 4.00 10.00
192 Brian Boucher 4.00 10.00
193 Sergei Berezin 3.00 8.00
194 Kris Beech 3.00 8.00
195 Vincent Damphousse 3.00 8.00
196 Fred Brathwaite 4.00 10.00
197 Ben Clymer 3.00 8.00
198 Wade Belak 6.00 15.00
199 Ed Jovanovski 4.00 10.00
200 Sergei Gonchar 3.00 8.00
201 Dan Blackburn 4.00 10.00
202 Daniel Tjarnqvist 3.00 8.00
203 Andreas Salomonsson 5.00 12.00
204 Vaclav Nedorost 3.00 8.00
205 Justin Kurtz 3.00 8.00
206 Jiri Dopita 3.00 8.00
207 Ilya Kovalchuk 6.00 15.00
208 Richard Jackman 3.00 8.00
209 Scott Nichol 3.00 8.00
210 Brad Larsen 3.00 8.00
211 Jason Williams 3.00 8.00
212 Kristian Huselius 3.00 8.00
213 Andreas Lilja 3.00 8.00
214 Nick Schultz 3.00 8.00
215 Marc Moro 3.00 8.00
216 Scott Clemmensen 4.00 10.00
217 Brad Tapper 3.00 8.00
218 Barrett Heisten 3.00 8.00
219 Chris Neil 3.00 8.00
220 Pavel Brendl 3.00 8.00
221 Miikka Kiprusoff 8.00 20.00
222 Jimmie Olvestad 3.00 8.00
223 Brian Sutherby 5.00 12.00
224 Timo Parssinen 3.00 8.00
225 Sascha Goc 3.00 8.00
226 Dany Heatley 6.00 15.00
227 Nick Boynton 3.00 8.00
228 Steve Begin 3.00 8.00
229 Erik Cole 5.00 12.00
230 Mark Bell 3.00 8.00
231 Rick Berry 3.00 8.00
232 Niko Kapanen 3.00 8.00
233 Pavel Datsyuk 40.00 100.00
234 Niklas Hagman 3.00 8.00
235 Jaroslav Bednar 3.00 8.00
236 Pascal Dupuis 4.00 10.00
237 Mike Ribeiro 3.00 8.00
238 Martin Erat 3.00 8.00
239 Jiri Bicek 3.00 8.00
240 Radek Martinek 3.00 8.00
241 Ivan Ciernik 3.00 8.00
242 Jesse Boulerice 3.00 8.00
243 Krystofer Kolanos 3.00 8.00
244 Toby Petersen 3.00 8.00
245 Jeff Jillson 3.00 8.00
246 Mark Rycroft 3.00 8.00
247 Kamil Piros 3.00 8.00
248 Nikita Alexeev 3.00 8.00
249 Stephen Peat 3.00 8.00
250 Pierre Dagenais 3.00 8.00
LAM Al MacInnis SP 8.00 20.00
LBD Byron Dafoe SP 10.00 25.00
LBG Bill Guerin SP 8.00 20.00
LBL Brian Leetch SP 12.50 30.00
LBS Brendan Shanahan SP 20.00 50.00
LCD Chris Drury SP 8.00 20.00
LCG Chris Gratton SP 8.00 20.00
LCJ Curtis Joseph SP 20.00 40.00
LCP Chris Pronger SP 8.00 20.00
LDA Donald Audette SP 8.00 20.00
LDW Doug Weight SP 10.00 25.00
LEB Ed Belfour SP 20.00 50.00
LJAL Jason Allison SP 8.00 20.00
LJL John LeClair SP 12.50 30.00
LJO Jeff O'Neill SP 8.00 20.00
LJR Jeremy Roenick SP 15.00 40.00
LJS Joe Sakic SP 25.00 60.00
LJT Joe Thornton SP 12.50 30.00
LKM Kyle McLaren SP 8.00 20.00
LLR Luc Robitaille SP 10.00 25.00
LMH Milan Hejduk SP 12.50 30.00
LML Martin Lapointe SP 8.00 20.00
LMR Mark Recchi SP 8.00 20.00
LOK Olaf Kolzig SP 8.00 20.00
LPBO Peter Bondra SP 8.00 20.00
LPBU Pavel Bure SP 12.50 30.00
LPK Paul Kariya SP 15.00 40.00
LPT Pierre Turgeon SP 8.00 20.00
LRB Rob Blake SP 8.00 20.00
LRF Ron Francis SP 8.00 20.00
LRT Roman Turek SP 8.00 20.00
LSF Sergei Fedorov SP 15.00 40.00
LSK Sami Kapanen SP 8.00 20.00
LSSA Sergei Samsonov SP 8.00 20.00
LSST Scott Stevens SP 12.00 30.00
LSY Steve Yzerman SP 40.00 80.00
LTA Tony Amonte SP 8.00 20.00
LTS Teemu Selanne SP 12.50 30.00
LTSA Tommy Salo SP 8.00 20.00
LVL Vincent Lecavalier SP 12.50 30.00
LZP Zigmund Palffy SP 10.00 25.00
XLDH Dominik Hasek SP 100.00 200.00
XLML Mario Lemieux SP 200.00 350.00
XLMM Mark Messier SP 75.00 150.00
XLMV Mike Vernon SP 25.00 60.00
XLON Owen Nolan SP 30.00 80.00
XLPF Peter Forsberg SP 75.00 125.00
XLPR Patrick Roy SP 200.00 350.00
XLWG Wayne Gretzky SP 300.00 800.00

2001-02 BAP Signature Series Autographs Gold

*GOLD: .5X TO 1.2X BASE AUTO
11 Anson Carter 25.00 60.00
21 Brent Johnson 40.00 100.00
46 Peter White 50.00 100.00
59 Jiri Fischer 40.00 100.00
82 Jan Hlavac 25.00 60.00
XLDH Dominik Hasek SP 250.00 400.00
XLML Mario Lemieux SP 250.00 400.00
XLWG Wayne Gretzky SP 500.00 1200.00

2001-02 BAP Signature Series Department of Defense

DD1 Rob Blake 10.00 25.00
DD2 Brian Leetch 10.00 25.00
DD3 Nicklas Lidstrom 12.00 30.00
DD4 Oleg Tverdovsky 10.00 25.00
DD5 Chris Pronger 10.00 25.00
DD6 Al MacInnis 10.00 25.00
DD7 Kyle McLaren 10.00 25.00
DD8 Sergei Gonchar 10.00 25.00
DD9 Tomas Kaberle 10.00 25.00
DD10 Sandis Ozolinsh 10.00 25.00
DD11 Darius Kasparaitis 10.00 25.00
DD12 Rostislav Klesla 10.00 25.00

2001-02 BAP Signature Series 500 Goal Scorers

2 Steve Yzerman/30 50.00 120.00
3 Jean Beliveau/20 40.00 80.00
4 Frank Mahovlich/30 40.00 80.00
5 Stan Mikita/30 40.00 80.00
6 Guy Lafleur/30 25.00 60.00
7 Marcel Dionne/30 15.00 40.00
8 Bobby Hull/20 25.00 60.00
9 Phil Esposito/30 40.00 80.00
10 Mike Bossy/50 20.00 50.00
11 Luc Robitaille/30 25.00 60.00
12 Jari Kurri/90 10.00 25.00
13 Dave Andreychuk/90 10.00 25.00
14 Mike Gartner/90 10.00 25.00
15 John Bucyk/30 25.00 60.00
16 Michel Goulet/90 10.00 25.00
17 Dino Ciccarelli/90 10.00 25.00
18 Pat Verbeek/90 10.00 25.00
19 Bryan Trottier/50 10.00 25.00
20 Dale Hawerchuk/90 10.00 25.00
21 Gilbert Perreault/90 12.00 30.00
22 Joe Mullen/90 12.00 30.00
23 Lanny McDonald/90 10.00 25.00
24 Brett Hull/30 30.00 80.00
25 Mark Messier/30 30.00 80.00
26 Mario Lemieux/20 100.00 200.00

2001-02 BAP Signature Series Franchise Jerseys

FP1 Paul Kariya 12.50 30.00
FP2 Ilya Kovalchuk 20.00 50.00
FP3 Joe Thornton 15.00 40.00
FP4 Miroslav Satan 12.50 30.00
FP5 Jarome Iginla 15.00 40.00
FP6 Sami Kapanen 12.50 30.00
FP7 Tony Amonte 12.50 30.00
FP8 Joe Sakic 20.00 50.00
FP9 Rostislav Klesla 12.50 30.00
FP10 Mike Modano 20.00 50.00
FP11 Steve Yzerman 15.00 40.00
FP12 Tommy Salo 15.00 40.00
FP13 Pavel Bure 12.50 30.00
FP14 Zigmund Palffy 12.50 30.00
FP15 Marian Gaborik 15.00 40.00
FP16 Jose Theodore 15.00 40.00
FP17 David Legwand 12.50 30.00
FP18 Martin Brodeur 20.00 50.00
FP19 Eric Lindros 12.50 30.00
FP20 Alexei Yashin 12.50 30.00
FP21 Daniel Alfredsson 12.50 30.00
FP22 John LeClair 12.50 30.00
FP23 Sean Burke 12.50 30.00
FP24 Mario Lemieux 30.00 80.00
FP25 Owen Nolan 12.50 30.00
FP26 Doug Weight 12.50 30.00
FP27 Vincent Lecavalier 12.50 30.00
FP28 Mats Sundin 12.50 30.00
FP29 Markus Naslund 12.50 30.00
FP30 Jaromir Jagr 20.00 50.00

2001-02 BAP Signature Series He Shoots He Scores Points

1 Tony Amonte 1pt. .20 .50
2 Sergei Fedorov 1pt. .30 .75
3 Bill Guerin 1pt. .25 .60
4 John Leclair 1pt. .25 .60
5 Eric Lindros 1pt. .30 .75
6 Mark Messier 1 pt. .30 .75
7 Mike Modano 1pt. .30 .75
8 Luc Robitaille 1pt. .20 .50
9 Jeremy Roenick 1pt. .25 .60
10 Teemu Selanne 1pt. .25 .60
11 Mats Sundin 1pt. .20 .50
12 Pavel Bure 2 pts. .30 .75
13 Jarome Iginla 2 pts. .30 .75
14 Jaromir Jagr 2 pts. .30 .75
15 Paul Kariya 2 pts. .25 .60
16 Ilya Kovalchuk 2 pts. .30 .75
17 Brendan Shanahan 2 pts. .30 .75
18 Mario Lemieux 3 pts. 1.50 4.00
19 Joe Sakic 3 pts. .30 .75
20 Steve Yzerman 3 pts. .50 1.25

2001-02 BAP Signature Series International Medals

IB1 Nikolai Khabibulin 12.50 30.00
IB2 Sergei Samsonov 12.50 30.00
IB3 Darius Kasparaitis 12.50 30.00
IB4 Alexei Yashin 12.50 30.00
IB5 Oleg Tverdovsky 12.50 30.00
IB6 Pavel Bure 12.50 30.00
IB7 Ilya Kovalchuk 15.00 40.00
IB8 Alexei Kovalev 12.50 30.00
IS1 Mike Richter 12.50 30.00
IS2 Tony Amonte 12.50 30.00
IS3 Chris Chelios 12.50 30.00
IS4 Doug Weight 12.50 30.00
IS5 John LeClair 12.50 30.00
IS6 Mike Modano 15.00 40.00
IS7 Bill Guerin 12.50 30.00
IS8 Brian Rolston 12.50 30.00
IG1 Martin Brodeur 20.00 50.00
IG2 Rob Blake 12.50 30.00
IG3 Al MacInnis 12.50 30.00
IG4 Theo Fleury 25.00 60.00
IG5 Paul Kariya 12.50 30.00
IG6 Mario Lemieux 30.00 80.00
IG7 Eric Lindros 15.00 40.00
IG8 Steve Yzerman 30.00 80.00

2001-02 BAP Signature Series Jerseys

GJ1 Paul Kariya 8.00 20.00
GJ2 Rostislav Klesla 5.00 12.00
GJ3 Joe Thornton 12.00 30.00
GJ4 Martin Havlat 6.00 15.00
GJ5 Byron Dafoe 6.00 15.00
GJ6 Dominik Hasek 12.00 30.00
GJ7 Miroslav Satan 6.00 15.00
GJ8 Teemu Selanne 15.00 40.00
GJ9 Jarome Iginla 10.00 25.00
GJ10 Ron Francis 10.00 25.00
GJ11 Pierre Turgeon 6.00 15.00
GJ12 Tony Amonte 6.00 15.00
GJ13 Henrik Sedin 10.00 25.00
GJ14 Alex Tanguay 6.00 15.00
GJ15 Marian Gaborik 8.00 20.00
GJ16 Joe Sakic 15.00 40.00
GJ17 Patrick Roy 20.00 50.00
GJ18 Chris Drury 6.00 15.00
GJ19 Rob Blake 8.00 20.00
GJ20 Mike Modano 12.00 30.00
GJ21 Sergei Fedorov 12.00 30.00
GJ22 Nicklas Lidstrom 8.00 20.00
GJ23 Steve Yzerman 20.00 50.00
GJ24 Milan Hejduk 6.00 15.00
GJ25 Jeff O'Neill 6.00 15.00
GJ26 Luc Robitaille 8.00 20.00
GJ27 Brendan Shanahan 8.00 20.00
GJ28 Pavel Bure 8.00 20.00
GJ29 Roberto Luongo 12.00 30.00
GJ30 Zigmund Palffy 8.00 20.00
GJ31 Brian Savage 5.00 12.00
GJ32 Saku Koivu 8.00 20.00
GJ33 Scott Stevens 8.00 20.00
GJ34 Scott Gomez 6.00 15.00
GJ35 Martin Brodeur 20.00 50.00
GJ36 Jason Arnott 6.00 15.00
GJ37 Scott Niedermayer 8.00 20.00
GJ38 Eric Lindros 12.00 30.00
GJ39 Brian Leetch 6.00 15.00
GJ40 Mark Messier 15.00 40.00
GJ41 Mike Richter 8.00 20.00
GJ42 Kenny Jonsson 5.00 12.00
GJ43 Alexei Yashin 6.00 15.00
GJ44 Radek Bonk 5.00 12.00
GJ45 Ilya Kovalchuk 25.00 60.00
GJ46 Marian Hossa 8.00 20.00
GJ47 Roman Cechmanek 6.00 15.00
GJ48 Mark Recchi 10.00 25.00
GJ49 John LeClair 8.00 20.00
GJ50 Brian Boucher 6.00 15.00
GJ51 Keith Primeau 6.00 15.00
GJ52 Jeremy Roenick 12.00 30.00
GJ53 Jaromir Jagr 25.00 60.00
GJ54 Mario Lemieux 30.00 80.00
GJ55 Owen Nolan 8.00 20.00
GJ56 Doug Weight 8.00 20.00
GJ57 Chris Pronger 8.00 20.00
GJ58 Al MacInnis 10.00 25.00
GJ59 Vincent Lecavalier 8.00 20.00
GJ60 Brad Richards 8.00 20.00
GJ61 Curtis Joseph 10.00 25.00
GJ62 Mats Sundin 8.00 20.00
GJ63 Daniel Sedin 10.00 25.00
GJ64 Peter Bondra 8.00 20.00
GJ65 Adam Oates 8.00 20.00
GJ66 Olaf Kolzig 8.00 20.00
GJ67 Sergei Gonchar 5.00 12.00
GJ68 Todd Bertuzzi 8.00 20.00
GJ69 Theo Fleury 10.00 25.00
GJ70 Markus Naslund 8.00 20.00
GJ71 Alexander Mogilny 6.00 15.00
GJ72 Nikolai Khabibulin 8.00 20.00
GJ73 Ed Belfour 8.00 20.00
GJ74 Petr Sykora 5.00 12.00
GJ75 Peter Forsberg 15.00 40.00
GJ76 Patrick Lalime 6.00 15.00
GJ77 Keith Tkachuk 8.00 20.00
GJ78 Daniel Alfredsson 8.00 20.00
GJ79 Chris Chelios 8.00 20.00
GJ80 Sean Burke 5.00 12.00
GJ81 Eric Daze 6.00 15.00
GJ82 Patrik Elias 8.00 20.00
GJ83 Adam Foote 6.00 15.00
GJ84 Bill Guerin 8.00 20.00
GJ85 Jose Theodore 8.00 20.00
GJ86 Sandis Ozolinsh 5.00 12.00
GJ87 Felix Potvin 12.00 30.00
GJ88 Tommy Salo 6.00 15.00
GJ89 Martin Straka 5.00 12.00
GJ90 Jocelyn Thibault 6.00 15.00
GJ91 Pavel Bure 8.00 20.00
GJ92 Roman Turek 6.00 15.00
GJ93 Sergei Samsonov 6.00 15.00
GJ94 Dan Cloutier 6.00 15.00
GJ95 Kristian Huselius 8.00 20.00
GJ96 Arturs Irbe 6.00 15.00
GJ97 Sami Kapanen 5.00 12.00
GJ98 Evgeni Nabokov 6.00 15.00

2001-02 BAP Signature Series Jersey and Stick

GSJ1 Paul Kariya 8.00 20.00
GSJ2 Rostislav Klesla 5.00 12.00
GSJ3 Joe Thornton 12.00 30.00
GSJ4 Martin Havlat 6.00 15.00
GSJ5 Byron Dafoe 6.00 15.00
GSJ6 Dominik Hasek 12.00 30.00
GSJ7 Miroslav Satan 6.00 15.00
GSJ8 Teemu Selanne 15.00 40.00
GSJ9 Jarome Iginla 10.00 25.00
GSJ10 Ron Francis 10.00 25.00
GSJ11 Pierre Turgeon 6.00 15.00
GSJ12 Tony Amonte 6.00 15.00
GSJ13 Henrik Sedin 10.00 25.00
GSJ14 Alex Tanguay 6.00 15.00
GSJ15 Marian Gaborik 8.00 20.00
GSJ16 Joe Sakic 15.00 40.00
GSJ17 Patrick Roy 20.00 50.00
GSJ18 Chris Drury 6.00 15.00
GSJ19 Rob Blake 8.00 20.00
GSJ20 Mike Modano 12.00 30.00
GSJ21 Sergei Fedorov 12.00 30.00
GSJ22 Nicklas Lidstrom 8.00 20.00
GSJ23 Steve Yzerman 20.00 50.00
GSJ24 Milan Hejduk 6.00 15.00
GSJ25 Jeff O'Neill 6.00 15.00
GSJ26 Luc Robitaille 8.00 20.00
GSJ27 Brendan Shanahan 8.00 20.00
GSJ28 Pavel Bure 8.00 20.00
GSJ29 Roberto Luongo 12.00 30.00
GSJ30 Zigmund Palffy 8.00 20.00
GSJ31 Brian Savage 5.00 12.00
GSJ32 Saku Koivu 8.00 20.00
GSJ33 Scott Stevens 8.00 20.00
GSJ34 Scott Gomez 6.00 15.00
GSJ35 Martin Brodeur 20.00 50.00
GSJ36 Jason Arnott 6.00 15.00
GSJ37 Scott Niedermayer 8.00 20.00
GSJ38 Eric Lindros 12.00 30.00
GSJ39 Brian Leetch 6.00 15.00
GSJ40 Mark Messier 15.00 40.00
GSJ41 Mike Richter 8.00 20.00
GSJ42 Kenny Jonsson 5.00 12.00
GSJ43 Alexei Yashin 6.00 15.00
GSJ44 Radek Bonk 5.00 12.00
GSJ45 Ilya Kovalchuk 25.00 60.00
GSJ46 Marian Hossa 8.00 20.00
GSJ47 Roman Cechmanek 6.00 15.00
GSJ48 Mark Recchi 10.00 25.00
GSJ49 John LeClair 8.00 20.00
GSJ50 Brian Boucher 6.00 15.00

GSJ51 Keith Primeau 6.00 15.00
GSJ52 Jeremy Roenick 12.00 30.00
GSJ53 Jaromir Jagr 25.00 60.00
GSJ54 Mario Lemieux 30.00 80.00
GSJ55 Owen Nolan 8.00 20.00
GSJ56 Doug Weight 8.00 20.00
GSJ57 Chris Pronger 8.00 20.00
GSJ58 Al MacInnis 10.00 25.00
GSJ59 Vincent Lecavalier 8.00 20.00
GSJ60 Brad Richards 8.00 20.00
GSJ61 Curtis Joseph 10.00 25.00
GSJ62 Mats Sundin 8.00 20.00
GSJ63 Daniel Sedin 10.00 25.00
GSJ64 Peter Bondra 8.00 20.00
GSJ65 Adam Oates 8.00 20.00
GSJ66 Olaf Kolzig 8.00 20.00
GSJ67 Sergei Gonchar 5.00 12.00
GSJ68 Todd Bertuzzi 8.00 20.00
GSJ69 Theo Fleury 10.00 25.00
GSJ70 Markus Naslund 8.00 20.00

2001-02 BAP Signature Series Teammates Jerseys

TM1 P.Kariya/J.Friesen 6.00 15.00
TM2 P.Stefan/I.Kovalchuk 20.00 50.00
TM3 B.Guerin/B.Dafoe 6.00 15.00
TM4 M.Biron/M.Satan 5.00 12.00
TM5 J.Iginla/R.Turek 8.00 20.00
TM6 R.Francis/S.Kapanen 8.00 20.00
TM7 T.Amonte/E.Daze 5.00 12.00
TM8 J.Sakic/P.Roy 15.00 40.00
TM9 C.Drury/M.Hejduk 5.00 12.00
TM10 M.Modano/E.Belfour 10.00 25.00
TM11 S.Yzerman/B.Shanahan 15.00 40.00
TM12 L.Robitaille/D.Hasek 10.00 25.00
TM13 P.Bure/R.Luongo 10.00 25.00
TM14 Z.Palffy/F.Potvin 10.00 25.00
TM15 M.Gaborik/M.Fernandez 6.00 15.00
TM16 B.Savage/J.Theodore 6.00 15.00
TM17 J.Arnott/M.Brodeur 15.00 40.00
TM18 S.Niedermayer/S.Stevens 6.00 15.00
TM19 M.Messier/E.Lindros 12.00 30.00
TM20 K. Jonsson/A.Yashin 5.00 12.00
TM21 D.Alfredsson/P.Lalime 6.00 15.00
TM22 M.Recchi/J.Roenick 10.00 25.00
TM23 J.LeClair/B.Boucher 6.00 15.00
TM24 M.Lemieux/M.Kraft 25.00 60.00
TM25 O.Nolan/T.Selanne 12.00 30.00
TM26 D.Weight/K.Tkachuk 6.00 15.00
TM27 V.Lecavalier/N.Khabibulin 6.00 15.00
TM28 M.Sundin/C.Joseph 8.00 20.00
TM29 D.Sedin/M.Naslund 8.00 20.00
TM30 P.Bondra/J.Jagr 20.00 50.00

2001-02 BAP Signature Series Vintage Autographs

VA1 Tony Esposito/60 25.00 60.00
VA2 Phil Esposito/40 25.00 60.00
VA3 Gordie Howe/20 100.00 250.00
VA4 Gordie Howe/20 100.00 250.00
VA5 Jean Beliveau/40 20.00 50.00
VA6 Jean Beliveau/40 20.00 50.00
VA7 Bobby Hull/40 30.00 80.00
VA8 Bobby Hull/40 30.00 80.00
VA9 Ted Lindsay/40 15.00 40.00
VA10 Johnny Bower/60 15.00 40.00
VA11 Milt Schmidt/80 12.00 30.00
VA12 Red Kelly/80 15.00 40.00
VA13 Glenn Hall/40 15.00 40.00
VA14 Chuck Rayner/40 10.00 25.00
VA15 Elmer Lach/80 12.00 30.00
VA17 Gerry Cheevers/40 15.00 40.00
VA18 Gump Worsley/40 20.00 50.00
VA19 Butch Bouchard/80 12.00 30.00
VA20 Henri Richard/80 20.00 50.00
VA21 Henri Richard/80 20.00 50.00
VA22 Bernie Geoffrion/80 20.00 50.00
VA23 Dollard St. Laurent/80 12.00 30.00
VA24 Dickie Moore/70 12.00 30.00
VA25 Jean-Guy Talbot/80 12.00 30.00
VA26 Bill Gadsby/80 12.00 30.00
VA27 Frank Mahovlich/40 15.00 40.00
VA28 Dino Ciccarelli/70 15.00 40.00
VA29 Jari Kurri/70 15.00 40.00
VA30 Mike Bossy/70 15.00 40.00
VA31 Johnny Bucyk/90 15.00 40.00
VA32 Michel Goulet/90 12.00 30.00
VA33 Stan Mikita/40 25.00 60.00
VA34 Bryan Trottier/70 15.00 40.00
VA35 Dale Hawerchuk/70 20.00 50.00
VA36 Gilbert Perreault/40 15.00 40.00
VA37 Marcel Dionne/40 20.00 50.00
VA38 Mike Gartner/70 20.00 50.00
VA39 Lanny McDonald/70 12.00 30.00
VA40 Guy Lafleur/40 20.00 50.00

2001-02 BAP Signature Series Beckett Promos

*SINGLES: 1.5X TO 4X BASIC CARDS

2002-03 BAP Signature Series

1 Dany Heatley .25 .60
2 Alexei Zhamnov .25 .60
3 Mike Comrie .30 .75
4 Dwayne Roloson .20 .50
5 Mike Dunham .25 .60
6 Simon Gagne .30 .75
7 Evgeni Nabokov .25 .60
8 Bryan McCabe .20 .50
9 Todd Bertuzzi .30 .75
10 Alex Kovalev .25 .60
11 Dave Andreychuk .30 .75
12 Daniel Alfredsson .30 .75
13 Marian Gaborik .30 .75
14 J-S Aubin .20 .50
15 Andy McDonald .30 .75
16 Brad Richards .30 .75
17 Henrik Sedin .40 1.00
18 Mark Bell .20 .50
19 Adam Deadmarsh .20 .50
20 Marc Denis .25 .60
21 Mike York .20 .50
22 Johan Hedberg .30 .75
23 Vincent Damphousse .25 .60
24 Marian Hossa .30 .75
25 Richard Zednik .20 .50
26 Alexei Yashin .25 .60
27 Sergei Gonchar .25 .60
28 Martin Straka .25 .60
29 Ed Jovanovski .25 .60
30 Robert Lang .20 .50
31 Markus Naslund .30 .75
32 Mike Sillinger .20 .50
33 Jamie Storr .25 .60
34 Kimmo Timonen .20 .50
35 Patrick Lalime .25 .60
36 Alyn McCauley .20 .50
37 Scott Walker .20 .50
38 Trevor Linden .30 .75
39 Ilya Kovalchuk .40 1.00
40 Jarome Iginla .40 1.00
41 Alex Tanguay .25 .60
42 Yanic Perreault .20 .50
43 Jocelyn Thibault .25 .60
44 Eric Brewer .20 .50
45 Ray Whitney .25 .60
46 Ryan Smyth .25 .60
47 Steven Reinprecht .20 .50
48 Phil Housley .25 .60
49 Milan Hnilicka .25 .60
50 Maxim Afinogenov .20 .50
51 Andrew Brunette .20 .50
52 Miroslav Satan .30 .75
53 Glen Murray .25 .60
54 Mark Parrish .20 .50
55 Daniel Sedin .40 1.00
56 Brendan Morrison .25 .60
57 Brian Rafalski .20 .50
58 Dan Cloutier .25 .60
59 Espen Knutsen .20 .50
60 Radim Vrbata .20 .50
61 Patrik Stefan .25 .60
62 Eric Daze .20 .50
63 Felix Potvin .50 1.25
64 Darcy Tucker .20 .50
65 Jose Theodore .30 .75
66 Scott Hartnell .20 .50
67 Martin Havlat .25 .60
68 Radek Bonk .25 .60
69 Patrick Marleau .30 .75
70 Andy Delmore .20 .50
71 Rostislav Klesla .20 .50
72 David Aebischer .25 .60
73 Steve Shields .25 .60
74 Stu Barnes .20 .50
75 Tim Connolly .20 .50
76 Jean-Sebastien Giguere .30 .75
77 Shane Doan .25 .60
78 Brian Rolston .25 .60
79 Shawn McEachern .20 .50
80 Martin Biron .25 .60
81 Craig Conroy .20 .50
82 Mika Noronen .25 .60
83 Brian Boucher .25 .60
84 Kyle Calder .20 .50
85 Cliff Ronning .20 .50
86 Brian Gionta .20 .50
87 Shawn Bates .20 .50
88 Michal Handzus .25 .60
89 Daniel Briere .25 .60
90 Adam Graves .25 .60
91 Martin St. Louis .30 .75
92 Ladislav Nagy .20 .50
93 Oleg Tverdovsky .20 .50
94 Pavel Brendl .20 .50
95 Alexei Morozov .20 .50
96 Daymond Langkow .25 .60
97 Krys Kolanos .20 .50
98 Sean Burke .20 .50
99 Chris Drury .30 .75
100 Steve Sullivan .20 .50
101 Paul Kariya .30 .75
102 Peter Forsberg .60 1.50
103 Ron Tugnutt .25 .60
104 Manny Legace .30 .75
105 Tommy Salo .25 .60
106 Kristian Huselius .20 .50
107 Jason Allison .25 .60
108 Mariusz Czerkawski .20 .50
109 Jeff Friesen .20 .50
110 Chris Osgood .30 .75
111 Martin Prusek .20 .50
112 Steve Yzerman .75 2.00
113 John LeClair .30 .75
114 Jan Hrdina .20 .50
115 Tony Amonte .25 .60
116 Teemu Selanne .60 1.50
117 Cory Stillman .20 .50
118 Nikolai Khabibulin .30 .75
119 Mats Sundin .30 .75
120 Olaf Kolzig .30 .75
121 Petr Sykora .25 .60
122 Joe Thornton .50 1.25
123 Roman Turek .30 .75
124 Derek Morris .20 .50
125 Bill Guerin .30 .75
126 Brendan Shanahan .30 .75
127 Roberto Luongo .50 1.25
128 Zigmund Palffy .30 .75
129 Pavol Demitra .40 1.00
130 Saku Koivu .30 .75
131 Joe Nieuwendyk .25 .60
132 Mike Peca .25 .60
133 Petr Schastlivy .20 .50
134 Jeremy Roenick .50 1.25
135 Mario Lemieux 1.25 3.00
136 Petr Cajanek .20 .50
137 Vincent Lecavalier .30 .75
138 Peter Bondra .30 .75
139 Brent Johnson .25 .60
140 Sergei Samsonov .25 .60
141 Joe Sakic .60 1.50
142 Brenden Morrow .25 .60
143 Arturs Irbe .25 .60
144 Chris Chelios .30 .75
145 Sandis Ozolinsh .20 .50
146 Doug Gilmour .40 1.00
147 Scott Stevens .30 .75
148 Sergei Fedorov .50 1.25
149 Keith Primeau .25 .60
150 Eric Boguniecki .20 .50
151 Shane Willis .20 .50
152 Rob Blake .30 .75
153 Luc Robitaille .30 .75
154 Pierre Turgeon .25 .60
155 Curtis Joseph .40 1.00
156 Stephen Weiss .30 .75
157 Patrik Elias .30 .75
158 Mark Recchi .40 1.00
159 Al MacInnis .40 1.00
160 Patrick Roy .75 2.00
161 Darryl Sydor .20 .50
162 Nicklas Lidstrom .30 .75
163 Doug Weight .30 .75
164 Roman Cechmanek .25 .60
165 Marty Turco .30 .75
166 Pavel Datsyuk .50 1.25
167 Chris Pronger .30 .75
168 Scott Young .20 .50
169 Igor Larionov .30 .75
170 Keith Tkachuk .30 .75
171 Ron Francis .40 1.00
172 Dan Blackburn .25 .60
173 Jeff O'Neill .20 .50
174 Bobby Holik .20 .50
175 Erik Cole .20 .50
176 Pavel Bure .30 .75
177 Brian Leetch .25 .60
178 Curtis Sanford RC .60 1.50
179 Carlo Colaiacovo RC .60 1.50
180 Dennis Seidenberg RC .60 1.50
181 Adam Hall RC .40 1.00
182 Ivan Majesky RC .40 1.00
183 Rick Nash RC 2.50 6.00
184 Alexei Smirnov RC .50 1.25
185 Chuck Kobasew RC .50 1.25
186 Ron Hainsey RC .40 1.00
187 Stephane Veilleux RC .40 1.00
188 Scottie Upshall RC .50 1.25
189 Lasse Pirjeta RC .40 1.00
190 Henrik Zetterberg RC 4.00 10.00
191 Jay Bouwmeester RC 1.25 3.00
192 Alexander Frolov RC 1.00 2.50
193 Dmitri Bykov RC .40 1.00
194 Stanislav Chistov RC .40 1.00
195 Jordan Leopold RC .60 1.50
196 P-M Bouchard RC .60 1.50
197 Mike Cammalleri RC 1.25 3.00
198 Anton Volchenkov RC .40 1.00
199 Lynn Loyns RC .40 1.00
200 Steve Eminger RC .40 1.00

2002-03 BAP Signature Series All-Rookie

AR1 Ryan Miller 15.00 40.00
AR2 Jay Bouwmeester 12.50 30.00
AR3 Dennis Seidenberg 10.00 25.00
AR4 Stephen Weiss 12.50 30.00
AR5 Marcel Hossa 12.50 30.00
AR6 Radovan Somik 10.00 25.00
AR7 Jan Lasak 10.00 25.00
AR8 Jordan Leopold 10.00 25.00
AR9 Barret Jackman 10.00 25.00
AR10 Mike Cammalleri 15.00 40.00
AR11 Henrik Zetterberg Skate 20.00 50.00
AR12 Rick Nash 20.00 50.00

2002-03 BAP Signature Series Autographs

*GOLD: .75X TO 1.25X
1 Dany Heatley 4.00 10.00
2 Alexei Zhamnov 2.50 6.00
3 Mike Comrie 2.50 6.00
4 Dwayne Roloson 3.00 8.00
5 Mike Dunham 2.00 5.00
6 Simon Gagne 6.00 15.00
7 Evgeni Nabokov 4.00 10.00
8 Bryan McCabe 2.00 5.00
9 Todd Bertuzzi 4.00 10.00
10 Alexei Kovalev 3.00 8.00
11 Dave Andreychuk 3.00 8.00
12 Daniel Alfredsson 3.00 8.00
13 Marian Gaborik 6.00 15.00
14 J-S Aubin 2.00 5.00
15 Andy McDonald 2.00 5.00
16 Brad Richards 3.00 8.00
17 Henrik Sedin 5.00 12.00
18 Mark Bell 2.00 5.00
19 Adam Deadmarsh 2.00 5.00
20 Marc Denis 4.00 10.00
21 Mike York 2.00 5.00
22 Johan Hedberg 2.00 5.00
23 Vincent Damphousse 2.00 5.00
24 Marian Hossa 5.00 12.00
25 Richard Zednik 2.00 5.00
26 Alexei Yashin 2.00 5.00
27 Sergei Gonchar 2.00 5.00
28 Martin Straka 2.00 5.00
29 Ed Jovanovski 4.00 10.00
30 Robert Lang 2.00 5.00
31 Markus Naslund 6.00 15.00
32 Mike Sillinger 2.00 5.00
33 Jamie Storr 2.00 5.00
34 Kimmo Timonen 2.00 5.00
35 Patrick Lalime 2.00 5.00
36 Alyn McCauley 2.00 5.00
37 Scott Walker 2.00 5.00
38 Trevor Linden 4.00 10.00
39 Ilya Kovalchuk 12.50 30.00
40 Jarome Iginla 8.00 20.00
41 Alex Tanguay 4.00 10.00
42 Yanic Perreault 2.00 5.00
43 Jocelyn Thibault 2.00 5.00
44 Eric Brewer 2.00 5.00
45 Ray Whitney 2.00 5.00
46 Ryan Smyth 2.00 5.00
47 Steven Reinprecht 2.00 5.00
48 Phil Housley 2.00 5.00
49 Milan Hnilicka 2.00 5.00
50 Maxim Afinogenov 2.00 5.00
51 Andrew Brunette 2.00 5.00
52 Miroslav Satan 4.00 10.00
53 Glen Murray 2.00 5.00
54 Mark Parrish 2.00 5.00
55 Daniel Sedin 5.00 12.00
56 Brendan Morrison 2.00 5.00
57 Brian Rafalski 2.00 5.00
58 Dan Cloutier 4.00 10.00
59 Espen Knutsen 2.00 5.00
60 Radim Vrbata 2.00 5.00
61 Patrik Stefan 2.00 5.00
62 Eric Daze 2.00 5.00
63 Felix Potvin 6.00 15.00
64 Darcy Tucker 2.00 5.00
65 Jose Theodore 6.00 15.00
66 Scott Hartnell 3.00 8.00
67 Martin Havlat 4.00 10.00
68 Radek Bonk 2.00 5.00
69 Patrick Marleau 4.00 10.00
70 Andy Delmore 2.00 5.00
71 Rostislav Klesla 2.00 5.00
72 David Aebischer 4.00 10.00
73 Steve Shields 2.00 5.00
74 Stu Barnes 2.00 5.00
75 Tim Connolly 2.00 5.00
76 Jean-Sebastien Giguere 4.00 10.00
77 Shane Doan 3.00 8.00
78 Brian Rolston 2.00 5.00
79 Shawn McEachern 2.00 5.00
80 Martin Biron 2.00 5.00
81 Craig Conroy 2.00 5.00
82 Mika Noronen 2.00 5.00
83 Brian Boucher 2.00 5.00
84 Kyle Calder 2.00 5.00
85 Cliff Ronning 2.00 5.00
86 Brian Gionta 2.00 5.00
87 Shawn Bates 2.00 5.00
88 Michal Handzus 2.00 5.00
89 Daniel Briere 4.00 10.00
90 Adam Graves 2.00 5.00
91 Martin St. Louis 6.00 15.00
92 Ladislav Nagy 2.00 5.00
93 Oleg Tverdovsky 2.00 5.00
94 Pavel Brendl 2.00 5.00
95 Alexei Morozov 2.00 5.00
96 Daymond Langkow 2.00 5.00
97 Krys Kolanos 2.00 5.00
98 Sean Burke 4.00 10.00
99 Chris Drury 4.00 10.00
100 Steve Sullivan 2.00 5.00
101 Paul Kariya SP 20.00 50.00
102 Peter Forsberg SP 25.00 60.00
103 Ron Tugnutt SP 8.00 20.00
104 Manny Legace 4.00 10.00
105 Tommy Salo SP 8.00 20.00
106 Kristian Huselius 2.00 5.00
107 Jason Allison SP 8.00 20.00
108 Mariusz Czerkawski 2.00 5.00
109 Jeff Friesen SP 8.00 20.00
110 Chris Osgood SP 8.00 20.00
111 Martin Prusek 2.00 5.00
112 Steve Yzerman SP 30.00 80.00
113 John LeClair SP 8.00 20.00
114 Jan Hrdina 2.00 5.00
115 Tony Amonte SP 8.00 20.00
116 Teemu Selanne SP 12.00 30.00
117 Cory Stillman 2.00 5.00
118 Nikolai Khabibulin SP 10.00 25.00
119 Mats Sundin SP 20.00 50.00
120 Olaf Kolzig SP 12.00 30.00
121 Petr Sykora 8.00 20.00
122 Joe Thornton SP 15.00 40.00
123 Roman Turek SP 8.00 20.00
124 Derek Morris SP 8.00 20.00
125 Bill Guerin SP 8.00 20.00
126 Brendan Shanahan SP 15.00 40.00
127 Roberto Luongo 8.00 20.00
128 Zigmund Palffy SP 8.00 20.00
129 Pavol Demitra SP 8.00 20.00
130 Saku Koivu SP 6.00 15.00
131 Joe Nieuwendyk SP 8.00 20.00
132 Mike Peca SP 8.00 20.00
133 Petr Schastlivy 2.00 5.00
134 Jeremy Roenick SP 15.00 40.00
135 Mario Lemieux SP 125.00 250.00
136 Petr Cajanek 2.00 5.00
137 Vincent Lecavalier SP 10.00 25.00
138 Peter Bondra SP 8.00 20.00
139 Brent Johnson SP 6.00 15.00
140 Sergei Samsonov SP 8.00 20.00
141 Joe Sakic SP 20.00 50.00
142 Brenden Morrow 4.00 10.00
143 Arturs Irbe 2.00 5.00
144 Chris Chelios SP 12.50 30.00
145 Sandis Ozolinsh 2.00 5.00
146 Doug Gilmour SP 8.00 20.00
147 Scott Stevens SP 10.00 25.00
148 Sergei Fedorov SP 15.00 40.00
149 Keith Primeau SP 8.00 20.00
150 Eric Boguniecki 2.00 5.00
151 Shane Willis 2.00 5.00
152 Rob Blake SP 8.00 20.00
153 Luc Robitaille SP 12.50 30.00
154 Pierre Turgeon SP 8.00 20.00
155 Curtis Joseph SP 12.50 30.00
156 Stephen Weiss 3.00 8.00
157 Patrik Elias SP 8.00 20.00
158 Mark Recchi SP 8.00 20.00
159 Al MacInnis SP 8.00 20.00
160 Patrick Roy SP 30.00 80.00
161 Darryl Sydor SP 8.00 20.00
162 Nicklas Lidstrom SP 12.00 30.00
163 Doug Weight SP 8.00 20.00
164 Roman Cechmanek 2.00 5.00
165 Marty Turco 4.00 10.00
166 Pavel Datsyuk 12.50 30.00
167 Chris Pronger SP 8.00 20.00
168 Scott Young 2.00 5.00
169 Igor Larionov SP 10.00 25.00
170 Keith Tkachuk SP 8.00 20.00
171 Ron Francis SP 8.00 20.00
172 Dan Blackburn 2.00 5.00
173 Jeff O'Neill SP 8.00 20.00
174 Bobby Holik SP 8.00 20.00
175 Erik Cole 2.00 5.00
176 Pavel Bure SP 10.00 25.00
177 Brian Leetch SP 8.00 20.00
178 Curtis Sanford 4.00 10.00
179 Carlo Colaiacovo 2.00 5.00
180 Dennis Seidenberg 3.00 8.00
181 Adam Hall 2.00 5.00
182 Ivan Majesky 2.00 5.00
183 Rick Nash 10.00 25.00
184 Alexei Smirnov 2.00 5.00
185 Chuck Kobasew 2.00 5.00
186 Ron Hainsey 2.00 5.00
187 Stephane Veilleux 2.00 5.00
188 Scottie Upshall 4.00 10.00
189 Lasse Pirjeta 2.00 5.00
190 Henrik Zetterberg 20.00 40.00
191 Jay Bouwmeester 6.00 15.00
192 Alexander Frolov 6.00 15.00
193 Dmitri Bykov 2.00 5.00
194 Stanislav Chistov 2.00 5.00
195 Jordan Leopold 2.00 5.00
196 P-M Bouchard 4.00 10.00
197 Mike Cammalleri 4.00 10.00
198 Anton Volchenkov 2.00 5.00
199 Lynn Loyns 2.00 5.00
200 Steve Eminger 2.00 5.00

2002-03 BAP Signature Series Autograph Buybacks 1998

*BUYBACKS: .6X TO 1.5X ORIGINAL VALUES
174 Ron Francis 12.00 30.00

2002-03 BAP Signature Series Autograph Buybacks 1999

*BUYBACKS: .6X TO 1.5X ORIGINAL VALUES

2002-03 BAP Signature Series Autograph Buybacks 2000

*BUYBACKS: .6X TO 1.5X ORIGINAL VALUES
158 Ron Francis 15.00 40.00

2002-03 BAP Signature Series Autograph Buybacks 2001

*BUYBACKS: .6X TO 1.5X ORIGINAL VALUES
LRF Ron Francis 12.00 30.00

2002-03 BAP Signature Series Defensive Wall

DW1 Colorado Avalanche 40.00 100.00
DW2 Toronto Maple Leafs 25.00 60.00
DW3 Philadelphia Flyers 15.00 40.00
DW4 NY Rangers 15.00 40.00
DW5 Dallas Stars 20.00 50.00
DW6 NJ Devils 20.00 50.00
DW7 St. Louis Blues 15.00 40.00
DW8 Ottawa Senators 15.00 40.00
DW9 Washington Capitals 15.00 40.00
DW10 Vancouver Canucks 15.00 40.00

2002-03 BAP Signature Series Famous Scraps

FS1 D.Schultz/T.Williams 20.00 50.00
FS2 B.Probert/W.Clark 25.00 60.00
FS3 I.Laperriere/B.Guerin 12.00 30.00
FS4 P.Worrell/C.Gratton 15.00 40.00
FS5 B.Guerin/J.Iginla 15.00 40.00
FS6 T.Domi/R.Ray 30.00 80.00
FS7 M.Comrie/I.Kovalchuk 20.00 50.00
FS8 F.Potvin/R.Hextall 20.00 50.00
FS9 O.Nolan/B.Probert 20.00 50.00
FS10 P.Roy/C.Osgood 30.00 80.00
FS11 D.Brashear/G.Laraque 20.00 50.00
FS12 M.Johnson/S.McCarthy 15.00 40.00

2002-03 BAP Signature Series Franchise Players

FJ1 Paul Kariya 8.00 20.00
FJ2 Dany Heatley 12.50 30.00
FJ3 Joe Thornton 15.00 40.00
FJ4 Miroslav Satan 8.00 20.00
FJ5 Jarome Iginla 10.00 25.00
FJ6 Ron Francis 8.00 20.00
FJ7 Jocelyn Thibault 8.00 20.00
FJ8 Rick Nash 15.00 40.00
FJ9 Joe Sakic 15.00 40.00
FJ10 Mike Modano 12.50 30.00
FJ11 Steve Yzerman 20.00 50.00
FJ12 Mike Comrie 8.00 20.00
FJ13 Roberto Luongo 12.50 30.00
FJ14 Jason Allison 8.00 20.00
FJ15 Marian Gaborik 15.00 40.00
FJ16 Jose Theodore 8.00 20.00
FJ17 David Legwand 8.00 20.00
FJ18 Martin Brodeur 20.00 50.00
FJ19 Mike Peca 8.00 20.00
FJ20 Pavel Bure 8.00 20.00
FJ21 Marian Hossa 8.00 20.00
FJ22 Jeremy Roenick 10.00 25.00
FJ23 Daniel Briere 8.00 20.00
FJ24 Mario Lemieux 15.00 40.00
FJ25 Teemu Selanne 8.00 20.00
FJ26 Chris Pronger 8.00 20.00
FJ27 Vincent Lecavalier 8.00 20.00
FJ28 Mats Sundin 8.00 20.00
FJ29 Markus Naslund 8.00 20.00
FJ30 Jaromir Jagr 12.50 30.00

2002-03 BAP Signature Series Golf

COMPLETE SET (100) 50.00 100.00
GS1 Adam Foote .50 1.25
GS2 Adam Oates .50 1.25
GS3 Adrian Aucoin .30 .75
GS4 Alex Tanguay .50 1.25
GS5 Alexander Mogilny .50 1.25
GS6 Alexei Yashin .30 .75
GS7 Alyn McCauley .30 .75
GS8 Andy McDonald .30 .75
GS9 Brian Leetch .50 1.25
GS10 Bates Battaglia .30 .75
GS11 Bobby Holik .30 .75
GS12 Brad Isbister .30 .75
GS13 Brendan Morrison .50 1.25
GS14 Arturs Irbe .50 1.25
GS15 Brian Savage .30 .75
GS16 Bryan Marchment .30 .75
GS17 Bryan McCabe .30 .75
GS18 Carlo Colaiacovo .30 .75
GS19 Chris Drury .50 1.25
GS20 Chris Gratton .30 .75
GS21 Chris Neil .30 .75
GS22 Chris Osgood .50 1.25
GS23 Chris Simon .30 .75
GS24 Curtis Joseph .60 1.50
GS25 Daniel Sedin .30 .75
GS26 Darius Kasparaitis .30 .75
GS27 Darren McCarty .30 .75
GS28 Darryl Sittler .60 1.50
GS29 David Aebischer .50 1.25
GS30 David Legwand .50 1.25
GS31 Denis Arkhipov .30 .75
GS32 Derek Morris .30 .75
GS33 Donald Brashear .30 .75
GS34 Doug Gilmour .50 1.25
GS35 Ed Belfour .60 1.50
GS36 Ed Jovanovski .50 1.25
GS37 Erik Cole .30 .75
GS38 Eric Lindros .60 1.50
GS39 Grant Fuhr .50 1.25
GS40 Jaroslav Svoboda .30 .75
GS41 Jeff O'Neill .30 .75
GS42 Jarome Iginla .75 2.00
GS43 Joe Sakic 1.25 3.00
GS44 Johan Hedberg .50 1.25
GS45 Josef Vasicek .30 .75
GS46 Jean-Sebastien Giguere .50 1.25
GS47 Kenny Jonsson .30 .75
GS48 Luc Robitaille .50 1.25
GS49 Mario Lemieux 4.00 10.00
GS50 Mark Parrish .30 .75
GS51 Martin Brodeur 1.50 4.00
GS52 Martin Erat .30 .75
GS53 Martin Skoula .30 .75
GS54 Mats Sundin .60 1.50
GS55 Matt Cooke .30 .75
GS56 Mattias Ohlund .30 .75
GS57 Mike Dunham .50 1.25
GS58 Mike Fisher .30 .75
GS59 Mike Keane .30 .75
GS60 Mike Peca .30 .75
GS61 Mike Ricci .30 .75
GS62 Milan Hejduk .60 1.50
GS63 Miroslav Satan .50 1.25
GS64 Nik Antropov .30 .75
GS65 Olaf Kolzig .50 1.25
GS66 Owen Nolan .50 1.25
GS67 Pat Verbeek .30 .75
GS68 Patrick Marleau .50 1.25
GS69 Patrick Roy 3.00 8.00
GS70 Paul Kariya .60 1.50
GS71 Peter Bondra .50 1.25
GS72 Peter Forsberg 1.50 4.00
GS73 Petr Sykora .30 .75
GS74 Radek Dvorak .30 .75
GS75 Rick DiPietro .50 1.25
GS76 Rob Blake .50 1.25
GS77 Robert Lang .30 .75
GS78 Roman Hamrlik .30 .75
GS79 Dany Heatley .50 1.25
GS80 Ron Francis .50 1.25
GS81 Ryan Smyth .30 .75
GS82 Sami Kapanen .30 .75
GS83 Scott Hartnell .30 .75
GS84 Scott Stevens .50 1.25
GS85 Scott Walker .30 .75
GS86 Stan Mikita .75 2.00
GS87 Stanislav Chistov .30 .75
GS88 Steve Konowalchuk .30 .75
GS89 Steve Rucchin .30 .75
GS90 Steve Yzerman 3.00 8.00
GS91 Stephen Peat .30 .75
GS92 Steven Reinprecht .30 .75
GS93 Teemu Selanne .60 1.50
GS94 Tie Domi .50 1.25
GS95 Todd Bertuzzi .60 1.50
GS96 Todd White .30 .75
GS97 Tom Poti .30 .75
GS98 Trent Klatt .30 .75
GS99 Trevor Kidd .50 1.25
GS100 Wade Redden .30 .75

2002-03 BAP Signature Series Jerseys

SGJ1 Mario Lemieux 20.00 50.00
SGJ2 Steve Yzerman 20.00 50.00
SGJ3 Peter Forsberg 12.50 30.00
SGJ4 Patrick Roy 20.00 50.00
SGJ5 Jarome Iginla 10.00 25.00
SGJ6 Pavel Bure 8.00 20.00
SGJ7 Jaromir Jagr 10.00 25.00
SGJ8 Eric Lindros 8.00 20.00
SGJ9 Paul Kariya 8.00 20.00
SGJ10 Ilya Kovalchuk 10.00 25.00
SGJ11 Mike Modano 10.00 25.00
SGJ12 Joe Thornton 12.50 30.00
SGJ13 Jose Theodore 8.00 20.00
SGJ14 Jeremy Roenick 10.00 25.00
SGJ15 Martin Brodeur 15.00 40.00
SGJ16 Mats Sundin 8.00 20.00
SGJ17 Mark Messier 8.00 20.00
SGJ18 Alexei Yashin 6.00 15.00
SGJ19 Marian Gaborik 12.50 30.00
SGJ20 Brendan Shanahan 8.00 20.00
SGJ21 Owen Nolan 6.00 15.00
SGJ22 Joe Sakic 12.50 30.00
SGJ23 Daniel Alfredsson 6.00 15.00
SGJ24 Teemu Selanne 8.00 20.00
SGJ25 Nicklas Lidstrom 8.00 20.00
SGJ26 John LeClair 8.00 20.00
SGJ27 Keith Tkachuk 8.00 20.00
SGJ28 Brian Leetch 6.00 15.00
SGJ29 Milan Hejduk 8.00 20.00
SGJ30 Dany Heatley 10.00 25.00
SGJ31 Sergei Samsonov 6.00 15.00
SGJ32 Todd Bertuzzi 8.00 20.00
SGJ33 Markus Naslund 8.00 20.00
SGJ34 Chris Chelios 8.00 20.00
SGJ35 Rob Blake 6.00 15.00
SGJ36 Sergei Fedorov 10.00 25.00
SGJ37 Al MacInnis 6.00 15.00
SGJ38 Luc Robitaille 6.00 15.00
SGJ39 Martin Havlat 6.00 15.00
SGJ40 Ron Francis 6.00 15.00
SGJ41 Alexander Mogilny 6.00 15.00
SGJ42 Chris Pronger 6.00 15.00
SGJ43 Doug Weight 6.00 15.00
SGJ44 Zigmund Palffy 8.00 20.00
SGJ45 Peter Bondra 6.00 15.00
SGJ46 Mike Comrie 6.00 15.00
SGJ47 Pavel Datsyuk 12.50 30.00
SGJ48 Marian Hossa 8.00 20.00
SGJ49 Saku Koivu 8.00 20.00
SGJ50 Dan Blackburn 6.00 15.00
SGJ51 Steve Shields 6.00 15.00
SGJ52 Bill Guerin 6.00 15.00
SGJ53 Doug Gilmour 6.00 15.00
SGJ54 Jason Spezza 12.50 30.00
SGJ55 Jay Bouwmeester 6.00 15.00
SGJ56 Alexei Smirnov 6.00 15.00
SGJ57 Stanislav Chistov 6.00 15.00
SGJ58 Chuck Kobasew 6.00 15.00
SGJ59 Jordan Leopold 6.00 15.00
SGJ60 Niko Kapanen 6.00 15.00
SGJ61 Scottie Upshall 6.00 15.00
SGJ62 Ron Hainsey 6.00 15.00
SGJ63 Alexander Frolov 6.00 15.00
SGJ64 Mike Cammalleri 6.00 15.00
SGJ65 Dennis Seidenberg 6.00 15.00
SGJ66 Rick Nash 10.00 25.00
SGJ67 Carlo Colaiacovo 6.00 15.00
SGJ68 Marty Turco 6.00 15.00
SGJ69 Alex Kovalev 6.00 15.00
SGJ70 Vincent Lecavalier 6.00 15.00

2002-03 BAP Signature Series Magnificent Inserts

MI1 2000-01 Season 30.00 80.00
MI2 1985-86 Season 30.00 80.00
MI3 2002 NHL All-Star 30.00 80.00
MI4 1987 Canada Cup 30.00 80.00
MI5 Dual Jersey 50.00 125.00

2002-03 BAP Signature Series Phenoms

YP1 Simon Gagne 12.00 30.00
YP2 Scott Gomez 12.00 30.00
YP3 David Legwand 10.00 25.00
YP4 Patrik Stefan 10.00 25.00
YP5 Brad Stuart 10.00 25.00
YP6 Alex Tanguay 10.00 25.00
YP7 Brent Johnson 8.00 20.00
YP8 Roberto Luongo 20.00 50.00
YP9 Evgeni Nabokov 12.00 30.00
YP10 Nik Antropov 12.00 30.00

2002-03 BAP Signature Series Triple Memorabilia

TM1 Mario Lemieux 100.00 250.00
TM2 Mats Sundin 20.00 50.00
TM3 Steve Yzerman 50.00 120.00
TM4 Joe Thornton 30.00 80.00
TM5 Eric Lindros 20.00 50.00
TM6 Patrick Roy 50.00 125.00
TM7 Brett Hull 30.00 80.00
TM8 Sergei Fedorov 30.00 80.00
TM9 Martin Brodeur 50.00 125.00
TM10 Joe Sakic 30.00 80.00

2000-01 BAP Ultimate Memorabilia Autographs

1 Theo Fleury 15.00 40.00
2 Brendan Shanahan 15.00 40.00
3 Curtis Joseph 15.00 40.00
4 Saku Koivu 15.00 40.00
5 Olaf Kolzig 10.00 25.00
6 Al MacInnis 12.00 30.00
7 John LeClair 15.00 40.00
8 Teemu Selanne 15.00 40.00
9 Wayne Gretzky 250.00 600.00
10 Pavel Bure 15.00 40.00
11 Mario Lemieux 100.00 200.00
12 Milan Hejduk 15.00 40.00
13 Ray Bourque 25.00 60.00
14 Daniel Alfredsson 10.00 25.00
15 Mats Sundin 20.00 50.00
16 Paul Kariya 15.00 40.00
17 Scott Gomez 10.00 25.00
18 Eric Lindros 15.00 40.00
19 Sergei Fedorov 20.00 50.00
20 Peter Forsberg 25.00 60.00
21 Vincent Lecavalier 12.00 30.00
22 Tony Amonte 10.00 25.00
23 Patrick Roy 60.00 150.00
24 Ed Belfour 15.00 40.00
25 Martin Brodeur 40.00 100.00
26 Brian Leetch 10.00 25.00
27 Mike Modano 20.00 50.00
28 Joe Sakic 30.00 80.00
29 Jeremy Roenick 15.00 40.00
30 Steve Yzerman 60.00 150.00
31 Nikolai Khabibulin 10.00 25.00
32 Roman Turek 10.00 25.00
33 Keith Primeau 12.00 30.00
34 Mike Richter 15.00 40.00
35 Patrik Stefan 10.00 25.00
36 Scott Stevens 10.00 25.00
37 Valeri Bure 10.00 25.00
38 Doug Weight 10.00 25.00
39 Nicklas Lidstrom 15.00 40.00
40 Chris Drury 10.00 25.00
41 Mike Peca 10.00 25.00
42 Chris Pronger 12.00 30.00
43 Rob Blake 10.00 25.00
44 Luc Robitaille 12.00 30.00
45 Joe Thornton 25.00 60.00
46 Jason Arnott 10.00 25.00
47 Daniel Sedin 20.00 40.00
48 Pierre Turgeon 10.00 25.00
49 Brad Stuart 10.00 25.00
50 Adam Oates 10.00 25.00

2000-01 BAP Ultimate Memorabilia Active Eight

AE1 Messier/Yzerman/Lemieux 200.00 400.00
AE2 Messier/Yzerman/Francis 60.00 150.00
AE3 Lemieux/Hull/Bure 75.00 200.00
AE4 Lemieux/Lindros/Jagr 100.00 200.00
AE5 Roy/Vernon/VBK 60.00 150.00
AE6 Belfour/Roy/Hasek 60.00 150.00
AE7 Brodeur/Hasek/Osgood 60.00 150.00
AE8 Hasek/Brodeur/Hebert 60.00 150.00

2000-01 BAP Ultimate Memorabilia Dynasty Jerseys

D1 Wayne Gretzky 150.00 300.00
D2 Mark Messier 40.00 100.00
D3 Grant Fuhr 30.00 80.00
D4 Paul Coffey 25.00 60.00
D5 Bill Ranford 30.00 80.00
D6 Mario Lemieux 100.00 200.00
D7 Paul Coffey 25.00 60.00
D8 Jaromir Jagr 40.00 100.00
D9 Tom Barrasso 25.00 60.00
D10 Ron Francis 25.00 60.00
D11 Larry Murphy 25.00 60.00
D12 Ulf Samuelsson 25.00 60.00
D13 Steve Yzerman 60.00 120.00
D14 Chris Osgood 25.00 60.00
D15 Nicklas Lidstrom 25.00 60.00
D16 Sergei Fedorov 30.00 80.00
D17 Brendan Shanahan 25.00 60.00
D18 Darren McCarty 25.00 60.00
D19 Slava Kozlov 20.00 50.00
D20 Mike Vernon 25.00 60.00

2000-01 BAP Ultimate Memorabilia Game-Used Jerseys

*STICK/90: .4X TO 1X JERSEY/60
GJ1 Theo Fleury 15.00 40.00
GJ2 Brendan Shanahan 10.00 25.00
GJ3 Curtis Joseph 10.00 25.00
GJ4 Roman Turek 10.00 25.00
GJ5 Dominik Hasek 20.00 50.00
GJ6 Al MacInnis 10.00 25.00
GJ7 John LeClair 10.00 25.00
GJ8 Teemu Selanne 10.00 25.00
GJ9 Wayne Gretzky 50.00 120.00
GJ10 Pavel Bure 10.00 25.00
GJ11 Mark Messier 10.00 25.00
GJ12 Jaromir Jagr 15.00 40.00
GJ13 Arturs Irbe 8.00 20.00
GJ14 Vincent Lecavalier 10.00 25.00
GJ15 Mats Sundin 12.50 30.00
GJ16 Paul Kariya 10.00 25.00
GJ17 Marian Hossa 10.00 25.00
GJ18 Owen Nolan 8.00 20.00
GJ19 Sergei Fedorov 12.00 30.00
GJ20 Peter Forsberg 20.00 50.00
GJ21 Brett Hull 12.50 30.00
GJ22 Tony Amonte 8.00 20.00
GJ23 Patrick Roy 30.00 80.00
GJ24 Ed Belfour 10.00 25.00
GJ25 Martin Brodeur 30.00 80.00
GJ26 Brian Leetch 8.00 20.00
GJ27 Mike Modano 15.00 40.00
GJ28 Joe Sakic 20.00 50.00
GJ29 Jeremy Roenick 12.50 30.00
GJ30 Steve Yzerman 30.00 80.00
GJ31 Jason Allison 8.00 20.00
GJ32 Milan Hejduk 10.00 25.00
GJ33 Mike Richter 10.00 25.00
GJ34 Patrik Stefan 8.00 20.00
GJ35 Kyle McLaren 8.00 20.00
GJ36 Valeri Bure 8.00 20.00
GJ37 Felix Potvin 20.00 50.00
GJ38 Chris Pronger 8.00 20.00
GJ39 Scott Stevens 8.00 20.00
GJ40 Luc Robitaille 8.00 20.00
GJ41 Roberto Luongo 15.00 40.00
GJ42 Chris Osgood 8.00 20.00
GJ43 Olaf Kolzig 8.00 20.00
GJ44 Scott Gomez 8.00 20.00
GJ45 Jason Arnott 8.00 20.00
GJ46 Rob Blake 8.00 20.00
GJ47 Keith Tkachuk 10.00 25.00
GJ48 Saku Koivu 8.00 20.00
GJ49 Alexei Yashin 8.00 20.00
GJ50 Nicklas Lidstrom 10.00 25.00

2000-01 BAP Ultimate Memorabilia Goalie Memorabilia

GM1 J.Plante/P.Roy 60.00 150.00
GM2 T.Sawchuk/P.Roy 60.00 150.00
GM3 M.Vernon/C.Osgood 25.00 60.00
GM4 C.Joseph/F.Potvin 40.00 100.00
GM5 T.Esposito/E.Belfour 25.00 60.00
GM6 T.Broda/J.Bower 30.00 80.00
GM7 B.Parent/B.Boucher 25.00 60.00
GM8 T.Esposito/G.Cheevers 30.00 80.00
GM9 B.Parent/G.Cheevers 40.00 100.00
GM10 Jacques Plante G/J 60.00 150.00
GM11 P.Roy/E.Belfour 60.00 150.00
GM12 C.Joseph/D.Hasek 30.00 80.00
GM13 R.Turek/E.Belfour 25.00 60.00
GM14 M.Brodeur/J.Plante 60.00 150.00
GM15 M.Richter/J.Vanbiesbrouck 25.00 60.00
GM16 Jacques Plante G/S/J 60.00 150.00
GM17 T.Esposito/Parent/Tretiak 60.00 150.00
GM18 Brimsek/Dafoe/Cheevers 50.00 125.00
GM19 Bower/Broda/Sawchuk 75.00 200.00
GM20 Roy/Vezina/Sawchuk 250.00 400.00

2000-01 BAP Ultimate Memorabilia Goalie Memorabilia Autographed

UG1 Gerry Cheevers 40.00 100.00
UG2 Vladislav Tretiak 75.00 200.00
UG3 Tony Esposito 40.00 100.00
UG4 Johnny Bower 40.00 100.00
UG5 Bernie Parent 50.00 125.00

2000-01 BAP Ultimate Memorabilia Goalie Sticks

G1 Guy Hebert 12.50 30.00
G2 Damian Rhodes 12.50 30.00
G3 Byron Dafoe 12.50 30.00
G4 Dominik Hasek 15.00 40.00
G5 Mike Vernon 12.50 30.00
G6 Arturs Irbe 12.50 30.00
G7 Jocelyn Thibault 12.50 30.00
G8 Patrick Roy 50.00 125.00
G9 Marc Denis 12.50 30.00
G10 Ed Belfour 12.50 30.00
G11 Chris Osgood 12.50 30.00
G12 Tommy Salo 12.50 30.00
G13 Roberto Luongo 15.00 40.00
G14 Jamie Storr 12.50 30.00
G15 Manny Fernandez 12.50 30.00
G16 Jeff Hackett 12.50 30.00
G17 Mike Dunham 12.50 30.00
G18 Martin Brodeur 30.00 80.00
G19 John Vanbiesbrouck 20.00 50.00
G20 Mike Richter 12.50 30.00
G21 Patrick Lalime 12.50 30.00
G22 Brian Boucher 12.50 30.00
G23 Nikolai Khabibulin 12.50 30.00
G24 J-S Aubin 12.50 30.00
G25 Roman Turek 12.50 30.00
G26 Steve Shields 12.50 30.00
G27 Dan Cloutier 12.50 30.00
G28 Curtis Joseph 12.50 30.00
G29 Felix Potvin 15.00 40.00
G30 Olaf Kolzig 12.50 30.00

2000-01 BAP Ultimate Memorabilia Gordie Howe No. 9

COMMON JSY/AU/20 125.00 250.00
9-1 Detroit 50.00 125.00
9-2 New England 50.00 125.00
9-3 Houston 50.00 125.00

2000-01 BAP Ultimate Memorabilia Gordie Howe Retrospective Jerseys

HL1 Detroit 60.00 150.00
HL2 New England 60.00 150.00
HL3 Houston 60.00 150.00
HL4 Detroit/New England 75.00 200.00
HL5 Houston/Detroit 75.00 200.00
HL6 Houston/New England 75.00 200.00
HL7 Detroit/Houston/N.Eng. 100.00 250.00

2000-01 BAP Ultimate Memorabilia Gordie Howe Retrospective Jerseys Autograph

GH1 Detroit 125.00 250.00
GH2 New England 125.00 250.00
GH3 Houston 125.00 250.00
GH4 Detroit/New England 125.00 250.00
GH5 Houston/Detroit 125.00 250.00
GH6 Houston/New England 125.00 250.00
GH7 Detroit/Houston/N.England 400.00 800.00

2000-01 BAP Ultimate Memorabilia Hart Trophy

H1 Chris Pronger 20.00 50.00
H2 Jaromir Jagr 40.00 100.00
H3 Dominik Hasek 30.00 80.00
H4 Dominik Hasek 30.00 80.00
H5 Mario Lemieux 60.00 150.00
H6 Eric Lindros 30.00 80.00
H7 Sergei Fedorov 30.00 80.00
H8 Mario Lemieux 60.00 150.00
H9 Mark Messier 50.00 125.00
H10 Brett Hull 25.00 60.00
H11 Mark Messier 50.00 125.00
H12 Wayne Gretzky 75.00 150.00
H13 Mario Lemieux 60.00 120.00
H14 Wayne Gretzky 60.00 120.00
H15 Wayne Gretzky 60.00 120.00
H16 Wayne Gretzky 60.00 120.00
H17 Wayne Gretzky 60.00 120.00
H18 Wayne Gretzky 60.00 120.00
H19 Wayne Gretzky 60.00 120.00
H20 Wayne Gretzky 60.00 120.00

2000-01 BAP Ultimate Memorabilia Jacques Plante Jerseys

*SKATES/20: .6X TO 1.5X JSY/30
PJ1 Patrick Roy 75.00 200.00
PJ2 Ed Belfour 25.00 60.00
PJ3 Martin Brodeur 50.00 120.00
PJ4 Dominik Hasek 40.00 100.00
PJ5 Chris Osgood 25.00 60.00
PJ6 Curtis Joseph 25.00 60.00
PJ7 Tommy Salo 25.00 60.00
PJ8 Mike Richter 25.00 60.00
PJ9 Byron Dafoe 25.00 60.00
PJ10 Roberto Luongo 25.00 60.00
PJ11 Roman Turek 25.00 60.00
PJ12 Olaf Kolzig 25.00 60.00
PJ13 Felix Potvin 25.00 60.00
PJ14 Jocelyn Thibault 25.00 60.00
PJ15 Brian Boucher 20.00 50.00

2000-01 BAP Ultimate Memorabilia Jacques Plante Skate

PS1 Patrick Roy 75.00 200.00
PS2 Ed Belfour 40.00 100.00
PS3 Martin Brodeur 75.00 200.00
PS4 Dominik Hasek 60.00 150.00
PS5 Chris Osgood 40.00 100.00
PS6 Curtis Joseph 40.00 80.00
PS7 Jeff Hackett 40.00 80.00
PS8 Mike Richter 25.00 60.00
PS9 Guy Hebert 30.00 80.00
PS10 Roberto Luongo 40.00 100.00
PS11 Roman Turek 40.00 100.00
PS12 Olaf Kolzig 30.00 80.00
PS13 Felix Potvin 60.00 125.00
PS14 Jocelyn Thibault 40.00 80.00
PS15 Brian Boucher 25.00 60.00

2000-01 BAP Ultimate Memorabilia Journey Jerseys

JJ1 Wayne Gretzky 150.00 350.00
JJ2 Mark Messier 25.00 60.00
JJ3 Pavel Bure 20.00 50.00
JJ4 Jeff Hackett 20.00 50.00
JJ5 Mats Sundin 20.00 50.00
JJ6 Curtis Joseph 20.00 50.00
JJ7 Ed Belfour 20.00 50.00
JJ8 Mike Modano 20.00 50.00
JJ9 Brett Hull 25.00 60.00
JJ10 Teemu Selanne 20.00 50.00
JJ11 Keith Tkachuk 20.00 50.00
JJ12 Patrick Roy 125.00 300.00
JJ13 Chris Chelios 20.00 50.00
JJ14 Al MacInnis 20.00 50.00
JJ15 Theo Fleury 25.00 60.00
JJ16 Jason Allison 20.00 50.00
JJ17 Jeremy Roenick 25.00 60.00
JJ18 Brendan Shanahan 20.00 50.00
JJ19 Owen Nolan 15.00 40.00
JJ20 Felix Potvin 30.00 80.00

2000-01 BAP Ultimate Memorabilia Magnificent Ones

ML1 S.Yzerman/M.Lemieux 60.00 150.00
ML2 J.Jagr/M.Lemieux 50.00 120.00
ML3 M.Brodeur/M.Lemieux 60.00 150.00
ML4 M.Messier/M.Lemieux 40.00 100.00
ML5 P.Roy/M.Lemieux 50.00 120.00
ML6 R.Bourque/M.Lemieux 60.00 150.00
ML7 R.Francis/M.Lemieux 25.00 60.00
ML8 D.Hasek/M.Lemieux 60.00 150.00
ML9 W.Gretzky/M.Lemieux 125.00 300.00
ML10 P.Coffey/M.Lemieux 30.00 80.00

2000-01 BAP Ultimate Memorabilia Maurice Richard Autographs

R1 Maurice Richard 200.00 400.00
R2 Maurice Richard 200.00 400.00
R3 Maurice Richard 200.00 400.00
R4 Maurice Richard 200.00 400.00
R5 Maurice Richard 200.00 400.00

2000-01 BAP Ultimate Memorabilia NHL Records

R1 Terry Sawchuk 50.00 120.00
R2 Patrick Roy 40.00 100.00
R3 Tony Esposito 25.00 60.00
R4 Jacques Plante 40.00 100.00
R5 Bill Mosienko 25.00 60.00
R6 Teemu Selanne 25.00 60.00
R7 Mario Lemieux 40.00 100.00
R8 Ray Bourque 30.00 80.00
R9 Gordie Howe 40.00 100.00
R10 Wayne Gretzky 60.00 150.00

2000-01 BAP Ultimate Memorabilia Norris Trophy

N1 Chris Pronger 15.00 40.00
N2 Al MacInnis 20.00 50.00
N3 Rob Blake 15.00 40.00
N4 Brian Leetch 15.00 40.00
N5 Chris Chelios 20.00 50.00
N6 Paul Coffey 20.00 50.00
N7 Ray Bourque 30.00 80.00
N8 Chris Chelios 20.00 50.00
N9 Brian Leetch 15.00 40.00
N10 Ray Bourque 30.00 80.00

2000-01 BAP Ultimate Memorabilia Retro-Active

RA1 G.Howe/C.Pronger 40.00 100.00
RA2 T.Sawchuk/P.Roy 100.00 200.00
RA3 T.Esposito/M.Lemieux 40.00 100.00
RA4 T.Esposito/E.Belfour 30.00 80.00
RA5 B.Parent/S.Yzerman 50.00 125.00
RA6 G.Howe/M.Lemieux 100.00 200.00
RA7 B.Mosienko/P.Kariya 40.00 100.00
RA8 J.Plante/P.Roy 100.00 200.00
RA9 G.Howe/J.Jagr 40.00 100.00
RA10 W.Gretzky/M.Messier 150.00 400.00

2000-01 BAP Ultimate Memorabilia Teammates

TM1 S.Yzerman/S.Fedorov 20.00 50.00
TM2 B.Shanahan/S.Kozlov 12.00 30.00
TM3 S.Yzerman/C.Chelios 20.00 50.00
TM4 S.Yzerman/B.Shanahan 30.00 80.00
TM5 J.Roenick/K.Tkachuk 12.00 30.00
TM6 N.Lidstom/S.Fedorov 15.00 40.00
TM7 N.Lidstrom/C.Osgood 12.00 30.00
TM8 N.Lidstrom/B.Shanahan 15.00 40.00
TM9 C.Osgood/S.Fedorov 12.00 30.00
TM10 N.Khabibulin/J.Roenick 8.00 20.00
TM11 S.Gonchar/A.Oates 8.00 20.00
TM12 C.Joseph/M.Sundin 12.00 30.00
TM13 C.Joseph/T.Domi 8.00 20.00
TM14 M.Sundin/T.Domi 8.00 20.00
TM15 P.Forsberg/P.Roy 40.00 100.00
TM16 P.Forsberg/J.Sakic 20.00 50.00
TM17 J.Sakic/P.Roy 40.00 100.00
TM18 B.Mironov/T.Amonte 8.00 20.00
TM19 P.Bure/P.Laus 8.00 20.00
TM20 M.Peca/D.Hasek 15.00 40.00
TM21 P.Kariya/T.Selanne 15.00 40.00
TM22 T.Selanne/G.Hebert 8.00 20.00
TM23 P.Kariya/G.Hebert 8.00 20.00
TM24 B.Hull/M.Modano 15.00 40.00
TM25 B.Hull/E.Belfour 12.00 30.00
TM26 E.Belfour/M.Modano 15.00 40.00
TM27 S.Zubov/E.Belfour 8.00 20.00
TM28 B.Hull/D.Sydor 8.00 20.00
TM29 E.Desjardins/J.LeClair 8.00 20.00
TM30 J.Arnott/M.Brodeur 15.00 40.00
TM31 S.Yzerman/M.Vernon 20.00 50.00
TM32 B.Hull/C.Joseph 20.00 50.00
TM33 K.Tkachuk/T.Selanne 12.00 30.00
TM34 M.Sundin/O.Nolan 12.00 30.00
TM35 E.Belfour/C.Chelios 12.00 30.00
TM36 M.Messier/W.Gretzky 100.00 250.00
TM37 T.Fleury/A.MacInnis 10.00 25.00
TM38 F.Potvin/M.Sundin 15.00 40.00
TM39 M.Lemieux/J.Jagr 40.00 100.00
TM40 R.Bourque/A.Oates 20.00 50.00

2001-02 BAP Ultimate Memorabilia Active Eight

1 Kariya/Lemieux/Sakic 60.00 150.00
2 Roy/Vernon/Barrasso 50.00 100.00
3 Francis/Messier/Yzerman 40.00 100.00
4 Lemieux/Robitaille/Jagr 50.00 125.00
5 Messier/Hull/Lemieux 60.00 150.00
6 Selanne/Nieuwendyk/Robitaille 40.00 100.00
7 Messier/Francis/Stevens 40.00 100.00
8 Lemieux/Sundin/Yzerman 40.00 100.00

2001-02 BAP Ultimate Memorabilia All-Star History

1 Turk Broda 20.00 50.00
2 Frank Brimsek 15.00 40.00
3 Ted Kennedy 15.00 40.00
4 Maurice Richard 60.00 120.00
5 Chuck Rayner 15.00 40.00
6 Bill Mosienko 15.00 40.00
7 Jean Beliveau 30.00 80.00
8 Doug Harvey 15.00 40.00
9 Ted Lindsay 15.00 40.00
10 Henri Richard 20.00 50.00
11 Jacques Plante 30.00 80.00
12 Glenn Hall 15.00 40.00
13 Terry Sawchuk 40.00 100.00
14 Bobby Hull 15.00 40.00
15 Johnny Bower 15.00 40.00
16 Tim Horton 40.00 100.00
17 Johnny Bucyk 12.50 30.00
18 Stan Mikita 15.00 40.00
19 Bill Gadsby 15.00 40.00
20 Gordie Howe 40.00 100.00
21 Ed Giacomin 15.00 40.00
22 Bernie Parent 40.00 80.00
23 Bobby Clarke 15.00 40.00
24 Gilbert Perreault 12.50 30.00
25 Frank Mahovlich 15.00 40.00
26 Tony Esposito 25.00 60.00
27 Denis Potvin 15.00 40.00
28 Guy Lafleur 25.00 60.00
29 Bryan Trottier 15.00 40.00
30 Lanny McDonald 12.50 30.00
31 Marcel Dionne 15.00 40.00
32 Wayne Gretzky 80.00 200.00
33 Mike Bossy 15.00 40.00
34 Mark Messier 15.00 40.00
35 Paul Coffey 25.00 60.00
36 Steve Yzerman 40.00 100.00
37 Mario Lemieux 40.00 100.00
38 Grant Fuhr 15.00 40.00
39 Patrick Roy 40.00 100.00
40 Brett Hull 25.00 60.00
41 Brian Leetch 15.00 40.00
42 Jeremy Roenick 20.00 50.00
43 Jaromir Jagr 25.00 60.00
44 Luc Robitaille 15.00 40.00
45 Joe Sakic 30.00 80.00
46 Eric Lindros 15.00 40.00
47 Paul Kariya 15.00 40.00
48 Mike Modano 15.00 40.00
49 Peter Forsberg 25.00 60.00
50 Pavel Bure 15.00 40.00
51 Milan Hejduk 15.00 40.00
52 Mats Sundin 15.00 40.00

2001-02 BAP Ultimate Memorabilia Autographs

1 Alexei Yashin/40 15.00 40.00
2 Brian Leetch/40 25.00 60.00
3 Daniel Alfredsson/40 15.00 40.00
4 Keith Tkachuk/40 25.00 60.00
5 Milan Hejduk/40 25.00 60.00
6 Mark Recchi/40 15.00 40.00
7 Paul Kariya/40 25.00 60.00
8 Scott Stevens/40 15.00 40.00
9 Joe Sakic/40 40.00 100.00
10 Al MacInnis/30 15.00 40.00
11 Peter Bondra/40 15.00 40.00
12 John LeClair/40 25.00 60.00
13 Brendan Shanahan/40 25.00 60.00
14 Rob Blake/40 15.00 40.00
15 Luc Robitaille/40 15.00 40.00
16 Jarome Iginla/40 30.00 80.00
17 Pavel Bure/40 25.00 60.00
18 Marcel Dionne/40 15.00 40.00
19 Gordie Howe/40 50.00 125.00
20 Phil Esposito/40 15.00 40.00
21 Guy Lafleur/40 30.00 80.00
22 Gilbert Perreault/40 15.00 40.00
23 Bobby Hull/40 30.00 80.00
24 Jean Beliveau/40 25.00 60.00
25 Stan Mikita/40 30.00 80.00
26 Ted Lindsay/20 25.00 60.00
27 Frank Mahovlich/30 25.00 60.00
28 Mario Lemieux/30 100.00 250.00
29 Tony Amonte/30 15.00 40.00
30 Jeremy Roenick/30 30.00 80.00
31 Owen Nolan/40 15.00 40.00
32 Mark Messier/40 40.00 100.00
33 Steve Yzerman/40 60.00 120.00
34 Sergei Fedorov/40 30.00 80.00
35 Wayne Gretzky/30 300.00 800.00

2001-02 BAP Ultimate Memorabilia Calder Trophy

1 Evgeni Nabokov 15.00 40.00
2 Scott Gomez 15.00 40.00
3 Chris Drury 10.00 25.00
4 Sergei Samsonov 15.00 40.00
5 Bryan Berard 10.00 25.00
6 Daniel Alfredsson 15.00 40.00
7 Peter Forsberg 25.00 60.00
8 Martin Brodeur 40.00 100.00
9 Teemu Selanne 20.00 50.00
10 Pavel Bure 20.00 50.00
11 Ed Belfour 20.00 50.00
12 Tom Barrasso 15.00 40.00
13 Brian Leetch 15.00 40.00
14 Joe Nieuwendyk 15.00 40.00
15 Luc Robitaille 15.00 40.00
16 Mario Lemieux 40.00 100.00
17 Dale Hawerchuk 15.00 40.00
18 Mike Bossy 20.00 50.00
19 Bryan Trottier 15.00 40.00
20 Denis Potvin 20.00 50.00
21 Gilbert Perreault 15.00 40.00
22 Tony Esposito 20.00 50.00
23 Glenn Hall 20.00 50.00
24 Terry Sawchuk 40.00 100.00
25 Frank Brimsek 20.00 50.00

2001-02 BAP Ultimate Memorabilia Decades

1 Chuck Rayner 20.00 50.00
2 Frank Brimsek 20.00 50.00
3 Terry Sawchuk 40.00 100.00
4 Jacques Plante 50.00 125.00
5 Doug Harvey 20.00 50.00
6 Bill Gadsby 20.00 50.00
7 Gordie Howe 40.00 100.00
8 Ted Lindsay 20.00 50.00
9 Johnny Bower 20.00 50.00
10 Glenn Hall 20.00 50.00
11 Bobby Hull 25.00 60.00
12 Stan Mikita 20.00 50.00
13 Tony Esposito 25.00 60.00
14 Gerry Cheevers 20.00 50.00
15 Guy Lafleur 25.00 60.00
16 Bobby Clarke 20.00 50.00
17 Denis Potvin 20.00 50.00
18 Serge Savard 20.00 50.00
19 Patrick Roy 40.00 100.00
20 Grant Fuhr 20.00 50.00
21 Larry Robinson 20.00 50.00
22 Al MacInnis 20.00 50.00
23 Cam Neely 30.00 80.00
24 Mike Bossy 20.00 50.00

2001-02 BAP Ultimate Memorabilia Dynamic Duos

1 M.Modano/W.Gretzky 50.00 125.00
2 J.Jagr/J.LeClair 20.00 50.00
3 L.Robitaille/J.Sakic 25.00 60.00
4 M.Hejduk/B.Hull 25.00 60.00
5 P.Bure/Yahsin 20.00 50.00
6 S.Yzerman/M.Sundin 30.00 80.00
7 P.Kariya/P.Forsberg 25.00 60.00
8 Selanne/Shanahan 20.00 50.00
9 M.Messier/J.Iginla 25.00 60.00
10 Mogilny/Recchi 20.00 50.00
11 Bondra/Fleury 20.00 50.00
12 Roenick/Lemieux 60.00 150.00
13 E.Lindros/I.Kovalchuk 25.00 60.00
14 Tkachuk/Amonte 20.00 50.00
15 Weight/Alfredsson 20.00 50.00
16 Damphousse/Fedorov 20.00 50.00

2001-02 BAP Ultimate Memorabilia Dynasty Jerseys

1 Bill Barber 20.00 50.00
2 Mike Bossy 20.00 50.00
3 Bobby Clarke 20.00 50.00
4 Yvan Cournoyer 20.00 50.00
5 Bob Gainey 20.00 50.00
6 Guy Lafleur 25.00 60.00
7 Guy Lapointe 20.00 50.00
8 Reggie Leach 20.00 50.00
9 Bob Nystrom 20.00 50.00
10 Bernie Parent 20.00 50.00
11 Denis Potvin 20.00 50.00
12 Larry Robinson 20.00 50.00
13 Serge Savard 20.00 50.00
14 Dave Schultz 20.00 50.00
15 Steve Shutt 20.00 50.00
16 Billy Smith 20.00 50.00
17 Bryan Trottier 20.00 50.00
18 Joe Watson 20.00 50.00

2001-02 BAP Ultimate Memorabilia 500 Goal Scorers

5 Mike Bossy/30 5.00 12.00
6 Guy Lafleur/30 6.00 15.00
8 Stan Mikita/30 8.00 20.00
9 Marcel Dionne/30 6.00 15.00
10 Phil Esposito/30 8.00 20.00
12 Mark Messier/30 10.00 25.00
13 Steve Yzerman/30 12.00 30.00
14 Brett Hull/30 10.00 25.00
15 Mike Gartner/30 6.00 15.00
16 Bryan Trottier/30 5.00 12.00
17 Gilbert Perreault/30 5.00 12.00
18 Lanny McDonald/30 4.00 10.00
19 Jari Kurri/30 5.00 12.00
20 Dale Hawerchuk/30 6.00 15.00
21 Luc Robitaille/30 5.00 12.00
22 Dave Andreychuk/30 5.00 12.00
23 John Bucyk/30 5.00 12.00
24 Michel Goulet/30 4.00 10.00
25 Joe Mullen/30 4.00 10.00
26 Dino Ciccarelli/30 5.00 12.00
27 Pat Verbeek/30 4.00 10.00
29 Ron Francis/30 6.00 15.00
30 Brendan Shanahan/30 5.00 12.00

2001-02 BAP Ultimate Memorabilia 500 Goal Scorers Autographs

1 Bobby Hull/25 75.00 150.00
2 Bryan Trottier/15 15.00 40.00
3 Dale Hawerchuk/25 30.00 60.00
4 Dave Andreychuk/30 30.00 60.00
6 Frank Mahovlich/25 40.00 100.00
8 Guy Lafleur/20 40.00 80.00
10 Jean Beliveau/15 40.00 80.00
11 John Bucyk/25 30.00 60.00
12 Lanny McDonald/20 25.00 50.00
14 Marcel Dionne/25 30.00 60.00
16 Michel Goulet/30 25.00 50.00
17 Mike Bossy/25 50.00 125.00
18 Mike Gartner/30 30.00 60.00
21 Phil Esposito/15 60.00 100.00
23 Stan Mikita/25 30.00 60.00
25 Joe Mullen/20 15.00 40.00

2001-02 BAP Ultimate Memorabilia 500 Goal Scorers Jerseys and Sticks

*JSY/STICK/40: .5X TO 1.2X JSY/30
7 Jean Beliveau/40 25.00 60.00
11 Frank Mahovlich/40 25.00 60.00

2001-02 BAP Ultimate Memorabilia Gloves Are Off

1 Rocket Richard 30.00 80.00
2 Gordie Howe 40.00 100.00
3 Mario Lemieux 30.00 80.00
4 Wayne Gretzky 40.00 100.00
5 Bill Gadsby 20.00 50.00
6 Doug Harvey 15.00 40.00
7 Ted Kennedy 20.00 50.00
8 King Clancy 25.00 60.00
9 Joe Sakic 30.00 80.00
10 Guy Lafleur 25.00 60.00
11 Eric Lindros 15.00 40.00
13 Mats Sundin 15.00 40.00
14 Al MacInnis 15.00 40.00
15 Doug Weight 15.00 40.00
16 Simon Gagne 15.00 40.00
17 Scott Niedermayer 15.00 40.00
18 Sergei Samsonov 15.00 40.00
19 Alexei Yashin 15.00 40.00
20 John LeClair 15.00 40.00
21 Sergei Fedorov 25.00 60.00
22 Chris Chelios 15.00 40.00
23 Jarome Iginla 25.00 60.00
24 Ace Bailey 30.00 80.00
25 Dickie Moore 15.00 40.00

2001-02 BAP Ultimate Memorabilia Jerseys

1 Paul Kariya 5.00 12.00
2 Martin Brodeur 12.00 30.00
3 John LeClair 5.00 12.00
4 Ilya Kovalchuk 15.00 40.00
5 Bill Guerin 5.00 12.00
6 Dominik Hasek 8.00 20.00
7 Keith Tkachuk 5.00 12.00
8 Pavel Bure 5.00 12.00
9 Brian Leetch 4.00 10.00
10 Mario Lemieux 20.00 50.00
11 Mats Sundin 5.00 12.00
12 Owen Nolan 5.00 12.00
13 Mark Messier 10.00 25.00
14 Jaromir Jagr 15.00 40.00
15 Joe Sakic 10.00 25.00
16 Rob Blake 5.00 12.00
17 Brendan Shanahan 5.00 12.00
18 Eric Lindros 8.00 20.00
19 Mike Modano 8.00 20.00
20 Sergei Fedorov 8.00 20.00
21 Nicklas Lidstrom 5.00 12.00
22 Steve Yzerman 12.00 30.00
23 Teemu Selanne 10.00 25.00
24 Alexei Yashin 4.00 10.00
25 Doug Weight 5.00 12.00
26 Chris Pronger 5.00 12.00
27 Patrick Roy 12.00 30.00
28 Curtis Joseph 6.00 15.00
29 Jeremy Roenick 8.00 20.00
30 Luc Robitaille 5.00 12.00

2001-02 BAP Ultimate Memorabilia Jerseys and Sticks

1 Paul Kariya 5.00 12.00
2 Martin Brodeur 12.00 30.00
3 John LeClair 5.00 12.00
4 Ilya Kovalchuk 15.00 40.00
5 Bill Guerin 5.00 12.00
6 Dominik Hasek 8.00 20.00
7 Keith Tkachuk 5.00 12.00
8 Pavel Bure 5.00 12.00
9 Brian Leetch 4.00 10.00
10 Mario Lemieux 20.00 50.00
11 Mats Sundin 5.00 12.00
12 Owen Nolan 5.00 12.00
13 Mark Messier 10.00 25.00
14 Jaromir Jagr 15.00 40.00
15 Joe Sakic 10.00 25.00
16 Rob Blake 5.00 12.00
17 Brendan Shanahan 5.00 12.00
18 Eric Lindros 8.00 20.00
19 Mike Modano 8.00 20.00
20 Sergei Fedorov 8.00 20.00
21 Nicklas Lidstrom 5.00 12.00
22 Steve Yzerman 12.00 30.00
23 Teemu Selanne 10.00 25.00
24 Alexei Yashin 4.00 10.00
25 Doug Weight 5.00 12.00
26 Chris Pronger 5.00 12.00
27 Patrick Roy 12.00 30.00
28 Curtis Joseph 6.00 15.00
29 Jeremy Roenick 8.00 20.00
30 Luc Robitaille 5.00 12.00

2001-02 BAP Ultimate Memorabilia Journey Jerseys

1 Mark Messier 15.00 40.00
2 Curtis Joseph 15.00 40.00
3 Alexei Yashin 12.50 30.00
4 Gordie Howe 50.00 125.00
5 Felix Potvin 15.00 40.00
6 Rob Blake 12.50 30.00
7 Pavel Bure 20.00 50.00
8 Mats Sundin 15.00 40.00
9 Ed Belfour 15.00 40.00
10 Mike Modano 20.00 50.00
11 Brett Hull 20.00 50.00
12 Brendan Shanahan 15.00 40.00
13 Teemu Selanne 15.00 40.00
14 Keith Tkachuk 12.50 30.00
15 Patrick Roy 60.00 150.00
16 Luc Robitaille 15.00 40.00
17 Jeremy Roenick 20.00 50.00
18 Alexander Mogilny 12.50 30.00
19 Dominik Hasek 20.00 50.00
20 Jaromir Jagr 25.00 60.00
21 Roman Turek 12.50 30.00
22 Wayne Gretzky 150.00 350.00

2001-02 BAP Ultimate Memorabilia Legend Terry Sawchuk

1 Patrick Roy
Terry Sawchuk 40.00 80.00
2 Martin Brodeur
Terry Sawchuk 40.00 80.00
7 Ed Belfour
Terry Sawchuk 20.00 40.00
8 Mike Richter
Terry Sawchuk 25.00 50.00
9 Felix Potvin
Terry Sawchuk 30.00 60.00
11 Roberto Luongo
Terry Sawchuk 20.00 40.00
14 Jocelyn Thibault
Terry Sawchuk 20.00 40.00
15 Evgeni Nabokov
Terry Sawchuk 20.00 40.00
16 Olaf Kolzig
Terry Sawchuk 20.00 40.00

2001-02 BAP Ultimate Memorabilia Les Canadiens

1 Mark Recchi 20.00 50.00
2 Yvan Cournoyer 20.00 50.00
3 Steve Shutt 20.00 50.00
4 Maurice Richard 75.00 200.00
5 Bob Gainey 25.00 60.00
6 Larry Robinson 20.00 50.00
7 Henri Richard 20.00 50.00
8 Jose Theodore 25.00 60.00
9 Saku Koivu 20.00 50.00
10 Patrick Roy 50.00 125.00
11 Jean Beliveau 30.00 80.00
12 Doug Harvey 20.00 50.00
13 Frank Mahovlich 20.00 50.00
14 Peter Mahovlich 20.00 50.00
15 Guy Lafleur 25.00 60.00
16 Serge Savard 20.00 50.00
17 Guy Lapointe 20.00 50.00
18 Jacques Plante 50.00 125.00

2001-02 BAP Ultimate Memorabilia Name Plates

1 Wayne Gretzky LA/40 100.00 200.00
2 Mario Lemieux/50 40.00 100.00
3 Paul Kariya/40 15.00 40.00
4 Pavel Bure/40 15.00 40.00
5 Mats Sundin/40 15.00 40.00
6 Mark Recchi/40 10.00 25.00
7 Dominik Hasek/40 20.00 50.00
8 Luc Robitaille/50 10.00 25.00
9 Bill Guerin/50 10.00 25.00
10 Eric Lindros/50 15.00 40.00
11 Patrick Roy/40 30.00 80.00
12 Nikolai Khabibulin/50 15.00 40.00
13 Teemu Selanne/50 15.00 40.00
14 Mark Messier/50 15.00 40.00
15 Steve Yzerman/50 30.00 80.00
16 Brian Leetch/50 10.00 25.00
17 Owen Nolan/50 10.00 25.00
18 Jarome Iginla/50 20.00 50.00
19 Gordie Howe Aeros/50 30.00 80.00
20 Roman Cechmanek/50 10.00 25.00
21 Joe Thornton/50 20.00 50.00
22 Ilya Kovalchuk/50 20.00 50.00
23 Curtis Joseph/50 15.00 40.00
24 Jeremy Roenick/50 20.00 50.00
25 Keith Tkachuk/50 15.00 40.00
26 Joe Sakic/50 15.00 40.00
27 Jaromir Jagr/50 20.00 50.00
28 Rob Blake/40 10.00 25.00
29 Mike Modano/50 20.00 50.00
30 Martin Brodeur/50 30.00 80.00
31 Nicklas Lidstrom/50 15.00 40.00
32 John LeClair/50 15.00 40.00
33 Gordie Howe NE/50 30.00 80.00
34 Chris Pronger/50 10.00 25.00
35 Sergei Fedorov/50 20.00 50.00
36 Jason Arnott/50 10.00 25.00
37 Marcel Dionne/40 10.00 25.00
38 Phil Esposito/50 20.00 50.00
39 Wayne Gretzky NYR/50 75.00 200.00
40 Doug Weight/40 10.00 25.00

2001-02 BAP Ultimate Memorabilia Playoff Records

1 Patrick Roy/50 20.00 50.00
2 Patrick Roy/50 20.00 50.00
3 Larry Robinson/50 12.00 30.00
4 Mark Messier/50 15.00 40.00
5 Wayne Gretzky/50 40.00 80.00
6 Reggie Leach/50 12.00 30.00
7 Jari Kurri/50 15.00 40.00
8 Jari Kurri/50 15.00 40.00
9 Wayne Gretzky/50 40.00 80.00
13 Wayne Gretzky/50 40.00 80.00
15 Mario Lemieux/50 30.00 60.00
16 Mike Bossy/50 12.00 30.00
17 Mark Messier/50 15.00 40.00
19 Joe Sakic/50 30.00 60.00

2001-02 BAP Ultimate Memorabilia Prototypical Players

1 J.Plante/P.Roy 40.00 100.00
2 J.Plante/M.Brodeur 40.00 100.00
3 J.Plante/D.Hasek 40.00 100.00
4 D.Harvey/C.Pronger 20.00 50.00
5 D.Harvey/R.Blake 20.00 50.00
6 D.Harvey/N.Lidstrom 25.00 60.00
7 J.Beliveau/S.Yzerman 40.00 100.00
8 J.Beliveau/M.Lemieux 40.00 100.00
9 J.Beliveau/J.Sakic 25.00 60.00
10 Bo.Hull/L.Robitaille 25.00 60.00
11 Bo.Hull/P.Kariya 25.00 60.00
12 Bo.Hull/B.Shanahan 25.00 60.00
13 G.Howe/J.Jagr 30.00 80.00
14 G.Howe/P.Bure 25.00 60.00
15 G.Howe/Br. Hull 25.00 60.00

2001-02 BAP Ultimate Memorabilia Retro Trophies

1 W.Gretzky/J.Sakic 60.00 150.00
2 G.Howe/J.Jagr 40.00 100.00
3 W.Gretzky/J.Jagr 60.00 150.00
4 W.Gretzky/M.Lemieux 75.00 200.00
5 B.Clarke/M.Lemieux 50.00 125.00
6 M.Bossy/J.Sakic 30.00 80.00
7 J.Kurri/P.Kariya 25.00 60.00
8 L.McDonald/C.Joseph 25.00 60.00
9 T.Sawchuk/D.Hasek 40.00 100.00
10 G.Hall/P.Roy 40.00 100.00
11 T.Sawchuk/E.Nabokov 30.00 80.00
12 T.Esposito/M.Brodeur 40.00 100.00
13 B.Clarke/S.Yzerman 30.00 80.00
14 G.Hall/P.Roy 30.00 80.00
15 B.Parent/P.Roy 40.00 80.00
16 W.Gretzky/M.Lemieux 75.00 200.00
17 G.Lafleur/M.Lemieux 50.00 125.00
18 D.Harvey/N.Lidstrom 25.00 60.00
19 W.Gretzky/M.Lemieux 75.00 200.00
20 G.Lafleur/J.Sakic 30.00 80.00

2001-02 BAP Ultimate Memorabilia Retro Teammates

3 Howe/Lindsay/Sawchuk/30 100.00 250.00
5 Bossy/Trottier/Potvin/30 40.00 80.00
6 Clarke/Barber/Schultz/30 40.00 80.00
7 Hull/Hall/Mikita/30 75.00 150.00
8 Horton/Bower/Sawchuk/30 75.00 150.00
9 Lapointe/Savard/Mahovlich/30 40.00 80.00
10 Lafleur/Cournoyer/Beliveau/30 60.00 120.00
11 Lemieux/Coffey/Jagr/30 50.00 100.00
12 Gretzky/Leetch/Messier/30 125.00 250.00
13 Gretzky/Kurri/Robitaille/30 100.00 200.00

2001-02 BAP Ultimate Memorabilia Scoring Leaders

1 Wayne Gretzky 1982 75.00 150.00
2 Wayne Gretzky 1983 75.00 150.00
3 Wayne Gretzky 1984 75.00 150.00
4 Wayne Gretzky 1985 75.00 150.00
5 Jari Kurri 1986 25.00 60.00
6 Wayne Gretzky 1987 75.00 150.00
7 Mario Lemieux 1988 30.00 80.00
8 Mario Lemieux 1989 30.00 80.00
9 Brett Hull 1990 12.00 30.00
10 Brett Hull 1991 12.00 30.00
11 Brett Hull 1992 12.00 30.00
12 T.Selanne
A.Mogilny 1993 15.00 40.00
13 Pavel Bure 1994 15.00 40.00
14 Peter Bondra 1995 15.00 40.00
15 Mario Lemieux 1996 30.00 80.00
16 Keith Tkachuk 1997 15.00 40.00
17 T.Selanne
P.Bondra 1998 20.00 50.00
18 Teemu Selanne 1999 20.00 50.00
19 Pavel Bure 2000 15.00 40.00
20 Pavel Bure 2001 15.00 40.00
21 Jarome Iginla 2002 20.00 50.00

2001-02 BAP Ultimate Memorabilia Stanley Cup Winners

1 Henri Richard 25.00 60.00
2 Jean Beliveau 30.00 80.00
3 Yvan Cournoyer 20.00 50.00
4 Red Kelly 20.00 50.00
5 Maurice Richard 60.00 150.00
6 Serge Savard 15.00 40.00
8 Johnny Bower 20.00 50.00

9 Bryan Trottier 20.00 50.00
10 Larry Robinson 20.00 50.00
11 Mark Messier 30.00 80.00
12 Jacques Laperriere 20.00 50.00
13 Doug Harvey 20.00 50.00
14 Frank Mahovlich 20.00 50.00
15 Guy Lapointe 12.00 30.00
16 Jari Kurri 25.00 60.00
17 Guy Lafleur 25.00 60.00
18 Bob Gainey 30.00 80.00
19 Grant Fuhr 20.00 50.00
21 Ted Kennedy 20.00 50.00
22 Steve Shutt 20.00 50.00
23 Wayne Gretzky 75.00 200.00
24 Terry Sawchuk 40.00 100.00
25 Denis Potvin 20.00 50.00
26 Ted Lindsay 20.00 50.00
27 Billy Smith 20.00 50.00

2001-02 BAP Ultimate Memorabilia Waving the Flag

1 Mario Lemieux 30.00 80.00
2 Joe Sakic 20.00 50.00
3 Steve Yzerman 25.00 60.00
4 Paul Kariya 15.00 40.00
5 Curtis Joseph 12.50 30.00
6 Martin Brodeur 25.00 60.00
7 Eric Lindros 12.50 30.00
8 Chris Pronger 10.00 25.00
9 Jaromir Jagr 15.00 40.00
10 Milan Hejduk 12.50 30.00
11 Dominik Hasek 20.00 50.00
12 Martin Havlat 10.00 25.00
13 Teemu Selanne 15.00 40.00
14 Jani Hurme 10.00 25.00
15 Miikka Kiprusoff 15.00 40.00
16 Sami Kapanen 10.00 25.00
17 Mats Sundin 12.50 30.00
18 Nicklas Lidstrom 12.50 30.00
19 Tommy Salo 10.00 25.00
20 Markus Naslund 12.50 30.00
21 Jeremy Roenick 15.00 40.00
22 Doug Weight 10.00 25.00
23 Tony Amonte 10.00 25.00
24 Brian Leetch 12.00 30.00
25 Mike Modano 15.00 40.00
26 Brett Hull 15.00 40.00
27 John Leclair 12.50 30.00
28 Keith Tkachuk 12.50 30.00
29 Alexei Yashin 10.00 25.00
30 Pavel Bure 12.50 30.00
31 Nikolai Khabibulin 12.50 30.00
32 Darius Kasparaitis 10.00 25.00

2002-03 BAP Ultimate Memorabilia

COMPLETE SET (100)
1 P-M Bouchard 3.00 8.00
2 Rick Nash 12.00 30.00
3 Dennis Seidenberg 3.00 8.00
4 Jay Bouwmeester 6.00 15.00
5 Stanislav Chistov 2.00 5.00
6 Kurt Sauer 2.00 5.00
7 Ivan Majesky 2.00 5.00
8 Chuck Kobasew 2.50 6.00
9 Jordan Leopold 3.00 8.00
10 Steve Ott 2.00 5.00
11 Ales Hemsky 8.00 20.00
12 Patrick Sharp 6.00 15.00
13 Kari Haakana 2.00 5.00
14 Dmitri Bykov 2.00 5.00
15 Alex Henry 2.50 6.00
16 Henrik Zetterberg 20.00 50.00
17 Alexander Frolov 5.00 12.00
18 Steve Eminger 2.00 5.00
19 Scottie Upshall 2.50 6.00
20 Tom Koivisto 2.00 5.00
21 Ari Ahonen 2.00 5.00
22 Ron Hainsey 2.00 5.00
23 Martin Gerber 3.00 8.00
24 Adam Hall 2.00 5.00
25 Lasse Pirjeta 2.00 5.00
26 Anton Volchenkov 2.00 5.00
27 Jeff Paul 2.00 5.00
28 Carlo Colaiacovo 3.00 8.00
29 Alexander Svitov 2.00 5.00
30 Alexei Smirnov 2.50 6.00
31 Jeff Taffe 2.00 5.00
32 Mikael Tellqvist 2.00 5.00
33 Radovan Somik 2.00 5.00
34 Mike Komisarek 3.00 8.00
35 Chris Schmidt 2.00 5.00
36 Dick Tarnstrom 2.00 5.00
37 Ryan Bayda 2.00 5.00
38 Sylvain Blouin 2.00 5.00
39 Ray Emery 6.00 15.00
40 Stephane Veilleux 2.00 5.00
41 Curtis Sanford 3.00 8.00
42 Eric Godard 2.00 5.00
43 Pascal Leclaire 2.50 6.00
44 Patrick Boileau 2.00 5.00
45 Tim Thomas 8.00 20.00
46 Mike Cammalleri 6.00 15.00
47 Jason Spezza 12.00 30.00
48 Cody Rudkowsky 2.00 5.00
49 Darren Haydar 2.00 5.00
50 Ryan Miller 12.00 30.00
51 Brandon Reid 2.00 5.00
52 Christian Backman 2.00 5.00
53 Niko Dimitrakos 2.00 5.00
54 Garnet Exelby 2.00 5.00
55 Jason King 3.00 8.00
56 Martin Samuelsson 2.00 5.00
57 Miroslav Zalesak 2.00 5.00
58 Tomas Malec 2.00 5.00
59 Michael Garnett 2.00 5.00
60 Matt Walker 2.00 5.00
61 Shaone Morrisonn 2.00 5.00
62 Chad Wiseman 2.00 5.00
63 Michael Leighton 3.00 8.00
64 Tomas Surovy 2.00 5.00
65 Jason Bacashihua 2.50 6.00
66 Jim Vandermeer 2.00 5.00
67 Konstantin Koltsov 2.50 6.00
68 Fernando Pisani 2.00 5.00
69 Rickard Wallin 2.00 5.00
70 Brooks Orpik 2.00 5.00
71 Tomas Zizka 2.00 5.00
72 Jarret Stoll 8.00 20.00
73 Cristobal Huet 4.00 10.00
74 Levente Szuper 3.00 8.00
75 Jared Aulin 2.00 5.00
76 Simon Gamache 2.00 5.00
77 Kris Vernarsky 2.00 5.00
78 Radoslav Hecl 2.00 5.00
79 Jamie Hodson 2.00 5.00
80 Marc-Andre Bergeron 2.50 6.00
81 Mike Siklenka 5.00 12.00
82 Igor Radulov 2.00 5.00
83 Paul Manning 2.00 5.00
84 John Tripp 2.00 5.00
85 Ian MacNeil 2.00 5.00
86 Jim Fahey 2.00 5.00
87 Dany Sabourin 2.00 5.00
88 Alexei Semenov 2.00 5.00
89 Curtis Murphy 2.00 5.00
90 Jerred Smithson 2.00 5.00
91 Francois Beauchemin 3.00 8.00
92 Vernon Fiddler 2.50 6.00
93 Cam Severson 2.00 5.00
94 Burke Henry 2.00 5.00
95 Brad Defauw 2.00 5.00
96 Craig Andersson 6.00 15.00
97 Frederic Cloutier 2.00 5.00
98 Tomas Kurka 2.00 5.00
99 Jonathan Hedstrom 2.00 5.00
100 Valeri Kharlamov 6.00 15.00

2002-03 BAP Ultimate Memorabilia Active Eight

1 Messier/Francis/Yzerman 40.00 100.00
2 Lemieux/Forsberg/Oates 40.00 100.00
3 Roy/Belfour/Brodeur 50.00 120.00
4 Hull/Messier/Yzerman 40.00 100.00
5 Messier/Francis/Yzerman 40.00 100.00
6 Roy/Belfour/Joseph 50.00 120.00
7 Lemieux/Sakic/Leetch 50.00 120.00
8 Lemieux/Yzerman/Oates 60.00 150.00

2002-03 BAP Ultimate Memorabilia All-Star MVP

1 Bill Guerin 12.50 30.00
2 Bobby Hull 15.00 40.00
3 Bobby Hull 15.00 40.00
4 Brett Hull 20.00 50.00
5 Dany Heatley 15.00 40.00
6 Eric Daze 12.50 30.00
7 Frank Mahovlich 15.00 40.00
8 Grant Fuhr 15.00 40.00
9 Henri Richard 12.50 30.00
10 Jean Beliveau 25.00 60.00
11 Mario Lemieux 25.00 60.00
12 Mario Lemieux 25.00 60.00
13 Mario Lemieux 25.00 60.00
14 Mark Recchi 12.50 30.00
15 Mike Bossy 12.50 30.00
16 Mike Gartner 12.50 30.00
17 Mike Richter 12.50 30.00
18 Pavel Bure 12.50 30.00
19 Peter Mahovlich 15.00 40.00
20 Reggie Leach 12.50 30.00
21 Vincent Damphousse 12.50 30.00
22 Teemu Selanne 15.00 40.00

2002-03 BAP Ultimate Memorabilia Autographs

COMMON CARD (1-30) 12.50 30.00
1 Alexander Frolov 15.00 35.00
2 Alexei Smirnov 12.50 30.00
3 Anton Volchenkov 12.50 30.00
4 Carlo Colaiacovo 12.50 30.00
5 Chuck Kobasew 12.50 30.00
6 Jay Bouwmeester 20.00 50.00
7 Jordan Leopold 12.50 30.00
8 Mike Cammalleri 12.50 30.00
9 P-M Bouchard 15.00 35.00
10 Rick Nash 40.00 80.00
11 Ron Hainsey 12.50 30.00
12 Scottie Upshall 12.50 30.00
13 Stanislav Chistov 12.00 30.00
14 Sergei Fedorov 25.00 60.00
15 Patrick Roy 100.00 250.00
16 Mario Lemieux 100.00 250.00
17 Brian Leetch 20.00 50.00
18 Dany Heatley 20.00 50.00
19 Jarome Iginla 25.00 60.00
20 Joe Sakic 50.00 125.00
21 Joe Thornton 30.00 80.00
22 Jose Theodore 25.00 60.00
23 Pavel Bure 20.00 50.00
24 Peter Forsberg 40.00 100.00
25 Saku Koivu 20.00 50.00
26 Alexander Svitov 12.50 30.00
27 Stephane Veilleux 12.50 30.00
28 Adam Hall 12.50 30.00
29 Henrik Zetterberg 40.00 100.00
30 Steve Eminger 12.50 30.00

2002-03 BAP Ultimate Memorabilia Calder Candidates

COMMON CARD (1-20) 12.50 30.00
1 Henrik Zetterberg 30.00 80.00
2 Niko Kapanen 12.50 30.00
3 Ron Hainsey 12.50 30.00
4 Jason Spezza 30.00 80.00
5 Anton Volchenkov 12.50 30.00
6 Ivan Huml 12.50 30.00
7 Tyler Arnason 12.50 30.00
8 Dennis Seidenberg 12.50 30.00
9 Alexander Frolov 12.50 30.00
10 Alexei Smirnov 12.50 30.00
11 Jay Bouwmeester 15.00 30.00
12 Ales Hemsky 15.00 35.00
13 Rick Nash 30.00 80.00
14 Jordan Leopold 12.50 30.00
15 Stephen Weiss 12.50 30.00
16 Ryan Miller 20.00 30.00
17 Chuck Kobasew 12.50 30.00
18 Alexander Svitov 12.50 30.00
19 Adam Hall 12.50 30.00
20 Stanislav Chistov 12.50 30.00

2002-03 BAP Ultimate Memorabilia Conn Smythe

1 Jean Beliveau 30.00 80.00
2 Roger Crozier 15.00 40.00
3 Glenn Hall 20.00 50.00
4 Serge Savard 15.00 40.00
5 Yvan Cournoyer 15.00 40.00
6 Bernie Parent 20.00 50.00
7 Bernie Parent 20.00 50.00
8 Reggie Leach 15.00 40.00
9 Guy Lafleur 25.00 60.00
10 Larry Robinson 15.00 40.00
11 Bryan Trottier 15.00 40.00
12 Mike Bossy 15.00 40.00
13 Billy Smith 15.00 40.00
14 Mark Messier 25.00 60.00
15 Patrick Roy 40.00 100.00
16 Ron Hextall 20.00 50.00
17 Al MacInnis 15.00 40.00
18 Bill Ranford 15.00 40.00
19 Mario Lemieux 40.00 100.00
20 Mario Lemieux 40.00 100.00
21 Patrick Roy 40.00 100.00
22 Brian Leetch 20.00 50.00
23 Claude Lemieux 15.00 40.00
24 Joe Sakic 30.00 80.00
25 Mike Vernon 25.00 60.00
26 Steve Yzerman 30.00 80.00
27 Joe Nieuwendyk 15.00 40.00
28 Scott Stevens 15.00 40.00
29 Patrick Roy 40.00 100.00
30 Nicklas Lidstrom 20.00 40.00

2002-03 BAP Ultimate Memorabilia Cup Duels

1 G.Hainsworth/T.Thompson 30.00 80.00
2 T.Sawchuk/J.Plante 60.00 150.00
3 J.Plante/J.Bower 25.00 60.00
4 G.Hall/T.Sawchuk 30.00 80.00
5 J.Bower/T.Sawchuk 25.00 60.00
6 R.Crozier/G.Worsley 15.00 40.00
7 G.Cheevers/E.Giacomin 15.00 40.00
8 G.Gilbert/B.Parent 15.00 40.00
9 B.Smith/G.Fuhr 15.00 40.00
10 P.Roy/M.Vernon 30.00 80.00
11 R.Hextall/G.Fuhr 15.00 40.00
12 A.Moog/G.Fuhr 20.00 50.00
13 P.Roy/M.Vernon 30.00 80.00
14 A.Moog/B.Ranford 15.00 40.00
15 T.Barrasso/E.Belfour 20.00 50.00
16 M.Brodeur/M.Vernon 30.00 80.00
17 J.Vanbiesbrouck/P.Roy 30.00 80.00
18 O.Kolzig/C.Osgood 20.00 50.00
19 M.Brodeur/E.Belfour 30.00 80.00
20 P.Roy/M.Brodeur 50.00 125.00

2002-03 BAP Ultimate Memorabilia Customer Appreciation

1 Henrik Zetterberg 40.00 100.00

2002-03 BAP Ultimate Memorabilia Dynamic Duos

1 M.Lemieux/J.Thornton 25.00 60.00
2 P.Forsberg/M.Sundin 20.00 50.00
3 I.Kovalchuk/S.Fedorov 25.00 60.00
4 S.Yzerman/D.Heatley 30.00 80.00
5 M.Modano/B.Hull 25.00 60.00
6 B.Shanahan/P.Kariya 20.00 50.00
7 J.Sakic/E.Lindros 20.00 50.00
8 S.Koivu/T.Selanne 20.00 50.00
9 J.Jagr/M.Gaborik 25.00 60.00
10 P.Bure/S.Samsonov 20.00 50.00

2002-03 BAP Ultimate Memorabilia Dynasty Jerseys

COMMON CARD (1-20) 15.00 50.00
1 Brendan Shanahan 25.00 60.00
2 Brett Hull 30.00 80.00
3 Chris Chelios 25.00 60.00
4 Chris Osgood 15.00 40.00
5 Darren McCarty 15.00 50.00
6 Igor Larionov 15.00 50.00
7 Jiri Fischer 15.00 50.00
8 Kirk Maltby 15.00 40.00
9 Kris Draper 15.00 50.00
10 Luc Robitaille 20.00 50.00
11 Manny Legace 20.00 50.00
12 Martin Lapointe 15.00 50.00
13 Mathieu Dandenault 15.00 40.00
14 Mike Vernon 20.00 50.00
15 Nicklas Lidstrom 25.00 60.00
16 Pavel Datsyuk 25.00 60.00
17 Sergei Fedorov 25.00 60.00
18 Steve Yzerman 40.00 100.00
19 Tomas Holmstrom 20.00 50.00
20 Slava Kozlov 15.00 40.00

2002-03 BAP Ultimate Memorabilia Finals Showdown

1 A.Delvecchio/D.Harvey 20.00 50.00
2 B.Geoffrion/T.Lindsay 20.00 50.00
3 H.Richard/T.Horton 30.00 80.00
4 M.Richard/F.Mahovlich 40.00 100.00
5 S.Mikita/T.Sawchuk 30.00 80.00
6 F.Mahovlich/B.Hull 20.00 50.00
7 R.Kelly/T.Sawchuk 25.00 60.00
8 T.Horton/A.Delvecchio 30.00 80.00
9 J.Beliveau/G.Hall 20.00 50.00
10 J.Beliveau/R.Crozier 20.00 50.00
11 J.Bower/J.Ferguson 20.00 50.00
12 P.Mahovlich/B.Hull 20.00 50.00
13 G.Cheevers/R.Gilbert 20.00 50.00
14 Y.Cournoyer/B.Hull 20.00 50.00
15 B.Parent/J.Bucyk 20.00 50.00
16 B.Clarke/G.Perreault 20.00 50.00
17 S.Shutt/D.Schultz 20.00 50.00
18 G.Lapointe/G.Cheevers 20.00 50.00
19 L.Robinson/G.Cheevers 15.00 40.00
20 G.Lafleur/P.Esposito 40.00 100.00
21 B.Smith/B.Clarke 25.00 60.00
22 B.Trottier/G.Fuhr 25.00 60.00
23 M.Messier/D.Potvin 20.00 50.00
24 P.Roy/L.McDonald 30.00 80.00
25 J.Kurri/R.Hextall 30.00 80.00
26 K.Lowe/C.Neely 20.00 50.00
27 A.MacInnis/P.Roy 30.00 80.00
28 M.Messier/C.Neely 20.00 50.00
29 M.Lemieux/M.Modano 40.00 100.00
30 J.Jagr/J.Roenick 25.00 60.00
31 P.Roy/L.Robitaille 30.00 80.00
32 M.Messier/P.Bure 30.00 80.00
33 M.Brodeur/S.Yzerman 40.00 100.00
34 P.Roy/R.Niedermayer 40.00 100.00
35 S.Yzerman/E.Lindros 40.00 100.00
36 S.Fedorov/O.Kolzig 20.00 50.00
37 B.Hull/M.Peca 20.00 50.00
38 J.Arnott/E.Belfour 20.00 50.00
39 J.Sakic/M.Brodeur 30.00 80.00
40 N.Lidstrom/R.Francis 20.00 50.00

2002-03 BAP Ultimate Memorabilia 500 Goal Scorers

1 Joe Nieuwendyk 15.00 40.00
2 Joe Sakic 30.00 80.00
3 Jaromir Jagr 25.00 60.00

2002-03 BAP Ultimate Memorabilia 500 Goal Scorers Jersey and Stick

1 Joe Nieuwendyk 5.00 12.00
2 Joe Sakic 12.00 30.00
3 Jaromir Jagr 20.00 50.00

2002-03 BAP Ultimate Memorabilia Global Dominators

COMMON CARD (1-10) 15.00 40.00
1 Mario Lemieux 40.00 100.00
2 Al MacInnis 10.00 25.00
3 Rob Blake 15.00 40.00
4 Peter Forsberg 15.00 40.00
5 Igor Larionov 15.00 40.00
6 Joe Sakic 30.00 80.00
7 Steve Yzerman 40.00 100.00
8 Alexander Mogilny 15.00 40.00
9 Theo Fleury 15.00 40.00
10 Brendan Shanahan 20.00 50.00

2002-03 BAP Ultimate Memorabilia Gloves Are Off

COMMON CARD (1-20) 15.00 40.00
1 Ace Bailey 40.00 100.00
2 Mario Lemieux 30.00 80.00
3 Joe Sakic 20.00 50.00
4 Aurel Joliat 40.00 100.00
5 Guy Lafleur 30.00 80.00
6 Al MacInnis 15.00 40.00
7 Dickie Moore 15.00 40.00
8 Chris Chelios 15.00 40.00
9 Sergei Fedorov 20.00 50.00
10 Eddie Shore 20.00 50.00
11 Ted Kennedy 25.00 60.00
12 Eric Lindros 15.00 40.00
13 Mats Sundin 15.00 40.00
14 Doug Harvey 12.00 30.00
15 Bill Gadsby 20.00 50.00
16 Jarome Iginla 20.00 50.00
17 Joe Thornton 20.00 50.00
18 Maurice Richard 30.00 80.00
19 Brett Hull 15.00 40.00
20 King Clancy 25.00 60.00

2002-03 BAP Ultimate Memorabilia Great Moments

COMMON CARD (1-20) 25.00 60.00
4 Mario Lemieux 50.00 125.00
5 Darryl Sittler/27 50.00 125.00
7 Frank Brimsek 25.00 60.00
8 Teemu Selanne 25.00 60.00
9 Mark Messier 25.00 60.00
10 Patrick Roy 50.00 125.00
11 Jacques Plante 30.00 80.00
12 Jean Beliveau 30.00 80.00
13 Glenn Hall 25.00 60.00
14 M.Richard/Five Playoff Goals 40.00 100.00
16 M.Richard/Habs 5th Cup 40.00 100.00
17 Bill Mosienko 25.00 60.00
18 M.Richard/Fifty in Fifty 40.00 100.00
19 Terry Sawchuk 40.00 100.00
20 Stan Mikita 25.00 60.00

2002-03 BAP Ultimate Memorabilia Hat Tricks

COMMON CARD (1-20) 10.00 25.00
UNLISTED STARS 15.00 40.00
1 Simon Gagne 20.00 50.00
2 John LeClair 15.00 40.00
3 Adam Deadmarsh 10.00 25.00
4 Jeff O'Neill 10.00 25.00
5 Keith Tkachuk 15.00 40.00
6 Joe Thornton 25.00 60.00
7 Rob Blake 10.00 25.00
8 Alexei Yashin 10.00 25.00
9 Sergei Fedorov 25.00 60.00
10 Mario Lemieux 60.00 150.00
11 Jarome Iginla 25.00 60.00
12 Doug Weight 15.00 40.00
13 Brett Hull 30.00 80.00
14 Joe Sakic 50.00 125.00
15 Sergei Samsonov 10.00 25.00
16 Al MacInnis 15.00 40.00
17 Eric Lindros 20.00 50.00
18 Steve Yzerman 60.00 150.00
19 Mats Sundin 20.00 50.00
20 Chris Chelios 20.00 50.00

2002-03 BAP Ultimate Memorabilia Jerseys

COMMON CARD (1-40) 10.00 25.00
1 Bill Guerin 10.00 25.00
2 Jarome Iginla 20.00 50.00
3 Jose Theodore 15.00 40.00
4 Mario Lemieux 30.00 80.00
5 Martin Brodeur 20.00 50.00
6 Brendan Shanahan 25.00 60.00
7 Brett Hull 20.00 50.00
8 Dany Heatley 12.50 30.00
9 Ed Belfour 8.00 20.00
10 Eric Lindros 10.00 25.00
11 Ilya Kovalchuk 15.00 40.00
12 Jaromir Jagr 15.00 40.00
13 Jason Spezza 15.00 40.00
14 Jay Bouwmeester 15.00 40.00
15 Jeremy Roenick 12.50 30.00
16 Joe Sakic 15.00 40.00
17 Joe Thornton 15.00 40.00
18 John LeClair 10.00 25.00
19 Marian Gaborik 20.00 50.00
20 Marian Hossa 10.00 25.00
21 Mark Messier 10.00 25.00
22 Markus Naslund 10.00 25.00
23 Marty Turco 10.00 25.00
24 Mats Sundin 10.00 25.00
25 Mike Modano 12.50 30.00
26 Milan Hejduk 10.00 25.00
27 Nicklas Lidstrom 15.00 40.00
28 Patrick Roy 30.00 75.00
29 Paul Kariya 10.00 25.00
30 Pavel Bure 10.00 25.00
31 Peter Forsberg 25.00 60.00
32 Rick Nash 25.00 60.00
33 Saku Koivu 10.00 25.00
34 Sergei Fedorov 15.00 40.00
35 Sergei Samsonov 10.00 25.00
36 Steve Yzerman 25.00 60.00
37 Teemu Selanne 15.00 40.00
38 Todd Bertuzzi 10.00 25.00
39 Valeri Kharlamov 25.00 60.00
40 Vincent Lecavalier 15.00 40.00

2002-03 BAP Ultimate Memorabilia Jersey and Stick

COMMON CARD (1-30) 12.50 30.00
SEMISTARS 15.00 40.00
*JSY/STK: .5X TO 1.25X JSY
1 Patrick Roy 20.00 50.00
2 Mike Modano 12.50 40.00
3 Peter Forsberg 20.00 50.00
4 Mark Messier 15.00 40.00
5 Brett Hull 25.00 60.00
6 Martin Brodeur 30.00 80.00
7 Joe Thornton 15.00 40.00
8 Ilya Kovalchuk 20.00 50.00
9 Pavel Bure 12.50 30.00
10 Rick Nash 25.00 60.00
11 Marty Turco 12.50 30.00
12 Jay Bouwmeester 12.50 30.00
13 Nicklas Lidstrom 15.00 40.00
14 Jaromir Jagr 20.00 50.00
15 Mario Lemieux 40.00 100.00
16 Markus Naslund 12.50 30.00
17 Brendan Shanahan 15.00 40.00
18 Paul Kariya 12.50 30.00
19 Roberto Luongo 20.00 50.00
20 Joe Sakic 15.00 40.00
21 Mats Sundin 12.50 30.00
22 Steve Yzerman 30.00 80.00
23 Dany Heatley 15.00 40.00
24 Jose Theodore 12.50 30.00
25 Saku Koivu 12.50 30.00
26 Marian Hossa 12.50 30.00
27 Marian Gaborik 25.00 60.00
28 Sergei Fedorov 15.00 40.00
29 Todd Bertuzzi 15.00 30.00
30 Teemu Selanne 12.50 30.00

2002-03 BAP Ultimate Memorabilia Journey Jerseys

COMMON CARD (1-10) 15.00 40.00
1 Patrick Roy 40.00 100.00
2 Ed Belfour 20.00 60.00
3 Jaromir Jagr 20.00 50.00
4 Brett Hull 30.00 80.00
5 Adam Oates 15.00 40.00
6 Eric Lindros 20.00 50.00
7 Bill Guerin 15.00 40.00
8 Jeremy Roenick 20.00 50.00
9 Pavel Bure 15.00 40.00
10 Alexander Mogilny 15.00 40.00

2002-03 BAP Ultimate Memorabilia Lifetime Achievers

COMMON CARD (1-20) 10.00 25.00
UNLISTED STARS 12.50 30.00
1 Sergei Fedorov 15.00 40.00
2 Nicklas Lidstrom 12.50 25.00
3 Brendan Shanahan 10.00 25.00
4 Ed Belfour 12.50 25.00
5 Doug Gilmour 10.00 25.00
6 Jaromir Jagr 20.00 50.00
7 Patrick Roy 30.00 80.00
8 Eric Lindros 12.50 25.00
9 Brian Leetch 12.50 30.00
10 Pavel Bure 12.50 30.00
11 Brett Hull 20.00 50.00
12 Martin Brodeur 30.00 80.00
13 Curtis Joseph 12.50 30.00
14 Mario Lemieux 30.00 80.00
15 Steve Yzerman 30.00 80.00
16 Luc Robitaille 12.50 30.00
17 Mark Messier 12.50 30.00
18 Chris Chelios 12.50 30.00
19 Ron Francis 10.00 25.00
20 Joe Sakic 25.00 60.00

2002-03 BAP Ultimate Memorabilia Magnificent Inserts

1 1985-86 Season 40.00 100.00
2 2000-01 Season 40.00 100.00
3 2002 NHL All-Star 40.00 100.00
4 1987 Canada Cup 40.00 100.00
5 Dual Jersey 50.00 120.00

2002-03 BAP Ultimate Memorabilia Magnificent Ones

1 M.Lemieux/P.Roy 60.00 120.00
2 M.Lemieux/S.Yzerman 50.00 100.00
3 M.Lemieux/J.Jagr 25.00 60.00
4 M.Lemieux/M.Modano 25.00 60.00
5 M.Lemieux/M.Brodeur 50.00 100.00
6 M.Lemieux/P.Kariya 25.00 60.00
7 M.Lemieux/J.Sakic 25.00 60.00
8 M.Lemieux/P.Forsberg 30.00 80.00
9 M.Lemieux/P.Bure 25.00 60.00
10 M.Lemieux/B.Shanahan 30.00 80.00

2002-03 BAP Ultimate Memorabilia Nameplates

COMMON CARD (1-20) 10.00 25.00
UNLISTED STARS 12.50 30.00
1 Jaromir Jagr 30.00 80.00
2 Mike Modano 15.00 40.00
3 Joe Thornton 20.00 50.00
4 Nicklas Lidstrom 12.50 30.00
5 Jay Bouwmeester 10.00 25.00
6 Jason Spezza 25.00 60.00
7 Patrick Roy 40.00 100.00
8 Peter Forsberg 25.00 60.00
9 Steve Yzerman 40.00 100.00
10 Marian Hossa 10.00 25.00
11 Ilya Kovalchuk 25.00 60.00
12 Ed Belfour 12.50 30.00
13 Mario Lemieux 40.00 100.00
14 Joe Sakic 25.00 60.00
15 Marian Gaborik 25.00 60.00
16 Pavel Bure 12.50 30.00
17 Martin Brodeur 25.00 60.00
18 Markus Naslund 10.00 25.00
19 Curtis Joseph 12.50 30.00
20 Paul Kariya 10.00 25.00

2002-03 BAP Ultimate Memorabilia Numerology

COMMON CARD (1-30) 12.50 30.00
1 G.Hall/J.Hedberg 12.50 30.00
2 T.Sawchuk/R.Turek 30.00 80.00
3 J.Plante/S.Burke 20.00 50.00
4 B.Parent/R.Luongo 20.00 50.00
5 D.Harvey/B.Leetch 12.50 30.00
6 J.Beliveau/V.Lecavalier 30.00 80.00
7 R.Kelly/R.Blake 12.50 30.00
8 D.Potvin/N.Lidstrom 12.50 30.00
9 P.Esposito/K.Tkachuk 30.00 80.00
10 R.Gilbert/G.Roberts 12.50 30.00
11 M.Richard/P.Kariya 40.00 100.00
12 B.Hull/M.Modano 15.00 40.00
13 J.Bucyk/P.Bure 12.50 30.00
14 G.Lafleur/M.Gaborik 40.00 100.00
15 A.Delvecchio/R.Francis 12.50 30.00
16 G.Perreault/M.Messier 15.00 40.00
17 Y.Cournoyer/J.Iginla 15.00 40.00
18 M.Dionne/T.Linden 15.00 40.00
19 V.Kharlamov/I.Kovalchuk 40.00 100.00
20 S.Savard/M.Hossa 12.50 30.00
21 L.Robinson/S.Yzerman 30.00 80.00
22 B.Trottier/J.Sakic 15.00 40.00
23 V.Tretiak/E.Belfour 25.00 60.00
24 S.Mikita/P.Forsberg 15.00 40.00
25 M.Bossy/K.Huselius 12.50 30.00
26 B.Nystrom/M.Hejduk 12.50 30.00
27 F.Mahovlich/M.Peca 12.50 30.00
28 B.Smith/C.Joseph 15.00 40.00
29 G.Fuhr/D.Blackburn 40.00 100.00
30 T.Esposito/M.Turco 15.00 40.00

2002-03 BAP Ultimate Memorabilia Playoff Scorers

1 Peter Forsberg 12.00 30.00
2 Joe Sakic 12.00 30.00
3 Brett Hull 12.00 30.00
4 Peter Forsberg 12.00 30.00
5 Steve Yzerman 15.00 40.00
6 Eric Lindros 10.00 25.00
7 Joe Sakic 12.00 30.00
8 Sergei Fedorov 10.00 25.00
9 Brian Leetch 5.00 12.00
10 Mario Lemieux 25.00 60.00
11 Mark Messier 12.00 30.00
12 Mike Bossy 6.00 15.00
13 Maurice Richard 12.00 30.00
14 Jean Beliveau 6.00 15.00
15 Brett Hull 12.00 30.00
16 Bryan Trottier 6.00 15.00
17 Mario Lemieux 25.00 60.00
18 Bobby Hull 12.00 30.00
19 Phil Esposito 10.00 25.00
20 Steve Yzerman 15.00 40.00

2002-03 BAP Ultimate Memorabilia Retro Teammates

1 Sittler/McDonald/Williams 30.00 80.00
2 G.Gilbert/Cheevers/Bucyk 30.00 80.00
3 Hull/Mikita/Hall 30.00 80.00
4 Lafleur/Cournoyer/Savard 75.00 200.00
5 R.Gilbert/Giacomin/P.Esposito 30.00 80.00
6 Lemieux/Jagr/Francis 75.00 200.00
7 Richard/Plante/Beliveau 75.00 200.00
8 Horton/Bower/Kelly 60.00 150.00
9 Schultz/Clarke/Parent 30.00 80.00
10 Delvecchio/Sawchuk/Abel 30.00 80.00

2002-03 BAP Ultimate Memorabilia Retro Trophies

COMMON CARD (1-20) 20.00 50.00
1 D.Heatley/M.Lemieux 30.00 80.00
2 P.Roy/T.Sawchuk 75.00 150.00
3 M.Peca/B.Clarke 20.00 50.00
4 S.Koivu/H.Richard 20.00 50.00
5 P.Kariya/M.Dionne 20.00 50.00
6 J.Jagr/S.Mikita 20.00 50.00
7 S.Yzerman/J.Beliveau 25.00 60.00
8 E.Belfour/G.Hall 20.00 50.00
10 J.Theodore/J.Plante 30.00 80.00
11 N.Lidstrom/L.Robinson 20.00 50.00
12 M.Lemieux/P.Esposito 40.00 100.00
13 J.Iginla/B.Hull 20.00 50.00
14 M.Messier/R.Hextall 20.00 50.00
15 M.Brodeur/F.Brimsek 40.00 100.00
16 N.Lidstrom/R.Crozier 20.00 50.00
17 M.Lemieux/L.McDonald 40.00 100.00
18 P.Forsberg/B.Trottier 20.00 50.00
19 Br.Hull/Bo.Hull 30.00 80.00
20 J.Sakic/M.Richard 40.00 100.00

2002-03 BAP Ultimate Memorabilia Scoring Leaders

1 Peter Forsberg 2002-03 25.00 60.00
2 Jarome Iginla 2001-02 15.00 40.00
3 Jaromir Jagr 2000-01 15.00 40.00
4 Jaromir Jagr 1999-00 15.00 40.00
5 Jaromir Jagr 1998-99 15.00 40.00
6 Jaromir Jagr 1997-98 15.00 40.00
7 Mario Lemieux 1996-97 20.00 50.00
8 Mario Lemieux 1995-96 20.00 50.00
9 Jaromir Jagr 1994-95 15.00 40.00
10 Mario Lemieux 1992-93 20.00 50.00
11 Mario Lemieux 1991-92 20.00 50.00
12 Mario Lemieux 1988-89 20.00 50.00
13 Mario Lemieux 1987-88 20.00 50.00
14 Marcel Dionne 1979-80 12.50 30.00
15 Bryan Trottier 1978-79 12.50 30.00
16 Guy Lafleur 1977-78 12.50 30.00
17 Guy Lafleur 1976-77 12.50 30.00
18 Guy Lafleur 1975-76 12.50 30.00
19 Phil Esposito 1973-74 20.00 50.00
20 Phil Esposito 1972-73 20.00 50.00
21 Phil Esposito 1971-72 20.00 50.00
22 Phil Esposito 1970-71 20.00 50.00
23 Phil Esposito 1968-69 12.00 30.00
24 Stan Mikita 1967-68 12.50 30.00
25 Stan Mikita 1966-67 12.50 30.00
26 Bobby Hull 1965-66 20.00 50.00
27 Stan Mikita 1964-65 12.50 30.00
28 Stan Mikita 1963-64 12.50 30.00
29 Bobby Hull 1961-62 20.00 50.00
30 Bernie Geoffrion 1960-61 12.50 30.00
31 Bobby Hull 1959-60 20.00 50.00
32 Dickie Moore 1958-59 12.50 30.00
33 Dickie Moore 1957-58 12.50 30.00
34 Jean Beliveau 1956-57 20.00 50.00
35 Bernie Geoffrion 1955-56 12.50 30.00

2002-03 BAP Ultimate Memorabilia Vintage Jerseys

1 Stan Mikita 15.00 40.00
2 Alex Delvecchio 15.00 40.00
3 Aurel Joliat 30.00 80.00
4 Bernie Parent 15.00 40.00
5 Bill Barber 12.50 30.00
6 Bobby Clarke 12.50 30.00
7 Bobby Hull 12.50 30.00
8 Bryan Trottier 12.50 30.00
9 Dennis Hull 12.50 30.00
10 Doug Harvey 12.50 30.00
11 Ed Giacomin 12.50 30.00
12 Frank Brimsek 12.50 30.00
13 Frank Mahovlich 12.50 30.00
14 George Hainsworth 20.00 50.00
15 Gerry Cheevers 12.50 30.00
16 Gilbert Perreault 12.50 30.00
17 Glenn Hall 12.50 30.00
18 Guy Lafleur 12.50 30.00
19 Harry Lumley 20.00 50.00
20 Henri Richard 12.50 30.00
21 Jacques Plante 30.00 80.00
22 Jean Beliveau 25.00 60.00
23 John Bucyk 12.50 30.00
24 Lanny McDonald 12.50 30.00
25 Larry Robinson 12.50 30.00
26 Marcel Dionne 12.50 30.00
27 Maurice Richard 30.00 80.00
28 Mike Bossy 12.50 30.00
29 Peter Mahovlich 12.50 30.00
30 Phil Esposito 12.50 30.00
31 Red Kelly 20.00 50.00
32 Roger Crozier 12.50 30.00
33 Roy Worters 20.00 50.00
34 Sid Abel 12.50 30.00
35 Ted Lindsay 12.50 30.00
36 Terry Sawchuk 50.00 125.00
37 Tim Horton 30.00 80.00
38 Tony Esposito 12.50 30.00
39 Valeri Kharlamov 25.00 60.00
40 Vladislav Tretiak 40.00 100.00

2003-04 BAP Ultimate Memorabilia Autographs

1 Alexei Kovalev 6.00 15.00
2 Shane Doan 6.00 15.00
3 Ales Hemsky 6.00 15.00
4 Ray Whitney 6.00 15.00
5 Alexander Frolov 6.00 15.00
6 Mike Peca 6.00 15.00
7 Chris Drury 6.00 15.00
8 Chris Osgood 6.00 15.00
9 Andrew Raycroft 8.00 20.00
10 Rick DiPietro 6.00 15.00
11 Chuck Kobasew 6.00 15.00
12 Vincent Lecavalier 8.00 20.00
13 Olaf Kolzig 8.00 20.00
14 Erik Cole 6.00 15.00
15 Ryan Smyth 6.00 15.00
16 Anson Carter 6.00 15.00
17 Jocelyn Thibault 6.00 15.00
18 Alexei Yashin 6.00 15.00
19 David Aebischer 6.00 15.00
20 Chris Pronger 6.00 15.00
21 Ron Francis 10.00 25.00
22 Markus Naslund 8.00 20.00
23 Tommy Salo 6.00 15.00
24 Patrick Lalime 6.00 15.00
25 Joe Nieuwendyk 8.00 20.00
26 Vincent Damphousse 6.00 15.00
27 Bill Guerin 6.00 15.00
28 Jeremy Roenick 12.00 30.00
29 Barret Jackman 6.00 15.00
30 Curtis Joseph 8.00 20.00
31 Jason Spezza 15.00 40.00
32 Sergei Fedorov 15.00 40.00
33 Gary Roberts 6.00 15.00
34 Glen Murray 6.00 15.00
35 Adam Oates 6.00 15.00
36 Felix Potvin 10.00 25.00
37 Eric Brewer 6.00 15.00
38 Jeff O'Neill 6.00 15.00
39 Tomas Vokoun 8.00 20.00
40 Olli Jokinen 6.00 15.00
41 Martin Prusek 6.00 15.00
42 Sergei Gonchar 6.00 15.00
43 Kevin Weekes 6.00 15.00
44 Roman Cechmanek 6.00 15.00
45 Scott Stevens 6.00 15.00
46 Dwayne Roloson 6.00 15.00
47 Martin Biron 6.00 15.00
48 Keith Tkachuk 6.00 15.00
49 Pasi Nurminen 6.00 15.00
50 Saku Koivu 8.00 20.00
51 David Legwand 6.00 15.00
52 Jay Bouwmeester 6.00 15.00
53 Patrik Elias 6.00 15.00
54 Zigmund Palffy 6.00 15.00
55 Tyler Arnason 6.00 15.00
56 Sergei Samsonov 6.00 15.00
57 Ryan Miller 15.00 40.00
58 Mike Dunham 6.00 15.00
59 Nikolai Khabibulin 8.00 20.00
60 Roman Turek 6.00 15.00
61 Marian Hossa 8.00 20.00
62 Marc Denis 6.00 15.00
63 Peter Bondra 8.00 20.00
64 Marty Turco 8.00 20.00
65 John LeClair 8.00 20.00
66 Johan Hedberg 6.00 15.00
67 Sean Burke 6.00 15.00
68 Ed Jovanovski 6.00 15.00
69 Tony Amonte 6.00 15.00
70 Daymond Langkow 6.00 15.00
71 Miroslav Satan 6.00 15.00
72 Jean-Sebastien Giguere 6.00 15.00
73 Evgeni Nabokov 8.00 20.00
74 Rostislav Klesla 6.00 15.00

75 Al MacInnis 6.00 15.00
76 Niko Kapanen 6.00 15.00
77 Manny Fernandez 6.00 15.00
78 Milan Hejduk 8.00 20.00
79 Doug Weight 6.00 15.00
80 Jarome Iginla 12.50 30.00
81 Martin St. Louis 8.00 20.00
82 Daniel Alfredsson 6.00 15.00
83 Marian Gaborik 12.50 30.00
84 Rob Blake 6.00 15.00
85 Dan Cloutier 6.00 15.00
86 Simon Gagne 10.00 25.00
87 Mark Recchi 6.00 15.00
88 Teemu Selanne 10.00 25.00
89 Todd Bertuzzi 8.00 20.00
90 Chris Kunitz 10.00 25.00
91 Eric Staal 40.00 100.00
92 Nathan Horton 12.50 30.00
93 Andrew Peters 8.00 20.00
94 Alexander Semin 25.00 60.00
95 Matthew Lombardi 8.00 20.00
96 Joffrey Lupul 12.50 30.00
97 John-Michael Liles 10.00 25.00
98 Jiri Hudler 12.50 30.00
99 Tuomo Ruutu 12.50 30.00
100 Anton Babchuk 8.00 20.00
101 Dan Fritsche 8.00 20.00
102 Derek Roy 8.00 20.00
103 Paul Martin 8.00 20.00
104 Pavel Vorobiev 8.00 20.00
105 Matthew Spiller 8.00 20.00
106 Patrice Bergeron 25.00 60.00
107 Chris Higgins 10.00 25.00
108 Noah Clarke 8.00 20.00
109 Nikolai Zherdev 15.00 30.00
110 Brent Burns 10.00 25.00
111 Dustin Brown 12.00 30.00
112 Michael Ryder 20.00 50.00
113 Joni Pitkanen 8.00 20.00
114 Jordin Tootoo 20.00 50.00
115 Ryan Malone 10.00 25.00
116 David Hale 8.00 20.00
117 Antti Miettinen 8.00 20.00
118 Doug Lynch 8.00 20.00
119 Tim Gleason 8.00 20.00
120 Dan Hamhuis 10.00 25.00
121 Fredrik Sjostrom 8.00 20.00
122 Kari Lehtonen 30.00 80.00
123 Marc-Andre Fleury 30.00 80.00
124 Marek Zidlicky 10.00 25.00
125 Milan Michalek 15.00 40.00
126 Matt Stajan 10.00 25.00
127 Peter Sarno 8.00 20.00
128 Antoine Vermette 10.00 25.00
129 Boyd Gordon 8.00 20.00
130 Kyle Wellwood 10.00 25.00
131 Steve Yzerman 100.00 200.00
132 Rick Nash 50.00 100.00
133 Roberto Luongo 25.00 50.00
134 Joe Thornton 40.00 80.00
135 Joe Sakic 50.00 100.00
136 Pavel Datsyuk 40.00 80.00
138 Mike Modano 30.00 60.00
139 Brian Leetch 40.00 80.00
140 Peter Forsberg 50.00 100.00
141 Owen Nolan 25.00 50.00
142 Brett Hull 50.00 100.00
143 Jaromir Jagr 40.00 80.00
144 Dominik Hasek 40.00 80.00
145 Ilya Kovalchuk 40.00 80.00
146 Jose Theodore 75.00 125.00
147 Mario Lemieux 100.00 200.00
148 Mats Sundin 40.00 80.00
149 Eric Lindros 50.00 100.00
150 Henrik Zetterberg 50.00 100.00
151 Dany Heatley 30.00 80.00
152 Nicklas Lidstrom 40.00 80.00
153 Bobby Orr 75.00 150.00
154 Ted Kennedy 40.00 80.00
155 Ray Bourque 40.00 80.00
156 Jean Beliveau 40.00 80.00
157 Tony Esposito 30.00 60.00
158 Patrick Roy 150.00 300.00
159 Ted Lindsay 40.00 80.00
160 Frank Mahovlich 30.00 60.00
161 Guy Lafleur 30.00 60.00
162 Henri Richard 25.00 50.00
163 Maurice Richard 100.00 200.00
164 Phil Esposito 30.00 60.00
165 Johnny Bower 25.00 50.00

2003-04 BAP Ultimate Memorabilia Autographs Gold

*1-89 GOLD/35: 1X TO 2.5X BASIC AU
*90-130 GOLD/20: .6X TO 1.5X BASIC AU

2003-04 BAP Ultimate Memorabilia Autographed Jerseys

10 Rick DiPietro 20.00 50.00
12 Vincent Lecavalier 30.00 80.00
13 Olaf Kolzig 25.00 60.00
17 Jocelyn Thibault 20.00 50.00
19 David Aebischer 20.00 50.00
20 Chris Pronger 20.00 50.00
21 Ron Francis 40.00 80.00
22 Markus Naslund 20.00 50.00
24 Patrick Lalime 20.00 50.00
27 Bill Guerin 20.00 50.00
28 Jeremy Roenick 25.00 60.00
29 Barret Jackman 20.00 50.00
30 Curtis Joseph 15.00 40.00
31 Jason Spezza 25.00 60.00
33 Gary Roberts 20.00 50.00
39 Tomas Vokoun 20.00 50.00
48 Keith Tkachuk 25.00 60.00
50 Saku Koivu 25.00 60.00
52 Jay Bouwmeester 20.00 50.00
56 Sergei Samsonov 25.00 60.00
57 Ryan Miller 25.00 60.00
58 Mike Dunham 20.00 50.00
59 Nikolai Khabibulin 25.00 60.00
60 Roman Turek 20.00 50.00
61 Marian Hossa 25.00 60.00
62 Marc Denis 20.00 50.00
65 John LeClair 25.00 60.00
66 Johan Hedberg 20.00 50.00
68 Ed Jovanovski 20.00 50.00
69 Tony Amonte 20.00 50.00
72 Jean-Sebastien Giguere 20.00 50.00
75 Al MacInnis 20.00 50.00
77 Manny Fernandez 20.00 50.00
78 Milan Hejduk 25.00 60.00
79 Doug Weight 20.00 50.00
81 Martin St.Louis 25.00 60.00
82 Daniel Alfredsson 20.00 50.00
83 Marian Gaborik 25.00 60.00
85 Dan Cloutier 20.00 50.00
86 Simon Gagne 20.00 50.00
87 Mark Recchi 20.00 50.00
88 Teemu Selanne 60.00 125.00
89 Todd Bertuzzi 25.00 60.00
91 Eric Staal 30.00 80.00
96 Joffrey Lupul 15.00 40.00
106 Patrice Bergeron 50.00 100.00
107 Christopher Higgins 20.00 50.00
109 Nikolai Zherdev 40.00 100.00
110 Brent Burns 12.00 30.00
111 Dustin Brown 10.00 25.00
112 Michael Ryder 20.00 50.00
113 Joni Pitkanen 12.00 30.00
131 Steve Yzerman 50.00 125.00
132 Rick Nash 30.00 80.00
133 Roberto Luongo 25.00 60.00
134 Joe Thornton 25.00 60.00
135 Joe Sakic 40.00 100.00
136 Pavel Datsyuk 30.00 80.00
137 Martin Brodeur 100.00 200.00
138 Mike Modano 25.00 60.00
139 Brian Leetch 20.00 50.00
140 Peter Forsberg 40.00 100.00
141 Owen Nolan 20.00 50.00
142 Brett Hull 25.00 60.00
144 Dominik Hasek 40.00 100.00
145 Ilya Kovalchuk 20.00 50.00
146 Jose Theodore 20.00 50.00
147 Mario Lemieux 75.00 200.00
148 Mats Sundin 25.00 60.00
149 Eric Lindros 25.00 60.00
150 Henrik Zetterberg 25.00 60.00
151 Dany Heatley 30.00 80.00
152 Nicklas Lidstrom 25.00 60.00
153 Bobby Orr 125.00 250.00
155 Ray Bourque 40.00 100.00
157 Tony Esposito 50.00 100.00
158 Patrick Roy 125.00 250.00
165 Johnny Bower 30.00 80.00

2003-04 BAP Ultimate Memorabilia Autographed Sticks

32 Sergei Fedorov 25.00 60.00
45 Scott Stevens 25.00 60.00
56 Sergei Samsonov 12.00 30.00
86 Simon Gagne 20.00 50.00
123 Marc-Andre Fleury 30.00 80.00
131 Steve Yzerman 60.00 150.00
132 Rick Nash 25.00 60.00
134 Joe Thornton 25.00 60.00
135 Joe Sakic 30.00 80.00
136 Pavel Datsyuk 30.00 80.00
138 Mike Modano 20.00 50.00
140 Peter Forsberg 25.00 60.00
142 Brett Hull 25.00 60.00
143 Jaromir Jagr 30.00 80.00
145 Ilya Kovalchuk 25.00 60.00
147 Mario Lemieux 75.00 200.00
151 Dany Heatley 25.00 60.00
153 Bobby Orr 125.00 250.00
158 Patrick Roy 75.00 200.00
165 Johnny Bower 25.00 60.00

2003-04 BAP Ultimate Memorabilia Active Eight

1 Belfour/Brodeur/Hasek 40.00 100.00
2 Belfour/Joseph/Brodeur 40.00 100.00
3 Lemieux/Hull/Mogilny 30.00 80.00
4 Sundin/Lidstrom/Forsberg 25.00 60.00
5 Lemieux/Messier/Forsberg 40.00 100.00
6 Yzerman/Sakic/Stevens 30.00 80.00
7 Roenick/Modano/Leetch 25.00 60.00
8 Lemieux/Hull/Yzerman 40.00 100.00

2003-04 BAP Ultimate Memorabilia Always An All-Star

1 Martin Brodeur 25.00 60.00
2 Mike Modano 15.00 40.00
3 Brian Leetch 12.50 30.00
4 Brett Hull 20.00 50.00
5 Al MacInnis 12.50 30.00
6 Paul Kariya 12.50 30.00
7 Eric Lindros 12.50 30.00
8 Teemu Selanne 12.50 30.00
9 Nicklas Lidstrom 12.50 30.00
10 Sergei Fedorov 20.00 50.00
11 Patrick Roy 30.00 80.00
12 Peter Forsberg 20.00 50.00
13 Mark Messier 20.00 50.00
14 Jaromir Jagr 15.00 40.00
15 Ray Bourque 25.00 60.00
16 Mario Lemieux 40.00 100.00
17 Brendan Shanahan 12.50 30.00
18 Chris Pronger 12.50 30.00
19 Dominik Hasek 15.00 40.00
20 Mats Sundin 12.50 30.00

2003-04 BAP Ultimate Memorabilia Blades of Steel

2 Henrik Zetterberg 15.00 40.00
3 Al MacInnis 12.00 30.00
4 Pavel Bure 20.00 50.00
5 Jarome Iginla 12.00 30.00
6 Raymond Bourque 20.00 50.00
7 Pavel Datsyuk 20.00 50.00

2003-04 BAP Ultimate Memorabilia Calder Candidates

1 Andrew Raycroft 8.00 20.00
2 Eric Staal 10.00 25.00
3 Michael Ryder 10.00 25.00
4 Marc-Andre Fleury 20.00 50.00
5 Ryan Malone 8.00 20.00
6 Trent Hunter 8.00 20.00
7 Patrice Bergeron 12.00 30.00
8 Joni Pitkanen 8.00 20.00
9 Matthew Lombardi 8.00 20.00
10 Nikolai Zherdev 12.50 30.00
11 Tuomo Ruutu 8.00 20.00
12 Joffrey Lupul 10.00 25.00

2003-04 BAP Ultimate Memorabilia Career Year

1 Martin Brodeur 30.00 80.00
2 Cam Neely 15.00 40.00
3 Ray Bourque 15.00 40.00
4 Patrick Roy 30.00 80.00
5 Rick Nash 15.00 40.00
6 Steve Yzerman 30.00 80.00
7 Bobby Orr 60.00 125.00
8 Mario Lemieux 40.00 100.00

2003-04 BAP Ultimate Memorabilia Complete Jersey

1 Joe Thornton 30.00 80.00
2 Mario Lemieux 100.00 200.00
3 Marian Gaborik 40.00 100.00
4 Brett Hull 30.00 80.00
5 Dany Heatley 30.00 80.00
6 Joe Sakic 50.00 120.00
7 Paul Kariya 25.00 60.00
8 Steve Yzerman 50.00 120.00
9 Rick Nash 40.00 100.00
10 Nicklas Lidstrom 25.00 60.00
11 Sergei Fedorov 25.00 60.00
12 Patrick Roy 50.00 120.00
13 Peter Forsberg 40.00 100.00
14 Henrik Zetterberg 25.00 60.00
15 Dominik Hasek 30.00 80.00
16 Martin Brodeur 50.00 120.00
17 Mike Modano 25.00 60.00
18 Brendan Shanahan 25.00 60.00
19 Ilya Kovalchuk 40.00 100.00
20 Saku Koivu 25.00 60.00

2003-04 BAP Ultimate Memorabilia Cornerstones

1 Vezina/Plnt/Roy/Theodre 100.00 200.00
2 Plante/Richrd/Harve/Belivu 75.00 150.00
3 H.Richard/Laflr/Rbnsn/Svrd 40.00 80.00
4 Bower/F.Mahvlch/Kelly/Hrtn 50.00 100.00
5 Shore/Orr/Bourq/Thrntn 75.00 150.00
6 Brimsk/Lumly/Hall/Espo 40.00 80.00
7 Lndsy/Swchk/Delvc/Yzrmn 40.00 100.00
8 Bossy/Trottr/Potvn/Smith 50.00 80.00

2003-04 BAP Ultimate Memorabilia Dynamic Duos

1 T.Selanne
S.Koivu 20.00 50.00
2 M.Sundin/P.Forsberg 20.00 50.00
3 M.Lemieux/S.Yzerman 40.00 100.00
4 J.Sakic/B.Shanahan 20.00 50.00
5 E.Lindros/P.Kariya 20.00 50.00
6 J.Roenick/K.Tkachuk 20.00 50.00
7 I.Kovalchuk/S.Fedorov 20.00 50.00
8 R.Nash/J.Thornton 20.00 50.00
9 B.Hull/M.Modano 15.00 40.00
10 M.Messier/J.Spezza 20.00 50.00

2003-04 BAP Ultimate Memorabilia Franchise Present and Future

1 S.Fedorov/J.Lupul 15.00 40.00
2 I.Kovalchuk/D.Heatley 25.00 60.00
3 J.Thornton/P.Bergeron 20.00 50.00
4 M.Satan/D.Roy 12.50 30.00
5 J.Iginla/M.Lombardi 15.00 40.00
6 J.O'Neill/E.Staal 15.00 40.00
7 J.Thibault/T.Ruutu 12.50 30.00
8 P.Forsberg/D.Aebischer 15.00 40.00
9 R.Nash/N.Zherdev 20.00 50.00
10 M.Modano/S.Ott 15.00 40.00
11 S.Yzerman/P.Datsyuk 30.00 80.00
12 R.Smyth/A.Hemsky 12.50 30.00
13 R.Luongo/J.Bouwmeester 20.00 50.00
14 Z.Palffy/A.Frolov 15.00 40.00
15 M.Gaborik/P.Bouchard 15.00 40.00
16 J.Theodore/M.Ryder 15.00 40.00
17 D.Legwand/J.Tootoo 15.00 40.00
18 M.Brodeur/P.Martin 30.00 80.00
19 A.Yashin/R.DiPietro 15.00 40.00
20 M.Messier/F.Tyutin 15.00 40.00
21 M.Hossa/J.Spezza 20.00 50.00
22 J.LeClair/J.Pitkanen 12.50 30.00
23 S.Doan/B.Boucher 12.50 30.00
24 M.Lemieux/M.Fleury 50.00 125.00
25 C.Pronger/B.Jackman 12.50 30.00
26 E.Nabokov/J.Cheechoo 15.00 40.00
27 N.Khabibulin/V.Lecavalier 15.00 40.00
28 M.Sundin/M.Stajan 15.00 40.00
29 M.Naslund/A.Auld 15.00 40.00
30 O.Kolzig/A.Semin 15.00 40.00

2003-04 BAP Ultimate Memorabilia Gloves Are Off

1 Joe Thornton 20.00 50.00
2 Brett Hull 20.00 50.00
3 Mario Lemieux 30.00 80.00
4 Joe Sakic 20.00 50.00
5 Jarome Iginla 20.00 50.00
6 Sergei Samsonov 15.00 40.00
7 Mats Sundin 15.00 40.00
8 Eric Lindros 15.00 40.00
9 Rob Blake 15.00 40.00
10 John LeClair 15.00 40.00
11 Stan Mikita 15.00 40.00
12 Bill Gadsby 15.00 40.00
13 Aurel Joliat 25.00 60.00
14 Bernie Geoffrion 15.00 40.00
15 Dickie Moore 15.00 40.00
16 Howie Morenz 50.00 125.00
17 Doug Harvey 20.00 50.00
18 King Clancy 30.00 80.00
19 Ray Bourque 15.00 40.00
20 Eddie Shore 30.00 80.00

2003-04 BAP Ultimate Memorabilia Great Moments

COMMON CARD(1-12) 12.50 30.00
UNLISTED STARS 15.00
1 Bobby Orr 40.00 100.00
2 S.Mikita
B.Hull 25.00 60.00
3 Patrick Roy 30.00 80.00
4 Steve Yzerman 25.00 60.00
5 M.Messier
J.Theodore 25.00 60.00
6 Ray Bourque 15.00 40.00
7 B.Clarke
B.Barber 15.00 40.00
8 Henri Richard 12.50 30.00
9 Mike Bossy 15.00 40.00
10 Maurice Richard 30.00 80.00
11 Mark Messier 25.00 60.00
12 Cam Neely 15.00 40.00

2003-04 BAP Ultimate Memorabilia Hat Tricks

1 Keith Tkachuk 15.00 40.00
2 Henrik Zetterberg 25.00 60.00
3 Alexei Yashin 12.50 30.00
4 Mats Sundin 15.00 40.00
5 Joe Thornton 25.00 60.00
6 Pavel Datsyuk 30.00 80.00
7 Joe Sakic 25.00 60.00
8 Mario Lemieux 50.00 125.00
9 Milan Hejduk 15.00 40.00
10 Eric Lindros 15.00 40.00
11 Jarome Iginla 25.00 60.00
12 Steve Yzerman 40.00 100.00
13 Sergei Samsonov 12.50 30.00
14 Brett Hull 15.00 40.00
15 Chris Chelios 15.00 40.00
16 Al MacInnis 12.50 30.00
17 Doug Weight 12.50 30.00
18 John LeClair 15.00 40.00
19 Rob Blake 12.50 30.00
20 Scott Niedermayer 15.00 40.00

2003-04 BAP Ultimate Memorabilia Heroes

1 I.Kovalchuk/V.Kharlamov 30.00 80.00
2 J.Thornton/S.Yzerman 25.00 60.00
3 J.Iginla/M.Messier 20.00 50.00
4 S.Yzerman/B.Trottier 25.00 60.00
5 M.Lemieux/G.Lafleur 40.00 100.00
6 R.Nash/M.Sundin 20.00 50.00
7 D.Heatley/B.Hull 20.00 50.00
8 P.Roy/J.Plante 50.00 125.00
9 T.Sawchuk/G.Hainsworth 40.00 100.00
10 J.Theodore/P.Roy 40.00 100.00
11 R.Luongo/P.Roy 40.00 100.00
12 E.Belfour/V.Tretiak 30.00 80.00
13 M.Brodeur/P.Roy 40.00 100.00
14 M.Richter/G.Cheevers 20.00 50.00
15 T.Selanne/J.Kurri 30.00 80.00
16 A.Tanguay/J.Sakic 20.00 50.00
17 P.Marleau/M.Lemieux 30.00 80.00
18 V.Lecavalier/S.Yzerman 25.00 60.00
19 M.St.Louis/M.Lemieux 30.00 80.00
20 T.Ruutu/P.Forsberg 20.00 50.00

2003-04 BAP Ultimate Memorabilia Hometown Heroes

1 M.Richard
H.Richard 30.00 80.00
2 M.Brodeur/R.Luongo 25.00 60.00
3 R.Bourque/D.Harvey 20.00 50.00
4 P.Forsberg/M.Naslund 15.00 40.00
5 M.Gaborik/Z.Chara 15.00 40.00
6 G.Hainsworth/B.Park 15.00 40.00
7 M.Dionne/Y.Cournoyer 12.50 30.00
8 E.Staal/A.Delvecchio 20.00 50.00
9 F.Mahovlich/P.Mahovlich 15.00 40.00
10 R.Blake/R.Kelly 15.00 40.00
11 B.Hull/A.Raycroft 15.00 40.00
12 J.Theodore/M.St.Louis 20.00 50.00
13 J.Thornton/E.Lindros 15.00 40.00
14 M.Messier/J.Iginla 15.00 40.00
15 B.Durnan/C.Conacher 20.00 50.00
16 P.Esposito/T.Esposito 20.00 50.00
17 J.Kurri/K.Lehtonen 25.00 60.00
18 T.Sawchuk/B.Mosienko 25.00 60.00
19 A.Joliat/D.Potvin 20.00 50.00
20 M.Bossy/M.Lemieux 30.00 80.00

2003-04 BAP Ultimate Memorabilia Jerseys

1 Paul Kariya 10.00 25.00
2 Teemu Selanne 10.00 25.00
3 Sergei Fedorov 12.50 30.00
4 Mario Lemieux 25.00 60.00
5 Dany Heatley 15.00 40.00
6 Joe Thornton 15.00 40.00
7 Steve Yzerman 25.00 60.00
8 Bill Guerin 8.00 20.00
9 Ilya Kovalchuk 15.00 40.00
10 Chris Pronger 8.00 20.00
11 Mats Sundin 10.00 25.00
12 Peter Forsberg 12.50 30.00
13 Rick Nash 15.00 40.00
14 Mike Modano 12.50 30.00
15 Martin Brodeur 25.00 60.00
16 Jason Spezza 15.00 40.00
17 Brett Hull 12.50 30.00
18 Jeremy Roenick 12.50 30.00
19 Joe Sakic 12.50 30.00
20 Ed Belfour 10.00 25.00
21 Jose Theodore 12.50 30.00
22 Roberto Luongo 12.50 30.00
23 Henrik Zetterberg 15.00 40.00
24 Dominik Hasek 12.50 30.00
25 Jarome Iginla 12.50 30.00
26 Eric Lindros 10.00 25.00
27 Keith Tkachuk 10.00 25.00
28 Marian Gaborik 12.50 30.00
29 Nicklas Lidstrom 10.00 25.00
30 John LeClair 10.00 25.00
31 Pavel Datsyuk 15.00 30.00
32 Vincent Lecavalier 10.00 25.00
33 Markus Naslund 10.00 25.00
34 Milan Hejduk 10.00 25.00
35 Todd Bertuzzi 10.00 25.00
36 Marty Turco 8.00 20.00
37 Rob Blake 8.00 20.00
38 Andrew Raycroft 8.00 20.00
39 Martin St. Louis 8.00 20.00
40 Saku Koivu 10.00 25.00

2003-04 BAP Ultimate Memorabilia Jersey and Stick

1 Jason Spezza 15.00 40.00
2 Brian Leetch 10.00 25.00
3 Dany Heatley 12.00 30.00
4 Mario Lemieux 30.00 80.00
5 Mats Sundin 10.00 25.00
6 Jarome Iginla 20.00 50.00
7 Mike Modano 12.00 30.00
8 Rick Nash 15.00 40.00
9 Steve Yzerman 30.00 80.00
10 Keith Tkachuk 15.00 40.00
11 Joe Thornton 15.00 40.00
12 Martin Brodeur 30.00 80.00
13 Dominik Hasek 20.00 50.00
14 Nikolai Khabibulin 15.00 40.00
15 Joe Sakic 15.00 40.00
16 Vincent Lecavalier 15.00 40.00
17 Peter Forsberg 15.00 40.00
18 Brendan Shanahan 12.00 30.00
19 Marc-Andre Fleury 20.00 50.00
20 Chris Pronger 10.00 25.00
21 Patrick Roy 30.00 80.00
22 Johnny Bower 25.00 60.00
23 Ray Bourque 20.00 50.00
24 Jacques Plante 25.00 60.00
25 Jean Beliveau 20.00 50.00
26 Gump Worsley 25.00 60.00
27 Gilbert Perreault 15.00 40.00
28 Bryan Trottier 12.00 30.00
29 Mike Bossy 12.00 30.00
30 Marcel Dionne 10.00 25.00

2003-04 BAP Ultimate Memorabilia Journey Jerseys

1 Sergei Fedorov 12.50 30.00
2 Paul Kariya 12.50 30.00
3 Teemu Selanne 12.50 30.00
4 Ed Belfour 20.00 50.00
5 Brian Leetch 12.50 30.00
6 Patrick Roy 40.00 100.00
7 Brett Hull 20.00 50.00
8 Mark Messier 20.00 50.00
9 Jeremy Roenick 15.00 40.00
10 Ray Bourque 25.00 60.00

2003-04 BAP Ultimate Memorabilia Lifetime Achievers

1 Mario Lemieux 30.00 80.00
2 Patrick Roy 30.00 80.00
3 Bobby Orr 50.00 125.00
4 Ray Bourque 15.00 40.00
5 Mark Messier 25.00 60.00
6 Brett Hull 15.00 40.00
7 Brian Leetch 15.00 40.00
8 Steve Yzerman 30.00 80.00

2003-04 BAP Ultimate Memorabilia Magnificent Career

1 Mario Lemieux
A Grand Entrance 30.00 80.00
2 Mario Lemieux
Twice Is Nice 30.00 80.00
3 Mario Lemieux
A Scoring Machine 30.00 80.00
4 Mario Lemieux
A Canadian Hero 30.00 80.00
5 Mario Lemieux
A Hoard Of Hardware 30.00 80.00
6 Mario Lemieux
Farewell For Now 30.00 80.00
7 Mario Lemieux/600-Goal Man 30.00 80.00
8 Mario Lemieux
International Star 30.00 80.00
9 Mario Lemieux/1,700th Point 30.00 80.00
10 Quad Jersey 75.00 150.00

2003-04 BAP Ultimate Memorabilia Magnificent Prospects

1 M.Lemieux/M.Fleury 75.00 150.00
2 M.Lemieux/E.Staal 30.00 80.00
3 M.Lemieux/P.Bergeron 40.00 100.00
4 M.Lemieux/M.Ryder 30.00 80.00
5 M.Lemieux/R.Malone 30.00 80.00
6 M.Lemieux/T.Ruutu 30.00 80.00
7 M.Lemieux/J.Lupul 30.00 80.00
8 M.Lemieux/J.Tootoo 30.00 80.00
9 M.Lemieux/A.Raycroft 30.00 80.00
10 M.Lemieux/N.Zherdev 30.00 80.00

2003-04 BAP Ultimate Memorabilia Nameplates

1 Sergei Fedorov 15.00 40.00
2 Dominik Hasek 15.00 40.00
3 Dany Heatley 15.00 40.00
4 Markus Naslund 12.50 30.00
5 Curtis Joseph 12.50 30.00
6 Mike Modano 15.00 40.00
7 Paul Kariya 12.50 30.00
8 Mark Messier 20.00 50.00
9 Teemu Selanne 12.50 30.00
10 Martin Brodeur 30.00 80.00
11 Brian Leetch 15.00 40.00
12 Joe Thornton 15.00 40.00
13 Mario Lemieux 40.00 100.00
14 Steve Yzerman 25.00 60.00
15 Eric Lindros 12.50 30.00
16 Peter Forsberg 25.00 60.00
17 Zigmund Palffy 12.50 30.00
18 Jeremy Roenick 15.00 40.00
19 Chris Pronger 12.50 30.00
20 Nicklas Lidstrom 15.00 40.00
21 Mats Sundin 12.50 30.00
22 Brendan Shanahan 12.50 30.00
23 Henrik Zetterberg 20.00 50.00
24 Jose Theodore 15.00 40.00
25 Marc-Andre Fleury 25.00 60.00
26 Kari Lehtonen 15.00 40.00
27 Andrew Raycroft 15.00 40.00
28 Ray Bourque 25.00 60.00
29 Cam Neely 15.00 40.00
30 Patrick Roy/20 50.00 120.00

2003-04 BAP Ultimate Memorabilia Perennial Powerhouse Jersey

1 Patrick Roy 30.00 80.00
2 Joe Sakic 20.00 50.00
3 Peter Forsberg 15.00 40.00
4 Ray Bourque 20.00 50.00
5 Rob Blake 12.50 30.00
6 Alex Tanguay 12.50 30.00
7 Milan Hejduk 12.50 30.00
8 David Aebischer 12.50 30.00
9 Paul Kariya 12.50 30.00
10 Teemu Selanne 12.50 30.00

2003-04 BAP Ultimate Memorabilia Perennial Powerhouse Jersey and Stick

*JSY/STK: .6X TO 1.5X JSY HI

2003-04 BAP Ultimate Memorabilia Raised to the Rafters

1 Cam Neely 25.00 60.00
2 Doug Harvey 25.00 60.00
3 Mike Richter 25.00 60.00
4 Bobby Orr 100.00 200.00
5 Johnny Bower 20.00 50.00
6 Ray Bourque 25.00 60.00
7 Sid Abel 20.00 50.00
8 Ted Lindsay 20.00 50.00
9 Rod Gilbert 20.00 50.00
10 Maurice Richard 30.00 80.00
11 Jean Beliveau 30.00 80.00
12 Bobby Hull 20.00 50.00
13 Stan Mikita 15.00 40.00
14 Bobby Clarke 25.00 60.00
15 Bernie Parent 25.00 60.00
16 Jacques Plante 30.00 80.00
17 Mike Bossy 20.00 50.00
18 Marcel Dionne 20.00 50.00
19 Bryan Trottier 20.00 50.00
20 Eddie Shore 30.00 80.00

2003-04 BAP Ultimate Memorabilia Retro Teammates

1 Bourque/Neely/Oates 40.00 100.00
2 M.Richard/Harvey/Plante 75.00 200.00
3 Sawchuk/Lindsay/Abel 40.00 100.00
4 Messier/Richter/Leetch 60.00 150.00
5 Orr/Cheevers/Bucyk 125.00 300.00
6 Trottier/Bossy/Potvin 40.00 100.00
7 Beliveau/H.Richard/Worsley 40.00 100.00
8 Clarke/Barber/Parent 40.00 100.00
9 Sittler/McDonald/Salming 40.00 100.00
10 Shore/Thomspon/Stewart 40.00 100.00

2003-04 BAP Ultimate Memorabilia Retro-Active Trophies

1 T.Lindsay/J.Iginla 15.00 40.00
2 B.Orr/P.Forsberg 30.00 80.00
3 J.Beliveau/M.Lemieux 30.00 80.00
4 R.Bourque/P.Forsberg 25.00 60.00
5 B.Orr/M.Lemieux 75.00 200.00
6 T.Sawchuk/M.Brodeur 30.00 80.00
7 R.Worters/D.Hasek 15.00 40.00
8 E.Shore/M.Messier 15.00 40.00
9 M.Richard/M.Lemieux 40.00 100.00
10 D.Harvey/N.Lidstrom 15.00 40.00
11 B.Orr/B.Leetch 40.00 100.00
12 R.Bourque/C.Pronger 15.00 40.00
13 B.Mosienko/J.Sakic 20.00 50.00
14 M.Dionne/Br.Hull 15.00 40.00
15 J.Plante/M.Brodeur 30.00 80.00
16 J.Bower/E.Belfour 15.00 40.00
17 P.Roy/J.Theodore 30.00 80.00
18 J.Beliveau/S.Yzerman 25.00 60.00
19 P.Roy/J.Sakic 30.00 80.00
20 G.Lafleur/M.Lemieux 30.00 80.00

2003-04 BAP Ultimate Memorabilia Seams Unbelievable

1 Mario Lemieux 25.00 60.00
2 Patrick Roy 25.00 60.00
3 Steve Yzerman 30.00 60.00
4 Bobby Orr 20.00 50.00
5 Raymond Bourque 20.00 50.00
6 Martin Brodeur 25.00 60.00
7 Ilya Kovalchuk 12.00 30.00
8 Rick Nash 20.00 50.00

2003-04 BAP Ultimate Memorabilia The Goal

1 Bobby Orr JSY 50.00 120.00
3 Noel Picard JSY 20.00 50.00
4 Glenn Hall JSY 20.00 50.00
5 B.Orr/N.Picard JSY/30 100.00 250.00
6 B.Orr/G.Hall JSY/30 125.00 250.00
8 Bobby Orr STK 75.00 200.00
9 Glenn Hall STK 25.00 60.00
10 Noel Picard STK 20.00 50.00
14 N.Picard/G.Hall JSY/29 25.00 60.00

2003-04 BAP Ultimate Memorabilia Triple Threads

1 Brodeur/Potvin/DiPietro 40.00 100.00
2 Hasek/Cloutier/Aebischer 25.00 60.00
3 Jean-Sebastien Giguere 20.00 50.00
4 Belfour/Turco/Cechmanek 15.00 40.00
5 Theodore/Osgood/Luongo 20.00 50.00
6 Kolzig/Biron/Nabokov 15.00 40.00
7 Roy/Crozier/Bower 20.00 50.00
8 Sawchuk/Lumley/Plante 40.00 100.00
9 Hainsworth/Brimsek/Worters 30.00 80.00
10 Blake/Bouwmeester/Pronger 12.50 30.00
11 Lidstrom/Brewer/MacInnis 12.50 30.00
12 Leetch/Chara/Foote 15.00 40.00
13 Orr/T.Horton/Robinson 75.00 200.00
14 Harvey/Bourque/Salming 20.00 50.00
15 Sundin/Modano/Alfredsson 15.00 40.00
16 Lemieux/Hossa/Hull 40.00 100.00
17 St.Louis/Mogilny/Kovalchuk 20.00 50.00
18 Heatley/Thornton/Koivu 30.00 80.00
19 Weight/Palffy/Kariya 12.50 30.00
20 Selanne/Lindros/Tkachuk 15.00 40.00
21 Sakic/Bertuzzi/Yzerman 30.00 80.00
22 Forsberg/Amonte/Naslund 20.00 50.00
23 Nolan/Roenick/Zetterberg 12.00 30.00
24 Nash/Shanahan/Arnott 15.00 40.00
25 Gaborik/Elias/LeClair 15.00 40.00
26 Beliveau/F.Mahovlich/Bossy 25.00 60.00
27 Lindsay/H.Richard/Clarke 20.00 50.00
28 Neely/P.Esposito/McDonald 30.00 80.00
29 Bergeron/Horton/Bergenheim 25.00 60.00
30 Hunter/Gordon/Hale 12.50 30.00
31 Ruutu/Semin/Martin 12.50 30.00
32 Tootoo/Lombardi/Pitkanen 12.00 30.00
33 Staal/Ryder/Brown 25.00 60.00
34 Fleury/Zherdev/Raycroft 25.00 60.00

2003-04 BAP Ultimate Memorabilia Ultimate Goaltender

1 Patrick Roy
Jersey 30.00 60.00
2 Patrick Roy
Jersey 30.00 60.00
3 Patrick Roy
Jersey
Stick 50.00 100.00
4 Patrick Roy
Number 40.00 80.00
5 Patrick Roy
Pad 40.00 80.00
6 Patrick Roy
Triple Memorabilia 40.00 100.00

2003-04 BAP Ultimate Memorabilia Vintage Blades of Steel

1 Bill Barilko 40.00 80.00
2 Georges Vezina 175.00 300.00
3 Rocket Richard 40.00 80.00
4 Cyclone Taylor 50.00 100.00
5 Frank Patrick 40.00 80.00
6 Frank Nighbor 30.00 60.00
7 Hap Day 50.00 100.00
8 Clint Benedict 40.00 80.00
9 Elmer Lach 30.00 60.00
10 Busher Jackson 30.00 60.00
11 Eddie Shore 30.00 60.00
12 Jacques Plante 40.00 80.00
13 Toe Blake 40.00 80.00
14 Jack Adams 30.00 60.00
15 Bobby Orr 75.00 150.00
16 Tim Horton 40.00 80.00
17 Aurel Joliat 40.00 80.00
18 Nels Stewart 30.00 60.00
19 Paddy Moran 30.00 60.00
20 Jean Beliveau 25.00 50.00

2003-04 BAP Ultimate Memorabilia Vintage Jerseys

1 Aurel Joliat 30.00 80.00
2 Bobby Orr 75.00 150.00
3 Doug Harvey 12.50 30.00
4 Roy Worters 20.00 50.00
5 Jacques Plante 20.00 50.00
6 Jean Beliveau 25.00 60.00
7 Johnny Bower 15.00 40.00
8 George Hainsworth 15.00 40.00
9 Frank Brimsek 15.00 40.00
10 Roger Crozier 12.50 30.00
11 Harry Lumley 20.00 50.00
12 Sid Abel 12.50 30.00
13 Bill Mosienko 12.50 30.00
14 John Bucyk 12.50 30.00
15 Ted Lindsay 12.50 30.00
16 Alex Delvecchio 12.50 30.00
17 Phil Esposito 15.00 40.00
18 Frank Mahovlich 12.50 30.00
19 Maurice Richard 30.00 80.00
20 Dennis Hull 12.50 30.00
21 Marcel Dionne 12.50 30.00
22 Terry O'Reilly 15.00 40.00
23 Vladislav Tretiak 25.00 60.00
24 Henri Richard 12.50 30.00
25 Larry Robinson 12.50 30.00
26 Mike Bossy 12.50 30.00
27 Bryan Trottier 12.50 30.00
28 Gump Worsley 12.50 30.00
29 Bobby Clarke 12.50 30.00
30 Red Kelly 15.00 40.00
31 Gilbert Perreault 12.50 30.00
32 Lanny McDonald 12.50 30.00
33 Ray Bourque 15.00 40.00
34 Ed Giacomin 12.50 30.00
35 Valeri Kharlamov 20.00 50.00
36 Stan Mikita 12.50 30.00
37 Denis Potvin 12.50 30.00
38 Bobby Hull 20.00 50.00
39 Patrick Roy 15.00 40.00
40 Cam Neely 12.50 30.00

2003-04 BAP Ultimate Memorabilia Vintage Lumber

1 Bernie Geoffrion 15.00 40.00
2 Henri Richard 20.00 50.00
3 Joe Primeau 15.00 40.00
4 Georges Vezina 100.00 250.00
5 Jean Beliveau 15.00 40.00
6 Maurice Richard 50.00 125.00
7 Tim Horton 30.00 80.00
8 Doug Harvey 15.00 40.00
9 Terry Sawchuk 30.00 80.00
10 Jacques Plante 25.00 60.00
11 Harry Lumley 20.00 50.00
12 Howie Morenz 40.00 100.00

2001-02 BAP Update He Shoots He Scores Points

1 Todd Bertuzzi 1 pt. .20 .50
2 Theo Fleury 1 pt. .25 .60
3 Marian Gaborik 1 pt. .25 .60
4 Bill Guerin 1 pt. .25 .60
5 Martin Havlat 1 pt. .20 .50
6 Marian Hossa 1 pt. .25 .60
7 Nicklas Lidstrom 1 pt. .30 .75
8 Joe Thornton 1 pt. .25 .60
9 Alexei Yashin 1 pt. .20 .50
10 Ed Belfour 2 pts. .25 .60
11 Martin Brodeur 2 pts. .40 1.00
12 Pavel Bure 2 pts. .30 .75
13 Ron Francis 2 pts. .25 .60
14 Luc Robitaille 2 pts. .20 .50
15 Jose Theodore 2 pts. .25 .60
16 Peter Forsberg 3 pts. .30 .75
17 Dominik Hasek 3 pts. .60 1.50
18 Curtis Joseph 3 pts. .60 1.50
19 Patrick Roy 3 pts. 1.50 4.00

2001-02 BAP Update Heritage

H1 Wayne Gretzky 30.00 80.00
H2 Curtis Joseph 10.00 25.00
H3 Felix Potvin 12.00 30.00
H4 Mark Messier 12.50 30.00
H5 Doug Gilmour 10.00 25.00
H6 Keith Tkachuk 10.00 25.00
H7 Teemu Selanne 8.00 20.00

H8 Adam Oates 10.00 25.00
H9 Pavel Bure 6.00 15.00
H10 Mats Sundin 10.00 25.00
H11 Ed Belfour 10.00 25.00
H12 Mike Modano 8.00 20.00
H13 Brett Hull 12.50 30.00
H14 Brendan Shanahan 10.00 25.00
H15 Al MacInnis 10.00 25.00
H16 Theo Fleury 10.00 25.00
H17 Ed Jovanovski 6.00 15.00
H18 Keith Primeau 6.00 15.00
H19 Patrick Roy 20.00 50.00
H20 Jeff Hackett 6.00 15.00
H21 Owen Nolan 10.00 25.00
H22 Jeremy Roenick 12.50 30.00
H23 Mark Recchi 10.00 25.00
H24 Roman Turek 10.00 25.00
H25 Alexander Mogilny 10.00 25.00
H26 Jason Allison 6.00 15.00
H27 Luc Robitaille 10.00 25.00
H28 Bill Guerin 10.00 25.00
H29 Rob Blake 10.00 25.00
H30 Gary Roberts 6.00 15.00

2001-02 BAP Update Passing the Torch

PTT1 Bucyk/Neely/Thornton 20.00 50.00
PTT2 Hull/Goulet/Amonte 20.00 50.00
PTT3 Abel/Howe/Yzerman 60.00 150.00
PTT4 Richard/Lafleur/Koivu 60.00 150.00
PTT5 Giacomin/Gilbert/Leetch 20.00 50.00
PTT6 Clancy/Horton/Sundin 60.00 150.00

2001-02 BAP Update Rocket's Rivals

RR2 Ted Lindsay/30 40.00 100.00
RR3 Johnny Bower/30 40.00 100.00
RR4 Terry Sawchuk/30 40.00 100.00
RR5 Frank Brimsek/40 20.00 50.00
RR7 Bill Gadsby/30 15.00 40.00
RR9 Glenn Hall/30 20.00 50.00
RR10 Bill Mosienko/40 30.00 80.00

2001-02 BAP Update Tough Customers

TC1 D.Schultz/T.Williams 20.00 50.00
TC2 B.Probert/T.Domi 15.00 40.00
TC3 I.Laperriere/S.Grimson 10.00 25.00
TC4 P.Worrell/C.Berube 8.00 20.00
TC5 J.Mayers/K.Belanger 8.00 20.00
TC6 S.Grimson/B.Probert 25.00 60.00
TC7 P.Laus/M.Johnson 8.00 20.00
TC8 R.Ray/C.Neil 12.00 30.00
TC9 A.Nazarov/B.Brown 8.00 20.00
TC10 J.Tetarenko/D.Langdon 8.00 20.00
TC11 T.Domi/R.Ray 12.00 30.00
TC12 K.Oliwa/P.Worrell 8.00 20.00
TC13 L.Richardson/J.Odgers 8.00 20.00
TC14 P.J.Stock/M.Barnaby 8.00 20.00
TC15 W.Belak/S.McCarthy 8.00 20.00
TC16 D.Brashear/G.Laraque 15.00 40.00
TC17 A.Roy/J.Odgers 8.00 20.00
TC18 A.Roy/T.Domi 8.00 20.00
TC19 D.Brashear/B.Probert 15.00 40.00
TC20 D.Langdon/R.Thompson 8.00 20.00
TC21 R.Vandenbussche/C.Simon 10.00 25.00
TC22 M.Johnson/C.Berube 8.00 20.00
TC23 S.Parker/D.Lambert 8.00 20.00
TC24 G.Laraque/J.Odgers 8.00 20.00
TC25 L.Richardson/W.Belak 8.00 20.00
TC26 C.Dingman/P.Laus 8.00 20.00
TC27 G.Odjick/C.Simon 8.00 20.00
TC28 I.Laperriere/A.Nazarov 8.00 20.00
TC29 G.Laraque/P.Laus 8.00 20.00
TC30 K.Oliwa/E.Cairns 8.00 20.00
TC31 M.Richard/T.Lindsay 50.00 125.00
TC32 G.Howe/S.Mikita 75.00 150.00
TC33 D.Lambert/A.Roy 8.00 20.00
TC34 W.Clark/B.Probert 20.00 50.00
TC35 R.Vandenbussche/J.Mayers 8.00 20.00
TC36 R.Thompson/P.J.Stock 8.00 20.00
TC37 S.Parker/K.Belanger 8.00 20.00
TC38 C.Neil/M.Barnaby 8.00 20.00
TC39 C.Dingman/S.McCarthy 15.00 40.00
TC40 G.Odjick/E.Cairns 8.00 20.00

2001-02 BAP Update Travel Plans

TP1 Jaromir Jagr 20.00 50.00
TP2 Dominik Hasek 20.00 50.00
TP3 Roman Turek 8.00 20.00
TP4 Teemu Selanne 15.00 40.00
TP5 Keith Tkachuk 12.50 30.00
TP6 Rob Blake 12.50 30.00
TP7 Alexander Mogilny 8.00 20.00
TP8 Luc Robitaille 12.50 30.00
TP9 Alexei Yashin 8.00 20.00
TP10 Eric Lindros 15.00 40.00
TP11 Jeremy Roenick 15.00 40.00
TP12 Doug Weight 8.00 20.00
TP13 Felix Potvin 15.00 40.00
TP14 Nikolai Khabibulin 15.00 40.00
TP15 Dave Andreychuk 8.00 20.00
TP16 Dan Cloutier 8.00 20.00

1934-44 Beehive Group I Photos

COMMON PHOTO 7.50 15.00
1 Bobby Bauer 7.50 15.00
2 Red Beattie 12.50 25.00
4 Yank Boyd 75.00 150.00
5A Frankie Brimsek
(With Net) 12.50 25.00
5B Frankie Brimsek
(Without Net) 15.00 30.00
8 Dit Clapper 10.00 20.00
9 Roy Conacher 10.00 20.00
10 Bun Cook 10.00 20.00
11 Bill Cowley 10.00 20.00
12 John Crawford 7.50 15.00
13 Woody Dumart 12.50 25.00
14 Don Gallinger 87.50 175.00
15 Ray Getliffe 15.00 30.00
17 Bep Guidolin 50.00 100.00
18 Red Hamill 15.00 30.00
19 Mel Hill 10.00 20.00
24 Pat McReavy 7.50 15.00
25 Alex Motter 15.00 30.00
26 Peggy O'Neil 10.00 20.00
29 Charlie Sands 10.00 20.00
30 Jackie Schmidt 87.50 175.00
31 Milt Schmidt 10.00 20.00
32 Jack Shewchuk 10.00 20.00
33 Eddie Shore 50.00 100.00
35 Tiny Thompson 25.00 50.00
36 Cooney Weiland 10.00 20.00
38 George Allen 12.50 25.00
39 Doug Bentley 15.00 30.00
40 Max Bentley 20.00 40.00
42 Glenn Brydson 62.50 125.00
43 Marty Burke 7.50 15.00
44 Bill Carse 7.50 15.00
45 Bob Carse 7.50 15.00
46 Lorne Chabot 25.00 50.00
47 John Chad 15.00 30.00
49 Les Cunningham 15.00 30.00
50 Cully Dahlstrom 10.00 20.00
53 Leroy Goldsworthy 12.50 25.00
54 Paul Goodman 20.00 40.00
55 Johnny Gottselig 12.50 25.00
56 Philip Hergesheimer 7.50 15.00
58 George(Wingy) Johnston 87.50 175.00
59 Alex Kaleta 15.00 30.00
60 Mike Karakas 15.00 30.00
63 Alex Levinsky 12.50 25.00
64 Sam LoPresti 25.00 50.00
65 Dave Mackay 125.00 250.00
67 Mush March 7.50 15.00
68 John Mariucci 25.00 50.00
69 Joe Matte 62.50 125.00
70 Red Mitchell UER
(Name misspelled
Mitchel) 87.50 175.00
72 Peter Palangio 40.00 80.00
73 Joe Papike 50.00 100.00
75 Cliff Purpur 87.50 175.00
77 Doc Romnes 25.00 50.00
78 Earl Seibert 10.00 20.00
81 Paul Thompson 15.00 30.00
83 Louis Trudel UER
(Name misspelled
Trudell) 20.00 40.00
84 Audley Tuten 87.50 175.00
85 Art Wiebe 12.50 25.00
86 Sid Abel 15.00 30.00
87 Larry Aurie 7.50 15.00
88 Marty Barry 12.50 25.00
89 Ralph Bowman 12.50 25.00
90 Adam Brown 40.00 80.00
91 Connie Brown 50.00 100.00
92 Jerry Brown 150.00 300.00
93 Mud Bruneteau 10.00 20.00
94 Eddie Bush 125.00 250.00
95 Joe Carveth 7.50 15.00
99 Les Douglas 50.00 100.00
100 Gus Biesebrecht UER
(Name misspelled
Geisebrech) 7.50 15.00
101 Ebbie Goodfellow 10.00 20.00
102 Don Grosso 7.50 15.00
104 Syd Howe 10.00 20.00
105 Bill Jennings 40.00 80.00
106 Jack Keating 15.00 30.00
107 Pete Kelly 10.00 20.00
108 Hec Kilrea 10.00 20.00
109 Ken Kilrea 10.00 20.00
110 Wally Kilrea 10.00 20.00
111 Herb Lewis 10.00 20.00
112 Carl Liscombe 7.50 15.00
114 Douglas McCaig 40.00 80.00
115A Bucko McDonald
(Ice photo) 50.00 100.00
115B Bucko McDonald
(Dressing room photo) 50.00 100.00
116 Pat McReavy 40.00 80.00
118 Johnny Mowers 12.50 25.00
119 Jimmy Orlando 7.50 15.00
120 Gord Pettinger 20.00 40.00
121 John Sherf 20.00 40.00
123 Norm Smith 15.00 30.00
124 John Sorrell 12.50 25.00
125 Jack Stewart 20.00 40.00
128 Carl Voss 50.00 100.00
129 Eddie Wares 12.00 30.00
131 Arch Wilder 12.50 25.00
132 Douglas Young 12.50 25.00
133 Jack Adams 12.50 25.00
134 Marty Barry 200.00 400.00
135 Joe Benoit 10.00 20.00
136 Paul Bibeault 25.00 50.00
137 Toe Blake 15.00 30.00
138 Butch Bouchard 7.50 15.00
139 Claude Bourque 20.00 40.00
140 George Allan Brown 62.50 125.00
141 Walt Buswell 20.00 40.00
143 Murph Chamberlain 25.00 50.00
144 Wilf Cude 15.00 30.00
145 Bunny Dame 25.00 50.00
146 Tony DeMeres UER
(Name misspelled
Dremers) 7.50 15.00
147 Joffre Desilets 10.00 20.00
148 Gordie Drillon 350.00 700.00
149 Polly Drouin 7.50 15.00
151 Johnny Gagnon 7.50 15.00
152 Bert Gardiner 15.00 30.00
153 Ray Getliffe 40.00 80.00
154 Red Goupille 10.00 20.00
155 Tony Graboski 10.00 20.00
157 Paul Haynes 7.50 15.00
158 Gerry Heffernan 75.00 150.00
160 Roger Jenkins 30.00 60.00
161 Aurel Joliat 20.00 40.00
162 Elmer Lach 20.00 40.00
163 Leo Lamoreux UER
(Name misspelled
Camoreaux) 62.50 125.00
164 Pit Lepine 7.50 15.00
165 Rod Lorraine 15.00 30.00
166 Georges Mantha 10.00 20.00
167 Sylvio Mantha 10.00 20.00
169 Armand Mondou 7.50 15.00
170 Howie Morenz 375.00 750.00
171 Pete Morin 75.00 150.00
172 Buddy O'Connor 75.00 150.00
175 Jack Portland 7.50 15.00
176 John Quilty 12.50 25.00
177 Ken Reardon 20.00 40.00
178 Terry Reardon 50.00 100.00
179 Maurice Richard 20.00 40.00
180 Earl Robinson 200.00 400.00
181 Charlie Sands 30.00 60.00
182 Babe Siebert 20.00 40.00
183 Alex Singbush 50.00 100.00
184 Bill Summerhill 87.50 175.00
185 Louis Trudel 40.00 80.00
187 Cy Wentworth 1500.00 3000.00
188 Douglas Young 50.00 100.00
189 Bill Beveridge 30.00 60.00
190 Russ Blinco 20.00 40.00
191 Herb Cain 30.00 60.00
192 Gerry Carson UER
(Name misspelled
Jerry) 87.50 175.00
194 Alex Connell 30.00 60.00
195 Tom Cook 20.00 40.00
196 Stewart Evans 15.00 30.00
197 Bob Gracie 50.00 100.00
198 Max Kaminsky 87.50 175.00
199 Bill MacKenzie 62.50 125.00
200 Gus Marker 100.00 200.00
201 Baldy Northcott 30.00 60.00
202 Earl Robinson 25.00 50.00
203 Paul Runge 87.50 175.00
204 Gerry Shannon UER
(Name misspelled
Jerry) 87.50 175.00
206 Des Smith 20.00 40.00
207 Hooley Smith 20.00 40.00
208 Dave Trottier 50.00 100.00
209 Jimmy Ward 20.00 40.00
210 Cy Wentworth 25.00 50.00
211 Viv Allen 30.00 60.00
212 Tom Anderson 20.00 40.00
215 Bill Benson 25.00 50.00
218 Lorne Carr 25.00 50.00
219 Art Chapman 20.00 40.00
222 Red Dutton 25.00 50.00
223 Pat Egan 20.00 40.00
224 Happy Emms 40.00 80.00
225 Wilf Field 20.00 40.00
226 John Gallagher 20.00 40.00
232 Joe Jerwa 25.00 50.00
234 Jim Klein 50.00 100.00
236 Joe Krol 625.00 1250.00
237 Joe Lamb 40.00 80.00
238 Red Heron 20.00 40.00
241 Hazen McAndrew 750.00 1500.00
243 Ken Mosdell 200.00 400.00
244 Al Murray 15.00 30.00
245 John O'Flaherty 30.00 60.00
246 Chuck Rayner 100.00 200.00
247 Earl Robertson 25.00 50.00
249 Sweeny Schriner 20.00 40.00
250 Al Shields 50.00 100.00
252 Pete Slobodzian UER
(Name misspelled
Slobodian) 30.00 60.00
255 Nels Stewart 25.00 50.00
256 Fred Thurier 62.50 125.00
257 Harry Watson 112.50 225.00
258 Eddie Wiseman 15.00 30.00
259 Roy Worters 30.00 60.00
260 Ralph Wycherly 30.00 60.00
261 Frank Boucher 20.00 40.00
263 Norm Burns 50.00 100.00
265 Mac Colville 7.50 15.00
266 Neil Colville 10.00 20.00
267 Bill Cook 12.50 25.00
268 Joe Cooper 7.50 15.00
269 Art Coulter 7.50 15.00
270 Gord Davidson 30.00 60.00
271 Cecil Dillon 10.00 20.00
272 Jim Franks 100.00 200.00
273 Red Garrett 75.00 150.00
275 Ott Heller 7.50 15.00
276A Jim Henry
(Vertical photo) 50.00 100.00
276B Jim Henry
(Horizontal photo) 30.00 60.00
277 Bryan Hextall Sr. 15.00 30.00
278 Dutch Hiller 10.00 20.00
279 Ching Johnson 12.50 25.00
280 Bill Juzda 10.00 20.00
281 Butch Keeling 10.00 20.00
282 Davey Kerr 15.00 30.00
283 Bobby Kirk 50.00 100.00
284 Bob Kirkpatrick 50.00 100.00
285 Kilby MacDonald 10.00 20.00
286 Larry Molyneaux 15.00 30.00
287 John Murray Murdoch 20.00 40.00
288 Vic Myles 87.50 175.00
289 Lynn Patrick 10.00 20.00
290 Murray Patrick 7.50 15.00
291 Alf Pike 7.50 15.00
292 Babe Pratt 12.50 25.00
293 Alex Shibicky 7.50 15.00
294 Clint Smith 7.50 15.00
295 Norman Tustin 50.00 100.00
296 Grant Warwick 50.00 100.00
297 Phil Watson 7.50 15.00
298 Syl Apps Sr. 12.50 25.00
299 Murray Armstrong 7.50 15.00
300 Andy Blair 10.00 20.00
301 Buzz Boll 10.00 20.00
302 George Boothman 125.00 250.00
303 Turk Broda 12.50 25.00
304 Lorne Carr 30.00 60.00
305 Murph Chamberlain 7.50 15.00
306 Lex Chisholm 10.00 20.00
307 Jack Church 10.00 20.00
308 Francis Clancy 15.00 30.00
309 Charlie Conacher 12.50 25.00
310 Bob Copp 30.00 60.00
311 Baldy Cotton 10.00 20.00
312 Bob Davidson 7.50 15.00
313 Hap Day 7.50 15.00
314 Ernie Dickens 100.00 200.00
315 Gordie Drillon 7.50 15.00
316 Frank Finnigan 12.50 25.00
317 Jack Forsey 100.00 200.00
318 Jimmy Fowler UER
(Name misspelled Jimmie) 7.50 15.00
319 Bob Goldham 100.00 200.00
320 Hank Goldup 7.50 15.00
321 George Hainsworth 20.00 40.00
322 Reg Hamilton 7.50 15.00
323 Red Heron 10.00 20.00
324 Mel Hill 150.00 300.00
325 Frank Hollett 7.50 15.00
326 Red Horner 10.00 20.00
327 Art Jackson 7.50 15.00
328 Harvey Jackson 7.50 15.00
329 Bingo Kampman 20.00 40.00
330 Reg Kelly 10.00 20.00
331 William Kendall 40.00 80.00
332 Hec Kilrea 25.00 50.00
333 Pete Langelle 10.00 20.00
334 Bucko McDonald 10.00 20.00
335A Norm Mann 12.50 25.00
335B Norm Mann
(Name overlaps stick) 87.50 175.00
336 Gus Marker 7.50 15.00
337 Johnny McCreedy 20.00 40.00
338 Jack McLean 50.00 100.00
339 Don Metz 7.50 15.00
340 Nick Metz 7.50 15.00
341 George Parsons 12.50 25.00
342 Bud Poile 87.50 175.00
343 Babe Pratt 125.00 250.00
344 Joe Primeau 12.50 25.00
345 Doc Romnes 25.00 50.00
346 Sweeny Schriner 15.00 30.00
347 Jack Shill 12.50 25.00
348 Wally Stanowski UER
(Name misspelled
Stanowsky) 7.50 15.00
349 Phil Stein 25.00 50.00
350A Gaye Stewart
(Home Sweater) 175.00 350.00
350B Gaye Stewart
(Away Sweater) 100.00 200.00
351 Billy Taylor 7.50 15.00
352 Rhys Thompson 200.00 400.00
353 Bill Thoms 7.50 15.00
354 1944-45 Maple Leafs 150.00 300.00
355 1937 Winnipeg Monarchs 75.00 150.00
356 Foster Hewitt 40.00 80.00
357 Wes McKnight 62.50 125.00
358A Allan Cup
(Dated on back) 30.00 60.00
358B Allan Cup
(Blank Back) 62.50 125.00
359A Lady Byng Trophy
(Dated on back) 30.00 60.00
359B Lady Byng Trophy
(Blank back) 62.50 125.00
360A Calder Trophy
(Dated on back) 30.00 60.00
360B Calder Trophy
(Blank back) 62.50 125.00
361A Hart Trophy
(Dated on back) 30.00 60.00
361B Hart Trophy
(Blank back) 62.50 125.00
362A Memorial Cup
(Dated on back) 40.00 80.00
362B Memorial Cup
(Blank back) 75.00 150.00
363A Prince of Wales Trophy
(Dated on back) 87.50 175.00
363B Prince of Wales Trophy
(Blank back) 100.00 200.00
364A Stanley Cup
(Dated on back) 30.00 60.00
364B Stanley Cup
(Blank back) 50.00 100.00
364C Stanley Cup
(Name horizontal) 50.00 100.00
365A Georges Vezina Trophy
(Dated on back) 30.00 60.00
365B Georges Vezina Trophy
(Blank back) 62.50 125.00

1944-63 Beehive Group II Photos

1 Bob Armstrong 5.00 10.00
2 Pete Babando 25.00 50.00
3 Ray Barry 25.00 50.00
4 Gus Bodnar 40.00 80.00
5 Leo Boivin 6.00 12.00
6 Frankie Brimsek 12.50 25.00
8 John Bucyk 7.50 15.00
9 Charlie Burns 5.00 10.00
10 Jack Caffery 30.00 60.00
11 Real Chevrefils 5.00 10.00
12A Wayne Connelly 10.00 20.00
12B Wayne Connelly
(Name overlaps skate) 30.00 60.00
14 John Crawford 10.00 20.00
15A Dave Creighton
(White sweater) 6.00 12.00
15B Dave Creighton
(Photo on ice) 30.00 60.00
16 Woody Dumart 12.50 25.00
17 Pat Egan 15.00 30.00
19 Lorne Ferguson 6.00 12.00
20 Fern Flaman 5.00 10.00
21 Bruce Gamble 6.00 12.00
22 Cal Gardner 6.00 12.00
23 Ray Gariepy 10.00 20.00
24 Jack Gelineau 12.50 25.00
25 Jean-Guy Gendron 5.00 10.00
26A Warren Godfrey
(A on sweater) 6.00 12.00
26B Warren Godfrey
(With puck) 30.00 60.00
26C Warren Godfrey
(Without puck) 50.00 100.00
27 Ed Harrison 5.00 10.00
28 Don Head 5.00 10.00
29 Andy Hebenton 7.50 15.00
30 Murray Henderson 7.50 15.00
31 Jim Henry 15.00 30.00
32 Larry Hillman 20.00 40.00
33 Pete Horeck 10.00 20.00
34 Bronco Horvath 5.00 10.00
35 Tom Johnson 6.00 12.00
36 Eddie Johnston 7.50 15.00
38 Joe Klukay 90.00 175.00
39 Edward Kryznowski 6.00 12.00
40 Orland Kurtenbach 20.00 40.00
41 Leo Labine 5.00 10.00
42 Hal Laycoe 5.00 10.00
43 Harry Lumley 7.50 15.00
44 Pentti Lund 500.00 1000.00
45 Fleming Mackell 5.00 10.00
46 Phil Maloney 10.00 20.00
47 Frank Martin 10.00 20.00
48 Jack McIntyre 10.00 20.00
49 Don McKenney 5.00 10.00
50 Dick Meissner 5.00 10.00
51 Doug Mohns 5.00 10.00
52 Murray Oliver 5.00 10.00
53 Willie O'Ree 80.00 200.00
54A John Peirson 6.00 12.00
54B Johnny Peirson 50.00 100.00
55A Cliff Pennington
(Name away from skate) 10.00 20.00
55B Cliff Pennington
(Name near skate) 50.00 100.00
56A Bob Perreault
(Name away from skate) 12.50 25.00
56B Bob Perreault
(Name overlaps skate) 50.00 100.00
57 Jim Peters 10.00 20.00
58 Dean Prentice 6.00 12.00
59 Andre Pronovost 5.00 10.00
60 Bill Quackenbush 10.00 20.00
61 Larry Regan 25.00 50.00
62 Earl Reibel 20.00 40.00
63 Paul Ronty 6.00 12.00
64 Ed Sandford 5.00 10.00
65 Terry Sawchuk 60.00 125.00
66A Norm Defelice ERR
(name on front is Don Simmons) 75.00 150.00
66B Norm Defelice COR 5.00 10.00
67 Kenny Smith 6.00 12.00
68A Pat Stapleton
(Name away from skate) 10.00 20.00
68B Pat Stapleton
(Name near skate) 50.00 100.00
69 Vic Stasiuk 7.50 15.00
70 Red Sullivan 12.50 25.00
71 Jerry Toppazzini 5.00 10.00
72 Zellio Toppazzini 6.00 12.00
73 Grant Warwick 20.00 40.00
74 Tom Williams 5.00 10.00
75 Al Arbour 6.00 12.00
76 Pete Babando 10.00 20.00
77 Earl Balfour 5.00 10.00
78 Murray Balfour 5.00 10.00
79 Jim Bedard 10.00 20.00
80 Doug Bentley 12.50 25.00
81 Gus Bodnar 6.00 12.00
82 Frankie Brimsek 20.00 40.00
83 Adam Brown 10.00 20.00
84 Hank Ciesla 20.00 40.00
85 Jim Conacher 7.50 15.00
86 Pete Conacher 5.00 10.00
87 Roy Conacher 5.00 10.00
88 Joe Conn 40.00 80.00
89 Murray Costello 40.00 80.00
90 Gerry Couture 12.50 25.00
91 Al Dewsbury 6.00 12.00
92 Ernie Dickens 5.00 10.00
93 Jack Evans 5.00 10.00
94 Reggie Fleming 5.00 10.00
95 Lee Fogolin 7.50 15.00
96 Bill Gadsby 5.00 10.00
97 George Gee 6.00 12.00
98 Bob Goldham 12.50 25.00
99 Bep Guidolin 6.00 12.00
100 Glenn Hall 6.00 12.00
101 Murray Hall 15.00 30.00
102 Red Hamill 15.00 30.00
103 Bill Hay 5.00 10.00
104 Jim Henry 15.00 30.00
105 Wayne Hillman 12.50 25.00
107 Bronco Horvath 6.00 12.00
108 Fred Hucul 12.50 25.00
109A Bobby Hull
(Jersey 9) 100.00 200.00
109B Bobby Hull
(Jersey 16) 20.00 50.00
110 Lou Jankowski 12.50 25.00
111 Forbes Kennedy 25.00 50.00
112 Ted Lindsay 7.50 15.00
113 Ed Litzenberger 5.00 10.00
114 Harry Lumley Goalie 20.00 40.00
115A Len Lunde
(Name away from stick) 30.00 60.00
115B Len Lunde
(Name overlaps stick) 10.00 20.00
116 Pat Lundy 7.50 15.00
118A Al MacNeil
(Name overlaps
stick and skate) 20.00 40.00
118B Al MacNeil
(Name overlaps stick) 6.00 12.00
119A Chico Maki
(Name away from stick) 7.50 15.00
119B Chico Maki
(Name overlaps stick) 60.00 125.00
120 Doug McCaig 12.50 25.00
121 Ab McDonald 5.00 10.00
122 Jim McFadden 20.00 40.00
124 Gerry Melnyk UER
(Name misspelled Jerry) 5.00 10.00
125 Stan Mikita 6.00 12.00
127 Gus Mortson 5.00 10.00
128 Bill Mosienko 7.50 15.00
129 Ron Murphy 5.00 10.00
130 Ralph Nattrass 12.50 25.00
131 Eric Nesterenko 5.00 10.00
132 Bert Olmstead 12.50 25.00
133 Jim Peters 20.00 40.00
134 Pierre Pilote 5.00 10.00
135 Metro Prystai 6.00 12.00
137 Clare Raglan 15.00 30.00
138A Al Rollins
(Vertical photo) 50.00 100.00
138B Al Rollins
(Horizontal photo) 15.00 30.00
139 Tod Sloan 5.00 10.00
140 Dollard St. Laurent 5.00 10.00
141 Gaye Stewart 10.00 20.00
142 Jack Stewart 20.00 40.00
143A Bob Turner
(Name away from stick) 25.00 50.00
143B Bob Turner
(Name overlaps stick) 15.00 30.00
144 Elmer Vasko 5.00 10.00
145 Kenny Wharram 5.00 10.00
146 Larry Wilson 10.00 20.00
147 Howie Young 12.50 25.00
149 Sid Abel 10.00 20.00
150 Al Arbour 20.00 40.00
151 Pete Babando 12.50 25.00
152A Doug Barkley
(Stick blade showing) 30.00 60.00
152B Doug Barkley
(No blade showing) 10.00 20.00
153 Hank Bassen 6.00 12.00
154 Stephen Black 15.00 30.00
155 Marcel Bonin 7.50 15.00
156 John Bucyk 25.00 50.00
157 John Conacher 100.00 200.00
158 Gerry Couture UER
(Name misspelled Jerry) 6.00 12.00
159 Billy Dea 12.50 25.00
160B Alex Delvecchio COR 5.00 10.00
162 Bill Dineen 5.00 10.00
163 Jim Enio 30.00 60.00
164 Alex Faulkner 25.00 50.00
165 Lee Fogolin 6.00 12.00
166 Val Fonteyne 5.00 10.00
167 Bill Gadsby 7.50 15.00
168 Fern Gauthier 20.00 40.00
169 George Gee 7.50 15.00
170 Fred Glover 5.00 10.00
171 Howie Glover 5.00 10.00
172 Warren Godfrey 5.00 10.00
173 Peter Goegan 5.00 10.00
174 Bob Goldham 6.00 12.00
175 Glenn Hall 40.00 80.00
176 Larry Hillman 25.00 50.00
177 Pete Horeck 20.00 40.00
178A Gordie Howe 30.00 80.00
178B Gordie Howe
(C on sweater) 30.00 80.00
179 Ron Ingram 20.00 40.00
180 Larry Jeffrey 15.00 30.00
181 Al Johnson 5.00 10.00
182 Red Kelly 5.00 10.00
183 Forbes Kennedy 5.00 10.00
184 Leo Labine 5.00 10.00
185 Tony Leswick 5.00 10.00
186 Ted Lindsay 6.00 12.00
187 Ed Litzenberger 15.00 30.00
188 Harry Lumley 12.50 25.00
189 Len Lunde 5.00 10.00
190 Parker MacDonald 5.00 10.00
191 Bruce MacGregor 5.00 10.00
192 Clare Martin 12.50 25.00
193 Jim McFadden 7.50 15.00
194 Max McNab 12.50 25.00
195 Gerry Melnyk UER
(Name misspelled Jerry) 5.00 10.00
196 Don Morrison 12.50 25.00
197 Rod Morrison 25.00 50.00
198 Gerry Odrowski 5.00 10.00
199 Murray Oliver 5.00 10.00
200 Marty Pavelich 5.00 10.00
201 Jim Peters 25.00 50.00
202 Bud Poile 75.00 150.00
203 Andre Pronovost 6.00 12.00
204 Marcel Pronovost 5.00 10.00
205 Metro Prystai 5.00 10.00
206 Bill Quackenbush 25.00 50.00
207 Earl Reibel 5.00 10.00
208 Leo Reise Jr. 6.00 12.00
209A Terry Sawchuk ERR
(name misspelled Sawchuck) 20.00 50.00
209B Terry Sawchuk COR
(name spelled correctly;
different photo) 12.00 30.00
210 Glen Skov 5.00 10.00
211 Floyd Smith 6.00 12.00
212A Vic Stasiuk
(Home sweater;
full stick showing) 12.50 25.00
212B Vic Stasiuk
(Home sweater;
partial stick showing) 20.00 40.00
212C Vic Stasiuk
(Away sweater) 7.50 15.00
213 Gaye Stewart 15.00 30.00
214 Jack Stewart 15.00 30.00
215 Norm Ullman 5.00 10.00
216 Johnny Wilson 5.00 10.00
217 Benny Woit 5.00 10.00
218 Howie Young 6.00 12.00
219 Larry Zeidel 12.50 25.00
220 Ralph Backstrom 5.00 10.00
221 Dave Balon 5.00 10.00
222 Jean Beliveau 10.00 20.00
223A Red Berenson
(White script) 12.50 25.00
223B Red Berenson
(Black script) 100.00 200.00
224 Marcel Bonin 5.00 10.00
225 Butch Bouchard 5.00 10.00
226 Tod Campeau 50.00 100.00
227 Joe Carveth 6.00 12.00
228 Murph Chamberlain 25.00 50.00
229 Doc Couture 20.00 40.00
230 Floyd Curry UER
(Name misspelled Currie) 5.00 10.00
231 Ian Cushenan 7.50 15.00
232 Lorne Davis 6.00 12.00
233 Eddie Dorohoy 12.50 25.00
234 Gilles Dube 30.00 60.00
235 Bill Durnan 20.00 40.00
236 Norm Dussault 12.50 25.00
237 John Ferguson 6.00 12.00
238 Bob Fillion 7.50 15.00
239 Louie Fontinato 5.00 10.00
240 Dick Gamble 10.00 20.00
241 Bernard Geoffrion 7.50 15.00
242 Phil Goyette 5.00 10.00
243 Leo Gravelle 12.50 25.00
244 John Hanna 30.00 60.00
245 Glen Harmon 10.00 20.00
246 Terry Harper 5.00 10.00
247 Doug Harvey 7.50 15.00
248 Bill Hicke 5.00 10.00
251A Charlie Hodge
(White script) 40.00 80.00
251B Charlie Hodge
(Black script) 6.00 12.00
252 Tom Johnson 6.00 12.00
253 Vern Kaiser 20.00 40.00
254 Frank King 20.00 40.00
255 Elmer Lach 6.00 12.00
256 Al Langlois 5.00 10.00
257 Jacques Laperriere 5.00 10.00
258 Hal Laycoe 6.00 12.00
259 Jackie Leclair 5.00 10.00
260 Roger Leger 10.00 20.00
261 Ed Litzenberger 12.50 25.00
262 Ross Lowe 20.00 40.00
263 Al MacNeil 5.00 10.00
264 Bud MacPherson 5.00 10.00
265 Cesare Maniago 6.00 12.00
266 Don Marshall 5.00 10.00
267 Paul Masnick 5.00 10.00
268 Eddie Mazur 10.00 20.00
269 John McCormack 6.00 12.00
270 Alvin McDonald 5.00 10.00
271 Calum MacKay 6.00 12.00
272 Gerry McNeil 7.50 15.00
273 Paul Meger 10.00 20.00
274 Dickie Moore 6.00 12.00
275 Kenny Mosdell 10.00 20.00
276 Bert Olmstead 5.00 10.00
277 Gerry Plamondon 10.00 20.00
278 Jacques Plante 20.00 50.00
279 Andre Pronovost 5.00 10.00
280 Claude Provost 5.00 10.00
281 Ken Reardon 12.50 25.00
282 Billy Reay 6.00 12.00
283 Henri Richard 10.00 20.00
284 Maurice Richard 30.00 80.00
285 Rip Riopelle 15.00 30.00
286 George Robertson 50.00 100.00
287 Bobby Rousseau 5.00 10.00
288 Dollard St. Laurent 5.00 10.00
289 Jean-Guy Talbot 5.00 10.00
290A Gilles Tremblay
(Dark background) 5.00 10.00
290B Gilles Tremblay
(Light background) 100.00 200.00
291A J.C. Tremblay
(Dark background) 5.00 10.00
291B J.C. Tremblay
(Light background) 100.00 200.00
292 Bob Turner 5.00 10.00
293 Grant Warwick 20.00 40.00
294 Gump Worsley 12.50 25.00
295 Clint Albright 6.00 12.00
296A Dave Balon
(Name high on photo) 12.50 25.00
296B Dave Balon
(Name low on photo) 5.00 10.00
297A Andy Bathgate
(Home sweater) 6.00 12.00
297B Andy Bathgate
(Away sweater) 10.00 20.00
298 Max Bentley 25.00 50.00
299 Johnny Bower 25.00 50.00
300 Hy Buller 10.00 20.00
301A Larry Cahan
(Home sweater) 6.00 12.00
301B Larry Cahan
(Away sweater) 12.50 25.00
302 Bob Crystal 15.00 30.00
304 Brian Cullen 5.00 10.00
305 Ian Cushenan 5.00 10.00
306 Billy Dea 15.00 30.00
307 Frank Eddolls 5.00 10.00
308 Pat Egan 20.00 40.00
309A Jack Evans
(Name parallel to bottom) 5.00 10.00
309B Jack Evans
(Name printed diagonally) 20.00 40.00
310 Dunc Fisher 7.50 15.00
311 Louie Fontinato 5.00 10.00
312 Bill Gadsby 5.00 10.00
313 Jean-Guy Gendron 5.00 10.00
314 Rod Gilbert 6.00 12.00
315 Howie Glover 20.00 40.00
317 Phil Goyette 5.00 10.00
318 Aldo Guidolin 25.00 50.00
319 Vic Hadfield 6.00 12.00
320 Ted Hampson 5.00 10.00
321 Doug Harvey 6.00 12.00
322 Andy Hebenton 5.00 10.00
323 Camille Henry 5.00 10.00
324 Wally Hergesheimer 5.00 10.00
325 Ike Hildebrand 15.00 30.00
326 Bronco Horvath 6.00 12.00
327 Harry Howell 5.00 10.00
328A Earl Ingarfield Sr.
(Name away from stick) 5.00 10.00
328B Earl Ingarfield Sr.
(Name near stick) 12.50 25.00
329 Bing Juckes 15.00 30.00
330 Alex Kaleta 7.50 15.00
331 Stephen Kraftcheck 20.00 40.00
332 Eddie Kullman 7.50 15.00
333 Gus Kyle 6.00 12.00
334 Gord Labossiere 25.00 50.00
335 Al Langlois 5.00 10.00
336 Edgar Laprade 7.50 15.00
337 Tony Leswick 6.00 12.00
338 Danny Lewicki 5.00 10.00
339 Pentti Lund 10.00 20.00
340 Don Marshall 12.50 25.00
341 Jack McCartan 6.00 12.00
342 Bill McDonagh 12.50 25.00
343 Don McKenney 10.00 20.00
344 Jackie McLeod 10.00 20.00
345 Nick Mickoski 6.00 12.00
346 Billy Moe 7.50 15.00
348 Ron Murphy 5.00 10.00
349 Buddy O'Connor 7.50 15.00
350 Marcel Paille 50.00 100.00
351 Jacques Plante 50.00 100.00
352 Bud Poile 20.00 40.00
353 Larry Popein 5.00 10.00
354A Dean Prentice
(Home sweater) 5.00 10.00
354B Dean Prentice

Card	Low	High
(Away sweater)	7.50	15.00
355 Don Raleigh	7.50	15.00
356A Jean Ratelle ERR (Name misspelled John)	25.00	50.00
356B Jean Ratelle COR	20.00	40.00
357 Chuck Rayner	12.50	25.00
358 Leo Reise Jr.	6.00	12.00
359 Paul Ronty	6.00	12.00
360 Ken Schinkel	5.00	10.00
361 Eddie Shack	15.00	30.00
362 Fred Shero	15.00	30.00
363 Reg Sinclair	20.00	40.00
364 Eddie Slowinski	7.50	15.00
365 Allan Stanley	5.00	10.00
366 Wally Stanowski	6.00	12.00
367 Red Sullivan	5.00	10.00
369 Gump Worsley	5.00	10.00
370 Gary Aldcorn	10.00	20.00
371 Syl Apps Sr.	40.00	100.00
372 Al Arbour	5.00	10.00
373A George Armstrong	6.00	12.00
373B George Armstrong (Dark background)	10.00	25.00
373C George Armstrong (Light background)	100.00	200.00
374 Bob Bailey	20.00	40.00
375 Earl Balfour	10.00	20.00
376 Bill Barilko	25.00	50.00
377 Andy Bathgate	25.00	50.00
378 Bob Baun	5.00	10.00
379 Max Bentley	12.50	25.00
380 Jack Bionda	75.00	150.00
381 Garth Boesch	6.00	12.00
382 Leo Boivin	7.50	15.00
383 Hugh Bolton	5.00	10.00
384 Johnny Bower	10.00	20.00
385 Carl Brewer	5.00	10.00
386 Turk Broda	12.50	25.00
387 Larry Cahan	7.50	15.00
388 Ray Ceresino	50.00	100.00
389 Ed Chadwick	6.00	12.00
390 Pete Conacher	50.00	100.00
391 Les Costello	20.00	40.00
392 Dave Creighton	10.00	20.00
393 Barry Cullen	12.50	25.00
394 Brian Cullen	5.00	10.00
395 Robert Dawes	12.50	25.00
396 Kent Douglas	5.00	10.00
397 Dick Duff	5.00	10.00
398 Gary Edmundson	5.00	10.00
399 Gerry Ehman	5.00	10.00
400 Bill Ezinicki	10.00	20.00
401 Fern Flaman	25.00	50.00
402 Cal Gardner	10.00	20.00
403 Ted Hampson	5.00	10.00
404 Gord Hannigan	10.00	20.00
405 Billy Harris	5.00	10.00
406 Bob Hassard	40.00	80.00
407 Larry Hillman	5.00	10.00
408 Tim Horton	12.50	25.00
409 Bronco Horvath	10.00	20.00
410 Ron Hurst	75.00	150.00
411 Gerry James UER (Name misspelled Jerry)	15.00	30.00
412 Bill Juzda	7.50	15.00
413A Red Kelly (Bare-headed)	6.00	12.00
413B Red Kelly (Wearing helmet)	15.00	30.00
414 Ted Kennedy	10.00	20.00
415 Dave Keon	7.50	15.00
416 Joe Klukay	6.00	12.00
417 Stephen Kraftcheck	20.00	40.00
418 Danny Lewicki	12.50	25.00
419 Ed Litzenberger	6.00	12.00
420 Harry Lumley	12.50	25.00
421 Vic Lynn	6.00	12.00
422 Fleming MacKell	7.50	15.00
423 John MacMillan	5.00	10.00
424 Al MacNeil	10.00	20.00
425 Frank Mahovlich	12.50	25.00
426 Phil Maloney	75.00	150.00
427 Cesare Maniago	6.00	12.00
428 Frank Mathers	20.00	40.00
429 John McCormack	30.00	60.00
430 Parker MacDonald	12.50	25.00
431 Don McKenney	20.00	40.00
432 Howie Meeker	7.50	15.00
433 Don Metz	150.00	300.00
434 Nick Metz	100.00	200.00
435 Rudy Migay	5.00	10.00
436 Jim Mikol	5.00	10.00
437 Jim Morrison	5.00	10.00
438 Gus Mortson	6.00	12.00
439 Eric Nesterenko	7.50	15.00
440 Bob Nevin	5.00	10.00
441 Mike Nykoluk	25.00	50.00
442 Bert Olmstead	6.00	12.00
443 Bob Pulford	5.00	10.00
444 Marc Reaume	7.50	15.00
445 Larry Regan	5.00	10.00
446 Dave Reid	75.00	150.00
447 Al Rollins	15.00	30.00
448 Eddie Shack	6.00	15.00
449 Don Simmons	6.00	12.00
450 Tod Sloan	5.00	10.00
451 Sid Smith	5.00	10.00
452 Bob Solinger	30.00	60.00
453A Allan Stanley ERR (Name misspelled Alan; dark background)	6.00	12.00
453B Allan Stanley COR (Light background)	12.50	25.00
454 Wally Stanowski	200.00	400.00
455 Ron Stewart	5.00	10.00
456 Harry Taylor	20.00	40.00
457 Jim Thomson	6.00	12.00
458 Ray Timgren	7.50	15.00
459 Harry Watson	6.00	12.00
460 Johnny Wilson	5.00	10.00
461 1962-63 Maple Leafs (Team picture)	200.00	400.00
462A Lady Byng Trophy (Four white borders)	150.00	300.00
462B Lady Byng Trophy (White bottom border only)	60.00	125.00
463A Calder Memorial Trophy (Four white borders)	150.00	300.00
463B Calder Memorial Trophy (White bottom border only)	60.00	125.00
464A Hart Trophy (Four white borders)	150.00	300.00
464B Hart Trophy (White bottom border only)	60.00	125.00
465A James Norris Memorial Trophy (Four white borders)	150.00	300.00
465B James Norris Memorial Trophy (White bottom border only)	60.00	125.00
466A Prince of Wales Trophy (Four white borders)	150.00	300.00
466B Prince of Wales Trophy (White bottom border only)	60.00	125.00
467A Art Ross Trophy (Four white borders)	150.00	300.00
467B Art Ross Trophy (White bottom border only)	60.00	125.00
468A Stanley Cup (Four white borders)	150.00	300.00
468B Stanley Cup (White bottom border only)	60.00	125.00
469A Georges Vezina Trophy (Four white borders)	150.00	300.00
469B Georges Vezina Trophy (White bottom border only)	60.00	125.00

1964-67 Beehive Group III Photos

Card	Low	High
1 Murray Balfour	12.50	25.00
2 Leo Boivin	6.00	12.00
3 John Bucyk	7.50	15.00
4 Wayne Connelly	75.00	150.00
5 Bob Dillabaugh	6.00	12.00
6 Gary Dornhoefer	7.50	15.00
7 Reggie Fleming	6.00	12.00
8 Guy Gendron	60.00	125.00
9 Warren Godfrey	150.00	300.00
10 Ted Green	6.00	12.00
11 Andy Hebenton	90.00	175.00
12 Eddie Johnston	7.50	15.00
13 Tom Johnson	7.50	15.00
14 Forbes Kennedy	10.00	20.00
15 Orland Kurtenbach	20.00	40.00
16 Bobby Leiter	6.00	12.00
17 Parker MacDonald	6.00	12.00
18 Bob McCord	10.00	20.00
19 Ab McDonald	6.00	12.00
20 Murray Oliver	6.00	12.00
21 Bernie Parent	40.00	80.00
22 Cliff Pennington	100.00	225.00
23 Bob Perreault	175.00	350.00
24 Dean Prentice	6.00	12.00
25 Ron Schock UER	6.00	12.00
26 Pat Stapleton	25.00	50.00
27 Ron Stewart	7.50	15.00
28 Ed Westfall	6.00	12.00
29 Tom Williams	6.00	12.00
30 Lou Angotti	6.00	12.00
31 Wally Boyer	6.00	12.00
32 Denis DeJordy	7.50	15.00
33 Dave Dryden	15.00	30.00
34A Phil Esposito	40.00	80.00
34B Phil Esposito	10.00	20.00
35 Glenn Hall ERR	10.00	20.00
36 Murray Hall	100.00	225.00
37 Bill Hay	6.00	12.00
38 Camille Henry	10.00	20.00
39 Wayne Hillman	75.00	150.00
40 Ken Hodge Sr.	7.50	15.00
41A Bobby Hull	100.00	225.00
41B Bobby Hull	200.00	400.00
41C Bobby Hull	15.00	30.00
41D Bobby Hull	15.00	30.00
41E Bobby Hull	200.00	400.00
41F Bobby Hull	15.00	30.00
42 Dennis Hull	6.00	12.00
43 Doug Jarrett	6.00	12.00
44 Len Lunde	6.00	12.00
45 Al MacNeil	6.00	12.00
46A Chico Maki	50.00	100.00
46B Chico Maki	6.00	12.00
47 John McKenzie	15.00	30.00
49 Stan Mikita	10.00	20.00
50 Doug Mohns	6.00	12.00
51A Eric Nesterenko	100.00	225.00
51B Eric Nesterenko	6.00	12.00
52A Pierre Pilote	125.00	250.00
52B Pierre Pilote	7.50	15.00
53 Matt Ravlich	6.00	12.00
55A Fred Stanfield	75.00	150.00
55B Fred Stanfield	50.00	100.00
56 Pat Stapleton	6.00	12.00
57 Bob Turner	125.00	250.00
58 Ed Van Impe	6.00	12.00
59 Elmer Vasko	7.50	15.00
60 Kenny Wharram	6.00	12.00
61 Doug Barkley	6.00	12.00
62 Hank Bassen	7.50	15.00
63A Andy Bathgate	6.00	12.00
63B Andy Bathgate	6.00	12.00
64 Gary Bergman	6.00	12.00
65 Leo Boivin	7.50	15.00
66 Roger Crozier	7.50	15.00
67A Alex Delvecchio	10.00	20.00
67B Alex Delvecchio	150.00	300.00
68 Alex Faulkner	175.00	350.00
69 Val Fonteyne	6.00	12.00
70 Bill Gadsby	6.00	12.00
71 Warren Godfrey	12.50	25.00
72 Pete Goegan	12.50	25.00
73 Murray Hall	6.00	12.00
74 Ted Hampson	6.00	12.00
75 Billy Harris	15.00	30.00
76 Paul Henderson	10.00	20.00
77A Gordie Howe	20.00	40.00
77B Gordie Howe	100.00	225.00
78 Ron Ingram	150.00	300.00
79A Larry Jeffrey	50.00	100.00
79B Larry Jeffrey	30.00	60.00
80A Eddie Joyal	12.50	25.00
80B Eddie Joyal	100.00	225.00
81 Al Langlois	6.00	12.00
82 Ted Lindsay	10.00	20.00
83 Parker MacDonald	6.00	12.00
84A Bruce MacGregor	7.50	15.00
84B Bruce MacGregor	50.00	100.00
85 Pete Mahovlich	6.00	12.00
86 Bert Marshall	6.00	12.00
87 Pit Martin	6.00	12.00
89 Ab McDonald	6.00	12.00
90 Ron Murphy	6.00	12.00
91 Dean Prentice	6.00	12.00
92 Andre Pronovost	10.00	20.00
93 Marcel Pronovost	5.00	10.00
94A Floyd Smith	7.50	15.00
94B Floyd Smith	100.00	225.00
94C Floyd Smith	90.00	175.00
95 Norm Ullman	10.00	20.00
96 Bob Wall	6.00	12.00
97 Ralph Backstrom	6.00	12.00
98 Dave Balon	6.00	12.00
99 Jean Beliveau	12.50	25.00
100 Red Berenson	6.00	12.00
101 Yvan Cournoyer	10.00	20.00
102 Dick Duff	7.50	15.00
103 John Ferguson	6.00	12.00
104 John Hanna	100.00	200.00
105A Terry Harper	6.00	12.00
105B Terry Harper IA	100.00	225.00
106 Ted Harris	6.00	12.00
107 Bill Hicke	7.50	15.00
108 Charlie Hodge	10.00	20.00
109 Jacques Laperriere	6.00	12.00
110A Claude Larose	6.00	12.00
110B Claude Larose	300.00	500.00
111 Claude Provost	6.00	12.00
112 Henri Richard	12.50	25.00
113 Maurice Richard	30.00	60.00
114 Jim Roberts	6.00	12.00
115 Bobby Rousseau	6.00	12.00
116 Jean-Guy Talbot	6.00	12.00
117A Gilles Tremblay	6.00	12.00
117B Gilles Tremblay	50.00	100.00
118 J.C. Tremblay	6.00	12.00
119 Gump Worsley	10.00	20.00
120 Lou Angotti	6.00	12.00
121 Arnie Brown	6.00	12.00
122 Larry Cahan	150.00	300.00
124 Reggie Fleming	6.00	12.00
125 Bernie Geoffrion	10.00	20.00
126 Ed Giacomin	12.50	25.00
127 Rod Gilbert	10.00	20.00
128 Phil Goyette	6.00	12.00
129 Vic Hadfield	7.50	15.00
131 Camille Henry	75.00	150.00
132 Bill Hicke	6.00	12.00
133 Wayne Hillman	6.00	12.00
134 Harry Howell	7.50	15.00
135 Earl Ingarfield Sr.	6.00	12.00
137 Orland Kurtenbach	10.00	20.00
138 Gord Labossiere	75.00	150.00
139 Al MacNeil	6.00	12.00
140 Cesare Maniago	10.00	20.00
141 Don Marshall	6.00	12.00
143 Jim Neilson	6.00	12.00
144 Bob Nevin	6.00	12.00
145 Marcel Paille	20.00	40.00
146 Jacques Plante	40.00	80.00
147 Jean Ratelle	12.50	25.00
148 Rod Seiling	6.00	12.00
151 George Armstrong	10.00	20.00
152 Andy Bathgate	10.00	20.00
153A Bob Baun	60.00	125.00
153B Bob Baun	10.00	20.00
154A Johnny Bower	90.00	175.00
154B Johnny Bower	12.50	25.00
155 Wally Boyer	15.00	30.00
156 John Brenneman	6.00	12.00
157 Carl Brewer	12.50	25.00
158 Turk Broda	15.00	30.00
159 Brian Conacher	6.00	12.00
160 Kent Douglas	6.00	12.00
161 Ron Ellis	6.00	12.00
162 Bruce Gamble	10.00	20.00
163A Billy Harris	50.00	100.00
163B Billy Harris	100.00	225.00
164 Larry Hillman	12.50	25.00
165A Tim Horton	90.00	175.00
165B Tim Horton	15.00	30.00
166 Bronco Horvath	90.00	175.00
167 Larry Jeffrey	15.00	30.00
168 Eddie Joyal	20.00	40.00
169 Red Kelly	10.00	20.00
170 Ted Kennedy	10.00	20.00
171A Dave Keon	75.00	150.00
171B Dave Keon	12.50	25.00
172 Orland Kurtenbach	7.50	20.00
173 Ed Litzenberger	10.00	20.00
174A Frank Mahovlich	90.00	175.00
174B Frank Mahovlich	15.00	30.00
175A Don McKenney	50.00	100.00
175B Don McKenney	10.00	20.00
176 Dickie Moore	10.00	20.00
177 Jim Pappin	6.00	12.00
178A Marcel Pronovost	7.50	15.00
178B Marcel Pronovost	15.00	30.00
180A Bob Pulford	50.00	100.00
180B Bob Pulford	10.00	20.00
181 Terry Sawchuk	15.00	30.00
182 Brit Selby	6.00	12.00
183 Eddie Shack	12.50	25.00
184 Don Simmons	12.50	25.00
185 Allan Stanley	10.00	20.00
186 Pete Stemkowski	6.00	12.00
187A Ron Stewart	90.00	175.00
187B Ron Stewart	30.00	60.00
188 Mike Walton	15.00	30.00
189 Bernie Geoffrion	25.00	50.00
190 Byng Trophy	60.00	125.00
191 Calder Memorial Trophy	60.00	125.00
192 Hart Trophy	60.00	125.00
193 Prince of Wales Trophy	60.00	125.00
194 James Norris Trophy	60.00	125.00
195 Art Ross Trophy	60.00	125.00
196 Stanley Cup	60.00	125.00
197 Vezina Trophy	60.00	125.00

1997-98 Beehive

Card	Low	High
COMPLETE SET (75)	25.00	60.00
1 Eric Lindros	1.00	2.50
2 Teemu Selanne	1.25	3.00
3 Brendan Shanahan	.60	1.50
4 Joe Sakic	1.25	3.00
5 John LeClair	.60	1.50
6 Brett Hull	1.25	3.00
7 Jaromir Jagr	2.00	5.00
8 Bryan Berard	.40	1.00
9 Peter Forsberg	1.25	3.00
10 Ed Belfour	.60	1.50
11 Steve Yzerman	1.50	4.00
12 Curtis Joseph	.75	2.00
13 Saku Koivu	.60	1.50
14 Keith Tkachuk	.60	1.50
15 Pavel Bure	.60	1.50
16 Felix Potvin	1.00	2.50
17 Ray Bourque	1.00	2.50
18 Theo Fleury	.75	2.00
19 Patrick Roy	1.50	4.00
20 Joe Nieuwendyk	.50	1.25
21 Alexei Yashin	.50	1.25
22 Owen Nolan	.60	1.50
23 Mark Recchi	.75	2.00
24 Dominik Hasek	1.00	2.50
25 Chris Chelios	.60	1.50
26 Mike Modano	1.00	2.50
27 John Vanbiesbrouck	.60	1.50
28 Brian Leetch	.50	1.25
29 Dino Ciccarelli	.60	1.50
30 Mark Messier	1.25	3.00
31 Paul Kariya	.60	1.50
32 Jocelyn Thibault	.50	1.25
33 Wayne Gretzky	4.00	10.00
34 Doug Weight	.60	1.50
35 Yanic Perreault	.50	1.25
36 Luc Robitaille	.60	1.50
37 Chris Osgood	.60	1.50
38 Adam Oates	.60	1.50
39 Mats Sundin	.60	1.50
40 Trevor Linden	.60	1.50
41 Mike Richter	.60	1.50
42 Zigmund Palffy	.60	1.50
43 Pat LaFontaine	.60	1.50
44 Grant Fuhr	1.00	2.50
45 Martin Brodeur	1.50	4.00
46 Sergei Fedorov	1.00	2.50
47 Doug Gilmour	.75	2.00
48 Daniel Alfredsson	.60	1.50
49 Ron Francis	.75	2.00
50 Geoff Sanderson	.50	1.25
51 Joe Thornton	1.00	2.50
52 Vaclav Prospal RC	.50	1.25
53 Patrik Elias RC	1.00	2.50
54 Mike Johnson RC	.50	1.25
55 Alyn McCauley	.50	1.25
56 Brendan Morrison RC	.75	2.00
57 Johnny Bower GO	.60	1.50
58 John Bucyk GO	.60	1.50
59 Stan Mikita GO	.75	2.00
60 Ted Lindsay GO	.60	1.50
61 Maurice Richard GO	1.00	2.50
62 Andy Bathgate GO	.60	1.50
63 Stefan Cherneski JLS RC	.50	1.25
64 Craig Hillier JLS RC	.60	1.50
65 Daniel Tkaczuk JLS	.60	1.50
66 Josh Holden JLS	.50	1.25
67 Marian Cisar JLS RC	.60	1.50
68 J-P Dumont JLS RC	.60	1.50
69 Roberto Luongo JLS RC	6.00	15.00
70 Aren Miller JLS RC	.60	1.50
71 Mathieu Garon JLS	.60	1.50
72 Charlie Stephens JLS RC	.60	1.50
73 Sergei Varlamov JLS RC	.50	1.25
74 Pierre Dagenais JLS RC	.60	1.50
75 Willie O'Ree CC RC	1.00	2.50
R1 Redemption EXPIRED	.08	.25

1997-98 Beehive Authentic Autographs

Card	Low	High
51 Joe Thornton	10.00	25.00
52 Vaclav Prospal	3.00	8.00
53 Patrik Elias	6.00	15.00
54 Mike Johnson	2.00	5.00
55 Alyn McCauley	15.00	40.00
56 Brendan Morrison	4.00	10.00
63 Stefan Cherneski	2.00	5.00
64 Craig Hillier	2.00	5.00
65 Daniel Tkaczuk	2.00	5.00
66 Josh Holden	2.00	5.00
67 Marian Cisar	2.00	5.00
68 J-P Dumont	4.00	10.00
69 Roberto Luongo	12.00	30.00
70 Aren Miller	2.00	5.00
71 Mathieu Garon	4.00	10.00
72 Charlie Stephens	2.00	5.00
73 Sergei Varlamov	2.00	5.00
74 Pierre Dagenais	2.00	5.00
75 Willie O'Ree	12.00	30.00

1997-98 Beehive Golden Portraits

*VETS: 2X TO 5X BASIC CARDS
*ROOKIES: 1X TO 2.5X BASIC CARD

1997-98 Beehive Golden Originals Autographs

Card	Low	High
57 Johnny Bower	8.00	20.00
58 John Bucyk	8.00	20.00
59 Stan Mikita	15.00	30.00
60 Ted Lindsay	8.00	20.00
61 Maurice Richard	50.00	100.00
62 Andy Bathgate	8.00	20.00

1997-98 Beehive Team

COMPLETE SET (25) 60.00 150.00
*GOLD TEAM: 1X TO 2.5X BASIC INSERTS

Card	Low	High
1 Paul Kariya	2.50	6.00
2 Mark Messier	3.00	8.00
3 Mike Modano	3.00	8.00
4 Brendan Shanahan	3.00	8.00
5 John Vanbiesbrouck	2.50	6.00
6 Martin Brodeur	6.00	15.00
7 Wayne Gretzky	12.00	30.00
8 Eric Lindros	3.00	8.00
9 Peter Forsberg	2.50	6.00
10 Jaromir Jagr	4.00	10.00
11 Teemu Selanne	2.50	6.00
12 John LeClair	2.50	6.00
13 Saku Koivu	2.50	6.00
14 Brett Hull	3.00	8.00
15 Patrick Roy	8.00	20.00
16 Steve Yzerman	8.00	20.00
17 Keith Tkachuk	2.00	5.00
18 Pat LaFontaine	2.00	5.00
19 Joe Sakic	5.00	12.00
20 Patrik Elias	2.00	5.00
21 Vaclav Prospal	1.50	4.00
22 Joe Thornton	4.00	10.00
23 Sergei Samsonov	2.00	5.00
24 Alexei Morozov UER	1.50	4.00
25 Marco Sturm	1.50	4.00

2003-04 Beehive

Card	Low	High
COMPLETE SET (250)	30.00	80.00
COMP.SET w/o SP's (200)	8.00	20.00
1 Petr Sykora	.25	.60
2 Martin Gerber	.20	.50
3 Vaclav Prospal	.20	.50
4 Jean-Sebastien Giguere	.30	.75
5 Sergei Fedorov	.50	1.25
6 Stanislav Chistov	.20	.50
7 Sandis Ozolinsh	.20	.50
8 Pasi Nurminen	.25	.60
9 Marc Savard	.20	.50
10 Vyacheslav Kozlov	.25	.60
11 Dany Heatley	.25	.60
12 Ilya Kovalchuk	.30	.75
13 Andrew Raycroft	.25	.60
14 Glen Murray	.25	.60
15 Brian Rolston	.25	.60
16 Jeff Jillson	.20	.50
17 Don Cherry	.60	1.50
18 Nick Boynton	.20	.50
19 Felix Potvin	.50	1.25
20 Joe Thornton	.50	1.25
21 Sergei Samsonov	.25	.60
22 Ales Kotalik	.20	.50
23 Alexei Zhitnik	.25	.60
24 Maxim Afinogenov	.20	.50
25 Chris Drury	.25	.60
26 Daniel Briere	.30	.75
27 Martin Biron	.25	.60
28 Steve Reinprecht	.20	.50
29 Jamie McLennan	.20	.50
30 Martin Gelinas	.20	.50
31 Jarome Iginla	.40	1.00
32 Roman Turek	.25	.60
33 Jeff O`Neill	.20	.50
34 Danny Markov	.20	.50
35 Erik Cole	.20	.50
36 Rod Brind'Amour	.30	.75
37 Jamie Storr	.25	.60
38 Ron Francis	.40	1.00
39 Bryan Berard	.25	.60
40 Eric Daze	.25	.60
41 Kyle Calder	.20	.50
42 Michael Leighton	.20	.50
44 Jocelyn Thibault	.25	.60
45 Tyler Arnason	.20	.50
46 Philippe Sauve	.25	.60
47 Teemu Selanne	.60	1.50
48 Alex Tanguay	.25	.60
49 Derek Morris	.20	.50
50 Milan Hejduk	.25	.60
51 Patrick Roy	.75	2.00
52 David Aebischer	.25	.60
53 Joe Sakic	.60	1.50
54 Paul Kariya	.30	.75
55 Peter Forsberg	.60	1.50
56 Darryl Sydor	.20	.50
57 Trevor Letowski	.20	.50
58 Marc Denis	.25	.60
59 Rick Nash	.30	.75
60 Todd Marchant	.20	.50
61 Brenden Morrow	.25	.60
62 Jere Lehtinen	.25	.60
63 Sergei Zubov	.25	.60
64 Stu Barnes	.20	.50
65 Teppo Numminen	.20	.50
66 Bill Guerin	.30	.75
67 Marty Turco	.30	.75
68 Mike Modano	.50	1.25
69 Gordie Howe	1.00	2.50
70 Brendan Shanahan	.30	.75
71 Brett Hull	.60	1.50
72 Nicklas Lidstrom	.30	.75
73 Dominik Hasek	.50	1.25
74 Henrik Zetterberg	.40	1.00
75 Steve Yzerman	.75	2.00
76 Eric Brewer	.20	.50
77 Adam Oates	.30	.75
78 Ryan Smyth	.25	.60
79 Ales Hemsky	.30	.75
80 Raffi Torres	.20	.50
81 Wayne Gretzky	2.00	5.00
82 Tommy Salo	.25	.60
83 Steve Shields	.25	.60
84 Jay Bouwmeester	.20	.50
85 Olli Jokinen	.30	.75
86 Roberto Luongo	.50	1.25
87 Marcel Dionne	.40	1.00
88 Alexander Frolov	.25	.60
89 Adam Deadmarsh	.20	.50
90 Jason Allison	.25	.60
91 Luc Robitaille	.30	.75
92 Roman Cechmanek	.25	.60
93 Zigmund Palffy	.30	.75
94 Andrew Brunette	.20	.50
95 Dwayne Roloson	.25	.60
96 Pascal Dupuis	.20	.50
97 Wes Walz	.20	.50
98 Manny Fernandez	.20	.50
99 Marian Gaborik	.30	.75
100 Pierre-Marc Bouchard	.30	.75
101 Andrei Markov	.30	.75
102 Guy Lafleur	.40	1.00
103 Mike Ribeiro	.20	.50
104 Jose Theodore	.30	.75
105 Marcel Hossa	.20	.50
106 Michael Ryder	.25	.60
107 Saku Koivu	.30	.75
108 Greg Johnson	.20	.50
109 David Legwand	.25	.60
110 Tomas Vokoun	.25	.60
111 Jamie Langenbrunner	.25	.60
112 Jeff Friesen	.20	.50
113 John Madden	.20	.50
114 Scott Niedermayer	.30	.75
115 Martin Brodeur	.75	2.00
116 Patrik Elias	.30	.75
117 Scott Gomez	.25	.60
118 Scott Stevens	.30	.75
119 Brian Gionta	.20	.50
119B Alexei Zhamnov	.25	.60
120 Mariusz Czerkawski	.20	.50
121 Eric Godard	.20	.50
122 Jason Blake	.20	.50
123 Mark Parrish	.20	.50
124 Alexei Yashin	.25	.60
125 Michael Peca	.25	.60
126 Rick DiPietro	.25	.60
127 Alex Kovalev	.25	.60
128 Anson Carter	.25	.60
129 Brian Leetch	.25	.60
130 Petr Nedved	.20	.50
131 Eric Lindros	.50	1.25
132 Mark Messier	.60	1.50
133 Mike Dunham	.25	.60
134 Daniel Alfredsson	.30	.75
135 Zdeno Chara	.30	.75
136 Jason Spezza	.30	.75
137 Marian Hossa	.30	.75
138 Patrick Lalime	.25	.60
139 Bobby Clarke	.50	1.25
140 John LeClair	.30	.75
141 Justin Williams	.25	.60
142 Mark Recchi	.40	1.00
143 Robert Esche	.20	.50
144 Tony Amonte	.25	.60
145 Jeff Hackett	.25	.60
146 Jeremy Roenick	.50	1.25
147 Simon Gagne	.30	.75
148 Brian Boucher	.25	.60
149 Chris Gratton	.20	.50
150 David Tanabe	.20	.50
151 Jan Hrdina	.20	.50
152 Mike Johnson	.20	.50
153 Sean Burke	.20	.50
154 Brooks Orpik	.20	.50
155 Konstantin Koltsov	.20	.50
156 Rico Fata	.20	.50
157 Sebastien Caron	.25	.60
158 Mario Lemieux	1.25	3.00
159 Martin Straka	.20	.50
160 Jonathan Cheechoo	.25	.60
161 Kyle McLaren	.20	.50
162 Niko Dimitrakos	.20	.50
163 Evgeni Nabokov	.25	.60
164 Patrick Marleau	.30	.75
165 Vincent Damphousse	.25	.60
166 Chris Pronger	.30	.75
167 Reed Low	.20	.50
168 Chris Osgood	.30	.75
169 Doug Weight	.30	.75
170 Keith Tkachuk	.30	.75
171 Pavol Demitra	.40	1.00
172 Dave Andreychuk	.30	.75
173 Martin St. Louis	.30	.75
174 Nikolai Khabibulin	.30	.75
175 Vincent Lecavalier	.30	.75
176 Brad Richards	.30	.75
177 Fredrik Modin	.20	.50
178 Gary Roberts	.20	.50
179 Joe Nieuwendyk	.25	.60
180 Tie Domi	.25	.60
181 Alexander Mogilny	.25	.60
182 Ed Belfour	.30	.75
183 Mats Sundin	.30	.75
184 Owen Nolan	.30	.75
185 Daniel Sedin	.40	1.00
186 Magnus Arvedson	.20	.50
187 Dan Cloutier	.25	.60
188 Henrik Sedin	.40	1.00
189 Brendan Morrison	.25	.60
190 Jason King	.20	.50
191 Trevor Linden	.30	.75
192 Ed Jovanovski	.25	.60
193 Johan Hedberg	.25	.60
194 Markus Naslund	.30	.75
195 Todd Bertuzzi	.30	.75
196 Robert Lang	.20	.50
197 Sergei Gonchar	.20	.50
198 Jaromir Jagr	1.00	2.50
199 Olaf Kolzig	.30	.75
200 Peter Bondra	.30	.75
201 Joffrey Lupul RC	2.00	5.00
202 Patrice Bergeron RC	4.00	10.00
203 Niklas Kronwall RC	1.50	4.00
204 Eric Staal RC	4.00	10.00
205 Pavel Vorobiev RC	1.00	2.50
206 Tuomo Ruutu RC	1.25	3.00
207 Tomas Plekanec RC	2.50	6.00
208 Timofei Shishkanov RC	.75	2.00
209 Tuomas Pihlman RC	1.00	2.50
210 Dan Fritsche RC	.75	2.00
211 Antti Miettinen RC	1.25	3.00
212 Jiri Hudler RC	2.00	5.00
213 Nathan Horton RC	2.00	5.00
214 Dustin Brown RC	2.00	5.00
215 Kyle Wellwood RC	1.25	3.00
216 Mike Smith RC	2.50	6.00
217 Ryan Kesler RC	3.00	8.00
218 Fredrik Sjostrom RC	1.25	3.00
219 Chris Higgins RC	1.50	4.00
220 Dan Hamhuis RC	1.00	2.50
221 Jordin Tootoo RC	1.50	4.00
222 Carl Corazzini RC	.75	2.00
223 Tony Martensson RC	.75	2.00
224 Aaron Johnson RC	.75	2.00
225 Anton Babchuk RC	.75	2.00
226 Jozef Balej RC	.75	2.00
227 Joni Pitkanen RC	1.25	3.00
228 Aleksander Suglobov RC	.75	2.00
229 Marc-Andre Fleury RC	5.00	12.00
230 Nikolai Zherdev RC	1.50	4.00
231 Gavin Morgan RC	1.00	2.50
232 Milan Michalek RC	1.50	4.00
233 Peter Sejna RC	1.00	2.50
234 Matt Stajan RC	1.25	3.00
235 Maxim Kondratiev RC	.75	2.00
236 Alexander Semin RC	2.50	6.00
237 Zbynek Michalek RC	.75	2.00
238 Jeff Hamilton RC	.75	2.00
239 Andrew Hutchinson RC	.75	2.00
240 Mikhail Yakubov RC	.75	2.00
241 Sergei Zinovjev RC	.75	2.00
242 Noah Clarke RC	.75	2.00
243 Tim Jackman RC	1.00	2.50
244 Jason Pominville RC	2.00	5.00
245 Tony Salmelainen RC	.75	2.00
246 Rastislav Stana RC	1.25	3.00
247 Darryl Bootland RC	1.00	2.50
248 Trevor Daley RC	1.25	3.00
249 Peter Sarno RC	.75	2.00
250 Nathan Smith RC	.75	2.00
NNO Checklist Card	.08	.20

2003-04 Beehive Variations

Card	Low	High
5 Sergei Fedorov	1.00	2.50
12 Ilya Kovalchuk	.60	1.50
17 Don Cherry	1.25	3.00
20 Joe Thornton	1.00	2.50
21 Sergei Samsonov	.50	1.25
25 Chris Drury	.50	1.25
31 Jarome Iginla	.75	2.00
35 Erik Cole	.40	1.00
44 Jocelyn Thibault	.50	1.25
51 Patrick Roy	1.50	4.00
53 Joe Sakic	1.25	3.00
55 Peter Forsberg	1.25	3.00
59 Rick Nash	.60	1.50
67 Marty Turco	.60	1.50
68 Mike Modano	1.00	2.50
69 Gordie Howe	2.00	5.00
74 Henrik Zetterberg	.75	2.00
75 Steve Yzerman	1.50	4.00
79 Ales Hemsky	.60	1.50
80 Raffi Torres	.40	1.00
81 Wayne Gretzky	4.00	10.00
86 Roberto Luongo	1.00	2.50
87 Marcel Dionne	.75	2.00
91 Luc Robitaille	.60	1.50
93 Zigmund Palffy	.60	1.50
99 Marian Gaborik	.60	1.50
102 Guy Lafleur	.75	2.00
104 Jose Theodore	.60	1.50
107 Saku Koivu	.60	1.50
110 Tomas Vokoun	.50	1.25
115 Martin Brodeur	1.50	4.00
120 Mariusz Czerkawski	.40	1.00
126 Rick DiPietro	.50	1.25
132 Mark Messier	1.25	3.00
136 Jason Spezza	.60	1.50
137 Marian Hossa	.60	1.50
139 Bobby Clarke	1.00	2.50
144 Tony Amonte	.50	1.25
146 Jeremy Roenick	1.00	2.50
153 Sean Burke	.40	1.00
158 Mario Lemieux	2.50	6.00
164 Patrick Marleau	.60	1.50
170 Keith Tkachuk	.60	1.50
174 Nikolai Khabibulin	.60	1.50
175 Vincent Lecavalier	.60	1.50
182 Ed Belfour	.60	1.50
183 Mats Sundin	.60	1.50
190 Jason King	.40	1.00
195 Todd Bertuzzi	.60	1.50
198 Jaromir Jagr	2.00	5.00

2003-04 Beehive Gold

*1-200 VETS/15: 8X TO 20X BASIC CARDS
*201-250 ROOKIE/15: 2X TO 5X BASIC RC

2003-04 Beehive Silver

*1-200 VETS/67: 5X TO 12X BASIC CARDS
*201-250 ROOKIE/67: 1.2X TO 3X BASIC RC

2003-04 Beehive Jumbos

Card	Low	High
1 Jean-Sebastien Giguere	1.00	2.50
2 Sergei Fedorov	1.25	3.00
3 Ilya Kovalchuk	1.50	4.00
4 Joe Thornton	2.00	5.00
5 Don Cherry	3.00	8.00
6 Ron Francis	1.00	2.50
7 Jocelyn Thibault	1.00	2.50
8 Peter Forsberg	3.00	8.00
9 Rick Nash	1.50	4.00
10 Marty Turco	1.00	2.50
11 Gordie Howe	4.00	10.00
12 Steve Yzerman	4.00	10.00
13 Roberto Luongo	1.50	4.00
14 Don Cherry	2.50	6.00
15 Marian Gaborik	2.50	6.00
16 Guy Lafleur	1.50	4.00
17 Scotty Bowman	1.50	4.00
18 Martin Brodeur	4.00	10.00
19 Jason Spezza	2.00	5.00
20 Marian Hossa	1.00	2.50
21 Jeremy Roenick	1.50	4.00
22 Mario Lemieux	5.00	12.00
23 Ed Belfour	1.25	3.00
24 Markus Naslund	1.00	2.50
25 Todd Bertuzzi	1.00	2.50

2003-04 Beehive Jumbo Variations

Card	Low	High
1 Joffrey Lupul	3.00	8.00
2 Sergei Fedorov	4.00	10.00
3 Ilya Kovalchuk	4.00	10.00
4 Joe Thornton	5.00	12.00
5 Don Cherry	8.00	20.00
6 Eric Staal	4.00	10.00
7 Tuomo Ruutu	2.50	6.00
8 Peter Forsberg	8.00	20.00
9 Rick Nash	4.00	10.00
10 Marty Turco	2.50	6.00
11 Gordie Howe	10.00	25.00
12 Jiri Hudler	4.00	10.00
13 Nathan Horton	4.00	10.00
14 Don Cherry	8.00	20.00
15 Marian Gaborik	6.00	15.00
16 Guy Lafleur	4.00	10.00
17 Scotty Bowman	4.00	10.00
18 Martin Brodeur	10.00	25.00
19 Jason Spezza	3.00	8.00
20 Marian Hossa	3.00	8.00
21 Joni Pitkanen	3.00	8.00
22 Marc-Andre Fleury	8.00	20.00

23 Ed Belfour 3.00 8.00
24 Markus Naslund 3.00 8.00
25 Todd Bertuzzi 3.00 8.00

2003-04 Beehive Jumbo Jerseys

BH1 Jeremy Roenick 6.00 15.00
BH2 Marty Turco 5.00 12.00
BH3 Mario Lemieux 40.00 100.00
BH4 Todd Bertuzzi 5.00 12.00
BH5 Jarome Iginla 6.00 15.00
BH6 Dominik Hasek 10.00 25.00
BH7 Chris Drury 5.00 12.00
BH8 Jose Theodore 8.00 20.00
BH9 Joe Sakic 8.00 20.00
BH10 Mike Modano 6.00 15.00
BH11 Mats Sundin 6.00 15.00
BH12 Sergei Fedorov 6.00 15.00
BH13 Keith Tkachuk 6.00 15.00
BH14 Ed Belfour 6.00 15.00
BH15 Sean Burke 5.00 12.00
BH16 Tony Amonte 5.00 12.00
BH17 Joe Thornton 8.00 20.00
BH18 Vincent Lecavalier 5.00 12.00
BH19 Roberto Luongo 8.00 20.00
BH20 Steve Yzerman 15.00 40.00
BH21 Jason Spezza 8.00 20.00
BH22 Rick Nash 8.00 20.00

2003-04 Beehive Jerseys

JT1 Mike Modano 5.00 12.00
JT2 Zigmund Palffy 3.00 8.00
JT3 Jason Spezza 5.00 12.00
JT4 Tony Amonte 3.00 8.00
JT5 Jeremy Roenick 5.00 12.00
JT6 Vincent Lecavalier 3.00 8.00
JT7 Marian Gaborik 8.00 20.00
JT8 Alexei Yashin 3.00 8.00
JT9 Ilya Kovalchuk 5.00 12.00
JT10 Keith Tkachuk 4.00 10.00
JT11 Markus Naslund 4.00 10.00
JT12 Bill Guerin 3.00 8.00
JT13 Brendan Shanahan 4.00 10.00
JT14 Dominik Hasek 6.00 15.00
JT15 Jose Theodore 5.00 12.00
JT16 Eric Lindros 4.00 10.00
JT17 Martin Brodeur 10.00 25.00
JT18 Patrick Lalime 3.00 8.00
JT19 Rick Nash 5.00 12.00
JT20 Ryan Smyth 3.00 8.00
JT21 Marty Turco 3.00 8.00
JT22 Roberto Luongo 5.00 12.00
JT23 Jean-Sebastien Giguere 3.00 8.00
JT24 Ed Belfour 6.00 15.00
JT25 Joe Thornton 5.00 12.00
JT26 Todd Bertuzzi 4.00 10.00
JT27 Steve Yzerman 10.00 25.00
JT28 Saku Koivu 4.00 10.00
JT29 Jarome Iginla 5.00 12.00
JT30 Chris Drury 3.00 8.00
JT31 Joe Sakic 8.00 20.00
JT32 Paul Kariya 4.00 10.00
JT33 Marian Hossa 4.00 10.00
JT34 Doug Weight 3.00 8.00
JT35 Sergei Fedorov 5.00 12.00
JT36 Mats Sundin 4.00 10.00
JT37 Mario Lemieux 12.50 30.00
JT38 Teemu Selanne 4.00 10.00
JT39 Jocelyn Thibault 4.00 10.00
JT40 Ron Francis 3.00 8.00

2003-04 Beehive Jersey Autographs

SJ1 Martin Brodeur/20 75.00 125.00
SJ2 Saku Koivu/25 30.00 80.00
SJ3 Ilya Kovalchuk/25 30.00 80.00
SJ4 Eric Lindros/25 60.00 120.00
SJ5 Patrick Roy/25 100.00 200.00
SJ6 Jason Spezza/25 50.00 125.00
SJ7 Marty Turco/25 20.00 50.00
SJ8 Jarome Iginla/30 20.00 50.00
SJ10 Marian Hossa/50 20.00 50.00
SJ12 Roberto Luongo/50 20.00 50.00
SJ13 Zigmund Palffy/25 15.00 40.00
SJ14 Jeremy Roenick/50 25.00 60.00
SJ15 Jose Theodore/25 25.00 60.00
SJ16 Joe Thornton/50 40.00 100.00
SJ17 David Aebischer/50 15.00 40.00
SJ18 Todd Bertuzzi/75 15.00 40.00
SJ19 Mike Comrie/75 12.50 30.00
SJ20 Marcel Hossa/75 12.50 30.00
SJ21 Markus Naslund/75 15.00 40.00
SJ22 Rick DiPietro/50 25.00 60.00
SJ23 Scott Hartnell/50 15.00 40.00
SJ24 Ales Hemsky/90 12.00 30.00
SJ25 Henrik Zetterberg/90 15.00 40.00

2003-04 Beehive Signatures

RF3 Jason Spezza/25 75.00 150.00
RF6 Jose Theodore/25 30.00 80.00
RF7 David Aebischer/25 15.00 40.00
RF8 Marian Gaborik/25 15.00 40.00
RF9 Jarome Iginla/25 50.00 125.00
RF10 Marian Hossa/50 25.00 60.00
RF11 Joe Thornton/100 15.00 40.00
RF12 Anson Carter/25 15.00 40.00
RF13 Chuck Kobasew/50 12.50 30.00
RF14 Roberto Luongo/25 20.00 50.00
RF15 Jeremy Roenick/25 50.00 125.00
RF16 Mike Comrie/100 8.00 20.00
RF17 Markus Naslund/100 12.50 30.00
RF18 Rick DiPietro/50 25.00 60.00
RF19 Henrik Zetterberg/100 15.00 40.00
RF20 Jared Aulin/50 12.50 30.00
RF21 Rick Nash/25 25.00 60.00
RF22 Owen Nolan/25 15.00 40.00
RF23 Marcel Hossa/50 6.00 15.00
RF24 Scott Hartnell/90 12.50 30.00
RF25 Ales Hemsky/75 6.00 15.00

2003-04 Beehive Sticks Beige Border

BE1 Jarome Iginla 5.00 12.00
BE2 Jean-Sebastien Giguere 2.50 6.00
BE3 Keith Tkachuk 4.00 10.00
BE4 Jocelyn Thibault 2.50 6.00
BE5 Martin Brodeur 10.00 25.00
BE6 Joe Sakic 8.00 20.00
BE7 Mike Modano 6.00 15.00
BE8 Johan Hedberg 2.50 6.00
BE9 Mats Sundin 4.00 10.00
BE10 Brendan Shanahan 4.00 10.00
BE11 Owen Nolan 2.50 6.00
BE12 Marc Denis 2.50 6.00
BE13 Teemu Selanne 4.00 10.00
BE14 Curtis Joseph 4.00 10.00
BE15 Patrik Stefan 2.50 6.00
BE16 Mike Comrie 2.50 6.00
BE17 Milan Hejduk 6.00 15.00
BE18 Ed Jovanovski 2.50 6.00
BE19 Luc Robitaille 2.50 6.00
BE20 Olaf Kolzig 2.50 6.00
BE21 Mika Noronen 2.50 6.00
BE22 Jeremy Roenick 6.00 15.00
BE23 Mike Dunham 2.50 6.00
BE24 Rick DiPietro 2.50 6.00
BE25 Peter Bondra 2.50 6.00
BE26 Ed Belfour 4.00 10.00
BE27 Felix Potvin 4.00 10.00
BE28 Peter Forsberg 10.00 25.00
BE29 Gordie Howe 10.00 25.00
BE30 Brian Boucher 2.50 6.00
BE31 Brett Hull 6.00 15.00
BE32 Sean Burke 2.50 6.00
BE33 Ilya Kovalchuk 6.00 15.00
BE34 Roman Cechmanek 2.50 6.00
BE35 Jaromir Jagr 6.00 15.00
BE36 David Aebischer 2.50 6.00
BE37 Dominik Hasek 8.00 20.00
BE38 Tommy Salo 2.50 6.00
BE39 Guy Lafleur 2.50 6.00
BE40 Jose Theodore 5.00 12.00
BE41 Marcel Dionne 2.50 6.00
BE42 Vincent Lecavalier 4.00 10.00

2003-04 Beehive Sticks Blue Border

BL1 Sean Burke 3.00 8.00
BL2 Zigmund Palffy 3.00 8.00
BL3 Simon Gagne 5.00 12.00
BL4 Justin Williams 3.00 8.00
BL5 Jean-Sebastien Giguere 4.00 10.00
BL6 Chris Chelios 5.00 12.00
BL7 John LeClair 5.00 12.00
BL8 Rick DiPietro 3.00 8.00
BL9 Peter Bondra 3.00 8.00
BL10 Pavel Bure 8.00 20.00
BL11 Mark Messier 6.00 15.00
BL12 Olaf Kolzig 3.00 8.00
BL13 Martin Brodeur 12.50 30.00
BL14 Felix Potvin 6.00 15.00
BL15 Owen Nolan 3.00 8.00
BL16 Patrik Stefan 3.00 8.00
BL17 Jaromir Jagr 8.00 20.00
BL18 Tommy Salo 3.00 8.00
BL19 Mark Recchi 3.00 8.00
BL20 Ed Belfour 5.00 12.00
BL21 Roman Cechmanek 3.00 8.00

2003-04 Beehive Sticks Red Border

RE1 Dominik Hasek 10.00 25.00
RE2 Brett Hull 8.00 20.00
RE3 Peter Forsberg 12.50 30.00
RE4 Jose Theodore 6.00 15.00
RE5 Marc Denis 3.00 8.00
RE6 Mike Modano 10.00 25.00
RE7 Mark Messier 6.00 15.00
RE8 Mats Sundin 5.00 12.00
RE9 Brendan Shanahan 5.00 12.00
RE10 Eric Lindros 5.00 12.00
RE11 Ron Francis 6.00 15.00
RE12 Jeremy Roenick 8.00 20.00
RE13 Ilya Kovalchuk 8.00 20.00
RE14 Martin Brodeur 12.50 30.00
RE15 Joe Sakic 10.00 25.00
RE16 Keith Tkachuk 5.00 12.00
RE17 David Aebischer 3.00 8.00
RE18 Marcel Dionne 3.00 8.00
RE19 Owen Nolan 3.00 8.00
RE20 Sergei Fedorov 8.00 20.00
RE21 Gordie Howe 12.50 30.00

2003-04 Beehive UD Promos

*UD PROMOS: 1X TO 2.5X BASIC CARDS
132 Mark Messier 1.50 4.00

2005-06 Beehive

COMP.SET w/o SP's (90) 10.00 25.00
1 Teemu Selanne .60 1.50
2 Joffrey Lupul .20 .50
3 Jean-Sebastien Giguere .30 .75
4 Ilya Kovalchuk .30 .75
5 Kari Lehtonen .25 .60
6 Marian Hossa .30 .75
7 Patrice Bergeron .40 1.00
8 Sergei Samsonov .25 .60
9 Andrew Raycroft .25 .60
10 Brian Leetch .25 .60
11 Glen Murray .25 .60
12 Chris Drury .25 .60
13 Daniel Briere .30 .75
14 Jarome Iginla .40 1.00
15 Miikka Kiprusoff .30 .75
16 Tony Amonte .25 .60
17 Erik Cole .20 .50
18 Eric Staal .40 1.00
19 Nikolai Khabibulin .30 .75
20 Tuomo Ruutu .20 .50
21 Eric Daze .25 .60
22 Joe Sakic .60 1.50
23 Milan Hejduk .25 .60
24 Alex Tanguay .30 .75
25 Rob Blake .30 .75
26 Rick Nash .30 .75
27 Sergei Fedorov .50 1.25
28 Mike Modano .50 1.25
29 Bill Guerin .30 .75
30 Marty Turco .30 .75
31 Steve Yzerman .75 2.00
32 Brendan Shanahan .30 .75
33 Pavel Datsyuk .50 1.25
34 Nicklas Lidstrom .30 .75
35 Ty Conklin .25 .60
36 Chris Pronger .30 .75
37 Ryan Smyth .25 .60
38 Roberto Luongo .50 1.25
39 Jay Bouwmeester .20 .50
40 Olli Jokinen .30 .75
41 Luc Robitaille .30 .75
42 Jeremy Roenick .50 1.25
43 Pavol Demitra .40 1.00
44 Marian Gaborik .30 .75
45 Dwayne Roloson .25 .60
46 Saku Koivu .30 .75
47 Jose Theodore .30 .75
48 Michael Ryder .25 .60
49 Mike Ribeiro .20 .50
50 Paul Kariya .30 .75
51 Tomas Vokoun .25 .60
52 Martin Brodeur .75 2.00
53 Patrik Elias .30 .75
54 Scott Gomez .25 .60
55 Alexander Mogilny .25 .60
56 Miroslav Satan .25 .60
57 Alexei Yashin .25 .60
58 Rick DiPietro .25 .60
59 Jaromir Jagr 1.00 2.50
60 Dominik Hasek .50 1.25
61 Dany Heatley .25 .60
62 Martin Havlat .30 .75
63 Jason Spezza .30 .75
64 Daniel Alfredsson .30 .75
65 Peter Forsberg .60 1.50
66 Robert Esche .25 .60
67 Keith Primeau .25 .60
68 Simon Gagne .30 .75
69 Curtis Joseph .40 1.00
70 Shane Doan .25 .60
71 Mario Lemieux 1.25 3.00
72 Mark Recchi .40 1.00
73 Zigmund Palffy .30 .75
74 Joe Thornton .50 1.25
75 Patrick Marleau .30 .75
76 Jonathan Cheechoo .25 .60
77 Evgeni Nabokov .25 .60
78 Doug Weight .30 .75
79 Keith Tkachuk .30 .75
80 Martin St. Louis .30 .75
81 Vincent Lecavalier .30 .75
82 Brad Richards .30 .75
83 Mats Sundin .30 .75
84 Ed Belfour .30 .75
85 Eric Lindros .50 1.25
86 Jason Allison .25 .60
87 Markus Naslund .30 .75
88 Brendan Morrison .20 .50
89 Todd Bertuzzi .30 .75
90 Olaf Kolzig .30 .75
91 Brandon Bochenski RC 1.50 4.00
92 Patrick Eaves RC 1.50 4.00
93 Derek Boogaard RC 2.50 6.00
94 Brad Richardson RC 1.50 4.00
95 Ole-Kristian Tollefsen RC 1.25 3.00
96 Dennis Wideman RC 1.00 2.50
97 Lee Stempniak RC 1.50 4.00
98 Maxim Lapierre RC 1.50 4.00
99 Andrei Kostitsyn RC 2.00 5.00
100 Rob McVicar RC 1.25 3.00
101 Sidney Crosby RC UER
Typo 'talent it tow' 25.00 50.00
102 Alexander Ovechkin RC 80.00 200.00
103 Jeff Carter RC 2.50 6.00
104 Corey Perry RC 5.00 12.00
105 Rostislav Olesz RC 1.25 3.00
106 Gilbert Brule RC 1.50 4.00
107 Zach Parise RC 4.00 10.00
108 Alexander Perezhogin RC 1.25 3.00
109 Hannu Toivonen RC 1.50 4.00
110 Wojtek Wolski RC 1.25 3.00
111 Jeff Woywitka RC 1.00 2.50
112 Alexander Steen RC 2.50 6.00
113 Ryan Getzlaf RC 4.00 10.00
114 Dion Phaneuf RC 2.50 6.00
115 Ryan Suter RC 2.00 5.00
116 Mike Richards RC 3.00 8.00
117 Cam Ward RC 2.50 6.00
118 Robert Nilsson RC 1.50 4.00
119 Jim Howard RC 4.00 10.00
120 Thomas Vanek RC 3.00 8.00
121 Braydon Coburn RC 1.50 4.00
122 Brent Seabrook RC 3.00 8.00
123 Peter Budaj RC 2.00 5.00
124 Yann Danis RC 1.25 3.00
125 David Leneveu RC 1.25 3.00
126 Henrik Lundqvist RC 8.00 20.00
127 Johan Franzen RC 2.50 6.00
128 Andrej Meszaros RC 1.25 3.00
129 Jussi Jokinen RC 1.50 4.00
130 Rene Bourque RC 1.50 4.00
131 Jay McClement RC 1.00 2.50
132 Keith Ballard RC 1.25 3.00
133 Evgeny Artyukhin RC 1.25 3.00
134 R.J. Umberger RC 1.50 4.00
135 Petteri Nokelainen RC 1.00 2.50
136 Petr Prucha RC 1.50 4.00
137 Ryan Whitney RC 1.50 4.00
138 Matt Foy RC 1.00 2.50
139 Ryane Clowe RC 2.00 5.00
140 Andrew Wozniewski RC 1.25 3.00
141 Maxime Talbot RC 1.50 4.00
142 Anthony Stewart RC 1.25 3.00
143 Andrew Alberts RC 1.00 2.50
144 Jakub Klepis RC 1.00 2.50
145 Mikko Koivu RC 2.00 5.00
146 Ryan Hollweg RC 1.00 2.50
147 Jim Slater RC 1.00 2.50
148 Chris Campoli RC 1.00 2.50
149 Jordan Sigalet RC 1.00 2.50
150 Steve Bernier RC 1.50 4.00
151 Tomas Fleischmann RC 1.50 4.00
152 Matt Jones RC 1.00 2.50
153 Barry Tallackson RC 1.25 3.00
154 Ben Eager RC 1.25 3.00
155 Danny Richmond RC 1.00 2.50
156 Andrew Ladd RC 2.00 5.00
157 Jeremy Colliton RC 1.00 2.50
158 Bruno Gervais RC 1.00 2.50
159 Jeff Tambellini RC 1.00 2.50
160 Gerald Coleman RC 1.00 2.50
161 Paul Ranger RC 1.00 2.50
162 Staffan Kronwall RC 1.00 2.50
163 Dustin Penner RC 1.50 4.00
164 Kyle Brodziak RC 1.00 2.50
165 Greg Jacina RC 1.00 2.50
166 Erik Christensen RC 1.00 2.50
167 Kyle Quincey RC 1.25 3.00
168 Chris Thorburn RC 1.25 3.00
169 Christoph Schubert RC 1.00 2.50
170 Dimitri Patzold RC 1.00 2.50
171 Junior Lessard RC 1.00 2.50
172 Vojtech Polak RC 1.00 2.50
173 Adam Berkhoel RC 1.25 3.00
174 Cam Barker RC 1.25 3.00
175 Kevin Dallman RC 1.25 3.00
176 Milan Jurcina RC 1.25 3.00
177 Brad Winchester RC 1.50 4.00
178 George Parros RC 1.00 2.50
179 Al Montoya RC 1.50 4.00
180 Brett Lebda RC 1.00 2.50
181 Joe Sakic .60 1.50
182 Alex Tanguay .75 2.00
183 Milan Hejduk .60 1.50
184 Rick Nash .75 2.00
185 Mike Modano 1.25 3.00
186 Bill Guerin .75 2.00
187 Steve Yzerman 2.00 5.00
188 Brendan Shanahan .75 2.00
189 Chris Pronger .75 2.00
190 Roberto Luongo 1.25 3.00
191 Jeremy Roenick 1.25 3.00
192 Luc Robitaille .75 2.00
193 Marian Gaborik .75 2.00
194 Saku Koivu .75 2.00
195 Jose Theodore .75 2.00
196 Paul Kariya .75 2.00
197 Martin Brodeur 2.00 5.00
198 Patrik Elias .75 2.00
199 Miroslav Satan .60 1.50
200 Alexei Yashin .60 1.50
201 Jaromir Jagr 2.50 6.00
202 Dominik Hasek 1.25 3.00
203 Dany Heatley .60 1.50
204 Jason Spezza .75 2.00
205 Peter Forsberg 1.50 4.00
206 Keith Primeau .60 1.50
207 Curtis Joseph 1.00 2.50
208 Brett Hull 1.50 4.00
209 Mario Lemieux 3.00 8.00
210 Evgeni Nabokov .60 1.50
211 Jonathan Cheechoo .60 1.50
212 Keith Tkachuk .75 2.00
213 Doug Weight .75 2.00
214 Martin St. Louis .75 2.00
215 Vincent Lecavalier .75 2.00
216 Mats Sundin .75 2.00
217 Ed Belfour .75 2.00
218 Eric Lindros 1.25 3.00
219 Markus Naslund .75 2.00
220 Olaf Kolzig .75 2.00
221 Mike Bossy .75 2.00
222 Wayne Cashman .50 1.25
223 Gerry Cheevers .75 2.00
224 Bobby Clarke 1.25 3.00
225 Phil Esposito 1.25 3.00
226 Tony Esposito 1.25 3.00
227 Grant Fuhr 1.25 3.00
228 Glenn Hall .75 2.00
229 Jari Kurri .75 2.00
230 Guy Lafleur 1.00 2.50
231 Lanny McDonald .75 2.00
232 Gilbert Perreault .75 2.00
233 Jean Beliveau .75 2.00
234 Johnny Bucyk .75 2.00
235 Gordie Howe 2.50 6.00
236 Wayne Gretzky 5.00 12.00
237 Bernie Geoffrion .60 1.50
238 Red Kelly .75 2.00
239 Stan Mikita 1.00 2.50
240 Bryan Trottier .75 2.00
241 Jean-Sebastien Giguere .75 2.00
242 Sergei Fedorov 1.25 3.00
243 Teemu Selanne 1.50 4.00
244 Ilya Kovalchuk .75 2.00
245 Marian Hossa .75 2.00
246 Patrice Bergeron .75 2.00
247 Joe Thornton 1.25 3.00
248 Jarome Iginla 1.00 2.50
249 Miikka Kiprusoff .75 2.00
250 Nikolai Khabibulin .75 2.00

2005-06 Beehive Beige

*1-90 VETS: 5X TO 12X BASIC CARDS
*101-150 ROOKIES: 1X TO 2.5X RC

2005-06 Beehive Blue

*1-90 VETS: 4X TO 10X BASIC CARDS
*101-150 ROOKIES: .6X TO 1.5X RC

2005-06 Beehive Gold

*1-90 VETS: 5X TO 12X BASIC CARDS
*101-150 ROOKIES: 1X TO 2.5X RC
101 Sidney Crosby UER
Typo 'talent it tow' 80.00 200.00

2005-06 Beehive Red

*1-90 VETS: 2X TO 5X BASIC CARDS
*101-150 ROOKIES: .4X TO 1X BASIC RC
101 Sidney Crosby 40.00 100.00

2005-06 Beehive Rookie Jumbos

COMPLETE SET (5) 20.00 40.00
COMMON CARD (R1-R5) 1.50 4.00
R1 Sidney Crosby 10.00 25.00
R2 Alexander Ovechkin 15.00 40.00
R3 Jeff Carter 2.50 6.00
R4 Alexander Perezhogin 1.50 4.00
R5 Corey Perry 2.50 6.00

2005-06 Beehive Matte

*1-90 VETS: 6X TO 15X BASIC CARDS
*91-180 ROOKIES: 1.5X TO 4X
101 Sidney Crosby UER
Typo 'talent it tow' 400.00 700.00

2005-06 Beehive Matted Materials

MMAF Adam Foote 3.00 8.00
MMAH Ales Hemsky 4.00 10.00
MMAK Alex Kovalev 4.00 10.00
MMAR Andrew Raycroft 4.00 10.00
MMAY Alexei Yashin 4.00 10.00
MMBG Bill Guerin 5.00 12.00
MMBM Brendan Morrison 3.00 8.00
MMBR Brad Richards 5.00 12.00
MMBW Brendan Witt 3.00 8.00
MMCD Chris Drury 4.00 10.00
MMCJ Curtis Joseph 6.00 15.00
MMCO Chris Osgood 5.00 12.00
MMDA Daniel Alfredsson 5.00 12.00
MMDB Dustin Brown 5.00 12.00
MMDC Dan Cloutier 4.00 10.00
MMDE Pavol Demitra 6.00 15.00
MMDH Dany Heatley 4.00 10.00
MMDR Dwayne Roloson 4.00 10.00
MMDW Doug Weight 5.00 12.00
MMEL Eric Lindros 8.00 20.00
MMGA Mathieu Garon 4.00 10.00
MMGI Brian Gionta 3.00 8.00
MMGL Guy Lafleur 6.00 15.00
MMGM Glen Murray 4.00 10.00
MMGO Scott Gomez 4.00 10.00
MMHJ Milan Hejduk 4.00 10.00
MMHO Marian Hossa 5.00 12.00
MMHS Henrik Sedin 6.00 15.00
MMHZ Henrik Zetterberg 6.00 15.00
MMIK Ilya Kovalchuk 5.00 12.00
MMJB Jay Bouwmeester 3.00 8.00
MMJG Jean-Sebastien Giguere 5.00 12.00
MMJO Jose Theodore 5.00 12.00
MMJR Jeremy Roenick 8.00 20.00
MMJS Jason Spezza 5.00 12.00
MMJT Joe Thornton 8.00 20.00
MMJW Jason Williams 3.00 8.00
MMKP Keith Primeau 4.00 10.00
MMKT Keith Tkachuk 5.00 12.00
MMLN Ladislav Nagy 3.00 8.00
MMLR Luc Robitaille 5.00 12.00
MMLU Joffrey Lupul 3.00 8.00
MMMB Martin Brodeur 8.00 20.00
MMMC Bryan McCabe 3.00 8.00
MMMD Marc Denis 4.00 10.00
MMMF Manny Fernandez 3.00 8.00
MMMG Martin Gerber 4.00 10.00
MMMH Marcel Hossa 3.00 8.00
MMMI Milan Michalek 3.00 8.00
MMMK Miikka Kiprusoff 5.00 12.00
MMML Mario Lemieux 20.00 50.00
MMMM Mike Modano 8.00 20.00
MMMN Markus Naslund 8.00 20.00
MMMP Mark Parrish 3.00 8.00
MMMR Michael Ryder 4.00 10.00
MMMS Mats Sundin 5.00 12.00
MMMT Marty Turco 5.00 12.00
MMMW Brenden Morrow 4.00 10.00
MMNA Nik Antropov 4.00 10.00
MMNH Nathan Horton 5.00 12.00
MMNK Nikolai Khabibulin 5.00 12.00
MMOJ Olli Jokinen 5.00 12.00
MMPA Patrik Elias 5.00 12.00
MMPB Pierre-Marc Bouchard 5.00 12.00
MMPD Pavel Datsyuk 8.00 20.00
MMPE Michael Peca 4.00 10.00
MMPF Peter Forsberg 10.00 25.00
MMRB Rob Blake 5.00 12.00
MMRE Robert Esche 4.00 10.00
MMRM Ryan Miller 5.00 12.00
MMRN Rick Nash 5.00 12.00
MMSA Joe Sakic 10.00 25.00
MMSC Sidney Crosby 15.00 40.00
MMSF Sergei Fedorov 8.00 20.00
MMSG Simon Gagne 5.00 12.00
MMSK Saku Koivu 5.00 12.00
MMSL Martin St. Louis 5.00 12.00
MMSS Sergei Samsonov 4.00 10.00
MMST Matt Stajan 3.00 8.00
MMSY Steve Yzerman 10.00 25.00
MMTB Todd Bertuzzi 5.00 12.00
MMTC Ty Conklin 4.00 10.00
MMWG Wayne Gretzky 30.00 60.00

2005-06 Beehive Matted Materials Remarkable

UNLISTED STARS 12.00 30.00
RMBM Brendan Morrison 12.00 30.00
RMBR Brad Richards 10.00 25.00
RMCO Chris Osgood 15.00 40.00
RMDH Dany Heatley 25.00 60.00
RMDW Doug Weight 12.00 30.00
RMGL Guy Lafleur 30.00 80.00
RMHO Marian Hossa 12.00 30.00
RMHZ Henrik Zetterberg 15.00 40.00
RMIK Ilya Kovalchuk 40.00 100.00
RMJO Jose Theodore 15.00 40.00
RMJR Jeremy Roenick 15.00 40.00
RMJS Jason Spezza 25.00 60.00
RMJT Joe Thornton 12.50 30.00
RMLR Luc Robitaille 25.00 60.00
RMMB Martin Brodeur 40.00 100.00
RMMH Marcel Hossa 15.00 40.00
RMMN Markus Naslund 25.00 60.00
RMMP Mark Parrish 12.00 30.00
RMPE Michael Peca 12.00 30.00
RMRB Rob Blake 15.00 40.00
RMRN Rick Nash 25.00 60.00
RMSC Sidney Crosby 400.00 700.00
RMSL Martin St. Louis 20.00 50.00
RMTB Todd Bertuzzi 15.00 40.00
RMWG Wayne Gretzky 250.00 600.00

2005-06 Beehive PhotoGraphs

PGAO Alexander Ovechkin 200.00 500.00
PGBH Bobby Hull 40.00 80.00
PGCO Corey Perry 4.00 10.00
PGCP Chris Pronger 10.00 25.00
PGDW Doug Weight 8.00 20.00
PGES Eric Staal 8.00 20.00
PGGH Gordie Howe 50.00 125.00
PGGL Guy Lafleur 30.00 80.00
PGJC Jeff Carter 8.00 20.00
PGJI Jarome Iginla 15.00 40.00
PGJS Jason Spezza 12.00 30.00
PGJT Joe Thornton 8.00 20.00
PGLA Guy Lapointe 8.00 20.00
PGMB Mike Bossy 10.00 25.00
PGMD Marcel Dionne 10.00 25.00
PGMM Mike Modano 12.00 30.00
PGMN Markus Naslund 8.00 20.00
PGMT Marty Turco 6.00 15.00
PGPE Phil Esposito SP 40.00 80.00
PGRB Ray Bourque 30.00 80.00
PGRN Rick Nash 8.00 20.00
PGSC Sidney Crosby 100.00 200.00
PGSL Martin St. Louis 8.00 20.00
PGTE Tony Esposito 15.00 40.00
PGWG Wayne Gretzky SP 250.00 600.00

2005-06 Beehive Signature Scrapbook

SSAA Andrew Alberts 3.00 8.00
SSAM Andrej Meszaros 3.00 8.00
SSAO Alexander Ovechkin 1200.00 3000.00
SSAP Alexander Perezhogin 6.00 15.00
SSAR Andrew Raycroft 6.00 15.00
SSAS Anthony Stewart 8.00 20.00
SSBA Matthew Barnaby 3.00 8.00
SSBB Brandon Bochenski 3.00 8.00
SSBC Bobby Clarke 15.00 40.00
SSBE Steve Bernier 8.00 20.00
SSBM Brenden Morrow 8.00 20.00
SSBO Mike Bossy SP 20.00 50.00
SSBP Brad Park 6.00 15.00
SSBR Brad Richards 6.00 15.00
SSBS Borje Salming 8.00 20.00
SSBU Peter Budaj 6.00 15.00
SSCB Cam Barker 3.00 8.00
SSCC Chris Campoli 3.00 8.00
SSCH Jonathan Cheechoo 8.00 20.00
SSCK Chris Kunitz 6.00 15.00
SSCL Ryane Clowe 5.00 12.00
SSCN Craig Conroy 3.00 8.00
SSCO Braydon Coburn 10.00 25.00
SSCP Corey Perry 8.00 20.00
SSCS Cory Stillman 3.00 8.00
SSCW Cam Ward 15.00 40.00
SSDA Daniel Alfredsson 8.00 20.00
SSDC Don Cherry 12.00 30.00
SSDF Dan Fritsche 3.00 8.00
SSDH Dany Heatley SP 20.00 50.00
SSDI Dickie Moore 6.00 15.00
SSDK Duncan Keith 3.00 8.00
SSDL David Leneveu 8.00 20.00
SSDM Darren McCarty 6.00 15.00
SSDP Dion Phaneuf 12.00 30.00
SSDS Derek Sanderson 8.00 20.00
SSDT Dave Taylor 5.00 12.00
SSEA Patrick Eaves 6.00 15.00
SSED Eric Daze 3.00 8.00
SSFC Fred Cusick 8.00 25.00
SSFT Fedor Tyutin 3.00 8.00
SSGB Gilbert Brule 5.00 12.00
SSGH Gordie Howe SP 60.00 150.00
SSGL Guy Lafleur SP 50.00 100.00
SSGP Gilbert Perreault 10.00 25.00
SSHO Marian Hossa 8.00 20.00
SSHV Martin Havlat 10.00 25.00
SSHZ Henrik Zetterberg 10.00 25.00
SSJB Jay Bouwmeester SP 15.00 40.00
SSJC Jeff Carter 10.00 25.00
SSJF Johan Franzen 8.00 20.00
SSJH Jim Howard 25.00 60.00
SSJI Jarome Iginla SP 10.00 25.00
SSJM Jay McClement 3.00 8.00
SSJO Jeff O'Neill 3.00 8.00
SSJR Jeremy Roenick 30.00 80.00
SSJS Jason Spezza SP 30.00 60.00
SSJT Joe Thornton SP 20.00 40.00
SSJV Josef Vasicek 3.00 8.00
SSKM Ken Morrow 3.00 8.00
SSKN Kevin Nastiuk 6.00 15.00
SSKP Keith Primeau SP 8.00 20.00
SSLM Lanny McDonald 5.00 12.00
SSLR Luc Robitaille SP 25.00 60.00
SSLS Lee Stempniak 3.00 8.00
SSLU Roberto Luongo SP 25.00 60.00
SSMB Martin Brodeur SP 75.00 150.00
SSMC Mike Cammalleri 8.00 20.00
SSMD Marcel Dionne SP 20.00 50.00
SSMG Marian Gaborik SP 30.00 60.00
SSMH Marcel Hossa 3.00 8.00
SSMJ Milan Jurcina 3.00 8.00
SSMK Mikko Koivu 8.00 20.00
SSMM Mike Modano SP 20.00 50.00
SSMN Markus Naslund SP 10.00 25.00
SSMP Michael Peca 3.00 8.00
SSMR Mike Ribeiro SP 8.00 20.00
SSMS Marco Sturm 3.00 8.00
SSMT Marty Turco 6.00 15.00
SSMU Larry Murphy 3.00 8.00
SSNH Nathan Horton 4.00 10.00
SSNK Nikolai Khabibulin 8.00 20.00
SSNY Michael Nylander 3.00 8.00
SSNZ Nikolai Zherdev 6.00 15.00
SSON Owen Nolan 10.00 25.00
SSPB Patrice Bergeron SP 10.00 25.00
SSPE Phil Esposito SP 25.00 50.00
SSPN Petteri Nokelainen 3.00 8.00
SSPP Petr Prucha 8.00 20.00
SSRB Rob Blake 10.00 25.00
SSRE Robert Esche 3.00 8.00
SSRI Mike Richards 10.00 25.00
SSRL Reggie Leach 5.00 12.00
SSRM Ryan Miller 8.00 20.00
SSRN Rick Nash SP 15.00 40.00
SSRS Ryan Smyth 12.00 30.00
SSRV Rogie Vachon 8.00 20.00
SSRW Ryan Whitney 6.00 15.00
SSRY Michael Ryder 6.00 15.00
SSSB Scotty Bowman SP 20.00 40.00
SSSC Sidney Crosby SP 400.00 1000.00
SSSD Shane Doan 3.00 8.00
SSSE Brent Seabrook 5.00 12.00
SSSG Simon Gagne 10.00 25.00
SSSL Martin St. Louis SP 10.00 25.00
SSST Alexander Steen 15.00 30.00
SSSZ Sergei Zubov 3.00 8.00
SSTA Tyler Arnason 3.00 8.00
SSTB Todd Bertuzzi SP 10.00 25.00
SSTE Tony Esposito SP 20.00 40.00
SSTO Terry O'Reilly 8.00 20.00
SSTV Thomas Vanek 20.00 50.00
SSVP Vaclav Prospal 3.00 8.00
SSWC Wayne Cashman 6.00 15.00
SSYD Yann Danis 6.00 15.00
SSZC Zdeno Chara 10.00 25.00
SSZP Zach Parise 8.00 20.00

2006-07 Beehive

COMPLETE SET w/o SPs (100) 10.00 25.00
1 Alexander Ovechkin 1.50 4.00
2 Olaf Kolzig .40 1.00
3 Markus Naslund .40 1.00
4 Roberto Luongo .60 1.50
5 Mats Sundin .40 1.00
6 Michael Peca .30 .75
7 Alexander Steen .25 .60
8 Andrew Raycroft .30 .75
9 Vincent Lecavalier .40 1.00
10 Brad Richards .40 1.00
11 Martin St. Louis .40 1.00
12 Manny Legace .30 .75
13 Keith Tkachuk .40 1.00
14 Doug Weight .40 1.00
15 Joe Thornton .60 1.50
16 Patrick Marleau .40 1.00
17 Jonathan Cheechoo .30 .75
18 Vesa Toskala .30 .75
19 Sidney Crosby 1.50 4.00
20 Mark Recchi .50 1.25
21 Marc-Andre Fleury .75 2.00
22 Colby Armstrong .30 .75
23 Shane Doan .30 .75
24 Ed Jovanovski .30 .75
25 Jeremy Roenick .60 1.50
26 Owen Nolan .40 1.00
27 Peter Forsberg .75 2.00
28 Simon Gagne .40 1.00
29 Jeff Carter .30 .75
30 Joni Pitkanen .25 .60
31 Jason Spezza .40 1.00
32 Dany Heatley .30 .75
33 Martin Gerber .30 .75
34 Daniel Alfredsson .40 1.00
35 Jaromir Jagr 1.25 3.00
36 Brendan Shanahan .40 1.00
37 Henrik Lundqvist 1.00 2.50
38 Alexei Yashin .30 .75
39 Rick DiPietro .30 .75
40 Miroslav Satan .30 .75
41 Martin Brodeur 1.00 2.50
42 Patrik Elias .40 1.00
43 Brian Gionta .25 .60
44 Paul Kariya .40 1.00
45 Tomas Vokoun .30 .75
46 Jason Arnott .30 .75
47 Saku Koivu .40 1.00
48 Cristobal Huet .30 .75
49 Michael Ryder .25 .60
50 Alexei Kovalev .30 .75
51 Marian Gaborik .40 1.00
52 Manny Fernandez .25 .60
53 Pavol Demitra .50 1.25
54 Mark Parrish .25 .60
55 Alexander Frolov .25 .60
56 Rob Blake .40 1.00
57 Ed Belfour .40 1.00
58 Todd Bertuzzi .30 .75
59 Olli Jokinen .40 1.00
60 Ales Hemsky .30 .75
61 Jarret Stoll .30 .75
62 Ryan Smyth .30 .75
63 Joffrey Lupul .30 .75
64 Henrik Zetterberg .50 1.25
65 Dominik Hasek .60 1.50
66 Pavel Datsyuk .60 1.50
67 Nicklas Lidstrom .60 1.50
68 Mike Modano .60 1.50
69 Marty Turco .40 1.00
70 Eric Lindros .60 1.50
71 Rick Nash .40 1.00
72 Pascal LeClaire .30 .75
73 Gilbert Brule .30 .75
74 Sergei Fedorov .60 1.50
75 Joe Sakic .75 2.00
76 Milan Hejduk .30 .75
77 Jose Theodore .40 1.00
78 Marek Svatos .25 .60
79 Nikolai Khabibulin .40 1.00
80 Tuomo Ruutu .40 1.00
81 Martin Havlat .25 .60
82 Eric Staal .50 1.25
83 Cam Ward .40 1.00
84 Rod Brind'Amour .40 1.00
85 Jarome Iginla .50 1.25
86 Miikka Kiprusoff .50 1.25
87 Alex Tanguay .25 .60
88 Dion Phaneuf .30 .75
89 Chris Drury .30 .75
90 Ryan Miller .40 1.00
91 Patrice Bergeron .50 1.25
92 Hannu Toivonen .30 .75
93 Brad Boyes .25 .60
94 Zdeno Chara .40 1.00
95 Ilya Kovalchuk .40 1.00
96 Kari Lehtonen .30 .75
97 Marian Hossa .40 1.00
98 Teemu Selanne .75 2.00
99 Chris Pronger .40 1.00
100 Jean-Sebastien Giguere .40 1.00
101 David McKee RC 1.25 3.00
102 Ryan Shannon RC 1.25 3.00
103 Shane O'Brien RC 1.25 3.00
104 Matt Lashoff RC 1.25 3.00
105 Phil Kessel RC 4.00 10.00
106 Mark Stuart RC 1.25 3.00
107 Yan Stastny RC 1.25 3.00
108 Clarke MacArthur RC 1.50 4.00
109 Drew Stafford RC 2.00 5.00
110 Brandon Prust RC 1.25 3.00
111 Dustin Boyd RC 1.25 3.00
112 Michael Blunden RC 1.25 3.00
113 Dave Bolland RC 2.00 5.00
114 Paul Stastny RC 3.00 8.00
115 Fredrik Norrena RC 1.25 3.00
116 Loui Eriksson RC 2.50 6.00
117 Tomas Kopecky RC 1.50 4.00
118 Stefan Liv RC 1.25 3.00
119 Jeff Drouin-Deslauriers RC 1.25 3.00
120 Alexei Mikhnov RC 1.25 3.00
121 Ladislav Smid RC 1.25 3.00
122 Patrick Thoresen RC 1.25 3.00
123 Marc-Antoine Pouliot RC 1.25 3.00
124 David Booth RC 1.50 4.00
125 Alexei Kopitar RC 4.00 10.00
126 Patrick O'Sullivan RC 2.00 5.00
127 Konstantin Pushkarev RC 1.50 4.00
128 Benoit Pouliot RC 1.25 3.00
129 Mikhail Grabovski RC 2.50 6.00
130 Guillaume Latendresse RC 2.00 5.00
131 Alexander Radulov RC 2.50 6.00

132 Shea Weber RC 3.00 8.00
133 Travis Zajac RC 2.50 6.00
134 Johnny Oduya RC 2.00 5.00
135 Blake Comeau RC 2.00 5.00
136 Nigel Dawes RC 1.25 3.00
137 Jarkko Immonen RC 1.50 4.00
138 Josh Hennessy RC 1.25 3.00
139 Kelly Guard RC 1.50 4.00
140 Martin Houle RC 1.50 4.00
141 Ryan Potulny RC 1.25 3.00
142 Enver Lisin RC 1.25 3.00
143 Keith Yandle RC 3.00 8.00
144 Evgeni Malkin RC 8.00 20.00
145 Kristopher Letang RC 5.00 12.00
146 Jordan Staal RC 3.00 8.00
147 Michel Ouellet RC 1.50 4.00
148 Noah Welch RC 1.25 3.00
149 Joe Pavelski RC 6.00 15.00
150 Marc-Edouard Vlasic RC 2.00 5.00
151 Matt Carle RC 1.25 3.00
152 Marek Schwarz RC 2.00 5.00
153 Blair Jones RC 1.25 3.00
154 Ian White RC 1.50 4.00
155 Brendan Bell RC 1.25 3.00
156 Kris Newbury RC 1.25 3.00
157 Jesse Schultz RC 1.25 3.00
158 Alexander Edler RC 2.00 5.00
159 Luc Bourdon RC 2.00 5.00
160 Eric Fehr RC 2.00 5.00
161 Alexander Ovechkin 5.00 12.00
162 Roberto Luongo 2.00 5.00
163 Markus Naslund 1.25 3.00
164 Michael Peca 1.00 2.50
165 Mats Sundin 1.25 3.00
166 Vincent Lecavalier 1.25 3.00
167 Joe Thornton 2.00 5.00
168 Jonathan Cheechoo 1.00 2.50
169 Sidney Crosby 5.00 12.00
170 Mario Lemieux 5.00 12.00
171 Marc-Andre Fleury 2.50 6.00
172 Jeremy Roenick 2.00 5.00
173 Shane Doan 1.00 2.50
174 Bobby Clarke 2.00 5.00
175 Peter Forsberg 2.50 6.00
176 Simon Gagne 1.25 3.00
177 Jason Spezza 1.25 3.00
178 Dany Heatley 1.00 2.50
179 Jaromir Jagr 4.00 10.00
180 Brendan Shanahan 1.25 3.00
181 Henrik Lundqvist 3.00 8.00
182 Mike Bossy 1.25 3.00
183 Billy Smith 1.25 3.00
184 Miroslav Satan 1.00 2.50
185 Martin Brodeur 3.00 8.00
186 Patrik Elias 1.25 3.00
187 Paul Kariya 1.25 3.00
188 Tomas Vokoun 1.00 2.50
189 Patrick Roy 3.00 8.00
190 Michael Ryder .75 2.00
191 Saku Koivu 1.25 3.00
192 Guy Lafleur 1.50 4.00
193 Marian Gaborik 1.25 3.00
194 Manny Fernandez .75 2.00
195 Rob Blake 1.25 3.00
196 Alexander Frolov .75 2.00
197 Luc Robitaille 1.25 3.00
198 Marcel Dionne 1.50 4.00
199 Ed Belfour 1.25 3.00
200 Todd Bertuzzi 1.25 3.00
201 Ryan Smyth 1.00 2.50
202 Ales Hemsky 1.00 2.50
203 Grant Fuhr 2.00 5.00
204 Gordie Howe 4.00 10.00
205 Henrik Zetterberg 1.50 4.00
206 Nicklas Lidstrom 1.25 3.00
207 Dominik Hasek 2.00 5.00
208 Mike Modano 2.00 5.00
209 Marty Turco 1.25 3.00
210 Eric Lindros 2.00 5.00
211 Rick Nash 1.25 3.00
212 Pascal LeClaire 1.00 2.50
213 Joe Sakic 2.50 6.00
214 Milan Hejduk 1.00 2.50
215 Jose Theodore 1.25 3.00
216 Ray Bourque 2.00 5.00
217 Bobby Hull 2.50 6.00
218 Tony Esposito 1.25 3.00
219 Martin Havlat .75 2.00
220 Cam Ward 1.25 3.00
221 Eric Staal 1.50 4.00
222 Jarome Iginla 1.50 4.00
223 Dion Phaneuf 1.00 2.50
224 Miikka Kiprusoff 1.25 3.00
225 Alex Tanguay .75 2.00
226 Chris Drury 1.00 2.50
227 Ryan Miller 1.25 3.00
228 Patrice Bergeron 1.50 4.00
229 Cam Neely 1.25 3.00
230 Brad Boyes .75 2.00
231 Bobby Orr 5.00 12.00
232 Ilya Kovalchuk 1.25 3.00
233 Kari Lehtonen 1.00 2.50
234 Teemu Selanne 2.50 6.00
235 Chris Pronger 1.25 3.00

2006-07 Beehive Blue

*BLUE (1-100): 2.5X TO 6X
*BLUE (101-160): .6X TO 1.5X

2006-07 Beehive Gold

*GOLD (1-100): 5X TO 12X
*GOLD (101-160): 2X TO 5X
COMMON TROPHY 15.00 40.00

2006-07 Beehive Matte

*MATTE (1-100): 4X TO 10X
*MATTER (101-160): 1X TO 2.5X

2006-07 Beehive Red Facsimile Signatures

*RED (1-100): 2X TO 5X
*RED (101-160): .5X TO 1.2XI

2006-07 Beehive Wood

*STARS: 1.5X TO 4X BASE HI
*RCs: .15X TO .4X BASE HI

2006-07 Beehive 5x7 Black and White

5 Mats Sundin 2.50 6.00
17 Jonathan Cheechoo 2.00 5.00
28 Simon Gagne 2.50 6.00
45 Tomas Vokoun 2.00 5.00
47 Saku Koivu 2.50 6.00
49 Michael Ryder 1.50 4.00
51 Marian Gaborik 2.50 6.00
57 Ed Belfour 2.50 6.00
67 Nicklas Lidstrom 2.50 6.00
74 Sergei Fedorov 4.00 10.00
83 Cam Ward 2.50 6.00
85 Jarome Iginla 3.00 8.00
91 Patrice Bergeron 3.00 8.00
96 Kari Lehtonen 2.00 5.00
98 Teemu Selanne 5.00 12.00
100 Jean-Sebastien Giguere 2.50 6.00
174 Bobby Clarke 3.00 8.00
182 Mike Bossy 2.00 5.00
183 Billy Smith 2.00 5.00
192 Guy Lafleur 2.50 6.00
203 Grant Fuhr 3.00 8.00
216 Ray Bourque 3.00 8.00
217 Bobby Hull 4.00 10.00
218 Tony Esposito 2.00 5.00
229 Cam Neely 2.00 5.00

2006-07 Beehive 5x7 Cherry Wood

PT President's Trophy 12.00 30.00
SC Stanley Cup 40.00 80.00
VT Vezina Trophy 25.00 50.00
ART Art Ross Trophy 40.00 80.00
BMT Masterton Trophy 12.00 30.00
CCT Campbell Trophy 12.00 30.00
CMT Calder Trophy 12.00 30.00
CST Conn Smythe Trophy 12.00 30.00
FST Selke Trophy 12.00 30.00
JAA Jack Adams Award 12.00 30.00
JNT James Norris Trophy 15.00 40.00
KCT King Clancy Trophy 20.00 50.00
LBP Pearson Award 12.00 30.00
LBT Lady Byng Trophy 12.00 30.00
MRT Rocket Richard Trophy 12.00 30.00
PWT Prince of Wales Trophy 12.00 30.00
WJT Jennings Trophy 12.00 30.00

2006-07 Beehive 5x7 Dark Wood

3 Markus Naslund 6.00 15.00
4 Roberto Luongo 10.00 25.00
9 Vincent Lecavalier 6.00 15.00
19 Sidney Crosby 25.00 60.00
21 Marc-Andre Fleury 12.00 30.00
31 Jason Spezza 6.00 15.00
32 Dany Heatley 5.00 12.00
36 Brendan Shanahan 6.00 15.00
37 Henrik Lundqvist 15.00 40.00
44 Paul Kariya 6.00 15.00
64 Henrik Zetterberg 8.00 20.00
68 Mike Modano 10.00 25.00
71 Rick Nash 6.00 15.00
82 Eric Staal 8.00 20.00
86 Miikka Kiprusoff 6.00 15.00
90 Ryan Miller 6.00 15.00
95 Ilya Kovalchuk 6.00 15.00
105 Phil Kessel 10.00 25.00
144 Evgeni Malkin 20.00 50.00
146 Jordan Staal 8.00 20.00
170 Mario Lemieux 20.00 50.00
189 Patrick Roy 12.00 30.00
198 Marcel Dionne 6.00 15.00
204 Gordie Howe 15.00 40.00
231 Bobby Orr 20.00 50.00

2006-07 Beehive Matted Materials

MMAE David Aebischer 5.00 12.00
MMAF Alexander Frolov 4.00 10.00
MMAH Ales Hemsky 5.00 12.00
MMAO Alexander Ovechkin 25.00 60.00
MMAS Alexander Steen 4.00 10.00
MMAT Alex Tanguay 4.00 10.00
MMBB Brad Boyes 4.00 10.00
MMBO Pierre-Marc Bouchard 6.00 15.00
MMCD Chris Drury 5.00 12.00
MMCN Cam Neely 6.00 15.00
MMCP Corey Perry 10.00 25.00
MMCS Cory Stillman 4.00 10.00
MMCW Cam Ward 6.00 15.00
MMDA Daniel Alfredsson 6.00 15.00
MMDH Dany Heatley 5.00 12.00
MMDR Dwayne Roloson 5.00 12.00
MMEB Ed Belfour 6.00 15.00
MMES Eric Staal 8.00 20.00
MMHA Martin Havlat 4.00 10.00
MMHT Hannu Toivonen 5.00 12.00
MMHZ Henrik Zetterberg 8.00 20.00
MMIK Ilya Kovalchuk 6.00 15.00
MMJB Jay Bouwmeester 4.00 10.00
MMJC Jeff Carter 5.00 12.00
MMJI Jarome Iginla 8.00 20.00
MMJJ Jaromir Jagr 20.00 50.00
MMJL Joffrey Lupul 4.00 10.00
MMJS Joe Sakic 12.00 30.00
MMJT Joe Thornton 10.00 25.00
MMLE Jere Lehtinen 4.00 10.00
MMLN Ladislav Nagy 4.00 10.00
MMMB Martin Brodeur 15.00 40.00
MMMG Marian Gaborik 6.00 15.00
MMMH Milan Hejduk 5.00 12.00
MMML Mario Lemieux SP 15.00 40.00
MMMM Mike Modano 10.00 25.00
MMMP Michael Peca 5.00 12.00
MMMS Mats Sundin 6.00 15.00
MMMT Marty Turco 6.00 15.00
MMNL Nicklas Lidstrom 6.00 15.00
MMPB Patrice Bergeron 8.00 20.00
MMPF Peter Forsberg 12.00 30.00
MMPK Paul Kariya 6.00 15.00
MMPM Patrick Marleau 6.00 15.00
MMRB Ray Bourque 10.00 25.00
MMRL Roberto Luongo 10.00 25.00
MMRM Ryan Miller 6.00 15.00
MMRN Rick Nash 6.00 15.00
MMRS Ryan Smyth 5.00 12.00
MMSA Marc Savard 4.00 10.00
MMSC Sidney Crosby SP 25.00 60.00
MMSG Scott Gomez 5.00 12.00
MMSK Saku Koivu 6.00 15.00
MMSS Sergei Samsonov 5.00 12.00
MMST Jarret Stoll 5.00 12.00
MMSV Marek Svatos 4.00 10.00
MMSZ Sergei Zubov 5.00 12.00
MMTH Tomas Holmstrom 5.00 12.00
MMTV Tomas Vokoun 5.00 12.00
MMZC Zdeno Chara 6.00 15.00

2006-07 Beehive PhotoGraphs

PGAR Andrew Raycroft 8.00 20.00
PGBO Bobby Orr SP 100.00 200.00
PGDH Dominik Hasek SP 60.00 125.00
PGES Eric Staal 12.00 30.00
PGGH Gordie Howe 75.00 125.00
PGGL Guy Lafleur 12.00 30.00
PGHE Dany Heatley 8.00 20.00
PGJI Jarome Iginla 12.00 30.00
PGJT Joe Thornton 15.00 40.00
PGKL Kari Lehtonen 8.00 20.00
PGMB Martin Brodeur 50.00 100.00
PGMG Marian Gaborik 10.00 25.00
PGMM Mike Modano 15.00 40.00
PGMR Michael Ryder 6.00 15.00
PGNL Nicklas Lidstrom 15.00 30.00
PGPB Patrice Bergeron 12.00 30.00
PGPR Patrick Roy 60.00 125.00
PGRB Ray Bourque 15.00 40.00
PGRL R. Luongo EXCH 15.00 40.00
PGRN Rick Nash 10.00 25.00
PGSC Sidney Crosby 75.00 150.00
PGTE Tony Esposito 10.00 25.00
PGVL Vincent Lecavalier 10.00 25.00
PGWG W. Gretzky EXCH 200.00 500.00

2006-07 Beehive Signature Scrapbook

SSAF Alexander Frolov 3.00 8.00
SSAH Ales Hemsky 4.00 10.00
SSBB Brad Boyes 3.00 8.00
SSBG Brian Gionta 3.00 8.00
SSCA Colby Armstrong 4.00 10.00
SSCC Chris Campoli 3.00 8.00
SSCH Chris Higgins 3.00 8.00
SSCP Chris Phillips 3.00 8.00
SSDC Don Cherry 12.00 30.00
SSDL David Leneveu 4.00 10.00
SSDR Dwayne Roloson 4.00 10.00
SSDS Darryl Sittler 6.00 15.00
SSDT Darcy Tucker 4.00 10.00
SSES Eric Staal SP 20.00 50.00
SSGE Martin Gerber 4.00 10.00
SSGH Gordie Howe SP 40.00 80.00
SSHE Milan Hejduk 4.00 10.00
SSHU Cristobal Huet 4.00 10.00
SSJA Jason Arnott 4.00 10.00
SSJB Johnny Bucyk 5.00 12.00
SSJC J. Cheechoo EXCH 4.00 10.00
SSJI Jarome Iginla 6.00 15.00
SSJP Joni Pitkanen 3.00 8.00
SSJS Jarret Stoll 4.00 10.00
SSJT Jose Theodore SP 15.00 40.00
SSKD Kris Draper 3.00 8.00
SSLN Ladislav Nagy 3.00 8.00
SSMB Mike Bossy SP 15.00 40.00
SSMC Mike Cammalleri 3.00 8.00
SSMF Marc-Andre Fleury 6.00 15.00
SSMG Marian Gaborik 5.00 12.00
SSMH Martin Havlat 3.00 8.00
SSMP Michael Peca 4.00 10.00
SSMR Mike Richards 4.00 10.00
SSMS Marek Svatos 3.00 8.00
SSPA J.P. Parise 3.00 8.00
SSPB Pierre-Marc Bouchard 5.00 12.00
SSPE Patrik Elias 5.00 12.00
SSPM Patrick Marleau SP 15.00 40.00
SSPP Petr Prucha 4.00 10.00
SSPR Patrick Roy SP 75.00 150.00
SSPS Peter Stastny 4.00 10.00
SSRB Rene Bourque 3.00 8.00
SSRM Ryan Miller 5.00 12.00
SSRW Ryan Whitney 4.00 10.00
SSSA Marc Savard 3.00 8.00
SSSB Steve Bernier 3.00 8.00
SSSS Sergei Samsonov SP 12.00 30.00
SSTH Tomas Holmstrom 4.00 10.00
SSTL Ted Lindsay SP 15.00 40.00
SSTO Terry O'Reilly SP 10.00 25.00
SSVT Vesa Toskala SP 12.00 30.00
SSWG Wayne Gretzky SP 250.00 600.00

2001-02 Between the Pipes

COMPLETE SET (150) 50.00 100.00
COMP.SET w/UPDATE (170) 75.00 150.00
1 Patrick Roy 1.50 4.00
2 Jean-Sebastien Giguere .60 1.50
3 Ron Tugnutt .50 1.25
4 Rick DiPietro .50 1.25
5 Milan Hnilicka .50 1.25
6 Jean-Sebastien Aubin .50 1.25
7 Craig Billington .40 1.00
8 Byron Dafoe .50 1.25
9 Maxime Ouellet .60 1.50
10 Ed Belfour .60 1.50
11 John Grahame .50 1.25
12 Mathieu Garon .50 1.25
13 Martin Biron .50 1.25
14 Dan Cloutier .50 1.25
15 Tomas Vokoun .50 1.25
16 Arturs Irbe .50 1.25
17 Curtis Joseph .75 2.00
18 Jocelyn Thibault .50 1.25
19 Roman Cechmanek .50 1.25
20 Miikka Kiprusoff .60 1.50
21 Olaf Kolzig .60 1.50
22 Jani Hurme .50 1.25
23 David Aebischer .50 1.25
24 Damian Rhodes .50 1.25
25 Marc Denis .50 1.25
26 Marty Turco .60 1.50
27 Evgeni Nabokov .50 1.25
28 Manny Legace .50 1.25
29 Mike Dunham .50 1.25
30 Tommy Salo .50 1.25
31 Sean Burke .40 1.00
32 Andrew Raycroft .50 1.25
33 Roberto Luongo 1.00 2.50
34 Johan Holmqvist .50 1.25
35 Felix Potvin 1.00 2.50
36 Martin Brodeur 1.50 4.00
37 Gregg Naumenko .40 1.00
38 Travis Scott .40 1.00
39 Manny Fernandez .40 1.00
40 Kevin Weekes .50 1.25
41 Steve Passmore .40 1.00
42 Johan Hedberg .50 1.25
43 Patrick Lalime .50 1.25
44 Jose Theodore .60 1.50
45 Mika Noronen .40 1.00
46 Brent Johnson .50 1.25
47 Chris Mason .40 1.00
48 Mike Fountain .40 1.00
49 Jamie McLennan .40 1.00
50 Mike Richter .60 1.50
51 Eric Fichaud .40 1.00
52 Steve Shields .50 1.25
53 Rich Parent .40 1.00
54 Mike Vernon .50 1.25
55 Jason LaBarbera .40 1.00
56 Dominik Hasek 1.00 2.50
57 Dan Blackburn RC 2.00 5.00
58 Robert Esche .40 1.00
59 Joaquin Gage .40 1.00
60 Jamie Storr .50 1.25
61 Brian Boucher .50 1.25
62 Trevor Kidd .40 1.00
63 Nikolai Khabibulin .60 1.50
64 Norm Maracle .40 1.00
65 Roman Turek .50 1.25
66 Tyler Moss .40 1.00
67 Fred Brathwaite .50 1.25
68 Garth Snow .50 1.25
69 Dieter Kochan .40 1.00
70 Bob Essensa .50 1.25
71 Kirk McLean .50 1.25
72 Chris Osgood .60 1.50
73 Jeff Hackett .50 1.25
74 Stephane Fiset .50 1.25
75 Dominic Roussel .40 1.00
76 Corey Hirsch .40 1.00
77 Vitali Yeremeyev .40 1.00
78 Tom Barrasso .50 1.25
79 Scott Clemmensen RC 1.50 4.00
80 Martin Brochu .40 1.00
81 Corey Schwab .40 1.00
82 Ty Conklin RC 2.50 6.00
83 Dwayne Roloson .50 1.25
84 Ilja Bryzgalov RC 4.00 10.00
85 Olivier Michaud RC 2.50 6.00
86 Vesa Toskala .40 1.00
87 Jussi Markkanen .40 1.00
88 Patrick Desrochers .40 1.00
89 Peter Skudra .50 1.25
90 J-F Damphousse .40 1.00
91 Mike Dunham .50 1.25
92 Mike Richter .60 1.50
93 Brian Boucher .50 1.25
94 Patrick Roy 1.50 4.00
95 Martin Biron .50 1.25
96 Jean-Sebastien Aubin .50 1.25
97 Curtis Joseph .75 2.00
98 Martin Brodeur 1.50 4.00
99 Arturs Irbe .50 1.25
100 Jeff Hackett .50 1.25
101 Ed Belfour .60 1.50
102 Jocelyn Thibault .50 1.25
103 Roman Cechmanek .50 1.25
104 Patrick Lalime .50 1.25
105 Olaf Kolzig .60 1.50
106 Byron Dafoe .50 1.25
107 Johan Hedberg .50 1.25
108 Dan Cloutier .50 1.25
109 Dominik Hasek 1.00 2.50
110 Olaf Kolzig .60 1.50
111 Patrick Roy 2.00 5.00
112 Ed Belfour .75 2.00
113 Grant Fuhr 1.25 3.00
114 Ron Hextall .75 2.00
115 Pelle Lindbergh .75 2.00
116 Tom Barrasso .60 1.50
117 Billy Smith .75 2.00
118 Bernie Parent 1.00 2.50
119 Tony Esposito 1.25 3.00
120 Gump Worsley 1.00 2.50
121 Glenn Hall .75 2.00
122 Jacques Plante 1.25 3.00
123 Johnny Bower .75 2.00
124 Terry Sawchuk 1.25 3.00
125 Harry Lumley .75 2.00
126 Bill Durnan .75 2.00
127 Turk Broda .60 1.50
128 Frank Brimsek .60 1.50
129 Tiny Thompson .60 1.50
130 George Hainsworth .60 1.50
131 Gump Worsley 1.00 2.50
132 Georges Vezina 1.25 3.00
133 Vladislav Tretiak .60 1.50
134 Tiny Thompson .60 1.50
135 Terry Sawchuk 1.25 3.00
136 Jacques Plante 1.25 3.00
137 Chuck Rayner .50 1.25
138 Bernie Parent 1.00 2.50
139 Harry Lumley .75 2.00
140 Glenn Hall .75 2.00
141 George Hainsworth .60 1.50
142 Ed Giacomin .75 2.00
143 Charlie Gardiner .50 1.25
144 Tony Esposito 1.25 3.00
145 Bill Durnan .75 2.00
146 Gerry Cheevers .75 2.00
147 Turk Broda .60 1.50
148 Frank Brimsek .60 1.50
149 Johnny Bower .75 2.00
150 Roy Worters .60 1.50
151 Pasi Nurminen RC 1.50 4.00
152 Alex Auld .40 1.00
153 John Vanbiesbrouck .60 1.50
154 Wade Flaherty .40 1.00
155 Kevin Weekes .50 1.25
156 Tom Barrasso .50 1.25
157 Stephane Fiset .50 1.25
158 Sebastien Centomo RC 1.50 4.00
159 Jean-Francois Labbe .50 1.25
160 Simon Lajeunesse .40 1.00
161 Frederic Cassivi RC 1.50 4.00
162 Martin Prusek RC 1.50 4.00
163 Dominik Hasek 1.00 2.50
164 David Aebischer .50 1.25
165 Dan Cloutier .50 1.25
166 Byron Dafoe .50 1.25
167 Curtis Joseph .75 2.00
168 Ed Belfour .60 1.50
169 Tommy Salo .50 1.25
170 Jose Theodore .60 1.50

2001-02 Between the Pipes All-Star Jerseys

ASJ1 Ed Belfour 10.00 25.00
ASJ2 Arturs Irbe 10.00 25.00
ASJ3 Martin Brodeur 25.00 60.00
ASJ4 Roman Cechmanek 10.00 25.00
ASJ5 Dominik Hasek 15.00 40.00
ASJ6 Olaf Kolzig 10.00 25.00
ASJ7 Curtis Joseph 10.00 25.00
ASJ8 Mike Richter 10.00 25.00
ASJ9 Patrick Roy 30.00 80.00
ASJ10 Evgeni Nabokov 10.00 25.00
ASJ11 Tommy Salo 10.00 25.00
ASJ12 Curtis Joseph 10.00 25.00
ASJ13 Dominik Hasek 12.00 30.00
ASJ14 Roman Turek 10.00 25.00
ASJ15 Nikolai Khabibulin 10.00 25.00
ASJ16 Patrick Roy 15.00 30.00

2001-02 Between the Pipes Double Memorabilia

DM1 Felix Potvin 15.00 40.00
DM2 Mike Vernon 15.00 40.00
DM3 Johan Hedberg 15.00 40.00
DM4 Olaf Kolzig 15.00 40.00
DM5 Jeff Hackett 15.00 40.00
DM6 Martin Brodeur 20.00 50.00
DM7 Mike Dunham 15.00 40.00
DM8 Trevor Kidd 12.00 30.00
DM9 Damian Rhodes 15.00 40.00
DM10 John Grahame 15.00 40.00
DM11 Roberto Luongo 15.00 40.00
DM12 Manny Legace 15.00 40.00
DM13 Evgeni Nabokov 15.00 40.00
DM14 Jose Theodore 15.00 40.00
DM15 Robert Esche 15.00 40.00
DM16 Chris Osgood 12.00 30.00
DM17 Sean Burke 15.00 40.00
DM18 Martin Biron 15.00 40.00
DM19 Jocelyn Thibault 15.00 40.00
DM20 Brian Boucher 20.00 40.00
DM21 Curtis Joseph 12.00 30.00
DM22 Roman Turek 15.00 40.00
DM23 Gerry Cheevers 15.00 40.00
DM24 Terry Sawchuk 75.00 150.00
DM25 Grant Fuhr 15.00 40.00
DM26 Bernie Parent 20.00 50.00
DM27 Ron Hextall 15.00 40.00
DM28 Gump Worsley 30.00 80.00
DM29 Tony Esposito 40.00 100.00
DM30 Ed Giacomin 15.00 40.00

2001-02 Between the Pipes Future Wave

FW1 Johan Hedberg 20.00 50.00
FW2 Martin Biron 15.00 40.00
FW3 Patrick Lalime 30.00 60.00
FW4 Roberto Luongo 30.00 60.00
FW5 J.Holmqvist
D.Blackburn 25.00 50.00
FW6 Dan Cloutier 12.50 30.00
FW7 M.Kiprusoff
E.Nabokov 12.50 30.00
FW8 Brian Boucher 12.50 30.00
FW9 Mathieu Garon 20.00 50.00
FW10 Rick DiPietro 25.00 60.00

2001-02 Between the Pipes Goalie Gear

GG1 Felix Potvin 12.50 30.00
GG2 Jeff Hackett 10.00 25.00
GG3 Mike Vernon 10.00 25.00
GG4 Sean Burke 10.00 25.00
GG5 Johan Hedberg 12.50 30.00
GG6 Jose Theodore 12.50 30.00
GG7 Robert Esche 10.00 25.00
GG8 Dan Cloutier 10.00 25.00
GG9 Olaf Kolzig 12.50 30.00
GG10 Roberto Luongo 15.00 40.00
GG11 Manny Legace 10.00 25.00
GG12 Martin Brodeur 25.00 60.00
GG13 Marty Turco 12.50 30.00
GG14 Arturs Irbe 12.50 30.00
GG15 Damian Rhodes 10.00 25.00
GG16 Trevor Kidd 10.00 25.00
GG17 Mike Dunham 10.00 25.00
GG18 Evgeni Nabokov 12.50 30.00
GG19 Roman Turek 10.00 25.00
GG20 Brian Boucher 10.00 25.00
GG21 Jocelyn Thibault 10.00 25.00
GG22 Dominik Hasek/20 15.00 40.00
GG23 Patrick Roy/20 25.00 50.00
GG24 Curtis Joseph/20 50.00 100.00
GG25 Brent Johnson 10.00 25.00
GG26 Patrick Lalime 10.00 25.00
GG27 J-S Aubin 10.00 25.00
GG28 Martin Biron 10.00 25.00
GG29 Chris Osgood 12.50 30.00
GG30 Rick DiPietro 12.50 30.00

2001-02 Between the Pipes He Shoots He Saves Points

1 Brian Boucher 1pt. .20 .50
2 Sean Burke 1pt. .20 .50
3 Byron Dafoe 1pt. .20 .50
4 Nikoali Khabibulin 1pt. .25 .60
5 Olaf Kolzig 1pt. .20 .50
6 Roberto Luongo 1pt. .25 .60
7 Evgeni Nabokov 1pt. .20 .50
8 Jose Theodore 1pt. .30 .75
9 Jocelyn Thibault 1 pt. .25 .60
10 Roman Turek 1pt. .20 .50
11 Ed Belfour 2 pts. .25 .60
12 Martin Brodeur 2 pts. .40 1.00
13 Grant Fuhr 2 pts. .30 .75
14 Glenn Hall 2 pts. .20 .50
15 Jacques Plante 2 pts. .25 .60
16 Tommy Salo 2 pts. .20 .50
17 Dominik Hasek 3 pts. .50 1.25
18 Curtis Joseph 3 pts. .30 .75
19 Patrick Roy 3 pts. 1.50 4.00
20 Terry Sawchuk 3 pts. .30 .75

2001-02 Between the Pipes Jerseys

*JSY-STICK/90: .5X TO 1.2X BASIC JSY
GJ1 Byron Dafoe 6.00 15.00
GJ2 Dominik Hasek 12.50 30.00
GJ3 Mike Vernon 10.00 25.00
GJ4 Arturs Irbe 10.00 25.00
GJ5 Jocelyn Thibault 6.00 15.00
GJ6 Patrick Roy 25.00 60.00
GJ7 Ed Belfour 10.00 25.00
GJ8 Chris Osgood 10.00 25.00
GJ9 Johan Hedberg 6.00 15.00
GJ10 Roberto Luongo 12.50 30.00
GJ11 Jose Theodore 12.50 30.00
GJ12 Mike Dunham 6.00 15.00
GJ13 Martin Brodeur 20.00 50.00
GJ14 Mike Richter 10.00 25.00
GJ15 Roman Cechmanek 6.00 15.00
GJ16 J-S Aubin 6.00 15.00
GJ17 Roman Turek 6.00 15.00
GJ18 Curtis Joseph 10.00 25.00
GJ19 Olaf Kolzig 10.00 25.00
GJ20 Felix Potvin 25.00 60.00
GJ21 Trevor Kidd 8.00 20.00
GJ22 Tommy Salo 6.00 15.00
GJ23 Jeff Hackett 8.00 20.00
GJ24 Brian Boucher 6.00 15.00
GJ25 Dan Cloutier 6.00 15.00
GJ26 Damian Rhodes 6.00 15.00
GJ27 Ron Tugnutt 6.00 15.00
GJ28 Marty Turco 8.00 20.00
GJ29 Manny Fernandez 6.00 15.00
GJ30 Marc Denis 6.00 15.00
GJ31 Evgeni Nabokov 10.00 25.00
GJ32 Nikolai Khabibulin 10.00 25.00
GJ33 Sean Burke 6.00 15.00
GJ34 Gregg Naumenko 6.00 15.00
GJ35 Steve Shields 6.00 15.00
GJ36 Mathieu Garon 6.00 15.00
GJ37 Manny Legace 6.00 15.00
GJ38 Johan Holmqvist 6.00 15.00
GJ39 Martin Biron 6.00 15.00
GJ40 David Aebischer 6.00 15.00
GJ41 Miikka Kiprusoff 10.00 25.00
GJ42 John Grahame 6.00 15.00

2001-02 Between the Pipes Emblems

GUE1 Dominik Hasek 50.00 120.00
GUE2 Jocelyn Thibault 25.00 60.00
GUE3 Patrick Roy 50.00 120.00
GUE4 Johan Hedberg 75.00 150.00
GUE5 Roman Turek 25.00 60.00
GUE6 Curtis Joseph 25.00 60.00
GUE7 Olaf Kolzig 25.00 60.00
GUE8 Tommy Salo 30.00 80.00
GUE9 Brian Boucher 25.00 60.00
GUE10 Evgeni Nabokov 30.00 80.00

2001-02 Between the Pipes Numbers

ITN1 Dominik Hasek 60.00 125.00
ITN3 Patrick Roy 60.00 125.00
ITN4 Johan Hedberg 40.00 80.00
ITN5 Roman Turek 25.00 60.00
ITN6 Curtis Joseph 40.00 80.00
ITN7 Olaf Kolzig 25.00 60.00
ITN8 Tommy Salo 15.00 40.00
ITN9 Brian Boucher 15.00 40.00
ITN10 Evgeni Nabokov 25.00 60.00

2001-02 Between the Pipes Masks

COMPLETE SET (40) 75.00 150.00
SILVER/300: .8X TO 2X BASIC INSERT
GOLD/30: 2X TO 5X BASIC INSERT
1 Murray Bannerman 2.50 6.00
2 Ed Belfour Stars 5.00 12.00
3 Martin Biron 3.00 8.00
4 Sean Burke 3.00 8.00
5 Roman Cechmanek 2.50 6.00
6 Gerry Cheevers 6.00 15.00
7 Byron Dafoe 3.00 8.00
8 Mike Dunham 2.50 6.00
9 Manny Fernandez 3.00 8.00
10 Ed Giacomin 5.00 12.00
11 Gilles Gratton 2.50 6.00
12 Johan Hedberg 3.00 8.00
13 Brent Johnson 3.00 8.00
14 Curtis Joseph Blues 5.00 12.00
15 Curtis Joseph Leafs 5.00 12.00
16 Olaf Kolzig 3.00 8.00
17 Patrick Lalime 3.00 8.00
18 Manny Legace 2.50 6.00
19 Roberto Luongo 5.00 12.00
20 Evgeni Nabokov 4.00 10.00
21 Jacques Plante 8.00 20.00
22 Felix Potvin 6.00 15.00
23 Damian Rhodes 2.50 6.00
24 Mike Richter 5.00 12.00
25 Patrick Roy 8.00 20.00
26 Tommy Salo 3.00 8.00
27 Steve Shields 2.50 6.00
28 Jose Theodore 4.00 10.00
29 Roman Turek 3.00 8.00
30 John Vanbiesbrouck 4.00 10.00
31 Ed Belfour Blackhawks 5.00 12.00
32 Rick DiPietro 3.00 8.00
33 Grant Fuhr 4.00 10.00
34 Jeff Hackett 3.00 8.00
35 Brian Hayward 2.50 6.00
36 Milan Hnilicka 2.50 6.00
37 Nikolai Khabibulin 4.00 10.00
38 Miikka Kiprusoff 3.00 8.00
39 Jocelyn Thibault 3.00 8.00
40 Ron Tugnutt 4.00 10.00

2001-02 Between the Pipes Record Breakers

RB1 Patrick Roy 25.00 60.00
RB2 Sawchuk/Brodeur/Plante 150.00 300.00
RB3 Jacques Plante 25.00 60.00
RB4 Martin Brodeur 25.00 60.00
RB5 Terry Sawchuk 30.00 80.00
RB6 Bernie Parent 15.00 40.00
RB7 Tony Esposito 15.00 40.00
RB8 Ed Belfour 15.00 40.00
RB9 Grant Fuhr 15.00 40.00
RB10 Patrick Roy 25.00 60.00
RB11 Patrick Roy 25.00 60.00
RB12 Ed Belfour 15.00 40.00
RB13 Jacques Plante 25.00 60.00
RB14 Gerry Cheevers 15.00 40.00
RB15 Terry Sawchuk 30.00 80.00
RB16 Patrick Roy 25.00 60.00
RB17 Patrick Roy 25.00 60.00
RB18 Chris Osgood 15.00 40.00
RB19 Tony Esposito 15.00 40.00
RB20 Glenn Hall 15.00 40.00

2001-02 Between the Pipes Tandems

GT1 E.Nabokov
M.Kiprusoff 30.00 80.00
GT2 R.Cechmanek/B.Boucher 12.00 30.00
GT3 J.Theodore/J.Hackett 20.00 50.00
GT4 R.Luongo/T.Kidd 15.00 40.00
GT5 P.Roy/D.Aebischer 50.00 125.00
GT6 S.Shields/J.Giguere 15.00 40.00
GT7 E.Belfour/M.Turco 15.00 40.00
GT8 R.Turek/M.Vernon 15.00 40.00
GT9 D.Hasek/M.Legace 15.00 40.00
GT10 B.Dafoe/J.Grahame 12.00 30.00
GT11 S.Burke/R.Esche 12.00 30.00
GT12 J.Thibault/S.Passmore 20.00 50.00
GT13 J.Aubin/J.Hedberg 15.00 40.00

2001-02 Between the Pipes Trophy Winners

TW1 Patrick Roy 50.00 125.00
TW2 Dominik Hasek 20.00 50.00
TW3 Evgeni Nabokov 30.00 80.00
TW4 Jacques Plante 40.00 100.00
TW5 Olaf Kolzig 15.00 40.00
TW6 Terry Sawchuk 60.00 150.00
TW7 Glenn Hall 15.00 40.00
TW8 Billy Smith 15.00 40.00
TW9 Turk Broda 40.00 100.00
TW10 Ron Hextall 15.00 40.00
TW11 Tiny Thompson 30.00 80.00
TW12 Bill Durnan 15.00 40.00
TW13 Glenn Hall 15.00 40.00
TW14 Terry Sawchuk 40.00 100.00
TW15 Tony Esposito 20.00 50.00
TW16 Glenn Hall 15.00 40.00
TW17 Martin Brodeur 25.00 60.00
TW18 Jacques Plante 25.00 60.00
TW19 Dominik Hasek 20.00 50.00
TW20 Billy Smith 15.00 40.00
TW21 Bernie Parent 15.00 40.00
TW22 Ed Belfour 20.00 50.00
TW23 Frank Brimsek 15.00 40.00
TW24 Dominik Hasek 20.00 50.00

2001-02 Between the Pipes Vintage Memorabilia

VM1 Grant Fuhr 15.00 40.00
VM2 Turk Broda 25.00 60.00
VM3 Gerry Cheevers 15.00 40.00
VM4 Bernie Parent 15.00 40.00
VM5 Jacques Plante 30.00 80.00
VM6 Terry Sawchuk 40.00 100.00
VM7 Frank Brimsek 20.00 50.00
VM8 Glenn Hall 15.00 40.00
VM9 Tony Esposito 15.00 40.00
VM10 Vladislav Tretiak 30.00 80.00
VM11 Billy Smith 15.00 40.00
VM12 Johnny Bower 40.00 100.00
VM13 Georges Vezina 300.00 600.00
VM14 Ron Hextall 15.00 40.00
VM15 Ed Giacomin 15.00 40.00
VM16 Gump Worsley 20.00 50.00
VM17 Bill Durnan 20.00 50.00
VM18 Rogie Vachon 25.00 60.00
VM19 Tiny Thompson 15.00 40.00
VM20 Charlie Gardner 15.00 40.00

2002-03 Between the Pipes

1 Patrick Roy .75 2.00
2 Jose Theodore .40 1.00
3 Olaf Kolzig .40 1.00
4 Roberto Luongo .60 1.50
5 Tommy Salo .30 .75
6 Dan Blackburn .30 .75
7 Patrick Lalime .30 .75
8 Martin Brodeur .75 2.00
9 Evgeni Nabokov .30 .75
10 Jani Hurme .30 .75
11 Dan Cloutier .30 .75
12 Mike Dunham .30 .75
13 Miikka Kiprusoff .40 1.00
14 Rick DiPietro .30 .75
15 Martin Biron .30 .75
16 Steve Passmore .20 .50
17 Curtis Joseph .40 1.00
18 Manny Fernandez .20 .50
19 Kevin Weekes .30 .75
20 Stephane Fiset .20 .50
21 Jocelyn Thibault .30 .75
22 David Aebischer .30 .75
23 Marty Turco .40 1.00
24 Jamie Storr .30 .75
25 Marc Denis .30 .75
26 Arturs Irbe .30 .75
27 Felix Potvin .60 1.50
28 Manny Legace .40 1.00
29 Mike Richter .40 1.00
30 J-S Aubin .20 .50
31 Sean Burke .20 .50
32 Milan Hnilicka .30 .75
33 Ed Belfour .40 1.00
34 Roman Turek .40 1.00
35 Frederic Cassivi .20 .50
36 Tomas Vokoun .30 .75
37 Travis Scott .20 .50
38 Dwayne Roloson .20 .50
39 Roman Cechmanek .30 .75
40 Johan Hedberg .40 1.00
41 Neil Little .20 .50
42 Jeff Hackett .30 .75
43 John Grahame .20 .50
44 Norm Maracle .20 .50
45 Ty Conklin .30 .75
46 Trevor Kidd .20 .50
47 Nikolai Khabibulin .40 1.00
48 Dieter Kochan .20 .50
49 Robert Esche .20 .50

50 Chris Osgood .40 1.00
51 Jean-Sebastien Giguere .40 1.00
52 Steve Shields .30 .75
53 Wade Flaherty .20 .50
54 Peter Skudra .20 .50
55 Brent Johnson .30 .75
56 Brian Boucher .30 .75
57 Garth Snow .30 .75
58 Fred Brathwaite .30 .75
59 Ron Tugnutt .30 .75
60 Craig Billington .20 .50
61 Martin Brochu .20 .50
62 Corey Schwab .30 .75
63 Tim Thomas RC .75 2.00
64 J-F Labbe .20 .50
65 Damian Rhodes .20 .50
66 Kevin Hodson .20 .50
67 Jamie McLennan .20 .50
68 Tyler Moss .20 .50
69 Tom Barrasso .30 .75
70 Corey Hirsch .20 .50
71 Eric Fichaud .20 .50
72 Byron Dafoe .30 .75
73 Mika Noronen .30 .75
74 Alex Auld .20 .50
75 Curtis Sanford RC .40 1.00
76 Martin Gerber RC .40 1.00
77 Mikael Tellqvist RC .20 .50
78 J-M Pelletier .20 .50
79 J-F Damphousse .30 .75
80 Johan Holmqvist .20 .50
81 Mathieu Garon .30 .75
82 Martin Prusek .20 .50
83 Ilya Bryzgalov .30 .75
84 Andrew Raycroft .30 .75
85 Derek Gustafson .20 .50
86 Jason LaBarbera .20 .50
87 Marc Lamothe .30 .75
88 Scott Clemmensen .20 .50
89 Cody Rudkowsky RC .20 .50
90 Craig Andersson RC .75 2.00
91 Maxime Ouellet .30 .75
92 Jan Lasak .30 .75
93 Patrick DesRochers .20 .50
94 Pasi Nurminen .20 .50
95 Sebastien Centomo .20 .50
96 Jussi Markkanen .20 .50
97 Sebastien Charpentier .20 .50
98 Reinhard Divis .20 .50
99 Simon Lajeunesse .20 .50
100 Vesa Toskala .20 .50
101 Olivier Michaud .20 .50
102 Levente Szuper RC .40 1.00
103 Philippe Sauve .20 .50
104 Dany Sabourin RC .20 .50
105 Ryan Miller RC 1.50 4.00
106 Chris Mason .20 .50
107 Steve Valiquette .20 .50
108 Pascal Leclaire RC .30 .75
109 Jason Elliott RC .20 .50
110 Michael Garnett RC .20 .50
111 Tiny Thompson EN .30 .75
112 Frank Brimsek EN .20 .50
113 Jacques Plante EN .40 1.00
114 Terry Sawchuk EN .75 2.00
115 Georges Vezina EN .40 1.00
116 Chuck Rayner EN .30 .75
117 Glenn Hall EN .40 1.00
118 Turk Broda EN .30 .75
119 George Hainsworth EN .30 .75
120 Roy Worters EN .30 .75
121 Jean-Sebastien Giguere HA .40 1.00
122 Milan Hnilicka HA .30 .75
123 Steve Shields HA .30 .75
124 Martin Biron HA .30 .75
125 Roman Turek HA .40 1.00
126 Arturs Irbe HA .30 .75
127 Jocelyn Thibault HA .30 .75
128 Patrick Roy HA .75 2.00
129 Marc Denis HA .30 .75
130 Marty Turco HA .40 1.00
131 Curtis Joseph HA .40 1.00
132 Tommy Salo HA .30 .75
133 Roberto Luongo HA .60 1.50
134 Felix Potvin HA .60 1.50
135 Manny Fernandez HA .20 .50
136 Jose Theodore HA .40 1.00
137 Tomas Vokoun HA .30 .75
138 Martin Brodeur HA .75 2.00
139 Chris Osgood HA .40 1.00
140 Mike Richter HA .40 1.00
141 Patrick Lalime HA .30 .75
142 Roman Cechmanek HA .30 .75
143 Sean Burke HA .20 .50
144 Johan Hedberg HA .40 1.00
145 Brent Johnson HA .30 .75
146 Evgeni Nabokov HA .30 .75
147 Nikolai Khabibulin HA .40 1.00
148 Ed Belfour HA .40 1.00
149 Dan Cloutier HA .30 .75
150 Olaf Kolzig HA .40 1.00

2002-03 Between the Pipes Silver

*STARS: 3X TO 8X BASE HI
*ROOKIES: .75X TO 2X

2002-03 Between the Pipes All-Star Stick and Jersey

COMMON CARD (1-16) 10.00 25.00
1 Ed Belfour 15.00 40.00
2 Curtis Joseph 15.00 40.00
3 Martin Brodeur 30.00 80.00
4 Patrick Roy 40.00 100.00
5 Mike Richter 15.00 40.00
6 Evgeni Nabokov 15.00 40.00
7 Olaf Kolzig 15.00 40.00
8 Felix Potvin 15.00 40.00
9 Tommy Salo 15.00 40.00
10 Jose Theodore 15.00 40.00
11 Nikolai Khabibulin 15.00 40.00
12 Roman Turek 10.00 25.00
13 Sean Burke 15.00 40.00
14 Roman Cechmanek 10.00 25.00
15 Arturs Irbe 15.00 40.00
16 Chris Osgood 15.00 40.00

2002-03 Between the Pipes Behind the Mask

COMMON CARD (1-20) 12.50 30.00
1 Marty Turco 12.50 30.00
2 Martin Brodeur 20.00 40.00
3 Patrick Roy 25.00 60.00
4 Roberto Luongo 20.00 50.00
5 Tommy Salo 12.50 30.00
6 Nikolai Khabibulin 12.50 30.00
7 Sean Burke 12.50 30.00
8 Patrick Lalime 12.50 30.00
9 Arturs Irbe 12.50 30.00
10 Jocelyn Thibault 12.50 30.00
11 Jose Theodore 15.00 40.00
12 Rick DiPietro 15.00 40.00
13 Marc Denis 12.50 30.00
14 Mike Dunham 12.50 30.00
15 Johan Hedberg 12.50 30.00
16 Olaf Kolzig 15.00 40.00
17 Dan Cloutier 12.50 30.00
18 Felix Potvin 20.00 50.00
19 Ed Belfour 15.00 40.00
20 Steve Shields 12.50 30.00

2002-03 Between the Pipes Blockers

COMMON CARD (1-18) 8.00 20.00
1 Curtis Joseph 10.00 40.00
2 Jani Hurme 8.00 20.00
3 Evgeni Nabokov 10.00 25.00
4 Felix Potvin 15.00 40.00
5 Jean-Sebastien Giguere 10.00 25.00
6 Jocelyn Thibault 8.00 25.00
7 Marty Turco 12.50 30.00
8 Mike Dunham 8.00 25.00
9 Johan Hedberg 8.00 20.00
10 Roman Cechmanek 8.00 25.00
11 Olaf Kolzig 10.00 25.00
12 Patrick Lalime 8.00 25.00
13 Roberto Luongo 15.00 30.00
14 Roman Turek 8.00 25.00
15 Nikolai Khabibulin 10.00 25.00
16 Tommy Salo 8.00 25.00
17 Trevor Kidd 8.00 25.00
18 Sean Burke 10.00 25.00

2002-03 Between the Pipes Double Memorabilia

COMMON CARD (1-20) 10.00 25.00
1 Martin Brodeur 30.00 80.00
2 Sean Burke 12.50 30.00
3 Dan Cloutier 10.00 25.00
4 Chris Osgood 15.00 40.00
5 Jose Theodore 20.00 50.00
6 Olaf Kolzig 12.50 30.00
7 Patrick Roy 30.00 80.00
8 Tommy Salo 10.00 25.00
9 Marty Turco 10.00 25.00
10 Roman Turek 10.00 25.00
11 Mike Dunham 10.00 25.00
12 Manny Legace 12.00 30.00
13 Jocelyn Thibault 10.00 25.00
14 Nikolai Khabibulin 12.50 30.00
15 Johan Hedberg 10.00 25.00
16 Trevor Kidd 10.00 25.00
17 J-S Aubin 12.50 30.00
18 Jacques Plante 40.00 100.00
19 Terry Sawchuk 40.00 100.00
20 Roger Crozier 12.50 30.00

2002-03 Between the Pipes Future Wave

COMMON CARD (1-12) 8.00 20.00
1 Miikka Kiprusoff 10.00 30.00
2 Jose Theodore 8.00 25.00
3 Roberto Luongo 20.00 50.00
4 Rick DiPietro 10.00 30.00
5 Dan Blackburn 8.00 20.00
6 Mathieu Garon 8.00 20.00
7 Johan Hedberg 8.00 20.00
8 Dan Cloutier 8.00 20.00
9 Martin Biron 8.00 20.00
10 Marty Turco 10.00 30.00
11 Alex Auld 10.00 25.00
12 Brent Johnson 8.00 20.00

2002-03 Between the Pipes Goalie Autographs

1 Martin Biron/50* 12.50 30.00
2 Dan Blackburn/50* 12.50 30.00
3 Sean Burke/50* 12.50 30.00
4 Dan Cloutier/50* 12.50 30.00
5 Marc Denis/50* 12.50 30.00
6 Jean-Sebastien Giguere/50* 12.50 30.00
7 Johan Hedberg/50* 12.50 30.00
8 Milan Hnilicka/50* 12.50 30.00
9 Arturs Irbe/50* 25.00 50.00
10 Brent Johnson/50* 12.50 30.00
11 Curtis Joseph/50* 15.00 40.00
12 Nikolai Khabibulin/50* 15.00 40.00
13 Olaf Kolzig/50* 12.50 30.00
14 Patrick Lalime/50* 12.50 30.00
15 Roberto Luongo/50* 20.00 50.00
16 Evgeni Nabokov/50* 12.50 30.00
17 Chris Osgood/50* 15.00 40.00
18 Felix Potvin/50* 20.00 50.00
19 Dwayne Roloson/50* 15.00 40.00
20 Tommy Salo/50* 12.50 30.00
21 Steve Shields/50* 12.50 30.00
22 Jose Theodore/50* 20.00 50.00
23 Jocelyn Thibault/50* 12.50 30.00
24 Marty Turco/50* 12.50 30.00
25 Roman Turek/50* 12.50 30.00
26 Johnny Bower/90* 15.00 40.00
27 Bernie Parent/90* 15.00 40.00
28 Ed Giacomin/90* 15.00 40.00
29 Gerry Cheevers/90* 15.00 40.00
30 Vladislav Tretiak/90* 40.00 100.00
31 Gump Worsley/40* 25.00 60.00
32 Tony Esposito/90* 20.00 50.00
33 John Davidson/90* 15.00 40.00
34 Glenn Hall/90* 15.00 40.00
35 Charlie Hodge/90* 15.00 40.00
36 Rogie Vachon/90* 15.00 40.00

2002-03 Between the Pipes He Shoots He Saves Points

1 Sean Burke 1 pt. .40 1.00
2 Roman Cechmanek 1 pt. .40 1.00
3 Dan Cloutier 1 pt. .40 1.00
4 Johan Hedberg 1 pt. .40 1.00
5 Arturs Irbe 1 pt. .40 1.00
6 Patrick Lalime 1 pt. .40 1.00
7 Evgeni Nabokov 1 pt. .40 1.00
8 Felix Potvin 1 pt. .40 1.00
9 Mike Richter 1 pt. .40 1.00
10 Marty Turco 1 pt. .40 1.00
11 Roman Turek 1 pt. .40 1.00
12 Dan Blackburn 2 pt. .40 1.00
13 Nikolai Khabibulin 2 pt. .40 1.00
14 Olaf Kolzig 2 pt. .40 1.00
15 Roberto Luongo 2 pt. .40 1.00
16 Tommy Salo 2 pt. .40 1.00
17 Jocelyn Thibault 2 pt. .40 1.00
18 Martin Brodeur 3 pt. .40 1.00
19 Patrick Roy 3 pt. .40 1.00
20 Jose Theodore 3 pt. .40 1.00

2002-03 Between the Pipes Inspirations

I1 P.Roy/J.Plante 30.00 80.00
I2 T.Sawchuk/G.Hainsworth 50.00 125.00
I3 J.Theodore/P.Roy 40.00 100.00
I4 R.Luongo/P.Roy 20.00 50.00
I5 S.Burke/B.Parent 20.00 50.00
I6 E.Belfour/V.Tretiak 25.00 60.00
I7 D.Blackburn/C.Joseph 20.00 50.00
I8 M.Brodeur/P.Roy 25.00 60.00
I9 M.Richter/G.Cheevers 25.00 60.00
I10 R.DiPietro/R.Hextall 20.00 50.00

2002-03 Between the Pipes Jerseys

*STK/JSY: .5X TO 1.25X BASE JERSEY
1 Arturs Irbe 8.00 20.00
2 Miikka Kiprusoff 8.00 20.00
3 Rick DiPietro 10.00 25.00
4 Dan Blackburn 8.00 20.00
5 Dan Cloutier 8.00 20.00
6 David Aebischer 8.00 20.00
7 Evgeni Nabokov 8.00 20.00
8 Felix Potvin 8.00 20.00
9 Manny Fernandez 8.00 20.00
10 J-S Aubin 10.00 25.00
11 Jean-Sebastien Giguere 10.00 25.00
12 Jani Hurme 8.00 20.00
13 Jocelyn Thibault 8.00 20.00
14 Jose Theodore 12.50 30.00
15 Mike Dunham 8.00 20.00
16 Martin Biron 8.00 20.00
17 Johan Hedberg 8.00 20.00
18 Martin Brodeur 15.00 40.00
19 Marty Turco 8.00 20.00
20 Mika Noronen 8.00 20.00
21 Mike Richter 10.00 25.00
22 Nikolai Khabibulin 10.00 25.00
23 Olaf Kolzig 10.00 25.00
24 Patrick Lalime 8.00 20.00
25 Patrick Roy 15.00 40.00
26 Roberto Luongo 15.00 40.00
27 Roman Cechmanek 8.00 20.00
28 Roman Turek 8.00 20.00
29 Sean Burke 10.00 25.00
30 Tommy Salo 8.00 20.00
31 Maxime Ouellet 8.00 20.00
32 Ed Belfour 10.00 25.00
33 Sebastien Charpentier 8.00 20.00
34 Robert Esche 8.00 20.00
35 Curtis Sanford 8.00 20.00
36 Milan Hnilicka 8.00 20.00
37 Steve Shields 8.00 20.00
38 Tim Thomas 12.50 30.00
39 Trevor Kidd 8.00 20.00
40 Fred Brathwaite 8.00 20.00
41 Martin Prusek 8.00 20.00
42 John Grahame 8.00 20.00
43 Jamie Storr 8.00 20.00
44 Sebastien Centomo 8.00 20.00
45 Ron Tugnutt 8.00 20.00
46 Martin Gerber 8.00 20.00
47 Jussi Markkanen 8.00 20.00
48 Simon Lajeunesse 8.00 20.00
49 Reinhard Divis 8.00 20.00
50 Jeff Hackett 8.00 20.00

2002-03 Between the Pipes Masks II

COMPLETE SET (30) 30.00 60.00
*SILVER: 1.25X TO 3X BASE HI
*GOLD: 3X TO 8X BASE HI
1 Jean-Sebastien Giguere 2.00 5.00
2 Milan Hnilicka 2.00 5.00
3 Steve Shields 2.00 5.00
4 Martin Biron 2.00 5.00
5 Roman Turek 2.00 5.00
6 Kevin Weekes 2.00 5.00
7 Jocelyn Thibault 2.00 5.00
8 Patrick Roy 4.00 10.00
9 Marc Denis 2.00 5.00
10 Marty Turco 2.00 5.00
11 Curtis Joseph 3.00 8.00
12 Tommy Salo 2.00 5.00
13 Roberto Luongo 4.00 10.00
14 Felix Potvin 3.00 8.00
15 Manny Fernandez 2.00 5.00
16 Jose Theodore 3.00 8.00
17 Mike Dunham 2.00 5.00
18 Mike Richter 2.50 6.00
19 Rick DiPietro 2.00 5.00
20 Patrick Lalime 2.00 5.00
21 Roman Cechmanek 2.00 5.00
22 Sean Burke 2.00 5.00
23 Johan Hedberg 2.00 5.00
24 Evgeni Nabokov 2.00 5.00
25 Miikka Kiprusoff 3.00 8.00
26 Brent Johnson 2.00 5.00
27 Nikolai Khabibulin 2.50 6.00
28 Ed Belfour 3.00 8.00
29 Jeff Hackett 2.00 5.00
30 Olaf Kolzig 2.00 5.00

2002-03 Between the Pipes Nightmares

GN1 D.Blackburn/I.Kovalchuk 12.50 30.00
GN2 M.Richter/M.Lemieux 20.00 50.00
GN3 T.Salo/J.Jagr 12.50 30.00
GN4 F.Potvin/S.Yzerman 25.00 60.00
GN5 S.Fiset/P.Bure 10.00 25.00
GN6 M.Richter/J.Iginla 12.50 30.00
GN7 T.Salo/P.Forsberg 12.50 30.00
GN8 C.Joseph/J.Sakic 15.00 40.00
GN9 O.Kolzig/E.Lindros 12.50 30.00
GN10 T.Barrasso/M.Sundin 10.00 25.00

2002-03 Between the Pipes Pads

1 Martin Brodeur 15.00 40.00
2 Patrick Roy 20.00 50.00
3 Marty Turco 8.00 20.00
4 Curtis Joseph 15.00 40.00
5 Ed Belfour 12.50 30.00
6 Jose Theodore 10.00 25.00
7 Sean Burke 8.00 20.00
8 Dan Cloutier 8.00 20.00
9 Chris Osgood 10.00 25.00
10 Nikolai Khabibulin 10.00 25.00
11 J-S Aubin 10.00 25.00
12 Steve Shields 8.00 20.00
13 Mike Dunham 8.00 20.00
14 Jocelyn Thibault 8.00 20.00

2002-03 Between the Pipes Record Breakers

1 Terry Sawchuk 30.00 80.00
2 Patrick Roy 15.00 40.00
3 George Hainsworth 20.00 50.00
4 Jacques Plante 25.00 60.00
5 Patrick Roy 20.00 50.00
6 Glenn Hall 12.50 30.00
7 Tony Esposito 12.50 30.00
8 Gerry Cheevers 12.50 30.00
9 Martin Brodeur 20.00 50.00
10 Bernie Parent 25.00 60.00
11 Terry Sawchuk 30.00 80.00
12 Patrick Roy 20.00 50.00
13 Johnny Bower 12.50 30.00
14 Ed Belfour 12.50 30.00
15 Patrick Roy 15.00 40.00
16 Terry Sawchuk 30.00 80.00

2002-03 Between the Pipes Stick and Jerseys

1 Arturs Irbe 10.00 25.00
2 Miikka Kiprusoff 10.00 25.00
3 Rick DiPietro 10.00 25.00
4 Dan Blackburn 10.00 25.00
5 Dan Cloutier 10.00 25.00
6 David Aebischer 10.00 25.00
7 Evgeni Nabokov 10.00 25.00
8 Felix Potvin 12.50 30.00
9 Manny Fernandez 10.00 25.00
10 J-S Aubin 10.00 25.00
11 Jean-Sebastien Giguere 10.00 25.00
12 Jani Hurme 10.00 25.00
13 Jocelyn Thibault 10.00 25.00
14 Jose Theodore 15.00 40.00
15 Mike Dunham 10.00 25.00
16 Martin Biron 10.00 25.00
17 Johan Hedberg 10.00 25.00
18 Martin Brodeur 15.00 40.00
19 Marty Turco 10.00 25.00
20 Mika Noronen 10.00 25.00
21 Mike Richter 10.00 25.00
22 Nikolai Khabibulin 10.00 25.00
23 Olaf Kolzig 10.00 25.00
24 Patrick Lalime 10.00 25.00
25 Patrick Roy 25.00 60.00
26 Roberto Luongo 12.00 30.00
27 Roman Cechmanek 10.00 25.00
28 Roman Turek 10.00 25.00
29 Sean Burke 10.00 25.00
30 Tommy Salo 10.00 25.00

2002-03 Between the Pipes Tandems

1 M.Richter/D.Blackburn 10.00 25.00
2 P.Roy/D.Aebischer 50.00 100.00
3 J.Thibault/S.Passmore 10.00 25.00
4 E.Nabokov/M.Kiprusoff 12.50 30.00
5 P.Lalime/M.Prusek 10.00 25.00
6 M.Biron/M.Noronen 10.00 25.00
7 J.Hedberg/J-S Aubin 10.00 25.00
8 R.Cechmanek/R.Esche 10.00 25.00
9 J.Theodore/J.Hackett 12.50 30.00
10 F.Potvin/J.Storr 15.00 40.00
11 M.Dunham/T.Voukon 10.00 25.00
12 D.Cloutier/A.Auld 10.00 25.00
13 J-S Giguere/M.Gerber 12.50 30.00
14 E.Belfour/T.Kidd 12.50 30.00
15 B.Johnson/F.Brathwaite 10.00 25.00
16 C.Osgood/R.Dipietro 30.00 80.00
17 S.Shields/J.Grahame 12.00 30.00
18 T.Salo/J.Markkanen 10.00 25.00
19 M.Turco/R.Tugnutt 10.00 25.00
20 O.Kolzig/M.Ouellet 12.50 30.00

2002-03 Between the Pipes Trappers

GT1 Vladislav Tretiak 20.00 50.00
GT2 Bill Durnan 20.00 50.00
GT3 Dan Cloutier 8.00 20.00
GT4 Byron Dafoe 8.00 20.00
GT5 Johan Hedberg 8.00 20.00
GT6 Charlie Hodge 20.00 50.00
GT7 Nikolai Khabibulin 8.00 20.00
GT8 Jacques Plante 30.00 80.00
GT9 Olaf Kolzig 12.00 30.00
GT10 Harry Lumley 12.00 30.00
GT11 Bernie Parent 20.00 60.00
GT12 Patrick Roy 25.00 60.00
GT13 Terry Sawchuk 30.00 80.00
GT14 Jocelyn Thibault 8.00 20.00
GT15 Marty Turco 8.00 20.00
GT16 Roger Crozier 15.00 40.00
GT17 Sean Burke 8.00 20.00
GT18 Grant Fuhr 20.00 50.00

2002-03 Between the Pipes Vintage Memorabilia

1 Johnny Bower 30.00 60.00
2 Harry Lumley 25.00 50.00
3 Roger Crozier 30.00 60.00
4 Ed Giacomin 30.00 60.00
5 Bill Durnan 25.00 60.00
6 George Hainsworth 30.00 60.00
7 Gerry Cheevers 40.00 80.00
8 Bernie Parent 30.00 60.00
9 Tony Esposito 20.00 50.00
10 Jacques Plante 30.00 60.00
11 Charlie Hodge 25.00 50.00
12 Glenn Hall 30.00 80.00
13 Roy Worters 25.00 60.00
14 Tiny Thompson 40.00 80.00
15 Charlie Gardiner 25.00 50.00
16 Terry Sawchuk 50.00 120.00
17 Frank Brimsek 25.00 50.00
18 Vladislav Tretiak 30.00 60.00
19 Bernie Parent 30.00 60.00
20 Ed Giacomin 75.00 150.00

2005-06 Between the Pipes

COMPLETE SET (25) 6.00 15.00
1 Johnny Bower .40 1.00
2 Turk Broda .40 1.00
3 Martin Brodeur 1.25 3.00
4 Richard Brodeur .20 .50
5 Gerry Cheevers .40 1.00
6 Tony Esposito .40 1.00
7 Grant Fuhr .40 1.00
8 Ed Giacomin .30 .75
9 Glenn Hall .30 .75
10 Ron Hextall .40 1.00
11 Charlie Hodge .20 .50
12 Mike Palmateer .30 .75
13 Bernie Parent .40 1.00
14 Jacques Plante .75 2.00
15 Bill Ranford .20 .50
16 Chico Resch .20 .50
17 Patrick Roy 1.25 3.00
18 Terry Sawchuk .75 2.00
19 Billy Smith .40 1.00
20 Jose Theodore .40 1.00
21 Tiny Thompson .40 1.00
22 Vladislav Tretiak .40 1.00
23 Rogie Vachon .30 .75
24 Georges Vezina .40 1.00
25 Gump Worsley .40 1.00

2005-06 Between the Pipes Autographs

ABP Bernie Parent 12.00 30.00
ABR Bill Ranford 6.00 15.00
ABS Billy Smith 10.00 25.00
ACH Charlie Hodge 8.00 20.00
ACR Chico Resch 6.00 15.00
AEG Ed Giacomin 10.00 25.00
AGC Gerry Cheevers 10.00 25.00
AGH Glenn Hall 10.00 25.00
AGR Grant Fuhr 10.00 25.00
AGW Gump Worsley 10.00 25.00
AJB Johnny Bower 12.00 30.00
AJT Jose Theodore 10.00 25.00
AMB Martin Brodeur 60.00 100.00
AMP Mike Palmateer 10.00 25.00
APR Patrick Roy 60.00 100.00
ARB Richard Brodeur 6.00 15.00
ARH Ron Hextall 10.00 25.00
ARV Rogie Vachon 8.00 20.00
ATO Tony Esposito 12.00 30.00
AVT Vladislav Tretiak 15.00 40.00

2005-06 Between the Pipes Complete Package

CP1 Grant Fuhr 30.00 60.00
CP2 Patrick Roy 40.00 80.00
CP3 Jacques Plante 60.00 120.00
CP4 Gerry Cheevers 25.00 60.00
CP5 Terry Sawchuk 40.00 100.00
CP6 Bernie Parent 40.00 80.00
CP7 Jose Theodore 25.00 60.00

2005-06 Between the Pipes Double Memorabilia

DM1 Patrick Roy 20.00 50.00
DM2 Patrick Roy 20.00 50.00
DM3 Martin Brodeur 15.00 40.00
DM4 Ron Hextall 10.00 25.00
DM5 Tony Esposito 10.00 25.00
DM6 Gerry Cheevers 10.00 25.00
DM7 Vladislav Tretiak 20.00 50.00
DM8 Jose Theodore 12.00 30.00

2005-06 Between the Pipes Gloves

GUG1 Tony Esposito 10.00 25.00
GUG2 Patrick Roy 15.00 40.00
GUG3 Gilles Gilbert 10.00 25.00
GUG4 Vladislav Tretiak 20.00 50.00
GUG5 Jose Theodore 10.00 25.00
GUG6 Rogie Vachon 8.00 20.00
GUG7 Charlie Hodge 8.00 20.00
GUG8 Grant Fuhr 10.00 25.00

2005-06 Between the Pipes Jerseys

GOLD/20: .8X TO 2X BASIC JSY
GUJ1 Patrick Roy 12.00 30.00
GUJ2 Patrick Roy 12.00 30.00
GUJ3 Martin Brodeur 12.00 30.00
GUJ4 Tony Esposito 8.00 20.00
GUJ5 Vladislav Tretiak 8.00 20.00
GUJ6 Glenn Hall 8.00 20.00
GUJ7 Mike Richter 8.00 20.00
GUJ8 Jose Theodore 8.00 20.00
GUJ9 Billy Smith 8.00 20.00
GUJ10 Grant Fuhr 8.00 20.00
GUJ11 Bill Ranford 5.00 12.00
GUJ12 Richard Brodeur 5.00 12.00

2005-06 Between the Pipes Jersey and Sticks

SJ1 Patrick Roy 15.00 40.00
SJ2 Patrick Roy 15.00 40.00
SJ3 Martin Brodeur 15.00 40.00
SJ4 Ed Giacomin 10.00 25.00
SJ5 Johnny Bower 10.00 25.00
SJ6 Tony Esposito 10.00 25.00
SJ7 Mike Richter 10.00 25.00
SJ8 Ron Hextall 10.00 25.00
SJ9 Jose Theodore 10.00 25.00
SJ10 Grant Fuhr 10.00 25.00

2005-06 Between the Pipes Pads

GUP1 Bernie Parent 12.00 30.00
GUP2 Grant Fuhr 12.00 30.00
GUP3 Gerry Cheevers 12.00 30.00
GUP4 Ron Hextall 12.00 30.00
GUP5 Martin Brodeur 15.00 40.00
GUP6 Patrick Roy 20.00 50.00
GUP7 Jacques Plante 25.00 60.00
GUP8 Jose Theodore 12.00 30.00

2005-06 Between the Pipes Signed Memorabilia

SM1 Patrick Roy 50.00 100.00
SM2 Patrick Roy 50.00 100.00
SM3 Martin Brodeur 40.00 80.00
SM4 Glenn Hall 20.00 40.00
SM5 Johnny Bower 20.00 40.00
SM6 Gerry Cheevers 20.00 40.00
SM7 Ed Giacomin 20.00 40.00
SM8 Jose Theodore 20.00 40.00
SM9 Grant Fuhr 40.00 80.00
SM10 Bernie Parent 30.00 60.00

2006-07 Between The Pipes

COMPLETE SET (150) 15.00 40.00
1 Al Montoya .30 .75
2 Andrew Penner .25 .60
3 Barry Brust .25 .60
4 Brent Krahn .25 .60
5 Bryan Pitton .25 .60
6 Brian Finley .25 .60
7 Carey Price 1.25 3.00
8 Chris Beckford-Tseu .30 .75
9 Corey Crawford .30 .75
10 Craig Anderson .30 .75
11 Curtis McElhinney .25 .60
12 David LeNeveu .25 .60
13 Frank Doyle .25 .60
14 Frederic Cassivi .25 .60
15 Gerald Coleman .25 .60
16 Hannu Toivonen .25 .60
17 Jaroslav Halak .60 1.50
18 Jason Bacashihua .25 .60
19 Jason LaBarbera .25 .60
20 Jeff Glass .25 .60
21 J-F Racine .25 .60
22 Jimmy Howard .50 1.25
23 John Murray .25 .60
24 Jonathan Bernier .60 1.50
25 Jordan Parise .50 1.25
26 Josh Harding .30 .75
27 J-P Levasseur .25 .60
28 Julien Ellis .25 .60
29 Justin Leclerc .25 .60
30 Justin Pogge .25 .60
31 Kelly Guard .25 .60
32 Kevin Lalande .25 .60
33 Kurt Mucha .25 .60
34 Kyle Moir .25 .60
35 Leland Irving .40 1.00
36 Marek Schwarz .30 .75
37 Martin Houle .25 .60
38 Michael Leighton .25 .60
39 Mikael Tellqvist .30 .75
40 Mike Smith .50 1.25
41 Nicola Riopel .25 .60
42 Pekka Rinne .30 .75
43 Philippe Sauve .25 .60
44 Rejean Beauchemin .25 .60
45 Ryan Daniels .25 .60
46 Stefan Liv .20 .50
47 Tobias Stephan .25 .60
48 Steve Mason .60 1.50
49 Trevor Cann .25 .60
50 Tuukka Rask .75 2.00
51 Tyler Plante .25 .60
52 Tyson Sexsmith .25 .60
53 Wade Dubielewicz .25 .60
54 Yann Danis .25 .60
55 Yutaka Fukufuji .25 .60
56 Alex Auld .20 .50
57 Antero Niittymaki .25 .60
58 Cam Ward .30 .75
59 Cristobal Huet .25 .60
60 Peter Budaj .25 .60
61 Dominik Hasek .50 1.25
62 Dwayne Roloson .25 .60
63 Henrik Lundqvist .75 2.00
64 Ilya Bryzgalov .30 .75
65 Ed Belfour .30 .75
66 Johan Holmqvist .30 .75
67 Kari Lehtonen .25 .60
68 Manny Fernandez .20 .50
69 Marc-Andre Fleury .60 1.50
70 Martin Brodeur .75 2.00
71 Martin Gerber .25 .60
72 Pascal Leclaire .25 .60
73 Ray Emery .25 .60
74 Rick DiPietro .25 .60
75 Roberto Luongo .50 1.25
76 Ryan Miller .30 .75
77 Tim Thomas .30 .75
78 Andy Moog .30 .75
79 Bernie Parent .40 1.00
80 Billy Smith .30 .75
81 Brian Hayward .25 .60
82 Charlie Hodge .40 1.00
83 Chico Resch .30 .75
84 Dan Bouchard .30 .75
85 Doug Favell .30 .75
86 Ed Giacomin .50 1.25
87 Emile Francis .30 .75
88 Felix Potvin .50 1.25
89 Gerry Cheevers .30 .75
90 Gilles Gilbert .25 .60
91 Glenn Hall .30 .75
92 Grant Fuhr .50 1.25
93 Gump Worsley .30 .75
94 John Davidson .30 .75
95 Johnny Bower .30 .75
96 Ken Wregget .25 .60
97 Mike Palmateer .30 .75
98 Patrick Roy .75 2.00
99 Richard Brodeur .25 .60
100 Rogie Vachon .40 1.00
101 Ron Hextall .30 .75
102 Tom Barrasso .30 .75
103 Tony Esposito .30 .75
104 Vladislav Tretiak .25 .60
105 Al Montoya .30 .75
106 Cam Ward .30 .75
107 Carey Price 1.25 3.00
108 Grant Fuhr .50 1.25
109 Hannu Toivonen .25 .60
110 Kari Lehtonen .25 .60
111 Leland Irving .40 1.00
112 Marc-Andre Fleury .60 1.50
113 Marek Schwarz .30 .75
114 Martin Brodeur .75 2.00
115 Rick DiPietro .25 .60
116 Tuukka Rask .75 2.00
117 Martin Brodeur .75 2.00
118 Patrick Roy .75 2.00
119 Roberto Luongo .50 1.25
120 Marc-Andre Fleury .60 1.50
121 Carey Price 1.25 3.00
122 Justin Pogge .25 .60
123 Jeff Glass .25 .60
124 Bill Ranford .30 .75
125 Ed Belfour .30 .75
126 George Hainsworth .30 .75
127 Georges Vezina .50 1.25
128 Jacques Plante .30 .75
129 Pelle Lindbergh .25 .60
130 Roger Crozier .30 .75
131 Roy Worters .30 .75
132 Terry Sawchuk .40 1.00
133 Tiny Thompson .30 .75
134 Turk Broda .30 .75
135 Bower/Sawchuk .40 1.00
136 Parent/Favell .40 1.00
137 Smith/Resch .30 .75
138 Worsley/Vachon .40 1.00
139 Belfour/Hasek .50 1.25
140 Giacomin/Davidson .50 1.25
141 Plante/Hall .30 .75
142 Hasek/Fuhr .50 1.25
143 Patrick Roy .75 2.00
144 Terry Sawchuk .40 1.00
145 Bernie Parent .40 1.00
146 George Hainsworth .30 .75
147 Glenn Hall .30 .75
148 Grant Fuhr .50 1.25
149 Martin Brodeur .75 2.00
150 Gerry Cheevers .30 .75

2006-07 Between The Pipes Aspiring

AS01 M.Brodeur/C.Ward 20.00 50.00
AS02 P.Roy/C.Huet 20.00 50.00
AS03 D.Hasek/R.Miller 12.00 30.00
AS04 R.Luongo/L.Irving 10.00 25.00
AS05 P.Roy/C.Price 30.00 80.00
AS06 D.Hasek/M.Schwarz 12.00 30.00
AS07 G.Fuhr/R.Emery 12.00 30.00
AS08 P.Lindbergh/H.Lundqvist 20.00 50.00
AS09 M.Brodeur/J.Glass 20.00 50.00
AS10 P.Roy/J.Bernier 20.00 50.00

2006-07 Between The Pipes Autographs

COMMON CARD 3.00 8.00
SEMISTARS 4.00 10.00
UNLISTED STARS 5.00 12.00
AAA Alex Auld 3.00 8.00
AAM Al Montoya 5.00 12.00
AAM2 Al Montoya SP 12.00 30.00
AAMO Andy Moog 5.00 12.00
AAN Antero Niittymaki 4.00 10.00
AAP Andrew Penner 4.00 10.00
ABB Barry Brust 4.00 10.00
ABF Brian Finley 4.00 10.00
ABH Brian Hayward 4.00 10.00
ABK Brent Krahn 4.00 10.00
ABP Bernie Parent 8.00 20.00
ABPI Bryan Pitton 4.00 10.00
ABR Bill Ranford 8.00 20.00
ABS Billy Smith 5.00 12.00
ACA Craig Anderson 5.00 12.00
ACBT Chris Beckford-Tseu 5.00 12.00
ACC Corey Crawford 8.00 20.00
ACH Cristobal Huet 4.00 10.00
ACHO Charlie Hodge 6.00 15.00
ACM Curtis McElhinney 4.00 10.00
ACP Carey Price 25.00 50.00
ACP2 Carey Price SP 50.00 100.00
ACP3 Carey Price 60.00 125.00
ACR Chico Resch 5.00 12.00
ACW Cam Ward 5.00 12.00
ACW2 Cam Ward SP 12.00 30.00
ADB Dan Bouchard 5.00 12.00
ADD Devan Dubnyk 6.00 15.00
ADF Doug Favell 5.00 12.00
ADH Dominik Hasek 15.00 40.00
ADL David LeNeveu 4.00 10.00
ADR Dwayne Roloson 4.00 10.00
AEB Ed Belfour 25.00 50.00
AEB2 Ed Belfour 25.00 50.00
AEF Emile Francis 5.00 12.00
AEG Ed Giacomin 8.00 20.00
AFC Frederic Cassivi 4.00 10.00
AFD Frank Doyle 4.00 10.00
AFP Felix Potvin 8.00 20.00
AGC Gerry Cheevers 5.00 12.00
AGF Grant Fuhr 8.00 20.00
AGF2 Grant Fuhr SP 12.00 30.00
AGG Gilles Gilbert 4.00 10.00
AGH Glenn Hall 5.00 12.00
AGW Gump Worsley 8.00 20.00
AHL Henrik Lundqvist 15.00 40.00
AHT Hannu Toivonen 4.00 10.00
AHT2 Hannu Toivonen SP 8.00 20.00
AIB Ilya Bryzgalov 5.00 12.00
AJB Johnny Bower 8.00 20.00
AJBA Jason Bacashihua 4.00 10.00
AJBE Jonathan Bernier 10.00 25.00
AJD John Davidson 8.00 20.00
AJDL Jeff Deslauriers 3.00 8.00
AJE Julien Ellis 4.00 10.00
AJFR J-F Racine 4.00 10.00
AJG Jeff Glass 4.00 10.00
AJG2 Jeff Glass 8.00 20.00
AJH Jimmy Howard 10.00 25.00
AJHA Jaroslav Halak 10.00 25.00
AJHO Johan Holmqvist 5.00 12.00
AJHR Josh Harding 5.00 12.00
AJL Justin Leclerc 4.00 10.00
AJLB Jason LaBarbera 4.00 10.00
AJM John Murray 4.00 10.00
AJP Justin Pogge 4.00 10.00
AJP2 Justin Pogge 25.00 50.00
AJPA Jordan Parise 8.00 20.00
AJPL J-P Levasseur 4.00 10.00
AJV John Vanbiesbrouck 12.00 30.00
AKG Kelly Guard 4.00 10.00

AKL Kari Lehtonen 4.00 10.00
AKL2 Kari Lehtonen 15.00 40.00
AKLA Kevin Lalande 4.00 10.00
AKM Kyle Moir 4.00 10.00
AKMU Kurt Mucha 4.00 10.00
AKW Ken Wregget 4.00 10.00
ALI Leland Irving 6.00 15.00
ALI2 Leland Irving SP 25.00 60.00
AMB Martin Brodeur 60.00 120.00
AMB2 Martin Brodeur 60.00 120.00
AMB3 Martin Brodeur 40.00 100.00
AMF Marc-Andre Fleury 40.00 80.00
AMF2 Marc-Andre Fleury SP 40.00 80.00
AMF3 Marc-Andre Fleury 40.00 80.00
AMFR Manny Fernandez 3.00 8.00
AMG Martin Gerber 4.00 10.00
AMH Martin Houle 4.00 10.00
AML Michael Leighton 4.00 10.00
AMP Mike Palmateer 5.00 12.00
AMS Marek Schwarz 5.00 12.00
AMS2 Marek Schwarz 25.00 50.00
AMSM Mike Smith 8.00 20.00
ANR Nicola Riopel 4.00 10.00
APL Pascal Leclaire 4.00 10.00
APR Patrick Roy 60.00 120.00
APR2 Patrick Roy 60.00 120.00
APRI Pekka Rinne 5.00 12.00
APS Philippe Sauve 4.00 10.00
ARB Rejean Beauchemin 4.00 10.00
ARBR Richard Brodeur 4.00 10.00
ARD Ryan Daniels 4.00 10.00
ARDI Rick DiPietro 25.00 50.00
ARE Ray Emery 4.00 10.00
ARH Ron Hextall 5.00 12.00
ARL Roberto Luongo 8.00 20.00
ARL2 Roberto Luongo 25.00 60.00
ARM Ryan Miller 12.00 30.00
ARV Rogie Vachon 6.00 15.00
ASL Stefan Liv 6.00 15.00
ASM Steve Mason 8.00 20.00
ATB Tom Barrasso 12.00 30.00
ATC Trevor Cann 4.00 10.00
ATE Tony Esposito 8.00 20.00
ATM Thomas McCollum 5.00 12.00
ATP Tyler Plante 4.00 10.00
ATR Tuukka Rask 12.00 30.00
ATR2 Tuukka Rask 30.00 60.00
ATS Tyson Sexsmith 4.00 10.00
ATST Tobias Stephan 4.00 10.00
ATT Tim Thomas 10.00 25.00
AVT Vladislav Tretiak 25.00 60.00
AWD Wade Dubielewicz 4.00 10.00
AYD Yann Danis 4.00 10.00
AYFA Yutaka Fukufuji ENG 20.00 50.00
AYFB Yutaka Fukufuji KANJI 60.00 150.00

2006-07 Between The Pipes Double Jerseys

DJ01 A.Montoya/J.Davidson 10.00 25.00
DJ02 D.Roloson/M.Fernandez 8.00 20.00
DJ03 R.Hextall/B.Parent 20.00 50.00
DJ04 C.Ward/M.Brodeur 15.00 40.00
DJ05 C.Huet/P.Roy 20.00 50.00
DJ06 D.Hasek/R.Miller 15.00 40.00
DJ07 D.Hasek/T.Sawchuk 15.00 40.00
DJ08 E.Giacomin/H.Lundqvist 25.00 60.00
DJ09 V.Tretiak/V.Myshkin 15.00 40.00
DJ10 G.Cheevers/T.Thomas 12.00 30.00
DJ11 G.Hall/T.Esposito 12.00 30.00
DJ12 G.Fuhr/B.Ranford 15.00 40.00
DJ13 J.Plante/G.Worsley 25.00 50.00
DJ14 J.Davidson/M.Richter 12.00 30.00
DJ15 F.Potvin/J.Pogge 20.00 50.00
DJ16 A.Niittymaki/K.Lehtonen 8.00 20.00
DJ17 D.Bouchard/P.Roy 25.00 60.00
DJ18 M.Fleury/T.Barrasso 15.00 40.00
DJ19 M.Brodeur/T.Sawchuk 25.00 60.00
DJ20 I.Bryzgalov/V.Tretiak 15.00 40.00
DJ21 P.Roy/C.Price 25.00 60.00
DJ22 P.Roy/M.Brodeur 30.00 80.00
DJ23 R.Emery/D.Hasek 12.00 30.00
DJ24 R.DiPietro/B.Smith 12.00 30.00
DJ25 R.Luongo/M.Brodeur 15.00 40.00
DJ26 R.Worters/F.Brimsek 8.00 20.00
DJ27 J.Vanbiesbrouck/M.Richter 20.00 50.00
DJ28 F.Potvin/A.Raycroft 15.00 40.00
DJ29 R.Luongo/P.Roy 25.00 60.00

2006-07 Between The Pipes Double Memorabilia

COMMON CARD 8.00 20.00
SEMISTARS 10.00 25.00
UNLISTED STARS 12.00 30.00
DM01 Rogie Vachon 10.00 25.00
DM02 Martin Brodeur 20.00 50.00
DM03 Gerry Cheevers 12.00 30.00
DM04 Tony Esposito 8.00 20.00
DM05 Marc-Andre Fleury 10.00 25.00
DM06 Ed Giacomin 15.00 40.00
DM07 Dominik Hasek 12.00 30.00
DM08 Ron Hextall 15.00 40.00
DM09 Leland Irving 12.00 30.00
DM10 Roberto Luongo 10.00 25.00
DM11 Al Montoya 8.00 20.00
DM12 Bernie Parent 12.00 30.00
DM13 Jacques Plante 15.00 40.00
DM14 Patrick Roy (COL) 20.00 50.00
DM15 Patrick Roy (MTL) 20.00 50.00
DM16 Terry Sawchuk 20.00 50.00
DM17 Tiny Thompson 10.00 25.00
DM18 Hannu Toivonen 8.00 20.00
DM19 Vladislav Tretiak 15.00 40.00
DM20 Felix Potvin 15.00 40.00

2006-07 Between The Pipes Forgotten Franchises

COMPLETE SET (10) 10.00 25.00
COMMON CARD 1.50 4.00
FF01 Chuck Rayner 1.50 4.00
FF02 Hap Holmes 1.50 4.00
FF03 Alex Connell 1.50 4.00
FF04 Vernon Jake Forbes 1.50 4.00
FF05 Lorne Chabot 1.50 4.00
FF06 Earl Robertson 1.50 4.00
FF07 Clint Benedict 1.50 4.00
FF08 Wilf Cude 1.50 4.00
FF09 Roy Worters 1.50 4.00
FF10 Paddy Moran 1.50 4.00

2006-07 Between The Pipes Gloves

GG01 Martin Brodeur 8.00 20.00
GG02 Rick DiPietro 2.50 6.00
GG03 Tony Esposito 3.00 8.00
GG04 Marc-Andre Fleury 6.00 15.00
GG05 Grant Fuhr 5.00 12.00
GG06 Ed Giacomin 5.00 12.00
GG07 Gilles Gilbert 2.50 6.00
GG08 David LeNeveu 2.50 6.00
GG09 Dominik Hasek 5.00 12.00
GG10 Charlie Hodge 4.00 10.00
GG11 Leland Irving 4.00 10.00
GG12 Curtis Joseph 4.00 10.00
GG13 Felix Potvin 5.00 12.00
GG14 Al Montoya 3.00 8.00
GG15 Jacques Plante 3.00 8.00
GG16 Patrick Roy 8.00 20.00
GG17 Hannu Toivonen 2.50 6.00
GG18 Gump Worsley 3.00 8.00
GG19 Glenn Hall 3.00 8.00

2006-07 Between The Pipes Jerseys

GUJ01 Rogie Vachon 6.00 15.00
GUJ02 Marc-Andre Fleury 12.00 30.00
GUJ03 Henrik Lundqvist 10.00 25.00
GUJ04 Tony Esposito 6.00 15.00
GUJ05 Manny Fernandez 4.00 10.00
GUJ06 Jeff Glass 5.00 12.00
GUJ07 Kelly Guard 5.00 12.00
GUJ08 Ron Hextall 6.00 15.00
GUJ09 Kari Lehtonen 5.00 12.00
GUJ10 Roberto Luongo 10.00 25.00
GUJ11 Antero Niittymaki 5.00 12.00
GUJ12 Billy Smith 6.00 15.00
GUJ13 Mike Smith 6.00 15.00
GUJ14 Hannu Toivonen 5.00 12.00
GUJ15 Gump Worsley 10.00 25.00
GUJ16 Tom Barrasso 6.00 15.00
GUJ17 Richard Brodeur 5.00 12.00
GUJ18 Barry Brust 5.00 12.00
GUJ19 Dwayne Roloson 5.00 12.00
GUJ20 Martin Gerber 5.00 12.00
GUJ21 Jason Bacashihua 5.00 12.00
GUJ22 Jonathan Bernier 8.00 20.00
GUJ23 Rejean Beauchemin 5.00 12.00
GUJ24 Ryan Daniels 5.00 12.00
GUJ25 Yann Danis 5.00 12.00
GUJ26 Curtis McElhinney 5.00 12.00
GUJ27 Brian Finley 5.00 12.00
GUJ28 Mathieu Garon 5.00 12.00
GUJ29 Johan Holmqvist 6.00 15.00
GUJ30 Mikael Tellqvist 6.00 15.00
GUJ31 Pekka Rinne 6.00 15.00
GUJ32 Bill Ranford 6.00 15.00
GUJ33 Andrew Penner 5.00 12.00
GUJ34 Corey Crawford 6.00 15.00
GUJ35 Andy Moog 6.00 15.00
GUJ36 Jimmy Howard 6.00 15.00
GUJ37 Josh Harding 6.00 15.00
GUJ38 Martin Houle 5.00 12.00
GUJ39 Pascal Leclaire 5.00 12.00
GUJ40 Vladislav Tretiak 10.00 25.00
GUJ41 Leland Irving 5.00 12.00
GUJ42 Philippe Sauve 5.00 12.00
GUJ43 Brent Krahn 5.00 12.00
GUJ44 Maxime Ouellet 5.00 12.00
GUJ45 Grant Fuhr 10.00 25.00
GUJ46 Cristobal Huet 8.00 20.00
GUJ47 Ryan Miller 6.00 15.00
GUJ48 Carey Price 12.00 30.00
GUJ49 Terry Sawchuk 10.00 25.00
GUJ50 Tim Thomas 6.00 15.00
GUJ51 Justin Pogge 3.00 8.00
GUJ52 Ed Giacomin 10.00 25.00
GUJ53 Andrew Raycroft 5.00 12.00
GUJ54 Frank Brimsek 5.00 12.00
GUJ55 Glenn Hall 6.00 15.00
GUJ56 Ray Emery 5.00 12.00
GUJ57 J-S Aubin 5.00 12.00
GUJ58 Ilya Bryzgalov 6.00 15.00
GUJ59 Marek Schwarz 6.00 15.00
GUJ60 Peter Budaj 5.00 12.00
GUJ61 Dominik Hasek 10.00 25.00
GUJ62 Curtis Joseph 8.00 20.00
GUJ63 Felix Potvin 6.00 15.00
GUJ64 Cam Ward 6.00 15.00
GUJ65 Mike Richter 6.00 15.00
GUJ66 Patrick Roy 15.00 40.00
GUJ67 David LeNeveu 5.00 12.00
GUJ68 Alex Auld 4.00 10.00
GUJ69 Rick DiPietro 5.00 12.00
GUJ70 Martin Brodeur 12.00 30.00
GUJ71 Ed Belfour 6.00 15.00

2006-07 Between The Pipes Pads

COMMON CARD 8.00 20.00
SEMISTARS 10.00 25.00
UNLISTED STARS 12.00 30.00
GP01 Martin Brodeur 12.00 30.00
GP02 Gerry Cheevers 8.00 20.00
GP03 Grant Fuhr 8.00 20.00
GP04 Bernie Parent 8.00 20.00
GP05 Jacques Plante 12.00 30.00
GP06 Patrick Roy 15.00 40.00
GP07 Tiny Thompson 8.00 20.00
GP08 Vladislav Tretiak 25.00 60.00
GP09 Curtis Joseph 10.00 25.00
GP10 Ron Hextall 10.00 25.00
GP11 Ed Belfour 10.00 25.00

2006-07 Between The Pipes Playing For Your Country

PC01 Jonathan Bernier 15.00 40.00
PC02 Martin Brodeur 12.00 30.00
PC03 Ilya Bryzgalov 8.00 20.00
PC04 Roberto Luongo 12.00 30.00
PC05 Tom Barrasso 10.00 25.00
PC06 Vladimir Dzurilla 8.00 20.00
PC07 Grant Fuhr 12.00 30.00
PC08 Dominik Hasek 10.00 25.00
PC09 Cristobal Huet 8.00 20.00
PC10 Marc-Andre Fleury 10.00 25.00
PC11 Carey Price 15.00 40.00
PC12 John Vanbiesbrouck 8.00 20.00
PC13 Henrik Lundqvist 10.00 25.00
PC14 Rogie Vachon 8.00 20.00
PC15 Al Montoya 8.00 20.00
PC16 Vladimir Myshkin 12.00 30.00
PC17 Antero Niittymaki 8.00 20.00
PC18 Justin Pogge 10.00 25.00
PC19 Tony Esposito 10.00 25.00
PC20 Mike Richter 8.00 20.00
PC21 Patrick Roy 12.00 30.00
PC22 Marek Schwarz 6.00 15.00
PC23 Hannu Toivonen 8.00 20.00
PC24 Vladislav Tretiak 15.00 40.00
PC25 Curtis Joseph 8.00 20.00
PC26 Kari Lehtonen 8.00 20.00

2006-07 Between The Pipes Prospect Trios

PT01 Thomas/Finley/Toivo 12.00 30.00
PT02 Leclaire/Budaj/Hard 12.00 30.00
PT03 Emery/Glass/Guard 15.00 40.00
PT04 Niitty/Houle/Beauch 15.00 40.00
PT05 McEl/Lalande/Irving 10.00 25.00
PT06 Irving/Bernier/Cann 15.00 40.00
PT07 Price/Levass/Mason 20.00 50.00
PT08 Ellis/LaCosta/Peters 8.00 20.00
PT09 Price/Westblom/Irving 20.00 50.00
PT10 Lalande/Plante/Moir 10.00 25.00
PT11 Daniels/Vincent/Ellis 10.00 25.00
PT12 Price/Boutin/Bernier 20.00 50.00
PT13 Fleury/Auld/Lehtonen 15.00 40.00
PT14 Bernier/Brust/Labarb 12.00 30.00
PT15 Huet/Price/Danis 20.00 50.00
PT16 Beck/Schwarz/Baca 10.00 25.00
PT17 Aubin/Coleman/Craw 12.00 30.00
PT18 Pogge/Bryz/Montoya 10.00 25.00
PT19 Thomp/Boutin/Munro 10.00 25.00
PT20 LeNev/Cassivi/Ouellet 10.00 25.00

2006-07 Between The Pipes Roy vs. Brodeur

RB01 Roy (MTL)/Brodeur JSY 40.00 80.00
RB02 Roy (COL)/Brodeur JSY 40.00 80.00
RB03 Roy (MTL)/Brodeur JSY 40.00 80.00
RB04 Roy (COL)/Brodeur JSY 40.00 80.00
RB05 Roy/Brodeur JSY 40.00 80.00
RB06 Roy/Brodeur GLV 40.00 80.00

2006-07 Between The Pipes Shooting Gallery

SG01 Vezina/Plante/Vach etc 250.00 400.00
SG02 Bower/Sawch/Palm etc 125.00 250.00
SG03 Thomp/Cheev/Gilb etc 75.00 175.00
SG04 Gard/Francis/Brims etc 75.00 175.00
SG05 Giac/Davids/VBK etc 150.00 300.00
SG06 Sawch/Croz/Giac etc 100.00 200.00
SG07 Parent/Lind/Hexy etc 125.00 250.00
SG08 Tret/Hasek/Richt etc 125.00 250.00
SG09 Sawch/Plant/Bow etc 75.00 150.00
SG10 Durn/Plante/Hall etc 200.00 350.00

2006-07 Between The Pipes Stick and Jersey

SJ01 Manny Fernandez 10.00 25.00
SJ02 Johnny Bower 10.00 25.00
SJ03 Martin Brodeur 15.00 40.00
SJ04 Gerry Cheevers 12.00 30.00
SJ05 John Davidson 10.00 25.00
SJ06 Rick DiPietro 12.50 30.00
SJ07 Ray Emery 8.00 20.00
SJ08 Tony Esposito 12.00 30.00
SJ09 Marc-Andre Fleury 15.00 40.00
SJ10 Grant Fuhr 12.00 30.00
SJ11 Ed Giacomin 12.00 30.00
SJ12 Glenn Hall 12.00 30.00
SJ13 Dominik Hasek 12.00 30.00
SJ14 Ron Hextall 15.00 40.00
SJ15 Cristobal Huet 10.00 25.00
SJ16 Leland Irving 12.00 30.00
SJ17 Jason LaBarbera 10.00 25.00
SJ18 Roberto Luongo 15.00 40.00
SJ19 Henrik Lundqvist 12.00 30.00
SJ20 Ryan Miller 12.50 30.00
SJ21 Al Montoya 10.00 25.00
SJ22 Antero Niittymaki 10.00 25.00
SJ23 Felix Potvin 10.00 40.00
SJ24 Bernie Parent 15.00 40.00
SJ25 Jacques Plante 25.00 60.00
SJ26 Andrew Raycroft 10.00 25.00
SJ27 Mike Richter 10.00 25.00
SJ28 Pekka Rinne 10.00 25.00
SJ29 Patrick Roy (COL) 15.00 40.00
SJ30 Patrick Roy (MTL) 20.00 50.00
SJ31 Terry Sawchuk 20.00 50.00
SJ32 Billy Smith 12.00 30.00
SJ33 Roger Crozier 10.00 25.00
SJ34 Tim Thomas 10.00 25.00
SJ35 Hannu Toivonen 10.00 25.00
SJ36 Rogie Vachon 12.00 30.00
SJ37 John Vanbiesbrouck 12.00 30.00
SJ38 Gump Worsley 12.00 30.00
SJ39 Richard Brodeur 12.00 30.00
SJ40 Tom Barrasso 12.00 30.00

2006-07 Between The Pipes Stick Work

SW01 Roy/Brodeur/Luongo 50.00 120.00
SW02 Crozier/Hasek/Miller 40.00 80.00
SW03 Parent/Lind/Hextall 40.00 80.00
SW04 Worsley/Roy/Huet 40.00 100.00
SW05 Espo/Cheesy/Giaco 12.00 30.00
SW06 Bower/Palma/Potvin 60.00 120.00

2006-07 Between The Pipes The Mask

COMPLETE SET (40) 125.00 250.00
M01 Al Montoya 4.00 10.00
M02 Kari Lehtonen 5.00 12.00
M03 Miikka Kiprusoff 5.00 12.00
M04 Antero Niittymaki 3.00 8.00
M05 Ray Emery 3.00 8.00
M06 Andrew Raycroft 3.00 8.00
M07 Ryan Miller 5.00 12.00
M08 Martin Gerber 3.00 8.00
M09 Ken Dryden 8.00 20.00
M10 Marc-Andre Fleury 6.00 15.00
M11 Joey MacDonald 3.00 8.00
M12 Henrik Lundqvist 5.00 12.00
M13 Cam Ward 4.00 10.00
M14 Cristobal Huet 5.00 12.00
M15 Rick DiPietro 4.00 10.00
M16 Ilya Bryzgalov 3.00 8.00
M17 Jose Theodore 4.00 10.00
M18 Dominik Hasek 8.00 20.00
M19 Nikolai Khabibulin 4.00 10.00
M20 Marty Turco 4.00 10.00
M21 Marek Schwarz 3.00 8.00
M22 Patrick Roy 10.00 25.00
M23 Dominik Hasek 8.00 20.00
M24 Ed Belfour 4.00 10.00
M25 Manny Legace 3.00 8.00
M26 Curtis Joseph 5.00 12.00
M27 Hannu Toivonen 3.00 8.00
M28 Martin Biron 3.00 8.00
M29 Dan Cloutier 3.00 8.00
M30 Kevin Weekes 3.00 8.00
M31 Jimmy Howard 4.00 10.00
M32 Devan Dubnyk 3.00 8.00
M33 Mikael Tellqvist 3.00 8.00
M34 Jacques Plante 6.00 15.00
M35 Jeff Glass 3.00 8.00
M36 Henrik Lundqvist 5.00 12.00
M37 Vesa Toskala 3.00 8.00
M38 Johan Hedberg 3.00 8.00
M39 Tomas Vokoun 4.00 10.00
M40 Carey Price 10.00 25.00

2006-07 Between The Pipes The Mask Silver

*SILVER: .5X to 1.5X MASK HI

2006-07 Between The Pipes The Mask Game-Used

MGU01 Martin Biron 15.00 40.00
MGU02 Ilya Bryzgalov 15.00 40.00
MGU03 Rick DiPietro 20.00 50.00
MGU04 Ken Dryden 100.00 200.00
MGU05 Ray Emery 15.00 40.00
MGU06 Marc-Andre Fleury 30.00 60.00
MGU07 Dominik Hasek 40.00 80.00
MGU08 Cristobal Huet 20.00 50.00
MGU09 Miikka Kiprusoff 40.00 80.00
MGU10 Kari Lehtonen 20.00 50.00
MGU11 Henrik Lundqvist 30.00 60.00
MGU12 Ryan Miller 20.00 50.00
MGU13 Al Montoya 15.00 40.00
MGU14 Antero Niittymaki 15.00 40.00
MGU15 Jacques Plante 30.00 80.00
MGU16 Andrew Raycroft 20.00 50.00
MGU17 Patrick Roy 40.00 100.00
MGU18 Marty Turco 15.00 40.00
MGU19 Cam Ward 15.00 40.00
MGU20 Hannu Toivonen 15.00 40.00

2007-08 Between The Pipes

COMPLETE SET (100) 12.00 30.00
1 Adam Courchaine .25 .60
2 Adam Dennis .25 .60
3 Al Montoya .25 .60
4 Antoine Lafleur .25 .60
5 Braden Holtby .75 2.00
6 Brian Elliott .40 1.00
7 Carey Price 1.25 3.00
8 Corey Crawford .30 .75
9 Cory Schneider .60 1.50
10 Curtis McElhinney .30 .75
11 Daren Machesney .25 .60
12 Devan Dubnyk .40 1.00
13 Dustin Tokarski .30 .75
14 Erik Ersberg .30 .75
15 Hannu Toivonen .25 .60
16 Jaroslav Halak .60 1.50
17 Jeff Deslauriers .25 .60
18 Jeff Glass .25 .60
19 Jeremy Smith .30 .75
20 Jimmy Howard .50 1.25
21 John Murray .25 .60
22 Jonas Hiller .40 1.00
23 Jonathan Bernier .40 1.00
24 Jordan Parise .30 .75
25 Jordan Sigalet .25 .60
26 Josh Tordjman .50 1.25
27 Josh Unice .30 .75
28 Justin Peters .25 .60
29 Justin Pogge .25 .60
30 Karri Ramo .30 .75
31 Kevin Desfosses .25 .60
32 Kevin Poulin .30 .75
33 Kyle Gajewski .25 .60
34 Leland Irving .30 .75
35 Linden Rowat .30 .75
36 Marek Schwarz .30 .75
37 Matt Keetley .20 .50
38 Maxime Daigneault .25 .60
39 Michal Neuvirth .40 1.00
40 Mike Murphy .30 .75
41 Ondrej Pavelec .40 1.00
42 Pekka Rinne .30 .75
43 Peter Delmas .20 .50
44 Riku Helenius .25 .60
45 Robert Mayer .30 .75
46 Ryan Munce .25 .60
47 Scott Munroe .25 .60
48 Simeon Varlamov .60 1.50
49 Steve Mason 2.50 6.00
50 Taylor Dakers .25 .60
51 Thomas Greiss .40 1.00
52 Thomas McCollum .30 .75
53 Tobias Stephan .25 .60
54 Tomas Popperle .20 .50
55 Tomi Karhunen .25 .60
56 Torrie Jung .25 .60
57 Trevor Cann .25 .60
58 Tuukka Rask .75 2.00
59 Tyler Weiman .25 .60
60 Tyson Sexsmith .25 .60
61 Cam Ward .30 .75
62 Dan Cloutier .25 .60
63 Dominik Hasek .50 1.25
64 Jean-Sebastien Giguere .30 .75
65 Kari Lehtonen .25 .60
66 Tim Thomas .30 .75
67 Martin Brodeur .75 2.00
68 Marty Turco .30 .75
69 Pascal Leclaire .25 .60
70 Peter Budaj .25 .60
71 Ray Emery .25 .60
72 Roberto Luongo .50 1.25
73 Ryan Miller .30 .75
74 Tomas Vokoun .25 .60
75 Terry Sawchuk .40 1.00
76 Billy Smith .30 .75
77 Felix Potvin .50 1.25
78 Glenn Hall .30 .75
79 Grant Fuhr .50 1.25
80 Gump Worsley .40 1.00
81 John Davidson .25 .60
82 Johnny Bower .30 .75
83 Mike Palmateer .30 .75
84 Patrick Roy .75 2.00
85 Rogie Vachon .40 1.00
86 Ron Hextall .30 .75
87 Tom Barrasso .30 .75
88 Ed Giacomin .30 .75
89 Tony Esposito .30 .75
90 Gerry Cheevers .30 .75
91 Joe Daley .30 .75
92 Gilles Gratton .30 .75
93 Richard Brodeur .25 .60
94 Bernie Parent .40 1.00
95 Les Binkley .25 .60
96 Ernie Wakely .25 .60
97 Michel Dion .25 .60
98 John Garrett .25 .60
99 Mike Liut .20 .50
100 Ed Mio .25 .60

2007-08 Between The Pipes Autographs

AAC Adam Courchaine 4.00 10.00
AAD Adam Dennis 4.00 10.00
AAL Antoine Lafleur 4.00 10.00
AAM Al Montoya 4.00 10.00
ABE Brian Elliott 6.00 15.00
ABH Braden Holtby 12.00 30.00
ABP Bernie Parent SP 25.00 60.00
ABS Billy Smith SP 15.00 40.00
ACC Corey Crawford 12.00 30.00
ACM Curtis McElhinney 5.00 12.00
ACO Chris Osgood SP 5.00 12.00
ACP Carey Price 20.00 50.00
ACS Cory Schneider 10.00 25.00
ACW Cam Ward 5.00 12.00
ADC Dan Cloutier 4.00 10.00
ADD Devan Dubnyk 6.00 15.00
ADH Dominik Hasek SP 10.00 25.00
ADMA1 Daren Machesney 4.00 10.00
ADMA2 Drew MacIntyre 3.00 8.00
ADT Dustin Tokarski 5.00 12.00
AEE Erik Ersberg 5.00 12.00
AEM Ed Mio 4.00 10.00
AEW Ernie Wakely 4.00 10.00
AFP Felix Potvin SP 8.00 20.00
AGC Gerry Cheevers SP 15.00 40.00
AGE Grant Fuhr SP 8.00 20.00
AGG Gilles Gratton 5.00 12.00
AGH Glenn Hall SP 20.00 50.00
AGW Gump Worsley SP 20.00 50.00
AHT Hannu Toivonen 4.00 10.00
AJB Johnny Bower SP 8.00 20.00
AJBE Jonathan Bernier 6.00 15.00
AJD Jeff Deslauriers 4.00 10.00
AJDA Joe Daley 5.00 12.00
AJG Jeff Glass 4.00 10.00
AJGA John Garrett 4.00 10.00
AJH Jaroslav Halak 10.00 25.00
AJHA Josh Harding SP 15.00 40.00
AJHI Jonas Hiller 6.00 15.00
AJHO Jimmy Howard 8.00 20.00
AJM John Murray 4.00 10.00
AJP Justin Pogge 4.00 10.00
AJPA Jordan Parise 5.00 12.00
AJPE Justin Peters 4.00 10.00
AJS Jordan Sigalet 4.00 10.00
AJSG Jean-Sebastien Giguere SP 5.00 12.00
AJSM Jeremy Smith 5.00 12.00
AJT Josh Tordjman 8.00 20.00
AJU Josh Unice 5.00 12.00
AKD Kevin Desfosses 4.00 10.00
AKG Kyle Gajewski 4.00 10.00
AKL Kari Lehtonen 4.00 10.00
AKP Kevin Poulin 5.00 12.00
AKR Karri Ramo 5.00 12.00
ALB Les Binkley 4.00 10.00
ALI Leland Irving 5.00 12.00
ALR Linden Rowat 5.00 12.00
AMB Martin Brodeur SP 25.00 60.00
AMD Michel Dion 4.00 10.00
AMDA Maxime Daigneault 4.00 10.00
AMG Martin Gerber SP 4.00 10.00
AMK Matt Keetley 3.00 8.00
AML Mike Liut 3.00 8.00
AMM Mike Murphy 5.00 12.00
AMN Michal Neuvirth 6.00 15.00
AMP Mike Palmateer SP 12.00 30.00
AMS Marek Schwarz 5.00 12.00
AMT Marty Turco SP 5.00 12.00
AOP Ondrej Pavelec 6.00 15.00
APB Peter Budaj 4.00 10.00
APD Peter Delmas 3.00 8.00
APL Pascal Leclaire 4.00 10.00
APR Patrick Roy SP 30.00 80.00
APRI Pekka Rinne 8.00 20.00
ARB Richard Brodeur 4.00 10.00
ARE Ray Emery SP 8.00 20.00
ARH Riku Helenius 4.00 10.00
ARHE Ron Hextall SP 5.00 12.00
ARL Roberto Luongo SP 10.00 25.00
ARM Ryan Miller SP 12.00 30.00
ARMA Robert Mayer 5.00 12.00
ARMU Ryan Munce 4.00 10.00
ARV Rogie Vachon SP 12.00 30.00
ASM Scott Munroe 4.00 10.00
ASMA Steve Mason 10.00 25.00
ATB Tom Barrasso SP 8.00 20.00
ATC Trevor Cann 4.00 10.00
ATD Taylor Dakers 4.00 10.00
ATE Tony Esposito SP 12.00 30.00
ATG Thomas Greiss 6.00 15.00
ATJ Torrie Jung 4.00 10.00
ATK Tomi Karhunen 4.00 10.00
ATMC Thomas McCollum 5.00 12.00
ATP Tomas Popperle 3.00 8.00
ATR Tuukka Rask 15.00 40.00
ATS Tobias Stephan 4.00 10.00
ATSE Tyson Sexsmith 4.00 10.00
ATT Tim Thomas SP 10.00 25.00
ATV Tomas Vokoun SP 8.00 20.00
ATW Tyler Weiman 4.00 10.00
AVT Vladislav Tretiak SP 20.00 50.00
AYD Yann Danis 4.00 10.00
AJDAV John Davidson SP 4.00 10.00

2007-08 Between The Pipes First Round Goalies Jerseys

FRG01 Leland Irving 5.00 12.00
FRG02 John Davidson 4.00 10.00
FRG03 Jonathan Bernier 6.00 15.00
FRG04 Tuukka Rask 12.00 30.00
FRG05 Carey Price 20.00 50.00
FRG06 Marek Schwarz 5.00 12.00
FRG07 Devan Dubnyk 6.00 15.00
FRG08 Al Montoya 4.00 10.00
FRG09 Marc-Andre Fleury 10.00 25.00
FRG10 Cam Ward 5.00 12.00
FRG11 Kari Lehtonen 4.00 10.00
FRG12 Adam Munro 4.00 10.00
FRG13 Hannu Toivonen 4.00 10.00
FRG14 Pascal Leclaire 4.00 10.00
FRG15 Dan Cloutier 4.00 10.00
FRG16 Jean-Sebastien Giguere 5.00 12.00
FRG17 Roberto Luongo 8.00 20.00
FRG18 Grant Fuhr 8.00 20.00
FRG19 Tom Barrasso 5.00 12.00
FRG20 Martin Brodeur 12.00 30.00

2007-08 Between The Pipes Flashbacks

COMPLETE SET (10) 15.00 40.00
FB01 Martin Brodeur 5.00 12.00
FB02 Dominik Hasek 3.00 8.00
FB03 Ray Emery 1.50 4.00
FB04 Patrick Roy 5.00 12.00
FB05 Ryan Miller 2.00 5.00
FB06 Ed Belfour 2.00 5.00
FB07 Jean-Sebastien Giguere 2.00 5.00
FB08 Roberto Luongo 3.00 8.00
FB09 Cam Ward 2.00 5.00
FB10 Kari Lehtonen 1.50 4.00

2007-08 Between The Pipes Goaltending Traditions

COMPLETE SET (10) 20.00 50.00
GT01 J.Bernier/R.Vachon 2.50 6.00
GT02 C.Price/P.Roy 8.00 20.00
GT03 T.Cann/P.Roy 5.00 12.00
GT04 J.Howard/D.Hasek 3.00 8.00
GT05 L.Irving/M.Vernon 2.50 6.00
GT06 A.Montoya/M.Richter 2.00 5.00
GT07 C.Schneider/R.Luongo 4.00 10.00
GT08 J.Pogge/F.Potvin 3.00 8.00
GT09 T.Rask/G.Cheevers 5.00 12.00
GT10 M.Schwarz/G.Hall 2.00 5.00

2007-08 Between The Pipes Jerseys

CCJ01 Adam Munro 4.00 10.00
CCJ02 Barry Brust 4.00 10.00
CCJ03 Brian Elliott 6.00 15.00
CCJ04 Cam Ward 5.00 12.00
CCJ05 Carey Price 15.00 40.00
CCJ06 Corey Crawford 5.00 12.00
CCJ07 David LeNeveu 4.00 10.00
CCJ08 Gerald Coleman 4.00 10.00
CCJ09 Jeremy Smith 5.00 12.00
CCJ10 John Murray 4.00 10.00
CCJ11 Jonathan Boutin 4.00 10.00
CCJ12 Karri Ramo 5.00 12.00
CCJ13 Kevin Nastiuk 4.00 10.00
CCJ14 Leland Irving 5.00 12.00
CCJ15 Linden Rowat 5.00 12.00
CCJ16 Michael Leighton 4.00 10.00
CCJ17 Pascal Leclaire 4.00 10.00
CCJ18 Pekka Rinne 5.00 12.00
CCJ19 Peter Budaj 4.00 10.00
CCJ20 Ray Emery 4.00 10.00
CCJ21 Roberto Luongo 8.00 20.00
CCJ22 Steve Mason 10.00 25.00
CCJ23 Thomas McCollum 5.00 12.00
CCJ24 Trevor Cann 4.00 10.00
CCJ25 Tuukka Rask 12.00 30.00
CCJ26 Tyson Sexsmith 4.00 10.00
CCJ27 Adam Dennis 4.00 10.00
CCJ28 Curtis McElhinney 5.00 12.00
CCJ29 Dan Cloutier 4.00 10.00
CCJ30 Hannu Toivonen 4.00 10.00
CCJ31 Jason Bacashihua 4.00 10.00
CCJ32 Jonathan Bernier 6.00 15.00
CCJ33 Manny Fernandez 3.00 8.00
CCJ34 Marty Turco 5.00 12.00
CCJ35 Patrick Roy (MON) 12.00 30.00
CCJ36 Patrick Roy (COL) 12.00 30.00
CCJ37 Richard Brodeur 4.00 10.00
CCJ38 Ryan Miller 6.00 15.00
CCJ39 Tim Thomas 5.00 12.00
CCJ40 Tyler Weiman 4.00 10.00
CCJ41 Dominik Hasek 8.00 20.00
CCJ42 Felix Potvin 8.00 20.00
CCJ43 Grant Fuhr 8.00 20.00
CCJ44 Josh Harding 5.00 12.00
CCJ45 Jean-Sebastien Giguere 5.00 12.00
CCJ46 Kari Lehtonen 4.00 10.00
CCJ47 Marek Schwarz 5.00 12.00
CCJ48 Martin Brodeur 12.00 30.00
CCJ49 Mike Richter 5.00 12.00
CCJ50 Ron Hextall 5.00 12.00
CCJ51 Ed Belfour 6.00 15.00
CCJ52 Dan Bouchard 4.00 10.00
CCJ53 Curtis Sanford 4.00 10.00
CCJ54 Tomas Vokoun 4.00 10.00
CCJ55 Philippe Sauve 4.00 10.00
CCJ56 Brent Krahn 4.00 10.00
CCJ57 Kevin Lalande 4.00 10.00
CCJ58 Alex Auld 3.00 8.00
CCJ59 Ryan Daniels 4.00 10.00
CCJ60 John Vanbiesbrouck 5.00 12.00
CCJ61 Mathieu Garon 4.00 10.00
CCJ62 Mike Smith 5.00 12.00
CCJ63 Ilya Bryzgalov 5.00 12.00
CCJ64 Vladislav Tretiak 10.00 25.00

2007-08 Between The Pipes Tandem Threads

TT01 D.Hasek/R.Miller 10.00 25.00
TT03 F.Potvin/J.Pogge 15.00 40.00
TT04 P.Roy/C.Price 30.00 80.00
TT05 C.McElhinney/L.Irving 6.00 15.00
TT06 G.Cheevers/T.Thomas 10.00 25.00
TT07 P.Roy/P.Budaj 15.00 40.00
TT08 G.Worsley/R.Vachon 12.00 30.00
TT09 E.Giacomin/A.Montoya 10.00 25.00
TT10 M.Turco/M.Smith 6.00 15.00
TT11 P.Roy/M.Brodeur 20.00 40.00
TT12 B.Parent/R.Hextall 20.00 40.00
TT13 T.Vokoun/R.Luongo 10.00 20.00
TT14 Beezer/Richter 10.00 25.00
TT15 T.Esposito/E.Belfour 10.00 25.00
TT16 T.Sawchuk/J.Bernier 10.00 25.00
TT17 G.Fuhr/M.Garon 10.00 25.00
TT18 M.Gerber/R.Emery 6.00 15.00
TT19 C.Ward/M.Leighton 6.00 15.00
TT20 J.Giguere/K.Lehtonen 6.00 15.00

2007-08 Between The Pipes The Future of Goaltending

COMPLETE SET (10) 6.00 15.00
FOG01 Carey Price 2.50 6.00
FOG02 Leland Irving .60 1.50
FOG03 Trevor Cann .50 1.25
FOG04 Tuukka Rask 1.50 4.00
FOG05 Jaroslav Halak 1.25 3.00
FOG06 Al Montoya .50 1.25
FOG07 Justin Pogge .50 1.25
FOG08 Jonathan Bernier .75 2.00
FOG09 Marek Schwarz .60 1.50
FOG10 Tyson Sexsmith .50 1.25

2007-08 Between The Pipes The Mask

COMPLETE SET (30) 75.00 150.00
M1 Nikolai Khabibulin 3.00 8.00
M2 Manny Legace 2.50 6.00
M3 Dominik Hasek 5.00 12.00
M4 Carey Price 12.00 30.00
M5 Roberto Luongo 5.00 12.00
M6 Jean-Sebastien Giguere 3.00 8.00
M7 Mathieu Garon 2.50 6.00
M8 Marc-Andre Fleury 6.00 15.00
M9 Marc Denis 2.50 6.00
M10 Evgeni Nabokov 2.50 6.00
M11 Manny Fernandez 2.00 5.00
M12 Niklas Backstrom 3.00 8.00
M13 Josh Harding 3.00 8.00
M14 Miikka Kiprusoff 3.00 8.00
M15 Martin Biron 2.50 6.00
M16 Chris Mason 2.50 6.00
M17 Cam Ward 3.00 8.00
M18 Tim Thomas 5.00 12.00
M19 Marty Turco 3.00 8.00
M20 Johan Hedberg 2.50 6.00
M21 Henrik Lundqvist 8.00 20.00
M22 Martin Gerber 2.50 6.00
M23 Johan Holmqvist 2.50 6.00
M24 Pascal Leclaire 2.50 6.00
M25 Cristobal Huet 2.50 6.00
M26 David Aebischer 2.50 6.00
M27 Peter Budaj 2.50 6.00
M28 Mikael Tellqvist 2.50 6.00
M29 Ryan Miller 3.00 8.00
M30 Ty Conklin 2.50 6.00

2007-08 Between The Pipes The Mask Game-Used

MGU01 Manny Legace 8.00 20.00
MGU02 Dominik Hasek 15.00 40.00
MGU03 Ryan Miller 10.00 25.00
MGU04 Roberto Luongo 15.00 40.00
MGU05 Jean-Sebastien Giguere 10.00 25.00
MGU06 Cristobal Huet 8.00 20.00
MGU07 Marc-Andre Fleury 20.00 50.00
MGU08 Evgeni Nabokov 8.00 20.00
MGU09 Miikka Kiprusoff 10.00 25.00
MGU10 Martin Biron 6.00 15.00
MGU11 Chris Mason 8.00 20.00
MGU12 Cam Ward 10.00 25.00
MGU13 Tim Thomas 10.00 25.00
MGU14 Pascal Leclaire 8.00 20.00
MGU15 Marty Turco 10.00 25.00
MGU16 Jacques Plante 25.00 60.00
MGU17 Henrik Lundqvist 25.00 60.00
MGU18 Martin Gerber 8.00 20.00
MGU19 Peter Budaj 8.00 20.00
MGU20 Carey Price 30.00 60.00

2008-09 Between The Pipes

1 Adam Courchaine .20 .50
2 Al Montoya .20 .50
3 Andrew Engelage .20 .50
4 Antoine Lafleur .20 .50
5 Ben Bishop .40 1.00
6 Braden Holtby .60 1.50
7 Brian Elliott .20 .50
8 Simeon Varlamov .50 1.25
9 Chet Pickard .25 .60
10 Chris Carrozzi .20 .50
11 Corey Crawford .30 .75
12 Cory Schneider .60 1.50
13 Curtis McElhinney .15 .40
14 Daren Machesney .20 .50
15 Dustin Tokarski .25 .60
16 Erik Ersberg .20 .50
17 Jacob DeSerres .20 .50
18 Jake Allen .40 1.00
19 Jaroslav Janus .20 .50
20 Jeremy Smith .25 .60
21 Jimmy Howard .40 1.00
22 John Curry .25 .60
23 Jonathan Bernier .20 .50
24 Jonathan Quick .30 .75
25 Josh Unice .20 .50
26 Justin Pogge .20 .50
27 Kevin Poulin .25 .60
28 Kurtis Mucha .20 .50
29 Kyle Gajewski .20 .50
30 Leland Irving .25 .60
31 Linden Rowat .20 .50
32 Marek Schwarz .25 .60
33 Michael Hutchinson .30 .75
34 Miika Wiikman .25 .60
35 Mike Murphy .25 .60
36 Nolan Schaefer .20 .50
37 Ondrej Pavelec .30 .75
38 Patrick Killeen .20 .50
39 Pekka Rinne .25 .60
40 Peter Delmas .25 .60
41 Raffaele D'Orso .20 .50
42 Robert Mayer .25 .60

43 Steve Mason	.40	1.00
44 Steven Stanford	.20	.50
45 Thomas McCollum	.25	.60
46 Tobias Stephan	.20	.50
47 Trevor Cann	.20	.50
48 Tuukka Rask	.30	.75
49 Tyler Beskorowany	.20	.50
50 Tyson Sexsmith	.30	.75
51 Nicola Riopel	.20	.50
52 Peter Di Salvo	.20	.50
53 Jhonas Enroth	.20	.50
54 Brandon Foote	.20	.50
55 Alain Valiquette	.20	.50
56 Jamie Tucker	.20	.50
57 J.P. Anderson	.20	.50
58 Travis Yonkman	.20	.50
59 Timo Pielmeier	.20	.50
60 Evgeni Nabokov	.20	.50
61 Chris Osgood	.25	.60
62 Jonas Hiller	.20	.50
63 Carey Price	.50	1.25
64 Jean-Sebastien Giguere	.25	.60
65 Vesa Toskala	.30	.75
66 Martin Brodeur	.60	1.50
67 Niklas Backstrom	.25	.60
68 Manny Fernandez	.15	.40
69 Tim Thomas	.25	.60
70 Olaf Kolzig	.25	.60
71 Cristobal Huet	.20	.50
72 Roberto Luongo	.40	1.00
73 Bill Durnan	.25	.60
74 Glenn Hall	.25	.60
75 Gump Worsley	.20	.50
76 Jacques Plante	.40	1.00
77 Johnny Bower	.25	.60
78 Roger Crozier	.20	.50
79 Terry Sawchuk	.30	.75
80 Turk Broda	.25	.60
81 Bernie Parent	.30	.75
82 Rogie Vachon	.30	.75
83 Dominik Hasek	.40	1.00
84 Ed Giacomin	.30	.75
85 Gerry Cheevers	.25	.60
86 Grant Fuhr	.40	1.00
87 John Vanbiesbrouck	.25	.60
88 Patrick Roy	.60	1.50
89 Pelle Lindbergh	.20	.50
90 Tony Esposito	.25	.60
91 Ed Belfour	.25	.60
92 Gary Smith	.20	.50
93 Gerry Desjardins	.20	.50
94 Jacques Plante	.40	1.00
95 Al Smith	.20	.50
96 Gilles Gratton	.25	.60
97 Marcel Paille	.20	.50
98 George Gardner	.20	.50
99 Les Binkley	.40	1.00
100 Ernie Wakely	.25	.60

2008-09 Between The Pipes Autographs

AAA Alain Valiquette	3.00	8.00
AAC Adam Courchaine	3.00	8.00
AAE Andrew Engelage	3.00	8.00
AAL Antoine Lafleur	3.00	8.00
AAM Al Montoya	3.00	8.00
ABE Brian Elliott	3.00	8.00
ABF Brandon Foote	3.00	8.00
ABH Braden Holtby	10.00	25.00
ABP Bernie Parent SP	6.00	15.00
ACC Chris Carrozzi	3.00	8.00
ACCR Corey Crawford	10.00	25.00
ACH Cristobal Huet	3.00	8.00
ACM Curtis McElhinney	2.50	6.00
ACO Chris Osgood SP	8.00	20.00
ACP Carey Price SP	25.00	60.00
ACPI Chet Pickard	4.00	10.00
ACPR Carey Price SP	25.00	60.00
ACS Cory Schneider	10.00	25.00
ADH Dominik Hasek	15.00	40.00
ADM Daren Machesney	3.00	8.00
ADT Dustin Tokarski	4.00	10.00
AEB Ed Belfour SP	15.00	40.00
AEE Erik Ersberg	3.00	8.00
AEW Ernie Wakely	4.00	10.00
AFP Felix Potvin SP	6.00	15.00
AGC Gerry Cheevers	8.00	20.00
AGD Gerry Desjardins	3.00	8.00
AGF Grant Fuhr	10.00	25.00
AGG Gilles Gratton	4.00	10.00
AGS Gary Smith	3.00	8.00
AJA Jake Allen	6.00	15.00
AJB Jonathan Bernier	3.00	8.00
AJC John Curry	4.00	10.00
AJD Jacob DeSerres	3.00	8.00
AJH Jimmy Howard	6.00	15.00
AJHI Jonas Hiller SP	3.00	8.00
AJJ Jaroslav Janus	3.00	8.00
AJP Justin Pogge	3.00	8.00
AJPA J.P. Anderson	3.00	8.00
AJQ Jonathan Quick	15.00	40.00
AJS Jeremy Smith	4.00	10.00
AJSG Jean-Sebastien Giguere SP	8.00	20.00
AJT Jamie Tucker	3.00	8.00
AJU Josh Unice	3.00	8.00
AJV John Vanbiesbrouck SP	20.00	50.00
AKM Kurtis Mucha	3.00	8.00
AKP Kevin Poulin	4.00	10.00
ALB Les Binkley	6.00	15.00
ALI Leland Irving	4.00	10.00
ALR Linden Rowat	3.00	8.00
AMB Martin Brodeur SP	25.00	60.00
AMF Manny Fernandez SP	2.50	6.00
AMH Michael Hutchinson	5.00	12.00
AMM Mike Murphy	4.00	10.00
AMS Marek Schwarz	4.00	10.00
AMT Marty Turco	4.00	10.00
AMW Miika Wiikman	4.00	10.00
ANB Niklas Backstrom SP	6.00	15.00
ANS Nolan Schaefer	3.00	8.00
AOK Olaf Kolzig	4.00	10.00
AOP Ondrej Pavelec	5.00	12.00
APB Peter Budaj	3.00	8.00
APD Peter Delmas	4.00	10.00
APDI Peter Di Salvo	3.00	8.00
APK Patrick Killeen	3.00	8.00
APR Pekka Rinne	4.00	10.00
APRO Patrick Roy SP	25.00	60.00
ARD Raffaele D'Orso	3.00	8.00
ARG Ed Giacomin SP	12.00	30.00
ARL Roberto Luongo SP	15.00	40.00
ARM Robert Mayer	4.00	10.00
ARV Rogie Vachon SP	8.00	20.00
ASM Steve Mason	6.00	15.00
ASS Steven Stanford	3.00	8.00
ASV Simeon Varlamov	12.00	30.00
ATB Tyler Beskorowany	3.00	8.00
ATC Trevor Cann	3.00	8.00
ATE Tony Esposito SP	25.00	60.00
ATM Thomas McCollum	4.00	10.00
ATR Tuukka Rask	12.00	30.00
ATS Tobias Stephan	3.00	8.00
ATSE Tyson Sexsmith	5.00	12.00
ATT Tim Thomas SP	4.00	10.00
ATY Travis Yonkman	3.00	8.00
AVT Vesa Toskala SP	5.00	12.00
AVTR Vladislav Tretiak	3.00	8.00

2008-09 Between The Pipes Draft Day Duos

DDD01 C.Pickard/T.McCollum	5.00	12.00
DDD02 T.Cann/T.Sexsmith	6.00	15.00
DDD03 J.Bernier/L.Irving	5.00	12.00
DDD04 S.Mason/S.Varlamov	10.00	25.00
DDD05 C.Price/T.Rusk	10.00	25.00
DDD06 A.Montoya/M.Schwarz	5.00	12.00
DDD07 C.Crawford/J.Howard	8.00	20.00
DDD08 J.Harding/H.Toivonen	5.00	12.00
DDD09 P.Leclaire/P.Budaj	4.00	10.00
DDD10 P.Sauve/J.LeBarbera	4.00	10.00
DDD11 R.Luongo/S.Clemmensen	8.00	20.00
DDD12 J.Giguere/B.Boucher	5.00	12.00
DDD13 M.Turco/D.Cloutier	5.00	12.00
DDD14 G.Fuhr/M.Vernon	8.00	20.00
DDD15 M.Brodeur/F.Potvin	12.00	30.00
DDD16 M.Richter/S.Burke	5.00	12.00
DDD17 P.Roy/K.McLean	12.00	30.00
DDD18 D.Hasek/V.Tretiak	8.00	20.00
DDD19 K.Wregget/R.Hextall	5.00	12.00
DDD20 T.Thomas/E.Nabokov	5.00	12.00

2008-09 Between The Pipes Emblems

GUE01 Martin Brodeur	12.00	30.00
GUE02 Peter Budaj	4.00	10.00
GUE03 Corey Crawford	6.00	15.00
GUE04 John Curry	5.00	12.00
GUE05 Peter Delmas	5.00	12.00
GUE06 Brian Elliott	4.00	10.00
GUE07 Tony Esposito	5.00	12.00
GUE08 Manny Fernandez	3.00	8.00
GUE09 Jean-Sebastien Giguere	5.00	12.00
GUE10 Jaroslav Halak	5.00	12.00
GUE11 Dominik Hasek	8.00	20.00
GUE12 Riku Helenius	4.00	10.00
GUE13 Jonas Hiller	4.00	10.00
GUE14 Braden Holtby	12.00	30.00
GUE15 Tim Thomas	5.00	12.00
GUE16 Torrie Jung	3.00	8.00
GUE17 Kris Lazaruk	5.00	12.00
GUE18 Pelle Lindbergh	4.00	10.00
GUE19 Roberto Luongo	8.00	20.00
GUE20 Daren Machesney	4.00	10.00
GUE21 Steve Mason	8.00	20.00
GUE22 Cristobal Huet	4.00	10.00
GUE23 Drew MacIntyre	5.00	12.00
GUE24 Simeon Varlamov	10.00	25.00
GUE25 Mike Murphy	5.00	12.00
GUE26 Chris Osgood	5.00	12.00
GUE27 Chet Pickard	5.00	12.00
GUE28 Justin Pogge	4.00	10.00
GUE29 Felix Potvin	8.00	20.00
GUE30 Carey Price	10.00	25.00
GUE31 Jonathan Quick	6.00	15.00
GUE32 Pekka Rinne	5.00	12.00
GUE33 Olivier Roy	5.00	12.00
GUE34 Patrick Roy	12.00	30.00
GUE35 Patrick Roy	12.00	30.00
GUE36 Marek Schwarz	5.00	12.00
GUE37 Dustin Tokarski	5.00	12.00
GUE38 Vesa Toskala	6.00	15.00
GUE39 Vladislav Tretiak	4.00	10.00
GUE40 Marty Turco	5.00	12.00
GUE41 Josh Unice	4.00	10.00
GUE42 John Vanbiesbrouck	5.00	12.00
GUE43 Kristofer Westblom	4.00	10.00
GUE44 Miika Wiikman	5.00	12.00
GUE45 Evgeni Nabokov	4.00	10.00

2008-09 Between The Pipes Goaltending Evolution

GE01 Roy/Price/Halak	12.00	30.00
GE02 Hasek/Elliott/Glass	8.00	20.00
GE03 Potvin/Toskala/Pogge	8.00	20.00
GE04 Cheevers/Thomas/Rask	6.00	15.00
GE05 Roy/Budaj/Delmas	12.00	30.00
GE06 Belfour/Turco/Stephan	5.00	12.00
GE07 Plante/Price/Halak	10.00	25.00
GE08 Sawchuk/Osgood/Howard	8.00	20.00
GE09 Brodeur/Luongo/Ellis	8.00	20.00
GE10 Sawchuk/Quick/Bernier	6.00	15.00

2008-09 Between The Pipes Great Moments

GM01 Jacques Plante	12.00	30.00
GM02 Glenn Hall	8.00	20.00
GM03 Billy Smith	8.00	20.00
GM04 Vladislav Tretiak	6.00	15.00
GM05 Terry Sawchuk	10.00	25.00
GM06 Patrick Roy	20.00	50.00
GM07 Martin Brodeur	20.00	50.00
GM08 Clint Benedict	10.00	25.00

2008-09 Between The Pipes He Shoots He Saves

HSHS01 P.Roy/M.Brodeur	20.00	50.00
HSHS02 O.Kolzig/Varlamov	15.00	40.00
HSHS03 Cheevers/Fernandez	8.00	20.00
HSHS04 T.Esposito/C.Huet	8.00	20.00
HSHS05 T.Thompson/Gardiner	6.00	15.00
HSHS06 R.Brodeur/R.Luongo	12.00	30.00
HSHS07 D.Tokarski/C.Pickard	8.00	20.00
HSHS08 F.Potvin/V.Toskala	12.00	30.00
HSHS09 D.Hasek/C.Osgood	12.00	30.00
HSHS10 Lindbergh/B.Parent	10.00	25.00
HSHS11 P.Roy/C.Price	20.00	50.00
HSHS12 Tretiak/E.Nabokov	6.00	15.00
HSHS13 E.Belfour/M.Turco	8.00	20.00
HSHS14 J.Bower/J.Pogge	8.00	20.00
HSHS15 T.Thomas/T.Rask	10.00	25.00
HSHS16 J.Plante/P.Roy	20.00	50.00
HSHS17 S.Mason/J.Quick	12.00	30.00
HSHS18 P.Roy/P.Budaj	20.00	50.00
HSHS19 Sawchuk/J.Bernier	10.00	25.00
HSHS20 D.Hasek/B.Elliott	12.00	30.00
HSHS21 J.Plante/J.Halak	12.00	30.00
HSHS22 R.Hextall/J.Vanbies	8.00	20.00
HSHS23 G.Hall/C.Crawford	10.00	25.00
HSHS24 M.Brodeur/T.Sawchuk	20.00	50.00
HSHS25 R.Luongo/E.Nabokov	12.00	30.00
HSHS26 J.Giguere/J.Hiller	8.00	20.00
HSHS27 R.Crozier/J.Howard	12.00	30.00
HSHS28 Hainsworth/R.Worters	10.00	25.00
HSHS29 S.Mason/S.Varlamov	15.00	40.00
HSHS30 C.Price/R.Vachon	15.00	40.00

2008-09 Between The Pipes Jerseys

GUJ01 Martin Brodeur SP	12.00	30.00
GUJ02 Peter Budaj	4.00	10.00
GUJ03 Corey Crawford	6.00	15.00
GUJ04 John Curry	5.00	12.00
GUJ05 Peter Delmas	5.00	12.00
GUJ06 Brian Elliott	4.00	10.00
GUJ07 Tony Esposito	5.00	12.00
GUJ08 Manny Fernandez	3.00	8.00
GUJ09 Jean-Sebastien Giguere	5.00	12.00
GUJ10 Jaroslav Halak	5.00	12.00
GUJ11 Dominik Hasek	8.00	20.00
GUJ12 Riku Helenius	4.00	10.00
GUJ13 Jonas Hiller	4.00	10.00
GUJ14 Braden Holtby	12.00	30.00
GUJ15 Tim Thomas	5.00	12.00
GUJ16 Torrie Jung	3.00	8.00
GUJ17 Kris Lazaruk	5.00	12.00
GUJ18 Pelle Lindbergh SP	20.00	50.00
GUJ19 Roberto Luongo SP	10.00	25.00
GUJ20 Daren Machesney	4.00	10.00
GUJ21 Steve Mason	8.00	20.00
GUJ22 Cristobal Huet	4.00	10.00
GUJ23 Drew MacIntyre	5.00	12.00
GUJ24 Simeon Varlamov	10.00	25.00
GUJ25 Mike Murphy	5.00	12.00
GUJ26 Chris Osgood	5.00	12.00
GUJ27 Chet Pickard	5.00	12.00
GUJ28 Justin Pogge	4.00	10.00
GUJ29 Felix Potvin	8.00	20.00
GUJ30 Carey Price	10.00	25.00
GUJ31 Jonathan Quick	6.00	15.00
GUJ32 Pekka Rinne	5.00	12.00
GUJ33 Olivier Roy	5.00	12.00
GUJ34 Patrick Roy SP	15.00	40.00
GUJ35 Patrick Roy SP	15.00	40.00
GUJ36 Marek Schwarz	5.00	12.00
GUJ37 Dustin Tokarski	5.00	12.00
GUJ38 Vesa Toskala	6.00	15.00
GUJ39 Vladislav Tretiak	4.00	10.00
GUJ40 Marty Turco	5.00	12.00
GUJ41 Josh Unice	4.00	10.00
GUJ42 John Vanbiesbrouck	5.00	12.00
GUJ43 Kristofer Westblom	4.00	10.00
GUJ44 Miika Wiikman	5.00	12.00
GUJ45 Evgeni Nabokov	4.00	10.00

2008-09 Between The Pipes Masked Men

MM01 Chet Pickard	3.00	8.00
MM02 Timo Pielmeier	2.50	6.00
MM03 Carey Price	6.00	15.00
MM04 Corey Crawford	4.00	10.00
MM05 Cory Schneider	8.00	20.00
MM06 Jimmy Howard	5.00	12.00
MM07 Jonathan Bernier	2.50	6.00
MM08 Marek Schwarz	3.00	8.00
MM09 Robert Mayer	3.00	8.00
MM10 Thomas McCollum	3.00	8.00
MM11 Antoine Tardif	3.00	8.00
MM12 Gabriel Girard	2.50	6.00
MM13 Karel St. Laurent	3.00	8.00
MM14 Brent Krahn	4.00	10.00
MM15 Jean-Philippe Levasseur	4.00	10.00
MM16 Peter Delmas	3.00	8.00
MM17 Cristobal Huet	2.50	6.00
MM18 Evgeni Nabokov	2.50	6.00
MM19 Jean-Sebastien Giguere	3.00	8.00
MM20 Martin Brodeur	8.00	20.00
MM21 Patrick Roy	8.00	20.00
MM22 Patrick Roy	8.00	20.00
MM23 Steve Mason	5.00	12.00
MM24 Vesa Toskala	4.00	10.00
MM25 Manny Fernandez	2.00	5.00
MM26 Marty Turco	3.00	8.00
MM27 Justin Pogge	2.50	6.00
MM28 Niklas Backstrom	3.00	8.00
MM29 Olivier Roy	3.00	8.00
MM30 Tim Thomas	3.00	8.00
MM31 Travis Fullerton	2.50	6.00
MM32 Devan Dubnyk	4.00	10.00
MM33 Jacob DeSerres	2.50	6.00
MM34 Marek Benda	3.00	8.00
MM35 Nathan Dunnett	2.50	6.00
MM36 Linden Rowat	2.50	6.00
MM37 Adam Courchaine	2.50	6.00
MM38 Dustin Tokarski	3.00	8.00
MM39 Daniel Larsson	5.00	12.00
MM40 Josh Tordjman	5.00	12.00
MM41 Roberto Luongo	5.00	12.00
MM42 Brian Elliott	2.50	6.00
MM43 Trevor Cann	2.50	6.00
MM44 Ed Belfour	3.00	8.00
MM45 Felix Potvin	5.00	12.00
MM46 Dominik Hasek	5.00	12.00
MM47 Frederic Piche	2.50	6.00
MM48 Jhonas Enroth	2.50	6.00
MM49 Kurtis Mucha	2.50	6.00
MM50 Nolan Schaefer	2.50	6.00

2008-09 Between The Pipes Numbers

GUN01 Martin Brodeur	15.00	40.00
GUN02 Peter Budaj	5.00	12.00
GUN03 Corey Crawford	8.00	20.00
GUN04 John Curry	6.00	15.00
GUN05 Peter Delmas	6.00	15.00
GUN06 Brian Elliott	5.00	12.00
GUN07 Tony Esposito	6.00	15.00
GUN08 Manny Fernandez	4.00	10.00
GUN09 Jean-Sebastien Giguere	6.00	15.00
GUN10 Jaroslav Halak	6.00	15.00
GUN11 Dominik Hasek	10.00	25.00
GUN12 Riku Helenius	5.00	12.00
GUN13 Jonas Hiller	5.00	12.00
GUN14 Braden Holtby	15.00	40.00
GUN15 Tim Thomas	6.00	15.00
GUN16 Torrie Jung	4.00	10.00
GUN17 Kris Lazaruk	6.00	15.00
GUN18 Pelle Lindbergh	5.00	12.00
GUN19 Roberto Luongo	10.00	25.00
GUN20 Daren Machesney	5.00	12.00
GUN21 Steve Mason	10.00	25.00
GUN22 Cristobal Huet	5.00	12.00
GUN23 Drew MacIntyre	6.00	15.00
GUN24 Simeon Varlamov	12.00	30.00
GUN25 Mike Murphy	6.00	15.00
GUN26 Chris Osgood	6.00	15.00
GUN27 Chet Pickard	6.00	15.00
GUN28 Justin Pogge	5.00	12.00
GUN29 Felix Potvin	10.00	25.00
GUN30 Carey Price	12.00	30.00
GUN31 Jonathan Quick	8.00	20.00
GUN32 Pekka Rinne	6.00	15.00
GUN33 Olivier Roy	6.00	15.00
GUN34 Patrick Roy	15.00	40.00
GUN35 Patrick Roy	15.00	40.00
GUN36 Marek Schwarz	6.00	15.00
GUN37 Dustin Tokarski	6.00	15.00
GUN38 Vesa Toskala	8.00	20.00
GUN39 Vladislav Tretiak	5.00	12.00
GUN40 Marty Turco	6.00	15.00
GUN41 Josh Unice	5.00	12.00
GUN42 John Vanbiesbrouck	6.00	15.00
GUN43 Kristofer Westblom	5.00	12.00
GUN44 Miika Wiikman	6.00	15.00
GUN45 Evgeni Nabokov	5.00	12.00

2008-09 Between The Pipes Prospect Combos

PC01 J.Pogge/M.Murphy	5.00	12.00
PC02 B.Elliott/T.Cann	4.00	10.00
PC03 J.Howard/T.McCollum	8.00	20.00
PC04 J.Halak/B.Holtby	10.00	25.00
PC05 M.Schwarz/K.Westblom	5.00	12.00
PC06 P.Rinne/T.Sexsmith	6.00	15.00
PC07 S.Varlamov/N.Riopel	10.00	25.00
PC08 J.Harding/D.Tokarski	5.00	12.00
PC09 J.Quick/O.Roy	6.00	15.00
PC10 C.Crawford/C.Pickard	6.00	15.00
PC11 A.Montoya/S.Mason	8.00	20.00
PC12 L.Irving/K.Lazaruk	5.00	12.00

2008-09 Between The Pipes Super-Sized Pads

SSP01 Patrick Roy	30.00	80.00
SSP02 Patrick Roy	30.00	80.00
SSP03 Martin Brodeur	30.00	80.00
SSP04 Pelle Lindbergh	60.00	120.00
SSP05 Ed Belfour	12.00	30.00
SSP06 Gerry Cheevers	20.00	50.00
SSP07 Grant Fuhr	20.00	50.00
SSP08 Chris Osgood	25.00	60.00
SSP09 Marty Turco	12.00	30.00
SSP10 Vladislav Tretiak	40.00	100.00
SSP11 Ron Hextall	25.00	60.00
SSP12 Bernie Parent	40.00	100.00

2008-09 Between The Pipes Super Glove

SG01 Martin Brodeur	30.00	80.00
SG02 Peter Budaj	8.00	20.00
SG03 Rick DiPietro	15.00	40.00
SG04 Marc-Andre Fleury	15.00	40.00
SG05 Jean-Sebastien Giguere	10.00	25.00
SG06 Dominik Hasek	15.00	40.00
SG07 Miikka Kiprusoff	15.00	40.00
SG08 Chris Osgood	15.00	40.00
SG09 Felix Potvin	15.00	40.00
SG10 Jose Theodore	10.00	25.00
SG11 Jocelyn Thibault	8.00	20.00
SG12 Vesa Toskala	20.00	50.00
SG13 Marty Turco	10.00	25.00
SG14 Tomas Vokoun	8.00	20.00
SG15 Cam Ward	10.00	25.00
SG16 Roberto Luongo	15.00	40.00
SG17 Patrick Roy	60.00	120.00
SG18 Sean Burke	6.00	15.00
SG19 Olaf Kolzig	15.00	40.00
SG20 Evgeni Nabokov	8.00	20.00

2009-10 Between The Pipes

1 Alexander Salak	.25	.60
2 Alex Stalock	.25	.60
3 Anton Khudobin	.50	1.25
4 Ben Bishop	.25	.60
5 Cedrick Desjardins	.50	1.25
6 Chad Johnson	.30	.75
7 Chet Pickard	.40	1.00
8 Cory Schneider	.30	.75
9 Daniel Larsson	.25	.60
10 Devan Dubnyk	.50	1.25
11 Dustin Tokarski	.30	.75
12 James Reimer	.75	2.00
13 Jhonas Enroth	.40	1.00
14 Joe Fallon	.25	.60
15 Johan Backlund	.30	.75
16 John Curry	.25	.60
17 Jonathan Bernier	.25	.60
18 Justin Pogge	.30	.75
19 Kevin Lalande	.25	.60
20 Leland Irving	.30	.75
21 Mark Dekanich	.25	.60
22 Matt Climie	.25	.60
23 Michal Neuvirth	.50	1.25
24 Mike Brodeur	.25	.60
25 Mike McKenna	.25	.60
26 Mike Murphy	.30	.75
27 Nathan Lawson	.25	.60
28 Thomas McCollum	.30	.75
29 Trevor Cann	.40	1.00
30 Tyler Weiman	.30	.75
31 Andrew Hayes	.25	.60
32 Adam Brown	.25	.60
33 Adam Morrison	.25	.60
34 Calvin Pickard	.50	1.25
35 Darcy Kuemper	.60	1.50
36 Drew Owsley	.25	.60
37 Garrett Zemlak	.25	.60
38 James Reid	.30	.75
39 Jamie Tucker	.25	.60
40 Kent Simpson	.25	.60
41 Linden Rowat	.25	.60
42 Martin Jones	.50	1.25
43 Nathan Lieuwen	.40	1.00
44 Torrie Jung	.25	.60
45 Tyler Bunz	.25	.60
46 Antoine Tardif	.25	.60
47 Jake Allen	.50	1.25
48 Kevin Poulin	.30	.75
49 Louis Domingue	.40	1.00
50 Marc-Antoine Gelinas	.30	.75
51 Marco Cousineau	.25	.60
52 Mathieu Corbeil-Theriault	.25	.60
53 Matthew Dopud	.25	.60
54 Maxime Clermont	.25	.60
55 Mickael Audette	.25	.60
56 Nathan Dunnett	.25	.60
57 Nicolas Champion	.25	.60
58 Olivier Roy	.30	.75
59 Peter Delmas	.25	.60
60 Jacob Markstrom	.60	1.50
61 Brandon Maxwell	.25	.60
62 Chris Carrozzi	.30	.75
63 Edward Pasquale	.30	.75
64 Jason Missiaen	.25	.60
65 J.P. Anderson	.25	.60
66 Matt Hackett	.40	1.00
67 Michael Houser	.40	1.00
68 Michael Hutchinson	.40	1.00
69 Patrick Killeen	.25	.60
70 Peter Di Salvo	.30	.75
71 Philipp Grubauer	.40	1.00
72 Robin Lehner	.60	1.50
73 Scott Stajcer	.25	.60
74 Troy Passingham	.25	.60
75 Tyler Beskorowany	.25	.60
76 Antti Niemi	.50	1.25
77 Cam Ward	.30	.75
78 Carey Price	.60	1.50
79 Chris Osgood	.30	.75
80 Evgeni Nabokov	.25	.60
81 Ilya Bryzgalov	.25	.60
82 Jean-Sebastien Giguere	.30	.75
83 Jaroslav Halak	.30	.75
84 Jimmy Howard	.40	1.00
85 Jonas Hiller	.25	.60
86 Josh Harding	.30	.75
87 Kari Lehtonen	.25	.60
88 Manny Legace	.25	.60
89 Marc-Andre Fleury	.60	1.50
90 Martin Brodeur	.75	2.00
91 Marty Turco	.30	.75
92 Miikka Kiprusoff	.30	.75
93 Niklas Backstrom	.30	.75
94 Tuukka Rask	.40	1.00
95 Ondrej Pavelec	.40	1.00
96 Pascal Leclaire	.30	.75
97 Ray Emery	.25	.60
98 Rick DiPietro	.25	.60
99 Roberto Luongo	.50	1.25
100 Ryan Miller	.30	.75
101 Scott Clemmensen	.25	.60
102 Simeon Varlamov	.30	.75
103 Cristobal Huet	.30	.75
104 Tim Thomas	.30	.75
105 Tomas Vokoun	.25	.60
106 Vesa Toskala	.30	.75
107 Allan Bester	.25	.60
108 Andy Moog	.30	.75
109 Bernie Parent	.40	1.00
110 Bill Durnan	.30	.75
111 Billy Smith	.30	.75
112 Brian Hayward	.25	.60
113 Bunny Larocque	.25	.60
114 Dan Bouchard	.25	.60
115 Dominik Hasek	.50	1.25
116 Charlie Hodge	.25	.60
117 Ed Giacomin	.40	1.00
118 Ed Johnston	.50	1.25
119 Felix Potvin	.50	1.25
120 Gerry Cheevers	.30	.75
121 Gilles Meloche	.30	.75
122 Gilles Villemure	.40	1.00
123 Glenn Hall	.30	.75
124 Grant Fuhr	.50	1.25
125 Gump Worsley	.50	1.25
126 Harry Lumley	.30	.75
127 Jacques Plante	.50	1.25
128 Georges Vezina	.40	1.00
129 Johnny Bower	.30	.75
130 Mike Liut	.20	.50
131 Patrick Roy	.75	2.00
132 Pelle Lindbergh	.25	.60
133 Pete Peeters	.50	1.25
134 Richard Brodeur	.30	.75
135 Rogie Vachon	.40	1.00
136 Ron Hextall	.30	.75
137 Terry Sawchuk	.40	1.00
138 Tony Esposito	.30	.75
139 Turk Broda	.30	.75
140 Vladislav Tretiak	.25	.60
141 Don McLeod	.30	.75
142 Pat Riggin	.40	1.00
143 Jim Corsi	.40	1.00
144 Gary Bromley	.40	1.00
145 George Gardner	.25	.60
146 Ron Grahame	.25	.60
147 Gary Inness	.50	1.25
148 Mike Curran	.25	.60
149 Ken Brown	.25	.60
150 Wayne Rutledge	.25	.60

2009-10 Between The Pipes AHL Rookies

COMPLETE SET (9)	15.00	40.00
AR01 Chad Johnson	2.50	6.00
AR02 Braden Holtby	6.00	15.00
AR03 Anton Khudobin	4.00	10.00
AR04 Dustin Tokarski	2.50	6.00
AR05 Alexander Salak	2.00	5.00
AR06 Alex Stalock	2.00	5.00
AR07 Chet Pickard	3.00	8.00
AR08 Mike Murphy	2.50	6.00
AR09 Thomas McCollum	2.50	6.00

2009-10 Between The Pipes Autographs

AAA Alex Auld SP	5.00	12.00
AAB Allan Bester SP	6.00	15.00
AAK Anton Khudobin	6.00	15.00
AAM Andy Moog	4.00	10.00
AAN Antero Niittymaki SP	10.00	25.00
AAS Alexander Salak	3.00	8.00
ABB Ben Bishop	3.00	8.00
ABH Brian Hayward	3.00	8.00
ABM Brandon Maxwell	3.00	8.00
ABP Bernie Parent SP	8.00	20.00
ABS Billy Smith	4.00	10.00
ACC Chris Carrozzi SP	6.00	15.00
ACD Cedrick Desjardins	6.00	15.00
ACH Cristobal Huet	4.00	10.00
ACJ Chad Johnson	4.00	10.00
ACO Chris Osgood	4.00	10.00
ACP Chet Pickard SP	8.00	20.00
ACS Cory Schneider	4.00	10.00
ADB Dan Bouchard	3.00	8.00
ADH Dominik Hasek SP	12.00	30.00
ADL Daniel Larsson	3.00	8.00
ADM Don McLeod	4.00	10.00
ADO Drew Owsley	3.00	8.00
ADT Dustin Tokarski SP	6.00	15.00
AEE Erik Ersberg	3.00	8.00
AEG Ed Giacomin SP	5.00	12.00
AEJ Ed Johnston	6.00	15.00
AEN Evgeni Nabokov	3.00	8.00
AEP Edward Pasquale	4.00	10.00
AFP Felix Potvin SP	8.00	20.00
AGB Gary Bromley	5.00	12.00
AGC Gerry Cheevers SP	6.00	15.00
AGF Grant Fuhr	6.00	15.00
AGH Glenn Hall SP	8.00	20.00
AGI Gary Inness	6.00	15.00
AGM Gilles Meloche	4.00	10.00
AGV Gilles Villemure	5.00	12.00
AGW Gump Worsley SP	12.00	30.00
AGZ Garrett Zemlak	3.00	8.00
AHT Hannu Toivonen	4.00	10.00
AJA Jake Allen	6.00	15.00
AJB Johan Backlund	4.00	10.00
AJC Jim Corsi	5.00	12.00
AJE Jhonas Enroth	5.00	12.00
AJG Jean-Sebastien Giguere	4.00	10.00
AJL Jason Labarbera	3.00	8.00
AJM Jason Missiaen	3.00	8.00
AJP Justin Pogge SP	5.00	12.00
AJQ Jonathan Quick	5.00	12.00
AJR James Reimer	10.00	25.00
AJT Jamie Tucker SP	5.00	12.00
AKP Kevin Poulin	4.00	10.00
AKS Kent Simpson	3.00	8.00
ALD Louis Domingue	5.00	12.00
ALI Leland Irving	4.00	10.00
ALR Linden Rowatt SP	5.00	12.00
AMA Mickael Audette	3.00	8.00
AMC Matt Climie	3.00	8.00
AMG Marc-Antoine Gelinas	4.00	10.00
AMH Matt Hackett	5.00	12.00
AMJ Martin Jones	6.00	15.00
AMK Miikka Kiprusoff	4.00	10.00
AML Mike Liut	2.50	6.00
AMM Mike McKenna	3.00	8.00
AMN Michal Neuvirth	6.00	15.00
AMT Marty Turco	4.00	10.00
ANB Niklas Backstrom	4.00	10.00
ANL Nathan Lawson	3.00	8.00
AOP Ondrej Pavelec	5.00	12.00
AOR Olivier Roy	4.00	10.00
APB Peter Budaj	3.00	8.00
APD Peter Delmas	3.00	8.00
APG Philipp Grubauer	5.00	12.00
APK Patrick Killeen	3.00	8.00
APP Pete Peeters	0.00	15.00
APR Patrick Roy SP	20.00	50.00
ARB Richard Brodeur SP	5.00	12.00
ARE Ray Emery	3.00	8.00
ARG Ron Grahame	3.00	8.00
ARH Ron Hextall	4.00	10.00
ARL Robin Lehner	8.00	20.00
ARV Rogie Vachon SP	8.00	20.00
ASS Scott Stajcer	3.00	8.00
ASV Simeon Varlamov	4.00	10.00
ATB Tyler Beskorowany	3.00	8.00
ATC Trevor Cann SP	12.00	30.00
ATE Tony Esposito SP	15.00	40.00
ATM Thomas McCollum SP	5.00	12.00
ATP Troy Passingham	3.00	8.00
ATR Tuukka Rask SP	6.00	15.00
ATT Tim Thomas SP	8.00	20.00
ATV Tomas Vokoun	3.00	8.00
ATW Tyler Weiman	4.00	10.00
AVT Vesa Toskala	4.00	10.00
AAM2 Andy Moog	4.00	10.00
AAST Alex Stalock	3.00	8.00
ABH2 Brian Hayward	3.00	8.00
ABP2 Bernie Parent SP	12.00	30.00
ACHO Charlie Hodge SP	8.00	20.00
ACPI Calvin Pickard	6.00	15.00
ACPR Carey Price	8.00	20.00
ADB2 Dan Bouchard	3.00	8.00
ADH2 Dominik Hasek SP	15.00	40.00
AEG2 Ed Giacomin SP	10.00	25.00
AGB2 Gary Bromley	5.00	12.00
AGC2 Gerry Cheevers SP	15.00	40.00
AGH2 Glenn Hall SP	10.00	25.00
AGI2 Gary Inness	6.00	15.00
AGM2 Gilles Meloche	4.00	10.00
AGW2 Gump Worsley SP	15.00	40.00
AJAN J.P. Anderson SP	5.00	12.00
AJBE Jonathan Bernier	3.00	8.00
AJBO Johnny Bower SP	15.00	40.00
AJMA Jacob Markstrom	8.00	20.00
AJRE James Reid	4.00	10.00
AMBR Martin Brodeur SP	20.00	50.00
AMCL Maxime Clermont	3.00	8.00
AMCO Marco Cousineau	3.00	8.00
AMHU Michael Hutchinson	5.00	12.00
AML2 Mike Liut	2.50	6.00
ANLI Nathan Lieuwen	5.00	12.00
APDI Peter Di Salvo	4.00	10.00
APP2 Pete Peeters	6.00	15.00
APR2 Pat Riggin	5.00	12.00
APRI Pat Riggin	5.00	12.00
ARB2 Richard Brodeur SP	6.00	15.00
ARLU Roberto Luongo SP	12.00	30.00
ARV2 Rogie Vachon SP	8.00	20.00
ATE2 Tony Esposito SP	20.00	50.00
AVTR Vladislav Tretiak	3.00	8.00
ACHO2 Charlie Hodge SP	6.00	15.00
AJBO2 Johnny Bower SP	15.00	40.00

2009-10 Between The Pipes Brodeur Tribute

COMMON BRODEUR	3.00	8.00

2009-10 Between The Pipes CHL Rookies

COMPLETE SET (9)	15.00	40.00
CR01 Michael Houser	3.00	8.00
CR02 Petr Mrazek	6.00	15.00
CR03 Tyson Teichmann	2.00	5.00
CR04 Brandon Anderson	2.00	5.00
CR05 Hudson Stremmel	3.00	8.00
CR06 Jordan Binnington	4.00	10.00
CR07 Guillaume Nadeau	3.00	8.00
CR08 Philippe Tremblay	2.00	5.00
CR09 Robin Gusse	2.50	6.00

2009-10 Between The Pipes Complete Package Silver

CP01 Pelle Lindbergh	10.00	25.00
CP02 Bernie Parent	15.00	40.00
CP03 Jacques Plante	20.00	50.00
CP04 Vladislav Tretiak	10.00	25.00
CP05 Patrick Roy	30.00	80.00
CP06 Gerry Cheevers	12.00	30.00
CP07 Patrick Roy	30.00	80.00
CP08 Martin Brodeur	30.00	80.00
CP09 Marc-Andre Fleury	25.00	60.00
CP10 Marty Turco	12.00	30.00

2009-10 Between The Pipes Glove Save Black

GS01 Cam Ward	8.00	20.00
GS02 Chris Osgood	8.00	20.00
GS03 Dominik Hasek	12.00	30.00
GS04 Ed Belfour	8.00	20.00
GS05 Evgeni Nabokov	6.00	15.00
GS06 Felix Potvin	12.00	30.00
GS07 Gerry Cheevers	8.00	20.00
GS08 Grant Fuhr	12.00	30.00
GS09 Hannu Toivonen	8.00	20.00
GS10 Jose Theodore	8.00	20.00
GS11 Jean-Sebastien Giguere	8.00	20.00
GS12 Kirk McLean	15.00	40.00
GS13 Leland Irving	8.00	20.00
GS14 Manny Fernandez	5.00	12.00
GS15 Manny Legace	6.00	15.00
GS16 Marc-Andre Fleury	15.00	40.00
GS17 Martin Brodeur	20.00	50.00
GS18 Marty Turco	8.00	20.00
GS19 Miikka Kiprusoff	8.00	20.00
GS20 Olaf Kolzig	8.00	20.00
GS21 Patrick Roy	20.00	50.00
GS22 Peter Budaj	6.00	15.00
GS23 Rick DiPietro	6.00	15.00
GS24 Roberto Luongo	12.00	30.00
GS25 Ron Hextall	8.00	20.00
GS26 Ryan Miller	8.00	20.00
GS27 Sean Burke	5.00	12.00
GS28 Tomas Vokoun	6.00	15.00
GS29 Tony Esposito	8.00	20.00
GS30 Vesa Toskala	8.00	20.00

2009-10 Between The Pipes Gold Medal Masks

GMM01 Tomas Vokoun	1.50	4.00
GMM02 Martin Brodeur	5.00	12.00
GMM03 Ilya Bryzgalov	1.50	4.00
GMM04 Jonas Hiller	1.50	4.00
GMM05 Miikka Kiprusoff	2.00	5.00
GMM06 Ryan Miller	2.00	5.00
GMM07 Roberto Luongo	3.00	8.00
GMM08 Jaroslav Halak	2.00	5.00
GMM09 Evgeni Nabokov	1.50	4.00

2009-10 Between The Pipes He Shoots He Saves Prizes

HS02 Ron Hextall	40.00	80.00
HS03 Ron Hextall	40.00	80.00
HS04 Chris Osgood	15.00	30.00
HS05 Martin Brodeur	40.00	80.00
HS06 Damian Rhodes	15.00	30.00
HS07 Martin Brodeur	40.00	80.00
HS08 Jose Theodore	15.00	40.00
HS09 Evgeni Nabokov	12.00	30.00
HS10 Mika Noronen	10.00	25.00
HS11 Chris Mason	15.00	40.00

2009-10 Between The Pipes Homegrown Black

HG1 Martin Brodeur	10.00	25.00
HG2 Marc-Andre Fleury	8.00	20.00
HG3 Marty Turco	4.00	10.00
HG4 Roberto Luongo	6.00	15.00
HG5 Carey Price	8.00	20.00
HG6 Tomas Vokoun	3.00	8.00
HG7 Kari Lehtonen	3.00	8.00
HG8 Tuukka Rask	5.00	12.00
HG9 Miikka Kiprusoff	4.00	10.00
HG10 Niklas Backstrom	4.00	10.00
HG11 Vesa Toskala	4.00	10.00
HG12 Olaf Kolzig	4.00	10.00
HG13 Peter Budaj	3.00	8.00
HG14 Jaroslav Halak	4.00	10.00
HG15 Jacob Markstrom	8.00	20.00
HG16 Pelle Lindbergh	3.00	8.00
HG17 Evgeni Nabokov	3.00	8.00
HG18 Jonas Hiller	3.00	8.00
HG19 Tim Thomas	4.00	10.00
HG20 Rick DiPietro	3.00	8.00
HG21 Ryan Miller	4.00	10.00
HG22 Jonathan Quick	5.00	12.00
HG23 Ilya Bryzgalov	3.00	8.00
HG24 Simeon Varlamov	4.00	10.00

2009-10 Between The Pipes International Crease Black

IC01 Brodeur/Luongo/Roy	12.00	30.00
IC02 Thomas/Miller/Craig	5.00	12.00
IC03 Markstrom/Lundqvist/Lindbergh	12.00	30.00
IC04 Kiprusoff/Lehtonen/Toskala	5.00	12.00
IC05 Varlamov/Bryzgalov/Tretiak	5.00	12.00
IC06 Pavelec/Vokoun/Hasek	8.00	20.00

2009-10 Between The Pipes Jerseys Black

M01 J.P. Anderson 2.00 5.00
M02 Martin Brodeur 6.00 15.00
M03 Peter Budaj 2.00 5.00
M04 Trevor Cann 3.00 8.00
M05 Maxime Clermont 2.00 5.00
M06 John Curry 2.00 5.00
M07 Peter Delmas 2.00 5.00
M08 Cedrick Desjardins 4.00 10.00
M09 Louis Domingue 3.00 8.00
M10 Brian Elliott 2.00 5.00
M11 Andrew Engelage 5.00 12.00
M12 Marc-Andre Fleury 5.00 12.00
M13 Jean-Sebastien Giguere 2.50 6.00
M14 Jacob Markstrom 5.00 12.00
M15 Dominik Hasek 4.00 10.00
M16 Riku Helenius 2.50 6.00
M17 Braden Holtby 6.00 15.00
M18 Torrie Jung 2.00 5.00
M19 Anton Khudobin 4.00 10.00
M20 Kari Lehtonen 2.00 5.00
M21 Nathan Lieuwen 3.00 8.00
M22 Roberto Luongo 4.00 10.00
M23 Daren Machesney 2.00 5.00
M24 Drew MacIntyre 4.00 10.00
M25 Ryan Miller 2.50 6.00
M26 Mike Murphy 2.50 6.00
M27 Evgeni Nabokov 2.00 5.00
M28 Edward Pasquale 2.50 6.00
M29 Calvin Pickard 4.00 10.00
M30 Chet Pickard 3.00 8.00
M31 Felix Potvin 4.00 10.00
M32 Carey Price 5.00 12.00
M33 Jonathan Quick 3.00 8.00
M34 Nicola Riopel 2.00 5.00
M35 Olivier Roy 2.50 6.00
M36 Patrick Roy 6.00 15.00
M37 Patrick Roy 6.00 15.00
M38 Scott Stajcer 2.00 5.00
M39 Tim Thomas 2.50 6.00
M40 Dustin Tokarski 2.50 6.00
M41 Jamie Tucker 2.00 5.00
M42 Simeon Varlamov 2.50 6.00
M43 Mark Visentin 2.00 5.00
M44 Cam Ward 2.50 6.00
M45 Miika Wiikman 2.50 6.00
M46 Tony Esposito/40* 6.00 15.00
M47 Bernie Parent/40* 5.00 12.00
M48 Glenn Hall/40* 6.00 15.00
M49 Ed Giacomin/40* 6.00 15.00
M50 Ron Hextall/40* 5.00 12.00

2009-10 Between The Pipes Masked Men II

*GOLD/20: 1.5X TO 4X BASIC INSERTS
MM01 Gilles Gratton 3.00 8.00
MM02 Brian Hayward 2.50 6.00
MM03 Denis Herron 2.50 6.00
MM04 Patrick Roy 8.00 20.00
MM05 Felix Potvin 5.00 12.00
MM06 Ed Belfour 3.00 8.00
MM07 Ron Hextall 3.00 8.00
MM08 Martin Brodeur 8.00 20.00
MM09 Jimmy Howard 4.00 10.00
MM10 Evgeni Nabokov 2.50 6.00
MM11 Michael Houser 4.00 10.00
MM12 Mike McKenna 2.50 6.00
MM13 Tuukka Rask 4.00 10.00
MM14 Michal Neuvirth 5.00 12.00
MM15 Chet Pickard 4.00 10.00
MM16 James Reimer 8.00 20.00
MM17 Jean-Francois Berube 2.50 6.00
MM18 Evan Mosher 2.50 6.00
MM19 Olivier Roy 3.00 8.00
MM20 Frederic Piche 2.50 6.00
MM21 Patrick Roy 8.00 20.00
MM22 Jacques Plante 5.00 12.00
MM23 Grant Fuhr 5.00 12.00
MM24 Mark Dekanich 2.50 6.00
MM25 Chris Carrozzi 3.00 8.00
MM26 Riku Helenius 3.00 8.00
MM27 Braden Holtby 8.00 20.00
MM28 Dan LaCosta 2.50 6.00
MM29 Peter Mannino 3.00 8.00
MM30 Kevin Regan 3.00 8.00
MM31 Jeff Zatkoff 3.00 8.00
MM32 Jean-Philipp Gagnon 2.50 6.00
MM33 Tim Thomas 3.00 8.00
MM34 Miikka Kiprusoff 3.00 8.00
MM35 Roberto Luongo 5.00 12.00
MM36 Carey Price 6.00 15.00
MM37 Cristobal Huet 3.00 8.00
MM38 Ilya Bryzgalov 2.50 6.00
MM39 Scott Clemmensen 2.50 6.00
MM40 Louis Domingue 4.00 10.00
MM41 Craig Anderson 3.00 8.00
MM42 Ed Giacomin 4.00 10.00
MM43 Jason LaBarbera 2.50 6.00
MM44 Marc-Andre Fleury 6.00 15.00
MM45 Simeon Varlamov 3.00 8.00
MM46 Ryan Miller 3.00 8.00
MM47 Matthew Hackett 4.00 10.00
MM48 Chris Perugini 2.50 6.00
MM49 Cody St. Jacques 2.50 6.00
MM50 Doug Favell 3.00 8.00

2009-10 Between The Pipes Mega Stars Black

MS01 Patrick Roy 12.00 30.00
MS02 Felix Potvin 8.00 20.00
MS03 Chris Osgood 5.00 12.00
MS04 Ed Belfour 5.00 12.00
MS05 Martin Brodeur 12.00 30.00
MS06 Dominik Hasek 8.00 20.00
MS07 Martin Brodeur 12.00 30.00
MS08 Ed Belfour 5.00 12.00
MS09 Dominik Hasek 8.00 20.00
MS10 Patrick Roy 12.00 30.00
MS11 Arturs Irbe 5.00 12.00
MS12 Dominik Hasek 8.00 20.00
MS13 Olaf Kolzig 5.00 12.00
MS14 Martin Brodeur 12.00 30.00
MS15 Mike Richter 5.00 12.00
MS16 Tommy Salo 4.00 10.00
MS17 Dominik Hasek 8.00 20.00
MS18 Martin Brodeur 12.00 30.00
MS19 Patrick Roy 12.00 30.00
MS20 Evgeni Nabokov 4.00 10.00
MS21 Patrick Roy 12.00 30.00
MS22 Dominik Hasek 8.00 20.00
MS23 Patrick Roy 12.00 30.00
MS24 Rick DiPietro 4.00 10.00

2009-10 Between The Pipes Net Brawlers

NB01 A.Montoya/R.DiPietro 4.00 10.00
NB02 T.Conklin/P.Nurminen 3.00 8.00
NB03 C.Osgood/P.Roy 10.00 25.00
NB04 J.Hurme/F.Potvin 6.00 15.00
NB05 O.Kolzig/B.Dafoe 4.00 10.00
NB06 T.Voukon/M.Kiprusoff 4.00 10.00
NB07 C.Crawford/A.Montoya 5.00 12.00
NB08 M.Leighton/J.Howard 5.00 12.00
NB09 R.Hextall/F.Potvin 6.00 15.00

2009-10 Between The Pipes Origins Black

O01 Gerry Cheevers 5.00 12.00
O02 Tony Esposito 5.00 12.00
O03 Bernie Parent 6.00 15.00
O04 Billy Smith 5.00 12.00
O05 Rogie Vachon 6.00 15.00
O06 Ed Belfour 5.00 12.00
O07 Miikka Kiprusoff 5.00 12.00
O08 Dominik Hasek 8.00 20.00
O09 Roberto Luongo 8.00 20.00
O10 Jean-Sebastien Giguere 5.00 12.00

2009-10 Between The Pipes Pad Save Black

PS01 David Aebischer 5.00 12.00
PS02 Ed Belfour 4.00 10.00
PS03 Brian Boucher 3.00 8.00
PS04 Martin Brodeur 10.00 25.00
PS05 Sean Burke 2.50 6.00
PS06 Gerry Cheevers 4.00 10.00
PS07 Dan Cloutier 3.00 8.00
PS08 Robert Esche 4.00 10.00
PS09 Grant Fuhr 6.00 15.00
PS10 Ron Hextall 4.00 10.00
PS11 Leland Irving 4.00 10.00
PS12 Curtis Joseph 5.00 12.00
PS13 Nikolai Khabibulin 4.00 10.00
PS14 Patrick Lalime 3.00 8.00
PS15 Pelle Lindbergh 3.00 8.00
PS16 Chris Osgood 4.00 10.00
PS17 Bernie Parent 5.00 12.00
PS18 Patrick Roy 10.00 25.00
PS19 Patrick Roy 10.00 25.00
PS20 Jose Theodore 4.00 10.00
PS21 Tim Thomas 4.00 10.00
PS22 Vladislav Tretiak 3.00 8.00
PS23 Marty Turco 4.00 10.00
PS24 Mike Vernon 3.00 8.00
PS25 Tomas Vokoun 3.00 8.00

2009-10 Between The Pipes Stick Save Black

SS01 Carey Price 10.00 25.00
SS02 Chris Osgood 5.00 12.00
SS03 Evgeni Nabokov 4.00 10.00
SS04 Steve Mason 4.00 10.00
SS05 Ilya Bryzgalov 4.00 10.00
SS06 Jimmy Howard 6.00 15.00
SS07 John Vanbiesbrouck 5.00 12.00
SS08 Jonas Gustavsson 6.00 15.00
SS09 Jonas Hiller 4.00 10.00
SS10 Mike Richter 5.00 12.00
SS11 Jean-Sebastien Giguere 5.00 12.00
SS12 Cristobal Huet 5.00 12.00
SS13 Ken Dryden 5.00 12.00
SS14 Marc-Andre Fleury 10.00 25.00
SS15 Martin Brodeur 12.00 30.00
SS16 Marty Turco 5.00 12.00
SS17 Miikka Kiprusoff 5.00 12.00
SS18 Mike Smith 5.00 12.00
SS19 Niklas Backstrom 5.00 12.00
SS20 Pascal Leclaire 5.00 12.00
SS21 Patrick Roy 12.00 30.00
SS22 Pekka Rinne 5.00 12.00
SS23 Pelle Lindbergh 4.00 10.00
SS24 Roberto Luongo 8.00 20.00
SS25 Ed Belfour 5.00 12.00
SS26 Nikolai Khabibulin 5.00 12.00
SS27 Tim Thomas 5.00 12.00
SS28 Tomas Vokoun 4.00 10.00
SS29 Tuukka Rask 10.00 25.00
SS30 Vesa Toskala 5.00 12.00

2010-11 Between The Pipes

COMPLETE SET (200) 20.00 50.00
1 Adam Brown .20 .50
2 Mickael Audette .20 .50
3 Antonio Mastropietro .20 .50
4 Brandon Maxwell .20 .50
5 Calvin Pickard .25 .60
6 Cam Lanigan .20 .50
7 Christopher Gibson .30 .75
8 Darcy Kuemper .50 1.25
9 David Honzik .20 .50
10 Drew Owsley .20 .50
11 Evan Mosher .20 .50
12 Frederic Piche .20 .50
13 Gabriel Girard .20 .50
14 Guillaume Nadeau .25 .60
15 Igor Bobkov .40 1.00
16 Jack Campbell .25 .60
17 James Reid .20 .50
18 Jean-Francois Berube .25 .60
19 Jordan Binnington .40 1.00
20 J.P. Anderson .25 .60
21 Kent Simpson .20 .50
22 Liam Liston .20 .50
23 Louis Domingue .25 .60
24 Mac Carruth .20 .50
25 Malcolm Subban .50 1.25
26 Mark Friesen .20 .50
27 Mark Segal .20 .50
28 Mark Visentin .25 .60
29 Mavric Parks .20 .50
30 Maxime Clermont .20 .50
31 Michael Houser .20 .50
32 Nathan Lieuwen .20 .50
33 Nicolas Champion .20 .50
34 Olivier Roy .25 .60
35 Petr Mrazek .50 1.25
36 Philipp Grubauer .30 .75
37 Ramis Sadikov .25 .60
38 Robin Gusse .25 .60
39 Scott Stajcer .20 .50
40 Scott Wedgewood .20 .50
41 Steven Stanford .20 .50
42 Thomas Heemskerk .20 .50
43 Ty Rimmer .20 .50
44 Tyler Bunz .20 .50
45 Tyson Teichmann .20 .50
46 Alec Richards .20 .50
47 Alex Stalock .20 .50
48 Anton Khudobin .25 .60
49 Ben Bishop .20 .50
50 Brad Thiessen .25 .60
51 Braden Holtby .30 .75
52 Carter Hutton .50 1.25
53 Cedrick Desjardins .25 .60
54 Chad Johnson .20 .50
55 Chet Pickard .20 .50
56 David Leggio .20 .50
57 Dustin Tokarski .20 .50
58 Eddie Lack .25 .60
59 Jacob Markstrom .50 1.25
60 Jake Allen .40 1.00
61 James Reimer .25 .60
62 Jean-Philippe Levasseur .20 .50
63 Jeff Deslauriers .15 .40
64 Jeff Frazee .30 .75
65 Jeff Zatkoff .25 .60
66 Jeremy Smith .25 .60
67 Jhonas Enroth .25 .60
68 Johan Backlund .20 .50
69 John Curry .20 .50
70 Jussi Rynnas .25 .60
71 Justin Pogge .20 .50
72 Kevin Poulin .25 .60
73 Leland Irving .25 .60
74 Mark Dekanich .20 .50
75 Martin Jones .40 1.00
76 Matt Climie .20 .50
77 Matt Hackett .25 .60
78 Michael Hutchinson .30 .75
79 Mike Murphy .25 .60
80 Mikko Koskinen .25 .60
81 Richard Bachman .25 .60
82 Robert Mayer .25 .60
83 Robin Lehner .40 1.00
84 Thomas McCollum .25 .60
85 Timo Pielmeier RC .25 .60
86 Tyler Weiman .20 .50
87 Alex Auld .20 .50
88 Andrew Raycroft .20 .50
89 Antero Niittymaki .20 .50
90 Antti Niemi .20 .50
91 Brian Boucher .20 .50
92 Brian Elliott .20 .50
93 Cam Ward .25 .60
94 Carey Price .50 1.25
95 Chris Mason .20 .50
96 Chris Osgood .25 .60
97 Corey Crawford .30 .75
98 Cory Schneider .25 .60
99 Craig Anderson .25 .60
100 Curtis McElhinney .15 .40
101 Dan Ellis .20 .50
102 Devan Dubnyk .20 .50
103 Dwayne Roloson .20 .50
104 Evgeni Nabokov .20 .50
105 Henrik Lundqvist .60 1.50
106 Ilya Bryzgalov .20 .50
107 Jean-Sebastien Giguere .25 .60
108 Jaroslav Halak .25 .60
109 Jason LaBarbera .20 .50
110 Jimmy Howard .30 .75
111 Johan Hedberg .20 .50
112 Jonas Hiller .20 .50
113 Jonathan Bernier .20 .50
114 Jonathan Quick .30 .75
115 Josh Harding .25 .60
116 Justin Peters .20 .50
117 Kari Lehtonen .20 .50
118 Marc-Andre Fleury .50 1.25
119 Martin Biron .20 .50
120 Martin Brodeur .60 1.50
121 Martin Gerber .20 .50
122 Marty Turco .25 .60
123 Mathieu Garon .20 .50
124 Michal Neuvirth .20 .50
125 Miikka Kiprusoff .25 .60
126 Mike Brodeur .20 .50
127 Mike Smith .25 .60
128 Niklas Backstrom .25 .60
129 Ondrej Pavelec .25 .60
130 Pascal Leclaire .20 .50
131 Patrick Lalime .20 .50
132 Pekka Rinne .25 .60
133 Peter Budaj .20 .50
134 Rick DiPietro .20 .50
135 Roberto Luongo .40 1.00
136 Ryan Miller .25 .60
137 Scott Clemmensen .20 .50
138 Semyon Varlamov .25 .60
139 Sergei Bobrovsky .75 2.00
140 Tim Thomas .25 .60
141 Tomas Vokoun .20 .50
142 Tuukka Rask .30 .75
143 Ty Conklin .20 .50
144 Andy Moog .25 .60
145 Rick Wamsley .25 .60
146 Bernie Parent .30 .75
147 Billy Smith .25 .60
148 Murray Bannerman .25 .60
149 Bob Sauve .25 .60
150 Cesare Maniago .30 .75
151 Chico Resch .25 .60
152 Curtis Joseph .30 .75
153 Dan Bouchard .20 .50
154 Darren Pang .25 .60
155 Denis Herron .20 .50
156 Dominik Hasek .40 1.00
157 Don Beaupre .20 .50
158 Ed Giacomin .40 1.00
159 Felix Potvin .40 1.00
160 Frank Pietrangelo .30 .75
161 Gerry Cheevers .25 .60
162 Gilles Gilbert .20 .50
163 Glenn Hall .25 .60
164 Grant Fuhr .40 1.00
165 Greg Millen .20 .50
166 John Garrett .25 .60
167 John Vanbiesbrouck .25 .60
168 Johnny Bower .25 .60
169 Kelly Hrudey .20 .50
170 Kirk McLean .25 .60
171 Michel Dion .20 .50
172 Mike Richter .25 .60
173 Mike Vernon .20 .50
174 Olaf Kolzig .25 .60
175 Patrick Roy .60 1.50
176 Phil Myre .20 .50
177 Pokey Reddick .20 .50
178 Richard Brodeur .25 .60
179 Roger Crozier .20 .50
180 Rogie Vachon .30 .75
181 Ron Low .25 .60
182 Sean Burke .15 .40
183 Steve Penney .25 .60
184 Tom Barrasso .25 .60
185 Tony Esposito .25 .60
186 Vladislav Tretiak .20 .50
187 Sami Jo Small .30 .75
188 Kim St. Pierre .40 1.00
189 Charline Labonte .30 .75
190 Manon Rheaume .60 1.50
191 Terry Sawchuk .30 .75
192 George Hainsworth .25 .60
193 Georges Vezina .30 .75
194 Gump Worsley .25 .60
195 Jacques Plante .30 .75
196 Pelle Lindbergh .20 .50
197 Clint Benedict .20 .50
198 Tiny Thompson .25 .60
199 Turk Broda .25 .60
200 Tom Fenton .30 .75

2010-11 Between The Pipes Autographs

AAK Anton Khudobin 5.00 12.00
AAM Andy Moog 5.00 12.00
AAR Alec Richards 4.00 10.00
AAS Alex Stalock 4.00 10.00
ABH Braden Holtby 10.00 25.00
ABP Bernie Parent SP 12.00 30.00
ABS Billy Smith SP 10.00 25.00
ABT Brad Thiessen 5.00 12.00
ACC Corey Crawford SP 12.00 30.00
ACD Cedrick Desjardins 5.00 12.00
ACG Christopher Gibson 6.00 15.00
ACJ Chad Johnson 4.00 10.00
ACL Charline Labonte 6.00 15.00
ACO Chris Osgood SP 10.00 25.00
ACP Calvin Pickard 5.00 12.00
ACR Chico Resch 5.00 12.00
ACS Cory Schneider SP 10.00 25.00
ADB Dan Bouchard 4.00 10.00
ADH Denis Herron 4.00 10.00
ADK Darcy Kuemper 10.00 25.00
ADL David LeNeveu SP 8.00 20.00
ADR Dwayne Roloson SP 8.00 20.00
ADT Dustin Tokarski 4.00 10.00
AEG Ed Giacomin SP 12.00 30.00
AEL Eddie Lack 5.00 12.00
AEM Evan Mosher 4.00 10.00
AFP Frederic Piche 4.00 10.00
AGC Gerry Cheevers SP 15.00 40.00
AGF Grant Fuhr SP 15.00 40.00
AGH Glenn Hall SP 10.00 25.00
AGM Greg Millen 4.00 10.00
AGN Guillaume Nadeau 5.00 12.00
AGW Gump Worsley SP 12.00 30.00
AHL Henrik Lundqvist SP 25.00 60.00
AIB Igor Bobkov 8.00 20.00
AJA Jake Allen 8.00 20.00
AJB Johan Backlund 4.00 10.00
AJC Jack Campbell 5.00 12.00
AJE Jhonas Enroth 5.00 12.00
AJF Jeff Frazee 6.00 15.00
AJG John Garrett 5.00 12.00
AJH Jaroslav Halak SP 10.00 25.00
AJM Jacob Markstrom 10.00 25.00
AJQ Jonathan Quick SP 15.00 30.00
AJR Jussi Rynnas 5.00 12.00
AJZ Jeff Zatkoff 5.00 12.00
AKH Kelly Hrudey 4.00 10.00
AKM Kirk McLean SP 10.00 25.00
AKS Kent Simpson 4.00 10.00
ALD Louis Domingue 5.00 12.00
ALI Leland Irving 5.00 12.00
AMC Matt Climie 4.00 10.00
AMD Mark Dekanich 4.00 10.00
AMG Martin Gerber SP 8.00 20.00
AMH Michael Hutchinson 6.00 15.00
AML Mike Liut SP 6.00 15.00
AMM Mike Murphy 5.00 12.00
AMN Michal Neuvirth SP 8.00 20.00
AMR Manon Rheaume SP 40.00 80.00
AMR Mike Richter SP 10.00 25.00
AMS Malcolm Subban 10.00 25.00
AMT Marty Turco 5.00 12.00
AMV Mark Visentin 5.00 12.00
ANB Niklas Backstrom SP 10.00 25.00
ANK Nikolai Khabibulin SP 8.00 20.00
AOK Olaf Kolzig 5.00 12.00
AOP Ondrej Pavelec 5.00 12.00
AOR Olivier Roy 5.00 12.00
APB Peter Budaj SP 8.00 20.00
APG Philipp Grubauer 6.00 15.00
APL Patrick Lalime SP 8.00 20.00
APM Phil Myre 4.00 10.00
APR Pekka Rinne SP 10.00 25.00
ARB Richard Brodeur 5.00 12.00
ARE Ray Emery SP 8.00 20.00
ARG Robin Gusse 5.00 12.00
ARH Ron Hextall SP 12.00 30.00
ARL Roberto Luongo SP 15.00 40.00
ARM Robert Mayer 5.00 12.00
ARS Ramis Sadikov 5.00 12.00
ARW Rick Wamsley 6.00 15.00
ASB Sergei Bobrovsky SP 15.00 40.00
ASP Steve Penney 6.00 15.00
ASS Steven Stanford 4.00 10.00
ASV Semyon Varlamov SP 12.00 30.00
ASW Scott Wedgewood 4.00 10.00
ATB Tyler Bunz 4.00 10.00
ATE Tony Esposito SP 15.00 30.00
ATF Tom Fenton 6.00 15.00
ATP Timo Pielmeier 5.00 12.00
ATR Tuukka Rask 10.00 25.00
ATT Tyson Teichmann 4.00 10.00
ATV Tomas Vokoun SP 8.00 20.00
AVT Vladislav Tretiak SP 15.00 40.00
AANI Antti Niemi SP 8.00 20.00
ABSA Bob Sauve 5.00 12.00
ACJO Curtis Joseph SP 12.00 30.00
ACMA Cesare Maniago 6.00 15.00
ACME Curtis McElhinney SP 6.00 15.00
ACPR Carey Price SP 20.00 50.00
ACSA Curtis Sanford 4.00 10.00
ADBE Don Beaupre SP 8.00 20.00
ADHA Dominik Hasek SP 15.00 40.00
AFPI Frank Pietrangelo 6.00 15.00
AFPO Felix Potvin SP 15.00 40.00
AJBE Jonathan Bernier 5.00 12.00
AJBI Jordan Binnington 8.00 20.00
AJBO Johnny Bower SP 10.00 25.00
AJFB Jean-Francois Berube 5.00 12.00
AJHE Johan Hedberg 5.00 12.00
AJHI Jonas Hiller 4.00 10.00
AJHO Jimmy Howard SP 12.00 30.00
AJPA J.P. Anderson 5.00 12.00
AJPO Justin Pogge 4.00 10.00
AJSG Jean-Sebastien Giguere SP 12.00 30.00
AJSM Jeremy Smith 5.00 12.00
AKSP Kim St. Pierre 8.00 20.00
AMAF Marc-Andre Fleury SP 15.00 40.00
AMBA Murray Bannerman 5.00 12.00
AMBR Martin Brodeur SP 25.00 60.00
AMCL Maxime Clermont 4.00 10.00
AMDI Michel Dion 4.00 10.00
AMIB Mike Brodeur 4.00 10.00
AMSE Mark Segal 4.00 10.00
AMVE Mike Vernon 4.00 10.00
APMR Petr Mrazek 10.00 25.00
APRE Pokey Reddick SP 8.00 20.00
APRO Patrick Roy SP 40.00 100.00
ARBA Richard Bachman 5.00 12.00
ARLO Ron Low 5.00 12.00
ASBU Sean Burke SP 6.00 15.00
ASJS Sami Jo Small 6.00 15.00
ATBA Tom Barrasso SP 12.00 30.00
ATMC Thomas McCollum 5.00 12.00
ATRI Ty Rimmer 4.00 10.00
ATTH Tim Thomas SP 10.00 25.00

2010-11 Between The Pipes Countrymen Quad Memorabilia Silver

CM01 Flry/Fuhr/Josph/Price 30.00 80.00
CM02 Vachn/Roy/Brdr/Longo 20.00 50.00
CM03 T.Espo/Barrso/Rchtr/Mllr 30.00 80.00
CM04 DiPtr/Vnbies/Thmas/Qck 30.00 80.00
CM05 Kipr/Lhtn/Bckstrm/Rask 15.00 40.00
CM06 Lndbrg/Hdbrg/Lndq/Mrkst 25.00 60.00
CM07 Trtk/Vrlmv/Bryz/Bbrvsky 20.00 50.00
CM08 Dzrilla/Hsek/Vokn/Halak 30.00 80.00

2010-11 Between The Pipes Deep In The Crease

COMPLETE SET (30) 50.00 100.00
DC01 Hiller/Lvsur/Emry/Bobkv 4.00 10.00
DC02 Pav/Masn/Mnno/Psqle 2.50 6.00
DC03 Thmas/Rask/Dltn/Htch 3.00 8.00
DC04 Miller/Lme/Enrth/Leggio 2.50 6.00
DC05 Kipr/Klley/Irvng/Lamr 2.50 6.00
DC06 Ward/Petrs/Pgge/Mrphy 2.50 6.00
DC07 Crwfrd/Trco/Rchrds/Smp 3.00 8.00
DC08 Budaj/Elliott/Grhme/Pick 2.50 6.00
DC09 Garn/Wsl/LNv/Corbl-Thr 2.00 5.00
DC10 Leht/Rycrft/Bchmn/Cmp 2.50 6.00
DC11 Howrd/Osgd/McCl/Mrz 5.00 12.00
DC12 Khab/Dbnyk/Dslr/Roy 2.50 6.00
DC13 Vokn/Clmsn/Mrks/Plnte 5.00 12.00
DC14 Quick/Bernr/Jns/Berb 4.00 10.00
DC15 Bckstr/Hrdng/Hcktt/Kmpr 5.00 12.00
DC16 Price/Auld/Sanford/Mayer 5.00 12.00
DC17 Brodr/Hdbrg/Frze/Wdge 6.00 15.00
DC18 Rinn/Dknch/Smth/Pckrd 2.50 6.00
DC19 DiPietro/Plin/Lwsn/Kskn 2.50 6.00
DC20 Lndqv/Birn/Jhnsn/Stjcr 6.00 15.00
DC21 Andrsn/Lclre/Brdr/Lhnr 4.00 10.00
DC22 Bobrvs/Bchr/Lghtn/Bcklnd 5.00 12.00
DC23 Bryz/LaBrb/Clim/Dmig 2.50 6.00
DC24 Flry/Jhnsn/Crry/Thsen 5.00 12.00
DC25 Nimi/Niitty/Stlck/Andr 2.50 6.00
DC26 Halk/Cnkln/Alln/Bshp 4.00 10.00
DC27 Rolsn/Smth/Tkrsk/Jnus 2.50 6.00
DC28 Gigre/Gustv/Rmer/Ryns 3.00 8.00
DC29 Lungo/Schn/Lck/Wman 4.00 10.00
DC30 Varlmv/Nvith/Hltby/Grbr 3.00 8.00

2010-11 Between The Pipes Franchise Leaders Jerseys Silver

FL01 Jean-Sebastien Giguere 10.00 25.00
FL02 Kari Lehtonen 5.00 12.00
FL04 Dominik Hasek 10.00 25.00
FL05 Mike Vernon 5.00 12.00
FL06 Cam Ward 6.00 15.00
FL07 Tony Esposito 6.00 15.00
FL08 Patrick Roy 15.00 40.00
FL10 Marty Turco 6.00 15.00
FL12 Grant Fuhr 10.00 25.00
FL13 Roberto Luongo 10.00 25.00
FL14 Rogie Vachon 8.00 20.00
FL15 Niklas Backstrom 10.00 25.00
FL17 Tomas Vokoun 10.00 25.00
FL18 Martin Brodeur 15.00 40.00
FL19 Billy Smith 6.00 15.00
FL20 Mike Richter 10.00 25.00
FL21 Patrick Lalime 5.00 12.00
FL22 Ron Hextall 6.00 15.00
FL23 Ilya Bryzgalov 5.00 12.00
FL24 Tom Barrasso 6.00 15.00
FL26 Mike Liut 15.00 40.00
FL27 Nikolai Khabibulin 8.00 20.00
FL29 Kirk McLean 15.00 40.00
FL30 Olaf Kolzig 6.00 15.00

2010-11 Between The Pipes Full Gear Silver

FG01 Martin Brodeur 25.00 60.00
FG02 Carey Price 30.00 80.00
FG03 Patrick Roy 30.00 80.00
FG04 Niklas Backstrom 20.00 50.00
FG05 Curtis Joseph 20.00 50.00
FG06 Pelle Lindbergh 40.00 80.00

2010-11 Between The Pipes Golden Goalies Jerseys Black

SILVER/20: .6X TO 1.5X BLACK/80*
GG01 Charline Labonte 6.00 15.00
GG02 Kim St. Pierre 8.00 20.00
GG03 Sami-Jo Small 6.00 15.00
GG04 Roberto Luongo 8.00 20.00
GG05 Martin Brodeur 12.00 30.00
GG06 Ed Belfour 5.00 12.00
GG07 Dominik Hasek 8.00 20.00
GG08 Vladimir Myshkin 5.00 12.00
GG09 Vladislav Tretiak/30* 8.00 20.00
GG10 Jim Craig/30* 15.00 40.00
GG11 Tomas Vokoun 4.00 10.00
GG12 Evgeni Nabokov 4.00 10.00
GG13 Henrik Lundqvist 12.00 30.00
GG14 Bill Ranford 5.00 12.00
GG15 Curtis Joseph 6.00 15.00
GG16 Vladimir Dzurilla 10.00 25.00
GG17 Jonas Hiller 4.00 10.00
GG18 Ilya Bryzgalov 4.00 10.00
GG19 Dwayne Roloson 4.00 10.00
GG20 Cam Ward 5.00 12.00
GG21 Jean-Sebastien Giguere 5.00 12.00
GG22 Marc Denis 4.00 10.00
GG23 Martin Biron 4.00 10.00
GG24 Johan Hedberg 4.00 10.00
GG25 Carey Price 10.00 25.00
GG26 Justin Pogge 4.00 10.00
GG27 Leland Irving 5.00 12.00
GG28 Dustin Tokarski 4.00 10.00
GG29 Mike Richter 5.00 12.00
GG30 Chet Pickard 4.00 10.00
GG31 Jonathan Bernier 4.00 10.00
GG32 Devan Dubnyk 4.00 10.00
GG33 Grant Fuhr 8.00 20.00

2010-11 Between The Pipes Guarding the Bleu Blanc et Rouge Net

COMPLETE SET (10) 25.00 60.00
BBR01 Georges Vezina 3.00 8.00
BBR02 George Hainsworth 2.50 6.00
BBR03 Wilf Cude 3.00 8.00
BBR04 Bill Durnan 2.50 6.00
BBR05 Gerry McNeil 1.50 4.00
BBR06 Jacques Plante 3.00 8.00
BBR07 Rogie Vachon 3.00 8.00
BBR08 Gump Worsley 2.50 6.00
BBR09 Patrick Roy 6.00 15.00
BBR10 Carey Price 5.00 12.00

2010-11 Between The Pipes Guarding the Blue and White Net

COMPLETE SET (10) 15.00 40.00
BW01 Lorne Chabot 2.00 5.00
BW02 Turk Broda 2.50 6.00
BW03 Harry Lumley 2.50 6.00
BW04 Johnny Bower 2.50 6.00
BW05 Mike Palmateer 2.50 6.00
BW06 Allan Bester 2.00 5.00
BW07 Felix Potvin 4.00 10.00
BW08 Curtis Joseph 3.00 8.00
BW09 Jean-Sebastien Giguere 2.50 6.00
BW10 James Reimer 2.50 6.00

2010-11 Between The Pipes Inspired Mask

COMPLETE SET (13) 60.00 120.00
IM01 Ray Emery 5.00 12.00
IM02 Tim Thomas 6.00 15.00
IM03 James Reimer 6.00 15.00
IM04 Antero Niittymaki 5.00 12.00
IM05 Jason Labarbera 5.00 12.00
IM06 Jaroslav Halak 6.00 15.00
IM07 Alex Auld 5.00 12.00
IM08 Carey Price 15.00 40.00
IM09 Mikael Tellqvist 6.00 15.00
IM10 Kari Lehtonen 5.00 12.00
IM11 Wade Dubielewicz 5.00 12.00
IM12 Carey Price 15.00 40.00
IM13 Ray Emery 5.00 12.00

2010-11 Between The Pipes Jerseys Black

M01 Antti Niemi 4.00 10.00
M02 Brian Boucher 4.00 10.00
M03 Calvin Pickard 5.00 12.00
M04 Chet Pickard 4.00 10.00
M05 Chris Osgood 5.00 12.00
M06 Christopher Gibson 6.00 15.00
M07 Corey Crawford 6.00 15.00
M08 Cory Schneider 5.00 12.00
M09 Darcy Kuemper 10.00 25.00
M10 Darren Pang 5.00 12.00
M11 David Honzik 4.00 10.00
M12 Devan Dubnyk 4.00 10.00
M13 Don Beaupre 4.00 10.00
M14 Ed Johnston/30* 12.00 30.00
M15 Evgeni Nabokov 4.00 10.00
M16 Felix Potvin 8.00 20.00
M17 Gilles Meloche 5.00 12.00
M18 Henrik Lundqvist 12.00 30.00
M19 Ilya Bryzgalov 4.00 10.00
M20 Jack Campbell 5.00 12.00
M21 Jacob Markstrom 10.00 25.00
M22 Jake Allen 8.00 20.00
M23 James Reimer 12.00 30.00
M24 Jamie Tucker 4.00 10.00
M25 Jeff Deslauriers 3.00 8.00
M26 Jean-Francois Berube 5.00 12.00
M27 Jhonas Enroth 5.00 12.00
M28 Ty Conklin 4.00 10.00
M29 Jonas Gustavsson 6.00 15.00
M30 Jonas Hiller 4.00 10.00
M31 Jonathan Quick 6.00 15.00
M32 Jordan Binnington 8.00 20.00
M33 Michael Leighton 4.00 10.00
M34 J.P. Anderson 5.00 12.00
M35 Kari Lehtonen 4.00 10.00
M36 Kent Simpson 4.00 10.00
M37 Mike Richter 5.00 12.00
M38 Liam Liston 4.00 10.00
M39 Marc-Andre Fleury 10.00 25.00
M40 Mark Visentin 5.00 12.00
M41 Martin Brodeur 10.00 25.00
M42 Mike Brodeur 4.00 10.00
M43 Mike Murphy 5.00 12.00
M44 Miikka Kiprusoff 5.00 12.00
M45 Mikko Koskinen 5.00 12.00
M46 Olivier Roy 5.00 12.00
M47 Pascal Leclaire 4.00 10.00
M48 Pekka Rinne 5.00 12.00
M49 Philipp Grubauer 6.00 15.00
M50 Pokey Reddick 4.00 10.00
M51 Roberto Luongo 8.00 20.00
M52 Roger Crozier/30* 6.00 15.00
M53 Ryan Miller 5.00 12.00
M54 Scott Stajcer 4.00 10.00
M55 Cam Ward 5.00 12.00
M56 Carey Price 10.00 25.00
M57 Jaroslav Halak 5.00 12.00
M58 Jean-Sebastien Giguere 5.00 12.00
M59 Niklas Backstrom 5.00 12.00
M60 Keith Hamilton 4.00 10.00
M61 Rick DiPietro 4.00 10.00
M62 Robin Lehner 8.00 20.00
M63 Semyon Varlamov 5.00 12.00
M64 Sergei Bobrovsky 10.00 25.00
M65 Tim Thomas 6.00 15.00
M66 Tom Barrasso 5.00 12.00
M67 Tuukka Rask 6.00 15.00
M68 Dominik Hasek/30* 12.00 30.00
M69 Ed Giacomin/30* 12.00 30.00
M70 Andy Moog/30* 12.00 30.00
M71 Grant Fuhr/30* 12.00 30.00
M72 Billy Smith/30 8.00 20.00
M73 John Vanbiesbrouck/30* 8.00 20.00
M74 Patrick Roy/30* 20.00 50.00
M75 Patrick Roy/30* 20.00 50.00
M76 Rogie Vachon/30* 10.00 25.00
M77 Tony Esposito/30* 10.00 25.00
M78 Ron Hextall/30* 8.00 20.00

2010-11 Between The Pipes Jerseys Silver

SILVER/20-30: .5X TO 1.2X BLACK

2010-11 Between The Pipes Leaders Jerseys Silver

L01 Martin Brodeur 15.00 40.00
L02 Martin Brodeur 15.00 40.00
L03 Dominik Hasek 10.00 25.00
L04 Patrick Roy 15.00 40.00
L05 Tom Barrasso 6.00 15.00
L06 Patrick Roy 12.00 30.00
L07 Ron Hextall 6.00 15.00
L08 Martin Brodeur 15.00 40.00
L09 Glenn Hall 6.00 15.00
L10 Jacques Plante 8.00 20.00

2010-11 Between The Pipes Masked Men III Emerald

MM01 Alex Auld 2.50 6.00
MM02 Andrew Raycroft 2.50 6.00
MM03 Antero Niittymaki 2.50 6.00
MM04 Antti Niemi 2.50 6.00
MM05 Brent Johnson 2.50 6.00
MM06 Brian Boucher 2.50 6.00
MM07 Brian Elliott 2.50 6.00
MM08 Cam Ward 3.00 8.00
MM09 Carey Price 6.00 15.00
MM10 Chris Mason 2.50 6.00
MM11 Corey Crawford 4.00 10.00
MM12 Cory Schneider 3.00 8.00
MM13 Craig Anderson 3.00 8.00
MM14 Scott Clemmensen 2.50 6.00
MM15 Ty Conklin 2.50 6.00
MM16 Devan Dubnyk 2.50 6.00
MM17 Dwayne Roloson 2.50 6.00
MM18 Henrik Lundqvist 8.00 20.00
MM19 Ilya Bryzgalov 2.50 6.00
MM20 James Reimer 8.00 20.00
MM21 Jaroslav Halak 3.00 8.00
MM22 Jason LaBarbera 2.50 6.00
MM23 Jean-Sebastien Giguere 3.00 8.00
MM24 Jimmy Howard 4.00 10.00
MM25 Johan Hedberg 2.50 6.00
MM26 Jhonas Enroth 3.00 8.00
MM27 Jonas Hiller 2.50 6.00
MM28 Jonathan Bernier 2.50 6.00
MM29 Jonathan Quick 4.00 10.00
MM30 Kari Lehtonen 2.50 6.00
MM31 Marc-Andre Fleury 6.00 15.00
MM32 Martin Brodeur 6.00 15.00
MM33 Marty Turco 6.00 15.00
MM34 Mathieu Garon 2.50 6.00
MM35 Michal Neuvirth 2.50 6.00
MM36 Miikka Kiprusoff 3.00 8.00
MM37 Niklas Backstrom 3.00 8.00
MM38 Ondrej Pavelec 3.00 8.00
MM39 Pascal Leclaire 2.50 6.00
MM40 Patrick Lalime 2.50 6.00
MM41 Pekka Rinne 3.00 8.00
MM42 Peter Budaj 2.50 6.00
MM43 Rick DiPietro 2.50 6.00
MM44 Roberto Luongo 5.00 12.00
MM45 Ryan Miller 3.00 8.00
MM46 Semyon Varlamov 4.00 10.00
MM47 Sergei Bobrovsky 6.00 15.00
MM48 Tim Thomas 3.00 8.00
MM49 Tomas Vokoun 2.50 6.00
MM50 Tuukka Rask 4.00 10.00

2010-11 Between The Pipes Masked Men III Silver

*SILVER: .5X TO 1.2X EMERALD

2010-11 Between The Pipes Ready Willing and Able Jerseys Black

SILVER/30: .5X TO 1.2X BLACK
RWA01 C.Price/A.Auld 15.00 40.00
RWA02 T.Thomas/T.Rask 10.00 25.00
RWA03 R.Miller/J.Enroth 8.00 20.00
RWA04 M.Fleury/B.Johnson 15.00 40.00
RWA05 R.Luongo/C.Schneider 12.00 30.00
RWA06 J.Quick/J.Bernier 10.00 25.00
RWA07 I.IBryzgalov/J.LaBarbera 6.00 15.00
RWA08 J-S Giguere/J.Reimer 12.00 30.00
RWA09 M.Brodeur/J.Hedberg 12.00 30.00
RWA10 B.Boucher/S.Bobrovsky 12.00 30.00
RWA11 C.Ward/J.Peters 8.00 20.00
RWA12 J.Halak/T.Conklin 8.00 20.00

2010-11 Between The Pipes School Is Out Jerseys Silver

SO01 K.McLean/P.Budaj 6.00 15.00
SO02 R.Wamsley/P.Leclaire 6.00 15.00
SO03 B.Parent/P.Lindbergh 25.00 60.00
SO04 G.Hall/M.Vernon 6.00 15.00
SO05 V.Tretiak/E.Belfour 6.00 15.00
SO06 A.Moog/M.Turco 6.00 15.00
SO07 G.Fuhr/I.Bryzgalov 10.00 25.00
SO08 P.Peeters/J.Hiller 6.00 15.00
SO09 T.Barrasso/C.Ward 6.00 15.00
SO10 B.Ranford/J.Quick 8.00 20.00
SO11 G.Meloche/M.Fleury 12.00 30.00
SO12 J.Plante/B.Parent 8.00 20.00

2010-11 Between The Pipes Showdown Dual Jerseys Silver

SD01 P.Roy/J.Vanbiesbrouck 20.00 50.00
SD02 R.Luongo/R.Miller 12.00 30.00
SD03 K.McLean/M.Richter 15.00 40.00
SD04 G.Fuhr/R.Hextall 12.00 30.00
SD05 M.Vernon/P.Roy 20.00 50.00
SD06 M.Brodeur/J.Giguere 20.00 50.00
SD07 B.Parent/G.Gilbert 10.00 25.00
SD08 V.Tretiak/T.Esposito 12.00 30.00

2010-11 Between The Pipes Stick Save Silver

SS01 Bernie Parent 20.00 50.00
SS02 Brent Johnson 12.00 30.00
SS03 Chris Osgood 15.00 40.00
SS04 Felix Potvin 25.00 60.00
SS05 Jaroslav Halak 15.00 40.00
SS06 John Vanbiesbrouck 15.00 40.00
SS07 Jonas Gustavsson 15.00 40.00
SS08 Kari Lehtonen 12.00 30.00
SS09 Mark Visentin 15.00 40.00
SS10 Martin Brodeur 40.00 100.00
SS11 Olaf Kolzig 15.00 40.00
SS12 Patrick Roy 40.00 100.00
SS13 Patrick Roy 40.00 100.00
SS14 Rick DiPietro 12.00 30.00
SS15 Ryan Miller 15.00 40.00
SS16 Tim Thomas 15.00 40.00
SS17 Tom Barrasso 15.00 40.00
SS18 Tomas Vokoun 12.00 30.00

2010-11 Between The Pipes Their Country's Finest

COMPLETE SET (9) 15.00 40.00
CF01 Martin Brodeur 6.00 15.00
CF02 Ryan Miller 2.50 6.00
CF03 Henrik Lundqvist 6.00 15.00
CF04 Miikka Kiprusoff 2.50 6.00
CF05 Ilya Bryzgalov 2.00 5.00
CF06 Tomas Vokoun 2.00 5.00
CF07 Jaroslav Halak 2.50 6.00
CF08 Jonas Hiller 2.00 5.00
CF09 Olaf Kolzig 2.50 6.00

2011-12 Between The Pipes

COMPLETE SET (200) 15.00 40.00
1 Jimmy Appleby .20 .50
2 J.P. Anderson .25 .60
3 Jordan Binnington .40 1.00
4 Laurent Brossoit .25 .60
5 Tyler Bunz .20 .50
6 Jack Campbell .25 .60
7 Mac Carruth .20 .50
8 Cole Cheveldave .20 .50
9 Mathieu Corbeil .20 .50
10 Andrew D'Agostini .20 .50
11 Louis Domingue .15 .40
12 Chris Driedger .20 .50
13 Alex Dubeau .25 .60
14 Christopher Gibson .25 .60
15 Gabriel Girard .20 .50
16 Domenic Graham .20 .50
17 Keith Hamilton .20 .50
18 Matt Hewitt .20 .50
19 David Honzik .25 .60
20 Michael Houser .20 .50
21 Nathan Liuewen .25 .60
22 Andrey Makarov .20 .50
23 Brandon Maxwell .20 .50
24 Adam Morrison .20 .50
25 Petr Mrazek .50 1.25
26 Matt Murray .30 .75
27 Mathias Niederberger .20 .50
28 Drew Owsley .20 .50
29 Calvin Pickard .25 .60
30 Ty Rimmer .20 .50
31 Luke Siemens .20 .50
32 Malcolm Subban .40 1.00
33 Francois Tremblay .15 .40
34 Mark Visentin .20 .50
35 Scott Wedgewood .25 .60
36 Roman Will .15 .40
37 Jake Allen .40 1.00
38 Richard Bachman .20 .50
39 Cedrick Desjardins .20 .50
40 Matt Hackett .25 .60
41 Braden Holtby .30 .75
42 Leland Irving .20 .50
43 Chad Johnson .20 .50
44 Martin Jones .40 1.00
45 Anton Khudobin .25 .60
46 Keith Kinkaid .20 .50
47 Darcy Kuemper .50 1.25
48 Eddie Lack .20 .50
49 Robin Lehner .20 .50
50 Jacob Markstrom .25 .60
51 Robert Mayer .25 .60
52 Mike Murphy .20 .50
53 Edward Pasquale .20 .50
54 Jordan Pearce .20 .50
55 Timo Pielmeier .25 .60
56 Alec Richards .20 .50
57 Jussi Rynnas .25 .60
58 Harri Sateri .20 .50
59 Ben Scrivens .20 .50
60 Tyson Sexsmith .20 .50
61 Jeremy Smith .25 .60
62 Iiro Tarkki .25 .60
63 Jeff Zatkoff .25 .60
64 Craig Anderson SG .25 .60
65 Niklas Backstrom SG .25 .60
66 Jonathan Bernier SG .20 .50
67 Sergei Bobrovsky SG .40 1.00
68 Ilya Bryzgalov SG .25 .60
69 Peter Budaj SG .20 .50
70 Corey Crawford SG .30 .75
71 Brian Elliott SG .20 .50
72 Dan Ellis SG .20 .50
73 Ray Emery SG .20 .50
74 Jhonas Enroth SG .25 .60
75 Marc-Andre Fleury SG .50 1.25
76 Mathieu Garon SG .20 .50
77 Thomas Greiss SG .20 .50
78 Jonas Gustavsson SG .25 .60
79 Jaroslav Halak SG .25 .60
80 Jonas Hiller SG .20 .50
81 Jimmy Howard SG .30 .75
82 Kari Lehtonen SG .20 .50
83 Henrik Lundqvist SG .60 1.50
84 Roberto Luongo SG .40 1.00
85 Tim Thomas SG .25 .60
86 Ryan Miller SG .25 .60
87 Michal Neuvirth SG .20 .50
88 Antti Niemi SG .20 .50
89 Antero Niittymaki SG .20 .50
90 Carey Price SG .50 1.25
91 Jonathan Quick SG .30 .75
92 Tuukka Rask SG .30 .75
93 James Reimer SG .25 .60
94 Pekka Rinne SG .25 .60
95 Dwayne Roloson SG .20 .50
96 Cory Schneider SG .25 .60
97 Mike Smith SG .25 .60
98 Semyon Varlamov SG .25 .60
99 Tomas Vokoun SG .20 .50
100 Don Beaupre DEC .20 .50
101 Ed Belfour DEC .25 .60
102 Dan Bouchard DEC .20 .50
103 Johnny Bower DEC .25 .60
104 Richard Brodeur DEC .25 .60
105 Gary Bromley DEC .30 .75
106 Sean Burke DEC .15 .40
107 Jim Carey DEC .20 .50
108 Ed Chadwick DEC .25 .60
109 Gerry Cheevers DEC .25 .60
110 Dan Cloutier DEC .20 .50
111 Byron Dafoe DEC .25 .60
112 Joe Daley DEC .20 .50
113 Denis DeJordy DEC .20 .50
114 Michel Dion DEC .20 .50
115 Tony Esposito DEC .25 .60
116 Emile Francis DEC .20 .50
117 Grant Fuhr DEC .40 1.00
118 Ed Giacomin DEC .25 .60
119 Gilles Gilbert DEC .20 .50
120 Glenn Hall DEC .25 .60
121 Glen Hanlon DEC .20 .50
122 Dominik Hasek DEC .40 1.00
123 Denis Herron DEC .20 .50
124 Charlie Hodge DEC .20 .50
125 Arturs Irbe DEC .20 .50
126 Curtis Joseph DEC .30 .75
127 Reggie Lemelin DEC .15 .40
128 Mike Liut DEC .15 .40
129 Cesare Maniago DEC .25 .60
130 Jack McCartan DEC .25 .60
131 Rollie Melanson DEC .15 .40
132 Gilles Meloche DEC .25 .60
133 Greg Millen DEC .20 .50
134 Phil Myre DEC .20 .50
135 Chris Osgood DEC .25 .60
136 Darren Pang DEC .25 .60
137 Bernie Parent DEC .30 .75
138 Pete Peeters DEC .25 .60
139 Felix Potvin DEC .40 1.00
140 Bill Ranford DEC .25 .60
141 Chico Resch DEC .25 .60
142 Damian Rhodes DEC .25 .60
143 Mike Richter DEC .25 .60
144 Patrick Roy DEC .60 1.50
145 Gary Simmons DEC .25 .60
146 Billy Smith DEC .25 .60
147 Doug Soetaert DEC .15 .40
148 Greg Stefan DEC .15 .40
149 Rogie Vachon DEC .30 .75
150 John Vanbiesbrouck DEC .25 .60
151 Mike Veisor DEC .15 .40
152 Mike Vernon DEC .20 .50
153 Gilles Villemure DEC .20 .50
154 Rick Wamsley DEC .25 .60
155 Craig Anderson SS .25 .60
156 Tom Barrasso SS .25 .60
157 Brian Boucher SS .20 .50
158 Jim Carey SS .20 .50
159 Ty Conklin SS .20 .50
160 Jim Craig SS .40 1.00
161 Jimmy Howard SS .30 .75
162 Brent Johnson SS .20 .50
163 Ryan Miller SS .25 .60
164 Jonathan Quick SS .30 .75
165 Damian Rhodes SS .25 .60
166 Mike Richter SS .25 .60
167 Cory Schneider SS .25 .60
168 Tim Thomas SS .25 .60
169 John Vanbiesbrouck SS .25 .60
170 Jonathan Bernier LBP .20 .50
171 Dan Bouchard LBP .20 .50
172 Richard Brodeur LBP .25 .60
173 Dan Cloutier LBP .20 .50
174 Corey Crawford LBP .30 .75
175 Denis DeJordy LBP .20 .50
176 Michel Dion LBP .20 .50
177 Gilles Gilbert LBP .20 .50
178 Denis Herron LBP .20 .50
179 Charlie Hodge LBP .20 .50
180 Reggie Lemelin LBP .15 .40
181 Roberto Luongo LBP .40 1.00
182 Gilles Meloche LBP .25 .60
183 Phil Myre LBP .20 .50
184 Bernie Parent LBP .30 .75
185 Felix Potvin LBP .40 1.00
186 Patrick Roy LBP .60 1.50
187 Rogie Vachon LBP .30 .75
188 Georges Vezina LBP .25 .60
189 Gilles Villemure LBP .20 .50
190 T.Sawchuk ET/W.Rutledge .25 .60
191 C.Maniago ET/G.Bauman .25 .60
192 C.Hodge ET/G.Smith .20 .50
193 L.Binkley ET/H.Bassen .20 .50
194 B.Parent ET/D.Favell .30 .75
195 G.Hall ET/S.Martin .25 .60
196 Jack McCartan IP .25 .60
197 Seth Martin IP .25 .60
198 Leif Holmqvist IP .20 .50
199 Vladimir Dzurilla IP .25 .60
200 Paul Deutsch OGW .25 .60

2011-12 Between The Pipes 10th Anniversary

BTPA01 Jonas Hiller 1.50 4.00
BTPA02 Tim Thomas 2.00 5.00
BTPA03 Ryan Miller 2.00 5.00
BTPA04 Miikka Kiprusoff 2.00 5.00
BTPA05 Cam Ward 2.00 5.00
BTPA06 Corey Crawford 2.50 6.00
BTPA07 Semyon Varlamov 2.00 5.00
BTPA08 Kari Lehtonen 1.50 4.00
BTPA09 Jim Howard 2.50 6.00
BTPA10 Nikolai Khabibulin 1.50 4.00
BTPA11 Jose Theodore 2.00 5.00
BTPA12 Jonathan Quick 2.50 6.00
BTPA13 Niklas Backstrom 2.00 5.00
BTPA14 Carey Price 4.00 10.00
BTPA15 Pekka Rinne 2.00 5.00
BTPA16 Evgeni Nabokov 1.50 4.00
BTPA17 Henrik Lundqvist 5.00 12.00
BTPA18 Craig Anderson 2.00 5.00
BTPA19 Ilya Bryzgalov 2.00 5.00
BTPA20 Mike Smith 2.00 5.00
BTPA21 Marc-Andre Fleury 4.00 10.00
BTPA22 Brian Elliott 1.50 4.00
BTPA23 Jaroslav Halak 2.00 5.00
BTPA24 Antti Niemi 1.50 4.00
BTPA25 Dwayne Roloson 1.50 4.00
BTPA26 Jonas Gustavsson 2.00 5.00
BTPA27 James Reimer 2.00 5.00
BTPA28 Roberto Luongo 3.00 8.00
BTPA29 Tomas Vokoun 1.50 4.00
BTPA30 Ondrej Pavelec 2.00 5.00
BTPA31 Bernie Parent 2.50 6.00
BTPA32 Curtis Joseph 2.50 6.00
BTPA33 Dominik Hasek 3.00 8.00
BTPA34 Ed Belfour 2.00 5.00
BTPA35 Georges Vezina 2.00 5.00
BTPA36 Gerry Cheevers 2.00 5.00
BTPA37 Glenn Hall 2.00 5.00
BTPA38 Grant Fuhr 3.00 8.00
BTPA39 Jacques Plante 2.50 6.00
BTPA40 Johnny Bower 2.00 5.00
BTPA41 Patrick Roy 5.00 12.00
BTPA42 Pelle Lindbergh 1.50 4.00
BTPA43 Terry Sawchuk 2.00 5.00
BTPA44 Tony Esposito 2.00 5.00
BTPA45 Turk Broda 2.00 5.00

2011-12 Between The Pipes Aspire Jerseys Silver

AS01 N.Lieuwen/R.Miller 4.00 10.00
AS02 L.Irving/M.Kiprusoff 4.00 10.00
AS03 A.Khudobin/T.Thomas 4.00 10.00
AS04 T.Cann/P.Roy 10.00 25.00
AS05 L.Brossoit/M.Kiprusoff 4.00 10.00
AS06 M.Murphy/C.Ward 4.00 10.00
AS07 K.Simpson/C.Crawford 5.00 12.00
AS08 J.Campbell/K.Lehtonen 4.00 10.00
AS09 P.Mrazek/J.Howard 8.00 20.00
AS10 J.Markstrom/H.Lundqvist 10.00 25.00
AS11 O.Roy/D.Dubnyk 3.00 8.00
AS12 C.Gibson/J.Quick 5.00 12.00
AS13 M.Hackett/N.Backstrom 4.00 10.00
AS14 R.Mayer/C.Price 8.00 20.00
AS15 C.Pickard/P.Rinne 4.00 10.00
AS16 S.Stajcer/H.Lundqvist 10.00 25.00
AS17 R.Lehner/C.Anderson 4.00 10.00
AS18 M.Visentin/M.Smith 4.00 10.00
AS19 J.Binnington/J.Halak 6.00 15.00
AS20 J.Anderson/A.Niemi 4.00 10.00
AS21 D.Honzik/R.Luongo 6.00 15.00
AS22 B.Holtby/T.Vokoun 5.00 12.00
AS23 J.Gervais-Chouinard/P.Roy 10.00 25.00
AS24 M.Koskinen/E.Nabokov 4.00 10.00
AS25 T.Bunz/N.Khabibulin 3.00 8.00
AS26 T.Rimmer/C.Price 8.00 20.00
AS27 S.Wedgewood/R.Luongo 6.00 15.00
AS28 E.Pasquale/O.Pavelec 4.00 10.00
AS29 M.Jones/J.Bernier 6.00 15.00
AS30 D.Tokarski/D.Roloson 4.00 10.00

2011-12 Between The Pipes Autographs

AAD Andrew D'Agostini 5.00 12.00
AADU Alex Dubeau 6.00 15.00
AAI Arturs Irbe DEC 5.00 12.00
AAK Anton Khudobin 6.00 15.00
AAM Adam Morrison 5.00 12.00
AAN Antti Niemi SG 5.00 12.00
AANI Antero Niittymaki SG 5.00 12.00
AAR Alec Richards 5.00 12.00
ABD Byron Dafoe DEC 6.00 15.00
ABM Brandon Maxwell 5.00 12.00
ABP Bernie Parent DEC 8.00 20.00
ABP2 Bernie Parent LBP SP 8.00 20.00
ABR Bill Ranford DEC 6.00 15.00
ABS Ben Scrivens 5.00 12.00
ABSM Billy Smith DEC 6.00 15.00
ACC Corey Crawford SG 8.00 20.00
ACC2 Corey Crawford LBP SP 8.00 20.00
ACD Cedrick Desjardins 5.00 12.00
ACG Christopher Gibson 6.00 15.00
ACH Charlie Hodge DEC 5.00 12.00
ACH2 Charlie Hodge LBP SP 5.00 12.00
ACJ Chad Johnson 5.00 12.00
ACJO Curtis Joseph DEC SP 8.00 20.00
ACM Cesare Maniago DEC 6.00 15.00
ACO Chris Osgood DEC 6.00 15.00
ACP Calvin Pickard 6.00 15.00
ACPR Carey Price SG 12.00 30.00
ACR Chico Resch DEC 6.00 15.00
ACS Curtis Sanford 5.00 12.00
ACS2 Cory Schneider SS 6.00 15.00
ADB Don Beaupre DEC 5.00 12.00
ADBO Dan Bouchard DEC 5.00 12.00
ADBO2 Dan Bouchard LBP SP 5.00 12.00
ADC Dan Cloutier DEC 5.00 12.00
ADC2 Dan Cloutier LBP SP 5.00 12.00
ADD Denis DeJordy DEC 5.00 12.00
ADD2 Denis DeJordy LBP SP 5.00 12.00
ADF Doug Favell DEC 6.00 15.00
ADG Domenic Graham 5.00 12.00
ADH David Honzik 6.00 15.00
ADH2 D.Herron LBP SP UER 5.00 12.00
ADHA Dominik Hasek DEC SP 10.00 25.00
ADHE Denis Herron DEC 5.00 12.00
ADM Drew MacIntyre 6.00 15.00
ADO Drew Owsley 5.00 12.00
ADP Darren Pang DEC 6.00 15.00
ADR Dwayne Roloson SG 5.00 12.00
ADR1 Damian Rhodes DEC 6.00 15.00
ADR2 Damian Rhodes SS SP 6.00 15.00
ADS Doug Soetaert DEC 4.00 10.00
AEB Ed Belfour DEC 6.00 15.00
AEC Ed Chadwick DEC 6.00 15.00
AEF Emile Francis DEC 5.00 12.00
AEG Ed Giacomin DEC 6.00 15.00
AEL Eddie Lack 5.00 12.00
AEP Edward Pasquale 5.00 12.00
AFP Felix Potvin DEC 10.00 25.00
AFP2 Felix Potvin LBP SP 10.00 25.00
AFT Francois Tremblay 4.00 10.00
AGB Gary Bromley DEC 8.00 20.00
AGC Gerry Cheevers DEC 6.00 15.00
AGF Grant Fuhr DEC 10.00 25.00
AGG Gilles Gilbert DEC 5.00 12.00
AGG2 Gilles Gilbert LBP SP 5.00 12.00
AGH Glenn Hall DEC 6.00 15.00
AGHA Glen Hanlon DEC 5.00 12.00
AGM Gilles Meloche DEC 6.00 15.00
AGM2 Gilles Meloche LBP SP 6.00 15.00
AGMI Greg Millen DEC 5.00 12.00
AGS Gary Simmons DEC 6.00 15.00
AGST Greg Stefan DEC 4.00 10.00
AGV Gilles Villemure DEC 5.00 12.00
AGV2 Gilles Villemure LBP SP 5.00 12.00
AHL Henrik Lundqvist SG 15.00 40.00
AIB Ilya Bryzgalov SG 6.00 15.00
AJA Jake Allen 10.00 25.00
AJB Jordan Binnington 10.00 25.00
AJBA Jason Bacashihua 5.00 12.00
AJBA2 Jason Bacashihua SS SP 5.00 12.00
AJBE Jonathan Bernier SG SP 5.00 12.00
AJBE2 Jonathan Bernier LBP SP 5.00 12.00
AJBO Johnny Bower DEC 6.00 15.00
AJC Jack Campbell 6.00 15.00
AJCA Jim Carey DEC 5.00 12.00
AJCA2 Jim Carey SS 5.00 12.00
AJCR Jim Craig SS 10.00 25.00
AJD Joe Daley DEC 5.00 12.00
AJE Jhonas Enroth SG 6.00 15.00
AJH Jaroslav Halak SG 6.00 15.00
AJHI Jonas Hiller SG 5.00 12.00
AJHO Jimmy Howard SG 8.00 20.00
AJHO2 Jimmy Howard SS SP 8.00 20.00
AJM Jacob Markstrom 6.00 15.00
AJMC Jack McCartan DEC 6.00 15.00
AJMC2 Jack McCartan IP SP 6.00 15.00
AJP Jordan Pearce 5.00 12.00
AJQ Jonathan Quick SG 8.00 20.00
AJQ2 Jonathan Quick SS SP 8.00 20.00
AJR Jussi Rynnas 6.00 15.00
AJV John Vanbiesbrouck DEC SP 6.00 15.00
AJV2 John Vanbiesbrouck SS SP 6.00 15.00
AJZ Jeff Zatkoff 6.00 15.00
AKH Keith Hamilton 5.00 12.00
AKK Keith Kinkaid 5.00 12.00
AKL Kari Lehtonen SG 5.00 12.00
AKS Kent Simpson 6.00 15.00
ALB Laurent Brossoit 6.00 15.00
ALD Louis Domingue 4.00 10.00
ALI Leland Irving 5.00 12.00
AMAF Marc-Andre Fleury SG SP 12.00 30.00
AMC Mac Carruth 5.00 12.00
AMCO Mathieu Corbeil 5.00 12.00
AMD Michel Dion DEC 5.00 12.00
AMD2 Michel Dion LBP SP 5.00 12.00
AMDF Mark Dekanich 4.00 10.00
AMG Mathieu Garon SG 5.00 12.00
AMH Michael Houser 5.00 12.00
AMHA Matt Hackett 6.00 15.00
AMJ Martin Jones 10.00 25.00
AML Michael Leighton 5.00 12.00
AMLI Mike Liut DEC 4.00 10.00
AMM Matt Murray 8.00 20.00
AMMU Mike Murphy 5.00 12.00
AMN Mathias Niederberger 5.00 12.00
AMR Mike Richter DEC SP 6.00 15.00
AMR2 Mike Richter SS SP 6.00 15.00
AMS Malcolm Subban 10.00 25.00
AMV Mike Veisor DEC 4.00 10.00
AMVE Mike Vernon DEC 5.00 12.00
AMVI Mark Visentin 5.00 12.00
ANL Nathan Lieuwen 4.00 10.00
APD Paul Deutsch OGW 6.00 15.00
APM Petr Mrazek 12.00 30.00
APM2 Phil Myre LBP SP 5.00 12.00
APMY Phil Myre DEC 5.00 12.00
APP Pete Peeters DEC 6.00 15.00
APR Patrick Roy DEC SP 15.00 40.00
APR2 Patrick Roy LBP SP 15.00 40.00
ARB Richard Bachman 5.00 12.00
ARBR Richard Brodeur DEC 6.00 15.00
ARBR2 Richard Brodeur LBP 6.00 15.00
ARE Ray Emery SG 5.00 12.00
ARG Robin Gusse 4.00 10.00
ARL Roberto Luongo SG SP 10.00 25.00
ARL2 Roberto Luongo LBP SP 10.00 25.00
ARLE Reggie Lemelin DEC 4.00 10.00
ARLE2 Reggie Lemelin LBP SP 4.00 10.00
ARM Rollie Melanson DEC 4.00 10.00
ARMA Robert Mayer 6.00 15.00
ARV Rogie Vachon DEC 8.00 20.00
ARV2 Rogie Vachon LBP 8.00 20.00
ARW Rick Wamsley DEC 6.00 15.00
ARW2 Roman Will 4.00 10.00
ASB Sean Burke DEC 4.00 10.00
ASBO Sergei Bobrovsky SG 10.00 25.00
ASM Seth Martin IP 6.00 15.00
ASV Semyon Varlamov SG 6.00 15.00
ASW Scott Wedgewood 6.00 15.00
ATB Tyler Bunz 5.00 12.00
ATB Tom Barrasso SS SP 6.00 15.00
ATE Tony Esposito DEC SP 6.00 15.00
ATG Thomas Greiss SG 5.00 12.00
ATP Timo Pielmeier 6.00 15.00
ATR Ty Rimmer 5.00 12.00
ATRA Tuukka Rask SG 8.00 20.00
ATS Tyson Sexsmith 5.00 12.00
ATT Tim Thomas SS SP 6.00 15.00
ATV Tomas Vokoun SG SP 5.00 12.00

2011-12 Between The Pipes Countrymen Quad Memorabilia Silver

CM01 Miikka Kiprusoff 8.00 20.00
CM02 Mike Richter 8.00 20.00
CM03 Roberto Luongo 12.00 30.00
CM04 Henrik Lundqvist 20.00 50.00
CM05 Olaf Kolzig 8.00 20.00
CM06 Ilya Bryzgalov 8.00 20.00
CM07 Jonas Hiller 6.00 15.00
CM08 Vladislav Tretiak 15.00 40.00
CM09 Vladimir Dzurilla 10.00 25.00

2011-12 Between The Pipes Cup Tandems Jerseys Silver

CT01 P.Roy/D.Soetaert 12.00 30.00
CT02 B.Ranford/G.Fuhr 8.00 20.00
CT03 P.Roy/A.Racicot 12.00 30.00
CT04 P.Roy/S.Fiset 12.00 30.00
CT05 M.Vernon/C.Osgood 5.00 12.00
CT06 E.Belfour/R.Turek 5.00 12.00
CT07 P.Roy/D.Aebischer 12.00 30.00
CT08 D.Hasek/M.Legace 8.00 20.00
CT09 N.Khabibulin/J.Grahame 4.00 10.00
CT10 C.Ward/M.Gerber 5.00 12.00
CT11 J.Giguere/I.Bryzgalov 5.00 12.00
CT12 C.Osgood/D.Hasek 8.00 20.00
CT13 M.Fleury/M.Garon 10.00 25.00
CT14 A.Niemi/C.Huet 4.00 10.00
CT15 T.Thomas/T.Rask 6.00 15.00

2011-12 Between The Pipes Decades Quad Memorabilia Silver

D01 Wrtrs/Grdin/Hains/Thmpsn 6.00 15.00
D02 Durnan/Rynr/Brim/Lumley 6.00 15.00
D03 Swchk/Plante/Hall/Hodge 8.00 20.00
D04 Sawchuk/Giacm/Hall/Croz 6.00 15.00
D05 Espo/Melche/Chvrs/Vchon 8.00 20.00
D06 Tretiak/Myre/Parent/Gilbert 8.00 20.00
D07 Fuhr/Roy/Vernon/Beaupre 15.00 40.00
D08 Smith/Bchrd/Hextall/Brodr 6.00 15.00
D09 Belfour/Roy/Hasek/Richter 15.00 40.00
D10 Joseph/Potvin/Irbe/Osgood 10.00 25.00
D11 Fleury/Ward/Gig/Nabokov 12.00 30.00
D12 Price/Miller/Luongo/Thomas 12.00 30.00

2011-12 Between The Pipes Franchise Jerseys Silver

F01 Hiller/Bryzgalov/Giguere 12.00 30.00
F02 Thomas/Moog/Cheevers 12.00 30.00
F03 Miller/Hasek/Barrasso 12.00 30.00
F04 Kiprusoff/Giguere/Vernon 12.50 30.00
F05 Crawford/Belfour/Esposito 10.00 25.00
F06 Lehtonen/Smith/Belfour 8.00 20.00
F07 Howard/Hasek/Crozier 12.00 30.00
F08 Dubnyk/Ranford/Fuhr 12.00 30.00
F09 Quick/Cloutier/Vachon 10.00 25.00
F10 Price/Roy/Vachon 25.00 60.00
F11 Lundqvist/Richter/Giacomin 12.00 30.00
F12 Bryzgalov/Hextall/Parent 10.00 25.00
F13 Fleury/Aubin/Barrasso 15.00 40.00
F14 Niemi/Nabokov/Vernon 15.00 40.00
F15 Halak/Joseph/Hall 15.00 40.00
F16 Reimer/Joseph/Potvin 15.00 40.00
F17 Luongo/Cloutier/Brodeur 12.00 30.00
F18 Vokoun/Varlamov/Riggin 10.00 25.00

2011-12 Between The Pipes Full Gear Silver

FG01 Miikka Kiprusoff 15.00 40.00
FG02 Patrick Roy 30.00 80.00
FG03 Dominik Hasek 25.00 60.00
FG04 Patrick Roy 30.00 80.00
FG05 Curtis Joseph 25.00 60.00
FG06 Carey Price 30.00 80.00

2011-12 Between The Pipes He Shoots He Saves Points

CJ1 Curtis Joseph UL .30 .75
CP1 Carey Price UL .50 1.25
GC1 Gerry Cheevers UL .30 .75
GV1 Georges Vezina UL .30 .75
HL1 Henrik Lundqvist UL .60 1.50
JB1 Johnny Bower UL .30 .75
JP1 Jacques Plante UL .40 1.00
PR1 Patrick Roy UL .60 1.50
RL1 Roberto Luongo UL .40 1.00
TE1 Tony Esposito UL .30 .75
TS1 Terry Sawchuk UL .30 .75

2011-12 Between The Pipes He Shoots He Saves Prizes

HSHS-01 Ilya Bryzgalov 10.00 25.00
HSHS-02 J.Reimer/J.Gustavsson 12.00 30.00
HSHS-03 Hltby/Vkoun/Klzig 15.00 40.00
HSHS-04 Jaroslav Halak 10.00 25.00
HSHS-05 J.Quick/J.Bernier 15.00 40.00
HSHS-06 Price/Mayer/Roy 30.00 80.00
HSHS-07 Roberto Luongo 15.00 40.00
HSHS-08 C.Crawford/R.Emery 15.00 40.00
HSHS-09 Thmas/Rask/Chvers 20.00 50.00
HSHS-10 Nikolai Khabibulin 8.00 20.00
HSHS-11 I.Bryzgalov/S.Bobrovsky 20.00 50.00
HSHS-12 Rmer/Gstvssn/Ptvin 20.00 50.00
HSHS-13 Braden Holtby 12.00 30.00
HSHS-14 J.Halak/B.Elliott 12.00 30.00
HSHS-15 Quick/Brnier/Vchon 15.00 40.00
HSHS-16 Carey Price 20.00 50.00
HSHS-17 R.Luongo/C.Schneider 20.00 50.00
HSHS-18 Crwfrd/Emery/Espsto 15.00 40.00
HSHS-19 Tim Thomas 10.00 25.00
HSHS-20 N.Khabibulin/D.Dubnyk 10.00 25.00
HSHS-21 Bryzglv/Bbrvsky/Prent 30.00 60.00
HSHS-22 James Reimer 10.00 25.00
HSHS-23 B.Hltby/Vkoun 15.00 40.00
HSHS-24 Hlak/Elltt/Jseph 15.00 40.00
HSHS-25 Jonathan Quick 12.00 30.00
HSHS-26 C.Price/R.Mayer 25.00 60.00
HSHS-27 Lngo/Schnder/Brdeur 20.00 50.00
HSHS-28 Corey Crawford 12.00 30.00
HSHS-29 T.Thomas/T.Rask 15.00 40.00
HSHS-30 Khbbln/Dbnyk/Fuhr 20.00 50.00

2011-12 Between The Pipes Jerseys Silver

SILVER PATCH/19: .8X TO 2X BASIC JSY
M01 Alex Auld 4.00 10.00
M02 Antero Niittymaki 4.00 10.00
M03 Antti Niemi 6.00 15.00
M04 Carey Price 10.00 25.00
M05 Kent Simpson 5.00 12.00
M06 Cory Schneider 5.00 12.00
M07 Craig Anderson 5.00 12.00
M08 Henrik Lundqvist 12.00 30.00
M09 Ilya Bryzgalov 5.00 12.00
M10 James Reimer 8.00 20.00
M11 Jaroslav Halak 5.00 12.00
M12 John Vanbiesbrouck 5.00 12.00
M13 Jonas Gustavsson 5.00 12.00
M14 Mikko Koskinen 5.00 12.00
M15 Jonathan Quick 6.00 15.00
M16 Josh Harding 5.00 12.00
M17 Kevin Bailie 5.00 12.00
M18 Niklas Backstrom 5.00 12.00
M19 Roberto Luongo 8.00 20.00
M20 Jonathan Bernier 4.00 10.00
M21 Tim Thomas 6.00 15.00
M22 Tomas Vokoun 4.00 10.00
M23 Patrick Roy 12.00 30.00
M24 Ed Belfour 6.00 15.00
M25 Dominik Hasek 8.00 20.00
M26 Grant Fuhr 8.00 20.00
M27 Keith Hamilton 4.00 10.00
M28 Marc-Andre Fleury 10.00 25.00
M29 Jonas Hiller 4.00 10.00
M30 Devan Dubnyk 4.00 10.00
M31 Ryan Miller 5.00 12.00
M32 J.P. Anderson 5.00 12.00
M33 Jack Campbell 5.00 12.00
M34 Sean Burke 3.00 8.00
M35 Curtis Joseph 6.00 15.00
M36 Don Beaupre 4.00 10.00
M37 Greg Stefan 3.00 8.00
M38 Byron Dafoe 5.00 12.00
M39 Arturs Irbe 8.00 20.00
M40 Dan Cloutier 4.00 10.00
M41 Thomas Greiss 4.00 10.00
M42 Robert Mayer 5.00 12.00
M43 Jacob Markstrom 5.00 12.00
M44 Jake Allen 8.00 20.00
M45 Darcy Kuemper 10.00 25.00
M46 Mike Murphy 4.00 10.00
M47 Robin Lehner 4.00 10.00
M48 Martin Jones 8.00 20.00
M49 Laurent Brossoit 5.00 12.00
M50 Tyler Bunz 6.00 15.00
M51 J.P. Cesario 4.00 10.00
M52 Andrew D'Agostini 4.00 10.00
M53 Mac Engel 3.00 8.00
M54 Jacob Gervais-Chouinard 3.00 8.00
M55 Maxime Lagace 5.00 12.00
M56 Petr Mrazek 10.00 25.00
M57 Matt Murray 6.00 15.00
M58 Drew Owsley 4.00 10.00
M59 Ty Rimmer 4.00 10.00
M60 Anthony Terenzio 3.00 8.00

2011-12 Between The Pipes Journey Dual Jerseys Silver

JJ01 Curtis Joseph 12.00 30.00
JJ02 Dominik Hasek 10.00 25.00
JJ03 Roberto Luongo 12.00 30.00
JJ04 John Vanbiesbrouck 8.00 20.00
JJ05 Ilya Bryzgalov 8.00 20.00
JJ06 J-S Giguere 8.00 20.00
JJ07 Chris Osgood 8.00 20.00
JJ08 Miikka Kiprusoff 8.00 20.00
JJ09 Tomas Vokoun 6.00 15.00
JJ10 Kari Lehtonen 6.00 15.00
JJ11 Glenn Hall 10.00 25.00
JJ12 Damian Rhodes 8.00 20.00
JJ13 Patrick Roy 20.00 50.00
JJ14 Rogie Vachon 10.00 25.00
JJ15 Ed Belfour 8.00 20.00
JJ10 Phil Myre 8.00 20.00
JJ17 Felix Potvin 12.00 30.00
JJ18 Mike Vernon 6.00 15.00
JJ19 Don Beaupre 8.00 20.00
JJ20 Grant Fuhr 12.00 30.00
JJ21 Jaroslav Halak 8.00 20.00

2011-12 Between The Pipes Masked Men IV Ruby Die Cuts

SILVER/90: .8X TO 2X BASIC INSERTS
MM01 Craig Anderson 2.50 6.00
MM02 Alex Auld 2.00 5.00
MM03 Niklas Backstrom 2.50 6.00
MM04 Murray Bannerman 2.00 5.00
MM05 Ed Belfour 2.50 6.00
MM06 Jonathan Bernier 2.00 5.00
MM07 Martin Biron 2.00 5.00
MM08 Sergei Bobrovsky 4.00 10.00
MM09 Gary Bromley 3.00 8.00
MM10 Ilya Bryzgalov 2.50 6.00
MM11 Jack Campbell 2.50 6.00
MM12 Scott Clemmensen 2.00 5.00
MM13 Corey Crawford 3.00 8.00
MM14 Rick DiPietro 2.00 5.00
MM15 Devan Dubnyk 2.00 5.00
MM16 Ray Emery 2.00 5.00
MM17 Marc-Andre Fleury 5.00 12.00
MM18 Grant Fuhr 4.00 10.00
MM19 Mathieu Garon 2.00 5.00
MM20 Martin Gerber 2.00 5.00
MM21 Ed Giacomin 2.50 6.00
MM22 Jonas Hiller 2.00 5.00
MM23 Jim Howard 3.00 8.00
MM24 Curtis Joseph 3.00 8.00
MM25 Miikka Kiprusoff 2.50 6.00
MM26 Kari Lehtonen 2.00 5.00
MM27 Henrik Lundqvist 6.00 15.00
MM28 Roberto Luongo 4.00 10.00
MM29 Chris Mason 2.00 5.00
MM30 Kirk McLean 2.00 5.00
MM31 Ryan Miller 2.50 6.00
MM32 Evgeni Nabokov 2.00 5.00
MM33 Bernie Parent 3.00 8.00
MM34 Felix Potvin 4.00 10.00
MM35 Carey Price 5.00 12.00
MM36 Jonathan Quick 3.00 8.00
MM37 James Reimer 2.50 6.00
MM38 Mike Richter 2.50 6.00
MM39 Dwayne Roloson 2.00 5.00
MM40 Patrick Roy 4.00 10.00
MM41 Patrick Roy 4.00 10.00
MM42 Curtis Sanford 2.00 5.00
MM43 Mike Smith 2.50 6.00
MM44 Tim Thomas 2.50 6.00
MM45 Rogie Vachon 3.00 8.00
MM46 John Vanbiesbrouck 2.50 6.00
MM47 Semyon Varlamov 2.50 6.00
MM48 Tomas Vokoun 2.00 5.00
MM49 Cam Ward 2.50 6.00
MM50 Gerry Cheevers 2.50 6.00

2011-12 Between The Pipes Stick and Jersey Silver

SJ01 Patrick Roy 40.00 100.00
SJ02 Billy Smith 15.00 40.00
SJ03 Mike Richter 15.00 40.00
SJ04 Felix Potvin 25.00 60.00
SJ05 Bill Ranford 15.00 40.00
SJ06 Chris Osgood 15.00 40.00
SJ07 John Vanbiesbrouck 25.00 60.00
SJ08 Pelle Lindbergh 30.00 75.00
SJ09 Ryan Miller 15.00 40.00
SJ10 Henrik Lundqvist 15.00 40.00
SJ11 Roberto Luongo 15.00 40.00
SJ12 Curtis Joseph 20.00 50.00
SJ13 Arturs Irbe 12.00 30.00
SJ14 Rogie Vachon 20.00 50.00
SJ15 Dominik Hasek 25.00 60.00
SJ16 Ed Belfour 15.00 40.00
SJ17 Marc-Andre Fleury 30.00 80.00
SJ18 Tony Esposito 15.00 40.00
SJ19 Rick DiPietro 12.00 30.00
SJ20 Carey Price 30.00 80.00
SJ21 Mike Vernon 12.00 30.00

2012-13 Between The Pipes

1 Jacob Brennan .15 .40
2 Philippe Cadorette .15 .40
3 Mathias Niederberger .15 .40
4 Malcolm Subban .25 .60
5 Etienne Marcoux .15 .40
6 Storm Phaneuf .15 .40
7 Matej Machovsky .15 .40
8 Corbin Boes .15 .40
9 Chris Driedger .15 .40
10 Alex Bureau .15 .40
11 Christopher Gibson .20 .50
12 Louis-Philip Guindon .12 .30
13 Domenic Graham .15 .40
14 Laurent Brossoit .20 .50
15 Tristan Jarry .20 .50
16 Devin Williams .12 .30
17 Oscar Dansk .25 .60
18 Austin Lotz .12 .30
19 Daniel Cotton .12 .30
20 Robert Steeves .12 .30
21 Garret Sparks .20 .50
22 Jaroslav Pavelka .15 .40
23 Zachary Fucale .25 .60
24 Cole Cheveldave .15 .40
25 Taran Kozun .12 .30
26 Jackson Whistle .12 .30
27 Jordon Cooke .15 .40
28 Mike Morrison .12 .30
29 Joel Vienneau .15 .40
30 John Gibson .30 .75
31 Mackenzie Skapski .15 .40
32 Ty Rimmer .15 .40
33 Anthony Stolarz .25 .60
34 Jake Patterson .25 .60
35 Marek Langhamer .20 .50
36 Spencer Martin .15 .40
37 Alex Dubeau .20 .50
38 Justin Paulic .12 .30
30 Daniel Wapplo .12 .30
40 Christopher Festarini .12 .30
41 Daniel Altshuller .15 .40
42 Clint Windsor .12 .30
43 Jacob Blair .12 .30
44 Brandon Hope .12 .30
45 Jordan Binnington .30 .75
46 Antoine Bibeau .12 .30
47 Maxime Lagace .15 .40
48 Andrew D'Agostini .15 .40
49 Michael Giugovaz .12 .30
50 Matt Mahalak .15 .40
51 Brendan Burke .15 .40
52 Mac Carruth .15 .40
53 Luke Siemens .15 .40
54 Brett Zarowny .12 .30
55 Mac Engel .20 .50
56 Francois Brassard .12 .30
57 Patrik Bartosak .20 .50
58 Matt Hewitt .15 .40
59 Philippe Desrosiers .15 .40
60 Robin Gusse .15 .40
61 Alexandre Belanger .15 .40
62 Jake Paterson .25 .60
63 Nikita Serebryakov .20 .50
64 Sebastien Auger .20 .50
65 J.P. Anderson .15 .40
66 Andrey Makarov .20 .50
67 Matt Murray .20 .50
68 Brandon Glover .20 .50
69 Marvin Cupper .12 .30
70 Jacob Gervais-Chouinard .15 .40
71 Eric Williams .12 .30
72 Franky Palazzese .12 .30
73 Eetu Laurikainen .20 .50
74 Eric Comrie .20 .50
75 Francois Tremblay .15 .40
76 Brandon Whitney .20 .50
77 Payton Lee .12 .30
78 Patrik Polivka .20 .50
79 Ondrej Pavelec SG .20 .50
80 Semyon Varlamov SG .20 .50
81 Antti Niemi SG .15 .40
82 Brian Elliott SG .15 .40
83 Carey Price SG .40 1.00
84 Corey Crawford SG .25 .60
85 Evgeni Nabokov SG .15 .40
86 Henrik Lundqvist SG .50 1.25
87 Ilya Bryzgalov SG .20 .50
88 Jonas Hiller SG .15 .40
89 Jonathan Quick SG .25 .60

90 Kari Lehtonen SG .15 .40
91 Marc-Andre Fleury SG .40 1.00
92 Jimmy Howard SG .25 .60
93 Nikolai Khabibulin SG .20 .50
94 Rick DiPietro SG .15 .40
95 Roberto Luongo SG .30 .75
96 Tomas Vokoun SG .15 .40
97 Arturs Irbe DEC .15 .40
98 Bill Ranford DEC .20 .50
99 Bob Essensa DEC .20 .50
100 Brian Hayward DEC .15 .40
101 Byron Dafoe DEC .15 .40
102 Chris Osgood DEC .20 .50
103 Chris Terreri DEC .15 .40
104 Craig Billington DEC .12 .30
105 Curtis Joseph DEC .25 .60
106 Damian Rhodes DEC .20 .50
107 Dan Cloutier DEC .15 .40
108 Dominik Hasek DEC .30 .75
109 Ed Belfour DEC .20 .50
110 Garth Snow DEC .15 .40
111 Jim Carey DEC .15 .40
112 John Vanbiesbrouck DEC .20 .50
113 Kirk McLean DEC .15 .40
114 Mike Richter DEC .20 .50
115 Olaf Kolzig DEC .20 .50
116 Peter Sidorkiewicz DEC .15 .40
117 Rick Wamsley DEC .20 .50
118 Ron Tugnutt DEC .15 .40
119 Sean Burke DEC .12 .30
120 Tim Cheveldae DEC .20 .50
121 Wendell Young DEC .12 .30
122 Allan Bester DEC .15 .40
123 Andy Moog DEC .20 .50
124 Billy Smith DEC .20 .50
125 Bob Froese DEC .15 .40
126 Corrado Micalef DEC .12 .30
127 Don Beaupre DEC .15 .40
128 Ed Mio DEC .20 .50
129 Glen Hanlon DEC .15 .40
130 Grant Fuhr DEC .30 .75
131 Jim Craig DEC .25 .60
132 Jiri Crha DEC .12 .30
133 John Garrett DEC .20 .50
134 Kelly Hrudey DEC .15 .40
135 Michel Dion DEC .15 .40
136 Mike Liut DEC .12 .30
137 Patrick Roy DEC .50 1.25
138 Rejean Lemelin DEC .12 .30
139 Richard Brodeur DEC .20 .50
140 Richard Sevigny DEC .15 .40
141 Rick St. Croix DEC .12 .30
142 Ron Hextall DEC .20 .50
143 Doug Favell DEC .15 .40
144 Bernie Parent DEC .25 .60
145 Chico Resch DEC .20 .50
146 Gary Bromley DEC .15 .40
147 Gary Inness DEC .20 .50
148 Gerry Cheevers DEC .20 .50
149 Gilles Gilbert DEC .15 .40
150 Gilles Gratton DEC .20 .50
151 Gilles Meloche DEC .20 .50
152 Gilles Villemure DEC .15 .40
153 Bobby Taylor DEC .12 .30
154 Mike Palmateer DEC .20 .50
155 Rogie Vachon DEC .25 .60
156 Ron Grahame DEC .15 .40
157 Ron Low DEC .15 .40
158 Tony Esposito DEC .20 .50
159 Vladislav Tretiak DEC .15 .40
160 Cesare Maniago DEC .20 .50
161 Charlie Hodge DEC .15 .40
162 Denis DeJordy DEC .15 .40
163 Ed Giacomin DEC .20 .50
164 Glenn Hall DEC .20 .50
165 Johnny Bower DEC .20 .50
166 Roger Crozier DEC .15 .40
167 Gump Worsley DEC .20 .50
168 Jacques Plante DEC .25 .60
169 Terry Sawchuk DEC .20 .50
170 Bill Durnan DEC .20 .50
171 Chuck Rayner DEC .12 .30
172 Emile Francis DEC .15 .40
173 Frank Brimsek DEC .15 .40
174 Harry Lumley DEC .20 .50
175 Turk Broda DEC .20 .50
176 Charlie Gardiner DEC .15 .40
177 George Hainsworth DEC .20 .50
178 Lorne Chabot DEC .15 .40
179 Roy Worters DEC .20 .50
180 Tiny Thompson DEC .20 .50
181 Patrick Roy RB .50 1.25
182 Grant Fuhr RB .30 .75
183 Glenn Hall RB .20 .50
184 George Hainsworth RB .20 .50
185 Henrik Lundqvist RB .50 1.25
186 Gerry Cheevers RB .20 .50
187 Alec Connell RB .15 .40
188 Sam LoPresti RB .12 .30
189 Dominik Hasek RB .30 .75
190 Ron Tugnutt RB .15 .40
191 Vladislav Tretiak IS .15 .40
192 Tony Esposito IS .20 .50
193 Rogie Vachon IS .25 .60
194 Jim Craig IS .25 .60
195 Grant Fuhr IS .30 .75
196 Bill Ranford IS .20 .50
197 Mike Richter IS .20 .50
198 Dominik Hasek IS .30 .75
199 Henrik Lundqvist IS .50 1.25
200 Roberto Luongo IS .30 .75

2012-13 Between The Pipes Aspire Jerseys Silver

ASP01 E.Comrie/C.Price 4.00 10.00
ASP02 J.Binnington/C.Joseph 3.00 8.00
ASP03 J.Gibson/J.Hiller 3.00 8.00
ASP04 O.Dansk/H.Lundqvist 5.00 12.00
ASP05 J.Anderson/A.Niemi 1.50 4.00
ASP06 M.Murray/M.Fleury 4.00 10.00
ASP07 C.Gibson/J.Quick 2.50 6.00
ASP08 G.Sparks/F.Potvin 3.00 8.00
ASP09 J.Paterson/J.Howard 2.50 6.00
ASP10 B.Whitney/E.Belfour 2.00 5.00
ASP11 L.Brossoit/M.Vernon 2.00 5.00
ASP12 M.Subban/A.Moog 2.50 6.00
ASP13 M.Lagace/K.Lehtonen 1.50 4.00
ASP14 D.Honzik/R.Luongo 3.00 8.00
ASP15 D.Altshuller/A.Irbe 1.50 4.00
ASP16 R.DiPietro/B.Smith 2.00 5.00
ASP17 I.Bryzgalov/R.Hextall 2.00 5.00
ASP18 C.Price/P.Roy 5.00 12.00
ASP19 H.Lundqvist/M.Richter 5.00 12.00
ASP20 P.Roy/D.Bouchard 5.00 12.00

2012-13 Between The Pipes Autographs

AABE Allan Bester DEC 5.00 12.00
AABI Antoine Bibeau 4.00 10.00
AAD Alex Dubeau 6.00 15.00
AAI Arturs Irbe DEC 5.00 12.00
AAM Andrey Makarov 6.00 15.00
AAMO Andy Moog DEC 6.00 15.00
AAN Antti Niemi SG 5.00 12.00
AAS Anthony Stolarz 8.00 20.00
ABB Brendan Burke 5.00 12.00
ABBI Ben Bishop SG SP 5.00 12.00
ABD Byron Dafoe DEC 5.00 12.00
ABE Bob Essensa DEC 6.00 15.00
ABEL Brian Elliott SG SP 5.00 12.00
ABF Bob Froese DEC 5.00 12.00
ABH Brian Hayward DEC 5.00 12.00
ABP Bernie Parent DEC SP 8.00 20.00
ABT Bobby Taylor DEC 4.00 10.00
ABW Brandon Whitney 6.00 15.00
ACB Corbin Boes 5.00 12.00
ACBI Craig Billington DEC 4.00 10.00
ACC Cole Cheveldave 5.00 12.00
ACCR Corey Crawford SG SP 8.00 20.00
ACD Chris Driedger 5.00 12.00
ACG Christopher Gibson 6.00 15.00
ACJ Curtis Joseph DEC SP 8.00 20.00
ACM Corrado Micalef DEC 4.00 10.00
ACMA Cesare Maniago DEC SP 6.00 15.00
ACP Carey Price SG SP 12.00 30.00
ACR Chico Resch DEC SP 6.00 15.00
ACT Chris Terreri DEC SP 5.00 12.00
ADA Daniel Altshuller 5.00 12.00
ADB Don Beaupre DEC 5.00 12.00
ADC Dan Cloutier DEC SP 5.00 12.00
ADD Denis DeJordy DEC SP 5.00 12.00
ADF Doug Favell DEC SP 5.00 12.00
ADG Domenic Graham 5.00 12.00
ADH Denis Herron DEC 5.00 12.00
ADHA Dominik Hasek DEC SP 10.00 25.00
ADR Damian Rhodes DEC 6.00 15.00
ADRI Dennis Riggin DEC 6.00 15.00
AEC Eric Comrie 6.00 15.00
AEF Emile Francis DEC SP 5.00 12.00
AEG Ed Giacomin DEC 6.00 15.00
AEL Eetu Laurikainen 6.00 15.00
AEM Etienne Marcoux 5.00 12.00
AEMI Ed Mio DEC 6.00 15.00
AEN Evgeni Nabokov SG SP 5.00 12.00
AFB Francois Brassard 4.00 10.00
AFT Francois Tremblay 5.00 12.00
AGB Gary Bromley DEC 5.00 12.00
AGG Gilles Gilbert DEC 5.00 12.00
AGGR Gilles Gratton DEC 6.00 15.00
AGH Glen Hanlon DEC 5.00 12.00
AGHE Guy Hebert DEC SP 5.00 12.00
AGI Gary Inness DEC 6.00 15.00
AGM Gilles Meloche DEC 6.00 15.00
AGS Greg Stefan DEC 5.00 12.00
AGSN Garth Snow DEC 5.00 12.00
AGSP Garret Sparks 6.00 15.00
AGV Gilles Villemure DEC 5.00 12.00
AHL Henrik Lundqvist SG SP 15.00 40.00
AIB Ilya Bryzgalov SG SP 6.00 15.00
AJA J.P. Anderson 5.00 12.00
AJB Jacob Brennan 5.00 12.00
AJBI Jordan Binnington 10.00 25.00
AJBO Johnny Bower DEC SP 6.00 15.00
AJC Jordon Cooke 5.00 12.00
AJCA Jim Carey DEC SP 5.00 12.00
AJCR Jiri Crha DEC 4.00 10.00
AJCRA Jim Craig DEC SP 8.00 20.00
AJG John Gibson 10.00 25.00
AJGA John Garrett DEC 6.00 15.00
AJGC Jacob Gervais-Chouinard 5.00 12.00
AJH Jonas Hiller SG 5.00 12.00
AJHO Jimmy Howard SG 8.00 20.00
AJP Jake Paterson 8.00 20.00
AJPA Jaroslav Pavelka 5.00 12.00
AJPAT Jake Patterson 8.00 20.00
AJQ Jonathan Quick SG 8.00 20.00
AJV John Vanbiesbrouck DEC SP 6.00 15.00
AKB Kevin Bailie 6.00 15.00
AKH Kelly Hrudey DEC 5.00 12.00
AKL Kari Lehtonen SG 5.00 12.00
AKM Kirk McLean DEC 5.00 12.00
ALB Laurent Brossoit 6.00 15.00
ALL Liam Liston 5.00 12.00
AMC Mac Carruth SP 5.00 12.00
AMD Michel Dion DEC 5.00 12.00
AME Mac Engel 6.00 15.00
AMF Marc-Andre Fleury SG SP 12.00 30.00
AMH Matt Hewitt 5.00 12.00
AML Manny Legace DEC 5.00 12.00
AMLI Mike Liut DEC SP 4.00 10.00
AMM Matt Mahalak 5.00 12.00
AMMU Matt Murray 6.00 15.00
AMN Mathias Niederberger 5.00 12.00
AMP Mike Palmateer DEC SP 6.00 15.00
AMS Malcolm Subban 8.00 20.00
ANK Nikolai Khabibulin SG SP 6.00 15.00
AOD Oscar Dansk 8.00 20.00
AOK Olaf Kolzig DEC SP 6.00 15.00
AOP Ondrej Pavelec SG 6.00 15.00
APB Patrik Bartosak 6.00 15.00
APC Philippe Cadorette 5.00 12.00
APD Philippe Desrosiers 5.00 12.00
APP Patrik Polivka 6.00 15.00
APR Patrick Roy DEC SP 25.00 60.00
APS Peter Sidorkiewicz DEC 5.00 12.00
ARB Richard Brodeur DEC SP 6.00 15.00
ARD Rick DiPietro SG SP 5.00 12.00
ARE Ray Emery SG SP 5.00 12.00
ARG Robin Gusse 5.00 12.00
ARGR Ron Grahame DEC SP 5.00 12.00
ARH Ron Hextall DEC SP 6.00 15.00
ARL Rejean Lemelin DEC 4.00 10.00
ARLO Ron Low DEC 5.00 12.00
ARLU Roberto Luongo SG SP 10.00 25.00
ARS Richard Sevigny DEC 5.00 12.00
ARST Rick St. Croix DEC SP 4.00 10.00
ART Ron Tugnutt DEC 5.00 12.00
ASA Sebastien Auger 6.00 15.00
ASB Sean Burke DEC 4.00 10.00
ASM Spencer Martin 5.00 12.00
ASP Storm Phaneuf 5.00 12.00
ASV Semyon Varlamov SG SP 6.00 15.00
ATC Tim Cheveldae DEC 6.00 15.00
ATE Tony Esposito DEC SP 6.00 15.00
ATJ Tristan Jarry 6.00 15.00
ATR Ty Rimmer 5.00 12.00
ATV Tomas Vokoun SG 5.00 12.00
AVT Vladislav Tretiak DEC SP 5.00 12.00
AWY Wendell Young DEC 4.00 10.00
AZF Zachary Fucale 8.00 20.00

2012-13 Between The Pipes Big League Debut Jerseys Silver

BL01 Carey Price/100* 5.00 12.00
BL02 Chris Osgood/100* 2.50 6.00
BL03 Curtis Joseph/100* 3.00 8.00
BL04 Dan Cloutier/100* 2.00 5.00
BL05 Ed Belfour/100* 2.50 6.00
BL06 Evgeni Nabokov/100* 2.00 5.00
BL07 Felix Potvin/100* 4.00 10.00
BL08 Don Beaupre/100* 2.00 5.00
BL09 Jimmy Howard/100* 3.00 8.00
BL10 Jonathan Quick/100* 3.00 8.00
BL11 Kari Lehtonen/100* 2.00 5.00
BL12 Marc-Andre Fleury/100* 5.00 12.00
BL13 Mike Richter/100* 2.50 6.00
BL14 Nikolai Khabibulin/100* 2.50 6.00
BL15 Olaf Kolzig/100* 2.50 6.00
BL16 Ondrej Pavelec/100* 2.50 6.00
BL17 Ray Emery/100* 2.00 5.00
BL18 Rick DiPietro/100* 2.00 5.00
BL19 Ron Hextall/100* 2.50 6.00
BL20 Ron Tugnutt/100* 2.00 5.00
BL21 Brian Elliott/100* 2.00 5.00
BL22 Antti Niemi/100* 2.00 5.00
BL23 Jonas Hiller/100* 2.00 5.00
BL24 John Vanbiesbrouck/100* 2.50 6.00
BL25 Chris Terreri/100* 2.00 5.00
BL26 Mike Vernon/100* 2.00 5.00
BL27 Patrick Roy/100* 6.00 15.00
BL28 Tim Cheveldae/100* 2.50 6.00
BL29 Allan Bester/100* 2.00 5.00
BL30 Tom Barrasso/100* 2.50 6.00
BL31 Ed Giacomin/19* 8.00 20.00
BL32 Jacques Plante/19* 10.00 25.00
BL33 Rogie Vachon/19* 10.00 25.00
BL34 Terry Sawchuk/19* 8.00 20.00
BL35 Grant Fuhr/19* 12.00 30.00
BL36 Mike Palmateer/19* 8.00 20.00
BL37 Tony Esposito/19* 8.00 20.00
BL38 Bernie Parent/19* 10.00 25.00
BL39 Corey Crawford/19* 10.00 25.00
BL40 Henrik Lundqvist/19* 20.00 50.00

2012-13 Between The Pipes Draft Day Jerseys Silver

DD01 M.Subban/D.Altshuller 5.00 12.00
DD02 M.Murray/J.Paterson 5.00 12.00
DD03 O.Dansk/B.Whitney 5.00 12.00
DD04 J.Gibson/C.Gibson 6.00 15.00
DD05 L.Brossoit/J.Binnington 6.00 15.00
DD06 D.Honzik/G.Sparks 4.00 10.00
DD07 C.Price/J.Quick 8.00 20.00
DD08 B.Bishop/O.Pavelec 4.00 10.00
DD09 M.Fleury/J.Howard 8.00 20.00
DD10 I.Bryzgalov/H.Lundqvist 10.00 25.00
DD11 E.Nabokov/D.Cloutier 3.00 8.00
DD12 O.Kolzig/A.Irbe 4.00 10.00
DD13 S.Burke/M.Richter 4.00 10.00
DD14 P.Roy/K.McLean 10.00 25.00
DD15 V.Tretiak/T.Barrasso 4.00 10.00
DD16 A.Bester/D.Hasek 6.00 15.00
DD17 G.Fuhr/M.Vernon 6.00 15.00
DD18 J.Vanbiesbrouck/G.Stefan 4.00 10.00
DD19 R.Lemelin/M.Palmateer 4.00 10.00
DD20 G.Meloche/B.Smith 4.00 10.00

2012-13 Between The Pipes He Shoots He Saves Points

BP1 Bernie Parent UL .25 .60
BP2 Bernie Parent UM .25 .50
BP3 Bernie Parent UR .25 .50
BP4 Bernie Parent CL .25 .50
BP5 Bernie Parent C .25 .50
BP6 Bernie Parent CR .25 .50
BP7 Bernie Parent LL .25 .50
BP8 Bernie Parent LM .25 .50
BP9 Bernie Parent LR .25 .50
CP1 Carey Price UL .25 1.50
CP2 Carey Price UM .25 1.50
CP3 Carey Price UR .25 1.50
CP4 Carey Price CL .25 1.50
CP5 Carey Price C .25 1.50
CP6 Carey Price CR .25 1.50
CP7 Carey Price LL .25 1.50
CP8 Carey Price LM .25 1.50
CP9 Carey Price LR .25 1.50
DH1 Dominik Hasek UL .25 1.00
DH2 Dominik Hasek UM .25 1.00
DH3 Dominik Hasek UR .25 1.00
DH4 Dominik Hasek CL .25 1.00
DH5 Dominik Hasek C .25 1.00
DH6 Dominik Hasek CR .25 1.00
DH7 Dominik Hasek LL .25 1.00
DH8 Dominik Hasek LM .25 1.00
DH9 Dominik Hasek LR .25 1.00
EB1 Ed Belfour UL .25 .50
EB2 Ed Belfour UM .25 .50
EB3 Ed Belfour UR .25 .50
EB4 Ed Belfour CL .25 .50
EB5 Ed Belfour C .25 .50
EB6 Ed Belfour CR .25 .50
EB7 Ed Belfour LL .25 .50
EB8 Ed Belfour LM .25 .50
EB9 Ed Belfour LR .25 .50
FP1 Felix Potvin UL .25 .75
FP2 Felix Potvin UM .25 .75
FP3 Felix Potvin UE .25 .75
FP4 Felix Potvin CL .25 .75
FP5 Felix Potvin C .25 .75
FP6 Felix Potvin CR .25 .75
FP7 Felix Potvin LL .25 .75
FP8 Felix Potvin LM .25 .75
FP9 Felix Potvin LR .25 .75
GF1 Grant Fuhr UL .25 .50
GF2 Grant Fuhr UM .25 .50
GF3 Grant Fuhr UR .25 .50
GF4 Grant Fuhr CL .25 .50
GF5 Grant Fuhr C .25 .50
GF6 Grant Fuhr CR .25 .50
GF7 Grant Fuhr LL .25 .50
GF8 Grant Fuhr LM .25 .50
GF9 Grant Fuhr LR .25 .50
HL1 Henrik Lundqvist UL .25 .60
HL2 Henrik Lundqvist UM .25 .60
HL3 Henrik Lundqvist UR .25 .60
HL4 Henrik Lundqvist CL .25 .60
HL5 Henrik Lundqvist C .25 .60
HL6 Henrik Lundqvist CR .25 .60
HL7 Henrik Lundqvist LL .25 .60
HL8 Henrik Lundqvist LM .25 .60
HL9 Henrik Lundqvist LR .25 .60
JQ1 Jonathan Quick UL .25 .75
JQ2 Jonathan Quick UM .25 .75
JQ3 Jonathan Quick UR .25 .75
JQ4 Jonathan Quick CL .25 .75
JQ5 Jonathan Quick C .25 .75
JQ6 Jonathan Quick CR .25 .75
JQ7 Jonathan Quick LL .25 .75
JQ8 Jonathan Quick LM .25 .75
JQ9 Jonathan Quick LR .25 .75
PR1 Patrick Roy UL .25 1.25
PR2 Patrick Roy UM .25 1.25
PR3 Patrick Roy UR .25 1.25
PR4 Patrick Roy CL .25 1.25
PR5 Patrick Roy C .25 1.25
PR6 Patrick Roy CR .25 1.25
PR7 Patrick Roy LL .25 1.25
PR8 Patrick Roy LM .25 1.25
PR9 Patrick Roy LR .25 1.25
RL1 Roberto Luongo UL .25 .50
RL2 Roberto Luongo UM .25 .50
RL3 Roberto Luongo UR .25 .50
RL4 Roberto Luongo CL .25 .50
RL5 Roberto Luongo C .25 .50
RL6 Roberto Luongo CR .25 .50
RL7 Roberto Luongo LL .25 .50
RL8 Roberto Luongo LM .25 .50
RL9 Roberto Luongo LR .25 .50
MAF1 Marc-Andre Fleury UL .25 .75
MAF2 Marc-Andre Fleury UM .25 .75
MAF3 Marc-Andre Fleury UR .25 .75
MAF4 Marc-Andre Fleury CL .25 .75
MAF5 Marc-Andre Fleury C .25 .75
MAF6 Marc-Andre Fleury CR .25 .75
MAF7 Marc-Andre Fleury LL .25 .75
MAF8 Marc-Andre Fleury LM .25 .75
MAF9 Marc-Andre Fleury LR .25 .75

2012-13 Between The Pipes He Shoots He Saves Prizes

HSHS01 Bernie Parent 20.00 50.00
HSHS02 John Vanbiesbrouck 15.00 40.00
HSHS03 Curtis Joseph 20.00 50.00
HSHS04 Chris Osgood 15.00 40.00
HSHS05 Dominik Hasek 25.00 60.00
HSHS06 Nikolai Khabibulin 15.00 40.00
HSHS07 Terry Sawchuk 15.00 40.00
HSHS08 Mike Vernon 12.00 30.00
HSHS09 Felix Potvin 25.00 60.00
HSHS10 Ron Hextall 15.00 40.00
HSHS11 Carey Price 30.00 80.00
HSHS12 Tony Esposito 15.00 40.00
HSHS13 Henrik Lundqvist 40.00 100.00
HSHS14 Rick DiPietro 12.00 30.00
HSHS15 Patrick Roy 40.00 100.00
HSHS16 Ed Giacomin 15.00 40.00
HSHS17 Sean Burke 10.00 25.00
HSHS18 Arturs Irbe 12.00 30.00
HSHS19 Marc-Andre Fleury 30.00 80.00
HSHS20 Mike Richter 15.00 40.00
HSHS21 Jacques Plante 20.00 50.00
HSHS22 Dan Cloutier 12.00 30.00
HSHS23 Vladislav Tretiak 12.00 30.00
HSHS24 Jonas Hiller 12.00 30.00
HSHS25 Pelle Lindbergh 12.00 30.00
HSHS26 Bill Ranford 15.00 40.00
HSHS27 Ilya Bryzgalov 15.00 40.00
HSHS28 Grant Fuhr 25.00 60.00
HSHS29 Patrick Roy 40.00 100.00
HSHS30 Kirk McLean 12.00 30.00

2012-13 Between The Pipes Jerseys Silver

PATCH/19: .8X TO 2X BASIC JSY/140*
M01 Daniel Altshuller 2.50 6.00
M02 J.P. Anderson 2.50 6.00
M03 Kevin Bailie 3.00 8.00
M04 Don Beaupre 2.50 6.00
M05 Ed Belfour 3.00 8.00
M06 Jordan Binnington 5.00 12.00
M07 Laurent Brossoit 3.00 8.00
M08 Ilya Bryzgalov 3.00 8.00
M09 Sean Burke 2.00 5.00
M10 Tim Cheveldae 3.00 8.00
M11 Cole Cheveldave 2.50 6.00
M12 Dan Cloutier 2.50 6.00
M13 Eric Comrie 3.00 8.00
M14 Jordon Cooke 2.50 6.00
M15 Andrew D'Agostini 2.50 6.00
M16 Byron Dafoe 2.50 6.00
M17 Oscar Dansk 4.00 10.00
M18 Rick DiPietro 2.50 6.00
M19 Alex Dubeau 3.00 8.00
M20 Mac Engel 3.00 8.00
M21 Marc-Andre Fleury 6.00 15.00
M22 Zachary Fucale 4.00 10.00
M23 Grant Fuhr 5.00 12.00
M24 John Garrett 3.00 8.00
M25 Jacob Gervais-Chouinard 2.50 6.00
M26 Christopher Gibson 3.00 8.00
M27 John Gibson 5.00 12.00
M28 Michael Giugovaz 2.00 5.00
M29 Robin Gusse 2.50 6.00
M30 Dominik Hasek 5.00 12.00
M31 David Honzik 3.00 8.00
M32 Gary Inness 3.00 8.00
M33 Arturs Irbe 2.50 6.00
M34 Tristan Jarry 3.00 8.00
M35 Curtis Joseph 4.00 10.00
M36 Nikolai Khabibulin 3.00 8.00
M37 Olaf Kolzig 3.00 8.00
M38 Maxime Lagace 2.50 6.00
M39 Manny Legace 2.50 6.00
M40 Kari Lehtonen 2.50 6.00
M41 Rejean Lemelin 2.00 5.00
M42 Liam Liston 2.50 6.00
M43 Henrik Lundqvist 8.00 20.00
M44 Roberto Luongo 5.00 12.00
M45 Spencer Martin 2.50 6.00
M46 Matt Murray 3.00 8.00
M47 Antti Niemi 2.50 6.00
M48 Jake Paterson 4.00 10.00
M49 Ondrej Pavelec 3.00 8.00
M50 Storm Phaneuf 2.50 6.00
M51 Carey Price 6.00 15.00
M52 Jonathan Quick 4.00 10.00
M53 Ty Rimmer 2.50 6.00
M54 Patrick Roy 8.00 20.00
M55 Garret Sparks 3.00 8.00
M56 Malcolm Subban 4.00 10.00
M57 Francois Tremblay 2.50 6.00
M58 John Vanbiesbrouck 3.00 8.00
M59 Brandon Whitney 3.00 8.00
M60 Ray Emery 2.50 6.00

2012-13 Between The Pipes Junior Gems Silver

JG01 M.Subban/J.Gibson 5.00 12.00
JG02 J.Binnington/G.Sparks 5.00 12.00
JG03 M.Engel/T.Rimmer 3.00 8.00
JG04 M.Lagace/A.Dubeau 3.00 8.00
JG05 J.Anderson/M.Murray 3.00 8.00
JG06 C.Cheveldave/J.Cooke 2.50 6.00
JG07 A.D'Agostini/M.Giugovaz 2.50 6.00
JG08 S.Phaneuf/B.Whitney 3.00 8.00
JG09 L.Brossoit/T.Jarry 3.00 8.00
JG10 E.Comrie/Z.Fucale 4.00 10.00

2012-13 Between The Pipes Masked Men V Rainbow

SILVER/50: .8X TO 2X RAINBOW
MM1 Murray Bannerman 1.50 4.00
MM2 Ed Belfour 2.00 5.00
MM3 Dan Bouchard 1.50 4.00
MM4 Gary Bromley 1.50 4.00
MM5 Gerry Cheevers 2.00 5.00
MM6 Michel Dion 1.50 4.00
MM7 Ray Emery 1.50 4.00
MM8 Doug Favell 1.50 4.00
MM9 Marc-Andre Fleury 4.00 10.00
MM10 Marc-Andre Fleury 4.00 10.00
MM11 Grant Fuhr 3.00 8.00
MM12 Corey Crawford 2.50 6.00
MM13 John Garrett 2.00 5.00
MM14 Gilles Gratton 2.00 5.00
MM15 Dominik Hasek 3.00 8.00
MM16 Brian Hayward 1.50 4.00
MM17 Rick DiPietro 1.50 4.00
MM18 Ron Hextall 2.00 5.00
MM19 Jimmy Howard 2.50 6.00
MM20 Arturs Irbe 1.50 4.00
MM21 Curtis Joseph 2.50 6.00
MM22 Nikolai Khabibulin 2.00 5.00
MM23 Olaf Kolzig 2.00 5.00
MM24 Manny Legace 1.50 4.00
MM25 Ron Low 1.50 4.00
MM26 Denis Herron 1.50 4.00
MM27 Roberto Luongo 3.00 8.00
MM28 Kirk McLean 1.50 4.00
MM29 Gilles Meloche 2.00 5.00
MM30 Ed Mio 2.00 5.00
MM31 Andy Moog 2.00 5.00
MM32 Evgeni Nabokov 1.50 4.00
MM33 Mike Palmateer 2.00 5.00
MM34 Bernie Parent 2.50 6.00
MM35 Ondrej Pavelec 2.00 5.00
MM36 Felix Potvin 3.00 8.00
MM37 Carey Price 4.00 10.00
MM38 Jonathan Quick 2.50 6.00
MM39 Bill Ranford 2.00 5.00
MM40 Chico Resch 2.00 5.00
MM41 Damian Rhodes 2.00 5.00
MM43 Mike Richter 2.00 5.00
MM43 Patrick Roy 5.00 12.00
MM44 Gary Simmons 2.00 5.00
MM45 Billy Smith 2.00 5.00
MM46 Garth Snow 1.50 4.00
MM47 Wayne Stephenson 1.50 4.00
MM48 Rogie Vachon 2.50 6.00
MM49 John Vanbiesbrouck 2.00 5.00
MM50 Semyon Varlamov 2.00 5.00

2012-13 Between The Pipes Masked Men V Memorabilia

MM01 Ed Belfour 8.00 20.00
MM02 Gerry Cheevers 8.00 20.00
MM03 Ray Emery 6.00 15.00
MM04 Marc-Andre Fleury 15.00 40.00
MM05 Grant Fuhr 12.00 30.00
MM06 Dominik Hasek 12.00 30.00
MM07 Rick DiPietro 6.00 15.00
MM08 Ron Hextall 8.00 20.00
MM09 Jimmy Howard 10.00 25.00
MM10 Arturs Irbe 6.00 15.00
MM11 Curtis Joseph 10.00 25.00
MM12 Olaf Kolzig 8.00 20.00
MM13 Henrik Lundqvist 20.00 50.00
MM14 Roberto Luongo 12.00 30.00
MM15 Andy Moog 8.00 20.00
MM16 Evgeni Nabokov 6.00 15.00
MM17 Felix Potvin 12.00 30.00
MM18 Carey Price 15.00 40.00
MM19 Jonathan Quick 10.00 25.00
MM20 Bill Ranford 8.00 20.00
MM21 Patrick Roy 20.00 50.00
MM22 Billy Smith 8.00 20.00
MM23 Garth Snow 6.00 15.00
MM24 John Vanbiesbrouck 8.00 20.00

2012-13 Between The Pipes Masked Men V Memorabilia Toronto Spring Expo

BTPR01 Ed Belfour JSY/19* 8.00 20.00
BTPR02 Gerry Cheevers JSY/19* 8.00 20.00
BTPR05 Ray Emery JSY/19* 6.00 15.00
BTPR07 Marc-Andre Fleury JSY/19* 15.00 40.00
BTPR09 Marc-Andre Fleury JSY/19* 15.00 40.00
BTPR11 Grant Fuhr JSY/19* 12.00 30.00
BTPR14 Dominik Hasek JSY/19* 12.00 30.00
BTPR16 Rick DiPietro JSY/19* 6.00 15.00
BTPR18 Ron Hextall JSY/19* 8.00 20.00
BTPR21 Jimmy Howard JSY/19* 10.00 25.00
BTPR22 Arturs Irbe JSY/19* 6.00 15.00
BTPR24 Curtis Joseph JSY/19* 10.00 25.00
BTPR29 Olaf Kolzig JSY/19* 8.00 20.00
BTPR31 Manny Legace JSY/19* 6.00 15.00
BTPR33 Roberto Luongo JSY/19* 12.00 30.00
BTPR36 Andy Moog JSY/19* 8.00 20.00
BTPR37 Evgeni Nabokov JSY/19* 6.00 15.00
BTPR39 Bernie Parent JSY/19* 10.00 25.00
BTPR42 Felix Potvin JSY/19* 12.00 30.00
BTPR44 Carey Price JSY/19* 15.00 40.00
BTPR47 Jonathan Quick JSY/19* 10.00 25.00
BTPR49 Bill Ranford JSY/19* 8.00 20.00
BTPR50 Damian Rhodes JSY/19* 8.00 20.00
BTPR51 Mike Richter JSY/19* 8.00 20.00
BTPR52 Patrick Roy JSY/19* 20.00 50.00
BTPR55 Billy Smith JSY/19* 8.00 20.00
BTPR56 Garth Snow JSY/19* 6.00 15.00
BTPR58 Rogie Vachon JSY/19* 10.00 25.00
BTPR59 John Vanbiesbrouck JSY/19* 8.00 20.00
BTPR60 Semyon Varlamov JSY/19* 8.00 20.00

2012-13 Between The Pipes Rivals Silver

R01 P.Roy/R.Tugnutt 10.00 25.00
R02 M.Richter/R.Hextall 4.00 10.00
R03 A.Bester/G.Stefan 3.00 8.00
R04 R.Lemelin/G.Fuhr 6.00 15.00
R05 E.Belfour/C.Joseph 5.00 12.00
R06 F.Potvin/P.Roy 10.00 25.00
R07 A.Moog/P.Roy 10.00 25.00
R08 J.Vanbiesbrouck/B.Smith 4.00 10.00
R09 A.Niemi/R.Luongo 6.00 15.00
R10 P.Roy/C.Osgood 10.00 25.00

2012-13 Between The Pipes Stick and Jersey Silver

SJ01 Mike Vernon 8.00 20.00
SJ02 John Vanbiesbrouck 10.00 25.00
SJ03 Rogie Vachon 12.00 30.00
SJ04 Patrick Roy 25.00 60.00
SJ05 Bill Ranford 10.00 25.00
SJ06 Chris Osgood 10.00 25.00
SJ07 Grant Fuhr 15.00 40.00
SJ08 Dominik Hasek 15.00 40.00
SJ09 Arturs Irbe 8.00 20.00
SJ10 Curtis Joseph 12.00 30.00
SJ11 Olaf Kolzig 10.00 25.00
SJ12 Allan Bester 8.00 20.00
SJ13 Roger Crozier 8.00 20.00
SJ14 Billy Smith 10.00 25.00
SJ15 Sean Burke 6.00 15.00
SJ16 Rick DiPietro 8.00 20.00
SJ17 Marc-Andre Fleury 20.00 50.00
SJ18 Richard Brodeur 10.00 25.00
SJ19 Bernie Parent 12.00 30.00
SJ20 Henrik Lundqvist 25.00 60.00

2013-14 Between the Pipes

1 Antti Niemi SG .25 .60
2 Antti Raanta SG .60 1.50
3 Ben Bishop SG .25 .60
4 Carey Price SG .60 1.50
5 Corey Crawford SG .40 1.00
6 Eddie Lack SG .25 .60
7 Evgeni Nabokov SG .30 .75
8 Jake Allen SG .30 .75
9 Jimmy Howard SG .40 1.00
10 Jonas Hiller SG .25 .60
11 Marc-Andre Fleury SG .60 1.50
12 Martin Jones SG .50 1.25
13 Mike Smith SG .30 .75
14 Ray Emery SG .25 .60
15 Semyon Varlamov SG .30 .75
16 Steve Mason SG .25 .60
17 Tomas Vokoun SG .25 .60
18 Tuukka Rask SG .40 1.00
19 Viktor Fasth SG .30 .75
20 Ondrej Pavelec SG .30 .75
21 Jonas Gustavsson SG .25 .60
22 Nikolai Khabibulin SG .30 .75
23 Peter Budaj SG .25 .60
24 Andrew D'Agostini CHL .25 .60
25 Sebastien Auger CHL .25 .60
26 Robert Steeves CHL .20 .50
27 Troy Trombley CHL .20 .50
28 Jake Patterson CHL .30 .75
29 Franky Palazzese CHL .20 .50
30 Danny Mumaugh CHL .25 .60
31 Alex Bureau CHL .25 .60
32 Alex Dubeau CHL .25 .60
33 Alex Nedeljkovic CHL .30 .75
34 Alexandre Belanger CHL .25 .60
35 Anthony Brodeur CHL .40 1.00
36 Anthony Stolarz CHL .40 1.00
37 Antoine Bibeau CHL .20 .50
38 Austin Lotz CHL .20 .50
39 Brandon Hope CHL .20 .50
40 Brandon Whitney CHL .30 .75
41 Brendan Burke CHL .20 .50
42 Brent Moran CHL .25 .60
43 Charlie Graham CHL .20 .50
44 Chris Driedger CHL .25 .60
45 Daniel Altshuller CHL .25 .60
46 Dawson MacAuley CHL .25 .60
47 Eetu Laurikainen CHL .30 .75
48 Eric Comrie CHL .25 .60
49 Eric Williams CHL .20 .50
50 Etienne Marcoux CHL .20 .50
51 Francois Brassard CHL .20 .50
52 Francois Tremblay CHL .25 .60
53 Jake Paterson CHL .30 .75
54 Jake Smith CHL .25 .60
55 Jordon Cooke CHL .20 .50
56 Julio Billia CHL .30 .75
57 Justin Nichols CHL .25 .60
58 Justin Paulic CHL .30 .75
59 Louis-Philip Guindon CHL .20 .50
60 Mackenzie Blackwood CHL .40 1.00
61 Mackenzie Skapski CHL .25 .60
62 Marek Langhamer CHL .30 .75
63 Mason McDonald CHL .30 .75
64 Matt Mahalak CHL .25 .60
65 Matt Murray CHL .30 .75
66 Michael Giugovaz CHL .30 .75
67 Nikita Serebryakov CHL .30 .75
68 Oscar Dansk CHL .40 1.00
69 Patrik Bartosak CHL .20 .50
70 Patrik Polivka CHL .30 .75
71 Payton Lee CHL .25 .60
72 Philippe Cadorette CHL .25 .60
73 Philippe Desrosiers CHL .25 .60
74 Spencer Martin CHL .30 .75
75 Storm Phaneuf CHL .20 .50
76 Taylor Dupuis CHL .20 .50
77 Tristan Jarry CHL .30 .75
78 Ty Edmonds CHL .30 .75
79 Zachary Fucale CHL .40 1.00
80 Coleman Vollrath CHL .30 .75
81 Andre Racicot GOTG .20 .50
82 Arturs Irbe GOTG .25 .60
83 Bernie Parent GOTG .40 1.00
84 Bill Ranford GOTG .30 .75
85 Billy Smith GOTG .30 .75
86 Blaine Lacher GOTG .20 .50
87 Byron Dafoe GOTG .25 .60
88 Charlie Hodge GOTG .25 .60
89 Chris Osgood GOTG .30 .75
90 Clint Malarchuk GOTG .20 .50
91 Corey Hirsch GOTG .20 .50
92 Cristobal Huet GOTG .25 .60
93 Curt Ridley GOTG .20 .50
94 Curtis Joseph GOTG .40 1.00
95 Dan Bouchard GOTG .25 .60
96 Daniel Berthiaume GOTG .20 .50
97 Andy Moog GOTG .30 .75
98 Dominic Roussel GOTG .20 .50
99 Dominik Hasek GOTG .50 1.25
100 Doug Soetaert GOTG .20 .50
101 Dwayne Roloson GOTG .20 .50
102 Ed Belfour GOTG .30 .75
103 Ed Giacomin GOTG .30 .75
104 Ed Staniowski GOTG .20 .50
105 Emile Francis GOTG .25 .60
106 Felix Potvin GOTG .50 1.25
107 Gerry Cheevers GOTG .30 .75
108 Gilles Villemure GOTG .25 .60
109 Glenn Hall GOTG .30 .75
110 Grant Fuhr GOTG .50 1.25
111 Guy Hebert GOTG .25 .60
112 Hardy Astrom GOTG .20 .50
113 Jamie Storr GOTG .20 .50
114 Jeff Hackett GOTG .25 .60
115 Jim Rutherford GOTG .25 .60
116 Jimmy Waite GOTG .25 .60
117 Mike Palmateer GOTG .30 .75
118 Johan Hedberg GOTG .25 .60
119 John Blue GOTG .20 .50
120 John Garrett GOTG .30 .75
121 John Vanbiesbrouck GOTG .30 .75
122 Johnny Bower GOTG .30 .75
123 Kelly Hrudey GOTG .25 .60
124 Tim Cheveldae GOTG .30 .75
125 Kirk McLean GOTG .25 .60
126 Mario Gosselin GOTG .20 .50
127 Mario Lessard GOTG .20 .50
128 Martin Prusek GOTG .20 .50
129 Marty Turco GOTG .30 .75
130 Mike Liut GOTG .20 .50
131 Mike Richter GOTG .30 .75
132 Olaf Kolzig GOTG .30 .75
133 Patrick Lalime GOTG .25 .60
134 Patrick Roy GOTG .75 2.00
135 Pete LoPresti GOTG .20 .50
136 Pete Peeters GOTG .25 .60
137 Richard Brodeur GOTG .30 .75
138 Tommy Salo GOTG .25 .60
139 Rick Wamsley GOTG .30 .75
140 Rogie Vachon GOTG .40 1.00
141 Roman Turek GOTG .25 .60
142 Ron Grahame GOTG .25 .60
143 Ron Hextall GOTG .30 .75
144 Sean Burke GOTG .20 .50
145 Steve Baker GOTG .20 .50
146 Steve Penney GOTG .20 .50
147 Tom Barrasso GOTG .30 .75
148 Tony Esposito GOTG .30 .75
149 Ty Conklin GOTG .25 .60
150 Vladislav Tretiak GOTG .25 .60

2013-14 Between the Pipes Aspire Jerseys Silver

ASP01 Z.Fucale/C.Price 3.00 8.00
ASP02 S.Martin/S.Varlamov 1.50 4.00
ASP03 B.Burke/M.Smith 1.50 4.00
ASP04 A.Stolarz/S.Mason 2.00 5.00
ASP05 M.Murray/M.A.Fleury 3.00 8.00
ASP06 J.Paterson/J.Howard 2.00 5.00
ASP07 T.Jarry/M.A.Fleury 3.00 8.00
ASP08 B.Whitney/C.Crawford 2.00 5.00

2013-14 Between the Pipes Autographs

AAB Alex Bureau 3.00 8.00
AABI Antoine Bibeau 2.50 6.00
AABR Anthony Brodeur 5.00 12.00
AAD Alex Dubeau 3.00 8.00
AAI Arturs Irbe 3.00 8.00
AAL Austin Lotz 2.50 6.00
AAN Alex Nedeljkovic 4.00 10.00
AAR Antti Raanta 8.00 20.00
AARA Andre Racicot 2.50 6.00
AAS Anthony Stolarz 5.00 12.00
ABB Ben Bishop 3.00 8.00
ABBR Brendan Burke 2.50 6.00
ABD Byron Dafoe SP 8.00 20.00
ABL Blaine Lacher 2.50 6.00
ABM Brent Moran 3.00 8.00
ABP Bernie Parent SP 12.00 30.00
ABS Billy Smith 4.00 10.00
ACC Corey Crawford 5.00 12.00
ACD Chris Driedger 3.00 8.00
ACG Charlie Graham 2.50 6.00
ACH Charlie Hodge SP 8.00 20.00
ACHI Corey Hirsch 2.50 6.00
ACHI2 Corey Hirsch 2.50 6.00
ACHU Cristobal Huet 3.00 8.00
ACHU2 Cristobal Huet 3.00 8.00
ACJ Curtis Joseph 5.00 12.00
ACM Clint Malarchuk 2.50 6.00
ACM2 Clint Malarchuk 2.50 6.00
ACO Chris Osgood SP 8.00 20.00
ACO2 Chris Osgood SP 8.00 20.00
ACP Carey Price 8.00 20.00
ACR Curt Ridley 2.50 6.00
ACR2 Curt Ridley 2.50 6.00

ACV Coleman Vollrath 4.00 10.00
ADA Daniel Altshuller 3.00 8.00
ADBE Daniel Berthiaume 2.50 6.00
ADBE2 Daniel Berthiaume 2.50 6.00
ADH Denis Herron 3.00 8.00
ADHA Dominik Hasek SP 15.00 40.00
ADR Dominic Roussel 2.50 6.00
ADS Doug Soetaert 2.50 6.00
AEB Ed Belfour SP 20.00 50.00
AEC Eric Comrie 3.00 8.00
AEF Emile Francis SP 8.00 20.00
AEG Ed Giacomin SP 15.00 40.00
AEL Eddie Lack 3.00 8.00
AEM Etienne Marcoux 2.50 6.00
AEN Evgeni Nabokov 4.00 10.00
AES Ed Staniowski 2.50 6.00
AES2 Ed Staniowski 2.50 6.00
AGC Gerry Cheevers SP 8.00 20.00
AGF Grant Fuhr SP 10.00 25.00
AGH Glenn Hall SP 10.00 25.00
AGV Gilles Villemure 3.00 8.00
AHA Hardy Astrom 2.50 6.00
AHA2 Hardy Astrom 2.50 6.00
AHL Henrik Lundqvist 10.00 25.00
AIB Ilya Bryzgalov SP 12.00 30.00
AJB Julio Billia 4.00 10.00
AJBL John Blue 2.50 6.00
AJBO Johnny Bower 4.00 10.00
AJC Jordon Cooke 2.50 6.00
AJG John Garrett 4.00 10.00
AJGU Jonas Gustavsson 3.00 8.00
AJH Jimmy Howard 5.00 12.00
AJHA Jeff Hackett 3.00 8.00
AJHE1 Johan Hedberg 3.00 8.00
AJHE2 Johan Hedberg 3.00 8.00
AJHI Jonas Hiller 3.00 8.00
AJN Justin Nichols 3.00 8.00
AJP Jake Patterson 4.00 10.00
AJPA Justin Paulic 4.00 10.00
AJR Jim Rutherford 3.00 8.00
AJR2 Jim Rutherford 3.00 8.00
AJS Jamie Storr 2.50 6.00
AJT Jocelyn Thibault SP 4.00 10.00
AJV John Vanbiesbrouck SP 6.00 15.00
AJW Jimmy Waite 3.00 8.00
AKM Kirk McLean SP 8.00 20.00
ALG Louis-Philip Guindon 2.50 6.00
AMF Marc-Andre Fleury 8.00 20.00
AMG Michael Giugovaz 4.00 10.00
AMGO Mario Gosselin 2.50 6.00
AMGO2 Mario Gosselin 2.50 6.00
AMJ Martin Jones 6.00 15.00
AMLE Mario Lessard 2.50 6.00
AMM Matt Murray 4.00 10.00
AMMA Mason McDonald 4.00 10.00
AMP Martin Prusek 2.50 6.00
AMSK Mackenzie Skapski 3.00 8.00
AMT Marty Turco 4.00 10.00
ANK Nikolai Khabibulin 4.00 10.00
ANS Nikita Serebryakov 4.00 10.00
AOD Oscar Dansk 5.00 12.00
AOK Olaf Kolzig 4.00 10.00
AOP Ondrej Pavelec 4.00 10.00
APB Patrik Bartosak 2.50 6.00
APC Philippe Cadorette 3.00 8.00
APD Philippe Desrosiers 3.00 8.00
APL Payton Lee 3.00 8.00
APLA Patrick Lalime 3.00 8.00
APLO Pete LoPresti 2.50 6.00
APLO2 Pete LoPresti 2.50 6.00
APP Pete Peeters 3.00 8.00
APR Patrick Roy SP 30.00 80.00
APR2 Patrick Roy SP 30.00 80.00
ARB Richard Brodeur SP 4.00 10.00
ARD Rick DiPietro 3.00 8.00
ARE Ray Emery 3.00 8.00
ARG Ron Grahame 3.00 8.00
ARL Roberto Luongo 6.00 15.00
ART Roman Turek SP 6.00 15.00
ARV Rogie Vachon SP 8.00 20.00
ARW Rick Wamsley SP 4.00 10.00
ASBA Steve Baker 2.50 6.00
ASM Steve Mason 3.00 8.00
ASMA Spencer Martin 4.00 10.00
ASP Storm Phaneuf 2.50 6.00
ASPE Steve Penney 2.50 6.00
ASV Semyon Varlamov 4.00 10.00
ATB Tom Barrasso SP 4.00 10.00
ATB2 Tom Barrasso SP 4.00 10.00
ATC Ty Conklin 3.00 8.00
ATC2 Ty Conklin 3.00 8.00
ATE Tony Esposito SP 12.00 30.00
ATJ Tristan Jarry 4.00 10.00
AVF Viktor Fasth 4.00 10.00
AVT Vladislav Tretiak 3.00 8.00
AZF Zachary Fucale 5.00 12.00

2013-14 Between the Pipes Big League Debut Jerseys Silver

BLD01 Steve Mason/180* 3.00 8.00
BLD02 Ed Belfour/180* 4.00 10.00
BLD03 Evgeni Nabokov/180* 4.00 10.00
BLD04 Patrick Roy/180* 10.00 25.00
BLD05 Ron Hextall/180* 4.00 10.00
BLD06 Mike Richter/180* 4.00 10.00
BLD07 Mike Vernon/180* 3.00 8.00
BLD08 Carey Price/180* 8.00 20.00
BLD09 Dan Cloutier/180* 3.00 8.00
BLD10 Semyon Varlamov/180* 4.00 10.00
BLD11 Viktor Fasth/180* 4.00 10.00
BLD12 Marty Turco/180* 4.00 10.00
BLD13 Marc-Andre Fleury/180* 8.00 20.00
BLD14 Don Beaupre/180* 2.50 6.00
BLD15 Cristobal Huet/180* 3.00 8.00
BLD16 Ray Emery/180* 3.00 8.00
BLD17 Olaf Kolzig/180* 4.00 10.00
BLD18 Rick Wamsley/180* 4.00 10.00

2013-14 Between the Pipes Current Crop Jerseys Silver

CC01 Corey Crawford 8.00 20.00
CC02 Ray Emery 4.00 10.00
CC03 Viktor Fasth 5.00 12.00
CC04 Marc-Andre Fleury 10.00 25.00
CC05 Antti Niemi 4.00 10.00
CC06 Steve Mason 4.00 10.00
CC07 Carey Price 6.00 15.00
CC08 Tuukka Rask 6.00 15.00
CC09 Evgeni Nabokov 5.00 12.00
CC10 Semyon Varlamov 5.00 12.00

2013-14 Between the Pipes Draft Day Jerseys Silver

DD01 Marc-Andre Fleury 5.00 12.00
DD02 Tuukka Rask 6.00 15.00
DD03 Carey Price 8.00 20.00
DD04 Corey Crawford 6.00 15.00
DD05 Ray Emery 4.00 10.00
DD06 Steve Mason 4.00 10.00
DD07 Ben Bishop 5.00 12.00
DD09 Jake Allen 5.00 12.00

2013-14 Between the Pipes He Shoots He Saves Points

AN1 Antti Niemi UL .20 .50
AN2 Antti Niemi UM .20 .50
AN3 Antti Niemi UR .20 .50
AN4 Antti Niemi CL .20 .50
AN5 Antti Niemi C .20 .50
AN6 Antti Niemi CR .20 .50
AN7 Antti Niemi LL .20 .50
AN8 Antti Niemi LM .20 .50
AN9 Antti Niemi LR .20 .50
AR1 Antti Raanta UL .50 1.25
AR2 Antti Raanta UM .50 1.25
AR3 Antti Raanta UR .50 1.25
AR4 Antti Raanta CL .50 1.25
AR5 Antti Raanta C .50 1.25
AR6 Antti Raanta CR .50 1.25
AR7 Antti Raanta LL .50 1.25
AR8 Antti Raanta LM .50 1.25
AR9 Antti Raanta LR .50 1.25
CC1 Corey Crawford UL .30 .75
CC2 Corey Crawford UM .30 .75
CC3 Corey Crawford UR .30 .75
CC4 Corey Crawford CL .30 .75
CC5 Corey Crawford C .30 .75
CC6 Corey Crawford CR .30 .75
CC7 Corey Crawford LL .30 .75
CC8 Corey Crawford LM .30 .75
CC9 Corey Crawford LR .30 .75
CP1 Carey Price UL .50 1.25
CP2 Carey Price UM .50 1.25
CP3 Carey Price UR .50 1.25
CP4 Carey Price CL .50 1.25
CP5 Carey Price C .50 1.25
CP6 Carey Price CR .50 1.25
CP7 Carey Price LL .50 1.25
CP8 Carey Price LM .50 1.25
CP9 Carey Price LR .50 1.25
EL1 Eddie Lack UL .20 .50
EL2 Eddie Lack UM .20 .50
EL3 Eddie Lack UR .20 .50
EL4 Eddie Lack CL .20 .50
EL5 Eddie Lack C .20 .50
EL6 Eddie Lack CR .20 .50
EL7 Eddie Lack LL .20 .50
EL8 Eddie Lack LM .20 .50
EL9 Eddie Lack LR .20 .50
JH1 Jimmy Howard UL .30 .75
JH2 Jimmy Howard UM .30 .75
JH3 Jimmy Howard UR .30 .75
JH4 Jimmy Howard CL .30 .75
JH5 Jimmy Howard C .30 .75
JH6 Jimmy Howard CR .30 .75
JH7 Jimmy Howard LL .30 .75
JH8 Jimmy Howard LM .30 .75
JH9 Jimmy Howard LR .30 .75
MS1 Mike Smith UL .25 .60
MS2 Mike Smith UM .25 .60
MS3 Mike Smith UR .25 .60
MS4 Mike Smith CL .25 .60
MS5 Mike Smith C .25 .60
MS6 Mike Smith CR .25 .60
MS7 Mike Smith LL .25 .60
MS8 Mike Smith LM .25 .60
MS9 Mike Smith LR .25 .60
SM1 Steve Mason UL .20 .50
SM2 Steve Mason UM .20 .50
SM3 Steve Mason UR .20 .50
SM4 Steve Mason CL .20 .50
SM5 Steve Mason C .20 .50
SM6 Steve Mason CR .20 .50
SM7 Steve Mason LL .20 .50
SM8 Steve Mason LM .20 .50
SM9 Steve Mason LR .20 .50
SV1 Semyon Varlamov UL .25 .60
SV2 Semyon Varlamov UM .25 .60
SV3 Semyon Varlamov UR .25 .60
SV4 Semyon Varlamov CL .25 .60
SV5 Semyon Varlamov C .25 .60
SV6 Semyon Varlamov CR .25 .60
SV7 Semyon Varlamov LL .25 .60
SV8 Semyon Varlamov LM .25 .60
SV9 Semyon Varlamov LR .25 .60
TR1 Tuukka Rask UL .30 .75
TR2 Tuukka Rask UM .30 .75
TR3 Tuukka Rask UR .30 .75
TR4 Tuukka Rask CL .30 .75
TR5 Tuukka Rask C .30 .75
TR6 Tuukka Rask CR .30 .75
TR7 Tuukka Rask LL .30 .75
TR8 Tuukka Rask LM .30 .75
TR9 Tuukka Rask LR .30 .75
MAF1 Marc-Andre Fleury UL .50 1.25
MAF2 Marc-Andre Fleury UM .50 1.25
MAF3 Marc-Andre Fleury UR .50 1.25
MAF4 Marc-Andre Fleury CL .50 1.25
MAF5 Marc-Andre Fleury C .50 1.25
MAF6 Marc-Andre Fleury CR .50 1.25
MAF7 Marc-Andre Fleury LL .50 1.25
MAF8 Marc-Andre Fleury LM .50 1.25
MAF9 Marc-Andre Fleury LR .50 1.25

2013-14 Between the Pipes Immortals

1 Georges Vezina 1.00 2.50
2 Clint Benedict .75 2.00
3 Hap Holmes .75 2.00
4 Hugh Lehman .75 2.00
5 Alec Connell .75 2.00
6 John Ross Roach .75 2.00
7 Doc Stewart 1.25 3.00
8 Lorne Chabot .75 2.00
9 George Hainsworth 1.00 2.50
10 Charlie Gardiner .75 2.00
11 Hal Winkler .75 2.00
12 Tiny Thompson 1.00 2.50
13 Roy Worters 1.00 2.50
14 Wilf Cude 1.25 3.00
15 Andy Aitkenhead 1.00 2.50
16 Norm Smith .75 2.00
17 Dave Kerr .60 1.50
18 Mike Karakas .60 1.50
19 Turk Broda 1.00 2.50
20 Bill Beveridge .60 1.50
21 Frank Brimsek .75 2.00
22 Bill Durnan 1.00 2.50
23 Paul Bibeault .75 2.00
24 Johnny Mowers .60 1.50
25 Chuck Rayner .75 2.00
26 Steve Buzinski 1.00 2.50
27 Frank McCool .75 2.00
28 Ken McAuley .60 1.50
29 Harry Lumley 1.00 2.50
30 Jim Henry .60 1.50
31 Jack Gelineau 1.25 3.00
32 Al Rollins .75 2.00
33 Gerry McNeil .60 1.50
34 Terry Sawchuk 1.00 2.50
35 Gump Worsley 1.00 2.50
36 Jacques Plante 1.25 3.00
37 Bruce Gamble .60 1.50
38 Hank Bassen .75 2.00
39 Roger Crozier .75 2.00
40 Wayne Rutledge .75 2.00
41 Gary Bauman .75 2.00
42 Al Smith .60 1.50
43 Roy Edwards .60 1.50
44 Bunny Larocque .75 2.00
45 Pelle Lindbergh .75 2.00

2013-14 Between the Pipes Jerseys Silver

GUM01 Alex Nedeljkovic 4.00 10.00
GUM02 Alex Dubeau 3.00 8.00
GUM03 Andrew D'Agostini 3.00 8.00
GUM04 Anthony Brodeur 5.00 12.00
GUM05 Anthony Stolarz 5.00 12.00
GUM06 Antoine Bibeau 2.50 6.00
GUM07 Brandon Whitney 4.00 10.00
GUM08 Brendan Burke 2.50 6.00
GUM09 Cole Cheveldave 4.00 10.00
GUM10 Daniel Altshuller 3.00 8.00
GUM11 Eric Comrie 3.00 8.00
GUM12 Etienne Marcoux 2.50 6.00
GUM13 Francois Tremblay 3.00 8.00
GUM14 Jake Patterson 4.00 10.00
GUM15 Jordon Cooke 2.50 6.00
GUM16 Julio Billia 4.00 10.00
GUM17 Matt Murray 4.00 10.00
GUM18 Michael Giugovaz 4.00 10.00
GUM19 Oscar Dansk 5.00 12.00
GUM20 Patrik Bartosak 2.50 6.00
GUM21 Payton Lee 3.00 8.00
GUM22 Philippe Desrosiers 3.00 8.00
GUM23 Spencer Martin 4.00 10.00
GUM24 Storm Phaneuf 2.50 6.00
GUM25 Tristan Jarry 4.00 10.00
GUM26 Arturs Irbe 3.00 8.00
GUM27 Mike Vernon 3.00 8.00
GUM28 Bill Ranford 4.00 10.00
GUM29 Chris Osgood 4.00 10.00
GUM30 Cristobal Huet 5.00 12.00
GUM31 Corey Hirsch 4.00 10.00
GUM32 Ron Hextall 4.00 10.00
GUM33 Andy Moog 4.00 10.00
GUM34 Daniel Berthiaume 4.00 10.00
GUM35 Dominic Roussel 2.50 6.00
GUM36 Dominik Hasek 6.00 15.00
GUM37 Ed Belfour 4.00 10.00
GUM38 Don Beaupre 3.00 8.00
GUM39 Grant Fuhr 6.00 15.00
GUM40 Jamie Storr 2.50 6.00
GUM41 Jim Rutherford 4.00 10.00
GUM42 Johan Hedberg 3.00 8.00
GUM43 John Vanbiesbrouck 4.00 10.00
GUM44 Kirk McLean 10.00 25.00
GUM45 Marty Turco 4.00 10.00
GUM46 Mike Richter 6.00 15.00
GUM47 Patrick Lalime 3.00 8.00
GUM48 Patrick Roy 6.00 15.00
GUM49 Tim Cheveldae 4.00 10.00
GUM50 Chico Resch 5.00 12.00
GUM51 Rick Wamsley 4.00 10.00
GUM52 Ty Conklin 3.00 8.00
GUM53 Dwayne Roloson 3.00 8.00
GUM54 Jeff Hackett 3.00 8.00

2013-14 Between the Pipes Pack Your Bags Jerseys Silver

PYB01 Curtis Joseph 8.00 20.00
PYB02 Curtis Joseph 8.00 20.00
PYB03 Dan Cloutier 5.00 12.00
PYB04 Dominik Hasek 10.00 25.00
PYB05 Dominik Hasek 10.00 25.00
PYB06 Ed Belfour 6.00 15.00
PYB07 Semyon Varlamov 6.00 15.00
PYB08 Evgeni Nabokov 6.00 15.00
PYB09 Felix Potvin 10.00 25.00
PYB10 Johan Hedberg 6.00 15.00
PYB11 Grant Fuhr 10.00 25.00
PYB12 Chris Osgood 6.00 15.00
PYB13 John Vanbiesbrouck 6.00 15.00
PYB14 Mike Vernon 5.00 12.00
PYB15 Byron Dafoe 5.00 12.00
PYB16 Patrick Roy 8.00 20.00
PYB17 Ray Emery 5.00 12.00
PYB18 Damian Rhodes 4.00 10.00
PYB19 Manny Fernandez 6.00 15.00
PYB20 Steve Mason 5.00 12.00
PYB21 Tom Barrassso 6.00 15.00

2013-14 Between the Pipes Rivals Jerseys Silver

R01 E.Belfour/D.Hasek 8.00 20.00
R02 J.Howard/C.Crawford 6.00 15.00
R03 C.Price/T.Rask 10.00 25.00
R04 P.Roy/C.Osgood 12.00 30.00
R05 R.Hextall/F.Potvin 8.00 20.00
R06 C.Joseph/P.Lalime 6.00 15.00

2013-14 Between the Pipes Top Prospects Jerseys Silver

TP01 Corey Crawford 5.00 12.00
TP02 Marc-Andre Fleury 8.00 20.00
TP03 Carey Price 8.00 20.00
TP04 Zachary Fucale 5.00 12.00
TP05 Tristan Jarry 4.00 10.00
TP06 Spencer Martin 4.00 10.00
TP07 Ty Edmonds 4.00 10.00
TP08 Mason McDonald 4.00 10.00
TP09 Alex Nedeljkovic 4.00 10.00

1996-97 Black Diamond

1 Roman Turek RC .40 1.00
2 Slava Fetisov .25 .60
3 Mike Dunham .25 .60
4 Jean-Francois Fortin RC .40 1.00
5 Keith Primeau .30 .75
6 Zigmund Palffy .40 1.00
7 Curtis Leschyshyn .25 .60
8 Vladimir Tsyplakov RC .40 1.00
9 Adam Graves .25 .60
10 Ian Laperriere .40 1.00
11 Bill Lindsay .25 .60
12 Brian Leetch .30 .75
13 Martin Lapointe .25 .60
14 Scott Barney RC .40 1.00
15 Mike Grier RC .50 1.25
16 Vladimir Konstantinov .30 .75
17 Rem Murray RC .40 1.00
18 Ed Jovanovski .30 .75
19 Chris O'Sullivan .25 .60
20 Steve Rucchin .25 .60
21 Jay Pandolfo .40 1.00
22 Nick Boynton RC .40 1.00
23 Greg Adams .25 .60
24 Adam Colagiacomo RC .40 1.00
25 Vincent Damphousse .30 .75
26 Shane Willis RC .40 1.00
27 Alexei Kovalev .30 .75
28 Doug Gilmour .50 1.25
29 Joel Otto .25 .60
30 Donald Audette .25 .60
31 Tommy Salo .30 .75
32 Rob Ray .25 .60
33 Kris Draper .25 .60
34 Ed Belfour .40 1.00
35 Mike Richter .40 1.00
36 Nikolai Khabibulin .30 .75
37 Eric Desjardins .30 .75
38 Daniel Tkaczuk RC .40 1.00
39 Keith Jones .25 .60
40 Per Gustafsson RC .40 1.00
41 Jocelyn Thibault .30 .75
42 Mike Gartner .50 1.25
43 Vitali Yachmenev .25 .60
44 Jonas Hoglund .25 .60
45 Craig Janney .30 .75
46 Daymond Langkow .30 .75
47 Mattias Timander RC .40 1.00
48 Scott Young .25 .60
49 Mikael Renberg .30 .75
50 Nicklas Lidstrom .50 1.25
51 Andrei Kovalenko .25 .60
52 Adam Foote .25 .60
53 Guy Hebert .30 .75
54 Kevin Hatcher .25 .60
55 Rick Tocchet .30 .75
56 Sergei Zubov .30 .75
57 Chris Phillips .40 1.00
58 Denis Savard .40 1.00
59 Bernie Nicholls .30 .75
60 Jozef Stumpel .25 .60
61 Darius Kasparaitis .25 .60
62 Kelly Hrudey .30 .75
63 Marcel Cousineau RC .25 .60
64 Brian Skrudland .25 .60
65 Byron Dafoe .30 .75
66 Ray Sheppard .30 .75
67 Chris Simon .25 .60
68 Dainius Zubrus RC .50 1.25
69 Ethan Moreau RC .40 1.00
70 Theo Fleury .75 2.00
71 Damian Rhodes .30 .75
72 Kevin Dineen .25 .60
73 Kenny Jonsson .25 .60
74 Ray Ferraro .25 .60
75 Jaromir Jagr 1.25 3.00
76 Wayne Primeau .25 .60
77 Chris Gratton .30 .75
78 Alyn McCauley .40 1.00
79 Christian Dube .25 .60
80 Bill Ranford .30 .75
81 Adam Deadmarsh .25 .60
82 Dale Hunter .30 .75
83 Derek Plante .25 .60
84 Todd Bertuzzi .40 1.00
85 Stephane Fiset .30 .75
86 Boyd Devereaux RC .40 1.00
87 Jere Lehtinen .25 .60
88 Peter Schaefer RC .30 .75
89 Alexander Mogilny .30 .75
90 Joe Juneau .25 .60
91 Alexandre Daigle .50 1.25
92 Jeff O'Neill .50 1.25
93 Todd Warriner .50 1.25
94 Sergei Berezin RC 1.25 3.00
95 Petr Nedved .60 1.50
96 Phil Housley .60 1.50
97 Jason Arnott .60 1.50
98 Sandis Ozolinsh .50 1.25
99 Mike Modano 1.25 3.00
100 Mark Messier 1.50 4.00
101 Ron Francis 1.00 2.50
102 Oleg Tverdovsky .60 1.50
103 Patrick Marleau RC 40.00 100.00
104 Brian Bellows .60 1.50
105 Eric Fichaud .60 1.50
106 Alexei Zhamnov .60 1.50
107 Wendel Clark 1.25 3.00
108 Dimitri Khristich .50 1.25
109 Mike Ricci .50 1.25
110 John LeClair .75 2.00
111 Owen Nolan .75 2.00
112 Bill Guerin .75 2.00
113 Vyacheslav Kozlov .50 1.25
114 Brendan Shanahan .75 2.00
115 Trevor Linden .75 2.00
116 Jose Theodore 1.00 2.50
117 Rod Brind'Amour .75 2.00
118 Brian Holzinger .60 1.50
119 Shayne Corson .60 1.50
120 Bryan Smolinski .50 1.25
121 Tony Granato .50 1.25
122 Mariusz Czerkawski .50 1.25
123 Andrew Cassels .50 1.25
124 Scott Stevens .75 2.00
125 Mike Ridley .50 1.25
126 Jamie Langenbrunner .50 1.25
127 Scott Mellanby .60 1.50
128 Grant Fuhr 1.25 3.00
129 Felix Potvin 1.25 3.00
130 Marc Denis .75 2.00
131 Corey Hirsch .60 1.50
132 Chris Osgood .75 2.00
133 Peter Bondra .75 2.00
134 Martin Brodeur 2.00 5.00
135 Pierre Turgeon .60 1.50
136 Pat Verbeek .50 1.25
137 Scott Niedermayer .75 2.00
138 Geoff Sanderson .60 1.50
139 Jason Dawe .50 1.25
140 Rob Niedermayer .60 1.50
141 Daniel Alfredsson .75 2.00
142 Jim Campbell .50 1.25
143 Roman Hamrlik .50 1.25
144 Rob Blake .75 2.00
145 Chris Chelios .75 2.00
146 Teemu Selanne 1.50 4.00
147 Jim Carey .75 2.00
148 Dino Ciccarelli .75 2.00
149 Mark Recchi 1.00 2.50
150 Chris Pronger .75 2.00
151 Paul Coffey 6.00 15.00
152 Adam Oates 6.00 15.00
153 Keith Tkachuk 6.00 15.00
154 Janne Niinimaa 6.00 15.00
155 Sergei Fedorov 10.00 25.00
156 Dominik Hasek 10.00 25.00
157 Eric Lindros 10.00 25.00
158 Curtis Joseph 8.00 20.00
159 Alexei Yashin 5.00 12.00
160 Joe Thornton RC 200.00 500.00
161 Bryan Berard 6.00 15.00
162 Steve Yzerman 15.00 40.00
163 Mats Sundin 6.00 15.00
164 Jarome Iginla 8.00 20.00
165 John Vanbiesbrouck 6.00 15.00
166 Mario Lemieux 25.00 60.00
167 Jeremy Roenick 10.00 25.00
168 Patrick Lalime RC 12.00 30.00
169 Joe Sakic 12.00 30.00
170 Brett Hull 12.00 30.00
171 Peter Forsberg 12.00 30.00
172 Doug Weight 6.00 15.00
173 Tony Amonte 5.00 12.00
174 Patrick Roy 15.00 40.00
175 Paul Kariya 6.00 15.00
176 Pavel Bure 6.00 15.00
177 Ray Bourque 10.00 25.00
178 Saku Koivu 6.00 15.00
179 Wade Redden 4.00 10.00
180 Wayne Gretzky 40.00 100.00
P180 Wayne Gretzky Promo 40.00 100.00

1996-97 Black Diamond Gold

*SINGLE VETS: 3X TO 8X BASIC CARDS
*SINGLE ROOKIES: 1.2X TO 3X
*DOUBLE VETS: 1.2X TO 3X BASIC CARDS
*DOUBLE ROOKIES: .8X TO 2X
*TRIPLE VETS: 1.5X TO 4X BASIC CARDS
*TRIPLE ROOKIES: 1.2X TO 3X

1996-97 Black Diamond Run for the Cup

RC1 Wayne Gretzky 200.00 350.00
RC2 Saku Koivu 30.00 80.00
RC3 Mario Lemieux 150.00 250.00
RC4 Patrick Roy 600.00 1500.00
RC5 Jaromir Jagr 50.00 120.00
RC6 John Vanbiesbrouck 20.00 50.00
RC7 Peter Forsberg 30.00 80.00
RC8 Paul Kariya 40.00 100.00
RC9 Steve Yzerman 125.00 250.00
RC10 Joe Sakic 75.00 150.00
RC11 Mark Messier 150.00 400.00
RC12 Sergei Fedorov 40.00 100.00
RC13 Mats Sundin 30.00 80.00
RC14 Pavel Bure 60.00 120.00
RC15 Ed Jovanovski 25.00 60.00
RC16 Mike Modano 30.00 80.00
RC17 Curtis Joseph 25.00 60.00
RC18 Teemu Selanne 30.00 80.00
RC19 Jarome Iginla 30.00 80.00
RC20 Eric Lindros 60.00 120.00

1997-98 Black Diamond

COMPLETE SET (150) 50.00 100.00
1 Alexei Zhitnik .25 .60
2 Adam Graves .25 .60
3 Keith Primeau .30 .75
4 Mike Richter .40 1.00
5 Felix Potvin .60 1.50
6 Valeri Bure .25 .60
7 Mark Messier .75 2.00
8 Dainius Zubrus .30 .75
9 Owen Nolan .40 1.00
10 Kenny Jonsson .30 .75
11 Ron Francis .50 1.25
12 Bryan Berard .25 .60
13 Eric Messier RC .40 1.00
14 Paul Kariya .40 1.00
15 Teemu Elomo RC .30 .75
16 Joe Nieuwendyk .30 .75
17 Scott Stevens .40 1.00
18 Zigmund Palffy .40 1.00
19 Brett Hull .75 2.00
20 Dominik Hasek .60 1.50
21 Dino Ciccarelli .40 1.00
22 Rob Niedermayer .25 .60
23 Mark Recchi .50 1.25
24 Brad Isbister .30 .75
25 Timo Vertala RC .30 .75
26 Mika Noronen RC .30 .75
27 Sandis Ozolinsh .25 .60
28 Chris Phillips .30 .75
29 Chris Chelios .40 1.00
30 Jason Dawe .30 .75
31 Kirk McLean .30 .75
32 Jason Allison .30 .75
33 Brian Leetch .30 .75
34 Guy Hebert .30 .75
35 David Legwand RC .50 1.25
36 Pierre Hedin RC .30 .75
37 Sergei Samsonov .30 .75
38 Bill Guerin .40 1.00
39 Chris Osgood .40 1.00
40 Jere Lehtinen .30 .75
41 Patrick Roy 1.00 2.50
42 John Vanbiesbrouck .40 1.00
43 Maxim Afinogenov RC .50 1.25
44 Patrik Elias RC 1.50 4.00
45 Josh Holden .30 .75
46 Saku Koivu .40 1.00
47 Maxim Balmochnykh RC .50 1.25
48 Pasi Petrilainen .25 .60
49 Robert Reichel .30 .75
50 Wade Redden .25 .60
51 Richard Zednik .30 .75
52 Ty Jones RC .30 .75
53 Nikolai Khabibulin .40 1.00
54 Kyle McLaren .25 .60
55 Daniel Tkaczuk .40 1.00
56 Alexei Zhamnov .25 .60
57 Donald MacLean RC .40 1.00
58 Dave Gagner .25 .60
59 Jeremy Roenick .60 1.50
60 Ray Bourque .60 1.50
61 Rod Brind'Amour .40 1.00
62 Miroslav Satan .25 .60
63 Eric Daze .25 .60
64 Mike Ricci .25 .60
65 John LeClair .40 1.00
66 Bryan Marchment .40 1.00
67 Henrik Petre RC .30 .75
68 John MacLean .25 .60
69 Artem Chubarov RC .30 .75
70 Doug Gilmour .50 1.25
71 Marco Sturm RC .40 1.00
72 Jaromir Jagr 1.25 3.00
73 Daniel Alfredsson .40 1.00
74 Daren Puppa .30 .75
75 Adam Deadmarsh .25 .60
76 Luc Robitaille .40 1.00
77 Mats Sundin .40 1.00
78 Dan Cloutier .25 .60
79 Manny Malhotra RC .50 1.25
80 Mike Modano .60 1.50
81 Espen Knutsen RC .40 1.00
82 Sergei Fedorov .60 1.50
83 Chris Pronger .40 1.00
84 Doug Weight .40 1.00
85 Dmitri Nabokov .30 .75
86 Gary Roberts .30 .75
87 Peter Bondra .40 1.00
88 Robert Dome RC .25 .60
89 Jan Bulis RC .40 1.00
90 Eric Brewer RC .50 1.25
91 Nikos Tselios RC .30 .75
92 Scott Mellanby .30 .75
93 Vitali Vishnevsky RC .50 1.25
94 Derian Hatcher .30 .75
95 Teemu Selanne .75 2.00
96 Joe Sakic .75 2.00
97 Alexander Mogilny .30 .75
98 Jesse Boulerice RC .50 1.25
99 Johan Forsander RC .30 .75
100 Pierre Turgeon .30 .75
101 Tony Amonte .30 .75
102 Timo Ahmaoja RC .30 .75
103 Rob Blake .40 1.00
104 Derek Morris RC .40 1.00
105 Alex Tanguay RC 1.00 2.50
106 Peter Forsberg .75 2.00
107 Shayne Corson .30 .75
108 Tyler Moss RC .30 .75
109 Adam Oates .40 1.00
110 Keith Tkachuk .40 1.00
111 Alexei Yashin .30 .75
112 Joe Thornton .60 1.50
113 Andy Moog .40 1.00
114 Daniel Sedin RC 4.00 10.00
115 Pavel Bure .40 1.00
116 Denis Shvidki RC .50 1.25
117 Jason Arnott .30 .75
118 Mike Johnson RC .30 .75
119 Nicklas Lidstrom .40 1.00
120 Mattias Ohlund .30 .75
121 Alexander Selivanov .25 .60
122 Martin Brodeur 1.00 2.50
123 Steve Yzerman 1.00 2.50
124 Dimitri Vlassenkov RC .40 1.00
125 Jeff Farkas RC .50 1.25
126 Curtis Joseph .50 1.25
127 Yanic Perreault .30 .75
128 Alyn McCauley .30 .75
129 Vyacheslav Kozlov .30 .75
130 Alexei Morozov .30 .75
131 Roberto Luongo RC 3.00 8.00
132 Jarome Iginla .50 1.25
133 Pat LaFontaine .40 1.00
134 Ed Belfour .40 1.00
135 Toby Petersen RC .50 1.25
136 Henrik Sedin RC 8.00 20.00
137 Marcus Nilson .30 .75
138 Cameron Mann .30 .75
139 Eero Somervuori RC .30 .75
140 Patrick Marleau .40 1.00
141 Ed Jovanovski .25 .60
142 Roman Hamrlik .25 .60
143 Theo Fleury .50 1.25
144 Wayne Gretzky 2.50 6.00
145 Eric Lindros .60 1.50
146 Boyd Deveraux .30 .75
147 Sami Kapanen .30 .75
148 Grant Fuhr .60 1.50
149 Brendan Shanahan .40 1.00
150 Vincent Lecavalier RC 2.50 6.00

1997-98 Black Diamond Double Diamond

*VETS: .75X TO 2X BASIC CARDS
*ROOKIES: .6X TO 1.5X

1997-98 Black Diamond Triple Diamond

*VETS: 3X TO 8X BASIC CARDS
*ROOKIES: 1.2X TO 3X

1997-98 Black Diamond Quadruple Diamond

*VETS: 15X TO 40X BASIC CARDS
*ROOKIES: 4X TO 10X

1997-98 Black Diamond Premium Cut

COMPLETE SET (30) 30.00 80.00
*DOUBLE DIAM: .5X TO 1.2X SINGLE
*TRIPLE DIAM: .8X TO 2X SINGLE
*QUAD VERTICAL: 3X TO 8X SINGLE
PC1 Wayne Gretzky 10.00 25.00
PC2 Patrick Roy 6.00 15.00
PC3 Brendan Shanahan 1.50 4.00
PC4 Ray Bourque 1.50 4.00
PC5 Alexei Morozov 1.00 2.50
PC6 John LeClair 1.50 4.00
PC7 Steve Yzerman 4.00 10.00
PC8 Patrik Elias 1.00 2.50
PC9 Pavel Bure 1.50 4.00
PC10 Brian Leetch 1.50 4.00
PC11 Peter Forsberg 2.00 5.00
PC12 Marco Sturm 1.00 2.50
PC13 Eric Lindros 1.50 4.00
PC14 Keith Tkachuk 1.00 2.50
PC15 Teemu Selanne 1.50 4.00
PC16 Bryan Berard 1.00 2.50
PC17 Joe Thornton 2.50 6.00
PC18 Brett Hull 2.00 5.00
PC19 Nicklas Lidstrom 1.50 4.00
PC20 Jaromir Jagr 2.50 6.00
PC21 Vaclav Prospal 1.00 2.50
PC22 Pat LaFontaine 1.50 4.00
PC23 Mark Messier 1.50 4.00
PC24 Martin Brodeur 4.00 10.00
PC25 Mike Modano 2.50 6.00
PC26 Paul Kariya 1.50 4.00
PC27 Mike Johnson 1.00 2.50
PC28 Sergei Samsonov 1.00 2.50
PC29 Joe Sakic 2.50 6.00
PC30 Mats Sundin 1.50 4.00

1997-98 Black Diamond Premium Cut Quadruple Diamond Horizontal

*HORIZONTAL 1:30: .8X TO 2X SINGLE
*HORIZONTAL 1:90: 1.2X TO 3X SINGLE
*HORIZONTAL 1:2000: 6X TO 15X SINGLE
PC1 Wayne Gretzky 300.00 800.00
PC2 Patrick Roy 200.00 400.00
PC13 Eric Lindros 60.00 150.00

1998-99 Black Diamond

1 Paul Kariya .25 .60
2 Teemu Selanne .50 1.25
3 Johan Davidsson .15 .40
4 Ray Bourque .40 1.00
5 Sergei Samsonov .20 .50
6 Jason Allison .20 .50
7 Joe Thornton .40 1.00
8 Miroslav Satan .20 .50
9 Brian Holzinger .15 .40
10 Dominik Hasek .40 1.00
11 Rico Fata .20 .50
12 Jarome Iginla .30 .75
13 Theo Fleury .30 .75
14 Ron Francis .30 .75
15 Gary Roberts .15 .40
16 Keith Primeau .20 .50
17 Sami Kapanen .15 .40
18 Doug Gilmour .30 .75
19 Chris Chelios .25 .60
20 Tony Amonte .20 .50
21 Peter Forsberg .50 1.25
22 Patrick Roy .60 1.50
23 Joe Sakic .50 1.25
24 Chris Drury .20 .50
25 Brett Hull .50 1.25
26 Ed Belfour .25 .60
27 Mike Modano .40 1.00
28 Darryl Sydor .15 .40
29 Sergei Fedorov .40 1.00
30 Steve Yzerman .60 1.50
31 Nicklas Lidstrom .30 .75
32 Chris Osgood .25 .60
33 Brendan Shanahan .25 .60
34 Doug Weight .25 .60
35 Bill Guerin .25 .60
36 Tom Poti .15 .40
37 Pavel Bure .25 .60
38 Mark Parrish RC .40 1.00
39 Rob Niedermayer .15 .40
40 Pavel Rosa RC .15 .40
41 Rob Blake .25 .60
42 Olli Jokinen .20 .50
43 Vincent Damphousse .20 .50
44 Mark Recchi .30 .75
45 Terry Ryan .15 .40
46 Saku Koivu .25 .60
47 Mike Dunham .20 .50
48 Sergei Krivokrasov .15 .40
49 Scott Stevens .25 .60
50 Martin Brodeur .60 1.50
51 Brendan Morrison .15 .40
52 Eric Brewer .25 .60
53 Zigmund Palffy .25 .60
54 Felix Potvin .40 1.00
55 Wayne Gretzky 1.50 4.00
56 Brian Leetch .20 .50
57 Manny Malhotra .25 .60
58 Mike Richter .25 .60
59 Alexei Yashin .20 .50
60 Wade Redden .15 .40
61 Daniel Alfredsson .25 .60
62 Eric Lindros .40 1.00
63 John LeClair .25 .60
64 John Vanbiesbrouck .25 .60
65 Rod Brind'Amour .25 .60
66 Keith Tkachuk .25 .60
67 Daniel Briere .20 .50
68 Jeremy Roenick .40 1.00
69 Jaromir Jagr .75 2.00
70 German Titov .15 .40
71 Alexei Morozov .15 .40
72 Patrick Marleau .25 .60
73 Andrei Zyuzin .15 .40
74 Mike Vernon .20 .50
75 Owen Nolan .25 .60

76 Marty Reasoner .25 .60
77 Al MacInnis .30 .75
78 Chris Pronger .25 .60
79 Wendel Clark .40 1.00
80 Vincent Lecavalier .50 1.25
81 Craig Janney .15 .40
82 Tomas Kaberle RC .30 .75
83 Curtis Joseph .30 .75
84 Mats Sundin .25 .60
85 Mark Messier .50 1.25
86 Bill Muckalt RC .15 .40
87 Mattias Ohlund .15 .40
88 Peter Bondra .25 .60
89 Olaf Kolzig .25 .60
90 Richard Zednik .15 .40
91 Harold Druken SP 1.00 2.50
92 Roberto Luongo SP 2.50 6.00
93 Daniel Tkaczuk SP 1.00 2.50
94 Brenden Morrow SP RC 2.50 6.00
95 Mike Van Ryn SP 1.00 2.50
96 Brian Finley SP RC 1.00 2.50
97 Jani Rita SP RC 1.00 2.50
98 Ilkka Mikkola SP RC 1.00 2.50
99 Mikko Jokela SP RC 1.00 2.50
100 Tommi Santala SP RC 1.00 2.50
101 Teemu Virkkunnen SP RC 1.00 2.50
102 Arto Laatikainen SP RC 1.00 2.50
103 Kirill Safronov SP RC 1.00 2.50
104 Alexei Volkov SP RC 1.00 2.50
105 Denis Arkhipov SP RC 1.00 2.50
106 Alexander Zevakhin SP RC 1.00 2.50
107 Denis Shvidki SP 1.00 2.50
108 Maxim Afinogenov SP 1.00 2.50
109 Daniel Sedin SP 1.50 4.00
110 Henrik Sedin SP 1.50 4.00
111 Jimmie Olvestad SP RC 1.00 2.50
112 Mattias Weinhandl SP RC 1.00 2.50
113 Mathias Tjarnqvist SP RC 1.00 2.50
115 David Legwand SP 1.00 2.50
116 Barrett Heisten SP RC 1.00 2.50
117 Tim Connolly SP RC 1.00 2.50
118 Andy Hilbert SP RC 1.00 2.50
119 Joe Blackburn SP RC 1.00 2.50
120 Dave Tanabe SP RC 1.00 2.50

1998-99 Black Diamond Double Diamond
*1-90 SINGLES: 2X TO 5X BASIC CARDS
*91-120 SINGLES: .6X TO 1.5X BASIC SP

1998-99 Black Diamond Triple Diamond
*1-90 TRIPLE: 3X TO 8X BASIC CARDS
*91-120 TRIPLE: 1.2X TO 3X BASIC SP

1998-99 Black Diamond Quadruple Diamond
*1-90 QUADS: 30X TO 80X BASIC CARDS
*91-120 QUADS: 4X TO 10X BASIC SP

1998-99 Black Diamond Myriad
COMPLETE SET (30)
M1 Vincent Lecavalier 6.00 15.00
M2 John Vanbiesbrouck 2.00 5.00
M3 Paul Kariya 2.50 6.00
M4 Keith Tkachuk 2.50 6.00
M5 Mike Modano 4.00 10.00
M6 Dominik Hasek 5.00 12.00
M7 Teemu Selanne 2.50 6.00
M8 Manny Malhotra 1.00 2.50
M9 Brendan Shanahan 2.50 6.00
M10 Pavel Bure 2.50 6.00
M11 Chris Drury 2.00 5.00
M12 Curtis Joseph 2.50 6.00
M13 Joe Sakic 5.00 12.00
M14 Eric Lindros 2.50 6.00
M15 Peter Bondra 2.00 5.00
M16 Brett Hull 4.00 10.00
M17 Ray Bourque 4.00 10.00
M18 Jaromir Jagr 4.00 10.00
M19 Steve Yzerman 12.50 30.00
M20 Mark Parrish 4.00 10.00
M21 Martin Brodeur 6.00 15.00
M22 Saku Koivu 2.50 6.00
M23 Patrick Roy 12.50 30.00
M24 John LeClair 2.50 6.00
M25 Doug Gilmour 2.00 5.00
M26 Sergei Fedorov 4.00 10.00
M27 Wayne Gretzky 15.00 40.00
M28 Peter Forsberg 6.00 15.00
M29 Eric Brewer 1.00 2.50
M30 Sergei Samsonov 2.00 5.00

1998-99 Black Diamond Winning Formula Gold
COMPLETE SET (30) 125.00 250.00
WF1 Paul Kariya/850 3.00 8.00
WF2 Teemu Selanne/2600 3.00 8.00
WF3 Sergei Samsonov/1100 2.50 6.00
WF4 Dominik Hasek/1650 6.00 15.00
WF5 Vincent Lecavalier/2200 5.00 12.00
WF6 Patrick Roy/1550 15.00 40.00
WF7 Peter Forsberg/1250 8.00 20.00
WF8 Joe Sakic/1350 5.00 12.00
WF9 Ed Belfour/1850 3.00 8.00
WF10 Brendan Shanahan/1400 3.00 8.00
WF11 Steve Yzerman/1200 20.00 50.00
WF12 Chris Osgood/1650 2.50 6.00
WF13 Curtis Joseph/1450 3.00 8.00
WF14 Manny Malhotra/800 2.50 6.00
WF15 Martin Brodeur/2150 6.00 15.00
WF16 Chris Drury/1400 2.50 6.00
WF17 Zigmund Palffy/2250 2.50 6.00
WF18 Wayne Gretzky/1150 15.00 40.00
WF19 Theo Fleury/1350 2.50 6.00
WF20 Alexei Yashin/1650 2.50 6.00
WF21 Eric Lindros/1500 3.00 8.00
WF22 John LeClair/2550 2.50 6.00
WF23 Keith Tkachuk/2000 3.00 8.00
WF24 Mark Messier/1100 3.00 8.00
WF25 Jaromir Jagr/1750 5.00 12.00
WF26 Brett Hull/1350 5.00 12.00
WF27 Mats Sundin/1650 3.00 8.00
WF28 Pavel Bure/2550 3.00 8.00
WF29 Peter Bondra/2600 2.50 6.00
WF30 Mike Modano/1050 8.00 20.00

1998-99 Black Diamond Winning Formula Platinum
WF2 Teemu Selanne/52 50.00 100.00
WF4 Dominik Hasek/33 100.00 200.00
WF5 Vincent Lecavalier/44 100.00 200.00
WF6 Patrick Roy/31 250.00 500.00
WF9 Ed Belfour/37 60.00 120.00
WF12 Chris Osgood/33 75.00 150.00
WF14 Manny Malhotra/16 25.00 60.00
WF15 Martin Brodeur/43 100.00 200.00
WF17 Zigmund Palffy/45 60.00 120.00
WF20 Alexei Yashin/33 25.00 60.00
WF21 Eric Lindros/30 50.00 100.00
WF22 John LeClair/51 40.00 100.00
WF23 Keith Tkachuk/40 75.00 150.00
WF25 Jaromir Jagr/35 60.00 150.00
WF27 Mats Sundin/33 50.00 100.00
WF28 Pavel Bure/51 50.00 100.00
WF29 Peter Bondra/52 50.00 100.00

1998-99 Black Diamond Year of the Great One
COMMON YOTG (1-99) 125.00 250.00

1999-00 Black Diamond
1 Paul Kariya .25 .60
2 Teemu Selanne .50 1.25
3 Guy Hebert .25 .60
4 Damian Rhodes .15 .40
5 Patrik Stefan RC .25 .60
6 Dean Sylvester RC .15 .40
7 Sergei Samsonov .20 .50
8 Byron Dafoe .20 .50
9 Ray Bourque .40 1.00
10 Joe Thornton .40 1.00
11 Dominik Hasek .40 1.00
12 Michael Peca .20 .50
13 Miroslav Satan .20 .50
14 Martin Biron .20 .50
15 Oleg Saprykin RC .25 .60
16 Valeri Bure .15 .40
17 Robyn Regehr .15 .40
18 Dave Tanabe .15 .40
19 Arturs Irbe .20 .50
20 Sami Kapanen .15 .40
21 Kyle Calder RC .20 .50
22 Tony Amonte .20 .50
23 Doug Gilmour .30 .75
24 Patrick Roy .60 1.50
25 Joe Sakic .50 1.25
26 Peter Forsberg .50 1.25
27 Chris Drury .25 .60
28 Milan Hejduk .20 .50
29 Mike Modano .40 1.00
30 Brett Hull .50 1.25
31 Ed Belfour .25 .60
32 Jon Sim RC .25 .60
33 Nicklas Lidstrom .25 .60
34 Sergei Fedorov .40 1.00
35 Brendan Shanahan .25 .60
36 Steve Yzerman .60 1.50
37 Chris Osgood .25 .60
38 Paul Comrie RC .40 1.00
39 Bill Guerin .25 .60
40 Doug Weight .25 .60
41 Pavel Bure .25 .60
42 Ivan Novoseltsev RC .30 .75
43 Trevor Kidd .15 .40
44 Zigmund Palffy .25 .60
45 Luc Robitaille .25 .60
46 Stephane Fiset .20 .50
47 Mike Ribeiro .15 .40
48 Saku Koivu .25 .60
49 David Legwand .15 .40
50 Rob Valicevic RC .20 .50
51 Martin Brodeur .60 1.50
52 Scott Gomez .20 .50
53 Brian Rafalski RC .25 .60
54 Tim Connolly .15 .40
55 Jorgen Jonsson RC .20 .50
56 Theo Fleury .30 .75
57 Brian Leetch .20 .50
58 Mike Richter .25 .60
59 Marian Hossa .25 .60
60 Radek Bonk .15 .40
61 Mike Fisher RC .25 .60
62 Eric Lindros .40 1.00
63 Keith Primeau .20 .50
64 John LeClair .25 .60
65 Jeremy Roenick .40 1.00
66 Keith Tkachuk .25 .60
67 Mika Alatalo RC .20 .50
68 Jaromir Jagr .75 2.00
69 Martin Straka .15 .40
70 Alexei Kovalev .20 .50
71 Jochen Hecht RC .40 1.00
72 Pavol Demitra .30 .75
73 Chris Pronger .25 .60
74 Patrick Marleau .25 .60
75 Owen Nolan .25 .60
76 Jeff Friesen .20 .50
77 Steve Shields .20 .50
78 Vincent Lecavalier .25 .60
79 Dan Cloutier .15 .40
80 Adam Mair RC .15 .40
81 Mike Johnson .20 .50
82 Mats Sundin .25 .60
83 Nikolai Antropov RC .60 1.50
84 Curtis Joseph .30 .75
85 Steve Kariya RC .25 .60
86 Mark Messier .50 1.25
87 Alexander Mogilny .20 .50
88 Olaf Kolzig .25 .60
89 Peter Bondra .25 .60
90 Alexandre Volchkov RC .15 .40
91 Pavel Brendl SP RC .40 1.00
92 Jamie Lundmark SP .20 .50
93 Kris Beech SP .15 .40
94 Michael Zigomanis SP .15 .40
95 Branislav Mezei SP RC .15 .40
96 Sheldon Keefe SP RC .25 .60
97 Brian Finley SP .25 .60
98 Taylor Pyatt SP .20 .50
99 Denis Shvidki SP .20 .50
100 Barret Jackman SP .15 .40
101 Maxime Ouellet SP .25 .60
102 Milan Kraft SP RC .20 .50
103 Brad Ralph SP RC .20 .50
104 Alexei Volkov SP .20 .50
105 Mathieu Chouinard SP .15 .40
106 Mark Bell SP .15 .40
107 Ryan Jardine SP RC .20 .50
108 Kristian Kudroc SP RC .15 .40
109 Norm Milley SP .15 .40
110 Jeff Heerema SP .15 .40
111 Jaroslav Kristek SP RC .20 .50
112 Luke Sellars SP RC .25 .60
113 Bryan Kazarian SP RC .20 .50
114 Brett Lysak SP RC .20 .50
115 Andrei Shefer SP RC .20 .50
116 Michal Sivek SP RC .20 .50
117 Justin Papineau SP .15 .40
118 Mattias Weinhandl SP .15 .40
119 Daniel Sedin SP .60 1.50
120 Henrik Sedin SP .60 1.50

1999-00 Black Diamond Diamond Cut
*VETERANS 1-90: 2X TO 5X BASIC CARDS
*ROOKIES 1-90: 1.2X TO 3X BASIC CARDS
*ROOKIES 91-20: .8X TO 2X BASIC CARDS

1999-00 Black Diamond Final Cut
*VETERANS 1-90: 10X TO 25X BASIC CARDS
*ROOKIES 1-90: 5X TO 12X
*ROOKIES 91-120: 4X TO 10X

1999-00 Black Diamond A Piece of History
*DOUBLE: .8X TO 2X SINGLE
BH Brett Hull 6.00 15.00
DH Dominik Hasek 5.00 12.00
EB Ed Belfour 3.00 8.00
EL Eric Lindros 5.00 12.00
GH Gordie Howe 12.00 30.00
JJ Jaromir Jagr 10.00 25.00
JL John LeClair 3.00 8.00
JS Joe Sakic 6.00 15.00
KT Keith Tkachuk 3.00 8.00
MB Martin Brodeur 8.00 20.00
MM Mike Modano 5.00 12.00
PB Pavel Bure 3.00 8.00
PF Peter Forsberg 6.00 15.00
PK Paul Kariya 3.00 8.00
PR Patrick Roy 8.00 20.00
RB Ray Bourque 5.00 12.00
SY Steve Yzerman 8.00 20.00
TC Tim Connolly 2.00 5.00
TS Teemu Selanne 6.00 15.00
WG Wayne Gretzky 20.00 50.00

1999-00 Black Diamond Diamonation
COMPLETE SET (20) 12.00 30.00
D1 Paul Kariya .50 1.25
D2 Patrik Stefan .75 2.00
D3 Sergei Samsonov .50 1.25
D4 Teemu Selanne .50 1.25
D5 Patrick Roy 2.50 6.00
D6 Mike Modano .75 2.00
D7 Sergei Fedorov 1.00 2.50
D8 Pavel Bure .60 1.50
D9 David Legwand .50 1.25
D10 Martin Brodeur 1.25 3.00
D11 Theo Fleury .50 1.25
D12 Eric Lindros .75 2.00
D13 Keith Tkachuk .50 1.25
D14 Jaromir Jagr .75 2.00
D15 Mats Sundin .50 1.25
D16 Steve Kariya .60 1.50
D17 Peter Bondra .50 1.25
D18 Peter Forsberg 1.25 3.00
D19 Steve Yzerman 2.50 6.00
D20 Zigmund Palffy .50 1.25

1999-00 Black Diamond Diamond Might
COMPLETE SET (10) 8.00 15.00
DM1 Peter Forsberg 1.50 4.00
DM2 Brendan Shanahan 1.00 2.50
DM3 Eric Lindros 1.00 2.50
DM4 John LeClair .75 2.00
DM5 Jaromir Jagr 1.00 2.50
DM6 Keith Tkachuk .60 1.50
DM7 Teemu Selanne .60 1.50
DM8 Mats Sundin .60 1.50
DM9 Mark Messier .75 2.00
DM10 Theo Fleury .60 1.50

1999-00 Black Diamond Diamond Skills
COMPLETE SET (10) 25.00 50.00
DS1 Teemu Selanne 1.25 3.00
DS2 Paul Kariya 3.00 8.00
DS3 Patrick Roy 6.00 15.00
DS4 Pavel Bure 1.50 4.00
DS5 Sergei Fedorov 2.50 6.00
DS6 Eric Lindros 2.00 5.00
DS7 Jaromir Jagr 2.00 5.00
DS8 Martin Brodeur 3.00 8.00
DS9 Theo Fleury 1.25 3.00
DS10 Curtis Joseph 1.25 3.00

1999-00 Black Diamond Gordie Howe Gallery
COMPLETE SET (10) 30.00 80.00
COMMON HOWE (GH1-GH10) 5.00 12.00

1999-00 Black Diamond Myriad
COMPLETE SET (10) 20.00 40.00
M1 Patrik Stefan 2.00 5.00
M2 Teemu Selanne 1.25 3.00
M3 Sergei Samsonov 1.25 3.00
M4 Joe Sakic 2.50 6.00
M5 Brett Hull 1.50 4.00
M6 Pavel Bure 1.50 4.00
M7 Steve Yzerman 6.00 15.00
M8 Jaromir Jagr 2.00 5.00
M9 Eric Lindros 2.00 5.00
M10 Paul Kariya 3.00 8.00

2000-01 Black Diamond
COMPLETE SET (90) 300.00 600.00
COMP.SET w/o SP's (82) 15.00 30.00
1 Paul Kariya .30 .75
2 Teemu Selanne .60 1.50
3 Patrik Stefan .25 .60
4 Joe Thornton .50 1.25
5 Sergei Samsonov .25 .60
6 Dominik Hasek .50 1.25
7 Maxim Afinogenov .20 .50
8 Valeri Bure .25 .60
9 Marc Savard .20 .50
10 Ron Francis .40 1.00
11 Jeff O'Neill .25 .60
12 Tony Amonte .25 .60
13 Michal Grosek .20 .50
14 Patrick Roy .75 2.00
15 Ray Bourque .50 1.25
16 Milan Hejduk .25 .60
17 Peter Forsberg .60 1.50
18 Brett Hull .60 1.50
19 Ed Belfour .30 .75
20 Mike Modano .50 1.25
21 Brendan Shanahan .30 .75
22 Chris Osgood .30 .75
23 Steve Yzerman .75 2.00
24 Doug Weight .30 .75
25 Tommy Salo .25 .60
26 Pavel Bure .30 .75
27 Trevor Kidd .20 .50
28 Rob Blake .30 .75
29 Luc Robitaille .30 .75
30 Jose Theodore .30 .75
31 Saku Koivu .30 .75
32 David Legwand .30 .75
33 Martin Brodeur .75 2.00
34 Scott Gomez .25 .60
35 Scott Stevens .30 .75
36 Tim Connolly .20 .50
37 Mariusz Czerkawski .20 .50
38 Mark Messier .60 1.50
39 Theo Fleury .40 1.00
40 Marian Hossa .30 .75
41 Radek Bonk .25 .60
42 Brian Boucher .25 .60
43 John LeClair .30 .75
44 Simon Gagne .30 .75
45 Jeremy Roenick .50 1.25
46 Keith Tkachuk .30 .75
47 Jaromir Jagr 1.00 2.50
48 Martin Straka UER .20 .50
49 Steve Shields .20 .50
50 Jeff Friesen .20 .50
51 Chris Pronger .30 .75
52 Roman Turek .25 .60
53 Vincent Lecavalier .30 .75
54 Dan Cloutier .25 .60
55 Curtis Joseph .40 1.00
56 Mats Sundin .30 .75
57 Markus Naslund .30 .75
58 Felix Potvin .50 1.25
59 Olaf Kolzig .30 .75
60 Jeff Halpern .20 .50
61 Matt Pettinger RC 1.50 4.00
62 Chris Nielsen RC 1.50 4.00
63 Dany Heatley RC 5.00 12.00
64 Matt Zultek RC 1.50 4.00
65 Dmitri Afanasenkov RC 1.50 4.00
66 Tyler Bouck RC 1.50 4.00
67 Jonas Andersson RC 1.50 4.00
68 Marc-Andre Thinel RC 1.50 4.00
69 Jaroslav Svoboda RC 1.50 4.00
70 Josef Vasicek RC 4.00 10.00
71 Andrew Raycroft RC 4.00 10.00
72 Juraj Kolnik RC 1.50 4.00
73 Zdenek Blatny RC 1.50 4.00
74 Sebastien Caron RC 2.00 5.00
75 Michael Ryder RC 6.00 15.00
76 Eric Nickulas RC 2.00 5.00
77 Jeff Cowan RC 2.00 5.00
78 Steven Reinprecht RC 3.00 8.00
79 David Gosselin RC 2.00 5.00
80 Colin White RC 2.00 5.00
81 Steve Valiquette RC 2.50 6.00
82 Jani Hurme RC 2.00 5.00
83 Jean-Guy Trudel RC 2.00 5.00
84 Dieter Kochan RC 2.00 5.00
85 Paul Kariya PG 6.00 15.00
86 Patrick Roy PG 15.00 40.00
87 Steve Yzerman PG 12.00 30.00
88 Pavel Bure PG 6.00 15.00
89 Martin Brodeur PG 10.00 25.00
90 Jaromir Jagr PG 12.00 30.00
91 Samuel Pahlsson .20 .50
92 Eric Boulton RC .30 .75
93 Daniel Tkaczuk .25 .60
94 Rob Shearer RC .40 1.00
95 David Vyborny .20 .50
96 Tyler Bouck .20 .50
97 Mike Comrie RC 3.00 8.00
98 Anson Carter .25 .60
99 Roman Simicek RC .30 .75
100 Andrei Markov .40 1.00
101 Jason Arnott .25 .60
102 Mike Mottau .20 .50
103 Taylor Pyatt .20 .50
104 Alexei Yashin .25 .60
105 Todd Fedoruk RC .30 .75
106 Milan Kraft .20 .50
107 Mario Lemieux 1.25 3.00
108 Evgeni Nabokov .30 .75
109 Brad Richards .30 .75
110 Daniel Sedin .25 .60
111 Henrik Sedin .40 1.00
112 Petr Tenkrat RC 1.50 4.00
113 Lee Goren RC 1.50 4.00
114 David Aebischer RC 3.00 8.00
115 Yuri Babenko RC 1.50 4.00
116 Rostislav Klesla RC 4.00 10.00
117 Marty Turco RC 3.00 8.00
118 Jason Williams RC 2.50 6.00
119 Michel Riesen RC 2.00 5.00
120 Lubomir Visnovsky RC 3.00 8.00
121 Travis Scott RC 2.00 5.00
122 Peter Bartos RC 2.00 5.00
123 Marian Gaborik RC 6.00 15.00
124 Scott Hartnell RC 4.00 10.00
125 Rick DiPietro RC 6.00 15.00
126 Vitali Yeremeyev RC 2.00 5.00
127 Martin Havlat RC 5.00 12.00
128 Roman Cechmanek RC 2.00 5.00
129 Justin Williams RC 4.00 10.00
130 Ruslan Fedotenko RC 4.00 10.00
131 Alexander Kharitonov RC 1.50 4.00
132 Alexei Ponikarovsky RC 2.50 6.00

2000-01 Black Diamond Gold
*1-60/91-111 VETS/100: 8X TO 20X
*61-75 ROOK/100: 1X TO 2.5X RC/1999
*76-84 ROOK/100: .8X TO 2X RC/1250
*85-90 PG/100: .6X TO 1.5X PG/500

2000-01 Black Diamond Diamonation
COMPLETE SET (9) 15.00 30.00
IG1 Paul Kariya 1.00 2.50
IG2 Patrick Roy 5.00 12.00
IG3 Sergei Fedorov 2.00 5.00
IG4 Pavel Bure 1.25 3.00
IG5 Scott Gomez 1.00 2.50
IG6 John LeClair 1.25 3.00
IG7 Jaromir Jagr 1.50 4.00
IG8 Vincent Lecavalier 1.00 2.50
IG9 Curtis Joseph 1.00 2.50

2000-01 Black Diamond Diamond Might
COMPLETE SET (9) 15.00 30.00
FP1 Teemu Selanne 1.25 3.00
FP2 Peter Forsberg 2.50 6.00
FP3 Ray Bourque 2.00 5.00
FP4 Mike Modano 1.50 4.00
FP5 Brendan Shanahan 1.50 4.00
FP6 Pavel Bure 1.25 3.00
FP7 Martin Brodeur 2.50 6.00
FP8 John LeClair 1.25 3.00
FP9 Jaromir Jagr 1.50 4.00

2000-01 Black Diamond Diamond Skills
COMPLETE SET (6) 20.00 40.00
IC1 Patrick Roy 6.00 15.00
IC2 Mike Modano 2.00 5.00
IC3 Steve Yzerman 6.00 15.00
IC4 Martin Brodeur 3.00 8.00
IC5 John LeClair 1.50 4.00
IC6 Jaromir Jagr 2.00 5.00

2000-01 Black Diamond Game Gear
BJV J.Vanbiesbrouck Blocker 8.00 20.00
BSB Sean Burke Blocker 6.00 15.00
BTB Tom Barrasso Blocker 6.00 15.00
BTS Tommy Salo Blocker 6.00 15.00
CJV J.Vanbiesbrouck Glove 6.00 15.00
CKM Kirk McLean Glove 6.00 15.00
CSB Sean Burke Glove 6.00 15.00
CTB Tom Barrasso Glove 6.00 15.00
CTS Tommy Salo Glove 6.00 15.00
GEL Eric Lindros Glove SP 8.00 20.00
GTS Teemu Selanne Glove SP 10.00 25.00
GWG Wayne Gretzky Glove SP 40.00 100.00
LBD Byron Dafoe Pad 6.00 15.00
LCJ Curtis Joseph Pad 6.00 15.00
LDH Dominik Hasek Pad 10.00 25.00
LGF Grant Fuhr Pad 20.00 50.00
LJV J.Vanbiesbrouck Pad 6.00 15.00
LMB Martin Biron Pad 6.00 15.00
LOK Olaf Kolzig Pad 6.00 15.00
LRL Roberto Luongo Pad 6.00 15.00
LSS Steve Shields Pad 6.00 15.00
SMM Mark Messier Skate SP 30.00 80.00
GDR Chris Drury Glove Upd 6.00 15.00
GFE S.Fedorov Glove Upd 20.00 50.00
GSA Joe Sakic Glove Upd 12.50 30.00
GTH J.Thornton Glove Upd 8.00 20.00
GYA Alexei Yashin Glove Upd 6.00 15.00
LAU J-S Aubin Pad Upd 6.00 15.00
LDE Marc Denis Pad Upd 5.00 12.00
LOS Chris Osgood Pad Upd 6.00 15.00
LTU Roman Turek Pad Upd 6.00 15.00
SJA J.Jagr Skate Upd 15.00 40.00

2000-01 Black Diamond Myriad
COMPLETE SET (6) 12.00 25.00
CC1 Paul Kariya 1.50 4.00
CC2 Peter Forsberg 3.00 8.00
CC3 Pavel Bure 1.50 4.00
CC4 Scott Gomez 1.50 4.00
CC5 Jaromir Jagr 2.00 5.00
CC6 Curtis Joseph 1.50 4.00

2003-04 Black Diamond
COMPLETE SET (198) 200.00 400.00
COMP.SET w/o SP's (126) 40.00 80.00
1 Mike York .25 .60
2 Pavel Bure .40 1.00
3 Steve Reinprecht .25 .60
4 Vincent Lecavalier .40 1.00
5 Alex Auld .25 .60
6 Eric Daze .30 .75
7 Jeff Hackett .30 .75
8 Manny Fernandez .25 .60
9 Alexei Zhamnov .40 1.00
10 Bryan Marchment .25 .60
11 Jason Allison .30 .75
12 Tony Amonte .30 .75
13 David Legwand .30 .75
14 Geoff Sanderson .25 .60
15 Olaf Kolzig .40 1.00
16 Vaclav Prospal .25 .60
17 Sebastien Caron .25 .60
18 Daniel Alfredsson .40 1.00
19 Martin Biron .40 1.00
20 Jay Bouwmeester .25 .60
21 Nikolai Khabibulin .40 1.00
22 Keith Tkachuk .40 1.00
23 Miroslav Satan .30 .75
24 Rick DiPietro .30 .75
25 Ryan Smyth .30 .75
26 Alexander Mogilny .30 .75
27 Daniil Markov .20 .50
28 Jason Spezza .40 1.00
29 Roman Cechmanek .30 .75
30 Brendan Morrison .30 .75
31 Chris Gratton .25 .60
32 Joe Sakic .75 2.00
33 Jose Theodore .60 1.50
34 Dwayne Roloson .30 .75
35 Ed Jovanovski .30 .75
36 Peter Forsberg .75 2.00
37 Robert Esche .25 .60
38 Daniel Briere .40 1.00
39 Doug Weight .40 1.00
40 Mike Comrie .30 .75
41 Michael Peca .30 .75
42 Ales Kotalik .25 .60
43 Alexei Kovalev .30 .75
44 Tommy Salo .30 .75
45 Pavol Demitra .50 1.25
46 Alex Tanguay .30 .75
47 Johan Hedberg .30 .75
48 Jan Hrdina .25 .60
49 Mike Komisarek .25 .60
50 Petr Sykora .30 .75
51 Ilya Kovalchuk .40 1.00
52 Mike Modano .60 1.50
53 Scottie Upshall .30 .75
54 Rico Fata .25 .60
55 Sergei Gonchar .25 .60
56 Mike Dunham .30 .75
57 Olli Jokinen .40 1.00
58 Roman Turek .30 .75
59 Alexander Svitov .25 .60
60 Bill Guerin .40 1.00
61 Byron Dafoe .30 .75
62 Patrick Marleau .40 1.00
63 Patrik Elias .40 1.00
64 Brett Hull .75 2.00
65 Marco Sturm .25 .60
66 Andrew Raycroft .30 .75
67 Scott Gomez .30 .75
68 John LeClair .40 1.00
69 Kyle Calder .25 .60
70 Pierre-Marc Bouchard .40 1.00
71 Nikolai Antropov .25 .60
72 Jean-Sebastien Giguere .40 1.00
73 Marc Denis .30 .75
74 Martin Straka .25 .60
75 Peter Bondra .40 1.00
76 Ron Hainsey .25 .60
77 Brendan Shanahan .40 1.00
78 Evgeni Nabokov .30 .75
79 Glen Murray .30 .75
80 Martin Brodeur 1.00 2.50
81 Adam Deadmarsh .25 .60
82 Kevin Weekes .30 .75
83 Owen Nolan .40 1.00
84 Zdeno Chara .40 1.00
85 Andrew Cassels .50 1.25
86 Simon Gagne .75 2.00
87 Derian Hatcher .50 1.25
88 Mats Sundin .75 2.00
89 Chris Osgood .75 2.00
90 Henrik Zetterberg 1.00 2.50
91 Saku Koivu .75 2.00
92 Sergei Samsonov .60 1.50
93 Arron Asham .50 1.25
94 Teppo Numminen .50 1.25
95 Philippe Sauve .60 1.50
96 Jeff O'Neill .50 1.25
97 Luc Robitaille .75 2.00
98 Marty Turco .75 2.00
99 Niko Dimitrakos .50 1.25
100 Markus Naslund .75 2.00
101 Stephen Weiss .50 1.25
102 Ed Belfour .75 2.00
103 Roberto Luongo 1.25 3.00
104 Eric Lindros 1.25 3.00
105 Jocelyn Thibault .60 1.50
106 Marian Hossa .75 2.00
107 Teemu Selanne 1.50 4.00
108 Jaromir Jagr 2.50 6.00
109 Stanislav Chistov .50 1.25
110 Zigmund Palffy .75 2.00
111 P.J. Axelsson .50 1.25
112 Denis Arkhipov .50 1.25
113 Sean Burke .50 1.25
114 Todd Marchant .50 1.25
115 Maxim Afinogenov .50 1.25
116 Tomas Vokoun .60 1.50
117 Jason Blake .50 1.25
118 Jordan Leopold .50 1.25
119 Martin St. Louis .75 2.00
120 Pavel Datsyuk 1.25 3.00
121 Marc Savard .50 1.25
122 Marian Gaborik .75 2.00
123 Jamie Langenbrunner .60 1.50
124 Jarome Iginla 1.00 2.50
125 Al MacInnis 1.00 2.50
126 Nicklas Lidstrom .75 2.00
127 Georges Laraque 2.00 5.00
128 Justin Williams 2.00 5.00
129 Anson Carter 2.00 5.00
130 Chris Drury 2.00 5.00
131 Willie Mitchell 1.50 4.00
132 Rick Nash 2.50 6.00
133 Scott Stevens 2.50 6.00
134 Chris Pronger 2.50 6.00
135 Mario Lemieux 10.00 25.00
136 Steve Ott 1.50 4.00
137 Steve Yzerman 6.00 15.00
138 Dany Heatley 2.00 5.00
139 Ron Francis 3.00 8.00
140 Alexander Frolov 2.00 5.00
141 Tyler Arnason 1.50 4.00
142 Rob Blake 2.50 6.00
143 Patrick Lalime 2.00 5.00
144 Joe Thornton 4.00 10.00
145 David Aebischer 2.00 5.00
146 Alexei Yashin 2.00 5.00
147 Felix Potvin 4.00 10.00
148 Boyd Gordon RC 2.50 6.00
149 Tom Preissing RC 2.50 6.00
150 Brent Burns RC 6.00 15.00
151 Antoine Vermette RC 4.00 10.00
152 Antti Miettinen RC 3.00 8.00
153 Maxim Kondratiev RC 2.00 5.00
154 Christian Ehrhoff RC 2.50 6.00
155 Jiri Hudler RC 5.00 12.00
156 David Hale RC 2.00 5.00
157 Marek Svatos RC 4.00 10.00
158 Matthew Lombardi RC 2.50 6.00
159 Alexander Semin RC 6.00 15.00
160 John-Michael Liles RC 2.50 6.00
161 Dan Fritsche RC 2.00 5.00
162 Esa Pirnes RC 2.00 5.00
163 Cody McCormick RC 2.50 6.00
164 Lasse Kukkonen RC 2.00 5.00
165 Tim Gleason RC 2.00 5.00
166 Marek Zidlicky RC 2.50 6.00
167 Christoph Brandner RC 2.50 6.00
168 Sean Bergenheim RC 2.50 6.00
169 Mike Johnson 3.00 8.00
170 Eric Cole 3.00 8.00
171 Barret Jackman 3.00 8.00
172 Marcel Hossa 3.00 8.00
173 Tie Domi 4.00 10.00
174 Michael Rupp 3.00 8.00
175 Jeremy Roenick 8.00 20.00
176 Sergei Fedorov 8.00 20.00
177 Paul Kariya 5.00 12.00
178 Mike Ricci 3.00 8.00
179 Brenden Morrow 4.00 10.00
180 Dominik Hasek 8.00 20.00
181 P.J. Stock 3.00 8.00
182 Ales Hemsky 5.00 12.00
183 Todd Bertuzzi 5.00 12.00
184 Patrice Bergeron RC 10.00 25.00
185 Pavel Vorobiev RC 4.00 10.00
186 Milan Michalek RC 6.00 15.00
187 Matt Stajan RC 5.00 12.00
188 Dan Hamhuis RC 4.00 10.00
189 Joffrey Lupul RC 8.00 20.00
190 Eric Staal RC 12.00 30.00
191 Tuomo Ruutu RC 5.00 12.00
192 Nathan Horton RC 8.00 20.00
193 Dustin Brown RC 8.00 20.00
194 Jordin Tootoo RC 6.00 15.00
195 Joni Pitkanen RC 5.00 12.00
196 Peter Sejna RC 4.00 10.00
197 Chris Higgins RC 6.00 15.00
198 Marc-Andre Fleury RC 15.00 40.00
NNO Joe Thornton 5X7 PREVIEW 1.50 4.00

2003-04 Black Diamond Green
*1-84 SINGLE/100: 4X TO 10X
*85-126 DOUBLE/100: 2X TO 5X
*127-147 TRIPLE/100: .6X TO 1.5X
*148-168 TRIP.ROOK/100: .5X TO 1.2X
*169-183 QUAD/100: .3X TO .8X
*184-198 QUAD ROOK/100: .4X TO 1X

2003-04 Black Diamond Red
*1-84 SINGLE/50: 6X TO 15X
*85-126 DOUBLE/50: 3X TO 8X
*127-147 TRIPLE/50: 1X TO 2.5X
*148-168 TRIP.ROOK/50: .8X TO 2X
*169-183 QUAD/50: .5X TO 1.2X
*184-198 QUAD ROOK/50: .6X TO 1.5X

2003-04 Black Diamond Signature Gems
SG1 Maxim Afinogenov 6.00 15.00
SG2 Ray Bourque 15.00 40.00
SG4 Pavel Bure 10.00 25.00
SG5 Eric Cole 6.00 15.00
SG6 Mike Comrie 6.00 15.00
SG7 Simon Gagne 8.00 20.00
SG8 Rick Nash 12.50 30.00
SG9 Wayne Gretzky 150.00 400.00
SG10 Scott Hartnell 8.00 20.00
SG11 Martin Havlat 6.00 15.00
SG12 Ilya Kovalchuk 8.00 20.00
SG13 Gordie Howe 50.00 125.00
SG14 Curtis Joseph 8.00 20.00
SG15 Alexander Svitov 6.00 15.00
SG16 John LeClair 6.00 15.00
SG17 Steve Ott 6.00 15.00
SG18 Bobby Orr 100.00 200.00
SG19 Joe Thornton 15.00 40.00
SG20 Henrik Zetterberg 10.00 25.00
SG21 Marty Turco 8.00 20.00
SG22 Marian Hossa 12.00 30.00
SG23 Patrick Roy/24 200.00 400.00
SG24 Jean-Sebastien Giguere 6.00 15.00
SG25 Marian Gaborik 10.00 25.00
SG26 Todd Bertuzzi 8.00 20.00
SG27 Jason Spezza 12.50 30.00
SG28 Jarome Iginla 15.00 40.00
SG29 Sergei Samsonov 6.00 15.00
SG30 Jose Theodore 12.50 30.00
SG31 Justin Williams 6.00 15.00
SG32 Alexander Frolov 6.00 15.00
SG33 Brooks Orpik 6.00 15.00
SG34 Kurt Sauer 6.00 15.00
SG35 Steve Yzerman 25.00 60.00
SG36 Ed Belfour 20.00 50.00
SG37 Jeff Taffe 6.00 15.00

2003-04 Black Diamond Threads
*GREEN/99: .6X TO 1.5X BASIC JSY
*RED/50: 1X TO 2.5X BASIC JSY
DTDH Dany Heatley 8.00 20.00
DTPF Peter Forsberg 8.00 20.00
DTRN Rick Nash 8.00 20.00
DTIK Ilya Kovalchuk 8.00 20.00
DTJS Jason Spezza 6.00 15.00
DTJT Joe Thornton 8.00 20.00
DTML Mario Lemieux 10.00 25.00
DTMN Markus Naslund 6.00 15.00
DTMB Martin Brodeur 10.00 25.00
DTMO Mike Modano 8.00 20.00
DTAZ Alexei Zhamnov 5.00 12.00
DTAF Alexander Frolov 5.00 12.00
DTAS Alexander Svitov 5.00 12.00
DTKC Kyle Calder 5.00 12.00
DTMA Maxim Afinogenov 5.00 12.00
DTSN Scott Niedermayer 5.00 12.00
DTDB Daniel Briere 5.00 12.00
DTJB Jay Bouwmeester 5.00 12.00
DTMT Marty Turco 6.00 15.00
DTEJ Ed Jovanovski 5.00 12.00
DTED Eric Daze 5.00 12.00
DTJG Jean-Sebastien Giguere 5.00 12.00
DTTH Jocelyn Thibault 5.00 12.00
DTKP Keith Primeau 5.00 12.00
DTMD Marc Denis 5.00 12.00
DTDU Mike Dunham 5.00 12.00
DTCP Chris Pronger 5.00 12.00
DTDA David Aebischer 5.00 12.00
DTDW Doug Weight 5.00 12.00
DTAT Alex Tanguay 5.00 12.00
DTBM Brenden Morrow 5.00 12.00
DTPB Peter Bondra 5.00 12.00
DTJR Jeremy Roenick 5.00 12.00
DTMM Mark Messier 12.50 30.00
DTEB Ed Belfour 6.00 15.00
DTRL Roberto Luongo 8.00 20.00
DTTE Jose Theodore 8.00 20.00
DTPK Paul Kariya 6.00 15.00
DTEL Eric Lindros 6.00 15.00

DTMS Mats Sundin 6.00 15.00
DTBS Brendan Shanahan 6.00 15.00
DTMH Marian Hossa 6.00 15.00

2005-06 Black Diamond

COMP.SET w/o SP's (84) 10.00 20.00
1 Joffrey Lupul .15 .40
2 Steve Rucchin .15 .40
3 Riku Hahl .15 .40
4 Shawn McEachern .15 .40
5 Marc Savard .15 .40
6 Philippe Sauve .20 .50
7 Nick Boynton .15 .40
8 Martin Lapointe .15 .40
9 Maxim Afinogenov .15 .40
10 Chris Drury .20 .50
11 Mike Grier .15 .40
12 Jordan Leopold .15 .40
13 Darren McCarty .15 .40
14 Martin Gelinas .15 .40
15 Eric Staal .30 .75
16 Jeff O'Neill .15 .40
17 Erik Cole .15 .40
18 Rod Brind'Amour .25 .60
19 Jocelyn Thibault .20 .50
20 Tyler Arnason .15 .40
21 Bryan Berard .15 .40
22 Eric Daze .20 .50
23 Rob Blake .25 .60
24 Nikolai Zherdev .15 .40
25 Marc Denis .20 .50
26 Justin Williams .20 .50
27 Brenden Morrow .20 .50
28 Sergei Zubov .20 .50
29 Jere Lehtinen .20 .50
30 Henrik Zetterberg .30 .75
31 Ty Conklin .20 .50
32 Ryan Smyth .20 .50
33 Jason Smith .15 .40
34 Chris Chelios .25 .60
35 Stephen Weiss .15 .40
36 Olli Jokinen .25 .60
37 Gary Roberts .15 .40
38 Alexander Frolov .15 .40
39 Mathieu Garon .20 .50
40 Lubomir Visnovsky .15 .40
41 Dwayne Roloson .20 .50
42 Pascal Dupuis .15 .40
43 Brian Rolston .20 .50
44 Filip Kuba .15 .40
45 Richard Zednik .15 .40
46 Sheldon Souray .15 .40
47 Steve Sullivan .15 .40
48 Jordin Tootoo .25 .60
49 Tomas Vokoun .20 .50
50 Scott Walker .15 .40
51 Martin Brodeur .60 1.50
52 Scott Niedermayer .25 .60
53 Brian Rafalski .20 .50
54 Alexander Mogilny .20 .50
55 Bobby Holik .15 .40
56 Kevin Weekes .20 .50
57 Jamie Lundmark .15 .40
58 Michael Peca .20 .50
59 Mark Parrish .15 .40
60 Adrian Aucoin .15 .40
61 Wade Redden .15 .40
62 Zdeno Chara .25 .60
63 Simon Gagne .25 .60
64 Robert Esche .20 .50
65 Mike Comrie .20 .50
66 Shane Doan .20 .50
67 Derian Hatcher .15 .40
68 Ladislav Nagy .15 .40
69 Milan Kraft .15 .40
70 Ryan Malone .15 .40
71 Marco Sturm .15 .40
72 Brad Stuart .15 .40
73 Alyn McCauley .15 .40
74 Patrick Lalime .20 .50
75 Dustin Brown .25 .60
76 Fredrik Modin .15 .40
77 Dave Andreychuk .25 .60
78 Brian Leetch .20 .50
79 Tie Domi .20 .50
80 Ed Jovanovski .20 .50
81 Brendan Morrison .15 .40
82 Dan Cloutier .20 .50
83 Brendan Witt .15 .40
84 Martin Biron .20 .50
85 Manny Legace 1.00 2.50
86 Jean-Sebastien Giguere 1.00 2.50
87 Sergei Fedorov 1.50 4.00
88 Andrew Raycroft .75 2.00
89 Sergei Samsonov .75 2.00
90 Miroslav Satan .75 2.00
91 Miikka Kiprusoff 1.00 2.50
92 David Aebischer .75 2.00
93 Milan Hejduk .75 2.00
94 Marty Turco 1.00 2.50
95 Curtis Joseph 1.25 3.00
96 Nicklas Lidstrom 1.00 2.50
97 Roberto Luongo 1.50 4.00
98 Zigmund Palffy 1.00 2.50
99 Luc Robitaille 1.00 2.50
100 Mike Ribeiro .60 1.50
101 Michael Ryder .75 2.00
102 Scott Gomez .75 2.00
103 Patrik Elias 1.00 2.50
104 Alexei Yashin .75 2.00
105 Daniel Alfredsson 1.00 2.50
106 Martin Havlat 1.00 2.50
107 Tony Amonte .75 2.00
108 John LeClair 1.00 2.50
109 Brett Hull 2.00 5.00
110 Marc-Andre Fleury 2.00 5.00
111 Mark Recchi 1.25 3.00
112 Patrick Marleau 1.00 2.50
113 Jonathan Cheechoo .75 2.00
114 Chris Pronger 1.00 2.50
115 Doug Weight 1.00 2.50
116 Brad Richards 1.00 2.50
117 Glen Murray .75 2.00
118 Tuomo Ruutu 1.00 2.50
119 Pavol Demitra 1.25 3.00
120 David Legwand .75 2.00
121 Eric Lindros 1.50 4.00
122 Rick DiPietro .75 2.00
123 Al MacInnis 1.25 3.00
124 Joe Nieuwendyk .75 2.00
125 Trevor Linden 1.00 2.50
126 Olaf Kolzig 1.00 2.50
127 Dany Heatley 1.50 4.00
128 Kari Lehtonen 1.50 4.00
129 Patrice Bergeron 2.50 6.00
130 Alex Tanguay 2.00 5.00
131 Paul Kariya 2.00 5.00
132 Mike Modano 3.00 8.00
133 Bill Guerin 2.00 5.00
134 Pavel Datsyuk 3.00 8.00
135 Brendan Shanahan 2.00 5.00
136 Saku Koivu 2.00 5.00
137 Marian Hossa 2.00 5.00
138 Jason Spezza 2.00 5.00
139 Jeremy Roenick 3.00 8.00
140 Keith Primeau 1.50 4.00
141 Evgeni Nabokov 1.50 4.00
142 Vincent Lecavalier 2.00 5.00
143 Ed Belfour 2.00 5.00
144 Jason Allison 1.50 4.00
145 Markus Naslund 2.00 5.00
146 Keith Tkachuk 2.00 5.00
147 Nikolai Khabibulin 2.00 5.00
148 Andrew Alberts RC 2.00 5.00
149 Andy Wozniewski RC 2.50 6.00
150 Brandon Bochenski RC 3.00 8.00
151 Brent Seabrook RC 6.00 15.00
152 Cam Ward RC 5.00 12.00
153 Chris Campoli RC 2.00 5.00
154 David Leneveu RC 2.50 6.00
155 Duncan Keith RC 6.00 15.00
156 Henrik Lundqvist RC 15.00 40.00
157 Jay McClement RC 2.00 5.00
158 Johan Franzen RC 5.00 12.00
159 Jussi Jokinen RC 3.00 8.00
160 Keith Ballard RC 2.50 6.00
161 Kevin Dallman RC 2.50 6.00
162 Maxime Talbot RC 3.00 8.00
163 Niklas Nordgren RC 3.00 8.00
164 Peter Budaj RC 4.00 10.00
165 Petteri Nokelainen RC 2.00 5.00
166 Rene Bourque RC 3.00 8.00
167 Jeff Woywitka RC 2.00 5.00
168 Ryan Hollweg RC 2.00 5.00
169 Ilya Kovalchuk 3.00 8.00
170 Joe Thornton 5.00 12.00
171 Jarome Iginla 4.00 10.00
172 Joe Sakic 6.00 15.00
173 Peter Forsberg 6.00 15.00
174 Rick Nash 3.00 8.00
175 Steve Yzerman 8.00 20.00
176 Marian Gaborik 3.00 8.00
177 Jose Theodore 3.00 8.00
178 Jaromir Jagr 10.00 25.00
179 Mark Messier 6.00 15.00
180 Dominik Hasek 5.00 12.00
181 Mario Lemieux 12.00 30.00
182 Martin St. Louis 3.00 8.00
183 Mats Sundin 3.00 8.00
184 Wayne Gretzky 20.00 50.00
185 Gordie Howe 10.00 25.00
186 Ray Bourque 5.00 12.00
187 Patrick Roy 8.00 20.00
188 Bryan Trottier 3.00 8.00
189 Cam Neely 3.00 8.00
190 Gilbert Brule RC 5.00 12.00
191 Alexander Ovechkin RC 250.00 600.00
192 Zach Parise RC 8.00 20.00
193 Sidney Crosby RC 300.00 800.00
194 Dion Phaneuf RC 8.00 20.00
195 Jeff Carter RC 8.00 20.00
196 Corey Perry RC 15.00 40.00
197 Thomas Vanek RC 10.00 25.00
198 Ryan Getzlaf RC 12.00 30.00
199 Mike Richards RC 10.00 25.00
200 Robert Nilsson RC 5.00 12.00
201 Alexander Steen RC 8.00 20.00
202 Rostislav Olesz RC 4.00 10.00
203 Wojtek Wolski RC 4.00 10.00
204 Ryan Suter RC 6.00 15.00
205 Hannu Toivonen RC 5.00 12.00
206 Yann Danis RC 4.00 10.00
207 Jim Howard RC 8.00 20.00
208 Andrej Meszaros RC 4.00 10.00
209 Braydon Coburn RC 5.00 12.00
210 Alexander Perezhogin RC 4.00 10.00
211 Dustin Penner RC 5.00 12.00
212 Zenon Konopka RC 2.00 5.00
213 Jim Slater RC 2.50 6.00
214 Adam Berkhoel RC 2.50 6.00
215 Jordan Sigalet RC 2.00 5.00
216 Milan Jurcina RC 2.50 6.00
217 Ben Walter RC 2.00 5.00
218 Chris Thorburn RC 2.50 6.00
219 Daniel Paille RC 3.00 8.00
220 Nathan Paetsch RC 2.50 6.00
221 Andrew Ladd RC 4.00 10.00
222 Kevin Nastiuk RC 2.00 5.00
223 Danny Richmond RC 2.00 5.00
224 Cam Barker RC 2.50 6.00
225 Corey Crawford RC 10.00 25.00
226 James Wisniewski RC 2.50 6.00
227 Brad Richardson RC 3.00 8.00
228 Vitaly Kolesnik RC 2.50 6.00
229 Ole-Kristian Tollefsen RC 2.50 6.00
230 Jaroslav Balastik RC 2.00 5.00
231 Geoff Platt RC 2.50 6.00
232 Alexandre Picard RC 2.00 5.00
233 Joakim Lindstrom RC 2.00 5.00
234 Junior Lessard RC 2.00 5.00
235 Vojtech Polak RC 2.00 5.00
236 Kyle Quincey RC 2.50 6.00
237 Valtteri Filppula RC 4.00 10.00
238 Brett Lebda RC 2.00 5.00
239 Kyle Brodziak RC 2.00 5.00
240 Brad Winchester RC 3.00 8.00
241 Danny Syvret RC 2.00 5.00
242 Matt Greene RC 2.00 5.00
243 J-F Jacques RC 2.00 5.00
244 Anthony Stewart RC 2.50 6.00
245 Rob Globke RC 2.00 5.00
246 Petr Taticek RC 2.50 6.00
247 Jeff Tambellini RC 2.00 5.00
248 Petr Kanko RC 3.00 8.00
249 George Parros RC 2.00 5.00
250 Yanick Lehoux RC 3.00 8.00
251 Richard Petiot RC 2.50 6.00
252 Mikko Koivu RC 4.00 10.00
253 Derek Boogaard RC 5.00 12.00
254 Matt Foy RC 2.00 5.00
255 Andrei Kostitsyn RC 4.00 10.00
256 Maxim Lapierre RC 3.00 8.00
257 Kevin Klein RC 2.00 5.00
258 Pekka Rinne RC 5.00 12.00
259 Barry Tallackson RC 2.50 6.00
260 Jason Ryznar RC 2.00 5.00
261 Jeremy Colliton RC 3.00 8.00
262 Bruno Gervais RC 2.00 5.00
263 Petr Prucha RC 3.00 8.00
264 Al Montoya RC 3.00 8.00
265 Christoph Schubert RC 2.00 5.00
266 Patrick Eaves RC 3.00 8.00
267 R.J. Umberger RC 3.00 8.00
268 Ben Eager RC 2.50 6.00
269 Alexandre Picard RC 2.00 5.00
270 Stefan Ruzicka RC 2.00 5.00
271 Ryan Whitney RC 3.00 8.00
272 Erik Christensen RC 2.00 5.00
273 Colby Armstrong RC 3.00 8.00
274 Steve Bernier RC 3.00 8.00
275 Dimitri Patzold RC 2.00 5.00
276 Ryane Clowe RC 4.00 10.00
277 Josh Gorges RC 2.50 6.00
278 Grant Stevenson RC 2.00 5.00
279 Lee Stempniak RC 3.00 8.00
280 Colin Hemingway RC 2.00 5.00
281 Dennis Wideman RC 2.00 5.00
282 Evgeny Artyukhin RC 2.50 6.00
283 Ryan Craig RC 2.00 5.00
284 Paul Ranger RC 2.00 5.00
285 Darren Reid RC 2.00 5.00
286 Gerald Coleman RC 2.00 5.00
287 Staffan Kronwall RC 2.00 5.00
288 Jay Harrison RC 2.50 6.00
289 Kevin Bieksa RC 5.00 12.00
290 Rob McVicar RC 3.00 8.00
291 Tomas Mojzis RC 2.00 5.00
292 Jakub Klepis RC 2.00 5.00
293 Tomas Fleischmann RC 3.00 8.00
294 Mike Green RC 4.00 10.00

2005-06 Black Diamond Emerald

*1-84 VET/25.: 12X TO 30X BASIC SNGL
*85-126 VET/25.: 3X TO 8X BASIC DBLE
*127-147 VET/25: 1.5X TO 4X BASIC TRPL
*148-168 ROOK/25: 1.5X TO 4X BASIC RC
*169-189 VET/25: 1X TO 2.5X BASIC QUAD
*QUAD ROOKIE: 1X TO 2.5X
156 Henrik Lundqvist 75.00 150.00
194 Dion Phaneuf 40.00 100.00

2005-06 Black Diamond Ruby

*1-84 VET/100: 8X TO 20X BASIC SNGL
*85-126 VET/100: 2X TO 5X BASIC DBLE
*127-147 VET/100: 1X TO 2.5X BASIC TRPL
*148-168 ROOK/100: .8X TO 2X BASIC RC
*169-189 VET/100: .6X TO 1.5X BASIC QUAD
*190-210 ROOK/100: .5X TO 1.2X BASIC RC

2005-06 Black Diamond Gemography

COMMON CARD 4.00 10.00
SEMISTARS 5.00 12.00
UNLISTED STARS 6.00 15.00
GAC Anson Carter 5.00 12.00
GAV Antoine Vermette 6.00 12.00
GBA Milan Bartovic 4.00 10.00
GBB Brad Boyes 6.00 12.00
GBI Martin Biron 6.00 12.00
GCD Chris Drury 6.00 12.00
GDB Dustin Brown 6.00 15.00
GDH Dany Heatley 12.00 30.00
GEC Erik Cole 6.00 15.00
GFS Fredrik Sjostrom 4.00 10.00
GGH Gordie Howe 40.00 100.00
GHA Dominik Hasek 15.00 40.00
GHO Marcel Hossa 4.00 10.00
GIK Ilya Kovalchuk 15.00 40.00
GJC Jonathan Cheechoo 12.50 30.00
GJI Jarome Iginla 15.00 40.00
GJR Jeremy Roenick 10.00 25.00
GJT Joe Thornton 20.00 50.00
GKD Kris Draper 5.00 12.00
GLR Luc Robitaille 10.00 25.00
GMB Martin Brodeur 50.00 125.00
GMC Mike Comrie 4.00 10.00
GMF Marc-Andre Fleury 15.00 40.00
GMG Marian Gaborik 20.00 50.00
GMH Martin Havlat 6.00 15.00
GMN Markus Naslund 6.00 12.00
GMP Mark Popovic 4.00 10.00
GMR Michael Ryder 8.00 15.00
GNK Nikolai Khabibulin 8.00 15.00
GNZ Nikolai Zherdev 4.00 10.00
GPB Patrice Bergeron 6.00 15.00
GRB Ray Bourque 30.00 80.00
GRE Robert Esche 4.00 10.00
GRK Ryan Kesler 10.00 25.00
GSB Sean Bergenheim 4.00 10.00
GSL Martin St. Louis 6.00 15.00
GSP Jason Spezza 12.00 30.00
GSS Sheldon Souray 4.00 10.00
GTM Travis Moen 4.00 10.00
GTR Tuomo Ruutu 6.00 12.00
GTS Timofei Shishkanov 4.00 10.00
GWG Wayne Gretzky 250.00 600.00

2005-06 Black Diamond Gemography Emerald

*EMERALD: .6X TO 1.5X
GWG Wayne Gretzky 400.00 1000.00

2005-06 Black Diamond Gemography Ruby

*RUBY: .5X TO 1.2X

2005-06 Black Diamond Jerseys

*RUBY/100: .5X TO 1.2X BASIC JSY
JAM Al MacInnis 4.00 10.00
JBH Brett Hull 5.00 12.00
JBO Mike Bossy 5.00 12.00
JBS Brendan Shanahan 5.00 12.00
JCC Chris Chelios 5.00 12.00
JCJ Curtis Joseph 5.00 12.00
JEB Ed Belfour 5.00 12.00
JEJ Ed Jovanovski 3.00 8.00
JGL Guy Lafleur 6.00 15.00
JHA Dominik Hasek 6.00 15.00
JJF Jeff Friesen 3.00 8.00
JJI Jarome Iginla 6.00 15.00
JJJ Jaromir Jagr 6.00 15.00
JJN Joe Nieuwendyk 3.00 8.00
JJO Jose Theodore 4.00 10.00
JJR Jeremy Roenick 5.00 12.00
JJS Joe Sakic 8.00 20.00
JJT Joe Thornton 6.00 15.00
JKP Keith Primeau 3.00 8.00
JMB Martin Brodeur 10.00 25.00
JMG Marian Gaborik 6.00 15.00
JMH Milan Hejduk 3.00 8.00
JML Mario Lemieux 15.00 40.00
JMM Mike Modano 5.00 12.00
JMS Mark Messier 8.00 20.00
JOJ Olli Jokinen 3.00 8.00
JON Owen Nolan 4.00 8.00
JPB Pavel Bure 5.00 12.00
JPE Peter Bondra 4.00 10.00
JPF Peter Forsberg 6.00 15.00
JPK Paul Kariya 5.00 12.00
JPL Patrick Lalime 3.00 8.00
JRL Roberto Luongo 6.00 15.00
JRN Rick Nash 5.00 12.00
JSF Sergei Fedorov 5.00 12.00
JSK Saku Koivu 5.00 12.00
JSL Martin St. Louis 4.00 10.00
JSU Mats Sundin 5.00 12.00
JSY Steve Yzerman 12.00 30.00
JTS Teemu Selanne 5.00 12.00
JWG Wayne Gretzky 15.00 40.00

2005-06 Black Diamond Jersey Duals

*DUAL: 1.25X TO 3X SINGLE
DJDH Dany Heatley 12.50 30.00

2006-07 Black Diamond

1 Corey Perry .50 1.25
2 Ilya Bryzgalov .30 .75
3 Scott Niedermayer .30 .75
4 Slava Kozlov .20 .50
5 Jim Slater .20 .50
6 Hannu Toivonen .25 .60
7 Marc Savard .20 .50
8 Zdeno Chara .30 .75
9 Glen Murray .25 .60
10 Daniel Briere .30 .75
11 Maxim Afinogenov .20 .50
12 Thomas Vanek .25 .60
13 Daymond Langkow .20 .50
14 Chuck Kobasew .20 .50
15 Rod Brind'Amour .30 .75
16 Justin Williams .25 .60
17 Mike Commodore .20 .50
18 Michal Handzus .25 .60
19 Brent Seabrook .20 .50
20 Nikolai Khabibulin .30 .75
21 Peter Budaj .25 .60
22 Wojtek Wolski .25 .60
23 Fredrik Modin .20 .50
24 Pascal Leclaire .25 .60
25 Bryan Berard .20 .50
26 Brenden Morrow .25 .60
27 Sergei Zubov .25 .60
28 Jere Lehtinen .20 .50
29 Kris Draper .20 .50
30 Tomas Holmstrom .25 .60
31 Dwayne Roloson .25 .60
32 Jarret Stoll .25 .60
33 Shawn Horcoff .20 .50
34 Fernando Pisani .20 .50
35 Olli Jokinen .30 .75
36 Nathan Horton .30 .75
37 Todd Bortuzzi .30 .76
38 Mike Cammalleri .20 .50
39 Craig Conroy .20 .50
40 Pavol Demitra .40 1.00
41 Mark Parrish .20 .50
42 Manny Fernandez .20 .50
43 Pierre-Marc Bouchard .30 .75
44 Sergei Samsonov .25 .60
45 Alex Kovalev .25 .60
46 Jason Arnott .25 .60
47 Steve Sullivan .20 .50
48 Scott Hartnell .20 .50
49 Scott Gomez .25 .60
50 Brian Gionta .20 .50
51 Zach Parise .30 .75
52 Rick DiPietro .25 .60
53 Robert Nilsson .20 .50
54 Jason Blake .20 .50
55 Petr Prucha .25 .60
56 Martin Straka .20 .50
57 Martin Gerber .25 .60
58 Wade Redden .20 .50
59 Patrick Eaves .20 .50
60 Joni Pitkanen .20 .50
61 Mike Richards .25 .60
62 Antero Niittymaki .25 .60
63 Curtis Joseph .40 1.00
64 Ladislav Nagy .20 .50
65 Ed Jovanovski .25 .60
66 Colby Armstrong .25 .60
67 Ryan Whitney .25 .60
68 Ryan Malone .20 .50
69 Steve Bernier .20 .50
70 Evgeni Nabokov .25 .60
71 Vesa Toskala .25 .60
72 Keith Tkachuk .30 .75
73 Bill Guerin .30 .75
74 Manny Legace .25 .60
75 Vaclav Prospal .20 .50
76 Marc Denis .25 .60
77 Martin St. Louis .30 .75
78 Andrew Raycroft .25 .60
79 Darcy Tucker .25 .60
80 Daniel Sedin .40 1.00
81 Henrik Sedin .40 1.00
82 Brendan Morrison .20 .50
83 Dainius Zubrus .20 .50
84 Olaf Kolzig .30 .75
85 Teemu Selanne 2.50 6.00
86 Jean-Sebastien Giguere 1.25 3.00
87 Chris Pronger 1.25 3.00
88 Marian Hossa 1.25 3.00
89 Brad Boyes .75 2.00
90 Chris Drury 1.00 2.50
91 Ryan Miller 1.25 3.00
92 Alex Tanguay .75 2.00
93 Erik Cole .75 2.00
94 Tuomo Ruutu 1.25 3.00
95 Martin Havlat .75 2.00
96 Jose Theodore 1.25 3.00
97 Marek Svatos .75 2.00
98 Sergei Fedorov 2.00 5.00
99 Gilbert Brule 1.00 2.50
100 Eric Lindros 2.00 5.00
101 Marty Turco 1.25 3.00
102 Pavel Datsyuk 2.00 5.00
103 Ales Hemsky 1.00 2.50
104 Ryan Smyth 1.00 2.50
105 Jay Bouwmeester .75 2.00
106 Rob Blake 1.25 3.00
107 Alexander Frolov .75 2.00
108 Mikko Koivu 1.00 2.50
109 Cristobal Huet 1.00 2.50
110 Mike Ribeiro .75 2.00
111 Tomas Vokoun 1.00 2.50
112 Patrik Elias 1.25 3.00
113 Alexei Yashin 1.00 2.50
114 Miroslav Satan 1.00 2.50
115 Henrik Lundqvist 3.00 8.00
116 Daniel Alfredsson 1.25 3.00
117 Simon Gagne 1.25 3.00
118 Jeff Carter 1.00 2.50
119 Shane Doan 1.00 2.50
120 Jeremy Roenick 2.00 5.00
121 Mark Recchi 1.50 4.00
122 Patrick Marleau 1.25 3.00
123 Doug Weight 1.25 3.00
124 Brad Richards 1.25 3.00
125 Alexander Steen .75 2.00
126 Michael Peca 1.00 2.50
127 Kari Lehtonen 1.50 4.00
128 Patrice Bergeron 2.50 6.00
129 Miikka Kiprusoff 2.00 5.00
130 Dion Phaneuf 1.50 4.00
131 Eric Staal 2.50 6.00
132 Cam Ward 2.00 5.00
133 Milan Hejduk 1.50 4.00
134 Mike Modano 3.00 8.00
135 Henrik Zetterberg 2.50 6.00
136 Nicklas Lidstrom 2.00 5.00
137 Ed Belfour 2.00 5.00
138 Saku Koivu 2.00 5.00
139 Michael Ryder 1.25 3.00
140 Paul Kariya 2.00 5.00
141 Brendan Shanahan 2.00 5.00
142 Dany Heatley 1.50 4.00
143 Marc-Andre Fleury 4.00 10.00
144 Jonathan Cheechoo 1.50 4.00
145 Vincent Lecavalier 2.00 5.00
146 Markus Naslund 2.00 5.00
147 Roberto Luongo 3.00 8.00
148A Roman Polak RC 1.50 4.00
148B Ilya Kovalchuk 2.50 6.00
149A Joel Perrault RC 1.25 3.00
149B Ray Bourque 4.00 10.00
150A Yan Stastny RC 1.25 3.00
150B Cam Neely 2.50 6.00
151A Konstantin Pushkarev RC 1.50 4.00
151B Jarome Iginla 3.00 8.00
152A Jarkko Immonen RC 1.50 4.00
152B Joe Sakic 5.00 12.00
153A Marc-Antoine Pouliot RC 1.25 3.00
153B Patrick Roy 6.00 15.00
154A Jeremy Williams RC 1.25 3.00
154B Rick Nash 2.50 6.00
155A Michel Ouellet RC 1.50 4.00
155B Dominik Hasek 4.00 10.00
156A Tomas Kopecky RC 1.50 4.00
156B Gordie Howe 5.00 12.00
157A Keith Yandle RC 3.00 8.00
157B Wayne Gretzky 8.00 20.00
158A Marc-Edouard Vlasic RC 2.00 5.00
158B Marian Gaborik 2.50 6.00
159A Shane O'Brien RC 1.25 3.00
159B Jean Beliveau 2.50 6.00
160A Ryan Shannon RC 1.25 3.00
160B Martin Brodeur 6.00 15.00
161A John Oduya RC 2.00 5.00
161B Jaromir Jagr 8.00 20.00
162A Fredrik Norrena RC 1.25 3.00
162B Jason Spezza 2.50 6.00
163A Kristopher Letang RC 5.00 12.00
163B Peter Forsberg 5.00 12.00
164A Niklas Backstrom RC 2.50 6.00
164B Sidney Crosby 10.00 25.00
165A D.J. King RC 1.25 3.00
165B Mario Lemieux 10.00 25.00
166A Patrick Thoresen RC 1.25 3.00
166B Joe Thornton 4.00 10.00
167A Patrick Fischer RC 1.25 3.00
167B Mats Sundin 2.50 6.00
168A Mikko Lehtonen RC 1.50 4.00
168B Alexander Ovechkin 10.00 25.00
190 Mark Stuart RC 2.50 6.00
191 Eric Fehr RC 4.00 10.00
192 Ryan Potulny RC 2.50 6.00
193 Ian White RC 3.00 8.00
194 Alexei Kaigorodov RC 2.50 6.00
195 Noah Welch RC 2.50 6.00
196 Shea Weber RC 6.00 15.00
197 Enver Lisin RC 2.50 6.00
198 Matt Carle RC 2.50 6.00
199 Patrick O'Sullivan RC 4.00 10.00
200 Anze Kopitar RC 12.00 30.00
201 Travis Zajac RC 5.00 12.00
202 Phil Kessel RC 8.00 20.00
203 G. Latendresse RC 4.00 10.00
204 Nigel Dawes RC 2.50 6.00
205 Jordan Staal RC 8.00 20.00
206 Paul Stastny RC 6.00 15.00
207 Luc Bourdon RC 4.00 10.00
208 Ladislav Smid RC 2.50 6.00
209 Loui Eriksson RC 5.00 12.00
210 Evgeni Malkin RC 25.00 60.00

2006-07 Black Diamond Ruby

*1-84 VETS/100: 6X TO 15X BASIC CARDS
*85-126 VET/100: 1.5X TO 4X BASIC CARDS
*86-147 VET/100: 1X TO 2.5X BASIC CARDS
*148-210 VET/100: 1.2X TO 3X BASIC CARD
*148-210 ROOK/100: 1.5X TO 4X BASIC RC

2006-07 Black Diamond Gemography

GAB Adam Berkhoel 3.00 8.00
GAL Andrew Ladd 3.00 8.00
GAO Alexander Ovechkin SP 125.00 300.00
GBB Brandon Bochenski 3.00 8.00
GBL Brian Leetch SP 25.00 60.00
GBM Bryan McCabe EXCH 3.00 8.00
GBW Brad Winchester 3.00 8.00
GCA Jeff Carter 6.00 15.00
GCB Cam Barker 3.00 8.00
GCK Chuck Kobasew 3.00 8.00
GCP Chris Phillips 3.00 8.00
GCS Cory Stillman 3.00 8.00
GDA David Aebischer 4.00 10.00
GDP Dion Phaneuf 8.00 20.00
GDR Danny Richmond 3.00 8.00
GDW Doug Weight 3.00 8.00
GEC Erik Christensen 4.00 10.00
GGH Gordie Howe SP 50.00 100.00
GGL Georges Laraque 3.00 8.00
GGM Glen Murray 4.00 10.00
GHA Scott Hartnell 3.00 8.00
GHZ Henrik Zetterberg SP 10.00 25.00
GJC Jonathan Cheechoo 6.00 15.00
GJG Josh Gorges 3.00 8.00
GJH Jim Howard 6.00 15.00
GJI Jarome Iginla SP 12.00 30.00
GJJ Jussi Jokinen 4.00 10.00
GJO Jeff O'Neill 3.00 8.00
GJP Joni Pitkanen SP 8.00 20.00
GJS Jim Slater 3.00 8.00
GJT Jose Theodore 6.00 15.00
GKD Kris Draper SP 10.00 25.00
GKL Kari Lehtonen SP 10.00 25.00
GKT Kimmo Timonen 3.00 8.00
GMG Marian Gaborik SP 15.00 40.00
GMH Marian Hossa SP 10.00 25.00
GMK Miikka Kiprusoff SP 15.00 40.00
GML Mario Lemieux SP 60.00 120.00
GMP Mark Parrish 3.00 8.00
GMR Mike Ribeiro 3.00 8.00
GMS Miroslav Satan 4.00 10.00
GMT Marty Turco SP 10.00 25.00
GMV Mike Van Ryn 3.00 8.00
GMZ Marek Zidlicky 3.00 8.00
GNH Nathan Horton 5.00 12.00
GPB Patrice Bergeron SP 10.00 25.00
GPM Patrick Marleau 5.00 12.00
GPP Petr Prucha 3.00 8.00
GPR Paul Ranger 3.00 8.00
GRB Rene Bourque 3.00 8.00
GRM Ryan Miller SP 10.00 25.00
GRN Rick Nash SP 15.00 40.00
GSC Sidney Crosby 75.00 150.00
GSH Shawn Horcoff 3.00 8.00
GTC Ty Conklin 4.00 10.00
GVT Vesa Toskala 4.00 10.00
GWG Wayne Gretzky SP 200.00 500.00

2006-07 Black Diamond Jerseys

JAA Arron Asham 2.50 6.00
JAF Alexander Frolov 2.50 6.00
JAH Ales Hemsky 3.00 8.00
JAK Alex Kovalev 3.00 8.00
JAL Jason Allison 3.00 8.00
JAM Andrej Meszaros 2.50 6.00
JAO Alexander Ovechkin SP 15.00 40.00
JAS Alexander Steen 2.50 6.00
JAT Alex Tanguay 2.50 6.00
JBB Brad Boyes 2.50 6.00
JBE Patrice Bergeron 5.00 12.00
JBG Bill Guerin 4.00 10.00
JBJ Barret Jackman 2.50 6.00
JBL Brian Leetch 3.00 8.00
JBM Brendan Morrison 2.50 6.00
JBO Brandon Bochenski 2.50 6.00
JBR Martin Brodeur 10.00 25.00
JBS Brad Stuart 2.50 6.00
JBU Peter Budaj 3.00 8.00
JCD Chris Drury 3.00 8.00
JCJ Curtis Joseph 5.00 12.00
JCK Chuck Kobasew 2.50 6.00
JCO Mike Comrie 3.00 8.00
JCP Corey Perry 6.00 15.00
JCW Cam Ward 4.00 10.00
JDB Donald Brashear 2.50 6.00
JDC Dan Cloutier 3.00 8.00
JDE Pavol Demitra 5.00 12.00
JDH Dan Hamhuis 3.00 8.00
JDK Duncan Keith 3.00 8.00
JDP Dion Phaneuf 3.00 8.00
JDW Doug Weight 4.00 10.00
JEA Evgeni Artyukhin 2.50 6.00
JEB Ed Belfour 4.00 10.00
JEL Eric Lindros 6.00 15.00
JGA Simon Gagne 4.00 10.00
JHE Milan Hejduk 3.00 8.00
JHZ Henrik Zetterberg 5.00 12.00
JIK Ilya Kovalchuk 4.00 10.00
JJA Jason Arnott 3.00 8.00
JJB Jay Bouwmeester 2.50 6.00
JJF Jeff Friesen 2.50 6.00
JJG Jean-Sebastien Giguere 4.00 10.00
JJH Jeff Hoggan 2.50 6.00
JJJ Jaromir Jagr 12.00 30.00
JJK Jakub Klepis 2.50 6.00
JJL Joffrey Lupul 2.50 6.00
JJN Joe Nieuwendyk 3.00 8.00
JJS Joe Sakic 8.00 20.00
JJT Joe Thornton 6.00 15.00
JKD Kris Draper 2.50 6.00
JKO Andrei Kostitsyn 3.00 8.00
JKT Keith Tkachuk 4.00 10.00
JLA Andrew Ladd 2.50 6.00
JLE Jere Lehtinen 2.50 6.00
JMA Mark Bell 2.50 6.00
JMB Martin Biron 3.00 8.00
JMC Mike Cammalleri 2.50 6.00
JMH Marian Hossa 4.00 10.00
JMI Mike Komisarek 2.50 6.00
JMJ Milan Jurcina 2.50 6.00
JMK Miikka Kiprusoff 4.00 10.00
JMM Mike Modano 6.00 15.00
JMN Markus Naslund 4.00 10.00
JMO Shaone Morrisonn 2.50 6.00
JMP Michael Peca 3.00 8.00
JMR Mark Recchi 5.00 12.00
JMS Marek Svatos 2.50 6.00
JNH Nathan Horton 4.00 10.00
JNK Nikolai Khabibulin 4.00 10.00
JPA Daniel Paille 3.00 8.00
JPB Peter Bondra 4.00 10.00
JPD Pavel Datsyuk 6.00 15.00
JPF Peter Forsberg 8.00 20.00
JPK Paul Kariya 4.00 10.00
JRB Rod Brind'Amour 4.00 10.00
JRC Ryan Craig 2.50 6.00
JRD Rick DiPietro 3.00 8.00
JRH Ryan Hollweg 2.50 6.00
JRK Rostislav Klesla 2.50 6.00
JRM Ryan Miller 4.00 10.00
JRO Rob Blake 4.00 10.00
JRU R.J. Umberger 2.50 6.00
JRY Michael Ryder 2.50 6.00
JSA Miroslav Satan 3.00 8.00
JSC Sidney Crosby SP 25.00 60.00
JSF Sergei Fedorov 6.00 15.00
JSG Scott Gomez 3.00 8.00
JSH Jody Shelley 2.50 6.00
JSM Mats Sundin 4.00 10.00
JSN Brendan Shanahan 4.00 10.00
JSS Sergei Samsonov 3.00 8.00
JST Matt Stajan 2.50 6.00
JSU Scottie Upshall 2.50 6.00
JSW Stephen Weiss 2.50 6.00
JTC Ty Conklin 3.00 8.00
JTH Tomas Holmstrom 3.00 8.00
JTP Tom Poti 2.50 6.00
JVN Ville Nieminen 2.50 6.00
JWG Wayne Gretzky 25.00 60.00

2006-07 Black Diamond Jerseys Ruby

*RUBY: .5X TO 1.5X BASE HI
JSC Sidney Crosby/25 75.00 150.00
JWG Wayne Gretzky/25 80.00 200.00

2007-08 Black Diamond

COMP.SET w/o SPs (84) 15.00 40.00
COMMON QUAD (169-189) 3.00 8.00
1 Scott Niedermayer .30 .75
2 Andy McDonald .25 .60
3 Bobby Holik .20 .50
4 Marc Savard .20 .50
5 Zdeno Chara .30 .75
6 Glen Murray .25 .60
7 Tim Thomas .30 .75
8 Manny Fernandez .20 .50
9 Jason Pominville .20 .50
10 Derek Roy .20 .50
11 Daymond Langkow .20 .50
12 Matthew Lombardi .20 .50
13 Justin Williams .25 .60
14 Rod Brind`Amour .30 .75
15 Erik Cole .20 .50
16 Nikolai Khabibulin .30 .75
17 Duncan Keith .25 .60
18 Brent Seabrook .20 .50
19 Tuomo Ruutu .30 .75
20 Peter Budaj .25 .60
21 Marek Svatos .20 .50
22 Wojtek Wolski .25 .60
23 Pascal LeClaire .25 .60
24 David Vyborny .20 .50
25 Gilbert Brule .25 .60
26 Brenden Morrow .25 .60
27 Mike Ribeiro .20 .50
28 Jussi Jokinen .20 .50
29 Jere Lehtinen .20 .50
30 Tomas Holmstrom .25 .60
31 Kris Draper .20 .50
32 Jarret Stoll .25 .60
33 Shawn Horcoff .20 .50
34 Joni Pitkanen .20 .50
35 Stephen Weiss .20 .50
36 Nathan Horton .30 .75
37 Jozef Stumpel .20 .50
38 Jay Bouwmeester .20 .50
39 Mike Cammalleri .25 .60
40 Rob Blake .30 .75
41 Patrick O'Sullivan .25 .60
42 Ladislav Nagy .20 .50
43 Pierre-Marc Bouchard .30 .75
44 Pavol Demitra .40 1.00
45 Brian Rolston .25 .60
46 Alexei Kovalev .25 .60
47 Chris Higgins .20 .50
48 Cristobal Huet .25 .60
49 Steve Sullivan .20 .50
50 Jason Arnott .25 .60
51 Travis Zajac .20 .50
52 Bill Guerin .30 .75
53 Scott Gomez .25 .60
54 Martin Straka .20 .50
55 Wade Redden .20 .50
56 Antoine Vermette .20 .50
57 Joffrey Lupul .20 .50
58 Mike Richards .25 .60
59 Martin Biron .25 .60
60 Mike Knuble .20 .50
61 Ed Jovanovski .25 .60
62 David Aebischer .25 .60
63 Keith Ballard .20 .50
64 Mark Recchi .40 1.00
65 Colby Armstrong .20 .50
66 Milan Michalek .20 .50
67 Steve Bernier .20 .50
68 Joe Pavelski .40 1.00
69 Keith Tkachuk .30 .75
70 Lee Stempniak .20 .50
71 Brad Boyes .20 .50
72 Johan Holmqvist .25 .60
73 Marc Denis .25 .60
74 Alexander Steen .20 .50
75 Tomas Kaberle .20 .50
76 Jason Blake .20 .50
77 Henrik Sedin .40 1.00
78 Daniel Sedin .40 1.00
79 Brendan Morrison .20 .50
80 Mattias Ohlund .20 .50
81 Michael Nylander .20 .50
82 Alexander Semin .30 .75

Card	Low	High
83 Olaf Kolzig	.30	.75
84 Viktor Kozlov	.20	.50
85 Ryan Getzlaf	1.25	3.00
86 Chris Pronger	1.25	3.00
87 Phil Kessel	1.25	3.00
88 Drew Stafford	.75	2.00
89 Alex Tanguay	1.00	2.50
90 Dion Phaneuf	1.00	2.50
91 Cam Ward	1.25	3.00
92 Martin Havlat	1.25	3.00
93 Milan Hejduk	1.00	2.50
94 Paul Stastny	1.00	2.50
95 Sergei Fedorov	2.00	5.00
96 Marty Turco	1.25	3.00
97 Nicklas Lidstrom	1.25	3.00
98 Pavel Datsyuk	2.00	5.00
99 Dwayne Roloson	1.00	2.50
100 Ales Hemsky	1.00	2.50
101 Olli Jokinen	1.00	2.50
102 Tomas Vokoun	1.00	2.50
103 Anze Kopitar	2.00	5.00
104 Alexander Frolov	.75	2.00
105 Mikko Koivu	1.00	2.50
106 Guillaume Latendresse	1.00	2.50
107 Alexander Radulov	1.25	3.00
108 Patrik Elias	1.25	3.00
109 Brian Gionta	.75	2.00
110 Zach Parise	1.25	3.00
111 Rick DiPietro	1.00	2.50
112 Miroslav Satan	1.00	2.50
113 Chris Drury	1.00	2.50
114 Ray Emery	1.00	2.50
115 Daniel Alfredsson	1.25	3.00
116 Daniel Briere	1.25	3.00
117 Jeff Carter	1.00	2.50
118 Shane Doan	1.00	2.50
119 Jordan Staal	1.00	2.50
120 Patrick Marleau	1.25	3.00
121 Doug Weight	1.25	3.00
122 Manny Legace	1.00	2.50
123 Brad Richards	1.25	3.00
124 Andrew Raycroft	1.00	2.50
125 Darcy Tucker	1.00	2.50
126 Markus Naslund	1.25	3.00
127 Jean-Sebastien Giguere	2.00	5.00
128 Teemu Selanne	4.00	10.00
129 Marian Hossa	2.00	5.00
130 Kari Lehtonen	1.50	4.00
131 Patrice Bergeron	2.50	6.00
132 Thomas Vanek	1.50	4.00
133 Miikka Kiprusoff	2.00	5.00
134 Rick Nash	2.00	5.00
135 Mike Modano	3.00	8.00
136 Dominik Hasek	3.00	8.00
137 Henrik Zetterberg	2.50	6.00
138 Marian Gaborik	2.00	5.00
139 Saku Koivu	2.00	5.00
140 Michael Ryder	1.25	3.00
141 Henrik Lundqvist	5.00	12.00
142 Jason Spezza	2.00	5.00
143 Simon Gagne	2.00	5.00
144 Evgeni Malkin	4.00	10.00
145 Jonathan Cheechoo	1.50	4.00
146 Paul Kariya	2.00	5.00
147 Martin St. Louis	2.00	5.00
148 Petr Kalus RC	1.25	3.00
149 Rob Schremp RC	1.50	4.00
150 Matt Smaby RC	1.25	3.00
151 Andy Greene RC	1.50	4.00
152 Drew Miller RC	1.50	4.00
153 Daniel Winnik RC	1.50	4.00
154 Frans Nielsen RC	2.00	5.00
155 Lauri Tukonen RC	1.25	3.00
156 Ryan Callahan RC	2.50	6.00
157 Jaroslav Halak RC	6.00	15.00
158 David Krejci RC	4.00	10.00
159 Mason Raymond RC	2.00	5.00
160 Curtis McElhinney RC	2.00	5.00
161 Jared Boll RC	1.50	4.00
162 Torrey Mitchell RC	1.50	4.00
163 David Perron RC	2.50	6.00
164 Milan Lucic RC	5.00	12.00
165 Jaroslav Hlinka RC	1.50	4.00
166 Brandon Dubinsky RC	2.50	6.00
167 Brian Elliott RC	2.50	6.00
168 Brett Sterling RC	1.25	3.00
169 Ilya Kovalchuk	3.00	8.00
170 Bobby Orr	12.00	30.00
171 Ryan Miller	3.00	8.00
172 Jarome Iginla	4.00	10.00
173 Eric Staal	4.00	10.00
174 Joe Sakic	6.00	15.00
175 Gordie Howe	10.00	25.00
176 Wayne Gretzky	12.00	30.00
177 Mark Messier	6.00	15.00
178 Peter Forsberg	6.00	15.00
179 Martin Brodeur	8.00	20.00
180 Jaromir Jagr	10.00	25.00
181 Dany Heatley	2.50	6.00
182 Sidney Crosby	8.00	20.00
183 Marc-Andre Fleury	6.00	15.00
184 Mario Lemieux	12.00	30.00
185 Joe Thornton	5.00	12.00
186 Vincent Lecavalier	3.00	8.00
187 Mats Sundin	3.00	8.00
188 Roberto Luongo	5.00	12.00
189 Alexander Ovechkin	12.00	30.00
190 Jack Johnson RC	4.00	10.00
191 Jonathan Toews RC	25.00	60.00
192 Bobby Ryan RC	8.00	20.00
193 Sam Gagner RC	6.00	15.00
194 Carey Price RC	30.00	80.00
195 Erik Johnson RC	5.00	12.00
196 Nicklas Bergfors RC	3.00	8.00
197 Jonathan Bernier RC	8.00	20.00
198 Nicklas Backstrom RC	10.00	25.00
199 Bryan Little RC	5.00	12.00
200 Patrick Kane RC	40.00	100.00
201 Andrew Cogliano RC	4.00	10.00
202 Marc Staal RC	5.00	12.00
203 Nick Foligno RC	6.00	15.00
204 Peter Mueller RC	4.00	10.00
205 Devin Setoguchi RC	5.00	12.00
206 Kris Russell RC	5.00	12.00
207 James Sheppard RC	3.00	8.00
208 Matt Niskanen RC	5.00	12.00
209 Kyle Chipchura RC	5.00	12.00
210 Martin Hanzal RC	4.00	10.00

2007-08 Black Diamond Ruby

*SINGLE RUBY: 5X TO 12X BASE
*DOUBLE RUBY: 1.5X TO 4X BASE DOUBLE
*TRIPLE RUBY: 1X TO 2.5X BASE TRIPLE
*TRIPLE RUBY ROOKIE: 1.2X TO 3X BASE
*DOUBLE RUBY: .8X TO 2X BASE QUADS
*DOUBLE RUBY ROOK: .6X TO 1.5X BASE

Card	Low	High
191 Jonathan Toews	100.00	200.00
194 Carey Price	100.00	200.00
198 Nicklas Backstrom	12.00	30.00
200 Patrick Kane	60.00	150.00
204 Peter Mueller	20.00	50.00

2007-08 Black Diamond Gemography

Card	Low	High
GAF Maxim Afinogenov	3.00	8.00
GAH Ales Hemsky	4.00	10.00
GAK Andrei Kostitsyn	4.00	10.00
GAO Alexander Ovechkin SP	80.00	200.00
GBL Michael Blunden	3.00	8.00
GBM Brenden Morrow	4.00	10.00
GBP Benoit Pouliot SP	15.00	40.00
GBR Martin Brodeur SP	60.00	120.00
GCA Colby Armstrong	3.00	8.00
GCB Cam Barker SP	5.00	12.00
GCH Jonathan Cheechoo	4.00	10.00
GCK Chuck Kobasew	3.00	8.00
GCO Erik Cole	3.00	8.00
GCP Corey Perry	8.00	20.00
GCT Chris Thorburn	3.00	8.00
GDB Daniel Briere	5.00	12.00
GDH Dominik Hasek SP	15.00	40.00
GDL David Leneveu	4.00	10.00
GDP Dion Phaneuf	4.00	10.00
GDR Dwayne Roloson SP	6.00	15.00
GDU Dustin Brown	5.00	12.00
GEC Erik Christensen	3.00	8.00
GEF Eric Fehr	3.00	8.00
GEM Evgeni Malkin	25.00	60.00
GEN Evgeni Nabokov	4.00	10.00
GES Eric Staal	6.00	15.00
GFO Matt Foy	3.00	8.00
GFP Fernando Pisani	3.00	8.00
GGB Gilbert Brule	4.00	10.00
GGE Martin Gerber	4.00	10.00
GGL Georges Laraque	4.00	10.00
GGO Scott Gomez	4.00	10.00
GHZ Henrik Zetterberg	6.00	15.00
GIK Ilya Kovalchuk	5.00	12.00
GJC Jeff Carter	4.00	10.00
GJH Josh Hennessy	3.00	8.00
GJI Jarome Iginla SP	25.00	60.00
GJL John-Michael Liles	3.00	8.00
GJM Jay McClement	3.00	8.00
GJP Joni Pitkanen SP	5.00	12.00
GJS Jarret Stoll	4.00	10.00
GJW Justin Williams SP	6.00	15.00
GKC Kyle Calder	3.00	8.00
GKG Kelly Guard	3.00	8.00
GKL Kristopher Letang	10.00	25.00
GKO Mikko Koivu	4.00	10.00
GKQ Kyle Quincey	3.00	8.00
GLA Guillaume Latendresse	4.00	10.00
GLE Loui Eriksson	6.00	15.00
GLN Ladislav Nagy	3.00	8.00
GMB Martin Biron	4.00	10.00
GMC Mike Cammalleri	4.00	10.00
GMF Marc-Andre Fleury SP	10.00	25.00
GMG Marian Gaborik SP	25.00	60.00
GMH Milan Hejduk	4.00	10.00
GMI Mike Richards	4.00	10.00
GMK Miikka Kiprusoff	5.00	12.00
GML Matt Lashoff	3.00	8.00
GMP Mark Parrish	3.00	8.00
GMR Mike Ribeiro	3.00	8.00
GMT Marty Turco	5.00	12.00
GND Nigel Dawes	3.00	8.00
GNH Nathan Horton	5.00	12.00
GPB Patrice Bergeron	8.00	20.00
GPE Patrik Elias	5.00	12.00
GPK Phil Kessel	5.00	12.00
GPM Paul Mara	3.00	8.00
GPO Patrick O'Sullivan	4.00	10.00
GPP Petr Prucha	3.00	8.00
GRB Rene Bourque SP	5.00	12.00
GRF Ruslan Fedotenko	3.00	8.00
GRI Brad Richardson	3.00	8.00
GRK Rostislav Klesla	3.00	8.00
GRM Ryan Malone	3.00	8.00
GRN Rick Nash	5.00	12.00
GSB Steve Bernier	3.00	8.00
GSC Sidney Crosby	100.00	175.00
GSG Simon Gagne	5.00	12.00
GSS Steve Sullivan	3.00	8.00
GST Mark Stuart	3.00	8.00
GSW Stephen Weiss	3.00	8.00
GTH Tomas Holmstrom	4.00	10.00
GVF Valtteri Filppula	3.00	8.00
GVT Vesa Toskala SP	6.00	15.00
GWI Jeremy Williams	3.00	8.00
GWR Wade Redden	3.00	8.00
GZC Zdeno Chara	8.00	20.00

2007-08 Black Diamond Jerseys

Card	Low	High
BDJAA Arron Asham	3.00	8.00
BDJAE David Aebischer	4.00	10.00
BDJAF Alexander Frolov	3.00	8.00
BDJAH Adam Hall	3.00	8.00
BDJAK Alexei Kovalev	4.00	10.00
BDJAM Andrej Meszaros	3.00	8.00
BDJAO Alex Ovechkin SP	20.00	50.00
BDJAR Alexander Radulov	5.00	12.00
BDJAS Alexander Steen	3.00	8.00
BDJAT Alex Tanguay	4.00	10.00
BDJAU Alexander Auld	3.00	8.00
BDJBB Brad Boyes	3.00	8.00
BDJBE Patrice Bergeron	6.00	15.00
BDJBG Bill Guerin	5.00	12.00
BDJBI Martin Biron	4.00	10.00
BDJBJ Barret Jackman	3.00	8.00
BDJBL Jason Blake	3.00	8.00
BDJBM Brendan Morrison	3.00	8.00
BDJBO Brandon Bochenski	3.00	8.00
BDJBR Brad Richards	5.00	12.00
BDJBS Brad Stuart	3.00	8.00
BDJCD Chris Drury	4.00	10.00
BDJCH Chris Higgins	3.00	8.00
BDJCK Chuck Kobasew	3.00	8.00
BDJCO Chris Osgood	5.00	12.00
BDJCP Chris Phillips	3.00	8.00
BDJDA Daniel Alfredsson	5.00	12.00
BDJDE Pavol Demitra	6.00	15.00
BDJDH Dany Heatley SP	4.00	10.00
BDJDL David Legwand	4.00	10.00
BDJDR Dwayne Roloson	4.00	10.00
BDJDT Darcy Tucker	4.00	10.00
BDJDW Doug Weight	5.00	12.00
BDJEB Ed Belfour	5.00	12.00
BDJEJ Ed Jovanovski	4.00	10.00
BDJEN Evgeni Nabokov	4.00	10.00
BDJES Eric Staal	6.00	15.00
BDJFP Fernando Pisani	3.00	8.00
BDJGE Martin Gerber	4.00	10.00
BDJGM Glen Murray	4.00	10.00
BDJHA Dominik Hasek SP	8.00	20.00
BDJHE Milan Hejduk	4.00	10.00
BDJHM Martin Havlat	5.00	12.00
BDJHS Henrik Sedin	6.00	15.00
BDJHT Hannu Toivonen	4.00	10.00
BDJIK Ilya Kovalchuk	5.00	12.00
BDJJA Jason Arnott	4.00	10.00
BDJJB Jay Bouwmeester	3.00	8.00
BDJJC Jeff Carter	4.00	10.00
BDJJG Jean-Sebastien Giguere	5.00	12.00
BDJJI Jarome Iginla	6.00	15.00
BDJJJ Jaromir Jagr	15.00	40.00
BDJJL Jere Lehtinen	3.00	8.00
BDJJO Jonathan Cheechoo	4.00	10.00
BDJJS Jarret Stoll	4.00	10.00
BDJJT Joe Thornton	8.00	20.00
BDJJU Jussi Jokinen	3.00	8.00
BDJJW Jason Williams	3.00	8.00
BDJKC Kyle Calder	3.00	8.00
BDJKT Keith Tkachuk	5.00	12.00
BDJLU Joffrey Lupul	3.00	8.00
BDJMA Martin Brodeur	12.00	30.00
BDJMB Mark Bell	3.00	8.00
BDJMC Bryan McCabe	3.00	8.00
BDJMD Marc Denis	4.00	10.00
BDJMF Manny Fernandez	3.00	8.00
BDJMG Marian Gaborik SP	5.00	12.00
BDJMH Marian Hossa	5.00	12.00
BDJMI Michael Peca	4.00	10.00
BDJMJ Milan Jurcina	3.00	8.00
BDJML Manny Legace	4.00	10.00
BDJMM Milan Michalek	3.00	8.00
BDJMN Markus Naslund	5.00	12.00
BDJMO Brenden Morrow	4.00	10.00
BDJMP Mark Parrish	3.00	8.00
BDJMR Mike Ribeiro	3.00	8.00
BDJMS Marc Savard	3.00	8.00
BDJMT Marty Turco	5.00	12.00
BDJNL Nicklas Lidstrom	5.00	12.00
BDJNZ Nikolai Zherdev	3.00	8.00
BDJOH Mattias Ohlund	3.00	8.00
BDJOJ Olli Jokinen	4.00	10.00
BDJPB Pierre-Marc Bouchard	5.00	12.00
BDJPC Corey Perry	8.00	20.00
BDJPD Pavel Datsyuk SP	8.00	20.00
BDJPE Patrik Elias	5.00	12.00
BDJPF Peter Forsberg	10.00	25.00
BDJPM Patrick Marleau	5.00	12.00
BDJRA Andrew Raycroft	4.00	10.00
BDJRL Roberto Luongo	8.00	20.00
BDJRM Ryan Miller	5.00	12.00
BDJRN Rick Nash SP	5.00	12.00
BDJSA Joe Sakic	10.00	25.00
BDJSC Sidney Crosby SP	12.00	30.00
BDJSG Simon Gagne	5.00	12.00
BDJSH Brendan Shanahan	5.00	12.00
BDJSP Jason Spezza SP	5.00	12.00
BDJSU Mats Sundin	5.00	12.00
BDJTH Jose Theodore	5.00	12.00
BDJWI Justin Williams	4.00	10.00

2007-08 Black Diamond Jerseys Ruby Dual

*RUBY DUAL: .5X TO 1.2X

2007-08 Black Diamond Jerseys Gold Triple

*GOLD TRIPLE: 1X TO 2.5X

2007-08 Black Diamond Run for the Cup

Card	Low	High
CUP1 Jean-Sebastien Giguere	10.00	25.00
CUP2 Ilya Kovalchuk	10.00	25.00
CUP3 Thomas Vanek	8.00	20.00
CUP4 Jarome Iginla	12.00	30.00
CUP5 Eric Staal	12.00	30.00
CUP6 Joe Sakic	20.00	50.00
CUP7 Mike Modano	15.00	40.00
CUP8 Henrik Zetterberg	12.00	30.00
CUP9 Ales Hemsky	8.00	20.00
CUP10 Marian Gaborik	10.00	25.00
CUP11 Saku Koivu	10.00	25.00
CUP12 Martin Brodeur	15.00	40.00
CUP13 Jaromir Jagr	12.00	30.00
CUP14 Dany Heatley	8.00	20.00
CUP15 Sidney Crosby	25.00	60.00
CUP16 Joe Thornton	15.00	40.00
CUP17 Paul Kariya	10.00	25.00
CUP18 Vincent Lecavalier	10.00	25.00
CUP19 Mats Sundin	10.00	25.00
CUP20 Roberto Luongo	15.00	40.00
CUP21 Alexander Ovechkin	150.00	400.00

2008-09 Black Diamond

Card	Low	High
COMP.SET w/o SPs (84)	10.00	25.00
1 Bobby Ryan	.20	.50
2 Corey Perry	.40	1.00
3 Bryan Little	.20	.50
4 Marco Sturm	.15	.40
5 Patrice Bergeron	.30	.75
6 Tim Thomas	.25	.60
7 Zdeno Chara	.25	.60
8 Jason Pominville	.15	.40
9 Daymond Langkow	.15	.40
10 Mike Cammalleri	.20	.50
11 Justin Williams	.20	.50
12 Ray Whitney	.20	.50
13 Rod Brind'Amour	.25	.60
14 Brian Campbell	.20	.50
15 Cristobal Huet	.20	.50
16 Dustin Byfuglien	.25	.60
17 Darcy Tucker	.20	.50
18 Marek Svatos	.15	.40
19 Wojtek Wolski	.20	.50
20 Pascal Leclaire	.20	.50
21 Brenden Morrow	.20	.50
22 Sean Avery	.15	.40
23 Sergei Zubov	.20	.50
24 Valtteri Filppula	.15	.40
25 Dan Cleary	.20	.50
26 Johan Franzen	.20	.50
27 Niklas Kronwall	.20	.50
28 Dustin Penner	.20	.50
29 Dwayne Roloson	.20	.50
30 Erik Cole	.15	.40
31 Gilbert Brule	.15	.40
32 Mathieu Garon	.20	.50
33 Andrew Cogliano	.15	.40
34 Jay Bouwmeester	.15	.40
35 Dustin Brown	.25	.60
36 Jack Johnson	.15	.40
37 Josh Harding	.25	.60
38 Pierre-Marc Bouchard	.25	.60
39 Alex Kovalev	.20	.50
40 Jaroslav Halak	.25	.60
41 Andrei Markov	.25	.60
42 Guillaume Latendresse	.15	.40
43 Sergei Kostitsyn	.15	.40
44 Tomas Plekanec	.15	.40
45 Dan Ellis	.15	.40
46 Brian Gionta	.15	.40
47 Brian Rolston	.20	.50
48 Patrik Elias	.25	.60
49 Bill Guerin	.25	.60
50 Mark Streit	.15	.40
51 Mike Comrie	.20	.50
52 Brendan Shanahan	.25	.60
53 Chris Drury	.20	.50
54 Marc Staal	.15	.40
55 Nikolai Zherdev	.15	.40
56 Scott Gomez	.20	.50
57 Wade Redden	.15	.40
58 Antoine Vermette	.15	.40
59 Martin Gerber	.20	.50
60 Jeff Carter	.20	.50
61 Mike Knuble	.15	.40
62 Scott Hartnell	.15	.40
63 Daniel Carcillo	.15	.40
64 Ed Jovanovski	.20	.50
65 Ilya Bryzgalov	.20	.50
66 Sergei Gonchar	.15	.40
67 Milan Michalek	.15	.40
68 Patrick Marleau	.25	.60
69 Andy McDonald	.20	.50
70 Brad Boyes	.15	.40
71 Manny Legace	.25	.60
72 Paul Kariya	.25	.60
73 Radim Vrbata	.15	.40
74 Ryan Malone	.15	.40
75 Vaclav Prospal	.15	.40
76 Jason Blake	.15	.40
77 Nikolai Antropov	.20	.50
78 Tomas Kaberle	.15	.40
79 Kevin Bieksa	.20	.50
80 Mattias Ohlund	.15	.40
81 Alexander Semin	.25	.60
82 Jose Theodore	.25	.60
83 Michael Nylander	.15	.40
84 Mike Green	.20	.50
85 Chris Pronger	.40	1.00
86 Teemu Selanne	.75	2.00
87 Kari Lehtonen	.50	1.25
88 Marc Savard	.25	.60
89 Derek Roy	.25	.60
90 Cam Ward	.40	1.00
91 Patrick Kane	.75	2.00
92 Patrick Sharp	.40	1.00
93 Milan Hejduk	.30	.75
94 Brad Richards	.40	1.00
95 Marty Turco	.40	1.00
96 Mike Ribeiro	.25	.60
97 Mike Modano	.60	1.50
98 Chris Osgood	.40	1.00
99 Ales Hemsky	.30	.75
100 Shawn Horcoff	.25	.60
101 Nathan Horton	.30	.75
102 Tomas Vokoun	.30	.75
103 Anze Kopitar	.60	1.50
104 Alexander Frolov	.25	.60
105 Niklas Backstrom	.40	1.00
106 Andrei Kostitsyn	.30	.75
107 Sam Gagner	.25	.60
108 Jason Arnott	.30	.75
109 J.P. Dumont	.25	.60
110 Zach Parise	.40	1.00
111 Rick DiPietro	.30	.75
112 Markus Naslund	.40	1.00
113 Simon Gagne	.40	1.00
114 Daniel Briere	.40	1.00
115 Mike Richards	.30	.75
116 Martin Biron	.30	.75
117 Shane Doan	.30	.75
118 Peter Mueller	.30	.75
119 Olli Jokinen	.30	.75
120 Jordan Staal	.30	.75
121 Evgeni Nabokov	.30	.75
122 Jonathan Cheechoo	.30	.75
123 Erik Johnson	.25	.60
124 Vesa Toskala	.50	1.25
125 Daniel Sedin	.50	1.25
126 Henrik Sedin	.50	1.25
127 Ryan Getzlaf	1.00	2.50
128 Jean-Sebastien Giguere	1.00	2.50
129 Ryan Miller	1.00	2.50
130 Thomas Vanek	.75	2.00
131 Dion Phaneuf	.75	2.00
132 Miikka Kiprusoff	1.00	2.50
133 Eric Staal	1.25	3.00
134 Jonathan Toews	1.50	4.00
135 Peter Forsberg	2.00	5.00
136 Paul Stastny	.75	2.00
137 Rick Nash	1.00	2.50
138 Marian Hossa	1.00	2.50
139 Pavel Datsyuk	1.50	4.00
140 Nicklas Lidstrom	1.00	2.50
141 Marian Gaborik	1.00	2.50
142 Saku Koivu	1.00	2.50
143 Dany Heatley	.75	2.00
144 Jason Spezza	1.00	2.50
145 Daniel Alfredsson	1.00	2.50
146 Martin St. Louis	1.00	2.50
147 Nicklas Backstrom	1.00	2.50
148 Viktor Tikhonov RC	1.50	4.00
149 Steve Mason RC	3.00	8.00
150 Mark Fistric RC	1.50	4.00
151 Justin Abdelkader RC	3.00	8.00
152 Mattias Ritola RC	1.50	4.00
153 Darren Helm RC	2.00	5.00
154 Claude Giroux RC	6.00	15.00
155 Tom Sestito RC	2.00	5.00
156 Shawn Matthias RC	2.00	5.00
157 Luca Sbisa RC	1.25	3.00
158 Oscar Moller RC	1.50	4.00
159 Erik Ersberg RC	1.50	4.00
160 Patric Hornqvist RC	2.00	5.00
161 Brian Lee RC	1.50	4.00
162 Ilya Zubov RC	1.50	4.00
163 Alex Goligoski RC	2.50	6.00
164 Jon Filewich RC	1.50	4.00
165 Vladimir Mihalik RC	1.25	3.00
166 Nikolai Kulemin RC	2.00	5.00
167 Robbie Earl RC	1.25	3.00
168 Mike Brown RC	2.00	5.00
169 Ilya Kovalchuk	3.00	8.00
170 Bobby Orr	12.00	30.00
171 Jarome Iginla	4.00	10.00
172 Joe Sakic	6.00	15.00
173 Gordie Howe	10.00	25.00
174 Henrik Zetterberg	4.00	10.00
175 Wayne Gretzky	20.00	50.00
176 Mark Messier	6.00	15.00
177 Patrick Roy	8.00	20.00
178 Carey Price	6.00	15.00
179 Martin Brodeur	8.00	20.00
180 Henrik Lundqvist	8.00	20.00
181 Mario Lemieux	12.00	30.00
182 Sidney Crosby	12.00	30.00
183 Evgeni Malkin	6.00	15.00
184 Marc-Andre Fleury	6.00	15.00
185 Joe Thornton	5.00	12.00
186 Vincent Lecavalier	3.00	8.00
187 Mats Sundin	3.00	8.00
188 Roberto Luongo	5.00	12.00
189 Alexander Ovechkin	12.00	30.00
190 Zach Bogosian RC	6.00	15.00
191 Blake Wheeler RC	12.00	30.00
192 Brandon Sutter RC	5.00	12.00
193 Jakub Voracek RC	10.00	25.00
194 Derick Brassard RC	5.00	12.00
195 James Neal RC	10.00	25.00
196 Michael Frolik RC	5.00	12.00
197 Drew Doughty RC	10.00	25.00
198 Colton Gillies RC	4.00	10.00
199 Kyle Okposo RC	6.00	15.00
200 Lauri Korpikoski RC	3.00	8.00
201 Fabian Brunnstrom RC	4.00	10.00
202 Zach Boychuk RC	5.00	12.00
203 Mikkel Boedker RC	6.00	15.00
204 Kyle Turris RC	8.00	20.00
205 Nikita Filatov RC	5.00	12.00
206 Alex Pietrangelo RC	8.00	20.00
207 T.J. Oshie RC	6.00	15.00
208 Patrik Berglund RC	4.00	10.00
209 Steven Stamkos RC	15.00	40.00
210 Luke Schenn RC	6.00	15.00

2008-09 Black Diamond Ruby

*RUBY (1-84): 6X TO 15X BASE
*RUBY (85-126): 4X TO 10X BASE
*RUBY (127-147): 1.5X TO 4X BASE
*RUBY RCs (148-168): .6X TO 1.5X BASE
*RUBY (169-189): .5X TO 1.2X BASE
*RUBY RCs (190-210): .6X TO 1.5X BASE

Card	Low	High
147 Nicklas Backstrom	4.00	10.00
209 Steven Stamkos	50.00	120.00

2008-09 Black Diamond Gemography

Card	Low	High
GAC Andrew Cogliano	5.00	12.00
GAO Alexander Ovechkin	30.00	80.00
GAT Alex Tanguay	5.00	12.00
GBA Cam Barker	5.00	12.00
GBB Brendan Bell	5.00	12.00
GBC Blake Comeau	5.00	12.00
GBD Brandon Dubinsky	5.00	12.00
GBE Jonathan Bernier	6.00	15.00
GBO Brad Boyes	5.00	12.00
GBR Bobby Ryan	6.00	15.00
GCA Ryan Carter	5.00	12.00
GCB Casey Borer	8.00	20.00
GCD Chris Drury	6.00	15.00
GCK Chris Kunitz	8.00	20.00
GCO Corey Perry	12.00	30.00
GCP Chris Phillips	5.00	12.00
GDC Dan Cleary	6.00	15.00
GDG Daniel Girardi	5.00	12.00
GDH Dany Heatley	6.00	15.00
GDM Drew Miller	8.00	20.00
GDP Daniel Paille	5.00	12.00
GDS Daniel Sedin	10.00	25.00
GDU Dustin Penner	6.00	15.00
GEJ Erik Johnson	5.00	12.00
GHA Josh Harding	8.00	20.00
GHS Henrik Sedin	10.00	25.00
GJB Jay Bouwmeester	5.00	12.00
GJG Jean-Sebastien Giguere	8.00	20.00
GJH Jannik Hansen	8.00	20.00
GJI Jarome Iginla	10.00	25.00
GJL John-Michael Liles	5.00	12.00
GJO Johnny Boychuk	6.00	15.00
GJS Jordan Staal	6.00	15.00
GJT Joe Thornton	12.00	30.00
GJW Justin Williams	6.00	15.00
GKD Kris Draper	5.00	12.00
GKE Phil Kessel	8.00	20.00
GKQ Kyle Quincey	5.00	12.00
GLE Loui Eriksson	5.00	12.00
GLK Lukas Kaspar	5.00	12.00
GLT Lauri Tukonen	5.00	12.00
GMA Drew MacIntyre	8.00	20.00
GMB Martin Biron	6.00	15.00
GMC Marco Sturm	5.00	12.00
GMG Martin Gerber	6.00	15.00
GMH Michal Handzus	6.00	15.00
GMK Mike Knuble	5.00	12.00
GML Milan Lucic	12.00	30.00
GMM Mark Mancari	6.00	15.00
GMN Markus Naslund	8.00	20.00
GMO Mike Modano	12.00	30.00
GMP Marc-Antoine Pouliot	5.00	12.00
GMR Mason Raymond	5.00	12.00
GMS Matt Stajan	5.00	12.00
GNB Nicklas Bergfors	12.00	30.00
GNI Nicklas Backstrom	8.00	20.00
GNW Noah Welch	5.00	12.00
GNZ Nikolai Zherdev	5.00	12.00
GPB Pierre-Marc Bouchard	8.00	20.00
GPE Rod Pelley	5.00	12.00
GPJ Jason Pominville	5.00	12.00
GPK Patrick Kane	15.00	40.00
GPO Ryan Potulny	5.00	12.00
GPR Carey Price	15.00	40.00
GPS Paul Stastny SP	6.00	15.00
GRC Ryane Clowe	5.00	12.00
GRG Ryan Getzlaf	8.00	20.00
GRI Mike Richards SP	6.00	15.00
GRK Rostislav Klesla	5.00	12.00
GRO Rob Schremp	6.00	15.00
GRP Rich Peverley	6.00	15.00
GRS Ryan Smyth	6.00	15.00
GSC Sidney Crosby	60.00	150.00
GSE Devin Setoguchi	6.00	15.00
GSM Stefan Meyer	5.00	12.00
GST Drew Stafford	5.00	12.00
GSW Stephen Weiss	5.00	12.00
GSZ Marek Schwarz	8.00	20.00
GTG Tom Gilbert	5.00	12.00
GTH Tomas Holmstrom	6.00	15.00
GTI Jussi Timonen	5.00	12.00
GTK Tyler Kennedy	6.00	15.00
GTL Jiri Tlusty	5.00	12.00
GTP Tomas Plihal	6.00	15.00
GTV Thomas Vanek SP	6.00	15.00
GTZ Travis Zajac	5.00	12.00

2008-09 Black Diamond Jerseys Quad

*GOLD/25: .6X TO 1.5X BASIC QUAD
*RUBY/100: .5X TO 1.2X BASIC QUAD

Card	Low	High
BDJAK Anze Kopitar	10.00	25.00
BDJAM Andrej Meszaros	4.00	10.00
BDJAO Alexander Ovechkin	12.00	30.00
BDJAR Andrew Raycroft	5.00	12.00
BDJAS Alexander Semin	6.00	15.00
BDJBB Brad Boyes	4.00	10.00
BDJBD Brandon Dubinsky	4.00	10.00
BDJBG Brian Gionta	4.00	10.00
BDJBM Brenden Morrow	5.00	12.00
BDJBO Brandon Bochenski	4.00	10.00
BDJBR Brad Richardson	4.00	10.00
BDJBW Brendan Witt	4.00	10.00
BDJCA Jeff Carter	5.00	12.00
BDJCC Chris Chelios	6.00	15.00
BDJCD Chris Drury	5.00	12.00
BDJCH Chris Higgins	4.00	10.00
BDJCK Chuck Kobasew	4.00	10.00
BDJCW Cam Ward	6.00	15.00
BDJDA Daniel Alfredsson	6.00	15.00
BDJDB Daniel Briere	6.00	15.00
BDJDH Dany Heatley	5.00	12.00
BDJDP Dion Phaneuf	5.00	12.00
BDJDR Dwayne Roloson	5.00	12.00
BDJDT Darcy Tucker	5.00	12.00
BDJDW Doug Weight	6.00	15.00
BDJEC Erik Cole	4.00	10.00
BDJEF Eric Fehr	4.00	10.00
BDJEJ Ed Jovanovski	5.00	12.00
BDJEN Evgeni Nabokov	5.00	12.00
BDJES Eric Staal	8.00	20.00
BDJGB Gilbert Brule	4.00	10.00
BDJGE Martin Gerber	5.00	12.00
BDJGL Guillaume Latendresse	4.00	10.00
BDJGU Bill Guerin	6.00	15.00
BDJHL Henrik Lundqvist	15.00	40.00
BDJHZ Henrik Zetterberg	8.00	20.00
BDJIK Ilya Kovalchuk	6.00	15.00
BDJIW Ian White	4.00	10.00
BDJJA Jason Arnott	5.00	12.00
BDJJB Jay Bouwmeester	4.00	10.00
BDJJC Jonathan Cheechoo	5.00	12.00
BDJJG Jean-Sebastien Giguere	6.00	15.00
BDJJI Jarome Iginla	8.00	20.00
BDJJM John-Michael Liles	4.00	10.00
BDJJP Joni Pitkanen	4.00	10.00
BDJJS Joe Sakic	12.00	30.00
BDJJT Joe Thornton	10.00	25.00
BDJKL Kari Lehtonen	8.00	20.00
BDJKO Alex Kovalev	5.00	12.00
BDJLE Manny Legace	6.00	15.00
BDJLS Lee Stempniak	4.00	10.00
BDJMA Mark Stuart	4.00	10.00
BDJMB Martin Brodeur	10.00	25.00
BDJMC Mike Cammalleri	5.00	12.00
BDJMF Manny Fernandez	4.00	10.00
BDJMG Marian Gaborik	6.00	15.00
BDJMI Milan Michalek	4.00	10.00
BDJML Mario Lemieux	12.00	30.00
BDJMM Mark Messier	12.00	30.00
BDJMN Markus Naslund	6.00	15.00
BDJMO Mike Modano	10.00	25.00
BDJMR Michael Ryder	4.00	10.00
BDJMS Martin St. Louis	6.00	15.00
BDJMU Joe Mullen	5.00	12.00
BDJMV Andrei Markov	6.00	15.00
BDJMZ Marek Zidlicky	4.00	10.00
BDJNZ Nikolai Zherdev	4.00	10.00
BDJOJ Olli Jokinen	5.00	12.00
BDJPB Patrice Bergeron	8.00	20.00
BDJPD Pavel Datsyuk	10.00	25.00
BDJPF Peter Forsberg	12.00	30.00
BDJPI Pierre-Marc Bouchard	6.00	15.00
BDJPK Paul Kariya	6.00	15.00
BDJPL Pascal Leclaire	5.00	12.00
BDJPR Patrick Roy	15.00	40.00
BDJPS Paul Stastny	5.00	12.00
BDJRD Rick DiPietro	5.00	12.00
BDJRE Mark Recchi	8.00	20.00
BDJRI Mike Richards	5.00	12.00
BDJRJ R.J. Umberger	4.00	10.00
BDJRL Roberto Luongo	10.00	25.00
BDJRN Rick Nash	6.00	15.00
BDJSA Marc Savard	4.00	10.00
BDJSC Sidney Crosby	15.00	40.00
BDJSG Simon Gagne	6.00	15.00
BDJSH Jody Shelley	4.00	10.00
BDJSP Jason Spezza	6.00	15.00
BDJST Alexander Steen	4.00	10.00
BDJSU Mats Sundin	5.00	12.00
BDJSW Shea Weber	5.00	12.00
BDJTH Jose Theodore	6.00	15.00
BDJTK Keith Tkachuk	6.00	15.00
BDJTP Tomas Plekanec	4.00	10.00
BDJTS Teemu Selanne	12.00	30.00
BDJTT Tim Thomas	6.00	15.00
BDJTV Thomas Vanek	5.00	12.00
BDJWG Wayne Gretzky	40.00	100.00
BDJZP Zach Parise	6.00	15.00

2008-09 Black Diamond Premier Die-Cut

Card	Low	High
PDC1 Scott Niedermayer	6.00	15.00
PDC2 Marian Hossa	6.00	15.00
PDC3 Jason Spezza	6.00	15.00
PDC4 Daniel Alfredsson	6.00	15.00
PDC5 Ryan Getzlaf	6.00	15.00
PDC6 Chris Pronger	6.00	15.00
PDC7 Ryan Malone	4.00	10.00
PDC8 Brenden Morrow	5.00	12.00
PDC9 Mike Ribeiro	4.00	10.00
PDC10 Alex Kovalev	5.00	12.00
PDC11 Alexander Frolov	4.00	10.00
PDC12 Mike Richards	5.00	12.00
PDC13 Daniel Briere	6.00	15.00
PDC14 Peter Mueller	5.00	12.00
PDC15 Shane Doan	5.00	12.00
PDC16 Olli Jokinen	5.00	12.00
PDC17 Henrik Sedin	8.00	20.00
PDC18 Daniel Sedin	8.00	20.00
PDC19 Patrick Marleau	6.00	15.00
PDC20 J.P. Dumont	4.00	10.00
PDC21 Zach Parise	6.00	15.00
PDC22 Andrew Cogliano	4.00	10.00
PDC23 Brad Richards	6.00	15.00
PDC24 Chris Drury	5.00	12.00
PDC25 Chris Osgood	6.00	15.00
PDC26 Dany Heatley	5.00	12.00
PDC27 Dion Phaneuf	5.00	12.00
PDC28 Eric Staal	8.00	20.00
PDC29 Henrik Lundqvist	15.00	40.00
PDC30 Jean-Sebastien Giguere	6.00	15.00
PDC31 Jonathan Cheechoo	5.00	12.00
PDC32 Marc-Andre Fleury	12.00	30.00
PDC33 Marian Gaborik	6.00	15.00
PDC34 Martin St. Louis	6.00	15.00
PDC35 Nicklas Lidstrom	6.00	15.00
PDC36 Patrik Elias	6.00	15.00
PDC37 Paul Stastny	5.00	12.00
PDC38 Rick Nash	6.00	15.00
PDC39 Roberto Luongo	10.00	25.00
PDC40 Ryan Miller	6.00	15.00
PDC41 Sam Gagner	4.00	10.00
PDC42 Thomas Vanek	5.00	12.00
PDC43 Carey Price	12.00	30.00
PDC44 Evgeni Malkin	12.00	30.00
PDC45 Henrik Zetterberg	8.00	20.00
PDC46 Ilya Kovalchuk	6.00	15.00
PDC47 Jarome Iginla	8.00	20.00
PDC48 Joe Thornton	10.00	25.00
PDC49 Jonathan Toews	10.00	25.00
PDC50 Mark Messier	12.00	30.00
PDC51 Martin Brodeur	15.00	40.00
PDC52 Nicklas Backstrom	6.00	15.00
PDC53 Patrick Kane	12.00	30.00
PDC54 Patrick Roy	15.00	40.00
PDC55 Alexander Ovechkin	25.00	60.00
PDC56 Bobby Orr	25.00	60.00
PDC57 Gordie Howe	20.00	50.00
PDC58 Mario Lemieux	25.00	60.00
PDC59 Sidney Crosby	25.00	60.00
PDC60 Wayne Gretzky	40.00	100.00

2008-09 Black Diamond Run for the Cup

Card	Low	High
CUP1 Jean-Sebastien Giguere	8.00	20.00
CUP2 Ilya Kovalchuk	8.00	20.00
CUP3 Marc Savard	5.00	12.00
CUP4 Ryan Miller	8.00	20.00
CUP5 Dion Phaneuf	6.00	15.00
CUP6 Jarome Iginla	10.00	25.00
CUP7 Eric Staal	10.00	25.00
CUP8 Jonathan Toews	12.00	30.00
CUP9 Patrick Kane	15.00	40.00
CUP10 Paul Stastny	6.00	15.00
CUP11 Joe Sakic	15.00	40.00
CUP12 Rick Nash	8.00	20.00
CUP13 Marty Turco	8.00	20.00
CUP14 Mike Modano	12.00	30.00
CUP15 Pavel Datsyuk	12.00	30.00
CUP16 Marian Hossa	8.00	20.00
CUP17 Henrik Zetterberg	12.00	30.00
CUP18 Shawn Horcoff	5.00	12.00
CUP19 Tomas Vokoun	6.00	15.00
CUP20 Anze Kopitar	12.00	30.00
CUP21 Marian Gaborik	8.00	20.00
CUP22 Carey Price	15.00	40.00
CUP23 Saku Koivu	8.00	20.00
CUP24 Martin Brodeur	20.00	50.00
CUP25 Rick DiPietro	6.00	15.00
CUP26 Daniel Alfredsson	8.00	20.00
CUP27 Jason Spezza	8.00	20.00
CUP28 Dany Heatley	6.00	15.00
CUP29 Mike Richards	6.00	15.00
CUP30 Shane Doan	6.00	15.00
CUP31 Olli Jokinen	6.00	15.00
CUP32 Peter Mueller	6.00	15.00
CUP33 Evgeni Malkin	15.00	40.00
CUP34 Marc-Andre Fleury	15.00	40.00
CUP35 Sidney Crosby	30.00	80.00
CUP36 Joe Thornton	12.00	30.00
CUP37 Paul Kariya	8.00	20.00
CUP38 Vincent Lecavalier	8.00	20.00
CUP39 Martin St. Louis	8.00	20.00
CUP40 Roberto Luongo	12.00	30.00
CUP41 Nicklas Backstrom	8.00	20.00
CUP42 Alexander Ovechkin	30.00	80.00

2009-10 Black Diamond

Card	Low	High
1 Jonas Hiller	.25	.60
2 Sean Avery	.25	.60
3 Peter Mueller	.25	.60
4 Alexander Frolov	.25	.60
5 Phil Kessel	.30	.75
6 Mikhail Grabovski	.20	.50
7 Teemu Selanne	.60	1.50
8 Justin Abdelkader	.25	.60

9 Daniel Sedin .40 1.00
10 Brent Burns .30 .75
11 Sheldon Souray .20 .50
12 Scott Gomez .25 .60
13 Evgeni Nabokov .25 .60
14 Joe Pavelski .40 1.00
15 Kyle Turris .30 .75
16 Martin Havlat .25 .60
17 Andrew Cogliano .20 .50
18 Marian Gaborik .30 .75
19 Darren Helm .20 .50
20 Niklas Kronwall .25 .60
21 Ryan Suter .25 .60
22 Mike Knuble .20 .50
23 Shea Weber .25 .60
24 Semyon Varlamov .30 .75
25 Chris Kunitz .30 .75
26 Nik Antropov .25 .60
27 Mikkel Boedker .20 .50
28 Ryan Malone .20 .50
29 Ilya Bryzgalov .25 .60
30 Drew Doughty .40 1.00
31 Tim Thomas .30 .75
32 Andrei Kostitsyn .25 .60
33 Paul Kariya .30 .75
34 Sam Gagner .25 .60
35 Patrik Elias .30 .75
36 Devin Setoguchi .20 .50
37 Scott Hartnell .20 .50
38 Derek Roy .20 .50
39 Brian Campbell .25 .60
40 Derick Brassard .15 .40
41 Todd White .20 .50
42 Jack Johnson .20 .50
43 Milan Hejduk .25 .60
44 Andrei Markov .30 .75
45 Marc Savard .20 .50
46 Jean-Sebastien Giguere .30 .75
47 Chris Mason .25 .60
48 Niklas Backstrom .30 .75
49 Jussi Jokinen .20 .50
50 Steve Ott .20 .50
51 Jonathan Cheechoo .25 .60
52 Pekka Rinne .30 .75
53 Ian Laperriere .20 .50
54 Steve Mason .25 .60
55 Kari Lehtonen .25 .60
56 Zdeno Chara .30 .75
57 Matt Stajan .20 .50
58 Dan Ellis .20 .50
59 Antti Miettinen .20 .50
60 Brian Gionta .20 .50
61 Sergei Gonchar .20 .50
62 Ryan Kesler .30 .75
63 Rene Bourque .20 .50
64 R.J. Umberger .25 .60
65 Alex Kovalev .25 .60
66 Tomas Kaberle .25 .60
67 Jaroslav Halak .30 .75
68 Chris Pronger .30 .75
69 David Booth .20 .50
70 Valtteri Filppula .20 .50
71 Henrik Sedin .40 1.00
72 Erik Cole .20 .50
73 Mike Ribeiro .20 .50
74 Daniel Carcillo .20 .50
75 Jamie Langenbrunner .20 .50
76 Jason Pominville .20 .50
77 Patrick Sharp .30 .75
78 Mike Cammalleri .25 .60
79 Jakub Voracek .25 .60
80 Scott Niedermayer .30 .75
81 David Krejci .30 .75
82 Marian Hossa .30 .75
83 Dustin Penner .20 .50
84 Tomas Vokoun .25 .60
85 Nikolai Khabibulin .30 .75
86 Loui Eriksson .20 .50
87 Rob Blake .30 .75
88 Martin St. Louis .30 .75
89 Ethan Moreau .20 .50
90 Dan Boyle .20 .50
91 Ales Hemsky .20 .50
92 Johan Franzen .25 .60
93 Ryan Smyth .25 .60
94 Pascal Leclaire .20 .50
95 Simon Gagne .30 .75
96 Brenden Morrow .25 .60
97 Vincent Lecavalier .30 .75
98 Mikko Koivu .30 .75
99 Jean Beliveau .30 .75
100 Zach Parise .30 .75
101 Patrick Marleau .30 .75
102 Luc Robitaille .30 .75
103 Paul Stastny .25 .60
104 Chris Drury .25 .60
105 Doug Gilmour .40 1.00
106 Bobby Ryan .25 .60
107 Shane Doan .25 .60
108 Corey Perry .50 1.25
109 Jason Arnott .20 .50
110 Henrik Lundqvist .75 2.00
111 Milan Lucic .25 .60
112 Ryan Getzlaf .30 .75
113 Anze Kopitar .50 1.25
114 Guy Carbonneau .50 1.25
115 Mats Sundin .30 .75
116 Jason Spezza .30 .75
117 Olli Jokinen .25 .60
118 Ryan Miller .30 .75
119 Mike Green .25 .60
120 Marty Turco .20 .50
121 Rogie Vachon .40 1.00
122 Alexandre Burrows .20 .50
123 Alexander Semin .20 .50
124 Johnny Bucyk .30 .75
125 Daniel Alfredsson .30 .75
126 Brendan Shanahan .30 .75
127 J.P. Dumont .20 .50
128 Clark Gillies .20 .50
129 Dion Phaneuf .25 .60
130 David Backes .20 .50
131 Eric Staal .40 1.00
132 Luke Schenn .30 .75
133 Bob Bourne .20 .50
134 Pavel Datsyuk .50 1.25
135 Cam Ward .30 .75
136 Dale Hawerchuk 1.25 3.00
137 Stan Mikita 1.25 3.00
138 Jeff Carter .75 2.00
139 Ilya Kovalchuk 1.00 2.50
140 Steven Stamkos 2.00 5.00
141 Dany Heatley .75 2.00
142 Carey Price 2.00 5.00
143 Henrik Zetterberg 1.25 3.00
144 Mike Richards .75 2.00
145 Harry Howell .75 2.00
146 Rick Nash 1.00 2.50
147 Gilbert Perreault 1.00 2.50
148 Patrick Kane 2.00 5.00
149 Joe Thornton 1.50 4.00
150 Miikka Kiprusoff 1.00 2.50
151 Jordan Staal .75 2.00
152 Tony Esposito 1.00 2.50
153 Nicklas Lidstrom .60 1.50
154 Nicklas Backstrom 1.00 2.50
155 Thomas Vanek .75 2.00
156 Phil Esposito 1.50 4.00
157 Marc-Andre Fleury 2.00 5.00
158 Brian Salcido RC 1.25 3.00
159 Luca Caputi RC 2.00 5.00
160 Yannick Weber RC 2.00 5.00
161 Kris Chucko RC 1.25 3.00
162 Riku Helenius RC 2.00 5.00
163 Ivan Vishnevskiy RC 1.25 3.00
164 T.J. Galiardi RC 2.00 5.00
165 Benn Ferriero RC 2.00 5.00
166 Cody Franson RC 2.00 5.00
167 Byron Bitz RC 1.50 4.00
168 Taylor Chorney RC 2.00 5.00
169 John Negrin RC 2.00 5.00
170 Jesse Joensuu RC 1.50 4.00
171 Cal O'Reilly RC 1.50 4.00
172 Spencer Machacek RC 2.00 5.00
173 Christian Hanson RC 2.00 5.00
174 Matt Beleskey RC 1.50 4.00
175 Jay Rosehill RC 2.00 5.00
176 Michael Sauer RC 1.50 4.00
177 Michael Grabner RC 2.00 5.00
178 Dmitry Kulikov RC 2.00 5.00
179 Alec Martinez RC 2.50 6.00
180 Matt Hendricks RC 1.50 4.00
181 Peter Stastny 2.00 5.00
182 Bobby Hull 5.00 12.00
183 Joe Sakic 5.00 12.00
184 Jarome Iginla 3.00 8.00
185 Don Cherry 2.50 6.00
186 Roberto Luongo 4.00 10.00
187 Jonathan Toews 5.00 12.00
188 Jari Kurri 2.50 6.00
189 Evgeni Malkin 5.00 12.00
190 Scotty Bowman 2.50 6.00
191 Martin Brodeur 6.00 15.00
192 Ray Bourque 4.00 10.00
193 Steve Yzerman 6.00 15.00
194 Sidney Crosby 10.00 25.00
195 Alexander Ovechkin 10.00 25.00
196 Bobby Orr 10.00 25.00
197 Mark Messier 5.00 12.00
198 Patrick Roy 6.00 15.00
199 Mario Lemieux 10.00 25.00
200 Gordie Howe 8.00 20.00
201 Wayne Gretzky 10.00 25.00
202 Tyler Bozak RC 4.00 10.00
203 Michael Del Zotto RC 2.50 6.00
204 Colin Wilson RC 2.50 6.00
205 Tyler Myers RC 4.00 10.00
206 Jamie Benn RC 8.00 20.00
207 Erik Karlsson RC 8.00 20.00
208 Viktor Stalberg RC 2.50 6.00
209 Matt Gilroy RC 2.50 6.00
210 Antti Niemi RC 4.00 10.00
211 Jhonas Enroth RC 3.00 8.00
212 Artem Anisimov RC 1.50 4.00
213 Ryan O'Reilly RC 5.00 12.00
214 Mikael Backlund RC 4.00 10.00
215 Ville Leino RC 2.00 5.00
216 Jonas Gustavsson RC 6.00 15.00
217 Sergei Shirokov RC 1.50 4.00
218 Victor Hedman RC 6.00 15.00
219 Evander Kane RC 5.00 12.00
220 James van Riemsdyk RC 5.00 12.00
221 Matt Duchene RC 5.00 12.00
222 John Tavares RC 12.00 30.00

2009-10 Black Diamond Ruby

*RUBY SINGLE DIAMOND: 8X TO 20X BASE
*RUBY DOUBLE DIAMOND: 5X TO 12X BASE
*RUBY TRIPLE DIAMOND: 4X TO 10X BASE
*RUBY TRIPLE D ROOKIES: 1X TO 2.5X BASE
*RUBY QUAD DIAMOND: .6X TO 1.5X BASE
*RUBY QUAD D ROOKIES: .5X TO 1.2X BASE

2009-10 Black Diamond Gemography

GAE Andrew Ebbett 4.00 10.00
GAF Alexander Frolov 5.00 12.00
GAM Al MacInnis 8.00 20.00
GAO Adam Oates 6.00 15.00
GAT Alex Tanguay 4.00 10.00
GBB Brian Boyle 4.00 10.00
GBD Brandon Dubinsky 4.00 10.00
GBE Brendan Bell 4.00 10.00
GBM Bryan McCabe 5.00 12.00
GBO Bobby Orr 60.00 150.00
GBW Blake Wheeler 6.00 15.00
GCP Carey Price 12.00 30.00
GDB David Backes 4.00 10.00
GDD Drew Doughty 8.00 20.00
GDH Darren Helm 4.00 10.00
GDL Dan LaCosta 5.00 12.00
GDU J.P. Dumont 4.00 10.00
GEL Patrik Elias 6.00 15.00
GEM Evgeni Malkin 12.00 30.00
GFL Marc-Andre Fleury 12.00 30.00
GFR Mark Fraser 4.00 10.00
GGH Gordie Howe 60.00 150.00
GHZ Henrik Zetterberg 8.00 20.00
GJA Jason Arnott 5.00 12.00
GJD Jeff Drouin-Deslauriers 4.00 10.00
GJE Jonathan Ericsson 4.00 10.00
GJG Jean-Sebastien Giguere 6.00 15.00
GJI Jarome Iginla 8.00 20.00
GJK Jari Kurri 6.00 15.00
GJO Joel Perrault 4.00 10.00
GJT Jiri Tlusty 4.00 10.00
GKN Patrick Kane 12.00 30.00
GKT Kyle Turris 6.00 15.00
GMD Matt D'Agostini 5.00 12.00
GMF Mark Fistric 4.00 10.00
GMH Michal Handzus 5.00 12.00
GMP Michael Peca 5.00 12.00
GMR Mattias Ritola 5.00 12.00
GMS Miroslav Satan 4.00 10.00
GNG Nathan Gerbe 5.00 12.00
GNK Nikolai Khabibulin 6.00 15.00
GNW Noah Welch 4.00 10.00
GOV Alexander Ovechkin 25.00 60.00
GPA Max Pacioretty 6.00 15.00
GPI Joni Pitkanen 5.00 12.00
GPK Phil Kessel 6.00 15.00
GPO Marc-Antoine Pouliot 5.00 12.00
GPR Patrick Roy 60.00 150.00
GRC Ryane Clowe 4.00 10.00
GRK Rostislav Klesla 6.00 15.00
GRP Rich Peverley 5.00 12.00
GSC Sidney Crosby 50.00 125.00
GSM Stefan Meyer 5.00 12.00
GSS Steven Stamkos 12.00 30.00
GTO Jonathan Toews 15.00 40.00
GTV Thomas Vanek 5.00 12.00
GTZ Travis Zajac 4.00 10.00
GWG Wayne Gretzky 200.00 500.00
GYZ Steve Yzerman 30.00 80.00
GZB Zach Bogosian 5.00 12.00

2009-10 Black Diamond Hardware Heroes

HH1 Patrick Kane 6.00 15.00
HH2 Evgeni Malkin 6.00 15.00
HH3 Dale Hawerchuk 4.00 10.00
HH4 Peter Stastny 2.50 6.00
HH5 Luc Robitaille 3.00 8.00
HH6 Mike Bossy 3.00 8.00
HH7 Gilbert Perreault 3.00 8.00
HH8 Steve Mason 2.50 6.00
HH9 Evgeni Malkin 6.00 15.00
HH10 Henrik Zetterberg 4.00 10.00
HH11 Steve Yzerman 8.00 20.00
HH12 Brad Richards 3.00 8.00
HH13 Wayne Gretzky 20.00 50.00
HH14 Wayne Gretzky 20.00 50.00
HH15 Mario Lemieux 12.00 30.00
HH16 Mark Messier 6.00 15.00
HH17 Mark Messier 6.00 15.00
HH18 Joe Sakic 6.00 15.00
HH19 Sidney Crosby 12.00 30.00
HH20 Phil Esposito 5.00 12.00
HH21 Gordie Howe 10.00 25.00
HH22 Bobby Hull 6.00 15.00
HH23 Stan Mikita 4.00 10.00
HH24 Bobby Clarke 5.00 12.00
HH25 Alexander Ovechkin 12.00 30.00
HH26 Steve Yzerman 8.00 20.00
HH27 Jarome Iginla 4.00 10.00
HH28 Sidney Crosby 12.00 30.00
HH29 Bobby Orr 12.00 30.00
HH30 Nicklas Lidstrom 2.00 5.00
HH31 Ray Bourque 5.00 12.00
HH32 Brian Leetch 2.50 6.00
HH33 Zdeno Chara 3.00 8.00
HH34 Pavel Datsyuk 5.00 12.00
HH35 Martin Brodeur 8.00 20.00
HH36 Patrick Roy 8.00 20.00
HH37 Ron Hextall 3.00 8.00
HH38 Grant Fuhr 5.00 12.00
HH39 Miikka Kiprusoff 3.00 8.00
HH40 Jose Theodore 3.00 8.00
HH41 Teemu Selanne 6.00 15.00
HH42 Tim Thomas 3.00 8.00

2009-10 Black Diamond Horizontal

*HORIZ: .5X TO 1.2X DIE-CUTS
BD1 Ilya Kovalchuk 4.00 10.00
BD2 Steven Stamkos 8.00 20.00
BD3 Carey Price 8.00 20.00
BD4 Henrik Zetterberg 5.00 12.00
BD5 Patrick Kane 8.00 20.00
BD6 Joe Thornton 6.00 15.00
BD7 Miikka Kiprusoff 4.00 10.00
BD8 Nicklas Lidstrom 2.50 6.00
BD9 Phil Esposito 6.00 15.00
BD10 Peter Stastny 3.00 8.00
BD11 Bobby Hull 8.00 20.00
BD12 Joe Sakic 8.00 20.00
BD13 Jarome Iginla 5.00 12.00
BD14 Don Cherry 4.00 10.00
BD15 Roberto Luongo 6.00 15.00
BD16 Jonathan Toews 6.00 15.00
BD17 Jari Kurri 4.00 10.00
BD18 Evgeni Malkin 8.00 20.00
BD19 Scotty Bowman 4.00 10.00
BD20 Ray Bourque 6.00 15.00
BD21 Martin Brodeur SP 10.00 25.00
BD22 Steve Yzerman SP 10.00 25.00
BD23 Sidney Crosby SP 15.00 40.00
BD24 Alexander Ovechkin SP 15.00 40.00
BD25 Bobby Orr SP 15.00 40.00
BD26 Mark Messier SP 8.00 20.00
BD27 Patrick Roy SP 10.00 25.00
BD28 Mario Lemieux SP 15.00 40.00
BD29 Gordie Howe SP 12.00 30.00
BD30 Wayne Gretzky SP 25.00 60.00

2009-10 Black Diamond Horizontal Perimeter Die-Cut

BD1 Ilya Kovalchuk 2.50 6.00
BD2 Steven Stamkos 5.00 12.00
BD3 Carey Price 5.00 12.00
BD4 Henrik Zetterberg 3.00 8.00
BD5 Patrick Kane 5.00 12.00
BD6 Joe Thornton 4.00 10.00
BD7 Miikka Kiprusoff 2.50 6.00
BD8 Nicklas Lidstrom 1.50 4.00
BD9 Phil Esposito 4.00 10.00
BD10 Peter Stastny 2.00 5.00
BD11 Bobby Hull 5.00 12.00
BD12 Joe Sakic 5.00 12.00
BD13 Jarome Iginla 3.00 8.00
BD14 Don Cherry 2.50 6.00
BD15 Roberto Luongo 4.00 10.00
BD16 Jonathan Toews 4.00 10.00
BD17 Jari Kurri 2.50 6.00
BD18 Evgeni Malkin 5.00 12.00
BD19 Scotty Bowman 2.50 6.00
BD20 Ray Bourque 4.00 10.00
BD21 Martin Brodeur SP 6.00 15.00
BD22 Steve Yzerman SP 6.00 15.00
BD23 Sidney Crosby SP 10.00 25.00
BD24 Alexander Ovechkin SP 10.00 25.00
BD25 Bobby Orr SP 10.00 25.00
BD26 Mark Messier SP 5.00 12.00
BD27 Patrick Roy SP 6.00 15.00
BD28 Mario Lemieux SP 10.00 25.00
BD29 Gordie Howe SP 8.00 20.00
BD30 Wayne Gretzky SP 15.00 40.00

2009-10 Black Diamond Jerseys Quad

*GOLD/25: .8X TO 2X BASIC JSY
*RUBY/50: .5X TO 1.2X BASIC JSY
QJAF Alexander Frolov 2.00 5.00
QJAK Anze Kopitar 3.00 8.00
QJAO Alexander Ovechkin 10.00 25.00
QJBD Brandon Dubinsky 1.50 4.00
QJBR Derick Brassard 1.50 4.00
QJCH Cristobal Huet 2.50 6.00
QJCP Carey Price 5.00 12.00
QJDB David Booth 1.50 4.00
QJDD Drew Doughty 3.00 8.00
QJDH Dale Hawerchuk 3.00 8.00
QJDP David Perron 2.00 5.00
QJDS Drew Stafford 1.50 4.00
QJDU Dustin Brown 2.50 6.00
QJEM Evgeni Malkin 5.00 12.00
QJFB Francis Bouillon 1.50 4.00
QJGA Glenn Anderson 2.00 5.00
QJJB Jay Bouwmeester 1.50 4.00
QJJL Jordan Leopold 1.50 4.00
QJJP Jason Pominville 1.50 4.00
QJJT Jeff Tambellini 1.50 4.00
QJJV Jakub Voracek 2.00 5.00
QJKA Sami Kapanen 1.50 4.00
QJLM Lanny McDonald 2.50 6.00
QJMB Martin Brodeur 6.00 15.00
QJMH Marian Hossa 2.50 6.00
QJMK Mike Komisarek 2.00 5.00
QJMS Marc Staal 1.50 4.00
QJNH Nathan Horton 2.50 6.00
QJPH Dion Phaneuf 2.00 5.00
QJPK Patrick Kane 5.00 12.00
QJPO Patrick O'Sullivan 2.00 5.00
QJPS Patrick Sharp 2.50 6.00
QJRD Rick DiPietro 2.00 5.00
QJRM Ryan Miller 2.50 6.00
QJRN Rick Nash 2.50 6.00
QJSC Sidney Crosby 10.00 25.00
QJSD Shane Doan 2.00 5.00
QJSG Simon Gagne 2.50 6.00
QJSK Saku Koivu 2.50 6.00
QJSS Steve Shutt 2.50 6.00
QJST Jordan Staal 2.00 5.00
QJSW Shea Weber 2.00 5.00
QJTO Jonathan Toews 4.00 10.00
QJTV Thomas Vanek 2.00 5.00
QJVL Vincent Lecavalier 2.50 6.00
QJVO Tomas Vokoun 2.00 5.00
QJWE Stephen Weiss 1.50 4.00
QJWR Wade Redden 1.50 4.00
QJZB Zach Bogosian 2.00 5.00
QJZP Zach Parise 2.50 6.00

2010-11 Black Diamond

COMP.SET w/o SPS (90) 8.00 20.00
1 Ales Hemsky .20 .50
2 Craig Anderson .25 .60
3 Tomas Plekanec .15 .40
4 Wojtek Wolski .15 .40
5 Olli Jokinen .20 .50
6 Mike Smith .25 .60
7 Ville Leino .20 .50
8 Marty Turco .20 .50
9 Daniel Alfredsson .25 .60
10 Nathan Horton .20 .50
11 Martin Havlat .20 .50
12 Steve Mason .20 .50
13 Mike Knuble .15 .40
14 Dustin Brown .25 .60
15 Bryan McCabe .15 .40
16 J.P. Dumont .15 .40
17 Mike Modano .40 1.00
18 Loui Eriksson .15 .40
19 Brandon Dubinsky .15 .40
20 Nik Antropov .20 .50
21 Patrick Sharp .25 .60
22 Lee Stempniak .15 .40
23 Brad Boyes .15 .40
24 Claude Giroux .25 .60
25 Mark Streit .15 .40
26 Dustin Penner .15 .40
27 Jason Pominville .15 .40
28 Devin Setoguchi .20 .50
29 Evander Kane .25 .60
30 Andrew Brunette .15 .40
31 Tomas Holmstrom .15 .40
32 Sam Gagner .15 .40
33 Alex Tanguay .15 .40
34 Blake Wheeler .25 .60
35 Brent Seabrook .15 .40
36 Ryan Kesler .25 .60
37 Jonas Hiller .20 .50
38 Jonathan Quick .30 .75
39 Nikolai Kulemin .15 .40
40 Pekka Rinne .25 .60
41 Brian Elliott .20 .50
42 Brenden Morrow .20 .50
43 Rich Peverley .25 .60
44 Kari Lehtonen .20 .50
45 Shawn Horcoff .15 .40
46 Tim Gleason .15 .40
47 Jamie Langenbrunner .15 .40
48 Antoine Vermette .15 .40
49 Milan Hejduk .20 .50
50 Alexander Semin .25 .60
51 Kyle Okposo .15 .40
52 Jean-Sebastien Giguere .25 .60
53 Pascal Dupuis .15 .40
54 Milan Michalek .15 .40
55 Bryan Little .25 .60
56 David Booth .15 .40
57 Michael Leighton .20 .50
58 Milan Lucic .25 .60
59 Andy McDonald .25 .60
60 Semyon Varlamov .25 .60
61 Andrei Markov .25 .60
62 Rene Bourque .15 .40
63 Josh Bailey .20 .50
64 Victor Hedman .30 .75
65 Tomas Kaberle .15 .40
66 Patric Hornqvist .15 .40
67 Mike Fisher .15 .40
68 Joe Pavelski .30 .75
69 Guillaume Latendresse .15 .40
70 Stephen Weiss .20 .50
71 Travis Zajac .15 .40
72 Jakub Voracek .20 .50
73 Alexandre Burrows .15 .40
74 David Backes .15 .40
75 James van Riemsdyk .20 .50
76 Rick DiPietro .20 .50
77 Ryan Smyth .20 .50
78 Ryan Suter .20 .50
79 Alex Kovalev .15 .40
80 Mike Ribeiro .15 .40
81 Scott Hartnell .15 .40
82 Ryan Malone .15 .40
83 T.J. Oshie .25 .60
84 Mikael Samuelsson .15 .40
85 Jay Bouwmeester .15 .40
86 Vaclav Prospal .15 .40
87 Valtteri Filppula .15 .40
88 Saku Koivu .25 .60
89 Jussi Jokinen .15 .40
90 Brian Gionta .15 .40
91 Chris Pronger .60 1.50
92 Antti Niemi .50 1.25
93 Cam Ward .60 1.50
94 Zdeno Chara .60 1.50
95 Shane Doan .50 1.25
96 Tomas Vokoun .50 1.25
97 Tyler Myers .40 1.00
98 Chris Drury .50 1.25
99 Dion Phaneuf .50 1.25
100 Niklas Backstrom .60 1.50
101 Drew Doughty .75 2.00
102 Miikka Kiprusoff .60 1.50
103 Vincent Lecavalier .60 1.50
104 Mike Cammalleri .60 1.50
105 Marian Hossa .60 1.50
106 Matt Duchene .60 1.50
107 Ilya Bryzgalov .50 1.25
108 Corey Perry 1.00 2.50
109 Phil Kessel .60 1.50
110 Shea Weber .50 1.25
111 Dan Boyle .40 1.00
112 Luke Schenn .60 1.50
113 Patrice Bergeron .75 2.00
114 Daniel Briere .60 1.50
115 Johan Franzen .50 1.25
116 Patrick Marleau .60 1.50
117 Brad Richards .60 1.50
118 Tuukka Rask .75 2.00
119 Teemu Selanne 1.25 3.00
120 Duncan Keith .50 1.25
121 Patrik Elias .60 1.50
122 Jordan Staal .60 1.50
123 Jimmy Howard .75 2.00
124 Anze Kopitar 1.00 2.50
125 Bobby Ryan .50 1.25
126 Derek Roy .40 1.00
127 Jason Spezza .60 1.50
128 Carey Price 1.25 3.00
129 Marc Savard .40 1.00
130 Scott Gomez .50 1.25
131 Daniel Sedin 1.25 3.00
132 Nicklas Lidstrom 1.00 2.50
133 John Tavares 1.50 4.00
134 Nicklas Backstrom 1.00 2.50
135 Tony Esposito 1.00 2.50
136 Mike Green .75 2.00
137 Zach Parise 1.00 2.50
138 Pavel Datsyuk 1.50 4.00
139 Paul Stastny .75 2.00
140 Ilya Kovalchuk 1.00 2.50
141 Henrik Sedin 1.25 3.00
142 Mark Messier 1.50 4.00
143 Luc Robitaille 1.00 2.50
144 Henrik Lundqvist 2.50 6.00
145 Ryan Getzlaf 1.50 4.00
146 Patrick Kane 2.00 5.00
147 Phil Esposito 2.00 5.00
148 Martin St. Louis 1.00 2.50
149 Mike Bossy 1.00 2.50
150 Marc-Andre Fleury 2.00 5.00
151 Marian Gaborik 1.00 2.50
152 Dany Heatley .75 2.00
153 Ryan Miller 1.00 2.50
154 Mikko Koivu 1.00 2.50
155 Thomas Vanek .75 2.00
156 Maxim Noreau RC 1.25 3.00
157 Arturs Kulda RC 1.50 4.00
158 Jacob Josefson RC 1.50 4.00
159 Brayden Irwin RC 1.50 4.00
160 Cody Almond RC 1.50 4.00
161 Alexander Urbom RC 1.50 4.00
162 Matt Taormina RC 1.50 4.00
163 Tommy Wingels RC 1.50 4.00
164 Nick Palmieri RC 1.50 4.00
165 Nick Johnson RC 1.25 3.00
166 T.J. Brodie RC 1.50 4.00
167 Casey Wellman RC 1.50 4.00
168 Alex Plante RC 1.50 4.00
169 Philip Larsen RC 1.50 4.00
170 Dustin Tokarski RC 1.50 4.00
171 Justin Falk RC 1.25 3.00
172 Anders Lindback RC 1.50 4.00
173 Brandon Pirri RC 1.50 4.00
174 Jake Muzzin RC 4.00 10.00
175 Kyle Clifford RC 2.00 5.00
176 Dana Tyrell RC 1.50 4.00
177 Mark Olver RC 1.50 4.00
178 Henrik Karlsson RC 1.50 4.00
179 Nick Leddy RC 2.00 5.00
180 Jamie McBain RC 1.50 4.00
181 Joe Thornton 4.00 10.00
182 Bobby Orr 10.00 25.00
183 Eric Staal 3.00 8.00
184 Steve Yzerman 6.00 15.00
185 Mario Lemieux 10.00 25.00
186 Jarome Iginla 3.00 8.00
187 Patrick Roy 6.00 15.00
188 Jonathan Toews 4.00 10.00
189 Jeff Carter 2.00 5.00
190 Steven Stamkos 5.00 12.00
191 Henrik Zetterberg 3.00 8.00
192 Alexander Ovechkin 10.00 25.00
193 Martin Brodeur 6.00 15.00
194 Guy Lafleur 3.00 8.00
195 Rick Nash 2.50 6.00
196 Mike Richards 2.00 5.00
197 Evgeni Malkin 5.00 12.00
198 Roberto Luongo 4.00 10.00
199 Sidney Crosby 10.00 25.00
200 Wayne Gretzky 15.00 40.00
201 Gordie Howe 8.00 20.00
202 Jared Cowen RC 2.50 6.00
203 Marcus Johansson RC 4.00 10.00
204 Sergei Bobrovsky RC 6.00 15.00
205 Zac Dalpe RC 3.00 8.00
206 Cam Fowler RC 6.00 15.00
207 Alexander Burmistrov RC 2.50 6.00
208 Nino Niederreiter RC 4.00 10.00
209 Oliver Ekman-Larsson RC 4.00 10.00
210 Zach Hamill RC 2.50 6.00
211 Brandon Yip RC 2.50 6.00
212 Jordan Caron RC 2.50 6.00
213 Jeff Skinner RC 10.00 25.00
214 Magnus Paajarvi RC 3.00 8.00
215 Brayden Schenn RC 6.00 15.00
216 Eric Tangradi RC 2.50 6.00
217 Derek Stepan RC 3.00 8.00
218 P.K. Subban RC 12.00 30.00
219 Nazem Kadri RC 8.00 20.00
220 Jordan Eberle RC 6.00 15.00
221 Tyler Seguin RC 20.00 40.00
222 Taylor Hall RC 10.00 25.00

2010-11 Black Diamond Ruby

*1-90 SINGLE: 8X TO 20X BASIC CARDS
*91-130 DOUBLE: 3X TO 8X BASIC CARDS
*131-155 TRIPLE: 2X TO 5X BASIC CARDS
*156-180 TRIP.ROOK: 1X TO 2.5X BASIC RC
*181-201 QUAD: .6X TO 1.5X BASIC CARDS
*202-222 QUAD ROOK: .6X TO 1.5X BASIC RC
213 Jeff Skinner 30.00 60.00
218 P.K. Subban 30.00 60.00
220 Jordan Eberle 15.00 40.00
221 Tyler Seguin 30.00 80.00
222 Taylor Hall 30.00 80.00

2010-11 Black Diamond Gemography

GBM Barry Melrose 5.00 12.00
GBO Bobby Orr 125.00 200.00
GBS Bobby Sanguinetti 4.00 10.00
GBU Peter Budaj 5.00 12.00
GCG Clark Gillies 6.00 15.00
GCL David Clarkson 4.00 10.00
GDC Daniel Carcillo 4.00 10.00
GEK Erik Karlsson 12.00 30.00
GEN Eric Nystrom 4.00 10.00
GET Eric Tangradi 5.00 12.00
GFR Mark Fraser 4.00 10.00
GGF Grant Fuhr SP 15.00 40.00
GGH Gordie Howe 60.00 120.00
GGI Claude Giroux 15.00 40.00
GHS Henrik Sedin 8.00 20.00
GIV Ivan Vishnevskiy 4.00 10.00
GJB Jamie Benn 10.00 25.00
GJC Jared Cowen 5.00 12.00
GJG Jean-Sebastien Giguere 10.00 25.00
GJK Jari Kurri 6.00 15.00
GJT John Tavares 15.00 30.00
GJV Jakub Voracek 5.00 12.00
GKA Evander Kane 8.00 20.00
GKC Kris Chucko 4.00 10.00
GLR Luc Robitaille 12.00 30.00
GMD Matt Duchene 20.00 50.00
GMF Mark Fistric 4.00 10.00
GMG Matt Gilroy 4.00 10.00
GMM Mark Messier 50.00 100.00
GMN Michal Neuvirth 5.00 12.00
GMP Matt Pelech 4.00 10.00
GMS Marek Svatos 4.00 10.00
GNG Nathan Gerbe 4.00 10.00
GNH Nathan Horton 5.00 12.00
GNK Nazem Kadri 15.00 40.00
GPB Patrice Bergeron 8.00 20.00
GPE Phil Esposito 15.00 30.00
GPH Patric Hornqvist 4.00 10.00
GPM Peter Mueller 5.00 12.00
GPS P.K. Subban 30.00 80.00
GRP Ryan Parent 4.00 10.00
GSC Sidney Crosby 60.00 120.00
GSG Simon Gagne 6.00 15.00
GSM Spencer Machacek 4.00 10.00
GSS Steven Stamkos 25.00 50.00
GST Peter Stastny 5.00 12.00
GSV Sergei Shirokov 5.00 12.00
GSW Stephen Weiss 5.00 12.00
GTJ T.J. Galiardi 5.00 12.00
GTM Tyler Myers 8.00 20.00
GVL Ville Leino 10.00 25.00
GVR James van Riemsdyk 5.00 12.00
GWG Wayne Gretzky 200.00 500.00
GYW Yannick Weber 4.00 10.00
GZH Zach Hamill 8.00 20.00

2010-11 Black Diamond Hardware Heroes

HHAO Alexander Ovechkin 20.00 50.00
HHBC Bobby Clarke 5.00 12.00
HHBL Brian Leetch 4.00 10.00
HHBO Bobby Orr 20.00 50.00
HHBR Martin Brodeur 12.00 30.00
HHCP Chris Pronger 5.00 12.00
HHCR Sidney Crosby 25.00 50.00
HHDC Don Cherry 10.00 25.00
HHDK Duncan Keith 4.00 10.00
HHGH Gordie Howe 10.00 25.00
HHGL Guy Lafleur 5.00 12.00
HHGR Wayne Gretzky 40.00 80.00
HHHS Henrik Sedin 12.00 30.00
HHJT Jonathan Toews 12.00 30.00
HHLG Guy Lafleur 10.00 25.00
HHLM Lanny McDonald 5.00 12.00
HHLR Larry Robinson 5.00 12.00
HHMB Martin Brodeur 12.00 30.00
HHML Mario Lemieux 20.00 50.00
HHMM Mark Messier 10.00 25.00
HHMS Martin St. Louis 5.00 12.00
HHOV Alexander Ovechkin 20.00 50.00
HHPD Pavel Datsyuk 8.00 20.00
HHPE Phil Esposito 8.00 20.00
HHPK Patrick Kane 10.00 25.00
HHPR Patrick Roy 12.00 30.00
HHRB Ray Bourque 8.00 20.00
HHRK Red Kelly 5.00 12.00
HHRM Ryan Miller 8.00 20.00
HHSB Scotty Bowman 5.00 12.00
HHSC Sidney Crosby 25.00 60.00
HHSD Shane Doan 4.00 10.00
HHSE Henrik Sedin 12.00 30.00
HHSM Stan Mikita 8.00 20.00
HHSS Steven Stamkos 10.00 25.00
HHSY Steve Yzerman 15.00 40.00
HHTE Tony Esposito 6.00 15.00
HHTH Jose Theodore 8.00 20.00
HHTM Tyler Myers 3.00 8.00
HHTS Teemu Selanne 10.00 25.00
HHWG Wayne Gretzky 40.00 80.00
HHYS Steve Yzerman 15.00 40.00

2010-11 Black Diamond Jerseys Quad

QJAK Alex Kovalev 3.00 8.00
QJAO Alexander Ovechkin 8.00 20.00
QJBL Brian Leetch 3.00 8.00
QJBR Bobby Ryan 3.00 8.00
QJBW Blake Wheeler 4.00 10.00
QJCC Chris Campoli 2.50 6.00
QJCN Cam Neely 4.00 10.00
QJCP Carey Price 8.00 20.00
QJDG Doug Gilmour 5.00 12.00
QJDH Dale Hawerchuk 5.00 12.00
QJDR Derek Roy 2.50 6.00
QJES Eric Staal 5.00 12.00
QJGA Glenn Anderson 3.00 8.00
QJHL Henrik Lundqvist 10.00 25.00
QJHZ Henrik Zetterberg 5.00 12.00
QJIB Ilya Bryzgalov 3.00 8.00
QJIK Ilya Kovalchuk 4.00 10.00
QJJA Jason Arnott 3.00 8.00
QJJC Jeff Carter 3.00 8.00
QJJT John Tavares 8.00 20.00
QJJV Jakub Voracek 3.00 8.00
QJJW Justin Williams 3.00 8.00
QJLM Lanny McDonald 4.00 10.00
QJMA Ryan Malone 2.50 6.00
QJMF Michael Frolik 2.50 6.00
QJMG Marian Gaborik 4.00 10.00
QJMJ Milan Jurcina 2.50 6.00
QJMK Mikko Koivu 4.00 10.00
QJML Mario Lemieux 8.00 20.00
QJNB Nicklas Backstrom 4.00 10.00
QJNH Nathan Horton 3.00 8.00
QJNK Nikolai Kulemin 2.50 6.00
QJPD Pavel Datsyuk 6.00 15.00
QJPM Peter Mueller 3.00 8.00
QJPS Peter Stastny 3.00 8.00
QJRB Ray Bourque 8.00 20.00
QJRM Ryan Miller 4.00 10.00
QJRN Rick Nash 4.00 10.00
QJSB Steve Bernier 2.50 6.00
QJSC Sidney Crosby 15.00 40.00
QJSG Scott Gomez 3.00 8.00
QJSM Steve Mason 6.00 15.00
QJSV Steve Shutt 4.00 10.00
QJSW Stephen Weiss 3.00 8.00
QJTB Todd Bertuzzi 3.00 8.00
QJTO Jonathan Toews 6.00 15.00
QJTT Tim Thomas 5.00 12.00
QJTV Thomas Vanek 3.00 8.00
QJVO Tomas Vokoun 3.00 8.00
QJWG Wayne Gretzky 25.00 60.00

2010-11 Black Diamond Jerseys Quad Gold

*SINGLES: .6X TO 1.5X BASIC INSERTS

2010-11 Black Diamond Jerseys Quad Ruby

*SINGLES: .5X TO 1.2X BASIC INSERTS

2010-11 Black Diamond Team Canada Die Cuts

COMPLETE SET (16) 150.00 300.00
TCBO Bobby Orr 15.00 40.00
TCDD Drew Doughty 5.00 12.00
TCDK Duncan Keith 5.00 12.00
TCGH Gordie Howe 8.00 20.00
TCJI Jarome Iginla 5.00 12.00
TCMB Martin Brodeur 10.00 25.00
TCMF Marc-Andre Fleury 8.00 20.00
TCML Mario Lemieux 15.00 40.00
TCMM Mark Messier 8.00 20.00
TCMR Mike Richards 3.00 8.00
TCPM Patrick Marleau 4.00 10.00
TCRL Roberto Luongo 6.00 15.00
TCSC Sidney Crosby 15.00 40.00
TCTO Jonathan Toews 6.00 15.00
TCWG Wayne Gretzky 12.00 30.00
TCYZ Steve Yzerman 8.00 20.00

2011-12 Black Diamond

COMP.SET w/o SPs (100) 8.00 20.00
1 Wayne Gretzky 1.25 3.00
2 Saku Koivu .25 .60
3 Nathan Gerbe .15 .40
4 Rene Bourque .15 .40
5 Patrik Elias .25 .60
6 Dustin Brown .25 .60
7 Brian Gionta .15 .40
8 Craig Anderson .25 .60
9 Chris Kunitz .25 .60
10 Bobby Orr 1.00 2.50
11 Kevin Shattenkirk .15 .40
12 Tobias Enstrom .15 .40
13 Michael Grabner .20 .50
14 Travis Zajac .15 .40
15 Guillaume Latendresse .20 .50
16 Ryan Smyth .20 .50
17 Loui Eriksson .15 .40
18 Patrick Sharp .25 .60
19 Alex Tanguay .15 .40

20 Gordie Howe .75 2.00
21 Tuukka Rask .30 .75
22 Tyler Myers .15 .40
23 Jussi Jokinen .15 .40
24 Semyon Varlamov .25 .60
25 Ales Hemsky .20 .50
26 Stephen Weiss .20 .50
27 Lars Eller .15 .40
28 Matt Moulson .15 .40
29 Milan Michalek .15 .40
30 Pascal Dupuis .15 .40
31 Martin Havlat .20 .50
32 Dwayne Roloson .20 .50
33 Tomas Vokoun .20 .50
34 Chris Pronger .25 .60
35 Marc Staal .15 .40
36 Kyle Okposo .15 .40
37 Patric Hornqvist .15 .40
38 Jonathan Bernier .20 .50
39 Sam Gagner .15 .40
40 Patrick Roy .60 1.50
41 Mike Ribeiro .15 .40
42 Steve Mason .20 .50
43 Milan Hejduk .20 .50
44 Brent Seabrook .15 .40
45 Matt Stajan .15 .40
46 Olli Jokinen .20 .50
47 Tyler Ennis .15 .40
48 Drew Stafford .15 .40
49 Mario Lemieux 1.00 2.50
50 Mark Messier .50 1.25
51 Jean-Sebastien Giguere .25 .60
52 Erik Johnson .15 .40
53 Valtteri Filppula .15 .40
54 Tomas Plekanec .15 .40
55 Derek Stepan .15 .40
56 Josh Bailey .20 .50
57 Ryan Callahan .15 .40
58 Daniel Briere .25 .60
59 James Neal .15 .40
60 Teemu Selanne .50 1.25
61 Dustin Penner .20 .50
62 Scott Clemmensen .20 .50
63 Ville Leino .20 .50
64 Nikolai Kulemin .15 .40
65 Antoine Vermette .15 .40
66 Milan Lucic .25 .60
67 Ryan Suter .20 .50
68 Jay Bouwmeester .15 .40
69 Ryane Clowe .15 .40
70 Jonathan Toews .40 1.00
71 Alexandre Burrows .15 .40
72 Jordan Eberle .25 .60
73 Dennis Seidenberg .15 .40
74 Brandon Dubinsky .15 .40
75 Corey Crawford .30 .75
76 Jason Pominville .15 .40
77 Rich Peverley .25 .60
78 David Booth .15 .40
79 Henrik Sedin .30 .75
80 Carey Price .50 1.25
81 T.J. Oshie .25 .60
82 Cam Fowler .25 .60
83 Thomas Vanek .20 .50
84 Bobby Ryan .20 .50
85 James van Riemsdyk .20 .50
86 Simon Gagne .25 .60
87 David Perron .20 .50
88 Travis Hamonic .20 .50
89 Michael Frolik .15 .40
90 Alexander Ovechkin 1.00 2.50
91 Nicklas Backstrom .25 .60
92 Darren Helm .15 .40
93 Daniel Sedin .30 .75
94 Sergei Bobrovsky .40 1.00
95 Andrei Markov .15 .40
96 Scott Hartnell .15 .40
97 Tyler Seguin .30 .75
98 Patrik Berglund .15 .40
99 Jonathan Ericsson .15 .40
100 Sidney Crosby 1.00 2.50
101 Evander Kane .60 1.50
102 Jordan Staal .50 1.25
103 Antti Niemi .50 1.25
104 Mikko Koivu .50 1.25
105 Chris Stewart .50 1.25
106 Erik Karlsson .75 2.00
107 Phil Kessel .60 1.50
108 Shea Weber .50 1.25
109 Duncan Keith .50 1.25
110 Brenden Morrow .50 1.25
111 Eric Staal .75 2.00
112 Dany Heatley .50 1.25
113 Jim Howard .75 2.00
114 Jaroslav Halak .60 1.50
115 Ilya Bryzgalov .60 1.50
116 Shane Doan .50 1.25
117 Jacob Markstrom .60 1.50
118 Alex Goligoski .50 1.25
119 Patrice Bergeron .75 2.00
120 Claude Giroux .60 1.50
121 Joe Pavelski .75 2.00
122 Victor Hedman .75 2.00
123 David Backes .40 1.00
124 Kristopher Letang .75 2.00
125 David Krejci .60 1.50
126 Jeff Skinner .75 2.00
127 Marian Hossa .60 1.50
128 Pekka Rinne .60 1.50
129 Jakub Voracek .50 1.25
130 Alexander Semin .60 1.50
131 Marc-Andre Fleury 1.25 3.00
132 Anze Kopitar 1.00 2.50
133 Johan Franzen .50 1.25
134 Joe Thornton 1.00 2.50
135 Mike Green .50 1.25
136 Michael Cammalleri .50 1.25
137 Jonas Hiller .50 1.25
138 Vincent Lecavalier .60 1.50
139 Devin Setoguchi .50 1.25
140 Cam Ward .60 1.50
141 Ondrej Pavelec .60 1.50
142 Nathan Horton .60 1.50
143 Matt Duchene .60 1.50
144 Daniel Alfredsson .60 1.50
145 Jonathan Quick .75 2.00
146 Ryan Getzlaf .60 1.50
147 Kari Lehtonen .50 1.25
148 Paul Stastny .50 1.25
149 Marian Gaborik .60 1.50
150 James Reimer .60 1.50
151 Corey Perry 1.50 4.00
152 Zach Parise 1.00 2.50
153 Miikka Kiprusoff 1.00 2.50
154 Pavel Datsyuk 1.50 4.00
155 Ryan Kesler 1.00 2.50
156 Ryan Miller 1.00 2.50
157 Henrik Lundqvist 2.50 6.00
158 Brad Marchand 2.00 5.00
159 Jeff Carter .75 2.00
160 Logan Couture 1.25 3.00
161 Patrick Kane 2.00 5.00
162 Zdeno Chara 1.00 2.50
163 Dustin Byfuglien 1.00 2.50
164 Rick Nash 1.00 2.50
165 Brayden Schenn 1.00 2.50
166 P.K. Subban 1.25 3.00
167 Jarome Iginla 1.25 3.00
168 Drew Doughty 1.25 3.00
169 John Tavares 1.50 4.00
170 Mike Richards .75 2.00
171 Dion Phaneuf .75 2.00
172 Ilya Kovalchuk 1.00 2.50
173 Taylor Hall 1.00 2.50
174 Henrik Zetterberg 1.25 3.00
175 Jason Spezza 1.00 2.50
176 Roman Horak RC 1.50 4.00
177 Maxime Macenauer RC 1.50 4.00
178 John Moore RC 1.50 4.00
179 Colin Greening RC 1.50 4.00
180 Cam Atkinson RC 4.00 10.00
181 Tomas Vincour RC 1.50 4.00
182 Yann Sauve RC 1.50 4.00
183 Alexei Emelin RC 1.50 4.00
184 Erik Condra RC 1.50 4.00
185 Justin Faulk RC 2.50 6.00
186 Cameron Gaunce RC 1.25 3.00
187 Joe Vitale RC 1.50 4.00
188 David Rundblad RC 1.50 4.00
189 Erik Gustafsson RC 2.00 5.00
190 Raphael Diaz RC 1.50 4.00
191 David Savard RC 1.50 4.00
192 Tim Erixon RC 1.50 4.00
193 Teemu Hartikainen RC 1.50 4.00
194 Ben Scrivens RC 1.50 4.00
195 Paul Postma RC 1.50 4.00
196 Craig Smith RC 2.00 5.00
197 Patrick Wiercioch RC 1.50 4.00
198 Alex Stalock 1.25 3.00
199 Brett Bulmer RC 1.50 4.00
200 Stephane Da Costa RC 1.50 4.00
201 Sidney Crosby AS 10.00 25.00
202 Alexander Ovechkin AS 10.00 25.00
203 Martin Brodeur AS 6.00 15.00
204 Steven Stamkos AS 5.00 12.00
205 Jonathan Toews AS 4.00 10.00
206 Carey Price AS 5.00 12.00
207 Tim Thomas AS 2.50 6.00
208 Nicklas Lidstrom AS 1.50 4.00
209 Roberto Luongo AS 4.00 10.00
210 Jaromir Jagr AS 8.00 20.00
211 Evgeni Malkin AS 5.00 12.00
212 Teemu Selanne AS 5.00 12.00
213 Mike Gartner AS 3.00 8.00
214 Brett Hull AS 5.00 12.00
215 Jari Kurri AS 2.50 6.00
216 Brendan Shanahan AS 2.50 6.00
217 Joe Sakic AS 5.00 12.00
218 Eric Lindros AS 4.00 10.00
219 Paul Coffey AS 2.50 6.00
220 Patrick Roy AS 6.00 15.00
221 Mark Messier AS 5.00 12.00
222 Mario Lemieux AS 10.00 25.00
223 Gordie Howe AS 8.00 20.00
224 Bobby Orr AS 10.00 25.00
225 Wayne Gretzky AS 15.00 40.00
226 Cody Hodgson RC 8.00 20.00
227 Jake Gardiner RC 5.00 12.00
228 Carl Klingberg RC 3.00 8.00
229 Mika Zibanejad RC 10.00 25.00
230 Mark Scheifele RC 12.00 30.00
231 Aaron Palushaj RC 3.00 8.00
232 Adam Larsson RC 4.00 10.00
233 Matt Read RC 4.00 10.00
234 Matt Frattin RC 3.00 8.00
235 Blake Geoffrion RC 3.00 8.00
236 Devante Smith-Pelly RC 4.00 10.00
237 Erik Gudbranson RC 4.00 10.00
238 Jonathon Blum RC 3.00 8.00
239 Anton Lander RC 3.00 8.00
240 Brandon Saad RC 6.00 15.00
241 Adam Henrique RC 8.00 20.00
242 Brett Connolly RC 3.00 8.00
243 Harri Sateri RC 3.00 8.00
244 Joe Colborne RC 3.00 8.00
245 Marcus Kruger RC 5.00 12.00
246 Greg Nemisz RC 3.00 8.00
247 Ryan Johansen RC 10.00 25.00
248 Sean Couturier RC 6.00 15.00
249 Gabriel Landeskog RC 8.00 20.00
250 Ryan Nugent-Hopkins RC 15.00 30.00

2011-12 Black Diamond Ruby

*1-100 SINGLE: 8X TO 20X BASIC CARDS
*101-150 DOUBLE: 3X TO 8X BASIC DBLE
*151-175 TRIPLE: 2X TO 5X BASIC TRIPLE
*176-200 TRIPLE ROOKIE: 1X TO 2.5X BASE
*201-225 QUAD: .8X TO 2X BASIC QUAD
*226-250 QUAD ROOKIE: .6X TO 1.5X BASE
226 Cody Hodgson 30.00 60.00
249 Gabriel Landeskog 25.00 60.00
250 Ryan Nugent-Hopkins 40.00 100.00

2011-12 Black Diamond All-Time Greats Championship Rings

ATG1 Duncan Keith 12.00 30.00
ATG2 Jonathan Toews 12.00 30.00
ATG3 Patrick Kane 15.00 40.00
ATG4 Patrick Sharp 10.00 25.00
ATG5 Henrik Zetterberg 12.00 30.00
ATG6 Johan Franzen 10.00 25.00
ATG7 Nicklas Lidstrom 6.00 15.00
ATG8 Pavel Datsyuk 15.00 40.00
ATG9 Glenn Anderson 10.00 25.00
ATG10 Grant Fuhr 15.00 40.00
ATG11 Jari Kurri 10.00 25.00
ATG12 Mark Messier 10.00 25.00
ATG13 Paul Coffey 10.00 25.00
ATG14 Wayne Gretzky 20.00 50.00
ATG15 Evgeni Malkin 10.00 25.00
ATG16 Jaromir Jagr 30.00 80.00
ATG17 Mario Lemieux 15.00 40.00
ATG18 Sidney Crosby 40.00 100.00

2011-12 Black Diamond Boston Bruins Championship Rings

CRB1 Tim Thomas 25.00 50.00
CRB2 Patrice Bergeron 20.00 50.00
CRB3 Zdeno Chara 15.00 40.00
CRB4 Brad Marchand 30.00 80.00
CRB5 Milan Lucic 15.00 40.00
CRB6 Nathan Horton 8.00 20.00
CRB7 David Krejci 12.00 30.00
CRB8 Michael Ryder 8.00 20.00
CRB9 Chris Kelly 12.00 30.00
CRB10 Dennis Seidenberg 10.00 25.00
CRB11 Mark Recchi 20.00 50.00
CRB12 Rich Peverley 15.00 40.00
CRB13 Tyler Seguin 15.00 40.00
CRB14 Andrew Ference 6.00 15.00
CRB15 Tomas Kaberle 10.00 25.00
CRB16 Johnny Boychuk 12.00 30.00
CRB17 Adam McQuaid 12.00 30.00
CRB18 Daniel Paille 6.00 15.00
CRB19 Gregory Campbell 6.00 15.00
CRB20 Shawn Thornton 10.00 25.00
CRB21 Shane Hnidy 10.00 25.00
CRB22 Steve Kampfer 10.00 25.00
CRB23 Jordan Caron 15.00 40.00
CRB24 Tuukka Rask 20.00 50.00

2011-12 Black Diamond Dual Jerseys

09TCCH Cody Hodgson C 3.00 8.00
09TCDT Dustin Tokarski E 4.00 10.00
09TCJE Jordan Eberle D 8.00 20.00
09TCJT John Tavares B 10.00 25.00
09TCPK P.K. Subban E 5.00 12.00
09TCTM Tyler Myers E 2.50 6.00
BOSNH Nathan Horton F 4.00 10.00
BOSTR Tuukka Rask F 5.00 12.00
BOSTT Tim Thomas F 5.00 12.00
BOSZC Zdeno Chara F 4.00 10.00
CGYJB Jay Bouwmeester F 2.50 6.00
CGYJI Jarome Iginla D 5.00 12.00
CGYMK Miikka Kiprusoff F 4.00 10.00
CGYRB Rene Bourque F 2.50 6.00
DETHZ Henrik Zetterberg F 5.00 12.00
DETJE Jonathan Ericsson F 2.50 6.00
DETJH Jim Howard E 5.00 12.00
DETNK Niklas Kronwall E 3.00 8.00
GR8GP Gilbert Perreault E 4.00 10.00
GR8ML Mario Lemieux C 15.00 40.00
GR8MM Mark Messier C 8.00 20.00
GR8WG Wayne Gretzky A 40.00 80.00
MTLAK Andrei Kostitsyn F 3.00 8.00
MTLAM Andrei Markov F 2.50 6.00
MTLCP Carey Price A 20.00 50.00
MTLPK P.K. Subban B 5.00 12.00
PHICG Claude Giroux F 4.00 10.00
PHICP Chris Pronger E 4.00 10.00
PHIJV James van Riemsdyk E 3.00 8.00
PHISH Scott Hartnell F 2.50 6.00
TORJG Jonas Gustavsson F 4.00 10.00
TORNK Nikolai Kulemin F 2.50 6.00
TORPK Phil Kessel E 4.00 10.00
TORTB Tyler Bozak F 2.50 6.00
VANAE Alexander Edler E 2.50 6.00
VANDS Daniel Sedin D 5.00 12.00
VANRK Ryan Kesler F 4.00 10.00
VANRL Roberto Luongo F 6.00 15.00
PITTJS Jordan Staal F 3.00 8.00
PITTKL Kristopher Letang D 5.00 12.00
PITTMF Marc-Andre Fleury E 8.00 20.00
PITTSC Sidney Crosby D 15.00 40.00
WASHAS Alexander Semin C 4.00 10.00
WASHMG Mike Green F 3.00 8.00
WASHNB Nicklas Backstrom C 4.00 10.00
WASHOV Alexander Ovechkin C 15.00 40.00
GOALIEMB Martin Brodeur E 6.00 15.00
GOALIEPR Patrick Roy E 6.00 15.00
GOALIERB Richard Brodeur F 4.00 10.00
GOALIETE Tony Esposito B 8.00 20.00

2011-12 Black Diamond Gemography

GEMAB Andy Bathgate B 50.00 100.00
GEMAH Ales Hemsky C 8.00 20.00
GEMAK Arturs Kulda D 4.00 10.00
GEMAO Alexander Ovechkin B 30.00 80.00
GEMBA Josh Bailey C 5.00 12.00
GEMBE Patrice Bergeron B 20.00 40.00
GEMBH Brett Hull B 30.00 60.00
GEMBL Brian Lee D 5.00 12.00
GEMBM Brett MacLean D 4.00 10.00
GEMBO Bobby Orr A 125.00 200.00
GEMBS Brayden Schenn C 8.00 20.00
GEMCA Cody Almond D 4.00 10.00
GEMCH Cody Hodgson B 40.00 80.00
GEMCN Cam Neely B 20.00 40.00
GEMCO Cal O'Reilly D 4.00 10.00
GEMCS Cory Schneider C 6.00 15.00
GEMDB Drayson Bowman D 4.00 10.00
GEMDC Daniel Carcillo C 8.00 20.00
GEMGH Gordie Howe B 60.00 120.00
GEMGL Guillaume Latendresse B 8.00 20.00
GEMJA Jamie Arniel D 5.00 12.00
GEMJB Jonathon Blum C 5.00 12.00
GEMJC John Carlson D 6.00 15.00
GEMJD Jason Demers D 4.00 10.00
GEMJE Jordan Eberle C 20.00 50.00
GEMJM Jacob Markstrom D 6.00 15.00
GEMJN John Negrin D 5.00 12.00
GEMKA Keith Aulie D 6.00 15.00
GEMKD Kaspars Daugavins D 5.00 12.00
GEMKT Kyle Turris C 4.00 10.00
GEMLC Luca Caputi D 4.00 10.00
GEMLO Logan Couture B 12.00 30.00
GEMMA Rick MacLeish B 30.00 60.00
GEMMH Matthew Halischuk D 4.00 10.00
GEMMM Mark Messier A 50.00 120.00
GEMMN Markus Naslund B 25.00 50.00
GEMMO Mark Olver D 4.00 10.00
GEMMS Marco Scandella D 4.00 10.00
GEMMZ Mats Zuccarello-Aasen D 6.00 15.00
GEMNP Nick Palmieri D 5.00 12.00
GEMOB Oskars Bartulis D 5.00 12.00
GEMPB Patrik Berglund D 4.00 10.00
GEMPC Patrice Cormier D 4.00 10.00
GEMPK Patrick Kane B 25.00 60.00
GEMPL Philip Larsen D 4.00 10.00
GEMPM Peter Mueller B 8.00 20.00
GEMRB Richard Bachman D 5.00 12.00
GEMRM Ryan McDonagh D 5.00 12.00
GEMSC Sidney Crosby B 75.00 150.00
GEMSH Steve Shutt A 50.00 100.00
GEMSS Steven Stamkos B 50.00 100.00
GEMST Chris Stewart C 5.00 12.00
GEMTE Tyler Ennis C 8.00 20.00
GEMTL Trevor Lewis D 4.00 10.00
GEMTM Thomas McCollum D 5.00 12.00
GEMTT Tomas Tatar D 6.00 15.00
GEMVH Victor Hedman B 12.00 30.00
GEMWG Wayne Gretzky B 200.00 500.00

2011-12 Black Diamond Hardware Heroes

HHBH Brett Hull 10.00 25.00
HHBO Bobby Orr 30.00 60.00
HHBP Bernie Parent 12.00 30.00
HHCP Corey Perry 15.00 40.00
HHCS Cory Schneider 10.00 25.00
HHDS Daniel Sedin 12.00 30.00
HHDW Doug Weight 8.00 20.00
HHEL Eric Lindros 15.00 40.00
HHHM Howie Morenz 12.00 30.00
HHIL Ian Laperriere 6.00 15.00
HHJA Jaromir Jagr 12.00 30.00
HHJG Jaromir Jagr 12.00 30.00
HHJJ Jaromir Jagr 12.00 30.00
HHJS Jeff Skinner 10.00 25.00
HHML Mario Lemieux 15.00 40.00
HHMS Martin St. Louis 10.00 25.00
HHNL Nicklas Lidstrom 6.00 15.00
HHPE Corey Perry 15.00 40.00
HHRK Ryan Kesler 10.00 25.00
HHSC Milt Schmidt 8.00 20.00
HHSE Daniel Sedin 8.00 20.00
HHTH Tim Thomas 12.00 30.00
HHTT Tim Thomas 12.00 30.00
HHWG Wayne Gretzky 50.00 100.00

2011-12 Black Diamond Lustrous Rookies

LR1 Devante Smith-Pelly 10.00 25.00
LR2 Greg Nemisz 8.00 20.00
LR3 Brandon Saad 15.00 40.00
LR4 Marcus Kruger 10.00 25.00
LR5 Gabriel Landeskog 25.00 60.00
LR6 Ryan Johansen 25.00 60.00
LR7 Anton Lander 8.00 20.00
LR8 Ryan Nugent-Hopkins 75.00 150.00
LR9 Erik Gudbranson 10.00 25.00
LR10 Adam Larsson 10.00 25.00
LR11 Adam Henrique 20.00 50.00
LR12 Mika Zibanejad 25.00 60.00
LR13 Sean Couturier 12.00 30.00
LR14 Brett Connolly 8.00 20.00
LR15 Jake Gardiner 10.00 25.00
LR16 Joe Colborne 8.00 20.00
LR17 Cody Hodgson 12.00 30.00
LR18 Mark Scheifele 30.00 80.00

2012-13 Black Diamond

1 Sidney Crosby .75 2.00
2 Jonathan Ericsson .12 .30
3 Patrik Berglund .12 .30
4 Tyler Seguin .25 .60
5 Scott Hartnell .12 .30
6 Tomas Fleischmann .12 .30
7 Ilya Bryzgalov .20 .50
8 Daniel Sedin .25 .60
9 Darren Helm .12 .30
10 Alexander Ovechkin .75 2.00
11 Nicklas Backstrom .20 .50
12 Eric Staal .25 .60
13 Evgeni Nabokov .15 .40
14 David Perron .15 .40
15 Jeff Carter .15 .40
16 James van Riemsdyk .15 .40
17 Bobby Ryan .15 .40
18 Thomas Vanek .15 .40
19 Scott Niedermayer .20 .50
20 Jonathan Quick .25 .60
21 Joe Thornton .30 .75
22 Henrik Sedin .25 .60
23 Dustin Byfuglien .20 .50
24 Jonas Hiller .15 .40
25 Jason Pominville .12 .30
26 Corey Crawford .25 .60
27 Jason Spezza .20 .50
28 Nathan Horton .20 .50
29 Taylor Hall .20 .50
30 Jonathan Toews .30 .75
31 Alexandre Burrows .12 .30
32 Joe Pavelski .25 .60
33 Jay Bouwmeester .12 .30
34 Ryan Suter .15 .40
35 Phil Esposito .30 .75
36 Mikkel Boedker .12 .30
37 Phil Kessel .20 .50
38 P.A. Parenteau .12 .30
39 Jacob Markstrom .20 .50
40 Jeff Skinner .25 .60
41 Dany Heatley .15 .40
42 Kristopher Letang .25 .60
43 Daniel Briere .20 .50
44 Ondrej Pavelec .20 .50
45 Andrew Ladd .12 .30
46 Derek Stepan .12 .30
47 Tomas Plekanec .12 .30
48 Valtteri Filppula .12 .30
49 Erik Johnson .12 .30
50 Steven Stamkos .40 1.00
51 Steve Ott .12 .30
52 James Neal .12 .30
53 Cody Hodgson .12 .30
54 Tyler Ennis .12 .30
55 Olli Jokinen .15 .40
56 Matt Stajan .12 .30
57 Kari Lehtonen .15 .40
58 Derek Roy .12 .30
59 Steve Mason .15 .40
60 Patrick Roy .50 1.25
61 Mike Ribeiro .12 .30
62 Sam Gagner .12 .30
63 Jack Johnson .12 .30
64 Patric Hornqvist .12 .30
65 Kyle Okposo .12 .30
66 Marc Staal .12 .30
67 Brian Elliott .15 .40
68 Mike Green .15 .40
69 Vincent Lecavalier .20 .50
70 Mario Lemieux .75 2.00
71 Mike Smith .20 .50
72 Milan Michalek .12 .30
73 Matt Moulson .12 .30
74 Lars Eller .12 .30
75 Stephen Weiss .15 .40
76 Ales Hemsky .15 .40
77 Semyon Varlamov .20 .50
78 Jordan Staal .15 .40
79 Tyler Myers .12 .30
80 Joe Sakic .40 1.00
81 Zdeno Chara .20 .50
82 Alex Tanguay .15 .40
83 Patrick Sharp .20 .50
84 Loui Eriksson .12 .30
85 Ryan Smyth .15 .40
86 Zach Parise .20 .50
87 Travis Zajac .12 .30
88 Michael Grabner .15 .40
89 Evander Kane .20 .50
90 Bobby Orr .75 2.00
91 Logan Couture .25 .60
92 Chris Kunitz .20 .50
93 Craig Anderson .20 .50
94 Niklas Backstrom .15 .40
95 Dustin Brown .20 .50
96 Patrik Elias .20 .50
97 Cam Ward .20 .50
98 Nathan Gerbe .12 .30
99 Ryan Getzlaf .20 .50
100 Wayne Gretzky 1.25 3.00
101 Tuukka Rask .75 2.00
102 Johnny Bucyk .60 1.50
103 Shea Weber .50 1.25
104 Saku Koivu .60 1.50
105 Ryan Miller .60 1.50
106 Ryan Callahan .40 1.00
107 Roberto Luongo 1.00 2.50
108 Rick Nash .60 1.50
109 Pekka Rinne .60 1.50
110 Paul Coffey .60 1.50
111 Patrick Marleau .60 1.50
112 Patrick Kane 1.25 3.00
113 Patrice Bergeron .75 2.00
114 P.K. Subban .75 2.00
115 Niklas Backstrom .50 1.25
116 Milan Lucic .60 1.50
117 Mikko Koivu .50 1.25
118 Mike Richards .50 1.25
119 Braden Holtby .75 2.00
120 Matt Duchene .60 1.50
121 Jordan Eberle .60 1.50
122 Marian Hossa .60 1.50
123 Marian Gaborik .60 1.50
124 Marcel Dionne .75 2.00
125 Marc-Andre Fleury 1.25 3.00
126 Luc Robitaille .60 1.50
127 Johan Franzen .50 1.25
128 Jim Howard .75 2.00
129 Jaroslav Halak .60 1.50
130 Jaromir Jagr 2.00 5.00
131 Joe Mullen .50 1.25
132 Jari Kurri .60 1.50
133 Jamie Benn .60 1.50
134 Jacob Markstrom .60 1.50
135 Henrik Zetterberg .75 2.00
136 Ryan Nugent-Hopkins .75 2.00
137 Gilbert Perreault .60 1.50
138 Paul Stastny .50 1.25
139 Erik Karlsson .75 2.00
140 Duncan Keith .50 1.25
141 Drew Doughty .75 2.00
142 Dion Phaneuf .50 1.25
143 David Clarkson .40 1.00
144 Daniel Alfredsson .60 1.50
145 Ron Hextall .60 1.50
146 Brendan Smith .40 1.00
147 Brayden Schenn .60 1.50
148 Bill Ranford .60 1.50
149 Anze Kopitar 1.00 2.50
150 Adam Henrique .50 1.25
151 Bobby Hull 1.25 3.00
152 Brad Park .50 1.25
153 Brendan Shanahan .60 1.50
154 Dino Ciccarelli .60 1.50
155 Dominik Hasek 1.00 2.50
156 Doug Gilmour .75 2.00
157 Gabriel Landeskog .75 2.00
158 Guy Lafleur .75 2.00
159 Jean Beliveau .60 1.50
160 Howie Morenz .50 1.25
161 Brian Leetch .50 1.25
162 Miikka Kiprusoff .60 1.50
163 Mike Gartner .75 2.00
164 John Tavares 1.00 2.50
165 Mike Modano 1.00 2.50
166 Neal Broten .50 1.25
167 Pelle Lindbergh .50 1.25
168 Mark Messier 1.25 3.00
169 Antti Niemi .50 1.25
170 Ron Francis .75 2.00
171 Claude Giroux .60 1.50
172 Martin St. Louis .60 1.50
173 Stan Mikita .75 2.00
174 Ted Lindsay .60 1.50
175 Tony Esposito .60 1.50
176 Mat Clark RC 1.50 4.00
177 Carter Camper RC 1.25 3.00
178 Lane MacDermid RC 1.50 4.00
179 Torey Krug RC 4.00 10.00
180 Michael Hutchinson RC 2.00 5.00
181 Travis Turnbull RC 1.25 3.00
182 Jeremy Welsh RC 1.50 4.00
183 Brandon Bollig RC 1.25 3.00
184 Mike Connolly RC 1.50 4.00
185 Dalton Prout RC 1.25 3.00
186 Andrew Joudrey RC 1.50 4.00
187 Shawn Hunwick RC 1.25 3.00
188 Ryan Garbutt RC 1.25 3.00
189 Mark Messier RG 4.00 10.00
190 Philippe Cornet RC 1.50 4.00
191 Colby Robak RC 1.25 3.00
192 Kristopher Foucault RC 1.25 3.00
193 Chay Genoway RC 1.25 3.00
194 Robert Mayer RC 2.00 5.00
195 Aaron Ness RC 1.25 3.00
196 Matt Donovan RC 1.50 4.00
197 Brandon Manning RC 1.50 4.00
198 Michael Stone RC 1.50 4.00
199 Matt Watkins RC 1.25 3.00
200 Tyson Sexsmith RC 1.25 3.00
201 Alexander Ovechkin AS 8.00 20.00
202 Bobby Clarke AS 3.00 8.00
203 Bobby Orr AS 8.00 20.00
204 Brett Hull AS 4.00 10.00
205 Carey Price AS 4.00 10.00
206 Curtis Joseph AS 2.50 6.00
207 Ed Belfour AS 2.00 5.00
208 Eric Lindros AS 3.00 8.00
209 Evgeni Malkin AS 4.00 10.00
210 Henrik Lundqvist AS 5.00 12.00
211 Ilya Kovalchuk AS 2.00 5.00
212 Jarome Iginla AS 2.50 6.00
213 Jeff Skinner AS 2.50 6.00
214 Joe Sakic AS 4.00 10.00
215 Jonathan Quick AS 2.50 6.00
216 Jonathan Toews AS 3.00 8.00
217 Mario Lemieux AS 8.00 20.00
218 Martin Brodeur AS 5.00 12.00
219 Nicklas Lidstrom AS 2.00 5.00
220 Patrick Roy AS 5.00 12.00
221 Pavel Datsyuk AS 3.00 8.00
222 Sidney Crosby AS 8.00 20.00
223 Steven Stamkos AS 4.00 10.00
224 Teemu Selanne AS 4.00 10.00
225 Wayne Gretzky AS 12.00 30.00
226 Maxime Sauve RC 1.25 3.00
227 Sven Baertschi RC 2.00 5.00
228 Akim Aliu RC 1.50 4.00
229 Tyson Barrie RC 4.00 10.00
230 Cody Goloubef RC 1.25 3.00
231 Brenden Dillon RC 1.50 4.00
232 Reilly Smith RC 4.00 10.00
233 Scott Glennie RC 1.50 4.00
234 Riley Sheahan RC 2.00 5.00
235 Wayne Gretzky RG 12.00 30.00
236 Jordan Nolan RC 1.25 3.00
237 Jason Zucker RC 3.00 8.00
238 Tyler Cuma RC 1.25 3.00
239 Gabriel Dumont RC 1.50 4.00
240 Chet Pickard RC 1.50 4.00
241 Casey Cizikas RC 1.50 4.00
242 Chris Kreider RC 5.00 12.00
243 Mark Stone RC 5.00 12.00
244 Jakob Silfverberg RC 2.50 6.00
245 Jake Allen RC 4.00 10.00
246 Jaden Schwartz RC 4.00 10.00
247 J.T. Brown RC 1.50 4.00
248 Ryan Hamilton RC 1.25 3.00
249 Carter Ashton RC 1.25 3.00
250 Jussi Rynnas RC 1.25 3.00

2012-13 Black Diamond Ruby

*1-100 SINGLE: 6X TO 15X BASIC CARDS
*101-150 DOUBLE: 3X TO 8X BASIC DBLE
*151-175 TRIPLE: 2X TO 5X BASIC TRIPLE
*176-200 TRIPLE ROOKIE: 1X TO 2.5X
*201-225 QUAD: .8X TO 2X BASIC QUAD
*226-250 QUAD ROOKIE: .6X TO 1.5X
242 Chris Kreider 15.00 40.00
246 Jaden Schwartz 12.00 30.00

2012-13 Black Diamond All-Time Greats Championship Rings

ATG1 Jean Beliveau 5.00 12.00
ATG2 Guy Lafleur 6.00 15.00
ATG3 Howie Morenz 4.00 10.00
ATG4 Patrick Roy 12.00 30.00
ATG5 Brendan Shanahan 5.00 12.00
ATG6 Brett Hull 10.00 25.00
ATG7 Nicklas Lidstrom 5.00 12.00
ATG8 Luc Robitaille 5.00 12.00
ATG9 Mike Bossy 5.00 12.00
ATG10 Clark Gillies 5.00 12.00
ATG11 Bryan Trottier 5.00 12.00
ATG12 Denis Potvin 5.00 12.00
ATG13 Patrick Roy 12.00 30.00
ATG14 Joe Sakic 10.00 25.00
ATG15 Ray Bourque 8.00 20.00
ATG16 Chris Drury 4.00 10.00
ATG17 Milan Hejduk 4.00 10.00
ATG18 Alex Tanguay 4.00 10.00
CRB1 Drew Doughty 6.00 15.00
CRB2 Jonathan Quick 6.00 15.00
CRB3 Anze Kopitar 8.00 20.00
CRB4 Jeff Carter 4.00 10.00
CRB5 Mike Richards 4.00 10.00
CRB6 Simon Gagne 5.00 12.00
CRB7 Rob Scuderi 4.00 10.00
CRB8 Matt Greene 4.00 10.00
CRB9 Dwight King 4.00 10.00
CRB10 Jordan Nolan 3.00 8.00
CRB11 Viatcheslav Voynov 5.00 12.00
CRB12 Justin Williams 4.00 10.00
CRB13 Dustin Brown 5.00 12.00
CRB14 Jarret Stoll 4.00 10.00
CRB15 Dustin Penner 4.00 10.00
CRB16 Trevor Lewis 3.00 8.00
CRB17 Jonathan Bernier 4.00 10.00
CRB18 Brad Richardson 3.00 8.00
CRB19 Kyle Clifford 3.00 8.00
CRB20 Colin Fraser 4.00 10.00
CRB21 Willie Mitchell 4.00 10.00
CRB22 Alec Martinez 4.00 10.00
CRB23 Andrei Loktionov 4.00 10.00
CRB24 Luc Robitaille 5.00 12.00

2012-13 Black Diamond Dual Jerseys

84BH Brett Hull C 6.00 15.00
84LR Luc Robitaille B 3.00 8.00
84ML Mario Lemieux B 12.00 30.00
84PR Patrick Roy B 8.00 20.00
ANABR Bobby Ryan F 2.50 6.00
ANACP Corey Perry D 5.00 12.00
ANAJH Jonas Hiller E 2.50 6.00
ANARG Ryan Getzlaf F 3.00 8.00
BEESBP Brad Park C 2.50 6.00
BEESCN Cam Neely F 3.00 8.00
BEESPE Phil Esposito C 5.00 12.00
BEESRB Ray Bourque D 5.00 12.00
BOSBM Brad Marchand F 6.00 15.00
BOSML Milan Lucic C 3.00 8.00
BOSPB Patrice Bergeron D 4.00 10.00
BOSTR Tuukka Rask F 4.00 10.00
BOSTS Tyler Seguin D 4.00 10.00
BOSZC Zdeno Chara D 3.00 8.00
BUFFCH Cody Hodgson E 2.00 5.00
BUFFDS Drew Stafford F 2.00 5.00
BUFFRM Ryan Miller F 3.00 8.00
BUFFTM Tyler Myers D 2.00 5.00
CBJDB Derick Brassard F 2.00 5.00
CBJJJ Jack Johnson B 2.00 5.00
CBJRJ Ryan Johansen F 2.50 6.00
CBJSM Steve Mason E 2.50 6.00
DALLJB Jamie Benn A 3.00 8.00
DALLKL Kari Lehtonen C 2.50 6.00
DALLLE Loui Eriksson F 2.00 5.00
DALLMR Michael Ryder C 2.00 5.00
DETHZ Henrik Zetterberg C 4.00 10.00
DETJF Johan Franzen D 2.50 6.00
DETJH Jim Howard D 4.00 10.00
DETNK Niklas Kronwall C 2.50 6.00
DETNL Nicklas Lidstrom E 3.00 8.00
DETPV Pavel Datsyuk C 5.00 12.00
EDMJE Jordan Eberle C 3.00 8.00
EDMLO Linus Omark C 2.50 6.00
EDMMP Magnus Paajarvi D 2.50 6.00
EDMRN Ryan Nugent-Hopkins C 4.00 10.00
EDMTH Taylor Hall D 3.00 8.00
EDMWG Wayne Gretzky A 20.00 50.00
GOALIEMB Martin Brodeur C 8.00 20.00
GOALIEPR Pekka Rinne D 3.00 8.00
GOALIERL Roberto Luongo B 5.00 12.00
LAKAK Anze Kopitar F 5.00 12.00
LAKDB Dustin Brown F 3.00 8.00
LAKJQ Jonathan Quick D 4.00 10.00
LAKJW Justin Williams F 2.50 6.00
NYRBB Brian Boyle D 2.00 5.00
NYRCK Chris Kreider C 8.00 20.00
NYRHL Henrik Lundqvist C 8.00 20.00
NYRMG Marian Gaborik C 3.00 8.00
NYRMS Marc Staal D 2.00 5.00
NYRRC Ryan Callahan E 2.00 5.00
PHICG Claude Giroux E 3.00 8.00
PHICP Chris Pronger E 3.00 8.00
PHIIB Ilya Bryzgalov D 3.00 8.00
PHISH Scott Hartnell D 2.00 5.00
PITTEM Evgeni Malkin E 6.00 15.00
PITTJN James Neal A 2.00 5.00
PITTKL Kristopher Letang C 4.00 10.00
PITTMF Marc-Andre Fleury D 6.00 15.00
PITTML Mario Lemieux B 12.00 30.00
PITTSC Sidney Crosby E 12.00 30.00
STARAO Alexander Ovechkin C 12.00 30.00
STARIK Ilya Kovalchuk C 3.00 8.00
STARJI Jarome Iginla B 4.00 10.00
STARJT Jonathan Toews C 5.00 12.00
STARSC Sidney Crosby D 12.00 30.00
STARSS Steven Stamkos D 6.00 15.00
STLCS Chris Stewart F 2.50 6.00
STLDB David Backes F 2.00 5.00
STLJH Jaroslav Halak E 3.00 8.00
STLPB Patrik Berglund D 2.00 5.00
TC1BC Brett Connolly TC E 2.00 5.00
TC1BS Brayden Schenn TC E 3.00 8.00
TC1CA Carter Ashton TC E 2.00 5.00
TC1CC Casey Cizikas TC E 2.50 6.00
TC1CE Cody Eakin TC E 2.00 5.00
TC1DO Dylan Olsen TC E 2.00 5.00
TC2EG Erik Gudbranson TC E 2.00 5.00
TC2JS Jaden Schwartz TC E 6.00 15.00
TC2LL Louis Leblanc TC C 2.00 5.00
TC2RE Ryan Ellis TC E 2.00 5.00
TC2SD Simon Despres TC E 2.50 6.00
TC2TB Tyson Barrie TC E 6.00 15.00
TORCO Colton Orr D 3.00 8.00
TORDP Dion Phaneuf A 2.50 6.00
TORNK Nikolai Kulemin E 2.00 5.00
TORPK Phil Kessel C 3.00 8.00
TOUGHCO Colton Orr E 3.00 8.00
TOUGHDC Daniel Carcillo F 2.00 5.00
TOUGHGP George Parros F 2.50 6.00
TOUGHMC Matt Carkner D 2.00 5.00
VANAB Alexandre Burrows C 2.00 5.00
VANDS Daniel Sedin C 4.00 10.00
VANRK Ryan Kesler C 3.00 8.00
VANRL Roberto Luongo D 5.00 12.00
GOALIERM Ryan Miller E 3.00 8.00

2012-13 Black Diamond Gemography

GEMAO Alexander Ovechkin A 80.00 150.00
GEMBM Brendan Mikkelson D 4.00 10.00
GEMBO Bobby Orr A 60.00 150.00
GEMBT Bryan Trottier A 6.00 15.00
GEMCA Carter Ashton D 4.00 10.00
GEMCE Cody Eakin D 4.00 10.00
GEMCF Cam Fowler D 6.00 15.00
GEMCJ Curtis Joseph B 8.00 20.00
GEMCK Chris Kunitz B 6.00 15.00
GEMCP Chet Pickard C 5.00 12.00
GEMCZ Casey Cizikas C 5.00 12.00
GEMDB Drayson Bowman D 4.00 10.00
GEMDG Daniel Girardi D 4.00 10.00
GEMDP David Perron B 5.00 12.00
GEMEN Evgeni Nabokov D 5.00 12.00
GEMGL Gabriel Landeskog A 8.00 20.00
GEMJB Jamie Benn B 6.00 15.00
GEMJE Jordan Eberle B 6.00 15.00
GEMJK Jake Allen C 12.00 30.00
GEMJM John Moore D 4.00 10.00
GEMKR Chris Kreider B 15.00 40.00
GEMLA Maxim Lapierre D 4.00 10.00
GEMMN Michal Neuvirth D 5.00 12.00
GEMMS Matt Stajan B 4.00 10.00
GEMNG Nicklas Grossman D 4.00 10.00
GEMRN Ryan Nugent-Hopkins A 8.00 20.00
GEMRY Jussi Rynnas C 4.00 10.00
GEMSC Sidney Crosby A 100.00 250.00
GEMSG Scott Glennie B 5.00 12.00
GEMSH Jaden Schwartz C 12.00 30.00
GEMSS Steven Stamkos A 40.00 100.00

GEMSV Sven Baertschi B 6.00 15.00
GEMSW Stephen Weiss C 5.00 12.00
GEMTA John Tavares A 30.00 80.00
GEMTS Tim Stapleton D 4.00 10.00
GEMTW Tom Wandell D 4.00 10.00
GEMVF Valtteri Filppula D 4.00 10.00
GEMWG Wayne Gretzky A 250.00 600.00
GEMZK Zack Kassian B 4.00 10.00

2012-13 Black Diamond Hardware Heroes

HHBC Brian Campbell 2.50 6.00
HHBE Brian Elliott 3.00 8.00
HHBH Bobby Hull 8.00 20.00
HHBT Bryan Trottier 4.00 10.00
HHDA Daniel Alfredsson 4.00 10.00
HHDP Denis Potvin 4.00 10.00
HHEK Erik Karlsson 5.00 12.00
HHEM Evgeni Malkin Ross 8.00 20.00
HHEV Evgeni Malkin Lindsay 8.00 20.00
HHGL Gabriel Landeskog 5.00 12.00
HHHL Henrik Lundqvist 10.00 25.00
HHJQ Jonathan Quick 5.00 12.00
HHMA Evgeni Malkin 8.00 20.00
HHMB Mike Bossy 4.00 10.00
HHMP Max Pacioretty 4.00 10.00
HHPB Patrice Bergeron 5.00 12.00
HHSS Steven Stamkos 8.00 20.00
HHWG Wayne Gretzky 25.00 60.00

2012-13 Black Diamond Lustrous

LGBO Bobby Orr G 15.00 40.00
LGML Mario Lemieux G 15.00 40.00
LGPR Patrick Roy G 10.00 25.00
LGWG Wayne Gretzky G 25.00 60.00
LRCA Carter Ashton R 2.50 6.00
LRCC Casey Cizikas R 3.00 8.00
LRCG Cody Goloubef R 2.50 6.00
LRCK Chris Kreider R 10.00 25.00
LRJA Jake Allen R 8.00 20.00
LRJR Jussi Rynnas R 2.50 6.00
LRJS Jakob Silfverberg R 5.00 12.00
LRJZ Jason Zucker R 6.00 15.00
LRSB Sven Baertschi R 4.00 10.00
LRSC Jaden Schwartz R 8.00 20.00
LRSG Scott Glennie R 3.00 8.00
LRTB Tyson Barrie R 8.00 20.00
LSAO Alexander Ovechkin S 15.00 40.00
LSCP Carey Price S 8.00 20.00
LSJE Jordan Eberle S 4.00 10.00
LSJS Jeff Skinner S 5.00 12.00
LSJT Jonathan Toews S 6.00 15.00
LSSC Sidney Crosby S 15.00 40.00
LSSS Steven Stamkos S 8.00 20.00
LSTH Taylor Hall S 4.00 10.00

2013-14 Black Diamond

COMP.SET w/o SP's (100) 10.00 25.00
1 Brad Richards .25 .60
2 Alex Tanguay .15 .40
3 Derek Roy .15 .40
4 Max Pacioretty .25 .60
5 Sergei Kostitsyn .15 .40
6 Ray Whitney .20 .50
7 Paul Stastny .20 .50
8 Cory Schneider .25 .60
9 Nicklas Backstrom .25 .60
10 Slava Voynov .20 .50
11 Jack Johnson .15 .40
12 Jonathan Bernier .20 .50
13 Devin Setoguchi .20 .50
14 David Krejci .25 .60
15 Jim Howard .30 .75
16 Martin Hanzal .15 .40
17 Mikael Backlund .20 .50
18 Dustin Jeffrey .15 .40
19 Alexander Semin .25 .60
20 David Backes .15 .40
21 Kyle Turris .15 .40
22 Sam Gagner .15 .40
23 Teddy Purcell .15 .40
24 Michael Ryder .15 .40
25 Bobby Ryan .20 .50
26 Andrew Ladd .15 .40
27 Raffi Torres .15 .40
28 Logan Couture .30 .75
29 David Clarkson .15 .40
30 Shea Weber .20 .50
31 Nathan Horton .25 .60
32 Steve Ott .15 .40
33 Joe Pavelski .30 .75
34 Ryan Suter .20 .50
35 Zdeno Chara .25 .60
36 Wayne Simmonds .30 .75
37 Ryan O'Reilly .25 .60
38 Jakob Silfverberg .15 .40
39 Jakub Voracek .15 .40
40 Alexandre Burrows .15 .40
41 Frazer McLaren .15 .40
42 Dan Boyle .15 .40
43 Kris Versteeg .15 .40
44 Evgeni Nabokov .20 .50
45 Henrik Sedin .30 .75
46 Patrick Marleau .25 .60
47 Jeff Skinner .30 .75
48 Michael Grabner .20 .50
49 Johan Franzen .20 .50
50 Andrew Shaw .15 .40
51 Ryan Johansen .20 .50
52 Lars Eller .15 .40
53 Tyler Ennis .15 .40
54 Niklas Kronwall .20 .50
55 Ales Hemsky .15 .40
56 Brent Seabrook .15 .40
57 Mike Ribeiro .15 .40
58 Tomas Vokoun .20 .50
59 Adam Henrique .20 .50
60 Justin Williams .20 .50
61 Justin Faulk .20 .50
62 Jiri Tlusty .15 .40
63 Mike Fisher .15 .40
64 Shawn Horcoff .15 .40
65 Chris Kunitz .25 .60
66 Kari Lehtonen .20 .50
67 Simon Despres .20 .50
68 Marian Hossa .25 .60
69 Cody Hodgson .20 .50
70 Brandon Saad .20 .50
71 Derek Stepan .15 .40
72 P.A. Parenteau .15 .40
73 Sergei Bobrovsky .40 1.00
74 Lee Stempniak .15 .40
75 David Legwand .20 .50
76 Oliver Ekman-Larsson .25 .60
77 Jake Muzzin .25 .60
78 Eric Staal .30 .75
79 Alex Pietrangelo .25 .60
80 Evander Kane .25 .60
81 Jonas Hiller .20 .50
82 Tyler Bozak .15 .40
83 Saku Koivu .25 .60
84 Matt Duchene .25 .60
85 Jacob Markstrom .25 .60
86 Martin St. Louis .25 .60
87 Ray Emery .20 .50
88 Matt Moulson .15 .40
89 Craig Anderson .25 .60
90 Pascal Dupuis .15 .40
91 Jason Pominville .15 .40
92 Joe Thornton .40 1.00
93 Ondrej Pavelec .25 .60
94 Chris Stewart .20 .50
95 Jamie Benn .25 .60
96 Brian Elliott .20 .50
97 Blake Wheeler .25 .60
98 James van Riemsdyk .20 .50
99 Patrik Elias .25 .60
100 Tomas Fleischmann .15 .40
101 Daniel Sedin .75 2.00
102 Andy Moog .60 1.50
103 Antti Niemi .50 1.25
104 Anze Kopitar 1.00 2.50
105 Bill Ranford .60 1.50
106 Brad Marchand 1.25 3.00
107 Braden Holtby .75 2.00
108 Brayden Schenn .60 1.50
109 Cam Neely .60 1.50
110 Roberto Luongo 1.00 2.50
111 Daniel Alfredsson .60 1.50
112 Dave Schultz .60 1.50
113 Dion Phaneuf .50 1.25
114 Corey Crawford .75 2.00
115 Erik Karlsson .75 2.00
116 Gabriel Landeskog .75 2.00
117 Grant Fuhr 1.00 2.50
118 Steve Mason .50 1.25
119 James Neal .60 1.50
120 Jari Kurri .60 1.50
121 Jarome Iginla .75 2.00
122 Jaroslav Halak .60 1.50
123 Jason Spezza .60 1.50
124 Jeff Carter .60 1.50
125 Jordan Staal .50 1.25
126 Kris Letang .75 2.00
127 Larry Robinson .60 1.50
128 Luc Robitaille .60 1.50
129 Marc-Andre Fleury 1.25 3.00
130 Marian Gaborik .60 1.50
131 Markus Naslund .60 1.50
132 Mike Richards .60 1.50
133 Milan Hejduk .50 1.25
134 Dany Heatley .50 1.25
135 Pekka Rinne .60 1.50
136 Peter Stastny .50 1.25
137 Phil Kessel .60 1.50
138 Ron Hextall .60 1.50
139 Terry O'Reilly .50 1.25
140 Ryan Getzlaf .60 1.50
141 Ryan Kesler .60 1.50
142 Ryan Smyth .60 1.50
143 Corey Perry 1.00 2.50
144 Scott Hartnell .40 1.00
145 Thomas Vanek .50 1.25
146 Tony Esposito .60 1.50
147 Tuukka Rask .75 2.00
148 Vincent Damphousse .50 1.25
149 Vincent Lecavalier .60 1.50
150 Wendel Clark 1.00 2.50
151 Bobby Hull 2.00 5.00
152 Gilbert Perreault 1.00 2.50
153 Carey Price 2.00 5.00
154 Chris Kunitz 1.00 2.50
155 Claude Giroux 1.00 2.50
156 P.K. Subban 1.25 3.00
157 Peter Forsberg 2.00 5.00
158 Doug Gilmour 1.25 3.00
159 Guy Lafleur 1.25 3.00
160 Felix Potvin 1.50 4.00
161 Jonathan Quick 1.25 3.00
162 Jordan Eberle 1.25 3.00
163 Mikko Koivu .75 2.00
164 Nicklas Lidstrom 1.00 2.50
165 Patrice Bergeron 1.25 3.00
166 Paul Coffey 1.00 2.50
167 Pavel Datsyuk 1.50 4.00
168 Phil Esposito 1.50 4.00
169 Rick Nash 1.00 2.50
170 Rogie Vachon 1.25 3.00
171 Ron Francis 1.25 3.00
172 Taylor Hall 1.25 3.00
173 Teemu Selanne 2.00 5.00
174 Tyler Seguin 1.25 3.00
175 Zach Parise 1.25 3.00
176 Charlie Coyle RC 2.50 6.00
177 Jack Campbell RC 4.00 10.00
178 Drew Shore RC 1.25 3.00
179 Lucas Lessio RC 1.25 3.00
180 Eric Gelinas RC 1.50 4.00
181 Igor Bobkov RC 1.25 3.00
182 Ryan Murphy RC 1.50 4.00
183 Beau Bennett RC 1.50 4.00
184 Tom Wilson RC 3.00 8.00
185 Nathan Beaulieu RC 1.00 2.50
186 Carl Soderberg RC 1.50 4.00
187 Tanner Pearson RC 1.50 4.00
188 Emerson Etem RC 1.50 4.00
189 Frank Corrado RC 1.00 2.50
190 Zach Redmond RC 1.25 3.00
191 Rickard Rakell RC 1.50 4.00
192 Scott Laughton RC 2.00 5.00
193 Johan Larsson RC 1.50 4.00
194 Austin Watson RC 1.50 4.00
195 Michael Sgarbossa RC 1.50 4.00
196 Joakim Nordstrom RC 2.00 5.00
197 Sami Vatanen RC 1.50 4.00
198 Filip Forsberg RC 5.00 12.00
199 Seth Jones RC 3.00 8.00
200 Nicklas Jensen RC 1.25 3.00
201 Alexander Ovechkin AS 8.00 20.00
202 Bobby Orr AS 8.00 20.00
203 Brett Hull AS 4.00 10.00
204 Dale Hawerchuk AS 2.50 6.00
205 Eric Lindros AS 3.00 8.00
206 Evgeni Malkin AS 4.00 10.00
207 Steve Yzerman AS 5.00 12.00
208 Jean Beliveau AS 2.00 5.00
209 Joe Sakic AS 4.00 10.00
210 John Tavares AS 3.00 8.00
211 Jonathan Toews AS 3.00 8.00
212 Mario Lemieux AS 8.00 20.00
213 Mark Messier AS 4.00 10.00
214 Martin Brodeur AS 5.00 12.00
215 Mats Sundin AS 2.00 5.00
216 Mike Bossy AS 2.50 6.00
217 Dominik Hasek AS 3.00 8.00
218 Patrick Kane AS 4.00 10.00
219 Patrick Roy AS 5.00 12.00
220 Pavel Bure AS 2.50 6.00
221 Ryan Miller AS 2.00 5.00
222 Sidney Crosby AS 8.00 20.00
223 Steven Stamkos AS 4.00 10.00
224 Theoren Fleury AS 2.50 6.00
225 Wayne Gretzky AS 6.00 15.00
226 Nail Yakupov RC 4.00 10.00
227 Tomas Hertl RC 4.00 10.00
228 Elias Lindholm RC 8.00 20.00
229 Nathan MacKinnon RC 20.00 50.00
230 Morgan Rielly RC 5.00 12.00
231 Brendan Gallagher RC 5.00 12.00
232 Cory Conacher RC 1.25 3.00
233 Justin Schultz RC 2.00 5.00
234 Mikael Granlund RC 3.00 8.00
235 Vladimir Tarasenko RC 5.00 12.00
236 Zemgus Girgensons RC 3.00 8.00
237 Alex Galchenyuk RC 8.00 20.00
238 Jonathan Huberdeau RC 5.00 12.00
239 Jonas Brodin RC 2.50 6.00
240 J.T. Miller RC 2.50 6.00
241 Dougie Hamilton RC 3.00 8.00
242 Boone Jenner RC 4.00 10.00
243 Tyler Toffoli RC 4.00 10.00
244 Aleksander Barkov RC 6.00 15.00
245 Rasmus Ristolainen RC 3.00 8.00
246 Ryan Murray RC 2.00 5.00
247 Valeri Nichushkin RC 4.00 10.00
248 Mikhail Grigorenko RC 1.25 3.00
249 Jacob Trouba RC 3.00 8.00
250 Sean Monahan RC 8.00 20.00

2013-14 Black Diamond Emerald

*176-200 ROOK/25: 2.5X TO 6X BASIC RC
*227-250 ROOK/25: 1.5X TO 4X BASIC RC
183 Beau Bennett AU 12.00 30.00
184 Tom Wilson AU 30.00 80.00
187 Tanner Pearson AU 15.00 40.00
192 Scott Laughton AU 20.00 50.00
194 Austin Watson AU 12.00 30.00
227 Tomas Hertl AU 30.00 80.00
229 Nathan MacKinnon AU 250.00 400.00
230 Morgan Rielly AU 60.00 120.00
231 Brendan Gallagher AU 40.00 100.00
232 Cory Conacher AU 10.00 25.00
233 Justin Schultz AU 15.00 40.00
237 Alex Galchenyuk AU 75.00 150.00
238 Jonathan Huberdeau AU 40.00 100.00
241 Dougie Hamilton AU 50.00 100.00
242 Boone Jenner AU 30.00 80.00
243 Tyler Toffoli AU 30.00 80.00
244 Aleksander Barkov AU 60.00 120.00
246 Ryan Murray AU 15.00 40.00
248 Mikhail Grigorenko AU 10.00 25.00
250 Sean Monahan AU 60.00 120.00

2013-14 Black Diamond Ruby

*1-100 VETS/50: 8X TO 20X BASIC CARD
*101-150 VETS/50: 3X TO 8X BASIC CARD
*151-175 VETS/50: 2X TO 5X BASIC CARD
*201-225 VET AS/50: 1.2X TO 3X BASIC CARD
*176-200 ROOK/150: 1.2X TO 3X BASIC RC
*226-250 ROOK/150: .8X TO 2X BASIC RC
114 Corey Crawford 6.00 15.00
229 Nathan MacKinnon 40.00 100.00

2013-14 Black Diamond All-Time Greats Championship Rings

ATG19 Wayne Gretzky 15.00 40.00
ATG20 Steve Yzerman 20.00 50.00
ATG21 Grant Fuhr 12.00 30.00
ATG22 Ron Francis 10.00 25.00
ATG23 Mike Bossy 8.00 20.00
ATG24 Bobby Hull 10.00 25.00
ATG25 Martin Brodeur 20.00 50.00
ATG26 Andy Moog 8.00 20.00
ATG27 Mark Messier 15.00 40.00

2013-14 Black Diamond Dual Jerseys

1984BH Brett Hull F 5.00 12.00
1984LR Luc Robitaille D 4.00 10.00
1984ML Mario Lemieux D 10.00 25.00
1984PR Patrick Roy C 15.00 40.00
ASBH Brett Hull B 15.00 30.00
ASJJ Jaromir Jagr F 5.00 12.00
ASMB Martin Brodeur F 10.00 25.00
ASML Mario Lemieux D 10.00 25.00
ASPR Patrick Roy D 10.00 25.00
ASWG Wayne Gretzky B 40.00 80.00
BEESBP Brad Park G 3.00 8.00
BEESCN Cam Neely H 4.00 10.00
BEESGM Glen Murray H 4.00 10.00
BEESPE Phil Esposito D 6.00 15.00
BEESRB Ray Bourque G 6.00 15.00
BRUINSDH Dougie Hamilton H 4.00 10.00
BRUINSPB Patrice Bergeron G 5.00 12.00
BRUINSTR Tuukka Rask C 8.00 20.00
BRUINSZC Zdeno Chara G 4.00 10.00
BUFFCH Cody Hodgson G 2.50 6.00
BUFFMG Mikhail Grigorenko G 1.25 3.00
BUFFRM Ryan Miller G 4.00 10.00
BUFFTV Thomas Vanek B 5.00 12.00
DALLJB Jamie Benn F 4.00 10.00
DALLJC Jack Campbell H 5.00 12.00
DALLJO Jamie Oleksiak G 3.00 8.00
DALLKL Kari Lehtonen H 3.00 8.00
EDMDD Devan Dubnyk H 3.00 8.00
EDMJE Jordan Eberle G 4.00 10.00
EDMJS Justin Schultz H 2.00 5.00
EDMNY Nail Yakupov G 6.00 15.00
EDMRN Ryan Nugent-Hopkins E 6.00 15.00
EDMTH Taylor Hall E 4.00 10.00
LAKAK Anze Kopitar F 6.00 15.00
LAKDB Dustin Brown F 4.00 10.00
LAKDD Drew Doughty E 5.00 12.00
LAKJQ Jonathan Quick D 5.00 12.00
LBBRCP Carey Price G 8.00 20.00
LBBRLR Larry Robinson F 4.00 10.00
LBBRPK P.K. Subban G 5.00 12.00
LBBRPR Patrick Roy C 10.00 25.00
NETCP Carey Price G 8.00 20.00
NETMB Martin Brodeur D 10.00 25.00
NETPR Pekka Rinne G 4.00 10.00
NETRM Ryan Miller F 4.00 10.00
NYRHL Henrik Lundqvist D 10.00 25.00
NYRJT J.T. Miller H 5.00 12.00
NYRRC Ryan Callahan B 10.00 25.00
NYRRN Rick Nash G 4.00 10.00
PENSBB Beau Bennett H 2.50 6.00
PENSEM Evgeni Malkin E 8.00 20.00
PENSJN James Neal G 2.50 6.00
PENSKL Kris Letang E 5.00 12.00
PENSMF Marc-Andre Fleury F 8.00 20.00
PENSML Mario Lemieux D 10.00 25.00
PHICG Claude Giroux F 4.00 10.00
PHIEL Eric Lindros D 6.00 15.00
PHIPF Peter Forsberg G 8.00 20.00
PHISL Scott Laughton H 2.50 6.00
PHIWS Wayne Simmonds G 5.00 12.00
RFWDAG Alex Galchenyuk H 8.00 20.00
RFWDJH Jonathan Huberdeau H 4.00 10.00
RFWDNY Nail Yakupov G 6.00 15.00
RFWDVT Vladimir Tarasenko G 5.00 12.00
ROOKBG Brendan Gallagher H 6.00 15.00
ROOKDH Dougie Hamilton R 4.00 10.00
ROOKDH Dougie Hamilton H 4.00 10.00
ROOKDJS Justin Schultz H 2.00 5.00
ROOKDJT Jarred Tinordi H 2.00 5.00
ROOKDNB Nathan Beaulieu H 1.25 3.00
ROOKJH Jonathan Huberdeau H 4.00 10.00
ROOKJO Jamie Oleksiak H 2.50 6.00
ROOKMP Mark Pysyk H 2.50 6.00
ROOKNB Nathan Beaulieu H 1.25 3.00
STARAO Alexander Ovechkin E 15.00 40.00
STARIK Ilya Kovalchuk G 4.00 10.00
STARJT Jonathan Toews G 5.00 12.00
STARRG Ryan Getzlaf D 4.00 10.00
STLCS Chris Stewart H 3.00 8.00
STLJH Jaroslav Halak F 4.00 10.00
STLPB Patrik Berglund D 2.50 6.00
STLVT Vladimir Tarasenko G 6.00 15.00
TORDP Dion Phaneuf G 3.00 8.00
TORNK Nikolai Kulemin D 2.50 6.00
TORPK Phil Kessel G 4.00 10.00
VANHS Henrik Sedin F 5.00 12.00
VANJS Jordan Schroeder H 2.50 6.00
VANRL Roberto Luongo G 6.00 15.00
WINGSDB Damien Brunner H 4.00 10.00
WINGSJF Johan Franzen E 3.00 8.00
WINGSJH Jim Howard G 3.00 8.00
WINGSNK Niklas Kronwall E 3.00 8.00
WINGSPV Pavel Datsyuk E 6.00 15.00
WINGSZT Henrik Zetterberg E 4.00 10.00

2013-14 Black Diamond Gemography

GEMAB Adam Burish E 5.00 12.00
GEMAK Arturs Kulda E 5.00 12.00
GEMAL Anders Lindback E 5.00 12.00
GEMAO Alexander Ovechkin A 80.00 150.00
GEMBO Bobby Orr C 50.00 125.00
GEMBS Brandon Saad E 6.00 15.00
GEMCS Clayton Stoner E 5.00 12.00
GEMDJ Dustin Jeffrey E 5.00 12.00
GEMDP Daniel Paille E 5.00 12.00
GEMEG Erik Gudbranson D 5.00 12.00
GEMEN Evgeni Nabokov A 8.00 20.00
GEMFB Fabian Brunnstrom D 5.00 12.00
GEMFM Frazer McLaren E 5.00 12.00
GEMJT John Tavares B 12.00 30.00
GEMKE Keaton Ellerby E 5.00 12.00
GEMML Mario Lemieux A 50.00 125.00
GEMMS Mats Sundin A 30.00 80.00
GEMPB Pavel Bure A 20.00 50.00
GEMPO Patrick O'Sullivan D 5.00 12.00
GEMPP Paul Postma E 5.00 12.00
GEMRE Ray Emery E 6.00 15.00
GEMRM Ryan McDonagh E 5.00 12.00
GEMSA Michael Sauer E 5.00 12.00
GEMSC Sidney Crosby A 100.00 200.00
GEMSK Sergei Kostitsyn E 5.00 12.00
GEMSS Steven Stamkos B 15.00 40.00
GEMTK Tim Kennedy E 5.00 12.00
GEMTR Tuukka Rask C 10.00 25.00
GEMWG Wayne Gretzky B 150.00 400.00
GEMZK Zenon Konopka D 6.00 15.00

2013-14 Black Diamond Hardware Heroes

HHAL Alexander Ovechkin 30.00 80.00
HHAO Alexander Ovechkin 30.00 80.00
HHBO Bobby Orr 12.00 30.00
HHCC Corey Crawford 10.00 25.00
HHDK Duncan Keith 10.00 25.00
HHHZ Henrik Zetterberg 8.00 20.00
HHJH Jonathan Huberdeau 10.00 25.00
HHJT Jonathan Toews 12.00 30.00
HHKA Patrick Kane 12.00 30.00
HHMB Martin Brodeur 20.00 50.00
HHPB Pavel Bure 8.00 20.00
HHPC Paul Coffey 8.00 20.00
HHPF Peter Forsberg 10.00 25.00
HHPK P.K. Subban 15.00 40.00
HHPR Patrick Roy 20.00 50.00
HHSB Sergei Bobrovsky 8.00 20.00
HHSC Sidney Crosby 30.00 80.00
HHZC Zdeno Chara 8.00 20.00

2013-14 Black Diamond Lustrous

L1 Nathan MacKinnon R 15.00 40.00
L2 Justin Schultz R 5.00 12.00
L3 Seth Jones R 10.00 25.00
L4 Jonathan Huberdeau R 10.00 25.00
L5 Cory Conacher R 3.00 8.00
L6 Nail Yakupov R 15.00 40.00
L7 Damien Brunner R 4.00 10.00
L8 Tyler Toffoli R 10.00 25.00
L9 Brendan Gallagher R 12.00 30.00
L10 Dougie Hamilton R 8.00 20.00
L11 Vladimir Tarasenko R 12.00 30.00
L12 Alex Galchenyuk R 12.00 30.00
L13 Sidney Crosby S 15.00 40.00
L14 Alexander Ovechkin S 30.00 80.00
L15 Steven Stamkos S 10.00 25.00
L16 Jonathan Toews S 10.00 25.00
L17 John Tavares S 12.00 30.00
L18 Patrice Bergeron S 10.00 25.00
L19 Henrik Lundqvist S 20.00 50.00
L20 Phil Kessel S 8.00 20.00
L21 Wayne Gretzky G 30.00 80.00
L22 Bobby Orr G 60.00 150.00
L23 Dominik Hasek G 25.00 60.00
L24 Bobby Hull G 8.00 20.00

2013-14 Black Diamond Stanley Cup Champs Championship Rings

CRB1 Andrew Shaw 6.00 15.00
CRB2 Ben Smith 8.00 20.00
CRB3 Brandon Bollig 8.00 20.00
CRB4 Brandon Saad 12.00 30.00
CRB5 Brent Seabrook 6.00 15.00
CRB6 Bryan Bickell 10.00 25.00
CRB7 Corey Crawford 12.00 30.00
CRB8 Daniel Carcillo 5.00 12.00
CRB9 Dave Bolland 6.00 15.00
CRB10 Duncan Keith 10.00 25.00
CRB11 Jamal Mayers 6.00 15.00
CRB12 Johnny Oduya 8.00 20.00
CRB13 Jonathan Toews 15.00 40.00
CRB14 Marcus Kruger 6.00 15.00
CRB15 Marian Hossa 10.00 25.00
CRB16 Michael Frolik 6.00 15.00
CRB17 Michal Handzus 8.00 20.00
CRB18 Michal Rozsival 6.00 15.00
CRB19 Nick Leddy 6.00 15.00
CRB20 Niklas Hjalmarsson 8.00 20.00
CRB21 Patrick Kane 20.00 50.00
CRB22 Patrick Sharp 10.00 25.00
CRB23 Ray Emery 8.00 20.00
CRB24 Viktor Stalberg 6.00 15.00

2014-15 Black Diamond

COMP.SET w/o SP's (100) 12.00 30.00
1 Valtteri Filppula .15 .40
2 Jiri Hudler .20 .50
3 Claude Lemieux .20 .50
4 Brandon Dubinsky .15 .40
5 Ryan Callahan .15 .40
6 Joe Pavelski .30 .75
7 Wayne Simmonds .30 .75
8 Mike Smith .25 .60
9 Chris Kreider .30 .75
10 Jack Johnson .15 .40
11 Nathan MacKinnon 1.00 2.50
12 Morgan Rielly .25 .60
13 Brandon Saad .20 .50
14 Evander Kane .25 .60
15 Justin Williams .20 .50
16 Jordan Eberle .25 .60
17 Eddie Lack .25 .60
18 Oliver Ekman-Larsson .25 .60
19 Marc-Andre Fleury .50 1.25
20 Andrew Ladd .15 .40
21 Pascal Dupuis .15 .40
22 Carter Hutton .20 .50
23 Patrik Berglund .15 .40
24 Matt Moulson .15 .40
25 Pierre Turgeon .20 .50
26 Mikko Koivu .20 .50
27 Alex Pietrangelo .20 .50
28 Niklas Kronwall .20 .50
29 Tomas Plekanec .15 .40
30 Johan Franzen .20 .50
31 Cam Fowler .25 .60
32 Blake Wheeler .25 .60
33 Cody Hodgson .20 .50
34 Mike Fisher .15 .40
35 Braden Holtby .30 .75
36 Tyler Johnson .15 .40
37 Nick Bjugstad .15 .40
38 Andrew Cogliano .15 .40
39 Mike Richards .20 .50
40 Aleksander Barkov .40 1.00
41 Glen Murray .15 .40
42 Alex Stalock .15 .40
43 Olli Maatta .15 .40
44 Tomas Hertl .25 .60
45 Jay Bouwmeester .15 .40
46 Brian Elliott .20 .50
47 Tyler Ennis .15 .40
48 Alec Martinez .15 .40
49 Zdeno Chara .25 .60
50 Travis Zajac .15 .40
51 Ryan McDonagh .25 .60
52 Jeff Skinner .30 .75
53 Slava Voynov .25 .60
54 Milan Lucic .25 .60
55 Doug Wilson .20 .50
56 Craig Smith .15 .40
57 Adam Henrique .20 .50
58 T.J. Oshie .25 .60
59 Tyler Toffoli .20 .50
60 Jason Pominville .15 .40
61 Matt Carle .15 .40
62 Kyle Turris .25 .60
63 John Carlson .20 .50
64 Antoine Vermette .15 .40
65 Bryan Little .20 .50
66 Ben Scrivens .20 .50
67 Patrik Elias .25 .60
68 Bill Barber .25 .60
69 Eric Staal .30 .75
70 Josh Bailey .15 .40
71 Daniel Sedin .30 .75
72 Kari Lehtonen .20 .50
73 Dion Phaneuf .20 .50
74 Patrick Marleau .25 .60
75 Derek Stepan .20 .50
76 Clarke MacArthur .15 .40
77 Vladimir Tarasenko .30 .75
78 David Perron .20 .50
79 Brayden Schenn .25 .60
80 Valeri Nichushkin .25 .60
81 Dustin Brown .25 .60
82 Erik Johnson .15 .40
83 Drew Stafford .15 .40
84 Shane Doan .20 .50
85 Marian Hossa .25 .60
86 Bryan Bickell .15 .40
87 Semyon Varlamov .25 .60
88 Sergei Bobrovsky .40 1.00
89 Mike Green .20 .50
90 Dwayne Roloson .15 .40
91 Jonathan Huberdeau .30 .75
92 Doug Harvey .25 .60
93 Kevin Shattenkirk .15 .40
94 Patrick Sharp .25 .60
95 Chris Higgins .15 .40
96 Colin Greening .15 .40
97 Vincent Damphousse .20 .50
98 Max Pacioretty .25 .60
99 Ryan O'Reilly .25 .60
100 Sean Monahan .15 .40
101 Nathan Horton .60 1.50
102 Nicklas Backstrom .60 1.50
103 Ryan Suter .50 1.25
104 Erik Karlsson .75 2.00
105 Jeff Carter .50 1.25
106 Henrik Sedin .75 2.00
107 Keith Yandle .40 1.00
108 Roberto Luongo 1.00 2.50
109 Bobby Ryan .50 1.25
110 Brian Bellows .50 1.25
111 Jakub Voracek .50 1.25
112 Jamie Benn .60 1.50
113 Antti Niemi .50 1.25
114 P.K. Subban .75 2.00
115 Tony Esposito .60 1.50
116 John LeClair .60 1.50
117 Taylor Hall .60 1.50
118 Brent Seabrook .40 1.00
119 Corey Crawford .75 2.00
120 Logan Couture .75 2.00
121 Pekka Rinne .60 1.50
122 Kyle Okposo .40 1.00
123 Zach Parise .60 1.50
124 Cory Schneider .60 1.50
125 Nazem Kadri .75 2.00
126 Mike Richter .60 1.50
127 Joe Thornton 1.00 2.50
128 David Backes .40 1.00
129 Trevor Linden .60 1.50
130 Brad Marchand 1.25 3.00
131 Doug Gilmour .75 2.00
132 Rick Nash .60 1.50
133 Ben Bishop .50 1.25
134 Guy Lafleur .75 2.00
135 Vincent Lecavalier .60 1.50
136 Jim Howard .75 2.00
137 Mike Modano 1.00 2.50
138 Corey Perry 1.00 2.50
139 Chris Kunitz .60 1.50
140 Phil Esposito 1.00 2.50
141 Arturs Irbe .50 1.25
142 Dustin Byfuglien .60 1.50
143 Duncan Keith .50 1.25
144 Nicklas Lidstrom .60 1.50
145 James van Riemsdyk .50 1.25
146 Alexander Steen .40 1.00
147 Craig Anderson .50 1.25
148 Gabriel Landeskog .75 2.00
149 Adam Oates .60 1.50
150 John Gibson .60 1.50
151 Pavel Datsyuk 1.50 4.00
152 Patrice Bergeron 1.25 3.00
153 Ron Francis 1.25 3.00
154 Jonathan Quick 1.25 3.00
155 Tyler Seguin 1.25 3.00
156 Jonathan Bernier .75 2.00
157 Grant Fuhr 1.25 3.00
158 Patrick Kane 1.50 4.00
159 Jari Kurri 1.00 2.50
160 Henrik Zetterberg 1.00 2.50
161 Phil Kessel 1.00 2.50
162 Shea Weber 1.00 2.50
163 Martin St. Louis 1.00 2.50
164 Ryan Getzlaf 1.00 2.50
165 Bobby Hull 2.00 5.00
166 Carey Price 2.00 5.00
167 Jeremy Roenick 1.50 4.00
168 Drew Doughty 1.25 3.00
169 Anze Kopitar 1.50 4.00
170 Ryan Nugent-Hopkins 1.25 3.00
171 Felix Potvin 1.50 4.00
172 Tuukka Rask 1.25 3.00
173 Matt Duchene 1.00 2.50
174 Theoren Fleury 1.00 2.50
175 Claude Giroux 1.00 2.50
176 Trevor van Riemsdyk RC 2.50 6.00
177 Nicolas Deslauriers RC 1.50 4.00
178 Vincent Trocheck RC 3.00 8.00
179 Mark Visentin RC 1.50 4.00
180 Mirco Mueller RC 1.50 4.00
181 Kristers Gudlevskis RC 1.50 4.00
182 Markus Granlund RC 2.50 6.00
183 Greg McKegg RC 1.25 3.00
184 Colton Sissons RC 1.50 4.00
185 Ryan Sproul RC 1.50 4.00
186 Andrey Makarov RC 1.50 4.00
187 William Karlsson RC 5.00 12.00
188 Laurent Brossoit RC 1.50 4.00
189 Pierre-Edouard Bellemare RC 1.50 4.00
190 Christian Folin RC 1.50 4.00
191 Corban Knight RC 1.50 4.00
192 Teemu Pulkkinen RC 2.00 5.00
193 Michael Zalewski RC 1.25 3.00
194 Jake McCabe RC 1.50 4.00
195 Patrick Brown RC 1.50 4.00
196 Patrik Nemeth RC 1.25 3.00
197 Brandon Kozun RC 1.25 3.00
198 Jori Lehtera RC 2.00 5.00
199 Dennis Everberg RC 1.50 4.00
200 Marko Dano RC 1.50 4.00
201 Jonathan Toews AS 3.00 8.00
202 Teemu Selanne AS 4.00 10.00
203 Peter Forsberg AS 4.00 10.00
204 John Tavares AS 3.00 8.00
205 Mats Sundin AS 2.00 5.00
206 Mario Lemieux AS 8.00 20.00
207 Stan Mikita AS 2.50 6.00
208 Martin Brodeur AS 5.00 12.00
209 Pavel Bure AS 2.00 5.00
210 Mark Messier AS 4.00 10.00
211 Bobby Orr AS 4.00 10.00
212 Mike Bossy AS 2.00 5.00
213 Steven Stamkos AS 4.00 10.00
214 Joe Sakic AS 4.00 10.00
215 Ray Bourque AS 3.00 8.00
216 Patrick Roy AS 5.00 12.00
217 Henrik Lundqvist AS 5.00 12.00
218 Evgeni Malkin AS 4.00 10.00
219 Sidney Crosby AS 5.00 12.00
220 Wayne Gretzky AS 12.00 30.00
221 Dominik Hasek AS 3.00 8.00
222 Jarome Iginla AS 2.50 6.00
223 Steve Yzerman AS 5.00 12.00
224 Jaromir Jagr AS 6.00 15.00
225 Alexander Ovechkin AS 8.00 20.00
226 Sam Reinhart RC 10.00 25.00
227 Brandon Gormley RC 2.50 6.00
228 Adam Lowry RC 4.00 10.00
229 Evgeny Kuznetsov RC 6.00 15.00
230 Vladislav Namestnikov RC 4.00 10.00
231 Johnny Gaudreau RC 8.00 20.00
232 Anthony Duclair RC 8.00 20.00
233 Damon Severson RC 2.50 6.00
234 Jiri Sekac RC 2.00 5.00
235 Teuvo Teravainen RC 4.00 10.00
236 Oscar Klefbom RC 5.00 12.00
237 Calle Jarnkrok RC 2.50 6.00
238 Alexander Khokhlachev RC 2.50 6.00
239 Griffin Reinhart RC 2.50 6.00
240 Andre Burakovsky RC 4.00 10.00
241 Ty Rattie RC 2.50 6.00
242 Alexander Wennberg RC 4.00 10.00
243 Aaron Ekblad RC 5.00 12.00
244 Joey Hishon RC 3.00 8.00
245 Jonathan Drouin RC 8.00 20.00
246 Chris Tierney RC 2.50 6.00
247 Victor Rask RC 2.50 6.00
248 Leon Draisaitl RC 15.00 40.00
249 Stuart Percy RC 2.50 6.00
250 Curtis Lazar RC 2.50 6.00

2014-15 Black Diamond Emerald

*176-200 ROOK/25: 2.5X TO 6X BASIC RC
*227-250 ROOK/25: 1.5X TO 4X BASIC RC
178 Vincent Trocheck AU 30.00 80.00
179 Mark Visentin AU 25.00 50.00
180 Mirco Mueller AU 15.00 40.00
182 Markus Granlund AU 25.00 60.00
183 Greg McKegg AU 12.00 30.00
184 Colton Sissons AU 15.00 40.00
185 Ryan Sproul AU 15.00 40.00
188 Laurent Brossoit AU 15.00 40.00
191 Corban Knight AU 15.00 40.00
194 Jake McCabe AU 15.00 40.00
226 Sam Reinhart AU 100.00 200.00
227 Brandon Gormley AU 15.00 40.00
229 Evgeny Kuznetsov AU 50.00 100.00
230 Vladislav Namestnikov AU 25.00 60.00
231 Johnny Gaudreau AU 150.00 250.00
235 Teuvo Teravainen AU 100.00 175.00
236 Oscar Klefbom AU 30.00 80.00
238 Alexander Khokhlachev AU 15.00 40.00
239 Griffin Reinhart AU 15.00 40.00
240 Andre Burakovsky AU 50.00 100.00
241 Ty Rattie AU 15.00 40.00
242 Alexander Wennberg AU 25.00 60.00
243 Aaron Ekblad AU 100.00 200.00
244 Joey Hishon AU 20.00 50.00
245 Jonathan Drouin AU 125.00 200.00
246 Chris Tierney AU 15.00 40.00
248 Leon Draisaitl AU 80.00 200.00

2014-15 Black Diamond Orange

*1-100 VETS: 3X TO 8X BASIC CARD
*101-150 VETS: 2X TO 5X BASIC CARD
*151-175 VET: 1.5X TO 4X BASIC CARD
*176-200 ROOK: 1.5X TO 4X BASIC RC
*201-225 VET AS: 1X TO 2.5X BASIC CARD
*226-250 ROOK: .8X TO 2X BASIC RC
102 Nicklas Backstrom 3.00 8.00
220 Wayne Gretzky AS 25.00 50.00
231 Johnny Gaudreau 20.00 50.00
248 Leon Draisaitl 20.00 50.00

2014-15 Black Diamond Ruby

*1-100 VETS/50: 6X TO 15X BASIC CARD
*101-150 VETS/50: 2.5X TO 6X BASIC CARD
*151-175 VETS/50: 1.5X TO 4X BASIC CARD
*176-200 ROOK/150: 1X TO 2.5X BASIC RC
*201-225 VET AS/50: 1.2X TO 3X BASIC CARD
*226-250 ROOK/150: .6X TO 1.5X BASIC RC
102 Nicklas Backstrom 4.00 10.00
220 Wayne Gretzky AS 25.00 50.00
231 Johnny Gaudreau 25.00 60.00
243 Aaron Ekblad 20.00 50.00
245 Jonathan Drouin 20.00 50.00
248 Leon Draisaitl 25.00 60.00

2014-15 Black Diamond Championship Rings

CRB1 Drew Doughty 12.00 30.00
CRB2 Anze Kopitar 15.00 40.00
CRB3 Willie Mitchell 6.00 15.00
CRB4 Kyle Clifford 6.00 15.00
CRB5 Slava Voynov 10.00 25.00
CRB6 Tanner Pearson 6.00 15.00
CRB7 Trevor Lewis 6.00 15.00
CRB8 Dustin Brown 10.00 25.00
CRB9 Mike Richards 8.00 20.00
CRB10 Matt Greene 6.00 15.00
CRB11 Tyler Toffoli 10.00 25.00
CRB12 Jeff Schultz 6.00 15.00
CRB13 Jeff Carter 8.00 20.00
CRB14 Jarret Stoll 8.00 20.00
CRB15 Jonathan Quick 12.00 30.00
CRB16 Jake Muzzin 10.00 25.00
CRB17 Alec Martinez 6.00 15.00
CRB18 Justin Williams 8.00 20.00
CRB19 Robyn Regehr 6.00 15.00
CRB20 Dwight King 6.00 15.00
CRB21 Marian Gaborik 10.00 25.00

2014-15 Black Diamond Dual Jerseys

ASEM Evgeni Malkin E 5.00 12.00
ASLC Logan Couture E 3.00 8.00
ASRN Rick Nash E 3.00 8.00

ASVL Vincent Lecavalier F 2.50 6.00
ANABL Ben Lovejoy F 1.50 4.00
ANACF Cam Fowler E 2.50 6.00
ANACP Corey Perry D 4.00 10.00
ANARG Ryan Getzlaf E 2.50 6.00
CHIBS Brent Seabrook F 1.50 4.00
CHIJT Jonathan Toews C 4.00 10.00
CHIPS Patrick Sharp F 2.50 6.00
CHISA Brandon Saad E 2.00 5.00
DALCE Cody Eakin E 1.50 4.00
DALKL Kari Lehtonen E 2.00 5.00
DALPN Patrik Nemeth F 2.50 6.00
DALTS Tyler Seguin E 3.00 8.00
LAKCF Colin Fraser E 1.50 4.00
LAKJM Jake Muzzin E 2.50 6.00
LAKJN Jordan Nolan E 2.50 6.00
LAKKC Kyle Clifford F 1.50 4.00
MONAG Alex Galchenyuk F 1.50 4.00
MONBG Brendan Gallagher E 2.50 6.00
MONCP Carey Price F 5.00 12.00
MONMP Max Pacioretty E 2.50 6.00
NJDAG Andy Greene F 1.50 4.00
NJDAH Adam Henrique E 2.00 5.00
NJDCS Cory Schneider E 2.50 6.00
NJDSG Stephen Gionta E 1.50 4.00
NYIFN Frans Nielsen F 1.50 4.00
NYIMD Matt Donovan F 1.50 4.00
NYIMG Michael Grabner E 2.00 5.00
NYITH Thomas Hickey E 1.50 4.00
OTTBR Bobby Ryan E 2.00 5.00
OTTEK Erik Karlsson E 3.00 8.00
OTTKT Kyle Turris A 2.50 6.00
OTTRL Robin Lehner E 2.00 5.00
PHIBC Braydon Coburn D 1.50 4.00
PHIJV Jakub Voracek B 2.00 5.00
PHIMR Matt Read B 1.50 4.00
PHISC Sean Couturier E 2.00 5.00
PHISM Steve Mason E 2.00 5.00
PHIWS Wayne Simmonds E 3.00 8.00
PITBG Brian Gibbons F 1.50 4.00
PITBS Brandon Sutter E 1.50 4.00
PITCK Chris Kunitz F 2.50 6.00
PITJZ Jeff Zatkoff E 2.00 5.00
PITMF Marc-Andre Fleury F 5.00 12.00
PITOM Olli Maatta F 1.50 4.00
TOREB Ed Belfour F 2.50 6.00
TORJB Jonathan Bernier E 2.00 5.00
TORPK Phil Kessel E 2.50 6.00
TORRF Ron Francis F 3.00 8.00
WASAO Alexander Ovechkin E 10.00 25.00
WASJC John Carlson D 2.50 6.00
WASMG Mike Green E 2.00 5.00
WASNB Nicklas Backstrom D 2.50 6.00
BUFFDS Drew Stafford C 1.50 4.00
BUFFMM Matt Moulson F 1.50 4.00
BUFFTE Tyler Ennis E 1.50 4.00
BUFFTM Tyler Myers E 1.50 4.00
LBBRBB Brian Bellows F 2.00 5.00
LBBRLR Larry Robinson F 2.50 6.00
LBBRPT Pierre Turgeon E 2.00 5.00
LBBRVD Vincent Damphousse F 2.00 5.00
DUCKSCP Corey Perry E 4.00 10.00
DUCKSHL Hampus Lindholm E 1.50 4.00
DUCKSRG Ryan Getzlaf E 2.50 6.00
DUCKSTS Teemu Selanne F 5.00 12.00
KINGSAK Anze Kopitar F 4.00 10.00
KINGSDB Dustin Brown E 2.50 6.00
KINGSDD Drew Doughty F 3.00 8.00
KINGSSV Slava Voynov E 2.50 6.00
WINGSJH Jim Howard E 3.00 8.00
WINGSNK Niklas Kronwall C 2.00 5.00
WINGSPD Pavel Datsyuk E 4.00 10.00
WINGSSY Steve Yzerman E 6.00 15.00
KINGS2JC Jeff Carter B 2.00 5.00
KINGS2JW Justin Williams E 2.00 5.00
KINGS2MG Matt Greene E 1.50 4.00
KINGS2MR Mike Richards E 2.00 5.00

2014-15 Black Diamond Gemography

GEMAW Austin Watson C 4.00 10.00
GEMBD Brenden Dillon D 3.00 8.00
GEMBO Bobby Orr B 90.00 150.00
GEMBR Bobby Ryan B 8.00 20.00
GEMBS Brandon Sutter C 4.00 10.00
GEMCC Connor Carrick D 3.00 8.00
GEMCK Chris Kreider C 8.00 20.00
GEMCT Colten Teubert C 5.00 12.00
GEMDB David Backes C 4.00 10.00
GEMDS Drew Shore D 3.00 8.00
GEMHS Harri Sateri D 20.00 40.00
GEMJB Johnny Bucyk B 15.00 40.00
GEMJC Jared Cowen C 4.00 10.00
GEMJG John Gibson D 5.00 12.00
GEMJM Jon Merrill D 3.00 8.00
GEMJO Jamie Oleksiak C 5.00 12.00
GEMJT Jarred Tinordi D 8.00 20.00
GEMLE Lars Eller C 4.00 10.00
GEMLL Lucas Lessio D 4.00 10.00
GEMLS Luke Schenn C 6.00 15.00
GEMML Michael Latta D 5.00 12.00
GEMPP Paul Postma D 3.00 8.00
GEMRF Ron Francis B 15.00 40.00
GEMRM Ryan Murphy D 3.00 8.00
GEMRP Richard Panik D 3.00 8.00
GEMSB Sergei Bobrovsky C 10.00 25.00
GEMTA John Tavares B 30.00 60.00
GEMTW Tom Wilson A 50.00 100.00
GEMWG Wayne Gretzky B 200.00 500.00

2014-15 Black Diamond Hardware Heroes

HHAO Alexander Ovechkin 30.00 80.00
HHDH Dominik Hasek 12.00 30.00
HHJS Joe Sakic 15.00 40.00
HHJT Joe Thornton 12.00 30.00
HHJW Justin Williams 8.00 20.00
HHMS Martin St. Louis 8.00 20.00
HHNM Nathan MacKinnon 15.00 40.00
HHPD Pavel Datsyuk 12.00 30.00
HHPF Peter Forsberg 12.00 30.00
HHRO Ryan O'Reilly 8.00 20.00
HHSC Sidney Crosby 30.00 80.00
HHTR Tuukka Rask 10.00 25.00
HHWG Wayne Gretzky 50.00 125.00

2014-15 Black Diamond UD Black Lustrous Rookies Previews

LRP1 Aaron Ekblad 12.00 30.00
LRP2 Evgeny Kuznetsov 6.00 15.00
LRP3 Curtis Lazar 5.00 12.00
LRP4 Leon Draisaitl 15.00 40.00
LRP5 Sam Reinhart 12.00 30.00
LRP6 Jonathan Drouin 12.00 30.00
LRP7 Alexander Wennberg 8.00 20.00
LRP8 Anthony Duclair 5.00 12.00

2015-16 Black Diamond

BDBAE Aaron Ekblad 3.00 8.00
BDBAK Anze Kopitar 4.00 10.00
BDBAL Andrew Ladd 1.50 4.00
BDBAO Alexander Ovechkin 10.00 25.00
BDBBD Brandon Dubinsky 1.50 4.00
BDBBE Jamie Benn 2.50 6.00
BDBBO Bobby Orr 10.00 25.00
BDBCG Claude Giroux 2.50 6.00
BDBCP Carey Price 5.00 12.00
BDBCS Cory Schneider 2.50 6.00
BDBEK Erik Karlsson 3.00 8.00
BDBEM Evgeni Malkin 5.00 12.00
BDBES Eric Staal 3.00 8.00
BDBFF Filip Forsberg 4.00 10.00
BDBHL Henrik Lundqvist 6.00 15.00
BDBHS Henrik Sedin 3.00 8.00
BDBHZ Henrik Zetterberg 3.00 8.00
BDBJB Jonathan Bernier 2.00 5.00
BDBJJ Jaromir Jagr 8.00 20.00
BDBJP Joe Pavelski 3.00 8.00
BDBJQ Jonathan Quick 3.00 8.00
BDBJT Jonathan Toews 4.00 10.00
BDBMD Matt Duchene 2.50 6.00
BDBML Mario Lemieux 10.00 25.00
BDBNA Rick Nash 2.50 6.00
BDBNB Nicklas Backstrom 2.50 6.00
BDBNM Nathan MacKinnon 10.00 25.00
BDBPB Patrice Bergeron 3.00 8.00
BDBPD Pavel Datsyuk 4.00 10.00
BDBPE Corey Perry 4.00 10.00
BDBPK Patrick Kane 5.00 12.00
BDBPR Patrick Roy 6.00 15.00
BDBPS P.K. Subban 3.00 8.00
BDBRG Ryan Getzlaf 2.50 6.00
BDBRM Ryan Miller 2.50 6.00
BDBRN Ryan Nugent-Hopkins 3.00 8.00
BDBSC Sidney Crosby 10.00 25.00
BDBSD Shane Doan 2.00 5.00
BDBSM Sean Monahan 1.50 4.00
BDBSS Steven Stamkos 5.00 12.00
BDBSW Shea Weber 2.50 6.00
BDBSY Steve Yzerman 6.00 15.00
BDBTA John Tavares 4.00 10.00
BDBTH Taylor Hall 2.50 6.00
BDBTR Tuukka Rask 3.00 8.00
BDBTS Tyler Seguin 3.00 8.00
BDBVT Vladimir Tarasenko 3.00 8.00
BDBWG Wayne Gretzky 15.00 40.00
BDBZG Zemgus Girgensons 2.00 5.00
BDBZP Zach Parise 2.50 6.00
BDRAC Andrew Copp RC 25.00 60.00
BDRAP Artemi Panarin RC 100.00 250.00
BDRCH Connor Hellebuyck RC 100.00 250.00
BDRCM Connor McDavid RC 3000.00 8000.00
BDRDL Dylan Larkin RC 80.00 200.00
BDRDS Daniel Sprong RC 30.00 80.00
BDREP Emile Poirier RC 20.00 50.00
BDRHS Henrik Samuelsson RC 15.00 40.00
BDRJE Jack Eichel RC 250.00 400.00
BDRJR Jacob de la Rose RC 25.00 60.00
BDRJV Jake Virtanen RC 30.00 80.00
BDRKF Kevin Fiala RC 30.00 80.00
BDRMD Max Domi RC 50.00 125.00
BDRMP Matt Puempel RC 20.00 50.00
BDRMS Malcolm Subban RC 40.00 100.00
BDRNE Nikolaj Ehlers RC 50.00 125.00
BDRNG Nikolay Goldobin RC 25.00 60.00
BDRNH Noah Hanifin RC 40.00 100.00
BDRNR Nick Ritchie RC 25.00 60.00
BDRNS Nick Shore RC 15.00 40.00
BDRRA Mikko Rantanen RC 50.00 125.00
BDRRF Robby Fabbri RC 30.00 80.00
BDRRH Ryan Hartman RC 30.00 80.00
BDRRK Ronalds Kenins RC 15.00 40.00
BDRSB Sam Bennett RC 50.00 125.00
BDRSP Shane Prince RC 15.00 40.00
BDRRWG Wayne Gretzky RR 150.00 350.00

2015-16 Black Diamond Pure Black

BDBAE Aaron Ekblad AU/99 6.00 15.00
BDBAK Anze Kopitar AU/99 8.00 20.00
BDBAL Andrew Ladd AU/99 3.00 8.00
BDBAO Alexander Ovechkin AU/25 40.00 100.00
BDBBD Brandon Dubinsky AU/99 3.00 8.00
BDBBE Jamie Benn/99 5.00 12.00
BDBBO Bobby Orr AU/25 60.00 150.00
BDBCG Claude Giroux/99 5.00 12.00
BDBCP Carey Price AU/25 50.00 125.00
BDBCS Cory Schneider/99 5.00 12.00
BDBEK Erik Karlsson/99 6.00 15.00
BDBEM Evgeni Malkin AU/99 10.00 25.00
BDBES Eric Staal AU/99 6.00 15.00
BDBFF Filip Forsberg/99 8.00 20.00
BDBHL Henrik Lundqvist/99 12.00 30.00
BDBHS Henrik Sedin/99 5.00 12.00
BDBHZ Henrik Zetterberg/99 5.00 12.00
BDBJB Jonathan Bernier AU/99 4.00 10.00
BDBJJ Jaromir Jagr/99 15.00 40.00
BDBJP Joe Pavelski AU/99 6.00 15.00
BDBJQ Jonathan Quick/99 6.00 15.00
BDBJT Jonathan Toews AU/25 30.00 80.00
BDBMD Matt Duchene AU/99 5.00 12.00
BDBML Mario Lemieux AU/25 50.00 125.00
BDBNA Rick Nash AU/99 5.00 12.00
BDBNB Nicklas Backstrom/99 5.00 12.00
BDBNM Nathan MacKinnon AU/99 20.00 50.00
BDBPB Patrice Bergeron/99 6.00 15.00
BDBPD Pavel Datsyuk AU/99 8.00 20.00
BDBPE Corey Perry/99 8.00 20.00
BDBPK Patrick Kane/99 10.00 25.00
BDBPR Patrick Roy AU/25 50.00 125.00
BDBPS P.K. Subban/99 8.00 20.00
BDBRG Ryan Getzlaf/99 5.00 12.00
BDBRM Ryan Miller/99 5.00 12.00
BDBRN Ryan Nugent-Hopkins/99 6.00 15.00
BDBSC Sidney Crosby
AU/25 EXCH 100.00 200.00
BDBSD Shane Doan/99 4.00 10.00
BDBSM Sean Monahan/99 3.00 8.00
BDBSS Steven Stamkos/99 10.00 25.00
BDBSW Shea Weber AU/99 4.00 10.00
BDBSY Steve Yzerman AU/25 40.00 100.00
BDBTA John Tavares AU/99 8.00 20.00
BDBTH Taylor Hall AU/99 6.00 15.00
BDBTR Tuukka Rask/99 6.00 15.00
BDBTS Tyler Seguin/99 6.00 15.00
BDBVT Vladimir Tarasenko/99 6.00 15.00
BDBWG Wayne Gretzky AU/25 200.00 500.00
BDBZG Zemgus Girgensons AU/99 4.00 10.00
BDBZP Zach Parise/99 5.00 12.00

2015-16 Black Diamond Championship Rings

CRAD Andrew Desjardins 3.00 8.00
CRAS Andrew Shaw 3.00 8.00
CRAV Antoine Vermette 3.00 8.00
CRBB Bryan Bickell 3.00 8.00
CRBR Brad Richards 5.00 12.00
CRBS Brent Seabrook 3.00 8.00
CRCC Corey Crawford 6.00 15.00
CRDK Duncan Keith 4.00 10.00
CRDR David Rundblad 3.00 8.00
CRJN Joakim Nordstrom 3.00 8.00
CRJO Johnny Oduya 4.00 10.00
CRJT Jonathan Toews 8.00 20.00
CRKC Kyle Cumiskey 3.00 8.00
CRKT Kimmo Timonen 3.00 8.00
CRKV Kris Versteeg 3.00 8.00
CRMH Marian Hossa 5.00 12.00
CRMK Marcus Kruger 3.00 8.00
CRMR Michal Rozsival 3.00 8.00
CRNH Niklas Hjalmarsson 3.00 8.00
CRPK Patrick Kane 10.00 25.00
CRPS Patrick Sharp 5.00 12.00
CRSA Brandon Saad 4.00 10.00
CRSD Scott Darling 4.00 10.00
CRTR Trevor van Riemsdyk 4.00 10.00
CRTT Teuvo Teravainen 5.00 12.00

2015-16 Black Diamond Diamond Mine Memorabilia

DMAG Alex Galchenyuk Ptch/50 3.00 8.00
DMAK Anze Kopitar Glv/25 8.00 20.00
DMAO Alexander Ovechkin Ptch/25 20.00 50.00
DMAT Alex Tanguay Ptch/75 3.00 8.00
DMBG Brendan Gallagher Ptch/25 5.00 12.00
DMBL Rob Blake Pants/75 5.00 12.00
DMBR Bill Ranford Pads/75 5.00 12.00
DMCC Chris Chelios Ptch/50 5.00 12.00
DMCG Claude Giroux Jsy/125 5.00 12.00
DMCP Carey Price Pants/25 10.00 25.00
DMCR Corey Crawford Ptch/50 6.00 15.00
DMDB Dustin Brown Glv/25 5.00 12.00
DMDG Doug Gilmour Stk/25 6.00 15.00
DMDS Daniel Sedin Ptch/50 5.00 12.00
DMEM Evgeni Malkin Skate/25 10.00 25.00
DMGM Glen Murray Ptch/75 4.00 10.00
DMGR Wayne Gretzky Socks/25 30.00 80.00
DMHL Henrik Lundqvist Jsy/125 12.00 30.00
DMHS Henrik Sedin Stk/50 6.00 15.00
DMHZ Henrik Zetterberg Ptch/25 6.00 15.00
DMJA James van Riemsdyk Jsy/125 4.00 10.00
DMJC Jeff Carter Glv/25 4.00 10.00
DMJG Johnny Gaudreau Jsy/125 8.00 20.00
DMJP Jason Spezza Ptch/25 5.00 12.00
DMJQ Jonathan Quick Blkr/50 8.00 20.00
DMJR Jeremy Roenick Ptch/50 8.00 20.00
DMJT Jonathan Toews Jsy/125 8.00 20.00
DMMD Marcel Dionne Ptch/25 6.00 15.00
DMMF Marc-Andre Fleury Pads/50 10.00 25.00
DMNM Nathan MacKinnon Jsy/125 20.00 50.00
DMPB Patrice Bergeron Jsy/125 6.00 15.00
DMPD Pavel Datsyuk Pads/25 8.00 20.00
DMPS P.K. Subban Jsy/125 6.00 15.00
DMPT Pierre Turgeon Ptch/50 4.00 10.00
DMRG Ryan Getzlaf Jsy/125 5.00 12.00
DMRL Roberto Luongo Glv/25 8.00 20.00
DMRN Rick Nash Jsy/125 5.00 12.00
DMRO Rod Brind'Amour Ptch/75 4.00 10.00
DMRY Bobby Ryan Ptch/50 4.00 10.00
DMSH Scott Hartnell Ptch/50 3.00 8.00
DMSS Steven Stamkos Jsy/125 10.00 25.00
DMTA John Tavares Jsy/125 8.00 20.00
DMTS Tyler Seguin Jsy/125 6.00 15.00
DMVT Vladimir Tarasenko Jsy/125 6.00 15.00
DMZC Zdeno Chara Ptch/50 5.00 12.00
DMZP Zach Parise Skate/25 5.00 12.00

2015-16 Black Diamond Double Diamond Jersey Booklets

DDBBK J.Bernier/N.Kadri/99 8.00 20.00
DDBBS J.Benn/T.Seguin/99 8.00 20.00
DDBBT D.Backes/Tarasenko/99 8.00 20.00
DDBCB R.Bourque/Z.Chara/99 10.00 25.00
DDBCT J.Carter/T.Toffoli/99 6.00 15.00
DDBFI T.Fleury/J.Iginla/99 6.00 15.00
DDBID J.Iginla/M.Duchene/99 8.00 20.00
DDBKM E.Malkin/C.Kunitz/99 12.00 30.00
DDBMC Brodeur/Schneider/99 15.00 40.00
DDBMG Monahan/Gaudreau/99 10.00 25.00
DDBNZ R.Nash/M.Zuccarello/99 6.00 15.00
DDBPG R.Getzlaf/C.Perry/99 10.00 25.00
DDBPP Z.Parise/J.Pominville/99 6.00 15.00
DDBPS C.Price/P.Subban/99 12.00 30.00
DDBRF B.Ranford/G.Fuhr/99 10.00 25.00
DDBRG W.Gretzky/R.Blake/25 40.00 100.00
DDBSK D.Savard/M.Keane/99 6.00 15.00
DDBSS D.Sedin/H.Sedin/99 6.00 15.00
DDBVG C.Giroux/J.Voracek/99 6.00 15.00

2015-16 Black Diamond Jerseys

*PRIME/25-35: .6X TO 1.5X BASIC INSERTS
BDBAE Aaron Ekblad/85 5.00 12.00
BDBAK Anze Kopitar/85 6.00 15.00
BDBAL Andrew Ladd/85 2.50 6.00
BDBAO Alexander Ovechkin/35 15.00 40.00
BDBBD Brandon Dubinsky/85 2.50 6.00
BDBBE Jamie Benn/85 6.00 15.00
BDBCG Claude Giroux/85 4.00 10.00
BDBCP Carey Price/35 8.00 20.00
BDBCS Cory Schneider/85 4.00 10.00
BDBEK Erik Karlsson/85 6.00 15.00
BDBEM Evgeni Malkin/35 8.00 20.00
BDBES Eric Staal/85 5.00 12.00
BDBHL Henrik Lundqvist/35 10.00 25.00
BDBHS Henrik Sedin/85 5.00 12.00
BDBHZ Henrik Zetterberg/85 5.00 12.00
BDBJB Jonathan Bernier/85 3.00 8.00
BDBJP Joe Pavelski/85 5.00 12.00
BDBJQ Jonathan Quick/85 6.00 15.00
BDBJT Jonathan Toews/35 6.00 15.00
BDBMD Matt Duchene/85 4.00 10.00
BDBML Mario Lemieux/35 15.00 40.00
BDBNA Rick Nash/85 4.00 10.00
BDBNB Nicklas Backstrom/85 4.00 10.00
BDBNM Nathan MacKinnon/35 15.00 40.00
BDBPB Patrice Bergeron/85 5.00 12.00
BDBPD Pavel Datsyuk/35 6.00 15.00
BDBPE Corey Perry/85 6.00 15.00
BDBPK Patrick Kane/35 8.00 20.00
BDBPR Patrick Roy/35 10.00 25.00
BDBPS P.K. Subban/85 5.00 12.00
BDBRG Ryan Getzlaf/35 4.00 10.00
BDBRM Ryan Miller/85 4.00 10.00
BDBSC Sidney Crosby/35 15.00 40.00
BDBSD Shane Doan/85 3.00 8.00
BDBSM Sean Monahan/85 2.50 6.00
BDBSS Steven Stamkos/85 8.00 20.00
BDBSW Shea Weber/85 3.00 8.00
BDBSY Steve Yzerman/35 10.00 25.00
BDBTA John Tavares/35 6.00 15.00
BDBTR Tuukka Rask/85 5.00 12.00
BDBTS Tyler Seguin/85 5.00 12.00
BDBVT Vladimir Tarasenko/85 5.00 12.00
BDBWG Wayne Gretzky/35 25.00 60.00
BDBZG Zemgus Girgensons/85 3.00 8.00
BDBZP Zach Parise/85 4.00 10.00

2015-16 Black Diamond Retired Numbers

RNBC Bobby Clarke/84 10.00 25.00
RNBH Bobby Hull/80 12.00 30.00
RNBO Bobby Orr/79 25.00 60.00
RNBS Borje Salming/90 6.00 15.00
RNDG Doug Gilmour/103 8.00 20.00
RNGF Grant Fuhr/100 10.00 25.00
RNHU Brett Hull/106 12.00 30.00
RNJS Joe Sakic/109 12.00 30.00
RNLR Larry Robinson/92 6.00 15.00
RNMB Mike Bossy/87 6.00 15.00
RNMD Marcel Dionne/89 8.00 20.00
RNME Mark Messier/104 12.00 30.00
RNMG Mike Gartner/98 8.00 20.00
RNML Mario Lemieux/106 25.00 60.00
RNMM Mike Modano/111 10.00 25.00
RNMN Markus Naslund/109 6.00 15.00
RNPR Patrick Roy/103 15.00 40.00
RNRB Ray Bourque/101 10.00 25.00
RNSA Terry Sawchuk/70 6.00 15.00
RNTS Teemu Selanne/114 12.00 30.00
RNWG Wayne Gretzky/99 40.00 100.00

2015-16 Black Diamond Retired Numbers Autographs

RNBC Bobby Clarke/49 15.00 40.00
RNBH Bobby Hull/25 25.00 60.00
RNBS Borje Salming/49 10.00 25.00
RNDG Doug Gilmour/49 12.00 30.00
RNGF Grant Fuhr/49 15.00 40.00
RNHU Brett Hull/25 20.00 50.00
RNJS Joe Sakic/25 20.00 50.00
RNLR Larry Robinson/25 10.00 25.00
RNMB Mike Bossy/49 10.00 25.00
RNMD Marcel Dionne/49 12.00 30.00
RNMG Mike Gartner/49 8.00 20.00
RNMM Mike Modano/25 15.00 40.00
RNMN Markus Naslund/49 10.00 25.00
RNRB Ray Bourque/25 15.00 40.00
RNTS Teemu Selanne/25 20.00 50.00

2015-16 Black Diamond Rookie Gems

RGCH Connor Hellebuyck 12.00 30.00
RGCM Connor McDavid 50.00 125.00
RGDL Dylan Larkin 10.00 25.00
RGEP Emile Poirier 2.50 6.00
RGHS Henrik Samuelsson 2.00 5.00
RGJE Jack Eichel 12.00 30.00
RGJR Jacob de la Rose 3.00 8.00
RGKF Kevin Fiala 4.00 10.00
RGMD Max Domi 6.00 15.00
RGMS Malcolm Subban 6.00 15.00
RGNE Nikolaj Ehlers 6.00 15.00
RGNH Noah Hanifin 5.00 12.00
RGRH Ryan Hartman 4.00 10.00
RGRK Ronalds Kenins 2.00 5.00
RGSB Sam Bennett 10.00 25.00
RGSG Stanislav Galiev 3.00 8.00

2015-16 Black Diamond Rookie Gems Pure Black

*BLACK/25: .8X TO 2X BASIC INSERTS/399
RGCM Connor McDavid 200.00 350.00
RGJE Jack Eichel 40.00 100.00

2015-16 Black Diamond Rookie Gems Pure Black Autographs

RGCM Connor McDavid/49 EXCH 250.00 450.00
RGEP Emile Poirier/99 6.00 15.00
RGJR Jacob de la Rose/99 8.00 20.00
RGKF Kevin Fiala/99 10.00 25.00
RGMD Max Domi/99 15.00 40.00
RGMS Malcolm Subban/99 12.00 30.00
RGNE Nikolaj Ehlers/99 15.00 40.00
RGNH Noah Hanifin/99 15.00 40.00
RGRH Ryan Hartman/99 10.00 25.00
RGSB Sam Bennett/49 25.00 60.00

2015-16 Black Diamond Rookie Jersey Booklets

RBRCH Connor Hellebuyck 20.00 50.00
RBRCM Connor McDavid 60.00 150.00
RBREP Emile Poirier 4.00 10.00
RBRJD Jacob de la Rose 5.00 12.00
RBRJE Jack Eichel 20.00 50.00
RBRJV Jake Virtanen 6.00 15.00
RBRKF Kevin Fiala 6.00 15.00
RBRMD Max Domi 10.00 25.00
RBRMP Matt Puempel 4.00 10.00
RBRNE Nikolaj Ehlers 10.00 25.00
RBRNH Noah Hanifin 8.00 20.00
RBRRH Ryan Hartman 6.00 15.00
RBRSB Sam Bennett 15.00 40.00
RBRSP Shane Prince 3.00 8.00

2015-16 Black Diamond Rookie Jersey Booklets Patch

RBRCH Connor Hellebuyck AU 60.00 150.00
RBRCM Connor McDavid AU 250.00 400.00
RBREP Emile Poirier AU 12.00 30.00
RBRJD Jacob de la Rose AU 15.00 40.00
RBRJE Jack Eichel 60.00 150.00
RBRJV Jake Virtanen AU 20.00 50.00
RBRKF Kevin Fiala AU 20.00 50.00
RBRMD Max Domi AU 30.00 80.00
RBRMP Matt Puempel AU 12.00 30.00
RBRNE Nikolaj Ehlers AU 30.00 80.00
RBRNH Noah Hanifin AU 25.00 60.00
RBRRH Ryan Hartman AU 20.00 50.00
RBRSB Sam Bennett AU 50.00 125.00
RBRSP Shane Prince AU 10.00 25.00

2015-16 Black Diamond Rookie Jersey Placards

*PATCH/25: .8X TO 2X BASIC JSY/299
RMPCM Connor McDavid 30.00 80.00
RMPJE Jack Eichel 12.00 30.00
RMPJR Jacob de la Rose 3.00 8.00
RMPKF Kevin Fiala 4.00 10.00
RMPMD Max Domi 6.00 15.00
RMPSB Sam Bennett 10.00 25.00

2015-16 Black Diamond Rookie Jersey Placards Autographs

*PATCH/15: X TO X BASIC AUTO/125
RMPCM Connor McDavid 200.00 400.00
RMPJR Jacob de la Rose 5.00 12.00
RMPKF Kevin Fiala 6.00 15.00
RMPMD Max Domi 10.00 25.00
RMPNE Nikolaj Ehlers 10.00 25.00
RMPSB Sam Bennett 15.00 40.00

2015-16 Black Diamond Rookie Signature Placards

RSPCM Connor McDavid/149 175.00 300.00
RSPEP Emile Poirier/249 4.00 10.00
RSPJR Jacob de la Rose/249 5.00 12.00
RSPKF Kevin Fiala/249 6.00 15.00
RSPMC Nikolaj Ehlers/149 10.00 25.00
RSPMD Max Domi/249 10.00 25.00
RSPMS Malcolm Subban/249 8.00 20.00
RSPNH Noah Hanifin/249 8.00 20.00
RSPRH Ryan Hartman/249 6.00 15.00
RSPSB Sam Bennett/249 15.00 40.00

2015-16 Black Diamond Rookie Team Logo Jumbos

RTLCM Connor McDavid 200.00 500.00
RTLJD Jacob de la Rose 4.00 10.00
RTLJE Jack Eichel 15.00 40.00
RTLJV Jake Virtanen 5.00 12.00
RTLKF Kevin Fiala 5.00 12.00
RTLMD Max Domi 8.00 20.00
RTLMP Matt Puempel 3.00 8.00
RTLMS Malcolm Subban 6.00 15.00
RTLNE Nikolaj Ehlers 8.00 20.00
RTLRH Ryan Hartman 5.00 12.00
RTLSB Sam Bennett 12.00 30.00

2015-16 Black Diamond Rookie Team Logo Jumbos Autographs Gold

RTLCM Connor McDavid 300.00 500.00
RTLJD Jacob de la Rose 8.00 20.00
RTLJV Jake Virtanen 10.00 25.00
RTLKF Kevin Fiala 10.00 25.00
RTLMD Max Domi 15.00 40.00
RTLMP Matt Puempel 6.00 15.00
RTLMS Malcolm Subban 12.00 30.00
RTLNE Nikolaj Ehlers 15.00 40.00
RTLRH Ryan Hartman 10.00 25.00
RTLSB Sam Bennett 25.00 60.00

2015-16 Black Diamond Signature Placards

SPAG Alex Galchenyuk B 6.00 15.00
SPAL Anders Lee E 10.00 25.00
SPBB Brent Burns C 10.00 25.00
SPBG Brendan Gallagher B 10.00 25.00
SPBH Bo Horvat D 12.00 30.00
SPBS Brandon Saad C 8.00 20.00
SPCN Cam Neely A 10.00 25.00
SPCO Chris Osgood B 10.00 25.00
SPCP Carey Price A 20.00 50.00
SPDH Dougie Hamilton C 8.00 20.00
SPFA Frederik Andersen E 12.00 30.00
SPGA Glenn Anderson A 8.00 20.00
SPGN Gustav Nyquist C 6.00 15.00
SPJC John Carlson D 10.00 25.00
SPJG Johnny Gaudreau D 15.00 40.00
SPJK John Klingberg E 10.00 25.00
SPJP Joe Pavelski A 12.00 30.00
SPJV James van Riemsdyk B 8.00 20.00
SPMK Mike Keane B 8.00 20.00
SPMM Marty McSorley B 8.00 20.00
SPON Owen Nolan B 6.00 15.00
SPTA Tomas Tatar E 6.00 15.00
SPTK Torey Krug E 8.00 20.00
SPTT Tyler Toffoli D 8.00 20.00
SPZG Zemgus Girgensons D 8.00 20.00
SPZP Zach Parise A 12.00 30.00

2015-16 Black Diamond Silver on Black Autographs

SBAK Anze Kopitar/50 20.00 50.00
SBAO Alexander Ovechkin/20 40.00 80.00
SBFP Felix Potvin/65 20.00 50.00
SBJB Jamie Benn/50 12.00 30.00
SBJT Jonathan Toews/35 60.00 100.00
SBKY Keith Yandle/65 6.00 15.00
SBMF Marc-Andre Fleury/35 25.00 60.00
SBMM Mark Messier/20 30.00 60.00
SBMP Max Pacioretty/65 10.00 25.00
SBNL Nicklas Lidstrom/35 12.00 30.00
SBPE Phil Esposito/35 25.00 50.00
SBRB Ray Bourque/35 20.00 50.00
SBSY Steve Yzerman/20 40.00 80.00
SBTH Taylor Hall/65 20.00 40.00

2015-16 Black Diamond Silver on Black Rookie Autographs

SBRSCM Connor McDavid/99 300.00 500.00
SBRSEP Emile Poirier/199 4.00 10.00
SBRSJR Jacob de la Rose/199 5.00 12.00
SBRSKF Kevin Fiala/199 6.00 15.00
SBRSMD Max Domi/199 15.00 40.00
SBRSMS Malcolm Subban/199 8.00 20.00
SBRSNE Nikolaj Ehlers/99 12.00 30.00
SBRSNH Noah Hanifin/199 8.00 20.00
SBRSRH Ryan Hartman/199 6.00 15.00
SBRSSB Sam Bennett/199 15.00 40.00

2015-16 Black Diamond Team Logo Jumbos

TLBBAO Adam Oates 8.00 20.00
TLBBBO Bobby Orr 30.00 80.00
TLBBCN Cam Neely 8.00 20.00
TLBBGC Gerry Cheevers 8.00 20.00
TLBBPB Patrice Bergeron 10.00 25.00
TLBBPE Phil Esposito 12.00 30.00
TLBBRB Ray Bourque 12.00 30.00
TLBBTR Tuukka Rask 10.00 25.00
TLBBZC Zdeno Chara 8.00 20.00
TLCBBH Bobby Hull 15.00 40.00
TLCBCC Chris Chelios 8.00 20.00
TLCBCR Corey Crawford 10.00 25.00
TLCBDK Duncan Keith 6.00 15.00
TLCBDS Denis Savard 8.00 20.00
TLCBGH Glenn Hall 8.00 20.00
TLCBJR Jeremy Roenick 12.00 30.00
TLCBJT Jonathan Toews 12.00 30.00
TLCBSL Steve Larmer 6.00 15.00
TLMCAG Alex Galchenyuk 5.00 12.00
TLMCBG Brendan Gallagher 8.00 20.00
TLMCCA Carey Price 15.00 40.00
TLMCGL Guy Lafleur 10.00 25.00
TLMCLR Larry Robinson 8.00 20.00
TLMCMP Max Pacioretty 8.00 20.00
TLMCPR Patrick Roy 20.00 50.00
TLMCPS P.K. Subban 10.00 25.00
TLMCVD Vincent Damphousse 6.00 15.00
TLNYBL Brian Leetch 8.00 20.00
TLNYDS Derek Stepan 5.00 12.00
TLNYHL Henrik Lundqvist 20.00 50.00
TLNYJV John Vanbiesbrouck 8.00 20.00
TLNYMG Mike Gartner 10.00 25.00
TLNYMM Mark Messier 15.00 40.00
TLNYMR Mike Richter 8.00 20.00
TLNYRN Rick Nash 8.00 20.00
TLNYWG Wayne Gretzky 50.00 125.00
TLPPCK Chris Kunitz 8.00 20.00
TLPPEM Evgeni Malkin 15.00 40.00
TLPPJJ Jaromir Jagr 25.00 60.00
TLPPKL Kris Letang 10.00 25.00
TLPPMF Marc-Andre Fleury 15.00 40.00
TLPPML Mario Lemieux 30.00 80.00
TLPPPC Paul Coffey 8.00 20.00
TLPPSC Sidney Crosby 30.00 80.00
TLPPTB Tom Barrasso 8.00 20.00
TLRWCC Chris Chelios 8.00 20.00
TLRWCO Chris Osgood 8.00 20.00
TLRWGN Gustav Nyquist 5.00 12.00
TLRWHZ Henrik Zetterberg 10.00 25.00
TLRWNL Nicklas Lidstrom 8.00 20.00
TLRWPD Pavel Datsyuk 12.00 30.00
TLRWSY Steve Yzerman 20.00 50.00
TLRWTS Terry Sawchuk 8.00 20.00
TLRWTT Tomas Tatar 5.00 12.00

2016-17 Black Diamond

BDBAH Adam Henrique 1.50 4.00
BDBAK Anze Kopitar 3.00 8.00
BDBAO Alexander Ovechkin 8.00 20.00
BDBBB Brent Burns 2.00 5.00
BDBBH Braden Holtby 2.50 6.00
BDBBS Brandon Saad 1.50 4.00
BDBBW Blake Wheeler 2.00 5.00
BDBCG Claude Giroux 2.00 5.00
BDBCM Connor McDavid 10.00 25.00
BDBCP Carey Price 4.00 10.00
BDBCS Cory Schneider 2.00 5.00
BDBDD Drew Doughty 2.50 6.00
BDBDK David Krejci 2.00 5.00
BDBEK Erik Karlsson 2.50 6.00
BDBEM Evgeni Malkin 4.00 10.00
BDBGI John Gibson 2.00 5.00
BDBHL Henrik Lundqvist 5.00 12.00
BDBHO Bo Horvat 2.00 5.00
BDBHZ Henrik Zetterberg 2.50 6.00
BDBJA Jake Allen 2.00 5.00
BDBJB Jamie Benn 2.50 6.00
BDBJE Jack Eichel 3.00 8.00
BDBJG Johnny Gaudreau 3.00 8.00
BDBJJ Jaromir Jagr 6.00 15.00
BDBJK John Klingberg 2.00 5.00
BDBJO Roman Josi 2.00 5.00
BDBJP Joe Pavelski 2.50 6.00
BDBJS Jeff Skinner 2.50 6.00
BDBJT Jonathan Toews 3.00 8.00
BDBKA Patrick Kane 4.00 10.00
BDBML Mario Lemieux 8.00 20.00
BDBMP Max Pacioretty 2.50 6.00
BDBMR Morgan Rielly 2.50 6.00
BDBMS Mark Scheifele 3.00 8.00
BDBNK Nikita Kucherov 4.00 10.00
BDBNM Nathan MacKinnon 8.00 20.00
BDBOE Oliver Ekman-Larsson 2.00 5.00
BDBPR Patrick Roy 6.00 15.00
BDBRB Ray Bourque 3.00 8.00
BDBRJ Ryan Johansen 1.50 4.00
BDBRN Rick Nash 2.00 5.00
BDBRO Ryan O'Reilly 2.00 5.00
BDBSC Sidney Crosby 8.00 20.00
BDBSG Shayne Gostisbehere 2.00 5.00
BDBSS Steven Stamkos 4.00 10.00
BDBSY Steve Yzerman 6.00 15.00
BDBTA John Tavares 3.00 8.00
BDBVT Vladimir Tarasenko 3.00 8.00
BDBWG Wayne Gretzky 12.00 30.00
BDBZP Zach Parise 2.00 5.00
BDRAM Auston Matthews RC 1000.00 1500.00
BDRBA Mathew Barzal RC 100.00 200.00
BDRBL Brendan Leipsic RC 20.00 50.00
BDRCB Connor Brown RC 40.00 100.00
BDRCD Christian Dvorak RC 30.00 80.00
BDRCL Charlie Lindgren RC 40.00 100.00
BDRDS Dylan Strome RC 80.00 200.00
BDRHF Hudson Fasching RC 25.00 60.00
BDRIP Ivan Provorov RC 40.00 100.00
BDRJB Joshua Bailey RC 25.00 60.00
BDRJD Jason Dickinson RC 20.00 50.00
BDRJE Joel Eriksson Ek RC 40.00 100.00
BDRJP Jesse Puljujarvi RC 50.00 125.00
BDRKC Kyle Connor RC 80.00 200.00
BDRKK Kasperi Kapanen RC 40.00 100.00
BDRLC Lawson Crouse RC 20.00 50.00
BDRMA Anthony Mantha RC 50.00 125.00
BDRMM Mitch Marner RC 80.00 200.00
BDRMO Tyler Motte RC 25.00 60.00
BDRMS Mikhail Sergachev RC 60.00 150.00
BDRMT Matthew Tkachuk RC 60.00 150.00
BDRMW Miles Wood RC 20.00 50.00
BDRNS Nikita Soshnikov RC 15.00 40.00
BDROB Oliver Bjorkstrand RC 30.00 80.00
BDRPB Pavel Buchnevich RC 40.00 100.00
BDRPL Patrik Laine RC 350.00 500.00
BDRPZ Pavel Zacha RC 40.00 100.00
BDRSA Sebastian Aho RC 80.00 200.00
BDRSC Nick Schmaltz RC 30.00 80.00
BDRSM Sonny Milano RC 30.00 80.00
BDRSS Steven Santini RC 20.00 50.00
BDRTK Travis Konecny RC 50.00 125.00
BDRTM Timo Meier 50.00 125.00
BDRVE Jimmy Vesey RC 40.00 100.00
BDRWN William Nylander RC 150.00 300.00
BDRZW Zach Werenski RC 50.00 125.00

2016-17 Black Diamond Championship Banners

CBAK Anze Kopitar/112 8.00 20.00
CBBC Bobby Clarke/74 8.00 20.00
CBCP Corey Perry/107 8.00 20.00
CBCW Cam Ward/106 5.00 12.00
CBGH Glenn Hall/61 5.00 12.00
CBIL Igor Larionov/97 5.00 12.00
CBJK Jari Kurri/87 5.00 12.00
CBJL John LeClair/93 5.00 12.00
CBJT Jonathan Toews/110 8.00 20.00
CBLM Lanny McDonald/89 5.00 12.00
CBLR Larry Robinson/79 5.00 12.00
CBMB Martin Brodeur/95 12.00 30.00
CBMF Marc-Andre Fleury/109 10.00 25.00
CBML Mario Lemieux/92 20.00 50.00
CBMM Mark Messier/94 10.00 25.00
CBMS Milt Schmidt/39 5.00 12.00
CBNL Nicklas Lidstrom/98 5.00 12.00
CBPR Patrick Roy/86 12.00 30.00
CBST Martin St. Louis/104 5.00 12.00
CBWG Wayne Gretzky/84 30.00 80.00

2016-17 Black Diamond Championship Banners Gold

CBAK Anze Kopitar AU/99 20.00 50.00
CBBC Bobby Clarke AU/99 20.00 50.00
CBCP Corey Perry AU/99 20.00 50.00
CBCW Cam Ward AU/99 12.00 30.00
CBGH Glenn Hall AU/99 12.00 30.00
CBIL Igor Larionov AU/25 12.00 30.00
CBJK Jari Kurri AU/99 12.00 30.00
CBJL John LeClair AU/99 12.00 30.00
CBJT Jonathan Toews AU/25 60.00 150.00
CBLM Lanny McDonald AU/25 12.00 30.00
CBLR Larry Robinson AU/99 12.00 30.00
CBMB Martin Brodeur AU/25 50.00 125.00
CBMF Marc-Andre Fleury AU/25 30.00 80.00
CBMM Mark Messier AU/25 25.00 60.00
CBNL Nicklas Lidstrom AU/25 20.00 50.00
CBST Martin St. Louis AU/25 12.00 30.00

2016-17 Black Diamond Championship Rings

CRBB Beau Bennett 4.00 10.00
CRBD Brian Dumoulin 4.00 10.00
CRBL Ben Lovejoy 3.00 8.00
CRBR Bryan Rust 5.00 12.00
CRCH Carl Hagelin 3.00 8.00
CRCK Chris Kunitz 5.00 12.00
CRCS Conor Sheary 5.00 12.00
CRDP Derrick Pouliot 3.00 8.00
CREF Eric Fehr 3.00 8.00
CREM Evgeni Malkin 10.00 25.00
CRIC Ian Cole 3.00 8.00
CRJS Justin Schultz 4.00 10.00
CRJZ Jeff Zatkoff 3.00 8.00
CRKL Kris Letang 6.00 15.00
CRMC Matt Cullen 5.00 12.00
CRMF Marc-Andre Fleury 10.00 25.00
CRMM Matt Murray 8.00 20.00
CRNB Nick Bonino 3.00 8.00
CROM Olli Maatta 3.00 8.00
CROS Oskar Sundqvist 5.00 12.00
CRPH Patric Hornqvist 3.00 8.00
CRPK Phil Kessel 5.00 12.00
CRSC Sidney Crosby 20.00 50.00
CRTD Trevor Daley 4.00 10.00
CRTK Tom Kuhnhackl 4.00 10.00

2016-17 Black Diamond Diamond Mine Relics

DMAE Aaron Ekblad/50 5.00 12.00
DMAS Alexander Steen/50 2.50 6.00
DMBB Brent Burns/199 4.00 10.00
DMBE Patrice Bergeron/199 5.00 12.00
DMBR Bill Ranford/35 4.00 10.00
DMCC Corey Crawford/199 5.00 12.00
DMCS Cory Schneider/50 4.00 10.00
DMDK Duncan Keith/199 3.00 8.00
DMDS Daniel Sedin/199 3.00 8.00
DMEM Evgeni Malkin/35 8.00 20.00
DMFF Filip Forsberg/50 6.00 15.00
DMHS Henrik Sedin/50 5.00 12.00
DMJB Jamie Benn/50 4.00 10.00
DMJC Jeff Carter/35 3.00 8.00
DMJH Jonathan Huberdeau/50 5.00 12.00
DMJO Joe Thornton/35 6.00 15.00
DMJR Jeremy Roenick/199 6.00 15.00
DMJW Justin Williams/50 3.00 8.00
DMKU Evgeny Kuznetsov/199 5.00 12.00
DMMB Martin Brodeur/199 15.00 40.00
DMMF Marc-Andre Fleury/50 8.00 20.00
DMMN Nathan MacKinnon/50 4.00 10.00
DMMR Morgan Rielly/50 4.00 10.00
DMOE Oliver Ekman-Larsson/199 4.00 10.00
DMPB Pavel Bure/199 4.00 10.00
DMPC Paul Coffey/199 4.00 10.00
DMRG Ryan Getzlaf/199 4.00 10.00
DMRL Roberto Luongo/35 6.00 15.00
DMRN Rick Nash/50 4.00 10.00
DMSB Sam Bennett/199 6.00 15.00
DMSK Jeff Skinner/50 5.00 12.00
DMTA John Tavares/35 6.00 15.00
DMVH Victor Hedman/35 5.00 12.00
DMVT Vladimir Tarasenko/35 5.00 12.00

2016-17 Black Diamond Pure Black

COMMON CARD 5.00 12.00
SEMISTARS 6.00 15.00
UNLISTED STARS 8.00 20.00
BDBCP Carey Price AU/25 50.00 125.00
BDBHL Henrik Lundqvist AU/25 50.00 125.00
BDBJJ Jaromir Jagr AU/25 40.00 100.00
BDBJT Jonathan Toews AU/25 40.00 100.00
BDBML Mario Lemieux AU/25 60.00 150.00
BDBPR Patrick Roy AU/25 50.00 125.00
BDBRB Ray Bourque AU/25 25.00 60.00
BDBSC Sidney Crosby AU/25 150.00 250.00
BDBSY Steve Yzerman AU/25 50.00 125.00
BDBWG Wayne Gretzky AU/25 250.00 600.00

2016-17 Black Diamond Pure Black Relics

BDBAH Adam Henrique/149 4.00 10.00
BDBAK Anze Kopitar/149 8.00 20.00
BDBAO Alexander Ovechkin/149 20.00 50.00
BDBBB Brent Burns/149 5.00 12.00
BDBBH Braden Holtby/149 6.00 15.00
BDBBS Brandon Saad/149 4.00 10.00
BDBBW Blake Wheeler/149 5.00 12.00
BDBCG Claude Giroux/149 5.00 12.00
BDBCM Connor McDavid/149 25.00 60.00
BDBCP Carey Price/149 10.00 25.00
BDBCS Cory Schneider/149 5.00 12.00
BDBDK David Krejci/49 5.00 12.00
BDBEM Evgeni Malkin/149 10.00 25.00
BDBGI John Gibson/149 5.00 12.00
BDBHO Bo Horvat/149 6.00 15.00
BDBHZ Henrik Zetterberg/149 6.00 15.00
BDBJA Jake Allen/149 5.00 12.00
BDBJB Jamie Benn/149 5.00 12.00
BDBJE Jack Eichel/149 8.00 20.00
BDBJG Johnny Gaudreau/149 8.00 20.00
BDBJJ Jaromir Jagr/149 15.00 40.00
BDBJK John Klingberg/149 5.00 12.00
BDBJP Joe Pavelski/149 6.00 15.00
BDBJS Jeff Skinner/149 6.00 15.00
BDBJT Jonathan Toews/149 8.00 20.00
BDBKA Patrick Kane/149 10.00 25.00
BDBML Mario Lemieux/49 20.00 50.00
BDBMP Max Pacioretty/149 5.00 12.00
BDBMR Morgan Rielly/149 5.00 12.00
BDBMS Mark Scheifele/149 8.00 20.00
BDBNK Nikita Kucherov/149 10.00 25.00
BDBPR Patrick Roy/49 12.00 30.00
BDBRB Ray Bourque/49 8.00 20.00
BDBRN Rick Nash/149 5.00 12.00
BDBRO Ryan O'Reilly/149 5.00 12.00
BDBSC Sidney Crosby/149 20.00 50.00
BDBSS Steven Stamkos/149 10.00 25.00
BDBSY Steve Yzerman/49 12.00 30.00
BDBTA John Tavares/149 8.00 20.00
BDBVT Vladimir Tarasenko/149 6.00 15.00
BDBWG Wayne Gretzky/49 30.00 80.00
BDBZP Zach Parise/149 5.00 12.00

2016-17 Black Diamond Rookie Booklet Relics

RBRAM Auston Matthews 30.00 80.00
RBRCD Christian Dvorak 6.00 15.00
RBRDS Dylan Strome 12.00 30.00
RBRHF Hudson Fasching 5.00 12.00
RBRIP Ivan Provorov 8.00 20.00
RBRJD Jason Dickinson 4.00 10.00
RBRJM Josh Morrissey 12.00 30.00
RBRJP Jesse Puljujarvi 10.00 25.00
RBRKK Kasperi Kapanen 8.00 20.00
RBRMA Anthony Mantha 10.00 25.00
RBRMM Mitch Marner 15.00 40.00
RBRMT Matthew Tkachuk 20.00 50.00
RBRPL Patrik Laine 12.00 30.00
RBRPZ Pavel Zacha 8.00 20.00
RBRSM Sonny Milano 6.00 15.00
RBRWN William Nylander 20.00 50.00

2016-17 Black Diamond Rookie Booklet Relics Jersey Autographs

RBRAM Auston Matthews 200.00 400.00
RBRCD Christian Dvorak 12.00 30.00
RBRDS Dylan Strome 25.00 60.00
RBRHF Hudson Fasching 10.00 25.00
RBRIP Ivan Provorov 15.00 40.00
RBRJD Jason Dickinson 8.00 20.00
RBRJM Josh Morrissey 25.00 60.00
RBRJP Jesse Puljujarvi 20.00 50.00
RBRKK Kasperi Kapanen 15.00 40.00
RBRMA Anthony Mantha 20.00 50.00
RBRMM Mitch Marner 30.00 80.00
RBRMT Matthew Tkachuk 40.00 100.00
RBRPL Patrik Laine 25.00 60.00
RBRPZ Pavel Zacha 15.00 40.00
RBRSM Sonny Milano 12.00 30.00
RBRWN William Nylander 50.00 125.00

2016-17 Black Diamond Rookie Gems

RGAM Auston Matthews 60.00 150.00
RGCL Charlie Lindgren 5.00 12.00
RGDS Dylan Strome 8.00 20.00
RGHF Hudson Fasching 3.00 8.00
RGIP Ivan Provorov 5.00 12.00
RGJD Jason Dickinson 2.50 6.00
RGJP Jesse Puljujarvi 6.00 15.00
RGJV Jimmy Vesey 5.00 12.00
RGLC Lawson Crouse 2.50 6.00
RGMA Anthony Mantha 6.00 15.00
RGMM Mitch Marner 10.00 25.00
RGNS Nikita Soshnikov 2.00 5.00
RGOB Oliver Bjorkstrand 4.00 10.00
RGPL Patrik Laine 8.00 20.00
RGPZ Pavel Zacha 5.00 12.00
RGTM Tyler Motte 3.00 8.00
RGWN William Nylander 12.00 30.00
RGZW Zach Werenski 10.00 25.00

2016-17 Black Diamond Rookie Gems Pure Black

*BLACK/25: 1X TO 2.5X BASIC INSERTS
RGAM Auston Matthews 150.00 300.00
RGPL Patrik Laine 80.00 200.00

2016-17 Black Diamond Rookie Gems Pure Black Signatures

RGCL Charlie Lindgren/199 12.00 30.00
RGDS Dylan Strome/199 20.00 50.00
RGHF Hudson Fasching/199 8.00 20.00
RGIP Ivan Provorov/199 12.00 30.00
RGJD Jason Dickinson/199 6.00 15.00
RGJP Jesse Puljujarvi/199 15.00 40.00
RGJV Jimmy Vesey/199 12.00 30.00
RGLC Lawson Crouse/199 6.00 15.00
RGMA Anthony Mantha/99 15.00 40.00
RGMM Mitch Marner/99 25.00 60.00
RGNS Nikita Soshnikov/199 5.00 12.00
RGOB Oliver Bjorkstrand/199 10.00 25.00
RGPL Patrik Laine/99 60.00 150.00
RGPZ Pavel Zacha/99 12.00 30.00
RGTM Tyler Motte/199 8.00 20.00
RGWN William Nylander/99 30.00 80.00
RGZW Zach Werenski/199 25.00 60.00

2016-17 Black Diamond Rookie Team Logo Jumbos Autographs Alternate Logo

RTLAM Auston Matthews 400.00 800.00
RTLIP Ivan Provorov 60.00 150.00
RTLMA Anthony Mantha 60.00 150.00
RTLSM Sonny Milano 40.00 100.00
RTLWN William Nylander 60.00 150.00

2016-17 Black Diamond Run for the Cup

RUNAK Anze Kopitar 8.00 20.00
RUNAM Auston Matthews 80.00 200.00
RUNAO Alexander Ovechkin 20.00 50.00
RUNAP Alex Pietrangelo 4.00 10.00
RUNBH Braden Holtby 6.00 15.00
RUNCM Connor McDavid 80.00 200.00
RUNCP Carey Price 10.00 25.00
RUNDD Drew Doughty 6.00 15.00
RUNDL Dylan Larkin 6.00 15.00
RUNEK Erik Karlsson 6.00 15.00
RUNFF Filip Forsberg 8.00 20.00
RUNHL Henrik Lundqvist 12.00 30.00
RUNJB Jamie Benn 5.00 12.00
RUNJE Jack Eichel 8.00 20.00
RUNJP Joe Pavelski 6.00 15.00
RUNJT John Tavares 8.00 20.00
RUNMA Anthony Mantha 10.00 25.00
RUNML Mario Lemieux 20.00 50.00
RUNNK Nikita Kucherov 10.00 25.00
RUNPA Artemi Panarin 10.00 25.00
RUNPK Patrick Kane 10.00 25.00
RUNRG Ryan Getzlaf 5.00 12.00
RUNSC Sidney Crosby 20.00 50.00
RUNSM Sean Monahan 3.00 8.00
RUNSS Steven Stamkos 10.00 25.00
RUNSY Steve Yzerman 12.00 30.00
RUNTH Joe Thornton 8.00 20.00
RUNTS Tyler Seguin 6.00 15.00
RUNVT Vladimir Tarasenko 6.00 15.00
RUNWG Wayne Gretzky 30.00 80.00

2016-17 Black Diamond Signature Placards

SPAH Andrew Hammond D 5.00 12.00
SPBC Bobby Clarke B 20.00 50.00
SPBG Brendan Gallagher B 12.00 30.00
SPBO Bo Horvat D 10.00 25.00
SPCH Carl Hagelin D 12.00 30.00
SPGN Gustav Nyquist B 10.00 25.00
SPHL Henrik Lundqvist B 30.00 80.00
SPHU Jonathan Huberdeau C 15.00 40.00
SPJK Jari Kurri C 15.00 40.00
SPJT Jacob Trouba D 8.00 20.00
SPKP Kyle Palmieri D 6.00 15.00
SPMD Matt Duchene A 25.00 60.00
SPMG Mikael Granlund D 10.00 25.00
SPMS Mark Stone C 6.00 15.00
SPNF Nick Foligno C 10.00 25.00
SPPR Pekka Rinne B 10.00 25.00
SPRJ Roman Josi D 8.00 20.00
SPRO Ryan O'Reilly D 8.00 20.00
SPTL Trevor Linden C 12.00 30.00
SPTT Tyler Toffoli C 15.00 40.00
SPZP Zach Parise B 12.00 30.00

2016-17 Black Diamond Signature Rookie Materials Jersey

SRJAM Auston Matthews/25 200.00 400.00
SRJDS Dylan Strome/99 20.00 50.00
SRJDV Christian Dvorak/99 10.00 25.00
SRJHF Hudson Fasching/99 8.00 20.00
SRJIP Ivan Provorov/99 12.00 30.00
SRJJD Jason Dickinson/99 6.00 15.00
SRJJP Jesse Puljujarvi/99 15.00 40.00
SRJKK Kasperi Kapanen/99 12.00 30.00
SRJLC Lawson Crouse/99 6.00 15.00
SRJMA Anthony Mantha/99 15.00 40.00
SRJMI Michael Matheson/99 8.00 20.00
SRJMM Mitch Marner/99 25.00 60.00
SRJMR Mike Reilly/99 6.00 15.00
SRJOB Oliver Bjorkstrand/99 10.00 25.00
SRJPL Patrik Laine/99 20.00 50.00
SRJPZ Pavel Zacha/99 12.00 30.00
SRJSM Sonny Milano/99 10.00 25.00
SRJWN William Nylander/99 30.00 80.00

2016-17 Black Diamond Silver on Black Rookie Signatures

SBRSAM Auston Matthews/35 250.00 450.00
SBRSCD Christian Dvorak/125 8.00 20.00
SBRSDS Dylan Strome/125 15.00 40.00
SBRSHF Hudson Fasching/125 6.00 15.00
SBRSIP Ivan Provorov/125 10.00 25.00
SBRSJP Jesse Puljujarvi/125 20.00 50.00
SBRSJV Jimmy Vesey/125 10.00 25.00
SBRSMA Anthony Mantha/49 12.00 30.00
SBRSMB Mathew Barzal/125 20.00 50.00
SBRSPL Patrik Laine/49 80.00 200.00
SBRSPZ Pavel Zacha/125 10.00 25.00
SBRSSM Sonny Milano/125 8.00 20.00
SBRSWL William Nylander/49 25.00 60.00

2016-17 Black Diamond Silver on Black Signatures

SBAH Adam Henrique/125 8.00 20.00
SBBP Peter Bondra/125 10.00 25.00
SBCM Connor McDavid/25 200.00 300.00
SBCP Carey Price/25 100.00 200.00
SBDA Dave Andreychuk/125 10.00 25.00
SBJG John Gibson/125 10.00 25.00
SBPM Patrick Marleau/125 10.00 25.00
SBRN Rick Nash/125 10.00 25.00
SBSB Sam Bennett/125 15.00 40.00
SBSM Sean Monahan/125 6.00 15.00
SBTA John Tavares/125 15.00 40.00

2016-17 Black Diamond Team Logo Jumbos

TLEOCM Connor McDavid 40.00 100.00
TLEOGF Grant Fuhr 12.00 30.00
TLEOJE Jordan Eberle 8.00 20.00
TLEOJK Jari Kurri 8.00 20.00
TLEOLD Leon Draisaitl 25.00 60.00
TLEOMM Mark Messier 15.00 40.00
TLEOPC Paul Coffey 8.00 20.00
TLEORN Ryan Nugent-Hopkins 10.00 25.00
TLEOWG Wayne Gretzky SP 60.00 150.00
TLNIBB Bob Bourne 5.00 12.00
TLNIBN Bob Nystrom 6.00 15.00
TLNIBS Billy Smith 8.00 20.00
TLNICG Clark Gillies 8.00 20.00
TLNIJT John Tavares 12.00 30.00
TLNIMB Mike Bossy SP 15.00 40.00
TLNINE Brock Nelson 8.00 20.00
TLNINL Nick Leddy 5.00 12.00
TLNITH Travis Hamonic 5.00 12.00
TLSBAM Al MacInnis 10.00 25.00
TLSBAP Alex Pietrangelo 6.00 15.00
TLSBAS Alexander Steen 5.00 12.00
TLSBBH Brett Hull SP 15.00 40.00
TLSBCP Colton Parayko 6.00 15.00
TLSBDG Doug Gilmour 10.00 25.00
TLSBJA Jake Allen 8.00 20.00
TLSBRF Robby Fabbri 5.00 12.00
TLSBVT Vladimir Tarasenko 10.00 25.00
TLVCAE Alexander Edler 5.00 12.00
TLVCBO Bo Horvat 10.00 25.00
TLVCDS Daniel Sedin 10.00 25.00
TLVCHS Henrik Sedin 10.00 25.00
TLVCJV Jake Virtanen 10.00 25.00
TLVCKM Kirk McLean 8.00 20.00
TLVCPB Pavel Bure SP 30.00 80.00
TLVCRL Roberto Luongo 12.00 30.00
TLVCTL Trevor Linden 8.00 20.00
TLWCAB Andre Burakovsky 5.00 12.00
TLWCAO Alexander Ovechkin SP 20.00 50.00
TLWCBH Braden Holtby 10.00 25.00
TLWCEK Evgeny Kuznetsov 10.00 25.00
TLWCJC John Carlson 8.00 20.00
TLWCJW Justin Williams 6.00 15.00
TLWCMG Mike Gartner 10.00 25.00
TLWCNB Nicklas Backstrom 8.00 20.00
TLWCPB Peter Bondra 8.00 20.00
TLWJBL Bryan Little 6.00 15.00
TLWJBW Blake Wheeler SP 20.00 50.00
TLWJCH Connor Hellebuyck 15.00 40.00
TLWJDB Dustin Byfuglien 8.00 20.00
TLWJJT Jacob Trouba 6.00 15.00
TLWJMP Mathieu Perreault 5.00 12.00
TLWJMS Mark Scheifele 12.00 30.00
TLWJNE Nikolaj Ehlers 8.00 20.00
TLWJTM Tyler Myers 5.00 12.00

2017-18 Black Diamond

BDBAM Auston Matthews 12.00 30.00
BDBAO Alexander Ovechkin 12.00 30.00
BDBBM Brad Marchand 6.00 15.00
BDBBO Bobby Orr 12.00 30.00
BDBCM Connor McDavid 15.00 40.00
BDBCP Carey Price 6.00 15.00
BDBDD Devan Dubnyk 2.50 6.00
BDBDH Dale Hawerchuk 4.00 10.00
BDBDO Max Domi 3.00 8.00
BDBEK Erik Karlsson 4.00 10.00
BDBEM Evgeni Malkin 6.00 15.00
BDBFA Frederik Andersen 4.00 10.00
BDBGL Guy Lafleur 4.00 10.00
BDBHL Henrik Lundqvist 8.00 20.00
BDBHS Henrik Sedin 4.00 10.00
BDBHZ Henrik Zetterberg 4.00 10.00
BDBJC Jeff Carter 2.50 6.00
BDBJD Jonathan Drouin 2.50 6.00
BDBJE Jack Eichel 5.00 12.00
BDBJG Jake Guentzel 5.00 12.00
BDBJP Joe Pavelski 4.00 10.00
BDBJS Jaden Schwartz 4.00 10.00
BDBJT John Tavares 5.00 12.00
BDBLC Logan Couture 4.00 10.00
BDBLD Leon Draisaitl 10.00 25.00
BDBMA Mitch Marner 5.00 12.00
BDBMF Marc-Andre Fleury 8.00 20.00
BDBMH Mike Hoffman 2.00 5.00
BDBML Mario Lemieux 12.00 30.00
BDBMM Matt Murray 5.00 12.00
BDBMT Matthew Tkachuk 6.00 15.00
BDBNE Nikolaj Ehlers 3.00 8.00
BDBNK Nikita Kucherov 6.00 15.00
BDBNM Nathan MacKinnon 12.00 30.00
BDBPK Patrick Kane 6.00 15.00
BDBPL Patrik Laine 4.00 10.00
BDBPS P.K. Subban 4.00 10.00
BDBRG Ryan Getzlaf 3.00 8.00
BDBRL Roberto Luongo 5.00 12.00
BDBSB Sergei Bobrovsky 5.00 12.00
BDBSC Sidney Crosby 12.00 30.00
BDBSS Steven Stamkos 6.00 15.00
BDBTH Taylor Hall 3.00 8.00
BDBTS Tyler Seguin 4.00 10.00
BDBVH Victor Hedman 4.00 10.00
BDBVR Victor Rask 2.00 5.00
BDBVT Vladimir Tarasenko 4.00 10.00
BDBWG Wayne Gretzky 20.00 50.00
BDBWN William Nylander 6.00 15.00
BDBWS Wayne Simmonds 4.00 10.00
BDRAB Anders Bjork RC 30.00 80.00
BDRAD Alex DeBrincat RC 60.00 150.00
BDRAK Adrian Kempe RC 50.00 125.00
BDRAN Alexander Nylander RC 40.00 100.00
BDRBB Brock Boeser RC 250.00 450.00
BDRCF Christian Fischer RC 30.00 80.00
BDRCK Clayton Keller RC 80.00 200.00
BDRCM Charlie McAvoy RC 100.00 250.00
BDRCW Colin White RC 30.00 80.00
BDRDG Denis Gurianov RC 60.00 150.00
BDREC Eric Comrie RC 20.00 50.00
BDRES Evgeny Svechnikov RC 50.00 125.00
BDRIB Ivan Barbashev RC 30.00 80.00
BDRJC J.T. Compher RC 25.00 60.00
BDRJD Jake DeBrusk RC 60.00 150.00
BDRJF Jakob Forsbacka-Karlsson RC 25.0060.00
BDRJG Jon Gillies RC 25.00 60.00
BDRJH Josh Ho-Sang RC 30.00 80.00
BDRJR Jack Roslovic RC 40.00 100.00
BDRLK Luke Kunin RC 25.00 60.00
BDRMB Madison Bowey RC 15.00 40.00
BDRNH Nico Hischier RC 150.00 250.00
BDRNP Nolan Patrick RC 50.00 125.00
BDRNS Nikita Scherbak RC 30.00 80.00
BDROT Owen Tippett RC 50.00 125.00
BDRPC Peter Cehlarik RC 25.00 60.00
BDRPD Pierre-Luc Dubois RC 60.00 150.00
BDRSM Samuel Morin RC 15.00 40.00
BDRTJ Tyson Jost RC 50.00 125.00
BDRTS Travis Sanheim RC 25.00 60.00
BDRVK Vladislav Kamenev RC 25.00 60.00
BDRVS Vadim Shipachyov RC 30.00 80.00
BDRRMR Maurice Richard RR 150.00 250.00

2017-18 Black Diamond Championship Banners

CBBO Bobby Orr/70 15.00 40.00
CBDA Dave Andreychuk/104 10.00 25.00
CBDG Doug Gilmour/89 12.00 30.00
CBDP Denis Potvin/81 10.00 25.00
CBEB Ed Belfour/99 12.00 30.00
CBJB Johnny Bower/64 10.00 25.00
CBJM Jake Muzzin/114 10.00 25.00
CBJS Joe Sakic/96 20.00 50.00
CBMU Matt Murray/116 15.00 40.00
CBVD Vincent Damphousse/93 8.00 20.00

2017-18 Black Diamond Championship Banners Gold

CBDA Dave Andreychuk AU/99 20.00 50.00
CBDG Doug Gilmour AU/25 25.00 60.00
CBJB Johnny Bower AU/25 40.00 100.00
CBJM Jake Muzzin AU/99 20.00 50.00
CBVD Vincent Damphousse AU/99 15.00 40.00

2017-18 Black Diamond Championship Rings

CRBR Bryan Rust 10.00 25.00
CRCH Carl Hagelin 6.00 15.00
CRCK Chris Kunitz 10.00 25.00
CRCS Conor Sheary 10.00 25.00
CREM Evgeni Malkin 12.00 30.00
CRJG Jake Guentzel 15.00 40.00
CRJS Justin Schultz 10.00 25.00
CRMC Matt Cullen 8.00 20.00
CRMF Marc-Andre Fleury 20.00 50.00
CRMM Matt Murray 15.00 40.00
CRNB Nick Bonino 6.00 15.00
CRPH Patric Hornqvist 6.00 15.00
CRPK Phil Kessel 10.00 25.00
CRRH Ron Hainsey 8.00 20.00
CRSC Sidney Crosby 40.00 100.00

2017-18 Black Diamond Diamond Cutters

DCBH Braden Holtby 12.00 30.00
DCBM Brad Marchand 20.00 50.00
DCCM Connor McDavid 50.00 125.00
DCEK Erik Karlsson 12.00 30.00
DCNM Nathan MacKinnon 40.00 100.00
DCVT Vladimir Tarasenko 12.00 30.00
DCRCW Colin White 25.00 60.00
DCRES Evgeny Svechnikov 40.00 100.00
DCRJH Josh Ho-Sang 25.00 60.00
DCRJR Jack Roslovic 25.00 60.00
DCRNH Nico Hischier 60.00 150.00
DCRNP Nolan Patrick 40.00 100.00

2017-18 Black Diamond Diamond Debut Relics

DDAN Alexander Nylander 3.00 8.00
DDBB Brock Boeser 5.00 12.00
DDCK Clayton Keller 5.00 12.00
DDCM Charlie McAvoy 5.00 12.00
DDCW Colin White 2.50 6.00
DDNH Nico Hischier 6.00 15.00
DDNP Nolan Patrick 4.00 10.00
DDNS Nikita Scherbak 2.50 6.00
DDPD Pierre-Luc Dubois 3.00 8.00

2017-18 Black Diamond Hardware Heroes

HHAD Alex Delvecchio 10.00 25.00
HHAM Auston Matthews 40.00 100.00
HHBB Brent Burns 10.00 25.00
HHBH Braden Holtby 12.00 30.00
HHCM Connor McDavid 50.00 125.00
HHCP Carey Price 20.00 50.00
HHEB Ed Belfour 12.00 30.00
HHES Eddie Shore 10.00 25.00
HHJB Johnny Bower 10.00 25.00
HHMR Maurice Richard 20.00 50.00
HHPK Patrick Kane 20.00 50.00
HHSC Sidney Crosby 40.00 100.00

2017-18 Black Diamond Pure Black

*PURE BLACK/25-99: .6X TO 1.50X BASIC CARDS
BDBDD Devan Dubnyk AU/99 8.00 20.00
BDBEM Evgeni Malkin AU/99 25.00 60.00
BDBGL Guy Lafleur AU/25 40.00 100.00
BDBJG Jake Guentzel AU/99 25.00 60.00
BDBJP Joe Pavelski AU/99 8.00 20.00
BDBJT John Tavares AU/99 12.00 30.00
BDBLC Logan Couture AU/99 8.00 20.00
BDBMF Marc-Andre Fleury AU/99 25.00 60.00
BDBML Mario Lemieux AU/25 60.00 150.00
BDBNK Nikita Kucherov AU/99 12.00 30.00
BDBPL Patrik Laine AU/99 30.00 80.00
BDBRL Roberto Luongo AU/25 20.00 50.00
BDBSS Steven Stamkos AU/99 15.00 40.00
BDBTS Tyler Seguin AU/99 10.00 25.00
BDBWN William Nylander AU/99 30.00 80.00

2017-18 Black Diamond Relics Pure Black Premium

*BLACK/50: .75X TO 2X BASIC CARDS
*BLACK/25: 2X TO 5X BASIC CARDS
BDBJG Jake Guentzel/50 20.00 50.00

2017-18 Black Diamond Rookie Booklet Relics

RBRAN Alexander Nylander 6.00 15.00
RBRBB Brock Boeser 10.00 25.00
RBRCK Clayton Keller 10.00 25.00
RBRCM Charlie McAvoy 10.00 25.00
RBRES Evgeny Svechnikov 8.00 20.00
RBRHF Haydn Fleury 4.00 10.00
RBRIB Ivan Barbashev 5.00 12.00
RBRJH Josh Ho-Sang 5.00 12.00
RBRLK Luke Kunin 4.00 10.00
RBRMB Madison Bowey 2.50 6.00
RBRNH Nico Hischier 12.00 30.00
RBRNP Nolan Patrick 8.00 20.00
RBRNS Nikita Scherbak 5.00 12.00
RBRPD Pierre-Luc Dubois 6.00 15.00
RBRTJ Tyson Jost 8.00 20.00
RBRVS Vadim Shipachyov 5.00 12.00

2017-18 Black Diamond Rookie Booklet Relics Patch Autographs

RBRBB Brock Boeser 100.00 200.00
RBRCK Clayton Keller 100.00 200.00
RBRCM Charlie McAvoy 50.00 125.00
RBRES Evgeny Svechnikov 20.00 50.00
RBRHF Haydn Fleury 10.00 25.00
RBRIB Ivan Barbashev 12.00 30.00
RBRJH Josh Ho-Sang 12.00 30.00
RBRLK Luke Kunin 10.00 25.00
RBRMB Madison Bowey 6.00 15.00
RBRNS Nikita Scherbak 30.00 80.00
RBRPD Pierre-Luc Dubois 15.00 40.00
RBRTJ Tyson Jost 20.00 50.00
RBRVS Vadim Shipachyov 30.00 80.00

2017-18 Black Diamond Rookie Gems

RGAN Alexander Nylander 5.00 12.00
RGBB Brock Boeser 8.00 20.00
RGCK Clayton Keller 8.00 20.00
RGCM Charlie McAvoy 8.00 20.00
RGCW Colin White 4.00 10.00
RGES Evgeny Svechnikov 6.00 15.00
RGIB Ivan Barbashev 4.00 10.00
RGJH Josh Ho-Sang 4.00 10.00
RGJR Jack Roslovic 4.00 10.00
RGLK Luke Kunin 3.00 8.00
RGNH Nico Hischier 10.00 25.00
RGNP Nolan Patrick 6.00 15.00
RGNS Nikita Scherbak 4.00 10.00
RGOT Owen Tippett 6.00 15.00
RGPD Pierre-Luc Dubois 5.00 12.00
RGTJ Tyson Jost 6.00 15.00
RGVS Vadim Shipachyov 4.00 10.00

2017-18 Black Diamond Rookie Team Logo Jumbos

RTLBB Brock Boeser 12.00 30.00
RTLCK Clayton Keller 12.00 30.00
RTLCM Charlie McAvoy 12.00 30.00
RTLES Evgeny Svechnikov 10.00 25.00
RTLIB Ivan Barbashev 6.00 15.00
RTLJH Josh Ho-Sang 6.00 15.00
RTLNH Nico Hischier 15.00 40.00
RTLNP Nolan Patrick 10.00 25.00
RTLTJ Tyson Jost 10.00 25.00
RTLVS Vadim Shipachyov 6.00 15.00

2017-18 Black Diamond Run for the Cup

RUNCK Clayton Keller 12.00 30.00
RUNNH Nico Hischier 15.00 40.00
RUNNP Nolan Patrick 10.00 25.00

2017-18 Black Diamond Signature Placards

SPAM Anthony Mantha C 12.00 30.00
SPCD Christian Dvorak C 6.00 15.00
SPDD Devan Dubnyk B 6.00 15.00
SPDS Derek Sanderson C 20.00 50.00
SPJC John Carlson B 8.00 20.00
SPMD Matt Duchene A 8.00 20.00
SPMT Matthew Tkachuk A 15.00 40.00
SPNE Nikolaj Ehlers B 8.00 20.00
SPWS Wayne Simmonds A 10.00 25.00
SPZW Zach Werenski B 12.00 30.00

2017-18 Black Diamond Silver on Black Rookie Signatures

SBRSAB Anders Bjork/125 10.00 25.00
SBRSAD Alex DeBrincat/125 40.00 100.00
SBRSBB Brock Boeser/49 100.00 200.00
SBRSCK Clayton Keller/49 100.00 200.00
SBRSCM Charlie McAvoy/49 100.00 200.00
SBRSCW Colin White/125 10.00 25.00
SBRSHS Josh Ho-Sang/49 10.00 25.00
SBRSOT Owen Tippett/125 15.00 40.00
SBRSTJ Tyson Jost/49 15.00 40.00
SBRSVS Vadim Shipachyov/125 25.00 60.00

2017-18 Black Diamond Silver on Black Signatures

SBCM Connor McDavid/50 150.00 250.00
SBFM Frank Mahovlich/99 12.00 30.00
SBJJ Joe Thornton/99 12.00 30.00
SBJT John Tavares/99 12.00 30.00
SBPP Pierre Pilote/99 10.00 25.00
SBRV Rogie Vachon/50 12.00 30.00

2017-18 Black Diamond Team Logo Jumbos

SCFLBR Martin Brodeur 40.00 100.00
SCFLJT Jonathan Toews 25.00 60.00
SCFLMB Mike Bossy 15.00 40.00
SCFLML Mario Lemieux 60.00 150.00
SCFLMM Mark Messier 30.00 80.00
SCFLPR Patrick Roy 40.00 100.00
SCFLSC Sidney Crosby 60.00 150.00
SCFLTS Teemu Selanne 30.00 80.00
SCFLWG Wayne Gretzky 100.00 250.00
TLCFDG Doug Gilmour 20.00 50.00
TLCFJG Johnny Gaudreau 25.00 60.00
TLCFJI Jarome Iginla 20.00 50.00
TLCFLM Lanny McDonald 15.00 40.00
TLCFMG Mark Giordano 15.00 40.00
TLCFMT Matthew Tkachuk 30.00 80.00
TLCFSB Sam Bennett 25.00 60.00
TLCFSM Sean Monahan 10.00 25.00
TLCFTF Theoren Fleury 15.00 40.00
TLLAAK Anze Kopitar 25.00 60.00
TLLACS Charlie Simmer 10.00 25.00
TLLADD Drew Doughty 20.00 50.00
TLLADT Dave Taylor 8.00 20.00
TLLAJQ Jonathan Quick 20.00 50.00
TLLAMD Marcel Dionne 20.00 50.00
TLLARB Rob Blake 15.00 40.00
TLLARV Rogie Vachon 20.00 50.00
TLLAWG Wayne Gretzky 100.00 250.00
TLMLAM Auston Matthews 40.00 100.00
TLMLDG Doug Gilmour 20.00 50.00
TLMLDS Darryl Sittler 20.00 50.00
TLMLFM Frank Mahovlich 15.00 40.00
TLMLFP Felix Potvin 25.00 60.00
TLMLJB Johnny Bower 15.00 40.00
TLMLKC King Clancy 12.00 30.00
TLMLSA Syl Apps 12.00 30.00
TLMLWC Wendel Clark 25.00 60.00

2018-19 Black Diamond

BDBAB Aleksander Barkov 3.00 8.00
BDBAD Alex DeBrincat 2.50 6.00
BDBAE Aaron Ekblad 2.50 6.00
BDBAK Anze Kopitar 3.00 8.00
BDBAM Auston Matthews 8.00 20.00
BDBAO Alexander Ovechkin 8.00 20.00
BDBAP Artemi Panarin 4.00 10.00
BDBAR Alexander Radulov 2.00 5.00
BDBAV Andrei Vasilevskiy 3.00 8.00
BDBBA Mathew Barzal 2.50 6.00
BDBBB Brock Boeser 2.50 6.00
BDBBH Bo Horvat 2.50 6.00
BDBBO Bobby Orr 8.00 20.00
BDBCG Claude Giroux 2.00 5.00
BDBCK Clayton Keller 2.50 6.00
BDBCM Connor McDavid 10.00 25.00
BDBCP Carey Price 4.00 10.00
BDBDP David Pastrnak 5.00 12.00
BDBES Eric Staal 2.00 5.00
BDBFA Frederik Andersen 2.50 6.00
BDBFF Filip Forsberg 3.00 8.00
BDBGI John Gibson 2.00 5.00
BDBHL Henrik Lundqvist 5.00 12.00
BDBIP Ivan Provorov 1.50 4.00
BDBJB Jean Beliveau 2.00 5.00
BDBJE Jack Eichel 3.00 8.00
BDBJG Johnny Gaudreau 3.00 8.00
BDBJM Jonathan Marchessault 2.50 6.00
BDBJP Joe Pavelski 2.50 6.00
BDBJQ Jonathan Quick 2.50 6.00
BDBJT John Tavares 3.00 8.00
BDBLC Logan Couture 2.50 6.00
BDBMA Anthony Mantha 1.50 4.00
BDBMB Martin Brodeur 5.00 12.00
BDBMF Marc-Andre Fleury 4.00 10.00
BDBMG Mikael Granlund 1.50 4.00
BDBML Mario Lemieux 8.00 20.00
BDBMS Mark Stone 2.50 6.00
BDBMZ Mats Zuccarello 2.00 5.00
BDBNK Nikita Kucherov 4.00 10.00
BDBNM Nathan MacKinnon 8.00 20.00
BDBPI Alex Pietrangelo 1.50 4.00
BDBPK Patrick Kane 4.00 10.00
BDBPL Patrik Laine 2.50 6.00
BDBPR Pekka Rinne 2.00 5.00
BDBSA Sebastian Aho 3.00 8.00
BDBSC Sidney Crosby 8.00 20.00
BDBSS Steven Stamkos 4.00 10.00
BDBTH Taylor Hall 2.00 5.00
BDBWG Wayne Gretzky 12.00 30.00
BDRAC Anthony Cirelli RC 30.00 80.00
BDRAG Adam Gaudette RC 30.00 80.00
BDRAJ Andreas Johnsson RC 25.00 60.00
BDRAS Andrei Svechnikov RC 50.00 125.00
BDRBH Blake Hillman RC 20.00 50.00
BDRBT Brady Tkachuk RC 60.00 150.00
BDRCM Casey Mittelstadt RC 40.00 100.00
BDRDB Daniel Brickley RC 20.00 50.00
BDRDD Dillon Dube RC 25.00 60.00
BDRDG Dylan Gambrell RC 20.00 50.00
BDRDO Ryan Donato RC 30.00 80.00
BDRDS Dylan Sikura RC 25.00 60.00
BDREB Ethan Bear RC 30.00 80.00
BDREP Elias Pettersson RC 400.00 800.00
BDRET Eeli Tolvanen RC 40.00 100.00
BDRHB Henrik Borgstrom RC 30.00 80.00
BDRJG Jordan Greenway RC 20.00 50.00
BDRJK Jesperi Kotkaniemi RC 40.00 100.00
BDRJK Jordan Kyrou RC 40.00 100.00
BDRLA Lias Andersson RC 30.00 80.00
BDRMB Mackenzie Blackwood RC 40.00 100.00
BDRMD Michael Dal Colle RC 20.00 50.00
BDRMH Miro Heiskanen RC 50.00 125.00
BDRMK Morgan Klimchuk RC 20.00 50.00
BDRMR Michael Rasmussen RC 25.00 60.00
BDRNJ Noah Juulsen RC 20.00 50.00
BDRNR Nicolas Roy RC 12.00 30.00
BDROL Oskar Lindblom RC 30.00 80.00
BDRRD Rasmus Dahlin RC 150.00 300.00
BDRRT Robert Thomas RC 40.00 100.00
BDRSM Samuel Montembeault RC 40.00 100.00
BDRSN Sami Niku RC 15.00 40.00
BDRSS Sam Steel RC 20.00 50.00
BDRTD Travis Dermott RC 30.00 80.00
BDRTH Tomas Hyka RC 20.00 50.00
BDRTT Troy Terry RC 30.00 80.00
BDRVE Victor Ejdsell RC 15.00 40.00
BDRWF Warren Foegele RC 20.00 50.00
BDRZA Zach Aston-Reese RC 30.00 80.00
BDRZW Zach Whitecloud RC 15.00 40.00
BDRRPR Patrick Roy RR 250.00 450.00

2018-19 Black Diamond Championship Banners

CBAD Alex Delvecchio/55 6.00 15.00
CBDK David Krejci/111 6.00 15.00
CBFM Frank Mahovlich/67 6.00 15.00
CBJB Jean Beliveau/56 6.00 15.00
CBMB Mike Bossy/80 6.00 15.00
CBPK Patrick Kane/115 12.00 30.00
CBRB Ray Bourque/101 10.00 25.00
CBSC Sidney Crosby/117 25.00 60.00
CBTS Teemu Selanne/107 12.00 30.00
CBWG Wayne Gretzky/88 40.00 100.00

2018-19 Black Diamond Championship Banners Gold Autographs

CBAD Alex Delvecchio/25 20.00 50.00
CBDK David Krejci/25 20.00 50.00
CBFM Frank Mahovlich/25 20.00 50.00
CBMB Mike Bossy/25 20.00 50.00
CBPK Patrick Kane/25 40.00 100.00
CBRB Ray Bourque/25 30.00 80.00
CBTS Teemu Selanne/25 40.00 100.00

2018-19 Black Diamond Diamond Cutters

DCAO Alexander Ovechkin 20.00 50.00
DCAV Andrei Vasilevskiy 8.00 20.00
DCCG Claude Giroux 5.00 12.00
DCCM Casey Mittelstadt 10.00 25.00
DCDD Drew Doughty 6.00 15.00
DCDO Ryan Donato 8.00 20.00
DCEP Elias Pettersson 15.00 40.00
DCJG Johnny Gaudreau 8.00 20.00
DCRD Rasmus Dahlin 12.00 30.00
DCSC Sidney Crosby 20.00 50.00

2018-19 Black Diamond Diamond Debut Relics

DDAG Adam Gaudette 3.00 8.00
DDAS Andrei Svechnikov 5.00 12.00
DDCM Casey Mittelstadt 4.00 10.00
DDDO Ryan Donato 3.00 8.00
DDEP Elias Pettersson 15.00 40.00
DDET Eeli Tolvanen 4.00 10.00
DDRD Rasmus Dahlin 15.00 40.00
DDTT Troy Terry 3.00 8.00

2018-19 Black Diamond Diamond Debut Relics Patch

*PATCH/49: 1X TO 2.5X BASIC INSERTS
DDEP Elias Pettersson 30.00 80.00

2018-19 Black Diamond Diamond Might

DMAM Auston Matthews 15.00 40.00
DMAS Andrei Svechnikov 10.00 25.00
DMBO Bobby Orr 15.00 40.00
DMCM Connor McDavid 20.00 50.00
DMDD Drew Doughty 5.00 12.00
DMDO Ryan Donato 6.00 15.00
DMML Mario Lemieux 15.00 40.00
DMMR Maurice Richard 8.00 20.00
DMPL Patrik Laine 5.00 12.00
DMPR Patrick Roy 10.00 25.00
DMPS P.K. Subban 5.00 12.00
DMRA Mikko Rantanen 10.00 25.00
DMRD Rasmus Dahlin 10.00 25.00
DMSC Sidney Crosby 15.00 40.00
DMSS Steven Stamkos 8.00 20.00
DMTH Taylor Hall 4.00 10.00
DMVH Victor Hedman 5.00 12.00
DMWG Wayne Gretzky 25.00 60.00

2018-19 Black Diamond Diamond Mine Relics

DMAK Anze Kopitar C 6.00 15.00
DMBW Blake Wheeler C 4.00 10.00
DMCM Connor McDavid B 20.00 50.00
DMLR Larry Robinson A 4.00 10.00
DMNM Nathan MacKinnon C 15.00 40.00
DMPB Patrice Bergeron C 5.00 12.00
DMPR Pekka Rinne C 4.00 10.00
DMSC Sidney Crosby B 15.00 40.00
DMTH Taylor Hall C 4.00 10.00
DMWG Wayne Gretzky A 25.00 60.00

2018-19 Black Diamond Gemography

GAD Alex Delvecchio A 10.00 25.00
GAO Alexander Ovechkin A 40.00 100.00
GBP Brian Propp D 8.00 20.00
GCA Cam Atkinson C 10.00 25.00
GCH Connor Hellebuyck C 20.00 50.00
GCP Carey Price A 20.00 50.00
GEK Evgeny Kuznetsov B 12.00 30.00
GHL Henrik Lundqvist A 25.00 60.00
GJG Jake Gardiner D 6.00 15.00
GJM Jonathan Marchessault C 12.00 30.00
GLD Leon Draisaitl B 30.00 80.00
GMM Michael Matheson C 8.00 20.00
GMR Mikko Rantanen B 25.00 60.00
GNE Nikolaj Ehlers C 10.00 25.00
GPB Pavel Buchnevich D 8.00 20.00
GRE Ryan Ellis C 8.00 20.00
GSM Sean Monahan B 6.00 15.00
GTA Tony Amonte D 8.00 20.00
GTP Tanner Pearson D 8.00 20.00
GVH Victor Hedman B 12.00 30.00

2018-19 Black Diamond Hall of Fame Rings

HRAO Adam Oates 3.00 8.00
HRBL Brian Leetch 2.50 6.00
HRCP Chris Pronger 3.00 8.00
HRDG Doug Gilmour 4.00 10.00
HRDH Dominik Hasek 5.00 12.00
HREB Ed Belfour 3.00 8.00
HRLR Larry Robinson 3.00 8.00
HRLU Luc Robitaille 3.00 8.00
HRML Mario Lemieux 12.00 30.00
HRMS Mats Sundin 3.00 8.00
HRPB Pavel Bure 3.00 8.00
HRPR Patrick Roy 8.00 20.00
HRSY Steve Yzerman 8.00 20.00
HRTS Teemu Selanne 6.00 15.00
HRWG Wayne Gretzky 20.00 50.00

2018-19 Black Diamond Hardware Heroes

HHAO Alexander Ovechkin 20.00 50.00
HHBA Mathew Barzal 6.00 15.00
HHCC Chris Chelios 5.00 12.00
HHJB Jean Beliveau 5.00 12.00
HHMB Martin Brodeur 12.00 30.00
HHNM Nathan MacKinnon 20.00 50.00
HHPB Patrice Bergeron 6.00 15.00
HHPC Paul Coffey 5.00 12.00
HHSB Sergei Bobrovsky 8.00 20.00
HHSS Steven Stamkos 10.00 25.00
HHTH Taylor Hall 5.00 12.00
HHWG Wayne Gretzky 30.00 80.00

2018-19 Black Diamond Rookie Booklet Relics
RBRAC Anthony Cirelli 6.00 15.00
RBRAG Adam Gaudette 6.00 15.00
RBRAS Andrei Svechnikov 10.00 25.00
RBRCM Casey Mittelstadt 8.00 20.00
RBRDO Ryan Donato 6.00 15.00
RBRDS Dylan Sikura 5.00 12.00
RBREP Elias Pettersson 30.00 80.00
RBRET Eeli Tolvanen 8.00 20.00
RBRHB Henrik Borgstrom 6.00 15.00
RBRJG Jordan Greenway 4.00 10.00
RBRNJ Noah Juulsen 4.00 10.00
RBRRD Rasmus Dahlin 10.00 25.00
RBRTD Travis Dermott 6.00 15.00
RBRTT Troy Terry 6.00 15.00
RBRZA Zach Aston-Reese 6.00 15.00

2018-19 Black Diamond Rookie Booklet Relics Patch Autographs
RBRAC Anthony Cirelli 15.00 40.00
RBRAG Adam Gaudette 15.00 40.00
RBRAS Andrei Svechnikov 25.00 60.00
RBRCM Casey Mittelstadt 20.00 50.00
RBRDO Ryan Donato 15.00 40.00
RBRDS Dylan Sikura 12.00 30.00
RBREP Elias Pettersson 150.00 300.00
RBRET Eeli Tolvanen 20.00 50.00
RBRHB Henrik Borgstrom 15.00 40.00
RBRJG Jordan Greenway 10.00 25.00
RBRNJ Noah Juulsen 10.00 25.00
RBRTD Travis Dermott 15.00 40.00
RBRTT Troy Terry 15.00 40.00
RBRZA Zach Aston-Reese 15.00 40.00

2018-19 Black Diamond Rookie Gems
RGAC Anthony Cirelli 5.00 12.00
RGAG Adam Gaudette 5.00 12.00
RGAS Andrei Svechnikov 8.00 20.00
RGCM Casey Mittelstadt 6.00 15.00
RGDO Ryan Donato 5.00 12.00
RGDS Dylan Sikura 4.00 10.00
RGEP Elias Pettersson 10.00 25.00
RGET Eeli Tolvanen 6.00 15.00
RGHB Henrik Borgstrom 5.00 12.00
RGJG Jordan Greenway 3.00 8.00
RGLA Lias Andersson 5.00 12.00
RGMD Michael Dal Colle 3.00 8.00
RGRD Rasmus Dahlin 8.00 20.00
RGTD Travis Dermott 5.00 12.00
RGTT Troy Terry 5.00 12.00

2018-19 Black Diamond Rookie Gems Pure Black Signatures
RGAC Anthony Cirelli/199 15.00 40.00
RGAG Adam Gaudette/199 15.00 40.00
RGAS Andrei Svechnikov/99 25.00 60.00
RGCM Casey Mittelstadt/99 20.00 50.00
RGDO Ryan Donato/199 15.00 40.00
RGDS Dylan Sikura/199 12.00 30.00
RGEP Elias Pettersson/99 100.00 200.00
RGET Eeli Tolvanen/199 20.00 50.00
RGHB Henrik Borgstrom/199 15.00 40.00
RGJG Jordan Greenway/199 10.00 25.00
RGLA Lias Andersson/199 15.00 40.00
RGMD Michael Dal Colle/199 10.00 25.00
RGTD Travis Dermott/199 15.00 40.00
RGTT Troy Terry/199 15.00 40.00

2018-19 Black Diamond Rookie Team Logo Jumbos
RTLAG Adam Gaudette A 5.00 12.00
RTLAS Andrei Svechnikov D 8.00 20.00
RTLCM Casey Mittelstadt B 6.00 15.00
RTLDO Ryan Donato D 5.00 12.00
RTLEP Elias Pettersson C 10.00 25.00
RTLET Eeli Tolvanen D 6.00 15.00
RTLJG Jordan Greenway D 3.00 8.00
RTLNJ Noah Juulsen D 3.00 8.00
RTLRD Rasmus Dahlin B 8.00 20.00

2018-19 Black Diamond Run for the Cup
RUNAS Andrei Svechnikov 15.00 40.00
RUNRD Rasmus Dahlin 12.00 30.00

2018-19 Black Diamond Silver on Black Rookie Signatures
SBRSAG Adam Gaudette/249 15.00 40.00
SBRSAS Andrei Svechnikov/99 25.00 60.00
SBRSCM Casey Mittelstadt/99 20.00 50.00
SBRSDS Dylan Sikura/249 12.00 30.00
SBRSEP Elias Pettersson/99 150.00 250.00
SBRSET Eeli Tolvanen/249 20.00 50.00
SBRSHB Henrik Borgstrom/249 15.00 40.00
SBRSJG Jordan Greenway/249 10.00 25.00
SBRSRD Ryan Donato/99 15.00 40.00
SBRSZA Zach Aston-Reese/249 15.00 40.00

2018-19 Black Diamond Silver on Black Signatures
SBAM Andy Moog/125 10.00 25.00
SBBB Bob Baun/50 10.00 25.00
SBCC Chris Chelios/125 10.00 25.00
SBJG Jake Guentzel/125 15.00 40.00
SBMM Mitch Marner/50 15.00 40.00
SBPD Pavel Datsyuk/50 15.00 40.00
SBPL Pierre-Luc Dubois/125 8.00 20.00
SBRH Ron Hextall/125 10.00 25.00
SBRK Red Kelly/50 10.00 25.00

2018-19 Black Diamond Team Logo Jumbos
ASTLAM Auston Matthews 10.00 25.00
ASTLAO Alexander Ovechkin 10.00 25.00
ASTLBB Brock Boeser 3.00 8.00
ASTLCM Connor McDavid 12.00 30.00
ASTLJT John Tavares 4.00 10.00
ASTLNK Nikita Kucherov 5.00 12.00
ASTLPS P.K. Subban 3.00 8.00
ASTLSC Sidney Crosby 10.00 25.00
ASTLSS Steven Stamkos 5.00 12.00
TLCABL Rob Blake 2.50 6.00
TLCAGL Gabriel Landeskog 3.00 8.00
TLCAJS Joe Sakic 5.00 12.00
TLCAMR Mikko Rantanen 6.00 15.00
TLCANM Nathan MacKinnon 10.00 25.00
TLCAPF Peter Forsberg 5.00 12.00
TLCAPR Patrick Roy 6.00 15.00
TLCARB Ray Bourque 4.00 10.00
TLCATJ Tyson Jost 2.00 5.00
TLGKAT Alex Tuch 2.50 6.00
TLGKCM Colin Miller 1.50 4.00
TLGKDE Deryk Engelland 2.00 5.00
TLGKJM Jonathan Marchessault 3.00 8.00
TLGKMF Marc-Andre Fleury 5.00 12.00
TLGKNS Nate Schmidt 2.00 5.00
TLGKRS Reilly Smith 2.50 6.00
TLGKST Shea Theodore 3.00 8.00
TLGKWK William Karlsson 3.00 8.00
TLPFBB Bill Barber 2.50 6.00
TLPFBC Bobby Clarke 4.00 10.00
TLPFBP Bernie Parent 3.00 8.00
TLPFCG Claude Giroux 2.50 6.00
TLPFJV Jakub Voracek 2.00 5.00
TLPFPL Pelle Lindbergh 2.00 5.00
TLPFPR Brian Propp 2.00 5.00
TLPFRH Ron Hextall 2.50 6.00
TLPFSC Sean Couturier 2.00 5.00

2019-20 Black Diamond
BDBAD Alex DeBrincat 2.50 6.00
BDBAE Aaron Ekblad 2.50 6.00
BDBAK Anze Kopitar 3.00 8.00
BDBAL Anders Lee 1.50 4.00
BDBAM Auston Matthews 8.00 20.00
BDBAO Alexander Ovechkin 8.00 20.00
BDBAP Artemi Panarin 4.00 10.00
BDBBA Mathew Barzal 2.50 6.00
BDBBB Brent Burns 2.00 5.00
BDBBH Bo Horvat 2.50 6.00
BDBBM Brad Marchand 4.00 10.00
BDBBO Bobby Orr 8.00 20.00
BDBBS Brady Skjei 1.50 4.00
BDBBT Brady Tkachuk 3.00 8.00
BDBBW Blake Wheeler 2.00 5.00
BDBCA Cam Atkinson 2.00 5.00
BDBCG Claude Giroux 2.00 5.00
BDBCM Connor McDavid 10.00 25.00
BDBCP Carey Price 4.00 10.00
BDBDD Devan Dubnyk 1.50 4.00
BDBDG Doug Gilmour 2.50 6.00
BDBDL Dylan Larkin 2.50 6.00
BDBED Evgenii Dadonov 1.25 3.00
BDBEK Evgeny Kuznetsov 2.50 6.00
BDBEP Elias Pettersson 3.00 8.00
BDBES Eric Staal 2.00 5.00
BDBGI John Gibson 2.00 5.00
BDBHA Noah Hanifin 2.00 5.00
BDBHL Henrik Lundqvist 5.00 12.00
BDBJE Jack Eichel 3.00 8.00
BDBJG Jake Guentzel 3.00 8.00
BDBJI Jarome Iginla 2.50 6.00
BDBJV Jakub Voracek 1.50 4.00
BDBKA Erik Karlsson 2.50 6.00
BDBLD Leon Draisaitl 6.00 15.00
BDBMA Mitch Marner 3.00 8.00
BDBMB Martin Brodeur 5.00 12.00
BDBMD Max Domi 2.00 5.00
BDBMF Marc-Andre Fleury 4.00 10.00
BDBML Mario Lemieux 8.00 20.00
BDBMM Mike Modano 3.00 8.00
BDBMR Mikko Rantanen 5.00 12.00
BDBMS Mark Scheifele 3.00 8.00
BDBNH Nico Hischier 3.00 8.00
BDBNK Nikita Kucherov 4.00 10.00
BDBNM Nathan MacKinnon 8.00 20.00
BDBOE Oliver Ekman-Larsson 2.00 5.00
BDBPK Patrick Kane 4.00 10.00
BDBPR Patrick Roy 5.00 12.00
BDBRD Rasmus Dahlin 2.50 6.00
BDBRE Ryan Ellis 1.50 4.00
BDBRG Ryan Getzlaf 2.00 5.00
BDBRO Ryan O'Reilly 2.00 5.00
BDBSA Sebastian Aho 3.00 8.00
BDBSC Sidney Crosby 8.00 20.00
BDBSE Teemu Selanne 4.00 10.00
BDBSJ Seth Jones 2.00 5.00
BDBSM Sean Monahan 1.25 3.00
BDBSS Steven Stamkos 4.00 10.00
BDBSY Steve Yzerman 5.00 12.00
BDBTA John Tavares 3.00 8.00
BDBTC Thomas Chabot 2.00 5.00
BDBTH Taylor Hall 2.00 5.00
BDBTO Jonathan Toews 3.00 8.00
BDBTS Tyler Seguin 2.50 6.00
BDBTT Teuvo Teravainen 2.00 5.00
BDBVA Viktor Arvidsson 1.25 3.00
BDBVT Vladimir Tarasenko 2.50 6.00
BDBWG Wayne Gretzky 12.00 30.00
BDBWK William Karlsson 2.50 6.00
BDRAF Adam Fox RC 125.00 300.00
BDRAT Alexandre Texier RC 20.00 50.00
BDRBH Barrett Hayton RC 40.00 100.00
BDRBL Teddy Blueger RC 20.00 50.00
BDRCF Cody Glass RC 30.00 80.00
BDRCG Carl Grundstrom RC 20.00 50.00
BDRCM Cale Makar RC 150.00 400.00
BDRDF Dante Fabbro RC 20.00 50.00
BDRDK Dominik Kubalik RC 40.00 100.00
BDREB Erik Brannstrom RC 20.00 50.00
BDREM Elvis Merzlikins RC 40.00 100.00
BDRFZ Filip Zadina RC 30.00 80.00
BDRIM Ilya Mikheyev RC 30.00 80.00
BDRJB Jesper Boqvist RC 15.00 40.00
BDRJF Joel Farabee RC 30.00 80.00
BDRJH Jack Hughes RC 100.00 250.00
BDRKD Kirby Dach RC 40.00 100.00
BDRKK Kaapo Kakko RC 30.00 80.00
BDRKU Karson Kuhlman RC 20.00 50.00
BDRMJ Max Jones RC 20.00 50.00
BDRMV Max Veronneau RC 15.00 40.00
BDRND Noah Dobson RC 50.00 125.00
BDRNG Nikita Gusev RC 30.00 80.00
BDRNK Nikolay Prokhorkin RC 15.00 40.00
BDRNS Nick Suzuki RC 80.00 200.00
BDRPI Rem Pitlick RC 20.00 50.00
BDRPM Philippe Myers RC 15.00 40.00
BDRQH Quinn Hughes RC 100.00 250.00
BDRRP Ryan Poehling RC 30.00 80.00
BDRRS Rasmus Sandin RC 30.00 80.00
BDRTF Trent Frederic RC 20.00 50.00
BDRTH Taro Hirose RC 20.00 50.00
BDRVA Vitaly Abramov RC 20.00 50.00
BDRVO Victor Olofsson RC 40.00 100.00
BDRZS Zach Senyshyn RC 20.00 50.00

2019-20 Black Diamond Championship Banners
CBAO Alexander Ovechkin/118 25.00 60.00
CBBB Bill Barber/75 6.00 15.00
CBBM Brad Marchand/111 12.00 30.00
CBBO Bobby Orr/72 25.00 60.00
CBBR Bill Ranford/90 5.00 12.00
CBCC Chris Chelios/102 6.00 15.00
CBEM Evgeni Malkin/117 12.00 30.00
CBJL Jacques Lemaire/79 5.00 12.00
CBJQ Jonathan Quick/112 8.00 20.00
CBMM Mike Modano/99 10.00 25.00
CBPR Patrick Roy/96 15.00 40.00
CBWG Wayne Gretzky/85 40.00 100.00
CBYC Yvan Cournoyer/73 6.00 15.00

2019-20 Black Diamond Championship Banners Gold
CBBB Bill Barber AU/99 25.00 60.00
CBBM Brad Marchand AU/25 50.00 125.00
CBBR Bill Ranford AU/99 20.00 50.00
CBCC Chris Chelios AU/25 25.00 60.00
CBEM Evgeni Malkin AU/25 50.00 125.00
CBJQ Jonathan Quick AU/25 30.00 80.00
CBMM Mike Modano AU/25 40.00 100.00
CBYC Yvan Cournoyer AU/99 25.00 60.00

2019-20 Black Diamond Diamond Cutters
DCAM Auston Matthews 20.00 50.00
DCBO Bobby Orr 20.00 50.00
DCBW Blake Wheeler 5.00 12.00
DCCG Cody Glass 8.00 20.00
DCCM Connor McDavid 25.00 60.00
DCCP Carey Price 10.00 25.00
DCEK Evgeny Kuznetsov 6.00 15.00
DCFZ Filip Zadina 8.00 20.00
DCJH Jack Hughes 25.00 60.00
DCJT John Tavares 8.00 20.00
DCKK Kaapo Kakko 8.00 20.00
DCML Mario Lemieux 20.00 50.00
DCMR Mikko Rantanen 12.00 30.00
DCNK Nikita Kucherov 10.00 25.00
DCPF Peter Forsberg 10.00 25.00
DCPL Pat LaFontaine 5.00 12.00
DCQH Quinn Hughes 25.00 60.00
DCVH Victor Hedman 6.00 15.00
DCWG Wayne Gretzky 30.00 80.00
DCWK William Karlsson 6.00 15.00

2019-20 Black Diamond Diamond Debut Relics
*PATCH/49: .8X TO 2X BASIC INSERTS
DDAT Alexandre Texier 2.50 6.00
DDBH Barrett Hayton 5.00 12.00
DDCG Cody Glass 4.00 10.00
DDCM Cale Makar 12.00 30.00
DDDF Dante Fabbro 2.50 6.00
DDEB Erik Brannstrom 2.50 6.00
DDFZ Filip Zadina 4.00 10.00
DDGR Carl Grundstrom- 2.50 6.00
DDJH Jack Hughes 12.00 30.00
DDMJ Max Jones 2.50 6.00
DDPM Philippe Myers 2.00 5.00
DDQH Quinn Hughes 15.00 40.00
DDRP Ryan Poehling 4.00 10.00

2019-20 Black Diamond Diamond in the Rough Relics
*PATCH/25: .8X TO 2X BASIC INSERTS
DRBG Brendan Gallagher 3.00 8.00
DRBH Braden Holtby 4.00 10.00
DRCA Cam Atkinson 3.00 8.00
DRCH Connor Hellebuyck 6.00 15.00
DRDB Dustin Byfuglien 3.00 8.00
DRHL Henrik Lundqvist 8.00 20.00
DRJB Jamie Benn 3.00 8.00
DRJG Johnny Gaudreau 5.00 12.00
DRPR Pekka Rinne 3.00 8.00

2019-20 Black Diamond Diamond Might
DMAO Alexander Ovechkin 15.00 40.00
DMBA Mathew Barzal 5.00 12.00
DMBB Brent Burns 4.00 10.00
DMBI Ben Bishop 3.00 8.00
DMCN Cam Neely 4.00 10.00
DMCP Carey Price 8.00 20.00
DMEM Evgeni Malkin 8.00 20.00
DMEP Elias Pettersson 6.00 15.00
DMFZ Filip Zadina 6.00 15.00
DMHL Henrik Lundqvist 10.00 25.00
DMJG Johnny Gaudreau 6.00 15.00
DMJH Jack Hughes 20.00 50.00
DMJL Jacques Lemaire 3.00 8.00
DMKK Kaapo Kakko 6.00 15.00
DMMB Martin Brodeur 10.00 25.00
DMMF Marc-Andre Fleury 8.00 20.00
DMMM Mitch Marner 6.00 15.00
DMMS Mark Scheifele 6.00 15.00
DMNK Nikita Kucherov 8.00 20.00
DMNM Nathan MacKinnon 15.00 40.00
DMPK Patrick Kane 8.00 20.00
DMPR Patrick Roy 10.00 25.00
DMQH Quinn Hughes 20.00 50.00
DMWG Wayne Gretzky 25.00 60.00

2019-20 Black Diamond Diamond Mine Relics
*PATCH/30: .6X TO 1.5X BASIC INSERTS
DMAM Auston Matthews B 15.00 40.00
DMCG Claude Giroux C 4.00 10.00
DMCM Connor McDavid B 20.00 50.00
DMDS Daniel Sedin C 5.00 12.00
DMGL Gabriel Landeskog D 5.00 12.00
DMHS Henrik Sedin C 5.00 12.00
DMJB Josh Bailey C 3.00 8.00
DMJG John Gibson D 4.00 10.00
DMJS Jaden Schwartz C 5.00 12.00
DMJT John Tavares C 6.00 15.00
DMKC Kyle Connor C 6.00 15.00
DMMH Mike Hoffman D 2.50 6.00
DMML Mario Lemieux A 15.00 40.00
DMNP Nolan Patrick D 4.00 10.00
DMOE Oliver Ekman-Larsson D 4.00 10.00
DMPB Patrice Bergeron D 5.00 12.00
DMPR Patrick Roy A 10.00 25.00
DMRO Ryan O'Reilly D 4.00 10.00
DMRS Ryan Suter D 3.00 8.00
DMSC Sidney Crosby B 15.00 40.00
DMSI Jakob Silfverberg D 2.50 6.00
DMSW Shea Weber D 4.00 10.00
DMVH Victor Hedman C 5.00 12.00
DMZP Zach Parise C 4.00 10.00

2019-20 Black Diamond Gemography
GBO Bobby Orr 80.00 200.00
GCA Cale Makar 100.00 250.00
GCM Connor McDavid 150.00 250.00
GEM Evgeni Malkin 40.00 100.00
GGH Gordie Howe 60.00 150.00
GJG Johnny Gaudreau 30.00 80.00
GJH Jack Hughes 300.00 400.00
GJT Jonathan Toews 30.00 80.00
GMA Mitch Marner 30.00 80.00
GMB Martin Brodeur 50.00 125.00
GMF Marc-Andre Fleury 60.00 150.00
GMM Mark Messier 40.00 100.00
GNH Nico Hischier 30.00 80.00
GPD Pierre-Luc Dubois 15.00 40.00
GQH Quinn Hughes 300.00 400.00
GRP Ryan Poehling 30.00 80.00
GSJ Seth Jones 20.00 50.00
GSS Steven Stamkos 40.00 100.00
GWG Wayne Gretzky 250.00 600.00

2019-20 Black Diamond Hall of Fame Rings
*GOLD.SPECTRUM: .5X TO 1.25X BASIC INSERTS
HRBP Brad Park 2.50 6.00
HRBS Brendan Shanahan 3.00 8.00
HRCN Cam Neely 3.00 8.00
HRGA Glenn Anderson 2.50 6.00
HRIL Igor Larionov 3.00 8.00
HRJN Joe Nieuwendyk 2.50 6.00
HRMB Martin Brodeur 8.00 20.00
HRMG Mike Gartner 4.00 10.00
HRMM Mark Messier 6.00 15.00
HRMO Mike Modano 5.00 12.00
HRNS Joe Sakic 6.00 15.00
HRPF Peter Forsberg 6.00 15.00
HRPL Pat LaFontaine 3.00 8.00
HRRB Rob Blake 3.00 8.00
HRRV Rogie Vachon 3.00 8.00
HRSN Scott Niedermayer 3.00 8.00
HRTE Tony Esposito 3.00 8.00
HRWO Willie O'Ree 4.00 10.00

2019-20 Black Diamond Hall of Fame Rings Gold Spectrum Autographs
HRCN Cam Neely/99 12.00 30.00
HRJS Joe Sakic/25 25.00 60.00
HRMO Mike Modano/50 20.00 50.00
HRPF Peter Forsberg/25 25.00 60.00
HRPL Pat LaFontaine/99 12.00 30.00
HRWO Willie O'Ree/99 15.00 40.00

2019-20 Black Diamond Hardware Heroes
HHAB Aleksander Barkov 8.00 20.00
HHAO Alexander Ovechkin 20.00 50.00
HHAV Andrei Vasilevskiy 8.00 20.00
HHBG Bernie Geoffrion 4.00 10.00
HHBR Bill Ranford 4.00 10.00
HHBS Brendan Shanahan 5.00 12.00
HHCJ Curtis Joseph 6.00 15.00
HHCM Connor McDavid 25.00 60.00
HHDG Dirk Graham 4.00 10.00
HHEP Elias Pettersson 8.00 20.00
HHHH Harry Howell 4.00 10.00
HHMG Mark Giordano 5.00 12.00
HHNK Nikita Kucherov 10.00 25.00
HHRH Ron Hextall 5.00 12.00
HHRR Ryan O'Reilly 5.00 12.00
HHSL Steve Larmer 4.00 10.00
HHSN Scott Niedermayer 5.00 12.00
HHTL Ted Lindsay 5.00 12.00
HHVH Victor Hedman 6.00 15.00
HHWK William Karlsson 6.00 15.00

2019-20 Black Diamond Jewels of the Draft Patch Autographs
JDAT Alexandre Texier 15.00 40.00
JDBG Brandon Gignac 12.00 30.00
JDBH Barrett Hayton 30.00 80.00
JDCG Cody Glass 25.00 60.00
JDCM Cale Makar 150.00 400.00
JDDF Dante Fabbro 15.00 40.00
JDFZ Filip Zadina 25.00 60.00
JDJF Joel Farabee 25.00 60.00
JDJH Jack Hughes 80.00 200.00
JDKD Kirby Dach 30.00 80.00
JDMJ Max Jones 15.00 40.00
JDNB Nathan Bastian 15.00 40.00
JDPI Rem Pitlick 15.00 40.00
JDQH Quinn Hughes 80.00 200.00
JDRP Ryan Poehling 25.00 60.00
JDTB Teddy Blueger 15.00 40.00
JDTF Trent Frederic 15.00 40.00
JDVO Victor Olofsson 30.00 80.00
JDZS Zach Senyshyn 15.00 40.00

2019-20 Black Diamond Pure Black
BDBAD Alex DeBrincat AU/99 10.00 25.00
BDBAE Aaron Ekblad AU/99 10.00 25.00
BDBAK Anze Kopitar/99 5.00 12.00
BDBAL Anders Lee AU/25 12.00 30.00
BDBAM Auston Matthews AU/25 60.00 150.00
BDBAO Alexander Ovechkin/99 12.00 30.00
BDBAP Artemi Panarin/99 6.00 15.00
BDBBA Mathew Barzal/99 4.00 10.00
BDBBB Brent Burns AU/25 15.00 40.00
BDBBH Bo Horvat AU/99 10.00 25.00
BDBBM Brad Marchand AU/25 30.00 80.00
BDBBO Bobby Orr AU/25 60.00 150.00
BDBBT Brady Tkachuk AU/99 12.00 30.00
BDBBW Blake Wheeler/99 3.00 8.00
BDBCA Cam Atkinson AU/99 8.00 20.00
BDBCG Claude Giroux/99 3.00 8.00
BDBCM Connor McDavid AU/25 150.00 250.00
BDBDL Dylan Larkin/99 4.00 10.00
BDBED Evgenii Dadonov AU/99 5.00 12.00
BDBEK Evgeny Kuznetsov AU/99 10.00 25.00
BDBES Eric Staal AU/99 8.00 20.00
BDBGI John Gibson AU/99 8.00 20.00
BDBHA Noah Hanifin AU/99 8.00 20.00
BDBHL Henrik Lundqvist AU/25 40.00 100.00
BDBJG Jake Guentzel AU/99 12.00 30.00
BDBJV Jakub Voracek/99 2.50 6.00
BDBMA Mitch Marner AU/25 25.00 60.00
BDBMB Martin Brodeur AU/25 40.00 100.00
BDBMF Marc-Andre Fleury AU/25 30.00 80.00
BDBMS Mark Scheifele AU/25 25.00 60.00
BDBNH Nico Hischier AU/99 12.00 30.00
BDBNM Nathan MacKinnon/99 12.00 30.00
BDBOE Oliver Ekman-Larsson/99 3.00 8.00
BDBPK Patrick Kane AU/25 30.00 80.00
BDBPR Patrick Roy AU/25 40.00 100.00
BDBRD Rasmus Dahlin/99 4.00 10.00
BDBRE Ryan Ellis AU/99 6.00 15.00
BDBRG Ryan Getzlaf/99 3.00 8.00
BDBRO Ryan O'Reilly AU/99 8.00 20.00
BDBSC Sidney Crosby AU/25 200.00 300.00
BDBSJ Seth Jones AU/25 15.00 40.00
BDBSM Sean Monahan AU/99 5.00 12.00
BDBSS Steven Stamkos AU/25 30.00 80.00
BDBSY Steve Yzerman AU/25 40.00 100.00
BDBTA John Tavares AU/25 25.00 60.00
BDBTC Thomas Chabot/99 3.00 8.00
BDBTH Taylor Hall AU/25 15.00 40.00
BDBTT Teuvo Teravainen AU/99 8.00 20.00
BDBVA Viktor Arvidsson AU/99 5.00 12.00
BDBWG Wayne Gretzky AU/25 250.00 600.00

2019-20 Black Diamond Rookie Gems
RGAF Adam Fox 8.00 20.00
RGBH Barrett Hayton 6.00 15.00
RGCG Cody Glass 5.00 12.00
RGCM Cale Makar 15.00 40.00
RGDF Dante Fabbro 3.00 8.00
RGEB Erik Brannstrom 3.00 8.00
RGFZ Filip Zadina 5.00 12.00
RGJH Jack Hughes 15.00 40.00
RGKD Kirby Dach 6.00 15.00
RGKK Kaapo Kakko 5.00 12.00
RGMJ Max Jones 3.00 8.00
RGNG Nikita Gusev 5.00 12.00
RGNP Nikolay Prokhorkin 2.50 6.00
RGNS Nick Suzuki 12.00 30.00
RGPM Philippe Myers 2.50 6.00
RGQH Quinn Hughes 15.00 40.00
RGRP Ryan Poehling 5.00 12.00
RGTF Trent Frederic 3.00 8.00
RGTH Taro Hirose 3.00 8.00
RGVA Vitaly Abramov 3.00 8.00
RGVO Victor Olofsson 6.00 15.00
RGZS Zach Senyshyn 3.00 8.00

2019-20 Black Diamond Rookie Gems Pure Black Signatures
RGAF Adam Fox/199 50.00 125.00
RGBH Barrett Hayton/199 20.00 50.00
RGCG Cody Glass/99 15.00 40.00
RGCM Cale Makar/99 50.00 125.00
RGDF Dante Fabbro/199 10.00 25.00
RGEB Erik Brannstrom/199 10.00 25.00
RGFZ Filip Zadina/199 15.00 40.00
RGJH Jack Hughes/99 50.00 125.00
RGMJ Max Jones/199 10.00 25.00
RGNG Nikita Gusev/199 15.00 40.00
RGNS Nick Suzuki/199 40.00 100.00
RGPM Philippe Myers/199 8.00 20.00
RGRP Ryan Poehling/99 15.00 40.00
RGTF Trent Frederic/199 10.00 25.00
RGTH Taro Hirose/199 10.00 25.00
RGVO Victor Olofsson/199 20.00 50.00
RGZS Zach Senyshyn/199 10.00 25.00

2019-20 Black Diamond Rookie Team Logo Jumbo Patch Autographs Alternate Logo
RTLCG Cody Glass/99 25.00 60.00
RTLCM Cale Makar/49 80.00 200.00
RTLEB Erik Brannstrom/99 15.00 40.00
RTLFZ Filip Zadina/99 25.00 60.00
RTLJH Jack Hughes/49 80.00 200.00
RTLKD Kirby Dach/99 30.00 80.00
RTLNS Nick Suzuki/99 60.00 150.00
RTLQH Quinn Hughes/99 80.00 200.00
RTLRP Ryan Poehling/99 25.00 60.00

2019-20 Black Diamond Rookie Team Logo Jumbo Patches
*RETRO: .8X TO 2X BASIC
RTLCG Cody Glass 15.00 40.00
RTLCM Cale Makar 50.00 120.00
RTLEB Erik Brannstrom 12.00 30.00
RTLFZ Filip Zadina 8.00 20.00
RTLJH Jack Hughes 25.00 60.00
RTLKD Kirby Dach 10.00 25.00
RTLKK Kaapo Kakko 15.00 40.00
RTLNS Nick Suzuki 25.00 60.00
RTLQH Quinn Hughes 20.00 50.00
RTLRP Ryan Poehling 15.00 40.00

2019-20 Black Diamond Run for the Cup
RUNBB Brent Burns 4.00 10.00
RUNBR Bill Ranford 3.00 8.00
RUNCM Cale Makar 25.00 60.00
RUNGH Gordie Howe 12.00 30.00
RUNJG Johnny Gaudreau 6.00 15.00
RUNJH Jack Hughes 20.00 50.00
RUNJT Jonathan Toews 6.00 15.00
RUNKK Kaapo Kakko 6.00 15.00
RUNMB Mathew Barzal 5.00 12.00
RUNMF Marc-Andre Fleury 8.00 20.00
RUNMM Mitch Marner 6.00 15.00
RUNMS Mark Scheifele 6.00 15.00
RUNNK Nikita Kucherov 8.00 20.00
RUNPB Patrice Bergeron 5.00 12.00
RUNPR Patrick Roy 10.00 25.00
RUNRJ Ryan Johansen 3.00 8.00

2019-20 Black Diamond Silver on Black Rookie Signatures
SBRSBH Barrett Hayton/249 20.00 50.00
SBRSCG Cody Glass/99 15.00 40.00
SBRSCM Cale Makar/99 50.00 125.00
SBRSDF Dante Fabbro/249 10.00 25.00
SBRSEB Erik Brannstrom/249 10.00 25.00
SBRSFZ Filip Zadina/249 15.00 40.00
SBRSJF Joel Farabee/249 15.00 40.00
SBRSJH Jack Hughes/99 80.00 200.00
SBRSMJ Max Jones/249 10.00 25.00
SBRSQH Quinn Hughes/99 50.00 125.00
SBRSRP Ryan Poehling/249 15.00 40.00
SBRSTH Taro Hirose/249 10.00 25.00

2019-20 Black Diamond Silver on Black Signatures
SBAB Aleksander Barkov/50 12.00 30.00
SBBM Brad Marchand/125 15.00 40.00
SBJE Jack Eichel/50 12.00 30.00
SBNU Norm Ullman/125 8.00 20.00
SBSM Sean Monahan/50 5.00 12.00
SBTS Tyler Seguin/50 10.00 25.00

2019-20 Black Diamond Sparkling Scripts
*SPECTRUM/25: .6X TO 1.5X BASIC INSERTS
SCBB Ben Bishop C 8.00 20.00
SCBN Bernie Nicholls C 8.00 20.00
SCCA Cam Atkinson C 10.00 25.00
SCCM Connor McDavid A 100.00 250.00
SCCN Cam Neely B 10.00 25.00
SCEK Evgeny Kuznetsov B 12.00 30.00
SCML Mike Liut C 6.00 15.00
SCMM Mitch Marner A 15.00 40.00
SCMS Mark Scheifele B 15.00 40.00
SCMU Matt Murray C 10.00 25.00

2019-20 Black Diamond Team Logo Jumbo Patches
TLASAM Auston Matthews 10.00 25.00
TLASBW Blake Wheeler 2.50 6.00
TLASCM Connor McDavid 12.00 30.00
TLASEP Elias Pettersson 4.00 10.00
TLASHL Henrik Lundqvist 6.00 15.00
TLASJE Jack Eichel 4.00 10.00
TLASMB Mathew Barzal 3.00 8.00
TLASPK Patrick Kane 5.00 12.00
TLASSC Sidney Crosby 10.00 25.00
TLBSDA Dave Andreychuk 2.50 6.00
TLBSDG Danny Gare 2.00 5.00
TLBSDH Dominik Hasek 4.00 10.00
TLBSJE Jack Eichel 4.00 10.00
TLBSPH Phil Housley 2.00 5.00
TLBSPL Pat LaFontaine 2.50 6.00
TLBSRD Rasmus Dahlin 3.00 8.00
TLBSRM Ryan Miller 2.50 6.00
TLBSSR Sam Reinhart 5.00 12.00
TLNYAB Andy Bathgate 2.00 5.00
TLNYAG Adam Graves 2.00 5.00
TLNYBL Brian Leetch 2.00 5.00
TLNYEG Ed Giacomin 2.00 5.00
TLNYHH Harry Howell 2.00 5.00
TLNYHL Henrik Lundqvist 6.00 15.00
TLNYJR Jean Ratelle 2.00 5.00
TLNYMM Mark Messier 5.00 12.00
TLNYMR Mike Richter 2.50 6.00
TLSJAI Arturs Irbe 2.00 5.00
TLSJBB Brent Burns 2.50 6.00
TLSJEK Erik Karlsson 3.00 8.00
TLSJEN Evgeni Nabokov 2.00 5.00
TLSJJP Joe Pavelski 3.00 8.00
TLSJJT Joe Thornton 4.00 10.00
TLSJLC Logan Couture 3.00 8.00
TLSJON Owen Nolan 2.50 6.00
TLSJPM Patrick Marleau 2.50 6.00
TLVCBB Brock Boeser 3.00 8.00
TLVCBH Bo Horvat 3.00 8.00
TLVCDS Daniel Sedin 3.00 8.00
TLVCEP Elias Pettersson 4.00 10.00
TLVCHS Henrik Sedin 3.00 8.00
TLVCKM Kirk McLean 2.00 5.00
TLVCMN Markus Naslund 2.50 6.00
TLVCRL Roberto Luongo 4.00 10.00
TLVCTL Trevor Linden 2.50 6.00

2020-21 Black Diamond
BDBAB Aleksander Barkov 3.00 8.00
BDBAK Anze Kopitar 3.00 8.00
BDBAL Anders Lee 1.50 4.00
BDBAM Auston Matthews 8.00 20.00
BDBAO Alex Ovechkin 8.00 20.00
BDBAP Artemi Panarin 4.00 10.00
BDBAS Andrei Svechnikov 2.50 6.00
BDBBG Brendan Gallagher 2.00 5.00
BDBBH Bo Horvat 2.50 6.00
BDBBM Brad Marchand 4.00 10.00
BDBBO Bobby Orr 8.00 20.00
BDBBT Brady Tkachuk 3.00 8.00
BDBCG Claude Giroux 2.00 5.00
BDBCH Connor Hellebuyck 4.00 10.00
BDBCK Clayton Keller 2.50 6.00
BDBCM Cale Makar 5.00 12.00
BDBCP Carey Price 4.00 10.00
BDBDK Dominik Kubalik 2.00 5.00
BDBDL Dylan Larkin 2.50 6.00
BDBDP David Pastrnak 5.00 12.00
BDBEP Elias Pettersson 3.00 8.00
BDBGU Jake Guentzel 3.00 8.00
BDBHU Jack Hughes 5.00 12.00
BDBJB Jordan Binnington 3.00 8.00
BDBJE Jack Eichel 3.00 8.00
BDBJG John Gibson 2.00 5.00
BDBJH Jonathan Huberdeau 2.50 6.00
BDBJT Joe Thornton 3.00 8.00
BDBKF Kevin Fiala 1.50 4.00
BDBKP Kyle Palmieri 1.50 4.00
BDBLD Leon Draisaitl 6.00 15.00
BDBMA Mark Scheifele 3.00 8.00
BDBMC Connor McDavid 10.00 25.00
BDBMH Miro Heiskanen 2.50 6.00
BDBML Mario Lemieux 8.00 20.00
BDBMM Mitch Marner 3.00 8.00
BDBMT Matthew Tkachuk 4.00 10.00
BDBMZ Mika Zibanejad 2.50 6.00
BDBNK Nikita Kucherov 4.00 10.00
BDBNM Nathan MacKinnon 8.00 20.00
BDBOK Olaf Kolzig 2.00 5.00
BDBPA Colton Parayko 1.50 4.00
BDBPD Pierre-Luc Dubois 1.50 4.00
BDBPK Patrick Kane 4.00 10.00
BDBPR Patrick Roy 5.00 12.00
BDBQH Quinn Hughes 5.00 12.00
BDBRI Pekka Rinne 2.00 5.00
BDBRJ Roman Josi 2.00 5.00
BDBRN Ryan Nugent-Hopkins 2.50 6.00
BDBRO Ryan O'Reilly 2.00 5.00
BDBRS Ryan Suter 1.50 4.00
BDBSA Sebastian Aho 3.00 8.00
BDBSC Sidney Crosby 8.00 20.00
BDBSM Sean Monahan 1.25 3.00
BDBSR Sam Reinhart 4.00 10.00
BDBSS Steven Stamkos 4.00 10.00
BDBST Mark Stone 2.50 6.00
BDBTB Tyler Bertuzzi 1.50 4.00
BDBTC Thomas Chabot 2.00 5.00
BDBTH Tomas Hertl 2.00 5.00
BDBTK Travis Konecny 2.00 5.00
BDBTS Tyler Seguin 2.50 6.00
BDBTT Teuvo Teravainen 2.00 5.00
BDBWG Wayne Gretzky 12.00 30.00
BDBWK William Karlsson 2.50 6.00
BDRAA Alexander Alexeyev RC 20.00 50.00
BDRAL Alexis Lafreniere RC 250.00 600.00
BDRAR Alexander Romanov RC 30.00 80.00
BDRBB Bowen Byram RC 125.00 300.00
BDRBE Alex Belzile RC 20.00 50.00
BDRBH Brandon Hagel RC 30.00 80.00
BDRCF Cal Foote RC 30.00 80.00
BDRCI Connor Ingram RC 20.00 50.00
BDRCM Connor McMichael RC 40.00 100.00
BDRDC Dylan Cozens RC 125.00 300.00
BDREK Egor Korshkov RC 15.00 40.00
BDREZ Egor Zamula RC 20.00 50.00
BDRGV Gabe Vilardi RC 40.00 100.00
BDRIM Ian Mitchell RC 20.00 50.00
BDRIS Ilya Sorokin RC 150.00 400.00
BDRJE Jake Evans RC 25.00 60.00
BDRJJ Jonas Johansson RC 25.00 60.00
BDRJN Josh Norris RC 40.00 100.00
BDRJO Jake Oettinger RC 60.00 150.00
BDRJR Jason Robertson RC 30.00 80.00
BDRJW Joseph Woll RC 50.00 125.00
BDRKA Kirill Kaprizov RC 200.00 500.00
BDRKB Kieffer Bellows RC 20.00 50.00
BDRKM K'Andre Miller RC 50.00 125.00
BDRKU Philipp Kurashev RC 30.00 80.00
BDRLC Lucas Carlsson RC 20.00 50.00
BDRLF Liam Foudy RC 25.00 60.00
BDRMA Mikey Anderson RC 25.00 60.00
BDRMB Mikhail Berdin RC 25.00 60.00
BDRMD Michael DiPietro RC 30.00 80.00
BDRMG Morgan Geekie RC 25.00 60.00
BDRMK Martin Kaut RC 25.00 60.00
BDRNB Nicolas Beaudin RC 25.00 60.00
BDRNR Nick Robertson RC 40.00 100.00
BDROJ Olli Juolevi RC 25.00 60.00
BDRPB Philip Broberg RC 60.00 150.00
BDRPF Pavel Francouz RC 30.00 80.00
BDRPJ Pierre-Olivier Joseph RC 25.00 60.00
BDRPK Peyton Krebs RC 80.00 200.00
BDRRM Ryan McLeod RC 20.00 50.00
BDRSB Shane Bowers RC 20.00 50.00
BDRSM Ty Smith RC 40.00 100.00
BDRTB Tyler Benson RC 25.00 60.00
BDRTD Ty Dellandrea RC 25.00 60.00
BDRTH Thomas Harley RC 40.00 100.00
BDRTL Timothy Liljegren RC 25.00 60.00
BDRTS Tim Stutzle RC 200.00 500.00
BDRVK Vitali Kravtsov RC 50.00 125.00
BDRVS Victor Soderstrom RC 20.00 50.00
BDRVV Vitek Vanecek RC 40.00 100.00

2020-21 Black Diamond Diamond Relics Ruby
*RUBY: .5X TO 1.25X BASIC
BDRAL Alexis Lafreniere 400.00 1000.00
BDRKA Kirill Kaprizov 250.00 600.00
BDRPB Philip Broberg 125.00 300.00
BDRPF Pavel Francouz 80.00 200.00
BDRTS Tim Stutzle 300.00 800.00

2020-21 Black Diamond Pure Black
BDBAB Aleksander Barkov AU/50 15.00 40.00
BDBAL Anders Lee AU/99 8.00 20.00
BDBAM Auston Matthews AU/25 60.00 150.00
BDBAO Alex Ovechkin/99 12.00 30.00
BDBAP Artemi Panarin/99 6.00 15.00
BDBAS Andrei Svechnikov AU/50 12.00 30.00
BDBBG Brendan Gallagher AU/50 10.00 25.00
BDBBH Bo Horvat AU/50 12.00 30.00
BDBBM Brad Marchand AU/25 30.00 80.00
BDBBO Bobby Orr AU/25 60.00 150.00
BDBCG Claude Giroux/99 3.00 8.00
BDBCH Connor Hellebuyck AU/50 20.00 50.00
BDBCP Carey Price AU/25 30.00 80.00
BDBDK Dominik Kubalik AU/99 25.00 60.00
BDBDP David Pastrnak/99 8.00 20.00
BDBHU Jack Hughes AU/25 40.00 100.00
BDBJB Jordan Binnington AU/99 20.00 50.00
BDBJE Jack Eichel/99 5.00 12.00
BDBJG John Gibson AU/25 15.00 40.00
BDBJH Jonathan Huberdeau/99 4.00 10.00
BDBJT Joe Thornton AU/25 25.00 60.00
BDBKP Kyle Palmieri AU/99 8.00 20.00
BDBMA Mark Scheifele AU/50 15.00 40.00
BDBMC Connor McDavid AU/25 200.00 500.00
BDBMH Miro Heiskanen AU/50 12.00 30.00
BDBML Mario Lemieux AU/25 60.00 150.00
BDBMM Mitch Marner AU/25 25.00 60.00
BDBMT Matthew Tkachuk AU/50 20.00 50.00
BDBMZ Mika Zibanejad/99 4.00 10.00
BDBNM Nathan MacKinnon/99 12.00 30.00
BDBOK Olaf Kolzig AU/50 10.00 25.00
BDBPA Colton Parayko AU/99 20.00 50.00
BDBPK Patrick Kane/99 6.00 15.00
BDBPR Patrick Roy AU/25 100.00 250.00
BDBRI Pekka Rinne AU/50 10.00 25.00
BDBRJ Roman Josi AU/99 10.00 25.00
BDBRN Ryan Nugent-Hopkins/99 4.00 10.00
BDBRS Ryan Suter AU/50 8.00 20.00
BDBSR Sam Reinhart AU/99 20.00 50.00
BDBSS Steven Stamkos AU/25 30.00 80.00
BDBST Mark Stone AU/50 12.00 30.00
BDBTB Tyler Bertuzzi AU/99 8.00 20.00
BDBTC Thomas Chabot AU/99 10.00 25.00
BDBTH Tomas Hertl AU/99 10.00 25.00
BDBTS Tyler Seguin AU/25 20.00 50.00
BDBTT Teuvo Teravainen AU/99 10.00 25.00
BDBWG Wayne Gretzky AU/25 400.00 1000.00

2020-21 Black Diamond Pure Black Premium Relics

BDBAB Aleksander Barkov/50 10.00 25.00
BDBAK Anze Kopitar/50 10.00 25.00
BDBAL Anders Lee/50 5.00 12.00
BDBAM Auston Matthews/25 25.00 60.00
BDBAP Artemi Panarin/25 12.00 30.00
BDBBG Brendan Gallagher/50 6.00 15.00
BDBBH Bo Horvat/50 8.00 20.00
BDBBM Brad Marchand/25 12.00 30.00
BDBCG Claude Giroux/50 6.00 15.00
BDBCH Connor Hellebuyck/50 12.00 30.00
BDBCK Clayton Keller/50 8.00 20.00
BDBCM Cale Makar/50 15.00 40.00
BDBCP Carey Price/50 12.00 30.00
BDBDP David Pastrnak/25 15.00 40.00
BDBEP Elias Pettersson/50 10.00 25.00
BDBGU Jake Guentzel/50 10.00 25.00
BDBHU Jack Hughes/50 15.00 40.00
BDBJB Jordan Binnington/50 10.00 25.00
BDBJG John Gibson/50 6.00 15.00
BDBJH Jonathan Huberdeau/50 8.00 20.00
BDBKP Kyle Palmieri/50 5.00 12.00
BDBLD Leon Draisaitl/25 20.00 50.00
BDBMA Mark Scheifele/50 10.00 25.00
BDBMH Miro Heiskanen/50 8.00 20.00
BDBMM Mitch Marner/50 10.00 25.00
BDBMT Matthew Tkachuk/50 12.00 30.00
BDBMZ Mika Zibanejad/50 8.00 20.00
BDBNK Nikita Kucherov/25 12.00 30.00
BDBNM Nathan MacKinnon/25 25.00 60.00
BDBOK Olaf Kolzig/25 6.00 15.00
BDBPA Colton Parayko/50 5.00 12.00
BDBPD Pierre-Luc Dubois/50 5.00 12.00
BDBPK Patrick Kane/25 12.00 30.00
BDBQH Quinn Hughes/50 15.00 40.00
BDBRI Pekka Rinne/50 6.00 15.00
BDBRJ Roman Josi/50 6.00 15.00
BDBRN Ryan Nugent-Hopkins/50 8.00 20.00
BDBRO Ryan O'Reilly/50 6.00 15.00
BDBRS Ryan Suter/50 5.00 12.00
BDBSM Sean Monahan/50 4.00 10.00
BDBSR Sam Reinhart/50 12.00 30.00
BDBSS Steven Stamkos/25 12.00 30.00
BDBST Mark Stone/50 8.00 20.00
BDBTB Tyler Bertuzzi/50 5.00 12.00
BDBTC Thomas Chabot/50 6.00 15.00
BDBTH Tomas Hertl/50 6.00 15.00
BDBTK Travis Konecny/50 6.00 15.00
BDBTS Tyler Seguin/50 8.00 20.00
BDBTT Teuvo Teravainen/50 6.00 15.00
BDBWK William Karlsson/50 8.00 20.00

2020-21 Black Diamond Diamonation

DAL Alexis Lafreniere 20.00 50.00
DAM Auston Matthews 20.00 50.00
DAO Alex Ovechkin 15.00 40.00
DAV Andrei Vasilevskiy 10.00 25.00
DBO Bobby Orr 15.00 40.00
DCM Connor McDavid 30.00 80.00
DDP David Pastrnak 15.00 40.00
DEP Elias Pettersson 10.00 25.00
DGL Guy Lafleur 8.00 20.00
DJJ Jaromir Jagr 20.00 50.00
DJS Joe Sakic 12.00 30.00
DNL Nicklas Lidstrom 6.00 15.00
DNM Nathan MacKinnon 25.00 60.00
DNR Nick Robertson 12.00 30.00
DPK Patrick Kane 12.00 30.00
DPR Patrick Roy 15.00 40.00
DSC Sidney Crosby 20.00 50.00
DSY Steve Yzerman 15.00 40.00
DWG Wayne Gretzky 30.00 80.00

2020-21 Black Diamond Diamond Cutters

DCAL Alexis Lafreniere 20.00 50.00
DCAS Andrei Svechnikov 6.00 15.00
DCGF Grant Fuhr 8.00 20.00
DCGH Glenn Hall 5.00 12.00
DCGV Gabe Vilardi 10.00 25.00
DCIS Igor Shesterkin 10.00 25.00
DCJN Josh Norris 10.00 25.00
DCLD Leon Draisaitl 15.00 40.00
DCLF Liam Foudy 6.00 15.00
DCMS Mats Sundin 5.00 12.00
DCNS Nick Suzuki 10.00 25.00
DCTL Trevor Linden 5.00 12.00
DCWG Wayne Gretzky 30.00 80.00

2020-21 Black Diamond Diamond Debut Relics

DDAL Alexis Lafreniere 8.00 20.00
DDAT Alexander True 2.00 5.00
DDBB Bowen Byram 5.00 12.00
DDDC Dylan Cozens 4.00 10.00
DDGV Gabe Vilardi 4.00 10.00
DDJE Jake Evans 2.50 6.00
DDJN Josh Norris 8.00 20.00
DDJR Jason Robertson 6.00 15.00
DDLF Liam Foudy 2.50 6.00
DDMA Mikey Anderson 2.50 6.00
DDMG Morgan Geekie 2.50 6.00
DDMK Martin Kaut 2.50 6.00
DDNR Nick Robertson 4.00 10.00
DDPK Peyton Krebs 4.00 10.00
DDTB Tyler Benson 2.50 6.00
DDTL Timothy Liljegren 2.50 6.00

2020-21 Black Diamond Diamond Debut Relics Patch Autographs

DDAL Alexis Lafreniere/25 40.00 1000.00
DDAT Alexander True/49 15.00 40.00
DDBB Bowen Byram/25 40.00 100.00
DDDC Dylan Cozens/25 30.00 80.00
DDGV Gabe Vilardi/49 30.00 80.00
DDJE Jake Evans/49 30.00 80.00
DDJN Josh Norris/25 30.00 80.00
DDJR Jason Robertson/49 100.00 250.00
DDLF Liam Foudy/49 20.00 50.00
DDMA Mikey Anderson/49 20.00 50.00
DDMG Morgan Geekie/49 20.00 50.00
DDMK Martin Kaut/49 20.00 50.00
DDNR Nick Robertson/49 30.00 80.00
DDPK Peyton Krebs/49 30.00 80.00
DDTB Tyler Benson/49 20.00 50.00
DDTL Timothy Liljegren/49 20.00 50.00

2020-21 Black Diamond Diamond Futures

BDFAL Alexis Lafreniere 8.00 20.00
BDFAT Alexander True 2.00 5.00
BDFBB Bowen Byram 5.00 12.00
BDFBE Tyler Benson 2.50 6.00
BDFCM Connor McMichael 8.00 20.00
BDFDC Dylan Cozens 10.00 25.00
BDFGV Gabe Vilardi 4.00 10.00
BDFIS Ilya Sorokin 15.00 40.00
BDFJE Jake Evans 2.50 6.00
BDFJN Josh Norris 4.00 10.00
BDFJO Jake Oettinger 5.00 12.00
BDFJR Jason Robertson 6.00 15.00
BDFKB Kieffer Bellows 2.00 5.00
BDFKK Kirill Kaprizov 25.00 60.00
BDFLF Liam Foudy 2.50 6.00
BDFMA Mikey Anderson 2.50 6.00
BDFMG Morgan Geekie 2.50 6.00
BDFMK Martin Kaut 2.50 6.00
BDFNR Nick Robertson 4.00 10.00
BDFOJ Olli Juolevi 4.00 10.00
BDFPK Peyton Krebs 4.00 10.00
BDFTL Timothy Liljegren 2.50 6.00
BDFVS Victor Soderstrom 2.00 5.00

2020-21 Black Diamond Diamond Futures Autographs

BDFAL Alexis Lafreniere/49 125.00 300.00
BDFAT Alexander True/99 10.00 25.00
BDFBB Bowen Byram/99 25.00 60.00
BDFBE Tyler Benson/99 12.00 30.00
BDFDC Dylan Cozens/99 60.00 150.00
BDFIS Ilya Sorokin/99 60.00 150.00
BDFJE Jake Evans/99 12.00 30.00
BDFJN Josh Norris/99 20.00 50.00
BDFJO Jake Oettinger/99 30.00 80.00
BDFKB Kieffer Bellows/99 10.00 25.00
BDFKK Kirill Kaprizov/99 200.00 500.00
BDFLF Liam Foudy/99 12.00 30.00
BDFMA Mikey Anderson/99 12.00 30.00
BDFMG Morgan Geekie/99 12.00 30.00
BDFMK Martin Kaut/99 12.00 30.00
BDFNR Nick Robertson/99 20.00 50.00
BDFOJ Olli Juolevi/99 12.00 30.00
BDFPK Peyton Krebs/99 20.00 50.00
BDFTL Timothy Liljegren/99 12.00 30.00
BDFVS Victor Soderstrom/99 10.00 25.00

2020-21 Black Diamond Diamond Futures Relic Autographs Premium

BDFAT Alexander True/25 15.00 40.00
BDFBB Bowen Byram/25 80.00 200.00
BDFBE Tyler Benson/25 20.00 50.00
BDFCM Connor McMichael/25 30.00 80.00
BDFDC Dylan Cozens/25 80.00 200.00
BDFGV Gabe Vilardi/25 20.00 50.00
BDFIS Ilya Sorokin/25 150.00 400.00
BDFJE Jake Evans/25 20.00 50.00
BDFJN Josh Norris/25 30.00 80.00
BDFJO Jake Oettinger/25 50.00 125.00
BDFJR Jason Robertson/25 300.00 800.00
BDFKB Kieffer Bellows/25 15.00 40.00
BDFLF Liam Foudy/25 20.00 50.00
BDFMA Mikey Anderson/25 20.00 50.00
BDFMG Morgan Geekie/25 20.00 50.00
BDFMK Martin Kaut/25 20.00 50.00
BDFNR Nick Robertson/25 80.00 200.00
BDFOJ Olli Juolevi/25 20.00 50.00
BDFPK Peyton Krebs/25 30.00 80.00
BDFTL Timothy Liljegren/25 20.00 50.00
BDFVS Victor Soderstrom/25 15.00 40.00

2020-21 Black Diamond Diamond Gallery

DGAL Alexis Lafreniere 15.00 40.00
DGAM Auston Matthews 15.00 40.00
DGAO Alex Ovechkin 15.00 40.00
DGBB Bowen Byram 10.00 25.00
DGBH Brett Hull 8.00 20.00
DGBP Bernie Parent 5.00 12.00
DGEP Elias Pettersson 6.00 15.00
DGGV Gabe Vilardi 8.00 20.00
DGJE Jack Eichel 6.00 15.00
DGLR Luc Robitaille 4.00 10.00
DGPC Paul Coffey 4.00 10.00
DGPK Patrick Kane 8.00 20.00
DGSS Steven Stamkos 8.00 20.00
DGTE Tony Esposito 4.00 10.00
DGTS Terry Sawchuk 4.00 10.00

2020-21 Black Diamond Diamond Legends

BDLDH Dominik Hasek 6.00 15.00
BDLMS Martin St. Louis 4.00 10.00
BDLNL Nicklas Lidstrom 4.00 10.00
BDLPR Patrick Roy 12.00 30.00
BDLWG Wayne Gretzky 15.00 40.00

2020-21 Black Diamond Diamond Legends Autographs

BDLMS Martin St. Louis 20.00 50.00
BDLNL Nicklas Lidstrom 25.00 60.00

2020-21 Black Diamond Diamond Legends Relic Autographs Premium

BDLMS Martin St. Louis 25.00 60.00
BDLNL Nicklas Lidstrom 30.00 80.00

2020-21 Black Diamond Diamond Might

DMAL Alexis Lafreniere 25.00 60.00
DMAP Artemi Panarin 25.00 60.00
DMBB Bowen Byram 20.00 50.00
DMBH Bobby Hull 8.00 20.00
DMCM Cale Makar 15.00 40.00
DMDC Dylan Cozens 15.00 40.00
DMDH Dominik Hasek 20.00 50.00
DMDP David Pastrnak 20.00 50.00
DMDS Darryl Sittler 10.00 25.00
DMJE Jack Eichel 12.00 30.00
DMLD Leon Draisaitl 25.00 60.00
DMMM Mark Messier 15.00 40.00
DMNR Nick Robertson 15.00 40.00
DMSY Steve Yzerman 20.00 50.00

2020-21 Black Diamond Diamond Mine Dual Relics

DMDRAS S.Aho/A.Svechnikov 8.00 20.00
DMDRCO J.Carlson/A.Ovechkin 20.00 50.00
DMDRGB S.Gomez/M.Brodeur 12.00 30.00
DMDRLR K.McLean/R.Luongo 8.00 20.00
DMDRMM N.MacKinnon/C.Makar 20.00 50.00
DMDRND R.Nugent-Hopkins/L.Draisaitl 15.00 40.00
DMDRPA F.Potvin/F.Andersen 8.00 20.00
DMDRRP D.Pastrnak/T.Rask 12.00 30.00
DMDRSD A.DeBrincat/D.Strome 6.00 15.00
DMDRTC T.Chabot/B.Tkachuk 8.00 20.00

2020-21 Black Diamond Diamond Mine Relics

*PREMIUM/25: .75X TO 2X BASIC
DMRAV Andrei Vasilevskiy 5.00 12.00
DMRCH Connor Hellebuyck 6.00 15.00
DMRDP David Pastrnak 8.00 20.00
DMREM Evgeni Malkin 6.00 15.00
DMREP Elias Pettersson 5.00 12.00
DMRHZ Henrik Zetterberg 4.00 10.00
DMRJH Jonathan Huberdeau 4.00 10.00
DMRJI Jarome Iginla 4.00 10.00
DMRLD Leon Draisaitl 10.00 25.00
DMRMM Mitch Marner 5.00 12.00
DMRMS Mark Stone 8.00 20.00
DMRMZ Mika Zibanejad 4.00 10.00
DMRNM Nathan MacKinnon 12.00 30.00
DMRRO Ryan O'Reilly 3.00 8.00
DMRZW Zach Werenski 5.00 12.00

2020-21 Black Diamond Diamond Mine Triple Relics

DMTRCAL Tanguay/Iginla/Giordano 8.00 20.00
DMTRDET Zetterberg/Larkin/Mantha 30.00 80.00
DMTRPHI LeClair/Gagne/Giroux 6.00 15.00
DMTRTBL St. Louis Stamkos/Kucherov 12.00 30.00
DMTRVAN Linden/Sedin/Horvat 15.00 40.00

2020-21 Black Diamond Diamond Stars

BDSBM Brad Marchand 5.00 12.00
BDSCM Connor McDavid 12.00 30.00
BDSMM Mitch Marner 4.00 10.00
BDSMS Mark Stone 3.00 8.00
BDSSC Sidney Crosby 10.00 25.00

2020-21 Black Diamond Diamond Stars Autographs

BDSBM Brad Marchand/25 40.00 100.00
BDSMM Mitch Marner/25 30.00 80.00
BDSMS Mark Stone/25 25.00 60.00

2020-21 Black Diamond Diamond Stars Relic Autographs Premium

BDSBM Brad Marchand/25 50.00 125.00
BDSMM Mitch Marner/25 40.00 100.00
BDSMS Mark Stone/25 30.00 80.00

2020-21 Black Diamond Gemography

GAK Anze Kopitar 30.00 80.00
GAL Alexis Lafreniere 200.00 500.00
GAP Artemi Panarin 40.00 100.00
GAV Andrei Vasilevskiy 30.00 80.00
GBB Bowen Byram 80.00 200.00
GBH Bobby Hull 50.00 125.00
GBM Brad Marchand 40.00 100.00
GCH Carter Hart 60.00 150.00
GDS Darryl Sittler 25.00 60.00
GEP Elias Pettersson 30.00 80.00
GGF Grant Fuhr 30.00 80.00
GHE Connor Hellebuyck 30.00 80.00
GKK Kirill Kaprizov 300.00 800.00
GMH Miro Heiskanen 30.00 80.00
GML Mario Lemieux 80.00 200.00
GMS Mark Stone 25.00 60.00
GNR Nick Robertson 40.00 100.00
GPR Patrick Roy 80.00 200.00
GRO Ryan O'Reilly 25.00 60.00
GSC Sidney Crosby 125.00 300.00
GTC Thomas Chabot 20.00 50.00
GTS Tyler Seguin 40.00 100.00
GWG Wayne Gretzky 400.00 1000.00

2020-21 Black Diamond Jewels of the Draft Patch Autographs

JDAL Alexis Lafreniere/49 300.00 800.00
JDAR Alexander Romanov/99 125.00 300.00
JDBB Bowen Byram/99 40.00 100.00
JDBE Tyler Benson/99 20.00 50.00
JDDC Dylan Cozens/99 30.00 80.00
JDGV Gabe Vilardi/99 30.00 80.00
JDIS Ilya Sorokin/99 150.00 400.00
JDJE Jake Evans/99 20.00 50.00
JDJO Jake Oettinger/99 60.00 150.00
JDJR Jason Robertson/99 50.00 125.00
JDKB Kieffer Bellows/99 15.00 40.00
JDLF Liam Foudy/99 20.00 50.00
JDMG Morgan Geekie/99 20.00 50.00
JDMK Martin Kaut/99 20.00 50.00
JDNR Nick Robertson/99 30.00 80.00
JDOJ Olli Juolevi/99 20.00 50.00
JDPJ Pierre-Olivier Joseph/99 20.00 50.00
JDPK Peyton Krebs/99 30.00 80.00
JDSB Shane Bowers/99 15.00 40.00
JDST Tim Stutzle/99 125.00 300.00
JDTL Timothy Liljegren/99 20.00 50.00
JDTS Ty Smith/99 30.00 80.00
JDVS Victor Soderstrom/99 15.00 40.00

2020-21 Black Diamond Retired Numbers Patches

RNBF Bernie Federko 8.00 20.00
RNBL Brian Leetch 25.00 60.00
RNBS Billy Smith 15.00 40.00
RNDH Dominik Hasek 30.00 80.00
RNDS Daniel Sedin 12.00 30.00
RNGH Gordie Howe 30.00 80.00
RNHS Henrik Sedin 12.00 30.00
RNJB Jean Beliveau 30.00 80.00
RNJI Jarome Iginla 15.00 40.00
RNPF Peter Forsberg 25.00 60.00
RNRL Roberto Luongo 15.00 40.00
RNSN Scott Niedermayer 10.00 25.00
RNWG Wayne Gretzky 60.00 150.00

2020-21 Black Diamond Retired Numbers Patches Gold

*GOLD: .75X TO 2X BASIC
RNBS Billy Smith AU/31 30.00 80.00
RNDH Dominik Hasek AU/39 200.00 500.00
RNDS Daniel Sedin AU/22 50.00 125.00
RNHS Henrik Sedin AU/33 50.00 125.00

2020-21 Black Diamond Rookie Gems

RGAL Alexis Lafreniere 12.00 30.00
RGAR Alexander Romanov 12.00 30.00
RGBB Bowen Byram 8.00 20.00
RGDC Dylan Cozens 12.00 30.00
RGIS Ilya Sorokin 15.00 40.00
RGJE Jake Evans 4.00 10.00
RGKB Kieffer Bellows 3.00 8.00
RGKK Kirill Kaprizov 30.00 80.00
RGKU Philipp Kurashev 5.00 12.00
RGLF Liam Foudy 4.00 10.00
RGMG Morgan Geekie 4.00 10.00
RGMK Martin Kaut 4.00 10.00
RGNB Nicolas Beaudin 4.00 10.00
RGNR Nick Robertson 6.00 15.00
RGOJ Olli Juolevi 4.00 10.00
RGPK Peyton Krebs 6.00 15.00
RGPO Pierre-Olivier Joseph 4.00 10.00
RGTB Tyler Benson 4.00 10.00
RGTH Thomas Harley 6.00 15.00
RGTL Timothy Liljegren 4.00 10.00
RGTR Alexander True 3.00 8.00
RGTS Tim Stutzle 25.00 60.00
RGVS Victor Soderstrom 3.00 8.00

2020-21 Black Diamond Rookie Gems Spectrum

*SPECTRUM: .75X TO 2X BASIC
RGKK Kirill Kaprizov 125.00 300.00

2020-21 Black Diamond Rookie Gems Pure Black Signatures

COMMON CARD 4.00 10.00
SEMISTARS 5.00 12.00
UNLISTED STARS 6.00 15.00
RGAR Alexander Romanov/199 30.00 80.00
RGBB Bowen Byram/99 40.00 100.00
RGDC Dylan Cozens/99 40.00 100.00
RGIS Ilya Sorokin/99 80.00 200.00
RGJE Jake Evans/199 8.00 20.00
RGKB Kieffer Bellows/199 6.00 15.00
RGKK Kirill Kaprizov/99 125.00 300.00
RGKU Philipp Kurashev/199 10.00 25.00
RGLF Liam Foudy/199 8.00 20.00
RGMG Morgan Geekie/199 8.00 20.00
RGMK Martin Kaut/199 8.00 20.00
RGNB Nicolas Beaudin/199 8.00 20.00
RGNR Nick Robertson/99 12.00 30.00
RGOJ Olli Juolevi/199 8.00 20.00
RGPK Peyton Krebs/99 30.00 80.00
RGPO Pierre-Olivier Joseph/199 20.00 50.00
RGTB Tyler Benson/199 8.00 20.00
RGTH Thomas Harley/199 12.00 30.00
RGTL Timothy Liljegren/199 8.00 20.00
RGTR Alexander True/199 6.00 15.00
RGTS Tim Stutzle/99 125.00 300.00
RGVS Victor Soderstrom/199 6.00 15.00

2020-21 Black Diamond Rookie Team Logo Jumbo Patch Autographs Full Logo 1

RTLAL Alexis Lafreniere/49 200.00 500.00
RTLBB Bowen Byram/99 40.00 100.00
RTLDC Dylan Cozens/99 80.00 200.00
RTLJN Josh Norris/99 40.00 100.00
RTLJR Jason Robertson/99 60.00 150.00
RTLKK Kirill Kaprizov/99 250.00 600.00
RTLLA Alexis Lafreniere/49 200.00 500.00
RTLLF Liam Foudy/99 25.00 60.00
RTLNR Nick Robertson/99 40.00 100.00

2020-21 Black Diamond Rookie Team Logo Jumbo Patch Autographs Full Logo 2

*LOGO.2: .5X TO 1.25X BASIC
RTLAL Alexis Lafreniere/25 300.00 800.00
RTLLA Alexis Lafreniere/25 300.00 800.00

2020-21 Black Diamond Rookie Team Logo Jumbo Patch Autographs Full Logo 3

*LOGO.3: .6X TO 1.5X BASIC
RTLJR Jason Robertson/25 150.00 400.00

2020-21 Black Diamond Rookie Team Logo Jumbo Puzzle Patches

*RETRO: .6X TO 1.5X BASIC
RTLAL Alexis Lafreniere 20.00 50.00
RTLBB Bowen Byram 12.00 30.00
RTLDC Dylan Cozens 10.00 25.00
RTLGV Gabe Vilardi 10.00 25.00
RTLJN Josh Norris 10.00 25.00
RTLJR Jason Robertson 15.00 40.00
RTLKK Kirill Kaprizov 25.00 60.00
RTLLA Alexis Lafreniere 20.00 50.00
RTLLF Liam Foudy 6.00 15.00
RTLNR Nick Robertson 10.00 25.00

2020-21 Black Diamond Run for the Cup

RUNAL Alexis Lafreniere 15.00 40.00
RUNBB Bowen Byram 10.00 25.00
RUNBM Brad Marchand 8.00 20.00
RUNBO Bobby Orr 25.00 60.00
RUNCH Carter Hart 15.00 40.00
RUNEP Elias Pettersson 20.00 50.00
RUNJB Jordan Binnington 12.00 30.00
RUNKC Kyle Connor 6.00 15.00
RUNMP Max Pacioretty 8.00 20.00
RUNMZ Mika Zibanejad 5.00 12.00
RUNNL Nicklas Lidstrom 5.00 12.00
RUNNM Nathan MacKinnon 15.00 40.00
RUNNR Nick Robertson 8.00 20.00
RUNSS Steven Stamkos 8.00 20.00
RUNTS Teemu Selanne 10.00 25.00
RUNTT Teuvo Teravainen 4.00 10.00

2020-21 Black Diamond Silver on Black Rookie Signatures

*SPECTRUM/25: .6X TO 1.5X BASIC
SBRSAL Alexis Lafreniere/49 150.00 400.00
SBRSAT Alexander True/149 10.00 25.00
SBRSBB Bowen Byram/99 25.00 60.00
SBRSBE Tyler Benson/149 12.00 30.00
SBRSDC Dylan Cozens/99 60.00 150.00
SBRSEK Egor Korshkov/149 8.00 20.00
SBRSGV Gabe Vilardi/149 20.00 50.00
SBRSIS Ilya Sorokin/149 60.00 150.00
SBRSJO Jake Oettinger/149 30.00 80.00
SBRSJR Jason Robertson/149 30.00 80.00
SBRSLF Liam Foudy/149 12.00 30.00
SBRSMG Morgan Geekie/149 12.00 30.00
SBRSMK Martin Kaut/149 12.00 30.00
SBRSNR Nick Robertson/99 20.00 50.00
SBRSPK Peyton Krebs/149 30.00 80.00
SBRSSB Shane Bowers/149 10.00 25.00
SBRSTL Timothy Liljegren/149 12.00 30.00
SBRSVS Victor Soderstrom/149 20.00 50.00

2020-21 Black Diamond Silver on Black Signatures

SBAV Andrei Vasilevskiy/50 25.00 60.00
SBBH Bo Horvat/100 25.00 60.00
SBBS Billy Smith/100 20.00 50.00
SBDG Doug Gilmour/50 25.00 60.00
SBJH Jack Hughes/50 50.00 125.00
SBMR Mike Richter/100 25.00 60.00
SBMS Martin St. Louis/50 20.00 50.00
SBMT Matthew Tkachuk/50 12.00 30.00
SBPB Peter Bondra/100 20.00 50.00
SBPL Pat LaFontaine/100 20.00 50.00
SBRJ Roman Josi/100 12.00 30.00
SBTL Trevor Linden/100 20.00 50.00
SBTT Tomas Tatar/100 12.00 30.00

2020-21 Black Diamond Silver on Black Signatures Spectrum

*SPECTRUM: .5X TO 1.25X BASIC
SBDG Doug Gilmour/25 40.00 100.00
SBJH Jack Hughes/25 80.00 200.00
SBMT Matthew Tkachuk/25 50.00 125.00
SBPB Peter Bondra/25 25.00 60.00
SBTL Trevor Linden/25 40.00 100.00

2020-21 Black Diamond Sparkling Rookie Scripts

RSCAL Alexis Lafreniere A 150.00 400.00
RSCAT Alexander True B 8.00 20.00
RSCBB Bowen Byram A 20.00 50.00
RSCCI Connor Ingram B 8.00 20.00
RSCDC Dylan Cozens A 30.00 80.00
RSCIS Ilya Sorokin A 25.00 60.00
RSCJO Jake Oettinger B 25.00 60.00
RSCKR Peyton Krebs B 15.00 40.00
RSCLF Liam Foudy B 10.00 25.00
RSCMG Morgan Geekie B 10.00 25.00
RSCNB Nicolas Beaudin B 10.00 25.00
RSCNR Nick Robertson B 15.00 40.00
RSCPJ Pierre-Olivier Joseph B 10.00 25.00
RSCPK Philipp Kurashev B 12.00 30.00
RSCTB Tyler Benson B 10.00 25.00
RSCTD Ty Dellandrea B 10.00 25.00
RSCTL Timothy Liljegren A 10.00 25.00

2020-21 Black Diamond Sparkling Rookie Scripts Spectrum

*SINGLES: .6X TO 1.5X BASIC
RSCKR Peyton Krebs 40.00 100.00
RSCNR Nick Robertson 50.00 125.00
RSCTB Tyler Benson 30.00 80.00

2020-21 Black Diamond Sparkling Scripts

SCAB Aleksander Barkov B 20.00 50.00
SCAE Aaron Ekblad B 15.00 40.00
SCAF Adam Fox B 30.00 80.00
SCAS Andrei Svechnikov C 15.00 40.00
SCBG Brendan Gallagher B 12.00 30.00
SCBO Bobby Orr A 80.00 200.00
SCCA Cam Atkinson A 12.00 30.00
SCCM Connor McDavid A 150.00 400.00
SCCN Cam Neely B 12.00 30.00
SCDG Dirk Graham C 10.00 25.00
SCDH Dany Heatley B 10.00 25.00
SCFP Felix Potvin C 20.00 50.00
SCGF Grant Fuhr A 20.00 50.00
SCGS Gary Suter B 8.00 20.00
SCIP Ivan Provorov B 20.00 50.00
SCIS Ilya Samsonov B 20.00 50.00
SCJK Jesperi Kotkaniemi B 12.00 30.00
SCJT Jonathan Toews B 30.00 80.00
SCKD Kirby Dach B 12.00 30.00
SCKY Keith Yandle B 8.00 20.00
SCMM Mitch Marner B 30.00 80.00
SCMR Mike Richter C 20.00 50.00
SCMS Martin St. Louis B 12.00 30.00
SCNG Nikita Gusev C 10.00 25.00
SCNL Nicklas Lidstrom B 25.00 60.00
SCNS Nick Suzuki C 25.00 60.00
SCPB Peter Bondra B 10.00 25.00
SCPE Phil Esposito B 20.00 50.00
SCPR Patrick Roy B 60.00 150.00
SCRH Ron Hextall B 12.00 30.00
SCRJ Roman Josi B 12.00 30.00
SCSJ Seth Jones C 12.00 30.00
SCSU Mats Sundin B 50.00 125.00
SCTH Tomas Hertl C 12.00 30.00
SCTS Teemu Selanne B 25.00 60.00
SCTT Teuvo Teravainen C 12.00 30.00

2020-21 Black Diamond Sparkling Scripts Spectrum

*SPECTRUM: .5X TO 1.25X BASIC
SCMR Mike Richter 30.00 80.00
SCPB Peter Bondra 50.00 125.00

2020-21 Black Diamond Team Logo Jumbo Patches Puzzle

TLASAK Anze Kopitar 6.00 15.00
TLASCM Connor McDavid 20.00 50.00
TLASDP David Pastrnak 10.00 25.00
TLASJB Jordan Binnington 6.00 15.00
TLASLD Leon Draisaitl 12.00 30.00
TLASMT Matthew Tkachuk 8.00 20.00
TLASQH Quinn Hughes 10.00 25.00
TLASSJ Seth Jones 4.00 10.00
TLASTH Tomas Hertl 4.00 10.00
TLBOBM Brad Marchand 8.00 20.00
TLBOBO Bobby Orr 15.00 40.00
TLBOCN Cam Neely 4.00 10.00
TLBODP David Pastrnak 10.00 25.00
TLBOGC Gerry Cheevers 4.00 10.00
TLBOPB Patrice Bergeron 5.00 12.00
TLBOPE Phil Esposito 6.00 15.00
TLBORB Ray Bourque 6.00 15.00
TLBOZC Zdeno Chara 4.00 10.00
TLCOCD Christian Dvorak 3.00 8.00
TLCOCK Clayton Keller 5.00 12.00
TLCOJR Jeremy Roenick 6.00 15.00
TLCOKT Keith Tkachuk 4.00 10.00
TLCOMS Mike Smith 2.50 6.00
TLCONS Nick Schmaltz 3.00 8.00
TLCOOE Oliver Ekman-Larsson 4.00 10.00
TLCOPK Phil Kessel 4.00 10.00
TLCOTN Teppo Numminen 2.50 6.00
TLEDCM Connor McDavid 20.00 50.00
TLEDGA Glenn Anderson 3.00 8.00
TLEDGF Grant Fuhr 6.00 15.00
TLEDJK Jari Kurri 4.00 10.00
TLEDLD Leon Draisaitl 12.00 30.00
TLEDMM Mark Messier 8.00 20.00
TLEDPC Paul Coffey 4.00 10.00
TLEDRN Ryan Nugent-Hopkins 5.00 12.00
TLEDWG Wayne Gretzky 25.00 60.00
TLSTAM Al MacInnis 5.00 12.00
TLSTAP Alex Pietrangelo 3.00 8.00
TLSTBH Brett Hull 8.00 20.00
TLSTCP Chris Pronger 4.00 10.00
TLSTDP David Perron 3.00 8.00
TLSTJB Jordan Binnington 6.00 15.00
TLSTJS Jaden Schwartz 5.00 12.00
TLSTRO Ryan O'Reilly 4.00 10.00
TLSTVT Vladimir Tarasenko 5.00 12.00

2020-21 Black Diamond Winter Classic Memories

*GOLD/17-19: .75X TO 2X BASIC
WCAO Alex Ovechkin 20.00 50.00
WCBR Troy Brouwer 3.00 8.00
WCDP David Pastrnak 12.00 30.00
WCHL Henrik Lundqvist 12.00 30.00
WCHZ Henrik Zetterberg 6.00 15.00
WCJH Jim Howard 6.00 15.00
WCJM J.T. Miller 6.00 15.00
WCPK Patrick Kane 10.00 25.00
WCRM Ryan Miller 5.00 12.00
WCTB Tyler Bozak 3.00 8.00
WCVT Vladimir Tarasenko 6.00 15.00

2021-22 Black Diamond

BDBAB Aleksander Barkov 3.00 8.00
BDBAD Alex DeBrincat 2.50 6.00
BDBAE Aaron Ekblad 2.50 6.00
BDBAF Adam Fox 2.50 6.00
BDBAK Anze Kopitar 3.00 8.00
BDBAL Alexis Lafreniere 3.00 8.00
BDBAM Anthony Mantha 1.50 4.00
BDBAO Alex Ovechkin 8.00 20.00
BDBAP Artemi Panarin 4.00 10.00
BDBAS Andrei Svechnikov 2.50 6.00
BDBAU Auston Matthews 8.00 20.00
BDBAV Andrei Vasilevskiy 3.00 8.00
BDBBA Mathew Barzal 2.50 6.00
BDBBB Brent Burns 2.00 5.00
BDBBH Brett Hull 3.00 8.00
BDBBI Jordan Binnington 3.00 8.00
BDBBM Brad Marchand 4.00 10.00
BDBBO Brock Boeser 2.50 6.00
BDBBP Brayden Point 2.50 6.00
BDBBT Brady Tkachuk 3.00 8.00
BDBCA John Carlson 2.00 5.00
BDBCH Carter Hart 2.00 5.00
BDBCM Connor McDavid 10.00 25.00
BDBCN Cam Neely 1.50 4.00
BDBCO Sean Couturier 1.50 4.00
BDBCP Carey Price 4.00 10.00
BDBCR Sidney Crosby 8.00 20.00
BDBDH Dominik Hasek 3.00 8.00
BDBDL Dylan Larkin 2.50 6.00
BDBDN Darnell Nurse 1.50 4.00
BDBDP David Pastrnak 5.00 12.00
BDBEI Jack Eichel 3.00 8.00
BDBEK Erik Karlsson 2.50 6.00
BDBEL Elias Lindholm 2.00 5.00
BDBEM Evgeni Malkin 4.00 10.00
BDBEP Elias Pettersson 3.00 8.00
BDBGL Guy Lafleur 2.50 6.00
BDBGU Jake Guentzel 3.00 8.00
BDBHE Connor Hellebuyck 4.00 10.00
BDBHO Bo Horvat 2.50 6.00
BDBHU Jack Hughes 5.00 12.00
BDBJB Josh Bailey 1.50 4.00
BDBJC Jakob Chychrun 2.00 5.00
BDBJE Jordan Eberle 2.00 5.00
BDBJF Joel Farabee 2.00 5.00
BDBJG John Gibson 2.00 5.00
BDBJH Jonathan Huberdeau 2.50 6.00
BDBJJ Jaromir Jagr 6.00 15.00
BDBJM Jacob Markstrom 2.00 5.00
BDBJN Josh Norris 2.00 5.00
BDBJP Joe Pavelski 2.50 6.00
BDBJR Jason Robertson 3.00 8.00
BDBJS Juuse Saros 2.50 6.00
BDBJT John Tavares 3.00 8.00
BDBJV Jakub Vrana 1.50 4.00
BDBKE Phil Kessel 2.50 6.00
BDBKF Kevin Fiala 1.50 4.00
BDBKK Kirill Kaprizov 6.00 15.00
BDBLA Patrik Laine 2.50 6.00
BDBLD Leon Draisaitl 6.00 15.00
BDBLE Anders Lee 1.50 4.00
BDBMA Cale Makar 5.00 12.00
BDBMB Mackenzie Blackwood 2.00 5.00
BDBMC Maxime Comtois 1.50 4.00
BDBMD Marcel Dionne 2.50 6.00
BDBMF Marc-Andre Fleury 4.00 10.00
BDBMG Mark Giordano 2.00 5.00
BDBMH Miro Heiskanen 2.50 6.00
BDBMM Mitch Marner 3.00 8.00
BDBMP Max Pacioretty 2.00 5.00
BDBMR Mikko Rantanen 5.00 12.00
BDBMS Mats Sundin 2.00 5.00
BDBMT Matthew Tkachuk 4.00 10.00
BDBMZ Mats Zuccarello 2.00 5.00
BDBNE Nikolaj Ehlers 2.00 5.00
BDBNK Nikita Kucherov 4.00 10.00
BDBNM Nathan MacKinnon 8.00 20.00
BDBNS Nick Suzuki 4.00 10.00
BDBPB Patrice Bergeron 2.50 6.00
BDBPD Phillip Danault 2.00 5.00
BDBPE David Perron 1.50 4.00
BDBPG Philipp Grubauer 2.00 5.00
BDBPK Patrick Kane 4.00 10.00
BDBPL Pat LaFontaine 2.00 5.00
BDBQH Quinn Hughes 5.00 12.00
BDBRJ Roman Josi 2.00 5.00
BDBRO Ryan O'Reilly 2.00 5.00
BDBSA Sebastian Aho 3.00 8.00
BDBSC Mark Scheifele 3.00 8.00
BDBSM Mark Stone 2.50 6.00
BDBSS Steven Stamkos 4.00 10.00
BDBST Shea Theodore 2.50 6.00
BDBSY Steve Yzerman 5.00 12.00
BDBTH Tomas Hertl 2.00 5.00
BDBTI Tim Stutzle 2.50 6.00
BDBTS Ty Smith 2.00 5.00
BDBTT Teuvo Teravainen 2.00 5.00
BDBVO Victor Olofsson 2.00 5.00
BDBWG Wayne Gretzky 12.00 30.00
BDBZW Zach Werenski 2.00 5.00
BDRAB Alex Barre-Boulet RC 20.00 50.00
BDRAH Alexander Holtz RC 30.00 80.00
BDRAL Anton Lundell RC 40.00 100.00
BDRAN Alex Newhook RC 30.00 80.00
BDRAT Alex Turcotte RC 25.00 60.00
BDRBA Morgan Barron RC 15.00 40.00
BDRBD Jacob Bernard-Docker RC 20.00 50.00
BDRBG Benoit-Olivier Groulx RC 20.00 50.00
BDRBR Jacob Bryson RC 20.00 50.00
BDRCA Calen Addison RC 20.00 50.00
BDRCC Cole Caufield RC 400.00 1000.00
BDRCP Cole Perfetti RC 80.00 200.00
BDRCS Cole Sillinger RC 30.00 80.00
BDRCY Cam York RC 20.00 50.00
BDRDF David Farrance RC 20.00 50.00
BDRDM Dawson Mercer RC 50.00 125.00
BDRFG Filip Gustavsson RC 40.00 100.00
BDRGD Grigori Denisenko RC 25.00 60.00
BDRGP Garrett Pilon RC 25.00 60.00
BDRHL Hendrix Lapierre RC 20.00 50.00
BDRIP Ivan Prosvetov RC 20.00 50.00
BDRJA Jack Ahcan RC 20.00 50.00
BDRJD Jamie Drysdale RC 30.00 80.00
BDRJJ Jan Jenik RC 25.00 60.00
BDRJK Joey Keane RC 15.00 40.00
BDRJN Jake Neighbours RC 40.00 100.00
BDRJV Joe Veleno RC 25.00 60.00
BDRJW Jasper Weatherby RC 20.00 50.00
BDRJY Jesse Ylonen RC 20.00 50.00
BDRKL Kole Lind RC 25.00 60.00
BDRLT Logan Thompson RC 50.00 125.00
BDRMH Mike Hardman RC 20.00 50.00
BDRMM Mason McTavish RC 100.00 250.00
BDRMP Matthew Phillips RC 20.00 50.00
BDRMS Moritz Seider RC 150.00 400.00
BDRMT Mattias Samuelsson RC 20.00 50.00
BDRNL Nils Lundkvist RC 20.00 50.00
BDRPK Parker Kelly RC 20.00 50.00
BDRPT Philip Tomasino RC 25.00 60.00
BDRQB Quinton Byfield RC 80.00 200.00
BDRRA Lucas Raymond RC 100.00 250.00
BDRRC Ross Colton RC 25.00 60.00
BDRRD Riley Damiani RC 20.00 50.00
BDRRK Rasmus Kupari RC 20.00 50.00
BDRRM Ryan Merkley RC 25.00 60.00
BDRRU Arttu Ruotsalainen RC 20.00 50.00
BDRRZ Radim Zohorna RC 20.00 50.00
BDRSJ Seth Jarvis RC 50.00 125.00
BDRSK Spencer Knight RC 150.00 400.00
BDRSP Shane Pinto RC 30.00 80.00
BDRSR Sampo Ranta RC 20.00 50.00
BDRST Marian Studenic RC 20.00 50.00
BDRSW Jeremy Swayman RC 60.00 150.00
BDRTT Tyce Thompson RC 20.00 50.00
BDRTZ Trevor Zegras RC 150.00 400.00
BDRUL Ukko-Pekka Luukkonen RC 30.00 80.00
BDRVP Vasily Podkolzin RC 25.00 60.00
BDRWA Wade Allison RC 20.00 50.00
BDRWE William Eklund RC 80.00 200.00
BDRWK Wyatt Kalynuk RC 20.00 50.00
BDRYC Yegor Chinakhov RC 30.00 80.00
BDRZJ Zac Jones RC 25.00 60.00

2021-22 Black Diamond Pure Black

BDBAB Aleksander Barkov/50 6.00 15.00
BDBAD Alex DeBrincat/50 5.00 12.00
BDBAE Aaron Ekblad/50 5.00 12.00
BDBAF Adam Fox/50 5.00 12.00
BDBAK Anze Kopitar/50 6.00 15.00
BDBAL Alexis Lafreniere/50 6.00 15.00
BDBAM Anthony Mantha AU/99 12.00 30.00
BDBAO Alex Ovechkin/50 15.00 40.00
BDBAP Artemi Panarin/50 8.00 20.00
BDBAS Andrei Svechnikov/50 5.00 12.00
BDBAU Auston Matthews AU/25 150.00 400.00
BDBAV Andrei Vasilevskiy AU/25 25.00 60.00
BDBBA Mathew Barzal/50 5.00 12.00
BDBBB Brent Burns AU/25 15.00 40.00
BDBBH Brett Hull AU/25 25.00 60.00
BDBBI Jordan Binnington/50 6.00 15.00
BDBBM Brad Marchand AU/25 30.00 80.00
BDBBO Brock Boeser AU/25 20.00 50.00
BDBBP Brayden Point/50 5.00 12.00
BDBBT Brady Tkachuk/50 6.00 15.00
BDBCA John Carlson/50 4.00 10.00
BDBCH Carter Hart/50 4.00 10.00
BDBCM Connor McDavid AU/25 200.00 500.00
BDBCN Cam Neely AU/25 12.00 30.00
BDBCO Sean Couturier/50 3.00 8.00
BDBCP Carey Price AU/25 30.00 80.00
BDBCR Sidney Crosby/50 15.00 40.00
BDBDH Dominik Hasek AU/25 25.00 60.00
BDBDL Dylan Larkin/50 5.00 12.00
BDBDN Darnell Nurse/50 3.00 8.00
BDBDP David Pastrnak/50 10.00 25.00
BDBEI Jack Eichel/50 6.00 15.00
BDBEK Erik Karlsson/50 5.00 12.00
BDBEL Elias Lindholm/50 4.00 10.00
BDBEM Evgeni Malkin/50 8.00 20.00
BDBEP Elias Pettersson/50 6.00 15.00

BDBGL Guy Lafleur/50 5.00 12.00
BDBGU Jake Guentzel/50 6.00 15.00
BDBHE Connor Hellebuyck AU/25 30.00 80.00
BDBHO Bo Horvat/50 5.00 12.00
BDBHU Jack Hughes/50 10.00 25.00
BDBJB Josh Bailey AU/99 12.00 30.00
BDBJC Jakob Chychrun/50 4.00 10.00
BDBJF Joel Farabee/50 4.00 10.00
BDBJG John Gibson AU/99 15.00 40.00
BDBJH Jonathan Huberdeau AU/25 20.00 50.00
BDBJJ Jaromir Jagr AU/25 50.00 125.00
BDBJM Jacob Markstrom/50 4.00 10.00
BDBJN Josh Norris AU/99 15.00 40.00
BDBJP Joe Pavelski AU/25 20.00 50.00
BDBJR Jason Robertson AU/99 25.00 60.00
BDBJS Juuse Saros/50 5.00 12.00
BDBJT John Tavares/50 6.00 15.00
BDBJV Jakub Vrana/50 3.00 8.00
BDBKE Phil Kessel/50 4.00 10.00
BDBKF Kevin Fiala AU/99 12.00 30.00
BDBLA Patrik Laine/50 5.00 12.00
BDBLD Leon Draisaitl/50 12.00 30.00
BDBLE Anders Lee AU/99 12.00 30.00
BDBMA Cale Makar AU/25 40.00 100.00
BDBMC Maxime Comtois/50 3.00 8.00
BDBMF Marc-Andre Fleury/50 8.00 20.00
BDBMH Miro Heiskanen AU/25 20.00 50.00
BDBMM Mitch Marner AU/25 25.00 60.00
BDBMP Max Pacioretty AU/99 15.00 40.00
BDBMR Mikko Rantanen/50 10.00 25.00
BDBMS Mats Sundin AU/25 15.00 40.00
BDBMT Matthew Tkachuk AU/25 30.00 80.00
BDBNE Nikolaj Ehlers AU/99 15.00 40.00
BDBNK Nikita Kucherov/50 8.00 20.00
BDBNM Nathan MacKinnon/50 15.00 40.00
BDBNS Nick Suzuki/50 8.00 20.00
BDBPB Patrice Bergeron/50 5.00 12.00
BDBPD Phillip Danault AU/99 15.00 40.00
BDBPE David Perron AU/99 12.00 30.00
BDBPG Philipp Grubauer AU/99 15.00 40.00
BDBPK Patrick Kane AU/25 30.00 80.00
BDBPL Pat LaFontaine AU/25 15.00 40.00
BDBRJ Roman Josi/50 4.00 10.00
BDBRO Ryan O'Reilly AU/25 15.00 40.00
BDBSA Sebastian Aho/50 6.00 15.00
BDBSC Mark Scheifele AU/25 25.00 60.00
BDBSM Mark Stone AU/25 20.00 50.00
BDBSS Steven Stamkos/50 8.00 20.00
BDBST Shea Theodore/50 5.00 12.00
BDBTH Tomas Hertl AU/99 15.00 40.00
BDBTI Tim Stutzle AU/25 20.00 50.00
BDBTS Ty Smith AU/99 15.00 40.00
BDBTT Teuvo Teravainen AU/99 15.00 40.00
BDBWG Wayne Gretzky AU/25 200.00 500.00
BDBZW Zach Werenski/50 6.00 15.00

2021-22 Black Diamond '15-16 Diamond Relic Rookie Gems Tribute

BDRRCC Cole Caufield 125.00 300.00
BDRRCP Cole Perfetti 60.00 150.00
BDRRQB Quinton Byfield 80.00 200.00
BDRRSK Spencer Knight 60.00 150.00
BDRRTZ Trevor Zegras 60.00 150.00

2021-22 Black Diamond Band of Color

BCAM Auston Matthews 300.00 800.00
BCAO Alex Ovechkin 300.00 800.00
BCAP Artemi Panarin 150.00 400.00
BCBO Bobby Orr 300.00 800.00
BCBR Martin Brodeur 200.00 500.00
BCBT Brady Tkachuk 125.00 300.00
BCCM Connor McDavid 400.00 1000.00
BCCP Carey Price 150.00 400.00
BCDP David Pastrnak 200.00 500.00
BCEP Elias Pettersson 125.00 300.00
BCGH Gordie Howe 250.00 600.00
BCKK Kirill Kaprizov 250.00 600.00
BCMB Mathew Barzal 100.00 250.00
BCMF Marc-Andre Fleury 150.00 400.00
BCML Mario Lemieux 300.00 800.00
BCMS Mark Stone 100.00 250.00
BCNK Nikita Kucherov 150.00 400.00
BCNM Nathan MacKinnon 300.00 800.00
BCSC Sidney Crosby 300.00 800.00
BCWG Wayne Gretzky 500.00 1250.00

2021-22 Black Diamond Band of Color Rookies

BCRAB Alex Barre-Boulet 80.00 200.00
BCRAH Alexander Holtz 125.00 300.00
BCRAL Anton Lundell 150.00 400.00
BCRAN Alex Newhook 125.00 300.00
BCRAT Alex Turcotte 100.00 250.00
BCRCA Calen Addison 80.00 200.00
BCRCC Cole Caufield 300.00 800.00
BCRCP Cole Perfetti 150.00 400.00
BCRCY Cam York 80.00 200.00
BCRGD Grigori Denisenko 100.00 250.00
BCRJB Jacob Bernard-Docker 80.00 200.00
BCRJD Jamie Drysdale 125.00 300.00
BCRJJ Jan Jenik 100.00 250.00
BCRJS Jeremy Swayman 500.00 1250.00
BCRJV Joe Veleno 100.00 250.00
BCRKL Kole Lind 100.00 250.00
BCRLR Lucas Raymond 250.00 600.00
BCRMM Mason McTavish 150.00 400.00
BCRMM David Farrance 80.00 200.00
BCRMP Matthew Phillips 80.00 200.00
BCRMS Moritz Seider 200.00 500.00
BCRNL Nils Lundkvist 80.00 200.00
BCRPI Shane Pinto 125.00 300.00
BCRPT Philip Tomasino 100.00 250.00
BCRQB Quinton Byfield 200.00 500.00
BCRRC Ross Colton 100.00 250.00
BCRSK Spencer Knight 150.00 400.00
BCRSR Sampo Ranta 80.00 200.00
BCRTZ Trevor Zegras 150.00 400.00
BCRUL Ukko-Pekka Luukkonen 125.00 300.00
BCRVP Vasily Podkolzin 100.00 250.00
BCRWA Wade Allison 80.00 200.00
BCRWE William Eklund 200.00 500.00
BCRWK Wyatt Kalynuk 80.00 200.00
BCRYC Yegor Chinakhov 125.00 300.00
BCRZJ Zac Jones 100.00 250.00

2021-22 Black Diamond Cup Winners Patches

CWAO Alex Ovechkin 25.00 60.00
CWAV Andrei Vasilevskiy 10.00 25.00
CWBO Bobby Orr 25.00 60.00
CWGF Grant Fuhr 10.00 25.00
CWGH Gordie Howe 20.00 50.00
CWGL Guy Lafleur 8.00 20.00
CWLM Lanny McDonald 6.00 15.00
CWML Mario Lemieux 25.00 60.00
CWMM Mark Messier 12.00 30.00
CWMO Mike Modano 10.00 25.00
CWNL Nicklas Lidstrom 6.00 15.00
CWPK Patrick Kane 12.00 30.00
CWRO Ryan O'Reilly 6.00 15.00
CWSC Sidney Crosby 25.00 60.00
CWWG Wayne Gretzky 40.00 100.00

2021-22 Black Diamond Cup Winners Patches Gold

*GOLD/25-49: .6X TO 1.5X BASIC INSERTS
CWML Mario Lemieux/25 50.00 125.00
CWWG Wayne Gretzky/25 150.00 400.00

2021-22 Black Diamond Cup Winners Patches Gold Autographs

CWAV Andrei Vasilevskiy/49 25.00 60.00
CWGF Grant Fuhr/25 25.00 60.00
CWLM Lanny McDonald/25 15.00 40.00
CWMO Mike Modano/25 25.00 60.00
CWRO Ryan O'Reilly/49 15.00 40.00

2021-22 Black Diamond Diamonation

DAB Aleksander Barkov 5.00 12.00
DCC Cole Caufield 25.00 60.00
DCH Connor Hellebuyck 6.00 15.00
DCP Cole Perfetti 6.00 15.00
DKK Kirill Kaprizov 10.00 25.00
DLD Leon Draisaitl 10.00 25.00
DLR Lucas Raymond 10.00 25.00
DMA Cale Makar 8.00 20.00
DMB Mathew Barzal 4.00 10.00
DMS Moritz Seider 8.00 20.00
DPT Philip Tomasino 4.00 10.00
DQB Quinton Byfield 8.00 20.00
DRO Ryan O'Reilly 3.00 8.00
DSA Sebastian Aho 5.00 12.00
DSK Spencer Knight 6.00 15.00
DSP Shane Pinto 5.00 12.00
DSS Steven Stamkos 6.00 15.00
DTH Taylor Hall 3.00 8.00
DTZ Trevor Zegras 6.00 15.00
DWE William Eklund 8.00 20.00

2021-22 Black Diamond Diamond Cutters

DCAD Alex DeBrincat 8.00 20.00
DCAF Adam Fox 8.00 20.00
DCAH Alexander Holtz 10.00 25.00
DCAN Alex Newhook 10.00 25.00
DCAO Alex Ovechkin 25.00 60.00
DCBB Brock Boeser 8.00 20.00
DCBP Brayden Point 8.00 20.00
DCCC Cole Caufield 25.00 60.00
DCCM Cale Makar 15.00 40.00
DCCS Cole Sillinger 10.00 25.00
DCJS Jeremy Swayman 20.00 50.00
DCKC Kyle Connor 10.00 25.00
DCMC Mason McTavish 12.00 30.00
DCMM Mitch Marner 10.00 25.00
DCMT Matthew Tkachuk 12.00 30.00
DCPB Patrice Bergeron 8.00 20.00
DCQB Quinton Byfield 15.00 40.00
DCSK Spencer Knight 12.00 30.00
DCTS Tim Stutzle 8.00 20.00
DCTZ Trevor Zegras 12.00 30.00

2021-22 Black Diamond Diamond Debut Relics

DDCC Cole Caufield 8.00 20.00
DDCY Cam York 2.00 5.00
DDDF David Farrance 2.00 5.00
DDJD Jamie Drysdale 3.00 8.00
DDJJ Jan Jenik 2.50 6.00
DDJS Jeremy Swayman 6.00 15.00
DDMS Moritz Seider 5.00 12.00
DDNL Nils Lundkvist 2.00 5.00
DDPT Philip Tomasino 2.50 6.00
DDQB Quinton Byfield 5.00 12.00
DDRC Ross Colton 2.50 6.00
DDRK Rasmus Kupari 2.00 5.00
DDRZ Radim Zohorna 2.00 5.00
DDSJ Seth Jarvis 5.00 12.00
DDSK Spencer Knight 4.00 10.00
DDTL Tanner Laczynski 2.00 5.00
DDTZ Trevor Zegras 4.00 10.00
DDWK Wyatt Kalynuk 2.00 5.00
DDZJ Zac Jones 2.50 6.00

2021-22 Black Diamond Diamond Debut Relics Patch Autographs

DDCC Cole Caufield/25 60.00 150.00
DDDF David Farrance/49 15.00 40.00
DDJD Jamie Drysdale/49 25.00 60.00
DDJJ Jan Jenik/49 20.00 50.00
DDJS Jeremy Swayman/49 80.00 200.00
DDMS Moritz Seider/25 40.00 100.00
DDNL Nils Lundkvist/49 15.00 40.00
DDQB Quinton Byfield/25 40.00 100.00
DDRC Ross Colton/49 20.00 50.00
DDRK Rasmus Kupari/49 15.00 40.00
DDSK Spencer Knight/49 30.00 80.00
DDTZ Trevor Zegras/25 30.00 80.00
DDWK Wyatt Kalynuk/49 15.00 40.00

2021-22 Black Diamond Diamond Futures

BDFAH Alexander Holtz 10.00 25.00
BDFAL Anton Lundell 12.00 30.00
BDFAN Alex Newhook 10.00 25.00
BDFAT Alex Turcotte 8.00 20.00
BDFCA Calen Addison 6.00 15.00
BDFCC Cole Caufield 25.00 60.00
BDFCP Cole Perfetti 12.00 30.00
BDFCS Cole Sillinger 10.00 25.00
BDFCY Cam York 6.00 15.00
BDFDF David Farrance 6.00 15.00
BDFDR Jamie Drysdale 10.00 25.00
BDFFG Filip Gustavsson 12.00 30.00
BDFGD Grigori Denisenko 8.00 20.00
BDFHL Hendrix Lapierre 6.00 15.00
BDFIP Ivan Prosvetov 6.00 15.00
BDFJB Jacob Bernard-Docker 6.00 15.00
BDFJL Jake Leschyshyn 6.00 15.00
BDFJS Jeremy Swayman 20.00 50.00
BDFJV Joe Veleno 8.00 20.00
BDFKL Kole Lind 8.00 20.00
BDFLR Lucas Raymond 20.00 50.00
BDFMM Mason McTavish 25.00 60.00
BDFMP Matthew Phillips 6.00 15.00
BDFMS Moritz Seider 30.00 80.00
BDFNL Nils Lundkvist 6.00 15.00
BDFPT Philip Tomasino 8.00 20.00
BDFQB Quinton Byfield 15.00 40.00
BDFRC Ross Colton 8.00 20.00
BDFSK Spencer Knight 12.00 30.00
BDFSP Shane Pinto 10.00 25.00
BDFSR Sampo Ranta 6.00 15.00
BDFTZ Trevor Zegras 12.00 30.00
BDFUL Ukko-Pekka Luukkonen 10.00 25.00
BDFVP Vasily Podkolzin 8.00 20.00
BDFWA Wade Allison 6.00 15.00
BDFWE William Eklund 15.00 40.00
BDFWK Wyatt Kalynuk 6.00 15.00
BDFZJ Zac Jones 8.00 20.00

2021-22 Black Diamond Diamond Futures Autographs

BDFAH Alexander Holtz/99 15.00 40.00
BDFAL Anton Lundell/99 20.00 50.00
BDFAN Alex Newhook/99 15.00 40.00
BDFAT Alex Turcotte/99 12.00 30.00
BDFCA Calen Addison/99 10.00 25.00
BDFCC Cole Caufield/25 80.00 200.00
BDFCP Cole Perfetti/49 20.00 50.00
BDFCS Cole Sillinger/99 15.00 40.00
BDFDF David Farrance/99 10.00 25.00
BDFDR Jamie Drysdale/99 15.00 40.00
BDFFG Filip Gustavsson/99 20.00 50.00
BDFGD Grigori Denisenko/49 12.00 30.00
BDFIP Ivan Prosvetov/99 10.00 25.00
BDFJB Jacob Bernard-Docker/99 10.00 25.00
BDFJL Jake Leschyshyn/99 10.00 25.00
BDFJS Jeremy Swayman/99 30.00 80.00
BDFJV Joe Veleno/99 12.00 30.00
BDFKL Kole Lind/99 12.00 30.00
BDFLR Lucas Raymond/99 60.00 150.00
BDFMM Mason McTavish/49 20.00 50.00
BDFMP Matthew Phillips/99 10.00 25.00
BDFMS Moritz Seider/49 25.00 60.00
BDFNL Nils Lundkvist/99 10.00 25.00
BDFPT Philip Tomasino/99 12.00 30.00
BDFQB Quinton Byfield/49 25.00 60.00
BDFRC Ross Colton/99 12.00 30.00
BDFSK Spencer Knight/49 20.00 50.00
BDFSP Shane Pinto/99 15.00 40.00
BDFSR Sampo Ranta/99 10.00 25.00
BDFTZ Trevor Zegras/49 80.00 200.00
BDFUL Ukko-Pekka Luukkonen/99 15.00 40.00
BDFVP Vasily Podkolzin/99 12.00 30.00
BDFWA Wade Allison/99 10.00 25.00
BDFWE William Eklund/99 25.00 60.00
BDFWK Wyatt Kalynuk/99 10.00 25.00

2021-22 Black Diamond Diamond Futures Relic Autographs

BDFAH Alexander Holtz 30.00 80.00
BDFAL Anton Lundell 40.00 100.00
BDFAN Alex Newhook 30.00 80.00
BDFAT Alex Turcotte 150.00 400.00
BDFCA Calen Addison 20.00 50.00
BDFCC Cole Caufield 500.00 1250.00
BDFCP Cole Perfetti 40.00 100.00
BDFCS Cole Sillinger 30.00 80.00
BDFDF David Farrance 20.00 50.00
BDFDR Jamie Drysdale 30.00 80.00
BDFFG Filip Gustavsson 40.00 100.00
BDFGD Grigori Denisenko 25.00 60.00
BDFIP Ivan Prosvetov 20.00 50.00
BDFJB Jacob Bernard-Docker 20.00 50.00
BDFJL Jake Leschyshyn 20.00 50.00
BDFJS Jeremy Swayman 400.00 1000.00
BDFJV Joe Veleno 25.00 60.00
BDFLR Lucas Raymond 60.00 150.00
BDFMP Matthew Phillips 20.00 50.00
BDFMS Moritz Seider 50.00 125.00
BDFNL Nils Lundkvist 20.00 50.00
BDFPT Philip Tomasino 25.00 60.00
BDFQB Quinton Byfield 50.00 125.00
BDFRC Ross Colton 25.00 60.00
BDFSK Spencer Knight 150.00 400.00
BDFSP Shane Pinto 30.00 80.00
BDFSR Sampo Ranta 20.00 50.00
BDFTZ Trevor Zegras 250.00 600.00
BDFUL Ukko-Pekka Luukkonen 30.00 80.00
BDFWA Wade Allison 20.00 50.00
BDFWK Wyatt Kalynuk 20.00 50.00

2021-22 Black Diamond Diamond Gallery

DGAM Auston Matthews 15.00 40.00
DGAS Andrei Svechnikov 5.00 12.00
DGCC Cole Caufield 15.00 40.00
DGCM Connor McDavid 20.00 50.00
DGCP Carey Price 8.00 20.00
DGCY Cam York 4.00 10.00
DGDP David Pastrnak 10.00 25.00
DGGD Grigori Denisenko 5.00 12.00
DGJD Jamie Drysdale 6.00 15.00
DGJR Jason Robertson 6.00 15.00
DGJS Jeremy Swayman 12.00 30.00
DGKK Kirill Kaprizov 12.00 30.00
DGLR Lucas Raymond 12.00 30.00
DGMR Mikko Rantanen 10.00 25.00
DGMS Mark Scheifele 6.00 15.00
DGNK Nikita Kucherov 8.00 20.00
DGQB Quinton Byfield 10.00 25.00
DGSC Sidney Crosby 15.00 40.00
DGSK Spencer Knight 8.00 20.00
DGST Shea Theodore 5.00 12.00

2021-22 Black Diamond Diamond Legends

BDLBH Brett Hull 6.00 15.00
BDLBR Martin Brodeur 10.00 25.00
BDLBS Billy Smith 4.00 10.00
BDLCN Cam Neely 3.00 8.00
BDLDH Dominik Hasek 6.00 15.00
BDLJS Joe Sakic 8.00 20.00
BDLKT Keith Tkachuk 4.00 10.00
BDLMM Mark Messier 8.00 20.00
BDLMS Mats Sundin 4.00 10.00
BDLNL Nicklas Lidstrom 4.00 10.00
BDLPC Paul Coffey 5.00 12.00
BDLPE Phil Esposito 6.00 15.00
BDLPL Pat LaFontaine 4.00 10.00
BDLPR Patrick Roy 10.00 25.00
BDLSK Saku Koivu 4.00 10.00
BDLSY Steve Yzerman 10.00 25.00
BDLTF Theoren Fleury 4.00 10.00
BDLTS Teemu Selanne 8.00 20.00
BDLWG Wayne Gretzky 25.00 60.00

2021-22 Black Diamond Diamond Legends Autographs

BDLBS Billy Smith/25 20.00 50.00
BDLCN Cam Neely/25 15.00 40.00
BDLKT Keith Tkachuk/25 20.00 50.00
BDLPL Pat LaFontaine/25 20.00 50.00
BDLSK Saku Koivu/25 20.00 50.00

2021-22 Black Diamond Diamond Legends Relic Autographs

BDLBS Billy Smith/25 40.00 100.00
BDLKT Keith Tkachuk/25 40.00 100.00
BDLPC Paul Coffey/25 50.00 125.00
BDLPL Pat LaFontaine/25 40.00 100.00
BDLSK Saku Koivu/25 40.00 100.00

2021-22 Black Diamond Diamond Might

DMAN Alex Newhook 4.00 10.00
DMBM Brad Marchand 5.00 12.00
DMBO Bobby Orr 10.00 25.00
DMCC Cole Caufield 10.00 25.00
DMCG Claude Giroux 2.50 6.00
DMCM Connor McDavid 12.00 30.00
DMHU Jack Hughes 6.00 15.00
DMJC Jakob Chychrun 2.50 6.00
DMJG Jake Guentzel 4.00 10.00
DMJH Jonathan Huberdeau 3.00 8.00
DMJV Jakub Vrana 2.00 5.00
DMLR Lucas Raymond 8.00 20.00
DMMG Mark Giordano 2.50 6.00
DMMH Miro Heiskanen 3.00 8.00
DMMM Mike Modano 4.00 10.00
DMMO Moritz Seider 6.00 15.00
DMMP Max Pacioretty 2.50 6.00
DMPC Paul Coffey 3.00 8.00
DMPL Patrik Laine 3.00 8.00
DMQB Quinton Byfield 6.00 15.00
DMSK Spencer Knight 5.00 12.00
DMSP Shane Pinto 4.00 10.00
DMTH Tomas Hertl 2.50 6.00
DMTZ Trevor Zegras 5.00 12.00

2021-22 Black Diamond Diamond Mine Dual Relics

DMDRGC Claude Giroux
Sean Couturier 4.00 10.00
DMDRHH Nico Hischier
Jack Hughes 10.00 25.00
DMDRKC Saku Koivu
Shayne Corson 4.00 10.00
DMDRKD Anze Kopitar
Drew Doughty 6.00 15.00
DMDRLB Dylan Larkin
Tyler Bertuzzi 5.00 12.00
DMDRMB Ken Morrow
Bob Bourne 4.00 10.00
DMDRMK Jonathan Marchessault
William Karlsson 5.00 12.00
DMDRMR Nathan MacKinnon
Mikko Rantanen 15.00 40.00
DMDRSS Daniel Sedin
Henrik Sedin 5.00 12.00
DMDRZS Mika Zibanejad
Igor Shesterkin 8.00 20.00

2021-22 Black Diamond Diamond Mine Relics

DMRBB Brent Burns 3.00 8.00
DMRBH Bo Horvat 4.00 10.00
DMRCH Connor Hellebuyck 6.00 15.00
DMRHA Carter Hart 3.00 8.00
DMRIS Igor Shesterkin 6.00 15.00
DMRJG Johnny Gaudreau 5.00 12.00
DMRJT John Tavares 5.00 12.00
DMRLD Leon Draisaitl 10.00 25.00
DMRMB Mathew Barzal 4.00 10.00
DMRRD Rasmus Dahlin 4.00 10.00
DMRRG Ryan Getzlaf 3.00 8.00
DMRSC Sidney Crosby 12.00 30.00
DMRTS Tyler Seguin 4.00 10.00
DMRVH Victor Hedman 4.00 10.00

2021-22 Black Diamond Diamond Mine Relics Premium

*SINGLES: .6X TO 1.5X BASIC INSERTS
DMRSC Sidney Crosby 40.00 100.00

2021-22 Black Diamond Diamond Mine Triple Relics

DMTRBRU Patrice Bergeron
Brad Marchand
David Pastrnak 20.00 50.00
DMTRMON Carey Price
Tyler Toffoli
Nick Suzuki 15.00 40.00
DMTRTBL Andrei Vasilevskiy
Steven Stamkos
Nikita Kucherov 15.00 40.00
DMTRTOR Auston Matthews
Mitch Marner
William Nylander 30.00 80.00
DMTRWAS Alex Ovechkin
Nicklas Backstrom
John Carlson 30.00 80.00

2021-22 Black Diamond Diamond Stars

BDSAB Aleksander Barkov 3.00 8.00
BDSAD Alex DeBrincat 2.50 6.00
BDSAK Anze Kopitar 3.00 8.00
BDSAM Auston Matthews 8.00 20.00
BDSAO Alex Ovechkin 8.00 20.00
BDSAP Artemi Panarin 4.00 10.00
BDSAV Andrei Vasilevskiy 3.00 8.00
BDSBB Brock Boeser 2.50 6.00
BDSBM Brad Marchand 4.00 10.00
BDSBT Brady Tkachuk 3.00 8.00
BDSCA Cale Makar 5.00 12.00
BDSCH Carter Hart 2.00 5.00
BDSCM Connor McDavid 10.00 25.00
BDSCP Carey Price 4.00 10.00
BDSEL Elias Lindholm 2.00 5.00
BDSEP Elias Pettersson 3.00 8.00
BDSGI John Gibson 2.00 5.00
BDSGU Jake Guentzel 3.00 8.00
BDSHE Connor Hellebuyck 4.00 10.00
BDSHU Jack Hughes 5.00 12.00
BDSJH Jonathan Huberdeau 2.50 6.00
BDSJP Joe Pavelski 2.50 6.00
BDSKK Kirill Kaprizov 6.00 15.00
BDSLD Leon Draisaitl 6.00 15.00
BDSMA Mark Scheifele 3.00 8.00
BDSMF Marc-Andre Fleury 4.00 10.00
BDSMH Miro Heiskanen 2.50 6.00
BDSMM Mitch Marner 3.00 8.00
BDSMP Max Pacioretty 2.00 5.00
BDSMS Mark Stone 2.50 6.00
BDSNM Nathan MacKinnon 8.00 20.00
BDSNS Nick Suzuki 4.00 10.00
BDSPK Patrick Kane 4.00 10.00
BDSQH Quinn Hughes 5.00 12.00
BDSRO Ryan O'Reilly 2.00 5.00
BDSSA Sebastian Aho 3.00 8.00
BDSSC Sidney Crosby 8.00 20.00
BDSSS Steven Stamkos 4.00 10.00
BDSTH Tomas Hertl 2.00 5.00
BDSTT Teuvo Teravainen 2.00 5.00

2021-22 Black Diamond Diamond Stars Autographs

BDSAB Aleksander Barkov/25 25.00 60.00
BDSBT Brady Tkachuk/25 25.00 60.00
BDSCH Carter Hart/25 15.00 40.00
BDSEL Elias Lindholm/25 15.00 40.00
BDSGI John Gibson/25 15.00 40.00
BDSHE Connor Hellebuyck/25 30.00 80.00
BDSJH Jonathan Huberdeau/25 20.00 50.00
BDSJP Joe Pavelski/25 20.00 50.00
BDSMA Mark Scheifele/25 25.00 60.00
BDSMH Miro Heiskanen/25 20.00 50.00
BDSMP Max Pacioretty/25 15.00 40.00
BDSMS Mark Stone/25 20.00 50.00
BDSNS Nick Suzuki/25 30.00 80.00
BDSRO Ryan O'Reilly/25 15.00 40.00
BDSTH Tomas Hertl/25 15.00 40.00
BDSTT Teuvo Teravainen/25 15.00 40.00

2021-22 Black Diamond Diamond Stars Relic Autographs

BDSAB Aleksander Barkov/25 30.00 80.00
BDSAV Andrei Vasilevskiy/25 30.00 80.00
BDSCH Carter Hart/25 20.00 50.00
BDSEL Elias Lindholm/25 20.00 50.00
BDSGI John Gibson/25 20.00 50.00
BDSGU Jake Guentzel/25 30.00 80.00
BDSHE Connor Hellebuyck/25 40.00 100.00
BDSJH Jonathan Huberdeau/25 25.00 60.00
BDSJP Joe Pavelski/25 25.00 60.00
BDSMA Mark Scheifele/25 30.00 80.00
BDSMH Miro Heiskanen/25 25.00 60.00
BDSMP Max Pacioretty/25 20.00 50.00
BDSMS Mark Stone/25 25.00 60.00
BDSRO Ryan O'Reilly/25 20.00 50.00
BDSTH Tomas Hertl/25 20.00 50.00

2021-22 Black Diamond Gemography

GAM Auston Matthews 150.00 400.00
GAN Alex Newhook 60.00 150.00
GAV Andrei Vasilevskiy 60.00 150.00
GBO Bobby Orr 150.00 400.00
GCC Cole Caufield 150.00 400.00
GCM Connor McDavid 200.00 500.00
GCN Cam Neely 30.00 80.00
GCP Carey Price 80.00 200.00
GJE Jack Eichel 60.00 150.00
GJT John Tavares 60.00 150.00
GLD Leon Draisaitl 125.00 300.00
GMS Mark Stone 50.00 125.00
GMT Matthew Tkachuk 80.00 200.00
GNS Nick Suzuki 80.00 200.00
GPR Patrick Roy 100.00 250.00
GQB Quinton Byfield 100.00 250.00
GRO Ryan O'Reilly 40.00 100.00
GSK Spencer Knight 80.00 200.00
GSS Steven Stamkos 80.00 200.00
GSY Steve Yzerman 100.00 250.00
GTZ Trevor Zegras 80.00 200.00

2021-22 Black Diamond Jewels of the Draft Patch Autographs

JDAN Alex Newhook/99 60.00 150.00
JDAT Alex Turcotte/99 50.00 125.00
JDCA Calen Addison/99 40.00 100.00
JDCC Cole Caufield/99 400.00 1000.00
JDCP Cole Perfetti/99 80.00 200.00
JDDF David Farrance/99 40.00 100.00
JDGD Grigori Denisenko/99 50.00 125.00
JDJB Jacob Bernard-Docker/99 40.00 100.00
JDJD Jamie Drysdale/99 60.00 150.00
JDJJ Jan Jenik/99 50.00 125.00
JDJS Jeremy Swayman/99 125.00 300.00
JDJV Joe Veleno/99 50.00 125.00
JDMP Matthew Phillips/99 40.00 100.00
JDMS Mattias Samuelsson/99 40.00 100.00
JDQB Quinton Byfield/99 100.00 250.00
JDRC Ross Colton/99 50.00 125.00
JDRK Rasmus Kupari/99 40.00 100.00
JDSE Moritz Seider/49 1000.00 2500.00
JDSK Spencer Knight/99 80.00 200.00
JDSP Shane Pinto/99 60.00 150.00
JDSR Sampo Ranta/99 40.00 100.00
JDTZ Trevor Zegras/99 400.00 1000.00
JDUL Ukko-Pekka Luukkonen/99 60.00 150.00
JDWA Wade Allison/99 40.00 100.00

2021-22 Black Diamond Jewels of the Draft Stars Patch Autographs

VJDBB Brock Boeser/49 40.00 100.00
VJDBT Brady Tkachuk/49 50.00 125.00
VJDCM Cale Makar/25 80.00 200.00
VJDJG John Gibson/99 30.00 80.00
VJDJH Jonathan Huberdeau/49 40.00 100.00
VJDMC Connor McDavid/25 150.00 400.00
VJDMM Mitch Marner/25 50.00 125.00
VJDPK Patrick Kane/25 60.00 150.00
VJDTH Tomas Hertl/99 30.00 80.00

2021-22 Black Diamond Maple Leafs Retired Numbers Patches

TMRNBS Börje Salming 15.00 40.00
TMRNDG Doug Gilmour 20.00 50.00
TMRNDS Darryl Sittler 15.00 40.00
TMRNFM Frank Mahovlich 15.00 40.00
TMRNJB Johnny Bower 15.00 40.00
TMRNKC King Clancy 15.00 40.00
TMRNMS Mats Sundin 15.00 40.00
TMRNTB Turk Broda 15.00 40.00
TMRNTH Tim Horton 25.00 60.00
TMRNWC Wendel Clark 25.00 60.00

2021-22 Black Diamond Maple Leafs Retired Numbers Patches Gold

*GOLD/1-27: .75X TO 2X BASIC INSERTS
TMRNWC Wendel Clark AU/17 50.00 125.00

2021-22 Black Diamond Premium Relics

BDBAB Aleksander Barkov/50 12.00 30.00
BDBAD Alex DeBrincat/50 10.00 25.00
BDBAE Aaron Ekblad/50 10.00 25.00
BDBAK Anze Kopitar/50 12.00 30.00
BDBAP Artemi Panarin/25 15.00 40.00
BDBAV Andrei Vasilevskiy/25 12.00 30.00
BDBBA Mathew Barzal/50 10.00 25.00
BDBBB Brent Burns/50 8.00 20.00
BDBBI Jordan Binnington/50 12.00 30.00
BDBBM Brad Marchand/25 15.00 40.00
BDBBO Brock Boeser/25 10.00 25.00
BDBCA John Carlson/50 8.00 20.00
BDBCO Sean Couturier/50 6.00 15.00
BDBDL Dylan Larkin/50 10.00 25.00
BDBDN Darnell Nurse/50 6.00 15.00
BDBDP David Pastrnak/25 20.00 50.00
BDBEI Jack Eichel/25 12.00 30.00
BDBEK Erik Karlsson/50 10.00 25.00
BDBEL Elias Lindholm/50 8.00 20.00
BDBEM Evgeni Malkin/25 15.00 40.00
BDBEP Elias Pettersson/25 12.00 30.00
BDBGU Jake Guentzel/50 12.00 30.00
BDBHE Connor Hellebuyck/50 15.00 40.00
BDBHO Bo Horvat/50 10.00 25.00
BDBHU Jack Hughes/25 20.00 50.00
BDBJB Josh Bailey/50 6.00 15.00
BDBJC Jakob Chychrun/50 8.00 20.00
BDBJF Joel Farabee/50 8.00 20.00
BDBJG John Gibson/50 8.00 20.00
BDBJH Jonathan Huberdeau/50 10.00 25.00
BDBJM Jacob Markstrom/50 8.00 20.00
BDBJP Joe Pavelski/50 10.00 25.00
BDBJT John Tavares/25 12.00 30.00
BDBKE Phil Kessel/50 8.00 20.00
BDBKF Kevin Fiala/50 6.00 15.00
BDBLA Patrik Laine/50 10.00 25.00
BDBLD Leon Draisaitl/25 25.00 60.00
BDBLE Anders Lee/50 6.00 15.00
BDBMB Mackenzie Blackwood/50 8.00 20.00
BDBMH Miro Heiskanen/50 10.00 25.00
BDBMM Mitch Marner/25 12.00 30.00
BDBMP Max Pacioretty/50 8.00 20.00
BDBMR Mikko Rantanen/50 20.00 50.00
BDBMZ Mats Zuccarello/50 8.00 20.00
BDBNE Nikolaj Ehlers/50 8.00 20.00
BDBNK Nikita Kucherov/25 15.00 40.00
BDBNS Nick Suzuki/50 15.00 40.00
BDBPB Patrice Bergeron/25 10.00 25.00
BDBQH Quinn Hughes/25 20.00 50.00
BDBRJ Roman Josi/50 8.00 20.00
BDBRO Ryan O'Reilly/25 8.00 20.00
BDBSA Sebastian Aho/25 12.00 30.00
BDBSC Mark Scheifele/50 12.00 30.00
BDBSM Mark Stone/25 10.00 25.00
BDBSS Steven Stamkos/25 15.00 40.00
BDBST Shea Theodore/50 10.00 25.00
BDBTH Tomas Hertl/50 8.00 20.00
BDBTI Tim Stutzle/25 10.00 25.00
BDBTS Ty Smith/50 8.00 20.00
BDBVO Victor Olofsson/50 8.00 20.00
BDBZW Zach Werenski/50 12.00 30.00

2021-22 Black Diamond Rookie Gems

RGAL Anton Lundell 6.00 15.00
RGAN Alex Newhook 5.00 12.00
RGAT Alex Turcotte 4.00 10.00
RGBO Benoit-Olivier Groulx 3.00 8.00
RGBR Jacob Bryson 3.00 8.00
RGCA Calen Addison 3.00 8.00
RGCC Cole Caufield 60.00 150.00
RGCP Cole Perfetti 6.00 15.00
RGCS Cole Sillinger 5.00 12.00
RGCY Cam York 3.00 8.00
RGDF David Farrance 3.00 8.00
RGDM Dawson Mercer 8.00 20.00
RGFG Filip Gustavsson 6.00 15.00
RGHL Hendrix Lapierre 3.00 8.00
RGJD Jamie Drysdale 5.00 12.00
RGJL Jake Leschyshyn 3.00 8.00
RGJS Jeremy Swayman 10.00 25.00
RGJV Joe Veleno 4.00 10.00
RGLR Lucas Raymond 25.00 60.00
RGMM Mason McTavish 25.00 60.00
RGMP Matthew Phillips 3.00 8.00
RGMS Moritz Seider 30.00 80.00
RGNL Nils Lundkvist 3.00 8.00
RGPT Philip Tomasino 4.00 10.00
RGQB Quinton Byfield 8.00 20.00
RGRC Ross Colton 4.00 10.00
RGSJ Seth Jarvis 8.00 20.00
RGSK Spencer Knight 6.00 15.00
RGSP Shane Pinto 5.00 12.00
RGSR Sampo Ranta 3.00 8.00
RGTZ Trevor Zegras 25.00 60.00
RGWA Wade Allison 3.00 8.00
RGWE William Eklund 8.00 20.00
RGWK Wyatt Kalynuk 3.00 8.00
RGZJ Zac Jones 4.00 10.00

2021-22 Black Diamond Rookie Gems Spectrum

*SPECTRUM/99: .75X TO 2X BASIC INSERTS
RGCC Cole Caufield 80.00 200.00
RGCS Cole Sillinger 40.00 100.00
RGMM Mason McTavish 60.00 150.00
RGMS Moritz Seider 60.00 150.00
RGTZ Trevor Zegras 60.00 150.00

2021-22 Black Diamond Rookie Gems Pure Black Signatures

RGAL Anton Lundell/99 30.00 80.00
RGAN Alex Newhook/99 25.00 60.00
RGAT Alex Turcotte/99 20.00 50.00
RGBO Benoit-Olivier Groulx/199 15.00 40.00
RGBR Jacob Bryson/199 15.00 40.00
RGCA Calen Addison/199 15.00 40.00
RGCC Cole Caufield/25 200.00 500.00
RGCP Cole Perfetti/99 30.00 80.00
RGCS Cole Sillinger/99 25.00 60.00
RGDF David Farrance/199 15.00 40.00
RGDM Dawson Mercer/199 40.00 100.00
RGFG Filip Gustavsson/199 30.00 80.00
RGJD Jamie Drysdale/99 25.00 60.00
RGJL Jake Leschyshyn/199 15.00 40.00
RGJS Jeremy Swayman/199 50.00 125.00
RGJV Joe Veleno/199 20.00 50.00
RGLR Lucas Raymond/99 50.00 125.00
RGMP Matthew Phillips/199 15.00 40.00
RGMS Moritz Seider/99 40.00 100.00
RGNL Nils Lundkvist/199 15.00 40.00
RGPT Philip Tomasino/199 20.00 50.00
RGQB Quinton Byfield/99 40.00 100.00
RGRC Ross Colton/199 20.00 50.00
RGSJ Seth Jarvis/99 40.00 100.00
RGSK Spencer Knight/99 30.00 80.00
RGSP Shane Pinto/199 25.00 60.00
RGSR Sampo Ranta/199 15.00 40.00
RGTZ Trevor Zegras/99 30.00 80.00
RGWA Wade Allison/199 15.00 40.00
RGWE William Eklund/99 40.00 100.00
RGWK Wyatt Kalynuk/199 15.00 40.00

2021-22 Black Diamond Rookie Team Logo Jumbo Patch Autographs Full Logo 1

*LOGO/49: X TO 1.25X BASIC INSERTS
*LOGO/25: .6X TO 1.5X BASIC INSERTS
RTLAH Alexander Holtz 60.00 150.00
RTLAN Alex Newhook 60.00 150.00
RTLCC Cole Caufield 150.00 400.00
RTLCP Cole Perfetti 80.00 200.00
RTLJS Jeremy Swayman 125.00 300.00
RTLMS Moritz Seider 100.00 250.00
RTLQB Quinton Byfield 100.00 250.00
RTLRC Ross Colton 50.00 125.00
RTLSK Spencer Knight 80.00 200.00
RTLSP Shane Pinto 60.00 150.00
RTLTZ Trevor Zegras 80.00 200.00
RTLVP Vasily Podkolzin 50.00 125.00

2021-22 Black Diamond Rookie Team Logo Jumbo Puzzle Patches

*RETRO: .6X TO 1.5X BASIC INSERTS
RTLAH Alexander Holtz 8.00 20.00
RTLAN Alex Newhook 8.00 20.00
RTLCC Cole Caufield 20.00 50.00
RTLCP Cole Perfetti 10.00 25.00
RTLCY Cam York 5.00 12.00
RTLJS Jeremy Swayman 15.00 40.00
RTLMS Moritz Seider 12.00 30.00
RTLQB Quinton Byfield 12.00 30.00
RTLRC Ross Colton 6.00 15.00
RTLSK Spencer Knight 10.00 25.00
RTLSP Shane Pinto 8.00 20.00
RTLTZ Trevor Zegras 10.00 25.00
RTLVP Vasily Podkolzin 6.00 15.00

2021-22 Black Diamond Run for the Cup

RUNAM Auston Matthews 15.00 40.00
RUNAO Alex Ovechkin 15.00 40.00
RUNAP Artemi Panarin 8.00 20.00
RUNBH Brett Hull 6.00 15.00
RUNCC Cole Caufield 15.00 40.00
RUNCP Carey Price 25.00 60.00
RUNDH Dominik Hasek 6.00 15.00
RUNJS Jeremy Swayman 25.00 60.00
RUNLD Leon Draisaitl 12.00 30.00
RUNMF Marc-Andre Fleury 25.00 60.00
RUNMS Mark Stone 5.00 12.00
RUNPF Peter Forsberg 8.00 20.00
RUNQH Quinn Hughes 10.00 25.00
RUNRC Ross Colton 5.00 12.00
RUNSK Spencer Knight 8.00 20.00
RUNVH Victor Hedman 5.00 12.00

2021-22 Black Diamond Silver on Black Rookie Signatures

*SPECTRUM/10-25: .6X TO 1.5X BASIC INSERTS
SBAL Anton Lundell/99 20.00 50.00
SBAN Alex Newhook/99 15.00 40.00
SBCS Cole Sillinger/99 15.00 40.00
SBJB Jacob Bryson/149 10.00 25.00
SBJS Jeremy Swayman/99 30.00 80.00
SBJV Joe Veleno/149 12.00 30.00
SBMC Mason McTavish/149 20.00 50.00
SBMP Matthew Phillips/149 10.00 25.00
SBMS Moritz Seider/49 25.00 60.00
SBNL Nils Lundkvist/149 10.00 25.00
SBPT Philip Tomasino/149 12.00 30.00
SBQB Quinton Byfield/49 25.00 60.00
SBSP Shane Pinto/149 15.00 40.00
SBTZ Trevor Zegras/49 125.00 300.00
SBWE William Eklund/99 25.00 60.00

2021-22 Black Diamond Silver on Black Signatures

*SPECTRUM/5-25: .6X TO 1.5X BASIC INSERTS
SBAK Anze Kopitar/50 15.00 40.00
SBAV Andrei Vasilevskiy/50 15.00 40.00
SBBH Bo Horvat/50 12.00 30.00
SBHU Brett Hull/25 15.00 40.00

SBJH Jack Hughes/25 25.00 60.00
SBJL John LeClair/100 10.00 25.00
SBMM Mitch Marner/25 15.00 40.00
SBMT Matthew Tkachuk/50 20.00 50.00
SBPE Phil Esposito/50 15.00 40.00

2021-22 Black Diamond Sparkling Rookie Scripts

*SPECTRUM/25: .75X TO 2X BASIC INSERTS
SCAD Calen Addison 10.00 25.00
SCBA Morgan Barron 8.00 20.00
SCCC Cole Caufield 40.00 100.00
SCJA Jack Ahcan 10.00 25.00
SCJD Jamie Drysdale 15.00 40.00
SCJJ Jan Jenik 12.00 30.00
SCJS Jeremy Swayman 30.00 80.00
SCLR Lucas Raymond 30.00 80.00
SCMS Moritz Seider 25.00 60.00
SCNL Nils Lundkvist 10.00 25.00
SCPE Cole Perfetti 20.00 50.00
SCPK Parker Kelly 10.00 25.00
SCPT Philip Tomasino 12.00 30.00
SCQB Quinton Byfield 25.00 60.00
SCRC Ross Colton 12.00 30.00
SCRK Rasmus Kupari 10.00 25.00
SCRU Arttu Ruotsalainen 10.00 25.00
SCSK Spencer Knight 20.00 50.00
SCSP Shane Pinto 15.00 40.00
SCTL Tanner Laczynski 10.00 25.00
SCTY Tyce Thompson 10.00 25.00

2021-22 Black Diamond Sparkling Scripts

*SPECTRUM/25: .6X TO 1.5X BASIC INSERTS
SCAL Anders Lee 8.00 20.00
SCAM Anthony Mantha 8.00 20.00
SCAT Alex Tuch 10.00 25.00
SCAV Andrei Vasilevskiy 15.00 40.00
SCBB Brent Burns 10.00 25.00
SCBH Bobby Hull 15.00 40.00
SCBN Bernie Nicholls 8.00 20.00
SCCA Cam Atkinson 10.00 25.00
SCCP Cal Petersen 6.00 15.00
SCEM Elvis Merzlikins 10.00 25.00
SCGA Mike Gartner 12.00 30.00
SCGL Guy Lafleur 12.00 30.00
SCGV Gabe Vilardi 10.00 25.00
SCJM Josh Morrissey 12.00 30.00
SCJR Jason Robertson 15.00 40.00
SCKF Kevin Fiala 8.00 20.00
SCKY Kailer Yamamoto 10.00 25.00
SCMC Maxime Comtois 8.00 20.00
SCMI J.T. Miller 12.00 30.00
SCMM Mike Modano 15.00 40.00
SCPR Carey Price 20.00 50.00
SCRT Robert Thomas 10.00 25.00
SCST Shea Theodore 12.00 30.00
SCTC Thomas Chabot 10.00 25.00
SCTT Teuvo Teravainen 10.00 25.00
SCVN Vladislav Namestnikov 6.00 15.00
SCWO Willie O'Ree 12.00 30.00
SCYS Yegor Sharangovich 10.00 25.00

2021-22 Black Diamond Team Logo Jumbo Puzzle Patches

TLASBS Brendan Shanahan 3.00 8.00
TLASDH Dominik Hasek 6.00 15.00
TLASMM Mark Messier 8.00 20.00
TLASPC Paul Coffey 5.00 12.00
TLASPR Patrick Roy 10.00 25.00
TLASSY Steve Yzerman 10.00 25.00
TLASTF Theoren Fleury 4.00 10.00
TLASTS Teemu Selanne 8.00 20.00
TLASWG Wayne Gretzky 25.00 60.00
TLDSBH Brett Hull 6.00 15.00
TLDSEB Ed Belfour 4.00 10.00
TLDSJB Jamie Benn 4.00 10.00
TLDSJN Joe Nieuwendyk 3.00 8.00
TLDSJR Jason Robertson 6.00 15.00
TLDSMH Miro Heiskanen 5.00 12.00
TLDSMM Mike Modano 6.00 15.00
TLDSMT Marty Turco 3.00 8.00
TLDSTS Tyler Seguin 5.00 12.00
TLNJBH Bobby Holik 3.00 8.00
TLNJCL Claude Lemieux 3.00 8.00
TLNJJH Jack Hughes 10.00 25.00
TLNJJM John MacLean 3.00 8.00
TLNJKD Ken Daneyko 3.00 8.00
TLNJMB Martin Brodeur 10.00 25.00
TLNJNH Nico Hischier 6.00 15.00
TLNJSG Scott Gomez 3.00 8.00
TLNJSN Scott Niedermayer 4.00 10.00
TLQNDB Dan Bouchard 3.00 8.00
TLQNGL Guy Lafleur 5.00 12.00
TLQNJS Joe Sakic 8.00 20.00
TLQNMG Michel Goulet 3.00 8.00
TLQNMM Mario Marois 3.00 8.00
TLQNMS Mats Sundin 4.00 10.00
TLQNON Owen Nolan 3.00 8.00
TLQNPF Peter Forsberg 8.00 20.00
TLQNPS Peter Stastny 3.00 8.00
TLTBAK Alex Killorn 2.50 6.00
TLTBAV Andrei Vasilevskiy 6.00 15.00
TLTBBP Brayden Point 5.00 12.00
TLTBNK Nikita Kucherov 8.00 20.00
TLTBOP Ondrej Palat 3.00 8.00
TLTBRC Ross Colton 5.00 12.00
TLTBSS Steven Stamkos 8.00 20.00
TLTBSS Mikhail Sergachev 3.00 8.00
TLTBVH Victor Hedman 5.00 12.00

2022-23 Black Diamond

BDBAB Aleksander Barkov 3.00 8.00
BDBAH Sebastian Aho 3.00 8.00
BDBAK Anze Kopitar 3.00 8.00
BDBAL Alexis Lafreniere 3.00 8.00
BDBAM Auston Matthews 8.00 20.00
BDBAO Alex Ovechkin 8.00 20.00
BDBAP Artemi Panarin 4.00 10.00
BDBAR Aatu Raty/349 RC 2.00 5.00
BDBAS Andrei Svechnikov 2.50 6.00
BDBAV Andrei Vasilevskiy 3.00 8.00
BDBBA Mathew Barzal 2.50 6.00
BDBBC Brandt Clarke/349 RC 4.00 10.00
BDBBM Brad Marchand 4.00 10.00
BDBBO Matt Boldy/349 RC 6.00 15.00
BDBBR Martin Brodeur 5.00 12.00
BDBBS Braden Schneider/349 RC 3.00 8.00
BDBBT Brady Tkachuk 3.00 8.00
BDBCA Cam Atkinson 2.00 5.00
BDBCC Cole Caufield 4.00 10.00
BDBCG Conor Garland 1.50 4.00
BDBCK Clayton Keller 2.50 6.00
BDBCM Connor McDavid 10.00 25.00
BDBCO Connor McMichael 2.00 5.00
BDBCP Carey Price 4.00 10.00
BDBDC Dylan Cozens 2.00 5.00
BDBDG Dylan Guenther/349 RC 5.00 12.00
BDBDH Dylan Holloway/349 RC 4.00 10.00
BDBDP David Pastrnak 5.00 12.00
BDBDR Leon Draisaitl 6.00 15.00
BDBEI Jack Eichel 3.00 8.00
BDBEM Evgeni Malkin 4.00 10.00
BDBES Elmer Soderblom/349 RC 4.00 10.00
BDBFF Filip Forsberg 3.00 8.00
BDBHA Dominik Hasek 3.00 8.00
BDBHU Jonathan Huberdeau 2.50 6.00
BDBHZ Henrik Zetterberg 2.50 6.00
BDBIS Igor Shesterkin 4.00 10.00
BDBJE Jordan Eberle 2.00 5.00
BDBJH Jack Hughes 5.00 12.00
BDBJK Jordan Kyrou 2.00 5.00
BDBJM Jared McCann 1.50 4.00
BDBJN Josh Norris 2.00 5.00
BDBJP Joe Pavelski 2.50 6.00
BDBJQ Jack Quinn/349 RC 3.00 8.00
BDBJR Jason Robertson 3.00 8.00
BDBJS Juraj Slafkovsky/349 RC 10.00 25.00
BDBKC Kyle Connor 3.00 8.00
BDBKD Kirby Dach 2.00 5.00
BDBKG Kaiden Guhle/349 RC 4.00 10.00
BDBKJ Kent Johnson/349 RC 4.00 10.00
BDBKK Kirill Kaprizov 6.00 15.00
BDBKT Keith Tkachuk 2.00 5.00
BDBKU Andrei Kuzmenko/349 RC 4.00 10.00
BDBLM Marc McLaughlin/349 RC 2.00 5.00
BDBLD Lukas Dostal/349 RC 4.00 10.00
BDBLR Lucas Raymond 3.00 8.00
BDBMA Jacob Markstrom 2.00 5.00
BDBMB Matty Beniers/349 RC 5.00 12.00
BDBMC Cale Makar 5.00 12.00
BDBMH Miro Heiskanen 2.50 6.00
BDBMI Mike Bossy 2.00 5.00
BDBML Mario Lemieux 8.00 20.00
BDBMM Mitch Marner 3.00 8.00
BDBMR Marco Rossi/349 RC 5.00 12.00
BDBMS Mark Scheifele 3.00 8.00
BDBMT Matthew Tkachuk 4.00 10.00
BDBNA Nick Abruzzese/349 RC 2.50 6.00
BDBNM Nathan MacKinnon 8.00 20.00
BDBOP Owen Power/349 RC 4.00 10.00
BDBPE Jacob Perreault/349 RC 2.00 5.00
BDBPK Patrick Kane 4.00 10.00
BDBPL Patrik Laine 2.50 6.00
BDBPO Samuel Poulin/349 RC 2.50 6.00
BDBQH Quinn Hughes 2.00 5.00
BDBRB Ray Bourque 3.00 8.00
BDBRD Rasmus Dahlin 2.50 6.00
BDBRE Lukas Reichel/349 RC 4.00 10.00
BDBRJ Roman Josi 2.00 5.00
BDBRO Ryan O'Reilly 2.00 5.00
BDBSA Joe Sakic 4.00 10.00
BDBSC Sidney Crosby 8.00 20.00
BDBSE Moritz Seider 2.50 6.00
BDBSF Samuel Fagemo/349 RC 1.50 4.00
BDBSJ Jake Sanderson/349 RC 5.00 12.00
BDBSK Spencer Knight 2.00 5.00
BDBSO Mads Sogaard/349 RC 2.50 6.00
BDBSP Jordan Spence/349 RC 2.00 5.00
BDBSS Steven Stamkos 4.00 10.00
BDBST Martin St. Louis 2.00 5.00
BDBSW Shane Wright/349 RC 5.00 12.00
BDBTA John Tavares 3.00 8.00
BDBTB Thomas Bordeleau/349 RC 2.00 5.00
BDBTH Tomas Hertl 2.00 5.00
BDBTM Timo Meier 2.00 5.00
BDBTR Brayden Tracey/349 RC 1.50 4.00
BDBTZ Trevor Zegras 5.00 12.00
BDBVL Alex Vlasic/349 RC 1.50 4.00
BDBWG Wayne Gretzky 12.00 30.00
BDBWK William Karlsson 2.50 6.00
BDRAK Andrei Kuzmenko/99 60.00 150.00
BDRAR Aatu Raty/99 20.00 50.00
BDRAV Alex Vlasic/99 15.00 40.00
BDRAX Arber Xhekaj/99 RC 40.00 100.00
BDRBB Bobby Brink/99 RC 20.00 50.00
BDRBC Brandt Clarke/99 40.00 100.00
BDRBO Matt Boldy/99 60.00 150.00
BDRBS Braden Schneider/99 30.00 80.00
BDRBT Brayden Tracey/99 15.00 40.00
BDRDG Dylan Guenther/99 50.00 125.00
BDRDH Dylan Holloway/99 40.00 100.00
BDRDJ David Jiricek/99 RC 40.00 100.00
BDRDS Dylan Samberg/99 RC 20.00 50.00
BDREK Erik Kallgren/99 RC 20.00 50.00
BDRFH Filip Hallander/99 RC 20.00 50.00
BDRFW Trey Fix-Wolansky/99 RC 20.00 50.00
BDRIR Isaac Ratcliffe/99 RC 20.00 50.00
BDRJB Jonatan Berggren/99 RC 30.00 80.00
BDRJC Jake Christiansen/99 RC 20.00 50.00
BDRJH Jordan Harris/99 RC 25.00 60.00
BDRJL Jakub Lauko/99 RC 25.00 60.00
BDRJM Jack McBain/99 RC 20.00 50.00
BDRJO Jordan Spence/99 20.00 50.00
BDRJP Jacob Perreault/99 20.00 50.00
BDRJQ Jack Quinn/99 30.00 80.00
BDRJS Juraj Slafkovsky/99 125.00 300.00
BDRKG Kaiden Guhle/99 40.00 100.00
BDRKJ Kent Johnson/99 40.00 100.00
BDRKK Kaedan Korczak/99 RC 15.00 40.00
BDRKM Kirill Marchenko/99 RC 50.00 125.00
BDRLD Lukas Dostal/99 40.00 100.00
BDRLR Lukas Reichel/99 80.00 200.00
BDRMA Matias Maccelli/99 RC 30.00 80.00
BDRMB Matty Beniers/99 100.00 250.00
BDRMC Mitchell Chaffee/99 RC 15.00 40.00
BDRMK Mark Kastelic/99 RC 15.00 40.00
BDRMM Marc McLaughlin/99 20.00 50.00
BDRMR Marco Rossi/99 50.00 125.00
BDRMS Mads Sogaard/99 25.00 60.00
BDRNA Nick Abruzzese/99 25.00 60.00
BDRNB Nick Blankenburg/99 RC 15.00 40.00
BDRNC Noah Cates/99 RC 20.00 50.00
BDRNS Nathan Smith/99 RC 15.00 40.00
BDROP Owen Power/99 40.00 100.00
BDRPA Juuso Parssinen/99 RC 20.00 50.00
BDRPK Pyotr Kochetkov/99 RC 40.00 100.00
BDRRA Ronnie Attard/99 RC 20.00 50.00
BDRRW Reilly Walsh/99 RC 20.00 50.00
BDRSA Jake Sanderson/99 50.00 125.00
BDRSE Samuel Ersson/99 RC 40.00 100.00
BDRSF Samuel Fagemo/99 15.00 40.00
BDRSP Samuel Poulin/99 25.00 60.00
BDRSW Shane Wright/99 125.00 300.00
BDRTB Thomas Bordeleau/99 20.00 50.00
BDRVK Vladislav Kolyachonok/99 RC 15.00 40.00
BDRVL Viktor Lodin/99 RC 20.00 50.00
BDRVP Valtteri Puustinen/99 RC 15.00 40.00
BDRWJ Wyatt Johnston/99 RC 60.00 150.00

2022-23 Black Diamond Blue

*BLUE/25: .75X TO 2X BASIC

2022-23 Black Diamond Diamond Relics Purple

*PURPLE/25: .6X TO 1.5X BASIC
BDRAK Andrei Kuzmenko 125.00 300.00
BDRBO Matt Boldy 200.00 500.00
BDRJS Juraj Slafkovsky 200.00 500.00
BDRLR Lukas Reichel 125.00 300.00
BDRSW Shane Wright 200.00 500.00
BDRWJ Wyatt Johnston 125.00 300.00

2022-23 Black Diamond Ruby

*RUBY: .5X TO 1.2X BASIC
BDRAK Andrei Kuzmenko 80.00 200.00
BDRJS Juraj Slafkovsky 150.00 400.00
BDRLR Lukas Reichel 100.00 250.00
BDRMB Matty Beniers 400.00 1000.00
BDRSW Shane Wright 150.00 400.00
BDRWJ Wyatt Johnston 80.00 200.00

2022-23 Black Diamond Band of Color

BCAM Auston Matthews 150.00 400.00
BCAO Alex Ovechkin 150.00 400.00
BCAV Andrei Vasilevskiy 60.00 150.00
BCBO Bobby Orr 150.00 400.00
BCCM Connor McDavid 200.00 500.00
BCCP Carey Price 80.00 200.00
BCDP David Pastrnak 100.00 250.00
BCEP Elias Pettersson 60.00 150.00
BCIS Igor Shesterkin 80.00 200.00
BCJH Jonathan Huberdeau 50.00 125.00
BCJJ Jaromir Jagr 125.00 300.00
BCJR Jason Robertson 60.00 150.00
BCKK Kirill Kaprizov 125.00 300.00
BCLD Leon Draisaitl 125.00 300.00
BCMA Cale Makar 100.00 250.00
BCML Mario Lemieux 150.00 400.00
BCMM Mitch Marner 60.00 150.00
BCMT Matthew Tkachuk 80.00 200.00
BCNM Nathan MacKinnon 150.00 400.00
BCPK Patrick Kane 80.00 200.00
BCPR Patrick Roy 100.00 250.00
BCSA Sebastian Aho 60.00 150.00
BCSC Sidney Crosby 150.00 400.00
BCSS Steven Stamkos 80.00 200.00
BCWG Wayne Gretzky 250.00 600.00

2022-23 Black Diamond Band of Color Rookies

BCRAB Nick Abruzzese 50.00 125.00
BCRAK Andrei Kuzmenko 100.00 250.00
BCRAR Aatu Raty 50.00 125.00
BCRBB Bobby Brink 50.00 125.00
BCRBC Brandt Clarke 100.00 250.00
BCRBO Matt Boldy 150.00 400.00
BCRBS Braden Schneider 80.00 200.00
BCRDG Dylan Guenther 125.00 300.00
BCRDH Dylan Holloway 100.00 250.00
BCRES Elmer Soderblom 100.00 250.00
BCRJB Jonatan Berggren 80.00 200.00
BCRJP Jacob Perreault 50.00 125.00
BCRJQ Jack Quinn 80.00 200.00
BCRJS Juraj Slafkovsky 250.00 600.00
BCRKG Kaiden Guhle 100.00 250.00
BCRKJ Kent Johnson 100.00 250.00
BCRLD Lukas Dostal 100.00 250.00
BCRLR Lukas Reichel 100.00 250.00
BCRMB Matty Beniers 125.00 300.00
BCRMM Matias Maccelli 80.00 200.00
BCRMR Marco Rossi 125.00 300.00
BCRMS Mads Sogaard 60.00 150.00
BCROP Owen Power 100.00 250.00
BCRPK Pyotr Kochetkov 100.00 250.00
BCRSA Jake Sanderson 125.00 300.00
BCRSF Samuel Fagemo 40.00 100.00
BCRSW Shane Wright 125.00 300.00
BCRTB Thomas Bordeleau 50.00 125.00
BCRWJ Wyatt Johnston 200.00 500.00

2022-23 Black Diamond Cup Winners Patches

*GOLD: 1X TO 2.5X BASIC
CWBP Brayden Point 5.00 12.00
CWBS Denis Potvin 4.00 10.00
CWHZ Henrik Zetterberg 5.00 12.00
CWJB Johnny Bucyk 4.00 10.00
CWJJ Jaromir Jagr 12.00 30.00
CWJS Joe Sakic 8.00 20.00
CWKL Kris Letang 5.00 12.00
CWMB Martin Brodeur 10.00 25.00
CWPC Paul Coffey 4.00 10.00
CWPK Patrick Kane 8.00 20.00
CWPR Patrick Roy 12.00 30.00
CWRB Rod Brind'Amour 4.00 10.00
CWRT Robert Thomas 4.00 10.00
CWTS Teemu Selanne 8.00 20.00
CWWG Wayne Gretzky 25.00 60.00

2022-23 Black Diamond Diamonation

DAM Auston Matthews 20.00 50.00
DAO Alex Ovechkin 20.00 50.00
DAP Artemi Panarin 10.00 25.00
DBO Matt Boldy 15.00 40.00
DCM Connor McDavid 25.00 60.00
DCP Carey Price 10.00 25.00
DJG Johnny Gaudreau 8.00 20.00
DJQ Jack Quinn 8.00 20.00
DJS Juraj Slafkovsky 25.00 60.00
DKJ Kent Johnson 10.00 25.00
DKK Kirill Kaprizov 15.00 40.00
DLR Lukas Reichel 10.00 25.00
DMB Matty Beniers 25.00 60.00
DMR Marco Rossi 12.00 30.00
DNM Nathan MacKinnon 20.00 50.00
DOP Owen Power 10.00 25.00
DPK Patrick Kane 10.00 25.00
DSC Sidney Crosby 20.00 50.00
DSW Shane Wright 20.00 50.00
DWJ Wyatt Johnston 20.00 50.00

2022-23 Black Diamond Diamond Debut Relics

DDBC Brandt Clarke 4.00 10.00
DDBO Matt Boldy 6.00 15.00
DDBS Braden Schneider 3.00 8.00
DDDG Dylan Guenther 5.00 12.00
DDJP Jacob Perreault 2.00 5.00
DDJQ Jack Quinn 3.00 8.00
DDJS Juraj Slafkovsky 10.00 25.00
DDKG Kaiden Guhle 4.00 10.00
DDKJ Kent Johnson 4.00 10.00
DDLD Lukas Dostal 4.00 10.00
DDLR Lukas Reichel 4.00 10.00
DDMB Matty Beniers 5.00 12.00
DDMR Marco Rossi 5.00 12.00
DDOP Owen Power 4.00 10.00
DDSW Shane Wright 5.00 12.00
DDTB Thomas Bordeleau 2.00 5.00

2022-23 Black Diamond Diamond Debut Relics Patch Autographs

DDBC Brandt Clarke/49 40.00 100.00
DDBO Matt Boldy/49 60.00 150.00
DDBS Braden Schneider/49 30.00 80.00
DDDG Dylan Guenther/49 50.00 125.00
DDJQ Jack Quinn/49 30.00 80.00
DDKG Kaiden Guhle/49 40.00 100.00
DDKJ Kent Johnson/49 40.00 100.00
DDLD Lukas Dostal/49 40.00 100.00
DDLR Lukas Reichel/49 40.00 100.00
DDOP Owen Power/25 40.00 100.00
DDSW Shane Wright/25 50.00 125.00

2022-23 Black Diamond Diamond Facet

DFAM Auston Matthews 12.00 30.00
DFAO Alex Ovechkin 12.00 30.00
DFAV Andrei Vasilevskiy 5.00 12.00
DFBB Shane Wright 8.00 20.00
DFBE Matty Beniers 8.00 20.00
DFBO Matt Boldy 10.00 25.00
DFCP Carey Price 6.00 15.00
DFJQ Jack Quinn 5.00 12.00
DFJS Juraj Slafkovsky 15.00 40.00
DFKJ Kent Johnson 6.00 15.00
DFKK Kirill Kaprizov 10.00 25.00
DFLD Leon Draisaitl 10.00 25.00
DFLR Lukas Reichel 6.00 15.00
DFMB Michael Bunting 3.00 8.00
DFMR Marco Rossi 8.00 20.00
DFMS Moritz Seider 8.00 20.00
DFOP Owen Power 6.00 15.00
DFPK Patrick Kane 6.00 15.00
DFSC Sidney Crosby 12.00 30.00
DFTZ Trevor Zegras 3.00 8.00

2022-23 Black Diamond Diamond Futures

*PURPLE/49: .6X TO 1.5X BASIC
BDFAK Andrei Kuzmenko 6.00 15.00
BDFAR Aatu Raty 3.00 8.00
BDFAV Alex Vlasic 2.50 6.00
BDFBB Bobby Brink 3.00 8.00
BDFBC Brandt Clarke 6.00 15.00
BDFBE Matty Beniers 8.00 20.00
BDFBS Braden Schneider 5.00 12.00
BDFBT Brayden Tracey 2.50 6.00
BDFDG Dylan Guenther 8.00 20.00
BDFDH Dylan Holloway 6.00 15.00
BDFDS Dylan Samberg 3.00 8.00
BDFEK Erik Kallgren 3.00 8.00
BDFIR Isaac Ratcliffe 3.00 8.00
BDFJB Jonatan Berggren 5.00 12.00
BDFJH Jordan Harris 4.00 10.00
BDFJP Jacob Perreault 3.00 8.00
BDFJQ Jack Quinn 5.00 12.00
BDFJS Jordan Spence 3.00 8.00
BDFKJ Kent Johnson 6.00 15.00
BDFLD Lukas Dostal 6.00 15.00
BDFLR Lukas Reichel 6.00 15.00
BDFMB Matt Boldy 10.00 25.00
BDFMC Marc McLaughlin 3.00 8.00
BDFMM Matias Maccelli 5.00 12.00
BDFMR Marco Rossi 8.00 20.00
BDFMS Mads Sogaard 4.00 10.00
BDFNA Nick Abruzzese 3.00 8.00
BDFNC Noah Cates 3.00 8.00
BDFOP Owen Power 6.00 15.00
BDFPK Pyotr Kochetkov 6.00 15.00
BDFSA Jake Sanderson 8.00 20.00
BDFSF Samuel Fagemo 2.50 6.00
BDFSL Juraj Slafkovsky 15.00 40.00
BDFSW Shane Wright 8.00 20.00
BDFTF Trey Fix-Wolansky 3.00 8.00
BDFWJ Wyatt Johnston 12.00 30.00

2022-23 Black Diamond Diamond Futures Autographs

BDFAR Aatu Raty/65 12.00 30.00
BDFAV Alex Vlasic/65 10.00 25.00
BDFBB Bobby Brink/99 12.00 30.00
BDFBC Brandt Clarke/99 25.00 60.00
BDFBE Matty Beniers/35 150.00 400.00
BDFBS Braden Schneider/65 20.00 50.00
BDFBT Brayden Tracey/65 8.00 20.00
BDFDG Dylan Guenther/65 30.00 80.00
BDFDH Dylan Holloway/65 20.00 50.00
BDFDS Dylan Samberg/65 12.00 30.00
BDFEK Erik Kallgren/99 12.00 30.00
BDFJB Jonatan Berggren/65 15.00 40.00
BDFJH Jordan Harris/65 10.00 25.00
BDFJQ Jack Quinn/65 20.00 50.00
BDFKJ Kent Johnson/35 25.00 60.00
BDFLD Lukas Dostal/65 25.00 60.00
BDFLR Lukas Reichel/35 25.00 60.00
BDFMB Matt Boldy/35 80.00 200.00
BDFMC Marc McLaughlin/99 12.00 30.00
BDFMS Mads Sogaard/99 15.00 40.00
BDFNA Nick Abruzzese/65 12.00 30.00
BDFNC Noah Cates/99 12.00 30.00
BDFOP Owen Power/35 100.00 250.00
BDFPK Pyotr Kochetkov/65 60.00 150.00
BDFSA Jake Sanderson/65 30.00 80.00
BDFSF Samuel Fagemo/65 10.00 25.00
BDFSL Juraj Slafkovsky/35 125.00 300.00
BDFSW Shane Wright/35 100.00 250.00
BDFWJ Wyatt Johnston/65 60.00 150.00

2022-23 Black Diamond Diamond Futures Premium Relic Autographs

BDFAR Aatu Raty 20.00 50.00
BDFAV Alex Vlasic 15.00 40.00
BDFBB Bobby Brink 20.00 50.00
BDFBC Brandt Clarke 40.00 100.00
BDFBE Matty Beniers 200.00 500.00
BDFBS Braden Schneider 30.00 80.00
BDFBT Brayden Tracey 15.00 40.00
BDFDG Dylan Guenther 50.00 125.00
BDFDH Dylan Holloway 100.00 250.00
BDFDS Dylan Samberg 20.00 50.00
BDFEK Erik Kallgren 20.00 50.00
BDFIR Isaac Ratcliffe 20.00 50.00
BDFJB Jonatan Berggren 30.00 80.00
BDFJH Jordan Harris 25.00 60.00
BDFJP Jacob Perreault 20.00 50.00
BDFJQ Jack Quinn 30.00 80.00
BDFKJ Kent Johnson 100.00 250.00
BDFLD Lukas Dostal 40.00 100.00
BDFLR Lukas Reichel 40.00 100.00
BDFMB Matt Boldy 60.00 150.00
BDFMC Marc McLaughlin 20.00 50.00
BDFMS Mads Sogaard 25.00 60.00
BDFNA Nick Abruzzese 20.00 50.00
BDFNC Noah Cates 20.00 50.00
BDFOP Owen Power 200.00 500.00
BDFPK Pyotr Kochetkov 100.00 250.00
BDFSA Jake Sanderson 50.00 125.00
BDFSF Samuel Fagemo 15.00 40.00
BDFSL Juraj Slafkovsky 150.00 400.00
BDFSW Shane Wright 80.00 200.00
BDFTF Trey Fix-Wolansky 20.00 50.00
BDFWJ Wyatt Johnston 80.00 200.00

2022-23 Black Diamond Diamond Gallery

DGAO Alex Ovechkin 15.00 40.00
DGAP Artemi Panarin 8.00 20.00
DGBC Brandt Clarke 8.00 20.00
DGBO Matt Boldy 12.00 30.00
DGCM Cale Makar 10.00 25.00
DGJH Jonathan Huberdeau 5.00 12.00
DGJS Juraj Slafkovsky 25.00 60.00
DGKJ Kent Johnson 8.00 20.00
DGKK Kirill Kaprizov 12.00 30.00
DGLD Leon Draisaitl 12.00 30.00
DGMB Matty Beniers 10.00 25.00
DGMM Mitch Marner 6.00 15.00
DGMT Matthew Tkachuk 8.00 20.00
DGOP Owen Power 8.00 20.00
DGRJ Roman Josi 4.00 10.00
DGSA Jake Sanderson 10.00 25.00
DGSC Sidney Crosby 15.00 40.00
DGSS Steven Stamkos 8.00 20.00
DGSW Shane Wright 10.00 25.00
DGVT Vladimir Tarasenko 5.00 12.00

2022-23 Black Diamond Diamond Legends

BDLBH Brett Hull 6.00 15.00
BDLBO Bobby Orr 12.00 30.00
BDLBR Martin Brodeur 8.00 20.00
BDLCN Cam Neely 3.00 8.00
BDLDH Dominik Hasek 5.00 12.00
BDLGH Gordie Howe 10.00 25.00
BDLGL Guy Lafleur 4.00 10.00
BDLJS Joe Sakic 6.00 15.00
BDLMB Mike Bossy 3.00 8.00
BDLMD Marcel Dionne 4.00 10.00
BDLML Mario Lemieux 12.00 30.00
BDLNL Nicklas Lidstrom 3.00 8.00
BDLPC Paul Coffey 3.00 8.00
BDLPF Peter Forsberg 6.00 15.00
BDLPR Patrick Roy 8.00 20.00
BDLRB Ray Bourque 5.00 12.00
BDLSC Shayne Corson 2.50 6.00
BDLSK Saku Koivu 3.00 8.00
BDLSY Steve Yzerman 8.00 20.00
BDLWG Wayne Gretzky 20.00 50.00

2022-23 Black Diamond Diamond Legends Purple

*PURPLE/49: .6X TO 1.5X BASIC
BDLGL Guy Lafleur 30.00 80.00
BDLML Mario Lemieux 30.00 80.00
BDLRB Ray Bourque 12.00 30.00
BDLSY Steve Yzerman 25.00 60.00

2022-23 Black Diamond Diamond Legends Autographs

BDLSK Saku Koivu/25 25.00 60.00

2022-23 Black Diamond Diamond Might

DMAK Andrei Kuzmenko 10.00 25.00
DMAM Auston Matthews 20.00 50.00
DMAO Alex Ovechkin 20.00 50.00
DMBE Matty Beniers 12.00 30.00
DMBO Matt Boldy 15.00 40.00
DMGL Guy Lafleur 6.00 15.00
DMIS Igor Shesterkin 10.00 25.00
DMJE Jeremy Swayman 8.00 20.00
DMJG Johnny Gaudreau 8.00 20.00
DMJQ Jack Quinn 8.00 20.00
DMJR Jason Robertson 8.00 20.00
DMJS Juraj Slafkovsky 25.00 60.00
DMKJ Kent Johnson 10.00 25.00
DMKK Kirill Kaprizov 15.00 40.00
DMLR Lukas Reichel 10.00 25.00
DMMB Michael Bunting 5.00 12.00
DMMI Mike Bossy 5.00 12.00
DMMR Marco Rossi 12.00 30.00
DMOP Owen Power 10.00 25.00
DMRJ Roman Josi 5.00 12.00
DMSK Spencer Knight 5.00 12.00
DMSW Shane Wright 12.00 30.00
DMTH Taylor Hall 5.00 12.00
DMTT Troy Terry 4.00 10.00

2022-23 Black Diamond Diamond Mine Dual Relics

DMDRBP D.Pastrnak/P.Bergeron 10.00 25.00
DMDRBS M.Barzal/I.Sorokin 6.00 15.00
DMDRCN C.Makar/N.MacKinnon 15.00 40.00
DMDRKQ A.Kopitar/J.Quick 6.00 15.00
DMDRMD C.McDavid/L.Draisaitl 20.00 50.00
DMDRML E.Malkin/K.Letang 8.00 20.00
DMDRMM A.Matthews/M.Marner 15.00 40.00
DMDRPH E.Pettersson/Q.Hughes 10.00 25.00
DMDRPS A.Panarin/I.Shesterkin 8.00 20.00
DMDRTS B.Tkachuk/T.Stutzle 6.00 15.00

2022-23 Black Diamond Diamond Mine Relics

DMRAM Auston Matthews 12.00 30.00
DMRAO Alex Ovechkin 12.00 30.00
DMRCM Connor McDavid 15.00 40.00
DMRDP David Pastrnak 8.00 20.00
DMRKK Kirill Kaprizov 10.00 25.00
DMRLR Larry Robinson 3.00 8.00
DMRMA Cale Makar 8.00 20.00
DMRMB Martin Brodeur 8.00 20.00
DMRNM Nathan MacKinnon 12.00 30.00
DMRPK Patrick Kane 6.00 15.00
DMRPR Patrick Roy 8.00 20.00
DMRRB Ray Bourque 5.00 12.00
DMRRD Rasmus Dahlin 4.00 10.00
DMRRI Pekka Rinne 3.00 8.00
DMRSC Sidney Crosby 12.00 30.00
DMRSS Steven Stamkos 6.00 15.00

2022-23 Black Diamond Diamond Mine Relics Premium

*PREMIUM/25: .75X TO 2X BASIC
DMRCM Connor McDavid 60.00 150.00
DMRPR Patrick Roy 40.00 100.00

2022-23 Black Diamond Diamond Mine Triple Relics

DMTRBCO Ovechkin
Carlson/Backstrom 30.00 80.00
DMTRGTZ Terry/Zegras/Getzlaf 8.00 20.00
DMTRKQD Kopitar/Doughty/Quick 12.00 30.00
DMTRLSR Seider/Raymond/Larkin 12.00 30.00
DMTROPT Thomas/Parayko/O'Reilly 8.00 20.00
DMTRPLS Shesterkin
Panarin/Lafreniere 15.00 40.00
DMTRPRO Robertson
Oettinger/Pavelski 12.00 30.00
DMTRRSF Roy/Sakic/Forsberg 20.00 50.00

2022-23 Black Diamond Diamond Plate Rookie Autographs

DPRAV Alex Vlasic/149 6.00 15.00
DPRBB Bobby Brink/99 8.00 20.00
DPRBS Braden Schneider/99 12.00 30.00
DPRBT Brayden Tracey/99 6.00 15.00
DPRDS Dylan Samberg/149 8.00 20.00
DPRJQ Jack Quinn/49 12.00 30.00
DPRKJ Kent Johnson/49 50.00 125.00
DPRLD Lukas Dostal/99 15.00 40.00
DPRLR Lukas Reichel/49 15.00 40.00
DPRMM Marc McLaughlin/149 8.00 20.00
DPRNA Nick Abruzzese/149 8.00 20.00
DPRNC Noah Cates/149 8.00 20.00
DPRSF Samuel Fagemo/99 6.00 15.00

2022-23 Black Diamond Diamond Plate Rookie Autographs Spectrum

*SPECTRUM/25: .75X TO 2X BASIC
DPRLD Lukas Dostal/25 25.00 60.00

2022-23 Black Diamond Diamond Stars

*PURPLE/49: .6X TO 1.5X BASIC
BDSAB Aleksander Barkov 3.00 8.00
BDSAL Alexis Lafreniere 3.00 8.00
BDSAM Auston Matthews 8.00 20.00
BDSAO Alex Ovechkin 8.00 20.00
BDSAS Andrei Svechnikov 2.50 6.00
BDSAV Andrei Vasilevskiy 3.00 8.00
BDSBP Brayden Point 2.50 6.00
BDSBT Brady Tkachuk 3.00 8.00
BDSCC Cole Caufield 3.00 8.00
BDSCM Connor McDavid 10.00 25.00
BDSCP Carey Price 4.00 10.00
BDSDP David Pastrnak 5.00 12.00
BDSIS Igor Shesterkin 4.00 10.00
BDSJB Jesper Bratt 2.00 5.00
BDSJG Jake Guentzel 3.00 8.00
BDSJH Jonathan Huberdeau 2.50 6.00
BDSJM Jared McCann 1.50 4.00
BDSJR Jason Robertson 3.00 8.00
BDSKC Kyle Connor 3.00 8.00
BDSKK Kirill Kaprizov 6.00 15.00
BDSKL Kris Letang 2.50 6.00
BDSKR Peyton Krebs 1.50 4.00
BDSLD Leon Draisaitl 6.00 15.00
BDSMA Cale Makar 6.00 15.00
BDSMB Mathew Barzal 2.50 6.00
BDSMF Marc-Andre Fleury 4.00 10.00
BDSMM Mitch Marner 3.00 8.00
BDSMT Matthew Tkachuk 4.00 10.00
BDSNE Nikolaj Ehlers 2.00 5.00
BDSPK Patrick Kane 4.00 10.00
BDSQH Quinn Hughes 5.00 12.00
BDSRJ Roman Josi 2.00 5.00
BDSSA Sebastian Aho 3.00 8.00
BDSSC Sidney Crosby 8.00 20.00
BDSSO Ilya Sorokin 3.00 8.00
BDSSS Steven Stamkos 4.00 10.00
BDSTD Thatcher Demko 2.50 6.00
BDSTH Taylor Hall 2.00 5.00
BDSTS Tim Stutzle 2.50 6.00
BDSTT Troy Terry 1.50 4.00

2022-23 Black Diamond Diamond Stars Autographs

BDSJG Jake Guentzel/25 25.00 60.00
BDSJM Jared McCann/25 12.00 30.00
BDSKR Peyton Krebs/25 12.00 30.00
BDSSO Ilya Sorokin/25 25.00 60.00
BDSTD Thatcher Demko/25 20.00 50.00

2022-23 Black Diamond Diamond Stars Premium Relic Autographs

BDSJM Jared McCann/25 25.00 60.00
BDSKR Peyton Krebs/25 20.00 50.00

2022-23 Black Diamond Gemography

GAL Alexis Lafreniere 60.00 150.00
GAM Auston Matthews 150.00 400.00
GAV Andrei Vasilevskiy 60.00 150.00
GBE Matty Beniers 100.00 250.00
GBM Brad Marchand 80.00 200.00
GBO Matt Boldy 125.00 300.00
GCM Connor McDavid 200.00 500.00
GCP Carey Price 80.00 200.00
GJH Jonathan Huberdeau 50.00 125.00
GJS Juraj Slafkovsky 200.00 500.00
GKL Kris Letang 50.00 125.00
GMB Michael Bunting 40.00 100.00
GMF Marc-Andre Fleury 80.00 200.00
GMT Matthew Tkachuk 80.00 200.00
GOP Owen Power 80.00 200.00
GSW Shane Wright 100.00 250.00
GTH Taylor Hall 40.00 100.00

2022-23 Black Diamond Habs Retired Numbers Patches

HRNGL Guy Lafleur 40.00 100.00
HRNHM Howie Morenz 20.00 50.00
HRNHR Henri Richard 20.00 50.00
HRNJB Jean Beliveau 20.00 50.00
HRNJP Jacques Plante 20.00 50.00
HRNLR Larry Robinson 12.00 30.00
HRNMR Guy Lapointe 15.00 40.00
HRNPR Patrick Roy 40.00 100.00
HRNSS Serge Savard 20.00 50.00
HRNYC Yvan Cournoyer 20.00 50.00

2022-23 Black Diamond Habs Retired Numbers Patches Gold

HRNPR Patrick Roy/33 40.00 100.00

2022-23 Black Diamond Jewels of the Draft Patch Autographs

JDAV Alex Vlasic/99 15.00 40.00
JDBC Brandt Clarke/49 40.00 100.00
JDBO Matt Boldy/49 60.00 150.00
JDBS Braden Schneider/99 30.00 80.00
JDBT Brayden Tracey/99 15.00 40.00
JDDG Dylan Guenther/49 50.00 125.00
JDDH Dylan Holloway/49 100.00 250.00
JDDS Dylan Samberg/99 20.00 50.00
JDIR Isaac Ratcliffe/99 20.00 50.00
JDJQ Jack Quinn/49 30.00 80.00
JDKG Kaiden Guhle/99 40.00 100.00
JDKJ Kent Johnson/49 100.00 250.00
JDLD Lukas Dostal/99 40.00 100.00
JDLR Lukas Reichel/49 125.00 300.00
JDMB Matty Beniers/49 200.00 500.00
JDMS Mads Sogaard/99 25.00 60.00
JDNA Nick Abruzzese/99 20.00 50.00
JDOP Owen Power/49 125.00 300.00
JDPK Pyotr Kochetkov/49 60.00 150.00
JDSA Jake Sanderson/49 50.00 125.00
JDSF Samuel Fagemo/99 15.00 40.00
JDSP Samuel Poulin/99 25.00 60.00
JDSW Shane Wright/49 125.00 300.00

2022-23 Black Diamond Pure Black Autographs

BDBAB Aleksander Barkov/49 25.00 60.00
BDBAL Alexis Lafreniere/25 25.00 60.00
BDBAR Aatu Raty/49 15.00 40.00
BDBBC Brandt Clarke/49 30.00 80.00
BDBBM Brad Marchand/25 30.00 80.00
BDBBO Matt Boldy/49 50.00 125.00
BDBBS Braden Schneider/49 20.00 50.00
BDBCA Cam Atkinson/25 15.00 40.00
BDBCO Connor McMichael/49 15.00 40.00
BDBDG Dylan Guenther/49 40.00 100.00
BDBDH Dylan Holloway/49 30.00 80.00
BDBHU Jonathan Huberdeau/25 20.00 50.00
BDBJE Jordan Eberle/49 15.00 40.00
BDBJK Jordan Kyrou/25 15.00 40.00
BDBJM Jared McCann/49 12.00 30.00
BDBJN Josh Norris/49 15.00 40.00
BDBJP Joe Pavelski/49 20.00 50.00
BDBJQ Jack Quinn/49 25.00 60.00
BDBJS Juraj Slafkovsky/49 80.00 200.00
BDBKG Kaiden Guhle/49 30.00 80.00
BDBKJ Kent Johnson/49 30.00 80.00
BDBKT Keith Tkachuk/25 15.00 40.00
BDBLA Marc McLaughlin/99 15.00 40.00
BDBLD Lukas Dostal/99 30.00 80.00
BDBMA Jacob Markstrom/25 15.00 40.00
BDBMH Miro Heiskanen/25 20.00 50.00
BDBMT Matthew Tkachuk/25 30.00 80.00
BDBNA Nick Abruzzese/49 15.00 40.00
BDBOP Owen Power/49 30.00 80.00
BDBPO Samuel Poulin/49 25.00 60.00
BDBRE Lukas Reichel/49 30.00 80.00
BDBSF Samuel Fagemo/49 12.00 30.00
BDBSJ Jake Sanderson/49 40.00 100.00
BDBSO Mads Sogaard/99 20.00 50.00
BDBST Martin St. Louis/25 25.00 60.00
BDBSW Shane Wright/49 40.00 100.00
BDBTA John Tavares/25 25.00 60.00
BDBTH Tomas Hertl/49 15.00 40.00
BDBTR Brayden Tracey/99 12.00 30.00
BDBVL Alex Vlasic/99 12.00 30.00
BDBWK William Karlsson/49 20.00 50.00

2022-23 Black Diamond Pure Black Premium Relics

BDBAB Aleksander Barkov/25 12.00 30.00
BDBAL Alexis Lafreniere/25 12.00 30.00
BDBAR Aatu Raty/25 8.00 20.00
BDBAS Andrei Svechnikov/25 10.00 25.00
BDBBC Brandt Clarke/25 15.00 40.00
BDBBO Matt Boldy/25 25.00 60.00
BDBBS Braden Schneider/25 12.00 30.00
BDBCA Cam Atkinson/25 8.00 20.00
BDBCG Conor Garland/25 6.00 15.00
BDBCK Clayton Keller/25 10.00 25.00
BDBCO Connor McMichael/25 8.00 20.00
BDBDC Dylan Cozens/25 8.00 20.00
BDBDG Dylan Guenther/25 20.00 50.00
BDBDH Dylan Holloway/25 15.00 40.00

2022-23 Black Diamond Pure Black Premium Relics

BDBES Elmer Soderblom/25 15.00 40.00
BDBFF Filip Forsberg/25 12.00 30.00
BDBHU Jonathan Huberdeau/25 10.00 25.00
BDBJK Jordan Kyrou/25 8.00 20.00
BDBJM Jared McCann/25 6.00 15.00
BDBJN Josh Norris/25 8.00 20.00
BDBJP Joe Pavelski/25 10.00 25.00
BDBJQ Jack Quinn/25 12.00 30.00
BDBJS Juraj Slafkovsky/25 40.00 100.00
BDBKC Kyle Connor/25 12.00 30.00
BDBKD Kirby Dach/25 8.00 20.00
BDBKG Kaiden Guhle/25 15.00 40.00
BDBKJ Kent Johnson/25 15.00 40.00
BDBKU Andrei Kuzmenko/25 15.00 40.00
BDBLA Marc McLaughlin/25 8.00 20.00
BDBLD Lukas Dostal/25 15.00 40.00
BDBMA Jacob Markstrom/25 8.00 20.00
BDBMB Matty Beniers/25 20.00 50.00
BDBMH Miro Heiskanen/25 10.00 25.00
BDBMR Marco Rossi/25 20.00 50.00
BDBMS Mark Scheifele/25 12.00 30.00
BDBNA Nick Abruzzese/25 8.00 20.00
BDBOP Owen Power/25 15.00 40.00
BDBPE Jacob Perreault/25 8.00 20.00
BDBPO Samuel Poulin/25 10.00 25.00
BDBRE Lukas Reichel/25 15.00 40.00
BDBRJ Roman Josi/25 8.00 20.00
BDBRO Ryan O'Reilly/25 8.00 20.00
BDBSF Samuel Fagemo/25 6.00 15.00
BDBSJ Jake Sanderson/25 20.00 50.00
BDBSK Spencer Knight/25 8.00 20.00
BDBSO Mads Sogaard/25 10.00 25.00
BDBSW Shane Wright/25 20.00 50.00
BDBTB Thomas Bordeleau/25 8.00 20.00
BDBTH Tomas Hertl/25 8.00 20.00
BDBTM Timo Meier/25 8.00 20.00
BDBTR Brayden Tracey/25 6.00 15.00
BDBVL Alex Vlasic/25 6.00 15.00
BDBWK William Karlsson/25 10.00 25.00

2022-23 Black Diamond Rookie Gems

*RED/100: .75X TO 2X BASIC
RGAK Andrei Kuzmenko 6.00 15.00
RGAR Aatu Raty 3.00 8.00
RGAV Alex Vlasic 2.50 6.00
RGBB Bobby Brink 3.00 8.00
RGBC Brandt Clarke 6.00 15.00
RGBE Matty Beniers 8.00 20.00
RGBS Braden Schneider 5.00 12.00
RGBT Brayden Tracey 2.50 6.00
RGDG Dylan Guenther 8.00 20.00
RGDH Dylan Holloway 6.00 15.00
RGDS Dylan Samberg 3.00 8.00
RGES Elmer Soderblom 6.00 15.00
RGIR Isaac Ratcliffe 3.00 8.00
RGJB Jonatan Berggren 5.00 12.00
RGJM Jack McBain 3.00 8.00
RGJP Jacob Perreault 3.00 8.00
RGJQ Jack Quinn 5.00 12.00
RGJS Jordan Spence 3.00 8.00
RGKG Kaiden Guhle 6.00 15.00
RGKJ Kent Johnson 6.00 15.00
RGKM Kirill Marchenko 8.00 20.00
RGLD Lukas Dostal 6.00 15.00
RGLR Lukas Reichel 6.00 15.00
RGMB Matt Boldy 10.00 25.00
RGMM Matias Maccelli 5.00 12.00
RGMR Marco Rossi 8.00 20.00
RGMS Mads Sogaard 4.00 10.00
RGNA Nick Abruzzese 3.00 8.00
RGOP Owen Power 6.00 15.00
RGPK Pyotr Kochetkov 6.00 15.00
RGRA Ronnie Attard 3.00 8.00
RGSA Jake Sanderson 8.00 20.00
RGSF Samuel Fagemo 2.50 6.00
RGSL Juraj Slafkovsky 15.00 40.00
RGSW Shane Wright 8.00 20.00
RGTB Thomas Bordeleau 3.00 8.00

2022-23 Black Diamond Rookie Gems Signatures

RGAR Aatu Raty/99 15.00 40.00
RGAV Alex Vlasic/149 12.00 30.00
RGBB Bobby Brink/99 15.00 40.00
RGBC Brandt Clarke/149 30.00 80.00
RGBE Matty Beniers/25 200.00 500.00
RGBS Braden Schneider/49 25.00 60.00
RGBT Brayden Tracey/49 12.00 30.00
RGDG Dylan Guenther/49 40.00 100.00
RGDH Dylan Holloway/49 30.00 80.00
RGDS Dylan Samberg/149 15.00 40.00
RGJB Jonatan Berggren/49 25.00 60.00
RGJM Jack McBain/149 15.00 40.00
RGJQ Jack Quinn/49 25.00 60.00
RGKG Kaiden Guhle/99 30.00 80.00
RGKJ Kent Johnson/149 30.00 80.00
RGLD Lukas Dostal/99 30.00 80.00
RGLR Lukas Reichel/49 30.00 80.00
RGMB Matt Boldy/25 50.00 125.00
RGNA Nick Abruzzese/149 15.00 40.00
RGOP Owen Power/25 30.00 80.00
RGPK Pyotr Kochetkov/49 50.00 125.00
RGRA Ronnie Attard/149 15.00 40.00
RGSA Jake Sanderson/49 40.00 100.00
RGSF Samuel Fagemo/49 12.00 30.00
RGSL Juraj Slafkovsky/25 80.00 200.00
RGSW Shane Wright/25 100.00 250.00

2022-23 Black Diamond Rookie Team Logo Jumbo Patch Autographs Full Logo 1

RTLBC Brandt Clarke 60.00 150.00
RTLBO Matt Boldy 100.00 250.00
RTLBS Braden Schneider 60.00 150.00
RTLJQ Jack Quinn 50.00 125.00
RTLJS Jake Sanderson 80.00 200.00
RTLKG Kaiden Guhle 60.00 150.00
RTLKJ Kent Johnson 60.00 150.00
RTLLD Lukas Dostal 60.00 150.00
RTLLR Lukas Reichel 60.00 150.00
RTLMB Matty Beniers 150.00 400.00
RTLOP Owen Power 60.00 150.00
RTLSL Juraj Slafkovsky 150.00 400.00
RTLSW Shane Wright 80.00 200.00

2022-23 Black Diamond Rookie Team Logo Jumbo Patch Autographs Full Logo 2

*LOGO 2/49: .5X TO 1.2X BASIC
RTLMB Matty Beniers 250.00 600.00
RTLSL Juraj Slafkovsky 250.00 600.00
RTLSW Shane Wright 150.00 400.00

2022-23 Black Diamond Rookie Team Logo Jumbo Patch Autographs Full Logo 3

*LOGO 3/25: .6X TO 1.5X BASIC
RTLMB Matty Beniers 300.00 800.00
RTLSL Juraj Slafkovsky 300.00 800.00
RTLSW Shane Wright 200.00 500.00

2022-23 Black Diamond Rookie Team Logo Jumbo Patches

RTLBC Brandt Clarke 12.00 30.00
RTLBO Matt Boldy 20.00 50.00
RTLBS Braden Schneider 10.00 25.00
RTLJP Jacob Perreault 6.00 15.00
RTLJQ Jack Quinn 10.00 25.00
RTLJS Jake Sanderson 15.00 40.00
RTLKG Kaiden Guhle SP 12.00 30.00
RTLKJ Kent Johnson 12.00 30.00
RTLLD Lukas Dostal 12.00 30.00
RTLLR Lukas Reichel 12.00 30.00
RTLMB Matty Beniers 40.00 100.00
RTLMR Marco Rossi 15.00 40.00
RTLOP Owen Power 12.00 30.00
RTLSL Juraj Slafkovsky SP 40.00 100.00
RTLSW Shane Wright 15.00 40.00

2022-23 Black Diamond Rookie Team Logo Jumbo Patches Retro

*RETRO: .6X TO 1.5X BASIC
RTLMB Matty Beniers 50.00 125.00
RTLSL Juraj Slafkovsky SP 50.00 125.00

2022-23 Black Diamond Run for the Cup

RUNBC Brandt Clarke 8.00 20.00
RUNBO Matt Boldy 12.00 30.00
RUNCC Cole Caufield 8.00 20.00
RUNCM Connor McDavid 20.00 50.00
RUNJH Jonathan Huberdeau 5.00 12.00
RUNJK Jordan Kyrou 4.00 10.00
RUNJR Jason Robertson 6.00 15.00
RUNJS Juraj Slafkovsky 20.00 50.00
RUNKJ Kent Johnson 8.00 20.00
RUNKK Kirill Kaprizov 12.00 30.00
RUNMA Cale Makar 10.00 25.00
RUNMB Matty Beniers 10.00 25.00
RUNMM Mitch Marner 6.00 15.00
RUNOP Owen Power 8.00 20.00
RUNSC Sidney Crosby 15.00 40.00
RUNSW Shane Wright 10.00 25.00

2022-23 Black Diamond Shimmering Signatures

SSCH Connor Hellebuyck 20.00 50.00
SSCN Cam Neely 20.00 50.00
SSDT Devon Toews 8.00 20.00
SSJM Jared McCann 8.00 20.00
SSJS Jeremy Swayman 30.00 80.00
SSMB Michael Bunting 10.00 25.00
SSMF Marc-Andre Fleury 20.00 50.00
SSNR Nick Robertson 10.00 25.00
SSPC Paul Coffey 10.00 25.00
SSPG Philipp Grubauer 10.00 25.00
SSTD Thatcher Demko 12.00 30.00
SSTF Theoren Fleury 10.00 25.00

2022-23 Black Diamond Shimmering Signatures Spectrum

*SPECTRUM/25: .6X TO 1.5X BASIC
SSJS Jeremy Swayman/25 40.00 100.00

2022-23 Black Diamond Sparkling Rookie Scripts

SCRAV Alex Vlasic 6.00 15.00
SCRBB Bobby Brink 8.00 20.00
SCRBO Matt Boldy 50.00 125.00
SCRBS Braden Schneider 12.00 30.00
SCRBT Brayden Tracey 6.00 15.00
SCRDS Dylan Samberg 8.00 20.00
SCREK Erik Kallgren 8.00 20.00
SCRJH Jordan Harris 10.00 25.00
SCRJQ Jack Quinn 12.00 30.00
SCRKJ Kent Johnson 30.00 80.00
SCRLD Lukas Dostal 15.00 40.00
SCRLR Lukas Reichel 25.00 60.00
SCRMM Marc McLaughlin 8.00 20.00
SCRMS Mads Sogaard 10.00 25.00
SCRNA Nick Abruzzese 8.00 20.00
SCROP Owen Power 50.00 125.00
SCRPK Pyotr Kochetkov 40.00 100.00
SCRRA Ronnie Attard 8.00 20.00
SCRRW Reilly Walsh 8.00 20.00
SCRSF Samuel Fagemo 6.00 15.00
SCRSW Shane Wright 40.00 100.00

2022-23 Black Diamond Sparkling Rookie Scripts Spectrum

*SPECTRUM/25: .75X TO 2X BASIC
SCRBO Matt Boldy 80.00 200.00
SCRKJ Kent Johnson 80.00 200.00
SCRLR Lukas Reichel 50.00 125.00
SCROP Owen Power 80.00 200.00
SCRPK Pyotr Kochetkov 60.00 150.00
SCRSW Shane Wright 80.00 200.00

2022-23 Black Diamond Sparkling Scripts

SCAB Anthony Beauvillier 5.00 12.00
SCAC Andrew Copp 5.00 12.00
SCAK Arthur Kaliyev 8.00 20.00
SCAL Anton Lundell 8.00 20.00
SCAN Alex Newhook 6.00 15.00
SCBD Brandon Duhaime 5.00 12.00
SCBH Brandon Hagel 6.00 15.00
SCCC Charlie Coyle 8.00 20.00
SCCM Connor McMichael 8.00 20.00
SCCO Connor McDavid 125.00 300.00
SCCP Cole Perfetti 8.00 20.00
SCDM Dawson Mercer 12.00 30.00
SCDT Devon Toews 6.00 15.00
SCDV Dan Vladar 6.00 15.00
SCHL Hendrix Lapierre 5.00 12.00
SCIL Isac Lundestrom 5.00 12.00
SCJC Jack Campbell 8.00 20.00
SCJM Jared McCann 6.00 15.00
SCKB Kieffer Bellows 5.00 12.00
SCKC Kyle Connor 12.00 30.00
SCKM K'Andre Miller 6.00 15.00
SCMC Maxime Comtois 6.00 15.00
SCNH Noah Hanifin 8.00 20.00
SCPF Pavel Francouz 6.00 15.00
SCPS Pius Suter 6.00 15.00
SCRK Rasmus Kupari 5.00 12.00
SCSD Sean Durzi 5.00 12.00
SCTJ Tanner Jeannot 5.00 12.00
SCTK Torey Krug 6.00 15.00
SCVN Vladislav Namestnikov 5.00 12.00

2022-23 Black Diamond Sparkling Scripts Spectrum

*SPECTRUM/25: .6X TO 1.5X BASIC
SCBH Brandon Hagel 15.00 40.00
SCJC Jack Campbell 25.00 60.00
SCKM K'Andre Miller 30.00 80.00

2022-23 Black Diamond Team Logo Jumbo Patches

*RETRO: .6X TO 1.5X BASIC
TLAB Aleksander Barkov 6.00 15.00
TLAE Aaron Ekblad 5.00 12.00
TLAL Anton Lundell 4.00 10.00
TLAM Auston Matthews AS 15.00 40.00
TLAU Auston Matthews 15.00 40.00
TLAV Andrei Vasilevskiy AS 6.00 15.00
TLBB Brent Burns 4.00 10.00
TLBS Borje Salming 4.00 10.00
TLCM Connor McDavid AS 20.00 50.00
TLCP Corey Perry 6.00 15.00
TLDG Doug Gilmour 5.00 12.00
TLDS Darryl Sittler 4.00 10.00
TLFM Frank Mahovlich 4.00 10.00
TLGI Jean-Sebastien Giguere 4.00 10.00
TLJD Jamie Drysdale 3.00 8.00
TLJG John Gibson 4.00 10.00
TLJH Jonathan Huberdeau AS 5.00 12.00
TLJK Jordan Kyrou AS 4.00 10.00
TLJS Jared Spurgeon 4.00 10.00
TLJT John Tavares 6.00 15.00
TLJV John Vanbiesbrouck 4.00 10.00
TLKA Kirill Kaprizov 12.00 30.00
TLKF Kevin Fiala 3.00 8.00
TLLD Leon Draisaitl AS 12.00 30.00
TLMA Cale Makar AS 10.00 25.00
TLMD Matt Dumba 2.50 6.00
TLMF Marc-Andre Fleury 8.00 20.00
TLMM Mitch Marner 6.00 15.00
TLMS Mats Sundin 4.00 10.00
TLMT Matthew Tkachuk 8.00 20.00
TLMZ Mats Zuccarello 4.00 10.00
TLPR Chris Pronger 4.00 10.00
TLRJ Roman Josi AS 4.00 10.00
TLRS Ryan Suter 3.00 8.00
TLSB Sergei Bobrovsky 6.00 15.00
TLSK Spencer Knight 4.00 10.00
TLSM Scott Mellanby 3.00 8.00
TLSN Scott Niedermayer 4.00 10.00
TLSR Sam Reinhart 8.00 20.00
TLSS Steven Stamkos AS 8.00 20.00
TLTS Teemu Selanne 8.00 20.00
TLTT Troy Terry 3.00 8.00
TLTZ Trevor Zegras 4.00 10.00
TLWN William Nylander 8.00 20.00
TLZP Zach Parise 4.00 10.00

2022-23 Black Diamond Veteran Jewels of the Draft Patch Autographs

VJDAL Alexis Lafreniere/25 50.00 125.00
VJDAS Andrei Svechnikov/25 40.00 100.00
VJDCM Connor McDavid/25 400.00 1000.00
VJDPG Philipp Grubauer/49 30.00 80.00
VJDTS Tim Stutzle/25 40.00 100.00
VJDTT Tage Thompson/49 40.00 100.00

2023-24 Black Diamond

BDBAI Aidan McDonough/349 RC 1.50 4.00
BDBAK Andrei Kuzmenko 2.00 5.00
BDBAM Auston Matthews 8.00 20.00
BDBAO Alex Ovechkin 8.00 20.00
BDBAS Andrei Svechnikov 2.50 6.00
BDBAT Alex Tuch 2.00 5.00
BDBAV Andrei Vasilevskiy 3.00 8.00
BDBBB Brent Burns 2.00 5.00
BDBBF Brock Faber/349 RC 5.00 12.00
BDBBH Bo Horvat 2.50 6.00
BDBBM Brad Marchand 4.00 10.00
BDBBO Matt Boldy 3.00 8.00
BDBBP Brayden Point 2.50 6.00
BDBBT Brady Tkachuk 3.00 8.00
BDBCB Connor Bedard/349 RC 100.00 250.00
BDBCC Cole Caufield 4.00 10.00
BDBCH Chris Chelios 2.00 5.00
BDBCK Clayton Keller 2.50 6.00
BDBCM Connor McDavid 10.00 25.00
BDBCV Carter Verhaeghe 2.00 5.00
BDBDL Devon Levi/349 RC 5.00 12.00
BDBDP David Pastrnak 5.00 12.00
BDBDU William Dufour/349 RC 1.50 4.00
BDBDW Dustin Wolf/349 RC 6.00 15.00
BDBEA Egor Afanasyev/349 RC 2.00 5.00
BDBED Simon Edvinsson/349 RC 4.00 10.00
BDBEK Erik Karlsson 2.50 6.00
BDBEL Eric Lindros 3.00 8.00
BDBEM Evgeni Malkin 4.00 10.00
BDBEP Elias Pettersson 3.00 8.00
BDBFP Felix Potvin 3.00 8.00
BDBHA Carter Hart 2.00 5.00
BDBHI Akito Hirose/349 RC 1.50 4.00
BDBIS Ilya Sorokin 3.00 8.00
BDBJE Jack Eichel 3.00 8.00
BDBJH Jack Hughes 5.00 12.00
BDBJK Jordan Kyrou 2.00 5.00
BDBJM Josh Morrissey 2.50 6.00
BDBJO Jake Oettinger 3.00 8.00
BDBJP Jiri Patera/349 RC 3.00 8.00
BDBJQ Jonathan Quick 2.50 6.00
BDBJR Jason Robertson 3.00 8.00
BDBJS Juuse Saros 2.50 6.00
BDBKC Kyle Connor 3.00 8.00
BDBKF Kevin Fiala 1.50 4.00
BDBKK Kirill Kaprizov 6.00 15.00
BDBKM Kirill Marchenko 2.50 6.00
BDBKN Matthew Knies/349 RC 8.00 20.00
BDBKO Anze Kopitar 3.00 8.00
BDBKU Evgeny Kuznetsov 2.50 6.00
BDBLA Pat LaFontaine 2.00 5.00
BDBLD Leon Draisaitl 6.00 15.00
BDBLE Luke Evangelista/349 RC 3.00 8.00
BDBLH Luke Hughes/349 RC 6.00 15.00
BDBLR Lukas Reichel 2.00 5.00
BDBMA Cale Makar 5.00 12.00
BDBMB Matty Beniers 2.50 6.00
BDBMC Matthew Coronato/349 RC 3.00 8.00
BDBME Mark Messier 4.00 10.00
BDBMK Marco Kasper/349 RC 5.00 12.00
BDBMM Mitch Marner 3.00 8.00
BDBMO Mike Modano 3.00 8.00
BDBMR Mikko Rantanen 5.00 12.00
BDBMS Moritz Seider 2.50 6.00
BDBMT Matthew Tkachuk 4.00 10.00
BDBNK Nazem Kadri 2.50 6.00
BDBNN Nikita Nesterenko/349 RC 2.00 5.00
BDBNS Nick Suzuki 4.00 10.00
BDBOB Owen Beck/349 RC 3.00 8.00
BDBPA Brad Park 1.50 4.00
BDBPB Pavel Buchnevich 1.50 4.00
BDBPE Jakob Pelletier/349 RC 2.50 6.00
BDBPG Philipp Grubauer 2.00 5.00
BDBPK Patrick Kane 4.00 10.00
BDBPL Patrik Laine 2.50 6.00
BDBRA Lucas Raymond 3.00 8.00
BDBRG Ridly Greig/349 RC 3.00 8.00
BDBRJ Roman Josi 2.00 5.00
BDBRO Lukas Rousek/349 RC 1.50 4.00
BDBSB Samuel Bolduc/349 RC 2.00 5.00
BDBSC Sidney Crosby 8.00 20.00
BDBSE Teemu Selanne 4.00 10.00
BDBSF Sean Farrell/349 RC 2.00 5.00
BDBSH Igor Shesterkin 4.00 10.00
BDBSJ Seth Jones 2.00 5.00
BDBSS Stanislav Svozil/349 RC 1.50 4.00
BDBSY Steve Yzerman 5.00 12.00
BDBTF Tyson Foerster/349 RC 4.00 10.00
BDBTH Tage Thompson 2.50 6.00
BDBTK Tye Kartye/349 RC 3.00 8.00
BDBTM Timo Meier 2.00 5.00
BDBTR Tristen Robins/349 RC 2.00 5.00
BDBTS Tim Stutzle 2.50 6.00
BDBTT Tyler Toffoli 2.00 5.00
BDBTZ Trevor Zegras 2.00 5.00
BDBVD Vincent Desharnais/349 RC 2.50 6.00
BDBVI Vincent Iorio/349 RC 2.00 5.00
BDBWC Will Cuylle/349 RC 3.00 8.00
BDBWG Wayne Gretzky 12.00 30.00
BDBYA Yaroslav Askarov/349 RC 5.00 12.00
BDRAD Arnaud Durandeau/99 RC 20.00 50.00
BDRAF Adam Fantilli/99 RC 60.00 150.00
BDRAH Akito Hirose/99 15.00 40.00
BDRAL Alex Laferriere/99 RC 30.00 80.00
BDRAM Aidan McDonough/99 15.00 40.00
BDRBF Brock Faber/99 50.00 120.00
BDRBM Bobby McMann/99 RC 30.00 80.00
BDRBS Billy Sweezey/99 RC 20.00 50.00
BDRCB Connor Bedard/99 500.00 1200.00
BDRCG Cole Guttman/99 RC 20.00 50.00
BDRCO Logan Cooley/99 RC 60.00 150.00
BDRCZ Connor Zary/99 RC 40.00 100.00
BDRDG Danil Gushchin/99 RC 20.00 50.00
BDRDH Drew Helleson/99 RC 20.00 50.00
BDRDL Devon Levi/99 50.00 125.00
BDRDW Dustin Wolf/99 60.00 150.00
BDREA Egor Afanasyev/99 20.00 50.00
BDRED Elliot Desnoyers/99 RC 20.00 50.00
BDRGR Jonathan Gruden/99 RC 20.00 50.00
BDRGU David Gust/99 RC 20.00 50.00
BDRHT Henry Thrun/99 RC 20.00 50.00
BDRJL Jackson LaCombe/99 RC 20.00 50.00
BDRJP Jakob Pelletier/99 25.00 60.00
BDRKA Marco Kasper/99 50.00 125.00
BDRKE Milos Kelemen/99 RC 20.00 50.00
BDRKK Kevin Korchinski/99 RC 30.00 80.00
BDRKL Tyler Kleven/99 RC 20.00 50.00
BDRKN Matthew Knies/99 80.00 200.00
BDRLC Leo Carlsson/99 RC 60.00 150.00
BDRLE Luke Evangelista/99 30.00 80.00
BDRLH Luke Hughes/99 60.00 150.00
BDRLI Jake Livingstone/99 RC 20.00 50.00
BDRLM Leevi Merilainen/99 RC 20.00 50.00
BDRLR Lukas Rousek/99 15.00 40.00
BDRMC Matthew Coronato/99 30.00 80.00
BDRMK Michael Kesselring/99 RC 20.00 50.00
BDRMM Matt Murray/99 RC 20.00 50.00
BDRMP Matthew Poitras/99 RC 40.00 100.00
BDRMS Matt Savoie/99 RC 40.00 100.00
BDRNN Nikita Nesterenko/99 20.00 50.00
BDROB Owen Beck/99 30.00 80.00
BDROE Olle Eriksson Ek/99 RC 20.00 50.00
BDRPA Jiri Patera/99 30.00 80.00
BDRPM Pavel Mintyukov/99 RC 30.00 80.00
BDRRG Ridly Greig/99 30.00 80.00
BDRSA Mackie Samoskevich/99 RC 30.00 80.00
BDRSB Samuel Bolduc/99 20.00 50.00
BDRSE Simon Edvinsson/99 40.00 100.00
BDRSF Sean Farrell/99 20.00 50.00
BDRSN Simon Nemec/99 RC 40.00 100.00
BDRSV Stanislav Svozil/99 15.00 40.00
BDRTF Tyson Foerster/99 40.00 100.00
BDRTK Tye Kartye/99 30.00 80.00
BDRTR Tristen Robins/99 20.00 50.00
BDRVI Vincent Iorio/99 20.00 50.00
BDRWC Will Cuylle/99 30.00 80.00
BDRWD William Dufour/99 15.00 40.00
BDRWK Wyatt Kaiser/99 RC 20.00 50.00
BDRYA Yaroslav Askarov/99 50.00 125.00
BDRZA Zach Benson/99 RC 30.00 80.00

2023-24 Black Diamond Blue

*BLUE/25: .75X TO 2X BASIC
BDBCB Connor Bedard 300.00 800.00

2023-24 Black Diamond Diamond Relics Purple

*PURPLE/25: .6X TO 1.5X BASIC
BDRCB Connor Bedard 2500.00 6000.00

2023-24 Black Diamond Diamond Relics Ruby

*RUBY/49: .5X TO 1.2X BASIC
BDRCB Connor Bedard 800.00 2000.00

2023-24 Black Diamond Red

*RED/75: .5X TO 1.2X BASIC
BDBCB Connor Bedard 150.00 400.00

2023-24 Black Diamond Band of Color

BCAM Auston Matthews 150.00 400.00
BCAO Alex Ovechkin 150.00 400.00
BCCH Connor Hellebuyck 80.00 200.00
BCCM Cale Makar 100.00 250.00
BCJH Jack Hughes 100.00 250.00
BCKK Kirill Kaprizov 125.00 300.00
BCLD Leon Draisaitl 125.00 300.00
BCMA Mitch Marner 60.00 150.00
BCMB Mike Bossy 40.00 100.00
BCMC Connor McDavid 200.00 500.00
BCML Mario Lemieux 150.00 400.00
BCMM Mark Messier 80.00 200.00
BCMR Maurice Richard 80.00 200.00
BCMS Moritz Seider 50.00 125.00
BCNM Nathan MacKinnon 150.00 400.00
BCPB Patrice Bergeron 50.00 125.00
BCPK Patrick Kane 80.00 200.00
BCSA Borje Salming 40.00 100.00
BCSC Sidney Crosby 150.00 400.00
BCSU Mats Sundin 40.00 100.00
BCSY Steve Yzerman 100.00 250.00
BCTE Tony Esposito 40.00 100.00
BCTS Teemu Selanne 80.00 200.00
BCTT Tage Thompson 50.00 125.00
BCWG Wayne Gretzky 250.00 600.00

2023-24 Black Diamond Band of Color Rookies

BCRAF Adam Fantilli 125.00 300.00
BCRDL Devon Levi 100.00 250.00
BCRKN Matthew Knies 150.00 400.00
BCRLC Logan Cooley 120.00 300.00
BCRLH Luke Hughes 125.00 300.00
BCRMC Matthew Coronato 60.00 150.00
BCRMK Marco Kasper 100.00 250.00
BCRMS Matt Savoie 80.00 200.00
BCROB Owen Beck 60.00 150.00
BCRRG Ridly Greig 60.00 150.00
BCRSE Simon Edvinsson 80.00 200.00
BCRSN Simon Nemec 80.00 200.00
BCRTF Tyson Foerster 80.00 200.00
BCRYA Yaroslav Askarov 100.00 250.00

2023-24 Black Diamond Cup Winner Patches

*GOLD: 1X TO 2.5X BASIC
CWAK Anze Kopitar 6.00 15.00
CWCM Cale Makar 10.00 25.00
CWDG Doug Gilmour 5.00 12.00
CWJK Jari Kurri 4.00 10.00
CWJM Joe Mullen 4.00 10.00
CWJP Jacques Plante 4.00 10.00
CWJT Jonathan Toews 6.00 15.00
CWMF Marc-Andre Fleury 15.00 40.00
CWMR Mark Recchi 4.00 10.00
CWPB Patrice Bergeron 5.00 12.00
CWPF Peter Forsberg 8.00 20.00
CWRG Ryan Getzlaf 4.00 10.00
CWSY Steve Yzerman 10.00 25.00
CWSZ Sergei Zubov 3.00 8.00

2023-24 Black Diamond Diamonation Rookies

DRAH Akito Hirose 2.00 5.00
DRBF Brock Faber 6.00 15.00
DRDL Devon Levi 6.00 15.00
DRDW Dustin Wolf 8.00 20.00
DRJL Jackson LaCombe 2.50 6.00
DRJP Jakob Pelletier 3.00 8.00
DRKN Matthew Knies 10.00 25.00
DRLE Luke Evangelista 4.00 10.00
DRLH Luke Hughes 8.00 20.00
DRMC Matthew Coronato 4.00 10.00
DRMK Marco Kasper 6.00 15.00
DROB Owen Beck 4.00 10.00
DRRG Ridly Greig 4.00 10.00
DRSB Samuel Bolduc 2.50 6.00
DRSE Simon Edvinsson 5.00 12.00
DRTF Tyson Foerster 5.00 12.00
DRTK Tye Kartye 4.00 10.00
DRWC Will Cuylle 4.00 10.00
DRWD William Dufour 2.00 5.00
DRYA Yaroslav Askarov 6.00 15.00

2023-24 Black Diamond Diamond Debut Relics

DDBF Brock Faber 6.00 15.00
DDDW Dustin Wolf 8.00 20.00
DDJP Jakob Pelletier 3.00 8.00
DDKA Marco Kasper 6.00 15.00
DDLE Luke Evangelista 4.00 10.00
DDLH Luke Hughes 8.00 20.00
DDLR Lukas Rousek 2.00 5.00
DDMC Matthew Coronato 4.00 10.00
DDMK Matthew Knies 10.00 25.00
DDOB Owen Beck 4.00 10.00
DDRG Ridly Greig 4.00 10.00
DDSE Simon Edvinsson 5.00 12.00
DDSF Sean Farrell 2.50 6.00
DDTF Tyson Foerster 5.00 12.00
DDWD William Dufour 2.00 5.00

2023-24 Black Diamond Diamond Debut Relics Patch Autographs

DDBF Brock Faber/49 50.00 125.00
DDDW Dustin Wolf/49 60.00 150.00
DDKA Marco Kasper/49 50.00 125.00
DDLE Luke Evangelista/49 30.00 80.00
DDLH Luke Hughes/25 60.00 150.00
DDLR Lukas Rousek/49 15.00 40.00
DDMC Matthew Coronato/49 30.00 80.00
DDMK Matthew Knies/25 80.00 200.00
DDOB Owen Beck/49 30.00 80.00
DDRG Ridly Greig/49 30.00 80.00
DDSE Simon Edvinsson/25 40.00 100.00
DDSF Sean Farrell/49 20.00 50.00
DDTF Tyson Foerster/49 40.00 100.00
DDWD William Dufour/49 15.00 40.00

2023-24 Black Diamond Diamond Facet

DFBO Matt Boldy 4.00 10.00
DFCG Claude Giroux 2.50 6.00
DFDL Dylan Larkin 3.00 8.00
DFEK Erik Karlsson 3.00 8.00
DFEM Evgeni Malkin 5.00 12.00
DFJP Jakob Pelletier 3.00 8.00
DFJT Jonathan Toews 4.00 10.00
DFLE Devon Levi 6.00 15.00
DFLH Luke Hughes 8.00 20.00
DFLU Linus Ullmark 2.50 6.00
DFMB Mathew Barzal 3.00 8.00
DFMK Matthew Knies 10.00 25.00
DFOB Owen Beck 4.00 10.00
DFPL Patrik Laine 3.00 8.00
DFQH Quinn Hughes 6.00 15.00
DFRT Robert Thomas 2.50 6.00
DFSA Sebastian Aho 4.00 10.00
DFSE Simon Edvinsson 5.00 12.00
DFSF Sean Farrell 2.50 6.00
DFTF Tyson Foerster 5.00 12.00

2023-24 Black Diamond Diamond Futures

*PURPLE/49: 1X TO 2.5X BASIC
BDFBF Brock Faber 5.00 12.00
BDFDL Devon Levi 5.00 12.00
BDFDW Dustin Wolf 6.00 15.00
BDFJP Jakob Pelletier 2.50 6.00
BDFKA Tye Kartye 3.00 8.00
BDFKN Matthew Knies 8.00 20.00
BDFLE Luke Evangelista 3.00 8.00
BDFLH Luke Hughes 6.00 15.00
BDFMC Matthew Coronato 3.00 8.00
BDFMK Marco Kasper 5.00 12.00
BDFOB Owen Beck 3.00 8.00
BDFRG Ridly Greig 3.00 8.00
BDFSE Simon Edvinsson 4.00 10.00
BDFSF Sean Farrell 2.00 5.00
BDFTF Tyson Foerster 4.00 10.00
BDFWC Will Cuylle 3.00 8.00
BDFYA Yaroslav Askarov 5.00 12.00

2023-24 Black Diamond Diamond Futures Autographs

BDFAH Akito Hirose/99 10.00 25.00
BDFAM Aidan McDonough/99 10.00 25.00
BDFBF Brock Faber/99 30.00 80.00
BDFBM Bobby McMann/99 20.00 50.00
BDFBS Billy Sweezey/99 12.00 30.00
BDFDW Dustin Wolf/99 40.00 100.00
BDFKA Tye Kartye/99 20.00 50.00
BDFKN Matthew Knies/35 40.00 100.00
BDFKO Joona Koppanen/99 10.00 25.00
BDFLE Luke Evangelista/99 20.00 50.00
BDFLI Jake Livingstone/99 12.00 30.00
BDFLP Luke Philp/99 12.00 30.00
BDFLR Lukas Rousek/99 10.00 25.00
BDFMC Matthew Coronato/65 20.00 50.00
BDFMK Marco Kasper/65 30.00 80.00
BDFMM Matt Murray/99 12.00 30.00
BDFNN Nikita Nesterenko/99 12.00 30.00
BDFOB Owen Beck/65 20.00 50.00
BDFPA Jiri Patera/99 20.00 50.00
BDFRG Ridly Greig/99 20.00 50.00
BDFSB Samuel Bolduc/65 12.00 30.00
BDFSE Simon Edvinsson/35 30.00 80.00
BDFSF Sean Farrell/99 12.00 30.00
BDFTF Tyson Foerster/65 25.00 60.00
BDFTK Tyler Kleven/99 12.00 30.00
BDFTR Tristen Robins/99 12.00 30.00
BDFVD Vincent Desharnais/99 15.00 40.00
BDFVI Vincent Iorio/99 12.00 30.00
BDFWD William Dufour/99 10.00 25.00
BDFYA Yaroslav Askarov/65 50.00 125.00

2023-24 Black Diamond Diamond Futures Premium Relic Autographs

BDFAH Akito Hirose 15.00 40.00
BDFAM Aidan McDonough 15.00 40.00
BDFBF Brock Faber 50.00 120.00
BDFBM Bobby McMann 30.00 80.00
BDFBS Billy Sweezey 20.00 50.00
BDFDW Dustin Wolf 60.00 150.00
BDFKA Tye Kartye 30.00 80.00
BDFKN Matthew Knies 80.00 200.00
BDFKO Joona Koppanen 15.00 40.00
BDFLE Luke Evangelista 30.00 80.00
BDFLH Luke Hughes 60.00 150.00
BDFLI Jake Livingstone 20.00 50.00
BDFLP Luke Philp 20.00 50.00
BDFLR Lukas Rousek 15.00 40.00
BDFMC Matthew Coronato 30.00 80.00
BDFMK Marco Kasper 50.00 125.00
BDFMM Matt Murray 20.00 50.00
BDFNN Nikita Nesterenko 20.00 50.00
BDFOB Owen Beck 30.00 80.00
BDFPA Jiri Patera 30.00 80.00
BDFRG Ridly Greig 30.00 80.00
BDFSB Samuel Bolduc 20.00 50.00
BDFSE Simon Edvinsson 40.00 100.00
BDFSF Sean Farrell 20.00 50.00
BDFSS Stanislav Svozil 15.00 40.00
BDFTF Tyson Foerster 40.00 100.00
BDFTK Tyler Kleven 20.00 50.00
BDFTR Tristen Robins 20.00 50.00
BDFVD Vincent Desharnais 25.00 60.00
BDFVI Vincent Iorio 20.00 50.00
BDFWC Will Cuylle 30.00 80.00
BDFWD William Dufour 15.00 40.00
BDFYA Yaroslav Askarov 50.00 125.00

2023-24 Black Diamond Diamond Gallery

DGAK Adrian Kempe 3.00 8.00
DGAM Auston Matthews 12.00 30.00
DGAO Alex Ovechkin 12.00 30.00
DGAV Andrei Vasilevskiy 5.00 12.00
DGCC Cole Caufield 6.00 15.00
DGCM Connor McDavid 15.00 40.00
DGDL Devon Levi 8.00 20.00
DGJP Jakob Pelletier 4.00 10.00
DGJS Juuse Saros 4.00 10.00
DGKN Matthew Knies 12.00 30.00
DGLH Luke Hughes 10.00 25.00
DGMA Cale Makar 8.00 20.00
DGMC Matthew Coronato 5.00 12.00
DGMH Miro Heiskanen 4.00 10.00
DGMK Marco Kasper 8.00 20.00
DGMM Mason McTavish 3.00 8.00
DGMS Moritz Seider 4.00 10.00
DGRG Ridly Greig 5.00 12.00
DGSE Simon Edvinsson 6.00 15.00
DGYA Yaroslav Askarov 8.00 20.00

2023-24 Black Diamond Diamond Legends

*PURPLE/49: .75X TO 2X BASIC
BDLAG Adam Graves 2.00 5.00
BDLBN Bernie Nicholls 2.00 5.00
BDLBS Brendan Shanahan 2.50 6.00
BDLBT Bryan Trottier 2.50 6.00
BDLEL Eric Lindros 4.00 10.00
BDLFP Felix Potvin 4.00 10.00
BDLHL Henrik Lundqvist 6.00 15.00
BDLJI Jarome Iginla 3.00 8.00
BDLJK Jari Kurri 2.50 6.00
BDLKT Keith Tkachuk 2.50 6.00
BDLLR Larry Robinson 2.50 6.00
BDLMB Martin Brodeur 6.00 15.00
BDLML Mario Lemieux 10.00 25.00
BDLMM Mike Modano 4.00 10.00
BDLPE Phil Esposito 4.00 10.00
BDLPL Pat LaFontaine 2.50 6.00
BDLPR Patrick Roy 6.00 15.00
BDLRF Ron Francis 3.00 8.00
BDLWG Wayne Gretzky 15.00 40.00
BDLYC Yvan Cournoyer 2.50 6.00

2023-24 Black Diamond Diamond Legends Autographs

BDLAG Adam Graves/25 15.00 40.00
BDLBN Bernie Nicholls/25 15.00 40.00
BDLBT Bryan Trottier/25 20.00 50.00
BDLHL Henrik Lundqvist/25 50.00 125.00
BDLJK Jari Kurri/25 20.00 50.00
BDLKT Keith Tkachuk/25 20.00 50.00
BDLLR Larry Robinson/25 20.00 50.00
BDLMM Mike Modano/25 30.00 80.00
BDLYC Yvan Cournoyer/25 20.00 50.00

2023-24 Black Diamond Diamond Might

DMAF Adam Fox 4.00 10.00
DMBB Brent Burns 3.00 8.00
DMCK Clayton Keller 4.00 10.00
DMCM Connor McDavid 15.00 40.00
DMDL Devon Levi 8.00 20.00
DMDP David Pastrnak 8.00 20.00
DMIS Ilya Sorokin 5.00 12.00
DMKA Marco Kasper 8.00 20.00
DMKD Kirby Dach 3.00 8.00
DMKF Kevin Fiala 2.50 6.00
DMLE Luke Evangelista 5.00 12.00
DMLH Luke Hughes 10.00 25.00
DMMB Matty Beniers 4.00 10.00
DMMC Matthew Coronato 5.00 12.00
DMMK Matthew Knies 12.00 30.00
DMML Mario Lemieux 12.00 30.00
DMMM Mitch Marner 5.00 12.00
DMNM Nathan MacKinnon 12.00 30.00
DMRG Ridly Greig 5.00 12.00
DMSC Sidney Crosby 12.00 30.00
DMSE Simon Edvinsson 6.00 15.00
DMSY Steve Yzerman 8.00 20.00
DMTF Tyson Foerster 6.00 15.00
DMYA Yaroslav Askarov 8.00 20.00

2023-24 Black Diamond Diamond Mine Dual Relics

DMDRBK K.Kaprizov/M.Boldy 12.00 30.00
DMDRBM B.Marchand/P.Bergeron 8.00 20.00
DMDRCP K.Connor/C.Perfetti 6.00 15.00
DMDRCS C.Caufield/J.Slafkovsky 8.00 20.00
DMDRKO A.Ovechkin/E.Kuznetsov 15.00 40.00
DMDRLS M.Seider/D.Larkin 5.00 12.00
DMDRMB M.Beniers/J.McCann 5.00 12.00
DMDRMH J.Hughes/D.Hamilton 10.00 25.00
DMDRNM W.Nylander/M.Marner 8.00 20.00
DMDRSK C.Keller/N.Schmaltz 5.00 12.00

2023-24 Black Diamond Diamond Mine Relics

*PREMIUM/25: 1X TO 2.5X BASIC
DMRAB Aleksander Barkov 4.00 10.00
DMRAF Adam Fox 3.00 8.00
DMRBS Brendan Shanahan 2.50 6.00
DMRCH Connor Hellebuyck 5.00 12.00
DMREP Elias Pettersson 4.00 10.00
DMRFF Filip Forsberg 4.00 10.00
DMRJM Jacob Markstrom 2.50 6.00
DMRJS Joe Sakic 5.00 12.00
DMRLD Leon Draisaitl 8.00 20.00
DMRMH Miro Heiskanen 3.00 8.00
DMRNK Nikita Kucherov 5.00 12.00
DMRNS Nick Suzuki 5.00 12.00
DMROP Owen Power 2.50 6.00
DMRPL Patrik Laine 3.00 8.00
DMRTK Travis Konecny 2.50 6.00
DMRZH Zach Hyman 4.00 10.00

2023-24 Black Diamond Diamond Mine Triple Relics

DMTRHHH Hughes/Hughes/Hughes 20.00 50.00
DMTRJSF Josi/Saros/Forsberg 10.00 25.00
DMTRKHT Toffoli/Huberdeau/Kadri 8.00 20.00
DMTRMTM Matthews/Tavares/Marner 25.0060.00
DMTRSME Eichel/Stone Marchessault 10.00 25.00
DMTRTDC Thompson/Dahlin/Cozens 8.00 20.00
DMTRTTT Tkachuk/Tkachuk/Tkachuk 12.0030.00

2023-24 Black Diamond Diamond Plate Rookie Autographs

*SPECTRUM/25: .75X TO 2X BASIC
DPRAD Arnaud Durandeau/149 8.00 20.00
DPRBF Brock Faber/99 20.00 50.00
DPRDW Dustin Wolf/99 25.00 60.00
DPRLE Luke Evangelista/99 12.00 30.00
DPRLH Luke Hughes/25 100.00 250.00
DPRLR Lukas Rousek/149 6.00 15.00
DPRMC Matthew Coronato/49 12.00 30.00
DPRMK Marco Kasper/49 20.00 50.00
DPROB Owen Beck/99 12.00 30.00
DPRSE Simon Edvinsson/25 30.00 80.00
DPRSF Sean Farrell/99 8.00 20.00
DPRTF Tyson Foerster/99 15.00 40.00
DPRVD Vincent Desharnais/149 10.00 25.00
DPRVI Vincent Iorio/149 8.00 20.00
DPRWD William Dufour/149 6.00 15.00

2023-24 Black Diamond Diamond Stars

*PURPLE/49: .75X TO 2X BASIC
BDSAK Anze Kopitar 3.00 8.00
BDSAL Anton Lundell 2.00 5.00
BDSAM Auston Matthews 8.00 20.00
BDSAO Alex Ovechkin 8.00 20.00
BDSBB Brent Burns 2.00 5.00
BDSBE Matty Beniers 2.50 6.00
BDSBG Brendan Gallagher 2.00 5.00
BDSBH Bo Horvat 2.50 6.00
BDSBT Brady Tkachuk 3.00 8.00
BDSCM Connor McDavid 10.00 25.00
BDSCS Chandler Stephenson 1.50 4.00
BDSDC Dylan Cozens 2.00 5.00
BDSDK Darcy Kuemper 2.00 5.00
BDSEB Jordan Eberle 2.00 5.00
BDSHA Brandon Hagel 1.50 4.00
BDSIS Ilya Sorokin 3.00 8.00
BDSJA Jacob Markstrom 2.00 5.00
BDSJE Jack Eichel 3.00 8.00
BDSJG John Gibson 2.00 5.00
BDSJM J.T. Miller 2.50 6.00
BDSJO Jake Oettinger 3.00 8.00
BDSJS Juuse Saros 2.50 6.00
BDSKF Kevin Fiala 1.50 4.00
BDSKM K'Andre Miller 1.50 4.00
BDSMA Cale Makar 5.00 12.00
BDSMB Michael Bunting 2.00 5.00
BDSMD Matt Duchene 2.00 5.00
BDSMR Mikko Rantanen 5.00 12.00
BDSMT Matthew Tkachuk 4.00 10.00
BDSNE Nikolaj Ehlers 2.00 5.00
BDSNS Nick Suzuki 4.00 10.00
BDSQB Quinton Byfield 2.50 6.00
BDSRH Roope Hintz 2.50 6.00
BDSSA Sebastian Aho 3.00 8.00
BDSSC Sidney Crosby 8.00 20.00
BDSTO Tyler Toffoli 2.00 5.00
BDSTS Tim Stutzle 2.50 6.00
BDSTT Tage Thompson 2.50 6.00
BDSTW Tom Wilson 2.00 5.00
BDSZH Zach Hyman 3.00 8.00

2023-24 Black Diamond Diamond Stars Autographs

BDSAL Anton Lundell/25 15.00 40.00
BDSBB Brent Burns/25 15.00 40.00
BDSBE Matty Beniers/25 20.00 50.00
BDSBG Brendan Gallagher/25 15.00 40.00
BDSBT Brady Tkachuk/25 25.00 60.00
BDSCS Chandler Stephenson/25 12.00 30.00
BDSDC Dylan Cozens/25 15.00 40.00
BDSEB Jordan Eberle/25 15.00 40.00
BDSIS Ilya Sorokin/25 25.00 60.00
BDSJE Jack Eichel/25 25.00 60.00
BDSJG John Gibson/25 15.00 40.00
BDSJO Jake Oettinger/25 25.00 60.00
BDSJS Juuse Saros/25 20.00 50.00
BDSKF Kevin Fiala/25 12.00 30.00
BDSKM K'Andre Miller/25 12.00 30.00
BDSMB Michael Bunting/25 15.00 40.00
BDSMD Matt Duchene/25 15.00 40.00
BDSMR Mikko Rantanen/25 40.00 100.00
BDSTO Tyler Toffoli/25 15.00 40.00
BDSTS Tim Stutzle/25 20.00 50.00

2023-24 Black Diamond Diamond Stars Premium Relic Autographs

BDSAL Anton Lundell/25 20.00 50.00
BDSBB Brent Burns/25 20.00 50.00
BDSBE Matty Beniers/25 25.00 60.00
BDSBG Brendan Gallagher/25 20.00 50.00
BDSBT Brady Tkachuk/25 30.00 80.00
BDSCS Chandler Stephenson/25 15.00 40.00
BDSDC Dylan Cozens/25 20.00 50.00
BDSED Jordan Eberle/25 20.00 50.00
BDSIS Ilya Sorokin/25 30.00 80.00
BDSJA Jacob Markstrom/25 20.00 50.00
BDSJE Jack Eichel/25 30.00 80.00
BDSJG John Gibson/25 20.00 50.00
BDSJO Jake Oettinger/25 40.00 100.00
BDSJS Juuse Saros/25 25.00 60.00
BDSKF Kevin Fiala/25 12.00 30.00
BDSKM K'Andre Miller/25 15.00 40.00
BDSMB Michael Bunting/25 20.00 50.00
BDSMD Matt Duchene/25 20.00 50.00
BDSMR Mikko Rantanen/25 50.00 125.00
BDSNS Nick Suzuki/25 40.00 100.00
BDSTO Tyler Toffoli/25 20.00 50.00
BDSTS Tim Stutzle/25 25.00 60.00

2023-24 Black Diamond Gemography

GAK Andrei Kuzmenko 25.00 60.00
GBB Brent Burns 25.00 60.00
GCB Connor Bedard 1200.00 3000.00
GCC Chris Chelios 25.00 60.00
GCM Connor McDavid 250.00 600.00
GEP Elias Pettersson 40.00 100.00
GIS Ilya Sorokin 40.00 100.00
GJH Jack Hughes 60.00 150.00
GLC Logan Cooley 80.00 200.00
GMK Matthew Knies 80.00 200.00
GMM Mike Modano 40.00 100.00
GMR Mikko Rantanen 60.00 150.00
GTM Timo Meier 25.00 60.00
GTS Tim Stutzle 30.00 80.00
GWG Wayne Gretzky 250.00 600.00

2023-24 Black Diamond Glistening Graphs

GGGL Gabriel Landeskog 15.00 40.00
GGOP Owen Power 12.00 30.00
GGPC Paul Coffey 12.00 30.00
GGRB Rod Brind'Amour 12.00 30.00
GGYC Yvan Cournoyer 20.00 50.00

2023-24 Black Diamond Jewels of the Draft Patch Autographs

JDAM Aidan McDonough/99 15.00 40.00
JDBF Brock Faber/99 50.00 120.00
JDCB Connor Bedard/49 2000.00 5000.00
JDCZ Connor Zary/49 40.00 100.00
JDDW Dustin Wolf/49 60.00 150.00
JDJK Joona Koppanen/99 15.00 40.00
JDKN Matthew Knies/49 60.00 150.00
JDLE Luke Evangelista/49 30.00 80.00
JDLH Luke Hughes/49 60.00 150.00
JDLR Lukas Rousek/99 15.00 40.00
JDMC Matthew Coronato/49 30.00 80.00
JDMK Marco Kasper/49 50.00 125.00
JDMS Matt Savoie/49 40.00 100.00
JDNN Nikita Nesterenko/99 20.00 50.00
JDOB Owen Beck/49 30.00 80.00
JDRG Ridly Greig/49 30.00 80.00
JDSE Simon Edvinsson/49 40.00 100.00
JDSF Sean Farrell/99 20.00 50.00
JDSS Stanislav Svozil/99 15.00 40.00
JDTF Tyson Foerster/49 40.00 100.00
JDTK Tyler Kleven/99 20.00 50.00
JDTR Tristen Robins/99 20.00 50.00
JDVD Vincent Desharnais/99 25.00 60.00
JDVI Vincent Iorio/99 20.00 50.00
JDWC Will Cuylle/99 30.00 80.00
JDWD William Dufour/99 15.00 40.00
JDYA Yaroslav Askarov/49 50.00 125.00

2023-24 Black Diamond Pure Black Autographs

BDBAI Aidan McDonough/99 12.00 30.00
BDBAK Andrei Kuzmenko/25 15.00 40.00
BDBAS Andrei Svechnikov/25 20.00 50.00
BDBAT Alex Tuch/49 15.00 40.00
BDBAV Andrei Vasilevskiy/25 25.00 60.00
BDBBB Brent Burns/25 15.00 40.00
BDBBF Brock Faber/99 40.00 100.00
BDBBM Brad Marchand/25 30.00 80.00
BDBBO Matt Boldy/25 25.00 60.00
BDBBT Brady Tkachuk/25 25.00 60.00
BDBCB Connor Bedard/49 800.00 2000.00
BDBCC Cole Caufield/25 30.00 80.00
BDBDU William Dufour/49 12.00 30.00
BDBDW Dustin Wolf/99 50.00 125.00
BDBED Simon Edvinsson/49 30.00 80.00
BDBEP Elias Pettersson/49 25.00 60.00
BDBHA Carter Hart/25 15.00 40.00
BDBHI Akito Hirose/99 12.00 30.00
BDBIS Ilya Sorokin/25 25.00 60.00
BDBJH Jack Hughes/49 40.00 100.00
BDBJK Jordan Kyrou/25 15.00 40.00
BDBJM Josh Morrissey/49 20.00 50.00
BDBJO Jake Oettinger/25 25.00 60.00
BDBJP Jiri Patera/99 25.00 60.00
BDBJQ Jonathan Quick/25 20.00 50.00
BDBJS Juuse Saros/25 20.00 50.00
BDBKC Kyle Connor/25 25.00 60.00
BDBKF Kevin Fiala/25 12.00 30.00
BDBKM Kirill Marchenko/49 20.00 50.00
BDBKN Matthew Knies/49 60.00 150.00
BDBKU Evgeny Kuznetsov/49 20.00 50.00
BDBLE Luke Evangelista/99 25.00 60.00
BDBLH Luke Hughes/49 50.00 125.00
BDBLR Lukas Reichel/99 15.00 40.00
BDBMB Matty Beniers/25 20.00 50.00
BDBMC Matthew Coronato/99 25.00 60.00
BDBMK Marco Kasper/49 40.00 100.00
BDBMR Mikko Rantanen/25 40.00 100.00
BDBNN Nikita Nesterenko/99 15.00 40.00
BDBOB Owen Beck/99 25.00 60.00
BDBRG Ridly Greig/99 25.00 60.00
BDBRO Lukas Rousek/99 12.00 30.00
BDBSB Samuel Bolduc/99 12.00 30.00
BDBSF Sean Farrell/99 25.00 60.00
BDBTF Tyson Foerster/99 30.00 80.00
BDBTK Tye Kartye/99 25.00 60.00
BDBTM Timo Meier/25 25.00 60.00
BDBTR Tristen Robins/99 15.00 40.00
BDBTS Tim Stutzle/25 20.00 50.00
BDBTT Tyler Toffoli/49 15.00 40.00
BDBVD Vincent Desharnais/99 20.00 50.00
BDBVI Vincent Iorio/99 15.00 40.00
BDBYA Yaroslav Askarov/49 40.00 100.00

2023-24 Black Diamond Pure Black Premium Relics

BDBAI Aidan McDonough/50 6.00 15.00
BDBAS Andrei Svechnikov/25 10.00 25.00
BDBAV Andrei Vasilevskiy/25 12.00 30.00
BDBBB Brent Burns/25 8.00 20.00
BDBBF Brock Faber/50 20.00 50.00
BDBBM Brad Marchand/25 20.00 50.00
BDBBO Matt Boldy/25 12.00 30.00
BDBBP Brayden Point/25 20.00 50.00
BDBBT Brady Tkachuk/25 20.00 50.00
BDBCC Cole Caufield/25 15.00 40.00
BDBCK Clayton Keller/25 10.00 25.00
BDBCV Carter Verhaeghe/25 8.00 20.00
BDBDU William Dufour/50 6.00 15.00
BDBDW Dustin Wolf/25 25.00 60.00
BDBEA Egor Afanasyev/50 8.00 20.00
BDBED Simon Edvinsson/25 12.00 30.00
BDBEK Erik Karlsson/25 10.00 25.00
BDBEM Evgeni Malkin/25 20.00 50.00
BDBEP Elias Pettersson/25 12.00 30.00
BDBHA Carter Hart/25 8.00 20.00
BDBHI Akito Hirose/99 6.00 15.00
BDBIS Ilya Sorokin/25 12.00 30.00
BDBJE Jack Eichel/25 15.00 40.00
BDBJK Jordan Kyrou/25 8.00 20.00
BDBJO Jake Oettinger/25 12.00 30.00
BDBJP Jiri Patera/50 12.00 30.00
BDBJS Juuse Saros/25 10.00 25.00
BDBKC Kyle Connor/25 12.00 30.00
BDBKF Kevin Fiala/25 6.00 15.00
BDBKN Matthew Knies/25 30.00 80.00
BDBKO Anze Kopitar/25 12.00 30.00
BDBKU Evgeny Kuznetsov/50 10.00 25.00
BDBLE Luke Evangelista/25 12.00 30.00
BDBLH Luke Hughes/25 25.00 60.00
BDBMB Matty Beniers/25 10.00 25.00
BDBMC Matthew Coronato/25 12.00 30.00
BDBMK Marco Kasper/25 20.00 50.00
BDBMR Mikko Rantanen/25 20.00 50.00
BDBMS Moritz Seider/25 12.00 30.00
BDBMT Matthew Tkachuk/25 15.00 40.00
BDBNK Nazem Kadri/25 10.00 25.00
BDBNN Nikita Nesterenko/50 8.00 20.00
BDBNS Nick Suzuki/25 15.00 40.00
BDBOB Owen Beck/25 10.00 25.00
BDBPB Pavel Buchnevich/25 6.00 15.00
BDBPE Jakob Pelletier/25 10.00 25.00
BDBPG Philipp Grubauer/50 8.00 20.00
BDBPL Patrik Laine/25 10.00 25.00
BDBRA Lucas Raymond/25 12.00 30.00
BDBRG Ridly Greig/25 12.00 30.00
BDBRJ Roman Josi/25 8.00 20.00
BDBRO Lukas Rousek/50 6.00 15.00
BDBSB Samuel Bolduc/50 8.00 20.00
BDBSF Sean Farrell/50 8.00 20.00
BDBSH Igor Shesterkin/25 15.00 40.00
BDBSJ Seth Jones/50 8.00 20.00
BDBSS Stanislav Svozil/25 6.00 15.00
BDBTF Tyson Foerster/25 15.00 40.00
BDBTH Tage Thompson/25 10.00 25.00
BDBTK Tye Kartye/50 12.00 30.00
BDBTR Tristen Robins/50 8.00 20.00
BDBTS Tim Stutzle/25 10.00 25.00
BDBTT Tyler Toffoli/50 8.00 20.00
BDBTZ Trevor Zegras/25 8.00 20.00
BDBVD Vincent Desharnais/50 10.00 25.00
BDBVI Vincent Iorio/50 8.00 20.00
BDBWC Will Cuylle/50 12.00 30.00
BDBYA Yaroslav Askarov/25 20.00 50.00

2023-24 Black Diamond Rangers Retired Number Patches

RRNPAB Andy Bathgate 12.00 30.00
RRNPAG Adam Graves 12.00 30.00
RRNPBL Brian Leetch 12.00 30.00
RRNPEG Ed Giacomin 15.00 40.00
RRNPHL Henrik Lundqvist 30.00 80.00
RRNPJR Jean Ratelle 12.00 30.00
RRNPMM Mark Messier 30.00 80.00
RRNPMR Mike Richter 15.00 40.00
RRNPRG Rod Gilbert 15.00 40.00
RRNPVH Vic Hadfield 12.00 30.00
RRNPWG Wayne Gretzky 50.00 125.00

2023-24 Black Diamond Rangers Retired Numbers Patches Gold

RRNPHL Henrik Lundqvist AU/30 125.00 300.00
RRNPJR Jean Ratelle/19 50.00 125.00
RRNPWG Wayne Gretzky/99 60.00 150.00

2023-24 Black Diamond Rookie Gems

RGAF Adam Fantilli 8.00 20.00
RGBF Brock Faber 6.00 15.00
RGCB Connor Bedard 125.00 300.00
RGCO Matthew Coronato 4.00 10.00
RGCU Will Cuylle 4.00 10.00
RGDL Devon Levi 6.00 15.00
RGDW Dustin Wolf 8.00 20.00
RGJP Jakob Pelletier 3.00 8.00
RGKA Marco Kasper 6.00 15.00
RGKT Tye Kartye 4.00 10.00
RGLE Luke Evangelista 4.00 10.00
RGLH Luke Hughes 8.00 20.00
RGMK Matthew Knies 10.00 25.00
RGMS Matt Savoie 5.00 12.00
RGOB Owen Beck 4.00 10.00
RGRG Ridly Greig 4.00 10.00
RGSE Simon Edvinsson 5.00 12.00
RGSF Sean Farrell 2.50 6.00
RGSN Simon Nemec 8.00 20.00
RGTF Tyson Foerster 5.00 12.00
RGYA Yaroslav Askarov 6.00 15.00

2023-24 Black Diamond Rookie Gems Red

*RED/100: .75X TO 2X BASIC
RGCB Connor Bedard 500.00 1200.00

2023-24 Black Diamond Rookie Gems Signatures

RGAH Akito Hirose/99 12.00 30.00
RGAM Aidan McDonough/199 12.00 30.00
RGBF Brock Faber/99 40.00 100.00
RGBM Bobby McMann/99 25.00 60.00
RGCB Connor Bedard/25 1000.00 2500.00
RGCO Matthew Coronato/49 25.00 60.00
RGCU Will Cuylle/99 25.00 60.00
RGDW Dustin Wolf/99 50.00 125.00
RGHM Hugh McGing/99 15.00 40.00
RGKA Marco Kasper/49 40.00 100.00
RGKO Joona Koppanen/99 12.00 30.00
RGKT Tye Kartye/49 25.00 60.00
RGLE Luke Evangelista/99 25.00 60.00
RGLH Luke Hughes/25 50.00 125.00
RGLR Lukas Rousek/199 12.00 30.00
RGMC Cole McWard/99 15.00 40.00
RGMK Matthew Knies/99 60.00 150.00
RGMS Matt Savoie/49 30.00 80.00
RGNN Nikita Nesterenko/199 15.00 40.00
RGOB Owen Beck/99 25.00 60.00
RGPA Jiri Patera/25 25.00 60.00
RGRG Ridly Greig/99 25.00 60.00
RGSB Samuel Bolduc/99 15.00 40.00
RGSE Simon Edvinsson/49 30.00 80.00
RGSF Sean Farrell/99 15.00 40.00
RGSN Simon Nemec/49 30.00 80.00
RGTF Tyson Foerster/99 30.00 80.00
RGTR Tristen Robins/199 15.00 40.00
RGVD Vincent Desharnais/199 20.00 50.00
RGVI Vincent Iorio/199 15.00 40.00
RGWD William Dufour/99 12.00 30.00
RGYA Yaroslav Askarov/49 40.00 100.00

2023-24 Black Diamond Rookie Team Logo Jumbo Patch Autographs Full Logo 1

*LOGO 2/49: .5X TO 1.2X BASIC
*LOGO 3/25: .6X TO 1.5X BASIC
RTLCB Connor Bedard 1000.00 2500.00
RTLKN Matthew Knies 125.00 300.00
RTLLC Leo Carlsson 100.00 250.00
RTLLE Luke Evangelista 50.00 120.00
RTLMC Matthew Coronato 50.00 120.00
RTLMK Marco Kasper 80.00 200.00
RTLMS Matt Savoie 60.00 150.00
RTLOB Owen Beck 50.00 120.00
RTLRG Ridly Greig 50.00 125.00
RTLTF Tyson Foerster 60.00 150.00
RTLWD William Dufour 25.00 60.00

2023-24 Black Diamond Rookie Team Logo Jumbo Patches

*RETRO: .6X TO 1.5X BASIC
RTLCB Connor Bedard 150.00 400.00
RTLDL Devon Levi SP 15.00 40.00
RTLJP Jakob Pelletier 8.00 20.00
RTLKN Matthew Knies 25.00 60.00
RTLLC Leo Carlsson 20.00 50.00
RTLLE Luke Evangelista 10.00 25.00
RTLMC Matthew Coronato 10.00 25.00
RTLMK Marco Kasper 15.00 40.00
RTLMS Matt Savoie SP 12.00 30.00
RTLOB Owen Beck 10.00 25.00
RTLRG Ridly Greig SP 10.00 25.00
RTLSE Simon Edvinsson 12.00 30.00
RTLTF Tyson Foerster 12.00 30.00
RTLWD William Dufour 5.00 12.00

2023-24 Black Diamond Run for the Cup

RUNAM Auston Matthews 15.00 40.00
RUNAO Alex Ovechkin 15.00 40.00
RUNBF Brock Faber 10.00 25.00
RUNCM Cale Makar 10.00 25.00
RUNJH Jack Hughes 10.00 25.00
RUNKA Marco Kasper 10.00 25.00
RUNKK Kirill Kaprizov 10.00 25.00
RUNLD Leon Draisaitl 12.00 30.00
RUNLH Luke Hughes 12.00 30.00
RUNMC Matthew Coronato 6.00 15.00
RUNMK Matthew Knies 15.00 40.00
RUNNK Nikita Kucherov 8.00 20.00
RUNPK Patrick Kane 8.00 20.00
RUNRG Ridly Greig 6.00 15.00
RUNSE Simon Edvinsson 8.00 20.00
RUNYA Yaroslav Askarov 10.00 25.00

2023-24 Black Diamond Sparkling Rookie Scripts

SCDW Dustin Wolf SP 25.00 60.00
SCKA Tye Kartye 12.00 30.00
SCKN Matthew Knies 40.00 100.00
SCMA Matthew Coronato SP 12.00 30.00
SCOB Owen Beck 12.00 30.00
SCSE Simon Edvinsson SP 15.00 40.00

2023-24 Black Diamond Sparkling Scripts

*SPECTRUM/25: .6X TO 1.5X BASIC
SCAI Alex Iafallo 5.00 12.00
SCAL Anders Lee 6.00 15.00
SCAO Alex Ovechkin SP 125.00 300.00
SCBC Blake Coleman 6.00 15.00
SCBJ Boone Jenner 8.00 20.00
SCBR Bryan Rust 8.00 20.00
SCBS Brandon Saad 6.00 15.00
SCBU Michael Bunting 8.00 20.00
SCCO Maxime Comtois 6.00 15.00
SCDG Dylan Guenther 10.00 25.00
SCEB Jordan Eberle 8.00 20.00
SCFE Mario Ferraro 5.00 12.00
SCJA Jacob Middleton 5.00 12.00
SCJE Jack Eichel SP 30.00 80.00
SCJM Jonathan Marchessault 10.00 25.00
SCJP Jeff Petry 8.00 20.00
SCJS Jaccob Slavin 6.00 15.00
SCKM Kirill Marchenko 10.00 25.00
SCKR Torey Krug 6.00 15.00
SCPK Peyton Krebs 6.00 15.00
SCRS Ryan Strome 8.00 20.00
SCSA Juuse Saros 10.00 25.00
SCSC Sidney Crosby SP 125.00 300.00
SCSR Sam Reinhart 15.00 40.00

2023-24 Black Diamond Team Logo Jumbo Patches

*RETRO: .6X TO 1.5X BASIC
TLAD Alex DeBrincat 5.00 12.00
TLAO Alex Ovechkin 15.00 40.00
TLAS Andrei Svechnikov 5.00 12.00
TLBB Brent Burns 4.00 10.00
TLBS Brendan Shanahan 6.00 15.00
TLBT Brady Tkachuk 6.00 15.00
TLCC Chris Chelios 4.00 10.00
TLCG Claude Giroux 4.00 10.00
TLCM Connor McDavid 20.00 50.00
TLDL Dylan Larkin 5.00 12.00
TLDP David Perron 3.00 8.00
TLEK Erik Karlsson 5.00 12.00
TLFF Filip Forsberg 6.00 15.00
TLIS Igor Shesterkin 8.00 20.00
TLJA Jake Sanderson 5.00 12.00
TLJB Jonatan Berggren 3.00 8.00
TLJC Jakob Chychrun 4.00 10.00
TLJH Jack Hughes 10.00 25.00
TLJN Josh Norris 4.00 10.00
TLJR Jason Robertson 6.00 15.00
TLJS Juuse Saros 5.00 12.00
TLKK Kirill Kaprizov 12.00 30.00
TLKP Keith Primeau 3.00 8.00
TLLR Lucas Raymond 6.00 15.00
TLMD Matt Duchene 4.00 10.00
TLMH Marian Hossa 4.00 10.00
TLMN Martin Necas 6.00 15.00
TLMS Moritz Seider 5.00 12.00
TLMT Matthew Tkachuk 8.00 20.00
TLNM Nathan MacKinnon 15.00 40.00
TLPF Peter Forsberg 8.00 20.00
TLPK Pyotr Kochetkov 4.00 10.00
TLPR Pekka Rinne 4.00 10.00
TLRB Rod Brind'Amour 4.00 10.00
TLRD Rasmus Dahlin 5.00 12.00
TLRF Ron Francis 3.00 8.00
TLRJ Roman Josi 4.00 10.00
TLRM Ryan McDonagh 2.50 6.00
TLSA Sebastian Aho 6.00 15.00
TLSJ Seth Jarvis 5.00 12.00
TLSY Steve Yzerman 10.00 25.00
TLTN Thomas Novak 2.50 6.00
TLTS Tim Stutzle 5.00 12.00
TLVA Viktor Arvidsson 2.50 6.00
TLVH Ville Husso 2.50 6.00

2023-24 Black Diamond Veteran Jewels of the Draft Patch Autographs

VJDAB Aleksander Barkov/49 30.00 80.00
VJDAD Alex DeBrincat/25 25.00 60.00
VJDKM K'Andre Miller/49 15.00 40.00
VJDLD Leon Draisaitl/25 60.00 150.00
VJDMH Miro Heiskanen/49 25.00 60.00
VJDNS Nick Suzuki/25 80.00 200.00
VJDRT Robert Thomas/49 20.00 50.00
VJDTT Troy Terry/49 15.00 40.00

2024-25 Black Diamond

BDBAB Aleksander Barkov 3.00 8.00
BDBAD Alex DeBrincat 2.50 6.00
BDBAF Adam Fantilli 3.00 8.00
BDBAK Anze Kopitar 3.00 8.00
BDBAM Auston Matthews 8.00 20.00
BDBAO Alex Ovechkin 8.00 20.00
BDBAP Artemi Panarin 4.00 10.00
BDBAS Andrei Svechnikov 2.50 6.00
BDBAT Akil Thomas/349 RC 2.00 5.00
BDBAV Andrei Vasilevskiy 3.00 8.00
BDBBB Brendan Brisson/349 RC 2.50 6.00
BDBBF Brock Faber 2.50 6.00
BDBBL Brad Lambert/349 RC 2.50 6.00
BDBBM Brad Marchand 4.00 10.00
BDBBN Bradly Nadeau/349 RC 2.50 6.00
BDBBO Brennan Othmann/349 RC 4.00 10.00
BDBBP Brayden Point 2.50 6.00
BDBBQ Mavrik Bourque/349 RC 4.00 10.00
BDBBR Brock Boeser 2.50 6.00
BDBBT Brady Tkachuk 3.00 8.00
BDBCA Leo Carlsson 3.00 8.00
BDBCB Connor Bedard 6.00 15.00
BDBCC Cole Caufield 4.00 10.00
BDBCG Cutter Gauthier/349 RC 5.00 12.00
BDBCK Clayton Keller 2.50 6.00
BDBCM Cale Makar 5.00 12.00
BDBCR Sidney Crosby 8.00 20.00
BDBDL Dylan Larkin 2.50 6.00
BDBDP Denis Potvin 2.50 6.00
BDBDR Leon Draisaitl 6.00 15.00
BDBEM Evgeni Malkin 4.00 10.00
BDBEP Elias Pettersson 3.00 8.00
BDBFF Filip Forsberg 3.00 8.00
BDBFN Frank Nazar/349 RC 6.00 15.00
BDBGB Gavin Brindley/349 RC 2.00 5.00
BDBGE Conor Geekie/349 RC 3.00 8.00
BDBHU Jack Hughes 5.00 12.00
BDBJD Josh Doan/349 RC 4.00 10.00
BDBJE Jack Eichel 3.00 8.00
BDBJP JJ Peterka 2.00 5.00
BDBJT Joe Thornton 2.50 6.00
BDBJW Jesper Wallstedt/349 RC 5.00 12.00
BDBKC Kyle Connor 3.00 8.00
BDBKH Marat Khusnutdinov/349 RC 2.00 5.00
BDBKK Kirill Kaprizov 6.00 15.00
BDBLE Brian Leetch 1.50 4.00
BDBLH Lane Hutson/349 RC 25.00 60.00
BDBLO Liam Ohgren/349 RC 4.00 10.00
BDBLS Logan Stankoven/349 RC 5.00 12.00
BDBLU Luke Hughes 3.00 8.00
BDBMA Mason McTavish 2.00 5.00
BDBMB Matt Boldy 3.00 8.00
BDBMC Macklin Celebrini/349 RC 30.00 80.00
BDBMD Connor McDavid 10.00 25.00
BDBMI Stan Mikita 2.00 5.00
BDBML Mario Lemieux 8.00 20.00
BDBMM Mitch Marner 3.00 8.00
BDBMS Mats Sundin 2.00 5.00
BDBMT Matthew Tkachuk 4.00 10.00
BDBMV Matvei Michkov/349 RC 8.00 20.00
BDBNK Nikita Kucherov 4.00 10.00
BDBNL Nicklas Lidstrom 2.00 5.00
BDBNM Nathan MacKinnon 8.00 20.00
BDBNS Nick Suzuki 4.00 10.00
BDBOW Olen Zellweger/349 RC 4.00 10.00
BDBPA David Pastrnak 5.00 12.00
BDBPR Patrick Roy 5.00 12.00
BDBQH Quinn Hughes 5.00 12.00
BDBRA Mikko Rantanen 5.00 12.00
BDBRD Rasmus Dahlin 2.50 6.00
BDBRO Jason Robertson 3.00 8.00
BDBSA Sebastian Aho 3.00 8.00
BDBSE Moritz Seider 2.50 6.00
BDBSM Shakir Mukhamadullin/349 RC 2.50 6.00
BDBTK Travis Konecny 2.00 5.00
BDBTS Tim Stutzle 2.50 6.00
BDBTT Tage Thompson 2.50 6.00
BDBWG Wayne Gretzky 10.00 25.00
BDBWJ Wyatt Johnston 4.00 10.00
BDBWS Will Smith/349 RC 6.00 15.00
BDBZB Zachary Bolduc/349 RC 3.00 8.00
BDBZC Zdeno Chara 2.00 5.00
BDBZD Zach Dean/349 RC 3.00 8.00
BDBZH Zach Hyman 3.00 8.00
BDBZI Mika Zibanejad 2.50 6.00
BDRAT Akil Thomas/99 12.00 30.00
BDRBB Brendan Brisson/99 RC 15.00 40.00
BDRBL Brad Lambert/99 15.00 40.00
BDRBN Bradly Nadeau/99 15.00 40.00
BDRBO Brennan Othmann/99 25.00 60.00
BDRCG Cutter Gauthier/99 30.00 80.00
BDRCO Sam Colangelo/99 RC 12.00 30.00
BDRDC Drew Commesso/99 RC 15.00 40.00
BDREC Ethan Cardwell/99 RC 10.00 25.00
BDRFN Frank Nazar/99 40.00 100.00
BDRGB Gavin Brindley/99 12.00 30.00
BDRGC Graeme Clarke/99 RC 12.00 30.00
BDRGE Conor Geekie/99 20.00 50.00
BDRGG Gage Goncalves/99 RC 15.00 40.00
BDRIF Ivan Fedotov/99 RC 20.00 50.00
BDRJB Joel Blomqvist/99 RC 15.00 40.00
BDRJD Josh Doan/99 25.00 60.00
BDRJR Joshua Roy/99 RC 25.00 60.00
BDRJT Jack Thompson/99 RC 12.00 30.00
BDRJW Jesper Wallstedt/99 30.00 80.00
BDRLD Luca Del Bel Belluz/99 RC 12.00 30.00
BDRLH Lane Hutson/99 100.00 250.00
BDRLO Liam Ohgren/99 25.00 60.00
BDRLS Logan Stankoven/99 30.00 80.00
BDRMB Mavrik Bourque/99 25.00 60.00
BDRMC Macklin Celebrini/99 250.00 600.00
BDRMK Marat Khusnutdinov/99 12.00 30.00
BDRMM Matvei Michkov/99 100.00 250.00
BDRMR Matt Rempe/99 RC 25.00 60.00
BDRMU Shakir Mukhamadullin/99 15.00 40.00
BDRNC Nikita Chibrikov/99 RC 15.00 40.00
BDRNK Nikolai Kovalenko/99 RC 10.00 25.00
BDROZ Olen Zellweger/99 25.00 60.00
BDRRI Ruslan Iskhakov/99 RC 12.00 30.00
BDRRM Rutger McGroarty/99 RC 25.00 60.00
BDRSL Landon Slaggert/99 RC 12.00 30.00
BDRSM Scott Morrow/99 RC 15.00 40.00
BDRWS Will Smith/99 40.00 100.00
BDRYK Yan Kuznetsov/99 RC 12.00 30.00
BDRZB Zachary Bolduc/99 20.00 50.00
BDRZD Zach Dean/99 12.00 30.00
BDRZL Zachary L'Heureux/99 RC 15.00 40.00
BDRZO Zack Ostapchuk/99 RC 12.00 30.00

2024-25 Black Diamond '15 Retro Diamond Relic Rookies

BDRRCG Cutter Gauthier 60.00 150.00
BDRRLS Logan Stankoven 60.00 150.00
BDRRMC Macklin Celebrini 200.00 500.00
BDRRMM Matvei Michkov 200.00 500.00
BDRRWS Will Smith 80.00 200.00

2024-25 Black Diamond Autographs

BDBAB Aleksander Barkov/49 20.00 50.00
BDBAK Anze Kopitar/49 20.00 50.00
BDBAS Andrei Svechnikov/49 15.00 40.00
BDBAT Akil Thomas/99 12.00 30.00
BDBAV Andrei Vasilevskiy/25 20.00 50.00
BDBBB Brendan Brisson/99 15.00 40.00
BDBBN Bradly Nadeau/99 15.00 40.00
BDBBO Brennan Othmann/99 25.00 60.00
BDBBQ Mavrik Bourque/49 25.00 60.00
BDBBR Brock Boeser/49 15.00 40.00
BDBBT Brady Tkachuk/49 20.00 50.00
BDBCG Cutter Gauthier/49 30.00 80.00
BDBDP Denis Potvin/25 12.00 30.00
BDBFN Frank Nazar/49 40.00 100.00
BDBFZ Fabian Zetterlund/99 8.00 20.00
BDBGE Conor Geekie/49 20.00 50.00
BDBJD Josh Doan/49 25.00 60.00
BDBJH Jonathan Huberdeau/49 15.00 40.00
BDBJM Jared McCann/49 10.00 25.00
BDBJT Joe Thornton/25 20.00 50.00
BDBJW Jesper Wallstedt/99 30.00 80.00
BDBKC Kyle Connor/49 20.00 50.00
BDBKH Marat Khusnutdinov/99 12.00 30.00
BDBLE Brian Leetch/25 15.00 40.00
BDBLH Lane Hutson/99 250.00 600.00
BDBLO Liam Ohgren/49 25.00 60.00
BDBLS Logan Stankoven/49 30.00 80.00
BDBLU Luke Hughes/25 40.00 100.00
BDBMA Mason McTavish/49 12.00 30.00
BDBMB Matt Boldy/25 20.00 50.00
BDBNE Brock Nelson/49 12.00 30.00
BDBOW Olen Zellweger/49 25.00 60.00
BDBRA Mikko Rantanen/25 40.00 100.00
BDBRO Jason Robertson/25 20.00 50.00
BDBRT Robert Thomas/49 12.00 30.00
BDBSM Shakir Mukhamadullin/99 15.00 40.00
BDBTH Tomas Hertl/49 12.00 30.00
BDBTK Travis Konecny/49 12.00 30.00
BDBTS Tim Stutzle/25 25.00 60.00
BDBTT Tage Thompson/49 15.00 40.00
BDBWJ Wyatt Johnston/49 25.00 60.00
BDBWS Will Smith/25 125.00 300.00
BDBZB Zachary Bolduc/49 20.00 50.00
BDBZD Zach Dean/99 12.00 30.00

2024-25 Black Diamond Band of Color

BCAM Auston Matthews 150.00 400.00
BCAO Alex Ovechkin 150.00 400.00
BCBP Brayden Point 50.00 125.00
BCCB Connor Bedard 200.00 500.00
BCCC Cole Caufield 80.00 200.00
BCCK Chris Kreider 50.00 125.00
BCCM Connor McDavid 200.00 500.00
BCCP Chris Pronger 40.00 100.00
BCDP David Pastrnak 100.00 250.00
BCEL Eric Lindros 60.00 150.00
BCFF Filip Forsberg 60.00 150.00
BCGL Guy Lafleur 50.00 125.00
BCHR Henri Richard 40.00 100.00
BCJE Jack Eichel 60.00 150.00
BCJS Joe Sakic 80.00 200.00
BCKC Kyle Connor 60.00 150.00
BCNM Nathan MacKinnon 150.00 400.00
BCQH Quinn Hughes 100.00 250.00
BCRB Ray Bourque 60.00 150.00
BCSC Sidney Crosby 150.00 400.00
BCTH Tim Horton 60.00 150.00
BCTL Ted Lindsay 40.00 100.00
BCTS Tim Stutzle 50.00 125.00
BCWG Wayne Gretzky 250.00 600.00

2024-25 Black Diamond Band of Color Rookies

BCRBL Brad Lambert 50.00 125.00
BCRBO Brennan Othmann 80.00 200.00
BCRCG Cutter Gauthier 100.00 250.00
BCRJD Josh Doan 80.00 200.00
BCRLO Liam Ohgren 80.00 200.00
BCRLS Logan Stankoven 100.00 250.00
BCRMB Mavrik Bourque 80.00 200.00
BCRMC Macklin Celebrini 250.00 600.00
BCROZ Olen Zellweger 80.00 200.00
BCRSM Shakir Mukhamadullin 50.00 125.00
BCRWS Will Smith 125.00 300.00
BCRZB Zachary Bolduc 60.00 150.00

2024-25 Black Diamond Diamond Debut Relics Jersey

DDBL Brad Lambert 3.00 8.00
DDBO Brennan Othmann 5.00 12.00
DDCG Cutter Gauthier 6.00 15.00
DDFN Frank Nazar 8.00 20.00
DDJD Josh Doan 6.00 15.00
DDJW Jesper Wallstedt 6.00 15.00
DDLH Lane Hutson 25.00 60.00
DDLO Liam Ohgren 6.00 15.00
DDLS Logan Stankoven 6.00 15.00
DDMB Mavrik Bourque 5.00 12.00
DDMC Macklin Celebrini 25.00 60.00
DDSM Shakir Mukhamadullin 3.00 8.00
DDWS Will Smith 8.00 20.00
DDZB Zachary Bolduc 4.00 10.00

2024-25 Black Diamond Diamond Debut Relics Patch Autographs

DDBO Brennan Othmann/49 30.00 80.00
DDFN Frank Nazar/25 60.00 150.00
DDJD Josh Doan/49 30.00 80.00
DDJW Jesper Wallstedt/49 40.00 100.00
DDLH Lane Hutson/49 200.00 500.00
DDLO Liam Ohgren/49 30.00 80.00
DDLS Logan Stankoven/25 40.00 100.00
DDMB Mavrik Bourque/49 30.00 80.00
DDSM Shakir Mukhamadullin/49 20.00 50.00
DDWS Will Smith/49 80.00 200.00
DDZB Zachary Bolduc/49 25.00 60.00

2024-25 Black Diamond Diamond Facet

DFAB Aleksander Barkov 4.00 10.00
DFAK Anze Kopitar 4.00 10.00
DFAV Andrei Vasilevskiy 4.00 10.00
DFCG Cutter Gauthier 6.00 15.00
DFDP David Pastrnak 6.00 15.00
DFFN Frank Nazar 8.00 20.00
DFJD Josh Doan 5.00 12.00
DFJH Jack Hughes 6.00 15.00
DFLD Leon Draisaitl 8.00 20.00
DFLS Logan Stankoven 6.00 15.00
DFMC Macklin Celebrini 20.00 50.00
DFMS Moritz Seider 3.00 8.00
DFWJ Wyatt Johnston 5.00 12.00
DFWS Will Smith 8.00 20.00

2024-25 Black Diamond Diamond Futures

BDFBB Brendan Brisson 2.50 6.00
BDFBL Brad Lambert 2.50 6.00
BDFBN Bradly Nadeau 2.50 6.00
BDFBO Brennan Othmann 4.00 10.00
BDFCG Cutter Gauthier 5.00 12.00
BDFFN Frank Nazar 6.00 15.00
BDFGB Gavin Brindley 2.00 5.00
BDFIF Ivan Fedotov 3.00 8.00
BDFJD Josh Doan 4.00 10.00
BDFJR Joshua Roy 4.00 10.00
BDFJW Jesper Wallstedt 5.00 12.00
BDFLH Lane Hutson 25.00 60.00
BDFLO Liam Ohgren 4.00 10.00
BDFLS Logan Stankoven 5.00 12.00
BDFMB Mavrik Bourque 4.00 10.00
BDFMR Matt Rempe 4.00 10.00
BDFOZ Olen Zellweger 4.00 10.00
BDFZB Zachary Bolduc 3.00 8.00

2024-25 Black Diamond Diamond Futures Autographs

BDFAB Arshdeep Bains/99 12.00 30.00
BDFAK Adam Klapka/99 10.00 25.00
BDFAR Aku Raty/99 10.00 25.00
BDFAT Akil Thomas/65 10.00 25.00
BDFBB Brendan Brisson/65 12.00 30.00
BDFBN Bradly Nadeau/65 12.00 30.00
BDFBO Brennan Othmann/35 30.00 80.00
BDFCG Cutter Gauthier/35 30.00 80.00
BDFED Ethan Del Mastro/99 10.00 25.00
BDFFN Frank Nazar/35 30.00 80.00
BDFGC Graeme Clarke/99 10.00 25.00
BDFGG Gage Goncalves/99 10.00 25.00
BDFGR Collin Graf/99 10.00 25.00
BDFIF Ivan Fedotov/65 15.00 40.00
BDFJD Josh Doan/35 25.00 60.00
BDFJR Joshua Roy/65 20.00 50.00
BDFJW Jesper Wallstedt/35 30.00 80.00
BDFLC Lukas Cormier/99 10.00 25.00
BDFLH Lane Hutson/35 150.00 400.00
BDFLO Liam Ohgren/35 20.00 50.00
BDFLS Logan Stankoven/35 40.00 100.00
BDFMB Mavrik Bourque/35 25.00 60.00
BDFMK Marat Khusnutdinov/65 10.00 25.00
BDFML Logan Morrison/99 10.00 25.00
BDFMM Mason Morelli/99 10.00 25.00
BDFMO Scott Morrow/65 12.00 30.00
BDFMR Matt Rempe/65 30.00 80.00
BDFNC Nikita Chibrikov/65 10.00 25.00
BDFOZ Olen Zellweger/35 20.00 50.00
BDFSC Sam Colangelo/99 10.00 25.00
BDFSM Shakir Mukhamadullin/65 12.00 30.00
BDFYK Yan Kuznetsov/99 10.00 25.00
BDFZB Zachary Bolduc/65 15.00 40.00
BDFZD Zach Dean/65 10.00 25.00
BDFZO Zack Ostapchuk/99 10.00 25.00

2024-25 Black Diamond Diamond Futures Premium Relic Autographs

BDFAB Arshdeep Bains 20.00 50.00
BDFAK Adam Klapka 15.00 40.00
BDFAR Aku Raty 15.00 40.00
BDFAT Akil Thomas 15.00 40.00
BDFBB Brendan Brisson 20.00 50.00
BDFBN Bradly Nadeau 20.00 50.00
BDFBO Brennan Othmann 30.00 80.00
BDFCG Cutter Gauthier 40.00 100.00
BDFED Ethan Del Mastro 15.00 40.00
BDFFN Frank Nazar 60.00 150.00
BDFGB Gavin Brindley 15.00 40.00
BDFGC Graeme Clarke 15.00 40.00
BDFGG Gage Goncalves 20.00 50.00
BDFGR Collin Graf 15.00 40.00
BDFIF Ivan Fedotov 50.00 125.00
BDFJD Josh Doan 30.00 80.00
BDFJR Joshua Roy 30.00 80.00
BDFJW Jesper Wallstedt 40.00 100.00
BDFLC Lukas Cormier 15.00 40.00
BDFLH Lane Hutson 800.00 2000.00
BDFLO Liam Ohgren 50.00 125.00
BDFLS Logan Stankoven 60.00 150.00
BDFMB Mavrik Bourque 30.00 80.00
BDFML Logan Morrison 15.00 40.00
BDFMM Mason Morelli 15.00 40.00
BDFMO Scott Morrow 20.00 50.00
BDFMR Matt Rempe 30.00 80.00
BDFNC Nikita Chibrikov 15.00 40.00
BDFOZ Olen Zellweger 30.00 80.00
BDFSC Sam Colangelo 15.00 40.00
BDFSM Shakir Mukhamadullin 20.00 50.00
BDFYK Yan Kuznetsov 15.00 40.00
BDFZB Zachary Bolduc 25.00 60.00
BDFZD Zach Dean 15.00 40.00
BDFZO Zack Ostapchuk 15.00 40.00

2024-25 Black Diamond Diamond Gallery

DGBL Brad Lambert 2.50 6.00
DGBM Brad Marchand 4.00 10.00
DGCC Cole Caufield 4.00 10.00
DGCG Cutter Gauthier 5.00 12.00
DGFN Frank Nazar 6.00 15.00
DGGE Conor Geekie 3.00 8.00
DGJO Jake Oettinger 3.00 8.00
DGLS Logan Stankoven 5.00 12.00
DGMB Matt Boldy 3.00 8.00
DGMC Macklin Celebrini 20.00 50.00
DGZH Zach Hyman 3.00 8.00

2024-25 Black Diamond Diamond Legends
BDLAM Al MacInnis 2.50 6.00
BDLBC Bobby Clarke 3.00 8.00
BDLBO Bobby Orr 8.00 20.00
BDLCC Corey Crawford 2.00 5.00
BDLDG Doug Gilmour 2.50 6.00
BDLDS Darryl Sittler 2.00 5.00
BDLGH Gordie Howe 6.00 15.00
BDLHR Henri Richard 2.00 5.00
BDLJK Jari Kurri 2.00 5.00
BDLJP Jacques Plante 2.00 5.00
BDLLR Luc Robitaille 2.00 5.00
BDLMB Mike Bossy 2.00 5.00
BDLMG Mike Gartner 2.50 6.00
BDLMM Mark Messier 4.00 10.00
BDLPF Peter Forsberg 4.00 10.00
BDLPS Peter Stastny 1.50 4.00
BDLSN Scott Niedermayer 2.00 5.00
BDLSY Steve Yzerman 5.00 12.00
BDLWG Wayne Gretzky 12.00 30.00

2024-25 Black Diamond Diamond Legends Autographs
BDLCC Corey Crawford/25 30.00 80.00
BDLMG Mike Gartner/25 12.00 30.00

2024-25 Black Diamond Diamond Might
DMAM Auston Matthews 10.00 25.00
DMAO Alex Ovechkin 10.00 25.00
DMBB Brock Boeser 3.00 8.00
DMCG Cutter Gauthier 6.00 15.00
DMCM Cale Makar 6.00 15.00
DMDL Dylan Larkin 3.00 8.00
DMFN Frank Nazar 8.00 20.00
DMHZ Henrik Zetterberg 3.00 8.00
DMKK Kirill Kaprizov 8.00 20.00
DMLH Lane Hutson 30.00 80.00
DMLS Logan Stankoven 6.00 15.00
DMMC Macklin Celebrini 30.00 80.00
DMMD Connor McDavid 12.00 30.00
DMMM Matvei Michkov 40.00 100.00
DMMT Matthew Tkachuk 5.00 12.00
DMNK Nikita Kucherov 5.00 12.00
DMRB Rob Blake 2.50 6.00
DMTT Tage Thompson 3.00 8.00
DMWS Will Smith 15.00 40.00
DMZH Zach Hyman 4.00 10.00

2024-25 Black Diamond Diamond Mine Dual Relics
DMDRCE L.Couture/W.Eklund 5.00 12.00
DMDRCO A.Ovechkin/S.Crosby 15.00 40.00
DMDRHC K.Connor/C.Hellebuyck 8.00 20.00
DMDRKP N.Kucherov/B.Point 8.00 20.00
DMDRLS I.Shesterkin/H.Lundqvist 10.00 25.00
DMDRMD C.McDavid/L.Draisaitl 20.00 50.00
DMDRMP E.Pettersson/J.Miller 6.00 15.00
DMDRRH J.Robertson/R.Hintz 6.00 15.00
DMDRRS J.Saros/P.Rinne 5.00 12.00
DMDRSC C.Caufield/N.Suzuki 8.00 20.00

2024-25 Black Diamond Diamond Mine Relics
*PREMIUM/25: 1.2X TO 3X BASIC
DMRAF Adam Fox 3.00 8.00
DMRAS Andrei Svechnikov 3.00 8.00
DMRBE Jamie Benn 2.50 6.00
DMRCB Connor Bedard 15.00 40.00
DMREM Evgeni Malkin 5.00 12.00
DMRFF Filip Forsberg 4.00 10.00
DMRJB Jesper Bratt 2.50 6.00
DMRJS Juraj Slafkovsky 5.00 12.00
DMRMR Mikko Rantanen 6.00 15.00
DMRMS Mark Scheifele 4.00 10.00
DMRMZ Mika Zibanejad 3.00 8.00
DMRPB Patrice Bergeron 3.00 8.00
DMRRG Ryan Getzlaf 2.50 6.00
DMRVH Victor Hedman 3.00 8.00
DMRZC Zdeno Chara 2.50 6.00

2024-25 Black Diamond Diamond Mine Triple Relics
DMTRBKD Byfield/Kopitar/Doughty 10.00 25.00
DMTRBTB Barkov/Tkachuk/Bobrovsky 12.00 30.00
DMTRDBH Demko/Boeser/Hughes 15.00 40.00
DMTRKTP Panarin/Kreider/Trouba 12.00 30.00
DMTRMPM Pastrnak Marchand/McAvoy 15.00 40.00
DMTRRMM MacKinnon/Makar/Roy 25.00 60.00
DMTRSKE Eichel/Stone/Karlsson 10.00 25.00
DMTRZMC Zegras McTavish/Carlsson 10.00 25.00

2024-25 Black Diamond Diamond Plate Rookie Autographs
*SPECTRUM/25: .6X TO 1.5X BASIC
DPRAK Adam Klapka/149 8.00 20.00
DPRBN Bradly Nadeau/99 10.00 25.00
DPRBO Brennan Othmann/49 15.00 40.00
DPRCG Collin Graf/149 8.00 20.00
DPRCO Sam Colangelo/149 8.00 20.00
DPRFN Frank Nazar/25 40.00 100.00
DPRGA Cutter Gauthier/25 80.00 200.00
DPRJD Josh Doan/49 15.00 40.00
DPRJW Jesper Wallstedt/99 20.00 50.00
DPRLH Lane Hutson/49 150.00 400.00
DPRLS Logan Stankoven/25 60.00 150.00
DPRMB Mavrik Bourque/99 15.00 40.00
DPRMC Macklin Celebrini/25 300.00 800.00
DPROZ Olen Zellweger/99 15.00 40.00
DPRPK Phil Kemp/149 8.00 20.00
DPRZB Zachary Bolduc/99 12.00 30.00

2024-25 Black Diamond Diamond Stars
BDSAM Auston Matthews 8.00 20.00
BDSAO Alex Ovechkin 8.00 20.00
BDSCB Connor Bedard 6.00 15.00
BDSCM Connor McDavid 10.00 25.00
BDSDP David Pastrnak 5.00 12.00
BDSEM Evgeni Malkin 4.00 10.00
BDSJH Jack Hughes 5.00 12.00
BDSJR Jason Robertson 3.00 8.00
BDSKK Kirill Kaprizov 6.00 15.00
BDSLD Leon Draisaitl 6.00 15.00
BDSMA Cale Makar 5.00 12.00
BDSMM Mitch Marner 3.00 8.00
BDSMT Matthew Tkachuk 4.00 10.00
BDSNK Nikita Kucherov 4.00 10.00
BDSNM Nathan MacKinnon 8.00 20.00
BDSPK Patrick Kane 4.00 10.00
BDSQH Quinn Hughes 5.00 12.00
BDSSC Sidney Crosby 8.00 20.00

2024-25 Black Diamond Diamond Stars Autographs
BDSCH Connor Hellebuyck/25 20.00 50.00
BDSCP Colton Parayko/25 8.00 20.00
BDSIS Ilya Sorokin/25 15.00 40.00
BDSJS Juuse Saros/25 12.00 30.00
BDSLC Logan Cooley/25 20.00 50.00
BDSMS Mark Stone/25 12.00 30.00
BDSND Noah Dobson/25 12.00 30.00
BDSNH Nico Hischier/25 15.00 40.00
BDSWK William Karlsson/25 12.00 30.00

2024-25 Black Diamond Diamond Stars Premium Relic Autographs
BDSCP Colton Parayko/25 10.00 25.00
BDSIS Ilya Sorokin/25 20.00 50.00
BDSJS Juuse Saros/25 15.00 40.00
BDSWK William Karlsson/25 25.00 60.00

2024-25 Black Diamond Gemography
GAM Auston Matthews 100.00 250.00
GAO Alex Ovechkin 125.00 300.00
GBP Brian Propp 20.00 50.00
GCG Cutter Gauthier 60.00 150.00
GCM Cale Makar 80.00 200.00
GEP Elias Pettersson 40.00 100.00
GFN Frank Nazar 80.00 200.00
GJB Johnny Bucyk 25.00 60.00
GKK Kirill Kaprizov 80.00 200.00
GLD Leon Draisaitl 80.00 200.00
GLR Larry Robinson 25.00 60.00
GLS Logan Stankoven 60.00 150.00
GMC Macklin Celebrini 300.00 800.00
GMD Connor McDavid 250.00 600.00
GMI Matvei Michkov 250.00 600.00
GMM Mitch Marner 40.00 100.00
GSY Steve Yzerman 60.00 150.00

2024-25 Black Diamond Hockey History Patches
*GOLD/25: .8X TO 2X BASIC
HHPAM Alec Martinez 3.00 8.00
HHPAO Alex Ovechkin 20.00 50.00
HHPBH Brett Hull 15.00 40.00
HHPBO Bobby Orr 20.00 50.00
HHPCB Connor Bedard 40.00 100.00
HHPCM Connor McDavid 25.00 60.00
HHPDS Darryl Sittler 5.00 12.00
HHPHU Bobby Hull 10.00 25.00
HHPMB Martin Brodeur 12.00 30.00
HHPMF Marc-Andre Fleury 20.00 50.00
HHPML Mario Lemieux 20.00 50.00
HHPMM Mark Messier 10.00 25.00
HHPPK Patrick Kane 10.00 25.00
HHPSC Sidney Crosby 20.00 50.00
HHPTS Teemu Selanne 20.00 50.00
HHPWG Wayne Gretzky 40.00 100.00
HHPWO Willie O'Ree 6.00 15.00

2024-25 Black Diamond Jewels of the Draft Patch Autographs
VJDIS Igor Shesterkin/25 125.00 300.00
VJDJD Joey Daccord/99 20.00 50.00
VJDJO Jake Oettinger/49 40.00 100.00
VJDJS Jeremy Swayman/49 50.00 125.00
VJDKM Kirill Marchenko/99 30.00 80.00
VJDMR Marco Rossi/49 40.00 100.00
VJDNS Timo Meier/25 20.00 50.00
VJDRA Mikko Rantanen/99 50.00 125.00
VJDTT Tage Thompson/25 40.00 100.00
VJDTY Troy Terry/49 15.00 40.00
VJDVD Vince Dunn/99 15.00 40.00

2024-25 Black Diamond Jewels of the Draft Patch Autographs Rookies
JDAT Akil Thomas/99 15.00 40.00
JDBB Brendan Brisson/99 15.00 40.00
JDBN Bradly Nadeau/99 20.00 50.00
JDBO Brennan Othmann/99 20.00 50.00
JDCG Cutter Gauthier/49 80.00 200.00
JDFN Frank Nazar/49 50.00 125.00
JDGC Graeme Clarke/99 15.00 40.00
JDIF Ivan Fedotov/99 25.00 60.00
JDJD Josh Doan/49 30.00 80.00
JDJW Jesper Wallstedt/49 60.00 150.00
JDLC Lukas Cormier/99 15.00 40.00
JDLH Lane Hutson/99 300.00 800.00
JDLO Liam Ohgren/49 30.00 80.00
JDLS Logan Stankoven/49 60.00 150.00
JDMB Mavrik Bourque/99 30.00 80.00
JDMC Macklin Celebrini/49 250.00 600.00
JDMM Matvei Michkov/49 300.00 800.00
JDMO Scott Morrow/99 25.00 60.00
JDMR Matt Rempe/99 100.00 250.00
JDNC Nikita Chibrikov/99 15.00 40.00
JDOZ Olen Zellweger/99 30.00 80.00
JDSC Sam Colangelo/99 15.00 40.00
JDSM Shakir Mukhamadullin/99 20.00 50.00
JDZB Zachary Bolduc/99 15.00 40.00
JDZD Zach Dean/99 15.00 40.00
JDZO Zack Ostapchuk/99 15.00 40.00

2024-25 Black Diamond Oilers Retired Number Patches
ORNPAH Al Hamilton 6.00 15.00
ORNPGA Glenn Anderson 8.00 20.00
ORNPGF Grant Fuhr 15.00 40.00
ORNPJK Jari Kurri 10.00 25.00
ORNPKL Kevin Lowe 10.00 25.00
ORNPMM Mark Messier 20.00 50.00
ORNPPC Paul Coffey 10.00 25.00
ORNPWG Wayne Gretzky 60.00 150.00

2024-25 Black Diamond Oilers Retired Numbers Patches Gold
ORNPGF Grant Fuhr/31 50.00 125.00
ORNPJK Jari Kurri/17 60.00 150.00

2024-25 Black Diamond Premium Relics
BDBAB Aleksander Barkov/50 12.00 30.00
BDBAD Alex DeBrincat/50 10.00 25.00
BDBAF Adam Fantilli/50 12.00 30.00
BDBAK Anze Kopitar/50 12.00 30.00
BDBAM Auston Matthews/25 30.00 80.00
BDBAO Alex Ovechkin/25 60.00 150.00
BDBAP Artemi Panarin/50 15.00 40.00
BDBAS Andrei Svechnikov/50 12.00 30.00
BDBAT Akil Thomas/50 8.00 20.00
BDBAV Andrei Vasilevskiy/50 12.00 30.00
BDBBB Brendan Brisson/50 10.00 25.00
BDBBF Brock Faber/50 10.00 25.00
BDBBH Bo Horvat/50 10.00 25.00
BDBBL Brad Lambert/25 10.00 25.00
BDBBM Brad Marchand/50 15.00 40.00
BDBBN Bradly Nadeau/50 10.00 25.00
BDBBO Brennan Othmann/50 15.00 40.00
BDBBP Brayden Point/50 10.00 25.00
BDBBR Brock Boeser/50 10.00 25.00
BDBBT Brady Tkachuk/50 12.00 30.00
BDBCA Leo Carlsson/50 12.00 30.00
BDBCB Connor Bedard/25 80.00 200.00
BDBCC Cole Caufield/50 15.00 40.00
BDBCG Cutter Gauthier/50 20.00 50.00
BDBCK Clayton Keller/50 10.00 25.00
BDBCM Cale Makar/25 20.00 50.00
BDBCR Sidney Crosby/25 60.00 150.00
BDBDL Dylan Larkin/50 10.00 25.00
BDBDR Leon Draisaitl/25 25.00 60.00
BDBEM Evgeni Malkin/50 15.00 40.00
BDBEP Elias Pettersson/50 12.00 30.00
BDBFF Filip Forsberg/50 12.00 30.00
BDBFN Frank Nazar/50 25.00 60.00
BDBFZ Fabian Zetterlund/50 5.00 12.00
BDBGB Gavin Brindley/50 8.00 20.00
BDBHU Jack Hughes/25 20.00 50.00
BDBJD Josh Doan/50 15.00 40.00
BDBJE Jack Eichel/50 12.00 30.00
BDBJH Jonathan Huberdeau/50 10.00 25.00
BDBJM Jared McCann/50 6.00 15.00
BDBJP JJ Peterka/50 8.00 20.00
BDBJW Jesper Wallstedt/50 20.00 50.00
BDBKC Kyle Connor/50 12.00 30.00
BDBKK Kirill Kaprizov/25 25.00 60.00
BDBLH Lane Hutson/50 100.00 250.00
BDBLO Liam Ohgren/50 15.00 40.00
BDBLS Logan Stankoven/50 20.00 50.00
BDBLU Luke Hughes/50 12.00 30.00
BDBMA Mason McTavish/50 8.00 20.00
BDBMB Matt Boldy/50 12.00 30.00
BDBMC Macklin Celebrini/25 100.00 250.00
BDBMD Connor McDavid/25 80.00 200.00
BDBMM Mitch Marner/25 12.00 30.00
BDBMS Mats Sundin/25 8.00 20.00
BDBMT Matthew Tkachuk/25 15.00 40.00
BDBMV Matvei Michkov/25 150.00 400.00
BDBNE Brock Nelson/50 8.00 20.00
BDBNK Nikita Kucherov/50 15.00 40.00
BDBNM Nathan MacKinnon/25 30.00 80.00
BDBNS Nick Suzuki/50 15.00 40.00
BDBOW Olen Zellweger/50 15.00 40.00
BDBPA David Pastrnak/25 40.00 100.00
BDBQH Quinn Hughes/25 20.00 50.00
BDBRA Mikko Rantanen/50 20.00 50.00
BDBRD Rasmus Dahlin/50 10.00 25.00
BDBRO Jason Robertson/50 12.00 30.00
BDBRT Robert Thomas/50 8.00 20.00
BDBSA Sebastian Aho/50 12.00 30.00
BDBSE Moritz Seider/50 12.00 30.00
BDBSM Shakir Mukhamadullin/50 10.00 25.00
BDBTK Travis Konecny/50 8.00 20.00
BDBTS Tim Stutzle/25 10.00 25.00
BDBTT Tage Thompson/25 10.00 25.00
BDBWJ Wyatt Johnston/50 15.00 40.00
BDBWS Will Smith/50 25.00 60.00
BDBZB Zachary Bolduc/50 12.00 30.00
BDBZD Zach Dean/50 8.00 20.00
BDBZH Zach Hyman/25 10.00 25.00
BDBZI Mika Zibanejad/50 10.00 25.00

2024-25 Black Diamond Rookie Diamond Cutters
RDCBB Brendan Brisson 2.50 6.00
RDCBL Brad Lambert 2.50 6.00
RDCBN Bradly Nadeau 2.50 6.00
RDCBO Brennan Othmann 4.00 10.00
RDCCG Cutter Gauthier 8.00 20.00
RDCFN Frank Nazar 6.00 15.00
RDCJW Jesper Wallstedt 6.00 15.00
RDCLH Lane Hutson 25.00 60.00
RDCLO Liam Ohgren 4.00 10.00
RDCLS Logan Stankoven 10.00 25.00
RDCMB Mavrik Bourque 4.00 10.00
RDCMC Macklin Celebrini 40.00 100.00
RDCMM Matvei Michkov 50.00 125.00
RDCOZ Olen Zellweger 4.00 10.00
RDCWS Will Smith 15.00 40.00
RDCZA Zachary Bolduc 3.00 8.00
RDCZO Zack Ostapchuk 2.00 5.00

2024-25 Black Diamond Rookie Gems
RGBB Brendan Brisson 2.50 6.00
RGBL Brad Lambert 2.50 6.00
RGBN Bradly Nadeau 2.50 6.00
RGBO Brennan Othmann 4.00 10.00
RGCG Cutter Gauthier 5.00 12.00
RGCO Sam Colangelo 2.00 5.00
RGFN Frank Nazar 6.00 15.00
RGGB Gavin Brindley 5.00 12.00
RGGE Conor Geekie 3.00 8.00
RGIF Ivan Fedotov 3.00 8.00
RGJD Josh Doan 4.00 10.00
RGJW Jesper Wallstedt 5.00 12.00
RGLH Lane Hutson 25.00 60.00
RGLO Liam Ohgren 4.00 10.00
RGLS Logan Stankoven 5.00 12.00
RGMB Mavrik Bourque 4.00 10.00
RGMC Macklin Celebrini 20.00 50.00
RGMM Matvei Michkov 40.00 100.00
RGMO Scott Morrow 3.00 8.00
RGOZ Olen Zellweger 3.00 8.00
RGSM Shakir Mukhamadullin 2.50 6.00
RGWS Will Smith 5.00 12.00
RGZB Zachary Bolduc 3.00 8.00

2024-25 Black Diamond Rookie Gems Red
*RED/100: .6X TO 1.5X BASIC
RGLH Lane Hutson 50.00 125.00
RGLS Logan Stankoven 15.00 40.00
RGWS Will Smith 15.00 40.00

2024-25 Black Diamond Rookie Gems Signatures
RGSAT Akil Thomas/199 6.00 15.00
RGSBB Brendan Brisson/99 8.00 20.00
RGSBN Bradly Nadeau/199 10.00 25.00
RGSBO Brennan Othmann/99 15.00 40.00
RGSFN Frank Nazar/49 25.00 60.00
RGSGA Cutter Gauthier/49 20.00 50.00
RGSGC Graeme Clarke/199 6.00 15.00
RGSIF Ivan Fedotov/199 10.00 25.00
RGSJB Jackson Blake/199 40.00 100.00
RGSJD Josh Doan/99 12.00 30.00
RGSJW Jesper Wallstedt/99 15.00 40.00
RGSLH Lane Hutson/99 150.00 400.00
RGSLO Liam Ohgren/99 12.00 30.00
RGSLS Logan Stankoven/49 20.00 50.00
RGSMB Mavrik Bourque/199 12.00 30.00
RGSMC Macklin Celebrini/25 300.00 800.00
RGSMM Matvei Michkov/25 200.00 500.00
RGSMU Shakir Mukhamadullin/199 8.00 20.00
RGSNC Nikita Chibrikov/199 6.00 15.00
RGSOZ Olen Zellweger/99 12.00 30.00
RGSSC Sam Colangelo/199 6.00 15.00
RGSSM Scott Morrow/199 8.00 20.00
RGSWS Will Smith/25 150.00 400.00
RGSZB Zachary Bolduc/99 10.00 25.00
RGSZD Zach Dean/199 6.00 15.00

2024-25 Black Diamond Rookie Team Logo Jumbo Patch Autographs Full Logo 1
RTLBB Brendan Brisson 25.00 60.00
RTLBO Brennan Othmann 40.00 100.00
RTLCG Cutter Gauthier 50.00 125.00
RTLFN Frank Nazar 60.00 150.00
RTLJD Josh Doan 40.00 100.00
RTLLH Lane Hutson 200.00 500.00
RTLLO Liam Ohgren 40.00 100.00
RTLLS Logan Stankoven 50.00 125.00
RTLMC Macklin Celebrini 250.00 600.00
RTLMM Matvei Michkov 200.00 500.00
RTLOZ Olen Zellweger 40.00 100.00
RTLWS Will Smith 60.00 150.00
RTLZB Zachary Bolduc 30.00 80.00

2024-25 Black Diamond Rookie Team Logo Jumbo Patch Autographs Full Logo 2
*LOGO 2: .5X TO 1.2X BASIC
RTLLH Lane Hutson 250.00 600.00
RTLMC Macklin Celebrini 300.00 800.00
RTLMM Matvei Michkov 250.00 600.00

2024-25 Black Diamond Rookie Team Logo Jumbo Patch Autographs Full Logo 3
*LOGO 3: .6X TO 1.5X BASIC
RTLLH Lane Hutson 300.00 800.00
RTLMC Macklin Celebrini 400.00 1000.00
RTLMM Matvei Michkov 250.00 600.00

2024-25 Black Diamond Rookie Team Logo Jumbo Puzzle Patch
*RETRO: .6X TO 1.5X BASIC
RTLBB Brendan Brisson 10.00 25.00
RTLBO Brennan Othmann 12.00 30.00
RTLCG Cutter Gauthier 15.00 40.00
RTLFN Frank Nazar 20.00 50.00
RTLJD Josh Doan 12.00 30.00
RTLLH Lane Hutson 50.00 125.00
RTLLO Liam Ohgren 12.00 30.00
RTLLS Logan Stankoven 15.00 40.00
RTLMC Macklin Celebrini 30.00 80.00
RTLOZ Olen Zellweger 12.00 30.00
RTLWS Will Smith 20.00 50.00
RTLZB Zachary Bolduc 10.00 25.00

2024-25 Black Diamond Run for the Cup
RUNCB Connor Bedard 12.00 30.00
RUNCG Cutter Gauthier 20.00 50.00
RUNCK Chris Kreider 5.00 12.00
RUNEP Elias Pettersson 6.00 15.00
RUNGE Conor Geekie 6.00 15.00
RUNJD Josh Doan 8.00 20.00
RUNJE Jack Eichel 6.00 15.00
RUNKC Kyle Connor 6.00 15.00
RUNLS Logan Stankoven 10.00 25.00
RUNMC Macklin Celebrini 25.00 60.00
RUNMM Matvei Michkov 40.00 100.00
RUNNM Nathan MacKinnon 15.00 40.00
RUNSC Sidney Crosby 15.00 40.00
RUNTS Tim Stutzle 5.00 12.00
RUNWS Will Smith 12.00 30.00

2024-25 Black Diamond Sparkling Rookie Scripts
SRSAK Adam Klapka 6.00 15.00
SRSAT Akil Thomas 6.00 15.00
SRSBB Brendan Brisson 8.00 20.00
SRSCG Cutter Gauthier SP 15.00 40.00
SRSDC Devin Cooley 6.00 15.00
SRSFN Frank Nazar SP 20.00 50.00
SRSIF Ivan Fedotov 10.00 25.00
SRSJD Josh Doan 12.00 30.00
SRSJR Joshua Roy 10.00 25.00
SRSJT Jack Thompson 6.00 15.00
SRSJW Jesper Wallstedt SP 15.00 40.00
SRSLH Lane Hutson SP 100.00 250.00
SRSLM Logan Morrison 6.00 15.00
SRSLO Liam Ohgren SP 12.00 30.00
SRSLS Logan Stankoven SP 20.00 50.00
SRSMB Mavrik Bourque 12.00 30.00
SRSMK Marat Khusnutdinov 6.00 15.00
SRSMR Matt Rempe 30.00 80.00
SRSOZ Olen Zellweger 12.00 30.00
SRSPK Phil Kemp 6.00 15.00
SRSSM Scott Morrow 8.00 20.00
SRSZB Zachary Bolduc 10.00 25.00
SRSZD Zach Dean 6.00 15.00
SRSZO Zack Ostapchuk 6.00 15.00

2024-25 Black Diamond Sparkling Scripts
SSAM Auston Matthews SP 80.00 200.00
SSBB Brock Boeser 10.00 25.00
SSBJ Boone Jenner 8.00 20.00
SSBO Matt Boldy 12.00 30.00
SSBP Brian Propp 6.00 15.00
SSBU Michael Bunting 8.00 20.00
SSCM Casey Mittelstadt 8.00 20.00
SSCO Chris Osgood 8.00 20.00
SSCS Cole Sillinger 6.00 15.00
SSDC Dylan Cozens 8.00 20.00
SSDH Dany Heatley 6.00 15.00
SSFG Filip Gustavsson 8.00 20.00
SSFP Felix Potvin SP 40.00 100.00
SSGV Gabe Vilardi 8.00 20.00
SSHL Henrik Lundqvist SP 20.00 50.00
SSJB Johnny Boychuk SP 6.00 15.00
SSJC J.T. Compher 5.00 12.00
SSJN Jake Neighbours 8.00 20.00
SSJR Jason Robertson SP 12.00 30.00
SSKM K'Andre Miller 6.00 15.00
SSKT Keith Tkachuk 8.00 20.00
SSMB Mikael Backlund 6.00 15.00
SSMK Matthew Knies 20.00 50.00
SSMM Mason Marchment 6.00 15.00
SSPA Brad Park 6.00 15.00
SSPB Patrice Bergeron 30.00 80.00
SSPE Peter Bondra 8.00 20.00
SSPZ Pavel Zacha 6.00 15.00
SSSC Sidney Crosby SP 125.00 300.00
SSSS Stuart Skinner 15.00 40.00
SSTT Tim Thomas 8.00 20.00
SSTW Tom Wilson 8.00 20.00

2024-25 Black Diamond Sparkling Scripts Spectrum
*SPECTRUM/25: .6X TO 1.5X BASIC
SSFP Felix Potvin 50.00 125.00
SSMK Matthew Knies 25.00 60.00
SSPB Patrice Bergeron 40.00 100.00
SSSS Stuart Skinner 20.00 50.00
SSTT Tim Thomas 25.00 60.00
SSTW Tom Wilson 20.00 50.00

2024-25 Black Diamond Team Logo Jumbo Patch Puzzle
*RETRO: .5X TO 1.2X BASIC
TLAF Adam Fantilli 20.00 50.00
TLAM Auston Matthews AS 20.00 50.00
TLBH Bo Horvat 15.00 40.00
TLBJ Boone Jenner 12.00 30.00
TLBN Brock Nelson 12.00 30.00
TLBO Mike Bossy 12.00 30.00
TLBS Billy Smith 12.00 30.00
TLBT Bryan Trottier 12.00 30.00
TLCC Cole Caufield 25.00 60.00
TLCM Connor McDavid AS 25.00 60.00
TLCR Sidney Crosby 50.00 125.00
TLCS Cole Sillinger 10.00 25.00
TLDP David Pastrnak AS 12.00 30.00
TLEK Erik Karlsson 15.00 40.00
TLEM Evgeni Malkin 25.00 60.00
TLEP Elias Pettersson AS 8.00 20.00
TLGL Guy Lafleur 15.00 40.00
TLHR Henri Richard 12.00 30.00
TLJB Jean Beliveau 12.00 30.00
TLKJ Kent Johnson 12.00 30.00
TLKL Kris Letang 15.00 40.00
TLKM Kirill Marchenko 12.00 30.00
TLLA Pat LaFontaine 12.00 30.00
TLLR Larry Robinson 12.00 30.00
TLMA Cale Makar AS 12.00 30.00
TLMB Mathew Barzal 15.00 40.00
TLMF Marc-Andre Fleury 25.00 60.00
TLML Mario Lemieux 50.00 125.00
TLMR Maurice Richard 25.00 60.00
TLND Noah Dobson 15.00 40.00
TLNK Nikita Kucherov AS 20.00 50.00
TLNM Nathan MacKinnon AS 20.00 50.00
TLNS Nick Suzuki 25.00 60.00
TLPD Denis Potvin 12.00 30.00
TLPR Patrick Roy 30.00 80.00
TLRF Ron Francis 15.00 40.00
TLRN Rick Nash 12.00 30.00
TLSB Sergei Bobrovsky 20.00 50.00
TLSC Sidney Crosby AS 20.00 50.00
TLTB Tom Barrasso 10.00 25.00
TLWN William Nylander AS 10.00 25.00
TLYC Yvan Cournoyer 12.00 30.00
TLZW Zach Werenski 20.00 50.00

1968-69 Blackhawks Team Issue
COMPLETE SET (8) 25.00 50.00
1 Dennis Hull 4.00 8.00
2 Doug Jarrett 2.50 5.00
3 Chico Maki 3.00 6.00
4 Gilles Marotte 2.50 5.00
5 Stan Mikita 10.00 20.00
6 Jim Pappin 2.50 5.00
7 Pat Stapleton 2.50 5.00
8 Ken Wharram 3.00 6.00

1970-71 Blackhawks Postcards
COMPLETE SET (14) 25.00 50.00
1 Lou Angotti 1.50 3.00
2 Bryan Campbell 1.50 3.00
3 Bobby Hull
Bill Wirtz
Stan Mikita 10.00 20.00
4 Dennis Hull 3.00 6.00
5 Tommy Ivan GM
Billy Reay CO 1.50 3.00
6 Doug Jarrett 1.50 3.00
7 Keith Magnuson 2.50 5.00
8 Pit Martin 1.50 3.00
9 Stan Mikita 5.00 10.00
10 Eric Nesterenko 2.50 5.00
11 Jim Pappin 2.00 4.00
12 Allan Pinder 1.50 3.00
13 Paul Shmyr 1.50 3.00
14 Bill White 2.00 4.00

1979-80 Blackhawks Postcards
COMPLETE SET (22) 12.50 25.00
1 Keith Brown .50 1.00
2 J.P. Bordeleau .50 1.00
3 Ted Bulley .50 1.00
4 Alain Daigle .50 1.00
5 Tony Esposito 3.00 6.00
6 Greg Fox .50 1.00
7 Tim Higgins .50 1.00
8 Eddie Johnston CO .40 1.00
9 Reggie Kerr .50 1.00
10 Cliff Koroll .50 1.00
11 Tom Lysiak .50 1.00
12 Keith Magnuson 1.00 2.00
13 John Marks .50 1.00
14 Stan Mikita 4.00 8.00
15 Grant Mulvey 1.00 2.00
16 Bob Murray 1.00 2.00
17 Mike O'Connell .50 1.00
18 Rich Preston .50 1.00
19 Bob Pulford 1.00 2.00
20 Terry Ruskowski .50 1.00
21 Mike Veisor .50 1.00
22 Doug Wilson 2.00 4.00

1980-81 Blackhawks Postcards
COMPLETE SET (16) 12.50 25.00
1 Keith Brown .75 2.00
2 Greg Fox .40 1.00
3 Dave Hutchison .40 1.00
4 Cliff Koroll ACO .40 1.00
5 Keith Magnuson CO .60 1.50
6 Peter Marsh .60 1.50
7 Grant Mulvey .60 1.50
8 Rich Preston .40 1.00
9 Florent Robidoux .40 1.00
10 Terry Ruskowski .60 1.50
11 Denis Savard 2.50 5.00
12 Al Secord .75 2.00
13 Ron Sedlbauer .40 1.00
14 Glen Sharpley .40 1.00
15 Darryl Sutter .75 2.00
16 Miles Zaharko .40 1.00

1980-81 Blackhawks White Border
COMPLETE SET (14) 10.00 20.00
1 Murray Bannerman .60 1.50
2 J.P. Bordeleau .40 1.00
3 Keith Brown .75 2.00
4 Tony Esposito 2.50 5.00
5 Greg Fox .40 1.00
6 Tim Higgins .40 1.00
7 Doug Lecuyer .40 1.00
8 John Marks .40 1.00
9 Grant Mulvey .60 1.50
10 Rich Preston .40 1.00
11 Terry Ruskowski .60 1.50
12 Denis Savard 2.50 5.00
13 Darryl Sutter .75 2.00
14 Tim Trimper .40 1.00

1981-82 Blackhawks Borderless Postcards
COMPLETE SET (28) 12.00 30.00
1 Murray Bannerman .60 1.50
2 Keith Brown .60 1.50
3 Ted Bulley .30 .75
4 Doug Crossman .60 1.50
5 Jerome Dupont .30 .75
6 Tony Esposito 2.00 5.00
7 Greg Fox .30 .75
8 Bill Gardner .30 .75
9 Tim Higgins .30 .75
10 Dave Hutchison .30 .75
11 Reg Kerr .30 .75
12 Cliff Koroll ACO .30 .75
13 Tom Lysiak .60 1.50
14 Keith Magnuson CO .60 1.50
15 John Marks .30 .75
16 Peter Marsh .30 .75
17 Grant Mulvey .30 .75
18 Bob Murray .30 .75
19 Rick Paterson .30 .75
20 Rich Preston .30 .75
21 Bob Pulford GM .60 1.50
22 Terry Ruskowski .30 .75
23 Denis Savard 2.00 5.00
24 Al Secord .75 2.00
25 Glen Sharpley .30 .75
26 Darryl Sutter .75 2.00
27 Toni Tanti .75 2.00
28 Doug Wilson 1.25 3.00

1981-82 Blackhawks Brown Background
COMPLETE SET (17) 10.00 25.00
1 Keith Brown .75 2.00
2 Greg Fox .40 1.00
3 Dave Hutchison .40 1.00
4 Cliff Koroll ACO .40 1.00
5 Keith Magnuson CO .75 2.00
6 Peter Marsh .75 2.00
7 Grant Mulvey .75 2.00
8 Bob Pulford GM CO 1.25 3.00
9 Rich Preston .40 1.00
10 Florent Robidoux .40 1.00
11 Terry Ruskowski .75 2.00
12 Denis Savard 3.00 8.00
13 Al Secord .75 2.00
14 Ron Sedlbauer .40 1.00
15 Glen Sharpley .40 1.00
16 Darryl Sutter 1.25 3.00
17 Miles Zaharko .40 1.00

1982-83 Blackhawks Postcards
COMPLETE SET (23) 12.00 30.00
1 Murray Bannerman .50 1.25
2 Keith Brown .50 1.25
3 Doug Crossman .40 1.00
4 Dennis Cyr .30 .75
5 Tony Esposito 1.50 4.00
6 Dave Feamster .30 .75
7 Bill Gardner .30 .75
8 Greg Fox .30 .75
9 Tim Higgins .30 .75
10 Steve Larmer 2.00 5.00
11 Steve Ludzik .60 1.50
12 Tom Lysiak .50 1.25
13 Peter Marsh .30 .75
14 Grant Mulvey .30 .75
15 Bob Murray .30 .75
16 Troy Murray .40 1.00
17 Rick Paterson .30 .75
18 Rich Preston .30 .75
19 Denis Savard 1.50 4.00
20 Al Secord .75 2.00
21 Darryl Sutter .60 1.50
22 Orval Tessier CO .40 1.00
23 Doug Wilson 1.00 2.50

1983-84 Blackhawks Postcards
COMPLETE SET (27) 14.00 35.00
1 Murray Bannerman .60 1.50
2 Keith Brown .40 1.00
3 Denis Cyr .30 .75
4 Jerome Dupont .30 .75
5 Tony Esposito 1.50 4.00
6 Dave Feamster .30 .75
7 Curt Fraser .40 1.00
8 Bill Gardner .30 .75
9 Bob Janecyk .60 1.50
10 Cliff Koroll ACO .20 .50
11 Steve Larmer 3.00 8.00
12 Steve Ludzik .60 1.50
13 Tom Lysiak .60 1.50
14 Peter Marsh .30 .75
15 Bob Murray .30 .75
16 Troy Murray .60 1.50
17 Jack O'Callahan .30 .75
18 Rick Paterson .30 .75
19 Rich Preston .30 .75
20 Denis Savard 1.50 4.00
21 Al Secord .75 2.00
22 Darryl Sutter .75 2.00
23 Orval Tessier CO .20 .50
24 Behn Wilson .30 .75
25 Doug Wilson 1.00 2.50
26 Ken Yaremchuk .30 .75
27 Title Card .20 .50

1985-86 Blackhawks Team Issue
COMPLETE SET (26) 20.00 40.00
1 Steve Larmer 1.25 3.00
2 Keith Brown .75 2.00
3 Cliff Koroll .40 1.00
4 Roger Neilson .40 1.00
5 Bob Pulford .40 1.00
6 Behn Wilson .75 2.00
7 Jerome Dupont .75 2.00
8 Rick Paterson .40 1.00
9 Al Secord 1.25 3.00
10 Marc Bergevin .40 1.00
11 Darryl Sutter 1.25 3.00
12 Murray Bannerman .75 2.00
13 Bruce Cassidy .40 1.00
14 Bill Watson .40 1.00
15 Curt Fraser .40 1.00
16 Warren Skorodenski .75 2.00
17 Troy Murray .40 1.00
18 Bill Gardner .40 1.00
19 Ken Yaremchuk .40 1.00
20 Steve Ludzik .40 1.00
21 Jack O'Callahan .75 2.00
22 Tom Lysiak .40 1.00
23 Bob Murray .40 1.00
24 Ed Olczyk .75 2.00
25 Denis Savard 1.25 3.00
26 Doug Wilson 1.25 3.00

1986-87 Blackhawks Coke
COMPLETE SET (24) 8.00 20.00
1 Murray Bannerman .40 1.00
2 Marc Bergevin .30 .75
3 Keith Brown .30 .75
4 Dave Donnelly .30 .75
5 Curt Fraser .30 .75
6 Steve Larmer 1.25 3.00
7 Steve Ludzik .30 .75
8 Dave Manson .60 1.50
9 Bob Murray .30 .75
10 Troy Murray .30 .75
11 Gary Nylund .30 .75
12 Jack O'Callahan .30 .75
13 Ed Olczyk .40 1.00
14 Rick Paterson .30 .75
15 Wayne Presley .30 .75
16 Rich Preston .30 .75
17 Bob Sauve .40 1.00
18 Denis Savard 1.25 3.00
19 Al Secord .30 .75
20 Mike Stapleton .30 .75
21 Darryl Sutter .40 1.00
22 Bill Watson .30 .75
23 Behn Wilson .30 .75
24 Doug Wilson .60 1.50

1987-88 Blackhawks Coke
COMPLETE SET (30) 8.00 20.00
1 Murray Bannerman .40 1.00
2 Marc Bergevin .30 .75
3 Keith Brown .30 .75
4 Glen Cochrane .30 .75
5 Curt Fraser .30 .75
6 Steve Larmer 1.00 2.50
7 Mark LaVarre .30 .75
8 Steve Ludzik .30 .75
9 Dave Manson .60 1.50
10 Bob Mason .40 1.00
11 Bob McGill .30 .75
12 Bob Murdoch CO .30 .75
13 Bob Murray .30 .75
14 Troy Murray .40 1.00
15 Brian Noonan .30 .75
16 Gary Nylund .30 .75
17 Darren Pang .60 1.50
18 Wayne Presley .30 .75
19 Everett Sanipass .30 .75
20 Denis Savard 1.00 2.50
21 Mike Stapleton .30 .75
22 Darryl Sutter CO .30 .75
23 Duane Sutter .40 1.00
24 Steve Thomas .50 1.25
25 Wayne Thomas CO .30 .75
26 Rick Vaive .40 1.00
27 Dan Vincelette .30 .75
28 Bill Watson .30 .75
29 Behn Wilson .30 .75
30 Doug Wilson .60 1.50

1988-89 Blackhawks Coke
COMPLETE SET (25) 8.00 20.00
1 Ed Belfour 4.00 10.00
2 Keith Brown .20 .50

3 Bruce Cassidy .20 .50
4 Mike Eagles .20 .50
5 Dirk Graham .40 1.00
6 Mike Hudson .20 .50
7 Mike Keenan CO .60 1.50
8 Steve Larmer .60 1.50
9 Dave Manson .40 1.00
10 Jacques Martin CO .08 .25
11 Bob McGill .20 .50
12 E.J. McGuire CO .08 .25
13 Troy Murray .40 1.00
14 Brian Noonan .20 .50
15 Darren Pang .30 .75
16 Wayne Presley .20 .50
17 Everett Sanipass .20 .50
18 Denis Savard .75 2.00
19 Duane Sutter .30 .75
20 Steve Thomas .40 1.00
21 Rick Vaive .30 .75
22 Dan Vincelette .20 .50
23 Jimmy Waite .30 .75
24 Doug Wilson .40 1.00
25 Trent Yawney .20 .50

1989-90 Blackhawks Coke

COMPLETE SET (27) 8.00 20.00
1 Denis Savard .75 2.00
2 Troy Murray .30 .75
3 Steve Larmer .60 1.50
4 Doug Wilson .60 1.50
5 Bob Murray .20 .50
6 Jeremy Roenick 3.00 8.00
7 Duane Sutter .30 .75
8 Greg Gilbert .20 .50
9 Trent Yawney .20 .50
10 Bob McGill .20 .50
11 Jacques Cloutier .30 .75
12 Bob Bassen .20 .50
13 Steve Thomas .40 1.00
14 Adam Creighton .30 .75
15 Wayne Van Dorp .20 .50
16 Dirk Graham .40 1.00
17 Mike Hudson .20 .50
18 Al Secord .30 .75
19 Alain Chevrier .30 .75
20 Wayne Presley .20 .50
21 Steve Konroyd .20 .50
22 Everett Sanipass .20 .50
23 Keith Brown .20 .50
24 Dave Manson .40 1.00
25 Mike Keenan CO .40 1.00
26 E.J. McGuire CO .08 .25
27 Jacques Martin CO .08 .25

1990-91 Blackhawks Coke

COMPLETE SET (28) 8.00 20.00
1 Dirk Graham .30 .75
2 Troy Murray .30 .75
3 Steve Larmer .40 1.00
4 Doug Wilson .40 1.00
5 Chris Chelios 1.00 2.50
6 Jeremy Roenick 2.00 5.00
7 Steve Thomas .30 .75
8 Greg Gilbert .20 .50
9 Trent Yawney .20 .50
10 Bob McGill .20 .50
11 Jacques Cloutier .25 .60
12 Jocelyn Lemieux .20 .50
13 Michel Goulet .40 1.00
14 Adam Creighton .25 .60
15 Mike McNeill .20 .50
16 Ed Belfour 2.50 6.00
17 Mike Hudson .20 .50
18 Greg Millen .30 .75
19 Stu Grimson .30 .75
20 Wayne Presley .20 .50
21 Steve Konroyd .20 .50
22 Mike Peluso .30 .75
23 Keith Brown .20 .50
24 Dave Manson .30 .75
25 Mike Keenan CO .30 .75
26 Darryl Sutter CO .30 .75
27 E.J. McGuire CO .08 .25
28 Vladislav Tretiak CO 1.00 2.50

1991-92 Blackhawks Coke

COMPLETE SET (28) 8.00 20.00
1 Ed Belfour 1.25 3.00
2 Keith Brown .20 .50
3 Rod Buskas .20 .50
4 Chris Chelios .75 2.00
5 Karl Dykhuis .20 .50
6 Greg Gilbert .20 .50
7 Michel Goulet .30 .75
8 Dirk Graham .30 .75
9 Stu Grimson .40 1.00
10 Mike Hudson .20 .50
11 Mike Keenan GM/CO .40 1.00
12 Steve Konroyd .20 .50
13 Frantisek Kucera .20 .50
14 Steve Larmer .40 1.00
15 Brad Lauer .20 .50
16 Jocelyn Lemieux .20 .50
17 Bryan Marchment .20 .50
18 Dave McDowall CO .08 .25
19 Brian Noonan .20 .50
20 Mike Peluso .20 .50
21 Rich Preston CO .08 .25
22 Jeremy Roenick 1.25 3.00
23 Steve Smith .30 .75
24 Mike Stapleton .20 .50
25 Brent Sutter .30 .75
26 Darryl Sutter CO .30 .75
27 John Tonelli .30 .75
28 Jimmy Waite .30 .75

1992-93 Blackhawks Coke

COMPLETE SET (20) 10.00 25.00
1 Adam Bennett .30 .75
2 Cam Russell .30 .75
3 Christian Ruuttu .30 .75
4 Stu Grimson .75 2.00
5 Brent Sutter .75 2.00
6 Dave Christian .40 1.00
7 Mike Hudson .30 .75
8 Rob Brown .30 .75
9 Steve Larmer .75 2.00
10 Bryan Marchment .30 .75
11 Igor Kravchuk .30 .75
12 Paul Baxter .30 .75
13 Vladislav Tretiak .75 2.00
14 Rich Preston .30 .75
15 Darryl Sutter .75 2.00
16 Keith Brown .30 .75
17 Bob Pulford .30 .75
18 Jimmy Waite .40 1.00
19 Ed Belfour 1.25 3.00
20 Jeremy Roenick 1.25 3.00

1993-94 Blackhawks Coke

COMPLETE SET (30) 6.00 15.00
1 Joe Murphy .30 .75
2 Chris Chelios .75 2.00
3 Rich Sutter .20 .50
4 Frantisek Kucera .20 .50
5 Jeff Shantz .20 .50
6 Brian Noonan .20 .50
7 Michel Goulet .30 .75
8 Jeremy Roenick .75 2.00
9 Dave Christian .20 .50
10 Patrick Poulin .20 .50
11 Brent Sutter .20 .50
12 Cam Russell .20 .50
13 Stephane Matteau .20 .50
14 Ed Belfour 1.00 2.50
15 Neil Wilkinson .20 .50
16 Eric Weinrich .20 .50
17 Christian Ruuttu .20 .50
18 Kevin Todd .20 .50
19 Jeff Hackett .40 1.00
20 Steve Smith .25 .60
21 Jocelyn Lemieux .20 .50
22 Keith Carney .20 .50
23 Troy Murray .20 .50
24 Darin Kimble .20 .50
25 Dirk Graham .30 .75
26 Bob Pulford GM .20 .50
27 Darryl Sutter CO .20 .50
28 Paul Baxter ACO .08 .25
29 Rich Preston ACO .08 .25
30 Phil Myre ACO .08 .25

1994-95 Blackhawks Coke

COMPLETE SET(21) 6.00 15.00
1 Tony Amonte .75 2.00
2 Ed Belfour 1.00 2.50
3 Keith Carney .20 .50
4 Chris Chelios .75 2.00
5 Dirk Graham .30 .75
6 Brent Grieve .20 .50
7 Jeff Hackett .40 1.00
8 Roger Johansson .20 .50
9 Darin Kimble .20 .50
10 Sergei Krivokrasov .20 .50
11 Joe Murphy .20 .50
12 Bernie Nicholls .40 1.00
13 Patrick Poulin .20 .50
14 Bob Probert .40 1.00
15 Cam Russell .20 .50
16 Jeff Shantz .20 .50
17 Steve Smith .20 .50
18 Greg Smyth .20 .50
19 Gary Suter .30 .75
20 Brent Sutter .20 .50
21 Eric Weinrich .20 .50

1995-96 Blackhawks Coke

COMPLETE SET (19) 6.00 15.00
1 Tony Amonte .75 2.00
2 Ed Belfour 1.00 2.50
3 Keith Carney .20 .50
4 Chris Chelios .75 2.00
5 Murray Craven .20 .50
6 Jim Cummins .20 .50
7 Eric Daze .40 1.00
8 Jeff Hackett .40 1.00
9 Sergei Krivokrasov .20 .50
10 Joe Murphy .20 .50
11 Bernie Nicholls .40 1.00
12 Bob Probert .40 1.00
13 Cam Russell .20 .50
14 Denis Savard .40 1.00
15 Jeff Shantz .20 .50
16 Steve Smith .20 .50
17 Gary Suter .20 .50
18 Brent Sutter .20 .50
19 Eric Weinrich .20 .50

1998 Blackhawks Legends

COMPLETE SET (5) 4.80 12.00
1 Tony Esposito 1.25 3.00
2 Glenn Hall 1.25 3.00
3 Bobby Hull 2.00 5.00
4 Steve Larmer .60 1.50
5 Denis Savard .60 1.50

1998-99 Blackhawks Chicago Sun-Times

COMPLETE SET 3.00 8.00
1 Chris Chelios 1.25 3.00
2 Mark Fitzpatrick .40 1.00
3 Doug Gilmour .75 2.00
4 Christian Laflamme .40 1.00
5 Bob Probert 1.25 3.00
6 Jocelyn Thibault .40 1.00

1999-00 Blackhawks Chicago Sun-Times

COMPLETE SET (12) 4.00 10.00
1 Tony Amonte .75 2.00
2 Brad Brown .40 1.00
3 Mark Janssens .40 1.00
4 Jean-Yves Leroux .40 1.00
5 Dave Manson .40 1.00
6 Bryan McCabe .40 1.00
7 Boris Mironov .40 1.00
8 Michael Nylander .40 1.00
9 Doug Zmolek .40 1.00
10 Coaches .40 1.00
11 Team photo .40 1.00

1999-00 Blackhawks Lineup Cards

COMPLETE SET (10) 8.00 20.00
1 Tony Amonte 1.50 4.00
2 Brad Brown .40 1.00
3 Eric Daze 1.25 3.00
4 Doug Gilmour 1.50 4.00
5 Dean McAmmond .40 1.00
6 Bryan McCabe .40 1.00
7 Boris Mironov .40 1.00
8 Steve Sullivan .75 2.00
9 Jocelyn Thibault 1.25 3.00
10 Alexei Zhamnov .40 1.00

2002-03 Blackhawks Postcards

1 Eric Daze .40 1.00
2 Steve Poapst .40 1.00
3 Jason Strudwick .40 1.00
4 Brian Sutter CO .40 1.00
5 Jocelyn Thibault .75 2.00
6 Ryan Vandenbussche .40 1.00
7 Alexei Zhamnov .40 1.00

2003-04 Blackhawks Postcards

COMPLETE SET (31) 10.00 25.00
1 Craig Andersson .40 1.00
2 Tyler Arnason .30 .75
3 Anton Babchuk .20 .50
4 Mark Bell .40 1.00
5 Kyle Calder .40 1.00
6 Eric Daze .40 1.00
7 Nathan Dempsey .20 .50
8 Alexander Karpovtsev .20 .50
9 Igor Korolev .20 .50
10 Lasse Kukkonen .20 .50
11 Michael Leighton .40 1.00
12 Al MacAdam ACO .04 .10
13 Steve McCarthy .20 .50
14 Brett McLean .20 .50
15 Travis Moen .20 .50
16 Scott Nichol .20 .50
17 Ville Nieminen .20 .50
18 Steve Passmore .40 1.00
19 Steve Poapst .20 .50
20 Deron Quint .20 .50
21 Igor Radulov .40 1.00
22 Tuomo Ruutu 2.00 5.00
23 Denis Savard ACO .30 .75
24 Jason Strudwick .20 .50
25 Steve Sullivan .40 1.00
26 Brent Sutter CO .10 .25
27 Jocelyn Thibault .75 2.00
28 Vladislav Tretiak ACO .40 1.00
29 Ryan VandenBussche .20 .50
30 Pavel Vorobiev .20 .50
31 Alexei Zhamnov .20 .50

2006-07 Blackhawks Postcards

COMPLETE SET (23) 10.00 20.00
1 Adrian Aucoin .40 1.00
2 Denis Arkhipov .40 1.00
3 Jeff Hamilton .40 1.00
4 Martin Lapointe .40 1.00
5 Tony Salmelainen .40 1.00
6 Jassen Cullimore .40 1.00
7 Martin Havlat .60 1.50
8 Patrick Sharp .40 1.00
9 Michael Holmqvist .40 1.00
10 Brent Seabrook .40 1.00
11 Rene Bourque .40 1.00
12 Jim Vandermeer .40 1.00
13 Duncan Keith .40 1.00
14 Nikolai Khabibulin .75 2.00
15 Michal Handzus .40 1.00
16 Tuomo Ruutu .75 2.00
17 Radim Vrbata .40 1.00
18 Brian Boucher .60 1.50
19 Bryan Smolinski .40 1.00
20 Lasse Kukkonen .40 1.00
21 Denis Savard CO .75 2.00
22 Mark Hardy CO .20 .50
23 Stephane Waite ACO .20 .50

2006-07 Blackhawks Postcards Glossy

1 Troy Brouwer .75 2.00
2 Peter Bondra 1.00 2.50
3 James Wisniewski .75 2.00
4 Karl Stewart .75 2.00
5 Ryan Stewart CO .75 2.00

2007-08 Blackhawks Team Issue

COMPLETE SET (28) 8.00 20.00
1 Kevyn Adams .30 .75
2 Rene Bourque .30 .75
3 Adam Burish .30 .75
4 Martin Havlat .30 .75
5 Magnus Johansson .30 .75
6 Patrick Kane 1.50 4.00
7 Duncan Keith .30 .75
8 Nikolai Khabibulin .40 1.00
9 David Koci .75 2.00
10 Patrick Lalime .40 1.00
11 Robert Lang .30 .75
12 Martin Lapointe .30 .75
13 Yanic Perreault .30 .75
14 Danny Richmond .30 .75
15 Tuomo Ruutu .40 1.00
16 Sergei Samsonov .30 .75
17 Brent Seabrook .30 .75
18 Patrick Sharp .30 .75
19 Brent Sopel .30 .75
20 Jonathan Toews 1.50 4.00
21 Jason Williams .30 .75
22 James Wisniewski .30 .75
23 Andrei Zyuzin .30 .75
24 Denis Savard HC .30 .75
25 Mark Hardy AC .10 .25
26 Ryan Stewart AC .10 .25
27 John Torchetti AC .10 .25
28 Stephane Waite CO .10 .25

2012-13 Blackhawks Upper Deck Stanley Cup Champions

COMPLETE SET (31) 12.00 20.00
1 Bryan Bickell .25 .60
2 Dave Bolland .30 .75
3 Brandon Bollig .25 .60
4 Sheldon Brookbank .25 .60
5 Daniel Carcillo .25 .60
6 Corey Crawford .50 1.25
7 Ray Emery .30 .75
8 Michael Frolik .25 .60
9 Michal Handzus .25 .60
10 Niklas Hjalmarsson .25 .60
11 Marian Hossa .40 1.00
12 Patrick Kane .75 2.00
13 Duncan Keith .30 .75
14 Marcus Kruger .25 .60
15 Nick Leddy .25 .60
16 Jamal Mayers .25 .60
17 Johnny Oduya .30 .75
18 Michal Rozsival .25 .60
19 Brandon Saad .30 .75
20 Brent Seabrook .25 .60
21 Patrick Sharp .40 1.00
22 Andrew Shaw .25 .60
23 Ben Smith .30 .75
24 Viktor Stalberg .25 .60
25 Jonathan Toews .60 1.50
26 No Loss SH .25 .60
27 Marian Hossa SH .40 1.00
28 Brent Seabrook SH .25 .60
29 Patrick Kane SH .75 2.00
30 Corey Crawford SH .50 1.25
CB Celebration Photo 1.25 3.00

1993 Bleachers 23K Manon Rheaume

COMPLETE SET (4) 8.00 20.00
COMMON CARD 2.00 5.00

1996 Bleachers Lemieux

1 Mario Lemieux 2.00 5.00

2001-02 Blizzak Kim St. Pierre

NNO Kim St. Pierre 2.00 5.00

2001-02 Blue Jackets Donatos Pizza

COMPLETE SET (24) 5.00 12.00
1 Geoff Sanderson .20 .50
2 Grant Marshall .20 .50
3 Serge Aubin .20 .50
4 Robert Kron .20 .50
5 Blake Sloan .20 .50
6 Mattias Timander .20 .50
7 Tyler Wright .20 .50
8 Espen Knutsen .40 1.00
9 Rostislav Klesla .40 1.00
10 Kevin Dineen .20 .50
11 Deron Quint .20 .50
12 Ron Tugnutt .40 1.00
13 Marc Denis .40 1.00
14 David Vyborny .20 .50
15 Lyle Odelein .20 .50
16 Jean-Luc Grand-Pierre .20 .50
17 Radim Bicanek .20 .50
18 Geoff Sanderson .20 .50
19 Ron Tugnutt .40 1.00
20 Ray Whitney .20 .50
21 Mike Sillinger .20 .50
22 Chris Nielsen .20 .50
23 Jamie Pushor .20 .50
24 Jamie Heward .20 .50

2013-14 Blue Jackets Buffalo Wild Wings

COMPLETE SET (8)

1970-71 Blues Postcards

COMPLETE SET (20) 20.00 40.00
1 Red Berenson 1.50 3.00
2 Chris Bordeleau 1.00 2.00
3 Craig Cameron 1.00 2.00
4 Tim Ecclestone 1.00 2.00
5 Glenn Hall 5.00 10.00
6 Fran Huck 1.00 2.00
7 Jim Lorentz 1.00 2.00
8 Bill McCreary AGM 1.00 2.00
9 Ab McDonald 1.50 3.00
10 George Morrison 1.00 2.00
11 Noel Picard 1.50 3.00
12 Barclay Plager 2.00 4.00
13 Bill Plager 1.50 3.00
14 Bob Plager 2.00 4.00
15 Jim Roberts 1.00 2.00
16 Gary Sabourin 1.00 2.00
17 Frank St. Marseille 1.50 3.00
18 Bill Sutherland 1.00 2.00
19 Ernie Wakely 1.50 3.00
20 Bob Wall 1.00 2.00

1971-72 Blues Postcards

COMPLETE SET (30) 35.00 70.00
1 Al Arbour CO 2.50 5.00
2 John Arbour 1.00 2.00
3 Curt Bennett 1.00 2.00
4 Chris Bordeleau 1.00 2.00
5 Carl Brewer 1.50 3.00
6 Jacques Caron 1.00 2.00
7 Terry Crisp 2.00 4.00
8 Andre Dupont 1.50 3.00
9 Jack Egers 1.00 2.00
10 Larry Hornung 1.00 2.00
11 Brian Lavender 1.00 2.00
11 Mike Murphy 1.00 2.00
12 G.Marchant/A.McPherson 1.00 2.00
12 Gerry Odrowski 1.00 2.00
13 Bill McCreary AGM .50 1.00
14 Danny O'Shea 1.00 2.00
15 Mike Parizeau 1.00 2.00
16 Noel Picard 1.50 3.00
17 Barclay Plager 2.00 4.00
18 Bill Plager 1.50 3.00
19 Bob Plager 2.00 4.00
20 Phil Roberto 1.50 3.00
21 Gary Sabourin 1.00 2.00
22 Jim Shires 1.00 2.00
23 Frank St. Marseille 1.50 3.00
24 Floyd Thomson 1.00 2.00
25 Garry Unger 2.50 5.00
26 Garry Unger action 2.50 5.00
27 Ernie Wakely 1.50 3.00
28 Tom Woodcock TR 1.00 2.00

1972-73 Blues White Border

COMPLETE SET (22) 30.00 60.00
1 Jacques Caron 1.50 3.00
2 Steve Durbano 2.00 4.00
3 Jack Egers 1.50 3.00
4 Chris Evans 1.50 3.00
5 Jean Hamel 1.50 3.00
6 Fran Huck 1.50 3.00
7 Brent Hughes 1.50 3.00
8 Bob Johnson 2.00 4.00
9 Mike Lampman 1.50 3.00
10 Bob McCord 1.50 3.00
11 Wayne Merrick 2.00 4.00
12 Mike Murphy 1.50 3.00
13 Danny O'Shea 1.50 3.00
14 Barclay Plager 2.50 5.00
15 Bob Plager 2.50 5.00
16 Pierre Plante 1.50 3.00
17 Phil Roberto 2.00 4.00
18 Gary Sabourin 1.50 3.00
19 Wayne Stephenson 2.50 5.00
20 Jean-Guy Talbot CO 1.50 3.00
21 Floyd Thomson 1.50 3.00
22 Garry Unger 2.50 5.00
AC1 Garry Unger 2.50 5.00
AC2 Phil Roberto 2.00 4.00

1973-74 Blues White Border

COMPLETE SET (24) 25.00 50.00
1 Lou Angotti .75 1.50
2 Don Awrey .75 1.50
3 John Davidson 2.50 5.00
4 Ab Demarco .75 1.50
5 Steve Durbano .75 1.50
6 Chris Evans .75 1.50
7 Larry Giroux .75 1.50
8 Jean Hamel .75 1.50
9 Nick Harbaruk .75 1.50
10 J.Bob Kelly 1.00 2.00
11 Mike Lampman .75 1.50
12 Wayne Merrick .75 1.50
13 Barclay Plager 2.00 4.00
14 Bob Plager 2.00 4.00
15 Pierre Plante 1.50 3.00
16 Phil Roberto 2.50 5.00
17 Gary Sabourin .75 1.50
18 Glen Sather 2.00 4.00
19 Wayne Stephenson 2.00 4.00
20 Jean-Guy Talbot CO .75 1.50
21 Floyd Thomson .75 1.50
22 Garry Unger 1.25 2.50
23 Garry Unger action 1.25 2.50
24 Team Photo (1972-73 team) 1.50 3.00

1978-79 Blues Postcards

COMPLETE SET (24) 15.00 30.00
1 Wayne Babych 1.00 2.00
2 Curt Bennett 1.00 2.00
3 Harvey Bennett .50 1.00
4 Red Berenson 1.50 3.00
5 Blue Angels 1.00 2.00
6 Jack Brownschidle 1.00 2.00
7 Mike Crombeen .50 1.00
8 Tony Currie .50 1.00
9 Fanvan .10 .25
10 Bernie Federko 2.00 4.00
11 Barry Gibbs .50 1.00
12 Larry Giroux .50 1.00
13 Inge Hammarstrom 1.00 2.00
14 Neil Labatte .50 1.00
15 Bob Murdoch .50 1.00
16 Phil Myre 1.00 2.00
17 Larry Patey .50 1.00
18 Barclay Plager CO 1.00 2.00
19 Rick Shinske .50 1.00
20 John Smrke .50 1.00
21 Ed Staniowski .50 1.00
22 Bob Stewart .50 1.00
23 Brian Sutter 2.00 4.00
24 Garry Unger 1.50 3.00

1987-88 Blues Team Photos

COMPLETE SET (20) 6.00 15.00
1 1967-68 Team Photo .60 1.50
2 1968-69 Team Photo .40 1.00
3 1969-70 Team Photo .40 1.00
4 1970-71 Team Photo .40 1.00
5 1971-72 Team Photo .40 1.00
6 1972-73 Team Photo .40 1.00
7 1973-74 Team Photo .40 1.00
8 1974-75 Team Photo .40 1.00
9 1975-76 Team Photo .40 1.00
10 1976-77 Team Photo .40 1.00
11 1977-78 Team Photo .40 1.00
12 1978-79 Team Photo .40 1.00
13 1979-80 Team Photo .40 1.00
14 1900-01 Team Photo .40 1.00
15 1981-82 Team Photo .40 1.00
16 1982-83 Team Photo .40 1.00
17 1983-84 Team Photo .40 1.00
18 1984-85 Team Photo .40 1.00
19 1985-86 Team Photo .40 1.00
20 1986-87 Team Photo .40 1.00

1987-88 Blues Kodak

COMPLETE SET (26) 12.00 30.00
1 Brian Benning .40 1.00
2 Tim Bothwell .30 .75
3 Charlie Bourgeois .30 .75
4 Paul Cavallini .40 1.00
5 Gino Cavallini .40 1.00
6 Michael Dark .30 .75
7 Doug Evans .30 .75
8 Todd Ewen .60 1.50
9 Bernie Federko 1.25 3.00
10 Ron Flockhart .30 .75
11 Doug Gilmour 2.50 6.00
12 Gaston Gingras .30 .75
13 Tony Hrkac .40 1.00
14 Mark Hunter .40 1.00
15 Jocelyn Lemieux .30 .75
16 Tony McKegney .40 1.00
17 Rick Meagher .40 1.00
18 Greg Millen .60 1.50
19 Robert Nordmark .30 .75
20 Greg Paslawski .30 .75
21 Herb Raglan .30 .75
22 Rob Ramage .40 1.00
23 Cliff Ronning 1.00 2.50
24 Brian Sutter .60 1.50
25 Perry Turnbull .30 .75
26 Rick Wamsley .60 1.50

1987-88 Blues Team Issue

COMPLETE SET (24) 14.00 35.00
1 Brian Benning .40 1.00
2 Mike Bullard .75 2.00
3 Gino Cavallini .40 1.00
4 Paul Cavallini .40 1.00
5 Craig Coxe .30 .75
6 Robert Dirk .30 .75
7 Doug Evans .30 .75
8 Todd Ewen .60 1.50
9 Bernie Federko 1.25 3.00
10 Gaston Gingras .30 .75
11 Tony Hrkac .40 1.00
12 Brett Hull 6.00 15.00
13 Tony McKegney .40 1.00
14 Rick Meagher .40 1.00
15 Greg Millen .60 1.50
16 Sergio Momesso .30 .75
17 Greg Paslawski .30 .75
18 Herb Raglan .30 .75
19 Dave Richter .30 .75
20 Vincent Riendeau .40 1.00
21 Gordie Roberts .40 1.00
22 Brian Sutter CO .60 1.50
23 Tom Tilley .30 .75
24 Steve Tuttle .30 .75

1988-89 Blues Kodak

COMPLETE SET (25) 10.00 25.00
1 Brian Benning .30 .75
2 Tim Bothwell .30 .75
3 Gino Cavallini .30 .75
4 Paul Cavallini .30 .75
5 Craig Coxe .30 .75
6 Doug Evans .30 .75
7 Todd Ewen .40 1.00
8 Bernie Federko .75 2.00
9 Gaston Gingras .30 .75
10 Tony Hrkac .40 1.00
11 Brett Hull 5.00 12.00
12 Mike Lalor .30 .75
13 Tony McKegney .40 1.00
14 Rick Meagher .30 .75
15 Greg Millen .40 1.00
16 Sergio Momesso .30 .75
17 Greg Paslawski .30 .75
18 Herb Raglan .30 .75
19 Vincent Riendeau .40 1.00
20 Dave Richter .30 .75
21 Gordie Roberts .30 .75
22 Cliff Ronning .75 2.00
23 Tom Tilley .30 .75
24 Steve Tuttle .30 .75
25 Peter Zezel .40 1.00

1988-89 Blues Team Issue

COMPLETE SET (24) 10.00 25.00
1 Brian Benning .30 .75
2 Mike Bullard .60 1.50
3 Gino Cavallini .30 .75
4 Paul Cavallini .30 .75
5 Craig Coxe .30 .75
6 Robert Dirk .30 .75
7 Doug Evans .30 .75
8 Todd Ewen .40 1.00
9 Bernie Federko .75 2.00
10 Gaston Gingras .30 .75
11 Tony Hrkac .40 1.00
12 Brett Hull 5.00 12.00
13 Tony McKegney .40 1.00
14 Rick Meagher .30 .75
15 Greg Millen .40 1.00
16 Sergio Momesso .30 .75
17 Greg Paslawski .30 .75
18 Herb Raglan .30 .75
19 Dave Richter .30 .75
20 Vincent Riendeau .40 1.00
21 Gordie Roberts .30 .75
22 Brian Sutter CO .40 1.00
23 Tom Tilley .30 .75
24 Steve Tuttle .30 .75

1989-90 Blues Kodak

COMPLETE SET (25) 10.00 25.00
1 Pat Jablonski .40 1.00
4 Gordie Roberts .20 .50
6 Tony Twist .60 1.50
9 Peter Zezel .30 .75
10 Dave Lowry .20 .50
12 Adam Oates 1.25 3.00
14 Paul Cavallini .20 .50
15 Paul MacLean .30 .75
16 Brett Hull 2.00 5.00
17 Gino Cavallini .20 .50
19 Rod Brind'Amour 1.25 3.00
20 Tom Tilley .20 .50
21 Jeff Brown .40 1.00
22 Rick Meagher .20 .50
23 Adrien Plavsic .20 .50
25 Herb Raglan .20 .50
26 Mike Lalor .20 .50
27 Sergio Momesso .20 .50
30 Vincent Riendeau .40 1.00
31 Curtis Joseph 4.00 10.00
35 Steve Tuttle .20 .50
38 Dominic Lavoie .20 .50
39 Kelly Chase .20 .50
40 Dave Thomlinson .20 .50
NNO Brian Sutter CO .30 .75

1990-91 Blues Kodak

COMPLETE SET (25) 10.00 25.00
1 Bob Bassen .20 .50
2 Rod Brind'Amour 1.25 3.00
3 Jeff Brown .30 .75
4 David Bruce .20 .50
5 Gino Cavallini .20 .50
6 Paul Cavallini .20 .50
7 Geoff Courtnall .40 1.00
8 Robert Dirk .20 .50
9 Glen Featherstone .20 .50
10 Brett Hull 2.00 5.00
11 Curtis Joseph 1.25 3.00
12 Dave Lowry .20 .50
13 Paul MacLean .20 .50
14 Mario Marois .20 .50
15 Rick Meagher .20 .50
16 Sergio Momesso .20 .50
17 Adam Oates 1.25 3.00
18 Vincent Riendeau .30 .75
19 Cliff Ronning .50 1.25
20 Harold Snepsts .40 1.00
21 Scott Stevens .60 1.50
22 Brian Sutter CO .20 .50
23 Rich Sutter .20 .50
24 Steve Tuttle .20 .50
25 Ron Wilson .20 .50

1991-92 Blues Postcards

COMPLETE SET (22) 8.00 20.00
1 Murray Baron .20 .50
2 Bob Bassen .20 .50
3 Jeff Brown .40 1.00
4 Garth Butcher .30 .75
5 Gino Cavallini .20 .50
6 Paul Cavallini .20 .50
7 Kelly Chase .25 .60
8 Dave Christian .30 .75
9 Nelson Emerson .30 .75
10 Brett Hull 1.50 4.00
11 Pat Jablonski .30 .75
12 Curtis Joseph 1.25 3.00
13 Darin Kimble .20 .50
14 Dave Lowry .20 .50
15 Michel Mongeau .20 .50
16 Adam Oates .75 2.00
17 Rob Robinson .20 .50
18 Brendan Shanahan 1.50 4.00
19 Rich Sutter .30 .75
20 Ron Sutter .30 .75
21 Ron Wilson .20 .50
22 Rick Zombo .20 .50

1992-93 Blues UD Best of the Blues

COMPLETE SET (28) 12.00 30.00
1 Glenn Hall 1.25 3.00
2 Doug Gilmour 1.25 3.00
3 Al Arbour .40 1.00
4 Mike Liut .40 1.00
5 Blake Dunlop .20 .50
6 Noel Picard .20 .50
7 Bob Plager .40 1.00
8 Ab McDonald .20 .50
9 Curtis Joseph 2.00 5.00
10 Wayne Babych .20 .50
11 Red Berenson .40 1.00
12 Brett Hull 1.50 4.00
13 Bob Gassoff .40 1.00
14 Bernie Federko .40 1.00
15 Gary Sabourin .20 .50
16 Joe Mullen .40 1.00
17 Adam Oates .75 2.00
18 Jorgen Pettersson .20 .50
19 Frank St. Marseille .30 .75
20 Scott Stevens .60 1.50
21 Rob Ramage .40 1.00
22 Jacques Plante 1.25 3.00
23 Rick Meagher .20 .50
24 Barclay Plager .40 1.00
25 Brian Sutter .40 1.00
26 Perry Turnbull .20 .50
27 Garry Unger .40 1.00
28 Checklist SP 2.00 5.00
NNO Brett Hull AU 60.00 150.00

1996-97 Blues Dispatch 30th Anniversary

COMPLETE SET (5) 4.00 10.00
1 Grant Fuhr .75 2.00
2 Brett Hull 1.50 4.00
3 Al MacInnis .75 2.00
4 Chris Pronger .75 2.00
5 Tony Twist .75 2.00

1999-00 Blues Taco Bell

COMPLETE SET (24) 6.00 15.00
1 Marc Bergevin .08 .25
2 Jochen Hecht .20 .50
3 Jamie McLennan .20 .50
4 Pierre Turgeon .30 .75
5 Scott Young .20 .50
6 Dave Ellett .08 .25
7 Lubos Bartecko .08 .25
8 Pavol Demitra .40 1.00
9 Michal Handzus .20 .50
10 Jeff Finley .08 .25
11 Ricard Persson .08 .25
12 Bob Bassen .08 .25
13 Craig Conroy .08 .25
14 Mike Eastwood .08 .25
15 Scott Pellerin .08 .25
16 Chris Pronger 1.25 3.00
17 Todd Reirden .08 .25
18 Roman Turek .30 .75
19 Kelly Chase .20 .50
20 Al MacInnis .75 2.00
21 Jamal Mayers .20 .50
22 Pascal Rheaume .08 .25
23 Tyson Nash .75 2.00
24 Stephane Richer .08 .25

2002-03 Blues Magnets

1 Pavol Demitra 2.00 5.00
2 Martin Rucinsky 1.25 3.00
3 Doug Weight 2.00 5.00

2002-03 Blues Team Issue

COMPLETE SET (24) 8.00 20.00
1 Fred Brathwaite .30 .75
2 Petr Cajanek .20 .50
3 Daniel Corso .20 .50
4 Pavol Demitra .40 1.00
5 Dallas Drake .20 .50
6 Mike Eastwood .20 .50
7 Jeff Finley .20 .50
8 Barret Jackman .75 2.00
9 Brent Johnson .40 1.00
10 Alexander Khavanov .20 .50
11 Tom Koivisto .20 .50
12 Christian Laflamme .20 .50
13 Reed Low .20 .50
14 Al MacInnis .60 1.50
15 Jamal Mayers .30 .75
16 Scott Mellanby .20 .50
17 Tyson Nash .40 1.00
18 Shjon Podein .20 .50
19 Chris Pronger .60 1.50
20 Bryce Salvador .20 .50
21 Cory Stillman .20 .50
22 Keith Tkachuk .75 2.00
23 Mike Van Ryn .20 .50
24 Doug Weight .60 1.50

2005-06 Blues Team Set

COMPLETE SET (24) 6.00 15.00
1 Christian Backman .30 .75
2 Eric Boguniecki .30 .75

3 Eric Brewer .30 .75
4 Petr Cajanek .30 .75
5 Aaron Downey .30 .75
6 Dallas Drake .30 .75
7 Jeff Hoggan .30 .75
8 Barret Jackman .30 .75
9 Ryan Johnson .30 .75
10 Patrick LaLime .40 1.00
11 Jamal Mayers .30 .75
12 Dean McAmmond .30 .75
13 Jay McClement .30 .75
14 Mark Rycroft .30 .75
15 Bryce Salvador .30 .75
16 Curtis Sanford .40 1.00
17 Mike Sillinger .30 .75
18 Lee Stempniak .50 1.25
19 Keith Tkachuk .50 1.25
20 Matt Walker .30 .75
21 Doug Weight .50 1.25
22 Eric Weinrich .30 .75
23 Dennis Wideman .30 .75
24 Scott Young .30 .75

1990-91 Bowman

1 Jeremy Roenick RC .40 1.00
2 Doug Wilson .10 .25
3 Greg Millen .10 .25
4 Steve Thomas .07 .20
5 Steve Larmer .10 .25
6 Denis Savard .12 .30
7 Ed Belfour RC .40 1.00
8 Dirk Graham .10 .25
9 Adam Creighton .07 .20
10 Keith Brown .10 .25
11 Jacques Cloutier RC .10 .25
12 Al Secord .10 .25
13 Troy Murray .10 .25
14 Kelly Chase RC .25 .60
15 Dave Lowry RC .10 .25
16 Adam Oates .12 .30
17 Sergio Momesso RC .10 .25
18 Paul MacLean .10 .25
19 Peter Zezel .12 .30
20 Vincent Riendeau RC .12 .30
21 Dave Thomlinson RC .10 .25
22 Paul Cavallini .10 .25
23 Rod Brind'Amour RC .25 .60
24 Brett Hull .25 .60
25 Jeff Brown .12 .30
26 Dominic Lavoie RC .10 .25
27 Andy Brickley .07 .20
28 Bob Sweeney .07 .20
29 Cam Neely .12 .30
30 Bob Carpenter .10 .25
31 Ray Bourque .20 .50
32 Rejean Lemelin .07 .20
33 Craig Janney .12 .30
34 Bob Beers RC .10 .25
35 Andy Moog .12 .30
36 Dave Poulin .12 .30
37 Brian Propp .12 .30
38 John Byce RC .10 .25
39 John Carter RC .10 .25
40 Dave Christian .07 .20
41 Shayne Corson .10 .25
42 Chris Chelios .12 .30
43 Mike McPhee .10 .25
44 Guy Carbonneau .07 .20
45 Stephane Richer .12 .30
46 Petr Svoboda
Chris Chelios actually pictured .12 .30
47 Russ Courtnall .12 .30
48 Sylvain Lefebvre RC .10 .25
49 Brian Skrudland .10 .25
50 Patrick Roy .30 .75
51 Bobby Smith .10 .25
52 Mathieu Schneider RC .10 .25
53 Stephan Lebeau RC .10 .25
54 Petri Skriko .12 .30
55 Jim Sandlak .12 .30
56 Doug Lidster .12 .30
57 Kirk McLean .07 .20
58 Brian Bradley .10 .25
59 Greg Adams .07 .20
60 Paul Reinhart .12 .30
61 Trevor Linden .12 .30
62 Adrien Plavsic RC .12 .30
63 Igor Larionov RC .25 .60
64 Steve Bozek .10 .25
65 Dan Quinn .10 .25
66 Mike Liut .07 .20
67 Nick Kypreos RC .12 .30
68 Michal Pivonka RC .10 .25
69 Dino Ciccarelli .12 .30
70 Kevin Hatcher .10 .25
71 Dale Hunter .12 .30
72 Don Beaupre .07 .20
73 Geoff Courtnall .10 .25
74 Rob Murray RC .07 .20
75 Calle Johansson .12 .30
76 Kelly Miller .07 .20
77 Mike Ridley .07 .20
78 Alan May RC .07 .20
79 Bob Brooke .07 .20
80 Slava Fetisov RC .25 .60
81 Sylvain Turgeon .10 .25
82 Kirk Muller .10 .25
83 John MacLean .10 .25
84 Jon Morris RC .07 .20
85 Brendan Shanahan .12 .30
86 Peter Stastny .10 .25
87 Bruce Driver .12 .30
88 Neil Brady RC .10 .25
89 Patrik Sundstrom .10 .25
90 Eric Weinrich RC .12 .30
91 Joe Nieuwendyk .10 .25
92 Sergei Makarov RC .25 .60
93 Al MacInnis .15 .40
94 Mike Vernon .10 .25
95 Gary Roberts .12 .30
96 Doug Gilmour .15 .40
97 Joe Mullen .10 .25
98 Rick Wamsley .12 .30
99 Joel Otto .10 .25
100 Paul Ranheim RC .12 .30
101 Gary Suter .07 .20
102 Theo Fleury .15 .40
103 Sergei Priakin RC .07 .20
104 Tony Horacek RC .07 .20
105 Ron Hextall .12 .30
106 Gord Murphy RC .12 .30
107 Pelle Eklund .07 .20
108 Rick Tocchet .12 .30
109 Murray Craven .12 .30
110 Doug Sulliman .10 .25
111 Kjell Samuelsson .10 .25
112 Ilkka Sinisalo .10 .25
113 Keith Acton .12 .30
114 Mike Bullard .10 .25
115 Doug Crossman .10 .25
116 Tom Fitzgerald RC .10 .25
117 Don Maloney .12 .30
118 Alan Kerr .10 .25
119 Mark Fitzpatrick RC .10 .25
120 Hubie McDonough RC .10 .25
121 Randy Wood .07 .20
122 Jeff Norton .12 .30
123 Pat LaFontaine .12 .30
124 Pat Flatley .12 .30
125 Joe Reekie RC .07 .20
126 Brent Sutter .10 .25
127 David Volek .12 .30
128 Shawn Cronin RC .07 .20
129 Dale Hawerchuk .15 .40
130 Brent Ashton .12 .30
131 Bob Essensa RC .20 .50
132 Dave Ellett .07 .20
133 Thomas Steen .10 .25
134 Doug Smail .10 .25
135 Fredrik Olausson .10 .25
136 Dave McLlwain .12 .30
137 Pat Elynuik .10 .25
138 Teppo Numminen RC .25 .60
139 Paul Fenton .12 .30
140 Tony Granato .07 .20
141 Tomas Sandstrom .12 .30
142 Rob Blake RC .20 .50
143 Wayne Gretzky .75 2.00
144 Kelly Hrudey .07 .20
145 Mike Krushelnyski .12 .30
146 Steve Duchesne .07 .20
147 Steve Kasper .07 .20
148 John Tonelli .10 .25
149 Dave Taylor .12 .30
150 Larry Robinson .12 .30
151 Todd Elik RC .12 .30
152 Luc Robitaille .12 .30
153 Al Iafrate .07 .20
154 Allan Bester .12 .30
155 Gary Leeman .10 .25
156 Mark Osborne .10 .25
157 Tom Fergus .07 .20
158 Brad Marsh .10 .25
159 Wendel Clark .20 .50
160 Daniel Marois .10 .25
161 Ed Olczyk .12 .30
162 Rob Ramage .12 .30
163 Vincent Damphousse .10 .25
164 Lou Franceschetti RC .12 .30
165 Paul Gillis .10 .25
166 Craig Wolanin RC .10 .25
167 Marc Fortier .10 .25
168 Tony McKegney .07 .20
169 Joe Sakic .40 1.00
170 Michel Petit .10 .25
171 Scott Gordon RC .07 .20
172 Tony Hrkac .07 .20
173 Bryan Fogarty RC .07 .20
174 Mike Hough .10 .25
175 Claude Loiselle RC .07 .20
176 Ulf Dahlen .12 .30
177 Larry Murphy .10 .25
178 Neal Broten .07 .20
179 Don Barber RC .10 .25
180 Shawn Chambers .10 .25
181 Clark Donatelli RC .07 .20
182 Brian Bellows .10 .25
183 Jon Casey .12 .30
184 Neil Wilkinson RC .10 .25
185 Aaron Broten .10 .25
186 Dave Gagner .12 .30
187 Basil McRae .07 .20
188 Mike Modano RC .40 1.00
189 Grant Fuhr .20 .50
190 Martin Gelinas RC .25 .60
191 Jari Kurri .15 .40
192 Geoff Smith RC .12 .30
193 Craig MacTavish .10 .25
194 Esa Tikkanen .10 .25
195 Glenn Anderson .10 .25
196 Joe Murphy RC .10 .25
197 Petr Klima .07 .20
198 Kevin Lowe .12 .30
199 Mark Messier .25 .60
200 Steve Smith .10 .25
201 Craig Simpson .10 .25
202 Rob Brown .25 .60
203 Wendell Young RC .12 .30
204 Mario Lemieux .50 1.25
205 Phil Bourque .10 .25
206 Mark Recchi RC .40 1.00
207 Zarley Zalapski .10 .25
208 Kevin Stevens RC .25 .60
209 Tom Barrasso .10 .25
210 John Cullen .12 .30
211 Paul Coffey .12 .30
212 Bob Errey .10 .25
213 Tony Tanti .10 .25
214 Carey Wilson .10 .25
215A Brian Leetch ERR .15 .40
215B Brian Leetch COR .15 .40
216 Darren Turcotte RC .10 .25
217 Brian Mullen .12 .30
218 Mike Richter RC .40 1.00
219 Troy Mallette RC .10 .25
220 Mike Gartner .15 .40
221 Bernie Nicholls .10 .25
222 John Vanbiesbrouck .12 .30
223 John Ogrodnick .12 .30
224 Paul Broten .10 .25
225 James Patrick .12 .30
226 Mark Janssens RC .12 .30
227 Randy McKay RC .10 .25
228 Marc Habscheid .10 .25
229 Jimmy Carson .10 .25
230 Yves Racine RC .12 .30
231 Dave Barr .12 .30
232 Shawn Burr .10 .25
233 Steve Yzerman .40 1.00
234 Steve Chiasson .07 .20
235 Daniel Shank RC .12 .30
236 John Chabot .12 .30
237 Gerard Gallant .07 .20
238 Bernie Federko .10 .25
239 Phil Housley .10 .25
240 Alexander Mogilny RC .40 1.00
241 Pierre Turgeon .10 .25
242 Daren Puppa .10 .25
243 Scott Arniel .07 .20
244 Christian Ruuttu .10 .25
245 Doug Bodger .10 .25
246 Dave Andreychuk .12 .30
247 Mike Foligno .10 .25
248 Dean Kennedy RC .07 .20
249 Dave Snuggerud RC .10 .25
250 Rick Vaive .10 .25
251 Todd Krygier RC .10 .25
252 Adam Burt RC .10 .25
253 Scott Young .07 .20
254 Ron Francis .15 .40
255 Peter Sidorkiewicz .12 .30
256 Dave Babych .07 .20
257 Pat Verbeek .10 .25
258 Ray Ferraro .10 .25
259 Chris Govedaris RC .10 .25
260 Brad Shaw RC .10 .25
261 Kevin Dineen .12 .30
262 Dean Evason .10 .25
263 Checklist 1-132 .10 .25
264 Checklist 133-264 .10 .25

1990-91 Bowman Tiffany

COMPLETE SET (264) 50.00 100.00
*TIFFANY: 5X TO 12X BASIC CARDS
254 Ron Francis .60 1.50

1990-91 Bowman Hat Tricks

*TIFFANY: 3X TO 8X BASIC INSERTS
1 Brett Hull .30 .75
2 Mario Lemieux .75 2.00
3 Rob Brown .30 .75
4 Mark Messier .30 .75
5 Steve Yzerman .75 2.00
6 Vincent Damphousse .12 .30
7 Kevin Dineen .15 .40
8 Mike Gartner .20 .50
9 Pat LaFontaine .15 .40
10 Gary Leeman .12 .30
11 Stephane Richer .15 .40
12 Luc Robitaille .15 .40
13 Steve Thomas .10 .25
14 Rick Tocchet .15 .40
15 Dino Ciccarelli .15 .40
16 John Druce .15 .40
17 Mike Gartner .20 .50
18 Tony Granato .10 .25
19 Jari Kurri .20 .50
20 Bernie Nicholls .12 .30
21 Tomas Sandstrom .15 .40
22 Dave Taylor .15 .40

1991-92 Bowman

1 John Cullen .10 .25
2 Todd Krygier .10 .25
3 Kay Whitmore .10 .25
4 Terry Yake .10 .25
5 Randy Ladouceur .10 .25
6 Kevin Dineen .10 .25
7 Jim McKenzie RC .12 .30
8 Brad Shaw .07 .20
9 Mark Hunter .10 .25
10 Dean Evason .10 .25
11 Mikael Andersson .10 .25
12 Pat Verbeek .10 .25
13 Peter Sidorkiewicz .10 .25
14 Mike Tomlak .10 .25
15 Zarley Zalapski .10 .25
16 Rob Brown .10 .25
17 Sylvain Cote .10 .25
18 Bobby Holik .12 .30
19 Daryl Reaugh .10 .25
20 Paul Cyr .10 .25
21 Doug Bodger .10 .25
22 Dave Andreychuk .12 .30
23 Clint Malarchuk .10 .25
24 Darrin Shannon .10 .25
25 Christian Ruuttu .10 .25
26 Uwe Krupp .10 .25
27 Pierre Turgeon .10 .25
28 Kevin Haller RC .12 .30
29 Dave Snuggerud .07 .20
30 Alexander Mogilny .10 .25
31 Dale Hawerchuk .15 .40
32 Mike Ramsey .10 .25
33 Darcy Wakaluk RC .12 .30
34 Tony Tanti .10 .25
35 Jay Wells .10 .25
36 Mikko Makela .10 .25
37 Daren Puppa .10 .25
38 Benoit Hogue .10 .25
39 Rick Vaive .07 .20
40 Grant Ledyard .10 .25
41 Steve Yzerman HT .40 1.00
42 Steve Yzerman .40 1.00
43 Shawn Burr .10 .25
44 Yves Racine .10 .25
45 Johan Garpenlov .10 .25
46 Keith Primeau .10 .25
47 Tim Cheveldae .10 .25
48 Brad McCrimmon .10 .25
49 Dave Barr .10 .25
50 Sergei Fedorov .20 .50
51 Brent Fedyk .10 .25
52 Jimmy Carson .10 .25
53 Paul Ysebaert .10 .25
54 Rick Zombo .10 .25
55 Bob Probert .12 .30
56 Gerard Gallant .07 .20
57 Kevin Miller .10 .25
58 Randy Moller .10 .25
59 Kris King .10 .25
60 Corey Millen RC .12 .30
61 Brian Mullen .10 .25
62 Darren Turcotte .10 .25
63 Ray Sheppard .10 .25
64 David Shaw .10 .25
65 Troy Mallette .10 .25
66 James Patrick .10 .25
67 Mark Janssens .10 .25
68 John Vanbiesbrouck .12 .30
69 Joey Kocur .07 .20
70 Mike Richter .12 .30
71 John Ogrodnick .10 .25
72 Kelly Kisio .10 .25
73 Normand Rochefort .10 .25
74 Mike Gartner .15 .40
75 Brian Leetch .10 .25
76 Bernie Nicholls .10 .25
77 Jan Erixon .10 .25
78 Larry Murphy .10 .25
79 Joe Mullen .10 .25
80 Tom Barrasso .10 .25
81 Paul Coffey .12 .30
82 Jiri Hrdina .10 .25
83 Mark Recchi .15 .40
84 Randy Gilhen .10 .25
85 Bob Errey .10 .25
86 Scott Young .10 .25
87 Mario Lemieux .50 1.25
88 Ulf Samuelsson .10 .25
89 Frank Pietrangelo .10 .25
90 Ron Francis .15 .40
91 Paul Stanton .10 .25
92 Kevin Stevens .10 .25
93 Bryan Trottier .12 .30
94 Phil Bourque .10 .25
95 Jaromir Jagr .40 1.00
96 Petr Klima HT .10 .25
97 Adam Graves .10 .25
98 Esa Tikkanen .10 .25
99 Norm Maciver RC .12 .30
100 Craig MacTavish .10 .25
101 Bill Ranford .10 .25
102 Martin Gelinas .10 .25
103 Charlie Huddy .10 .25
104 Petr Klima .10 .25
105 Ken Linseman .10 .25
106 Steve Smith .12 .30
107 Craig Simpson .07 .20
108 Chris Joseph .10 .25
109 Joe Murphy .10 .25
110 Jeff Beukeboom .10 .25
111 Grant Fuhr .20 .50
112 Geoff Smith .10 .25
113 Anatoli Semenov .10 .25
114 Mark Messier .25 .60
115 Kevin Lowe .10 .25
116 Glenn Anderson .10 .25
117 Bobby Smith .10 .25
118 Doug Smail .10 .25
119 Jon Casey .10 .25
120 Gaetan Duchesne .07 .20
121 Neal Broten .10 .25
122 Brian Hayward .10 .25
123 Brian Propp .10 .25
124 Mark Tinordi .10 .25
125 Mike Modano .25 .60
126 Marc Bureau .10 .25
127 Ulf Dahlen .10 .25
128 Chris Dahlquist .10 .25
129 Brian Bellows .10 .25
130 Mike Craig .10 .25
131 Dave Gagner .10 .25
132 Brian Glynn .10 .25
133 Joe Sakic .40 1.00
134 Owen Nolan .12 .30
135 Everett Sanipass .10 .25
136 Jamie Baker RC .10 .25
137 Mats Sundin .12 .30
138 Craig Wolanin .10 .25
139 Kip Miller .10 .25
140 Steven Finn .07 .20
141 Tony Hrkac .10 .25
142 Curtis Leschyshyn .10 .25
143 Mike McNeil .10 .25
144 Mike Hough .10 .25
145 Alexei Gusarov RC .10 .25
146 Jacques Cloutier .10 .25
147 Shawn Anderson .10 .25
148 Stephane Morin .10 .25
149 Bryan Fogarty .10 .25
150 Scott Pearson .10 .25
151 Ron Tugnutt .10 .25
152 Randy Velischek .10 .25
153 David Reid .07 .20
154 Rob Ramage .10 .25
155 Dave Hannan .10 .25
156 Wendel Clark .20 .50
157 Peter Ing .10 .25
158 Michel Petit .10 .25
159 Brian Bradley .10 .25
160 Rob Cimetta .10 .25
161 Gary Leeman .10 .25
162 Aaron Broten .10 .25
163 Dave Ellett .10 .25
164 Peter Zezel .07 .20
165 Daniel Marois .10 .25
166 Mike Krushelnyski .10 .25
167 Luke Richardson .10 .25
168 Scott Thornton .10 .25
169 Mike Foligno .12 .30
170 Vincent Damphousse .10 .25
171 Todd Gill .10 .25
172 Kevin Maguire .10 .25
173 Wayne Gretzky HT .75 2.00
174 Tomas Sandstrom HT .10 .25
175 John Tonelli .10 .25
176 Wayne Gretzky .75 2.00
177 Larry Robinson .12 .30
178 Jay Miller .10 .25
179 Tomas Sandstrom .10 .25
180 John McIntyre .10 .25
181 Brad Jones .10 .25
182 Rob Blake .12 .30
183 Kelly Hrudey .10 .25
184 Marty McSorley .10 .25
185 Todd Elik .10 .25
186 Dave Taylor .10 .25
187 Steve Kasper .07 .20
188 Luc Robitaille .12 .30
189 Bob Kudelski .07 .20
190 Daniel Berthiaume .10 .25
191 Steve Duchesne .07 .20
192 Tony Granato .07 .20
193 Bob Essensa .10 .25
194 Phil Sykes .10 .25
195 Paul MacDermid .10 .25
196 Dave McLlwain .10 .25
197 Phil Housley .10 .25
198 Pat Elynuik .10 .25
199 Randy Carlyle .10 .25
200 Thomas Steen .10 .25
201 Teppo Numminen .10 .25
202 Danton Cole .07 .20
203 Doug Evans .07 .20
204 Ed Olczyk .10 .25
205 Moe Mantha .10 .25
206 Scott Arniel .07 .20
207 Rick Tabaracci .10 .25
208 Bryan Marchment RC .10 .25
209 Mark Osborne .10 .25
210 Fredrik Olausson .10 .25
211 Brent Ashton .10 .25
212 Ray Ferraro .10 .25
213 Mark Fitzpatrick .10 .25
214 Hubie McDonough .10 .25
215 Joe Reekie .10 .25
216 Bill Berg .10 .25
217 Wayne McBean .07 .20
218 Pat Flatley .10 .25
219 Jeff Hackett .10 .25
220 Derek King .07 .20
221 Craig Ludwig .10 .25
222 Pat LaFontaine .12 .30
223 David Volek .10 .25
224 Glenn Healy .12 .30
225 Jeff Norton .10 .25
226 Brent Sutter .10 .25
227 Randy Wood .10 .25
228 Gary Nylund .10 .25
229 Dave Chyzowski .07 .20
230 Rick Tocchet .10 .25
231 Ken Wregget .10 .25
232 Terry Carkner .10 .25
233 Martin Hostak .07 .20
234 Ron Hextall .12 .30
235 Gord Murphy .10 .25
236 Scott Mellanby .10 .25
237 Pete Peeters .07 .20
238 Ron Sutter .10 .25
239 Murray Craven .10 .25
240 Kjell Samuelsson .10 .25
241 Pelle Eklund .10 .25
242 Mark Pederson .10 .25
243 Murray Baron .10 .25
244 Keith Acton .10 .25
245 Derrick Smith .10 .25
246 Mike Ricci .07 .20
247 Dale Kushner .10 .25
248 Normand Lacombe .10 .25
249 Theo Fleury HT .10 .25
250 Sergei Makarov HT .10 .25
251 Paul Ranheim .12 .30
252 Joe Nieuwendyk .10 .25
253 Mike Vernon .10 .25
254 Gary Suter .07 .20
255 Doug Gilmour .15 .40
256 Paul Fenton .10 .25
257 Roger Johansson .10 .25
258 Stephane Matteau .10 .25
259 Frank Musil .10 .25
260 Joel Otto .10 .25
261 Tim Sweeney .10 .25
262 Al MacInnis .15 .40
263 Gary Roberts .10 .25
264 Sergei Makarov .10 .25
265 Carey Wilson .10 .25
266 Ric Nattress .10 .25
267 Robert Reichel .25 .60
268 Rick Wamsley .07 .20
269 Brian MacLellan .10 .25
270 Theo Fleury .10 .25
271 Claude Lemieux .10 .25
272 John MacLean .10 .25
273 Slava Fetisov .10 .25
274 Kirk Muller .07 .20
275 Sean Burke .12 .30
276 Alexei Kasatonov .07 .20
277 Claude Lemieux .10 .25
278 Eric Weinrich .12 .30
279 Patrik Sundstrom .10 .25
280 Zdeno Ciger .10 .25
281 Bruce Driver .10 .25
282 Laurie Boschman .10 .25
283 Chris Terreri .10 .25
284 Ken Daneyko .10 .25
285 Doug Brown .10 .25
286 Jon Morris .10 .25
287 Peter Stastny .10 .25
288 Brendan Shanahan .12 .30
289 John MacLean .10 .25
290 Mike Liut .07 .20
291 Michal Pivonka .10 .25
292 Kelly Miller .10 .25
293 John Druce .10 .25
294 Calle Johansson .10 .25
295 Alan May .10 .25
296 Kevin Hatcher .10 .25
297 Tim Bergland .10 .25
298 Mikhail Tatarinov .10 .25
299 Peter Bondra .12 .30
300 Al Iafrate .10 .25
301 Nick Kypreos .10 .25
302 Dino Ciccarelli .10 .25
303 Dale Hunter .10 .25
304 Don Beaupre .10 .25
305 Jim Hrivnak .10 .25
306 Stephen Leach .10 .25
307 Dimitri Khristich FBC .10 .25
308 Mike Ridley .10 .25
309 Sergio Momesso .10 .25
310 Kirk McLean .10 .25
311 Greg Adams .10 .25
312 Adrien Plavsic .10 .25
313 Cliff Ronning .07 .20
314 Garry Valk .10 .25
315 Troy Gamble .07 .20
316 Gino Odjick .07 .20
317 Doug Lidster .10 .25
318 Geoff Courtnall .10 .25
319 Tom Kurvers .10 .25
320 Robert Kron .10 .25
321 Jyrki Lumme .10 .25
322 Jay Mazur .07 .20
323 Dave Capuano .10 .25
324 Petr Nedved .10 .25
325 Steve Bozek .10 .25
326 Igor Larionov .10 .25
327 Trevor Linden .12 .30
328 Shayne Corson .10 .25
329 Eric Desjardins .12 .30
330 Stephane Richer .10 .25
331 Brian Skrudland .10 .25
332 Sylvain Lefebvre .10 .25
333 Stephan Lebeau .10 .25
334 Mike Keane .07 .20
335 Patrick Roy UER .30 .75
336 Brent Gilchrist .10 .25
337 Andre Racicot RC .10 .25
338 Guy Carbonneau .10 .25
339 Mike McPhee .10 .25
340 Andrew Cassels .10 .25
341 Petr Svoboda .10 .25
342 Denis Savard .12 .30
343 Mathieu Schneider .10 .25
344 John LeClair RC .30 .75
345 Tom Chorske .10 .25
346 Russ Courtnall .10 .25
347 Ken Hodge Jr. HT .10 .25
348 Cam Neely HT .12 .30
349 Randy Burridge .10 .25
350 Glen Wesley .10 .25
351 Chris Nilan .07 .20
352 Jeff Lazaro .10 .25
353 Wes Walz .10 .25
354 Rejean Lemelin .07 .20
355 Craig Janney .10 .25
356 Ray Bourque .20 .50
357 Bob Sweeney .07 .20
358 Dave Christian .07 .20
359 Dave Poulin .10 .25
360 Garry Galley .10 .25
361 Andy Moog .12 .30
362 Ken Hodge Jr. .10 .25
363 Jim Wiemer .10 .25
364 Petri Skriko .07 .20
365 Don Sweeney .07 .20
366 Cam Neely .12 .30
367 Brett Hull HT .25 .60
368 Gino Cavallini .10 .25
369 Scott Stevens .12 .30
370 Rich Sutter .10 .25
371 Glen Featherstone .07 .20
372 Vincent Riendeau .10 .25
373 Dave Lowry .10 .25
374 Rod Brind'Amour .10 .25
375 Brett Hull .25 .60
376 Dan Quinn .10 .25
377 Tom Tilley .07 .20
378 Paul Cavallini .10 .25
379 Bob Bassen .10 .25
380 Mario Marois .10 .25
381 Darin Kimble .10 .25
382 Ron Wilson .10 .25
383 Garth Butcher .10 .25
384 Adam Oates .12 .30
385 Jeff Brown .10 .25
386 Jeremy Roenick HT .20 .50
387 Tony McKegney .10 .25
388 Troy Murray .10 .25
389 Dave Manson .10 .25
390 Ed Belfour .30 .75
391 Steve Thomas .10 .25
392 Michel Goulet .10 .25
393 Trent Yawney .10 .25
394 Adam Creighton .10 .25
395 Steve Larmer .10 .25
396 Jim Waite .10 .25
397 Dirk Graham .10 .25
398 Chris Chelios .12 .30
399 Mike Hudson .10 .25
400 Doug Wilson .10 .25
401 Greg Gilbert .10 .25
402 Wayne Presley .10 .25
403 Jeremy Roenick .20 .50
404 Frantisek Kucera .10 .25
405 Blackhawks
North Stars .10 .25
406 Blues
Red Wings .12 .30
407 Flames
Oilers .20 .50
408 Penguins
Devils .10 .25
409 Rangers
Capitals .10 .25
410 Bruins
Whalers .05 .15
411 Canadiens
Sabres .10 .25
412 Kings
Canucks .05 .15
413 Penguins
Capitals .10 .25
414 Bruins
Canadiens .10 .25
415 North Stars
Blues .25 .60
416 Kings
Oilers .05 .15
417 North Stars
Oilers .12 .30
418 Bruins
Penguins .12 .30
419 Game 1 Cup Finals .10 .25
420 Game 2 Cup Finals .10 .25
421 Game 3 Cup Finals .10 .25
422 Game 4 Cup Finals .10 .25
423 Game 5 Cup Finals .10 .25
424 Game 6 Cup Finals .10 .25
425 Mario Lemieux Smythe .50 1.25
426 Checklist 1-108 .05 .15
427 Checklist 109-216 .05 .15
428 Checklist 217-324 .05 .15
429 Checklist 325-429 .05 .15

1992-93 Bowman

1 Wayne Gretzky 2.50 6.00
2 Mike Krushelnyski .07 .20
3 Ray Bourque .50 1.25
4 Keith Brown .10 .25
5 Bob Sweeney .07 .20
6 Dave Christian .07 .20
7 Frantisek Kucera .10 .25
8 John LeClair .12 .30
9 Jamie Macoun .10 .25
10 Bob Carpenter .10 .25
11 Garry Galley .07 .20
12 Bob Kudelski .10 .25
13 Doug Bodger .07 .20
14 Craig Janney .10 .25
15 Glen Wesley .07 .20
16 Daren Puppa .10 .25
17 Andy Brickley .07 .20
18 Steve Konroyd .10 .25
19 Dave Poulin .07 .20
20 Phil Housley .10 .25
21 Kevin Todd .07 .20
22 Tomas Sandstrom .10 .25
23 Pierre Turgeon .10 .25
24 Steve Smith .07 .20
25 Ray Sheppard .07 .20
26 Stu Barnes .07 .20
27 Grant Ledyard .07 .20
28 Benoit Hogue .07 .20
29 Randy Burridge .07 .20
30 Clint Malarchuk .07 .20
31 Steve Duchesne .07 .20
32 Guy Hebert RC 2.00 5.00
33 Steve Kasper .07 .20
34 Alexander Mogilny .10 .25
35 Marty McSorley .10 .25
36 Doug Weight .25 .60
37 Dave Taylor .10 .25
38 Guy Carbonneau .10 .25
39 Brian Benning .07 .20
40 Nelson Emerson .07 .20
41 Craig Wolanin .07 .20
42 Kelly Hrudey .10 .25
43 Chris Chelios .12 .30
44 Dave Andreychuk .12 .30
45 Russ Courtnall .07 .20
46 Stephane Richer .10 .25
47 Petr Svoboda .10 .25
48 Barry Pederson .07 .20
49 Claude Lemieux .07 .20
50 Tony Granato .07 .20
51 Al MacInnis .15 .40
52 Luciano Borsato .07 .20
53 Sergei Makarov .07 .20
54 Bobby Smith .10 .25
55 Gary Suter .07 .20
56 Tom Draper .07 .20
57 Corry Millen .07 .20
58 Joe Mullen .10 .25
59 Joe Nieuwendyk .10 .25
60 Brian Hayward .07 .20
61 Steve Larmer .07 .20
62 Cam Neely .12 .30
63 Ric Nattress .10 .25
64 Denis Savard .12 .30
65 Gerald Diduck .10 .25
66 Pat Jablonski .10 .25
67 Brad McCrimmon .07 .20
68 Dirk Graham .07 .20
69 Joel Otto .07 .20
70 Luc Robitaille .12 .30
71 Dana Murzyn .07 .20
72 Jocelyn Lemieux .07 .20
73 Mike Hudson .07 .20
74 Patrick Roy 2.00 6.00
75 Doug Wilson .10 .25
76 Wayne Presley .07 .20
77 Felix Potvin .25 .60
78 Jeremy Roenick .20 .50
79 Andy Moog .12 .30
80 Joey Kocur .07 .20
81 Neal Broten .10 .25
82 Shayne Corson .10 .25
83 Doug Gilmour .15 .40
84 Rob Zettler .07 .20
85 Bob Probert .12 .30
86 Mike Vernon .10 .25
87 Rick Zombo .07 .20
88 Adam Creighton .07 .20
89 Mike McPhee .07 .20
90 Ed Belfour .12 .30
91 Steve Chiasson .07 .20
92 Dominic Roussel .10 .25
93 Troy Murray .07 .20
94 Jari Kurri .12 .30
95 Geoff Smith .07 .20
96 Paul Ranheim .07 .20
97 Rick Wamsley .07 .20
98 Brian Noonan .07 .20
99 Kevin Lowe .10 .25
100 Josef Beranek .07 .20
101 Michel Petit .07 .20
102 Craig Billington .10 .25
103 Steve Yzerman .75 2.00
104 Glenn Anderson .10 .25
105 Perry Berezan .07 .20
106 Bill Ranford .10 .25
107 Randy Ladouceur .07 .20
108 Jimmy Carson .07 .20
109 Gary Roberts .07 .20
110 Checklist 1-110 .08 .25
111 Brad Shaw .07 .20
112 Pat Verbeek .07 .20
113 Mark Messier .25 .60
114 Grant Fuhr .20 .50
115 Sylvain Cote .10 .25
116 Mike Sullivan .07 .20
117 Steve Thomas .10 .25
118 Craig MacTavish .07 .20
119 Dave Babych .10 .25
120 Jim Waite .10 .25
121 Kevin Dineen .07 .20
122 Shawn Burr .07 .20
123 Ron Francis .15 .40
124 Garth Butcher .10 .25
125 Jarmo Myllys .07 .20
126 Doug Brown .10 .25

127 James Patrick .07 .20
128 Ray Ferraro .07 .20
129 Terry Carkner .10 .25
130 John MacLean .10 .25
131 Randy Velischek .07 .20
132 John Vanbiesbrouck .12 .30
133 Dean Evason .07 .20
134 Patrick Flatley .10 .25
135 Petr Klima .07 .20
136 Geoff Sanderson .10 .25
137 Joe Reekie .07 .20
138 Kirk Muller .07 .20
139 Brian Mullen .07 .20
140 Daniel Berthiaume .10 .25
141 David Shaw .10 .25
142 Pat LaFontaine .12 .30
143 Ulf Dahlen .07 .20
144 Esa Tikkanen .07 .20
145 Slava Fetisov .07 .20
146 Mike Gartner .15 .40
147 Brent Sutter .07 .20
148 Darcy Wakaluk .10 .25
149 Brian Leetch .10 .25
150 Craig Simpson .07 .20
151 Mike Modano .30 .75
152 Bryan Trottier .12 .30
153 Larry Murphy .10 .25
154 Pavel Bure .12 .30
155 Kay Whitmore .10 .25
156 Darren Turcotte .07 .20
157 Frank Musil .10 .25
158 Mikael Andersson .07 .20
159 Rick Tocchet .10 .25
160 Scott Stevens .12 .30
161 Bernie Nicholls .10 .25
162 Peter Sidorkiewicz .07 .20
163 Scott Mellanby .07 .20
164 Alexander Semak .07 .20
165 Kjell Samuelsson .10 .25
166 Kelly Kisio .10 .25
167 Sylvain Turgeon .07 .20
168 Rob Brown .07 .20
169 Gerard Gallant .07 .20
170 Jyrki Lumme .07 .20
171 Dave Gagner .10 .25
172 Tony Tanti .07 .20
173 Zarley Zalapski .07 .20
174 Joe Murphy .07 .20
175 Ron Sutter .07 .20
176 Dino Ciccarelli .10 .25
177 Jim Johnson .10 .25
178 Mike Hough .10 .25
179 Pelle Eklund .10 .25
180 John Druce .07 .20
181 Paul Coffey .12 .30
182 Ken Wregget .10 .25
183 Brendan Shanahan .12 .30
184 Keith Acton .10 .25
185 Steven Finn .07 .20
186 Brett Hull .25 .60
187 Rollie Melanson .07 .20
188 Derek King .07 .20
189 Mario Lemieux .50 1.25
190 Mathieu Schneider .07 .20
191 Claude Vilgrain .10 .25
192 Gary Leeman .07 .20
193 Paul Cavallini .07 .20
194 John Cullen .07 .20
195 Ron Hextall .12 .30
196 David Volek .07 .20
197 Gordie Roberts .10 .25
198 Dale Craigwell .07 .20
199 Ed Belfour FOIL 2.00 6.00
200 Brian Bellows FOIL SP .10 .25
201 Chris Chelios FOIL .12 .30
202 Tim Cheveldae FOIL SP .07 .20
203A V.Damphousse FOIL ERR .10 .25
203B V.Damphousse FOIL COR .10 .25
204 Dave Ellett FOIL .07 .20
205 Sergei Fedorov FOIL SP 4.00 10.00
206 Theo Fleury FOIL 1.50 4.00
207 Wayne Gretzky FOIL 6.00 15.00
208 Phil Housley FOIL .10 .25
209 Brett Hull FOIL 2.00 5.00
210 Trevor Linden FOIL SP .12 .30
211 Al MacInnis FOIL .15 .40
212 Kirk McLean FOIL SP .07 .20
213 Adam Oates FOIL .12 .30
214 Gary Roberts FOIL SP .07 .20
215 Larry Robinson FOIL .12 .30
216 Luc Robitaille FOIL .12 .30
217 Jeremy Roenick FOIL SP 3.00 8.00
218 Mark Tinordi FOIL .07 .20
219 Doug Wilson FOIL .10 .25
220 Steve Yzerman FOIL 3.00 8.00
221 Checklist 111-220 .08 .25
222 Don Beaupre FOIL SP .10 .25
223 Ray Bourque FOIL 2.00 5.00
224 Rod Brind'Amour FOIL SP .07 .20
225 Randy Burridge FOIL SP .07 .20
226 Paul Coffey FOIL SP .12 .30
227 John Cullen FOIL .07 .20
228 Eric Desjardins FOIL SP .10 .25
229 Ray Ferraro FOIL .07 .20
230 Kevin Hatcher FOIL .07 .20
231 Jaromir Jagr FOIL 2.50 6.00
232 Brian Leetch FOIL SP .10 .25
233 Mario Lemieux FOIL 3.00 8.00
234 Mark Messier FOIL .25 .60
235 Alexander Mogilny FOIL .10 .25
236 Kirk Muller FOIL .07 .20
237 Owen Nolan FOIL .12 .30
238 Mike Richter FOIL .12 .30
239 Patrick Roy FOIL 4.00 10.00
240 Joe Sakic FOIL SP 6.00 15.00
241 Kevin Stevens FOIL .10 .25
242 Scott Stevens FOIL .12 .30
243 Bryan Trottier FOIL SP .12 .30
244 Joe Sakic .25 .60
245 Daniel Marois .07 .20
246 Randy Wood .07 .20
247 Jeff Brown .10 .25
248 Peter Bondra .12 .30
249 Peter Stastny .10 .25
250 Tom Barrasso .10 .25
251 Al Iafrate .10 .25
252 James Black .07 .20
253 Jan Erixon .10 .25
254 Brian Lawton .10 .25
255 Luke Richardson .10 .25
256 Rich Sutter .07 .20
257 Jeff Chychrun .07 .20
258 Adam Oates .12 .30
259 Tom Kurvers .07 .20
260 Brian Bellows .10 .25
261 Trevor Linden .12 .30
262 Vincent Riendeau .10 .25
263 Peter Zezel .07 .20
264 Rich Pilon .07 .20
265 Paul Broten .07 .20
266 Gaetan Duchesne .07 .20
267 Doug Lidster .10 .25
268 Rod Brind'Amour .07 .20
269 Jon Casey .07 .20
270 Pat Elynuik .07 .20
271 Kevin Hatcher .07 .20
272 Brian Propp .07 .20
273 Tom Fergus .07 .20
274 Steve Weeks .07 .20
275 Calle Johansson .07 .20
276 Russ Romaniuk .07 .20
277 Greg Paslawski .07 .20
278 Ed Olczyk .07 .20
279 Rod Langway .10 .25
280 Murray Craven .07 .20
281 Guy Larose .07 .20
282 Paul MacDermid .10 .25
283 Brian Bradley .07 .20
284 Paul Stanton .07 .20
285 Kirk McLean .07 .20
286 Andrei Lomakin .07 .20
287 Randy Carlyle .10 .25
288 Donald Audette .10 .25
289 Dan Quinn .10 .25
290 Mike Keane .07 .20
291 Dave Ellett .07 .20
292 Joe Juneau UER .07 .20
293 Phil Bourque .07 .20
294 Michal Pivonka .07 .20
295 Fredrik Olausson .07 .20
296 Randy McKay .10 .25
297 Don Beaupre .10 .25
298 Steve Leach .07 .20
299 Teppo Numminen .07 .20
300 Slava Kozlov .10 .25
301 Kevin Haller .07 .20
302 Jaromir Jagr .25 .60
303 Dale Hunter .10 .25
304 Bob Errey .10 .25
305 Nicklas Lidstrom .10 .25
306 Bob Essensa .10 .25
307 Sylvain Lefebvre .07 .20
308 Dale Hawerchuk .15 .40
309 Dave Snuggerud .07 .20
310 Michel Goulet .10 .25
311 Eric Desjardins .10 .25
312 Thomas Steen .07 .20
313 Scott Niedermayer .12 .30
314 Mark Recchi .15 .40
315 Gord Murphy .10 .25
316 Sergio Momesso .07 .20
317 Todd Elik .07 .20
318 Louie DeBrusk .07 .20
319 Mike Lalor .10 .25
320 Jamie Leach .07 .20
321 Darryl Sydor .07 .20
322 Brent Gilchrist .07 .20
323 Alexei Kasatonov .07 .20
324 Rick Tabaracci .07 .20
325 Wendel Clark .20 .50
326 Vladimir Konstantinov .12 .30
327 Randy Gilhen .07 .20
328 Owen Nolan .12 .30
329 Vincent Damphousse .10 .25
330 Checklist 221-331 .08 .25
331 Yves Racine .07 .20
332 Jacques Cloutier .10 .25
333 Greg Adams .07 .20
334 Mike Craig .07 .20
335 Curtis Leschyshyn .10 .25
336 John McIntyre .07 .20
337 Stephane Quintal .07 .20
338 Kelly Miller .07 .20
339 Dave Manson .07 .20
340 Stephane Matteau .07 .20
341 Christian Ruuttu .07 .20
342 Mike Donnelly .07 .20
343 Eric Weinrich .07 .20
344 Mats Sundin .12 .30
345 Geoff Courtnall .07 .20
346 Stephan Lebeau .07 .20
347 Jeff Beukeboom .07 .20
348 Jeff Hackett .10 .25
349 Uwe Krupp .07 .20
350 Igor Larionov .07 .20
351 Ulf Samuelsson .07 .20
352 Marty McInnis .07 .20
353 Peter Ahola .07 .20
354 Mike Richter .12 .30
355 Theo Fleury .20 .50
356 Dan Lambert .07 .20
357 Brent Ashton .07 .20
358 David Bruce .07 .20
359 Chris Dahlquist .10 .25
360 Mike Ridley .07 .20
361 Pat Falloon .07 .20
362 Doug Smail .07 .20
363 Adrien Plavsic .07 .20
364 Ron Wilson .10 .25
365 Derian Hatcher .07 .20
366 Kevin Stevens .10 .25
367 Rob Blake .10 .25
368 Curtis Joseph .15 .40
369 Tom Fitzgerald .07 .20
370 Dave Lowry .10 .25
371 J.J. Daigneault .07 .20
372 Jim Hrivnak .10 .25
373 Adam Graves .07 .20
374 Brad May .07 .20
375 Todd Gill .07 .20
376 Paul Ysebaert .07 .20
377 David Williams RC .07 .20
378 Bob Bassen .07 .20
379 Brian Glynn .07 .20
380 Kris King .07 .20
381 Rob Pearson .07 .20
382 Marc Bureau .10 .25
383 Jim Paek .10 .25
384 Tomas Forslund .07 .20
385 Darrin Shannon .07 .20
386 Chris Terreri .10 .25
387 Andrew Cassels .07 .20
388 Jay More .07 .20
389 Tony Amonte .10 .25
390 Mark Pederson .07 .20
391 Kevin Miller .07 .20
392 Igor Ulanov .07 .20
393 Kelly Buchberger .07 .20
394 Mark Fitzpatrick .10 .25
395 Mikhail Tatarinov .07 .20
396 Petr Nedved .10 .25
397 Jeff Odgers .07 .20
398 Stephane Fiset .07 .20
399 Mark Tinordi .07 .20
400 Johan Garpenlov .07 .20
401 Robert Reichel .07 .20
402 Don Sweeney UER .07 .20
403 Rob DiMaio .07 .20
404 Bill Lindsay RC .07 .20
405 Steph Beauregard .10 .25
406 Mike Ricci .07 .20
407 Bobby Holik .10 .25
408 Igor Kravchuk .07 .20
409 Murray Baron .07 .20
410 Troy Gamble .07 .20
411 Cliff Ronning .07 .20
412 Jeff Reese .07 .20
413 Robert Kron .07 .20
414 Benoit Brunet .07 .20
415 Shawn McEachern .07 .20
416 Sergei Fedorov .20 .50
417 Joe Sacco .07 .20
418 Bryan Marchment .10 .25
419 John LeBlanc RC .10 .25
420 Tim Cheveldae .07 .20
421 Claude LaPointe .07 .20
422 Ken Sutton .07 .20
423 Anatoli Semenov .07 .20
424 Mike McNeil .10 .25
425 Norm Maciver .07 .20
426 Sergei Nemchinov .07 .20
427 Dimitri Khristich .07 .20
428 Dominik Hasek .20 .50
429 Bob McGill .07 .20
430 Valeri Zelepukin .07 .20
431 Vladimir Ruzicka .07 .20
432 Valeri Kamensky .07 .20
433 Pat MacLeod .07 .20
434 Glenn Healy .10 .25
435 Patrice Brisebois .07 .20
436 James Baker .07 .20
437 Michel Picard .10 .25
438 Scott Lachance UER .07 .20
439 Gilbert Dionne .07 .20
440 M.Lemieux Smythe FOIL 3.00 8.00
441 Checklist 332-441 .08 .25
442 Eric Lindros UER .20 .50

1995-96 Bowman

1 Wayne Gretzky 1.00 2.50
2 Ray Bourque .25 .60
3 Craig Janney .10 .25
4 Andrew Cassels .10 .25
5 Alexander Mogilny .12 .30
6 Pierre Turgeon .12 .30
7 Dave Andreychuk .15 .40
8 Mark Messier .30 .75
9 Igor Korolev .10 .25
10 Tomas Sandstrom .12 .30
11 Shayne Corson .12 .30
12 Chris Chelios .15 .40
13 Claude Lemieux .15 .40
14 Stephane Richer .12 .30
15 Patrick Roy .40 1.00
16 Al MacInnis .20 .50
17 Cam Neely .15 .40
18 Doug Gilmour .20 .50
19 Steve Thomas .12 .30
20 Jeremy Roenick .25 .60
21 Steve Yzerman .40 1.00
22 Petr Klima .10 .25
23 Luc Robitaille .15 .40
24 Bill Ranford .12 .30
25 Grant Fuhr .25 .60
26 Sean Burke .10 .25
27 John MacLean .12 .30
28 Brendan Shanahan .15 .40
29 Pat LaFontaine .15 .40
30 John Vanbiesbrouck .15 .40
31 Ron Francis .20 .50
32 Brian Leetch .12 .30
33 Dave Gagner .10 .25
34 Larry Murphy .12 .30
35 Mike Modano .25 .60
36 Rick Tocchet .12 .30
37 Scott Mellanby .12 .30
38 Ron Hextall .15 .40
39 Joe Juneau .10 .25
40 Mario Lemieux .60 1.50
41 Paul Coffey .15 .40
42 Joe Sakic .30 .75
43 Brett Hull .30 .75
44 Adam Oates .15 .40
45 Wendel Clark .25 .60
46 Trevor Linden .15 .40
47 Tom Barrasso .12 .30
48 Kevin Hatcher .12 .30
49 Mats Sundin .15 .40
50 Scott Stevens .15 .40
51 Mark Recchi .20 .50
52 Theo Fleury .20 .50
53 Ed Belfour .12 .30
54 Adam Graves .12 .30
55 Peter Bondra .15 .40
56 Dominik Hasek .25 .60
57 Jaromir Jagr .50 1.25
58 Owen Nolan .15 .40
59 Kevin Stevens .12 .30
60 Alexei Zhamnov .15 .40
61 Dimitri Khristich .10 .25
62 Chris Pronger .15 .40
63 John LeClair .15 .40
64 Scott Niedermayer .15 .40
65 Pavel Bure .15 .40
66 Chris Osgood .15 .40
67 Geoff Sanderson .10 .25
68 Doug Weight .15 .40
69 Keith Tkachuk .15 .40
70 Martin Brodeur .40 1.00
71 Eric Lindros .25 .60
72 Martin Straka .10 .25
73 Alexander Selivanov .12 .30
74 Jim Carey .12 .30
75 Teemu Selanne .30 .75
76 Rob Niedermayer .12 .30
77 Vyacheslav Kozlov .12 .30
78 Todd Harvey .10 .25
79 Felix Potvin .25 .60
80 Sergei Fedorov .25 .60
81 Mathieu Schneider .10 .25
82 Roman Hamrlik .10 .25
83 Mikael Renberg .12 .30
84 Jeff Friesen .10 .25
85 Peter Forsberg .30 .75
86 Kenny Jonsson .15 .40
87 Brian Savage .10 .25
88 Oleg Tverdovsky .15 .40
89 Nikolai Khabibulin .12 .30
90 Paul Kariya .15 .40
91 Zdenek Nedved .10 .25
92 Darren Langdon RC .30 .75
93 Lonny Bohonos RC .12 .30
94 Mike Wilson RC .30 .75
95 Landon Wilson RC .10 .25
96 Bryan McCabe .15 .40
97 Byron Dafoe .12 .30
98 Denny Lambert RC .12 .30
99 Craig Mills .10 .25
100 Ed Jovanovski .15 .40
101 Jason Bonsignore .10 .25
102 Clayton Beddoes UER RC .12 .30
103 Jamie Pushor .12 .30
104 Drew Bannister .12 .30
105 Ed Ward .12 .30
106 Todd Warriner .12 .30
107 Deron Quint .12 .30
108 Rhett Warrener .10 .25
109 Marko Kiprusoff .12 .30
110 Daniel Alfredsson RC .75 2.00
111 Marcus Ragnarsson UER RC .20 .50
112 Miroslav Satan RC .20 .50
113 Niklas Sundstrom .15 .40
114 Mathieu Dandenault .30 .75
115 Vitali Yachmenev .15 .40
116 Petr Sykora RC .40 1.00
117 Antti Tormanen .10 .25
118 Jeff O'Neill .15 .40
119 David Nemirovsky RC .12 .30
120 Jason Doig .15 .40
121 Aaron Gavey .10 .25
122 Ladislav Kohn .12 .30
123 Richard Park .15 .40
124 Stephane Yelle .12 .30
125 Eric Daze .30 .75
126 Niclas Andersson .12 .30
127 Brendan Witt .15 .40
128 Jamie Storr .12 .30
129 Darby Hendrickson .10 .25
130 Radek Dvorak RC .20 .50
131 Cory Stillman .10 .25
132 Jamie Rivers .10 .25
133 Ville Peltonen .10 .25
134 Peter Ferraro .12 .30
135 Trent McCleary RC .12 .30
136 Chris Wells .12 .30
137 Chad Kilger RC .15 .40
138 Denis Pederson .10 .25
139 Roman Vopat .10 .25
140 Shean Donovan .10 .25
141 Alex Stojanov .10 .25
142 Mark Kolesar RC .12 .30
143 Scott Walker RC .10 .25
144 Dave Roche RC .12 .30
145 Corey Hirsch .12 .30
146 Aki Berg .15 .40
147 Stefan Ustorf .10 .25
148 Saku Koivu .15 .40
149 Shane Doan RC .50 1.25
150 Jere Lehtinen .12 .30
151 Kyle McLaren RC .10 .25
152 Marty Murray .15 .40
153 Sean Pronger RC .12 .30
154 Joaquin Gage RC .12 .30
155 Eric Fichaud .12 .30
156 Todd Bertuzzi RC .20 .50
157 Wayne Primeau .10 .25
158 Scott Bailey RC .20 .50
159 Viktor Kozlov .12 .30
160 Valeri Bure .10 .25
161 Dody Wood .10 .25
162 Grant Marshall .10 .25
163 Ken Klee RC .10 .25
164 Corey Schwab RC .30 .75
165 Brian Holzinger RC .30 .75

1995-96 Bowman Foil

*VETS: 3X TO 8X BASIC CARDS
*ROOKIES: 1.2X TO 3X BASIC CARDS

1995-96 Bowman Draft Prospects

P1 Johnathan Aitken .15 .40
P2 Chris Allen .15 .40
P3 Matt Bradley .15 .40
P4 Daniel Briere .40 1.00
P5 Jeff Brown .15 .40
P6 Jan Bulis .15 .40
P7 Daniel Corso .40 1.00
P8 Luke Curtin .15 .40
P9 Matthieu Descoteaux .15 .40
P10 Boyd Devereaux .15 .40
P11 Jason Doyle .15 .40
P12 Etienne Drapeau .15 .40
P13 J-P Dumont .15 .40
P14 Mathieu Garon .50 1.25
P15 Josh Green .15 .40
P16 Chris Hajt .15 .40
P17 Matt Higgins .15 .40
P18 Craig Hillier .15 .40
P19 Josh Holden .12 .30
P20 Dan Focht .15 .40
P21 Henry Kuster .15 .40
P22 Francis Larivee .15 .40
P23 Mario Larocque .15 .40
P24 Wes Mason .15 .40
P25 Francois Methot .12 .30
P26 Geoff Peters .12 .30
P27 Randy Petruk .15 .40
P28 Chris Phillips .20 .50
P29 Boris Protsenko .15 .40
P30 Remi Royer .15 .40
P31 Cory Sarich .15 .40
P32 Jaroslav Svejkovsky .15 .40
P33 Curtis Tipler .15 .40
P34 Darren Van Oene .12 .30
P35 Jesse Wallin .15 .40
P36 Kurt Walsh .15 .40
P37 Lance Ward .15 .40
P38 Steve Wasylko .15 .40
P39 Trevor Wasyluk .20 .50
P40 Jon Zukiwsky .15 .40

1995-96 Bowman Bowman's Best

*REFRACTOR: 1X TO 2.5X BASIC INSERTS
BB1 Peter Forsberg 3.00 8.00
BB2 Teemu Selanne 3.00 8.00
BB3 Eric Lindros 2.50 6.00
BB4 Scott Stevens 1.50 4.00
BB5 Wayne Gretzky 10.00 25.00
BB6 Mark Messier 3.00 8.00
BB7 Jaromir Jagr 5.00 12.00
BB8 Martin Brodeur 4.00 10.00
BB9 Alexander Mogilny 1.25 3.00
BB10 Mario Lemieux 6.00 15.00
BB11 Joe Sakic 3.00 8.00
BB12 Sergei Fedorov 2.50 6.00
BB13 Pavel Bure 1.50 4.00
BB14 Brian Leetch 1.25 3.00
BB15 Paul Kariya 1.50 4.00
BB16 Daniel Alfredsson 8.00 20.00
BB17 Saku Koivu 1.50 4.00
BB18 Eric Daze 3.00 8.00
BB19 Ed Jovanovski 1.50 4.00
BB20 Vitali Yachmenev 1.50 4.00
BB21 Niklas Sundstrom 1.50 4.00
BB22 Radek Dvorak 2.00 5.00
BB23 Byron Dafoe 1.25 3.00
BB24 Shane Doan 5.00 12.00
BB25 Chad Kilger 1.50 4.00
BB26 Jeff O'Neill 1.50 4.00
BB27 Cory Stillman 1.00 2.50
BB28 Valeri Bure 1.00 2.50
BB29 Marcus Ragnarsson 2.00 5.00
BB30 Todd Bertuzzi 2.00 5.00

1998-99 Bowman's Best

1 Steve Yzerman .60 1.50
2 Paul Kariya .25 .60
3 Wayne Gretzky 1.50 4.00
4 Jaromir Jagr .75 2.00
5 Mark Messier .50 1.25
6 Keith Tkachuk .25 .60
7 John LeClair .25 .60
8 Martin Brodeur .60 1.50
9 Rob Blake .25 .60
10 Brett Hull .50 1.25
11 Dominik Hasek .40 1.00
12 Peter Forsberg .50 1.25
13 Doug Gilmour .30 .75
14 Vincent Damphousse .20 .50
15 Zigmund Palffy .25 .60
16 Daniel Alfredsson .25 .60
17 Mike Vernon .20 .50
18 Chris Pronger .25 .60
19 Wendel Clark .40 1.00
20 Curtis Joseph .30 .75
21 Peter Bondra .25 .60
22 Grant Fuhr .40 1.00
23 Nikolai Khabibulin .25 .60
24 Kevin Hatcher .15 .40
25 Brian Leetch .20 .50
26 Patrik Elias .25 .60
27 Chris Osgood .25 .60
28 Patrick Roy .60 1.50
29 Chris Chelios .25 .60
30 Trevor Kidd .15 .40
31 Theo Fleury .30 .75
32 Michael Peca .15 .40
33 Ray Bourque .40 1.00
34 Ed Belfour .25 .60
35 Sergei Fedorov .40 1.00
36 Adrian Aucoin .15 .40
37 Alexei Yashin .20 .50
38 Rick Tocchet .20 .50
39 Mats Sundin .25 .60
40 Alexander Mogilny .20 .50
41 Jeff Friesen .15 .40
42 Eric Lindros .40 1.00
43 Mike Richter .25 .60
44 Saku Koivu .25 .60
45 Teemu Selanne .50 1.25
46 Doug Weight .25 .60
47 Nicklas Lidstrom .30 .75
48 Mike Modano .40 1.00
49 Joe Sakic .50 1.25
50 Ron Francis .30 .75
51 Jason Allison .20 .50
52 Brendan Shanahan .25 .60
53 Bobby Holik .15 .40
54 Damian Rhodes .25 .60
55 Jeremy Roenick .40 1.00
56 Tom Barrasso .20 .50
57 Al MacInnis .30 .75
58 Pavel Bure .25 .60
59 Olaf Kolzig .25 .60
60 Patrick Marleau .25 .60
61 Cliff Ronning .15 .40
62 Joe Nieuwendyk .20 .50
63 Jeff Hackett .15 .40
64 Keith Primeau .20 .50
65 Jarome Iginla .30 .75
66 Sergei Samsonov .20 .50
67 Rod Brind'Amour .25 .60
68 Dino Ciccarelli .25 .60
69 Ryan Smyth .20 .50
70 Owen Nolan .25 .60
71 Mike Johnson .15 .40
72 Adam Oates .25 .60
73 Mattias Ohlund .15 .40
74 Jamie Heward RC .15 .40
75 Mike Dunham .20 .50
76 Jere Lehtinen .20 .50
77 Tony Amonte .20 .50
78 Derek Morris .15 .40
79 Darren McCarty .15 .40
80 Bryan Berard .20 .50
81 Adam Graves .15 .40
82 John Vanbiesbrouck .25 .60
83 Marco Sturm .15 .40
84 Joe Thornton .40 1.00
85 Wade Redden .15 .40
86 Pierre Turgeon .20 .50
87 Bill Ranford .20 .50
88 Alexei Zhitnik .15 .40
89 Valeri Kamensky .15 .40
90 Dean McAmmond .15 .40
91 Jozef Stumpel .15 .40
92 Jocelyn Thibault .20 .50
93 Joe Juneau .15 .40
94 Craig Janney .15 .40
95 Robert Reichel .15 .40
96 Mark Recchi .30 .75
97 Sami Kapanen .15 .40
98 Shayne Corson .20 .50
99 Scott Niedermayer .25 .60
100 Trevor Linden .25 .60
101 Olli Jokinen SP .75 2.00
102 Chris Drury SP .75 2.00
103 Daniel Cleary SP .60 1.50
104 Yan Golubovsky SP RC .75 2.00
105 Brendan Morrison SP .60 1.50
106 Manny Malhotra SP 1.00 2.50
107 Marian Hossa SP 1.00 2.50
108 Daniel Briere SP .75 2.00
109 Vincent Lecavalier SP 2.00 5.00
110 Milan Hejduk SP RC 1.50 4.00
111 Tom Poti SP .60 1.50
112 Mike Maneluk SP RC .60 1.50
113 Marty Reasoner SP 1.00 2.50
114 Rico Fata SP .75 2.00
115 Eric Brewer SP 1.00 2.50
116 Dan Cloutier SP .75 2.00
117 Mike Leclerc SP .60 1.50
118 Dimitri Tertyshny SP RC .60 1.50
119 Josh Green SP RC 1.00 2.50
120 Mark Parrish SP RC 1.50 4.00
121 Jamie Wright SP .60 1.50
122 Fred Lindquist SP RC .60 1.50
123 Daniil Markov SP RC .75 2.00
124 Bill Muckalt SP RC .60 1.50
125 Johan Davidsson SP .60 1.50
126 Oleg Kvasha SP RC 1.00 2.50
127 Cameron Mann SP .60 1.50
128 Pascal Trepanier SP RC .60 1.50
129 Clarke Wilm SP RC .60 1.50
130 Alain Nasreddine SP RC .60 1.50
131 Bryan Helmer SP RC .60 1.50
132 Michal Handzus SP RC 1.25 3.00
133 Pavel Kubina SP RC .75 2.00
134 Zdeno Chara SP 1.00 2.50
135 Matt Higgins SP RC .60 1.50
136 David Legwand SP .60 1.50
137 Brad Stuart SP RC .60 1.50
138 Mark Bell SP RC .60 1.50
139 Eric Chouinard SP .60 1.50
140 Simon Gagne SP 1.00 2.50
141 Ramzi Abid SP RC .60 1.50
142 Sergei Varlamov SP .60 1.50
143 Mike Ribeiro SP .75 2.00
144 Derrick Walser SP RC .60 1.50
145 Mathieu Garon SP .60 1.50
146 Daniel Tkaczuk SP .60 1.50
147 Jeff Heerema SP RC .60 1.50
148 Sebastien Roger SP RC .60 1.50
149 Bret DeCecco SP .60 1.50
150 Checklist SP .40 1.00

1998-99 Bowman's Best Refractors

*1-100 REFRACTOR: 8X TO 20X BASIC CARDS
*101-150 REFRACTOR: 3X TO 6X BASIC SP

1998-99 Bowman's Best Atomic Refractors

*1-100 ATOMIC REF: 20X TO 50X BASIC CARDS
*101-150 ATOMIC REF: 6X TO 15X BASIC SP
1 Steve Yzerman 40.00 100.00
3 Wayne Gretzky 60.00 150.00
28 Patrick Roy 40.00 100.00

1998-99 Bowman's Best Autographs

*REFRACTOR: .8X TO 2X BASIC AUTO
*ATOMIC REF: 1.5X TO 4X BASIC AUTO
A1A Dominik Hasek 12.00 30.00
A1B Dominik Hasek 12.00 30.00
A2A Jaromir Jagr 25.00 60.00
A2B Jaromir Jagr 25.00 60.00
A3A Peter Bondra 8.00 20.00
A3B Peter Bondra 8.00 20.00
A4A Sergei Fedorov 12.00 30.00
A4B Sergei Fedorov 12.00 30.00
A5A Ray Bourque 12.00 30.00
A5B Ray Bourque 12.00 30.00
A6A Bill Muckalt 5.00 12.00
A6B Bill Muckalt 5.00 12.00
A7A Brendan Morrison 5.00 12.00
A7B Brendan Morrison 5.00 12.00
A8A Chris Drury 6.00 15.00
A8B Chris Drury 6.00 15.00
A9A Mark Parrish 12.00 30.00
A9B Mark Parrish 12.00 30.00
A10A Manny Malhotra 8.00 20.00
A10B Manny Malhotra 8.00 20.00

1998-99 Bowman's Best Mirror Image Fusion

*REFRACTOR/100: 4X TO 10X BASIC INSERTS
*ATOMIC REF/25: 10X TO 25X BASIC INSERTS
F1 J.LeClair/B.Battaglia .60 1.50
F2 P.Kariya/M.LeClerc .60 1.50
F3 J.Jagr/M.Parrish 2.00 5.00
F4 Selanne/Lindquist 1.25 3.00
F5 Lindros/Lecavalier 1.25 3.00
F6 P.Forsberg/O.Jokinen 1.25 3.00
F7 B.Leetch/D.Markov .50 1.25
F8 Lidstrom/Golubovsky .75 2.00
F9 D.Hasek/D.Cloutier 1.00 2.50
F10 P.Roy/T.Moss 1.50 4.00
F11 S.Samsonov/M.Watt .50 1.25
F12 K.Tkachuk/J.Wright .60 1.50
F13 P.Bondra/M.Hossa .60 1.50
F14 P.Bure/B.Muckalt .60 1.50
F15 Gretzky/Morrison 4.00 10.00
F16 Fedorov/Reasoner 1.00 2.50
F17 R.Bourque/E.Brewer 1.00 2.50
F18 C.Pronger/T.Poti .60 1.50
F19 Brodeur/Theodore 1.50 4.00
F20 C.Osgood/J.Storr .60 1.50

1998-99 Bowman's Best Performers

*REFRACTOR/200: 4X TO 10X BASIC INSERTS
*ATOMIC REF/50: 10X TO 25X BASIC INSERTS
BP1 Mike Johnson .40 1.00
BP2 Sergei Samsonov .50 1.25
BP3 Patrik Elias .60 1.50
BP4 Patrick Marleau .60 1.50
BP5 Mattias Ohlund .40 1.00
BP6 Manny Malhotra .60 1.50
BP7 Chris Drury .50 1.25
BP8 Daniel Briere .50 1.25
BP9 Brendan Morrison .40 1.00
BP10 Vincent Lecavalier 1.25 3.00

1998-99 Bowman's Best Scotty Bowman's Best

*REFRACT/200: 2.5X TO 6X BASIC INSERTS
*ATOMIC REF/50: 5X TO 12X BASIC INSERTS
SB1 Dominik Hasek 1.00 2.50
SB2 Martin Brodeur 1.50 4.00
SB3 Chris Osgood .60 1.50
SB4 Nicklas Lidstrom .75 2.00
SB5 Eric Lindros 1.00 2.50
SB6 Jaromir Jagr 2.00 5.00
SB7 Steve Yzerman 1.50 4.00
SB8 Peter Forsberg 1.25 3.00
SB9 Paul Kariya .60 1.50
SB10 Ray Bourque 1.00 2.50
SB11 Scotty Bowman 1.25 3.00
SB11S Scotty Bowman AU/100 20.00 50.00

2001-02 Bowman YoungStars

1 Patrick Roy .75 2.00
2 Brett Hull .60 1.50
3 Mario Lemieux 1.25 3.00
4 Jaromir Jagr 1.00 2.50
5 Mats Sundin .30 .75
6 Mike Modano .50 1.25
7 Jarome Iginla .40 1.00
8 Jason Allison .25 .60
9 Mike Richter .30 .75
10 Chris Pronger .30 .75
11 Patrik Elias .30 .75
12 Tommy Salo .25 .60
13 Tony Amonte .25 .60
14 Joe Thornton .50 1.25
15 Joe Sakic .60 1.50
16 Pavel Bure .30 .75
17 Teemu Selanne .60 1.50
18 Markus Naslund .30 .75
19 Nikolai Khabibulin .30 .75
20 Paul Kariya .30 .75
21 Dominik Hasek .50 1.25
22 Ron Francis .40 1.00
23 Ray Ferraro .20 .50
24 Miroslav Satan .25 .60
25 Milan Hejduk .25 .60
26 Jose Theodore .30 .75
27 Daniel Alfredsson .30 .75
28 Michael Peca .25 .60
29 Keith Primeau .25 .60
30 Doug Weight .30 .75
31 Sean Burke .20 .50
32 Adam Oates .30 .75
33 Brian Rolston .25 .60
34 Rob Blake .30 .75
35 Steve Yzerman .75 2.00
36 Eric Lindros .50 1.25
37 Keith Tkachuk .30 .75
38 Dan Cloutier .25 .60
39 Chris Osgood .30 .75
40 Zigmund Palffy .30 .75
41 Jocelyn Thibault .25 .60
42 Roman Turek .25 .60
43 Ed Belfour .30 .75
44 Adam Deadmarsh .20 .50
45 Marian Hossa .30 .75
46 Owen Nolan .30 .75
47 Curtis Joseph .40 1.00
48 Peter Bondra .30 .75
49 Jeremy Roenick .50 1.25
50 Brendan Shanahan .30 .75
51 Eric Daze .25 .60
52 J-P Dumont .20 .50
53 Bill Guerin .30 .75
54 Jukka Hentunen RC .40 1.00
55 Brian Leetch .25 .60
56 Alexei Kovalev .25 .60
57 Olaf Kolzig .30 .75
58 Mike York .20 .50
59 Felix Potvin .50 1.25
60 Pierre Turgeon .25 .60
61 Luc Robitaille .30 .75
62 Sami Kapanen .20 .50
63 Byron Dafoe .25 .60
64 Ryan Smyth .25 .60
65 John LeClair .30 .75
66 Pavol Demitra .40 1.00
67 Alexei Yashin .25 .60
68 Vincent Lecavalier .30 .75
69 Chris Drury .25 .60
70 Mike Dunham .25 .60
71 Patrick Lalime .25 .60
72 Derek Morris .20 .50
73 Peter Forsberg .60 1.50
74 Sergei Fedorov .50 1.25
75 Mark Parrish .20 .50
76 Simon Gagne .30 .75
77 Jeff O'Neill .25 .60
78 Alexander Mogilny .25 .60
79 Johan Hedberg .25 .60
80 Martin Brodeur .75 2.00
81 Claude Lemieux .25 .60
82 Mark Messier .60 1.50
83 Nicklas Lidstrom .30 .75

84 Stu Barnes .25 .60
85 Steve Sullivan .20 .50
86 Jeff Friesen .20 .50
87 Brent Johnson .25 .60
88 Marc Denis .25 .60
89 Jason Arnott .25 .60
90 Brendan Morrison .25 .60
91 Jere Lehtinen .25 .60
92 Craig Conroy .20 .50
93 Petr Sykora .20 .50
94 Gary Roberts .20 .50
95 Saku Koivu .30 .75
96 Scott Stevens .30 .75
97 Radek Bonk .20 .50
98 Roman Cechmanek .25 .60
99 Robert Lang .20 .50
100 Tom Barrasso .25 .60
101 Yanic Perreault .20 .50
102 Joe Nieuwendyk .25 .60
103 Al MacInnis .40 1.00
104 Vincent Damphousse .25 .60
105 Anson Carter .25 .60
106 Sergei Samsonov .25 .60
107 Theo Fleury .40 1.00
108 Mark Recchi .40 1.00
109 Marco Sturm .20 .50
110 Jiri Dopita RC .40 1.00
111 Tim Connolly .20 .50
112 Mike Fisher .20 .50
113 Alex Tanguay .25 .60
114 Christian Berglund RC .50 1.25
115 Olivier Michaud RC .60 1.50
116 John Erskine RC .40 1.00
117 Mikael Samuelsson RC .50 1.25
118 Radek Martinek RC .40 1.00
119 Mark Rycroft RC .50 1.25
120 Mike Ribeiro .20 .50
121 Vaclav Pletka RC .40 1.00
122 Toni Dahlman RC .40 1.00
123 Brian Sutherby RC .40 1.00
124 Karel Rachunek .20 .50
125 Robyn Regehr .20 .50
126 Martin Erat RC .50 1.25
127 Nick Boynton .20 .50
128 Nick Schultz RC .40 1.00
129 Timo Parssinen RC .50 1.25
130 Jaroslav Bednar RC .40 1.00
131 Roberto Luongo .50 1.25
132 Pascal Dupuis RC .60 1.50
133 Dave Tanabe .20 .50
134 Dany Heatley .25 .60
135 Jeff Jillson RC .40 1.00
136 Marian Gaborik .30 .75
137 Radim Vrbata .20 .50
138 Andrew Ference .20 .50
139 Rostislav Klesla .20 .50
140 Dan Blackburn RC .50 1.25
141 Andy Hilbert .20 .50
142 Martin Havlat .25 .60
143 Niko Kapanen RC .60 1.50
144 Brenden Morrow .25 .60
145 Scott Hartnell .20 .50
146 Raffi Torres RC .60 1.50
147 Vaclav Nedorost RC .40 1.00
148 Krys Kolanos RC .40 1.00
149 Kyle Calder .20 .50
150 Niklas Hagman RC .50 1.25
151 Brian Gionta .25 .60
152 Kristian Huselius RC .60 1.50
153 Mike Comrie .25 .60
154 Ty Conklin RC .60 1.50
155 Justin Williams .25 .60
156 Erik Cole RC .75 2.00
157 Nikita Alexeev RC .40 1.00
158 Paul Mara .20 .50
159 Ilya Kovalchuk RC 4.00 10.00
160 David Legwand .25 .60
161 Ilja Bryzgalov RC 1.00 2.50
162 Brad Richards .30 .75
163 Evgeni Nabokov .25 .60
164 Kris Beech .20 .50
165 Pavel Datsyuk RC 3.00 8.00

2001-02 Bowman YoungStars Gold

*VETS/250: 1.5X TO 4X BASIC CARDS
*ROOKIES/250: 1X TO 2.5X BASIC CARDS

2001-02 Bowman YoungStars Ice Cubed

*ICE CUBED: .5X TO 1.2X BASIC CARDS

2001-02 Bowman YoungStars Autographs

AF Andrew Ference 6.00 15.00
BM Brenden Morrow 8.00 20.00
BR Brad Richards 10.00 25.00
DB Dan Blackburn 8.00 20.00
DH Dany Heatley 8.00 20.00
DL David Legwand 8.00 20.00
DT Dave Tanabe 6.00 15.00
IK Ilya Kovalchuk 30.00 80.00
JW Justin Williams 8.00 20.00
KC Kyle Calder 6.00 15.00
KH Kristian Huselius 10.00 25.00
KR Karel Rachunek 6.00 15.00
MC Mike Comrie 8.00 20.00
MF Mike Fisher 6.00 15.00
MG Marian Gaborik 10.00 25.00
MR Mike Ribeiro 6.00 15.00
NB Nick Boynton 6.00 15.00
PD Pavel Datsyuk 500.00 1200.00
PM Paul Mara 6.00 15.00
RL Roberto Luongo 15.00 40.00
RR Robyn Regehr 6.00 15.00
SH Scott Hartnell 6.00 15.00
TC Tim Connolly 6.00 15.00

2001-02 Bowman YoungStars Relics

JAF Andrew Ference J 2.00 5.00
JBM Brenden Morrow J 3.00 8.00
JBR Brad Richards J 3.00 8.00
JDB Dan Blackburn J 2.00 5.00
JDH Dany Heatley J 4.00 10.00
JDL David Legwand J 2.00 5.00
JDT Dave Tanabe J 2.00 5.00
JIK Ilya Kovalchuk J 6.00 15.00
JJW Justin Williams J 2.00 5.00
JKC Kyle Calder J 2.00 5.00
JKH Kristian Huselius J 2.00 5.00
JKR Karel Rachunek J 2.00 5.00
JMC Mike Comrie J 2.00 5.00
JMF Mike Fisher J 2.00 5.00
JMG Marian Gaborik J 12.00 30.00
JMR Mike Ribeiro J 2.00 5.00
JNB Nick Boynton J 2.00 5.00
JPD Pavel Datsyuk J 6.00 15.00
JPM Paul Mara J 2.00 5.00
JRL Roberto Luongo J 4.00 10.00
JRR Robyn Regehr J 2.00 5.00
JSH Scott Hartnell J 2.00 5.00
JTC Tim Connolly J 2.00 5.00
SAF Andrew Ference S 8.00 20.00
SBM Brenden Morrow S 10.00 25.00
SBR Brad Richards S 8.00 20.00
SDB Dan Blackburn S 8.00 20.00
SDH Dany Heatley S 10.00 25.00
SDL David Legwand S 8.00 20.00
SDT Dave Tanabe S 8.00 20.00
SIK Ilya Kovalchuk S 20.00 50.00
SJW Justin Williams S 10.00 25.00
SKC Kyle Calder S 8.00 20.00
SKH Kristian Huselius S 8.00 20.00
SKR Karel Rachunek S 8.00 20.00
SMC Mike Comrie S 8.00 20.00
SMF Mike Fisher S 8.00 20.00
SMG Marian Gaborik S 10.00 25.00
SMR Mike Ribeiro S 8.00 20.00
SNB Nick Boynton S 8.00 20.00
SPD Pavel Datsyuk S 12.00 30.00
SPM Paul Mara S 8.00 20.00
SRL Roberto Luongo S 10.00 25.00
SRR Robyn Regehr S 8.00 20.00
SSH Scott Hartnell S 8.00 20.00
STC Tim Connolly S 8.00 20.00
DSAF Andrew Ference J-S 15.00 40.00
DSBM Brenden Morrow J-S 15.00 40.00
DSBR Brad Richards J-S 25.00 60.00
DSDB Dan Blackburn J-S 25.00 60.00
DSDH Dany Heatley J-S 50.00 125.00
DSDL David Legwand J-S 12.00 30.00
DSDT Dave Tanabe J-S 15.00 40.00
DSIK Ilya Kovalchuk J-S 75.00 200.00
DSJW Justin Williams J-S 15.00 40.00
DSKC Kyle Calder J-S 15.00 40.00
DSKH Kristian Huselius J-S 15.00 40.00
DSKR Karel Rachunek J-S 15.00 40.00
DSMC Mike Comrie J-S 25.00 60.00
DSMF Mike Fisher J-S 15.00 40.00
DSMG Marian Gaborik J-S 50.00 125.00
DSMR Mike Ribeiro J-S 25.00 60.00
DSNB Nick Boynton J-S 15.00 40.00
DSPD Pavel Datsyuk J-S 50.00 125.00
DSPM Paul Mara J-S 15.00 40.00
DSRL Roberto Luongo J-S 40.00 100.00
DSRR Robyn Regehr J-S 15.00 40.00
DSSH Scott Hartnell J-S 15.00 40.00
DSTC Tim Connolly J-S 15.00 40.00

2001-02 Bowman YoungStars Rivals

R1 R.Luongo/D.Blackburn 15.00 40.00
R2 K.Rachunek/B.Richards 12.00 30.00
R3 A.Ference/D.Tanabe 10.00 25.00
R4 N.Boynton/R.Regehr 12.00 30.00
R5 M.Gaborik/I.Kovalchuk 20.00 50.00
R6 M.Comrie/D.Heatley 15.00 40.00
R7 M.Ribeiro/J.Williams 10.00 25.00
R8 T.Connolly/D.Legwand 10.00 25.00
R9 M.Fisher/P.Datsyuk 15.00 40.00
R10 S.Hartnell/B.Morrow 12.00 30.00
R11 K.Huselius/K.Calder 10.00 25.00

2002 Bowman Toronto Spring Expo

COMPLETE SET (10) 10.00 25.00
1 Ilya Kovalchuk/200* 6.00 15.00
1B Ilya Kovalchuk AU/300* 15.00 40.00
2 Curtis Joseph .80 2.00
3 Pavel Datsyuk 2.00 5.00
4 Jose Theodore .80 2.00
5 Jarome Iginla .40 1.00
6 Martin Brodeur .80 2.00
7 Patrick Roy 1.20 3.00
8 Dany Heatley 1.20 3.00
9 Dan Blackburn 1.20 3.00
10 Mats Sundin .40 1.00

2002-03 Bowman YoungStars

1 Nicklas Lidstrom .30 .75
2 Martin Brodeur .75 2.00
3 Tony Amonte .25 .60
4 Todd Bertuzzi .30 .75
5 Joe Thornton .50 1.25
6 Ron Francis .40 1.00
7 Paul Kariya .30 .75
8 Eric Lindros .50 1.25
9 John LeClair .30 .75
10 Doug Weight .30 .75
11 Jaromir Jagr 1.00 2.50
12 Mats Sundin .30 .75
13 Saku Koivu .30 .75
14 Peter Forsberg .60 1.50
15 Alexei Yashin .25 .60
16 Mike Modano .50 1.25
17 Chris Drury .30 .75
18 Ryan Smyth .25 .60
19 Tomas Vokoun .30 .75
20 Marian Hossa .30 .75
21 Owen Nolan .30 .75
22 Vincent Lecavalier .30 .75
23 Jocelyn Thibault .25 .60
24 Marc Denis .25 .60
25 Roberto Luongo .50 1.25
26 Mario Lemieux 1.25 3.00
27 Keith Tkachuk .30 .75
28 Radek Bonk .25 .60
29 Bill Guerin .30 .75
30 Jason Allison .25 .60
31 Jeff O'Neill .25 .60
32 Alexei Zhamnov .25 .60
33 Scott Stevens .30 .75
34 Mark Recchi .40 1.00
35 Alexander Mogilny .25 .60
36 Olaf Kolzig .30 .75
37 Sean Burke .20 .50
38 Brett Hull .60 1.50
39 Andrew Cassels .20 .50
40 Jarome Iginla .40 1.00
41 Joe Sakic .60 1.50
42 Brian Leetch .25 .60
43 Simon Gagne .30 .75
44 Dan Cloutier .25 .60
45 Brian Rolston .25 .60
46 Milan Hejduk .25 .60
47 Steve Yzerman .75 2.00
48 Martin Havlat .25 .60
49 Alexei Kovalev .25 .60
50 Pavol Demitra .40 1.00
51 Mark Parrish .20 .50
52 Felix Potvin .50 1.25
53 Brenden Morrow .25 .60
54 Steve Sullivan .20 .50
55 Patrick Roy .75 2.00
56 Manny Fernandez .20 .50
57 Vincent Damphousse .25 .60
58 Michael Peca .20 .50
59 Anson Carter .25 .60
60 Kevin Weekes .25 .60
61 Peter Bondra .30 .75
62 Brad Richards .30 .75
63 Johan Hedberg .30 .75
64 Olli Jokinen .30 .75
65 Miroslav Satan .30 .75
66 Petr Sykora .25 .60
67 Al MacInnis .40 1.00
68 Markus Naslund .30 .75
69 Mark Messier .60 1.50
70 Rob Blake .30 .75
71 Sergei Samsonov .25 .60
72 Jose Theodore .20 .50
73 Eric Boguniecki .20 .50
74 Nikolai Khabibulin .30 .75
75 Marco Sturm .20 .50
76 Patrick Lalime .25 .60
77 Jeremy Roenick .50 1.25
78 John Madden .20 .50
79 Steve Rucchin .20 .50
80 Jere Lehtinen .30 .75
81 Stu Barnes .20 .50
82 Roman Turek .30 .75
83 Curtis Joseph .40 1.00
84 Evgeni Nabokov .25 .60
85 Daniel Alfredsson .30 .75
86 Brendan Morrison .25 .60
87 Roman Cechmanek .25 .60
88 Chris Osgood .30 .75
89 Tommy Salo .25 .60
90 Craig Conroy .25 .60
91 Zigmund Palffy .25 .60
92 Pavel Bure .30 .75
93 Brent Johnson .25 .60
94 Ed Belfour .30 .75
95 Shane Doan .25 .60
96 David Legwand .25 .60
97 Sergei Fedorov .50 1.25
98 Jason Arnott .25 .60
99 Keith Primeau .25 .60
100 Martin St. Louis .30 .75
101 Teemu Selanne .60 1.50
102 Patrik Elias .30 .75
103 Ray Whitney .25 .60
104 Brendan Shanahan .30 .75
105 Taylor Pyatt .30 .75
106 Niklas Hagman .30 .75
107 Henrik Tallinder .20 .50
108 Rostislav Klesla .30 .75
109 David Aebischer .25 .60
110 Marcel Hossa .20 .50
111 Pavel Brendl .20 .50
112 Ossi Vaananen .20 .50
113 Erik Cole .30 .75
114 Marian Gaborik .30 .75
115 Alexander Svitov RC .20 .50
116 Stanislav Chistov RC .20 .50
117 Jordan Leopold RC .30 .75
118 Ryan Miller RC 1.25 3.00
119 Kurt Sauer RC .20 .50
120 Jonathan Cheechoo .20 .50
121 Radovan Somik RC .20 .50
122 Anton Volchenkov RC .20 .50
123 Pavel Datsyuk .50 1.25
124 Alexander Frolov RC .50 1.25
125 Steve Ott RC .20 .50
126 Jason Spezza RC 1.25 3.00
127 Barret Jackman .20 .50
128 Steve Eminger RC .20 .50
129 Pascal Dupuis .20 .50
130 Brian Sutherby .20 .50
131 Dan Blackburn .25 .60
132 Ron Hainsey RC .20 .50
133 Jay Bouwmeester RC .60 1.50
134 Adam Hall RC .20 .50
135 Mike Comrie .25 .60
136 Nick Schultz .20 .50
137 Henrik Zetterberg RC 2.00 5.00
138 Radim Vrbata .20 .50
139 Jaroslav Svoboda .20 .50
140 Tyler Arnason .30 .75
141 Dany Heatley .25 .60
142 Ivan Huml .20 .50
143 Kristian Huselius .20 .50
144 Martin Gerber RC .30 .75
145 Tom Koivisto RC .20 .50
146 Mikael Tellqvist RC .20 .50
147 Dennis Seidenberg RC .30 .75
148 Mike Cammalleri RC .60 1.50
149 Niko Kapanen .20 .50
150 Shawn Thornton RC .25 .60
151 Alexei Smirnov RC .25 .60
152 Jamie Lundmark .25 .60
153 Shawn Horcoff .20 .50
154 Branko Radivojevic .20 .50
155 Rick Nash RC 1.25 3.00
156 Mattias Weinhandl .20 .50
157 Stephen Weiss .30 .75
158 Dmitri Bykov RC .20 .50
159 Ales Hemsky RC .75 2.00
160 Chuck Kobasew RC .20 .50
161 P-M Bouchard RC .30 .75
162 Scottie Upshall RC .25 .60
163 Patrick Sharp RC .60 1.50
164 Derrick Walser .20 .50
165 Ilya Kovalchuk .40 1.00
NNO Jerry Walsh
Honorary Eqmt. Mgr. .08 .25

2002-03 Bowman YoungStars Gold

69 Mark Messier 1.50 4.00

2002-03 Bowman YoungStars Silver

*VETS: .8X TO 2X BASIC CARDS
*ROOKIES: .6X TO 1.5X
69 Mark Messier 1.25 3.00

2002-03 Bowman YoungStars Autographs

AF Alexander Frolov 12.00 30.00
AH Adam Hall 5.00 12.00
AS Alexander Svitov 5.00 12.00
AV Anton Volchenkov 5.00 12.00
BJ Barret Jackman 5.00 12.00
BR Branko Radivojevic 5.00 12.00
BS Brian Sutherby 5.00 12.00
DA David Aebischer 6.00 15.00
DS Dennis Seidenberg 8.00 20.00
HT Henrik Tallinder 5.00 12.00
JB Jay Bouwmeester 15.00 40.00
JL Jordan Leopold 8.00 20.00
MH Marcel Hossa 5.00 12.00
MW Mattias Weinhandl 5.00 12.00
NH Niklas Hagman 5.00 12.00
NK Niko Kapanen 6.00 15.00
NS Nick Schultz 5.00 12.00
OV Ossi Vaananen 5.00 12.00
PB Pavel Brendl 5.00 12.00
RK Rostislav Klesla 5.00 12.00
RM Ryan Miller 30.00 80.00
RN Rick Nash 30.00 80.00
SC Stanislav Chistov 5.00 12.00
SH Shawn Horcoff 6.00 15.00
SW Stephen Weiss 8.00 20.00
TA Tyler Arnason 8.00 20.00
TP Taylor Pyatt 5.00 12.00

2002-03 Bowman YoungStars Jerseys

AF Alexander Frolov 3.00 8.00
AH Adam Hall 1.25 3.00
AS Alexander Svitov 1.25 3.00
AV Anton Volchenkov 1.25 3.00
BJ Barret Jackman 1.25 3.00
BR Branko Radivojevic 1.25 3.00
BS Brian Sutherby 1.25 3.00
DA David Aebischer 1.50 4.00
DS Dennis Seidenberg 2.00 5.00
HT Henrik Tallinder 1.25 3.00
JB Jay Bouwmeester 4.00 10.00
JL Jordan Leopold 2.00 5.00
MH Marcel Hossa 1.25 3.00
MW Mattias Weinhandl 1.25 3.00
NH Niklas Hagman 1.25 3.00
NK Niko Kapanen 1.50 4.00
NS Nick Schultz 1.25 3.00
OV Ossi Vaananen 1.25 3.00
PB Pavel Brendl 1.25 3.00
RK Rostislav Klesla 1.25 3.00
RM Ryan Miller 8.00 20.00
RN Rick Nash 8.00 20.00
SC Stanislav Chistov 1.25 3.00
SH Shawn Horcoff 1.50 4.00
SW Stephen Weiss 2.00 5.00
TA Tyler Arnason 2.00 5.00
TP Taylor Pyatt 1.25 3.00

2002-03 Bowman YoungStars MVP Puck Relic

1 Brian Sutherby 20.00 50.00

2002-03 Bowman YoungStars Rivals

AFAS A.Frolov/A.Svitov 4.00 10.00
AHMW A.Hall/M.Weinhandl 1.50 4.00
BJDS B.Jackman/D.Seidenberg 2.50 6.00
BRPB B.Radivojevic/P.Brendl 1.50 4.00
DARM D.Aebischer/R.Miller 10.00 25.00
JLTP J.Leopold/T.Pyatt 2.50 6.00
NKMH N.Kapanen/M.Hossa 2.00 5.00
NSNH N.Schultz/N.Hagman 1.50 4.00
OVHT O.Vaananen/H.Tallinder 1.50 4.00
RKAV R.Klesla/A.Volchenkov 1.50 4.00
RNJB R.Nash/J.Bouwmeester 10.00 25.00
SCSW S.Chistov/S.Weiss 2.50 6.00
TABS T.Arnason/B.Sutherby 2.50 6.00

2003-04 Bowman

COMP.SET w/o SP's (110) 20.00 40.00
1 Rick Nash .25 .60
2 Brian Leetch .20 .50
3 Pasi Nurminen .20 .50
4 Vincent Lecavalier .25 .60
5 Nicklas Lidstrom .25 .60
6 Barret Jackman .15 .40
7 Stanislav Chistov .15 .40
8 Patrick Marleau .25 .60
9 Paul Kariya .25 .60
10 Joe Thornton .40 1.00
11 Daniel Alfredsson .25 .60
12 Bill Guerin .25 .60
13 Tyler Arnason .15 .40
14 Dwayne Roloson .20 .50
15 Dany Heatley .20 .50
16 Brett Hull .50 1.25
17 Ilya Kovalchuk .25 .60
18 Marian Hossa .25 .60
19 Joe Sakic .50 1.25
20 Henrik Zetterberg .30 .75
21 Peter Forsberg .50 1.25
22 Ales Kotalik .15 .40
23 Jamie Lundmark .15 .40
24 Brian Sutherby .15 .40
25 Patrik Elias .25 .60
26 Tomas Vokoun .20 .50
27 Jeremy Roenick .40 1.00
28 Alexander Svitov .15 .40
29 Josef Vasicek .15 .40
30 Martin Brodeur .60 1.50
31 Chuck Kobasew .15 .40
32 Kyle Calder .15 .40
33 Daymond Langkow .15 .40
34 Marc Denis .20 .50
35 Sergei Samsonov .20 .50
36 Chris Pronger .25 .60
37 Sebastien Caron .20 .50
38 Markus Naslund .25 .60
39 Dominik Hasek .40 1.00
40 Alex Kovalev .20 .50
41 Roman Turek .20 .50
42 Petr Sykora .20 .50
43 Niko Kapanen .15 .40
44 Todd Bertuzzi .20 .50
45 Aleksey Morozov .15 .40
46 Ed Belfour .25 .60
47 David Aebischer .20 .50
48 Mike Johnson .15 .40
49 Jose Theodore .25 .60
50 Marian Gaborik .25 .60
51 Evgeni Nabokov .20 .50
52 Eric Brewer .15 .40
53 Chris Osgood .20 .50
54 Sergei Gonchar .15 .40
55 Michael Rupp .15 .40
56 Olaf Kolzig .25 .60
57 Jan Bulis .15 .40
58 Dan Cloutier .20 .50
59 Nik Antropov .20 .50
60 Roberto Luongo .40 1.00
61 Ales Hemsky .25 .60
62 Robert Esche .15 .40
63 Adam Hall .15 .40
64 Chris Drury .20 .50
65 Alyn McCauley .15 .40
66 Mario Lemieux 1.00 2.50
67 Pierre-Marc Bouchard .25 .60
68 Jaromir Jagr .75 2.00
69 Alexei Yashin .20 .50
70 Patrick Lalime .20 .50
71 Miroslav Satan .20 .50
72 Michael Peca .20 .50
73 Ziggy Palffy .25 .60
74 Jason Spezza .25 .60
75 Jay Bouwmeester .15 .40
76 Tommy Salo .20 .50
77 Simon Gagne .25 .60
78 Nick Schultz .15 .40
79 Scott Stevens .25 .60
80 Jarome Iginla .30 .75
81 Roman Cechmanek .20 .50
82 Alexander Mogilny .20 .50
83 Ron Francis .30 .75
84 Mike Dunham .20 .50
85 Glen Murray .20 .50
86 Rick DiPietro .20 .50
87 David Legwand .20 .50
88 Nikolai Khabibulin .25 .60
89 Mike Comrie .20 .50
90 Marty Turco .25 .60
91 Sergei Fedorov .40 1.00
92 Brian Boucher .20 .50
93 Kristian Huselius .15 .40
94 Saku Koivu .25 .60
95 Justin Papineau .15 .40
96 Martin Biron .20 .50
97 Derian Hatcher .15 .40
98 Martin St. Louis .25 .60
99 Mike Modano .40 1.00
100 Jean-Sebastien Giguere .25 .60
101 Pavol Demitra .30 .75
102 Olli Jokinen .25 .60
103 Kevin Weekes .20 .50
104 Steve Shields .20 .50
105 Mats Sundin .25 .60
106 Artem Chubarov .15 .40
107 Alexander Frolov .20 .50
108 Jocelyn Thibault .20 .50
109 Martin Havlat .25 .60
110 Milan Hejduk .25 .60
111 Nathan Horton RC 1.50 4.00
112 Joffrey Lupul RC 1.00 2.50
113 Tuomo Ruutu RC 1.00 2.50
114 Jiri Hudler RC 1.50 4.00
115 Marek Svatos RC 1.25 3.00
116 Milan Michalek RC 1.25 3.00
117 Maxim Kondratiev RC .60 1.50
118 Dan Hamhuis RC .75 2.00
119 Boyd Gordon RC .75 2.00
120 Eric Staal RC 5.00 12.00
121 Dan Fritsche RC .60 1.50
122 Matthew Spiller RC .75 2.00
123 Ryan Malone RC 1.25 3.00
124 Cody McCormick RC .75 2.00
125 Tom Preissing RC .75 2.00
126 Dominic Moore RC .60 1.50
127 Matthew Lombardi RC .75 2.00
128 Chris Higgins RC 1.25 3.00
129 Pavel Vorobiev RC .75 2.00
130 Wade Brookbank RC .75 2.00
131 Tim Gleason RC .75 2.00
132 Matt Murley RC .75 2.00
133 Andrew Peters RC .75 2.00
134 Gregory Campbell RC .60 1.50
135 John-Michael Liles RC .75 2.00
136 Sergei Zinovjev RC .60 1.50
137 Alexander Semin RC 2.00 5.00
138 Lasse Kukkonen RC .60 1.50
139 Marek Zidlicky RC .60 1.50
140 Tony Salmelainen RC .60 1.50
141 Travis Moen RC .60 1.50
142 Nikolai Zherdev RC 1.25 3.00
143 Paul Martin RC .75 2.00
144 Peter Sarno RC .60 1.50
145 David Hale RC .60 1.50
146 Dustin Brown RC 1.50 4.00
147 Matt Stajan AU RC 6.00 15.00
148 Peter Sejna AU RC 5.00 12.00
149 S.Bergenheim AU RC 5.00 12.00
150 Antti Miettinen AU RC 6.00 15.00
151 Patrice Bergeron AU RC 125.00 300.00
152 Marc-Andre Fleury AU RC 50.00 125.00
153 Antoine Vermette AU RC 8.00 20.00
154 Jordin Tootoo AU RC 8.00 20.00
155 Rick Mrozik AU RC 4.00 10.00
156 Joni Pitkanen AU RC 6.00 15.00

2003-04 Bowman Gold

*1-110 VETS: 2.5X TO 6X BASIC CARDS
*111-146 ROOKIES: .5X TO 1.2X BASIC RC
147 Matt Stajan 1.50 4.00
148 Peter Sejna 1.25 3.00
149 Sean Bergenheim 1.25 3.00
150 Antti Miettinen 1.50 4.00
151 Patrice Bergeron 5.00 12.00
152 Marc-Andre Fleury 6.00 15.00
153 Antoine Vermette 2.00 5.00
154 Jordin Tootoo 2.00 5.00
155 Rick Mrozik 1.00 2.50
156 Joni Pitkanen 1.50 4.00

2003-04 Bowman Future Fabrics

FFDA David Aebischer 5.00 12.00
FFAF Alexander Frolov 5.00 12.00
FFJS Jason Spezza 8.00 20.00
FFDB Dan Blackburn 4.00 10.00
FFRM Ryan Miller 8.00 20.00
FFSHO Shawn Horcoff 3.00 8.00
FFMW Mattias Weinhandl 3.00 8.00
FFNK Niko Kapanen 3.00 8.00
FFAH Adam Hall 3.00 8.00
FFAS Alexander Svitov 3.00 8.00
FFKH Kristian Huselius 3.00 8.00
FFNH Niklas Hagman 3.00 8.00
FFJB Jay Bouwmeester 3.00 8.00
FFJL Jordan Leopold 3.00 8.00
FFBS Brian Sutherby 3.00 8.00
FFSC Stanislav Chistov 3.00 8.00
FFSH Scott Hartnell 3.00 8.00
FFBJ Barret Jackman 3.00 8.00
FFTA Tyler Arnason 3.00 8.00
FFJLU Jamie Lundmark 3.00 8.00

2003-04 Bowman Future Rivals

AK T.Arnason/N.Kapanen 4.00 10.00
AT D.Aebischer/M.Turco 6.00 15.00
CH S.Chistov/M.Hejduk 4.00 10.00
CI M.Comrie/J.Iginla 8.00 20.00
GH M.Gaborik/D.Heatley 12.00 30.00
HD M.Hejduk/P.Datsyuk 10.00 25.00
HG K.Huselius/S.Gagne 4.00 10.00
HH S.Horcoff/A.Hall 4.00 10.00
JF B.Jackman/A.Frolov 4.00 10.00
KD N.Kapanen/P.Datsyuk 6.00 15.00
LK V. Lecavalier/I.Kovalchuk 10.00 25.00
LT P.Lalime/J.Theodore 6.00 15.00
ML R.Miller/R.Luongo 10.00 25.00
MM P.Marleau/B.Morrison 6.00 15.00
NC R.Nash/S.Chistov 10.00 25.00
NG R.Nash/M.Gaborik 12.00 30.00
RS B.Richards/B.Sutherby 6.00 15.00
SH J.Spezza/N.Hagman 8.00 20.00
WL M. Weinhandl/J.Lundmark 4.00 10.00

2003-04 Bowman Goal to Goal

AY D.Alfredsson/A.Yashin 12.00 30.00
GC M.Gaborik/S.Chistov 15.00 40.00
HG D.Heatley/B.Guerin 12.00 30.00
JH J.Jagr/M.Hejduk 20.00 50.00
KN N.Kapanen/R.Nash 15.00 40.00
MN M.Modano/M.Naslund 15.00 40.00
SG J.Spezza/S.Gagne 15.00 40.00
SI M.Satan/J.Iginla 12.00 30.00
TK J.Thornton/I.Kovalchuk 25.00 60.00

2003-04 Bowman Premier Performance Jerseys

PPMSTO Matt Stajan 4.00 10.00
PPNH Nathan Horton 4.00 10.00
PPPS Peter Sejna 2.50 6.00
PPAM Antti Miettinen 2.50 6.00
PPMS Marek Svatos 5.00 12.00
PPJP Joni Pitkanen 2.50 6.00
PPJL Joffrey Lupul 3.00 8.00
PPAV Antoine Vermette 2.50 6.00
PPDH Dan Hamhuis 2.50 6.00
PPSB Sean Bergenheim 3.00 8.00

2003-04 Bowman Premier Performance Patches

*PATCHES: .75X TO 2X JSY HI

2003-04 Bowman Signs of the Future

SOFES Eric Staal 8.00 20.00
SOFMS Matt Stajan 8.00 20.00
SOFRN Rick Nash 10.00 25.00
SOFMAF Marc-Andre Fleury 40.00 100.00
SOFAM Antti Miettinen 4.00 10.00
SOFAV Antoine Vermette 4.00 10.00
SOFMZ Miroslav Zalesak 4.00 10.00
SOFPMB Pierre-Marc Bouchard 5.00 12.00
SOFPS Peter Sejna 4.00 10.00

2003-04 Bowman Chrome

COMP.SET w/o SP's (110) 30.00 60.00
1 Rick Nash .40 1.00
2 Brian Leetch .30 .75
3 Pasi Nurminen .30 .75
4 Vincent Lecavalier .40 1.00
5 Nicklas Lidstrom .40 1.00
6 Barret Jackman .25 .60
7 Stanislav Chistov .25 .60
8 Patrick Marleau .40 1.00
9 Paul Kariya .40 1.00
10 Joe Thornton .60 1.50
11 Daniel Alfredsson .40 1.00
12 Bill Guerin .40 1.00
13 Tyler Arnason .25 .60
14 Dwayne Roloson .30 .75
15 Dany Heatley .30 .75
16 Brett Hull .75 2.00
17 Ilya Kovalchuk .40 1.00
18 Marian Hossa .40 1.00
19 Joe Sakic .75 2.00
20 Henrik Zetterberg .50 1.25
21 Peter Forsberg .75 2.00
22 Ales Kotalik .25 .60
23 Jamie Lundmark .25 .60
24 Brian Sutherby .25 .60
25 Patrik Elias .40 1.00
26 Tomas Vokoun .30 .75
27 Jeremy Roenick .60 1.50
28 Alexander Svitov .25 .60
29 Josef Vasicek .25 .60
30 Martin Brodeur 1.00 2.50
31 Chuck Kobasew .25 .60
32 Kyle Calder .25 .60
33 Daymond Langkow .25 .60
34 Marc Denis .30 .75
35 Sergei Samsonov .30 .75
36 Chris Pronger .40 1.00
37 Sebastien Caron .30 .75
38 Markus Naslund .40 1.00
39 Dominik Hasek .60 1.50
40 Alex Kovalev .30 .75
41 Roman Turek .30 .75
42 Petr Sykora .30 .75
43 Niko Kapanen .25 .60
44 Todd Bertuzzi .40 1.00
45 Aleksey Morozov .25 .60
46 Ed Belfour .40 1.00
47 David Aebischer .30 .75
48 Mike Johnson .25 .60
49 Jose Theodore .40 1.00
50 Marian Gaborik .40 1.00
51 Evgeni Nabokov .30 .75
52 Eric Brewer .25 .60
53 Chris Osgood .40 1.00
54 Sergei Gonchar .25 .60
55 Michael Rupp .25 .60
56 Olaf Kolzig .40 1.00
57 Jan Bulis .25 .60
58 Dan Cloutier .30 .75
59 Nik Antropov .30 .75
60 Roberto Luongo .60 1.50
61 Ales Hemsky .40 1.00
62 Robert Esche .25 .60
63 Adam Hall .25 .60
64 Chris Drury .30 .75
65 Alyn McCauley .25 .60
66 Mario Lemieux 1.50 4.00
67 Pierre-Marc Bouchard .40 1.00
68 Jaromir Jagr 1.25 3.00
69 Alexei Yashin .30 .75
70 Patrick Lalime .30 .75
71 Miroslav Satan .30 .75
72 Michael Peca .30 .75
73 Ziggy Palffy .40 1.00
74 Jason Spezza .40 1.00
75 Jay Bouwmeester .25 .60
76 Tommy Salo .30 .75
77 Simon Gagne .40 1.00
78 Nick Schultz .25 .60
79 Scott Stevens .40 1.00
80 Jarome Iginla .50 1.25
81 Roman Cechmanek .30 .75
82 Alexander Mogilny .30 .75
83 Ron Francis .50 1.25
84 Mike Dunham .30 .75
85 Glen Murray .30 .75
86 Rick DiPietro .30 .75
87 David Legwand .30 .75
88 Nikolai Khabibulin .40 1.00
89 Mike Comrie .30 .75
90 Marty Turco .40 1.00
91 Sergei Fedorov .60 1.50
92 Brian Boucher .30 .75
93 Kristian Huselius .25 .60
94 Saku Koivu .40 1.00
95 Justin Papineau .25 .60
96 Martin Biron .30 .75
97 Derian Hatcher .25 .60
98 Martin St. Louis .40 1.00
99 Mike Modano .60 1.50
100 Jean-Sebastien Giguere .40 1.00
101 Pavol Demitra .50 1.25
102 Olli Jokinen .40 1.00
103 Kevin Weekes .30 .75
104 Steve Shields .30 .75
105 Mats Sundin .40 1.00
106 Artem Chubarov .25 .60
107 Alexander Frolov .30 .75
108 Jocelyn Thibault .30 .75
109 Martin Havlat .40 1.00
110 Milan Hejduk .30 .75
111 Nathan Horton RC 2.00 5.00
112 Joffrey Lupul RC 2.00 5.00
113 Tuomo Ruutu RC 1.25 3.00
114 Jiri Hudler RC 2.00 5.00
115 Marek Svatos RC 1.50 4.00
116 Milan Michalek RC 1.50 4.00
117 Maxim Kondratiev RC .75 2.00
118 Dan Hamhuis RC 1.00 2.50
119 Boyd Gordon RC 1.00 2.50
120 Eric Staal RC 4.00 10.00
121 Dan Fritsche RC .75 2.00
122 Matthew Spiller RC 1.00 2.50
123 Ryan Malone RC 1.50 4.00
124 Cody McCormick RC 1.00 2.50
125 Tom Preissing RC 1.00 2.50
126 Dominic Moore RC .75 2.00
127 Matthew Lombardi RC 1.00 2.50
128 Chris Higgins RC 1.50 4.00
129 Pavel Vorobiev RC 1.00 2.50
130 Wade Brookbank RC 1.00 2.50
131 Tim Gleason RC 1.00 2.50
132 Matt Murley RC 1.00 2.50
133 Andrew Peters RC 1.00 2.50
134 Gregory Campbell RC .75 2.00
135 John-Michael Liles RC .75 2.00
136 Sergei Zinovjev RC .75 2.00
137 Alexander Semin RC 2.50 6.00
138 Lasse Kukkonen RC .75 2.00
139 Marek Zidlicky RC .75 2.00
140 Tony Salmelainen RC .75 2.00
141 Travis Moen RC 1.00 2.50
142 Nikolai Zherdev RC 1.50 4.00
143 Paul Martin RC 1.00 2.50
144 Peter Sarno RC .75 2.00
145 David Hale RC .75 2.00
146 Dustin Brown RC 2.00 5.00
147 Matt Stajan AU RC 8.00 20.00
148 Peter Sejna AU RC 6.00 15.00
149 Sean Bergenheim AU RC 6.00 15.00
150 Antti Miettinen AU RC 8.00 20.00
151 Patrice Bergeron AU RC 150.00 400.00
152 Marc-Andre Fleury AU RC 125.00 300.00
153 Antoine Vermette AU RC 10.00 25.00
154 Jordin Tootoo AU RC 10.00 25.00
155 Rick Mrozik AU RC 5.00 12.00
156 Joni Pitkanen AU RC 8.00 20.00

2003-04 Bowman Chrome Refractors

*1-110 VETS/300: 2.5X TO 6X BASIC CARDS
*111-146 ROOKIE/300: .8X TO 2X BASIC RC
*ROOKIE AU/50: .5X TO 1.2X BASIC AU
151 Patrice Bergeron 250.00 600.00
152 Marc-Andre Fleury 200.00 500.00

2003-04 Bowman Chrome Gold Refractors
*1-110 VETS/50: 6X TO 15X BASIC CARDS
*111-146 ROOKIES/50: 2X TO 5X BASIC RC

2003-04 Bowman Chrome Xfractors
*1-110 VETS/150: 4X TO 10X BASIC CARDS
*111-146 ROOKIE/150: 1.2X TO 3X BASIC RC
*ROOKIE AU/25: .6X TO 1.5X BASIC AU
151 Patrice Bergeron AU 300.00 800.00
152 Marc-Andre Fleury AU 250.00 600.00

1938-39 Bruins Garden Magazine Supplement
COMPLETE SET (9) 350.00 700.00
1 Red Beattie 20.00 40.00
2 Walter Galbraith 20.00 40.00
3 Lionel Hitchman 40.00 80.00
4 Joseph Lamb 20.00 40.00
5 Harry Oliver 20.00 40.00
6 Art Ross 75.00 150.00
7 Eddie Shore 125.00 250.00
8 Nels Stewart 40.00 80.00
9 Tiny Thompson 50.00 100.00

1955-56 Bruins Photos
COMPLETE SET (17) 100.00 200.00
1 Bob Armstrong 5.00 10.00
2 Marcel Bonin 5.00 10.00
3 Leo Boivin 7.50 15.00
4 Real Chevrefils 5.00 10.00
5 Fern Flaman 7.50 15.00
6 Cal Gardner 2.50 5.00
7 Lionel Heinrich 2.50 5.00
8 Leo Labine 7.50 15.00
9 Hal Laycoe 5.00 10.00
10 Fleming Mackell 5.00 10.00
11 Don McKenney 5.00 10.00
12 Doug Mohns 7.50 15.00
13 Bill Quackenbush 7.50 15.00
14 Johnny Peirson 5.00 10.00
15 Terry Sawchuk 25.00 50.00
16 Vic Stasiuk 5.00 10.00
17 Jerry Toppazzini 5.00 10.00
NNO Envelope 10.00 20.00

1957-58 Bruins Photos
COMPLETE SET (20) 100.00 200.00
1 Bob Armstrong 5.00 10.00
2 Jack Bionda 2.50 5.00
3 Leo Boivin 5.00 10.00
4 Johnny Bucyk 25.00 50.00
5 Real Chevrefils 4.00 8.00
6 Fern Flaman 6.00 12.00
7 Jean-Guy Gendron 5.00 10.00
8 Larry Hillman 5.00 10.00
9 Bronco Horvath 6.00 12.00
10 Norm Johnson 6.00 12.00
11 Leo Labine 5.00 10.00
12 Fleming Mackell 4.00 8.00
13 Don McKenney 4.00 8.00
14 Doug Mohns 6.00 12.00
15 Jim Morrison 2.50 5.00
16 Johnny Peirson 2.50 5.00
17 Larry Regan 2.50 5.00
18 Milt Schmidt CO 10.00 20.00
19 Vic Stasiuk 6.00 12.00
20 Jerry Toppazzini 2.50 5.00

1958-59 Bruins Photos
COMPLETE SET (15) 75.00 150.00
1 Bob Armstrong 5.00 10.00
2 Johnny Bucyk 15.00 30.00
3 Real Chevrefils 5.00 10.00
4 Fern Flaman 6.00 12.00
5 Jean-Guy Gendron 5.00 10.00
6 Larry Hillman 5.00 10.00
7 Leo Labine 5.00 10.00
8 Fleming Mackell 5.00 10.00
9 Don McKenney 5.00 10.00
10 Jim Morrison 5.00 10.00
11 Larry Regan 5.00 10.00
12 Dutch Reibel 5.00 10.00
13 Don Simmons 10.00 20.00
14 Vic Stasiuk 5.00 10.00
15 Jerry Toppazzini 5.00 10.00

1970-71 Bruins Postcards
COMPLETE SET (21) 75.00 150.00
1 Team Photo 2.50 5.00
2 Ed Johnston 2.50 5.00
3 Gerry Cheevers 7.50 15.00
4 Wayne Cashman 2.50 5.00
5 Garnet Bailey 5.00 10.00
6 Don Marcotte 1.50 3.00
7 John Bucyk 5.00 10.00
8 Wayne Carleton 1.50 3.00
9 Reggie Leach 4.00 8.00
10 Ken Hodge 2.50 5.00
11 Ed Westfall 2.00 4.00
12 John McKenzie 2.00 4.00
13 Phil Esposito 10.00 20.00
14 Fred Stanfield 1.50 3.00
15 Derek Sanderson 5.00 10.00
16 Bobby Orr 25.00 50.00
17 Dallas Smith 2.00 4.00
18 Rick Smith 1.50 3.00
19 Ted Green 2.00 4.00
20 Don Awrey 1.50 3.00
21 Tom Johnson CO 2.00 4.00

1970-71 Bruins Team Issue
COMPLETE SET (18) 50.00 100.00
1 Garnet Bailey 5.00 10.00
2 Johnny Bucyk 5.00 10.00
3 Gary Doak 2.00 4.00
4 Phil Esposito 10.00 20.00
5 Ed Johnston 2.50 5.00
6 Don Marcotte 1.50 3.00
7 Derek Sanderson 5.00 10.00
8 Dallas Smith 2.00 4.00
9 Ed Westfall 2.00 4.00
10 Don Awrey 1.50 3.00
11 Wayne Carleton 1.50 3.00
12 Wayne Cashman 2.50 5.00
13 Gerry Cheevers 7.50 15.00
14 Ken Hodge 2.50 5.00
15 John McKenzie 2.00 4.00
16 Bobby Orr 25.00 50.00
17 Rick Smith 1.50 3.00
18 Fred Stanfield 1.50 3.00

1971-72 Bruins Postcards
COMPLETE SET (20) 50.00 100.00
1 Ed Johnston 2.00 4.00
2 Bobby Orr 20.00 40.00
3 Teddy Green 1.50 3.00
4 Phil Esposito 10.00 20.00
5 Ken Hodge 2.00 4.00
6 John Bucyk 4.00 8.00
7 Rick Smith 1.00 2.00
8 Mike Walton 1.50 3.00
9 Wayne Cashman 2.00 4.00
10 Ace Bailey 5.00 10.00
11 Derek Sanderson 4.00 8.00
12 Fred Stanfield 1.00 2.00
13 Ed Westfall 1.50 3.00
14 John McKenzie 1.50 3.00
15 Dallas Smith 1.00 2.00
16 Don Marcotte 1.00 2.00
17 Garry Peters 1.00 2.00
18 Don Awrey 1.00 2.00
19 Reggie Leach 2.00 4.00
20 Gerry Cheevers 5.00 10.00

1983-84 Bruins Team Issue
COMPLETE SET (17) 10.00 25.00
1 Ray Bourque 4.00 10.00
2 Bruce Crowder .40 1.00
3 Keith Crowder .60 1.50
4 Luc Dufour .40 1.00
5 Tom Fergus .40 1.00
6 Randy Hillier .40 1.00
7 Steve Kasper .60 1.50
8 Gord Kluzak .60 1.50
9 Mike Krushelnyski .40 1.00
10 Peter McNab .60 1.50
11 Rick Middleton 1.25 3.00
12 Mike Milbury .60 1.50
13 Mike O'Connell .60 1.50
14 Terry O'Reilly .75 2.00
15 Brad Palmer .40 1.00
16 Barry Pederson .60 1.50
17 Pete Peeters .75 2.00

1984-85 Bruins Postcards
COMPLETE SET (20) 12.00 30.00
1 Pete Peeters .75 2.00
2 Lou Sleigher .60 1.50
3 Ray Bourque 3.00 8.00
4 Mike Milbury .60 1.50
5 Keith Crowder .60 1.50
6 Steve Kasper .60 1.50
7 Mats Thelin .40 1.00
8 Ken Linseman .60 1.50
9 Terry O'Reilly 1.25 3.00
10 Barry Pederson .60 1.50
11 Nevin Markwart .60 1.50
12 Mike O'Connell .40 1.00
13 Geoff Courtnall .75 2.00
14 Doug Keans .60 1.50
15 Charlie Simmer .60 1.50
16 Rick Middleton 1.25 3.00
17 Tom Fergus .40 1.00
18 Mike Gillis .40 1.00
19 Gord Kluzak .60 1.50
20 Lyndon Byers 1.25 3.00

1988-89 Bruins Sports Action
COMPLETE SET (24) 6.00 15.00
1 Ray Bourque 1.25 3.00
2 Randy Burridge .15 .40
3 Lyndon Byers .40 1.00
4 Keith Crowder .20 .50
5 Craig Janney .20 .50
6 Bob Joyce .08 .25
7 Steve Kasper .20 .50
8 Gord Kluzak .20 .50
9 Reed Larson .08 .25
10 Rejean Lemelin .30 .75
11 Ken Linseman .20 .50
12 Tom McCarthy .08 .25
13 Rick Middleton .60 1.50
14 Jay Miller .40 1.00
15 Andy Moog .60 1.50
16 Cam Neely 1.00 2.50
17 Terry O'Reilly CO .20 .50
18 Allen Pederson .08 .25
19 Willi Plett .08 .25
20 Bob Sweeney .08 .25
21 Michael Thelven .08 .25
22 Glen Wesley .20 .50
23 Bob Joyce
Craig Janney .20 .50
24 Dynamic Duo
Ray Bourque
Cam Neely .75 2.00

1988-89 Bruins Sports Action Postcards
COMPLETE SET (20) 8.00 20.00
1 Ray Bourque 1.50 4.00
2 Andy Brickley .20 .50
3 John Carter .20 .50
4 Garry Galley .30 .75
5 Craig Janney .60 1.50
6 Greg Johnston .20 .50
7 Bob Joyce .20 .50
8 Steve Kasper .30 .75
9 Gord Kluzak .30 .75
10 Rejean Lemelin .40 1.00
11 Ken Linseman .30 .75
12 Rick Middleton .60 1.50
13 Andy Moog 1.00 2.50
14 Cam Neely 1.50 4.00
15 Bill O'Dwyer .20 .50
16 Allen Pedersen .20 .50
17 Stephane Quintal .20 .50
18 Bob Sweeney .20 .50
19 Michael Thelven .20 .50
20 Glen Wesley .40 1.00

1989-90 Bruins Sports Action
COMPLETE SET (24) 4.80 12.00
1 Ray Bourque .75 2.00
2 Andy Brickley .20 .50
3 Randy Burridge .20 .50
4 Lyndon Byers .20 .50
5 Bob Carpenter .20 .50
6 John Carter .20 .50
7 Rob Cimetta .20 .50
8 Garry Galley .30 .75
9 Bob Gould .20 .50
10 Greg Hawgood .20 .50
11 Craig Janney .30 .75
12 Bob Joyce .20 .50
13 Rejean Lemelin .30 .75
14 Ken Linseman .20 .50
15 Andy Moog .40 1.00
16 Nevin Markwart .20 .50
17 Cam Neely .60 1.50
18 Allen Pedersen .20 .50
19 Stephane Quintal .20 .50
20 Bob Sweeney .20 .50
21 Michael Thelven .20 .50
22 Glen Wesley .30 .75
23 Bruins Top 10 Scorers .40 1.00
24 Stanley Cup Champions .40 1.00

1989-90 Bruins Sports Action Update
COMPLETE SET (12) 3.00 8.00
1 Ray Bourque .75 2.00
2 Dave Christian .30 .75
3 Peter Douris .20 .50
4 Gord Kluzak .30 .75
5 Brian Lawton .20 .50
6 Mike Millar .20 .50
7 Dave Poulin .30 .75
8 Brian Propp .30 .75
9 Don Sweeney .30 .75
10 Graeme Townshend .20 .50
11 Jim Wiemer .20 .50
12 Bruins Leaders
Ray Bourque
Rejean Lemelin
Cam Neely .75 2.00

1990-91 Bruins Sports Action
COMPLETE SET (26) 8.00 20.00
1 Bob Beers .20 .50
2 Ray Bourque 1.25 3.00
3 Andy Brickley .20 .50
4 Randy Burridge .25 .60
5 John Byce .20 .50
6 Lyndon Byers .30 .75
7 Bob Carpenter .20 .50
8 John Carter .20 .50
9 Dave Christian .25 .60
10 Peter Douris .20 .50
11 Garry Galley .20 .50
12 Ken Hodge Jr. .20 .50
13 Craig Janney .30 .75
14 Rejean Lemelin .30 .75
15 Nevin Markwart SP 1.25 3.00
16 Andy Moog .60 1.50
17 Cam Neely .75 2.00
18 Chris Nilan .25 .60
19 Allen Pedersen .20 .50
20 Dave Poulin .25 .60
21 Stephane Quintal SP 1.25 3.00
22 Bob Sweeney .20 .50
23 Don Sweeney .25 .60
24 Wes Walz .20 .50
25 Glen Wesley .30 .75
26 Rejean Lemelin
Andy Moog .40 1.00

1991-92 Bruins Sports Action
COMPLETE SET (24) 4.80 12.00
1 Brent Ashton .15 .40
2 Bob Beers .15 .40
3 Daniel Berthiaume .20 .50
4 Ray Bourque 1.00 2.50
5 Bob Carpenter .15 .40
6 Peter Douris .08 .25
7 Glen Featherstone .08 .25
8 Ken Hodge Jr .08 .25
9 Jeff Lazaro .08 .25
10 Stephen Leach .15 .40
11 Andy Moog .40 1.00
12 Gord Murphy .08 .25
13 Cam Neely .75 2.00
14 Adam Oates .40 1.00
15 Dave Poulin .20 .50
16 David Reid .15 .40
17 Vladimir Ruzicka .15 .40
18 Bob Sweeney .15 .40
19 Don Sweeney .15 .40
20 Jim Vesey .08 .25
21 Glen Wesley .15 .40
22 Jim Wiemer .08 .25
23 Chris Winnes .08 .25
24 The Big Three
Andy Moog
Ray Bourque
Cam Neely .60 1.50

1991-92 Bruins Sports Action Legends
COMPLETE SET (36) 6.00 15.00
1 Bob Armstrong .08 .25
2 Leo Boivin .15 .40
3 Ray Bourque .75 2.00
4 Frank Brimsek .30 .75
5 Johnny Bucyk .40 1.00
6 Wayne Cashman .08 .25
7 Gerry Cheevers .40 1.00
8 Dit Clapper .30 .75
9 Bill Cowley .08 .25
10 Phil Esposito .50 1.25
11 Fernie Flaman .15 .40
12 Mel Hill
Bill Cowley
Roy Conacher .15 .40
13 Lionel Hitchman .15 .40
14 Fleming Mackell .08 .25
15 Don Marcotte .08 .25
16 Don McKenney .08 .25
17 Rick Middleton .20 .50
18 Doug Mohns .08 .25
19 Terry O'Reilly .15 .40
20 Bobby Orr 1.25 3.00
21 Brad Park .30 .75
22 John Peirson .08 .25
23 Bill Quackenbush .20 .50
24 Jean Ratelle .30 .75
25 Art Ross CO
GM .20 .50
26 Ed Sandford .08 .25
27 Terry Sawchuk .60 1.50
28 Milt Schmidt .40 1.00
29 Milt Schmidt
Cooney Weiland
Bill Cowley .20 .50
30 Eddie Shore .40 1.00
31 Harry Sinden CO
GM
and President .20 .50
32 Tiny Thompson .15 .40
33 Cooney Weiland .15 .40
34 Ed Westfall .08 .25
35 Bruins Defense/1955-56
Bill Quackenbush
Fern Flaman
Terry Sawchuk
Bob Armstrong
Leo Boivin .20 .50
36 The Kraut Line
Milt Schmidt
Woody Dumart
Bobby Bauer .30 .75

1992-93 Bruins Postcards
COMPLETE SET (12) 4.00 10.00
1 Ray Bourque 1.25 3.00
2 Ted Donato .20 .50
3 Joe Juneau .30 .75
4 Dimitri Kvartalnov .20 .50
5 Stephen Leach .20 .50
6 Andy Moog .75 2.00
7 Adam Oates .75 2.00
8 Dave Poulin .30 .75
9 Gordie Roberts .20 .50
10 Vladimir Ruzicka .20 .50
11 Don Sweeney .30 .75
12 Glen Wesley .30 .75

1998 Bruins Alumni
COMPLETE SET (35) 8.00 20.00
1 Reggie Lemelin .20 .50
2 Harry Sinden .08 .25
3 Jim Craig .20 .50
4 Bobby Orr 2.00 5.00
5 Ferny Flaman .20 .50
6 Bob Beers .08 .25
7 Ken Hodge .20 .50
8 Cam Neely 1.25 3.00
9 John Bucyk .40 1.00
10 Jean Ratelle .20 .50
11 Bob Miller .02 .10
12 Ed Sandford .02 .10
13 Ken Linseman .20 .50
14 Woody Dumart .20 .50
15 Milt Schmidt .30 .75
16 Derek Sanderson .40 1.00
17 Fred Stanfield .08 .25
18 Garnet Bailey .75 2.00
19 John McKenzie .20 .50
20 Dallas Smith .08 .25
21 Don Marcotte .08 .25
22 Brad Park .30 .75
23 Matt Glennon .02 .10
24 Terry O'Reilly .40 1.00
25 Gary Doak .08 .25
26 Don Awrey .08 .25
27 Billy O'Dwyer .02 .10
28 Dave Hynes .02 .10
29 Tom Songin .02 .10
30 Gerry Cheevers .40 1.00
31 Don McKenney .08 .25
32 Frank Simonetti .02 .10
33 Bronco Horvath .08 .25
34 Doug Mohns .08 .25
35 Header Card .02 .10

1998 Bruins Alumni Autographs
COMPLETE SET (35) 120.00 300.00
1 Reggie Lemelin 4.00 10.00
2 Harry Sinden 4.00 10.00
3 Jim Craig 6.00 15.00
5 Ferny Flaman 2.00 5.00
6 Bob Beers .75 2.00
7 Ken Hodge 3.00 8.00
9 John Bucyk 10.00 25.00
10 Jean Ratelle 8.00 20.00
11 Bob Miller .40 1.00
12 Ed Sandford .40 1.00
13 Ken Linseman 2.00 5.00
14 Woody Dumart 15.00 40.00
15 Milt Schmidt 10.00 25.00
16 Derek Sanderson 15.00 40.00
17 Fred Stanfield 1.25 3.00
18 Garnet Bailey 15.00 40.00
19 John McKenzie 3.00 8.00
20 Dallas Smith 4.00 10.00
21 Don Marcotte 1.25 3.00
22 Brad Park 6.00 15.00
23 Matt Glennon .40 1.00
24 Terry O'Reilly 15.00 40.00
25 Gary Doak 1.25 3.00
26 Don Awrey 1.25 3.00
27 Billy O'Dwyer .40 1.00
28 Dave Hynes .40 1.00
29 Tom Songin .40 1.00
30 Gerry Cheevers 10.00 25.00
31 Don McKenney 1.25 3.00
32 Frank Simonetti .40 1.00
33 Bronco Horvath 4.00 10.00
34 Doug Mohns 2.00 5.00
35 Header Card .40 1.00

1999-00 Bruins Season Ticket Offer
COMPLETE SET (2) 25.00 60.00
1 Joe Thornton 20.00 50.00
2 Sergei Samsonov 6.00 15.00

2002-03 Bruins Team Issue
COMPLETE SET (8) 6.00 15.00
1 Blades MASCOT .20 .50
2 Nick Boynton .40 1.00
3 Hal Gill .40 1.00
4 Glen Murray .75 2.00
5 Brian Rolston .75 2.00
6 Sergei Samsonov 1.25 3.00
7 P.J. Stock 1.25 3.00
8 Joe Thornton 2.00 5.00

2003-04 Bruins Team Issue
COMPLETE SET (14) 8.00 20.00
1 Nick Boynton .40 1.00
2 Hal Gill .40 1.00
3 Mike Knuble .40 1.00
4 Martin Lapointe .60 1.50
5 Dan McGillis .40 1.00
6 Glen Murray .60 1.50
7 Sean O'Donnell .40 1.00
8 Felix Potvin .40 1.00
9 Andrew Raycroft 1.25 3.00
10 Sergei Samsonov 1.25 3.00
11 Mike Sullivan CO .10 .25
12 Joe Thornton 2.00 5.00
13 Blades MASCOT .10 .25
14 Team photo .40 1.00

2005-06 Bruins Boston Globe
COMPLETE SET (24) 8.00 20.00
1 Glen Murray .20 .50
2 Hannu Toivonen 1.00 2.50
3 Andrew Alberts .20 .50
4 Hal Gill .20 .50
5 Tom Fitzgerald .20 .50
6 Milan Jurcina .20 .50
7 Brad Boyes .30 .75
8 David Tanabe .20 .50
9 Wayne Primeau .20 .50
10 Brad Stuart .20 .50
11 Alexei Zhamnov .20 .50
12 Brian Leetch .75 2.00
13 Patrice Bergeron .75 2.00
14 Marco Sturm .20 .50
15 Nick Boynton .20 .50
16 Brad Isbister .20 .50
17 Sergei Samsonov .40 1.00
18 Pat Leahy .20 .50
19 Andrew Raycroft .40 1.00
20 Tim Thomas .75 2.00
21 Travis Green .20 .50
22 Josh Langfeld .20 .50
23 Dan LaCouture .20 .50
24 P.J. Axelsson .20 .50

2010-11 Bruins Upper Deck Stanley Cup Champions
COMPLETE SET (31) 8.00 20.00
1 Patrice Bergeron .30 .75
2 Tim Thomas .25 .60
3 Zdeno Chara .25 .60
4 Brad Marchand .50 1.25
5 Milan Lucic .25 .60
6 Nathan Horton .20 .50
7 David Krejci .25 .60
8 Michael Ryder .15 .40
9 Chris Kelly .20 .50
10 Dennis Seidenberg .15 .40
11 Mark Recchi .30 .75
12 Rich Peverley .25 .60
13 Tyler Seguin .60 1.50
14 Andrew Ference .15 .40
15 Tomas Kaberle .15 .40
16 Johnny Boychuk .20 .50
17 Adam McQuaid .25 .60
18 Daniel Paille .15 .40
19 Gregory Campbell .15 .40
20 Shawn Thornton .15 .40
21 Shane Hnidy .15 .40
22 Marc Savard .15 .40
23 Steve Kampfer .30 .75
24 Jordan Caron .25 .60
25 Tuukka Rask .30 .75
26 Milan Lucic HL .25 .60
27 Tim Thomas HL .25 .60
28 Zdeno Chara HL .25 .60
29 Tim Thomas HL .25 .60
30 Tyler Seguin HL .60 1.50
BOS Team Photo 2.00 5.00

1911-12 C55
COMPLETE SET (45) 12000.00 30000.00
1 Paddy Moran 400.00 1000.00
2 Joe Hall RC 250.00 600.00
3 Barney Holden 100.00 250.00
4 Joe Malone RC 500.00 1200.00
5 Ed Oatman RC 300.00 800.00
6 Tom Dunderdale 250.00 600.00
7 Ken Mallen RC 100.00 250.00
8 Jack MacDonald RC 100.00 250.00
9 Fred Lake 100.00 250.00
10 Albert Kerr RC 150.00 400.00
11 Marty Walsh 200.00 500.00
12 Hamby Shore RC 150.00 400.00
13 Alex Currie RC 100.00 250.00
14 Bruce Ridpath 125.00 300.00
15 Bruce Stuart 250.00 600.00
16 Percy Lesueur 200.00 500.00
17 Jack Darragh RC 150.00 400.00
18 Steve Vair RC 100.00 250.00
19 Don Smith RC 100.00 250.00
20 Cyclone Taylor 500.00 1200.00
21 Bert Lindsay RC 125.00 300.00
22 H.L. Gilmour RC 125.00 300.00
23 Bobby Rowe RC 200.00 500.00
24 Sprague Cleghorn RC 500.00 1200.00
25 Odie Cleghorn RC 125.00 300.00
26 Skene Ronan RC 100.00 250.00
27A Walter Smaill RC 300.00 700.00
27B Walter Smaill RC 500.00 800.00
28 Ernest Johnson 150.00 400.00
29 Jack Marshall 125.00 300.00
30 Harry Hyland 125.00 300.00
31 Art Ross 600.00 1500.00
32 Riley Hern 200.00 500.00
33 Gordon Roberts 300.00 800.00
34 Frank Glass 100.00 250.00
35 Ernest Russell 200.00 500.00
36 James Gardner UER RC 250.00 600.00
37 Art Bernier 100.00 250.00
38 Georges Vezina RC 10000.00 25000.00
39 Henri Dallaire RC 125.00 300.00
40 R.(Rocket) Power RC 125.00 300.00
41 Didier Pitre 125.00 300.00
42 Newsy Lalonde 600.00 1500.00
43 Eugene Payan RC 100.00 250.00
44 George Poulin RC 100.00 250.00
45 Jack Laviolette 200.00 500.00

1910-11 C56
COMPLETE SET (36) 8000.00 20000.00
1 Frank Patrick RC 250.00 600.00
2 Percy Lesueur RC 200.00 500.00
3 Gordon Roberts RC 300.00 800.00
4 Barney Holden RC 250.00 600.00
5 Frank Glass RC 150.00 400.00
6 Edgar Dey RC 200.00 500.00
7 Marty Walsh RC 250.00 600.00
8 Art Ross RC 2500.00 6000.00
9 Angus Campbell RC 80.00 200.00
10 Harry Hyland RC 250.00 600.00
11 Herb Clark RC 80.00 200.00
12 Art Ross RC 400.00 1000.00
13 Ed Decary RC 300.00 800.00
14 Tom Dunderdale RC 250.00 600.00
15 Cyclone Taylor RC 600.00 1500.00
16 Joseph Cattarinich RC 250.00 600.00
17 Bruce Stuart RC 150.00 400.00
18 Nick Bawlf RC 125.00 300.00
19 Joseph Jones RC 200.00 500.00
20 Ernest Russell RC 250.00 600.00
21 Jack Laviolette RC 1200.00 3000.00
22 Riley Hern RC 250.00 600.00
23 Didier Pitre RC 300.00 800.00
24 Skinner Poulin RC 300.00 800.00
25 Art Bernier RC 250.00 600.00
26 Lester Patrick RC 1000.00 2500.00
27 Fred Lake RC 60.00 150.00
28 Paddy Moran RC 300.00 800.00
29 C.Toms RC 250.00 600.00
30 Ernest Johnson RC 300.00 800.00
31 Horace Gaul RC 100.00 250.00
32 Harold McNamara RC 125.00 300.00
33 Jack Marshall RC 600.00 1500.00
34 Bruce Ridpath RC 600.00 1500.00
35 Jack Marshall RC 600.00 1500.00
36 Newsy Lalonde RC 400.00 1000.00

1912-13 C57
COMPLETE SET (50) 12000.00 20000.00
1 Georges Vezina 2500.00 5000.00
2 Punch Broadbent RC 350.00 600.00
3 Clint Benedict RC 350.00 600.00
4 A. Atchinson RC 150.00 300.00
5 Tom Dunderdale 200.00 400.00
6 Art Bernier 150.00 300.00
7 Henri Dallaire 150.00 300.00
8 George Poulin 150.00 300.00
9 Eugene Payan 150.00 300.00
10 Steve Vair 150.00 300.00
11 Bobby Rowe 150.00 300.00
12 Don Smith 150.00 300.00
13 Bert Lindsay 150.00 300.00
14 Skene Ronan 150.00 300.00
15 Sprague Cleghorn 350.00 600.00
16 Joe Hall 200.00 400.00
17 Jack MacDonald 150.00 300.00
18 Paddy Moran 300.00 500.00
19 Harry Hyland 150.00 300.00
20 Art Ross 800.00 1200.00
21 Frank Glass 150.00 300.00
22 Walter Smaill 150.00 300.00
23 Gordon Roberts 150.00 300.00
24 James Gardner 200.00 400.00
25 Ernest Johnson 200.00 400.00
26 Ernie Russell 200.00 400.00
27 Percy Lesueur 300.00 500.00
28 Bruce Ridpath 150.00 300.00
29 Jack Darragh 200.00 400.00
30 Hamby Shore 150.00 300.00
31 Fred Lake 150.00 300.00
32 Alex Currie 150.00 300.00
33 Albert Kerr 150.00 300.00
34 Eddie Gerard RC 200.00 400.00
35 Carl Kendall RC 150.00 300.00
36 Jack Fournier RC 150.00 300.00
37 Goldie Prodgers RC 200.00 400.00
38 Jack Marks RC 150.00 300.00
39 George Broughton RC 150.00 300.00
40 Arthur Boyce RC 150.00 300.00
41 Lester Patrick 500.00 1000.00
42 Joe Dennison RC 150.00 300.00
43 Cyclone Taylor 700.00 1200.00
44 Newsy Lalonde 800.00 1200.00
45 Didier Pitre 150.00 300.00
46 Jack Laviolette 150.00 300.00
47 Ed Oatman 150.00 300.00
48 Joe Malone 500.00 1000.00
49 Marty Walsh 300.00 600.00
50 Odie Cleghorn 400.00 1000.00

1912 Imperial Tobacco Lacrosse C61
1 Charlie Querrie 150.00 400.00
2 Dolly Durkin 60.00 150.00
3 Fred Rowntree 60.00 150.00
4 Fred Graydon 60.00 150.00
5 Kid Kinsman 60.00 150.00
6 Al Dade 60.00 150.00
7 Jimmy Hogan 60.00 150.00
8 A. Kenna 60.00 150.00
9 W. O'Kane 60.00 150.00
10 F. Scott 60.00 150.00
11 Newsy Lalonde 500.00 800.00
12 Mickey Ions 100.00 200.00
13 Mag MacGregor 60.00 150.00
14 Dot Phelan 60.00 150.00
15 Spike Griffiths 60.00 150.00
16 Whitey Eastwood 60.00 150.00
17 Red McCarthy 60.00 150.00
18 Jack Shea 60.00 150.00
19 Clint Benedict 250.00 500.00
20 Bobby Pringle 60.00 150.00
21 A. Ranson 60.00 150.00
22 Lawrence Degray 60.00 150.00
23 Francis Cummings 60.00 150.00
24 Fred Degan 60.00 150.00
25 Don Cameron 60.00 150.00
26 James Gifford 60.00 150.00
27 Archie Hall 60.00 150.00
28 W. Turnbull 60.00 150.00
29 Punk Wintermute 60.00 150.00
30 Tom Gifford 60.00 150.00
31 O. Secours 60.00 150.00
32 Dr. LaChapelle 60.00 150.00
33 Joe Cattarinich 100.00 200.00
34 Dare Devil Gauthier 60.00 150.00
35 Jack Laviolette 100.00 200.00
36 George Roberts 60.00 150.00
37 Steve Rochford 60.00 150.00
38 Henry Scott 60.00 150.00
39 J. McIlwane 60.00 150.00
40 Nick Neville 60.00 150.00
41 P.J. Brennan 60.00 150.00
42 Howie McIntyre 60.00 150.00
43 Gus Dillon 60.00 150.00
44 J. Barry 60.00 150.00
45 Johnny Howard 60.00 150.00
46 Eddie Powers 60.00 150.00
47 Art Warwick 60.00 150.00
48 Ernie Menary 60.00 150.00
49 Georgie Kalls 60.00 150.00
50 Fred Stagg 60.00 150.00

1924-25 C144 Champ's Cigarettes
COMPLETE SET (60) 10000.00 20000.00
1 Jack Adams 150.00 250.00
2 Lloyd Andrews RC 125.00 200.00
3 Clint Benedict 250.00 400.00
4 Louis Berlinquette RC 125.00 200.00
5 Eddie Bouchard 125.00 200.00
6 Billy Boucher 150.00 250.00
7 Bob Boucher RC 125.00 200.00
8 Punch Broadbent 200.00 350.00
9 Billy Burch 200.00 350.00
10 Dutch Cain RC 125.00 200.00
11 Earl Campbell RC 125.00 200.00
12 George Carroll RC 125.00 200.00
13 King Clancy 1000.00 1750.00
14 Odie Cleghorn 150.00 250.00
15 Sprague Cleghorn 250.00 400.00
16 Alex Connell RC 250.00 400.00
17 Carson Cooper RC 125.00 200.00
18 Bert Corbeau 150.00 250.00
19 Billy Coutu 125.00 200.00
20 Hap Day RC 250.00 400.00
21 Cy Denneny 200.00 350.00
22 Charlie Dinsmore RC 125.00 200.00
23 Babe Dye 200.00 350.00
24 Frank Finnigan RC 200.00 350.00
25 Vernon Forbes 125.00 200.00
26 Norman Hec Fowler RC 150.00 250.00
27 Red Green 125.00 200.00
28 Shorty Green 200.00 350.00
29 Curly Headley RC 125.00 200.00
30 Jim Herberts RC 125.00 200.00
31 Fred Hitchman RC 125.00 200.00
32 Albert Holway RC 125.00 200.00
33 Stan Jackson 125.00 200.00
34 Aurel Joliat 800.00 1400.00
35 Louis C. Langlois RC 125.00 200.00
36 Fred Lowrey RC 125.00 200.00
37 Sylvio Mantha 200.00 350.00
38 Albert McCaffrey RC 125.00 200.00
39 Robert McKinnon RC 125.00 200.00
40 Herbie Mitchell RC 125.00 200.00
41 Howie Morenz 2000.00 3500.00
42 Dunc Munro RC 150.00 250.00
43 Gerald J.M. Munro RC 125.00 200.00
44 Frank Nighbor 250.00 400.00
45 Reg Noble 200.00 350.00
46 Mickey O'Leary RC 125.00 200.00
47 Goldie Prodgers 125.00 200.00
48 Ken Randall 125.00 200.00
49 George Redding RC 125.00 200.00
50 John Ross Roach 150.00 250.00
51 Mickey Roach 125.00 200.00
52 Sam Rothschild RC 150.00 250.00
53 Werner Schnarr RC 125.00 200.00
54 Ganton Scott RC 125.00 200.00
55 Alf Skinner RC 125.00 200.00
56 Hooley Smith RC 200.00 350.00
57 Chris Speyers RC 125.00 200.00
58 Jesse Spring 125.00 200.00
59 The Stanley Cup 350.00 600.00
60 Georges Vezina 1200.00 2000.00

1930 Campbell's Soup
COMPLETE SET (1) 50.00 100.00
NNO Hockey Player 50.00 100.00

1994-95 Canada Games NHL POGS
COMPLETE SET (376) 40.00 100.00
1 Kini-Kings .20 .50
2 Kini-Rangers .20 .50
3 Kini-Penguins .20 .50
4 Kini-Stars .20 .50
5 Kini-Senators .20 .50
6 Kini-Jets .20 .50
7 Kini-Canucks .20 .50
8 Kini-Capitals .20 .50
9 Kini-Ducks .20 .50
10 Kini-Bruins .20 .50
11 Kini-Sabres .20 .50
12 Kini-Flames .20 .50
13 Kini-Blackhawks .20 .50
14 Kini-Red Wings .20 .50
15 Kini-Oilers .20 .50
16 Kini-Panthers .20 .50
17 Kini-Whalers .20 .50
18 Kini-Canadiens .20 .50
19 Kini-Devils .20 .50
20 Kini-Islanders .20 .50
21 Kini-Flyers .20 .50
22 Kini-Nordiques .20 .50
23 Kini-Sharks .20 .50
24 Kini-Blues .20 .50
25 Kini-Lightning .20 .50
26 Kini-Leafs .20 .50
27 Cliff Ronning .02 .10
28 Bob Corkum .02 .10
29 Joe Sacco .02 .10
30 Peter Douris .02 .10
31 Shaun Van Allen .02 .10
32 Stephan Lebeau .02 .10
33 Stu Grimson .02 .10
34 Tim Sweeney .02 .10
35 Adam Oates .20 .50
36 Al Iafrate .05 .15
37 Alexei Kastanov .02 .10
38 Bryan Smolinski .08 .25
39 Cam Neely .30 .75
40 Don Sweeney .02 .10
41 Glen Murray .02 .10

42 Ray Bourque .40 1.00
43 Ted Donato .02 .10
44 Alexander Mogilny .40 1.00
45 Doug Gilmour .40 1.00
46 Dale Hawerchuk .20 .50
47 Derek Plante .08 .25
48 Donald Audette .08 .25
49 Doug Bodger .02 .10
50 Pat LaFontaine .20 .50
51 Randy Wood .02 .10
52 Richard Smehlik .02 .10
53 Yuri Khmylev .02 .10
54 Theo Fleury .30 .75
55 Kelly Kisio .02 .10
56 Joe Nieuwendyk .08 .25
57 Michael Nylander .02 .10
58 Joel Otto .02 .10
59 James Patrick .02 .10
60 Robert Reichel .08 .25
61 Gary Roberts .08 .25
62 Wes Walz .02 .10
63 Ulf Dahlen .02 .10
64 Zarley Zalapski .02 .10
65 Tony Amonte .30 .75
66 Dirk Graham .02 .10
67 Joe Murphy .05 .15
68 Bernie Nicholls .08 .25
69 Patrick Poulin .02 .10
70 Jeremy Roenick .40 1.00
71 Christian Ruutu .02 .10
72 Brent Sutter .02 .10
73 Chris Chelios .60 1.50
74 Steve Smith .02 .10
75 Gary Suter .02 .10
76 Neil Broten .05 .15
77 Russ Courtnall .02 .10
78 Dean Evason .02 .10
79 Dave Gagner .05 .15
80 Mike McPhee .02 .10
81 Mike Modano .30 .75
82 Paul Cavallini .02 .10
83 Derian Hatcher .02 .10
84 Grant Ledyard .02 .10
85 Mark Tinordi .02 .10
86 Dino Ciccarelli .15 .40
87 Sergei Fedorov 1.25 3.00
88 Slava Kozlov .08 .25
89 Darren McCarty .08 .25
90 Keith Primeau .08 .25
91 Ray Sheppard .08 .25
92 Steve Yzerman 2.00 5.00
93 Paul Coffey .40 1.00
94 Vladimir Konstantinov .02 .10
95 Nicklas Lidstrom .15 .40
96 Greg Adams .02 .10
97 Jason Arnott .30 .75
98 Kelly Buchberger .02 .10
99 Shayne Corson .02 .10
100 Scott Pearson .02 .10
101 Doug Weight .20 .50
102 Boris Mironov .08 .25
103 Fredrik Olausson .02 .10
104 Stu Barnes .02 .10
105 Bob Kudelski .02 .10
106 Andrei Lomakin .02 .10
107 Dave Lowry .02 .10
108 Scott Mellanby .08 .25
109 Rob Niedermayer .20 .50
110 Brian Skrudland .02 .10
111 Brian Benning .02 .10
112 Gord Murphy .02 .10
113 Andrew Cassels .02 .10
114 Robert Kron .02 .10
115 Jocelyn Lemieux .02 .10
116 Paul Ranheim .02 .10
117 Geoff Sanderson .20 .50
118 Jim Sandlak .02 .10
119 Darren Turcotte .02 .10
120 Pat Verbeek .08 .25
121 Chris Pronger .15 .40
122 Pat Conacher .02 .10
123 Mike Donnelly .04 .10
124 John Druce .02 .10
125 Tony Granato .05 .15
126 Wayne Gretzky 4.00 10.00
127 Jari Kurri .08 .25
128 Warren Rychel .02 .10
129 Rob Blake .07 .20
130 Marty McSorley .08 .25
131 Alexei Zhitnik .02 .10
132 Brian Bellows .02 .10
133 Vince Damphousse .20 .50
134 Gilbert Dionne .02 .10
135 Mike Keane .02 .10
136 John LeClair 1.00 2.50
137 Kirk Muller .08 .25
138 Oleg Petrov .02 .10
139 Eric Desjardins .02 .10
140 Lyle Odelein .02 .10
141 Peter Popovic .02 .10
142 Mathieu Schneider .02 .10
143 Trent Klatt .02 .10
144 Bobby Holik .02 .10
145 Claude Lemieux .15 .40
146 John MacLean .07 .20
147 Corey Millen .02 .10
148 Stephane Richer .05 .15
149 Valeri Zelepukin .02 .10
150 Bruce Driver .02 .10
151 Gino Odjick .02 .10
152 Scott Stevens .08 .25
153 Brad Dalgarno .02 .10
154 Ray Ferraro .02 .10
155 Pat Flatley .02 .10
156 Travis Green .05 .15
157 Derek King .02 .10
158 Marty McInnis .02 .10
159 Steve Thomas .08 .25
160 Pierre Turgeon .20 .50
161 Darius Kasparaitis .02 .10
162 Vladimir Malakhov .02 .10
163 Alexei Kovalev .08 .25
164 Steve Larmer .08 .25
165 Stephane Matteau .02 .10
166 Mark Messier .75 2.00
167 Sergei Nemchinov .02 .10
168 Brian Noonan .02 .10
169 Petr Nedved .08 .25
170 Brian Leetch .60 1.50
171 Kevin Lowe .02 .10
172 Sergei Zubov .02 .10
173 Sylvain Turgeon .02 .10
174 Alexei Yashin .20 .50
175 Norm Maciver .02 .10
176 Brad Shaw .02 .10
177 Brent Fedyk .02 .10
178 Mark Lamb .02 .10
179 Don McSween .02 .10
180 Mark Recchi .20 .50
181 Mikael Renberg .30 .75
182 Gary Galley .02 .10
183 Ron Francis .20 .50
184 Jaromir Jagr 2.00 5.00
185 Mario Lemieux 3.00 8.00
186 Shawn McEachern .02 .10
187 Joe Mullen .07 .20
188 Tomas Sandstrom .05 .15
189 Kevin Stevens .07 .20
190 Martin Straka .02 .10
191 Larry Murphy .08 .25
192 Kjell Samuelsson .02 .10
193 Ulf Samuelsson .02 .10
194 Wendel Clark .15 .40
195 Valeri Kamensky .15 .40
196 Andrei Kovalenko .02 .10
197 Owen Nolan .20 .50
198 Mike Ricci .02 .10
199 Joe Sakic 1.25 3.00
200 Scott Young .02 .10
201 Uwe Krupp .02 .10
202 Curtis Leschyshyn .02 .10
203 Brett Hull .75 2.00
204 Craig Janney .08 .25
205 Kevin Miller .02 .10
206 Vitali Prokhorov .02 .10
207 Brendan Shanahan 1.25 3.00
208 Peter Stastny .08 .25
209 Esa Tikkanen .07 .20
210 Steve Duchesne .02 .10
211 Gaetan Duchesne .02 .10
212 Todd Elik .02 .10
213 Pogman .20 .50
214 Pat Falloon .02 .10
215 Johan Garpenlov .02 .10
216 Igor Larionov .08 .25
217 Sergei Makarov .05 .15
218 Jeff Norton .02 .10
219 Sandis Ozolinsh .20 .50
220 Mikael Andersson .02 .10
221 Brian Bradley .08 .25
222 Danton Cole .02 .10
223 Chris Gratton .20 .50
224 Petr Klima .02 .10
225 Denis Savard .08 .25
226 John Tucker .02 .10
227 Shawn Chambers .02 .10
228 Chris Joseph .02 .10
229 Dave Andreychuk .08 .25
230 Nikolai Borschevsky .02 .10
231 Mike Craig .02 .10
232 Mike Eastwood .02 .10
233 Mike Gartner .20 .50
234 Doug Gilmour .40 1.00
235 Kent Manderville .02 .10
236 Mike Ridley .20 .50
237 Mats Sundin .30 .75
238 Dave Ellett .02 .10
239 Todd Gill .02 .10
240 Jamie Macoun .02 .10
241 Dmitri Mironov .02 .10
242 Peter Bondra .40 1.00
243 Randy Burridge .02 .10
244 Dale Hunter .20 .50
245 Joe Juneau .15 .40
246 Dmitri Khristich .08 .25
247 Kelly Miller .02 .10
248 Michal Pivonka .02 .10
249 Sylvain Cote .02 .10
250 Tie Domi .20 .50
251 Dallas Drake .02 .10
252 Nelson Emerson .02 .10
253 Teemu Selanne 1.25 3.00
254 Darrin Shannon .02 .10
255 Thomas Steen .02 .10
256 Keith Tkachuk .60 1.50
257 Dave Manson .02 .10
258 Stephane Quintal .02 .10
259 Adam Graves AS .08 .25
260 Brian Leetch AS .40 1.00
261 John Vanbiesbrouck AS .60 1.50
262 Scott Stevens AS .08 .25
263 Ray Bourque AS .40 1.00
264 Al MacInnis AS .08 .25
265 Brendan Shanahan AS 1.25 3.00
266 Pavel Bure AS 1.50 4.00
267 Sergei Fedorov AS 1.25 3.00
268 Wayne Gretzky AS 4.00 10.00
269 Guy Hebert .02 .10
270 Kirk McLean .20 .50
271 John Blue .08 .25
272 Vincent Riendeau .08 .25
273 Grant Fuhr .20 .50
274 Dominik Hasek 1.25 3.00
275 Trevor Kidd .15 .40
276 Ed Belfour .60 1.50
277 Andy Moog .20 .50
278 Mike Vernon .20 .50
279 Bill Ranford .20 .50
280 John Vanbiesbrouck 1.00 2.50
281 Sean Burke .20 .50
282 Kelly Hrudey .20 .50
283 Patrick Roy 3.00 8.00
284 Martin Brodeur 1.50 4.00
285 Chris Terreri .05 .15
286 Jamie McLennan .07 .20
287 Glenn Healy .08 .25
288 Mike Richter .60 1.50
289 Craig Billington .08 .25
290 Dominic Roussel .07 .20
291 Tom Barrasso .08 .25
292 Stephane Fiset .08 .25
293 Curtis Joseph .75 2.00
294 Arturs Irbe .40 1.00
295 Darren Puppa .20 .50
296 Felix Potvin .60 1.50
297 Tim Cheveldae .08 .25
298 Don Beaupre .08 .25
299 Rick Tabaracci .07 .20
300 Anaheim Mighty Ducks .15 .40
301 Boston Bruins .15 .40
302 Buffalo Sabres .02 .10
303 Calgary Flames .02 .10
304 Chicago Blackhawks .08 .25
305 Dallas Stars .02 .10
306 Detroit Red Wings .15 .40
307 Edmonton Oilers .02 .10
308 Florida Panthers .02 .10
309 Hartford Whalers .02 .10
310 Los Angeles Kings .15 .40
311 Montreal Canadiens .15 .40
312 New Jersey Devils .02 .10
313 New York Islanders .02 .10
314 New York Rangers .15 .40
315 Ottawa Senators .02 .10
316 Philadelphia Flyers .02 .10
317 Pittsburgh Penguins .02 .10
318 Quebec Nordiques .02 .10
319 St. Louis Blues .02 .10
320 San Jose Sharks .08 .25
321 Tampa Bay Lightning .02 .10
322 Toronto Maple Leafs .08 .25
323 Vancouver Canucks .02 .10
324 Washington Capitals .02 .10
325 Winnipeg Jets .02 .10
326 Calder Trophy 1.50 4.00
327 Norris Trophy .40 1.00
328 Game Winning Goals .30 .75
329 Geoff Courtnall .02 .10
330 Pogman .20 .50
331 Art Ross Trophy 1.25 3.00
332 Vezina Trophy 1.25 3.00
333 Jennings Trophy 1.25 3.00
334 Brian Leetch .40 1.00
335 Martin Gelinas .07 .20
336 Cam Neely .20 .50
337 Mike Richter .60 1.50
338 Luke Richardson .02 .10
339 Jyrkki Lumme .02 .10
340 Nathan Lafayette .02 .10
341 Pavel Bure 1.00 2.50
342 Sergio Momesso .02 .10
343 Trevor Linden .20 .50
344 Tie Domi .15 .40
345 Scott Stevens .08 .25
346 Teppo Numminen .02 .10
347 Anatoli Semenov .02 .10
348 Steve Heinze .02 .10
349 Tom Chorske .02 .10
350 Bill Guerin .07 .20
351 Scott Niedermayer .08 .25
352 Adam Graves .08 .25
353 Alexandre Daigle .20 .50
354 Troy Mallette .02 .10
355 Dave McLlwain .02 .10
356 Josef Beranek .02 .10
357 Kevin Dineen .02 .10
358 Eric Lindros 1.50 4.00
359 Bob Rouse .02 .10
360 Sergei Fedorov AW 1.25 3.00
361 Bob Errey .02 .10
362 Brad May .02 .10
363 Kevin Hatcher .02 .10
364 New York Islanders .02 .10
365 Randy Ladouceur .02 .10
366 Bobby Dollas .02 .10
367 Igor Kravchuk .02 .10
368 Jesse Belanger .02 .10
369 Pogman .20 .50
370 Gary Valk .02 .10
371 Pogman .20 .50
372 Ron Hextall .20 .50
373 Rod Brind'Amour .20 .50
374 Benoit Hogue .02 .10
375 Alexei Zhamnov .08 .25
376 Goal Scoring Leader 1.50 4.00
NNO Checklist 1-47 .02 .10
NNO Checklist 48-94 .02 .10
NNO Checklist 95-141 .02 .10
NNO Checklist 142-188 .02 .10
NNO Checklist 189-235 .02 .10
NNO Checklist 236-282 .02 .10
NNO Checklist 283-329 .02 .10
NNO Checklist 330-376 .02 .10

1995-96 Canada Games NHL POGS

COMPLETE SET (296) 32.00 80.00
1 Wayne Gretzky 2.50 6.00
2 Mario Lemieux 2.00 5.00
3 Cam Neely .40 1.00
4 Ray Bourque .75 2.00
5 Patrick Roy 1.50 4.00
6 Mark Messier .50 1.25
7 Brett Hull .50 1.25
8 Grant Fuhr .30 .75
9 Eric Lindros 1.00 2.50
10 John LeClair .60 1.50
11 Jaromir Jagr 1.25 3.00
12 Chris Chelios .30 .75
13 Paul Coffey .40 1.00
14 Dominik Hasek .75 2.00
15 Alexei Zhamnov .02 .10
16 Keith Tkachuk .40 1.00
17 Theo Fleury .40 1.00
18 Ray Bourque .75 2.00
19 Larry Murphy .30 .75
20 Ed Belfour .40 1.00
21 Pavel Bure 1.00 2.50
22 Doug Gilmour .40 1.00
23 Brett Hull .50 1.25
24 Mark Messier .50 1.25
25 Cam Neely .40 1.00
26 Jeremy Roenick .40 1.00
27 Patrick Roy 1.50 4.00
28 Jim Carey .30 .75
29 Peter Forsberg 1.00 2.50
30 Jeff Friesen .02 .10
31 Kenny Jonsson .02 .10
32 Paul Kariya 1.25 3.00
33 Ian Laperriere .02 .10
34 David Oliver .02 .10
35 Kyle McLaren .30 .75
36 Ray Bourque .50 1.25
37 Alexei Kasatonov .02 .10
38 Blaine Lacher .30 .75
39 Brian Holzinger .30 .75
40 Derek Plante .02 .10
41 Mike Peca .02 .10
42 Pat LaFontaine .40 1.00
43 Jason Dawe .02 .10
44 Brad May .02 .10
45 Yuri Khmylev .02 .10
46 Garry Galley .02 .10
47 Alexei Zhitnik .02 .10
48 Dominik Hasek .75 2.00
49 Joe Nieuwendyk .02 .10
50 German Titov .02 .10
51 Cory Stillman .02 .10
52 Theo Fleury .40 1.00
53 Paul Kruse .02 .10
54 Michael Nylander .02 .10
55 Gary Roberts .02 .10
56 Phil Housley .02 .10
57 Steve Chiasson .02 .10
58 Zarley Zalapski .02 .10
59 Ron Stern .02 .10
60 Trevor Kidd .30 .75
61 Jeremy Roenick .40 1.00
62 Denis Savard .40 1.00
63 Tony Amonte .40 1.00
64 Bernie Nicholls .02 .10
65 Sergei Krivokrasov .02 .10
66 Joe Murphy .02 .10
67 Patrick Poulin .02 .10
68 Bob Probert .30 .75
69 Gary Suter .02 .10
70 Chris Chelios .40 1.00
71 Ed Belfour .40 1.00
72 Joe Sakic .75 2.00
73 Mike Ricci .02 .10
74 Valeri Kamensky .30 .75
75 Andrei Kovalenko .02 .10
76 Owen Nolan .30 .75
77 Peter Forsberg 1.00 2.50
78 Scott Young .02 .10
79 Uwe Krupp .02 .10
80 Curtis Leschyshyn .02 .10
81 Adam Deadmarsh .30 .75
82 Stephane Fiset .02 .10
83 Bob Bassen .02 .10
84 Corey Millen .02 .10
85 Mike Modano .50 1.25
86 Dave Gagner .30 .75
87 Mike Donnelly .02 .10
88 Trent Klatt .02 .10
89 Kevin Hatcher .02 .10
90 Grant Ledyard .02 .10
91 Greg Adams .02 .10
92 Andy Moog .30 .75
93 Keith Primeau .30 .75
94 Kris Draper .02 .10
95 Sergei Fedorov .75 2.00
96 Steve Yzerman 1.25 3.00
97 Vyacheslav Kozlov .02 .10
98 Ray Sheppard .30 .75
99 Dino Ciccarelli .30 .75
100 Slava Fetisov .02 .10
101 Nicklas Lidstrom .40 1.00
102 Paul Coffey .40 1.00
103 Darren McCarty .30 .75
104 Mike Vernon .30 .75
105 Doug Weight .30 .75
106 Jason Arnott .30 .75
107 Todd Marchant .02 .10
108 David Oliver .02 .10
109 Igor Kravchuk .02 .10
110 Jiri Slegr .02 .10
111 Kelly Buchberger .02 .10
112 Scott Thornton .02 .10
113 Bill Ranford .30 .75
114 Jesse Belanger .02 .10
115 Stu Barnes .02 .10
116 Scott Mellanby .30 .75
117 Bill Lindsay .02 .10
118 Dave Lowry .02 .10
119 Gaetan Duchesne .02 .10
120 Johan Garpenlov .02 .10
121 Paul Laus .02 .10
122 Gord Murphy .02 .10
123 John Vanbiesbrouck .40 1.00
124 Andrew Cassels .02 .10
125 Geoff Sanderson .30 .75
126 Brendan Shanahan .75 2.00
127 Paul Ranheim .02 .10
128 Steven Rice .02 .10
129 Frantisek Kucera .02 .10
130 Glen Wesley .02 .10
131 Sean Burke .30 .75
132 Wayne Gretzky 2.50 6.00
133 Dimitri Khristich .02 .10
134 Jari Kurri .30 .75
135 John Druce .02 .10
136 Pat Conacher .02 .10
137 Rick Tocchet .30 .75
138 Rob Blake .30 .75
139 Tony Granato .02 .10
140 Marty McSorley .02 .10
141 Darryl Sydor .30 .75
142 Eric Lacroix .02 .10
143 Kelly Hrudey .30 .75
144 Brian Savage .02 .10
145 Pierre Turgeon .30 .75
146 Benoit Brunet .02 .10
147 Valeri Bure .30 .75
148 Vincent Damphousse .30 .75
149 Mike Keane .02 .10
150 Mark Recchi .30 .75
151 Vladimir Malakhov .02 .10
152 Patrice Brisebois .02 .10
153 J.J. Daigneault .02 .10
154 Yves Racine .02 .10
155 Patrick Roy 1.50 4.00
156 Bob Carpenter .02 .10
157 Neal Broten .02 .10
158 Steve Thomas .30 .75
159 Bobby Holik .30 .75
160 John MacLean .30 .75
161 Mike Peluso .02 .10
162 Randy McKay .02 .10
163 Stephane Richer .30 .75
164 Scott Niedermayer .30 .75
165 Scott Stevens .30 .75
166 Bill Guerin .30 .75
167 Martin Brodeur 1.00 2.50
168 Kirk Muller .02 .10
169 Zigmund Palffy .40 1.00
170 Travis Green .02 .10
171 Brett Lindros .02 .10
172 Derek King .02 .10
173 Pat Flatley .02 .10
174 Wendel Clark .30 .75
175 Bryan McCabe .02 .10
176 Mathieu Schneider .02 .10
177 Eric Fichaud .30 .75
178 Ray Ferraro .02 .10
179 Adam Graves .30 .75
180 Mark Messier .50 1.25
181 Sergei Nemchinov .02 .10
182 Pat Verbeek .30 .75
183 Luc Robitaille .30 .75
184 Alexei Kovalev .30 .75
185 Jeff Beukeboom .02 .10
186 Brian Leetch .40 1.00
187 Ulf Samuelsson .02 .10
188 Alexander Karpovtsev .02 .10
189 Mike Richter .40 1.00
190 Alexandre Daigle .30 .75
191 Alexei Yashin .30 .75
192 Dan Quinn .02 .10
193 Martin Straka .02 .10
194 Radek Bonk .02 .10
195 Pavol Demitra .30 .75
196 Steve Duchesne .30 .75
197 Chris Dahlquist .02 .10
198 Sean Hill .02 .10
199 Stanislav Neckar .02 .10
200 Don Beaupre .02 .10
201 Eric Lindros 1.00 2.50
202 Rod Brind'Amour .30 .75
203 Shjon Podein .02 .10
204 Brent Fedyk .02 .10
205 Joel Otto .02 .10
206 John LeClair .60 1.50
207 Kevin Dineen .02 .10
208 Petr Svoboda .02 .10
209 Eric Desjardins .02 .10
210 Ron Hextall .30 .75
211 Mario Lemieux 2.00 5.00
212 Petr Nedved .30 .75
213 Bryan Smolinski .30 .75
214 Tomas Sandstrom .30 .75
215 Ron Francis .30 .75
216 Jaromir Jagr 1.25 3.00
217 Sergei Zubov .02 .10
218 Drake Berehowsky .02 .10
219 Dmitri Mironov .02 .10
220 Ken Wregget .30 .75
221 Tom Barrasso .30 .75
222 Igor Larionov .30 .75
223 Jeff Friesen .30 .75
224 Kevin Miller .02 .10
225 Ray Whitney .30 .75
226 Craig Janney .30 .75
227 Pat Falloon .02 .10
228 Ulf Dahlen .02 .10
229 Viktor Kozlov .02 .10
230 Michal Sykora .02 .10
231 Sandis Ozolinsh .30 .75
232 Jamie Baker .02 .10
233 Arturs Irbe .30 .75
234 Adam Creighton .02 .10
235 Ian Laperriere .02 .10
236 Brett Hull .50 1.25
237 Brian Noonan .02 .10
238 Dale Hawerchuk .02 .10
239 Esa Tikkanen .30 .75
240 Geoff Courtnall .02 .10
241 Shayne Corson .02 .10
242 Al MacInnis .30 .75
243 Chris Pronger .30 .75
244 Jeff Norton .02 .10
245 Grant Fuhr .30 .75
246 Brian Bradley .30 .75
247 Chris Gratton .30 .75
248 John Cullen .02 .10
249 John Tucker .02 .10
250 Paul Ysebaert .02 .10
251 Petr Klima .02 .10
252 Alexander Selivanov .02 .10
253 Brian Bellows .02 .10
254 Enrico Ciccone .02 .10
255 Roman Hamrlik .30 .75
256 Daren Puppa .30 .75
257 Doug Gilmour .40 1.00
258 Benoit Hogue .02 .10
259 Mats Sundin .40 1.00
260 Dave Andreychuk .30 .75
261 Mike Gartner .30 .75
262 Randy Wood .02 .10
263 Tie Domi .02 .10
264 Dave Ellett .02 .10
265 Todd Gill .02 .10
266 Larry Murphy .30 .75
267 Kenny Jonsson .30 .75
268 Felix Potvin .40 1.00
269 Cliff Ronning .02 .10
270 Mike Ridley .02 .10
271 Trevor Linden .02 .10
272 Alexander Mogilny .30 .75
273 Martin Gelinas .02 .10
274 Pavel Bure .75 2.00
275 Russ Courtnall .02 .10
276 Jeff Brown .02 .10
277 Jyrki Lumme .02 .10
278 Kirk McLean .30 .75
279 Steve Konowalchuk .02 .10
280 Kelly Miller .02 .10
281 Peter Bondra .40 1.00
282 Keith Jones .02 .10
283 Joe Juneau .02 .10
284 Mark Tinordi .02 .10
285 Calle Johansson .02 .10
286 Sergei Gonchar .02 .10
287 Jim Carey .02 .10
288 Dallas Drake .02 .10
289 Alexei Zhamnov .30 .75
290 Mike Eastwood .02 .10
291 Igor Korolev .02 .10
292 Teemu Selanne .75 2.00
293 Keith Tkachuk .40 1.00
294 Teppo Numminen .02 .10
295 Dave Manson .02 .10
296 Tim Cheveldae .30 .75
K1 Lester B. Pearson .30 .75
K2 Art Ross .30 .75
K3 Bill Masterton .30 .75
K4 Calder .30 .75
K5 Clarence S. Campbell .30 .75
K6 Conn Smythe .30 .75
K7 Frank J. Selke .30 .75
K8 Hart .30 .75
K9 Jack Adams .30 .75
K10 James Norris .30 .75
K11 King Clancy .30 .75
K12 Lady Byng .30 .75
K13 Prince of Wales .30 .75
K14 Stanley Cup .30 .75
K15 Vezina .30 .75
K16 William M. Jennings .30 .75

1983 Canadian National Juniors

COMPLETE SET (21) 50.00 125.00
1 Dave Andreychuk 3.00 8.00
2 Joe Cirella .75 2.00
3 Paul Cyr .40 1.00
4 Dale Derkatch .40 1.00
5 Mike Eagles .40 1.00
6 Pat Flatley UER
(Misspelled Flately) .75 2.00
7 Mario Gosselin .75 2.00
8 Gary Leeman .75 2.00
9 Mario Lemieux 30.00 75.00
10 Mark Morrison .40 1.00
11 James Patrick .75 2.00
12 Mike Sands .60 1.50
13 Gord Sherven .40 1.00
14 Tony Tanti .75 2.00
15 Larry Trader .40 1.00
16 Sylvain Turgeon .60 1.50
17 Pat Verbeek 3.00 8.00
18 Mike Vernon 3.00 8.00
19 Steve Yzerman 30.00 60.00
20 Checklist Card .20 .50
21 Title Card .20 .50
NNO Team Card
(Regular size 3.00 8.00
NNO Large Team Card 4.00 10.00
NNO Team Card '82 2.00 5.00
NNO Celebration '82
(Troy Murray 2.00 5.00

2003 Canada Post

COMPLETE SET (24) 30.00 60.00
1 Wayne Gretzky 4.00 10.00
2 Gordie Howe 3.00 8.00
3 Maurice Richard 2.00 5.00
4 Doug Harvey 1.25 3.00
5 Bobby Orr 3.00 8.00
6 Jacques Plante 1.50 4.00
7 Jean Beliveau 2.00 5.00
8 Terry Sawchuk 2.00 5.00
9 Eddie Shore 1.50 4.00
10 Denis Potvin 1.25 3.00
11 Bobby Hull 2.00 5.00
12 Syl Apps 1.25 3.00
13 Tim Horton 1.50 4.00
14 Guy Lafleur 1.50 4.00
15 Howie Morenz 1.50 4.00
16 Glenn Hall 1.50 4.00
17 Red Kelly 1.25 3.00
18 Phil Esposito 1.50 4.00
19 Frank Mahovlich 1.25 3.00
20 Ray Bourque 1.50 4.00
21 Serge Savard 1.25 3.00
22 Stan Mikita 1.25 3.00
23 Mike Bossy 1.25 3.00
24 Bill Durnan 1.50 4.00

2003 Canada Post Autographs

COMPLETE SET (4) 150.00 300.00
7 Jean Beliveau 40.00 100.00
11 Bobby Hull 40.00 100.00
14 Guy Lafleur 40.00 80.00
16 Glenn Hall 30.00 60.00

2004 Canada Post

COMPLETE SET (6) 6.00 15.00
25 Johnny Bower 1.50 4.00
26 Marcel Dionne 1.25 3.00
27 Ted Lindsay 1.25 3.00
28 Brad Park 1.25 3.00
29 Larry Robinson 1.00 2.50
30 Milt Schmidt 1.25 3.00

2004 Canada Post Autographs

COMPLETE SET (6) 150.00 250.00
1 Johnny Bower 25.00 50.00
2 Marcel Dionne 20.00 40.00
3 Larry Robinson 20.00 40.00
4 Milt Schmidt 20.00 40.00
5 Ted Lindsay 25.00 50.00
6 Brad Park 20.00 40.00

2005 Canada Post

COMPLETE SET (6) 6.00 15.00
31 Henri Richard 1.25 3.00
32 Grant Fuhr 1.50 4.00
33 Allan Stanley 1.00 2.50
34 Pierre Pilote 1.25 3.00
35 Bryan Trottier 1.50 4.00
36 John Bucyk 1.25 3.00

2005 Canada Post Autographs

COMPLETE SET (6) 125.00 200.00
31 Henri Richard 12.00 30.00
32 Grant Fuhr 15.00 40.00
33 Allan Stanley 10.00 25.00
34 Pierre Pilote 15.00 40.00
35 Bryan Trottier 15.00 40.00
36 John Bucyk 15.00 40.00

2014 Canada Post Original 6 Defensemen

1 Doug Harvey 1.25 3.00
2 Tim Horton 1.25 3.00
3 Harry Howell 1.00 2.50
4 Red Kelly 1.00 2.50
5 Bobby Orr 1.50 4.00
6 Pierre Pilote 1.00 2.50

2015 Canada Post Great Canadian Goalies

1 Johnny Bower 1.00 2.50
2 Martin Brodeur 1.25 3.00
3 Ken Dryden 1.00 2.50
4 Tony Esposito 1.00 2.50
5 Bernie Parent 1.25 3.00
6 Gump Worsley 1.00 2.50

1992 Canadian Summer Olympics

COMPLETE SET (263) 3.00 8.00
136 Alain Cote .08 .25

2004 Canadian Women's World Championship Team

COMPLETE SET (22) 25.00
1 Dana Antal .40 1.00
2 Gillian Apps .60 1.50
3 Kelly Bechard .40 1.00
4 Jennifer Botterill .40 1.00
5 Therese Brisson .40 1.00
6 Cassie Campbell 1.25 3.00
7 Delaney Collins .40 1.00
8 Gillian Ferrari .40 1.00
9 Danielle Goyette .40 1.00
10 Jayna Hefford .75 2.00
11 Becky Kellar .40 1.00
12 Gina Kingsbury .40 1.00
13 Charline Labonte 1.25 3.00
14 Caroline Ouellette .40 1.00
15 Cherie Piper .40 1.00
16 Cheryl Pounder .40 1.00
17 Sami Jo Small .75 2.00
18 Colleen Sostorics .40 1.00
19 Kim St. Pierre .75 2.00
20 Vicky Sunohara .75 2.00
21 Sarah Vaillancourt .40 1.00
22 Hayley Wickenheiser 1.25 3.00

1964-65 Canadiens Postcards

COMPLETE SET (24) 100.00 200.00
1 Ralph Backstrom 2.50 5.00
2 Jean Beliveau 12.50 25.00
3 Toe Blake 5.00 10.00
4 Yvan Cournoyer 15.00 30.00
5 Dick Duff 2.50 5.00
6 John Ferguson 5.00 10.00
7 Danny Grant 2.50 5.00
8 Terry Harper 2.50 5.00
9 Ted Harris 2.50 5.00
10 Jacques Laperriere 4.00 8.00
11 Claude Larose 2.50 5.00
12 Jacques Lemaire 10.00 20.00
13 Garry Monahan 2.50 5.00
14 Claude Provost 2.50 5.00
15 Mickey Redmond 10.00 20.00
16 Henri Richard 7.50 15.00
17 Bobby Rousseau 2.50 5.00
18 Serge Savard 5.00 10.00
19 Gilles Tremblay 2.50 5.00
20 J.C. Tremblay 2.50 5.00
21 Carol Vadnais 1.50 3.00
22 Rogatien Vachon 15.00 30.00
23 Bryan Watson 1.50 3.00
24 Gump Worsley 5.00 10.00

1965-66 Canadiens Steinberg Glasses

COMPLETE SET (12) 75.00 150.00
1 Ralph Backstrom 5.00 10.00
2 Jean Beliveau 15.00 30.00
3 John Ferguson 7.50 15.00
4 Charlie Hodge 7.50 15.00
5 Jacques Laperierre 5.00 10.00
6 Claude Provost 5.00 10.00
7 Henri Richard 10.00 20.00
8 Bob Rousseau 5.00 10.00
9 Jean Guy Talbot 5.00 10.00
10 Gilles Trembley 5.00 10.00
11 J.C. Trembley 6.00 12.00
12 Gump Worsley 10.00 20.00

1966-67 Canadiens IGA

COMPLETE SET (10) 150.00 300.00
1 J.C. Tremblay 15.00 30.00
2 Ralph Backstrom 15.00 30.00
3 Dick Duff 15.00 30.00
4 Ted Harris 12.50 25.00
5 Claude Larose 12.50 25.00
6 Bobby Rousseau 12.50 25.00
7 Terry Harper 15.00 30.00
8 Gilles Tremblay 12.50 25.00
9 John Ferguson 12.50 25.00
10 Gump Worsley 40.00 80.00

1967-68 Canadiens IGA

COMPLETE SET (30) 325.00 650.00
1 Gump Worsley 25.00 50.00
2 Jacques Laperriere 15.00 30.00
3 J.C. Tremblay 12.50 25.00
4 Jean Beliveau 40.00 80.00
5 Gilles Tremblay 10.00 20.00
6 Ralph Backstrom 10.00 20.00
8 Dick Duff 12.50 25.00
10 Ted Harris 10.00 20.00
11 Claude Larose 10.00 20.00
12 Yvan Cournoyer 20.00 40.00
14 Claude Provost 10.00 20.00
15 Bobby Rousseau 10.00 20.00
16 Henri Richard 25.00 50.00
17 Carol Vadnais 10.00 20.00
18 Serge Savard 25.00 50.00
19 Terry Harper 12.50 25.00
20 Garry Monahan 10.00 20.00
22 John Ferguson 12.50 25.00
23 Danny Grant 12.50 25.00
24 Mickey Redmond 20.00 40.00
25 Jacques Lemaire 30.00 60.00
30 Rogatien Vachon 40.00 80.00
NNO Toe Blake CO 15.00 30.00

1968-69 Canadiens IGA

COMPLETE SET (30) 300.00 600.00
1 Gump Worsley 30.00 60.00
2 Jacques Laperriere 15.00 30.00
3 J.C. Tremblay 12.50 25.00
4 Jean Beliveau 40.00 80.00

5 Gilles Tremblay 10.00 20.00
6 Ralph Backstrom 12.50 25.00
8 Dick Duff 12.50 25.00
10 Ted Harris 10.00 20.00
12 Yvan Cournoyer 25.00 50.00
14 Claude Provost 10.00 20.00
15 Bobby Rousseau 12.50 25.00
16 Henri Richard 25.00 50.00
18 Serge Savard 20.00 40.00
19 Terry Harper 12.50 25.00
20 Garry Monahan 10.00 20.00
22 John Ferguson 15.00 30.00
24 Mickey Redmond 20.00 40.00
25 Jacques Lemaire 30.00 60.00
30 Rogatien Vachon 30.00 60.00

1968-69 Canadiens Postcards BW

COMPLETE SET (20) 40.00 80.00
1 Ralph Backstrom 1.50 3.00
2 Jean Beliveau 7.50 15.00
3 Yvan Cournoyer 4.00 8.00
4 Dick Duff 1.50 3.00
5 John Ferguson 2.50 5.00
6 Terry Harper 1.50 3.00
7 Ted Harris 1.25 2.50
8 Jacques Laperriere 2.00 4.00
9 Jacques Lemaire 5.00 10.00
10 Garry Monahan 1.25 2.50
11 Claude Provost 1.25 2.50
12 Mickey Redmond 4.00 8.00
13 Henri Richard 4.00 8.00
14 Bobby Rousseau 1.50 3.00
15 Claude Ruel CO 1.25 2.50
16 Serge Savard 4.00 8.00
17 Gilles Tremblay 1.25 2.50
18 J.C. Tremblay 1.50 3.00
19 Rogatien Vachon 5.00 10.00
20 Gump Worsley 5.00 10.00

1969-71 Canadiens Postcards Color

COMPLETE SET (31) 50.00 100.00
1 Ralph Backstrom 1.50 3.00
2 Jean Beliveau 6.00 12.00
3 Chris Bordeleau 1.25 2.50
4 Pierre Bouchard 1.25 2.50
5 Guy Charron 1.25 2.50
6 Bill Collins 1.25 2.50
7 Yvan Cournoyer 4.00 8.00
8 John Ferguson 2.00 4.00
9 Terry Harper 1.50 3.00
10 Ted Harris 1.25 2.50
11 Rejean Houle 2.00 4.00
12 Jacques Laperriere 2.00 4.00
13 Guy Lapointe 3.00 6.00
14 Claude Larose 1.25 2.50
15 Jacques Lemaire 4.00 8.00
16 Al MacNeil CO 1.25 2.50
17 Frank Mahovlich 4.00 8.00
18 Peter Mahovlich 3.00 6.00
19 Phil Myre 2.00 4.00
20 Larry Pleau 1.50 3.00
21 Claude Provost 1.50 3.00
22 Mickey Redmond 4.00 8.00
23 Henri Richard 4.00 8.00
24 Phil Roberto 1.25 2.50
25 Jim Roberts 1.25 2.50
26 Bobby Rousseau 1.50 3.00
27 Claude Ruel CO 1.25 2.50
28 Serge Savard 4.00 8.00
29 Marc Tardif 1.50 3.00
30 J.C. Tremblay 1.50 3.00
31 Rogatien Vachon 5.00 10.00

1970-72 Canadiens Pins

COMPLETE SET (22) 75.00 150.00
1 Jean Beliveau 10.00 20.00
2 Yvan Cournoyer 4.00 8.00
3 Ken Dryden 20.00 40.00
4 John Ferguson 2.50 5.00
5 Terry Harper 2.00 4.00
6 Guy Lafleur 12.50 25.00
7 Jacques Laperriere 2.50 5.00
8 Guy Lapointe 2.50 5.00
9 Jacques Lemaire 4.00 8.00
10 Frank Mahovlich 5.00 10.00
11 Peter Mahovlich 2.50 5.00
12 Henri Richard 5.00 10.00
13 Bobby Rousseau 2.50 5.00
14 Claude Ruel CO 1.50 3.00
15 Serge Savard 2.50 5.00
16 J.C. Tremblay 2.00 4.00
17 Rogatien Vachon 4.00 8.00
18 Ted Harris 2.50 5.00
19 Claude Provost 2.50 5.00
20 Mickey Redmond 3.00 6.00
21 Ralph Backstrom 2.50 5.00
22 Gump Worsley 5.00 10.00

1971-72 Canadiens Postcards

COMPLETE SET (25) 75.00 150.00
1 Pierre Bouchard .75 1.50
2 Scotty Bowman CO 4.00 8.00
3 Yvan Cournoyer 4.00 8.00
4 Denis DeJordy 1.50 3.00
5 Ken Dryden 20.00 40.00
6 Terry Harper 1.00 2.00
7 Dale Hoganson .75 1.50
8 Rejean Houle 1.00 2.00
9 Guy Lafleur 15.00 30.00
10 Jacques Laperriere 2.00 4.00
11 Guy Lapointe 2.00 4.00
12 Claude Larose .75 1.50
13 Jacques Lemaire 4.00 8.00
14 Frank Mahovlich 4.00 8.00
15 Peter Mahovlich 1.50 3.00
16 Phil Myre 1.50 3.00
17 Larry Pleau 1.00 2.00
18 Henri Richard 4.00 8.00
19 Phil Roberto .75 1.50
20 Jim Roberts .75 1.50
21 Leon Rochefort .75 1.50
22 Serge Savard 2.00 4.00
23 Marc Tardif 1.25 2.50
24 J.C. Tremblay 1.25 2.50
25 Rogatien Vachon 4.00 8.00

1972-73 Canadiens Postcards

COMPLETE SET (22) 62.50 125.00
1 Chuck Arnason 1.00 2.00
2 Pierre Bouchard 1.50 3.00
3 Scotty Bowman CO 5.00 10.00
4 Yvan Cournoyer 2.50 5.00
5 Ken Dryden 17.50 35.00
6 Rejean Houle 1.50 3.00
7 Guy Lafleur 10.00 20.00
8 Jacques Laperriere 2.00 4.00
9 Guy Lapointe 2.00 4.00
10 Claude Larose 1.00 2.00
11 Chuck Lefley 1.00 2.00
12 Jacques Lemaire 2.50 5.00
13 Frank Mahovlich 2.50 5.00
14 Peter Mahovlich 2.00 4.00
15 Bob Murdoch 1.00 2.00
16 Michel Plasse 2.00 4.00
17 Henri Richard 2.50 5.00
18 Jim Roberts 1.00 2.00
19 Serge Savard 2.00 4.00
20 Steve Shutt 4.00 8.00
21 Marc Tardif 1.50 3.00
22 Murray Wilson 1.00 2.00

1972 Canadiens Great West Life Prints

COMPLETE SET (6) 50.00 100.00
1 Pierre Bouchard 5.00 10.00
2 Yvan Cournoyer 5.00 10.00
3 Ken Dryden 20.00 40.00
4 Pete Mahovlich 5.00 10.00
5 Guy Lafleur 12.50 25.00
6 Steve Shutt 5.00 10.00

1973-74 Canadiens Postcards

COMPLETE SET (24) 40.00 80.00
1 Jean Beliveau (Portrait) 6.00 12.00
2 Pierre Bouchard .75 1.50
3 Scotty Bowman CO 3.00 6.00
4 Yvan Cournoyer 2.50 5.00
5 Bob Gainey 4.00 8.00
6 Dave Gardner .75 1.50
7 Guy Lafleur 5.00 10.00
8 Yvon Lambert .75 1.50
9 Jacques Laperriere 1.25 2.50
10 Guy Lapointe 1.25 2.50
11 Michel Larocque 1.50 3.00
12 Claude Larose SP 2.50 5.00
13 Chuck Lefley .75 1.50
14 Jacques Lemaire 1.50 3.00
15 Frank Mahovlich 2.50 5.00
16 Peter Mahovlich 1.25 2.50
17 Michel Plasse SP 2.50 5.00
18 Henri Richard 2.50 5.00
19 Jim Roberts SP 2.50 5.00
20 Larry Robinson 5.00 10.00
21 Serge Savard 1.25 2.50
22 Steve Shutt 2.50 5.00
23 Wayne Thomas 1.25 2.50
24 Murray Wilson SP 2.50 5.00

1974-75 Canadiens Postcards

COMPLETE SET (27) 37.50 75.00
1 Pierre Bouchard .75 1.50
2 Scotty Bowman CO 2.00 4.00
3 Rick Chartraw .75 1.50
4 Yvan Cournoyer 2.00 4.00
5 Ken Dryden 6.00 12.00
6 Bob Gainey 4.00 8.00
7 Glenn Goldup .75 1.50
8 Guy Lafleur 4.00 8.00
9 Yvon Lambert .75 1.50
10 Jacques Laperriere 1.00 2.00
11 Guy Lapointe 1.50 3.00
12 Michel Larocque 1.00 2.00
13 Claude Larose SP 1.50 3.00
14 Chuck Lefley SP 1.50 3.00
15 Jacques Lemaire 2.00 4.00
16 Peter Mahovlich 1.00 2.00
17 Henri Richard 2.00 4.00
18 Doug Risebrough 1.00 2.00
19 Jim Roberts SP 1.50 3.00
20 Larry Robinson 4.00 8.00
21 Glen Sather 1.50 3.00
22 Serge Savard 1.00 2.00
23 Steve Shutt 2.00 4.00
24 Wayne Thomas 1.00 2.00
25 Mario Tremblay 1.00 2.00
26 John Van Boxmeer .75 1.50
27 Murray Wilson SP 1.50 3.00

1975-76 Canadiens Postcards

COMPLETE SET (20) 25.00 50.00
1 Don Awrey .75 1.50
2 Pierre Bouchard .75 1.50
3 Scotty Bowman CO 2.00 4.00
4 Yvan Cournoyer 2.00 4.00
5 Ken Dryden 6.00 12.00
6 Bob Gainey 2.00 4.00
7 Doug Jarvis 2.00 4.00
8 Guy Lafleur 4.00 8.00
9 Yvon Lambert .75 1.50
10 Guy Lapointe 1.25 2.50
11 Michel Larocque 1.00 2.00
12 Jacques Lemaire 2.00 4.00
13 Peter Mahovlich 1.00 2.00
14 Doug Risebrough .75 1.50
15 Jim Roberts .75 1.50
16 Larry Robinson 3.00 6.00
17 Serge Savard 1.25 2.50
18 Steve Shutt 2.00 4.00
19 Mario Tremblay 1.00 2.00
20 Murray Wilson .75 1.50

1976-77 Canadiens Postcards

COMPLETE SET (23) 25.00 50.00
1 Pierre Bouchard .75 1.50
2 Scotty Bowman CO 2.00 4.00
3 Rick Chartraw .75 1.50
4 Yvan Cournoyer 1.50 3.00
5 Ken Dryden 5.00 10.00
6 Bob Gainey 2.00 4.00
7 Rejean Houle .75 1.50
8 Doug Jarvis 1.00 2.00
9 Guy Lafleur 4.00 8.00
10 Yvon Lambert .75 1.50
11 Guy Lapointe 1.00 2.00
12 Michel Larocque 1.25 2.50
13 Jacques Lemaire 1.50 3.00
14 Peter Mahovlich 1.00 2.00
15 Bill Nyrop .75 1.50
16 Doug Risebrough .75 1.50
17 Jim Roberts .75 1.50
18 Larry Robinson 2.50 5.00
19 Claude Ruel CO .50 1.00
20 Serge Savard 1.00 2.00
21 Steve Shutt 1.50 3.00
22 Mario Tremblay 1.00 2.00
23 Murray Wilson .75 1.50

1977-78 Canadiens Postcards

COMPLETE SET (25) 25.00 50.00
1 Pierre Bouchard .50 1.00
2 Scotty Bowman CO 1.50 3.00
3 Rick Chartraw .50 1.00
4 Yvan Cournoyer 1.50 3.00
5 Ken Dryden 4.50 9.00
6 Brian Engblom .75 1.50
7 Bob Gainey 1.50 3.00
8 Rejean Houle .50 1.00
9 Doug Jarvis .75 1.50
10 Guy Lafleur 3.00 6.00
11 Yvon Lambert .50 1.00
12 Guy Lapointe 1.00 2.00
13 Michel Larocque .75 1.50
14 Pierre Larouche 1.00 2.00
15 Jacques Lemaire 1.25 2.50
16 Gilles Lupien .50 1.00
17 Pierre Mondou .50 1.00
18 Bill Nyrop .50 1.00
19 Doug Risebrough .50 1.00
20 Larry Robinson 2.00 4.00
21 Claude Ruel CO .50 1.00
22 Serge Savard 1.00 2.00
23 Steve Shutt 1.50 3.00
24 Mario Tremblay .75 1.50
25 Murray Wilson .50 1.00

1978-79 Canadiens Postcards

COMPLETE SET (26) 25.00 50.00
1 Scotty Bowman CO 1.50 3.00
2 Rick Chartraw .50 1.00
3 Cam Connor .50 1.00
4 Yvan Cournoyer 1.50 3.00
5 Ken Dryden 4.00 8.00
6 Brian Engblom .50 1.00
7 Bob Gainey 1.50 3.00
8 Rejean Houle .50 1.00
9 Pat Hughes .50 1.00
10 Doug Jarvis .50 1.00
11 Guy Lafleur 3.00 6.00
12 Yvon Lambert .50 1.00
13 Rod Langway 2.00 4.00
14 Guy Lapointe 1.00 2.00
15 Michel Larocque .75 1.50
16 Pierre Larouche 1.00 2.00
17 Jacques Lemaire 1.25 2.50
18 Gilles Lupien .50 1.00
19 Pierre Mondou .50 1.00
20 Mark Napier .50 1.00
21 Doug Risebrough .50 1.00
22 Larry Robinson 2.00 4.00
23 Claude Ruel CO .50 1.00
24 Serge Savard 1.00 2.00
25 Steve Shutt 1.50 3.00
26 Mario Tremblay .50 1.00

1979-80 Canadiens Postcards

COMPLETE SET (25) 20.00 40.00
1 Rick Chartraw .50 1.00
2 Normand Dupont .50 1.00
3 Brian Engblom .50 1.00
4 Bob Gainey 1.50 3.00
5 Bernie Geoffrion CO SP 2.50 5.00
6 Danny Geoffrion .50 1.00
7 Denis Herron .75 1.50
8 Rejean Houle .50 1.00
9 Doug Jarvis .50 1.00
10 Guy Lafleur 2.50 5.00
11 Yvon Lambert .50 1.00
12 Rod Langway 1.00 2.00
13 Guy Lapointe 1.00 2.00
14 Michel Larocque .75 1.50
15 Pierre Larouche 1.00 2.00
16 Gilles Lupien .50 1.00
17 Pierre Mondou .50 1.00
18 Mark Napier .75 1.50
19 Doug Risebrough .75 1.50
20 Larry Robinson 1.50 3.00
21 Claude Ruel CO .50 1.00
22 Serge Savard .75 1.50
23 Richard Sevigny SP 2.50 5.00
24 Steve Shutt 1.00 2.00
25 Mario Tremblay .50 1.00

1980-81 Canadiens Postcards

COMPLETE SET (26) 17.50 35.00
1 Keith Acton .60 1.50
2 Bill Baker .40 1.00
3 Rick Chartraw .40 1.00
4 Brian Engblom .40 1.00
5 Bob Gainey .75 2.00
6 Gaston Gingras .40 1.00
7 Denis Herron .75 2.00
8 Rejean Houle .60 1.50
9 Doug Jarvis .40 1.00
10 Guy Lafleur 2.50 5.00
11 Yvon Lambert .40 1.00
12 Rod Langway .60 1.50
13 Guy Lapointe .60 1.50
14 Michel Larocque .75 2.00
15 Pierre Larouche .60 1.50
16 Pierre Mondou .40 1.00
17 Mark Napier .40 1.00
18 Chris Nilan .75 2.00
19 Doug Risebrough .40 1.00
20 Larry Robinson 1.25 3.00
21 Claude Ruel CO .40 1.00
22 Serge Savard .60 1.50
23 Richard Sevigny .40 1.00
24 Steve Shutt .75 2.00
25 Mario Tremblay .60 1.50
26 Doug Wickenheiser .40 1.00

1981-82 Canadiens Postcards

COMPLETE SET (28) 14.00 35.00
1 Team Photo 1.25 3.00
2 Keith Acton .40 1.00
3 Bob Berry CO .30 .75
4 Jeff Brubaker .30 .75
5 Gilbert Delorme SP 1.50 4.00
6 Brian Engblom .30 .75
7 Bob Gainey .75 2.00
8 Gaston Gingras .30 .75
9 Denis Herron .50 1.25
10 Rejean Houle .40 1.00
11 Mark Hunter .30 .75
12 Doug Jarvis .30 .75
13 Guy Lafleur 2.00 5.00
14 Rod Langway .60 1.50
15 Jacques Laperriere .60 1.50
16 Guy Lapointe .60 1.50
17 Craig Laughlin .30 .75
18 Pierre Mondou .30 .75
19 Mark Napier .40 1.00
20 Chris Nilan .40 1.00
21 Robert Picard .30 .75
22 Doug Risebrough .30 .75
23 Larry Robinson 1.25 3.00
24 Richard Sevigny .50 1.25
25 Steve Shutt .75 2.00
26 Mario Tremblay .40 1.00
27 Rick Wamsley .50 1.25
28 Doug Wickenheiser .30 .75

1982-83 Canadiens Postcards

COMPLETE SET (28) 12.00 30.00
1 Keith Acton .30 .75
2 Bob Berry CO .30 .75
3 Guy Carbonneau 1.50 4.00
4 Dan Daoust .30 .75
5 Gilbert Delorme .30 .75
6 Bob Gainey .75 2.00
7 Gaston Gingras .30 .75
8 Rick Green .30 .75
9 Rejean Houle .30 .75
10 Mark Hunter .30 .75
11 Guy Lafleur 2.00 5.00
12 Jacques Laperriere .40 1.00
13 Craig Ludwig .60 1.50
14 Pierre Mondou .30 .75
15 Mark Napier .40 1.00
16 Mats Naslund 1.25 3.00
17 Ric Nattress .30 .75
18 Chris Nilan .40 1.00
19 Robert Picard .30 .75
20 Henri Richard 1.25 3.00
21 Larry Robinson 1.25 3.00
22 Bill Root SP .75 2.00
23 Richard Sevigny .50 1.25
24 Steve Shutt .75 2.00
25 Mario Tremblay .40 1.00
26 Ryan Walter .40 1.00
27 Rick Wamsley .50 1.25
28 Doug Wickenheiser .30 .75

1982-83 Canadiens Steinberg

COMPLETE SET (24) 10.00 25.00
1 Keith Acton .20 .50
2 Guy Carbonneau 1.25 3.00
3 Gilbert Delorme (French bio) .20 .50
4 Bob Gainey .60 1.50
5 Rick Green .20 .50
6 Mark Hunter .20 .50
7 Rejean Houle .20 .50
8 Guy Lafleur 1.50 4.00
9 Craig Ludwig .40 1.00
10 Pierre Mondou .20 .50
11 Mark Napier .30 .75
12 Mats Naslund .75 2.00
13 Ric Nattress (French bio) .20 .50
14 Chris Nilan .30 .75
15 Robert Picard .20 .50
16 Larry Robinson .75 2.00
17 Bill Root .20 .50
18 Richard Sevigny .40 1.00
19 Steve Shutt .60 1.50
20 Mario Tremblay .30 .75
21 Ryan Walter .30 .75
22 Rick Wamsley (French bio) .40 1.00
23 Doug Wickenheiser .20 .50
24 Team Photo .50 1.25
xx Vinyl Card Album 2.00 5.00

1983-84 Canadiens Postcards

COMPLETE SET (33) 16.00 40.00
1 Jean Beliveau 1.25 3.00
2 Bob Berry CO .30 .75
3 Guy Carbonneau .75 2.00
4 Kent Carlson .30 .75
5 John Chabot .30 .75
6 Chris Chelios 4.00 10.00
7 Gilbert Delorme SP 1.25 3.00
8 Bob Gainey .60 1.50
9 Rick Green .30 .75
10 Jean Hamel .30 .75
11 Mark Hunter .30 .75
12 Guy Lafleur 1.50 4.00
13 Jacques Lemaire .60 1.50
14 Jacques Laperriere (Action shot) .40 1.00
15 Jacques Laperriere (Head shot) .40 1.00
16 Craig Ludwig .40 1.00
17 Pierre Mondou .30 .75
18 Mats Naslund .75 2.00
19 Ric Nattress .30 .75
20 Chris Nilan .40 1.00
21 Steve Penney .40 1.00
22 Jacques Plante 1.25 3.00
23 Larry Robinson 1.00 2.50
24 Bill Root .30 .75
25 Richard Sevigny .40 1.00
26 Steve Shutt .60 1.50
27 Bobby Smith .60 1.50
28 Mario Tremblay .40 1.00
29 Alfie Turcotte .30 .75
30 Perry Turnbull .30 .75
31 Ryan Walter .30 .75
32 Rick Wamsley .50 1.25
33 Doug Wickenheiser SP 1.25 3.00

1984-85 Canadiens Postcards

COMPLETE SET (31) 12.00 30.00
1 Guy Carbonneau (Action on ice) .60 1.50
2 Guy Carbonneau (Still) .60 1.50
3 Kent Carlson .30 .75
4 Chris Chelios (Same card as 1983-84& but with facsimile auto) 2.50 6.00
5 Lucien Deblois .30 .75
6 Ron Flockhart .30 .75
7 Bob Gainey .60 1.50
8 Rick Green .30 .75
9 Jean Hamel .30 .75
10 Mark Hunter .30 .75
11 Tom Kurvers .30 .75
12 Guy Lafleur 1.50 4.00
13 Jacques Laperriere .40 1.00
14 Jacques Lemaire .60 1.50
15 Craig Ludwig .40 1.00
16 Mike McPhee .60 1.50
17 Pierre Mondou .30 .75
18 Mats Naslund .75 2.00
19 Ric Nattress .30 .75
20 Chris Nilan .40 1.00
21 Steve Penney (Same card as 1983-84) .40 1.00
22 Steve Penney .40 1.00
23 Jean Perron .30 .75
24 Larry Robinson 1.00 2.50
25 Bobby Smith .60 1.50
26 Doug Soetaert .40 1.00
27 Petr Svoboda .60 1.50
28 Mario Tremblay .30 .75
29 Alfie Turcotte (Same card as 1983-84) .30 .75
30 Alfie Turcotte (Facsimile autograph on front) .30 .75
31 Ryan Walter .40 1.00

1985-86 Canadiens Placemats

COMPLETE SET (7) 8.00 20.00
1 Bob Gainey Guy Carbonneau 1.50 4.00
2 Mats Naslund Tom Kurvers .75 2.00
3 Chris Nilan Petr Svoboda .75 2.00
4 Steve Penney Chris Chelios 2.00 5.00
5 Larry Robinson Serge Boisvert 1.50 4.00
6 Mario Tremblay Bobby Smith .75 2.00
7 Hockey Stars Steve Penney Chris Chelios Larry Robinson Serge Boisvert Mario Tremblay Bobby Smith Mats Naslund Tom Kurvers Bob Gainey Guy Carbonneau Chris Nilan Petr Svoboda 2.00 5.00

1985-86 Canadiens Postcards

COMPLETE SET (40) 24.00 60.00
1 Serge Boisvert SP (No red line or autograph) .60 1.50
2 Serge Boisvert SP (Portrait) .60 1.50
3 Randy Bucyk SP (No red line or autograph) .60 1.50
4 Guy Carbonneau .40 1.00
5 Chris Chelios 1.50 4.00
6 Kjell Dahlin (J in autograph on stick) .20 .50
7 Kjell Dahlin (E in autograph on stick) .20 .50
8 Lucien Deblois .20 .50
9 Bob Gainey (B in autograph on stick) .60 1.50
10 Bob Gainey (G in autograph on stick) .60 1.50
11 Gaston Gingras SP .60 1.50
12 Rick Green (No letters on stick) .20 .50
13 Rick Green (C in autograph on stick) .20 .50
14 John Kordic SP (No red line or autograph) 2.00 5.00
15 Tom Kurvers .20 .50
16 Mike Lalor .20 .50
17 Claude Lemieux SP (No red line or autograph) 3.00 8.00
18 Craig Ludwig .30 .75
19 David Maley SP (No red line or autograph) .60 1.50
20 Mike McPhee .40 1.00
21 Sergio Momesso .30 .75
22 Mats Naslund .60 1.50
23 Chris Nilan (Dot from i in Nilan touching toe) .30 .75
24 Chris Nilan (Dot from i in Nilan away from toe) .30 .75
25 Steve Penney .30 .75
26 Jean Perron (Portrait) .20 .50
27 Stephane Richer .75 2.00
28 Larry Robinson 1.00 2.50
29 Steve Rooney (Loop in R through skate toe) .20 .50
30 Steve Rooney (Loop in R through skate laces) .20 .50
31 Patrick Roy 10.00 25.00
32 Brian Skrudland .75 2.00
33 Bobby Smith (B in autograph touching stick) .40 1.00
34 Bobby Smith (0 in autograph on stick) .40 1.00
35 Doug Soetaert (T at end of name by pad) .30 .75
36 Doug Soetaert (T at end of name away from pad) .30 .75
37 Petr Svoboda .30 .75
38 Mario Tremblay (T in autograph touching blade) .30 .75
39 Mario Tremblay (T in autograph away from blade) .30 .75
40 Ryan Walter .30 .75

1985-86 Canadiens Provigo

COMPLETE SET (25) 16.00 40.00
1 Guy Carbonneau 21 .50 1.25
2 Chris Chelios 24 1.50 4.00
3 Kjell Dahlin 20 .20 .50
4 Lucien Deblois 27 .20 .50
5 Bob Gainey 23 .60 1.50
6 Rick Green 5 .20 .50
7 Tom Kurvers 18 .20 .50
8 Mike Lalor 38 .20 .50
9 Craig Ludwig 17 .30 .75
10 Mike McPhee 35 .40 1.00
11 Sergio Momesso 36 .30 .75
12 Mats Naslund 26 .60 1.50
13 Chris Nilan 30 .30 .75
14 Steve Penney 37 .30 .75
15 Jean Perron CO .20 .50
16 Stephane Richer 44 .75 2.00
17 Larry Robinson 19 1.00 2.50
18 Steve Rooney 28 .20 .50
19 Patrick Roy 33 10.00 25.00
20 Brian Skrudland 39 .75 2.00
21 Bobby Smith 15 .40 1.00
22 Doug Soetaert 1 .30 .75
23 Petr Svoboda 25 .30 .75
24 Mario Tremblay 14 .30 .75
25 Ryan Walter 11 .30 .75
NNO Provigo Poster 2.00 5.00

1986-87 Canadiens Postcards

COMPLETE SET (25) 14.00 35.00
1 Guy Carbonneau 21 .40 1.00
2 Chris Chelios 24 1.25 3.00
3 Shayne Corson 34 .75 2.00
4 Kjell Dahlin 20 .20 .50
5 Bob Gainey 23 .40 1.00
6 Rick Green 5 .20 .50
7 Brian Hayward 1 .40 1.00
8 John Kordic 31 .60 1.50
9 Mike Lalor 38 .20 .50
10 Jacques Laperriere ACO .20 .50
11 Claude Lemieux 1.50 4.00
12 Craig Ludwig 17 .20 .50
13 Mike McPhee 35 .30 .75
14 Sergio Momesso 36 .30 .75
15 Mats Naslund 26 .40 1.00
16 Chris Nilan 30 .30 .75
17 Jean Perron CO .20 .50
18 Stephane Richer 44 .75 2.00
19 Larry Robinson 19 .75 2.00
20 Patrick Roy 33 6.00 15.00
21 Scott Sandelin 3 .20 .50
22 Brian Skrudland 39 .60 1.50
23 Bobby Smith 15 .30 .75
24 Petr Svoboda 25 .20 .50
25 Ryan Walter 11 .20 .50

1987 Canadiens Kodak

COMPLETE SET (7) 2.50 6.00
1 Guy Carbonneau .40 1.00
2 Bob Gainey .50 1.25
3 Mike McPhee .30 .75
4 Mats Naslund .40 1.00
5 Chris Nilan .30 .75
6 Larry Robinson .75 2.00
7 Bobby Smith .30 .75

1987-88 Canadiens Postcards

COMPLETE SET (35) 12.00 30.00
1 Francois Allaire ACO .08 .25
2 Guy Carbonneau .30 .75
3 Jose Charbonneau .20 .50
4 Chris Chelios 1.00 2.50
5 Shayne Corson .40 1.00
6 Kjell Dahlin .20 .50
7 Bob Gainey .50 1.25
8 Rick Green .20 .50
9 Gaston Gingras .20 .50
10 Brian Hayward .30 .75
11 John Kordic .60 1.50
12 Mike Lalor .20 .50
13 Jacques Laperriere ACO .20 .50
14 Claude Lemieux 1.25 3.00
15 Craig Ludwig .20 .50
16 David Maley .20 .50
17 Mike McPhee .30 .75
18 Sergio Momesso .20 .50
19 Claude Mouton ANN .08 .25
20 Mats Naslund .40 1.00
21 Chris Nilan .30 .75
22 Jean Perron CO .08 .25
23A Stephane Richer (With moustache) .60 1.50
23B Stephane Richer (No moustache) .60 1.50
24 Larry Robinson .75 2.00
25 Steve Rooney .20 .50
26 Patrick Roy 6.00 15.00
27 Scott Sandelin .20 .50
28 Serge Savard DIR .20 .50
29 Brian Skrudland .50 1.25
30 Bobby Smith .30 .75
31 Petr Svoboda .20 .50
32 Gilles Thibaudeau .20 .50
33 Larry Trader .20 .50
34 Ryan Walter .30 .75

1987-88 Canadiens Vachon Stickers

COMPLETE SET (88) 16.00 40.00
1 Canadiens Team Photo (Top left) .08 .25
2 Canadiens Team Photo (Top middle) .08 .25
3 Canadiens Team Photo (Top right) .08 .25
4 Canadiens Team Photo (Bottom left) .08 .25
5 Canadiens Team Photo (Bottom middle) .08 .25
6 Canadiens Team Photo (Bottom right) .08 .25
7 Jean Perron CO .08 .25
8 Jacques Laperriere ACO .08 .25
9 Francois Allaire ACO .08 .25
10 Jean Perron CO .08 .25
11 Jacques Laperriere .08 .25
12 Bob Gainey .30 .75
13 Bob Gainey .30 .75
14 Guy Carbonneau .15 .40
15 Guy Carbonneau .15 .40
16 Guy Carbonneau .15 .40
17 Michael McPhee .15 .40
18 Bob Gainey .30 .75
19 Chris Nilan .15 .40
20 Chris Nilan .15 .40
21 Guy Carbonneau .15 .40
22 Mike Lalor .08 .25
23 Patrick Roy and Guy Carbonneau 1.50 4.00
24 Ryan Walter .08 .25
25 Ryan Walter .08 .25
26 Bobby Smith .15 .40
27 Mats Naslund .15 .40
28 Bobby Smith .15 .40
29 Mike McPhee .15 .40
30 Bobby Smith .15 .40
31 Claude Lemieux .75 2.00
32 Brian Skrudland .08 .25
33 Craig Ludwig .15 .40
34 Brian Skrudland .08 .25
35 Craig Ludwig .15 .40
36 Brian Skrudland .15 .40
37 Mike McPhee .15 .40
38 Mike McPhee .15 .40
39 Kjell Dahlin .08 .25
40 Kjell Dahlin .08 .25
41 Bobby Smith .15 .40
42 Patrick Roy 2.00 5.00
43 Patrick Roy 2.00 5.00
44 Larry Trader .08 .25
45 Mats Naslund .20 .50
46 Mats Naslund .20 .50
47 Mats Naslund .20 .50
48 Mats Naslund .20 .50
49 Shayne Corson .20 .50
50 Shayne Corson .20 .50
51 Stephane Richer .20 .50
52 Stephane Richer .20 .50
53 Bob Gainey .30 .75
54 Stephane Richer .20 .50
55 Sergio Momesso .08 .25
56 Sergio Momesso .08 .25
57 John Kordic .40 1.00
58 John Kordic .40 1.00
59 Mike Lalor .08 .25
60 Mike Lalor .08 .25
61 Brian Hayward .15 .40
62 Guy Carbonneau .15 .40
63 Guy Carbonneau .15 .40
64 Brian Hayward .15 .40
65 Rick Green .08 .25
66 Rick Green .08 .25
67 Brian Hayward .15 .40
68 Rick Green .08 .25
69 Patrick Roy 2.00 5.00
70 Rick Green .08 .25
71 Patrick Roy 2.00 5.00
72 Larry Robinson .40 1.00
73 Larry Robinson .40 1.00
74 Patrick Roy 2.00 5.00
75 Petr Svoboda .08 .25
76 Patrick Roy 2.00 5.00
77 Petr Svoboda .08 .25
78 Chris Chelios .60 1.50
79 Chris Chelios .60 1.50
80 Craig Ludwig .15 .40
81 Craig Ludwig .15 .40
82 Chris Chelios .60 1.50
83 Chris Chelios .60 1.50
84 Brian Hayward .15 .40
85 Craig Ludwig .15 .40
86 Bobby Smith .15 .40
87 Mats Naslund .15 .40
88 Bob Gainey .30 .75
xx Sticker Album 2.00 5.00

1988-89 Canadiens Postcards

COMPLETE SET (30) 10.00 25.00
1 Francois Allaire ACO .08 .25
2 Pat Burns CO .40 1.00
3 Guy Carbonneau .40 1.00
4 Jose Charbonneau .20 .50
5 Chris Chelios .75 2.00
6 Ronald Corey PRES .08 .25
7 Shayne Corson .40 1.00
8 Russ Courtnall .40 1.00
9 Eric Desjardins .60 1.50
10 Bob Gainey .40 1.00
11 Brent Gilchrist .30 .75
12 Rick Green .20 .50
13 Brian Hayward .30 .75
14 Mike Keane .40 1.00
15 Mike Lalor .20 .50
16 Jacques Laperriere ACO .20 .50
17 Claude Lemieux .60 1.50
18 Craig Ludwig .30 .75
19 Steven Martinson .20 .50
20 Mike McPhee .30 .75
21 Mats Naslund .40 1.00
22 Stephane Richer .40 1.00
23 Larry Robinson .75 2.00
24 Patrick Roy 4.00 10.00
25 Serge Savard DIR .40 1.00

26 Brian Skrudland .40 1.00
27 Bobby Smith .30 .75
28 Petr Svoboda .20 .50
30 Ryan Walter .20 .50
39 Gilles Thibaudeau .20 .50

1989-90 Canadiens Kraft
COMPLETE SET (24) 10.00 25.00
1 Pat Burns CO .40 1.00
2 Guy Carbonneau .40 1.00
3 Chris Chelios 1.00 2.50
4 Shayne Corson .60 1.50
5 Russ Courtnall .30 .75
6 J.J. Daigneault .30 .75
7 Eric Desjardins .40 1.00
8 Todd Ewen .30 .75
9 Brent Gilchrist .30 .75
10 Brian Hayward .30 .75
11 Mike Keane .40 1.00
12 Stephan Lebeau .50 1.25
13 Sylvain Lefebvre .30 .75
14 Claude Lemieux .75 2.00
15 Craig Ludwig .40 1.00
16 Mike McPhee .30 .75
17 Mats Naslund .60 1.50
18 Stephane Richer .60 1.50
19 Patrick Roy 3.00 8.00
20 Mathieu Schneider .60 1.50
21 Brian Skrudland .30 .75
22 Bobby Smith .30 .75
23 Petr Svoboda .30 .75
24 Ryan Walter .30 .75

1989-90 Canadiens Postcards
COMPLETE SET (32) 10.00 25.00
1 Francois Allaire ACO .08 .25
2 Pat Burns CO .40 1.00
3 Guy Carbonneau .30 .75
4 Chris Chelios .60 1.50
5 Tom Chorske .20 .50
6 Ronald Corey PR .08 .25
7 Shayne Corson .40 1.00
8 Russ Courtnall .40 1.00
9 Jean-Jacques Daigneault .20 .50
10 Eric Desjardins .40 1.00
11 Martin Desjardins .20 .50
12 Donald Dufresne .20 .50
13 Brent Gilchrist .20 .50
14 Brian Hayward .30 .75
15 Mike Keane .30 .75
16 Jacques Laperriere ACO .20 .50
17 Stephan Lebeau .30 .75
18 Sylvain Lefebvre .40 1.00
19 Claude Lemieux .40 1.00
20 Jocelyn Lemieux .20 .50
21 Craig Ludwig .20 .50
22 Jyrki Lumme .40 1.00
23 Steven Martinson .20 .50
24 Mike McPhee .30 .75
25 Mats Naslund .40 1.00
26 Stephane Richer .40 1.00
27 Patrick Roy 2.50 6.00
28 Serge Savard DIR .20 .50
29 Brian Skrudland .40 1.00
30 Bobby Smith .30 .75
31 Petr Svoboda .30 .75
32 Ryan Walter .20 .50

1989-90 Canadiens Provigo Figurines
COMPLETE SET (13) 28.00 70.00
6 Russ Courtnall 1.50 4.00
15 Bobby Smith 1.50 4.00
17 Craig Ludwig 1.25 3.00
21 Guy Carbonneau 1.50 4.00
23 Bob Gainey 2.00 5.00
24 Chris Chelios 3.00 8.00
25 Petr Svoboda 1.25 3.00
26 Mats Naslund 2.00 5.00
27 Shayne Corson 2.00 5.00
33 Patrick Roy 10.00 25.00
35 Mike McPhee 1.25 3.00
39 Brian Skrudland 1.50 4.00
44 Stephane Richer 2.00 5.00

1990-91 Canadiens Postcards
COMPLETE SET (33) 10.00 25.00
1 Francois Allaire ACO .08 .25
2 Jean-Claude Bergeron .30 .75
3 Benoit Brunet .20 .50
4 Pat Burns CO .30 .75
5 Guy Carbonneau .30 .75
6 Andrew Cassels .30 .75
7 Tom Chorske .20 .50
8 Ronald Corey PR .08 .25
9 Shayne Corson .40 1.00
10 Russ Courtnall .30 .75
11 Jean-Jacques Daigneault .20 .50
12 Eric Desjardins .40 1.00
13 Gerald Diduck .20 .50
14 Donald Dufresne .20 .50
15 Todd Ewen .25 .60
16 Brent Gilchrist .20 .50
17 Mike Keane .30 .75
18 Jacques Laperriere ACO .20 .50
19 Stephan Lebeau .20 .50
20 Sylvain Lefebvre .30 .75
21 Mike McPhee .30 .75
22 Lyle Odelein .40 1.00
23 Mark Pederson .20 .50
24 Stephane Richer .30 .75
25 Patrick Roy 2.50 6.00
26 Denis Savard .60 1.50
27 Serge Savard DIR .30 .75
28 Mathieu Schneider .40 1.00
29 Brian Skrudland .40 1.00
30 Petr Svoboda .30 .75
31 Charles Thiffault ACO .08 .25
32 Sylvain Turgeon .20 .50
33 Ryan Walter .20 .50

1991 Canadiens Panini Team Stickers
COMPLETE SET (32) 2.00 5.00
1 Jean-Claude Bergeron .02 .10
2 Guy Carbonneau .02 .10
3 Andrew Cassels .05 .15
4 Tom Chorske .01 .05
5 Shayne Corson .05 .15
6 Russ Courtnall .05 .15
7 Jean-Jacques Daigneault .02 .10
8 Eric Desjardins .02 .10
9 Gerald Diduck .01 .05
10 Donald Dufresne .01 .05
11 Todd Ewen .01 .05
12 Brent Gilchrist .02 .10
13 Mike Keane .02 .10
14 Stephan Lebeau .02 .10
15 Sylvain Lefebvre .02 .10
16 Mike McPhee .02 .10
17 Mark Pederson .01 .05
18 Stephane Richer .08 .25
19 Patrick Roy 1.00 2.50
20 Denis Savard .15 .40
21 Mathieu Schneider .02 .10
22 Brian Skrudland .02 .10
23 Petr Svoboda .02 .10
24 Ryan Walter .02 .10
A Team Logo Left Side .05 .15
B Team Logo Right Side .05 .15
C Canadiens in Action Upper Left Corner .05 .15
D Canadiens in Action Lower Left Corner .05 .15
E Game Action Upper Right Corner .05 .15
F Game Action Lower Right Corner .05 .15
G Patrick Roy .75 2.00
H Game Action .08 .25

1991-92 Canadiens Postcards
COMPLETE SET (31) 10.00 25.00
1 Francois Allaire ACO .08 .25
2 Patrice Brisebois .30 .75
3 Pat Burns CO .30 .75
4 Guy Carbonneau .30 .75
5 Ronald Corey PRES .08 .25
6 Shayne Corson .40 1.00
7 Alain Cote .20 .50
8 Russ Courtnall .40 1.00
9 Jean-Jacques Daigneault .20 .50
10 Eric Desjardins .30 .75
11 Donald Dufresne .20 .50
12 Todd Ewen .20 .50
13 Brent Gilchrist .30 .75
14 Mike Keane .30 .75
15 Jacques Laperriere ACO .20 .50
16 Stephan Lebeau .20 .50
17 John LeClair 2.50 6.00
18 Sylvain Lefebvre .30 .75
19 Mike McPhee .30 .75
20 Kirk Muller .40 1.00
21 Lyle Odelein .30 .75
22 Andre Racicot .30 .75
23 Mario Roberge .20 .50
24 Patrick Roy 2.00 5.00
25 Denis Savard .40 1.00
26 Serge Savard DIR .30 .75
27 Mathieu Schneider .30 .75
28 Brian Skrudland .30 .75
29 Petr Svoboda .20 .50
30 Charles Thiffault ACO .08 .25
31 Sylvain Turgeon .20 .50

1992-93 Canadiens Postcards
COMPLETE SET (27) 7.20 18.00
1 Brian Bellows .30 .75
2 Patrice Brisebois .20 .50
3 Benoit Brunet .20 .50
4 Guy Carbonneau .30 .75
5 Jean-Jacques Daigneault .20 .50
6 Vincent Damphousse .40 1.00
7 Eric Desjardins .30 .75
8 Jacques Demers CO .30 .75
9 Gilbert Dionne .20 .50
10 Donald Dufresne .20 .50
11 Todd Ewen .20 .50
12 Kevin Haller .20 .50
13 Sean Hill .20 .50
14 Mike Keane .30 .75
15 Patric Kjellberg .20 .50
16 Stephan Lebeau .20 .50
17 John LeClair 1.25 3.00
18 Kirk Muller .40 1.00
19 Lyle Odelein .30 .75
20 Oleg Petrov .20 .50
21 Andre Racicot .25 .60
22 Mario Roberge .20 .50
23 Ed Ronan .20 .50
24 Patrick Roy 1.50 4.00
25 Denis Savard .40 1.00
26 Mathieu Schneider .30 .75
27 Brian Skrudland .30 .75

1993-94 Canadiens Molson
COMPLETE SET (10) 20.00 50.00
1 Brian Bellows 2.50 6.00
2 Benoit Brunet 2.00 5.00
3 Guy Carbonneau 2.50 6.00
4 Vincent Damphousse 4.00 10.00
5 Jean-Jacques Daigneault 3.00 8.00
6 Kevin Haller 2.00 5.00
7 Mike Keane 2.50 6.00
8 Kirk Muller 2.50 6.00
9 Peter Popovic 2.00 5.00
10 Mathieu Schneider 2.50 6.00

1993-94 Canadiens Postcards
COMPLETE SET (26) 8.00 20.00
1 Brian Bellows .30 .75
2 Patrice Brisebois .25 .60
3 Benoit Brunet .20 .50
4 Guy Carbonneau .30 .75
5 Jean-Jacques Daigneault .20 .50
6 Vincent Damphousse .40 1.00
7 Jacques Demers CO .20 .50
8 Eric Desjardins .30 .75
9 Gilbert Dionne .20 .50
10 Paul DiPietro .20 .50
11 Kevin Haller .20 .50
12 Mike Keane .25 .60
13 Stephan LeBeau .20 .50
14 John LeClair 1.00 2.50
15 Gary Leeman .20 .50
16 Kirk Muller .30 .75
17 Lyle Odelein .30 .75
18 Peter Popovic .20 .50
19 Andre Racicot .25 .60
20 Rob Ramage .20 .50
21 Mario Roberge .20 .50
22 Ed Ronan .20 .50
23 Patrick Roy 2.00 5.00
24 Mathieu Schneider .30 .75
25 Pierre Sevigny .20 .50
26 Ron Wilson .20 .50

1994-95 Canadiens Postcards
COMPLETE SET (27) 6.00 15.00
1 Brian Bellows .30 .75
2 Donald Brashear .20 .50
3 Patrice Brisebois .20 .50
4 Benoit Brunet .20 .50
5 Jean-Jacques Daigneault .20 .50
6 Vincent Damphousse .30 .75
7 Jacques Demers CO .20 .50
8 Eric Desjardins .30 .75
9 Gilbert Dionne .20 .50
10 Paul Dipietro .20 .50
11 Gerry Fleming .20 .50
12 Bryan Fogarty .20 .50
13 Mike Keane .20 .50
14 John LeClair .75 2.00
15 Jim Montgomery .20 .50
16 Kirk Muller .30 .75
17 Lyle Odelein .30 .75
18 Oleg Petrov .20 .50
19 Peter Popovic .20 .50
20 Yves Racine .20 .50
21 Ed Ronan .20 .50
22 Patrick Roy 1.50 4.00
23 Brian Savage .30 .75
24 Mathieu Schneider .30 .75
25 Pierre Sevigny .20 .50
26 Turner Stevenson .20 .50
27 Ron Tugnutt .40 1.00

1995-96 Canadiens Postcards
COMPLETE SET (20) 6.00 15.00
NNO Donald Brashear .20 .50
NNO Patrice Brisebois .20 .50
NNO Benoit Brunet .20 .50
NNO Valeri Bure .20 .50
NNO Marc Bureau .20 .50
NNO Vincent Damphousse .40 1.00
NNO Mike Keane .25 .60
NNO Saku Koivu 1.50 4.00
NNO Vladimir Malakhov .20 .50
NNO Lyle Odelein .20 .50
NNO Oleg Petrov .20 .50
NNO Peter Popovic .20 .50
NNO Stephane Quintal .20 .50
NNO Yves Racine .20 .50
NNO Mark Recchi .40 1.00
NNO Patrick Roy 1.50 4.00
NNO Brian Savage .25 .60
NNO Turner Stevenson .20 .50
NNO Mario Tremblay CO .20 .50
NNO Pierre Turgeon .40 1.00

1995-96 Canadiens Sheets
COMPLETE SET (12) 48.00 120.00
1 Valeri Bure 8.00 20.00
2 Benoit Brunet 4.00 10.00
3 Peter Popovic 4.00 10.00
4 Saku Koivu 6.00 15.00
5 Turner Stevenson 4.00 10.00
6 Mark Recchi 5.00 12.00
7 Vladimir Malakhov 4.00 10.00
8 Stephane Quintal 4.00 10.00
9 Brian Savage 4.00 10.00
10 Patrice Brisebois 4.00 10.00
11 Vincent Damphousse 5.00 12.00
12 Pierre Turgeon 5.00 12.00

1996-97 Canadiens Postcards
COMPLETE SET (33) 8.00 20.00
1 Murray Baron .20 .50
2 Sebastien Bordeleau .20 .50
3 Patrice Brisebois .20 .50
4 Benoit Brunet .20 .50
5 Valeri Bure .20 .50
6 Marc Bureau .20 .50
7 Ronald Corey PRES .20 .50
8 Shayne Corson .40 1.00
9 Yvan Cournoyer .60 1.50
10 Jassen Cullimore .20 .50
11 Vincent Damphousse .40 1.00
12 Rejean Houle .20 .50
13 Pat Jablonski .30 .75
14 Saku Koivu 1.25 3.00
15 Jacques Laperierre .30 .75
16 Vladimir Malakhov .20 .50
17 Dave Manson .20 .50
18 Chris Murray .20 .50
19 Peter Popovic .20 .50
20 Stephane Qunital .20 .50
21 Mark Recchi .40 1.00
22 Stephane Richer .40 1.00
23 Craig Rivet .20 .50
24 Martin Rucinsky .30 .75
25 Brian Savage .30 .75
26 Steve Shutt .30 .75
27 Turner Stevenson .20 .50
28 Jose Theodore 4.00 10.00
29 Jocelyn Thibault .75 2.00
30 Scott Thornton .20 .50
31 Mario Trembley .20 .50
32 Darcy Tucker .40 1.00
33 David Wilkie .20 .50

1996-97 Canadiens Sheets
COMPLETE SET (28) 40.00 100.00
1 Patrice Brisebois 1.25 3.00
2 Benoit Brunet 1.25 3.00
3 Valeri Bure 1.50 4.00
4 Marc Bureau 1.25 3.00
5 Shayne Corson 1.50 4.00
6 Jassen Cullimore 1.25 3.00
7 Vincent Damphousse 2.00 5.00
8 Rory Fitzpatrick 1.25 3.00
9 Saku Koivu 4.00 10.00
10 Vladimir Malakhov 1.25 3.00
11 Dave Manson 1.50 4.00
12 Chris Murray 1.25 3.00
13 Peter Popovic 1.25 3.00
14 Stephane Quintal 1.25 3.00
15 Mark Recchi 2.00 5.00
16 Stephane Richer 1.50 4.00
17 Craig Rivet 1.25 3.00
18 Martin Rucinsky 1.50 4.00
19 Brian Savage 1.50 4.00
20 Turner Stevenson 1.25 3.00
21 Jose Theodore 8.00 20.00
22 Jocelyn Thibault 3.00 8.00
23 Scott Thornton 1.25 3.00
24 Darcy Tucker 1.50 4.00
25 Pierre Turgeon 2.00 5.00
26 David Wilkie 1.25 3.00
27 Centre Molson First Anniversary .40 1.00
28 Canadiens Line-up 1.25 3.00

1997-98 Canadiens Postcards
COMPLETE SET (26) 6.00 15.00
1 Sebastien Bordeleau .20 .50
2 Patrice Brisebois .20 .50
3 Benoit Brunet .20 .50
4 Valeri Bure .20 .50
5 Marc Bureau .20 .50
6 Brett Clark .20 .50
7 Shayne Corson .40 1.00
8 Jassen Cullimore .20 .50
9 Vincent Damphousse .40 1.00
10 Saku Koivu 1.25 3.00
11 Vladimir Malakhov .20 .50
12 Dave Manson .20 .50
13 Andy Moog .40 1.00
14 Peter Popovic .20 .50
15 Stephane Quintal .20 .50
16 Mark Recchi .30 .75
17 Stephane Richer .40 1.00
18 Craig Rivet .20 .50
19 Martin Rucinsky .30 .75
20 Brian Savage .30 .75
21 Turner Stevenson .20 .50
22 Jocelyn Thibault .40 1.00
23 Scott Thornton .20 .50
24 Darcy Tucker .20 .50
25 Alain Vigneault .20 .50
26 David Wilkie .20 .50

1998-99 Canadiens Team Issue
COMPLETE SET (26) 4.00 15.00
1 Benoit Brunet .20 .50
2 Brett Clark .20 .50
3 Shayne Corson .20 .50
4 Vincent Damphousse .40 1.00
5 Jeff Hackett .40 1.00
6 Matt Higgins .20 .50
7 Jonas Hoglund .20 .50
8 Eric Houde .20 .50
9 Saku Koivu .75 2.00
10 Vladimir Malakhov .20 .50
11 Trent McCleary .20 .50
12 Dave Morissette .20 .50
13 Alain Nasreddine .20 .50
14 Patrick Poulin .20 .50
15 Stephane Quintal .20 .50
16 Marc Recchi .30 .75
17 Craig Rivet .20 .50
18 Martin Rucinsky .20 .50
19 Brian Savage .30 .75
20 Turner Stevenson .20 .50
21 Jose Theodore 1.25 3.00
22 Scott Thornton .20 .50
23 Igor Ulanov .20 .50
24 Alain Vigneault .20 .50
25 Eric Weinrich .20 .50
26 Sergei Zholtok .20 .50

2000-01 Canadiens Postcards
COMPLETE SET (34) 8.00 20.00
1 Francois Bouillon .20 .50
2 Andrei Bashkirov .20 .50
3 Mathieu Garon .60 1.50
4 Karl Dykhuis .20 .50
5 Xavier Delisle .20 .50
6 Patrice Brisebois .20 .50
7 Benoit Brunet .20 .50
8 Jose Theodore 1.20 3.00
9 Craig Darby .20 .50
10 Eric Chouinard .30 .75
11 Jeff Hackett .40 1.00
12 Chad Kilger .20 .50
13 Jim Campbell .20 .50
14 Christian Laflamme .20 .50
15 Eric Landry .20 .50
16 Juha Lind .20 .50
17 Trevor Linden .40 1.00
18 Andrei Markov .60 1.50
19 Gino Odjick .30 .75
20 Patrick Poulin .20 .50
21 Oleg Petrov .20 .50
22 Craig Rivet .20 .50
23 Stephane Robidas .20 .50
24 Martin Rucinsky .20 .50
25 Brian Savage .40 1.00
26 Sheldon Souray .20 .50
27 Saku Koivu .60 1.50
28 Johan Witehall .20 .50
29 Eric Weinrich .20 .50
30 Dainius Zubrus .20 .50
31 Michel Therrien CO .10 .25
32 Guy Carbonneau CO .40 1.00
33 Rick Green CO .10 .25
34 Andre Savard GM .20 .50

2000-01 Canadiens Team Issue
COMPLETE SET (22) 5.00 12.00
1 Arron Asham .40 1.00
2 Patrice Brisebois .40 1.00
3 Benoit Brunet .40 1.00
4 Craig Darby .40 1.00
5 Karl Dykhuis .40 1.00
6 Jeff Hackett .40 1.00
7 Chad Kilger .60 1.50
8 Saku Koivu 2.00 5.00
9 Christian LaFlamme .40 1.00
10 Eric Landry .40 1.00
11 Juha Lind .40 1.00
12 Andrei Markov 1.00 2.50
13 Gino Odjick .40 1.00
14 Oleg Petrov .40 1.00
15 Patrick Poulin .40 1.00
16 Craig Rivet .40 1.00
17 Stephane Robidas .40 1.00
18 Martin Rucinsky .40 1.00
19 Brian Savage .40 1.00
20 Sheldon Souray .75 2.00
21 Jose Theodore 2.00 5.00
22 Johan Witehall .40 1.00

2001-02 Canadiens Postcards
COMPLETE SET (32) 10.00 24.44
1 Donald Audette .30 .75
2 Shaun Van Allen .30 .75
3 Patrice Brisebois .30 .75
4 Benoit Brunet .30 .75
5 Jan Bulis .30 .75
6 Andreas Dackell .30 .75
7 Karl Dykhuis .30 .75
8 Mathieu Garon .60 1.50
9 Doug Gilmour .75 2.00
10 Jeff Hackett .60 1.50
11 Joe Juneau .30 .75
12 Chad Kilger .30 .75
13 Saku Koivu .75 2.00
14 Gino Odjick .30 .75
15 Yanic Perreault .30 .75
16 Oleg Petrov .30 .75
17 Patrick Poulin .30 .75
18 Stephane Quintal .30 .75
19 Mike Ribeiro .40 1.00
20 Craig Rivet .30 .75
21 Stephane Robidas .30 .75
22 Martin Rucinsky .30 .75
23 Jose Theodore 1.25 3.00
24 Brian Savage .30 .75
25 Reid Simpson .30 .75
26 Sheldon Souray .30 .75
27 Patrick Traverse .30 .75
28 Richard Zednik .30 .75
29 Michel Therrien HCO .10 .25
30 Guy Carbonneau CO .30 .75
31 Rick Green CO .10 .25
32 Roland Melanson CO .20 .50

2002 Canadiens AGF
COMPLETE SET (4) 2.00 5.00
NNO Yvan Cournoyer .80 2.00
NNO Steve Shutt .80 2.00
NNO Henri Richard .80 2.00
NNO Rejean Houle .40 1.00

2002-03 Canadiens Postcards
COMPLETE SET (31) 7.20 18.00
1 Stephane Quintal .20 .50
2 Saku Koivu .75 2.00
3 Oleg Petrov .20 .50
4 Richard Zednik .20 .50
5 Randy McKay .20 .50
6 Bill Lindsay .20 .50
7 Andreas Dackell .20 .50
8 Chad Kilger .20 .50
9 Sylvain Blouin .20 .50
10 Mariusz Czerkawski .20 .50
11 Karl Dykhuis .20 .50
12 Mathieu Garon .40 1.00
13 Jeff Hackett .40 1.00
14 Jan Bulis .20 .50
15 Patrice Brisebois .20 .50
16 Sheldon Souray .20 .50
17 Craig Rivet .20 .50
18 Patrick Traverse .20 .50
19 Jose Theodore .75 2.00
20 Ron Hainsey .60 1.50
21 Mike Ribeiro .20 .50
22 Andrei Markov .20 .50
23 Donald Audette .20 .50
24 Joe Juneau .20 .50
25 Doug Gilmour .40 1.00
26 Yanic Perreault .20 .50
27 Michel Therrien HCO .04 .10
28 Guy Charron ACO .04 .10
29 Rick Green ACO .04 .10
30 Clement Jodoin ACO .04 .10
31 Roland Melanson ACO .10 .25

2003-04 Canadiens Postcards
COMPLETE SET (30) 10.00 25.00
1 Donald Audette .20 .50
2 Steve Begin .20 .50
3 Francois Bouillon .20 .50
4 Patrice Brisebois .20 .50
5 Jan Bulis .20 .50
6 Andreas Dackell .20 .50
7 Karl Dykhuis .20 .50
8 Bob Gainey GM .20 .50
9 Mathieu Garon .40 1.00
10 Ron Hainsey .20 .50
11 Chris Higgins 1.00 2.50
12 Marcel Hossa .40 1.00
13 Claude Julien CO .10 .25
14 Joe Juneau .20 .50
15 Chad Kilger .20 .50
16 Saku Koivu .75 2.00
17 Mike Komisarek .40 1.00
18 Darren Langdon .40 1.00
19 Andrei Markov .20 .50
20 Yanic Perreault .20 .50
21 Stephane Quintal .20 .50
22 Mike Ribeiro .40 1.00
23 Craig Rivet .20 .50
24 Michael Ryder 1.25 3.00
25 Sheldon Souray .40 1.00
26 Niklas Sundstrom .20 .50
27 Jose Theodore 1.25 3.00
28 Jason Ward .20 .50
29 Richard Zednik .20 .50
30 Team Photo .20 .50

2005-06 Canadiens Team Issue
COMPLETE SET (25) 15.00 30.00
1 Steve Begin .40 1.00
2 Radek Bonk .40 1.00
3 Francis Bouillon .40 1.00
4 Jan Bulis .40 1.00
5 Pierre Dagenais .40 1.00
6 Mathieu Dandenault .40 1.00
7 Yann Danis .60 1.50
8 Chris Higgins .40 1.00
9 Cristobal Huet 1.00 2.50
10 Raitis Ivanans .75 2.00
11 Saku Koivu .75 2.00
12 Mike Komisarek .40 1.00
13 Alexei Kovalev .40 1.00
14 Andrei Markov .40 1.00
15 Alexander Perezhogin .40 1.00
16 Tomas Plekanec .40 1.00
17 Mike Ribeiro .40 1.00
18 Craig Rivet .40 1.00
19 Michael Ryder .75 2.00
20 Sheldon Souray .40 1.00
21 Mark Streit .40 1.00
22 Niklas Sundstrom .40 1.00
23 Jose Theodore 1.00 2.50
24 Richard Zednik .40 1.00
25 Youppi MASCOT .10 .25

2006-07 Canadiens Postcards
1 David Aebischer .60 1.50
2 Cristobal Huet .75 2.00
3 Steve Begin .40 1.00
4 Radek Bonk .40 1.00
5 Francis Bouillon .40 1.00
6 Mathieu Dandenault .40 1.00
7 Aaron Downey .60 1.50
8 Christopher Higgins .60 1.50
9 Mike Johnson .40 1.00
10 Mike Komisarek .40 1.00
11 Alex Kovalev .40 1.00
12 Guillaume Latendresse 1.25 3.00
13 Andrei Markov .40 1.00
14 Garth Murray .40 1.00
15 Janne Niinimaa .40 1.00
16 Alexander Perezhogin .40 1.00
17 Tomas Plekanec .40 1.00
18 Craig Rivet .40 1.00
19 Michael Ryder .60 1.50
20 Mark Streit .75 2.00
21 Sheldon Souray .40 1.00
22 Sergei Samsonov .40 1.00
23 Team Photo .40 1.00
24 Youppi MASCOT .10 .25

2007-08 Canadiens Postcards
COMPLETE SET (24) 7.50 15.00
1 Saku Koivu .50 1.25
2 Carey Price 2.00 5.00
3 Josh Gorges .30 .75
4 Mike Komisarek .30 .75
5 Andrei Kostitsyn .40 1.00
6 Christopher Higgins .30 .75
7 Kyle Chipchura .50 1.25
8 Steve Begin .30 .75
9 Alex Kovalev .40 1.00
10 Guillaume Latendresse .40 1.00
11 Francis Bouillon .30 .75
12 Tomas Plekanec .30 .75
13 Mikhail Grabovski .30 .75
14 Mark Streit .30 .75
15 Michael Ryder .30 .75
16 Roman Hamrlik .30 .75
17 Maxim Lapierre .30 .75
18 Andrei Markov .50 1.25
19 Garth Murray .30 .75
20 Bryan Smolinski .30 .75
21 Mathieu Dandenault .30 .75
22 Tom Kostopoulos .30 .75
23 Patrice Brisebois .30 .75
24 Cristobal Huet .40 1.00

2007-08 Canadiens Team Issue
COMPLETE SET (25) 10.00 25.00
1 Steve Begin .30 .75
2 Francis Bouillon .30 .75
3 Patrice Brisebois .30 .75
4 Kyle Chipchura .50 1.25
5 Mathieu Dandenault .30 .75
6 Josh Gorges .30 .75
7 Mikhail Grabovski .30 .75
8 Roman Hamrlik .30 .75
9 Christopher Higgins .30 .75
10 Cristobal Huet .40 1.00
11 Saku Koivu .50 1.25
12 Mike Komisarek .30 .75
13 Andrei Kostitsyn .40 1.00
14 Tom Kostopoulos .30 .75
15 Alex Kovalev .40 1.00
16 Maxim Lapierre .30 .75
17 Guillaume Latendresse .40 1.00
18 Andrei Markov .50 1.25
19 Garth Murray .30 .75
20 Tomas Plekanec .30 .75
21 Carey Price 2.00 5.00
22 Michael Ryder .30 .75
23 Bryan Smolinski .30 .75
24 Mark Streit .30 .75
25 Youppi! MASCOT .30 .75

2008-09 Canadiens Postcards
COMPLETE SET (24) 7.50 15.00
1 Steve Begin .30 .75
2 Francis Bouillon .40 1.00
4 Josh Gorges .30 .75
5 Jaroslav Halak .50 1.25
6 Roman Hamrlik .30 .75
7 Chris Higgins .30 .75
8 Saku Koivu .50 1.25
9 Mike Komisarek .30 .75
10 Andrei Kostitsyn .40 1.00
11 Sergei Kostitsyn .30 .75
13 Alex Kovalev .40 1.00
15 Maxim Lapierre .30 .75
16 Georges Laraque .40 1.00
17 Guillaume Latendresse .30 .75
18 Andrei Markov .50 1.25
19 Ryan O'Byrne .30 .75
20 Tomas Plekanec .30 .75
21 Carey Price 1.00 2.50
22 Alex Tanguay .30 .75

2009-10 Canadiens Postcards
COMPLETE SET (37) 10.00 20.00
1 Marc-Andre Bergeron .30 .75
2 Mike Cammalleri .40 1.00
3 Matt D'Agostini .40 1.00
4 Hal Gill .30 .75
5 Brian Gionta .30 .75
6 Scott Gomez .40 1.00
7 Josh Gorges .30 .75
8 Jaroslav Halak .50 1.25
9 Roman Hamrlik .30 .75
10 Andrei Kostitsyn .40 1.00
11 Maxim Lapierre .30 .75
12 Georges Laraque .40 1.00
13 Guillaume Latendresse .40 1.00
14 Paul Mara .30 .75
15 Andrei Markov .50 1.25
17 Travis Moen .30 .75
19 Max Pacioretty .50 1.25
20 Tomas Plekanec .30 .75
21 Carey Price 1.00 2.50
22 Jaroslav Spacek .30 .75
23 Greg Stewart .30 .75
24 Youppi MASCOT .30 .75
25 Mathieu Carle .50 1.25
26 Kyle Chipchura .40 1.00
27 Ben Maxwell .40 1.00
28 Benoit Pouliot .30 .75
29 Tom Pyatt .50 1.25
30 Curtis Sanford .30 .75
31 P.K. Subban 1.50 4.00
32 Yannick Weber .50 1.25
33 Jacques Martin CO .30 .75
34 Perry Pearn ACO .30 .75
35 Kirk Muller ACO .30 .75
36 Pierre Groulx ACO .30 .75
37 Bob Gainey GM .40 1.00

2011-12 Canadiens Postcards
COMPLETE SET (25) 6.00 12.00
1 Peter Budaj .40 1.00
2 Mike Cammalleri .40 1.00
3 Chris Campoli .30 .75
4 Erik Cole .30 .75
5 Mathieu Darche .40 1.00
6 David Desharnais .30 .75
7 Raphael Diaz .40 1.00
8 Lars Eller .30 .75
9 Alexei Emelin .40 1.00
10 Andreas Engqvist .40 1.00
11 Hal Gill .30 .75
12 Brian Gionta .30 .75
13 Scott Gomez .40 1.00
14 Josh Gorges .30 .75
15 Andrei Kostitsyn .40 1.00
16 Andrei Markov .30 .75
17 Travis Moen .30 .75
18 Max Pacioretty .50 1.25
19 Aaron Palushaj .40 1.00
20 Tomas Plekanec .30 .75
21 Carey Price 1.00 2.50
22 Jaroslav Spacek .30 .75
23 P.K. Subban .60 1.50
24 Yannick Weber .30 .75
25 Ryan White .30 .75

2012-13 Canadiens Postcards
COMPLETE SET (24) 6.00 12.00
1 Colby Armstrong .30 .75
2 Mike Blunden .30 .75
3 Francis Bouillon .30 .75
4 Rene Bourque .30 .75
5 Peter Budaj .40 1.00
6 David Desharnais .30 .75
7 Raphael Diaz .30 .75
8 Lars Eller .30 .75
9 Alexei Emelin .30 .75
10 Alex Galchenyuk 1.50 4.00
11 Brendan Gallagher 1.50 4.00
12 Brian Gionta .30 .75
13 Josh Gorges .40 1.00
14 Tomas Kaberle .30 .75
15 Andrei Markov .30 .75
16 Travis Moen .30 .75
17 Petteri Nokelainen .30 .75
18 Max Pacioretty .50 1.25
19 Carey Price 1.00 2.50
20 Brandon Prust .30 .75
21 P.K. Subban .60 1.50
22 Yannick Weber .30 .75
23 Ryan White .30 .75
24 Youppi MASCOT .30 .75

2013-14 Canadiens Postcards
COMPLETE SET (26) 5.00 10.00
1 Francis Bouillon .30 .75
2 Michael Bournival .50 1.25
3 Rene Bourque .30 .75
4 Daniel Briere .50 1.25
5 Peter Budaj .40 1.00
6 David Desharnais .30 .75
7 Raphael Diaz .30 .75
8 Davis Drewiske .30 .75
9 Lars Eller .30 .75
10 Alexei Emelin .30 .75
11 Alex Galchenyuk 1.25 3.00
12 Brendan Gallagher 1.25 3.00
13 Brian Gionta .30 .75
14 Josh Gorges .40 1.00
15 Andrei Markov .30 .75
16 Travis Moen .30 .75
17 Douglas Murray .30 .75
18 Max Pacioretty .50 1.25
19 George Parros .40 1.00
20 Tomas Plekanec .30 .75
21 Carey Price 1.00 2.50
22 Brandon Prust .30 .75
23 P.K. Subban .60 1.50
24 Jarred Tinordi .50 1.25
25 Ryan White .30 .75
26 Youppi MASCOT .30 .75

2014-15 Canadiens Postcards
COMPLETE SET (24) 6.00 12.00
1 Nathan Beaulieu .30 .75
2 Michael Bournival .40 1.00
3 Rene Bourque .30 .75
4 David Desharnais .30 .75
5 Lars Eller .30 .75
6 Alexei Emelin .30 .75
7 Alex Galchenyuk .30 .75
8 Brendan Gallagher .50 1.25
9 Tom Gilbert .30 .75
10 Manny Malhotra .30 .75
11 Andrei Markov .30 .75
12 Travis Moen .30 .75
13 Max Pacioretty .50 1.25
14 P.A. Parenteau .30 .75
15 Tomas Plekanec .30 .75
16 Carey Price 1.00 2.50
17 Brandon Prust .30 .75
18 Jiri Sekac .40 1.00

Card	Low	High
19 P.K. Subban	.60	1.50
20 Jarred Tinordi	.75	2.00
21 Dustin Tokarski	.30	.75
22 Mike Weaver	.30	.75
23 Dale Weise	.30	.75
24 Youppi! Mascot	.30	.75

2015-16 Canadiens Postcards

Card	Low	High
COMPLETE SET (25)	6.00	12.00
1 Nathan Beaulieu	.30	.75
2 Marc Bergevin	.30	.75
3 Paul Byron	.30	.75
4 Mike Condon	.30	.75
5 David Desharnais	.30	.75
6 Lars Eller	.30	.75
7 Alexei Emelin	.30	.75
8 Tomas Fleischmann	.30	.75
9 Brian Flynn	.30	.75
10 Alex Galchenyuk	.30	.75
11 Brendan Gallagher	.50	1.25
12 Tom Gilbert	.30	.75
13 Andrei Markov	.30	.75
14 Torrey Mitchell	.30	.75
15 Geoff Molson OWN	.30	.75
16 Max Pacioretty	.50	1.25
17 Greg Pateryn	.30	.75
18 Jeff Petry	.50	1.25
19 Tomas Plekanec	.30	.75
20 Carey Price	1.00	2.50
21 Alexander Semin	.50	1.25
22 Devante Smith-Pelly	.40	1.00
23 P.K. Subban	.60	1.50
24 Dale Weise	.30	.75
25 Youppi MASCOT	.30	.75

1970-71 Canucks Royal Bank

Card	Low	High
COMPLETE SET (20)	30.00	60.00
1 Andre Boudrias	2.00	4.00
2 Mike Corrigan	1.50	3.00
3 Ray Cullen	2.50	5.00
4 Gary Doak	1.50	3.00
5 George Gardner	1.50	3.00
6 Murray Hall	1.50	3.00
7 Charlie Hodge	4.00	8.00
8 Danny Johnson	1.50	3.00
9 Orland Kurtenbach	2.50	5.00
10 Wayne Maki	1.50	3.00
11 Rosaire Paiement	2.00	4.00
12 Paul Popiel	2.00	4.00
13 Pat Quinn	4.00	8.00
14 Marc Reaume	1.50	3.00
15 Darryl Sly	1.50	3.00
16 Dale Tallon	2.50	5.00
17 Ted Taylor	1.50	3.00
18 Barry Wilkins	1.50	3.00
19 Dunc Wilson	2.50	5.00
20 Jim Wiste	1.50	3.00

1971-72 Canucks Royal Bank

Card	Low	High
COMPLETE SET (20)	25.00	50.00
1 Bobby Lalonde	1.00	2.00
2 Mike Corrigan	1.00	2.00
3 Murray Hall	1.00	2.00
4 Jocelyn Guevremont	2.00	4.00
5 Pat Quinn	3.00	6.00
6 Orland Kurtenbach	2.00	4.00
7 Paul Popiel	2.00	4.00
8 Ron Ward	1.00	2.00
9 Rosaire Paiement	1.50	3.00
11 Dale Tallon	2.00	4.00
12 Bobby Schmautz	2.00	4.00
13 Dennis Kearns	1.00	2.00
14 Barry Wilkins	1.00	2.00
15 Dunc Wilson	2.50	5.00
16 Andre Boudrias	2.00	4.00
17 Ted Taylor	1.50	3.00
18 George Gardner	1.00	2.00
19 John Schella	1.00	2.00
20 Wayne Maki	1.50	3.00
21 Gary Doak	1.00	2.00

1972-73 Canucks Nalley's

Card	Low	High
COMPLETE SET (6)	62.50	125.00
1 Andre Boudrias	10.00	20.00
2 George Gardner	10.00	20.00
3 Wayne Maki	12.50	25.00
4 Rosaire Paiement	12.50	25.00
5 Pat Quinn	20.00	40.00
6 Barry Wilkins	10.00	20.00

1972-73 Canucks Royal Bank

Card	Low	High
COMPLETE SET (21)	20.00	40.00
1 Dave Balon	1.50	3.00
2 Gregg Boddy	1.00	2.00
3 Larry Bolonchuk	1.00	2.00
4 Andre Boudrias	1.00	2.00
5 Ed Dyck	1.00	2.00
6 Jocelyn Guevremont	1.50	3.00
7 James Hargreaves	1.00	2.00
8 Dennis Kearns	1.00	2.00
9 Orland Kurtenbach	1.50	3.00
10 Bobby Lalonde	1.00	2.00
11 Richard Lemieux	1.00	2.00
12 Don Lever	1.50	3.00
13 Wayne Maki	1.50	3.00
14 Bryan McSheffrey	1.00	2.00
15 Gerry O'Flaherty	1.00	2.00
16 Bobby Schmautz	1.50	3.00
17 Dale Tallon	1.50	3.00
18 Don Tannahill	1.00	2.00
19 Barry Wilkins	1.00	2.00
20 Dunc Wilson	1.50	3.00
21 John Wright	1.00	2.00

1973-74 Canucks Royal Bank

Card	Low	High
COMPLETE SET (21)	20.00	40.00
1 Paulin Bordeleau	1.00	2.00
2 Andre Boudrias	1.00	2.00
3 Jacques Caron	1.00	2.00
4 Bob Dailey	1.00	2.00
5 Dave Dunn	1.00	2.00
6 Jocelyn Guevremont	1.50	3.00
7 Dennis Kearns	1.00	2.00
8 Jerry Korab	1.00	2.00
9 Orland Kurtenbach	2.00	4.00
10 Bobby Lalonde	1.00	2.00
11 Richard Lemieux	1.00	2.00
12 Don Lever	1.50	3.00
13 Bill McCreary	1.00	2.00
14 Bryan McSheffrey	1.00	2.00
15 Gerry O'Flaherty	1.00	2.00
16 Bobby Schmautz	2.00	4.00
17 Gary Smith	2.00	4.00
18 Don Tannahill	1.00	2.00
19 Dennis Ververgaert	1.50	3.00
20 Barry Wilkins	1.00	2.00
21 John Wright	1.00	2.00

1974-75 Canucks Royal Bank

Card	Low	High
COMPLETE SET (20)	20.00	40.00
1 Gregg Boddy	1.00	2.00
2 Paulin Bordeleau	1.50	3.00
3 Andre Boudrias	1.50	3.00
4 Bob Dailey	1.00	2.00
5 Ab DeMarco	1.00	2.00
6 John Gould	1.00	2.00
7 John Grisdale	1.00	2.00
8 Dennis Kearns	1.00	2.00
9 Bobby Lalonde	1.00	2.00
10 Don Lever	1.50	3.00
11 Ken Lockett	1.00	2.00
12 Gerry Meehan	1.50	3.00
13 Garry Monahan	1.00	2.00
14 Chris Oddleifson	1.00	2.00
15 Gerry O'Flaherty	1.00	2.00
16 Tracy Pratt	1.00	2.00
17 Mike Robitaille	1.00	2.00
18 Leon Rochefort	1.00	2.00
19 Gary Smith	1.50	3.00
20 Dennis Ververgaert	1.50	3.00

1975-76 Canucks Royal Bank

Card	Low	High
COMPLETE SET (22)	20.00	40.00
1 Rick Blight	1.00	2.00
2 Gregg Boddy	1.00	2.00
3 Paulin Bordeleau	1.00	2.00
4 Andre Boudrias	1.00	2.00
5 Bob Dailey	1.00	2.00
6 Ab DeMarco	1.00	2.00
7 John Gould	1.00	2.00
8 John Grisdale	1.00	2.00
9 Dennis Kearns	1.00	2.00
10 Bobby Lalonde	1.00	2.00
11 Don Lever	1.50	3.00
12 Ken Lockett	1.00	2.00
13 Garry Monahan	1.00	2.00
14 Bob Murray	1.00	2.00
15 Chris Oddleifson	1.00	2.00
16 Gerry O'Flaherty	1.00	2.00
17 Tracy Pratt	1.00	2.00
18 Mike Robitaille	1.00	2.00
19 Ron Sedlbauer	1.00	2.00
20 Gary Smith	1.50	3.00
21 Harold Snepsts	3.00	6.00
22 Dennis Ververgaert	1.50	3.00

1976-77 Canucks Royal Bank

Card	Low	High
COMPLETE SET (23)	20.00	40.00
1 Rick Blight	1.00	2.00
2 Bob Dailey	1.00	2.00
3 Dave Fortier	1.00	2.00
4 Brad Gassoff	1.00	2.00
5 John Gould	1.00	2.00
6 John Grisdale	1.00	2.00
7 Dennis Kearns	1.00	2.00
8 Bobby Lalonde	1.00	2.00
9 Don Lever	1.50	3.00
10 Cesare Maniago	2.00	4.00
11 Garry Monahan	1.00	2.00
12 Bob Murray	1.00	2.00
13 Chris Oddleifson	1.00	2.00
14 Gerry O'Flaherty	1.00	2.00
15 Curt Ridley	1.00	2.00
16 Mike Robitaille	1.00	2.00
17 Ron Sedlbauer	1.00	2.00
18 Harold Snepsts	2.50	5.00
19 Andy Spruce	1.00	2.00
20 Ralph Stewart	1.00	2.00
21 Dennis Ververgaert	1.50	3.00
22 Mike Walton	1.50	3.00
23 Jim Wiley	1.50	3.00

1977-78 Canucks Canada Dry Oans

Card	Low	High
COMPLETE SET (16)	20.00	40.00
1 Rick Blight	1.00	2.00
2 Brad Gassoff	1.00	2.00
3 Jere Gillis	1.00	2.00
4 Larry Goodenough	1.00	2.00
5 Hilliard Graves	1.00	2.00
6 Dennis Kearns	1.00	2.00
7 Don Lever	1.00	2.00
8 Cesare Maniago	2.50	5.00
9 Jack McIlhargey	1.00	2.00
10 Garry Monahan	1.00	2.00
11 Chris Oddleifson	1.00	2.00
12 Curt Ridley	1.00	2.00
13 Derek Sanderson	2.50	5.00
14 Harold Snepsts	2.00	4.00
15 Mike Walton	1.00	2.00
16 Dennis Ververgaert	1.00	2.00

1977-78 Canucks Royal Bank

Card	Low	High
COMPLETE SET (21)	20.00	40.00
1 Rick Blight	1.00	2.00
2 Larry Carriere	1.00	2.00
3 Rob Flockhart	1.00	2.00
4 Brad Gassoff	1.00	2.00
5 Jere Gillis	1.00	2.00
6 Larry Goodenough	1.00	2.00
7 Hilliard Graves	1.00	2.00
8 John Grisdale	1.00	2.00
9 Dennis Kearns	1.00	2.00
10 Don Lever	1.50	3.00
11 Cesare Maniago	2.00	4.00
12 Bob Manno	1.00	2.00
13 Jack McIlhargey	1.00	2.00
14 Garry Monahan	1.00	2.00
15 Chris Oddleifson	1.00	2.00
16 Gerry O'Flaherty	1.00	2.00
17 Curt Ridley	1.50	3.00
18 Ron Sedlbauer	1.00	2.00
19 Harold Snepsts	2.00	4.00
20 Dennis Ververgaert	1.50	3.00
21 Mike Walton	1.00	2.00

1978-79 Canucks Royal Bank

Card	Low	High
COMPLETE SET (23)	20.00	40.00
1 Rick Blight	.75	1.50
2 Gary Bromley	1.00	2.00
3 Bill Derlago	.75	1.50
4 Roland Eriksson	.75	1.50
5 Curt Fraser	1.00	2.00
6 Jere Gillis	.75	1.50
7 Thomas Gradin	2.00	4.00
8 Hilliard Graves	.75	1.50
9 John Grisdale	.75	1.50
10 Glen Hanlon	1.25	2.50
11 Randy Holt	.75	1.50
12 Dennis Kearns	.75	1.50
13 Don Lever	1.00	2.00
14 Lars Lindgren	.75	1.50
15 Bob Manno	.75	1.50
16 Pit Martin	1.00	2.00
17 Jack McIlhargey	.75	1.50
18 Chris Oddleifson	.75	1.50
19 Ron Sedlbauer	.75	1.50
20 Stan Smyl	2.00	4.00
21 Harold Snepsts	2.00	4.00
22 Dennis Ververgaert	1.00	2.00
23 Lars Zetterstrom	.75	1.50

1979-80 Canucks Royal Bank

Card	Low	High
COMPLETE SET (22)	15.00	30.00
1 Brent Ashton	1.00	2.00
2 Rick Blight	.75	1.50
3 Gary Bromley	1.00	2.00
4 Drew Callander	.75	1.50
5 Bill Derlago	1.00	2.00
6 Curt Fraser	1.00	2.00
7 Jere Gillis	.75	1.50
8 Thomas Gradin	1.50	3.00
9 Glen Hanlon	1.25	2.50
10 John Hughes	.75	1.50
11 Dennis Kearns	.75	1.50
12 Don Lever	1.00	2.00
13 Lars Lindgren	.75	1.50
14 Bob Manno	.75	1.50
15 Kevin McCarthy	.75	1.50
16 Jack McIlhargey	.75	1.50
17 Chris Oddleifson	.75	1.50
18 Curt Ridley	.75	1.50
19 Ron Sedlbauer	.75	1.50
20 Stan Smyl	1.50	3.00
21 Harold Snepsts	1.50	3.00
22 Rick Vaive	1.25	2.50

1980-81 Canucks Silverwood Dairies

Card	Low	High
COMPLETE SET (24)	20.00	40.00
1 Brent Ashton	.75	2.00
2 Ivan Boldirev	.75	2.00
3 Per-Olov Brasar	.60	1.50
4 Richard Brodeur	1.50	4.00
5 Gary Bromley	.75	2.00
6 Jerry Butler	.60	1.50
7 Colin Campbell	1.00	2.50
8 Curt Fraser	.75	2.00
9 Thomas Gradin	1.00	2.50
10 Glen Hanlon	1.00	2.50
11 Dennis Kearns	.60	1.50
12 Rick Lanz	.60	1.50
13 Lars Lindgren	.60	1.50
14 Dave Logan	.60	1.50
15 Gary Lupul	.60	1.50
16 Bob Manno	.60	1.50
17 Kevin McCarthy	.60	1.50
18 Gerry Minor	.60	1.50
19 Kevin Primeau	.60	1.50
20 Darcy Rota	.60	1.50
21 Stan Smyl	1.25	3.00
22 Harold Snepsts	1.25	3.00
23 Bobby Schmautz	.60	1.50
24 Tiger Williams	1.50	4.00

1980-81 Canucks Team Issue

Card	Low	High
COMPLETE SET (22)	15.00	30.00
1 Brent Ashton	.75	2.00
2 Ivan Boldirev	.75	2.00
3 Per-Olov Brasar	.60	1.50
4 Richard Brodeur	1.50	4.00
5 Gary Bromley	.75	2.00
6 Jerry Butler	.60	1.50
7 Colin Campbell	1.00	2.50
8 Curt Fraser	.75	2.00
9 Thomas Gradin	1.00	2.50
10 Glen Hanlon	1.00	2.50
11 Dennis Kearns	.60	1.50
12 Rick Lanz	.60	1.50
13 Lars Lindgren	.60	1.50
14 Dave Logan	.60	1.50
15 Gary Lupul	.60	1.50
16 Kevin McCarthy	.60	1.50
17 Gerry Minor	.60	1.50
18 Darcy Rota	.60	1.50
19 Bobby Schmautz	.60	1.50
20 Stan Smyl	1.25	3.00
21 Harold Snepsts	1.25	3.00
22 Tiger Williams	1.50	4.00

1981-82 Canucks Silverwood Dairies

Card	Low	High
COMPLETE SET (24)	10.00	25.00
1 Per-Olov Brasar	.40	1.00
2 Richard Brodeur	1.00	2.50
3 Ivan Boldirev	.50	1.25
4 Jiri Bubla	.40	1.00
5 Jerry Butler	.40	1.00
6 Colin Campbell	.60	1.50
7 Marc Crawford	.75	2.00
8 Anders Eldebrink	.40	1.00
9 Curt Fraser	.40	1.00
10 Thomas Gradin	.75	2.00
11 Doug Halward	.40	1.00
12 Darcy Rota	.40	1.00
12 Glen Hanlon	.60	1.50
13 Ivan Hlinka	.40	1.00
13 Stan Smyl	1.00	2.50
14 Rick Lanz	.40	1.00
15 Lars Lindgren	.40	1.00
16 Blair MacDonald	.40	1.00
17 Gerry Minor	.40	1.00
18 Gary Lupul	.40	1.00
22 Kevin McCarthy	.40	1.00
24 Dave(Tiger) Williams	1.00	2.50
24 Lars Molin	.40	1.00
25 Harold Snepsts	1.00	2.50

1981-82 Canucks Team Issue

Card	Low	High
COMPLETE SET (20)	8.00	20.00
1 Ivan Boldirev	.60	1.50
2 Per-Olov Brasar	.40	1.00
3 Richard Brodeur	1.00	2.50
4 Jiri Bubla	.40	1.00
5 Jerry Butler	.40	1.00
6 Colin Campbell	1.00	2.50
7 Anders Eldebrink	.40	1.00
8 Curt Fraser	.60	1.50
9 Thomas Gradin	.75	2.00
10 Doug Halward	.40	1.00
11 Glen Hanlon	.60	1.50
12 Rick Lanz	.40	1.00
13 Gary Lupul	.40	1.00
14 Blair MacDonald	.40	1.00
15 Kevin McCarthy	.40	1.00
16 Gerry Minor	.40	1.00
17 Lars Molin	.40	1.00
18 Darcy Rota	.40	1.00
19 Stan Smyl	.75	2.00
20 Tiger Williams	1.00	2.50

1982-83 Canucks Team Issue

Card	Low	High
COMPLETE SET (23)	8.00	20.00
1 Ivan Boldirev	.40	1.00
2 Richard Brodeur	1.00	2.50
3 Jiri Bubla	.30	.75
4 Garth Butcher	.40	1.00
5 Ron Delorme	.30	.75
6 Ken Ellacott	.30	.75
7 Curt Fraser	.30	.75
8 Thomas Gradin	.60	1.50
9 Doug Halward	.30	.75
10 Ivan Hlinka	.30	.75
11 Rick Lanz	.30	.75
12 Moe Lemay	.30	.75
13 Lars Lindgren	.30	.75
14 Kevin McCarthy	.30	.75
15 Gerry Minor	.30	.75
16 Lars Molin	.30	.75
17 Jim Nill	.30	.75
18 Darcy Rota	.30	.75
19 Stan Smyl	.60	1.50
20 Harold Snepsts	1.00	2.50
21 Patrik Sundstrom	.75	2.00
22 Tiger Williams	.75	2.00
23 Team Photo	.30	.75

1983-84 Canucks Team Issue

Card	Low	High
COMPLETE SET (23)	10.00	25.00
1 Richard Brodeur 35	.75	2.00
2 Jiri Bubla 29	.20	.50
3 Garth Butcher 5	.40	1.00
4 Marc Crawford 28	.40	1.00
5 Ron Delorme 19	.20	.50
6 John Garrett 31	.40	1.00
7 Jere Gillis 4	.20	.50
8 Thomas Gradin 23	.60	1.50
9 Doug Halward 2	.20	.50
10 Mark Kirton 16	.20	.50
11 Rick Lanz 4	.20	.50
12 Gary Lupul 7	.20	.50
13 Kevin McCarthy 25	.20	.50
14 Lars Molin 26	.20	.50
15 Jim Nill 8	.20	.50
16 Michel Petit 3	.40	1.00
17 Darcy Rota 18	.20	.50
18 Stan Smyl 12	.60	1.50
19 Harold Snepsts 27	.75	2.00
20 Patrik Sundstrom 17	.60	1.50
21 Tony Tanti 9	.60	1.50
22 Tiger Williams 22	.75	2.00
23 Team Photo	.40	1.00

1984-85 Canucks Team Issue

Card	Low	High
COMPLETE SET (26)	10.00	25.00
1 Neil Belland	.20	.50
2 Richard Brodeur	.60	1.50
3 Jiri Bubla	.20	.50
4 Garth Butcher	.30	.75
5 Frank Caprice	.30	.75
6 J.J. Daigneault	.30	.75
7 Ron Delorme	.20	.50
8 John Garrett	.40	1.00
9 Thomas Gradin	.60	1.50
10 Taylor Hall	.20	.50
11 Doug Halward	.20	.50
12 Rick Lanz	.20	.50
13 Moe Lemay	.20	.50
14 Doug Lidster	.30	.75
15 Gary Lupul	.20	.50
16 Al MacAdam	.20	.50
17 Peter McNab	.30	.75
18 Cam Neely	4.00	10.00
19 Michel Petit	.30	.75
20 Darcy Rota	.20	.50
21 Petri Skriko	.40	1.00
22 Stan Smyl	.40	1.00
23 Patrik Sundstrom	.40	1.00
24 Tony Tanti	.40	1.00
25 Team Photo (Large size)	.60	1.50
26 Air Canucks (Advertisement)	.08	.25

1985-86 Canucks Team Issue

Card	Low	High
COMPLETE SET (25)	7.20	18.00
1 Richard Brodeur	.60	1.50
2 Jiri Bubla	.20	.50
3 Garth Butcher	.30	.75
4 Frank Caprice	.30	.75
5 Glen Cochrane	.20	.50
6 Craig Coxe	.20	.50
7 J.J. Daigneault	.30	.75
8 Thomas Gradin	.40	1.00
9 Taylor Hall	.20	.50
10 Doug Halward	.20	.50
11 Jean-Marc Lanthier	.20	.50
12 Rick Lanz	.20	.50
13 Moe Lemay	.20	.50
14 Doug Lidster	.30	.75
15 Dave Lowry	.20	.50
16 Gary Lupul	.20	.50
17 Cam Neely	3.00	8.00
18 Brent Peterson	.20	.50
19 Jim Sandlak	.30	.75
20 Petri Skriko	.40	1.00
21 Stan Smyl	.40	1.00
22 Patrik Sundstrom	.40	1.00
23 Steve Tambellini	.20	.50
24 Tony Tanti	.40	1.00
25 Team Photo (Large size)	1.25	3.00

1986-87 Canucks Team Issue

Card	Low	High
COMPLETE SET (24)	4.80	12.00
1 Richard Brodeur 35	.60	1.50
2 Garth Butcher 5	.30	.75
3 Frank Caprice 30	.30	.75
4 Glen Cochrane 29	.20	.50
5 Craig Coxe 32	.20	.50
6 Taylor Hall 8	.20	.50
7 Stu Kulak 16	.20	.50
8 Moe Lemay 14	.20	.50
9 Dave Lowry 22	.20	.50
10 Brad Maxwell 27	.20	.50
11 Petri Skriko 26	.30	.75
12 Barry Pederson 7	.40	1.00
13 Rick Lanz 4	.20	.50
14 Doug Lidster 3	.30	.75
15 Brent Peterson 10	.20	.50
16 Michel Petit 24	.30	.75
17 Dave Richter 6	.20	.50
18 Stan Smyl 12	.40	1.00
19 Jim Sandlak 33	.20	.50
20 Patrik Sundstrom 17	.40	1.00
21 Rich Sutter 15	.20	.50
22 Steve Tambellini 20	.20	.50
23 Tony Tanti 9	.40	1.00
24 Wendell Young 1	.40	1.00

1987-88 Canucks Shell Oil

Card	Low	High
COMPLETE SET (24)	3.00	8.00
1 Greg Adams	.30	.75
2 Jim Benning	.08	.25
3 Randy Boyd	.08	.25
4 Richard Brodeur	.40	1.00
5 David Bruce	.08	.25
6 Garth Butcher	.08	.25
7 Frank Caprice	.15	.40
8 Craig Coxe	.08	.25
9 Willie Huber	.08	.25
10 Doug Lidster	.20	.50
11 Dave Lowry	.08	.25
12 Kirk McLean	1.00	2.50
13 Larry Melnyk	.08	.25
14 Barry Pederson	.20	.50
15 Dave Richter	.08	.25
16 Jim Sandlak	.08	.25
17 Dave Saunders	.08	.25
18 Petri Skriko	.20	.50
19 Stan Smyl	.30	.75
20 Daryl Stanley	.08	.25
21 Rich Sutter	.08	.25
22 Steve Tambellini	.08	.25
23 Tony Tanti	.30	.75
24 Doug Wickenheiser	.08	.25

1988-89 Canucks Mohawk

Card	Low	High
COMPLETE SET (24)	6.00	15.00
1 Greg Adams 8	.40	1.00
2 Jim Benning 4	.20	.50
3 Ken Berry 18	.20	.50
4 Randy Boyd 29	.20	.50
5 Steve Bozek 14	.20	.50
6 Brian Bradley 10	.60	1.50
7 David Bruce 25	.20	.50
8 Garth Butcher 5	.20	.50
9 Kevan Guy 2	.20	.50
10 Doug Lidster 3	.20	.50
11 Trevor Linden 16	2.00	5.00
12 Kirk McLean 1	1.25	3.00
13 Larry Melnyk 24	.20	.50
14 Robert Nordmark 6	.20	.50
15 Barry Pederson 7	.30	.75
16 Paul Reinhart 23	.30	.75
17 Jim Sandlak 19	.20	.50
18 Petri Skriko 26	.30	.75
19 Stan Smyl 12	.30	.75
20 Harold Snepsts 27	.60	1.50
21 Ronnie Stern 20	.20	.50
22 Rich Sutter 15	.20	.50
23 Tony Tanti 9	.30	.75
24 Steve Weeks 31	.30	.75

1989-90 Canucks Mohawk

Card	Low	High
COMPLETE SET (24)	6.00	15.00
1 Greg Adams 8	.30	.75
2 Jim Benning 4	.20	.50
3 Steve Bozek 14	.20	.50
4 Brian Bradley 10	.40	1.00
5 Garth Butcher 5	.20	.50
6 Craig Coxe 22	.20	.50
7 Vladimir Krutov 17	.40	1.00
8 Igor Larionov 18	.75	2.00
9 Doug Lidster 3	.20	.50
10 Trevor Linden 16	1.50	4.00
11 Kirk McLean 1	.75	2.00
12 Larry Melnyk 24	.20	.50
13 Robert Nordmark 6	.20	.50
14 Barry Pederson 7	.30	.75
15 Paul Reinhart 23	.30	.75
16 Jim Sandlak 19	.20	.50
17 Petri Skriko 26	.30	.75
18 Doug Smith	.20	.50
19 Stan Smyl 12	.40	1.00
20 Harold Snepsts 27	.40	1.00
21 Daryl Stanley 29	.20	.50
22 Rich Sutter 15	.20	.50
23 Tony Tanti 9	.30	.75
24 Steve Weeks 31	.30	.75

1990-91 Canucks Mohawk

Card	Low	High
COMPLETE SET (29)	6.00	15.00
1 Greg Adams	.30	.75
2 Jim Agnew	.20	.50
3 Steve Bozek	.20	.50
4 Garth Butcher	.20	.50
5 Dave Capuano	.20	.50
6 Craig Coxe	.20	.50
7 Gerald Diduck	.20	.50
8 Troy Gamble	.30	.75
9 Don Gibson	.20	.50
10 Kevan Guy	.20	.50
11 Robert Kron	.20	.50
12 Tom Kurvers	.20	.50
13 Igor Larionov	.60	1.50
14 Doug Lidster	.20	.50
15 Trevor Linden	.75	2.00
16 Jyrki Lumme	.30	.75
17 Jay Mazur	.20	.50
18 Andrew McBain	.20	.50
19 Kirk McLean	.60	1.50
20 Rob Murphy	.20	.50
21 Petr Nedved	.60	1.50
22 Robert Nordmark	.20	.50
23 Gino Odjick	.30	.75
24 Adrien Plavsic	.20	.50
25 Dan Quinn	.20	.50
26 Jim Sandlak	.20	.50
27 Stan Smyl	.30	.75
28 Ronnie Stern	.20	.50
29 Garry Valk	.20	.50

1990-91 Canucks Molson

Card	Low	High
COMPLETE SET (6)	16.00	40.00
1 Brian Bradley	2.00	5.00
2 Troy Gamble	2.00	5.00
3 Doug Lidster	2.00	5.00
4 Trevor Linden	4.00	10.00
5 Kirk McLean (Facing right)	3.00	8.00
6 Kirk McLean (Facing front)	3.00	8.00

1991 Canucks Panini Team Stickers

Card	Low	High
COMPLETE SET (32)	1.50	4.00
1 Greg Adams	.02	.10
2 Jim Agnew	.01	.05
3 Steve Bozek	.01	.05
4 Brian Bradley	.07	.20
5 Garth Butcher	.01	.05
6 Dave Capuano	.01	.05
7 Craig Coxe	.01	.05
8 Troy Gamble	.02	.10
9 Kevan Guy	.01	.05
10 Robert Kron	.01	.05
11 Igor Larionov	.08	.25
12 Doug Lidster	.02	.10
13 Trevor Linden	.20	.50
14 Jyrki Lumme	.02	.10
15 Andrew McBain	.01	.05
16 Rob Murphy	.01	.05
17 Petr Nedved	.20	.50
18 Robert Nordmark	.01	.05
19 Adrien Plavsic	.01	.05
20 Dan Quinn	.02	.10
21 Jim Sandlak	.01	.05
22 Petri Skriko	.02	.10
23 Stan Smyl	.07	.20
24 Ronnie Stern	.01	.05
A Team Logo Left Side	.05	.15
B Team Logo Right Side	.05	.15
C Canucks in Action Upper Left Corner	.05	.15
D Canucks in Action Lower Left Corner	.05	.15
E Game Action Upper Right Corner	.05	.15
F Game Action Lower Right Corner	.05	.15
G Kirk McLean	.20	.50
H Trevor Linden	.20	.50

1991-92 Canucks Autograph Cards

Card	Low	High
COMPLETE SET (23)	10.00	25.00
1 Greg Adams	.40	1.00
2 Pavel Bure	3.00	8.00
3 Dave Babych	.40	1.00
4 Geoff Courtnall	.40	1.00
5 Gerald Diduck	.20	.50
6 Robert Dirk	.20	.50
7 Troy Gamble	.30	.75
8 Randy Gregg	.20	.50
9 Robert Kron	.20	.50
10 Igor Larionov	.60	1.50
11 Doug Lidster	.20	.50
12 Trevor Linden	1.00	2.50
13 Jyrki Lumme	.30	.75
14 Kirk McLean	1.25	3.00
15 Sergio Momesso	.20	.50
16 Rob Murphy	.20	.50
17 Dana Murzyn	.20	.50
18 Petr Nedved	1.25	3.00
19 Gino Odjick	.30	.75
20 Adrien Plavsic	.20	.50
21 Cliff Ronning	.60	1.50
22 Jim Sandlak	.20	.50
23 Ryan Walter	.20	.50
24 Garry Valk	.20	.50

1991-92 Canucks Molson

Card	Low	High
COMPLETE SET (7)	20.00	50.00
1 Greg Adams	1.50	4.00
2 Pavel Bure (White uniform)	6.00	15.00
3 Pavel Bure POY (Black uniform)	6.00	15.00
4 Igor Larionov	2.50	6.00
5 Trevor Linden	3.00	8.00
6 Kirk McLean	3.00	8.00
7 Cliff Ronning	2.00	5.00

1991-92 Canucks Team Issue 8x10

Card	Low	High
COMPLETE SET (23)	30.00	75.00
1 Greg Adams	1.50	4.00
2 Pavel Bure	6.00	15.00
3 Dave Babych	1.25	3.00
4 Geoff Courtnall	1.50	4.00
5 Gerald Diduck	1.25	3.00
6 Robert Dirk	1.25	3.00
7 Troy Gamble	1.50	4.00
8 Randy Gregg	1.25	3.00
9 Robert Kron	1.25	3.00
10 Igor Larionov	1.50	4.00
11 Doug Lidster	1.25	3.00
12 Trevor Linden	2.00	5.00
13 Jyrki Lumme	1.25	3.00
14 Kirk McLean	2.00	5.00
15 Sergio Momesso	1.25	3.00
16 Rob Murphy	1.25	3.00
17 Dana Murzyn	1.25	3.00
18 Petr Nedved	2.00	5.00
19 Gino Odjick	1.50	4.00
20 Adrien Plavsic	1.25	3.00
21 Cliff Ronning	2.00	5.00
22 Jim Sandlak	1.25	3.00
23 Ryan Walter	1.25	3.00

1992-93 Canucks Road Trip Art

Card	Low	High
COMPLETE SET (25)	6.00	15.00
1 Greg Adams W1	.30	.75
2 Shawn Antoski W5	.20	.50
3 Dave Babych W5	.30	.75
4 Pavel Bure W3	2.00	5.00
5 Geoff Courtnall W5	.30	.75
6 Gerald Diduck W4	.20	.50
7 Robert Dirk W5	.20	.50
8 Tom Fergus W3	.20	.50
9 Robert Kron W2	.20	.50
10 Doug Lidster W2	.20	.50
11 Trevor Linden W1	.60	1.50
12 Jyrki Lumme W1	.30	.75
13 Kirk McLean W2	.60	1.50
14 Sergio Momesso W2	.20	.50
15 Dana Murzyn W3	.20	.50
16 Petr Nedved W4	.60	1.50
17 Gino Odjick W4	.40	1.00
18 Adrien Plavsic W6	.20	.50
19 Cliff Ronning W6	.30	.75
20 Jim Sandlak W6	.20	.50
21 Jiri Slegr W1	.20	.50
22 Garry Valk W4	.20	.50
23 Ryan Walter W5	.20	.50
24 Dixon Ward W3	.20	.50
25 Kay Whitmore W6	.30	.75

1994-95 Canucks Program Inserts

Card	Low	High
COMPLETE SET (22)	32.00	80.00
1 Greg Adams	1.50	4.00
2 Shawn Antoski	1.50	4.00
3 Dave Babych	1.50	4.00
4 Jeff Brown	1.50	4.00
5 Pavel Bure	4.00	10.00
6 Geoff Courtnall	1.50	4.00
7 Gerald Diduck	1.50	4.00
8 Robert Dirk	1.50	4.00
9 Martin Gelinas	1.50	4.00
10 Brian Glynn	1.50	4.00
11 Tim Hunter	1.50	4.00
12 Nathan LaFayette	1.50	4.00
13 Trevor Linden	2.00	5.00
14 Jyrki Lumme	1.50	4.00
15 Kirk McLean	2.00	5.00
16 Dana Murzyn	1.50	4.00
17 Gino Odjick	1.50	4.00
18 Adrien Plavsic	1.50	4.00
19 Cliff Ronning	1.50	4.00
20 Jiri Slegr	1.50	4.00
21 Dixon Ward	1.50	4.00
22 Kay Whitmore	2.00	5.00

1995-96 Canucks Building the Dream Art

Card	Low	High
COMPLETE SET (18)	6.00	15.00
1 Kirk McLean	.40	1.00
2 Kay Whitmore	.25	.60
3 Bret Hedican	.20	.50
4 Tim Hunter	.20	.50
5 Dana Murzyn	.20	.50
6 Jyrki Lumme	.25	.60
7 Cliff Ronning	.30	.75
8 Jeff Brown	.30	.75
9 Martin Gelinas	.40	1.00
10 Pavel Bure	2.00	5.00
11 Jiri Slegr	.20	.50
12 Sergio Momesso	.20	.50
13 Gino Odjick	.40	1.00
14 Geoff Courtnall	.20	.50
15 John McIntyre	.20	.50
16 Trevor Linden	.75	2.00
17 Mike Peca	.40	1.00
18 Dave Babych	.20	.50

1990-97 Canucks Postcards

Card	Low	High
COMPLETE SET (27)	6.00	15.00
1 Kirk McLean	.30	.75
3 Bret Hedican	.08	.25
4 Mark Wotton	.08	.25
5 Dana Murzyn	.08	.25
6 Adrian Aucoin	.08	.25
7 David Roberts	.08	.25
8 Donald Brashear	.08	.25
9 Russ Courtnall	.20	.50
10 Esa Tikkanen	.20	.50
16 Trevor Linden	.30	.75
17 Mike Ridley	.20	.50
18 Troy Crowder	.08	.25
19 Markus Naslund	.20	.50
20 Alexander Semak	.08	.25
21 Jyrki Lumme	.20	.50
23 Martin Gelinas	.30	.75
24 Scott Walker	.20	.50
26 Mike Sillinger	.08	.25
27 Leif Rohlin	.08	.25
29 Gino Odjick	.30	.75
30 Mike Fountain	.20	.50
31 Corey Hirsch	.30	.75
32 Chris Joseph	.08	.25
44 Dave Babych	.20	.50
89 Alexander Mogilny	.60	1.50
96 Pavel Bure	1.50	4.00
NNO Team Photo	.20	.50

2001-02 Canucks Postcards

Card	Low	High
COMPLETE SET (11)	4.00	10.00
1 Todd Bertuzzi	.40	1.00
2 Murray Baron	.40	1.00
3 Artem Chubarov	.40	1.00
4 Dan Cloutier	.60	1.50
5 Matt Cooke	.40	1.00
6 Ed Jovanovski	.60	1.50
7 Scott Lachance	.40	1.00
8 Trevor Linden	.75	2.00
9 Brendan Morrison	.60	1.50
10 Markus Naslund	.60	1.50
11 Peter Skudra	.40	1.00

2002-03 Canucks Team Issue

Card	Low	High
COMPLETE SET		
1 Murray Baron	.40	1.00

2 Todd Bertuzzi 2.00 5.00
3 Dan Cloutier 1.25 3.00
4 Matt Cooke 1.25 3.00
6 Ed Jovanovski 1.25 3.00
8 Trevor Linden 1.25 3.00
10 Brendan Morrison 1.25 3.00
11 Markus Naslund 2.00 5.00
12 Mattias Ohlund .40 1.00
14 Daniel Sedin 1.25 3.00
15 Henrik Sedin 1.25 3.00

2003-04 Canucks Postcards
COMPLETE SET (28) 20.00
1 Bryan Allen .20 .50
2 Magnus Arvedson .20 .50
3 Todd Bertuzzi .40 1.00
4 Brian Burke GM .04 .10
5 Artem Chubarov .20 .50
6 Dan Cloutier .40 1.00
7 Matt Cooke .40 1.00
8 Marc Crawford CO .10 .25
9 Johan Hedberg .20 .50
10 Mike Johnston ACO .04 .10
11 Ed Jovanovski .40 1.00
12 Mike Keane .20 .50
13 Jason King .20 .50
14 Trevor Linden .40 1.00
15 Mats Lindgren .20 .50
16 Marek Malik .20 .50
17 Brad May .20 .50
18 Jack McIlhargey ACO .04 .10
19 Brendan Morrison .40 1.00
20 Markus Naslund .75 2.00
21 Mattias Ohlund .20 .50
22 Jarkko Ruutu .20 .50
23 Sami Salo .20 .50
24 Daniel Sedin .40 1.00
25 Henrik Sedin .40 1.00
26 Jiri Slegr .20 .50
27 Brent Sopel .20 .50
28 Finn MASCOT .04 .10

2003-04 Canucks Sav-on-Foods
COMPLETE SET (30) 6.00 15.00
1 Trevor Linden .60 1.50
2 Johan Hedberg .20 .50
3 Mike Keane .20 .50
4 Todd Bertuzzi
Brendan Morrison
Markus Naslund .40 1.00
5 Markus Naslund .60 1.50
6 Daniel Sedin .40 1.00
7 Marek Malik .20 .50
8 Brad May .20 .50
9 Brendan Morrison .20 .50
10 Mattias Ohlund .20 .50
11 Magnus Arvedson .20 .50
12 Bryan Allen .20 .50
13 Jason King .20 .50
14 Henrik Sedin .40 1.00
15 Brent Sopel .20 .50
16 Ed Jovanovski
Dan Cloutier
Mattias Ohlund .40 1.00
17 Dan Cloutier .40 1.00
18 Artem Chubarov .20 .50
19 Jarkko Ruutu .20 .50
20 Daniel Sedin
Henrik Sedin
Jason King .40 1.00
21 Ed Jovanovski .40 1.00
22 Todd Bertuzzi .40 1.00
23 Matt Cooke .40 1.00
24 Sami Salo .20 .50

2006-07 Canucks Postcards
COMPLETE SET (25) 15.00 25.00
1 Kevin Bieksa .60 1.50
2 Luc Bourdon .40 1.00
3 Jan Bulis .40 1.00
4 Alexandre Burrows .40 1.00
5 Marc Chouinard .40 1.00
6 Matt Cooke .60 1.50
7 Rory Fitzpatrick .40 1.00
8 Josh Green .40 1.00
9 Ryan Kesler .40 1.00
10 Lukas Krajicek .40 1.00
11 Trevor Linden .75 2.00
12 Roberto Luongo 1.25 3.00
13 Willie Mitchell .40 1.00
14 Brendan Morrison .40 1.00
15 Markus Naslund .75 2.00
16 Mattias Ohlund .40 1.00
17 Taylor Pyatt .40 1.00
18 Dany Sabourin .40 1.00
19 Sami Salo .40 1.00
20 Tommi Santala .40 1.00
21 Daniel Sedin .75 2.00
22 Henrik Sedin .75 2.00
23 Alain Vigneault CO .10 .25
24 Fin MASCOT .10 .25
25 Logo Card .10 .25

2007-08 Canucks Team Issue
COMPLETE SET (21) 5.00 12.00
1 Logo Card .30 .75
2 Kevin Bieksa .40 1.00
3 Alexandre Burrows .30 .75
4 Jeff Cowan .30 .75
5 Matt Cooke .30 .75
6 Brad Isbister .30 .75
7 Ryan Kesler .50 1.25
8 Lukas Krajicek .30 .75
9 Trevor Linden .50 1.25
10 Roberto Luongo .75 2.00
11 Willie Mitchell .30 .75
12 Aaron Miller .30 .75
13 Brendan Morrison .30 .75
14 Markus Naslund .50 1.25
15 Mattias Ohlund .30 .75
16 Taylor Pyatt .30 .75
17 Byron Ritchie .30 .75
18 Sami Salo .30 .75
19 Daniel Sedin .60 1.50
20 Henrik Sedin .60 1.50
21 Curtis Sanford .40 1.00

2010-11 Canucks Oversized Team Issue
COMPLETE SET (25) 60.00 120.00
1 Andrew Alberts 2.50 6.00
2 Keith Ballard 2.50 6.00
3 Kevin Bieksa 4.00 10.00
4 Alex Bolduc 2.50 6.00
5 Alexandre Burrows 2.50 6.00
6 Guillaume Desbiens 4.00 10.00
7 Christian Ehrhoff 2.50 6.00
8 Tanner Glass 2.50 6.00
9 Dan Hamhuis 3.00 8.00
10 Jannik Hansen 3.00 8.00
11 Ryan Kesler 4.00 10.00
12 Roberto Luongo 6.00 15.00
13 Manny Malhotra 3.00 8.00
14 Mason Raymond 2.50 6.00
15 Aaron Rome 2.50 6.00
16 Rick Rypien 4.00 10.00
17 Sami Salo 2.50 6.00
18 Mikael Samuelsson 2.50 6.00
19 Cory Schneider 4.00 10.00
20 Daniel Sedin 5.00 12.00
21 Henrik Sedin 5.00 12.00
22 Jeff Tambellini 2.50 6.00
23 Raffi Torres 2.50 6.00
24 Alain Vigneault 4.00 10.00
25 Kyle Wellwood 3.00 8.00

1974-75 Capitals White Borders
COMPLETE SET (25) 30.00 60.00
1 John Adams 1.00 2.00
2 Jim Anderson CO 1.00 2.00
3 Ron Anderson 1.00 2.00
4 Steve Atkinson 1.00 2.00
5 Michel Belhumeur 2.00 4.00
6 Mike Bloom 1.00 2.00
7 Gord Brooks 1.00 2.00
8 Bruce Cowick 1.00 2.00
9 Denis Dupere 1.00 2.00
10 Jack Egers 1.00 2.00
11 Jim Hrycuik 1.00 2.00
12 Greg Joly 1.50 3.00
13 Dave Kryskow 1.00 2.00
14 Yvon Labre 1.50 3.00
15 Pete Laframboise 1.00 2.00
16 Bill Lesuk 1.00 2.00
17 Ron Low 2.00 4.00
18 Joe Lundrigan 1.00 2.00
19 Mike Marson 1.50 3.00
20 Bill Mikkelson 1.00 2.00
21 Doug Mohns 2.00 4.00
22 Andre Peloffy 1.00 2.00
23 Milt Schmidt GM 2.50 5.00
24 Gord Smith 1.00 2.00
25 Tom Williams 1.50 3.00

1978-79 Capitals Team Issue
COMPLETE SET (18) 7.50 15.00
1 Michel Bergeron .75 1.50
2 Greg Carroll .50 1.00
3 Guy Charron .50 1.00
4 Rolf Edberg .50 1.00
5 Rick Green .50 1.00
6 Gordie Lane .50 1.00
7 Mark Lofthouse .50 1.00
8 Jack Lynch .50 1.00
9 Dennis Maruk .75 1.50
10 Paul Mulvey .50 1.00
11 Robert Picard .50 1.00
12 Bill Riley .50 1.00
13 Tom Rowe .50 1.00
14 Bob Sirois .50 1.00
15 Gord Smith .50 1.00
16 Leif Svensson .75 1.50
17 Ryan Walter .50 1.00
18 Bernie Wolfe .50 1.00

1979-80 Capitals Team Issue
COMPLETE SET (23) 20.00 40.00
1 Pierre Bouchard .50 1.00
2 Guy Charron .50 1.00
3 Rolf Edberg .50 1.00
4 Mike Gartner 12.50 25.00
5 Rick Green .50 1.00
6 Bengt Gustafsson .75 1.50
7 Dennis Hextall .75 1.50
8 Gary Inness .50 1.00
9 Yvon Labre .50 1.00
10 Antero Lehtonen .50 1.00
11 Mark Lofthouse .50 1.00
12 Paul McKinnon .50 1.00
13 Dennis Maruk .75 1.50
14 Paul Mulvey .50 1.00
15 Robert Picard .75 1.50
16 Greg Polis .50 1.00
17 Errol Rausse .50 1.00
18 Tom Rowe .50 1.00
19 Peter Scamurra .50 1.00
20 Bob Sirois .50 1.00
21 Wayne Stephenson .50 1.00
22 Leif Svensson .75 1.50
23 Ryan Walter .50 1.00

1981-82 Capitals Team Issue
COMPLETE SET (21) 12.00 30.00
1 Timo Blomqvist .40 1.00
2 Bobby Carpenter 1.25 3.00
3 Glen Currie .40 1.00
4 Gaetan Duchesne .60 1.50
5 Mike Gartner 4.00 10.00
6 Rick Green .60 1.50
7 Randy Holt .40 1.00
8 Wes Jarvis .40 1.00
9 Al Jensen .60 1.50
10 Dennis Maruk 1.25 3.00
11 Terry Murray .40 1.00
12 Lee Norwood .40 1.00
13 Mike Palmateer 1.25 3.00
14 Dave Parro .60 1.50
15 Torrie Robertson .60 1.50
16 Greg Theberge .40 1.00
17 Chris Valentine .40 1.00
18 Darren Veitch .40 1.00
20 Howard Walker .40 1.00
21 Ryan Walter .75 2.00

1982-83 Capitals Team Issue
COMPLETE SET (25) 16.00 40.00
1 Timo Blomqvist .40 1.00
2 Ted Bulley .40 1.00
3 Bobby Carpenter .75 2.00
4 Glen Currie .40 1.00
5 Brian Engblom .60 1.50
6 Mike Gartner 3.00 8.00
7 Bob Gould .40 1.00
8 Bengt Gustafsson .75 2.00
9 Alan Haworth .40 1.00
10 Randy Holt .40 1.00
11 Ken Houston .40 1.00
12 Doug Jarvis .75 2.00
13 Rod Langway 1.50 4.00
14 Craig Laughlin .40 1.00
15 Dennis Maruk .75 2.00
16 Bryan Murray CO .40 1.00
17 Terry Murray ACO .40 1.00
18 Lee Norwood .40 1.00
19 Milan Novy .40 1.00
20 Dave Parro .60 1.50
21 David Poile GM .40 1.00
22 Pat Riggin 1.00 2.50
23 Scott Stevens 4.00 10.00
24 Chris Valentine .40 1.00
25 Darren Veitch .40 1.00

1984-85 Capitals Pizza Hut
COMPLETE SET (15) 14.00 35.00
1 Bob Carpenter .75 2.00
2 Dave Christian 1.00 2.50
3 Glen Currie .60 1.50
4 Gaetan Duchesne .60 1.50
5 Mike Gartner 3.00 8.00
6 Bob Gould .60 1.50
7 Bengt Gustafsson .75 2.00
8 Alan Haworth .60 1.50
9 Doug Jarvis .75 2.00
10 Al Jensen .75 2.00
11 Rod Langway 1.25 3.00
12 Craig Laughlin .60 1.50
13 Larry Murphy 2.00 5.00
14 Pat Riggin .75 2.00
15 Scott Stevens 3.00 8.00

1985-86 Capitals Pizza Hut
COMPLETE SET (15) 14.00 35.00
1 Bob Carpenter .75 2.00
2 Dave Christian 1.00 2.50
3 Gaetan Duchesne .60 1.50
4 Mike Gartner 2.50 6.00
5 Bob Gould .60 1.50
6 Bengt Gustafsson .75 2.00
7 Alan Haworth .60 1.50
8 Doug Jarvis SP 1.50 4.00
9 Al Jensen .75 2.00
10 Rod Langway 1.25 3.00
11 Craig Laughlin .60 1.50
12 Larry Murphy 2.00 5.00
13 Pat Riggin SP 2.00 5.00
14 Scott Stevens 2.50 6.00
15 Darren Veitch SP 1.50 4.00

1986-87 Capitals Kodak
COMPLETE SET (26) 12.00 30.00
1 Greg Adams .60 1.50
2 John Barrett .30 .75
3 John Blum .30 .75
4 Dave Christian .40 1.00
5 Bob Crawford .30 .75
6 Gaetan Duchesne .30 .75
7 Lou Franceschetti .30 .75
8 Mike Gartner 1.50 4.00
9 Bob Gould .30 .75
10 Jeff Greenlaw .30 .75
11 Kevin Hatcher .75 2.00
12 Alan Haworth .30 .75
13 David A. Jensen .30 .75
14 Rod Langway .75 2.00
15 Craig Laughlin .30 .75
16 Bob Mason .40 1.00
17 Kelly Miller .40 1.00
18 Larry Murphy 1.00 2.50
19 Bryan Murray CO .30 .75
20 Pete Peeters .75 2.00
21 Michal Pivonka 1.25 3.00
22 Mike Ridley .75 2.00
23 Gary Sampson .30 .75
24 Greg Smith .30 .75
25 Scott Stevens 1.50 4.00
26 Large Team Photo .75 2.00

1986-87 Capitals Police
COMPLETE SET (24) 6.00 15.00
1 Greg Adams 22 .40 1.00
2 John Barrett 6 .20 .50
3 Bob Carpenter 10 .20 .50
4 Dave Christian 27 .30 .75
5 Yvon Corriveau 26 .20 .50
6 Gaetan Duchesne 14 .20 .50
7 Lou Franceschetti 32 .20 .50
8 Mike Gartner 11 1.25 3.00
9 Bob Gould 23 .20 .50
10 Kevin Hatcher 4 .60 1.50
11 Alan Haworth 15 .20 .50
12 Al Jensen 35 .25 .60
13 David A. Jensen 9 .20 .50
14 Rod Langway 5 .60 1.50
15 Craig Laughlin 18 .20 .50
16 Stephen Leach 21 .20 .50
17 Larry Murphy 8 .75 2.00
18 Bryan Murray CO .20 .50
19 Pete Peeters 1 .60 1.50
20 Jorgen Pettersson 12 .20 .50
21 Michal Pivonka 17 .75 2.00
22 David Poile VP
GM .20 .50
23 Greg Smith 19 .20 .50
24 Scott Stevens 3 1.25 3.00

1987-88 Capitals Kodak
COMPLETE SET (26) 8.00 20.00
1 Pete Peeters .40 1.00
2 Garry Galley .40 1.00
3 Scott Stevens .75 2.00
4 Kevin Hatcher .75 2.00
5 Rod Langway .40 1.00
6 John Barrett .20 .50
8 Larry Murphy .60 1.50
10 Kelly Miller .30 .75
11 Mike Gartner 1.00 2.50
12 Peter Sundstrom .30 .75
16 Bengt Gustafsson .30 .75
17 Mike Ridley .60 1.50
18 Craig Laughlin .20 .50
19 Greg Smith .20 .50
20 Michal Pivonka .60 1.50
22 Greg Adams .40 1.00
23 Bob Gould .20 .50
25 Lou Franceschetti .20 .50
27 Dave Christian .40 1.00
29 Ed Kastelic .20 .50
30 Clint Malarchuk .40 1.00
32 Dale Hunter .60 1.50
34 Bill Houlder .30 .75
xx Bryan Murray CO .20 .50
XX Team Photo .20 .50
xx David Poile VP
GM .20 .50

1987-88 Capitals Team Issue
COMPLETE SET (23) 10.00 25.00
1 Greg Adams .50 1.25
2 John Barrett .30 .75
3 Dave Christian .50 1.25
4 Lou Franceschetti .30 .75
5 Garry Galley .60 1.50
6 Mike Gartner 1.25 3.00
7 Bob Gould .30 .75
8 Bengt Gustafsson .40 1.00
9 Kevin Hatcher 1.25 3.00
10 Dale Hunter .75 2.00
11 David Jensen .30 .75
12 Ed Kastelic .30 .75
13 Rod Langway .50 1.25
14 Craig Laughlin .30 .75
15 Clint Malarchuk .50 1.25
16 Kelly Miller .40 1.00
17 Larry Murphy .75 2.00
18 Pete Peeters .60 1.50
19 Michal Pivonka .75 2.00
20 Mike Ridley .75 2.00
21 Greg Smith .30 .75
22 Scott Stevens 1.00 2.50
23 Peter Sundstrom .40 1.00

1988-89 Capitals Borderless
COMPLETE SET (21) 6.00 15.00
1 Dave Christian .40 1.00
2 Yvon Corriveau .30 .75
3 Geoff Courtnall .75 2.00
4 Lou Franceschetti .30 .75
5 Mike Gartner .75 2.00
6 Bob Gould .30 .75
7 Bengt Gustafsson .30 .75
8 Kevin Hatcher .60 1.50
9 Dale Hunter .60 1.50
10 Rod Langway .60 1.50
11 Stephen Leach .30 .75
12 Grant Ledyard .30 .75
13 Clint Malarchuk .40 1.00
14 Kelly Miller .30 .75
15 Larry Murphy .60 1.50
16 Pete Peeters .40 1.00
17 Michal Pivonka .75 2.00
18 Mike Ridley .60 1.50
19 Neil Sheehy .30 .75
20 Scott Stevens .75 2.00
21 Peter Sundstrom .40 1.00

1988-89 Capitals Smokey
COMPLETE SET (24) 6.00 15.00
1 Dave Christian 27 .30 .75
2 Yvon Corriveau 26 .20 .50
3 Geoff Courtnall 14 .60 1.50
4 Lou Franceschetti 25 .20 .50
5 Mike Gartner 11 .60 1.50
6 Bob Gould 23 .20 .50
7 Bengt Gustafsson 16 .30 .75
8 Kevin Hatcher 4 .60 1.50
9 Dale Hunter 32 .40 1.00
10 Rod Langway 5 .40 1.00
11 Stephen Leach 21 .20 .50
12 Grant Ledyard 6 .20 .50
13 Clint Malarchuk 30 .30 .75
14 Kelly Miller 10 .30 .75
15 Larry Murphy 8 .40 1.00
16 Bryan Murray CO .20 .50
17 Pete Peeters 1 .30 .75
18 Michal Pivonka 20 .60 1.50
19 David Poile VP
GM .20 .50
20 Mike Ridley 17 .40 1.00
21 Neil Sheehy 15 .20 .50
22 Scott Stevens 3 .60 1.50
23 Peter Sundstrom 12 .30 .75
24 Title Card
Smokey the Bear .20 .50

1989-90 Capitals Kodak
COMPLETE SET (25) 8.00 20.00
1 Mike Liut .40 1.00
3 Scott Stevens .75 2.00
4 Kevin Hatcher .60 1.50
5 Rod Langway .60 1.50
6 Calle Johansson .40 1.00
8 Bob Rouse .30 .75
10 Kelly Miller .30 .75
11 Tim Bergland .30 .75
12 John Tucker .30 .75
14 Geoff Courtnall .60 1.50
15 Neil Sheehy .30 .75
16 Alan May .30 .75
17 Mike Ridley .40 1.00
19 John Druce .30 .75
20 Michal Pivonka .40 1.00
21 Stephen Leach .30 .75
22 Dino Ciccarelli .75 2.00
26 Steve Maltais .30 .75
27 Bob Joyce .30 .75
29 Scot Kleinendorst .30 .75
32 Dale Hunter .60 1.50
33 Don Beaupre .40 1.00
xx Rob Laird ACO .20 .50
xx Terry Murray CO .20 .50
xx David Poile VP/GM .20 .50

1989-90 Capitals Team Issue
COMPLETE SET (23) 7.20 18.00
1 Don Beaupre .30 .75
2 Dave Christian .30 .75
3 Dino Ciccarelli .60 1.50
4 Yvon Corriveau .20 .50
5 Geoff Courtnall .40 1.00
6 Kevin Hatcher .40 1.00
7 Bill Houlder .30 .75
8 Dale Hunter .40 1.00
9 Calle Johansson .30 .75
10 Dimitri Khristich .60 1.50
11 Scot Kleinendorst .20 .50
12 Nick Kypreos .20 .50
13 Rod Langway .40 1.00
14 Stephen Leach .20 .50
15 Bob Mason .30 .75
16 Alan May .30 .75
17 Kelly Miller .30 .75
18 Michal Pivonka .30 .75
19 Mike Ridley .30 .75
20 Bob Rouse .20 .50
21 Neil Sheehy .20 .50
22 Scott Stevens .60 1.50
23 Doug Wickenheiser .20 .50

1990-91 Capitals Kodak
COMPLETE SET (25) 6.00 15.00
1 Don Beaupre .40 1.00
2 Tim Bergland .20 .50
3 Peter Bondra 2.00 5.00
4 Dino Ciccarelli .40 1.00
5 John Druce .20 .50
6 Kevin Hatcher .40 1.00
7 Dale Hunter .40 1.00
8 Al Iafrate .60 1.50
9 Calle Johansson .30 .75
10 Dimitri Khristich .40 1.00
11 Nick Kypreos .20 .50
12 Mike Lalor .20 .50
13 Rod Langway .40 1.00
14 Stephen Leach .20 .50
15 Mike Liut .40 1.00
16 Alan May .20 .50
17 Kelly Miller .20 .50
18 Terry Murray CO .08 .25
19 John Perpich .20 .50
20 Michal Pivonka .40 1.00
21 David Poile VP
GM .08 .25
22 Mike Ridley .40 1.00
23 Ken Sabourin .20 .50
24 Mikhail Tatarinov .20 .50
25 Dave Tippett .20 .50

1990-91 Capitals Postcards
COMPLETE SET (22) 8.00 20.00
1 Don Beaupre .40 1.00
2 Tim Bergland .20 .50
3 Peter Bondra 2.00 5.00
4 Dino Ciccarelli .40 1.00
5 John Druce .20 .50
6 Kevin Hatcher .40 1.00
7 Jim Hrivnak .25 .60
8 Dale Hunter .40 1.00
9 Al Iafrate .60 1.50
10 Calle Johansson .30 .75
11 Nick Kypreos .20 .50
12 Mike Lalor .20 .50
13 Rod Langway .40 1.00
14 Steve Leach .20 .50
15 Mike Liut .40 1.00
16 Alan May .20 .50
17 Kelly Miller .20 .50
18 Rob Murray .20 .50
19 Michal Pivonka .40 1.00
20 Mike Ridley .40 1.00
21 Neil Sheehy .20 .50
22 Dave Tippett .20 .50

1990-91 Capitals Smokey
COMPLETE SET (22) 4.80 12.00
1 Don Beaupre .30 .75
2 Tim Bergland .15 .40
3 Peter Bondra 1.50 4.00
4 Dino Ciccarelli .40 1.00
5 John Druce .15 .40
6 Kevin Hatcher .30 .75
7 Jim Hrivnak .20 .50
8 Dale Hunter .30 .75
9 Calle Johansson .20 .50
10 Nick Kypreos .15 .40
11 Mike Lalor .15 .40
12 Rod Langway .30 .75
13 Stephen Leach .20 .50
14 Mike Liut .40 1.00
15 Alan May .15 .40
16 Kelly Miller .15 .40
17 Rob Murray .15 .40
18 Michal Pivonka .40 1.00
19 Mike Ridley .30 .75
20 Neil Sheehy .15 .40
21 Mikhail Tatarinov .15 .40
22 Dave Tippett .15 .40

1991-92 Capitals Junior 5x7
COMPLETE SET (25) 7.20 18.00
1 Don Beaupre .40 1.00
2 Tim Bergland .20 .50
3 Peter Bondra 1.50 4.00
4 Randy Burridge .30 .75
5 Shawn Chambers .20 .50
6 Dino Ciccarelli .60 1.50
7 Sylvain Cote .20 .50
8 John Druce .20 .50
9 Jeff Greenlaw .20 .50
10 Kevin Hatcher .60 1.50
11 Dale Hunter .60 1.50
12 Al Iafrate .60 1.50
13 Calle Johansson .30 .75
14 Dimitri Khristich .60 1.50
15 Todd Krygier .20 .50
16 Nick Kypreos .20 .50
17 Mike Lalor .20 .50
18 Rod Langway .40 1.00
19 Mike Liut .40 1.00
20 Alan May .20 .50
21 Kelly Miller .20 .50
22 Michal Pivonka .60 1.50
23 Mike Ridley .40 1.00
24 Ken Sabourin .20 .50
25 Dave Tippett .20 .50

1991-92 Capitals Kodak
COMPLETE SET (25) 4.80 12.00
1 Don Beaupre .30 .75
2 Tim Bergland .15 .40
3 Peter Bondra 1.00 2.50
4 Randy Burridge .20 .50
5 Shawn Chambers .15 .40
6 Dino Ciccarelli .40 1.00
7 Sylvain Cote .20 .50
8 John Druce .15 .40
9 Kevin Hatcher .30 .75
10 Jim Hrivnak .30 .75
11 Dale Hunter .30 .75
12 Al Iafrate .40 1.00
13 Calle Johansson .20 .50
14 Dimitri Khristich .40 1.00
15 Todd Krygier .15 .40
16 Nick Kypreos .15 .40
17 Rod Langway .30 .75
18 Mike Liut .30 .75
19 Paul MacDermid .15 .40
20 Alan May .15 .40
21 Kelly Miller .15 .40
22 Michal Pivonka .30 .75
23 Mike Ridley .30 .75
24 Brad Schlegel .15 .40
25 Dave Tippett .15 .40

1992-93 Capitals Kodak
COMPLETE SET (25) 6.00 15.00
1 Shawn Anderson .20 .50
2 Don Beaupre .40 1.00
3 Peter Bondra 1.00 2.50
4 Randy Burridge .25 .60
5 Bobby Carpenter .25 .60
6 Paul Cavallini .20 .50
7 Sylvain Cote .20 .50
8 Pat Elynuik .20 .50
9 Kevin Hatcher .30 .75
10 Jim Hrivnak .25 .60
11 Dale Hunter .40 1.00
12 Al Iafrate .40 1.00
13 Calle Johansson .25 .60
14 Keith Jones .25 .60
15 Dimitri Khristich .40 1.00
16 Steve Konowalchuk .30 .75
17 Todd Krygier .20 .50
18 Rod Langway .30 .75
19 Paul MacDermid .20 .50
20 Alan May .20 .50
21 Kelly Miller .20 .50
22 Michal Pivonka .40 1.00
23 Mike Ridley .30 .75
24 Reggie Savage .20 .50
25 Jason Woolley .25 .60

1995-96 Capitals Team Issue
COMPLETE SET (28) 4.80 12.00
1 Jason Allison .60 1.50
2 Craig Berube .15 .40
3 Peter Bondra 1.25 3.00
4 Jim Carey .20 .50
5 Sylvain Cote .15 .40
6 Mike Eagles .15 .40
7 Martin Gendron .15 .40
8 Sergei Gonchar .15 .40
9 Dale Hunter .30 .75
10 Calle Johansson .20 .50
11 Jim Johnson .15 .40
12 Keith Jones .15 .40
13 Joe Juneau .30 .75
14 Kevin Kaminski .15 .40
15 Ken Klee .15 .40
16 Olaf Kolzig .60 1.50
17 Steve Konowalchuk .15 .40
18 Kelly Miller .15 .40
19 Jeff Nelson .15 .40
20 Pat Peake .15 .40
21 Michal Pivonka .30 .75
22 Joe Reekie .15 .40
23 Jim Schoenfeld CO .08 .25
24 Slapshot
Mascot .02 .10
25 Slapshot
Mascot .02 .10
26 Mark Tinordi .15 .40
27 Stefan Ustorf .15 .40
28 Brendan Witt .20 .50

1998-99 Capitals Kids and Cops
COMPLETE SET (7) 4.00 10.00
1 Olaf Kolzig 1.25 3.00
2 Peter Bondra 1.25 3.00
3 Adam Oates .75 2.00
4 Dale Hunter .75 2.00
5 Calle Johansson .40 1.00
6 Steve Konowalchuk .40 1.00
7 Slapshot MAS .40 1.00

2002-03 Capitals Team Issue
1 Peter Bondra .60 1.50
2 Jason Doig .40 1.00
3 Sergei Gonchar .40 1.00
4 Jaromir Jagr 1.25 3.00
5 Olaf Kolzig 1.25 3.00
6 Steve Konowalchuk .40 1.00
7 Robert Lang .40 1.00
8 Brendan Witt .40 1.00
9 Dainius Zubrus .40 1.00

1949 Carrera Ltd Sports Series
44 Les Anning 15.00 40.00
46 Duke Campbell 15.00 40.00

1934-35 CCM Brown Border Photos
COMPLETE SET (12) 500.00 1000.00
1 Boston Bruins 50.00 100.00
2 Chicago Blackhawks 50.00 100.00
3 Detroit Red Wings 50.00 100.00
4 Montreal Canadiens 62.50 125.00
5 Montreal Maroons 62.50 125.00
6 New York Americans 62.50 125.00
7 New York Rangers 50.00 100.00
8 Toronto Maple Leafs 50.00 100.00
9 All-Star Game 75.00 150.00
10 Allan Cup Moncton 25.00 50.00
11 Can-Am Providence 30.00 60.00
12 Memorial Cup St. Mike's 25.00 50.00

1935-36 CCM Green Border Photos
COMPLETE SET (10) 375.00 750.00
1 Boston Cubs
(Can-Am champs) 25.00 50.00
2 Boston Bruins 62.50 125.00
3 Halifax (Allan Cup) 25.00 50.00
4 Montreal Maroons 75.00 150.00
5 Toronto Maple Leafs 62.50 125.00
6 Winnipeg (Memorial Cup) 25.00 50.00
7 Frank Boucher 37.50 75.00
8 Lorne Chabot 50.00 100.00
9 Charlie Conacher 50.00 100.00
10 Foster Hewitt 37.50 75.00

2010 Certified National Convention
COMPLETE SET (2) 3.00 6.00
AO Alex Ovechkin 1.25 3.00
SC Sidney Crosby 1.50 4.00

2010 Certified National Convention Blue
COMPLETE SET (2) 7.50 15.00
*BLUE: 1X TO 2.5X BASIC CARDS

2010-11 Certified
COMP.SET w/o SPs (150) 20.00 50.00
1 Ryan Getzlaf .40 1.00
2 Corey Perry .60 1.50
3 Teemu Selanne .75 2.00
4 Bobby Ryan .30 .75
5 Jonas Hiller .30 .75
6 Evander Kane .40 1.00
7 Zach Bogosian .30 .75
8 Dustin Byfuglien .30 .75
9 Nik Antropov .30 .75
10 Ondrej Pavelec .40 1.00
11 Milan Lucic .40 1.00
12 Patrice Bergeron .50 1.25
13 Zdeno Chara .40 1.00
14 Nathan Horton .30 .75
15 Tuukka Rask .50 1.25
16 Ryan Miller .40 1.00
17 Thomas Vanek .30 .75
18 Tyler Myers .25 .60
19 Nathan Gerbe .25 .60
20 Derek Roy .25 .60
21 Jarome Iginla .50 1.25
22 Miikka Kiprusoff .40 1.00
23 Rene Bourque .25 .60
24 Mikael Backlund .30 .75
25 Jay Bouwmeester .25 .60
26 Brandon Sutter .25 .60
27 Eric Staal .50 1.25
28 Cam Ward .40 1.00
29 Zach Boychuk .30 .75
30 Drayson Bowman .30 .75
31 Jonathan Toews .60 1.50
32 Patrick Kane .75 2.00
33 Duncan Keith .30 .75
34 Marty Turco .40 1.00
35 Patrick Sharp .40 1.00
36 Marian Hossa .40 1.00
37 Craig Anderson .40 1.00
38 Matt Duchene .40 1.00
39 Chris Stewart .30 .75
40 Peter Mueller .30 .75
41 Paul Stastny .30 .75
42 Rick Nash .40 1.00
43 Steve Mason .30 .75
44 Jakub Voracek .30 .75
45 Antoine Vermette .25 .60
46 James Neal .25 .60
47 Jamie Benn .50 1.25
48 Steve Ott .25 .60
49 Kari Lehtonen .30 .75
50 Brad Richards .40 1.00
51 Pavel Datsyuk .60 1.50
52 Henrik Zetterberg .50 1.25
53 Jimmy Howard .50 1.25
54 Nicklas Lidstrom .40 1.00
55 Johan Franzen .30 .75
56 Tomas Holmstrom .25 .60
57 Ales Hemsky .30 .75
58 Sam Gagner .25 .60
59 Dustin Penner .25 .60
60 Jeff Deslauriers .25 .60
61 Nikolai Khabibulin .30 .75
62 Tomas Vokoun .30 .75
63 Stephen Weiss .25 .60
64 Dmitri Kulikov .30 .75
65 Michael Frolik .25 .60
66 Drew Doughty .50 1.25
67 Anze Kopitar .60 1.50
68 Jonathan Quick .50 1.25
69 Wayne Simmonds .50 1.25
70 Ryan Smyth .30 .75
71 Mikko Koivu .40 1.00
72 Cal Clutterbuck .25 .60
73 Niklas Backstrom .40 1.00
74 Guillaume Latendresse .30 .75
75 Carey Price .75 2.00
76 Tomas Plekanec .25 .60
77 Scott Gomez .30 .75
78 Michael Cammalleri .40 1.00
79 Brian Gionta .25 .60
80 Pekka Rinne .40 1.00
81 Patric Hornqvist .25 .60
82 Shea Weber .30 .75
83 Colin Wilson .30 .75
84 Jordin Tootoo .30 .75
85 Martin Brodeur 1.00 2.50
86 Zach Parise .30 .75
87 Ilya Kovalchuk .40 1.00
88 Travis Zajac .25 .60
89 Andy Greene .25 .60
90 John Tavares .60 1.50
91 Matt Moulson .30 .75
92 Kyle Okposo .25 .60
93 Josh Bailey .25 .60
94 Dwayne Roloson .30 .75
95 Henrik Lundqvist 1.00 2.50
96 Marian Gaborik .40 1.00
97 Artem Anisimov .25 .60
98 Michael Del Zotto .30 .75
99 Marc Staal .25 .60
100 Daniel Alfredsson .40 1.00
101 Jason Spezza .40 1.00
102 Mike Fisher .25 .60
103 Brian Elliott .30 .75
104 Erik Karlsson .50 1.25
105 Mike Richards .30 .75
106 Jeff Carter .30 .75
107 Chris Pronger .40 1.00

108 Claude Giroux .40 1.00
109 Simon Gagne .40 1.00
110 Michael Leighton .30 .75
111 Ilya Bryzgalov .30 .75
112 Shane Doan .30 .75
113 Wojtek Wolski .25 .60
114 Mikkel Boedker .25 .60
115 Sidney Crosby 1.50 4.00
116 Evgeni Malkin .75 2.00
117 Marc-Andre Fleury .75 2.00
118 Jordan Staal .30 .75
119 Alex Goligoski .30 .75
120 Dany Heatley .30 .75
121 Joe Thornton .60 1.50
122 Dan Boyle .25 .60
123 Patrick Marleau .40 1.00
124 Joe Pavelski .50 1.25
125 T.J. Oshie .40 1.00
126 David Backes .25 .60
127 Erik Johnson .25 .60
128 David Perron .30 .75
129 Jaroslav Halak .40 1.00
130 Steven Stamkos .75 2.00
131 Vincent Lecavalier .40 1.00
132 Martin St. Louis .40 1.00
133 Steve Downie .25 .60
134 Phil Kessel .40 1.00
135 Jonas Gustavsson .50 1.25
136 Jean-Sebastien Giguere .40 1.00
137 Dion Phaneuf .30 .75
138 Luca Caputi .30 .75
139 Henrik Sedin .50 1.25
140 Daniel Sedin .50 1.25
141 Alexandre Burrows .25 .60
142 Roberto Luongo .60 1.50
143 Ryan Kesler .40 1.00
144 Cory Schneider .40 1.00
145 Alexander Ovechkin 1.50 4.00
146 Mike Green .30 .75
147 Semyon Varlamov .40 1.00
148 John Carlson .40 1.00
149 Nicklas Backstrom .40 1.00
150 Alexander Semin .40 1.00
151 Cam Neely 2.00 5.00
152 Steve Yzerman 5.00 12.00
153 Bobby Hull 4.00 10.00
154 Ed Giacomin 3.00 8.00
155 Jean Beliveau 2.00 5.00
156 Mario Lemieux 8.00 20.00
157 Ray Bourque 3.00 8.00
158 Gilbert Perreault 2.00 5.00
159 Patrick Roy 5.00 12.00
160 Bryan Trottier 2.00 5.00
161 Stan Mikita 2.50 6.00
162 Pat LaFontaine 2.00 5.00
163 Grant Fuhr 3.00 8.00
164 Phil Esposito 3.00 8.00
165 Tony Esposito 2.00 5.00
166 Guy Lafleur 2.50 6.00
167 Glenn Hall 2.00 5.00
168 Lanny McDonald 2.00 5.00
169 Eric Lindros 3.00 8.00
170 Trevor Linden 2.00 5.00
171 Nick Bonino AU RC 3.00 8.00
172 Justin Mercier AU RC 2.50 6.00
173 Philip Larsen AU RC 2.50 6.00
174 Casey Wellman AU RC 2.50 6.00
175 Jamie McBain AU RC 2.50 6.00
176 Brandon Yip AU RC 2.50 6.00
177 Nick Palmieri AU RC 2.50 6.00
178 Maxim Noreau AU RC 2.00 5.00
179 Nick Spaling AU RC 2.50 6.00
180 Nick Johnson AU RC 2.00 5.00
181 Zach Hamill AU RC 2.50 6.00
182 Dustin Tokarski AU RC 2.50 6.00
183 Bobby Butler AU RC 2.50 6.00
184 Jared Cowen AU RC 2.50 6.00
185 Nazem Kadri AU RC 10.00 25.00
186 P.K. Subban AU RC 12.00 30.00
187 Brayden Irwin AU RC 3.00 8.00
188 Eric Tangradi AU RC 3.00 8.00
189 Taylor Hall JSY AU RC 25.00 50.00
190 Tyler Seguin JSY AU RC 25.00 50.00
191 Cam Fowler JSY AU RC 12.00 30.00
192 Jordan Eberle JSY AU RC 15.00 40.00
193 M.Paajarvi JSY AU RC 6.00 15.00
194 A.Burmistrov JSY AU RC 5.00 12.00
195 M.Tedenby JSY AU RC 5.00 12.00
196 K.Shattenkirk JSY AU RC 10.00 25.00
197 Derek Stepan JSY AU RC 6.00 15.00
198 B.Schenn JSY AU RC 12.00 30.00
199 Jeff Skinner JSY AU RC 12.00 30.00
200 N.Niederreiter JSY AU RC 8.00 20.00
201 Brad Thiessen AU RC 6.00 15.00
202 James Wyman AU RC 4.00 10.00
203 Corey Elkins AU RC 3.00 8.00
204 Jerome Samson AU RC 4.00 10.00
205 Jeremy Duchesne AU RC 5.00 12.00
206 Derek Smith AU RC 4.00 10.00
207 Bryan Pitton AU RC 5.00 12.00
208 Carter Hutton AU RC 10.00 25.00
209 Matt Martin AU RC 6.00 15.00
210 Jean-Philippe Levasseur AU RC 4.00 10.00
211 Marc-Andre Cliche AU RC 3.00 8.00
212 Brock Trotter NO AU RC 40.00 80.00
RM Ryan Miller Preview .50 1.25

2010-11 Certified Mirror Blue

*BLUE (1-150): 2.5X TO 6X BASE
*BLUE (151-170): .5X TO 1.2X BASE
*BLUE AU (171-184): .8X TO 2X BASE
*BLUE AU (185-188): .6X TO 1.5X BASE
*BLUE JSY AU (189-200): .6X TO 1.5X BASE
*BLUE AU (201-212): .6X TO 1.5X BASE
149 Nicklas Backstrom 2.50 6.00
186 P.K. Subban AU 25.00 60.00
189 Taylor Hall JSY AU 30.00 80.00
192 Jordan Eberle JSY AU 20.00 50.00

2010-11 Certified Mirror Blue Materials

1 Ryan Getzlaf 3.00 8.00
2 Corey Perry 5.00 12.00
3 Teemu Selanne 6.00 15.00
4 Bobby Ryan 2.50 6.00
5 Jonas Hiller 2.50 6.00
6 Evander Kane 3.00 8.00
7 Zach Bogosian 2.50 6.00
8 Dustin Byfuglien 3.00 8.00
9 Nik Antropov 2.50 6.00
10 Ondrej Pavelec 3.00 8.00
11 Milan Lucic 3.00 8.00
12 Patrice Bergeron 4.00 10.00
13 Zdeno Chara 3.00 8.00
14 Nathan Horton 2.50 6.00
15 Tuukka Rask 4.00 10.00
16 Ryan Miller 3.00 8.00
17 Thomas Vanek 2.50 6.00
18 Tyler Myers 2.00 5.00
19 Nathan Gerbe 2.00 5.00
20 Derek Roy 2.00 5.00
21 Jarome Iginla 4.00 10.00
22 Miikka Kiprusoff 3.00 8.00
23 Rene Bourque 2.00 5.00
24 Mikael Backlund 2.50 6.00
25 Jay Bouwmeester 2.00 5.00
26 Brandon Sutter 2.00 5.00
27 Eric Staal 4.00 10.00
28 Cam Ward 3.00 8.00
29 Zach Boychuk 2.50 6.00
30 Drayson Bowman 2.50 6.00
31 Jonathan Toews 5.00 12.00
32 Patrick Kane 6.00 15.00
33 Duncan Keith 2.50 6.00
34 Marty Turco 3.00 8.00
35 Patrick Sharp 3.00 8.00
36 Marian Hossa 3.00 8.00
37 Craig Anderson 3.00 8.00
38 Matt Duchene 3.00 8.00
39 Chris Stewart 2.50 6.00
40 Peter Mueller 2.50 6.00
41 Paul Stastny 2.50 6.00
42 Rick Nash 3.00 8.00
43 Steve Mason 2.50 6.00
44 Jakub Voracek 2.50 6.00
45 Antoine Vermette 2.00 5.00
46 James Neal 2.00 5.00
47 Jamie Benn 4.00 10.00
48 Steve Ott 2.00 5.00
49 Kari Lehtonen 2.50 6.00
50 Brad Richards 3.00 8.00
51 Pavel Datsyuk 5.00 12.00
52 Henrik Zetterberg 4.00 10.00
53 Jimmy Howard 4.00 10.00
54 Nicklas Lidstrom 3.00 8.00
55 Johan Franzen 2.50 6.00
56 Tomas Holmstrom 2.00 5.00
57 Ales Hemsky 2.50 6.00
58 Sam Gagner 2.00 5.00
59 Dustin Penner 2.00 5.00
60 Jeff Deslauriers 2.00 5.00
61 Nikolai Khabibulin 2.50 6.00
62 Tomas Vokoun 2.50 6.00
63 Stephen Weiss 2.50 6.00
64 Dmitri Kulikov 2.50 6.00
65 Michael Frolik 2.00 5.00
66 Drew Doughty 4.00 10.00
67 Anze Kopitar 5.00 12.00
68 Jonathan Quick 4.00 10.00
69 Wayne Simmonds 4.00 10.00
70 Ryan Smyth 2.50 6.00
71 Mikko Koivu 3.00 8.00
72 Cal Clutterbuck 2.00 5.00
73 Niklas Backstrom 3.00 8.00
74 Guillaume Latendresse 2.50 6.00
75 Carey Price 6.00 15.00
76 Tomas Plekanec 2.00 5.00
77 Scott Gomez 2.50 6.00
78 Michael Cammalleri 3.00 8.00
79 Brian Gionta 2.00 5.00
80 Pekka Rinne 3.00 8.00
81 Patric Hornqvist 2.00 5.00
82 Shea Weber 2.50 6.00
83 Colin Wilson 2.50 6.00
84 Jordin Tootoo 2.50 6.00
85 Martin Brodeur 8.00 20.00
86 Zach Parise 3.00 8.00
87 Ilya Kovalchuk 3.00 8.00
88 Travis Zajac 2.00 5.00
89 Andy Greene 2.00 5.00
90 John Tavares 5.00 12.00
91 Matt Moulson 2.50 6.00
92 Kyle Okposo 2.00 5.00
93 Josh Bailey 2.50 6.00
94 Dwayne Roloson 2.50 6.00
95 Henrik Lundqvist 8.00 20.00
96 Marian Gaborik 3.00 8.00
97 Artem Anisimov 2.00 5.00
98 Michael Del Zotto 2.50 6.00
99 Marc Staal 2.00 5.00
100 Daniel Alfredsson 3.00 8.00
101 Jason Spezza 3.00 8.00
102 Mike Fisher 2.00 5.00
103 Brian Elliott 2.50 6.00
104 Erik Karlsson 4.00 10.00
105 Mike Richards 2.50 6.00
106 Jeff Carter 2.50 6.00
107 Chris Pronger 3.00 8.00
108 Claude Giroux 3.00 8.00
109 Simon Gagne 3.00 8.00
110 Michael Leighton 2.50 6.00
111 Ilya Bryzgalov 2.50 6.00
112 Shane Doan 2.50 6.00
113 Wojtek Wolski 2.00 5.00
114 Mikkel Boedker 2.00 5.00
115 Sidney Crosby 12.00 30.00
116 Evgeni Malkin 6.00 15.00
117 Marc-Andre Fleury 6.00 15.00
118 Jordan Staal 2.50 6.00
119 Alex Goligoski 2.50 6.00
120 Dany Heatley 2.50 6.00
121 Joe Thornton 5.00 12.00
122 Dan Boyle 2.00 5.00
123 Patrick Marleau 3.00 8.00
124 Joe Pavelski 4.00 10.00
125 T.J. Oshie 3.00 8.00
126 David Backes 2.00 5.00
127 Erik Johnson 2.00 5.00
128 David Perron 2.50 6.00
129 Jaroslav Halak 3.00 8.00
130 Steven Stamkos 6.00 15.00
131 Vincent Lecavalier 3.00 8.00
132 Martin St. Louis 3.00 8.00
133 Steve Downie 2.00 5.00
134 Phil Kessel 3.00 8.00
135 Jonas Gustavsson 4.00 10.00
136 Jean-Sebastien Giguere 3.00 8.00
137 Dion Phaneuf 2.50 6.00
138 Luca Caputi 2.50 6.00
139 Henrik Sedin 4.00 10.00
140 Daniel Sedin 4.00 10.00
141 Alexandre Burrows 2.00 5.00
142 Roberto Luongo 5.00 12.00
143 Ryan Kesler 3.00 8.00
144 Cory Schneider 3.00 8.00
145 Alexander Ovechkin 12.00 30.00
146 Mike Green 2.50 6.00
147 Semyon Varlamov 3.00 8.00
148 John Carlson 3.00 8.00
149 Nicklas Backstrom 3.00 8.00
150 Alexander Semin 3.00 8.00
151 Cam Neely 3.00 8.00
152 Steve Yzerman 8.00 20.00
153 Bobby Hull 6.00 15.00
154 Ed Giacomin 5.00 12.00
155 Jean Beliveau 3.00 8.00
156 Mario Lemieux 12.00 30.00
157 Ray Bourque 5.00 12.00
158 Gilbert Perreault 3.00 8.00
159 Patrick Roy 8.00 20.00
160 Bryan Trottier 3.00 8.00
161 Stan Mikita 4.00 10.00
162 Pat LaFontaine 3.00 8.00
163 Grant Fuhr 5.00 12.00
164 Phil Esposito 5.00 12.00
165 Tony Esposito 3.00 8.00
166 Guy Lafleur 4.00 10.00
167 Glenn Hall 3.00 8.00
168 Lanny McDonald 3.00 8.00
169 Eric Lindros 5.00 12.00
170 Trevor Linden 3.00 8.00

2010-11 Certified Mirror Blue Signatures

5 Jonas Hiller 5.00 12.00
7 Zach Bogosian 5.00 12.00
8 Dustin Byfuglien 6.00 15.00
19 Nathan Gerbe 4.00 10.00
26 Brandon Sutter 4.00 10.00
29 Zach Boychuk 5.00 12.00
37 Craig Anderson 6.00 15.00
40 Peter Mueller 5.00 12.00
41 Paul Stastny 5.00 12.00
45 Antoine Vermette 4.00 10.00
46 James Neal 4.00 10.00
47 Jamie Benn 8.00 20.00
49 Kari Lehtonen 5.00 12.00
53 Jimmy Howard 8.00 20.00
58 Sam Gagner 4.00 10.00
59 Dustin Penner 4.00 10.00
60 Jeff Deslauriers 4.00 10.00
65 Michael Frolik 4.00 10.00
74 Guillaume Latendresse 5.00 12.00
79 Brian Gionta 4.00 10.00
81 Patric Hornqvist 4.00 10.00
83 Colin Wilson 5.00 12.00
91 Matt Moulson 5.00 12.00
93 Josh Bailey 5.00 12.00
94 Dwayne Roloson 5.00 12.00
97 Artem Anisimov 4.00 10.00
99 Marc Staal 4.00 10.00
102 Mike Fisher 4.00 10.00
103 Brian Elliott 5.00 12.00
108 Claude Giroux 6.00 15.00
110 Michael Leighton 5.00 12.00
113 Wojtek Wolski 4.00 10.00
114 Mikkel Boedker 4.00 10.00
119 Alex Goligoski 5.00 12.00
122 Dan Boyle 4.00 10.00
124 Joe Pavelski 8.00 20.00
126 David Backes 4.00 10.00
133 Steve Downie 4.00 10.00
138 Luca Caputi 5.00 12.00
141 Alexandre Burrows 12.00 30.00
143 Ryan Kesler 6.00 15.00
144 Cory Schneider 6.00 15.00
148 John Carlson 10.00 25.00

2010-11 Certified Mirror Gold

*GOLD (1-150): 4X TO 10X BASE
*GOLD (151-170): .8X TO 2X BASE
*GOLD AU (171-184): 1.2X TO 3X BASE
*GOLD AU (185-188): 1X TO 2.5X BASE
*GOLD JSY AU (189-200): 1X TO 2.5X BASE
*GOLD AU (201-212): .8X TO 2X BASE
149 Nicklas Backstrom 4.00 10.00
186 P.K. Subban AU 40.00 100.00
189 Taylor Hall JSY AU 60.00 120.00
192 Jordan Eberle JSY AU 50.00 120.00

2010-11 Certified Mirror Gold Materials Prime

*GOLD: 1X TO 2.5X MIRROR BLUE MATERIALS
149 Nicklas Backstrom 10.00 25.00

2010-11 Certified Mirror Gold Signatures

1 Ryan Getzlaf 15.00 40.00
2 Corey Perry 12.00 30.00
3 Teemu Selanne 12.00 30.00
4 Bobby Ryan 6.00 15.00
5 Jonas Hiller 6.00 15.00
6 Evander Kane 8.00 20.00
7 Zach Bogosian 6.00 15.00
8 Dustin Byfuglien 8.00 20.00
9 Nik Antropov 6.00 15.00
13 Zdeno Chara 8.00 20.00
14 Nathan Horton 6.00 15.00
16 Ryan Miller 8.00 20.00
17 Thomas Vanek 6.00 15.00
18 Tyler Myers 5.00 12.00
19 Nathan Gerbe 5.00 12.00
20 Derek Roy 5.00 12.00
21 Jarome Iginla 15.00 40.00
23 Rene Bourque 5.00 12.00
24 Mikael Backlund 8.00 20.00
25 Jay Bouwmeester 12.00 30.00
26 Brandon Sutter 5.00 12.00
27 Eric Staal 10.00 25.00
28 Cam Ward 10.00 25.00
29 Zach Boychuk 6.00 15.00
30 Drayson Bowman 6.00 15.00
31 Jonathan Toews 10.00 25.00
32 Patrick Kane 25.00 60.00
35 Patrick Sharp 15.00 40.00
36 Marian Hossa 15.00 40.00
37 Craig Anderson 15.00 40.00
38 Matt Duchene 20.00 50.00
39 Chris Stewart 6.00 15.00
40 Peter Mueller 6.00 15.00
41 Paul Stastny 6.00 15.00
42 Rick Nash 12.00 30.00
43 Steve Mason 6.00 15.00
44 Jakub Voracek 6.00 15.00
45 Antoine Vermette 5.00 12.00
46 James Neal 5.00 12.00
47 Jamie Benn 10.00 25.00
48 Steve Ott 5.00 12.00
51 Pavel Datsyuk 15.00 40.00
53 Jimmy Howard 10.00 25.00
54 Nicklas Lidstrom 15.00 40.00
55 Johan Franzen 10.00 25.00
56 Tomas Holmstrom 12.00 30.00
57 Ales Hemsky 6.00 15.00
59 Dustin Penner 5.00 12.00
60 Jeff Deslauriers 5.00 12.00
62 Tomas Vokoun 6.00 15.00
63 Stephen Weiss 8.00 20.00
65 Michael Frolik 5.00 12.00
66 Drew Doughty 20.00 50.00
67 Anze Kopitar 12.00 30.00
68 Jonathan Quick 20.00 40.00
69 Wayne Simmonds 8.00 20.00
70 Ryan Smyth 6.00 15.00
72 Cal Clutterbuck 5.00 12.00
73 Niklas Backstrom 8.00 20.00
74 Guillaume Latendresse 6.00 15.00
75 Carey Price 20.00 50.00
77 Scott Gomez 6.00 15.00
78 Michael Cammalleri 8.00 20.00
79 Brian Gionta 5.00 12.00
80 Pekka Rinne 12.00 30.00
81 Patric Hornqvist 5.00 12.00
82 Shea Weber 6.00 15.00
84 Jordin Tootoo 6.00 15.00
85 Martin Brodeur 40.00 80.00
86 Zach Parise 10.00 30.00
87 Ilya Kovalchuk 15.00 40.00
89 Andy Greene 5.00 12.00
90 John Tavares 12.00 30.00
91 Matt Moulson 6.00 15.00
93 Josh Bailey 6.00 15.00
94 Dwayne Roloson 6.00 15.00
95 Henrik Lundqvist 20.00 50.00
97 Artem Anisimov 5.00 12.00
99 Marc Staal 5.00 12.00
100 Daniel Alfredsson 8.00 20.00
101 Jason Spezza 12.00 30.00
102 Mike Fisher 5.00 12.00
104 Erik Karlsson 15.00 40.00
105 Mike Richards 15.00 40.00
106 Jeff Carter 15.00 40.00
107 Chris Pronger 8.00 20.00
108 Claude Giroux 15.00 40.00
109 Simon Gagne 8.00 20.00
110 Michael Leighton 6.00 15.00
111 Ilya Bryzgalov 6.00 15.00
112 Shane Doan 6.00 15.00
113 Wojtek Wolski 5.00 12.00
115 Sidney Crosby 75.00 150.00
116 Evgeni Malkin 15.00 40.00
118 Jordan Staal 15.00 40.00
119 Alex Goligoski 10.00 25.00
120 Dany Heatley 6.00 15.00
121 Joe Thornton 15.00 40.00
122 Dan Boyle 5.00 12.00
123 Patrick Marleau 8.00 20.00
124 Joe Pavelski 15.00 40.00
125 T.J. Oshie 8.00 20.00
126 David Backes 5.00 12.00
127 Erik Johnson 5.00 12.00
128 David Perron 6.00 15.00
130 Steven Stamkos 25.00 60.00
131 Vincent Lecavalier 8.00 20.00
132 Martin St. Louis 12.00 30.00
133 Steve Downie 5.00 12.00
134 Phil Kessel 8.00 20.00
135 Jonas Gustavsson 10.00 25.00
137 Dion Phaneuf 6.00 15.00
138 Luca Caputi 6.00 15.00
139 Henrik Sedin 10.00 25.00
140 Daniel Sedin 12.00 30.00
141 Alexandre Burrows 15.00 40.00
143 Ryan Kesler 15.00 40.00
144 Cory Schneider 12.00 30.00
145 Alexander Ovechkin 50.00 100.00
146 Mike Green 6.00 15.00
147 Semyon Varlamov 8.00 20.00
148 John Carlson 12.00 30.00
150 Alexander Semin 8.00 20.00
151 Cam Neely 15.00 30.00
152 Steve Yzerman 50.00 100.00
153 Bobby Hull 20.00 50.00
155 Jean Beliveau 25.00 60.00
156 Mario Lemieux 60.00 120.00
157 Ray Bourque 12.00 30.00
160 Bryan Trottier 6.00 15.00
162 Pat LaFontaine 10.00 25.00
163 Grant Fuhr 10.00 25.00
164 Phil Esposito 20.00 40.00
165 Tony Esposito 12.00 30.00
166 Guy Lafleur 12.00 30.00
167 Glenn Hall 8.00 20.00
168 Lanny McDonald 8.00 20.00
169 Eric Lindros 20.00 50.00
170 Trevor Linden 25.00 60.00

2010-11 Certified Mirror Red

*RED (1-150): 2X TO 5X BASE
*RED (151-170): .4X TO 1X BASE
*RED AU (171-184): .6X TO 1.5X BASE
*RED AU (185-188): .5X TO 1.2X BASE
*RED JSY AU (189-200): .5X TO 1.2X BASE
*RED AU (201-212): .5X TO 1.2X BASE
149 Nicklas Backstrom 2.00 5.00
189 Taylor Hall JSY AU 30.00 80.00
192 Jordan Eberle JSY AU 15.00 40.00

2010-11 Certified Mirror Red Materials Dual

*SINGLES: .4X TO 1X MIRROR BLUE MATERIALS
149 Nicklas Backstrom 4.00 10.00

2010-11 Certified Platinum Blue

*SINGLES: 2X TO 5X BASIC CARDS
149 Nicklas Backstrom 2.00 5.00

2010-11 Certified Platinum Gold

*SINGLES: 4X TO 10X BASIC CARDS
149 Nicklas Backstrom 4.00 10.00

2010-11 Certified Platinum Red

*SINGLES: 1.2X TO 3X BASIC CARDS
149 Nicklas Backstrom 1.25 3.00

2010-11 Certified Big Men On Campus Jerseys

*PRIME/25: 1X TO 2.5X BASIC JSY/150-250
*PRIME/25: .6X TO 1.5X BASIC JSY/100
1 Joe Pavelski 5.00 12.00
2 Michael Cammalleri/100 6.00 15.00
3 Jonathan Quick 5.00 12.00
4 Brian Gionta 8.00 20.00
5 Zach Parise 4.00 10.00
6 Jonathan Toews/150 6.00 15.00
7 Ryan Miller 4.00 10.00
8 Tim Thomas 5.00 12.00
9 Kyle Okposo 2.50 6.00
10 Paul Stastny 3.00 8.00
11 Tyler Bozak 2.50 6.00
12 Travis Zajac 4.00 10.00
13 Martin St. Louis 4.00 10.00
14 Colin Wilson 3.00 8.00
15 Brett Hull 8.00 20.00

2010-11 Certified Champions

1 Jonathan Toews 3.00 8.00
2 Patrick Kane 4.00 10.00
3 Antti Niemi 1.50 4.00
4 Dustin Byfuglien 2.00 5.00
5 Patrick Sharp 2.00 5.00
6 Marc-Andre Fleury 4.00 10.00
7 Sidney Crosby 6.00 15.00
8 Evgeni Malkin 4.00 10.00
9 Jordan Staal 1.50 4.00
10 Nicklas Lidstrom 2.00 5.00
11 Dan Boyle 1.25 3.00
12 Teemu Selanne 4.00 10.00
13 Ryan Getzlaf 2.00 5.00
14 Corey Perry 3.00 8.00
15 Cam Ward 2.00 5.00
16 Eric Staal 2.50 6.00
17 Martin St. Louis 2.00 5.00
18 Vincent Lecavalier 2.00 5.00
19 Nikolai Khabibulin 1.50 4.00
20 Luc Robitaille 2.50 6.00
21 Mario Lemieux 5.00 12.00
22 Tom Barrasso 2.50 6.00
23 Paul Coffey 2.50 6.00
24 Patrick Roy 6.00 15.00
25 Brett Hull 5.00 12.00
JT Jonathan Toews Preview 1.00 2.50

2010-11 Certified Champions Autographs

1 Jonathan Toews 20.00 50.00
2 Patrick Kane 20.00 50.00
4 Dustin Byfuglien 8.00 20.00
5 Patrick Sharp 25.00 60.00
6 Marc-Andre Fleury 12.00 30.00
8 Evgeni Malkin 20.00 50.00
9 Jordan Staal 10.00 25.00
10 Nicklas Lidstrom 12.00 30.00
11 Dan Boyle 5.00 12.00
12 Teemu Selanne 15.00 40.00
13 Ryan Getzlaf 8.00 20.00
14 Corey Perry 12.00 30.00
15 Cam Ward 8.00 20.00
16 Eric Staal 10.00 25.00
17 Martin St. Louis 8.00 20.00
20 Luc Robitaille 12.00 30.00
22 Tom Barrasso 10.00 25.00
23 Paul Coffey 8.00 20.00
25 Brett Hull 15.00 40.00

2010-11 Certified Champions Materials

1 Jonathan Toews 8.00 20.00
2 Patrick Kane 10.00 25.00
3 Antti Niemi 4.00 10.00
5 Patrick Sharp 10.00 25.00
6 Marc-Andre Fleury 8.00 20.00
7 Sidney Crosby 20.00 50.00
8 Evgeni Malkin 8.00 20.00
9 Jordan Staal 4.00 10.00
10 Nicklas Lidstrom 5.00 12.00
12 Teemu Selanne 6.00 15.00
13 Ryan Getzlaf 5.00 12.00
14 Corey Perry 8.00 20.00
16 Eric Staal 6.00 15.00
17 Martin St. Louis 5.00 12.00
18 Vincent Lecavalier 5.00 12.00
19 Nikolai Khabibulin 4.00 10.00
20 Luc Robitaille 6.00 15.00
21 Mario Lemieux 10.00 25.00
22 Tom Barrasso 6.00 15.00
23 Paul Coffey 6.00 15.00
24 Patrick Roy 15.00 40.00
25 Brett Hull 12.00 30.00

2010-11 Certified Champions Mirror Blue

*SINGLES: .6X TO 1.5X BASIC INSERTS

2010-11 Certified Champions Mirror Gold

*SINGLES: 1X TO 2.5X BASIC INSERTS

2010-11 Certified Champions Mirror Red

*SINGLES: .5X TO 1.2X BASIC INSERTS

2010-11 Certified Collision Course

*BLUE/100: .6X TO 1.5X BASIC INSERTS
*GOLD/25: 1X TO 2.5X BASIC INSERTS
*RED/250: .5X TO 1.2X BASIC INSERTS
1 Cal Clutterbuck 1.50 4.00
2 David Backes 1.50 4.00
3 Dustin Byfuglien 2.50 6.00
4 Steve Ott 1.50 4.00
5 Zenon Konopka 2.00 5.00
6 Colton Orr 1.50 4.00
7 Daniel Carcillo 1.50 4.00
8 George Parros 2.00 5.00
9 Milan Lucic 2.50 6.00
10 Drew Doughty 3.00 8.00

2010-11 Certified Collision Course Autographs

1 Cal Clutterbuck 5.00 12.00
2 David Backes 5.00 12.00
3 Dustin Byfuglien 10.00 25.00
4 Steve Ott 5.00 12.00
5 Zenon Konopka 6.00 15.00
6 Colton Orr 12.00 30.00
7 Daniel Carcillo 10.00 25.00
8 George Parros 6.00 15.00
9 Milan Lucic 8.00 20.00
10 Drew Doughty 10.00 25.00

2010-11 Certified Fabric of the Game

*PRIME/25: 1X TO 2.5X BASIC FOTG
*JSY NUM/25: .8X TO 2X BASIC FOTG
*NHL DC/25: .8X TO 2X BASIC FOTG
*TEAM DC/25: .8X TO 2X BASIC FOTG
AB Alexandre Burrows 2.00 5.00
AG Andy Greene 2.00 5.00
AGO Alex Goligoski 2.50 6.00
AH Ales Hemsky 2.50 6.00
AK Anze Kopitar 5.00 12.00
AN Antti Niemi 2.50 6.00
AO Alexander Ovechkin 8.00 20.00
AS Alexander Semin 3.00 8.00
BE Brian Elliott 2.50 6.00
BG Brian Gionta 2.00 5.00
BR Brad Richards 3.00 8.00
CA Craig Anderson 3.00 8.00
CAP Carey Price 6.00 15.00
CG Claude Giroux 3.00 8.00
COS Cory Schneider 3.00 8.00
COW Colin Wilson 2.50 6.00
CP Corey Perry 5.00 12.00
CPR Chris Pronger 3.00 8.00
CS Chris Stewart 2.50 6.00
DA Daniel Alfredsson 3.00 8.00
DD Drew Doughty 4.00 10.00
DIP Dion Phaneuf 2.50 6.00
DK Dmitri Kulikov 2.50 6.00
DR Derek Roy 2.00 5.00
DS Daniel Sedin 4.00 10.00
DUK Duncan Keith 2.50 6.00
DUP Dustin Penner 2.00 5.00
EK Erik Karlsson 4.00 10.00
EM Evgeni Malkin 6.00 15.00
ES Eric Staal 4.00 10.00
EVK Evander Kane 3.00 8.00
HL Henrik Lundqvist 8.00 20.00
HS Henrik Sedin 4.00 10.00
HZ Henrik Zetterberg 4.00 10.00
IK Ilya Kovalchuk 3.00 8.00
JAB Jay Bouwmeester 2.00 5.00
JB Jamie Benn 4.00 10.00
JC Jeff Carter 2.50 6.00
JD Jeff Deslauriers 2.00 5.00
JG Jean-Sebastien Giguere 3.00 8.00
JH Jaroslav Halak 3.00 8.00
JI Jarome Iginla 4.00 10.00
JN James Neal 2.00 5.00
JOB Josh Bailey 2.50 6.00
JOC John Carlson 3.00 8.00
JOG Jonas Gustavsson 4.00 10.00
JOH Jonas Hiller 2.50 6.00
JOS Jordan Staal 2.50 6.00
JP Joe Pavelski 4.00 10.00
JQ Jonathan Quick 5.00 12.00
JS Jason Spezza 3.00 8.00
JT Jordin Tootoo 2.50 6.00
JTA John Tavares 5.00 12.00
JTO Jonathan Toews 5.00 12.00
KO Kyle Okposo 2.00 5.00
LC Luca Caputi 2.50 6.00
MAB Martin Brodeur 8.00 20.00
MB Mikael Backlund 2.50 6.00
MC Michael Cammalleri 3.00 8.00
MD Matt Duchene 3.00 8.00
MF Marc-Andre Fleury 6.00 15.00
MFI Mike Fisher 2.00 5.00
MG Marian Gaborik 3.00 8.00
MID Michael Del Zotto 2.50 6.00
MIG Mike Green 2.50 6.00
MIK Miikka Kiprusoff 3.00 8.00
MLU Milan Lucic 3.00 8.00
MM Matt Moulson 2.50 6.00
MS Marc Staal 2.00 5.00
MSL Martin St. Louis 3.00 8.00
NA Nik Antropov 2.50 6.00
NCB Nicklas Backstrom 3.00 8.00
NH Nathan Horton 2.50 6.00
NL Nicklas Lidstrom 3.00 8.00
OP Ondrej Pavelec 3.00 8.00
PB Patrice Bergeron 4.00 10.00
PD Pavel Datsyuk 5.00 12.00
PEM Peter Mueller 2.50 6.00
PH Patric Hornqvist 2.00 5.00
PK Patrick Kane 6.00 15.00
PKE Phil Kessel 3.00 8.00
PM Patrick Marleau 3.00 8.00
PR Pekka Rinne 3.00 8.00
PS Patrick Sharp 3.00 8.00
PST Paul Stastny 2.50 6.00
RB Rene Bourque 2.00 5.00
RG Ryan Getzlaf 3.00 8.00
RK Ryan Kesler 3.00 8.00
RL Roberto Luongo 5.00 12.00
RM Ryan Miller 3.00 8.00
RN Rick Nash 3.00 8.00
SC Sidney Crosby 12.00 30.00
SCG Scott Gomez 2.50 6.00
SD Shane Doan 2.50 6.00
SG Sam Gagner 2.00 5.00
SM Steve Mason 2.50 6.00
SO Steve Ott 2.00 5.00
SS Steven Stamkos 6.00 15.00
STD Steve Downie 2.00 5.00
STW Stephen Weiss 2.50 6.00
SV Semyon Varlamov 3.00 8.00
SW Shea Weber 2.50 6.00
TOV Tomas Vokoun 2.50 6.00
TP Tomas Plekanec 2.00 5.00
TR Tuukka Rask 4.00 10.00
TS Teemu Selanne 5.00 12.00
TZ Travis Zajac 2.00 5.00
VL Vincent Lecavalier 3.00 8.00
ZB Zach Bogosian 2.50 6.00
ZC Zdeno Chara 3.00 8.00
ZP Zach Parise 3.00 8.00

2010-11 Certified Fabric of the Game Jersey Number Autographs

AB Alexandre Burrows 15.00 40.00
AGO Alex Goligoski 25.00 60.00
AH Ales Hemsky 15.00 40.00
AK Anze Kopitar 15.00 40.00
AO Alexander Ovechkin 40.00 80.00
AS Alexander Semin 10.00 25.00
BE Brian Elliott 8.00 20.00
BG Brian Gionta 6.00 15.00
BR Brad Richards 12.00 30.00
CA Craig Anderson 20.00 50.00
CAP Carey Price 40.00 80.00
CG Claude Giroux 20.00 40.00
COS Cory Schneider 15.00 40.00
COW Colin Wilson 8.00 20.00
CP Corey Perry 15.00 40.00
CPR Chris Pronger 20.00 50.00
DA Daniel Alfredsson 10.00 25.00
DS Daniel Sedin 12.00 30.00
DUP Dustin Penner 8.00 20.00
EM Evgeni Malkin 30.00 60.00
HL Henrik Lundqvist 25.00 60.00
IK Ilya Kovalchuk 12.00 30.00
JAB Jay Bouwmeester 6.00 15.00
JB Jamie Benn 12.00 30.00
JC Jeff Carter 12.00 30.00
JD Jeff Deslauriers 6.00 15.00
JH Jaroslav Halak 10.00 25.00
JI Jarome Iginla 12.00 30.00
JOB Josh Bailey 8.00 20.00
JOG Jonas Gustavsson 12.00 30.00
JOH Jonas Hiller 8.00 20.00
JOS Jordan Staal 15.00 40.00
JP Joe Pavelski 15.00 40.00
JQ Jonathan Quick 30.00 60.00
JS Jason Spezza 15.00 40.00
JTO Jonathan Toews 15.00 40.00
MAB Martin Brodeur 40.00 80.00
MC Michael Cammalleri 15.00 40.00
MD Matt Duchene 12.00 30.00
MF Marc-Andre Fleury 20.00 50.00
MFI Mike Fisher 6.00 15.00
MG Marian Gaborik 10.00 25.00
MM Matt Moulson 8.00 20.00
MS Marc Staal 6.00 15.00
MSL Martin St. Louis 10.00 25.00
NL Nicklas Lidstrom 15.00 40.00
PEM Peter Mueller 15.00 40.00
PH Patric Hornqvist 10.00 25.00
PKE Phil Kessel 15.00 40.00
PM Patrick Marleau 10.00 25.00
PR Pekka Rinne 15.00 40.00
PS Patrick Sharp 25.00 60.00
PST Paul Stastny 10.00 25.00
RK Ryan Kesler 20.00 50.00
RM Ryan Miller 10.00 25.00
RN Rick Nash 10.00 25.00
SC Sidney Crosby 60.00 120.00
SCG Scott Gomez 8.00 20.00
SG Sam Gagner 6.00 15.00
SO Steve Ott 6.00 15.00
STD Steve Downie 6.00 15.00
TOV Tomas Vokoun 12.00 30.00
VL Vincent Lecavalier 10.00 25.00
ZB Zach Bogosian 8.00 20.00
ZP Zach Parise 12.00 30.00

2010-11 Certified Junior Legacy Combos

1 Crosby/Lecavalier/50 15.00 40.00
2 C.Perry/R.Nash 6.00 15.00
3 Trottier/Sakic/50 12.00 30.00
4 J.Benn/L.Schenn 5.00 12.00
5 J.Theodore/L.Robitaille 4.00 10.00
6 D.Carcillo/S.Stamkos 8.00 20.00
7 P.Mueller/Z.Hamill 3.00 8.00
8 J.Spezza/M.Duchene 4.00 10.00
9 D.Hamhuis/Z.Chara 4.00 10.00
10 C.Armstrong/D.Phaneuf 3.00 8.00
11 J.Iginla/S.Doan 5.00 12.00
12 J.Spezza/S.Ott 4.00 10.00
13 J.Carter/P.Coffey 4.00 10.00
14 Pronger/Staal/50 8.00 20.00
15 R.Getzlaf/T.Galiardi 4.00 10.00
16 D.Roy/N.Kadri 6.00 15.00
17 C.Price/S.Gomez 8.00 20.00
18 J.Neal/S.Weiss 3.00 8.00
19 C.Anderson/D.Doughty 5.00 12.00
20 E.Lindros/J.Tavares/50 10.00 25.00

2010-11 Certified Junior Legacy Combos Prime

*SINGLES: 1X TO 2.5X BASIC INSERTS/250
*SINGLES: .6X TO 1.5X BASIC INSERTS/50
5 J.Theodore/L.Robitaille 12.00 30.00
18 J.Neal/S.Weiss 8.00 20.00

2010-11 Certified Legends

*BLUE/100: .6X TO 1.5X BASIC INSERTS
*GOLD/25: 1X TO 2.5X BASIC INSERTS
*RED/250: .5X TO 1.2X BASIC INSERTS
1 Ray Bourque 3.00 8.00
2 Bernie Parent 2.50 6.00
3 Bobby Clarke 3.00 8.00
4 Mario Lemieux 8.00 20.00
5 Steve Yzerman 5.00 12.00
6 Jean Beliveau 2.00 5.00
7 Henri Richard 2.00 5.00
8 Patrick Roy 5.00 12.00
9 Darryl Sittler 2.50 6.00
10 Paul Coffey 2.00 5.00
11 Bobby Hull 4.00 10.00
12 Jim Craig 1.50 4.00

2010-11 Certified Legends Autographs

1 Ray Bourque/100 20.00 50.00
2 Bernie Parent/95 12.00 30.00
3 Bobby Clarke/100 15.00 40.00
4 Mario Lemieux/25 80.00 200.00
5 Steve Yzerman/25 50.00 125.00

6 Jean Beliveau/100 25.00 50.00
7 Henri Richard/100 10.00 25.00
8 Patrick Roy/25 40.00 100.00
9 Darryl Sittler/100 12.00 30.00
10 Paul Coffey/50 15.00 40.00
11 Bobby Hull/50 30.00 80.00
12 Jim Craig/99 15.00 40.00

2010-11 Certified Masked Marvels

*BLUE/100: .6X TO 1.5X BASIC INSERTS
*GOLD/25: 1X TO 2.5X BASIC INSERTS
*RED/250: .5X TO 1.2X BASIC INSERTS
1 Antti Niemi 1.50 4.00
2 Semyon Varlamov 2.00 5.00
3 Jonas Gustavsson 2.50 6.00
4 Ryan Miller 2.00 5.00
5 Brian Elliott 1.50 4.00
6 Cam Ward 2.00 5.00
7 Jimmy Howard 2.50 6.00
8 Craig Anderson 2.00 5.00
9 Steve Mason 1.50 4.00
10 Jonathan Quick 2.50 6.00
11 Tuukka Rask 2.50 6.00
12 Steve Valiquette 1.50 4.00
13 Pekka Rinne 2.00 5.00
14 Henrik Lundqvist 5.00 12.00
15 Brad Thiessen 2.00 5.00
16 Ondrej Pavelec 2.00 5.00
17 Curtis McElhinney 1.25 3.00
18 Mathieu Garon 1.50 4.00
19 Carey Price 4.00 10.00
20 Pascal Leclaire 1.50 4.00
21 Michael Leighton 1.50 4.00
22 Ilya Bryzgalov 1.50 4.00
23 Jason Labarbera 1.50 4.00
24 Mike Smith 2.00 5.00
25 Michal Neuvirth 1.50 4.00
AN Antti Niemi Preview 1.00 2.50

2010-11 Certified Masked Marvels Materials

1 Antti Niemi 3.00 8.00
2 Semyon Varlamov 4.00 10.00
3 Jonas Gustavsson 5.00 12.00
4 Ryan Miller 4.00 10.00
5 Brian Elliott 3.00 8.00
8 Craig Anderson 4.00 10.00
10 Jonathan Quick 5.00 12.00
11 Tuukka Rask 8.00 20.00
12 Steve Valiquette 3.00 8.00
13 Pekka Rinne 4.00 10.00
14 Henrik Lundqvist 10.00 25.00
16 Ondrej Pavelec 4.00 10.00
17 Curtis McElhinney 2.50 6.00
19 Carey Price 8.00 20.00
22 Ilya Bryzgalov 3.00 8.00
24 Mike Smith 4.00 10.00

2010-11 Certified Masked Marvels Materials Autographs

2 Semyon Varlamov 10.00 25.00
3 Jonas Gustavsson 12.00 30.00
4 Ryan Miller 10.00 25.00
5 Brian Elliott 8.00 20.00
6 Cam Ward 10.00 25.00
8 Craig Anderson 10.00 25.00
10 Jonathan Quick 30.00 60.00
13 Pekka Rinne 12.00 30.00
14 Henrik Lundqvist 30.00 60.00
15 Brad Thiessen 10.00 25.00
16 Ondrej Pavelec 10.00 25.00
17 Curtis McElhinney 6.00 15.00
18 Mathieu Garon 8.00 20.00
19 Carey Price 30.00 60.00
20 Pascal Leclaire 8.00 20.00
21 Michael Leighton 8.00 20.00
22 Ilya Bryzgalov 10.00 25.00
24 Mike Smith 10.00 25.00

2010-11 Certified Potential

*BLUE/100: .6X TO 1.5X BASIC INSERTS
*GOLD/25: 1X TO 2.5X BASIC INSERTS
*RED/250: .5X TO 1.2X BASIC INSERTS
1 Nazem Kadri 6.00 15.00
2 Philip Larsen 1.50 4.00
3 Nick Bonino 2.00 5.00
4 Eric Tangradi 1.50 4.00
5 Bobby Butler 1.50 4.00
6 Nick Palmieri 1.50 4.00
7 Jared Cowen 1.50 4.00
8 P.K. Subban 5.00 12.00
9 Zach Hamill 1.50 4.00
10 John Tavares 3.00 8.00
11 Matt Duchene 2.00 5.00
12 Tyler Myers 1.25 3.00
13 Jimmy Howard 2.50 6.00
14 Jamie Benn 2.50 6.00
15 Tuukka Rask 2.50 6.00
16 Tyler Bozak 1.25 3.00
17 Colin Wilson 1.50 4.00
18 John Carlson 2.00 5.00
PS P.K. Subban Preview 2.00 5.00

2010-11 Certified Potential Materials

1 Nazem Kadri 10.00 25.00
2 Philip Larsen 3.00 8.00
5 Bobby Butler 3.00 8.00
6 Nick Palmieri 3.00 8.00
7 Jared Cowen 3.00 8.00
9 Zach Hamill 6.00 15.00
10 John Tavares 6.00 15.00
11 Matt Duchene 4.00 10.00
14 Jamie Benn 5.00 12.00
15 Tuukka Rask 5.00 12.00
16 Tyler Bozak 2.50 6.00
17 Colin Wilson 3.00 8.00
18 John Carlson 4.00 10.00

2010-11 Certified Potential Materials Autographs

1 Nazem Kadri 15.00 40.00
2 Philip Larsen 6.00 15.00
5 Bobby Butler 6.00 15.00
10 John Tavares 12.00 30.00
11 Matt Duchene 20.00 50.00
14 Jamie Benn 10.00 25.00
16 Tyler Bozak 12.00 30.00
18 John Carlson 12.00 30.00

2010-11 Certified Shirt Off My Back Combos

*PRIME/25: .6X TO 1.5X BASIC INSERTS
*PRIME/25: .5X TO 1.2X BASIC INSERTS/50
1 J.Iginla/S.Crosby 15.00 40.00
2 R.Miller/S.Crosby 15.00 40.00
3 Brodeur/Luongo/100 10.00 25.00
4 R.Luongo/R.Miller 6.00 15.00
5 J.Tavares/N.Kadri 10.00 25.00
6 J.Carlson/M.Green 4.00 10.00
7 Ovechkin/Backstrom/100 15.00 40.00
8 C.Perry/R.Getzlaf 6.00 15.00
9 R.Bourque/Z.Chara 6.00 15.00
10 D.Doughty/R.Bourque 6.00 15.00
11 Miller/Parise/50 5.00 12.00
12 B.Trottier/J.Toews 6.00 15.00
13 C.Price/P.Roy/100 10.00 25.00
14 S.Crosby/S.Stamkos/51 20.00 50.00
15 Lemieux/Roy/50 20.00 50.00

2010-11 Certified Throwback Threads

*BLUE/100: .6X TO 1.5X BASIC INSERTS
*GOLD/25: 1X TO 2.5X BASIC INSERTS
*RED/250: .5X TO 1.2X BASIC INSERTS
1 Ray Ferraro 2.00 5.00
2 Dale Hawerchuk 2.50 6.00
3 Peter Stastny 1.50 4.00
4 Guy Lafleur 2.50 6.00
5 Charlie Hodge 1.50 4.00
6 Dennis Maruk 1.50 4.00
7 Simon Nolet 1.50 4.00
8 Dan Bouchard 1.50 4.00
9 Lanny McDonald 2.00 5.00
10 Dino Ciccarelli 2.00 5.00

2010-11 Certified Throwback Threads Autographs

1 Ray Ferraro 10.00 25.00
2 Dale Hawerchuk 10.00 25.00
3 Peter Stastny 12.00 30.00
4 Guy Lafleur/25 40.00 100.00
5 Charlie Hodge 10.00 25.00
6 Dennis Maruk 10.00 25.00
7 Simon Nolet 10.00 25.00
8 Dan Bouchard 12.00 30.00
9 Lanny McDonald 10.00 25.00
10 Dino Ciccarelli 10.00 25.00

2010-11 Certified Top Choice

*BLUE/100: .6X TO 1.5X BASIC INSERTS
*GOLD/25: 1X TO 2.5X BASIC INSERTS
*RED/250: .5X TO 1.2X BASIC INSERTS
1 John Tavares 3.00 8.00
2 Steven Stamkos 4.00 10.00
3 Patrick Kane 4.00 10.00
4 Erik Johnson 1.25 3.00
5 Sidney Crosby 6.00 15.00
6 Alexander Ovechkin 5.00 12.00
7 Marc-Andre Fleury 4.00 10.00
8 Rick Nash 2.00 5.00
9 Ilya Kovalchuk 2.00 5.00
10 Joe Thornton 3.00 8.00
11 Vincent Lecavalier 2.00 5.00
12 Mario Lemieux 8.00 20.00
SC Sidney Crosby Preview 2.00 5.00

2010-11 Certified Top Choice Materials

*PRIME/25: .8X TO 2X BASIC JSY
1 John Tavares 6.00 15.00
2 Steven Stamkos 8.00 20.00
3 Patrick Kane 8.00 20.00
4 Erik Johnson 2.50 6.00
5 Sidney Crosby 15.00 40.00
6 Alexander Ovechkin 15.00 40.00
7 Marc-Andre Fleury 8.00 20.00
8 Rick Nash 4.00 10.00
9 Ilya Kovalchuk 4.00 10.00
10 Joe Thornton 6.00 15.00
11 Vincent Lecavalier 4.00 10.00
12 Mario Lemieux 15.00 40.00

2011-12 Certified

COMP.SET w/o SPs (150) 20.00 50.00
1 Jeff Skinner .50 1.25
2 Danny Briere .40 1.00
3 Patrice Bergeron .50 1.25
4 Patrick Sharp .40 1.00
5 Ryan Miller .40 1.00
6 Mikhail Grabovski .25 .60
7 Paul Bissonette .25 .60
8 Andy McDonald .30 .75
9 Mike Richards .30 .75
10 Milan Lucic .40 1.00
11 Eric Staal .50 1.25
12 Patrick Kane .75 2.00
13 Jonathan Quick .50 1.25
14 Pekka Rinne .40 1.00
15 Dwayne Roloson .30 .75
16 Michael Cammalleri .30 .75
17 Cam Ward .40 1.00
18 Andrei Markov .25 .60
19 David Backes .25 .60
20 Matt Moulson .25 .60
21 Steve Mason .30 .75
22 Andrew Ladd .25 .60
23 Jamie Benn .40 1.00
24 Ryan Callahan .25 .60
25 Erik Karlsson .50 1.25
26 Drew Doughty .50 1.25
27 Nicklas Backstrom .40 1.00
28 Patrick Marleau .40 1.00
29 Cal Clutterbuck .25 .60
30 Miikka Kiprusoff .40 1.00
31 Jeff Carter .30 .75
32 Kris Letang .50 1.25
33 Joe Thornton .60 1.50
34 Alex Ovechkin 1.50 4.00
35 David Krejci .40 1.00
36 Rene Bourque .25 .60
37 Brandon Dubinsky .25 .60
38 Evander Kane .40 1.00
39 John Tavares .60 1.50
40 Paul Stastny .30 .75
41 Brad Richards .40 1.00
42 Shane Doan .30 .75
43 Alex Steen .25 .60
44 Ales Hemsky .30 .75
45 Nik Antropov .30 .75
46 Kari Lehtonen .30 .75
47 Daniel Alfredsson .40 1.00
48 Nicklas Lidstrom .25 .60
49 Corey Perry .60 1.50
50 Jordan Eberle .40 1.00
51 Thomas Vanek .30 .75
52 Martin Brodeur 1.00 2.50
53 Mark Giordano .40 1.00
54 Mikko Koivu .30 .75
55 Ryan Getzlaf .40 1.00
56 Ryan Kesler .40 1.00
57 Drew Stafford .25 .60
58 Joffrey Lupul .25 .60
59 Teddy Purcell .25 .60
60 Sam Gagner .25 .60
61 Max Pacioretty .40 1.00
62 Ray Whitney .30 .75
63 Taylor Hall .40 1.00
64 Alexandre Burrows .25 .60
65 Michal Neuvirth .30 .75
66 Travis Zajac .25 .60
67 Marc-Andre Fleury .75 2.00
68 Sergei Bobrovsky .60 1.50
69 Antti Niemi .30 .75
70 Sidney Crosby 1.50 4.00
71 Claude Giroux .40 1.00
72 Tyler Seguin .50 1.25
73 Ryan Smyth .30 .75
74 Mike Fisher .25 .60
75 Michael Grabner .30 .75
76 Keith Yandle .25 .60
77 Jacob Markstrom .40 1.00
78 Milan Hejduk .30 .75
79 Brian Gionta .25 .60
80 Kyle Okposo .25 .60
81 Vincent Lecavalier .40 1.00
82 Ondrej Pavelec .40 1.00
83 James Reimer .40 1.00
84 Brenden Morrow .30 .75
85 Sergei Kostitsyn .25 .60
86 Derek Roy .25 .60
87 Henrik Lundqvist 1.00 2.50
88 Cory Schneider .40 1.00
89 Valtteri Filppula .25 .60
90 Anze Kopitar .60 1.50
91 Teemu Selanne .75 2.00
92 Eric Fehr .25 .60
93 Corey Crawford .50 1.25
94 Joe Pavelski .50 1.25
95 Mattias Tedenby .25 .60
96 Tim Thomas .40 1.00
97 Brent Burns .40 1.00
98 Jordan Staal .30 .75
99 Curtis Glencross .25 .60
100 James van Riemsdyk .30 .75
101 Evgeni Malkin .75 2.00
102 Niklas Backstrom .40 1.00
103 Zach Parise .40 1.00
104 Ryane Clowe .25 .60
105 Dion Phaneuf .30 .75
106 Ilya Bryzgalov .40 1.00
107 Erik Johnson .25 .60
108 Jaroslav Halak .40 1.00
109 Carey Price .75 2.00
110 Derick Brassard .25 .60
111 Martin St. Louis .40 1.00
112 Dustin Byfuglien .40 1.00
113 Loui Eriksson .25 .60
114 Tyler Ennis .25 .60
115 Pavel Datsyuk .60 1.50
116 Jonathan Toews .60 1.50
117 Dany Heatley .30 .75
118 Ilya Kovalchuk .40 1.00
119 Martin Havlat .30 .75
120 Jarome Iginla .50 1.25
121 Mike Green .30 .75
122 Cam Fowler .40 1.00
123 Henrik Zetterberg .50 1.25
124 Marc Staal .25 .60
125 Phil Kessel .40 1.00
126 Steven Stamkos .75 2.00
127 Antoine Vermette .25 .60
128 P.K. Subban .50 1.25
129 Matt Duchene .40 1.00
130 Stephen Weiss .30 .75
131 Daniel Sedin .50 1.25
132 Henrik Sedin .50 1.25
133 Marian Gaborik .40 1.00
134 Shea Weber .30 .75
135 Luke Schenn .40 1.00
136 Brad Marchand .75 2.00
137 Marian Hossa .40 1.00
138 Johan Franzen .30 .75
139 Rick Nash .40 1.00
140 Tomas Plekanec .25 .60
141 Brandon Sutter .25 .60
142 David Booth .25 .60
143 Barret Jackman .25 .60
144 Roberto Luongo .60 1.50
145 Jimmy Howard .50 1.25
146 Bobby Ryan .30 .75
147 Logan Couture .50 1.25
148 Craig Anderson .40 1.00
149 Jason Spezza .40 1.00
150 Derek Stepan .25 .60
151 Brendan Shanahan 1.50 4.00
152 Eric Lindros 2.50 6.00
153 Pat LaFontaine 1.50 4.00
154 Grant Fuhr 2.50 6.00
155 Ron Francis 2.00 5.00
156 Joe Mullen 1.25 3.00
157 Patrick Roy 4.00 10.00
158 Ray Bourque 2.50 6.00
159 Bryan Trottier 1.50 4.00
160 Darryl Sittler 2.00 5.00
161 Luc Robitaille 1.50 4.00
162 Mario Lemieux 6.00 15.00
163 Johnny Bucyk 1.50 4.00
164 Joe Sakic 3.00 8.00
165 Curtis Joseph 2.00 5.00
166 Guy Lafleur 2.00 5.00
167 Jeremy Roenick 2.50 6.00
168 Doug Gilmour 2.00 5.00
169 Mark Messier 3.00 8.00
170 Joe Nieuwendyk 1.25 3.00
171 Patrick Wiercioch AU RC 3.00 8.00
172 Brian Strait AU RC 4.00 10.00
173 Yann Sauve AU RC 3.00 8.00
174 Ben Scrivens AU RC 3.00 8.00
175 Ben Holmstrom AU RC 3.00 8.00
176 Paul Postma AU RC 3.00 8.00
177 Lance Bouma AU RC 3.00 8.00
178 Stephane Da Costa AU RC 3.00 8.00
179 Matt Frattin AU RC 3.00 8.00
180 Mark Katic AU RC 3.00 8.00
181 Brendon Nash AU RC 3.00 8.00
182 Erik Condra AU RC 3.00 8.00
183 Mikko Koskinen AU RC 4.00 10.00
184 Justin DiBenedetto AU RC 2.50 6.00
185 Brandon Saad AU SP RC 20.00 40.00
186 C.Smith AU SP RC 8.00 20.00
187 Colin Greening AU RC 3.00 8.00
188 Matt Read AU SP RC 40.00 80.00
189 Joe Vitale AU RC 3.00 8.00
190 Cam Talbot AU RC 8.00 20.00
191 Zac Rinaldo AU RC 3.00 8.00
192 Scott Timmins AU RC 3.00 8.00
193 Cameron Gaunce AU RC 2.50 6.00
194 Tomas Kubalik AU RC 3.00 8.00
195 Erik Gustafsson AU RC 4.00 10.00
196 Sean Couturier AU SP RC 20.00 50.00
197 Chris Vande Velde AU SP RC 8.00 20.00
198 Drew Bagnall AU SP RC 5.00 12.00
199 Mark Scheifele AU SP RC 10.00 25.00
200 Connie Madigan AU SP RC 80.00 200.00
201 Colton Sceviour AU SP RC 5.00 12.00
202 Teemu Hartikainen AU SP RC 5.00 12.00
203 A.Larsson AU SP RC EXCH 30.00 60.00
204 Hugh Jessiman AU SP RC 5.00 12.00
205 Carson McMillan AU SP RC 6.00 15.00
206 Tomas Vincour AU SP RC 5.00 12.00
207 Dylan Olsen AU RC 5.00 12.00
208 Colten Teubert AU RC 3.00 8.00
209 Cody Hodgson JSY AU RC 8.00 20.00
210 Blake Geoffrion JSY AU RC 5.00 12.00
211 Jonathon Blum JSY AU RC 5.00 12.00
212 Joe Colborne JSY AU RC 5.00 12.00
213 Adam Henrique JSY AU RC 12.00 30.00
214 Greg Nemisz JSY AU RC 5.00 12.00
215 Carl Klingberg JSY AU RC 5.00 12.00
216 John Moore JSY AU RC 5.00 12.00
217 Marcus Kruger JSY AU RC 8.00 20.00
218 Aaron Palushaj JSY AU RC 5.00 12.00
219 Nugent-Hopkins JSY AU RC 20.00 50.00
220 Ryan Johansen JSY AU RC 15.00 40.00
221 Brett Connolly JSY AU RC 5.00 12.00
222 Gabriel Landeskog JSY AU RC 15.00 40.00
223 Mika Zibanejad JSY AU RC 15.00 40.00
224 Jake Gardiner JSY AU RC 8.00 20.00
225 Justin Faulk JSY AU RC 8.00 20.00
226 Brett Bulmer AU RC 3.00 8.00
227 Anders Nilsson AU RC 3.00 8.00
228 Corey Tropp AU RC 3.00 8.00
229 Andy Miele AU RC 3.00 8.00
230 Anton Lander AU RC 3.00 8.00
231 T.J. Brennan AU RC 3.00 8.00
232 Brayden McNabb AU RC 3.00 8.00
233 Leland Irving AU RC 3.00 8.00
234 Roman Josi AU RC 8.00 20.00
235 Brad Malone AU RC 3.00 8.00
236 Stefan Elliott AU RC 3.00 8.00
237 Jimmy Hayes AU RC 4.00 10.00
238 Joe Finley AU RC 3.00 8.00
239 Marcus Foligno AU RC 5.00 12.00
240 Peter Holland AU RC 3.00 8.00
241 Keith Kinkaid AU RC 3.00 8.00
242 Riley Nash AU RC 3.00 8.00
243 Dmitry Orlov AU RC 8.00 20.00
244 Cody Eakin JSY AU/299 RC 10.00 25.00
245 Tim Erixon JSY AU/299 RC 6.00 15.00
246 Kassian JSY AU/299 RC 8.00 20.00
247 Ryan Ellis JSY AU/299 RC 6.00 15.00
248 D.Rundblad JSY AU/299 RC 6.00 15.00
249 B.Smith JSY AU/299 RC 6.00 15.00
250 Despres JSY AU/299 RC 6.00 15.00
251 Smith-Pelly JSY AU/99 RC 10.00 25.00
252 C.de Haan JSY AU/299 RC 6.00 15.00
253 L.Leblanc JSY AU/299 RC 6.00 15.00
254 Gudbranson JSY AU/99 RC 10.00 25.00
255 Allen York JSY AU/99 RC 10.00 25.00
256 C.Gaunce JSY AU/99 RC 6.00 15.00
257 R.Diaz JSY AU/99 RC 8.00 20.00
258 Zolnierczyk JSY AU/299 RC 6.00 15.00
259 Eddie Lack JSY AU/299 RC 6.00 15.00
260 Harri Sateri JSY AU/299 RC 6.00 15.00
261 D.Savard JSY AU/299 RC 6.00 15.00
262 Nyquist JSY AU/299 RC 15.00 40.00
263 Voynov JSY AU/299 RC 6.00 15.00
264 Hagelin JSY AU/299 RC 10.00 25.00
265 Atkinson JSY AU/150 RC 20.00 50.00
266 Emelin JSY AU/99 RC 8.00 20.00
267 R.Bortuzzo JSY AU/299 RC 6.00 15.00
268 R.Horak JSY AU/299 RC 6.00 15.00

2011-12 Certified Mirror Blue

*MIRROR BLUE/99: 2X TO 5X BASIC CARDS
*MIR.BLU IMM/99: .5X TO 1.2X BASIC CARDS
93 Corey Crawford 2.50 6.00

2011-12 Certified Mirror Gold

*GOLD VETS: 4X TO 10X BASIC CARDS
*GOLD IMMORT: 1X TO 2.5X BASIC IMM
*GOLD AU: 1X TO 2.5X BASIC AU RC
*GOLD AU SP: .6X TO 1.5X BASIC AU SP
*GOLD JSY AU: 1X TO 2.5X JSY AU/499
*GOLD JSY AU: .8X TO 2X JSY AU/299
*GOLD JSY AU: .6X TO 1.5X JSY AU/99
93 Corey Crawford 6.00 15.00
200 Connie Madigan AU/25 125.00 300.00
219 Nugent-Hopkins JSY AU/25 125.00 250.00

2011-12 Certified Mirror Red

*MIRROR RED/199: 1.5X TO 4X BASIC
*MIRROR RED IMM/199: .4X TO 1X BASIC
93 Corey Crawford 2.00 5.00

2011-12 Certified Totally Silver

*TOTALLY SILVER: 1X TO 2.5X BASIC CARDS
*TOTALLY SILVER IMM: .25X TO .6X BASIC CARDS
27 Nicklas Backstrom 1.00 2.50
93 Corey Crawford 1.25 3.00

2011-12 Certified Champions

*MIRROR GOLD/25: 1.5X TO 4X BASIC INSERTS
1 Tim Thomas 1.50 4.00
2 Zdeno Chara 1.50 4.00
3 Tyler Seguin 2.00 5.00
4 Patrice Bergeron 2.00 5.00
5 Brad Marchand 3.00 8.00
6 Brent Seabrook 1.00 2.50
7 Duncan Keith 1.25 3.00
8 Sidney Crosby 6.00 15.00
9 Max Talbot 1.00 2.50
10 Pavel Datsyuk 2.50 6.00
11 Henrik Zetterberg 2.00 5.00
12 Jean-Sebastien Giguere 1.50 4.00
13 Chris Pronger 1.50 4.00
14 Tomas Holmstrom 1.00 2.50
15 Scott Niedermayer 1.50 4.00
16 Milt Schmidt 1.25 3.00
17 Al Arbour 1.25 3.00
18 Bernie Parent 2.00 5.00
19 Mark Messier 3.00 8.00
20 Jean Beliveau 1.50 4.00

2011-12 Certified Champions Autographs

2 Zdeno Chara/25 25.00 50.00
3 Tyler Seguin/25 40.00 100.00
5 Brad Marchand/25 15.00 40.00
6 Brent Seabrook/25 10.00 25.00
8 Sidney Crosby/50 75.00 125.00
9 Max Talbot/25 10.00 25.00
10 Pavel Datsyuk/25 20.00 50.00
14 Tomas Holmstrom/25 20.00 50.00
15 Scott Niedermayer/25 15.00 40.00
16 Milt Schmidt/25 15.00 40.00
17 Al Arbour/25 12.00 30.00
18 Bernie Parent/25 10.00 25.00
20 Jean Beliveau/25 30.00 80.00

2011-12 Certified Champions Materials

*PRIME/25: .8X TO 2X MATERIAL/99
1 Tim Thomas 12.00 30.00
2 Zdeno Chara 8.00 20.00
3 Tyler Seguin 10.00 25.00
4 Patrice Bergeron 8.00 20.00
5 Brad Marchand 12.00 30.00
6 Brent Seabrook 4.00 10.00
7 Duncan Keith 5.00 12.00
8 Sidney Crosby 12.00 30.00
9 Max Talbot 4.00 10.00
10 Pavel Datsyuk 10.00 25.00
11 Henrik Zetterberg 8.00 20.00
12 Jean-Sebastien Giguere 6.00 15.00
13 Chris Pronger 6.00 15.00
14 Tomas Holmstrom 5.00 12.00
15 Scott Niedermayer 6.00 15.00
19 Mark Messier 12.00 30.00

2011-12 Certified Collision Course

*MIRROR GOLD/25: 1X TO 2.5X BASIC INSERTS
1 Tuomo Ruutu 1.25 3.00
2 Ryan Callahan 1.00 2.50
3 Brenden Morrow 1.25 3.00
4 Shea Weber 1.25 3.00
5 Tim Thomas 1.50 4.00
6 P.K. Subban 2.00 5.00
7 Ryan Kesler 1.50 4.00
8 Travis Hamonic 1.25 3.00
9 Dustin Brown 1.50 4.00
10 Alex Ovechkin 6.00 15.00

2011-12 Certified Collision Course Autographs

1 Tuomo Ruutu/100 6.00 15.00
2 Ryan Callahan/100 8.00 20.00
3 Brenden Morrow/100 6.00 15.00
4 Shea Weber/100 6.00 15.00
5 Tim Thomas/100 15.00 40.00
6 P.K. Subban/100 10.00 25.00
7 Ryan Kesler/100 8.00 20.00
8 Travis Hamonic/100 6.00 15.00
9 Dustin Brown/100 8.00 20.00
10 Alex Ovechkin/50 30.00 80.00

2011-12 Certified Eternals

*MIRROR GOLD/25: 1X TO 2.5X BASIC INSERTS
1 Joe Sakic 3.00 8.00
2 Ron Francis 2.00 5.00
3 Stan Mikita 2.00 5.00
4 Tim Kerr 1.00 2.50
5 Bill Ranford 1.50 4.00
6 Mark Messier 3.00 8.00
7 Adam Graves 1.25 3.00
8 Milt Schmidt 1.25 3.00
9 Marcel Dionne 2.00 5.00
10 Denis Potvin 1.50 4.00
11 Felix Potvin 2.50 6.00
12 Emile Bouchard 1.50 4.00

2011-12 Certified Eternals Autographs

1 Joe Sakic/25 50.00 100.00
2 Ron Francis/25 15.00 40.00
3 Stan Mikita/25 12.00 30.00
4 Tim Kerr/100 6.00 15.00
5 Bill Ranford/100 10.00 25.00
7 Adam Graves/100 8.00 20.00
8 Milt Schmidt/100 8.00 20.00
9 Marcel Dionne/100 12.00 30.00
10 Denis Potvin/100 10.00 25.00
11 Felix Potvin/100 25.00 60.00
12 Emile Bouchard/100 10.00 25.00

2011-12 Certified Fabric of the Game

1 Corey Perry/99 6.00 15.00
2 Ryan Getzlaf/399 3.00 8.00
3 Brandon McMillan/399 2.00 5.00
4 Cam Fowler/399 3.00 8.00
5 Bobby Ryan/99 3.00 8.00
6 Andrew Ladd/399 2.00 5.00
7 Evander Kane/399 3.00 8.00
9 Ondrej Pavelec/399 3.00 8.00
10 Alexander Burmistrov/399 2.50 6.00
11 Patrice Bergeron/399 4.00 10.00
12 Milan Lucic/299 3.00 8.00
13 David Krejci/399 3.00 8.00
14 Tyler Seguin/399 4.00 10.00
15 Tim Thomas/399 4.00 10.00
16 Jordan Caron/399 4.00 10.00
17 Ryan Miller/99 4.00 10.00
18 Thomas Vanek/99 3.00 8.00
19 Drew Stafford/399 2.00 5.00
20 Derek Roy/399 2.00 5.00
21 Tyler Ennis/25 4.00 10.00
22 Nathan Gerbe/399 2.00 5.00
23 Miikka Kiprusoff/99 4.00 10.00
24 Rene Bourque/399 2.00 5.00
25 Mark Giordano/99 4.00 10.00
26 Henrik Karlsson/399 2.50 6.00
27 Jarome Iginla/99 5.00 12.00
28 Jeff Skinner/399 4.00 10.00
29 Eric Staal/99 5.00 12.00
30 Cam Ward/25 6.00 15.00
31 Brandon Sutter/399 2.00 5.00
32 Patrick Sharp/99 4.00 10.00
34 Corey Crawford/99 5.00 12.00
35 Duncan Keith/99 3.00 8.00
36 Troy Brouwer/399 2.00 5.00
37 Paul Stastny/399 2.50 6.00
38 Milan Hejduk/99 3.00 8.00
39 Ryan O'Reilly/399 3.00 8.00
40 Matt Duchene/99 4.00 10.00
41 Derick Brassard/25 4.00 10.00
42 Rick Nash/99 4.00 10.00
43 Jamie Benn/399 3.00 8.00
44 Brad Richards/399 3.00 8.00
45 Kari Lehtonen/399 2.50 6.00
46 Brenden Morrow/399 2.50 6.00
47 Loui Eriksson/399 2.00 5.00
48 Kris Draper/399 2.00 5.00
49 Nicklas Lidstrom/99 2.50 6.00
50 Valtteri Filppula/25 10.00 25.00
51 Pavel Datsyuk/399 5.00 12.00
52 Tomas Tatar/399 4.00 10.00
53 Johan Franzen/25 5.00 12.00
54 Brian Rafalski/399 2.00 5.00
55 Jimmy Howard/399 4.00 10.00
56 Shawn Horcoff/399 2.00 5.00
57 Ales Hemsky/99 3.00 8.00
58 Jordan Eberle/399 3.00 8.00
59 Sam Gagner/25 4.00 10.00
60 Taylor Hall/399 8.00 20.00
61 Magnus Paajarvi/399 2.50 6.00
62 Jacob Markstrom/399 3.00 8.00
63 Stephen Weiss/399 2.50 6.00
64 David Booth/399 3.00 8.00
65 Jonathan Quick/399 4.00 10.00
66 Drew Doughty/99 5.00 12.00
67 Ryan Smyth/399 2.50 6.00
68 Anze Kopitar/399 5.00 12.00
69 Cal Clutterbuck/99 5.00 12.00
70 Mikko Koivu/99 3.00 8.00
71 Brent Burns/399 3.00 8.00
72 Niklas Backstrom/399 3.00 8.00
73 Martin Havlat/399 2.50 6.00
74 Michael Cammalleri/25 5.00 12.00
75 Andrei Markov/399 2.00 5.00
76 Max Pacioretty/25 6.00 15.00
77 Brian Gionta/99 2.50 6.00
78 Carey Price/99 8.00 20.00
79 Lars Eller/399 2.00 5.00
80 P.K. Subban/399 4.00 10.00
81 Tomas Plekanec/399 2.00 5.00
82 Andrei Kostitsyn/399 2.50 6.00
83 Ryan Suter/399 2.50 6.00
84 Sergei Kostitsyn/399 2.00 5.00
85 Shea Weber/99 3.00 8.00
86 Martin Brodeur/99 10.00 25.00
87 Patrik Elias/399 3.00 8.00
88 Mattias Tedenby/399 2.00 5.00
89 Zach Parise/99 4.00 10.00
90 Ilya Kovalchuk/99 4.00 10.00
91 Matt Moulson/25 4.00 10.00
92 John Tavares/25 10.00 25.00
94 Kyle Okposo/399 2.00 5.00
95 Ryan Callahan/399 2.00 5.00
96 Brandon Dubinsky/399 2.00 5.00
97 Henrik Lundqvist/99 10.00 25.00
98 Marc Staal/399 2.00 5.00
99 Marian Gaborik/99 4.00 10.00
100 Erik Karlsson/25 8.00 20.00
101 Daniel Alfredsson/399 3.00 8.00
102 Bobby Butler/399 2.50 6.00
103 Jason Spezza/399 3.00 8.00
104 Danny Briere/399 3.00 8.00
105 Mike Richards/399 2.50 6.00
106 Jody Shelley/399 2.50 6.00
107 Jeff Carter/399 2.50 6.00
108 Chris Pronger/399 3.00 8.00
109 Sergei Bobrovsky/399 5.00 12.00
110 Claude Giroux/25 12.00 30.00
111 James van Riemsdyk/99 3.00 8.00
112 Shane Doan/99 3.00 8.00
113 Keith Yandle/25 4.00 10.00
114 Ilya Bryzgalov/399 3.00 8.00
115 Kris Letang/99 5.00 12.00
116 Marc-Andre Fleury/25 12.00 30.00
117 Mark Letestu/399 2.50 6.00
118 Sidney Crosby/99 15.00 40.00
119 Jordan Staal/99 3.00 8.00
120 Evgeni Malkin/99 5.00 12.00
121 Max Talbot/399 2.00 5.00
122 Patrick Marleau/25 6.00 15.00
123 Joe Thornton/25 10.00 25.00
124 Torrey Mitchell/399 2.00 5.00
125 Ryane Clowe/99 2.50 6.00
126 David Backes/99 2.50 6.00
127 T.J. Oshie/25 6.00 15.00
128 Jaroslav Halak/99 4.00 10.00
129 Victor Hedman/25 8.00 20.00
131 Teddy Purcell/399 2.00 5.00
132 Vincent Lecavalier/25 6.00 15.00
133 Martin St. Louis/99 4.00 10.00
134 Steven Stamkos/99 8.00 20.00
135 Mikhail Grabovski/399 2.00 5.00
136 Nikolai Kulemin/399 2.00 5.00
137 James Reimer/99 4.00 10.00
138 Phil Kessel/99 4.00 10.00
139 Luke Schenn/25 6.00 15.00
140 Ryan Kesler/399 3.00 8.00
142 Cory Schneider/399 3.00 8.00
143 Daniel Sedin/25 8.00 20.00
144 Henrik Sedin/399 4.00 10.00
145 Roberto Luongo/99 6.00 15.00
146 Nicklas Backstrom/99 4.00 10.00
147 Alex Ovechkin/99 6.00 15.00
148 Michal Neuvirth/399 2.50 6.00
149 Eric Fehr/399 2.00 5.00
150 Mike Green/99 3.00 8.00

2011-12 Certified Fabric of the Game Claim To Fame Die Cut

*CLAIM FAME/25: .8X TO 2X FOTG/299-399
*CLAIM FAME/25: .6X TO 1.5X FOTG/99
*CLAIM FAME/25: .5X TO 1.2X FOTG/25
33 Patrick Kane 12.00 30.00

2011-12 Certified Fabric of the Game Jersey Number

*JSY NUM/25: 1X TO 2.5X FOTG/299-399
*JSY NUM/25: .8X TO 2X FOTG/99
*JSY NUM/25: .6X TO 1.5X FOTG/25
33 Patrick Kane/25 15.00 40.00

2011-12 Certified Fabric of the Game National Die Cut

*NATL DC/20-25: 1X TO 2.5X FOTG/299-399
*NATL DC/20-25: .8X TO 2X FOTG/99
*NATL DC/20-25: .6X TO 1.5X FOTG/25
33 Patrick Kane/25 15.00 40.00

2011-12 Certified Fabric of the Game NHL Die Cut

*NHL DC/20-25: 1X TO 2.5X FOTG/299-399
*NHL DC/20-25: .8X TO 2X FOTG/99
*NHL DC/20-25: .6X TO 1.5X FOTG/25
33 Patrick Kane 15.00 40.00

2011-12 Certified Fabric of the Game Prime

*PRIME/25: .8X TO 2X FOTG/299-399
*PRIME/25: .6X TO 1.5X FOTG/99
*PRIME/25: .5X TO 1.2X FOTG/25
33 Patrick Kane 12.00 30.00

2011-12 Certified Fabric of the Game Jersey Number Autographs

3 Brandon McMillan/25 6.00 15.00
5 Bobby Ryan/25 15.00 40.00
6 Andrew Ladd/25 6.00 15.00
7 Evander Kane/25 10.00 25.00
9 Ondrej Pavelec/25 10.00 25.00
14 Tyler Seguin/25 30.00 80.00
15 Tim Thomas/25 15.00 40.00
16 Jordan Caron/25 10.00 25.00
18 Thomas Vanek/25 8.00 20.00
20 Derek Roy/25 6.00 15.00
21 Tyler Ennis/25 6.00 15.00
22 Nathan Gerbe/25 6.00 15.00
26 Henrik Karlsson/25 8.00 20.00
27 Jarome Iginla/25 10.00 25.00
28 Jeff Skinner/25 12.00 30.00
29 Eric Staal/25 12.00 30.00
32 Patrick Sharp/25 20.00 50.00
33 Patrick Kane/25 30.00 60.00
36 Troy Brouwer/25 12.00 30.00
37 Paul Stastny/25 8.00 20.00
39 Ryan O'Reilly/25 10.00 25.00
42 Rick Nash/25 15.00 40.00
43 Jamie Benn/25 10.00 25.00
44 Brad Richards/25 10.00 25.00
45 Kari Lehtonen/25 8.00 20.00
46 Brenden Morrow/25 8.00 20.00
49 Nicklas Lidstrom/25 15.00 40.00
51 Pavel Datsyuk/25 30.00 60.00
52 Tomas Tatar/25 6.00 15.00
53 Johan Franzen/25 8.00 20.00
54 Brian Rafalski/25 6.00 15.00
55 Jimmy Howard/25 12.00 30.00
56 Shawn Horcoff/25 6.00 15.00
57 Ales Hemsky/25 10.00 25.00
60 Taylor Hall/25 10.00 25.00
61 Magnus Paajarvi/25 8.00 20.00
62 Jacob Markstrom/25 20.00 50.00
63 Stephen Weiss/25 8.00 20.00
65 Jonathan Quick/25 15.00 40.00
66 Drew Doughty/25 12.00 30.00
67 Ryan Smyth/25 8.00 20.00
68 Anze Kopitar/25 15.00 40.00
69 Cal Clutterbuck/25 40.00 80.00
71 Brent Burns/25 10.00 25.00
72 Niklas Backstrom/25 10.00 25.00
74 Michael Cammalleri/25 8.00 20.00
77 Brian Gionta/25 6.00 15.00
78 Carey Price/25 15.00 40.00
79 Lars Eller/25 20.00 40.00
80 P.K. Subban/25 12.00 30.00
82 Andrei Kostitsyn/25 8.00 20.00
83 Ryan Suter/25 8.00 20.00
85 Shea Weber/25 10.00 25.00
86 Martin Brodeur/25 50.00 100.00
87 Patrik Elias/25 10.00 25.00
88 Mattias Tedenby/25 10.00 25.00
89 Zach Parise/25 10.00 25.00
92 John Tavares/25 25.00 50.00
95 Ryan Callahan/25 15.00 40.00
97 Henrik Lundqvist/25 30.00 80.00
98 Marc Staal/25 6.00 15.00
99 Marian Gaborik/25 15.00 30.00
100 Erik Karlsson/25 12.00 30.00
101 Daniel Alfredsson/24 10.00 25.00
102 Bobby Butler/25 8.00 20.00
103 Jason Spezza/25 EXCH 10.00 25.00
104 Danny Briere/25 10.00 25.00
105 Mike Richards/25 8.00 20.00
106 Jody Shelley/25 25.00 50.00
108 Chris Pronger/25 10.00 25.00
109 Sergei Bobrovsky/25 15.00 40.00
110 Claude Giroux/25 10.00 25.00
111 James van Riemsdyk/25 8.00 20.00
113 Keith Yandle/25 6.00 15.00
114 Ilya Bryzgalov/25 10.00 25.00
115 Kris Letang/25 25.00 50.00
116 Marc-Andre Fleury/25 12.00 30.00
117 Mark Letestu/25 12.00 30.00
118 Sidney Crosby/25 75.00 135.00
120 Evgeni Malkin/25 30.00 80.00
121 Max Talbot/25 20.00 50.00
123 Joe Thornton/25 12.00 30.00
124 Torrey Mitchell/25 6.00 15.00
126 David Backes/25 6.00 15.00
127 T.J. Oshie/25 20.00 50.00
128 Jaroslav Halak/25 10.00 25.00
129 Victor Hedman/25 12.00 30.00
131 Teddy Purcell/25 6.00 15.00
132 Vincent Lecavalier/25 12.00 30.00
133 Martin St. Louis/25 10.00 25.00

134 Steven Stamkos/25 25.00 50.00
137 James Reimer/25 30.00 60.00
139 Luke Schenn/25 10.00 25.00
140 Ryan Kesler/25 40.00 80.00
143 Daniel Sedin/25 12.00 30.00
144 Henrik Sedin/25 12.00 30.00
145 Roberto Luongo/25 15.00 40.00
147 Alex Ovechkin/25 40.00 100.00
148 Michal Neuvirth/25 8.00 20.00
149 Eric Fehr/25 6.00 15.00

2011-12 Certified Gold Team

*MIR.GOLD/25: 1X TO 2.5X BASIC INSERTS
1 Martin St. Louis 1.50 4.00
2 Daniel Sedin 2.00 5.00
3 Corey Perry 2.50 6.00
4 Jarome Iginla 2.00 5.00
5 Steven Stamkos 3.00 8.00
6 Claude Giroux 1.50 4.00
7 Henrik Sedin 2.00 5.00
8 Shea Weber 1.25 3.00
9 Zdeno Chara 1.50 4.00
10 Nicklas Lidstrom 1.00 2.50
11 Tim Thomas 1.50 4.00
12 Pekka Rinne 1.50 4.00

2011-12 Certified Gold Team Autographs

1 Martin St. Louis 10.00 25.00
2 Daniel Sedin 15.00 40.00
3 Corey Perry 20.00 50.00
4 Jarome Iginla 15.00 40.00
5 Steven Stamkos 25.00 60.00
6 Claude Giroux 12.00 30.00
7 Henrik Sedin 15.00 40.00
8 Shea Weber 10.00 25.00
11 Tim Thomas 12.00 30.00
12 Pekka Rinne 12.00 30.00

2011-12 Certified Masked Marvels

*MIR.GOLD/25: 1X TO 2.5X BASIC INSERTS
1 Sergei Bobrovsky 2.50 6.00
2 Tim Thomas 1.50 4.00
3 Carey Price 3.00 8.00
4 Cam Ward 1.50 4.00
5 Corey Crawford 2.00 5.00
6 Marc-Andre Fleury 3.00 8.00
7 Pekka Rinne 1.50 4.00
8 Jonathan Quick 2.00 5.00
9 James Reimer 1.50 4.00
10 Kari Lehtonen 1.25 3.00
11 Roberto Luongo 2.50 6.00
12 Michal Neuvirth 1.25 3.00
13 Ilya Bryzgalov 1.50 4.00
14 Ondrej Pavelec 1.50 4.00
15 Henrik Lundqvist 4.00 10.00
16 Niklas Backstrom 1.50 4.00
17 Miikka Kiprusoff 1.50 4.00
18 Jonas Hiller 1.25 3.00
19 Jacob Markstrom 1.50 4.00
20 Jimmy Howard 2.00 5.00

2011-12 Certified Masked Marvels Materials

*PRIME/25: .8X TO 2X BASIC MATERIAL/99
1 Sergei Bobrovsky 6.00 15.00
2 Tim Thomas 5.00 12.00
3 Carey Price 8.00 20.00
4 Cam Ward 4.00 10.00
5 Corey Crawford 5.00 12.00
6 Marc-Andre Fleury 8.00 20.00
7 Pekka Rinne 4.00 10.00
8 Jonathan Quick 5.00 12.00
9 James Reimer 4.00 10.00
10 Kari Lehtonen 3.00 8.00
11 Roberto Luongo 6.00 15.00
12 Michal Neuvirth 3.00 8.00
14 Ondrej Pavelec 4.00 10.00
15 Henrik Lundqvist 10.00 25.00
16 Niklas Backstrom 3.00 8.00
17 Miikka Kiprusoff 4.00 10.00
18 Jonas Hiller 3.00 8.00
19 Jacob Markstrom 4.00 10.00
20 Jimmy Howard 5.00 12.00

2011-12 Certified Masked Marvels Materials Autographs

1 Sergei Bobrovsky 20.00 50.00
2 Tim Thomas 15.00 40.00
3 Carey Price 15.00 40.00
4 Cam Ward 12.00 30.00
6 Marc-Andre Fleury 20.00 50.00
7 Pekka Rinne 12.00 30.00
8 Jonathan Quick 15.00 40.00
10 Kari Lehtonen 10.00 25.00
11 Roberto Luongo 20.00 50.00
12 Michal Neuvirth 10.00 25.00
13 Ilya Bryzgalov 12.00 30.00
15 Henrik Lundqvist 30.00 60.00
16 Niklas Backstrom 12.00 30.00
18 Jonas Hiller 10.00 25.00
19 Jacob Markstrom 20.00 50.00
20 Jimmy Howard 15.00 40.00

2011-12 Certified Mirror Blue Materials

1 Jeff Skinner/99 5.00 12.00
2 Danny Briere/99 4.00 10.00
3 Patrice Bergeron/99 5.00 12.00
4 Patrick Sharp/99 4.00 10.00
5 Ryan Miller/99 4.00 10.00
9 Mike Richards/99 3.00 8.00
10 Milan Lucic/99 4.00 10.00
11 Eric Staal/99 5.00 12.00
13 Jonathan Quick/99 5.00 12.00
14 Pekka Rinne/99 4.00 10.00
16 Michael Cammalleri/99 3.00 8.00
17 Cam Ward/99 4.00 10.00
18 Andrei Markov/99 2.50 6.00
19 David Backes/99 2.50 6.00
22 Andrew Ladd/99 2.50 6.00
23 Jamie Benn/99 4.00 10.00
24 Ryan Callahan/99 2.50 6.00
25 Erik Karlsson/99 4.00 10.00
26 Drew Doughty/99 5.00 12.00
27 Nicklas Backstrom/99 4.00 10.00
28 Patrick Marleau/99 4.00 10.00
29 Cal Clutterbuck/99 2.50 6.00
30 Miikka Kiprusoff/99 4.00 10.00
31 Jeff Carter/99 3.00 8.00
32 Kris Letang/99 5.00 12.00
34 Alex Ovechkin/99 15.00 40.00
36 Rene Bourque/99 2.50 6.00
38 Evander Kane/99 4.00 10.00
40 Paul Stastny/99 3.00 8.00
41 Brad Richards/99 4.00 10.00
42 Shane Doan/99 3.00 8.00
44 Ales Hemsky/99 3.00 8.00
45 Nik Antropov/40 3.00 8.00
46 Kari Lehtonen/99 5.00 12.00
47 Daniel Alfredsson/99 4.00 10.00
48 Nicklas Lidstrom/99 5.00 12.00
49 Corey Perry/99 6.00 15.00
50 Jordan Eberle/99 6.00 15.00
51 Thomas Vanek/99 3.00 8.00
52 Martin Brodeur/99 10.00 25.00
53 Mark Giordano/99 4.00 10.00
54 Mikko Koivu/99 6.00 15.00
55 Ryan Getzlaf/99 4.00 10.00
56 Ryan Kesler/99 4.00 10.00
59 Teddy Purcell/99 2.50 6.00
60 Sam Gagner/99 2.50 6.00
63 Taylor Hall/99 8.00 20.00
65 Michal Neuvirth/99 3.00 8.00
66 Travis Zajac/99 2.50 6.00
67 Marc-Andre Fleury/99 8.00 20.00
70 Sidney Crosby/99 15.00 40.00
71 Claude Giroux/99 4.00 10.00
72 Tyler Seguin/99 5.00 12.00
73 Ryan Smyth/99 3.00 8.00
74 Mike Fisher/99 2.50 6.00
76 Keith Yandle/99 2.50 6.00
77 Jacob Markstrom/99 4.00 10.00
78 Milan Hejduk/99 3.00 8.00
80 Kyle Okposo/99 2.50 6.00
81 Vincent Lecavalier/99 4.00 10.00
82 Ondrej Pavelec/99 4.00 10.00
83 James Reimer/99 8.00 20.00
84 Brenden Morrow/99 3.00 8.00
85 Sergei Kostitsyn/99 2.50 6.00
86 Derek Roy/99 2.50 6.00
87 Henrik Lundqvist/99 10.00 25.00
88 Cory Schneider/99 6.00 15.00
89 Valtteri Filppula/99 20.00 50.00
90 Anze Kopitar/99 6.00 15.00
92 Eric Fehr/99 2.50 6.00
94 Joe Pavelski/99 5.00 12.00
95 Mattias Tedenby/99 2.50 6.00
96 Tim Thomas/99 4.00 10.00
97 Brent Burns/99 4.00 10.00
98 Jordan Staal/99 3.00 8.00
99 Curtis Glencross/99 2.50 6.00
100 James van Riemsdyk/99 3.00 8.00
101 Evgeni Malkin/99 8.00 20.00
102 Niklas Backstrom/99 4.00 10.00
103 Zach Parise/99 4.00 10.00
105 Dion Phaneuf/99 3.00 8.00
106 Ilya Bryzgalov/99 4.00 10.00
107 Erik Johnson/99 2.50 6.00
108 Jaroslav Halak/99 4.00 10.00
109 Carey Price/99 8.00 20.00
110 Derick Brassard/99 2.50 6.00
111 Martin St. Louis/99 4.00 10.00
112 Dustin Byfuglien/99 4.00 10.00
113 Loui Eriksson/99 2.50 6.00
114 Tyler Ennis/99 2.50 6.00
115 Pavel Datsyuk/99 6.00 15.00
117 Dany Heatley/99 3.00 8.00
118 Ilya Kovalchuk/99 4.00 10.00
119 Martin Havlat/99 3.00 8.00
120 Jarome Iginla/99 5.00 12.00
121 Mike Green/99 3.00 8.00
122 Cam Fowler/99 4.00 10.00
123 Henrik Zetterberg/99 5.00 12.00
124 Marc Staal/99 2.50 6.00
125 Phil Kessel/99 4.00 10.00
126 Steven Stamkos/99 8.00 20.00
127 Antoine Vermette/99 2.50 6.00
128 P.K. Subban/99 6.00 15.00
129 Matt Duchene/99 4.00 10.00
130 Stephen Weiss/99 3.00 8.00
131 Daniel Sedin/99 5.00 12.00
132 Henrik Sedin/99 5.00 12.00
133 Marian Gaborik/99 4.00 10.00
134 Shea Weber/99 3.00 8.00
135 Luke Schenn/99 4.00 10.00
136 Brad Marchand/99 8.00 20.00
139 Rick Nash/99 4.00 10.00
140 Tomas Plekanec/99 2.50 6.00
141 Brandon Sutter/99 2.50 6.00
143 Barret Jackman/99 2.50 6.00
144 Roberto Luongo/99 6.00 15.00
145 Jimmy Howard/99 5.00 12.00
146 Bobby Ryan/99 3.00 8.00
147 Logan Couture/99 5.00 12.00
148 Craig Anderson/99 4.00 10.00
149 Jason Spezza/99 4.00 10.00
150 Derek Stepan/99 2.50 6.00
151 Brendan Shanahan/49 4.00 10.00
152 Eric Lindros/49 6.00 15.00
153 Pat LaFontaine/49 6.00 15.00
155 Ron Francis/49 10.00 25.00
156 Joe Mullen/49 3.00 8.00
157 Patrick Roy/49 10.00 25.00
158 Ray Bourque/49 10.00 25.00
159 Bryan Trottier/49 4.00 10.00
160 Darryl Sittler/49 8.00 20.00
161 Luc Robitaille/49 4.00 10.00
162 Mario Lemieux/49 12.00 30.00
163 Johnny Bucyk/49 4.00 10.00
165 Curtis Joseph/49 5.00 12.00
166 Guy Lafleur/49 8.00 20.00
167 Jeremy Roenick/49 8.00 20.00
168 Doug Gilmour/49 6.00 15.00

2011-12 Certified Mirror Gold Materials Prime

1 Jeff Skinner 8.00 20.00
2 Danny Briere 6.00 15.00
3 Patrice Bergeron 6.00 15.00
4 Patrick Sharp 6.00 15.00
5 Ryan Miller 6.00 15.00
6 Mikhail Grabovski 10.00 25.00
9 Mike Richards 5.00 12.00
10 Milan Lucic 6.00 15.00
11 Eric Staal 8.00 20.00
12 Patrick Kane 12.00 30.00
13 Jonathan Quick 8.00 20.00
14 Pekka Rinne 6.00 15.00
17 Cam Ward 6.00 15.00
19 David Backes 4.00 10.00
23 Jamie Benn 6.00 15.00
24 Ryan Callahan 4.00 10.00
25 Erik Karlsson 8.00 20.00
26 Drew Doughty 8.00 20.00
27 Nicklas Backstrom 6.00 15.00
28 Patrick Marleau 6.00 15.00
29 Cal Clutterbuck 8.00 20.00
30 Miikka Kiprusoff 6.00 15.00
31 Jeff Carter 5.00 12.00
32 Kris Letang 8.00 20.00
33 Joe Thornton 10.00 25.00
34 Alex Ovechkin 12.00 30.00
35 David Krejci 6.00 15.00
36 Rene Bourque 4.00 10.00
37 Brandon Dubinsky 4.00 10.00
38 Evander Kane 6.00 15.00
39 John Tavares 12.00 30.00
40 Paul Stastny 5.00 12.00
41 Brad Richards 12.00 30.00
42 Shane Doan 5.00 12.00
44 Ales Hemsky 5.00 12.00
45 Nik Antropov 5.00 12.00
46 Kari Lehtonen 8.00 20.00
47 Daniel Alfredsson 6.00 15.00
48 Nicklas Lidstrom 8.00 20.00
49 Corey Perry 10.00 25.00
50 Jordan Eberle 6.00 15.00
52 Martin Brodeur 15.00 40.00
53 Mark Giordano 6.00 15.00
54 Mikko Koivu 5.00 12.00
56 Ryan Kesler 6.00 15.00
57 Drew Stafford 4.00 10.00
59 Teddy Purcell 4.00 10.00
60 Sam Gagner 4.00 10.00
61 Max Pacioretty 6.00 15.00
63 Taylor Hall 6.00 15.00
65 Michal Neuvirth 5.00 12.00
66 Travis Zajac 4.00 10.00
69 Antti Niemi 5.00 12.00
70 Sidney Crosby 25.00 60.00
72 Tyler Seguin 8.00 20.00
73 Ryan Smyth 5.00 12.00
74 Mike Fisher 4.00 10.00
75 Michael Grabner 5.00 12.00
76 Keith Yandle 4.00 10.00
78 Milan Hejduk 5.00 12.00
80 Kyle Okposo 4.00 10.00
82 Ondrej Pavelec 6.00 15.00
83 James Reimer 6.00 15.00
84 Brenden Morrow 5.00 12.00
85 Sergei Kostitsyn 4.00 10.00
86 Derek Roy 4.00 10.00
87 Henrik Lundqvist 15.00 40.00
88 Cory Schneider 6.00 15.00
90 Anze Kopitar 10.00 25.00
93 Corey Crawford 8.00 20.00
94 Joe Pavelski 8.00 20.00
96 Tim Thomas 8.00 20.00
97 Brent Burns 6.00 15.00
99 Curtis Glencross 4.00 10.00
100 James van Riemsdyk 5.00 12.00
101 Evgeni Malkin 12.00 30.00
102 Niklas Backstrom 10.00 25.00
103 Zach Parise 8.00 20.00
104 Ryane Clowe 12.00 30.00
105 Dion Phaneuf 20.00 50.00
107 Erik Johnson 4.00 10.00
108 Jaroslav Halak 8.00 20.00
109 Carey Price 25.00 50.00
110 Derick Brassard 4.00 10.00
111 Martin St. Louis 6.00 15.00
112 Dustin Byfuglien 15.00 40.00
114 Tyler Ennis 6.00 15.00
115 Pavel Datsyuk 10.00 25.00
116 Jonathan Toews 10.00 25.00
117 Dany Heatley 5.00 12.00
118 Ilya Kovalchuk 8.00 20.00
119 Martin Havlat 5.00 12.00
121 Mike Green 5.00 12.00
123 Henrik Zetterberg 8.00 20.00
125 Phil Kessel 6.00 15.00
126 Steven Stamkos 12.00 30.00
128 P.K. Subban 10.00 25.00
129 Matt Duchene 6.00 15.00
130 Stephen Weiss 5.00 12.00
131 Daniel Sedin 8.00 20.00
132 Henrik Sedin 10.00 25.00
133 Marian Gaborik 6.00 15.00
134 Shea Weber 5.00 12.00
136 Brad Marchand 12.00 30.00
137 Marian Hossa 6.00 15.00
138 Johan Franzen 5.00 12.00
139 Rick Nash 6.00 15.00
140 Tomas Plekanec 4.00 10.00
141 Brandon Sutter 4.00 10.00
142 David Booth 4.00 10.00
143 Barret Jackman 4.00 10.00
144 Roberto Luongo 10.00 25.00
145 Jimmy Howard 8.00 20.00
147 Logan Couture 8.00 20.00
148 Craig Anderson 6.00 15.00
150 Derek Stepan 4.00 10.00
151 Brendan Shanahan 12.00 30.00
152 Eric Lindros 12.00 30.00
153 Pat LaFontaine 10.00 25.00
154 Grant Fuhr 10.00 25.00
155 Ron Francis 8.00 20.00
156 Joe Mullen 8.00 20.00
157 Patrick Roy 15.00 40.00
158 Ray Bourque 10.00 25.00
159 Bryan Trottier 6.00 15.00
160 Darryl Sittler 12.00 30.00
162 Mario Lemieux 20.00 50.00
164 Joe Sakic 12.00 30.00
165 Curtis Joseph 8.00 20.00
166 Guy Lafleur 8.00 20.00
167 Jeremy Roenick 15.00 40.00
169 Mark Messier 8.00 20.00

2011-12 Certified Mirror Red Materials Dual

1 Jeff Skinner/150 5.00 12.00
2 Danny Briere/150 4.00 10.00
3 Patrice Bergeron/150 5.00 12.00
4 Patrick Sharp/150 4.00 10.00
5 Ryan Miller/150 4.00 10.00
6 Mikhail Grabovski/150 2.50 6.00
9 Mike Richards/150 3.00 8.00
10 Milan Lucic/150 4.00 10.00
11 Eric Staal/150 5.00 12.00
12 Patrick Kane/25 10.00 25.00
13 Jonathan Quick/99 5.00 12.00
14 Pekka Rinne/150 4.00 10.00
16 Michael Cammalleri/150 3.00 8.00
18 Andrei Markov/150 2.50 6.00
19 David Backes/150 2.50 6.00
22 Andrew Ladd/150 2.50 6.00
23 Jamie Benn/150 4.00 10.00
24 Ryan Callahan/150 2.50 6.00
25 Erik Karlsson/150 5.00 12.00
26 Drew Doughty/150 5.00 12.00
27 Nicklas Backstrom/150 4.00 10.00
28 Patrick Marleau/150 4.00 10.00
29 Cal Clutterbuck/150 2.50 6.00
30 Miikka Kiprusoff/25 5.00 12.00
31 Jeff Carter/150 3.00 8.00
32 Kris Letang/150 5.00 12.00
34 Alex Ovechkin/25 20.00 50.00
36 Rene Bourque/150 2.50 6.00
37 Brandon Dubinsky/150 2.50 6.00
38 Evander Kane/150 4.00 10.00
39 John Tavares/25 8.00 20.00
40 Paul Stastny/150 3.00 8.00
41 Brad Richards/150 4.00 10.00
42 Shane Doan/150 3.00 8.00
44 Ales Hemsky/150 3.00 8.00
45 Nik Antropov/150 3.00 8.00
46 Kari Lehtonen/150 3.00 8.00
47 Daniel Alfredsson/150 4.00 10.00
49 Corey Perry/150 6.00 15.00
50 Jordan Eberle/25 10.00 25.00
51 Thomas Vanek/150 3.00 8.00
52 Martin Brodeur/25 12.00 30.00
53 Mark Giordano/150 4.00 10.00
54 Mikko Koivu/150 3.00 8.00
55 Ryan Getzlaf/150 4.00 10.00
56 Ryan Kesler/150 4.00 10.00
57 Drew Stafford/150 2.50 6.00
59 Teddy Purcell/150 2.50 6.00
60 Sam Gagner/150 2.50 6.00
61 Max Pacioretty/25 5.00 12.00
63 Taylor Hall/25 15.00 30.00
65 Michal Neuvirth/150 3.00 8.00
66 Travis Zajac/150 2.50 6.00
67 Marc-Andre Fleury/150 8.00 20.00
68 Sergei Bobrovsky/150 6.00 15.00
69 Antti Niemi/150 3.00 8.00
70 Sidney Crosby/75 15.00 40.00
71 Claude Giroux/150 4.00 10.00
72 Tyler Seguin/25 6.00 15.00
73 Ryan Smyth/150 3.00 8.00
74 Mike Fisher/150 2.50 6.00
76 Keith Yandle/150 2.50 6.00
77 Jacob Markstrom/150 4.00 10.00
78 Milan Hejduk/25 4.00 10.00
79 Brian Gionta/150 2.50 6.00
81 Vincent Lecavalier/150 4.00 10.00
82 Ondrej Pavelec/150 4.00 10.00
83 James Reimer/150 8.00 20.00
84 Brenden Morrow/150 3.00 8.00
85 Sergei Kostitsyn/150 2.50 6.00
86 Derek Roy/150 2.50 6.00
87 Henrik Lundqvist/150 10.00 25.00
88 Cory Schneider/25 5.00 12.00
89 Valtteri Filppula/150 20.00 50.00
90 Anze Kopitar/150 6.00 15.00
92 Eric Fehr/150 2.50 6.00
93 Corey Crawford/25 6.00 15.00
94 Joe Pavelski/150 5.00 12.00
95 Mattias Tedenby/150 2.50 6.00
96 Tim Thomas/150 5.00 12.00
97 Brent Burns/150 4.00 10.00
98 Jordan Staal/150 3.00 8.00
99 Curtis Glencross/150 2.50 6.00
100 James van Riemsdyk/150 3.00 8.00
101 Evgeni Malkin/25 10.00 25.00
102 Niklas Backstrom/150 4.00 10.00
103 Zach Parise/150 4.00 10.00
104 Ryane Clowe/150 2.50 6.00
105 Dion Phaneuf/150 3.00 8.00
106 Ilya Bryzgalov/150 4.00 10.00
107 Erik Johnson/150 2.50 6.00
108 Jaroslav Halak/150 4.00 10.00
109 Carey Price/150 6.00 15.00
112 Dustin Byfuglien/150 4.00 10.00
113 Loui Eriksson/150 2.50 6.00
114 Tyler Ennis/25 3.00 8.00
115 Pavel Datsyuk/150 6.00 15.00
117 Dany Heatley/150 3.00 8.00
118 Ilya Kovalchuk/150 4.00 10.00
119 Martin Havlat/150 3.00 8.00
120 Jarome Iginla/150 5.00 12.00
121 Mike Green/150 3.00 8.00
122 Cam Fowler/150 4.00 10.00
123 Henrik Zetterberg/25 6.00 15.00
124 Marc Staal/150 2.50 6.00
125 Phil Kessel/25 5.00 12.00
126 Steven Stamkos/25 10.00 25.00
127 Antoine Vermette/25 3.00 8.00
128 P.K. Subban/150 8.00 20.00
129 Matt Duchene/99 4.00 10.00
130 Stephen Weiss/25 4.00 10.00
131 Daniel Sedin/15 6.00 15.00
132 Henrik Sedin/150 5.00 12.00
133 Marian Gaborik/99 4.00 10.00
134 Shea Weber/75 3.00 8.00
135 Luke Schenn/150 4.00 10.00
136 Brad Marchand/150 8.00 20.00
137 Marian Hossa/25 5.00 12.00
138 Johan Franzen/25 4.00 10.00
139 Rick Nash/150 4.00 10.00
140 Tomas Plekanec/150 2.50 6.00
141 Brandon Sutter/150 2.50 6.00
142 David Booth/150 2.50 6.00
143 Barret Jackman/150 2.50 6.00
144 Roberto Luongo/150 6.00 15.00
146 Bobby Ryan/150 3.00 8.00
147 Logan Couture/150 5.00 12.00
148 Craig Anderson/150 4.00 10.00
149 Jason Spezza/150 4.00 10.00
150 Derek Stepan/150 2.50 6.00
151 Brendan Shanahan/50 4.00 10.00
152 Eric Lindros/50 6.00 15.00
153 Pat LaFontaine/50 6.00 15.00
154 Grant Fuhr/50 6.00 15.00
155 Ron Francis/50 10.00 25.00
156 Joe Mullen/50 3.00 8.00
157 Patrick Roy/50 10.00 25.00
158 Ray Bourque/50 10.00 25.00
159 Bryan Trottier/50 4.00 10.00
160 Darryl Sittler/50 8.00 20.00
161 Luc Robitaille/50 4.00 10.00
162 Mario Lemieux/50 12.00 30.00
163 Johnny Bucyk/25 10.00 25.00
164 Joe Sakic/50 8.00 20.00
165 Curtis Joseph/50 5.00 12.00
166 Guy Lafleur/50 8.00 20.00
167 Jeremy Roenick/50 10.00 25.00
168 Doug Gilmour/50 6.00 15.00
169 Mark Messier/25 8.00 20.00

2011-12 Certified Mirror Blue Signatures

1 Jeff Skinner/99 10.00 25.00
15 Dwayne Roloson/99 6.00 15.00
19 David Backes/99 5.00 12.00
21 Steve Mason/99 6.00 15.00
24 Ryan Callahan/99 8.00 20.00
26 Drew Doughty/99 10.00 25.00
29 Cal Clutterbuck/99 5.00 12.00
50 Jordan Eberle/99 20.00 50.00
61 Max Pacioretty/99 8.00 20.00
65 Michal Neuvirth/99 6.00 15.00
69 Antti Niemi/99 6.00 15.00
73 Ryan Smyth/99 6.00 15.00
97 Brent Burns/99 8.00 20.00
98 Jordan Staal/99 6.00 15.00
100 James van Riemsdyk/99 6.00 15.00
103 Zach Parise/99 8.00 20.00
106 Ilya Bryzgalov/99 8.00 20.00
107 Erik Johnson/99 5.00 12.00
108 Jaroslav Halak/99 8.00 20.00
112 Dustin Byfuglien/99 8.00 20.00
117 Dany Heatley/99 6.00 15.00
124 Marc Staal/99 6.00 15.00
130 Stephen Weiss/99 6.00 15.00
131 Daniel Sedin/99 10.00 25.00
132 Henrik Sedin/99 10.00 25.00
134 Shea Weber/99 6.00 15.00
150 Derek Stepan/99 5.00 12.00
153 Pat LaFontaine/99 12.00 30.00
161 Luc Robitaille/50 20.00 40.00
168 Doug Gilmour/50 10.00 25.00

2011-12 Certified Mirror Gold Signatures

1 Jeff Skinner/25 12.00 30.00
2 Danny Briere/25 10.00 25.00
4 Patrick Sharp/25 25.00 60.00
5 Ryan Miller/25 8.00 20.00
6 Mikhail Grabovski/25 6.00 15.00
11 Eric Staal/25 12.00 30.00
12 Patrick Kane/25 20.00 50.00
13 Jonathan Quick/25 25.00 50.00
14 Pekka Rinne/25 15.00 40.00
15 Dwayne Roloson/25 8.00 20.00
16 Michael Cammalleri/25 8.00 20.00
17 Cam Ward/25 8.00 20.00
20 Matt Moulson/25 6.00 15.00
21 Steve Mason/25 8.00 20.00
23 Jamie Benn/25 8.00 20.00
24 Ryan Callahan/25 6.00 15.00
25 Erik Karlsson/25 20.00 40.00
26 Drew Doughty/25 12.00 30.00
28 Patrick Marleau/25 10.00 25.00
29 Cal Clutterbuck/25 6.00 15.00
31 Jeff Carter/25 8.00 20.00
32 Kris Letang/25 12.00 30.00
33 Joe Thornton/25 15.00 40.00
34 Alex Ovechkin/25 40.00 100.00
36 Rene Bourque/25 10.00 25.00
37 Brandon Dubinsky/25 6.00 15.00
38 Evander Kane/25 10.00 25.00
39 John Tavares/25 15.00 40.00
40 Paul Stastny/25 8.00 20.00
41 Brad Richards/25 10.00 25.00
42 Shane Doan/25 8.00 20.00
46 Kari Lehtonen/25 8.00 20.00
47 Daniel Alfredsson/25 10.00 25.00
48 Nicklas Lidstrom/25 15.00 30.00
49 Corey Perry/25 15.00 40.00
50 Jordan Eberle/25 20.00 50.00
51 Thomas Vanek/25 8.00 20.00
52 Martin Brodeur/25 25.00 60.00
53 Mark Giordano/25 12.00 30.00
56 Ryan Kesler/25 10.00 25.00
57 Drew Stafford/25 6.00 15.00
59 Teddy Purcell/25 6.00 15.00
60 Sam Gagner/25 12.00 30.00
61 Max Pacioretty/25 12.00 30.00
63 Taylor Hall/25 30.00 60.00
64 Alexandre Burrows/25 15.00 40.00
65 Michal Neuvirth/25 8.00 20.00
67 Marc-Andre Fleury/25 20.00 50.00
68 Sergei Bobrovsky/25 15.00 40.00
70 Sidney Crosby/25 60.00 120.00
71 Claude Giroux/25 20.00 40.00
72 Tyler Seguin/25 20.00 50.00
73 Ryan Smyth/25 8.00 20.00
74 Mike Fisher/25 6.00 15.00
77 Jacob Markstrom/25 10.00 25.00
79 Brian Gionta/25 6.00 15.00
80 Kyle Okposo/25 6.00 15.00
81 Vincent Lecavalier/25 10.00 25.00
82 Ondrej Pavelec/25 6.00 15.00
84 Brenden Morrow/25 8.00 20.00
87 Henrik Lundqvist/25 25.00 60.00
88 Cory Schneider/25 10.00 25.00
90 Anze Kopitar/25 10.00 25.00
96 Tim Thomas/25 15.00 40.00
97 Brent Burns/25 10.00 25.00
98 Jordan Staal/25 8.00 20.00
100 James van Riemsdyk/25 8.00 20.00
101 Evgeni Malkin/25 25.00 50.00
102 Niklas Backstrom/25 10.00 25.00
103 Zach Parise/25 8.00 20.00
104 Ryane Clowe/25 EXCH 15.00 40.00
105 Dion Phaneuf/25 8.00 20.00
106 Ilya Bryzgalov/25 15.00 30.00
107 Erik Johnson/25 6.00 15.00
108 Jaroslav Halak/25 10.00 25.00
109 Carey Price/25 20.00 50.00
110 Derick Brassard/25 6.00 15.00
111 Martin St. Louis/25 10.00 25.00
112 Dustin Byfuglien/25 10.00 25.00
113 Loui Eriksson/25 10.00 25.00
114 Tyler Ennis/25 6.00 15.00
115 Pavel Datsyuk/25 15.00 40.00
116 Jonathan Toews/25 15.00 40.00
117 Dany Heatley/25 8.00 20.00
120 Jarome Iginla/25 12.00 30.00
124 Marc Staal/25 8.00 20.00
126 Steven Stamkos/25 25.00 50.00
127 Antoine Vermette/25 6.00 15.00
128 P.K. Subban/25 25.00 60.00
129 Matt Duchene/25 10.00 25.00
131 Daniel Sedin/25 12.00 30.00
132 Henrik Sedin/25 12.00 30.00
133 Marian Gaborik/25 10.00 25.00
134 Shea Weber/25 8.00 20.00
135 Luke Schenn/25 10.00 25.00
136 Brad Marchand/25 15.00 40.00
137 Marian Hossa/25 12.00 30.00
138 Johan Franzen/25 8.00 20.00
139 Rick Nash/25 10.00 25.00
141 Brandon Sutter/25 10.00 25.00
144 Roberto Luongo/25 15.00 30.00
145 Jimmy Howard/25 15.00 30.00
146 Bobby Ryan/25 8.00 20.00
147 Logan Couture/25 12.00 30.00
150 Derek Stepan/25 20.00 50.00
152 Eric Lindros/25 30.00 80.00
153 Pat LaFontaine/25 12.00 30.00
154 Grant Fuhr/25 15.00 40.00
155 Ron Francis/25 15.00 40.00
156 Joe Mullen/25 8.00 20.00
157 Patrick Roy/25 40.00 80.00
158 Ray Bourque/20 15.00 40.00
159 Bryan Trottier/25 20.00 40.00
161 Luc Robitaille/25 15.00 40.00
162 Mario Lemieux/25 50.00 100.00
163 Johnny Bucyk/25 10.00 25.00
164 Joe Sakic/25 20.00 50.00
165 Curtis Joseph/25 12.00 30.00
166 Guy Lafleur/25 20.00 50.00
167 Jeremy Roenick/25 20.00 50.00
168 Doug Gilmour/25 12.00 30.00

2011-12 Certified Potential

*MIR.GOLD/25: 1X TO 2.5X BASIC INSERTS
1 Taylor Hall 1.50 4.00
2 Jordan Eberle 1.50 4.00
3 Jeff Skinner 2.00 5.00
4 Tyler Seguin 2.00 5.00
5 Sergei Bobrovsky 2.50 6.00
6 Blake Geoffrion 1.25 3.00
7 Cody Hodgson 2.00 5.00
8 Joe Colborne 1.25 3.00
9 Logan Couture 2.00 5.00
10 Marcus Kruger 2.00 5.00

2011-12 Certified Potential Materials

*PRIME/25: 1X TO 2.5X BASIC MATERIAL/99
1 Taylor Hall 6.00 15.00
2 Jordan Eberle 3.00 8.00
3 Jeff Skinner 4.00 10.00
4 Tyler Seguin 4.00 10.00
5 Sergei Bobrovsky 5.00 12.00
6 Blake Geoffrion 2.50 6.00
7 Cody Hodgson 8.00 20.00
8 Joe Colborne 2.50 6.00
9 Logan Couture 4.00 10.00
10 Marcus Kruger 4.00 10.00

2011-12 Certified Potential Materials Autographs

*PRIME AU/25: .5X TO 1.2X BASIC AU/25-50
1 Taylor Hall/50 50.00 100.00
2 Jordan Eberle/50 30.00 60.00
3 Jeff Skinner/50 15.00 40.00
4 Tyler Seguin/50 EXCH 15.00 40.00
5 Sergei Bobrovsky/50 12.00 30.00
6 Blake Geoffrion/50 6.00 15.00
7 Cody Hodgson/25 40.00 80.00
8 Joe Colborne/50 10.00 25.00
9 Logan Couture/50 10.00 25.00
10 Marcus Kruger/50 10.00 25.00

2011-12 Certified Shirt Off My Back Combos

*PRIME/25: 1.2X TO 3X BASIC SHIRT 25-99
1 J.Eberle/T.Hall 4.00 10.00
3 M.St.Louis/T.Thomas 5.00 12.00
4 C.Joseph/J.Reimer 5.00 12.00
5 C.Price/J.Halak 8.00 20.00
6 S.Weber/Z.Chara 4.00 10.00
7 Yzerman/S.Stamkos/25 10.00 25.00
8 N.Leveille/R.Bourque 6.00 15.00
9 B.Leetch/M.Messier 6.00 15.00
10 J.Iginla/J.Nieuwendyk 6.00 15.00
11 J.Sakic/M.Duchene 8.00 20.00
12 M.Koivu/S.Koivu 4.00 10.00
13 G.Fuhr/J.Quick 6.00 15.00
14 C.Neely/R.Middleton 6.00 15.00
15 P.Roy/R.Vachon/25 60.00 120.00

2011-12 Certified Shirt Off My Back Combos Autographs

4 C.Joseph/J.Reimer 50.00 100.00
5 C.Price/J.Halak 30.00 80.00
6 S.Weber/Z.Chara 15.00 40.00
7 S.Yzerman/S.Stamkos 75.00 150.00
8 N.Leveille/R.Bourque 25.00 60.00
9 B.Leetch/M.Messier 30.00 80.00
10 J.Iginla/J.Nieuwendyk 40.00 80.00
11 J.Sakic/M.Duchene 50.00 100.00
13 G.Fuhr/J.Quick 40.00 80.00
14 C.Neely/R.Middleton 25.00 60.00
15 P.Roy/R.Vachon 60.00 120.00

2011-12 Certified Stars of the NHL

1 Corey Perry 12.00 30.00
2 Dustin Byfuglien 8.00 20.00
3 Milan Lucic 8.00 20.00
4 Ryan Miller 8.00 20.00
5 Jarome Iginla 10.00 25.00
6 Jeff Skinner 10.00 25.00
7 Jonathan Toews 12.00 30.00
8 Matt Duchene 8.00 20.00
9 Rick Nash 8.00 20.00
10 Jamie Benn 8.00 20.00
11 Henrik Zetterberg 10.00 25.00
12 Taylor Hall 8.00 20.00
13 Jacob Markstrom 8.00 20.00
14 Anze Kopitar 12.00 30.00
15 Niklas Backstrom 8.00 20.00
16 P.K. Subban 10.00 25.00
17 Shea Weber 6.00 15.00
18 Martin Brodeur 20.00 50.00
19 John Tavares 12.00 30.00
20 Henrik Lundqvist 20.00 50.00
21 Daniel Alfredsson 8.00 20.00
22 Claude Giroux 8.00 20.00
23 Shane Doan 6.00 15.00
24 Sidney Crosby 30.00 80.00
25 Joe Thornton 6.00 15.00
26 Chris Stewart 6.00 15.00
27 Steven Stamkos 15.00 40.00
28 James Reimer 8.00 20.00
29 Roberto Luongo 12.00 30.00
30 Alex Ovechkin 30.00 80.00

2011-12 Certified Stick Em

1 Derek Stepan 6.00 15.00
2 Marian Gaborik 10.00 25.00
3 Sidney Crosby 20.00 50.00
4 Evgeni Malkin 20.00 50.00
5 Ilya Kovalchuk 10.00 25.00
6 Jarome Iginla 12.00 30.00
7 Andrei Kostitsyn 8.00 20.00
8 Alex Ovechkin 30.00 80.00
9 David Krejci 15.00 40.00
10 Tyler Seguin 10.00 25.00
11 Jaromir Jagr 15.00 40.00
12 Mario Lemieux 40.00 100.00
16 Teemu Selanne 12.00 30.00
17 Brett Hull 20.00 50.00
18 Paul Coffey 10.00 25.00
19 Pavel Datsyuk 12.00 30.00
20 Ryan Getzlaf 10.00 25.00

2011-12 Certified Throwback Threads

*MIRROR GOLD/25: .8X TO 2X BASIC INSERTS
1 Joel Quenneville 1.25 3.00
2 Randy Moller 1.25 3.00
3 Charlie Simmer 1.25 3.00
4 Chris Pronger 2.00 5.00
5 Guy Chouinard 1.50 4.00
6 Gary Bromley 2.50 6.00
7 Mike Modano 3.00 8.00
8 Nikolai Khabibulin 1.50 4.00
10 Gary Simmons 2.00 5.00

2011-12 Certified Throwback Threads Autographs

1 Joel Quenneville/100 8.00 20.00
2 Randy Moller/100 5.00 12.00
3 Charlie Simmer/100 5.00 12.00
4 Chris Pronger/100 8.00 20.00
5 Guy Chouinard/100 6.00 15.00
6 Gary Bromley/50 10.00 25.00
7 Mike Modano/100 15.00 40.00
8 Nikolai Khabibulin/100 10.00 25.00
10 Gary Simmons/50 8.00 20.00

2012-13 Certified

1 Jonas Hiller .25 .60
2 Brendan Smith .20 .50
3 Dion Phaneuf .25 .60
4 Taylor Hall .30 .75
5 Nicklas Lidstrom .30 .75
6 Erik Johnson .20 .50
7 Jack Johnson .20 .50
8 Alex Ovechkin 1.25 3.00
9 Bobby Ryan .25 .60
10 Marian Gaborik .30 .75
11 Daniel Alfredsson .30 .75
12 Jarome Iginla .40 1.00
13 Pavol Datsyuk .50 1.25
14 Jamie Benn .30 .75
15 Dany Heatley .25 .60
16 Andrew Ladd .20 .50
17 Ilya Kovalchuk .30 .75
18 Marc Staal .20 .50
19 Shane Doan .25 .60
20 Chris Pronger .30 .75
21 Loui Eriksson .20 .50
22 Daniel Sedin .40 1.00
23 Dustin Brown .30 .75
24 Ryan Callahan .20 .50
25 Nick Johnson .25 .60
26 Patrik Elias .30 .75
27 Rene Bourque .20 .50
28 Claude Giroux .30 .75
29 Jason Pominville .20 .50
30 Scott Clemmensen .25 .60
31 Antti Niemi .25 .60
32 Kris Versteeg .20 .50
33 Henrik Sedin .40 1.00
34 James Reimer .30 .75
35 Jean-Sebastien Giguere .30 .75
36 Patrick Kaleta .20 .50
37 Patrice Bergeron .40 1.00
38 Jonathan Toews .50 1.25
39 Logan Couture .40 1.00
40 Henrik Zetterberg .40 1.00
41 Craig Anderson .30 .75
42 David Backes .20 .50
43 Nazem Kadri .40 1.00
44 Jason Arnott .25 .60
45 Jonathan Bernier .25 .60
46 Andrei Kostitsyn .25 .60
47 T.J. Oshie .30 .75
48 Danny Briere .30 .75
49 Ryan Ellis .20 .50
50 Antoine Vermette .20 .50
51 Ryan Getzlaf .30 .75
52 Mike Green .25 .60
53 Jeff Skinner .40 1.00
54 Vincent Lecavalier .30 .75
55 Sergei Gonchar .20 .50
56 Brian Boucher .25 .60
57 Tyler Myers .20 .50
58 Kris Letang .40 1.00
59 Steve Mason .25 .60

2012-13 Certified

60 Shea Weber .25 .60
61 Rick Nash .30 .75
62 Carl Hagelin .20 .50
63 Brad Marchand .60 1.50
64 Zach Parise .30 .75
65 Erik Karlsson .40 1.00
66 James Neal .20 .50
67 Max Pacioretty .30 .75
68 Jaromir Jagr 1.00 2.50
69 Zdeno Chara .30 .75
70 Matt Martin .20 .50
71 Evgeni Malkin .60 1.50
72 Mikael Backlund .25 .60
73 Mikko Koivu .25 .60
74 John Carlson .30 .75
75 Nicklas Backstrom .30 .75
76 P.K. Subban .40 1.00
77 Jeff Carter .25 .60
78 Martin St. Louis .30 .75
79 Andrei Markov .20 .50
80 Nik Antropov .25 .60
81 Marian Hossa .30 .75
82 Drew Doughty .40 1.00
83 Ales Hemsky .25 .60
84 Mikhail Grabovski .20 .50
85 Dustin Byfuglien .30 .75
86 Wojtek Wolski .20 .50
87 Sidney Crosby 1.25 3.00
88 Patrick Kane .60 1.50
89 Sam Gagner .20 .50
90 John Tavares .50 1.25
91 Steven Stamkos .60 1.50
92 Gabriel Landeskog .40 1.00
93 Ryan Nugent-Hopkins .40 1.00
94 Michael Cammalleri .25 .60
95 Michael Grabner .25 .60
96 Eric Staal .40 1.00
97 Ryan Kesler .30 .75
98 Mikkel Boedker .20 .50
99 Martin Havlat .25 .60
100 Brenden Morrow .25 .60
101 Henrik Lundqvist MM 2.50 6.00
102 Jonathan Quick MM 1.25 3.00
103 Pekka Rinne MM 1.00 2.50
104 Mike Smith MM 1.00 2.50
105 Braden Holtby MM 1.25 3.00
106 Ilya Bryzgalov MM 1.00 2.50
107 Kari Lehtonen MM .75 2.00
108 Marc-Andre Fleury MM 2.00 5.00
109 Brian Elliott MM .75 2.00
110 Cory Schneider MM 1.00 2.50
111 Ondrej Pavelec MM 1.00 2.50
112 Carey Price MM 2.00 5.00
113 Miikka Kiprusoff MM 1.00 2.50
114 Tim Thomas MM 1.00 2.50
115 Ryan Miller MM 1.00 2.50
116 Niklas Backstrom MM .75 2.00
117 Corey Crawford MM 1.25 3.00
118 Cam Ward MM 1.00 2.50
119 Martin Brodeur MM 2.50 6.00
120 Jimmy Howard MM 1.25 3.00
121 Gordie Howe IMM 3.00 8.00
122 Bobby Clarke IMM 1.50 4.00
123 Patrick Roy IMM 2.50 6.00
124 Ray Bourque IMM 1.50 4.00
125 Jean Beliveau IMM 1.00 2.50
126 Steve Yzerman IMM 2.50 6.00
127 Joe Sakic IMM 2.00 5.00
128 Johnny Bower IMM 1.00 2.50
129 Mike Bossy IMM 1.00 2.50
130 Phil Esposito IMM 1.50 4.00
131 Mario Lemieux IMM 4.00 10.00
132 Ron Francis IMM 1.25 3.00
133 Brendan Shanahan IMM 1.00 2.50
134 Doug Gilmour IMM 1.25 3.00
135 Bernie Parent IMM 1.25 3.00
136 Gilbert Perreault IMM 1.00 2.50
137 Brian Leetch IMM .75 2.00
138 Mike Modano IMM 1.50 4.00
139 Brett Hull IMM 2.00 5.00
140 Ed Belfour IMM 1.00 2.50
141 Andrew Joudrey RC 2.00 5.00
142 Travis Turnbull RC 1.50 4.00
143 Gabriel Dumont RC 2.00 5.00
144 Jason Zucker RC 4.00 10.00
145 Jeremy Welsh RC 2.00 5.00
146 Ryan Hamilton RC 1.50 4.00
147 Lane MacDermid RC 2.00 5.00
148 Matt Watkins RC 1.50 4.00
149 Akim Aliu RC 2.00 5.00
150 Shawn Hunwick RC 1.50 4.00
151 Riley Sheahan RC 2.50 6.00
152 Ryan Garbutt RC 1.50 4.00
153 Torey Krug AU RC 5.00 12.00
154 Tyler Cuma AU RC 1.50 4.00
155 Mark Stone AU RC 6.00 15.00
156 Aaron Ness AU RC 1.50 4.00
157 Tyson Sexsmith AU RC 1.50 4.00
158 Brandon Bollig AU RC 1.50 4.00
159 Brandon Manning AU RC 2.00 5.00
160 Brenden Dillon AU RC 2.00 5.00
161 Carter Camper AU RC 1.50 4.00
162 Casey Cizikas AU RC 2.00 5.00
163 Chay Genoway AU RC 1.50 4.00
164 Cody Goloubef AU RC 1.50 4.00
165 Colby Robak AU RC 1.50 4.00
166 Dalton Prout AU RC 1.50 4.00
167 Jordan Nolan AU RC 1.50 4.00
168 Kristopher Foucault AU RC 1.50 4.00
169 Mat Clark AU RC 2.00 5.00
170 Matt Donovan AU RC 2.00 5.00
171 Max Sauve AU RC 1.50 4.00
172 Michael Hutchinson AU RC 2.50 6.00
173 Michael Stone AU RC 2.00 5.00
174 Mike Connolly AU RC 2.00 5.00
175 Philippe Cornet AU RC 2.00 5.00
176 Robert Mayer AU RC 2.50 6.00
177 Sven Baertschi JSY AU RC 2.50 6.00
178 J.T. Brown JSY AU RC 2.00 5.00
179 Reilly Smith JSY AU RC 5.00 12.00
180 Tyson Barrie JSY AU RC 5.00 12.00
181 Carter Ashton JSY AU RC 1.50 4.00
182 Chet Pickard JSY AU RC 2.00 5.00
183 Chris Kreider JSY AU RC 8.00 20.00
184 J.Schwartz JSY AU RC 8.00 20.00
185 Jake Allen JSY AU RC 5.00 12.00
186 Silfverberg JSY AU RC 3.00 8.00
187 Jussi Rynnas JSY AU RC 1.50 4.00
188 S.Glennie JSY AU RC 2.00 5.00

2012-13 Certified Fabric of the Game

*RED/25-150: .6X TO 1.5X BASIC INSERTS
*HOT BOX/25-75: .6X TO 1.5X BASIC INSERTS
*GOLD/25: .8X TO 2X BASIC INSERTS
FOGAB Alexander Burmistrov/299 2.00 5.00
FOGABU Alexandre Burrows/299 1.50 4.00
FOGAE Alexander Edler/299 1.50 4.00
FOGALI Anders Lindback/299 1.50 4.00
FOGAO Alex Ovechkin/299 10.00 25.00
FOGAP Alex Pietrangelo/199 2.00 5.00
FOGBEL Ed Belfour/299 2.50 6.00
FOGBER Jonathan Bernier/299 2.00 5.00
FOGBET Brian Elliott/299 2.00 5.00
FOGBJC B.J. Crombeen/299 1.50 4.00
FOGBLI Bryan Little/299 2.50 6.00
FOGBOR Brooks Orpik/299 1.50 4.00
FOGBR Bobby Ryan/299 2.00 5.00
FOGBRO Dustin Brown/299 2.50 6.00
FOGBS2 Brendan Shanahan/299 2.50 6.00
FOGBSC Brayden Schenn/150 2.50 6.00
FOGBSU Brandon Sutter/100 1.50 4.00
FOGBUR Brent Burns/299 2.50 6.00
FOGCFO Cam Fowler/299 2.50 6.00
FOGCG Claude Giroux/299 2.50 6.00
FOGCKU Chris Kunitz/299 2.50 6.00
FOGCNE Chris Neil/299 1.50 4.00
FOGCPI Chet Pickard/299 2.00 5.00
FOGDB David Backes/299 1.50 4.00
FOGDD Drew Doughty/299 3.00 8.00
FOGDH Dany Heatley/299 2.00 5.00
FOGDSE Devin Setoguchi/299 2.00 5.00
FOGDSP Devante Smith-Pelly/299 2.00 5.00
FOGDWI Dennis Wideman/299 1.50 4.00
FOGEJ Erik Johnson/299 1.50 4.00
FOGEK Erik Karlsson/299 3.00 8.00
FOGEL Eric Lindros/299 4.00 10.00
FOGFN Frans Nielsen/299 1.50 4.00
FOGFP Felix Potvin/299 4.00 10.00
FOGGAB Marian Gaborik/299 2.50 6.00
FOGGLE Scott Glennie/299 2.00 5.00
FOGHAL Jaroslav Halak/299 2.50 6.00
FOGHEM Ales Hemsky/299 2.00 5.00
FOGHZ Henrik Zetterberg/299 3.00 8.00
FOGIB Ilya Bryzgalov/299 2.50 6.00
FOGIK Ilya Kovalchuk/299 2.50 6.00
FOGJA Jake Allen/299 5.00 12.00
FOGJAG Jaromir Jagr/299 8.00 20.00
FOGJC Jeff Carter/299 2.00 5.00
FOGJHE Jhonas Enroth/299 2.50 6.00
FOGJI Jarome Iginla/299 3.00 8.00
FOGJJ Jack Johnson/299 1.50 4.00
FOGJL Joffrey Lupul/299 1.50 4.00
FOGJPO Jason Pominville/299 1.50 4.00
FOGJS Joe Sakic/299 5.00 12.00
FOGJSG Jean-Sebastien Giguere/299 2.50 6.00
FOGJTO Jonathan Toews/299 4.00 10.00
FOGJVO Jakub Voracek/299 2.00 5.00
FOGKAN Patrick Kane/299 5.00 12.00
FOGKHA Nikolai Khabibulin/299 2.50 6.00
FOGKL Kari Lehtonen/299 2.00 5.00
FOGKS Kevin Shattenkirk/299 1.50 4.00
FOGKV Kris Versteeg/299 1.50 4.00
FOGLC Logan Couture/299 3.00 8.00
FOGLE Loui Eriksson/299 1.50 4.00
FOGLEM Mario Lemieux/299 10.00 25.00
FOGLET Kris Letang/299 3.00 8.00
FOGMAF Marc-Andre Fleury/299 5.00 12.00
FOGMAR Patrick Marleau/299 2.50 6.00
FOGMBA Mikael Backlund/299 2.00 5.00
FOGMBI Martin Biron/299 2.00 5.00
FOGMD Matt Duchene/299 2.50 6.00
FOGMGR Matt Greene/299 2.00 5.00
FOGMRI Mike Richards/299 2.00 5.00
FOGMRU Mike Rupp/299 1.50 4.00
FOGNF Nick Foligno/199 2.00 5.00
FOGNG Nathan Gerbe/299 1.50 4.00
FOGNLI Nicklas Lidstrom/299 2.50 6.00
FOGOP Ondrej Pavelec/299 2.50 6.00
FOGPBE Patrik Berglund/299 1.50 4.00
FOGPK Phil Kessel/299 2.50 6.00
FOGPRO Chris Pronger/299 2.50 6.00
FOGRDP Rick DiPietro/299 2.00 5.00
FOGRN Rick Nash/299 2.50 6.00
FOGRO Ryan O'Reilly/299 2.50 6.00
FOGSC2 Sidney Crosby/299 10.00 25.00
FOGSCL Scott Clemmensen/299 2.00 5.00
FOGSD Simon Despres/299 2.00 5.00
FOGSED Daniel Sedin/299 3.00 8.00
FOGSEM Alexander Semin/299 2.50 6.00
FOGSGA Simon Gagne/299 2.50 6.00
FOGSHA Scott Hartnell/299 1.50 4.00
FOGSM Steve Mason/199 2.00 5.00
FOGSTA Marc Staal/299 1.50 4.00
FOGSY Steve Yzerman/299 6.00 15.00
FOGTE Tyler Ennis/299 1.50 4.00
FOGTH Taylor Hall/299 2.50 6.00
FOGTM Tyler Myers/299 1.50 4.00
FOGTO T.J. Oshie/299 2.50 6.00
FOGTR Tuukka Rask/299 3.00 8.00
FOGTS Tyler Seguin/299 3.00 8.00
FOGTT Tim Thomas/299 2.50 6.00
FOGWIL Colin Wilson/299 2.00 5.00
FOGZB Zach Boychuk/299 1.50 4.00
FOGZP Zach Parise/299 2.50 6.00

2012-13 Certified Fabric of the Game Mirror Blue Jersey Autographs

FOGAB Alexander Burmistrov/50 8.00 20.00
FOGABU Alexandre Burrows/50 8.00 20.00
FOGAO Alex Ovechkin/25 60.00 120.00
FOGAP Alex Pietrangelo/25 10.00 25.00
FOGBEL Ed Belfour/25 12.00 30.00
FOGBER Jonathan Bernier/50 8.00 20.00
FOGBR Bobby Ryan/50 8.00 20.00
FOGBRO Dustin Brown/50 10.00 25.00
FOGBS2 Brendan Shanahan/25 40.00 80.00
FOGBUR Brent Burns/50 8.00 20.00
FOGCFO Cam Fowler/50 10.00 25.00
FOGCG Claude Giroux/50 12.00 30.00
FOGCNE Chris Neil/50 6.00 15.00
FOGCPI Chet Pickard/50 8.00 20.00
FOGDB David Backes/50 6.00 15.00
FOGDD Drew Doughty/50 15.00 30.00
FOGDH Dany Heatley/50 8.00 20.00
FOGDSE Devin Setoguchi/50 10.00 25.00
FOGDSP Devante Smith-Pelly/50 8.00 20.00
FOGEJ Erik Johnson/50 6.00 15.00
FOGEL Eric Lindros/25 25.00 50.00
FOGFN Frans Nielsen/50 6.00 15.00
FOGFP Felix Potvin/50 25.00 50.00
FOGGAB Marian Gaborik/50 12.00 30.00
FOGGLE Scott Glennie/50 8.00 20.00
FOGHAL Jaroslav Halak/50 10.00 25.00
FOGHEM Ales Hemsky/50 8.00 20.00
FOGJA Jake Allen/50 20.00 50.00
FOGJAG Jaromir Jagr/25 30.00 60.00
FOGJI Jarome Iginla/25 12.00 30.00
FOGJJ Jack Johnson/50 6.00 15.00
FOGJS Joe Sakic/25 25.00 60.00
FOGJSG Jean-Sebastien Giguere/50 15.00 40.00
FOGJTO Jonathan Toews/50 30.00 60.00
FOGKAN Patrick Kane/25 25.00 60.00
FOGKHA Nikolai Khabibulin/50 10.00 25.00
FOGKL Kari Lehtonen/50 8.00 20.00
FOGKS Kevin Shattenkirk/50 6.00 15.00
FOGLC Logan Couture/50 12.00 30.00
FOGLE Loui Eriksson/50 6.00 15.00
FOGLET Kris Letang/50 EXCH 25.00 50.00
FOGMAF Marc-Andre Fleury/50 20.00 50.00
FOGMAR Patrick Marleau/50 10.00 25.00
FOGMD Matt Duchene/50 10.00 25.00
FOGNG Nathan Gerbe/50 6.00 15.00
FOGNLI Nicklas Lidstrom/25 12.00 30.00
FOGOP Ondrej Pavelec/50 6.00 15.00
FOGPK Phil Kessel/50 10.00 25.00
FOGPRO Chris Pronger/50 10.00 25.00
FOGRN Rick Nash/50 12.00 30.00
FOGRO Ryan O'Reilly/50 15.00 30.00
FOGSD Simon Despres/50 8.00 20.00
FOGSED Daniel Sedin/50 12.00 30.00
FOGSEM Alexander Semin/50 10.00 25.00
FOGSM Steve Mason/50 8.00 20.00
FOGSTA Marc Staal/50 6.00 15.00
FOGTE Tyler Ennis/25 12.00 30.00
FOGTH Taylor Hall/50 10.00 25.00
FOGTO T.J. Oshie/50 10.00 25.00
FOGTR Tuukka Rask/50 12.00 30.00
FOGTS Tyler Seguin/50 25.00 50.00
FOGWIL Colin Wilson/50 8.00 20.00
FOGZP Zach Parise/50 10.00 25.00

2012-13 Certified Face Off Dual Sticks

1 A.Ovechkin/E.Malkin/50 10.00 25.00
2 B.Shanahan/P.Roy/50 12.00 30.00
3 C.Price/J.Halak/50 10.00 25.00
4 L.Robitaille/S.Yzerman/20 12.00 30.00
5 C.Neely/D.Gilmour/50 6.00 15.00
6 E.Lindros/M.Lemieux/50 20.00 50.00
7 H.Lundqvist/M.Streit/50 12.00 30.00
8 J.Sakic/L.Eriksson/20 10.00 25.00
9 R.McDonagh/Z.Parise/50 5.00 12.00
10 R.Kesler/V.Lecavalier/20 5.00 12.00

2012-13 Certified Goalie Pulls

*JERSEYS/25: 1X TO 2.5X BASIC INSERT
1 James Reimer 2.50 6.00
2 Jake Allen 5.00 12.00
3 Chet Pickard 2.00 5.00
4 Mike Smith 2.50 6.00
5 Kari Lehtonen 2.00 5.00
6 Brian Elliott 2.00 5.00
7 Curtis Joseph 3.00 8.00
8 Carey Price 5.00 12.00
9 Ed Belfour 2.50 6.00
10 Nikolai Khabibulin 2.50 6.00
11 Jaroslav Halak 2.50 6.00
12 Steve Mason 2.00 5.00
13 Brent Johnson 2.00 5.00
14 Ondrej Pavelec 2.50 6.00
15 Antti Niemi 2.00 5.00
16 Jonathan Quick 3.00 8.00
17 Tom Barrasso 2.50 6.00
18 Ron Hextall 2.50 6.00
19 Grant Fuhr 4.00 10.00
20 Marc-Andre Fleury 5.00 12.00
21 Jonas Hiller 2.00 5.00
22 Ilya Bryzgalov 2.50 6.00
23 Patrick Roy COL 6.00 15.00
24 Anders Lindback 1.50 4.00
25 Semyon Varlamov 2.50 6.00
26 Cam Ward 2.50 6.00
27 Roberto Luongo 4.00 10.00
28 Evgeni Nabokov 2.00 5.00
29 Niklas Backstrom 2.00 5.00
30 Tim Thomas 2.50 6.00
31 Tomas Vokoun 2.00 5.00
32 Craig Anderson 2.50 6.00
33 Jhonas Enroth 2.50 6.00
34 Patrick Roy MON 6.00 15.00
35 Rogie Vachon 3.00 8.00
36 Robin Lehner 2.00 5.00
37 Miikka Kiprusoff 2.50 6.00
38 Ryan Miller 2.50 6.00
39 Sergei Bobrovsky 4.00 10.00
40 Martin Brodeur 6.00 15.00
41 Jonathan Bernier 2.00 5.00
42 Scott Clemmensen 2.00 5.00
43 Jussi Rynnas 1.50 4.00
44 Tuukka Rask 3.00 8.00
45 Felix Potvin 4.00 10.00
46 Jimmy Howard 3.00 8.00
47 Henrik Lundqvist 6.00 15.00
48 Pekka Rinne 2.50 6.00
49 Braden Holtby 3.00 8.00
50 Cory Schneider 2.50 6.00

2012-13 Certified Icons

SEMISTARS/250 1.25 3.00
UNLISTED STARS/250 1.50 4.00
1 Gordie Howe 5.00 12.00
2 Jean Beliveau 1.50 4.00
3 Alex Delvecchio 1.50 4.00
4 Stan Mikita 2.00 5.00
5 Johnny Bower 1.50 4.00
6 Bobby Clarke 2.50 6.00
7 Denis Potvin 1.50 4.00
8 Lanny McDonald 1.50 4.00
9 Bobby Hull 3.00 8.00
10 Johnny Bucyk 1.50 4.00
11 Gilbert Perreault 1.50 4.00
12 Bernie Parent 2.00 5.00
13 Marcel Dionne 2.00 5.00
14 Phil Esposito 2.50 6.00
15 Guy Lafleur 2.00 5.00

2012-13 Certified Icons Signatures

SEMISTARS 10.00 25.00
UNLISTED STARS 12.00 30.00
2 Jean Beliveau/25 20.00 50.00
3 Alex Delvecchio/25 12.00 30.00
4 Stan Mikita/25 15.00 40.00
5 Johnny Bower/25 12.00 30.00
6 Bobby Clarke/25 30.00 60.00
7 Denis Potvin/25 12.00 30.00
8 Lanny McDonald/25 12.00 30.00
9 Bobby Hull/25 30.00 60.00
10 Johnny Bucyk/25 12.00 30.00
11 Gilbert Perreault/25 EXCH 12.00 30.00
12 Bernie Parent/25 15.00 40.00
13 Marcel Dionne/25 15.00 40.00
14 Phil Esposito/25 EXCH 15.00 40.00
15 Guy Lafleur/25 15.00 40.00

2012-13 Certified Junior Class Signatures

UNLISTED STARS /100 10.00 25.00
UNLISTED STARS /25-75 12.00 30.00
1 C.Hodgson/M.Duchene/50 12.00 30.00
2 B.Shanahan/R.Nash/25 30.00 60.00
3 Landeskog/M.Boedker/75 12.00 30.00
4 Phaneuf/Nugent-Hpkns/100 15.00 40.00
5 C.Neely/S.Baertschi/100 10.00 25.00
7 A.Henrique/T.Hall/100 15.00 40.00
8 J.Staal/S.Yzerman/20 30.00 60.00
9 D.Doughty/D.Brown/100 12.00 30.00
10 C.Price/C.Pickard/50 15.00 40.00
11 E.Lindros/R.Middleton/100 20.00 40.00
12 D.Byfuglien/S.Glennie/100 10.00 25.00
13 Pietrangelo/Scheifele/100 20.00 40.00
14 D.Dubnyk/J.Iginla/50 15.00 40.00
15 T.Linden/T.Ennis/25 25.00 50.00
16 B.Trottier/J.Sakic/25 30.00 80.00
17 C.Perry/P.Kane/25 25.00 50.00
18 C.Simmer/J.Thornton/100 15.00 40.00
19 A.Shaw/B.Ryan/100 8.00 20.00
20 C.Giroux/L.Robitaille/50 12.00 30.00

2012-13 Certified Mirror Blue

*BLUE VETS/99: 2X TO 5X BASIC CARDS
*BLUE MM/IMM/50: .8X TO 2X BASIC CARDS
*BLUE ROOKIE/50: .6X TO 1.5X BASIC RC
*BLUE AU/99: .6X TO 1.5X BASIC AU RC
*BLUE JSY AU/50: .8X TO 2X JSY AU

2012-13 Certified Mirror Gold

*GOLD VETS/25: 4X TO 10X BASIC CARDS
*GOLD MM/IMM/25: 1.2X TO 3X BASIC IMM
*GOLD AU/25: 1X TO 2.5X BASIC AU RC
*GOLD JSY AU/25: 1X TO 2.5X BASE JSY AU

2012-13 Certified Mirror Hot Box

*HB VETS(1-100): 1X TO 2.5X BASIC CARDS
*HB MM/IMM/75: .6X TO 1.5X BASIC MM/IMM
*HB ROOKIE/99: .5X TO 1.2X BASIC RC
*HB AU: .8X TO 2X BASIC AU RC /50

2012-13 Certified Mirror Red

*RED VETS/199: 1.5X TO 4X BASIC CARDS
*RED MM/IMM/100: .6X TO 1.5X BASIC MM/IMM
*RED ROOKIE/100: .5X TO 1.2X BASIC RC
*RED AU/199: .5X TO 1.2X BASIC AU RC
*RED JSY AU/100: .6X TO 1.5X JSY AU RC

2012-13 Certified Path to the Cup Conference Finals

1 D.Brown/S.Doan 1.50 4.00
2 J.Carter/K.Yandle 1.25 3.00
3 A.Martinez/P.Bissonnette 1.25 3.00
4 J.Quick/M.Smith 2.00 5.00
5 D.Doughty/M.Hanzal 2.00 5.00
6 C.Kreider/S.Bernier 4.00 10.00
7 H.Lundqvist/M.Brodeur 4.00 10.00
8 P.Elias/R.Callahan 1.50 4.00
9 R.Fedotenko/Z.Parise 1.50 4.00
10 I.Kovalchuk/M.Gaborik 1.50 4.00
11 B.Richards/M.Brodeur 4.00 10.00

2012-13 Certified Path to the Cup Conference Finals Dual Jerseys

1 D.Brown/S.Doan 6.00 15.00
2 J.Carter/K.Yandle 5.00 12.00
3 A.Martinez/P.Bissonnette 5.00 12.00
4 J.Quick/M.Smith 8.00 20.00
5 D.Doughty/M.Hanzal 8.00 20.00
6 C.Kreider/S.Bernier 15.00 40.00
7 H.Lundqvist/M.Brodeur 15.00 40.00
8 P.Elias/R.Callahan 6.00 15.00
9 R.Fedotenko/Z.Parise 6.00 15.00
10 I.Kovalchuk/M.Gaborik 6.00 15.00
11 B.Richards/M.Brodeur 15.00 40.00

2012-13 Certified Path to the Cup Conference Trophy

1 Zach Parise 6.00 15.00
2 Dustin Brown 6.00 15.00

2012-13 Certified Path to the Cup Conn Smythe

1 Jonathan Quick 5.00 12.00

2012-13 Certified Path to the Cup Quarter Finals

1 D.Penner/R.Luongo 2.00 5.00
2 H.Sedin/T.Lewis 1.50 4.00
3 C.Schneider/J.Williams 1.25 3.00
4 R.Kesler/W.Mitchell 1.25 3.00
5 D.Sedin/J.Stoll 1.50 4.00
6 M.Havlat/P.Berglund 1.00 2.50
7 J.Halak/J.Thornton 2.00 5.00
8 J.Arnott/L.Couture 1.50 4.00
9 A.Niemi/B.Crombeen 1.00 2.50
10 J.Langenbrunner/P.Marleau 1.25 3.00
11 A.Vermette/J.Toews 2.00 5.00
12 K.Yandle/P.Sharp 1.25 3.00
13 M.Frolik/M.Boedker .75 2.00
14 D.Keith/M.Smith 1.25 3.00
15 P.Kane/S.Doan 2.50 6.00
16 B.Seabrook/M.Smith 1.25 3.00
17 B.Yip/H.Zetterberg 1.50 4.00
18 A.Kostitsyn/J.Howard 1.50 4.00
19 P.Hornqvist/P.Datsyuk 2.00 5.00
20 M.Erat/N.Lidstrom 1.25 3.00
21 D.Legwand/T.Holmstrom 1.00 2.50
22 A.Anisimov/D.Alfredsson 1.25 3.00
23 E.Karlsson/M.Del Zotto 1.50 4.00
24 B.Boyle/C.Anderson 1.25 3.00
25 M.Michalek/R.McDonagh .75 2.00
26 D.Girardi/J.Spezza 1.25 3.00
27 B.Prust/C.Neil .75 2.00
28 C.Kreider/N.Foligno 3.00 8.00
29 K.Alzner/T.Thomas 1.25 3.00
30 D.Krejci/N.Backstrom 1.25 3.00
31 M.Green/Z.Chara 1.25 3.00
32 D.Wideman/M.Lucic 1.25 3.00
33 M.Johansson/P.Bergeron 1.50 4.00
34 A.Ovechkin/T.Seguin 5.00 12.00
35 B.Marchand/J.Carlson 2.50 6.00
36 K.Versteeg/P.Elias 1.25 3.00
37 M.Samuelsson/T.Zajac .75 2.00
38 S.Clemmensen/Z.Parise 1.25 3.00
39 M.Brodeur/S.Weiss 3.00 8.00
40 B.Campbell/S.Bernier .75 2.00
41 D.Kulikov/I.Kovalchuk 1.25 3.00
42 J.Theodore/M.Brodeur 3.00 8.00
43 J.Voracek/K.Letang 1.50 4.00
44 E.Malkin/S.Couturier 2.50 6.00
45 D.Briere/J.Staal 1.00 2.50
46 K.Timonen/S.Despres 1.00 2.50
47 M.Fleury/S.Hartnell 2.50 6.00
48 I.Bryzgalov/J.Neal 1.25 3.00

2012-13 Certified Path to the Cup Quarter Finals Dual Jerseys

1 D.Penner/R.Luongo 5.00 12.00
2 H.Sedin/T.Lewis 4.00 10.00
3 C.Schneider/J.Williams 3.00 8.00
4 R.Kesler/W.Mitchell 3.00 8.00
5 D.Sedin/J.Stoll 4.00 10.00
6 M.Havlat/P.Berglund 2.50 6.00
7 J.Halak/J.Thornton 5.00 12.00
8 J.Arnott/L.Couture 4.00 10.00
9 A.Niemi/B.Crombeen 2.50 6.00
10 J.Langenbrunner/P.Marleau 3.00 8.00
11 A.Vermette/J.Toews 5.00 12.00
12 K.Yandle/P.Sharp 3.00 8.00
13 M.Frolik/M.Boedker 2.00 5.00
14 D.Keith/M.Smith 3.00 8.00
15 P.Kane/S.Doan 6.00 15.00
16 B.Seabrook/M.Smith 3.00 8.00
17 B.Yip/H.Zetterberg 4.00 10.00
18 A.Kostitsyn/J.Howard 4.00 10.00
19 P.Hornqvist/P.Datsyuk 5.00 12.00
20 M.Erat/N.Lidstrom 3.00 8.00
21 D.Legwand/T.Holmstrom 2.50 6.00
22 A.Anisimov/D.Alfredsson 3.00 8.00
23 E.Karlsson/M.Del Zotto 4.00 10.00
24 B.Boyle/C.Anderson 3.00 8.00
25 M.Michalek/R.McDonagh 2.00 5.00
26 D.Girardi/J.Spezza 3.00 8.00
27 B.Prust/C.Neil 2.00 5.00
28 C.Kreider/N.Foligno 8.00 20.00
29 K.Alzner/T.Thomas 3.00 8.00
30 D.Krejci/N.Backstrom 3.00 8.00
31 M.Green/Z.Chara 3.00 8.00
32 D.Wideman/M.Lucic 3.00 8.00
33 M.Johansson/P.Bergeron 4.00 10.00
34 A.Ovechkin/T.Seguin 12.00 30.00
35 B.Marchand/J.Carlson 6.00 15.00
36 K.Versteeg/P.Elias 3.00 8.00
37 M.Samuelsson/T.Zajac 2.00 5.00
38 S.Clemmensen/Z.Parise 3.00 8.00
39 M.Brodeur/S.Weiss 8.00 20.00
40 B.Campbell/S.Bernier 2.00 5.00
41 D.Kulikov/I.Kovalchuk 3.00 8.00
42 J.Theodore/M.Brodeur 8.00 20.00
43 J.Voracek/K.Letang 4.00 10.00
44 E.Malkin/S.Couturier 6.00 15.00
45 D.Briere/J.Staal 2.50 6.00
46 K.Timonen/S.Despres 2.50 6.00
47 M.Fleury/S.Hartnell 6.00 15.00
48 I.Bryzgalov/J.Neal 3.00 8.00

2012-13 Certified Path to the Cup Semifinals

1 D.Backes/M.Greene 1.25 3.00
2 J.Allen/M.Richards 3.00 8.00
3 A.Pietrangelo/A.Kopitar 2.50 6.00
4 J.Quick/T.Oshie 2.00 5.00
5 C.Wilson/M.Hanzal 1.25 3.00
6 A.Vermette/R.Suter 1.25 3.00
7 K.Yandle/P.Rinne 1.50 4.00
8 P.Hornqvist/S.Doan 1.25 3.00
9 M.Smith/S.Weber 1.50 4.00
10 A.Semin/B.Richards 1.50 4.00
11 A.Ovechkin/M.Del Zotto 6.00 15.00
12 J.Carlson/M.Gaborik 1.50 4.00
13 C.Hagelin/M.Green 1.25 3.00
14 D.Wideman/H.Lundqvist 4.00 10.00
15 B.Holtby/D.Stepan 2.00 5.00
16 M.Rupp/N.Backstrom 1.50 4.00
17 J.van Riemsdyk/Z.Parise 1.50 4.00
18 A.Larsson/B.Schenn 1.50 4.00
19 I.Kovalchuk/J.Jagr 5.00 12.00
20 C.Giroux/M.Brodeur 4.00 10.00
21 P.Elias/W.Simmonds 2.00 5.00

2012-13 Certified Path to the Cup Semifinals Dual Jerseys

1 D.Backes/M.Greene 5.00 12.00
2 J.Allen/M.Richards 8.00 20.00
3 A.Pietrangelo/A.Kopitar 6.00 15.00
4 J.Quick/T.Oshie 5.00 12.00
5 C.Wilson/M.Hanzal 3.00 8.00
6 A.Vermette/R.Suter 3.00 8.00
7 K.Yandle/P.Rinne 4.00 10.00
8 P.Hornqvist/S.Doan 3.00 8.00
9 M.Smith/S.Weber 4.00 10.00
10 A.Semin/B.Richards 4.00 10.00
11 A.Ovechkin/M.Del Zotto 15.00 40.00
12 J.Carlson/M.Gaborik 4.00 10.00
13 C.Hagelin/M.Green 3.00 8.00
14 D.Wideman/H.Lundqvist 10.00 25.00
15 B.Holtby/D.Stepan 5.00 12.00
16 M.Rupp/N.Backstrom 4.00 10.00
17 J.van Riemsdyk/Z.Parise 4.00 10.00
18 A.Larsson/B.Schenn 4.00 10.00
19 I.Kovalchuk/J.Jagr 12.00 30.00
20 C.Giroux/M.Brodeur 10.00 25.00
21 P.Elias/W.Simmonds 5.00 12.00

2012-13 Certified Path to the Cup Stanley Cup Finals

1 A.Kopitar/P.Elias 5.00 12.00
2 I.Kovalchuk/J.Carter 3.00 8.00
3 J.Quick/Z.Parise 4.00 10.00
4 D.Doughty/I.Kovalchuk 4.00 10.00
5 J.Williams/M.Brodeur 8.00 20.00
6 M.Richards/T.Zajac 2.50 6.00

2012-13 Certified Path to the Cup Stanley Cup Finals Dual Jerseys

1 A.Kopitar/P.Elias 8.00 20.00
2 I.Kovalchuk/J.Carter 5.00 12.00
3 J.Quick/Z.Parise 6.00 15.00
4 D.Doughty/I.Kovalchuk 6.00 15.00
5 J.Williams/M.Brodeur 12.00 30.00
6 M.Richards/T.Zajac 4.00 10.00

2012-13 Certified Path to the Cup Stanley Cup Winner

1 Dustin Brown 5.00 12.00
2 Jonathan Quick 6.00 15.00
3 Anze Kopitar 8.00 20.00
4 Willie Mitchell 4.00 10.00
5 Simon Gagne 5.00 12.00
6 Drew Doughty 6.00 15.00
7 Dustin Penner 4.00 10.00
8 Mike Richards 4.00 10.00
9 Matt Greene 4.00 10.00
10 Justin Williams 4.00 10.00
11 Jarret Stoll 4.00 10.00

2012-13 Certified Rookie Redemption

1 Nail Yakupov 10.00 25.00
2 Alex Galchenyuk 10.00 25.00
3 Jonathan Huberdeau 8.00 20.00
4 Brendan Gallagher 10.00 25.00
5 Dougie Hamilton 6.00 15.00
6 Vladimir Tarasenko 8.00 20.00
7 Mikhail Grigorenko 6.00 15.00
8 Sean Monahan 6.00 15.00
9 Seth Jones 6.00 15.00
10 Morgan Rielly 4.00 10.00
11 Tomas Hertl 6.00 15.00
12 Jacob Trouba 5.00 12.00
13 Ryan Murray 4.00 10.00
14 Aleksander Barkov 12.00 30.00
15 Nathan MacKinnon 10.00 25.00

2012-13 Certified Signatures

COMMON CARD 4.00 10.00
SEMISTARS 5.00 12.00
UNLISTED STARS 6.00 15.00
1 Gabriel Landeskog 8.00 20.00
2 Colten Teubert 4.00 10.00
3 Dustin Byfuglien 6.00 15.00
4 Max Sauve 4.00 10.00
5 Brendan Shanahan 6.00 15.00
6 Brad Richards 6.00 15.00
7 Tuukka Rask 8.00 20.00
8 Keith Aulie 4.00 10.00
9 Allen York 4.00 10.00
10 Eddie Lack 6.00 15.00
11 Bryan Trottier 6.00 15.00
12 Tyler Seguin 8.00 20.00
13 Jaden Schwartz 12.00 30.00
14 Cody Eakin 4.00 10.00
15 Nick Palmieri 5.00 12.00
16 Roman Horak 5.00 12.00
17 Cam Neely 6.00 15.00
18 Pavel Datsyuk 10.00 25.00
19 Ryan Nugent-Hopkins 8.00 20.00
20 Peter Holland 4.00 10.00
21 Alexei Emelin 4.00 10.00
22 Stefan Elliott 5.00 12.00
23 Clarke MacArthur 4.00 10.00
24 Robert Bortuzzo 4.00 10.00
25 Tyler Bozak 4.00 10.00
26 Alex Ovechkin 25.00 60.00
27 Corey Tropp 5.00 12.00
28 Gustav Nyquist 4.00 10.00
29 Chris Kreider 15.00 40.00
30 Dmitry Orlov 6.00 15.00
31 Alexander Semin 6.00 15.00
32 David Savard 4.00 10.00
33 Harry Zolnierczyk 4.00 10.00
34 Anton Lander 5.00 12.00
35 Andy Miele 4.00 10.00
36 Anders Nilsson 4.00 10.00
37 Cody Almond 4.00 10.00
38 Dylan Olsen 4.00 10.00
39 Andrew Shaw 4.00 10.00
40 Brenden Dillon 5.00 12.00
41 Chris Vande Velde 4.00 10.00
42 Marcus Foligno 5.00 12.00
43 Cory Emmerton 4.00 10.00
44 Brendan Smith 4.00 10.00
45 Jimmy Hayes 4.00 10.00
46 Carl Hagelin 4.00 10.00
47 Carson McMillan 4.00 10.00
48 Matt Read 5.00 12.00
49 Harri Sateri 5.00 12.00
50 Brayden McNabb 6.00 15.00

2012-13 Certified Stars

S1 Claude Giroux 1.00 2.50
S2 Evgeni Malkin 2.00 5.00
S3 Steven Stamkos 2.00 5.00
S4 Henrik Lundqvist 2.50 6.00
S5 Jonathan Quick 1.25 3.00
S6 Tyler Seguin 1.25 3.00
S7 Alex Ovechkin 4.00 10.00
S8 Jordan Eberle 1.00 2.50
S9 Jonathan Toews 1.50 4.00
S10 John Tavares 1.50 4.00
S11 Jarome Iginla 1.25 3.00
S12 Carey Price 2.00 5.00
S13 Sidney Crosby 4.00 10.00
S14 Rick Nash 1.00 2.50
S15 Ilya Kovalchuk 1.00 2.50
S16 Erik Karlsson 1.25 3.00
S17 Phil Kessel 1.00 2.50
S18 Henrik Sedin 1.25 3.00
S19 Joe Thornton 1.50 4.00
S20 Henrik Zetterberg 1.25 3.00

2012-13 Certified Stars Materials Mirror Red Jersey

*BLUE/50: .8X TO 2X RED/100
*GOLD/25: 1.X TO 2.5X RED/100
S1 Claude Giroux 2.50 6.00
S2 Evgeni Malkin 5.00 12.00
S3 Steven Stamkos 5.00 12.00
S4 Henrik Lundqvist 6.00 15.00
S5 Jonathan Quick 3.00 8.00
S6 Tyler Seguin 3.00 8.00
S7 Alex Ovechkin 10.00 25.00
S8 Jordan Eberle 2.50 6.00
S9 Jonathan Toews 4.00 10.00
S10 John Tavares 4.00 10.00
S11 Jarome Iginla 3.00 8.00
S12 Carey Price 4.00 10.00
S13 Sidney Crosby 10.00 25.00
S14 Rick Nash 2.50 6.00
S15 Ilya Kovalchuk 2.50 6.00
S16 Erik Karlsson 3.00 8.00
S17 Phil Kessel 2.50 6.00
S18 Henrik Sedin 3.00 8.00
S19 Joe Thornton 4.00 10.00
S20 Henrik Zetterberg 3.00 8.00

1936 Champion Postcards

COMPLETE SET (10) 875.00 1750.00
1 Marty Barry
Boston Bruins/18/1/36 40.00 80.00
2 Mush March
Chicago Blackhawks/8/2/36 40.00 80.00
3 Reg(Hooley) Smith
Montreal Canadiens/18/1/36 87.50 175.00
4 Sweeney Schriner/22/2/36 87.50 175.00
5 King Clancy
Toronto Maple Leafs/18/1/36 250.00 500.00
6 Bill Cook
New York Rangers/1/2/36 100.00 200.00
7 Pep Kelly
Toronto Maple Leafs/25/1/36 40.00 80.00
8 Aurel Joliat
Montreal Canadiens/15/2/36 225.00 450.00
9 Charles Conacher
Toronto Maple Leafs/29/2/36 200.00 400.00
10 Bun Cook
New York Rangers/7/3/36 100.00 200.00

1963-65 Chex Photos

COMPLETE SET (60) 1000.00 2000.00
1 George Armstrong 20.00 40.00
2 Ralph Backstrom 10.00 20.00
3 Dave Balon 7.50 15.00
4 Bob Baun 12.50 25.00
5A Jean Beliveau 50.00 100.00
5B Jean Beliveau 50.00 100.00
6 Red Berenson 10.00 20.00
7 Toe Blake CO 15.00 30.00
8 Johnny Bower 25.00 50.00
9 Alex Delvecchio 20.00 40.00
10 Kent Douglas 7.50 15.00
11 Dick Duff 10.00 20.00
12 Phil Esposito 75.00 150.00
13 John Ferguson 12.50 25.00
14 Bill Gadsby 15.00 30.00
15 Jean Gauthier 7.50 15.00
16 BoomBoom Geoffrion 30.00 60.00
17 Glenn Hall 25.00 50.00
18 Terry Harper 10.00 20.00
19 Billy Harris 7.50 15.00
20 Bill Hay 7.50 15.00
21 Paul Henderson 20.00 40.00
22 Bill Hicke 7.50 15.00
23 Wayne Hillman 7.50 15.00
24 Charlie Hodge 12.50 25.00
25 Tim Horton 50.00 100.00
26 Gordie Howe 112.50 225.00
27 Bobby Hull 100.00 200.00
28 Punch Imlach CO 10.00 20.00
29 Red Kelly 20.00 40.00
30 Dave Keon 30.00 60.00
31 Jacques Laperriere 12.50 25.00
32 Ed Litzenberger 7.50 15.00
33 Parker MacDonald 7.50 15.00
34 Bruce MacGregor 7.50 15.00
35 Frank Mahovlich 30.00 60.00
36 Chico Maki 10.00 20.00
37 Pit Martin 10.00 20.00
38 John MacMillan 7.50 15.00
39 Stan Mikita 30.00 60.00
40 Bob Nevin 7.50 15.00
41 Pierre Pilote 12.50 25.00
42 Marcel Pronovost 15.00 30.00
43 Claude Provost 7.50 15.00
44 Bob Pulford 15.00 30.00
45 Marc Reaume 7.50 15.00
46 Henri Richard 30.00 60.00
47A Bobby Rousseau 10.00 20.00
47B Bob Rousseau 15.00 30.00
48 Eddie Shack 20.00 40.00
49 Don Simmons 10.00 20.00
50 Allan Stanley 15.00 30.00
51 Ron Stewart 7.50 15.00
52 Jean-Guy Talbot 10.00 20.00
53 Gilles Tremblay 7.50 15.00
54 J.C. Tremblay 10.00 20.00
55 Norm Ullman 20.00 40.00
56 Elmer Vasko 7.50 15.00
57 Ken Wharram 10.00 20.00
58 Gump Worsley 25.00 50.00

2018-19 Chronology

1 Johnny Bower 4.00 10.00
2 Al MacInnis 5.00 12.00
3 Wendel Clark 6.00 15.00
4 Bobby Orr 15.00 40.00
5 Bernie Geoffrion 3.00 8.00
6 Phil Housley 3.00 8.00
7 Phil Esposito 6.00 15.00
8 Teemu Selanne 8.00 20.00
9 Maurice Richard 8.00 20.00
10 Guy Lafleur 5.00 12.00
11 Mark Messier 8.00 20.00
12 Scott Niedermayer 4.00 10.00
13 Mats Sundin 4.00 10.00
14 Cam Neely 4.00 10.00
15 Alex Delvecchio 4.00 10.00
16 Marcel Dionne 5.00 12.00
17 Jari Kurri 4.00 10.00

18 Serge Savard 4.00 10.00
19 Steve Yzerman 10.00 25.00
20 Jean Beliveau 4.00 10.00
21 Stan Mikita 4.00 10.00
22 Mike Bossy 4.00 10.00
23 Peter Forsberg 8.00 20.00
24 Curtis Joseph 5.00 12.00
25 Dave Andreychuk 4.00 10.00
26 Peter Stastny 3.00 8.00
27 Darryl Sittler 5.00 12.00
28 Howie Morenz 4.00 10.00
29 Rogie Vachon 4.00 10.00
30 Martin Brodeur 10.00 25.00
31 Grant Fuhr 6.00 15.00
32 Gerry Cheevers 4.00 10.00
33 Patrick Roy 10.00 25.00
34 John Vanbiesbrouck 4.00 10.00
35 Tony Esposito 4.00 10.00
36 Bobby Clarke 6.00 15.00
37 Tim Horton 6.00 15.00
38 Eddie Shore 4.00 10.00
39 Dominik Hasek 6.00 15.00
40 Scotty Bowman 4.00 10.00
41 Trevor Linden 4.00 10.00
42 Jacques Plante 4.00 10.00
43 Yvan Cournoyer 4.00 10.00
44 Chris Pronger 4.00 10.00
45 Ted Lindsay 4.00 10.00
46 Jean Ratelle 3.00 8.00
47 Joe Nieuwendyk 3.00 8.00
48 Elmer Lach 3.00 8.00
49 Sid Abel 3.00 8.00
50 Henri Richard 3.00 8.00
51 Bobby Hull 8.00 20.00
52 Bill Barber 4.00 10.00
53 Terry Sawchuk 4.00 10.00
54 Lanny McDonald 4.00 10.00
55 Larry Murphy 3.00 8.00
56 Tie Domi 3.00 8.00
57 Rod Langway 3.00 8.00
58 Johnny Bucyk 4.00 10.00
59 Andy Bathgate 3.00 8.00
60 Steve Shutt 4.00 10.00
61 Brett Hull 8.00 20.00
62 Theoren Fleury 4.00 10.00
63 Michel Goulet 4.00 10.00
64 Brendan Shanahan 4.00 10.00
65 Ed Belfour 4.00 10.00
66 Mario Lemieux 15.00 40.00
67 Turk Broda 4.00 10.00
68 Daniel Sedin 5.00 12.00
69 Tom Barrasso 4.00 10.00
70 Chris Chelios 4.00 10.00
71 Ron Hextall 4.00 10.00
72 Keith Tkachuk 4.00 10.00
73 Borje Salming 4.00 10.00
74 Bernie Parent 5.00 12.00
75 Henrik Sedin 5.00 12.00
76 Denis Potvin 3.00 8.00
77 Ray Bourque 6.00 15.00
78 Larry Robinson 4.00 10.00
79 Bryan Trottier 4.00 10.00
80 Ed Giacomin 4.00 10.00
81 Denis Savard 4.00 10.00
82 Dale Hawerchuk 5.00 12.00
83 Billy Smith 4.00 10.00
84 Brad Park 3.00 8.00
85 Paul Coffey 4.00 10.00
86 Clark Gillies 4.00 10.00
87 Luc Robitaille 4.00 10.00
88 Frank Mahovlich 4.00 10.00
89 Glenn Hall 4.00 10.00
90 Mike Gartner 5.00 12.00
91 Joe Sakic 8.00 20.00
92 Mike Modano 8.00 20.00
93 Doug Gilmour 5.00 12.00
94 Brian Leetch 3.00 8.00
95 Pat LaFontaine 4.00 10.00
96 Pavel Bure 4.00 10.00
97 Jeremy Roenick 6.00 15.00
98 Glenn Anderson 4.00 10.00
99 Wayne Gretzky 8.00 20.00
100 Charlie Conacher 3.00 8.00

2018-19 Chronology 0 Celsius

0C1 Kirk McLean 6.00 15.00
0C2 Brian Leetch 6.00 15.00
0C3 Jean Beliveau 8.00 20.00
0C4 Bobby Orr 30.00 80.00
0C5 Nicklas Lidstrom 8.00 20.00
0C6 Bobby Hull 15.00 40.00
0C7 Phil Esposito 12.00 30.00
0C8 Teemu Selanne 15.00 40.00
0C9 Maurice Richard 15.00 40.00
0C10 Guy Lafleur 10.00 25.00
0C11 Mark Messier 15.00 40.00
0C12 Joe Nieuwendyk 6.00 15.00
0C13 Mats Sundin 8.00 20.00
0C14 Theoren Fleury 8.00 20.00
0C15 Brett Hull 15.00 40.00
0C16 Marcel Dionne 10.00 25.00
0C17 Wendel Clark 12.00 30.00
0C18 Doug Gilmour 10.00 25.00
0C19 Steve Yzerman 20.00 50.00
0C20 Luc Robitaille 8.00 20.00
0C21 Stan Mikita 8.00 20.00
0C22 Mike Bossy 8.00 20.00
0C23 Ray Bourque 12.00 30.00
0C24 Brendan Shanahan 8.00 20.00
0C25 Jaromir Jagr 25.00 60.00
0C26 Peter Stastny 6.00 15.00
0C27 Ron Hextall 8.00 20.00
0C28 Peter Forsberg 15.00 40.00
0C29 Billy Smith 8.00 20.00
0C30 Martin Brodeur 20.00 50.00
0C31 Grant Fuhr 12.00 30.00
0C32 Al MacInnis 10.00 25.00
0C33 Patrick Roy 20.00 50.00
0C34 Paul Coffey 8.00 20.00
0C35 Evgeni Nabokov 6.00 15.00
0C36 Pat LaFontaine 8.00 20.00
0C37 Pelle Lindbergh 6.00 15.00
0C38 Curtis Joseph 10.00 25.00
0C39 Dominik Hasek 12.00 30.00
0C40 Mario Lemieux 30.00 80.00
0C41 Mike Gartner 10.00 25.00
0C42 Martin St. Louis 8.00 20.00
0C43 Ed Belfour 8.00 20.00
0C44 Chris Pronger 8.00 20.00
0C45 Dale Hawerchuk 10.00 25.00
0C46 Joe Sakic 15.00 40.00
0C47 Pavel Bure 8.00 20.00
0C48 Scott Niedermayer 8.00 20.00
0C49 Mike Modano 15.00 40.00
0C50 Wayne Gretzky 50.00 125.00

2018-19 Chronology 1 In 100

100AM Al MacInnis STK 12.00 30.00
100BC Bobby Clarke AU 15.00 40.00
100BL Brian Leetch AU 25.00 60.00
100BO Bobby Orr AU 100.00 200.00
100BP Bernie Parent AU 15.00 40.00
100CC Chris Chelios AU 15.00 40.00
100DG Doug Gilmour JSY AU 12.00 30.00
100DH Dale Hawerchuk JSY AU 12.00 30.00
100DP Denis Potvin PATCH AU 12.00 30.00
100GJ Bobby Hull AU 30.00 80.00
100JJ Jaromir Jagr PATCH 100.00 200.00
100JO Johnny Bower JSY 10.00 25.00
100LR Larry Robinson PATCH AU 10.00 25.00
100LU Luc Robitaille JSY AU 10.00 25.00
100MD Marcel Dionne SKT AU 20.00 50.00
100MS Mats Sundin PATCH 10.00 25.00
100PB Pavel Bure PATCH 10.00 25.00
100PC Paul Coffey JSY AU 10.00 25.00
100PD Pavel Datsyuk JSY 15.00 40.00
100PF Peter Forsberg PATCH 20.00 50.00
100SN Scott Niedermayer PATCH AU 10.00 25.00
100TS Teemu Selanne PATCH AU 30.00 80.00
100WC Wendel Clark AU 15.00 40.00

2018-19 Chronology Canvas Autographs

CAAO Adam Oates A 6.00 15.00
CABB Bill Barber A 6.00 15.00
CABF Bernie Federko C 5.00 12.00
CABS Billy Smith C 6.00 15.00
CADP Denis Potvin A 5.00 12.00
CAKL Kevin Lowe B 6.00 15.00
CAMC Lanny McDonald B 6.00 15.00
CAPH Phil Housley B 5.00 12.00
CARL Reggie Leach C 5.00 12.00
CASC Shayne Corson C 5.00 12.00
CASL Steve Larmer B 6.00 15.00
CASN Scott Niedermayer A 6.00 15.00
CAWC Wendel Clark A 10.00 25.00

2018-19 Chronology Canvas Masterpiece Autographs

CMABC Bobby Clarke B 15.00 40.00
CMABH Bobby Hull C 20.00 50.00
CMABL Brian Leetch B 8.00 20.00
CMABO Bobby Orr C 40.00 100.00
CMABP Brad Park B 8.00 20.00
CMABT Bryan Trottier B 10.00 25.00
CMACC Chris Chelios B 10.00 25.00
CMACJ Curtis Joseph B 12.00 30.00
CMACP Chris Pronger B 10.00 25.00
CMADG Doug Gilmour B 12.00 30.00
CMADH Dale Hawerchuk B 12.00 30.00
CMADO Dominik Hasek B 15.00 40.00
CMADS Darryl Sittler C 12.00 30.00
CMAGB Wayne Gretzky A 125.00 300.00
CMAGF Grant Fuhr B 15.00 40.00
CMAGK Wayne Gretzky A 125.00 300.00
CMAGL Guy Lafleur B 12.00 30.00
CMAGO Wayne Gretzky A 125.00 300.00
CMAGR Wayne Gretzky A 125.00 300.00
CMAHU Brett Hull B 20.00 50.00
CMAJJ Jaromir Jagr C 30.00 80.00
CMAJK Jari Kurri B 10.00 25.00
CMAJM Joe Mullen B 10.00 25.00
CMAJS Joe Sakic C 20.00 50.00
CMALR Larry Robinson B 10.00 25.00
CMALU Luc Robitaille B 10.00 25.00
CMAMB Martin Brodeur C 25.00 60.00
CMAMD Marcel Dionne B 12.00 30.00
CMAMI Mike Bossy B 10.00 25.00
CMAML Mario Lemieux C 40.00 100.00
CMAMM Mark Messier B 20.00 50.00
CMAMO Mike Modano B 20.00 50.00
CMAMS Mats Sundin C 10.00 25.00
CMAPC Paul Coffey B 10.00 25.00
CMAPE Phil Esposito B 15.00 40.00
CMAPL Pat LaFontaine C 10.00 25.00
CMARA Patrick Roy B 25.00 60.00
CMARB Ray Bourque B 15.00 40.00
CMARC Patrick Roy B 25.00 60.00
CMARL Rod Langway C 8.00 20.00
CMASY Steve Yzerman C 25.00 60.00
CMATD Tie Domi B 8.00 20.00
CMATS Teemu Selanne B 20.00 50.00

2018-19 Chronology Diamond Relics

1 Johnny Bower 15.00 40.00
2 Al MacInnis 20.00 50.00
3 Wendel Clark 25.00 60.00
4 Bobby Orr 60.00 150.00
5 Bernie Geoffrion 12.00 30.00
6 Phil Housley 12.00 30.00
7 Phil Esposito 25.00 60.00
8 Teemu Selanne 30.00 80.00
9 Maurice Richard 30.00 80.00
10 Guy Lafleur 20.00 50.00
11 Mark Messier 30.00 80.00
12 Scott Niedermayer 15.00 40.00
13 Mats Sundin 15.00 40.00
14 Cam Neely 15.00 40.00
15 Alex Delvecchio 15.00 40.00
16 Marcel Dionne 20.00 50.00
17 Jari Kurri 15.00 40.00
18 Serge Savard 15.00 40.00
19 Steve Yzerman 40.00 100.00
20 Jean Beliveau 15.00 40.00
21 Stan Mikita 15.00 40.00
22 Mike Bossy 15.00 40.00
23 Peter Forsberg 30.00 80.00
24 Curtis Joseph 20.00 50.00
25 Dave Andreychuk 15.00 40.00
26 Peter Stastny 12.00 30.00
27 Darryl Sittler 20.00 50.00
28 Howie Morenz 15.00 40.00
29 Rogie Vachon 15.00 40.00
30 Martin Brodeur 40.00 100.00
31 Grant Fuhr 25.00 60.00
32 Gerry Cheevers 15.00 40.00
33 Patrick Roy 40.00 100.00
34 John Vanbiesbrouck 15.00 40.00
35 Tony Esposito 15.00 40.00
36 Bobby Clarke 25.00 60.00
37 Tim Horton 25.00 60.00
38 Eddie Shore 15.00 40.00
39 Dominik Hasek 25.00 60.00
40 Scotty Bowman 15.00 40.00
41 Trevor Linden 15.00 40.00
42 Jacques Plante 15.00 40.00
43 Yvan Cournoyer 15.00 40.00
44 Chris Pronger 15.00 40.00
45 Ted Lindsay 15.00 40.00
46 Jean Ratelle 12.00 30.00
47 Joe Nieuwendyk 12.00 30.00
48 Elmer Lach 12.00 30.00
49 Sid Abel 12.00 30.00
50 Henri Richard 12.00 30.00
51 Bobby Hull 30.00 80.00
52 Bill Barber 15.00 40.00
53 Terry Sawchuk 15.00 40.00
54 Lanny McDonald 15.00 40.00
55 Larry Murphy 12.00 30.00
56 Tie Domi 12.00 30.00
57 Rod Langway 12.00 30.00
58 Johnny Bucyk 15.00 40.00
59 Andy Bathgate 12.00 30.00
60 Steve Shutt 15.00 40.00
61 Brett Hull 30.00 80.00
62 Theoren Fleury 15.00 40.00
63 Michel Goulet 15.00 40.00
64 Brendan Shanahan 15.00 40.00
65 Ed Belfour 15.00 40.00
66 Mario Lemieux 60.00 150.00
67 Turk Broda 15.00 40.00
68 Daniel Sedin 20.00 50.00
69 Tom Barrasso 15.00 40.00
70 Chris Chelios 15.00 40.00
71 Ron Hextall 15.00 40.00
72 Keith Tkachuk 15.00 40.00
73 Borje Salming 15.00 40.00
74 Bernie Parent 20.00 50.00
75 Henrik Sedin 20.00 50.00
76 Denis Potvin 12.00 30.00
77 Ray Bourque 25.00 60.00
78 Larry Robinson 15.00 40.00
79 Bryan Trottier 15.00 40.00
80 Ed Giacomin 15.00 40.00
81 Denis Savard 15.00 40.00
82 Dale Hawerchuk 20.00 50.00
83 Billy Smith 15.00 40.00
84 Brad Park 12.00 30.00
85 Paul Coffey 15.00 40.00
86 Clark Gillies 15.00 40.00
87 Luc Robitaille 15.00 40.00
88 Frank Mahovlich 15.00 40.00
89 Glenn Hall 15.00 40.00
90 Mike Gartner 20.00 50.00
91 Joe Sakic 30.00 80.00
92 Mike Modano 30.00 80.00
93 Doug Gilmour 20.00 50.00
94 Brian Leetch 12.00 30.00
95 Pat LaFontaine 15.00 40.00
96 Pavel Bure 15.00 40.00
97 Jeremy Roenick 25.00 60.00
98 Glenn Anderson 12.00 30.00
99 Wayne Gretzky 100.00 250.00
100 Charlie Conacher 12.00 30.00

2018-19 Chronology Dual Autographs

DAGK W.Gretzky/J.Kurri 400.00 1000.00
DAGM W.Gretzky/M.Messier 400.00 1000.00
DALR G.Lafleur/L.Robinson 40.00 100.00
DARB P.Roy/M.Brodeur 80.00 200.00
DAYL S.Yzerman/N.Lidstrom 80.00 200.00

2018-19 Chronology Franchise History Autographs

FHAFCB Curt Bennett 6.00 15.00
FHANGH Guy Hebert E 10.00 25.00
FHANJG Jean-Sebastien Giguere D 10.00 25.00
FHANKB Ken Baumgartner G 6.00 15.00
FHANSG Stu Grimson D 10.00 25.00
FHANSN Scott Niedermayer C 10.00 25.00
FHANTS Teemu Selanne C 25.00 60.00
FHATJH Johan Hedberg E 8.00 20.00
FHBOBO Bobby Orr C 80.00 200.00
FHBOBP Brad Park B 8.00 20.00
FHBODI Rob DiMaio G 8.00 20.00
FHBODM Don Marcotte F 6.00 15.00
FHBOGC Gerry Cheevers E 10.00 25.00
FHBOGS Greg Sheppard G 8.00 20.00
FHBOPE Phil Esposito A 15.00 40.00
FHBORB Ray Bourque B 15.00 40.00
FHBORD Dave Reid F 8.00 20.00
FHBORS Rick Smith G 8.00 20.00
FHBOSH Steve Heinze E 8.00 20.00
FHBOWO Willie O'Ree D 12.00 30.00
FHBUBH Benoit Hogue F 8.00 20.00
FHBUBI Martin Biron F 8.00 20.00
FHBUBM Brad May G 8.00 20.00
FHBUDG Danny Gare G 8.00 20.00
FHBUDH Dale Hawerchuk B 12.00 30.00
FHBUHA Dominik Hasek B 15.00 40.00
FHBUJK Jerry Korab G 8.00 20.00
FHBUMB Matthew Barnaby E 6.00 15.00
FHBUMP Michael Peca G 8.00 20.00
FHBUPH Phil Housley C 8.00 20.00
FHBUPL Pat LaFontaine C 10.00 25.00
FHBUPT Pierre Turgeon C 8.00 20.00
FHBUSB Scotty Bowman B 40.00 100.00
FHBUWP Wayne Primeau G 8.00 20.00
FHCAAM Al MacInnis A 12.00 30.00
FHCACG Curtis Glencross G 8.00 20.00
FHCACH Cale Hulse G 8.00 20.00
FHCACK Chuck Kobasew G 8.00 20.00
FHCAJM Joe Mullen C 10.00 25.00
FHCAJO Joel Otto F 8.00 20.00
FHCAKN Kent Nilsson E 8.00 20.00
FHCALM Lanny McDonald D 10.00 25.00
FHCAMA Jamie Macoun E 8.00 20.00
FHCARR Robyn Regehr G 8.00 20.00
FHCATF Theoren Fleury B 10.00 25.00
FHCATS Todd Simpson G 8.00 20.00
FHCHAS Al Secord F 8.00 20.00
FHCHBH Bobby Hull C 25.00 60.00
FHCHBO Bobby Orr C 80.00 200.00
FHCHCC Chris Chelios B 10.00 25.00
FHCHCK Cliff Koroll G 8.00 20.00
FHCHDH Dennis Hull D 8.00 20.00
FHCHDS Denis Savard D 10.00 25.00
FHCHEB Ed Belfour A 10.00 25.00
FHCHED Eric Daze F 8.00 20.00
FHCHEO Ed Olczyk F 8.00 20.00
FHCHGH Glenn Hall D 10.00 25.00
FHCHJR Jeremy Roenick B 40.00 100.00
FHCHPP Pierre Pilote C 10.00 25.00
FHCHSL Steve Larmer D 10.00 25.00
FHCHSM Stan Mikita A 10.00 25.00
FHCHST Steve Thomas F 8.00 20.00
FHCHTM Troy Murray F 6.00 15.00
FHCOJS Joe Sakic C 20.00 50.00
FHCOPR Patrick Roy B 100.00 250.00
FHCORB Ray Bourque A 15.00 40.00
FHCOSY Stephane Yelle F 8.00 20.00
FHCRRB Rod Brind'Amour D 10.00 25.00
FHCRSH Sean Hill G 8.00 20.00
FHDABH Brett Hull B 20.00 50.00
FHDACL Craig Ludwig E 8.00 20.00
FHDAEB Ed Belfour A 10.00 25.00
FHDAGL Grant Ledyard G 8.00 20.00
FHDAJE Jere Lehtinen F 8.00 20.00
FHDAJL Jamie Langenbrunner D 8.00 20.00
FHDAMT Marty Turco G 8.00 20.00
FHDEBS Brendan Shanahan D 10.00 25.00
FHDECC Chris Chelios B 10.00 25.00
FHDEDH Dominik Hasek A 15.00 40.00
FHDEJK Joey Kocur E 8.00 20.00
FHDENL Nick Libett G 8.00 20.00
FHDERL Reed Larson G 8.00 20.00
FHDESB Scotty Bowman B 40.00 100.00
FHDESY Steve Yzerman C 60.00 150.00
FHDEWM Walt McKechnie G 8.00 20.00
FHEDAM Andy Moog C 10.00 25.00
FHEDCH Charlie Huddy G 8.00 20.00
FHEDCS Craig Simpson G 8.00 20.00
FHEDGF Grant Fuhr B 15.00 40.00
FHEDGL Georges Laraque G 8.00 20.00
FHEDJK Jari Kurri A 60.00 150.00
FHEDKL Kevin Lowe D 10.00 25.00
FHEDKM Kevin McClelland G 8.00 20.00
FHEDMK Mike Krushelnyski G 8.00 20.00
FHEDMM Mark Messier B 50.00 120.00
FHEDMR Marty Reasoner F 6.00 15.00
FHEDPC Paul Coffey B 10.00 25.00
FHEDSS Steve Staios G 8.00 20.00
FHEDTM Todd Marchant D 8.00 20.00
FHEDWG Wayne Gretzky B 400.00 1000.00
FHFLJV John Vanbiesbrouck B 10.00 25.00
FHFLOJ Olli Jokinen G 8.00 20.00
FHFLRW Rhett Warrener G 8.00 20.00
FHHABS Brendan Shanahan C 10.00 25.00
FHHARF Ray Ferraro F 8.00 20.00
FHHASB Sean Burke E 8.00 20.00
FHLABG Butch Goring C 8.00 20.00
FHLABN Bernie Nicholls G 8.00 20.00
FHLACS Charlie Simmer G 6.00 15.00
FHLADH Dave Hutchison G 8.00 20.00
FHLADT Dave Taylor B 8.00 20.00
FHLAJC Jimmy Carson F 8.00 20.00
FHLAJW Jay Wells G 8.00 20.00
FHLAKH Kelly Hrudey E 8.00 20.00
FHLALR Luc Robitaille B 10.00 25.00
FHLAMD Marcel Dionne B 12.00 30.00
FHLAMM Marty McSorley D 8.00 20.00
FHLARV Rogie Vachon B 8.00 20.00
FHLAWG Wayne Gretzky B 400.00 1000.00
FHMNBG Barry Gibbs G 8.00 20.00
FHMNCH Craig Hartsburg G 8.00 20.00
FHMNDG Danny Grant G 10.00 25.00
FHMNGR Gordie Roberts F 6.00 15.00
FHMNLN Lou Nanne G 8.00 20.00
FHMNMA Brad Maxwell F 6.00 15.00
FHMNTR Tom Reid G 8.00 20.00
FHMOBH Brian Hayward E 8.00 20.00
FHMOCC Chris Chelios B 8.00 20.00
FHMOCN Chris Nilan D 6.00 15.00
FHMOGC Guy Carbonneau D 10.00 25.00
FHMOGL Guy Lafleur B 12.00 30.00
FHMOJB Jean Beliveau A 10.00 25.00
FHMOLR Larry Robinson A 10.00 25.00
FHMOMG Mathieu Garon G 8.00 20.00
FHMOMN Mark Napier G 8.00 20.00
FHMOPR Patrick Roy B 100.00 250.00
FHMORH Rejean Houle G 8.00 20.00
FHMORV Rogie Vachon B 8.00 20.00
FHMOSB Scotty Bowman A 40.00 100.00
FHMOSC Shayne Corson D 8.00 20.00
FHMOSR Stephane Richer F 8.00 20.00
FHMOSS Steve Shutt C 10.00 25.00
FHMOYC Yvan Cournoyer D 8.00 20.00
FHMWDR Dwayne Roloson F 8.00 20.00
FHNAAH Adam Hall G 8.00 20.00
FHNADH Darcy Hordichuk G 8.00 20.00
FHNASW Scott Walker G 8.00 20.00
FHNJAB Aaron Broten E 8.00 20.00
FHNJBD Bruce Driver F 8.00 20.00
FHNJCL Claude Lemieux B 10.00 25.00
FHNJJD Jim Dowd G 8.00 20.00
FHNJJM John MacLean D 8.00 20.00
FHNJKD Ken Daneyko E 8.00 20.00
FHNJMB Martin Brodeur C 25.00 60.00
FHNJSN Scott Niedermayer C 10.00 25.00
FHNJTA Tommy Albelin E 8.00 20.00
FHOTCP Chris Phillips D 8.00 20.00
FHPCJR Jeremy Roenick B 40.00 100.00
FHPCKT Keith Tkachuk C 10.00 25.00
FHPCMJ Mike Johnson G 8.00 20.00
FHPHBB Bill Barber D 10.00 25.00
FHPHBC Bobby Clarke B 15.00 40.00
FHPHBM Brad Marsh G 8.00 20.00
FHPHBP Bernie Parent B 12.00 30.00
FHPHCL Bill Clement F 8.00 20.00
FHPHDB Daniel Briere G 8.00 20.00
FHPHDC Doug Crossman G 8.00 20.00
FHPHGD Gary Dornhoefer F 6.00 15.00
FHPHKP Keith Primeau E 8.00 20.00
FHPHPH Paul Holmgren G 8.00 20.00
FHPHPR Brian Propp E 8.00 20.00
FHPHRB Rod Brind'Amour F 10.00 25.00
FHPHRH Ron Hextall C 8.00 20.00
FHPHRL Reggie Leach D 8.00 20.00
FHPIDQ Dan Quinn F 6.00 15.00
FHPIGM Greg Malone F 6.00 15.00
FHPIJM Joe Mullen C 10.00 25.00
FHPIML Mario Lemieux C 40.00 100.00
FHPIRB Rob Brown G 8.00 20.00
FHPISB Scotty Bowman B 40.00 100.00
FHPITB Tom Barrasso D 10.00 25.00
FHQUMG Michel Goulet B 10.00 25.00
FHQUPS Peter Stastny C 8.00 20.00
FHQURM Randy Moller G 8.00 20.00
FHSABM Bryan Marchment G 8.00 20.00
FHSADM Douglas Murray G 8.00 20.00
FHSAEN Evgeni Nabokov E 8.00 20.00
FHSAJO Jeff Odgers F 6.00 15.00
FHSAON Owen Nolan C 10.00 25.00
FHSAST Scott Thornton G 8.00 20.00
FHSATH Todd Harvey G 8.00 20.00
FHSTAM Al MacInnis A 12.00 30.00
FHSTAO Adam Oates C 10.00 25.00
FHSTBA Bob Bassen G 8.00 20.00
FHSTBB Brian Benning G 8.00 20.00
FHSTBF Bernie Federko D 8.00 20.00
FHSTBH Brett Hull B 20.00 50.00
FHSTBO Brad Boyes G 6.00 15.00
FHSTCJ Curtis Joseph F 12.00 30.00
FHSTCP Chris Pronger B 10.00 25.00
FHSTGU Garry Unger E 8.00 20.00
FHSTJM Jamal Mayers E 8.00 20.00
FHSTKT Keith Tkachuk C 10.00 25.00
FHSTME Mike Eastwood G 8.00 20.00
FHSTPC Paul Cavallini G 8.00 20.00
FHSTSB Scotty Bowman B 40.00 100.00
FHSTWG Wayne Gretzky B 400.00 1000.00
FHTABB Brian Bradley D 8.00 20.00
FHTACC Cory Cross G 8.00 20.00
FHTAFM Fredrik Modin G 8.00 20.00
FHTARF Ruslan Fedotenko F 6.00 15.00
FHTATT Tim Taylor G 8.00 20.00
FHTOAI Al Iafrate E 8.00 20.00
FHTOAM Alyn McCauley G 8.00 20.00
FHTOBB Bob Baun G 10.00 25.00
FHTOBM Bob McGill G 8.00 20.00
FHTOBS Borje Salming B 10.00 25.00
FHTODA Dan Daoust G 8.00 20.00
FHTODG Doug Gilmour B 12.00 30.00
FHTODS Darryl Sittler C 12.00 30.00
FHTODT Darcy Tucker G 8.00 20.00
FHTOET Errol Thompson G 8.00 20.00
FHTOFM Frank Mahovlich C 10.00 25.00
FHTOFP Felix Potvin F 15.00 40.00
FHTOJB Johnny Bower A 10.00 25.00
FHTOLM Lanny McDonald D 10.00 25.00
FHTOMS Mats Sundin C 10.00 25.00
FHTOMW Mike Walton G 8.00 20.00
FHTORE Ron Ellis F 8.00 20.00
FHTORV Rick Vaive F 8.00 20.00
FHTOTD Tie Domi C 8.00 20.00
FHTOWC Wendel Clark B 15.00 40.00
FHVABM Brendan Morrison G 8.00 20.00
FHVADS Daniel Sedin D 12.00 30.00
FHVAGA Greg Adams G 8.00 20.00
FHVAGB Garth Butcher G 8.00 20.00
FHVAGS Gary Smith G 8.00 20.00
FHVAHS Henrik Sedin D 12.00 30.00
FHVAJL Jyrki Lumme G 8.00 20.00
FHVAJS Jason Strudwick G 8.00 20.00
FHVAMN Markus Naslund F 10.00 25.00
FHVARS Rich Sutter F 8.00 20.00
FHVATL Trevor Linden B 10.00 25.00
FHVATP Taylor Pyatt G 8.00 20.00
FHVATT Tony Tanti E 6.00 15.00
FHWAAO Adam Oates C 10.00 25.00
FHWABC Bob Carpenter G 8.00 20.00
FHWADM Dennis Maruk G 8.00 20.00
FHWAGC Guy Charron G 8.00 20.00
FHWAKJ Keith Jones G 8.00 20.00
FHWAMG Mike Gartner B 12.00 30.00
FHWANK Nick Kypreos G 8.00 20.00
FHWARL Rod Langway C 8.00 20.00
FHWASG Sergei Gonchar E 8.00 20.00
FHWIDB Dave Babych G 8.00 20.00
FHWIDE Dave Ellett G 8.00 20.00
FHWIDH Dale Hawerchuk B 12.00 30.00
FHWIKK Kris King G 8.00 20.00
FHWIML Morris Lukowich G 8.00 20.00
FHWIST Thomas Steen E 8.00 20.00
FHWITS Teemu Selanne C 25.00 60.00
FHWITW Tim Watters G 8.00 20.00
FHNYIBN Bob Nystrom E 8.00 20.00
FHNYIBS Billy Smith D 10.00 25.00
FHNYIBT Bryan Trottier B 10.00 25.00
FHNYIDP Denis Potvin B 8.00 20.00
FHNYIDS Duane Sutter G 8.00 20.00
FHNYIGD Gord Dineen F 6.00 15.00
FHNYIGG Greg Gilbert G 8.00 20.00
FHNYIMB Mike Bossy B 10.00 25.00
FHNYIMF Mark Fitzpatrick F 6.00 15.00
FHNYIPL Pat LaFontaine C 10.00 25.00
FHNYRAB Andy Bathgate B 8.00 20.00
FHNYRAG Adam Graves E 10.00 25.00
FHNYRBL Brian Leetch B 10.00 25.00
FHNYRBP Brad Park B 8.00 20.00
FHNYREG Ed Giacomin F 10.00 25.00
FHNYRGH Glenn Healy G 8.00 20.00
FHNYRJB Jeff Beukeboom D 8.00 20.00
FHNYRMM Mark Messier B 50.00 120.00
FHNYRPL Pierre Larouche F 6.00 15.00
FHNYRSG Rod Seiling G 8.00 20.00
FHNYRVH Vic Hadfield E 8.00 20.00
FHNYRWG Wayne Gretzky B 400.00 1000.00

2018-19 Chronology Letterman Patches

LANGH Guy Hebert AU/20 10.00 25.00
LATJH Johan Hedberg AU/20 8.00 20.00
LBODR Dave Reid AU/20 8.00 20.00
LBOES Eddie Shore/35 10.00 25.00
LBOSH Steve Heinze AU/20 8.00 20.00
LBUBH Benoit Hogue AU/20 8.00 20.00
LBUMA Matthew Barnaby AU/20 6.00 15.00
LBUMB Martin Biron AU/20 8.00 20.00
LCAJO Joel Otto AU/20 8.00 20.00
LCAMA Jamie Macoun AU/20 8.00 20.00
LCHAS Al Secord AU/20 8.00 20.00
LCHDH Dennis Hull AU/20 8.00 20.00
LCHED Eric Daze AU/20 8.00 20.00
LCHSM Stan Mikita/35 10.00 25.00
LCOSY Stephane Yelle AU/20 8.00 20.00
LDACL Craig Ludwig AU/20 8.00 20.00
LDEBP Bob Probert/35 10.00 25.00
LDESA Sid Abel/35 8.00 20.00
LDETL Ted Lindsay/35 10.00 25.00
LDETS Terry Sawchuk/35 10.00 25.00
LEDKL Kevin Lowe AU/20 10.00 25.00
LEDTM Todd Marchant AU/20 8.00 20.00
LLAKH Kelly Hrudey AU/20 8.00 20.00
LLAMM Marty McSorley AU/20 8.00 20.00
LMIDR Dwayne Roloson AU/20 8.00 20.00
LMOBG Bernie Geoffrion/35 8.00 20.00
LMOBH Brian Hayward AU/20 8.00 20.00
LMOEL Elmer Lach/35 8.00 20.00
LMOHM Howie Morenz/35 10.00 25.00
LMOHR Henri Richard/35 8.00 20.00
LMOJB Jean Beliveau/35 10.00 25.00
LMOJP Jacques Plante/35 10.00 25.00
LMOMR Maurice Richard/35 20.00 50.00
LMOSC Shayne Corson AU/20 8.00 20.00
LMOSR Stephane Richer AU/20 8.00 20.00
LMOYC Yvan Cournoyer/35 10.00 25.00
LNJAB Aaron Broten AU/20 8.00 20.00
LNJBD Bruce Driver AU/20 8.00 20.00
LNJTA Tommy Albelin AU/20 8.00 20.00
LOTCP Chris Phillips AU/20 8.00 20.00
LPHCL Bill Clement AU/20 8.00 20.00
LPHKP Keith Primeau AU/20 8.00 20.00
LPHMH Mark Howe/35 10.00 25.00
LPHPL Pelle Lindbergh/35 10.00 25.00
LSTAO Adam Oates AU/20 10.00 25.00
LSTBD Blake Dunlop AU/20 8.00 20.00
LSTGU Garry Unger AU/20 8.00 20.00
LSTJM Jamal Mayers AU/20 8.00 20.00
LTOAI Al Iafrate AU/20 8.00 20.00
LTOBB Bill Barilko/35 10.00 25.00
LTOCC Charlie Conacher/35 8.00 20.00
LTODD Dick Duff/35 8.00 20.00
LTOFP Felix Potvin AU/20 15.00 40.00
LTOJB Johnny Bower/35 10.00 25.00
LTOTB Turk Broda/35 10.00 25.00
LTOTD Tie Domi AU/20 8.00 20.00
LTOTH Tim Horton/35 15.00 40.00
LVARS Rich Sutter AU/20 8.00 20.00
LWASG Sergei Gonchar AU/20 8.00 20.00
LNYIBN Bob Nystrom AU/20 8.00 20.00
LNYRAB Andy Bathgate/35 8.00 20.00
LNYRAG Adam Graves AU/20 8.00 20.00
LNYRHH Harry Howell/35 8.00 20.00
LNYRJB Jeff Beukeboom AU/20 8.00 20.00

2018-19 Chronology Time Capsules

TC1 Stan Mikita 8.00 20.00
TC2 Peter Forsberg 15.00 40.00
TC3 Dale Hawerchuk 10.00 25.00
TC4 Ted Lindsay 8.00 20.00
TC5 Guy Lafleur 10.00 25.00
TC6 Jean Beliveau 8.00 20.00
TC7 Al MacInnis 10.00 25.00
TC8 Luc Robitaille 8.00 20.00
TC9 Bobby Orr 30.00 80.00
TC10 Alex Delvecchio 8.00 20.00
TC11 Darryl Sittler 10.00 25.00
TC12 Johnny Bower 8.00 20.00
TC13 Peter Stastny 6.00 15.00
TC14 Maurice Richard 15.00 40.00
TC15 Chris Chelios 8.00 20.00
TC16 Larry Robinson 8.00 20.00
TC17 Pat LaFontaine 8.00 20.00
TC18 Patrick Roy 20.00 50.00
TC19 Brian Leetch 6.00 15.00
TC20 Steve Yzerman 20.00 50.00
TC21 Jacques Plante 8.00 20.00
TC22 Bobby Hull 15.00 40.00
TC23 Terry Sawchuk 8.00 20.00
TC24 Wayne Gretzky 50.00 125.00
TC25 Teemu Selanne 15.00 40.00
TC26 Pavel Bure 8.00 20.00
TC27 Mario Lemieux 30.00 80.00
TC28 Mike Gartner 10.00 25.00
TC29 Bobby Clarke 12.00 30.00
TC30 Paul Coffey 8.00 20.00
TC31 Andy Bathgate 6.00 15.00
TC32 Marcel Dionne 10.00 25.00
TC33 Mike Modano 15.00 40.00
TC34 Phil Esposito 12.00 30.00
TC35 Charlie Conacher 6.00 15.00
TC36 Howie Morenz 8.00 20.00
TC37 Joe Sakic 15.00 40.00
TC38 Martin Brodeur 20.00 50.00
TC39 Dominik Hasek 12.00 30.00
TC40 Eddie Shore 8.00 20.00
TC41 Nicklas Lidstrom 8.00 20.00
TC42 Mats Sundin 8.00 20.00
TC43 Ray Bourque 12.00 30.00
TC44 Mark Messier 15.00 40.00
TC45 Bryan Trottier 8.00 20.00
TC46 Brett Hull 15.00 40.00
TC47 Mike Bossy 8.00 20.00
TC48 Jarome Iginla 10.00 25.00
TC49 Jaromir Jagr 25.00 60.00
TC50 Doug Gilmour 10.00 25.00

2018-19 Chronology Time Capsules Canvas Mini

M1 Johnny Bucyk 3.00 8.00
M2 Reggie Leach 2.50 6.00
M3 Lanny McDonald 3.00 8.00
M4 Dave Andreychuk 3.00 8.00
M5 Dominik Hasek 5.00 12.00
M6 Kirk Muller 2.50 6.00
M7 Mark Messier 6.00 15.00
M8 Patrick Roy 8.00 20.00
M9 Dwayne Roloson 2.50 6.00
M10 Johan Hedberg 2.50 6.00
M11 Borje Salming 3.00 8.00
M12 Mike Bossy 3.00 8.00
M13 Phil Housley 2.50 6.00
M14 Brad Park 2.50 6.00
M15 Bobby Holik 2.50 6.00
M16 Joe Mullen 3.00 8.00
M17 Adam Oates 3.00 8.00
M18 John MacLean 2.50 6.00
M19 Pierre Turgeon 2.50 6.00
M20 Joel Otto 2.50 6.00
M21 Brett Hull 6.00 15.00
M22 Johnny Bower 3.00 8.00
M23 Ron Hextall 3.00 8.00
M24 Joe Mullen 3.00 8.00
M25 Sid Abel 2.50 6.00
M26 Mats Sundin 3.00 8.00
M27 Michel Goulet 3.00 8.00
M28 Teemu Selanne 6.00 15.00
M29 Andy Bathgate 2.50 6.00
M30 Gary Roberts 3.00 8.00
M31 Mike Modano 6.00 15.00
M32 Brad Park 2.50 6.00
M33 Craig Ludwig 2.50 6.00
M34 Al Iafrate 2.50 6.00
M35 Georges Laraque 2.50 6.00
M36 Al MacInnis 4.00 10.00
M37 Steve Duchesne 2.50 6.00
M38 Patrick Roy 8.00 20.00
M39 Thomas Steen 2.50 6.00
M40 Andy Moog 3.00 8.00
M41 Scott Mellanby 2.50 6.00
M42 Bobby Hull 6.00 15.00
M43 Owen Nolan 3.00 8.00
M44 Rod Brind'Amour 3.00 8.00
M45 Larry Murphy 2.50 6.00
M46 Eric Daze 2.50 6.00
M47 Scotty Bowman 3.00 8.00
M48 Darryl Sittler 4.00 10.00
M49 Jaromir Jagr 10.00 25.00
M50 Ed Belfour 3.00 8.00
M51 Peter Forsberg 6.00 15.00
M52 Pavel Bure 3.00 8.00
M53 Theoren Fleury 3.00 8.00
M54 Ron Ellis 2.50 6.00
M55 Shayne Corson 2.50 6.00
M56 Curtis Joseph 4.00 10.00
M57 Dave Schultz 2.50 6.00
M58 Jere Lehtinen 2.50 6.00
M59 Pat LaFontaine 3.00 8.00
M60 Mike Krushelnyski 2.50 6.00
M61 Bobby Orr 12.00 30.00
M62 Kevin Lowe 3.00 8.00
M63 Denis Potvin 2.50 6.00
M64 Bill Barber 3.00 8.00
M65 John Vanbiesbrouck 3.00 8.00
M66 Jeremy Roenick 5.00 12.00
M67 Teemu Selanne 6.00 15.00
M68 Doug Gilmour 4.00 10.00
M69 Dave Andreychuk 3.00 8.00
M70 Bobby Orr 12.00 30.00
M71 Chris Pronger 3.00 8.00
M72 Scotty Bowman 3.00 8.00
M73 Harry Howell 2.50 6.00
M74 Dave Reid 2.50 6.00
M75 Chris Chelios 3.00 8.00
M76 Steve Larmer 3.00 8.00
M77 Butch Goring 2.50 6.00
M78 Jean Beliveau 3.00 8.00
M79 Wayne Gretzky 20.00 50.00
M80 Dominik Hasek 5.00 12.00
M81 Ted Lindsay 3.00 8.00
M82 Evgeni Nabokov 2.50 6.00
M83 Scotty Bowman 3.00 8.00
M84 Markus Naslund 3.00 8.00
M85 Matthew Barnaby 2.00 5.00
M86 Charlie Conacher 2.50 6.00
M87 Guy Lafleur 4.00 10.00
M88 Wayne Gretzky 20.00 50.00
M89 Henri Richard 2.50 6.00
M90 Chris Nilan 2.00 5.00
M91 Trevor Linden 3.00 8.00
M92 Ed Belfour 3.00 8.00
M93 Larry Murphy 2.50 6.00
M94 Al MacInnis 4.00 10.00
M95 Kent Nilsson 2.50 6.00
M96 Wayne Gretzky 20.00 50.00
M97 Guy Hebert 3.00 8.00
M98 Teppo Numminen 2.00 5.00
M99 Wayne Gretzky 20.00 50.00
M100 Grant Fuhr 5.00 12.00
M101 Mike Vernon 2.50 6.00
M102 Larry Murphy 2.50 6.00
M103 Scotty Bowman 3.00 8.00
M104 Sean Burke 2.50 6.00
M105 Bruce Driver 2.50 6.00
M106 Terry Sawchuk 3.00 8.00
M107 Luc Robitaille 3.00 8.00
M108 Brian Bellows 2.50 6.00
M109 Nicklas Lidstrom 3.00 8.00
M110 Chris Phillips 2.50 6.00
M111 Rick Vaive 2.50 6.00
M112 Steve Shutt 3.00 8.00
M113 Glenn Anderson 2.50 6.00
M114 Joe Sakic 6.00 15.00
M115 Chris Chelios 3.00 8.00
M116 Sergei Gonchar 2.50 6.00
M117 Serge Savard 3.00 8.00
M118 Aaron Broten 2.50 6.00
M119 Brian Bradley 2.50 6.00
M120 Denis Savard 3.00 8.00
M121 Jeremy Roenick 5.00 12.00
M122 Igor Larionov 3.00 8.00
M123 Adam Graves 3.00 8.00
M124 Bernie Federko 2.50 6.00
M125 Wendel Clark 5.00 12.00
M126 Tom Barrasso 3.00 8.00
M127 Mike Vernon 2.50 6.00
M128 Marty McSorley 2.50 6.00
M129 Pavel Bure 3.00 8.00
M130 Jamie Langenbrunner 2.50 6.00
M131 Peter Stastny 2.50 6.00
M132 Lanny McDonald 3.00 8.00
M133 Tie Domi 2.50 6.00
M134 Dennis Hull 2.50 6.00
M135 Pat LaFontaine 3.00 8.00
M136 Paul Coffey 3.00 8.00
M137 Guy Carbonneau 3.00 8.00
M138 Jimmy Carson 2.50 6.00
M139 Wade Redden 2.50 6.00
M140 Bob Nystrom 2.50 6.00
M141 Yvan Cournoyer 3.00 8.00
M142 Brian Leetch 2.50 6.00
M143 Claude Lemieux 3.00 8.00
M144 Cam Neely 3.00 8.00
M145 Steve Yzerman 8.00 20.00
M146 Ray Bourque 5.00 12.00
M147 Glenn Hall 3.00 8.00
M148 Bernie Geoffrion 2.50 6.00
M149 Jason Arnott 2.50 6.00
M150 Rogie Vachon 2.50 6.00
M151 Larry Robinson 2.50 6.00
M152 Rod Langway 2.50 6.00

M153 Tim Horton 5.00 12.00
M154 Marcel Dionne 4.00 10.00
M155 Maurice Richard 6.00 15.00
M156 Bill Ranford 2.50 6.00
M157 Bryan Trottier 3.00 8.00
M158 Clark Gillies 3.00 8.00
M159 Bernie Parent 4.00 10.00
M160 Jacques Plante 3.00 8.00
M161 Keith Tkachuk 3.00 8.00
M162 Jean Ratelle 2.50 6.00
M163 Rod Brind'Amour 3.00 8.00
M164 Ray Bourque 5.00 12.00
M165 Ray Ferraro 2.50 6.00
M166 Mike Gartner 4.00 10.00
M167 Brett Hull 6.00 15.00
M168 Howie Morenz 3.00 8.00
M169 Alex Delvecchio 3.00 8.00
M170 Joey Kocur 2.50 6.00
M171 Turk Broda 3.00 8.00
M172 Jarome Iginla 4.00 10.00
M173 Bobby Clarke 5.00 12.00
M174 Phil Esposito 5.00 12.00
M175 Bryan Berard 3.00 8.00
M176 Willie O'Ree 4.00 10.00
M177 Gerry Cheevers 3.00 8.00
M178 Dale Hawerchuk 4.00 10.00
M179 Dale Hawerchuk 4.00 10.00
M180 Jari Kurri 3.00 8.00
M181 Mario Lemieux 12.00 30.00
M182 Mark Messier 6.00 15.00
M183 Chris Chelios 3.00 8.00
M184 Mike Liut 2.00 5.00
M185 Stan Mikita 3.00 8.00
M186 Joe Nieuwendyk 2.50 6.00
M187 Ed Olczyk 2.50 6.00
M188 Tony Amonte 2.50 6.00
M189 Tony Esposito 3.00 8.00
M190 Rob Blake 3.00 8.00
M191 Ken Daneyko 2.50 6.00
M192 Rogie Vachon 3.00 8.00

2019-20 Chronology

101 Connor McDavid 15.00 40.00
102 Marian Gaborik 2.50 6.00
103 Mark Recchi 3.00 8.00
104 Erik Karlsson 3.00 8.00
105 Mark Scheifele 4.00 10.00
106 Patrick Marleau 2.50 6.00
107 John Carlson 2.50 6.00
108 Alex Ovechkin 6.00 15.00
109 Seth Jones 2.50 6.00
110 Jack Hughes RC 6.00 15.00
111 Jonathan Huberdeau 3.00 8.00
112 Matthew Tkachuk 5.00 12.00
113 Patrik Laine 3.00 8.00
114 Ryan Nugent-Hopkins 3.00 8.00
115 Andrei Svechnikov 3.00 8.00
116 Claude Giroux 2.50 6.00
117 Henrik Lundqvist 6.00 15.00
118 Tyler Seguin 3.00 8.00
119 William Karlsson 3.00 8.00
120 Sean Couturier 2.00 5.00
121 Mark Giordano 2.50 6.00
122 Pierre-Luc Dubois 2.00 5.00
123 Jordan Binnington 4.00 10.00
124 Artemi Panarin 5.00 12.00
125 Jonathan Toews 4.00 10.00
126 Pekka Rinne 2.50 6.00
127 Shea Weber 2.50 6.00
128 Filip Forsberg 4.00 10.00
129 Victor Hedman 3.00 8.00
130 Ryan O'Reilly 2.50 6.00
131 Jeff Skinner 2.50 6.00
132 Aleksander Barkov 4.00 10.00
133 Marc-Andre Fleury 5.00 12.00
134 Carey Price 8.00 20.00
135 Clayton Keller 3.00 8.00
136 Sergei Bobrovsky 4.00 10.00
137 Oliver Ekman-Larsson 2.50 6.00
138 Joe Thornton 4.00 10.00
139 Jonathan Quick 3.00 8.00
140 Nicklas Lidstrom 3.00 8.00
141 Nathan MacKinnon 5.00 12.00
142 Roberto Luongo 4.00 10.00
143 Mark Stone 3.00 8.00
144 Mitch Marner 4.00 10.00
145 Kaapo Kakko RC 8.00 20.00
146 Brock Boeser 3.00 8.00
147 Miro Heiskanen 3.00 8.00
148 Sebastian Aho 4.00 10.00
149 Quinn Hughes RC 6.00 15.00
150 Sidney Crosby 6.00 15.00
151 Jarome Iginla 3.00 8.00
152 Frederik Andersen 3.00 8.00
153 Morgan Rielly 2.50 6.00
154 Dylan Larkin 3.00 8.00
155 Leon Draisaitl 8.00 20.00
156 Andrei Vasilevskiy 4.00 10.00
157 Anze Kopitar 4.00 10.00
158 Kris Letang 3.00 8.00
159 Ryan Suter 2.00 5.00
160 Zach Parise 2.50 6.00
161 Mathew Barzal 3.00 8.00
162 Mikko Rantanen 6.00 15.00
163 Auston Matthews 5.00 12.00
164 Brad Marchand 5.00 12.00
165 Teuvo Teravainen 2.50 6.00
166 Nico Hischier 4.00 10.00
167 Patrick Kane 5.00 12.00
168 Johnny Gaudreau 4.00 10.00
169 Patrice Bergeron 3.00 8.00
170 Kirby Dach RC 15.00 40.00
171 Cam Atkinson 2.50 6.00
172 Ryan Getzlaf 2.50 6.00
173 Brendan Gallagher 2.50 6.00
174 Drew Doughty 3.00 8.00
175 Zdeno Chara 2.50 6.00
176 Steven Stamkos 5.00 12.00
177 Tuukka Rask 3.00 8.00
178 Cale Makar RC 6.00 15.00
179 Connor Hellebuyck 5.00 12.00
180 Brady Tkachuk 4.00 10.00
181 John Gibson 2.50 6.00
182 Evgeni Malkin 4.00 10.00
183 Nick Suzuki RC 8.00 20.00
184 David Pastrnak 6.00 15.00
185 Roman Josi 2.50 6.00
186 Anders Lee 2.00 5.00
187 Jack Eichel 4.00 10.00
188 Vladimir Tarasenko 3.00 8.00
189 Carter Hart 2.50 6.00
190 John Tavares 4.00 10.00
191 Anthony Mantha 2.00 5.00
192 Nikita Kucherov 5.00 12.00
193 Blake Wheeler 2.50 6.00
194 Duncan Keith 2.00 5.00
195 Thomas Chabot 2.50 6.00
196 Jamie Benn 2.50 6.00
197 Logan Couture 3.00 8.00
198 Elias Pettersson 4.00 10.00
199 Nicklas Backstrom 2.50 6.00
200 Gordie Howe 6.00 15.00

2019-20 Chronology Diamond Relics

*DIAMOND: 2.5X TO 6X BASIC
108 Alex Ovechkin 60.00 150.00
110 Jack Hughes 50.00 125.00
134 Carey Price 30.00 80.00
141 Nathan MacKinnon 30.00 80.00
145 Kaapo Kakko 25.00 60.00
149 Quinn Hughes 50.00 125.00
150 Sidney Crosby 60.00 150.00
163 Auston Matthews 60.00 150.00
178 Cale Makar 80.00 200.00
182 Evgeni Malkin 30.00 80.00
200 Gordie Howe 50.00 120.00

2019-20 Chronology Gold Premium

102 Marian Gaborik PATCH AU/25 15.00 40.00
103 Mark Recchi PATCH AU/25 40.00 100.00
104 Erik Karlsson PATCH/25 10.00 25.00
105 Mark Scheifele PATCH AU/25 25.00 60.00
107 John Carlson PATCH/25 8.00 20.00
111 Jonathan Huberdeau PATCH/25 10.00 25.00
112 Matthew Tkachuk PATCH AU/25 30.00 80.00
113 Patrik Laine PATCH/25 10.00 25.00
114 Ryan Nugent-Hopkins PATCH/25 10.00 25.00
115 Andrei Svechnikov PATCH AU/25 20.00 50.00
116 Claude Giroux PATCH/25 8.00 20.00
119 William Karlsson PATCH AU/25 20.00 50.00
120 Sean Couturier PATCH/25 6.00 15.00
121 Mark Giordano PATCH AU/25 15.00 40.00
123 Jordan Binnington PATCH/25 12.00 30.00
124 Artemi Panarin PATCH AU/25 30.00 80.00
128 Filip Forsberg PATCH/25 12.00 30.00
131 Jeff Skinner PATCH/25 8.00 20.00
135 Clayton Keller PATCH/25 10.00 25.00
137 Oliver Ekman-Larsson PATCH/25 8.00 20.00
139 Jonathan Quick PATCH AU/25 20.00 50.00
143 Mark Stone PATCH/25 10.00 25.00
144 Mitch Marner PATCH/25 12.00 30.00
146 Brock Boeser PATCH AU/25 20.00 50.00
149 Quinn Hughes PATCH AU/25 150.00 400.00
153 Morgan Rielly PATCH/25 8.00 20.00
156 Andrei Vasilevskiy PATCH AU/25 25.00 60.00
157 Anze Kopitar PATCH AU/25 25.00 60.00
158 Kris Letang PATCH/25 10.00 25.00
159 Ryan Suter PATCH/25 6.00 15.00
160 Zach Parise PATCH AU/25 15.00 40.00
161 Mathew Barzal PATCH/25 10.00 25.00
166 Nico Hischier PATCH AU/25 25.00 60.00
168 Johnny Gaudreau PATCH/25 12.00 30.00
169 Patrice Bergeron PATCH/25 10.00 25.00
170 Kirby Dach PATCH AU/25 30.00 80.00
171 Cam Atkinson PATCH AU/25 15.00 40.00
172 Ryan Getzlaf PATCH/25 8.00 20.00
173 Brendan Gallagher PATCH AU/25 15.00 40.00
175 Zdeno Chara PATCH/25 8.00 20.00
177 Tuukka Rask PATCH/25 10.00 25.00
178 Cale Makar PATCH AU/25 150.00 400.00
179 Connor Hellebuyck PATCH AU/25 30.00 80.00
180 Brady Tkachuk PATCH AU/25 25.00 60.00
181 John Gibson PATCH AU/25 15.00 40.00
183 Nick Suzuki PATCH AU/25 60.00 150.00
184 David Pastrnak PATCH/25 20.00 50.00
185 Roman Josi PATCH/25 8.00 20.00
186 Anders Lee PATCH AU/25 12.00 30.00
189 Carter Hart PATCH AU/25 60.00 150.00
193 Blake Wheeler PATCH/25 8.00 20.00
198 Elias Pettersson PATCH/25 12.00 30.00
199 Nicklas Backstrom PATCH/25 8.00 20.00

2019-20 Chronology 1 in 100

100AK Anze Kopitar PATCH AU/25 40.00 100.00
100BE Patrice Bergeron PATCH/100 12.00 30.00
100BM Brad Marchand PATCH AU/100 50.00 125.00
100BW Blake Wheeler PATCH/100 10.00 25.00
100CG Claude Giroux PATCH/100 15.00 40.00
100CM Connor McDavid PATCH AU/25 150.00 400.00
100CP Carey Price PATCH AU/25 50.00 125.00
100DD Drew Doughty PATCH/25 12.00 30.00
100DK Duncan Keith PATCH/100 8.00 20.00
100EK Erik Karlsson PATCH/100 12.00 30.00
100EP Elias Pettersson PATCH/100 15.00 40.00
100HL Henrik Lundqvist PATCH AU/25 60.00 150.00
100HS Henrik Sedin PATCH AU/25 30.00 80.00
100JE Jack Eichel PATCH/50 15.00 40.00
100JI Jarome Iginla PATCH AU/25 30.00 80.00
100JQ Jonathan Quick PATCH AU/50 30.00 80.00
100KA Patrick Kane PATCH AU/25 50.00 125.00
100KT Keith Tkachuk PATCH AU/50 15.00 40.00
100MA Auston Matthews PATCH AU/25 100.00 250.00
100MF Marc-Andre Fleury PATCH AU/25 50.00 125.00
100MK Mark Scheifele PATCH AU/100 40.00 100.00
100MR Mitch Marner PATCH/100 15.00 40.00
100NB Nicklas Backstrom PATCH/100 10.00 25.00
100NK Nikita Kucherov PATCH/50 20.00 50.00
100NM Nathan MacKinnon PATCH/25 40.00 100.00
100PA David Pastrnak PATCH/100 25.00 60.00
100PL Patrik Laine PATCH/100 10.00 25.00
100RG Ryan Getzlaf PATCH/100 10.00 25.00
100SE Daniel Sedin PATCH AU/25 40.00 100.00
100ST Mark Stone PATCH AU/100 30.00 80.00
100TA John Tavares PATCH AU/50 40.00 100.00
100TH Joe Thornton PATCH AU/25 40.00 100.00
100ZC Zdeno Chara PATCH/100 20.00 50.00

2019-20 Chronology Canvas Autographs

CAAD Adam Deadmarsh D 12.00 30.00
CAAK Anze Kopitar A 30.00 80.00
CAAL Anders Lee D 15.00 40.00
CAAS Andrei Svechnikov A 25.00 60.00
CABG Brendan Gallagher B 20.00 50.00
CABN Bernie Nicholls D 15.00 40.00
CABO Brooks Orpik D 12.00 30.00
CABS Bobby Smith D 12.00 30.00
CABT Brady Tkachuk A 20.00 50.00
CACH Carter Hart C 20.00 50.00
CACP Colton Parayko B 15.00 40.00
CADB Dustin Brown D 20.00 50.00
CADD Dick Duff A 15.00 40.00
CADE Alex DeBrincat A 25.00 60.00
CADW Doug Weight D 20.00 50.00
CAFP Felix Potvin B 30.00 80.00
CAGA Marian Gaborik B 20.00 50.00
CAHE Connor Hellebuyck C 40.00 100.00
CAJB Jay Bouwmeester C 12.00 30.00
CAJG Jake Guentzel C 25.00 60.00
CAJK Jesperi Kotkaniemi C 20.00 50.00
CAJL John LeClair B 20.00 50.00
CAJT Jacob Trouba C 15.00 40.00
CAJV James van Riemsdyk A 15.00 40.00
CAKP Kyle Palmieri D 8.00 20.00
CAKY Keith Yandle D 12.00 30.00
CAMG Mark Giordano C 20.00 50.00
CAMN Mats Naslund C 30.00 80.00
CAMT Matthew Tkachuk A 30.00 80.00
CANL Nicklas Lidstrom A 20.00 50.00
CAOK Olaf Kolzig D 25.00 60.00
CASG Scott Gomez C 15.00 40.00
CASR Sam Reinhart C 40.00 100.00
CAST Anton Stastny D 20.00 50.00
CATW Tom Wilson C 20.00 50.00
CAWI Doug Wilson C 20.00 50.00
CAWK William Karlsson C 25.00 60.00
CAZP Zach Parise A 20.00 50.00

2019-20 Chronology Canvas Autographs Red

*RED: .5X TO 1.25X BASIC
CADD Dick Duff AU 30.00 80.00

2019-20 Chronology Canvas Draft Masterpiece Autographs

*RED: .75X TO 2X BASIC
CDMABH Barrett Hayton B 20.00 50.00
CDMACG Cody Glass B 25.00 60.00
CDMACM Cale Makar A 80.00 200.00
CDMAJH Jack Hughes A 80.00 200.00
CDMAKD Kirby Dach B 30.00 80.00
CDMAQH Quinn Hughes A 80.00 200.00
CDMARP Ryan Poehling B 25.00 60.00
CDMARS Rasmus Sandin B 10.00 25.00

2019-20 Chronology Dual Autographs

DAGM C.McDavid/W.Gretzky 3000.00 8000.00
DALC S.Crosby/M.Lemieux 800.00 2000.00
DARP C.Price/P.Roy 125.00 300.00
DATM J.Tavares/A.Matthews 200.00 500.00

2019-20 Chronology Franchise Finds Patch Autographs

FFBH Barrett Hayton 60.00 150.00
FFCG Cody Glass 50.00 120.00
FFCM Cale Makar 150.00 400.00
FFDF Dante Fabbro 30.00 80.00
FFIM Ilya Mikheyev 50.00 125.00
FFIS Igor Shesterkin 125.00 300.00
FFJH Jack Hughes 150.00 400.00
FFKD Kirby Dach 60.00 150.00
FFMF Mario Ferraro 25.00 60.00
FFQH Quinn Hughes 150.00 400.00
FFRA Rasmus Asplund 25.00 60.00
FFRP Ryan Poehling 50.00 120.00
FFRS Rasmus Sandin 50.00 125.00
FFTB Tobias Bjornfot 30.00 80.00

2019-20 Chronology Franchise History '20 XRC Autograph Redemptions

I Redemption I 150.00 400.00
II Redemption II 150.00 400.00
III Redemption III 150.00 400.00

2019-20 Chronology Franchise History '20 XRC Redemptions

I Redemption I 100.00 250.00
II Redemption II 100.00 250.00
III Redemption III 100.00 250.00

2019-20 Chronology Letterman Patches

LANCP Corey Perry/35 15.00 40.00
LANJG John Gibson AU/25 20.00 50.00
LANRG Ryan Getzlaf/35 10.00 25.00
LBOBM Brad Marchand AU/15 40.00 100.00
LBODP David Pastrnak/35 25.00 60.00
LBOPB Patrice Bergeron/35 12.00 30.00
LBOTR Tuukka Rask/35 12.00 30.00
LBOZC Zdeno Chara/35 10.00 25.00
LBURD Rasmus Dahlin/35 12.00 30.00
LBURR Rob Ray AU/25 12.00 30.00
LBUSR Sam Reinhart AU/25 40.00 100.00
LCAJG Johnny Gaudreau/35 15.00 40.00
LCAMG Mark Giordano AU/15 20.00 50.00
LCAMT Matthew Tkachuk AU/15 40.00 100.00
LCHAD Alex DeBrincat AU/15 25.00 60.00
LCHBS Brent Seabrook/35 6.00 15.00
LCHCR Corey Crawford/35 10.00 25.00
LCHDG Dirk Graham AU/25 15.00 40.00
LCHDK Duncan Keith/35 8.00 20.00
LCHJT Jonathan Toews AU/10 30.00 80.00
LCHKD Kirby Dach AU/15 100.00 250.00
LCHPK Patrick Kane AU/10 40.00 100.00
LCOCM Cale Makar AU/10 150.00 400.00
LCOGL Gabriel Landeskog/35 12.00 30.00
LCONM Nathan MacKinnon/35 20.00 50.00
LCOPG Philipp Grubauer AU/25 20.00 50.00
LCYBH Barrett Hayton AU/25 30.00 80.00
LCYOE Oliver Ekman-Larsson/35 10.00 25.00
LDABM Brenden Morrow AU/25 15.00 40.00
LDEGH Gordie Howe/35 30.00 80.00
LEDCM Connor McDavid AU/10 200.00 500.00
LEDRN Ryan Nugent-Hopkins/35 12.00 30.00
LFLJH Jonathan Huberdeau/35 12.00 30.00
LFLKY Keith Yandle AU/25 12.00 30.00
LHAST Sylvain Turgeon AU/25 12.00 30.00
LHUAS Andrei Svechnikov AU/25 25.00 60.00
LLAAK Anze Kopitar AU/15 30.00 80.00
LLABN Bernie Nicholls AU/25 15.00 40.00
LLADB Dustin Brown AU/25 20.00 50.00
LLADD Drew Doughty/35 10.00 25.00
LLAJQ Jonathan Quick AU/15 25.00 60.00
LMIZP Zach Parise/35 10.00 25.00
LMNBS Bobby Smith AU/25 20.00 50.00
LMOCP Carey Price AU/10 40.00 100.00
LMOGA Brendan Gallagher/35 10.00 25.00
LMOJK Jesperi Kotkaniemi AU/15 20.00 50.00
LMOMD Max Domi/35 10.00 25.00
LMONS Nick Suzuki AU/15 80.00 200.00
LMORP Ryan Poehling AU/15 30.00 80.00
LMOSW Shea Weber/35 10.00 25.00
LNAFF Filip Forsberg/35 15.00 40.00
LNARJ Roman Josi/35 10.00 25.00
LNJJH Jack Hughes AU/10 100.00 250.00
LNJKP Kyle Palmieri AU/25 15.00 40.00
LNJNH Nico Hischier AU/15 30.00 80.00
LNJPK P.K. Subban/35 12.00 30.00
LNJSG Scott Gomez AU/25 15.00 40.00
LOTBT Brady Tkachuk AU/15 30.00 80.00
LPHBK Bob Kelly AU/25 12.00 30.00
LPHCG Claude Giroux/35 10.00 25.00
LPHCH Carter Hart AU/15 20.00 50.00
LPHTK Tim Kerr AU/25 12.00 30.00
LPIBO Brooks Orpik AU/25 12.00 30.00
LPIJG Jake Guentzel AU/15 30.00 80.00
LPISC Sidney Crosby AU/10 150.00 400.00
LQUAS Anton Stastny AU/25 12.00 30.00
LSABB Brent Burns AU/15 20.00 50.00
LSAJP Joe Pavelski AU/15 25.00 60.00
LSAJT Joe Thornton AU/10 40.00 100.00
LSAMV Marc-Edouard Vlasic/35 6.00 15.00
LSATH Tomas Hertl AU/25 20.00 50.00
LSTDW Doug Weight AU/25 20.00 50.00
LSTJB Jordan Binnington/35 15.00 40.00
LTAAV Andrei Vasilevskiy AU/15 30.00 80.00
LTANK Nikita Kucherov/35 20.00 50.00
LTASS Steven Stamkos AU/10 40.00 100.00
LTAVH Victor Hedman/35 12.00 30.00
LTOAM Auston Matthews AU/10 80.00 200.00
LTODS Darryl Sittler AU/10 25.00 60.00
LTOIM Ilya Mikheyev AU/25 30.00 80.00
LTOJT John Tavares AU/10 60.00 150.00
LTOMM Mitch Marner/35 15.00 40.00
LTOMR Morgan Rielly/35 10.00 25.00
LTOWN William Nylander/35 20.00 50.00
LVAAB Alexandre Burrows AU/25 12.00 30.00
LVADS Daniel Sedin AU/10 60.00 150.00
LVAHS Henrik Sedin AU/10 80.00 200.00
LVAQH Quinn Hughes AU/10 150.00 400.00
LVARL Roberto Luongo AU/15 80.00 200.00
LVECG Cody Glass AU/15 30.00 80.00
LVEMF Marc-Andre Fleury AU/10 40.00 100.00
LVEWK William Karlsson AU/25 25.00 60.00
LWAJC John Carlson/35 10.00 25.00
LWANB Nicklas Backstrom/35 10.00 25.00
LWAOK Olaf Kolzig AU/25 20.00 50.00
LWATW Tom Wilson AU/25 20.00 50.00
LWIBW Blake Wheeler/35 10.00 25.00
LWICH Connor Hellebuyck AU/15 40.00 100.00
LWIMS Mark Scheifele AU/25 30.00 80.00
LWIPL Patrik Laine/35 12.00 30.00
LCBJCA Cam Atkinson AU/25 20.00 50.00
LNYIAL Anders Lee AU/25 15.00 40.00
LNYIBA Mathew Barzal/35 12.00 30.00
LNYRAP Artemi Panarin AU/10 40.00 100.00
LNYRHL Henrik Lundqvist AU/10 50.00 125.00
LNYRIS Igor Shesterkin AU/15 80.00 200.00
LNYRJT Jacob Trouba AU/25 12.00 30.00
LNYRKK Kaapo Kakko/35 30.00 80.00

2019-20 Chronology Time Capsules

*GOLD: .5X TO 1.25X BASIC
TC51 Marc-Andre Fleury 25.00 60.00
TC52 Roberto Luongo 15.00 40.00
TC53 Cale Makar 30.00 80.00
TC54 Jack Hughes 25.00 60.00
TC55 Brad Marchand 15.00 40.00
TC56 Quinn Hughes 25.00 60.00
TC57 Nicklas Lidstrom 15.00 40.00
TC58 Patrick Kane 15.00 40.00
TC59 Drew Doughty 10.00 25.00
TC60 Henrik Lundqvist 20.00 50.00
TC61 Jarome Iginla 20.00 50.00
TC62 Nathan MacKinnon 30.00 80.00
TC63 Joe Thornton 20.00 50.00
TC64 Anze Kopitar 12.00 30.00
TC65 Artemi Panarin 20.00 50.00
TC66 Sidney Crosby 20.00 50.00
TC67 Gordie Howe 15.00 40.00
TC68 Johnny Gaudreau 10.00 25.00
TC69 Zdeno Chara 12.00 30.00
TC70 Auston Matthews 30.00 80.00
TC71 Evgeni Malkin 15.00 40.00
TC72 Claude Giroux 15.00 40.00
TC73 John Tavares 12.00 30.00
TC74 Connor McDavid 30.00 80.00
TC75 Carey Price 20.00 50.00
TC76 Pekka Rinne 8.00 20.00
TC77 Patrice Bergeron 10.00 25.00
TC78 Jonathan Toews 12.00 30.00
TC79 Alex Ovechkin 30.00 80.00
TC80 Steven Stamkos 10.00 25.00

2019-20 Chronology Time Capsules Canvas Mini

M193 Victor Hedman/60 6.00 15.00
M194 John LeClair/60 5.00 12.00
M195 Mike Fisher/60 3.00 8.00
M196 Doug Wilson/60 4.00 10.00
M197 Gary Suter/60 3.00 8.00
M198 Marian Gaborik/60 5.00 12.00
M199 Phil Kessel/60 5.00 12.00
M200 Scott Gomez/60 4.00 10.00
M201 Mark Recchi/60 6.00 15.00
M202 Rob Ray/60 3.00 8.00
M203 Jordan Staal/60 4.00 10.00
M204 Patrik Sundstrom/60 4.00 10.00
M205 Keith Yandle/60 3.00 8.00
M206 Mike Green/60 4.00 10.00
M207 Sam Reinhart/60 10.00 25.00
M208 Jacob Trouba/60 4.00 10.00
M209 Andrei Svechnikov/60 6.00 15.00
M210 Brady Tkachuk/60 8.00 20.00
M211 Doug Weight/60 5.00 12.00
M212 Zdeno Chara/60 5.00 12.00
M213 Nick Suzuki/90 12.00 30.00
M214 Auston Matthews/60 12.00 30.00
M215 Jeff Skinner/60 5.00 12.00
M216 Matthew Tkachuk/60 10.00 25.00
M217 Ben Bishop/60 4.00 10.00
M218 Adam Fox/90 12.00 30.00
M219 Gordie Howe/60 15.00 40.00
M220 Jonathan Toews/60 8.00 20.00
M221 Jonathan Huberdeau/60 6.00 15.00
M222 Duncan Keith/60 4.00 10.00
M223 Quinn Hughes/90 20.00 50.00
M224 Jack Hughes/90 20.00 50.00
M225 Steven Stamkos/60 10.00 25.00
M226 Claude Giroux/60 5.00 12.00
M227 Aleksander Barkov/60 8.00 20.00
M228 Cody Glass/90 8.00 20.00
M229 Cale Makar/90 20.00 50.00
M230 Sidney Crosby/60 15.00 40.00
M231 Patrice Bergeron/60 6.00 15.00
M232 Miro Heiskanen/60 6.00 15.00
M233 Morgan Rielly/60 5.00 12.00
M234 Nicklas Lidstrom/60 5.00 12.00
M235 Alex Ovechkin/60 15.00 40.00
M236 Mark Stone/60 6.00 15.00
M237 Ryan Poehling/90 8.00 20.00
M238 Ilya Kovalchuk/60 5.00 12.00
M239 Mikko Rantanen/60 12.00 30.00
M240 Marc-Andre Fleury/60 10.00 25.00
M241 Brad Marchand/60 10.00 25.00
M242 Mattias Ekholm/60 4.00 10.00
M243 Carey Price/60 12.00 30.00
M244 Pierre-Luc Dubois/60 4.00 10.00
M245 William Karlsson/60 6.00 15.00
M246 Thomas Chabot/60 5.00 12.00
M247 Shea Weber/60 5.00 12.00
M248 Roberto Luongo/60 8.00 20.00
M249 Seth Jones/60 5.00 12.00
M250 Anthony Mantha/60 4.00 10.00
M251 Roberto Luongo/60 8.00 20.00
M252 Adam Boqvist/90 5.00 12.00
M253 Roman Josi/60 5.00 12.00
M254 Nikolaj Ehlers/60 5.00 12.00
M255 John Tavares/60 8.00 20.00
M256 Leon Draisaitl/60 15.00 40.00
M257 Tyler Seguin/60 6.00 15.00
M258 Mark Scheifele/60 6.00 15.00
M259 Max Domi/60 5.00 12.00
M260 Aaron Ekblad/60 5.00 12.00
M261 Ryan Nugent-Hopkins/60 6.00 15.00
M262 Mark Giordano/60 5.00 12.00
M263 Jack Eichel/60 8.00 20.00
M264 Patrik Laine/60 8.00 20.00
M265 Filip Zadina/90 12.00 30.00
M266 Barrett Hayton/90 10.00 25.00
M267 Travis Konecny/60 5.00 12.00
M268 Brock Boeser/60 6.00 15.00
M269 Niklas Hjalmarsson/60 3.00 8.00
M270 Tomas Hertl/60 5.00 12.00
M271 Rasmus Sandin/90 8.00 20.00
M272 Nikita Kucherov/60 10.00 25.00
M273 Mathew Barzal/60 6.00 15.00
M274 Frederik Andersen/60 6.00 15.00
M275 Jamie Benn/60 5.00 12.00
M276 Vladimir Tarasenko/60 6.00 15.00
M277 Kaapo Kakko/90 15.00 40.00
M278 Dylan Larkin/60 6.00 15.00
M279 John Gibson/60 5.00 12.00
M280 Henrik Lundqvist/60 12.00 30.00
M281 Nicklas Backstrom/60 6.00 15.00
M282 Nathan MacKinnon/60 20.00 50.00
M283 Cam Atkinson/60 5.00 12.00
M284 Carter Hart/60 6.00 15.00
M285 Andrei Vasilevskiy/60 8.00 20.00
M286 Johnny Gaudreau/60 8.00 20.00
M287 Evgeni Malkin/60 10.00 25.00
M288 John Carlson/60 5.00 12.00
M289 Clayton Keller/60 6.00 15.00
M290 Joe Thornton/60 8.00 20.00
M291 Anders Lee/60 4.00 10.00
M292 Artemi Panarin/60 10.00 25.00
M293 Sean Couturier/60 4.00 10.00
M294 Pekka Rinne/60 5.00 12.00
M295 Ryan O'Reilly/60 5.00 12.00
M296 Patrick Marleau/60 5.00 12.00
M297 Max Pacioretty/60 6.00 15.00
M298 Connor McDavid/60 20.00 50.00
M299 Jarome Iginla/60 6.00 15.00
M300 Morgan Frost/90 8.00 20.00
M301 Logan Couture/60 6.00 15.00
M302 Mitch Marner/60 8.00 20.00
M303 Connor Hellebuyck/60 10.00 25.00
M304 Sebastian Aho/60 8.00 20.00
M305 Jonathan Quick/60 6.00 15.00
M306 Oliver Ekman-Larsson/60 5.00 12.00
M307 Brendan Gallagher/60 5.00 12.00
M308 Sergei Bobrovsky/60 8.00 20.00
M309 Igor Shesterkin/90 12.00 30.00
M310 Patrick Kane/60 10.00 25.00
M311 Victor Olofsson/90 12.00 30.00
M312 Kirby Dach/90 20.00 50.00
M313 Phillip Danault/60 5.00 12.00
M314 Olaf Kolzig/60 5.00 12.00
M315 Ryan Getzlaf/60 5.00 12.00
M316 Tuukka Rask/60 6.00 15.00
M317 Elias Pettersson/60 8.00 20.00
M318 Ryan Suter/60 4.00 10.00
M319 Anze Kopitar/60 8.00 20.00
M320 Zach Parise/60 5.00 12.00
M321 Jordan Binnington/60 8.00 20.00
M322 Nico Hischier/60 8.00 20.00
M323 Filip Forsberg/60 8.00 20.00
M324 Kris Letang/60 6.00 15.00
M325 David Pastrnak/60 12.00 30.00
M326 Drew Doughty/60 5.00 12.00
M327 Teuvo Teravainen/60 6.00 15.00
M328 Blake Wheeler/60 5.00 12.00

2019-20 Chronology Time Capsules Canvas Mini Autographs

M194 John LeClair/30 10.00 25.00
M195 Mike Fisher/30 6.00 15.00
M197 Gary Suter/30 6.00 15.00
M198 Marian Gaborik/30 10.00 25.00
M216 Matthew Tkachuk/30 20.00 50.00
M218 Adam Fox/60 25.00 60.00
M224 Jack Hughes/60 30.00 80.00
M228 Cody Glass/60 15.00 40.00
M237 Ryan Poehling/60 15.00 40.00
M258 Mark Scheifele/30 15.00 40.00
M262 Mark Giordano/30 10.00 25.00
M266 Barrett Hayton/60 20.00 50.00
M271 Rasmus Sandin/60 15.00 40.00
M303 Connor Hellebuyck/30 20.00 50.00
M312 Kirby Dach/60 20.00 50.00
M314 Olaf Kolzig/30 10.00 25.00
M322 Nico Hischier/30 15.00 40.00

2019-20 Chronology Time Capsules Mini Painting Redemptions

RED Redemption Card 250.00 600.00

1992-93 Clark Candy Mario Lemieux

COMPLETE SET (3) 2.50 6.00
COMMON CARD (1-3) 1.00 2.50

2012-13 Classics Signatures

1 Gordie Howe 2.50 6.00
2 Bobby Hull 1.50 4.00
3 Mike Bossy .75 2.00
4 Bill Barber .60 1.50
5 Dave Taylor .60 1.50
7 Gary Leeman .60 1.50
9 Bryan Trottier .75 2.00
10 Bobby Clarke 1.25 3.00
11 Marcel Dionne 1.00 2.50
12 Gilbert Perreault .75 2.00
13 Russ Courtnall .50 1.25
14 Eric Lindros 1.25 3.00
15 Clark Gillies .75 2.00
16 Reggie Leach .60 1.50
17 Charlie Simmer .50 1.25
19 Wendel Clark 1.25 3.00
20 John LeClair .75 2.00
22 Al Secord .60 1.50
23 Errol Thompson .50 1.25
25 Gordie Howe 2.50 6.00
26 Brian Mullen .50 1.25
27 Geoff Courtnall .50 1.25
28 Marian Stastny .50 1.25
31 Denis Savard .75 2.00
32 Darryl Sittler 1.00 2.50
35 Dale Hawerchuk 1.00 2.50
36 Cliff Ronning .50 1.25
37 Peter Stastny .60 1.50
38 Ron Francis 1.00 2.50
40 Steve Larmer .60 1.50
41 Lanny McDonald .75 2.00
43 Anders Hedberg .50 1.25
44 Paul MacLean .50 1.25
45 Trevor Linden .75 2.00
46 Anton Stastny .50 1.25
47 Kevin Dineen .50 1.25
48 Al Iafrate .60 1.50
49 Adam Foote .50 1.25
50 Johnny Bower .75 2.00
51 Stu Grimson .50 1.25
54 Valeri Bure .50 1.25
55 Richard Brodeur .50 1.25
57 Ray Ferraro .50 1.25
58 Bobby Hull 1.50 4.00
59 Nick Kypreos .50 1.25
60 Ron Hextall .75 2.00
61 Igor Larionov .75 2.00
62 Luc Robitaille .75 2.00
63 Tony Twist .50 1.25
64 Glenn Resch .60 1.50
65 Kirk Muller .60 1.50
66 Stan Mikita 1.00 2.50
67 Dave Schultz .75 2.00
68 Mario Lemieux 3.00 8.00
69 Brendan Shanahan .75 2.00
70 Joe Sakic 1.50 4.00
71 Steve Yzerman 2.00 5.00
73 Johnny Bucyk .75 2.00
74 Bernie Nicholls .60 1.50
75 Ed Belfour .75 2.00
76 Larry Robinson .75 2.00
77 Jim Craig 1.00 2.50
78 Rod Gilbert .75 2.00
79 Rick Tocchet .60 1.50
80 Kevin Weekes .60 1.50
81 Brian Leetch .60 1.50
82 Darren Pang .60 1.50
83 Marty McSorley .60 1.50
85 Craig Berube .50 1.25
86 Michel Goulet .60 1.50
87 Bruce Shoebottom .50 1.25
88 Bernie Federko .60 1.50
89 Andy Moog .75 2.00
90 Mark Messier 1.50 4.00
91 Neal Broten .60 1.50
92 Kris Draper .60 1.50
93 Doug Wilson .60 1.50
94 Reggie Lemelin .50 1.25
95 Jari Kurri .75 2.00
96 Darryl Sydor .50 1.25
97 Al MacInnis 1.00 2.50
98 Adam Graves .60 1.50
99 Denis Potvin .75 2.00
100 Guy Lafleur 1.00 2.50
101 Dave Tippett .50 1.25
102 Pat Verbeek .60 1.50
103 Guy Carbonneau .75 2.00
104 Tony Esposito .75 2.00
105 Dino Ciccarelli .75 2.00
106 John Vanbiesbrouck .75 2.00
107 Craig Patrick .50 1.25
108 Adam Oates .75 2.00
109 Phil Esposito 1.25 3.00
110 Brian Bellows .60 1.50
111 Dave Andreychuk .75 2.00
112 Serge Savard .75 2.00
113 Owen Nolan .60 1.50
114 Rick Middleton .60 1.50
115 Rod Brind'Amour .60 1.50
116 Curtis Joseph 1.00 2.50
118 Gerry Cheevers .75 2.00
119 Joe Mullen .60 1.50
120 Stephane Matteau .50 1.25
121 Craig Ramsay .60 1.50
122 Dirk Graham .50 1.25
123 Bill Clement .50 1.25
124 Jeff Hackett .60 1.50
125 Craig Hartsburg .50 1.25
126 Olaf Kolzig .75 2.00
127 Ken Morrow .50 1.25
128 Tim Kerr .50 1.25
130 Stu Barnes .50 1.25
131 Dennis Maruk .60 1.50
132 Grant Fuhr 1.25 3.00
133 Paul Coffey .75 2.00
134 Mike Richter .75 2.00
135 Billy Smith .75 2.00
136 Rod Langway .60 1.50
137 Pierre Pilote .60 1.50
138 Bob Baun .75 2.00
139 Sean Burke .50 1.25
140 Keith Primeau .60 1.50
141 Pierre Turgeon .60 1.50
142 Brad Park .60 1.50
144 Harry Howell .60 1.50
145 Ted Lindsay .75 2.00
146 Dave Babych .50 1.25
147 Dave Gagner .50 1.25
148 Bill Gadsby .75 2.00
149 Geoff Sanderson .50 1.25
151 Rich Sutter .50 1.25
152 Mike Gartner 1.00 2.50
154 Yvan Cournoyer .75 2.00
155 Duane Sutter .50 1.25
156 Milt Schmidt .60 1.50
157 Alex Delvecchio .75 2.00
158 Rogie Vachon 1.00 2.50
160 Andy Bathgate .75 2.00
161 Dan Cloutier .60 1.50
162 Ken Linseman .50 1.25
163 Jean Pronovost .50 1.25
164 Chris Chelios .75 2.00
165 John Ogrodnick .50 1.25
166 Mike Foligno .60 1.50
168 Bob Gainey .75 2.00
169 Dale Tallon .50 1.25
170 Orest Kindrachuk .50 1.25
171 Red Kelly .75 2.00
172 Pat Falloon .50 1.25
173 Dennis Hextall .50 1.25
175 Nick Fotiu .50 1.25
176 Guy Hebert .60 1.50
177 Mike Peca .50 1.25
179 Brent Sutter .50 1.25
180 Steve Shutt .60 1.50
181 Glenn Anderson .60 1.50
182 Darryl Sutter .75 2.00
183 Ron Sutter .50 1.25
184 Joe Juneau .50 1.25
185 Lou Fontinato .50 1.25
186 Terry O'Reilly .60 1.50
187 Mark Howe .75 2.00
188 Joe Nieuwendyk .60 1.50
189 Derian Hatcher .50 1.25
191 Bob Essensa .75 2.00
192 Norm Ullman .75 2.00
193 Rob Blake .75 2.00
194 Ulf Samuelsson .75 2.00
195 Kjell Samuelsson .50 1.25
196 Pat LaFontaine .75 2.00
198 Scott Mellanby .50 1.25
199 Ed Van Impe .50 1.25
200 Laurie Boschman .50 1.25

2012-13 Classics Signatures Autographs

1 Gordie Howe SP 500.00 800.00
2 Bobby Hull SP 60.00 150.00
3 Mike Bossy SP 60.00 150.00
4 Bill Barber 6.00 15.00
5 Dave Taylor 6.00 15.00
7 Gary Leeman 6.00 15.00
9 Bryan Trottier SP 30.00 80.00
10 Bobby Clarke SP 30.00 80.00
11 Marcel Dionne 10.00 25.00
12 Gilbert Perreault 8.00 20.00
13 Russ Courtnall 5.00 12.00
14 Eric Lindros SP 12.00 30.00
15 Clark Gillies 8.00 20.00
16 Reggie Leach 6.00 15.00
17 Charlie Simmer 5.00 12.00
19 Wendel Clark 12.00 30.00
20 John LeClair 8.00 20.00
22 Al Secord 6.00 15.00
23 Errol Thompson 5.00 12.00
25 Gordie Howe SP 500.00 800.00
26 Brian Mullen 5.00 12.00
27 Geoff Courtnall 5.00 12.00
28 Marian Stastny 5.00 12.00
31 Denis Savard 8.00 20.00
32 Darryl Sittler SP 15.00 40.00
35 Dale Hawerchuk 10.00 25.00
36 Cliff Ronning 5.00 12.00
37 Peter Stastny SP 30.00 80.00
38 Ron Francis SP 60.00 150.00
40 Steve Larmer 6.00 15.00
41 Lanny McDonald SP 30.00 80.00
43 Anders Hedberg 5.00 12.00
44 Paul MacLean 5.00 12.00
45 Trevor Linden 8.00 20.00
46 Anton Stastny 5.00 12.00
47 Kevin Dineen 5.00 12.00
48 Al Iafrate 6.00 15.00
49 Adam Foote 5.00 12.00
50 Johnny Bower 8.00 20.00
51 Stu Grimson 5.00 12.00
54 Valeri Bure 5.00 12.00
55 Richard Brodeur 8.00 20.00
57 Ray Ferraro 5.00 12.00
58 Bobby Hull SP 60.00 150.00
59 Nick Kypreos 5.00 12.00
60 Ron Hextall SP 25.00 60.00
61 Igor Larionov SP 50.00 125.00
62 Luc Robitaille SP 15.00 40.00
63 Tony Twist 5.00 12.00
64 Glenn Resch 6.00 15.00
65 Kirk Muller 6.00 15.00
66 Stan Mikita SP 25.00 60.00
67 Dave Schultz 8.00 20.00

68 Mario Lemieux SP 200.00 300.00
69 Brendan Shanahan SP 60.00 150.00
70 Joe Sakic SP 60.00 150.00
71 Steve Yzerman SP 200.00 300.00
73 Johnny Bucyk SP 8.00 20.00
74 Bernie Nicholls 6.00 15.00
75 Ed Belfour SP 25.00 60.00
76 Larry Robinson 8.00 20.00
77 Jim Craig 10.00 25.00
78 Rod Gilbert SP 8.00 20.00
79 Rick Tocchet 6.00 15.00
80 Kevin Weekes 6.00 15.00
81 Brian Leetch SP 15.00 40.00
82 Darren Pang 6.00 15.00
83 Marty McSorley 6.00 15.00
85 Craig Berube 5.00 12.00
86 Michel Goulet 6.00 15.00
87 Bruce Shoebottom 5.00 12.00
88 Bernie Federko 6.00 15.00
89 Andy Moog 8.00 20.00
90 Mark Messier SP 60.00 150.00
91 Neal Broten 6.00 15.00
92 Kris Draper 6.00 15.00
93 Doug Wilson 6.00 15.00
94 Reggie Lemelin 5.00 12.00
95 Jari Kurri SP 15.00 40.00
96 Darryl Sydor 5.00 12.00
97 Al MacInnis SP 10.00 25.00
98 Adam Graves 6.00 15.00
99 Denis Potvin SP 8.00 20.00
100 Guy Lafleur SP 25.00 60.00
101 Dave Tippett 5.00 12.00
102 Pat Verbeek 6.00 15.00
103 Guy Carbonneau 8.00 20.00
104 Tony Esposito SP 8.00 20.00
106 John Vanbiesbrouck 8.00 20.00
107 Craig Patrick 5.00 12.00
108 Adam Oates 8.00 20.00
109 Phil Esposito SP 12.00 30.00
110 Brian Bellows 6.00 15.00
111 Dave Andreychuk 8.00 20.00
112 Serge Savard 8.00 20.00
113 Owen Nolan 8.00 20.00
114 Rick Middleton 6.00 15.00
115 Rod Brind'Amour 6.00 15.00
116 Curtis Joseph 10.00 25.00
118 Gerry Cheevers 8.00 20.00
119 Joe Mullen 6.00 15.00
120 Stephane Matteau 5.00 12.00
121 Craig Ramsay 6.00 15.00
122 Dirk Graham 5.00 12.00
123 Bill Clement 5.00 12.00
124 Jeff Hackett 6.00 15.00
125 Craig Hartsburg 5.00 12.00
126 Olaf Kolzig 8.00 20.00
127 Ken Morrow 5.00 12.00
128 Tim Kerr 5.00 12.00
130 Stu Barnes 5.00 12.00
131 Dennis Maruk 6.00 15.00
132 Grant Fuhr 25.00 60.00
133 Paul Coffey 30.00 80.00
134 Mike Richter 8.00 20.00
135 Billy Smith 8.00 20.00
136 Rod Langway 6.00 15.00
137 Pierre Pilote 6.00 15.00
138 Bob Baun 8.00 20.00
139 Sean Burke 5.00 12.00
140 Keith Primeau 6.00 15.00
141 Pierre Turgeon 6.00 15.00
142 Brad Park 6.00 15.00
144 Harry Howell 6.00 15.00
145 Ted Lindsay 8.00 20.00
146 Dave Babych 5.00 12.00
147 Dave Gagner 5.00 12.00
148 Bill Gadsby 8.00 20.00
149 Geoff Sanderson 5.00 12.00
151 Rich Sutter 5.00 12.00
152 Mike Gartner SP 25.00 60.00
154 Yvan Cournoyer SP 25.00 60.00
155 Duane Sutter 5.00 12.00
156 Milt Schmidt 6.00 15.00
157 Alex Delvecchio 8.00 20.00
158 Rogie Vachon 10.00 25.00
160 Andy Bathgate 8.00 20.00
161 Dan Cloutier 6.00 15.00
162 Ken Linseman 5.00 12.00
163 Jean Pronovost 5.00 12.00
164 Chris Chelios SP 15.00 40.00
165 John Ogrodnick 5.00 12.00
166 Mike Foligno 6.00 15.00
168 Bob Gainey 8.00 20.00
169 Dale Tallon 5.00 12.00
170 Orest Kindrachuk 5.00 12.00
171 Red Kelly 8.00 20.00
173 Dennis Hextall 5.00 12.00
175 Nick Fotiu 5.00 12.00
176 Guy Hebert 6.00 15.00
177 Mike Peca 5.00 12.00
179 Brent Sutter 5.00 12.00
180 Steve Shutt 6.00 15.00
181 Glenn Anderson 40.00 100.00
182 Darryl Sutter 8.00 20.00
183 Ron Sutter 5.00 12.00
184 Joe Juneau 5.00 12.00
185 Lou Fontinato 5.00 12.00
186 Terry O'Reilly 6.00 15.00
187 Mark Howe SP 30.00 80.00
188 Joe Nieuwendyk SP 60.00 150.00
189 Derian Hatcher 5.00 12.00
191 Bob Essensa 8.00 20.00
192 Norm Ullman 8.00 20.00
193 Rob Blake 8.00 20.00
194 Ulf Samuelsson 8.00 20.00
195 Kjell Samuelsson 5.00 12.00
196 Pat LaFontaine 20.00 50.00
198 Scott Mellanby 5.00 12.00
199 Ed Van Impe 5.00 12.00
200 Laurie Boschman 5.00 12.00

2012-13 Classics Signatures Banner Numbers

1 Lanny McDonald SP 2.00 5.00
2 Stan Mikita SP 2.50 6.00
3 Paul Coffey SP 2.00 5.00
4 Gordie Howe SP 6.00 15.00
5 Patrick Roy SP 5.00 12.00
6 Billy Smith SP 2.00 5.00
7 Mark Messier SP 4.00 10.00
8 Bernie Parent SP 2.50 6.00
9 Mario Lemieux SP 8.00 20.00
10 Bobby Hull SP 4.00 10.00
11 Ray Bourque 3.00 8.00
12 Johnny Bucyk 2.00 5.00
13 Phil Esposito 3.00 8.00
14 Cam Neely 2.00 5.00
15 Terry O'Reilly 1.50 4.00
16 Milt Schmidt 1.50 4.00
17 Pat LaFontaine 2.00 5.00
18 Rick Martin 2.00 5.00
19 Gilbert Perreault 2.00 5.00
20 Al MacInnis 2.00 5.00
21 Ron Francis 2.50 6.00
22 Tony Esposito 2.00 5.00
23 Bobby Hull 4.00 10.00
24 Denis Savard 2.00 5.00
25 Ray Bourque 3.00 8.00
26 Patrick Roy 5.00 12.00
27 Joe Sakic 4.00 10.00
28 Neal Broten 1.50 4.00
29 Alex Delvecchio 2.00 5.00
30 Gordie Howe 6.00 15.00
31 Steve Yzerman 5.00 12.00
32 Glenn Anderson 1.50 4.00
33 Grant Fuhr 3.00 8.00
34 Jari Kurri 2.00 5.00
35 Mark Messier 4.00 10.00
36 Marcel Dionne 2.50 6.00
37 Luc Robitaille 2.00 5.00
38 Dave Taylor 1.50 4.00
39 Rogie Vachon 2.50 6.00
40 Jean Beliveau 2.00 5.00
41 Yvan Cournoyer 2.00 5.00
42 Guy Lafleur 2.50 6.00
43 Henri Richard 2.00 5.00
44 Larry Robinson 2.00 5.00
45 Serge Savard 2.00 5.00
46 Scott Niedermayer 2.00 5.00
47 Mike Bossy 2.00 5.00
48 Clark Gillies 2.00 5.00
49 Denis Potvin 2.00 5.00
50 Bryan Trottier 2.00 5.00
51 Andy Bathgate 2.00 5.00
52 Ed Giacomin 2.00 5.00
53 Rod Gilbert 2.00 5.00
54 Adam Graves 1.50 4.00
55 Brian Leetch 2.00 5.00
56 Mike Richter 2.00 5.00
57 Bill Barber 1.50 4.00
58 Bobby Clarke 3.00 8.00
59 Mark Howe 2.00 5.00
60 Jeremy Roenick 3.00 8.00
61 Keith Tkachuk 2.00 5.00
62 Michel Goulet 1.50 4.00
63 Bernie Federko 1.50 4.00
64 Brett Hull 4.00 10.00
65 Al MacInnis 2.50 6.00
66 Trevor Linden 2.00 5.00
67 Markus Naslund 2.00 5.00
68 Mike Gartner 2.50 6.00
69 Dale Hunter 1.50 4.00
70 Dale Hawerchuk 2.50 6.00
71 Thomas Steen 1.25 3.00
72 Harry Howell 1.50 4.00
73 Ted Lindsay 2.00 5.00
74 Pierre Pilote 1.50 4.00
75 Marc Tardif 1.25 3.00

2012-13 Classics Signatures Classic Combos Dual Autographs

1 B.Hull/B.Hull/50 50.00 125.00
2 B.Clarke/R.Leach/100 25.00 60.00
3 B.Parent/B.Barber/100 25.00 60.00
5 P.Esposito/R.Bourque/50 30.00 80.00
8 Belfour/Roenick/50 30.00 80.00
9 Cheevers/M.Schmidt/100 15.00 40.00
10 G.Howe/M.Howe/25 100.00 250.00
12 D.Gilmour/W.Clark/100 25.00 60.00
13 E.Lindros/R.Hextall/50 30.00 80.00
17 B.Leetch/S.Matteau/100 12.00 30.00
18 D.Schultz/T.O'Reilly/100 15.00 40.00
20 M.Gartner/R.Langway/100 20.00 50.00
21 Vanbiesbrck/Mellanby/100 15.00 40.00
22 K.Samuels/U.Samuels/100 15.00 40.00
23 A.Moog/G.Fuhr/50 25.00 60.00
24 Hawerchuk/Babych/100 20.00 50.00
25 Bellows/Modano/100 25.00 60.00
27 R.Tocchet/T.Kerr/100 12.00 30.00
28 R.Sutter/R.Sutter/100 10.00 25.00

2012-13 Classics Signatures Classic Combos Triple Autographs

2 Parent/Clarke/Schultz/50 40.00 100.00
4 Kurri/Robitaille/Dionne/50 40.00 100.00
6 Lafleur/Robinson/Cournoyer/50 60.00 150.00
7 Delvecchio/Howe/Kelly/25 150.00 250.00
8 Pang/Belfour/Esposito/25 100.00 200.00
9 Craig/Morrow/Broten/50 30.00 80.00
10 Andrsn/Fhr/Cffey/50 EXCH 40.00 100.00

2012-13 Classics Signatures Classic Lines Triple Autographs

1 Trottier/Gillies/Bossy 50.00 125.00
2 Barber/Clarke/Leach 50.00 125.00
3 Simmer/Taylor/Dionne 50.00 125.00
8 Secord/Savard/Larmer 50.00 125.00
9 Sittler/Thompson/McDonald 30.00 80.00
12 Mullen/Hawerchuk/MacLean 30.00 80.00
14 Stastny/Stastny/Stastny 150.00 250.00

2012-13 Classics Signatures Inaugural INKS

1 Gordie Howe/72 60.00 150.00
2 Bobby Hull/83 25.00 60.00
3 Mark Messier/100 25.00 60.00
4 Patrick Roy/100 30.00 80.00
5 Joe Nieuwendyk/100 10.00 25.00
6 Johnny Bower/76 20.00 50.00
7 Doug Gilmour/100 15.00 40.00
8 Jari Kurri/100 12.00 30.00
9 Adam Oates/100 12.00 30.00
10 Mario Lemieux/97 50.00 125.00
11 Gerry Cheevers/84 12.00 30.00
12 Brett Hull/100 25.00 60.00
13 Denis Potvin/91 12.00 30.00
14 Guy Lafleur/88 15.00 40.00
15 Ed Belfour/100 12.00 30.00
16 Tony Esposito/88 12.00 30.00
17 Bobby Clarke/87 20.00 50.00
18 Phil Esposito/84 EXCH 20.00 50.00
19 Dale Hawerchuk/100 15.00 40.00
20 Bernie Parent/84 15.00 40.00

2012-13 Classics Signatures Notable Nicknames

1 Al Iafrate 12.00 30.00
2 Bobby Hull 30.00 80.00
3 Johnny Bower 15.00 40.00
4 Stu Grimson 10.00 25.00
5 Eddie Shack 15.00 40.00
8 Richard Brodeur 15.00 40.00
10 Ray Ferraro 10.00 25.00
11 Ron Francis 20.00 50.00
12 Gordie Howe 100.00 200.00
13 Ron Hextall 15.00 40.00
14 Igor Larionov 15.00 40.00
15 Luc Robitaille 15.00 40.00
16 Tony Twist 10.00 25.00
17 Glenn Resch 12.00 30.00
19 Stan Mikita 20.00 50.00
20 Dave Schultz 15.00 40.00
21 Mario Lemieux 60.00 150.00
22 Brendan Shanahan 15.00 40.00
23 Joe Sakic 30.00 80.00
24 Steve Yzerman 40.00 100.00
25 Reggie Leach 12.00 30.00
26 Johnny Bucyk 15.00 40.00
27 John Vanbiesbrouck 15.00 40.00
28 Ed Belfour 15.00 40.00

2012-13 Classics Signatures Social Signatures

SSBN Bernie Nicholls 5.00 12.00
SSBP Bernie Parent SP 15.00 40.00
SSBS Brendan Shanahan SP 25.00 60.00
SSDG Doug Gilmour SP 8.00 20.00
SSKH Kelly Hrudey EXCH 5.00 12.00
SSKW Kevin Weekes 5.00 12.00
SSMB Mike Bossy SP 25.00 60.00
SSMM Mike Modano SP 25.00 60.00
SSNK Nick Kypreos 4.00 10.00
SSRG Rod Gilbert 6.00 15.00
SSRT Rick Tocchet 5.00 12.00
SSTL Trevor Linden 6.00 15.00
SSVB Valeri Bure 4.00 10.00
SSFOX Jim Fox 4.00 10.00
SSJIM Jim Craig 8.00 20.00
SSPAN Darren Pang 5.00 12.00
SSREA Daryl Reaugh 5.00 12.00

2012-13 Classics Signatures The Expansion

1 Gilbert Perreault/50 25.00 50.00
2 Craig Ramsay/100 8.00 20.00
5 Pat LaFontaine/50 20.00 40.00
6 Bobby Clarke/50 30.00 60.00
7 Bernie Parent/50 20.00 50.00
8 Reggie Leach/50 15.00 40.00
9 Bill Barber/50 15.00 40.00
10 Eric Lindros/50 30.00 60.00
11 Dave Taylor/50 15.00 40.00
12 Marcel Dionne/50 20.00 50.00
13 Charlie Simmer/50 12.00 30.00
14 Rogie Vachon/50 15.00 40.00
15 Luc Robitaille/50 15.00 30.00
16 Neal Broten/50 12.00 30.00
17 Brian Bellows/50 12.00 30.00
18 Dino Ciccarelli/50 12.00 30.00
19 Craig Hartsburg/50 10.00 25.00
20 Mike Modano/50 25.00 50.00
22 Orest Kindrachuk/100 8.00 20.00
23 Jean Pronovost/100 15.00 40.00
24 Ron Francis/50 30.00 60.00
25 Mario Lemieux/25 75.00 150.00
26 Dennis Maruk/100 10.00 25.00
27 Craig Patrick/100 8.00 20.00
28 Gary Simmons/100 12.00 30.00
29 Dennis Hextall/100 12.00 30.00
30 Bob Baun/100 12.00 30.00

2012-13 Classics Signatures The Originals

1 Jean Beliveau/50 EXCH 12.00 30.00
2 Larry Robinson/50 12.00 30.00
3 Guy Lafleur/50 15.00 40.00
4 Serge Savard/50 12.00 30.00
6 Yvan Cournoyer/50 12.00 30.00
7 Bob Gainey/50 12.00 30.00
8 Guy Carbonneau/100 12.00 30.00
9 Patrick Roy/25 60.00 150.00
11 Johnny Bower/100 12.00 30.00
13 Darryl Sittler/50 15.00 40.00
17 Doug Gilmour/50 15.00 40.00
18 Wendel Clark/50 20.00 50.00
19 Milt Schmidt/100 10.00 25.00
20 Bruce Shoebottom/100 8.00 20.00
21 Johnny Bucyk/50 12.00 30.00
22 Cam Neely/50 12.00 30.00
23 Gerry Cheevers/100 12.00 30.00
24 Adam Oates/50 12.00 30.00
25 Rick Middleton/50 12.00 30.00
26 Phil Esposito/25 EXCH 40.00 100.00
27 Ray Bourque/25 50.00 125.00
28 Stan Mikita/25 50.00 125.00
29 Tony Esposito/25 40.00 100.00
30 Pierre Pilote/100 10.00 25.00
31 Bill Gadsby/100 12.00 30.00
33 Denis Savard/50 12.00 30.00
34 Dirk Graham/100 8.00 20.00
35 Darryl Sutter/100 12.00 30.00
36 Chris Chelios/100 12.00 30.00
38 Lou Fontinato/100 12.00 30.00
39 Harry Howell/100 10.00 25.00
40 Andy Bathgate/100 12.00 30.00
41 Phil Esposito/25 40.00 100.00
42 Adam Graves/50 10.00 25.00
43 Brian Leetch/50 10.00 25.00
44 Mark Messier/25 50.00 125.00
45 Gordie Howe/25 200.00 300.00
46 Ted Lindsay/50 12.00 30.00
47 Red Kelly/100 12.00 30.00
48 Norm Ullman/50 12.00 30.00
49 Igor Larionov/50 12.00 30.00
50 Steve Yzerman/25 100.00 200.00

1972-73 Cleveland Crusaders WHA

COMPLETE SET (15) 25.00 50.00
1 Ron Buchanan 2.00 4.00
2 Ray Clearwater 2.00 4.00
3 Bob Dillabough 2.00 4.00
4 Grant Erickson 2.00 4.00
5 Ted Hodgson 2.00 4.00
6 Ralph Hopiavouri 2.00 4.00
7 Bill Horton 2.00 4.00
8 Gary Jarrett 2.00 4.00
9 Skip Krake 2.00 4.00
10 Wayne Muloin 2.00 4.00
11 Bill Needham CO 2.00 4.00
12 Rick Pumple 2.50 5.00
13 Paul Shmyr 2.00 4.00
14 Robert Whidden 2.00 4.00
15 Jim Wiste 2.50 5.00

1964-65 Coca-Cola Caps

COMPLETE SET (108) 375.00 750.00
1 Ed Johnston 1 2.50 5.00
2 Bob McCord 4 1.50 3.00
3 Ted Green 6 2.00 4.00
4 Orland Kurtenbach 7 2.00 4.00
5 Gary Dornhoefer 8 2.00 4.00
6 Johnny Bucyk 9 5.00 10.00
7 Tom Johnson 10 2.00 4.00
8 Tom Williams 11 1.50 3.00
9 Murray Balfour 12 1.50 3.00
10 Forbes Kennedy 14 1.50 3.00
11 Murray Oliver 16 1.50 3.00
12 Dean Prentice 17 2.00 4.00
13 Ed Westfall 18 2.00 4.00
14 Reg Fleming 19 1.50 3.00
15 Leo Boivin 20 2.00 4.00
16 Ab McDonald 21 1.50 3.00
17 Ron Schock 23 1.50 3.00
18 Bob Leiter 24 1.50 3.00
19 Glenn Hall 1 6.00 12.00
20 Doug Mohns 2 2.00 4.00
21 Pierre Pilote 3 2.50 5.00
22 Elmer Vasko 4 1.50 3.00
23 Fred Stanfield 6 1.50 3.00
24 Phil Esposito 7 20.00 40.00
25 Bobby Hull 9 25.00 50.00
26 Bill Hay 11 1.25 2.50
27 John Brenneman 12 1.25 2.50
28 Doug Robinson 14 1.50 3.00
29 Eric Nesterenko 15 2.00 4.00
30 Chico Maki 16 2.00 4.00
31 Ken Wharram 17 1.50 3.00
32 John McKenzie 18 1.50 3.00
33 Al MacNeil 19 1.50 3.00
34 Wayne Hillman 20 1.50 3.00
35 Stan Mikita 21 7.50 15.00
36 Denis DeJordy 30 2.00 4.00
37 Roger Crozier 1 2.50 5.00
38 Albert Langlois 2 1.50 3.00
39 Marcel Pronovost 3 2.00 4.00
40 Bill Gadsby 4 2.00 4.00
41 Doug Barkley 5 1.50 3.00
42 Norm Ullman 7 4.00 8.00
43 Pit Martin 8 2.00 4.00
44 Gordie Howe 9 30.00 60.00
45A Gordie Howe 10 40.00 80.00
45B Alex Delvecchio 10 15.00 30.00
46 Ron Murphy 12 1.50 3.00
47 Larry Jeffrey 14 1.50 3.00
48 Ted Lindsay 15 5.00 10.00
49 Bruce MacGregor 16 1.50 3.00
50 Floyd Smith 17 1.50 3.00
51 Gary Bergman 18 1.50 3.00
52 Paul Henderson 19 3.00 6.00
53 Parker MacDonald 20 1.50 3.00
54 Eddie Joyal 21 1.50 3.00
55 Charlie Hodge 1 2.00 4.00
56 Jacques Laperriere 2 2.50 5.00
57 J.C. Tremblay 3 2.00 4.00
58 Jean Beliveau 4 10.00 20.00
59 Ralph Backstrom 6 2.00 4.00
60 Bill Hicke 8 1.50 3.00
61 Ted Harris 10 1.50 3.00
62 Claude Larose 11 1.50 3.00
63 Yvan Cournoyer 12 7.50 15.00
64 Claude Provost 14 1.50 3.00
65 Bobby Rousseau 15 2.00 4.00
66 Henri Richard 16 6.00 12.00
67 Jean-Guy Talbot 17 2.00 4.00
68 Terry Harper 19 2.00 4.00
69 Dave Balon 20 1.50 3.00
70 Gilles Tremblay 21 1.50 3.00
71 John Ferguson 22 2.50 5.00
72 Jim Roberts 26 1.50 3.00
73 Jacques Plante 1 10.00 20.00
74 Harry Howell 3 2.00 4.00
75 Arnie Brown 4 1.50 3.00
76 Don Johns 6 1.50 3.00
77 Rod Gilbert 7 4.00 8.00
78 Bob Nevin 8 1.50 3.00
79 Dick Duff 9 2.00 4.00
80 Earl Ingarfield 10 1.50 3.00
81 Vic Hadfield 11 2.00 4.00
82 Jim Mikol 12 1.50 3.00
83 Val Fonteyne 14 1.50 3.00
84 Jim Neilson 15 1.50 3.00
85 Rod Seiling 16 1.50 3.00
86 Lou Angotti 17 1.50 3.00
87 Phil Goyette 20 1.50 3.00
88 Camille Henry 21 2.00 4.00
89 Don Marshall 22 2.00 4.00
90 Marcel Paille 23 2.00 4.00
91 Johnny Bower 1 5.00 10.00
92 Carl Brewer 2 2.00 4.00
93 Red Kelly 4 4.00 8.00
94 Tim Horton 7 7.50 15.00
95 George Armstrong 9 4.00 8.00
96 Andy Bathgate 10 4.00 8.00
97 Ron Ellis 11 2.00 4.00
98 Ralph Stewart 12 1.50 3.00
99 Dave Keon 14 4.00 8.00
100 Dickie Moore 16 2.50 5.00
101 Don McKenney 17 1.50 3.00
102 Kent Douglas 19 1.50 3.00
103 Bob Pulford 20 2.50 5.00
104 Bob Baun 21 2.50 5.00
105 Eddie Shack 23 4.00 8.00
106 Terry Sawchuk 24 10.00 20.00
107 Allan Stanley 26 2.50 5.00
108 Frank Mahovlich 6.00 12.00
xx Cap Holder (Plastic Rink 50.00 100.00

1965-66 Coca-Cola

COMPLETE SET (108) 250.00 500.00
1 Gerry Cheevers 15.00 40.00
2 Albert Langlois 1.25 3.00
3 Ted Green 1.00 2.50
4 Ron Stewart .75 2.00
5 Bob Woytowich 1.25 3.00
6 Johnny Bucyk 6.00 15.00
7 Tom Williams .75 2.00
8 Forbes Kennedy 1.25 3.00
9 Murray Oliver 1.50 4.00
10 Dean Prentice 1.25 3.00
11 Ed Westfall 1.00 2.50
12 Reg Fleming 1.00 2.50
13 Leo Boivin 2.00 5.00
14 Parker MacDonald 1.25 3.00
15 Bob Dillabough 2.00 5.00
16 Barry Ashbee 2.50 6.00
17 Don Awrey 2.00 5.00
18 Bernie Parent 15.00 40.00
19 Glenn Hall 5.00 12.00
20 Doug Mohns 1.50 4.00
21 Pierre Pilote 2.00 5.00
22 Elmer Vasko 1.00 2.50
23 Matt Ravlich 1.25 3.00
24 Fred Stanfield 1.25 3.00
25 Phil Esposito 15.00 40.00
26 Bobby Hull 15.00 40.00
27 Dennis Hull 3.00 8.00
28 Bill Hay 1.50 4.00
29 Ken Hodge 2.00 5.00
30 Eric Nesterenko 1.50 4.00
31 Chico Maki 1.00 2.50
32 Ken Wharram 1.00 2.50
33 Al MacNeil .75 2.00
34 Doug Jarrett 1.25 3.00
35 Stan Mikita 5.00 12.00
36 Dave Dryden 1.00 2.50
37 Roger Crozier 4.00 10.00
38 Warren Godfrey .75 2.00
39 Bert Marshall 2.00 5.00
40 Bill Gadsby 2.50 6.00
41 Doug Barkley .75 2.00
42 Norm Ullman 1.50 4.00
43 Gordie Howe 25.00 60.00
44 Alex Delvecchio 8.00 20.00
45 Val Fonteyne 2.00 5.00
46 Ron Murphy .75 2.00
47 Billy Harris 2.50 6.00
48 Bruce MacGregor .75 2.00
49 Floyd Smith 4.00 10.00
50 Paul Henderson 4.00 10.00
51 Andy Bathgate 6.00 15.00
52 Ab McDonald 2.50 6.00
53 Gary Bergman 2.00 5.00
54 Hank Bassen 1.00 2.50
55 Charlie Hodge 2.00 5.00
56 Jacques Laperriere 1.50 4.00
57 Jean-Claude Tremblay .75 2.00
58 Jean Beliveau 6.00 15.00
59 Ralph Backstrom 1.50 4.00
60 Dick Duff 1.25 3.00
61 Ted Harris .75 2.00
62 Claude Larose .75 2.00
63 Yvan Cournoyer 8.00 20.00
64 Claude Provost 1.50 4.00
65 Bobby Rousseau .75 2.00
66 Henri Richard 4.00 10.00
67 Jean-Guy Talbot 1.00 2.50
68 Terry Harper 2.00 5.00
69 Gilles Tremblay .75 2.00
70 John Ferguson 1.50 4.00
71 Jim Roberts 1.25 3.00
72 Gump Worsley 4.00 10.00
73 Ed Giacomin 10.00 25.00
74 Wayne Hillman 1.50 4.00
75 Harry Howell 2.00 5.00
76 Arnie Brown 1.25 3.00
77 Doug Robinson 1.25 3.00
78 Mike McMahon 1.25 3.00
79 Rod Gilbert 3.00 8.00
80 Bob Nevin 1.25 3.00
81 Earl Ingarfield 1.50 4.00
82 Vic Hadfield 1.50 4.00
83 Bill Hicke .75 2.00
84 John McKenzie 2.50 6.00
85 Jim Neilson .75 2.00
86 Jean Ratelle 2.00 5.00
87 Phil Goyette 1.50 4.00
88 Garry Peters 1.00 2.50
89 Don Marshall 1.25 3.00
90 Don Simmons 1.50 4.00
91 Johnny Bower 3.00 8.00
92 Marcel Pronovost .75 2.00
93 Red Kelly 1.50 4.00
94 Tim Horton 5.00 12.00
95 Ron Ellis 1.00 2.50
96 George Armstrong 1.50 4.00
97 Brit Selby 1.00 2.50
98 Pete Stemkowski .75 2.00
99 Dave Keon 4.00 10.00
100 Mike Walton 1.00 2.50
101 Kent Douglas 1.00 2.50
102 Bob Pulford 1.25 3.00
103 Bob Baun 1.50 4.00
104 Eddie Shack 1.50 4.00
105 Orland Kurtenbach .75 2.00
106 Allan Stanley 1.00 2.50
107 Frank Mahovlich 4.00 10.00
108 Terry Sawchuk 8.00 20.00
NNO Album 40.00 80.00

1965-66 Coca-Cola Booklets

COMPLETE SET (4) 75.00 150.00
A Johnny Bower How To Play Goal 25.00 50.00
B Dave Keon How To Play Forward/Defense 25.00 50.00
C Jacques Laperriere How to Play Defense 12.50 25.00
D Henri Richard How To Play Forward/Offense 25.00 50.00

1977-78 Coca-Cola

COMPLETE SET (30) 62.50 300.00
1 Syl Apps .75 3.00
2 Dave Burrows .75 3.00
3 Bobby Clarke 6.00 25.00
4 Yvan Cournoyer 2.50 10.00
5 John Davidson 1.50 10.00
6 Marcel Dionne 4.00 15.00
7 Doug Favell 1.25 5.00
8 Rod Gilbert 1.50 10.00
9 Brian Glennie .75 3.00
10 Butch Goring .75 3.00
11 Lorne Henning .75 3.00
12 Cliff Koroll .75 3.00
13 Guy Lapointe 1.50 5.00
14 Dave Maloney .75 3.00
15 Pit Martin .75 3.00
16 Lou Nanne .75 3.00
17 Bobby Orr 30.00 125.00
18 Brad Park 2.50 10.00
19 Craig Ramsay .75 3.00
20 Larry Robinson 5.00 20.00
21 Jim Rutherford 1.25 5.00
22 Don Saleski .75 3.00
23 Steve Shutt 2.50 8.00
24 Darryl Sittler 4.00 20.00
25 Billy Smith 3.00 10.00
26 Bob Stewart .75 3.00
27 Rogatien Vachon 2.50 10.00
28 Jimmy Watson .75 3.00
29 Joe Watson .75 3.00
30 Ed Westfall .75 3.00

1994 Coca-Cola Wayne Gretzky Cups

COMPLETE SET (5) 8.00 20.00
COMMON CUP 1.50 4.00

1994 Coke/Mac's Milk Gretzky POGs

COMPLETE SET (18) 6.00 15.00
COMMON POG (1-18) .40 1.00

1970-71 Colgate Stamps

COMPLETE SET (93) 100.00 200.00
1 Walt McKechnie .50 1.00
2 Bob Pulford 1.50 3.00
3 Mike Walton .50 1.00
4 Alex Delvecchio 2.50 5.00
5 Tom Williams .50 1.00
6 Derek Sanderson 5.00 10.00
7 Garry Unger 1.00 2.00
8 Lou Angotti .50 1.00
9 Ted Hampson .50 1.00
10 Phil Goyette .50 1.00
11 Juha Widing .50 1.00
12 Norm Ullman 2.00 4.00
13 Garry Monahan .50 1.00
14 Henri Richard 2.50 5.00
15 Ray Cullen .50 1.00
16 Danny O'Shea .50 1.00
17 Marc Tardif .75 1.50
18 Jude Drouin .50 1.00
19 Charlie Burns .50 1.00
20 Gerry Meehan .75 1.50
21 Ralph Backstrom .75 1.50
22 Frank St.Marseille .50 1.00
23 Orland Kurtenbach .50 1.00
24 Red Berenson 1.00 2.00
25 Jean Ratelle 2.00 4.00
26 Syl Apps .75 1.50
27 Don Marshall .50 1.00
28 Gilbert Perreault 5.00 10.00
29 Andre Lacroix .75 1.50
30 Jacques Lemaire 1.50 3.00
31 Pit Martin .75 1.50
32 Dennis Hull .75 1.50
33 Dave Balon .50 1.00
34 Keith McCreary .50 1.00
35 Bobby Rousseau .75 1.50
36 Danny Grant .75 1.50
37 Brit Selby .50 1.00
38 Bob Nevin .50 1.00
39 Rosaire Paiement .50 1.00
40 Gary Dornhoefer 1.00 2.00
41 Eddie Shack 2.00 4.00
42 Ron Schock .50 1.00
43 Jim Pappin .50 1.00
44 Mickey Redmond 1.50 3.00
45 Vic Hadfield .75 1.50
46 Johnny Bucyk 2.00 4.00
47 Gordie Howe 12.00 30.00
48 Ron Anderson .50 1.00
49 Gary Jarrett .50 1.00
50 Jean Pronovost .75 1.50
51 Simon Nolet .50 1.00
52 Bill Goldsworthy .75 1.50
53 Rod Gilbert 2.00 4.00
54 Ron Ellis .75 1.50
55 Mike Byers .50 1.00
56 Norm Ferguson .50 1.00
57 Gary Sabourin .50 1.00
58 Tim Ecclestone .50 1.00
59 John McKenzie .75 1.50
60 Yvan Cournoyer 2.00 4.00
61 Ken Schinkel .50 1.00
62 Ken Hodge 1.00 2.00
63 Cesare Maniago 1.50 3.00
64 J.C. Tremblay .75 1.50
65 Gilles Marotte .50 1.00
66 Bob Baun 1.00 2.00
67 Gerry Desjardins 1.00 2.00
68 Charlie Hodge 1.50 3.00
69 Matt Ravlich .50 1.00
70 Ed Giacomin 3.00 6.00
71 Gerry Cheevers 4.00 8.00
72 Pat Quinn .75 1.50
73 Gary Bergman .50 1.00
74 Serge Savard 1.00 2.00
75 Les Binkley 1.00 2.00
76 Arnie Brown .50 1.00
77 Pat Stapleton .50 1.00
78 Ed Van Impe .50 1.00
79 Jim Dorey .50 1.00
80 Dave Dryden 1.50 3.00
81 Dale Tallon .75 1.50
82 Bruce Gamble 1.50 3.00
83 Roger Crozier 1.50 3.00
84 Denis DeJordy 1.50 3.00
85 Rogatien Vachon 2.00 4.00
86 Carol Vadnais .50 1.00
87 Bobby Orr 20.00 50.00
88 Noel Picard .50 1.00
89 Gilles Villemure 1.50 3.00
90 Gary Smith 1.50 3.00
91 Doug Favell 1.50 3.00
92 Ernie Wakely 1.50 3.00
93 Bernie Parent 5.00 10.00
NNO Stamp Calendar Sheet 5.00 10.00

1971-72 Colgate Heads

COMPLETE SET (16) 100.00 200.00
1 Yvon Cournoyer 3.00 8.00
2 Marcel Dionne UER 6.00 15.00
3 Ken Dryden 8.00 20.00
4 Paul Henderson 2.50 6.00
5 Guy Lafleur 8.00 20.00
6 Frank Mahovlich 4.00 10.00
7 Richard Martin SP 15.00 30.00
8 Bobby Orr 20.00 40.00
9 Brad Park SP 20.00 40.00
10 Jacques Plante 6.00 15.00
11 Jean Ratelle 3.00 8.00
12 Derek Sanderson 6.00 15.00
13 Dale Tallon 2.00 5.00
14 Walt Tkaczuk 2.00 4.00
15A Norm Ullman ERR incorrectly spelled Ullmann 5.00 12.00
15B Norm Ullman COR Spelled Ullman 12.00 30.00
16 Garry Unger 2.00 5.00

1995-96 Collector's Choice

1 Wayne Gretzky .75 2.00
2 Darius Kasparaitis .07 .20
3 Scott Niedermayer .12 .30
4 Brendan Shanahan .12 .30
5 Doug Gilmour .15 .40
6 Lyle Odelein .07 .20
7 Dave Gagner .07 .20
8 Gary Suter .07 .20
9 Sandis Ozolinsh .07 .20
10 Sergei Zubov .10 .25
11 Don Beaupre .10 .25
12 Bill Lindsay .07 .20
13 David Oliver .07 .20
14 Bob Corkum .07 .20
15 German Titov .10 .25
16 Jari Kurri .12 .30
17 Cliff Ronning .07 .20
18 Paul Coffey .12 .30
19 Ian Laperriere .07 .20
20 Dave Andreychuk .12 .30
21 Andrei Nikolishin .07 .20
22 Blaine Lacher .10 .25
23 Yuri Khmylev .07 .20
24 Darren Turcotte .07 .20
25 Joe Mullen .10 .25
26 Peter Forsberg .25 .60
27 Paul Ysebaert .07 .20
28 Tommy Soderstrom .10 .25
29 Rod Brind'Amour .10 .25
30 Jim Carey .10 .25
31 Geoff Courtnall .07 .20
32 Slava Kozlov .10 .25
33 Ray Ferraro .07 .20
34 John MacLean .10 .25
35 Benoit Brunet .07 .20
36 Trent Klatt .07 .20
37 Chris Chelios .12 .30
38 Tom Pederson .12 .30
39 Pat Elynuik .10 .25
40 Rob Niedermayer .10 .25
41 Jason Arnott .10 .25
42 Patrik Carnback .07 .20
43 Steve Chiasson .07 .20
44 Marty McSorley .10 .25
45 Pavel Bure .12 .30
46 Glenn Anderson .10 .25
47 Doug Brown .07 .20
48 Mike Ridley .07 .20
49 Alexei Zhamnov .12 .30
50 Mariusz Czerkawski .07 .20
51 Derek Plante .07 .20
52 Andrew Cassels .07 .20
53 Tom Barrasso .10 .25
54 Andrei Kovalenko .07 .20
55 Pat Verbeek .10 .25
56 Alexander Semak .07 .20
57 Eric Lindros .20 .50
58 Peter Bondra .12 .30
59 Marty McInnis .07 .20
60 Bill Guerin .12 .30
61 Patrice Brisebois .07 .20
62 Andy Moog .12 .30
63 Eric Weinrich .07 .20
64 Arturs Irbe .10 .25
65 Sean Hill .07 .20
66 Jesse Belanger .07 .20
67 Bryan Marchment .07 .20
68 Joe Sacco .07 .20
69 Trevor Kidd .10 .25
70 Dan Quinn .07 .20
71 Kirk McLean .10 .25
72 Benoit Hogue .07 .20
73 Garry Galley .07 .20
74 Randy Wood .07 .20
75 Nikolai Khabibulin .10 .25
76 Ted Donato .07 .20
77 Doug Bodger .07 .20
78 Paul Ranheim .07 .20
79 Ulf Samuelsson .07 .20
80 Uwe Krupp .10 .25
81 Oleg Tverdovsky .12 .30
82 Kelly Miller .07 .20
83 Darryl Sydor .10 .25
84 Brian Bellows .07 .20
85 Jeremy Roenick .20 .50
86 Phil Bourque .10 .25
87 Louie DeBrusk .10 .25
88 Joel Otto .07 .20
89 Dino Ciccarelli .10 .25

90 Mats Sundin .12 .30
91 Don Sweeney .07 .20
92 Roman Hamrlik .07 .20
93 Petr Svoboda .07 .20
94 Zigmund Palffy .12 .30
95 Patrick Roy .30 .75
96 Sergei Krivokrasov .07 .20
97 Wade Flaherty RC .10 .25
98 Fredrik Olausson .10 .25
99 Sergio Momesso .07 .20
100 Mike Vernon .10 .25
101 Todd Gill .07 .20
102 Cam Neely .12 .30
103 Wendel Clark .20 .50
104 John Tucker .07 .20
105 Eric Desjardins .10 .25
106 Ed Olczyk .07 .20
107 Bob Beers .07 .20
108 Mark Recchi .15 .40
109 Ed Belfour .10 .25
110 Radek Bonk .07 .20
111 Cory Stillman .07 .20
112 Jeff Norton .07 .20
113 Terry Carkner .07 .20
114 Felix Potvin .20 .50
115 Alexei Kasatonov .07 .20
116 Brian Noonan .07 .20
117 Daren Puppa .10 .25
118 Joe Juneau .07 .20
119 Valeri Bure .07 .20
120 Murray Craven .07 .20
121 Marko Tuomainen .07 .20
122 Trevor Linden .12 .30
123 Zarley Zalapski .07 .20
124 Jeff Shantz .07 .20
125 Dmitri Mironov .07 .20
126 Jamie Huscroft .10 .25
127 Jaromir Jagr .40 1.00
128 Brian Bradley .10 .25
129 Brett Lindros .07 .20
130 Calle Johansson .07 .20
131 Pierre Turgeon .10 .25
132 Denis Savard .12 .30
133 Joe Nieuwendyk .10 .25
134 Petr Klima .07 .20
135 John Druce .10 .25
136 Chris Osgood .12 .30
137 Kenny Jonsson .12 .30
138 Jocelyn Lemieux .10 .25
139 Tomas Sandstrom .10 .25
140 Chris Gratton .07 .20
141 Mark Tinordi .07 .20
142 Kirk Muller .10 .25
143 Vladimir Malakhov .07 .20
144 Jiri Slegr .07 .20
145 Shawn McEachern .07 .20
146 Shayne Corson .10 .25
147 Kelly Hrudey .10 .25
148 Sergei Fedorov .20 .50
149 Mike Gartner .15 .40
150 Stephane Fiset .10 .25
151 Larry Murphy .10 .25
152 Enrico Ciccone .07 .20
153 Mike Keane .07 .20
154 Steve Larmer .10 .25
155 Dale Hunter .10 .25
156 Joe Murphy .07 .20
157 Pat LaFontaine .12 .30
158 Rob Gaudreau .07 .20
159 Paul Kariya .12 .30
160 Rob Blake .10 .25
161 Keith Primeau .10 .25
162 Dave Ellett .07 .20
163 Alexander Mogilny .10 .25
164 Luc Robitaille .12 .30
165 Alexander Selivanov .10 .25
166 Keith Jones .10 .25
167 Turner Stevenson .07 .20
168 Keith Tkachuk .12 .30
169 Bernie Nicholls .10 .25
170 Stanislav Neckar .07 .20
171 Scott Mellanby .10 .25
172 Doug Weight .12 .30
173 Shaun Van Allen .07 .20
174 Gary Roberts .07 .20
175 Robert Lang .07 .20
176 Martin Gelinas .07 .20
177 Ray Sheppard .10 .25
178 Bryan Smolinski .07 .20
179 Wayne Presley .07 .20
180 Jimmy Carson .10 .25
181 John Cullen .07 .20
182 Mikael Andersson .10 .25
183 Dimitri Khristich .07 .20
184 Chris Therien .07 .20
185 Bobby Holik .07 .20
186 Kevin Hatcher .10 .25
187 Patrick Poulin .07 .20
188 Pat Falloon .07 .20
189 Alexei Yashin .10 .25
190 Gord Murphy .07 .20
191 Kirk Maltby .10 .25
192 Dave Karpa .07 .20
193 Kelly Kisio .10 .25
194 Tony Granato .07 .20
195 Al Iafrate .10 .25
196 Nelson Emerson .07 .20
197 Adam Oates .12 .30
198 Rob Ray .07 .20
199 Sean Burke .07 .20
200 Ron Francis .15 .40
201 Theo Fleury .15 .40
202 Patrick Flatley .07 .20
203 Ron Hextall .12 .30
204 Martin Brodeur .30 .75
205 Mike Kennedy .10 .25
206 Tony Amonte .10 .25
207 Sergei Makarov .07 .20
208 Alexandre Daigle .07 .20
209 Stu Barnes .07 .20
210 Todd Marchant .07 .20
211 Valeri Karpov .07 .20
212 Phil Housley .10 .25
213 Jamie Storr .10 .25
214 Brett Hull .25 .60
215 Kris King .07 .20
216 Ray Bourque .20 .50
217 Donald Audette .10 .25
218 Steven Rice .07 .20
219 Kevin Stevens .10 .25
220 Mark Messier .25 .60
221 Valeri Kamensky .10 .25
222 Mikael Renberg .10 .25
223 Scott Stevens .12 .30
224 Derian Hatcher .10 .25
225 Ray Whitney .10 .25
226 Bob Kudelski .07 .20
227 Mikhail Shtalenkov .07 .20
228 Nicklas Lidstrom .12 .30
229 Adam Creighton .07 .20
230 Dave Manson .07 .20
231 Craig Simpson .10 .25
232 Chris Pronger .12 .30
233 Adrien Plavsic .10 .25
234 Alexei Kovalev .10 .25
235 Tommy Salo RC .20 .50
236 Patrik Juhlin .07 .20
237 Tom Chorske .07 .20
238 Mike Modano .20 .50
239 Igor Larionov .07 .20
240 Johan Garpenlov .07 .20
241 Todd Krygier .07 .20
242 Tie Domi .10 .25
243 Bill Houlder .07 .20
244 Teemu Selanne .25 .60
245 Dale Hawerchuk .15 .40
246 Bill Ranford .10 .25
247 Brian Leetch .10 .25
248 Steve Thomas .10 .25
249 Dimitri Yushkevich .07 .20
250 Stephane Richer .10 .25
251 Todd Harvey .07 .20
252 Viktor Kozlov .10 .25
253 John Vanbiesbrouck .12 .30
254 Rick Tocchet .10 .25
255 Bret Hedican .07 .20
256 Mario Lemieux .50 1.25
257 Igor Korolev .07 .20
258 Dominik Hasek .20 .50
259 Owen Nolan .12 .30
260 Michal Pivonka .07 .20
261 John LeClair .12 .30
262 Claude Lemieux .12 .30
263 Mike Donnelly .07 .20
264 Craig Janney .07 .20
265 Milos Holan .07 .20
266 Steve Yzerman .30 .75
267 Russ Courtnall .07 .20
268 Esa Tikkanen .07 .20
269 Dallas Drake .07 .20
270 Norm Maciver .10 .25
271 Scott Young .07 .20
272 Glenn Healy .10 .25
273 Brian Rolston .10 .25
274 Corey Millen .07 .20
275 Kevin Miller .10 .25
276 Eric LaCroix .07 .20
277 Adam Graves .10 .25
278 Christian Ruuttu .10 .25
279 Steve Duchesne .07 .20
280 Stephane Quintal .10 .25
281 Brent Gretzky .10 .25
282 Mike Ricci .07 .20
283 Sergei Nemchinov .07 .20
284 Sylvain Cote .07 .20
285 Neal Broten .10 .25
286 Greg Adams .07 .20
287 Guy Hebert .10 .25
288 Joe Sakic .25 .60
289 Bobby Dollas .07 .20
290 Gino Odjick .07 .20
291 Curtis Joseph .15 .40
292 Teppo Numminen .07 .20
293 Geoff Sanderson .07 .20
294 Adam Deadmarsh .07 .20
295 Kevin Haller .07 .20
296 Sergei Brylin .07 .20
297 Ulf Dahlen .07 .20
298 Robert Kron .07 .20
299 Dave Lowry .07 .20
300 Nikolai Borschevsky .07 .20
301 Jeff Brown .10 .25
302 Guy Carbonneau .12 .30
303 Alexei Zhitnik .07 .20
304 Frantisek Kucera .07 .20
305 Curtis Leschyshyn .07 .20
306 Mike Richter .12 .30
307 Dean Evason .07 .20
308 Jozef Stumpel .07 .20
309 Jeff Friesen .07 .20
310 Kelly Buchberger .07 .20
311 Michael Nylander .07 .20
312 Josef Beranek .07 .20
313 Al MacInnis .15 .40
314 Ken Wregget .10 .25
315 Glen Wesley .07 .20
316 Jocelyn Thibault .10 .25
317 Jeff Beukeboom .07 .20
318 Steve Konowalchuk .10 .25
319 Tim Cheveldae .10 .25
320 Vincent Damphousse .10 .25
321 Mats Naslund .07 .20
322 Mathieu Schneider .07 .20
323 Petr Nedved .10 .25
324 Brent Fedyk .07 .20
325 Jussi Tie RC .10 .25
326 Mikko Markkanen RC .10 .25
327 Timo Hakanen RC .10 .25
328 Sami Salonen RC .10 .25
329 Juha Viinikainen RC .10 .25
330 Jani Riihinen RC .10 .25
331 Teemu Riihijarvi RC .12 .30
332 Jaako Niskavaara RC .10 .25
333 Miika Elomo .12 .30
334 Tomi Kallio RC .30 .75
335 Vesa Toskala RC .12 .30
336 Tuomas Reijonen RC .12 .30
337 Aki Berg RC .12 .30
338 Tomi Hirvonen RC .12 .30
339 Jussi Salminen RC .12 .30
340 Andreas Sjolund RC .12 .30
341 Johan Ramstedt RC .12 .30
342 Bjorn Danielsson RC .12 .30
343 Per Gustavsson RC .12 .30
344 Niklas Anger RC .12 .30
345 Marcus Nilsson RC .25 .60
346 Per Anton Lundstrom RC .12 .30
347 Henrik Rehnberg RC .12 .30
348 Robert Borgqvist RC .12 .30
349 Ted Christensen RC .12 .30
350 Samuel Phalsson RC .12 .30
351 Fredrik Loven RC .12 .30
352 Patrik Wallenberg RC .12 .30
353 Jan Labraaten RC .12 .30
354 Peter Wallin RC .12 .30
355 Cam Neely WYG .12 .30
356 Keith Tkachuk WYG .12 .30
357 Chris Gratton WYG .07 .20
358 Adam Graves WYG .10 .25
359 Doug Gilmour WYG .15 .40
360 Adam Deadmarsh WYG .07 .20
361 Wayne Gretzky WYG .75 2.00
362 Joe Sakic WYG .25 .60
363 Paul Kariya WYG .12 .30
364 Brett Hull WYG .25 .60
365 Sergei Fedorov WYG .20 .50
366 Brian Rolston WYG .10 .25
367 Dominik Hasek WYG .20 .50
368 John Vanbiesbrouck WYG .12 .30
369 Jim Carey WYG .10 .25
370 Paul Kariya HH .12 .30
371 Peter Forsberg HH .25 .60
372 Jeff Friesen HH .07 .20
373 Kenny Jonsson HH .12 .30
374 Chris Therien HH .07 .20
375 Jim Carey HH .10 .25
376 John LeClair HH .12 .30
377 Eric Lindros HH .20 .50
378 Jaromir Jagr HH .40 1.00
379 Paul Coffey HH .12 .30
380 Chris Chelios HH .12 .30
381 Dominik Hasek HH .20 .50
382 Keith Tkachuk HH .12 .30
383 Alexei Zhamnov HH .12 .30
384 Theo Fleury HH .15 .40
385 Ray Bourque HH .20 .50
386 Larry Murphy HH .10 .25
387 Ed Belfour HH .10 .25
388 Eric Lindros HH .20 .50
389 Jaromir Jagr HH .40 1.00
390 Paul Coffey HH .12 .30
391 Peter Forsberg HH .25 .60
392 Claude Lemieux HH .12 .30
393 Ron Francis HH .15 .40
394 Dominik Hasek HH .20 .50
395 Checklist
Gretzky .75 2.00
396 Checklist
Gretzky .75 2.00
397 Saku Koivu YG 1.50 4.00
398 Radek Dvorak YG .60 1.50
399 Ed Jovanovski YG .50 1.25
400 Brendan Witt YG .50 1.25
401 Jeff O'Neill YG .50 1.25
402 Daymond Langkow YG .50 1.25
403 Shane Doan RC 1.50 4.00
404 Bryan McCabe YG .50 1.25
405 Marty Murray YG .50 1.25
406 Daniel Alfredsson YG 1.50 4.00
407 Jason Doig YG .50 1.25
408 Niklas Sundstrom YG .50 1.25
409 Vitali Yachmenev YG .50 1.25
410 Aki Berg YG .50 1.25
411 Eric Daze YG 1.00 2.50

1995-96 Collector's Choice Player's Club

COMPLETE SET (396) 40.00 100.00
*SINGLES: 3X TO 8X BASIC CARDS

1995-96 Collector's Choice Player's Club Platinum

*PLATINUM: 6X TO 15X BASIC CARDS

1995-96 Collector's Choice Crash the Game Silver

COMPLETE SET (90) 40.00 80.00
*GOLD STARS: 1.5X TO 4X BASIC CARDS
*EXCHANGE CARDS: .1X TO .25X BASIC CARDS
*GOLD EXCH.CARDS: .4X TO .8X BASIC CARDS
*BONUS CARDS: 1X TO 2X BASIC CARDS
*GOLD BONUS CARDS: 2.5X TO 5X BASIC CARDS
C1A Pavel Bure 10/12/95 .30 .75
C1B Pavel Bure 12/17/95 .30 .75
C1C Pavel Bure 3/23/96 .30 .75
C2A Sergei Fedorov 10/19/95 .50 1.25
C2B Sergei Fedorov 12/31/95 .50 1.25
C2C Sergei Fedorov 3/12/96 .50 1.25
C3A Wayne Gretzky 10/7/95 2.00 5.00
C3B Wayne Gretzky 12/31/95 2.00 5.00
C3C Wayne Gretzky 2/10/96 2.00 5.00
C4A Eric Lindros 11/12/95 .30 .75
C4B Eric Lindros 1/3/96 .30 .75
C4C Eric Lindros 3/3/96 .30 .75
C5A Brett Hull 10/10/95 .50 1.25
C5B Brett Hull 12/9/95 .50 1.25
C5C Brett Hull 3/24/96 .50 1.25
C6A Mark Messier 11/8/95 .30 .75
C6B Mark Messier 1/22/96 .30 .75
C6C Mark Messier 3/31/96 .30 .75
C7A Jaromir Jagr 10/14/95 .50 1.25
C7B Jaromir Jagr 12/17/95 .50 1.25
C7C Jaromir Jagr 3/5/96 .50 1.25
C8A Alexei Zhamnov 10/9/95 .25 .60
C8B Alexei Zhamnov 12/28/95 .25 .60
C8C Alexei Zhamnov 2/21/96 .25 .60
C9A Joe Sakic 10/6/95 .60 1.50
C9B Joe Sakic 12/9/95 .60 1.50
C9C Joe Sakic 2/3/96 .60 1.50
C10A Paul Kariya 10/18/95 .30 .75
C10B Paul Kariya 12/19/95 .30 .75
C10C Paul Kariya 3/17/96 .30 .75
C11A Theo Fleury 10/27/95 .20 .50
C11B Theo Fleury 12/11/95 .20 .50
C11C Theo Fleury 2/6/96 .20 .50
C12A Owen Nolan 11/1/95 .25 .60
C12B Owen Nolan 1/4/96 .25 .60
C12C Owen Nolan 3/17/96 .25 .60
C13A Peter Bondra 10/13/95 .25 .60
C13B Peter Bondra 12/2/95 .25 .60
C13C Peter Bondra 3/12/96 .25 .60
C14A Cam Neely 11/7/95 .30 .75
C14B Cam Neely 1/11/96 .30 .75
C14C Cam Neely 3/23/96 .30 .75
C15A Pierre Turgeon 10/25/95 .25 .60
C15B Pierre Turgeon 12/23/95 .25 .60
C15C Pierre Turgeon 2/21/96 .25 .60
C16A Mike Modano 11/1/95 .60 1.50
C16B Mike Modano 1/5/96 .60 1.50
C16C Mike Modano 2/22/96 .60 1.50
C17A Bernie Nicholls 10/10/95 .20 .50
C17B Bernie Nicholls 12/15/95 .20 .50
C17C Bernie Nicholls 3/24/96 .20 .50
C18A Alexei Yashin 11/4/95 .20 .50
C18B Alexie Yashin 12/23/95 .20 .50
C18C Alexei Yashin 3/21/96 .20 .50
C19A Jason Arnott 10/27/95 .20 .50
C19B Jason Arnott 12/18/95 .20 .50
C19C Jason Arnott 2/28/96 .20 .50
C20A Peter Forsberg 11/22/95 .75 2.00
C20B Peter Forsberg 2/15/96 .75 2.00
C20C Peter Forsberg 3/27/96 .75 2.00
C21A Doug Gilmour 10/17/95 .25 .60
C21B Doug Gilmour 12/16/95 .25 .60
C21C Doug Gilmour 2/18/96 .25 .60
C22A Geoff Sanderson/ 10/11/95 .20 .50
C22B Geoff Sanderson/ 12/18/95 .20 .50
C22C Geoff Sanderson/ 3/6/96 .20 .50
C23A John LeClair 10/15/95 .30 .75
C23B John LeClair 12/16/95 .30 .75
C23C John LeClair 2/19/96 .30 .75
C24A Ray Bourque 10/11/95 .20 .50
C24B Ray Bourque 12/16/95 .20 .50
C24C Ray Bourque 2/6/96 .20 .50
C25A Mario Lemieux 11/1/95 1.50 4.00
C25B Mario Lemieux 12/1/95 1.50 4.00
C25C Mario Lemieux 2/6/96 1.50 4.00
C26A Steve Yzerman 11/7/95 1.50 4.00
C26B Steve Yzerman 1/24/96 1.50 4.00
C26C Steve Yzerman 2/27/96 1.50 4.00
C27A Pat LaFontaine 10/20/95 .30 .75
C27B Pat LaFontaine 12/27/95 .30 .75
C27C Pat LaFontaine 2/17/96 .30 .75
C28A Claude Lemieux 10/7/95 .20 .50
C28B Claude Lemieux 12/15/95 .20 .50
C28C Claude Lemieux 2/10/96 .20 .50
C29A Paul Coffey 10/15/95 .30 .75
C29B Paul Coffey 12/5/95 .30 .75
C29C Paul Coffey 2/13/96 .30 .75
C30A Mats Sundin 11/7/95 .30 .75
C30B Mats Sundin 1/3/96 .30 .75
C30C Mats Sundin 3/15/96 .30 .75

1996-97 Collector's Choice

COMPLETE SET (348) 10.00 25.00
1 Paul Kariya .15 .40
2 Teemu Selanne .30 .75
3 Steve Rucchin .10 .25
4 Mikhail Shtalenkov .10 .25
5 Guy Hebert .12 .30
6 Shaun Van Allen .10 .25
7 Anatoli Semenov .10 .25
8 J.F. Jomphe RC .15 .40
9 Alex Hicks .15 .40
10 Roman Oksiuta .10 .25
11 Todd Ewen .10 .25
12 Adam Oates .15 .40
13 Ray Bourque .25 .60
14 Don Sweeney .10 .25
15 Kyle McLaren .10 .25
16 Cam Neely .15 .40
17 Bill Ranford .12 .30
18 Rick Tocchet .12 .30
19 Ted Donato .10 .25
20 Shawn McEachern .10 .25
21 Jon Rohloff .10 .25
22 Joe Mullen .12 .30
23 Pat LaFontaine .15 .40
24 Brian Holzinger .12 .30
25 Wayne Primeau .10 .25
26 Alexei Zhitnik .10 .25
27 Derek Plante .10 .25
28 Randy Burridge .10 .25
29 Brad May .10 .25
30 Dominik Hasek .25 .60
31 Jason Dawe .10 .25
32 Mike Peca .10 .25
33 Matthew Barnaby .10 .25
34 Trevor Kidd .10 .25
35 Theo Fleury .30 .75
36 Cale Hulse .10 .25
37 Bob Sweeney .10 .25
38 Michael Nylander .10 .25
39 German Titov .10 .25
40 Cory Stillman .10 .25
41 Zarley Zalapski .10 .25
42 Jocelyn Lemieux .10 .25
43 Sandy McCarthy .10 .25
44 Steve Chiasson .10 .25
45 Eric Daze .12 .30
46 Jeremy Roenick .25 .60
47 Chris Chelios .15 .40
48 Joe Murphy .10 .25
49 Tony Amonte .12 .30
50 Bernie Nicholls .12 .30
51 Eric Weinrich .10 .25
52 Gary Suter .10 .25
53 Jeff Shantz .10 .25
54 Jeff Hackett .12 .30
55 Ed Belfour .15 .40
56 Uwe Krupp .10 .25
57 Claude Lemieux .10 .25
58 Adam Deadmarsh .10 .25
59 Stephane Fiset .12 .30
60 Sandis Ozolinsh .10 .25
61 Stephane Yelle .10 .25
62 Valeri Kamensky .12 .30
63 Peter Forsberg .30 .75
64 Joe Sakic .30 .75
65 Patrick Roy .40 1.00
66 Chris Simon .10 .25
67 Todd Harvey .10 .25
68 Joe Nieuwendyk .12 .30
69 Mike Modano .25 .60
70 Derian Hatcher .10 .25
71 Kevin Hatcher .10 .25
72 Benoit Hogue .10 .25
73 Guy Carbonneau .15 .40
74 Jamie Langenbrunner .10 .25
75 Jere Lehtinen .10 .25
76 Craig Ludwig .10 .25
77 Grant Marshall .10 .25
78 Greg Johnson .10 .25
79 Steve Yzerman .40 1.00
80 Sergei Fedorov .25 .60
81 Vyacheslav Kozlov .10 .25
82 Vladimir Konstantinov .12 .30
83 Igor Larionov .15 .40
84 Chris Osgood .15 .40
85 Paul Coffey .15 .40
86 Nicklas Lidstrom .20 .50
87 Keith Primeau .12 .30
88 Dino Ciccarelli .15 .40
89 Darren McCarty .10 .25
90 Curtis Joseph .20 .50
91 Doug Weight .15 .40
92 Jason Arnott .12 .30
93 Mariusz Czerkawski .10 .25
94 Kelly Buchberger .10 .25
95 Zdeno Ciger .10 .25
96 David Oliver .10 .25
97 Todd Marchant .10 .25
98 Miroslav Satan .10 .25
99 Bryan Marchment .10 .25
100 Louie DeBrusk .10 .25
101 John Vanbiesbrouck .15 .40
102 Scott Mellanby .12 .30
103 Rob Niedermayer .12 .30
104 Robert Svehla .10 .25
105 Ed Jovanovski .12 .30
106 Johan Garpenlov .10 .25
107 Jody Hull .10 .25
108 Bill Lindsay .10 .25
109 Terry Carkner .10 .25
110 Stu Barnes .10 .25
111 Ray Sheppard .12 .30
112 Brendan Shanahan .15 .40
113 Geoff Sanderson .12 .30
114 Andrei Nikolishin .10 .25
115 Andrew Cassels .10 .25
116 Nelson Emerson .10 .25
117 Jason Muzzatti .12 .30
118 Marek Malik .10 .25
119 Sean Burke .10 .25
120 Jeff Brown .10 .25
121 Jeff O'Neill .10 .25
122 Kelly Chase .10 .25
123 Dimitri Khristich .10 .25
124 Kevin Stevens .12 .30
125 Vitali Yachmenev .10 .25
126 Yanic Perreault .10 .25
127 Kevin Todd .10 .25
128 Aki Berg .10 .25
129 Craig Johnson .10 .25
130 Mattias Norstrom .10 .25
131 Ray Ferraro .10 .25
132 Steven Finn .10 .25
133 Pierre Turgeon .12 .30
134 Saku Koivu .15 .40
135 Mark Recchi .20 .50
136 Jocelyn Thibault .12 .30
137 Andrei Kovalenko .10 .25
138 Vincent Damphousse .12 .30
139 Vladimir Malakhov .10 .25
140 Brian Savage .10 .25
141 Valeri Bure .10 .25
142 Patrice Brisebois .10 .25
143 Martin Rucinsky .10 .25
145 Steve Thomas .10 .25
146 Bill Guerin .15 .40
147 Petr Sykora .10 .25
148 Scott Stevens .15 .40
149 Scott Niedermayer .15 .40
150 Phil Housley .12 .30
151 Brian Rolston .12 .30
152 Neal Broten .12 .30
153 Dave Andreychuk .15 .40
154 Randy McKay .10 .25
155 Eric Fichaud .12 .30
156 Zigmund Palffy .15 .40
157 Travis Green .12 .30
158 Darby Hendrickson .10 .25
159 Kenny Jonsson .10 .25
160 Marty McInnis .10 .25
161 Bryan McCabe .10 .25
162 Darius Kasparaitis .10 .25
163 Alexander Semak .10 .25
164 Todd Bertuzzi .15 .40
165 Niclas Andersson .10 .25
166 Mark Messier .30 .75
167 Mike Richter .15 .40
168 Niklas Sundstrom .10 .25
169 Brian Leetch .12 .30
170 Wayne Gretzky 1.00 2.50
171 Luc Robitaille .15 .40
172 Marty McSorley .12 .30
173 Jari Kurri .15 .40
174 Adam Graves .10 .25
175 Sergei Nemchinov .10 .25
176 Alexei Kovalev .12 .30
177 Daniel Alfredsson .15 .40
178 Randy Cunneyworth .10 .25
179 Alexei Yashin .12 .30
180 Alexandre Daigle .10 .25
181 Radek Bonk .10 .25
182 Steve Duchesne .10 .25
183 Ted Drury .10 .25
184 Antti Tormanen .10 .25
185 Stan Neckar .10 .25
186 Damian Rhodes .12 .30
187 Janne Laukkanen .10 .25
188 Eric Lindros .25 .60
189 Mikael Renberg .12 .30
190 John LeClair .15 .40
191 Ron Hextall .15 .40
192 Rod Brind'Amour .15 .40
193 Joel Otto .10 .25
194 Pat Falloon .10 .25
195 Eric Desjardins .12 .30
196 Dale Hawerchuk .20 .50
197 Chris Therien .10 .25
198 Dan Quinn .10 .25
199 Oleg Tverdovsky .12 .30
200 Chad Kilger .10 .25
201 Keith Tkachuk .15 .40
202 Igor Korolev .10 .25
203 Alexei Zhamnov .12 .30
204 Nikolai Khabibulin .12 .30
205 Shane Doan .12 .30
206 Deron Quint .10 .25
207 Craig Janney .12 .30
208 Norm MacIver .10 .25
209 Teppo Numminen .10 .25
210 Mario Lemieux .60 1.50
211 Jaromir Jagr .50 1.25
212 Ron Francis .20 .50
213 Tom Barrasso .12 .30
214 Sergei Zubov .12 .30
215 Tomas Sandstrom .10 .25
216 Joe Dziedzic .10 .25
217 Richard Park .10 .25
218 Bryan Smolinski .10 .25
219 Petr Nedved .12 .30
220 Ken Wregget .12 .30
221 Dmitri Mironov .10 .25
222 Peter Zezel .10 .25
223 Brett Hull .30 .75
224 Grant Fuhr .25 .60
225 Shayne Corson .12 .30
226 Chris Pronger .15 .40
227 Craig MacTavish .10 .25
228 Al MacInnis .20 .50
229 Geoff Courtnall .10 .25
230 Stephane Matteau .10 .25
231 Tony Twist .10 .25
232 Brian Noonan .10 .25
233 Owen Nolan .15 .40
234 Shean Donovan .10 .25
235 Darren Turcotte .10 .25
236 Marcus Ragnarsson .10 .25
237 Viktor Kozlov .10 .25
238 Jeff Friesen .10 .25
239 Chris Terreri .12 .30
240 Ray Whitney .10 .25
241 Ville Peltonen .10 .25
242 Andrei Nazarov .10 .25
243 Ulf Dahlen .10 .25
244 Roman Hamrlik .10 .25
245 Chris Gratton .12 .30
246 Petr Klima .10 .25
247 Daren Puppa .12 .30
248 Rob Zamuner .10 .25
249 Aaron Gavey .10 .25
250 Brian Bradley .10 .25
251 Paul Ysebaert .10 .25
252 Igor Ulanov .10 .25
253 Alexander Selivanov .10 .25
254 Shawn Burr .10 .25
255 Mats Sundin .15 .40
256 Doug Gilmour .20 .50
257 Felix Potvin .25 .60
258 Wendel Clark .25 .60
259 Kirk Muller .10 .25
260 Dave Gagner .15 .40
261 Tie Domi .12 .30
262 Mathieu Schneider .10 .25
263 Dimitri Yushkevich .10 .25
264 Don Beaupre .12 .30
265 Larry Murphy .12 .30
266 Pavel Bure .15 .40
267 Alexander Mogilny .12 .30
268 Trevor Linden .15 .40
269 Jyrki Lumme .10 .25
270 Cliff Ronning .10 .25
271 Kirk McLean .12 .30
272 Corey Hirsch .12 .30
273 Esa Tikkanen .10 .25
274 Gino Odjick .10 .25
275 Markus Naslund .15 .40
276 Russ Courtnall .10 .25
277 Joe Juneau .10 .25
278 Jim Carey .15 .40
279 Peter Bondra .15 .40
280 Michal Pivonka .10 .25
281 Steve Konowalchuk .10 .25
282 Pat Peake .10 .25
283 Brendan Witt .10 .25
284 Stefan Ustorf .10 .25
285 Keith Jones .10 .25
286 Sergei Gonchar .10 .25
287 Sylvain Cote .10 .25
288 Dale Hunter .12 .30
289 Paul Kariya SB .15 .40
290 Wayne Gretzky SB 1.00 2.50
291 Eric Lindros SB .25 .60
292 Steve Yzerman SB .40 1.00
293 Mario Lemieux SB .60 1.50
294 Jaromir Jagr SB .50 1.25
295 Keith Tkachuk SB .15 .40
296 Mark Messier SB .30 .75
297 Jeremy Roenick SB .25 .60
298 Peter Forsberg SB .30 .75
299 Joe Sakic SB .30 .75
300 Theo Fleury SB .30 .75
301 Chris Chelios SB .15 .40
302 Vlad Konstantinov SB .12 .30
303 Brian Leetch SB .12 .30
304 Ray Bourque SB .25 .60
305 Scott Stevens SB .15 .40
306 Martin Brodeur SB .40 1.00
307 Patrick Roy SB .40 1.00
308 Scotty Bowman .15 .40
309 Kariya
Selanne
Hebert .30 .75
310 Oates
Bourque
Neely .25 .60
311 LaFontaine
Zhitnik
Hasek .25 .60
312 Fleury
Nylander
Kidd .30 .75
313 Roenick
Chelios
Daze .25 .60
314 Sakic/Roy/Forsberg .40 1.00
315 Modano
Nieuwendyk
Harvey .25 .60
316 Fedorov
Konstantinov
Coffey .25 .60
317 Weight/Arnott/Joseph .20 .50
318 Jovan
VBK
Nieder. .15 .40
319 Shanahan
Sanderson
Burke .15 .40
320 Yachmenev
Khristich
Ferraro .10 .25
321 Thibault
Turgeon
Koivu .15 .40
322 Brodeur
Thomas
Stevens .40 1.00
323 Bertuzzi
Fichaud
Palffy .15 .40
324 Leetch
Graves
Richter .15 .40
325 Daigle
Yashin
Rhodes .12 .30
326 Hextall
LeClair
Renberg .15 .40
327 Zhamnov
Tkachuk
Tverdovsky .15 .40
328 Jagr
Nedved
Francis .50 1.25
329 Gretzky/Hull/MacInnis 1.00 2.50
330 Nolan
Turcotte
Terreri .15 .40
331 Hamrlik
Gratton
Puppa .12 .30
332 Gilmour
Potvin
Sundin .25 .60
333 Mogilny
Bure
Linden .15 .40
334 Carey
Juneau
Bondra .15 .40
335 Lemieux
Messier
Lindros .60 1.50
336 Gretzky/Selanne/Sakic 1.00 2.50
337 Chad Kilger .10 .25
338 Todd Bertuzzi .15 .40
339 Petr Sykora .10 .25
340 Ed Jovanovski CT .12 .30
341 Kyle McLaren .10 .25
342 Brian Holzinger .12 .30
343 Jeff O'Neill .10 .25
344 Daniel Alfredsson .15 .40
345 Brendan Witt .10 .25
346 Daymond Langkow .12 .30
347 Checklist .10 .25
348 Checklist .10 .25
349 Jarome Iginla YG .60 1.50
350 Sergei Berezin YG .75 2.00
351 Jose Theodore YG .60 1.50
352 Rem Murray YG .50 1.25
353 Daniel Goneau YG .50 1.25
354 Ethan Moreau YG .50 1.25
355 Jonas Hoglund YG .30 .75
356 Anders Eriksson YG .30 .75
357 Christian Dube YG .30 .75
358 Roman Turek YG .50 1.25
359 Bryan Berard YG .50 1.25
360 Jim Campbell YG .30 .75
361 Janne Niinimaa YG .50 1.25
362 Wade Redden YG .30 .75
363 Marc Denis YG .50 1.25
P222 Wayne Gretzky PROMO 1.00 2.50
NNO1 Wayne Gretzky '79-80 1.00 2.50
NNO2 Wayne Gretzky 802 1.00 2.50

1996-97 Collector's Choice Jumbos 5x7

COMPLETE SET (5) 3.00 8.00
1 Theo Fleury .75 2.00
2 Curtis Joseph 1.00 2.50
3 Jose Theodore 1.00 2.50
4 Wade Redden .40 1.00
5 Mats Sundin 1.00 2.50

1996-97 Collector's Choice MVP

COMPLETE SET (45) 25.00 60.00
*GOLD: 2.5X TO 6X BASIC INSERTS
UD1 Wayne Gretzky 3.00 8.00
UD2 Ron Francis .60 1.50
UD3 Peter Forsberg 1.00 2.50
UD4 Alexander Mogilny .40 1.00
UD5 Joe Sakic 1.00 2.50
UD6 Claude Lemieux .30 .75
UD7 Teemu Selanne 1.00 2.50
UD8 John LeClair .50 1.25
UD9 Doug Weight .50 1.25
UD10 Paul Kariya .50 1.25
UD11 Theo Fleury 1.00 2.50
UD12 John Vanbiesbrouck .50 1.25
UD13 Sergei Fedorov .75 2.00
UD14 Steve Yzerman 1.25 3.00
UD15 Adam Oates .50 1.25
UD16 Keith Tkachuk .50 1.25
UD17 Mike Modano .75 2.00
UD18 Jeremy Roenick .75 2.00
UD19 Patrick Roy 1.25 3.00
UD20 Felix Potvin .75 2.00
UD21 Martin Brodeur 1.25 3.00
UD22 Pavel Bure .50 1.25
UD23 Peter Bondra .50 1.25
UD24 Zigmund Palffy .50 1.25
UD25 Roman Hamrlik .30 .75
UD26 Brendan Shanahan .50 1.25
UD27 Ray Bourque .75 2.00
UD28 Paul Coffey .50 1.25
UD29 Brett Hull 1.00 2.50
UD30 Brian Leetch .40 1.00

UD31 Chris Chelios .50 1.25
UD32 Vitali Yachmenev .40 1.00
UD33 Nicklas Lidstrom .60 1.50
UD34 Ed Jovanovski .40 1.00
UD35 Sandis Ozolinsh .30 .75
UD36 Scott Stevens .50 1.25
UD37 Eric Daze .40 1.00
UD38 Saku Koivu .50 1.25
UD39 Daniel Alfredsson .50 1.25
UD40 Pat LaFontaine .50 1.25
UD41 Cam Neely .50 1.25
UD42 Owen Nolan .50 1.25
UD43 Jaromir Jagr 1.50 4.00
UD44 Mats Sundin .50 1.25
UD45 Doug Gilmour .60 1.50

1996-97 Collector's Choice Stick'Ums

COMPLETE SET (30) 10.00 20.00
S1 Wayne Gretzky 2.00 5.00
S2 Brett Hull .60 1.50
S3 Peter Forsberg .60 1.50
S4 Patrick Roy .75 2.00
S5 Cam Neely .30 .75
S6 Jeremy Roenick .50 1.25
S7 Mario Lemieux 1.25 3.00
S8 Jaromir Jagr 1.00 2.50
S9 Eric Lindros .50 1.25
S10 Mark Messier .60 1.50
S11 Felix Potvin .50 1.25
S12 Brendan Shanahan .30 .75
S13 Teemu Selanne .60 1.50
S14 Paul Kariya .30 .75
S15 Mike Modano .50 1.25
S16 Pavel Bure .30 .75
S17 Jim Carey .30 .75
S18 Roman Hamrlik .20 .50
S19 Pierre Turgeon .25 .60
S20 Theo Fleury .60 1.50
S21 Pat LaFontaine .30 .75
S22 Steve Yzerman .75 2.00
S23 Sergei Fedorov .50 1.25
S24 Martin Brodeur .75 2.00
S25 Owen Nolan .30 .75
S26 Ice Machine .20 .50
S27 Champions .20 .50
S28 Slap Shot .20 .50
S29 Stripes .20 .50
S30 Goal .20 .50

1996-97 Collector's Choice Crash the Game Silver

COMPLETE SET (88) 30.00 80.00
*GOLD: 1.25X TO 3X BASIC INSERTS
*EXCH.STARS: 1.25X TO 3X BASIC INSERTS
*GOLD EXCH: 4X TO 10X BASIC INSERTS
C1A Wayne Gretzky 2.00 5.00
C1B Wayne Gretzky 2.00 5.00
C1C Wayne Gretzky 2.00 5.00
C2A Doug Gilmour .25 .60
C2B Doug Gilmour .25 .60
C2C Doug Gilmour .25 .60
C3A Alexander Mogilny .25 .60
C3B Alexander Mogilny .25 .60
C3C Alexander Mogilny .25 .60
C4A Peter Bondra .25 .60
C4B Peter Bondra .25 .60
C4C Peter Bondra .25 .60
C5A Mario Lemieux 1.50 4.00
C5B Mario Lemieux 1.50 4.00
C5C Mario Lemieux 1.50 4.00
C6A Jaromir Jagr .50 1.25
C6B Jaromir Jagr .50 1.25
C6C Jaromir Jagr .50 1.25
C7A Joe Sakic .60 1.50
C7B Joe Sakic .60 1.50
C8A Vitali Yachmenev .20 .50
C8B Vitali Yachmenev .20 .50
C8C Vitali Yachmenev .20 .50
C9A Doug Weight .25 .60
C9B Doug Weight .25 .60
C9C Doug Weight .25 .60
C10A Steve Yzerman 1.50 4.00
C10B Steve Yzerman 1.50 4.00
C10C Steve Yzerman 1.50 4.00
C11A Alexei Zhamnov .20 .50
C11B Alexei Zhamnov .20 .50
C11C Alexei Zhamnov .20 .50
C12A John LeClair .30 .75
C12B John LeClair .30 .75
C12C John LeClair .30 .75
C13A Daniel Alfredsson .25 .60
C13B Daniel Alfredsson .25 .60
C13C Daniel Alfredsson .25 .60
C14A Brendan Shanahan .30 .75
C14B Brendan Shanahan .50 1.25
C14C Brendan Shanahan .50 1.25
C15A Saku Koivu .30 .75
C15B Saku Koivu .30 .75
C15C Saku Koivu .30 .75
C16A Steve Thomas .20 .50
C16B Steve Thomas .20 .50
C16C Steve Thomas .20 .50
C17A Pavel Bure .30 .75
C17B Pavel Bure .50 1.25
C17C Pavel Bure .50 1.25
C18A Slava Kozlov .20 .50
C18B Slava Kozlov .20 .50
C18C Slava Kozlov .20 .50
C19A Teemu Selanne .30 .75
C19B Teemu Selanne .30 .75
C19C Teemu Selanne .30 .75
C20A Eric Daze .20 .50
C20B Eric Daze .20 .50
C20C Eric Daze .20 .50
C21A Adam Oates .25 .60
C21B Adam Oates .25 .60
C22A Ray Bourque .50 1.25
C22B Ray Bourque .50 1.25
C22C Ray Bourque .50 1.25
C23A Jason Arnott .20 .50
C23B Jason Arnott .20 .50
C23C Jason Arnott .20 .50
C24A Paul Kariya .30 .75
C24B Paul Kariya .30 .75
C24C Paul Kariya .30 .75
C25A Mikael Renberg .20 .50
C25B Mikael Renberg .20 .50
C25C Mikael Renberg .20 .50
C26A Keith Tkachuk .30 .75
C26B Keith Tkachuk .30 .75
C26C Keith Tkachuk .30 .75
C27A Brian Leetch .25 .60
C27B Brian Leetch .25 .60
C27C Brian Leetch .25 .60
C28A Eric Lindros .30 .75
C28B Eric Lindros .50 1.25
C28C Eric Lindros .50 1.25
C29A Mats Sundin .30 .75
C29B Mats Sundin .30 .75
C29C Mats Sundin .30 .75
C30A Mark Messier .40 1.00
C30B Mark Messier .40 1.00
C30C Mark Messier .40 1.00

1996-97 Collector's Choice Jumbos

COMPLETE SET (10) 10.00 25.00
13 Ray Bourque .75 2.00
23 Pat LaFontaine .50 1.25
35 Theo Fleury .60 1.50
62 Valeri Kamensky .50 1.25
69 Mike Modano .75 2.00
84 Chris Osgood .60 1.50
133 Pierre Turgeon .50 1.25
170 Wayne Gretzky 4.00 10.00
244 Roman Hamrlik .40 1.00
257 Felix Potvin .50 1.25

1996-97 Collector's Choice Jumbos Bi-Way

COMPLETE SET (8) 6.00 15.00
1 Wayne Gretzky 4.00 10.00
2 Theo Fleury .60 1.50
3 Jason Arnott .50 1.25
4 Saku Koivu .60 1.50
5 Pierre Turgeon .50 1.25
6 Daniel Alfredsson .50 1.25
7 Felix Potvin .50 1.25
8 Alexander Mogilny .50 1.25

1997-98 Collector's Choice

COMPLETE SET (320) 8.00 20.00
1 Guy Hebert .07 .20
2 Sean Pronger .05 .15
3 Dmitri Mironov .07 .20
4 Darren Van Impe .07 .20
5 Joe Sacco .07 .20
6 Ted Drury .07 .20
7 Steve Rucchin .07 .20
8 Teemu Selanne .20 .50
9 Paul Kariya .10 .25
10 Jari Kurri .10 .25
11 Kevin Todd .05 .15
12 Ray Bourque .15 .40
13 Anson Carter .05 .15
14 Ted Donato .05 .15
15 Kyle McLaren .05 .15
16 Jason Allison .07 .20
17 Jim Carey .05 .15
18 Jozef Stumpel .05 .15
19 Jean-Yves Roy .05 .15
20 Steve Heinze .05 .15
21 Sheldon Kennedy .05 .15
22 Dominik Hasek .15 .40
23 Rob Ray .05 .15
24 Derek Plante .07 .20
25 Brian Holzinger .07 .20
26 Mike Peca .07 .20
27 Matthew Barnaby .07 .20
28 Donald Audette .07 .20
29 Alexei Zhitnik .05 .15
30 Garry Galley .05 .15
31 Pat LaFontaine .10 .25
32 Jason Dawe .07 .20
33 Hnat Domenichelli .07 .20
34 Jarome Iginla .12 .30
35 Chris O'Sullivan .07 .20
36 Todd Simpson .07 .20
37 Trevor Kidd .05 .15
38 Dave Gagner .05 .15
39 German Titov .05 .15
40 Theo Fleury .12 .30
41 Dwayne Roloson .07 .20
42 Marty McInnis .05 .15
43 Jonas Hoglund .07 .20
44 Tony Amonte .07 .20
45 Gary Suter .05 .15
46 Chris Chelios .10 .25
47 Jeff Hackett .05 .15
48 Ulf Dahlen .05 .15
49 Bob Probert .10 .25
50 Kevin Miller .05 .15
51 Ethan Moreau .05 .15
52 Eric Weinrich .05 .15
53 Eric Daze .05 .15
54 Peter Forsberg .20 .50
55 Joe Sakic .20 .50
56 Patrick Roy .25 .60
57 Adam Deadmarsh .07 .20
58 Valeri Kamensky .07 .20
59 Keith Jones .05 .15
60 Sandis Ozolinsh .05 .15
61 Mike Ricci .05 .15
62 Claude Lemieux .05 .15
63 Mike Keane .05 .15
64 Adam Foote .05 .15
65 Mike Modano .15 .40
66 Pat Verbeek .07 .20
67 Andy Moog .10 .25
68 Joe Nieuwendyk .07 .20
69 Jamie Langenbrunner .07 .20
70 Derian Hatcher .07 .20
71 Greg Adams .07 .20
72 Darryl Sydor .05 .15
73 Dave Reid .05 .15
74 Jere Lehtinen .07 .20
75 Todd Harvey .07 .20
76 Brendan Shanahan .10 .25
77 Mike Vernon .07 .20
78 Steve Yzerman .25 .60
79 Sergei Fedorov .15 .40
80 Chris Osgood .10 .25
81 Nicklas Lidstrom .10 .25
82 Vladimir Konstantinov .05 .15
83 Darren McCarty .07 .20
84 Kirk Maltby .05 .15
85 Vyacheslav Kozlov .07 .20
86 Martin Lapointe .05 .15
87 Doug Weight .10 .25
88 Mike Grier .07 .20
89 Curtis Joseph .12 .30
90 Andrei Kovalenko .05 .15
91 Rem Murray .05 .15
92 Ryan Smyth .07 .20
93 Mariusz Czerkawski .05 .15
94 Drew Bannister .07 .20
95 Jason Arnott .07 .20
96 Luke Richardson .05 .15
97 Dean McAmmond .05 .15
98 Kirk Muller .05 .15
99 Ray Sheppard .07 .20
100 Scott Mellanby .07 .20
101 Ed Jovanovski .07 .20
102 John Vanbiesbrouck .10 .25
103 Radek Dvorak .07 .20
104 Robert Svehla .07 .20
105 Rob Niedermayer .05 .15
106 Dave Nemirovsky .05 .15
107 Steve Washburn .05 .15
108 Bill Lindsay .07 .20
109 Kevin Dineen .07 .20
110 Keith Primeau .07 .20
111 Sean Burke .05 .15
112 Derek King .07 .20
113 Andrew Cassels .05 .15
114 Glen Wesley .05 .15
115 Nelson Emerson .07 .20
116 Geoff Sanderson .07 .20
117 Jeff O'Neill .07 .20
118 Kent Manderville .05 .15
119 Dimitri Khristich .05 .15
120 Ian Laperriere .05 .15
121 Aki Berg .05 .15
122 Vladimir Tsyplakov .07 .20
123 Vitali Yachmenev .07 .20
124 Roman Vopat .07 .20
125 Rob Blake .10 .25
126 Jan Vopat .05 .15
127 Jeff Shevalier RC .05 .15
128 Byron Dafoe .07 .20
129 Saku Koivu .10 .25
130 Vincent Damphousse .07 .20
131 Brian Savage .07 .20
132 Valeri Bure .05 .15
133 Mark Recchi .12 .30
134 Jocelyn Thibault .07 .20
135 Jose Theodore .10 .25
136 Dave Manson .05 .15
137 Shayne Corson .07 .20
138 Stephane Richer .05 .15
139 Doug Gilmour .12 .30
140 Scott Stevens .10 .25
141 Martin Brodeur .25 .60
142 Dave Andreychuk .10 .25
143 Bobby Holik .05 .15
144 Brian Rolston .07 .20
145 Jay Pandolfo .07 .20
146 John MacLean .05 .15
147 Bill Guerin .10 .25
148 Scott Niedermayer .10 .25
149 Denis Pederson .05 .15
150 Zigmund Palffy .10 .25
151 Robert Reichel .07 .20
152 Bryan Smolinski .07 .20
153 Eric Fichaud .07 .20
154 Todd Bertuzzi .10 .25
155 Bryan Berard .05 .15
156 Niklas Anderson .05 .15
157 Bryan McCabe .05 .15
158 Tommy Salo .07 .20
159 Kenny Jonsson .07 .20
160 Travis Green .07 .20
161 Mike Richter .10 .25
162 Brian Leetch .07 .20
163 Adam Graves .07 .20
164 Vladimir Vorobiev RC .07 .20
165 Niklas Sundstrom .05 .15
166 Russ Courtnall .05 .15
167 Wayne Gretzky .60 1.50
168 Mark Messier .20 .50
169 Alexander Karpovtsev .05 .15
170 Luc Robitaille .10 .25
171 Ulf Samuelsson .10 .25
172 Daniel Alfredsson .10 .25
173 Alexei Yashin .07 .20
174 Alexandre Daigle .05 .15
175 Andreas Dackell .07 .20
176 Wade Redden .07 .20
177 Sergei Zholtok .07 .20
178 Damian Rhodes .07 .20
179 Steve Duchesne .05 .15
180 Shawn McEachern .05 .15
181 Ron Tugnutt .10 .25
182 John Leclair .10 .25
183 Janne Niinimaa .07 .20
184 Mikael Renberg .07 .20
185 Vaclav Prospal RC .07 .20
186 Eric Lindros .15 .40
187 Dainius Zubrus .07 .20
188 Ron Hextall .10 .25
189 Paul Coffey .10 .25
190 Dale Hawerchuk .12 .30
191 Trent Klatt .07 .20
192 Rod Brind'Amour .10 .25
193 Nikolai Khabibulin .10 .25
194 Keith Tkachuk .07 .20
195 Jeremy Roenick .15 .40
196 Mike Gartner .12 .30
197 Dallas Drake .07 .20
198 Oleg Tverdovsky .05 .15
199 Cliff Ronning .05 .15
200 Teppo Numminen .05 .15
201 Craig Janney .07 .20
202 Deron Quint .05 .15
203 Jason Wooley .05 .15
204 Ron Francis .12 .30
205 Jaromir Jagr .30 .75
206 Greg Johnson .05 .15
207 Kevin Hatcher .05 .15
208 Patrick Lalime .07 .20
209 Petr Nedved .10 .25
210 Ken Wregget .05 .15
211 Darius Kasparaitis .07 .20
212 Stu Barnes .05 .15
213 Joe Dziedzic .05 .15
214 Owen Nolan .10 .25
215 Jeff Friesen .07 .20
216 Ed Belfour .10 .25
217 Viktor Kozlov .07 .20
218 Tony Granato .05 .15
219 Darren Turcotte .07 .20
220 Stephen Guolla RC .05 .15
221 Marty McSorley .07 .20
222 Marcus Ragnarsson .05 .15
223 Al Iafrate .05 .15
224 Brett Hull .20 .50
225 Grant Fuhr .15 .40
226 Pierre Turgeon .07 .20
227 Geoff Courtnall .05 .15
228 Jim Campbell .05 .15
229 Harry York .07 .20
230 Tony Twist .07 .20
231 Joe Murphy .07 .20
232 Pavol Demitra .12 .30
233 Chris Pronger .10 .25
234 Al MacInnis .12 .30
235 Daren Puppa .07 .20
236 Chris Gratton .05 .15
237 Dino Ciccarelli .10 .25
238 Rob Zamuner .05 .15
239 Igor Ulanov .07 .20
240 Roman Hamrlik .05 .15
241 Alexander Selivanov .05 .15
242 Patrick Poulin .05 .15
243 Daymond Langkow .05 .15
244 Corey Schwab .07 .20
245 Mats Sundin .10 .25
246 Wendel Clark .15 .40
247 Sergei Berezin .07 .20
248 Steve Sullivan .07 .20
249 Fredrik Modin .07 .20
250 Darby Hendrickson .05 .15
251 Jason Podollan .07 .20
252 Felix Potvin .15 .40
253 Tie Domi .07 .20
254 Todd Warriner .07 .20
255 Pavel Bure .10 .25
256 Alexander Mogilny .07 .20
257 Martin Gelinas .05 .15
258 Corey Hirsch .07 .20
259 Trevor Linden .10 .25
260 Mike Sillinger .05 .15
261 Markus Naslund .10 .25
262 Jyrki Lumme .07 .20
263 Gino Odjick .05 .15
264 Mike Ridley .05 .15
265 Dave Roberts .05 .15
266 Adam Oates .10 .25
267 Bill Ranford .07 .20
268 Joe Juneau .05 .15
269 Chris Simon .07 .20
270 Peter Bondra .07 .20
271 Dale Hunter .07 .20
272 Jaroslav Svejkovski .07 .20
273 Sergei Gonchar .05 .15
274 Steve Konowalchuk .07 .20
275 Phil Housley .07 .20
276 Angela James RC .12 .30
277 Nancy Drolet RC .07 .20
278 Lesley Reddon RC .12 .30
279 Hayley Wickenheiser RC .12 .30
280 Vicky Sunohara RC .12 .30
281 Cassie Campbell RC .12 .30
282 Geraldine Heaney RC .07 .20
283 Judy Diduck RC .07 .20
284 France St. Louis RC .07 .20
285 Danielle Goyette RC .07 .20
286 Therese Brisson RC .07 .20
287 Stacey Wilson RC .07 .20
288 Danielle Dube RC .07 .20
289 Jayna Hefford RC .12 .30
290 Luce Letendre RC .07 .20
291 Lori Dupuis RC .07 .20
292 Rebecca Fahey RC .07 .20
293 Fiona Smith RC .07 .20
294 Laura Schuler RC .07 .20
295 Karen Nystrom RC .07 .20
296 Joe Thornton .15 .40
297 Peter Schaefer .07 .20
298 Daniel Tkaczuk .07 .20
299 Alyn McCauley .07 .20
300 Shane Willis .05 .15
301 Chris Phillips .07 .20
302 Marc Denis .10 .25
303 Jason Ward .05 .15
304 Patrick Marleau .10 .25
305 Brad Isbister .07 .20
306 Cameron Mann .07 .20
307 Daniel Cleary .07 .20
308 Brad Larsen .05 .15
309 Nick Boynton .05 .15
310 Scott Barney .05 .15
311 Boyd Devereaux .07 .20
312 Wayne Gretzky CL .60 1.50
313 Steve Yzerman CL .25 .60
314 Jaromir Jagr CL .30 .75
315 Jarome Iginla CL .12 .30
316 Patrick Roy CL .25 .60
317 John Vanbiesbrouck CL .10 .25
318 Paul Kariya CL .10 .25
319 Doug Weight CL .10 .25
320 Mats Sundin CL .10 .25

1997-98 Collector's Choice Blow-Ups

1 Wayne Gretzky 4.00 10.00
2 Tony Amonte 1.00 2.50
3 Zigmund Palffy 1.00 2.50

1997-98 Collector's Choice Crash the Game

COMPLETE SET (90) 15.00 40.00
COMP.PRIZE SET (30) 12.00 30.00
*PRIZE CARDS: 1.2X TO 3X BASIC INSERTS
C1A Wayne Gretzky COL W 1.50 4.00
C1B Wayne Gretzky DET L 1.50 4.00
C1C Wayne Gretzky EDM L 1.50 4.00
C2A Mike Modano FLO W .40 1.00
C2B Mike Modano NYI W .40 1.00
C2C Mike Modano NYR L .40 1.00
C3A Doug Weight BUF L .25 .60
C3B Doug Weight OTT W .25 .60
C3C Doug Weight NYR W .25 .60
C4A Brendan Shanahan MON W .25 .60
C4B Brendan Shanahan PIT W .25 .60
C4C Brendan Shanahan PHI W .25 .60
C5A Ray Sheppard ANA L .20 .50
C5B Ray Sheppard SET L .20 .50
C5C Ray Sheppard PHO W .20 .50
C6A Keith Primeau CAL W .20 .50
C6B Keith Primeau DET L .20 .50
C6C Keith Primeau TOR L .20 .50
C7A Ray Bourque DET L .40 1.00
C7B Ray Bourque LA L .40 1.00
C7C Ray Bourque VAN W .40 1.00
C8A Teemu Selanne NJ L .50 1.25
C8B Teemu Selanne NYI W .50 1.25
C8C Teemu Selanne WAS W .50 1.25
C9A Paul Kariya BOS L .25 .60
C9B Paul Kariya PIT L .25 .60
C9C Paul Kariya TB W .25 .60
C10A Tony Amonte MON L .20 .50
C10B Tony Amonte NYR W .20 .50
C10C Tony Amonte PHI L .20 .50
C11A Saku Koivu CAL L .25 .60
C11B Saku Koivu PHO L .25 .60
C11C Saku Koivu SJ W .25 .60
C12A Donald Audette ANA W .20 .50
C12B Donald Audette EDM L .20 .50
C12C Donald Audette STL L .20 .50
C13A Doug Gilmour CAL W .30 .75
C13B Doug Gilmour STL W .30 .75
C13C Doug Gilmour TOR W .30 .75
C14A Theo Fleury BUF L .30 .75
C14B Theo Fleury FLO L .30 .75
C14C Theo Fleury PHI W .30 .75
C15A Alexei Yashin COL W .20 .50
C15B Alexei Yashin LA L .20 .50
C15C Alexei Yashin TOR W .20 .50
C16A Zigmund Palffy CHI W .25 .60
C16B Zigmund Palffy DET W .25 .60
C16C Zigmund Palffy SJ W .25 .60
C17A Dimitri Khristich OTT W .20 .50
C17B Dimitri Khristich TB W .20 .50
C17C Dimitri Khristich WAS W .20 .50
C18A Joe Sakic NJ L .50 1.25
C18B Joe Sakic NYR L .50 1.25
C18C Joe Sakic PHI W .50 1.25
C19A Steve Yzerman BUF W .60 1.50
C19B Steve Yzerman MON L .60 1.50
C19C Steve Yzerman PHI W .60 1.50
C20A Eric Lindros ANA W .40 1.00
C20B Eric Lindros PHO W .40 1.00
C20C Eric Lindros TOR L .40 1.00
C21A Peter Forsberg FLO L .50 1.25
C21B Peter Forsberg PHI L .50 1.25
C21C Peter Forsberg WAS W .50 1.25
C22A Dino Ciccarelli DAL W .25 .60
C22B Dino Ciccarelli DET L .25 .60
C22C Dino Ciccarelli EDM L .25 .60
C23A Mats Sundin BUF L .25 .60
C23B Mats Sundin MOT L .25 .60
C23C Mats Sundin OTT L .25 .60
C24A Pavel Bure NYI W .25 .60
C24B Pavel Bure NYR W .25 .60
C24C Pavel Bure PIT W .25 .60
C25A Peter Bondra CHI L .25 .60
C25B Peter Bondra LA W .25 .60
C25C Peter Bondra VAN W .25 .60
C26A Brett Hull BOS W .50 1.25
C26B Brett Hull NYR L .50 1.25
C26C Brett Hull WAS W .50 1.25
C27A Keith Tkachuk BOS L .25 .60
C27B Keith Tkachuk NJ L .25 .60
C27C Keith Tkachuk TB W .25 .60
C28A Jaromir Jagr DET L .75 2.00
C28B Jaromir Jagr EDM W .75 2.00
C28C Jaromir Jagr STL L .75 2.00
C29A Jarome Iginla MON L .30 .75
C29B Jarome Iginla OTT L .30 .75
C29C Jarome Iginla WAS L .30 .75
C30A Owen Nolan BUF L .25 .60
C30B Owen Nolan FLO L .25 .60
C30C Owen Nolan NYI L .25 .60

1997-98 Collector's Choice Magic Men

COMMON GRETZKY (MM1-MM5) 5.00 10.00
COMMON ROY (MM6-MM10) 3.00 8.00

1997-98 Collector's Choice StarQuest

COMPLETE SET (90) 125.00 250.00
COMP.SERIES 1 (45) 3.00 8.00
SQ1 Bryan Berard .15 .40
SQ2 Robert Svehla .07 .20
SQ3 Petr Nedved .15 .40
SQ4 Steve Sullivan .07 .20
SQ5 Nicklas Lidstrom .15 .40
SQ6 Wade Redden .07 .20
SQ7 Jason Arnott .07 .20
SQ8 Martin Gelinas .07 .20
SQ9 Mikael Renberg .07 .20
SQ10 Jeff Friesen .07 .20
SQ11 Chris Chelios .15 .40
SQ12 Jarome Iginla .25 .60
SQ13 Vyacheslav Kozlov .07 .20
SQ14 Brian Holzinger .07 .20
SQ15 Eric Daze .15 .40
SQ16 Pat Verbeek .07 .20
SQ17 Jozef Stumpel .15 .40
SQ18 Rob Niedermayer .15 .40
SQ19 Sergei Fedorov .30 .75
SQ20 Brian Leetch .20 .50
SQ21 Bill Guerin .07 .20
SQ22 Dino Ciccarelli .07 .20
SQ23 Adam Oates .15 .40
SQ24 Mike Grier .07 .20
SQ25 Alexandre Daigle .07 .20
SQ26 Janne Niinimaa .15 .40
SQ27 Dimitri Khristich .07 .20
SQ28 Oleg Tverdovsky .07 .20
SQ29 Felix Potvin 1.00 2.50
SQ30 Mike Richter .20 .50
SQ31 Curtis Joseph .20 .50
SQ32 Vincent Damphousse .07 .20
SQ33 Vladimir Konstantinov .15 .40
SQ34 Andy Moog .15 .40
SQ35 Nikolai Khabibulin .15 .40
SQ36 Ed Belfour .20 .50
SQ37 Scott Mellanby .07 .20
SQ38 Sandis Ozolinsh .07 .20
SQ39 Travis Green .07 .20
SQ40 Patrick Lalime .15 .40
SQ41 Niklas Sundstrom .07 .20
SQ42 Guy Hebert .15 .40
SQ43 Vitali Yachmenev .07 .20
SQ44 Roman Hamrlik .07 .20
SQ45 Adam Deadmarsh .07 .20
SQ46 Alexei Zhamnov .60 1.50
SQ47 Saku Koivu 1.25 3.00
SQ48 Sergei Berezin 1.00 2.50
SQ49 Mark Messier 1.25 3.00
SQ50 Martin Brodeur 3.00 8.00
SQ51 Daniel Alfredsson 1.00 2.50
SQ52 John LeClair 1.25 3.00
SQ53 Mike Vernon 1.00 2.50
SQ54 Ron Francis 1.00 2.50
SQ55 Keith Primeau .60 1.50
SQ56 Pierre Turgeon 1.00 2.50
SQ57 Jim Carey 1.00 2.50
SQ58 Peter Bondra 1.00 2.50
SQ59 Pavel Bure 1.25 3.00
SQ60 Ray Sheppard .60 1.50
SQ61 Chris Gratton 1.00 2.50
SQ62 Derek Plante .60 1.50
SQ63 Joe Sakic 2.50 6.00
SQ64 Theo Fleury 1.00 2.50
SQ65 Tony Amonte 1.00 2.50
SQ66 Zigmund Palffy 1.50 4.00
SQ67 Steve Yzerman 10.00 25.00
SQ68 Doug Weight 2.00 5.00
SQ69 Alexander Mogilny 2.00 5.00
SQ70 Doug Gilmour 2.00 5.00
SQ71 Peter Forsberg 5.00 12.00
SQ72 Alexei Yashin 2.00 5.00
SQ73 Geoff Sanderson 2.00 5.00
SQ74 Brendan Shanahan 2.50 6.00
SQ75 Mark Recchi 2.50 6.00
SQ76 Brett Hull 3.00 8.00
SQ77 Ray Bourque 4.00 10.00
SQ78 Owen Nolan 2.00 5.00
SQ79 Jeremy Roenick 3.00 8.00
SQ80 Teemu Selanne 3.00 8.00
SQ81 Dominik Hasek 6.00 15.00
SQ82 Mike Modano 5.00 12.00
SQ83 Mats Sundin 4.00 10.00
SQ84 John Vanbiesbrouck 6.00 15.00
SQ85 Paul Kariya 3.00 8.00
SQ86 Patrick Roy 10.00 25.00
SQ87 Keith Tkachuk 4.00 10.00
SQ88 Eric Lindros 5.00 12.00
SQ89 Jaromir Jagr 6.00 15.00
SQ90 Wayne Gretzky 15.00 40.00

1997-98 Collector's Choice Stick 'Ums

COMPLETE SET (30) 15.00 30.00
S1 Wayne Gretzky 2.50 5.00
S2 John Vanbiesbrouck .25 .60
S3 Martin Brodeur .75 2.00
S4 Rob Blake .25 .60
S5 Saku Koivu .30 .75
S6 Curtis Joseph .30 .75
S7 Chris Chelios .30 .75
S8 Mike Modano .50 1.25
S9 Paul Kariya .30 .75
S10 Eric Lindros .30 .75
S11 Daniel Alfredsson .25 .60
S12 Jarome Iginla .40 1.00
S13 Jeremy Roenick .40 1.00
S14 Brendan Shanahan .30 .75
S15 Jaromir Jagr .50 1.25
S16 Zigmund Palffy .25 .60
S17 Mats Sundin .30 .75
S18 Teemu Selanne .30 .75
S19 Joe Sakic .60 1.50
S20 Ed Belfour .30 .75
S21 Peter Forsberg .75 2.00
S22 Dino Ciccarelli .25 .60
S23 Patrick Roy 1.50 4.00
S24 Doug Gilmour .25 .60
S25 Pavel Bure .30 .75
S26 Brett Hull .40 1.00
S27 Ray Bourque .50 1.25
S28 Adam Oates .25 .60
S29 Steve Yzerman 1.50 4.00
S30 Dominik Hasek .60 1.50

1997-98 Collector's Choice World Domination

COMPLETE SET (20) 25.00 50.00
W1 Wayne Gretzky 5.00 12.00
W2 Mark Messier .75 2.00
W3 Steve Yzerman 4.00 10.00
W4 Brendan Shanahan .75 2.00
W5 Paul Kariya .75 2.00
W6 Joe Sakic 1.50 4.00
W7 Eric Lindros .75 2.00
W8 Rod Brind'Amour .60 1.50
W9 Keith Primeau .60 1.50
W10 Trevor Linden .60 1.50
W11 Theo Fleury .60 1.50
W12 Scott Niedermeyer .60 1.50
W13 Rob Blake .60 1.50
W14 Chris Pronger .60 1.50
W15 Eric Desjardins .60 1.50
W16 Adam Foote .60 1.50
W17 Scott Stevens .60 1.50
W18 Patrick Roy 4.00 10.00
W19 Curtis Joseph .75 2.00
W20 Martin Brodeur 2.00 5.00

2008-09 Collector's Choice

COMPLETE SET (300) 30.00 60.00
COMP.SET w/o SPs (200) 12.00 30.00
1 Ales Hemsky .15 .40
2 Ales Kotalik .12 .30
3 Alex Kovalev .15 .40
4 Alex Tanguay .12 .30
5 Alexander Edler .12 .30
6 Alexander Frolov .12 .30
7 Alexander Ovechkin .75 2.00
8 Alexander Semin .20 .50
9 Alexander Steen .12 .30
10 Andrei Kostitsyn .12 .30
11 Andrew Cogliano .12 .30
12 Anze Kopitar .30 .75
13 Bill Guerin .20 .50
14 Brad Boyes .12 .30
15 Brad Richards .20 .50
16 Brendan Morrison .12 .30
17 Aaron Voros .12 .30
18 Brenden Morrow .15 .40
19 Brian Campbell .15 .40
20 Brian Gionta .12 .30
21 Brian Rolston .15 .40
22 Cam Ward .20 .50
23 Carey Price .40 1.00
24 Chris Drury .15 .40
25 Chris Higgins .12 .30
26 Chris Kunitz .20 .50
27 Chris Osgood .20 .50
28 Chris Pronger .20 .50
29 Colby Armstrong .12 .30
30 Corey Perry .30 .75
31 Cristobal Huet .15 .40
32 Dan Boyle .12 .30
33 Dan Cleary .15 .40
34 Dan Ellis .12 .30
35 Daniel Alfredsson .20 .50
36 Daniel Briere .20 .50
37 Daniel Carcillo .12 .30
38 Daniel Sedin .20 .50
39 Dany Heatley .15 .40
40 Darcy Tucker .15 .40
41 David Booth .12 .30
42 David Clarkson .12 .30
43 David Legwand .15 .40
44 Daymond Langkow .12 .30
45 Derek Roy .12 .30
46 Dion Phaneuf .15 .40
47 Doug Weight .20 .50
48 Drew Stafford .15 .40
49 Duncan Keith .15 .40
50 Dustin Brown .20 .50
51 Dustin Penner .15 .40
52 Dwayne Roloson .15 .40
53 Ed Jovanovski .15 .40
54 Eric Staal .25 .60
55 Erik Cole .12 .30
56 Erik Johnson .12 .30
57 Evgeni Malkin .40 1.00
58 Evgeni Nabokov .15 .40
59 George Parros .12 .30
60 Gilbert Brule .12 .30
61 Chuck Kobasew .12 .30
62 Guillaume Latendresse .12 .30
63 Henrik Lundqvist .50 1.25
64 Henrik Sedin .25 .60
65 Henrik Zetterberg .25 .60
66 Ilya Bryzgalov .15 .40
67 Ilya Kovalchuk .20 .50
68 J.P. Dumont .12 .30
69 Jack Johnson .12 .30
70 Jarome Iginla .25 .60
71 Jarret Stoll .15 .40
72 Jason Arnott .15 .40
73 Jason LaBarbera .15 .40
74 Jason Pominville .12 .30
75 Jason Spezza .20 .50
76 Jay Bouwmeester .12 .30
77 Jean-Sebastien Giguere .20 .50
78 Jeff Carter .15 .40
79 Jere Lehtinen .12 .30
80 Joe Sakic .40 1.00
81 Joe Thornton .30 .75
82 Johan Franzen .15 .40
83 Johan Hedberg .15 .40
84 Jaroslav Halak .20 .50
85 Jonathan Cheechoo .15 .40
86 Jonathan Toews .30 .75
87 Jordan Staal .15 .40
88 Josh Harding .20 .50
89 Jussi Jokinen .12 .30
90 Justin Williams .15 .40
91 Kari Lehtonen .25 .60
92 Keith Tkachuk .20 .50
93 Kristian Huselius .12 .30
94 Lee Stempniak .12 .30
95 Manny Legace .20 .50
96 Marc Savard .12 .30
97 Marc Staal .12 .30
98 Marc-Andre Fleury .40 1.00
99 Marek Zidlicky .12 .30
100 Marian Gaborik .20 .50
101 Marian Hossa .20 .50
102 Markus Naslund .20 .50
103 Martin Biron .15 .40
104 Martin Brodeur .50 1.25
105 Martin Erat .12 .30
106 Martin Gerber .15 .40
107 Martin Hanzal .15 .40
108 Martin Havlat .20 .50
109 Martin St. Louis .20 .50
110 Marty Turco .20 .50
111 Mats Sundin .20 .50
112 Matt Stajan .12 .30
113 Matthew Lombardi .12 .30
114 Michael Peca .15 .40
115 Michael Ryder .12 .30
116 Michal Rozsival .12 .30
117 Miikka Kiprusoff .20 .50
118 Mike Cammalleri .15 .40
119 Mike Comrie .15 .40
120 Mike Knuble .12 .30
121 Mike Modano .30 .75
122 Mike Ribeiro .12 .30
123 Mike Richards .15 .40
124 Mike Smith .20 .50
125 Mikko Koivu .15 .40
126 Milan Hejduk .15 .40
127 Milan Lucic .30 .75
128 Milan Michalek .15 .40
129 Miroslav Satan .20 .50
130 Nathan Horton .15 .40
131 Nicklas Backstrom .20 .50
132 Nicklas Lidstrom .20 .50
133 Niklas Backstrom .20 .50
134 Nikolai Antropov .15 .40
135 Nikolai Khabibulin .20 .50
136 Nikolai Zherdev .12 .30
137 Olli Jokinen .15 .40
138 Pascal Leclaire .15 .40
139 Patrice Bergeron .25 .60

140 Patrick Kane .40 1.00
141 Patrick Marleau .20 .50
142 Patrick O'Sullivan .15 .40
143 Patrick Sharp .20 .50
144 Patrik Elias .20 .50
145 Paul Kariya .20 .50
146 Paul Ranger .12 .30
147 Paul Stastny .15 .40
148 Pavel Datsyuk .30 .75
149 Peter Budaj .15 .40
150 Peter Forsberg .40 1.00
151 Peter Mueller .15 .40
152 Phil Kessel .20 .50
153 Pierre-Marc Bouchard .20 .50
154 R.J. Umberger .12 .30
155 Radim Vrbata .12 .30
156 Ray Whitney .15 .40
157 Rick DiPietro .15 .40
158 Rick Nash .20 .50
159 Robert Lang .12 .30
160 Roberto Luongo .30 .75
161 Rod Brind'Amour .20 .50
162 Ryan Getzlaf .20 .50
163 Ryan Kesler .20 .50
164 Ryan Malone .12 .30
165 Ryan Miller .20 .50
166 Ryan Smyth .15 .40
167 Ryan Suter .15 .40
168 Saku Koivu .20 .50
169 Sam Gagner .12 .30
170 Scott Gomez .15 .40
171 Scott Niedermayer .20 .50
172 Sergei Fedorov .30 .75
173 Sergei Zubov .15 .40
174 Shane Doan .15 .40
175 Shawn Horcoff .12 .30
176 Shea Weber .15 .40
177 Sidney Crosby .75 2.00
178 Simon Gagne .20 .50
179 Slava Kozlov .12 .30
180 Stephen Weiss .12 .30
181 Steve Bernier .12 .30
182 Teemu Selanne .40 1.00
183 Thomas Vanek .15 .40
184 Tim Thomas .20 .50
185 Tobias Enstrom .12 .30
186 Todd White .12 .30
187 Tomas Holmstrom .15 .40
188 Tomas Kaberle .12 .30
189 Tomas Vokoun .15 .40
190 Travis Zajac .12 .30
191 Trent Hunter .12 .30
192 Ty Conklin .15 .40
193 Vaclav Prospal .12 .30
194 Valtteri Filppula .12 .30
195 Vesa Toskala .25 .60
196 Vincent Lecavalier .20 .50
197 Wade Redden .12 .30
198 Wojtek Wolski .15 .40
199 Zach Parise .20 .50
200 Zdeno Chara .20 .50
201 Justin Abdelkader RC 1.00 2.50
202 Patrik Berglund RC .50 1.25
203 Mikkel Boedker RC .75 2.00
204 Zach Bogosian RC .75 2.00
205 Zach Boychuk RC .60 1.50
206 Derick Brassard RC .60 1.50
207 Fabian Brunnstrom RC .50 1.25
208 Matt D'Agostini RC .50 1.25
209 Drew Doughty RC 1.50 4.00
210 Robbie Earl RC .40 1.00
211 Andrew Ebbett RC .40 1.00
212 Jonathan Ericsson RC .60 1.50
213 Erik Ersberg RC .50 1.25
214 Nikita Filatov RC .60 1.50
215 Michael Frolik RC .60 1.50
216 Colton Gillies RC .50 1.25
217 Claude Giroux RC 1.25 3.00
218 Alex Goligoski RC .75 2.00
219 Darren Helm RC .60 1.50
220 Patric Hornqvist RC .60 1.50
221 Josh Bailey RC .75 2.00
222 Ryan Jones RC .60 1.50
223 Lauri Korpikoski RC .40 1.00
224 Nikolai Kulemin RC .60 1.50
225 Brian Lee RC .50 1.25
226 Shawn Matthias RC .60 1.50
227 Vladimir Mihalik RC .40 1.00
228 Oscar Moller RC .50 1.25
229 James Neal RC 1.25 3.00
230 Andreas Nodl RC .40 1.00
231 Kyle Okposo RC .75 2.00
232 T.J. Oshie RC 1.25 3.00
233 Nathan Oystrick RC .60 1.50
234 Alex Pietrangelo RC 1.00 2.50
235 Kevin Porter RC .50 1.25
236 Teddy Purcell RC .50 1.25
237 Tim Ramholt RC .50 1.25
238 Mattias Ritola RC .50 1.25
239 Luca Sbisa RC .40 1.00
240 Luke Schenn RC .75 2.00
241 Tom Sestito RC .60 1.50
242 Steven Stamkos RC 2.50 6.00
243 Brandon Sutter RC .60 1.50
244 Viktor Tikhonov RC .50 1.25
245 Kyle Turris RC 1.00 2.50
246 Boris Valabik RC .60 1.50
247 Jakub Voracek RC 1.25 3.00
248 Petr Vrana RC .40 1.00
249 Blake Wheeler RC 1.50 4.00
250 Ilya Zubov RC .50 1.25
251 Getzlaf/Giguere/Pronger .75 2.00
252 Kovalchuk/Lehtonen/Little 1.00 2.50
253 Savard/Thomas/Chara .75 2.00
254 Vanek/Miller/Roy .75 2.00
255 Iginla/Kiprusoff/Phaneuf 1.00 2.50
256 Staal/Ward/Whitney 1.00 2.50
257 Toews/Huet/Kane 1.50 4.00
258 Sakic/Budaj/Stastny 1.50 4.00
259 Nash/Leclaire/Huselius .75 2.00
260 Morrow/Turco/Richards .75 2.00
261 Zetterberg/Osgood/Datsyuk 1.25 3.00
262 Hemsky/Garon/Horcoff .60 1.50
263 Horton/Vokoun/Booth .60 1.50
264 Kopitar/LaBerbera/Frolov 1.25 3.00
265 Gaborik/Backstrom/Burns .75 2.00
266 Koivu/Price/Kovalev 1.50 4.00
267 Dumont/Ellis/Arnott .60 1.50
268 Parise/Brodeur/Elias 2.00 5.00
269 Comrie/DiPietro/Streit .60 1.50
270 Naslund/Lundqvist/Drury 2.00 5.00
271 Heatley/Gerber/Spezza .75 2.00
272 Richards/Biron/Carter .60 1.50
273 Doan/Bryzgalov/Jokinen .60 1.50
274 Crosby/Fleury/Malkin 3.00 8.00
275 Thornton/Nabokov/Cheechoo 1.25 3.00
276 Kariya/Legace/Boyes .75 2.00
277 Lecavalier/Smith/St. Louis .75 2.00
278 Antropov/Toskala/Kaberle 1.00 2.50
279 Sedin/Luongo/Sedsin 1.25 3.00
280 Ovechkin/Theodore/Green 3.00 8.00
281 Alexander Ovechkin 3.00 8.00
282 Brenden Morrow .60 1.50
283 Chris Pronger .75 2.00
284 Daniel Carcillo .50 1.25
285 Dion Phaneuf .60 1.50
286 Dustin Brown .75 2.00
287 Ed Jovanovski .60 1.50
288 Eric Staal 1.00 2.50
289 Henrik Lundqvist 2.00 5.00
290 Henrik Zetterberg 1.00 2.50
291 Ilya Kovalchuk .75 2.00
292 Jonathan Toews 1.25 3.00
293 Martin Brodeur 2.00 5.00
294 Rick Nash .75 2.00
295 Roberto Luongo 1.25 3.00
296 Ryan Getzlaf .75 2.00
297 Sidney Crosby 3.00 8.00
298 Vincent Lecavalier .75 2.00
299 Wade Redden .50 1.25
300 Zdeno Chara .75 2.00

2008-09 Collector's Choice Prime Reserve Gold

*GOLD (1-200): 5X TO 12X BASIC CARDS
*GOLD (201-250): 1.2X TO 3X BASIC CARDS
*GOLD (251-300): 1X TO 2.5X BASIC CARDS
131 Nicklas Backstrom 2.50 6.00

2008-09 Collector's Choice Reserve Silver

COMPLETE SET (300) 50.00 100.00
*SINGLES (1-200): .8X TO 2X BASIC CARDS
*SINGLES (201-250): 1X TO 2.5X BASIC CARDS
*SINGLES (251-300): .6X TO 1.5X BASIC CARDS
131 Nicklas Backstrom .40 1.00

2008-09 Collector's Choice Cup Quest

COMPLETE SET (90) 50.00 100.00
CQ1 Ales Hemsky FR .50 1.25
CQ2 Brian Rafalski FR .50 1.25
CQ3 Brian Rolston FR .50 1.25
CQ4 Corey Perry FR 1.00 2.50
CQ5 Cristobal Huet FR .50 1.25
CQ6 Daniel Sedin FR .75 2.00
CQ7 David Booth FR .40 1.00
CQ8 Derek Roy FR .40 1.00
CQ9 Ed Jovanovski FR .50 1.25
CQ10 J.P. Dumont FR .40 1.00
CQ11 Jason Arnott FR .50 1.25
CQ12 Jeff Carter FR .50 1.25
CQ13 Jere Lehtinen FR .40 1.00
CQ14 Jordan Staal FR .50 1.25
CQ15 Kari Lehtonen FR .75 2.00
CQ16 Manny Legace FR .60 1.50
CQ17 Marian Hossa FR .60 1.50
CQ18 Mark Streit FR .40 1.00
CQ19 Martin Biron FR .50 1.25
CQ20 Martin Gerber FR .50 1.25
CQ21 Mike Green FR .50 1.25
CQ22 Milan Hejduk FR .50 1.25
CQ23 Nathan Horton FR .50 1.25
CQ24 Niklas Backstrom FR .60 1.50
CQ25 Pascal Leclaire FR .50 1.25
CQ26 Pavol Demitra FR .75 2.00
CQ27 Rob Blake FR .60 1.50
CQ28 Rod Brind'Amour FR .60 1.50
CQ29 Ryan Malone FR .40 1.00
CQ30 Scott Gomez FR .50 1.25
CQ31 Todd Bertuzzi FR .60 1.50
CQ32 Tomas Holmstrom FR .50 1.25
CQ33 Tomas Kaberle FR .40 1.00
CQ34 Vesa Toskala FR .75 2.00
CQ35 Zdeno Chara FR .60 1.50
CQ36 Alex Kovalev SR .60 1.50
CQ37 Andrew Cogliano SR .50 1.25
CQ38 Anze Kopitar SR 1.25 3.00
CQ39 Brenden Morrow SR .60 1.50
CQ40 Carey Price SR 1.50 4.00
CQ41 Chris Drury SR .60 1.50
CQ42 Chris Osgood SR .75 2.00
CQ43 Henrik Lundqvist SR 2.00 5.00
CQ44 Henrik Sedin SR 1.00 2.50
CQ45 Jason Spezza SR .75 2.00
CQ46 Joe Sakic SR 1.50 4.00
CQ47 Jonathan Toews SR 1.25 3.00
CQ48 Miikka Kiprusoff SR .75 2.00
CQ49 Mike Ribeiro SR .50 1.25
CQ50 Mikko Koivu SR .60 1.50
CQ51 Nicklas Backstrom SR .75 2.00
CQ52 Olli Jokinen SR .60 1.50
CQ53 Patrick Kane SR 1.50 4.00
CQ54 Peter Mueller SR .60 1.50
CQ55 Ryan Miller SR .75 2.00
CQ56 Sam Gagner SR .50 1.25
CQ57 Shawn Horcoff SR .50 1.25
CQ58 Thomas Vanek SR .60 1.50
CQ59 Wade Redden SR .50 1.25
CQ60 Zach Parise SR .75 2.00
CQ61 Daniel Alfredsson SF 1.00 2.50
CQ62 Dany Heatley SF .75 2.00
CQ63 Dion Phaneuf SF .75 2.00
CQ64 Evgeni Nabokov SF .75 2.00
CQ65 Jean-Sebastien Giguere SF 1.00 2.50
CQ66 Jonathan Cheechoo SF .75 2.00
CQ67 Marc-Andre Fleury SF 2.00 5.00
CQ68 Marian Gaborik SF 1.00 2.50
CQ69 Johan Franzen SF .75 2.00
CQ70 Markus Naslund SF 1.00 2.50
CQ71 Martin St. Louis SF 1.00 2.50
CQ72 Mats Sundin SF 1.00 2.50
CQ73 Mike Modano SF 1.50 4.00
CQ74 Nicklas Lidstrom SF 1.00 2.50
CQ75 Paul Stastny SF .75 2.00
CQ76 Pavel Datsyuk SF 1.50 4.00
CQ77 Rick Nash SF 1.00 2.50
CQ78 Ryan Getzlaf SF 1.00 2.50
CQ79 Saku Koivu SF 1.00 2.50
CQ80 Shane Doan SF .75 2.00
CQ81 Alexander Ovechkin F 6.00 15.00
CQ82 Sidney Crosby F 6.00 15.00
CQ83 Evgeni Malkin F 3.00 8.00
CQ84 Jarome Iginla F 2.00 5.00
CQ85 Vincent Lecavalier F 1.50 4.00
CQ86 Roberto Luongo F 2.50 6.00
CQ87 Henrik Zetterberg F 2.00 5.00
CQ88 Ilya Kovalchuk F 1.50 4.00
CQ89 Joe Thornton F 2.50 6.00
CQ90 Martin Brodeur F 4.00 10.00

2008-09 Collector's Choice Stick-Ums

COMPLETE SET (30) 25.00 60.00
UMS1 Alexander Ovechkin 2.50 6.00
UMS2 Anze Kopitar 1.00 2.50
UMS3 Carey Price 1.25 3.00
UMS4 Dany Heatley .50 1.25
UMS5 Evgeni Malkin 1.25 3.00
UMS6 Henrik Lundqvist 1.50 4.00
UMS7 Henrik Zetterberg .75 2.00
UMS8 Ilya Kovalchuk .60 1.50
UMS9 Jarome Iginla .75 2.00
UMS10 Jean-Sebastien Giguere .60 1.50
UMS11 Joe Sakic 1.25 3.00
UMS12 Joe Thornton 1.00 2.50
UMS13 Jonathan Toews 1.00 2.50
UMS14 Marc-Andre Fleury 1.25 3.00
UMS15 Marian Gaborik .60 1.50
UMS16 Martin Brodeur 1.50 4.00
UMS17 Martin St. Louis .60 1.50
UMS18 Marty Turco .60 1.50
UMS19 Mike Modano 1.00 2.50
UMS20 Mike Richards .50 1.25
UMS21 Nicklas Backstrom .60 1.50
UMS22 Nicklas Lidstrom .60 1.50
UMS23 Patrick Kane 1.25 3.00
UMS24 Paul Stastny .50 1.25
UMS25 Pavel Datsyuk 1.00 2.50
UMS26 Rick Nash .60 1.50
UMS27 Roberto Luongo 1.00 2.50
UMS28 Ryan Miller .60 1.50
UMS29 Sidney Crosby 2.50 6.00
UMS30 Vincent Lecavalier .60 1.50

2009-10 Collector's Choice

1 Rick DiPietro .12 .30
2 Kyle Okposo .10 .25
3 Josh Bailey .12 .30
4 Mark Streit .10 .25
5 Doug Weight .15 .40
6 Trent Hunter .10 .25
7 Vincent Lecavalier .15 .40
8 Steven Stamkos .30 .75
9 Ryan Malone .10 .25
10 Mike Smith .15 .40
11 Vaclav Prospal .10 .25
12 Martin St. Louis .15 .40
13 Paul Stastny .12 .30
14 Peter Budaj .12 .30
15 John-Michael Liles .10 .25
16 Milan Hejduk .12 .30
17 Marek Svatos .10 .25
18 Wojtek Wolski .10 .25
19 Chris Stewart .12 .30
20 Ilya Kovalchuk .15 .40
21 Todd White .10 .25
22 Bryan Little .15 .40
23 Kari Lehtonen .12 .30
24 Colby Armstrong .10 .25
25 Zach Bogosian .12 .30
26 Anze Kopitar .25 .60
27 Dustin Brown .15 .40
28 Jonathan Quick .20 .50
29 Alexander Frolov .12 .30
30 Drew Doughty .20 .50
31 Ryan Smyth .12 .30
32 Peter Mueller .12 .30
33 Shane Doan .12 .30
34 Scottie Upshall .10 .25
35 Ilya Bryzgalov .12 .30
36 Keith Yandle .10 .25
37 Matthew Lombardi .10 .25
38 Nikolai Kulemin .10 .25
39 Mike Komisarek .12 .30
40 Vesa Toskala .15 .40
41 Matt Stajan .10 .25
42 Tomas Kaberle .10 .25
43 Mikhail Grabovski .10 .25
44 Luke Schenn .15 .40
45 Marty Turco .15 .40
46 James Neal .10 .25
47 Mike Ribeiro .10 .25
48 Steve Ott .10 .25
49 Brad Richards .15 .40
50 Loui Eriksson .10 .25
51 Mike Modano .25 .60
52 Jason Spezza .15 .40
53 Jarkko Ruutu .10 .25
54 Filip Kuba .10 .25
55 Daniel Alfredsson .15 .40
56 Alex Kovalev .12 .30
57 Nick Foligno .12 .30
58 Dany Heatley .12 .30
59 Ales Hemsky .12 .30
60 Patrick O'Sullivan .12 .30
61 Nikolai Khabibulin .15 .40
62 Sheldon Souray .10 .25
63 Shawn Horcoff .10 .25
64 Andrew Cogliano .10 .25
65 Sam Gagner .10 .25
66 Pekka Rinne .15 .40
67 Jason Arnott .12 .30
68 Shea Weber .12 .30
69 Jordin Tootoo .15 .40
70 Ryan Suter .12 .30
71 J.P. Dumont .10 .25
72 Mikko Koivu .15 .40
73 Martin Havlat .12 .30
74 Niklas Backstrom .15 .40
75 Marek Zidlicky .10 .25
76 Pierre-Marc Bouchard .15 .40
77 Andrew Brunette .10 .25
78 Thomas Vanek .12 .30
79 Tim Connolly .10 .25
80 Derek Roy .10 .25
81 Ryan Miller .15 .40
82 Jason Pominville .10 .25
83 Drew Stafford .10 .25
84 Clarke MacArthur .10 .25
85 Stephen Weiss .10 .25
86 Michael Frolik .12 .30
87 Keith Ballard .10 .25
88 David Booth .10 .25
89 Nathan Horton .15 .40
90 Tomas Vokoun .12 .30
91 Ryan Getzlaf .15 .40
92 Scott Niedermayer .15 .40
93 Corey Perry .25 .60
94 Saku Koivu .15 .40
95 Teemu Selanne .30 .75
96 Bobby Ryan .12 .30
97 Steve Mason .12 .30
98 Rick Nash .15 .40
99 Jakub Voracek .12 .30
100 Kris Russell .10 .25
101 R.J. Umberger .12 .30
102 Derick Brassard .10 .25
103 Paul Kariya .15 .40
104 David Perron .12 .30
105 T.J. Oshie .15 .40
106 Brad Boyes .10 .25
107 Andy McDonald .12 .30
108 David Backes .10 .25
109 Chris Mason .12 .30
110 Carey Price .30 .75
111 Andrei Markov .15 .40
112 Scott Gomez .12 .30
113 Mike Cammalleri .12 .30
114 Tomas Plekanec .10 .25
115 Maxim Lapierre .10 .25
116 Andrei Kostitsyn .12 .30
117 Chris Drury .12 .30
118 Brandon Dubinsky .10 .25
119 Henrik Lundqvist .40 1.00
120 Marc Staal .10 .25
121 Sean Avery .12 .30
122 Chris Higgins .10 .25
123 Marian Gaborik .15 .40
124 Olli Jokinen .12 .30
125 Dion Phaneuf .12 .30
126 Jay Bouwmeester .10 .25
127 Craig Conroy .10 .25
128 Miikka Kiprusoff .15 .40
129 Daymond Langkow .10 .25
130 Jarome Iginla .20 .50
131 Mike Richards .12 .30
132 Claude Giroux .15 .40
133 Braydon Coburn .10 .25
134 Jeff Carter .12 .30
135 Simon Gagne .15 .40
136 Chris Pronger .15 .40
137 Daniel Briere .15 .40
138 Roberto Luongo .25 .60
139 Henrik Sedin .20 .50
140 Kyle Wellwood .12 .30
141 Alexander Edler .10 .25
142 Ryan Kesler .15 .40
143 Daniel Sedin .20 .50
144 Mason Raymond .10 .25
145 Patrik Elias .15 .40
146 Paul Martin .10 .25
147 Martin Brodeur .40 1.00
148 Zach Parise .15 .40
149 Travis Zajac .10 .25
150 Jamie Langenbrunner .10 .25
151 David Clarkson .12 .30
152 Alexander Ovechkin .60 1.50
153 Semyon Varlamov .15 .40
154 Tomas Fleischmann .10 .25
155 Alexander Semin .15 .40
156 Nicklas Backstrom .15 .40
157 Brooks Laich .10 .25
158 Mike Green .12 .30
159 Tim Thomas .15 .40
160 Michael Ryder .10 .25
161 Marc Savard .10 .25
162 David Krejci .15 .40
163 Phil Kessel .15 .40
164 Zdeno Chara .15 .40
165 Patrice Bergeron .20 .50
166 Joe Thornton .25 .60
167 Ryane Clowe .10 .25
168 Dan Boyle .10 .25
169 Joe Pavelski .20 .50
170 Patrick Marleau .15 .40
171 Evgeni Nabokov .12 .30
172 Devin Setoguchi .12 .30
173 Eric Staal .20 .50
174 Jussi Jokinen .10 .25
175 Rod Brind`Amour .15 .40
176 Tuomo Ruutu .10 .25
177 Sergei Samsonov .12 .30
178 Ray Whitney .12 .30
179 Cam Ward .15 .40
180 Patrick Kane .30 .75
181 Brian Campbell .12 .30
182 Kris Versteeg .10 .25
183 Marian Hossa .15 .40
184 Cristobal Huet .15 .40
185 Patrick Sharp .15 .40
186 Jonathan Toews .25 .60
187 Sidney Crosby .60 1.50
188 Maxime Talbot .10 .25
189 Marc-Andre Fleury .30 .75
190 Evgeni Malkin .30 .75
191 Sergei Gonchar .10 .25
192 Kristopher Letang .20 .50
193 Jordan Staal .12 .30
194 Henrik Zetterberg .20 .50
195 Dan Cleary .15 .40
196 Chris Osgood .15 .40
197 Pavel Datsyuk .25 .60
198 Valtteri Filppula .10 .25
199 Niklas Kronwall .12 .30
200 Nicklas Lidstrom .10 .25
201 Koivu/Ryan/Getzlaf .60 1.50
202 Little/Lehtonen/Kovalchuk .60 1.50
203 Thomas/Savard/Chara .60 1.50
204 Miller/Roy/Vanek .60 1.50
205 Iginla/Kiprusoft/Phaneuf .75 2.00
206 Staal/Ward/Whitney .75 2.00
207 Sharp/Kane/Toews 1.25 3.00
208 Hejduk/Stastny/Wolski .50 1.25
209 Brassard/Mason/Nash .60 1.50
210 Turco/Eriksson/Ribeiro .60 1.50
211 Zetterberg/Lidstrom/Datsyuk 1.00 2.50
212 Gagner/Souray/Hemsky .50 1.25
213 Booth/Vokoun/Weiss .50 1.25
214 Frolov/Kopitar/Doughty 1.00 2.50
215 Koivu/Backstrom/Nolan .60 1.50
216 Gomez/Markov/Price 1.25 3.00
217 Arnott/Weber/Rinne .60 1.50
218 Brodeur/Parise/Elias 1.50 4.00
219 Streit/Okposo/Weight .60 1.50
220 Gaborik/Lundqvist/Drury 1.50 4.00
221 Spezza/Kovalev/Alfredsson .60 1.50
222 Pronger/Carter/Richards .60 1.50
223 Doan/Bryzgalov/Mueller .50 1.25
224 Crosby/Malkin/Fleury 2.50 6.00
225 Nabokov/Thornton/Marleau 1.00 2.50
226 Boyes/Mason/Perron .50 1.25
227 St. Louis/Lecavalier/Stamkos 1.25 3.00
228 Schenn/Kessel/Toskala .60 1.50
229 Luongo/Sedin/Sedin 1.00 2.50
230 Backstrom/Green/Ovechkin 2.50 6.00
231 Brian Salcido RC .50 1.25
232 Matt Beleskey RC .60 1.50
233 Spencer Machacek RC .75 2.00
234 Evander Kane RC 1.50 4.00
235 Brad Marchand RC 3.00 8.00
236 Byron Bitz RC .60 1.50
237 Jhonas Enroth RC 1.00 2.50
238 Tyler Myers RC 1.25 3.00
239 Chris Butler RC .75 2.00
240 Riley Armstrong RC .60 1.50
241 Mikael Backlund RC 1.25 3.00
242 Kris Chucko RC .50 1.25
243 Matt Pelech RC .75 2.00
244 John Negrin RC .75 2.00
245 Jakub Petruzalek RC .75 2.00
246 Antti Niemi RC 1.25 3.00
247 Chris Durno RC .60 1.50
248 T.J. Galiardi RC .75 2.00
249 Ray Macias RC .60 1.50
250 Matt Hendricks RC .60 1.50
251 Matt Duchene RC 1.50 4.00
252 Ryan O'Reilly RC 1.50 4.00
253 Ivan Vishnevskiy RC .50 1.25
254 Tom Wandell RC .75 2.00
255 Jamie Benn RC 2.50 6.00
256 Ville Leino RC .60 1.50
257 Taylor Chorney RC .75 2.00
258 Dmitry Kulikov RC .75 2.00
259 Davis Drewiske RC .75 2.00
260 Alec Martinez RC 1.00 2.50
261 Jaime Sifers RC .60 1.50
262 Mathieu Carle RC .75 2.00
263 Yannick Weber RC .75 2.00
264 Cal O'Reilly RC .60 1.50
265 Alexander Sulzer RC .50 1.25
266 Mike Santorelli RC .75 2.00
267 Colin Wilson RC .75 2.00
268 Teemu Laakso RC .50 1.25
269 Cody Franson RC .75 2.00
270 Jesse Joensuu RC .60 1.50
271 Andrew MacDonald RC .50 1.25
272 Joel Rechlicz RC .50 1.25
273 John Tavares RC 6.00 15.00
274 Michael Sauer RC .60 1.50
275 Artem Anisimov RC .50 1.25
276 Matt Gilroy RC .75 2.00
277 Michael Del Zotto RC .75 2.00
278 Peter Regin RC .60 1.50
279 Erik Karlsson RC 2.50 6.00
280 James van Riemsdyk RC 1.50 4.00
281 Mika Pyorala RC .60 1.50
282 David Schlemko RC .60 1.50
283 Luca Caputi RC .75 2.00
284 Jason Demers RC 1.25 3.00
285 Benn Ferriero RC .75 2.00
286 Frazer McLaren RC .60 1.50
287 Steven Zalewski RC .60 1.50
288 Logan Couture RC 1.50 4.00
289 Kevin Quick RC .50 1.25
290 Riku Helenius RC .75 2.00
291 James Wright RC .75 2.00
292 Victor Hedman RC 2.00 5.00
293 Christian Hanson RC .75 2.00
294 Viktor Stalberg RC .75 2.00
295 Tyler Bozak RC 1.25 3.00
296 Jonas Gustavsson RC 5.00 12.00
297 Sergei Shirokov RC .50 1.25
298 Guillaume Desbiens RC .75 2.00
299 Michael Grabner RC .75 2.00
300 Michal Neuvirth RC 1.25 3.00

2009-10 Collector's Choice Reserve

*SINGLES 1-200: .8X TO 2X BASIC
*SINGLES 201-230: .6X TO 1.5X BASIC
*ROOKIES 231-300: .6X TO 1.5X BASIC
156 Nicklas Backstrom .40 1.00

2009-10 Collector's Choice Reserve Prime

*SINGLES 1-200: 5X TO 12X BASIC
*SINGLES 201-230: 2X TO 5X BASIC
*SINGLES 231-300: 2X TO 5X BASIC
156 Nicklas Backstrom 2.50 6.00

2009-10 Collector's Choice Badge of Honor Tattoos

COMPLETE SET (30) 4.00 10.00
BH1 Anaheim Ducks .20 .50
BH2 Atlanta Thrashers .20 .50
BH3 Boston Bruins .20 .50
BH4 Buffalo Sabres .20 .50
BH5 Calgary Flames .20 .50
BH6 Carolina Hurricanes .20 .50
BH7 Chicago Blackhawks .20 .50
BH8 Colorado Avalanche .20 .50
BH9 Columbus Blue Jackets .20 .50
BH10 Dallas Stars .20 .50
BH11 Detroit Red Wings .20 .50
BH12 Edmonton Oilers .20 .50
BH13 Florida Panthers .20 .50
BH14 Los Angeles Kings .20 .50
BH15 Minnesota Wild .20 .50
BH16 Montreal Canadiens .20 .50
BH17 Nashville Predators .20 .50
BH18 New Jersey Devils .20 .50
BH19 New York Islanders .20 .50
BH20 New York Rangers .20 .50
BH21 Ottawa Senators .20 .50
BH22 Philadelphia Flyers .20 .50
BH23 Phoenix Coyotes .20 .50
BH24 Pittsburgh Penguins .20 .50
BH25 San Jose Sharks .20 .50
BH26 St. Louis Blues .20 .50
BH27 Tampa Bay Lightning .20 .50
BH28 Toronto Maple Leafs .20 .50
BH29 Vancouver Canucks .20 .50
BH30 Washington Capitals .20 .50

2009-10 Collector's Choice Cup Quest

COMPLETE SET (80) 150.00 300.00
CQ1 Chris Pronger FR .60 1.50
CQ2 Patrice Bergeron FR .75 2.00
CQ3 Dion Phaneuf FR .50 1.25
CQ4 Dany Heatley FR .50 1.25
CQ5 Marty Turco FR .60 1.50
CQ6 Nicklas Lidstrom FR .40 1.00
CQ7 Ales Hemsky FR .50 1.25
CQ8 Tomas Vokoun FR .50 1.25
CQ9 Anze Kopitar FR 1.00 2.50
CQ10 Owen Nolan FR .60 1.50
CQ11 Shea Weber FR .50 1.25
CQ12 Doug Weight FR .60 1.50
CQ13 Rick DiPietro FR .50 1.25
CQ14 Chris Drury FR .50 1.25
CQ15 Patrick Marleau FR .60 1.50
CQ16 Simon Gagne FR .60 1.50
CQ17 Shane Doan FR .50 1.25
CQ18 Devin Setoguchi FR .50 1.25
CQ19 David Perron FR .50 1.25
CQ20 Matt Stajan FR .40 1.00
CQ21 Mike Green FR .50 1.25
CQ22 Zdeno Chara FR .60 1.50
CQ23 Brian Campbell FR .50 1.25
CQ24 Brad Richards FR .60 1.50
CQ25 Andrew Cogliano FR .40 1.00
CQ26 David Booth FR .40 1.00
CQ27 Pekka Rinne FR .60 1.50
CQ28 Peter Mueller FR .50 1.25
CQ29 Paul Kariya FR .60 1.50
CQ30 Ryan Kesler FR .60 1.50
CQ31 Mikko Koivu SR .75 2.00
CQ32 Jeff Carter SR .60 1.50
CQ33 Jordan Staal SR .60 1.50
CQ34 Jason Spezza SR .75 2.00
CQ35 Nicklas Backstrom SR .75 2.00
CQ36 Marian Gaborik SR .75 2.00
CQ37 Bobby Ryan SR .60 1.50
CQ38 Phil Kessel SR .75 2.00
CQ39 Ryan Miller SR .75 2.00
CQ40 Miikka Kiprusoff SR .75 2.00
CQ41 Eric Staal SR 1.00 2.50
CQ42 Rick Nash SR .75 2.00
CQ43 Steve Mason SR .60 1.50
CQ44 Mike Modano SR 1.25 3.00
CQ45 Pavel Datsyuk SR 1.25 3.00
CQ46 Sam Gagner SR .50 1.25
CQ47 Drew Doughty SR 1.00 2.50
CQ48 Zach Parise SR .75 2.00
CQ49 Henrik Lundqvist SR 2.00 5.00
CQ50 Paul Stastny SR .60 1.50
CQ51 Mike Richards SR .60 1.50
CQ52 Marc-Andre Fleury SR 1.50 4.00
CQ53 Teemu Selanne SR 1.50 4.00
CQ54 Martin St. Louis SR .75 2.00
CQ55 Luke Schenn SR .75 2.00
CQ56 Ryan Getzlaf SR .75 2.00
CQ57 Thomas Vanek SR .60 1.50
CQ58 Cam Ward SR .75 2.00
CQ59 Steven Stamkos SR 1.50 4.00
CQ60 Saku Koivu SR .75 2.00
CQ61 Ilya Kovalchuk TR 1.00 2.50
CQ62 Jarome Iginla TR 1.50 4.00
CQ63 Jonathan Toews TR 2.00 5.00
CQ64 Joe Thornton TR 2.00 5.00
CQ65 Henrik Zetterberg TR 1.50 4.00
CQ66 Carey Price TR 2.50 6.00
CQ67 Evgeni Malkin TR 2.50 6.00
CQ68 Vincent Lecavalier TR 1.25 3.00
CQ69 Roberto Luongo TR 2.00 5.00
CQ70 Patrick Kane TR 2.50 6.00
CQ71 Martin Brodeur F/100 12.00 30.00
CQ72 Sidney Crosby F/100 20.00 50.00
CQ73 Alexander Ovechkin F/100 20.00 50.00
CQ74 Wayne Gretzky F/100 30.00 80.00
CQ75 Bobby Orr F/100 20.00 50.00
CQ76 Gordie Howe F/100 15.00 40.00
CQ77 Mario Lemieux F/100 20.00 50.00
CQ78 Steve Yzerman F/100 12.00 30.00
CQ79 Patrick Roy F/100 12.00 30.00
CQ80 Mark Messier F/100 10.00 25.00

2009-10 Collector's Choice Stick-Ums

COMPLETE SET (30) 12.00 30.00
SU1 Ilya Kovalchuk .40 1.00
SU2 Phil Kessel .40 1.00
SU3 Ryan Miller .40 1.00
SU4 Jarome Iginla .50 1.25
SU5 Eric Staal .50 1.25
SU6 Patrick Kane .75 2.00
SU7 Jonathan Toews .60 1.50
SU8 Paul Siastny .30 .75
SU9 Rick Nash .40 1.00
SU10 Henrik Zetterberg .50 1.25
SU11 Pavel Datsyuk .60 1.50
SU12 Drew Doughty .50 1.25
SU13 Carey Price .75 2.00
SU14 Shea Weber .30 .75
SU15 Martin Brodeur 1.00 2.50
SU16 Zach Parise .40 1.00
SU17 Henrik Lundqvist 1.00 2.50
SU18 Daniel Alfredsson .40 1.00
SU19 Jason Spezza .40 1.00
SU20 Jeff Carter .30 .75
SU21 Mike Richards .30 .75
SU22 Sidney Crosby 1.50 4.00
SU23 Evgeni Malkin .75 2.00
SU24 Marc-Andre Fleury .75 2.00
SU25 Joe Thornton .60 1.50
SU26 Vincent Lecavalier .40 1.00
SU27 Luke Schenn .40 1.00
SU28 Roberto Luongo .60 1.50
SU29 Alexander Ovechkin 1.50 4.00
SU30 Mike Green .30 .75

2009-10 Collector's Choice Warriors of Ice

COMPLETE SET (6) 4.00 10.00
W1 Alexander Ovechkin 1.50 4.00
W2 Henrik Zetterberg .50 1.25
W3 Jarome Iginla .50 1.25
W4 Martin Brodeur 1.00 2.50
W5 Sidney Crosby 1.50 4.00
W6 Zdeno Chara .40 1.00

1962-63 Cowan Ceramic Tiles

1 Charlie Burns 75.00 150.00
2 Red Berenson 100.00 200.00
3 Ralph Backstrom 100.00 200.00
4 Larry Cahan 75.00 150.00
5 Bernie Geoffrion 250.00 500.00
6 Phil Goyette 75.00 150.00
7 Doug Harvey 150.00 300.00
8 Bronco Horvath 75.00 150.00
9 Harry Howell 125.00 250.00
10 Andy Hebenton 75.00 150.00
11 Jim Langlois 75.00 150.00
12 Bert Marshall 75.00 150.00
13 Marcel Pronovost 150.00 300.00
14 Henri Richard 350.00 600.00
15 Bobby Rousseau 75.00 150.00
16 Gilles Tremblay 100.00 200.00
17 Jerry Toppazzini 100.00 200.00
18 Gump Worsley 250.00 500.00
19 Dave Balon 75.00 150.00
20 Jean Beliveau 500.00 800.00
21 Claude Provost 125.00 250.00
22 Vic Hadfield 75.00 150.00
23 Jean-Guy Talbot 100.00 200.00
24 Dickie Moore 100.00 200.00
25 Jean Ratelle 75.00 150.00
26 Tom Johnson 100.00 200.00
27 Earl Ingarfield 75.00 150.00
28 Lou Fontinato 100.00 200.00
29 Cesare Maniago 100.00 200.00
30 Ted Hampson 75.00 150.00
31 Muzz Patrick 75.00 150.00
32 Andy Bathgate 100.00 200.00
33 Bill Hicke 75.00 150.00
34 J.C. Tremblay 100.00 200.00

1996-97 Coyotes Coca-Cola

COMPLETE SET (37) 10.00 25.00
1 Bob Corkum .20 .50
2 Shane Doan .60 1.50
3 Dallas Drake .20 .50
4 Dallas Eakins .20 .50
5 Mike Eastwood .20 .50
6 Jeff Finley .20 .50
7 Mike Gartner .30 .75
8 Mike Gartner .30 .75
9 Mike Hudson .20 .50
10 Craig Janney .20 .50
11 Jim Johnson .20 .50
12 Nikolai Khabibulin .60 1.50
13 Nikolai Khabibulin .60 1.50
14 Chad Kilger .20 .50
15 Kris King .20 .50
16 Kris King .20 .50
17 Igor Korolev .20 .50
18 Norm Maciver .20 .50
19 Dave Manson .20 .50
20 Brad McCrimmon .20 .50
21 Jim McKenzie .20 .50
22 Teppo Numminen .30 .75
23 Deron Quint .20 .50
24 Jeremy Roenick .75 2.00
25 Jeremy Roenick .75 2.00
26 Jeremy Roenick .75 2.00
27 Cliff Ronning .20 .50
28 Darrin Shannon .20 .50
29 Mike Stapleton .20 .50
30 Keith Tkachuk .75 2.00
31 Keith Tkachuk .75 2.00
32 Oleg Tverdovsky .20 .50
33 Darcy Wakaluk .25 .60
34 Zinetula Bilyaletinov CO .08 .25
34 Don Hay CO .08 .25
34 Paul MacLean CO .08 .25
36 Team Photo .20 .50

2001-02 Coyotes Team Issue

COMPLETE SET (22) 10.00 25.00
1 Drake Berehowsky .40 1.00
2 Sergei Berezin .40 1.00
3 Daniel Briere .75 2.00
4 Sean Burke .75 2.00
5 Shane Doan .75 2.00
6 Robert Esche .75 2.00
7 Michal Handzus .40 1.00
8 Mike Johnson .40 1.00
9 Krys Kolanos 1.25 3.00
10 Daymond Langkow .75 2.00
11 Claude Lemieux .40 1.00
12 Paul Mara .40 1.00
13 Daniil Markov .40 1.00
14 Brad May .40 1.00
15 Ladislav Nagy .40 1.00
16 Teppo Numminen .40 1.00
17 Denis Pederson .40 1.00
18 Todd Simpson .40 1.00
19 Radoslav Suchy .40 1.00
20 Mike Sullivan .40 1.00
21 Ossi Vaananen .40 1.00
22 Landon Wilson .40 1.00

2002-03 Coyotes Team Issue

COMPLETE SET (25) 15.00 30.00
1 Header .10 .25
2 Todd Simpson .40 1.00
3 Ossi Vaananen .40 1.00
4 Drake Berehowsky .40 1.00
5 Deron Quint .40 1.00
6 Daymond Langkow .60 1.50
7 Mike Johnson .40 1.00
8 Radoslav Suchy .40 1.00
9 Kelly Buchberger .40 1.00
10 Ladislav Nagy .75 2.00

11 Shane Doan .75 2.00
12 Paul Mara .40 1.00
13 Teppo Numminen .40 1.00
14 Landon Wilson .40 1.00
15 Branko Radivojevic .60 1.50
16 Brian Boucher .60 1.50
17 Krys Kolanos .40 1.00
18 Andrei Nazarov .40 1.00
19 Brian Savage .40 1.00
20 Danny Markov .40 1.00
21 Sean Burke .75 2.00
22 Benoit Allaire ACO .10 .25
23 Pat Conacher ACO .10 .25
24 Rick Bowness ACO .10 .25
25 Bob Francis CO .10 .25
26 Scott Pellerin .40 1.00
27 Paul Ranheim .40 1.00
28 Zac Bierk .60 1.50
29 Tony Amonte .75 2.00
30 Charlie Simmer ANN .20 .50
31 Curt Keilback ANN .10 .25
32 Ramzi Abid .40 1.00
33 Dan Focht .40 1.00
34 Daniel Briere .75 2.00
35 Brad May .40 1.00

2003-04 Coyotes Postcards

COMPLETE SET (27) 10.00 20.00
1 Zac Bierk .40 1.00
2 Brian Boucher .30 .75
3 Sean Burke .40 1.00
4 Daniel Cleary .20 .50
5 Shane Doan 1.00 2.50
6 Brad Ference .20 .50
7 Dave Tanabe .20 .50
8 Jan Hrdina .20 .50
9 Cale Hulse .20 .50
10 Mike Johnson .20 .50
11 Krystofer Kolanos .20 .50
12 Daymond Langkow .30 .75
13 Paul Mara .20 .50
14 Ladislav Nagy .60 1.50
15 Tyson Nash .40 1.00
16 Andrei Nazarov .20 .50
17 Ivan Novoseltsev .20 .50
18 Branko Radivojevic .40 1.00
19 Brian Savage .20 .50
20 Mike Sillinger .20 .50
21 Fredrik Sjostrom .30 .75
22 Matthew Spiller .20 .50
23 Radoslav Suchy .20 .50
24 Jeff Taffe .20 .50
25 Dave Tanabe .20 .50
26 Ossi Vaananen .20 .50
27 Landon Wilson .20 .50

1924-25 Crescent Falcon-Tigers

COMPLETE SET (13) 1200.00 2400.00
1 Bill Cockburn 112.50 225.00
2 Wally Byron 100.00 200.00
3 Wally Fridfinson 100.00 200.00
4 Murray Murdoch 125.00 250.00
5 Oliver Redpath 100.00 200.00
7 Ward McVey 100.00 200.00
8 Tote Mitchell 100.00 200.00
9 Lorne Carrol 100.00 200.00
10 Tony Wise 100.00 200.00
11 Johnny Myres 100.00 200.00
12 Gordon McKenzie 100.00 200.00
13 Harry Neal 112.50 225.00
14 Blake Watson 112.50 225.00

1923-24 Crescent Selkirks

COMPLETE SET (13) 600.00 1200.00
1 Cliff O'Meara 62.50 125.00
2 Leo Benard 50.00 100.00
3 Pete Speirs 50.00 100.00
4 Howard Brandon 50.00 100.00
5 George A. Clark 50.00 100.00
7 Cecil Browne 50.00 100.00
8 Jack Connelly 50.00 100.00
9 Charlie Gardiner 100.00 200.00
10 Ward Turvey 50.00 100.00
11 Connie Johanneson 50.00 100.00
12 Frank Woodall 50.00 100.00
13 Harold McMunn 50.00 100.00
14 Connie Neil 62.50 125.00

1924-25 Crescent Selkirks

COMPLETE SET (14) 850.00 1700.00
1 Howard Brandon 50.00 100.00
2 Jack Hughes 50.00 100.00
3 Tony Baril 50.00 100.00
4 Bill Bowman 50.00 100.00
5 W. Roberts 50.00 100.00
6 Cecil Browne SP 375.00 750.00
7 Errol Gillis 50.00 100.00
8 Selkirks Team
On The Ice 100.00 200.00
9 Fred Comfort 50.00 100.00
10 Cliff O'Meara 50.00 100.00
11 Leo Benard 50.00 100.00
12 Pete Speirs 50.00 100.00
13 Peter Meurer 50.00 100.00
14 Bill Borland 50.00 100.00

1935-40 Crown Brand Photos

49 Montreal Maroons 1936-37 30.00 60.00
50 Montreal Canadiens 1936-37 30.00 60.00
51 Baldy Northcott 12.50 25.00
52 Dave Trottier 12.50 25.00
53 Russ Blinco 12.50 25.00
54 Earl Robinson Maroons 12.50 25.00
55 Bob Gracie 12.50 25.00
56 Gus Marker 12.50 25.00
57 Howie Morenz 150.00 250.00
58 Johnny Gagnon 12.50 25.00
59 Wilfred Cude 60.00 100.00
60 Georges Mantha 12.50 25.00
61 Paul Haynes 12.50 25.00
62 Marty Barry 20.00 40.00
63 Peter Kelly 12.50 25.00
64 Dave Kerr 12.50 25.00
65 Roy Worters 12.50 25.00
66 Ace Bailey 20.00 40.00
67 Art Lesieur 15.00 30.00
68 Frank Boucher 15.00 30.00
69 Marty Burke 12.50 25.00
70 Alex Levinsky 12.50 25.00
71 Father Leveque's Maple Leafs 40.00 80.00
72 Father Leveque's Six Stars 40.00 80.00
76 Father Leveque's Canadiens 20.00 40.00
77 Stewart Evans 12.50 25.00
78 Herb Cain 12.50 25.00
79 Carl Voss 20.00 40.00
80 Roger Jenkins 12.50 25.00
81 Jack McGill 12.50 25.00
82 Mush March 15.00 30.00
106 Montreal Maroons 1937-38 40.00 80.00
107 Montreal Canadiens 1937-38 30.00 60.00
108 Toe Blake 40.00 80.00
109 Joffre Desilets 12.50 25.00
110 Babe Siebert 20.00 40.00
111 Frank Clancy 300.00 500.00
112 Aurel Joliat 50.00 100.00
113 Walter Buswell 12.50 25.00
114 Bill MacKenzie 12.50 25.00
115 Pit Lepine 12.50 25.00
116 Cliff Goupille 12.50 25.00
117 Rod Lorrain 12.50 25.00
118 Polly Drouin 12.50 25.00
119 Marvin Wentworth 12.50 25.00
120 Allan Shields 12.50 25.00
121 Jimmy Ward 12.50 25.00
122 Bill Beveridge 12.50 25.00
123 Gerry Shannon 12.50 25.00
124 Des Smith 12.50 25.00
125 Armand Mondou 15.00 30.00
151 Montreal Canadiens 1938-39 40.00 80.00
152 Herb Cain 12.50 25.00
153 Bob Gracie 12.50 25.00
154 Jimmy Ward 12.50 25.00
155 Stew Evans 12.50 25.00
156 Louis Trudel 12.50 25.00
157 Cy Wentworth 12.50 25.00
195 Marty Barry 12.50 25.00
196 Earl Robinson Canadiens 12.50 25.00
197 Ray Getliffe 12.50 25.00
198 Charlie Sands 12.50 25.00
199 Claude Bourque 12.50 25.00
200 Doug Young 12.50 25.00
NNO Montreal Canadiens (1935-36) 40.00 80.00
NNO Montreal Canadiens 1939-40 30.00 60.00
NNO Stanley Cup Champs 1934-35 25.00 50.00
NNO Team Canada 1936 20.00 40.00
NNO Album 25.00 50.00

1997-98 Crown Royale

*SILVER: 2X TO 5X BASIC CARDS
*ICEBLUE: 3X TO 8X BSIC CARDS
1 Guy Hebert .25 .60
2 Paul Kariya .30 .75
3 Steve Rucchin .25 .60
4 Tomas Sandstrom .20 .50
5 Teemu Selanne .60 1.50
6 Jason Allison .25 .60
7 Ray Bourque .50 1.25
8 Anson Carter .20 .50
9 Byron Dafoe .20 .50
10 Ted Donato .20 .50
11 Joe Thornton .50 1.25
12 Jason Dawe .20 .50
13 Michal Grosek .20 .50
14 Dominik Hasek .50 1.25
15 Michael Peca .25 .60
16 Miroslav Satan .20 .50
17 Chris Dingman RC .30 .75
18 Theo Fleury .40 1.00
19 Jarome Iginla .40 1.00
20 Tyler Moss RC .25 .60
21 Cory Stillman .25 .60
22 Kevin Dineen .25 .60
23 Nelson Emerson .20 .50
24 Trevor Kidd .20 .50
25 Keith Primeau .25 .60
26 Geoff Sanderson .25 .60
27 Tony Amonte .25 .60
28 Chris Chelios .30 .75
29 Eric Daze .20 .50
30 Jeff Hackett .20 .50
31 Chris Terreri .20 .50
32 Adam Deadmarsh .20 .50
33 Peter Forsberg .60 1.50
34 Valeri Kamensky .25 .60
35 Jari Kurri .30 .75
36 Claude Lemieux .25 .60
37 Patrick Roy .75 2.00
38 Joe Sakic .60 1.50
39 Ed Belfour .30 .75
40 Derian Hatcher .20 .50
41 Mike Modano .50 1.25
42 Joe Nieuwendyk .25 .60
43 Pat Verbeek .25 .60
44 Sergei Zubov .25 .60
45 Sergei Fedorov .50 1.25
46 Vyacheslav Kozlov .25 .60
47 Nicklas Lidstrom .30 .75
48 Darren McCarty .25 .60
49 Chris Osgood .30 .75
50 Brendan Shanahan .30 .75
51 Steve Yzerman .75 2.00
52 Jason Arnott .25 .60
53 Curtis Joseph .40 1.00
54 Ryan Smyth .25 .60
55 Doug Weight .30 .75
56 Dave Gagner .20 .50
57 Ed Jovanovski .20 .50
58 Viktor Kozlov .25 .60
59 Scott Mellanby .25 .60
60 John Vanbiesbrouck .25 .60
61 Kevin Weekes RC .25 .60
62 Rob Blake .30 .75
63 Donald MacLean .20 .50
64 Yanic Perreault .25 .60
65 Luc Robitaille .30 .75
66 Jozef Stumpel .20 .50
67 Shayne Corson .25 .60
68 Vincent Damphousse .25 .60
69 Saku Koivu .30 .75
70 Andy Moog .20 .50
71 Mark Recchi .40 1.00
72 Stephane Richer .20 .50
73 Martin Brodeur .75 2.00
74 Patrik Elias RC .50 1.25
75 Doug Gilmour .40 1.00
76 Bobby Holik .20 .50
77 Scott Stevens .30 .75
78 Bryan Berard .20 .50
79 Zigmund Palffy .30 .75
80 Robert Reichel .25 .60
81 Tommy Salo .20 .50
82 Bryan Smolinski .25 .60
83 Adam Graves .20 .50
84 Wayne Gretzky 2.00 5.00
85 Pat LaFontaine .30 .75
86 Brian Leetch .25 .60
87 Mike Richter .30 .75
88 Niklas Sundstrom .25 .60
89 Daniel Alfredsson .30 .75
90 Alexandre Daigle .20 .50
91 Shawn McEachern .20 .50
92 Chris Phillips .25 .60
93 Ron Tugnutt .30 .75
94 Alexei Yashin .25 .60
95 Rod Brind'Amour .30 .75
96 Chris Gratton .20 .50
97 Ron Hextall .30 .75
98 John LeClair .30 .75
99 Eric Lindros .50 1.25
100 Vaclav Prospal RC .25 .60
101 Dainius Zubrus .25 .60
102 Mike Gartner .40 1.00
103 Brad Isbister .25 .60
104 Nikolai Khabibulin .30 .75
105 Jeremy Roenick .50 1.25
106 Cliff Ronning .20 .50
107 Keith Tkachuk .30 .75
108 Tom Barrasso .25 .60
109 Ron Francis .40 1.00
110 Jaromir Jagr 1.00 2.50
111 Alexei Morozov .25 .60
112 Ed Olczyk .20 .50
113 Jim Campbell .20 .50
114 Pavol Demitra .40 1.00
115 Steve Duchesne .20 .50
116 Grant Fuhr .50 1.25
117 Brett Hull .60 1.50
118 Pierre Turgeon .25 .60
119 Jeff Friesen .25 .60
120 Patrick Marleau .30 .75
121 Owen Nolan .30 .75
122 Marco Sturm RC .75 2.00
123 Mike Vernon .25 .60
124 Dino Ciccarelli .30 .75
125 Roman Hamrlik .20 .50
126 Daren Puppa .25 .60
127 Paul Ysebaert .25 .60
128 Sergei Berezin .25 .60
129 Wendel Clark .50 1.25
130 Alyn McCauley .25 .60
131 Felix Potvin .50 1.25
132 Mats Sundin .30 .75
133 Pavel Bure .30 .75
134 Martin Gelinas .20 .50
135 Trevor Linden .30 .75
136 Mark Messier .60 1.50
137 Alexander Mogilny .25 .60
138 Peter Bondra .30 .75
139 Dale Hunter .25 .60
140 Joe Juneau .20 .50
141 Olaf Kolzig .30 .75
142 Adam Oates .30 .75
143 Jaroslav Svejkovsky .25 .60
144 Richard Zednik .25 .60

1997-98 Crown Royale Blades of Steel Die-Cuts

COMPLETE SET (20) 50.00 125.00
1 Paul Kariya 2.00 5.00
2 Teemu Selanne 2.00 5.00
3 Joe Thornton 4.00 10.00
4 Chris Chelios 1.50 4.00
5 Peter Forsberg 4.00 10.00
6 Patrick Roy 10.00 25.00
7 Mike Modano 2.50 6.00
8 Sergei Fedorov 2.50 6.00
9 Brendan Shanahan 2.00 5.00
10 Steve Yzerman 8.00 20.00
11 Ryan Smyth 1.50 4.00
12 Saku Koivu 2.00 5.00
13 Bryan Berard .75 2.00
14 Wayne Gretzky 12.00 30.00
15 Brian Leetch 1.50 4.00
16 Eric Lindros 2.50 6.00
17 Jaromir Jagr 4.00 10.00
18 Brett Hull 2.50 6.00
19 Pavel Bure 2.00 5.00
20 Mark Messier 2.50 6.00

1997-98 Crown Royale Cramer's Choice Jumbos

COMPLETE SET (10) 15.00 40.00
*GOLD: 1.5X TO 4X BASIC CARDS
1 Paul Kariya 3.00 8.00
2 Teemu Selanne 2.50 6.00
3 Joe Thornton 5.00 12.00
4 Peter Forsberg 3.00 8.00
5 Patrick Roy 6.00 15.00
6 Steve Yzerman 5.00 12.00
7 Wayne Gretzky 8.00 20.00
8 Eric Lindros 3.00 8.00
9 Jaromir Jagr 3.00 8.00
10 Pavel Bure 2.50 6.00

1997-98 Crown Royale Freeze Out Die-Cuts

COMPLETE SET (20) 30.00 80.00
1 Guy Hebert 1.00 2.50
2 Byron Dafoe 1.00 2.50
3 Dominik Hasek 4.00 10.00
4 Tyler Moss 1.00 2.50
5 Patrick Roy 10.00 25.00
6 Ed Belfour 2.00 5.00
7 Chris Osgood 1.00 2.50
8 Curtis Joseph 3.00 8.00
9 John Vanbiesbrouck 2.00 5.00
10 Andy Moog 2.00 5.00
11 Martin Brodeur 6.00 15.00
12 Mike Richter 2.00 5.00
13 Ron Hextall 2.00 5.00
14 Garth Snow 1.00 2.50
15 Nikolai Khabibulin 2.00 5.00
16 Tom Barrasso 1.00 2.50
17 Grant Fuhr 2.00 5.00
18 Mike Vernon 2.00 5.00
19 Felix Potvin 3.00 8.00
20 Olaf Kolzig 2.00 5.00

1997-98 Crown Royale Hat Tricks Die-Cuts

COMPLETE SET (20) 40.00 100.00
1 Paul Kariya 2.50 6.00
2 Teemu Selanne 2.50 6.00
3 Joe Thornton 4.00 10.00
4 Peter Forsberg 4.00 10.00
5 Joe Sakic 5.00 12.00
6 Mike Modano 4.00 10.00
7 Brendan Shanahan 2.50 6.00
8 Steve Yzerman 6.00 15.00
9 Ryan Smyth 1.50 4.00
10 Zigmund Palffy 1.50 4.00
11 Wayne Gretzky 10.00 25.00
12 John LeClair 1.50 4.00
13 Eric Lindros 2.50 6.00
14 Keith Tkachuk 1.50 4.00
15 Jaromir Jagr 4.00 10.00
16 Brett Hull 3.00 8.00
17 Mats Sundin 2.00 5.00
18 Pavel Bure 2.00 5.00
19 Mark Messier 2.00 5.00
20 Peter Bondra 1.50 4.00

1997-98 Crown Royale Lamplighters Cel-Fusion Die-Cuts

COMPLETE SET (20) 40.00 100.00
1 Paul Kariya 2.00 5.00
2 Teemu Selanne 2.00 5.00
3 Joe Thornton 6.00 15.00
4 Michael Peca 1.00 2.50
5 Peter Forsberg 6.00 15.00
6 Joe Sakic 8.00 20.00
7 Mike Modano 4.00 10.00
8 Brendan Shanahan 2.00 5.00
9 Steve Yzerman 12.00 30.00
10 Saku Koivu 2.00 5.00
11 Wayne Gretzky 20.00 50.00
12 Pat LaFontaine 1.00 2.50
13 John LeClair 1.00 2.50
14 Eric Lindros 4.00 10.00
15 Dainius Zubrus 1.00 2.50
16 Keith Tkachuk 2.00 5.00
17 Jaromir Jagr 6.00 15.00
18 Brett Hull 2.00 5.00
19 Pavel Bure 2.00 5.00
20 Mark Messier 4.00 10.00

1998-99 Crown Royale

1 Travis Green .25 .60
2 Guy Hebert .30 .75
3 Paul Kariya .40 1.00
4 Tomas Sandstrom .25 .60
5 Teemu Selanne .75 2.00
6 Jason Allison .30 .75
7 Ray Bourque .60 1.50
8 Byron Dafoe .30 .75
9 Dimitri Khristich .25 .60
10 Sergei Samsonov .30 .75
11 Matthew Barnaby .25 .60
12 Michal Grosek .25 .60
13 Dominik Hasek .60 1.50
14 Michael Peca .25 .60
15 Miroslav Satan .30 .75
16 Andrew Cassels .25 .60
17 Rico Fata .30 .75
18 Theo Fleury .50 1.25
19 Jarome Iginla .50 1.25
20 Martin St. Louis RC 1.25 3.00
21 Ken Wregget .30 .75
22 Ron Francis .50 1.25
23 Arturs Irbe .30 .75
24 Sami Kapanen .25 .60
25 Trevor Kidd .25 .60
26 Keith Primeau .25 .60
27 Tony Amonte .30 .75
28 Chris Chelios .40 1.00
29 Eric Daze .30 .75
30 Doug Gilmour .50 1.25
31 Jocelyn Thibault .30 .75
32 Chris Drury .50 1.25
33 Peter Forsberg .75 2.00
34 Milan Hejduk RC .60 1.50
35 Patrick Roy 1.00 2.50
36 Joe Sakic .75 2.00
37 Ed Belfour .40 1.00
38 Brett Hull .75 2.00
39 Jamie Langenbrunner .25 .60
40 Jere Lehtinen .25 .60
41 Mike Modano .60 1.50
42 Joe Nieuwendyk .30 .75
43 Darryl Sydor .25 .60
44 Sergei Fedorov .60 1.50
45 Nicklas Lidstrom .50 1.25
46 Darren McCarty .25 .60
47 Chris Osgood .40 1.00
48 Brendan Shanahan .40 1.00
49 Steve Yzerman 1.00 2.50
50 Bob Essensa .30 .75
51 Bill Guerin .40 1.00
52 Janne Niinimaa .25 .60
53 Tom Poti .25 .60
54 Ryan Smyth .30 .75
55 Doug Weight .40 1.00
56 Sean Burke .25 .60
57 Dino Ciccarelli .40 1.00
58 Ed Jovanovski .30 .75
59 Viktor Kozlov .30 .75
60 Oleg Kvasha RC .40 1.00
61 Mark Parrish RC .60 1.50
62 Rob Blake .40 1.00
63 Manny Legace .30 .75
64 Yanic Perreault .25 .60
65 Luc Robitaille .40 1.00
66 Jozef Stumpel .25 .60
67 Shayne Corson .30 .75
68 Vincent Damphousse .30 .75
69 Jeff Hackett .25 .60
70 Saku Koivu .40 1.00
71 Mark Recchi .50 1.25
72 Andrew Brunette .30 .75
73 Mike Dunham .30 .75
74 Tom Fitzgerald .30 .75
75 Greg Johnson .25 .60
76 Sergei Krivokrasov .25 .60
77 Jason Arnott .30 .75
78 Martin Brodeur 1.00 2.50
79 Patrik Elias .40 1.00
80 Bobby Holik .25 .60
81 Brendan Morrison .25 .60
82 Bryan Berard .30 .75
83 Trevor Linden .40 1.00
84 Zigmund Palffy .40 1.00
85 Robert Reichel .25 .60
86 Tommy Salo .30 .75
87 Adam Graves .25 .60
88 Wayne Gretzky 2.50 6.00
89 Brian Leetch .30 .75
90 Manny Malhotra .40 1.00
91 Mike Richter .40 1.00
92 Daniel Alfredsson .40 1.00
93 Igor Kravchuk .25 .60
94 Shawn McEachern .25 .60
95 Damian Rhodes .25 .60
96 Alexei Yashin .30 .75
97 Rod Brind'Amour .40 1.00
98 Ron Hextall .40 1.00
99 John LeClair .40 1.00
100 Eric Lindros .60 1.50
101 John Vanbiesbrouck .40 1.00
102 Dainius Zubrus .25 .60
103 Nikolai Khabibulin .40 1.00
104 Jeremy Roenick .60 1.50
105 Keith Tkachuk .40 1.00
106 Rick Tocchet .30 .75
107 Oleg Tverdovsky .40 1.00
108 Tom Barrasso .30 .75
109 Jan Hrdina RC .50 1.25
110 Jaromir Jagr 1.25 3.00
111 Alexei Morozov .25 .60
112 German Titov .25 .60
113 Jim Campbell .25 .60
114 Grant Fuhr .60 1.50
115 Al MacInnis .50 1.25
116 Chris Pronger .40 1.00
117 Pierre Turgeon .30 .75
118 Jeff Friesen .25 .60
119 Patrick Marleau .40 1.00
120 Owen Nolan .40 1.00
121 Marco Sturm .25 .60
122 Mike Vernon .30 .75
123 Wendel Clark .60 1.50
124 Vincent Lecavalier .75 2.00
125 Bill Ranford .30 .75
126 Stephane Richer .25 .60
127 Rob Zamuner .25 .60
128 Sergei Berezin .30 .75
129 Tie Domi .30 .75
130 Mike Johnson .25 .60
131 Curtis Joseph .50 1.25
132 Mats Sundin .40 1.00
133 Donald Brashear .25 .60
134 Pavel Bure .40 1.00
135 Mark Messier .75 2.00
136 Alexander Mogilny .30 .75
137 Bill Muckalt RC .25 .60
138 Mattias Ohlund .25 .60
139 Garth Snow .30 .75
140 Peter Bondra .40 1.00
141 Matthew Herr RC .25 .60
142 Joe Juneau .25 .60
143 Olaf Kolzig .40 1.00
144 Adam Oates .40 1.00

1998-99 Crown Royale Limited Series

*VETERANS: 3X TO 8X BASIC CARDS
*ROOKIES: 2.5X TO 6X BASIC CARDS

1998-99 Crown Royale Cramer's Choice Jumbos

COMPLETE SET (10) 12.00 30.00
*DARK BLUE/35: 10X TO 20X BASIC INSERTS
*GOLD/10: 20X TO 50X BASIC INSERTS
*GREEN/30: 10X TO 25X BASIC INSERTS
*LT.BLUE/20: 15X TO 40X BASIC INSERTS
*RED/25: 10X TO 25X BASIC INSERTS
1 Paul Kariya 1.25 3.00
2 Teemu Selanne 1.25 3.00
3 Dominik Hasek 2.00 5.00
4 Peter Forsberg 2.50 6.00
5 Patrick Roy 3.00 8.00
6 Steve Yzerman 3.00 8.00
7 Martin Brodeur 3.00 8.00
8 Wayne Gretzky 4.00 10.00
9 Eric Lindros 1.25 3.00
10 Jaromir Jagr 1.50 4.00

1998-99 Crown Royale Living Legends

COMPLETE SET (10) 75.00 150.00
1 Paul Kariya 5.00 12.00
2 Teemu Selanne 4.00 10.00
3 Dominik Hasek 8.00 20.00
4 Peter Forsberg 8.00 20.00
5 Patrick Roy 10.00 25.00
6 Steve Yzerman 10.00 25.00
7 Martin Brodeur 8.00 20.00
8 Wayne Gretzky 12.00 30.00
9 Eric Lindros 6.00 15.00
10 Jaromir Jagr 6.00 15.00

1998-99 Crown Royale Master Performers

COMPLETE SET (20) 40.00 100.00
1 Paul Kariya 2.00 5.00
2 Teemu Selanne 2.00 5.00
3 Dominik Hasek 4.00 10.00
4 Peter Forsberg 3.00 8.00
5 Patrick Roy 6.00 15.00
6 Joe Sakic 4.00 10.00
7 Brett Hull 2.50 6.00
8 Mike Modano 3.00 8.00
9 Sergei Fedorov 2.50 6.00
10 Brendan Shanahan 2.00 5.00
11 Steve Yzerman 6.00 15.00
12 Saku Koivu 2.00 5.00
13 Martin Brodeur 5.00 12.00
14 Wayne Gretzky 8.00 20.00
15 John LeClair 1.50 4.00
16 Eric Lindros 2.00 5.00
17 Jaromir Jagr 3.00 8.00
18 Mats Sundin 2.00 5.00
19 Mark Messier 2.00 5.00
20 Peter Bondra 1.50 4.00

1998-99 Crown Royale Pillars of the Game

COMPLETE SET (25) 10.00 20.00
1 Teemu Selanne .30 .75
2 Ray Bourque .50 1.25
3 Michael Peca .25 .60
4 Theo Fleury .25 .60
5 Chris Chelios .30 .75
6 Doug Gilmour .25 .60
7 Patrick Roy 1.50 4.00
8 Joe Sakic .60 1.50
9 Ed Belfour .30 .75
10 Brett Hull .40 1.00
11 Mike Modano .50 1.25
12 Sergei Fedorov .50 1.25
13 Brendan Shanahan .30 .75
14 Steve Yzerman 1.50 4.00
15 Saku Koivu .30 .75
16 Martin Brodeur .75 2.00
17 John LeClair .30 .75
18 Eric Lindros .30 .75
19 John Vanbiesbrouck .25 .60
20 Keith Tkachuk .30 .75
21 Jaromir Jagr .50 1.25
22 Curtis Joseph .30 .75
23 Mats Sundin .30 .75
24 Mark Messier .30 .75
25 Peter Bondra .25 .60

1998-99 Crown Royale Pivotal Players

COMPLETE SET (25) 10.00 20.00
1 Paul Kariya .30 .75
2 Dominik Hasek .60 1.50
3 Michael Peca .25 .60
4 Peter Forsberg .75 2.00
5 Joe Sakic .60 1.50
6 Brett Hull .40 1.00
7 Mike Modano .50 1.25
8 Sergei Fedorov .50 1.25
9 Chris Osgood .25 .60
10 Brendan Shanahan .30 .75
11 Ryan Smyth .25 .60
12 Mark Parrish .40 1.00
13 Saku Koivu .30 .75
14 Martin Brodeur .75 2.00
15 Trevor Linden .30 .75
16 Wayne Gretzky 2.00 5.00
17 Alexei Yashin .25 .60
18 John LeClair .30 .75
19 John Vanbiesbrouck .25 .60
20 Keith Tkachuk .30 .75
21 Vincent Lecavalier .75 2.00
22 Mats Sundin .30 .75
23 Mark Messier .30 .75
24 Peter Bondra .25 .60
25 Olaf Kolzig .25 .60

1998-99 Crown Royale Rookie Class

COMPLETE SET (10) 15.00 40.00
1 Chris Drury 2.00 5.00
2 Milan Hejduk 2.00 5.00
3 Mark Parrish 1.25 3.00
4 Manny Legace 2.00 5.00
5 Brendan Morrison 1.25 3.00
6 Manny Malhotra 1.25 3.00
7 Daniel Briere 2.00 5.00
8 Vincent Lecavalier 4.00 10.00
9 Tomas Kaberle 1.25 3.00
10 Bill Muckalt 1.25 3.00

1999-00 Crown Royale

1 Guy Hebert .40 1.00
2 Paul Kariya .40 1.00
3 Steve Rucchin .40 1.00
4 Teemu Selanne .75 2.00
5 Andrew Brunette .25 .60
6 Scott Fankhouser RC .25 .60
7 Andreas Karlsson SP RC .25 .60
8 Damian Rhodes .25 .60
9 Patrik Stefan SP RC .40 1.00
10 Jason Allison .30 .75
11 Ray Bourque .60 1.50
12 Byron Dafoe .30 .75
13 Mikko Eloranta RC .30 .75
14 Sergei Samsonov .30 .75
15 Joe Thornton .60 1.50
16 Maxim Afinogenov SP .25 .60
17 Martin Biron SP .25 .60
18 Dominik Hasek .60 1.50
19 Michael Peca .25 .60
20 Miroslav Satan .30 .75
21 Valeri Bure .25 .60
22 Grant Fuhr .60 1.50
23 Jarome Iginla .50 1.25
24 Robyn Regehr SP .25 .60
25 Oleg Saprykin SP RC .40 1.00
26 Ron Francis .50 1.25
27 Arturs Irbe .30 .75
28 Sami Kapanen .25 .60
29 Jeff O'Neill .25 .60
30 Tony Amonte .30 .75
31 Kyle Calder SP RC .30 .75
32 Eric Daze .30 .75
33 Doug Gilmour .50 1.25
34 Jocelyn Thibault .30 .75
35 Marc Denis SP .30 .75
36 Chris Drury .30 .75
37 Peter Forsberg .75 2.00
38 Milan Hejduk .30 .75
39 Patrick Roy 1.00 2.50
40 Joe Sakic .75 2.00
41 Alex Tanguay SP .30 .75
42 Ed Belfour .40 1.00
43 Ryan Christie RC .30 .75
44 Brett Hull .75 2.00
45 Jere Lehtinen .30 .75
46 Mike Modano .60 1.50
47 Joe Nieuwendyk .30 .75
48 Chris Chelios .40 1.00
49 Sergei Fedorov .60 1.50
50 Nicklas Lidstrom .40 1.00
51 Chris Osgood .40 1.00
52 Brendan Shanahan .40 1.00
53 Steve Yzerman 1.00 2.50
54 Bill Guerin .40 1.00
55 Tommy Salo .30 .75
56 Alexander Selivanov .25 .60
57 Ryan Smyth .30 .75
58 Doug Weight .40 1.00
59 Pavel Bure .40 1.00
60 Trevor Kidd .25 .60
61 Ivan Novoseltsev SP RC .50 1.25
62 Ray Whitney .30 .75
63 Mike Vernon .30 .75
64 Rob Blake .40 1.00
65 Stephane Fiset .30 .75
66 Zigmund Palffy .40 1.00
67 Luc Robitaille .40 1.00
68 Brian Smolinski .25 .60
69 Jeff Hackett .25 .60
70 Saku Koivu .40 1.00
71 Trevor Linden .40 1.00
72 Brian Savage .25 .60
73 Jose Theodore .40 1.00
74 Mike Dunham .25 .60
75 Sergei Krivokrasov .25 .60
76 David Legwand SP .25 .60
77 Cliff Ronning .25 .60
78 Martin Brodeur 1.00 2.50
79 Patrik Elias .40 1.00
80 Scott Gomez SP .30 .75
81 Bobby Holik .25 .60
82 Claude Lemieux .25 .60
83 Petr Sykora .30 .75
84 Tim Connolly SP .25 .60
85 Mariusz Czerkawski .25 .60
86 Brad Isbister .25 .60
87 Kenny Jonsson .25 .60
88 Roberto Luongo SP .60 1.50
89 Theo Fleury .50 1.25
90 Milan Hnilicka RC .25 .60
91 Brian Leetch .30 .75
92 Mike Richter .40 1.00
93 Michael York SP .25 .60
94 Daniel Alfredsson .40 1.00
95 Radek Bonk .25 .60
96 Mike Fisher SP RC .40 1.00
97 Marian Hossa .40 1.00
98 Joe Juneau .25 .60
99 Ron Tugnutt .30 .75
100 Alexei Yashin .30 .75
101 Simon Gagne SP .40 1.00
102 John LeClair .40 1.00
103 Eric Lindros .60 1.50
104 Keith Primeau .30 .75
105 Mark Recchi .50 1.25
106 John Vanbiesbrouck .40 1.00
107 Travis Green .25 .60
108 Nikolai Khabibulin .40 1.00
109 Jeremy Roenick .60 1.50
110 Keith Tkachuk .40 1.00
111 Tom Barrasso .40 1.00
112 Jaromir Jagr 1.25 3.00
113 Alexei Kovalev .30 .75
114 Robert Lang .25 .60
115 Pavol Demitra .50 1.25
116 Jochen Hecht SP RC .60 1.50
117 Al MacInnis .50 1.25
118 Ladislav Nagy SP RC .25 .60
119 Chris Pronger .40 1.00
120 Roman Turek .30 .75
121 Pierre Turgeon .30 .75
122 Vincent Damphousse .30 .75
123 Jeff Friesen .30 .75
124 Patrick Marleau .40 1.00
125 Owen Nolan .40 1.00
126 Steve Shields .30 .75
127 Dan Cloutier .25 .60
128 Chris Gratton .25 .60
129 Vincent Lecavalier .40 1.00
130 Mike Sillinger .25 .60
131 Nikolai Antropov SP RC 1.00 2.50
132 Sergei Berezin .25 .60
133 Tie Domi .30 .75
134 Curtis Joseph .50 1.25
135 Mats Sundin .40 1.00
136 Steve Kariya SP RC .40 1.00
137 Mark Messier .75 2.00
138 Markus Naslund .40 1.00
139 Peter Schaefer SP .25 .60
140 Garth Snow .30 .75
141 Peter Bondra .40 1.00
142 Jan Bulis .25 .60
143 Olaf Kolzig .40 1.00
144 Adam Oates .40 1.00

1999-00 Crown Royale Limited Series

*LIMITED SER/99: 5X TO 12X BASIC CARDS
*LIMITED SER/99: 3X TO 8X BASIC SP

1999-00 Crown Royale Premiere Date

*PREM.DATE/73: 6X TO 15X BASIC CARDS
*PREM.DATE/73: 4X TO 10X BASIC SP

1999-00 Crown Royale Prospects Parallel

*PROSPECT PAR: 1.2X TO 3X BASIC CARDS

1999-00 Crown Royale Card-Supials

COMP.LARGE SET (20) 20.00 50.00
1 Paul Kariya 1.00 2.50
2 Teemu Selanne 1.00 2.50
3 Patrik Stefan 1.50 4.00
4 Joe Thornton 1.25 3.00
5 Dominik Hasek 2.00 5.00
6 Peter Forsberg 1.50 4.00
7 Patrick Roy 4.00 10.00
8 Alex Tanguay 1.00 2.50
9 Mike Modano 1.50 4.00
10 Brendan Shanahan 1.00 2.50
11 Steve Yzerman 3.00 8.00
12 Pave Bure 1.00 2.50
13 Martin Brodeur 2.50 6.00
14 Scott Gomez 1.00 2.50
15 Roberto Luongo 1.50 4.00
16 Eric Lindros 1.00 2.50
17 John Vanbiesbrouck 1.00 2.50
18 Jaromir Jagr 1.50 4.00
19 Mats Sundin 1.00 2.50
20 Steve Kariya 1.50 4.00

1999-00 Crown Royale Century 21

COMPLETE SET (10) 30.00 60.00
1 Paul Kariya 3.00 8.00
2 Patrik Stefan .75 2.00
3 Chris Drury 2.00 5.00
4 Peter Forsberg 5.00 12.00
5 Pave Bure 3.00 8.00
6 Scott Gomez 1.25 3.00
7 Roberto Luongo 4.00 10.00
8 Marian Hossa 2.00 5.00
9 Jaromir Jagr 5.00 12.00
10 Vincent Lecavalier 3.00 8.00

1999-00 Crown Royale Cramer's Choice Jumbos

COMPLETE SET (10) 15.00 30.00
*DARK BLUE/35: 5X TO 12X BASIC INSERTS
*GREEN/30: 5X TO 12X BASIC INSERTS
*LIGHT BLUE/20: 6X TO 15X BASIC INSERTS
*RED/25: 6X TO 15X BASIC CARDS
1 Paul Kariya 1.00 2.50
2 Teemu Selanne 1.00 2.50
3 Peter Forsberg 2.00 5.00
4 Patrick Roy 3.00 8.00
5 Mike Modano 1.25 3.00
6 Steve Yzerman 3.00 8.00
7 Pave Bure 1.00 2.50
8 Martin Brodeur 3.00 8.00
9 Eric Lindros 1.00 2.50
10 Jaromir Jagr 1.25 3.00

1999-00 Crown Royale Gold Crown Die-Cuts Jumbos

COMPLETE SET (6) 25.00 50.00
1 Teemu Selanne 3.00 8.00
2 Dominik Hasek 3.00 8.00
3 Patrick Roy 8.00 20.00
4 Steve Yzerman 8.00 20.00
5 Martin Brodeur 4.00 10.00
6 John LeClair 2.00 5.00

1999-00 Crown Royale Ice Elite

COMPLETE SET (25) 10.00 20.00
1 Paul Kariya .30 .75
2 Teemu Selanne .30 .75
3 Joe Thornton .50 1.25
4 Dominik Hasek .60 1.50
5 Tony Amonte .25 .60
6 Milan Hejduk .30 .75
7 Patrick Roy 1.50 4.00
8 Joe Sakic .60 1.50
9 Ed Belfour .30 .75
10 Brett Hull .40 1.00
11 Brendan Shanahan .30 .75
12 Steve Yzerman 1.50 4.00
13 Luc Robitaille .25 .60
14 Trevor Linden .25 .60
15 David Legwand .25 .60
16 Martin Brodeur .75 2.00
17 Theo Fleury .25 .60
18 Marian Hossa .30 .75
19 John LeClair .30 .75
20 Mark Recchi .25 .60
21 Jeremy Roenick .40 1.00
22 Owen Nolan .25 .60
23 Vincent Lecavalier .30 .75
24 Curtis Joseph .30 .75
25 Steve Kariya .25 .60

1999-00 Crown Royale International Glory

COMPLETE SET (25) 10.00 20.00
*PASSPORT/20: 30X TO 80X BASIC INSERTS
1 Teemu Selanne .30 .75
2 Patrik Stefan .25 .60
3 Dominik Hasek .60 1.50
4 Arturs Irbe .25 .60
5 Chris Drury .25 .60
6 Peter Forsberg .75 2.00
7 Patrick Roy 1.25 3.00
8 Mike Modano .50 1.25
9 Sergei Fedorov .50 1.25
10 Brendan Shanahan .30 .75
11 Pave Bure .30 .75
12 Zigmund Palffy .25 .60
13 Saku Koivu .30 .75
14 Martin Brodeur .75 2.00
15 Scott Gomez .25 .60
16 Theo Fleury .25 .60
17 Simon Gagne .30 .75
18 Eric Lindros .30 .75
19 John Vanbiesbrouck .30 .75
20 Keith Tkachuk .30 .75
21 Jaromir Jagr .50 1.25
22 Pavol Demitra .25 .60
23 Jochen Hecht .25 .60
24 Jeff Friesen .25 .60
25 Mats Sundin .30 .75

1999-00 Crown Royale Team Captain Die-Cuts

COMPLETE SET (10) 25.00 50.00
1 Paul Kariya 4.00 10.00
2 Ray Bourque 2.50 6.00
3 Joe Sakic 3.00 8.00
4 Steve Yzerman 8.00 20.00
5 Eric Lindros 2.50 6.00
6 Keith Tkachuk 1.50 4.00
7 Jaromir Jagr 2.50 6.00
8 Owen Nolan 1.25 3.00
9 Mats Sundin 1.50 4.00
10 Mark Messier 2.50 6.00

2000-01 Crown Royale

1 Guy Hebert .20 .50
2 Paul Kariya .25 .60
3 Teemu Selanne .50 1.25
4 Donald Audette .20 .50
5 Andrew Brunette .15 .40
6 Damian Rhodes .15 .40
7 Patrik Stefan .20 .50
8 Jason Allison .20 .50
9 Byron Dafoe .20 .50
10 Bill Guerin .25 .60
11 Sergei Samsonov .20 .50
12 Joe Thornton .40 1.00
13 Doug Gilmour .30 .75
14 Chris Gratton .15 .40
15 Dominik Hasek .40 1.00
16 Michael Peca .20 .50
17 Valeri Bure .20 .50
18 Jarome Iginla .30 .75
19 Marc Savard .15 .40
20 Ron Francis .30 .75
21 Arturs Irbe .20 .50
22 Sami Kapanen .15 .40
23 Tony Amonte .20 .50
24 Jocelyn Thibault .20 .50
25 Alexei Zhamnov .20 .50
26 Ray Bourque .40 1.00
27 Chris Drury .20 .50
28 Peter Forsberg .50 1.25
29 Milan Hejduk .20 .50
30 Patrick Roy .60 1.50
31 Joe Sakic .50 1.25
32 Geoff Sanderson .20 .50
33 Ron Tugnutt .20 .50
34 Ed Belfour .25 .60
35 Brett Hull .50 1.25
36 Mike Modano .40 1.00
37 Joe Nieuwendyk .20 .50
38 Sergei Fedorov .40 1.00
39 Chris Osgood .25 .60
40 Brendan Shanahan .25 .60
41 Steve Yzerman .60 1.50
42 Tommy Salo .20 .50
43 Ryan Smyth .20 .50
44 Doug Weight .25 .60
45 Pavel Bure .25 .60
46 Rob Niedermayer .20 .50
47 Ray Whitney .20 .50
48 Stephane Fiset .15 .40
49 Zigmund Palffy .25 .60
50 Luc Robitaille .25 .60
51 Jamie Storr .20 .50
52 Jim Dowd .15 .40
53 Jamie McLennan .15 .40
54 Scott Pellerin .15 .40
55 Saku Koivu .25 .60
56 Martin Rucinsky .15 .40
57 Brian Savage .15 .40
58 Jose Theodore .25 .60
59 Mike Dunham .15 .40
60 David Legwand .25 .60
61 Vitali Yachmenev .15 .40
62 Martin Brodeur .60 1.50
63 Patrik Elias .25 .60
64 Scott Gomez .20 .50
65 Alexander Mogilny .20 .50
66 Tim Connolly .15 .40
67 Brad Isbister .15 .40
68 John Vanbiesbrouck .25 .60
69 Theo Fleury .30 .75
70 Brian Leetch .20 .50
71 Mark Messier .50 1.25
72 Mike Richter .25 .60
73 Daniel Alfredsson .25 .60
74 Radek Bonk .20 .50
75 Marian Hossa .25 .60
76 Patrick Lalime .20 .50
77 Alexei Yashin .20 .50
78 Brian Boucher .20 .50
79 Simon Gagne .25 .60
80 John LeClair .25 .60
81 Eric Lindros .40 1.00
82 Sean Burke .15 .40
83 Shane Doan .20 .50
84 Jeremy Roenick .40 1.00
85 Keith Tkachuk .25 .60
86 Jaromir Jagr .75 2.00
87 Mario Lemieux 1.00 2.50
88 Martin Straka .20 .50
89 Chris Pronger .25 .60
90 Roman Turek .20 .50
91 Pierre Turgeon .20 .50
92 Scott Young .15 .40
93 Patrick Marleau .25 .60
94 Owen Nolan .25 .60
95 Steve Shields .15 .40
96 Vincent Lecavalier .25 .60
97 Fredrik Modin .15 .40
98 Kevin Weekes .15 .40
99 Sergei Berezin .15 .40
100 Curtis Joseph .30 .75
101 Gary Roberts .15 .40
102 Mats Sundin .25 .60
103 Andrew Cassels .15 .40
104 Markus Naslund .25 .60
105 Felix Potvin .40 1.00
106 Peter Bondra .25 .60
107 Olaf Kolzig .25 .60
108 Adam Oates .25 .60
109 Samuel Pahlsson SP 1.25 3.00
110 Tomi Kallio SP 1.25 3.00
111 Andrew Raycroft RC 3.00 8.00
112 Eric Boulton RC 1.25 3.00
113 Dimitri Kalinin SP 1.25 3.00
114 Oleg Saprykin SP 1.25 3.00
115 Josef Vasicek RC 3.00 8.00
116 Shane Willis SP 1.25 3.00
117 Steven McCarthy SP 1.25 3.00
118 David Aebischer RC 2.50 6.00
119 Serge Aubin RC 1.50 4.00
120 Marc Denis SP 1.50 4.00
121 David Vyborny SP 1.25 3.00
122 Marty Turco RC 8.00 20.00
123 Roberto Luongo SP 6.00 15.00
124 Ivan Novoseltsev SP 1.25 3.00
125 Denis Shvidki SP 1.25 3.00
126 Steven Reinprecht RC 2.00 5.00
127 Marian Gaborik RC 8.00 20.00
128 Filip Kuba SP 1.25 3.00
129 Andrei Markov SP 2.50 6.00
130 Scott Hartnell RC 3.00 8.00
131 Colin White RC 1.25 3.00
132 Rick DiPietro RC 2.50 6.00
133 Taylor Pyatt SP 1.25 3.00
134 Martin Havlat RC 4.00 10.00
135 Jani Hurme RC 1.25 3.00
136 Justin Williams RC 3.00 8.00
137 Robert Esche SP 1.25 3.00
138 Milan Kraft SP 1.25 3.00
139 Brent Johnson SP 1.50 4.00
140 Evgeni Nabokov SP 1.50 4.00
141 Sheldon Keefe SP 1.25 3.00
142 Brad Richards SP 2.00 5.00
143 Daniel Sedin SP 2.50 6.00
144 Henrik Sedin SP 2.50 6.00
S1 Rick DiPietro Sample 3.00 8.00

2000-01 Crown Royale Ice Blue

*1-108 BLUE/75: 6X TO 15X BASIC CARDS

2000-01 Crown Royale Limited Series

*1-108 LMTD/25: 15X TO 40X BASIC CARDS

2000-01 Crown Royale Premiere Date

*PREM.DATE/80: 6X TO 15X BASIC CARDS

2000-01 Crown Royale Red

*1-108 RED: .8X TO 2X BASIC CARDS

2000-01 Crown Royale 21st Century Rookies

1 Tomi Kallio .30 .75
2 Andrew Raycroft .75 2.00
3 Eric Boulton .30 .75
4 Oleg Saprykin .30 .75
5 Shane Willis .30 .75
6 Steven McCarthy .30 .75
7 David Aebischer .60 1.50
8 Marc Denis .40 1.00
9 Marty Turco .60 1.50
10 Roberto Luongo .75 2.00
11 Steven Reinprecht .50 1.25
12 Marian Gaborik 1.00 2.50
13 Andrei Markov .60 1.50
14 Colin White .30 .75
15 Rick DiPietro .60 1.50
16 Taylor Pyatt .30 .75
17 Martin Havlat 1.00 2.50
18 Jani Hurme .30 .75
19 Justin Williams .75 2.00
20 Milan Kraft .30 .75
21 Brent Johnson .40 1.00
22 Evgeni Nabokov .40 1.00
23 Brad Richards .50 1.25
24 Daniel Sedin .60 1.50
25 Henrik Sedin .60 1.50

2000-01 Crown Royale Game-Worn Jerseys

1 Byron Dafoe/602 3.00 8.00
2 Valeri Bure/599 3.00 8.00
3 Rico Fata/596 2.50 6.00
4 Phil Housley/599 3.00 8.00
5 Marc Savard/597 2.50 6.00
6 Peter Forsberg/624 8.00 20.00
7 Ed Belfour/608 4.00 10.00
8 Brett Hull/591 8.00 20.00
9 Jamie Langenbrunner/599 3.00 8.00
10 Grant Marshall/593 3.00 8.00
11 Mike Modano/587 6.00 15.00
12 Joe Nieuwendyk/597 3.00 8.00
13 Chris Chelios/1157 4.00 10.00
14 Chris Osgood/592 4.00 10.00
15 Brendan Shanahan/781 4.00 10.00
16 Patric Kjellberg/594 2.50 6.00
17 Mike Richter/596 4.00 10.00
18 Alexei Yashin/946 3.00 8.00
19 Eric Desjardins/594 3.00 8.00
20 John LeClair/594 4.00 10.00
21 Jyrki Lumme/592 2.50 6.00
22 Michal Rozsival/591 2.50 6.00
23 Martin Straka/581 3.00 8.00
24 Mats Sundin/343 4.00 10.00
25 Felix Potvin/585 6.00 15.00

2000-01 Crown Royale Game-Worn Jersey Patches

1 Byron Dafoe/141 6.00 15.00
2 Valeri Bure/145 6.00 15.00
3 Rico Fata/144 5.00 12.00
4 Phil Housley/144 6.00 15.00
5 Marc Savard/144 5.00 12.00
6 Peter Forsberg/141 15.00 40.00
7 Ed Belfour/145 8.00 20.00
8 Brett Hull/144 15.00 40.00
9 Jamie Langenbrunner/143 6.00 15.00
10 Grant Marshall/144 6.00 15.00
11 Mike Modano/143 12.00 30.00
12 Joe Nieuwendyk/142 6.00 15.00
13 Chris Chelios/192 8.00 20.00
14 Chris Osgood/143 8.00 20.00
15 Brendan Shanahan/163 8.00 20.00
16 Patric Kjellberg/136 5.00 12.00
17 Mike Richter/135 8.00 20.00
18 Alexei Yashin/283 6.00 15.00
19 Eric Desjardins/145 6.00 15.00
20 John LeClair/144 8.00 20.00
21 Jyrki Lumme/144 5.00 12.00
22 Michal Rozsival/144 5.00 12.00
23 Martin Straka/144 6.00 15.00
24 Mats Sundin/104 8.00 20.00
25 Felix Potvin/144 12.00 30.00

2000-01 Crown Royale Premium-Sized Game-Worn Jerseys

1 Byron Dafoe/343 10.00 25.00
2 Valeri Bure/349 6.00 15.00
3 Rico Fata/343 6.00 15.00
4 Phil Housley/344 6.00 15.00
5 Marc Savard/343 6.00 15.00
6 Peter Forsberg/95 15.00 40.00
7 Ed Belfour/352 10.00 25.00
8 Brett Hull/317 15.00 40.00
9 Jamie Langenbrunner/338 6.00 15.00
10 Grant Marshall/342 6.00 15.00
11 Mike Modano/320 10.00 25.00
12 Joe Nieuwendyk/333 8.00 20.00
13 Chris Chelios/94 15.00 40.00
14 Chris Osgood/351 8.00 20.00
15 Brendan Shanahan/96 10.00 25.00
16 Patric Kjellberg/327 6.00 15.00
17 Mike Richter/346 10.00 25.00
18 Alexei Yashin/345 6.00 15.00
19 Eric Desjardins/349 6.00 15.00
20 John LeClair/330 6.00 15.00
21 Jyrki Lumme/336 6.00 15.00
22 Michal Rozsival/357 6.00 15.00
23 Martin Straka/334 6.00 15.00
25 Felix Potvin/345 10.00 25.00

2000-01 Crown Royale Game-Worn Jersey Redemptions

1 Stu Barnes/475 6.00 15.00
2 Jarome Iginla/475 6.00 15.00
3 Joe Sakic/475 6.00 12.00
4 David Legwand/475 6.00 15.00
5 Scott Niedermayer/475 8.00 20.00
6 Theo Fleury/475 8.00 20.00
7 Daniel Alfredsson/475 5.00 12.00
8 Jeremy Roenick/475 5.00 12.00
9 Jaromir Jagr/475 12.00 30.00
10 Curtis Joseph/475 6.00 12.00
11 Mario Lemieux/100 30.00 80.00

2000-01 Crown Royale Jewels of the Crown

COMPLETE SET (25) 15.00 40.00
1 Paul Kariya .60 1.50
2 Teemu Selanne .60 1.50
3 Patrik Stefan .40 1.00
4 Jason Allison .40 1.00
5 Joe Thornton 1.00 2.50
6 Dominik Hasek 1.25 3.00
7 Ray Bourque 1.25 3.00
8 Peter Forsberg 1.50 4.00
9 Patrick Roy 3.00 8.00
10 Joe Sakic 1.25 3.00
11 Brett Hull .75 2.00
12 Mike Modano 1.00 2.50
13 Brendan Shanahan 1.00 2.50
14 Steve Yzerman 3.00 8.00
15 Doug Weight .40 1.00
16 Pavel Bure .75 2.00
17 Martin Brodeur 1.50 4.00
18 Mark Messier .75 2.00
19 John LeClair .75 2.00
20 Eric Lindros 1.00 2.50
21 Jaromir Jagr 1.00 2.50
22 Mario Lemieux 4.00 10.00
23 Vincent Lecavalier .60 1.50
24 Curtis Joseph .60 1.50
25 Mats Sundin .60 1.50

2000-01 Crown Royale Landmarks

COMPLETE SET (10) 75.00 150.00
1 Paul Kariya 6.00 15.00
2 Dominik Hasek 10.00 25.00
3 Peter Forsberg 12.50 30.00
4 Patrick Roy 25.00 60.00
5 Steve Yzerman 25.00 60.00
6 Pavel Bure 6.00 15.00
7 Martin Brodeur 12.50 30.00
8 Jaromir Jagr 8.00 20.00
9 Mario Lemieux 30.00 80.00
10 Curtis Joseph 6.00 15.00

2000-01 Crown Royale Now Playing

COMPLETE SET (20) 50.00 100.00
1 Paul Kariya 1.50 4.00
2 Teemu Selanne 1.50 4.00
3 Jason Allison 1.25 3.00
4 Ray Bourque 3.00 8.00
5 Peter Forsberg 3.00 8.00
6 Patrick Roy 8.00 20.00
7 Brett Hull 2.00 5.00
8 Steve Yzerman 6.00 15.00
9 Pavel Bure 2.00 5.00
10 Marian Gaborik 4.00 10.00
11 Martin Brodeur 4.00 10.00
12 Theo Fleury 1.25 3.00
13 John LeClair 1.50 4.00
14 Jaromir Jagr 2.50 6.00
15 Mario Lemieux 8.00 20.00
16 Vincent Lecavalier 1.50 4.00
17 Curtis Joseph 1.50 4.00
18 Mats Sundin 1.50 4.00
19 Daniel Sedin 1.25 3.00
20 Henrik Sedin 1.25 3.00

2001 Crown Royale Calder Collection All-Star Edition

COMPLETE SET (8) 20.00 50.00
*GOLD/1000: .5X TO 1.2X SILVER/2001
C1 David Aebischer 3.00 8.00
C2 Marian Gaborik 4.00 10.00
C3 Rick DiPietro 3.00 8.00
C4 Martin Havlat 4.00 10.00
C5 Evgeni Nabokov 3.00 8.00
C6 Brad Richards 1.50 4.00
C7 Daniel Sedin 1.50 4.00
C8 Henrik Sedin 1.25 3.00

2001-02 Crown Royale

1 Matt Cullen .20 .50
2 Jeff Friesen .20 .50
3 Jean-Sebastien Giguere .30 .75
4 Paul Kariya .30 .75
5 Ray Ferraro .20 .50
6 Dany Heatley .25 .60
7 Milan Hnilicka .25 .60
8 Patrik Stefan .25 .60
9 Byron Dafoe .25 .60
10 Glen Murray .25 .60
11 Brian Rolston .25 .60
12 Sergei Samsonov .25 .60
13 Joe Thornton .50 1.25
14 Stu Barnes .25 .60
15 Martin Biron .25 .60
16 Tim Connolly .20 .50
17 J-P Dumont .20 .50
18 Miroslav Satan .25 .60
19 Craig Conroy .20 .50
20 Jarome Iginla .40 1.00
21 Dean McAmmond .20 .50
22 Derek Morris .20 .50
23 Marc Savard .20 .50
24 Roman Turek .25 .60
25 Ron Francis .40 1.00
26 Arturs Irbe .25 .60
27 Sami Kapanen .20 .50
28 Jeff O'Neill .25 .60
29 Tony Amonte .25 .60
30 Mark Bell .20 .50
31 Kyle Calder .20 .50
32 Eric Daze .25 .60
33 Steve Sullivan .20 .50
34 Jocelyn Thibault .25 .60
35 Rob Blake .30 .75
36 Chris Drury .25 .60
37 Peter Forsberg .60 1.50
38 Milan Hejduk .25 .60
39 Patrick Roy .75 2.00
40 Joe Sakic .60 1.50
41 Alexei Tanguay .25 .60
42 Marc Denis .25 .60
43 Rostislav Klesla .20 .50
44 Geoff Sanderson .20 .50
45 Ron Tugnutt .25 .60
46 Ed Belfour .30 .75
47 Jere Lehtinen .25 .60
48 Mike Modano .50 1.25
49 Joe Nieuwendyk .25 .60
50 Pierre Turgeon .25 .60
51 Sergei Fedorov .50 1.25
52 Dominik Hasek .50 1.25
53 Brett Hull .60 1.50
54 Nicklas Lidstrom .30 .75
55 Luc Robitaille .30 .75
56 Brendan Shanahan .30 .75
57 Steve Yzerman .75 2.00
58 Anson Carter .25 .60
59 Daniel Cleary .25 .60
60 Mike Comrie .25 .60
61 Tommy Salo .25 .60
62 Ryan Smyth .25 .60
63 Pavel Bure .30 .75
64 Viktor Kozlov .20 .50
65 Roberto Luongo .50 1.25
66 Jason Allison .25 .60
67 Adam Deadmarsh .20 .50
68 Steve Heinze .20 .50
69 Zigmund Palffy .30 .75
70 Felix Potvin .50 1.25
71 Andrew Brunette .20 .50
72 Jim Dowd .20 .50
73 Manny Fernandez .20 .50
74 Marian Gaborik .30 .75
75 Doug Gilmour .40 1.00
76 Jeff Hackett .25 .60
77 Yanic Perreault .20 .50
78 Brian Savage .20 .50
79 Jose Theodore .30 .75
80 Mike Dunham .25 .60
81 David Legwand .25 .60
82 Cliff Ronning .20 .50
83 Scott Walker .20 .50
84 Jason Arnott .25 .60
85 Martin Brodeur .75 2.00
86 Patrik Elias .30 .75
87 Scott Stevens .30 .75
88 Petr Sykora .20 .50
89 Rick DiPietro .25 .60
90 Chris Osgood .30 .75
91 Mark Parrish .20 .50
92 Mike Peca .25 .60
93 Alexei Yashin .25 .60
94 Theo Fleury .40 1.00
95 Brian Leetch .25 .60
96 Eric Lindros .50 1.25
97 Mark Messier .60 1.50
98 Mike Richter .30 .75
99 Daniel Alfredsson .30 .75
100 Martin Havlat .25 .60
101 Marian Hossa .30 .75
102 Patrick Lalime .25 .60
103 Todd White .20 .50
104 Brian Boucher .25 .60
105 Roman Cechmanek .25 .60
106 Simon Gagne .30 .75
107 John LeClair .30 .75
108 Mark Recchi .40 1.00
109 Jeremy Roenick .50 1.25
110 Daniel Briere .25 .60
111 Sean Burke .20 .50
112 Shane Doan .25 .60
113 Claude Lemieux .25 .60
114 Johan Hedberg .25 .60
115 Alexei Kovalev .25 .60
116 Roberto Lang .20 .50
117 Mario Lemieux 1.25 3.00
118 Pavol Demitra .40 1.00
119 Brent Johnson .25 .60
120 Chris Pronger .30 .75
121 Keith Tkachuk .30 .75
122 Doug Weight .30 .75
123 Vincent Damphousse .25 .60
124 Evgeni Nabokov .25 .60
125 Owen Nolan .30 .75
126 Teemu Selanne .60 1.50
127 Nikolai Khabibulin .30 .75
128 Vincent Lecavalier .30 .75
129 Brad Richards .30 .75
130 Martin St. Louis .30 .75
131 Curtis Joseph .40 1.00
132 Alexander Mogilny .25 .60
133 Gary Roberts .20 .50
134 Mats Sundin .30 .75
135 Darcy Tucker .20 .50
136 Dan Cloutier .25 .60
137 Brendan Morrison .25 .60
138 Markus Naslund .30 .75
139 Daniel Sedin .40 1.00
140 Henrik Sedin .40 1.00
141 Peter Bondra .30 .75
142 Jaromir Jagr 1.00 2.50
143 Olaf Kolzig .30 .75
144 Adam Oates .30 .75
145 Ilja Bryzgalov RC 6.00 15.00
146 Timo Parssinen RC 3.00 8.00
147 Ilya Kovalchuk RC 15.00 40.00
148 Brian Pothier RC 2.50 6.00
149 Jukka Hentunen RC 2.50 6.00
150 Erik Cole RC 5.00 12.00
151 Vaclav Nedorost RC 2.50 6.00
152 Brian Gionta 3.00 8.00
153 Mathieu Darche RC 4.00 10.00
154 Jody Shelley RC 3.00 8.00
155 Martin Spanhel RC 2.50 6.00
156 Niko Kapanen RC 4.00 10.00
157 Pavel Datsyuk RC 15.00 40.00
158 Jason Chimera RC 2.50 6.00
159 Ty Conklin RC 4.00 10.00
160 Jussi Markkanen 2.50 6.00
161 Niklas Hagman RC 3.00 8.00
162 Kristian Huselius RC 4.00 10.00
163 Jaroslav Bednar RC 2.50 6.00
164 David Cullen RC 2.50 6.00
165 Pascal Dupuis RC 4.00 10.00
166 Nick Schultz RC 2.50 6.00
167 Martin Erat RC 3.00 8.00
168 Andreas Salomonsson RC 2.50 6.00
169 Radek Martinek RC 2.50 6.00
170 Raffi Torres RC 4.00 10.00
171 Dan Blackburn RC 3.00 8.00
172 Chris Neil RC 3.00 8.00
173 Jiri Dopita RC 2.50 6.00
174 Krystofer Kolanos RC 2.50 6.00
175 Billy Tibbetts RC 2.50 6.00
176 Mark Rycroft RC 3.00 8.00
177 Jeff Jillson RC 2.50 6.00
178 Nikita Alexeev RC 2.50 6.00
179 Chris Corrinet RC 2.50 6.00
180 Brian Sutherby RC 2.50 6.00

2001-02 Crown Royale Premiere Date

*PREM.DATE/60: 5X TO 12X BASIC CARDS
97 Mark Messier 10.00 25.00

2001-02 Crown Royale Retail Green

*RETAIL: .5X TO 1.2X HOBBY
97 Mark Messier 1.00 2.50

2001-02 Crown Royale All-Star Honors

COMPLETE SET (1-20) 20.00 50.00
1 Paul Kariya 2.00 5.00
2 Roman Turek 1.50 4.00
3 Rob Blake 1.50 4.00
4 Patrick Roy 10.00 25.00
5 Joe Sakic 4.00 10.00
6 Mike Modano 3.00 8.00
7 Dominik Hasek 4.00 10.00
8 Brett Hull 2.50 6.00
9 Brendan Shanahan 3.00 8.00
10 Steve Yzerman 10.00 25.00
11 Pavel Bure 3.00 8.00
12 Martin Brodeur 5.00 12.00
13 Patrik Elias 1.50 4.00
14 Alexei Yashin 1.50 4.00
15 Eric Lindros 3.00 8.00
16 Mark Messier 2.50 6.00
17 Mario Lemieux 12.50 30.00
18 Doug Weight 1.50 4.00
19 Curtis Joseph 2.00 5.00
20 Mats Sundin 2.00 5.00

2001-02 Crown Royale Crowning Achievement

COMPLETE SET (20) 15.00 40.00
1 Dany Heatley 2.00 5.00
2 Ilya Kovalchuk 8.00 10.00
3 Mark Bell .75 2.00
4 Rostislav Klesla .75 2.00
5 Kristian Huselius .75 2.00
6 Martin Erat .75 2.00
7 Rick Dipietro 1.25 3.00
8 Dan Blackburn .75 2.00
9 Krystofer Kolanos .75 2.00
10 Johan Hedberg .75 2.00
11 Jarome Iginla 2.50 6.00
12 Patrick Roy 6.00 15.00
13 Joe Sakic 2.00 5.00
14 Dominik Hasek 2.50 6.00
15 Steve Yzerman 4.00 10.00
16 Pavel Bure 1.25 3.00
17 Martin Brodeur 3.00 8.00
18 Eric Lindros 1.25 3.00
19 Mario Lemieux 6.00 15.00
20 Jaromir Jagr 2.00 5.00

2001-02 Crown Royale Jewels of the Crown

COMPLETE SET (1-30) 40.00 100.00
1 Paul Kariya 1.00 2.50
2 Joe Thornton 2.00 5.00
3 Jarome Iginla 1.50 4.00
4 Roman Turek .75 2.00
5 Jeff O'Neill .75 2.00
6 Peter Forsberg 2.00 5.00
7 Patrick Roy 6.00 15.00
8 Joe Sakic 2.50 6.00
9 Mike Modano 1.50 4.00
10 Dominik Hasek 2.50 6.00
11 Brendan Shanahan 1.25 3.00
12 Steve Yzerman 4.00 10.00
13 Ryan Smyth .75 2.00
14 Pavel Bure 1.25 3.00
15 Jason Allison .75 2.00
16 Marian Gaborik 2.00 5.00
17 Saku Koivu 1.00 2.50
18 Martin Brodeur 3.00 8.00
19 Patrik Elias .75 2.00
20 Alexei Yashin .75 2.00
21 Eric Lindros 1.25 3.00
22 Mark Messier 1.50 4.00
23 Marian Hossa 1.00 2.50
24 Jeremy Roenick 1.25 3.00
25 Mario Lemieux 6.00 15.00
26 Keith Tkachuk 1.00 2.50
27 Teemu Selanne 1.00 2.50
28 Curtis Joseph 1.00 2.50
29 Mats Sundin 1.00 2.50
30 Jaromir Jagr 2.00 5.00

2001-02 Crown Royale Legendary Heroes

1 Paul Kariya 20.00 50.00
2 Patrick Roy 30.00 80.00
3 Dominik Hasek 12.50 30.00
4 Steve Yzerman 40.00 100.00
5 Martin Brodeur 20.00 50.00
6 Eric Lindros 12.50 30.00
7 Mark Messier 10.00 25.00
8 Mario Lemieux 50.00 125.00
9 Curtis Joseph 10.00 25.00
10 Jaromir Jagr 15.00 40.00

2001-02 Crown Royale Rookie Royalty

COMPLETE SET (1-20) 10.00 25.00
1 Dany Heatley 4.00 10.00
2 Ilya Kovalchuk 8.00 20.00
3 Erik Cole 1.50 4.00
4 Mark Bell .75 2.00
5 Vaclav Nedorost .75 2.00
6 Brian Willsie .75 2.00
7 Rostislav Klesla .75 2.00
8 Pavel Datsyuk 8.00 20.00
9 Ty Conklin .75 2.00
10 Kristian Huselius .75 2.00
11 Jaroslav Bednar .75 2.00
12 Martin Erat .75 2.00
13 Rick Dipietro 2.00 5.00
14 Dan Blackburn .75 2.00
15 Krystofer Kolanos .75 2.00
16 Kris Beech .75 2.00
17 Johan Hedberg .75 2.00
18 Toby Petersen .75 2.00
19 Jeff Jillson .75 2.00
20 Nikita Alexeev .75 2.00

2001-02 Crown Royale Triple Threads

1 Anaheim Mighty Ducks 3.00 8.00
2 Calgary Flames 2.50 6.00
3 Samsonov/V.Bure/Zubov 2.50 6.00
4 Giguere/Theodore/Roy 8.00 20.00
5 Buffalo Sabres 2.00 5.00
6 Calder/Dandenault/Daze 2.50 6.00
7 Colorado Avalanche 8.00 20.00
8 Dallas Stars 5.00 12.00
9 Iginla/Hecht/Cassels 4.00 10.00
10 Nashville Predators 2.00 5.00
11 Yzerman/Sakic/Lindros 8.00 20.00
12 Koivu/Sundin/Turek 3.00 8.00
13 Niedermayer/Terreri/Malholtra 3.00 8.00
14 Czerkawski/Lindgren/Alatalo 2.00 5.00
15 New York Rangers 4.00 10.00
16 Nashville Predators 2.50 6.00
17 Pittsburgh Penguins 12.00 30.00
18 Young/McLennan/Eastwood 2.00 5.00
19 St. Louis Blues 2.50 6.00
20 Bondra/Jagr/Straka 10.00 25.00

2001 Crown Royale Toronto Expo Rookie Collection

COMPLETE SET (8) 32.00 80.00
G1 Marty Turco 4.80 12.00
G2 Mike Comrie 10.00 25.00
G3 Rick DiPietro 6.00 15.00
G4 Martin Havlat 8.00 20.00
G5 Roman Cechmanek 4.00 10.00
G6 Brent Johnson 3.20 8.00
G7 Evgeni Nabokov 4.00 10.00
G8 Brad Richards 4.00 10.00

2002-03 Crown Royale

1 Jean-Sebastien Giguere .40 1.00
2 Paul Kariya .40 1.00
3 Adam Oates .40 1.00
4 Dany Heatley .30 .75
5 Ilya Kovalchuk .50 1.25
6 Glen Murray .30 .75
7 Sergei Samsonov .30 .75
8 Steve Shields .30 .75
9 Joe Thornton .60 1.50
10 Martin Biron .30 .75
11 Chris Gratton .25 .60
12 Miroslav Satan .40 1.00
13 Chris Drury .40 1.00
14 Jarome Iginla .50 1.25
15 Roman Turek .40 1.00
16 Rod Brind'Amour .40 1.00
17 Ron Francis .50 1.25
18 Arturs Irbe .30 .75
19 Jeff O'Neill .25 .60
20 Eric Daze .25 .60
21 Jocelyn Thibault .30 .75
22 Alexei Zhamnov .30 .75
23 Peter Forsberg .75 2.00
24 Milan Hejduk .30 .75
25 Patrick Roy 1.00 2.50
26 Joe Sakic .75 2.00
27 Andrew Cassels .25 .60
28 Marc Denis .30 .75
29 Bill Guerin .40 1.00
30 Mike Modano .60 1.50
31 Marty Turco .40 1.00
32 Sergei Fedorov .60 1.50
33 Brett Hull .75 2.00
34 Curtis Joseph .50 1.25
35 Nicklas Lidstrom .40 1.00
36 Brendan Shanahan .40 1.00
37 Steve Yzerman 1.00 2.50
38 Anson Carter .30 .75
39 Mike Comrie .40 1.00
40 Tommy Salo .30 .75
41 Ryan Smyth .30 .75
42 Kristian Huselius .25 .60
43 Roberto Luongo .60 1.50
44 Jason Allison .30 .75
45 Zigmund Palffy .40 1.00
46 Felix Potvin .60 1.50
47 Manny Fernandez .25 .60
48 Marian Gaborik .40 1.00
49 Bill Muckalt .25 .60
50 Jeff Hackett .30 .75
51 Saku Koivu .40 1.00
52 Jose Theodore .40 1.00
53 Richard Zednik .25 .60
54 David Legwand .30 .75
55 Tomas Vokoun .30 .75
56 Martin Brodeur 1.00 2.50
57 Patrik Elias .40 1.00
58 Scott Gomez .30 .75
59 Joe Nieuwendyk .30 .75
60 Chris Osgood .40 1.00
61 Michael Peca .30 .75
62 Alexei Yashin .30 .75
63 Pavel Bure .40 1.00
64 Eric Lindros .60 1.50
65 Mike Richter .40 1.00
66 Daniel Alfredsson .40 1.00
67 Marian Hossa .40 1.00
68 Patrick Lalime .30 .75
69 Roman Cechmanek .30 .75
70 Simon Gagne .40 1.00
71 John LeClair .40 1.00
72 Jeremy Roenick .60 1.50
73 Tony Amonte .30 .75
74 Daniel Briere .30 .75

75 Sean Burke .25 .60
76 Johan Hedberg .40 1.00
77 Alexei Kovalev .30 .75
78 Mario Lemieux 1.50 4.00
79 Alexei Morozov .25 .60
80 Pavol Demitra .50 1.25
81 Brent Johnson .30 .75
82 Keith Tkachuk .40 1.00
83 Doug Weight .40 1.00
84 Vincent Damphousse .30 .75
85 Evgeni Nabokov .30 .75
86 Teemu Selanne .75 2.00
87 Nikolai Khabibulin .40 1.00
88 Vincent Lecavalier .40 1.00
89 Martin St. Louis .40 1.00
90 Ed Belfour .40 1.00
91 Trevor Kidd .25 .60
92 Alexander Mogilny .30 .75
93 Mats Sundin .40 1.00
94 Todd Bertuzzi .40 1.00
95 Dan Cloutier .30 .75
96 Brendan Morrison .30 .75
97 Markus Naslund .40 1.00
98 Peter Bondra .40 1.00
99 Jaromir Jagr 1.25 3.00
100 Olaf Kolzig .40 1.00
101 Stanislav Chistov RC .60 1.50
102 Martin Gerber RC 1.00 2.50
103 Alexei Smirnov RC .75 2.00
104 Tim Thomas RC 2.50 6.00
105 Ryan Miller RC 4.00 10.00
106 Chuck Kobasew RC .75 2.00
107 Jordan Leopold RC 1.00 2.50
108 Pascal Leclaire RC .75 2.00
109 Rick Nash RC 4.00 10.00
110 Lasse Pirjeta RC .60 1.50
111 Steve Ott RC .60 1.50
112 Dmitri Bykov RC .60 1.50
113 Henrik Zetterberg RC 6.00 15.00
114 Ales Hemsky RC 2.50 6.00
115 Jay Bouwmeester RC 2.00 5.00
116 Ivan Majesky RC .60 1.50
117 Mike Cammalleri RC 2.00 5.00
118 Alexander Frolov RC 1.50 4.00
119 P-M Bouchard RC 1.00 2.50
120 Stephane Veilleux RC .60 1.50
121 Kyle Wanvig SP .60 1.50
122 Sylvain Blouin RC .60 1.50
123 Ron Hainsey RC .60 1.50
124 Adam Hall RC .60 1.50
125 Scottie Upshall RC .75 2.00
126 Ray Schultz RC .60 1.50
127 Jason Spezza RC 4.00 10.00
128 Anton Volchenkov RC .60 1.50
129 Dennis Seidenberg RC 1.00 2.50
130 Patrick Sharp RC 2.00 5.00
131 Radovan Somik RC .60 1.50
132 Jeff Taffe RC .60 1.50
133 Dick Tarnstrom RC .60 1.50
134 Tom Koivisto RC .60 1.50
135 Curtis Sanford RC 1.00 2.50
136 Lynn Loyns RC .60 1.50
137 Alexander Svitov RC .60 1.50
138 Carlo Colaiacovo RC 1.00 2.50
139 Steve Eminger RC .60 1.50
140 Alex Henry RC .75 2.00

2002-03 Crown Royale Blue

*1-100 VETS: 1.2X TO 3X BASIC CARDS
*101-140 ROOKIES/350: .5X TO 1.2X

2002-03 Crown Royale Purple

*101-140 PURPLE/799: .4X TO 1X BASIC CARDS

2002-03 Crown Royale Red

*1-100 VETS: .8X TO 2X BASIC CARDS
*101-140 ROOKIES/350: .5X TO 1.2X

2002-03 Crown Royale Retail

*1-100 VETS: .4X TO 1X HOBBY
*101-140 ROKIE SP: .3X TO .8X HOB

2002-03 Crown Royale Jerseys

*GOLD/25: .8X TO 2X BASE JSY
1 Dany Heatley/755 5.00 12.00
2 Ilya Kovalchuk/762 8.00 20.00
3 Joe Sakic/513 6.00 15.00
4 Geoff Sanderson/758 4.00 10.00
5 Marty Turco/763 4.00 10.00
6 Mike Comrie/762 4.00 10.00
7 Valeri Bure/760 4.00 10.00
8 Zigmund Palffy/512 4.00 10.00
9 Jose Theodore/746 4.00 10.00
10 Martin Brodeur/511 10.00 25.00
11 Patrik Elias/503 4.00 10.00
12 Mike Peca/762 4.00 10.00
13 Brian Leetch/762 4.00 10.00
14 Martin Havlat/757 4.00 10.00
15 Jeremy Roenick/746 4.00 10.00
16 Mario Lemieux/752 10.00 25.00
17 Alexei Morozov/753 4.00 10.00
18 Chris Pronger/763 4.00 10.00
19 Sergei Varlamov/757 4.00 10.00
20 Owen Nolan/513 4.00 10.00
21 Fredrik Modin/759 4.00 10.00
22 Alexander Mogilny/762 4.00 10.00
23 Markus Naslund/754 4.00 10.00
24 Peter Bondra/761 4.00 10.00
25 Jaromir Jagr/763 8.00 20.00

2002-03 Crown Royale Dual Patches

1 Heatley/I.Kovalchuk/63 25.00 60.00
2 M.Biron/J-P Dumont/273 10.00 25.00
3 R.Brind'Amour/E.Cole/203 12.50 30.00
4 Zhamnov/S.Sullivan/209 8.00 20.00
5 P.Roy/P.Forsberg SP 40.00 100.00
6 J.Sakic/A.Tanguay/228 15.00 40.00
7 Sanderson/R.Klesla/403 10.00 25.00
8 Modano/P.Turgeon/133 15.00 40.00
9 Fedorov/L.Robitaille/177 15.00 40.00
10 T.Salo/R.Smyth/188 10.00 25.00
11 V.Bure/K.Huselius/403 10.00 25.00
12 Deadmarsh/Smolinski/403 10.00 25.00
13 Gaborik/Fernandez/303 15.00 40.00
14 M.Brodeur/P.Elias/153 25.00 60.00
15 M.Peca/A.Yashin/253 10.00 25.00
16 B.Leetch/M.Richter/213 15.00 40.00
17 M.Lemieux/Morozov/203 25.00 60.00
18 A.Kovalev/M.Straka/403 20.00 50.00
19 E.Nabokov/P.Marleau/163 15.00 40.00
20 Khabibulin/B.Richards/303 15.00 40.00
21 A.Mogilny/D.Tucker/203 12.50 30.00
22 D.Sedin/H.Sedin/243 20.00 50.00
23 P.Bondra/O.Kolzig/347 10.00 25.00

2002-03 Crown Royale Coats of Armor

COMPLETE SET (10) 8.00 20.00
COMMON CARD (1-10) .60 1.50
1 Patrick Roy 4.00 10.00
2 Marty Turco .60 1.50
3 Curtis Joseph .75 2.00
4 Roberto Luongo 1.50 3.50
5 Jose Theodore .60 1.50
6 Martin Brodeur 3.00 8.00
7 Mike Richter .75 2.00
8 Patrick Lalime .60 1.50
9 Nikolai Khabibulin .60 1.50
10 Ed Belfour .75 2.00

2002-03 Crown Royale Lords of the Rink

COMPLETE SET (20) 25.00 60.00
1 Paul Kariya .75 2.00
2 Dany Heatley .75 2.00
3 Ilya Kovalchuk 1.00 2.50
4 Joe Thornton 1.25 3.00
5 Jarome Iginla 1.00 2.50
6 Peter Forsberg 2.00 5.00
7 Joe Sakic 1.50 4.00
8 Mike Modano 1.25 3.00
9 Brendan Shanahan .75 2.00
10 Steve Yzerman 3.00 8.00
11 Zigmund Palffy .40 1.00
12 Marian Gaborik 1.50 4.00
13 Saku Koivu .75 2.00
14 Pavel Bure .75 2.00
15 Eric Lindros 1.00 2.50
16 Mario Lemieux 4.00 10.00
17 Teemu Selanne 1.00 2.50
18 Vincent Lecavalier .75 2.00
19 Mats Sundin .75 2.00
20 Jaromir Jagr 1.25 3.00

2002-03 Crown Royale Rookie Royalty

COMPLETE SET (20) 12.00 25.00
1 Stanislav Chistov .30 .75
2 Martin Gerber .50 1.25
3 Alexei Smirnov .40 1.00
4 Ivan Huml .30 .75
5 Chuck Kobasew .40 1.00
6 Tyler Arnason .50 1.25
7 Rick Nash 2.00 5.00
8 Dmitri Bykov .30 .75
9 Henrik Zetterberg 3.00 8.00
10 Ales Hemsky 1.25 3.00
11 Jay Bouwmeester 1.00 2.50
12 Stephen Weiss .50 1.25
13 Alexander Frolov .75 2.00
14 Scottie Upshall .40 1.00
15 Justin Mapletoft .30 .75
16 Jamie Lundmark .40 1.00
17 Jason Spezza 2.00 5.00
18 Petr Cajanek .30 .75
19 Jonathan Cheechoo .40 1.00
20 Alexander Svitov .30 .75

2002-03 Crown Royale Royal Portraits

1 Paul Kariya 2.50 6.00
2 Ilya Kovalchuk 3.00 8.00
3 Patrick Roy 10.00 25.00
4 Joe Sakic 5.00 12.00
5 Rick Nash 10.00 25.00
6 Steve Yzerman 6.00 15.00
7 Martin Brodeur 6.00 15.00
0 Jason Spezza 10.00 25.00
9 Mario Lemieux 10.00 25.00
10 Jaromir Jagr 6.00 15.00

2003-04 Crown Royale

COMP.SET w/o SP's (100) 20.00 50.00
1 Sergei Fedorov .75 2.00
2 Martin Gerber .30 .75
3 Jean-Sebastien Giguere .50 1.25
4 Ilya Kovalchuk .50 1.25
5 Pasi Nurminen .40 1.00
6 Marc Savard .30 .75
7 Glen Murray .40 1.00
8 Felix Potvin .75 2.00
9 Joe Thornton .75 2.00
10 Martin Biron .40 1.00
11 J-P Dumont .30 .75
12 Taylor Pyatt .30 .75
13 Jarome Iginla .60 1.50
14 Chuck Kobasew .30 .75
15 Roman Turek .40 1.00
16 Erik Cole .30 .75
17 Jeff O'Neill .30 .75
18 Kevin Weekes .40 1.00
19 Tyler Arnason .30 .75
20 Brett McLean .30 .75
21 Jocelyn Thibault .40 1.00
22 David Aebischer .40 1.00
23 Peter Forsberg 1.00 2.50
24 Milan Hejduk .40 1.00
25 Paul Kariya .50 1.25
26 Joe Sakic 1.00 2.50
27 Philippe Sauve .40 1.00
28 Marc Denis .40 1.00
29 Todd Marchant .30 .75
30 Rick Nash .50 1.25
31 Jason Arnott .40 1.00
32 Bill Guerin .50 1.25
33 Mike Modano .75 2.00
34 Marty Turco .50 1.25
35 Dominik Hasek .75 2.00
36 Nicklas Lidstrom .50 1.25
37 Brendan Shanahan .50 1.25
38 Ray Whitney .40 1.00
39 Steve Yzerman 1.25 3.00
40 Georges Laraque .40 1.00
41 Tommy Salo .40 1.00
42 Ryan Smyth .40 1.00
43 Jay Bouwmeester .30 .75
44 Olli Jokinen .50 1.25
45 Roberto Luongo .75 2.00
46 Jason Allison .40 1.00
47 Roman Cechmanek .40 1.00
48 Ziggy Palffy .50 1.25
49 Luc Robitaille .50 1.25
50 Pierre-Marc Bouchard .50 1.25
51 Marian Gaborik .50 1.25
52 Dwayne Roloson .40 1.00
53 Mathieu Garon .30 .75
54 Saku Koivu .50 1.25
55 Mike Ribeiro .30 .75
56 Jose Theodore .50 1.25
57 Scottie Upshall .40 1.00
58 Tomas Vokoun .40 1.00
59 Martin Brodeur 1.25 3.00
60 Patrik Elias .50 1.25
61 Jeff Friesen .30 .75
62 Scott Gomez .40 1.00
63 Mariusz Czerkawski .30 .75
64 Jason Blake .30 .75
65 Rick DiPietro .40 1.00
66 Mike Dunham .40 1.00
67 Alex Kovalev .40 1.00
68 Mark Messier 1.00 2.50
69 Daniel Alfredsson .50 1.25
70 Marian Hossa .50 1.25
71 Patrick Lalime .40 1.00
72 Jason Spezza .50 1.25
73 Jeff Hackett .40 1.00
74 Mark Recchi .60 1.50
75 Jeremy Roenick .75 2.00
76 Justin Williams .40 1.00
77 Sean Burke .30 .75
78 Ladislav Nagy .30 .75
79 Rico Fata .30 .75
80 Mario Lemieux 2.00 5.00
81 Chris Osgood .50 1.25
82 Chris Pronger .50 1.25
83 Keith Tkachuk .50 1.25
84 Doug Weight .50 1.25
85 Jonathan Cheechoo .40 1.00
86 Alyn McCauley .30 .75
87 Evgeni Nabokov .40 1.00
88 Nikolai Khabibulin .50 1.25
89 Vincent Lecavalier .50 1.25
90 Brad Richards .50 1.25
91 Martin St. Louis .50 1.25
92 Ed Belfour .50 1.25
93 Alexander Mogilny .40 1.00
94 Owen Nolan .50 1.25
95 Mats Sundin .50 1.25
96 Todd Bertuzzi .50 1.25
97 Jason King .30 .75
98 Markus Naslund .50 1.25
99 Jaromir Jagr 1.50 4.00
100 Olaf Kolzig .50 1.25
101 Garrett Burnett RC 1.00 2.50
102 Joffrey Lupul RC 2.50 6.00
103 Patrice Bergeron RC 15.00 40.00
104 Sergei Zinovjev RC 1.00 2.50
105 Brent Krahn RC 1.00 2.50
106 Matthew Lombardi RC 1.25 3.00
107 Eric Staal RC 6.00 15.00
108 Tuomo Ruutu RC 1.50 4.00
109 Pavel Vorobiev RC 1.25 3.00
110 John-Michael Liles RC 1.25 3.00
111 Cody McCormick RC 1.25 3.00
112 Dan Fritsche RC 1.00 2.50
113 Nikolai Zherdev RC 2.00 5.00
114 Trevor Daley RC 1.50 4.00
115 Antti Miettinen RC 1.50 4.00
116 Jiri Hudler RC 2.50 6.00
117 Gregory Campbell RC 1.00 2.50
118 Nathan Horton RC 2.50 6.00
119 Dustin Brown RC 2.50 6.00
120 Tim Gleason RC 1.25 3.00
121 Brent Burns RC 3.00 8.00
122 Christopher Higgins RC 2.00 5.00
123 Dan Hamhuis RC 1.25 3.00
124 Jordin Tootoo RC 2.00 5.00
125 Marek Zidlicky RC 1.00 2.50
126 Paul Martin RC 1.25 3.00
127 Sean Bergenheim RC 1.25 3.00
128 Antoine Vermette RC 2.00 5.00
129 Joni Pitkanen RC 1.50 4.00
130 Matthew Spiller RC 1.25 3.00
131 Marc-Andre Fleury RC 8.00 20.00
132 Peter Sejna RC 1.25 3.00
133 Milan Michalek RC 2.00 5.00
134 Tom Preissing RC 1.25 3.00
135 Matt Stajan RC 1.50 4.00
136 Boyd Gordon RC 1.25 3.00

2003-04 Crown Royale Blue

*BLUE/850: 1.2X TO 3X BASIC CARDS
68 Mark Messier 3.00 8.00

2003-04 Crown Royale Retail

*1-110 VETS: .4X TO 1X HOBBY
*111-136 ROOKIE/899: .3X TO .8X HOB.RC
68 Mark Messier 1.00 2.50

2003-04 Crown Royale Gauntlet of Glory

COMPLETE SET (20) 10.00 20.00
1 Jean-Sebastien Giguere .50 1.25
2 Pasi Nurminen .50 1.25
3 Felix Potvin .60 1.50
4 Martin Biron .50 1.25
5 Jocelyn Thibault .50 1.25
6 David Aebischer .50 1.25
7 Marc Denis .50 1.25
8 Marty Turco .50 1.25
9 Dominik Hasek 1.25 3.00
10 Roberto Luongo .75 2.00
11 Jose Theodore .75 2.00
12 Martin Brodeur 1.50 4.00
13 Rick DiPietro .50 1.25
14 Patrick Lalime .50 1.25
15 Sean Burke .50 1.25
16 Marc-Andre Fleury 1.50 4.00
17 Evgeni Nabokov .50 1.25
18 Nikolai Khabibulin .60 1.50
19 Ed Belfour .60 1.50
20 Dan Cloutier .50 1.25

2003-04 Crown Royale Global Conquest

1 M.Brodeur/M.Lemieux 2.00 5.00
2 D.Hasek/J.Jagr .75 2.00
3 T.Selanne/S.Koivu .60 1.50
4 O.Kolzig/M.Sturm .60 1.50
5 E.Nabokov/N.Antropov .60 1.50
6 S.Fedorov/I.Kovalchuk 1.25 3.00
7 M.Gaborik/M.Hossa 1.00 2.50
8 M.Naslund/P.Forsberg 1.25 3.00
9 D.Aebischer/M.Gerber .60 1.50
10 M.Modano/J.Roenick .60 1.50

2003-04 Crown Royale Jerseys

1 Sergei Fedorov 4.00 10.00
2 Ilya Kovalchuk 5.00 12.00
3 Joe Thornton 5.00 12.00
4 Ryan Miller 3.00 8.00
5 Matthew Lombardi 2.00 5.00
6 Peter Forsberg 6.00 15.00
7 Teemu Selanne 4.00 10.00
8 Mike Modano 4.00 10.00
9 Steve Yzerman 8.00 20.00
10 Ales Hemsky 2.50 6.00
11 Jay Bouwmeester 2.00 5.00
12 Nathan Horton 4.00 10.00
13 Saku Koivu 3.00 8.00
14 Martin Brodeur 8.00 20.00
15 Rick DiPietro 2.50 6.00
16 Eric Lindros 3.00 8.00
17 Jason Spezza 6.00 15.00
18 Antoine Vermette 2.00 5.00
19 Jeremy Roenick 4.00 10.00
20 Mario Lemieux 10.00 25.00
21 Barret Jackman 2.00 5.00
22 Vincent Lecavalier 3.00 8.00
23 Ed Belfour 3.00 8.00
24 Owen Nolan 2.50 6.00
25 Markus Naslund 3.00 8.00

2003-04 Crown Royale Patches

*PATCHES: .75X TO 2X JSY HI

2003-04 Crown Royale Lords of the Rink

COMPLETE SET (24) 15.00 40.00
1 Sergei Fedorov .75 2.00
2 Ilya Kovalchuk .75 2.00
3 Joe Thornton .75 2.00
4 Eric Staal .50 1.25
5 Peter Forsberg 1.50 4.00
6 Milan Hejduk .60 1.50
7 Paul Kariya .60 1.50
8 Joe Sakic 1.25 3.00
9 Rick Nash .75 2.00
10 Mike Modano .75 2.00
11 Steve Yzerman 2.00 5.00
12 Henrik Zetterberg .75 2.00
13 Jay Bouwmeester .50 1.25
14 Ziggy Palffy .50 1.25
15 Marian Hossa .60 1.50
16 Jason Spezza .75 2.00
17 Jeremy Roenick .60 1.50
18 Mario Lemieux 2.50 6.00
19 Keith Tkachuk .60 1.50
20 Vincent Lecavalier .50 1.25
21 Mats Sundin .60 1.50
22 Todd Bertuzzi .60 1.50
23 Markus Naslund .60 1.50
24 Jaromir Jagr .75 2.00

2003-04 Crown Royale Royal Portraits

COMPLETE SET (10) 12.50 25.00
1 Joffrey Lupul 1.00 2.50
2 Patrice Bergeron 10.00 25.00
3 Eric Staal 1.50 4.00
4 Jiri Hudler 1.00 2.50
5 Nathan Horton 1.25 3.00
6 Jordin Tootoo 1.00 2.50
7 Joni Pitkanen 1.00 2.50
8 Marc-Andre Fleury 2.50 6.00
9 Milan Michalek 1.00 2.50
10 Matt Stajan 1.00 2.50

2010-11 Crown Royale

COMP.SET w/o SPs (100) 40.00 80.00
1 Bobby Ryan .60 1.50
2 Ryan Getzlaf .75 2.00
3 Teemu Selanne 1.50 4.00
4 Corey Perry 1.25 3.00
5 Dustin Byfuglien .75 2.00
6 Nicklas Bergfors .60 1.50
7 Zach Bogosian .60 1.50
8 Nathan Horton .60 1.50
9 Tim Thomas .75 2.00
10 Zdeno Chara .75 2.00
11 Thomas Vanek .60 1.50
12 Tyler Myers .50 1.25
13 Tyler Ennis .50 1.25
14 Ryan Miller .75 2.00
15 Rene Bourque .50 1.25
16 Jarome Iginla 1.00 2.50
17 Jay Bouwmeester .50 1.25
18 Eric Staal 1.00 2.50
19 Cam Ward .75 2.00
20 Brandon Sutter .50 1.25
21 Jonathan Toews 1.25 3.00
22 Marty Turco .75 2.00
23 Patrick Kane 1.50 4.00
24 Marian Hossa .75 2.00
25 Paul Stastny .60 1.50
26 Matt Duchene .75 2.00
27 Craig Anderson .75 2.00
28 Rick Nash .75 2.00
29 Steve Mason .60 1.50
30 Jakub Voracek .60 1.50
31 Brenden Morrow .60 1.50
32 Brad Richards .75 2.00
33 Steve Ott .50 1.25
34 Mike Modano 1.25 3.00
35 Pavel Datsyuk 1.25 3.00
36 Jimmy Howard 1.00 2.50
37 Nicklas Lidstrom .75 2.00
38 Johan Franzen .60 1.50
39 Sam Gagner .50 1.25
40 Dustin Penner .50 1.25
41 Ales Hemsky .60 1.50
42 Tomas Vokoun .60 1.50
43 Shawn Matthias .50 1.25
44 David Booth .50 1.25
45 Drew Doughty 1.00 2.50
46 Jonathan Bernier .60 1.50
47 Anze Kopitar 1.25 3.00
48 Mikko Koivu .75 2.00
49 Niklas Backstrom .75 2.00
50 Matt Cullen .50 1.25
51 Carey Price 1.50 4.00
52 Tomas Plekanec .50 1.25
53 Michael Cammalleri .75 2.00
54 Brian Gionta .50 1.25
55 Pekka Rinne .75 2.00
56 Shea Weber .60 1.50
57 Colin Wilson .60 1.50
58 Ilya Kovalchuk .75 2.00
59 Martin Brodeur 2.00 5.00
60 Zach Parise .75 2.00
61 Dwayne Roloson .60 1.50
62 John Tavares 1.25 3.00
63 Josh Bailey .60 1.50
64 Marian Gaborik .75 2.00
65 Henrik Lundqvist 2.00 5.00
66 Brian Elliott .60 1.50
67 Jason Spezza .75 2.00
68 Daniel Alfredsson .75 2.00
69 Sergei Gonchar .50 1.25
70 Mike Richards .60 1.50
71 Jeff Carter .60 1.50
72 Chris Pronger .75 2.00
73 Claude Giroux .75 2.00
74 Wojtek Wolski .50 1.25
75 Ray Whitney .60 1.50
76 Ilya Bryzgalov .60 1.50
77 Evgeni Malkin 1.50 4.00
78 Marc-Andre Fleury 1.50 4.00
79 Sidney Crosby 3.00 8.00
80 Joe Pavelski 1.00 2.50
81 Joe Thornton 1.25 3.00
82 Antti Niemi .60 1.50
83 Dany Heatley .60 1.50
84 Alex Steen .50 1.25
85 Jaroslav Halak .75 2.00
86 Erik Johnson .50 1.25
87 Simon Gagne .75 2.00
88 Steven Stamkos 1.50 4.00
89 Vincent Lecavalier .75 2.00
90 Dion Phaneuf .60 1.50
91 Jonas Gustavsson 1.00 2.50
92 Phil Kessel .75 2.00
93 Tyler Bozak .50 1.25
94 Ryan Kesler .75 2.00
95 Henrik Sedin 1.00 2.50
96 Alexandre Burrows .50 1.25
97 Alex Ovechkin 3.00 8.00
98 Alexander Semin .75 2.00
99 Mike Green .60 1.50
100 Michal Neuvirth .60 1.50
101 Phil Esposito 2.50 6.00
102 Patrick Roy 4.00 10.00
103 Tony Esposito 1.50 4.00
104 Rogie Vachon 2.00 5.00
105 Rod Gilbert 1.50 4.00
106 Luc Robitaille 1.50 4.00
107 Lanny McDonald 1.50 4.00
108 Rick Middleton 1.50 4.00
109 Grant Fuhr 2.50 6.00
110 Johnny Bower 1.50 4.00
111 Mario Lemieux 6.00 15.00
112 Ken Hodge 1.25 3.00
113 Stan Mikita 2.00 5.00
114 Ed Belfour 1.50 4.00
115 Eric Lindros 2.50 6.00
116 Taylor Hall JSY AU RC 150.00 300.00
117 Tyler Seguin JSY AU RC 150.00 250.00
118 Jeff Skinner JSY AU RC 30.00 80.00
119 B.Schenn JSY AU RC 30.00 80.00
120 Jordan Eberle JSY AU RC 40.00 100.00
121 M.Paajarvi JSY AU RC 15.00 40.00
124 Derek Stepan JSY AU RC 40.00 100.00
125 Nazem Kadri JSY AU RC 40.00 80.00
126 M.Tedenby JSY AU RC 12.00 30.00
127 K.Shattenkirk JSY AU RC 25.00 60.00
128 Ekman-Larsson JSY AU RC 30.00 60.00
129 Zach Hamill JSY AU RC 12.00 30.00
130 Robin Lehner AU RC 8.00 20.00
131 A.Vasyunov AU RC 4.00 10.00
132 Jordan Caron AU RC 5.00 12.00
133 Sergei Bobrovsky AU RC 15.00 40.00
134 P.K. Subban AU RC 20.00 40.00
135 Eric Tangradi AU RC 4.00 10.00
136 Bobby Butler AU RC 4.00 10.00
137 Brandon Yip AU RC 4.00 10.00
138 Tommy Wingels AU RC 4.00 10.00
139 Kyle Clifford AU RC 5.00 12.00
140 Matt Taormina AU RC 4.00 10.00
141 Nick Bonino AU RC 5.00 12.00
142 Alexander Burmistrov AU RC 4.00 10.00
143 Nick Leddy AU RC 5.00 12.00
144 Zac Dalpe AU RC 5.00 12.00
145 Anders Lindback AU RC 4.00 10.00
146 Marcus Johansson AU RC 6.00 15.00
147 Jamie McBain AU RC 4.00 10.00
148 Brandon Pirri AU RC 4.00 10.00
149 Evgeny Grachev AU RC 4.00 10.00
150 Dana Tyrell AU RC 4.00 10.00
151 Jacob Josefson AU RC 4.00 10.00
152 Colby Cohen AU RC 4.00 10.00
153 Justin Falk AU RC 3.00 8.00
154 Mark Olver AU RC 4.00 10.00
155 Jake Muzzin AU RC 10.00 25.00
156 Henrik Karlsson AU RC 4.00 10.00
157 Ian Cole AU RC 4.00 10.00
158 John McCarthy AU RC 4.00 10.00
159 Ryan Reaves AU RC 5.00 12.00
160 Jeremy Morin AU RC 4.00 10.00
161 Eric Wellwood AU RC 5.00 12.00
162 Korbinian Holzer AU RC 4.00 10.00
163 Keith Aulie AU RC 4.00 10.00
164 Brandon McMillan AU RC 4.00 10.00
165 T.J. Brodie AU RC 4.00 10.00
166 Luke Adam AU RC 4.00 10.00
167 Nick Spaling AU RC 4.00 10.00
168 Dustin Tokarski AU RC 4.00 10.00
169 Maxim Noreau AU RC 3.00 8.00
170 Brayden Irwin AU RC 4.00 10.00
171 Nick Palmieri AU RC 4.00 10.00
172 Kyle Palmieri AU RC 8.00 20.00
173 Stephen Gionta AU RC 5.00 12.00
174 Brad Mills AU RC 4.00 10.00
175 Mike Moore AU RC 4.00 10.00

2010-11 Crown Royale Premiere Date

*PREMIERE DATE: 1.2X TO 3X BASE

2010-11 Crown Royale Premiere Date Signatures

1 Bobby Ryan/100 5.00 12.00
2 Ryan Getzlaf/50 8.00 20.00
3 Teemu Selanne/50 15.00 40.00
4 Corey Perry/50 10.00 25.00
5 Dustin Byfuglien/75 6.00 15.00
7 Zach Bogosian/50 5.00 12.00
8 Nathan Horton/100 5.00 12.00
9 Tim Thomas/100 12.00 30.00
10 Zdeno Chara/100 12.00 30.00
11 Thomas Vanek/100 5.00 12.00
12 Tyler Myers/100 4.00 10.00
13 Tyler Ennis/100 4.00 10.00
14 Ryan Miller/100 8.00 20.00
15 Rene Bourque/100 4.00 10.00
16 Jarome Iginla/25 10.00 25.00
17 Jay Bouwmeester/100 4.00 10.00
18 Eric Staal/75 8.00 20.00
19 Cam Ward/100 6.00 15.00
20 Brandon Sutter/100 4.00 10.00
21 Jonathan Toews/100 15.00 40.00
22 Marty Turco/100 12.00 30.00
23 Patrick Kane/75 15.00 40.00
24 Marian Hossa/100 12.00 30.00
25 Paul Stastny/50 5.00 12.00
26 Matt Duchene/100 6.00 15.00
29 Steve Mason/100 5.00 12.00
30 Jakub Voracek/100 5.00 12.00
31 Brenden Morrow/100 5.00 12.00
32 Brad Richards/75 6.00 15.00
33 Steve Ott/100 4.00 10.00
34 Mike Modano/25 25.00 60.00
35 Pavel Datsyuk/25 15.00 40.00
36 Jimmy Howard/100 10.00 25.00
37 Nicklas Lidstrom/25 12.00 30.00
38 Johan Franzen/100 6.00 15.00
39 Sam Gagner/100 4.00 10.00
40 Dustin Penner/50 5.00 12.00
41 Ales Hemsky/100 6.00 15.00
42 Tomas Vokoun/100 5.00 12.00
45 Drew Doughty/100 8.00 20.00
46 Jonathan Bernier/50 5.00 12.00
47 Anze Kopitar/75 10.00 25.00
49 Niklas Backstrom/50 8.00 20.00
51 Carey Price/25 15.00 40.00
53 Michael Cammalleri/75 8.00 20.00
54 Brian Gionta/100 4.00 10.00
55 Pekka Rinne/100 8.00 20.00
56 Shea Weber/75 8.00 20.00
57 Colin Wilson/100 5.00 12.00
58 Ilya Kovalchuk/25 20.00 50.00
60 Zach Parise/25 10.00 25.00
61 Dwayne Roloson/25 6.00 15.00
62 John Tavares/50 10.00 25.00
63 Josh Bailey/25 6.00 15.00
65 Henrik Lundqvist/100 15.00 40.00
66 Brian Elliott/50 8.00 20.00
67 Jason Spezza/100 6.00 15.00
68 Daniel Alfredsson/100 10.00 25.00
70 Mike Richards/100 12.00 30.00
72 Chris Pronger/75 12.00 30.00
73 Claude Giroux/50 6.00 15.00
74 Wojtek Wolski/100 4.00 10.00
76 Ilya Bryzgalov/50 5.00 12.00
77 Evgeni Malkin/50 12.00 30.00
78 Marc-Andre Fleury/75 15.00 40.00
79 Sidney Crosby/25 75.00 135.00
80 Joe Pavelski/100 8.00 20.00
81 Joe Thornton/50 10.00 25.00
83 Dany Heatley/100 5.00 12.00
85 Jaroslav Halak/100 6.00 15.00
86 Erik Johnson/100 4.00 10.00
87 Simon Gagne/75 6.00 15.00
89 Vincent Lecavalier/50 8.00 20.00
90 Dion Phaneuf/100 10.00 25.00
91 Jonas Gustavsson/100 8.00 20.00
92 Phil Kessel/50 8.00 20.00
93 Tyler Bozak/100 4.00 10.00
94 Ryan Kesler/25 12.00 30.00
95 Henrik Sedin/75 8.00 20.00
96 Alexandre Burrows/75 4.00 10.00
98 Alexander Semin/100 8.00 20.00
99 Mike Green/100 5.00 12.00

2010-11 Crown Royale Purple

*PURPLE: 2.5X TO 6X BASE

2010-11 Crown Royale Rookie Silhouettes Patch Autographs

*PATCH/1525: .5X TO 1.2X JSY AU/99
116 Taylor Hall/25 400.00 750.00
117 Tyler Seguin/25 150.00 300.00
118 Jeff Skinner/25 150.00 300.00
120 Jordan Eberle/25 40.00 100.00

2010-11 Crown Royale Calder Collection

1 Tyler Ennis 2.50 6.00
2 Tyler Seguin 15.00 40.00
3 Jonathan Bernier 3.00 8.00
4 John Carlson 4.00 10.00
5 P.K. Subban 20.00 50.00
6 Taylor Hall 25.00 60.00
7 Magnus Paajarvi 4.00 10.00
8 Nikita Filatov 2.50 6.00
9 Jeff Skinner 8.00 20.00
10 Michal Neuvirth 3.00 8.00
11 Derek Stepan 4.00 10.00
12 Cam Fowler 6.00 20.00

2010-11 Crown Royale Coat of Arms Materials

1 Alex Ovechkin/25 20.00 50.00
3 Steve Ott/25 12.00 30.00
4 Milan Lucic/25 15.00 30.00
5 Miikka Kiprusoff/25 12.00 30.00
6 Roberto Luongo/25 15.00 40.00
9 Henrik Zetterberg/25 30.00 60.00
10 Mike Green/25 15.00 40.00
11 Travis Zajac/25 8.00 20.00
12 Tuukka Rask/25 12.00 30.00
14 Brad Richards/25 10.00 25.00
15 Shane Doan/25 15.00 40.00
16 John Tavares/25 15.00 40.00
17 Luke Schenn/25 10.00 25.00
18 Chris Pronger/25 10.00 25.00
19 Jay McClement/25 6.00 15.00
20 Brayden Schenn/25 20.00 50.00
21 Rick DiPietro/25 10.00 25.00
23 Jeff Skinner/25 20.00 50.00
25 Taylor Hall/25 20.00 50.00
26 Sidney Crosby/25 40.00 100.00
27 Thomas Vanek/25 8.00 20.00
29 T.J. Galiardi/25 8.00 20.00
30 Jean-Sebastien Giguere/25 15.00 40.00
31 Jeff Carter/25 12.00 30.00
32 Mike Fisher/25 6.00 15.00
34 Steve Mason/25 15.00 40.00
35 Ryan Smyth/25 12.00 30.00
37 Stephen Weiss/25 8.00 20.00
38 Bryan Little/25 10.00 25.00
39 Artem Anisimov/25 10.00 25.00
40 Shea Weber/25 10.00 25.00
41 Duncan Keith/25 12.00 30.00
42 Joe Thornton/25 15.00 40.00
44 Matt Duchene/25 10.00 25.00
45 Alexander Frolov/25 15.00 40.00
46 Andrei Kostitsyn/25 8.00 20.00
47 Derek Roy/25 6.00 15.00
48 Jordan Staal/25 8.00 20.00
49 Matt Moulson/25 8.00 20.00
50 Mike Smith/25 15.00 40.00

2010-11 Crown Royale Heirs to the Throne Materials

*PRIME/30-50: .6X TO 1.5X BASIC JSY
AG Alex Goligoski 4.00 10.00
AR Andy Greene 3.00 8.00
BA Josh Bailey 4.00 10.00
BN Jamie Benn 6.00 15.00
BO Mikkel Boedker 3.00 8.00
BSC Brayden Schenn 6.00 15.00
CG Claude Giroux 5.00 12.00
CP Carey Price 10.00 25.00
CS Chris Stewart 4.00 10.00
CW Colin Wilson 4.00 10.00
DD Drew Doughty 6.00 15.00
DK David Krejci 5.00 12.00
EK Evander Kane 5.00 12.00
ER Erik Karlsson 6.00 15.00
FN Frans Nielsen 3.00 8.00
JB Jonathan Bernier 4.00 10.00
JE Jordan Eberle 6.00 15.00
JG Jonas Gustavsson 6.00 15.00
JN James Neal 3.00 8.00
JQ Jonathan Quick 6.00 15.00
JS Jordan Staal 4.00 10.00
JT John Tavares 8.00 20.00
JV Jakub Voracek 4.00 10.00
KL Kari Lehtonen 4.00 10.00
LE Loui Eriksson 3.00 8.00
MB Mikael Backlund 4.00 10.00
MD Matt Duchene/25 6.00 15.00
MF Marc-Andre Fleury 10.00 25.00
MP Magnus Paajarvi 3.00 8.00
MS Marc Staal 3.00 8.00
NB Nicklas Bergfors 4.00 10.00
NK Nazem Kadri 8.00 20.00
PH Patric Hornqvist 3.00 8.00
PR1 Peter Regin 4.00 10.00
PR2 Pekka Rinne 5.00 12.00
PS Paul Stastny 4.00 10.00
SG Sam Gagner 3.00 8.00
SK Jeff Skinner 6.00 15.00
TG T.J. Galiardi 4.00 10.00
TH Taylor Hall 12.00 30.00
TR Tuukka Rask 6.00 15.00
TS Tyler Seguin 8.00 20.00
ZB Zach Bogosian 4.00 10.00
ZH Zach Hamill 2.50 6.00
ZP Zach Parise/25 6.00 15.00

2010-11 Crown Royale Heirs to the Throne Materials Autographs

AG Alex Goligoski/25 5.00 12.00
AR Andy Greene 4.00 10.00
BA Josh Bailey 5.00 12.00
BN Jamie Benn 8.00 20.00
BO Mikkel Boedker 4.00 10.00
BS Brayden Schenn 12.00 30.00
CP Carey Price 30.00 80.00
CS Chris Stewart 5.00 12.00
CW Colin Wilson 5.00 12.00
DD Drew Doughty 8.00 20.00
EK Evander Kane 6.00 15.00
ER Erik Karlsson 30.00 80.00
FN Frans Nielsen 4.00 10.00
JB Jonathan Bernier 5.00 12.00
JE Jordan Eberle 12.00 30.00
JG Jonas Gustavsson 8.00 20.00
JN James Neal 4.00 10.00
JQ Jonathan Quick 8.00 20.00
JS Jordan Staal 5.00 12.00
JT John Tavares 10.00 25.00
KL Kari Lehtonen 5.00 12.00
LE Loui Eriksson 4.00 10.00
MB Mikael Backlund 5.00 12.00
MD Matt Duchene 6.00 15.00
MF Marc-Andre Fleury 12.00 30.00
MP Magnus Paajarvi 6.00 15.00
MS Marc Staal 4.00 10.00
NK Nazem Kadri 15.00 40.00
PH Patric Hornqvist 4.00 10.00
PR1 Peter Regin 5.00 12.00
PR2 Pekka Rinne 6.00 15.00
PS Paul Stastny 5.00 12.00
SG Sam Gagner 4.00 10.00
SK Jeff Skinner 12.00 30.00
TG T.J. Galiardi 5.00 12.00
TH Taylor Hall 12.00 30.00
TS Tyler Seguin 15.00 40.00
ZB Zach Bogosian 5.00 12.00
ZH Zach Hamill 5.00 12.00

2010-11 Crown Royale In Harm's Way

1 Ryan Miller 1.50 4.00
2 Pekka Rinne 1.50 4.00
3 Roberto Luongo 2.50 6.00
4 Jimmy Howard 2.00 5.00
5 Jonas Hiller 1.25 3.00

6 Jonathan Bernier 1.25 3.00
7 Tim Thomas 1.50 4.00
8 Semyon Varlamov 1.50 4.00
9 Carey Price 3.00 8.00
10 Cam Ward 1.50 4.00
11 Tomas Vokoun 1.25 3.00
12 Henrik Lundqvist 4.00 10.00
13 Nikolai Khabibulin 1.25 3.00
14 Jean-Sebastien Giguere 1.50 4.00
15 Miikka Kiprusoff 1.50 4.00
16 Jaroslav Halak 1.50 4.00
17 Antti Niemi 1.25 3.00
18 Marty Turco 1.50 4.00
19 Rick DiPietro 1.25 3.00
20 Martin Brodeur 4.00 10.00

2010-11 Crown Royale Lancers

1 Henrik Sedin 2.00 5.00
2 Steven Stamkos 3.00 8.00
3 Tomas Fleischmann 1.00 2.50
4 Alexandre Burrows 1.00 2.50
5 Patrick Marleau 1.50 4.00
6 Teemu Selanne 3.00 8.00
7 Mike Knuble 1.00 2.50
8 Dustin Penner 1.00 2.50
9 Jussi Jokinen 1.00 2.50
10 Ilya Kovalchuk 1.50 4.00
11 Alexander Semin 1.50 4.00
12 Dany Heatley 1.25 3.00
13 Zach Parise 1.50 4.00
14 Rick Nash 1.50 4.00
15 Bobby Ryan 1.25 3.00
16 Phil Kessel 1.50 4.00
17 Patrick Kane 3.00 8.00
18 Matt Moulson 1.25 3.00
19 Loui Eriksson 1.00 2.50
20 Eric Staal 2.00 5.00
21 Patric Hornqvist 1.00 2.50
22 Mike Richards 1.25 3.00
23 Anze Kopitar 2.50 6.00
24 Rene Bourque 1.00 2.50
25 James Neal 1.00 2.50

2010-11 Crown Royale Lancers Materials Prime

*PATCH/25: .6X TO 1.5X PRIME
1 Henrik Sedin 8.00 20.00
2 Steven Stamkos 12.00 30.00
4 Alexandre Burrows 4.00 10.00
5 Patrick Marleau 6.00 15.00
6 Teemu Selanne 12.00 30.00
7 Mike Knuble 4.00 10.00
8 Dustin Penner 4.00 10.00
10 Ilya Kovalchuk 6.00 15.00
11 Alexander Semin 6.00 15.00
12 Dany Heatley 5.00 12.00
13 Zach Parise 6.00 15.00
15 Bobby Ryan 5.00 12.00
16 Phil Kessel 6.00 15.00
17 Patrick Kane 12.00 30.00
18 Matt Moulson 5.00 12.00
19 Loui Eriksson 4.00 10.00
20 Eric Staal 8.00 20.00
21 Patric Hornqvist 4.00 10.00
23 Anze Kopitar 10.00 25.00
24 Rene Bourque 4.00 10.00
25 James Neal 4.00 10.00

2010-11 Crown Royale Legends

COMPLETE SET (12) 20.00 50.00
1 Brian Leetch 1.25 3.00
2 Johnny Bucyk 1.50 4.00
3 Luc Robitaille 1.50 4.00
4 Mario Lemieux 6.00 15.00
5 Martin Brodeur 4.00 10.00
6 Patrick Roy 4.00 10.00
7 Teemu Selanne 3.00 8.00
8 Joe Sakic 3.00 8.00
9 Mike Modano 2.50 6.00
10 Marcel Dionne 2.00 5.00
11 Lanny McDonald 1.50 4.00
12 Mark Recchi 2.00 5.00

2010-11 Crown Royale Legends Memorabilia

1 Brian Leetch 4.00 10.00
2 Johnny Bucyk 5.00 12.00
3 Luc Robitaille 5.00 12.00
4 Mario Lemieux 20.00 50.00
5 Martin Brodeur/50 12.00 30.00
6 Patrick Roy 12.00 30.00
8 Joe Sakic 10.00 25.00
9 Mike Modano 8.00 20.00
10 Marcel Dionne 6.00 15.00
11 Lanny McDonald 5.00 12.00
12 Mark Recchi 6.00 15.00

2010-11 Crown Royale Legends Signatures

1 Brian Leetch 12.00 30.00
2 Johnny Bucyk 8.00 20.00
3 Luc Robitaille 15.00 40.00
4 Mario Lemieux 40.00 100.00
5 Martin Brodeur 40.00 80.00
6 Patrick Roy 50.00 100.00
7 Teemu Selanne 15.00 40.00
8 Joe Sakic 40.00 80.00
9 Mike Modano 12.00 30.00
10 Marcel Dionne 20.00 50.00
11 Lanny McDonald 8.00 20.00
12 Mark Recchi 15.00 40.00

2010-11 Crown Royale Lords of the NHL

1 Alex Ovechkin 6.00 15.00
2 Henrik Sedin 2.00 5.00
3 Steven Stamkos 3.00 8.00
4 Sidney Crosby 6.00 15.00
5 Ryan Miller 1.50 4.00
6 Jonathan Toews 2.50 6.00
7 Evgeni Malkin 3.00 8.00
8 Pavel Datsyuk 2.50 6.00
9 Drew Doughty 2.00 5.00
10 Nicklas Lidstrom 1.50 4.00
11 Duncan Keith 1.25 3.00
12 Ilya Kovalchuk 1.50 4.00

2010-11 Crown Royale Lords of the NHL Memorabilia

*PRIME/15: 1X TO 2.5X BASIC JSY/49-99
*PRIME/15: .6X TO 1.5X BASIC JSY/19
1 Alex Ovechkin/49 20.00 50.00
2 Henrik Sedin/99 6.00 15.00
3 Steven Stamkos/49 10.00 25.00
4 Sidney Crosby/99 20.00 50.00
5 Ryan Miller/19 8.00 20.00
7 Evgeni Malkin/99 10.00 25.00
8 Pavel Datsyuk/99 8.00 20.00
9 Drew Doughty/99 6.00 15.00
10 Nicklas Lidstrom/49 5.00 12.00
11 Duncan Keith/99 4.00 10.00
12 Ilya Kovalchuk/99 5.00 12.00

2010-11 Crown Royale Loyalty

AH Ales Hemsky 1.25 3.00
AM Andrei Markov 1.50 4.00
BM Brenden Morrow 1.25 3.00
DA Daniel Alfredsson 1.50 4.00
DL David Legwand 1.25 3.00
DS Daniel Sedin 2.00 5.00
HS Henrik Sedin 2.00 5.00
HZ Henrik Zetterberg 2.00 5.00
JI Jarome Iginla 2.00 5.00
JS Jason Spezza 1.50 4.00
MB Martin Brodeur 4.00 10.00
NL Nicklas Lidstrom 1.50 4.00
PB Patrice Bergeron 2.00 5.00
PD Pavel Datsyuk 2.50 6.00
PE Patrik Elias 1.50 4.00
PM Patrick Marleau 1.50 4.00
RM Ryan Miller 1.50 4.00
RN Rick Nash 1.50 4.00
RR Robyn Regehr 1.00 2.50
SD Shane Doan 1.25 3.00
SW Stephen Weiss 1.25 3.00
TC Tim Connolly 1.00 2.50
TH Tomas Holmstrom 1.00 2.50
TK Tomas Kaberle 1.00 2.50
VL Vincent Lecavalier 1.50 4.00

2010-11 Crown Royale Loyalty Patches

AH Ales Hemsky 6.00 15.00
BM Brenden Morrow 6.00 15.00
DA Daniel Alfredsson 8.00 20.00
DL David Legwand 6.00 15.00
DS Daniel Sedin 10.00 25.00
HS Henrik Sedin 10.00 25.00
HZ Henrik Zetterberg 10.00 25.00
JI Jarome Iginla 10.00 25.00
MB Martin Brodeur 20.00 50.00
NL Nicklas Lidstrom 8.00 20.00
PB Patrice Bergeron 10.00 25.00
PD Pavel Datsyuk 15.00 40.00
PE Patrik Elias 8.00 20.00
RM Ryan Miller 8.00 20.00
RR Robyn Regehr 5.00 12.00
SD Shane Doan 6.00 15.00
SW Stephen Weiss 6.00 15.00
TC Tim Connolly 5.00 12.00
TH Tomas Holmstrom 6.00 15.00
TK Tomas Kaberle 5.00 12.00
VL Vincent Lecavalier 8.00 20.00

2010-11 Crown Royale Razor's Choice

1 Pavel Datsyuk 10.00 25.00
2 Chris Pronger 6.00 15.00
3 Mike Richards 5.00 12.00
4 Martin Brodeur 12.00 30.00
5 Tyler Myers 4.00 10.00
6 Martin St. Louis 6.00 15.00
7 Sidney Crosby 25.00 60.00
8 Jonathan Toews 10.00 25.00
9 Roberto Luongo 10.00 25.00
10 Mike Fisher 4.00 10.00
11 Ian Laperriere 8.00 20.00
12 Cal Clutterbuck 8.00 20.00

2010-11 Crown Royale Regal Achievements

1 Patrick Kane 3.00 8.00
2 Martin Brodeur 4.00 10.00
3 Jonathan Toews 2.50 6.00
4 Ilya Bryzgalov 1.25 3.00
5 Steve Mason 1.25 3.00
6 Tyler Myers 1.00 2.50
7 Marian Hossa 1.50 4.00
8 Matt Carkner 1.25 3.00
9 Steven Stamkos 3.00 8.00
10 Sidney Crosby 6.00 15.00
11 Nicklas Backstrom 1.50 4.00
12 Mikko Koivu 1.50 4.00
13 Evgeni Malkin 3.00 8.00
14 Mike Modano 2.50 6.00
15 Pavel Datsyuk 2.50 6.00
16 Eric Staal 2.00 5.00
17 Daniel Alfredsson 1.50 4.00
18 Mark Recchi 2.00 5.00
19 Nicklas Lidstrom 1.50 4.00
20 Roberto Luongo 2.50 6.00

2010-11 Crown Royale Royal Lineage Materials

*PRIME/50: .6X TO 1.5X MATRL/75-100
*PRIME/25: .8X TO 2X MATERIAL/100
*PATCH/15-25: .8X TO 2X MATERL/75-100
*PATCH/25: .6X TO 1.5X MATERIAL/25
ASE Alfredsson/Spezza/Elliott 6.00 15.00
BPK Brodeur/Parise/Kovalchuk 10.00 25.00
DKQ Doughty/Kopitar/Quick 12.00 30.00
GPR Getzlaf/Perry/Ryan 10.00 25.00
HEP Hall/Eberle/Paajarvi 10.00 25.00
HTS Hall/Tavares/Stamkos/25 12.00 30.00
IKT Iginla/Kiprusoff/Tanguay 8.00 20.00
KPG Kessel/Phaneuf/Giguere 6.00 15.00
KRB Kiprusoff/Rask/Backstrom 8.00 20.00
LGA Lundqvst/Gabork/Anismv 15.00 40.00
LMB Lucic/Morrow/Brown 6.00 15.00
MSC Malkin/Staal/Crosby 25.00 60.00
OKS Okposo/Kane/Simmonds 8.00 20.00
OSC Ovechkin/Stamkos/Crosby 25.00 60.00
PCG Price/Cammalleri/Gomez 12.00 30.00
SAD Stastny/Anderson/Duchene 6.00 15.00
SLS Sedin/Luongo/Sedin 10.00 25.00
SRM Selanne/Recchi/Modano 12.00 30.00
TMP Thrntn/Marlu/Pavlsk/75 10.00 25.00
TRS Thomas/Rask/Seguin 15.00 40.00
ZDL Zetterbr/Datsyuk/Lidstrm 10.00 25.00
SLSL Stamks/Lecavalr/St.Louis 12.00 30.00

2010-11 Crown Royale Royal Pains

1 Milan Lucic 1.50 4.00
2 Dustin Byfuglien 1.50 4.00
3 Dion Phaneuf 1.25 3.00
4 Brenden Morrow 1.25 3.00
5 Alex Ovechkin 6.00 15.00
6 David Backes 1.00 2.50
7 Ryan Getzlaf 1.50 4.00
8 James Neal 1.00 2.50
9 Michael Del Zotto 1.25 3.00
10 Mike Richards 1.25 3.00
11 Rick Nash 1.50 4.00
12 Steve Downie 1.00 2.50

2010-11 Crown Royale Scratching the Surface Signatures

2 Anze Kopitar 10.00 25.00
3 Bernie Parent/50 12.00 30.00
4 Bill Ranford/50 12.00 30.00
5 Bobby Clarke/50 12.00 30.00
6 Bobby Hull/50 25.00 60.00
7 Brandon Sutter 10.00 25.00
8 Brenden Morrow 6.00 15.00
9 Brian Gionta 12.00 30.00
10 Brian Leetch/25 15.00 40.00
11 Cam Fowler 12.00 30.00
12 Cam Neely/50 15.00 40.00
13 Cam Ward 10.00 25.00
14 Carey Price 25.00 60.00
15 Chris Neil 8.00 20.00
16 Chris Mason 5.00 12.00
17 Chris Pronger 12.00 30.00
18 Chris Stewart 5.00 12.00
19 Claude Giroux 12.00 30.00
20 Cody Almond 6.00 15.00
21 Colin Wilson 6.00 15.00
22 Corey Perry/50 8.00 20.00
23 Cory Schneider 8.00 20.00
24 Dale Tallon/50 12.00 30.00
25 Dan Hamhuis 12.00 30.00
26 Daniel Carcillo 8.00 20.00
27 David Backes 4.00 10.00
28 David Perron/99 5.00 12.00
29 Dany Heatley/25 6.00 15.00
30 Derek Dorsett/50 6.00 15.00
31 Dion Phaneuf 5.00 12.00
32 Drayson Bowman 8.00 20.00
33 Evander Kane 6.00 15.00
34 Evgeni Malkin/25 30.00 60.00
35 Guillaume Latendresse 6.00 15.00
36 Henrik Lundqvist/50 20.00 50.00
37 Henrik Sedin 12.00 30.00
38 Ilya Bryzgalov 10.00 25.00
39 Ilya Kovalchuk 8.00 20.00
40 Jakub Voracek 10.00 25.00
41 James Neal 4.00 10.00
42 James van Riemsdyk 5.00 12.00
43 Jamie Benn 8.00 20.00
44 Jarome Iginla 10.00 25.00
45 Jaroslav Halak 12.00 30.00
46 Jay Bouwmeester 4.00 10.00
47 Jeff Carter 12.00 30.00
48 Jimmy Howard 12.00 30.00
49 Joe Pavelski 8.00 20.00
50 Joe Thornton/25 20.00 50.00
51 Johan Franzen 10.00 25.00
25 John Carlson 10.00 25.00
53 John Tavares/50 20.00 40.00
54 Jonas Hiller/50 5.00 12.00
55 Jordan Staal 10.00 25.00
56 Jose Theodore 10.00 25.00
57 Josh Bailey 6.00 15.00
58 Justin Abdelkader 8.00 20.00
59 Kari Lehtonen 5.00 12.00
60 Keith Yandle 8.00 20.00
61 Luca Caputi 5.00 12.00
62 Marc Savard 4.00 10.00
63 Marc Staal 4.00 10.00
64 Marc-Andre Fleury 15.00 40.00
65 Marian Gaborik 6.00 15.00
66 Marian Hossa 12.00 30.00
67 Martin Brodeur/25 40.00 80.00
68 Matt Carkner 10.00 25.00
69 Mikael Samuelsson 6.00 15.00
70 Mike Brodeur 5.00 12.00
71 Mike Smith 8.00 20.00
72 Mikkel Boedker 6.00 15.00
73 Nathan Gerbe 6.00 15.00
74 Nicklas Lidstrom/25 15.00 40.00
75 Niklas Backstrom/50 6.00 15.00
76 Patric Hornqvist 4.00 10.00
77 Paul Stastny 10.00 25.00
78 Pekka Rinne 8.00 20.00
79 Phil Kessel 12.00 30.00
80 Rene Bourque 4.00 10.00
81 Rich Peverley/50 8.00 20.00
82 Rick Nash 10.00 25.00
83 Ryan Callahan 6.00 15.00
84 Ryan Getzlaf 10.00 25.00
85 Ryan Miller 12.00 30.00
86 Ryan Smyth 10.00 25.00
87 Ryan Stoa 4.00 10.00
88 Scott Gomez 8.00 20.00
89 Semyon Varlamov 6.00 15.00
90 Shea Weber 5.00 12.00
92 Simon Gagne 10.00 25.00
93 Stephen Weiss 5.00 12.00
94 Steve Mason 5.00 12.00
95 Steve Ott 8.00 20.00
96 Steven Stamkos 20.00 50.00
97 Thomas Vanek 5.00 12.00
98 Tomas Holmstrom 10.00 25.00
99 Tyler Bozak 4.00 10.00
100 Viktor Stalberg 8.00 20.00

2010-11 Crown Royale Voices of the Game Signatures

1 Charlie Simmer 10.00 25.00
2 Daryl Reaugh 6.00 15.00
3 Jim Fox 6.00 15.00
4 Pete Weber 6.00 15.00
5 Joe Bowen 10.00 25.00
6 Bob Miller 25.00 60.00
7 Rick Jeanneret 20.00 50.00
8 Randy Moller 6.00 15.00
9 Denis Potvin 6.00 15.00
10 Darren Pang 6.00 15.00
11 Cassie Campbell 10.00 25.00
12 Mike Milbury 6.00 15.00
13 Kelly Hrudey 6.00 15.00
14 Mike Lange 25.00 60.00
15 Don Cherry 25.00 60.00

2011-12 Crown Royale

COMP.SET w/o SP's (100) 25.00 50.00
1 Corey Perry 1.00 2.50
2 Ryan Getzlaf .60 1.50
3 Bobby Ryan .50 1.25
4 Saku Koivu .60 1.50
5 Tim Thomas .60 1.50
6 Brad Marchand 1.25 3.00
7 Tyler Seguin .75 2.00
8 Rich Peverley .60 1.50
9 Thomas Vanek .50 1.25
10 Ryan Miller .60 1.50
11 Tyler Ennis .40 1.00
12 Jarome Iginla .75 2.00
13 Miikka Kiprusoff .60 1.50
14 Curtis Glencross .40 1.00
15 Jeff Skinner .75 2.00
16 Eric Staal .75 2.00
17 Cam Ward .60 1.50
18 Patrick Kane 1.25 3.00
19 Jonathan Toews 1.00 2.50
20 Corey Crawford .75 2.00
21 Jean-Sebastien Giguere .60 1.50
22 Matt Duchene .60 1.50
23 Paul Stastny .50 1.25
24 Steve Mason .50 1.25
25 Rick Nash .60 1.50
26 Jeff Carter .50 1.25
27 Jamie Benn .60 1.50
28 Loui Eriksson .40 1.00
29 Kari Lehtonen .50 1.25
30 Henrik Zetterberg .75 2.00
31 Pavel Datsyuk 1.00 2.50
32 Jimmy Howard .75 2.00
33 Nicklas Lidstrom .40 1.00
34 Taylor Hall .60 1.50
35 Jordan Eberle .60 1.50
36 Nikolai Khabibulin .50 1.25
37 Jacob Markstrom .60 1.50
38 Mike Santorelli .40 1.00
39 Stephen Weiss .50 1.25
40 Mike Richards .50 1.25
41 Anze Kopitar 1.00 2.50
42 Drew Doughty .75 2.00
43 Jonathan Quick .75 2.00
44 Matt Kassian .40 1.00
45 Dany Heatley .50 1.25
46 Niklas Backstrom .60 1.50
47 Carey Price 1.25 3.00
48 P.K. Subban .75 2.00
49 David Desharnais .40 1.00
50 Lars Eller .40 1.00
51 Shea Weber .50 1.25
52 Pekka Rinne .60 1.50
53 Mike Fisher .40 1.00
54 Martin Brodeur 1.50 4.00
55 Zach Parise .60 1.50
56 Ilya Kovalchuk .60 1.50
57 Kyle Okposo .40 1.00
58 John Tavares 1.00 2.50
59 Michael Grabner .50 1.25
60 Brad Richards .60 1.50
61 Brandon Dubinsky .40 1.00
62 Henrik Lundqvist 1.50 4.00
63 Marian Gaborik .60 1.50
64 Jason Spezza .60 1.50
65 Erik Karlsson .75 2.00
66 Daniel Alfredsson .60 1.50
67 Brayden Schenn .60 1.50
68 Claude Giroux .60 1.50
69 Ilya Bryzgalov .60 1.50
70 James van Riemsdyk .50 1.25
71 Shane Doan .50 1.25
72 Ray Whitney .50 1.25
73 Paul Bissonnette .40 1.00
74 Evgeni Malkin 1.25 3.00
75 Marc-Andre Fleury 1.25 3.00
76 Sidney Crosby 2.50 6.00
77 Ryane Clowe .40 1.00
78 Logan Couture .75 2.00
79 Joe Thornton 1.00 2.50
80 Joe Pavelski .75 2.00
81 Alex Pietrangelo .50 1.25
82 Jaroslav Halak .60 1.50
83 T.J. Oshie .60 1.50
84 Steven Stamkos 1.25 3.00
85 Vincent Lecavalier .60 1.50
86 Martin St. Louis .60 1.50
87 James Reimer .60 1.50
88 Dion Phaneuf .50 1.25
89 Mikhail Grabovski .40 1.00
90 Roberto Luongo 1.00 2.50
91 Ryan Kesler .60 1.50
92 Henrik Sedin .75 2.00
93 Daniel Sedin .75 2.00
94 Alex Ovechkin 2.50 6.00
95 Tomas Vokoun .50 1.25
96 Nicklas Backstrom .60 1.50
97 Dustin Byfuglien .60 1.50
98 Andrew Ladd .40 1.00
99 Alexander Burmistrov .50 1.25
100 Ondrej Pavelec .60 1.50
101 Steve Yzerman 3.00 8.00
102 Patrick Roy 3.00 8.00
103 Mark Messier 2.50 6.00
104 Brett Hull 2.50 6.00
105 Cam Neely 1.25 3.00
106 Trevor Linden 1.25 3.00
107 Yvan Cournoyer 1.25 3.00
108 Tony Esposito 1.25 3.00
109 Stan Mikita 1.50 4.00
110 Ken Linseman 1.25 3.00
111 Don Cherry 1.25 3.00
112 Doug Gilmour 1.50 4.00
113 Ed Belfour 1.25 3.00
114 Doug Wilson 1.00 2.50
115 Brendan Shanahan 1.25 3.00
116 Bernie Parent 1.50 4.00
117 Phil Esposito 2.00 5.00
118 Manon Rheaume 3.00 8.00
119 Bobby Hull 1.50 4.00
120 Bobby Clarke 2.00 5.00
121 Thomas Steen .75 2.00
122 Luc Robitaille 1.25 3.00
123 Wendel Clark 2.00 5.00
124 Dale Hawerchuk 1.50 4.00
125 Dale Hunter 1.00 2.50
126 Bob McGill .75 2.00
126 Maxime Macenauer RC 1.50 4.00
127 Mikko Koskinen RC 2.00 5.00
128 Cam Talbot RC 4.00 10.00
129 Yann Sauve RC 1.50 4.00
130 Raphael Diaz RC 1.50 4.00
131 Erik Gustafsson RC 2.00 5.00
132 Colton Sceviour RC 1.50 4.00
133 Drew Bagnall RC 1.50 4.00
134 Brian Strait RC 2.00 5.00
135 Harri Sateri RC 1.50 4.00
136 Lance Bouma RC 1.50 4.00
137 T.Hartikainen RC 1.50 4.00
138 Brendon Nash RC 1.50 4.00
139 Mattias Ekholm RC 3.00 8.00
140 Lennart Petrell RC 2.00 5.00
141 Mark Scheifele AU RC 15.00 40.00
142 Tomas Kubalik AU RC 4.00 10.00
143 Anton Lander AU RC 4.00 10.00
144 Zac Rinaldo AU RC 4.00 10.00
145 Colin Greening AU SP RC 4.00 10.00
146 S.Da Costa AU RC 4.00 10.00
147 Erik Condra AU RC 4.00 10.00
148 Paul Postma AU RC 4.00 10.00
149 P.Wiercioch AU RC 4.00 10.00
150 Ben Scrivens AU RC 4.00 10.00
151 Greg Nemisz AU RC 4.00 10.00
152 Brett Bulmer AU RC 4.00 10.00
153 Cam Atkinson AU RC 10.00 25.00
154 Alexei Emelin AU RC 4.00 10.00
155 Roman Horak AU RC 4.00 10.00
156 Matt Frattin AU RC 4.00 10.00
157 D.Smith-Pelly AU RC 5.00 12.00
158 Justin Faulk AU SP RC 6.00 15.00
159 Craig Smith AU RC 5.00 12.00
160 Joe Vitale AU RC 4.00 10.00
161 David Savard AU RC 4.00 10.00
162 John Moore AU RC 4.00 10.00
163 Matt Read AU RC 5.00 12.00
164 Carl Klingberg AU RC 4.00 10.00
165 Tomas Vincour AU RC 4.00 10.00
166 J.Colborne JSY AU/99 RC 12.00 30.00
167 C.Hodgson JSY AU/49 RC 40.00 100.00
168 J.Blum JSY AU/99 RC 12.00 30.00
169 B.Geoffrion JSY AU/99 RC 12.00 30.00
170 Nugent-Hpk JSY AU/99 RC 150.00 300.00
171 A.Larsson JSY AU/99 RC 15.00 40.00
172 B.Saad JSY AU/99 RC 30.00 80.00
173 Landeskog JSY AU/99 RC 75.00 150.00
174 Johansen JSY AU/99 RC 40.00 100.00
175 J.Gardiner JSY AU/99 RC 20.00 50.00
176 Zibanejad JSY AU/99 RC 40.00 100.00
177 Gudbranson JSY AU/99 RC 15.00 40.00
178 S.Couturier JSY AU/99 RC 25.00 60.00
179 B.Connolly JSY AU/99 RC 12.00 30.00
180 Henrique JSY AU/99 RC 30.00 80.00
181 M.Kruger JSY AU/99 RC 20.00 50.00
182 Tim Erixon JSY AU/99 RC 12.00 30.00
183 Cody Eakin JSY AU/99 RC 20.00 50.00
184 A.Palushaj JSY AU/99 RC 12.00 30.00
185 Rundblad JSY AU/99 RC 12.00 30.00
186 Ryan Thang RC 1.00 2.50
187 Marc-Andre Bourdon RC 1.25 3.00
188 David Ullstrom RC 1.25 3.00
189 Jeremy Smith RC 1.50 4.00
190 Iiro Tarkki RC 1.50 4.00
191 Gabriel Bourque RC 1.25 3.00
192 Warren Peters RC 1.50 4.00
193 Patrick Maroon RC 1.25 3.00
194 Andrew Shaw RC 3.00 8.00
195 Mike Murphy RC 1.25 3.00
196 Milan Kytnar RC 1.50 4.00
197 Jarod Palmer RC 1.25 3.00
198 Stu Bickel RC 1.25 3.00
199 Cade Fairchild RC 1.00 2.50
200 Carl Sneep RC 1.25 3.00
201 Brian Foster RC 1.50 4.00
202 Mike Hoffman RC 5.00 12.00
203 Pierre-Cedric Labrie RC 1.25 3.00
204 Ryan Russell RC 1.50 4.00
205 Tomas Kundratek RC 1.50 4.00
206 Allen York AU RC 5.00 12.00
207 Colten Teubert AU RC 4.00 10.00
208 Keith Kinkaid AU RC 4.00 10.00
209 Harry Zolnierczyk AU RC 4.00 10.00
210 Jimmy Hayes AU RC 6.00 15.00
211 Marcus Foligno AU RC 6.00 15.00
212 Robert Bortuzzo AU RC 4.00 10.00
213 Slava Voynov AU RC 4.00 10.00
214 Corey Tropp AU RC 4.00 10.00
215 Roman Josi AU RC 10.00 25.00
216 Stefan Elliott AU RC 12.50 30.00
217 Anders Nilsson AU RC 4.00 10.00
218 Eddie Lack AU RC 4.00 10.00
219 Riley Nash AU RC 4.00 10.00
220 Dmitry Orlov AU RC 10.00 25.00
221 Dylan Olsen AU RC 5.00 12.00
222 Brayden McNabb AU RC 6.00 15.00
223 T.J. Brennan AU RC 4.00 10.00
224 Brad Malone AU RC 4.00 10.00
225 Andy Miele AU RC 4.00 10.00
226 Z.Kassian JSY AU/99 RC 15.00 40.00
227 Ryan Ellis JSY AU/99 RC 12.00 30.00
228 S.Despres JSY AU/99 RC 12.00 30.00
229 L.Leblanc JSY AU/99 RC 12.00 30.00
230 G.Nyquist JSY AU/99 RC 30.00 80.00
231 B.Smith JSY AU/99 RC 12.00 30.00
232 C.Hagelin JSY AU/99 RC 20.00 50.00
233 C.de Haan JSY AU/99 RC 12.00 30.00
234 P.Holland JSY AU/99 RC 12.00 30.00
235 C.Gaunce JSY AU/99 RC 10.00 25.00

2011-12 Crown Royale Red

*RED: 1.5X TO 4X BASIC CARDS
20 Corey Crawford 3.00 8.00
96 Nicklas Backstrom 2.50 6.00

2011-12 Crown Royale All The Kings Men Materials

*PATCH/25: 1X TO 2.5X BASIC JSY
*PRIME/50: .8X TO 2X BASIC JSY
*PRIME/25: 1X TO 2.5X BASIC JSY
1 Ales Hemsky 3.00 8.00
2 Alex Ovechkin 6.00 15.00
3 Antti Niemi 3.00 8.00
4 Anze Kopitar 6.00 15.00
5 Bobby Ryan 3.00 8.00
6 Joe Colborne 2.00 5.00
7 Cal Clutterbuck 2.50 6.00
8 Carey Price 8.00 20.00
9 Claude Giroux 4.00 10.00
10 Corey Perry 6.00 15.00
11 Curtis Glencross 2.50 6.00
12 Daniel Sedin 5.00 12.00
13 Danny Briere 4.00 10.00
14 David Rundblad 2.00 5.00
15 Derek Stepan 2.50 6.00
16 Charlie Simmer 2.50 6.00
17 Dion Phaneuf 3.00 8.00
18 Drew Doughty 5.00 12.00
19 Luc Robitaille 4.00 10.00
20 Dustin Brown 4.00 10.00
21 Dustin Byfuglien 4.00 10.00
22 Eric Staal 5.00 12.00
23 Evander Kane 4.00 10.00
24 Evgeni Malkin 6.00 15.00
25 George Parros 3.00 8.00
26 Henrik Lundqvist 10.00 25.00
27 Henrik Sedin 5.00 12.00
28 Marcel Dionne 5.00 12.00
29 Ilya Bryzgalov 4.00 10.00
30 Patrick Marleau 4.00 10.00
31 James Neal 2.50 6.00
32 Tyler Seguin 5.00 12.00
33 James van Riemsdyk 3.00 8.00
34 Jamie Benn 4.00 10.00
35 Jarome Iginla 5.00 12.00
36 Jaroslav Halak 4.00 10.00
37 Pat LaFontaine 4.00 10.00
38 Jeff Carter 3.00 8.00
39 Jeff Skinner 5.00 12.00
40 Joe Thornton 6.00 15.00
41 John Tavares 5.00 12.00
42 Jonathan Toews 6.00 15.00
43 Logan Couture 5.00 12.00
44 Marc-Andre Fleury 8.00 20.00
45 Dustin Penner 3.00 8.00
46 Ondrej Pavelec 4.00 10.00
47 P.K. Subban 5.00 12.00
48 Patrick Kane 8.00 20.00
49 Sidney Crosby 8.00 20.00
50 Taylor Hall 4.00 10.00

2011-12 Crown Royale All The Kings Men Materials Autographs

*PRIME/25: .8X TO 2X JSY AU/70-100
*PRIME/25: .6X TO 1.5X JSY AU/40
*PRIME/25: .5X TO 1.2X JSY AU/25
1 Ales Hemsky/100 6.00 15.00
2 Alex Ovechkin/100 20.00 50.00
3 Antti Niemi/100 6.00 15.00
4 Anze Kopitar/100 10.00 25.00
5 Bobby Ryan/100 6.00 15.00
6 Joe Colborne/100 6.00 15.00
8 Carey Price/100 25.00 50.00
11 Curtis Glencross/75 6.00 15.00
12 Daniel Sedin/100 10.00 25.00
13 Danny Briere/100 8.00 20.00
14 David Rundblad/100 6.00 15.00
15 Derek Stepan/100 5.00 12.00
16 Charlie Simmer/100 6.00 15.00
20 Dustin Brown/100 8.00 20.00
24 Evgeni Malkin/100 25.00 50.00
25 George Parros/100 6.00 15.00
26 Henrik Lundqvist/100 15.00 40.00
27 Henrik Sedin/100 10.00 25.00
29 Ilya Bryzgalov/100 8.00 20.00
33 James van Riemsdyk/100 6.00 15.00
34 Jamie Benn/100 8.00 20.00
35 Jarome Iginla/100 8.00 20.00
36 Jaroslav Halak/70 8.00 20.00
37 Pat LaFontaine/100 12.00 30.00
38 Jeff Carter/100 6.00 15.00
39 Jeff Skinner/25 8.00 20.00
40 Joe Thornton/100 12.00 30.00
41 John Tavares/100 15.00 40.00
42 Jonathan Toews/100 20.00 40.00
43 Logan Couture/100 8.00 20.00
44 Marc-Andre Fleury/100 15.00 30.00
45 Dustin Penner/100 6.00 15.00
48 Patrick Kane/100 15.00 40.00
49 Sidney Crosby/25 75.00 150.00

2011-12 Crown Royale Calder Collection

1 Craig Smith 2.00 5.00
2 Ryan Nugent-Hopkins 6.00 15.00
3 Gabriel Landeskog 5.00 12.00
4 Brett Connolly 1.50 4.00
5 Mika Zibanejad 5.00 12.00
6 Luke Adam 1.50 4.00
7 Adam Larsson 2.00 5.00
8 Brayden Schenn 2.00 5.00
9 Sean Couturier 3.00 8.00
10 Mark Scheifele 6.00 15.00

2011-12 Crown Royale Calder Collection Autographs

1 Craig Smith 6.00 15.00
2 Ryan Nugent-Hopkins 30.00 80.00
3 Gabriel Landeskog 15.00 40.00
4 Brett Connolly 5.00 12.00
6 Luke Adam 5.00 12.00
7 Adam Larsson 6.00 15.00
8 Brayden Schenn 10.00 25.00
9 Mark Scheifele 20.00 40.00
10 Sean Couturier 20.00 50.00

2011-12 Crown Royale Coat of Arms Patches

2 Tim Thomas/25 12.00 30.00
3 Brad Marchand/25 25.00 60.00
4 Ryan Miller/25 12.00 30.00
5 Tyler Ennis/25 8.00 20.00
6 Curtis Glencross/25 8.00 20.00
7 Jarome Iginla/25 15.00 40.00
8 Ryan Nugent-Hopkins/25 75.00 150.00
9 Marian Hossa/25 15.00 40.00
10 Matt Duchene/25 12.00 30.00
11 Gabriel Landeskog/25 15.00 40.00
12 Rick Nash/25 12.00 30.00
13 Loui Eriksson/25 12.00 30.00
14 Jamie Benn/25 10.00 25.00
15 Johan Franzen/25 10.00 25.00
16 Pavel Datsyuk/25 20.00 50.00
17 Nikolai Khabibulin/25 10.00 25.00
19 Stephen Weiss/25 10.00 25.00
20 Anze Kopitar/25 20.00 50.00
21 Dustin Brown/25 12.00 30.00
22 Niklas Backstrom/25 12.00 30.00
23 Carey Price/25 25.00 60.00
24 Jordan Eberle/25 12.00 30.00
25 Pekka Rinne/25 12.00 30.00
26 Martin Brodeur/25 30.00 80.00
27 Zach Parise/25 12.00 30.00
28 Brandon Dubinsky/25 8.00 20.00
29 Marian Gaborik/25 12.00 30.00
30 Erik Karlsson/25 15.00 40.00
31 James van Riemsdyk/25 10.00 25.00
32 Sergei Bobrovsky/25 20.00 50.00
33 Claude Giroux/25 12.00 30.00
34 Sidney Crosby/25 30.00 80.00
35 Marc-Andre Fleury/25 25.00 60.00
36 Jordan Staal/25 10.00 25.00
37 Joe Thornton/25 20.00 50.00
38 Patrick Marleau/25 12.00 30.00
39 David Rundblad/25 5.00 12.00
40 Vincent Lecavalier/25 12.00 30.00
41 Martin St. Louis/25 12.00 30.00
42 Nikolai Kulemin/25 8.00 20.00
43 Jonas Gustavsson/25 12.00 30.00
44 Roberto Luongo/25 20.00 50.00
45 Ryan Kesler/25 12.00 30.00
46 Alex Ovechkin/25 15.00 40.00
47 Alexander Semin/25 12.00 30.00
48 Alexander Burmistrov/25 10.00 25.00
49 Andrew Ladd/25 8.00 20.00
50 Shane Doan/25 10.00 25.00

2011-12 Crown Royale Crown Jewels

1 Alex Ovechkin 20.00 50.00
2 Martin Brodeur 12.00 30.00
3 Steven Stamkos 10.00 25.00
4 Carey Price 10.00 25.00
5 Sidney Crosby 20.00 50.00
6 Taylor Hall 5.00 12.00
7 Ryan Nugent-Hopkins 40.00 80.00
8 Tim Thomas 5.00 12.00
9 Corey Perry 8.00 20.00
10 Roberto Luongo 8.00 20.00

2011-12 Crown Royale Heirs To The Throne Materials

*PRIME/50: .8X TO 2X BASIC JSY
1 P.K. Subban 5.00 12.00
2 Jeff Skinner 5.00 12.00
3 Logan Couture 5.00 12.00
4 Derek Stepan 2.50 6.00
5 Tyler Ennis 2.50 6.00
6 Taylor Hall 4.00 10.00
7 John Carlson 4.00 10.00
8 Nazem Kadri 5.00 12.00
9 Blake Geoffrion 3.00 8.00
10 Jordan Eberle 5.00 12.00
11 Jamie Benn 4.00 10.00
12 Magnus Paajarvi 3.00 8.00
13 Jake Gardiner 4.00 10.00
14 Gabriel Landeskog 6.00 15.00
15 Devan Dubnyk 3.00 8.00
16 Tyler Seguin 5.00 12.00
17 James Reimer 4.00 10.00
18 Brayden Schenn 4.00 10.00
19 Joe Colborne 2.50 6.00
20 David Rundblad 2.50 6.00
21 Jonathon Blum 3.00 8.00
22 Aaron Palushaj 2.50 6.00
23 Ryan Nugent-Hopkins 8.00 20.00
24 Cody Hodgson 4.00 10.00
25 Greg Nemisz 3.00 8.00
26 James Neal 2.50 6.00
27 Erik Karlsson 5.00 12.00
28 Cody Eakin 4.00 10.00
29 Ryan Johansen 8.00 20.00
30 Erik Gudbranson 3.00 8.00

2011-12 Crown Royale Heirs To The Throne Materials Autographs

3 Logan Couture/100 10.00 25.00
4 Derek Stepan/100 10.00 25.00
5 Tyler Ennis/100 5.00 12.00
6 Taylor Hall/25 30.00 60.00
7 John Carlson/100 8.00 20.00
8 Nazem Kadri/100 15.00 40.00
11 Jamie Benn/100 10.00 25.00
12 Magnus Paajarvi/100 10.00 25.00
13 Jake Gardiner/100 8.00 20.00
17 James Reimer/100 15.00 30.00
18 Brayden Schenn/75 8.00 20.00
19 Joe Colborne/75 12.00 30.00
20 David Rundblad/100 6.00 15.00
21 Jonathon Blum/100 6.00 15.00
22 Aaron Palushaj/100 6.00 15.00
23 Ryan Nugent-Hopkins/100 40.00 100.00
24 Cody Hodgson/15 60.00 120.00
25 Greg Nemisz/100 6.00 15.00
26 James Neal/100 5.00 12.00
28 Cody Eakin/100 10.00 25.00
29 Ryan Johansen/100 12.00 30.00
30 Erik Gudbranson/100 8.00 20.00

2011-12 Crown Royale Heirs To The Throne Materials Prime Autographs

*PRIME/25: .8X TO 2X JSY AU/75-100
14 Gabriel Landeskog/25 20.00 50.00
16 Tyler Seguin/25 40.00 80.00
27 Erik Karlsson/25 30.00 60.00

2011-12 Crown Royale Ice Kings

1 Alex Ovechkin 10.00 25.00
2 Taylor Hall 2.50 6.00
3 Steven Stamkos 5.00 12.00
4 Daniel Sedin 3.00 8.00
5 Jeff Skinner 3.00 8.00
6 Sidney Crosby 10.00 25.00
7 Trevor Linden 2.50 6.00
8 Corey Perry 4.00 10.00

9 Ryan Nugent-Hopkins 5.00 12.00
10 Cam Ward 2.50 6.00
11 Nicklas Lidstrom 1.50 4.00
12 Tyler Seguin 3.00 8.00
13 Mario Lemieux 10.00 25.00
14 John Tavares 4.00 10.00
15 Gabriel Landeskog 4.00 10.00
16 Glenn Hall 2.50 6.00
17 Cody Hodgson 2.00 5.00
18 Gerry Cheevers 2.50 6.00
19 Henrik Lundqvist 6.00 15.00
20 Steve Yzerman 6.00 15.00

2011-12 Crown Royale Ice Kings Autographs

1 Alex Ovechkin/99 30.00 80.00
2 Taylor Hall/25 40.00 100.00
3 Steven Stamkos/99 20.00 50.00
4 Daniel Sedin/99 8.00 20.00
6 Sidney Crosby/25 60.00 120.00
7 Trevor Linden/99 20.00 40.00
9 Ryan Nugent-Hopkins/99 25.00 60.00
10 Cam Ward/99 8.00 20.00
11 Nicklas Lidstrom/99 15.00 40.00
12 Tyler Seguin/99 12.00 30.00
13 Mario Lemieux/25 60.00 120.00
14 John Tavares/99 15.00 40.00
15 Gabriel Landeskog/99 20.00 50.00
16 Glenn Hall/99 10.00 25.00
17 Cody Hodgson/99 10.00 25.00
19 Henrik Lundqvist/99 15.00 40.00
20 Steve Yzerman/25 40.00 100.00

2011-12 Crown Royale In Harms Way

1 Roberto Luongo 3.00 8.00
2 Carey Price 4.00 10.00
3 Cam Ward 2.00 5.00
4 Miikka Kiprusoff 2.00 5.00
5 Jimmy Howard 2.50 6.00
6 Henrik Lundqvist 5.00 12.00
7 Marc-Andre Fleury 4.00 10.00
8 Ilya Bryzgalov 2.00 5.00
9 Tim Thomas 2.00 5.00
10 Jonathan Quick 2.50 6.00
11 Antti Niemi 1.50 4.00
12 Ryan Miller 2.00 5.00
13 Martin Brodeur 5.00 12.00
14 Steve Mason 1.50 4.00
15 James Reimer 2.00 5.00
16 Tomas Vokoun 1.50 4.00
17 Ondrej Pavelec 2.00 5.00
18 Jonas Hiller 1.50 4.00
19 Jaroslav Halak 2.00 5.00
20 Corey Crawford 2.50 6.00

2011-12 Crown Royale Lords of the NHL

1 Alex Ovechkin 8.00 20.00
2 Steven Stamkos 4.00 10.00
3 Anze Kopitar 3.00 8.00
4 Rick Nash 2.00 5.00
5 Henrik Lundqvist 5.00 12.00
6 Eric Staal 2.50 6.00
7 P.K. Subban 2.50 6.00
8 Evgeni Malkin 4.00 10.00
9 Tim Thomas 2.00 5.00
10 Brad Richards 2.00 5.00
11 Henrik Sedin 2.50 6.00
12 Sidney Crosby 8.00 20.00
13 Carey Price 4.00 10.00
14 Corey Perry 3.00 8.00
15 Pavel Datsyuk 3.00 8.00
16 Jonathan Toews 3.00 8.00
17 Claude Giroux 2.00 5.00
18 Daniel Sedin 2.50 6.00
19 Martin St. Louis 2.00 5.00
20 Patrick Kane 4.00 10.00
21 Roberto Luongo 3.00 8.00
22 Zach Parise 2.00 5.00
23 Patrice Bergeron 2.00 5.00
24 Jeff Skinner 2.50 6.00
25 Dustin Byfuglien 2.00 5.00

2011-12 Crown Royale Lords of the NHL Materials Patches

*BASE JSY: .15X TO .4X PATCH/25
1 Alex Ovechkin 40.00 100.00
2 Steven Stamkos 15.00 40.00
3 Anze Kopitar 15.00 40.00
4 Rick Nash 10.00 25.00
5 Henrik Lundqvist 25.00 60.00
6 Eric Staal 12.00 30.00
7 P.K. Subban 12.00 30.00
8 Evgeni Malkin 15.00 40.00
9 Tim Thomas 10.00 25.00
10 Brad Richards 10.00 25.00
11 Henrik Sedin 12.00 30.00
12 Sidney Crosby 20.00 50.00
13 Carey Price 20.00 50.00
14 Corey Perry 15.00 40.00
15 Pavel Datsyuk 12.00 30.00
16 Jonathan Toews 15.00 40.00
17 Claude Giroux 12.00 30.00
18 Daniel Sedin 12.00 30.00
19 Martin St. Louis 10.00 25.00
20 Patrick Kane 20.00 50.00
21 Roberto Luongo 15.00 40.00
22 Zach Parise 12.00 30.00
23 Patrice Bergeron 12.00 30.00
24 Jeff Skinner 12.00 30.00
25 Dustin Byfuglien 10.00 25.00

2011-12 Crown Royale Mythology Materials

*PATCH/10: 1.5X TO 4X BASIC JSY
1 Steve Yzerman 10.00 25.00
2 Ron Francis 6.00 15.00
3 Curtis Joseph 5.00 12.00
4 Guy Lafleur 6.00 15.00
5 Brendan Shanahan 4.00 10.00
6 Eric Lindros 6.00 15.00
7 Patrick Roy 10.00 25.00
8 Grant Fuhr 6.00 15.00
9 Mario Lemieux 15.00 40.00
10 Charlie Simmer 3.00 8.00
11 Denis Savard 4.00 10.00
12 Wendel Clark 4.00 10.00
13 Joe Mullen 3.00 8.00
14 Ed Belfour 4.00 10.00
15 Joe Nieuwendyk 4.00 10.00
16 Cam Neely 4.00 10.00
17 Paul Coffey 4.00 10.00
18 Luc Robitaille 4.00 10.00
19 Adam Graves 3.00 8.00
20 Ray Bourque 6.00 15.00
21 Phil Esposito 5.00 12.00
22 Bryan Trottier 4.00 10.00
23 Ken Linseman 4.00 10.00
24 Joe Sakic 8.00 20.00
25 Jeremy Roenick 6.00 15.00

2011-12 Crown Royale Premiere Date Autographs

2 Ryan Getzlaf/25 12.00 30.00
3 Bobby Ryan/99 5.00 12.00
4 Saku Koivu/99 6.00 15.00
5 Tim Thomas/99 15.00 40.00
6 Brad Marchand/99 10.00 25.00
8 Rich Peverley/99 6.00 15.00
10 Ryan Miller/99 6.00 15.00
11 Tyler Ennis/99 4.00 10.00
12 Jarome Iginla/99 8.00 20.00
14 Curtis Glencross/99 6.00 15.00
16 Eric Staal/99 10.00 25.00
17 Cam Ward/99 8.00 20.00
18 Patrick Kane/95 15.00 40.00
19 Jonathan Toews/99 20.00 40.00
21 Jean-Sebastien Giguere/88 15.00 40.00
22 Matt Duchene/99 6.00 15.00
24 Steve Mason/99 5.00 12.00
25 Rick Nash/99 6.00 15.00
26 Jeff Carter/99 5.00 12.00
27 Jamie Benn/99 6.00 15.00
29 Kari Lehtonen/99 5.00 12.00
31 Pavel Datsyuk/99 20.00 40.00
32 Jimmy Howard/99 10.00 25.00
33 Nicklas Lidstrom/99 15.00 40.00
36 Nikolai Khabibulin/99 6.00 15.00
37 Jacob Markstrom/99 6.00 15.00
38 Mike Santorelli/99 4.00 10.00
39 Stephen Weiss/99 5.00 12.00
41 Anze Kopitar/99 8.00 20.00
44 Matt Kassian/99 4.00 10.00
45 Dany Heatley/99 5.00 12.00
47 Carey Price/99 15.00 40.00
50 Lars Eller/99 6.00 15.00
51 Shea Weber/99 5.00 12.00
52 Pekka Rinne/99 6.00 15.00
53 Mike Fisher/99 4.00 10.00
54 Martin Brodeur/25 40.00 80.00
55 Zach Parise/99 10.00 25.00
56 Ilya Kovalchuk/99 6.00 15.00
57 Kyle Okposo/99 4.00 10.00
58 John Tavares/99 15.00 40.00
59 Michael Grabner/99 12.00 30.00
60 Brad Richards/99 10.00 25.00
62 Henrik Lundqvist/99 10.00 25.00
65 Erik Karlsson/99 8.00 20.00
69 Ilya Bryzgalov/99 8.00 20.00
70 James van Riemsdyk/99 8.00 20.00
71 Shane Doan/99 5.00 12.00
73 Paul Bissonnette/99 5.00 12.00
74 Evgeni Malkin/99 20.00 40.00
75 Marc-Andre Fleury/99 12.00 30.00
78 Logan Couture/25 12.00 30.00
79 Joe Thornton/99 8.00 20.00
80 Joe Pavelski/99 8.00 20.00
81 Alex Pietrangelo/25 8.00 20.00
82 Jaroslav Halak/99 8.00 20.00
84 Steven Stamkos/99 15.00 40.00
85 Vincent Lecavalier/99 8.00 20.00
86 Martin St. Louis/99 6.00 15.00
87 James Reimer/25 15.00 40.00
91 Ryan Kesler/99 6.00 15.00
92 Henrik Sedin/99 8.00 20.00
93 Daniel Sedin/99 10.00 25.00
94 Alex Ovechkin/49 25.00 60.00
95 Tomas Vokoun/25 8.00 20.00
98 Andrew Ladd/98 8.00 20.00
99 Alexander Burmistrov/99 5.00 12.00

2011-12 Crown Royale Razor's Choice

1 Ryan Kesler 8.00 20.00
2 Pekka Rinne 8.00 20.00
3 Sheldon Souray 5.00 12.00
4 Ryan Smyth 6.00 15.00
5 Brendan Morrison 5.00 12.00
6 Ryane Clowe 5.00 12.00
7 Shawn Thornton 8.00 20.00
8 Matt Moulson 5.00 12.00
9 Nathan Gerbe 5.00 12.00
10 Teemu Selanne 15.00 40.00

2011-12 Crown Royale Rookie Silhouette Patch Autographs

*PATCH/25: .6X TO 1.5X BASIC JSY AU
167 Cody Hodgson 200.00 400.00
170 Ryan Nugent-Hopkins 400.00 800.00
172 Brandon Saad 75.00 150.00
173 Gabriel Landeskog 150.00 300.00

2011-12 Crown Royale Royal Lineage Materials

*PATCH/25: .8X TO 2X BASIC JSY
*PRIME: .6X TO 1.5X BASIC JSY
1 Bartkow/Brque/Chara 10.00 25.00
2 Staal/Skinner/Francis 8.00 20.00
3 Landskg/Dchne/Hjduk 8.00 20.00
4 Morrow/Benn/Modano 5.00 12.00
5 Ovech/Maruk/Johansn 10.00 25.00
6 Malkin/Jagr/Letestu 20.00 50.00
7 Thorntn/Couture/Clowe 10.00 25.00
8 Backes/Mullen/Oshie 6.00 15.00
9 Stepan/Gaborik/Messier 12.00 30.00
10 Fuhr/Bernier/Quick 8.00 20.00
11 Colbrne/Grabvski/Clark 10.00 25.00
12 Yzerman/Hlmstrm/Tatar 15.00 40.00
14 Eberle/Coffey/Hall 6.00 15.00
15 Henriq/Kvlchk/Nieuwen 6.00 15.00
16 Palshaj/Kostsyn/Pleknec 5.00 12.00
17 Nemisz/Iginla/Nieuwen 8.00 20.00
18 Savard/Toews/Kane 12.00 30.00
19 Clutter/Maruk/Modano 10.00 25.00
20 Giroux/Briere/Roenick 10.00 25.00

2011-12 Crown Royale Scratching The Surface Signatures

1 Adam Graves 6.00 15.00
2 Ales Hemsky 6.00 15.00
5 Alexander Semin 6.00 15.00
6 Adam Henrique 12.00 30.00
7 David Rundblad 4.00 10.00
8 Antti Niemi 15.00 30.00
9 Tyler Bozak 8.00 20.00
10 Bill Ranford 10.00 25.00
11 Blake Geoffrion 6.00 15.00
12 Bobby Ryan 5.00 12.00
13 Tim Erixon 5.00 12.00
14 Brad Marchand 12.00 30.00
15 Brad Mills 4.00 10.00
16 Brandon McMillan 4.00 10.00
17 Brayden Schenn 10.00 25.00
18 Brian Elliott 10.00 25.00
20 Cam Atkinson 12.00 30.00
22 Cody Almond 4.00 10.00
23 Cody Hodgson SP 30.00 60.00
24 Colin Wilson 5.00 12.00
25 Craig Anderson 6.00 15.00
26 Curtis Joseph 10.00 25.00
27 Dan Bouchard 10.00 25.00
28 Felix Potvin 15.00 30.00
29 Tomas Tatar 10.00 25.00
30 Sean Couturier 12.00 30.00
32 Jonas Gustavsson 8.00 20.00
35 Mike Komisarek 8.00 20.00
37 Pavel Datsyuk 15.00 40.00
39 Ray Ferraro SP 6.00 15.00
41 Simon Nolet 8.00 20.00
42 Teemu Selanne 15.00 30.00
43 Tom Barrasso 12.50 25.00
45 Wojtek Wolski 5.00 12.00
46 Ben Scrivens 5.00 12.00
48 Jaromir Jagr SP 40.00 100.00
49 Jeff Carter 5.00 12.00
50 Mats Zuccarello 6.00 15.00
51 Nazem Kadri 8.00 20.00
58 Michael Ontkean SP 6.00 15.00
60 Roman Horak 5.00 12.00

2011-12 Crown Royale Veteran Silhouette Patch Autographs

1 Sidney Crosby/25 150.00 250.00
2 Carey Price/25 40.00 80.00
3 Roberto Luongo/15 40.00 80.00
4 Alex Ovechkin/25 60.00 120.00
5 Martin Brodeur/25 60.00 120.00
6 Steven Stamkos/25 40.00 80.00
7 Tim Thomas/25 30.00 60.00
8 Henrik Lundqvist/25 40.00 100.00
9 Corey Perry/25 25.00 60.00
10 Jarome Iginla/25 50.00 100.00
11 Joe Thornton/25 40.00 100.00
12 Matt Duchene/25 20.00 50.00
13 Pavel Datsyuk/25 50.00 100.00
14 Claude Giroux/25 30.00 80.00
15 Marc-Andre Fleury/25 50.00 100.00
16 Jimmy Howard/25 20.00 50.00
17 Ryan Miller/25 20.00 50.00
18 Rick Nash/25 60.00 120.00
19 Vincent Lecavalier/25 15.00 40.00
20 Marian Gaborik/25 30.00 80.00
21 James van Riemsdyk/25 50.00 100.00
22 Evgeni Malkin/25 75.00 150.00
23 Ryan Getzlaf/25 25.00 60.00
27 Thomas Vanek/25 15.00 40.00
28 Anze Kopitar/25 EXCH 30.00 80.00
29 Zach Parise/25 30.00 80.00
31 Jordan Staal/25 15.00 40.00
32 Jonathan Quick/25 60.00 120.00
33 Tuukka Rask/25 EXCH 25.00 60.00
35 Phil Kessel/25 25.00 60.00

2011-12 Crown Royale Voices of the Game Signatures

1 Mike Doc Emrick 20.00 50.00
2 Dick Irvin 6.00 15.00
3 Pierre McGuire 8.00 20.00
4 Bill Clement 6.00 15.00
5 Peter Maher 8.00 20.00
6 Pierre Houde 6.00 15.00
7 John Forslund 6.00 15.00
8 Joe Beninati 10.00 25.00
9 Dennis Beyak 6.00 15.00
10 John Shorthouse 8.00 20.00

2012-13 Crown Royale All the Kings Men Materials

*PRIME/50: .8X TO 2X BASIC JSY
LAAK Anze Kopitar 5.00 12.00
LAAM Alec Martinez 2.50 6.00
LABR Brad Richardson 2.00 5.00
LADB Dustin Brown 3.00 8.00
LADD Drew Doughty 4.00 10.00
LADK Dwight King 2.50 6.00
LADP Dustin Penner 2.50 6.00
LAJB Jonathan Bernier 2.50 6.00
LAJC Jeff Carter 2.50 6.00
LAJQ Jonathan Quick 4.00 10.00
LAJS Jarret Stoll 2.50 6.00
LAJW Justin Williams 2.50 6.00
LAKC Kyle Clifford 2.00 5.00
LAMG Matt Greene 2.50 6.00
LAMR Mike Richards 2.50 6.00
LARS Rob Scuderi 2.50 6.00
LASG Simon Gagne 3.00 8.00
LASV Slava Voynov 3.00 8.00
LATL Trevor Lewis 2.00 5.00
LAWM Willie Mitchell 2.50 6.00

2012-13 Crown Royale Lords of the NHL Materials

*PRIME/25: 1X TO 2.5X BASIC JSY
LNAO Alex Ovechkin SP 12.00 30.00
LNBD Brandon Dubinsky 2.00 5.00
LNBR Bobby Ryan 2.50 6.00
LNCG Claude Giroux 3.00 8.00
LNCP Carey Price 6.00 15.00
LNDB David Backes 2.00 5.00
LNDBY Dustin Byfuglien 3.00 8.00
LNEK Erik Karlsson 4.00 10.00
LNES Eric Staal 4.00 10.00
LNHL Henrik Lundqvist SP 8.00 20.00
LNHS Henrik Sedin 4.00 10.00
LNJI Jarome Iginla 4.00 10.00
LNJQ Jonathan Quick 4.00 10.00
LNJT John Tavares 5.00 12.00
LNJTH Joe Thornton 5.00 12.00
LNJTO Jonathan Toews 5.00 12.00
LNLE Loui Eriksson 2.00 5.00
LNMB Martin Brodeur 8.00 20.00
LNMD Matt Duchene 3.00 8.00
LNPD Pavel Datsyuk 5.00 12.00
LNPK Phil Kessel 3.00 8.00
LNPR Pekka Rinne 3.00 8.00
LNRM Ryan Miller 3.00 8.00
LNSC Sidney Crosby 12.00 30.00
LNSD Shane Doan 2.50 6.00
LNSS Steven Stamkos 6.00 15.00
LNSW Stephen Weiss 2.50 6.00
LNTH Taylor Hall 3.00 8.00
LNTS Tyler Seguin 4.00 10.00
LNZP Zach Parise 3.00 8.00

2012-13 Crown Royale Rookie Silhouette Prime Autographs

*PATCH/25: .5X TO 1.2X BASIC JSY AU
41 Chris Kreider 30.00 80.00
42 J.T. Brown 15.00 40.00
43 Sven Baertschi 20.00 50.00
44 Jussi Rynnas 20.00 50.00
45 Tyson Barrie 40.00 100.00
46 Carter Ashton 15.00 40.00
47 Jaden Schwartz 30.00 80.00
48 Reilly Smith 25.00 60.00
49 Jake Allen 40.00 100.00
50 Jakob Silfverberg 20.00 50.00
51 Chet Pickard 12.00 30.00
52 Scott Glennie 12.00 30.00
53 Akim Aliu 15.00 40.00
54 Mat Clark 15.00 40.00
55 Michael Stone 15.00 40.00
56 Colby Robak 12.00 30.00
57 Brenden Dillon 12.00 30.00
58 Brandon Bollig 12.00 30.00
59 Robert Mayer 20.00 50.00
60 Ryan Hamilton 12.00 30.00
61 Matt Donovan 15.00 40.00
62 Kris Foucault 12.00 30.00
63 Jordan Nolan 12.00 30.00
64 Andrew Joudrey 15.00 40.00
65 Max Sauve 12.00 30.00
66 Jeremy Welsh 15.00 40.00
67 Jason Zucker 15.00 40.00
68 Brandon Manning 15.00 40.00
69 Aaron Ness 12.00 30.00
70 Dalton Prout 12.00 30.00
71 Michael Hutchinson 12.00 30.00
72 Philippe Cornet 15.00 40.00
73 Travis Turnbull 12.00 30.00
74 Gabriel Dumont 15.00 40.00
75 Chay Genoway 12.00 30.00
76 Casey Cizikas 15.00 40.00
77 Mark Stone 50.00 125.00
78 Ryan Garbutt 12.00 30.00
79 Riley Sheahan 20.00 50.00
80 Torey Krug 30.00 80.00
81 Cody Goloubef 12.00 30.00
82 Matt Watkins 12.00 30.00
83 Tyson Sexsmith 12.00 30.00
84 Shawn Hunwick 15.00 40.00
85 Mike Connolly 12.00 30.00
86 Carter Camper 12.00 30.00
87 Tyler Cuma 12.00 30.00
88 Lane MacDermid 15.00 40.00

2012-13 Crown Royale Royale Lineage Materials

*PRIME/50: .8X TO 2X BASIC INSERTS
*PRIME/25: 1X TO 2.5X BASIC INSERTS
RLANA Perry/Bonino/Selnne SP 5.00 12.00
RLBOS Neely/Bergrn/Seguin SP 3.00 8.00
RLBUF Andrychk/Pomnvl/Vnek 2.50 6.00
RLCAR Staal/Staal/Francis SP 3.00 8.00
RLCBJ Anisimov/Dubinsky/Boll 1.50 4.00
RLCGY Tanguay/Iginla/Stajan 3.00 8.00
RLCHI Chelios/Toews/Hossa 4.00 10.00
RLCOL Johnson/Bourque/Barrie 5.00 12.00
RLCOL2 Landeskog/Sakic/Hejduk 5.00 12.00
RLDAL Morrow/Eriksson/Glennie 2.00 5.00
RLDET Howard/Datsyk/Yzermn 6.00 15.00
RLEDM Hemsky/Eberle/Gagner 2.50 6.00
RLFLA Kulikov/Parros/Weiss 2.00 5.00
RLHRT Shanhn/Hwe/Vrbek SP 8.00 20.00
RLLAK Taylor/Williams/Clifford 2.00 5.00
RLMON Price/Lafleur/Pacioretty 5.00 12.00
RLNJD Larsson/Kovalchuk/Elias 2.50 6.00
RLNSH Pickard/Legwand/Rinne 2.50 6.00
RLNYI Boyes/Trottier/Tavares 4.00 10.00
RLNYR Kreider/Messier/Nash SP 6.00 15.00
RLPHI Giroux/Lindros/Couturier 4.00 10.00
RLPHX Yandle/Hanzal/Doan 2.00 5.00
RLPIT Kunitz/Neal/Lemieux SP 10.00 25.00
RLSJS Pavelski/Thornton/Clowe 4.00 10.00
RLSTL MacInn/Bcks/Schwtz 5.00 12.00
RLTBL Brown/Stamkos/Lecav 5.00 12.00
RLTOR Joseph/Potvin/Rynnas 4.00 10.00
RLVAN Burrows/Sedin/Luongo 4.00 10.00
RLWAS Ovech/Holtby/Johansn 10.00 25.00
RLWIN Burmist/Byfglien/Bogsn 2.50 6.00

2012-13 Crown Royale Scratching the Surface Signatures

1 Scott Glennie 3.00 8.00
2 Jake Allen 8.00 20.00
3 Chet Pickard 3.00 8.00
4 Jakob Silfverberg 8.00 20.00
5 Chris Kreider 10.00 25.00
6 Jussi Rynnas 6.00 15.00
7 Sven Baertschi 4.00 10.00
8 Carter Ashton 2.50 6.00
9 Jaden Schwartz 6.00 15.00
10 Brad Richards 6.00 15.00
11 Alex Urbom 15.00 40.00
12 Brett Hull 10.00 25.00
13 Cal Clutterbuck 6.00 15.00
14 Derek Stepan 8.00 20.00
15 Gabriel Landeskog 10.00 25.00
16 Jordan Eberle 12.00 30.00
17 Pat LaFontaine 15.00 30.00
18 Ryan Nugent-Hopkins 12.00 30.00
19 Steve Yzerman SP 50.00 100.00
21 Reilly Smith 8.00 20.00
22 Tyson Barrie 8.00 20.00

2012-13 Crown Royale Silhouette Materials

*PRIME/15-25: .8X TO 2X BASIC JSY
1 Nick Fotiu 4.00 10.00
2 Mike Richards 5.00 12.00
3 Zdeno Chara 6.00 15.00
4 Jason Pominville 4.00 10.00
5 Jack Johnson 4.00 10.00
6 Kari Lehtonen 5.00 12.00
7 Henrik Zetterberg 8.00 20.00
8 Teemu Selanne SP 12.00 30.00
9 Pekka Rinne 6.00 15.00
10 P.K. Subban 8.00 20.00
11 Keith Primeau 5.00 12.00
12 John Vanbiesbrouck 6.00 15.00
13 Kris Letang 8.00 20.00
14 Daniel Sedin 8.00 20.00
15 Mike Gartner 8.00 20.00
16 Chris Chelios 6.00 15.00
17 Jaroslav Halak 6.00 15.00
18 Mikhail Grabovski 4.00 10.00
19 Patrick Sharp 6.00 15.00
20 Milan Lucic 6.00 15.00

2012-13 Crown Royale Silhouette Materials Signatures

22 Jarome Iginla 15.00 40.00
23 Loui Eriksson 8.00 20.00
24 Jeremy Roenick SP B 20.00 50.00
25 Jonathan Toews 30.00 80.00
26 Eric Lindros SP B 30.00 80.00
27 Matt Duchene 12.00 30.00
28 Steve Yzerman 30.00 80.00
29 Dustin Brown 12.00 30.00
30 John Tavares 20.00 50.00
31 Mario Lemieux SP B 50.00 125.00
32 Brett Hull 25.00 60.00
33 Martin St. Louis 12.00 30.00
34 Antti Niemi 10.00 25.00
35 Gordie Howe SP A 150.00 250.00
36 Sam Gagner 8.00 20.00
37 Cory Schneider 12.00 30.00
38 Jonas Hiller 10.00 25.00
39 Brad Richards 12.00 30.00
40 Joe Sakic SP B 25.00 60.00

2012-13 Crown Royale Towering Defenders Materials

*PRIME/25: 1X TO 2.5X BASIC JSY
TDBB Brent Burns 2.50 6.00
TDCP Chris Pronger 2.50 6.00
TDDB Dustin Byfuglien 2.50 6.00
TDDP Dion Phaneuf 2.00 5.00
TDEJ Erik Johnson 1.50 4.00
TDHK Henrik Karlsson 2.00 5.00
TDIB Ilya Bryzgalov 2.50 6.00
TDJB Jay Bouwmeester 1.50 4.00
TDJC Jared Cowen 2.50 6.00
TDJG Jonas Gustavsson 2.50 6.00
TDJL Kari Lehtonen 2.00 5.00
TDJS Jeff Schultz 1.50 4.00
TDJSG Jean-Sebastien Giguere 2.50 6.00
TDMS Mike Smith 2.50 6.00
TDMST Marc Staal 1.50 4.00
TDPR Pekka Rinne 2.50 6.00
TDSW Shea Weber 2.00 5.00
TDTM Tyler Myers 1.50 4.00
TDTR Tuukka Rask 3.00 8.00
TDZC Zdeno Chara 2.50 6.00

2013-14 Crown Royale

1 Brian Gionta .40 1.00
2 Evander Kane .60 1.50
3 Jack Johnson .40 1.00
4 Mike Fisher .40 1.00
5 Evgeni Nabokov .60 1.50
6 Semyon Varlamov .60 1.50
7 Scott Hartnell .40 1.00
8 Teemu Selanne 1.25 3.00
9 Braden Holtby .75 2.00
10 Claude Giroux .60 1.50
11 Patrick Marleau .60 1.50
12 Marc-Andre Fleury 1.25 3.00
13 Pavel Datsyuk 1.00 2.50
14 Duncan Keith .50 1.25
15 Dany Heatley .50 1.25
16 Vincent Lecavalier .60 1.50
17 Thomas Vanek .50 1.25
18 Cory Schneider .60 1.50
19 Jonathan Toews 1.00 2.50
20 Alexander Steen .40 1.00
21 Curtis Glencross .40 1.00
22 Jacob Markstrom .60 1.50
23 Zdeno Chara .60 1.50
24 Shane Doan .50 1.25
25 Andrew Ladd .40 1.00
26 Martin St. Louis .60 1.50
27 Patrick Kane 1.25 3.00
28 Mark Giordano .60 1.50
29 Kari Lehtonen .50 1.25
30 Henrik Lundqvist 1.50 4.00
31 Cody Hodgson .40 1.00
32 Mike Smith .60 1.50
33 Kris Letang .75 2.00
34 Zach Parise .60 1.50
35 Eric Staal .75 2.00
36 Tyler Seguin .75 2.00
37 Mikko Koivu .50 1.25
38 Keith Yandle .40 1.00
39 Logan Couture .75 2.00
40 John Tavares 1.00 2.50
41 Niklas Kronwall .50 1.25
42 David Backes .40 1.00
43 Nazem Kadri .75 2.00
44 Henrik Zetterberg .75 2.00
45 Tuukka Rask .75 2.00
46 Alex Ovechkin 2.50 6.00
47 Matt Moulson .40 1.00
48 Pekka Rinne .60 1.50
49 Jay Bouwmeester .40 1.00
50 Joe Thornton 1.00 2.50
51 Ryan McDonagh .40 1.00
52 Matt Duchene .60 1.50
53 Evgeni Malkin 1.25 3.00
54 Jonathan Quick .75 2.00
55 Ryan Miller .60 1.50
56 Jason Spezza .60 1.50
57 Ben Bishop .50 1.25
58 Corey Perry 1.00 2.50
59 Joffrey Lupul .40 1.00
60 Jordan Eberle .60 1.50
61 Rick Nash .60 1.50
62 Martin Brodeur 1.50 4.00
63 Jordan Staal .50 1.25
64 Patrice Bergeron .75 2.00
65 Erik Karlsson .75 2.00
66 Daniel Sedin .75 2.00
67 Max Pacioretty .60 1.50
68 Shea Weber .50 1.25
69 Dustin Brown .60 1.50
70 Craig Anderson .60 1.50
71 Mike Cammalleri .50 1.25
72 Corey Crawford .75 2.00
73 Carey Price 1.25 3.00
74 Patrik Elias .60 1.50
75 Ryan Getzlaf .60 1.50
76 P.K. Subban .75 2.00
77 Taylor Hall .60 1.50
78 Ryan Kesler .60 1.50
79 Brian Campbell .40 1.00
80 Sergei Bobrovsky 1.00 2.50
81 Blake Wheeler .60 1.50
82 Ed Jovanovski .40 1.00
83 Henrik Sedin .75 2.00
84 Ryan Nugent-Hopkins .75 2.00
85 Jimmy Howard .75 2.00
86 Jamie Benn .60 1.50
87 Sidney Crosby 2.50 6.00
88 Phil Kessel .60 1.50
89 Sam Gagner .40 1.00
90 James Reimer .60 1.50
91 Steven Stamkos 1.25 3.00
92 Gabriel Landeskog .75 2.00
93 Milan Michalek .40 1.00
94 Mike Green .50 1.25
95 Roberto Luongo 1.00 2.50
96 Cam Ward .60 1.50
97 Anze Kopitar 1.00 2.50
98 Ryan Callahan .40 1.00
99 Marian Gaborik .60 1.50
100 Jarome Iginla .75 2.00
101 Sami Vatanen JSY AU RC 8.00 20.00
102 Carl Soderberg JSY AU RC 8.00 20.00
103 M.Grigorenko JSY AU RC 5.00 12.00
104 Max Reinhart JSY AU RC 8.00 20.00
105 Jared Staal JSY AU RC 6.00 15.00
106 Kuemper JSY AU RC EXCH 15.00 40.00
107 Antoine Roussel JSY AU RC 8.00 20.00
108 Alex Chiasson JSY AU RC 8.00 20.00
109 Brian Lashoff JSY AU RC 6.00 15.00
110 D.DeKeyser JSY AU RC 15.00 40.00
111 Petr Mrazek JSY AU RC 30.00 60.00
112 Nick Bjugstad JSY AU RC 12.00 30.00
113 Drew Shore JSY AU RC 6.00 15.00
114 Tanner Pearson JSY AU RC 8.00 20.00
115 R.Strome JSY AU RC 15.00 40.00
116 J.Brodin JSY AU RC EXCH 10.00 25.00
117 Mikael Granlund JSY AU RC 20.00 40.00
118 B.Gallagher JSY AU RC 20.00 50.00
119 Filip Forsberg JSY AU RC 30.00 60.00
120 Stefan Matteau JSY AU RC 6.00 15.00
121 Thomas Hickey JSY AU RC 6.00 15.00
122 J.T. Miller JSY AU RC 20.00 50.00
123 Matt Dumba JSY AU RC 10.00 25.00
124 Tarasenko JSY AU RC EXCH 75.00 150.00
125 Dmitrij Jaskin JSY AU RC 8.00 20.00
126 Alex Killorn JSY AU RC 12.00 30.00
127 Cory Conacher JSY AU RC 5.00 12.00
128 H.Lindholm JSY AU RC 12.00 30.00
129 Nicklas Jensen JSY AU RC 6.00 15.00
130 Tom Wilson JSY AU RC 15.00 40.00
131 Nail Yakupov JSY AU RC 30.00 60.00
132 D.Hamilton JSY AU RC 12.00 30.00
133 J.Huberdeau JSY AU RC 20.00 50.00
134 A.Galchenyuk JSY AU RC 40.00 100.00
135 Justin Schultz JSY AU RC 8.00 20.00
136 Q.Howden JSY AU RC 6.00 15.00
137 Tyler Toffoli JSY AU RC 25.00 50.00
138 Emerson Etem JSY AU RC 8.00 20.00
139 Scott Laughton JSY AU RC 10.00 25.00
140 Beau Bennett JSY AU RC 10.00 25.00
141 Viktor Fasth JSY AU RC 8.00 20.00
142 J.Schroeder JSY AU RC 8.00 20.00
143 Charlie Coyle JSY AU RC 12.00 30.00
144 Ryan Murphy JSY AU RC 8.00 20.00
145 Ryan Spooner JSY AU RC 8.00 20.00
146 Jarred Tinordi JSY AU RC 8.00 20.00
147 N.Beaulieu JSY AU RC 5.00 12.00
148 A.Watson JSY AU RC EXCH 6.00 15.00
149 Jack Campbell JSY AU RC 20.00 50.00
150 Igor Bobkov JSY AU RC 6.00 15.00
151 Tye McGinn JSY AU RC 8.00 20.00
152 Jamie Oleksiak JSY AU RC 6.00 15.00
153 F.Andersen JSY AU RC 30.00 80.00
154 Rickard Rakell JSY AU RC 8.00 20.00
155 Jamie Tardif JSY AU RC 5.00 12.00
156 Ben Street JSY AU RC 6.00 15.00
157 Brian Flynn JSY AU RC 6.00 15.00
158 Michal Jordan JSY AU RC 5.00 12.00
159 Calvin Pickard JSY AU RC 10.00 25.00
160 M.Sgarbossa JSY AU RC 8.00 20.00
161 Cristopher Nilstorp JSY AU RC 6.00 15.00
162 Mark Arcobello JSY AU RC 8.00 20.00
163 Brock Nelson JSY AU RC 15.00 40.00
164 Eric Hartzell JSY AU RC 8.00 20.00
165 Philipp Grubauer JSY AU RC 20.00 50.00
166 Michael Caruso JSY AU RC 5.00 12.00
167 Richard Panik JSY AU RC 8.00 20.00
168 Eric Gryba JSY AU RC 6.00 15.00
169 Matt Irwin JSY AU RC 6.00 15.00
170 Zach Redmond JSY AU RC 6.00 15.00
171 Johan Larsson JSY AU RC 10.00 25.00
172 Chris Brown JSY AU RC 5.00 12.00
173 Nick Petrecki JSY AU RC 5.00 12.00
174 Anthony Peluso JSY AU RC 5.00 12.00
175 Edward Pasquale JSY AU RC 5.00 12.00
176 Michael Kostka JSY AU RC EXCH 6.00 15.00
177 Christian Thomas JSY AU RC 6.00 15.00
178 Mark Pysyk JSY AU RC 8.00 20.00
179 Frank Corrado JSY AU RC 5.00 12.00
180 Jacob Trouba JSY AU RC EXCH 30.00 60.00
181 MacKinnon JSY AU RC EXCH 150.00 400.00
182 Girgensons JSY AU RC EXCH 12.00 30.00
183 J.Nordstrom JSY AU RC EXCH 6.00 15.00
184 Seth Jones JSY AU RC 25.00 50.00
185 Tomas Hertl JSY AU RC 40.00 80.00
186 Sean Monahan JSY AU RC 40.00 80.00
187 Nichushkin JSY AU RC EXCH 30.00 60.00
188 Olli Maatta JSY AU RC 30.00 60.00
189 Rasmus Ristolainen JSY AU RC 12.00 30.00
190 A.Barkov JSY AU RC 40.00 100.00
191 Boone Jenner JSY AU RC 15.00 40.00
192 R.Murray JSY AU RC EXCH 12.00 30.00
193 Morgan Rielly JSY AU RC 25.00 50.00
194 Matt Nieto JSY AU RC 6.00 15.00
195 Elias Lindholm JSY AU RC 20.00 50.00
196 Tomas Jurco JSY AU RC 10.00 25.00
197 J.Merrill JSY AU RC EXCH 8.00 20.00
198 Dylan McIlrath JSY AU RC 5.00 12.00
199 Cody Ceci JSY AU RC 6.00 15.00
200 Martin Jones JSY AU RC 12.00 30.00
201A Ben Hanowski RC 1.50 4.00
201B M.Mazanec JSY AU RC EXCH 8.00 20.00
202A Carter Bancks RC 1.50 4.00
202B M.Hellberg JSY AU RC EXCH 8.00 20.00
203A Brett Bellemore RC 1.50 4.00
203B Nikita Zadorov JSY AU RC 5.00 12.00
204A Nicolas Blanchard RC 1.50 4.00
204B Reto Berra JSY AU RC 8.00 20.00
205A Drew LeBlanc RC 1.25 3.00
205B J.Missiaen JSY AU RC EXCH 8.00 20.00
206A Sami Aittokallio RC 2.00 5.00
206B Jesper Fast JSY AU RC 8.00 20.00
207A Eric Selleck RC 1.50 4.00
207B J.Gustafsson JSY AU RC 10.00 25.00
208A Kevin Henderson RC 1.50 4.00
208B J.Gibson JSY AU RC EXCH 25.00 50.00
209A Matt Anderson RC 1.25 3.00
209B M.Bournival JSY AU RC 8.00 20.00
210A Eric Gelinas RC 2.00 5.00
210B Lucas Lessio JSY AU RC 5.00 12.00
211A Jean-Gabriel Pageau RC 2.00 5.00
211B C.Murphy JSY AU RC EXCH 6.00 15.00
212A Andrej Sustr RC 1.25 3.00
212B Jamie Devane JSY AU RC 6.00 15.00
213 Steven Pinizzotto RC 2.00 5.00
214 Damien Brunner RC 1.50 4.00
215 Connor Carrick RC 1.50 4.00
216 Mark Cundari AU/499 RC 2.00 5.00
217 Chris Terry AU/499 RC 2.00 5.00
218 Shawn Lalonde AU/499 RC 3.00 8.00
219 Ryan Stanton AU/499 RC 3.00 8.00
220 Greg Pateryn AU/499 RC 3.00 8.00
221 Jonathan Rheault AU/499 RC 2.00 5.00
222 Oliver Lauridsen AU/499 RC 2.50 6.00
223 Jeff Zatkoff AU/499 RC 3.00 8.00
224 Matt Tennyson AU/499 RC 2.00 5.00
225 Tyler Johnson AU/499 RC 6.00 15.00
226 Patrick Bordeleau AU/399 RC 3.00 8.00
227 Sean Collins AU/499 RC 2.50 6.00
228 Dave Dziurzynski AU/499 RC 2.50 6.00
229 Harri Pesonen AU/499 RC 2.50 6.00
230 Victor Bartley AU/499 RC 2.50 6.00
231 Derek Grant AU/499 RC 2.50 6.00
232 J.Marchessault AU/499 RC 8.00 20.00
233 Taylor Beck AU/399 RC 2.50 6.00
234 Ondrej Palat AU/499 RC 5.00 12.00
235 Radko Gudas AU/499 RC 3.00 8.00
236 John Muse AU/499 RC 3.00 8.00
237 Alex Petrovic AU/499 RC 2.50 6.00
238 Joonas Rask AU/499 RC 2.00 5.00
239 Steve Oleksy AU/499 RC 3.00 8.00
240 Matthew Konan AU/499 RC 3.00 8.00

2013-14 Crown Royale Red

*RED/99: 1.5X TO 4X BASIC CARDS
72 Corey Crawford 3.00 8.00

2013-14 Crown Royale Coat of Arms Materials

*PRIME/50: .6X TO 1.5X BASIC JSY
CAAR Antoine Roussel 2.50 6.00
CABG Brendan Gallagher 6.00 15.00
CABSC Brayden Schenn 2.50 6.00
CACC Cory Conacher 1.50 4.00
CACH Carl Hagelin 1.50 4.00
CACPE Corey Perry 5.00 12.00
CADBY Dustin Byfuglien 3.00 8.00
CADDK Danny DeKeyser 3.00 8.00
CADK Duncan Keith 2.50 6.00
CAGL Gabriel Landeskog 4.00 10.00
CAJFC Jeff Carter 2.50 6.00
CAJH Jonathan Huberdeau 6.00 15.00
CAMAF Marc-Andre Fleury 6.00 15.00
CAMGR Mikael Granlund 4.00 10.00
CAMIK Mikhail Grigorenko 1.50 4.00
CAMSL Martin St. Louis 3.00 8.00
CANCB Nicklas Backstrom 3.00 8.00
CANJ Nicklas Jensen 2.00 5.00
CANY Nail Yakupov 5.00 12.00
CAPM Patrick Marleau 3.00 8.00
CASJ Seth Jones 5.00 12.00
CATB Tyler Bozak 1.50 4.00
CATH Thomas Hickey 2.00 5.00
CAVT Vladimir Tarasenko 6.00 15.00
CAZC Zdeno Chara 3.00 8.00

2013-14 Crown Royale Fans of the Game Autographs

FGAP Audrina Patridge 25.00 60.00
FGCS Chantal Sutherland-Kruse 10.00 25.00
FGDO Dan O'Toole 8.00 20.00
FGGW Greg Wyshynski 25.00 60.00
FGJB John Buccigross 10.00 25.00
FGJBO Jennifer Botterill 10.00 25.00
FGJC Julie Chu 15.00 40.00
FGJM John C. McGinley 12.00 30.00
FGJO Jay Onrait 8.00 20.00
FGKB Katrina Bowden 15.00 40.00
FGMA Meghan Agosta 6.00 15.00
FGMC Melanie Collins 25.00 60.00
FGMD Meghan Duggan 40.00 100.00
FGSL Steve Levy 10.00 25.00
FGTB Tessa Bonhomme 15.00 40.00

2013-14 Crown Royale First Class Sigs

FCAG Alex Galchenyuk 15.00 40.00
FCCK Chris Kreider 8.00 20.00
FCDH Dougie Hamilton 10.00 25.00

FCEE Emerson Etem 6.00 15.00
FCJSC Jaden Schwartz 8.00 20.00
FCJUS Justin Schultz 6.00 15.00
FCNY Nail Yakupov 12.00 30.00
FCRMR Ryan Murray 10.00 25.00

2013-14 Crown Royale Heirs to the Throne Materials

*PRIME/50: .6X TO 1.5X BASIC JSY
HTAB Aleksander Barkov 8.00 20.00
HTAG Alex Galchenyuk 6.00 15.00
HTAK Alex Killorn 4.00 10.00
HTANP Anthony Peluso 1.50 4.00
HTAR Antoine Roussel 2.50 6.00
HTAW Austin Watson 2.00 5.00
HTBB Beau Bennett 3.00 8.00
HTBG Brendan Gallagher 6.00 15.00
HTCB Chris Brown 1.50 4.00
HTCC Cory Conacher 1.50 4.00
HTCOY Charlie Coyle 4.00 10.00
HTCSO Carl Soderberg 2.50 6.00
HTDDK Danny DeKeyser 3.00 8.00
HTDH Dougie Hamilton 4.00 10.00
HTEE Emerson Etem 2.50 6.00
HTFF Filip Forsberg 8.00 20.00
HTJAS Jared Staal 2.00 5.00
HTJB Jonas Brodin 3.00 8.00
HTJH Jonathan Huberdeau 5.00 12.00
HTJO Jamie Oleksiak 2.00 5.00
HTJSD Jordan Schroeder 2.50 6.00
HTJTM J.T. Miller 6.00 15.00
HTJTR Jacob Trouba 4.00 10.00
HTJUS Justin Schultz 2.50 6.00
HTMGR Mikael Granlund 4.00 10.00
HTMIK Mikhail Grigorenko 1.50 4.00
HTMXR Max Reinhart 2.50 6.00
HTNBJ Nick Bjugstad 3.00 8.00
HTNJ Nicklas Jensen 2.00 5.00
HTNMK Nathan MacKinnon 12.00 30.00
HTNP Nick Petrecki 1.50 4.00
HTNY Nail Yakupov 5.00 12.00
HTPMR Petr Mrazek 5.00 12.00
HTRLY Morgan Rielly 6.00 15.00
HTRMP Ryan Murphy 2.50 6.00
HTRMR Ryan Murray 4.00 10.00
HTRSP Ryan Spooner 2.50 6.00
HTSJ Seth Jones 5.00 12.00
HTSMA Stefan Matteau 2.00 5.00
HTSMO Sean Monahan 4.00 10.00
HTSV Sami Vatanen 2.50 6.00
HTTHE Tomas Hertl 5.00 12.00
HTTHI Thomas Hickey 2.00 5.00
HTTMG Tye McGinn 2.50 6.00
HTTP Tanner Pearson 2.50 6.00
HTTT Tyler Toffoli 5.00 12.00
HTTW Tom Wilson 5.00 12.00
HTVF Viktor Fasth 2.50 6.00
HTVT Vladimir Tarasenko 5.00 12.00
HTZG Zemgus Girgensons 4.00 10.00

2013-14 Crown Royale Heirs to the Throne Materials Patches

*PATCH/25: 1X TO 2.5X BASIC JSY
HTNMK Nathan MacKinnon 75.00 150.00

2013-14 Crown Royale Lords of the NHL Materials

*PRIME/25: .6X TO 1.5X BASIC JSY
*PRIME/25: .5X TO 1.2X BASIC JSY SP
LAH Adam Henrique SP 4.00 10.00
LCG Curtis Glencross 2.50 6.00
LCHO Cody Hodgson 2.50 6.00
LDS Daniel Sedin 5.00 12.00
LEK Erik Karlsson 5.00 12.00
LHL Henrik Lundqvist SP 12.00 30.00
LHZ Henrik Zetterberg 5.00 12.00
LJH Jonathan Huberdeau 4.00 10.00
LJQ Jonathan Quick 5.00 12.00
LJT John Tavares SP 5.00 12.00
LJTH Joe Thornton SP 8.00 20.00
LJTO Jonathan Toews SP 8.00 20.00
LKLE Kari Lehtonen 3.00 8.00
LMG Marian Gaborik 4.00 10.00
LNK Nazem Kadri 6.00 15.00
LNMK Nathan MacKinnon 8.00 20.00
LNY Nail Yakupov 5.00 12.00
LOVI Alex Ovechkin SP 20.00 50.00
LPKS P.K. Subban 5.00 12.00
LSC Sidney Crosby SP 20.00 50.00
LSCO Sean Couturier 3.00 8.00
LSJ Seth Jones 4.00 10.00
LSS Steven Stamkos SP 10.00 25.00
LTMU Teemu Selanne SP 10.00 25.00
LTR Tuukka Rask 5.00 12.00

2013-14 Crown Royale Majestic Marks

MJBPA Brad Park 5.00 12.00
MJBS Brendan Shanahan SP 15.00 40.00
MJGHA Glenn Hall SP 12.00 30.00
MJJE Jordan Eberle SP 12.00 30.00
MJML Mario Lemieux 40.00 80.00
MJMR Manon Rheaume 30.00 80.00
MJNK Nazem Kadri SP 8.00 20.00
MJOEL Oliver Ekman-Larsson SP 10.00 25.00
MJBOB Sergei Bobrovsky SP 15.00 40.00

2013-14 Crown Royale Mythology Materials

*PRIME/25: .5X TO 1.2X BASIC JSY
MYBH Brett Hull/100* 10.00 25.00
MYCN Cam Neely/100* 5.00 12.00
MYDG Doug Gilmour/100* 6.00 15.00
MYDSA Denis Savard/100* 5.00 12.00
MYEB Ed Belfour/100* 5.00 12.00
MYEL Eric Lindros/100* 8.00 20.00
MYGF Grant Fuhr/100* 8.00 20.00
MYGH Gordie Howe/25* 20.00 40.00
MYJN Joe Nieuwendyk/100* 4.00 10.00
MYJS Joe Sakic/100* 10.00 25.00
MYLM Lanny McDonald/100* 6.00 15.00
MYLUC Luc Robitaille/100* 5.00 12.00
MYML Mario Lemieux/100* 20.00 50.00
MYMM Mark Messier/50* 10.00 25.00
MYMO Mike Modano/100* 8.00 20.00
MYNL Nicklas Lidstrom/100* 5.00 12.00
MYPC Paul Coffey/100* 5.00 12.00
MYPE Phil Esposito/50* 6.00 15.00
MYPLF Pat LaFontaine/100* 5.00 12.00
MYPR Patrick Roy/100* 12.00 30.00
MYPT Pierre Turgeon/100* 4.00 10.00
MYRB Ray Bourque/50* 8.00 20.00
MYRBA Rod Brind'Amour/100* 5.00 12.00
MYRBL Rob Blake/100* 5.00 12.00
MYWC Wendel Clark/100* 8.00 20.00

2013-14 Crown Royale Pacific's Choice Autographs Bronze

PCCCH Chris Chelios 15.00 40.00
PCCGX Claude Giroux EXCH 15.00 40.00
PCCJ Curtis Joseph 15.00 40.00
PCDCI Dino Ciccarelli 10.00 25.00
PCDPH Dion Phaneuf EXCH 8.00 20.00
PCDPO Denis Potvin 10.00 25.00
PCDS Daniel Sedin 12.00 30.00
PCERS Eric Staal 12.00 30.00
PCGF Grant Fuhr 15.00 40.00
PCGNY Bob Gainey 10.00 25.00
PCHS Henrik Sedin 12.00 30.00
PCJRE James Reimer 10.00 25.00
PCLR Larry Robinson 10.00 25.00
PCMDU Matt Duchene EXCH 10.00 25.00
PCMSL Martin St. Louis 10.00 25.00
PCPRI Pekka Rinne 10.00 25.00
PCTH Taylor Hall 15.00 40.00
PCYC Yvan Cournoyer 10.00 25.00
PCZP Zach Parise 10.00 25.00

2013-14 Crown Royale Pacific's Choice Autographs Ruby

*RUBY HOLO/25: .8X TO 2X BASIC AU/199
*RUBY HOLO/25: .6X TO 1.5X BASIC AU/99
PCAD Alex Delvecchio/99 10.00 25.00
PCAH Adam Henrique/199 4.00 10.00
PCBE Brian Elliott/199 EXCH 4.00 10.00
PCKT Kyle Turris/199 3.00 8.00
PCMP Max Pacioretty /199 5.00 12.00
PCRL Robin Lehner/199 4.00 10.00
PCTC Tyler Cuma/199 3.00 8.00
PCZK Zack Kassian/199 3.00 8.00
PCBCO Brett Connolly/199 3.00 8.00
PCBHY Braden Holtby/199 6.00 15.00
PCCDH Calvin de Haan/199 3.00 8.00
PCCHO Cody Hodgson/99 4.00 10.00
PCJEN Jhonas Enroth/199 5.00 12.00
PCJL John LeClair/99 8.00 20.00
PCJZU Jason Zucker/199 5.00 12.00
PCMMO Matt Moulson/199 3.00 8.00
PCMXT Maxime Talbot/99 4.00 10.00
PCREL Ryan Ellis/199 4.00 10.00
PCRJU R.J. Umberger/199 3.00 8.00
PCTBA Tyson Barrie/199 5.00 12.00

2013-14 Crown Royale Pacific's Choice Autographs Sapphire

PCAL Andrew Ladd 5.00 12.00
PCAN Antti Niemi 6.00 15.00
PCBSC Brayden Schenn 8.00 20.00
PCBWR Johnny Bower 10.00 25.00
PCCGI Clark Gillies 8.00 20.00
PCCK Chris Kreider EXCH 10.00 25.00
PCJHA Jaroslav Halak 8.00 20.00
PCJHO Jimmy Howard 10.00 25.00
PCJNE James Neal 5.00 12.00
PCJP Joe Pavelski 12.00 30.00
PCJVR James van Riemsdyk 6.00 15.00
PCMC Mike Cammalleri 6.00 15.00
PCMF Mike Fisher 5.00 12.00
PCMS Mike Smith 8.00 20.00
PCRFE Ray Ferraro 5.00 12.00
PCRNH Ryan Nugent-Hopkins 10.00 25.00
PCSSA Serge Savard 8.00 20.00
PCTL Trevor Linden 10.00 25.00
PCVH Victor Hedman 10.00 25.00

2013-14 Crown Royale Regal Achievements Materials

*PRIME/25: .6X TO 1.5X BASIC JSY
*PRIME/25: .5X TO 1.2X BASIC JSY SP
RABGI Brian Gionta 2.50 6.00
RABH Brett Hull 5.00 12.00
RABSY Mike Bossy SP 5.00 12.00
RACCH Chris Chelios 4.00 10.00
RADA Dave Andreychuk 4.00 10.00
RADSI Darryl Sittler 5.00 12.00
RAJH Jonathan Huberdeau 4.00 10.00
RAJJ Jaromir Jagr 8.00 20.00
RAJS Joe Sakic 8.00 20.00
RALUC Luc Robitaille 4.00 10.00
RAMB Martin Brodeur SP 12.00 30.00
RAMGO Michel Goulet 3.00 8.00
RAMO Mike Modano 6.00 15.00
RAMRI Mike Richards 3.00 8.00
RAPK Patrick Kane 8.00 20.00
RAPM Patrick Marleau 4.00 10.00
RAPR Patrick Roy 10.00 25.00
RARB Ray Bourque 6.00 15.00
RARF Ron Francis 5.00 12.00
RARLE Reggie Leach SP 4.00 10.00
RASG Sam Gagner 2.50 6.00
RASS Steven Stamkos SP 6.00 15.00
RASY Steve Yzerman 10.00 25.00
RATKE Tim Kerr SP 5.00 12.00
RATMU Teemu Selanne SP 10.00 25.00

2013-14 Crown Royale Rookie Royalty

*ROOKIES/99: .8X TO 2X BASIC RC

2013-14 Crown Royale Rookie Royalty Autographs Ruby

*RUBY/99: .6X TO 1.5X BASIC AU/399-499

2013-14 Crown Royale Rookie Silhouette Patch Autographs

*PATCH AU/25: 1X TO 2.5X JSY AU/99
124 Vladimir Tarasenko EXCH 90.00 150.00
181 Nathan MacKinnon 200.00 500.00

2013-14 Crown Royale Royal Lineage Materials

*PRIME/25: .6X TO 1.5X BASIC INSERTS
RLANA Kvu/Prry/Etem 8.00 20.00
RLBOS Brque/Chra/Hmltn 8.00 20.00
RLCA1 Blke/Wber/Schltz 2.50 6.00
RLCA2 Brdr/Prce/Roy 12.00 30.00
RLCA3 Yzrmn/Hbrdu/Toews 8.00 20.00
RLCOL Skic/Lndskg/McKnnon 12.00 30.00
RLCZE Vkn/Pvlc/Mrzek 10.00 25.00
RLDAL Nwndyk/Sguin/Rssel 10.00 25.00
RLDEN Jnsn/Nlsn/Ellr 4.00 10.00
RLFIN Slnne/Lhtnn/Grnlnd 8.00 20.00
RLLAK Kptr/Prsn/Rbtlle 8.00 20.00
RLMTL Gney/Gnta/Gllghr 8.00 20.00
RLNYR Mssr/Nsh/Mller 8.00 20.00
RLPHI Clrke/Grx/Lghtn 10.00 25.00
RLRU1 Lrnov/Ovchkn/Ykpv SP 10.00 25.00
RLRU2 Mlkn/Grgrnko/Bre 10.00 25.00
RLSLO Mkta/Gbrik/Pnk 6.00 15.00
RLSTL Elltt/Trsnko/McInns 6.00 15.00
RLSW1 Alfrdsn/Sdin/Frsbrg 10.00 30.00
RLSW2 Krlssn/Brdin/Ldstrm 6.00 15.00
RLTOR Slmng/Phnf/Rlly 6.00 15.00
RLUS1 Byfgln/Ltch/Jnes 5.00 12.00
RLUS2 Rnck/Brwn/Glchnyk 10.00 25.00
RLUS3 Vnbsbrk/Cmpbll/Qck 12.00 30.00
RLVAN Ksler/Schrder/Bre 6.00 15.00

2013-14 Crown Royale Scratching the Surface Signatures

SCAG Alex Galchenyuk 15.00 40.00
SCAW Austin Watson 6.00 15.00
SCBB Beau Bennett 5.00 12.00
SCBG Brendan Gallagher 12.00 30.00
SCBNE Brock Nelson 8.00 20.00
SCCC Cory Conacher 5.00 12.00
SCCF Cam Fowler 4.00 10.00
SCCOY Charlie Coyle 6.00 15.00
SCDH Dougie Hamilton 12.00 30.00
SCEE Emerson Etem 4.00 10.00
SCJO Jamie Oleksiak 3.00 8.00
SCJTI Jarred Tinordi 4.00 10.00
SCJUS Justin Schultz 4.00 10.00
SCMGR Mikael Granlund 6.00 15.00
SCMIK Mikhail Grigorenko 2.50 6.00
SCNBE Nathan Beaulieu 2.50 6.00
SCNMK Nathan MacKinnon 30.00 80.00
SCNY Nail Yakupov 8.00 20.00
SCQH Quinton Howden 5.00 12.00
SCRLY Morgan Rielly 10.00 25.00
SCRMP Ryan Murphy 4.00 10.00
SCRMR Ryan Murray 6.00 15.00
SCRSP Ryan Spooner 4.00 10.00
SCSL Scott Laughton 6.00 15.00
SCTT Tyler Toffoli 8.00 20.00

2013-14 Crown Royale Silhouette Materials

PRIME/15-25: .8X TO 2X BASIC JSY/100
PRIME/15-25: .6X TO 1.5X BASIC JSY/50
SAAN Artem Anisimov/100* 3.00 8.00
SAF Adam Foote/100* 5.00 12.00
SAKH Anton Khudobin/100* 5.00 12.00
SAMI Al MacInnis/100* 6.00 15.00
SBBE Brian Bellows/50* 5.00 12.00
SBEN Jamie Benn/100* 5.00 12.00
SBGI Brian Gionta/100* 3.00 8.00
SBHY Braden Holtby/100* 6.00 15.00
SBN Bernie Nicholls/50* 6.00 15.00
SBRM Brad Marchand/100* 6.00 15.00
SBRS Tom Barrasso/100* 5.00 12.00
SBSA Borje Salming/50* 6.00 15.00
SBYL Brian Boyle/100* 3.00 8.00
SCG Curtis Glencross/100* 3.00 8.00
SCTA Chris Tanev/100* 6.00 15.00
SDA Dave Andreychuk/100* 5.00 12.00
SDB David Backes/100* 4.00 10.00
SDBO Dan Boyle/100* 3.00 8.00
SDC Daniel Cleary/100* 5.00 12.00
SDJE Dustin Jeffrey/100* 5.00 12.00
SDK Duncan Keith/100* 6.00 15.00
SDKR David Krejci/100* 6.00 15.00
SDT Dave Taylor/50* 6.00 15.00
SET Eric Tangradi/100* 5.00 12.00
SGF Grant Fuhr/100* 8.00 20.00
SGUY Guy Lafleur/50* 8.00 20.00
SJE Jordan Eberle/50* 6.00 15.00
SJHI Jonas Hiller/100* 4.00 10.00
SJHO Jimmy Howard/50* 8.00 20.00
SJJ Jaromir Jagr/100* 10.00 25.00
SJLU Joffrey Lupul/100* 3.00 8.00
SJST Jarret Stoll/100* 4.00 10.00
SKO Kyle Okposo/100* 3.00 8.00
SKY Keith Yandle/100* 3.00 8.00
SLAI Brooks Laich/100* 3.00 8.00
SLS Luke Schenn/100* 5.00 12.00
SLSB Luca Sbisa/100* 4.00 10.00
SMBA Mikael Backlund/100* 4.00 10.00
SMBI Martin Biron/100* 4.00 10.00
SMDZ Michael Del Zotto/100* 3.00 8.00
SMG Marian Gaborik/50* 6.00 15.00
SMLO Matthew Lombardi/100* 3.00 8.00
SMMS Marty McSorley/100* 4.00 10.00
SMXT Maxime Talbot/100* 3.00 8.00
SNKB Niklas Backstrom/100* 4.00 10.00
SNS Nick Spaling/100* 3.00 8.00
SPAP P.A. Parenteau/100* 3.00 8.00
SPAS Paul Stastny/100* 4.00 10.00
SPB Pavel Bure/50* 6.00 15.00
SPLF Pat LaFontaine/50* 6.00 15.00
SPT Pierre Turgeon/100* 4.00 10.00
SPV Pat Verbeek/100* 3.00 8.00
SRB Ray Bourque/50* 10.00 25.00
SRBA Rod Brind'Amour/50* 6.00 15.00
SRBL Rob Blake/100* 5.00 12.00
SRBO Robert Bortuzzo/100* 3.00 8.00
SRF Ron Francis/100* 6.00 15.00
SRLE Reggie Leach/25* 6.00 15.00
SRPO Roman Polak/100* 3.00 8.00
SRRE Robyn Regehr/100* 3.00 8.00
SRSU Ryan Suter/100* 4.00 10.00
SRT Rick Tocchet/100* 5.00 12.00
SSBR Sheldon Brookbank/100* 3.00 8.00
SSC Sidney Crosby/50* 25.00 60.00
SSD Shane Doan/100* 4.00 10.00
SSGR Stu Grimson/100* 3.00 8.00
SSHA Scott Hartnell/100* 3.00 8.00
SSK Saku Koivu/100* 5.00 12.00
STPL Tomas Plekanec/100* 3.00 8.00
STR Tuukka Rask/100* 6.00 15.00

2013-14 Crown Royale Silhouette Materials Signatures

*PRIME/25: .6X TO 1.5X JSY AU/99
SSAL Andrew Ladd/99* 6.00 15.00
SSBE Brian Elliott/99* 8.00 20.00
SSBP Bernie Parent/25* 20.00 50.00
SSBS Brendan Shanahan/25* 25.00 50.00
SSCN Cam Neely/25* 15.00 40.00
SSCP Carey Price/25* 30.00 80.00
SSHL Henrik Lundqvist/25* 40.00 100.00
SSIL Igor Larionov/25* 15.00 40.00
SSJN Joe Nieuwendyk/99* 8.00 20.00
SSJP Joe Pavelski/99* 10.00 25.00
SSJQ Jonathan Quick/99* 25.00 50.00
SSMB Martin Brodeur/25* 40.00 80.00
SSMC Mike Cammalleri/99* 8.00 20.00
SSNG Nathan Gerbe/99* 6.00 15.00
SSPR Patrick Roy/25* 50.00 100.00
SSRG Ryan Getzlaf/99* 10.00 25.00
SSRM Ryan Miller/99* 10.00 25.00
SSRV Rogie Vachon/25* 20.00 50.00
SSCGX Claude Giroux/99* 30.00 60.00
SSJTH Joe Thornton/99* 12.00 30.00
SSLUC Luc Robitaille/99* 10.00 25.00
SSMDU Matt Duchene/99* 10.00 25.00
SSMHE Milan Hejduk/99* 8.00 20.00
SSOVI Alex Ovechkin/25* 60.00 150.00
SSPKE Phil Kessel/99* 10.00 25.00
SSRJO Roman Josi/99* 8.00 20.00
SSRNH Ryan Nugent-Hopkins/99* 12.00 30.00

2013-14 Crown Royale Silver Chalice Materials

*PRIME/25: .8X TO 2X BASIC JSY
*PRIME/25: .6X TO 1.5X BASIC JSY SP
SIBC Bobby Clarke 6.00 15.00
SIBH Brett Hull 10.00 25.00
SIBS Brendan Shanahan 8.00 20.00
SIBSY Mike Bossy SP 8.00 20.00
SICCR Corey Crawford 6.00 15.00
SICPE Corey Perry 8.00 20.00
SIHZ Henrik Zetterberg 6.00 15.00
SIJN Joe Nieuwendyk 4.00 10.00
SIJQ Jonathan Quick 8.00 20.00
SIJS Joe Sakic 8.00 20.00
SIMB Martin Brodeur SP 15.00 40.00
SIMHE Milan Hejduk 4.00 10.00
SIML Mario Lemieux SP 25.00 60.00
SIMM Mark Messier SP 8.00 20.00
SIMSL Martin St. Louis 5.00 12.00
SINL Nicklas Lidstrom 8.00 20.00
SIPC Paul Coffey 6.00 15.00
SIPEL Patrik Elias 5.00 12.00
SIPK Patrick Kane SP 12.00 30.00
SIPR Patrick Roy 12.00 30.00
SIRBA Rod Brind'Amour 4.00 10.00
SISC Sidney Crosby 15.00 40.00
SISY Steve Yzerman 10.00 25.00
SIZC Zdeno Chara 5.00 12.00

2013-14 Crown Royale Sovereign Sigs

*RUBY/25: .6X TO 1.5X BASIC AU
SOAA Akim Aliu 2.50 6.00
SOAJO Andrew Joudrey 2.50 6.00
SOANE Aaron Ness 2.50 6.00
SOANL Anton Lander 2.50 6.00
SOASH Carter Ashton 2.50 6.00
SOBDU Brandon Dubinsky 2.50 6.00
SOBRB Brent Burns 4.00 10.00
SOBRS Brian Strait 2.50 6.00
SOCA Craig Anderson 4.00 10.00
SOCCL Cal Clutterbuck 2.50 6.00
SOCCM Carter Camper 2.50 6.00
SOCHP Chet Pickard 2.50 6.00
SOCK Chris Kreider 5.00 12.00
SOCTR Corey Tropp 2.50 6.00
SODBO Dan Boyle 4.00 10.00
SODDU Devan Dubnyk 3.00 8.00
SODHA Dan Hamhuis 3.00 8.00
SODHT Derian Hatcher 2.50 6.00
SODRU David Rundblad 3.00 8.00
SODSA Denis Savard 4.00 10.00
SODW Doug Wilson 3.00 8.00
SOEF Eric Fehr 2.50 6.00
SOGB Gabriel Bourque 3.00 8.00
SOGD Gabriel Dumont 4.00 10.00
SOGNY Gustav Nyquist 8.00 20.00
SOJA Jake Allen 4.00 10.00
SOJCO Joe Colborne 4.00 10.00
SOJF Joe Finley 2.50 6.00
SOJGA Jake Gardiner 5.00 12.00
SOJM Jacob Markstrom 4.00 10.00
SOJSC Jaden Schwartz 5.00 12.00
SOJSI Jakob Silfverberg 2.50 6.00
SOJVI Joe Vitale 2.50 6.00
SOJZU Jason Zucker 4.00 10.00
SOKA Karl Alzner 2.50 6.00
SOKPO Kevin Poulin 3.00 8.00
SOLI Leland Irving 3.00 8.00
SOLMD Lane MacDermid 3.00 8.00
SOMDZ Michael Del Zotto 2.50 6.00
SOMHV Marty Havlat 5.00 12.00
SOMIS Michael Stone 3.00 8.00
SOMST Mark Stone 5.00 12.00
SONKU Nikolai Kulemin 2.50 6.00
SORJ Ryan Johansen 3.00 8.00
SORMA Robert Mayer 2.50 6.00
SORMI Rick Middleton 3.00 8.00
SORRA Rob Ray 4.00 10.00
SORSH Riley Sheahan 2.50 6.00
SOSB Sven Baertschi 5.00 12.00
SOSCH Shane Churla 2.50 6.00
SOSDE Simon Despres 3.00 8.00
SOSVA Semyon Varlamov 5.00 12.00
SOTBA Tyson Barrie 2.50 6.00
SOTER Tim Erixon 2.50 6.00
SOTK Torey Krug 6.00 15.00
SOTM Torrey Mitchell 2.50 6.00
SOTOR Terry O'Reilly 5.00 12.00

2013-14 Crown Royale Voices of the Game Autographs

VGBF Bernie Federko 5.00 12.00
VGCR Celena Rae 12.00 30.00
VGDD Darren Dreger 6.00 15.00
VGGR Glenn Resch 6.00 15.00
VGHR Howie Rose 8.00 20.00
VGJC Jim Cornelison 10.00 25.00
VGJJ Jeff Jimerson 10.00 25.00
VGJR Jeremy Roenick 8.00 20.00
VGKJ Keith Jones 6.00 15.00
VGKT Kathryn Tappen 50.00 100.00
VGKW Kevin Weekes 5.00 12.00
VGMD Mark Donnelly 5.00 12.00
VGPT Pia Toscano 10.00 25.00
VGRFE Ray Ferraro 5.00 12.00
VGTC Terry Crisp 8.00 20.00

1970-71 Dad's Cookies

COMPLETE SET (144) 100.00 200.00
1 Lou Angotti .75 2.00
2 Don Awrey .50 1.00
3 Bob Baun 1.25 3.00
4 Jean Beliveau 6.00 15.00
5 Red Berenson .75 2.00
6 Gary Bergman .50 1.00
7 Les Binkley 1.00 2.50
8 Andre Boudrias .50 1.00
9 Wally Boyer .50 1.00
10 Arnie Brown .50 1.00
11 Johnny Bucyk 1.50 4.00
12 Charlie Burns .50 1.00
13 Larry Cahan .50 1.00
14 Gerry Cheevers 2.50 6.00
15 Bobby Clarke 5.00 12.00
16 Wayne Connelly .50 1.00
17 Yvan Cournoyer 1.50 4.00
18 Roger Crozier 1.00 2.50
19 Ray Cullen .50 1.00
20 Denis DeJordy 1.00 2.50
21 Alex Delvecchio 1.50 4.00
22 Bob Dillabough .50 1.00
23 Gary Doak .50 1.00
24 Gary Dornhoefer 1.00 2.50
25 Dick Duff .75 2.00
26 Tim Ecclestone .50 1.00
27 Roy Edwards 1.00 2.50
28 Gerry Ehman .50 1.00
29 Ron Ellis .75 2.00
30 Phil Esposito 5.00 12.00
31 Tony Esposito 5.00 12.00
32 Doug Favell 1.00 2.50
33 John Ferguson .75 2.00
34 Norm Ferguson .50 1.00
35 Reg Fleming .50 1.00
36 Bill Flett .50 1.00
37 Bruce Gamble 1.00 2.50
38 Jean-Guy Gendron .50 1.00
39 Ed Giacomin 2.00 5.00
40 Rod Gilbert 1.50 4.00
41 Bill Goldsworthy .75 2.00
42 Phil Goyette .50 1.00
43 Danny Grant .75 2.00
44 Ted Green .75 2.00
45 Vic Hadfield .75 2.00
46 Al Hamilton .50 1.00
47 Ted Hampson .50 1.00
48 Terry Harper .75 2.00
49 Ted Harris .50 1.00
50 Paul Henderson 2.50 6.00
51 Bryan Hextall .50 1.00
52 Bill Hicke .50 1.00
53 Larry Hillman .50 1.00
54 Wayne Hillman .50 1.00
55 Charlie Hodge 1.25 3.00
56 Ken Hodge .75 2.00
57 Gordie Howe 10.00 25.00
58 Harry Howell 1.00 2.50
59 Bobby Hull 8.00 20.00
60 Dennis Hull .75 2.00
61 Earl Ingarfield .50 1.00
62 Doug Jarrett .50 1.00
63 Gary Jarrett .50 1.00
64 Ed Johnston 1.00 2.50
65 Dave Keon 1.50 4.00
66 Skip Krake .50 1.00
67 Orland Kurtenbach .75 2.00
68 Andre Lacroix .75 2.00
69 Jacques Laperriere 1.25 3.00
70 Jacques Lemaire 1.50 4.00
71 Rick Ley .50 1.00
72 Bruce MacGregor .50 1.00
73 Keith Magnuson .75 2.00
74 Frank Mahovlich 2.00 5.00
75 Chico Maki .50 1.00
76 Gilles Marotte .50 1.00
77 Bert Marshall .50 1.00
78 Don Marshall .50 1.00
79 Pit Martin .75 2.00
80 Keith McCreary .50 1.00
81 Ab McDonald .50 1.00
82 Jim McKenny .75 2.00
83 John McKenzie .75 2.00
84 Mike McMahon .50 1.00
85 Larry Mickey .50 1.00
86 Stan Mikita 2.50 6.00
87 Doug Mohns .50 1.00
88 Wayne Muloin .50 1.00
89 Jim Neilson .50 1.00
90 Bob Nevin .50 1.00
91 Murray Oliver .50 1.00
92 Bobby Orr 20.00 40.00
93 Danny O'Shea .50 1.00
94 Rosaire Paiement .50 1.00
95 Bernie Parent 2.50 6.00
96 Jean-Paul Parise .50 1.00
97 Brad Park 4.00 10.00
98 Mike Pelyk .50 1.00
99 Gilbert Perreault 2.00 5.00
100 Noel Picard .50 1.00
101 Barclay Plager .75 2.00
102 Jacques Plante 6.00 15.00
103 Tracy Pratt .50 1.00
104 Dean Prentice .50 1.00
105 Jean Pronovost .75 2.00
106 Bob Pulford .75 2.00
107 Pat Quinn 1.00 2.50
108 Jean Ratelle 1.00 2.50
109 Matt Ravlich .50 1.00
110 Mickey Redmond 1.00 2.50
111 Henri Richard 2.50 6.00
112 Jim Roberts .50 1.00
113 Dale Rolfe .50 1.00
114 Bobby Rousseau .50 1.00
115 Gary Sabourin .50 1.00
116 Derek Sanderson 2.50 6.00
117 Glen Sather 1.50 4.00
118 Serge Savard 1.00 2.50
119 Ken Schinkel .50 1.00
120 Rod Selling .50 1.00
121 Brit Selby .50 1.00
122 Eddie Shack 1.50 4.00
123 Floyd Smith .50 1.00
124 Fred Stanfield .50 1.00
125 Pat Stapleton .60 1.50
126 Frank St.Marseille .50 1.00
127 Dale Tallon .60 1.50
128 Walt Tkaczuk .50 1.00
129 J.C. Tremblay .50 1.00
130 Norm Ullman .75 2.00
131 Garry Unger .75 2.00
132 Rogatien Vachon 2.00 5.00
133 Carol Vadnais .50 1.00
134 Ed Van Impe .50 1.00
135 Bob Wall .50 1.00
136 Mike Walton .50 1.00
137 Bryan Watson .50 1.00
138 Joe Watson .50 1.00
139 Tom Webster .50 1.00
140 Juha Widing 1.00 2.50
141 Tom Williams .50 1.00
142 Jim Wiste .50 1.00
143 Gump Worsley 2.50 6.00
144 Bob Woytowich .75 2.00

2009-10 Danone Foods Pee-Wee Quebec World Championship

COMPLETE SET (10) 4.00 10.00
1 Patrick Roy 1.00 2.50
2 Rick Nash .40 1.00
3 Vincent Lecavalier .40 1.00
4 Simon Gagne .40 1.00
5 Patrice Bergeron .50 1.25
6 Marc-Andre Fleury .75 2.00
7 Mike Cammalleri .30 .75
8 Mike Komisarek .30 .75
9 Anze Kopitar .60 1.50
10 Thomas Vanek .30 .75

1983-84 Devils Postcards

COMPLETE SET (25) 10.00 25.00
1 Mike Antonovich .20 .50
2 Mel Bridgman .30 .75
3 Aaron Broten .30 .75
4 Murray Bromwell .30 .75
5 Dave Cameron .30 .75
6 Rich Chernomaz .20 .50
7 Joe Cirella .20 .50
8 Ken Daneyko .60 1.50
9 Larry Floyd .20 .50
10 Paul Gagne .20 .50
11 Mike Kitchen .30 .75
12 Jeff Larmer .30 .75
13 Don Lever .20 .50
14 Dave Lewis .20 .50
15 Bob Lorimer .20 .50
16 Ron Low .30 .75
17 Jan Ludvig .20 .50
18 John Maclean 2.50 6.00
19 Bob MacMillan .30 .75
20 Hector Marini .20 .50
21 Rick Meagher .20 .50
22 Grant Mulvey .30 .75
23 Glenn Resch .60 1.50
24 Phil Russell .20 .50
25 Pat Verbeek 2.50 6.00

1984-85 Devils Postcards

COMPLETE SET (25) 8.00 20.00
1 Chico Resch .75 2.00
2 Joe Cirella .30 .75
4 Bob Lorimer .20 .50
5 Phil Russell .20 .50
8 Dave Pichette .20 .50
9 Don Lever .30 .75
10 Aaron Broten .20 .50
12 Pat Verbeek 2.00 5.00
14 Rich Chernomaz .20 .50
15 John MacLean 1.50 4.00
16 Rick Meagher .20 .50
17 Paul Gagne .20 .50
18 Mel Bridgman .30 .75
19 Rich Preston .20 .50
20 Tim Higgins .20 .50
21 Bob Hoffmeyer .20 .50
22 Doug Sulliman .20 .50
23 Bruce Driver .40 1.00
25 Dave Lewis .20 .50
27 Kirk Muller 2.00 5.00
28 Uli Hiemer .20 .50
29 Jan Ludvig .20 .50
30 Ron Low .30 .75
33 Hannu Kamppurri .30 .75
NNO Doug Carpenter CO .20 .50

1985-86 Devils Postcards

COMPLETE SET (10) 5.60 14.00
1 Greg Adams .60 1.50
2 Perry Anderson .40 1.00
3 Craig Billington .75 2.00
4 Alain Chevrier .60 1.50
5 Paul Gagne .40 1.00
6 Mark Johnson .40 1.00
7 Kirk Muller 1.50 4.00
8 Chico Resch 1.00 2.50
9 Randy Velischek .40 1.00
10 Craig Wolanin .40 1.00

1986-87 Devils Police

COMPLETE SET (20) 12.00 30.00
1 Greg Adams 24 .60 1.50
2 Perry Anderson 25 .40 1.00
3 Timo Blomqvist 5 .40 1.00
4 Andy Brickley 26 .40 1.00
5 Mel Bridgman 18 .60 1.50
6 Aaron Broten 10 .40 1.00
7 Alain Chevrier 30 .60 1.50
8 Joe Cirella 2 .60 1.50
9 Ken Daneyko 3 .60 1.50
10 Bruce Driver 23 .75 2.00
11 Uli Hiemer 28 .40 1.00
12 Mark Johnson 12 .60 1.50
13 Jan Ludvig 29 .40 1.00
14 John MacLean 15 1.50 4.00
15 Peter McNab 7 .60 1.50
16 Kirk Muller 9 2.00 5.00
17 Doug Sulliman 22 .40 1.00
18 Randy Velischek 27 .40 1.00
19 Pat Verbeek 2.00 5.00
20 Craig Wolanin 6 .40 1.00

1988-89 Devils Carretta

COMPLETE SET (30) 10.00 25.00
1 Perry Anderson 25 .20 .50
2 Bob Bellemore CO .20 .50
3 Aaron Broten 10 .20 .50
4 Doug Brown 24 .20 .50
5 Sean Burke 1 1.25 3.00
6 Anders Carlsson 20 .20 .50
7 Joe Cirella 2 .20 .50
8 Pat Conacher 32 .20 .50
9 Ken Daneyko 3 .30 .75
10 Bruce Driver 23 .30 .75
11 Bob Hoffmeyer CO .20 .50
12 Jamie Huscroft 4 .20 .50
13 Mark Johnson 12 .30 .75
14 Jim Korn 14 .20 .50
15 Tom Kurvers 5 .20 .50
16 Lou Lamoriello P/GM .08 .25
17 Claude Loiselle 19 .20 .50
18 John MacLean 15 .75 2.00
19 David Maley 8 .20 .50
20 Doug McKay CO .08 .25
21 Kirk Muller 9 .75 2.00
22 Jack O'Callahan 7 .20 .50
23 Steve Rooney 18 .20 .50
24 Bob Sauve 28 .30 .75
25 Jim Schoenfeld CO .40 1.00
26 Brendan Shanahan 11 6.00 15.00
27 Patrik Sundstrom 17 .30 .75
28 Randy Velischek 27 .20 .50
29 Pat Verbeek 16 .75 2.00
30 Craig Wolanin 6 .20 .50

1989-90 Devils Caretta

COMPLETE SET (29) 8.00 20.00
1 Tommy Albelin 26 .20 .50
2 Bob Bellemore CO .08 .25
3 Neil Brady 19 .20 .50
4 Aaron Broten 10 .20 .50
5 Doug Brown 24 .20 .50
6 Sean Burke 1 .75 2.00
7 Pat Conacher 32 .20 .50
8 John Cunniff CO .08 .25
9 Ken Daneyko 3 .20 .50
10 Bruce Driver 23 .40 1.00
11 Slava Fetisov 2 .75 2.00
12 Mark Johnson 12 .20 .50
13 Jim Korn 14 .20 .50
14 Lou Lamoriello P/GM .08 .25
15 Jim MacLean 15 .60 1.50
16 David Maley 8 .20 .50
17 Kirk Muller 9 .75 2.00
18 Janne Ojanen 22 .20 .50
19 Walt Poddubny 21 .20 .50
20 Reijo Ruotsalainen 29 .20 .50
21 Brendan Shanahan 11 2.00 5.00
22 Sergei Starikov 4 .20 .50
23 Patrik Sundstrom 17 .20 .50
24 Peter Sundstrom 20 .20 .50
25 Chris Terreri 31 .40 1.00
26 Sylvain Turgeon 16 .20 .50
27 Randy Velischek 27 .20 .50
28 Eric Weinrich 7 .20 .50
29 Craig Wolanin 6 .20 .50

1990-91 Devils Team Issue

COMPLETE SET (30) 6.00 15.00
1 Tommy Albelin .15 .40
2 Laurie Boschman .15 .40
3 Doug Brown .20 .50
4 Sean Burke .60 1.50
5 Tim Burke .15 .40
6 Zdeno Ciger .20 .50
7 Pat Conacher .15 .40
8 Troy Crowder .20 .50
9 John Cunniff CO .08 .25
10 Ken Daneyko .30 .75
11 Bruce Driver .20 .50
12 Slava Fetisov .30 .75
13 Alexei Kasatonov .20 .50
14 Lou Lamoriello P/GM .08 .25
15 Claude Lemieux .40 1.00
16 David Maley .15 .40
17 John MacLean .40 1.00
18 Jon Morris .15 .40
19 Kirk Muller .60 1.50
20 Lee Norwood .15 .40
21 Myles O'Connor .15 .40
22 Walt Poddubny .15 .40
23 Brendan Shanahan 2.00 5.00
24 Peter Stastny .60 1.50
25 Alan Stewart .15 .40
26 Warren Strelow .15 .40
27 Doug Sulliman .15 .40
28 Patrik Sundstrom .20 .50
29 Chris Terreri .20 .50
30 Eric Weinrich .20 .50

1991-92 Devils Teams Carvel

COMPLETE SET (10) 8.00 20.00
1 1982-83 Devils Team 1.25 3.00
2 1983-84 Devils Team 1.00 2.50
3 1984-85 Devils Team 1.00 2.50
4 1985-86 Devils Team 1.00 2.50
5 1986-87 Devils Team 1.00 2.50
6 1987-88 Devils Team 1.00 2.50
7 1988-89 Devils Team 1.00 2.50
8 1989-90 Devils Team 1.00 2.50
9 1990-91 Devils Team 1.00 2.50
10 1991-92 Devils Team 1.00 2.50

1996-97 Devils Team Issue

COMPLETE SET (30) 12.00 30.00
1 Mike Dunham .75 2.00
3 Ken Daneyko .20 .50
4 Scott Stevens .30 .75
6 Denis Pederson .20 .50
11 Steve Sullivan .40 1.00
12 Bill Guerin .75 2.00
14 Brian Rolston .30 .75
15 John MacLean .30 .75
16 Bobby Holik .30 .75
17 Petr Sykora .75 2.00
18 Sergei Brylin .20 .50
19 Bob Carpenter .08 .25
20 Jay Pandolfo .30 .75
21 Randy McKay .30 .75
22 Patrik Elias 4.00 10.00
23 Dave Andreychuk .20 .50

24 Lyle Odelein .20 .50
25 Valeri Zelepukin .08 .25
26 Jason Smith .20 .50
27 Scott Niedermayer .40 1.00
28 Kevin Dean .08 .25
29 Shawn Chambers .08 .25
30 Martin Brodeur 2.00 5.00
32 Steve Thomas .20 .50
33 Reid Simpson .08 .25
NNO John J. McMullen(Chairman) .02 .10
NNO Jacques Lemaire CO .20 .50
NNO Robbie Ftorek ASST CO .08 .25
NNO Lou Lamoriello GM .02 .10
NNO Jacques Caron ACO .02 .10

1997-98 Devils Team Issue

COMPLETE SET (32) 8.00 20.00
1 Mike Dunham .40 1.00
2 Sheldon Souray .15 .40
3 Ken Daneyko .15 .40
4 Scott Stevens .30 .75
5 Ken Sutton .15 .40
6 Brad Bombardir .15 .40
7 Vlastimil Kroupa .15 .40
8 Denis Pederson .15 .40
9 Bill Guerin .40 1.00
10 John MacLean .15 .40
11 Bobby Holik .20 .50
12 Petr Sykora .40 1.00
13 Sergei Brylin .15 .40
14 Bobby Carpenter .15 .40
15 Jay Pandolfo .15 .40
16 Randy McKay .20 .50
17 Scott Daniels .15 .40
18 Dave Andreychuk .20 .50
19 Lyle Odelein .15 .40
20 Valeri Zelepukin .15 .40
21 Patrik Elias 1.25 3.00
22 Kevin Dean .15 .40
23 Krzysztof Oliwa .30 .75
24 Martin Brodeur 1.25 3.00
25 Steve Thomas .20 .50
26 Reid Simpson .15 .40
27 Doug Gilmour .40 1.00
28 Jacques Lemaire CO .08 .25
29 Robbie Ftorek CO .02 .10
30 Jacques Caron CO .02 .10
31 Lou Lamoriello PRES .02 .10
32 John McMullen CHAIR .02 .10

1998-99 Devils Team Issue

COMPLETE SET (30) 20.00
1 Dave Andreychuk .30 .75
2 Jason Arnott .30 .75
3 Brad Bombardir .20 .50
4 Martin Brodeur 2.00 5.00
5 Sergei Brylin .20 .50
6 Jacques Caron ACO .02 .10
7 Bob Carpenter ACO .02 .10
8 Ken Daneyko .20 .50
9 Kevin Dean .20 .50
10 Patrik Elias .40 1.00
11 Slava Fetisov CO .08 .25
12 Robbie Ftorek HCO .02 .10
13 Bobby Holik .20 .50
14 Sasha Lakovic .20 .50
15 Lou Lamoriello GM .02 .10
16 John Madden .40 1.00
17 Randy McKay .20 .50
18 John McMullen OWN .02 .10
19 Brendan Morrison .40 1.00
20 Scott Niedermayer .30 .75
21 Lyle Odelein .20 .50
22 Krzysztof Oliwa .40 1.00
23 Jay Pandolfo .30 .75
24 Denis Pederson .20 .50
25 Brian Rolston .30 .75
26 Vadim Sharifijanov .20 .50
27 Sheldon Souray .20 .50
28 Scott Stevens .40 1.00
29 Petr Sykora .40 1.00
30 Chris Terreri .30 .75

1999-00 Devils Team Issue

COMPLETE SET (31) 8.00 20.00
1 Scott Stevens .30 .75
2 Sheldon Souray .15 .40
3 Ken Daneyko .15 .40
4 Brad Bombardir .15 .40
5 Vadim Sharifijanov .15 .40
6 Brendan Morrison .40 1.00
7 John Madden .40 1.00
8 Sergei Nemchinov .15 .40
9 Bobby Holik .20 .50
10 Petr Sykora .40 1.00
11 Sergei Brylin .15 .40
12 Denis Pederson .15 .40
13 Jay Pandolfo .15 .40
14 Randy McKay .20 .50
15 Claude Lemieux .30 .75
16 Scott Gomez .40 1.00
17 Lyle Odelein .15 .40
18 Jason Arnott .30 .75
19 Patrik Elias .60 1.50
20 Scott Niedermayer .30 .75
21 Brian Rafalski .20 .50
22 Krzysztof Oliwa .40 1.00
23 Martin Brodeur 1.50 4.00
24 Chris Terreri .20 .50
25 Robbie Ftorek CO .15 .40
26 Slava Fetisov CO .20 .50
27 Larry Robinson CO .20 .50
28 Jacques Caron CO .02 .10
29 Lou Lamoriello GM .02 .10
30 Dr. John J. McMullen .02 .10
31 PSEG Energy .02 .10

2000-01 Devils Team Issue

COMPLETE SET (30) 10.00 25.00
1 Jason Arnott .40 1.00
2 Martin Brodeur 2.00 5.00
3 Sergei Brylin .20 .50
4 Mike Commodore .30 .75
5 Ken Daneyko .20 .50
6 Patrik Elias .80 2.00
7 Sascha Goc .20 .50
8 Scott Gomez .40 1.00
9 Bobby Holik .30 .75
10 Steve Kelly .20 .50
11 John Madden .80 2.00
12 Randy McKay .30 .75
13 Jim McKenzie .20 .50
14 Alexander Mogilny .30 .75
15 Sergei Nemchinov .20 .50
16 Scott Niedermayer .40 1.00
17 Jay Pandolfo .20 .50
18 Brian Rafalski .20 .50
19 Scott Stevens .40 1.00
20 Turner Stevenson .20 .50
21 Ken Sutton .20 .50
22 Petr Sykora .80 2.00
23 Chris Terreri .30 .75
24 Colin White .30 .75
25 Larry Robinson CO .20 .50
26 Slava Fetisov ACO .20 .50
27 Kurt Kleinendorst ACO .04 .10
28 Jacques Caron ACO .04 .10
29 Lou Lamoriello GM .04 .10
30 2000 Stanley Cup Champions .20 .50

2001-02 Devils Team Issue

COMPLETE SET (25) 8.00 20.00
1 Jason Arnott .40 1.00
2 Martin Brodeur 2.00 5.00
3 Sergei Brylin .20 .50
4 Jacques Caron ACO .04 .10
5 Pierre Dagenais .20 .50
6 Patrik Elias .75 2.00
7 Slava Fetisov ACO .20 .50
8 Scott Gomez .40 1.00
9 Bobby Holik .30 .75
10 Lou Lamoriello GM .04 .10
11 Jay Leach ACO .04 .10
12 John Madden .40 1.00
13 Randy McKay .30 .75
14 Jim McKenzie .20 .50
15 Sergei Nemchinov .20 .50
16 Scott Niedermayer .40 1.00
17 Devil Mascot .04 .10
18 Jay Pandolfo .20 .50
19 Brian Rafalski .20 .50
20 Larry Robinson CO .20 .50
21 Andreas Salomonsson .75 2.00
22 Scott Stevens .40 1.00
23 Turner Stevenson .20 .50
24 Petr Sykora .75 2.00
NNO Title Card .04 .10

2002-03 Devils Team Issue

COMPLETE SET (30)
1 Ken Daneyko .15 .40
2 Scott Stevens .40 1.00
3 Colin White .15 .40
4 Tommy Albelin .15 .40
5 Steve Guolla .15 .40
6 Jiri Bicek .20 .50
7 Craig Darby .15 .40
8 Oleg Tverdovsky .15 .40
9 John Madden .40 1.00
10 Jeff Friesen .30 .75
11 Brian Gionta .40 1.00
12 Jamie Langenbrunner .30 .75
13 Christian Berglund .15 .40
14 Sergei Brylin .15 .40
15 Jim McKenzie .15 .40
16 Jay Pandolfo .15 .40
17 Scott Gomez .30 .75
18 Turner Stevenson .15 .40
19 Joe Nieuwendyk .40 1.00
20 Patrik Elias .30 .75
21 Scott Niedermayer .40 1.00
22 Brian Rafalski .20 .50
23 Martin Brodeur 2.00 5.00
24 Corey Schwab .30 .75
25 Lou Lamoriello GM .04 .10
26 Pat Burns HCO .04 .10
27 Bobby Carpenter ACO .04 .10
28 John MacLean ACO .04 .10
29 Jacques Caron CO .04 .10
30 Mascot .04 .10

2003-04 Devils Team Issue

2 Sean Brown .20 .50
4 Scott Stevens .30 .75
5 Colin White .20 .50
6 Tommy Albelin .20 .50
7 Paul Martin .40 1.00
8 Igor Larionov .30 .75
10 Erik Rasmussen .20 .50
11 John Madden .40 1.00
12 Jeff Friesen .30 .75
14 Brian Gionta .75 2.00
15 Jamie Langenbrunner .30 .75
16 Mike Rupp .20 .50
17 Christian Berglund .20 .50
18 Sergei Brylin .20 .50
20 Jay Pandolfo .20 .50
23 Scott Gomez .40 1.00
24 Turner Stevenson .20 .50
25 David Hale .20 .50
26 Patrik Elias .40 1.00
27 Scott Niedermayer .40 1.00
28 Brian Rafalski .20 .50
29 Grant Marshall .20 .50
30 Martin Brodeur 2.00 5.00
35 Corey Schwab .30 .75
40 Scott Clemmensen .30 .75
41 Lou Lamoriello GM .04 .10
42 Pat Burns HCO .04 .10
43 Bob Carpenter ACO .04 .10
44 John MacLean ACO .04 .10
45 Jacques Laperiere ACO .04 .10
46 Jacques Caron ACO .04 .10
47 Mascot .04 .10

2005-06 Devils Team Issue

COMPLETE SET (30) 10.00 20.00
1 N.J. Devil MASCOT .02 .10
2 Jacques Caron ACO .02 .10
3 John MacLean ACO .02 .10
4 Jacques Laperriere ACO .02 .10
5 Larry Robinson CO .02 .10
6 Lou Lamoriello GM .02 .10
7 Alexander Mogilny .30 .75
8 Scott Clemmensen .30 .75
9 Ari Ahonen .30 .75
10 Martin Brodeur 2.00 5.00
11 Grant Marshall .20 .50
12 Brian Rafalski .20 .50
13 Patrik Elias .30 .75
14 David Hale .20 .50
15 Richard Matvichuk .20 .50
16 Scott Gomez .30 .75
17 Viktor Kozlov .20 .50
18 Jay Pandolfo .20 .50
19 Sergei Brylin .20 .50
20 Darren Langdon .30 .75
21 Jamie Langenbrunner .20 .50
22 Brain Gionta .40 1.00
23 John Madden .20 .50
24 Erik Rasmussen .20 .50
25 Zach Parise 2.00 5.00
26 Sean Brown .20 .50
27 Paul Martin .20 .50
28 Dan McGillis .20 .50
29 Colin White .20 .50
30 Vladimir Malakhov .20 .50

2006-07 Devils Team Set

COMPLETE SET (41) 10.00 25.00
1 Martin Brodeur 2.00 5.00
2 Alex Brooks .20 .50
3 Sergei Brylin .20 .50
4 Scott Clemmensen .20 .50
5 Jim Dowd .20 .50
6 Patrik Elias .30 .75
7 Brian Gionta .40 1.00
8 Scott Gomez .40 1.00
9 David Hale .20 .50
10 Cam Janssen .40 1.00
11 Dan LaCouture .20 .50
12 Jamie Langenbrunner .20 .50
13 Brad Lukowich .20 .50
14 John Madden .20 .50
15 Paul Martin .20 .50
16 Richard Matvichuk .20 .50
17 Alexander Mogilny .30 .75
18 Johnny Oduya .20 .50
19 Jay Pandolfo .20 .50
20 Zach Parise .75 2.00
21 Brian Rafalski .20 .50
22 Erik Rasmussen .20 .50
23 Mike Rupp .20 .50
24 Barry Tallackson .20 .50
25 Colin White .20 .50
26 Jason Wiemer .20 .50
27 Travis Zajac .40 1.00
28 Lou Lamoriello GM .10 .25
29 Claude Julien CO .10 .25
30 Jacques Laperriere ACO .10 .25
31 John MacLean ACO .10 .25
32 Jacques Caron ACO .10 .25
33 Mel Bridgman .20 .50
34 Bruce Driver .20 .50
35 Patrik Elias .30 .75
36 Don Lever .20 .50
37 Kirk Muller .20 .50
38 Scott Niedermayer .30 .75
39 Scott Stevens .30 .75
40 Ken Daneyko .20 .50
41 Scott Stevens .30 .75

2013-14 Devils Score NHL Draft

COMPLETE SET (6) 4.00 8.00

1934-35 Diamond Matchbooks Silver

COMPLETE SET (60) 1500.00 2400.00
1 Taffy Abel 15.00 25.00
2 Marty Barry 15.00 25.00
3 Red Beattie 15.00 25.00
4 Frank Boucher 25.00 40.00
5 Doug Bronnan 15.00 25.00
6 Bill Brydge 15.00 25.00
7 Eddie Burke 35.00 50.00
8 Marty Burke 15.00 25.00
9 Gerald Carson 15.00 25.00
10 Lorne Chabot 35.00 50.00
11 Art Chapman 15.00 25.00
12 Dit Clapper 50.00 80.00
13 Lionel Conacher 50.00 80.00
14 Red Conn 15.00 25.00
15 Bill Cook 35.00 50.00
16 Bun Cook 35.00 50.00
17 Thomas Cook 18.00 30.00
18 Rosario Lolo Couture 15.00 25.00
19 Bob Davie 15.00 25.00
20 Cecil Dillon 15.00 25.00
21 Duke Dutkowski 15.00 25.00
22 Red Dutton 25.00 40.00
23 Johnny Gagnon 15.00 25.00
24 Chuck Gardiner 35.00 50.00
25 Johnny Gottselig 15.00 25.00
26 Robert Gracie 15.00 25.00
27 Lloyd Gross 15.00 25.00
28 Ott Heller 15.00 25.00
29 Normie Himes 15.00 25.00
30 Lionel Hitchman 35.00 50.00
31 Red Jackson 15.00 25.00
32 Roger Jenkins 15.00 25.00
33 Aurel Joliat 50.00 80.00
34 Butch Keeling 15.00 25.00
35 William Kendall 15.00 25.00
36 Jim Klein 15.00 25.00
37 Joe Lamb 15.00 25.00
38 Wildor Larochelle 18.00 30.00
39 Pit Lepine 15.00 25.00
40 Jack Leswick 15.00 25.00
41 Georges Mantha 35.00 50.00
42 Sylvio Mantha 35.00 50.00
43 Mush March 18.00 30.00
44 Ronnie Martin 15.00 25.00
45 Rabbitt McVeigh 15.00 25.00
46 Howie Morenz 200.00 350.00
47 Murray Murdoch 15.00 25.00
48 Harold Oliver 25.00 40.00
49 George Patterson 15.00 25.00
50 Hal Picketts 15.00 25.00
51 Victor Ripley 15.00 25.00
52 Doc Romnes 15.00 25.00
53 Johnny Sheppard 15.00 25.00
54 Eddie Shore 75.00 125.00
55 Art Somers 15.00 25.00
56 Chris Speyers 15.00 25.00
57 Nelson Stewart 35.00 50.00
58 Tiny Thompson 50.00 80.00
59 Louis Trudel 15.00 25.00
60 Roy Worters 35.00 50.00

1935-36 Diamond Matchbooks Tan 1

COMPLETE SET (69) 1100.00 1800.00
1 Andy Aitkenhead 15.00 25.00
2 Vern Ayres 15.00 25.00
3 Bill Beveridge 18.00 30.00
4 Ralph Bowman 15.00 25.00
5 Bill Brydge 15.00 25.00
6 Glenn Brydson 15.00 25.00
7 Eddie Burke 18.00 30.00
8 Marty Burke 15.00 25.00
9 Lorne Carr 15.00 25.00
10 Gerald Carson 15.00 25.00
11 Lorne Chabot 25.00 40.00
12 Art Chapman 15.00 25.00
13 Red Conn 15.00 25.00
14 Bert Connoly 15.00 25.00
15 Bun Cook 25.00 40.00
16 Tommy Cook 15.00 25.00
17 Art Coulter 15.00 25.00
18 Lolo Couture 15.00 25.00
19 Bill Cowley 18.00 30.00
20 Wilf Cude 18.00 30.00
21 Red Dutton 18.00 30.00
22 Frank Finnigan 15.00 25.00
23 Irv Frew 15.00 25.00
24 LeRoy Goldsworthy 15.00 25.00
25 Johnny Gottselig 15.00 25.00
26 Bob Gracie 15.00 25.00
27 Ott Heller 15.00 25.00
28 Normie Himes 15.00 25.00
29 Syd Howe 25.00 40.00
30 Roger Jenkins 15.00 25.00
31 Ching Johnson 30.00 50.00
32 Aurel Joliat 35.00 60.00
33 Max Kaminsky 15.00 25.00
34 Butch Keeling 15.00 25.00
35 Bill Kendall 15.00 25.00
36 Lloyd Klein 15.00 25.00
37 Joe Lamb 15.00 25.00
38 Wildor Larochelle 15.00 25.00
39 Pit Lepine 15.00 25.00
40 Norman Locking 15.00 25.00
41 Georges Mantha 25.00 40.00
42 Sylvio Mantha 25.00 40.00
43 Mush March 15.00 25.00
44 Charlie Mason 15.00 25.00
45 Donnie McFadyen 15.00 25.00
46 Jack McGill 15.00 25.00
47 Rabbit McVeigh 15.00 25.00
48 Armand Mondou 15.00 25.00
49 Howie Morenz 180.00 300.00
50 Murray Murdoch 15.00 25.00
51 Al Murray 15.00 25.00
52 Harry Oliver 25.00 40.00
53 Jean Pusie 15.00 25.00
54 Paul Marcel Raymond 15.00 25.00
55 Jack Riley 15.00 25.00
56 Vic Ripley 15.00 25.00
57 Desse Roche 15.00 25.00
58 Earl Roche 15.00 25.00
59 Doc Romnes 15.00 25.00
60 Sweeney Schriner 30.00 50.00
61 Earl Seibert 25.00 40.00
62 Gerald Shannon 15.00 25.00
63 Alex Smith 15.00 25.00
64 Joe Starke 15.00 25.00
65 Nels Stewart 30.00 50.00
66 Paul Thompson 15.00 25.00
67 Louis Trudel 15.00 25.00
68 Carl Voss 15.00 25.00
69 Art Wiebe 15.00 25.00
70 Roy Wortoro 25.00 40.00

1935-36 Diamond Matchbooks Tan 2

COMPLETE SET (63) 1100.00 1800.00
1 Tommy Anderson 15.00 25.00
2 Vern Ayres 15.00 25.00
3 Frank Boucher 25.00 40.00
4 Frank Boucher 25.00 40.00
5 Bill Brydge 15.00 25.00
6 Marty Burke 15.00 25.00
7 Lorne Carr 15.00 25.00
8 Lorne Chabot 25.00 40.00
9 Art Chapman 15.00 25.00
10 Bert Connolly 15.00 25.00
11 Bill Cook 25.00 40.00
12 Bill Cook 25.00 40.00
13 Bun Cook 25.00 40.00
14 Tommy Cook 15.00 25.00
15 Art Coulter 15.00 25.00
16 Lolo Couture 15.00 25.00
17 Wilf Cude 25.00 40.00
18 Cecil Dillon 15.00 25.00
19 Cecil Dillon 15.00 25.00
20 Red Dutton 25.00 40.00
21 Happy Emms 25.00 40.00
22 Irv Frew 15.00 25.00
23 Johnny Gagnon 15.00 25.00
24 Leroy Goldsworthy 15.00 25.00
25 Johnny Gottselig 15.00 25.00
26 Paul Haynes 15.00 25.00
27 Ott Heller 15.00 25.00
28 Irving Jaffee 15.00 25.00
29 Joe Jerwa 15.00 25.00
30 Ching Johnson 25.00 40.00
31 Aurel Joliat 30.00 50.00
32 Butch Keeling 15.00 25.00
33 William Kendall 15.00 25.00
34 Davey Kerr 25.00 40.00
35 Lloyd Klein 15.00 25.00
36 Wildor Larochelle 15.00 25.00
37 Pit Lepine 15.00 25.00
38 Arthur Lesieur 15.00 25.00
39 Alex Levinsky 15.00 25.00
40 Alex Levinsky 15.00 25.00
41 Norm Locking 15.00 25.00
42 Georges Mantha 25.00 40.00
43 Sylvio Mantha 25.00 40.00
44 Mush Marsh 15.00 25.00
45 Charlie Mason 15.00 25.00
46 Donnie McFadyen 15.00 25.00
47 Jack McGill 15.00 25.00
48 Armand Mondou 15.00 25.00
49 Howie Morenz 180.00 300.00
50 Murray Murdoch 15.00 25.00
51 Al Murray 15.00 25.00
52 Harry Oliver 25.00 40.00
53 Eddie Ouellette 15.00 25.00
54 Lynn Patrick 25.00 40.00
55 Lynn Patrick 25.00 40.00
56 Paul Runge 15.00 25.00
57 Sweeney Schriner 25.00 40.00
58 Art Somers 15.00 25.00
59 Harold Starr 15.00 25.00
60 Nels Stewart 30.00 50.00
61 Paul Thompson 15.00 25.00
62 Louis Trudel 15.00 25.00
63 Carl Voss 15.00 25.00
64 Art Wiebe 25.00 40.00
65 Roy Worters 25.00 40.00

1935-36 Diamond Matchbooks Tan 3

COMPLETE SET (60) 950.00 1600.00
1 Tommy Anderson 15.00 25.00
2 Vern Ayres 15.00 25.00
3 Frank Boucher 18.00 30.00
4 Bill Brydge 15.00 25.00
5 Marty Burke 15.00 25.00
6 Walter Buswell 15.00 25.00
7 Lorne Carr 15.00 25.00
8 Lorne Chabot 25.00 40.00
9 Art Chapman 15.00 25.00
10 Bert Connolly 15.00 25.00
11 Bill Cook 25.00 40.00
12 Bun Cook 25.00 40.00
13 Tommy Cook 18.00 30.00
14 Art Coulter 15.00 25.00
15 Lolo Couture 15.00 25.00
16 Wilf Cude 18.00 30.00
17 Cecil Dillon 15.00 25.00
18 Red Dutton 18.00 30.00
19 Happy Emms 18.00 30.00
20 Irvin Frew 15.00 25.00
21 Johnny Gagnon 15.00 25.00
22 Leroy Goldsworthy 15.00 25.00
23 Johnny Gottselig 15.00 25.00
24 Paul Haynes 15.00 25.00
25 Ott Heller 15.00 25.00
26 Joe Jerwa 15.00 25.00
27 Ching Johnson 25.00 40.00
28 Aurel Joliat 30.00 50.00
29 Mike Karakas 18.00 30.00
30 Butch Keeling 15.00 25.00
31 Dave Kerr 18.00 30.00
32 Lloyd Klein 15.00 25.00
33 Wildor Larochelle 18.00 30.00
34 Pit Lepine 15.00 25.00
35 Arthur Lesieur 15.00 25.00
36 Alex Levinsky 18.00 30.00
37 Norman Locking 15.00 25.00
38 George Mantha 25.00 40.00
39 Sylvio Mantha 25.00 40.00
40 Mush March 18.00 30.00
41 Charlie Mason 15.00 25.00
42 Charlie Mason 15.00 25.00
43 Donnie McFadyen 15.00 25.00
44 Jack McGill 15.00 25.00
45 Armand Mondou 15.00 25.00
46 Howie Morenz 180.00 300.00
47 Murray Murdoch 15.00 25.00
48 Al Murray 15.00 25.00
49 Harry Oliver 25.00 40.00
50 Eddie Ouellette 15.00 25.00
51 Lynn Patrick 25.00 40.00
52 Paul Runge 15.00 25.00
53 Sweeney Schriner 25.00 40.00
54 Harold Starr 15.00 25.00
55 Nels Stewart 30.00 50.00
56 Paul Thompson 15.00 25.00
57 Louis Trudel 15.00 25.00
58 Carl Voss 18.00 30.00
59 Art Wiebe 18.00 30.00
60 Roy Worters 18.00 30.00

1935-36 Diamond Matchbooks Tan 4

COMPLETE SET (15) 180.00 300.00
1 Andy Blair 15.00 25.00
2 Glenn Brydson 15.00 25.00
3 Marty Burke 15.00 25.00
4 Tommy Cook 18.00 30.00
5 Johnny Gottselig 15.00 25.00
6 Harold Jackson 15.00 25.00
7 Mike Karakas 18.00 30.00
8 Wildor Larochelle 18.00 30.00
9 Alex Levinsky 18.00 30.00
10 Clem Loughlin 15.00 25.00
11 Mush March 18.00 30.00
12 Earl Seibert 25.00 40.00
13 Paul Thompson 15.00 25.00
14 Louis Trudel 15.00 25.00
15 Art Wiebe 18.00 30.00

1935-36 Diamond Matchbooks Tan 5

COMPLETE SET (14) 125.00 200.00
1 Glenn Brydson 15.00 25.00
2 Marty Burke 15.00 25.00
3 Tommy Cook 15.00 25.00
4 Cully Dahlstrom 15.00 25.00
5 Johnny Gottselig 15.00 25.00
6 Vic Heyliger 15.00 25.00
7 Mike Karakas 15.00 25.00
8 Alex Levinsky 15.00 25.00
9 Mush March 15.00 25.00
10 Earl Seibert 15.00 25.00
11 William J. Stewart 15.00 25.00
12 Paul Thompson 15.00 25.00
13 Louis Trudel 15.00 25.00
14 Art Wiebe 15.00 25.00

1937 Diamond Matchbooks Tan 6

COMPLETE SET (14) 150.00 250.00
1 Glenn Brydson 15.00 25.00
2 Martin A. Burke 15.00 25.00
3 Tom Cook 15.00 25.00
4 Cully Dahlstrom 15.00 25.00
5 Johnny Gottselig 15.00 25.00
6 Vic Heyliger 15.00 25.00
7 Mike Karakas 15.00 25.00
8 Alex Levinsky 15.00 25.00
9 Mush March 15.00 25.00
10 Earl Seibert 18.00 30.00
11 William J. Stewart 15.00 25.00
12 Paul Thompson 15.00 25.00
13 Louis Trudel 15.00 25.00
14 Art Wiebe 15.00 25.00

1992 Disney Mighty Ducks Movie

COMPLETE SET (8) 16.00 40.00
1 Brandon Adams Jesse 2.00 5.00
2 Emilio Estevez Coach Bombay 2.50 6.00
3 Joshua Jackson Charlie 3.00 8.00
4 Marguerite Moreau Connie 2.00 5.00
5 Elden Ratliff Fulton 2.00 5.00
6 Shaun Weiss Goldberg 2.00 5.00
7 Rollerblading in Shopping Mall 2.00 5.00
8 Team Photo 2.00 5.00

2010-11 Dominion

1 Corey Perry 3.00 8.00
2 Ryan Getzlaf 2.00 5.00
3 Saku Koivu 2.00 5.00
4 Bobby Ryan 1.50 4.00
5 Dustin Byfuglien 2.00 5.00
6 Andrew Ladd 1.25 3.00
7 Evander Kane 2.00 5.00
8 Milan Lucic 2.00 5.00
9 Patrice Bergeron 2.50 6.00
10 Tim Thomas 2.00 5.00
11 Ryan Miller 2.00 5.00
12 Thomas Vanek 1.50 4.00
13 Drew Stafford 1.25 3.00
14 Miikka Kiprusoff 2.00 5.00
15 Jarome Iginla 2.50 6.00
16 Alex Tanguay 1.25 3.00
17 Cam Ward 2.00 5.00
18 Eric Staal 2.50 6.00
19 Brandon Sutter 1.25 3.00
20 Jonathan Toews 3.00 8.00
21 Patrick Kane 4.00 10.00
22 Patrick Sharp 2.00 5.00
23 Corey Crawford 2.50 6.00
24 Duncan Keith 1.50 4.00
25 Erik Johnson 1.25 3.00
26 Brian Elliott 1.50 4.00
27 Matt Duchene 2.00 5.00
28 Rick Nash 2.00 5.00
29 Steve Mason 1.50 4.00
30 Antoine Vermette 1.25 3.00
31 Brad Richards 2.00 5.00
32 Loui Eriksson 1.25 3.00
33 Kari Lehtonen 1.50 4.00
34 Jimmy Howard 2.50 6.00
35 Pavel Datsyuk 3.00 8.00
36 Nicklas Lidstrom 2.00 5.00
37 Henrik Zetterberg 2.50 6.00
38 Ales Hemsky 1.50 4.00
39 Sam Gagner 1.25 3.00
40 Andrew Cogliano 1.25 3.00
41 Stephen Weiss 1.50 4.00
42 David Booth 1.25 3.00
43 Tomas Vokoun 1.50 4.00
44 Anze Kopitar 3.00 8.00
45 Drew Doughty 2.50 6.00
46 Jonathan Quick 2.50 6.00
47 Brent Burns 2.00 5.00
48 Cal Clutterbuck 1.25 3.00
49 Mikko Koivu 2.00 5.00
50 Andrei Kostitsyn 1.50 4.00
51 Carey Price 4.00 10.00
52 Brian Gionta 1.25 3.00
53 Tomas Plekanec 1.25 3.00
54 Shea Weber 1.50 4.00
55 Pekka Rinne 2.00 5.00
56 Sergei Kostitsyn 1.25 3.00
57 Martin Brodeur 5.00 12.00
58 Travis Zajac 1.25 3.00
59 Ilya Kovalchuk 2.00 5.00
60 John Tavares 3.00 8.00
61 Matt Moulson 1.50 4.00
62 Michael Grabner 1.50 4.00
63 Henrik Lundqvist 5.00 12.00
64 Marian Gaborik 2.00 5.00
65 Marc Staal 1.25 3.00
66 Craig Anderson 2.00 5.00
67 Jason Spezza 2.00 5.00
68 Daniel Alfredsson 2.00 5.00
69 Chris Pronger 2.00 5.00
70 Claude Giroux 2.00 5.00
71 Jeff Carter 1.50 4.00
72 Mike Richards 1.50 4.00
73 Mikkel Boedker 1.25 3.00
74 Ilya Bryzgalov 1.50 4.00
75 Keith Yandle 1.25 3.00
76 Kris Letang 2.50 6.00
77 Sidney Crosby 8.00 20.00
78 Marc-Andre Fleury 4.00 10.00
79 Jordan Staal 1.50 4.00
80 Evgeni Malkin 4.00 10.00
81 Joe Thornton 3.00 8.00
82 Ryane Clowe 1.25 3.00
83 Dany Heatley 1.50 4.00
84 Logan Couture 2.50 6.00
85 T.J. Oshie 2.00 5.00
86 David Backes 1.25 3.00
87 Jaroslav Halak 2.00 5.00
88 Steven Stamkos 4.00 10.00
89 Vincent Lecavalier 2.00 5.00
90 Martin St. Louis 2.00 5.00
91 Dion Phaneuf 1.50 4.00
92 James Reimer 2.00 5.00
93 Phil Kessel 2.00 5.00
94 Roberto Luongo 3.00 8.00
95 Henrik Sedin 2.50 6.00
96 Daniel Sedin 2.50 6.00
97 Ryan Kesler 2.00 5.00
98 Alex Ovechkin 8.00 20.00
99 Nicklas Backstrom 2.00 5.00
100 Semyon Varlamov 2.00 5.00
101 Cam Neely 2.00 5.00
102 Derek Sanderson 2.00 5.00
103 Felix Potvin 3.00 8.00
104 Milt Schmidt 1.50 4.00
105 Normand Leveille 1.25 3.00
106 Ray Bourque 3.00 8.00
107 Reggie Lemelin 1.25 3.00
108 Rick Middleton 2.00 5.00
109 Dale Hawerchuk 2.50 6.00
110 Gilbert Perreault 2.00 5.00
111 Tom Barrasso 2.00 5.00
112 Doug Gilmour 2.50 6.00
113 Bobby Hull 4.00 10.00
114 Denis Savard 2.00 5.00
115 Paul Coffey 2.00 5.00
116 Phil Esposito 3.00 8.00
117 Stan Mikita 2.50 6.00
118 Tony Esposito 2.00 5.00
119 Ed Belfour 2.00 5.00
120 Steve Yzerman 5.00 12.00
121 Grant Fuhr 3.00 8.00
122 Mark Messier 4.00 10.00
123 Kelly Hrudey 1.50 4.00
124 Guy Lafleur 2.50 6.00
125 Henri Richard 2.00 5.00
126 Jean Beliveau 2.00 5.00
127 Patrick Roy 5.00 12.00
128 Denis Potvin 2.00 5.00
129 Mike Bossy 2.00 5.00
130 Brad Park 1.50 4.00
131 Brian Leetch 1.50 4.00
132 Adam Graves 1.50 4.00
133 Ed Giacomin 3.00 8.00
134 Rod Gilbert 2.00 5.00
135 Bernie Parent 2.50 6.00
136 Bobby Clarke 3.00 8.00
137 Eric Lindros 3.00 8.00
138 Luc Robitaille 2.00 5.00
139 Mario Lemieux 8.00 20.00
140 Joe Sakic 4.00 10.00
141 Ron Hextall 2.00 5.00
142 Jeremy Roenick 3.00 8.00
143 Brendan Shanahan 2.00 5.00
144 Brett Hull 4.00 10.00
145 Glenn Hall 2.00 5.00
146 Manon Rheaume 5.00 12.00
147 Curtis Joseph 2.50 6.00
148 Darryl Sittler 2.50 6.00
149 Johnny Bower 2.00 5.00
150 Trevor Linden 2.00 5.00
151 Brandon McMillan AU RC 5.00 12.00
152 Kyle Palmieri AU RC 10.00 25.00
153 Nick Bonino AU RC 6.00 15.00
154 Alexander Burmistrov AU RC 5.00 12.00
155 Patrice Cormier AU RC 6.00 15.00
156 Jordan Caron AU RC 6.00 15.00
157 Jamie Arniel AU RC 5.00 12.00
158 Matt Bartkowski AU RC 6.00 15.00
159 Zach Hamill AU RC 5.00 12.00
160 Colby Cohen AU RC 5.00 12.00
161 Luke Adam AU RC 5.00 12.00
162 T.J. Brodie AU RC 5.00 12.00
163 Henrik Karlsson AU RC 5.00 12.00
164 Zac Dalpe AU RC 6.00 15.00
165 Jamie McBain AU RC 5.00 12.00
166 Nick Leddy AU RC 6.00 15.00
167 Brandon Pirri AU RC 5.00 12.00
168 Evan Brophey AU RC 5.00 12.00
169 Jeremy Morin AU RC 5.00 12.00
170 Ben Smith AU RC 6.00 15.00
171 Mark Olver AU RC 5.00 12.00
172 Jonas Holos AU RC 5.00 12.00
173 Brandon Yip AU RC 5.00 12.00
174 Matt Calvert AU RC 8.00 20.00
175 Grant Clitsome AU RC 5.00 12.00
176 Richard Bachman AU RC 6.00 15.00
177 Philip Larsen AU RC 5.00 12.00
178 Jan Mursak AU RC 10.00 25.00
179 Thomas McCollum AU RC 6.00 15.00
180 Jordan Pearce AU RC 8.00 20.00
181 Dave Hanson AU 10.00 25.00
182 Jeff Petry AU RC 20.00 50.00
183 Evgeny Dadonov AU RC 6.00 15.00
184 Jake Muzzin AU RC 12.00 30.00
185 Kyle Clifford AU RC 6.00 15.00
186 Steve Carlson AU 10.00 25.00
187 Cody Almond AU RC 5.00 12.00
188 Justin Falk AU RC 4.00 10.00
189 Matt Hackett AU RC 6.00 15.00
190 Andreas Engqvist AU RC 8.00 20.00
191 Anders Lindback AU RC 5.00 12.00
192 Mark Dekanich AU RC 5.00 12.00
193 Nick Spaling AU RC 5.00 12.00
194 Alex Urbom AU RC 5.00 12.00
195 Matt Taormina AU RC 5.00 12.00
196 Jeff Frazee AU RC 8.00 20.00
197 Jacob Josefson AU RC 5.00 12.00
198 Brad Mills AU RC 5.00 12.00
199 Stephen Gionta AU RC 6.00 15.00
200 Alexander Vasyunov AU RC 5.00 12.00
201 Travis Hamonic AU RC 6.00 15.00
202 Rhett Rakhshani AU RC 5.00 12.00
203 Nathan Lawson AU RC 5.00 12.00
204 Kevin Poulin AU RC 6.00 15.00
205 Trevor Gillies AU RC 5.00 12.00
206 Evgeny Grachev AU RC 5.00 12.00
207 Brodie Dupont AU RC 6.00 15.00
208 Jim O'Brien AU RC 6.00 15.00
209 Robin Lehner AU RC 10.00 25.00
210 Jared Cowen AU RC 5.00 12.00
211 Chris Summers AU RC 5.00 12.00
212 Eric Wellwood AU RC 6.00 15.00
213 Nick Johnson AU RC 4.00 10.00
214 Eric Tangradi AU RC 5.00 12.00

215 Alex Stalock AU RC 5.00 12.00
216 Andrew Desjardins AU RC 5.00 12.00
217 Justin Braun AU RC 5.00 12.00
218 Mike Moore AU RC 5.00 12.00
219 Ryan Reaves AU RC 6.00 15.00
220 S.Della Rovere AU RC 5.00 12.00
221 Philip McRae AU RC 5.00 12.00
222 Linus Omark AU RC 6.00 15.00
223 Ian Cole AU RC 5.00 12.00
224 Dustin Tokarski AU RC 5.00 12.00
225 Cedrick Desjardins AU RC 6.00 15.00
226 Brayden Irwin AU RC 5.00 12.00
227 Keith Aulie AU RC 5.00 12.00
228 Korbinian Holzer AU RC 5.00 12.00
229 Marcel Mueller AU RC 6.00 15.00
230 Marcus Johansson AU RC 8.00 20.00
231 Taylor Hall JSY AU RC 60.00 150.00
232 Tyler Seguin JSY AU RC 60.00 150.00
233 N.Niederreiter JSY AU RC 20.00 50.00
234 Cory Emmerton JSY AU RC 15.00 40.00
235 Jordan Eberle JSY AU RC 30.00 80.00
236 Tomas Tatar JSY AU RC 30.00 80.00
237 J.Markstrom JSY AU RC 30.00 80.00
238 Magnus Paajarvi JSY AU RC 15.00 40.00
239 B.Schenn JSY AU RC 30.00 80.00
240 Nazem Kadri JSY AU RC 40.00 100.00
241 Cam Fowler JSY AU RC 30.00 80.00
242 Derek Stepan JSY AU RC 15.00 40.00
243 P.K. Subban JSY AU RC 40.00 100.00
244 S.Bobrovsky JSY AU RC 50.00 125.00
245 Mats Zuccarello JSY AU RC 25.00 60.00
246 Jeff Skinner JSY AU RC 30.00 80.00
247 K.Shattenkirk JSY AU RC 25.00 60.00
248 M.Tedenby JSY AU RC 12.00 30.00
249 Dana Tyrell JSY AU RC 12.00 30.00
250 Ekman-Larsson JSY AU RC 20.00 50.00

2010-11 Dominion Gold

*GOLD/19-25: .6X TO 1.5X BASIC CARDS
231 Taylor Hall JSY AU 100.00 200.00
232 Tyler Seguin JSY AU 150.00 250.00

2010-11 Dominion All Decade Jerseys

*PRIME/25: .6X TO 1.5X BASIC INSERTS
AO Alex Ovechkin 12.00 30.00
CP Chris Pronger 3.00 8.00
DA Daniel Alfredsson 3.00 8.00
DB Dan Boyle 2.00 5.00
DH Dany Heatley 2.50 6.00
EB Ed Belfour 3.00 8.00
EM Evgeni Malkin 6.00 15.00
ES Eric Staal 4.00 10.00
IK Ilya Kovalchuk 3.00 8.00
JI Jarome Iginla 4.00 10.00
JT Joe Thornton 5.00 12.00
MB Martin Brodeur 8.00 20.00
MH Marian Hossa 3.00 8.00
MK Miikka Kiprusoff 3.00 8.00
MS Martin St. Louis 3.00 8.00
NL Nicklas Lidstrom 3.00 8.00
PD Pavel Datsyuk 5.00 12.00
RM Ryan Miller 3.00 8.00
RN Rick Nash 3.00 8.00
SC Sidney Crosby 12.00 30.00
TV Tomas Vokoun 2.50 6.00
ZC Zdeno Chara 3.00 8.00

2010-11 Dominion All Decade Jerseys Autographs

AO Alex Ovechkin/24 40.00 100.00
CP Chris Pronger 10.00 25.00
DA Daniel Alfredsson 10.00 25.00
DB Dan Boyle 6.00 15.00
DH Dany Heatley 8.00 20.00
EM Evgeni Malkin 20.00 50.00
IK Ilya Kovalchuk 10.00 25.00
JI Jarome Iginla 12.00 30.00
JT Joe Thornton 15.00 40.00
MB Martin Brodeur/24 25.00 60.00
MH Marian Hossa 10.00 25.00
MS Martin St. Louis 10.00 25.00
NL Nicklas Lidstrom 10.00 25.00
PD Pavel Datsyuk 15.00 40.00
RM Ryan Miller 10.00 25.00
RN Rick Nash 10.00 25.00
SC Sidney Crosby/24 40.00 100.00
TV Tomas Vokoun 8.00 20.00
ZC Zdeno Chara 10.00 25.00

2010-11 Dominion All Decade Autographs

1 Martin Brodeur/24 20.00 50.00
3 Ryan Miller 8.00 20.00
4 Tomas Vokoun 6.00 15.00
5 Nicklas Lidstrom 8.00 20.00
6 Chris Pronger 8.00 20.00
7 Dan Boyle 5.00 12.00
8 Zdeno Chara 8.00 20.00
9 Pavel Datsyuk 12.00 30.00
10 Daniel Alfredsson 8.00 20.00
11 Jarome Iginla 10.00 25.00
12 Evgeni Malkin 15.00 40.00
13 Joe Thornton 12.00 30.00
14 Ilya Kovalchuk 8.00 20.00
15 Dany Heatley 6.00 15.00
16 Marian Hossa 8.00 20.00
17 Rick Nash 8.00 20.00
18 Martin St. Louis 8.00 20.00
19 Alex Ovechkin/24 30.00 80.00
20 Sidney Crosby/24 50.00 125.00

2010-11 Dominion All Decade Autographs Dual

1 M.Brodeur/R.Miller 25.00 60.00
2 N.Lidstrom/Z.Chara 10.00 25.00
3 C.Pronger/D.Boyle 10.00 25.00
4 J.Iginla/R.Nash 12.00 30.00
5 J.Thornton/D.Heatley 15.00 40.00
6 A.Ovechkin/I.Kovalchuk 40.00 100.00
7 E.Malkin/D.Alfredsson 20.00 50.00
8 P.Datsyuk/M.Hossa 15.00 40.00
9 M.St. Louis/B.Richards 10.00 25.00
10 E.Belfour/T.Vokoun 10.00 25.00

2010-11 Dominion All Decade Autographs Quads

1 Brodeur/Belfour/Miller/Vokoun 30.00 80.00
2 Lidstrom/Chara/Boyle/Pronger 12.00 30.00
3 Thornton/Heatley/Iginla/Nash 20.00 50.00
4 Datsyk/Koval/Malkn/Ovech 50.00 125.00
5 St.L/Alfredsn/Lecav/Richards 12.00 30.00

2010-11 Dominion All Decade Autographs Trios

1 Brodeur/Vokoun/Miller 30.00 80.00
2 Lidstrom/Pronger/Chara 12.00 30.00
3 Ovech/Koval/Datsyuk 50.00 125.00
4 Iginla/Heatley/St. Louis 15.00 40.00
5 Thornton/Nash/Alfredsn 20.00 50.00

2010-11 Dominion Benchmark Sticks

1 Brendan Shanahan 5.00 12.00
2 Brett Hull/25 10.00 25.00
3 Dale Hawerchuk/50 6.00 15.00
4 Dino Ciccarelli/50 5.00 12.00
5 Guy Lafleur/115 6.00 15.00
6 Joe Nieuwendyk 4.00 10.00
7 Lanny McDonald/50 5.00 12.00
8 Marcel Dionne/50 6.00 15.00
9 Mario Lemieux 20.00 50.00
10 Phil Esposito/25 8.00 20.00
11 Steve Yzerman/25 12.00 30.00
12 Stan Mikita/110 6.00 15.00
13 Joe Sakic 10.00 25.00

2010-11 Dominion Benchmark Sticks Autographs

1 Brendan Shanahan/25 15.00 40.00
2 Brett Hull/20 30.00 80.00
3 Dale Hawerchuk/45 20.00 50.00
4 Dino Ciccarelli/50 15.00 40.00
5 Guy Lafleur/50 20.00 50.00
6 Joe Nieuwendyk/50 12.00 30.00
7 Lanny McDonald/50 15.00 40.00
8 Marcel Dionne/50 20.00 50.00
9 Mario Lemieux/25 60.00 150.00
10 Phil Esposito/20 25.00 60.00
11 Steve Yzerman/25 40.00 100.00
12 Stan Mikita/50 20.00 50.00
13 Joe Sakic/25 30.00 80.00

2010-11 Dominion Bonded in Silver Dual Autographs

1 M.Lemieux/T.Barrasso 60.00 150.00
2 S.Yzerman/N.Lidstrom 40.00 100.00
3 B.Hull/E.Belfour 30.00 80.00
4 P.Roy/J.Sakic 40.00 100.00
5 E.Malkin/M.Fleury 30.00 80.00
6 J.Toews/P.Sharp 25.00 60.00
7 J.Beliveau/H.Richard 15.00 40.00
8 G.Lafleur/Y.Cournoyer 20.00 50.00
9 E.Staal/C.Ward 20.00 50.00
10 G.Cheevers/D.Sanderson 15.00 40.00
11 J.Bucyk/P.Esposito 25.00 60.00
12 J.Giguere/R.Getzlaf 15.00 40.00
13 M.Brodeur/S.Gomez 40.00 100.00
14 B.Hull/S.Mikita 30.00 80.00
15 M.Messier/B.Leetch 30.00 80.00
16 B.Parent/B.Clarke 25.00 60.00
17 D.Potvin/M.Bossy 15.00 40.00
18 V.Lecavalier/B.Richards 15.00 40.00
19 J.Nieuwendyk/D.Gilmour 20.00 50.00
20 G.Fuhr/P.Coffey 25.00 60.00

2010-11 Dominion Brass Bonanza Autographs

1 Bobby Hull/24 20.00 50.00
2 Brendan Shanahan/24 10.00 25.00
3 Keith Primeau 8.00 20.00
4 Nick Fotiu 12.00 30.00
5 Paul Coffey 10.00 25.00
6 Ray Ferraro 10.00 25.00
7 Tiger Williams 6.00 15.00
8 Daryl Reaugh 8.00 20.00
9 Ron Francis 12.00 30.00
10 Pat Verbeek 8.00 20.00

2010-11 Dominion Championship Gear

1 Patrick Kane 5.00 12.00
2 Sidney Crosby 12.00 30.00
3 Nicklas Lidstrom 3.00 8.00
4 Ryan Getzlaf 3.00 8.00
5 Eric Staal 4.00 10.00
6 Martin St. Louis 3.00 8.00
7 Vincent Lecavalier 3.00 8.00
8 Martin Brodeur 8.00 20.00
9 Patrick Sharp 3.00 8.00
10 Jonathan Toews 5.00 12.00
11 Jordan Staal 2.50 6.00
12 Max Talbot 2.00 5.00
13 Pavel Datsyuk 5.00 12.00
14 Jean-Sebastien Giguere 3.00 8.00
15 Cam Ward 3.00 8.00
16 Nikolai Khabibulin 2.50 6.00
17 Patrick Roy 8.00 20.00
18 Steve Yzerman 8.00 20.00
19 Joe Nieuwendyk 2.50 6.00
20 Yvan Cournoyer 3.00 8.00
21 Corey Perry 5.00 12.00
22 Marc-Andre Fleury 6.00 15.00
23 Mario Lemieux 12.00 30.00
24 Ed Belfour 3.00 8.00
25 Brian Leetch/25 2.50 6.00
26 Mike Modano 5.00 12.00
27 Evgeni Malkin 6.00 15.00
28 Brett Hull 6.00 15.00
29 Antti Niemi 2.50 6.00
30 Bryan Trottier 3.00 8.00
32 George Parros 2.50 6.00

2010-11 Dominion Eight Is Enough Jerseys

1 GP/SD/ZK/MC/KB/BP/JB/ST 10.00 25.00
2 Goalies East 30.00 80.00
3 Goalies West 20.00 50.00
4 Superstars/Legends 50.00 125.00
5 CP/MR/RN/JT/ES/JI/RG/PB 20.00 50.00

2010-11 Dominion Franchise Legends Jerseys

1 Yvan Cournoyer 3.00 8.00
2 Steve Yzerman 8.00 20.00
3 Charlie Simmer 2.00 5.00
4 Rick Middleton 3.00 8.00
5 Lanny McDonald 3.00 8.00
6 Johnny Bucyk 3.00 8.00
7 Guy Lafleur 4.00 10.00
8 Eric Lindros 5.00 12.00
9 Don Cherry 3.00 8.00
10 Brendan Shanahan 3.00 8.00
11 Mike Modano 5.00 12.00
12 Nicklas Lidstrom 3.00 8.00
13 Marcel Dionne 4.00 10.00
14 Martin Brodeur 8.00 20.00

2010-11 Dominion Franchise Legends Jerseys Autographs

1 Yvan Cournoyer/50 12.00 30.00
2 Steve Yzerman/19 30.00 80.00
3 Charlie Simmer/50 8.00 20.00
4 Rick Middleton/50 12.00 30.00
5 Lanny McDonald/50 12.00 30.00
6 Johnny Bucyk/50 12.00 30.00
7 Guy Lafleur/50 15.00 40.00
8 Eric Lindros/50 20.00 50.00
9 Don Cherry/50 12.00 30.00
10 Brendan Shanahan/19 12.00 30.00
11 Mike Modano/50 20.00 50.00
12 Nicklas Lidstrom/25 12.00 30.00
13 Marcel Dionne/50 15.00 40.00
14 Martin Brodeur/25 30.00 80.00

2010-11 Dominion Got Your Number Dual Autographs

1 J.Sakic/S.Yzerman/19 40.00 100.00
2 R.Vachon/M.Brodeur/30 40.00 100.00
3 D.Savard/M.Richards 15.00 40.00
4 H.Lundqvist/C.Ward 40.00 100.00
5 S.Stamkos/J.Tavares 30.00 80.00
6 Y.Cournoyer/J.Iginla 20.00 50.00
8 B.Morrow/P.Sharp 15.00 40.00
9 D.Alfredsson/A.Kopitar 25.00 60.00
10 B.Trottier/J.Toews 25.00 60.00

2010-11 Dominion Got Your Number Dual Jerseys

1 J.Sakic/S.Yzerman 12.00 30.00
2 R.Vachon/M.Brodeur 12.00 30.00
3 D.Savard/M.Richards 5.00 12.00
4 H.Lundqvist/C.Ward 12.00 30.00
5 S.Stamkos/J.Tavares 10.00 25.00
6 Y.Cournoyer/J.Iginla 6.00 15.00
7 B.Shanahan/R.Smyth 5.00 12.00
8 B.Morrow/P.Sharp 5.00 12.00
9 D.Alfredsson/A.Kopitar 8.00 20.00
10 B.Trottier/J.Toews 8.00 20.00

2010-11 Dominion Honoured Rivals Dual Jerseys

1 E.Malkin/A.Ovechkin 15.00 40.00
2 D.Doughty/R.Getzlaf 5.00 12.00
3 M.Staal/J.Tavares 6.00 15.00
4 C.Pronger/J.Toews 6.00 15.00
5 H.Lundqvist/M.Brodeur 10.00 25.00
6 H.Sedin/D.Keith 5.00 12.00
7 N.Lidstrom/M.Fleury 8.00 20.00
8 T.Hall/T.Seguin 10.00 25.00
9 D.Sittler/G.Lafleur 5.00 12.00
10 J.Bucyk/R.Vachon 5.00 12.00

2010-11 Dominion Jerseys

*PRIME/25: .6X TO 1.5X BASIC JSY
*PRIME PATCH/25: .8X TO 2X BASICJSY
*PRIME JSY #/23-25: .6X TO 1.5X BASIC JSY
*NAMEPLATE/15-25 .6X TO 1.5X BASIC JSY
1 Corey Perry 6.00 15.00
2 Ryan Getzlaf 4.00 10.00
3 Saku Koivu 4.00 10.00
4 Bobby Ryan 3.00 8.00
5 Dustin Byfuglien 4.00 10.00
6 Andrew Ladd 2.50 6.00
7 Evander Kane 4.00 10.00
8 Milan Lucic 4.00 10.00
9 Patrice Bergeron 5.00 12.00
10 Tim Thomas 4.00 10.00
11 Ryan Miller 4.00 10.00
12 Thomas Vanek 3.00 8.00
13 Drew Stafford 2.50 6.00
14 Miikka Kiprusoff 4.00 10.00
15 Jarome Iginla 5.00 12.00
16 Alex Tanguay 2.50 6.00
17 Cam Ward 4.00 10.00
18 Eric Staal 5.00 12.00
19 Brandon Sutter 2.50 6.00
20 Jonathan Toews 6.00 15.00
21 Patrick Kane 8.00 20.00
22 Patrick Sharp 4.00 10.00
23 Corey Crawford 5.00 12.00
24 Duncan Keith 3.00 8.00
25 Erik Johnson 2.50 6.00
26 Brian Elliott 3.00 8.00
27 Matt Duchene 4.00 10.00
28 Rick Nash 4.00 10.00
30 Antoine Vermette 2.50 6.00
31 Brad Richards 4.00 10.00
32 Loui Eriksson 2.50 6.00
33 Kari Lehtonen 3.00 8.00
34 Jimmy Howard 5.00 12.00
35 Pavel Datsyuk 6.00 15.00
36 Nicklas Lidstrom 4.00 10.00
37 Henrik Zetterberg 5.00 12.00
38 Ales Hemsky 3.00 8.00
39 Sam Gagner 2.50 6.00
40 Andrew Cogliano 2.50 6.00
41 Stephen Weiss 3.00 8.00
42 David Booth 2.50 6.00
43 Tomas Vokoun 3.00 8.00
44 Anze Kopitar 6.00 15.00
45 Drew Doughty 5.00 12.00
46 Jonathan Quick 5.00 12.00
47 Brent Burns 4.00 10.00
48 Cal Clutterbuck 2.50 6.00
49 Mikko Koivu 4.00 10.00
50 Andrei Kostitsyn 3.00 8.00
51 Carey Price 8.00 20.00
52 Brian Gionta 2.50 6.00
53 Tomas Plekanec 2.50 6.00
54 Shea Weber 3.00 8.00
55 Pekka Rinne 4.00 10.00
57 Martin Brodeur 10.00 25.00
58 Travis Zajac 2.50 6.00
59 Ilya Kovalchuk 4.00 10.00
60 John Tavares 6.00 15.00
61 Matt Moulson 3.00 8.00
62 Michael Grabner 3.00 8.00
63 Henrik Lundqvist 10.00 25.00
64 Marian Gaborik 4.00 10.00
65 Marc Staal 2.50 6.00
66 Craig Anderson 4.00 10.00
67 Jason Spezza 4.00 10.00
68 Daniel Alfredsson 4.00 10.00
69 Chris Pronger 4.00 10.00
70 Claude Giroux 4.00 10.00
71 Jeff Carter 3.00 8.00
72 Mike Richards 3.00 8.00
74 Ilya Bryzgalov 3.00 8.00
75 Keith Yandle 2.50 6.00
76 Kris Letang 5.00 12.00
77 Sidney Crosby 15.00 40.00
78 Marc-Andre Fleury 8.00 20.00
79 Jordan Staal 3.00 8.00
80 Evgeni Malkin 8.00 20.00
81 Joe Thornton 6.00 15.00
83 Dany Heatley/25 3.00 8.00
85 T.J. Oshie 4.00 10.00
86 David Backes 2.50 6.00
87 Jaroslav Halak 4.00 10.00
88 Steven Stamkos 8.00 20.00
89 Vincent Lecavalier 4.00 10.00
90 Martin St. Louis 4.00 10.00
91 Dion Phaneuf 3.00 8.00
92 James Reimer 4.00 10.00
93 Phil Kessel 4.00 10.00
94 Roberto Luongo 6.00 15.00
95 Henrik Sedin 5.00 12.00
96 Daniel Sedin 5.00 12.00
97 Ryan Kesler 4.00 10.00
98 Alex Ovechkin 15.00 40.00
99 Nicklas Backstrom 4.00 10.00
100 Semyon Varlamov 4.00 10.00
105 Normand Leveille 2.50 6.00
106 Ray Bourque 6.00 15.00
108 Rick Middleton 4.00 10.00
111 Tom Barrasso 4.00 10.00
114 Denis Savard 4.00 10.00
115 Paul Coffey 4.00 10.00
119 Ed Belfour 4.00 10.00
120 Steve Yzerman 10.00 25.00
124 Guy Lafleur 5.00 12.00
127 Patrick Roy/33 10.00 25.00
131 Brian Leetch 3.00 8.00
132 Adam Graves 3.00 8.00
137 Eric Lindros 6.00 15.00
138 Luc Robitaille 4.00 10.00
139 Mario Lemieux 15.00 40.00
140 Joe Sakic 8.00 20.00
143 Brendan Shanahan 4.00 10.00
144 Brett Hull 8.00 20.00
147 Curtis Joseph 5.00 12.00
148 Darryl Sittler 5.00 12.00

2010-11 Dominion Mammoth

1 Jacob Markstrom 20.00 50.00
2 Mattias Tedenby 8.00 20.00
3 Ryan McDonagh 20.00 50.00
4 Mats Zuccarello 15.00 40.00
7 Nazem Kadri 25.00 60.00
8 Kevin Shattenkirk 15.00 40.00
9 Zach Hamill 8.00 20.00
10 Jeff Skinner 20.00 50.00

2010-11 Dominion NHL Heritage Classics Embroidered Patches Autographs

1 Carey Price 20.00 50.00
2 Michael Cammalleri 10.00 25.00
3 P.K. Subban 25.00 60.00
5 Scott Gomez 8.00 20.00
6 Brian Gionta 6.00 15.00
8 Jarome Iginla 12.00 30.00
9 Jay Bouwmeester 6.00 15.00
10 Henrik Karlsson 8.00 20.00
11 Joe Nieuwendyk 8.00 20.00
12 Lanny McDonald 10.00 25.00

2010-11 Dominion Nifty 50 Autographs

1 Joe Nieuwendyk 8.00 20.00
2 Johnny Bucyk 10.00 25.00
3 Dino Ciccarelli 10.00 25.00
4 Adam Graves 8.00 20.00
5 Dany Heatley 8.00 20.00
6 Steven Stamkos 20.00 50.00
7 Jarome Iginla 12.00 30.00
8 Cam Neely 10.00 25.00
9 Jeremy Roenick 15.00 40.00
10 Rick Middleton 10.00 25.00
11 Lanny McDonald 10.00 25.00
12 Dennis Maruk/48 8.00 20.00
13 Charlie Simmer 6.00 15.00
14 Phil Esposito 15.00 40.00
15 Bobby Hull 20.00 50.00
16 Brett Hull 20.00 50.00
17 Guy Lafleur 12.00 30.00
18 Mike Bossy 10.00 25.00
19 Marcel Dionne 12.00 30.00
20 Dale Hawerchuk 12.00 30.00

2010-11 Dominion Notable Nicknames Autographs

1 Jean Beliveau 30.00 80.00
2 Mark Messier 25.00 60.00
3 Al Arbour 10.00 25.00
4 Dustin Byfuglien 12.00 30.00
5 Johan Franzen 10.00 25.00
6 Ken Linseman 12.00 30.00
7 Felix Potvin 20.00 50.00
8 Ed Belfour 12.00 30.00
9 Doug Gilmour 15.00 40.00
10 Jarome Iginla 15.00 40.00

2010-11 Dominion Peerless Patches

1 Shea Weber 12.00 30.00
2 Pekka Rinne 15.00 40.00
3 Rick Nash 15.00 40.00
4 Jonathan Toews 25.00 60.00
5 Patrick Kane 30.00 80.00
6 Michael Del Zotto 12.00 30.00
7 Eric Staal 20.00 50.00
8 Marc-Andre Fleury 30.00 80.00
9 Kris Draper 10.00 25.00
11 Dennis Maruk 12.00 30.00
12 Rogie Vachon 20.00 50.00
13 Alex Ovechkin 60.00 150.00
14 Milan Lucic 15.00 40.00
15 Jimmy Howard/19 20.00 50.00
16 Henrik Lundqvist 40.00 100.00
17 Dan Boyle 10.00 25.00
18 Cam Ward 15.00 40.00
19 Brent Burns 15.00 40.00
20 Ed Belfour 15.00 40.00
21 Evgeni Malkin 30.00 80.00
22 Mario Lemieux 60.00 150.00
23 Michael Grabner 12.00 30.00
24 Ryan Kesler 15.00 40.00
25 Sidney Crosby 60.00 150.00
26 Steven Stamkos 30.00 80.00
27 Ray Bourque 25.00 60.00
28 Miikka Kiprusoff 15.00 40.00
30 Duncan Keith 12.00 30.00
31 Matt Duchene 15.00 40.00
32 Lanny McDonald 15.00 40.00
33 Roberto Luongo 25.00 60.00
34 Teddy Purcell 10.00 25.00
35 Jaroslav Halak 15.00 40.00
36 Mikko Koivu 15.00 40.00
37 Denis Savard 15.00 40.00
38 Saku Koivu 15.00 40.00
39 Patrick Roy 40.00 100.00
40 Jason Pominville 10.00 25.00

2010-11 Dominion Peerless Patches Combos

1 M.Dionne/A.Kopitar 25.00 60.00
2 R.Middleton/M.Recchi 20.00 50.00
3 E.Lindros/M.Richards 25.00 60.00
4 A.Graves/T.Hall 30.00 80.00
5 J.Nieuwendyk/J.Iginla 20.00 50.00

2010-11 Dominion Pen Pals

1 M.Schmidt/J.Beliveau 10.00 25.00
2 R.Miller/J.Craig 10.00 25.00
3 C.Neely/E.Lindros 15.00 40.00
4 D.Hanson/C.Hanson 15.00 40.00
5 N.Leveille/R.Bourque 15.00 40.00
6 T.O'Reilly/D.Schultz 10.00 25.00
7 A.Graves/B.Leetch 8.00 20.00
8 M.Richards/C.Giroux 10.00 25.00
9 J.Halak/C.Price 20.00 50.00
10 L.McDonald/S.Nolet 10.00 25.00
11 A.Arbour/D.Cherry 10.00 25.00
12 R.Lemelin/D.Bouchard 8.00 20.00
13 D.Maruk/C.Simmer 8.00 20.00
14 D.Sanderson/G.Cheevers 10.00 25.00
15 K.Linseman/S.Ott 10.00 25.00
16 B.Shanahan/B.Hull 20.00 50.00
17 C.Joseph/F.Potvin 15.00 40.00
18 L.Schenn/B.Schenn 20.00 50.00
19 N.Lidstrom/Z.Chara 10.00 25.00
20 M.Duchene/P.Stastny 10.00 25.00
21 B.Ranford/G.Fuhr 15.00 40.00
22 P.Coffey/K.Letang 12.00 30.00
23 R.Francis/E.Staal 12.00 30.00
24 T.Kerr/C.Giroux 10.00 25.00
25 J.Nieuwendyk/J.Iginla 12.00 30.00

2010-11 Dominion Pen Pals Triples

1 Hall/Fowler/Wellwood 25.00 60.00
2 Sanderson/Neely/Lucic 12.00 30.00
3 Linden/Brodeur/Williams 12.00 30.00
4 Park/Staal/Leetch 10.00 25.00
5 Parent/Bobrovsky/Hextall 40.00 100.00
6 Beliveau/Cournoyer/Savard 12.00 30.00
7 Hall/Eberle/Paajarvi 25.00 60.00
8 Hanson/Carlson/Carlson 20.00 50.00
9 Dionne/Robitaille/Doughty 15.00 40.00
10 Hull/Hawerchuk/Doan 25.00 60.00

2010-11 Dominion Rookie Showcase Showdown Colossal Jerseys

*PRIME/75: .5X TO 1.2X BASIC JSY
*NAME-NMBR/25-50: .4X TO 1X BASIC JSY
*PATCH/19: .8X TO 2X BASIC JSY
1 Taylor Hall 6.00 15.00
2 Jeff Skinner 6.00 15.00
3 Tomas Tatar 6.00 15.00
4 Magnus Paajarvi 3.00 8.00
5 Ryan McDonagh 6.00 15.00
6 Mats Zuccarello 5.00 12.00
7 Mattias Tedenby 2.50 6.00

2010-11 Dominion Signatures Ruby

1 Corey Perry 10.00 25.00
2 Ryan Getzlaf 6.00 15.00
3 Saku Koivu 6.00 15.00
4 Bobby Ryan 5.00 12.00
5 Dustin Byfuglien 6.00 15.00
7 Evander Kane 6.00 15.00
10 Tim Thomas 6.00 15.00
11 Ryan Miller 6.00 15.00
12 Thomas Vanek 5.00 12.00
13 Drew Stafford 4.00 10.00
15 Jarome Iginla 8.00 20.00
17 Cam Ward 6.00 15.00
18 Eric Staal 8.00 20.00
19 Brandon Sutter 4.00 10.00
20 Jonathan Toews 10.00 25.00
21 Patrick Kane 12.00 30.00
22 Patrick Sharp 6.00 15.00
23 Corey Crawford 8.00 20.00
25 Erik Johnson 4.00 10.00
26 Brian Elliott 5.00 12.00
27 Matt Duchene 6.00 15.00
28 Rick Nash 6.00 15.00
29 Steve Mason 5.00 12.00
30 Antoine Vermette 4.00 10.00
31 Brad Richards 6.00 15.00
32 Loui Eriksson 4.00 10.00
33 Kari Lehtonen 5.00 12.00
34 Jimmy Howard 8.00 20.00
35 Pavel Datsyuk 10.00 25.00
36 Nicklas Lidstrom 6.00 15.00
38 Ales Hemsky 5.00 12.00
39 Sam Gagner 4.00 10.00
41 Stephen Weiss 5.00 12.00
43 Tomas Vokoun 5.00 12.00
44 Anze Kopitar 10.00 25.00
45 Drew Doughty 8.00 20.00
46 Jonathan Quick 8.00 20.00
47 Brent Burns 6.00 15.00
48 Cal Clutterbuck 4.00 10.00
50 Andrei Kostitsyn 5.00 12.00
51 Carey Price 12.00 30.00
52 Brian Gionta 4.00 10.00
54 Shea Weber 5.00 12.00
55 Pekka Rinne 6.00 15.00
57 Martin Brodeur/25 20.00 50.00
58 Travis Zajac 4.00 10.00
60 John Tavares 10.00 25.00
61 Matt Moulson 5.00 12.00
62 Michael Grabner 5.00 12.00
63 Henrik Lundqvist 15.00 40.00
64 Marian Gaborik 6.00 15.00
65 Marc Staal 4.00 10.00
66 Craig Anderson 6.00 15.00
67 Jason Spezza 6.00 15.00
68 Daniel Alfredsson 6.00 15.00
69 Chris Pronger 6.00 15.00
70 Claude Giroux 6.00 15.00
71 Jeff Carter 5.00 12.00
72 Mike Richards 5.00 12.00
73 Mikkel Boedker 4.00 10.00
74 Ilya Bryzgalov 5.00 12.00
75 Keith Yandle 4.00 10.00
76 Kris Letang 8.00 20.00
77 Sidney Crosby/25 50.00 125.00
78 Marc-Andre Fleury 12.00 30.00
79 Jordan Staal 5.00 12.00
80 Evgeni Malkin 12.00 30.00
81 Joe Thornton 10.00 25.00
82 Ryane Clowe 4.00 10.00
83 Dany Heatley 5.00 12.00
84 Logan Couture 8.00 20.00
85 T.J. Oshie 6.00 15.00
86 David Backes 4.00 10.00
87 Jaroslav Halak 6.00 15.00
88 Steven Stamkos 12.00 30.00
89 Vincent Lecavalier 6.00 15.00
90 Martin St. Louis 6.00 15.00
91 Dion Phaneuf 5.00 12.00
93 Phil Kessel 6.00 15.00
94 Roberto Luongo 10.00 25.00
95 Henrik Sedin 8.00 20.00
96 Daniel Sedin 8.00 20.00
97 Ryan Kesler 6.00 15.00
98 Alex Ovechkin/25 40.00 100.00
100 Semyon Varlamov 6.00 15.00
101 Cam Neely/45 12.00 30.00
102 Derek Sanderson 6.00 15.00
103 Felix Potvin 10.00 25.00
104 Milt Schmidt 5.00 12.00
105 Normand Leveille 4.00 10.00
106 Ray Bourque 10.00 25.00
107 Reggie Lemelin 4.00 10.00
108 Rick Middleton 6.00 15.00
109 Dale Hawerchuk 8.00 20.00
110 Gilbert Perreault 6.00 15.00
111 Tom Barrasso 6.00 15.00
112 Doug Gilmour 8.00 20.00
113 Bobby Hull 12.00 30.00
114 Denis Savard 6.00 15.00
116 Phil Esposito 10.00 25.00
117 Stan Mikita 8.00 20.00
118 Tony Esposito 6.00 15.00
119 Ed Belfour 6.00 15.00
120 Steve Yzerman/25 30.00 80.00
121 Grant Fuhr 10.00 25.00
122 Mark Messier/25 25.00 60.00
123 Kelly Hrudey 5.00 12.00
124 Guy Lafleur 8.00 20.00
125 Henri Richard 6.00 15.00
126 Jean Beliveau 6.00 15.00
127 Patrick Roy/25 30.00 80.00
128 Denis Potvin 6.00 15.00
129 Mike Bossy 6.00 15.00
130 Brad Park 5.00 12.00
131 Brian Leetch 5.00 12.00
132 Adam Graves 5.00 12.00
133 Ed Giacomin 10.00 25.00
134 Rod Gilbert 6.00 15.00
135 Bernie Parent 8.00 20.00
136 Bobby Clarke 10.00 25.00
137 Eric Lindros/25 30.00 80.00
138 Luc Robitaille 6.00 15.00
139 Mario Lemieux 25.00 60.00
140 Joe Sakic/25 20.00 50.00
141 Ron Hextall 6.00 15.00
142 Jeremy Roenick 10.00 25.00
143 Brendan Shanahan/25 15.00 40.00
144 Brett Hull 12.00 30.00
145 Glenn Hall 6.00 15.00
146 Manon Rheaume 15.00 40.00
147 Curtis Joseph 8.00 20.00
148 Darryl Sittler 8.00 20.00
149 Johnny Bower 6.00 15.00
150 Trevor Linden 6.00 15.00

2010-11 Dominion Stickside Signatures

1 Gerry Cheevers 12.00 30.00
2 Curtis Joseph 15.00 40.00
3 Ed Belfour 12.00 30.00
4 Johnny Bower 12.00 30.00
5 Patrick Roy 30.00 80.00
6 Jose Theodore 12.00 30.00
7 Marc-Andre Fleury 25.00 60.00
8 Martin Brodeur 30.00 80.00
9 Ilya Bryzgalov 10.00 25.00
10 Henrik Lundqvist 30.00 80.00
11 Jaroslav Halak 12.00 30.00
12 Tim Thomas 12.00 30.00
13 Carey Price/49 25.00 60.00
14 Marty Turco 12.00 30.00
15 Jonathan Bernier 10.00 25.00
16 Mike Smith 12.00 30.00
17 Tomas Vokoun 10.00 25.00
18 Rogie Vachon 15.00 40.00
19 Charlie Hodge 10.00 25.00
20 Grant Fuhr 20.00 50.00

2010-11 Dominion Strapping Lads

1 Sidney Crosby 25.00 60.00
2 Alex Ovechkin 25.00 60.00
3 Carey Price 12.00 30.00
4 Tim Thomas 6.00 15.00
5 Milan Lucic 6.00 15.00
6 Dion Phaneuf 5.00 12.00
7 Mike Green 5.00 12.00
8 Jarome Iginla 8.00 20.00
9 Evander Kane 6.00 15.00
10 Ilya Kovalchuk 6.00 15.00

2010-11 Dominion Tape to Tape Autographs

1 Marc-Andre Fleury 50.00 125.00
2 Johnny Bower 25.00 60.00
3 Alex Ovechkin 100.00 250.00
4 Gerry Cheevers 25.00 60.00
5 Henrik Lundqvist 60.00 150.00
6 Rogie Vachon 30.00 80.00
7 Steve Ott 15.00 40.00
8 Phil Kessel 25.00 60.00
9 Mario Lemieux 100.00 250.00
10 Brendan Shanahan 25.00 60.00
11 Tim Thomas/19 25.00 60.00
12 Patrick Roy 60.00 150.00
13 Marian Gaborik 25.00 60.00
15 Scott Gomez 20.00 50.00
17 Joe Nieuwendyk 20.00 50.00
18 Stan Mikita 30.00 80.00
19 Mark Messier/19 50.00 125.00

2011-12 Dominion

1 Evgeni Malkin 3.00 8.00
2 Claude Giroux 1.50 4.00
3 Steven Stamkos 3.00 8.00
4 James Reimer 1.50 4.00
5 Phil Kessel 1.50 4.00
6 Dustin Byfuglien 1.50 4.00
7 Henrik Sedin 2.00 5.00
8 Pavel Datsyuk 2.50 6.00
9 Gordie Howe 5.00 12.00
10 Jordan Eberle 1.50 4.00
11 John Tavares 2.50 6.00
12 Jonathan Toews 2.50 6.00
13 Daniel Sedin 2.00 5.00
14 Ryan Miller 1.50 4.00
15 Shea Weber 1.25 3.00
16 Brett Hull 3.00 8.00
17 Erik Karlsson 2.00 5.00
18 Zach Parise 1.50 4.00
19 Steve Yzerman 4.00 10.00
20 Sidney Crosby 6.00 15.00
21 Alex Ovechkin 6.00 15.00
22 Jimmy Howard 2.00 5.00
23 Patrice Bergeron 2.00 5.00
24 Jamie Benn 1.50 4.00
25 Joe Thornton 2.50 6.00
26 Patrick Kane 3.00 8.00
27 Jonathan Quick 2.00 5.00
28 Loui Eriksson 1.00 2.50
29 Vincent Lecavalier 1.50 4.00
30 Marian Gaborik 1.50 4.00
31 Carey Price 3.00 8.00
32 Corey Perry 2.50 6.00
33 Patrick Roy 4.00 10.00
34 Taylor Hall 1.50 4.00
35 Tyler Seguin 2.00 5.00
36 Martin Brodeur 4.00 10.00
37 Eric Staal 2.00 5.00
38 Marc-Andre Fleury 3.00 8.00
39 Dany Heatley 1.25 3.00
40 David Backes 1.00 2.50
41 Jaromir Jagr 5.00 12.00
42 Ryan Getzlaf 1.50 4.00
43 Henrik Lundqvist 4.00 10.00
44 Rick Nash 1.50 4.00
45 Matt Duchene 1.50 4.00
46 Shane Doan 1.25 3.00
47 Evander Kane 1.50 4.00
48 Tim Thomas 1.50 4.00
49 Saku Koivu 1.50 4.00
50 Nicklas Lidstrom 1.00 2.50
51 P.K. Subban 2.00 5.00
52 Kris Letang 2.00 5.00
53 Pekka Rinne 1.50 4.00
54 Cam Ward 1.50 4.00
55 Marian Hossa 1.50 4.00
56 Logan Couture 2.00 5.00
57 Matt Moulson 1.00 2.50
58 Bobby Ryan 1.25 3.00
59 Dion Phaneuf 1.25 3.00
60 Jose Theodore 1.50 4.00
61 Patrick Sharp 1.50 4.00
62 Henrik Zetterberg 2.00 5.00
63 T.J. Oshie 1.50 4.00
64 Jarome Iginla 2.00 5.00
65 Mikko Koivu 1.25 3.00
66 Mario Lemieux 6.00 15.00
67 Scott Hartnell 1.00 2.50
68 Jean-Sebastien Giguere 1.50 4.00
69 Jonas Gustavsson 1.50 4.00
70 Ray Whitney 1.25 3.00
71 Ryan Kesler 1.50 4.00
72 Kari Lehtonen 1.25 3.00
73 Brian Elliott 1.25 3.00
74 Miikka Kiprusoff 1.50 4.00
75 Patrick Marleau 1.50 4.00
76 Ilya Kovalchuk 1.50 4.00
77 Michael Grabner 1.25 3.00
78 David Krejci 1.50 4.00
79 Max Pacioretty 1.50 4.00
80 Jason Spezza 1.50 4.00
81 Jeff Skinner 2.00 5.00
82 Paul Stastny 1.25 3.00
83 Alexander Semin 1.50 4.00
84 Jaroslav Halak 1.50 4.00
85 Braden Holtby 2.00 5.00
86 Daniel Alfredsson 1.50 4.00
87 Brad Richards 1.50 4.00
88 Eric Lindros 2.50 6.00
89 Bobby Hull 3.00 8.00
90 Martin St. Louis 1.50 4.00
91 Anze Kopitar 2.50 6.00
92 Curtis Joseph 2.00 5.00
93 Roberto Luongo 2.50 6.00
94 Guy Lafleur 2.00 5.00

95 Thomas Vanek 1.25 3.00
96 Cam Neely 1.50 4.00
97 Ron Hextall 1.50 4.00
98 Joe Sakic 3.00 8.00
99 Mike Modano 2.50 6.00
100 Phil Esposito 2.50 6.00
101 P.Maroon AU/199 RC EX 5.00 12.00
102 T.J. Brennan AU/199 RC 5.00 12.00
103 Joe Finley AU/199 RC 5.00 12.00
104 Marcus Foligno AU/199 RC 8.00 20.00
105 Brayden McNabb AU/199 RC 5.00 12.00
106 Corey Tropp AU/199 RC 5.00 12.00
107 Leland Irving AU/199 RC 5.00 12.00
108 Lance Bouma AU/99 RC 6.00 15.00
109 Riley Nash AU/199 RC 5.00 12.00
110 Jimmy Hayes AU/199 RC 6.00 15.00
111 Dylan Olsen AU/199 RC 6.00 15.00
112 Andrew Shaw AU/199 RC 12.00 30.00
113 Brad Malone AU/199 RC 5.00 12.00
114 Elliott AU/199 RC EX 5.00 12.00
115 Matt Fraser AU/199 RC 6.00 15.00
116 C.Vande Velde AU/199 RC 8.00 20.00
117 Colten Teubert AU/199 RC 5.00 12.00
118 Lennart Petrell AU/199 RC 6.00 15.00
119 Hugh Jessiman AU/199 RC 5.00 12.00
120 Scott Timmins AU/199 RC 5.00 12.00
121 Carson McMillan AU/199 RC 6.00 15.00
122 Bagnall AU/150 RC 5.00 12.00
123 Roman Josi AU/199 RC 12.00 30.00
124 G.Bourque AU/199 RC 5.00 12.00
125 Keith Kinkaid AU/199 RC 5.00 12.00
126 A.Nilsson AU/199 RC 5.00 12.00
127 Mark Katic AU/199 RC 5.00 12.00
128 Mikko Koskinen AU/199 RC 6.00 15.00
129 Ben Holmstrom AU/199 RC 5.00 12.00
130 Paul Postma AU/199 RC 5.00 12.00
131 Peter Holland JSY AU/199 RC 5.00 12.00
133 Greg Nemisz JSY AU/199 RC 5.00 12.00
134 Roman Horak JSY AU/199 RC 5.00 12.00
135 J.Faulk JSY AU/199 RC 8.00 20.00
136 Kruger JSY AU/199 RC EX 8.00 20.00
137 C.Gaunce JSY AU/199 RC 4.00 10.00
138 John Moore JSY AU/199 RC 5.00 12.00
139 C.Atkinson JSY AU/199 RC 12.00 30.00
140 Allen York JSY AU/199 RC 6.00 15.00
141 Tomas Kubalik JSY AU/199 RC 5.00 12.00
142 Da.Savard JSY AU/199 RC 5.00 12.00
143 T.Vincour JSY AU/199 RC 5.00 12.00
144 Sceviour JSY AU/199 RC 5.00 12.00
145 G.Nyquist JSY AU/199 RC 12.00 30.00
146 B.Smith JSY AU/199 RC 5.00 12.00
147 Hartikainn JSY AU/199 RC 5.00 12.00
148 Lander JSY AU/199 RC 5.00 12.00
149 S.Voynov JSY AU/199 RC 5.00 12.00
150 B.Bulmer JSY AU/199 RC 5.00 12.00
151 R.Diaz JSY AU/199 RC 5.00 12.00
152 A.Emelin JSY AU/199 RC 5.00 12.00
153 Palushaj JSY AU/199 RC 5.00 12.00
154 Geoffrion JSY AU/199 RC 5.00 12.00
155 J.Blum JSY AU/199 RC 5.00 12.00
156 Craig Smith JSY AU/199 RC 6.00 15.00
157 Ryan Ellis JSY AU/199 RC 5.00 12.00
158 Calvin de Haan JSY AU/199 RC 5.00 12.00
159 Cam Talbot JSY AU/199 RC 12.00 30.00
160 Tim Erixon JSY AU/199 RC 5.00 12.00
161 P.Wiercioch JSY AU/199 RC 5.00 12.00
162 Erik Condra JSY AU/199 RC 5.00 12.00
163 S.Da Costa JSY AU/199 RC 5.00 12.00
164 Colin Greening JSY AU/199 RC 5.00 12.00
165 Zac Rinaldo JSY AU/199 RC 5.00 12.00
166 H.Zolnierczyk JSY AU/199 RC 5.00 12.00
167 Gustafsson JSY AU/199 RC 6.00 15.00
168 Rundblad JSY AU/199 RC 5.00 12.00
169 Andy Miele JSY AU/199 RC 5.00 12.00
170 Despres JSY AU/199 RC 5.00 12.00
171 R.Bortuzzo JSY AU/199 RC 5.00 12.00
172 Joe Vitale JSY AU/199 RC 5.00 12.00
173 H.Sateri JSY AU/199 RC 5.00 12.00
174 B.Connolly JSY AU/199 RC 5.00 12.00
175 Matt Frattin JSY AU/199 RC 5.00 12.00
176 J.Gardiner JSY AU/199 RC 8.00 20.00
177 Scrivens JSY AU/199 RC 5.00 12.00
178 E.Lack JSY AU/199 RC 5.00 12.00
179 Yann Sauve JSY AU/199 RC 5.00 12.00
180 Cody Eakin JSY AU/199 RC 8.00 20.00
181 D.Orlov JSY AU/199 RC 12.00 30.00
182 Carl Klingberg JSY AU/199 RC 5.00 12.00
183 M.Macenauer JSY AU/99 RC 5.00 12.00
184 Hodgson JSY AU/99 RC 8.00 20.00
185 B.Saad JSY AU/99 RC 25.00 60.00
186 Landeskog JSY AU/99 RC 40.00 100.00
187 Johansen JSY AU/99 RC 25.00 60.00
188 RNH JSY AU/99 RC 50.00 125.00
189 Gudbranson JSY AU/99 RC 10.00 25.00
190 L.Leblanc JSY AU/99 RC 5.00 12.00
191 Henrique JSY AU/99 RC 12.00 30.00
192 Larsson JSY AU/99 RC 6.00 15.00
193 Hagelin JSY AU/99 RC 8.00 20.00
194 Zibanejad JSY AU/99 RC 15.00 40.00
195 Couturier JSY AU/99 RC 10.00 25.00
196 M.Read JSY AU/99 RC 6.00 15.00
197 Brian Strait JSY AU/99 RC 6.00 15.00
198 Colborne JSY AU/99 RC 5.00 12.00
199 Kassian JSY AU/99 RC 6.00 15.00
200 Scheifele JSY AU/99 RC 20.00 50.00

2011-12 Dominion Gold

*1-100 VETS/25: .6X TO 1.5X BASIC CARDS
*101-130 RK.AU/25: .6X TO 1.5X AU/99-199
*131-182 JSY AU/25: .6X TO 1.5X JSY AU/199
*183-200 JSY AU/25: .4X TO 1X JSY AU RC/99
33 Patrick Roy 25.00 60.00
186 G.Landeskog JSY AU 100.00 200.00
188 R.Nugent-Hopkins JSY AU 300.00 600.00

2011-12 Dominion Autographed Rookie Patches Horizontal

131 Peter Holland/74 8.00 20.00
133 Greg Nemisz/48 8.00 20.00
134 Roman Horak/51 8.00 20.00
135 Justin Faulk/28 12.00 30.00
136 Marcus Kruger/16 EXCH 20.00 50.00
137 Cameron Gaunce/43 6.00 15.00
140 Allen York/41 10.00 25.00
141 Tomas Kubalik/33 8.00 20.00
142 David Savard/58 8.00 20.00
143 Tomas Vincour/81 8.00 20.00
144 Colton Sceviour/22 8.00 20.00
147 Teemu Hartikainen/56 8.00 20.00
148 Anton Lander/57 8.00 20.00
149 Slava Voynov/26 8.00 20.00
150 Brett Bulmer/19 8.00 20.00
151 Raphael Diaz/61 8.00 20.00
152 Alexei Emelin/74 8.00 20.00
153 Aaron Palushaj/60 8.00 20.00
154 Blake Geoffrion/57 8.00 20.00
157 Ryan Ellis/49 8.00 20.00
158 Calvin de Haan/44 8.00 20.00
159 Cam Talbot/81 20.00 50.00
160 Tim Erixon/53 8.00 20.00
161 Patrick Wiercioch/46 8.00 20.00
162 Erik Condra/22 8.00 20.00
163 Stephane Da Costa/24 8.00 20.00
165 Zac Rinaldo/36 8.00 20.00
166 Harry Zolnierczyk/29 8.00 20.00
167 Erik Gustafsson/26 10.00 25.00
169 Andy Miele/21 8.00 20.00
170 Simon Despres/47 8.00 20.00
171 Robert Bortuzzo/41 8.00 20.00
172 Joe Vitale/46 8.00 20.00
173 Harri Sateri/35 8.00 20.00
175 Matt Frattin/39 8.00 20.00
176 Jake Gardiner/51 12.00 30.00
177 Ben Scrivens/30 8.00 20.00
178 Eddie Lack/31 8.00 20.00
179 Yann Sauve/47 8.00 20.00
180 Cody Eakin/50 12.00 30.00
181 Dmitry Orlov/81 20.00 50.00
182 Carl Klingberg/48 8.00 20.00
183 Maxime Macenauer/49 8.00 20.00
184 Cody Hodgson/19 12.00 30.00
185 Brandon Saad/43 15.00 40.00
186 Gabriel Landeskog/92 25.00 60.00
187 Ryan Johansen/19 25.00 60.00
188 R.Nugent-Hopkins JSY 30.00 80.00
189 Erik Gudbranson/44 EXCH 10.00 25.00
190 Louis Leblanc/71 8.00 20.00
193 Carl Hagelin/62 12.00 30.00
194 Mika Zibanejad/93 25.00 60.00
196 Matt Read/24 10.00 25.00
197 Brian Strait/37 10.00 25.00
198 Joe Colborne/32 8.00 20.00
200 Mark Scheifele/55 30.00 80.00

2011-12 Dominion Benchmark Sticks

1 Martin Brodeur/50 25.00 60.00
2 Ron Francis/50 12.00 30.00
3 Mark Messier/50 20.00 50.00
4 Steve Yzerman/50 25.00 60.00
5 Gordie Howe/25 30.00 80.00
6 Marcel Dionne/25 12.00 30.00
7 Mario Lemieux/50 40.00 100.00
8 Joe Sakic/25 20.00 50.00
9 Jaromir Jagr/25 30.00 80.00
10 Ed Belfour/99 10.00 25.00
11 Tony Esposito/50 10.00 25.00
12 Patrick Roy/99 25.00 60.00
13 Martin Brodeur/50 25.00 60.00
14 Gordie Howe/25 30.00 80.00
15 Mark Messier/50 20.00 50.00
16 Jaromir Jagr/50 30.00 80.00
17 Bobby Hull/25 20.00 50.00
18 Mike Modano/25 15.00 40.00

2011-12 Dominion Complete Rookies Quad Jerseys

1 Devante Smith-Pelly/25 8.00 20.00
2 Cody Hodgson/25 10.00 25.00
3 Greg Nemisz/25 6.00 15.00
4 Justin Faulk/25 10.00 25.00
5 Brandon Saad/25 12.00 30.00
6 Marcus Kruger/25 10.00 25.00
7 Gabriel Landeskog/25 20.00 50.00
8 Cam Atkinson/25 15.00 40.00
9 Ryan Johansen/25 20.00 50.00
10 Brendan Smith/25 6.00 15.00
11 Gustav Nyquist/25 15.00 40.00
12 Anton Lander/25 6.00 15.00
13 Ryan Nugent-Hopkins/25 25.00 60.00
14 Erik Gudbranson/25 8.00 20.00
15 Slava Voynov/25 6.00 15.00
16 Brett Bulmer/25 6.00 15.00
17 Blake Geoffrion/25 6.00 15.00
18 Louis Leblanc/25 6.00 15.00
19 Craig Smith/25 8.00 20.00
20 Ryan Ellis/25 6.00 15.00
21 Adam Henrique/25 15.00 40.00
22 Adam Larsson/25 8.00 20.00
23 Calvin de Haan/25 6.00 15.00
24 Carl Hagelin/25 10.00 25.00
25 Tim Erixon/25 6.00 15.00
26 Colin Greening/25 6.00 15.00
27 Mika Zibanejad/25 20.00 50.00
28 Matt Read/25 8.00 20.00
29 Sean Couturier/25 12.00 30.00
30 David Rundblad/25 6.00 15.00
31 Simon Despres/25 6.00 15.00
32 Brett Connolly/25 6.00 15.00
33 Ben Scrivens/25 6.00 15.00
34 Jake Gardiner/25 10.00 25.00
35 Joe Colborne/25 6.00 15.00
36 Eddie Lack/25 6.00 15.00
37 Zack Kassian/25 8.00 20.00
38 Cody Eakin/25 10.00 25.00
39 Dmitry Orlov/25 15.00 40.00

2011-12 Dominion Crazy Eights Jerseys

1 Ovechkin/RNH/Kane/MAF 25.00 60.00
2 Goalie Young Stars 15.00 40.00
3 Forward Young Stars 12.00 30.00
4 Defense Stars 8.00 20.00
5 Physical Leaders 5.00 12.00
6 Colorado Avalanche 15.00 40.00
7 Toronto Maple Leafs 8.00 20.00
8 Ovechkin/Kane/Lindros 25.00 60.00
9 LA Kings 10.00 25.00
10 Boston Bruins 10.00 25.00
11 Lemieux/Lindros/Roy/Messier 25.00 60.00
12 Philadelphia Flyers Vets 10.00 25.00
13 RNH/Landeskog Young Stars 20.00 50.00
14 Larsson/Gudbranson/Voynov 12.00 30.00
15 Scheifele/Connolly/Saad 20.00 50.00
16 Detroit Red Wings 15.00 40.00
17 Pittsburgh Penguins 25.00 60.00
18 Flyers Young Stars 10.00 25.00
19 Star Captains 15.00 40.00
20 Czech Stars 20.00 50.00
21 Finnish Stars 12.00 30.00
22 Canada Vets 15.00 40.00
23 Canada Young Stars 10.00 25.00
24 USA Stars 12.00 30.00
25 Russian Stars 25.00 60.00
26 Sweeden Stars 15.00 40.00
27 Retired Stars 25.00 60.00

2011-12 Dominion Jerseys

*PRIME/25: .6X TO 1.5X BASIC INSERTS
1 Cam Fowler/100 4.00 10.00
2 D.Smith-Pelly/100 4.00 10.00
3 Teemu Selanne/100 8.00 20.00
4 Milan Lucic/100 4.00 10.00
5 Tuukka Rask/100 5.00 12.00
6 Ray Bourque/50 6.00 15.00
7 Brad Boyes/100 2.50 6.00
8 Cody Hodgson/100 5.00 12.00
9 Tyler Myers/100 2.50 6.00
10 Mike Cammalleri/100 3.00 8.00
11 Greg Nemisz/100 3.00 8.00
12 Mikael Backlund/100 3.00 8.00
13 Justin Faulk/100 5.00 12.00
14 Zach Boychuk/100 2.50 6.00
15 Brandon Saad/100 6.00 15.00
16 Marcus Kruger/100 5.00 12.00
17 Stan Mikita/50 5.00 12.00
18 Gabriel Landeskog/100 10.00 25.00
19 Joe Sakic/100 8.00 20.00
20 Paul Stastny/100 3.00 8.00
21 Steve Downie/50 2.50 6.00
22 Cam Atkinson/100 8.00 20.00
23 Jack Johnson/100 2.50 6.00
24 Ryan Johansen/100 10.00 25.00
25 Colton Sceviour/100 3.00 8.00
26 Brenden Morrow/100 3.00 8.00
27 Loui Eriksson/100 2.50 6.00
28 Brendan Smith/100 3.00 8.00
30 Niklas Kronwall/100 3.00 8.00
31 Pavel Datsyuk/100 6.00 15.00
32 Jordan Eberle/100 4.00 10.00
33 R.Nugent-Hopkins/100 12.00 30.00
34 Sam Gagner/100 2.50 6.00
35 Teemu Hartikainen/100 3.00 8.00
36 Dmitry Kulikov/100 2.50 6.00
37 Erik Gudbranson/100 4.00 10.00
38 Wojtek Wolski/100 2.50 6.00
39 Kris Versteeg/100 2.50 6.00
40 Ron Francis/50 5.00 12.00
41 Jeff Carter/100 3.00 8.00
42 Luc Robitaille/100 4.00 10.00
43 Mike Richards/100 3.00 8.00
44 Cal Clutterbuck/50 2.50 6.00
45 Dany Heatley/100 3.00 8.00
46 Devin Setoguchi/100 3.00 8.00
47 Blake Geoffrion/100 3.00 8.00
48 Louis Leblanc/100 3.00 8.00
49 Patrick Roy/50 10.00 25.00
50 Raphael Diaz/100 3.00 8.00
51 Anders Lindback/100 3.00 8.00
52 Craig Smith/100 4.00 10.00
53 Patric Hornqvist/100 2.50 6.00
54 Adam Larsson/100 4.00 10.00
55 Joe Nieuwendyk/100 3.00 8.00
56 Martin Brodeur/100 10.00 25.00
57 Bryan Trottier/100 4.00 10.00
58 Frans Nielsen/100 2.50 6.00
59 Pat LaFontaine/100 4.00 10.00
60 Brandon Dubinsky/100 2.50 6.00
61 Carl Hagelin/100 5.00 12.00
62 Marian Gaborik/100 4.00 10.00
63 Ryan Callahan/100 2.50 6.00
64 Daniel Alfredsson/100 4.00 10.00
65 Erik Condra/100 3.00 8.00
66 Robin Lehner/100 3.00 8.00
67 Brayden Schenn/100 4.00 10.00
68 Matt Read/100 4.00 10.00
69 Scott Hartnell/100 2.50 6.00
70 Sean Couturier/100 6.00 15.00
71 David Rundblad/100 3.00 8.00
72 Mike Smith/100 4.00 10.00
73 Shane Doan/100 3.00 8.00
74 Chris Kunitz/100 4.00 10.00
75 Mario Lemieux/50 15.00 40.00
76 Sidney Crosby/50 15.00 40.00
77 Simon Despres/100 3.00 8.00
78 Dan Boyle/100 2.50 6.00
79 Joe Pavelski/100 5.00 12.00
80 Patrick Marleau/100 4.00 10.00
81 Brett Hull/100 8.00 20.00
82 David Perron/100 3.00 8.00
83 Patrik Berglund/100 2.50 6.00
84 Brett Connolly/100 3.00 8.00
85 Martin St. Louis/100 4.00 10.00
86 Ryan Malone/100 2.50 6.00
87 Steven Stamkos/50 8.00 20.00
88 Jake Gardiner/100 5.00 12.00
89 Joe Colborne/100 3.00 8.00
90 Mikhail Grabovski/100 2.50 6.00
91 Wendel Clark/100 6.00 15.00
92 Alexandre Burrows/100 2.50 6.00
93 Eddie Lack/100 3.00 8.00
94 Zack Kassian/100 4.00 10.00
95 Alex Ovechkin/100 15.00 40.00
96 Braden Holtby/100 5.00 12.00
97 Mike Green/100 3.00 8.00
98 Carl Klingberg/100 3.00 8.00
99 Mark Scheifele/100 12.00 30.00
100 Tobias Enstrom/100 2.50 6.00

2011-12 Dominion Mammoth Jerseys

*PRIME/25: .5X TO 1.25X MAMMOTH/50
1 D.Smith-Pelly/50 6.00 15.00
2 Cody Hodgson/50 8.00 20.00
3 Greg Nemisz/50 5.00 12.00
4 Justin Faulk/50 8.00 20.00
5 Brandon Saad/50 10.00 25.00
6 Marcus Kruger/50 8.00 20.00
7 Cameron Gaunce/50 4.00 10.00
8 Gabriel Landeskog/50 15.00 40.00
9 Cam Atkinson/50 12.00 30.00
10 David Savard/50 5.00 12.00
11 John Moore/50 5.00 12.00
12 Ryan Johansen/50 15.00 40.00
13 Tomas Vincour/50 5.00 12.00
14 Brendan Smith/50 5.00 12.00
15 Gustav Nyquist/50 12.00 30.00
16 Anton Lander/50 5.00 12.00
17 R.Nugent-Hopkins/50 20.00 50.00
18 Teemu Hartikainen/50 5.00 12.00
19 Erik Gudbranson/50 6.00 15.00
20 Slava Voynov/50 5.00 12.00
21 Brett Bulmer/50 5.00 12.00
22 Blake Geoffrion/50 5.00 12.00
23 Louis Leblanc/50 5.00 12.00
24 Raphael Diaz/50 5.00 12.00
25 Craig Smith/50 6.00 15.00
26 Ryan Ellis/50 5.00 12.00
27 Adam Henrique/50 12.00 30.00
28 Adam Larsson/50 6.00 15.00
29 Calvin de Haan/50 5.00 12.00
30 Carl Hagelin/50 8.00 20.00
31 Tim Erixon/50 5.00 12.00
32 Colin Greening/50 5.00 12.00
33 Erik Condra/50 5.00 12.00
34 Mika Zibanejad/50 15.00 40.00
35 Matt Read/50 6.00 15.00
36 Sean Couturier/50 10.00 25.00
37 Zac Rinaldo/50 5.00 12.00
38 David Rundblad/50 5.00 12.00
39 Joe Vitale/50 5.00 12.00
40 Simon Despres/50 5.00 12.00
41 Harri Sateri/50 5.00 12.00
42 Ben Scrivens/50 5.00 12.00
43 Jake Gardiner/50 8.00 20.00
44 Joe Colborne/50 5.00 12.00
45 Matt Frattin/50 5.00 12.00
46 Yann Sauve/50 5.00 12.00
47 Zack Kassian/50 6.00 15.00
48 Cody Eakin/50 8.00 20.00
49 Dmitry Orlov/50 12.00 30.00
50 Mark Scheifele/50 20.00 50.00
51 Ray Bourque/25 10.00 25.00
52 Joe Sakic/25 12.00 30.00
53 Steve Yzerman/25 15.00 40.00
54 Patrick Roy/25 15.00 40.00
55 Martin Brodeur/25 15.00 40.00
56 Mark Messier/25 12.00 30.00
57 Jaromir Jagr/25 20.00 50.00
58 Sidney Crosby/25 25.00 60.00
59 Steven Stamkos/25 12.00 30.00
60 Alex Ovechkin/25 25.00 60.00

2011-12 Dominion Patches Autographs

1 Corey Perry/60 12.00 30.00
3 Ryan Getzlaf/60 12.00 30.00
4 Brad Marchand/60 12.00 30.00
5 Patrice Bergeron/60 20.00 50.00
6 Ray Bourque/25 40.00 80.00
7 Tim Thomas/60 15.00 40.00
8 Cody Hodgson/60 12.00 30.00
9 Ryan Miller/60 20.00 50.00
10 Curtis Glencross/60 10.00 25.00
11 Greg Nemisz/60 10.00 25.00
12 Jarome Iginla/60 15.00 40.00
13 Mark Scheifele/25 25.00 60.00
14 Justin Faulk/60 12.00 30.00
15 Ron Francis/60 15.00 40.00
16 Brandon Saad/60 30.00 80.00
17 Jonathan Toews/60 30.00 60.00
18 Marcus Kruger/60 12.00 30.00
19 Patrick Kane/60 20.00 50.00
21 Joe Sakic/25 50.00 100.00
22 Matt Duchene/60 10.00 25.00
24 Jack Johnson/60 10.00 25.00
25 Rick Nash/60 16.00 40.00
26 Ryan Johansen/60 15.00 40.00
27 Loui Eriksson/60 12.00 30.00
28 Mike Modano/25 30.00 60.00
29 Brendan Smith/60 15.00 40.00
31 Pavel Datsyuk/60 15.00 40.00
32 Steve Yzerman/25 60.00 120.00
33 Anton Lander/60 12.00 30.00
34 Jordan Eberle/60 40.00 80.00
35 Ryan Nugent-Hopkins/60 40.00 100.00
36 Taylor Hall/25 15.00 40.00
37 Ed Belfour/60 25.00 50.00
38 Erik Gudbranson/60 EXCH 12.00 30.00
39 Drew Doughty/60 EXCH 15.00 40.00
40 Dustin Brown/60 12.00 30.00
42 Jeremy Roenick/60 15.00 40.00
43 Luc Robitaille/60 12.00 30.00
44 Cal Clutterbuck/60 12.00 30.00
45 Niklas Backstrom/60 12.00 30.00
46 Brian Gionta/60 6.00 15.00
47 Carey Price/25 30.00 80.00
48 Louis Leblanc/60 8.00 20.00
49 Patrick Roy/25 60.00 120.00
50 Craig Smith/60 10.00 25.00
51 Pekka Rinne/60 15.00 40.00
52 Ryan Ellis/60 15.00 40.00
53 Adam Henrique/60 20.00 50.00
54 Adam Larsson/60 10.00 25.00
55 Joe Nieuwendyk/60 15.00 40.00
56 Martin Brodeur/25 90.00 150.00
57 Calvin de Haan/60 8.00 20.00
58 John Tavares/60 30.00 80.00
59 Pat LaFontaine/60 15.00 40.00
60 Carl Hagelin/60 12.00 30.00
61 Marc Staal/60 10.00 25.00
62 Marian Gaborik/60 12.00 30.00
63 Mark Messier/25 40.00 80.00
64 Colin Greening/60 8.00 20.00
65 Craig Anderson/60 10.00 25.00
66 Mika Zibanejad/60 25.00 60.00
67 Nick Foligno/60 8.00 20.00
68 Claude Giroux/60 EXCH 25.00 50.00
69 Eric Lindros/25 60.00 120.00
70 Jaromir Jagr/60 40.00 100.00
71 Matt Read/60 15.00 40.00
72 Sean Couturier/60 15.00 40.00
73 David Rundblad/60 12.00 30.00
74 Shane Doan/60 10.00 25.00
76 Joe Vitale/60 8.00 20.00
77 Mario Lemieux/25 100.00 175.00
78 Sidney Crosby/25 100.00 175.00
79 Dan Boyle/60 12.00 30.00
80 Joe Thornton/60 15.00 40.00
81 Patrick Marleau/60 12.00 30.00
82 Alex Pietrangelo/60 12.00 30.00
83 David Backes/60 12.00 30.00
84 Brett Connolly/60 8.00 20.00
85 Martin St. Louis/60 10.00 25.00
86 Steven Stamkos/25 30.00 80.00
87 Vincent Lecavalier/35 15.00 40.00
88 Curtis Joseph/60 15.00 40.00
89 Felix Potvin/60 15.00 40.00
90 Jake Gardiner/60 20.00 50.00
91 Joe Colborne/60 20.00 50.00
92 Phil Kessel/50 12.00 30.00
93 Cam Neely/25 30.00 60.00
94 Daniel Sedin/60 10.00 25.00
95 Henrik Sedin/60 15.00 40.00
96 Zack Kassian/60 10.00 25.00
97 Alex Ovechkin/25 60.00 120.00
98 Cody Eakin/60 12.00 30.00
99 Dustin Byfuglien/60 12.00 30.00

2011-12 Dominion Peerless Patches Autographs

1 Bobby Ryan/40 15.00 40.00
4 Tim Thomas/40 20.00 50.00
5 Tyler Seguin/40 30.00 80.00
6 Cam Neely/25 25.00 50.00
7 Ray Bourque/25 40.00 80.00
8 Ryan Miller/40 15.00 40.00
9 Henrik Sedin/40 25.00 50.00
10 Cody Hodgson/40 15.00 40.00
11 Jarome Iginla/40 25.00 50.00
12 Greg Nemisz/40 10.00 25.00
13 Ryan Kesler/40 15.00 40.00
15 Patrick Kane/40 75.00 150.00
16 Jonathan Toews/40 40.00 100.00
17 Brandon Saad/40 30.00 60.00
18 Denis Savard/25 30.00 60.00
19 Matt Duchene/40 20.00 50.00
20 Patrick Roy/25 150.00 300.00
21 Gabriel Landeskog/40 40.00 80.00
23 Ryan Johansen/40 30.00 80.00
24 Loui Eriksson/40 8.00 20.00
25 Jamie Benn/40 15.00 40.00
26 Ed Belfour/25 30.00 60.00
27 Mike Modano/40 30.00 80.00
30 Steve Yzerman/25 60.00 120.00
31 Brendan Smith/40 10.00 25.00
32 Brendan Shanahan/40 40.00 80.00
33 Nicklas Lidstrom/25 60.00 120.00
34 R.Nugent-Hopkins/40 50.00 100.00
35 Taylor Hall/40 60.00 120.00
37 Anton Lander/40 15.00 40.00
39 Stephen Weiss/40 10.00 25.00
40 Ron Francis/25 40.00 100.00
41 Anze Kopitar/40 25.00 50.00
44 Bernie Nicholls/25 30.00 80.00
45 Alex Ovechkin/40 60.00 120.00
46 Niklas Backstrom/40 15.00 40.00
47 Cal Clutterbuck/40 8.00 20.00
48 Louis Leblanc/40 10.00 25.00
49 Carey Price/40 40.00 100.00
50 Patrick Roy/25 125.00 250.00
51 Guy Lafleur/25 90.00 150.00
52 Blake Geoffrion/40 10.00 25.00
53 Craig Smith/40 8.00 20.00
54 Pekka Rinne/40 25.00 60.00
55 Adam Larsson/40 12.00 30.00
56 Adam Henrique/40 20.00 50.00
57 Martin Brodeur/25 60.00 125.00
58 John Tavares/40 50.00 100.00
59 Pat LaFontaine/25 15.00 40.00
60 Marian Gaborik/40 15.00 40.00
61 Brad Richards/40 12.50 30.00
62 Carl Hagelin/40 15.00 40.00
63 Marc Staal/40 12.00 30.00
64 Cody Eakin/40 15.00 40.00
65 Mark Messier/25 40.00 80.00
66 Colin Greening/40 10.00 25.00
67 Mika Zibanejad/40 15.00 40.00
68 Erik Karlsson/40 EXCH 30.00 80.00
69 Claude Giroux/40 40.00 80.00
70 Sean Couturier/40 15.00 40.00
71 Matt Read/40 12.00 30.00
72 Jaromir Jagr/40 40.00 100.00
73 Ron Hextall/25 15.00 40.00
74 Eric Lindros/25 60.00 120.00
76 Andy Miele/40 10.00 25.00
77 Mario Lemieux/25 150.00 300.00
79 Sidney Crosby/40 100.00 200.00
80 Marc-Andre Fleury/40 20.00 50.00
81 Joe Sakic/25 50.00 120.00
82 Joe Thornton/40 12.00 30.00
83 Patrick Marleau/40 15.00 40.00
84 Alex Pietrangelo/25 25.00 50.00
85 Jaroslav Halak/40 15.00 40.00
86 Brett Hull/25 50.00 100.00
87 Steven Stamkos/40 40.00 100.00
88 Brett Connolly/40 20.00 50.00
89 Martin St. Louis/40 12.00 30.00
90 Phil Kessel/40 12.00 30.00
91 Jake Gardiner/40 25.00 60.00
92 Joe Colborne/40 10.00 25.00
94 Zack Kassian/40 20.00 50.00
95 Daniel Sedin/40 15.00 40.00

2011-12 Dominion Peerless Patches Combos

1 J.Eberle/RNH/15 100.00 200.00
2 Alfredsson/Zetterberg/15 25.00 60.00
3 S.Koivu/T.Selanne/15 60.00 150.00
4 J.Carter/M.Richards/15 30.00 80.00
5 H.Lundqvist/M.Biron/15 60.00 125.00
6 Bryzgalov/Bobrovsky/15 50.00 100.00
7 A.Lindback/P.Rinne/15 60.00 150.00
8 J.Enroth/R.Miller/15 30.00 80.00
9 J.Bernier/J.Quick/15 50.00 120.00
11 C.Hagelin/C.Greening/15 40.00 100.00
12 C.Perry/P.Kane/15 60.00 120.00
13 J.Benn/M.Read/15 20.00 50.00
14 S.Stamkos/T.Thomas/15 40.00 100.00
16 D.Phaneuf/RNH/15 75.00 150.00
17 Landeskog/Eriksson/15 60.00 150.00
18 M.Read/S.Couturier/15 40.00 100.00
19 B.Saad/M.Kruger/15 100.00 200.00

2011-12 Dominion Pen Pals

2 Bourque/Thomas/50 15.00 40.00
3 C.Hodgson/P.LaFontaine 12.00 30.00
4 A.Shaw/B.Saad/50 20.00 50.00
5 R.Nash/R.Johansen/50 25.00 60.00
6 B.Smith/G.Nyquist/50 20.00 50.00
7 B.Hull/B.Shanahan 20.00 50.00
8 Lander/RNH/50 30.00 80.00
10 Geoffrn/Leblnc/50 8.00 20.00
11 C.Smith/R.Ellis/50 10.00 25.00
12 Henrique/Larsson/50 20.00 50.00
13 C.Hagelin/G.Landeskog 25.00 60.00
14 Ovchkin/Malkin/25 EXCH 40.00 100.00
16 B.Schenn/S.Couturier 15.00 40.00
17 C.Giroux/M.Read 10.00 25.00
18 E.Lindros/J.Jagr/50 30.00 80.00
19 Vitale/Tocchet/50 EXCH 8.00 20.00
20 C.Joseph/J.Halak/50 12.00 30.00
21 B.Connolly/S.Stamkos 20.00 50.00
22 Gardiner/Colborne/50 12.00 30.00
23 B.Scrivens/F.Potvin/50 15.00 40.00
24 R.Kesler/Z.Kassian/50 10.00 25.00
25 Hawerchuk/Scheifele/50 30.00 80.00
26 Landeskog/Eriksson/50 25.00 60.00
27 Gudbranson/Despres/50 10.00 25.00
28 M.Modano/J.Iginla 15.00 40.00
29 M.Gaborik/S.Mikita 12.00 30.00

2011-12 Dominion Quad Jerseys

1 Ducks/25 10.00 25.00
2 Bruins/25 8.00 20.00
3 Sabres/25 8.00 20.00
4 Flames/25 8.00 20.00
5 Blackhawks/25 10.00 25.00
6 Avalanche/25 15.00 40.00
7 Blue Jackets/25 15.00 40.00
8 Stars/25 5.00 12.00
9 Red Wings/25 12.00 30.00
10 Oilers/25 20.00 50.00
11 Panthers/25 6.00 15.00
12 Kings/25 10.00 25.00
13 Wild/25 6.00 15.00
14 Canadiens/25 5.00 12.00
15 Predators/25 6.00 15.00
16 Devils/25 15.00 40.00
17 Islanders/25 10.00 25.00
18 Rangers/25 15.00 40.00
19 Senators/25 15.00 40.00
20 Flyers/25 10.00 25.00
21 Coyotes/25 6.00 15.00
22 Penguins/25 6.00 15.00
23 Sharks/25 10.00 25.00
24 Blues/25 5.00 12.00
25 Lightning/25 12.00 30.00
26 Maple Leafs/25 8.00 20.00
27 Canucks/25 6.00 15.00
28 Capitals/25 25.00 60.00
29 Jets/25 6.00 15.00
31 Ovch/Giroux/Gabrk/Brodr/25 25.00 60.00
32 Backes/Brwn/Doan/Wber/25 6.00 15.00
33 Sedin/Lngo/Thms/Chra/25 10.00 25.00
34 Ebrle/Erksn/StLou/Moulsn/25 6.00 15.00
35 Backs/Bergrn/Dtsyk/Keslr/25 10.00 25.00
36 Lndqvst/Quick/Smth/Rnne/25 15.00 40.00
37 Karlssn/Lidst/Webr/Chara/25 8.00 20.00
38 Girx/Malkn/Lnqvst/Stmks/25 15.00 40.00
39 Henrq/Lndskg/Read/RNH/25 20.00 50.00
40 Joseph/Belfour/Roy/Hextll/25 15.00 40.00

2011-12 Dominion Rookie Showcase Autographed Pucks

*PRIME JSY/25: .4X TO 1X DUAL PUCK/25
1 Landeskog/RNH 75.00 150.00
4 Gardiner/Colborne 15.00 40.00
6 B.Smith/R.Ellis 10.00 25.00
8 J.Faulk/T.Erixon 15.00 40.00
9 Klingbrg/Lndeskg 30.00 80.00
11 B.Connolly/C.Eakin 15.00 40.00
12 A.Henrique/S.Despres 25.00 60.00
13 Connolly/Nugent-Hopkins 15.00 40.00
14 A.Henrique/G.Nemisz 25.00 60.00
15 A.Palushaj/J.Moore 10.00 25.00
16 Lndeskg/Zibnejad 30.00 80.00
18 Landeskog/Kruger EXCH 30.00 80.00
19 Nugent-Hopkins/Kassian 50.00 120.00

2011-12 Dominion RPS Pen Pals

1 Nugent-Hopkins/Hall/25 40.00 100.00
2 Landeskog/Duchene/99 20.00 50.00
3 R.Ellis/T.Hall/25 10.00 25.00
7 Landeskog/Zibanejad/99 12.00 30.00
9 Landeskog/RNH/25 50.00 120.00
10 B.Smith/N.Lidstrom/25 20.00 50.00
12 Eberle/RNH/25 40.00 100.00
13 Messier/RNH/25 40.00 100.00
14 RNH/Stamkos/25 75.00 150.00
15 Larsson/Lidstrom/25 30.00 60.00
16 Larsson/Niedermayer/25 20.00 50.00
17 Rundblad/Zibanejad/99 20.00 50.00
19 Geoffrion/Ellis/99 6.00 15.00

2011-12 Dominion RPS Pen Pals Triples

1 Tavares/RNH/Hall 100.00 200.00
2 Larsson/Landeskog/RNH 75.00 150.00
4 Larsson/Landskg/Zibanjd 50.00 100.00
8 Park/Smith/Lidstrom 12.00 30.00
9 Miller/Vanek/Kassian 15.00 40.00

2011-12 Dominion Stanley Cup Championship Signatures

1 Tim Thomas 30.00 60.00
2 Jonathan Toews 30.00 60.00
3 Sidney Crosby 100.00 175.00
6 Eric Staal 20.00 50.00
7 Martin St. Louis 25.00 50.00
9 Brendan Shanahan 40.00 80.00
10 Ray Bourque 40.00 80.00
11 Scott Niedermayer 15.00 40.00
12 Brett Hull 30.00 80.00
13 Steve Yzerman 60.00 120.00
14 Nicklas Lidstrom 40.00 80.00
15 Joe Sakic 50.00 100.00
16 Martin Brodeur 40.00 80.00
17 Mark Messier 30.00 60.00
18 Patrick Roy 75.00 150.00
19 Ron Francis 30.00 60.00
20 Mario Lemieux 60.00 120.00

2011-12 Dominion Stickside Signatures

1 Cam Neely/25 50.00 100.00
2 Dale Hawerchuk/25 40.00 100.00
3 Tyler Seguin/25 50.00 120.00
4 Alex Ovechkin/15 150.00 300.00
5 Pat LaFontaine/25 25.00 60.00
6 Bobby Hull/25 50.00 100.00
7 Ryan Kesler/25 40.00 100.00
8 Joe Sakic/25 60.00 120.00
9 Loui Eriksson/25 15.00 40.00
10 Mike Modano/15 50.00 100.00
12 Steve Yzerman/15 75.00 150.00
14 Ron Francis/25 30.00 80.00
15 Luc Robitaille/25 25.00 60.00
16 Marcel Dionne/25 30.00 80.00
17 Doug Gilmour/25 30.00 80.00
18 Vincent Lecavalier/25 15.00 40.00
19 Steven Stamkos/25 100.00 200.00
20 Denis Potvin/25 25.00 60.00
22 Marian Gaborik/25 25.00 60.00
23 Eric Lindros/25 40.00 100.00
25 Evgeni Malkin/25 EXCH 75.00 150.00
26 Jordan Staal/25 20.00 50.00
27 Mario Lemieux/15 150.00 300.00
28 Joe Thornton/25 40.00 80.00
29 Brett Hull/25 50.00 100.00

2011-12 Dominion Sweeter By The Dozen Jerseys

1 Young Stars 60.00 120.00
2 Superstar Vets 150.00 300.00
3 Goalie Stars 125.00 250.00
4 Bruins/Canucks 60.00 150.00
5 Wings/Avalanche 60.00 120.00
6 Rangers/Flyers 60.00 120.00
7 Capitals/Penguins 60.00 120.00
8 Leafs/Canadiens 75.00 150.00
9 Oilers/Flames 60.00 150.00

2011-12 Dominion Tape to Tape Autographs

3 Ed Belfour/16 30.00 80.00
4 Jonathan Toews/20 125.00 200.00
12 Carey Price/20 75.00 150.00
14 Martin Brodeur/18 75.00 150.00
18 Mike Smith/20 25.00 60.00
20 Sidney Crosby/15 150.00 300.00
21 Jaroslav Halak/20 25.00 60.00
25 Vincent Lecavalier/20 15.00 40.00
26 Curtis Joseph/20 40.00 100.00
29 Felix Potvin/20 60.00 120.00

2012-13 Dominion

*RC.PATCH.AU/4-74: .4X TO 1X BASE RC
1 Teemu Selanne 3.00 8.00
2 Corey Perry 2.50 6.00
3 Cam Fowler 1.50 4.00
4 Jarome Iginla 2.00 5.00
5 Miikka Kiprusoff 1.50 4.00
6 Al MacInnis 2.00 5.00
7 Patrick Kane 3.00 8.00
8 Jonathan Toews 2.50 6.00
9 Ed Belfour 1.50 4.00
10 Gabriel Landeskog 2.00 5.00
11 Joe Sakic 3.00 8.00
12 Matt Duchene 1.50 4.00
13 Artem Anisimov 1.00 2.50
14 Sergei Bobrovsky 2.50 6.00
15 Jack Johnson 1.00 2.50
16 Jaromir Jagr 5.00 12.00
17 Loui Eriksson 1.00 2.50
18 Mike Modano 2.50 6.00
19 Henrik Zetterberg 2.00 5.00
20 Gordie Howe 5.00 12.00
21 Steve Yzerman 4.00 10.00
22 Pavol Datsyuk 2.50 6.00
23 Mark Messier 3.00 8.00
24 Ryan Nugent-Hopkins 2.00 5.00
25 Taylor Hall 1.50 4.00
26 Jordan Eberle 1.50 4.00
27 Jonathan Quick 2.00 5.00
28 Anze Kopitar 2.50 6.00
29 Luc Robitaille 1.50 4.00
30 Dustin Brown 1.50 4.00
31 Zach Parise 1.50 4.00
32 Niklas Backstrom 1.25 3.00
33 Ryan Suter 1.25 3.00
34 Pekka Rinne 1.50 4.00
35 Craig Smith 1.00 2.50
36 Shea Weber 1.25 3.00
37 Mike Smith 1.50 4.00
38 Oliver Ekman-Larsson 1.50 4.00
39 Mikkel Boedker 1.00 2.50
40 Joe Thornton 2.50 6.00
41 Logan Couture 2.00 5.00
42 Jeremy Roenick 2.50 6.00
43 Alex Pietrangelo 1.25 3.00
44 T.J. Oshie 1.50 4.00
45 Brett Hull 3.00 8.00
46 Pavel Bure 1.50 4.00
47 Daniel Sedin 2.00 5.00
48 Cory Schneider 1.50 4.00
49 Tyler Seguin 2.00 5.00
50 Tuukka Rask 2.00 5.00
51 Cam Neely 1.50 4.00
52 Ryan Miller 1.50 4.00
53 Thomas Vanek 1.25 3.00
54 Pierre Turgeon 1.25 3.00
55 Cody Hodgson 1.00 2.50
56 Jordan Staal 1.25 3.00
57 Eric Staal 2.00 5.00
58 Cam Ward 1.50 4.00
59 Scott Clemmensen 1.25 3.00
60 George Parros 1.25 3.00
61 John Vanbiesbrouck 1.50 4.00
62 Carey Price 3.00 8.00
63 Patrick Roy 4.00 10.00
64 Michael Ryder 1.00 2.50
65 Ilya Kovalchuk 1.50 4.00
66 Adam Henrique 1.25 3.00
67 Martin Brodeur 4.00 10.00
68 John Tavares 2.50 6.00
69 Pat LaFontaine 1.50 4.00
70 Matt Moulson 1.00 2.50
71 Rick Nash 1.50 4.00

72 Henrik Lundqvist 4.00 10.00
73 Mike Richter 1.50 4.00
74 Marian Gaborik 1.50 4.00
75 Daniel Alfredsson 1.50 4.00
76 Mika Zibanejad 2.00 5.00
77 Erik Karlsson 2.00 5.00
78 Claude Giroux 1.50 4.00
79 Simon Gagne 1.50 4.00
80 Eric Lindros 2.50 6.00
81 Sidney Crosby 6.00 15.00
82 Mario Lemieux 6.00 15.00
83 Marc-Andre Fleury 3.00 8.00
84 Evgeni Malkin 3.00 8.00
85 Vincent Lecavalier 1.50 4.00
86 Steven Stamkos 3.00 8.00
87 Anders Lindback 1.00 2.50
88 James van Riemsdyk 1.25 3.00
89 Felix Potvin 2.50 6.00
90 Phil Kessel 1.50 4.00
91 Nazem Kadri 2.00 5.00
92 Alex Ovechkin 6.00 15.00
93 Nicklas Backstrom 1.50 4.00
94 Braden Holtby 2.00 5.00
95 Mike Gartner 2.00 5.00
96 Andrew Ladd 1.00 2.50
97 Mark Scheifele 2.50 6.00
98 Ondrej Pavelec 1.50 4.00
99 Dustin Byfuglien 1.50 4.00
100 Dale Hawerchuk 2.00 5.00
101 Mat Clark JSY AU RC 6.00 15.00
102 Max Sauve JSY AU RC 5.00 12.00
103 Michael Hutchinson JSY AU RC 8.00 20.00
104 Torey Krug JSY AU RC 15.00 40.00
105 Carter Camper JSY AU RC 5.00 12.00
106 Lane MacDermid JSY AU RC 6.00 15.00
107 Travis Turnbull JSY AU RC 5.00 12.00
108 Akim Aliu JSY AU RC 6.00 15.00
109 Sven Baertschi JSY AU RC 8.00 20.00
110 Jeremy Welsh JSY AU RC 6.00 15.00
111 Brandon Bollig JSY AU RC 5.00 12.00
112 Mike Connolly JSY AU RC 6.00 15.00
113 Tyson Barrie JSY AU RC 15.00 40.00
114 Andrew Joudrey JSY AU RC 6.00 15.00
115 Cody Goloubef JSY AU RC 5.00 12.00
116 Dalton Prout JSY AU RC 5.00 12.00
117 Shawn Hunwick JSY AU RC 5.00 12.00
118 Brenden Dillon JSY AU RC 6.00 15.00
119 Reilly Smith JSY AU RC 15.00 40.00
120 Ryan Garbutt JSY AU RC 5.00 12.00
121 Scott Glennie JSY AU RC 6.00 15.00
122 Riley Sheahan JSY AU RC 8.00 20.00
123 Philippe Cornet JSY AU RC 6.00 15.00
124 Colby Robak JSY AU RC 5.00 12.00
125 Jordan Nolan JSY AU RC 5.00 12.00
126 Chay Genoway JSY AU RC 5.00 12.00
127 Jason Zucker JSY AU RC 12.00 30.00
128 Kris Foucault JSY AU RC 5.00 12.00
129 Tyler Cuma JSY AU RC 5.00 12.00
130 Gabriel Dumont JSY AU RC 6.00 15.00
131 Robert Mayer JSY AU RC 8.00 20.00
132 Chet Pickard JSY AU RC 6.00 15.00
133 Aaron Ness JSY AU RC 5.00 12.00
134 Casey Cizikas JSY AU RC 6.00 15.00
135 Matt Donovan JSY AU RC 6.00 15.00
136 Matt Watkins JSY AU RC 5.00 12.00
137 Chris Kreider JSY AU RC 60.00 150.00
138 Jakob Silfverberg JSY AU RC 10.00 25.00
139 Mark Stone JSY AU RC 20.00 50.00
140 Brandon Manning JSY AU RC 6.00 15.00
141 Michael Stone JSY AU RC 6.00 15.00
142 Tyson Sexsmith JSY AU RC 5.00 12.00
143 Jaden Schwartz JSY AU RC 15.00 40.00
144 Jake Allen JSY AU RC 15.00 40.00
145 J.T. Brown JSY AU RC 6.00 15.00
146 Carter Ashton JSY AU RC 5.00 12.00
147 Jussi Rynnas JSY AU RC 5.00 12.00
148 Ryan Hamilton JSY AU RC 5.00 12.00

2012-13 Dominion Gold

*1-100 VETS/25: .8X TO 2X BASIC CARDS
93 Nicklas Backstrom 6.00 15.00

2012-13 Dominion Autographed Rookie Patches Parallel

137 Chris Kreider/20 80.00 200.00

2012-13 Dominion Patches Autographs

1 Chris Kreider/60 40.00 100.00
2 Jaden Schwartz/60 12.00 30.00
3 Jakob Silfverberg/60 10.00 25.00
4A Alex Ovechkin/25 40.00 80.00
4B Jake Allen/60 15.00 40.00
5 Reilly Smith/60 15.00 40.00
6 Jussi Rynnas/60 5.00 12.00
7 Sven Baertschi/60 8.00 20.00
8 Chet Pickard/60 6.00 15.00
9 J.T. Brown/60 10.00 25.00
10 Carter Ashton/60 5.00 12.00
11 Casey Cizikas/60 12.00 30.00
12 Jason Zucker/60 12.00 30.00
13 Michael Stone/60 6.00 15.00
14 Robert Mayer/60 8.00 20.00
15 Travis Turnbull/60 5.00 12.00
16 Tyler Cuma/60 5.00 12.00
17 Tyson Barrie/60 15.00 40.00
18 Andrew Joudrey/60 6.00 15.00
19 Ryan Hamilton/60 5.00 12.00
20 Brandon Manning/60 10.00 25.00
21 Matt Watkins/60 5.00 12.00
22 Matt Donovan/60 6.00 15.00
23 Mark Stone/60 20.00 50.00
24 Lane MacDermid/60 8.00 20.00
25 Kris Foucault/60 5.00 12.00
26 Jordan Nolan/60 5.00 12.00
27 Jeremy Welsh/60 6.00 15.00
28 Shawn Hunwick/60 5.00 12.00
29 Riley Sheahan/60 8.00 20.00
31 Joe Pavelski/60 12.00 30.00
32 Henrik Lundqvist/25 25.00 50.00
33 John Tavares/60 15.00 40.00
34 Gabriel Landeskog/60 10.00 25.00
35 Carl Hagelin/60 5.00 12.00
36 James Neal/60 10.00 25.00
37 Dustin Brown/60 10.00 25.00
39 Colin Wilson/60 8.00 20.00
40 Cory Schneider/60 10.00 25.00
41 Bobby Ryan/60 8.00 20.00
42 Patrick Kane/25 40.00 100.00
43 Milan Hejduk/60 8.00 20.00
44 Jonathan Quick/25 30.00 60.00
45 Marc-Andre Fleury/25 30.00 80.00
46 Loui Eriksson/60 6.00 15.00
48 Jay Bouwmeester/60 6.00 15.00
49 Stu Grimson/60 6.00 15.00
50 Richard Bachman/60 8.00 20.00
51 Stan Mikita/25 30.00 80.00
52 Cody Goloubef/60 6.00 15.00
53 Kevin Shattenkirk/60 6.00 15.00
54 Bernie Parent/25 40.00 80.00
55 Matt Duchene/60 12.00 30.00
56 Cody Hodgson/60 6.00 15.00
57 Patrik Elias/60 10.00 25.00
58 Pat LaFontaine/25 15.00 40.00
59 Phil Kessel/60 12.00 30.00
60 Ryan Nugent-Hopkins/60 20.00 50.00
61 Joe Thornton/25 25.00 60.00
62 Jamie Benn/40 10.00 25.00
63 Patrick Marleau/60 10.00 25.00
64 Nikolai Kulemin/60 6.00 15.00
65 Mason Raymond/60 6.00 15.00
66 Martin St. Louis/60 10.00 25.00
67 Devan Dubnyk/60 10.00 25.00
68 Semyon Varlamov/60 12.00 30.00
69 Ray Bourque/25 25.00 50.00
70 Reggie Leach/60 15.00 30.00
71 Logan Couture/60 12.00 30.00
72 Ryan Miller/25 15.00 40.00
73 Ryan Getzlaf/25 10.00 25.00
74 Pierre Turgeon/60 15.00 40.00
75 Pekka Rinne/60 10.00 25.00
79 Keith Yandle/60 6.00 15.00
80 Jordan Eberle/60 15.00 40.00
82 Martin Brodeur/25 40.00 80.00
83 John Carlson/60 10.00 25.00
84 Claude Giroux/60 15.00 40.00
88 Luc Robitaille/25 20.00 50.00
89 Taylor Hall/60 20.00 50.00
90 Brett Hull/25 50.00 100.00
91 Ed Belfour/25 25.00 50.00
92 Rod Brind'Amour/60 10.00 25.00
93 Ron Francis/25 12.00 30.00
94 Joe Sakic/25 30.00 80.00
96 Igor Larionov/25 15.00 40.00

2012-13 Dominion Peerless Patches Autographs

*1-29 ROOKIE/40: .6X TO 1.5X PATCH AU/60
1 Chris Kreider/40 40.00 100.00
2 Jaden Schwartz/40 20.00 50.00
3 Jakob Silfverberg/40 15.00 40.00
4B Jake Allen/40 25.00 60.00
5 Reilly Smith/40 15.00 40.00
6 Jussi Rynnas/40 8.00 20.00
7 Sven Baertschi/40 15.00 40.00
8 Chet Pickard/40 10.00 25.00
9 J.T. Brown/40 8.00 20.00
10 Carter Ashton/40 8.00 20.00
11 Casey Cizikas/40 15.00 40.00
12 Jason Zucker/40 20.00 50.00
13 Michael Stone/40 10.00 25.00
14 Robert Mayer/40 12.00 30.00
15 Travis Turnbull/40 8.00 20.00
16 Tyler Cuma/40 8.00 20.00
17 Tyson Barrie/40 25.00 60.00
18 Andrew Joudrey/40 10.00 25.00
19 Ryan Hamilton/40 8.00 20.00
20 Brandon Manning/40 15.00 40.00
21 Matt Watkins/40 8.00 20.00
22 Matt Donovan/40 15.00 40.00
23 Mark Stone/40 30.00 80.00
24 Lane MacDermid/40 12.00 30.00
25 Kris Foucault/40 8.00 20.00
26 Jordan Nolan/40 8.00 20.00
27 Jeremy Welsh/40 10.00 25.00
28 Shawn Hunwick/40 8.00 20.00
29 Riley Sheahan/40 15.00 40.00
31 Joe Pavelski/40 20.00 50.00
33 John Tavares/40 30.00 80.00
34 Gabriel Landeskog/40 20.00 50.00
35 Carl Hagelin/40 12.00 30.00
36 James Neal/40 10.00 25.00
37 Dustin Brown/40 15.00 40.00
39 Colin Wilson/40 12.00 30.00
40 Cory Schneider/40 15.00 40.00
41 Bobby Ryan/40 12.00 30.00
42 Patrick Kane/25 60.00 120.00
43 Milan Hejduk/40 12.00 30.00
44 Jonathan Quick/40 40.00 80.00
45 Marc-Andre Fleury/25 40.00 100.00
46 Loui Eriksson/40 10.00 25.00
47 Kevin Bieksa/40 12.00 30.00
48 Jay Bouwmeester/40 10.00 25.00
49 Sean Couturier/40 12.00 30.00
50 Richard Bachman/40 10.00 25.00
51 Jhonas Enroth/40 15.00 40.00
52 Henrik Lundqvist/25 25.00 60.00
53 Kevin Shattenkirk/40 10.00 25.00
54 Jonathan Bernier/40 12.00 30.00
55 Matt Duchene/40 10.00 25.00
56 Cody Hodgson/40 10.00 25.00
57 Stephen Weiss/30 15.00 40.00
58 David Backes/40 10.00 25.00
59 Phil Kessel/40 10.00 25.00
60 Ryan Nugent-Hopkins/40 40.00 100.00
61 Joe Thornton/25 30.00 80.00
62 Jamie Benn/40 20.00 50.00
63 Patrick Marleau/40 15.00 40.00
64 Nikolai Kulemin/40 10.00 25.00
65 Mason Raymond/40 10.00 25.00
66 Martin St. Louis/40 15.00 40.00
67 Devan Dubnyk/40 12.00 30.00
68 Semyon Varlamov/40 15.00 40.00
69 Matt Read/40 12.00 30.00
70 Kris Letang/40 20.00 50.00
71 Logan Couture/40 20.00 50.00
73 Ryan Getzlaf/40 15.00 40.00
74 Mikael Backlund/40 12.00 30.00
75 Pekka Rinne/40 15.00 40.00
76 Pavel Datsyuk/25 EXCH 40.00 80.00
79 Keith Yandle/40 10.00 25.00
80 Jordan Eberle/40 15.00 40.00
81 Evgeni Malkin/25 40.00 80.00
83 John Carlson/40 15.00 40.00
84 Claude Giroux/40 25.00 60.00
87 Felix Potvin/40 30.00 80.00
88 Luc Robitaille/25 25.00 60.00
89 John LeClair/40 12.00 30.00
90 Brett Hull/25 30.00 80.00
92 Keith Primeau/40 15.00 40.00
96 Ron Francis/25 25.00 60.00

2013-14 Dominion

1 Bobby Ryan 1.50 4.00
2 Ryan Getzlaf 2.00 5.00
3 Corey Perry 3.00 8.00
4 Cam Fowler 2.00 5.00
5 Brad Marchand 4.00 10.00
6 Tuukka Rask 2.50 6.00
7 Tyler Seguin 2.50 6.00
8 Torey Krug 1.50 4.00
9 Ryan Miller 2.00 5.00
10 Cody Hodgson 1.25 3.00
11 Thomas Vanek 1.50 4.00
12 Mike Cammalleri 1.50 4.00
13 Curtis Glencross 1.25 3.00
14 Miikka Kiprusoff 2.00 5.00
15 Eric Staal 2.50 6.00
16 Jeff Skinner 2.50 6.00
17 Cam Ward 2.00 5.00
18 Patrick Kane 4.00 10.00
19 Jonathan Toews 3.00 8.00
20 Brandon Saad 1.50 4.00
21 Corey Crawford 2.50 6.00
22 Gabriel Landeskog 2.50 6.00
23 Matt Duchene 2.00 5.00
24 P.A. Parenteau 1.25 3.00
25 Tyson Barrie 1.25 3.00
26 Marian Gaborik 2.00 5.00
27 Brandon Dubinsky 1.25 3.00
28 Sergei Bobrovsky 3.00 8.00
29 Jamie Benn 2.00 5.00
30 Loui Eriksson 1.25 3.00
31 Kari Lehtonen 1.50 4.00
32 Pavel Datsyuk 3.00 8.00
33 Henrik Zetterberg 2.50 6.00
34 Brendan Smith 1.25 3.00
35 Jimmy Howard 2.50 6.00
36 Taylor Hall 2.00 5.00
37 Ryan Nugent-Hopkins 2.50 6.00
38 Jordan Eberle 1.50 4.00
39 Devan Dubnyk 1.50 4.00
40 Jacob Markstrom 2.00 5.00
41 Tomas Fleischmann 1.25 3.00
42 Brian Campbell 1.25 3.00
43 Jonathan Quick 2.50 6.00
44 Jeff Carter 1.50 4.00
45 Drew Doughty 2.50 6.00
46 Anze Kopitar 3.00 8.00
47 Zach Parise 2.00 5.00
48 Ryan Suter 1.50 4.00
49 Mikko Koivu 1.50 4.00
50 Carey Price 4.00 10.00
51 P.K. Subban 2.50 6.00
52 Max Pacioretty 2.00 5.00
53 Pekka Rinne 2.00 5.00
54 Shea Weber 1.50 4.00
55 Mike Fisher 1.25 3.00
56 Martin Brodeur 4.00 10.00
57 Patrik Elias 2.00 5.00
58 Adam Henrique 1.50 4.00
59 John Tavares 3.00 8.00
60 Matt Moulson 1.25 3.00
61 Kyle Okposo 1.25 3.00
62 Rick Nash 2.00 5.00
63 Henrik Lundqvist 5.00 12.00
64 Derek Stepan 1.25 3.00
65 Ryan Callahan 1.25 3.00
66 Erik Karlsson 2.50 6.00
67 Mika Zibanejad 2.50 6.00
68 Jakob Silfverberg 1.25 3.00
69 Claude Giroux 2.00 5.00
70 Jakub Voracek 1.50 4.00
71 Brayden Schenn 2.00 5.00
72 Mike Smith 2.00 5.00
73 Keith Yandle 1.25 3.00
74 Mikkel Boedker 1.25 3.00
75 Sidney Crosby 6.00 15.00
76 Marc-Andre Fleury 4.00 10.00
77 Evgeni Malkin 4.00 10.00
78 Kris Letang 2.50 6.00
79 Logan Couture 2.50 6.00
80 Patrick Marleau 2.00 5.00
81 Joe Pavelski 2.50 6.00
82 Chris Stewart 1.50 4.00
83 David Backes 1.25 3.00
84 Alex Pietrangelo 1.50 4.00
85 Martin St. Louis 2.00 5.00
86 Steven Stamkos 4.00 10.00
87 Ben Bishop 1.50 4.00
88 James Reimer 2.00 5.00
89 Nazem Kadri 2.50 6.00
90 Phil Kessel 2.00 5.00
91 Dion Phaneuf 1.50 4.00
92 Henrik Sedin 2.50 6.00
93 Cory Schneider 2.00 5.00
94 Ryan Kesler 2.00 5.00
95 Alex Ovechkin 8.00 20.00
96 Braden Holtby 2.50 6.00
97 Mike Ribeiro 1.25 3.00
98 Andrew Ladd 1.25 3.00
99 Dustin Byfuglien 2.00 5.00
100 Evander Kane 2.00 5.00
101 Matt Anderson RC 1.50 4.00
102 Anders Lee RC 3.00 8.00
103 Steven Pinizzotto RC 2.00 5.00
104 Brett Bellemore RC 1.50 4.00
105 Eric Selleck RC 1.50 4.00
106 Alex Petrovic AU RC 4.00 10.00
107 Mark Pysyk AU RC 5.00 12.00
108 Jonathan Marchessault AU RC 12.00 30.00
109 Zach Redmond AU RC 4.00 10.00
110 Radko Gudas AU RC 5.00 12.00
111 Mark Cundari AU RC 3.00 8.00
112 Chris Terry AU RC 3.00 8.00
113 Shawn Lalonde AU RC 5.00 12.00
114 Ryan Stanton AU RC 5.00 12.00
115 Jonathan Rheault AU RC 3.00 8.00
116 Greg Pateryn AU RC 5.00 12.00
117 Oliver Lauridsen AU RC 4.00 10.00
118 Jeff Zatkoff AU RC 5.00 12.00
119 Matt Tennyson AU RC 3.00 8.00
120 Tyler Johnson AU RC 12.00 30.00
121 Ben Street AU RC 4.00 10.00
123 Sean Collins AU RC 4.00 10.00
124 Michael Caruso AU RC 3.00 8.00
125 Victor Bartley AU RC 4.00 10.00
126 Harri Pesonen AU RC 4.00 10.00
127 Dave Dziurzynski AU RC 4.00 10.00
128 Derek Grant AU RC 4.00 10.00
129 Eric Gryba AU RC 4.00 10.00
130 Ondrej Palat AU RC 8.00 20.00
131 Emerson Etem JSY AU/299 RC 6.00 15.00
132 T.Pearson JSY AU/299 RC 10.00 25.00
133 I.Bobkov JSY AU/299 RC 5.00 12.00
134 Rickard Rakell JSY AU/299 RC 6.00 15.00
135 Sami Vatanen JSY AU/299 RC 6.00 15.00
136 Viktor Fasth JSY AU/299 RC 6.00 15.00
137 Jamie Tardif JSY AU/299 RC 4.00 10.00
138 R.Spooner JSY AU/299 RC 8.00 20.00
139 Brian Flynn JSY AU/299 RC 5.00 12.00
140 M.Grigorenko JSY AU/299 RC 4.00 10.00
141 Carl Soderberg JSY AU/299 RC 6.00 15.00
142 Brock Nelson JSY AU/199 RC 12.00 30.00
143 Michal Jordan JSY AU/299 RC 4.00 10.00
144 Ryan Murphy JSY AU/299 RC 6.00 15.00
145 A.Barkov JSY AU/99 RC 30.00 80.00
146 Calvin Pickard JSY AU/299 RC 8.00 20.00
147 M.Sgarbossa JSY AU/299 RC 6.00 15.00
148 Antoine Roussel JSY AU/299 RC 6.00 15.00
149 Alex Chiasson JSY AU/299 RC 6.00 15.00
150 Jack Campbell JSY AU/299 RC 15.00 40.00
151 Jamie Oleksiak JSY AU/299 RC 5.00 12.00
152 Brian Lashoff JSY AU/299 RC 5.00 12.00
153 F.Andersen JSY AU/199 RC 12.00 30.00
154 D.DeKeyser JSY AU/299 RC 8.00 20.00
155 Petr Mrazek JSY AU/299 RC 12.00 30.00
156 Justin Schultz JSY AU/299 RC 6.00 15.00
157 Mark Arcobello JSY AU/299 RC 6.00 15.00
158 Drew Shore JSY AU/299 RC 5.00 12.00
159 N.Bjugstad JSY AU/299 RC 8.00 20.00
160 Q.Howden JSY AU/299 RC 5.00 12.00
161 Tyler Toffoli JSY AU/299 RC 15.00 40.00
162 Charlie Coyle JSY AU/299 RC 10.00 25.00
163 Ryan Strome JSY AU/199 RC 10.00 25.00
164 Jonas Brodin JSY AU/299 RC 8.00 20.00
165 M.Granlund JSY AU/299 RC 10.00 25.00
166 B.Gallagher JSY AU/299 RC 25.00 60.00
167 Jarred Tinordi JSY AU/299 RC 6.00 15.00
168 N.Beaulieu JSY AU/299 RC 4.00 10.00
169 Austin Watson JSY AU/299 RC 5.00 12.00
170 Filip Forsberg JSY AU/299 RC 40.00 80.00
171 S.Matteau JSY AU/299 RC 5.00 12.00
172 T.Hickey JSY AU/299 RC 5.00 12.00
173 C.Thomas JSY AU/299 RC 5.00 12.00
174 J.T. Miller JSY AU/299 RC 15.00 40.00
175 Cory Conacher JSY AU/299 RC 4.00 10.00
176 Jared Staal JSY AU/299 RC 5.00 12.00
177 S.Laughton JSY AU/199 RC 12.00 30.00
178 Tye McGinn JSY AU/299 RC 6.00 15.00
179 Chris Brown JSY AU/299 RC 4.00 10.00
180 Beau Bennett JSY AU/299 RC 8.00 20.00
181 Matt Irwin JSY AU/299 RC 5.00 12.00
182 Dmitrij Jaskin JSY AU/299 RC 6.00 15.00
183 Alex Killorn JSY AU/299 RC 10.00 25.00
184 Richard Panik JSY AU/299 RC 6.00 15.00
185 H.Lindholm JSY AU/199 RC 10.00 25.00
186 M.Kostka JSY AU/299 RC 5.00 12.00
187 J.Schroeder JSY AU/299 RC 6.00 15.00
188 N.Jensen JSY AU/299 RC 5.00 12.00
189 P.Grubauer JSY AU/299 RC 15.00 40.00
190 A.Peluso JSY AU/299 RC 4.00 10.00
191 E.Pasquale JSY AU/299 RC 4.00 10.00
192 Tom Wilson JSY AU/299 RC 12.00 30.00
193 F.Corrado JSY AU/199 RC 4.00 10.00
195 M.Reinhart JSY AU/299 RC 6.00 15.00
196 D.Hamilton JSY AU/199 RC 12.00 30.00
197 J.Huberdeau JSY AU/199 RC 25.00 60.00
198 Tarasenko JSY AU/199 RC EX 40.00 100.00
199 Galchenyuk JSY AU/199 RC 60.00 120.00
200 N.Ykupov JSY AU/199 RC 30.00 80.00
201 N.MacKinnon JSY AU/99 RC 600.00 1500.00
202 S.Monahan JSY AU/99 RC 75.00 150.00
203 V.Nichushkin JSY AU/99 RC 50.00 100.00
204 Seth Jones JSY AU/99 RC 50.00 120.00
205 Tomas Hertl JSY AU/99 RC 75.00 150.00
206 B.Jenner JSY AU/99 RC 40.00 100.00
207 Matt Dumba JSY AU/99 RC 20.00 50.00
208 J.Trouba JSY AU/99 RC 40.00 100.00
209 Elias Lindholm JSY AU/99 RC 25.00 60.00
211 J.Nordstrom JSY AU/199 RC 12.00 30.00
212 Jon Merrill JSY AU/199 RC (inserted in 2013-14 Panini Prime) 6.00 15.00
213 Tomas Jurco JSY AU/199 RC 8.00 20.00
214 Marek Mazanec JSY AU/199 RC (inserted in 2013-14 Panini Prime) 6.00 15.00
216 M.Bournival JSY AU/199 RC 6.00 15.00
217 M.Rielly JSY AU/199 RC 30.00 60.00
218 Martin Jones JSY AU/199 RC 10.00 25.00
219 Nikita Zadorov JSY AU/199 RC (inserted in 2013-14 Panini Prime) 4.00 10.00
220 Magnus Hellberg JSY AU/199 RC (inserted in 2013-14 Panini Prime) 6.00 15.00
222 Ryan Murray JSY AU/199 RC 10.00 25.00
223 Jamie Devane JSY AU/199 RC 5.00 12.00
224 D.McIlrath JSY AU/99 RC 12.00 30.00
225 John Gibson JSY AU/99 RC 100.00 200.00
226 Reto Berra JSY AU/199 RC 6.00 15.00

2013-14 Dominion Gold

*1-100 VETS/50: .8X TO 2X BASIC VET/299
*101-105 ROOKIE/50: .8X TO 2X RC/299
*106-130 ROOK.AU/50: .6X TO 1.5X AU RC/299
*131-192 JSY AU/50: .6X TO 1.5X JSY AU/199-299
*196-200 JSY AU/25: .6X TO 1.5X JSY AU/199
*201-209 JSY AU/25: .5X TO 1.2X JSY AU/99
21 Corey Crawford 5.00 12.00
197 Jonathan Huberdeau JSY AU 40.00 100.00
198 Vladimir Tarasenko JSY AU 60.00 150.00
199 Alex Galchenyuk JSY AU 90.00 150.00
200 Nail Yakupov JSY AU 75.00 150.00
201 Nathan MacKinnon JSY AU 800.00 2000.00
202 Sean Monahan JSY AU 125.00 250.00
203 Valeri Nichushkin JSY AU 75.00 150.00
205 Tomas Hertl JSY AU 75.00 150.00
225 John Gibson JSY AU/25 125.00 200.00

2013-14 Dominion Back to Back Beginnings Autographs

BBBM R.Murphy/N.Beaulieu/149 5.00 12.00
BBCL C.Coyle/S.Laughton/149 8.00 20.00
BBEP E.Etem/T.Pearson/99 5.00 12.00
BBES E.Etem/J.Schultz/99 10.00 25.00
BBGB A.Glchnyk/N.Beaulieu/99 12.00 30.00
BBGG A.Galchenyuk/B.Gallagher/99 30.00 80.00
BBGH A.Glchnyk/J.Hbrdeau/49 30.00 60.00
BBHE Q.Howden/E.Etem/149 5.00 12.00
BBHG B.Gallagher/J.Huberdeau/99 12.00 30.00
BBHH J.Huberdeau/Q.Howden/99 10.00 25.00
BBHM D.Hamilton/R.Murphy/99 10.00 25.00
BBHS D.Hamilton/J.Schultz/49 12.00 30.00
BBHS D.Hamilton/R.Spooner/149 12.00 30.00
BBLG S.Lghton/M.Grgrenko/149 6.00 15.00
BBMC J.Campbell/P.Mrazek/149 12.00 30.00
BBRM M.Rielly/R.Murray/149 15.00 40.00
BBSG R.Spooner/M.Grigorenko/149 5.00 12.00
BBSM J.Schultz/R.Murphy/99 8.00 20.00
BBWR T.Wilson/M.Rielly/149 12.00 30.00
BBYG N.Ykpov/A.Glchnyk/99 25.00 60.00
BBYH N.Yakupov/D.Hamilton/49 20.00 50.00
BBYO M.Grigorenko/N.Yakupov/25 40.00 80.00
BBYS N.Yakupov/J.Schultz/99 20.00 50.00
BBYU N.Yakupov/J.Huberdeau/99 15.00 40.00

2013-14 Dominion Complete Rookie Jerseys

CRAB Aleksander Barkov 30.00 80.00
CRAG Alex Galchenyuk 25.00 60.00
CRAK Alex Killorn 15.00 40.00
CRAR Antoine Roussel 12.00 30.00
CRAW Austin Watson 8.00 20.00
CRBB Beau Bennett 15.00 40.00
CRBG Brendan Gallagher 20.00 50.00
CRBJ Nick Bjugstad 12.00 30.00
CRBJE Boone Jenner 20.00 50.00
CRBL Brian Lashoff 8.00 20.00
CRBN Brock Nelson 20.00 50.00
CRCC Cody Ceci 8.00 20.00
CRCC Cory Conacher 6.00 15.00
CRCM Connor Murphy 8.00 20.00
CRCS Carl Soderberg 15.00 40.00
CRCT Christian Thomas 8.00 20.00
CRDD Danny DeKeyser 12.00 30.00
CRDH Dougie Hamilton 15.00 40.00
CRDI Jarred Tinordi 10.00 25.00
CRED Jared Staal 8.00 20.00
CREE Emerson Etem 10.00 25.00
CRFC Frank Corrado 8.00 20.00
CRFF Filip Forsberg 30.00 80.00
CRHI Thomas Hickey 8.00 20.00
CRHLI Hampus Lindholm 15.00 40.00
CRHY Ryan Murphy 10.00 25.00
CRJB Jonas Brodin 12.00 30.00
CRJC Jack Campbell 25.00 60.00
CRJH Jonathan Huberdeau 20.00 50.00
CRJM J.T. Miller 25.00 60.00
CRJME Jon Merrill 12.00 30.00
CRJTR Jacob Trouba 15.00 40.00
CRKO Mikhail Grigorenko 6.00 15.00
CRLK Leo Komarov 10.00 25.00
CRLV Calvin Pickard 12.00 30.00
CRMDB Matt Dumba 6.00 15.00
CRMG Mikael Granlund 15.00 40.00
CRMMZ Marek Mazanec 10.00 25.00
CRNU Nathan Beaulieu 6.00 15.00
CRNY Nail Yakupov 20.00 50.00
CRNZ Nikita Zadorov 6.00 15.00
CROE Jordan Schroeder 10.00 25.00
CROK Jamie Oleksiak 8.00 20.00
CROY Charlie Coyle 15.00 40.00
CRQH Quinton Howden 8.00 20.00
CRRBE Reto Berra 10.00 25.00
CRRC Roman Cervenka 10.00 25.00
CRRLY Morgan Rielly 25.00 60.00
CRRP Richard Panik 12.00 30.00
CRRR Rickard Rakell 10.00 25.00
CRRS Ryan Strome 20.00 50.00
CRSL Scott Laughton 15.00 40.00
CRSM Stefan Matteau 8.00 20.00
CRSMO Sean Monahan 15.00 40.00
CRSP Ryan Spooner 20.00 50.00
CRSZ Justin Schultz 10.00 25.00
CRTHE Tomas Hertl 25.00 60.00
CRTJU Tomas Jurco 12.00 30.00
CRTP Tanner Pearson 10.00 25.00
CRTT Tyler Toffoli 20.00 50.00
CRTW Tom Wilson 20.00 50.00
CRVF Viktor Fasth 10.00 25.00
CRVN Valeri Nichushkin 20.00 50.00
CRVT Vladimir Tarasenko 25.00 60.00
CRWE Drew Shore 8.00 20.00
CRYO Anthony Peluso 6.00 15.00

2013-14 Dominion Complete Sweaters

CSBC Bobby Clarke 30.00 60.00
CSBH Brett Hull 30.00 80.00
CSCP Carey Price 30.00 80.00
CSEM Evgeni Malkin 20.00 50.00
CSGH Gordie Howe 50.00 100.00
CSGL Gabriel Landeskog 20.00 50.00
CSGX Claude Giroux 15.00 40.00
CSHL Henrik Lundqvist 15.00 40.00
CSJQ Jonathan Quick 15.00 40.00
CSJR Jeremy Roenick 25.00 60.00
CSJS Joe Sakic 15.00 40.00
CSJT John Tavares 25.00 60.00
CSMB Martin Brodeur 40.00 100.00
CSML Mario Lemieux 60.00 150.00
CSMM Mark Messier 30.00 80.00
CSOV Alex Ovechkin 40.00 80.00
CSPB Pavel Bure 25.00 60.00
CSPR Patrick Roy 50.00 100.00
CSRB Ray Bourque 25.00 60.00
CSSC Sidney Crosby 40.00 80.00
CSSS Steven Stamkos 30.00 80.00
CSSY Steve Yzerman 30.00 60.00
CSTN Teemu Selanne 25.00 50.00
CSWS Jonathan Toews 25.00 60.00

2013-14 Dominion Engravatures Blackhawks

EC1 Chicago Blackhawks 200.00 350.00
EC2 Bryan Bickell 75.00 150.00
EC3 Dave Bolland 50.00 100.00
EC4 Brandon Bollig 50.00 100.00
EC5 Sheldon Brookbank 40.00 80.00
EC6 Corey Crawford 150.00 225.00
EC8 Michael Frolik 75.00 150.00
EC9 Michal Handzus 125.00 200.00
EC10 Niklas Hjalmarsson 125.00 200.00
EC11 Marian Hossa 150.00 225.00
EC12 Patrick Kane 150.00 250.00
EC13 Duncan Keith 125.00 250.00
EC14 Marcus Kruger 100.00 200.00
EC15 Nick Leddy 150.00 250.00
EC16 Johnny Oduya 100.00 200.00
EC17 Michal Rozsival 75.00 150.00
EC18 Brandon Saad 175.00 300.00
EC19 Brent Seabrook 125.00 250.00
EC20 Patrick Sharp 150.00 250.00
EC21 Andrew Shaw 100.00 200.00
EC22 Ben Smith 75.00 150.00
EC23 Viktor Stalberg 75.00 150.00
EC24 Daniel Carcillo 40.00 80.00
EC25 Jonathan Toews 250.00 400.00

2013-14 Dominion Frozen Moments Autographs

FMBC Bobby Clarke/50 25.00 60.00
FMBH Brett Hull/50 30.00 80.00
FMHX Ron Hextall/50 40.00 80.00
FMJQ Jonathan Quick/50 50.00 100.00
FMKP Keith Primeau/99 15.00 40.00
FMMB Martin Brodeur/50 50.00 100.00
FMML Mario Lemieux/25 60.00 150.00
FMMM Mark Messier/99 40.00 100.00
FMNY Nail Yakupov/99 20.00 50.00
FMOV Alex Ovechkin/99 60.00 125.00
FMPD Pavel Datsyuk/50 40.00 80.00
FMPK Patrick Kane/99 50.00 100.00
FMPN Patrice Bergeron/99 125.00 300.00
FMRB Ray Bourque/50 40.00 80.00
FMRM Ryan Miller/99 EXCH 25.00 60.00

2013-14 Dominion Hand Signed

HSBH Brett Hull 40.00 80.00
HSDX Derek Stepan 12.00 30.00
HSGX Claude Giroux 30.00 60.00
HSIC Brad Richards 20.00 50.00
HSIK Marian Gaborik 20.00 50.00
HSIL Igor Larionov 20.00 50.00
HSJO Joe Thornton 30.00 80.00
HSOS Chris Chelios 30.00 60.00
HSOU Sean Couturier 15.00 40.00
HSPK Patrick Kane 50.00 100.00
HSPV Joe Pavelski 25.00 60.00
HSRE Matt Read 12.00 30.00
HSVR James van Riemsdyk 15.00 40.00
HSWC Matthew Carle 12.00 30.00

2013-14 Dominion Ice Level Jersey Autographs

ILAG Alex Galchenyuk 75.00 150.00
ILAW Austin Watson 12.00 30.00
ILBB Beau Bennett 20.00 50.00
ILCK Chris Kreider EXCH 20.00 50.00
ILDH Dougie Hamilton 30.00 80.00
ILDI Jarred Tinordi EXCH 15.00 40.00
ILEE Emerson Etem 15.00 40.00
ILHY Ryan Murphy 15.00 40.00
ILJC Jack Campbell 40.00 100.00
ILNB Nathan Beaulieu 10.00 25.00
ILNY Nail Yakupov 25.00 60.00
ILOK Jamie Oleksiak 12.00 30.00
ILOY Charlie Coyle EXCH 15.00 40.00
ILQH Quinton Howden 12.00 30.00
ILSL Scott Laughton 30.00 60.00
ILSP Ryan Spooner 15.00 40.00
ILSZ Justin Schultz 15.00 40.00
ILTT Tyler Toffoli 30.00 80.00
ILTZ Jaden Schwartz 20.00 50.00

2013-14 Dominion Jerseys

*PRIME/25: .8X TO 2X BASIC JSY/99
DAB Aleksander Barkov 8.00 20.00
DAC Alex Chiasson 2.50 6.00
DAG Alex Galchenyuk 10.00 25.00
DAS Alexander Semin 4.00 10.00
DAW Austin Watson 3.00 8.00
DAZ Anze Kopitar 6.00 15.00
DBB Beau Bennett 3.00 8.00
DBE Brian Elliott 3.00 8.00
DBG Brendan Gallagher 8.00 20.00
DBR Bobby Ryan 3.00 8.00
DBY Dustin Byfuglien 4.00 10.00
DCC Cody Ceci 3.00 8.00
DCC Cory Conacher 5.00 12.00
DCG Curtis Glencross 2.50 6.00
DCI David Krejci 4.00 10.00
DCL Scott Clemmensen 4.00 10.00
DCM Connor Murphy 2.50 6.00
DCN Cam Neely 4.00 10.00
DCP Carey Price 8.00 20.00
DDH Dougie Hamilton 4.00 10.00
DDI Jarred Tinordi 2.50 6.00
DDS Daniel Sedin 5.00 12.00
DDU Brandon Dubinsky 2.50 6.00
DDY Drew Doughty 5.00 12.00
DEE Emerson Etem 4.00 10.00
DEI James Reimer 4.00 10.00
DEK Erik Karlsson 5.00 12.00
DEV Evander Kane 4.00 10.00
DFC Frank Corrado 2.50 6.00
DFF Filip Forsberg 6.00 15.00
DFL Marc-Andre Fleury 8.00 20.00
DGL Gabriel Landeskog 5.00 12.00
DGX Claude Giroux 5.00 12.00
DHB Braden Holtby 5.00 12.00
DHL Henrik Lundqvist 10.00 25.00
DHW Jimmy Howard 5.00 12.00
DHY Ryan Murphy 4.00 10.00
DHZ Martin Hanzal 2.50 6.00
DIC Brad Richards 4.00 10.00
DIK Marian Gaborik 5.00 12.00
DJB Jonas Brodin 5.00 12.00
DJE Jordan Eberle 4.00 10.00
DJH Jonathan Huberdeau 6.00 15.00
DJM J.T. Miller 6.00 15.00
DJO Joe Thornton 6.00 15.00
DJQ Jonathan Quick 5.00 12.00
DJS Joe Sakic 8.00 20.00
DKO Mikhail Grigorenko 1.50 4.00
DKY Keith Yandle 2.50 6.00
DLA Adam Larsson 4.00 10.00
DLK Leo Komarov 5.00 12.00
DLS Luke Schenn 4.00 10.00
DLU Roberto Luongo 6.00 15.00
DLV Calvin Pickard 5.00 12.00
DMB Martin Brodeur 8.00 20.00
DMG Mikael Granlund 4.00 10.00
DML Mario Lemieux 15.00 40.00
DMM Mark Messier 5.00 12.00
DMR Mike Richards 5.00 12.00
DMV Marc-Edouard Vlasic 2.50 6.00
DNB Nathan Beaulieu 1.50 4.00
DNH Ryan Nugent-Hopkins 5.00 12.00
DNL Nicklas Lidstrom 5.00 12.00
DNN Jamie Benn 4.00 10.00
DNY Nail Yakupov 10.00 25.00
DNZ Nikita Zadorov 1.50 4.00
DOE Jordan Schroeder 4.00 10.00
DOK Jamie Oleksiak 3.00 8.00
DOM Olli Maatta 10.00 25.00
DOR Ryan O'Reilly 4.00 10.00
DOV Alex Ovechkin 15.00 40.00
DOY Charlie Coyle 4.00 10.00
DPB Pavel Bure 6.00 15.00
DPD Pavel Datsyuk 6.00 15.00
DPR Patrick Roy 10.00 25.00
DPS Patrick Sharp 4.00 10.00
DPU Patrick Marleau 4.00 10.00
DQH Quinton Howden 3.00 8.00
DRK Ryan Kesler 4.00 10.00
DRM Ryan Miller 4.00 10.00
DRP Richard Panik 6.00 15.00
DRS Ryan Strome 5.00 12.00
DRZ Petr Mrazek 5.00 12.00
DSC Sidney Crosby 12.00 30.00
DSD Shane Doan 3.00 8.00
DSJ Seth Jones 5.00 12.00
DSL Scott Laughton 4.00 10.00
DSM Stefan Matteau 3.00 8.00
DSP Ryan Spooner 6.00 15.00
DSV Sami Vatanen 4.00 10.00
DSZ Justin Schultz 2.50 6.00
DTH Taylor Hall 4.00 10.00
DTS Tyler Seguin 5.00 12.00
DTT Tyler Toffoli 6.00 15.00
DUC Milan Lucic 4.00 10.00
DUF Dion Phaneuf 3.00 8.00
DUU Tuukka Rask 5.00 12.00
DUW Jay Bouwmeester 2.50 6.00
DVA Semyon Varlamov 5.00 12.00
DVF Viktor Fasth 4.00 10.00
DVL Vincent Lecavalier 4.00 10.00
DVN Valeri Nichushkin 5.00 12.00
DVT Vladimir Tarasenko 8.00 20.00
DWS Wayne Simmonds 5.00 12.00
DWS Jonathan Toews 6.00 15.00
DYR Ray Emery 3.00 8.00
DYR Cory Schneider 4.00 10.00
DYY Corey Perry 6.00 15.00
DBJE Boone Jenner 5.00 12.00
DELI Elias Lindholm 6.00 15.00
DHLI Hampus Lindholm 4.00 10.00
DJME Jon Merrill 5.00 12.00
DJTR Jacob Trouba 8.00 20.00
DMDB Matt Dumba 1.50 4.00
DMMZ Marek Mazanec 6.00 15.00
DNMK Nathan MacKinnon 20.00 50.00
DRBE Reto Berra 2.50 6.00
DRLY Morgan Rielly 6.00 15.00
DRMR Ryan Murray 4.00 10.00
DSMO Sean Monahan 6.00 15.00
DTHE Tomas Hertl 6.00 15.00
DTJU Tomas Jurco 8.00 20.00

2013-14 Dominion Mammoth Jerseys

*PRIME/15-25: .6X TO 1.5X BASIC JSY/50
MAB Aleksander Barkov/50 8.00 20.00
MAC Alex Chiasson/50 4.00 10.00
MAG Alex Galchenyuk/50 15.00 40.00
MAH Adam Henrique/50 5.00 12.00
MAK Alex Killorn/50 10.00 25.00
MAW Austin Watson/50 5.00 12.00
MBB Beau Bennett/50 5.00 12.00
MBG Brendan Gallagher/50 10.00 25.00
MBJE Boone Jenner/50 8.00 20.00
MBL Brian Lashoff/50 5.00 12.00
MBS Brendan Shanahan/50 8.00 20.00
MCC Cody Ceci/50 3.00 8.00
MCM Connor Murphy/50 3.00 8.00
MCS Cory Schneider/50 6.00 15.00
MDB David Backes/50 8.00 20.00
MDD Danny DeKeyser/50 5.00 12.00
MDH Dougie Hamilton/50 6.00 15.00
MDK Duncan Keith/50 8.00 20.00
MEE Emerson Etem/50 6.00 15.00
MEG Eric Gryba/50 5.00 12.00
MELI Elias Lindholm/50 10.00 25.00
MFC Frank Corrado/50 2.50 6.00
MFF Filip Forsberg/50 12.00 30.00
MGH Gordie Howe/25 25.00 50.00
MHL Henrik Lundqvist/50 15.00 40.00
MHLI Hampus Lindholm/50 6.00 15.00
MHX Ron Hextall/50 8.00 20.00
MHY Ryan Murphy/50 6.00 15.00
MJB Jonas Brodin/50 8.00 20.00
MJH Jonathan Huberdeau/50 10.00 25.00
MJM J.T. Miller/50 10.00 25.00
MJME Jon Merrill/50 6.00 15.00
MJN Joe Nieuwendyk/50 5.00 12.00
MJQ Jonathan Quick/50 8.00 20.00
MJTR Jacob Trouba/50 6.00 15.00
MKA Michael Kostka/50 5.00 12.00
MKL Kari Lehtonen/50 5.00 12.00
MKO Mikhail Grigorenko/50 2.50 6.00
MLR Luc Robitaille/50 6.00 15.00
MLV Calvin Pickard/50 8.00 20.00
MMDB Matt Dumba/50 2.50 6.00
MMG Mikael Granlund/50 6.00 15.00
MMH Milan Hejduk/50 5.00 12.00
MMK Miikka Kiprusoff/50 6.00 15.00
MMMZ Marek Mazanec/50 4.00 10.00
MNB Nicklas Backstrom/50 6.00 15.00
MNMK Nathan MacKinnon/50 15.00 40.00
MNY Nail Yakupov/50 12.00 30.00
MNZ Nikita Zadorov/50 2.50 6.00
MOM Olli Maatta/50 6.00 15.00
MOV Alex Ovechkin/50 25.00 60.00
MOY Charlie Coyle/50 6.00 15.00
MPG Philipp Grubauer/50 10.00 25.00
MPU Patrick Marleau/50 6.00 15.00
MQH Quinton Howden/50 5.00 12.00
MRBE Reto Berra/50 4.00 10.00

MRLY Morgan Rielly/50 10.00 25.00
MRMR Ryan Murray/50 6.00 15.00
MRS Ryan Strome/50 8.00 20.00
MSC Sidney Crosby/50 20.00 50.00
MSJ Seth Jones/50 8.00 20.00
MSM Stefan Matteau/50 5.00 12.00
MSMO Sean Monahan/50 6.00 15.00
MSZ Justin Schultz/50 4.00 10.00
MTHE Tomas Hertl/50 8.00 20.00
MTJU Tomas Jurco/50 5.00 12.00
MTM Tye McGinn/50 6.00 15.00
MTT Tyler Toffoli/50 8.00 20.00
MVN Valeri Nichushkin/50 8.00 20.00
MVT Vladimir Tarasenko/50 10.00 25.00
MXH Jonas Hiller/50 5.00 12.00
MZC Zdeno Chara/50 6.00 15.00
MZG Zemgus Girgensons/35 6.00 15.00

2013-14 Dominion Patches Autographs

APAB Aleksander Barkov/99 20.00 50.00
APAC Alex Chiasson/99 6.00 15.00
APAG Alex Galchenyuk/99 25.00 60.00
APAH Adam Henrique/99 8.00 20.00
APAK Alex Killorn/99 8.00 20.00
APAN Antti Niemi/99 12.00 30.00
APAR Antoine Roussel/99 8.00 20.00
APAW Austin Watson/99 8.00 20.00
APBB Beau Bennett/99 8.00 20.00
APBF Brian Flynn/99 8.00 20.00
APBG Brendan Gallagher/99 15.00 40.00
APBI Bill Barber/50 10.00 25.00
APBJ Nick Bjugstad/99 12.00 30.00
APBJE Boone Jenner/99 20.00 40.00
APBNE Brock Nelson/99 12.00 30.00
APBP Bernie Parent/50 20.00 50.00
APBR Bobby Ryan/99 8.00 20.00
APCC Cory Conacher/99 4.00 10.00
APCG Curtis Glencross/99 6.00 15.00
APCH Carl Hagelin/99 6.00 15.00
APCN Cam Neely/50 15.00 40.00
APCP Carey Price/50 30.00 60.00
APCT Christian Thomas/99 8.00 20.00
APDD Danny DeKeyser/99 12.00 30.00
APDE Dan Boyle/99 6.00 15.00
APDH Dougie Hamilton/99 15.00 40.00
APDI Jarred Tinordi/99 6.00 15.00
APDP David Perron/99 EXCH 8.00 20.00
APDQ Daniel Briere/99 10.00 25.00
APDS Daniel Sedin/99 12.00 30.00
APDX Derek Stepan/99 6.00 15.00
APED Jared Staal/99 8.00 20.00
APEE Emerson Etem/99 EXCH 10.00 25.00
APEG Eric Gryba/99 8.00 20.00
APEL Eric Lindros/50 20.00 50.00
APEL Elias Lindholm/99 15.00 40.00
APEP Edward Pasquale/99 6.00 15.00
APER Jonathan Bernier/99 8.00 20.00
APEY Bob Gainey/99 15.00 40.00
APFA Frederik Andersen/99 15.00 40.00
APFF Filip Forsberg/99 25.00 50.00
APFL Marc-Andre Fleury/50 12.00 30.00
APGF Grant Fuhr/99 15.00 40.00
APGI Mikhail Grabovski/99 EXCH 10.00 25.00
APGL Gabriel Landeskog/99 12.00 30.00
APGU Jean-Sebastien Giguere/99 10.00 25.00
APHI Thomas Hickey/99 8.00 20.00
APHK Jaroslav Halak/99 10.00 25.00
APHL Henrik Lundqvist/50 15.00 40.00
APHO Cody Hodgson/50 6.00 15.00
APHS Henrik Sedin/99 12.00 30.00
APHY Ryan Murphy/99 10.00 25.00
APIB Igor Bobkov/99 5.00 12.00
APIF Jamie Tardif/99 6.00 15.00
APIJ Dmitrij Jaskin/99 12.00 30.00
APJB Jonas Brodin/99 EXCH 12.00 30.00
APJC Jack Campbell/99 10.00 25.00
APJGI John Gibson/99 20.00 50.00
APJH Jonathan Huberdeau/99 15.00 40.00
APJI Jarome Iginla/99 10.00 25.00
APJJ Jaromir Jagr/50 50.00 100.00
APJK Jack Johnson/99 6.00 15.00
APJL Johan Larsson/99 12.00 30.00
APJM Jon Merrill/99 8.00 20.00
APJMI J.T. Miller/99 10.00 25.00
APJN Joakim Nordstrom/99 8.00 20.00
APJQ Jonathan Quick/99 25.00 50.00
APJT John Tavares/50 25.00 60.00
APJTR Jacob Trouba/99 10.00 25.00
APJX John Carlson/99 10.00 25.00
APKA Michael Kostka/99 5.00 12.00
APKL Karl Alzner/99 6.00 15.00
APKI Stan Mikita/25 20.00 40.00
APKN Pekka Rinne/99 EXCH 10.00 25.00
APKO Mikhail Grigorenko/99 4.00 10.00
APKS Kevin Shattenkirk/99 6.00 15.00
APLE Loui Eriksson/99 EXCH 6.00 15.00
APLO Mark Arcobello/99 6.00 15.00
APMD Matt Duchene/99 12.00 30.00
APMF Mike Fisher/99 6.00 15.00
APMG Mikael Granlund/99 10.00 25.00
APMJ Michal Jordan/99 6.00 15.00
APMO Martin Jones/99 15.00 40.00
APMM Mark Messier/50 25.00 50.00
APMP Max Pacioretty/99 EXCH 20.00 40.00
APNH Nugent-Hopkins/99 EXCH 12.00 30.00
APNJ Nicklas Jensen/99 8.00 20.00
APNK Nazem Kadri/50 12.00 30.00
APNL Nicklas Lidstrom/99 20.00 50.00
APNM Nathan MacKinnon/99 50.00 120.00
APNU Nathan Beaulieu/99 12.00 30.00
APNY Nail Yakupov/99 25.00 60.00
APOE Jordan Schroeder/99 8.00 20.00
APOF Brian Lashoff/99 8.00 20.00
APOK Jamie Oleksiak/99 8.00 20.00
APOS Chris Chelios/99 12.00 30.00
APOT Maxime Talbot/50 10.00 25.00
APOV Alex Ovechkin/50 40.00 100.00
APOW Brenden Morrow/99 8.00 20.00
APOY Charlie Coyle/99 EXCH 8.00 20.00
APPC Paul Coffey/99 15.00 40.00
APPD Pavel Datsyuk/99 20.00 40.00
APPE Phil Esposito/50 EXCH 15.00 40.00
APPG Philipp Grubauer/99 10.00 25.00
APPH Phil Kessel/99 10.00 25.00
APPV Joe Pavelski/99 12.00 30.00
APQD Simon Despres/99 8.00 20.00
APQG Michael Sgarbossa/99 10.00 25.00
APQH Quinton Howden/99 8.00 20.00
APRE Matt Read/99 EXCH 6.00 15.00
APRLY Morgan Rielly/99 15.00 40.00
APRM Ryan Miller/99 12.00 30.00
APRMR Ryan Murray/99 10.00 25.00
APRP Richard Panik/99 12.00 30.00
APRR Rickard Rakell/99 10.00 25.00
APRS Ryan Strome/99 25.00 60.00
APRZ Petr Mrazek/99 12.00 30.00
APSC Sidney Crosby/25 90.00 150.00
APSJ Seth Jones/99 25.00 60.00
APSM Stefan Matteau/99 8.00 20.00
APSMO Sean Monahan/99 50.00 100.00
APSO Carl Soderberg/99 10.00 25.00
APSP Ryan Spooner/99 12.00 30.00
APSQ Craig Smith/99 6.00 15.00
APSV Sami Vatanen/99 8.00 20.00
APSZ Justin Schultz/99 12.00 30.00
APTH Taylor Hall/99 15.00 40.00
APTHE Tomas Hertl/99 30.00 80.00
APTJU Tomas Jurco/99 8.00 20.00
APTM Tye McGinn/99 10.00 25.00
APTP Tanner Pearson/99 10.00 25.00
APTT Tyler Toffoli/99 8.00 20.00
APTW Tom Wilson/99 15.00 40.00
APVF Viktor Fasth/99 6.00 15.00
APVL Vincent Lecavalier/99 10.00 25.00
APVN V. Nichushkin/99 EXCH 15.00 40.00
APVO Slava Voynov/99 EXCH 8.00 20.00
APVT Vladimir Tarasenko/99 25.00 60.00
APWE Drew Shore/99 8.00 20.00
APWI Colin Wilson/99 8.00 20.00
APXA Alexander Semin/99 10.00 25.00
APXW Max Reinhart/99 6.00 15.00
APYO Anthony Peluso/99 8.00 20.00
APZL Ryan Getzlaf/99 15.00 40.00
APZR Zach Redmond/99 8.00 20.00

2013-14 Dominion Peerless Patches Autographs

PPAB Aleksander Barkov/50 30.00 80.00
PPAC Alex Chiasson/50 10.00 25.00
PPAG Alex Galchenyuk/50 60.00 120.00
PPAK Alex Killorn/50 25.00 60.00
PPAR Antoine Roussel/50 15.00 40.00
PPBB Beau Bennett/50 12.00 30.00
PPBG Brendan Gallagher/50 30.00 80.00
PPBH Brett Hull/50 30.00 60.00
PPBJ Nick Bjugstad/50 15.00 40.00
PPBJE Boone Jenner/50 20.00 50.00
PPBNE Brock Nelson/50 20.00 50.00
PPCC Cory Conacher/50 6.00 15.00
PPDD Danny DeKeyser/50 20.00 50.00
PPDH Dougie Hamilton/50 30.00 60.00
PPDS Drew Shore/50 12.00 30.00
PPED Jared Staal/50 12.00 30.00
PPEE Emerson Etem/50 15.00 40.00
PPELI E.Lindholm/50 EXCH 15.00 40.00
PPFA Frederik Andersen/50 25.00 60.00
PPFF Filip Forsberg/50 25.00 60.00
PPGL Gabriel Landeskog/50 20.00 50.00
PPHI Thomas Hickey/50 8.00 20.00
PPHL Henrik Lundqvist/50 40.00 100.00
PPHY Ryan Murphy/50 12.00 30.00
PPIJ Dmitrij Jaskin/50 12.00 30.00
PPJB Jonas Brodin/50 EXCH 12.00 30.00
PPJGI John Gibson/50 15.00 40.00
PPJH Jonathan Huberdeau/50 25.00 60.00
PPJM J.T. Miller/50 12.00 30.00
PPJN Joakim Nordstrom/50 20.00 50.00
PPJQ Jonathan Quick/50 20.00 50.00
PPJS Joe Sakic/50 30.00 80.00
PPJT John Tavares/50 25.00 60.00
PPJTR Jacob Trouba/50 15.00 40.00
PPKO Mikhail Grigorenko/50 6.00 15.00
PPMB Martin Brodeur/50 40.00 80.00
PPMG Mikael Granlund/50 12.00 30.00
PPMJO Martin Jones/50 15.00 40.00
PPML Mario Lemieux/50 60.00 120.00
PPMM Mark Messier/50 25.00 50.00
PPNJ Nicklas Jensen/50 12.00 30.00
PPNMK Nathan MacKinnon/50 125.00 250.00
PPNY Nail Yakupov/50 30.00 80.00
PPOE Jordan Schroeder/50 8.00 20.00
PPOV Alex Ovechkin/50 60.00 150.00
PPOY Charlie Coyle/50 EXCH 15.00 40.00
PPPR Patrick Roy/50 125.00 250.00
PPQH Quinton Howden/50 12.00 30.00
PPRLY Morgan Rielly/50 25.00 60.00
PPRMR Ryan Murray/50 15.00 40.00
PPRS Ryan Strome/50 20.00 50.00
PPRZ Petr Mrazek/50 15.00 40.00
PPSJ Seth Jones/50 60.00 120.00
PPSM Stefan Matteau/50 12.00 30.00
PPSMO Sean Monahan/50 15.00 40.00
PPSO Carl Soderberg/50 12.00 30.00
PPSP Ryan Spooner/50 12.00 30.00
PPSV Sami Vatanen/50 12.00 30.00
PPSY Steve Yzerman/50 50.00 100.00
PPSZ Justin Schultz/50 8.00 20.00
PPTHE Tomas Hertl/50 20.00 50.00
PPTJU Tomas Jurco/50 12.00 30.00
PPTP Tanner Pearson/50 12.00 30.00
PPTT Tyler Toffoli/50 20.00 50.00
PPTW Tom Wilson/50 25.00 60.00
PPVF Viktor Fasth/50 15.00 40.00
PPVN Valeri Nichushkin/50 30.00 80.00
PPVT Vladimir Tarasenko/50 30.00 80.00
PPWS Jonathan Toews/50 60.00 120.00
PPXW Max Reinhart/50 15.00 40.00

2013-14 Dominion Quad Jerseys

QALB Ykpv/Schltz/Strt/Crvnka/50 10.00 25.00
QANA Cglno/Bchmn/Hllr/Koivu/50 8.00 20.00
QARK Etem/Fsth/Rkll/Bbkv/50 8.00 20.00
QAVS Lnds/Skc/Jhnsn/Brq/50 15.00 40.00
QBGD Nwndyk/Olksk/Sydr/Benn/50 8.00 20.00
QBOS Mrch/Hmtn/Spnr/Chra/50 12.00 30.00
QBRU Lcic/Rask/Krjc/Sdrb/50 15.00 40.00
QBUF1 Grgn/Rstn/Pysk/Zdv/50 12.00 30.00
QBUF2 Hdgsn/Sttlrd/Flynn/Mller/50 8.00 20.00
QCAR Mrphy/Jrdn/Staal/Smin/50 8.00 20.00
QCBJ2 Mrry/Jnnr/Jhnsn/Erxn/50 15.00 40.00
QCBJ1 Gbrik/Ltstu/Dbnsky/Ansmv/50 8.00 20.00
QCGY2 Mnh/Cmlr/Grdn/Wdm/50 12.00 30.00
QCGY1 Glncrss/Bcklnd
Stjn/Kprsoff/50 8.00 20.00
QCHI1 Nrdstm/Vrstg/Kne/Rnta/50 8.00 20.00
QCHI2 Shrp/Tws/Ktn/Crwf/50 15.00 40.00
QCOL2 Sgrb/Dchne/Pckrd/Vrlmv/50 10.00 25.00
QCZE Hrtl/Mzn/Jskn/Mrzk/50 25.00 60.00
QDAL2 Nchsh/Sgn/Cle/Glioki/50 15.00 40.00
QDAL1 Chsson/Rssel
Nlstrp/Cmpbll/50 10.00 25.00
QDET Krnwl/Lshf/Mrzk/DKy/50 12.00 30.00
QEDM Ykpv/RNH/Hll/Ebrle/50 12.00 30.00
QFIN Brkv/Mtta/Rstln/Grnl/50 12.00 30.00
QFLA Hbrdeau/Hwdn/Shre/Crso/50 8.00 20.00
QFLY Groux/Tbt/Schnn/Smmnds/50 12.00 30.00
QHAB Eller/Armstrng/Mrkv/Sbbn/50 10.00 25.00
QHFD Hwe/Shn/Vrbk/Frnc/50 20.00 50.00
QKGR Rbte/Rnk/Nchls/Dne/50 20.00 50.00
QKNG Brwn/Rchr/Dght/Qck/50 15.00 30.00
QLAK Kptr/Tffli/Crtr/Prsn/50 10.00 25.00
QMIN Cyle/Brdn/Bckstrm/Htley/50 6.00 15.00
QMRK Glchnyk/Gllgh/Bli/Tnr/50 12.00 30.00
QMSG Byl/McDn/Grdi/Lndq/50 20.00 50.00
QMTL1 Brnvl/Brq/Plkn/Grges/50 8.00 20.00
QMTL2 Gnta/Lflr/Prce/Roy/50 20.00 50.00
QNJD Hnrque/Mttau/Lrssn/Zjac/50 8.00 20.00
QNSH2 Jns/Frsbrg/Mznc/Wtsn/50 15.00 40.00
QNSH1 Frsbrg/Smth/Wtsn/Lgwnd/50 25.00 60.00
QNYI1 Strm/Nlsn/Hcky/Vank/50 15.00 40.00
QNYI2 Tvres/Bley/Hmnc/Hcky/50 12.00 30.00
QNYR1 Fst/Stpn/Mcll/St.Lo/50 8.00 20.00
QNYR2 Nash/Mller/Brssrd/Staal/50 20.00 50.00
QOIL Ggnr/Schltz/Whtny/Dbnyk/50 10.00 25.00
QOTT Cncher/Spzza/Andrsn/Ryan/50 8.00 20.00
QPEN Neal/Mrrow/Ltng/Vitale/50 10.00 25.00
QPHI2 Girx/Dwn/Msn/Tmnen/50 10.00 25.00
QPHI1 Ctrier/Lghton/Read/McGnn/50 10.00 25.00
QPHX Doan/Hnzl/Brwn/Yndle/50 8.00 20.00
QPIT Mlkn/Bntt/Dsps/Flry/50 15.00 40.00
QRKD Mrphy/Brdin/Blu/Sch/50 12.00 30.00
QRKF Ykpv/Trsn/Hbrd/Gln/50 12.00 30.00
QRKG Mrzk/Cmp/Fsth/Psql/50 12.00 30.00
QRUS Ykpv/Nch/Trsn/Grig/50 15.00 40.00
QSC4 Sidney Crosby Quad/50 30.00 80.00
QSEN Mchlk/Neil/Gryba/Krlssn/50 10.00 25.00
QSJS Hrtl/Ptrcki/Irwn/Nieto/50 15.00 40.00
QSJS Mrleau/Irwn/Thrntn/Ptrcki/50 12.00 30.00
QSTL Trsn/Osh/Shttk/Ellt/50 12.00 30.00
QTBL Pnk/Kllrn/St.L/Stmk/50 15.00 40.00
QTOR Kssel/Kmrv/Phnf/Rmer/50 8.00 20.00
QUSA Glchn/Etm/Jns/Trba/50 15.00 40.00
QVAN1 Crrdo/Hgg/Hmhs/Tnv/50 6.00 15.00
QVAN2 Jnsn/Schrder/Sdin/Bksa/50 10.00 25.00
QWLD Pmnv/Prs/Grnln/Ster/50 12.00 30.00
QWPG2 Trba/Lttl/Whlr/Tngr/50 10.00 25.00
QWPG1 Plso/Rdmnd
Pvlec/Psquale/50 8.00 20.00
QWSH Ovch/Lch/Alzn/Grbr/50 30.00 80.00
QAMBH Andrs/Mzn/Brra/Hrtz/50 12.00 30.00
QJTLD Lndh/Jnes/Trba/Dmba/50 10.00 25.00
QLFLL Lndhm/Frsbrg/Lndh/Lrs/50 10.00 25.00
QMMHB McKin/Brkv/Hrtl/Mnh/50 25.00 60.00
QMSHJ McKn/Hbrd/Jnr/Strm/50 15.00 40.00
QRWML Jrco/Oullt/Rlly/Dvan/50 10.00 25.00

2013-14 Dominion Rookie Showcase Memorabilia

RSBE E.Etem/B.Nelson 10.00 25.00
RSBH B.Bennett/Q.Howden 6.00 15.00
RSBO T.Barrie/J.Oleksiak 5.00 12.00
RSBS T.Barrie/J.Schwartz 6.00 15.00
RSGB A.Glchnyk/N.Beaulieu 15.00 40.00
RSGY A.Glchnyk/N.Yakupov 15.00 40.00
RSHM D.Hamilton/R.Murphy 10.00 25.00
RSHO D.Hamilton/J.Oleksiak 10.00 25.00
RSLB S.Laughton/B.Bennett 8.00 20.00
RSLM S.Laughton/R.Murphy 6.00 15.00
RSMS R.Murphy/J.Schultz 8.00 20.00
RSNH R.NgntHpkns/J.Hbrdeau 10.00 25.00
RSOC J.Oleksiak/J.Campbell 12.00 30.00
RSSC R.Smith/J.Campbell 12.00 30.00
RSSH R.Spooner/D.Hamilton 10.00 25.00
RSSK J.Schwartz/C.Kreider 6.00 15.00
RSSK R.Smith/C.Kreider 6.00 15.00
RSSL R.Spooner/S.Laughton 6.00 15.00
RSTB J.Tinordi/N.Beaulieu 5.00 12.00
RSTG J.Tinordi/A.Galchenyuk 15.00 40.00
RSWH A.Watson/Q.Howden 6.00 15.00
RSYS N.Yakupov/J.Schultz 10.00 25.00
RSYW N.Yakupov/A.Watson 10.00 25.00

2013-14 Dominion Rookie Showcase Pen Pals

PPBC J.Brodin/C.Coyle 10.00 25.00
PPCK C.Conacher/A.Killorn 10.00 25.00
PPCO J.Campbell/J.Oleksiak 15.00 40.00
PPFW F.Forsberg/A.Watson 20.00 50.00
PPGG A.Galchenyuk/B.Gallagher 50.00 100.00
PPHH Q.Howden/J.Huberdeau 15.00 40.00
PPHS D.Hamilton/R.Spooner 10.00 25.00
PPJS N.Jensen/J.Schroeder 6.00 15.00
PPKM C.Kreider/J.Miller 15.00 40.00
PPMK P.Mrzaek/D.Kuemper 12.00 30.00
PPPT T.Pearson/T.Toffoli 12.00 30.00
PPRC A.Roussel/A.Chiasson 10.00 25.00
PPVE E.Etem/S.Vatanen 6.00 15.00
PPWM T.Wilson/S.Matteau 8.00 20.00

2013-14 Dominion Rookie Showcase Pen Pals Quad

PPCROC Chsn/Rssl/Olks/Cmpbl 40.00 100.00

2013-14 Dominion Rookie Showcase Pen Pals Triple

PPCROC Chssn/Rssel/Cmpbll 15.00 40.00

2013-14 Dominion Stickside Signatures

SSBC Bobby Clarke/25 40.00 80.00
SSBH Brett Hull/25 40.00 80.00
SSBO Mike Bossy/25 30.00 80.00
SSBR Bobby Ryan/25 12.00 30.00
SSBT Bryan Trottier/25 20.00 50.00
SSCH Carl Hagelin/25 25.00 60.00
SSCJ Curtis Joseph/25 20.00 50.00
SSCN Cam Neely/25 30.00 80.00
SSCP Carey Price/25 40.00 80.00
SSDA Dave Andreychuk/25 20.00 50.00
SSDG Doug Gilmour/25 30.00 80.00
SSDS Daniel Sedin/25 20.00 50.00
SSDX Derek Stepan/25 20.00 50.00
SSEL Eric Lindros/25 30.00 80.00
SSES Eric Staal/25 25.00 60.00
SSGH Gordie Howe/25 100.00 200.00
SSHK Jaroslav Halak/25 20.00 50.00
SSHL Henrik Lundqvist/25 75.00 150.00
SSHS Henrik Sedin/25 30.00 60.00
SSHU Bobby Hull/25 30.00 60.00
SSHW Jimmy Howard/25 25.00 60.00
SSIC Brad Richards/25 20.00 50.00
SSJN Joe Nieuwendyk/25 15.00 40.00
SSJO Joe Thornton/25 30.00 60.00
SSJS Joe Sakic/25 30.00 80.00
SSJT John Tavares/25 50.00 100.00
SSKA Karl Alzner/25 12.00 30.00
SSLR Luc Robitaille/25 20.00 50.00
SSLX Adam Larsson/25 20.00 50.00
SSMB Martin Brodeur/25 40.00 80.00
SSML Mario Lemieux/25 90.00 200.00
SSMM Mark Messier/25 30.00 80.00
SSMO Mike Modano/25 40.00 80.00
SSMP Max Pacioretty/25 20.00 50.00
SSMR Mike Richter/25 50.00 100.00
SSOV Alex Ovechkin/25 80.00 200.00
SSOW Brenden Morrow/25 15.00 40.00
SSPC Paul Coffey/25 50.00 100.00
SSPE Phil Esposito/25 30.00 60.00
SSPL Pat LaFontaine/25 20.00 50.00
SSPR Patrick Roy/25 50.00 100.00
SSPT Pierre Turgeon/25 40.00 80.00
SSPU Patrick Marleau/25 20.00 50.00
SSPV Joe Pavelski/25 20.00 50.00
SSRB Ray Bourque/25 50.00 100.00
SSRE Matt Read/25 12.00 30.00
SSRF Ron Francis/25 25.00 60.00
SSRK Ryan Kesler/25 30.00 80.00
SSST Martin St. Louis/25 20.00 50.00
SSSY Steve Yzerman/25 50.00 100.00
SSTA Brian Gionta/25 12.00 30.00
SSTE Tony Esposito/25 30.00 60.00
SSUD Marcel Dionne/25 40.00 80.00
SSVR James van Riemsdyk/25 EXCH 20.00 50.00
SSXA Alexander Semin/25 12.00 30.00
SSYE Brad Boyes/25 12.00 30.00
SSZL Ryan Getzlaf/25 20.00 50.00
SSZP Zach Parise/25 20.00 50.00

2013-14 Dominion Tape to Tape Autographs

TTBS Brendan Shanahan/25 25.00 50.00
TTCJ Curtis Joseph/25 30.00 60.00
TTDX Derek Stepan/25 20.00 50.00
TTEL Eric Lindros/25 50.00 100.00
TTFP Felix Potvin/20 30.00 80.00
TTHK Jaroslav Halak/25 25.00 50.00
TTHL Henrik Lundqvist/20 40.00 80.00
TTJI Jarome Iginla/19 25.00 50.00
TTML Mario Lemieux/25 60.00 120.00
TTMM Mark Messier/25 40.00 80.00
TTOV Alex Ovechkin/16 150.00 400.00
TTPD Pavel Datsyuk/22 50.00 100.00
TTVL Vincent Lecavalier/25 25.00 50.00

2013-14 Dominion Time Warp Patches

TWBL B.Bennett/M.Lemieux 15.00 40.00
TWCB E.Belfour/J.Campbell 25.00 60.00
TWDL D.DeKeyser/N.Lidstrom 12.00 30.00
TWGA D.Andrychk/M.Grgrnko 8.00 20.00
TWGG A.Galchenyuk/B.Gainey 20.00 40.00
TWGR B.Gallagher/P.Roy 25.00 60.00
TWHB D.Hamilton/R.Bourque 15.00 40.00
TWLK S.Laughton/T.Kerr 10.00 25.00
TWMF R.Murphy/R.Francis 12.00 30.00
TWML T.McGinn/E.Lindros 12.00 30.00
TWMM J.Miller/M.Messier 15.00 40.00
TWMV I.Larionov/P.Mrazek 15.00 40.00
TWNB B.Bellows/V.Nichushkin 15.00 40.00
TWOS J.Oleksiak/D.Sydor 6.00 15.00
TWPF C.Pickard/A.Foote 12.00 30.00
TWPN T.Pearson/B.Nicholls 10.00 25.00
TWRM A.Roussel/M.Modano 25.00 00.00
TWRN J.Nieuwendyk/M.Reinhart 8.00 20.00
TWSB J.Staal/R.Brind'Amour 8.00 20.00
TWSC J.Schultz/P.Coffey 12.00 30.00
TWSN R.Spooner/C.Neely 10.00 25.00
TWTH V.Tarasenko/B.Hull 15.00 40.00
TWTR T.Toffoli/L.Robitaille 12.00 30.00
TWWG M.Gartner/T.Wilson 15.00 40.00
TWYG N.Yakupov/A.Graves 12.00 30.00

1993-94 Donruss

1 Steven King .10 .25
2 Joe Sacco .10 .25
3 Anatoli Semenov .10 .25
4 Terry Yake .10 .25
5 Alexei Kasatonov .10 .25
6 Patrick Carnback RC .15 .40
7 Sean Hill .10 .25
8 Bill Houlder .10 .25
9 Todd Ewen .10 .25
10 Bob Corkum .10 .25
11 Tim Sweeney .10 .25
12 Ron Tugnutt .12 .30
13 Guy Hebert .12 .30
14 Shaun Van Allen .10 .25
15 Stu Grimson .10 .25
16 Jon Casey .12 .30
17 Dan Marois .10 .25
18 Adam Oates .15 .40
19 Glen Wesley .10 .25
20 Cam Stewart RC .15 .40
21 Don Sweeney .10 .25
22 Glen Murray .12 .30
23 Jozef Stumpel .10 .25
24 Ray Bourque .25 .60
25 Ted Donato .10 .25
26 Joe Juneau .10 .25
27 Dmitri Kvartalnov .10 .25
28 Steve Leach .10 .25
29 Cam Neely .15 .40
30 Bryan Smolinski .10 .25
31 Craig Simpson .10 .25
32 Donald Audette .10 .25
33 Doug Bodger .10 .25
34 Grant Fuhr .25 .60
35 Dale Hawerchuk .20 .50
36 Yuri Khmylev .10 .25
37 Pat LaFontaine .15 .40
38 Brad May .12 .30
39 Alexander Mogilny .12 .30
40 Richard Smehlik .10 .25
41 Petr Svoboda .10 .25
42 Matthew Barnaby .12 .30
43 Sergei Petrenko .10 .25
44 Mark Astley RC .15 .40
45 Derek Plante RC .15 .40
46 Theo Fleury .15 .40
47 Al MacInnis .20 .50
48 Joe Nieuwendyk .12 .30
49 Joel Otto .10 .25
50 Paul Ranheim .10 .25
51 Robert Reichel .10 .25
52 Gary Roberts .10 .25
53 Gary Suter .10 .25
54 Mike Vernon .12 .30
55 Kelly Kisio .10 .25
56 German Titov RC .15 .40
57 Wes Walz .10 .25
58 Ted Drury .10 .25
59 Sandy McCarthy .10 .25
60 Vesa Viitakoski RC .15 .40
61 Jeff Hackett .10 .25
62 Neil Wilkinson .10 .25
63 Dirk Graham .10 .25
64 Ed Belfour .15 .40
65 Chris Chelios .15 .40
66 Joe Murphy .10 .25
67 Jeremy Roenick .25 .60
68 Steve Smith .10 .25
69 Brent Sutter .10 .25
70 Steve Dubinsky RC .15 .40
71 Michel Goulet .10 .25
72 Christian Ruuttu .10 .25
73 Bryan Marchment .10 .25
74 Sergei Krivokrasov .10 .25
75 Jeff Shantz RC .15 .40
76 Mike Modano .25 .60
77 Derian Hatcher .10 .25
78 Ulf Dahlen .10 .25
79 Mark Tinordi .10 .25
80 Russ Courtnall .10 .25
81 Mike Craig .10 .25
82 Trent Klatt .10 .25
83 Dave Gagner .12 .30
84 Chris Tancill .10 .25
85 James Black .10 .25
86 Dean Evason .10 .25
87 Andy Moog .15 .40
88 Paul Cavallini .10 .25
89 Grant Ledyard .10 .25
90 Jarkko Varvio .10 .25
91 Slava Kozlov .12 .30
92 Mike Sillinger .10 .25
93 Aaron Ward RC .15 .40
94 Greg Johnson .10 .25
95 Steve Yzerman .40 1.00
96 Tim Cheveldae .12 .30
97 Steve Chiasson .10 .25
98 Dino Ciccarelli .12 .30
99 Paul Coffey .15 .40
100 Dallas Drake RC .15 .40
101 Sergei Fedorov .25 .60
102 Nicklas Lidstrom .15 .40
103 Darren McCarty RC .25 .60
104 Bob Probert .15 .40
105 Ray Sheppard .12 .30
106 Scott Pearson .10 .25
107 Steven Rice .10 .25
108 Louie DeBrusk .10 .25
109 Dave Manson .10 .25
110 Dean McAmmond .10 .25
111 Roman Oksiuta RC .15 .40
112 Geoff Smith .10 .25
113 Zdeno Ciger .10 .25
114 Shayne Corson .12 .30
115 Luke Richardson .10 .25
116 Igor Kravchuk .10 .25
117 Bill Ranford .15 .40
118 Doug Weight .12 .30
119 Fred Brathwaite RC .15 .40
120 Jason Arnott RC .30 .75
121 Tom Fitzgerald .10 .25
122 Mike Hough .10 .25
123 Jesse Belanger .10 .25
124 Brian Skrudland .10 .25
125 Dave Lowry .10 .25
126 Scott Mellanby .12 .30
127 Evgeny Davydov .10 .25
128 Andrei Lomakin .10 .25
129 Brian Benning .10 .25
130 Scott Levins RC .15 .40
131 Gord Murphy .10 .25
132 John Vanbiesbrouck .15 .40
133 Mark Fitzpatrick .10 .25
134 Rob Niedermayer .12 .30
135 Alexander Godynyuk .10 .25
136 Eric Weinrich .10 .25
137 Mark Greig .10 .25
138 Jim Sandlak .10 .25
139 Adam Burt .10 .25
140 Nick Kypreos .10 .25
141 Sean Burke .15 .40
142 Andrew Cassels .10 .25
143 Robert Kron .10 .25
144 Michael Nylander .10 .25
145 Robert Petrovicky .10 .25
146 Patrick Poulin .10 .25
147 Geoff Sanderson .12 .30
148 Pat Verbeek .10 .25
149 Zarley Zalapski .10 .25
150 Chris Pronger .15 .40
151 Jari Kurri .15 .40
152 Wayne Gretzky 1.00 2.50
153 Pat Conacher .10 .25
154 Shawn McEachern .10 .25
155 Mike Donnelly .10 .25
156 Warren Rychel .10 .25
157 Gary Shuchuk .10 .25
158 Rob Blake .12 .30
159 Jimmy Carson .10 .25
160 Tony Granato .10 .25
161 Kelly Hrudey .12 .30
162 Luc Robitaille .15 .40
163 Tomas Sandstrom .10 .25
164 Darryl Sydor .10 .25
165 Alexei Zhitnik .10 .25
166 Benoit Brunet .10 .25
167 Lyle Odelein .10 .25
168 Kevin Haller .10 .25
169 Pierre Sevigny .10 .25
170 Brian Bellows .12 .30
171 Patrice Brisebois .10 .25
172 Vincent Damphousse .12 .30
173 Eric Desjardins .10 .25
174 Gilbert Dionne .10 .25
175 Stephan Lebeau .10 .25
176 John LeClair .15 .40
177 Kirk Muller .10 .25
178 Patrick Roy .40 1.00
179 Mathieu Schneider .10 .25
180 Peter Popovic RC .15 .40
181 Corey Millen .10 .25
182 Jason Smith RC .10 .25
183 Bobby Holik .15 .40
184 John MacLean .12 .30
185 Bruce Driver .10 .25
186 Bill Guerin .15 .40
187 Claude Lemieux .10 .25
188 Bernie Nicholls .12 .30
189 Scott Niedermayer .15 .40
190 Stephane Richer .12 .30
191 Alexander Semak .15 .40
192 Scott Stevens .15 .40
193 Valeri Zelepukin .10 .25
194 Chris Terreri .12 .30
195 Martin Brodeur .40 1.00
196 Ron Hextall .15 .40
197 Brad Dalgarno .10 .25
198 Ray Ferraro .10 .25
199 Patrick Flatley .10 .25
200 Travis Green .12 .30
201 Benoit Hogue .10 .25
202 Steve Junker RC .15 .40
203 Darius Kasparaitis .10 .25
204 Derek King .10 .25
205 Uwe Krupp .10 .25
206 Scott Lachance .10 .25
207 Vladimir Malakhov .10 .25
208 Steve Thomas .10 .25
209 Pierre Turgeon .12 .30
210 Scott Scissons .10 .25
211 Glenn Healy .12 .30
212 Alexander Karpovtsev .10 .25
213 James Patrick .10 .25
214 Sergei Nemchinov .10 .25
215 Esa Tikkanen .10 .25
216 Corey Hirsch .12 .30
217 Tony Amonte .12 .30
218 Mike Gartner .20 .50
219 Adam Graves .10 .25
220 Alexei Kovalev .12 .30
221 Brian Leetch .15 .40
222 Mark Messier .30 .75
223 Mike Richter .15 .40
224 Darren Turcotte .10 .25
225 Sergei Zubov .12 .30
226 Craig Billington .12 .30
227 Troy Mallette .10 .25
228 Vladimir Ruzicka .10 .25
229 Darrin Madeley RC .15 .40
230 Mark Lamb .10 .25
231 Dave Archibald .10 .25
232 Bob Kudelski .10 .25
233 Norm Maciver .10 .25
234 Brad Shaw .10 .25
235 Sylvain Turgeon .10 .25
236 Brian Glynn .10 .25
237 Alexandre Daigle .10 .25
238 Alexei Yashin .15 .40
239 Dimitri Filimonov .10 .25
240 Pavol Demitra .20 .50
241 Jason Bowen .15 .40
242 Eric Lindros .25 .60
243 Dominic Roussel .12 .30
244 Milos Holan RC .15 .40
245 Greg Hawgood .10 .25
246 Yves Racine .10 .25
247 Josef Beranek .10 .25
248 Rod Brind'Amour .12 .30
249 Kevin Dineen .10 .25
250 Pelle Eklund .10 .25
251 Garry Galley .10 .25
252 Mark Recchi .20 .50
253 Tommy Soderstrom .12 .30
254 Dimitri Yushkevich .10 .25
255 Mikael Renberg .15 .40
256 Marty McSorley .12 .30
257 Joe Mullen .10 .25
258 Doug Brown .10 .25
259 Kjell Samuelsson .10 .25
260 Tom Barrasso .12 .30
261 Ron Francis .20 .50
262 Mario Lemieux .60 1.50
263 Larry Murphy .12 .30
264 Ulf Samuelsson .10 .25
265 Kevin Stevens .12 .30
266 Martin Straka .12 .30
267 Rick Tocchet .12 .30
268 Bryan Trottier .15 .40
269 Markus Naslund .15 .40
270 Jaromir Jagr .50 1.25
271 Martin Gelinas .10 .25
272 Adam Foote .10 .25
273 Curtis Leschyshyn .10 .25
274 Stephane Fiset .12 .30
275 Jocelyn Thibault RC .15 .40
276 Steve Duchesne .10 .25
277 Valeri Kamensky .12 .30
278 Andrei Kovalenko .10 .25
279 Owen Nolan .15 .40
280 Mike Ricci .10 .25
281 Martin Rucinsky .10 .25
282 Joe Sakic .30 .75
283 Mats Sundin .15 .40
284 Scott Young .10 .25
285 Claude Lapointe .12 .30
286 Brett Hull .30 .75
287 Vitali Karamnov .10 .25
288 Ron Sutter .12 .30
289 Garth Butcher .10 .25
290 Vitali Prokhorov .10 .25
291 Bret Hedican .10 .25
292 Tony Hrkac .10 .25
293 Jeff Brown .12 .30
294 Phil Housley .10 .25
295 Craig Janney .12 .30
296 Curtis Joseph .20 .50
297 Igor Korolev .10 .25
298 Kevin Miller .10 .25
299 Brendan Shanahan .15 .40
300 Jim Montgomery RC .15 .40
301 Gaetan Duchesne .10 .25
302 Jimmy Waite .12 .30
303 Jeff Norton .10 .25
304 Sergei Makarov .10 .25
305 Igor Larionov .10 .25
306 Mike Lalor .10 .25
307 Michal Sykora RC .15 .40
308 Pat Falloon .10 .25
309 Johan Garpenlov .10 .25
310 Rob Gaudreau RC .15 .40
311 Arturs Irbe .10 .25
312 Sandis Ozolinsh .10 .25
313 Doug Zmolek .10 .25
314 Mike Rathje .10 .25
315 Vlastimil Kroupa RC .15 .40
316 Daren Puppa .10 .25
317 Petr Klima .10 .25
318 Brent Gretzky RC .15 .40
319 Denis Savard .15 .40
320 Gerard Gallant .10 .25
321 Joe Reekie .10 .25
322 Mikael Andersson .10 .25
323 Bill McDougall RC .15 .40
324 Brian Bradley .10 .25
325 Shawn Chambers .10 .25
326 Adam Creighton .10 .25
327 Roman Hamrlik .10 .25
328 John Tucker .10 .25
329 Rob Zamuner .10 .25
330 Chris Gratton .12 .30
331 Sylvain Lefebvre .10 .25
332 Nikolai Borschevsky .10 .25
333 Bob Rouse .10 .25
334 John Cullen .10 .25
335 Todd Gill .10 .25
336 Drake Berehowsky .10 .25
337 Wendel Clark .25 .60
338 Peter Zezel .10 .25
339 Rob Pearson .10 .25
340 Glenn Anderson .12 .30
341 Doug Gilmour .20 .50
342 Dave Andreychuk .15 .40
343 Felix Potvin .30 .75
344 David Ellett .10 .25
345 Alexei Kudashov RC .15 .40
346 Gino Odjick .10 .25
347 Jyrki Lumme .10 .25
348 Dana Murzyn .10 .25
349 Sergio Momesso .10 .25
350 Greg Adams .10 .25
351 Pavel Bure .15 .40
352 Geoff Courtnall .10 .25
353 Murray Craven .10 .25
354 Trevor Linden .15 .40
355 Kirk McLean .12 .30
356 Petr Nedved .10 .25
357 Cliff Ronning .10 .25
358 Jiri Slegr .10 .25
359 Kay Whitmore .10 .25
360 Gerald Diduck .10 .25
361 Pat Peake .10 .25
362 Dave Poulin .10 .25
363 Rick Tabaracci .10 .25
364 Jason Woolley .10 .25
365 Kelly Miller .10 .25
366 Peter Bondra .15 .40
367 Sylvain Cote .10 .25
368 Pat Elynuik .10 .25
369 Kevin Hatcher .10 .25
370 Dale Hunter .10 .25
371 Al Iafrate .10 .25
372 Calle Johansson .10 .25
373 Dimitri Khristich .10 .25
374 Michal Pivonka .10 .25
375 Mike Ridley .10 .25
376 Paul Ysebaert .10 .25
377 Stu Barnes .10 .25
378 Sergei Bautin .10 .25
379 Kris King .10 .25
380 Alexei Zhamnov .12 .30
381 Tie Domi .12 .30
382 Bob Essensa .12 .30
383 Nelson Emerson .10 .25
384 Boris Mironov .10 .25
385 Teppo Numminen .10 .25
386 Fredrik Olausson .10 .25
387 Teemu Selanne .30 .75
388 Darrin Shannon .10 .25
389 Thomas Steen .10 .25
390 Keith Tkachuk .15 .40
391 Panthers Opening Night .10 .25
392 Ducks Opening Night .10 .25
393 Daig
Prong
Gratton .15 .40
394 T.Selanne
J.Juneau RB .30 .75
395 W.Gretzky
L.Robitaille RB 1.00 2.50
396 Inserts Checklist .05 .15
397 Atlantic Div. Checklist .05 .15
398 Northeast Div. Checklist .05 .15
399 Central Div. Checklist .05 .15
400 Pacific Div. Checklist .05 .15
401 Garry Valk .10 .25
402 Al Iarante .10 .25
403 David Reid .10 .25
404 Jason Dawe .10 .25
405 Craig Muni .10 .25
406 Dan Keczmer RC .10 .25
407 Michael Nylander .10 .25
408 James Patrick .10 .25
409 Andrei Trefilov .10 .25
410 Zarley Zalapski .10 .25
411 Tony Amonte .12 .30
412 Keith Carney .10 .25
413 Randy Cunneyworth .10 .25
414 Ivan Droppa RC .10 .25
415 Gary Suter .10 .25
416 Eric Weinrich .10 .25
417 Paul Ysebaert .10 .25

418 Richard Matvichuk .10 .25
419 Alan May .10 .25
420 Darcy Wakaluk .10 .25
421 Micah Aivazoff RC .15 .40
422 Terry Carkner .10 .25
423 Kris Draper .10 .25
424 Chris Osgood RC 1.00 2.50
425 Keith Primeau .12 .30
426 Bob Beers .10 .25
427 Ilya Byakin RC .10 .25
428 Kirk Maltby RC .15 .40
429 Boris Mironov .10 .25
430 Fredrik Olausson .10 .25
431 Peter White RC .10 .25
432 Stu Barnes .10 .25
433 Mike Foligno .10 .25
434 Bob Kudelski .10 .25
435 Geoff Smith .10 .25
436 Igor Chibirev RC .10 .25
437 Ted Drury .10 .25
438 Alexander Godynyuk .10 .25
439 Frank Kucera .10 .25
440 Jocelyn Lemieux .10 .25
441 Brian Propp .10 .25
442 Paul Ranheim .10 .25
443 Jeff Reese .10 .25
444 Kevin Smyth RC .10 .25
445 Jim Storm RC .10 .25
446 Phil Crowe RC .10 .25
447 Marty McSorley .12 .30
448 Keith Redmond RC .10 .25
449 Dixon Ward .10 .25
450 Guy Carbonneau .10 .25
451 Mike Keane .10 .25
452 Oleg Petrov .10 .25
453 Ron Tugnutt .12 .30
454 Randy McKay .10 .25
455 Jaroslav Modry RC .15 .40
456 Yan Kaminsky .10 .25
457 Marty McInnis .10 .25
458 Jamie McLennan RC .10 .25
459 Zigmund Palffy .10 .25
460 Glenn Anderson .12 .30
461 Steve Larmer .12 .30
462 Craig MacTavish .10 .25
463 Stephane Matteau .10 .25
464 Brian Noonan .10 .25
465 Mattias Norstrom RC .15 .40
466 Scott Levins .15 .40
467 Derek Mayer RC .10 .25
468 Andy Schneider RC .10 .25
469 Todd Hlushko RC .12 .30
470 Stewart Malgunas RC .15 .40
471 Justin Duberman RC .10 .25
472 Ladislav Karabin RC .15 .40
473 Shawn McEachern .10 .25
474 Ed Patterson RC .10 .25
475 Tomas Sandstrom .10 .25
476 Bob Bassen .10 .25
477 Garth Butcher .10 .25
478 Iain Fraser RC .15 .40
479 Mike McKee RC .10 .25
480 Dwayne Norris RC .10 .25
481 Garth Snow RC .10 .25
482 Ron Sutter .10 .25
483 Kelly Chase .10 .25
484 Steve Duchesne .10 .25
485 Daniel Laperrire .10 .25
486 Petr Nedved .10 .25
487 Peter Stastny .12 .30
488 Ulf Dahlen .10 .25
489 Todd Elik .10 .25
490 Andrei Nazarov RC .10 .25
491 Danton Cole .10 .25
492 Chris Joseph .10 .25
493 Chris LiPuma RC .10 .25
494 Mike Gartner .20 .50
495 Mark Greig .10 .25
496 David Harlock .12 .30
497 Matt Martin RC .15 .40
498 Shawn Antoski .10 .25
499 Jeff Brown .10 .25
500 Jimmy Carson .10 .25
501 Martin Gelinas .10 .25
502 Yevgeny Namestnikov RC .10 .25
503 Randy Burridge .10 .25
504 Joe Juneau .10 .25
505 Kevin Kaminski RC .10 .25
506 Arto Blomsten .10 .25
507 Tim Cheveldae .12 .30
508 Dallas Drake .15 .40
509 Dave Manson .10 .25
510 Update Checklist .05 .15

1993-94 Donruss Elite Inserts
COMPLETE SET (10) 30.00 60.00
1 Mario Lemieux 10.00 25.00
2 Alexandre Daigle 1.25 3.00
3 Teemu Selanne 2.00 5.00
4 Eric Lindros 4.00 10.00
5 Brett Hull 4.00 10.00
6 Jeremy Roenick 2.00 5.00
7 Doug Gilmour 4.00 10.00
8 Alexander Mogilny 1.50 4.00
9 Patrick Roy 10.00 25.00
10 Wayne Gretzky 12.00 30.00
U1 Mikael Renberg 1.25 3.00
U2 Sergei Fedorov 6.00 15.00
U3 Felix Potvin 3.00 8.00
U4 Cam Neely 2.00 5.00
U5 Alexei Yashin 1.25 3.00

1993-94 Donruss Ice Kings
COMPLETE SET (10) 10.00 25.00
1 Patrick Roy 1.50 4.00
2 Pat LaFontaine .60 1.50
3 Jaromir Jagr .75 2.00
4 Wayne Gretzky 2.00 5.00
5 Chris Chelios .60 1.50
6 Felix Potvin .75 2.00
7 Mario Lemieux 1.50 4.00
8 Pavel Bure .60 1.50
9 Eric Lindros .75 2.00
10 Teemu Selanne .60 1.50

1993-94 Donruss Rated Rookies
COMPLETE SET (15) 6.00 15.00
1 Alexandre Daigle .20 .50
2 Chris Gratton .30 .75
3 Chris Pronger .75 2.00
4 Rob Niedermayer .30 .75
5 Mikael Renberg .30 .75
6 Jarkko Varvio .20 .50
7 Alexei Yashin .20 .50
8 Markus Naslund .60 1.50
9 Boris Mironov .20 .50
10 Martin Brodeur 2.00 5.00
11 Jocelyn Thibault .60 1.50
12 Jason Arnott .75 2.00
13 Jim Montgomery .20 .50
14 Ted Drury .20 .50
15 Roman Oksiuta .20 .50

1993-94 Donruss Special Print
COMPLETE SET (26) 25.00 60.00
NNO Ron Tugnutt 1.00 2.50
NNO Adam Oates 1.25 3.00
NNO Alexander Mogilny 1.00 2.50
NNO Theo Fleury 1.00 2.50
NNO Jeremy Roenick 1.50 4.00
NNO Mike Modano 1.50 4.00
NNO Steve Yzerman 2.50 6.00
NNO Jason Arnott 1.00 2.50
NNO Rob Niedermayer 1.00 2.50
NNO Chris Pronger 1.00 2.50
NNO Wayne Gretzky 4.00 10.00
NNO Patrick Roy 3.00 8.00
NNO Scott Niedermayer 1.00 2.50
NNO Pierre Turgeon 1.00 2.50
NNO Mark Messier 1.25 3.00
NNO Alexandre Daigle 1.00 2.50
NNO Eric Lindros 1.50 4.00
NNO Mario Lemieux 4.00 10.00
NNO Mats Sundin 1.25 3.00
NNO Pat Falloon .75 2.00
NNO Brett Hull 1.50 4.00
NNO Chris Gratton .75 2.00
NNO Felix Potvin 1.50 4.00
NNO Pavel Bure 1.25 3.00
NNO Al Iafrate 1.00 2.50
NNO Teemu Selanne 1.25 3.00
NNO Luc Robitaille WC 1.50 4.00
NNO Mario Lemieux EC 5.00 12.00

1993-94 Donruss Team Canada
COMPLETE SET (22) 5.00 10.00
1 Jason Allison .40 1.00
2 Chris Armstrong .30 .75
3 Drew Bannister .30 .75
4 Jason Botterill .30 .75
5 Joel Bouchard .30 .75
6 Curtis Bowen .30 .75
7 Anson Carter .50 1.25
8 Brandon Convery .30 .75
9 Yanick Dube .30 .75
10 Manny Fernandez .50 1.25
11 Jeff Friesen .30 .75
12 Aaron Gavey .30 .75
13 Martin Gendron .30 .75
14 Rick Girard .30 .75
15 Todd Harvey .40 1.00
16 Bryan McCabe .40 1.00
17 Marty Murray .30 .75
18 Mike Peca .50 1.25
19 Nick Stajduhar .30 .75
20 Jamie Storr .40 1.00
21 Brent Tully .30 .75
22 Brendan Witt .40 1.00
NNO WJC Checklist .30 .75

1993-94 Donruss Team USA
COMPLETE SET (22) 3.00 8.00
1 Kevyn Adams .30 .75
2 Jason Bonsignore .30 .75
3 Andy Brink .30 .75
4 Jon Coleman .30 .75
5 Adam Deadmarsh .40 1.00
6 Aaron Ellis .30 .75
7 John Emmons .30 .75
8 Ashlin Halfnight .30 .75
9 Kevin Hilton .30 .75
10 Jason Karmanos .30 .75
11 Toby Kvalevog .30 .75
12 Bob Lachance .30 .75
13 Jamie Langenbrunner .40 1.00
14 Jason McBain .30 .75
15 Chris O'Sullivan .30 .75
16 Jay Pandolfo .30 .75
17 Richard Park .30 .75
18 Deron Quint .30 .75
19 Ryan Sittler .30 .75
20 Blake Sloan .30 .75
21 John Varga .30 .75
22 David Wilkie .30 .75
NNO WJC Checklist .30 .75

1994-95 Donruss
1 Steve Yzerman .40 1.00
2 Paul Ysebaert .10 .25
3 Doug Weight .12 .30
4 Trevor Kidd .12 .30
5 Mario Lemieux .60 1.50
6 Andrei Kovalenko .10 .25
7 Arturs Irbe .12 .30
8 Doug Gilmour .20 .50
9 Mark Messier .30 .75
10 Milos Holan .10 .25
11 Kevin Miller .10 .25
12 Felix Potvin .25 .60
13 Josef Beranek .10 .25
14 Mikael Andersson .10 .25
15 Stephane Matteau .10 .25
16 Todd Simon RC .10 .25
17 Darcy Wakaluk .12 .30
18 Kelly Buchberger .10 .25
19 Pavel Bure .15 .40
20 Dave Lowry .10 .25
21 Bryan Smolinski .10 .25
22 Kirk McLean .12 .30
23 Pierre Turgeon .12 .30
24 Martin Brodeur .40 1.00
25 Jason Arnott .12 .30
26 Steve Dubinsky .10 .25
27 Larry Murphy .12 .30
28 Craig Janney .12 .30
29 Patrik Carnback .10 .25
30 Derek King .10 .25
31 Peter Bondra .15 .40
32 Jason Bowen .10 .25
33 Maxim Bets .10 .25
34 Matt Martin .10 .25
35 Jeff Hackett .10 .25
36 Kevin Dineen .10 .25
37 Trent Klatt .10 .25
38 Joe Murphy .10 .25
39 Sandy McCarthy .10 .25
40 Brian Bradley .10 .25
41 Scott Lachance .10 .25
42 Scott Mellanby .12 .30
43 Adam Graves .10 .25
44 Dale Hawerchuk .20 .50
45 Owen Nolan .15 .40
46 Keith Primeau .12 .30
47 Jim Dowd .10 .25
48 Dan Plante RC .10 .25
49 Rick Tabaracci .12 .30
50 Geoff Courtnall .10 .25
51 Markus Naslund .15 .40
52 Kelly Miller .10 .25
53 Kirk Maltby .10 .25
54 Paul Coffey .15 .40
55 Gord Murphy .10 .25
56 Joe Nieuwendyk .12 .30
57 Ulf Dahlen .10 .25
58 Dmitri Mironov .10 .25
59 Kevin Smyth .10 .25
60 Tie Domi .12 .30
61 Oleg Petrov .10 .25
62 Bill Guerin .15 .40
63 Alexei Yashin .15 .40
64 Joe Sacco .10 .25
65 Aris Brimanis RC .10 .25
66 Randy Burridge .10 .25
67 Neal Broten .12 .30
68 Ray Bourque .25 .60
69 Ron Tugnutt .12 .30
70 Darryl Sydor .10 .25
71 Jocelyn Thibault .12 .30
72 Shawn Chambers .10 .25
73 Alexei Zhamnov .12 .30
74 Michael Nylander .12 .30
75 Travis Green .12 .30
76 Brad May .10 .25
77 Geoff Sanderson .12 .30
78 Derek Plante .10 .25
79 Stephane Richer .12 .30
80 Rod Brind'Amour .12 .30
81 Guy Hebert .12 .30
82 Claude Lemieux .15 .40
83 Pat Falloon .10 .25
84 Alexei Kudashov .10 .25
85 Andrei Lomakin .10 .25
86 Dino Ciccarelli .12 .30
87 John Tucker .10 .25
88 Jamie McLennan .12 .30
89 Peter Taglianetti .10 .25
90 Bobby Holik .10 .25
91 Sergei Krivokrasov .10 .25
92 Alexander Mogilny .12 .30
93 Jari Kurri .12 .30
94 Dominik Hasek .25 .60
95 Shawn McEachern .10 .25
96 Bob Corkum .10 .25
97 Dimitri Filimonov .10 .25
98 John LeClair .15 .40
99 Theo Fleury .15 .40
100 Daren Puppa .12 .30
101 Greg Adams .10 .25
102 Joel Otto .10 .25
103 Sergei Makarov .10 .25
104 Mike Ricci .10 .25
105 Sylvain Turgeon .10 .25
106 Igor Larionov .10 .25
107 Tony Amonte .12 .30
108 Andy Moog .15 .40
109 Jeff Brown .10 .25
110 Checklist 1-83 .10 .25
111 Mike Gartner .20 .50
112 Craig Simpson .10 .25
113 Rob Niedermayer .12 .30
114 Robert Kron .10 .25
115 Jason York RC .10 .25
116 Valeri Kamensky .12 .30
117 Ray Whitney .10 .25
118 Chris Chelios .15 .40
119 Scott Levins .10 .25
120 Sandis Ozolinsh .10 .25
121 Mark Recchi .20 .50
122 Ron Francis .20 .50
123 Dean McAmmond .10 .25
124 Terry Yake .10 .25
125 Sergei Nemchinov .10 .25
126 Vitali Prokhorov .10 .25
127 Wayne Gretzky 1.00 2.50
128 Roman Hamrlik .10 .25
129 Jarkko Varvio .10 .25
130 Brian Skrudland .10 .25
131 Murray Craven .10 .25
132 Jeff Norton .10 .25
133 Pavol Demitra .20 .50
134 Mike Keane .10 .25
135 Paul Cavallini .10 .25
136 Richard Smehlik .10 .25
137 Eric Lindros .25 .60
138 Mariusz Czerkawski RC .15 .40
139 Darrin Shannon .10 .25
140 Brian Noonan .10 .25
141 Joe Sakic .30 .75
142 Steve Thomas .10 .25
143 Gary Roberts .10 .25
144 Patrick Poulin .10 .25
145 Tony Granato .10 .25
146 Donald Brashear RC .10 .25
147 Ron Hextall .15 .40
148 Corey Millen .10 .25
149 Dale Hunter .10 .25
150 Greg Johnson .10 .25
151 John MacLean .12 .30
152 Brian Leetch .12 .30
153 Sylvain Cote .10 .25
154 Thomas Steen .10 .25
155 Ted Donato .10 .25
156 Nathan Lafayette .10 .25
157 Kelly Chase .10 .25
158 Sean Burke .12 .30
159 Jaromir Jagr .50 1.25
160 Checklist 84-166 .10 .25
161 Scott Niedermayer .15 .40
162 Ray Ferraro .10 .25
163 Todd Elik .10 .25
164 Dave Gagner .12 .30
165 Mike Richter .15 .40
166 Garry Galley .10 .25
167 Russ Courtnall .10 .25
168 Marty McSorley .12 .30
169 Robert Reichel .10 .25
170 Mike Rathje .10 .25
171 Bill Ranford .12 .30
172 Danton Cole .10 .25
173 Sergei Fedorov .25 .60
174 Brendan Shanahan .15 .40
175 Byron Dafoe RC .50 1.25
176 John Vanbiesbrouck .15 .40
177 Eric Desjardins .12 .30
178 Andrew Cassels .10 .25
179 John Gruden RC .10 .25
180 Slava Kozlov .12 .30
181 Trevor Linden .15 .40
182 Kris Draper .10 .25
183 Steve Smith .10 .25
184 Andre Faust .10 .25
185 James Patrick .10 .25
186 Ted Drury .10 .25
187 Dan Laperriere .10 .25
188 Benoit Hogue .10 .25
189 Chris Gratton .10 .25
190 Jyrki Lumme .10 .25
191 Peter Stastny .12 .30
192 Keith Tkachuk .15 .40
193 Mike Modano .25 .60
194 Nicklas Lidstrom .15 .40
195 Pierre Sevigny .10 .25
196 Scott Pearson .10 .25
197 Jaroslav Modry .10 .25
198 Garry Valk .10 .25
199 Kevin Hatcher .10 .25
200 Denis Tsygurov RC .15 .40
201 Paul Laus .10 .25
202 Alexander Godynyuk .10 .25
203 Brian Bellows .12 .30
204 Michal Sykora .10 .25
205 Al Iafrate .10 .25
206 Mark Tinordi .10 .25
207 Kelly Hrudey .12 .30
208 Tom Barrasso .12 .30
209 Craig Billington .12 .30
210 Teemu Selanne .30 .75
211 Alexandre Daigle .10 .25
212 Grant Fuhr .25 .60
213 Doug Brown .10 .25
214 Tim Sweeney .10 .25
215 Chris Pronger .15 .40
216 Alexei Gusarov .12 .30
217 Gary Suter .10 .25
218 Boris Mironov .10 .25
219 Sergei Zubov .12 .30
220 Checklist 167-249 .10 .25
221 Shayne Corson .12 .30
222 Jeremy Roenick .25 .60
223 John Druce .12 .30
224 Martin Straka .10 .25
225 Stephane Fiset .12 .30
226 Vincent Damphousse .12 .30
227 Bob Kudelski .10 .25
228 German Titov .10 .25
229 Kevin Stevens .12 .30
230 Dave Ellett .10 .25
231 Steve Larmer .12 .30
232 Glen Wesley .10 .25
233 Mathieu Schneider .10 .25
234 Stephan Lebeau .10 .25
235 Mark Fitzpatrick .12 .30
236 Mikael Renberg .12 .30
237 Darren McCarty .10 .25
238 Todd Nelson .10 .25
239 Igor Korolev .10 .25
240 Warren Rychel .10 .25
241 Gino Odjick .10 .25
242 Dave Manson .10 .25
243 Calle Johansson .10 .25
244 Andrei Trefilov .10 .25
245 Jason Dawe .10 .25
246 Glen Murray .12 .30
247 Jeff Shantz .10 .25
248 Zarley Zalapski .10 .25
249 Petr Klima .10 .25
250 Patrice Brisebois .10 .25
251 Chris Osgood .25 .60
252 Darius Kasparaitis .10 .25
253 Chris Joseph .10 .25
254 Glenn Anderson .12 .30
255 Kirk Muller .10 .25
256 Jason Smith .12 .30
257 Bob Bassen .10 .25
258 Joe Juneau .10 .25
259 Igor Kravchuk .10 .25
260 John Lilley .10 .25
261 Philippe Bozon .12 .30
262 Scott Stevens .15 .40
263 Dominic Roussel .12 .30
264 Dimitri Khristich .10 .25
265 Ed Patterson .10 .25
266 Mike Peca .12 .30
267 Teppo Numminen .10 .25
268 Alexei Kovalev .12 .30
269 Cam Neely .15 .40
270 Iain Fraser .10 .25
271 Tomas Sandstrom .10 .25
272 Lyle Odelein .12 .30
273 Norm Maciver .10 .25
274 Zdeno Ciger .10 .25
275 Ed Belfour .15 .40
276 Brian Savage .10 .25
277 Vlastimil Kroupa .10 .25
278 Cliff Ronning .10 .25
279 Alexei Zhitnik .12 .30
280 Jim Storm .12 .30
281 Don Sweeney .10 .25
282 Mike Donnelly .10 .25
283 Glenn Healy .12 .30
284 Denis Savard .15 .40
285 Chris Terreri .12 .30
286 Darren Turcotte .10 .25
287 Curtis Joseph .20 .50
288 Ken Baumgartner .10 .25
289 Matthew Barnaby .12 .30
290 Brent Sutter .12 .30
291 Valeri Zelepukin .10 .25
292 Michal Pivonka .10 .25
293 Ray Sheppard .12 .30
294 Jiri Slegr .10 .25
295 Vesa Viitakoski .12 .30
296 Ulf Samuelsson .10 .25
297 Nelson Emerson .10 .25
298 John Slaney .10 .25
299 Pat Verbeek .12 .30
300 Pat LaFontaine .15 .40
301 Johan Garpenlov .10 .25
302 Eric Weinrich .10 .25
303 Richard Matvichuk .10 .25
304 Steve Duchesne .10 .25
305 Donald Audette .10 .25
306 Stu Barnes .10 .25
307 Vladimir Malakhov .10 .25
308 Dimitri Yushkevich .10 .25
309 David Sacco .10 .25
310 Scott Young .10 .25
311 Marty McInnis .10 .25
312 Grant Ledyard .10 .25
313 Peter Popovic .10 .25
314 Mikhail Shtalenkov RC .10 .25
315 Dave McLlwain .10 .25
316 Cam Stewart .10 .25
317 Derian Hatcher .10 .25
318 Pat Peake .10 .25
319 Wes Walz .10 .25
320 Fred Brathwaite .10 .25
321 Jesse Belanger .10 .25
322 Jozef Stumpel .10 .25
323 Dave Andreychuk .15 .40
324 Yuri Khmylev .10 .25
325 Tim Cheveldae .12 .30
326 Anatoli Semenov .10 .25
327 Alexander Karpovtsev .10 .25
328 Patrick Roy .40 1.00
329 Troy Mallette .10 .25
330 Checklist 250-330 .10 .25

1994-95 Donruss Dominators
COMPLETE SET (8) 15.00 40.00
1 Messier/Lemieux/Lindros 3.00 8.00
2 Leetch/Bourque/Stevens 4.00 10.00
3 Roy/Hasek/Vanbiesbrouck 6.00 15.00
4 Jagr/Renberg/Neely 2.00 5.00
5 Gretzky/Roenick/Fedorov 6.00 15.00
6 Chelios/Coffey/MacInnis 2.00 5.00
7 Potvin/Belfour/Irbe 5.00 12.00
8 Bure/Hull/Selanne 4.00 10.00

1994-95 Donruss Elite Inserts
COMPLETE SET (10) 30.00 60.00
1 Jason Arnott .60 1.50
2 Martin Brodeur 5.00 12.00
3 Pavel Bure 3.00 8.00
4 Sergei Fedorov 2.00 5.00
5 Wayne Gretzky 12.00 30.00
6 Mario Lemieux 6.00 15.00
7 Eric Lindros 3.00 8.00
8 Felix Potvin 4.00 10.00
9 Jeremy Roenick 2.50 6.00
10 Patrick Roy 6.00 15.00

1994-95 Donruss Ice Masters
COMPLETE SET (10) 8.00 15.00
1 Ed Belfour .50 1.25
2 Sergei Fedorov .75 2.00
3 Doug Gilmour .25 .60
4 Wayne Gretzky 3.00 8.00
5 Mario Lemieux 2.50 6.00
6 Eric Lindros .50 1.25
7 Mark Messier .50 1.25
8 Mike Modano .75 2.00
9 Luc Robitaille .25 .60
10 John Vanbiesbrouck .25 .60

1994-95 Donruss Masked Marvels
COMPLETE SET (10) 15.00 30.00
1 Ed Belfour 1.00 2.50
2 Martin Brodeur 2.50 6.00
3 Dominik Hasek 2.00 5.00
4 Arturs Irbe .75 2.00
5 Curtis Joseph 1.25 3.00
6 Kirk McLean .75 2.00
7 Felix Potvin 1.00 2.50
8 Mike Richter 1.00 2.50
9 Patrick Roy 4.00 10.00
10 John Vanbiesbrouck 1.00 2.50

1995-96 Donruss
1 Eric Lindros .25 .60
2 Steve Larmer .12 .30
3 Oleg Tverdovsky .15 .40
4 Vladimir Malakhov .10 .25
5 Ian Laperriere .10 .25
6 Chris Marinucci RC .12 .30
7 Nelson Emerson .10 .25
8 David Oliver .10 .25
9 Felix Potvin .25 .60
10 Manny Fernandez .10 .25
11 Jason Wiemer .10 .25
12 Dale Hunter .12 .30
13 Wayne Gretzky 1.00 2.50
14 Todd Gill .10 .25
15 Radim Bicanek .12 .30
16 Kirk McLean .12 .30
17 Esa Tikkanen .10 .25
18 Yuri Khmylev .10 .25
19 Peter Bondra .15 .40
20 Brian Savage .10 .25
21 Mariusz Czerkawski .10 .25
22 Rob Blake .12 .30
23 Chris Osgood .15 .40
24 Bernie Nicholls .12 .30
25 Doug Weight .15 .40
26 Shaun Van Allen .10 .25
27 Jeremy Roenick .25 .60
28 Sean Burke .10 .25
29 Pat Verbeek .12 .30
30 Dino Ciccarelli .12 .30
31 Trevor Kidd .12 .30
32 Steve Thomas .12 .30
33 Dominik Hasek .25 .60
34 Sandis Ozolinsh .10 .25
35 Bill Guerin .15 .40
36 Scott Young .10 .25
37 Scott Mellanby .12 .30
38 Joe Mullen .12 .30
39 Steve Larouche RC .10 .25
40 Joe Nieuwendyk .12 .30
41 Rick Tocchet .12 .30
42 Keith Primeau .12 .30
43 Darren Turcotte .10 .25
44 Jason Arnott .12 .30
45 Brantt Myhres RC .10 .25
46 Murray Craven .10 .25
47 Martin Gendron .12 .30
48 Mark Recchi .20 .50
49 Uwe Krupp .12 .30
50 Alexei Zhitnik .10 .25
51 Rob Niedermayer .12 .30
52 Sergei Brylin .10 .25
53 Mats Naslund .10 .25
54 Glenn Healy .12 .30
55 Mathieu Schneider .10 .25
56 Marko Tuomainen .10 .25
57 Paul Kariya .15 .40
58 Dave Gagner .10 .25
59 Mike Richter .15 .40
60 Patrik Juhlin .10 .25
61 Pierre Turgeon .12 .30
62 Mike Modano .25 .60
63 Chris Pronger .15 .40
64 Chris Joseph .10 .25
65 Peter Forsberg .30 .75
66 Roman Oksiuta .10 .25
67 Jamie Storr .12 .30
68 Brett Hull .30 .75
69 Steve Chiasson .10 .25
70 Benoit Hogue .10 .25
71 Guy Hebert .12 .30
72 Chris Therien .10 .25
73 Darryl Sydor .12 .30
74 Phil Housley .12 .30
75 Jason Allison .12 .30
76 Richard Smehlik .12 .30
77 Shean Donovan .10 .25
78 Keith Tkachuk .15 .40
79 Cliff Ronning .10 .25
80 Mikael Renberg .12 .30
81 Steven Rice .10 .25
82 Adam Graves .12 .30
83 Nicklas Lidstrom .15 .40
84 Daren Puppa .12 .30
85 Todd Warriner .12 .30
86 Jon Rohloff .10 .25
87 Patrice Tardif .12 .30
88 John MacLean .12 .30
89 Ulf Samuelsson .10 .25
90 Alexander Selivanov .12 .30
91 Chris Chelios .15 .40
92 Ulf Dahlen .10 .25
93 Brad May .10 .25
94 Ron Francis .20 .50
95 Kevin Hatcher .12 .30
96 Steve Yzerman .40 1.00
97 Jocelyn Thibault .12 .30
98 Dave Andreychuk .15 .40
99 Gary Suter .10 .25
100 Teemu Selanne .30 .75
101 Don Sweeney .10 .25
102 Valeri Bure .10 .25
103 Todd Harvey .10 .25
104 Luc Robitaille .15 .40
105 Scott Niedermayer .15 .40
106 John Vanbiesbrouck .15 .40
107 Alexei Yashin .12 .30
108 Ed Belfour .12 .30
109 Jyrki Lumme .10 .25
110 Petr Klima .10 .25
111 Tony Granato .10 .25
112 Bob Corkum .10 .25
113 Chris McAlpine RC .12 .30
114 John LeClair .15 .40
115 Kenny Jonsson .15 .40
116 Garry Galley .10 .25
117 Jeff Norton .10 .25
118 Tomas Sandstrom .12 .30
119 Paul Coffey .15 .40
120 Mike Ricci .10 .25
121 Tony Amonte .12 .30
122 Chris Gratton .10 .25
123 Blaine Lacher .12 .30
124 Andrei Nikolishin .10 .25
125 Michal Grosek .10 .25
126 Shawn Chambers .10 .25
127 Ray Bourque .25 .60
128 Jeff Nelson .12 .30
129 Kirk Muller .12 .30
130 Sergei Zubov .12 .30
131 Stanislav Neckar .10 .25
132 Stu Barnes .10 .25
133 Jari Kurri .15 .40
134 Slava Kozlov .12 .30
135 Curtis Joseph .20 .50
136 Joe Juneau .10 .25
137 Craig Janney .10 .25
138 Bryan Smolinski .10 .25
139 Brian Bradley .12 .30
140 Steve Rucchin .12 .30
141 Donald Audette .12 .30
142 Jaromir Jagr .50 1.25
143 Mike Torchia RC .12 .30
144 Ray Ferraro .10 .25
145 Adam Deadmarsh .10 .25
146 Joe Murphy .10 .25
147 Ron Hextall .15 .40
148 Andrew Cassels .10 .25
149 Martin Brodeur .40 1.00
150 Marek Malik .10 .25
151 Eric Desjardins .12 .30
152 Cory Stillman .10 .25
153 Owen Nolan .15 .40
154 Randy Wood .10 .25
155 Alexei Zhamnov .15 .40
156 John Cullen .10 .25
157 Zdenek Nedved .10 .25
158 Greg Adams .10 .25
159 Kelly Miller .10 .25
160 Alexandre Daigle .10 .25
161 Gord Murphy .10 .25
162 Jeff Friesen .10 .25
163 Scott Stevens .15 .40
164 Denis Chasse .10 .25
165 Cam Neely .15 .40
166 Magnus Svensson RC .12 .30
167 Joe Sakic .30 .75
168 Kevin Brown .12 .30
169 Craig Conroy RC .12 .30
170 Pavel Bure .15 .40
171 Viktor Kozlov .12 .30
172 Pat LaFontaine .15 .40
173 Sergei Gonchar .10 .25
174 Brett Lindros .10 .25
175 Jassen Cullimore .12 .30
176 Mats Sundin .15 .40
177 Zarley Zalapski .10 .25
178 Stephane Richer .12 .30
179 Steve Smith .10 .25
180 Brendan Shanahan .15 .40
181 Brian Leetch .12 .30
182 Ken Wregget .12 .30
183 Jeff Brown .12 .30
184 Darby Hendrickson .10 .25
185 Nikolai Khabibulin .12 .30
186 Glen Wesley .10 .25
187 Andrei Nazarov .12 .30
188 Rod Brind'Amour .15 .40
189 Jim Carey .12 .30
190 Derek Plante .10 .25
191 Valeri Karpov .10 .25
192 Mike Kennedy .12 .30
193 Wendel Clark .25 .60
194 Radek Bonk .10 .25
195 Jozef Stumpel .10 .25
196 Tommy Salo RC .25 .60
197 Michal Pivonka .10 .25
198 Ray Sheppard .12 .30
199 Russ Courtnall .10 .25
200 Todd Marchant .10 .25
201 Geoff Sanderson .10 .25
202 Vincent Damphousse .12 .30
203 Sergei Krivokrasov .10 .25
204 Jesse Belanger .10 .25
205 Al MacInnis .20 .50
206 Philippe DeRouville .12 .30
207 Mike Eastwood .10 .25
208 Travis Green .12 .30
209 Jeff Shantz .10 .25
210 Shane Doan RC .50 1.25
211 Mike Sullivan .12 .30
212 Kevin Dineen .12 .30
213 Pat Falloon .10 .25
214 Rick Tabaracci .12 .30
215 Kelly Hrudey .12 .30
216 Alexei Kovalev .12 .30
217 Matt Johnson .12 .30
218 Turner Stevenson .10 .25
219 Mike Sillinger .10 .25
220 Bobby Holik .10 .25
221 Kevin Stevens .12 .30
222 Dave Lowry .10 .25
223 Martin Gelinas .10 .25
224 Darren Langdon RC .30 .75
225 Tie Domi .12 .30
226 Doug Bodger .10 .25
227 Patrick Flatley .10 .25
228 Anders Myrvold RC .12 .30
229 German Titov .12 .30
230 Pat Peake .10 .25
231 Robert Kron .10 .25
232 Mike Donnelly .10 .25
233 Denis Savard .15 .40
234 Mathieu Dandenault RC .30 .75
235 Joe Dziedzic .10 .25
236 Valeri Kamensky .12 .30
237 Joaquin Gage RC .12 .30
238 Geoff Courtnall .10 .25
239 Arturs Irbe .12 .30
240 Dan Quinn .12 .30
241 J.C. Bergeron .12 .30
242 Brian Noonan .10 .25
243 Ulf Samuelsson .10 .25
244 Jeff O'Neill .15 .40
245 Sandy Moger RC .10 .25
246 Don Beaupre .12 .30
247 Bob Probert .15 .40
248 Mattias Norstrom .12 .30
249 Jason Bonsignore .10 .25
250 Mike Ridley .10 .25
251 Joe Mullen .12 .30
252 Petr Nedved .12 .30
253 Jason Doig .15 .40
254 Olaf Kolzig .15 .40
255 Mark Tinordi .10 .25
256 Roman Hamrlik .10 .25
257 Denis Pederson .10 .25
258 Paul Ysebaert .10 .25
259 Neal Broten .12 .30
260 Jason Woolley .10 .25
261 Teppo Numminen .10 .25
262 Scott Thornton .12 .30
263 Ted Donato .10 .25
264 Marcus Ragnarsson RC .20 .50
265 Dimitri Khristich .10 .25
266 Mike Peca .12 .30
267 Dominic Roussel .10 .25
268 Owen Nolan .15 .40
269 Patrick Poulin .10 .25
270 Mario Lemieux .60 1.50
271 Mark Messier .30 .75
272 Slava Fetisov .12 .30
273 Andrei Trefilov .10 .25
274 Damian Rhodes .12 .30
275 Alexander Mogilny .12 .30
276 Ray Sheppard .12 .30
277 Radek Dvorak RC .20 .50
278 Steve Duchesne .10 .25
279 Jason Smith .12 .30
280 Wade Flaherty RC .12 .30
281 Lyle Odelein .10 .25
282 Keith Jones .12 .30
283 Saku Koivu .15 .40
284 Marty Murray .15 .40
285 Sergei Fedorov .25 .60
286 Brian Rolston .12 .30

287 Dave Roche RC .12 .30
288 Sylvain Lefebvre .10 .25
289 Theo Fleury .20 .50
290 Andy Moog .15 .40
291 Tom Barrasso .12 .30
292 Craig Mills RC .10 .25
293 Mike Gartner .20 .50
294 Stefan Ustorf .10 .25
295 Darren Turcotte .10 .25
296 Steve Konowalchuk .12 .30
297 Ray Ferraro .10 .25
298 Brian Holzinger RC .30 .75
299 Daniel Alfredsson RC .75 2.00
300 Derek King .12 .30
301 Mark Fitzpatrick .12 .30
302 Joe Sacco .10 .25
303 Scott Walker RC .10 .25
304 Ricard Persson RC .12 .30
305 Mike Rathje .12 .30
306 Petr Svoboda .10 .25
307 Roman Vopat RC .10 .25
308 Ray Whitney .12 .30
309 Calle Johansson .10 .25
310 Grant Fuhr .25 .60
311 John Tucker .10 .25
312 Anatoli Semenov .12 .30
313 Darren McCarty .12 .30
314 Stephane Quintal .12 .30
315 Jason Dawe .10 .25
316 Zigmund Palffy .15 .40
317 Dave Manson .10 .25
318 Vitali Yachmenev .10 .25
319 Chris Pronger .15 .40
320 Valeri Zelepukin .10 .25
321 Ryan Smyth .12 .30
322 Johan Garpenlov .10 .25
323 Bill Ranford .12 .30
324 Daymond Langkow RC .15 .40
325 Aki Berg RC .15 .40
326 Derian Hatcher .12 .30
327 Bryan Smolinski .10 .25
328 Michel Picard .12 .30
329 Alek Stojanov .10 .25
330 Trent Klatt .10 .25
331 Richard Park .15 .40
332 Jere Lehtinen .12 .30
333 Bryan McCabe .15 .40
334 Kyle McLaren RC .10 .25
335 Todd Krygier .10 .25
336 Adam Creighton .10 .25
337 Jamie Pushor .12 .30
338 Patrick Roy .40 1.00
339 Milos Holan .10 .25
340 Dave Ellett .10 .25
341 Brian Bellows .12 .30
342 Jamie Rivers .10 .25
343 Claude Lemieux .15 .40
344 Leif Rohlin RC .12 .30
345 Eric Daze .30 .75
346 Todd Bertuzzi RC .20 .50
347 Antti Tormanen RC .10 .25
348 Luc Robitaille .15 .40
349 Tim Taylor .10 .25
350 Stephane Yelle RC .12 .30
351 Marko Kiprusoff .12 .30
352 Igor Korolev .10 .25
353 Scott Lachance .10 .25
354 Marty McSorley .12 .30
355 Joel Otto .10 .25
356 Josef Beranek .10 .25
357 Sergei Zubov .12 .30
358 Rhett Warrener RC .10 .25
359 Jimmy Carson .12 .30
360 Zdeno Ciger .12 .30
361 Brendan Witt .15 .40
362 Byron Dafoe .12 .30
363 Steve Thomas .12 .30
364 Deron Quint .12 .30
365 Nelson Emerson .10 .25
366 Larry Murphy .12 .30
367 Benoit Brunet .10 .25
368 Kjell Samuelsson .10 .25
369 Aaron Gavey .10 .25
370 Robert Svehla RC .10 .25
371 Rene Corbet .10 .25
372 Gary Roberts .10 .25
373 Shawn McEachern .10 .25
374 Andrei Kovalenko .10 .25
375 Yanic Perreault .10 .25
376 Shayne Corson .12 .30
377 Brendan Shanahan .15 .40
378 Sergei Nemchinov .12 .30
379 Chad Kilger RC .15 .40
380 Sergio Momesso .10 .25
381 Craig Billington .12 .30
382 Niklas Sundstrom .15 .40
383 Matthew Barnaby .15 .40
384 Dale Hawerchuk .20 .50
385 Trevor Linden .15 .40
386 Adam Oates .15 .40
387 Dimitri Yushkevich .10 .25
388 Todd Elik .10 .25
389 Wendel Clark .25 .60
390 Stephane Fiset .12 .30
NNO Checklist Card 1 .07 .20
NNO Checklist Card 2 .07 .20
NNO Checklist Card 3 .07 .20
NNO Checklist Card 4 .07 .20
NNO Checklist Card 5 .07 .20
NNO Checklist Card 6 .07 .20
NNO Checklist Card 7 .07 .20
NNO Checklist Card 8 .07 .20

1995-96 Donruss Between the Pipes

COMPLETE SET (10) 25.00 60.00
COMPLETE SERIES 1 (5) 12.00 30.00
COMPLETE SERIES 2 (5) 12.00 30.00
1 Blaine Lacher 2.00 5.00
2 Dominik Hasek 4.00 10.00
3 Mike Vernon 2.00 5.00
4 Trevor Kidd 2.00 5.00
5 Martin Brodeur 5.00 12.00
6 Jim Carey 2.00 5.00
7 Patrick Roy 10.00 25.00
8 Sean Burke 2.00 5.00
9 Felix Potvin 3.00 8.00
10 Ed Belfour 3.00 8.00

1995-96 Donruss Canadian World Junior Team

COMPLETE SET (22) 5.00 12.00
COMP.SERIES 1 (11) 2.00 5.00
COMP.SERIES 2 (11) 3.00 8.00
1 Jamie Storr .60 1.50
2 Dan Cloutier .20 .50
3 Nolan Baumgartner .20 .50
4 Chad Allen .20 .50
5 Wade Redden .20 .50
6 Ed Jovanovski .60 1.50
7 Jamie Rivers .20 .50
8 Bryan McCabe .60 1.50
9 Lee Sorochan .20 .50
10 Marty Murray .20 .50
11 Larry Courville .20 .50
12 Jason Allison .20 .50
13 Darcy Tucker .20 .50
14 Jeff O'Neill .20 .50
15 Eric Daze .60 1.50
16 Alexandre Daigle .20 .50
17 Todd Harvey .60 1.50
18 Jason Botterill .20 .50
19 Shean Donovan .20 .50
20 Denis Pederson .20 .50
21 Jeff Friesen .20 .50
22 Ryan Smyth .40 1.00

1995-96 Donruss Dominators

COMPLETE SET (8) 20.00 50.00
1 Forsberg/Lindros/Lemieux 6.00 15.00
2 LeClair/Renberg/Jagr 5.00 12.00
3 Zubov/Bourque/Leetch 2.00 5.00
4 Carey/Brodeur/Hasek 5.00 12.00
5 Gilmour/Gretzky/Fedorov 6.00 15.00
6 Hull/Kariya/Bure 2.50 6.00
7 Coffey/Chelios/MacInnis 2.00 5.00
8 Potvin/Belfour/Kidd 5.00 12.00

1995-96 Donruss Elite Inserts

COMPLETE SET (10) 25.00 50.00
1 Alexei Zhamnov .60 1.50
2 Joe Sakic 2.50 6.00
3 Mikael Renberg .60 1.50
4 Sergei Fedorov 1.50 4.00
5 Paul Coffey 1.25 3.00
6 Paul Kariya 1.25 3.00
7 Wayne Gretzky 8.00 20.00
8 Eric Lindros 1.25 3.00
9 Mario Lemieux 6.00 15.00
10 Jaromir Jagr 2.00 5.00

1995-96 Donruss Igniters

COMPLETE SET (10) 15.00 30.00
1 Adam Oates 1.25 3.00
2 Paul Coffey 1.50 4.00
3 Doug Gilmour 1.25 3.00
4 Pierre Turgeon 1.25 3.00
5 Mark Messier 1.50 4.00
6 Alexei Zhamnov 1.25 3.00
7 Jeremy Roenick 2.00 5.00
8 Steve Yzerman 6.00 15.00
9 Joe Nieuwendyk 1.25 3.00
10 Ron Francis 1.25 3.00

1995-96 Donruss Marksmen

COMPLETE SET (8) 6.00 12.00
1 Peter Bondra .75 2.00
2 Owen Nolan .75 2.00
3 Eric Lindros .75 2.00
4 Ray Sheppard .75 2.00
5 Jaromir Jagr 1.25 3.00
6 Theo Fleury .75 2.00
7 Brett Hull 1.00 2.50
8 Brendan Shanahan .75 2.00

1995-96 Donruss Pro Pointers

COMPLETE SET (20) 3.00 6.00
1 Jeremy Roenick .12 .30
2 Pat LaFontaine .15 .40
3 Jason Bonsignore .02 .10
4 Chris Chelios .15 .40
5 Brian Leetch .07 .20
6 Brett Hull .12 .30
7 Keith Tkachuk .15 .40
8 Mike Modano .25 .60
9 Brian Rolston .02 .10
10 Darren Turcotte .02 .10
11 Jeff Friesen .02 .10
12 Theo Fleury .02 .10
13 Eric Lindros .15 .40
14 Mario Lemieux .75 2.00
15 Jamie Storr .07 .20
16 Trevor Kidd .07 .20
17 Chris Pronger .15 .40
18 Brendan Witt .02 .10
19 Paul Kariya .15 .40
20 Todd Harvey .07 .20

1995-96 Donruss Rated Rookies

COMPLETE SET (16) 15.00 40.00
1 Saku Koivu 4.00 10.00
2 Todd Bertuzzi 2.00 5.00
3 Niklas Sundstrom .75 2.00
4 Jeff O'Neill .75 2.00
5 Zdenek Nedved .75 2.00
6 Eric Daze .75 2.00
7 Chad Kilger .75 2.00
8 Shane Doan .75 2.00
9 Vitali Yachmenev .75 2.00
10 Radek Dvorak .75 2.00
11 Marty Murray .75 2.00
12 Cory Stillman .75 2.00
13 Marcus Ragnarsson .75 2.00
14 Daniel Alfredsson 2.00 5.00
15 Antti Tormanen .75 2.00
16 Petr Sykora 1.50 4.00

1995-96 Donruss Rookie Team

COMPLETE SET (9) 3.00 6.00
1 Jim Carey .20 .50
2 Peter Forsberg 1.00 2.50
3 Paul Kariya .40 1.00
4 David Oliver .10 .30
5 Blaine Lacher .20 .50
6 Oleg Tverdovsky .10 .30
7 Jeff Friesen .10 .30
8 Todd Marchant .10 .30
9 Todd Harvey .20 .50

1996-97 Donruss

1 Joe Sakic .40 1.00
2 Jeremy Roenick .30 .75
3 Kirk McLean .15 .40
4 Zarley Zalapski .12 .30
5 Jyrki Lumme .12 .30
6 Owen Nolan .20 .50
7 Luc Robitaille .20 .50
8 Bob Probert .20 .50
9 Ken Baumgartner .12 .30
10 Rick Tabaracci .15 .40
11 Alexei Zhitnik .12 .30
12 Al MacInnis .25 .60
13 Brian Leetch .15 .40
14 Valeri Kamensky .15 .40
15 Todd Gill .15 .40
16 Mark Messier .40 1.00
17 Pierre Turgeon .15 .40
18 Mathieu Schneider .12 .30
19 Vyacheslav Kozlov .12 .30
20 Milos Holan .12 .30
21 Yanic Perreault .12 .30
22 Mike Modano .30 .75
23 Claude Lemieux .12 .30
24 Rob Niedermayer .15 .40
25 Eric Desjardins .15 .40
26 Alexander Semak .12 .30
27 Mark Recchi .25 .60
28 Slava Fetisov .12 .30
29 Kevin Hatcher .12 .30
30 Mats Sundin .20 .50
31 Jeff Reese .12 .30
32 Alexander Selivanov .12 .30
33 Jim Carey .20 .50
34 Daren Puppa .15 .40
35 Vincent Damphousse .15 .40
36 John LeClair .20 .50
37 Jon Casey .15 .40
38 Chris Terreri .15 .40
39 Larry Murphy .15 .40
40 Geoff Sanderson .15 .40
41 Adam Oates .20 .50
42 Sandy McCarthy .12 .30
43 Jaromir Jagr .60 1.50
44 Roman Oksiuta .12 .30
45 Zigmund Palffy .20 .50
46 Doug Gilmour .25 .60
47 Cliff Ronning .12 .30
48 Curtis Leschyshyn .12 .30
49 Scott Mellanby .15 .40
50 Sergei Fedorov .30 .75
51 Denis Savard .20 .50
52 Mike Vernon .15 .40
53 Todd Marchant .12 .30
54 Geoff Courtnall .12 .30
55 Shayne Corson .15 .40
56 Dimitri Khristich .12 .30
57 Scott Stevens .20 .50
58 German Titov .12 .30
59 Darren Turcotte .12 .30
60 Michal Pivonka .12 .30
61 Ron Hextall .20 .50
62 Ed Belfour .20 .50
63 Chris Pronger .20 .50
64 Brian Bellows .15 .40
65 Pavel Bure .20 .50
66 Adam Graves .12 .30
67 Tom Barrasso .15 .40
68 Stu Barnes .12 .30
69 Norm MacIver .12 .30
70 Jesse Belanger .12 .30
71 Chris Chelios .20 .50
72 Tommy Soderstrom .15 .40
73 Nelson Emerson .12 .30
74 Kenny Jonsson .12 .30
75 Bill Lindsay .12 .30
76 Petr Nedved .15 .40
77 Robert Svehla .12 .30
78 Tomas Sandstrom .12 .30
79 Jeff Friesen .12 .30
80 Tony Amonte .15 .40
81 Sylvain Lefebvre .12 .30
82 Greg Adams .12 .30
83 Vladimir Konstantinov .15 .40
84 Roman Hamrlik .12 .30
85 Doug Weight .20 .50
86 Shaun Van Allen .12 .30
87 Bill Ranford .15 .40
88 Jeff Hackett .12 .30
89 Alexei Zhamnov .15 .40
90 Dale Hawerchuk .25 .60
91 Sergei Zubov .12 .30
92 Dan Quinn .12 .30
93 Wayne Gretzky 1.25 3.00
94 Todd Harvey .12 .30
95 Chris Osgood .20 .50
96 Felix Potvin .30 .75
97 Richard Matvichuk .12 .30
98 Wendel Clark .30 .75
99 Bryan Smolinski .12 .30
100 Rob Blake .12 .30
101 Jocelyn Thibault .20 .50
102 Trevor Linden .20 .50
103 Craig MacTavish .12 .30
104 Sandis Ozolinsh .12 .30
105 Oleg Tverdovsky .12 .30
106 Garry Galley .12 .30
107 Derek Plante .12 .30
108 Stephane Richer .15 .40
109 Dave Andreychuk .20 .50
110 Curtis Joseph .25 .60
111 Greg Johnson .12 .30
112 Patrick Roy .50 1.25
113 Pat LaFontaine .20 .50
114 Uwe Krupp .12 .30
115 Ulf Dahlen .12 .30
116 Brian Bradley .12 .30
117 Grant Fuhr .30 .75
118 Brian Skrudland .12 .30
119 Nicklas Lidstrom .25 .60
120 Steve Chiasson .12 .30
121 Sean Burke .12 .30
122 Rick Tocchet .15 .40
123 Martin Rucinsky .12 .30
124 Alexei Yashin .15 .40
125 Mikael Renberg .15 .40
126 Teppo Numminen .12 .30
127 Randy Burridge .12 .30
128 Radek Bonk .12 .30
129 Scott Young .12 .30
130 Gary Suter .12 .30
131 Mario Lemieux .75 2.00
132 Ray Bourque .30 .75
133 Martin Gelinas .12 .30
134 Keith Tkachuk .20 .50
135 Benoit Hogue .12 .30
136 Ken Wregget .15 .40
137 Eric Lindros .30 .75
138 Keith Primeau .15 .40
139 Peter Forsberg .40 1.00
140 Paul Coffey .20 .50
141 Mike Ridley .12 .30
142 Paul Kariya .20 .50
143 Jason Arnott .15 .40
144 Joe Murphy .12 .30
145 Adam Deadmarsh .12 .30
146 John MacLean .15 .40
147 Peter Bondra .20 .50
148 Martin Brodeur .50 1.25
149 Ron Francis .25 .60
150 Dino Ciccarelli .20 .50
151 Joe Juneau .12 .30
152 Matthew Barnaby .12 .30
153 Mark Tinordi .12 .30
154 Craig Janney .12 .30
155 Rod Brind'Amour .20 .50
156 Damian Rhodes .15 .40
157 Teemu Selanne .40 1.00
158 James Patrick .12 .30
159 Theo Fleury .40 1.00
160 Trevor Kidd .20 .50
161 Kirk Muller .12 .30
162 Andrew Cassels .12 .30
163 Brent Fedyk .12 .30
164 Guy Hebert .15 .40
165 Jason Dawe .12 .30
166 Andy Moog .20 .50
167 Igor Larionov .20 .50
168 Brian Savage .12 .30
169 Kris Draper .12 .30
170 Dave Gagner .20 .50
171 Steve Yzerman .50 1.25
172 Nikolai Khabibulin .15 .40
173 Chris Gratton .15 .40
174 Dave Lowry .12 .30
175 Travis Green .12 .30
176 Alexei Kovalev .15 .40
177 Mike Ricci .15 .40
178 Brendan Shanahan .20 .50
179 Corey Hirsch .12 .30
180 Bill Guerin .20 .50
181 Alexander Mogilny .15 .40
182 Steve Duchesne .12 .30
183 Ray Ferraro .12 .30
184 Mike Richter .20 .50
185 Yuri Khmylev .12 .30
186 Stephane Fiset .15 .40
187 John Vanbiesbrouck .20 .50
188 Scott Niedermayer .20 .50
189 Brad May .12 .30
190 Shawn McEachern .12 .30
191 Joe Mullen .15 .40
192 Dominik Hasek .30 .75
193 Steve Thomas .12 .30
194 Russ Courtnall .12 .30
195 Joe Nieuwendyk .15 .40
196 Petr Klima .12 .30
197 Brett Hull .40 1.00
198 Bernie Nicholls .12 .30
199 Dale Hunter .15 .40
200 Pat Verbeek .12 .30
201 Phil Housley .15 .40
202 Todd Krygier .12 .30
203 Zdeno Ciger .12 .30
204 Alexandre Daigle .12 .30
205 Cam Neely .20 .50
206 Mike Gartner .25 .60
207 Garth Snow .15 .40
208 Pat Falloon .12 .30
209 Kelly Hrudey .15 .40
210 Ray Sheppard .15 .40
211 Ted Donato .12 .30
212 Glenn Healy .15 .40
213 Radek Dvorak .15 .40
214 Niclas Andersson .12 .30
215 Miroslav Satan .12 .30
216 Roman Vopat .12 .30
217 Bryan McCabe .12 .30
218 Jamie Langenbrunner .12 .30
219 Kyle McLaren .12 .30
220 Stephane Yelle .12 .30
221 Byron Dafoe .15 .40
222 Grant Marshall .12 .30
223 Ryan Smyth .15 .40
224 Ville Peltonen .12 .30
225 Deron Quint .12 .30
226 Brian Holzinger .15 .40
227 Jose Theodore .25 .60
228 Ethan Moreau RC .20 .50
229 Steve Sullivan RC .15 .40
230 Kevin Hodson RC .12 .30
231 Cory Stillman .12 .30
232 Ralph Intranuovo .12 .30
233 Vitali Yachmenev .12 .30
234 Marcus Ragnarsson .12 .30
235 Nolan Baumgartner .12 .30
236 Chad Kilger .12 .30
237 Niklas Sundstrom .12 .30
238 Paul Coffey CL (1-120) .20 .50
239 Doug Gilmour CL (121-240) .25 .60
240 Steve Yzerman CL .50 1.25

1996-97 Donruss Press Proofs

*SINGLES: 4X TO 10X BASIC CARDS

1996-97 Donruss Between the Pipes

COMPLETE SET (10) 20.00 50.00
1 Patrick Roy 5.00 12.00
2 Martin Brodeur 3.00 8.00
3 Jim Carey 1.50 4.00
4 John Vanbiesbrouck 2.00 5.00
5 Chris Osgood 2.50 6.00
6 Ed Belfour 2.50 6.00
7 Jocelyn Thibault 2.00 5.00
8 Curtis Joseph 2.50 6.00
9 Nikolai Khabibulin 2.00 5.00
10 Felix Potvin 4.00 10.00

1996-97 Donruss Dominators

COMPLETE SET (10) 20.00 40.00
1 Carey/Brodeur/Beezer 1.50 4.00
2 Khabib./Osgood/Thibault 1.50 4.00
3 Chelios/Coffey/Bourque 2.00 5.00
4 Lemieux/Jagr/Francis 4.00 10.00
5 Lindros/Gretzky/Arnott 4.00 10.00
6 Gilmour/Clark/Turgeon 1.50 4.00
7 Mogilny/Bure/Linden 1.50 4.00
8 Kariya/Selanne/Tkachuk 1.50 4.00
9 Modano/Roenick/Fedorov 1.50 4.00
10 Daze/Koivu/Jovanovski 1.50 4.00

1996-97 Donruss Elite Inserts

COMPLETE SET (10) 15.00 40.00
*GOLD: 1.2X TO 3X BASIC INSERTS
1 Pavel Bure 1.25 3.00
2 Wayne Gretzky 8.00 20.00
3 Doug Weight 1.25 3.00
4 Brett Hull 2.00 5.00
5 Mark Messier 1.25 3.00
6 Brendan Shanahan 1.25 3.00
7 Joe Sakic 2.50 6.00
8 Sergei Fedorov 1.50 4.00
9 Eric Lindros 1.25 3.00
10 Patrick Roy 6.00 15.00

1996-97 Donruss Go Top Shelf

COMPLETE SET (10) 20.00 50.00
1 Mario Lemieux 8.00 20.00
2 Teemu Selanne 2.00 5.00
3 Joe Sakic 4.00 10.00
4 Alexander Mogilny 1.25 3.00
5 Jaromir Jagr 3.00 8.00
6 Brett Hull 2.50 6.00
7 Mike Modano 2.50 6.00
8 Paul Kariya 2.00 5.00
9 Eric Lindros 2.00 5.00
10 Peter Forsberg 3.00 8.00

1996-97 Donruss Hit List

COMPLETE SET (20) 10.00 25.00
1 Eric Lindros .75 2.00
2 Wendel Clark .40 1.00
3 Ed Jovanovski .20 .50
4 Jeremy Roenick 1.50 4.00
5 Doug Weight .40 1.00
6 Chris Chelios .75 2.00
7 Brendan Shanahan .75 2.00
8 Mark Messier 1.25 3.00
9 Scott Stevens .20 .50
10 Keith Tkachuk .60 1.50
11 Trevor Linden .60 1.50
12 Eric Daze .20 .50
13 John LeClair .60 1.50
14 Peter Forsberg 2.00 5.00
15 Doug Gilmour .60 1.50
16 Roman Hamrlik .20 .50
17 Owen Nolan .20 .50
18 Claude Lemieux .20 .50
19 Saku Koivu .75 2.00
20 Theo Fleury .20 .50
P1 Eric Lindros PROMO .40 1.00

1996-97 Donruss Rated Rookies

COMPLETE SET (10) 8.00 20.00
*PRESS PROOF: 4X TO 10X BASIC INSERTS
1 Eric Daze .75 2.00
2 Petr Sykora .75 2.00
3 Valeri Bure .75 2.00
4 Jere Lehtinen .75 2.00
5 Jeff O'Neill .75 2.00
6 Saku Koivu 1.50 4.00
7 Ed Jovanovski .75 2.00
8 Eric Fichaud .75 2.00
9 Todd Bertuzzi 1.50 4.00
10 Daniel Alfredsson 1.50 4.00

1997-98 Donruss

1 Peter Forsberg .30 .75
2 Steve Yzerman .40 1.00
3 Eric Lindros .25 .60
4 Mark Messier .30 .75
5 Patrick Roy .40 1.00
6 Jeremy Roenick .25 .60
7 Paul Kariya .15 .40
8 Valeri Bure .10 .25
9 Dominik Hasek .25 .60
10 Doug Gilmour .20 .50
11 Garth Snow .12 .30
12 Todd Bertuzzi .15 .40
13 Chris Osgood .15 .40
14 Jarome Iginla .20 .50
15 Lonny Bohonos .12 .30
16 Jeff O'Neill .12 .30
17 Daniel Alfredsson .15 .40
18 Daymond Langkow .10 .25
19 Alexei Yashin .12 .30
20 Byron Dafoe .12 .30
21 Mike Peca .12 .30
22 Jim Carey .10 .25
23 Pat Verbeek .12 .30
24 Terry Ryan .10 .25
25 Adam Oates .10 .25
26 Kevin Hatcher .10 .25
27 Ken Wregget .10 .25
28 Pierre Turgeon .10 .25
29 John LeClair .15 .40
30 Jere Lehtinen .12 .30
31 Jamie Storr .12 .30
32 Doug Weight .15 .40
33 Tommy Salo .10 .25
34 Bernie Nicholls .12 .30
35 Jocelyn Thibault .12 .30
36 Dale Hawerchuk .20 .50
37 Chris Chelios .15 .40
38 Kirk Muller .10 .25
39 Steve Sullivan .12 .30
40 Andy Moog .15 .40
41 Martin Gelinas .10 .25
42 Shayne Corson .12 .30
43 Curtis Joseph .20 .50
44 Donald Audette .12 .30
45 Rick Tocchet .10 .25
46 Craig Janney .10 .25
47 Geoff Courtnall .10 .25
48 Wade Redden .10 .25
49 Steve Rucchin .12 .30
50 Ethan Moreau .10 .25
51 Steve Shields RC .10 .25
52 Jamie Pushor .10 .25
53 Saku Koivu .15 .40
54 Oleg Tverdovsky .12 .30
55 Jeff Friesen .12 .30
56 Chris Gratton .10 .25
57 Wendel Clark .25 .60
58 John Vanbiesbrouck .12 .30
59 Trevor Kidd .10 .25
60 Sandis Ozolinsh .10 .25
61 Dave Andreychuk .12 .30
62 Travis Green .12 .30
63 Paul Coffey .15 .40
64 Roman Turek .12 .30
65 Vladimir Konstantinov .10 .25
66 Ray Bourque .25 .60
67 Wayne Primeau .12 .30
68 Todd Harvey .12 .30
69 Derek King .12 .30
70 Adam Graves .12 .30
71 Brett Hull .30 .75
72 Scott Niedermayer .15 .40
73 Mike Vernon .12 .30
74 Brian Holzinger .12 .30
75 Dainius Zubrus .12 .30
76 Patrick Lalime .12 .30
77 Corey Schwab .12 .30
78 Alexandre Daigle .10 .25
79 Geoff Sanderson .12 .30
80 Dave Gagner .10 .25
81 Jose Theodore .15 .40
82 Sergei Fedorov .25 .60
83 Keith Tkachuk .15 .40
84 Owen Nolan .12 .30
85 Brandon Convery .10 .25
86 Trevor Linden .15 .40
87 Landon Wilson .10 .25
88 Claude Lemieux .12 .30
89 Dimitri Khristich .12 .30
90 Luc Robitaille .15 .40
91 Todd Warriner .12 .30
92 Kelly Hrudey .15 .40
93 Mike Dunham .12 .30
94 Mike Grier .12 .30
95 Joe Juneau .12 .30
96 Alexei Zhamnov .12 .30
97 Jamie Langenbrunner .12 .30
98 Sean Pronger .10 .25
99 Janne Niinimaa .12 .30
100 Chris Pronger .12 .30
101 Ray Sheppard .12 .30
102 Tony Amonte .12 .30
103 Ron Tugnutt .12 .30
104 Mike Modano .25 .60
105 Dan Trebil .12 .30
106 Alexander Mogilny .12 .30
107 Darren McCarty .12 .30
108 Ted Donato .10 .25
109 Brian Savage .10 .25
110 Mike Gartner .20 .50
111 Jim Campbell .10 .25
112 Roman Hamrlik .10 .25
113 Andreas Dackell .12 .30
114 Ron Hextall .15 .40
115 Steve Washburn .12 .30
116 Jeff Hackett .10 .25
117 Joe Sakic .30 .75
118 Anson Carter .10 .25
119 Vyacheslav Kozlov .12 .30
120 Nikolai Khabibulin .15 .40
121 Tony Granato .10 .25
122 Al MacInnis .12 .30
123 Daren Puppa .12 .30
124 Mike Richter .15 .40
125 Zigmund Palffy .12 .30
126 Martin Brodeur .40 1.00
127 Rem Murray .10 .25
128 Sean Burke .12 .30
129 Aki Berg .10 .25
130 Dimitri Mironov .10 .25
131 Jamie Allison .12 .30
132 Valeri Kamensky .12 .30
133 Pat LaFontaine .15 .40
134 Jozef Stumpel .12 .30
135 Peter Bondra .15 .40
136 Mark Recchi .20 .50
137 Ron Francis .20 .50
138 Harry York .12 .30
139 Mats Sundin .20 .50
140 Bobby Holik .12 .30
141 Eric Desjardins .10 .25
142 Scott Lachance .12 .30
143 Wayne Gretzky 1.00 2.50
144 Ed Jovanovski .10 .25
145 Jason Arnott .10 .25
146 Andrew Cassels .12 .30
147 Roman Vopat .12 .30
148 Dwayne Roloson .12 .30
149 Derek Plante .12 .30
150 Phil Housley .12 .30
151 Mikael Renberg .12 .30
152 Petr Nedved .12 .30
153 Grant Fuhr .15 .40
154 Felix Potvin .25 .60
155 John MacLean .12 .30
156 Brian Leetch .15 .40
157 Rod Brind'Amour .15 .40
158 Ryan Smyth .12 .30
159 Teemu Selanne .30 .75
160 Theo Fleury .12 .30
161 Adam Deadmarsh .10 .25
162 Corey Hirsch .12 .30
163 Bryan Berard .10 .25
164 Ed Belfour .12 .30
165 Sergei Berezin .12 .30
166 Damian Rhodes .12 .30
167 Guy Hebert .12 .30
168 Derian Hatcher .12 .30
169 Jonas Hoglund .12 .30
170 Matthew Barnaby .10 .25
171 Scott Mellanby .12 .30
172 Bill Ranford .12 .30
173 Vincent Damphousse .12 .30
174 Anders Eriksson .12 .30
175 Chad Kilger .12 .30
176 Darren Turcotte .12 .30
177 Dino Ciccarelli .15 .40
178 Niklas Sundstrom .12 .30
179 Stephane Fiset .12 .30
180 Mike Ricci .10 .25
181 Brendan Shanahan .15 .40
182 Darcy Tucker .15 .40
183 Eric Fichaud .15 .40
184 Todd Marchant .12 .30
185 Keith Primeau .12 .30
186 Joe Nieuwendyk .12 .30
187 Pavel Bure .15 .40
188 Jaromir Jagr .50 1.25
189 Kirk McLean .12 .30
190 Daniel Goneau .12 .30
191 Rob Niedermayer .10 .25
192 Eric Daze .10 .25
193 Richard Matvichuk .12 .30
194 Scott Stevens .15 .40
195 Dale Hunter .12 .30
196 Hnat Domenichelli .12 .30
197 Philippe DeRouville .12 .30
198 Marcel Cousineau .12 .30
199 Kevin Hodson .12 .30
200 Jean-Sebastien Giguere .15 .40
201 Paxton Schafer RC .10 .25
202 Marc Denis .15 .40
203 Frank Banham RC .12 .30
204 Vadim Sharifijanov .12 .30
205 Paul Healey RC .12 .30
206 D.J. Smith RC .15 .40
207 Christian Matte RC .15 .40
208 Sean Brown RC .15 .40
209 Tomas Vokoun RC .15 .40
210 Vladimir Vorobiev RC .15 .40
211 Jean-Yves Leroux RC .15 .40
212 Domenic Pittis RC .15 .40
213 Derek Wilkinson RC .15 .40
214 Jason Holland .15 .40
215 Pascal Rheaume RC .12 .30
216 Steve Kelly .12 .30
217 Vaclav Varada .10 .25
218 Mike Fountain .12 .30
219 Vaclav Prospal RC .12 .30
220 Jaroslav Svejkovsky .12 .30
221 Marty Murray .12 .30
222 Wade Belak RC .15 .40
223 Jamal Mayers RC .15 .40
224 Shayne Toporowski RC .15 .40
225 Mike Knuble RC .15 .40
226 Jarome Iginla CL (1-60) .20 .50
227 Keith Tkachuk CL (61-120) .15 .40
228 Adam Oates CL (121-180) .15 .40
229 John LeClair CL (181-230) .15 .40
230 Brian Leetch CL (inserts) .12 .30

1997-98 Donruss Press Proofs Silver

*VETS: 8X TO 20X BASIC CARDS
*ROOKIES: 4X TO 10X BASIC CARDS

1997-98 Donruss Press Proofs Gold

*VETS: 15X TO 40X BASIC CARDS
*ROOKIES: 8X TO 20X BASIC CARDS

1997-98 Donruss Between the Pipes

1 Patrick Roy 4.00 10.00
2 Martin Brodeur 4.00 10.00
3 John Vanbiesbrouck 1.50 4.00
4 Dominik Hasek 2.50 6.00
5 Chris Osgood 1.50 4.00
6 Jose Theodore 1.50 4.00
7 Garth Snow 1.25 3.00
8 Curtis Joseph 2.00 5.00
9 Felix Potvin 2.50 6.00
10 Jocelyn Thibault 1.25 3.00

1997-98 Donruss Elite Inserts

COMPLETE SET (12) 20.00 50.00
1 Wayne Gretzky 8.00 20.00
2 Jaromir Jagr 2.00 5.00
3 Eric Lindros 1.25 3.00
4 Paul Kariya 1.25 3.00
5 Patrick Roy 6.00 15.00
6 Steve Yzerman 5.00 12.00
7 Peter Forsberg 3.00 8.00
8 John Vanbiesbrouck .75 2.00
9 Brendan Shanahan 1.25 3.00
10 Martin Brodeur 3.00 8.00
11 Dominik Hasek 2.50 6.00
12 Teemu Selanne 1.25 3.00
13P Martin Brodeur PROMO 2.00 5.00

1997-98 Donruss Line 2 Line

COMPLETE SET (24) 100.00 200.00
*RED DIE CUT: 2X TO 5X BASIC RED
*BLUE DIE CUT: 1.2X TO 3X BASIC BLUE
*GOLD DIE CUT: 1X TO 2.5X BASIC GOLD
*PROMO: 2X TO 5X BASIC INSERTS
1 Wayne Gretzky G 12.00 30.00
2 Teemu Selanne R 2.00 5.00
3 Brian Leetch B 4.00 10.00
4 Peter Forsberg R 3.00 8.00
5 Steve Yzerman R 8.00 20.00
6 Oleg Tverdovsky B 1.25 3.00
7 Doug Gilmour R 1.50 4.00
8 Eric Lindros G 3.00 8.00
9 Bryan Berard B 2.50 6.00
10 Brendan Shanahan R 1.50 4.00
11 Pavel Bure R 3.00 8.00
12 Joe Sakic R 6.00 15.00
13 Chris Chelios B 3.00 8.00
14 Mike Modano R 5.00 12.00
15 Paul Coffey B 5.00 12.00
16 Jaromir Jagr G 8.00 20.00
17 Jarome Iginla R 5.00 12.00
18 Brett Hull R 4.00 10.00
19 Wade Redden B 2.50 6.00
20 Paul Kariya G 8.00 20.00
21 Ray Bourque B 7.50 15.00
22 Ryan Smyth R 1.50 4.00
23 Mark Messier R 3.00 8.00
24 Sandis Ozolinsh B 1.25 3.00

1997-98 Donruss Rated Rookies

COMPLETE SET (10) 6.00 15.00
*MEDALIST: 1.5X TO 4X BASIC INSERTS

1 Tomas Vokoun 2.00 5.00
2 Paxton Schafer .40 1.00
3 Vaclav Prospal .75 2.00
4 Marc Denis .75 2.00
5 Domenic Pittis .40 1.00
6 Christian Matte .40 1.00
7 Marcel Cousineau .40 1.00
8 Steve Kelly .40 1.00
9 Jaroslav Svejkovsky .40 1.00
10 Jean-Sebastien Giguere 2.00 5.00

1997-98 Donruss Red Alert

COMPLETE SET (10) 30.00 80.00
1 Adam Deadmarsh 2.00 5.00
2 Ryan Smyth 4.00 10.00
3 Sergei Fedorov 6.00 15.00
4 Keith Tkachuk 4.00 10.00
5 Brett Hull 6.00 15.00
6 Pavel Bure 6.00 15.00
7 John LeClair 2.00 5.00
8 Zigmund Palffy 4.00 10.00
9 Mats Sundin 4.00 10.00
10 Peter Bondra 4.00 10.00

2010-11 Donruss

*RR GHOSTED BOX: .4X TO 1X
1 Teemu Selanne .40 1.00
2 Milan Lucic .20 .50
3 Zach Boychuk .15 .40
4 Robyn Regehr .12 .30
5 Derick Brassard .12 .30
6 Craig Anderson .20 .50
7 Shawn Horcoff .12 .30
8 Wayne Simmonds .25 .60
9 Shea Weber .15 .40
10 Matt Moulson .15 .40
11 Mike Richards .15 .40
12 Mikkel Boedker .12 .30
13 Evgeni Malkin .40 1.00
14 Alex Steen .12 .30
15 Simon Gagne .20 .50
16 Henrik Sedin .25 .60
17 Jeff Schultz .12 .30
18 Ryan Kesler .20 .50
19 Tyler Bozak .12 .30
20 Joe Pavelski .25 .60
21 Daniel Alfredsson .20 .50
22 Dwayne Roloson .15 .40
23 Andrei Markov .20 .50
24 Stephen Weiss .15 .40
25 Jimmy Howard .25 .60
26 Jonathan Toews .30 .75
27 Jamie Benn .25 .60
28 Martin Havlat .15 .40
29 Marian Gaborik .20 .50
30 Nikolai Zherdev .12 .30
31 Tim Connolly .12 .30
32 Corey Perry .30 .75
33 Rene Bourque .12 .30
34 Sean Avery .15 .40
35 Josh Bailey .15 .40
36 Wojtek Wolski .12 .30
37 Marc-Andre Fleury .40 1.00
38 Cam Janssen .12 .30
39 Dion Phaneuf .15 .40
40 Roberto Luongo .30 .75
41 Logan Couture .25 .60
42 Jonas Gustavsson .25 .60
43 Nicklas Lidstrom .20 .50
44 Miikka Kiprusoff .20 .50
45 Pavel Datsyuk .30 .75
46 Jarome Iginla .25 .60
47 Nathan Horton .15 .40
48 Zach Bogosian .15 .40
49 Rick Nash .20 .50
50 Matt Duchene .20 .50
51 Dan Boyle .12 .30
52 Colton Orr .12 .30
53 Alex Ovechkin .75 2.00
54 Brad Boyes .12 .30
55 Jordan Staal .15 .40
56 Victor Hedman .25 .60
57 Ilya Kovalchuk .20 .50
58 Michael Cammalleri .20 .50
59 Anze Kopitar .30 .75
60 Ryan Suter .15 .40
61 James Neal .12 .30
62 Marian Hossa .20 .50
63 Henrik Zetterberg .25 .60
64 Kris Russell .12 .30
65 Dustin Penner .12 .30
66 Evander Kane .20 .50
67 Tuukka Rask .25 .60
68 Ryan Miller .20 .50
69 Mikael Backlund .15 .40
70 Cam Barker .12 .30
71 Cory Stillman .12 .30
72 Carey Price .40 1.00
73 Henrik Lundqvist .50 1.25
74 Keith Yandle .12 .30
75 Kyle Okposo .12 .30
76 Ilya Bryzgalov .15 .40
77 Martin Brodeur .50 1.25
78 Marc Staal .12 .30
79 Michael Leighton .15 .40
80 Joe Thornton .30 .75
81 Steven Stamkos .40 1.00
82 Tyler Kennedy .12 .30
83 Alexander Semin .20 .50
84 Dan Hamhuis .15 .40
85 Brian Gionta .12 .30
86 Colin Wilson .15 .40
87 Cal Clutterbuck .12 .30
88 Jonathan Quick .25 .60
89 Matthew Lombardi .12 .30
90 Scott Gomez .15 .40
91 Steve Ott .12 .30
92 Paul Stastny .15 .40
93 Johan Franzen .15 .40
94 Duncan Keith .15 .40
95 Loui Eriksson .12 .30
96 Cam Ward .20 .50
97 Mark Recchi .25 .60
98 Dustin Byfuglien .20 .50
99 Brandon Sutter .12 .30
100 Saku Koivu .20 .50
101 Derek Roy .12 .30
102 Patrice Bergeron .25 .60
103 Luca Sbisa .15 .40
104 Daymond Langkow .12 .30
105 Chris Stewart .15 .40
106 Ales Hemsky .15 .40
107 Patrick Kane .40 1.00
108 Zack Stortini .12 .30
109 Mark Streit .12 .30
110 James van Riemsdyk .15 .40
111 Peter Regin .15 .40
112 Jamie Langenbrunner .12 .30
113 Ed Jovanovski .12 .30
114 David Backes .12 .30
115 Martin St. Louis .20 .50
116 Alexandre Burrows .12 .30
117 Dany Heatley .15 .40
118 Phil Kessel .20 .50
119 Tomas Fleischmann .12 .30
120 Ryan Getzlaf .20 .50
121 Thomas Vanek .15 .40
122 Joni Pitkanen .15 .40
123 Zdeno Chara .20 .50
124 Nicklas Bergfors .15 .40
125 T.J. Galiardi .15 .40
126 Kari Lehtonen .15 .40
127 Patrick Sharp .20 .50
128 Tomas Holmstrom .12 .30
129 R.J. Umberger .12 .30
130 Tom Gilbert .12 .30
131 Jordin Tootoo .15 .40
132 Travis Zajac .12 .30
133 Niklas Backstrom .20 .50
134 Drew Doughty .25 .60
135 Ryan Whitney .12 .30
136 Jean-Sebastien Giguere .20 .50
137 Vincent Lecavalier .20 .50
138 Max Talbot .12 .30
139 Jaroslav Halak .20 .50
140 Daniel Sedin .25 .60
141 Mike Green .15 .40
142 Chris Pronger .20 .50
143 Artem Anisimov .12 .30
144 Shane Doan .15 .40
145 Jason Spezza .20 .50
146 Pierre-Luc Leblond-Letourneau .12 .30
147 Mike Fisher .12 .30
148 Patric Hornqvist .12 .30
149 Zach Parise .20 .50
150 Guillaume Latendresse .15 .40
151 Steve Reinprecht .12 .30
152 Andrei Kostitsyn .15 .40
153 Sam Gagner .12 .30
154 Dave Bolland .15 .40
155 Mark Fistric .12 .30
156 Joffrey Lupul .12 .30
157 Ondrej Pavelec .20 .50
158 Matt Stajan .12 .30
159 Eric Staal .25 .60
160 David Krejci .20 .50
161 Josh Gorges .12 .30
162 Pekka Rinne .20 .50
163 Jonathan Bernier .15 .40
164 Chris Mason .15 .40
165 Dmitry Kulikov .15 .40
166 Alex Goligoski .15 .40
167 Patrick Marleau .20 .50
168 Luke Schenn .20 .50
169 Antero Niittymaki .15 .40
170 Semyon Varlamov .20 .50
171 Jeff Carter .15 .40
172 Andy Greene .12 .30
173 Chris Drury .15 .40
174 Brian Elliott .15 .40
175 Scottie Upshall .12 .30
176 Zenon Konopka .15 .40
177 Tomas Plekanec .12 .30
178 Ryan Smyth .15 .40
179 Jeff Deslauriers .12 .30
180 Mike Modano .30 .75
181 Steve Mason .15 .40
182 Nathan Gerbe .12 .30
183 Tim Gleason .12 .30
184 Marc Savard .12 .30
185 Brenden Morrow .15 .40
186 Troy Brouwer .12 .30
187 Valtteri Filppula .12 .30
188 Brent Burns .20 .50
189 Michael Grabner .15 .40
190 Benoit Pouliot .12 .30
191 Ray Whitney .15 .40
192 Claude Giroux .20 .50
193 John Tavares .30 .75
194 David Perron .15 .40
195 Colby Armstrong .12 .30
196 Mason Raymond .12 .30
197 Kristopher Letang .25 .60
198 Mike Komisarek .12 .30
199 Nicklas Backstrom .20 .50
200 Rick Rypien .20 .50
201 Daniel Briere .20 .50
202 Milan Michalek .12 .30
203 Steve Sullivan .12 .30
204 Brad Richards .20 .50
205 Derek Dorsett .12 .30
206 Tuomo Ruutu .15 .40
207 Bobby Ryan .15 .40
208 Antti Niemi .15 .40
209 David Booth .12 .30
210 Frans Nielsen .12 .30
211 Ryane Clowe .12 .30
212 Eric Fehr .12 .30
213 Rich Peverley .20 .50
214 Adam Foote .12 .30
215 Andrew Brunette .12 .30
216 Erik Karlsson .25 .60
217 Kris Versteeg .12 .30
218 Mike Knuble .12 .30
219 Jay Bouwmeester .12 .30
220 Milan Hejduk .15 .40
221 Mikko Koivu .20 .50
222 Sergei Gonchar .12 .30
223 Mike Smith .20 .50
224 Christian Ehrhoff .12 .30
225 Nik Antropov .15 .40
226 Antoine Vermette .12 .30
227 Jack Johnson .12 .30
228 Ryan Callahan .12 .30
229 Devin Setoguchi .15 .40
230 Michal Neuvirth .15 .40
231 Tyler Myers .12 .30
232 Jonas Hiller .15 .40
233 Jakub Voracek .15 .40
234 Michael Frolik .12 .30
235 Dustin Brown .20 .50
236 Tomas Vokoun .15 .40
237 Michael Del Zotto .15 .40
238 Dan Ellis .15 .40
239 Patrik Berglund .12 .30
240 Ryan Malone .12 .30
241 Tyler Ennis .12 .30
242 Tobias Enstrom .12 .30
243 Patrik Elias .20 .50
244 Erik Johnson .12 .30
245 Peter Mueller .15 .40
246 Jason Pominville .12 .30
247 Patrick Dwyer .12 .30
248 Jiri Hudler .15 .40
249 Andrei Loktionov .15 .40
250 Ville Leino .15 .40
251 Eric Tangradi RC .75 2.00
252 P.K. Subban RC 2.50 6.00
253 Brandon Yip RC .75 2.00
254 Jamie McBain RC .75 2.00
255 Bobby Butler RC .75 2.00
256 Nazem Kadri RC 2.50 6.00
257 Brayden Irwin RC .75 2.00
258 Nick Palmieri RC .75 2.00
259 Zach Hamill RC .75 2.00
260 Nick Bonino RC 1.00 2.50
261 Dustin Tokarski RC .75 2.00
262 Jared Cowen RC .75 2.00
263 Philip Larsen RC .75 2.00
264 Justin Mercier RC .75 2.00
265 Kyle Wilson RC 1.00 2.50
266 Nick Johnson RC .60 1.50
267 James Wyman RC .75 2.00
268 Nick Spaling RC .75 2.00
269 Maxim Noreau RC .60 1.50
270 Cody Almond RC .75 2.00
271 Casey Wellman RC .75 2.00
272 Evgeny Dadonov RC 1.00 2.50
273 Jerome Samson RC .75 2.00
274 Arturs Kulda RC .75 2.00
275 Jean Philippe Levasseur RC .75 2.00
276 Bryan Pitton RC 1.00 2.50
277 Alexander Pechurskiy RC 1.00 2.50
278 Carter Hutton RC 2.00 5.00
279 Matt Zaba RC 1.00 2.50
280 Brock Trotter RC 1.50 4.00
281 Jeff Skinner RC 2.00 5.00
282 Evan Oberg RC 1.00 2.50
283 Grant Clitsome RC .75 2.00
284 Derek Smith RC .75 2.00
285 Justin Falk RC .60 1.50
286 Marc-Andre Cliche RC .60 1.50
287 Jeff Penner RC 1.25 3.00
288 Taylor Hall RC 2.00 5.00
289 Trevor Frischmon RC .75 2.00
290 Oliver Ekman-Larsson RC 1.25 3.00
291 Corey Elkins RC .60 1.50
292 Adam McQuaid RC 1.00 2.50
293 Andrew Bodnarchuk RC .75 2.00
294 Magnus Paajarvi RC 1.00 2.50
295 Brayden Schenn RC 2.00 5.00
296 John McCarthy RC .75 2.00
297 Nino Niederreiter RC 1.25 3.00
298 Jordan Eberle RC 2.00 5.00
299 Tyler Seguin RC 2.50 6.00
300 Anton Klementyev RC .75 2.00

2010-11 Donruss Die-Cut Gems

*SINGLES: 6X TO 15X BASE
199 Nicklas Backstrom 4.00 10.00

2010-11 Donruss Die-Cut Gems Autographs

1 Teemu Selanne 12.00 30.00
6 Craig Anderson 8.00 20.00
9 Shea Weber 4.00 10.00
11 Mike Richards 25.00 60.00
12 Mikkel Boedker 3.00 8.00
15 Simon Gagne 5.00 12.00
16 Henrik Sedin 8.00 20.00
18 Ryan Kesler 12.00 30.00
19 Tyler Bozak 8.00 20.00
26 Jonathan Toews 25.00 60.00
27 Jamie Benn 8.00 20.00
29 Marian Gaborik 12.00 30.00
32 Corey Perry 8.00 20.00
33 Rene Bourque 8.00 20.00
35 Josh Bailey 4.00 10.00
37 Marc-Andre Fleury 15.00 40.00
38 Cam Janssen 12.00 30.00
42 Jonas Gustavsson 10.00 25.00
43 Nicklas Lidstrom 30.00 80.00
45 Pavel Datsyuk 10.00 25.00
46 Jarome Iginla 8.00 20.00
49 Rick Nash 20.00 50.00
50 Matt Duchene 10.00 25.00
52 Colton Orr 20.00 50.00
53 Alex Ovechkin 60.00 120.00
55 Jordan Staal 10.00 25.00
57 Ilya Kovalchuk 5.00 20.00
59 Anze Kopitar 10.00 25.00
61 James Neal 6.00 15.00
65 Dustin Penner 6.00 15.00
68 Ryan Miller 8.00 20.00
72 Carey Price 20.00 40.00
73 Henrik Lundqvist 15.00 40.00
76 Ilya Bryzgalov 4.00 10.00
79 Michael Leighton 15.00 40.00
81 Steven Stamkos 25.00 60.00
84 Dan Hamhuis 15.00 40.00
86 Colin Wilson 4.00 10.00
87 Cal Clutterbuck 8.00 20.00
90 Scott Gomez 10.00 25.00
91 Steve Ott 10.00 25.00
96 Cam Ward 5.00 12.00
98 Dustin Byfuglien 8.00 20.00
99 Brandon Sutter 12.00 30.00
106 Ales Hemsky 6.00 15.00
107 Patrick Kane 20.00 50.00
114 David Backes 10.00 25.00
116 Alexandre Burrows 10.00 25.00
117 Dany Heatley 4.00 10.00
118 Phil Kessel 10.00 25.00
120 Ryan Getzlaf 8.00 20.00
125 T.J. Galiardi 8.00 20.00
126 Kari Lehtonen 4.00 10.00
131 Jordin Tootoo 8.00 20.00
133 Niklas Backstrom 12.00 30.00
138 Max Talbot 6.00 15.00
142 Chris Pronger 12.00 30.00
144 Shane Doan 5.00 12.00
148 Patric Hornqvist 3.00 8.00
149 Zach Parise 12.00 30.00
153 Sam Gagner 10.00 25.00
159 Eric Staal 8.00 20.00
162 Pekka Rinne 6.00 15.00
163 Jonathan Bernier 8.00 20.00
166 Alex Goligoski 12.00 30.00
170 Semyon Varlamov 15.00 40.00
171 Jeff Carter 15.00 40.00
172 Andy Greene 3.00 8.00
174 Brian Elliott 8.00 20.00
178 Ryan Smyth 10.00 25.00
179 Jeff Deslauriers 3.00 8.00
180 Mike Modano 15.00 40.00
192 Claude Giroux 12.00 30.00
193 John Tavares 40.00 80.00
194 David Perron 8.00 20.00
205 Derek Dorsett 8.00 20.00
207 Bobby Ryan 8.00 20.00
213 Rich Peverley 5.00 12.00
219 Jay Bouwmeester 12.00 30.00
223 Mike Smith 8.00 20.00
226 Antoine Vermette 10.00 25.00
228 Ryan Callahan 3.00 8.00
231 Tyler Myers 3.00 8.00
241 Tyler Ennis 3.00 8.00

2010-11 Donruss Press Proofs

*SINGLES: 5X TO 12X BASE
199 Nicklas Backstrom 3.00 8.00

2010-11 Donruss Rated Rookies Autographs

251 Eric Tangradi/75 5.00 12.00
252 P.K. Subban/25 30.00 80.00
253 Brandon Yip 5.00 12.00
255 Bobby Butler 5.00 12.00
256 Nazem Kadri 15.00 40.00
257 Brayden Irwin 5.00 12.00
258 Nick Palmieri 5.00 12.00
259 Zach Hamill 5.00 12.00
260 Nick Bonino 6.00 15.00
262 Jared Cowen 8.00 20.00
263 Philip Larsen 5.00 12.00
264 Justin Mercier 5.00 12.00
273 Jerome Samson/50 5.00 12.00
276 Bryan Pitton/20 10.00 25.00
278 Carter Hutton/50 12.00 30.00
281 Jeff Skinner 20.00 50.00
284 Derek Smith/50 5.00 12.00
288 Taylor Hall 30.00 80.00
290 Oliver Ekman-Larsson 8.00 20.00
291 Corey Elkins/20 6.00 15.00
292 Adam McQuaid/75 6.00 15.00
294 Magnus Paajarvi 6.00 15.00
295 Brayden Schenn 15.00 40.00
297 Nino Niederreiter 8.00 20.00
298 Jordan Eberle 40.00 80.00
299 Tyler Seguin 40.00 80.00

2010-11 Donruss Boys of Winter

COMPLETE SET (80) 75.00 150.00
1 Alexandre Burrows 1.00 2.50
2 Sidney Crosby 6.00 15.00
3 Evander Kane 1.50 4.00
4 Daniel Carcillo 1.00 2.50
5 Niklas Backstrom 1.50 4.00
6 Tyler Bozak 1.00 2.50
7 Patric Hornqvist 1.00 2.50
8 Steve Downie 1.00 2.50
9 Zenon Konopka 1.25 3.00
10 Cory Schneider 1.50 4.00
11 Scott Hartnell 1.00 2.50
12 Scott Gomez 1.25 3.00
13 Craig Anderson 1.50 4.00
14 Mike Fisher 1.00 2.50
15 Steve Valiquette 1.25 3.00
16 Erik Karlsson 2.00 5.00
17 Jeff Carter 1.25 3.00
18 Anze Kopitar 2.50 6.00
19 James Neal 1.00 2.50
20 Mason Raymond 1.00 2.50
21 Mark Flood 1.00 2.50
22 Ales Hemsky 1.25 3.00
23 Evgeni Malkin 3.00 8.00
24 Jonas Gustavsson 2.00 5.00
25 Jose Theodore 1.50 4.00
26 Roberto Luongo 2.50 6.00
27 Marty Turco 1.50 4.00
28 Dan Hamhuis 1.25 3.00
29 Mikael Backlund 1.25 3.00
30 Daniel Sedin 2.00 5.00
31 Anton Klementyev 1.25 3.00
32 Rene Bourque 1.00 2.50
33 Johan Backlund 1.25 3.00
34 Mike Modano 2.50 6.00
35 Teddy Purcell 1.00 2.50
36 Matt Martin 2.00 5.00
37 Rich Peverley 1.50 4.00
38 Jonathan Toews 2.50 6.00
39 Mikael Samuelsson 1.00 2.50
40 Luke Schenn 1.50 4.00
41 Wade Redden 1.00 2.50
42 Shea Weber 1.25 3.00
43 Colton Orr 1.00 2.50
44 Corey Perry 2.50 6.00
45 Max Pacioretty 1.50 4.00
46 Zach Bogosian 1.25 3.00
47 Brian Elliott 1.25 3.00
48 Patrice Bergeron 2.00 5.00
49 Matt Carkner 1.25 3.00
50 Peter Budaj 1.25 3.00
51 Brian Boucher 1.25 3.00
52 Josh Gorges 1.00 2.50
53 Steve Ott 1.00 2.50
54 Jonas Hiller 1.25 3.00
55 Dustin Penner 1.00 2.50
56 Maxim Lapierre 1.00 2.50
57 Brenden Morrow 1.25 3.00
58 Dylan Reese 1.25 3.00
59 Tim Thomas 1.50 4.00
60 Tomas Plekanec 1.00 2.50
61 T.J. Galiardi 1.25 3.00
62 Michael Frolik 1.00 2.50
63 Carey Price 3.00 8.00
64 Travis Zajac 1.00 2.50
65 Kari Lehtonen 1.25 3.00
66 Alex Ovechkin 6.00 15.00
67 Colin Wilson 1.25 3.00
68 Ryan Smyth 1.25 3.00
69 Jordin Tootoo 1.25 3.00
70 Jay Rosehill 1.00 2.50
71 Martin Brodeur 4.00 10.00
72 Pavel Datsyuk 2.50 6.00
73 Zach Parise 1.50 4.00
74 Matt Moulson 1.25 3.00
75 Henrik Lundqvist 4.00 10.00
76 Daniel Briere 1.50 4.00
77 Jamie Benn 2.00 5.00
78 Jeremy Duchesne 1.50 4.00
79 Phil Kessel 1.50 4.00
80 Nathan Horton 1.25 3.00

2010-11 Donruss Boys of Winter Autographs

1 Alexandre Burrows 4.00 10.00
2 Sidney Crosby 75.00 200.00
3 Evander Kane 6.00 15.00
4 Daniel Carcillo 4.00 10.00
5 Niklas Backstrom 6.00 15.00
6 Tyler Bozak 4.00 10.00
7 Patric Hornqvist 4.00 10.00
8 Steve Downie 4.00 10.00
10 Cory Schneider 6.00 15.00
12 Scott Gomez 5.00 12.00
13 Craig Anderson 6.00 15.00
14 Mike Fisher 4.00 10.00
17 Jeff Carter 5.00 12.00
18 Anze Kopitar 10.00 25.00
19 James Neal 4.00 10.00
22 Ales Hemsky 5.00 12.00
23 Evgeni Malkin 10.00 25.00
24 Jonas Gustavsson 8.00 20.00
25 Jose Theodore 6.00 15.00
28 Dan Hamhuis 5.00 12.00
29 Mikael Backlund 5.00 12.00
30 Daniel Sedin 8.00 20.00
32 Rene Bourque 4.00 10.00
34 Mike Modano 10.00 25.00
36 Matt Martin/20 8.00 20.00
37 Rich Peverley 6.00 15.00
38 Jonathan Toews 10.00 25.00
42 Shea Weber 5.00 12.00
43 Colton Orr 4.00 10.00
44 Corey Perry 10.00 25.00
45 Max Pacioretty 6.00 15.00
46 Zach Bogosian 5.00 12.00
47 Brian Elliott 5.00 12.00
49 Matt Carkner 5.00 12.00
51 Brian Boucher 5.00 12.00
53 Steve Ott 4.00 10.00
54 Jonas Hiller 5.00 12.00
55 Dustin Penner 4.00 10.00
57 Brenden Morrow 5.00 12.00
59 Tim Thomas 6.00 15.00
61 T.J. Galiardi 5.00 12.00
62 Michael Frolik 4.00 10.00
63 Carey Price 12.00 30.00
65 Kari Lehtonen 5.00 12.00
66 Alex Ovechkin 25.00 60.00
67 Colin Wilson 5.00 12.00
68 Ryan Smyth 5.00 12.00
69 Jordin Tootoo 5.00 12.00
71 Martin Brodeur 15.00 40.00
72 Pavel Datsyuk 10.00 25.00
73 Zach Parise 6.00 15.00
74 Matt Moulson 5.00 12.00
75 Henrik Lundqvist 15.00 40.00
77 Jamie Benn 8.00 20.00
79 Phil Kessel 6.00 15.00

2010-11 Donruss Boys of Winter Threads

*PRIME/50-100: .6X TO 1.5X THREADS
*PRIME/25: .8X TO 2X THREADS
1 Alexandre Burrows 2.00 5.00
2 Sidney Crosby 12.00 30.00
3 Evander Kane 3.00 8.00
4 Daniel Carcillo 2.00 5.00
5 Niklas Backstrom 3.00 8.00
6 Tyler Bozak 2.00 5.00
7 Patric Hornqvist 2.00 5.00
8 Steve Downie 2.00 5.00
9 Zenon Konopka 2.50 6.00
10 Cory Schneider 3.00 8.00
11 Scott Hartnell 2.00 5.00
12 Scott Gomez 2.50 6.00
13 Craig Anderson 3.00 8.00
14 Mike Fisher 2.00 5.00
15 Steve Valiquette 2.50 6.00
16 Erik Karlsson 4.00 10.00
17 Jeff Carter 2.50 6.00
18 Anze Kopitar 5.00 12.00
19 James Neal 2.00 5.00
20 Mason Raymond 2.00 5.00
21 Mark Flood 2.00 5.00
22 Ales Hemsky 2.50 6.00
23 Evgeni Malkin 6.00 15.00
24 Jonas Gustavsson 4.00 10.00
25 Jose Theodore 3.00 8.00
26 Roberto Luongo 5.00 12.00
27 Marty Turco 3.00 8.00
28 Dan Hamhuis 2.50 6.00
29 Mikael Backlund 2.50 6.00
30 Daniel Sedin 4.00 10.00
31 Anton Klementyev 2.50 6.00
32 Rene Bourque 2.00 5.00
33 Johan Backlund 2.50 6.00
34 Mike Modano 5.00 12.00
35 Teddy Purcell 2.00 5.00
36 Matt Martin 4.00 10.00
37 Rich Peverley 3.00 8.00
38 Jonathan Toews 5.00 12.00
39 Mikael Samuelsson 2.00 5.00
40 Luke Schenn 3.00 8.00
41 Wade Redden 2.00 5.00
42 Shea Weber 2.50 6.00
43 Colton Orr 2.00 5.00
44 Corey Perry 5.00 12.00
45 Max Pacioretty 3.00 8.00
46 Zach Bogosian 2.50 6.00
47 Brian Elliott 2.50 6.00
48 Patrice Bergeron 4.00 10.00
49 Matt Carkner 2.50 6.00
50 Peter Budaj 2.50 6.00
51 Brian Boucher 2.50 6.00
52 Josh Gorges 2.00 5.00
53 Steve Ott 2.00 5.00
54 Jonas Hiller 2.50 6.00
55 Dustin Penner 2.00 5.00
56 Maxim Lapierre 2.00 5.00
57 Brenden Morrow 2.50 6.00
58 Dylan Reese 2.50 6.00
59 Tim Thomas 3.00 8.00
60 Tomas Plekanec 2.00 5.00
61 T.J. Galiardi 2.50 6.00
62 Michael Frolik 2.00 5.00
63 Carey Price 6.00 15.00
64 Travis Zajac 2.00 5.00
65 Kari Lehtonen 2.50 6.00
66 Alex Ovechkin 12.00 30.00
67 Colin Wilson 2.50 6.00
68 Ryan Smyth 2.50 6.00
69 Jordin Tootoo 2.50 6.00
70 Jay Rosehill 2.00 5.00
71 Martin Brodeur 8.00 20.00
72 Pavel Datsyuk 5.00 12.00
73 Zach Parise 3.00 8.00
74 Matt Moulson 2.50 6.00
75 Henrik Lundqvist 8.00 20.00
76 Daniel Briere 3.00 8.00
77 Jamie Benn 4.00 10.00
78 Jeremy Duchesne 3.00 8.00
79 Phil Kessel 3.00 8.00
80 Nathan Horton 2.50 6.00

2010-11 Donruss Elite

1 Sidney Crosby 20.00 50.00
2 Alex Ovechkin 20.00 50.00
3 Steven Stamkos 10.00 25.00
4 Jonathan Toews 8.00 20.00
5 Henrik Sedin 6.00 15.00
6 Ryan Miller 5.00 12.00
7 Martin Brodeur 12.00 30.00
8 Zach Parise 5.00 12.00
9 Patrick Kane 10.00 25.00
10 Nicklas Backstrom 5.00 12.00
11 Drew Doughty 6.00 15.00
12 Tuukka Rask 6.00 15.00
13 Marian Gaborik 5.00 12.00
14 Daniel Alfredsson 5.00 12.00
15 Pavel Datsyuk 8.00 20.00

2010-11 Donruss Ice Kings

COMPLETE SET (15) 15.00 40.00
1 Ray Bourque 2.50 6.00
2 Darryl Sittler 2.00 5.00
3 Patrick Roy 4.00 10.00
4 Cam Neely 1.50 4.00
5 Joe Sakic 3.00 8.00
6 Glenn Hall 1.50 4.00
7 Brett Hull 3.00 8.00
8 Jim Craig 1.25 3.00
9 Bobby Hull 3.00 8.00
10 Mike Bossy 1.50 4.00
11 Bobby Clarke 2.50 6.00
12 Mario Lemieux 6.00 15.00
13 Johnny Bucyk 1.50 4.00
14 Jean Beliveau 1.50 4.00
15 Gerry Cheevers 1.50 4.00

2010-11 Donruss Les Gardiens

COMPLETE SET (15) 15.00 40.00
1 Martin Brodeur 4.00 10.00
2 Roberto Luongo 2.50 6.00
3 Patrick Roy 4.00 10.00
4 Felix Potvin 2.50 6.00
5 Marc-Andre Fleury 3.00 8.00
6 Ryan Miller 1.50 4.00
7 Jonathan Quick 2.00 5.00
8 Craig Anderson 1.50 4.00
9 Jimmy Howard 2.00 5.00
10 Curtis Joseph 2.00 5.00
11 Tuukka Rask 2.00 5.00
12 Miikka Kiprusoff 1.50 4.00
13 Antti Niemi 1.25 3.00
14 Jonas Gustavsson 2.00 5.00
15 Jaroslav Halak 1.50 4.00

2010-11 Donruss Line of the Times

1 Toews/Kane/Hossa 8.00 20.00
2 Sedin/Sedin/Burrows 8.00 20.00
3 Richards/Neal/Eriksson 5.00 12.00
6 Cammalleri/Gomez/Gionta 8.00 20.00
7 Thornton/Heatley/Marleau 8.00 20.00
8 Ovechkin/Backstrom/Knuble 20.00 50.00
9 Stamkos/St. Louis/Malone 8.00 20.00
10 Tavares/Okposo/Moulson 8.00 20.00

2010-11 Donruss Rookie Showcase Threads

*PRIME/25: .8X TO 2X BASIC JSY
BS Brayden Schenn 6.00 15.00
JC Joe Colborne 3.00 8.00
JE Jordan Eberle 12.00 30.00
JS Jeff Skinner 10.00 25.00
MP Magnus Paajarvi 3.00 8.00
NK Nazem Kadri 8.00 20.00
TH Taylor Hall 25.00 60.00
TS Tyler Seguin 12.00 30.00
ZH Zach Hamill 2.50 6.00

2010-11 Donruss Rookie Showcase Threads Autographs

BS Brayden Schenn 12.00 30.00
JE Jordan Eberle 30.00 80.00
JS Jeff Skinner 12.00 30.00
MP Magnus Paajarvi 6.00 15.00
NK Nazem Kadri 15.00 40.00
TH Taylor Hall 40.00 100.00
TS Tyler Seguin 30.00 60.00
ZH Zach Hamill 10.00 25.00

2010-11 Donruss The Ultimate Draft

COMPLETE SET (30) 15.00 40.00
1 Marc-Andre Fleury 3.00 8.00
2 Eric Staal 2.00 5.00
3 Nathan Horton 1.25 3.00
4 Thomas Vanek 1.25 3.00
5 Milan Michalek 1.00 2.50
6 Ryan Suter 1.25 3.00
7 Braydon Coburn 1.00 2.50
8 Dion Phaneuf 1.25 3.00
9 Andrei Kostitsyn 1.25 3.00
10 Jeff Carter 1.25 3.00
11 Dustin Brown 1.50 4.00
12 Brent Seabrook 1.00 2.50
13 Zach Parise 1.50 4.00
14 Eric Fehr 1.00 2.50
15 Ryan Getzlaf 1.50 4.00
16 Brent Burns 1.50 4.00
17 Ryan Kesler 1.50 4.00
18 Mike Richards 1.25 3.00
19 Corey Perry 2.50 6.00
20 Loui Eriksson 1.00 2.50
21 Patrice Bergeron 2.00 5.00
22 David Backes 1.00 2.50
23 Jimmy Howard 2.00 5.00
24 Daniel Carcillo 1.00 2.50
25 Joe Pavelski 2.00 5.00
26 Tobias Enstrom 1.00 2.50
27 Dustin Byfuglien 1.50 4.00
28 Matt Moulson 1.25 3.00
29 Jaroslav Halak 1.50 4.00
30 Brian Elliott 1.25 3.00

2010-11 Donruss Tough Times

COMPLETE SET (9) 10.00 25.00
1 Lyndon Byers 1.50 4.00
2 Ron Hextall 1.50 4.00
3 Joey Kocur 1.50 4.00
4 Dave Brown 1.00 2.50
5 Basil McRae 1.00 2.50
6 Torrie Robertson 1.25 3.00
7 Paul Baxter 1.25 3.00
8 Jay Miller 1.50 4.00
9 Tim Hunter 1.00 2.50

2010-11 Donruss Tough Times Autographs

1 Lyndon Byers 10.00 25.00
2 Ron Hextall 10.00 25.00
3 Joey Kocur 10.00 25.00
4 Dave Brown 6.00 15.00
5 Basil McRae 6.00 15.00
6 Torrie Robertson 8.00 20.00
7 Paul Baxter 8.00 20.00
8 Jay Miller 10.00 25.00
9 Tim Hunter 6.00 15.00
10 Bob McGill 6.00 15.00

2010-11 Donruss Toronto Fall Expo

1 Alexander Ovechkin 5.00 12.00
2 Sidney Crosby 5.00 12.00
3 Ryan Miller 1.25 3.00
4 Nazem Kadri 3.00 8.00
5 Jonas Gustavsson 1.50 4.00
6 Henrik Sedin 1.50 4.00
TH Taylor Hall RR 3.00 8.00
TS Tyler Seguin RR 4.00 10.00

2010-11 Donruss Ice Kings Toronto Fall Expo

ML Mario Lemieux 8.00 20.00
RB Ray Bourque 3.00 8.00

1996-97 Donruss Canadian Ice

COMPLETE SET (150) 10.00 25.00
1 Jaromir Jagr .60 1.50
2 Jocelyn Thibault .15 .40
3 Paul Kariya .20 .50
4 Derian Hatcher .12 .30
5 Wayne Gretzky 1.25 3.00
6 Peter Forsberg .40 1.00
7 Eric Lindros .30 .75
8 Adam Oates .20 .50
9 Paul Coffey .20 .50
10 Chris Osgood .20 .50
11 Pat LaFontaine .20 .50
12 Mats Sundin .20 .50
13 Rob Niedermayer .15 .40
14 Doug Weight .20 .50
15 Al MacInnis .25 .60
16 Damian Rhodes .15 .40
17 Stephane Fiset .15 .40
18 Mike Gartner .25 .60
19 Patrick Roy .50 1.25
20 Eric Daze .15 .40
21 Ray Bourque .30 .75
22 Keith Tkachuk .20 .50
23 Mark Recchi .25 .60
24 Peter Bondra .20 .50
25 Mike Modano .30 .75
26 Mike Richter .20 .50
27 Keith Primeau .15 .40
28 Todd Bertuzzi .20 .50
29 Wendel Clark .30 .75
30 Scott Young .12 .30
31 Mario Lemieux .75 2.00
32 Valeri Kamensky .15 .40
33 Kirk McLean .15 .40
34 Daniel Alfredsson .20 .50
35 Ed Jovanovski .15 .40
36 Kelly Hrudey .15 .40
37 Trevor Kidd .12 .30
38 Joe Juneau .12 .30
39 Steve Yzerman .50 1.25
40 Saku Koivu .20 .50
41 Alexei Kovalev .15 .40

42 Rob Blake .20 .50
43 Shayne Corson .15 .40
44 Roman Hamrlik .12 .30
45 Stephane Yelle .12 .30
46 Martin Brodeur .50 1.25
47 Kirk Muller .12 .30
48 Pat Verbeek .12 .30
49 Jari Kurri .20 .50
50 Michal Pivonka .12 .30
51 Ron Hextall .20 .50
52 Trevor Linden .20 .50
53 Vincent Damphousse .15 .40
54 Owen Nolan .20 .50
55 Sergei Fedorov .30 .75
56 Chris Chelios .20 .50
57 Jeremy Roenick .30 .75
58 Zigmund Palffy .20 .50
59 Pavel Bure .20 .50
60 Dominik Hasek .30 .75
61 Alexei Yashin .15 .40
62 Chris Gratton .15 .40
63 Joe Nieuwendyk .15 .40
64 Luc Robitaille .20 .50
65 Brett Hull .40 1.00
66 Sean Burke .12 .30
67 Felix Potvin .30 .75
68 Jason Arnott .15 .40
69 Valeri Bure .12 .30
70 Tom Barrasso .15 .40
71 Vyacheslav Kozlov .12 .30
72 Petr Sykora .12 .30
73 Corey Hirsch .15 .40
74 Joe Sakic .40 1.00
75 Bill Ranford .15 .40
76 Yanic Perreault .12 .30
77 Mikael Renberg .15 .40
78 Theo Fleury .40 1.00
79 Jim Carey .20 .50
80 Vitali Yachmenev .12 .30
81 Martin Rucinsky .12 .30
82 Jeff O'Neill .12 .30
83 Marcus Ragnarsson .12 .30
84 John Vanbiesbrouck .20 .50
85 Teemu Selanne .40 1.00
86 Larry Murphy .15 .40
87 Mark Messier .40 1.00
88 Alexei Zhamnov .15 .40
89 Ryan Smyth .15 .40
90 Andy Moog .20 .50
91 Alexander Mogilny .15 .40
92 Kris Draper .12 .30
93 Ron Francis .25 .60
94 Mike Vernon .15 .40
95 Nikolai Khabibulin .15 .40
96 Mariusz Czerkawski .12 .30
97 Mathieu Schneider .12 .30
98 Stephane Richer .15 .40
99 Mike Ricci .12 .30
100 John LeClair .20 .50
101 Brendan Shanahan .20 .50
102 Daren Puppa .15 .40
103 Scott Stevens .20 .50
104 Alexandre Daigle .12 .30
105 Dimitri Khristich .12 .30
106 Bernie Nicholls .15 .40
107 Scott Mellanby .15 .40
108 Brian Leetch .15 .40
109 Grant Fuhr .30 .75
110 Pierre Turgeon .15 .40
111 Jere Lehtinen .12 .30
112 Doug Gilmour .25 .60
113 Ed Belfour .20 .50
114 Geoff Sanderson .15 .40
115 Claude Lemieux .12 .30
116 Curtis Joseph .25 .60
117 Igor Larionov .20 .50
118 Jamie Pushor .12 .30
119 Sergei Berezin RC .30 .75
120 Eric Fichaud .15 .40
121 Wade Redden .12 .30
122 Hnat Domenichelli .12 .30
123 Rem Murray RC .20 .50
124 Jarome Iginla .25 .60
125 Richard Zednik RC .25 .60
126 Daniel Goneau RC .20 .50
127 Ethan Moreau RC .20 .50
128 Janne Niinimaa .20 .50
129 Tomas Holmstrom RC .60 1.50
130 Fredrik Modin RC .20 .50
131 Bryan Berard .20 .50
132 Jim Campbell .12 .30
133 Chris O'Sullivan .12 .30
134 Andreas Dackell RC .20 .50
135 Daymond Langkow .15 .40
136 Kevin Hodson RC .20 .50
137 Jamie Langenbrunner .12 .30
138 Mattias Timander RC .20 .50
139 Tuomas Gronman .12 .30
140 Jonas Hoglund .12 .30
141 Mike Grier RC .25 .60
142 Terry Ryan RC .20 .50
143 Darcy Tucker .12 .30
144 Brandon Convery .12 .30
145 Anders Eriksson .12 .30
146 Christian Dube .12 .30
147 Dainius Zubrus RC .25 .60
148 Grant Fuhr CL .30 .75
149 Paul Coffey CL .20 .50
150 Ray Bourque CL .30 .75

1996-97 Donruss Canadian Ice Gold Press Proofs

*VETS: 12X TO 30X BASIC CARDS
*ROOKIES: 6X TO 15X BASIC CARDS

1996-97 Donruss Canadian Ice Red Press Proofs

*VETS: 6X TO 15X BASIC CARDS
*ROOKIES: 3X TO 8X

1996-97 Donruss Canadian Ice Les Gardiens

COMPLETE SET (10) 25.00 60.00
1 Patrick Roy 10.00 25.00
2 Jocelyn Thibault 2.00 5.00
3 Felix Potvin 3.00 8.00
4 Martin Brodeur 6.00 15.00
5 Stephane Fiset 2.00 5.00
6 Eric Fichaud 2.00 5.00
7 Dominic Roussel 2.00 5.00
8 Emmanuel Fernandez 2.00 5.00
9 Martin Biron 2.00 5.00
10 Jose Theodore 4.00 10.00

1996-97 Donruss Canadian Ice Mario Lemieux Scrapbook

COMPLETE SET (25) 30.00 80.00
COMMON CARD (1-25) 4.00 10.00
NNO1 M.Lemieux AU/500 100.00 250.00
NNO2 M.Lemieux AU/1200 30.00 80.00

1996-97 Donruss Canadian Ice O Canada

COMPLETE SET (16) 40.00 100.00
1 Joe Sakic 6.00 15.00
2 Paul Kariya 2.50 6.00
3 Mark Messier 2.50 6.00
4 Jarome Iginla 3.00 8.00
5 Theo Fleury .75 2.00
6 Ed Belfour 2.50 6.00
7 Wayne Gretzky 10.00 25.00
8 Chris Gratton .75 2.00
9 Doug Gilmour 2.00 5.00
10 Kirk Muller .75 2.00
11 Eric Lindros 2.50 6.00
12 Brendan Shanahan 2.50 6.00
13 Mario Lemieux 10.00 25.00
14 Eric Daze .75 2.00
15 Geoff Sanderson .75 2.00
16 Terry Ryan .75 2.00

1997-98 Donruss Canadian Ice

COMPLETE SET (150) 15.00 30.00
1 Patrick Roy 1.00 2.50
2 Paul Kariya .20 .50
3 Eric Lindros .20 .50
4 Steve Yzerman 1.00 2.50
5 Wayne Gretzky 1.25 3.00
6 Peter Forsberg .50 1.25
7 John Vanbiesbrouck .08 .25
8 Jaromir Jagr .30 .75
9 Jim Campbell .02 .10
10 Dominik Hasek .40 1.00
11 Ray Bourque .30 .75
12 Jarome Iginla .25 .60
13 Mike Modano .30 .75
14 Ed Jovanovski .08 .25
15 Jocelyn Thibault .08 .25
16 Keith Tkachuk .20 .50
17 Brett Hull .25 .60
18 Pavel Bure .20 .50
19 Saku Koivu .20 .50
20 Curtis Joseph .20 .50
21 Eric Daze .08 .25
22 Keith Primeau .08 .25
23 Theo Fleury .02 .10
24 Pierre Turgeon .08 .25
25 Peter Bondra .08 .25
26 Ed Belfour .20 .50
27 Pat Verbeek .02 .10
28 Chris Osgood .08 .25
29 Ray Sheppard .02 .10
30 Stephane Fiset .08 .25
31 Wade Redden .02 .10
32 Trevor Linden .08 .25
33 Zigmund Palffy .08 .25
34 Tony Amonte .08 .25
35 Derek Plante .02 .10
36 Jonas Hoglund .02 .10
37 Guy Hebert .08 .25
38 Garth Snow .08 .25
39 Chris Gratton .08 .25
40 Mats Sundin .20 .50
41 Geoff Sanderson .08 .25
42 Martin Brodeur .50 1.25
43 Jozef Stumpel .08 .25
44 Ron Francis .08 .25
45 Alexander Mogilny .08 .25
46 Bill Ranford .08 .25
47 Kirk Muller .02 .10
48 Ron Hextall .08 .25
49 Doug Gilmour .08 .25
50 Mark Messier .20 .50
51 Joe Nieuwendyk .08 .25
52 Ryan Smyth .08 .25
53 Mark Recchi .08 .25
54 Mike Gartner .08 .25
55 Al MacInnis .08 .25
56 Felix Potvin .20 .50
57 Rob Blake .08 .25
58 Dimitri Khristich .02 .10
59 Jim Carey .08 .25
60 Trevor Kidd .08 .25
61 Martin Gelinas .02 .10
62 Oleg Tverdovsky .02 .10
63 Ron Tugnutt .08 .25
64 Paul Coffey .20 .50
65 Travis Green .02 .10
66 Andrew Cassels .02 .10
67 Brendan Shanahan .20 .50
68 Luc Robitaille .08 .25
69 Pat LaFontaine .20 .50
70 Daymond Langkow .08 .25
71 Petr Nedved .08 .25
72 Sergei Fedorov .30 .75
73 Anson Carter .08 .25
74 Teemu Selanne .20 .50
75 Nikolai Khabibulin .20 .50
76 Ken Wregget .08 .25
77 Dino Ciccarelli .02 .10
78 Adam Oates .08 .25
79 Kirk McLean .08 .25
80 Wendel Clark .08 .25
81 Jeff Friesen .02 .10
82 Valeri Kamensky .08 .25
83 Ethan Moreau .02 .10
84 Matthew Barnaby .02 .10
85 Andy Moog .08 .25
86 Doug Weight .08 .25
87 Mike Dunham .08 .25
88 Brian Leetch .20 .50
89 Mike Peca .02 .10
90 Chris Pronger .08 .25
91 Alexei Zhamnov .02 .10
92 Bryan Berard .08 .25
93 John LeClair .20 .50
94 Steve Sullivan .02 .10
95 Grant Fuhr .08 .25
96 Mikael Renberg .08 .25
97 Adam Graves .02 .10
98 Ray Ferraro .02 .10
99 Sean Burke .08 .25
100 Jeremy Roenick .25 .60
101 Jeff Hackett .08 .25
102 Joe Sakic .40 1.00
103 Jamie Langenbrunner .02 .10
104 Stephane Richer .02 .10
105 Dave Andreychuk .02 .10
106 Tommy Salo .08 .25
107 Mike Richter .20 .50
108 Owen Nolan .08 .25
109 Corey Hirsch .08 .25
110 Daren Puppa .08 .25
111 Darcy Tucker .02 .10
112 Daniel Alfredsson .08 .25
113 Rod Brind'Amour .08 .25
114 Scott Stevens .08 .25
115 Vincent Damphousse .02 .10
116 Mathieu Schneider .02 .10
117 Jason Arnott .02 .10
118 Mike Vernon .08 .25
119 Sandis Ozolinsh .02 .10
120 Chris Chelios .20 .50
121 Mike Grier .02 .10
122 Alexandre Daigle .02 .10
123 Roman Hamrlik .02 .10
124 Derian Hatcher .02 .10
125 Damian Rhodes .08 .25
126 Adam Deadmarsh .02 .10
127 Alexei Yashin .02 .10
128 Terry Ryan .02 .10
129 Jeff Ware .02 .10
130 Steve Kelly .02 .10
131 Hnat Domenichelli .02 .10
132 Steve Shields RC .30 .75
133 Paxton Schafer RC .08 .25
134 Vadim Sharifijanov .02 .10
135 Vaclav Prospal RC .20 .50
136 Mike Fountain .02 .10
137 Christian Matte RC .02 .10
138 Tomas Vokoun RC .60 1.50
139 Vladimir Vorobiev RC .02 .10
140 Domenic Pittis RC .02 .10
141 Vaclav Varada .02 .10
142 D.J. Smith RC .02 .10
143 Jaroslav Svejkovsky .08 .25
144 Jason Holland .02 .10
145 Marc Denis .08 .25
146 Jean-Sebastien Giguere .08 .25
147 Marcel Cousineau .08 .25
148 Dave Andreychuk CL (1-75) .02 .10
149 Mike Gartner CL (76-150) .02 .10
150 Stanley Cup Team Picture CL (inserts) .02 .10

1997-98 Donruss Canadian Ice Dominion Series

*VETS: 8X TO 20X BASIC CARDS
*ROOKIES: 4X TO 10X BASIC CARDS

1997-98 Donruss Canadian Ice Provincial Series

*VETS: 5X TO 12X BASIC CARDS
*ROOKIES: 1X TO 2.5X BASIC CARDS

1997-98 Donruss Canadian Ice Les Gardiens

COMPLETE SET (12) 30.00 80.00
*PROMOS: .4X TO 1X BASIC INSERTS
1 Patrick Roy 12.00 30.00
2 Felix Potvin 6.00 15.00
3 Martin Brodeur 8.00 20.00
4 Jean-Sebastien Giguere 4.00 10.00
5 Stephane Fiset 2.00 5.00
6 Jose Theodore 4.00 10.00
7 Jocelyn Thibault 2.00 5.00
8 Eric Fichaud 2.00 5.00
9 Patrick Lalime 2.00 5.00
10 Marcel Cousineau 2.00 5.00
11 Philippe DeRouville 2.00 5.00
12 Marc Denis 2.00 5.00

1997-98 Donruss Canadian Ice National Pride

COMPLETE SET (30) 75.00 175.00
1 Wayne Gretzky 12.00 30.00
2 Mark Messier 3.00 8.00
3 Paul Kariya 3.00 8.00
4 Steve Yzerman 8.00 20.00
5 Brendan Shanahan 4.00 10.00
6 Chris Osgood 2.50 6.00
7 Adam Oates 2.50 6.00
8 Eric Lindros 4.00 10.00
9 Doug Gilmour 3.00 8.00
10 Ryan Smyth 2.50 6.00
11 Ray Bourque 5.00 12.00
12 Jason Arnott 2.00 5.00
13 Jarome Iginla 3.00 8.00
14 Geoff Sanderson 2.00 5.00
15 Alexandre Daigle 2.00 5.00
16 Trevor Linden 3.00 8.00
17 Joe Sakic 6.00 15.00
18 Mark Recchi 3.00 8.00
19 Theo Fleury 3.00 8.00
20 Ron Francis 2.50 6.00
21 Daymond Langkow 2.00 5.00
22 Ed Belfour 3.00 8.00
23 Paul Coffey 3.00 8.00
24 Pierre Turgeon 2.50 6.00
25 Claude Lemieux 2.00 5.00
26 Ron Hextall 3.00 8.00
27 Curtis Joseph 3.00 8.00
28 Mike Vernon 2.50 6.00
29 Vincent Damphousse 2.00 5.00
30 Owen Nolan 2.50 6.00

1997-98 Donruss Canadian Ice Stanley Cup Scrapbook

*FRAMED/500: .5X TO 1.2X BASIC INSERTS
1 Mike Modano Q 4.00 10.00
2 Curtis Joseph Q 4.00 10.00
3 Joe Sakic Q 8.00 20.00
4 Chris Chelios Q 2.50 6.00
5 Chris Osgood Q 2.50 6.00
6 Brett Hull Q 4.00 10.00
7 Jeremy Roenick Q 4.00 10.00
8 Teemu Selanne Q 4.00 10.00
9 Jaromir Jagr Q 6.00 15.00
10 Garth Snow Q 2.00 5.00
11 Alexei Yashin Q 2.00 5.00
12 Steve Shields Q 2.00 5.00
13 Doug Gilmour Q 3.00 8.00
14 Jose Theodore Q 4.00 10.00
15 Mike Richter Q 2.50 6.00
16 John Vanbiesbrouck Q 2.50 6.00
17 Ryan Smyth CS 2.50 6.00
18 Peter Forsberg CS 8.00 20.00
19 Steve Yzerman CS 12.00 30.00
20 Paul Kariya CS 4.00 10.00
21 Janne Niinimaa CS 2.00 5.00
22 Dominik Hasek CS 8.00 20.00
23 Mark Messier CS 4.00 10.00
24 Martin Brodeur CS 12.50 30.00
25 Slava Kozlov CF 2.50 6.00
26 Sergei Fedorov CF 8.00 20.00
27 Patrick Roy CF 15.00 40.00
28 Wayne Gretzky CF 25.00 60.00
29 John LeClair CF 2.50 6.00
30 Paul Coffey CF 4.00 10.00
31 Mike Vernon AU/750 10.00 25.00
32 Eric Lindros AU/750 20.00 40.00
33 B.Shanahan AU/250 40.00 80.00

1995-96 Donruss Elite

COMPLETE SET (110) 12.00 30.00
1 Jocelyn Thibault .12 .30
2 Nicklas Lidstrom .15 .40
3 Brendan Shanahan .15 .40
4 Kenny Jonsson .12 .30
5 Doug Weight .15 .40
6 Oleg Tverdovsky .15 .40
7 Brett Hull .30 .75
8 Larry Murphy .12 .30
9 Ray Bourque .15 .40
10 Adam Graves .12 .30
11 Gary Suter .10 .25
12 Bill Ranford .12 .30
13 Zigmund Palffy .15 .40
14 Cam Neely .15 .40
15 Al MacInnis .20 .50
16 Joe Sakic .30 .75
17 Kevin Hatcher .12 .30
18 Alexander Mogilny .12 .30
19 Radek Dvorak RC .20 .50
20 Ed Belfour .12 .30
21 Jeff O'Neill .15 .40
22 Valeri Kamensky .12 .30
23 John MacLean .12 .30
24 Zdeno Ciger .12 .30
25 Daniel Alfredsson RC .75 2.00
26 Owen Nolan .15 .40
27 Wendel Clark .25 .60
28 Brian Savage .10 .25
29 Alexei Zhamnov .15 .40
30 Dominik Hasek .25 .60
31 Paul Kariya .15 .40
32 Mike Modano .25 .60
33 Craig Janney .10 .25
34 Todd Harvey .10 .25
35 Jaromir Jagr .50 1.25
36 Roman Hamrlik .10 .25
37 Sergei Zubov .12 .30
38 Marcus Ragnarsson RC .20 .50
39 Peter Forsberg .30 .75
40 Ron Francis .20 .50
41 German Titov .12 .30
42 Grant Fuhr .25 .60
43 Martin Brodeur .40 1.00
44 Claude Lemieux .10 .25
45 Trevor Linden .15 .40
46 Mark Messier .30 .75
47 Jeremy Roenick .25 .60
48 Peter Bondra .15 .40
49 Donald Audette .12 .30
50 Joe Nieuwendyk .07 .20
51 Mario Lemieux CL .60 1.50
52 Vitali Yachmenev .15 .40
53 Sergei Fedorov .25 .60
54 Kirk Muller .12 .30
55 Chad Kilger RC .15 .40
56 John LeClair .15 .40
57 Todd Bertuzzi RC .20 .50
58 Wayne Gretzky .60 1.50
59 Curtis Joseph .20 .50
60 Niklas Sundstrom .15 .40
61 Chris Chelios .15 .40
62 Radek Bonk .10 .25
63 Eric Daze .30 .75
64 Patrick Roy .40 1.00
65 Rob Niedermayer .12 .30
66 Mario Lemieux .60 1.50
67 Saku Koivu .15 .40
68 Ed Jovanovski .15 .40
69 Jim Carey .12 .30
70 Scott Stevens .12 .30
71 Steve Thomas .12 .30
72 Mats Sundin .30 .75
73 Teemu Selanne .30 .75
74 Tomas Sandstrom .12 .30
75 Pat LaFontaine .12 .30
76 Pat Verbeek .12 .30
77 Pavel Bure .12 .30
78 Jeff Brown .12 .30
79 Alexei Yashin .12 .30
80 Adam Oates .15 .40
81 Keith Tkachuk .15 .40
82 Brian Bradley .12 .30
83 John Vanbiesbrouck .15 .40
84 Alexander Selivanov .12 .30
85 Paul Coffey .12 .30
86 Scott Mellanby .12 .30
87 Slava Kozlov .12 .30
88 Eric Lindros .25 .60
89 Deron Quint .12 .30
90 Pierre Turgeon .12 .30
91 Rod Brind'Amour .15 .40
92 Doug Gilmour .20 .50
93 Sandis Ozolinsh .10 .25
94 Mikael Renberg .12 .30
95 Kevin Stevens .12 .30
96 Vincent Damphousse .12 .30
97 Felix Potvin .25 .60
98 Brian Leetch .12 .30
99 Steve Yzerman .40 1.00
100 Dale Hawerchuk .20 .50
101 Jason Arnott .12 .30
102 Ray Sheppard .12 .30
103 Mark Recchi .20 .50
104 Joe Juneau .10 .25
105 Luc Robitaille .10 .25
106 Theo Fleury .20 .50
107 Sean Burke .10 .25
108 Ron Hextall .15 .40
109 Shane Doan RC .50 1.25
110 Eric Lindros CL .25 .60
NNO Cool Trade Exch. EXP. .05 .15

1995-96 Donruss Elite Die Cuts

*DIE CUT VETS: 12X TO 30X BASIC CARDS
*DIE CUT ROOKIES: 4X TO 10X

1995-96 Donruss Elite Die Cuts Uncut

*UNCUT VETS: 10X TO 25X BASIC CARDS
*UNCUT ROOKIES: 5X TO 12X

1995-96 Donruss Elite Cutting Edge

COMPLETE SET (15) 25.00 60.00
1 Eric Lindros 2.00 5.00
2 Mario Lemieux 5.00 12.00
3 Wayne Gretzky 8.00 20.00
4 Peter Forsberg 3.00 8.00
5 Paul Kariya 2.00 5.00
6 Jaromir Jagr 3.00 8.00
7 Alexander Mogilny 1.00 2.50
8 Mark Messier 2.00 5.00
9 Sergei Fedorov 2.00 5.00
10 Pierre Turgeon 1.00 2.50
11 Mats Sundin 2.00 5.00
12 Brett Hull 2.00 5.00
13 Paul Coffey 1.00 2.50
14 Jeremy Roenick 2.00 5.00
15 Teemu Selanne 2.00 5.00

1995-96 Donruss Elite Lemieux/Lindros Series

COMP LEMIEUX SET (7) 125.00 300.00
COMMON LEMIEUX (1-6) 8.00 20.00
COMP LINDROS SET (7) 75.00 200.00
COMMON LINDROS (1-6) 6.00 15.00
7 Mario Lemieux AU 30.00 80.00
7E Eric Lindros AU 10.00 25.00
NNO Lemieux/Lindros AU/500 50.00 120.00

1995-96 Donruss Elite Painted Warriors

COMPLETE SET (10) 25.00 60.00
1 Patrick Roy 6.00 15.00
2 Felix Potvin 4.00 10.00
3 Martin Brodeur 6.00 15.00
4 Ed Belfour 2.00 5.00
5 Guy Hebert 2.00 5.00
6 John Vanbiesbrouck 2.50 6.00
7 Jocelyn Thibault 2.00 5.00
8 Ron Hextall 3.00 8.00
9 Grant Fuhr 2.50 6.00
10 Jim Carey 2.00 5.00
P3 Martin Brodeur PROMO 2.50 6.00
P4 Ed Belfour PROMO 2.50 6.00
P9 Grant Fuhr PROMO 2.50 6.00
P10 Jim Carey PROMO 1.50 4.00

1995-96 Donruss Elite Rookies

COMPLETE SET (15) 15.00 40.00
1 Eric Daze 1.00 2.50
2 Vitali Yachmenev 1.00 2.50
3 Daniel Alfredsson 2.00 5.00
4 Todd Bertuzzi 2.00 5.00
5 Byron Dafoe 1.00 2.50
6 Eric Fichaud 1.00 2.50
7 Marcus Ragnarsson 1.00 2.50
8 Saku Koivu 3.00 8.00
9 Chad Kilger 1.00 2.50
10 Radek Dvorak 1.00 2.50
11 Ed Jovanovski 2.00 5.00
12 Jeff O'Neill 2.00 5.00
13 Shane Doan 2.00 5.00
14 Niklas Sundstrom 1.00 2.50
15 Kyle McLaren 1.00 2.50

1995-96 Donruss Elite World Juniors

COMPLETE SET (44) 125.00 200.00
1 Marc Denis 3.00 8.00
2 Jose Theodore 5.00 12.00
3 Chad Allan 2.00 5.00
4 Nolan Baumgartner 2.00 5.00
5 Denis Gauthier 2.00 5.00
6 Jason Holland 2.00 5.00
7 Chris Phillips 3.00 8.00
8 Wade Redden 4.00 10.00
9 Rhett Warrener 2.00 5.00
10 Jason Botterill 2.00 5.00
11 Curtis Brown 2.00 5.00
12 Hnat Domenichelli 2.00 5.00
13 Christian Dube 2.00 5.00
14 Robb Gordon 2.00 5.00
15 Jarome Iginla 10.00 25.00
16 Daymond Langkow 3.00 8.00
17 Brad Larsen 2.00 5.00
18 Alyn McCauley 2.00 5.00
19 Craig Mills 2.00 5.00
20 Jason Podollan 2.00 5.00
21 Mike Watt 2.00 5.00
22 Jamie Wright 2.00 5.00
23 Brian Boucher 3.00 8.00
24 Marc Magliarditi 2.00 5.00
25 Bryan Berard 2.00 5.00
26 Chris Bogas 2.00 5.00
27 Ben Clymer 2.00 5.00
28 Jeff Kealty 2.00 5.00
29 Mike McBain 2.00 5.00
30 Jeremiah McCarthy 2.00 5.00
31 Tom Poti 2.00 5.00
32 Reg Berg 2.00 5.00
33 Matt Cullen 3.00 8.00
34 Chris Drury 6.00 15.00
35 Jeff Farkas 2.00 5.00
36 Casey Hankinson 2.00 5.00
37 Matt Herr 2.00 5.00
38 Mark Parrish 3.00 8.00
39 Erik Rasmussen 2.00 5.00
40 Marty Reasoner 2.00 5.00
41 Wyatt Smith 2.00 5.00
42 Brian Swanson 2.00 5.00
43 Mike Sylvia 2.00 5.00
44 Mike York 3.00 8.00

1996-97 Donruss Elite

*DIECUT: 1.5X TO 4X BASIC CARDS
1 Paul Kariya .40 1.00
2 Ron Hextall .40 1.00
3 Andy Moog .40 1.00
4 Brett Hull .75 2.00
5 Felix Potvin .60 1.50
6 Jocelyn Thibault .30 .75
7 Eric Lindros .60 1.50
8 Jaromir Jagr 1.25 3.00
9 Sergei Fedorov .60 1.50
10 Wayne Gretzky 2.50 6.00
11 Peter Bondra .40 1.00
12 Peter Forsberg .75 2.00
13 Stephane Fiset .30 .75
14 Owen Nolan .40 1.00
15 Rob Niedermayer .30 .75
16 Martin Brodeur 1.00 2.50
17 Ray Bourque .60 1.50
18 Todd Bertuzzi .40 1.00
19 Jim Carey .40 1.00
20 Chris Chelios .40 1.00
21 Chris Osgood .40 1.00
22 Mark Messier .75 2.00
23 Roman Hamrlik .25 .60
24 Kevin Hatcher .25 .60
25 Doug Weight .40 1.00
26 Mark Recchi .50 1.25
27 Jeremy Roenick .60 1.50
28 Derian Hatcher .25 .60
29 Grant Fuhr .60 1.50
30 Scott Stevens .40 1.00
31 Adam Oates .40 1.00
32 Scott Mellanby .30 .75
33 Mikael Renberg .30 .75
34 Corey Hirsch .30 .75
35 Michal Pivonka .25 .60
36 Stephane Richer .30 .75
37 Dominik Hasek .60 1.50
38 Steve Yzerman 1.00 2.50
39 Jeff O'Neill .25 .60
40 Ron Francis .50 1.25
41 Alexei Yashin .30 .75
42 Pat Verbeek .25 .60
43 Geoff Courtnall .25 .60
44 Doug Gilmour .50 1.25
45 Trevor Kidd .25 .60
46 Jason Arnott .30 .75
47 Niklas Sundstrom .25 .60
48 Rob Blake .40 1.00
49 Nikolai Khabibulin .30 .75
50 Igor Larionov .40 1.00
51 Sean Burke .25 .60
52 Zigmund Palffy .40 1.00
53 Jeff Friesen .25 .60
54 Theo Fleury .75 2.00
55 Mats Sundin .40 1.00
56 Alexander Mogilny .30 .75
57 John LeClair .40 1.00
58 Shayne Corson .30 .75
59 Teemu Selanne .75 2.00
60 Kelly Hrudey .30 .75
61 Keith Tkachuk .40 1.00
62 Joe Nieuwendyk .30 .75
63 Tom Barrasso .30 .75
64 Aaron Gavey .25 .60
65 Alexei Zhamnov .30 .75
66 Patrick Roy 1.00 2.50
67 Al MacInnis .50 1.25
68 Trevor Linden .40 1.00
69 Bill Guerin .40 1.00
70 Dimitri Khristich .25 .60
71 Eric Daze .30 .75
72 Paul Coffey .40 1.00
73 Keith Primeau .30 .75
74 John Vanbiesbrouck .40 1.00
75 Bernie Nicholls .30 .75
76 Yanic Perreault .25 .60
77 Jere Lehtinen .25 .60
78 Luc Robitaille .40 1.00
79 Todd Gill .30 .75
80 Saku Koivu .40 1.00
81 Vyacheslav Kozlov .25 .60
82 Ed Jovanovski .25 .60
83 Brendan Witt .25 .60
84 Alexandre Daigle .25 .60
85 Jari Kurri .40 1.00
86 Mike Vernon .30 .75
87 Jeff Beukeboom .25 .60
88 Mathieu Schneider .25 .60
89 Niklas Andersson .25 .60
90 Joe Juneau .25 .60
91 Ed Belfour .40 1.00
92 Curtis Joseph .50 1.25
93 Rod Brind'Amour .40 1.00
94 Vitali Yachmenev .25 .60
95 Alexander Selivanov .25 .60
96 Mike Richter .40 1.00
97 Bill Ranford .30 .75
98 Wendel Clark .60 1.50
99 Slava Fetisov .25 .60
100 Daniel Alfredsson .40 1.00
101 Pat LaFontaine .40 1.00
102 Joe Murphy .25 .60
103 Pavel Bure .40 1.00
104 Craig Janney .30 .75
105 Radek Dvorak .30 .75
106 Cory Stillman .25 .60
107 Adam Graves .25 .60
108 Aki Berg .25 .60
109 Mario Lemieux 1.50 4.00
110 Claude Lemieux .25 .60
111 Sergei Zubov .30 .75
112 Pierre Turgeon .30 .75
113 Damian Rhodes .30 .75
114 Daren Puppa .30 .75
115 Alexei Zhitnik .25 .60
116 Mike Modano .60 1.50
117 Kenny Jonsson .25 .60
118 Valeri Kamensky .30 .75
119 Valeri Bure .25 .60
120 Joe Sakic .75 2.00
121 Kirk McLean .30 .75
122 Petr Sykora .25 .60
123 Mike Gartner .50 1.25
124 Ryan Smyth .30 .75
125 Brian Leetch .30 .75
126 Brendan Shanahan .40 1.00
127 Geoff Sanderson .30 .75
128 Corey Schwab .30 .75
129 Anders Eriksson .25 .60
130 Harry York RC .40 1.00
131 Jarome Iginla .50 1.25
132 Eric Fichaud .30 .75
133 Patrick Lalime RC .50 1.25
134 Daymond Langkow .30 .75
135 Mattias Timander RC .40 1.00
136 Ethan Moreau RC .40 1.00
137 Christian Dube .25 .60
138 Sergei Berezin RC .60 1.50
139 Jose Theodore .50 1.25
140 Wade Redden .25 .60
141 Dainius Zubrus RC .50 1.25
142 Jim Campbell .25 .60
143 Daniel Goneau RC .40 1.00
144 Jamie Langenbrunner .25 .60
145 Rem Murray RC .40 1.00
146 Jonas Hoglund .25 .60
147 Bryan Berard .40 1.00
148 Chris Osgood CL (1-75) .30 .75
149 Eric Lindros CL .60 1.50
150 Jason Arnott CL (inserts) .30 .75

1996-97 Donruss Elite Aspirations

1 Eric Daze .75 2.00
2 Daniel Alfredsson 1.00 2.50
3 Petr Sykora .60 1.50
4 Todd Bertuzzi 1.00 2.50
5 Saku Koivu 1.00 2.50
6 Ed Jovanovski .75 2.00
7 Jim Campbell .60 1.50
8 Valeri Bure .60 1.50
9 Jeff O'Neill .60 1.50
10 Jere Lehtinen .60 1.50
11 Terry Ryan 1.00 2.50
12 Jonas Hoglund .60 1.50
13 Daymond Langkow .75 2.00
14 Eric Fichaud .75 2.00
15 Dainius Zubrus 1.25 3.00
16 Janne Niinimaa 1.00 2.50
17 Sergei Berezin 1.50 4.00
18 Daniel Goneau 1.00 2.50
19 Jarome Iginla 1.25 3.00
20 Ethan Moreau 1.00 2.50
21 Jamie Langenbrunner .60 1.50
22 Rem Murray 1.00 2.50
23 Bryan Berard 1.00 2.50
24 Wade Redden .60 1.50
25 Christian Dube .60 1.50

1996-97 Donruss Elite Hart to Hart

COMPLETE LEMIEUX SET (6) 40.00 100.00
COMMON LEMIEUX 8.00 20.00
COMMON LEMIEUX AU 25.00 60.00
COMPLETE LINDROS SET (6) 30.00 80.00
COMMON LINDROS 6.00 15.00
COMMON LINDROS AU 20.00 50.00
ELML Lindros/Lemieux AU/500 50.00 125.00

1996-97 Donruss Elite Painted Warriors

COMPLETE SET (10) 30.00 80.00
1 Patrick Roy 8.00 20.00
2 Mike Richter 4.00 10.00
3 Jim Carey 2.00 5.00
4 John Vanbiesbrouck 4.00 10.00
5 Jocelyn Thibault 2.00 5.00
6 Felix Potvin 5.00 12.00
7 Ed Belfour 4.00 10.00
8 Martin Brodeur 6.00 15.00
9 Nikolai Khabibulin 4.00 10.00
10 Stephane Fiset 2.00 5.00

1996-97 Donruss Elite Painted Warriors Promos

COMPLETE SET (10) 30.00 75.00
P1 Patrick Roy 6.00 12.00
P2 Mike Richter 6.00 12.00
P3 Jim Carey 6.00 12.00
P4 John Vanbiesbrouck 6.00 12.00
P5 Jocelyn Thibault 6.00 12.00
P6 Felix Potvin 6.00 12.00
P7 Ed Belfour 6.00 12.00
P8 Martin Brodeur 6.00 12.00
P9 Nikolai Khabibulin 6.00 12.00
P10 Stephane Fiset 6.00 12.00

1996-97 Donruss Elite Perspective

COMPLETE SET (12) 40.00 100.00
1 Wayne Gretzky 15.00 40.00
2 Mark Messier 3.00 8.00
3 Steve Yzerman 10.00 25.00
4 Mario Lemieux 12.00 30.00
5 Paul Coffey 2.00 5.00
6 Doug Gilmour 2.00 5.00
7 Brendan Shanahan 3.00 8.00
8 Jaromir Jagr 5.00 12.00
9 Brett Hull 4.00 10.00
10 Pat LaFontaine 2.00 5.00
11 Chris Chelios 2.00 5.00
12 Grant Fuhr 2.00 5.00

1996-97 Donruss Elite Status

COMPLETE SET (12) 20.00 50.00
1 Pavel Bure 2.50 6.00
2 Keith Tkachuk 2.50 6.00
3 Sergei Fedorov 3.00 8.00
4 Doug Weight 1.25 3.00
5 Paul Kariya 2.50 6.00
6 Owen Nolan 1.25 3.00
7 Peter Forsberg 6.00 15.00
8 Eric Lindros 2.50 6.00
9 Alexander Mogilny 1.25 3.00
10 Teemu Selanne 2.50 6.00
11 Joe Sakic 5.00 12.00
12 Jeremy Roenick 3.00 8.00

1997-98 Donruss Elite

COMPLETE SET (150) 15.00 40.00
1 Peter Forsberg .40 1.00
2 Mike Modano .30 .75
3 John Vanbiesbrouck .20 .50
4 Pavel Bure .20 .50
5 Mark Messier .40 1.00
6 Joe Thornton .30 .75
7 Paul Kariya .20 .50
8 Martin Brodeur .50 1.25
9 Wayne Gretzky 1.25 3.00
10 Eric Lindros .30 .75
11 Jaromir Jagr .60 1.50
12 Brett Hull .40 1.00
13 Jarome Iginla .25 .60
14 Patrick Roy .50 1.25
15 Steve Yzerman .50 1.25
16 Sergei Samsonov .15 .40
17 Teemu Selanne .40 1.00
18 Brendan Shanahan .20 .50
19 Curtis Joseph .25 .60
20 Saku Koivu .20 .50
21 Ray Bourque .30 .75
22 Jaroslav Svejkovsky .15 .40
23 Keith Primeau .15 .40
24 Alexandre Daigle .12 .30
25 Vyacheslav Kozlov .15 .40
26 Jozef Stumpel .12 .30
27 Alexei Yashin .15 .40
28 Marian Hossa RC .25 .60
29 Bryan Berard .12 .30
30 Dominik Hasek .30 .75
31 Chris Chelios .20 .50
32 Derian Hatcher .15 .40
33 Ed Jovanovski .12 .30
34 Zigmund Palffy .20 .50
35 Ron Hextall .20 .50
36 Daymond Langkow .12 .30
37 Daniel Cleary .15 .40
38 Alyn McCauley .15 .40
39 Sean Burke .12 .30
40 Brian Leetch .15 .40
41 Joe Juneau .12 .30
42 Damian Rhodes .15 .40
43 Dino Ciccarelli .20 .50
44 Valeri Kamensky .15 .40
45 Guy Hebert .15 .40
46 Brad Isbister .15 .40
47 Adam Graves .12 .30
48 Andrew Cassels .12 .30
49 Joe Sakic .40 1.00
50 Dainius Zubrus .15 .40
51 Roberto Luongo RC 3.00 8.00
52 Ethan Moreau .12 .30
53 Chris Osgood .20 .50
54 Stephane Fiset .15 .40
55 Sergei Berezin .15 .40
56 Mike Richter .20 .50
57 Valeri Bure .12 .30
58 Mats Sundin .20 .50
59 Mike Dunham .15 .40
60 Byron Dafoe .15 .40
61 Joe Nieuwendyk .15 .40
62 Mike Grier .15 .40
63 Paul Coffey .20 .50
64 Chris Phillips .15 .40
65 Patrik Elias RC .30 .75
66 Andy Moog .20 .50
67 Geoff Sanderson .15 .40
68 Jere Lehtinen .15 .40
69 Alexander Mogilny .15 .40
70 Ryan Smyth .15 .40
71 John LeClair .20 .50
72 Olli Jokinen RC .25 .60
73 Doug Gilmour .25 .60
74 Theo Fleury .25 .60
75 Adam Deadmarsh .12 .30
76 Scott Mellanby .15 .40
77 Jeremy Roenick .30 .75
78 Jim Campbell .12 .30
79 Daren Puppa .15 .40
80 Vaclav Prospal RC .15 .40
81 Vincent Damphousse .15 .40
82 Derek Plante .15 .40
83 Sandis Ozolinsh .12 .30
84 Darren McCarty .15 .40
85 Luc Robitaille .20 .50
86 Wade Redden .12 .30
87 Eric Fichaud .15 .40
88 Jocelyn Thibault .15 .40
89 Trevor Linden .20 .50
90 Boyd Devereaux .15 .40
91 Chris Gratton .12 .30
92 Janne Niinimaa .15 .40
93 Jeff Friesen .15 .40
94 Roman Hamrlik .12 .30
95 Jason Arnott .15 .40
96 Sergei Fedorov .30 .75
97 Tony Amonte .15 .40
98 Mattias Ohlund .15 .40
99 Patrick Marleau .20 .50
100 Felix Potvin .30 .75
101 Tommy Salo .12 .30
102 Ed Belfour .20 .50
103 Doug Weight .20 .50
104 Daniel Alfredsson .20 .50
105 Pierre Turgeon .15 .40
106 Espen Knutsen RC .20 .50
107 Trevor Kidd .12 .30
108 Alexei Morozov .15 .40
109 Oleg Tverdovsky .15 .40
110 Grant Fuhr .30 .75
111 Pat LaFontaine .20 .50
112 Keith Tkachuk .20 .50
113 Ron Francis .25 .60
114 Derek Morris RC .20 .50
115 Joe Sakic G .40 1.00
116 Brian Leetch G .15 .40
117 Alyn McCauley G .15 .40
118 Pavel Bure G .20 .50
119 Eric Lindros G .30 .75
120 Teemu Selanne G .40 1.00
121 Jarome Iginla G .25 .60
122 Steve Yzerman G .50 1.25
123 Daniel Cleary G .15 .40
124 Bryan Berard G .12 .30
125 Jaromir Jagr G .60 1.50
126 John Vanbiesbrouck G .20 .50
127 Mark Messier G .40 1.00
128 Patrick Marleau G .20 .50
129 Mike Modano G .30 .75
130 Zigmund Palffy G .20 .50
131 Felix Potvin G .30 .75
132 Derek Morris G .20 .50
133 Brendan Shanahan G .20 .50
134 Sergei Samsonov G .15 .40
135 Dainius Zubrus G .15 .40
136 Paul Kariya G .20 .50
137 Martin Brodeur G .50 1.25
138 Joe Thornton G .30 .75
139 Mattias Ohlund G .15 .40
140 Ryan Smyth G .15 .40
141 Jaroslav Svejkovsky G .15 .40
142 Patrick Roy G .50 1.25
143 Wayne Gretzky G 1.25 3.00
144 Espen Knutsen G .20 .50
145 Patrick Marleau CL .20 .50
146 Pat Lafontaine CL .20 .50
147 Mike Gartner CL .25 .60
148 Joe Thornton CL .30 .75
149 Teemu Selanne CL .40 1.00
150 Mark Messier CL .40 1.00

1997-98 Donruss Elite Aspirations

*VETS: 4X TO 10X BASIC CARDS
*ROOKIE STAR: 2.5X TO 6X BASIC RC

1997-98 Donruss Elite Status

*VETS: 10X TO 25X BASIC CARDS
*ROOKIES: 6X TO 15X BASIC CARDS

1997-98 Donruss Elite Back to the Future

COMPLETE SET (8) 30.00 60.00
1 E.Lindros/J.Thornton 3.00 8.00
2 J.Thibault/M.Denis 3.00 8.00
3 T.Selanne/P.Marleau 3.00 8.00
4 J.Jagr/D.Cleary 4.00 10.00
5 S.Fedorov/P.Forsberg 5.00 12.00
6 B.Hull/B.Hull 4.00 10.00
7 M.Brodeur/R.Luongo 5.00 12.00
8 G.Howe/S.Yzerman 6.00 15.00

1997-98 Donruss Elite Back to the Future Autographs

1 E.Lindros/J.Thornton 60.00 150.00
2 J.Thibault/M.Denis 30.00 80.00
3 T.Selanne/P.Marleau 50.00 120.00
4 J.Jagr/D.Cleary 80.00 150.00
5 S.Fedorov/P.Forsberg 80.00 150.00
6 B.Hull/B.Hull 75.00 150.00
7 M.Brodeur/R.Luongo 150.00 300.00
8 G.Howe/S.Yzerman 200.00 400.00

1997-98 Donruss Elite Craftsmen

COMPLETE SET (30) 75.00 150.00
*MASTER/100: 2X TO 5X BASIC INSERTS
1 John Vanbiesbrouck 1.00 2.50
2 Eric Lindros 1.50 4.00
3 Joe Sakic 2.50 6.00
4 Mark Messier 2.00 5.00
5 Jaroslav Svejkovsky 1.00 2.50
6 Dominik Hasek 3.00 8.00
7 Chris Osgood 1.00 2.50
8 Martin Brodeur 4.00 10.00
9 Sergei Fedorov 2.00 5.00
10 Daniel Cleary 1.00 2.50
11 Patrick Marleau 1.50 4.00
12 Sergei Samsonov 1.25 3.00
13 Felix Potvin 1.50 4.00
14 Patrick Roy 8.00 20.00
15 Teemu Selanne 1.50 4.00
16 Steve Yzerman 8.00 20.00
17 Jarome Iginla 2.00 5.00
18 Mike Modano 2.50 6.00
19 Wayne Gretzky 6.00 15.00
20 Pavel Bure 1.50 4.00
21 Ryan Smyth 1.25 3.00
22 Paul Kariya 1.50 4.00
23 Peter Forsberg 4.00 10.00
24 Joe Thornton 2.50 6.00
25 Jaromir Jagr 2.50 6.00
26 Bryan Berard 1.00 2.50
27 Brendan Shanahan 1.50 4.00
28 Keith Tkachuk 1.50 4.00
29 Curtis Joseph 1.50 4.00
30 Brian Leetch 1.00 2.50

1997-98 Donruss Elite Prime Numbers

1A Peter Forsberg 2/54* 30.00 80.00
1B Peter Forsberg 5/204* 8.00 20.00
1C Peter Forsberg 4/250* 8.00 20.00
2A Patrick Roy 3/49* 40.00 100.00
2B Patrick Roy 4/309* 15.00 40.00
2C Patrick Roy 9/340* 15.00 40.00
3A Mark Messier 2/95* 8.00 20.00
3B Mark Messier 9/205* 4.00 10.00
3C Mark Messier 5/290* 4.00 10.00
4A Eric Lindros 4/36* 15.00 40.00
4B Eric Lindros 3/406* 4.00 10.00
4C Eric Lindros 6/430* 5.00 12.00
5A Paul Kariya 2/46* 30.00 80.00
5B Paul Kariya 4/206* 8.00 20.00
5C Paul Kariya 6/240* 4.00 10.00
6A Jaromir Jagr 2/66* 20.00 50.00
6B Jaromir Jagr 6/206* 10.00 25.00
6C Jaromir Jagr 6/260* 10.00 25.00
7A Teemu Selanne 2/37* 15.00 40.00
7B Teemu Selanne 3/207* 4.00 10.00
7C Teemu Selanne 7/230* 6.00 15.00
8A John Vanbiesbrouck 2/88* 6.00 15.00
8B John Vanbiesbrouck 8/208* 4.00 10.00
8C John Vanbiesbrouck 8/280* 4.00 10.00
9A Brendan Shanahan 3/35* 12.50 30.00
9B Brendan Shanahan 3/305* 4.00 10.00
9C Brendan Shanahan 5/330* 4.00 10.00
10A Steve Yzerman 5/39* 60.00 150.00
10B Steve Yzerman 3/509* 12.50 30.00
10C Steve Yzerman 9/530* 12.50 30.00
11B Joe Sakic 0/307* 6.00 15.00
11C Joe Sakic 7/300* 6.00 15.00
12A Pavel Bure 3/88* 8.00 20.00
12B Pavel Bure 8/308* 4.00 10.00
12C Pavel Bure 8/380* 4.00 10.00

1997-98 Donruss Elite Prime Numbers Die-Cuts

1A Peter Forsberg 2/200* 12.50 30.00
1B Peter Forsberg 5/50* 50.00 125.00
2A Patrick Roy 3/300* 15.00 40.00
2B Patrick Roy 4/40* 60.00 150.00
3A Mark Messier 2/200* 8.00 20.00
3B Mark Messier 9/90* 12.50 30.00
4A Eric Lindros 4/400* 8.00 20.00
4B Eric Lindros 3/30* 20.00 50.00
5A Paul Kariya 2/200* 12.50 30.00
5B Paul Kariya 4/40* 50.00 125.00
6A Jaromir Jagr 2/200* 10.00 25.00
6B Jaromir Jagr 6/60* 30.00 80.00
7A Teemu Selanne 2/200* 8.00 20.00
7B Teemu Selanne 3/30* 15.00 40.00
8A John Vanbiesbrouck 2/200* 8.00 20.00
8B John Vanbiesbrouck 8/80* 12.50 30.00
9A Brendan Shanahan 3/300* 8.00 20.00
9B Brendan Shanahan 3/30* 20.00 50.00
10A Steve Yzerman 5/500* 15.00 40.00
10B Steve Yzerman 3/30* 60.00 150.00
11A Joe Sakic 3/300* 10.00 25.00
12A Pavel Bure 3/300* 8.00 20.00
12B Pavel Bure 8/80* 12.50 30.00

1998-99 Donruss Elite Promos

1 John LeClair 10.00 25.00
2 Brett Hull 6.00 15.00
3 Saku Koivu 4.00 10.00
4 Mark Messier 10.00 25.00
5 Keith Tkachuk 6.00 15.00
6 Teemu Selanne 15.00 40.00
7 Sergei Samsonov 2.00 5.00
8 Pavel Bure 15.00 40.00
9 Brendan Shanahan 10.00 25.00
10 Dominik Hasek 2.00 5.00
11 Joe Thornton 20.00 50.00
12 Joe Sakic 20.00 50.00
13 Martin Brodeur 10.00 25.00
14 Peter Forsberg 20.00 50.00
15 Steve Yzerman 40.00 100.00
16 Patrick Roy 40.00 100.00
17 Jaromir Jagr 10.00 25.00
18 Paul Kariya 20.00 50.00
19 Eric Lindros 15.00 40.00
20 Wayne Gretzky 40.00 125.00

1997-98 Donruss Limited

COMPLETE SET (200) 150.00 400.00
COMP.COUNTERPART.SET (100) 10.00 25.00
1 Brendan Shanahan
Harry York C .25 .60
2 P.Forsberg/M.Knuble RC C .60 1.50
3 Chris Osgood
Kirk McLean C .25 .60
4 Wayne Gretzky S 20.00 50.00
5 John Vanbiesbrouck
Ed Jovanovski D 1.00 2.50
6 Paul Coffey
Darryl Sydor C .25 .60
7 Pavel Bure
Valeri Bure C .25 .60
8 Sergei Berezin
Jaromir Jagr U 2.00 5.00
9 Saku Koivu
Mats Sundin C .15 .40
10 Trevor Kidd
Corey Hirsch C .08 .25
11 Teemu Selanne S 2.50 6.00
12 Zigmund Palffy
Radek Bonk C .08 .25
13 Mats Sundin
Sergei Berezin D 1.00 2.50
14 Jim Carey
Bill Ranford C .08 .25
15 John LeClair
Claude Lemieux C .08 .25
16 Janne Niinimaa
Chris Chelios U 1.50 4.00
17 Kevin Hodson
Michael Knuble D 1.00 2.50
18 Adam Graves
Keith Jones C .08 .25
19 M.Modano/T.Linden C .40 1.00
20 Brett Hull S 4.00 10.00
21 Derian Hatcher
Kevin Hatcher C .08 .25
22 Daniel Alfredsson
Dave Andreychuk C .08 .25
23 Steve Shields
Vaclav Varada D 1.00 2.50
24 Theo Fleury
Geoff Courtnall C .08 .25
25 Mark Messier
Dino Ciccarelli C .25 .60
26 Ryan Smyth S 2.00 5.00
27 Mike Grier
Jason Arnott D 1.00 2.50
28 Ed Belfour
Andy Moog C .25 .60
29 Jarome Iginla
Ed Belfour
Martin St. Louis
Jean-Sebastien Giguere
Jose Theodore
Manny Legace 2.00 5.00
30 Eric Lindros
Todd Bertuzzi C .25 .60
31 Daymond Langkow
David Roberts C .08 .25
32 Mike Richter
Grant Fuhr C .15 .40
33 Adam Oates
Jaroslav Svejkovsky D 1.00 2.50
34 Saku Koivu
Darcy Tucker D 1.00 2.50
35 Paul Kariya S 2.50 6.00
36 J.Sakic/B.Nicholls C .50 1.25
37 Ed Jovanovski
D.J. Smith C RC .08 .25
38 Vaclav Prospal
Brendan Shanahan U 1.50 4.00
39 Mike Peca
Marty Murray C .08 .25
40 Mike Gartner
Wendel Clark C .08 .25
41 Steve Yzerman S 12.00 30.00
42 M.Modano/R.Turek D 1.50 4.00
43 Joe Nieuwendyk
Jarome Iginla C .08 .25
44 P.Roy/J.Thibault C 1.25 3.00
45 Hnat Domenichelli
Andrew Cassels C .08 .25
46 Christian Dube
Steve Sullivan C .08 .25
47 Marc Denis
Valeri Kamensky D 1.00 2.50
48 Peter Forsberg S 6.00 15.00
49 Derek Plante
Todd Harvey C .08 .25
50 Mike Grier
Eric Lindros U 2.50 6.00
51 B.Hull/J.Campbell D 1.25 3.00
52 Mark Recchi
Landon Wilson C .08 .25
53 Darcy Tucker
Pascal Rheaume C RC .08 .25
54 Chris O'Sullivan
Anders Eriksson C .08 .25
55 Jaromir Jagr S 6.00 15.00
56 Paul Kariya
Teemu Selanne D 1.00 2.50
57 Felix Potvin
Damian Rhodes C .25 .60
58 Brian Holzinger
Mike Ricci C .08 .25
59 Eric Fichaud
Travis Green D 1.00 2.50
60 Ethan Moreau
John MacLean C .08 .25
61 Joe Juneau
Jeff O'Neill C .08 .25
62 John Vanbiesbrouck S 2.00 5.00
63 Byron Dafoe
Steve Shields C RC .08 .25
64 Mikael Renberg
Niklas Sundstrom C .08 .25
65 Ryan Smyth
Eric Daze C .08 .25
66 Doug Gilmour
Pascal Rheaume D 1.00 2.50
67 Jim Campbell
Craig Janney C .08 .25
68 Alexander Mogilny
Mathew Barnaby C .08 .25
69 Alexei Yashin S 2.00 5.00
70 Bryan Berard
Brian Leetch U 1.50 4.00
71 Alexei Yashin
Brain Savage C .08 .25
72 Jeff Friesen
Darren McCarty C .08 .25
73 Dimitri Khristich
Chad Kilger C .08 .25
74 M.Brodeur/D.Andreychuk D 2.50 6.00
75 Luc Robitaille
Pat Verbeek C .08 .25
76 D.Hasek/J.Storr C .50 1.25
77 Felix Potvin S 2.50 6.00
78 Mike Dunham
Vadim Sharifijanov D 1.00 2.50
79 Jason Arnott
Rob Niedermayer C .08 .25
80 Eric Desjardins
Chris Phillips C .08 .25
81 Curtis Joseph
Jose Theodore C .25 .60
82 Doug Gilmour
Rod Brind'Amour C .08 .25
83 Keith Tkachuk
Rick Tocchet C .25 .60
84 Mark Messier S 2.50 6.00
85 Chris Pronger
Aki Berg C .08 .25
86 Marcel Cousineau
Dominik Hasek U 2.50 6.00
87 Ethan Moreau
Chris Chelios D 1.00 2.50
88 Jonas Hoglund
Rob Zamuner C .08 .25
89 Ron Hextall
Kevin Hodson C .08 .25
90 John LeClair S 2.50 6.00
91 Vaclav Prospal RC
Viktor Kozlov C .25 .60
92 R.Bourque/J.Thornton D 2.50 6.00
93 Oleg Tverdovsky
Sergei Zubov C .08 .25
94 Ethan Moreau
John LeClair U 1.50 4.00
95 Adam Deadmarsh S 2.00 5.00
96 Jaroslav Svejkovsky
Jozef Stumpel C .08 .25
97 W.Gretzky/V.Vorobiev D 6.00 15.00
98 Sergei Fedorov S 3.00 8.00
99 Jim Campbell
Ryan Smyth U 1.50 4.00
100 Vaclav Prospal
Paul Coffey D 1.00 2.50
101 Wayne Primeau
Sean Pronger C .08 .25
102 Jean Giguere
Felix Potvin U .08 .25
103 Curtis Joseph S 2.50 6.00
104 Pavel Bure
Alexander Mogilny D 1.00 2.50
105 Jeremy Roenick
Tony Amonte C .25 .60
106 Sandis Ozolinsh
Kirk McLaren C .08 .25
107 Anson Carter
Steve Kelly C .08 .25
108 Paul Coffey S 2.00 5.00
109 Dainius Zubrus
Peter Forsberg U 2.50 6.00
110 Travis Green
Scott Mellanby C .08 .25
111 Pat LaFontaine
Valeri Kamensky C .08 .25
112 Adam Oates S 2.00 5.00
113 John Vanbiesbrouck
Roman Turek C .08 .25
114 J.Iginla/P.Kariya U 4.00 10.00
115 S.Yzerman/C.Osgood D 4.00 10.00
116 Marcel Cousineau
Steve Sullivan D .60 1.50
117 Owen Nolan
Steve Rucchin C .08 .25
118 Donald Audette
Ted Donato C .08 .25
119 Geoff Sanderson
Sean Burke D .75 2.00
120 Jeremy Roenick S 4.00 10.00
121 Vladimir Vorobiev RC
Andreas Johansson .08 .25
122 Alexander Mogilny S 2.00 5.00
123 Jocelyn Thibault
Terry Ryan D 1.00 2.50
124 Eric Fichaud
Nikolai Khabibulin C .08 .25
125 R.Bourque/E.Messier RC C .50 1.25
126 S.Fedorov/K.Primeau C .30 .75
127 M.Denis/M.Brodeur U 4.00 10.00
128 Mats Sundin S 2.50 6.00
129 Peter Bondra
Roman Vopat C .08 .25
130 Tommy Salo
Corey Schwab C .08 .25
131 Sergei Samsonov
Jim Carey D 1.00 2.50
132 A.Deadmarsh/J.Sakic D 2.00 5.00
133 Daymond Langkow
Keith Tkachuk U 1.50 4.00
134 Mike Richter S 2.50 6.00
135 Geoff Sanderson
Jere Lehtinen C .08 .25
136 Janne Niinimaa
Jamie Pushor C .08 .25
137 Andreas Dackell
Vincent Damphousse C .08 .25
138 Keith Tkachuk S 2.00 5.00
139 Ray Bourque S 4.00 10.00
140 K.Tkachuk/J.Roenick D 1.25 3.00
141 Rem Murray
Ray Sheppard C .08 .25
142 Peter Schafer
Patrick Lalime C .08 .25
143 Jaroslav Svejkovsky
Teemu Selanne U 2.00 5.00
144 Todd Marchant
Tony Granato C .08 .25
145 Sandis Ozolinsh S 1.50 4.00
146 Roman Hamrlik
Nicklas Lidstrom C .25 .60
147 Dominik Hasek S 6.00 15.00
148 Chris Gratton
Daniel Goneau C .08 .25
149 Martin Brodeur S 8.00 20.00
150 M.Brodeur/S.Fiset C .60 1.50
151 J.Theodore/P.Roy U 8.00 20.00
152 Jose Theodore
Mark Recchi D 1.00 2.50
153 Pavel Bure S 2.50 6.00
154 Sergei Berezin
Denis Pederson C .08 .25
155 Doug Gilmour S 2.00 5.00
156 Peter Nedved
Kirk Muller C .08 .25
157 Theo Fleury S 2.00 5.00
158 Harry York
Pierre Turgeon D 1.00 2.50
159 Andreas Johansson
Patrick Lalime D 1.00 2.50
160 Marcel Cousineau
Jeff Hackett C .08 .25
161 Adam Deadmarsh
Alexandre Daigle C .08 .25
162 Adam Oates
Todd Warriner C .08 .25
163 Zigmund Palffy S 1.50 4.00
164 Ed Belfour S 2.50 6.00
165 S.Koivu/S.Yzerman U 6.00 15.00
166 Chris Chelios
Scott Lachance C .25 .60
167 Jamie Langenbrunner
Brandon Convery C .08 .25
168 Janne Niinimaa
John LeClair D .75 2.00
169 Brendan Shanahan S 2.50 6.00
170 Darren Puppa
Garth Snow C .08 .25
171 Chris Osgood S 2.00 5.00
172 Pierre Turgeon
Shane Corson C .08 .25
173 Doug Weight
Rem Murray D .75 2.00
174 Eric Fichaud
Curtis Joseph U 1.50 4.00
175 Chris Chelios S 2.00 5.00
176 Wade Redden
Scott Stevens C .08 .25
177 Jarome Iginla
Theo Fleury D 1.00 2.50
178 Vaclav Varada
Igor Larionov C .08 .25
179 Brian Leetch S 2.00 5.00
180 Stephane Fiset
Roman Vopat D 1.00 2.50
181 Zigmund Palffy
Bryan Berard D 1.00 2.50
182 Bryan Berard
Brian Leetch C 1.00 2.50
183 Eric Lindros S 2.50 6.00
184 Derek Plante
Brian Holzinger D .60 1.50
185 B.Hull/M.Gelinas C .30 .75
186 Daniel Alfredsson
Damian Rhodes D 1.00 2.50
187 J.Thornton/M.Messier U 4.00 10.00
188 Mike Vernon
Ken Wregget C .08 .25
189 Alexei Yashin
Wade Redden D .60 1.50
190 Joe Sakic S 8.00 20.00
191 Doug Weight
Darren Turcotte C .08 .25
192 Daymond Langkow
Darren Puppa C .08 .25
193 Mike Modano S 4.00 10.00
194 Sean Burke
Mike Dunham C .08 .25
195 Dainius Zubrus
Sebastien Bordeleau C .08 .25
196 Owen Nolan
Jeff Friesen D .75 2.00
197 Vladimir Vorobiev
Sergei Fedorov U 2.00 5.00
198 Patrick Roy S 15.00 40.00
199 Mike Grier
Ron Francis C .08 .25
200 P.Marleau/W.Gretzky U 12.00 30.00
P183 Eric Lindros PROMO .40 1.00

1997-98 Donruss Limited Exposure

*COUNTERPARTS: 5X TO 10X BASIC CARDS
*DOUBLE TEAM: 5X TO 10X BASIC CARDS
*STAR FACTOR: 2.5X TO 6X BASIC CARDS
*UNLIMITED: 2X TO 5X BASIC CARDS

1997-98 Donruss Limited Fabric of the Game

1 Wayne Gretzky HF 40.00 100.00
2 Martin Brodeur S 6.00 15.00
3 Dainius Zubrus M 1.00 2.50
4 Joe Sakic SS 8.00 20.00
5 Joe Sakic HF 12.00 30.00
6 Sergei Fedorov S 3.00 8.00
7 John Vanbiesbrouck HF 8.00 20.00
8 Saku Koivu M 2.50 6.00
9 Jean-Sebastien Giguere M 2.50 6.00
10 Paul Kariya S 3.00 8.00
11 Mike Richter SS 4.00 10.00
12 Paul Coffey L 10.00 25.00
13 Brendan Shanahan L 20.00 50.00
14 Jaromir Jagr SS 6.00 15.00
15 Felix Potvin SS 6.00 15.00
16 Mats Sundin SS 4.00 10.00
17 Mike Vernon HF 6.00 15.00
18 Keith Tkachuk S 2.00 5.00
19 Doug Gilmour HF 6.00 15.00
20 Patrick Roy L 40.00 100.00
21 Sergei Samsonov M 2.50 6.00
22 Mike Grier M 1.00 2.50
23 Curtis Joseph SS 3.00 8.00
24 Zigmund Palffy S 2.00 5.00
25 Chris Osgood S 2.00 5.00
26 Mats Sundin S 3.00 8.00
27 Kelly Hrudey HF 6.00 15.00
28 Brett Hull L 25.00 60.00
29 Ray Bourque HF 10.00 25.00
30 Nikolai Khabibulin S 2.00 5.00
31 Bryan Berard M 1.00 2.50
32 Jaroslav Svejkovsky M 1.00 2.50
33 Ed Belfour SS 4.00 10.00
34 Wayne Gretzky L 75.00 200.00
35 Jeremy Roenick SS 5.00 12.00
36 Andy Moog L 10.00 25.00
37 Eric Lindros S 3.00 8.00
38 Brett Hull SS 5.00 12.00
39 Marcel Cousineau M 1.00 2.50
40 Paul Kariya M 2.50 6.00
41 Mike Dunham M 1.00 2.50
42 Chris Phillips M 1.00 2.50
43 Teemu Selanne SS 6.00 15.00
44 Mark Messier L 15.00 40.00
45 Grant Fuhr L 15.00 40.00
46 Daniel Alfredsson M 1.50 4.00
47 Marc Denis M 1.00 2.50
48 Daymond Langkow M 1.00 2.50
49 Steve Yzerman HF 20.00 50.00
50 Ryan Smyth S 2.00 5.00
51 Alexander Mogilny HF 6.00 15.00
52 Ron Hextall HF 8.00 20.00
53 Brendan Shanahan S 3.00 8.00
54 Jim Carey S 2.00 5.00
55 Eric Lindros S 3.00 8.00
56 Eric Fichaud M 1.00 2.50
57 Sergei Berezin M 1.00 2.50
58 Chris Chelios HF 6.00 15.00
59 Mark Messier HF 10.00 25.00
60 Damian Rhodes M 2.50 6.00
61 Jarome Iginla M 3.00 8.00
62 Jocelyn Thibault S 2.00 5.00
63 John LeClair S 2.00 5.00
64 Brian Leetch SS 4.00 10.00
65 Dominik Hasek S 6.00 15.00
66 Pavel Bure SS 4.00 10.00
67 Mike Modano S 4.00 10.00
68 Daniel Cleary M 1.00 2.50
69 Janne Niinimaa M 1.00 2.50
70 Steve Yzerman L 40.00 100.00
71 Jose Theodore M 3.00 6.00
72 Peter Forsberg S 5.00 12.00

1997-98 Donruss Preferred

COMPLETE SET (200) 200.00 400.00
COMP.BRONZE SET (100) 12.50 30.00
1 Dominik Hasek G 8.00 20.00
2 Peter Forsberg G 10.00 25.00
3 Brendan Shanahan P 8.00 20.00
4 Wayne Gretzky P 20.00 50.00
5 Eric Lindros P 8.00 20.00
6 Keith Tkachuk G 4.00 10.00
7 Mark Messier P 8.00 20.00
8 Mike Modano G 6.00 15.00
9 John Vanbiesbrouck P 8.00 20.00
10 Paul Kariya P 8.00 20.00
11 Saku Koivu G 4.00 10.00
12 Paul Coffey B .25 .60
13 Joe Juneau B .20 .50
14 Jeff Friesen S .75 2.00
15 Brett Hull G 5.00 12.00
16 Martin Brodeur G 10.00 25.00
17 Jarome Iginla G 5.00 12.00
18 Keith Primeau S .75 2.00
19 Ed Jovanovski B .20 .50
20 Jamie Langenbrunner B .08 .25
21 Derian Hatcher S .75 2.00
22 Brian Leetch G 4.00 10.00
23 Daymond Langkow S 1.50 4.00
24 Ray Bourque S 3.00 8.00
25 Pavel Bure G 2.50 6.00
26 Janne Niinimaa S 1.50 4.00
27 Jamie Storr S 1.50 4.00
28 Darcy Tucker B .08 .25
29 Anson Carter B .20 .50
30 Jeff O'Neill B .08 .25
31 Jason Arnott G 1.50 4.00
32 Tommy Salo B .20 .50
33 Petr Nedved B .20 .50
34 Mike Peca B .20 .50
35 Ethan Moreau S .75 2.00
36 Ray Sheppard B .20 .50
37 Damian Rhodes B .20 .50
38 Mats Sundin S 2.00 5.00
39 Alexander Mogilny G 3.00 8.00
40 Mike Dunham S 1.50 4.00
41 Steve Yzerman P 15.00 40.00
42 Alexei Yashin S .75 2.00
43 Jim Carey S 1.50 4.00
44 Mike Grier S .75 2.00
45 Steve Rucchin B .08 .25
46 Mark Recchi S .75 2.00
47 Mike Gartner B .20 .50
48 Alexandre Daigle S 1.50 4.00
49 Eric Fichaud G 3.00 8.00
50 Harry York B .08 .25
51 Dino Ciccarelli B .20 .50
52 Bill Ranford B .20 .50
53 Adam Deadmarsh G 1.50 4.00
54 Ed Belfour B .25 .60
55 Jozef Stumpel S 1.50 4.00
56 Rem Murray B .08 .25
57 Pat Verbeek B .08 .25
58 Pat LaFontaine S 1.50 4.00
59 Dainius Zubrus S 1.50 4.00
60 Grant Fuhr B .20 .50
61 Rob Niedermayer B .20 .50
62 Brian Savage B .08 .25
63 Gary Roberts B .08 .25
64 Tony Amonte B .20 .50
65 Jere Lehtinen B .20 .50
66 Dave Andreychuk B .20 .50
67 Rod Brind'Amour B .20 .50
68 Mikael Renberg B .20 .50
69 Doug Gilmour S 1.50 4.00
70 Kevin Hatcher B .08 .25
71 Byron Dafoe B .20 .50
72 Derek Plante S .75 2.00
73 Trevor Kidd B .20 .50
74 Doug Weight S 1.50 4.00
75 Valeri Bure B .08 .25
76 John LeClair G 4.00 10.00
77 Sergei Berezin B .20 .50
78 Peter Bondra S 1.50 4.00
79 Bryan Berard G 3.00 8.00
80 Steve Shields B RC .25 .60
81 Chris Osgood G 3.00 8.00
82 Mike Vernon B .20 .50
83 Martin Gelinas B .20 .50
84 Curtis Joseph S 2.00 5.00
85 Geoff Sanderson S 1.50 4.00
86 Patrick Roy P 15.00 40.00
87 Jocelyn Thibault G 3.00 8.00
88 Jeremy Roenick S 2.50 6.00
89 Trevor Linden B .20 .50
90 Daniel Alfredsson S 1.50 4.00
91 Sergei Zubov B .08 .25
92 Dimitri Khristich S .75 2.00
93 Brian Holzinger B .08 .25
94 Andrew Cassels B .08 .25
95 Teemu Selanne G 4.00 10.00
96 Ron Hextall B .20 .50
97 Wade Redden B .08 .25
98 Jim Campbell B .08 .25
99 Felix Potvin G 5.00 12.00
100 Adam Oates S 1.50 4.00
101 Nikolai Khabibulin B .20 .50
102 Jose Theodore S 2.50 6.00
103 Sandis Ozolinsh S .75 2.00
104 Sean Burke B .20 .50
105 Vaclav Prospal G RC 3.00 8.00
106 Zigmund Palffy G 3.00 8.00
107 Kyle McLaren B .08 .25
108 Owen Nolan S 1.50 4.00
109 Chris Pronger S 1.50 4.00
110 Daren Puppa B .20 .50
111 Garth Snow B .20 .50
112 Aki Berg B .08 .25
113 Andy Moog B .20 .50
114 Darren McCarty B .08 .25
115 Joe Nieuwendyk B .20 .50
116 Eric Daze S 1.50 4.00
117 Pierre Turgeon S 1.50 4.00
118 Ken Wregget B .20 .50
119 Ryan Smyth G 3.00 8.00
120 Kirk Muller B .08 .25
121 Luc Robitaille B .20 .50
122 Sergei Fedorov G 6.00 15.00
123 Sean Pronger B .08 .25
124 Mike Richter S 2.00 5.00
125 Jaromir Jagr P 8.00 20.00
126 Claude Lemieux B .08 .25
127 Chris Chelios S 2.00 5.00
128 Joe Sakic P 12.50 30.00
129 Guy Hebert S 1.50 4.00
130 Chris Gratton S 1.50 4.00
131 Steve Sullivan B .08 .25
132 Al MacInnis B .20 .50
133 Adam Graves S .75 2.00
134 Vyacheslav Kozlov B .08 .25
135 Scott Mellanby S .75 2.00
136 Stephane Fiset B .20 .50
137 Oleg Tverdovsky S .75 2.00
138 Theo Fleury S .75 2.00
139 Jeff Hackett B .20 .50
140 Vincent Damphousse B .08 .25
141 Roman Hamrlik S .75 2.00
142 Ron Francis S 1.50 4.00
143 Scott Lachance B .08 .25
144 Todd Harvey B .08 .25
145 Marc Denis S 1.50 4.00
146 Jaroslav Svejkovsky G 3.00 8.00
147 Olli Jokinen S RC 6.00 15.00
148 Sergei Samsonov G 3.00 8.00
149 Chris Phillips G 1.50 4.00
150 Patrick Marleau G 8.00 20.00
151 Joe Thornton G 10.00 25.00
152 Daniel Cleary S 1.50 4.00
153 Alyn McCauley G 3.00 8.00
154 Brad Isbister S .75 2.00
155 Alexei Morozov S 2.00 5.00
156 Shawn Bates B RC .08 .25
157 Jean-Yves Leroux B RC .08 .25
158 Marcel Cousineau B .20 .50
159 Vaclav Varada B .08 .25

160 Jean-Sebastien Giguere S 1.50 4.00
161 Espen Knutsen B RC .75 2.00
162 Marian Hossa S RC 15.00 30.00
163 Robert Dome B RC .08 .25
164 Juha Lind B RC .08 .25
165 Sergei Fedorov NT B .40 1.00
166 Jarome Iginla NT B .30 .75
167 Jaroslav Svejkovsky NT B .20 .50
168 Patrick Roy NT S 10.00 25.00
169 Dominik Hasek NT B .50 1.25
170 Alexander Mogilny NT B .20 .50
171 Chris Chelios NT B .25 .60
172 Wayne Gretzky NT S 12.50 30.00
173 Peter Forsberg NT B .60 1.50
174 Ray Bourque NT B .40 1.00
175 Joe Sakic NT S 4.00 10.00
176 Mike Modano NT B .25 .60
177 Mark Messier NT B .25 .60
178 Teemu Selanne NT B .25 .60
179 Steve Yzerman NT S 10.00 25.00
180 Eric Lindros NT S 2.00 5.00
181 Doug Weight NT B .20 .50
182 John Vanbiesbrouck NT B .20 .50
183 Paul Kariya NT S 2.00 5.00
184 Brendan Shanahan NT S 2.00 5.00
185 Martin Brodeur NT B .60 1.50
186 Bryan Berard NT B .20 .50
187 Marc Denis NT B .20 .50
188 Brian Leetch NT B .25 .60
189 Ryan Smyth NT S 2.00 5.00
190 Dainius Zubrus NT B .20 .50
191 Keith Tkachuk NT B .25 .60
192 Jaromir Jagr NT S 3.00 8.00
193 Brett Hull NT B .30 .75
194 Pavel Bure NT B .25 .60
195 Sergei Samsonov B .20 .50
196 Olli Jokinen B .40 1.00
197 Chris Phillips B .20 .50
198 Patrick Marleau B .60 1.50
199 Daniel Cleary B .20 .50
200 Joe Thornton B .75 2.00

1997-98 Donruss Preferred Cut to the Chase

*BRONZE VETS: 4X TO 10X BASIC CARDS
*BRONZE ROOKIES: 2X TO 5X
*SILVER VETS: 1.5X TO 4X BASIC CARDS
*SILVER ROOKIES: 1X TO 2.5X
*GOLD: 1.2X TO 3X BASIC CARDS
*PLATINUM: 1X TO 2.5X BASIC CARDS
162 Marian Hossa S 60.00 100.00

1997-98 Donruss Preferred Color Guard

*PROMOS: .6X TO 1.5X BASIC INSERTS
1 Patrick Roy 12.00 30.00
2 Martin Brodeur 10.00 25.00
3 Curtis Joseph 5.00 12.00
4 John Vanbiesbrouck 3.00 8.00
5 Felix Potvin 5.00 12.00
6 Dominik Hasek 6.00 15.00
7 Chris Osgood 4.00 10.00
8 Eric Fichaud 3.00 8.00
9 Jocelyn Thibault 2.00 5.00
10 Marc Denis 3.00 8.00
11 Jose Theodore 5.00 12.00
12 Mike Vernon 3.00 8.00
13 Jim Carey 2.50 6.00
14 Ron Hextall 3.00 8.00
15 Mike Richter 4.00 10.00
16 Ed Belfour 4.00 10.00
17 Mike Dunham 2.50 6.00
18 Damian Rhodes 3.00 8.00

1997-98 Donruss Preferred Line of the Times

COMPLETE SET (24) 125.00 250.00
*PROMO: .3X TO .8X BASIC INSERTS
1A Ryan Smyth 2.50 6.00
1B Sergei Fedorov 5.00 12.00
1C Jaromir Jagr 5.00 12.00
2A Eric Lindros 4.00 10.00
2B Joe Thornton 4.00 10.00
2C Brendan Shanahan 4.00 10.00
3A John LeClair 3.00 8.00
3B Keith Tkachuk 3.00 8.00
3C Brett Hull 4.00 10.00
4A Pavel Bure 4.00 10.00
4B Sergei Samsonov 2.50 6.00
4C Paul Kariya 3.00 8.00
5A Mike Modano 4.00 10.00
5B Teemu Selanne 3.00 8.00
5C Patrick Marleau 2.50 6.00
6A Wayne Gretzky 12.00 30.00
6B Steve Yzerman 8.00 20.00
6C Daniel Cleary 2.50 6.00
7A Jarome Iginla 4.00 10.00
7B Peter Forsberg 3.00 8.00
7C Mark Messier 3.00 8.00
8A Joe Sakic 6.00 15.00
8B Jaroslav Svejkovsky 2.00 5.00
8C Dainius Zubrus 2.00 5.00

1997-98 Donruss Preferred Precious Metals

1 Brendan Shanahan P 50.00 100.00
2 Joe Thornton G 60.00 150.00
3 Wayne Gretzky P 200.00 400.00
4 Mark Messier P 75.00 150.00
5 Patrick Roy P 100.00 200.00
6 Martin Brodeur G 75.00 150.00
7 Eric Lindros P 60.00 120.00
8 Paul Kariya P 40.00 100.00
9 Teemu Selanne G 60.00 120.00
10 Jaromir Jagr P 75.00 150.00
11 Joe Sakic P 60.00 150.00
12 Peter Forsberg G 100.00 200.00
13 John Vanbiesbrouck P 60.00 120.00
14 Steve Yzerman P 125.00 250.00
15 Sergei Samsonov G 40.00 80.00

1997-98 Donruss Preferred Tin Packs

COMPLETE SET (24) 8.00 20.00
*GOLD PACK/499: 4X TO 10X BASIC TIN
*BLUE BOX/499: 2.5X TO 6X BASIC TIN
*RED PACK: .4X TO 1X BASIC TIN
*RED BOX/499: 2.5X TO 6X BASIC TIN
1 Eric Lindros .25 .60
2 Paul Kariya .50 1.25
3 Wayne Gretzky 1.00 2.50
4 Teemu Selanne .30 .75
5 Patrick Roy .75 2.00
6 John Vanbiesbrouck .25 .60
7 Mike Modano .25 .60
8 Joe Sakic .30 .75
9 Peter Forsberg .40 1.00
10 Martin Brodeur .40 1.00
11 Sergei Samsonov .40 1.00
12 Brendan Shanahan .25 .60
13 Steve Yzerman .60 1.50
14 Jaromir Jagr .40 1.00
15 Mark Messier .20 .50
16 Joe Thornton .40 1.00
17 Pavel Bure .40 1.00
18 Brett Hull .20 .50
19 Brendan Shanahan MC .25 .60
20 Jaromir Jagr MC .40 1.00
21 Eric Lindros MC .25 .60
22 Paul Kariya MC .50 1.25
23 Wayne Gretzky MC 1.00 2.50
24 Patrick Roy MC .75 2.00

1997-98 Donruss Preferred Tin Packs Double Wide

COMPLETE SET (12) 10.00 25.00
1 W.Gretzky/J.Thornton 1.25 3.00
2 P.Kariya/B.Hull .50 1.25
3 E.Lindros/J.Sakic .50 1.25
4 T.Selanne/P.Forsberg .60 1.50
5 P.Bure/M.Modano .60 1.50
6 S.Samsonov/S.Yzerman 1.50 4.00
7 J.Jagr/B.Shanahan .50 1.25
8 M.Messier/J.Vanbiesbrouck .40 1.00
9 P.Roy/M.Brodeur 1.25 3.00
10 B.Shanahan/E.Lindros .40 1.00
11 J.Jagr/P.Kariya 1.00 2.50
12 W.Gretzky/P.Roy 1.50 4.00

1997-98 Donruss Priority

COMPLETE SET (220) 25.00 50.00
1 Patrick Roy SP 1.25 3.00
2 Eric Lindros .20 .50
3 Keith Tkachuk SP .15 .40
4 Steve Yzerman .75 2.00
5 John Vanbiesbrouck SP .25 .60
6 Teemu Selanne .20 .50
7 Martin Brodeur SP .60 1.50
8 Peter Forsberg .40 1.00
9 Brett Hull SP .30 .75
10 Wayne Gretzky 1.00 2.50
11 Mike Modano SP .40 1.00
12 Sergei Fedorov .25 .60
13 Paul Kariya SP .60 1.50
14 Saku Koivu .20 .50
15 Pavel Bure SP .25 .60
16 Mark Messier .20 .50
17 Joe Sakic SP .50 1.25
18 Jaromir Jagr .25 .60
19 Brendan Shanahan SP .25 .60
20 Ray Bourque .25 .60
21 Daymond Langkow SP .10 .30
22 Alexandre Daigle .07 .20
23 Dainius Zubrus SP .10 .30
24 Ryan Smyth .10 .30
25 Derek Plante SP .10 .30
26 Eric Daze .10 .30
27 Ed Jovanovski SP .10 .30
28 Sergei Berezin .07 .20
29 Roman Turek SP .15 .40
30 Derian Hatcher .07 .20
31 Jarome Iginla SP .25 .60
32 Luc Robitaille .10 .30
33 Rod Brind'Amour SP .15 .40
34 Mathieu Schneider .07 .20
35 Olaf Kolzig SP .15 .40
36 Nikolai Khabibulin .10 .30
37 Scott Niedermayer SP .10 .30
38 Keith Primeau .07 .20
39 Dimitri Khristich SP .10 .30
40 Eric Fichaud .10 .30
41 Pierre Turgeon SP .15 .40
42 Kevin Stevens .07 .20
43 Nicklas Lidstrom SP .10 .30
44 Sean Burke .10 .30
45 Sandis Ozolinsh SP .10 .30
46 Owen Nolan .10 .30
47 Peter Bondra SP .25 .60
48 Ron Hextall .10 .30
49 Rob Blake SP .10 .30
50 Geoff Sanderson .10 .30
51 Sergei Zubov SP .10 .30
52 Doug Gilmour .10 .30
53 Oleg Tverdovsky SP .10 .30
54 Bryan Berard .07 .20
55 Bill Ranford SP .15 .40
56 Mats Sundin .20 .50
57 Damian Rhodes SP .15 .40
58 Zigmund Palffy .10 .30
59 Mike Grier SP .10 .30
60 Jozef Stumpel .10 .30
61 Mark Recchi SP .10 .30
62 Alexei Zhamnov .07 .20
63 Jere Lehtinen SP .10 .30
64 Andrew Cassels .07 .20
65 Kevin Hodson SP .15 .40
66 Dino Ciccarelli .10 .30
67 Niklas Sundstrom SP .10 .30
68 Jeff Hackett .10 .30
69 Brian Holzinger SP .15 .40
70 Jeff Friesen .07 .20
71 Ed Belfour SP .25 .60
72 Wayne Primeau .07 .20
73 Sami Kapanen SP .10 .30
74 Brian Leetch .10 .30
75 Mikael Renberg SP .15 .40
76 Ron Tugnutt .10 .30
77 Ron Francis SP .15 .40
78 Jocelyn Thibault .10 .30
79 Jamie Langenbrunner SP .10 .30
80 Dominik Hasek .30 .75
81 Chris Osgood SP .15 .40
82 Grant Fuhr .10 .30
83 Adam Graves SP .10 .30
84 Janne Niinimaa .10 .30
85 Kelly Hrudey SP .15 .40
86 Mike Dunham .10 .30
87 Valeri Kamensky SP .15 .40
88 Cory Stillman .07 .20
89 Anson Carter SP .10 .30
90 Igor Larionov .07 .20
91 Chris Pronger SP .15 .40
92 Steve Sullivan .07 .20
93 Mike Gartner SP .15 .40
94 Jim Campbell .10 .30
95 Valeri Bure SP .10 .30
96 Stephane Fiset .10 .30
97 Jason Arnott SP .10 .30
98 Trevor Kidd .10 .30
99 Chris Chelios SP .25 .60
100 Kevin Hatcher .07 .20
101 Felix Potvin SP .30 .75
102 Travis Green .07 .20
103 Dave Gagner SP .10 .30
104 Byron Dafoe .10 .30
105 Rick Tabaracci SP .15 .40
106 Gary Roberts .07 .20
107 Mike Ricci SP .10 .30
108 Andy Moog .10 .30
109 Sean Pronger SP .10 .30
110 Paul Coffey .10 .30
111 Trevor Linden SP .15 .40
112 Rob Zamuner .07 .20
113 Daniel Alfredsson SP .15 .40
114 Ray Sheppard .10 .30
115 Steve Shields SP RC .40 1.00
116 Ethan Moreau .07 .20
117 Tomas Sandstrom SP .10 .30
118 Chris Gratton .10 .30
119 Alexander Mogilny SP .15 .40
120 Roman Hamrlik .07 .20
121 Tommy Salo SP .15 .40
122 Jason Allison .07 .20
123 Curtis Joseph SP .25 .60
124 Guy Hebert .10 .30
125 Jeff O'Neill SP .10 .30
126 Donald Audette .07 .20
127 Claude Lemieux SP .10 .30
128 Brian Savage .07 .20
129 Scott Mellanby SP .10 .30
130 Vyacheslav Kozlov .10 .30
131 Wade Redden SP .10 .30
132 John LeClair .20 .50
133 Jeremy Roenick SP .25 .60
134 Andreas Johansson .07 .20
135 Nelson Emerson SP .10 .30
136 Daren Puppa .10 .30
137 Joe Juneau SP .15 .40
138 Garth Snow .10 .30
139 Tom Barrasso SP .15 .40
140 Joe Nieuwendyk .10 .30
141 Theo Fleury SP .10 .30
142 Yanic Perreault .07 .20
143 Mike Richter SP .25 .60
144 Al MacInnis .10 .30
145 Mike Peca SP .15 .40
146 Darren McCarty .07 .20
147 Alexei Yashin SP .10 .30
148 Rick Tocchet .10 .30
149 Adam Oates SP .15 .40
150 Wendel Clark .07 .20
151 Tony Amonte SP .15 .40
152 Dave Andreychuk .07 .20
153 Jamie Storr SP .15 .40
154 Craig Janney .10 .30
155 Todd Bertuzzi SP .10 .30
156 Harry York .07 .20
157 Todd Harvey SP .10 .30
158 Bobby Holik .07 .20
159 Mike Vernon SP .15 .40
160 Pat LaFontaine .10 .30
161 Doug Weight SP .15 .40
162 Kirk McLean .10 .30
163 Adam Deadmarsh SP .10 .30
164 Vincent Damphousse .07 .20
165 Vaclav Prospal SP RC .15 .40
166 Daniel Cleary .10 .30
167 Jaroslav Svejkovsky SP .15 .40
168 Marco Sturm RC .20 .50
169 Robert Dome SP RC .10 .30
170 Patrik Elias RC .50 1.25
171 Mattias Ohlund SP .15 .40
172 Espen Knutsen RC .20 .50
173 Joe Thornton SP .60 1.50
174 Jan Bulis RC .07 .20
175 Patrick Marleau SP .40 1.00
176 Brad Isbister .07 .20
177 Kevin Weekes SP RC 1.00 2.50
178 Sergei Samsonov .10 .30
179 Tyler Moss RC SP .10 .30
180 Chris Phillips .07 .20
181 Alyn McCauley SP .10 .30
182 Derek Morris RC .10 .30
183 Alexei Morozov SP .15 .40
184 Boyd Devereaux .07 .20
185 Peter Forsberg SP .15 .40
186 Brendan Shanahan .10 .30
187 Teemu Selanne SP .15 .40
188 Eric Lindros .10 .30
189 Mark Messier SP .15 .40
190 Vaclav Prospal .10 .30
191 Jarome Iginla SP .25 .60
192 Mike Modano .10 .30
193 John Vanbiesbrouck SP .15 .40
194 Bryan Berard .07 .20
195 Patrick Marleau SP .15 .40
196 Martin Brodeur .10 .30
197 Patrick Roy SP 1.25 3.00
198 Felix Potvin .25 .60
199 Wayne Gretzky SP 1.50 4.00
200 Sergei Samsonov .10 .30
201 Ryan Smyth SP .15 .40
202 Keith Tkachuk .20 .50
203 Chris Osgood SP .15 .40
204 Paul Kariya .10 .30
205 John LeClair SP .25 .60
206 Alyn McCauley .10 .30
207 Joe Thornton SP .40 1.00
208 Joe Sakic .10 .30
209 Steve Yzerman SP 1.25 3.00
210 Saku Koivu .20 .50
211 Pavel Bure SP .15 .40
212 Zigmund Palffy .10 .30
213 Alexei Yashin SP .10 .30
214 Sergei Fedorov .10 .30
215 Joe Thornton CL SP .40 1.00
216 Patrick Marleau CL .10 .30
217 Daniel Cleary CL SP .10 .30
218 Sergei Samsonov CL .10 .30
219 Jaroslav Svejkovsky CL SP .10 .30
220 Alyn McCauley CL .07 .20

1997-98 Donruss Priority Stamp of Approval

*EVEN CARD #: 20X TO 50X BASIC CARDS
*ODD CARD #: 15X TO 40X BASIC CARDS

1997-98 Donruss Priority Direct Deposit

COMPLETE SET (30) 100.00 200.00
*PROMOS: .3X TO .8X BASIC INSERTS
1 Brendan Shanahan 2.50 6.00
2 Steve Yzerman 8.00 20.00
3 Pavel Bure 2.50 6.00
4 Jaromir Jagr 4.00 10.00
5 Ryan Smyth 1.50 4.00
6 Sergei Samsonov 1.50 4.00
7 Mark Messier 2.50 6.00
8 Wayne Gretzky 10.00 25.00
9 Jarome Iginla 3.00 8.00
10 Peter Forsberg 6.00 15.00
11 Joe Sakic 5.00 12.00
12 Sergei Fedorov 4.00 10.00
13 Mike Modano 4.00 10.00
14 Paul Kariya 2.50 6.00
15 Teemu Selanne 2.50 6.00
16 Eric Lindros 2.50 6.00
17 Keith Tkachuk 2.50 6.00
18 Patrick Marleau 1.50 4.00
19 Jaroslav Svejkovsky 1.50 4.00
20 Alyn McCauley 1.50 4.00
21 Saku Koivu 2.50 6.00
22 Zigmund Palffy 1.50 4.00
23 Brett Hull 3.00 8.00
24 Patrik Elias 2.50 6.00
25 Joe Thornton 6.00 15.00
26 Espen Knutsen 1.50 4.00
27 Daniel Alfredsson 2.00 5.00
28 John LeClair 2.50 6.00
29 Dainius Zubrus 1.50 4.00
30 Jason Arnott 1.50 4.00

1997-98 Donruss Priority Postcards

COMPLETE SET (36) 20.00 50.00
*OPEN.DAY/1000: 2X TO 5X BASIC INSERTS
1 Patrick Roy 2.50 6.00
2 Brendan Shanahan .50 1.25
3 Steve Yzerman 2.50 6.00
4 Jaromir Jagr .75 2.00
5 Pavel Bure .60 1.50
6 Mark Messier .50 1.25
7 Wayne Gretzky 3.00 8.00
8 Eric Lindros .60 1.50
9 Joe Sakic 1.00 2.50
10 Peter Forsberg 1.25 3.00
11 John Vanbiesbrouck .50 1.25
12 Mike Modano .75 2.00
13 Paul Kariya .50 1.25
14 Teemu Selanne .50 1.25
15 Sergei Fedorov .75 2.00
16 Joe Thornton 1.25 3.00
17 Sergei Samsonov .40 1.00
18 Patrick Marleau .75 2.00
19 Ryan Smyth .40 1.00
20 Jarome Iginla .60 1.50
21 John LeClair .50 1.25
22 Brian Leetch .50 1.25
23 Chris Chelios .50 1.25
24 Martin Brodeur 1.25 3.00
25 Bryan Berard .40 1.00
26 Keith Tkachuk .50 1.25
27 Saku Koivu .50 1.25
28 Brett Hull .60 1.50
29 Felix Potvin 1.00 2.50
30 Chris Osgood .40 1.00
31 Dominik Hasek 1.00 2.50
32 Zigmund Palffy .40 1.00
33 Jeremy Roenick .60 1.50
34 Dainius Zubrus .40 1.00
35 Ray Bourque .75 2.00
36 Jocelyn Thibault .40 1.00

1997-98 Donruss Priority Postmaster Generals

COMPLETE SET (20) 40.00 80.00
*PROMO: .3X TO .8X BASIC INSERTS
1 Patrick Roy 12.00 30.00
2 John Vanbiesbrouck 2.00 5.00
3 Felix Potvin 3.00 8.00
4 Curtis Joseph 3.00 8.00
5 Mike Richter 2.00 5.00
6 Jocelyn Thibault 1.00 2.50
7 Ed Belfour 2.00 5.00
8 Chris Osgood 2.00 5.00
9 Ron Hextall 2.00 5.00
10 Martin Brodeur 8.00 20.00
11 Mike Vernon 2.00 5.00
12 Eric Fichaud 1.00 2.50
13 Dominik Hasek 6.00 15.00
14 Byron Dafoe 1.00 2.50
15 Tommy Salo 1.00 2.50
16 Garth Snow 1.00 2.50
17 Tom Barrasso 1.00 2.50
18 Marc Denis 1.00 2.50
19 Grant Fuhr 2.00 5.00
20 Guy Hebert 1.00 2.50

1997-98 Donruss Priority Stamps

COMPLETE SET (36) 20.00 40.00
*BRONZE: .8X TO 2X BASIC INSERTS
*SILVER: 1.5X TO 4X BASIC INSERTS
*GOLD: 3X TO 8X BASIC INSERTS
1 Patrick Roy 2.50 6.00
2 Brendan Shanahan .50 1.25
3 Steve Yzerman 2.50 6.00
4 Jaromir Jagr .75 2.00
5 Pavel Bure .50 1.25
6 Mark Messier .50 1.25
7 Wayne Gretzky 3.00 8.00
8 Eric Lindros .50 1.25
9 Joe Sakic 1.00 2.50
10 Peter Forsberg 1.25 3.00
11 John Vanbiesbrouck .40 1.00
12 Mike Modano .75 2.00
13 Paul Kariya .50 1.25
14 Teemu Selanne .50 1.25
15 Sergei Fedorov .75 2.00
16 Joe Thornton 1.25 3.00
17 Sergei Samsonov .40 1.00
18 Patrick Marleau 1.00 2.50
19 Ryan Smyth .40 1.00
20 Jarome Iginla .60 1.50
21 John LeClair .50 1.25
22 Brian Leetch .40 1.00
23 Chris Chelios .40 1.00
24 Martin Brodeur 1.25 3.00
25 Bryan Berard .40 1.00
26 Keith Tkachuk .50 1.25
27 Saku Koivu .50 1.25
28 Brett Hull .60 1.50
29 Felix Potvin .50 1.25
30 Chris Osgood .40 1.00
31 Dominik Hasek 1.00 2.50
32 Zigmund Palffy .40 1.00
33 Jeremy Roenick .60 1.50
34 Dainius Zubrus .40 1.00
35 Ray Bourque .75 2.00
36 Jocelyn Thibault .40 1.00

1993-94 Ducks Milk Caps

COMPLETE SET (6) 2.00 5.00
1 Tim Sweeney .40 1.00
2 Bobby Dollas .40 1.00
3 Stu Grimson .60 1.50
4 Terry Yake .40 1.00
5 Bob Corkum .40 1.00
NNO Inaugural Season First Win .40 1.00

1994-95 Ducks Carl's Jr.

COMPLETE SET (28) 6.00 15.00
1 Patrik Carnback .08 .25
2 Bob Corkum .08 .25
3 Robert Dirk .08 .25
4 Bobby Dollas .08 .25
5 Peter Douris .08 .25
6 Todd Ewen .20 .50
7 Shaun Van Allen .08 .25
8 Garry Valk .08 .25
9 Guy Hebert .60 1.50
10 Paul Kariya 3.00 8.00
11 Valeri Karpov .08 .25
12 Steven King .08 .25
13 Todd Krygier .08 .25
14 Tom Kurvers .08 .25
15 Randy Ladouceur .08 .25
16 Stephan Lebeau .20 .50
17 John Lilley .08 .25
18 Don McSween .08 .25
19 Steve Rucchin .30 .75
20 David Sacco .08 .25
21 Joe Sacco .08 .25
22 Mikhail Shtalenkov .30 .75
23 Jim Thomson .08 .25
24 Oleg Tverdovsky .30 .75
25 David Williams .08 .25
26 Wild Wing (Mascot) .08 .25
27 Carl Karcher (Sponsor Owner) .01 .05
28 Happy Star (Sponsor Logo) .01 .05

1995-96 Ducks Team Issue

COMPLETE SET (5) 1.25 3.00
1 Bobby Dollas .20 .50
2 David Karpa .20 .50
3 Steve Rucchin .30 .75
4 Mikhail Shtalenkov .30 .75
5 Garry Valk .20 .50

1996-97 Ducks Team Issue

COMPLETE SET (26) 8.00 20.00
1 Mikhail Shtalenkov .20 .50
2 Bobby Dollas .15 .40
3 Roman Oksiuta .15 .40
4 Kevin Todd .15 .40
5 Ted Drury .15 .40
6 Joe Sacco .15 .40
7 Dmitri Mironov .20 .50
8 Warren Rychel .20 .50
10 Shawn Antoski .15 .40
11 Steve Rucchin .20 .50
12 Ken Baumgartner .15 .40
13 Brian Bellows .15 .40
14 Nikolai Tsulygin .15 .40
15 Jason Marshall .15 .40
16 Darren Van Impe .15 .40
17 David Karpa .15 .40
18 Wild Wing .15 .40
19 J.F. Jomphe .15 .40
20 Sean Pronger .15 .40
21 Guy Hebert .60 1.50
22 Paul Kariya 2.50 6.00
23 Jari Kurri 1.00 2.50
24 Teemu Selanne 1.50 4.00
25 Southland .01 .05
26 Southland .01 .05
27 Ron Wilson CO .08 .25
28 Garry Valk .02 .10

2002-03 Ducks Team Issue

COMPLETE SET
1 Dan Bylsma .20 .50
1 Adam Oates .40 1.00
2 Jean-Sebastien Giguere 1.25 3.00
3 Paul Kariya 1.25 3.00
4 Ruslan Salei .20 .50
5 Petr Sykora .20 .50
6 Vitaly Vishnevski .20 .50

2005-06 Ducks Team Issue

COMPLETE SET (22) 6.00 15.00
1 Kip Brennan .20 .50
2 Ilya Bryzgalov .30 .75
3 Keith Carney .20 .50
4 Joe DiPenta .30 .75
5 Todd Fedoruk .20 .50
6 Ryan Getzlaf .75 2.00
7 Jean-Sebastien Giguere .40 1.00
8 Jonathan Hedstrom .20 .50
9 Joffrey Lupul .40 1.00
10 Jason Marshall .20 .50
11 Andy McDonald .20 .50
12 Travis Moen .20 .50
13 Rob Niedermayer .20 .50
14 Scott Niedermayer .20 .50
15 Sandis Ozolinsh .20 .50
16 Samuel Pahlsson .20 .50
17 Corey Perry .75 2.00
18 Ruslan Salei .20 .50
19 Teemu Selanne .75 2.00
20 Petr Sykora .20 .50
21 Vitali Vishnevsky .20 .50
22 Randy Carlyle HC .02 .10

1992-93 Durivage Panini

COMPLETE SET (50) 8.00 20.00
1 Guy Carbonneau .08 .25
2 Lucien Deblois .07 .20
3 Benoit Hogue .07 .20
4 Steve Kasper .07 .20
5 Mike Krushelnyski Toron .07 .20
6 Claude Lapointe Quebec .07 .20
7 Stephan Lebeau Montreal .07 .20
8 Mario Lemieux 1.50 4.00
9 Stephane Morin .07 .20
10 Denis Savard .08 .25
11 Pierre Turgeon .08 .25
12 Kevin Dineen .07 .20
13 Gord Donnelly .07 .20
14 Claude Lemieux .08 .25
15 Jocelyn Lemieux .07 .20
16 Daniel Marois .07 .20
17 Scott Mellanby .07 .20
18 Stephane Richer .08 .25
19 Benoit Brunet Montreal .08 .25
20 Vincent Damphousse .08 .25
21 Gilbert Dionne Montreal .08 .25
22 Gaetan Duchesne .07 .20
23 Bob Errey .07 .20
24 Michel Goulet .08 .25
25 Mike Hough .07 .20
26 Sergio Momesso .07 .20
27 Mario Roberge .07 .20
28 Luc Robitaille Los Ange .10 .30
29 Sylvain Turgeon .07 .20
30 Marc Bergevin .07 .20
31 Ray Bourque .50 1.25
32 Patrice Brisebois .07 .20
33 Jeff Chychrun .07 .20
34 Sylvain Cote .07 .20
35 J.J. Daigneault .07 .20
36 Eric Desjardins .08 .25
37 Gord Dineen .07 .20
38 Steve Duchesne .07 .20
39 Donald Dufresne .07 .20
40 Steven Finn .07 .20
41 Garry Galley .07 .20
42 Kevin Lowe .08 .25
43 Michel Petit .07 .20
44 Normand Rochefort .07 .20
45 Randy Velischek .07 .20
46 Jacques Cloutier Quebec .08 .25
47 Stephane Fiset Quebec N .10 .30
48 Rejean Lemelin Boston B .08 .25
49 Andre Racicot Montreal .08 .25
50 Patrick Roy Montreal Ca 3.00 8.00
NNO Patrick Roy AU 50.00 125.00

1993-94 Durivage Score

COMPLETE SET (50) 12.00 30.00
1 Alexandre Daigle .30 .75
2 Pierre Sevigny .10 .30
3 Jocelyn Thibault .50 1.25
4 Philippe Boucher .10 .30
5 Martin Brodeur New Jers 1.50 4.00
6 Martin Lapointe Detroit .40 1.00
7 Patrice Brisebois Montr .40 1.00
8 Benoit Brunet .10 .30
9 Guy Carbonneau Montreal .40 1.00
10 Jean-Jacques Daigneault .10 .30
11 Vincent Damphousse .40 1.00
12 Eric Desjardins .40 1.00
13 Gilbert Dionne Montreal .10 .30
14 Stephan Lebeau Montreal .40 1.00
15 Andre Racicot Montreal .40 1.00
16 Mario Roberge .10 .30
17 Patrick Roy Montreal Ca 3.00 8.00
18 Jacques Cloutier Quebec .40 1.00
19 Alain Cote .10 .30
20 Steven Finn .10 .30
21 Stephane Fiset .30 .75
22 Martin Gelinas .10 .30
23 Reggie Savage .10 .30
24 Claude Lapointe .10 .30
25 Denis Savard .50 1.25
26 Ray Bourque Boston Brui .75 2.00
27 Joe Juneau Boston Bruin .30 .75
28 Ron Stern .10 .30
29 Benoit Hogue New York I .40 1.00
30 Pierre Turgeon .50 1.25
31 Mike Krushelnyski .10 .30
32 Felix Potvin .50 1.25
33 Sergio Momesso .10 .30
34 Yves Racine .10 .30
35 Sylvain Cote .10 .30
36 Sylvain Turgeon .10 .30
37 Kevin Dineen Philadelph .40 1.00
38 Garry Galley Philadelph .40 1.00
39 Dominic Roussel .40 1.00
40 Gaetan Duchesne .10 .30
41 Luc Robitaille .50 1.25
42 Michel Goulet .50 1.25
43 Jocelyn Lemieux .10 .30
44 Stephane Matteau .10 .30
45 Mike Hough .10 .30
46 Scott Mellanby .50 1.25
47 Claude Lemieux .30 .75
48 Stephane Richer .50 1.25
49 Jimmy Waite San Jose Sh .10 .30
50 Patrick Poulin .40 1.00
NNO Patrick Roy AU 75.00 200.00
NNO Jocelyn Thibault AU 40.00 100.00

1996-97 Duracell All-Cherry Team

COMPLETE SET (22) 8.00 20.00
DC1 Paul Coffey .30 .75
DC2 Lyle Odelein .08 .25
DC3 Joe Sakic .50 1.25
DC4 Curtis Joseph .40 1.00
DC5 Brett Hull .40 1.00
DC6 Eric Lindros .60 1.50
DC7 Doug Gilmour .30 .75
DC8 Chris Chelios .30 .75
DC9 Marty McSorley .08 .25
DC10 Kirk Muller .08 .25
DC11 Trevor Linden .08 .25
DC12 Brendan Shanahan .60 1.50
DC13 Tie Domi .20 .50
DC14 Rick Tocchet .08 .25
DC15 Steve Yzerman 1.25 3.00
DC16 Scott Stevens .08 .25
DC17 Patrick Roy 1.50 4.00
DC18 Keith Tkachuk .30 .75
DC19 Owen Nolan .20 .50
DC20 Dale Hunter .08 .25
DC21 Don Cherry .40 1.00
DC22 Don Cherry .40 1.00

1996-97 Duracell L'Equipe Beliveau

COMPLETE SET (22) 14.00 35.00
JB1 Paul Coffey .40 1.00
JB2 Lyle Odelein .08 .25
JB3 Joe Sakic 1.00 2.50
JB4 Eric Daze .30 .75
JB5 Brett Hull .75 2.00
JB6 Martin Brodeur 1.25 3.00
JB7 Doug Gilmour .60 1.50
JB8 Peter Forsberg 1.25 3.00
JB9 Mike Gartner .20 .50
JB10 Saku Koivu .60 1.50
JB11 Trevor Linden .08 .25
JB12 Felix Potvin .40 1.00
JB13 Mats Sundin .40 1.00
JB14 Pierre Turgeon .20 .50
JB15 Vincent Damphousse .08 .25
JB16 Scott Stevens .08 .25
JB17 Patrick Roy 2.00 5.00
JB18 Keith Tkachuk .60 1.50
JB19 Ray Bourque .75 2.00
JB20 Paul Kariya 1.25 3.00
JB21 Jean Beliveau .40 1.00
JB22 Jean Beliveau .40 1.00

2003-04 Duracell

COMPLETE SET (15) 20.00
1 Jean-Sebastien Giguere .40 1.00
2 Patrick Lalime .20 .50
3 Curtis Joseph .75 2.00
4 Marty Turco .40 1.00
5 Ed Belfour .75 2.00
6 Sean Burke .20 .50
7 Roberto Luongo .75 2.00
8 Jose Theodore .75 2.00
9 Olaf Kolzig .20 .50
10 Martin Brodeur 1.25 3.00
11 Mike Richter .20 .50
12 Dan Blackburn .20 .50
13 Patrick Roy 1.50 4.00
14 Dwayne Roloson .20 .50
15 Dan Cloutier .20 .50

2023-24 E-X2000

1 Connor McDavid 3.00 8.00
2 Erik Karlsson .75 2.00
3 John Carlson .60 1.50
4 Zach Werenski 1.00 2.50
5 Tom Wilson .60 1.50
6 William Nylander 1.25 3.00
7 Seth Jarvis .75 2.00
8 Jeremy Swayman 1.00 2.50
9 Juraj Slafkovsky 1.25 3.00
10 Claude Giroux .60 1.50
11 Mark Stone .75 2.00
12 Jonathan Huberdeau .75 2.00
13 David Pastrnak 1.50 4.00
14 Brad Marchand 1.25 3.00
15 Andrei Vasilevskiy 1.00 2.50
16 Elias Pettersson 1.00 2.50
17 Brock Nelson .60 1.50
18 Alexandar Georgiev .60 1.50
19 Igor Shesterkin 1.25 3.00
20 Alex DeBrincat .75 2.00
21 Matthew Tkachuk 1.25 3.00
22 Jonathan Marchessault .75 2.00
23 Rasmus Dahlin .75 2.00
24 Johnny Gaudreau 1.00 2.50
25 Evgeni Malkin 1.25 3.00
26 Jordan Eberle .60 1.50
27 Jason Robertson 1.00 2.50
28 Patrick Kane 1.25 3.00
29 Casey Mittelstadt .60 1.50
30 Mikko Rantanen 1.50 4.00
31 Wyatt Johnston 1.25 3.00
32 Kris Letang .75 2.00
33 Aleksander Barkov 1.00 2.50
34 William Eklund .75 2.00
35 Dylan Larkin .75 2.00
36 Sean Couturier .50 1.25
37 Jack Hughes 1.50 4.00
38 Roman Josi .60 1.50

39 Nico Hischier 1.00 2.50
40 Jake Oettinger 1.00 2.50
41 Matt Boldy 1.00 2.50
42 Sebastian Aho 1.00 2.50
43 Matias Maccelli .50 1.25
44 Cale Makar 1.50 4.00
45 Jesper Bratt .60 1.50
46 Artemi Panarin 1.25 3.00
47 Quinn Hughes 1.50 4.00
48 Chris Kreider .75 2.00
49 Travis Konecny .60 1.50
50 Dylan Cozens .60 1.50
51 Brady Tkachuk 1.00 2.50
52 Jack Eichel 1.00 2.50
53 Nikolaj Ehlers .60 1.50
54 Nikita Kucherov 1.25 3.00
55 Seth Jones .60 1.50
56 Stuart Skinner .75 2.00
57 Nick Suzuki 1.25 3.00
58 Brock Boeser .75 2.00
59 Nazem Kadri .75 2.00
60 Anze Kopitar 1.00 2.50
61 Tim Stutzle .75 2.00
62 Andrei Svechnikov .75 2.00
63 Kirill Kaprizov 2.00 5.00
64 Alexis Lafreniere 1.00 2.50
65 Robert Thomas .60 1.50
66 Philipp Kurashev .50 1.25
67 Filip Forsberg 1.00 2.50
68 Kyle Connor 1.00 2.50
69 Nathan MacKinnon 2.50 6.00
70 Kevin Fiala .50 1.25
71 J.T. Miller .75 2.00
72 Matty Beniers .75 2.00
73 Steven Stamkos 1.25 3.00
74 Trevor Zegras .60 1.50
75 Alex Ovechkin 2.50 6.00
76 Joe Pavelski .75 2.00
77 Clayton Keller .75 2.00
78 Quinton Byfield .75 2.00
79 Linus Ullmark .60 1.50
80 Troy Terry .50 1.25
81 Marc-Andre Fleury 1.25 3.00
82 Auston Matthews 2.50 6.00
83 Moritz Seider .75 2.00
84 Leon Draisaitl 2.00 5.00
85 Cole Caufield 1.25 3.00
86 Sam Reinhart 1.25 3.00
87 Sidney Crosby 2.50 6.00
88 Mason McTavish .60 1.50
89 Tage Thompson .75 2.00
90 Mark Scheifele 1.00 2.50
91 Mitch Marner 1.00 2.50
92 Brayden Schenn .60 1.50
93 Zach Hyman 1.00 2.50
94 John Tavares 1.00 2.50
95 Ilya Sorokin 1.00 2.50
96 Shane Wright .75 2.00
97 Tomas Hertl .60 1.50
98 Jordan Kyrou .60 1.50
99 Mathew Barzal .75 2.00
100 MacKenzie Weegar .50 1.25
101 Zach Benson RC 1.50 4.00
102 Simon Nemec RC 2.00 5.00
103 William Dufour RC .75 2.00
104 Kevin Korchinski RC 1.50 4.00
105 Egor Afanasyev RC 1.00 2.50
106 Jakob Pelletier RC 1.25 3.00
107 Stanislav Svozil RC .75 2.00
108 Ivan Miroshnichenko RC 1.50 4.00
109 Connor Bedard RC 15.00 40.00
110 Luke Hughes RC 3.00 8.00
111 Justin Sourdif RC 1.00 2.50
112 Matthew Knies RC 4.00 10.00
113 Alex Laferriere RC 1.50 4.00
114 John Beecher RC 2.00 5.00
115 Samuel Bolduc RC 1.00 2.50
116 Matt Savoie RC 2.00 5.00
117 Tristen Robins RC 1.00 2.50
118 Fraser Minten RC 2.00 5.00
119 Sean Farrell RC 1.00 2.50
120 Logan Cooley RC 3.00 8.00
121 Matthew Coronato RC 1.50 4.00
122 Tye Kartye RC 1.50 4.00
123 Connor Zary RC 2.00 5.00
124 Milos Kelemen RC 1.00 2.50
125 Michael Kesselring RC 1.00 2.50
126 Adam Fantilli RC 3.00 8.00
127 Isak Rosen RC 1.00 2.50
128 Pavel Mintyukov RC 1.50 4.00
129 Henry Thrun RC 1.00 2.50
130 Ridly Greig RC 1.50 4.00
131 Ryker Evans RC 1.25 3.00
132 Mackie Samoskevich RC 1.50 4.00
133 Leo Carlsson RC 3.00 8.00
134 Yaroslav Askarov RC 2.50 6.00
135 Owen Beck RC 1.50 4.00
136 Tyson Foerster RC 2.00 5.00
137 Marco Kasper RC 2.50 6.00
138 Raphael Lavoie RC 1.00 2.50
139 Devon Levi RC 2.50 6.00
140 Tristan Luneau RC 1.00 2.50
141 Will Cuylle RC 1.50 4.00
142 Luke Evangelista RC 1.50 4.00
143 Jackson LaCombe RC 1.00 2.50
144 Jiri Kulich RC 2.00 5.00
145 Dustin Wolf RC 3.00 8.00
146 Drew Helleson RC 1.00 2.50
147 Matthew Poitras RC 2.00 5.00
148 Brock Faber RC 2.50 6.00
149 Hugh McGing RC 1.00 2.50
150 Simon Edvinsson RC 2.00 5.00

2023-24 E-X2000 All-Access Credentials

*ALL-ACCESS: 1.5X TO 4X BASIC
*ALL-ACCESS RC: 1.2X TO 3X BASIC
1 Connor McDavid 60.00 150.00
75 Alex Ovechkin 20.00 50.00
87 Sidney Crosby 15.00 40.00

2023-24 E-X2000 Credentials

*CRED/499: 1X TO 2.5X BASIC
*CRED RC/499: .8X TO 2X BASIC
1 Connor McDavid 20.00 50.00

2023-24 E-X2000 Credentials Blue

*CRED BLUE/299: 1.2X TO 3X BASIC
*CRED BLUE RC/299: 1X TO 2.5X BASIC
1 Connor McDavid 25.00 60.00
75 Alex Ovechkin 12.00 30.00
120 Logan Cooley 10.00 25.00
126 Adam Fantilli 10.00 25.00

2023-24 E-X2000 Essential Credentials

*ESSEN/99: 3X TO 8X BASIC
*ESSEN RC/99: 2X TO 5X BASIC
1 Connor McDavid 60.00 150.00
75 Alex Ovechkin 60.00 150.00
87 Sidney Crosby 80.00 200.00
109 Connor Bedard 200.00 500.00
120 Logan Cooley 30.00 80.00
122 Tye Kartye 15.00 40.00
126 Adam Fantilli 40.00 100.00
128 Pavel Mintyukov 12.00 30.00
148 Brock Faber 40.00 100.00

2023-24 E-X2000 Autographics

AGAG Adam Graves 8.00 20.00
AGBT Brady Tkachuk 15.00 40.00
AGCC Chris Chelios 15.00 40.00
AGCH Connor Hellebuyck 20.00 50.00
AGCS Cole Sillinger 8.00 20.00
AGDP David Perron 8.00 20.00
AGEP Elias Pettersson 15.00 40.00
AGFG Filip Gustavsson 10.00 25.00
AGFV Frank Vatrano 8.00 20.00
AGJA Jared McCann 8.00 20.00
AGJE Joel Eriksson Ek 8.00 20.00
AGJH Jonathan Huberdeau 12.00 30.00
AGJK Joonas Korpisalo 10.00 25.00
AGJU Juuse Saros 12.00 30.00
AGJZ Jason Zucker 10.00 25.00
AGKH Kevin Hayes 8.00 20.00
AGKL Kris Letang 12.00 30.00
AGLD Leon Draisaitl 30.00 80.00
AGLR Luc Robitaille 15.00 40.00
AGMB Mikael Backlund 8.00 20.00
AGMF Mario Ferraro 6.00 15.00
AGMI Michael Bunting 10.00 25.00
AGMM Mike Modano 15.00 40.00
AGMN Martin Necas 12.00 30.00
AGNH Nico Hischier 15.00 40.00
AGNL Nils Lundkvist 6.00 15.00
AGNS Nick Suzuki 20.00 50.00
AGRB Ray Bourque 15.00 40.00
AGRC Ross Colton 8.00 20.00
AGRJ Roman Josi 10.00 25.00
AGSR Sam Reinhart 20.00 50.00
AGTA Tony Amonte 20.00 50.00

2023-24 E-X2000 Autographics Rookies

AGAI Aidan McDonough 5.00 12.00
AGBF Brock Faber 50.00 125.00
AGDG Danil Gushchin 6.00 15.00
AGFM Fraser Minten 12.00 30.00
AGJB John Beecher 12.00 30.00
AGKN Matthew Knies 40.00 100.00
AGKO Kevin Korchinski 10.00 25.00
AGLA Alex Laferriere 10.00 25.00
AGLC Leo Carlsson 60.00 150.00
AGLM Leevi Merilainen 6.00 15.00
AGMC Matthew Coronato 10.00 25.00
AGMP Matthew Poitras 12.00 30.00
AGMS Matt Savoie 12.00 30.00
AGOB Owen Beck 10.00 25.00
AGPA Jiri Patera 10.00 25.00
AGRG Ridly Greig 10.00 25.00
AGRL Raphael Lavoie 6.00 15.00
AGRO Lukas Rousek 5.00 12.00
AGSB Samuel Bolduc 6.00 15.00
AGSE Simon Edvinsson 12.00 30.00
AGTF Tyson Foerster 12.00 30.00
AGTK Tye Kartye 10.00 25.00
AGVD Vincent Desharnais 8.00 20.00
AGWC Will Cuylle 10.00 25.00

2023-24 E-X2000 Double Helix

DH1 Wayne Gretzky 80.00 200.00
DH2 Connor McDavid 50.00 125.00
DH3 Jack Eichel 8.00 20.00
DH4 Brad Marchand 10.00 25.00
DH5 Martin Brodeur 12.00 30.00
DH6 Mikko Rantanen 12.00 30.00
DH7 Jack Hughes 12.00 30.00
DH8 Auston Matthews 20.00 50.00
DH9 Igor Shesterkin 10.00 25.00
DH10 Mario Lemieux 80.00 200.00
DH11 Ilya Sorokin 8.00 20.00
DH12 Matt Boldy 15.00 40.00
DH13 Nikita Kucherov 10.00 25.00
DH14 Jake Oettinger 20.00 50.00
DH15 Dominik Hasek 25.00 60.00
DH16 Sebastian Aho 8.00 20.00
DH17 Nick Suzuki 10.00 25.00
DH18 Alex Ovechkin 100.00 250.00
DH19 Sidney Crosby 80.00 200.00
DH20 Eric Lindros 25.00 60.00
DH21 Adam Fantilli 25.00 60.00
DH22 Leon Draisaitl 15.00 40.00
DH23 Matthew Knies 20.00 50.00
DH24 Logan Cooley 40.00 100.00
DH25 Connor Bedard 100.00 250.00

2023-24 E-X2000 E-Xceptional

1 Connor McDavid 150.00 400.00
2 Auston Matthews 50.00 125.00
3 Sidney Crosby 50.00 125.00
5 Nikita Kucherov 25.00 60.00
6 Nathan MacKinnon 50.00 125.00
8 David Pastrnak 30.00 80.00
9 Jack Hughes 30.00 80.00
10 Marc-Andre Fleury 25.00 60.00
11 Leon Draisaitl 40.00 100.00
12 Cale Makar 30.00 80.00
13 Quinn Hughes 30.00 80.00
14 Brad Marchand 25.00 60.00
15 Tage Thompson 15.00 40.00
16 Matthew Tkachuk 25.00 60.00
17 Kirill Kaprizov 40.00 100.00
18 Cole Caufield 25.00 60.00
19 Jason Robertson 20.00 50.00
20 Patrick Kane 25.00 60.00
21 Tim Stutzle 15.00 40.00
22 Mitch Marner 20.00 50.00
23 Leo Carlsson 40.00 100.00
24 Adam Fantilli 40.00 100.00
25 Wyatt Johnston 25.00 60.00
26 Igor Shesterkin 25.00 60.00
27 Trevor Zegras 12.00 30.00
28 Elias Pettersson 20.00 50.00
29 Jack Eichel 20.00 50.00
30 Artemi Panarin 25.00 60.00

2023-24 E-X2000 Hall or Nothing

*SPECKLE/99: 1X TO 2.5X BASIC
HN1 Alex Ovechkin 5.00 12.00
HN2 Sidney Crosby 5.00 12.00
HN3 Anze Kopitar 2.00 5.00
HN4 Steven Stamkos 2.50 6.00
HN5 Connor McDavid 6.00 15.00
HN6 Marc-Andre Fleury 4.00 10.00
HN7 Nathan MacKinnon 5.00 12.00
HN8 Andrei Vasilevskiy 2.00 5.00
HN9 Patrick Kane 2.50 6.00
HN10 Leon Draisaitl 4.00 10.00

2023-24 E-X2000 Index Movers

*SPECKLE/99: .6X TO 1.5X BASIC
IM1 Owen Power 1.00 2.50
IM2 Shane Wright 1.25 3.00
IM3 Anton Lundell 1.00 2.50
IM4 Bowen Byram 1.25 3.00
IM5 Andrei Kuzmenko 1.00 2.50
IM6 Dylan Cozens 1.00 2.50
IM7 Mason McTavish 1.00 2.50
IM8 Marco Rossi 1.25 3.00
IM9 Seth Jarvis 1.25 3.00
IM10 Arber Xhekaj 1.00 2.50
IM11 Cole Perfetti 1.00 2.50
IM12 Wyatt Johnston 2.00 5.00
IM13 Dakota Joshua .60 1.50
IM14 Dylan Holloway 1.00 2.50
IM15 Logan Thompson 1.25 3.00
IM16 David Jiricek 1.00 2.50
IM17 Evan Bouchard 1.25 3.00
IM18 Jake Sanderson 1.25 3.00
IM19 Thomas Bordeleau .60 1.50
IM20 Pyotr Kochetkov 1.00 2.50

2023-24 E-X2000 Index Movers Autographs Speckle

IM1 Owen Power SP 6.00 15.00
IM2 Shane Wright 8.00 20.00
IM5 Andrei Kuzmenko 6.00 15.00
IM8 Marco Rossi 8.00 20.00
IM11 Cole Perfetti 6.00 15.00
IM12 Wyatt Johnston 12.00 30.00
IM13 Dakota Joshua 4.00 10.00
IM14 Dylan Holloway 6.00 15.00
IM18 Jake Sanderson 10.00 25.00
IM20 Pyotr Kochetkov 20.00 50.00

2023-24 E-X2000 Net Assets

1 Ilya Sorokin 3.00 8.00
2 Sergei Bobrovsky 3.00 8.00
3 Alexandar Georgiev 2.00 5.00
4 Jordan Binnington 3.00 8.00
5 Thatcher Demko 2.50 6.00
6 Igor Shesterkin 4.00 10.00
7 Connor Hellebuyck 4.00 10.00
8 Marc-Andre Fleury 4.00 10.00
9 Jake Oettinger 3.00 8.00
10 Jeremy Swayman 3.00 8.00
11 Linus Ullmark 2.00 5.00
12 Jacob Markstrom 2.00 5.00
13 Stuart Skinner 2.50 6.00
14 Samuel Montembeault 2.00 5.00
15 Tristan Jarry 2.00 5.00
16 Juuse Saros 2.50 6.00
17 Petr Mrazek 1.50 4.00
18 Vitek Vanecek 2.00 5.00
19 Andrei Vasilevskiy 3.00 8.00
20 Logan Thompson 2.50 6.00
21 Cam Talbot 2.00 5.00
22 Samuel Ersson 2.00 5.00
23 Filip Gustavsson 2.00 5.00
24 Devon Levi 5.00 12.00
25 Joey Daccord 2.00 5.00
26 Jonathan Quick 2.50 6.00
27 Henrik Lundqvist 5.00 12.00
28 Patrick Roy 10.00 25.00
29 Martin Brodeur 5.00 12.00
30 Dominik Hasek 3.00 8.00

2023-24 E-X2000 Reverberation

1 Connor Bedard 12.00 30.00
2 David Pastrnak 2.50 6.00
3 Nikita Kucherov 2.00 5.00
4 Sidney Crosby 4.00 10.00
5 Auston Matthews 4.00 10.00
6 Connor McDavid 5.00 12.00
7 Alex Ovechkin 4.00 10.00
8 Nathan MacKinnon 4.00 10.00
9 Quinn Hughes 2.50 6.00
10 Jack Hughes 2.50 6.00
11 Luke Hughes 3.00 8.00
12 Jack Eichel 1.50 4.00
13 Cale Makar 2.50 6.00
14 Andrei Svechnikov 1.25 3.00
15 Jason Robertson 1.50 4.00
16 Alexis Lafreniere 1.50 4.00
17 Wyatt Johnston 2.00 5.00
18 Tim Stutzle 1.25 3.00
19 Nick Suzuki 2.00 5.00
20 William Nylander 2.00 5.00

2023-24 E-X2000 Star Date 3000

SD1 Sidney Crosby 3.00 8.00
SD2 Elias Pettersson 1.25 3.00
SD3 Alex DeBrincat 1.00 2.50
SD4 Auston Matthews 3.00 8.00
SD5 Cale Makar 2.00 5.00
SD6 Jake Walman .50 1.25
SD7 David Pastrnak 2.00 5.00
SD8 Jason Robertson 1.25 3.00
SD9 Tim Stutzle 1.00 2.50
SD10 Matthew Tkachuk 1.50 4.00
SD11 Alexis Lafreniere 1.25 3.00
SD12 Juraj Slafkovsky 1.50 4.00
SD13 Brandon Montour 1.00 2.50
SD14 Nick Schmaltz .60 1.50
SD15 Jack Hughes 2.00 5.00
SD16 Lukas Reichel .75 2.00
SD17 Tage Thompson 1.00 2.50
SD18 Jordan Kyrou .75 2.00
SD19 Mitch Marner 1.25 3.00
SD20 Kirill Kaprizov 2.50 6.00
SD21 Ryan O'Reilly .75 2.00
SD22 Jared Spurgeon .75 2.00
SD23 Andrei Vasilevskiy 1.25 3.00
SD24 Kyle Connor 1.25 3.00
SD25 Connor McDavid 4.00 10.00

2023-24 E-X2000 Star Date 3000 Speckle

*SPECKLE/99: 1X TO 2.5X BASIC
SD1 Sidney Crosby 20.00 50.00
SD25 Connor McDavid 25.00 60.00

2023-24 E-X2000 Star Date 3000 Autographs Speckle

SD2 Elias Pettersson 10.00 25.00
SD11 Alexis Lafreniere 10.00 25.00
SD13 Brandon Montour 8.00 20.00
SD17 Tage Thompson 15.00 40.00
SD18 Jordan Kyrou 6.00 15.00
SD21 Ryan O'Reilly 6.00 15.00
SD22 Jared Spurgeon 6.00 15.00
SD23 Andrei Vasilevskiy 10.00 25.00
SD24 Kyle Connor 10.00 25.00
SD25 Connor McDavid 200.00 500.00

1994 EA Sports

COMPLETE SET (225) 30.00 75.00
1 Alexei Kasatonov .01 .05
2 Randy Ladouceur .01 .05
3 Terry Yake .01 .05
4 Troy Loney .01 .05
5 Anatoli Semenov .01 .05
6 Guy Hebert .05 .15
7 Ray Bourque 1.25 3.00
8 Don Sweeney .01 .05
9 Adam Oates .20 .50
10 Joe Juneau .15 .40
11 Cam Neely .40 1.00
12 Andy Moog .08 .25
13 Doug Bodger .01 .05
14 Petr Svoboda .01 .05
15 Pat LaFontaine .20 .50
16 Dale Hawerchuk .08 .25
17 Alexander Mogilny .20 .50
18 Grant Fuhr .08 .25
19 Gary Suter .01 .05
20 Al MacInnis .05 .15
21 Joe Nieuwendyk .05 .15
22 Gary Roberts .05 .15
23 Theo Fleury .08 .25
24 Mike Vernon .05 .15
25 Chris Chelios .40 1.00
26 Steve Smith .01 .05
27 Jeremy Roenick .60 1.50
28 Michel Goulet .05 .15
29 Steve Larmer .05 .15
30 Ed Belfour .60 1.50
31 Mark Tinordi .01 .05
32 Tommy Sjodin .01 .05
33 Mike Modano .75 2.00
34 Dave Gagner .05 .15
35 Russ Courtnall .05 .15
36 Jon Casey .05 .15
37 Paul Coffey .40 1.00
38 Steve Chiasson .01 .05
39 Steve Yzerman 2.50 6.00
40 Sergei Fedorov 1.25 3.00
41 Dino Ciccarelli .05 .15
42 Tim Cheveldae .05 .15
43 Dave Manson .01 .05
44 Igor Kravchuk .01 .05
45 Doug Weight .08 .25
46 Shayne Corson .05 .15
47 Petr Klima .01 .05
48 Bill Ranford .05 .15
49 Joe Cirella .01 .05
50 Gord Murphy .01 .05
51 Brian Skrudland .01 .05
52 Andrei Lomakin .01 .05
53 Scott Mellanby .01 .05
54 John Vanbiesbrouck .40 1.00
55 Zarley Zalapski .01 .05
56 Eric Weinrich .01 .05
57 Andrew Cassels .01 .05
58 Geoff Sanderson .05 .15
59 Pat Verbeek .05 .15
60 Sean Burke .05 .15
61 Rob Blake .05 .15
62 Marty McSorley .05 .15
63 Wayne Gretzky 4.00 10.00
64 Luc Robitaille .20 .50
65 Tomas Sandstrom .05 .15
66 Kelly Hrudey .05 .15
67 Eric Desjardins .05 .15
68 Mathieu Schneider .05 .15
69 Kirk Muller .05 .15
70 Vincent Damphousse .08 .25
71 Brian Bellows .01 .05
72 Patrick Roy 3.00 8.00
73 Scott Stevens .05 .15
74 Slava Fetisov .05 .15
75 Alexander Semak .01 .05
76 Stephane Richer .05 .15
77 Claude Lemieux .08 .25
78 Chris Terreri .05 .15
79 Vladimir Malakhov .01 .05
80 Darius Kasparaitis .01 .05
81 Pierre Turgeon .20 .50
82 Steve Thomas .05 .15
83 Benoit Hogue .01 .05
84 Glenn Healy .05 .15
85 Brian Leetch .40 1.00
86 James Patrick .01 .05
87 Mark Messier .75 2.00
88 Designer Tip
The Wong
One-Timer From
Boards To .01 .05
89 Mike Gartner .05 .15
90 Mike Richter .40 1.00
91 Norm Maciver .01 .05
92 Brad Shaw .01 .05
93 Jamie Baker .01 .05
94 Sylvain Turgeon .01 .05
95 Bob Kudelski .01 .05
96 Peter Sidorkiewicz .01 .05
97 Garry Galley .01 .05
98 Dimitri Yushkevich .01 .05
99 Eric Lindros 1.50 4.00
100 Rod Brind'Amour .05 .15
101 Mark Recchi .20 .50
102 Tommy Soderstrom .01 .05
103 Larry Murphy .08 .25
104 Ulf Samuelsson .05 .15
105 Mario Lemieux 3.00 8.00
106 Kevin Stevens .05 .15
107 Jaromir Jagr 2.00 5.00
108 Tom Barrasso .08 .25
109 Steve Duchesne .05 .15
110 Curtis Leschyshyn .01 .05
111 Mats Sundin .40 1.00
112 Joe Sakic 1.25 3.00
113 Owen Nolan .20 .50
114 Ron Hextall .08 .25
115 Doug Wilson .05 .15
116 Neil Wilkinson .01 .05
117 Kelly Kisio .01 .05
118 Johan Garpenlov .01 .05
119 Pat Falloon .05 .15
120 Arturs Irbe .15 .40
121 Jeff Brown .05 .15
122 Garth Butcher .05 .15
123 Craig Janney .05 .15
124 Brendan Shanahan .75 2.00
125 Brett Hull .75 2.00
126 Curtis Joseph .75 2.00
127 Bob Beers .01 .05
128 Roman Hamrlik .08 .25
129 Brian Bradley .05 .15
130 Mikael Andersson .01 .05
131 Chris Kontos .01 .05
132 Wendell Young .01 .05
133 Todd Gill .01 .05
134 Dave Ellett .01 .05
135 Doug Gilmour .40 1.00
136 Dave Andreychuk .05 .15
137 Nikolai Borschevsky .01 .05
138 Felix Potvin .40 1.00
139 Jyrki Lumme .01 .05
140 Doug Lidster .01 .05
141 Cliff Ronning .05 .15
142 Geoff Courtnall .01 .05
143 Pavel Bure 1.50 4.00
144 Kirk McLean .05 .15
145 Phil Housley .05 .15
146 Teppo Numminen .01 .05
147 Alexei Zhamnov .05 .15
148 Thomas Steen .01 .05
149 Teemu Selanne 1.25 3.00
150 Bob Essensa .05 .15
151 Kevin Hatcher .01 .05
152 Al Iafrate .05 .15
153 Mike Ridley .01 .05
154 Dimitri Khristich .01 .05
155 Peter Bondra .08 .25
156 Don Beaupre .01 .05
157 All Stars East CL .05 .15
158 All Stars West CL .05 .15
159 Mighty Ducks Team CL .08 .25
160 Bruins Team CL .08 .25
161 Sabres Team CL .05 .15
162 Flames Team CL .05 .15
163 Blackhawks Team CL .08 .25
164 Red Wings Team CL .08 .25
165 Oilers Team CL .05 .15
166 Panthers Team CL .05 .15
167 Whalers Team CL .05 .15
168 Kings Team CL .08 .25
169 Stars Team CL .05 .15
170 Canadiens Team CL .08 .25
171 Devils Team CL .05 .15
172 Islanders Team CL .05 .15
173 Rangers Team CL .08 .25
174 Senators Team CL .05 .15
175 Flyers Team CL .05 .15
176 Penguins Team CL .05 .15
177 Nordiques Team CL .05 .15
178 Sharks Team CL .08 .25
179 Blues Team CL .05 .15
180 Lightning Team CL .05 .15
181 Leafs Team CL .08 .25
182 Canucks Team CL .05 .15
183 Capitals Team CL .05 .15
184 Jets Team CL .05 .15
185 Skill Leaders
Checking# .08 .25
186 Skill Leaders
Defense/ .08 .25
187 Skill Leaders
Goaltendi .40 1.00
188 Skill Leaders
Passing/ .08 .25
189 Skill Leaders
Shot Accu 1.50 4.00
190 Al Iafrate SL .05 .15
191 Skill Leaders
Skating/ .20 .50
192 Skill Leaders
Stickhand 2.00 5.00
193 New Feature .01 .05
194 Derian Hatcher .01 .05
195 Dmitri Kvartalnov .01 .05
196 Randy Wood .01 .05
197 Gord Murphy .01 .05
198 New Feature .01 .05
199 New Feature
Expansion T .08 .25
200 New Feature
Goalie Cont .08 .25
201 Terry Yake .01 .05
202 Mark Fitzpatrick .01 .05
203 Brad Shaw .01 .05
204 NHL Logos .01 .05
205 Jyrki Lumme .01 .05
206 New Feature
Penalty Sho .01 .05
207 Gord Murphy .01 .05
208 Slava Fetisov .01 .05
209 Stephan LeBeau .01 .05
210 Gord Murphy .01 .05
211 New Feature
Shootout Ga 1.25 3.00
212 New Feature
User Record .40 1.00
213 Designer Tips .01 .05
214 Designer Tips .01 .05
215 Designer Tips .01 .05
216 Designer Tips
The Lange
Use Goalie To Take
Out .01 .05
217 Designer Tips
The Lesser
Create A Screen
With D .01 .05
218 Designer Tips
The Matulac
Fake Outside&
Shoot I .01 .05
219 Designer Tips
The Scott
Fake Inside&
Shoot Outs .01 .05
220 Designer Tips
The Probin
Set Up One-Timer
In Th .01 .05
221 Designer Tips
The Rogers
Set Up One-Sider
Acros .01 .05
222 Designer Tips
The Rubinelli
Fake Outside&
Fake .01 .05
223 Designer Tips
The Shin
Wrap Around Goal&
Shoot .01 .05
224 Designer Tips
The White
Deflection At
Goal Mout .01 .05
225 Designer Tips
The Wike
Set Up One-Timer
From Be .01 .05

1964-67 Eaton's Sports Adviser

NNO Gordie Howe
action 10.00 25.00
NNO Gordie Howe
All-Star uniform 10.00 25.00
NNO Gordie Howe
standing 10.00 25.00

1935 Edwards, Ringer and Bigg Sports Games in Many Lands

3 Ice Hockey-Canada 30.00 60.00
3 Ice Hockey-Canada
same as above, but with
Imperial Tobacco 22.50 45.00

2011-12 Elite

COMP.SET w/o RC's (200) 15.00 40.00
1 Teemu Selanne .60 1.50
2 Evgeni Malkin .60 1.50
3 Jimmy Howard .40 1.00
4 Patrick Sharp .30 .75
5 Keith Yandle .20 .50
6 Michael Grabner .25 .60
7 Pascal Dupuis .20 .50
8 Ryan Getzlaf .30 .75
9 Steven Stamkos .60 1.50
10 Aaron Johnson .20 .50
11 Brian Gionta .20 .50
12 Dany Heatley .25 .60
13 Evander Kane .30 .75
14 Joe Pavelski .40 1.00
15 Kevin Shattenkirk .20 .50
16 Michal Neuvirth .25 .60
17 Patrice Bergeron .40 1.00
18 Ryan Kesler .30 .75
19 Taylor Hall .30 .75
20 Al Montoya .20 .50
21 Cal Clutterbuck .20 .50
22 David Backes .20 .50
23 Henrik Lundqvist .75 2.00
24 Joe Thornton .50 1.25
25 Kris Letang .40 1.00
26 Michael Ryder .20 .50
27 Patrick Kane .60 1.50
28 Ryan Miller .30 .75
29 Thomas Greiss .25 .60
30 Alexander Burmistrov .25 .60
31 Cam Fowler .30 .75
32 David Clarkson .20 .50
33 Henrik Sedin .40 1.00
34 Joel Ward .20 .50
35 Kris Versteeg .20 .50
36 Miikka Kiprusoff .30 .75
37 Patrick Marleau .30 .75
38 Ryan O'Reilly .30 .75
39 Thomas Vanek .25 .60
40 Alexandre Burrows .20 .50
41 Cam Ward .30 .75
42 David Desharnais .20 .50
43 Henrik Zetterberg .40 1.00
44 Joffrey Lupul .20 .50
45 Kyle Wellwood .25 .60
46 Mikhail Grabovski .20 .50
47 Patrik Elias .30 .75
48 Ryan Smyth .25 .60
49 Tim Connolly .20 .50
50 Alexander Edler .20 .50
51 Carey Price .60 1.50
52 David Legwand .25 .60
53 Ilya Bryzgalov .30 .75
54 Johan Franzen .25 .60
55 Loui Eriksson .20 .50
56 Mike Ribeiro .20 .50
57 Paul Bissonnette .20 .50
58 Ryan Suter .25 .60
59 Tim Thomas .30 .75
60 Alex Ovechkin 1.25 3.00
61 Chad LaRose .20 .50
62 Derek Stepan .20 .50
63 Ilya Kovalchuk .30 .75
64 Johan Hedberg .25 .60
65 Luke Adam .25 .60
66 Mike Richards .25 .60
67 Paul Stastny .25 .60
68 Ryan Wilson .25 .60
69 T.J. Oshie .30 .75
70 Alex Pietrangelo .25 .60
71 Chris Neil .20 .50
72 Devan Dubnyk .25 .60
73 James Neal .20 .50
74 John Tavares .50 1.25
75 Marc-Andre Bergeron .20 .50
76 Mike Smith .30 .75
77 Pavel Datsyuk .50 1.25
78 Ryane Clowe .20 .50
79 Tomas Fleischmann .20 .50
80 Alexander Semin .30 .75
81 Chris Pronger .30 .75
82 Devin Setoguchi .25 .60
83 James Reimer .30 .75
84 John-Michael Liles .20 .50
85 Marc-Andre Fleury .60 1.50
86 Mikko Koivu .25 .60
87 Pekka Rinne .30 .75
88 Saku Koivu .30 .75
89 Tomas Plekanec .20 .50
90 Alex Tanguay .20 .50
91 Clarke MacArthur .20 .50
92 Dion Phaneuf .25 .60
93 James van Riemsdyk .25 .60
94 Jonas Hiller .25 .60
95 Marian Gaborik .30 .75
96 Milan Lucic .30 .75
97 Phil Kessel .30 .75
98 Scott Hartnell .20 .50
99 Tomas Vokoun .25 .60
100 Alexander Steen .20 .50
101 Claude Giroux .30 .75
102 Drew Doughty .40 1.00
103 Jonathan Quick .40 1.00
104 James Wisniewski .20 .50
105 Marian Hossa .30 .75
106 Milan Michalek .20 .50
107 P.K. Subban .40 1.00
108 Semyon Varlamov .30 .75
109 Tuomo Ruutu .25 .60
110 Andrew Ladd .20 .50
111 Corey Crawford .40 1.00
112 Duncan Keith .25 .60
113 Jamie Benn .30 .75
114 Jonathan Toews .50 1.25
115 Mark Giordano .30 .75
116 Nathan Gerbe .20 .50
117 Pierre-Marc Bouchard .30 .75
118 Sergei Kostitsyn .20 .50
119 Ty Conklin .25 .60
120 Antti Niemi .25 .60
121 Corey Perry .50 1.25
122 Jarome Iginla .40 1.00
123 Jordan Eberle .30 .75
124 Mark Streit .20 .50
125 Nathan Horton .30 .75
126 Radim Vrbata .20 .50
127 Shane Doan .25 .60
128 Tyler Myers .20 .50
129 Anze Kopitar .50 1.25
130 Corey Potter .25 .60
131 Dustin Brown .30 .75
132 Jaromir Jagr 1.00 2.50
133 Jordan Staal .25 .60
134 Martin Brodeur .75 2.00
135 Nicklas Backstrom .30 .75
136 Ray Emery .25 .60
137 Shawn Horcoff .20 .50
138 Tyler Seguin .40 1.00
139 Bobby Ryan .25 .60
140 Cory Schneider .30 .75
141 Dustin Byfuglien .30 .75
142 Jaroslav Halak .30 .75
143 Jordin Tootoo .25 .60
144 Martin Havlat .25 .60
145 Nicklas Lidstrom .20 .50
146 Ray Whitney .25 .60
147 Shea Weber .25 .60
148 Valtteri Filppula .20 .50
149 Brad Marchand .60 1.50
150 Craig Anderson .30 .75
151 Dwayne Roloson .25 .60
152 Jason Pominville .20 .50
153 Jose Theodore .30 .75
154 Martin St. Louis .30 .75
155 Nik Antropov .25 .60
156 Sheldon Souray .20 .50
157 Victor Hedman .40 1.00
158 Brad Richards .30 .75
159 Curtis Glencross .20 .50
160 Ed Jovanovski .20 .50
161 Jason Spezza .30 .75
162 Josh Harding .30 .75
163 Matt Cullen .20 .50
164 Niklas Backstrom .30 .75
165 Rene Bourque .20 .50
166 Rich Peverley .30 .75
167 Sidney Crosby 1.25 3.00
168 Vincent Lecavalier .30 .75
169 Brandon Dubinsky .20 .50
170 Daniel Alfredsson .30 .75
171 Eric Staal .40 1.00
172 Jeff Carter .25 .60
173 Jean-Sebastien Giguere .30 .75
174 Matt Duchene .30 .75
175 Nikolai Khabibulin .25 .60
176 Rick Nash .30 .75
177 Simon Gagne .30 .75
178 Vinny Prospal .20 .50
179 Brenden Morrow .25 .60
180 Daniel Sedin .40 1.00
181 Erik Johnson .20 .50
182 Jeff Skinner .40 1.00
183 Jussi Jokinen .20 .50
184 Matt Moulson .20 .50
185 Ondrej Pavelec .30 .75
186 Roberto Luongo .50 1.25
187 Stephen Weiss .25 .60
188 Wayne Simmonds .40 1.00
189 Brian Campbell .20 .50
190 Danny Briere .30 .75
191 Erik Karlsson .40 1.00
192 Jhonas Enroth .30 .75
193 Kari Lehtonen .25 .60
194 Max Pacioretty .30 .75
195 P.A. Parenteau .20 .50

196 Ryan Callahan .20 .50
197 Steve Mason .25 .60
198 Zach Parise .30 .75
199 Brian Elliott .25 .60
200 Zdeno Chara .30 .75
201 Allen York RC 3.00 8.00
202 Brett Bulmer RC 2.50 6.00
203 Carl Hagelin RC 4.00 10.00
204 T.J. Brennan RC 2.50 6.00
205 Brayden McNabb RC 2.50 6.00
206 Roman Horak RC 2.50 6.00
207 Aaron Palushaj RC 2.50 6.00
208 Anton Lander RC 2.50 6.00
209 Cam Atkinson RC 6.00 15.00
210 Erik Condra RC 2.50 6.00
211 Joe Vitale RC 2.50 6.00
212 Marcus Kruger RC 4.00 10.00
213 Tomas Kubalik RC 2.50 6.00
214 Robert Bortuzzo RC 2.50 6.00
215 Bracken Kearns RC 2.50 6.00
216 Lance Bouma RC 2.50 6.00
217 David Rundblad RC 2.50 6.00
218 Yann Sauve RC 2.50 6.00
219 Adam Henrique RC 6.00 15.00
220 Carl Klingberg RC 2.50 6.00
221 Greg Nemisz RC 2.50 6.00
222 John Moore RC 2.50 6.00
223 Matt Read RC 3.00 8.00
224 Teemu Hartikainen RC 2.50 6.00
225 Tomas Vincour RC 2.50 6.00
226 Corey Tropp RC 2.50 6.00
227 Cam Talbot RC 6.00 15.00
228 Maxime Macenauer RC 2.50 6.00
229 Paul Postma RC 2.50 6.00
230 Marcus Foligno RC 6.00 15.00
231 Alexei Emelin RC 2.50 6.00
232 Ben Scrivens RC 2.50 6.00
233 Colin Greening RC 2.50 6.00
234 Harri Sateri RC 2.50 6.00
235 Jonathon Blum RC 2.50 6.00
236 Keith Kinkaid RC 2.50 6.00
237 Raphael Diaz RC 2.50 6.00
238 Zac Rinaldo RC 2.50 6.00
239 Peter Holland RC 2.50 6.00
240 Erik Gustafsson RC 3.00 8.00
241 Mikko Koskinen RC 3.00 8.00
242 Ryan Thang RC 2.00 5.00
243 Scott Timmins RC 2.50 6.00
244 Colten Teubert RC 2.50 6.00
245 Andy Miele RC 2.50 6.00
246 Brendon Nash RC 2.50 6.00
247 Brian Strait RC 3.00 8.00
248 David Savard RC 2.50 6.00
249 Erik Gudbranson RC 3.00 8.00
250 Harry Zolnierczyk RC 2.50 6.00
251 Justin Faulk RC 4.00 10.00
252 Slava Voynov RC 2.50 6.00
253 Stephane Da Costa RC 2.50 6.00
254 Mattias Ekholm RC 5.00 12.00
255 Tim Erixon RC 2.50 6.00
256 Drew Bagnall RC 2.50 6.00
257 Zack Kassian RC 3.00 8.00
258 Eddie Lack RC 2.50 6.00
259 Calvin de Haan RC 2.50 6.00
260 Kris Fredheim RC 2.50 6.00
261 Adam Larsson/99 RC 12.00 30.00
262 Cody Eakin/99 RC 15.00 40.00
263 Gustav Nyquist/99 RC 15.00 40.00
264 Mika Zibanejad/99 RC 30.00 80.00
265 Brendan Smith/99 RC 10.00 25.00
266 Brandon Saad/99 RC 15.00 40.00
267 Cody Hodgson/99 RC 15.00 40.00
268 Jake Gardiner/99 RC 15.00 40.00
269 R.Nugent-Hopkins/99 RC 40.00 100.00
270 Craig Smith/99 RC 12.00 30.00
271 Blake Geoffrion/99 RC 10.00 25.00
272 Louis Leblanc/99 RC 20.00 50.00
273 Joe Colborne/99 RC 12.00 30.00
274 Ryan Johansen/99 RC 30.00 80.00
275 Brett Connolly/99 RC 10.00 25.00
276 D.Smith-Pelly/99 RC 12.00 30.00
277 Mark Scheifele/99 RC 20.00 50.00
278 Sean Couturier/99 RC 25.00 50.00
279 Gabriel Landeskog/99 RC 15.00 40.00
280 Matt Frattin/99 RC 10.00 25.00

2011-12 Elite Aspirations

*1-200 VETS: 2X TO 5X BASIC CARDS
*201-260 ROOKIES: .8X TO 2X BASIC RC
*201-260 ROOKIES: .6X TO 1.5X BASIC RC
111 Corey Crawford 2.00 5.00
135 Nicklas Backstrom 1.50 4.00
275 Brett Connolly 12.00 30.00

2011-12 Elite Status Gold

*1-200 VETS: 6X TO 15X BASIC CARDS
111 Corey Crawford 6.00 15.00
135 Nicklas Backstrom 5.00 12.00

2011-12 Elite Materials

*PATCH/15: 1X TO 2.5X BASIC JSY
*PATCH/15: .8X TO 2X BASIC JSY SP
1 Ales Hemsky 3.00 8.00
2 Alex Ovechkin 15.00 40.00
3 Antoine Vermette 2.50 6.00
4 Antti Niemi 3.00 8.00
5 Anze Kopitar 6.00 15.00
6 Brad Marchand 8.00 20.00
7 Brenden Morrow 3.00 8.00
8 Chris Pronger 4.00 10.00
10 Corey Perry 6.00 15.00
11 Dan Boyle 2.50 6.00
12 Sean Couturier 6.00 15.00
13 Derek Roy 2.50 6.00
14 Derek Stepan 5.00 12.00
15 Dion Phaneuf 3.00 8.00
16 Dustin Brown 4.00 10.00
17 Erik Johnson 2.50 6.00
19 Henrik Lundqvist 6.00 15.00
20 Ilya Kovalchuk SP 5.00 12.00
21 James Neal 5.00 12.00
22 James van Riemsdyk 3.00 8.00
23 Jarome Iginla SP 6.00 15.00
24 Joe Pavelski 5.00 12.00
25 Joe Thornton SP 8.00 20.00
26 Johan Franzen 3.00 8.00
27 John Carlson 4.00 10.00
29 Jonathan Toews SP 8.00 20.00
31 Zdeno Chara 4.00 10.00
32 Marian Gaborik 4.00 10.00
33 Gabriel Landeskog 6.00 15.00
34 Martin Brodeur SP 12.00 30.00
35 Matt Duchene 4.00 10.00
36 Mike Fisher 2.50 6.00
37 Nikolai Khabibulin 5.00 12.00
38 Pavel Datsyuk 6.00 15.00
39 Rick Nash 4.00 10.00
40 Robin Lehner 3.00 8.00
41 Ryan Getzlaf 4.00 10.00
42 Ryan Nugent-Hopkins 8.00 20.00
43 Ryan O'Reilly 4.00 10.00
44 Scott Gomez 3.00 8.00
45 Sidney Crosby SP 12.00 30.00
46 Steve Ott 2.50 6.00
47 Shane Doan 3.00 8.00
48 Victor Hedman 5.00 12.00
49 Zach Parise SP 5.00 12.00
50 Ryan Kesler 5.00 12.00

2011-12 Elite Materials Autographs

1 Ales Hemsky/25 10.00 25.00
2 Alex Ovechkin/25 40.00 80.00
4 Antti Niemi/25 10.00 25.00
5 Anze Kopitar/25 20.00 50.00
6 Brad Marchand/25 25.00 60.00
8 Chris Pronger/25 12.00 30.00
9 Craig Anderson/25 12.00 30.00
10 Corey Perry/25 10.00 25.00
11 Dan Boyle/25 8.00 20.00
12 Sean Couturier/25 20.00 50.00
14 Derek Stepan/25 8.00 20.00
15 Dion Phaneuf/25 10.00 25.00
16 Dustin Brown/25 12.00 30.00
18 Evgeni Malkin/25 30.00 60.00
19 Henrik Lundqvist/25 25.00 50.00
20 Ilya Kovalchuk/25 12.00 30.00
21 James Neal/25 10.00 25.00
22 James van Riemsdyk/25 10.00 25.00
23 Jarome Iginla/25 15.00 40.00
24 Joe Pavelski/25 15.00 40.00
25 Joe Thornton/25 20.00 50.00
27 John Carlson/25 12.00 30.00
28 Jonas Gustavsson/25 12.00 30.00
29 Jonathan Toews/25 25.00 50.00
30 Loui Eriksson/25 8.00 20.00
31 Zdeno Chara/25 12.00 30.00
32 Marian Gaborik/25 12.00 30.00
33 Gabriel Landeskog/25 25.00 50.00
34 Martin Brodeur/25 40.00 80.00
35 Matt Duchene/20 12.00 30.00
37 Nikolai Khabibulin/25 12.00 30.00
38 Pavel Datsyuk/25 30.00 60.00
39 Rick Nash/25 10.00 25.00
40 Robin Lehner/25 10.00 25.00
41 Ryan Getzlaf/25 12.00 30.00
42 Ryan Nugent-Hopkins/25 60.00 125.00
43 Ryan O'Reilly/25 12.00 30.00
44 Scott Gomez/25 10.00 25.00
45 Sidney Crosby/25 75.00 150.00
46 Steve Ott/25 12.00 30.00
47 Shane Doan/25 10.00 25.00
48 Victor Hedman/25 20.00 40.00
49 Zach Parise/25 12.00 30.00
50 Ryan Kesler/25 20.00 40.00

2011-12 Elite New Breed Materials

*PATCH/25: 1.2X TO 3X BASIC INSERTS
*PRIME/25: 1.2X TO 3X BASIC INSERTS
1 Adam Larsson 2.50 6.00
2 Adam Henrique 5.00 12.00
3 Blake Geoffrion 2.00 5.00
4 Brandon Saad 3.00 8.00
5 Brett Connolly 2.00 5.00
6 Cody Eakin 3.00 8.00
7 Cody Hodgson 5.00 12.00
8 David Rundblad 2.00 5.00
9 Devante Smith-Pelly 2.50 6.00
10 Gabriel Landeskog 6.00 15.00
11 Gustav Nyquist 6.00 15.00
12 Jake Gardiner 3.00 8.00
13 Joe Colborne 2.50 6.00
14 Mark Scheifele 6.00 15.00
15 Matt Frattin 5.00 12.00
16 Mika Zibanejad 6.00 15.00
17 Ryan Johansen 6.00 15.00
18 Ryan Nugent-Hopkins 10.00 25.00
19 Sean Couturier 5.00 12.00
20 Tim Erixon 2.00 5.00
21 Aaron Palushaj 2.00 5.00
22 Greg Nemisz 2.00 5.00
23 Erik Gudbranson 2.50 6.00
24 John Moore 2.00 5.00
25 Jonathon Blum 2.00 5.00
26 Justin Faulk 3.00 8.00
27 Marcus Kruger 3.00 8.00
28 Simon Despres 2.00 5.00
29 Zack Kassian 2.50 6.00
30 Calvin de Haan 2.00 5.00
32 Tyler Seguin 4.00 10.00
33 Raphael Diaz 2.00 5.00
34 Tomas Vincour 2.00 5.00
35 Harri Sateri 2.00 5.00
36 Derek Stepan 1.50 4.00
38 Stephane Da Costa 2.00 5.00
39 Tomas Kubalik 2.00 5.00
40 Slava Voynov 2.00 5.00
41 Cam Atkinson 5.00 12.00
42 Patrick Wiercioch 2.00 5.00
43 Brendan Smith 2.00 5.00
45 Colin Greening 2.00 5.00
46 Zac Dalpe 2.00 5.00
48 Victor Hedman 4.00 10.00
49 Matt Read 2.50 6.00
50 Ben Scrivens 2.00 5.00

2011-12 Elite New Breed Materials Autographs

1 Adam Larsson/50 8.00 20.00
2 Adam Henrique/50 15.00 40.00
3 Blake Geoffrion/50 6.00 15.00
4 Brandon Saad/50 10.00 25.00
5 Brett Connolly/50 6.00 15.00
6 Cody Eakin/50 10.00 25.00
7 Cody Hodgson/50 10.00 25.00
8 David Rundblad/50 6.00 15.00
9 Devante Smith-Pelly/50 8.00 20.00
10 Gabriel Landeskog/50 20.00 50.00
11 Gustav Nyquist/50 15.00 40.00
12 Jake Gardiner/50 10.00 25.00
13 Joe Colborne/50 6.00 15.00
14 Mark Scheifele/50 25.00 60.00
15 Matt Frattin/50 6.00 15.00
16 Mika Zibanejad/50 20.00 50.00
17 Ryan Johansen/50 20.00 50.00
18 Ryan Nugent-Hopkins/50 25.00 60.00
19 Sean Couturier/50 12.00 30.00
20 Tim Erixon/50 6.00 15.00
21 Aaron Palushaj/50 6.00 15.00
22 Greg Nemisz/50 6.00 15.00
23 Erik Gudbranson/50 8.00 20.00
24 John Moore/50 6.00 15.00
25 Jonathon Blum /50 6.00 15.00
26 Justin Faulk/50 10.00 25.00
27 Marcus Kruger/50 10.00 25.00
28 Simon Despres/50 6.00 15.00
29 Zack Kassian/50 8.00 20.00
30 Calvin de Haan/50 6.00 15.00
33 Raphael Diaz/50 6.00 15.00
34 Tomas Vincour/50 6.00 15.00
35 Harri Sateri/50 6.00 15.00
36 Derek Stepan/50 5.00 12.00
38 Stephane Da Costa/50 6.00 15.00
39 Tomas Kubalik/50 6.00 15.00
40 Slava Voynov/50 6.00 15.00
41 Cam Atkinson/50 15.00 40.00
42 Patrick Wiercioch/50 6.00 15.00
43 Brendan Smith/50 6.00 15.00
45 Colin Greening/50 6.00 15.00
46 Zac Dalpe/50 5.00 12.00
48 Victor Hedman/50 10.00 25.00
49 Matt Read/50 8.00 20.00
50 Ben Scrivens/50 6.00 15.00

2011-12 Elite Passing the Torch Autographs

1 M.St. Louis/N.Gerbe 10.00 25.00
2 Gudbranson/Pronger 10.00 25.00
3 B.Smith/N.Lidstrom 20.00 50.00
4 H.Lundqvist/R.Lehner 20.00 50.00
5 D.Dubnyk/B.Ranford 15.00 40.00
6 S.Doan/A.Miele 12.00 30.00
7 C.Eakin/A.Semin 12.00 30.00
8 D.Graham/B.Saad 15.00 40.00
9 J.Anderson/A.Niemi 15.00 40.00
10 J.Howard/T.McCollum 12.00 30.00
11 S.Weber/J.Blum 12.00 30.00
12 C.Hodgson/R.Kesler 15.00 40.00
13 J.Shelley/Z.Rinaldo 12.00 30.00
14 J.Davidson/J.Halak 12.00 30.00
15 Belfour/Lehtonen 20.00 40.00
16 R.Clowe/D.Cleary 10.00 25.00
17 Scheifele/Hawerchuk 25.00 50.00
18 D.Gilmour/A.Henrique 15.00 40.00
19 B.Scrivens/C.Joseph 12.00 30.00
20 B.Clarke/S.Couturier 30.00 60.00

2011-12 Elite Passing the Torch Autographs SP

1 P.Roy/C.Price 75.00 150.00
2 Messier/Nugent-Hopkins 100.00 200.00
3 M.Lemieux/E.Malkin 100.00 200.00
4 V.Lecavalier/B.Connolly 25.00 50.00
5 S.Niedermayer/A.Larsson 25.00 50.00
6 M.Duchene/J.Sakic 50.00 100.00
7 F.Potvin/J.Reimer 60.00 120.00
8 B.Trottier/J.Tavares 50.00 120.00
9 S.Mikita/J.Toews 75.00 125.00
10 C.Neely/T.Seguin 60.00 120.00

2011-12 Elite Prime Number Autographs

1 Joe Sakic/20* 50.00 100.00
2 Steve Yzerman/90* 40.00 100.00
3 Ray Bourque/90* 30.00 60.00
4 Patrick Roy/50* 50.00 100.00
5 Ron Francis/40* 20.00 50.00
6 Mario Lemieux/70* 60.00 120.00
7 Bernie Nicholls/70* 12.00 30.00
8 Curtis Joseph/50* 20.00 50.00
9 Scott Niedermayer/70* 12.00 30.00
10 Luc Robitaille/50* 15.00 40.00
11 Ed Belfour/80* 15.00 40.00
13 Wendel Clark/30* 15.00 40.00
15 Zach Parise/40* 12.00 30.00
16 Tim Thomas/90* 15.00 40.00
19 Jarome Iginla/80* 20.00 50.00
20 Henrik Sedin/60* 20.00 50.00
22 Rick Nash/50* 15.00 40.00
23 Ilya Kovalchuk/60* EXCH 15.00 40.00
24 Marc-Andre Fleury/80* 30.00 80.00
25 Marian Gaborik/80* 12.00 30.00
26 Thomas Vanek/80* 12.00 30.00
28 Ryan Miller/50* 15.00 40.00
29 Anze Kopitar/50* 25.00 60.00
30 Patrick Marleau/50* 15.00 40.00
31 Nicklas Lidstrom/50* 40.00 80.00

2011-12 Elite Prime Number Jerseys

1 Joe Sakic/600* 10.00 25.00
2 Steve Yzerman/600* 12.00 30.00
3 Ray Bourque/300* 8.00 20.00
4 Patrick Roy/500* 12.00 30.00
5 Ron Francis/500* 6.00 15.00
6 Mario Lemieux/100* 20.00 50.00
7 Bernie Nicholls/400* 4.00 10.00
8 Curtis Joseph/400* 6.00 15.00
9 Scott Niedermayer/100* 5.00 12.00
10 Luc Robitaille/500* 5.00 12.00
11 Ed Belfour/400* 6.00 15.00
12 Bryan Trottier/500* 5.00 12.00
13 Wendel Clark/290* 5.00 12.00
14 Alex Ovechkin/290* 15.00 40.00
15 Zach Parise/300* 4.00 10.00
16 Tim Thomas/100* 5.00 12.00
17 Nikolai Khabibulin/300* 3.00 8.00
18 Joe Thornton/290* 6.00 15.00
19 Jarome Iginla/400* 6.00 15.00
20 Henrik Sedin/600* 6.00 15.00
21 Henrik Lundqvist/200* 10.00 25.00
22 Rick Nash/200* 4.00 10.00
23 Ilya Kovalchuk/300* 4.00 10.00
24 Marc-Andre Fleury/100* 8.00 20.00
25 Marian Gaborik/200* 4.00 10.00
26 Thomas Vanek/300* 3.00 8.00
27 Evgeni Malkin/400* 6.00 15.00
28 Ryan Miller/200* 6.00 15.00
29 Anze Kopitar/300* 6.00 15.00
30 Patrick Marleau/300* 4.00 10.00
31 Nicklas Lidstrom/200* 5.00 12.00
32 Sidney Crosby/200* 15.00 40.00
33 Martin Brodeur/100* 12.00 30.00

2011-12 Elite Rookie Autographs

202 Brett Bulmer 4.00 10.00
206 Roman Horak 4.00 10.00
207 Aaron Palushaj 4.00 10.00
209 Cam Atkinson 10.00 25.00
210 Erik Condra 4.00 10.00
212 Marcus Kruger 6.00 15.00
219 Adam Henrique 6.00 15.00
220 Carl Klingberg 4.00 10.00
221 Greg Nemisz 4.00 10.00
223 Matt Read 4.00 10.00
225 Tomas Vincour 4.00 10.00
229 Paul Postma 4.00 10.00
231 Alexei Emelin 4.00 10.00
232 Ben Scrivens 4.00 10.00
233 Colin Greening 4.00 10.00
235 Jonathon Blum 4.00 10.00
236 Keith Kinkaid 4.00 10.00
238 Zac Rinaldo 4.00 10.00
239 Peter Holland 4.00 10.00
241 Mikko Koskinen 5.00 12.00
245 Andy Miele 4.00 10.00
248 David Savard 4.00 10.00
249 Erik Gudbranson 5.00 12.00
251 Justin Faulk 6.00 15.00
252 Slava Voynov 4.00 10.00
253 Stephane Da Costa 4.00 10.00
255 Tim Erixon 4.00 10.00
258 Eddie Lack 4.00 10.00
259 Calvin de Haan 4.00 10.00
261 Adam Larsson SP 15.00 40.00
262 Cody Eakin SP 20.00 50.00
263 Gustav Nyquist SP 25.00 50.00
264 Mika Zibanejad SP 25.00 50.00
265 Brendan Smith SP 12.00 30.00
266 Brandon Saad SP 20.00 50.00
267 Cody Hodgson SP 30.00 60.00
268 Jake Gardiner SP 25.00 50.00
269 Nugent-Hopkins SP 250.00 400.00
270 Craig Smith SP 15.00 40.00
271 Blake Geoffrion SP 12.00 30.00
272 Louis Leblanc SP 8.00 20.00
273 Joe Colborne SP 15.00 40.00
274 Ryan Johansen SP 40.00 100.00
275 Brett Connolly SP 12.00 30.00
276 Devante Smith-Pelly SP 15.00 40.00
277 Mark Scheifele SP 12.00 30.00
278 Sean Couturier SP 15.00 40.00
279 Gabriel Landeskog SP 20.00 50.00
280 Matt Frattin SP 15.00 40.00

2011-12 Elite Rookie Stars

1 Ryan Nugent-Hopkins 4.00 10.00
2 Gabriel Landeskog 3.00 8.00
3 Brett Connolly 1.00 2.50
4 Sean Couturier 2.00 5.00
5 Craig Smith 1.25 3.00
6 Devante Smith-Pelly 1.25 3.00
7 Cody Hodgson 1.50 4.00
8 Adam Larsson 1.25 3.00
9 Matt Read 1.25 3.00
10 Ryan Johansen 3.00 8.00

2011-12 Elite Series Alexander Ovechkin

COMMON OVECHKIN (1-6) 2.00 5.00

2011-12 Elite Series Autographs

1 Joe Sakic/50 30.00 80.00
2 Alex Ovechkin/50 30.00 80.00
4 Sidney Crosby/50 75.00 150.00
5 Steven Stamkos/50 25.00 60.00
6 Steve Yzerman/50 40.00 80.00
7 Mark Messier/29 30.00 60.00

2011-12 Elite Series Dual

COMMON HALL/RYAN N-H 4.00 10.00

2011-12 Elite Series Dual Autographs

5 T.Hall/R.Nugent-Hopkins 100.00 200.00

2011-12 Elite Series Joe Sakic

COMMON SAKIC (1-6) 1.50 4.00

2011-12 Elite Series Mark Messier

COMMON MESSIER (1-6) 1.50 4.00

2011-12 Elite Series Sidney Crosby

COMMON CROSBY (1-6) 2.50 6.00

2011-12 Elite Series Steve Yzerman

COMMON YZERMAN (1-6) 2.00 5.00

2011-12 Elite Series Steven Stamkos

COMMON STAMKOS (1-6) 2.00 5.00

2011-12 Elite Signings

1 Zenon Konopka 4.00 10.00
2 Zach Boychuk 3.00 8.00
5 Vincent Lecavalier SP 15.00 30.00
6 Viktor Stalberg 3.00 8.00
8 Tyler Seguin 25.00 50.00
10 Tyler Bozak SP 10.00 25.00
11 Tuukka Rask SP 20.00 40.00
12 Trevor Linden 12.00 30.00
13 Trevor Gillies 4.00 10.00
14 Tony Esposito SP 12.00 30.00
15 Tomas Tatar 5.00 12.00
16 Taylor Hall 5.00 12.00
17 Teemu Selanne SP 25.00 50.00
18 Thomas Vanek SP 6.00 15.00
19 T.J. Galiardi 4.00 10.00
20 Steven Stamkos SP 25.00 50.00
21 Steven Kampfer EXCH 4.00 10.00
22 Steve Yzerman SP 50.00 100.00
23 Simon Gagne 8.00 20.00
24 Scott Gomez 6.00 15.00
25 Ryan Nugent-Hopkins SP 50.00 100.00
26 Ryan Miller SP 8.00 20.00
27 Ryan McDonagh 3.00 8.00
28 Rick Nash SP 8.00 20.00
29 Rhett Rakhshani 4.00 10.00
30 Ray Ferraro 5.00 12.00
31 Phil Esposito SP 12.00 30.00
33 Patrik Elias 5.00 12.00
34 Patrick Marleau SP 8.00 20.00
35 Patrick Kane 15.00 30.00
36 Patric Hornqvist 5.00 12.00
37 Ryan Johansen 12.00 30.00
38 Ondrej Pavelec 15.00 30.00
39 Patrick Roy SP 40.00 80.00
40 Nicklas Lidstrom SP 20.00 40.00
41 Nick Palmieri 4.00 10.00
42 Nick Johnson 4.00 10.00
43 Nazem Kadri 8.00 20.00
44 Nathan Horton 25.00 50.00
46 Mike Santorelli 3.00 8.00
47 Kris Letang 10.00 25.00
48 Michael Frolik 6.00 15.00
49 Max Pacioretty 6.00 15.00
50 Matt Duchene 8.00 20.00
51 Mats Zuccarello EXCH 5.00 12.00
52 Mark Scheifele SP 10.00 25.00
53 Mario Lemieux SP 50.00 100.00
54 David Rundblad 6.00 15.00
55 Magnus Paajarvi 8.00 20.00
56 Luke Adam 4.00 10.00
58 Lee Stempniak 3.00 8.00
59 Krys Barch 4.00 10.00
60 Kevin Shattenkirk 3.00 8.00
61 Kelly Hrudey SP 6.00 15.00
62 Kari Lehtonen 8.00 20.00
63 Jordan Eberle SP 10.00 25.00
64 Justin Abdelkader 5.00 12.00
65 Jonathan Quick 15.00 40.00
66 Jonas Gustavsson 5.00 12.00
67 John Tavares SP 15.00 30.00
68 John McCarthy 3.00 8.00
69 Joe Thornton SP 20.00 40.00
70 Joe Nieuwendyk SP 20.00 40.00
71 Brendan Smith 15.00 30.00
72 Jack Johnson 3.00 8.00
73 Ilya Bryzgalov SP 15.00 30.00
74 Stephane Da Costa SP 6.00 15.00
75 George Parros SP 6.00 15.00
76 Gabriel Landeskog SP 20.00 50.00
77 Evander Kane 6.00 15.00
80 Don Cherry SP 15.00 30.00
81 Adam Henrique 8.00 20.00
82 Dany Heatley SP 6.00 15.00
83 Dan Boyle SP 5.00 12.00
84 Colin Wilson 4.00 10.00
85 Chris Neil 4.00 10.00
86 Charlie Hodge SP 8.00 20.00
87 Carey Price SP 15.00 40.00
88 Cam Ward SP 8.00 20.00
90 Bryan Trottier SP 15.00 40.00
91 Bobby Hull SP 20.00 40.00
92 Bernie Parent SP 20.00 40.00
93 Andrew Ladd 5.00 12.00
94 Alex Urbom 4.00 10.00
96 Andre Dupont SP 30.00 60.00
97 Zack Kassian 5.00 12.00
98 Simon Despres 10.00 25.00
99 Jonathan Toews SP 25.00 50.00
100 Ed Belfour SP 20.00 40.00

2011-12 Elite Social Signatures

1 Paul Bissonnette 10.00 25.00
2 Bobby Ryan 12.00 30.00
3 Matt Duchene 10.00 25.00
4 Michael Grabner 12.00 30.00
5 Dustin Brown 12.00 30.00
6 James van Riemsdyk 10.00 25.00
7 Steven Stamkos SP 40.00 80.00
8 Nazem Kadri 8.00 20.00
9 Daniel Carcillo 10.00 25.00
10 Evander Kane 12.00 30.00

2011-12 Elite Stars

1 Alex Ovechkin 6.00 15.00
2 Martin Brodeur 4.00 10.00
3 Steven Stamkos 3.00 8.00
4 Tim Thomas 1.50 4.00
5 Tyler Seguin 2.00 5.00
6 Patrick Kane 3.00 8.00
7 Matt Duchene 1.50 4.00
8 Jaromir Jagr 5.00 12.00
9 Carey Price 3.00 8.00
10 Sidney Crosby 4.00 10.00

2012-13 Elite Inscriptions

EIAH Adam Henrique 6.00 15.00
EICH Carl Hagelin 5.00 12.00
EICO Sean Couturier 8.00 20.00
EICS Cory Schneider 8.00 20.00
EIDB Dustin Brown 8.00 20.00
EIES Eric Staal 10.00 25.00
EIJB Jamie Benn 6.00 15.00
EIJH Jonas Hiller 6.00 15.00
EIJQ Jonathan Quick 20.00 40.00
EIJT John Tavares SP B 12.00 30.00
EIMD Matt Duchene 8.00 20.00
EIMF Marcus Foligno 6.00 15.00
EIMS Mike Smith 8.00 20.00
EIMSL Martin St. Louis 8.00 20.00
EIPD Pavel Datsyuk 10.00 25.00
EIRG Ryan Getzlaf 8.00 20.00
EIRM Ryan Miller 8.00 20.00
EIRN Ryan Nugent-Hopkins 50.00 100.00
EISW Stephen Weiss 5.00 12.00
EIZP Zach Parise 12.00 30.00

2012-13 Elite Intensity

1 Jarome Iginla 3.00 8.00
2 Mark Messier 5.00 12.00
3 Martin Brodeur 6.00 15.00
4 Claude Giroux 2.50 6.00
5 Chris Kreider 4.00 10.00
6 Nicklas Lidstrom 3.00 8.00
7 Jonathan Quick 3.00 8.00
8 Patrick Roy 6.00 15.00
9 Henrik Lundqvist 6.00 15.00
10 Sidney Crosby 10.00 25.00
11 Bobby Clarke 4.00 10.00
12 Wendel Clark 4.00 10.00
13 Cam Neely 2.50 6.00
14 Teemu Selanne 5.00 12.00
15 Gordie Howe 8.00 20.00
16 Alex Ovechkin 10.00 25.00
17 Zdeno Chara 2.50 6.00
18 Steven Stamkos 5.00 12.00
19 Ryan Miller 2.50 6.00
20 Jonathan Toews 4.00 10.00
21 Doug Gilmour 3.00 8.00
22 Shea Weber 2.00 5.00
23 Carey Price 5.00 12.00
24 Eric Staal 3.00 8.00
25 Gabriel Landeskog 3.00 8.00
26 Chris Chelios 2.50 6.00
27 Steve Yzerman 6.00 15.00
28 Daniel Alfredsson 2.50 6.00
29 Brett Hull 5.00 12.00
30 Luc Robitaille 2.50 6.00

2012-13 Elite Rookies

1 Andrew Joudrey 1.50 4.00
2 Mike Connolly 1.50 4.00
3 Jordan Nolan 1.25 3.00
4 Ryan Garbutt 1.25 3.00
5 Casey Cizikas 1.50 4.00
6 Max Sauve 1.25 3.00
7 Jaden Schwartz 4.00 10.00
8 Travis Turnbull 1.25 3.00
9 Gabriel Dumont 1.50 4.00
10 Riley Sheahan 2.00 5.00
11 Tyson Barrie 4.00 10.00
12 Aaron Ness 1.25 3.00
13 Colby Robak 1.25 3.00
14 Michael Stone 1.50 4.00
15 Brandon Manning 1.50 4.00
16 Cody Goloubef 1.25 3.00
17 Mat Clark 1.50 4.00
18 Dalton Prout 1.25 3.00
19 Torey Krug 6.00 15.00
20 Matt Donovan 1.50 4.00
21 Tyler Cuma 1.25 3.00
22 Chay Genoway 1.25 3.00
23 Brenden Dillon 1.50 4.00
24 Tyson Sexsmith 1.25 3.00
25 Jussi Rynnas 1.25 3.00
26 Shawn Hunwick 1.25 3.00
27 Robert Mayer 2.00 5.00
28 Chet Pickard 1.50 4.00
29 Jake Allen 4.00 10.00
30 Michael Hutchinson 2.00 5.00
31 Philippe Cornet 1.50 4.00
32 Kris Foucault 1.25 3.00
33 Brandon Bollig 1.25 3.00
34 Lane MacDermid 1.50 4.00
35 Sven Baertschi 2.00 5.00
36 Ryan Hamilton 1.25 3.00
37 Jeremy Welsh 1.50 4.00
38 Chris Kreider 5.00 12.00
39 Jason Zucker 3.00 8.00
40 Jakob Silfverberg 2.50 6.00
41 Carter Camper 1.25 3.00
42 Carter Ashton 1.25 3.00
43 Reilly Smith 5.00 12.00
44 J.T. Brown 1.50 4.00
45 Akim Aliu 1.50 4.00
46 Scott Glennie 1.50 4.00
47 Matt Watkins 1.25 3.00
48 Mark Stone 5.00 12.00

2012-13 Elite Rookies Aspirations

ASPIR/50-96: .6X TO 1.5X BASIC INSERTS
ASPIR/30-49: .8X TO 2X BASIC INSERTS
ASPIR/26-29: 1X TO 2.5X BASIC INSERTS

2012-13 Elite Rookies Status

STATUS/50-74: .6X TO 1.5X BASIC INSERTS
STATUS/31-48: .8X TO 2X BASIC INSERTS
STATUS/15-29: 1X TO 2.5X BASIC INSERTS

2012-13 Elite The Great Outdoors

1 Sidney Crosby 10.00 25.00
2 Kris Letang 3.00 8.00
3 Jordan Staal 2.00 5.00
4 Ryan Miller 2.50 6.00
5 Thomas Vanek 2.00 5.00
6 Pavel Datsyuk 4.00 10.00
7 Henrik Zetterberg 3.00 8.00
8 Nicklas Lidstrom 3.00 8.00
9 Patrick Kane 5.00 12.00
10 Jonathan Toews 4.00 10.00
11 Mike Richards 2.00 5.00
12 Claude Giroux 2.50 6.00
13 Tim Thomas 2.50 6.00
14 Patrice Bergeron 3.00 8.00
15 Zdeno Chara 2.50 6.00
16 Alex Ovechkin 10.00 25.00
17 Nicklas Backstrom 2.50 6.00
18 Mike Green 2.00 5.00
19 Evgeni Malkin 5.00 12.00
20 Marc-Andre Fleury 5.00 12.00
21 Carl Hagelin 1.50 4.00
22 Henrik Lundqvist 6.00 15.00
23 Marian Gaborik 2.50 6.00
24 Brayden Schenn 2.50 6.00
25 Danny Briere 2.50 6.00
26 Scott Hartnell 1.50 4.00
27 Carey Price 6.00 15.00
28 P.K. Subban 3.00 8.00
29 Jarome Iginla 3.00 8.00
30 Miikka Kiprusoff 2.50 6.00
31 Ales Hemsky 2.00 5.00
32 Ryan Smyth 2.00 5.00
33 Jose Theodore 2.50 6.00
34 Saku Koivu 2.50 6.00
35 Guy Carbonneau 2.50 6.00
36 Guy Lafleur 3.00 8.00
37 Kirk Muller 2.00 5.00
38 Grant Fuhr 4.00 10.00
39 Mark Messier 5.00 12.00
40 Jari Kurri 3.00 8.00

1962-63 El Producto Discs

COMPLETE SET (6) 150.00 300.00
1 Jean Beliveau 30.00 60.00
2 Glenn Hall 25.00 50.00
3 Gordie Howe 75.00 150.00
4 Dave Keon 30.00 60.00
5 Frank Mahovlich 25.00 50.00
6 Henri Richard 25.00 50.00

1995-96 Emotion Promo Strip

1 Jeremy Roenick .40 1.00

1995-96 Emotion

1 Bobby Dollas .05 .15
2 Guy Hebert .12 .30
3 Paul Kariya .15 .40
4 Oleg Tverdovsky .15 .40
5 Shaun Van Allen .10 .25
6 Ray Bourque .25 .60
7 Al Iafrate .12 .30
8 Blaine Lacher .12 .30
9 Joe Mullen .12 .30
10 Cam Neely .15 .40
11 Adam Oates .15 .40
12 Kevin Stevens .12 .30
13 Don Sweeney .10 .25
14 Donald Audette .12 .30
15 Garry Galley .10 .25
16 Dominik Hasek .25 .60
17 Brian Holzinger RC .30 .75
18 Pat LaFontaine .15 .40
19 Alexei Zhitnik .10 .25
20 Steve Chiasson .10 .25
21 Theo Fleury .20 .50
22 Phil Housley .12 .30
23 Trevor Kidd .12 .30
24 Joe Nieuwendyk .12 .30
25 Gary Roberts .10 .25
26 Zarley Zalapski .10 .25
27 Ed Belfour .12 .30
28 Chris Chelios .15 .40
29 Sergei Krivokrasov .10 .25
30 Joe Murphy .10 .25
31 Bernie Nicholls .12 .30
32 Patrick Poulin .10 .25
33 Jeremy Roenick .25 .60
34 Gary Suter .10 .25
35 Rene Corbet .10 .25
36 Peter Forsberg .30 .75
37 Valeri Kamensky .12 .30
38 Uwe Krupp .12 .30
39 Curtis Leschyshyn .10 .25
40 Owen Nolan .15 .40
41 Mike Ricci .10 .25
42 Joe Sakic .30 .75
43 Jocelyn Thibault .12 .30
44 Bob Bassen .10 .25
45 Dave Gagner .10 .25
46 Todd Harvey .10 .25
47 Derian Hatcher .12 .30
48 Kevin Hatcher .12 .30
49 Mike Modano .25 .60
50 Andy Moog .15 .40
51 Dino Ciccarelli .12 .30
52 Paul Coffey .15 .40
53 Sergei Fedorov .25 .60
54 Vladimir Konstantinov .12 .30
55 Slava Kozlov .12 .30
56 Nicklas Lidstrom .15 .40
57 Keith Primeau .12 .30
58 Ray Sheppard .12 .30
59 Mike Vernon .12 .30
60 Steve Yzerman .40 1.00
61 Jason Arnott .12 .30
62 Curtis Joseph .20 .50
63 Igor Kravchuk .10 .25
64 Todd Marchant .10 .25
65 David Oliver .10 .25
66 Bill Ranford .12 .30
67 Doug Weight .15 .40
68 Stu Barnes .10 .25
69 Jesse Belanger .10 .25
70 Gord Murphy .10 .25
71 Magnus Svensson RC .12 .30
72 John Vanbiesbrouck .15 .40
73 Sean Burke .10 .25
74 Andrew Cassels .10 .25
75 Frantisek Kucera .10 .25
76 Andrei Nikolishin .10 .25
77 Geoff Sanderson .10 .25
78 Brendan Shanahan .15 .40
79 Darren Turcotte .10 .25
80 Rob Blake .12 .30
81 Wayne Gretzky 1.00 2.50
82 Dimitri Khristich .10 .25
83 Jari Kurri .15 .40
84 Jamie Storr .12 .30
85 Darryl Sydor .12 .30
86 Rick Tocchet .12 .30
87 Vincent Damphousse .12 .30
88 Vladimir Malakhov .10 .25
89 Stephane Quintal .12 .30
90 Mark Recchi .20 .50
91 Patrick Roy .40 1.00
92 Brian Savage .10 .25
93 Pierre Turgeon .12 .30
94 Martin Brodeur .40 1.00
95 Neal Broten .12 .30
96 Shawn Chambers .10 .25
97 Claude Lemieux .15 .40
98 John MacLean .12 .30
99 Randy McKay .10 .25
100 Scott Niedermayer .15 .40
101 Stephane Richer .12 .30
102 Scott Stevens .15 .40
103 Todd Bertuzzi RC .20 .50
104 Patrick Flatley .10 .25
105 Brett Lindros .10 .25
106 Kirk Muller .12 .30
107 Tommy Salo RC .25 .60
108 Mathieu Schneider .10 .25
109 Alexander Semak .10 .25
110 Dennis Vaske .10 .25
111 Ray Ferraro .10 .25
112 Adam Graves .12 .30
113 Alexei Kovalev .12 .30
114 Steve Larmer .12 .30
115 Brian Leetch .12 .30
116 Mark Messier .30 .75
117 Mike Richter .15 .40
118 Luc Robitaille .15 .40
119 Ulf Samuelsson .10 .25
120 Pat Verbeek .12 .30
121 Don Beaupre .12 .30
122 Radek Bonk .10 .25
123 Alexandre Daigle .10 .25
124 Steve Duchesne .10 .25

125 Steve Larouche .10 .25
126 Dan Quinn .12 .30
127 Martin Straka .10 .25
128 Alexei Yashin .12 .30
129 Rod Brind'Amour .15 .40
130 Eric Desjardins .12 .30
131 Ron Hextall .15 .40
132 John LeClair .15 .40
133 Eric Lindros .25 .60
134 Mikael Renberg .12 .30
135 Chris Therien .10 .25
136 Ron Francis .20 .50
137 Jaromir Jagr .50 1.25
138 Mario Lemieux .60 1.50
139 Dmitri Mironov .10 .25
140 Petr Nedved .12 .30
141 Tomas Sandstrom .12 .30
142 Bryan Smolinski .10 .25
143 Ken Wregget .12 .30
144 Sergei Zubov .12 .30
145 Shayne Corson .12 .30
146 Geoff Courtnall .10 .25
147 Dale Hawerchuk .20 .50
148 Brett Hull .30 .75
149 Ian Laperriere .10 .25
150 Al MacInnis .20 .50
151 Chris Pronger .15 .40
152 David Roberts .10 .25
153 Esa Tikkanen .10 .25
154 Ulf Dahlen .10 .25
155 Jeff Friesen .10 .25
156 Arturs Irbe .12 .30
157 Craig Janney .10 .25
158 Sergei Makarov .10 .25
159 Sandis Ozolinsh .10 .25
160 Mike Rathje .12 .30
161 Ray Whitney .12 .30
162 Brian Bradley .12 .30
163 Chris Gratton .10 .25
164 Roman Hamrlik .10 .25
165 Petr Klima .10 .25
166 Daren Puppa .12 .30
167 Paul Ysebaert .10 .25
168 Dave Andreychuk .15 .40
169 Mike Gartner .20 .50
170 Todd Gill .10 .25
171 Doug Gilmour .20 .50
172 Kenny Jonsson .15 .40
173 Larry Murphy .12 .30
174 Felix Potvin .25 .60
175 Mats Sundin .15 .40
176 Josef Beranek .10 .25
177 Jeff Brown .10 .25
178 Pavel Bure .15 .40
179 Russ Courtnall .10 .25
180 Trevor Linden .15 .40
181 Kirk McLean .12 .30
182 Alexander Mogilny .12 .30
183 Roman Oksiuta .10 .25
184 Mike Ridley .10 .25
185 Jason Allison .12 .30
186 Jim Carey .12 .30
187 Sergei Gonchar .12 .30
188 Dale Hunter .12 .30
189 Calle Johansson .10 .25
190 Joe Juneau .10 .25
191 Joe Reekie .10 .25
192 Nelson Emerson .10 .25
193 Nikolai Khabibulin .12 .30
194 Dave Manson .10 .25
195 Teppo Numminen .10 .25
196 Teemu Selanne .30 .75
197 Keith Tkachuk .15 .40
198 Alexei Zhamnov .15 .40
199 Checklist #1 .05 .15
200 Checklist #2 .05 .15
NNO Roenick Exch. EXPIRED 2.50 5.00
NNO J.Roenick SkyMotion 15.00 30.00

1995-96 Emotion generationNext

COMPLETE SET (10) 8.00 15.00
1 Brian Holzinger 1.00 2.50
2 Eric Daze .60 1.50
3 Jason Bonsignore .30 .75
4 Jamie Storr .60 1.50
5 Tommy Salo 2.00 5.00
6 Brendan Witt .30 .75
7 Saku Koivu 1.00 2.50
8 Todd Bertuzzi 3.00 8.00
9 Ed Jovanovski .30 .75
10 Chad Kilger .30 .75

1995-96 Emotion Ntense Power

COMPLETE SET (10) 10.00 20.00
1 Cam Neely 1.50 4.00
2 Keith Primeau .50 1.25
3 Mark Messier 1.50 4.00
4 Eric Lindros 1.50 4.00
5 Mikael Renberg 1.00 2.50
6 Owen Nolan 1.00 2.50
7 Brendan Shanahan 1.50 4.00
8 Kevin Stevens .50 1.25
9 Keith Tkachuk 1.50 4.00
10 Rick Tocchet 1.00 2.50

1995-96 Emotion Xcel

COMPLETE SET (10) 30.00 60.00
1 Adam Oates .75 2.00
2 Jeremy Roenick 2.00 5.00
3 Sergei Fedorov 2.00 5.00
4 Wayne Gretzky 8.00 20.00
5 Alexei Yashin .60 1.50
6 Eric Lindros 1.25 3.00
7 Ron Francis .75 2.00
8 Mario Lemieux 6.00 15.00
9 Joe Sakic 3.00 8.00
10 Alexei Zhamnov .60 1.50

1995-96 Emotion Xcited

COMPLETE SET (20) 15.00 30.00
1 Theo Fleury .20 .50
2 Jeremy Roenick .75 2.00
3 Mike Modano 1.00 2.50
4 Sergei Fedorov 1.00 2.50
5 Wayne Gretzky 5.00 12.00
6 Brian Leetch .40 1.00
7 Alexei Yashin .20 .50
8 Brett Hull .75 2.00
9 Jaromir Jagr 1.00 2.50
10 Mario Lemieux 3.00 8.00
11 Ron Francis .40 1.00
12 Keith Primeau .20 .50
13 Joe Sakic 1.25 3.00
14 Peter Forsberg 1.50 4.00
15 Paul Kariya .60 1.50
16 Pavel Bure .60 1.50
17 Alexei Zhamnov .60 1.50
18 Martin Brodeur 1.50 4.00
19 Jim Carey .40 1.00
20 Chris Chelios .60 1.50

1992-93 Enor Mark Messier

COMPLETE SET (10) 2.00 5.00
COMMON MESSIER (1-10) .20 .50

1969-73 Equitable Sports Hall of Fame

COMPLETE SET (6) 62.50 125.00
1 Phil Esposito 10.00 20.00
2 Bernie Geoffrion 10.00 20.00
3 Gordie Howe 25.00 50.00
4 Ching Johnson 7.50 15.00
5 Stan Mikita 10.00 20.00
6 Maurice Richard 12.50 25.00

1970-71 Esso Power Players

COMPLETE SET (252) 125.00 250.00
1 Rogatien Vachon 1 1.50 3.00
2 Jacques Laperriere 2 .38 .75
3 J.C. Tremblay 3 .25 .50
4 Jean Beliveau 4 4.00 8.00
5 Guy Lapointe 5 .50 1.00
6 Fran Huck 6 .20 .40
7 Bill Collins 10 .20 .40
8 Marc Tardif 11 .25 .50
9 Yvan Cournoyer 12 .75 1.50
10 Claude Larose 15 .20 .40
11 Henri Richard 16 2.00 4.00
12 Serge Savard 18 .38 .75
13 Terry Harper 19 .25 .50
14 Pete Mahovlich 20 .38 .75
15 John Ferguson 22 .50 1.00
16 Mickey Redmond 24 .63 1.25
17 Jacques Lemaire 25 .63 1.25
18 Phil Myre 30 .38 .75
19 Jacques Plante 1 4.00 8.00
20 Rick Ley 2 .25 .50
21 Mike Pelyk 4 .20 .40
22 Ron Ellis 6 .25 .50
23 Jim Dorey 8 .20 .40
24 Norm Ullman 9 1.00 2.00
25 Guy Trottier 11 .20 .40
26 Jim Harrison 12 .20 .40
27 Dave Keon 14 1.00 2.00
28 Mike Walton 16 .25 .50
29 Jim McKenny 18 .20 .40
30 Paul Henderson 19 .50 1.00
31 Garry Monahan 20 SP .50 1.00
32 Bob Baun 21 .38 .75
33 Bill MacMillan 23 .20 .40
34 Brian Glennie 24 .20 .40
35 Darryl Sittler 27 5.00 10.00
36 Bruce Gamble 30 .50 1.00
37 Charlie Hodge 1 .63 1.25
38 Gary Doak 2 .20 .40
39 Pat Quinn 3 .38 .75
40 Barry Wilkins 4 .20 .40
41 Darryl Sly 5 SP .50 1.00
42 Marc Reaume 6 .20 .40
43 Andre Boudrias 7 .20 .40
44 Danny Johnson 8 .20 .40
45 Ray Cullen 10 SP .50 1.00
46 Wayne Maki 11 .20 .40
47 Mike Corrigan 12 .20 .40
48 Rosaire Paiement 15 .20 .40
49 Paul Popiel 18 SP .38 .75
50 Dale Tallon 19 .25 .50
51 Murray Hall 23 SP .50 1.00
52 Len Lunde 24 .20 .40
53 Orland Kurtenbach 25 .25 .50
54 Dunc Wilson 30 SP .50 1.00
55 Ed Johnston 1 .50 1.00
56 Bobby Orr 4 12.50 25.00
57 Ted Green 6 .25 .50
58 Phil Esposito 7 2.50 5.00
59 Ken Hodge 8 .38 .75
60 Johnny Bucyk 9 1.00 2.00
61 Rick Smith 10 SP .50 1.00
62 Wayne Carleton 11 SP .50 1.00
63 Wayne Cashman 12 SP .75 1.50
64 Garnet Bailey 14 .20 .40
65 Derek Sanderson 16 2.00 4.00
66 Fred Stanfield 17 SP .50 1.00
67 Ed Westfall 18 .25 .50
68 John McKenzie 19 .20 .40
69 Dallas Smith 20 .20 .40
70 Don Marcotte 21 .20 .40
71 Don Awrey 26 SP .50 1.00
72 Gerry Cheevers 30 1.50 3.00
73 Roger Crozier 1 .75 1.50
74 Jim Watson 2 .25 .50
75 Tracy Pratt 3 .20 .40
76 Doug Barrie 5 SP .50 1.00
77 Al Hamilton 6 .25 .50
78 Cliff Schmautz 7 SP .50 1.00
79 Reg Fleming 9 .20 .40
80 Phil Goyette 10 .20 .40
81 Gilbert Perreault 11 2.50 5.00
82 Skip Krake 12 .20 .40
83 Gerry Meehan 15 .25 .50
84 Ron Anderson 16 .20 .40
85 Floyd Smith 17 SP .50 1.00
86 Steve Atkinson 19 .20 .40
87 Paul Andrea 21 SP .50 1.00
88 Don Marshall 22 .20 .40
89 Eddie Shack 23 SP 1.50 3.00
90 Larry Keenan 26 .20 .40
91 Gary Smith 1 .50 1.00
92 Doug Roberts 2 .20 .40
93 Harry Howell 3 .63 1.25
94 Wayne Muloin 4 .20 .40
95 Carol Vadnais 5 .20 .40
96 Dick Mattiussi 6 .20 .40
97 Earl Ingarfield 7 .20 .40
98 Gerry Ehman 8 .20 .40
99 Bill Hicke 9 .20 .40
100 Ted Hampson 10 .20 .40
101 Gary Jarrett 12 .20 .40
102 Joe Hardy 14 SP .50 1.00
103 Tony Featherstone 16 SP .50 1.00
104 Gary Croteau 18 .20 .40
105 Ernie Hicke 20 SP .50 1.00
106 Ron Stackhouse 21 .20 .40
107 Dennis Hextall 22 SP .75 1.50
108 Bob Sneddon 30 SP .50 1.00
109 Gerry Desjardins 1 SP .75 1.50
110 Bill White 2 .25 .50
111 Keith Magnuson 3 .25 .50
112 Doug Jarrett 4 SP .50 1.00
113 Lou Angotti 6 .20 .40
114 Pit Martin 7 .25 .50
115 Jim Pappin 8 .20 .40
116 Bobby Hull 9 5.00 10.00
117 Dennis Hull 10 SP 1.00 2.00
118 Doug Mohns 11 .25 .50
119 Pat Stapleton 12 .25 .50
120 Bryan Campbell 14 SP .50 1.00
121 Eric Nesterenko 15 .25 .50
122 Chico Maki 16 .25 .50
123 Gerry Pinder 18 .25 .50
124 Cliff Koroll 20 .20 .40
125 Stan Mikita 21 3.00 6.00
126 Tony Esposito 35 3.00 6.00
127 Jim Rutherford 1 SP 1.00 2.00
128 Gary Bergman 2 .25 .50
129 Dale Rolfe 3 .20 .40
130 Larry Brown 4 SP .50 1.00
131 Serge Lajeunesse 5 .20 .40
132 Garry Unger 7 .38 .75
133 Tom Webster 8 .25 .50
134 Gordie Howe 9 7.50 15.00
135 Alex Delvecchio 10 1.00 2.00
136 Don Luce 11 SP .50 1.00
137 Bruce MacGregor 12 .20 .40
138 Nick Libett 14 .25 .50
139 Al Karlander 15 .20 .40
140 Ron Harris 16 .20 .40
141 Wayne Connelly 17 SP .50 1.00
142 Billy Dea 21 SP .50 1.00
143 Frank Mahovlich 27 2.00 4.00
144 Roy Edwards 30 .38 .75
145 Jack Norris 1 .20 .40
146 Dale Hoganson 2 .20 .40
147 Larry Cahan 3 .20 .40
148 Gilles Marotte 4 SP .50 1.00
149 Noel Price 5 SP .50 1.00
150 Paul Curtis 6 SP .50 1.00
151 Ross Lonsberry 8 .20 .40
152 Gord Labossiere 9 .20 .40
153 Doug Robinson 11 SP .50 1.00
154 Larry Mickey 12 .20 .40
155 Juha Widing 15 .20 .40
156 Eddie Joyal 16 .20 .40
157 Bill Flett 17 .20 .40
158 Bob Berry 18 .25 .50
159 Bob Pulford 20 .38 .75
160 Matt Ravlich 21 .20 .40
161 Mike Byers 24 SP .50 1.00
162 Denis DeJordy 30 .50 1.00
163 Gump Worsley 1 2.00 4.00
164 Barry Gibbs 2 SP .50 1.00
165 Fred Barrett 3 .20 .40
166 Ted Harris 4 .20 .40
167 Danny O'Shea 7 .20 .40
168 Bill Goldsworthy 8 .25 .50
169 Charlie Burns 9 .20 .40
170 Murray Oliver 10 .20 .40
171 Jean-Paul Parise 11 .25 .50
172 Tom Williams 12 SP .50 1.00
173 Bobby Rousseau 15 .25 .50
174 Buster Harvey 18 SP .50 1.00
175 Tom Reid 20 SP .50 1.00
176 Danny Grant 21 .25 .50
177 Walt McKechnie 22 .20 .40
178 Lou Nanne 23 .25 .50
179 Danny Lawson 24 SP .50 1.00
180 Cesare Maniago 30 .50 1.00
181 Ed Giacomin 1 1.50 3.00
182 Brad Park 2 3.00 8.00
183 Tim Horton 3 2.50 5.00
184 Arnie Brown 4 .20 .40
185 Rod Gilbert 7 .75 1.50
186 Bob Nevin 8 .20 .40
187 Bill Fairbairn 10 SP .50 1.00
188 Vic Hadfield 11 .25 .50
189 Ron Stewart 12 .20 .40
190 Jim Neilson 15 .25 .50
191 Rod Seiling 16 SP .50 1.00
192 Dave Balon 17 SP .50 1.00
193 Walt Tkaczuk 18 .25 .50
194 Jean Ratelle 19 .75 1.50
195 Jack Egers 20 .20 .40
196 Pete Stemkowski 21 SP .50 1.00
197 Ted Irvine 27 .20 .40
198 Gilles Villemure 30 .50 1.00
199 Doug Favell 1 .75 1.50
200 Ed Van Impe 2 .20 .40
201 Larry Hillman 3 .20 .40
202 Barry Ashbee 4 .38 .75
203 Wayne Hillman 6 SP .50 1.00
204 Andre Lacroix 7 .25 .50
205 Lew Morrison 8 .20 .40
206 Bob Kelly 9 SP .50 1.00
207 Jean-Guy Gendron 11 .20 .40
208 Gary Dornhoefer 12 .38 .75
209 Joe Watson 14 .20 .40
210 Garry Peters 15 SP .50 1.00
211 Bobby Clarke 16 5.00 10.00
212 Earl Heiskala 19 SP .50 1.00
213 Jim Johnson 20 .20 .40
214 Serge Bernier 21 .20 .40
215 Larry Hale 23 SP .50 1.00
216 Bernie Parent 30 2.50 5.00
217 Al Smith 1 .38 .75
218 Duane Rupp 2 .20 .40
219 Bob Woytowich 3 .20 .40
220 Bob Blackburn 4 .20 .40
221 Bryan Watson 5 SP .50 1.00
222 Dunc McCallum 6 .25 .50
223 Bryan Hextall 7 .25 .50
224 Andy Bathgate 9 SP 1.25 2.50
225 Keith McCreary 10 SP .50 1.00
226 Nick Harbaruk 11 .20 .40
227 Ken Schinkel 12 .20 .40
228 Glen Sather 16 SP 1.25 2.50
229 Ron Schock 17 .20 .40
230 Wally Boyer 18 .20 .40
231 Jean Pronovost 19 .25 .50
232 Dean Prentice 20 .25 .50
233 Jim Morrison 27 .20 .40
234 Les Binkley 30 SP .75 1.50
235 Glenn Hall 1 2.00 4.00
236 Bob Wall 2 .20 .40
237 Noel Picard 4 .20 .40
238 Bob Plager 5 .25 .50
239 Jim Roberts 6 .25 .50
240 Red Berenson 7 .25 .50
241 Barclay Plager 8 .25 .50
242 Frank St.Marseille 9 .20 .40
243 George Morrison 10 SP .50 1.00
244 Gary Sabourin 11 .20 .40
245 Terry Crisp 12 SP 1.00 2.00
246 Tim Ecclestone 14 .20 .40
247 Bill McCreary 15 .20 .40
248 Brit Selby 18 SP .50 1.00
249 Jim Lorentz 19 SP .50 1.00
250 Ab McDonald 20 .20 .40
251 Chris Bordeleau 21 SP .50 1.00
252 Ernie Wakely 31 .50 1.00
xx Soft Cover Album 7.50 15.00
xx Hard Cover Album 25.00 50.00

1983-84 Esso

COMPLETE SET (21) 6.00 15.00
*FRENCH: .5X TO 1.2X ENGLISH
1 Glenn Anderson .40 1.00
2 John Anderson .20 .50
3 Dave Babych .20 .50
4 Richard Brodeur .40 1.00
5 Paul Coffey 1.50 4.00
6 Bill Derlago .20 .50
7 Bob Gainey .60 1.50
8 Michel Goulet .40 1.00
9 Dale Hawerchuk .75 2.00
10 Dale Hunter .30 .75
11 Morris Lukowich .20 .50
12 Lanny McDonald .60 1.50
13 Mark Messier 2.00 5.00
14 Jim Peplinski .20 .50
15 Paul Reinhart .20 .50
16 Larry Robinson .50 1.25
17 Stan Smyl .30 .75
18 Harold Snepsts .30 .75
19 Marc Tardif .20 .50
20 Mario Tremblay .20 .50
21 Rick Vaive .30 .75

1988-89 Esso All-Stars

COMPLETE SET (48) 6.00 15.00
1 Jean Beliveau .30 .75
2 Mike Bossy .30 .75
3 Ray Bourque .30 .75
4 Johnny Bower .15 .40
5 Bobby Clarke .20 .50
6 Paul Coffey .30 .75
7 Yvan Cournoyer .08 .25
8 Marcel Dionne .15 .40
9 Ken Dryden .40 1.00
10 Phil Esposito .30 .75
11 Tony Esposito .20 .50
12 Grant Fuhr .15 .40
13 Clark Gillies .07 .20
14 Michel Goulet .08 .25
15 Wayne Gretzky 1.50 4.00
16 Dale Hawerchuk .08 .25
17 Ron Hextall .15 .40
18 Gordie Howe .60 1.50
19 Mark Howe .07 .20
20 Bobby Hull .30 .75
21 Tim Kerr .07 .20
22 Jari Kurri .08 .25
23 Guy Lafleur .30 .75
24 Rod Langway .07 .20
25 Jacques Laperriere .07 .20
26 Guy Lapointe .08 .25
27 Mario Lemieux 1.00 2.50
28 Frank Mahovlich .20 .50
29 Lanny McDonald .08 .25
30 Mark Messier .40 1.00
31 Stan Mikita .20 .50
32 Mats Naslund .07 .20
33 Bobby Orr .75 2.00
34 Brad Park .08 .25
35 Gilbert Perreault .08 .25
36 Denis Potvin .08 .25
37 Larry Robinson .08 .25
38 Luc Robitaille .20 .50
39 Borje Salming .07 .20
40 Denis Savard .08 .25
41 Serge Savard .08 .25
42 Steve Shutt .08 .25
43 Darryl Sittler .08 .25
44 Billy Smith .08 .25
45 John Tonelli .07 .20
46 Bryan Trottier .08 .25
47 Norm Ullman .08 .25
48 Gump Worsley .20 .50
xx Album 1.25 3.00

1997-98 Esso Olympic Hockey Heroes

COMPLETE SET (60) 12.00 30.00
*FRENCH: .5X TO 1.2X ENGLISH
1 Header Card .02 .10
2 Olympic Hockey History .02 .10
3 CBC Broadcast Guide .02 .10
4 Olympic Hockey Bracket .02 .10
5 Team Canada .02 .10
6 Eric Lindros .75 2.00
7 Joe Sakic .60 1.50
8 Trevor Linden .15 .40
9 Paul Kariya .75 2.00
10 Brendan Shanahan .40 1.00
11 Rod Brind'Amour .15 .40
12 Theo Fleury .15 .40
13 Eric Desjardins .08 .25
14 Scott Niedermayer .08 .25
15 Chris Pronger .15 .40
16 Rob Blake .08 .25
17 Patrick Roy 1.00 2.50
18 Curtis Joseph .20 .50
19 Keith Primeau .15 .40
20 Mark Messier .30 .75
21 Adam Foote .08 .25
22 Team USA .02 .10
23 Keith Tkachuk .25 .60
24 Mike Modano .20 .50
25 John LeClair .30 .75
26 Doug Weight .15 .40
27 Brett Hull .25 .60
28 Jeremy Roenick .20 .50
29 Brian Leetch .20 .50
30 Chris Chelios .20 .50
31 Kevin Hatcher .08 .25
32 Derian Hatcher .08 .25
33 Mike Richter .20 .50
34 John Vanbiesbrouck .40 1.00
35 Team Russia .02 .10
36 Sergei Fedorov .40 1.00
37 Alexei Yashin .15 .40
38 Pavel Bure .40 1.00
39 Alexander Mogilny .15 .40
40 Nikolai Khabibulin .15 .40
41 Team Sweden .02 .10
42 Mats Sundin .20 .50
43 Peter Forsberg .60 1.50
44 Daniel Alfredsson .15 .40
45 Nicklas Lidstrom .15 .40
46 Kenny Jonsson .08 .25
47 Team Finland .02 .10
48 Saku Koivu .40 1.00
49 Esa Tikkanen .15 .40
50 Teemu Selanne .40 1.00
51 Team Czech Republic .02 .10
52 Jaromir Jagr .60 1.50
53 Roman Hamrlik .15 .40
54 Dominik Hasek .40 1.00
55 Women's Team Canada .02 .10
56 Nancy Drolet .20 .50
57 Geraldine Heaney .20 .50
58 Hayley Wickenheiser .20 .50
59 Cassie Campbell .20 .50
60 Stacy Wilson .20 .50
NNO Eric Lindros AU 40.00 100.00

2001-02 eTopps

COMMON CARD .75 2.00
SEMISTARS 1.00 2.50
UNLISTED STARS 1.25 3.00
1 Joe Sakic/782 2.50 6.00
2 Paul Kariya/1032 1.25 3.00
3 Curtis Joseph/714 1.50 4.00
4 Brendan Shanahan/2000 1.25 3.00
5 Patrik Elias/859 1.25 3.00
6 Evgeni Nabokov/549 1.00 2.50
7 Johan Hedberg/574 1.00 2.50
8 Patrick Roy/938 3.00 8.00
9 John LeClair/494 1.25 3.00
10 Martin Brodeur/663 3.00 8.00
11 Teemu Selanne/784 2.50 6.00
12 Mike Modano/559 2.00 5.00
13 Martin Havlat/510 1.00 2.50
14 Roberto Luongo/747 2.00 5.00
15 Peter Forsberg/598 2.50 6.00
16 Steve Yzerman/796 3.00 8.00
17 Pavel Bure/896 1.25 3.00
18 Mark Messier/618 2.50 6.00
19 Mike Comrie/809 1.00 2.50
20 Mats Sundin/717 1.25 3.00
21 Owen Nolan/457 1.25 3.00
22 Ed Belfour/730 1.25 3.00
23 Mario Lemieux/1116 5.00 12.00
24 Keith Tkachuk/751 1.25 3.00
25 Milan Hejduk/532 1.00 2.50
26 Rick Dipietro/579 1.00 2.50
27 Roman Cechmanek/511 1.00 2.50
28 Sergei Fedorov/710 2.00 5.00
29 Vincent Lecavalier/550 1.25 3.00
30 Eric Lindros/634 2.00 5.00
31 Ilya Kovalchuk/2513 4.00 10.00
32 Zigmund Palffy/550 1.25 3.00
33 Dominik Hasek/753 2.00 5.00
34 Jaromir Jagr/569 4.00 10.00
35 Doug Weight/521 1.25 3.00

1948-52 Exhibits Canadian

COMPLETE SET (65) 750.00 1500.00
1 Reggie Abbott 6.00 12.00
2 Jean Beliveau 37.50 75.00
3 Jean Beliveau 50.00 100.00
4 Toe Blake 20.00 40.00
5 Butch Bouchard 10.00 20.00
6 Bob Fillion 6.00 12.00
7 Dick Gamble 7.50 15.00
8 Bernie Geoffrion 25.00 50.00
9 Doug Harvey 20.00 40.00
10 Tom Johnson 10.00 20.00
11 Elmer Lach 20.00 40.00
12 Hal Laycoe 6.00 12.00
13 Jacques Locas 6.00 12.00
14 Bud McPherson 6.00 12.00
15 Paul Maznick 6.00 12.00
16 Gerry McNeil 20.00 40.00
17 Paul Meger 6.00 12.00
18 Dickie Moore 20.00 40.00
19 Ken Mosdell 6.00 12.00
20 Bert Olmstead 10.00 20.00
21 Ken Reardon 12.50 25.00
22 Billy Reay 7.50 15.00
23 Maurice Richard 50.00 100.00
24 Maurice Richard 50.00 100.00
25 Dollard St.Laurent 7.50 15.00
26 Grant Warwick 6.00 12.00
27 Floyd Curry 7.50 15.00
28 Bill Barilko 20.00 40.00
29 Turk Broda 20.00 40.00
30 Cal Gardner 10.00 20.00
31 Bill Juzda 6.00 12.00
32 Ted Kennedy 20.00 40.00
33 Joe Klukay 6.00 12.00
34 Fleming Mackell 6.00 12.00
35 Howie Meeker 15.00 30.00
36 Gus Mortson 6.00 12.00
37 Al Rollins 12.50 25.00
38 Sid Smith 7.50 15.00
39 Tod Sloan 6.00 12.00
40 Ray Timgren 6.00 12.00
41 Jim Thomson 6.00 12.00
42 Max Bentley 12.50 25.00
43 Sid Abel 10.00 20.00
44 Gordie Howe 62.50 125.00
45 Ted Lindsay 25.00 50.00
46 Harry Lumley 20.00 40.00
47 Jack Gelineau 6.00 12.00
48 Paul Ronty 6.00 12.00
49 Doug Bentley 12.50 25.00
50 Roy Conacher 7.50 15.00
51 Chuck Rayner 12.50 25.00
52 Boston vs. Montreal 10.00 20.00
53 Detroit vs. New York 30.00 60.00
54 Montreal vs. Toronto 30.00 60.00
55 New York vs. Montreal 30.00 60.00
56 New York vs. Montreal 10.00 20.00
57 Montreal vs. Boston 10.00 20.00
58 Detroit vs. Montreal 10.00 20.00
59 Chicago vs. Montreal 10.00 20.00
60 New York vs. Montreal 25.00 50.00
61 Chicago vs. Montreal 15.00 30.00
62 Detroit vs. Montreal 20.00 40.00
63 Detroit vs. Montreal 10.00 20.00
64 Toronto vs. Montreal 10.00 20.00
65 Chicago vs. Montreal 10.00 20.00

2013-14 Exquisite Collection Brilliance Autographs

BRN Ryan Nugent-Hopkins (inserted in 2015-16 The Cup) 6.00 15.00

2013-14 Exquisite Collection Enshrinements

CERN Ryan Nugent-Hopkins (inserted in 2015-16 The Cup) 12.00 30.00

2014-15 Exquisite Collection Brilliance Autographs

BAI Arturs Irbe C (inserted in 2015-16 The Cup) 6.00 15.00
BBH Bobby Hull A (inserted in 2015-16 The Cup) 15.00 40.00
BCP Corey Perry B (inserted in 2015-16 The Cup) 12.00 30.00
BNY Nail Yakupov C (inserted in 2015-16 The Cup) 5.00 12.00

2014-15 Exquisite Collection Gold Spectrum

144 Vladislav Namestnikov AU (inserted in 2015-16 The Cup) 10.00 25.00
145 Brett Ritchie AU (inserted in 2015-16 The Cup) 6.00 15.00
159 Chris Tierney AU (inserted in 2015-16 The Cup) 6.00 15.00
171 Anthony Duclair AU (inserted in 2015-16 The Cup) 10.00 25.00

2014-15 Exquisite Collection Honorable Numbers

HNCK Chris Kreider/20 (inserted in 2015-16 The Cup) 12.00 30.00
HNJN James Neal/18 (inserted in 2015-16 The Cup) 6.00 15.00
HNLC Logan Couture/39 (inserted in 2015-16 The Cup) 12.00 30.00
HNNM Nathan MacKinnon/29 (inserted in 2015-16 The Cup) 40.00 100.00
HNOP Ondrej Palat/18 (inserted in 2015-16 The Cup) 8.00 20.00
HNVN Valeri Nichushkin/43 (inserted in 2015-16 The Cup) 10.00 25.00

2014-15 Exquisite Collection Limited Logos Autographs

LLCO Sean Couturier/50 (inserted in 2015-16 The Cup) 6.00 15.00
LLEM Evgeni Malkin/25 (inserted in 2015-16 The Cup) 15.00 40.00
LLJV Jakub Voracek/50 (inserted in 2015-16 The Cup) 6.00 15.00
LLKR Chris Kreider/50 (inserted in 2015-16 The Cup) 10.00 25.00
LLMS Mats Sundin/25 (inserted in 2015-16 The Cup) 8.00 20.00
LLOP Ondrej Palat/50 (inserted in 2015-16 The Cup) 6.00 15.00
LLVN Valeri Nichushkin/50 (inserted in 2015-16 The Cup) 8.00 20.00

2014-15 Exquisite Collection Rookie Bookmarks Dual Autographs

DARBDN J.Drouin/V.Namestnikov 25.00 60.00

2014-15 Exquisite Collection Scripted Sticks

SSEM Evgeni Malkin (inserted in 2015-16 The Cup) 20.00 50.00
SSJV John Vanbiesbrouck (inserted in 2015-16 The Cup) 10.00 25.00
SSMS Mats Sundin (inserted in 2015-16 The Cup) 10.00 25.00
SSPF Peter Forsberg (inserted in 2015-16 The Cup) 20.00 50.00

2014-15 Exquisite Collection Scripted Swatches

SWDH Dale Hawerchuk (inserted in 2015-16 The Cup) 12.00 30.00
SWNY Nail Yakupov (inserted in 2015-16 The Cup) 6.00 15.00

2014-15 Exquisite Collection Signature Patches

SPBG Brendan Gallagher/99 (inserted in 2015-16 The Cup) 15.00 40.00
SPJN James Neal/99 (inserted in 2015-16 The Cup) 10.00 25.00
SPKR Chris Kreider/99 (inserted in 2015-16 The Cup) 20.00 50.00
SPLC Logan Couture/99 (inserted in 2015-16 The Cup) 20.00 50.00
SPNY Nail Yakupov/99 (inserted in 2015-16 The Cup) 10.00 25.00
SPOM Olli Maatta/99 (inserted in 2015-16 The Cup) 10.00 25.00
SPPF Peter Forsberg/25 (inserted in 2015-16 The Cup) 30.00 80.00

2014-15 Exquisite Collection Signature Patches Dual

DSPCO C.Chelios/C.Osgood/35 10.00 25.00
DSPGC C.Coyle/M.Granlund/35 10.00 25.00
DSPJJ J.Benn/J.Spezza/35 10.00 25.00
DSPKP C.Perry/R.Kesler/35 15.00 40.00
DSPRJ J.Sakic/R.Blake/35 20.00 50.00

2014-15 Exquisite Collection Signature Renditions

SRBH Bobby Hull B (inserted in 2015-16 The Cup) 25.00 60.00
SRCP Corey Perry D (inserted in 2015-16 The Cup) 20.00 50.00
SRJT Jonathan Toews C (inserted in 2015-16 The Cup) 20.00 50.00
SRMG Mike Gartner E (inserted in 2015-16 The Cup) 15.00 40.00
SRNM Nathan MacKinnon A (inserted in 2015-16 The Cup) 50.00 125.00

2014-15 Exquisite Collection Signature Renditions Combos

SRCGG W.Gretzky/W.Gretzky A 200.00 500.00
SRCNS M.St. Louis/R.Nash C 15.00 40.00
SRCSP C.Perry/T.Selanne B 30.00 80.00

2015-16 Exquisite Collection

1 Ryan Getzlaf 2.00 5.00
2 Shane Doan 1.50 4.00
3 Zdeno Chara 2.00 5.00
4 Tyler Ennis 1.25 3.00
5 Johnny Gaudreau 3.00 8.00
6 Eric Staal 2.50 6.00
7 Jonathan Toews 3.00 8.00
8 Nathan MacKinnon 8.00 20.00
9 Ryan Johansen 1.50 4.00
10 Tyler Seguin 2.50 6.00
11 Henrik Zetterberg 2.50 6.00
12 Taylor Hall 2.00 5.00
13 Aaron Ekblad 2.50 6.00
14 Anze Kopitar 3.00 8.00
15 Zach Parise 2.00 5.00
16 Carey Price 4.00 10.00
17 Shea Weber 1.50 4.00
18 Cory Schneider 2.00 5.00
19 John Tavares 3.00 8.00
20 Henrik Lundqvist 5.00 12.00
21 Erik Karlsson 2.50 6.00
22 Claude Giroux 2.00 5.00
23 Sidney Crosby 8.00 20.00
24 Joe Pavelski 2.50 6.00
25 Vladimir Tarasenko 2.50 6.00
26 Steven Stamkos 4.00 10.00
27 Jonathan Bernier 1.50 4.00
28 Ryan Miller 2.00 5.00
29 Alexander Ovechkin 8.00 20.00
30 Blake Wheeler 2.00 5.00
31 Bobby Orr 8.00 20.00
32 Bobby Hull 4.00 10.00
33 Mario Lemieux 8.00 20.00
34 Patrick Roy 5.00 12.00
35 Mark Messier 4.00 10.00
36 Doug Gilmour 2.50 6.00
37 Terry Sawchuk 2.00 5.00
38 Wayne Gretzky 12.00 30.00
39 Joe Sakic 4.00 10.00
40 Doug Harvey 2.00 5.00
41 Phil Esposito 3.00 8.00
42 Peter Forsberg 4.00 10.00
43 Ray Bourque 3.00 8.00
44 Mike Bossy 2.00 5.00
45 Guy Lafleur 2.50 6.00
R1 Artemi Panarin RC 8.00 20.00
R2 Kevin Fiala RC 2.50 6.00
R3 Andrew Copp RC 2.00 5.00
R4 Emile Poirier RC 1.50 4.00
R5 Mikko Rantanen RC 10.00 25.00
R6 Noah Hanifin RC 3.00 8.00
R7 Oscar Lindberg RC 2.00 5.00
R8 Brock McGinn RC 2.00 5.00
R9 Robby Fabbri RC 2.50 6.00
R10 Jared McCann RC 2.50 6.00
R11 Viktor Arvidsson RC 2.00 5.00
R12 Sergei Plotnikov RC 1.25 3.00
R13 Jake Virtanen RC 2.50 6.00
R14 Ronalds Kenins RC 1.25 3.00
R15 Ryan Hartman RC 2.50 6.00
R16 Nikolay Goldobin RC 2.00 5.00
R17 Radek Faksa RC 2.00 5.00
R18 Joonas Donskoi RC 2.00 5.00
R19 Colton Parayko RC 3.00 8.00
R20 Daniel Sprong RC 2.50 6.00
R21 Jordan Weal RC 1.25 3.00
R22 Mattias Janmark RC 2.00 5.00
R23 Nick Shore RC 1.25 3.00
R24 Nicolas Petan RC 2.00 5.00
R25 Jack Eichel RC 8.00 20.00
R26 Dylan Larkin RC 6.00 15.00
R27 Nikolaj Ehlers RC 4.00 10.00
R28 Max Domi RC 4.00 10.00
R29 Sam Bennett RC 6.00 15.00
R30 Connor McDavid RC 80.00 200.00
RCH Connor Hellebuyck JSY/299 15.00 40.00
RCM Connor McDavid JSY/199 125.00 250.00
RDL Dylan Larkin JSY/299 60.00 100.00
REP Emile Poirier JSY/299 5.00 12.00
RHS Henrik Samuelsson JSY/299 2.50 6.00
RJD Jacob de la Rose JSY/299 4.00 10.00
RJE Jack Eichel JSY/199 30.00 80.00
RJV Jake Virtanen JSY/299 5.00 12.00
RKF Kevin Fiala JSY/299 5.00 12.00
RMD Max Domi JSY/299 8.00 20.00
RMP Matt Puempel JSY/299 3.00 8.00
RNE Nikolaj Ehlers JSY/299 8.00 20.00
RNH Noah Hanifin JSY/299 6.00 15.00
RRH Ryan Hartman JSY/299 5.00 12.00
RSB Sam Bennett JSY/199 12.00 30.00
RSK Slater Koekkoek JSY/299 2.50 6.00
RSP Shane Prince JSY/299 2.50 6.00

2015-16 Exquisite Collection Materials Combos

EM2BB N.Bjugstad/A.Barkov 8.00 20.00
EM2DE S.Doan/Ekman-Lrsn 5.00 12.00
EM2EG T.Ennis/Girgensons 4.00 10.00
EM2FK C.Kunitz/M.Fleury 10.00 25.00
EM2GA J.Gibson/F.Andersen 6.00 15.00
EM2HD S.Hartnell/B.Dubinsky 3.00 8.00
EM2IL J.Iginla/G.Landeskog 6.00 15.00
EM2JK J.Spezza/K.Lehtonen 5.00 12.00
EM2MB Marchand/P.Bergeron 10.00 25.00
EM2OS K.Okposo/R.Strome 5.00 12.00
EM2PG Pacioretty/Galchenyuk 5.00 12.00
EM2SK D.Keith/B.Seabrook 4.00 10.00
EM2SL E.Lindholm/J.Skinner 6.00 15.00

2015-16 Exquisite Collection Material Dual (continued)

EM2SN T.Seguin/Nichushkin 6.00 15.00
EM2SP O.Palat/S.Stamkos 10.00 25.00
EM2TP T.Toffoli/T.Pearson 5.00 12.00
EM2ZN Zetterberg/G.Nyquist 6.00 15.00

2015-16 Exquisite Collection Material Signatures

EMSBR Bill Ranford/135 12.00 30.00
EMSCP Carey Price/135 25.00 60.00
EMSDG Doug Gilmour/25 25.00 60.00
EMSEM Evgeni Malkin/99 25.00 60.00
EMSGF Grant Fuhr/99 20.00 50.00
EMSGL Guy Lafleur/25 30.00 80.00
EMSJP Joe Pavelski/135 15.00 40.00
EMSJS Jason Spezza/135 12.00 30.00
EMSMF Marc-Andre Fleury/99 25.00 60.00
EMSMG Guy Carbonneau/135 10.00 25.00
EMSMK Mike Keane/135 10.00 25.00
EMSRB Rod Brind'Amour/135 10.00 25.00
EMSSE Tyler Seguin/99 15.00 40.00
EMSTS Teemu Selanne/25 25.00 60.00

2015-16 Exquisite Collection Materials Quads

EM4CGY Gdru/Mnhn/Hillr/Hdlr 15.00 40.00
EM4EDM RNH/Ebrle/Drstl/Ykpv 30.00 80.00
EM4FLY Schn/Ctrier/Vrck/Msn 10.00 25.00
EM4NYR Nsh/Krdr/St.Ls/Zcrlo 12.00 30.00
EM4OTT Andr/Krlsn/Trs/Ryn 12.00 30.00
EM4STL Bcks/Ststny/Trsn/Aln 12.00 30.00
EM4TML Bzk/Brnr/vn Rms/Kdr 12.00 30.00
EM4VAN Mlr/Brws/Sdin/Sdin 12.00 30.00
EM4WAS Hltby/Bksm/Crln/Kznt 12.00 30.00
EM4JETS Whlr/Schf/Pvlc/Trba 15.00 40.00
EM4PRED Jrnk/Nl/Webr/Jnes 10.00 25.00
EM4WILD Prse/Cyl/Pmnvl/Grnl 10.00 25.00

2015-16 Exquisite Collection Rookie Dual Jerseys

*DUAL SPECTRUM/25: .6X TO 1.5X DUAL/149
*QUAD/99: .5X TO 1.2X DUAL/149
R2CM Connor McDavid 600.00 1500.00
R2EP Emile Poirier 4.00 10.00
R2JE Jack Eichel 40.00 80.00
R2JR Jacob de la Rose 5.00 12.00
R2KF Kevin Fiala 6.00 15.00
R2MD Max Domi 10.00 25.00
R2NE Nikolaj Ehlers 10.00 25.00
R2NH Noah Hanifin 8.00 20.00

2015-16 Exquisite Collection Endorsements Relics

ERAO Alexander Ovechkin 50.00 125.00
ERCO Chris Osgood 12.00 30.00
ERCP Carey Price 25.00 60.00
ERDH Dale Hawerchuk 15.00 40.00
EREM Evgeni Malkin 25.00 60.00
ERJB Jamie Benn 12.00 30.00
ERJG Johnny Gaudreau 20.00 50.00
ERJI Jarome Iginla 15.00 40.00
ERJR Jeremy Roenick 20.00 50.00
ERJT Jonathan Toews 60.00 150.00
ERMB Martin Brodeur 60.00 150.00
ERMM Mike Modano 20.00 50.00
ERPC Paul Coffey 25.00 60.00
ERPD Pavel Datsyuk 30.00 80.00
ERPF Peter Forsberg 60.00 150.00
ERRB Rob Blake 12.00 30.00
ERSC Sidney Crosby 200.00 300.00
ERTS Teemu Selanne 25.00 60.00

2015-16 Exquisite Collection Endorsements Rookie Relics

ERCH Charles Hudon 15.00 40.00
ERCM Connor McDavid 3000.00 6000.00
ERDL Dylan Larkin 50.00 125.00
ERJM Jared McCann 20.00 50.00
ERJV Jake Virtanen 20.00 50.00
ERKF Kevin Fiala 20.00 50.00
ERMD Max Domi 30.00 80.00
ERMR Mikko Rantanen 125.00 300.00
ERNE Nikolaj Ehlers 30.00 80.00
ERNH Noah Hanifin 25.00 60.00
ERNR Nick Ritchie 15.00 40.00
ERRF Robby Fabbri 20.00 50.00
ERSB Sam Bennett 50.00 125.00
ERZF Zachary Fucale 12.00 30.00

2015-16 Exquisite Collection Rookie Jumbo Patches

RJCH Connor Hellebuyck/35 25.00 50.00
RJCM Connor McDavid/35 150.00 300.00
RJEP Emile Poirier/35 10.00 25.00
RJJR Jacob de la Rose/35 12.00 30.00
RJKF Kevin Fiala/35 15.00 40.00
RJMD Max Domi/35 25.00 60.00
RJNE Nikolaj Ehlers/35 25.00 60.00
RJNH Noah Hanifin/35 20.00 50.00
RJSB Sam Bennett/35 40.00 100.00
RJSP Shane Prince/35 8.00 20.00

2015-16 Exquisite Collection Rookie Signatures

ERSBM Brock McGinn/399 6.00 15.00
ERSCH Connor Hellebuyck/399 25.00 60.00
ERSCM Connor McDavid/149 300.00 500.00
ERSCS Chandler Stephenson/399 8.00 20.00
ERSDL Dylan Larkin/399 25.00 60.00
ERSDS Daniel Sprong/399 8.00 20.00
ERSEP Emile Poirier/399 5.00 12.00
ERSFA Radek Faksa/399 6.00 15.00
ERSJD Joonas Donskoi/399 6.00 15.00
ERSJM Jared McCann/399 8.00 20.00
ERSJV Jake Virtanen/199 8.00 20.00
ERSJW Jordan Weal/399 4.00 10.00
ERSKF Kevin Fiala/399 8.00 20.00
ERSMJ Mattias Janmark/399 6.00 15.00
ERSMR Mikko Rantanen/199 40.00 100.00
ERSNE Nikolaj Ehlers/199 12.00 30.00
ERSNG Nikolay Goldobin/399 6.00 15.00
ERSNH Noah Hanifin/399 10.00 25.00
ERSNP Nicolas Petan/399 6.00 15.00
ERSOL Oscar Lindberg/399 6.00 15.00
ERSRH Ryan Hartman/399 8.00 20.00
ERSSB Sam Bennett/199 20.00 50.00
ERSSP Sergei Plotnikov/399 4.00 10.00
ERSVA Viktor Arvidsson/399 6.00 15.00
ERSVH Vincent Hinostroza/399 4.00 10.00

2015-16 Exquisite Collection Rookie Signatures Gold Spectrum

*GOLD/35: .6X TO 1.5X BASIC INSERTS
ERSCM Connor McDavid 2500.00 6000.00
ERSDL Dylan Larkin 90.00 150.00
ERSRH Ryan Hartman 12.00 30.00

2015-16 Exquisite Collection '03-04 Rookie Tribute Patch Autographs

03TAP Artemi Panarin 250.00 400.00
03TCM Connor McDavid 3000.00 5000.00
03TDL Dylan Larkin 100.00 250.00
03TJV Jake Virtanen 40.00 100.00
03TMD Max Domi 60.00 150.00
03TMR Mikko Rantanen 150.00 400.00
03TNE Nikolaj Ehlers 60.00 150.00
03TNH Noah Hanifin 50.00 120.00
03TRF Robby Fabbri 40.00 100.00
03TSB Sam Bennett 100.00 250.00

2015-16 Exquisite Collection Signatures

ESAE Aaron Ekblad/125 15.00 40.00
ESAG Alex Galchenyuk/125 8.00 20.00
ESAI Arturs Irbe 10.00 25.00
ESAO Alexander Ovechkin/15 90.00 150.00
ESBC Bobby Clarke 25.00 60.00
ESBH Bobby Hull 40.00 100.00
ESCP Corey Perry/125 20.00 50.00
ESDK David Krejci 12.00 30.00
ESEM Evgeni Malkin/35 40.00 100.00
ESFP Felix Potvin/125 20.00 50.00
ESGA Glenn Anderson/35 15.00 40.00
ESGL Guy Lafleur/35 25.00 60.00
ESJB Jonathan Bernier/125 10.00 25.00
ESJF Justin Faulk/125 12.00 30.00
ESJG Johnny Gaudreau 20.00 50.00
ESJP Joe Pavelski/125 15.00 40.00
ESJS Joe Sakic/35 40.00 100.00
ESJT Jonathan Toews/35 30.00 80.00
ESLA Gabriel Landeskog 15.00 40.00
ESLR Larry Robinson/99 15.00 40.00
ESMB Martin Brodeur/15 70.00 150.00
ESML Mario Lemieux/15 70.00 150.00
ESMM Mark Messier/15 40.00 100.00
ESNL Nicklas Lidstrom/125 12.00 30.00
ESPB Pavel Bure/35 20.00 50.00
ESPD Pavel Datsyuk/35 30.00 80.00
ESRM Ryan Miller/99 15.00 40.00
ESSJ Seth Jones/125 10.00 25.00
ESSM Sean Monahan 8.00 20.00
ESSY Steve Yzerman/15 70.00 150.00
ESTH Taylor Hall/125 12.00 30.00
ESTJ Tyler Johnson/125 8.00 20.00
ESTS Teemu Selanne/35 40.00 100.00
ESWG Wayne Gretzky/15 300.00 800.00
ESZP Zach Parise/125 12.00 30.00

2015-16 Exquisite Collection Signatures Rookie Previews

ESRPCM Connor McDavid/99 450.00 600.00
ESRPDL Dylan Larkin/149 30.00 80.00
ESRPJM Jared McCann/249 12.00 30.00
ESRPJV Jake Virtanen/249 12.00 30.00
ESRPKF Kevin Fiala/249 12.00 30.00
ESRPMR Mikko Rantanen/249 40.00 100.00
ESRPNE Nikolaj Ehlers/149 20.00 50.00
ESRPNH Noah Hanifin/249 15.00 40.00
ESRPOL Oscar Lindberg/249 10.00 25.00
ESRPRF Robby Fabbri/249 12.00 30.00
ESRPSB Sam Bennett/149 30.00 80.00

2015-16 Exquisite Collection Rookie Spectrum

RCH Connor Hellebuyck/30 30.00 80.00
RCM Connor McDavid/97 500.00 1200.00
RDL Dylan Larkin/71 25.00 60.00
REP Emile Poirier/57 6.00 15.00
RHS Henrik Samuelsson/55 5.00 12.00
RJD Jacob de la Rose/25 8.00 20.00
RJV Jake Virtanen/18 10.00 25.00
RKF Kevin Fiala/56 10.00 25.00
RMD Max Domi/16 15.00 40.00
RMP Matt Puempel/26 6.00 15.00
RNE Nikolaj Ehlers/27 15.00 40.00
RRH Ryan Hartman/38 10.00 25.00
RSB Sam Bennett/93 25.00 60.00
RSK Slater Koekkoek/29 5.00 12.00

2016-17 Exquisite Collection

1 Ryan Getzlaf 3.00 8.00
2 Max Domi 3.00 8.00
3 Patrice Bergeron 4.00 10.00
4 Jack Eichel 5.00 12.00
5 Sean Monahan 2.00 5.00
6 Justin Faulk 2.50 6.00
7 Patrick Kane 6.00 15.00
8 Matt Duchene 3.00 8.00
9 Brandon Saad 2.50 6.00
10 Jamie Benn 3.00 8.00
11 Dylan Larkin 4.00 10.00
12 Connor McDavid 15.00 40.00
13 Aleksander Barkov 5.00 12.00
14 Drew Doughty 4.00 10.00
15 Ryan Suter 2.50 6.00
16 Carey Price 6.00 15.00
17 Ryan Johansen 2.50 6.00
18 Cory Schneider 3.00 8.00
19 John Tavares 5.00 12.00
20 Henrik Lundqvist 8.00 20.00
21 Erik Karlsson 4.00 10.00
22 Shayne Gostisbehere 3.00 8.00
23 Sidney Crosby 12.00 30.00
24 Brent Burns 3.00 8.00
25 Vladimir Tarasenko 4.00 10.00
26 Steven Stamkos 6.00 15.00
27 Morgan Rielly 3.00 8.00
28 Daniel Sedin 4.00 10.00
29 Alexander Ovechkin 12.00 30.00
30 Dustin Byfuglien 3.00 8.00
31 Wayne Gretzky 20.00 50.00
32 Martin Brodeur 8.00 20.00
33 Milt Schmidt 3.00 8.00
34 Mike Bossy 3.00 8.00
35 Bobby Orr 12.00 30.00
36 Pavel Bure 3.00 8.00
37 Paul Coffey 3.00 8.00
38 Red Kelly 3.00 8.00
39 Mike Modano 5.00 12.00
40 Mario Lemieux 12.00 30.00
41 Dominik Hasek 5.00 12.00
42 Steve Yzerman 8.00 20.00
43 Mark Messier 6.00 15.00
44 Luc Robitaille 3.00 8.00
45 Patrick Roy 8.00 20.00
49 Dylan Strome JSY AU/20 RC 60.00 150.00
50 Anthony Mantha JSY AU/39 RC 150.00250.00
51 Travis Konecny JSY AU/28 RC 100.00 200.00
52 Thomas Chabot JSY AU/72 RC 50.00 120.00
53 Sonny Milano JSY AU/92 RC 80.00 150.00
54 Artturi Lehkonen JSY AU/62 RC 30.00 80.00
55 Michael Matheson JSY AU/19 RC 60.00150.00
56 Jake Guentzel JSY AU/59 RC 150.00 400.00
57 Hudson Fasching JSY AU/52 RC 100.00 200.00
58 Pavel Buchnevich JSY AU/89 RC 80.00200.00
59 Matthew Tkachuk JSY AU/16 RC 200.00500.00
60 Kasperi Kapanen JSY AU/37 RC 300.00400.00
61 Brendan Perlini JSY AU/29 RC 30.00 80.00
62 Brendan Leipsic JSY AU/49 RC 60.00 150.00
64 Anthony DeAngelo JSY AU/77 RC 50.00120.00
67 Patrik Laine JSY AU/29 RC 2000.00 2500.00
68 Sebastian Aho JSY AU/20 RC 200.00 300.00
70 John Quenneville JSY AU/47 RC 25.00 60.00
71 Jimmy Vesey JSY AU/26 RC 120.00 300.00
72 Brandon Montour JSY AU/71 RC 30.00 80.00
73 Brandon Carlo JSY AU/25 RC 100.00 200.00
74 William Nylander JSY AU/29 RC 400.00 1000.00
76 Mikhail Sergachev JSY AU/22 RC 200.00 500.00
78 Kevin Labanc JSY AU/62 RC 30.00 80.00
79 Brayden Point JSY AU/21 RC 200.00 500.00
80 Auston Matthews JSY AU/34 RC 2500.00 3500.00
81 Oliver Bjorkstrand JSY AU/28 RC 80.00200.00
82 Josh Morrissey JSY AU/44 RC 40.00 100.00
83 Esa Lindell JSY AU/23 RC 40.00 100.00
84 Anthony Beauvillier JSY AU/72 RC 50.00 120.00
85 Jesse Puljujarvi JSY AU/98 RC 40.00 100.00
86 Tyler Motte JSY AU/64 RC 80.00 200.00
87 Christian Dvorak JSY AU/18 RC 20.00 50.00
88 Kyle Connor JSY AU/81 RC 100.00 250.00
89 Timo Meier JSY AU/28 RC 100.00 200.00
91 Mitch Marner JSY AU/16 RC 2500.00 3000.00
92 Thatcher Demko JSY AU/35 RC 200.00500.00
94 Pavel Zacha JSY AU/37 RC 80.00 200.00
95 Miles Wood JSY AU/44 RC 30.00 80.00

2016-17 Exquisite Collection '09-10 Rookie Auto Tribute

09TAM Auston Matthews 800.00 1000.00
09TDS Dylan Strome 80.00 150.00
09TJP Jesse Puljujarvi 50.00 125.00
09TJV Jimmy Vesey 40.00 100.00
09TMA Anthony Mantha 80.00 200.00
09TMM Mitch Marner 150.00 400.00
09TMT Matthew Tkachuk 150.00 400.00
09TPL Patrik Laine 250.00 500.00
09TWN William Nylander 350.00 500.00

2016-17 Exquisite Collection Gold Rookies

R1 Anthony Mantha/299 5.00 12.00
R2 Oliver Bjorkstrand/299 3.00 8.00
R3 Dominik Simon/299 2.00 5.00
R4 Kyle Connor/299 8.00 20.00
R5 Brendan Leipsic/299 2.00 5.00
R6 Ivan Provorov/299 4.00 10.00
R7 Matthew Tkachuk/299 10.00 25.00
R8 Josh Morrissey/299 6.00 15.00
R9 Joel Eriksson Ek/299 3.00 8.00
R10 Connor Brown/299 4.00 10.00
R11 Sonny Milano/299 3.00 8.00
R12 Esa Lindell/299 2.50 6.00
R13 Travis Konecny/299 5.00 12.00
R14 Pavel Zacha/299 4.00 10.00
R15 Hudson Fasching/299 2.50 6.00
R16 Charlie Lindgren/299 5.00 12.00
R17 William Nylander/200 10.00 25.00
R18 Mikhail Sergachev/299 4.00 10.00
R19 Chris Bigras/299 2.00 5.00
R20 Jason Dickinson/299 2.00 5.00
R21 Ryan Pulock/299 2.50 6.00
R22 Kasperi Kapanen/299 4.00 10.00
R23 Steven Santini/299 2.00 5.00
R24 Michael Matheson/299 2.50 6.00
R25 Patrik Laine/199 25.00 60.00
R26 Mitch Marner/199 20.00 50.00
R27 Jesse Puljujarvi/199 5.00 12.00
R28 Jimmy Vesey/199 4.00 10.00
R29 Dylan Strome/199 6.00 15.00
R30 Auston Matthews/199 60.00 150.00

2016-17 Exquisite Collection Gold Rookies Spectrum

COMMON CARD 3.00 8.00
SEMISTARS 4.00 10.00
UNLISTED STARS 5.00 12.00
R1 Anthony Mantha 40.00 100.00
R2 Oliver Bjorkstrand 20.00 50.00
R4 Kyle Connor 12.00 30.00
R7 Matthew Tkachuk 50.00 120.00
R8 Josh Morrissey 12.00 30.00
R9 Joel Eriksson Ek 40.00 100.00
R10 Connor Brown 25.00 60.00
R11 Sonny Milano 20.00 50.00
R12 Esa Lindell 15.00 40.00
R13 Travis Konecny 40.00 100.00
R16 Charlie Lindgren 20.00 50.00
R17 William Nylander 50.00 120.00
R18 Mikhail Sergachev 40.00 100.00
R20 Jason Dickinson 12.00 30.00
R22 Kasperi Kapanen 12.00 30.00
R24 Michael Matheson 25.00 60.00
R25 Patrik Laine 150.00 300.00
R26 Mitch Marner 150.00 400.00
R27 Jesse Puljujarvi 15.00 40.00
R28 Jimmy Vesey 15.00 40.00
R29 Dylan Strome 20.00 50.00
R30 Auston Matthews 200.00 500.00

2016-17 Exquisite Collection Material Combos

ECCE C.Crawford/T.Esposito 15.00 40.00
ECDB D.Doughty/R.Blake 15.00 40.00
ECED O.Ekman-Larsson/M.Domi 12.00 30.00
ECEO J.Eichel/R.O'Reilly 20.00 50.00
ECFR G.Fuhr/B.Ranford 20.00 50.00
ECKH E.Karlsson/M.Hoffman 8.00 20.00
ECKZ N.Kronwall/H.Zetterberg 15.00 40.00
ECLN H.Lundqvist/R.Nash 30.00 80.00
ECMG C.McDavid/W.Gretzky 80.00 200.00
ECOK A.Ovechkin/E.Kuznetsov 50.00 120.00
ECPG C.Price/A.Galchenyuk 25.00 60.00
ECRC T.Rask/G.Cheevers 15.00 40.00
ECSL H.Sedin/T.Linden 15.00 40.00
ECSM B.Salming/M.Rielly 12.00 30.00
ECWB B.Wheeler/D.Byfuglien 12.00 30.00

2016-17 Exquisite Collection Material Quads

EQBB Bergeron/Bourque Rask/Cheevers 25.00 60.00
EQCA MacKinnon/Sakic Duchene/Roy 60.00 150.00
EQFP Barkov/Bure/Ekblad/Luongo 25.00 60.00
EQLA Doughty/Quick/Kopitar/Carter 25.00 60.00
EQRW Kronwall/Zetterberg Mrazek/Hasek 25.00 60.00
EQST Tarasenko/Steen Pietrangelo/Allen 20.00 50.00

2016-17 Exquisite Collection Materials

EMAK Anze Kopitar 15.00 40.00
EMBB Brent Burns 10.00 25.00
EMBH Braden Holtby 12.00 30.00
EMCA John Carlson 10.00 25.00
EMCG Claude Giroux 10.00 25.00
EMCM Connor McDavid 80.00 200.00
EMCP Carey Price 20.00 50.00
EMDB Dustin Byfuglien 10.00 25.00
EMDK Duncan Keith 8.00 20.00
EMEK Erik Karlsson 10.00 25.00
EMEM Evgeni Malkin 20.00 50.00
EMGL Gabriel Landeskog 12.00 30.00
EMHL Henrik Lundqvist 25.00 60.00
EMJB Jamie Benn 10.00 25.00
EMJC Jeff Carter 8.00 20.00
EMJE Jack Eichel 15.00 40.00
EMJL John LeClair 10.00 25.00
EMJS Jeff Skinner 12.00 30.00
EMJV Jakub Voracek 8.00 20.00
EMKE Phil Kessel 10.00 25.00
EMMB Martin Brodeur 25.00 60.00
EMNK Nazem Kadri 12.00 30.00
EMNM Nathan MacKinnon 40.00 100.00
EMOE Oliver Ekman-Larsson 10.00 25.00
EMPR Patrick Roy 25.00 60.00
EMRB Rob Blake 10.00 25.00
EMRG Ryan Getzlaf 10.00 25.00
EMRI Pekka Rinne 10.00 25.00
EMRL Roberto Luongo 15.00 40.00
EMRN Rick Nash 10.00 25.00
EMSC Sidney Crosby 40.00 100.00
EMTA John Tavares 15.00 40.00
EMTR Tuukka Rask 12.00 30.00
EMVH Victor Hedman 12.00 30.00
EMVT Vladimir Tarasenko 12.00 30.00

2016-17 Exquisite Collection Material Signatures

EMSAK Anze Kopitar 20.00 50.00
EMSBB Brent Burns 25.00 60.00
EMSCP Corey Perry 20.00 50.00
EMSCS Cory Schneider 12.00 30.00
EMSDH Dale Hawerchuk 15.00 40.00
EMSFP Felix Potvin 30.00 80.00
EMSGL Guy Lafleur 40.00 100.00
EMSHZ Henrik Zetterberg 40.00 100.00
EMSIL Igor Larionov 25.00 60.00
EMSJJ Jaromir Jagr 80.00 150.00
EMSJS Joe Sakic 30.00 80.00
EMSJT John Tavares 20.00 50.00
EMSLD Leon Draisaitl 60.00 150.00
EMSMP Max Pacioretty 12.00 30.00
EMSPB Pavel Bure 12.00 30.00
EMSRJ Roman Josi 12.00 30.00
EMSTJ Tyler Johnson 8.00 20.00
EMSTL Trevor Linden 25.00 60.00

2016-17 Exquisite Collection Rookie Draft Day

RDDAM Auston Matthews 80.00 150.00
RDDDS Dylan Strome 8.00 20.00
RDDIP Ivan Provorov 6.00 15.00
RDDMA Anthony Mantha 8.00 20.00
RDDMM Mitch Marner 30.00 80.00
RDDPL Patrik Laine 10.00 25.00
RDDPZ Pavel Zacha 6.00 15.00
RDDSM Sonny Milano 5.00 12.00
RDDWN William Nylander 15.00 40.00

2016-17 Exquisite Collection Rookie Draft Day Spectrum

RDDMA Anthony Mantha/20 20.00 50.00
RDDSM Sonny Milano/16 10.00 25.00

2016-17 Exquisite Collection Rookie Dual Materials

RDAM Auston Matthews/25 150.00 300.00
RDDS Dylan Strome/99 15.00 40.00
RDHF Hudson Fasching/99 6.00 15.00
RDIP Ivan Provorov/99 12.00 30.00
RDJM Josh Morrissey/99 10.00 25.00
RDJP Jesse Puljujarvi/99 15.00 40.00
RDJV Jimmy Vesey/99 12.00 30.00
RDKC Kyle Connor/99 20.00 50.00
RDKK Kasperi Kapanen/99 15.00 40.00
RDMA Anthony Mantha/99 15.00 40.00
RDMM Mitch Marner/99 20.00 50.00
RDOB Oliver Bjorkstrand/99 8.00 20.00
RDPL Patrik Laine/99 15.00 40.00
RDPZ Pavel Zacha/99 10.00 25.00
RDSM Sonny Milano/99 8.00 20.00
RDWN William Nylander/99 25.00 60.00

2016-17 Exquisite Collection Rookie Patches

RPAM Auston Matthews/99 80.00 150.00
RPDS Dylan Strome/299 15.00 40.00
RPHF Hudson Fasching/299 6.00 15.00
RPIP Ivan Provorov/299 15.00 40.00
RPJD Jason Dickinson/299 5.00 12.00
RPJM Josh Morrissey/299 15.00 40.00
RPJP Jesse Puljujarvi/299 20.00 50.00
RPKC Kyle Connor/299 20.00 50.00
RPKK Kasperi Kapanen/299 10.00 25.00
RPLC Lawson Crouse/299 5.00 12.00
RPMA Anthony Mantha/299 12.00 30.00
RPMM Mitch Marner/299 20.00 50.00
RPMT Matthew Tkachuk/299 25.00 60.00
RPPL Patrik Laine/199 25.00 60.00
RPPZ Pavel Zacha/299 10.00 25.00
RPSM Sonny Milano/299 8.00 20.00
RPWN William Nylander/199 20.00 50.00

2016-17 Exquisite Collection Rookie Quad Materials

RQCD Christian Dvorak/49 15.00 40.00
RQCL Charlie Lindgren/49 20.00 50.00
RQHF Hudson Fasching/49 12.00 30.00
RQIP Ivan Provorov/49 20.00 50.00
RQJP Jesse Puljujarvi/49 25.00 60.00
RQKC Kyle Connor/49 40.00 100.00
RQKK Kasperi Kapanen/49 20.00 50.00
RQLC Lawson Crouse/49 10.00 25.00
RQMA Anthony Mantha/49 25.00 60.00
RQMI Michael Matheson/49 12.00 30.00
RQMM Mitch Marner/49 40.00 100.00
RQPL Patrik Laine/49 30.00 80.00
RQPZ Pavel Zacha/49 20.00 50.00
RQSM Sonny Milano/49 15.00 40.00
RQWN William Nylander/49 50.00 125.00

2016-17 Exquisite Collection Rookie Signatures

ERSAM Auston Matthews 500.00 900.00
ERSBL Brendan Leipsic 4.00 10.00
ERSCB Connor Brown 8.00 20.00
ERSCL Charlie Lindgren 8.00 20.00
ERSDS Dylan Strome 15.00 40.00
ERSHF Hudson Fasching 5.00 12.00
ERSIP Ivan Provorov 8.00 20.00
ERSJD Jason Dickinson 4.00 10.00
ERSJM Josh Morrissey 12.00 30.00
ERSJP Jesse Puljujarvi 15.00 40.00
ERSJV Jimmy Vesey 12.00 30.00
ERSKC Kyle Connor 15.00 40.00
ERSKK Kasperi Kapanen 8.00 20.00
ERSMA Anthony Mantha 10.00 25.00
ERSMB Mathew Barzal 15.00 40.00
ERSMI Michael Matheson 5.00 12.00
ERSMM Mitch Marner 125.00 300.00
ERSMT Matthew Tkachuk 25.00 60.00
ERSMW Miles Wood 4.00 10.00
ERSNI Nikita Soshnikov 3.00 8.00
ERSOK Oliver Kylington 4.00 10.00
ERSOS Oskar Sundqvist 5.00 12.00
ERSPL Patrik Laine 150.00 250.00
ERSRP Ryan Pulock 5.00 12.00
ERSTK Travis Konecny 10.00 25.00
ERSWN William Nylander 40.00 100.00
ERSZW Zach Werenski 25.00 60.00

2016-17 Exquisite Collection Signatures

ESBO Bobby Orr/49 80.00 150.00
ESBS Borje Salming/49 15.00 40.00
ESBU Johnny Bucyk/99 10.00 25.00
ESCG Clark Gillies/49 15.00 40.00
ESCH Carl Hagelin/125 6.00 15.00
ESDH Dominik Hasek/49 25.00 60.00
ESDK David Krejci/125 10.00 25.00
ESJB Jamie Benn/49 15.00 40.00
ESJH Jonathan Huberdeau/125 12.00 30.00
ESJI Jarome Iginla/99 12.00 30.00
ESJK Jari Kurri/125 10.00 25.00
ESJP Joe Pavelski/99 12.00 30.00
ESJR Jeremy Roenick/99 15.00 40.00
ESKP Kyle Palmieri/125 8.00 20.00
ESLR Luc Robitaille/25 20.00 50.00
ESMB Mike Bossy/25 20.00 50.00
ESMO Mike Modano/49 25.00 60.00
ESMU Matt Murray/99 15.00 40.00
ESNL Nicklas Lidstrom/25 20.00 50.00
ESRL Roberto Luongo/99 15.00 40.00
ESRN Rick Nash/99 10.00 25.00
ESTH Taylor Hall/49 15.00 40.00
ESTS Teemu Selanne/49 30.00 80.00
ESZP Zach Parise/99 10.00 25.00

2017-18 Exquisite Collection

1 Nicklas Backstrom 1.25 3.00
2 Carey Price 2.50 6.00
3 Jack Eichel 2.00 5.00
4 Aleksander Barkov 2.00 5.00
5 John Tavares 2.00 5.00
6 Brent Burns 1.25 3.00
7 Artemi Panarin 2.50 6.00
8 Ryan Getzlaf 1.25 3.00
9 Nikita Kucherov 2.50 6.00
10 Connor McDavid 8.00 20.00
11 Patrick Kane 2.50 6.00
12 Erik Karlsson 1.50 4.00
13 Vladimir Tarasenko 1.50 4.00
14 P.K. Subban 1.50 4.00
15 Jamie Benn 1.25 3.00
16 Patrice Bergeron 1.50 4.00
17 Sidney Crosby 10.00 25.00
18 Anze Kopitar 2.00 5.00
19 Marc-Andre Fleury 10.00 25.00
20 Johnny Gaudreau 2.00 5.00
21 Claude Giroux 1.25 3.00
22 Steven Stamkos 2.50 6.00
23 Patrik Laine 1.50 4.00
24 Kevin Shattenkirk .75 2.00
25 Auston Matthews 5.00 12.00
26 Pat LaFontaine 1.25 3.00
27 Frank Mahovlich 1.25 3.00
28 Jean Beliveau 1.25 3.00
29 Phil Esposito 1.25 3.00
30 Wayne Gretzky 12.00 30.00

2017-18 Exquisite Collection '07-08 Rookie Tribute

07TCM Connor McDavid PATCH AU 450.00 500.00
07TCP Carey Price PATCH AU 80.00 150.00
07TNH Nico Hischier 40.00 100.00
07TNP Nolan Patrick 40.00 100.00
08TAD Alex DeBrincat PATCH AU 150.00 250.00
08TCM Charlie McAvoy PATCH AU 200.00300.00
08TJH Josh Ho-Sang PATCH AU 80.00 150.00
08TNH Nico Hischier 40.00 100.00
08TNP Nolan Patrick 40.00 100.00
08TTT Tage Thompson PATCH AU 80.00 150.00

2017-18 Exquisite Collection Material Signatures

EMSAK Anze Kopitar/25 20.00 50.00
EMSBH Bo Horvat/49 15.00 40.00
EMSBP Brian Propp/25 10.00 25.00
EMSCP Colton Parayko/49 10.00 25.00
EMSGN Gustav Nyquist/49 8.00 20.00
EMSJC John Carlson/49 12.00 30.00
EMSJI Jarome Iginla/49 15.00 40.00
EMSJP Joe Pavelski/25 15.00 40.00
EMSPL Patrik Laine/25 15.00 40.00
EMSRL Rod Langway/49 12.00 30.00

2017-18 Exquisite Collection Material Quads

EQBJ Wennberg/Jenner Jones/Bobrovsky 15.00 40.00
EQMC Pacioretty/Galchenyuk Price/Weber 20.00 50.00
EQML Marner/Kadri/Rielly/Andersen 12.00 30.00
EQNP Johansen/Forsberg Subban/Rinne 25.00 60.00
EQPP Lemieux/Barrasso Malkin/Murray 40.00 100.00
EQWC Ovechkin/Backstrom Oshie/Holtby 40.00 100.00

2017-18 Exquisite Collection Materials

EMAO Alexander Ovechkin 30.00 80.00
EMBB Brent Burns 15.00 40.00
EMBH Brett Hull 25.00 60.00
EMCP Carey Price 25.00 60.00
EMDH Dominik Hasek 12.00 30.00
EMEK Erik Karlsson 10.00 25.00
EMHL Henrik Lundqvist 20.00 50.00
EMJB Jamie Benn 8.00 20.00
EMKL Kris Letang 10.00 25.00
EMNB Nicklas Backstrom 8.00 20.00
EMPK Patrick Kane 15.00 40.00
EMSS Steven Stamkos 15.00 40.00

2017-18 Exquisite Collection Rookie Dual Materials

RDBB Brock Boeser 30.00 80.00
RDCK Clayton Keller 15.00 40.00
RDCM Charlie McAvoy 12.00 30.00
RDHF Haydn Fleury 5.00 12.00
RDJG Jon Gillies 5.00 12.00
RDJR Jack Roslovic 6.00 15.00
RDLK Luke Kunin 5.00 12.00
RDOT Owen Tippett 15.00 40.00
RDPD Pierre-Luc Dubois 8.00 20.00
RDTJ Tyson Jost 10.00 25.00
RDTT Tage Thompson 12.00 30.00

2017-18 Exquisite Collection Rookie Patches

RPAB Anders Bjork/299 10.00 25.00
RPAD Alex DeBrincat/299 20.00 50.00
RPAN Alexander Nylander/299 12.00 30.00
RPBB Brock Boeser/99 20.00 50.00
RPCK Clayton Keller/99 12.00 30.00
RPCM Charlie McAvoy/299 20.00 50.00
RPCW Colin White/299 10.00 25.00
RPES Evgeny Svechnikov/299 15.00 40.00
RPHF Haydn Fleury/299 8.00 20.00
RPIB Ivan Barbashev/299 10.00 25.00
RPLK Luke Kunin/299 8.00 20.00
RPMB Madison Bowey/299 5.00 12.00
RPPD Pierre-Luc Dubois/299 12.00 30.00
RPTJ Tyson Jost/299 8.00 20.00
RPVS Vadim Shipachyov/99 10.00 25.00

2017-18 Exquisite Collection Rookie Signatures

ERSAD Alex DeBrincat/199 30.00 80.00
ERSAK Adrian Kempe/199 20.00 50.00
ERSAN Alexander Nylander/99 25.00 60.00
ERSAT Alex Tuch/199 30.00 80.00
ERSBB Brock Boeser/99 150.00 250.00
ERSCF Christian Fischer/199 12.00 30.00
ERSCH Filip Chlapik/199 8.00 20.00
ERSCK Clayton Keller/99 25.00 60.00
ERSCM Charlie McAvoy/99 25.00 60.00
ERSCW Colin White/199 12.00 30.00
ERSDG Denis Gurianov/199 25.00 60.00
ERSES Evgeny Svechnikov/199 20.00 50.00
ERSFC Filip Chytil/199 10.00 25.00
ERSHF Haydn Fleury/199 10.00 25.00
ERSJD Jake DeBrusk/199 25.00 60.00
ERSJH Josh Ho-Sang/199 30.00 80.00
ERSKY Kailer Yamamoto/199 25.00 60.00
ERSLK Luke Kunin/199 10.00 25.00
ERSOT Owen Tippett/199 20.00 50.00
ERSPD Pierre-Luc Dubois/99 15.00 40.00
ERSRH Robert Hagg/99 10.00 25.00
ERSSM Samuel Morin/199 6.00 15.00
ERSTJ Tyson Jost/199 20.00 50.00
ERSTT Tage Thompson/199 25.00 60.00
ERSVH Ville Husso/199 12.00 30.00
ERSVM Victor Mete/199 10.00 25.00
ERSWB Will Butcher/199 12.00 30.00

2017-18 Exquisite Collection Rookie Quad Materials

RQBB Brock Boeser 25.00 60.00
RQCK Clayton Keller 25.00 60.00
RQCM Charlie McAvoy 20.00 50.00
RQCW Colin White 12.00 30.00
RQIB Ivan Barbashev 12.00 30.00
RQJH Josh Ho-Sang 12.00 30.00
RQMB Madison Bowey 6.00 15.00
RQPD Pierre-Luc Dubois 15.00 40.00
RQTJ Tyson Jost 12.00 30.00
RQVS Vadim Shipachyov 10.00 25.00

2017-18 Exquisite Collection Rookies

R1 Tyson Jost 10.00 25.00
R2 Colin White 6.00 15.00
R3 Josh Ho-Sang 4.00 10.00
R4 Christian Fischer 4.00 10.00
R5 Alexander Nylander 5.00 12.00
R6 Adrian Kempe 6.00 15.00
R7 Evgeny Svechnikov 6.00 15.00
R8 Jack Roslovic 4.00 10.00
R9 Will Butcher 4.00 10.00
R10 Victor Mete 3.00 8.00
R11 Kailer Yamamoto 8.00 20.00
R12 Tage Thompson 8.00 20.00
R13 Jake DeBrusk 8.00 20.00
R14 Filip Chytil 3.00 8.00
R15 Travis Sanheim 3.00 8.00
R16 Logan Brown 3.00 8.00
R17 Alex DeBrincat 8.00 20.00
R18 Anders Bjork 4.00 10.00
R19 Haydn Fleury 3.00 8.00
R20 Nikita Scherbak 4.00 10.00
R21 Luke Kunin 3.00 8.00
R22 Alex Kerfoot 6.00 15.00
R23 Owen Tippett 6.00 15.00
R24 Alex Tuch 8.00 20.00
R25 Brock Boeser 8.00 20.00
R26 Clayton Keller 8.00 20.00
R27 Charlie McAvoy 8.00 20.00
R28 Pierre-Luc Dubois 5.00 12.00
R29 Nolan Patrick 6.00 15.00
R30 Nico Hischier 10.00 25.00
RAD Alex DeBrincat/299 8.00 20.00
RAN Alexander Nylander/299 5.00 12.00
RBB Brock Boeser/299 8.00 20.00
RCK Clayton Keller/199 8.00 20.00
RCM Charlie McAvoy/199 8.00 20.00
RCW Colin White/299 4.00 10.00
RES Evgeny Svechnikov/299 6.00 15.00
RJD Jake DeBrusk/299 8.00 20.00
RJH Josh Ho-Sang/299 4.00 10.00
RMB Madison Bowey/299 2.00 5.00
RNH Nico Hischier/199 10.00 25.00
RNP Nolan Patrick/199 6.00 15.00
RPD Pierre-Luc Dubois/299 5.00 12.00
RTJ Tyson Jost/299 6.00 15.00
RTT Tage Thompson/299 8.00 20.00
RVS Vadim Shipachyov/199 4.00 10.00

2017-18 Exquisite Collection Rookies Draft Day

RDDAN Alexander Nylander 8.00 20.00
RDDCK Clayton Keller 12.00 30.00
RDDCM Charlie McAvoy 12.00 30.00
RDDES Evgeny Svechnikov 10.00 25.00
RDDLK Luke Kunin 5.00 12.00
RDDNH Nico Hischier 15.00 40.00
RDDNP Nolan Patrick 15.00 40.00
RDDPD Pierre-Luc Dubois 8.00 20.00
RDDTJ Tyson Jost 10.00 25.00

2017-18 Exquisite Collection Rookies Spectrum

RAD Alex DeBrincat/12 150.00 225.00
RAN Alexander Nylander/70 25.00 60.00
RCK Clayton Keller/14 125.00 250.00
RCM Charlie McAvoy/73 15.00 40.00
RCW Colin White/82 12.00 30.00
RES Evgeny Svechnikov/37 15.00 40.00
RJD Jake DeBrusk/74 15.00 40.00
RJH Josh Ho-Sang/66 15.00 40.00
RMB Madison Bowey/22 12.00 30.00
RNH Nico Hischier/13 250.00 325.00
RNP Nolan Patrick/64 40.00 100.00
RTJ Tyson Jost/27 30.00 80.00
RTT Tage Thompson/32 30.00 80.00
RVS Vadim Shipachyov/87 12.00 30.00

2018-19 Exquisite Collection '03-04 Retro

03VAM Auston Matthews 12.00 30.00
03VAO Alexander Ovechkin 12.00 30.00
03VCM Connor McDavid 15.00 40.00
03VCP Carey Price 6.00 15.00
03VMF Marc-Andre Fleury 6.00 15.00
03VNK Nikita Kucherov 6.00 15.00
03VPK Patrick Kane 6.00 15.00
03VPL Patrik Laine 4.00 10.00
03VSC Sidney Crosby 12.00 30.00

2018-19 Exquisite Collection '03-04 Retro Rookies

03RAG Adam Gaudette 5.00 12.00
03RAS Andrei Svechnikov 8.00 20.00
03RCM Casey Mittelstadt 6.00 15.00
03RDO Ryan Donato 5.00 12.00
03RDS Dylan Sikura 4.00 10.00
03REP Elias Pettersson 25.00 60.00
03RET Eeli Tolvanen 6.00 15.00
03RHB Henrik Borgstrom 5.00 12.00
03RJG Jordan Greenway 3.00 8.00
03RLA Lias Andersson 5.00 12.00
03RNJ Noah Juulsen 3.00 8.00
03RRD Rasmus Dahlin 8.00 20.00
03RTD Travis Dermott 5.00 12.00
03RTT Troy Terry 5.00 12.00

2018-19 Exquisite Collection Materials

EMAM Auston Matthews/34 40.00 100.00
EMCH Connor Hellebuyck/37 20.00 50.00
EMCP Carey Price/31 20.00 50.00
EMHZ Henrik Zetterberg/40 12.00 30.00
EMJT Jonathan Toews/19 15.00 40.00
EMMA Mitch Marner/16 15.00 40.00
EMMB Martin Brodeur/30 25.00 60.00
EMMS Mark Scheifele/55 15.00 40.00
EMNM Nathan MacKinnon/29 40.00 100.00
EMPB Patrice Bergeron/37 12.00 30.00
EMRH Ron Hextall/27 10.00 25.00

2018-19 Exquisite Collection Platinum Rookies

R1 Maxime Lajoie/299 5.00 12.00
R2 Dennis Cholowski/299 3.00 8.00
R3 Dominik Kahun/299 3.00 8.00
R4 Noah Juulsen/299 3.00 8.00
R5 Casey Mittelstadt/299 6.00 15.00
R6 Miro Heiskanen/299 8.00 20.00
R7 Robert Thomas/299 6.00 15.00
R8 Jordan Greenway/299 3.00 8.00
R9 Henrik Borgstrom/299 5.00 12.00
R10 Lias Andersson/299 5.00 12.00
R11 Ryan Donato/299 5.00 12.00
R12 Maxime Comtois/299 3.00 8.00
R13 Kristian Vesalainen/299 3.00 8.00
R14 Michael Rasmussen/299 6.00 15.00
R15 Troy Terry/299 5.00 12.00
R16 Mathieu Joseph/299 4.00 10.00

R17 Jordan Kyrou/299 6.00 15.00
R18 Dillon Dube/299 4.00 10.00
R19 Evan Bouchard/299 8.00 20.00
R20 Brett Howden/299 4.00 10.00
R21 Henri Jokiharju/299 2.50 6.00
R22 Sam Steel/299 3.00 8.00
R23 Travis Dermott/299 5.00 12.00
R24 Juuso Valimaki/299 3.00 8.00
R25 Eeli Tolvanen/299 6.00 15.00
R26 Jesperi Kotkaniemi/199 6.00 15.00
R27 Andrei Svechnikov/199 8.00 20.00
R28 Brady Tkachuk/199 10.00 25.00
R29 Rasmus Dahlin/199 8.00 20.00
R30 Elias Pettersson/199 10.00 25.00

2018-19 Exquisite Collection Rookie Patches

RPAC Anthony Cirelli/299 10.00 25.00
RPAG Adam Gaudette/299 10.00 25.00
RPAS Andrei Svechnikov/99 15.00 40.00
RPCM Casey Mittelstadt/99 12.00 30.00
RPDO Ryan Donato/299 10.00 25.00
RPDS Dylan Sikura/299 8.00 20.00
RPEP Elias Pettersson/99 80.00 150.00
RPET Eeli Tolvanen/299 12.00 30.00
RPHB Henrik Borgstrom/299 10.00 25.00
RPJG Jordan Greenway/299 6.00 15.00
RPTD Travis Dermott/299 10.00 25.00
RPTT Troy Terry/299 10.00 25.00

2018-19 Exquisite Collection Rookie Patches Gold Spectrum

RPEP Elias Pettersson/25 250.00 350.00

2018-19 Exquisite Collection Rookies

RAC Anthony Cirelli/299 5.00 12.00
RAG Adam Gaudette/299 5.00 12.00
RAJ Andreas Johnsson/299 4.00 10.00
RAS Andrei Svechnikov/199 8.00 20.00
RBT Brady Tkachuk/199 10.00 25.00
RCM Casey Mittelstadt/299 6.00 15.00
RDO Ryan Donato/299 5.00 12.00
RDS Dylan Sikura/299 4.00 10.00
REP Elias Pettersson/199 10.00 25.00
RET Eeli Tolvanen/299 6.00 15.00
RHB Henrik Borgstrom/299 5.00 12.00
RJG Jordan Greenway/299 3.00 8.00
RLA Lias Andersson/299 5.00 12.00
RMR Michael Rasmussen/299 4.00 10.00
RNJ Noah Juulsen/299 3.00 8.00
ROL Oskar Lindblom/299 5.00 12.00
RRD Rasmus Dahlin/199 8.00 20.00
RTT Troy Terry/299 5.00 12.00

2018-19 Exquisite Collection Rookies Draft Day

RRD1 Connor McDavid 25.00 60.00
RDDAS Andrei Svechnikov 12.00 30.00
RDDCM Casey Mittelstadt 10.00 25.00
RDDDO Ryan Donato 8.00 20.00
RDDEP Elias Pettersson 15.00 40.00
RDDET Eeli Tolvanen 10.00 25.00
RDDHB Henrik Borgstrom 8.00 20.00
RDDLA Lias Andersson 8.00 20.00
RDDRD Rasmus Dahlin 12.00 30.00

2018-19 Exquisite Collection Signatures

ESCM Connor McDavid/25 200.00 300.00
ESJT John Tavares/25 40.00 100.00
ESRH Ron Hextall/99 20.00 50.00

2019-20 Exquisite Collection '03-04 Retro Extra Exquisite Jerseys

03XAT Alexandre Texier 3.00 8.00
03XBH Barrett Hayton 6.00 15.00
03XBK Brady Keeper 3.00 8.00
03XCG Cody Glass 5.00 12.00
03XCM Cale Makar 15.00 40.00
03XDF Dante Fabbro 3.00 8.00
03XEB Erik Brannstrom 3.00 8.00
03XFZ Filip Zadina 5.00 12.00
03XJH Jack Hughes 15.00 40.00
03XKD Kirby Dach 6.00 15.00
03XKK Kaapo Kakko 5.00 12.00
03XLH Libor Hajek 2.50 6.00
03XMJ Max Jones 3.00 8.00
03XMV Max Veronneau 2.50 6.00
03XPI Rem Pitlick 3.00 8.00
03XPM Philippe Myers 2.50 6.00
03XQH Quinn Hughes 15.00 40.00
03XRB Rudolfs Balcers 3.00 8.00
03XRP Ryan Poehling 5.00 12.00
03XRS Riley Stillman 3.00 8.00
03XTF Trent Frederic 3.00 8.00
03XTH Taro Hirose 3.00 8.00
03XVA Vitaly Abramov 3.00 8.00
03XZS Zach Senyshyn 3.00 8.00

2019-20 Extra Exquisite Collection '03-04 Rookie Tribute Patch Autographs

03TAT Alexandre Texier 60.00 150.00
03TCM Cale Makar 120.00 300.00
03TFZ Filip Zadina 100.00 250.00
03TJH Jack Hughes 300.00 600.00
03TQH Quinn Hughes 300.00 600.00
03TRP Ryan Poehling 40.00 100.00

2019-20 Exquisite Collection '05-06 Retro

05VAM Auston Matthews 3.00 8.00
05VCM Connor McDavid 4.00 10.00
05VCP Carey Price 1.50 4.00
05VJG Johnny Gaudreau 1.25 3.00
05VMS Mark Scheifele 1.25 3.00
05VNK Nikita Kucherov 1.50 4.00
05VNM Nathan MacKinnon 3.00 8.00
05VPK Patrick Kane 1.50 4.00
05VSC Sidney Crosby 3.00 8.00

2019-20 Exquisite Collection '05-06 Retro Rookies

*GOLD: 1X TO 2.5X BASIC
05RAF Adam Fox 5.00 12.00
05RBH Barrett Hayton 4.00 10.00
05RCG Cody Glass 3.00 8.00
05RCM Cale Makar 10.00 25.00
05RDF Dante Fabbro 2.00 5.00
05REB Erik Brannstrom 2.00 5.00
05RFZ Filip Zadina 3.00 8.00
05RJF Joel Farabee 3.00 8.00
05RJH Jack Hughes 10.00 25.00
05RKK Kaapo Kakko 5.00 12.00
05RMF Morgan Frost 3.00 8.00
05RMJ Max Jones 2.00 5.00
05RNG Nikita Gusev 3.00 8.00
05RNS Nick Suzuki 8.00 20.00
05RPM Philippe Myers 1.50 4.00
05RQH Quinn Hughes 10.00 25.00
05RRP Ryan Poehling 3.00 8.00
05RTH Taro Hirose 2.00 5.00
05RVA Vitaly Abramov 2.00 5.00

2019-20 Exquisite Collection '09-10 Rookie Tribute Autographs

09TCG Cody Glass 25.00 60.00
09TCM Cale Makar 100.00 250.00
09TDF Dante Fabbro 15.00 40.00
09TEB Erik Brannstrom 25.00 60.00
09TFZ Filip Zadina 30.00 80.00
09TJH Jack Hughes 80.00 200.00
09TKD Kirby Dach 60.00 150.00
09TQH Quinn Hughes 80.00 200.00
09TRP Ryan Poehling 15.00 40.00

2019-20 Exquisite Collection '09-10 Rookie Tribute Autographs Gold

*GOLD: .75X TO 2X BASIC
09TJH Jack Hughes 200.00 500.00

2019-20 Exquisite Collection Materials

EMAB Aleksander Barkov/49 8.00 20.00
EMAM Auston Matthews/25 20.00 50.00
EMBB Ben Bishop/49 4.00 10.00
EMBH Braden Holtby/49 6.00 15.00
EMBW Blake Wheeler/49 5.00 12.00
EMCA Cam Atkinson/49 5.00 12.00
EMCG Claude Giroux/49 5.00 12.00
EMCM Connor McDavid/25 25.00 60.00
EMCP Carey Price/49 10.00 25.00
EMDL Dylan Larkin/49 6.00 15.00
EMDP David Pastrnak/49 12.00 30.00
EMEP Elias Pettersson/49 8.00 20.00
EMFA Frederik Andersen/49 6.00 15.00
EMJG Johnny Gaudreau/49 8.00 20.00
EMNK Nikita Kucherov/25 10.00 25.00
EMPK Patrick Kane/25 10.00 25.00
EMSC Sidney Crosby/25 20.00 50.00
EMSJ Seth Jones/49 5.00 12.00
EMSS Steven Stamkos/49 10.00 25.00
EMVT Vladimir Tarasenko/49 6.00 15.00

2019-20 Exquisite Collection Material Signatures

EMSAB Aleksander Barkov/65 30.00 80.00
EMSAD Alex DeBrincat/65 25.00 60.00
EMSJM Jonathan Marchessault/65 25.00 60.00
EMSLD Leon Draisaitl/25 200.00 500.00
EMSTC Thomas Chabot/65 15.00 40.00

2019-20 Exquisite Collection Platinum Rookie Signatures

R1 Ilya Mikheyev/199 12.00 30.00
R2 Oliver Wahlstrom/199 12.00 30.00
R6 Noah Dobson/199 20.00 50.00
R7 Adam Fox/199 20.00 50.00
R9 Barrett Hayton/199 15.00 40.00
R10 Cody Glass/199 12.00 30.00
R11 Nikita Gusev/199 12.00 30.00
R12 Nick Suzuki/199 30.00 80.00
R15 Alexandre Texier/199 8.00 20.00
R16 Erik Brannstrom/199 8.00 20.00
R18 Dante Fabbro/199 8.00 20.00
R19 Philippe Myers/199 6.00 15.00
R20 Karson Kuhlman/199 8.00 20.00
R22 Quinn Hughes/99 60.00 150.00
R23 Cale Makar/99 80.00 200.00
R25 Jack Hughes/99 60.00 150.00

2019-20 Exquisite Collection Platinum Rookie Signatures Gold Foil

*GOLD: .6X TO 1.5X BASIC
R6 Noah Dobson 15.00 40.00
R10 Cody Glass 30.00 80.00
R12 Nick Suzuki 100.00 250.00
R15 Alexandre Texier 15.00 40.00
R22 Quinn Hughes 100.00 250.00
R23 Cale Makar 200.00 500.00

2019-20 Exquisite Collection Platinum Rookies

R1 Ilya Mikheyev/399 5.00 12.00
R2 Oliver Wahlstrom/399 5.00 12.00
R3 Joel Farabee/399 5.00 12.00
R4 Adam Boqvist/399 3.00 8.00
R5 Max Jones/399 3.00 8.00
R6 Noah Dobson/399 8.00 20.00
R7 Adam Fox/399 8.00 20.00
R8 Filip Zadina/399 5.00 12.00
R9 Barrett Hayton/399 6.00 15.00
R10 Cody Glass/399 5.00 12.00
R11 Nikita Gusev/399 5.00 12.00
R12 Nick Suzuki/399 12.00 30.00
R13 Taro Hirose/399 3.00 8.00
R14 Ryan Poehling/399 5.00 12.00
R15 Alexandre Texier/399 3.00 8.00
R16 Erik Brannstrom/399 3.00 8.00
R17 Victor Olofsson/399 6.00 15.00
R18 Dante Fabbro/399 3.00 8.00
R19 Philippe Myers/399 2.50 6.00
R20 Karson Kuhlman/399 3.00 8.00
R21 Kirby Dach/299 6.00 15.00
R22 Quinn Hughes/299 15.00 40.00
R23 Cale Makar/299 15.00 40.00
R24 Kaapo Kakko/299 5.00 12.00
R25 Jack Hughes/299 15.00 40.00

2019-20 Exquisite Collection Retro Rookie Draft Day

RVDJS Joe Sakic 6.00 15.00
RVDKT Keith Tkachuk 3.00 8.00
RVDMB Martin Brodeur 8.00 20.00
RVDPF Peter Forsberg 6.00 15.00
RVDPT Pierre Turgeon 2.50 6.00

2019-20 Exquisite Collection Rookie Draft Day

RDDCM Cale Makar 15.00 40.00
RDDJH Jack Hughes 15.00 40.00
RDDKK Kaapo Kakko 5.00 12.00
RDDQH Quinn Hughes 15.00 40.00

2019-20 Exquisite Collection Rookie Patches

*GOLD: .75X TO 2X BASIC
RPBH Barrett Hayton/299 10.00 25.00
RPCG Cody Glass/99 8.00 20.00
RPCM Cale Makar/99 25.00 60.00
RPDF Dante Fabbro/299 5.00 12.00
RPEB Erik Brannstrom/299 5.00 12.00
RPFZ Filip Zadina/299 8.00 20.00
RPJF Joel Farabee/299 8.00 20.00
RPJH Jack Hughes/99 25.00 60.00
RPMF Morgan Frost/299 8.00 20.00
RPMJ Max Jones/299 5.00 12.00
RPQH Quinn Hughes/99 30.00 80.00
RPRP Ryan Poehling/299 8.00 20.00
RPVA Vitaly Abramov/299 5.00 12.00

2019-20 Exquisite Collection Rookies

*GOLD: .75X TO 2X BASIC
RBH Barrett Hayton/299 5.00 12.00
RCG Cody Glass/299 4.00 10.00
RCM Cale Makar/199 12.00 30.00
RDF Dante Fabbro/299 2.50 6.00
REB Erik Brannstrom/299 2.50 6.00
RFZ Filip Zadina/299 4.00 10.00
RJF Joel Farabee/299 4.00 10.00
RJH Jack Hughes/199 12.00 30.00
RKD Kirby Dach/299 5.00 12.00
RKK Kaapo Kakko/199 4.00 10.00
RMF Morgan Frost/299 4.00 10.00
RMJ Max Jones/299 2.50 6.00
RND Noah Dobson/299 6.00 15.00
RNG Nikita Gusev/299 4.00 10.00
RNS Nick Suzuki/299 10.00 25.00
RQH Quinn Hughes/199 12.00 30.00
RRP Ryan Poehling/199 4.00 10.00
RTH Taro Hirose/299 2.50 6.00

2019-20 Exquisite Collection Signatures

ESBH Bobby Hull/25 15.00 40.00
ESBN Bernie Nicholls/99 4.00 10.00
ESJI Jarome Iginla/25 15.00 40.00
ESJT Joe Thornton/25 15.00 40.00
ESKM Kirk McLean/99 15.00 40.00
ESMM Mark Messier/25 40.00 100.00

2021-22 Exquisite Collection '07-08 Retro

*GOLD/99: .75X TO 2X BASIC INSERTS
*SPECTRUM/25: 3X TO 8X BASIC INSERTS
07VAM Auston Matthews 3.00 8.00
07VAO Alex Ovechkin 3.00 8.00
07VAP Artemi Panarin 1.50 4.00
07VCM Connor McDavid 4.00 10.00
07VCP Carey Price 1.50 4.00
07VDP David Pastrnak 2.00 5.00
07VKK Kirill Kaprizov 2.50 6.00
07VNM Nathan MacKinnon 3.00 8.00
07VPK Patrick Kane 1.50 4.00
07VSC Sidney Crosby 3.00 8.00

2021-22 Exquisite Collection '07-08 Retro Rookies

*GOLD/25: .75X TO 2X BASIC INSERTS
07RCC Cole Caufield 8.00 20.00
07RCP Cole Perfetti 4.00 10.00
07RCY Cam York 2.00 5.00
07RGD Grigori Denisenko 2.50 6.00
07RJD Jamie Drysdale 3.00 8.00
07RJS Jeremy Swayman 6.00 15.00
07RLR Lucas Raymond 6.00 15.00
07RMM Mason McTavish 4.00 10.00
07RMS Moritz Seider 5.00 12.00
07RQB Quinton Byfield 5.00 12.00
07RSK Spencer Knight 3.00 8.00
07RSP Shane Pinto 3.00 8.00
07RTZ Trevor Zegras 4.00 10.00
07RVP Vasily Podkolzin 2.50 6.00

2021-22 Exquisite Collection '07-08 Retro Rookies Gold Spectrum

*SPECTRUM/25: 1.5X TO 4X BASIC INSERTS
07RMS Moritz Seider 60.00 150.00

2021-22 Exquisite Collection Extra Exquisite Jerseys

ECEAS Andrei Svechnikov/99 5.00 12.00
ECECO Sean Couturier/99 3.00 8.00
ECEDL Dylan Larkin/99 5.00 12.00
ECEGU Jake Guentzel/99 6.00 15.00
ECEIS Igor Shesterkin/99 8.00 20.00
ECELC Logan Couture/99 5.00 12.00
ECEMC Charlie McAvoy/99 5.00 12.00
ECEMP Max Pacioretty/99 4.00 10.00
ECEMR Mikko Rantanen/99 10.00 25.00
ECENK Nikita Kucherov/99 8.00 20.00
ECERJ Roman Josi/99 5.00 12.00
ECETS Tyler Seguin/99 5.00 12.00
ECEZW Zach Werenski/99 6.00 15.00

2021-22 Exquisite Collection Extra Exquisite Rookie Jerseys

ECERAN Alex Newhook 4.00 10.00
ECERCC Cole Caufield 15.00 40.00
ECERCY Cam York 4.00 10.00
ECERDF David Farrance 4.00 10.00
ECERJD Jamie Drysdale 6.00 15.00
ECERJS Jeremy Swayman 8.00 20.00
ECERQB Quinton Byfield 10.00 25.00
ECERSK Spencer Knight 8.00 20.00
ECERTZ Trevor Zegras 8.00 20.00
ECERUL Ukko-Pekka Luukkonen 6.00 15.00

2021-22 Exquisite Collection Materials

EMAK Anze Kopitar/49 10.00 25.00
EMAV Andrei Vasilevskiy/49 10.00 25.00
EMBB Brock Boeser/49 8.00 20.00
EMBM Brad Marchand/49 12.00 30.00
EMCH Connor Hellebuyck/49 12.00 30.00
EMEM Evgeni Malkin/49 12.00 30.00
EMJE Jack Eichel/49 10.00 25.00
EMJH Jonathan Huberdeau/49 8.00 20.00
EMVH Victor Hedman/49 8.00 20.00

2021-22 Exquisite Collection Moments

ECMAL Alexis Lafreniere 5.00 12.00
ECMAM Auston Matthews 12.00 30.00
ECMAO Alex Ovechkin 12.00 30.00
ECMAV Andrei Vasilevskiy 5.00 12.00
ECMBO Bobby Orr 12.00 30.00
ECMCC Cole Caufield 12.00 30.00
ECMCM Connor McDavid 15.00 40.00
ECMEL Eric Lindros 5.00 12.00
ECMJS Jeremy Swayman 10.00 25.00
ECMKK Kirill Kaprizov 10.00 25.00
ECMKR Seattle Kraken 20.00 50.00
ECMMM Mike Modano 5.00 12.00
ECMPK Patrick Kane 6.00 15.00
ECMQB Quinton Byfield 8.00 20.00
ECMRO Ryan O'Reilly 3.00 8.00
ECMSC Sidney Crosby 12.00 30.00
ECMSK Spencer Knight 6.00 15.00
ECMSY Steve Yzerman 8.00 20.00
ECMTZ Trevor Zegras 6.00 15.00
ECMWG Wayne Gretzky 20.00 50.00

2021-22 Exquisite Collection Rookie Draft Day

RDDAN Alex Newhook 4.00 10.00
RDDCC Cole Caufield 25.00 60.00
RDDCY Cam York 2.50 6.00
RDDMS Moritz Seider 30.00 80.00
RDDSK Spencer Knight 5.00 12.00
RDDTZ Trevor Zegras 20.00 50.00
RDDVP Vasily Podkolzin 3.00 8.00

2021-22 Exquisite Collection Rookie Draft Day Gold

*GOLD/99: 1X TO 2.5X BASIC INSERTS
RDDCC Cole Caufield 40.00 100.00
RDDMS Moritz Seider 60.00 150.00

2021-22 Exquisite Collection Rookie Patch

RAN Alex Newhook 15.00 40.00
RCC Cole Caufield 125.00 300.00
RCP Cole Perfetti 20.00 50.00
RCY Cam York 10.00 25.00
RJD Jamie Drysdale 15.00 40.00
RJS Jeremy Swayman 30.00 80.00
RLR Lucas Raymond 30.00 80.00
RMS Moritz Seider 150.00 400.00
RNL Nils Lundkvist 10.00 25.00
RPT Philip Tomasino 12.00 30.00
RQB Quinton Byfield 25.00 60.00
RRC Ross Colton 12.00 30.00
RSK Spencer Knight 20.00 50.00
RSP Shane Pinto 15.00 40.00
RTZ Trevor Zegras 60.00 150.00
RUP Ukko-Pekka Luukkonen 15.00 40.00
RWK Wyatt Kalynuk 10.00 25.00

2021-22 Exquisite Collection Rookie Patch Gold

*GOLD/25: .6X TO 1.5X BASIC INSERTS
RCC Cole Caufield 200.00 500.00
RLR Lucas Raymond 125.00 300.00
RMS Moritz Seider 200.00 500.00

2021-22 Exquisite Collection Rookies

*GOLD/25: 2.5X TO 6X BASIC INSERTS
RAN Alex Newhook 6.00 15.00
RCC Cole Caufield 15.00 40.00
RCP Cole Perfetti 8.00 20.00
RCY Cam York 4.00 10.00
RJD Jamie Drysdale 6.00 15.00
RJS Jeremy Swayman 12.00 30.00
RLR Lucas Raymond 12.00 30.00
RMS Moritz Seider 10.00 25.00
RNL Nils Lundkvist 3.00 8.00
RPT Philip Tomasino 5.00 12.00
RQB Quinton Byfield 10.00 25.00
RRC Ross Colton 6.00 15.00
RSK Spencer Knight 8.00 20.00
RSP Shane Pinto 6.00 15.00
RTZ Trevor Zegras 6.00 15.00
RUP Ukko-Pekka Luukkonen 6.00 15.00
RVP Vasily Podkolzin 5.00 12.00
RWK Wyatt Kalynuk 4.00 10.00

2021-22 Exquisite Collection Rookies Gold

*GOLD/99: .75X TO 2X BASIC INSERTS
RCC Cole Caufield 100.00 250.00
RMS Moritz Seider 80.00 200.00
RTZ Trevor Zegras 125.00 300.00

2024-25 Exquisite Collection

RBB Brendan Brisson RC 2.50 6.00
RBL Brad Lambert RC 2.50 6.00
RCG Cutter Gauthier RC 5.00 12.00
RFN Frank Nazar RC 6.00 15.00
RGE Conor Geekie RC 4.00 10.00
RJD Josh Doan RC 3.00 8.00
RJW Jesper Wallstedt RC 5.00 12.00
RLH Lane Hutson RC 25.00 60.00
RLO Liam Ohgren RC 4.00 10.00
RLS Logan Stankoven RC 6.00 15.00
RMB Mavrik Bourque RC 4.00 10.00
RMC Macklin Celebrini RC 30.00 80.00
RMM Matvei Michkov RC 30.00 80.00
ROZ Olen Zellweger RC 4.00 10.00
RSM Shakir Mukhamadullin RC 2.50 6.00
RWS Will Smith RC 6.00 15.00
RZB Zachary Bolduc RC 4.00 10.00
RZO Zack Ostapchuk RC 2.00 5.00
VCB Connor Bedard 5.00 12.00
VCM Connor McDavid 8.00 20.00
VMM Mitch Marner 2.50 6.00
VNK Nikita Kucherov 3.00 8.00
VNM Nathan MacKinnon 6.00 15.00
VNS Nick Suzuki 3.00 8.00

2024-25 Exquisite Collection Gold

*GOLD/99: .5X TO 1.2X BASIC
RLH Lane Hutson 40.00 100.00
RMC Macklin Celebrini 60.00 150.00
RMM Matvei Michkov 50.00 125.00
RWS Will Smith 15.00 40.00
VCB Connor Bedard 15.00 40.00

2024-25 Exquisite Collection Gold Spectrum

*GOLD SPEC/25: 1.5X TO 4X BASIC
RLH Lane Hutson 125.00 300.00
RMC Macklin Celebrini 125.00 300.00
RMM Matvei Michkov 80.00 200.00
RWS Will Smith 40.00 100.00
VCB Connor Bedard 80.00 200.00

2024-25 Exquisite Collection Dual Swatch Rookies

*GOLD/25: .6X TO 1.5X BASIC
EDSBL Brad Lambert 6.00 15.00
EDSBO Brennan Othmann 10.00 25.00
EDSCG Cutter Gauthier 12.00 30.00
EDSFN Frank Nazar 15.00 40.00
EDSJD Josh Doan 10.00 25.00
EDSJW Jesper Wallstedt 12.00 30.00
EDSLO Liam Ohgren 10.00 25.00
EDSLS Logan Stankoven 12.00 30.00
EDSMC Macklin Celebrini 80.00 200.00
EDSWS Will Smith 15.00 40.00

2024-25 Exquisite Collection Extra Exquisite Jerseys

ECEAP Alex Pietrangelo/99 4.00 10.00
ECEBH Brandon Hagel/99 4.00 10.00
ECECG Claude Giroux/99 5.00 12.00
ECECM Cale Makar/99 12.00 30.00
ECECV Carter Verhaeghe/99 5.00 12.00
ECEDS Dylan Strome/99 6.00 15.00
ECEEK Evander Kane/99 5.00 12.00
ECEFP Felix Potvin/99 8.00 20.00
ECEJT Joe Thornton/49 8.00 20.00
ECEKM Kirill Marchenko/99 6.00 15.00
ECEMS Moritz Seider/99 6.00 15.00
ECEQB Quinton Byfield/99 6.00 15.00
ECERB Ray Bourque/25 15.00 40.00
ECERD Rasmus Dahlin/99 6.00 15.00
ECESJ Seth Jarvis/99 6.00 15.00
ECEST Martin St. Louis/25 12.00 30.00
ECETS Tyler Seguin/99 6.00 15.00
ECEVT Vincent Trocheck/99 5.00 12.00

2024-25 Exquisite Collection Extra Exquisite Rookie Jerseys

ECERBL Brad Lambert 3.00 8.00
ECERCG Cutter Gauthier 6.00 15.00
ECERFN Frank Nazar 8.00 20.00
ECERJD Josh Doan 5.00 12.00
ECERLO Liam Ohgren 5.00 12.00
ECERLS Logan Stankoven 6.00 15.00
ECERMC Macklin Celebrini 25.00 60.00
ECERMM Matvei Michkov 10.00 25.00
ECERWS Will Smith 8.00 20.00

2024-25 Exquisite Collection Materials

EMAO Alex Ovechkin/25 50.00 125.00
EMAP Artemi Panarin/49 12.00 30.00
EMBH Bo Horvat/49 8.00 20.00
EMCB Connor Bedard/49 125.00 300.00
EMCC Cole Caufield/49 40.00 100.00
EMCM Connor McDavid/49 40.00 100.00
EMJH Jack Hughes/49 15.00 40.00
EMJR Jason Robertson/49 10.00 25.00
EMNM Nathan MacKinnon/49 25.00 60.00
EMSB Sergei Bobrovsky/49 10.00 25.00
EMSC Sidney Crosby/25 30.00 80.00

2024-25 Exquisite Collection Moments

*GOLD/49: .6X TO 1.5X BASIC
MAK Anze Kopitar 4.00 10.00
MAM Auston Matthews 10.00 25.00
MAO Alex Ovechkin 10.00 25.00
MJT John Tavares 4.00 10.00
MKL Kris Letang 3.00 8.00
MMF Marc-Andre Fleury 8.00 20.00
MRO Ryan O'Reilly 2.50 6.00
MSC Sidney Crosby 10.00 25.00

2024-25 Exquisite Collection Moments Gold Spectrum

*GOLD SPEC/25: .8X TO 2X BASIC
MMF Marc-Andre Fleury 40.00 100.00

2024-25 Exquisite Collection Rookie Draft Day

RDDBL Brad Lambert 3.00 8.00
RDDCG Cutter Gauthier 6.00 15.00
RDDFN Frank Nazar 8.00 20.00
RDDJD Josh Doan 5.00 12.00
RDDLO Liam Ohgren 5.00 12.00
RDDLS Logan Stankoven 6.00 15.00
RDDMC Macklin Celebrini 30.00 80.00
RDDMM Matvei Michkov 30.00 80.00
RDDWS Will Smith 8.00 20.00

2024-25 Exquisite Collection Rookie Draft Day Gold

*GOLD/75: .6X TO 1.5X BASIC
RDDMC Macklin Celebrini 80.00 200.00
RDDMM Matvei Michkov 60.00 150.00
RDDWS Will Smith 20.00 50.00

2024-25 Exquisite Collection Rookie Patch

RPBB Brendan Brisson 5.00 12.00
RPBO Brennan Othmann 6.00 15.00
RPCG Cutter Gauthier 10.00 25.00
RPFN Frank Nazar 12.00 30.00
RPGB Gavin Brindley 4.00 10.00
RPJD Josh Doan 6.00 15.00
RPJW Jesper Wallstedt 10.00 25.00
RPLH Lane Hutson 30.00 80.00
RPLO Liam Ohgren 8.00 20.00
RPLS Logan Stankoven 10.00 25.00
RPMC Macklin Celebrini 125.00 300.00
RPOZ Olen Zellweger 8.00 20.00
RPWS Will Smith 10.00 25.00
RPZB Zachary Bolduc 6.00 15.00

2024-25 Exquisite Collection Rookie Patch Gold

*GOLD/25: .8X TO 2X BASIC
RPCG Cutter Gauthier 30.00 80.00
RPLH Lane Hutson 125.00 300.00

2024-25 Exquisite Collection Tandems

ETAS S.Aho/A.Svechnikov 3.00 8.00
ETBK M.Boldy/K.Kaprizov 6.00 15.00
ETBP M.Bossy/D.Potvin 2.00 5.00
ETBT M.Tkachuk/A.Barkov 4.00 10.00
ETEO B.Orr/P.Esposito 8.00 20.00
ETGM W.Gretzky/M.Messier 12.00 30.00
ETHB B.Horvat/M.Barzal 2.50 6.00
ETHL G.Howe/T.Lindsay 6.00 15.00
ETKT J.Kyrou/R.Thomas 2.00 5.00
ETLM K.Letang/E.Malkin 4.00 10.00
ETMB M.Modano/E.Belfour 3.00 8.00
ETMM A.Matthews/M.Marner 8.00 20.00
ETMR M.Rantanen/N.MacKinnon 8.00 20.00
ETPH R.Hextall/B.Propp 2.00 5.00
ETRB R.Blake/L.Robitaille 2.00 5.00
ETRS J.Sakic/P.Roy 5.00 12.00
ETSE M.Stone/J.Eichel 3.00 8.00
ETTP T.Thompson/J.Peterka 2.50 6.00
ETYL S.Yzerman/N.Lidstrom 5.00 12.00

2024-25 Exquisite Collection Tandems Gold

*GOLD/99: .8X TO 2X BASIC
ETRS J.Sakic/P.Roy 15.00 40.00

2024-25 Exquisite Collection Tandems Silver Spectrum

*SILVER/25: 1.2X TO 3X BASIC
ETBP M.Bossy/D.Potvin 15.00 40.00
ETRS J.Sakic/P.Roy 30.00 80.00

1995-96 Fanfest Phil Esposito

COMPLETE SET (5) 8.00 20.00
COMMON ESPO (1-5) 2.50 6.00

2008-09 Fathead Tradeables

COMPLETE SET (30) 40.00 100.00
1 Ales Hemsky .75 2.00
2 Alexander Ovechkin 4.00 10.00
3 Anze Kopitar 1.50 4.00
4 Carey Price 2.00 5.00
5 Daniel Alfredsson 1.00 2.50
6 Eric Staal 1.25 3.00
7 Henrik Lundqvist 2.50 6.00
8 Henrik Zetterberg 1.25 3.00
9 Ilya Kovalchuk 1.00 2.50
10 Jarome Iginla 1.25 3.00
11 Jason Arnott .75 2.00
12 Joe Sakic 2.00 5.00
13 Joe Thornton 1.50 4.00
14 Jonathan Toews 1.50 4.00
15 Luke Schenn 1.25 3.00
16 Martin Brodeur 2.50 6.00
17 Mike Modano 1.50 4.00
18 Mike Richards .75 2.00
19 Mikko Koivu .75 2.00
20 Nathan Horton .75 2.00
21 Paul Kariya 1.00 2.50
22 Rick DiPietro .75 2.00
23 Rick Nash 1.00 2.50
24 Roberto Luongo 1.50 4.00
25 Ryan Getzlaf 1.00 2.50
26 Ryan Miller 1.00 2.50
27 Shane Doan .75 2.00
28 Sidney Crosby 4.00 10.00
29 Vincent Lecavalier 1.00 2.50
30 Zdeno Chara 1.00 2.50

2009-10 Fathead Tradeables

1 Sidney Crosby 3.00 8.00
2 Nicklas Lidstrom .50 1.25
3 Alex Ovechkin 3.00 8.00
4 John Tavares 3.00 8.00
5 Henrik Lundqvist 2.00 5.00
6 Jarome Iginla 1.25 3.00
7 Ilya Kovalchuk .75 2.00
8 Henrik Sedin 1.00 2.50
9 Martin Brodeur 2.00 5.00
10 Corey Perry 1.25 3.00
11 Patrick Marleau .75 2.00
12 Steven Stamkos 1.50 4.00
13 Sam Gagner .50 1.25
14 Jonas Gustavsson 1.00 2.50
15 Shea Weber .60 1.50
16 Jeff Carter .60 1.50
17 Steve Mason .60 1.50
18 Scott Gomez .60 1.50
19 Martin Havlat .60 1.50
20 Roberto Luongo 1.25 3.00
21 Jason Spezza .75 2.00
22 Dion Phaneuf .60 1.50
23 Evgeni Malkin 1.50 4.00
24 Marian Hossa .75 2.00
25 Martin St. Louis .75 2.00
26 Milan Lucic .60 1.50
27 Zach Parise .75 2.00
28 Thomas Vanek .60 1.50
29 Marian Gaborik .75 2.00
30 Nathan Horton .75 2.00
31 Phil Kessel .75 2.00
32 Shane Doan .60 1.50
33 Niklas Backstrom .75 2.00
34 Mike Cammalleri .60 1.50
35 Rick Nash .75 2.00
36 Tim Thomas .75 2.00
37 Teemu Selanne 1.50 4.00
38 Patrick Kane 1.50 4.00
39 Dustin Penner .50 1.25
40 Erik Johnson .50 1.25
41 Matt Duchene 1.50 4.00
42 Cam Ward .50 1.25
43 Drew Doughty 1.00 2.50
44 Mike Green .50 1.25
45 Mike Fisher .50 1.25
46 Mike Richards .60 1.50
47 Derek Roy .50 1.25
48 Dany Heatley .60 1.50
49 Pavel Datsyuk 1.25 3.00
50 Brenden Morrow .60 1.50

2010-11 Fathead Tradeables

1 Jonathan Toews 1.50 4.00
2 Sidney Crosby 4.00 10.00
3 Alex Ovechkin 4.00 10.00
4 Ilya Kovalchuk 1.00 2.50
5 John Tavares 1.50 4.00
6 Miikka Kiprusoff 1.00 2.50
7 Milan Lucic 1.00 2.50
8 Dion Phaneuf .75 2.00
9 Shea Weber .75 2.00
10 Ryan Getzlaf 1.00 2.50
11 Joe Thornton 1.50 4.00
12 Phil Kessel 1.00 2.50
13 Henrik Zetterberg 1.25 3.00
14 Roberto Luongo 1.50 4.00
15 Brian Gionta .60 1.50
16 Mike Richards .75 2.00
17 Brad Richards 1.00 2.50
18 Pavel Datsyuk 1.50 4.00
19 Mikko Koivu 1.00 2.50
20 Henrik Sedin 1.25 3.00
21 Henrik Lundqvist 2.50 6.00
22 Jarome Iginla 1.25 3.00
23 Evgeni Malkin 2.00 5.00
24 Patrick Kane 2.00 5.00
25 Steven Stamkos 2.00 5.00
26 Zdeno Chara .75 2.00
27 Martin Brodeur 2.50 6.00
28 Thomas Vanek .75 2.00
29 Marian Gaborik 1.00 2.50
30 Stephen Weiss .75 2.00
31 Jonas Gustavsson 1.25 3.00
32 Shane Doan .75 2.00
33 Niklas Backstrom 1.00 2.50
34 Michael Cammalleri 1.00 2.50
35 Rick Nash 1.00 2.50
36 Patrice Bergeron 1.25 3.00
37 Evander Kane 1.00 2.50
38 Duncan Keith .75 2.00
39 Ales Hemsky .75 2.00
40 T.J. Oshie 1.00 2.50
41 Paul Stastny .75 2.00
42 Eric Staal 1.25 3.00
43 Drew Doughty 1.25 3.00
44 Nicklas Backstrom 1.00 2.50
45 Daniel Alfredsson 1.00 2.50
46 Jeff Carter .75 2.00
47 Ryan Miller 1.00 2.50
48 Marc-Andre Fleury 2.00 5.00
49 Taylor Hall 2.00 5.00
50 Winter Classic Logo .75 2.00

2013-14 Fathead Tradeables

COMPLETE SET (50) 20.00 50.00
3 Steven Stamkos 1.25 3.00
4 Henrik Sedin .75 2.00
5 Patrice Bergeron .75 2.00
6 Pekka Rinne .60 1.50
10 Ilya Kovalchuk .60 1.50
11 Jimmy Howard .75 2.00
12 Jarome Iginla .75 2.00
14 David Backes .40 1.00
15 Taylor Hall .60 1.50
17 Corey Perry 1.00 2.50
23 Dion Phaneuf .50 1.25
25 Zdeno Chara .60 1.50
27 Daniel Sedin .75 2.00
28 Brad Richards .60 1.50
29 Loui Eriksson .40 1.00
32 Andrew Ladd .40 1.00
34 Eric Staal .75 2.00
35 Jordan Eberle .60 1.50
38 Shane Doan .50 1.25
40 Tomas Fleischmann .40 1.00
42 Shea Weber .50 1.25
43 Pavel Datsyuk 1.00 2.50
48 Phil Kessel .60 1.50
AK Anze Kopitar 1.00 2.50
AO Alex Ovechkin 2.50 6.00
CG Claude Giroux .60 1.50
CP Carey Price 1.25 3.00
DB Danny Briere .60 1.50
DB Dustin Brown .60 1.50
EK Erik Karlsson .75 2.00
EM Evgeni Malkin 1.25 3.00
GL Gabriel Landeskog .75 2.00
HL Henrik Lundqvist 1.50 4.00
HZ Henrik Zetterberg .75 2.00
JJ Jack Johnson .40 1.00
JN James Neal .40 1.00
JQ Jonathan Quick .75 2.00
JT John Tavares 1.00 2.50
LC Logan Couture .75 2.00
MB Martin Brodeur 1.50 4.00
MK Mikko Koivu .50 1.25
PK Patrick Kane 1.25 3.00
PS Patrick Sharp .60 1.50
RM Ryan Miller .60 1.50
SC Sidney Crosby 2.50 6.00
TO T.J. Oshie .60 1.50
TS Tyler Seguin .75 2.00
JTO Johnathan Toews 1.00 2.50
MSL Martin St. Louis .60 1.50
PKS P.K. Subban .75 2.00

2014-15 Fathead Tradeables

1 Patrick Kane .75 2.00
2 Alex Ovechkin 1.50 4.00
3 Sergei Bobrovsky .60 1.50
4 P.K. Subban .50 1.25
5 Sidney Crosby 1.50 4.00
6 Jonathan Toews .60 1.50
7 Martin St. Louis .40 1.00
8 Patrice Bergeron .50 1.25
9 John Tavares .60 1.50
10 Henrik Lundqvist 1.00 2.50
11 Ryan Suter .30 .75
12 Pavel Datsyuk .60 1.50
13 Scott Hartnell .25 .60
14 Corey Perry .60 1.50
15 Marian Gaborik .40 1.00
16 Erik Karlsson .50 1.25
17 Joffrey Lupul .25 .60
18 Shea Weber .30 .75
19 Eric Staal .50 1.25
20 Jonathan Huberdeau .50 1.25
21 Claude Giroux .40 1.00
22 Logan Couture .50 1.25

23 Henrik Sedin .50 1.25
24 Dustin Brown .40 1.00
25 Patrick Sharp .40 1.00
26 Evgeni Malkin .75 2.00
27 Taylor Hall .40 1.00
28 Martin Brodeur 1.00 2.50
29 James Neal .25 .60
30 Steven Stamkos .75 2.00
31 Daniel Sedin .50 1.25
32 Zdeno Chara .40 1.00
33 Joe Thornton .60 1.50
34 Henrik Zetterberg .50 1.25
35 Carey Price .75 2.00
36 Thomas Vanek .30 .75
37 Andrew Ladd .25 .60
38 Jamie Benn .40 1.00
39 Ryan Getzlaf .40 1.00
40 Jordan Staal .30 .75
41 Zach Parise .40 1.00
42 Rick Nash .40 1.00
43 David Backes .25 .60
44 Phil Kessel .40 1.00
45 Nicklas Backstrom .40 1.00
46 Matt Duchene .40 1.00
47 Mike Cammalleri .30 .75
48 Jonathan Quick .50 1.25
49 Jordan Eberle .40 1.00
50 Shane Doan .30 .75

1994-95 Finest

1 Peter Forsberg .75 2.00
2 Oleg Tverdovsky .30 .75
3 Radek Bonk RC .25 .60
4 Brian Rolston .30 .75
5 Kenny Jonsson UER .40 1.00
6 Patrik Juhlin RC .25 .60
7 Paul Kariya .40 1.00
8 Janne Laukkanen .30 .75
9 Brett Lindros .25 .60
10 Andrei Nikolishin .25 .60
11 Jeff Friesen .25 .60
12 Jamie Storr .30 .75
13 Chris Therien .25 .60
14 Alexander Cherbayev .25 .60
15 Kevin Brown RC .40 1.00
16 Mark Messier .75 2.00
17 Kevin Hatcher .25 .60
18 Scott Stevens .40 1.00
19 Keith Tkachuk .40 1.00
20 Guy Hebert .30 .75
21 Jason Arnott .30 .75
22 Cam Neely .40 1.00
23 Adam Graves .25 .60
24 Pavel Bure .40 1.00
25 Mark Tinordi .25 .60
26 Felix Potvin .60 1.50
27 Nikolai Khabibulin .30 .75
28 Theo Fleury .40 1.00
29 Curtis Joseph .50 1.25
30 Patrick Roy 1.00 2.50
31 Adam Deadmarsh .25 .60
32 Pat Falloon .25 .60
33 Jaromir Jagr 1.25 3.00
34 Chris Chelios .40 1.00
35 Ray Bourque .60 1.50
36 Mike Vernon .30 .75
37 Steve Thomas .25 .60
38 Eric Lindros .60 1.50
39 Dave Andreychuk .40 1.00
40 John Vanbiesbrouck .40 1.00
41 Wayne Gretzky 2.50 6.00
42 Brett Hull .75 2.00
43 Dominik Hasek .60 1.50
44 Kirk Muller .25 .60
45 Rob Blake .40 1.00
46 Viktor Kozlov .25 .60
47 Todd Harvey .25 .60
48 Valeri Bure .25 .60
49 Brian Leetch .30 .75
50 Ray Sheppard .30 .75
51 Ed Belfour .50 1.25
52 Rick Tocchet .30 .75
53 Daren Puppa .30 .75
54 Russ Courtnall .25 .60
55 Jason Allison .30 .75
56 Alexei Yashin UER .40 1.00
57 Sandis Ozolinsh .25 .60
58 Chris Gratton .25 .60
59 Mike Peca .30 .75
60 Glen Wesley .25 .60
61 Kirk McLean .30 .75
62 Chris Pronger .40 1.00
63 Steve Larmer .30 .75
64 Michal Grosek RC .25 .60
65 Sergei Fedorov .60 1.50
66 Stu Barnes .25 .60
67 Adam Oates .40 1.00
68 Paul Coffey UER .40 1.00
69 Joe Sakic .75 2.00
70 Pat LaFontaine .40 1.00
71 Martin Brodeur 1.00 2.50
72 Bob Corkum .25 .60
73 Jeremy Roenick .60 1.50
74 Shayne Corson .30 .75
75 German Titov .25 .60
76 Teemu Selanne .75 2.00
77 Eric Fichaud RC .40 1.00
78 Pierre Turgeon .30 .75
79 Alexander Selivanov RC .30 .75
80 Kevin Stevens .30 .75
81 Jari Kurri .30 .75
82 Gary Roberts .25 .60
83 Geoff Courtnall .25 .60
84 Steve Yzerman 1.00 2.50
85 Rod Brind'Amour .30 .75
86 Mike Richter .40 1.00
87 Bernie Nicholls .30 .75
88 Alexandre Daigle .25 .60
89 Luc Robitaille .40 1.00
90 John MacLean .30 .75
91 Phil Housley .30 .75
92 Brendan Shanahan .40 1.00
93 Joe Juneau .30 .75
94 Stephane Richer .30 .75
95 Blaine Lacher RC .30 .75
96 Mike Gartner .50 1.25
97 Rene Corbet .25 .60
98 Vincent Damphousse .30 .75
99 Alexander Mogilny UER .30 .75
100 Doug Gilmour .50 1.25
101 Petr Nedved .30 .75
102 Alexei Zhamnov .30 .75
103 Wendel Clark .60 1.50
104 Arturs Irbe .30 .75
105 Brian Bellows .30 .75
106 Mike Modano .60 1.50
107 Ravil Gusmanov RC .25 .60
108 Geoff Sanderson .30 .75
109 Mark Recchi .50 1.25
110 Mats Sundin .40 1.00
111 Pavol Demitra .50 1.25
112 Richard Park .25 .60
113 Doug Bonner RC .40 1.00
114 Bryan Berard RC .60 1.50
115 Rory Fitzpatrick RC .40 1.00
116 Deron Quint .25 .60
117 Jason Bonsignore .40 1.00
118 Adam Deadmarsh .25 .60
119 Sean Haggerty RC .40 1.00
120 Jamie Langenbrunner .30 .75
121 Jeff Mitchell RC .30 .75
122 Antti Aalto RC .30 .75
123 Tommi Rajamaki RC .30 .75
124 J. Markkanen RC UER 1.25 3.00
125 Miikka Kiprusoff RC 6.00 15.00
126 Jere Karalahti RC .40 1.00
127 Petri Kokko RC .40 1.00
128 Janne Niinimaa .40 1.00
129 Kimmo Timonen .30 .75
130 Martti Jarventie RC .40 1.00
131 Mikko Helisten RC .40 1.00
132 Niko Halttunen RC .40 1.00
133 Tommi Miettinen .30 .75
134 Miska Kangasniemi RC .40 1.00
135 Veli-Pekka Nutikka RC .40 1.00
136 Jani Hassinen RC .40 1.00
137 Timo Salonen RC .40 1.00
138 Tommi Sova RC .40 1.00
139 Toni Makiaho RC .40 1.00
140 Tommi Hamalainen RC .40 1.00
141 Juha Vuorivirta RC .40 1.00
142 Jussi Tarvainen RC .40 1.00
143 Miikka Elomo RC .40 1.00
144 Jason Botterill .30 .75
145 Dan Cloutier RC .60 1.50
146 Jamie Storr .30 .75
147 Chad Allan RC .40 1.00
148 Nolan Baumgartner RC .40 1.00
149 Ed Jovanovski RC .60 1.50
150 Bryan McCabe .25 .60
151 Wade Redden RC .60 1.50
152 Jamie Rivers RC .40 1.00
153 Lee Sorochan RC .40 1.00
154 Jason Allison .30 .75
155 Alexandre Daigle .25 .60
156 Larry Courville RC .40 1.00
157 Eric Daze RC .60 1.50
158 Shean Donovan RC .40 1.00
159 Jeff Friesen .25 .60
160 Todd Harvey .25 .60
161 Marty Murray .30 .75
162 Jeff O'Neill RC .30 .75
163 Denis Pederson RC .30 .75
164 Darcy Tucker RC .60 1.50
165 Ryan Smyth RC 1.25 3.00

1994-95 Finest Super Team Winners

COMPLETE SET (165) 50.00 100.00
*SUPER TEAM: 1.2X TO 3X BASIC CARDS
125 Miikka Kiprusoff WJC 15.00 40.00

1994-95 Finest Refractors

*VETS: 4X TO 10X BASIC CARDS
*ROOKIES: 2.5X TO 6X BASIC CARDS
125 Miikka Kiprusoff WJC 30.00 80.00

1994-95 Finest Bowman's Best

COMPLETE SET (45) 40.00 100.00
*B1-B20 REF: 3X TO 8X BASIC INSERTS
*R1-R20 REF: 2X TO 5X BASIC INSERTS
*X21-X25 REF: 1.5X TO 4X BASIC INSERTS
B1 Ray Bourque 2.00 5.00
B2 Mark Messier 1.50 4.00
B3 Cam Neely 1.50 4.00
B4 Theo Fleury 1.25 3.00
B5 Jeremy Roenick 2.00 5.00
B6 Mike Modano 2.00 5.00
B7 Sergei Fedorov 2.00 5.00
B8 John Vanbiesbrouck 1.25 3.00
B9 Pierre Turgeon .40 1.00
B10 Kirk Muller .40 1.00
B11 Pavel Bure 2.00 5.00
B12 Brian Leetch 1.25 3.00
B13 Mike Richter 1.25 3.00
B14 Teemu Selanne 1.25 3.00
B15 Brett Hull 1.50 4.00
B16 Eric Lindros 1.25 3.00
B17 Keith Tkachuk 1.25 3.00
B18 Joe Sakic 3.00 8.00
B19 Doug Gilmour 1.25 3.00
B20 Jaromir Jagr 2.00 5.00
R1 Paul Kariya 1.25 3.00
R2 Oleg Tverdovsky .40 1.00
R3 Blaine Lacher .40 1.00
R4 Todd Harvey .40 1.00
R5 Roman Oksiuta .40 1.00
R6 David Oliver .40 1.00
R7 Jamie Storr .40 1.00
R8 Brian Savage .40 1.00
R9 Brian Rolston .40 1.00
R10 Brett Lindros .40 1.00
R11 Radek Bonk .40 1.00
R12 Peter Forsberg 2.00 5.00
R13 Adam Deadmarsh .40 1.00
R14 Jeff Friesen .40 1.00
R15 Denis Chasse .40 1.00
R16 Jason Wiemer .40 1.00
R17 Alexander Selivanov .40 1.00
R18 Kenny Jonsson .40 1.00
R19 Todd Marchant .40 1.00
R20 Mariusz Czerkawski .40 1.00
X21 T.Fleury/P.Kariya 1.25 3.00
X22 D.Gilmour/P.Forsberg 2.00 5.00
X23 J.Sakic/R.Bonk 1.25 3.00
X24 B.Leetch/O.Tverdovsky 1.25 3.00
X25 C.Neely/J.Weimer 1.25 3.00

1994-95 Finest Division's Finest Clear Cut

COMPLETE SET (20) 25.00 60.00
1 Patrick Roy 5.00 12.00
2 Ray Bourque 4.00 8.00
3 Adam Oates .60 1.50
4 Luc Robitaille .60 1.50
5 Mark Recchi .60 1.50
6 Mike Richter 1.25 3.00
7 Scott Stevens .60 1.50
8 Eric Lindros 1.50 4.00
9 Adam Graves .40 1.00
10 Stephane Richer .60 1.50
11 Ed Belfour 1.25 3.00
12 Al MacInnis .60 1.50
13 Sergei Fedorov 2.00 5.00
14 Brendan Shanahan 1.25 3.00
15 Brett Hull 2.00 5.00
16 Arturs Irbe .60 1.50
17 Sandis Ozolinsh .40 1.00
18 Wayne Gretzky 8.00 20.00
19 Gary Roberts .40 1.00
20 Pavel Bure 1.50 4.00

1994-95 Finest Ring Leaders

COMPLETE SET (20) 30.00 80.00
1 Mark Messier 3.00 8.00
2 Kevin Lowe 2.00 5.00
3 Jari Kurri 3.00 8.00
4 Grant Fuhr 3.00 8.00
5 Wayne Gretzky 12.00 30.00
6 Paul Coffey 3.00 8.00
7 Craig Simpson 2.00 5.00
8 Craig MacTavish 2.00 5.00
9 Jeff Beukeboom 2.00 5.00
10 Joe Mullen 2.50 6.00
11 Marty McSorley 2.50 6.00
12 Steve Smith 2.50 6.00
13 Kevin Stevens 2.50 6.00
14 Patrick Roy 6.00 15.00
15 Jaromir Jagr 4.00 10.00
16 Ron Francis 3.00 8.00
17 Bill Ranford 2.50 6.00
18 Larry Murphy 2.50 6.00
19 Tom Barrasso 2.50 6.00
20 Adam Graves 2.50 6.00

1995-96 Finest

1 Eric Lindros B .75 2.00
2 Ray Bourque G 8.00 20.00
3 Eric Daze B 1.00 2.50
4 Craig Janney S .30 .75
5 Wayne Gretzky B 4.00 10.00
6 Dave Andreychuk B .50 1.25
7 Phil Housley B .40 1.00
8 Mike Gartner B .60 1.50
9 Cam Neely B .50 1.25
10 Brett Hull B 1.00 2.50
11 Daren Puppa S .40 1.00
12 Tomas Sandstrom S .40 1.00
13 Patrick Roy G 12.00 30.00
14 Steve Thomas B .40 1.00
15 Joe Sakic B 1.00 2.50
16 Ray Sheppard S .40 1.00
17 Steve Duchesne B .30 .75
18 Shayne Corson S .40 1.00
19 Chris Chelios G 3.00 8.00
20 John Vanbiesbrouck B .50 1.25
21 Randy Burridge B .30 .75
22 Shane Doan B RC 1.50 4.00
23 Brian Savage B .30 .75
24 Luc Robitaille B .50 1.25
25 Jeremy Roenick G 8.00 20.00
26 Peter Forsberg B 1.00 2.50
27 Jeff Friesen S .30 .75
28 Aaron Gavey S .30 .75
29 Kenny Jonsson S .50 1.25
30 Theo Fleury G 6.00 15.00
31 Dave Gagner S .30 .75
32 Alexander Selivanov S .40 1.00
33 Scott Stevens B .50 1.25
34 Valeri Bure B .30 .75
35 Teemu Selanne G 5.00 12.00
36 Ray Ferraro S .30 .75
37 Sylvain Cote S .30 .75
38 John MacLean B .40 1.00
39 Brendan Shanahan B .50 1.25
40 Pat LaFontaine B .50 1.25
41 Brian Leetch G 4.00 10.00
42 Larry Murphy B .40 1.00
43 Adam Oates B .50 1.25
44 Rod Brind'Amour B .50 1.25
45 Martin Brodeur G 8.00 20.00
46 Pierre Turgeon B .40 1.00
47 Claude Lemieux B .50 1.25
48 Al MacInnis S .60 1.50
49 Geoff Courtnall S .30 .75
50 Mark Messier B 1.00 2.50
51 Bill Ranford B .40 1.00
52 Vincent Damphousse S .40 1.00
53 Jere Lehtinen B .40 1.00
54 Bryan McCabe S .50 1.25
55 Doug Gilmour G 4.00 10.00
56 Mathieu Schneider S .30 .75
57 Igor Larionov S .30 .75
58 Joe Murphy S .30 .75
59 Niklas Sundstrom B .50 1.25
60 John LeClair B .60 1.50
61 Cory Stillman B .30 .75
62 David Oliver B .30 .75
63 Nikolai Khabibulin B .40 1.00
64 Steve Rucchin B .40 1.00
65 Brendan Shanahan S .50 1.25
66 Jim Carey B .40 1.00
67 Brian Holzinger S RC 1.00 2.50
68 Stu Barnes S .30 .75
69 Nicklas Lidstrom B .50 1.25
70 Jaromir Jagr B 1.50 4.00
71 Donald Audette S .40 1.00
72 Dominik Hasek B .75 2.00
73 Peter Bondra S .50 1.25
74 Andrew Cassels B .30 .75
75 Pavel Bure B .50 1.25
76 Marcus Ragnarsson B RC .60 1.50
77 Ray Bourque S 5.00 12.00
78 Alexei Zhamnov B .50 1.25
79 Travis Green S .40 1.00
80 Joe Sakic B 1.00 2.50
81 Chad Kilger B RC .50 1.25
82 Bill Guerin S .50 1.25
83 Vyacheslav Kozlov B .40 1.00
84 Igor Korolev S .30 .75
85 Saku Koivu G 4.00 10.00
86 Ron Hextall B .50 1.25
87 Wendel Clark S .75 2.00
88 Eric Lindros G 5.00 12.00
89 Richard Park B .50 1.25
90 Dominik Hasek S 5.00 12.00
91 Shawn McEachern B .30 .75
92 Martin Straka S .30 .75
93 Roman Hamrlik B .30 .75
94 Roman Oksiuta S .30 .75
95 Sergei Fedorov B .75 2.00
96 Jeff O'Neill S .50 1.25
97 Todd Harvey S .30 .75
98 Rob Niedermayer B .40 1.00
99 Mark Messier G 5.00 12.00
100 Peter Forsberg G 8.00 20.00
101 Deron Quint B .40 1.00
102 Nelson Emerson S .30 .75
103 Scott Niedermayer B .50 1.25
104 Doug Weight S .50 1.25
105 Felix Potvin B .75 2.00
106 Brendan Witt B .50 1.25
107 Zdeno Ciger B .40 1.00
108 Ed Belfour S .40 1.00
109 Jody Hull B .30 .75
110 Cam Neely S .50 1.25
111 Kyle McLaren B RC .30 .75
112 Petr Klima S .30 .75
113 Grant Fuhr B .75 2.00
114 Todd Krygier B .30 .75
115 Brian Leetch B .40 1.00
116 Daniel Alfredsson S RC 6.00 15.00
117 Zigmund Palffy B .50 1.25
118 Antti Tormanen B .30 .75
119 Mark Recchi B .60 1.50
120 Mikael Renberg B .40 1.00
121 Chris Chelios B .50 1.25
122 Guy Hebert B .40 1.00
123 Keith Tkachuk G 5.00 12.00
124 Joe Juneau S .30 .75
125 Radek Dvorak S RC .60 1.50
126 Gary Suter B .30 .75
127 Ron Francis B .60 1.50
128 Mike Modano G 8.00 20.00
129 Tom Barrasso B .40 1.00
130 Pat LaFontaine B .50 1.25
131 Pat Verbeek B .50 1.25
132 Sean Burke S .30 .75
133 Rick Tocchet B .40 1.00
134 Petr Sykora B RC 1.25 3.00
135 Felix Potvin B .75 2.00
136 Scott Mellanby B .40 1.00
137 Paul Coffey B .50 1.25
138 Aki Berg G RC .50 1.25
139 Jason Arnott B .40 1.00
140 Alexander Mogilny G 6.00 15.00
141 Sandis Ozolinsh B .30 .75
142 Owen Nolan S .50 1.25
143 Brian Bradley B .40 1.00
144 Trevor Linden B .30 .75
145 Patrick Roy B 2.50 6.00
146 Todd Bertuzzi B RC 1.50 4.00
147 Michal Pivonka B .30 .75
148 Kevin Hatcher S .40 1.00
149 Chris Terreri B .40 1.00
150 Mario Lemieux B 2.00 5.00
151 Alexei Yashin S .40 1.00
152 Scott Stevens S .50 1.25
153 Dale Hawerchuk B .60 1.50
154 Markus Naslund B .75 2.00
155 Teemu Selanne B 1.00 2.50
156 Darcy Wakaluk S .30 .75
157 Vitali Yachmenev B .50 1.25
158 Jason Dawe B .30 .75
159 Chris Osgood B .50 1.25
160 Alexander Mogilny B .40 1.00
161 Kirk McLean S .40 1.00
162 Steve Yzerman G 8.00 20.00
163 Shean Donovan B .30 .75
164 Valeri Kamensky S .40 1.00
165 Paul Kariya B .50 1.25
166 Dimitri Khristich S .30 .75
167 Teppo Numminen B .30 .75
168 Joe Nieuwendyk S .40 1.00
169 Mike Richter S .60 1.50
170 Doug Gilmour B .60 1.50
171 Sergei Zubov B .40 1.00
172 Michael Nylander B .30 .75
173 Geoff Sanderson B .30 .75
174 Eric Desjardins S .30 .75
175 Jeremy Roenick B .75 2.00
176 Ed Jovanovski G 5.00 12.00
177 Mats Sundin B .50 1.25
178 Martin Brodeur B 1.25 3.00
179 John LeClair G 4.00 10.00
180 Wayne Gretzky G 15.00 40.00
181 Theo Fleury B .60 1.50
182 Pierre Turgeon S .40 1.00
183 Robert Svehla B RC .30 .75
184 Brett Hull G 5.00 12.00
185 Jaromir Jagr G 8.00 20.00
186 Sergei Fedorov B .75 2.00
187 Pavel Bure G 5.00 12.00
188 John Vanbiesbrouck B .50 1.25
189 Paul Kariya B .50 1.25
190 Mario Lemieux G 10.00 25.00
191 Checklist UER G .50 1.25

1995-96 Finest Refractors

1 Eric Lindros B 5.00 12.00
2 Ray Bourque G 20.00 50.00
3 Eric Daze B 2.50 6.00
4 Craig Janney S 2.00 5.00
5 Wayne Gretzky B 25.00 60.00
6 Dave Andreychuk B 2.50 6.00
7 Phil Housley B 2.00 5.00
8 Mike Gartner B 2.00 5.00
9 Cam Neely B 5.00 12.00
10 Brett Hull B 8.00 20.00
11 Daren Puppa S 2.00 5.00
12 Tomas Sandstrom S 5.00 12.00
13 Patrick Roy G 25.00 60.00
14 Steve Thomas B 2.00 5.00
15 Joe Sakic B 8.00 20.00
16 Ray Sheppard S 5.00 12.00
17 Steve Duchesne B 2.00 5.00
18 Shayne Corson S 5.00 12.00
19 Chris Chelios G 12.00 30.00
20 John Vanbiesbrouck B 2.50 6.00
21 Randy Burridge B 1.50 4.00
22 Shane Doan B 6.00 15.00
23 Brian Savage B 2.00 5.00
24 Luc Robitaille B 2.50 6.00
25 Jeremy Roenick G 12.00 30.00
26 Peter Forsberg B 6.00 15.00
27 Jeff Friesen S 5.00 12.00
28 Aaron Gavey S 4.00 10.00
29 Kenny Jonsson S 5.00 12.00
30 Theo Fleury G 12.00 30.00
31 Dave Gagner S 5.00 12.00
32 Alexander Selivanov S 5.00 12.00
33 Scott Stevens B 3.00 8.00
34 Valeri Bure B 3.00 8.00
35 Teemu Selanne G 20.00 50.00
36 Ray Ferraro S 4.00 10.00
37 Sylvain Cote S 5.00 12.00
38 John MacLean B 1.50 4.00
39 Brendan Shanahan B 3.00 8.00
40 Pat LaFontaine B 1.50 4.00
41 Brian Leetch G 10.00 25.00
42 Larry Murphy B 3.00 8.00
43 Adam Oates B 3.00 8.00
44 Rod Brind'Amour B 3.00 8.00
45 Martin Brodeur G 25.00 60.00
46 Pierre Turgeon B 1.50 4.00
47 Claude Lemieux B 2.50 6.00
48 Al MacInnis S 5.00 12.00
49 Geoff Courtnall S 5.00 12.00
50 Mark Messier B 5.00 12.00
51 Bill Ranford B 3.00 8.00
52 Vincent Damphousse S 5.00 12.00
53 Jere Lehtinen B 1.50 4.00
54 Bryan McCabe S 5.00 12.00
55 Doug Gilmour G 8.00 20.00
56 Mathieu Schneider S 5.00 12.00
57 Igor Larionov S 5.00 12.00
58 Joe Murphy S 6.00 15.00
59 Niklas Sundstrom B 1.25 3.00
60 John LeClair B 8.00 20.00
61 Cory Stillman B 2.00 5.00
62 David Oliver B 2.00 5.00
63 Nikolai Khabibulin B 5.00 12.00
64 Steve Rucchin B 2.50 6.00
65 Brendan Shanahan S 5.00 12.00
66 Jim Carey B 3.00 8.00
67 Brian Holzinger S 3.00 8.00
68 Stu Barnes S 4.00 10.00
69 Nicklas Lidstrom B 5.00 12.00
70 Jaromir Jagr B 8.00 20.00
71 Donald Audette S 5.00 12.00
72 Dominik Hasek B 10.00 25.00
73 Peter Bondra S 6.00 15.00
74 Andrew Cassels B 2.50 6.00
75 Pavel Bure B 12.00 30.00
76 Marcus Ragnarsson B 1.50 4.00
77 Ray Bourque S 8.00 20.00
78 Alexei Zhamnov B 1.50 4.00
79 Travis Green S 5.00 12.00
80 Joe Sakic B 12.00 30.00
81 Chad Kilger B 1.25 3.00
82 Bill Guerin S 2.00 5.00
83 Vyacheslav Kozlov B 2.50 6.00
84 Igor Korolev S 8.00 20.00
85 Saku Koivu G 12.00 30.00
86 Ron Hextall B 3.00 8.00
87 Wendel Clark S 6.00 15.00
88 Eric Lindros G 20.00 50.00
89 Richard Park B 2.50 6.00
90 Dominik Hasek S 12.00 30.00
91 Shawn McEachern B 1.50 4.00
92 Martin Straka S 6.00 15.00
93 Roman Hamrlik B 1.50 4.00
94 Roman Oksiuta S 5.00 12.00
95 Sergei Fedorov B 8.00 20.00
96 Jeff O'Neill S 5.00 12.00
97 Todd Harvey S 5.00 12.00
98 Rob Niedermayer B 2.50 6.00
99 Mark Messier G 15.00 40.00
100 Peter Forsberg G 20.00 50.00
101 Deron Quint B 1.25 3.00
102 Nelson Emerson S 5.00 12.00
103 Scott Niedermayer B 2.50 6.00
104 Doug Weight S 6.00 15.00
105 Felix Potvin B 6.00 15.00
106 Brendan Witt B 1.25 3.00
107 Zdeno Ciger B 2.50 6.00
108 Ed Belfour S 6.00 15.00
109 Jody Hull B 2.50 6.00
110 Cam Neely S 6.00 15.00
111 Kyle McLaren B 1.25 3.00
112 Petr Klima S 5.00 12.00
113 Grant Fuhr B 3.00 8.00
114 Todd Krygier B 1.50 4.00
115 Brian Leetch B 4.00 10.00
116 Daniel Alfredsson S 8.00 20.00
117 Zigmund Palffy B 2.00 5.00
118 Antti Tormanen B 2.00 5.00
119 Mark Recchi B 3.00 8.00
120 Mikael Renberg B 2.00 5.00
121 Chris Chelios B 5.00 12.00
122 Guy Hebert B 3.00 8.00
123 Keith Tkachuk G 10.00 25.00
124 Joe Juneau S 5.00 12.00
125 Radek Dvorak S 15.00 40.00
126 Gary Suter B 1.25 3.00
127 Ron Francis B 2.50 6.00
128 Mike Modano G 10.00 25.00
129 Tom Barrasso B 3.00 8.00
130 Pat LaFontaine B 2.00 5.00
131 Pat Verbeek B 2.00 5.00
132 Sean Burke S 8.00 20.00
133 Rick Tocchet B 1.50 4.00
134 Petr Sykora B 5.00 12.00
135 Felix Potvin B 6.00 15.00
136 Scott Mellanby B 2.50 6.00
137 Paul Coffey B 5.00 12.00
138 Aki Berg G 8.00 20.00
139 Jason Arnott B 1.25 3.00
140 Alexander Mogilny G 8.00 20.00
141 Sandis Ozolinsh B 1.50 4.00
142 Owen Nolan S 8.00 20.00
143 Brian Bradley B 1.25 3.00
144 Trevor Linden B 3.00 8.00
145 Patrick Roy B 12.00 30.00
146 Todd Bertuzzi B 10.00 25.00
147 Michal Pivonka B 2.00 5.00
148 Kevin Hatcher S 5.00 12.00
149 Chris Terreri B 3.00 8.00
150 Mario Lemieux B 12.00 30.00
151 Alexei Yashin S 4.00 10.00
152 Scott Stevens S 5.00 12.00
153 Dale Hawerchuk B 1.50 4.00
154 Markus Naslund B 5.00 12.00
155 Teemu Selanne B 6.00 15.00
156 Darcy Wakaluk S 5.00 12.00
157 Vitali Yachmenev B 1.25 3.00
158 Jason Dawe B 2.50 6.00
159 Chris Osgood B 5.00 12.00
160 Alexander Mogilny B 3.00 8.00
161 Kirk McLean S 5.00 12.00
162 Steve Yzerman G 30.00 80.00
163 Shean Donovan B 2.00 5.00
164 Valeri Kamensky S 5.00 12.00
165 Paul Kariya B 5.00 12.00
166 Dimitri Khristich S 5.00 12.00
167 Teppo Numminen B 1.25 3.00
168 Joe Nieuwendyk S 8.00 20.00
169 Mike Richter S 8.00 20.00
170 Doug Gilmour B 2.00 5.00
171 Sergei Zubov B 1.50 4.00
172 Michael Nylander B 2.00 5.00
173 Geoff Sanderson B 1.25 3.00
174 Eric Desjardins S 4.00 10.00
175 Jeremy Roenick B 6.00 15.00
176 Ed Jovanovski G 8.00 20.00
177 Mats Sundin B 5.00 12.00
178 Martin Brodeur B 10.00 25.00
179 John LeClair G 8.00 20.00
180 Wayne Gretzky G 50.00 125.00
181 Theo Fleury B 3.00 8.00
182 Pierre Turgeon S 5.00 12.00
183 Robert Svehla B 1.25 3.00
184 Brett Hull G 12.00 30.00
185 Jaromir Jagr G 30.00 80.00
186 Sergei Fedorov B 8.00 20.00
187 Pavel Bure G 12.00 30.00
188 John Vanbiesbrouck B 3.00 8.00
189 Paul Kariya B 5.00 12.00
190 Mario Lemieux G 25.00 60.00
191 Checklist G 6.00 15.00

1998-99 Finest

*REFRACTORS: 1.25X TO 3X BASIC CARDS
1 Teemu Selanne .40 1.00
2 Theo Fleury .25 .60
3 Ed Belfour .20 .50
4 Dominik Hasek .30 .75
5 Dino Ciccarelli .20 .50
6 Peter Forsberg .40 1.00
7 Rob Blake .20 .50
8 Martin Gelinas .12 .30
9 Vincent Damphousse .15 .40
10 Doug Brown .12 .30
11 Dave Andreychuk .20 .50
12 Bill Guerin .20 .50
13 Daniel Alfredsson .20 .50
14 Dainius Zubrus .12 .30
15 Nikolai Khabibulin .20 .50
16 Sergei Nemchinov .12 .30
17 Rod Brind'Amour .20 .50
18 Patrick Marleau .20 .50
19 Brett Hull .40 1.00
20 Rob Zamuner .12 .30
21 Anson Carter .15 .40
22 Chris Pronger .20 .50
23 Owen Nolan .20 .50
24 Alexandre Daigle .12 .30
25 Darius Kasparaitis .12 .30
26 Steve Rucchin .12 .30
27 Grant Fuhr .30 .75
28 Mike Sillinger .12 .30
29 Tony Amonte .15 .40
30 Jeremy Roenick .30 .75
31 Garry Galley .12 .30
32 Jeff Friesen .12 .30
33 Alexei Zhitnik .12 .30
34 Sergei Fedorov .30 .75
35 Martin Brodeur .50 1.25
36 Curtis Joseph .25 .60
37 Mike Johnson .12 .30
38 Mattias Ohlund .12 .30
39 Derian Hatcher .12 .30
40 Zigmund Palffy .20 .50
41 Rob Niedermayer .12 .30
42 Keith Primeau .15 .40
43 Valeri Kamensky .12 .30
44 Cliff Ronning .12 .30
45 Saku Koivu .20 .50
46 Jiri Slegr .12 .30
47 Igor Korolev .12 .30
48 Sergei Samsonov .15 .40
49 Vaclav Prospal .12 .30
50 Ron Francis .25 .60
51 John LeClair .20 .50
52 Peter Bondra .20 .50
53 Matt Cullen .12 .30
54 Doug Gilmour .25 .60
55 John Vanbiesbrouck .20 .50
56 Kevin Stevens .15 .40
57 Vladimir Malakhov .12 .30
58 Guy Hebert .12 .30
59 Patrik Elias .20 .50
60 Boris Mironov .12 .30
61 Rob DiMaio .12 .30
62 Pavol Demitra .25 .60
63 Michael Nylander .12 .30
64 Wayne Gretzky 1.25 3.00
65 Miroslav Satan .15 .40
66 Eric Daze .12 .30
67 Jozef Stumpel .12 .30
68 Mark Messier .40 1.00
69 Pat Verbeek .12 .30
70 Felix Potvin .30 .75
71 Ethan Moreau .12 .30
72 Steve Yzerman .50 1.25
73 Paul Ysebaert .12 .30
74 Jaromir Jagr .60 1.50
75 Mike Modano .30 .75
76 Chris Osgood .20 .50
77 Robert Svehla .12 .30
78 Joe Juneau .12 .30
79 Adam Deadmarsh .12 .30
80 Keith Tkachuk .20 .50
81 Mark Recchi .25 .60
82 Andrew Cassels .12 .30
83 Mike Hough .12 .30
84 Rem Murray .12 .30
85 Trevor Kidd .12 .30
86 Jeff Hackett .12 .30
87 Mikael Renberg .15 .40
88 Al MacInnis .20 .50
89 Mike Richter .20 .50
90 Markus Naslund .20 .50
91 Joe Sakic .40 1.00
92 Michael Peca .12 .30
93 Scott Thornton .12 .30
94 Vyacheslav Kozlov .15 .40
95 Bobby Holik .12 .30
96 Alexei Yashin .15 .40
97 Robert Kron .12 .30
98 Adam Oates .20 .50
99 Chris Simon .12 .30
100 Paul Kariya .20 .50
101 Ray Bourque .30 .75
102 Eric Desjardins .15 .40
103 Glen Murray .15 .40
104 Oleg Tverdovsky .20 .50
105 Pavel Bure .20 .50
106 Mats Sundin .20 .50
107 Bryan Berard .15 .40
108 Janne Niinimaa .12 .30
109 Wade Redden .12 .30
110 Trevor Linden .12 .30
111 Jarome Iginla .25 .60
112 Joe Nieuwendyk .15 .40
113 Alexei Kovalev .15 .40
114 Dave Gagner .12 .30
115 Dimitri Yushkevich .12 .30
116 Sandis Ozolinsh .12 .30
117 Dimitri Khristich .12 .30
118 Jim Campbell .12 .30
119 Nicklas Lidstrom .25 .60
120 Scott Niedermayer .20 .50
121 Niklas Sundstrom .12 .30
122 Karl Dykhuis .12 .30
123 Brendan Shanahan .25 .60
124 Sandy McCarthy .12 .30
125 Pierre Turgeon .15 .40
126 Olaf Kolzig .20 .50
127 Chris Chelios .20 .50
128 Luc Robitaille .20 .50
129 Alexander Mogilny .15 .40
130 Sami Kapanen .12 .30
131 Stu Barnes .12 .30
132 Scott Stevens .20 .50
133 Doug Weight .20 .50
134 Alexei Zhamnov .15 .40
135 Mike Vernon .15 .40
136 Derek Morris .12 .30
137 Brian Leetch .15 .40
138 Ray Whitney .12 .30
139 Chris Gratton .15 .40
140 Patrick Roy .50 1.25
141 Jason Allison .15 .40
142 Tom Barrasso .15 .40
143 Derek Plante .12 .30
144 Denis Pederson .12 .30
145 Mike Ricci .12 .30
146 Damian Rhodes .20 .50
147 Marco Sturm .12 .30
148 Darryl Sydor .12 .30
149 Eric Lindros .30 .75
150 Checklist .12 .30

1998-99 Finest No Protectors

*NO PROT REF: .6X TO 1.5X BASIC CARDS
1 Teemu Selanne .75 2.00
2 Theo Fleury .50 1.25
3 Ed Belfour .40 1.00
4 Dominik Hasek .60 1.50
5 Dino Ciccarelli .40 1.00
6 Peter Forsberg .75 2.00
7 Rob Blake .40 1.00
8 Martin Gelinas .25 .60
9 Vincent Damphousse .30 .75
10 Doug Brown .25 .60
11 Dave Andreychuk .40 1.00
12 Bill Guerin .40 1.00
13 Daniel Alfredsson .40 1.00
14 Dainius Zubrus .25 .60
15 Nikolai Khabibulin .40 1.00
16 Sergei Nemchinov .25 .60
17 Rod Brind'Amour .40 1.00
18 Patrick Marleau .40 1.00
19 Brett Hull .75 2.00
20 Rob Zamuner .25 .60
21 Anson Carter .30 .75
22 Chris Pronger .40 1.00
23 Owen Nolan .40 1.00
24 Alexandre Daigle .25 .60
25 Darius Kasparaitis .25 .60
26 Steve Rucchin .25 .60
27 Grant Fuhr .60 1.50
28 Mike Sillinger .25 .60
29 Tony Amonte .30 .75
30 Jeremy Roenick .60 1.50
31 Garry Galley .25 .60
32 Jeff Friesen .25 .60
33 Alexei Zhitnik .25 .60
34 Sergei Fedorov .60 1.50
35 Martin Brodeur 1.00 2.50
36 Curtis Joseph .50 1.25
37 Mike Johnson .25 .60
38 Mattias Ohlund .25 .60
39 Derian Hatcher .25 .60
40 Zigmund Palffy .40 1.00
41 Rob Niedermayer .25 .60
42 Keith Primeau .30 .75
43 Valeri Kamensky .25 .60
44 Cliff Ronning .25 .60
45 Saku Koivu .40 1.00
46 Jiri Slegr .25 .60
47 Igor Korolev .25 .60
48 Sergei Samsonov .30 .75
49 Vaclav Prospal .25 .60
50 Ron Francis .50 1.25
51 John LeClair .40 1.00

52 Peter Bondra .40 1.00
53 Matt Cullen .25 .60
54 Doug Gilmour .50 1.25
55 John Vanbiesbrouck .40 1.00
56 Kevin Stevens .30 .75
57 Vladimir Malakhov .25 .60
58 Guy Hebert .30 .75
59 Patrik Elias .40 1.00
60 Boris Mironov .25 .60
61 Rob DiMaio .25 .60
62 Pavol Demitra .50 1.25
63 Michael Nylander .30 .75
64 Wayne Gretzky 2.50 6.00
65 Miroslav Satan .30 .75
66 Eric Daze .30 .75
67 Jozef Stumpel .25 .60
68 Mark Messier .75 2.00
69 Pat Verbeek .25 .60
70 Felix Potvin .60 1.50
71 Ethan Moreau .25 .60
72 Steve Yzerman 1.00 2.50
73 Paul Ysebaert .25 .60
74 Jaromir Jagr 1.25 3.00
75 Mike Modano .60 1.50
76 Chris Osgood .40 1.00
77 Robert Svehla .25 .60
78 Joe Juneau .25 .60
79 Adam Deadmarsh .25 .60
80 Keith Tkachuk .40 1.00
81 Mark Recchi .50 1.25
82 Andrew Cassels .25 .60
83 Mike Hough .25 .60
84 Rem Murray .25 .60
85 Trevor Kidd .25 .60
86 Jeff Hackett .25 .60
87 Mikael Renberg .30 .75
88 Al MacInnis .50 1.25
89 Mike Richter .40 1.00
90 Markus Naslund .40 1.00
91 Joe Sakic .75 2.00
92 Michael Peca .25 .60
93 Scott Thornton .25 .60
94 Vyacheslav Kozlov .30 .75
95 Bobby Holik .25 .60
96 Alexei Yashin .25 .60
97 Robert Kron .25 .60
98 Adam Oates .40 1.00
99 Chris Simon .25 .60
100 Paul Kariya .40 1.00
101 Ray Bourque .60 1.50
102 Eric Desjardins .30 .75
103 Glen Murray .30 .75
104 Oleg Tverdovsky .40 1.00
105 Pavel Bure .40 1.00
106 Mats Sundin .40 1.00
107 Bryan Berard .30 .75
108 Janne Niinimaa .25 .60
109 Wade Redden .25 .60
110 Trevor Linden .40 1.00
111 Jarome Iginla .50 1.25
112 Joe Nieuwendyk .30 .75
113 Alexei Kovalev .30 .75
114 Dave Gagner .25 .60
115 Dimitri Yushkevich .25 .60
116 Sandis Ozolinsh .25 .60
117 Dimitri Khristich .25 .60
118 Jim Campbell .25 .60
119 Nicklas Lidstrom .50 1.25
120 Scott Niedermayer .40 1.00
121 Niklas Sundstrom .25 .60
122 Karl Dykhuis .25 .60
123 Brendan Shanahan .40 1.00
124 Sandy McCarthy .25 .60
125 Pierre Turgeon .30 .75
126 Olaf Kolzig .30 .75
127 Chris Chelios .40 1.00
128 Luc Robitaille .40 1.00
129 Alexander Mogilny .30 .75
130 Sami Kapanen .25 .60
131 Stu Barnes .25 .60
132 Scott Stevens .40 1.00
133 Doug Weight .40 1.00
134 Alexei Zhamnov .25 .60
135 Mike Vernon .30 .75
136 Derek Morris .25 .60
137 Brian Leetch .30 .75
138 Ray Whitney .25 .60
139 Chris Gratton .30 .75
140 Patrick Roy 1.00 2.50
141 Jason Allison .30 .75
142 Tom Barrasso .30 .75
143 Derek Plante .25 .60
144 Denis Pederson .25 .60
145 Mike Ricci .25 .60
146 Damian Rhodes .40 1.00
147 Marco Sturm .25 .60
148 Darryl Sydor .25 .60
149 Eric Lindros .60 1.50
150 Checklist .40 1.00

1998-99 Finest Centurion
*REFRACTOR/75: 1X TO 2.5X BASIC INSERTS
C1 Patrik Elias 2.00 5.00
C2 Bryan Berard 1.50 4.00
C3 Chris Osgood 2.00 5.00
C4 Saku Koivu 2.00 5.00
C5 Alexei Yashin 1.50 4.00
C6 Zigmund Palffy 2.00 5.00
C7 Peter Forsberg 4.00 10.00
C8 Jason Allison 1.50 4.00
C9 Wade Redden 1.25 3.00
C10 Paul Kariya 2.00 5.00
C11 Martin Brodeur 5.00 12.00
C12 Patrick Marleau 2.00 5.00
C13 Jaromir Jagr 6.00 15.00
C14 Mattias Ohlund 1.00 2.50
C15 Teemu Selanne 4.00 10.00
C16 Mike Johnson 1.25 3.00
C17 Joe Thornton 3.00 8.00
C18 Jocelyn Thibault 1.50 4.00
C19 Daniel Alfredsson 2.00 5.00
C20 Sergei Samsonov 1.50 4.00

1998-99 Finest Double Sided Mystery Finest
*REFRACTORS: .8X TO 2X BASIC INSERTS
M1 J.Jagr/W.Gretzky 12.00 30.00
M2 J.Jagr/D.Hasek 6.00 15.00
M3 J.Jagr/E.Lindros 6.00 15.00
M4 J.Jagr/J.Jagr 6.00 15.00
M5 D.Hasek/W.Gretzky 12.00 30.00
M6 D.Hasek/E.Lindros 3.00 8.00
M7 D.Hasek/D.Hasek 3.00 8.00
M8 W.Gretzky/E.Lindros 12.00 30.00
M9 W.Gretzky/W.Gretzky 12.00 30.00
M10 E.Lindros/E.Lindros 3.00 8.00
M11 P.Kariya/T.Selanne 4.00 10.00
M12 P.Kariya/R.Bourque 3.00 8.00
M13 P.Kariya/S.Samsonov 2.00 5.00
M14 P.Kariya/P.Kariya 2.00 5.00
M15 T.Selanne/R.Bourque 4.00 10.00
M16 T.Selanne/S.Samsonov 4.00 10.00
M17 T.Selanne/T.Selanne 4.00 10.00
M18 R.Bourque/S.Samsonov 3.00 8.00
M19 R.Bourque/R.Bourque 3.00 8.00
M20 S.Samsonov/S.Samsonov 1.50 4.00
M21 M.Brodeur/P.Forsberg 5.00 12.00
M22 M.Brodeur/P.Roy 5.00 12.00
M23 M.Brodeur/J.Sakic 5.00 12.00
M24 M.Brodeur/M.Brodeur 5.00 12.00
M25 P.Forsberg/P.Roy 5.00 12.00
M26 P.Forsberg/J.Sakic 4.00 10.00
M27 P.Forsberg/P.Forsberg 4.00 10.00
M28 P.Roy/J.Sakic 5.00 12.00
M29 P.Roy/P.Roy 5.00 12.00
M30 J.Sakic/J.Sakic 4.00 10.00
M31 M.Modano/S.Yzerman 5.00 12.00
M32 M.Modano/S.Fedorov 3.00 8.00
M33 M.Modano/B.Shanahan 3.00 8.00
M34 M.Modano/M.Modano 3.00 8.00
M35 S.Yzerman/S.Fedorov 5.00 12.00
M36 S.Yzerman/B.Shanahan 5.00 12.00
M37 S.Yzerman/S.Yzerman 5.00 12.00
M38 S.Fedorov/B.Shanahan 3.00 8.00
M39 S.Fedorov/S.Fedorov 3.00 8.00
M40 B.Shanahan/B.Shanahan 2.00 5.00
M41 M.Messier/J.Leclair 4.00 10.00
M42 M.Messier/K.Tkachuk 4.00 10.00
M43 M.Messier/P.Bure 4.00 10.00
M44 M.Messier/M.Messier 4.00 10.00
M45 J.Leclair/K.Tkachuk 2.00 5.00
M46 J.Leclair/P.Bure 2.00 5.00
M47 J.Leclair/J.Leclair 2.00 5.00
M48 P.Bure/K.Tkachuk 2.00 5.00
M49 P.Bure/P.Bure 2.00 5.00
M50 K.Tkachuk/K.Tkachuk 2.00 5.00

1998-99 Finest Futures Finest
*REFRACTOR/150: 1X TO 2X BASIC INSERTS
F1 David Legwand 1.25 3.00
F2 Manny Malhotra 2.00 5.00
F3 Vincent Lecavalier 4.00 10.00
F4 Brad Stuart 1.25 3.00
F5 Bryan Allen 1.25 3.00
F6 Rico Fata 1.50 4.00
F7 Mark Bell 1.25 3.00
F8 Michael Rupp 1.50 4.00
F9 Jeff Heerema 1.25 3.00
F10 Alex Tanguay 1.50 4.00
F11 Patrick Desrochers 1.25 3.00
F12 Mathieu Chouinard 1.25 3.00
F13 Eric Chouinard 1.25 3.00
F14 Martin Skoula 1.25 3.00
F15 Robyn Regehr 1.25 3.00
F16 Marian Hossa 2.00 5.00
F17 Daniel Cleary 1.25 3.00
F18 Olli Jokinen 1.50 4.00
F19 Brendan Morrison 1.25 3.00
F20 Erik Rasmussen 1.25 3.00

1998-99 Finest Oversize
*REFRACTORS: .6X TO 1.5X BASIC INSERTS
1 Teemu Selanne 1.50 4.00
2 Dominik Hasek 1.25 3.00
3 Martin Brodeur 2.00 5.00
4 Wayne Gretzky 5.00 12.00
5 Steve Yzerman 2.00 5.00
6 Jaromir Jagr 2.50 6.00
7 Eric Lindros 1.25 3.00

1998-99 Finest Promos
PP1 Scott Stevens .40 1.00
PP2 Michael Nylander .30 .75
PP3 Brendan Shanahan .40 1.00
PP4 Trevor Kidd .25 .60
PP5 Bill Guerin .40 1.00
PP6 Brian Leetch .30 .75

1998-99 Finest Red Lighters
*REFRACTORS: .6X TO 1.5X BASIC INSERTS
R1 Jaromir Jagr 3.00 8.00
R2 Mike Modano 1.25 3.00
R3 Paul Kariya 1.25 3.00
R4 Pavel Bure .75 2.00
R5 Peter Bondra .75 2.00
R6 Sergei Fedorov 1.25 3.00
R7 Steve Yzerman 2.00 5.00
R8 Teemu Selanne 1.50 4.00
R9 Wayne Gretzky 6.00 15.00
R10 Brendan Shanahan .75 2.00
R11 Eric Lindros 1.25 3.00
R12 Alexei Yashin .60 1.50
R13 Jason Allison .60 1.50
R14 Joe Nieuwendyk .60 1.50
R15 Joe Sakic 1.50 4.00
R16 John Leclair .75 2.00
R17 Keith Tkachuk .75 2.00
R18 Mark Messier 1.50 4.00
R19 Mats Sundin 1.00 2.50
R20 Zigmund Palffy .75 2.00

1994-95 Flair
1 Bob Corkum .10 .25
2 Bobby Dollas .10 .25
3 Guy Hebert .12 .30
4 Paul Kariya .15 .40
5 Anatoli Semenov .10 .25
6 Tim Sweeney .10 .25
7 Garry Valk .10 .25
8 Ray Bourque .25 .60
9 Mariusz Czerkawski RC .15 .40
10 Al Iafrate .10 .25
11 Cam Neely .15 .40
12 Adam Oates .15 .40
13 Vincent Riendeau .10 .25
14 Don Sweeney .10 .25
15 Donald Audette .10 .25
16 Doug Dodger .10 .25
17 Dominik Hasek .25 .60
18 Dale Hawerchuk .20 .50
19 Pat LaFontaine .15 .40
20 Alexander Mogilny .12 .30
21 Craig Muni .10 .25
22 Richard Smehlik .10 .25
23 Denis Tsygurov RC .15 .40
24 Theo Fleury .15 .40
25 Trevor Kidd .12 .30
26 James Patrick .10 .25
27 Robert Reichel .10 .25
28 Gary Roberts .10 .25
29 German Titov .10 .25
30 Zarley Zalapski .10 .25
31 Ed Belfour .15 .40
32 Chris Chelios .15 .40
33 Dirk Graham .10 .25
34 Joe Murphy .10 .25
35 Bernie Nicholls .12 .30
36 Jeremy Roenick .25 .60
37 Steve Smith .10 .25
38 Gary Suter .10 .25
39 Neal Broten .12 .30
40 Russ Courtnall .10 .25
41 Todd Harvey .10 .25
42 Grant Ledyard .10 .25
43 Mike Modano .25 .60
44 Andy Moog .15 .40
45 Mark Tinordi .10 .25
46 Dino Ciccarelli .12 .30
47 Paul Coffey .15 .40
48 Sergei Fedorov .25 .60
49 Vladimir Konstantinov .12 .30
50 Slava Kozlov .12 .30
51 Keith Primeau .10 .25
52 Ray Sheppard .12 .30
53 Mike Vernon .12 .30
54 Jason York RC .10 .25
55 Steve Yzerman .40 1.00
56 Jason Arnott .10 .25
57 Shayne Corson .12 .30
58 Igor Kravchuk .10 .25
59 Dean McAmmond .10 .25
60 David Oliver RC .10 .25
61 Bill Ranford .12 .30
62 Doug Weight .12 .30
63 Jesse Belanger .10 .25
64 Bob Kudelski .10 .25
65 Scott Mellanby .12 .30
66 Gord Murphy .10 .25
67 Rob Niedermayer .12 .30
68 Brian Skrudland .10 .25
69 John Vanbiesbrouck .15 .40
70 Sean Burke .12 .30
71 Andrew Cassels .10 .25
72 Alexander Godynyuk .10 .25
73 Chris Pronger .15 .40
74 Geoff Sanderson .12 .30
75 Darren Turcotte .10 .25
76 Pat Verbeek .10 .25
77 Rob Blake .15 .40
78 Mike Donnelly .10 .25
79 Wayne Gretzky 1.00 2.50
80 Kelly Hrudey .12 .30
81 Jari Kurri .12 .30
82 Marty McSorley .10 .25
83 Rick Tocchet .12 .30
84 Brian Bellows .10 .25
85 Patrice Brisebois .10 .25
86 Valeri Bure .10 .25
87 Vincent Damphousse .10 .25
88 Eric Desjardins .10 .25
89 Kirk Muller .10 .25
90 Oleg Petrov .10 .25
91 Patrick Roy .40 1.00
92 Martin Brodeur .40 1.00
93 David Emma .15 .40
94 Bill Guerin .12 .30
95 John MacLean .12 .30
96 Scott Niedermayer .15 .40
97 Stephane Richer .12 .30
98 Brian Rolston .12 .30
99 Alexander Semak .10 .25
100 Scott Stevens .15 .40
101 Valeri Zelepukin .10 .25
102 Patrick Flatley .10 .25
103 Derek King .10 .25
104 Brett Lindros .10 .25
105 Vladimir Malakhov .10 .25
106 Marty McInnis .10 .25
107 Jamie McLennan .12 .30
108 Steve Thomas .10 .25
109 Pierre Turgeon .12 .30
110 Jeff Beukeboom .10 .25
111 Adam Graves .10 .25
112 Alexei Kovalev .12 .30
113 Steve Larmer .12 .30
114 Brian Leetch .12 .30
115 Mark Messier .30 .75
116 Sergei Nemchinov .10 .25
117 Mike Richter .15 .40
118 Sergei Zubov .12 .30
119 Craig Billington .12 .30
120 Alexandre Daigle .10 .25
121 Sean Hill .10 .25
122 Norm Maciver .10 .25
123 Dave McLlwain .10 .25
124 Alexei Yashin .10 .25
125 Vladislav Boulin RC .15 .40
126 Rod Brind'Amour .15 .40
127 Ron Hextall .15 .40
128 Patrik Juhlin RC .10 .25
129 Eric Lindros .25 .60
130 Mark Recchi .20 .50
131 Mikael Renberg .15 .40
132 Chris Therien .10 .25
133 Tom Barrasso .12 .30
134 Ron Francis .20 .50
135 Mario Lemieux .60 1.50
136 Shawn McEachern .10 .25
137 Larry Murphy .12 .30
138 Luc Robitaille .15 .40
139 Ulf Samuelsson .10 .25
140 Kevin Stevens .10 .25
141 Martin Straka .10 .25
142 Wendel Clark .25 .60
143 Rene Corbet .10 .25
144 Adam Deadmarsh .10 .25
145 Stephane Fiset .12 .30
146 Peter Forsberg .30 .75
147 Valeri Kamensky .12 .30
148 Janne Laukkanen .12 .30
149 Sylvain Lefebvre .10 .25
150 Mike Ricci .10 .25
151 Joe Sakic .30 .75
152 Steve Duchesne .10 .25
153 Brett Hull .30 .75
154 Craig Janney .12 .30
155 Craig Johnson .10 .25
156 Curtis Joseph .20 .50
157 Al MacInnis .20 .50
158 Brendan Shanahan .15 .40
159 Peter Stastny .12 .30
160 Esa Tikkanen .10 .25
161 Ulf Dahlen .10 .25
162 Todd Elik .10 .25
163 Pat Falloon .10 .25
164 Jeff Friesen .10 .25
165 Johan Garpenlov .10 .25
166 Arturs Irbe .12 .30
167 Sergei Makarov .10 .25
168 Jeff Norton .10 .25
169 Sandis Ozolinsh .10 .25
170 Brian Bradley .15 .40
171 Shawn Chambers .10 .25
172 Aaron Gavey .10 .25
173 Chris Gratton .10 .25
174 Petr Klima .10 .25
175 Daren Puppa .12 .30
176 Jason Wiemer RC .10 .25
177 Dave Andreychuk .15 .40
178 Dave Ellett .10 .25
179 Eric Fichaud RC .15 .40
180 Mike Gartner .20 .50
181 Doug Gilmour .20 .50
182 Kenny Jonsson .10 .25
183 Dmitri Mironov .10 .25
184 Felix Potvin .25 .60
185 Mike Ridley .10 .25
186 Mats Sundin .15 .40
187 Greg Adams .10 .25
188 Jeff Brown .10 .25
189 Pavel Bure .15 .40
190 Nathan Lafayette .10 .25
191 Trevor Linden .15 .40
192 Jyrki Lumme .10 .25
193 Kirk McLean .12 .30
194 Cliff Ronning .10 .25
195 Jason Wilson .10 .25
196 Peter Bondra .15 .40
197 Randy Burridge .10 .25
198 Sylvain Cote .10 .25
199 Dale Hunter .10 .25
200 Joe Juneau .10 .25
201 Dimitri Khristich .10 .25
202 Todd Nelson .10 .25
203 Pat Peake .10 .25
204 Rick Tabaracci .12 .30
205 Tim Cheveldae .12 .30
206 Dallas Drake .10 .25
207 Dave Manson .10 .25
208 Teppo Numminen .10 .25
209 Teemu Selanne .30 .75
210 Darrin Shannon .10 .25
211 Keith Tkachuk .15 .40
212 Alexei Zhamnov .12 .30
213 Sergei Fedorov .25 .60
214 Sergei Fedorov .25 .60
215 Sergei Fedorov .25 .60
216 Sergei Fedorov .25 .60
217 Sergei Fedorov .25 .60
218 Sergei Fedorov .25 .60
219 Sergei Fedorov .25 .60
220 Sergei Fedorov .25 .60
221 Sergei Fedorov .25 .60
222 Sergei Fedorov .25 .60
223 Checklist .10 .25
224 Checklist .10 .25
225 Checklist .10 .25

1994-95 Flair Center Spotlight
COMPLETE SET (10) 10.00 20.00
1 Jason Arnott .15 .40
2 Sergei Fedorov 1.00 2.50
3 Doug Gilmour .30 .75
4 Wayne Gretzky 4.00 10.00
5 Pat LaFontaine .60 1.50
6 Mario Lemieux 3.00 8.00
7 Eric Lindros .60 1.50
8 Mark Messier .60 1.50
9 Mike Modano 1.00 2.50
10 Jeremy Roenick .75 2.00

1994-95 Flair Hot Numbers
COMPLETE SET (10) 20.00 40.00
1 Pavel Bure .75 2.00
2 Wayne Gretzky 5.00 12.00
3 Dominik Hasek 2.00 5.00
4 Brett Hull 1.00 2.50
5 Mario Lemieux 4.00 10.00
6 Adam Oates .40 1.00
7 Luc Robitaille .40 1.00
8 Patrick Roy 3.00 8.00
9 Brendan Shanahan .75 2.00
10 Steve Yzerman 3.00 8.00

1994-95 Flair Scoring Power
COMPLETE SET (10) 6.00 12.00
1 Pavel Bure .75 2.00
2 Alexandre Daigle .40 1.00
3 Sergei Fedorov 1.25 3.00
4 Alexei Kovalev .40 1.00
5 Brian Leetch .75 2.00
6 Eric Lindros .75 2.00
7 Mike Modano 1.25 3.00
8 Alexander Mogilny .40 1.00
9 Jeremy Roenick 1.00 2.50
10 Alexei Yashin .20 .50

1996-97 Flair
COMPLETE SET (125) 30.00 80.00
COMP BASE SET (100) 20.00 40.00
1 Guy Hebert .30 .75
2 Paul Kariya .40 1.00
3 Teemu Selanne .75 2.00
4 Ray Bourque .60 1.50
5 Adam Oates .40 1.00
6 Bill Ranford .30 .75
7 Jozef Stumpel .25 .60
8 Dominik Hasek .60 1.50
9 Pat LaFontaine .40 1.00
10 Alexei Zhitnik .25 .60
11 Theo Fleury .75 2.00
12 Dave Gagner .40 1.00
13 Trevor Kidd .25 .60
14 Tony Amonte .30 .75
15 Chris Chelios .40 1.00
16 Eric Daze .30 .75
17 Alexei Zhamnov .30 .75
18 Peter Forsberg .75 2.00
19 Sandis Ozolinsh .25 .60
20 Patrick Roy 1.00 2.50
21 Joe Sakic .75 2.00
22 Derian Hatcher .25 .60
23 Mike Modano .60 1.50
24 Andy Moog .40 1.00
25 Pat Verbeek .25 .60
26 Sergei Fedorov .60 1.50
27 Slava Fetisov .25 .60
28 Nicklas Lidstrom .50 1.25
29 Chris Osgood .40 1.00
30 Brendan Shanahan .40 1.00
31 Steve Yzerman 1.00 2.50
32 Jason Arnott .30 .75
33 Curtis Joseph .50 1.25
34 Boris Mironov .25 .60
35 Ryan Smyth .30 .75
36 Doug Weight .40 1.00
37 Ed Jovanovski .30 .75
38 Ray Sheppard .30 .75
39 Robert Svehla .25 .60
40 John Vanbiesbrouck .40 1.00
41 Andrew Cassels .25 .60
42 Jason Muzzatti .30 .75
43 Keith Primeau .30 .75
44 Geoff Sanderson .30 .75
45 Rob Blake .40 1.00
46 Dimitri Khristich .25 .60
47 Vincent Damphousse .30 .75
48 Saku Koivu .40 1.00
49 Mark Recchi .50 1.25
50 Martin Rucinsky .25 .60
51 Jocelyn Thibault .30 .75
52 Martin Brodeur 1.00 2.50
53 Bill Guerin .40 1.00
54 Scott Stevens .40 1.00
55 Scott Lachance .25 .60
56 Zigmund Palffy .40 1.00
57 Tommy Salo .30 .75
58 Bryan Smolinski .25 .60
59 Wayne Gretzky 2.50 6.00
60 Brian Leetch .40 1.00
61 Mark Messier .75 2.00
62 Mike Richter .40 1.00
63 Daniel Alfredsson .40 1.00
64 Damian Rhodes .30 .75
65 Alexei Yashin .30 .75
66 Paul Coffey .40 1.00
67 Dale Hawerchuk .50 1.25
68 Ron Hextall .40 1.00
69 John LeClair .40 1.00
70 Eric Lindros .60 1.50
71 Nikolai Khabibulin .40 1.00
72 Jeremy Roenick .60 1.50
73 Keith Tkachuk .40 1.00
74 Oleg Tverdovsky .30 .75
75 Ron Francis .50 1.25
76 Kevin Hatcher .25 .60
77 Jaromir Jagr 1.25 3.00
78 Mario Lemieux 1.50 4.00
79 Petr Nedved .30 .75
80 Grant Fuhr .60 1.50
81 Brett Hull .75 2.00
82 Al MacInnis .50 1.25
83 Ed Belfour .40 1.00
84 Tony Granato .25 .60
85 Owen Nolan .40 1.00
86 Dino Ciccarelli .40 1.00
87 John Cullen .30 .75
88 Roman Hamrlik .25 .60
89 Wendel Clark .60 1.50
90 Doug Gilmour .50 1.25
91 Felix Potvin .60 1.50
92 Mats Sundin .40 1.00
93 Pavel Bure .40 1.00
94 Corey Hirsch .30 .75
95 Trevor Linden .40 1.00
96 Alexander Mogilny .30 .75
97 Peter Bondra .40 1.00
98 Jim Carey .40 1.00
99 Dale Hunter .30 .75
100 Chris Simon .25 .60
101 Mattias Timander RC .60 1.50
102 Vaclav Varada RC .60 1.50
103 Jarome Iginla SP .75 2.00
104 Ethan Moreau RC .60 1.50
105 Jamie Langenbrunner SP .40 1.00
106 Roman Turek RC .60 1.50
107 Tomas Holmstrom RC 2.00 5.00
108 Kevin Hodson RC .60 1.50
109 Mats Lindgren SP .75 2.00
110 Mike Grier SP RC .75 2.00
111 Rem Murray RC .60 1.50
112 Jose Theodore SP .75 2.00
113 David Wilkie SP .40 1.00
114 Bryan Berard SP .60 1.50
115 Eric Fichaud SP .50 1.25
116 Daniel Goneau RC .60 1.50
117 Andreas Dackell RC .60 1.50
118 Wade Redden SP .40 1.00
119 Dainius Zubrus RC .75 2.00
120 Janne Niinimaa SP .60 1.50
121 Patrick Lalime RC .75 2.00
122 Harry York RC SP .60 1.50
123 Jim Campbell SP .40 1.00
124 Sergei Berezin RC 1.00 2.50
125 Jaro. Svejkovsky RC .75 2.00

1996-97 Flair Blue Ice
*VETS: 8X TO 20X BASIC CARDS
*SPs: 1.5X TO 3X
R59 Wayne Gretzky 300.00 800.00

1996-97 Flair Center Ice Spotlight
COMPLETE SET (10) 15.00 40.00
1 Pavel Bure 1.50 4.00
2 Sergei Fedorov 2.00 5.00
3 Peter Forsberg 2.00 5.00
4 Brett Hull 2.00 5.00
5 Jaromir Jagr 2.50 6.00
6 Paul Kariya 1.50 4.00
7 Joe Sakic 3.00 8.00
8 Teemu Selanne 1.50 4.00
9 Mats Sundin 1.50 4.00
10 Steve Yzerman 6.00 15.00

1996-97 Flair Hot Gloves
COMPLETE SET (12) 15.00 40.00
1 Ed Belfour 2.50 6.00
2 Martin Brodeur 6.00 15.00
3 Jim Carey 1.50 4.00
4 Dominik Hasek 5.00 12.00
5 Curtis Joseph 2.50 6.00
6 Patrick Lalime 3.00 8.00
7 Chris Osgood 2.00 5.00
8 Felix Potvin 4.00 10.00
9 Mike Richter 2.00 5.00
10 Patrick Roy 8.00 20.00
11 Jocelyn Thibault 2.00 5.00
12 John Vanbiesbrouck 8.00 20.00

1996-97 Flair Hot Numbers
COMPLETE SET (10) 25.00 50.00
1 Ray Bourque 2.50 6.00
2 Paul Coffey 1.50 4.00
3 Eric Daze 1.00 2.50
4 Wayne Gretzky 10.00 25.00
5 Ed Jovanovski 1.00 2.50
6 Saku Koivu 1.50 4.00
7 Mario Lemieux 8.00 20.00
8 Eric Lindros 1.50 4.00
9 Mark Messier 1.50 4.00
10 Owen Nolan 1.00 2.50

1996-97 Flair Now And Then
COMPLETE SET (3) 40.00 100.00
1 Gretzky/Messier/Gartner 15.00 40.00
2 Lemieux/Roy/Muller 15.00 40.00
3 Lindros/Forsberg/Nieder. 10.00 25.00

2006-07 Flair Showcase
COMP.SET w/o SPs (100) 12.00 30.00
1 Jean-Sebastien Giguere .50 1.25
2 Teemu Selanne 1.00 2.50
3 Corey Perry .75 2.00
4 Scott Niedermayer .50 1.25
5 Joffrey Lupul .30 .75
6 Ilya Kovalchuk .50 1.25
7 Marian Hossa .50 1.25
8 Kari Lehtonen .40 1.00
9 Patrice Bergeron .60 1.50
10 Marc Savard .30 .75
11 Brad Boyes .30 .75
12 Mark Stuart RC .30 .75
13 Chris Drury .40 1.00
14 Ryan Miller .50 1.25
15 Thomas Vanek .40 1.00
16 Jarome Iginla .60 1.50
17 Miikka Kiprusoff .50 1.25
18 Dion Phaneuf .40 1.00
19 Eric Staal .60 1.50
20 Cam Ward .50 1.25
21 Justin Williams .40 1.00
22 Erik Cole .30 .75
23 Doug Weight .50 1.25
24 Nikolai Khabibulin .50 1.25
25 Tuomo Ruutu .50 1.25
26 Dustin Byfuglien RC .75 2.00
27 Milan Hejduk .40 1.00
28 Alex Tanguay .30 .75
29 Jose Theodore .50 1.25
30 Marek Svatos .30 .75
31 Rob Blake .50 1.25
32 Rick Nash .50 1.25
33 Sergei Fedorov .75 2.00
34 Mike Modano .75 2.00
35 Marty Turco .50 1.25
36 Brenden Morrow .40 1.00
37 Jere Lehtinen .30 .75
38 Steve Yzerman 1.25 3.00
39 Tomas Kopecky RC .40 1.00
40 Henrik Zetterberg .60 1.50
41 Pavel Datsyuk .75 2.00
42 Tomas Holmstrom .40 1.00
43 Kris Draper .30 .75
44 M-A Pouliot RC .30 .75
45 Ales Hemsky .40 1.00
46 Roberto Luongo .75 2.00
47 Olli Jokinen .50 1.25
48 K. Pushkarev RC .40 1.00
49 Jeremy Roenick .75 2.00
50 Alexander Frolov .30 .75
51 Marian Gaborik .50 1.25
52 Manny Fernandez .30 .75
53 Saku Koivu .50 1.25
54 Michael Ryder .30 .75
55 Mike Ribeiro .30 .75
56 Cristobal Huet .40 1.00
57 Paul Kariya .50 1.25
58 Tomas Vokoun .40 1.00
59 Shea Weber RC .75 2.00
60 Patrik Elias .50 1.25
61 Masi Marjamaki RC .30 .75
62 Alexei Yashin .40 1.00
63 Rick DiPietro .40 1.00
64 Miroslav Satan .40 1.00
65 Henrik Lundqvist 1.25 3.00
66 Jarkko Immonen RC .40 1.00
67 Daniel Alfredsson .50 1.25
68 Martin Gerber .40 1.00
69 Jason Spezza .50 1.25
70 Dany Heatley .40 1.00
71 Martin Havlat .30 .75
72 Zdeno Chara .50 1.25
73 Simon Gagne .50 1.25
74 Ryan Potulny RC .30 .75
75 Jeff Carter .40 1.00
76 Peter Forsberg 1.00 2.50
77 Shane Doan .40 1.00
78 Ladislav Nagy .30 .75
79 Curtis Joseph .60 1.50
80 Marc-Andre Fleury 1.00 2.50
81 Noah Welch RC .30 .75
82 Matt Carle RC .30 .75
83 Evgeni Nabokov .40 1.00
84 Jonathan Cheechoo .40 1.00
85 Patrick Marleau .50 1.25
86 Keith Tkachuk .50 1.25
87 Vincent Lecavalier .50 1.25
88 Martin St. Louis .50 1.25
89 Brad Richards .50 1.25
90 Ian White RC .40 1.00
91 Ben Ondrus RC .30 .75
92 Eric Lindros .75 2.00
93 Alexander Steen .30 .75
94 Jeremy Williams RC .30 .75
95 Todd Bertuzzi .50 1.25
96 Markus Naslund .50 1.25
97 Ed Jovanovski .40 1.00
98 Eric Fehr RC .50 1.25
99 Alexander Ovechkin 2.00 5.00
100 Olaf Kolzig .50 1.25
101 Teemu Selanne 1.50 4.00
102 Scott Niedermayer .75 2.00
103 Corey Perry 1.25 3.00
104 Marian Hossa .75 2.00
105 Kari Lehtonen .60 1.50
106 Yan Stastny RC .50 1.25
107 Glen Murray .60 1.50
108 Brian Leetch .60 1.50
109 Brad Boyes .50 1.25
110 Chris Drury .60 1.50
111 Ryan Miller .75 2.00
112 Thomas Vanek .60 1.50
113 Dion Phaneuf .60 1.50
114 Erik Cole .50 1.25
115 Cam Ward .75 2.00
116 Mark Recchi 1.00 2.50
117 Nikolai Khabibulin .75 2.00
118 Tuomo Ruutu .75 2.00
119 Rob Blake .75 2.00
120 Milan Hejduk .60 1.50
121 Marek Svatos .50 1.25
122 Sergei Fedorov 1.25 3.00
123 Brenden Morrow .60 1.50
124 Marty Turco .75 2.00
125 Tomas Kopecky .60 1.50
126 Pavel Datsyuk 1.25 3.00
127 Henrik Zetterberg 1.00 2.50
128 M-A Pouliot RC .50 1.25
129 Ales Hemsky .60 1.50
130 Olli Jokinen .75 2.00
131 K. Pushkarev RC .60 1.50
132 Luc Robitaille .75 2.00
133 Jeremy Roenick 1.25 3.00
134 Alexander Frolov .50 1.25
135 Marian Gaborik .75 2.00
136 Michael Ryder .50 1.25
137 Shea Weber 1.25 3.00
138 Paul Kariya .75 2.00
139 Tomas Vokoun .60 1.50
140 Patrik Elias .75 2.00
141 Alexei Yashin .60 1.50
142 Rick DiPietro .60 1.50
143 Miroslav Satan .60 1.50
144 Henrik Lundqvist 2.00 5.00
145 Billy Thompson RC .50 1.25
146 Filip Novak RC .50 1.25
147 Daniel Alfredsson .75 2.00
148 Zdeno Chara .50 1.25
149 Martin Havlat .50 1.25
150 Simon Gagne .75 2.00
151 Keith Primeau .60 1.50
152 Jeff Carter .60 1.50
153 Shane Doan .60 1.50
154 Ladislav Nagy .50 1.25
155 Curtis Joseph 1.00 2.50
156 Noah Welch .60 1.50
157 Marc-Andre Fleury 1.50 4.00
158 Evgeni Nabokov .60 1.50
159 Jonathan Cheechoo .60 1.50
160 Patrick Marleau .75 2.00
161 Keith Tkachuk .75 2.00
162 Brad Richards .75 2.00
163 Ben Ondrus .50 1.25
164 Brendan Bell RC .50 1.25
165 Ian White .60 1.50
166 Eric Lindros 1.25 3.00
167 Todd Bertuzzi .75 2.00
168 Ed Jovanovski .60 1.50
169 Eric Fehr .75 2.00
170 Olaf Kolzig .75 2.00
171 Jean-Sebastien Giguere .75 2.00
172 Ilya Kovalchuk .75 2.00
173 Patrice Bergeron 1.00 2.50
174 Jarome Iginla 1.00 2.50
175 Miikka Kiprusoff .75 2.00
176 Eric Staal 1.00 2.50
177 Joe Sakic 1.50 4.00
178 Jose Theodore .75 2.00
179 Alex Tanguay .50 1.25
180 Rick Nash .75 2.00
181 Mike Modano 1.25 3.00
182 Steve Yzerman 2.00 5.00
183 Brendan Shanahan .75 2.00
184 Chris Pronger .75 2.00
185 Roberto Luongo 1.25 3.00
186 Saku Koivu .75 2.00
187 Martin Brodeur 2.00 5.00
188 Jaromir Jagr 2.50 6.00
189 Jason Spezza .75 2.00
190 Dany Heatley .60 1.50
191 Martin Gerber .60 1.50
192 Peter Forsberg 1.50 4.00
193 Sidney Crosby 3.00 8.00
194 Joe Thornton 1.25 3.00
195 Vincent Lecavalier .75 2.00
196 Martin St. Louis .75 2.00
197 Mats Sundin .75 2.00
198 Andrew Raycroft .60 1.50
199 Markus Naslund .75 2.00
200 Alexander Ovechkin 3.00 8.00
201 Jean-Sebastien Giguere 2.50 6.00
202 Teemu Selanne 5.00 12.00
203 Kari Lehtonen 2.00 5.00
204 Marian Hossa 2.50 6.00
205 Ilya Kovalchuk 2.50 6.00
206 Ray Bourque 4.00 10.00

207 Patrice Bergeron 3.00 8.00
208 Brian Leetch 2.00 5.00
209 Chris Drury 2.00 5.00
210 Ryan Miller 2.50 6.00
211 Jarome Iginla 3.00 8.00
212 Miikka Kiprusoff 2.50 6.00
213 Dion Phaneuf 2.00 5.00
214 Eric Staal 3.00 8.00
215 Cam Ward 2.50 6.00
216 Rod Brind'Amour 2.50 6.00
217 Nikolai Khabibulin 2.50 6.00
218 Joe Sakic 5.00 12.00
219 Alex Tanguay 1.50 4.00
220 Milan Hejduk 2.00 5.00
221 Jose Theodore 2.50 6.00
222 Marek Svatos 1.50 4.00
223 Rick Nash 2.50 6.00
224 Sergei Fedorov 4.00 10.00
225 Mike Modano 4.00 10.00
226 Marty Turco 2.50 6.00
227 Brenden Morrow 2.00 5.00
228 Steve Yzerman 6.00 15.00
229 Gordie Howe 8.00 20.00
230 Brendan Shanahan 2.50 6.00
231 Henrik Zetterberg 3.00 8.00
232 Pavel Datsyuk 4.00 10.00
233 Chris Pronger 2.50 6.00
234 Roberto Luongo 4.00 10.00
235 Olli Jokinen 2.50 6.00
236 Luc Robitaille 2.50 6.00
237 Jeremy Roenick 4.00 10.00
238 Marian Gaborik 2.50 6.00
239 Saku Koivu 2.50 6.00
240 Patrick Roy 6.00 15.00
241 Michael Ryder 1.50 4.00
242 Paul Kariya 2.50 6.00
243 Martin Brodeur 6.00 15.00
244 Patrik Elias 2.50 6.00
245 Alexei Yashin 2.00 5.00
246 Rick DiPietro 2.00 5.00
247 Jaromir Jagr 8.00 20.00
248 Henrik Lundqvist 6.00 15.00
249 Martin Gerber 2.00 5.00
250 Dany Heatley 2.00 5.00
251 Jason Spezza 2.50 6.00
252 Daniel Alfredsson 2.50 6.00
253 Peter Forsberg 5.00 12.00
254 Simon Gagne 2.50 6.00
255 Shane Doan 2.00 5.00
256 Mario Lemieux 10.00 25.00
257 Sidney Crosby 10.00 25.00
258 Marc-Andre Fleury 5.00 12.00
259 Evgeni Nabokov 2.00 5.00
260 Joe Thornton 4.00 10.00
261 Jonathan Cheechoo 2.00 5.00
262 Vincent Lecavalier 2.50 6.00
263 Martin St. Louis 2.50 6.00
264 Brad Richards 2.50 6.00
265 Andrew Raycroft 2.50 6.00
266 Mats Sundin 2.50 6.00
267 Markus Naslund 2.50 6.00
268 Todd Bertuzzi 2.50 6.00
269 Alexander Ovechkin 10.00 25.00
270 Olaf Kolzig 2.50 6.00
271 Jean-Sebastien Giguere 2.50 6.00
272 Ilya Kovalchuk 2.50 6.00
273 Ray Bourque 4.00 10.00
274 Jarome Iginla 3.00 8.00
275 Miikka Kiprusoff 2.50 6.00
276 Eric Staal 3.00 8.00
277 Joe Sakic 5.00 12.00
278 Rick Nash 2.50 6.00
279 Mike Modano 4.00 10.00
280 Steve Yzerman 6.00 15.00
281 Gordie Howe 8.00 20.00
282 Henrik Zetterberg 3.00 8.00
283 Roberto Luongo 4.00 10.00
284 Saku Koivu 2.50 6.00
285 Patrick Roy 6.00 15.00
286 Paul Kariya 2.50 6.00
287 Martin Brodeur 6.00 15.00
288 Jaromir Jagr 8.00 20.00
289 Daniel Alfredsson 2.50 6.00
290 Dany Heatley 2.00 5.00
291 Jason Spezza 2.50 6.00
292 Peter Forsberg 5.00 12.00
293 Mario Lemieux 10.00 25.00
294 Sidney Crosby 10.00 25.00
295 Joe Thornton 4.00 10.00
296 Vincent Lecavalier 2.50 6.00
297 Andrew Raycroft 2.00 5.00
298 Mats Sundin 2.50 6.00
299 Markus Naslund 2.50 6.00
300 Alexander Ovechkin 10.00 25.00
301 Ryan Shannon RC 2.50 6.00
302 David McKee RC 2.50 6.00
303 Phil Kessel RC 8.00 20.00
304 Matt Lashoff RC 2.50 6.00
305 Drew Stafford RC 4.00 10.00
306 Clarke MacArthur RC 3.00 8.00
307 Dustin Boyd RC 2.50 6.00
308 Brandon Prust RC 2.50 6.00
309 Dave Bolland RC 4.00 10.00
310 Paul Stastny RC 6.00 15.00
311 Loui Eriksson RC 5.00 12.00
312 Ladislav Smid RC 2.50 6.00
313 Patrick O'Sullivan RC 4.00 10.00
314 Anze Kopitar RC 12.00 30.00
315 Benoit Pouliot RC 3.00 8.00
316 G. Latendresse RC 4.00 10.00
317 Alexander Radulov RC 5.00 12.00
318 Travis Zajac RC 5.00 12.00
319 Nigel Dawes RC 2.50 6.00
320 Josh Hennessy RC 2.50 6.00
321 Enver Lisin RC 2.50 6.00
322 Evgeni Malkin RC 15.00 40.00
323 Jordan Staal RC 6.00 15.00
324 Kristopher Letang RC 10.00 25.00
325 Marc-Edouard Vlasic RC 4.00 10.00
326 Joe Pavelski RC 12.00 30.00
327 Marek Schwarz RC 2.50 6.00
328 Karri Ramo RC 2.50 6.00
329 Luc Bourdon RC 4.00 10.00
330 Jesse Schultz RC 2.50 6.00
FE301 Evgeni Malkin 15.00 40.00

2006-07 Flair Showcase Parallel

*PARALLEL 1-100: 3X TO 8X BASE
*PARALLEL 101-200: 2X TO 5X BASE
*PARALLEL 201-270: .8X TO 2X BASE
*PARALLEL 271-300: 1X TO 2.5X BASE

2006-07 Flair Showcase Hot Gloves

HG1 Jean-Sebastien Giguere 5.00 12.00
HG2 Kari Lehtonen 4.00 10.00
HG3 Hannu Toivonen 4.00 10.00
HG4 Ryan Miller 5.00 12.00
HG5 Miikka Kiprusoff 5.00 12.00
HG6 Martin Gerber 4.00 10.00
HG7 Nikolai Khabibulin 5.00 12.00
HG8 Jose Theodore 5.00 12.00
HG9 Marc Denis 4.00 10.00
HG10 Marty Turco 5.00 12.00
HG11 Cam Ward 5.00 12.00
HG12 Dwayne Roloson 4.00 10.00
HG13 Roberto Luongo 8.00 20.00
HG14 Mathieu Garon 4.00 10.00
HG15 Manny Fernandez 3.00 8.00
HG16 Cristobal Huet 4.00 10.00
HG17 Tomas Vokoun 4.00 10.00
HG18 Martin Brodeur 12.00 30.00
HG19 Rick DiPietro 4.00 10.00
HG20 Henrik Lundqvist 12.00 30.00
HG21 Pascal Leclaire 4.00 10.00
HG22 Antero Niittymaki 4.00 10.00
HG23 Curtis Joseph 6.00 15.00
HG24 Marc-Andre Fleury 10.00 25.00
HG25 Evgeni Nabokov 4.00 10.00
HG26 Curtis Sanford 4.00 10.00
HG27 Vesa Toskala 4.00 10.00
HG28 Andrew Raycroft 4.00 10.00
HG29 Alex Auld 3.00 8.00
HG30 Olaf Kolzig 5.00 12.00

2006-07 Flair Showcase Hot Numbers

HN1 Teemu Selanne 12.00 30.00
HN2 Kari Lehtonen 5.00 12.00
HN3 Ray Bourque 10.00 25.00
HN4 Miikka Kiprusoff 6.00 15.00
HN5 Jarome Iginla 8.00 20.00
HN6 Martin Gerber 5.00 12.00
HN7 Eric Staal 8.00 20.00
HN8 Nikolai Khabibulin 6.00 15.00
HN9 Alex Tanguay 4.00 10.00
HN10 Jose Theodore 6.00 15.00
HN11 Joe Sakic 12.00 30.00
HN12 Milan Hejduk 5.00 12.00
HN13 Rick Nash 6.00 15.00
HN14 Sergei Fedorov 10.00 25.00
HN15 Mike Modano 10.00 25.00
HN16 Henrik Zetterberg 8.00 20.00
HN17 Gordie Howe 20.00 50.00
HN18 Brendan Shanahan 6.00 15.00
HN19 Steve Yzerman 15.00 40.00
HN20 Ales Hemsky 5.00 12.00
HN21 Jeremy Roenick 10.00 25.00
HN22 Luc Robitaille 6.00 15.00
HN23 Marian Gaborik 6.00 15.00
HN24 Patrick Roy 15.00 40.00
HN25 Michael Ryder 4.00 10.00
HN26 Saku Koivu 6.00 15.00
HN27 Martin Brodeur 15.00 40.00
HN28 Alexei Yashin 5.00 12.00
HN29 Jaromir Jagr 20.00 50.00
HN30 Dominik Hasek 10.00 25.00
HN31 Dany Heatley 5.00 12.00
HN32 Peter Forsberg 12.00 30.00
HN33 Sidney Crosby 25.00 60.00
HN34 Mario Lemieux 25.00 60.00
HN35 Joe Thornton 10.00 25.00
HN36 Vincent Lecavalier 6.00 15.00
HN37 Martin St. Louis 6.00 15.00
HN38 Mats Sundin 6.00 15.00
HN39 Eric Lindros 10.00 25.00
HN40 Todd Bertuzzi 6.00 15.00
HN41 Markus Naslund 6.00 15.00
HN42 Alexander Ovechkin 25.00 60.00

2006-07 Flair Showcase Hot Numbers Parallel

*PARALLEL/60-97: .5X TO 1.2X BASIC
*PARALLEL/30-50: .6X TO 1.5X BASIC
*PARALLEL/20-29: .8X TO 2X BASIC

2006-07 Flair Showcase Inks

IAF Alexander Frolov 4.00 10.00
IAH Ales Hemsky 5.00 12.00
IAL Andrew Ladd 4.00 10.00
IAM Andy McDonald 5.00 12.00
IAN Antero Niittymaki 5.00 12.00
IAO Alexander Ovechkin SP 80.00 200.00
IBB Brad Boyes 4.00 10.00
IBE Ben Eager 5.00 12.00
IBG Brian Gionta 4.00 10.00
IBI Martin Biron 5.00 12.00
IBL Brian Leetch 5.00 12.00
IBR Brenden Morrow 5.00 12.00
ICD Chris Drury 5.00 12.00
ICH Cristobal Huet 5.00 12.00
ICK Chris Kunitz 6.00 15.00
IDA David Aebischer 5.00 12.00
IDB Daniel Briere 6.00 15.00
IDC Dan Cloutier 5.00 12.00
IDK Duncan Keith 5.00 12.00
IDL David Leneveu 5.00 12.00
IDP Dion Phaneuf 5.00 12.00
IDR Dwayne Roloson 5.00 12.00
IDU Dustin Brown 6.00 15.00
IED Eric Daze 4.00 10.00
IEN Evgeni Nabokov 5.00 12.00
IFP Fernando Pisani 4.00 10.00
IHA Michal Handzus 5.00 12.00
IHE Dany Heatley 5.00 12.00
IHJ Milan Hejduk 5.00 12.00
IHO Marcel Hossa 4.00 10.00
IHZ Henrik Zetterberg 15.00 40.00
IIK Ilya Kovalchuk SP 15.00 40.00
IJC Jonathan Cheechoo 5.00 12.00
IJI Jarome Iginla 8.00 20.00
IJL Joffrey Lupul 4.00 10.00
IJO Jeff O'Neill 4.00 10.00
IJP Joni Pitkanen 4.00 10.00
IJR Jeremy Roenick SP 15.00 40.00
IJT Jose Theodore 6.00 15.00
IKD Kris Draper 4.00 10.00
IKE Ryan Kesler 6.00 15.00
IKI Miikka Kiprusoff 6.00 15.00
IKL Kari Lehtonen 5.00 12.00
IKO Chuck Kobasew 4.00 10.00
ILR Luc Robitaille 6.00 15.00
ILX Mario Lemieux SP 75.00 150.00
IMA Maxim Afinogenov 4.00 10.00
IMB Martin Brodeur SP 50.00 100.00
IMC Mike Cammalleri 4.00 10.00
IMF Marc-Andre Fleury 10.00 25.00
IMG Marian Gaborik 6.00 15.00
IMH Martin Havlat 4.00 10.00
IMI Ryan Miller 6.00 15.00
IML Manny Legace 5.00 12.00
IMM Milan Michalek 4.00 10.00
IMN Markus Naslund 6.00 15.00
IMO Brendan Morrison 4.00 10.00
IMP Mark Parrish 4.00 10.00
IMR Mike Richards 5.00 12.00
IMS Marc Savard 4.00 10.00
IMT Marty Turco SP 6.00 15.00
INA Nikolai Antropov 5.00 12.00
IOJ Olli Jokinen 6.00 15.00
IOK Olaf Kolzig 6.00 15.00
IPA Jay McClement 4.00 10.00
IPB Pierre-Marc Bouchard 6.00 15.00
IPM Patrick Marleau SP 6.00 15.00
IRB Rob Blake 6.00 15.00
IRF Ruslan Fedotenko 4.00 10.00
IRI Mike Ribeiro 4.00 10.00
IRM Ryan Malone 4.00 10.00
IRS Ryan Smyth 5.00 12.00
IRY Michael Ryder 4.00 10.00
ISA Miroslav Satan 5.00 12.00
ISC Sidney Crosby SP 100.00 200.00
ISG Scott Gomez 5.00 12.00
ISH Shawn Horcoff 4.00 10.00
ISS Sergei Samsonov SP 5.00 12.00
ISV Marek Svatos SP 12.00 30.00
ITB Todd Bertuzzi SP 10.00 25.00
ITC Ty Conklin 5.00 12.00
ITE Mikael Tellqvist 6.00 15.00
ITH Joe Thornton SP 20.00 50.00
ITV Tomas Vokoun 5.00 12.00
IVL Vincent Lecavalier 6.00 15.00
IWR Wade Redden 4.00 10.00

2006-07 Flair Showcase Stitches

SSAH Ales Hemsky 4.00 10.00
SSAK Alex Kovalev 4.00 10.00
SSAO Alexander Ovechkin 12.00 30.00
SSAT Alex Tanguay 3.00 8.00
SSBG Bill Guerin 5.00 12.00
SSBL Rob Blake 5.00 12.00
SSBM Brenden Morrow 4.00 10.00
SSBO Radek Bonk 3.00 8.00
SSBR Martin Brodeur 10.00 25.00
SSBS Brad Stuart 3.00 8.00
SSCA Carlo Colaiacovo 3.00 8.00
SSCC Chris Chelios 5.00 12.00
SSCD Chris Drury 4.00 10.00
SSCO Chris Osgood 5.00 12.00
SSCP Chris Pronger 5.00 12.00
SSDA Daniel Alfredsson 5.00 12.00
SSDB Donald Brashear 3.00 8.00
SSDC Dan Cloutier 4.00 10.00
SSDE Pavol Demitra 6.00 15.00
SSDH Dan Hamhuis 4.00 10.00
SSDL David Legwand 4.00 10.00
SSDM Darren McCarty 3.00 8.00
SSDR Dwayne Roloson 4.00 10.00
SSEB Ed Belfour 8.00 20.00
SSED Eric Daze 3.00 8.00
SSEL Eric Lindros 8.00 20.00
SSEN Evgeni Nabokov 4.00 10.00
SSES Eric Staal 6.00 16.00
SSFP Fernando Pisani 3.00 8.00
SSGA Mathieu Garon 4.00 10.00
SSGM Glen Murray 4.00 10.00
SSGR Gary Roberts 3.00 8.00
SSHO Marcel Hossa 3.00 8.00
SSJA Jason Arnott 4.00 10.00
SSJB Jay Bouwmeester 3.00 8.00
SSJC Jonathan Cheechoo 4.00 10.00
SSJG Jean-Sebastien Giguere 5.00 12.00
SSJI Jarome Iginla 6.00 15.00
SSJJ Jaromir Jagr 15.00 40.00
SSJL Joffrey Lupul 3.00 8.00
SSJO Joe Thornton 8.00 20.00
SSJR Jeremy Roenick 8.00 20.00
SSJS Jason Spezza 5.00 12.00
SSJT Jose Theodore 5.00 12.00
SSJW Justin Williams 4.00 10.00
SSKP Keith Primeau 4.00 10.00
SSKT Keith Tkachuk 5.00 12.00
SSLE Jere Lehtinen 3.00 8.00
SSLM Mario Lemieux 12.00 30.00
SSLN Ladislav Nagy 3.00 8.00
SSLU Jamie Lundmark 3.00 8.00
SSMA Marian Gaborik 5.00 12.00
SSMB Martin Biron 3.00 8.00
SSMC Bryan McCabe 3.00 8.00
SSMG Martin Gerber 4.00 10.00
SSMH Marian Hossa 5.00 12.00
SSMK Miikka Kiprusoff 5.00 12.00
SSML Manny Legace 4.00 10.00
SSMM Mike Modano 8.00 20.00
SSMN Markus Naslund 5.00 12.00
SSMO Brendan Morrison 3.00 8.00
SSMP Michael Peca 4.00 10.00
SSMR Mike Ribeiro 3.00 8.00
SSMS Marek Svatos 3.00 8.00
SSNA Nikolai Antropov 4.00 10.00
SSOH Mattias Ohlund 3.00 8.00
SSOJ Olli Jokinen 5.00 12.00
SSPA Mark Parrish 3.00 8.00
SSPB Pierre-Marc Bouchard 5.00 12.00
SSPD Pavel Datsyuk 8.00 20.00
SSPE Patrik Elias 5.00 12.00
SSPF Peter Forsberg 10.00 25.00
SSRA Brian Rafalski 4.00 10.00
SSRB Rod Brind'Amour 5.00 12.00
SSRE Robert Esche 4.00 10.00
SSRL Robert Lang 3.00 8.00
SSRM Ryan Miller 5.00 12.00
SSRR Robyn Regehr 3.00 8.00
SSRT Raffi Torres 3.00 8.00
SSRY Michael Ryder 3.00 8.00
SSRZ Richard Zednik 3.00 8.00
SSSA Miroslav Satan 4.00 10.00
SSSC Sidney Crosby 15.00 40.00
SSSG Simon Gagne 5.00 12.00
SSSK Sami Kapanen 3.00 8.00
SSSM Matt Stajan 3.00 8.00
SSSN Scott Niedermayer 5.00 12.00
SSST Martin Straka 3.00 8.00
SSSU Mats Sundin 5.00 12.00
SSSW Stephen Weiss 3.00 8.00
SSSY Steve Yzerman 12.00 30.00
SSTA Tony Amonte 4.00 10.00
SSTC Ty Conklin 4.00 10.00
SSTH Tomas Holmstrom 4.00 10.00
SSTL Trevor Linden 5.00 12.00
SSTR Tuomo Ruutu 5.00 12.00
SSTS Teemu Selanne 10.00 25.00
SSWI Jason Williams 3.00 8.00
SSWR Wade Redden 3.00 8.00
SSZC Zdeno Chara 5.00 12.00

2006-07 Flair Showcase Wave of the Future

WF1 Joffrey Lupul 1.00 2.50
WF2 Kari Lehtonen 1.25 3.00
WF3 Ilya Kovalchuk 1.50 4.00
WF4 Patrice Bergeron 2.00 5.00
WF5 Brad Boyes 1.00 2.50
WF6 Ryan Miller 1.50 4.00
WF7 Dion Phaneuf 1.25 3.00
WF8 Eric Staal 2.00 5.00
WF9 Tuomo Ruutu 1.50 4.00
WF10 Marek Svatos 1.00 2.50
WF11 Rick Nash 1.50 4.00
WF12 Jussi Jokinen 1.25 3.00
WF13 Henrik Zetterberg 2.00 5.00
WF14 Ales Hemsky 1.25 3.00
WF15 Jarret Stoll 1.25 3.00
WF16 Nathan Horton 1.50 4.00
WF17 Dustin Brown 1.50 4.00
WF18 Alexander Frolov 1.00 2.50
WF19 Marian Gaborik 1.50 4.00
WF20 Mikko Koivu 1.25 3.00
WF21 Corey Perry 2.50 6.00
WF22 Thomas Vanek 1.25 3.00
WF23 Michael Ryder 1.00 2.50
WF24 Chris Higgins 1.00 2.50
WF25 Zach Parise 1.50 4.00
WF26 Rick DiPietro 1.00 2.50
WF27 Henrik Lundqvist 4.00 10.00
WF28 Petr Prucha 1.25 3.00
WF29 Jason Spezza 1.50 4.00
WF30 Dany Heatley 1.25 3.00
WF31 Martin Havlat 1.00 2.50
WF32 Jeff Carter 1.25 3.00
WF33 Joni Pitkanen 1.00 2.50
WF34 Mike Richards 1.25 3.00
WF35 Sidney Crosby 6.00 15.00
WF36 Marc-Andre Fleury 3.00 8.00
WF37 Steve Bernier 1.00 2.50
WF38 Alexander Steen 1.00 2.50
WF39 Kyle Wellwood 1.25 3.00
WF40 Andrew Raycroft 1.25 3.00
WF41 Ryan Kesler 1.50 4.00
WF42 Alexander Ovechkin 6.00 15.00

1972-73 Flames Postcards

COMPLETE SET (20) 30.00 60.00
1 Curt Bennett 1.00 2.00
2 Dan Bouchard 2.50 5.00
3 Rey Comeau 1.00 2.00
4 BoomBoom Geoffrion CO 5.00 10.00
5 Bob Leiter 1.00 2.00
6 Kerry Ketter 1.00 2.00
7 Billy MacMillan 1.00 2.00
8 Randy Manery 1.00 2.00
9 Keith McCreary 1.00 2.00
10 Lew Morrison 1.00 2.00
11 Phil Myre 3.00 6.00
12 Bob Paradise 1.00 2.00
13 Noel Picard 1.00 2.00
14 Bill Plager 1.50 3.00
15 Noel Price 1.50 3.00
16 Pat Quinn 2.50 5.00
17 Jacques Richard 1.50 3.00
18 Leon Rochefort 1.00 2.00
19 Larry Romanchych 1.00 2.00
20 John Stewart 1.00 2.00

1978-79 Flames Majik Market

COMPLETE SET (20) 15.00 30.00
1 Rejean Lemelin 1.50 3.00
2 Greg Fox .50 1.00
3 Pat Ribble SP 5.00 10.00
5 Brad Marsh 2.00 4.00
6 Ken Houston .50 1.00
7 Bobby LaLonde .50 1.00
8 David Shand .50 1.00
9 Jean Pronovost .75 1.50
10 Bill Clement 1.50 3.00
11 Bob MacMillan .50 1.00
12 Tom Lysiak 1.00 2.00
15 Rod Seiling .50 1.00
16 Guy Chouinard 1.00 2.00
17 Don Red Laurence .50 1.00
19 Ed Kea .50 1.00
20 Bob Murdoch .75 1.50
24 Harold Phillipoff .50 1.00
25 Willi Plett 1.00 2.00
27 Eric Vail 1.00 2.00
30 Daniel Bouchard 1.50 3.00

1979-80 Flames Postcards

COMPLETE SET (20) 15.00 30.00
1 Jim Craig 2.50 5.00
2 Curt Bennett .50 1.00
3 Phil Russell .50 1.00
4 Pekka Rautakallio .50 1.00
5 Brad Marsh 2.50 5.00
6 Ken Houston .50 1.00
7 Garry Unger 1.50 3.00
8 David Shand .50 1.00
9 Jean Pronovost .75 1.50
10 Bill Clement 2.00 4.00
11 Bob MacMillan .50 1.00
12 Don Lever .50 1.00
14 Kent Nilsson 2.50 5.00
16 Guy Chouinard 1.00 2.00
20 Bob Murdoch .75 1.50
23 Paul Reinhardt .75 1.50
25 Willi Plett 1.25 2.50
27 Eric Vail .75 1.50
30 Dan Bouchard 1.50 3.00
31 Pat Riggin 1.25 2.50

1979-80 Flames Team Issue

COMPLETE SET (22) 20.00 40.00
1 Curt Bennett .50 1.00
2 Ivan Boldirev .50 1.00
3 Dan Bouchard 1.50 3.00
4 Guy Chouinard 1.00 2.00
5 Bill Clement 1.50 3.00
6 Jim Craig 2.00 4.00
7 Ken Houston .50 1.00
8 Brad Marsh 1.50 3.00
9 Bob MacMillan .50 1.00
10 Al MacNeil .50 1.00
11 Bob Murdoch .75 1.50
12 Kent Nilsson 2.00 4.00
13 Willi Plett 1.00 2.00
14 Jean Pronovost .75 1.50
15 Pekka Rautakallio .50 1.00
16 Paul Reinhart .75 1.50
17 Pat Riggin 1.00 2.00
18 Darcy Rota .50 1.00
19 Phil Russell .50 1.00
20 David Shand .50 1.00
21 Garry Unger 1.25 2.50
22 Eric Vail 1.00 2.00

1980-81 Flames Postcards

COMPLETE SET (24) 20.00 40.00
1 Daniel Bouchard 1.25 3.00
2 Guy Chouinard .75 2.00
3 Bill Clement .75 2.00
4 Denis Cyr .40 1.00
5 Randy Holt .40 1.00
6 Ken Houston .40 1.00
7 Rejean Lemelin 2.50 5.00
8 Kevin Lavallee .40 1.00
9 Don Lever .40 1.00
10 Bob MacMillan .40 1.00
11 Bob Murdoch .40 1.00
12 Brad Marsh 1.00 2.50
13 Kent Nilsson 1.50 4.00
14 Willi Plett .60 1.50
15 Jim Peplinski 1.00 2.50
16 Pekka Rautakallio .75 2.00
17 Paul Reinhart 1.00 2.50
18 Pat Riggin .75 2.00
19 Phil Russell .40 1.00
20 Brad Smith .40 1.00
21 Jay Soleway .40 1.00
22 Eric Vail .60 1.50
23 Bert Wilson .40 1.00
24 Team Photo .60 1.50

1981-82 Flames Postcards

COMPLETE SET (20) 10.00 25.00
1 Charlie Bourgeois .30 .75
2 Mel Bridgman .40 1.00
3 Guy Chouinard .60 1.50
4 Bill Clement .60 1.50
5 Denis Cyr .30 .75
6 Jamie Hislop .30 .75
7 Ken Houston .30 .75
8 Steve Konroyd .30 .75
9 Dan Labraaten .30 .75
10 Kevin Lavallee .30 .75
11 Rejean Lemelin 1.25 3.00
12 Lanny McDonald 1.25 3.00
13 Gary McAdam .30 .75
14 Bob Murdoch .40 1.00
15 Jim Peplinski .75 2.00
16 Willi Plett .60 1.50
17 Pekka Rautakallio .40 1.00
18 Paul Reinhart .60 1.50
19 Pat Riggin .60 1.50
20 Phil Russell .30 .75

1982-83 Flames Dollars

COMPLETE SET (6) 10.00 25.00
1 Mel Bridgman 1.50 4.00
2 Don Edwards 1.50 4.00
3 Lanny McDonald DP 3.00 8.00
4 Kent Nilsson 2.50 6.00
5 Jim Peplinski 1.50 4.00
6 Paul Reinhart 2.00 5.00

1985-86 Flames Red Rooster

COMPLETE SET (30) 10.00 25.00
1 Paul Baxter .15 .40
2 Ed Beers .15 .40
3 Perry Berezan .15 .40
4 Charlie Bourgeois .15 .40
5 Steve Bozek .15 .40
6 Gino Cavallini .15 .40
7 Marc D'Amour .20 .50
8 Tim Hunter .40 1.00
9 Bob Johnson CO 1.00 2.50
10 Steve Konroyd .15 .40
11 Richard Kromm .15 .40
12 Rejean Lemelin .40 1.00
13 Hakan Loob .40 1.00
14 Lanny McDonald .75 2.00
15 Lanny McDonald .75 2.00
16 Al MacInnis 2.50 6.00
17 Jamie Macoun .20 .50
18 Bob Murdoch CO .15 .40
19 Joel Otto .60 1.50
20 Pierre Page CO .20 .50
21 Colin Patterson .15 .40
22 Jim Peplinski .30 .75
23 Dan Quinn .20 .50
24 Paul Reinhart .30 .75
25 Doug Risebrough .15 .40
26 Doug Risebrough .15 .40
27 Neil Sheehy .15 .40
28 Gary Suter .40 1.00
29 Mike Vernon
(No facsimile autograph 2.50 6.00
30 Carey Wilson .15 .40

1986-87 Flames Red Rooster

COMPLETE SET (30) 8.00 20.00
1 Paul Baxter .20 .50
2 Perry Berezan .20 .50
3 Steve Bozek .20 .50
4 Brian Bradley .40 1.00
5 Brian Engblom .20 .50
6 Nick Fotiu .20 .50
7 Tim Hunter .30 .75
8 Bob Johnson CO .75 2.00
9 Rejean Lemelin .40 1.00
10 Hakan Loob .40 1.00
11 Al MacInnis 1.25 3.00
12 Jamie Macoun .20 .50
13 Lanny McDonald .60 1.50
14 Lanny McDonald .60 1.50
15 Joe Mullen .60 1.50
16 Joe Mullen .60 1.50
17 Bob Murdoch CO .20 .50
18 Joel Otto .40 1.00
19 Pierre Page CO .20 .50
20 Colin Patterson .20 .50
21 Jim Peplinski .20 .50
22 Paul Reinhart .20 .50
23 Paul Reinhart .20 .50
24 Doug Risebrough .20 .50
25 Gary Roberts 1.50 4.00
26 Neil Sheehy .20 .50
27 Gary Suter .30 .75
28 John Tonelli .30 .75
29 Mike Vernon 1.25 3.00
30 Carey Wilson .20 .50

1987-88 Flames Red Rooster

COMPLETE SET (30) 20.00 50.00
1 Perry Berezan .15 .40
2 Steve Bozek .15 .40
3 Mike Bullard .20 .50
4 Shane Churla .30 .75
5 Terry Crisp CO .15 .40
6 Doug Dadswell .20 .50
7 Brian Glynn .15 .40
8 Brett Hull 12.00 30.00
9 Tim Hunter .20 .50
10 Hakan Loob .30 .75
11 Hakan Loob .30 .75
12 Al MacInnis .75 2.00
13 Brad McCrimmon .20 .50
14 Lanny McDonald .40 1.00
15 Lanny McDonald .40 1.00
16 Joe Mullen .40 1.00
17 Dana Murzyn .15 .40
18 Ric Nattress .15 .40
19 Joe Nieuwendyk 2.50 6.00
20 Joe Nieuwendyk 2.50 6.00
21 Joel Otto .30 .75
22 Pierre Page CO .15 .40
23 Colin Patterson .15 .40
24 Jim Peplinski .20 .50
25 Paul Reinhart .20 .50
26 Doug Risebrough CO .15 .40
27 Gary Roberts .75 2.00
28 Gary Suter .30 .75
29 John Tonelli .20 .50
30 Mike Vernon .75 2.00

1990-91 Flames IGA/McGavin's

COMPLETE SET (30) 14.00 35.00
1 Paul Baxter CO SP 1.25 3.00
2 Guy Charron CO SP 1.50 4.00
3 Theo Fleury 2.00 5.00
4 Doug Gilmour 2.00 5.00
5 Jiri Hrdina .20 .50
6 Mark Hunter .20 .50
7 Tim Hunter .40 1.00
8 Roger Johansson .20 .50
9 Al MacInnis .75 2.00
10 Brian MacLellan .20 .50
11 Jamie Macoun .30 .75
12 Sergei Makarov .60 1.50
13 Sergei Makarov
Al MacInnis .60 1.50
14 Stephane Matteau .30 .75
15 Dana Murzyn .20 .50
16 Frantisek Musil .20 .50
17 Ric Nattress .20 .50
18 Joe Nieuwendyk 1.25 3.00
19 Joel Otto .40 1.00
20 Colin Patterson .20 .50
21 Sergei Priakin .20 .50
22 Paul Ranheim .30 .75
23 Robert Reichel .60 1.50
24 Doug Risebrough CO/GM SP 1.25 3.00
25 Gary Roberts .75 2.00
26 Gary Suter .40 1.00
27 Tim Sweeney .20 .50
28 Mike Vernon .75 2.00
29 Rick Wamsley .40 1.00
30 Checklist Card SP 1.25 3.00

1991 Flames Panini Team Stickers

COMPLETE SET (32) 1.50 4.00
1 Theo Fleury .30 .75
2 Doug Gilmour .30 .75
3 Jiri Hrdina .01 .05
4 Mark Hunter .01 .05
5 Tim Hunter .02 .10
6 Roger Johansson .01 .05
7 Al MacInnis .15 .40
8 Brian MacLellan .01 .05
9 Jamie Macoun .01 .05
10 Sergei Makarov .08 .25
11 Stephane Matteau .01 .05
12 Dana Murzyn .01 .05
13 Ric Nattress .01 .05
14 Joe Nieuwendyk .15 .40
15 Joel Otto .05 .15
16 Colin Patterson .01 .05
17 Sergei Priakin .01 .05
18 Paul Ranheim .02 .10
19 Gary Roberts .15 .40
20 Ken Sabourin .01 .05
21 Gary Suter .02 .10
22 Tim Sweeney .01 .05
23 Mike Vernon .15 .40
24 Rick Wamsley .02 .10
A Team Logo
Left Side .01 .05
B Team Logo
Right Side .01 .05
C Flames' Time Out
Upper Left Corner .01 .05
D Flames' Time Out
Lower Left Corner .01 .05
E Flames' Time Out
Upper Right Corner .01 .05
F Flames' Time Out
Lower Right Corner .01 .05
G Joel Otto
Roger Johansson .02 .10
H Gary Suter .02 .10

1991-92 Flames IGA

COMPLETE SET (30) 10.00 25.00
1 Theo Fleury 1.00 2.50
2 Tomas Forslund .15 .40
3 Doug Gilmour 1.00 2.50
4 Marc Habscheid .15 .40
5 Tim Hunter .25 .60
6 Jim Kyte .15 .40
7 Al MacInnis .40 1.00
8 Jamie Macoun .15 .40
9 Sergei Makarov .40 1.00
10 Stephane Matteau .15 .40
11 Frantisek Musil .15 .40
12 Ric Nattress .15 .40
13 Joe Nieuwendyk .50 1.25
14 Mark Osiecki .75 2.00
15 Joel Otto .25 .60
16 Paul Ranheim .15 .40
17 Robert Reichel .30 .75
18 Gary Roberts .40 1.00
19 Neil Sheehy .15 .40
20 Martin Simard .15 .40
21 Ronnie Stern .15 .40
22 Gary Suter .30 .75
23 Tim Sweeney .15 .40
24 Mike Vernon .40 1.00
25 Rick Wamsley .30 .75
26 Carey Wilson .15 .40
27 Paul Baxter CO SP 1.00 2.50
28 Guy Charron CO SP 1.00 2.50
29 Doug Risebrough CO SP 1.00 2.50
30 Checklist Card SP 1.00 2.50

1992-93 Flames IGA

COMPLETE SET (30) 8.00 20.00
1 Checklist .02 .10
2 Craig Berube .20 .50
3 Gary Leeman .15 .40
4 Joel Otto .30 .75
5 Robert Reichel .40 1.00
6 Gary Roberts .40 1.00
7 Greg Smyth .15 .40
8 Gary Suter .30 .75
9 Jeff Reese .25 .60
10 Mike Vernon .40 1.00
11 Carey Wilson .15 .40
12 Trent Yawney .15 .40
13 Michel Petit .15 .40
14 Paul Ranheim .15 .40
15 Sergei Makarov .40 1.00
16 Frantisek Musil .15 .40
17 Joe Nieuwendyk .75 2.00
18 Alexander Godynyuk .15 .40
19 Roger Johansson .15 .40
20 Theo Fleury 1.00 2.50
21 Chris Lindberg .15 .40
22 Al MacInnis .60 1.50
23 Kevin Dahl .15 .40
24 Chris Dahlquist .15 .40
25 Ronnie Stern .20 .50
26 Dave King CO .15 .40
27 Guy Charron CO .02 .10
28 Slavomir Lener CO .02 .10
29 Jamie Hislop CO .02 .10
30 Franchise History .02 .10

1994-95 Fleer

1 Patrik Carnback .10 .25
2 Bob Corkum .10 .25
3 Paul Kariya .15 .40
4 Valeri Karpov RC .10 .25
5 Tom Kurvers .10 .25
6 John Lilley .10 .25
7 Mikhail Shtalenkov RC .10 .25
8 Oleg Tverdovsky .12 .30
9 Ray Bourque .25 .60
10 Mariusz Czerkawski RC .15 .40
11 John Gruden RC .10 .25
12 Al Iafrate .10 .25
13 Blaine Lacher RC .12 .30
14 Mats Naslund .10 .25
15 Cam Neely .15 .40
16 Adam Oates .15 .40
17 Bryan Smolinski .10 .25
18 Don Sweeney .10 .25
19 Donald Audette .10 .25
20 Dominik Hasek .25 .60
21 Dale Hawerchuk .20 .50
22 Yuri Khmylev .10 .25
23 Pat LaFontaine .15 .40
24 Brad May .10 .25
25 Alexander Mogilny .12 .30
26 Derek Plante .10 .25
27 Richard Smehlik .10 .25
28 Steve Chiasson .10 .25
29 Theo Fleury .15 .40
30 Phil Housley .12 .30
31 Trevor Kidd .12 .30
32 Joe Nieuwendyk .12 .30
33 James Patrick .10 .25
34 Robert Reichel .10 .25
35 Gary Roberts .10 .25
36 German Titov .10 .25
37 Tony Amonte .12 .30
38 Ed Belfour .15 .40
39 Chris Chelios .15 .40
40 Dirk Graham .10 .25
41 Sergei Krivokrasov .10 .25
42 Joe Murphy .10 .25
43 Bernie Nicholls .12 .30
44 Patrick Poulin .10 .25
45 Jeremy Roenick .25 .60
46 Steve Smith .10 .25
47 Gary Suter .10 .25
48 Russ Courtnall .10 .25
49 Dave Gagner .12 .30
50 Brent Gilchrist .10 .25
51 Todd Harvey .10 .25
52 Derian Hatcher .10 .25

53 Kevin Hatcher .10 .25
54 Mike Kennedy RC .15 .40
55 Mike Modano .25 .60
56 Andy Moog .15 .40
57 Dino Ciccarelli .12 .30
58 Paul Coffey .15 .40
59 Sergei Fedorov .25 .60
60 Vladimir Konstantinov .12 .30
61 Slava Kozlov .12 .30
62 Nicklas Lidstrom .15 .40
63 Chris Osgood .25 .60
64 Keith Primeau .12 .30
65 Ray Sheppard .12 .30
66 Mike Vernon .12 .30
67 Steve Yzerman .40 1.00
68 Jason Arnott .12 .30
69 Shayne Corson .12 .30
70 Igor Kravchuk .10 .25
71 Todd Marchant .10 .25
72 Roman Oksiuta .10 .25
73 Fredrik Olausson .10 .25
74 David Oliver RC .10 .25
75 Bill Ranford .12 .30
76 Stu Barnes .10 .25
77 Jesse Belanger .10 .25
78 Keith Brown .10 .25
79 Bob Kudelski .10 .25
80 Scott Mellanby .12 .30
81 Gord Murphy .10 .25
82 Rob Niedermayer .12 .30
83 John Vanbiesbrouck .15 .40
84 Sean Burke .12 .30
85 Jimmy Carson .10 .25
86 Andrew Cassels .10 .25
87 Andrei Nikolishin .10 .25
88 Chris Pronger .15 .40
89 Geoff Sanderson .12 .30
90 Darren Turcotte .10 .25
91 Pat Verbeek .12 .30
92 Glen Wesley .10 .25
93 Rob Blake .15 .40
94 Wayne Gretzky 1.00 2.50
95 Kelly Hrudey .12 .30
96 Jari Kurri .12 .30
97 Eric Lacroix .15 .40
98 Marty McSorley .12 .30
99 Jamie Storr .12 .30
100 Rick Tocchet .12 .30
101 Brian Bellows .12 .30
102 Patrice Brisebois .10 .25
103 Vincent Damphousse .12 .30
104 Kirk Muller .10 .25
105 Lyle Odelein .10 .25
106 Mark Recchi .20 .50
107 Patrick Roy .40 1.00
108 Brian Savage .10 .25
109 Mathieu Schneider .10 .25
110 Turner Stevenson .10 .25
111 Martin Brodeur .40 1.00
112 Bill Guerin .15 .40
113 Claude Lemieux .15 .40
114 John MacLean .12 .30
115 Scott Niedermayer .15 .40
116 Stephane Richer .12 .30
117 Brian Rolston .12 .30
118 Alexander Semak .10 .25
119 Scott Stevens .15 .40
120 Ray Ferraro .10 .25
121 Patrick Flatley .10 .25
122 Darius Kasparaitis .10 .25
123 Derek King .10 .25
124 Scott Lachance .10 .25
125 Brett Lindros .10 .25
126 Vladimir Malakhov .10 .25
127 Jamie McLennan .12 .30
128 Zigmund Palffy .12 .30
129 Steve Thomas .10 .25
130 Pierre Turgeon .12 .30
131 Jeff Beukeboom .10 .25
132 Adam Graves .10 .25
133 Alexei Kovalev .12 .30
134 Steve Larmer .12 .30
135 Brian Leetch .12 .30
136 Mark Messier .30 .75
137 Petr Nedved .12 .30
138 Sergei Nemchinov .10 .25
139 Mike Richter .15 .40
140 Sergei Zubov .12 .30
141 Don Beaupre .12 .30
142 Radek Bonk RC .10 .25
143 Alexandre Daigle .10 .25
144 Pavol Demitra .20 .50
145 Pat Elynuik .10 .25
146 Rob Gaudreau .10 .25
147 Sean Hill .10 .25
148 Sylvain Turgeon .10 .25
149 Alexei Yashin .15 .40
150 Rod Brind'Amour .12 .30
151 Eric Desjardins .12 .30
152 Gilbert Dionne .10 .25
153 Garry Galley .10 .25
154 Ron Hextall .15 .40
155 Patrik Juhlin RC .10 .25
156 John LeClair .15 .40
157 Eric Lindros .25 .60
158 Mikael Renberg .12 .30
159 Chris Therien .10 .25
160 Dimitri Yushkevich .10 .25
161 Len Barrie .10 .25
162 Ron Francis .20 .50
163 Jaromir Jagr .50 1.25
164 Shawn McEachern .10 .25
165 Joe Mullen .12 .30
166 Larry Murphy .12 .30
167 Luc Robitaille .15 .40
168 Ulf Samuelsson .10 .25
169 Tomas Sandstrom .10 .25
170 Kevin Stevens .12 .30
171 Martin Straka .10 .25
172 Ken Wregget .12 .30
173 Wendel Clark .25 .60
174 Adam Deadmarsh .10 .25
175 Stephane Fiset .12 .30
176 Peter Forsberg .30 .75
177 Valeri Kamensky .12 .30
178 Andrei Kovalenko .10 .25
179 Uwe Krupp .10 .25
180 Sylvain Lefebvre .10 .25
181 Owen Nolan .15 .40
182 Mike Ricci .10 .25
183 Joe Sakic .30 .75
184 Denis Chasse RC .15 .40
185 Adam Creighton .10 .25
186 Steve Duchesne .10 .25
187 Brett Hull .30 .75
188 Curtis Joseph .20 .50
189 Ian Laperriere RC .15 .40
190 Al MacInnis .20 .50
191 Brendan Shanahan .15 .40
192 Patrice Tardif RC .15 .40
193 Esa Tikkanen .10 .25
194 Ulf Dahlen .10 .25
195 Pat Falloon .10 .25
196 Jeff Friesen .10 .25
197 Arturs Irbe .12 .30
198 Sergei Makarov .10 .25
199 Andrei Nazarov .10 .25
200 Sandis Ozolinsh .10 .25
201 Michal Sykora .10 .25
202 Ray Whitney .10 .25
203 Brian Bradley .10 .25
204 Shawn Chambers .10 .25
205 Eric Charron .15 .40
206 Chris Gratton .10 .25
207 Roman Hamrlik .10 .25
208 Petr Klima .10 .25
209 Daren Puppa .12 .30
210 Alexander Selivanov RC .12 .30
211 Jason Wiemer RC .12 .30
212 Dave Andreychuk .15 .40
213 Dave Ellett .10 .25
214 Mike Gartner .20 .50
215 Doug Gilmour .20 .50
216 Kenny Jonsson .10 .25
217 Dmitri Mironov .10 .25
218 Felix Potvin .25 .60
219 Mike Ridley .10 .25
220 Mats Sundin .15 .40
221 Josef Beranek .10 .25
222 Jeff Brown .10 .25
223 Pavel Bure .15 .40
224 Geoff Courtnall .10 .25
225 Trevor Linden .15 .40
226 Jyrki Lumme .10 .25
227 Kirk McLean .12 .30
228 Gino Odjick .10 .25
229 Mike Peca .12 .30
230 Cliff Ronning .10 .25
231 Jason Allison .12 .30
232 Peter Bondra .15 .40
233 Jim Carey RC .15 .40
234 Sylvain Cote .10 .25
235 Dale Hunter .10 .25
236 Joe Juneau .10 .25
237 Dimitri Khristich .10 .25
238 Pat Peake .10 .25
239 Mark Tinordi .10 .25
240 Nelson Emerson .10 .25
241 Michal Grosek .10 .25
242 Nikolai Khabibulin .12 .30
243 Dave Manson .10 .25
244 Stephane Quintal .10 .25
245 Teemu Selanne .30 .75
246 Keith Tkachuk .15 .40
247 Alexei Zhamnov .12 .30
248 Checklist .07 .12
249 Checklist .07 .12
250 Checklist .07 .12

1994-95 Fleer Franchise Futures

COMPLETE SET (10) 5.00 10.00
1 Jason Arnott .40 1.00
2 Rob Blake .60 1.50
3 Adam Graves .40 1.00
4 Arturs Irbe .60 1.50
5 Joe Juneau .60 1.50
6 Sandis Ozolinsh .40 1.00
7 Mikael Renberg .60 1.50
8 Keith Tkachuk 1.25 3.00
9 Alexei Yashin .40 1.00
10 Sergei Zubov .40 1.00

1994-95 Fleer Headliners

COMPLETE SET (10) 8.00 15.00
1 Pavel Bure .60 1.50
2 Sergei Fedorov .75 2.00
3 Doug Gilmour .30 .75
4 Wayne Gretzky 3.00 8.00
5 Brian Leetch .60 1.50
6 Eric Lindros .60 1.50
7 Mark Messier .60 1.50
8 Cam Neely .60 1.50
9 Mark Recchi .30 .75
10 Brendan Shanahan .60 1.50

1994-95 Fleer Netminders

COMPLETE SET (10) 3.00 8.00
1 Ed Belfour .30 .75
2 Martin Brodeur .75 2.00
3 Dominik Hasek .60 1.50
4 Arturs Irbe .15 .40
5 Curtis Joseph .20 .50
6 Kirk McLean .15 .40
7 Felix Potvin .20 .50
8 Mike Richter .30 .75
9 Patrick Roy 1.50 4.00
10 John Vanbiesbrouck .15 .40

1994-95 Fleer Rookie Sensations

COMPLETE SET (10) 10.00 25.00
1 Radek Bonk .75 2.00
2 Peter Forsberg 4.00 10.00
3 Jeff Friesen .75 2.00
4 Todd Harvey .75 2.00
5 Paul Kariya 2.50 6.00
6 Blaine Lacher .75 2.00
7 Brett Lindros .75 2.00
8 Mike Peca .75 2.00
9 Jamie Storr .75 2.00
10 Oleg Tverdovsky .75 2.00

1994-95 Fleer Slapshot Artists

COMPLETE SET (10) 10.00 20.00
1 Wendel Clark .75 2.00
2 Brett Hull 2.00 5.00
3 Al Iafrate .50 1.25
4 Jaromir Jagr 2.50 6.00
5 Al MacInnis .75 2.00
6 Mike Modano .75 2.00
7 Stephane Richer .75 2.00
8 Jeremy Roenick 2.00 5.00
9 Geoff Sanderson .75 2.00
10 Steve Thomas .50 1.25

1996-97 Fleer Promo Sheet

COMPLETE SET (3) .40 1.00
1 John LeClair .20 .50
2 John LeClair
Art Ross insert .20 .50
3 Peter Ferraro .08 .25

1996-97 Fleer

1 Guy Hebert .12 .30
2 Paul Kariya .15 .40
3 Teemu Selanne .30 .75
4 Ray Bourque .25 .60
5 Kyle McLaren .10 .25
6 Adam Oates .10 .25
7 Bill Ranford .12 .30
8 Rick Tocchet .12 .30
9 Jason Dawe .10 .25
10 Dominik Hasek .25 .60
11 Pat LaFontaine .15 .40
12 Theo Fleury .30 .75
13 Trevor Kidd .10 .25
14 German Titov .10 .25
15 Ed Belfour .12 .30
16 Chris Chelios .15 .40
17 Eric Daze .12 .30
18 Jeremy Roenick .25 .60
19 Gary Suter .10 .25
20 Peter Forsberg .30 .75
21 Valeri Kamensky .12 .30
22 Claude Lemieux .10 .25
23 Sandis Ozolinsh .10 .25
24 Patrick Roy .40 1.00
25 Joe Sakic .30 .75
26 Derian Hatcher .10 .25
27 Mike Modano .25 .60
28 Sergei Zubov .10 .25
29 Paul Coffey .15 .40
30 Sergei Fedorov .25 .60
31 Vladimir Konstantinov .12 .30
32 Slava Kozlov .10 .25
33 Chris Osgood .15 .40
34 Keith Primeau .12 .30
35 Steve Yzerman .40 1.00
36 Jason Arnott .12 .30
37 Curtis Joseph .20 .50
38 Doug Weight .15 .40
39 Ed Jovanovski .15 .40
40 Scott Mellanby .10 .25
41 Rob Niedermayer .12 .30
42 Ray Sheppard .12 .30
43 Robert Svehla .10 .25
44 John Vanbiesbrouck .15 .40
45 Sean Burke .10 .25
46 Andrew Cassels .10 .25
47 Geoff Sanderson .12 .30
48 Brendan Shanahan .15 .40
49 Ray Ferraro .10 .25
50 Dimitri Khristich .10 .25
51 Vitali Yachmenev .10 .25
52 Valeri Bure .10 .25
53 Vincent Damphousse .12 .30
54 Saku Koivu .15 .40
55 Mark Recchi .20 .50
56 Jocelyn Thibault .12 .30
57 Pierre Turgeon .12 .30
58 Martin Brodeur .40 1.00
59 Phil Housley .12 .30
60 Scott Niedermayer .12 .30
61 Scott Stevens .15 .40
62 Steve Thomas .10 .25
63 Todd Bertuzzi .15 .40
64 Travis Green .12 .30
65 Kenny Jonsson .10 .25
66 Zigmund Palffy .15 .40
67 Adam Graves .12 .30
68 Wayne Gretzky 1.00 2.50
69 Alexei Kovalev .12 .30
70 Brian Leetch .12 .30
71 Mark Messier .30 .75
72 Niklas Sundstrom .10 .25
73 Daniel Alfredsson .15 .40
74 Radek Bonk .10 .25
75 Steve Duchesne .10 .25
76 Damian Rhodes .12 .30
77 Alexei Yashin .12 .30
78 Rod Brind'Amour .12 .30
79 Eric Desjardins .12 .30
80 Ron Hextall .15 .40
81 John LeClair .15 .40
82 Eric Lindros .25 .60
83 Mikael Renberg .12 .30
84 Tom Barrasso .12 .30
85 Ron Francis .20 .50
86 Jaromir Jagr .50 1.25
87 Mario Lemieux .60 1.50
88 Petr Nedved .12 .30
89 Bryan Smolinski .10 .25
90 Nikolai Khabibulin .12 .30
91 Teppo Numminen .10 .25
92 Keith Tkachuk .15 .40
93 Oleg Tverdovsky .12 .30
94 Alexei Zhamnov .12 .30
95 Shayne Corson .12 .30
96 Grant Fuhr .25 .60
97 Brett Hull .30 .75
98 Al MacInnis .20 .50
99 Chris Pronger .15 .40
100 Owen Nolan .15 .40
101 Marcus Ragnarsson .10 .25
102 Chris Terreri .12 .30
103 Brian Bradley .10 .25
104 Roman Hamrlik .10 .25
105 Daren Puppa .12 .30
106 Alexander Selivanov .10 .25
107 Doug Gilmour UER .20 .50
108 Larry Murphy .12 .30
109 Felix Potvin .25 .60
110 Mats Sundin .15 .40
111 Pavel Bure .15 .40
112 Trevor Linden .15 .40
113 Kirk McLean .12 .30
114 Alexander Mogilny .12 .30
115 Peter Bondra .15 .40
116 Jim Carey .15 .40
117 Sergei Gonchar .10 .25
118 Joe Juneau .10 .25
119 Michal Pivonka .10 .25
120 Brendan Witt .10 .25
121 Nolan Baumgartner .10 .25
122 Martin Biron RC .20 .50
123 Jason Bonsignore .10 .25
124 Andrew Brunette RC .20 .50
125 Jason Doig .10 .25
126 Peter Ferraro .10 .25
127 Eric Fichaud .12 .30
128 Ladislav Kohn RC .10 .25
129 Jamie Langenbrunner .10 .25
130 Daymond Langkow .12 .30
131 Jay McKee RC .10 .25
132 Wayne Primeau RC .10 .25
133 Jamie Storr RC .10 .25
134 Jose Theodore .20 .50
135 Roman Vopat .10 .25
136 Rookie Scor.Ldrs .05 .15
137 Points Ldrs. .05 .15
138 Goals Ldrs. .05 .15
139 Assists Ldrs. .05 .15
140 Def.Pts.Ldrs .05 .15
141 Pow.Play.Goal Ldrs .05 .15
142 Game.Winning.Goal Ldrs. .05 .15
143 Plus
Minus Ldrs. .05 .15
144 G.A.A. Ldrs. .05 .15
145 Games Won Ldrs. .05 .15
146 Shutouts Ldrs. .05 .15
147 Save Percentage Ldrs. .05 .15
148 Checklist (1-72) .05 .15
149 Checklist (73-150) .05 .15
150 Checklist (Inserts) .05 .15

1996-97 Fleer Art Ross

COMPLETE SET (25) 20.00 50.00
1 Pavel Bure .60 1.50
2 Sergei Fedorov .75 2.00
3 Theo Fleury .30 .75
4 Peter Forsberg 1.50 4.00
5 Ron Francis .30 .75
6 Wayne Gretzky 5.00 10.00
7 Brett Hull .75 2.00
8 Jaromir Jagr 1.00 2.50
9 Valeri Kamensky .30 .75
10 Paul Kariya .60 1.50
11 Pat LaFontaine .60 1.50
12 John LeClair .60 1.50
13 Mario Lemieux 4.00 8.00
14 Eric Lindros .60 1.50
15 Mark Messier .60 1.50
16 Alexander Mogilny .30 .75
17 Petr Nedved .30 .75
18 Adam Oates .30 .75
19 Jeremy Roenick .75 2.00
20 Joe Sakic 1.25 3.00
21 Teemu Selanne .60 1.50
22 Keith Tkachuk .60 1.50
23 Pierre Turgeon .30 .75
24 Doug Weight .30 .75
25 Steve Yzerman 4.00 8.00

1996-97 Fleer Calder Candidates

COMPLETE SET (10) 8.00 20.00
1 Andrew Brunette .75 2.00
2 Jason Doig .75 2.00
3 Peter Ferraro .75 2.00
4 Eric Fichaud .75 2.00
5 Ladislav Kohn .75 2.00
6 Jamie Langenbrunner 1.25 3.00
7 Daymond Langkow 1.25 3.00
8 Jamie Storr .75 2.00
9 Jose Theodore 3.00 8.00
10 Roman Vopat .75 2.00

1996-97 Fleer Norris

COMPLETE SET (10) 15.00 40.00
1 Ray Bourque 6.00 15.00
2 Chris Chelios 4.00 10.00
3 Paul Coffey 4.00 10.00
4 Eric Desjardins 1.25 3.00
5 Phil Housley 1.25 3.00
6 Vladimir Konstantinov 2.50 6.00
7 Brian Leetch 4.00 10.00
8 Teppo Numminen 1.25 3.00
9 Larry Murphy 1.25 3.00
10 Sandis Ozolinsh 1.25 3.00

1996-97 Fleer Pearson

COMPLETE SET (10) 50.00 125.00
1 Pavel Bure 3.00 8.00
2 Sergei Fedorov 3.00 8.00
3 Peter Forsberg 5.00 12.00
4 Wayne Gretzky 15.00 40.00
5 Jaromir Jagr 5.00 12.00
6 Paul Kariya 3.00 8.00
7 Mario Lemieux 10.00 25.00
8 Eric Lindros 3.00 8.00
9 Patrick Roy 10.00 25.00
10 Joe Sakic 6.00 15.00

1996-97 Fleer Rookie Sensations

COMPLETE SET (10) 6.00 15.00
1 Daniel Alfredsson .75 2.00
2 Todd Bertuzzi .75 2.00
3 Valeri Bure .40 1.00
4 Eric Daze .40 1.00
5 Sergei Gonchar .40 1.00
6 Ed Jovanovski .40 1.00
7 Saku Koivu .75 2.00
8 Marcus Ragnarsson .40 1.00
9 Petr Sykora .40 1.00
10 Vitali Yachmenev .40 1.00

1996-97 Fleer Vezina

COMPLETE SET (10) 30.00 80.00
1 Ed Belfour 3.00 8.00
2 Sean Burke 2.50 6.00
3 Jim Carey 3.00 8.00
4 Dominik Hasek 6.00 15.00
5 Ron Hextall 3.00 8.00
6 Chris Osgood 3.00 8.00
7 Felix Potvin 4.00 10.00
8 Daren Puppa 3.00 8.00
9 Patrick Roy 12.00 30.00
10 John Vanbiesbrouck 3.00 8.00

1996-97 Fleer Picks

COMPLETE SET (92) 4.00 10.00
2 Joe Sakic .20 .50
4 Eric Lindros .08 .25
6 Paul Kariya .08 .25
8 Wayne Gretzky 1.50 4.00
10 Chris Osgood .02 .10
12 Brian Leetch .08 .25
14 Ray Bourque .15 .40
16 Ron Francis .02 .10
18 Keith Tkachuk .08 .25
20 Paul Coffey .08 .25
22 Phil Housley .02 .10
24 Theo Fleury .01 .05
26 Sergei Zubov .01 .05
28 Adam Oates .01 .05
30 John LeClair .08 .25
32 Pierre Turgeon .02 .10
34 Nicklas Lidstrom .08 .25
36 Vincent Damphousse .01 .05
38 Pat LaFontaine .08 .25
40 Brendan Shanahan .08 .25
42 Robert Svehla .01 .05
44 Peter Bondra .02 .10
46 Mikael Renberg .02 .10
48 Alexei Yashin .01 .05
50 Zigmund Palffy .02 .10
52 Larry Murphy .02 .10
54 Rod Brind'Amour .02 .10
56 Alexei Zhamnov .02 .10
58 Jason Arnott .01 .05
60 Craig Janney .02 .10
62 Jason Woolley .01 .05
64 Jeff Brown .01 .05
66 Tomas Sandstrom .01 .05
68 Doug Gilmour .02 .10
70 Travis Green .02 .10
72 Teppo Numminen .01 .05
74 Petr Sykora .01 .05
76 Saku Koivu .08 .25
78 Daniel Alfredsson .02 .10
80 Ron Hextall .02 .10
82 Jocelyn Thibault .08 .25
84 Mike Richter .08 .25
86 Nikolai Khabibulin .02 .10
88 John Vanbiesbrouck .02 .10
90 Adam Graves .01 .05
92 Kenny Jonsson .01 .05
94 Jyrki Lumme .01 .05
96 Zdeno Ciger .01 .05
98 Ed Jovanovski .02 .10
100 Greg Johnson .01 .05
102 Pat Falloon .01 .05
104 Andrew Cassels .01 .05
106 German Titov .01 .05
108 Joe Juneau .01 .05
110 Igor Larionov .01 .05
112 Norm Maciver .01 .05
114 Chris Pronger .02 .10
116 Scott Niedermayer .01 .05
118 Vladimir Malakhov .01 .05
120 Dale Hawerchuk .02 .10
122 Jason Dawe .01 .05
124 Valeri Bure .01 .05
126 Marcus Ragnarsson .01 .05
128 Stephane Richer .02 .10
130 Wendel Clark .02 .10
132 Bryan Smolinski .01 .05
134 Dimitri Khristich .01 .05
136 Benoit Hogue .01 .05
138 Kirk Muller .01 .05
140 Peter Ferraro .01 .05
142 Vitali Yachmenev .01 .05
144 Jere Lehtinen .01 .05
146 Brandon Convery .01 .05
148 Darcy Tucker .01 .05
150 Curtis Brown .01 .05
152 Alexei Zhitnik .01 .05
154 John Slaney .01 .05
156 Bruce Driver .01 .05
158 Jeff O'Neill .01 .05
160 Patrice Brisebois .01 .05
162 Gord Murphy .01 .05
164 Doug Bodger .01 .05
166 Marty McSorley .01 .05
168 Nolan Baumgartner .01 .05
170 Mike Gartner .02 .10
172 Andrei Nikolishin .01 .05
174 Alexei Yegorov RC .01 .05
176 Dave Reid .01 .05
178 Marty Murray .01 .05
180 Anders Eriksson .01 .05
182 Checklist (2-180) .01 .05
184 Checklist (inserts) .01 .05

1996-97 Fleer Picks Captain's Choice

COMPLETE SET (10) 50.00 100.00
1 Eric Lindros 2.00 5.00
2 Steve Yzerman 10.00 25.00
3 Mario Lemieux 15.00 40.00
4 Wayne Gretzky 20.00 50.00
5 Mark Messier 3.00 8.00
6 Joe Sakic 6.00 15.00
7 Keith Tkachuk 2.00 5.00
8 Doug Gilmour 2.50 6.00
9 Trevor Linden 2.00 5.00
10 Brendan Shanahan 2.50 6.00

1996-97 Fleer Picks Dream Lines

COMPLETE SET (10) 40.00 80.00
1 Gretzky/Lemieux/Lindros 15.00 40.00
2 Roenick/Chelios/Richt. 3.00 8.00
3 Alfred./Forsberg/Brodeur 4.00 10.00
4 Fedorov/Mogilny/Bure 6.00 15.00
5 Selanne/Kariya/Tkachuk 5.00 12.00
6 Jagr/Hasek/Hamrlik 5.00 12.00
7 LeClair/Shan./Modano 4.00 10.00
8 Roy/Belfour/Beezer 10.00 25.00
9 Sakic/Kamensky/Ozol. 4.00 10.00
10 Hull/Verbeek/LaFont. 3.00 8.00

1996-97 Fleer Picks Fabulous 50

COMPLETE SET (50) 12.50 30.00
1 Daniel Alfredsson .20 .50
2 Peter Bondra .20 .50
3 Ray Bourque .50 1.25
4 Martin Brodeur .75 2.00
5 Pavel Bure .30 .75
6 Jim Carey .20 .50
7 Chris Chelios .30 .75
8 Paul Coffey .30 .75
9 Eric Daze .20 .50
10 Sergei Fedorov .40 1.00
11 Theo Fleury .07 .20
12 Peter Forsberg .75 2.00
13 Ron Francis .20 .50
14 Sergei Gonchar .07 .20
15 Wayne Gretzky 2.00 5.00
16 Roman Hamrlik .20 .50
17 Kevin Hatcher .07 .20
18 Ron Hextall .07 .20
19 Brett Hull .40 1.00
20 Jaromir Jagr .50 1.25
21 Ed Jovanovski .20 .50
22 Valeri Kamensky .07 .20
23 Paul Kariya .30 .75
24 John LeClair .30 .75
25 Brian Leetch .30 .75
26 Mario Lemieux 1.50 4.00
27 Trevor Linden .07 .20
28 Eric Lindros .30 .75
29 Mark Messier .30 .75
30 Mike Modano .50 1.25
31 Alexander Mogilny .20 .50
32 Petr Nedved .07 .20
33 Joe Nieuwendyk .07 .20
34 Owen Nolan .20 .50
35 Adam Oates .07 .20
36 Chris Osgood .20 .50
37 Sandis Ozolinsh .07 .20
38 Zigmund Palffy .20 .50
39 Jeremy Roenick .40 1.00
40 Patrick Roy 1.50 4.00
41 Joe Sakic .60 1.50
42 Teemu Selanne .30 .75
43 Brendan Shanahan .30 .75
44 Keith Tkachuk .30 .75
45 Pierre Turgeon .07 .20
46 John Vanbiesbrouck .20 .50
47 Doug Weight .07 .20
48 Alexei Yashin .07 .20
49 Steve Yzerman 1.50 4.00
50 Alexei Zhamnov .20 .50

1996-97 Fleer Picks Fantasy Force

COMPLETE SET (10) 25.00 60.00
1 John LeClair 1.25 3.00
2 Chris Osgood 1.25 3.00
3 Ron Hextall 1.25 3.00
4 Eric Daze .75 2.00
5 Jaromir Jagr 4.00 10.00
6 Brett Hull 2.00 5.00
7 Ron Francis 1.25 3.00
8 Martin Brodeur 6.00 15.00
9 Sergei Fedorov 3.00 8.00
10 Petr Nedved .75 2.00

1996-97 Fleer Picks Jagged Edge

COMPLETE SET (20) 10.00 25.00
1 Daniel Alfredsson 1.25 3.00
2 Theo Fleury 1.00 2.50
3 Alexander Mogilny 1.25 3.00
4 Doug Weight .75 2.00
5 Alexei Yashin .75 2.00
6 Paul Kariya 1.25 3.00
7 Saku Koivu 1.25 3.00
8 Sandis Ozolinsh .40 1.00
9 Petr Nedved .40 1.00
10 Jeremy Roenick 2.00 5.00
11 Mike Modano 2.00 5.00
12 Jim Carey .40 1.00
13 Ed Jovanovski .40 1.00
14 Alexei Zhamnov .40 1.00
15 Adam Oates .75 2.00
16 Ron Francis .75 2.00
17 Brian Leetch 1.25 3.00
18 Paul Coffey 1.25 3.00
19 Eric Daze .40 1.00
20 Zigmund Palffy .60 1.50

2006-07 Fleer

1 Jean-Sebastien Giguere .20 .50
2 Andy McDonald .15 .40
3 Teemu Selanne .40 1.00
4 Scott Niedermayer .20 .50
5 Chris Pronger .20 .50
6 Ilya Bryzgalov .20 .50
7 Ryan Getzlaf .20 .50
8 Corey Perry .30 .75
9 Jim Slater .12 .30
10 Ilya Kovalchuk .20 .50
11 Kari Lehtonen .15 .40
12 Marian Hossa .20 .50
13 Bobby Holik .12 .30
14 Slava Kozlov .12 .30
15 Patrice Bergeron .25 .60
16 Hannu Toivonen .15 .40
17 Brad Boyes .12 .30
18 Zdeno Chara .20 .50
19 Marco Sturm .12 .30
20 Glen Murray .15 .40
21 Marc Savard .12 .30
22 Maxim Afinogenov .12 .30
23 Chris Drury .15 .40
24 Ryan Miller .20 .50
25 Ales Kotalik .12 .30
26 Thomas Vanek .15 .40
27 Daniel Briere .20 .50
28 Jaroslav Spacek .12 .30
29 Jarome Iginla .25 .60
30 Miikka Kiprusoff .20 .50
31 Daymond Langkow .12 .30
32 Dion Phaneuf .15 .40
33 Chuck Kobasew .12 .30
34 Alex Tanguay .12 .30
35 Eric Staal .25 .60
36 Justin Williams .15 .40
37 Cam Ward .20 .50
38 Cory Stillman .12 .30
39 Rod Brind'Amour .20 .50
40 Mike Commodore .12 .30
41 Erik Cole .12 .30
42 Andrew Ladd .12 .30
43 Michal Handzus .15 .40
44 Tuomo Ruutu .20 .50
45 Nikolai Khabibulin .20 .50
46 Martin Havlat .12 .30
47 Rene Bourque .12 .30
48 Brent Seabrook .12 .30
49 Joe Sakic .40 1.00
50 Wojtek Wolski .15 .40
51 Milan Hejduk .15 .40
52 Marek Svatos .12 .30
53 Jose Theodore .20 .50
54 Pierre Turgeon .15 .40
55 Peter Budaj .15 .40
56 Sergei Fedorov .30 .75
57 Fredrik Modin .12 .30
58 Rick Nash .20 .50
59 Pascal Leclaire .15 .40
60 Bryan Berard .12 .30
61 David Vyborny .12 .30
62 Mike Modano .30 .75
63 Marty Turco .12 .30
64 Brenden Morrow .15 .40
65 Eric Lindros .30 .75
66 Jussi Jokinen .15 .40
67 Jere Lehtinen .12 .30
68 Sergei Zubov .15 .40
69 Pavel Datsyuk .30 .75
70 Tomas Holmstrom .15 .40
71 Henrik Zetterberg .25 .60
72 Nicklas Lidstrom .20 .50
73 Dominik Hasek .30 .75
74 Robert Lang .12 .30
75 Kris Draper .12 .30
76 Ales Hemsky .15 .40
77 Jeffrey Lupul .12 .30
78 Dwayne Roloson .15 .40
79 Ryan Smyth .15 .40
80 Jarret Stoll .15 .40
81 Shawn Horcoff .12 .30
82 Fernando Pisani .12 .30
83 Todd Bertuzzi .12 .30
84 Nathan Horton .20 .50
85 Jay Bouwmeester .12 .30
86 Olli Jokinen .20 .50
87 Joe Nieuwendyk .15 .40
88 Jozef Stumpel .12 .30
89 Alexander Frolov .12 .30
90 Mike Cammalleri .12 .30
91 Mathieu Garon .15 .40
92 Lubomir Visnovsky .12 .30
93 Craig Conroy .12 .30
94 Rob Blake .20 .50
95 Pavol Demitra .25 .60
96 Brian Rolston .15 .40
97 Manny Fernandez .15 .40
98 Marian Gaborik .20 .50
99 Pierre-Marc Bouchard .20 .50
100 Mikko Koivu .15 .40
101 Mark Parrish .12 .30
102 Cristobal Huet .15 .40
103 Saku Koivu .20 .50
104 Alex Kovalev .15 .40
105 Michael Ryder .12 .30
106 Mike Ribeiro .12 .30
107 Chris Higgins .15 .40
108 David Aebischer .12 .30
109 Paul Kariya .20 .50
110 Steve Sullivan .12 .30
111 Tomas Vokoun .15 .40
112 David Legwand .15 .40
113 Jason Arnott .15 .40
114 Scott Hartnell .12 .30
115 Martin Brodeur .50 1.25
116 Patrik Elias .20 .50
117 Brian Gionta .12 .30
118 Brian Rafalski .15 .40
119 Scott Gomez .15 .40
120 Zach Parise .20 .50
121 Alexei Yashin .15 .40
122 Jason Blake .12 .30
123 Rick DiPietro .15 .40
124 Miroslav Satan .15 .40
125 Trent Hunter .12 .30
126 Mike Sillinger .12 .30
127 Jaromir Jagr .60 1.50
128 Henrik Lundqvist .50 1.25
129 Martin Straka .12 .30
130 Brendan Shanahan .20 .50
131 Petr Prucha .20 .50
132 Matt Cullen .12 .30
133 Martin Gerber .15 .40
134 Antoine Vermette .15 .40
135 Daniel Alfredsson .20 .50
136 Jason Spezza .20 .50
137 Dany Heatley .20 .50
138 Wade Redden .15 .40
139 Patrick Eaves .12 .30
140 Ray Emery .15 .40
141 Simon Gagne .20 .50
142 Antero Niittymaki .15 .40
143 Peter Forsberg .40 1.00
144 Keith Primeau .15 .40
145 Jeff Carter .15 .40
146 Joni Pitkanen .12 .30
147 R.J. Umberger .12 .30
148 Shane Doan .15 .40
149 Curtis Joseph .25 .60
150 Ladislav Nagy .12 .30
151 Mike Comrie .15 .40
152 Jeremy Roenick .30 .75
153 Ed Jovanovski .12 .30
154 Sidney Crosby .75 2.00
155 Ryan Malone .12 .30
156 Colby Armstrong .15 .40
157 Marc-Andre Fleury .40 1.00
158 Sergei Gonchar .12 .30
159 John LeClair .20 .50
160 Patrick Marleau .20 .50
161 Jonathan Cheechoo .20 .50
162 Vesa Toskala .15 .40
163 Joe Thornton .30 .75
164 Evgeni Nabokov .15 .40
165 Steve Bernier .12 .30
166 Keith Tkachuk .20 .50
167 Manny Legace .15 .40

168 Doug Weight .20 .50
169 Petr Cajanek .12 .30
170 Lee Stempniak .12 .30
171 Bill Guerin .20 .50
172 Vincent Lecavalier .20 .50
173 Martin St. Louis .20 .50
174 Marc Denis .15 .40
175 Brad Richards .20 .50
176 Vaclav Prospal .12 .30
177 Ryan Craig .12 .30
178 Ruslan Fedotenko .12 .30
179 Mats Sundin .20 .50
180 Michael Peca .15 .40
181 Kyle Wellwood .15 .40
182 Bryan McCabe .12 .30
183 Alexander Steen .12 .30
184 Andrew Raycroft .15 .40
185 Darcy Tucker .15 .40
186 Tomas Kaberle .12 .30
187 Roberto Luongo .30 .75
188 Markus Naslund .20 .50
189 Daniel Sedin .25 .60
190 Henrik Sedin .25 .60
191 Mattias Ohlund .12 .30
192 Brendan Morrison .12 .30
193 Willie Mitchell .12 .30
194 Ryan Kesler .20 .50
195 Alexander Ovechkin .75 2.00
196 Olaf Kolzig .20 .50
197 Dainius Zubrus .12 .30
198 Brent Johnson .15 .40
199 Chris Clark .12 .30
200 Richard Zednik .12 .30
201 Shea Weber RC 1.50 4.00
202 Noah Welch RC .60 1.50
203 Eric Fehr RC 1.00 2.50
204 Mark Stuart RC .60 1.50
205 Matt Carle RC .60 1.50
206 Jarkko Immonen RC .75 2.00
207 Michel Ouellet RC .75 2.00
208 Konstantin Pushkarev RC .75 2.00
209 Marc-Antoine Pouliot RC .60 1.50
210 Ian White RC .75 2.00
211 Filip Novak RC .60 1.50
212 Tomas Kopecky RC .75 2.00
213 Billy Thompson RC .60 1.50
214 Dustin Byfuglien RC 1.50 4.00
215 Yan Stastny RC .60 1.50
216 Ben Ondrus RC .60 1.50
217 Brendan Bell RC .60 1.50
218 Steve Regier RC .60 1.50
219 Erik Reitz RC .60 1.50
220 Joel Perrault RC .60 1.50
221 Bill Thomas RC .60 1.50
222 Carsen Germyn RC .60 1.50
223 Rob Collins RC .60 1.50
224 Frank Doyle RC .75 2.00
225 Dan Jancevski RC .60 1.50
226 David Liffiton RC .60 1.50
227 Matt Koalska RC .60 1.50
228 Ryan Potulny RC .60 1.50
229 Ryan Caldwell RC .60 1.50
230 David Printz RC .60 1.50

2006-07 Fleer Oversized

COMPLETE SET (14) 12.00 30.00
15 Patrice Bergeron 1.50 4.00
30 Miikka Kiprusoff 1.25 3.00
35 Eric Staal 1.50 4.00
49 Joe Sakic 2.50 6.00
71 Henrik Zetterberg 1.50 4.00
103 Saku Koivu 1.25 3.00
115 Martin Brodeur 2.50 6.00
127 Jaromir Jagr 4.00 10.00
137 Dany Heatley 1.00 2.50
143 Peter Forsberg 1.50 4.00
154 Sidney Crosby 4.00 10.00
163 Joe Thornton 2.00 5.00
179 Mats Sundin 1.25 3.00
195 Alexander Ovechkin 3.00 8.00

2006-07 Fleer Tiffany

*1-200 VETS: 5X TO 12X BASIC CARDS
*201-300 ROOKIES: 1.5X TO 4X BASIC RC

2006-07 Fleer Fabricology

FAA Ari Ahonen 2.50 6.00
FAF Alexander Frolov 2.50 6.00
FAH Adam Hall 2.50 6.00
FAK Alex Kovalev 2.50 6.00
FAM Andrej Meszaros 2.50 6.00
FAO Alexander Ovechkin SP 15.00 40.00
FAR Andrew Raycroft 3.00 8.00
FAU Alex Auld 3.00 8.00
FBG Bill Guerin 2.50 6.00
FBJ Barret Jackman 2.50 6.00
FBM Brendan Morrison 2.50 6.00
FBO Jay Bouwmeester 2.50 6.00
FBR Brian Rolston 2.50 6.00
FBS Brad Stuart 2.50 6.00
FBT Barry Tallackson 2.50 6.00
FCC Chris Chelios 3.00 8.00
FCD Chris Drury 3.00 8.00
FCO Chris Osgood 4.00 10.00
FCP Chris Pronger 3.00 8.00
FDB Donald Brashear 2.50 6.00
FDE Pavol Demitra 2.50 6.00
FDH Dan Hamhuis 2.50 6.00
FDL David Legwand 2.50 6.00
FDM Dominic Moore 2.50 6.00
FDS Daniel Sedin 2.50 6.00
FDW Doug Weight 2.50 6.00
FEB Ed Belfour SP 8.00 20.00
FED Eric Daze 2.50 6.00
FEL Eric Lindros 4.00 10.00
FEP Patrik Elias 2.50 6.00
FGA Mathieu Garon 3.00 8.00
FGR Gary Roberts 2.50 6.00
FHO Marian Hossa 3.00 8.00
FIK Ilya Kovalchuk 6.00 15.00
FJA Jason Arnott 2.50 6.00
FJB Jason Bacashihua 3.00 8.00
FJG Jean-Sebastien Giguere 3.00 8.00
FJJ Jaromir Jagr 6.00 15.00
FJL Jamie Lundmark 2.50 6.00
FJR Jeremy Roenick 4.00 10.00
FJS Jason Spezza 4.00 10.00
FJT Joe Thornton 6.00 15.00
FJW Justin Williams 2.50 6.00
FKL Kari Lehtonen 4.00 10.00
FKO Mike Komisarek 2.50 6.00
FKP Keith Primeau 2.50 6.00
FKT Keith Tkachuk 3.00 8.00
FLE Jere Lehtinen 3.00 8.00
FMA Martin Brodeur 8.00 20.00
FMB Martin Biron 3.00 8.00
FMC Bryan McCabe 2.50 6.00
FMG Marian Gaborik 5.00 12.00
FMH Marcel Hossa 2.50 6.00
FMK Miikka Kiprusoff 4.00 10.00
FMM Mike Modano 5.00 12.00
FMN Markus Naslund 3.00 8.00
FMO Mattias Ohlund 2.50 6.00
FMP Mark Parrish 2.50 6.00
FMS Martin Straka 2.50 6.00
FMT Marty Turco 3.00 8.00
FNA Nikolai Antropov 2.50 6.00
FNO Mika Noronen 3.00 8.00
FOJ Olli Jokinen 2.50 6.00
FOK Olaf Kolzig 4.00 10.00
FPA Patrik Stefan 2.50 6.00
FPB Peter Bondra 3.00 8.00
FPD Pavel Datsyuk 4.00 10.00
FPE Michael Peca 2.50 6.00
FPF Peter Forsberg 6.00 15.00
FPL Patrick Lalime 3.00 8.00
FPM Patrick Marleau 3.00 8.00
FPS Patrick Sharp 3.00 8.00
FPT Pierre Turgeon 2.50 6.00
FRB Rob Blake 2.50 6.00
FRE Robert Esche 3.00 8.00
FRF Ruslan Fedotenko 2.50 6.00
FRH Ryan Hollweg 2.50 6.00
FRK Rostislav Klesla 2.50 6.00
FRL Robert Lang 2.50 6.00
FRM Ryan Miller 4.00 10.00
FRN Rob Niedermayer 2.50 6.00
FRO Rod Brind`Amour 2.50 6.00
FRT Raffi Torres 3.00 8.00
FSA Philippe Sauve 3.00 8.00
FSC Sidney Crosby SP 25.00 60.00
FSF Sergei Fedorov 6.00 15.00
FSG Simon Gagne 3.00 8.00
FSK Sami Kapanen 2.50 6.00
FSN Scott Niedermayer 2.50 6.00
FSS Sergei Samsonov 3.00 8.00
FST Matt Stajan 2.50 6.00
FSW Stephen Weiss 2.50 6.00
FTC Tim Connolly 2.50 6.00
FTH Tomas Holmstrom 3.00 8.00
FTO Jordin Tootoo 4.00 10.00
FTP Tom Poti 2.50 6.00
FTR Tuomo Ruutu 3.00 8.00
FTS Teemu Selanne 4.00 10.00
FTY Ty Conklin 3.00 8.00
FZC Zdeno Chara 2.50 6.00

2006-07 Fleer Hockey Headliners

COMPLETE SET (25) 10.00 25.00
HL1 Sidney Crosby 2.50 6.00
HL2 Alexander Ovechkin 1.00 2.50
HL3 Teemu Selanne .30 .75
HL4 Cam Ward .30 .75
HL5 Luc Robitaille .25 .60
HL6 Mario Lemieux 1.50 4.00
HL7 Joe Thornton .50 1.25
HL8 Ilya Kovalchuk .40 1.00
HL9 Daniel Alfredsson .25 .60
HL10 Henrik Lundqvist .40 1.00
HL11 Brian Leetch .30 .75
HL12 Pierre Turgeon .15 .40
HL13 Fernando Pisani .15 .40
HL14 Alexander Ovechkin 1.00 2.50
HL15 Sidney Crosby 2.50 6.00
HL16 Alexander Ovechkin 1.00 2.50
HL17 Dany Heatley .40 1.00
HL18 Martin Havlat .25 .60
HL19 Dion Phaneuf .40 1.00
HL20 Miikka Kiprusoff .30 .75
HL21 Jaromir Jagr .50 1.25
HL22 Jonathan Cheechoo .30 .75
HL23 Martin Brodeur 1.00 2.50
HL24 Ilya Bryzgalov .25 .60
HL25 Marek Svatos .15 .40

2006-07 Fleer Netminders

COMPLETE SET (25) 8.00 20.00
N1 Ilya Bryzgalov .75 2.00
N2 Kari Lehtonen .60 1.50
N3 Ryan Miller .75 2.00
N4 Dominik Hasek 1.25 3.00
N5 Miikka Kiprusoff .75 2.00
N6 Cam Ward .75 2.00
N7 Nikolai Khabibulin .75 2.00
N8 Jose Theodore .75 2.00
N9 Marty Turco 1.00 2.50
N10 Dwayne Roloson .60 1.50
N11 Roberto Luongo 1.25 3.00
N12 Manny Fernandez .50 1.25
N13 Cristobal Huet .75 2.00
N14 Tomas Vokoun .75 2.00
N15 Martin Brodeur 1.50 4.00
N16 Rick DiPietro .60 1.50
N17 Henrik Lundqvist 2.00 5.00
N18 Martin Gerber .60 1.50
N19 Antero Niittymaki .60 1.50
N20 Curtis Joseph 1.00 2.50
N21 Marc-Andre Fleury 2.00 5.00
N22 Andrew Raycroft .60 1.50
N23 Vesa Toskala .60 1.50
N24 Olaf Kolzig .75 2.00
N25 Marc Denis .60 1.50

2006-07 Fleer Signing Day

SDAA Adrian Aucoin 6.00 15.00
SDAF Alexander Frolov 6.00 15.00
SDAH Ales Hemsky 10.00 25.00
SDAO Alexander Ovechkin SP 150.00 400.00
SDBA Matthew Barnaby 6.00 15.00
SDBB Brad Boyes 6.00 15.00
SDBI Martin Biron 8.00 20.00
SDBL Brian Leetch 20.00 50.00
SDBR Dustin Brown 6.00 15.00
SDBS Brent Seabrook 8.00 20.00
SDCD Chris Drury 6.00 15.00
SDCK Chuck Kobasew 6.00 15.00
SDCP Chris Phillips 6.00 15.00
SDCW Cam Ward 12.00 30.00
SDDA David Aebischer 8.00 20.00
SDDB Daniel Briere 15.00 40.00
SDDP Dion Phaneuf 15.00 40.00
SDDR Dwayne Roloson 8.00 20.00
SDEA Evgeni Artyukhin 6.00 15.00
SDGL Georges Laraque 12.00 30.00
SDHO Marcel Hossa 6.00 15.00
SDJC Jonathan Cheechoo 10.00 25.00
SDJF Johan Franzen 6.00 15.00
SDJH Jeff Halpern 8.00 20.00
SDJI Jarome Iginla SP 15.00 40.00
SDJT Jose Theodore 12.00 30.00
SDKC Kyle Calder 6.00 15.00
SDKD Kris Draper 6.00 15.00
SDMB Martin Brodeur SP 20.00 50.00
SDMH Milan Hejduk 8.00 20.00
SDMJ Milan Jurcina 6.00 15.00
SDMK Mikko Koivu 10.00 25.00
SDMR Mike Ribeiro 6.00 15.00
SDMS Marc Savard 6.00 15.00
SDMT Mikael Tellqvist 10.00 25.00
SDPB Peter Budaj 10.00 25.00
SDPN Petteri Nokelainen 6.00 15.00
SDRB Rob Blake 8.00 20.00
SDRF Ruslan Fedotenko 6.00 15.00
SDRG Ryan Getzlaf 12.00 30.00
SDRI Raitis Ivanans 6.00 15.00
SDRO Rostislav Olesz 6.00 15.00
SDRS Ryan Suter 6.00 15.00
SDRY Michael Ryder 8.00 20.00
SDSC Sidney Crosby 125.00 250.00
SDSG Scott Gomez 6.00 15.00
SDSH Scott Hartnell 6.00 15.00
SDTA Jeff Tambellini 6.00 15.00
SDTC Ty Conklin 8.00 20.00
SDTV Thomas Vanek 12.00 30.00

2006-07 Fleer Speed Machines

COMPLETE SET (25) 6.00 15.00
SM1 Scott Niedermayer .50 1.25
SM2 Teemu Selanne 1.00 2.50
SM3 Ilya Kovalchuk .50 1.25
SM4 Marian Hossa .50 1.25
SM5 Erik Cole .30 .75
SM6 Chris Drury .40 1.00
SM7 Alex Tanguay .30 .75
SM8 Joe Sakic 1.00 2.50
SM9 Sergei Fedorov .75 2.00
SM10 Bill Guerin .50 1.25
SM11 Mike Modano .75 2.00
SM12 Pavel Datsyuk .75 2.00
SM13 Jay Bouwmeester .30 .75
SM14 Marian Gaborik .50 1.25
SM15 Alex Kovalev .40 1.00
SM16 Paul Kariya .50 1.25
SM17 Miroslav Satan .40 1.00
SM18 Dany Heatley .40 1.00
SM19 Sami Kapanen .30 .75
SM20 Simon Gagne .50 1.25
SM21 Patrick Marleau .50 1.25
SM22 Martin St. Louis .50 1.25
SM23 Mats Sundin .50 1.25
SM24 Markus Naslund .50 1.25
SM25 Alexander Ovechkin 2.00 5.00

2006-07 Fleer Total O

COMPLETE SET (25) 8.00 20.00
O1 Ilya Kovalchuk .50 1.25
O2 Patrice Bergeron .60 1.50
O3 Jarome Iginla .60 1.50
O4 Eric Staal .60 1.50
O5 Joe Sakic 1.00 2.50
O6 Rick Nash .50 1.25
O7 Mike Modano .75 2.00
O8 Pavel Datsyuk .75 2.00
O9 Henrik Zetterberg .60 1.50
O10 Ales Hemsky .40 1.00
O11 Olli Jokinen .50 1.25
O12 Saku Koivu .50 1.25
O13 Paul Kariya .50 1.25
O14 Patrik Elias .50 1.25
O15 Jaromir Jagr 1.50 4.00
O16 Dany Heatley .40 1.00
O17 Daniel Alfredsson .50 1.25
O18 Jason Spezza .50 1.25
O19 Peter Forsberg 1.00 2.50
O20 Sidney Crosby 2.00 5.00
O21 Joe Thornton .75 2.00
O22 Jonathan Cheechoo .40 1.00
O23 Mats Sundin .50 1.25
O24 Markus Naslund .50 1.25
O25 Alexander Ovechkin 2.00 5.00

2001-02 Fleer Legacy

1 Mario Lemieux SP 3.00 8.00
2 Bobby Hull SP 2.50 6.00
3 Guy Lafleur SP 3.00 8.00
4 Phil Esposito SP 2.50 6.00
5 Cam Neely SP 1.50 4.00
6 Jean Beliveau SP 2.00 5.00
7 Bryan Trottier SP 1.50 4.00
8 Jari Kurri SP 1.50 4.00
9 Jean Beliveau .25 .60
10 Bob Nystrom .15 .40
11 Phil Esposito .30 .75
12 Bobby Hull .40 1.00
13 Guy Lafleur .25 .60
14 Gilbert Perreault .20 .50
15 Henri Richard .25 .60
16 Marcel Dionne .25 .60
17 Tony Esposito .30 .75
18 Clark Gillies .20 .50
19 Grant Fuhr .30 .75
20 Brad Park .15 .40
21 Frank Mahovlich .20 .50
22 John Bucyk .20 .50
23 Billy Smith .20 .50
24 Ulf Samuelsson .15 .40
25 Mario Lemieux .75 2.00
26 Rod Gilbert .25 .60
27 Basil McRae .12 .30
28 Dave Semenko .12 .30
29 Neal Broten .15 .40
30 Terry Sawchuk .30 .75
31 Dino Ciccarelli .20 .50
32 Mike Bossy .20 .50
33 Borje Salming .20 .50
34 Stan Mikita .30 .75
35 Ted Lindsay .20 .50
36 Gerry Cheevers .20 .50
37 Michel Goulet .15 .40
38 Red Kelly .20 .50
39 Bobby Clarke .30 .75
40 Todd Ewen .12 .30
41 Denis Potvin .20 .50
42 Paul Henderson .15 .40
43 Butch Goring .20 .50
44 Nick Fotiu .12 .30
45 Denis Savard .20 .50
46 Larry Robinson .20 .50
47 Joe Kocur .15 .40
48 Bernie Parent .25 .60
49 Mike Liut .12 .30
50 Bernie Geoffrion .25 .60
51 Tony Twist .15 .40
52 Bryan Trottier .20 .50
53 Cam Neely .20 .50
54 Brent Sutter .15 .40
55 Dave Schultz .20 .50
56 Terry O'Reilly .15 .40
57 Jari Kurri .20 .50
58 Lanny McDonald .15 .40
59 Mike Gartner .25 .60
60 Alex Delvecchio .20 .50
61 Ron Hextall .20 .50
62 Darryl Sittler .25 .60
63 Dale Hunter .15 .40
64 John Vanbiesbrouck .20 .50

2001-02 Fleer Legacy Ultimate

*ULT 9-64: 4X TO 10X BASIC CARDS
*ULT 1-8: 1.2X TO 3X BASIC SP

2001-02 Fleer Legacy Autographed Puck Redemptions

COMMON EXPIRED CARD .30 .75

2001-02 Fleer Legacy In the Corners

1 Dino Ciccarelli 5.00 12.00
2 Jari Kurri 6.00 15.00
3 Guy Lafleur 6.00 15.00
4 Mario Lemieux 10.00 25.00
5 Lanny McDonald 5.00 12.00
6 Cam Neely 5.00 12.00
7 Denis Potvin 5.00 12.00
8 Larry Robinson 5.00 12.00
9 Borje Salming 5.00 12.00
10 Darryl Sittler 5.00 12.00
11 Billy Smith 5.00 12.00
12 Tony Twist 5.00 12.00

2001-02 Fleer Legacy Memorabilia

1 Dino Ciccarelli JSY 6.00 15.00
2 Tony Esposito JSY 8.00 20.00
3 Michel Goulet JSY 6.00 15.00
4 Guy Lafleur JSY 8.00 20.00
5 Mario Lemieux JSY 10.00 25.00
6 Larry Robinson JSY 6.00 15.00
7 Borje Salming JSY 6.00 15.00
8 Denis Savard JSY 6.00 15.00
9 Jean Beliveau STK 8.00 20.00
10 Marcel Dionne STK 5.00 12.00
11 Tony Esposito STK 6.00 15.00
12 Phil Esposito STK 10.00 25.00
13 Mike Gartner STK 6.00 15.00
14 Bobby Hull STK 10.00 25.00
15 Guy Lafleur STK 6.00 15.00
16 Mario Lemieux STK 12.50 30.00
17 Stan Mikita STK 10.00 25.00
18 Cam Neely STK 10.00 25.00
19 Brad Park STK 6.00 15.00
20 Gilbert Perreault STK 6.00 15.00
21 Henri Richard STK 6.00 15.00
22 Terry Sawchuk STK 20.00 50.00
23 Darryl Sittler STK 8.00 20.00
24 Bryan Trottier STK 6.00 15.00
25 John Vanbiesbrouck STK 6.00 15.00

2001-02 Fleer Legacy Memorabilia Autographs

1 Jean Beliveau 40.00 80.00
2 Phil Esposito 25.00 60.00
3 Bobby Hull 30.00 80.00
4 Guy Lafleur 20.00 50.00
5 Mario Lemieux 50.00 125.00
6 Stan Mikita 20.00 50.00
7 Darryl Sittler 20.00 50.00
8 Bryan Trottier 15.00 40.00

2002 Fleer Lemieux All-Star Fantasy

1 Mario Lemieux 2.00 5.00

2012-13 Fleer Retro

1 Dale Hawerchuk .40 1.00
2 Evander Kane .40 1.00
3 Alexander Burmistrov .30 .75
4 Alexander Ovechkin 1.50 4.00
5 Braden Holtby .40 1.00
6 Nicklas Backstrom .40 1.00
7 Pavel Bure .40 1.00
8 Alexandre Burrows .20 .50
9 Markus Naslund .40 1.00
10 Ryan Kesler .40 1.00
11 Trevor Linden .40 1.00
12 Doug Gilmour .40 1.00
13 Dion Phaneuf .30 .75
14 Phil Kessel .40 1.00
15 Mats Sundin .60 1.50
16 Steven Stamkos .75 2.00
17 Curtis Joseph .40 1.00
18 Brett Hull .75 2.00
19 David Backes .20 .50
20 Chris Stewart .30 .75
21 Alex Pietrangelo .30 .75
22 Joe Pavelski .40 1.00
23 Antti Niemi .30 .75
24 Logan Couture .40 1.00
25 Evgeni Malkin .75 2.00
26 Marc-Andre Fleury .75 2.00
27 Mario Lemieux 1.50 4.00
28 Sidney Crosby 1.50 4.00
29 Shane Doan .30 .75
30 Dave Schultz .40 1.00
31 Eric Lindros .60 1.50
32 Brayden Schenn .40 1.00
33 Bobby Clarke .60 1.50
34 Erik Karlsson .40 1.00
35 Jason Spezza .40 1.00
36 Rick Nash .40 1.00
37 Brad Richards .40 1.00
38 Theoren Fleury .40 1.00
39 Marian Gaborik .40 1.00
40 Mark Messier .75 2.00
41 Henrik Lundqvist .75 2.00
42 Clark Gillies .40 1.00
43 John Tavares .60 1.50
44 Bryan Trottier .40 1.00
45 Ilya Kovalchuk .40 1.00
46 Martin Brodeur .75 2.00
47 Pekka Rinne .40 1.00
48 Jean Beliveau .40 1.00
49 Lars Eller .20 .50
50 P.K. Subban .40 1.00
51 Carey Price .75 2.00
52 Dany Heatley .30 .75
53 Mike Modano .60 1.50
54 Anze Kopitar .60 1.50
55 Drew Doughty .40 1.00
56 Dustin Brown .40 1.00
57 Luc Robitaille .40 1.00
58 Jonathan Quick .40 1.00
59 Ron Francis .40 1.00
60 Stephen Weiss .30 .75
61 Grant Fuhr .60 1.50
62 Ryan Smyth .30 .75
63 Jordan Eberle .40 1.00
64 Jari Kurri .40 1.00
65 Paul Coffey .40 1.00
66 Ryan Nugent-Hopkins .40 1.00
67 Taylor Hall .40 1.00
68 Wayne Gretzky 2.00 5.00
69 Johan Franzen .30 .75
70 Nicklas Lidstrom .40 1.00
71 Pavel Datsyuk .60 1.50
72 Derek Roy .20 .50
73 Jamie Benn .40 1.00
74 Jaromir Jagr 1.25 3.00
75 Joe Sakic .75 2.00
76 Matt Duchene .40 1.00
77 Gabriel Landeskog .40 1.00
78 Bobby Hull .75 2.00
79 Doug Wilson .30 .75
80 Ed Belfour .40 1.00
81 Jonathan Toews .60 1.50
82 Marian Hossa .40 1.00
83 Patrick Kane .75 2.00
84 Jeff Skinner .40 1.00
85 Eric Staal .40 1.00
86 Jarome Iginla .40 1.00
87 Thomas Vanek .30 .75
88 Dominik Hasek .60 1.50
89 Bobby Orr 1.50 4.00
90 Cam Neely .40 1.00
91 Brad Marchand .75 2.00
92 Tuukka Rask .40 1.00
93 Patrice Bergeron .40 1.00
94 Ray Bourque .60 1.50
95 Terry O'Reilly .30 .75
96 Adam Oates .40 1.00
97 Bobby Ryan .30 .75
98 Ryan Getzlaf .40 1.00
99 Jonas Hiller .30 .75
100 Teemu Selanne .75 2.00

2012-13 Fleer Retro 1992-93 Ultra

921 Ryan Getzlaf 1.00 2.50
922 Patrice Bergeron 1.25 3.00
923 Tyler Seguin 1.25 3.00
924 Jeff Skinner 1.25 3.00
925 Jonathan Toews 1.50 4.00
926 Patrick Kane 2.00 5.00
927 Gabriel Landeskog 1.25 3.00
928 Pavel Datsyuk 1.50 4.00
929 Jordan Eberle 1.00 2.50
9210 Ryan Nugent-Hopkins 1.25 3.00
9211 Taylor Hall 1.00 2.50
9212 Jonathan Quick 1.25 3.00
9213 Carey Price 2.00 5.00
9214 Adam Larsson 1.00 2.50
9215 John Tavares 1.50 4.00
9216 Pekka Rinne 1.00 2.50
9217 Erik Karlsson 1.25 3.00
9218 Zach Parise 1.00 2.50
9219 Claude Giroux 1.00 2.50
9220 Evgeni Malkin 2.00 5.00
9221 Marc-Andre Fleury 2.00 5.00
9222 Sidney Crosby 4.00 10.00
9223 Steven Stamkos 2.00 5.00
9224 Dion Phaneuf .75 2.00
9225 Alexander Ovechkin 4.00 10.00

2012-13 Fleer Retro 1992-93 Ultra Autographs

921 Ryan Getzlaf B 12.00 30.00
922 Patrice Bergeron B 15.00 40.00
925 Jonathan Toews B 25.00 50.00
926 Patrick Kane C 25.00 50.00
928 Pavel Datsyuk B 20.00 40.00
9210 Ryan Nugent-Hopkins B 30.00 60.00
9211 Taylor Hall C 10.00 25.00
9212 Jonathan Quick A 15.00 40.00
9213 Carey Price B 20.00 50.00
9214 Adam Larsson C 10.00 25.00
9215 John Tavares C 20.00 40.00
9217 Erik Karlsson C 12.00 30.00
9219 Claude Giroux A 12.00 30.00
9221 Marc-Andre Fleury B 25.00 60.00
9223 Steven Stamkos C 20.00 40.00
9224 Dion Phaneuf C 8.00 20.00
9225 Alexander Ovechkin C 30.00 80.00

2012-13 Fleer Retro 1993-94 Ultra

931 Zdeno Chara 1.00 2.50
932 Patrice Bergeron 1.25 3.00
933 Marcus Foligno .75 2.00
934 Theoren Fleury 1.25 3.00
935 Jonathan Toews 1.50 4.00
936 Patrick Kane 2.00 5.00
937 Matt Duchene 1.00 2.50
938 Jamie Benn 1.00 2.50
939 Pavel Datsyuk 1.50 4.00
9310 Jordan Eberle 1.00 2.50
9311 Ryan Nugent-Hopkins 1.25 3.00
9312 Taylor Hall 1.00 2.50
9313 Carey Price 2.00 5.00
9314 P.K. Subban 1.25 3.00
9315 Martin Brodeur 2.50 6.00
9316 Adam Henrique .75 2.00
9317 John Tavares 1.50 4.00
9318 Marian Gaborik 1.00 2.50
9319 Chris Kreider 2.00 5.00
9320 Erik Karlsson 1.25 3.00
9321 Claude Giroux 1.00 2.50
9322 Evgeni Malkin 2.00 5.00
9323 Sidney Crosby 4.00 10.00
9324 Joe Pavelski 1.25 3.00
9325 Antti Niemi .75 2.00
9326 Alex Pietrangelo .75 2.00
9327 Steven Stamkos 2.00 5.00
9328 Mats Sundin 1.50 4.00
9329 Pavel Bure 1.00 2.50
9330 Alexandre Burrows .60 1.50
9331 Cory Schneider 1.00 2.50
9332 Ryan Kesler 1.00 2.50
9333 Alexander Ovechkin 4.00 10.00
9334 Alexander Burmistrov .75 2.00
9335 Evander Kane 1.00 2.50

2012-13 Fleer Retro 1993-94 Ultra Autographs

932 Patrice Bergeron C 15.00 30.00
933 Marcus Foligno C 8.00 20.00
935 Jonathan Toews A 30.00 60.00
936 Patrick Kane C 25.00 50.00
937 Matt Duchene B 10.00 25.00
938 Jamie Benn C 10.00 25.00
939 Pavel Datsyuk B 15.00 30.00
9310 Jordan Eberle A 25.00 60.00
9311 Ryan Nugent-Hopkins A 20.00 50.00
9312 Taylor Hall C 10.00 25.00
9313 Carey Price C 20.00 50.00
9314 P.K. Subban C 12.00 30.00
9316 Adam Henrique C 8.00 20.00
9317 John Tavares C 15.00 40.00
9318 Marian Gaborik B EXCH 12.00 30.00
9319 Chris Kreider C 25.00 50.00
9320 Erik Karlsson C 12.00 30.00
9321 Claude Giroux B 15.00 40.00
9322 Evgeni Malkin B 20.00 40.00
9323 Sidney Crosby A 75.00 125.00
9324 Joe Pavelski C 12.00 30.00
9325 Antti Niemi A 12.00 30.00
9326 Alex Pietrangelo C 8.00 20.00
9327 Steven Stamkos C 20.00 40.00
9328 Mats Sundin A 30.00 80.00
9329 Pavel Bure B 30.00 60.00
9331 Cory Schneider C 12.00 30.00
9332 Ryan Kesler A 25.00 60.00
9333 Alexander Ovechkin C 25.00 60.00
9335 Evander Kane C 8.00 20.00

2012-13 Fleer Retro 1994-95 Ultra

941 Corey Perry 1.50 4.00
942 Bobby Ryan .75 2.00
943 Zdeno Chara 1.00 2.50
944 Patrice Bergeron 1.25 3.00
945 Ryan Miller 1.00 2.50
946 Theoren Fleury 1.25 3.00
947 Sven Baertschi .75 2.00
948 Eric Staal 1.25 3.00
949 Jonathan Toews 1.50 4.00
9410 Patrick Kane 2.00 5.00
9411 Marian Hossa 1.00 2.50
9412 Johan Franzen .75 2.00
9413 Jordan Eberle 1.00 2.50
9414 Ryan Nugent-Hopkins 1.25 3.00
9415 Taylor Hall 1.00 2.50
9416 Jonathan Quick 1.25 3.00
9417 Anze Kopitar 1.50 4.00
9418 Zach Parise 1.00 2.50
9419 Josh Gorges .75 2.00
9420 Carey Price 2.00 5.00
9421 John Tavares 1.50 4.00
9422 Rick Nash 1.00 2.50
9423 Erik Karlsson 1.25 3.00
9424 Pekka Rinne 1.00 2.50
9425 Claude Giroux 1.00 2.50
9426 Shane Doan .75 2.00
9427 Evgeni Malkin 2.00 5.00
9428 Sidney Crosby 4.00 10.00
9429 Kris Letang 1.25 3.00
9430 Patrick Marleau 1.00 2.50
9431 Joe Pavelski 1.25 3.00
9432 Logan Couture 1.25 3.00
9433 Arturs Irbe .75 2.00
9434 Jaden Schwartz 1.50 4.00
9435 Steven Stamkos 2.00 5.00
9436 Martin St. Louis 1.00 2.50
9437 Jake Gardiner .60 1.50
9438 Dion Phaneuf .75 2.00
9439 Alexander Ovechkin 4.00 10.00
9440 Evander Kane 1.00 2.50

2012-13 Fleer Retro 1994-95 Ultra Autographs

941 Corey Perry B 15.00 40.00
942 Bobby Ryan B 8.00 20.00
944 Patrice Bergeron B 10.00 25.00
945 Ryan Miller B 8.00 20.00
946 Theoren Fleury C EXCH 15.00 30.00
947 Sven Baertschi D 6.00 15.00
948 Eric Staal B 12.00 30.00
949 Jonathan Toews B 25.00 50.00
9410 Patrick Kane D 20.00 40.00
9412 Johan Franzen C 8.00 20.00
9414 Ryan Nugent-Hopkins B 15.00 40.00
9415 Taylor Hall B 10.00 25.00
9416 Jonathan Quick B 25.00 50.00
9417 Anze Kopitar C 15.00 40.00
9419 Josh Gorges B 8.00 20.00
9420 Carey Price C 25.00 50.00
9421 John Tavares D 15.00 30.00
9422 Rick Nash C 15.00 30.00
9423 Erik Karlsson D 10.00 25.00
9424 Pekka Rinne B 10.00 25.00
9425 Claude Giroux C 10.00 25.00
9426 Shane Doan B 8.00 20.00
9427 Evgeni Malkin C 15.00 40.00
9428 Sidney Crosby B 75.00 125.00
9429 Kris Letang C EXCH 12.00 30.00
9430 Patrick Marleau B 15.00 40.00
9431 Joe Pavelski D 10.00 25.00
9432 Logan Couture C 12.00 30.00
9433 Arturs Irbe B 25.00 50.00
9434 Jaden Schwartz C 6.00 15.00
9435 Steven Stamkos C 20.00 40.00
9436 Martin St. Louis D 8.00 20.00
9437 Jake Gardiner B 6.00 15.00
9438 Dion Phaneuf D 6.00 15.00
9439 Alexander Ovechkin C 25.00 60.00
9440 Evander Kane C 6.00 15.00

2012-13 Fleer Retro Autographics 1996-97

96AL Adam Larsson B 6.00 15.00
96AO Alexander Ovechkin A 20.00 50.00
96BB Brett Bulmer E 2.50 6.00
96BF Benn Ferriero E 2.50 6.00
96BG Blake Geoffrion C 4.00 10.00
96BL Jonathon Blum E 3.00 8.00
96BM Brendan Mikkelson E 2.50 6.00
96BR Bobby Ryan D 3.00 8.00
96BS Brendan Smith D 5.00 12.00
96CA Cam Atkinson D 4.00 10.00
96CD Calvin de Haan E 2.50 6.00
96CK Chris Kunitz D 5.00 12.00
96CO Cal O'Reilly E 2.50 6.00
96DB Drayson Bowman E 2.50 6.00
96DH Dany Heatley C 3.00 8.00
96DP Daniel Paille D 6.00 15.00
96DS David Savard D 2.50 6.00
96JA Jason Arnott D 4.00 10.00
96JB Josh Bailey E 3.00 8.00
96JF Justin Falk D 2.50 6.00
96JG Jake Gardiner D 2.50 6.00
96JS James Sheppard E 2.50 6.00
96KA Keith Aulie E 2.50 6.00
96KL Carl Klingberg E 2.50 6.00
96KS Kevin Shattenkirk D 2.50 6.00
96LK Lauri Korpikoski D 2.50 6.00
96MH Matthew Halischuk E 2.50 6.00
96ML Maxim Lapierre D 3.00 8.00
96MM Matt Martin D 2.50 6.00
96MP Michael Peca E 3.00 8.00
96MS Michael Sauer E 2.50 6.00
96NG Nicklas Grossman E 2.50 6.00
96PH Dion Phaneuf B 10.00 25.00
96PL Pascal Leclaire D 3.00 8.00
96PM Peter Mueller C 3.00 8.00
96PO Patrick O'Sullivan E 2.50 6.00
96RE Ryan Ellis E 2.50 6.00
96RJ Ryan Jones D 3.00 8.00
96RO Ryan O'Marra D 2.50 6.00
96RW Roman Wick E 3.00 8.00
96SC Brayden Schenn C 4.00 10.00
96SD Simon Despres D 3.00 8.00
96SM Shawn Matthias D 2.50 6.00
96SS Steven Stamkos A 15.00 40.00
96TL Trevor Lewis E 2.50 6.00
96TW Tommy Wingels E 2.50 6.00
96VF Valtteri Filppula E 2.50 6.00
96VH Victor Hedman E 5.00 12.00
96WC Wendel Clark D 6.00 15.00

2012-13 Fleer Retro Autographics 1999

99AM Andrei Markov D 4.00 10.00
99AO Alexander Ovechkin C 25.00 60.00
99BH Ben Holmstrom D 3.00 8.00
99BS Ben Scrivens D 4.00 10.00
99CK Chris Kreider B 15.00 40.00
99CS Craig Smith D 2.50 6.00
99DB Dustin Byfuglien D 4.00 10.00
99EG Erik Gustafsson D 2.50 6.00
99EL Eric Lindros A 40.00 80.00
99GN Greg Nemisz D 2.50 6.00
99JB Josh Bailey C 4.00 10.00
99JC John Carlson D 4.00 10.00
99JS Jaden Schwartz C 8.00 20.00
99JV Joe Vitale D 4.00 10.00
99MF Michael Frolik D 4.00 10.00
99ML Mario Lemieux A 60.00 120.00
99MR Mike Ribeiro D 4.00 10.00
99MS Matt Stajan D 2.50 6.00
99NK Nikolai Kulemin D 2.50 6.00
99PE Patrik Elias D 4.00 10.00
99PW Patrick Wiercioch D 2.50 6.00
99RH Roman Horak D 3.00 8.00
99RJ Ryan Johansen D 3.00 8.00
99SA Jerome Samson D 2.50 6.00
99SB Sven Baertschi C 5.00 12.00
99SM Steve Mason D 3.00 8.00
99SS Steven Stamkos B 12.00 30.00
99TH Teemu Hartikainen D 3.00 8.00
99VS Viktor Stalberg D 2.50 6.00
99WG Wayne Gretzky A 250.00 600.00

2012-13 Fleer Retro Autographs

1 Dale Hawerchuk D 10.00 25.00
2 Evander Kane D 8.00 20.00
3 Alexander Burmistrov E 6.00 15.00
4 Alexander Ovechkin B 150.00 400.00
5 Braden Holtby D 10.00 25.00
6 Nicklas Backstrom E 8.00 20.00
7 Pavel Bure B 8.00 20.00
8 Alexandre Burrows D 5.00 12.00
9 Markus Naslund E 8.00 20.00
10 Ryan Kesler D 8.00 20.00
11 Trevor Linden D 8.00 20.00
12 Doug Gilmour C 10.00 25.00
13 Dion Phaneuf E 6.00 15.00
14 Phil Kessel D 8.00 20.00
15 Mats Sundin C 12.00 30.00
16 Steven Stamkos E 15.00 40.00
17 Curtis Joseph B 10.00 25.00
18 Brett Hull C 15.00 40.00
19 David Backes D 5.00 12.00
20 Chris Stewart E 6.00 15.00
21 Alex Pietrangelo D 6.00 15.00
22 Joe Pavelski E 10.00 25.00
23 Antti Niemi D 6.00 15.00
24 Logan Couture D 10.00 25.00
25 Evgeni Malkin E 15.00 40.00
26 Marc-Andre Fleury D 15.00 40.00
27 Mario Lemieux B 60.00 150.00
28 Sidney Crosby B 60.00 150.00
29 Shane Doan E 6.00 15.00

30 Dave Schultz D 8.00 20.00
31 Eric Lindros C 12.00 30.00
32 Brayden Schenn E 8.00 20.00
33 Bobby Clarke D 12.00 30.00
34 Erik Karlsson E 10.00 25.00
36 Rick Nash E 8.00 20.00
37 Brad Richards D 8.00 20.00
38 Theoren Fleury E 10.00 25.00
39 Marian Gaborik C 8.00 20.00
40 Mark Messier B 15.00 40.00
41 Henrik Lundqvist C 20.00 50.00
42 Clark Gillies C 8.00 20.00
43 John Tavares E 12.00 30.00
44 Bryan Trottier E 8.00 20.00
45 Ilya Kovalchuk C 8.00 20.00
46 Martin Brodeur A 20.00 50.00
47 Pekka Rinne C 8.00 20.00
48 Jean Beliveau C 8.00 20.00
49 Lars Eller E 5.00 12.00
50 P.K. Subban D 10.00 25.00
51 Carey Price D 15.00 40.00
52 Dany Heatley E 6.00 15.00
53 Mike Modano C 12.00 30.00
54 Anze Kopitar D 12.00 30.00
55 Drew Doughty C 10.00 25.00
56 Dustin Brown C 8.00 20.00
57 Luc Robitaille E 8.00 20.00
58 Jonathan Quick E 10.00 25.00
59 Ron Francis B 10.00 25.00
60 Stephen Weiss E 6.00 15.00
61 Grant Fuhr D 12.00 30.00
62 Ryan Smyth E 6.00 15.00
63 Jordan Eberle A 8.00 20.00
64 Jari Kurri D 8.00 20.00
65 Paul Coffey A 8.00 20.00
66 Ryan Nugent-Hopkins B 10.00 25.00
67 Taylor Hall E 8.00 20.00
68 Wayne Gretzky B 300.00 800.00
69 Johan Franzen D 6.00 15.00
70 Nicklas Lidstrom E 8.00 20.00
71 Pavel Datsyuk C 12.00 30.00
72 Derek Roy E 5.00 12.00
73 Jamie Benn E 8.00 20.00
74 Jaromir Jagr B 25.00 60.00
75 Joe Sakic B 15.00 40.00
76 Matt Duchene E 8.00 20.00
77 Gabriel Landeskog D 10.00 25.00
78 Bobby Hull E 15.00 40.00
79 Doug Wilson E 6.00 15.00
80 Ed Belfour D 8.00 20.00
81 Jonathan Toews C 12.00 30.00
82 Marian Hossa C 8.00 20.00
83 Patrick Kane E 15.00 40.00
84 Jeff Skinner D 10.00 25.00
85 Eric Staal C 10.00 25.00
86 Jarome Iginla C 10.00 25.00
87 Thomas Vanek E 6.00 15.00
88 Dominik Hasek C 12.00 30.00
89 Bobby Orr B 60.00 150.00
90 Cam Neely E 8.00 20.00
91 Brad Marchand D 15.00 40.00
92 Tuukka Rask E 10.00 25.00
93 Patrice Bergeron E 25.00 60.00
94 Ray Bourque D 12.00 30.00
96 Adam Oates E 8.00 20.00
97 Bobby Ryan E 6.00 15.00
98 Ryan Getzlaf D 8.00 20.00
99 Jonas Hiller E 6.00 15.00

2012-13 Fleer Retro Diamond Tribute

1 Bobby Orr 10.00 25.00
2 Sven Baertschi 2.00 5.00
3 Jonathan Toews 4.00 10.00
4 Joe Sakic 5.00 12.00
5 Ryan Nugent-Hopkins 3.00 8.00
6 Mark Messier 5.00 12.00
7 Jordan Eberle 2.50 6.00
8 Taylor Hall 2.50 6.00
9 Wayne Gretzky 15.00 40.00
10 Patrick Roy 6.00 15.00
11 Ilya Kovalchuk 2.50 6.00
12 Chris Kreider 4.00 10.00
13 Eric Lindros 4.00 10.00
14 Sidney Crosby 10.00 25.00
15 Mario Lemieux 10.00 25.00
16 Jaden Schwartz 4.00 10.00
17 Steven Stamkos 5.00 12.00
18 Mats Sundin 4.00 10.00
19 Pavel Bure 3.00 8.00
20 Alexander Ovechkin 5.00 12.00

2012-13 Fleer Retro E-X 2001

1 Sidney Crosby 12.00 30.00
2 Alexander Ovechkin 4.00 10.00
3 Ryan Nugent-Hopkins 2.50 6.00
4 Bobby Orr 8.00 20.00
5 Teemu Selanne 4.00 10.00
6 Mario Lemieux 8.00 20.00
7 Pavel Bure 2.00 5.00
8 Eric Lindros 3.00 8.00
9 Wayne Gretzky 12.00 30.00
10 Tyler Seguin 2.50 6.00
11 Mark Messier 4.00 10.00
12 Henrik Lundqvist 5.00 12.00
13 Mats Sundin 3.00 8.00
14 Jordan Eberle 2.00 5.00
15 Jason Spezza 2.00 5.00
16 Brett Hull 4.00 10.00
17 Gabriel Landeskog 2.50 6.00
18 Evgeni Malkin 4.00 10.00
19 Jonathan Toews 3.00 8.00
20 Jonathan Quick 2.50 6.00
21 John Tavares 3.00 8.00
22 Erik Karlsson 2.50 6.00
23 Ondrej Pavelec 2.00 5.00
24 Trevor Linden 2.00 5.00
25 Jeff Skinner 2.50 6.00
26 Pekka Rinne 2.00 5.00
27 Cory Schneider 2.00 5.00
28 Dominik Hasek 3.00 8.00
29 Mikko Koivu 1.50 4.00
30 Martin Brodeur 5.00 12.00
31 Carey Price 4.00 10.00
32 Pavel Datsyuk 3.00 8.00
33 Patrick Roy 6.00 15.00
34 Taylor Hall 2.00 5.00
35 Jaromir Jagr 5.00 12.00
36 Steven Stamkos 4.00 10.00
37 Patrice Bergeron 2.50 6.00
38 Joe Sakic 4.00 10.00
39 Jussi Rynnas 1.00 2.50
40 Jaden Schwartz 3.00 8.00
41 Sven Baertschi 1.50 4.00
42 Chris Kreider 5.00 12.00

2012-13 Fleer Retro E-X 2001 Essential Credentials Future

*FUTURE/30-42: 2X TO 5X BASIC INSERTS
*FUTURE/20-29: 3X TO 8X BASIC INSERTS
*FUTURE/15-19: 4X TO 10X BASIC INSERTS
1 Sidney Crosby/42 500.00 1200.00
7 Pavel Bure/36 125.00 300.00
9 Wayne Gretzky/34 75.00 150.00

2012-13 Fleer Retro E-X 2001 Essential Credentials Now

*NOW/30-42: 2.5X TO 5X BASIC INSERTS
*NOW/20-29: 3X TO 8X BASIC INSERTS
*NOW/15-19: 4X TO 10X BASIC INSERTS
33 Patrick Roy/33 40.00 100.00

2012-13 Fleer Retro E-X 2001 Jambalaya

1JB Teemu Selanne 50.00 100.00
2JB Bobby Orr 60.00 120.00
3JB Jonathan Toews 40.00 100.00
4JB Joe Sakic 40.00 100.00
5JB Patrick Roy 50.00 120.00
6JB Evgeni Malkin 30.00 80.00
7JB Taylor Hall 60.00 120.00
8JB Jordan Eberle 30.00 80.00
9JB Ryan Nugent-Hopkins 20.00 50.00
10JB Wayne Gretzky 150.00 300.00
11JB Carey Price 60.00 120.00
12JB Martin Brodeur 60.00 120.00
13JB Jonathan Quick 25.00 60.00
14JB Eric Lindros 40.00 100.00
15JB Mario Lemieux 60.00 120.00
16JB Sidney Crosby 75.00 150.00
17JB Brett Hull 40.00 100.00
18JB Pelle Lindbergh 50.00 100.00
19JB Mats Sundin 40.00 100.00
20JB Pavel Bure 30.00 80.00
21JB Alexander Ovechkin 40.00 100.00

2012-13 Fleer Retro Tradition Electrifying

1 Bobby Orr 60.00 150.00
2 Sven Baertschi 12.00 30.00
3 Ryan Nugent-Hopkins 60.00 150.00
4 Wayne Gretzky 200.00 500.00
5 Anze Kopitar 12.00 30.00
6 Patrick Roy 100.00 250.00
7 Martin Brodeur 60.00 150.00
8 Chris Kreider 12.00 30.00
9 Eric Lindros 50.00 125.00
10 Sidney Crosby 150.00 400.00
11 Mario Lemieux 80.00 200.00
12 Evgeni Malkin 40.00 100.00
13 Jaromir Jagr 80.00 200.00
14 Mats Sundin 40.00 100.00
15 Joe Sakic 50.00 125.00
16 Brett Hull 30.00 80.00
17 Jaden Schwartz 12.00 30.00
18 Steven Stamkos 40.00 100.00
19 Pavel Bure 40.00 100.00
20 Alexander Ovechkin 200.00 500.00

2012-13 Fleer Retro Flair Showcase Hot Shots

1 Ray Bourque 5.00 12.00
2 Bobby Orr 12.00 30.00
3 Zdeno Chara 3.00 8.00
4 Theoren Fleury 4.00 10.00
5 Bobby Hull 6.00 15.00
6 Nicklas Lidstrom 3.00 8.00
7 Paul Coffey 3.00 8.00
8 Wayne Gretzky 20.00 50.00
9 Mark Messier 6.00 15.00
10 Shea Weber 2.50 6.00
11 Ilya Kovalchuk 3.00 8.00
12 John Tavares 5.00 12.00
13 Teemu Selanne 6.00 15.00
14 Evgeni Malkin 6.00 15.00
15 Mario Lemieux 12.00 30.00
16 Sidney Crosby 10.00 25.00
17 Kris Letang 4.00 10.00
18 Brett Hull 6.00 15.00
19 Al MacInnis 4.00 10.00
20 Steven Stamkos 6.00 15.00
21 Phil Kessel 3.00 8.00
22 Dion Phaneuf 2.50 6.00
23 Trevor Linden 3.00 8.00
24 Pavel Bure 3.00 8.00
25 Alexander Ovechkin 6.00 15.00

2012-13 Fleer Retro Flair Showcase Row 2

*LEGACY/150: 1.2X TO 3X BASIC INSERTS
1 Steven Stamkos 2.50 6.00
2 Mats Sundin 2.00 5.00
3 Pavel Bure 1.50 4.00
4 Alexander Ovechkin 5.00 12.00
5 Brett Hull 2.50 6.00
6 Joe Sakic 2.50 6.00
7 Jaromir Jagr 4.00 10.00
8 Taylor Hall 1.25 3.00
9 Jordan Eberle 1.25 3.00
10 Ryan Nugent-Hopkins 1.50 4.00
11 Mario Lemieux 5.00 12.00
12 Carey Price 2.50 6.00
13 Martin Brodeur 3.00 8.00
14 Sidney Crosby 5.00 12.00
15 Henrik Lundqvist 3.00 8.00
16 Mark Messier 2.50 6.00
17 Eric Lindros 2.00 5.00
18 Bobby Orr 5.00 12.00
19 Wayne Gretzky 4.00 10.00
20 Patrick Roy 3.00 8.00
21 Erik Karlsson 1.50 4.00
22 Jake Allen 2.00 5.00
23 Claude Giroux 1.25 3.00
24 Marc-Andre Fleury 2.50 6.00
25 Jeff Skinner 1.50 4.00
26 Ondrej Pavelec 1.25 3.00
27 Trevor Linden 1.25 3.00
28 Nicklas Lidstrom 1.25 3.00
29 Pekka Rinne 1.25 3.00
30 Jaden Schwartz 2.00 5.00
31 Sven Baertschi 1.00 2.50
32 Chris Kreider 2.50 6.00
33 Cory Schneider 1.25 3.00
34 Jussi Rynnas .60 1.50
35 Antti Niemi 1.00 2.50
36 Dominik Hasek 2.00 5.00
37 Mikko Koivu 1.00 2.50
38 Zdeno Chara 1.25 3.00
39 Milan Lucic 1.25 3.00
40 Pavel Datsyuk 2.00 5.00
41 Anze Kopitar 2.00 5.00
42 Teemu Selanne 2.50 6.00
43 Patrice Bergeron 1.50 4.00
44 Tyler Seguin 1.50 4.00
45 Jonathan Toews 2.00 5.00
46 Gabriel Landeskog 1.50 4.00
47 Jonathan Quick 1.50 4.00
48 John Tavares 2.00 5.00
49 Jason Spezza 1.25 3.00
50 Evgeni Malkin 2.50 6.00

2012-13 Fleer Retro Premium Golden Touch

1GT Teemu Selanne 6.00 15.00
2GT Tyler Seguin 8.00 20.00
3GT Chris Kreider 5.00 12.00
4GT Jeff Skinner 8.00 20.00
5GT Jonathan Toews 10.00 25.00
6GT Matt Duchene 6.00 15.00
7GT Pavel Datsyuk 10.00 25.00
8GT Henrik Zetterberg 8.00 20.00
9GT Taylor Hall 6.00 15.00
10GT Jordan Eberle 6.00 15.00
11GT Ryan Nugent-Hopkins 10.00 25.00
12GT Mike Richards 5.00 12.00
13GT Wayne Gretzky 15.00 40.00
14GT John Tavares 5.00 12.00
15GT Marian Gaborik 6.00 15.00
16GT Jason Spezza 6.00 15.00
17GT Claude Giroux 6.00 15.00
18GT Evgeni Malkin 12.00 30.00
19GT Mario Lemieux 25.00 60.00
20GT Sidney Crosby 10.00 25.00
21GT James Neal 4.00 10.00
22GT Logan Couture 8.00 20.00
23GT Steven Stamkos 12.00 30.00
24GT Pavel Bure 6.00 15.00
25GT Alexander Ovechkin 25.00 60.00

2012-13 Fleer Retro Metal Universe

1 Bobby Orr 2.00 5.00
2 Teemu Selanne 1.50 4.00
3 Ryan Nugent-Hopkins 1.50 4.00
4 Eric Lindros 2.00 5.00
5 Tie Domi 1.00 2.50
6 Marc-Andre Fleury 1.50 4.00
7 Jaden Schwartz 2.00 5.00
8 Antti Niemi 1.00 2.50
9 Wayne Gretzky 4.00 10.00
10 Dominik Hasek 2.00 5.00
11 Chris Kreider 2.50 6.00
12 Arturs Irbe 1.00 2.50
13 Jeff Skinner 1.50 4.00
14 Pelle Lindbergh 1.00 2.50
15 Doug Gilmour 1.50 4.00
16 Alexander Ovechkin 5.00 12.00
17 Steven Stamkos 2.50 6.00
18 Jarome Iginla 1.50 4.00
19 Pavel Datsyuk 2.00 5.00
20 Saku Koivu 1.25 3.00
21 Zdeno Chara 1.25 3.00
22 Mikko Koivu 1.00 2.50
23 Jussi Rynnas .60 1.50
24 Sven Baertschi 1.00 2.50
25 Nicklas Lidstrom 1.25 3.00
26 Ondrej Pavelec 1.25 3.00
27 Ilya Kovalchuk 1.25 3.00
28 Erik Karlsson 1.50 4.00
29 P.K. Subban 1.50 4.00
30 Mats Sundin 2.00 5.00
31 Patrice Bergeron 1.50 4.00
32 Gabriel Landeskog 1.50 4.00
33 Patrick Roy 3.00 8.00
34 Henrik Lundqvist 3.00 8.00
35 Jason Spezza 1.25 3.00
36 Evgeni Malkin 2.50 6.00
37 Pavel Bure 1.25 3.00
38 Claude Giroux 1.25 3.00
39 Tyler Seguin 1.50 4.00
40 Mark Messier 2.50 6.00
41 Patrick Kane 2.50 6.00
42 Pekka Rinne 1.25 3.00
43 Cory Schneider 1.25 3.00
44 Daniel Sedin 1.50 4.00
45 Ray Bourque 2.00 5.00
46 Milan Lucic 1.25 3.00
47 Drew Doughty 1.50 4.00
48 Jonathan Toews 2.00 5.00
49 Jaromir Jagr 4.00 10.00
50 Mario Lemieux 5.00 12.00
51 Carey Price 2.50 6.00
52 Martin Brodeur 3.00 8.00
53 John Tavares 2.00 5.00
54 Jordan Eberle 1.25 3.00
55 Joe Sakic 2.50 6.00
56 Taylor Hall 1.25 3.00
57 Brett Hull 2.50 6.00
58 Jonathan Quick 1.50 4.00
59 Henrik Sedin 1.50 4.00
60 Sidney Crosby 2.00 5.00

2012-13 Fleer Retro Metal Universe Precious Metal Gems Blue

*BLUE/50: 2.5X TO 6X BASIC INSERTS
9 Wayne Gretzky 300.00 800.00
16 Alexander Ovechkin 200.00 500.00
33 Patrick Roy 125.00 300.00
60 Sidney Crosby 200.00 500.00

2012-13 Fleer Retro Metal Universe Precious Metal Gems Red

*RED/100: 1.5X TO 4X BASIC INSERTS
9 Wayne Gretzky 125.00 300.00
16 Alexander Ovechkin 80.00 200.00
60 Sidney Crosby 80.00 200.00

2012-13 Fleer Retro Metal Universe Championship Hardware

1CH Bobby Orr 15.00 40.00
2CH Tyler Seguin 5.00 12.00
3CH Sven Baertschi 3.00 8.00
4CH Patrick Kane 8.00 20.00
5CH Patrick Roy 10.00 25.00
6CH Ryan Nugent-Hopkins 5.00 12.00
7CH Jordan Eberle 4.00 10.00
8CH Taylor Hall 4.00 10.00
9CH Wayne Gretzky 25.00 60.00
10CH Henrik Lundqvist 10.00 25.00
11CH Chris Kreider 8.00 20.00
12CH Erik Karlsson 5.00 12.00
13CH Sidney Crosby 12.00 30.00
14CH Mario Lemieux 15.00 40.00
15CH Jaden Schwartz 6.00 15.00
16CH Steven Stamkos 8.00 20.00
17CH Henrik Sedin 5.00 12.00
18CH Daniel Sedin 5.00 12.00
19CH Alexander Ovechkin 8.00 20.00
20CH Ondrej Pavelec 4.00 10.00

2012-13 Fleer Retro Playmaker's Theatre

1 Bobby Orr 30.00 80.00
2 Tyler Seguin 10.00 25.00
3 Sven Baertschi 8.00 20.00
4 Jonathan Toews 20.00 50.00
5 Ryan Nugent-Hopkins 10.00 25.00
6 Mark Messier 20.00 50.00
7 Jordan Eberle 10.00 25.00
8 Taylor Hall 8.00 20.00
9 Wayne Gretzky 15.00 40.00
10 Jonathan Quick 10.00 25.00
11 Patrick Roy 20.00 50.00
12 Martin Brodeur 30.00 80.00
13 Chris Kreider 12.00 30.00
14 Eric Lindros 30.00 80.00
15 Sidney Crosby 20.00 40.00
16 Mario Lemieux 50.00 125.00
17 Evgeni Malkin 20.00 50.00
18 Carey Price 8.00 20.00
19 Mats Sundin 15.00 40.00
20 Joe Sakic 15.00 40.00
21 Brett Hull 20.00 50.00
22 Jaden Schwartz 8.00 20.00
23 Steven Stamkos 25.00 60.00
24 Pavel Bure 30.00 80.00
25 Alexander Ovechkin 150.00 400.00

2012-13 Fleer Retro Premium Intimidation Nation

1IN Alexander Ovechkin 20.00 50.00
2IN Pavel Bure 5.00 12.00
3IN Alexandre Burrows 3.00 8.00
4IN Tie Domi 4.00 10.00
5IN Steven Stamkos 10.00 25.00
6IN Jaden Schwartz 6.00 15.00
7IN Sidney Crosby 20.00 50.00
8IN Mario Lemieux 20.00 50.00
9IN Eric Lindros 8.00 20.00
10IN Dave Schultz 5.00 12.00
11IN Chris Kreider 8.00 20.00
12IN Patrick Roy 12.00 30.00
13IN Claude Lemieux 4.00 10.00
14IN Wayne Gretzky 30.00 80.00
15IN Ryan Nugent-Hopkins 6.00 15.00
16IN Jordan Eberle 5.00 12.00
17IN Taylor Hall 5.00 12.00
18IN Jeff Skinner 6.00 15.00
19IN Sven Baertschi 3.00 8.00
20IN Terry O'Reilly 4.00 10.00

2012-13 Fleer Retro Rookie Sensations Autographs

1 Akim Aliu C 3.00 8.00
2 Carter Ashton C 2.50 6.00
3 Casey Cizikas C 8.00 20.00
4 Chet Pickard C 3.00 8.00
5 Chris Kreider B 15.00 40.00
6 Cody Goloubef A 8.00 20.00
7 J.T. Brown C 3.00 8.00
8 Jaden Schwartz C 8.00 20.00
9 Jake Allen C 8.00 20.00
10 Jakob Silfverberg C 10.00 25.00
11 Jason Zucker C 6.00 15.00
12 Jussi Rynnas C 2.50 6.00
13 Mark Stone C 10.00 25.00
14 Reilly Smith C 8.00 20.00
15 Riley Sheahan C 6.00 15.00
16 Scott Glennie C 3.00 8.00
17 Sven Baertschi C 4.00 10.00
18 Tyson Barrie C 8.00 20.00

2012-13 Fleer Retro Thunder Noyz Boyz

1NB Evander Kane 15.00 40.00
2NB Alexander Ovechkin 600.00 1500.00
3NB Tie Domi 15.00 40.00
4NB Steven Stamkos 50.00 125.00
5NB Joe Sakic 200.00 500.00
6NB Mats Sundin 50.00 125.00
7NB Evgeni Malkin 50.00 125.00
8NB Mario Lemieux 300.00 800.00
9NB Sidney Crosby 600.00 1500.00
10NB Jaromir Jagr 50.00 125.00
11NB Claude Giroux 15.00 40.00
12NB Erik Karlsson 15.00 40.00
13NB Chris Kreider 30.00 80.00
14NB Henrik Lundqvist 30.00 80.00
15NB John Tavares 50.00 125.00
16NB Drew Doughty 15.00 40.00
17NB Jonathan Quick 15.00 40.00
18NB Pavel Bure 25.00 60.00
19NB Taylor Hall 15.00 40.00
20NB Jordan Eberle 12.00 30.00
21NB Ryan Nugent-Hopkins 12.00 30.00
22NB Wayne Gretzky 600.00 1500.00
23NB P.K. Subban 15.00 40.00
24NB Theoren Fleury 15.00 40.00
25NB Milan Lucic 12.00 30.00

2012-13 Fleer Retro Ultra Stars Gold

1US Bobby Orr 12.00 30.00
2US Sven Baertschi 2.00 5.00
3US Jeff Skinner 4.00 10.00
4US Ryan Nugent-Hopkins 4.00 10.00
5US Jordan Eberle 3.00 8.00
6US Taylor Hall 3.00 8.00
7US Wayne Gretzky 20.00 50.00
8US Patrick Roy 8.00 20.00
9US Pekka Rinne 3.00 8.00
10US John Tavares 5.00 12.00
11US Chris Kreider 5.00 12.00
12US Erik Karlsson 4.00 10.00
13US Sidney Crosby 12.00 30.00
14US Mario Lemieux 12.00 30.00
15US Jaden Schwartz 4.00 10.00
16US Steven Stamkos 6.00 15.00
17US Pavel Bure 4.00 10.00
18US Cory Schneider 3.00 8.00
19US Alexander Ovechkin 6.00 15.00
20US Teemu Selanne 4.00 10.00

2013-14 Fleer Showcase

COMP.SET w/o RC's (100) 10.00 25.00
1 Evgeni Malkin AS .75 2.00
2 Jeremy Roenick AS .60 1.50
3 Ryan Getzlaf .40 1.00
4 Corey Perry .60 1.50
5 Jonas Hiller .30 .75
6 Milan Lucic .40 1.00
7 Tuukka Rask .50 1.25
8 Zdeno Chara .40 1.00
9 Glen Murray .30 .75
10 Ryan Miller .40 1.00
11 Dominik Hasek .60 1.50
12 Matt Stajan .25 .60
13 Eric Staal .50 1.25
14 Cam Ward .40 1.00
15 Jonathan Toews .60 1.50
16 Patrick Kane .75 2.00
17 Duncan Keith .30 .75
18 Corey Crawford .50 1.25
19 Bryan Bickell .25 .60
20 Matt Duchene .40 1.00
21 Milan Hejduk .30 .75
22 Paul Stastny .30 .75
23 Patrick Roy 1.00 2.50
24 Peter Forsberg .75 2.00
25 Henrik Zetterberg .50 1.25
26 Jim Howard .50 1.25
27 Johan Franzen .30 .75
28 Pavel Datsyuk .60 1.50
29 Steve Yzerman 1.00 2.50
30 Ryan Nugent-Hopkins .50 1.25
31 Wayne Gretzky 2.50 6.00
32 Taylor Hall .40 1.00
33 Jordan Eberle .40 1.00
34 David Perron .30 .75
35 Ales Hemsky .25 .60
36 Sam Gagner .25 .60
37 Pavel Bure .40 1.00
38 Ed Belfour .40 1.00
39 Jonathan Quick .50 1.25
40 Mike Richards .30 .75
41 Anze Kopitar .60 1.50
42 Dustin Brown .40 1.00
43 Slava Voynov .30 .75
44 Zach Parise .40 1.00
45 Mikko Koivu .30 .75
46 Tomas Plekanec .25 .60
47 P.K. Subban .50 1.25
48 Max Pacioretty .40 1.00
49 Larry Robinson .40 1.00
50 Carey Price .75 2.00
51 David Desharnais .25 .60
52 David Legwand .30 .75
53 Pekka Rinne .40 1.00
54 Patrik Elias .40 1.00
55 Martin Brodeur 1.00 2.50
56 Travis Zajac .25 .60
57 Mike Bossy .40 1.00
58 Kyle Okposo .25 .60
59 John Tavares .60 1.50
60 Rick Nash .40 1.00
61 Mike Gartner .50 1.25
62 Derek Stepan .25 .60
63 Chris Kreider .50 1.25
64 Theoren Fleury .50 1.25
65 Carl Hagelin .25 .60
66 Bobby Ryan .30 .75
67 Robin Lehner .30 .75
68 Jason Spezza .40 1.00
69 Erik Karlsson .50 1.25
70 Simon Gagne .40 1.00
71 Claude Giroux .40 1.00
72 Bill Barber .40 1.00
73 Scott Hartnell .25 .60
74 Steve Mason .30 .75
75 Shane Doan .30 .75
76 Mario Lemieux 1.50 4.00
77 Kris Letang .50 1.25
78 Marc-Andre Fleury .75 2.00
79 Sidney Crosby 1.50 4.00
80 Logan Couture .50 1.25
81 Patrick Marleau .40 1.00
82 Antti Niemi .30 .75
83 Alexander Steen .25 .60
84 Patrik Berglund .25 .60
85 Brett Hull .75 2.00
86 Martin St. Louis .40 1.00
87 Steven Stamkos .75 2.00
88 Mats Sundin .40 1.00
89 Grant Fuhr .60 1.50
90 Eric Lindros .60 1.50
91 Phil Kessel .40 1.00
92 Nazem Kadri .50 1.25
93 Daniel Sedin .50 1.25
94 Henrik Sedin .50 1.25
95 Ryan Kesler .40 1.00
96 Alexandre Burrows .25 .60
97 Roberto Luongo .60 1.50
98 Braden Holtby .50 1.25
99 Nicklas Backstrom .40 1.00
100 Alexander Ovechkin 1.50 4.00
101 Trtmn/Flrk/Cnnghm RC 5.00 12.00
102 Bncks/Cndri/Brn RC 1.50 4.00
103 Sstr/Mgna/Hys RC 2.00 5.00
104 Rnhrt/Jhnsn/Ptrvc RC 3.00 8.00
105 Jnes/Brra/Rnta RC 3.00 8.00
106 Hnwski/LBlnc/Lrdsn RC 1.50 4.00
107 Rsk/Brtly/Hndrsn RC 1.50 4.00
108 Grba/Grnt/Dzzynski RC 1.50 4.00
109 Grbr/Crrck/Olksy RC 2.50 6.00
110 Dmln/Wey/Smlssn RC 3.00 8.00
111 Gds/Plt/Krbv RC 3.00 8.00
112 Chpt/Ady-Mrchsslt/Rssl RC 5.00 12.00
113 Ptryn/Glndning/Bllns RC 2.00 5.00
114 Vtnn/Lndhlm/Grnt RC 3.00 8.00
115 Albrt/Mlchri/O'Dll RC 2.00 5.00
116 Mllr/Gbbns/Wrsfsky RC 2.50 6.00
117 Cnntn/Olksk/Nlstrp RC 1.50 4.00
118 Llnde/Aksn/Cci RC 3.00 8.00
119 Jskn/Brbrio/Sll RC 2.00 5.00
120 Crrdo/Cnnta/Archbld RC 1.50 4.00
121 Irwn/Alln/Kstka RC 1.50 4.00
122 Stl/Sgrbssa/Chrt RC 2.00 5.00
123 Actn/Ptlck/Gzdc RC 2.00 5.00
124 Mrncn/Fdn/Hnt RC 2.50 6.00
125 Mse/Psqle/Bbkv RC 2.00 5.00
126 S.Abbott/J.D'Amigo RC 2.00 5.00
127 Bournival/P.Holland RC 3.00 8.00
128 N.Schmidt/E.Haula RC 6.00 15.00
129 C.Pickard/K.Simpson RC 2.50 6.00
130 R.Boucher/C.Murphy RC 2.50 6.00
131 J.Leivo/D.Broll RC 2.00 5.00
132 M.Raffl/M.Konan RC 2.50 6.00
133 J.Eriksson/N.Svedberg RC 4.00 10.00
134 Almqvist/Marchenko RC 2.50 6.00
135 E.Hartzell/J.Zatkoff RC 2.00 5.00
136 M.Mazanec/M.Hellberg RC 2.00 5.00
137 E.Gelinas/M.Sislo RC 2.00 5.00
138 O.Maatta/N.Zadorov RC 5.00 12.00
139 Frederik Andersen AU RC 8.00 20.00
140 Freddie Hamilton AU RC 4.00 10.00
141 John Gibson AU RC 25.00 50.00
142 Linden Vey AU RC 2.50 6.00
143 Rickard Rakell AU RC 4.00 10.00
144 Mathew Dumba AU RC 5.00 12.00
145 Zemgus Girgensons AU RC 6.00 15.00
146 Justin Fontaine AU RC 4.00 10.00
147 Jon Merrill AU RC 4.00 10.00
148 Matt Nieto AU RC 3.00 8.00
149 Alex Killorn AU RC 6.00 15.00
150 Tomas Jurco AU RC 8.00 20.00
151 Ryan Murphy JSY AU/375 RC 6.00 15.00
152 Mark Arcobello JSY AU/375 RC 6.00 15.00
153 T.Hickey JSY AU/375 RC 8.00 20.00
154 Tom Wilson JSY AU/375 RC 8.00 20.00
155 Brock Nelson JSY AU/375 RC 12.00 30.00
156 R.Ristolainen JSY AU/375 RC 10.00 25.00
157 J.G.Pageau JSY AU/175 RC 8.00 20.00
158 Nichushkin JSY AU/175 RC 15.00 40.00
159 Johan Larsson JSY AU/375 RC 8.00 20.00
160 M.Rielly JSY AU/175 RC 20.00 50.00
161 D.DeKeyser JSY AU/375 RC 8.00 20.00
162 Jacob Trouba JSY AU/375 RC 10.00 25.00
163 C.Thomas JSY AU/375 RC 5.00 12.00
164 Chris Brown JSY AU/375 RC 4.00 10.00
165 Richard Panik JSY AU/375 RC 6.00 15.00
166 J.Schroeder JSY AU/375 RC 6.00 15.00
167 Zach Redmond JSY AU/375 RC 5.00 12.00
168 Ryan Strome JSY AU/375 RC 10.00 25.00
169 C.Soderberg JSY AU/375 RC 6.00 15.00
170 Drew Shore JSY AU/175 RC 6.00 15.00
171 Dylan McIlrath JSY AU/375 RC 4.00 10.00
172 Maatta JSY AU/175 RC EXCH 20.00 50.00
173 M.Granlund JSY AU/375 RC 8.00 20.00
174 Grigorenko JSY AU/375 RC 4.00 10.00
175 N.Beaulieu JSY AU/375 RC 10.00 25.00
176 Charlie Coyle JSY AU/375 RC 10.00 25.00
177 D.Hamilton JSY AU/175 RC 15.00 40.00
178 E.Lindholm JSY AU/175 RC 15.00 40.00
179 Beau Bennett JSY AU/375 RC 10.00 25.00
180 Austin Watson JSY AU/375 RC 5.00 12.00
181 Ryan Murray JSY AU/375 RC 10.00 25.00
182 Emerson Etem JSY AU/375 RC 6.00 15.00
183 Jonas Brodin JSY AU/175 RC 10.00 25.00
184 Jack Campbell JSY AU/375 RC 15.00 40.00
185 Petr Mrazek JSY AU/375 RC 12.00 30.00
186 Q.Howden JSY AU/375 RC 5.00 12.00
187 Ryan Spooner JSY AU/175 RC 8.00 20.00
188 Scott Laughton JSY AU/375 RC 8.00 20.00
189 D.Brunner JSY AU/375 RC 5.00 12.00
190 Viktor Fasth JSY AU/375 RC 6.00 15.00
191 Jarred Tinordi JSY AU/375 RC 6.00 15.00
192 Cory Conacher JSY AU/375 RC 4.00 10.00
193 Nicklas Jensen JSY AU/375 RC 5.00 12.00
194 F.Forsberg JSY AU/375 RC 15.00 40.00
195 Boone Jenner JSY AU/175 RC 15.00 40.00
196 T.Pearson JSY AU/375 RC 6.00 15.00
197 Alex Chiasson JSY AU/375 RC 6.00 15.00
198 N.Bjugstad JSY AU/375 RC 8.00 20.00
199 N.Yakupov JSY AU/175 RC 25.00 60.00
200 Galchenyuk JSY AU/175 RC 40.00 100.00
201 J.Huberdeau JSY AU/175 RC 15.00 40.00
202 B.Gallagher JSY AU/175 RC 25.00 60.00
203 Tomas Hertl JSY AU/175 RC 15.00 40.00
204 S.Monahan JSY AU/175 RC 30.00 80.00
205 Justin Schultz JSY AU/175 RC 8.00 20.00
206 Tyler Toffoli JSY AU/175 RC 20.00 50.00
207 MacKinnon JSY AU/175 RC 150.00 400.00
208 Seth Jones JSY AU/175 RC 15.00 40.00
209 A.Barkov JSY AU/175 RC 40.00 100.00
210 V.Tarasenko JSY AU/175 RC 50.00 100.00

2013-14 Fleer Showcase Jambalaya

1JB Tony Esposito 15.00 40.00
2JB Mario Lemieux 25.00 60.00
3JB Ron Hextall 20.00 50.00
4JB Peter Forsberg 15.00 40.00
5JB Tuukka Rask 20.00 50.00
6JB Marcel Dionne 20.00 50.00
7JB Wayne Gretzky 60.00 120.00
8JB Pavel Bure 15.00 40.00
9JB Ray Bourque 15.00 40.00
10JB Ryan Nugent-Hopkins 15.00 40.00
11JB Steve Yzerman 20.00 50.00
12JB Nazem Kadri 20.00 50.00
13JB Corey Crawford 20.00 50.00
14JB Taylor Hall 12.00 30.00
15JB Zdeno Chara 15.00 40.00
16JB Jonathan Toews 25.00 60.00
17JB Zach Parise 12.00 30.00
18JB Carey Price 20.00 50.00
19JB P.K. Subban 15.00 40.00
20JB Evander Kane 12.00 30.00
21JB Sidney Crosby 60.00 120.00
22JB Jonathan Quick 12.00 30.00
23JB Antti Niemi 12.00 30.00
24JB James van Riemsdyk 12.00 30.00
25JB Anze Kopitar 12.00 30.00
26JB Patrick Roy 25.00 60.00
27JB Nathan MacKinnon 30.00 80.00
28JB Marc-Andre Fleury 12.00 30.00
29JB Henrik Lundqvist 40.00 100.00
30JB Sean Monahan 25.00 60.00
31JB Ryan Miller 15.00 40.00
32JB Doug Gilmour 20.00 50.00
33JB Teemu Selanne 30.00 80.00
34JB Evgeni Malkin 15.00 40.00
35JB Tomas Hertl 20.00 50.00
36JB Bobby Orr 30.00 60.00
37JB Alexander Ovechkin 30.00 80.00
38JB Alex Galchenyuk 40.00 80.00
39JB Brendan Gallagher 30.00 60.00
40JB Henrik Zetterberg 15.00 40.00
41JB Jonathan Huberdeau 15.00 40.00
42JB Nail Yakupov 15.00 40.00

2013-14 Fleer Showcase Metal Universe

MU1 Bobby Orr 1.50 4.00
MU2 Alex Galchenyuk 2.50 6.00
MU3 Claude Giroux .75 2.00
MU4 Zach Parise .75 2.00
MU5 Wayne Gretzky 5.00 12.00
MU6 Jonas Brodin .75 2.00
MU7 Brad Marchand 1.50 4.00
MU8 Nail Yakupov 1.25 3.00
MU9 Corey Crawford 1.00 2.50
MU10 Brendan Gallagher 1.50 4.00
MU11 Felix Potvin 1.25 3.00
MU12 Vladimir Tarasenko 2.50 6.00
MU13 Peter Forsberg 1.50 4.00
MU14 Aleksander Barkov 2.00 5.00
MU15 Tyler Seguin 1.00 2.50
MU16 Elias Lindholm 1.50 4.00
MU17 John Tavares 1.25 3.00
MU18 Dino Ciccarelli .75 2.00
MU19 Patrick Kane 1.50 4.00
MU20 Teemu Selanne 1.00 2.50
MU21 Paul Coffey .75 2.00
MU22 Sean Monahan 1.00 2.50
MU23 Nazem Kadri 1.00 2.50
MU24 Tomas Hertl 1.25 3.00
MU25 Matt Duchene .75 2.00
MU26 Mikhail Grigorenko .40 1.00
MU27 Brett Hull 1.50 4.00
MU28 Bobby Ryan .60 1.50
MU29 Guy Lafleur 1.00 2.50
MU30 Nathan MacKinnon 5.00 12.00
MU31 Doug Gilmour 1.00 2.50
MU32 Valeri Nichushkin 1.25 3.00
MU33 Tyler Toffoli 1.25 3.00
MU34 Beau Bennett .75 2.00
MU35 Sidney Crosby 3.00 8.00
MU36 Seth Jones 1.25 3.00
MU37 Patrick Roy 2.00 5.00
MU38 Ryan Strome 1.00 2.50
MU39 Cam Neely .75 2.00
MU40 Morgan Rielly 1.50 4.00
MU41 Nicklas Lidstrom .75 2.00
MU42 Justin Schultz .60 1.50

2013-14 Fleer Showcase Metal Universe Precious Metal Gems Blue

*BLUE/25: 3X TO 8X BASIC INSERTS
MU1 Bobby Orr 15.00 40.00
MU5 Wayne Gretzky 50.00 100.00
MU9 Corey Crawford 8.00 20.00
MU30 Nathan MacKinnon 50.00 120.00
MU33 Tyler Toffoli 20.00 50.00
MU35 Sidney Crosby 15.00 40.00

2013-14 Fleer Showcase Metal Universe Precious Metal Gems Red

MU1 Bobby Orr 12.00 30.00
MU5 Wayne Gretzky 15.00 40.00
MU9 Corey Crawford 3.00 8.00
MU30 Nathan MacKinnon 20.00 50.00
MU33 Tyler Toffoli 8.00 20.00
MU35 Sidney Crosby 15.00 40.00

2013-14 Fleer Showcase Red Glow

*101-138 ROOK/27: 1X TO 2.5X RC/299-399
*139-150 ROOK.AU/27: .6X TO 1.5X RC/149
*151-210 ROOK.JSY AU/18-27: .6X TO 1.5X
*1-100 WHITE/18: .8X TO 2X RED/36
1 Evgeni Malkin AS JSY 10.00 25.00
2 Jeremy Roenick AS JSY 8.00 20.00
3 Ryan Getzlaf JSY 5.00 12.00
4 Corey Perry JSY 8.00 20.00
5 Jonas Hiller JSY 4.00 10.00
6 Milan Lucic JSY 5.00 12.00
7 Tuukka Rask JSY 6.00 15.00
8 Zdeno Chara JSY 5.00 12.00
9 Glen Murray JSY 4.00 10.00
10 Ryan Miller JSY 5.00 12.00
11 Dominik Hasek JSY 8.00 20.00
12 Matt Stajan JSY 3.00 8.00
13 Eric Staal JSY 6.00 15.00
14 Cam Ward JSY 5.00 12.00
15 Jonathan Toews JSY 8.00 20.00
17 Duncan Keith JSY 4.00 10.00
18 Corey Crawford JSY 6.00 15.00
19 Bryan Bickell JSY 3.00 8.00
20 Matt Duchene JSY 5.00 12.00
21 Milan Hejduk JSY 4.00 10.00
22 Paul Stastny JSY 4.00 10.00
23 Patrick Roy JSY 12.00 30.00
24 Peter Forsberg JSY 10.00 25.00
25 Henrik Zetterberg JSY 6.00 15.00
26 Jim Howard JSY 6.00 15.00
27 Johan Franzen JSY 4.00 10.00
28 Pavel Datsyuk JSY 8.00 20.00
29 Steve Yzerman JSY 12.00 30.00
30 Ryan Nugent-Hopkins JSY 6.00 15.00
31 Wayne Gretzky JSY 25.00 60.00

32 Taylor Hall JSY 5.00 12.00
33 Jordan Eberle JSY 5.00 12.00
34 David Perron JSY 4.00 10.00
35 Ales Hemsky JSY 3.00 8.00
36 Sam Gagner JSY 3.00 8.00
37 Pavel Bure JSY 8.00 20.00
38 Ed Belfour JSY 5.00 12.00
39 Jonathan Quick JSY 6.00 15.00
40 Mike Richards JSY 4.00 10.00
41 Anze Kopitar JSY 8.00 20.00
42 Dustin Brown JSY 6.00 15.00
43 Slava Voynov JSY 4.00 10.00
45 Mikko Koivu JSY 4.00 10.00
46 Tomas Plekanec JSY 6.00 15.00
47 P.K. Subban JSY 6.00 15.00
48 Max Pacioretty JSY 5.00 12.00
50 Carey Price JSY 10.00 25.00
52 David Legwand JSY 4.00 10.00
53 Pekka Rinne JSY 5.00 12.00
54 Patrik Elias JSY 5.00 12.00
55 Martin Brodeur JSY 12.50 25.00
56 Travis Zajac JSY 3.00 8.00
58 Kyle Okposo JSY 3.00 8.00
59 John Tavares JSY 8.00 20.00
60 Rick Nash JSY 5.00 12.00
61 Mike Gartner JSY 6.00 15.00
62 Derek Stepan JSY 3.00 8.00
63 Chris Kreider JSY 6.00 15.00
64 Theoren Fleury JSY 6.00 15.00
65 Carl Hagelin JSY 3.00 8.00
67 Robin Lehner JSY 4.00 10.00
68 Jason Spezza JSY 5.00 12.00
69 Erik Karlsson JSY 6.00 15.00
70 Simon Gagne JSY 5.00 12.00
72 Bill Barber JSY 5.00 12.00
73 Scott Hartnell JSY 3.00 8.00
74 Steve Mason JSY 4.00 10.00
75 Shane Doan JSY 4.00 10.00
76 Mario Lemieux JSY 20.00 50.00
78 Marc-Andre Fleury JSY 10.00 25.00
79 Sidney Crosby JSY 15.00 40.00
80 Logan Couture JSY 6.00 15.00
81 Patrick Marleau JSY 5.00 12.00
82 Antti Niemi JSY 4.00 10.00
84 Patrik Berglund JSY 3.00 8.00
85 Brett Hull JSY 8.00 20.00
86 Martin St. Louis JSY 5.00 12.00
87 Steven Stamkos JSY 12.00 30.00
88 Mats Sundin JSY 5.00 12.00
89 Grant Fuhr JSY 8.00 20.00
90 Eric Lindros JSY 10.00 20.00
91 Phil Kessel JSY 5.00 12.00
92 Nazem Kadri JSY 6.00 15.00
93 Daniel Sedin JSY 6.00 15.00
95 Ryan Kesler JSY 5.00 12.00
97 Roberto Luongo JSY 8.00 20.00
98 Braden Holtby JSY 6.00 15.00
99 Nicklas Backstrom JSY 5.00 12.00
100 Alexander Ovechkin JSY 20.00 50.00
145 Zemgus Girgensons AU 30.00 60.00
207 N.MacKinnon GLV AU/18 400.00 800.00

2013-14 Fleer Showcase SkyBox Premium

*1-15 RUBY/50: 1.2X TO 3X BASIC INSERTS
*16-25 RUBY/50: .8X TO 2X BASIC INSERTS
*26-45 RBY/50: .8X TO 2X BAS.INSERT/299
1 Wayne Gretzky 8.00 20.00
2 Bobby Orr 2.50 6.00
3 Mario Lemieux 5.00 12.00
4 Eric Lindros 2.00 5.00
5 Steve Yzerman 3.00 8.00
6 Sidney Crosby 5.00 12.00
7 Alexander Ovechkin 5.00 12.00
8 Martin St. Louis 1.25 3.00
9 Jonathan Toews 2.00 5.00
10 Henrik Lundqvist 3.00 8.00
11 John Tavares 2.00 5.00
12 Steven Stamkos 2.50 6.00
13 Carey Price 2.50 6.00
14 P.K. Subban 1.50 4.00
15 Evgeni Malkin 2.50 6.00
16 Rick Nash SP 2.00 5.00
17 Ryan Getzlaf SP 2.00 5.00
18 Phil Kessel SP 2.00 5.00
19 Jordan Eberle SP 2.00 5.00
20 Anze Kopitar SP 3.00 8.00
21 Logan Couture SP 2.50 6.00
22 Henrik Zetterberg SP 2.50 6.00
23 Eric Staal SP 2.50 6.00
24 Patrice Bergeron SP 2.50 6.00
25 Martin Brodeur SP 5.00 12.00
26 Nail Yakupov/299 4.00 10.00
27 Alex Galchenyuk/299 6.00 15.00
28 Aleksander Barkov/299 5.00 12.00
29 Morgan Rielly/299 4.00 10.00
30 Nikita Kucherov/299 30.00 80.00
31 Sean Monahan/299 2.50 6.00
32 Justin Schultz/299 1.50 4.00
33 Taylor Beck/299 1.25 3.00
34 Seth Jones/299 3.00 8.00
35 Mikhail Grigorenko/299 1.00 2.50
36 Ryan Murray/299 2.50 6.00
37 Tomas Hertl/299 3.00 8.00
38 Dougie Hamilton/299 2.50 6.00
39 Philipp Grubauer/299 4.00 10.00
40 Valeri Nichushkin/299 3.00 8.00
41 Zemgus Girgensons/299 2.50 6.00
42 Nathan MacKinnon/299 8.00 20.00
43 Olli Maatta/299 2.50 6.00
44 Jonathan Huberdeau/299 4.00 10.00
45 Brendan Gallagher/299 5.00 12.00

2013-14 Fleer Showcase Stitches

SAG Alex Galchenyuk 5.00 12.00
SAK Anze Kopitar 3.00 8.00
SAN Antti Niemi 1.50 4.00
SBB Beau Bennett 2.00 5.00
SCA Carey Price 4.00 10.00
SDD Devan Dubnyk 1.50 4.00
SDK Duncan Keith 1.50 4.00
SDS Drew Stafford 1.00 2.50
SEM Evgeni Malkin 4.00 10.00
SHE Tomas Hertl 4.00 10.00
SJC Jack Campbell 4.00 10.00
SJE Jordan Eberle 2.00 5.00
SJM J.T. Miller 4.00 10.00
SMD Matt Duchene 2.00 5.00
SMS Martin St. Louis 2.00 5.00
SNB Nicklas Backstrom 2.00 5.00
SNM Nathan MacKinnon 8.00 20.00
SPK Phil Kessel 2.00 5.00
SPR Pekka Rinne 2.00 5.00
SPS P.K. Subban 2.50 6.00
SRG Ryan Getzlaf 2.00 5.00
SSJ Seth Jones 3.00 8.00
SSV Slava Voynov 1.50 4.00
STH Taylor Hall 2.00 5.00

2013-14 Fleer Showcase Ultra

*1-25 VETS/99: 1X TO 2.5X BASIC INSERTS
*26-35 VETS/99: .6X TO 1.5X BASIC INSERT
*36-65 ROOKIES/99: .8X TO 2X ROOKIE/499
1 Wayne Gretzky 8.00 20.00
2 Bobby Orr 2.50 6.00
3 Mario Lemieux 5.00 12.00
4 Peter Forsberg 2.50 6.00
5 Steve Yzerman 3.00 8.00
6 Patrick Roy 3.00 8.00
7 Bobby Clarke 2.00 5.00
8 Bobby Hull 2.50 6.00
9 Mike Bossy 1.25 3.00
10 Grant Fuhr 1.50 4.00
11 Sidney Crosby 5.00 12.00
12 Alexander Ovechkin 5.00 12.00
13 Ryan Nugent-Hopkins 1.50 4.00
14 Jonathan Toews 2.00 5.00
15 Henrik Lundqvist 3.00 8.00
16 John Tavares 2.00 5.00
17 Steven Stamkos 2.50 6.00
18 Carey Price 2.50 6.00
19 P.K. Subban 1.50 4.00
20 Evgeni Malkin 2.50 6.00
21 Rick Nash 1.25 3.00
22 Teemu Selanne 2.50 6.00
23 Phil Kessel 1.25 3.00
24 Jordan Eberle 1.25 3.00
25 Anze Kopitar 2.00 5.00
26 Logan Couture SP 2.50 6.00
27 Henrik Zetterberg SP 2.50 6.00
28 Eric Staal SP 2.50 6.00
29 Patrice Bergeron SP 2.50 6.00
30 Martin Brodeur SP 5.00 12.00
31 Drew Doughty SP 2.50 6.00
32 Claude Giroux SP 2.00 5.00
33 Tuukka Rask SP 2.50 6.00
34 Marian Gaborik SP 2.00 5.00
35 Pavel Datsyuk SP 3.00 8.00
36 Nail Yakupov/499 3.00 8.00
37 Alex Galchenyuk/499 5.00 12.00
38 Jonathan Huberdeau/499 3.00 8.00
39 Brendan Gallagher/499 4.00 10.00
40 Cory Conacher/499 .75 2.00
41 Aleksander Barkov/499 4.00 10.00
42 Justin Schultz/499 1.25 3.00
43 Vladimir Tarasenko/499 4.00 10.00
44 Mikael Granlund/499 2.00 5.00
45 John Gibson/499 6.00 15.00
46 Elias Lindholm/499 3.00 8.00
47 Charlie Coyle/499 2.00 5.00
48 Dougie Hamilton/499 2.00 5.00
49 Linden Vey/499 .75 2.00
50 Jon Merrill/499 1.25 3.00
51 Tyler Toffoli/499 2.50 6.00
52 Sean Monahan/499 2.00 5.00
53 Ryan Murray/499 2.00 5.00
54 Tomas Hertl/499 2.50 6.00
55 Valeri Nichushkin/499 2.50 6.00
56 J.T. Miller/499 3.00 8.00
57 Nikita Zadorov/499 .75 2.00
58 Jonas Brodin/499 1.50 4.00
59 Filip Forsberg/499 4.00 10.00
60 Ryan Strome/499 2.00 5.00
61 Martin Jones/499 2.00 5.00
62 Seth Jones/499 2.50 6.00
63 Nathan MacKinnon/499 30.00 80.00
64 Jacob Trouba/499 3.00 8.00
65 Morgan Rielly/499 3.00 8.00

2013-14 Fleer Showcase Ultra Platinum Medallion

*1-25 VETS/25: 2X TO 5X BASIC INSERTS
*26-35 VETS/25: 1.2X TO 3X BASIC INSERT
*36-65 ROOKIE/25: 1.5X TO 4X ROOKIE/499
45 John Gibson 40.00 80.00
63 Nathan MacKinnon 125.00 300.00

2013-14 Fleer Showcase Uniformity

UBN N.Bckstrm/M.Nvirth 2.00 5.00
UCN J.Cmpbll/V.Nchshkn 5.00 12.00
UDE D.Dubnyk/J.Eberle 2.00 5.00
UDM M.Dchne/N.McKnnon 8.00 20.00
UEH J.Eberle/T.Hall 2.00 5.00
UER E.Etem/R.Rakell 2.00 5.00
UGF R.Getzlaf/V.Fasth 2.00 5.00
UHB J.Huberdeau/A.Barkov 6.00 15.00
UHM C.Hagelin/J.Miller 5.00 12.00
UJF S.Jones/F.Forsberg 6.00 15.00
UKC D.Keith/C.Crawford 2.50 6.00
UKQ A.Kopitar/J.Quick 3.00 8.00
UMR R.Miller/R.Ristolainen 3.00 8.00
UNH R.Ngnt-Hpkns/T.Hall 2.50 6.00
UPJ P.Subban/J.Tinordi 2.50 6.00
USN R.Strome/B.Nelson 4.00 10.00
UST R.Strome/J.Tavares 3.00 8.00
UWJ A.Watson/S.Jones 4.00 10.00

2014-15 Fleer Showcase

1 Cam Ward .40 1.00
2 Andy Greene .25 .60
3 Jari Kurri .40 1.00
4 Adam Henrique .30 .75
5 Sean Couturier .30 .75
6 Jonathan Toews .60 1.50
7 Cory Schneider .40 1.00
8 Darcy Kuemper .40 1.00
9 Gabriel Landeskog .50 1.25
10 Max Pacioretty .40 1.00
11 Ondrej Pavelec .40 1.00
12 Ryan Miller .40 1.00
13 Taylor Hall .40 1.00
14 Matt Duchene .40 1.00
15 Tuukka Rask .50 1.25
16 T.J. Oshie .40 1.00
17 Dustin Brown .40 1.00
18 Chris Osgood .40 1.00
19 Ryan Johansen .30 .75
20 Brendan Gallagher .40 1.00
21 Pavel Datsyuk .60 1.50
22 Brett Hull .75 2.00
23 Steven Stamkos .75 2.00
24 Shea Weber .30 .75
25 Glen Murray .30 .75
26 Braden Holtby .50 1.25
27 Lars Eller .25 .60
28 Filip Forsberg .60 1.50
29 Curtis Joseph .50 1.25
30 Doug Weight .40 1.00
31 P.K. Subban .50 1.25
32 Patrick Marleau .40 1.00
33 Nail Yakupov .25 .60
34 Patrick Sharp .40 1.00
35 Zdeno Chara .40 1.00
36 John Tavares .60 1.50
37 Ed Belfour .40 1.00
38 Bobby Hull .75 2.00
39 Wayne Simmonds .50 1.25
40 Semyon Varlamov .40 1.00
41 Nathan MacKinnon 1.50 4.00
42 Roberto Luongo .60 1.50
43 Dale Hawerchuk .50 1.25
44 Dominik Hasek .60 1.50
45 Tyler Seguin .50 1.25
46 Steve Mason .30 .75
47 Antti Niemi .30 .75
48 Ryan Getzlaf .40 1.00
49 Jaromir Jagr 1.25 3.00
50 Zack Kassian .25 .60
51 Evander Kane .40 1.00
52 Karri Ramo .30 .75
53 Claude Giroux .40 1.00
54 Carey Price .75 2.00
55 Eric Staal .50 1.25
56 Johan Franzen .30 .75
57 Kris Letang .50 1.25
58 Alexandre Burrows .25 .60
59 Phil Kessel .40 1.00
60 Jonathan Bernier .30 .75
61 Jake Muzzin .40 1.00
62 Jonathan Quick .50 1.25
63 Mark Messier .75 2.00
64 Matt Moulson .25 .60
65 Corey Crawford .50 1.25
66 Jeremy Roenick .60 1.50
67 Henrik Zetterberg .50 1.25
68 Mats Zuccarello .40 1.00
69 Duncan Keith .30 .75
70 Sean Monahan .25 .60
71 Pete Peeters .30 .75
72 Cam Fowler .40 1.00
73 Marc-Andre Fleury .75 2.00
74 R.J. Umberger .25 .60
75 Ryan Nugent-Hopkins .50 1.25
76 Shane Doan .30 .75
77 Joe Thornton .60 1.50
78 Alexander Ovechkin 1.50 4.00
79 Steve Yzerman 1.00 2.50
80 Anze Kopitar .60 1.50
81 David Backes .25 .60
82 Brian Bellows .30 .75
83 Dominic Moore .25 .60
84 Sidney Crosby 1.50 4.00
85 Zach Parise .40 1.00
86 Chris Chelios .40 1.00
87 Adam Oates .40 1.00
88 Brett Hull .75 2.00
89 Wayne Gretzky 2.50 6.00
90 Milan Hejduk .30 .75
91 Drew Doughty .50 1.25
92 Denis Savard .40 1.00
93 Andrei Markov .25 .60
94 Alex Galchenyuk .25 .60
95 Pekka Rinne .40 1.00
96 Derek Stepan .25 .60
97 Alex Tanguay .25 .60
98 Kyle Clifford .25 .60
99 Mike Smith .40 1.00
100 Mike Richards .30 .75
101 Halmo/Persson/Gallant RC 1.50 4.00
102 A.Frsbrg/Hmnd/Grsnck RC 6.00 15.00
103 Lindbhm/Davdsn/Jokpka RC 2.00 5.00
104 Everberg/Agozzino/Carey RC 2.00 5.00
105 Uher/Rust/Farnham RC 1.50 4.00
106 Makarov/Knapp/Lieuwen RC 2.00 5.00
107 Paqtte/Gudlvsk/Kunyk RC 2.00 5.00
108 Sutter/Shinnimin/Varone RC 1.50 4.00
109 Payrl/Whtny/Pkarin RC 1.50 4.00
110 Agsti/Ferland/Van Brbt RC 2.50 6.00
111 B.Robins/M.Lindblad RC 1.50 4.00
112 S.Darling/M.Carey RC 4.00 10.00
113 S.Moser/M.Van Guilder RC 1.25 3.00
114 C.Wagner/J.Manson RC 2.00 5.00
115 M.Friberg/J.Armia RC 2.00 5.00
116 T.Graovac/T.Gaudet RC 1.50 4.00
117 S.Mayfield/K.Czuczman RC 1.50 4.00
118 B.Woods/J.Shugg RC 1.25 3.00
119 L.Ferraro/M.Callahan RC 1.25 3.00
120 J.Racine/G.Wilson RC 2.00 5.00
121 J.Johnson/J.Sundstrom RC 2.00 5.00
122 B.Rendulic/C.Smith RC 2.00 5.00
123 C.Gibson/R.Zepp RC 3.00 8.00
124 M.Zalewski/B.Defazio RC 1.50 4.00
125 P.Granberg/S.Carrick RC 2.00 5.00
126 Justin Hodgman AU/149 RC 3.00 8.00
127 S.Harrington AU/149 RC 4.00 10.00
128 Phillip Danault AU/149 RC 8.00 20.00
129 B.Goodrow AU/149 RC 4.00 10.00
130 Seth Helgeson AU/149 RC 3.00 8.00
131 John Klingberg AU/149 RC 8.00 20.00
132 Melker Karlsson AU/149 RC 4.00 10.00
133 Josh Jooris AU/149 RC 4.00 10.00
134 Joe Morrow AU/149 RC 5.00 12.00
135 Brett Ritchie AU/149 RC 4.00 10.00
136 Rocco Grimaldi AU/149 RC 4.00 10.00
137 T.van Riemsdyk AU/149 RC 6.00 15.00
138 Tobias Rieder AU/149 RC 4.00 10.00
139 S.Andrighetto AU/149 RC 5.00 12.00
140 Andrej Nestrasil AU/149 RC 4.00 10.00
151 K.Rychel JSY AU/375 RC 4.00 10.00
152 D.Severson JSY AU/375 RC 5.00 12.00
153 N.Deslauriers JSY AU/175 RC 6.00 15.00
154 C.Knight JSY AU/175 RC 6.00 15.00
155 Patrick Brown JSY AU/175 RC 6.00 15.00
156 Marko Dano JSY AU/375 RC 5.00 12.00
157 A.Vasilevskiy JSY AU/375 RC 60.00 150.00
158 Brandon Gormley JSY AU/375 RC 5.00 12.00
159 V.Trocheck JSY AU/175 RC 12.00 30.00
160 William Karlsson JSY AU/375 RC 15.00 40.00
161 Joonas Nattinen JSY AU/175 RC 6.00 15.00
162 J.Binnington JSY AU/375 RC 30.00 80.00
163 Greg McKegg JSY AU/175 RC 5.00 12.00
164 Curtis McKenzie JSY AU/175 RC 5.00 12.00
165 G.Reinhart JSY AU/175 RC 6.00 15.00
166 M.Granlund JSY AU/175 RC 10.00 25.00
167 Adam Lowry JSY AU/375 RC 10.00 25.00
168 A.Clendening JSY AU/375 RC 5.00 12.00
169 Dennis Everberg JSY AU/375 RC 5.00 12.00
170 K.Hayes JSY AU/175 RC 15.00 40.00
171 V.Namestnikov JSY AU/375 RC 8.00 20.00
172 M.Mueller JSY AU/375 RC 5.00 12.00
173 Ty Rattie JSY AU/175 RC 6.00 15.00
174 Wotherspoon JSY AU/175 RC 6.00 15.00
175 L.Brossoit JSY AU/175 RC 6.00 15.00
176 A.Andreoff JSY AU/175 RC EX 6.00 15.00
177 C.Sissons JSY AU/175 RC 8.00 20.00
178 Joey Hishon JSY AU/375 RC 6.00 15.00
179 D.Nurse JSY AU/375 RC 10.00 25.00
180 Jiri Sekac JSY AU/375 RC 4.00 10.00
181 S.Gostisbehere JSY AU/375 RC 10.00 25.00
182 Jake McCabe JSY AU/175 RC 6.00 15.00
183 B.Yakimov JSY AU/175 RC 6.00 15.00
184 Ryan Sproul JSY AU/375 RC 5.00 12.00
185 Derrick Pouliot JSY AU/375 RC 6.00 15.00
186 Oscar Klefbom JSY AU/175 RC 12.00 30.00
187 D.Pastrnak JSY AU/175 RC EX 300.00 800.00
188 Khokhlachev JSY AU/375 RC 5.00 12.00
189 T.Teravainen JSY AU/375 RC 8.00 20.00
190 T.Pulkkinen JSY AU/375 RC 6.00 15.00
191 Liam O'Brien JSY AU/175 RC 6.00 15.00
192 P.Nemeth JSY AU/375 RC 5.00 12.00
193 C.Tierney JSY AU/375 RC 5.00 12.00
194 A.Wennberg JSY AU/175 RC 10.00 25.00
195 Curtis Lazar JSY AU/375 RC 5.00 12.00
196 Victor Rask JSY AU/175 RC 6.00 15.00
197 M.Visentin JSY AU/375 RC 5.00 12.00
198 Stuart Percy JSY AU/375 RC 5.00 12.00
199 C.Jarnkrok JSY AU/175 RC 6.00 15.00
200 Seth Griffith JSY AU/375 RC 6.00 15.00
201 S.Reinhart JSY AU/175 RC 25.00 60.00
202 J.Gaudreau JSY AU/175 RC 50.00 125.00
203 L.Draisaitl JSY AU/175 RC 120.00 300.00
204 A.Ekblad JSY AU/175 RC 15.00 40.00
205 Jori Lehtera JSY AU/175 RC 8.00 20.00
206 A.Burakovsky JSY AU/175 RC 15.00 40.00
207 Bo Horvat JSY AU/175 RC 15.00 40.00
208 E.Kuznetsov JSY AU/175 RC 15.00 40.00
209 A.Duclair JSY AU/175 RC EX 10.00 25.00
210 Drouin JSY AU/175 RC EXCH 25.00 60.00

2014-15 Fleer Showcase Red Glow

*101-125 ROOK/27: 1X TO 2.5X RC/299-399
*126-140 ROOK.AU/27: .6X TO 1.5X RC/149
*151-210 ROOK.JSY AU/18-27: .8X TO 2X
1 Cam Ward JSY 5.00 12.00
3 Jari Kurri JSY 5.00 12.00
4 Adam Henrique JSY 4.00 10.00
5 Sean Couturier JSY 4.00 10.00
6 Jonathan Toews JSY 8.00 20.00
7 Cory Schneider JSY 5.00 12.00
8 Darcy Kuemper JSY 5.00 12.00
9 Gabriel Landeskog JSY 6.00 15.00
10 Max Pacioretty JSY 5.00 12.00
11 Ondrej Pavelec JSY 5.00 12.00
12 Ryan Miller JSY 5.00 12.00
13 Taylor Hall JSY 5.00 12.00
14 Matt Duchene JSY 5.00 12.00
15 Tuukka Rask JSY 6.00 15.00
16 T.J. Oshie JSY 5.00 12.00
17 Dustin Brown JSY 5.00 12.00
18 Chris Osgood JSY 5.00 12.00
19 Ryan Johansen JSY 4.00 10.00
20 Brendan Gallagher JSY 5.00 12.00
21 Pavel Datsyuk JSY 8.00 20.00
22 Brett Hull JSY 10.00 25.00
23 Steven Stamkos JSY 10.00 25.00
24 Shea Weber JSY 4.00 10.00
25 Glen Murray JSY 4.00 10.00
26 Braden Holtby JSY 6.00 15.00
27 Lars Eller JSY 3.00 8.00
29 Curtis Joseph JSY 6.00 15.00
31 P.K. Subban JSY 6.00 15.00
32 Patrick Marleau JSY 5.00 12.00
33 Nail Yakupov JSY 3.00 8.00
34 Patrick Sharp JSY 5.00 12.00
35 Zdeno Chara JSY 5.00 12.00
36 John Tavares JSY 8.00 20.00
37 Ed Belfour JSY 5.00 12.00
38 Bobby Hull JSY 10.00 25.00
39 Wayne Simmonds JSY 6.00 15.00
40 Semyon Varlamov JSY 5.00 12.00
41 Nathan MacKinnon JSY 20.00 50.00
42 Roberto Luongo JSY 8.00 20.00
43 Dale Hawerchuk JSY 6.00 15.00
44 Dominik Hasek JSY 8.00 20.00
45 Tyler Seguin JSY 8.00 20.00
46 Steve Mason JSY 4.00 10.00
47 Antti Niemi JSY 4.00 10.00
48 Ryan Getzlaf JSY 5.00 12.00
49 Jaromir Jagr JSY 15.00 40.00
50 Zack Kassian JSY 3.00 8.00
51 Evander Kane JSY 5.00 12.00
52 Karri Ramo JSY 4.00 10.00
53 Claude Giroux JSY 5.00 12.00
54 Carey Price JSY 15.00 30.00
55 Eric Staal JSY 6.00 15.00
56 Johan Franzen JSY 4.00 10.00
57 Kris Letang JSY 6.00 15.00
58 Alexandre Burrows JSY 3.00 8.00
59 Phil Kessel JSY 5.00 12.00
60 Jonathan Bernier JSY 4.00 10.00
61 Jake Muzzin JSY 5.00 12.00
62 Jonathan Quick JSY 6.00 15.00
63 Mark Messier JSY 10.00 25.00
64 Matt Moulson JSY 3.00 8.00
65 Corey Crawford JSY 6.00 15.00
66 Jeremy Roenick JSY 8.00 20.00
67 Henrik Zetterberg JSY 6.00 15.00
68 Mats Zuccarello JSY 5.00 12.00
69 Duncan Keith JSY 4.00 10.00
70 Sean Monahan JSY 3.00 8.00
71 Pete Peeters JSY 4.00 10.00
72 Cam Fowler JSY 5.00 12.00
73 Marc-Andre Fleury JSY 10.00 25.00
74 R.J. Umberger JSY 3.00 8.00
75 Ryan Nugent-Hopkins JSY 6.00 15.00
76 Shane Doan JSY 4.00 10.00
77 Joe Thornton JSY 8.00 20.00
78 Alexander Ovechkin JSY 20.00 50.00
79 Steve Yzerman JSY 15.00 30.00
80 Anze Kopitar JSY 8.00 20.00
81 David Backes JSY 3.00 8.00
82 Brian Bellows JSY 4.00 10.00
83 Dominic Moore JSY 3.00 8.00
84 Sidney Crosby JSY 20.00 50.00
86 Chris Chelios JSY 5.00 12.00
87 Adam Oates JSY 8.00 20.00
88 Brett Hull JSY 10.00 25.00
89 Wayne Gretzky JSY 20.00 40.00
90 Milan Hejduk JSY 4.00 10.00
91 Drew Doughty JSY 6.00 15.00
92 Denis Savard JSY 5.00 12.00
94 Alex Galchenyuk JSY 3.00 8.00
95 Pekka Rinne JSY 5.00 12.00
96 Derek Stepan JSY 3.00 8.00
99 Mike Smith JSY 5.00 12.00
100 Mike Richards JSY 4.00 10.00
202 Johnny Gaudreau GLV AU/18 100.00 250.00
204 Aaron Ekblad GLV AU/18 75.00 150.00
210 Jonathan Drouin GLV AU/18 40.00 100.00

2014-15 Fleer Showcase Flair

*BLUE ICE/99: 1X TO 2.5X FLAIR R2
*BLUE ICE/99: .6X TO 1.5X FLAIR R1-R0
1 Marian Hossa R2 1.25 3.00
2 Braden Holtby R2 1.50 4.00
3 Alex Pietrangelo R2 1.00 2.50
4 Alex Galchenyuk R2 .75 2.00
5 David Clarkson R2 .75 2.00
6 Corey Perry R2 2.00 5.00
7 Shane Doan R2 1.00 2.50
8 Nail Yakupov R2 .75 2.00
9 Mats Zuccarello R2 1.25 3.00
10 David Backes R2 .75 2.00
11 Kris Letang R2 1.50 4.00
12 Dougie Hamilton R2 1.00 2.50
13 Derek Stepan R2 .75 2.00
14 Dany Heatley R2 1.00 2.50
15 Darcy Kuemper R2 1.25 3.00
16 Drew Doughty R2 1.50 4.00
17 Brendan Gallagher R2 1.25 3.00
18 Karri Ramo R2 1.00 2.50
19 Patrick Marleau R2 1.25 3.00
20 R.J. Umberger R2 .75 2.00
21 Matt Moulson R2 .75 2.00
22 Milan Hejduk R2 1.00 2.50
23 Matt Duchene R2 1.25 3.00
24 Lars Eller R2 .75 2.00
25 Max Pacioretty R2 1.25 3.00
26 Mike Richards R2 1.00 2.50
27 Ryan McDonagh R2 .75 2.00
28 Marc-Andre Fleury R2 2.50 6.00
29 Semyon Varlamov R2 1.25 3.00
30 Cory Schneider R2 1.25 3.00
31 Anze Kopitar R1 3.00 8.00
32 Jonathan Quick R1 2.50 6.00
33 Joe Thornton R1 3.00 8.00
34 Phil Kessel R1 2.00 5.00
35 Evgeni Malkin R1 4.00 10.00
36 Jamie Benn R1 2.00 5.00
37 P.K. Subban R1 2.50 6.00
38 Sidney Crosby R1 8.00 20.00
39 Henrik Zetterberg R1 2.50 6.00
40 John Tavares R1 3.00 8.00
41 Teemu Selanne R1 4.00 10.00
42 Brett Hull R1 4.00 10.00
43 Joan Bolivoau R1 2.00 5.00
44 Mark Messier R1 4.00 10.00
45 Nicklas Lidstrom R1 2.00 5.00
46 Mats Sundin R1 2.00 5.00
47 Joe Sakic R1 4.00 10.00
48 Rob Blake R1 2.00 5.00
49 Patrick Roy R1 5.00 12.00
50 Steve Yzerman R1 5.00 12.00
51 Victor Rask R0 2.00 5.00
52 Evgeny Kuznetsov R0 5.00 12.00
53 Teuvo Teravainen R0 3.00 8.00
54 Aaron Ekblad R0 5.00 12.00
55 Jiri Sekac R0 1.50 4.00
56 Andrei Vasilevskiy R0 6.00 15.00
57 Jonathan Drouin R0 4.00 10.00
58 Curtis Lazar R0 2.00 5.00
59 Darnell Nurse R0 4.00 10.00
60 Andre Burakovsky R0 3.00 8.00
61 Kevin Hayes R0 5.00 12.00
62 Anthony Duclair R0 3.00 8.00
63 David Pastrnak R0 10.00 25.00
64 Griffin Reinhart R0 2.00 5.00
65 Jori Lehtera R0 2.50 6.00
66 Sam Reinhart R0 8.00 20.00
67 Johnny Gaudreau R0 6.00 15.00
68 Alexander Wennberg R0 3.00 8.00
69 Leon Draisaitl R0 10.00 25.00
70 Damon Severson R0 2.00 5.00

2014-15 Fleer Showcase Flair Hot Gloves

1 Ben Bishop 3.00 8.00
2 Corey Crawford 5.00 12.00
3 Tuukka Rask 5.00 12.00
4 Cory Schneider 4.00 10.00
5 Curtis Joseph 5.00 12.00
6 Ed Belfour 4.00 10.00
7 Jonathan Bernier 3.00 8.00
8 Kari Lehtonen 3.00 8.00
9 Dominik Hasek 6.00 15.00
10 Patrick Roy 10.00 25.00
11 Steve Mason 3.00 8.00
12 Pekka Rinne 4.00 10.00
13 Sergei Bobrovsky 6.00 15.00
14 Marc-Andre Fleury 8.00 20.00
15 Carey Price 8.00 20.00
16 Tony Esposito 4.00 10.00
17 Semyon Varlamov 4.00 10.00
18 Henrik Lundqvist 10.00 25.00
19 Antti Niemi 3.00 8.00
20 Jonathan Quick 5.00 12.00

2014-15 Fleer Showcase Flair Jerseys

1 Marian Hossa R2 2.50 6.00
2 Braden Holtby R2 3.00 8.00
3 Alex Pietrangelo R2 2.00 5.00
4 Alex Galchenyuk R2 1.50 4.00
5 David Clarkson R2 1.50 4.00
6 Corey Perry R2 4.00 10.00
7 Shane Doan R2 2.00 5.00
8 Nail Yakupov R2 1.50 4.00
9 Mats Zuccarello R2 2.50 6.00
10 David Backes R2 1.50 4.00
12 Dougie Hamilton R2 2.00 5.00
13 Derek Stepan R2 1.50 4.00
14 Dany Heatley R2 2.00 5.00
15 Darcy Kuemper R2 2.50 6.00
16 Drew Doughty R2 3.00 8.00
17 Brendan Gallagher R2 2.50 6.00
18 Karri Ramo R2 2.00 5.00
19 Patrick Marleau R2 2.50 6.00
20 R.J. Umberger R2 1.50 4.00
21 Matt Moulson R2 1.50 4.00
22 Milan Hejduk R2 2.00 5.00
23 Matt Duchene R2 2.50 6.00
24 Lars Eller R2 1.50 4.00
25 Max Pacioretty R2 2.50 6.00
26 Mike Richards R2 2.00 5.00
27 Ryan McDonagh R2 1.50 4.00
28 Marc-Andre Fleury R2 5.00 12.00
29 Semyon Varlamov R2 2.50 6.00
31 Anze Kopitar R1 6.00 15.00
32 Jonathan Quick R1 5.00 12.00
33 Joe Thornton R1 6.00 15.00
34 Phil Kessel R1 4.00 10.00
35 Evgeni Malkin R1 8.00 20.00
36 Jamie Benn R1 4.00 10.00
37 P.K. Subban R1 5.00 12.00
38 Sidney Crosby R1 15.00 40.00
39 Henrik Zetterberg R1 5.00 12.00
40 John Tavares R1 6.00 15.00
41 Teemu Selanne R1 8.00 20.00
42 Brett Hull R1 8.00 20.00
44 Mark Messier R1 8.00 20.00
45 Nicklas Lidstrom R1 4.00 10.00
47 Joe Sakic R1 8.00 20.00
48 Rob Blake R1 4.00 10.00
49 Patrick Roy R1 10.00 25.00
50 Steve Yzerman R1 10.00 25.00
52 Evgeny Kuznetsov R0 6.00 15.00
53 Teuvo Teravainen R0 4.00 10.00
54 Aaron Ekblad R1 4.00 10.00
55 Jiri Sekac R1 2.00 5.00
56 Andrei Vasilevskiy R0 8.00 20.00
57 Jonathan Drouin R0 5.00 12.00
58 Curtis Lazar R0 2.50 6.00
59 Darnell Nurse R0 5.00 12.00
60 Andre Burakovsky R0 4.00 10.00
64 Griffin Reinhart R0 2.50 6.00
65 Jori Lehtera R0 3.00 8.00
66 Sam Reinhart R0 10.00 25.00
67 Johnny Gaudreau R0 8.00 20.00
68 Alexander Wennberg R0 4.00 10.00
69 Leon Draisaitl R0 12.00 30.00
70 Damon Severson R0 2.50 6.00

2014-15 Fleer Showcase Flair Memorabilia Prime

53 Teuvo Teravainen AU R0 10.00 25.00
54 Aaron Ekblad AU R0 15.00 40.00
55 Jiri Sekac AU R0 5.00 12.00
56 Andrei Vasilevskiy AU R0 40.00 100.00
57 Jonathan Drouin AU R0 EXCH 12.00 30.00
58 Curtis Lazar AU R0 6.00 15.00
59 Darnell Nurse AU R0 12.00 30.00
60 Andre Burakovsky AU R0 10.00 25.00
64 Griffin Reinhart AU R0 6.00 15.00
65 Jori Lehtera AU R0 8.00 20.00
66 Sam Reinhart AU R0 25.00 60.00
67 Johnny Gaudreau AU R0 80.00 200.00
69 Leon Draisaitl AU R0 30.00 80.00
70 Damon Severson AU R0 6.00 15.00

2014-15 Fleer Showcase Flair Wave of the Future

1 Aaron Ekblad 10.00 25.00
2 Sam Reinhart 15.00 40.00
3 Griffin Reinhart 4.00 10.00
4 Darnell Nurse 8.00 20.00
5 Adam Lowry 6.00 15.00
6 Chris Tierney 4.00 10.00
7 Curtis Lazar 4.00 10.00
8 Damon Severson 4.00 10.00
9 Johnny Gaudreau 12.00 30.00
10 William Karlsson 12.00 30.00
11 Jiri Sekac 3.00 8.00
12 Victor Rask 4.00 10.00
13 Calle Jarnkrok 4.00 10.00
14 Andre Burakovsky 6.00 15.00
15 Anthony Duclair 6.00 15.00
16 Evgeny Kuznetsov 10.00 25.00
17 Teuvo Teravainen 6.00 15.00
18 Stuart Percy 4.00 10.00
19 Leon Draisaitl 20.00 50.00
20 Alexander Wennberg 6.00 15.00

2014-15 Fleer Showcase Metal Universe

BLUE/25: 3X TO 8X BASIC INSERTS
RED/65: 1.2X TO 3X BASIC INSERTS
1 Steven Stamkos 1.25 3.00
2 Alexander Ovechkin 2.50 6.00
3 Wayne Gretzky 4.00 10.00
4 Claude Giroux .60 1.50
5 John Tavares 1.00 2.50
6 Mario Lemieux 2.50 6.00
7 Ryan Getzlaf .60 1.50
8 Sidney Crosby 2.50 6.00
9 Steve Yzerman 1.50 4.00
10 Evgeni Malkin 1.25 3.00
11 Jonathan Toews 1.00 2.50
12 Tuukka Rask .75 2.00
13 Patrick Roy 1.50 4.00
14 Pavel Datsyuk 1.00 2.50
15 Tyler Seguin .75 2.00
16 P.K. Subban .75 2.00
17 Anze Kopitar 1.00 2.50
18 Patrick Kane 1.25 3.00
19 Phil Kessel .60 1.50
20 Bobby Hull 1.25 3.00
21 Taylor Hall .60 1.50
22 Teuvo Teravainen 1.00 2.50
23 Anthony Duclair 1.00 2.50
24 Jori Lehtera .75 2.00
25 David Pastrnak 3.00 8.00
26 Aaron Ekblad 1.50 4.00
27 Andre Burakovsky 1.00 2.50
28 Bo Horvat 1.50 4.00
29 Damon Severson .60 1.50
30 Evgeny Kuznetsov 1.50 4.00
31 Leon Draisaitl 15.00 40.00
32 Jiri Sekac .50 1.25
33 Sam Reinhart 2.50 6.00
34 Vladislav Namestnikov 1.00 2.50
35 Stuart Percy .60 1.50
36 Sven Andrighetto .75 2.00
37 Griffin Reinhart .60 1.50
38 Curtis Lazar .60 1.50
39 Alexander Wennberg 1.00 2.50
40 Ryan Sproul .60 1.50
41 Johnny Gaudreau 2.00 5.00
42 Jonathan Drouin 1.25 3.00

2014-15 Fleer Showcase Metal Universe Precious Metal Gems Blue

BLUE/25: 3X TO 8X BASIC INSERTS

2014-15 Fleer Showcase SkyBox Premium

1 Patrice Bergeron 2.00 5.00
2 Anze Kopitar 2.50 6.00
3 Jonathan Bernier 1.25 3.00
4 Brett Hull 3.00 8.00
5 Alexander Ovechkin 6.00 15.00
6 Evgeni Malkin 3.00 8.00
7 Pekka Rinne 1.50 4.00
8 Jordan Eberle 1.50 4.00
9 Ryan Getzlaf 1.50 4.00
10 Vladimir Tarasenko 2.00 5.00
11 Tyler Seguin 2.00 5.00
12 Henrik Sedin 2.00 5.00
13 P.K. Subban 2.00 5.00
14 Nathan MacKinnon 6.00 15.00
15 Thomas Vanek 1.25 3.00
16 Jamie Benn 1.50 4.00
17 Steven Stamkos 3.00 8.00
18 Filip Forsberg 2.50 6.00
19 Sergei Bobrovsky 2.50 6.00
20 John Tavares 2.50 6.00
21 Chris Chelios 1.50 4.00
22 Felix Potvin 2.50 6.00
23 Patrick Kane 3.00 8.00
24 Rick Nash 1.50 4.00
25 Claude Giroux 1.50 4.00
26 Henrik Zetterberg 2.00 5.00
27 Sidney Crosby 6.00 15.00
28 Wayne Gretzky 10.00 25.00
29 Jonathan Toews 2.50 6.00
30 Jaromir Jagr 5.00 12.00
31 Martin Brodeur 4.00 10.00
32 Tuukka Rask 2.00 5.00
33 Taylor Hall 1.50 4.00
34 Ryan Miller 1.50 4.00
35 Jakub Voracek 1.25 3.00
36 Damon Severson 1.50 4.00
37 Andre Burakovsky 2.50 6.00
38 Stuart Percy 1.50 4.00
39 Sam Reinhart 6.00 15.00
40 Curtis Lazar 1.50 4.00
41 Bo Horvat 4.00 10.00
42 Teuvo Teravainen 2.50 6.00
43 David Pastrnak 8.00 20.00
44 Leon Draisaitl 8.00 20.00
45 Aaron Ekblad 4.00 10.00
46 Shayne Gostisbehere 3.00 8.00
47 Anthony Duclair 2.50 6.00
48 Adam Clendening 1.50 4.00
49 Victor Rask 1.50 4.00
50 Evgeny Kuznetsov 4.00 10.00
51 Griffin Reinhart 1.50 4.00
52 Jonathan Drouin 3.00 8.00
53 Jiri Sekac 1.25 3.00
54 Johnny Gaudreau 5.00 12.00
55 Alexander Wennberg 2.50 6.00
56 Kerby Rychel 1.25 3.00
57 Josh Jooris 1.50 4.00
58 Jori Lehtera 2.00 5.00
59 Tobias Rieder 1.50 4.00
60 Colin Smith 1.50 4.00

2014-15 Fleer Showcase SkyBox Premium Star Rubies

*RUBIES: .8X TO 2X BASIC INSERTS
22 Felix Potvin 8.00 20.00
28 Wayne Gretzky 25.00 50.00
31 Martin Brodeur 15.00 30.00

2015-16 Fleer Showcase

1 Steven Stamkos .60 1.50
2 P.K. Subban .40 1.00
3 Ryan Getzlaf .30 .75
4 Daniel Sedin .40 1.00
5 Alexander Ovechkin 1.25 3.00
6 Sam Gagner .20 .50
7 Henrik Zetterberg .40 1.00
8 Jonathan Bernier .25 .60
9 Anze Kopitar .50 1.25
10 Rick Nash .30 .75
11 Jordan Eberle .30 .75
12 Evgeni Malkin .60 1.50
13 Corey Crawford .40 1.00
14 Jiri Hudler .25 .60
15 John Tavares .50 1.25
16 Joe Thornton .50 1.25
17 Patrice Bergeron .40 1.00
18 Bobby Ryan .25 .60
19 Claude Giroux .30 .75
20 Vladimir Tarasenko .40 1.00
21 Tyler Ennis .20 .50
22 Andrew Ladd .20 .50
23 Tyler Johnson .20 .50
24 Eric Staal .40 1.00
25 Tyler Seguin .40 1.00
26 Gabriel Landeskog .40 1.00
27 Filip Forsberg .50 1.25
28 Kris Letang .40 1.00
29 John Carlson .30 .75

30 Max Pacioretty .30 .75
31 Jonathan Quick .40 1.00
32 Nick Foligno .25 .60
33 Nazem Kadri .40 1.00
34 Johnny Gaudreau .50 1.25
35 Joe Pavelski .40 1.00
36 Justin Faulk .25 .60
37 Jonathan Toews .50 1.25
38 Oliver Ekman-Larsson .30 .75
39 Brock Nelson .30 .75
40 Derek Stepan .20 .50
41 Logan Couture .40 1.00
42 Henrik Sedin .40 1.00
43 Zemgus Girgensons .25 .60
44 Jaromir Jagr 1.00 2.50
45 Ryan Kesler .30 .75
46 Jarome Iginla .40 1.00
47 Loui Eriksson .20 .50
48 Braden Holtby .40 1.00
49 Taylor Hall .30 .75
50 Sidney Crosby 1.25 3.00
51 Carey Price .60 1.50
52 Ondrej Palat .25 .60
53 Marian Hossa .30 .75
54 Jeff Skinner .40 1.00
55 Jakub Voracek .25 .60
56 Mark Stone .40 1.00
57 Alexander Steen .20 .50
58 Pavel Datsyuk .50 1.25
59 Ryan Suter .25 .60
60 Sean Monahan .20 .50
61 Brendan Gallagher .30 .75
62 Jeff Carter .25 .60
63 Jaroslav Halak .30 .75
64 Patrick Kane .60 1.50
65 Corey Perry .50 1.25
66 Patrik Elias .30 .75
67 James van Riemsdyk .25 .60
68 David Backes .20 .50
69 Ben Bishop .25 .60
70 Matt Duchene .30 .75
71 Henrik Lundqvist .75 2.00
72 Matt Moulson .20 .50
73 Pekka Rinne .30 .75
74 Ryan Johansen .25 .60
75 Shane Doan .25 .60
76 Zach Parise .30 .75
77 Patric Hornqvist .20 .50
78 Erik Karlsson .40 1.00
79 Kyle Okposo .20 .50
80 Brad Marchand .60 1.50
81 Jamie Benn .30 .75
82 Mark Giordano .30 .75
83 Ryan Nugent-Hopkins .40 1.00
84 Shea Weber .25 .60
85 Nikita Kucherov .60 1.50
86 Gustav Nyquist .20 .50
87 Nathan MacKinnon 1.25 3.00
88 Jonathan Huberdeau .40 1.00
89 Adam Henrique .25 .60
90 Dustin Byfuglien .30 .75
91 Peter Forsberg .60 1.50
92 Bobby Hull .60 1.50
93 Ray Bourque .50 1.25
94 Mark Messier .60 1.50
95 Theoren Fleury .40 1.00
96 Steve Yzerman .75 2.00
97 Bobby Clarke .50 1.25
98 Guy Lafleur .40 1.00
99 Wayne Gretzky 2.00 5.00
100 Johnny Bucyk .30 .75
101 Korpisalo RC/Dansk RC/Hannikainen RC 6.00 15.00
102 O'Neill RC/Blandisi RC/Hrabarenka RC 3.00 8.00
103 Biega RC/Rissanen RC/Slavin RC 5.00 12.00
104 Mersch RC/Skjei RC/Shore RC 3.00 8.00
105 Alt RC/Straka RC/Medvedev RC 2.50 6.00
106 Biega RC/Grenier RC/Pedan RC 4.00 10.00
107 Pesce RC/Olofsson RC/Carr RC 3.00 8.00
108 Musil RC/Kulak RC/Oesterle RC 2.50 6.00
109 Murray RC/Hellebuyck RC/Berube RC 12.00 30.00
110 Carpenter RC/Dzingel RC/Di Giuseppe RC 3.00 8.00
111 Ranford RC/Holloway RC/Mouillierat RC 3.00 8.00
112 Martinsen RC/Thompson RC/Nosek RC 4.00 10.00
113 Hamilton RC/Khaira RC/Miller RC 3.00 8.00
114 Ferlin RC/Randell RC/Cross RC 3.00 8.00
115 Domingue RC/Dauphin RC/Langhamer RC 4.00 10.00
116 A.Bitetto RC/J.Saros RC 8.00 20.00
117 T.Kero RC/E.Gustafsson RC 4.00 10.00
118 R.Bourque RC/C.Sheary RC 10.00 25.00
119 B.Lerg RC/D.Tarasov RC 2.50 6.00
120 B.Froese RC/C.Bailey RC 3.00 8.00
121 L.Shaw RC/Y.Gourde RC 5.00 12.00
122 K.Gabriel RC/M.Keranen RC 2.50 6.00
123 C.Wideman RC/M.McCormick RC 3.00 8.00
124 D.Rasmussen RC/F.Claesson RC 4.00 10.00
125 J.Vermin RC/L.Witkowski RC 2.50 6.00
126 Adam Pelech AU RC 5.00 12.00
127 Linus Ullmark AU RC 12.00 30.00
128 Frank Vatrano AU RC 8.00 20.00
129 Garret Sparks AU RC 6.00 15.00
130 Joel Edmundson AU RC 5.00 12.00
131 Shea Theodore AU RC 10.00 25.00
132 Charles Hudon AU RC 6.00 15.00
133 Keegan Lowe AU RC 6.00 15.00
134 Devin Shore AU RC 6.00 15.00
135 Taylor Leier AU RC 6.00 15.00
136 Mike McCarron AU RC 8.00 20.00
137 Christoph Bertschy AU RC 5.00 12.00
138 Chris Driedger AU RC 5.00 12.00
139 Anton Slepyshev AU RC 4.00 10.00
140 Dylan DeMelo AU RC 5.00 12.00
141 Viktor Arvidsson JSY AU/499 RC 6.00 15.00
142 Colton Parayko JSY AU/499 RC 10.00 25.00
143 Matt O'Connor JSY AU/499 RC 5.00 12.00
144 Nikolay Goldobin JSY AU/499 RC 6.00 15.00
145 Mattias Janmark JSY AU/499 RC 6.00 15.00
146 Oscar Lindberg JSY AU/499 RC 6.00 15.00
147 Sergei Kalinin JSY AU/499 RC 4.00 10.00
148 Jordan Weal JSY AU/499 RC 4.00 10.00
149 Daniel Sprong JSY AU/499 RC 8.00 20.00
150 Stefan Noesen JSY AU/499 RC 4.00 10.00
151 Joonas Donskoi JSY AU/499 RC 6.00 15.00
152 Malcolm Subban JSY AU/499 RC 10.00 25.00
153 Kevin Fiala JSY AU/499 RC 8.00 20.00
154 Shane Prince JSY AU/499 RC 4.00 10.00
155 Andrew Copp JSY AU/499 RC 6.00 15.00
156 Emile Poirier JSY AU/499 RC 5.00 12.00
157 Jared McCann JSY AU/499 RC 8.00 20.00
158 Ben Hutton JSY AU/499 RC 6.00 15.00
159 Mike Condon JSY AU/499 RC 6.00 15.00
160 Colin Miller JSY AU/499 RC 5.00 12.00
161 Henrik Samuelsson JSY AU/499 RC 4.00 10.00
162 Anthony Stolarz JSY AU/499 RC 15.00 40.00
163 Jacob de la Rose JSY AU/499 RC 6.00 15.00
164 Ronalds Kenins JSY AU/499 RC 4.00 10.00
165 Antoine Bibeau JSY AU/499 RC 6.00 15.00
166 Slater Koekkoek JSY AU/499 RC 4.00 10.00
167 Matt Puempel JSY AU/499 RC 5.00 12.00
168 Nick Cousins JSY AU/499 RC 6.00 15.00
169 Brock McGinn JSY AU/499 RC 6.00 15.00
170 Derek Forbort JSY AU/499 RC 5.00 12.00
171 Mackenzie Skapski JSY AU/499 RC 6.00 15.00
172 Ryan Hartman JSY AU/499 RC 8.00 20.00
173 Radek Faksa JSY AU/499 RC 6.00 15.00
174 Kyle Baun JSY AU/499 RC 6.00 15.00
175 Brendan Gaunce JSY AU/499 RC 8.00 20.00
176 Joonas Kemppainen JSY AU/499 RC 4.00 10.00
177 Josh Anderson JSY AU/499 RC 12.00 30.00
178 Hunter Shinkaruk JSY AU/499 RC 6.00 15.00
179 Sam Brittain JSY AU/499 RC 6.00 15.00
180 Sergei Plotnikov JSY AU/499 RC 4.00 10.00
181 Stanislav Galiev JSY AU/499 RC 6.00 15.00
182 Viktor Svedberg JSY AU/499 RC 5.00 12.00
183 Vincent Hinostroza JSY AU/499 RC 4.00 10.00
184 Chandler Stephenson JSY AU/499 RC 8.00 20.00
185 Connor Brickley JSY AU/499 RC 5.00 12.00
186 Zachary Fucale JSY AU/499 RC 5.00 12.00
187 Mikko Rantanen JSY AU/499 RC 80.00 200.00
188 Andreas Athanasiou JSY AU/499 RC 15.00 40.00
189 Connor McDavid JSY AU/299 RC 600.00 1500.00
190 Dylan Larkin JSY AU/299 RC 30.00 80.00
191 Noah Hanifin JSY AU/299 RC 10.00 25.00
192 Artemi Panarin JSY AU/299 RC 30.00 80.00
193 Jake Virtanen JSY AU/299 RC 8.00 20.00
194 Robby Fabbri JSY AU/299 RC 8.00 20.00
195 Nikolaj Ehlers JSY AU/299 RC 12.00 30.00
196 Max Domi JSY AU/299 RC 12.00 30.00
197 Nicolas Petan JSY AU/299 RC 6.00 15.00
198 Sam Bennett JSY AU/299 RC 20.00 50.00
199 Nick Ritchie JSY AU/299 RC 6.00 15.00
200 Jack Eichel JSY RC 25.00 60.00

2015-16 Fleer Showcase Red Glow

*RED/25 (1-100): 4X TO 10X BASIC CARDS
*RED/25 (101-125): .6X TO 1.5X BASIC CARDS
*RED/25 (126-200): .8X TO 2X BASIC CARDS
189 Connor McDavid GLV AU 1000.00 2500.00

2015-16 Fleer Showcase Flair

1 Sidney Crosby R1 4.00 10.00
2 Corey Perry R1 1.50 4.00
3 Pekka Rinne R1 1.00 2.50
4 Blake Wheeler R1 1.00 2.50
5 Alexander Ovechkin R1 4.00 10.00
6 Erik Karlsson R1 1.25 3.00
7 Ryan Johansen R1 .75 2.00
8 Oliver Ekman-Larsson R1 1.00 2.50
9 Steven Stamkos R1 2.00 5.00
10 Vladimir Tarasenko R1 1.25 3.00
11 Anze Kopitar R1 1.50 4.00
12 Eric Staal R1 1.25 3.00
13 Jamie Benn R1 1.00 2.50
14 Henrik Lundqvist R1 2.50 6.00
15 P.K. Subban R1 1.25 3.00
16 Tuukka Rask R1 1.25 3.00
17 John Tavares R1 1.50 4.00
18 Joe Pavelski R1 1.25 3.00
19 Pavel Datsyuk R1 1.50 4.00
20 Jordan Eberle R1 1.00 2.50
21 James van Riemsdyk R1 .75 2.00
22 Jonathan Toews R1 1.50 4.00
23 Gabriel Landeskog R1 1.25 3.00
24 Zach Parise R1 1.00 2.50
25 Claude Giroux R1 1.00 2.50
26 Patrick Roy R1 2.50 6.00
27 Doug Gilmour R1 1.25 3.00
28 Larry Robinson R1 1.00 2.50
29 Mark Messier R1 2.00 5.00
30 Jeremy Roenick R1 1.50 4.00
31 Mike Bossy R1 1.00 2.50
32 Denis Savard R1 1.00 2.50
33 Guy Carbonneau R1 .75 2.00
34 Paul Coffey R1 1.00 2.50
35 Wayne Gretzky R1 6.00 15.00
36 Connor McDavid R0 60.00 150.00
37 Noah Hanifin R0 1.50 4.00
38 Dylan Larkin R0 3.00 8.00
39 Sam Bennett R0 3.00 8.00
40 Max Domi R0 2.00 5.00
41 Nikolaj Ehlers R0 2.00 5.00
42 Jake Virtanen R0 1.25 3.00
43 Malcolm Subban R0 1.50 4.00
44 Artemi Panarin R0 4.00 10.00
45 Daniel Sprong R0 1.25 3.00
46 Oscar Lindberg R0 1.00 2.50
47 Nick Cousins R0 1.00 2.50
48 Mattias Janmark R0 1.00 2.50
49 Jordan Weal R0 .60 1.50
50 Jared McCann R0 1.25 3.00
51 Robby Fabbri R0 1.25 3.00
52 Stefan Noesen R0 .60 1.50
53 Nick Ritchie R0 1.00 2.50
54 Mikko Rantanen R0 5.00 12.00
55 Nicolas Petan R0 1.00 2.50
56 Kevin Fiala R0 1.25 3.00
57 Henrik Samuelsson R0 .60 1.50
58 Nikolay Goldobin R0 1.00 2.50
59 Slater Koekkoek R0 .60 1.50
60 Emile Poirier R0 .75 2.00
61 Antoine Bibeau R0 1.00 2.50
62 Zachary Fucale R0 .75 2.00
63 Matt Puempel R0 .75 2.00
64 Jacob de la Rose R0 1.00 2.50
65 Jack Eichel R0 4.00 10.00

2015-16 Fleer Showcase Flair Blue Ice

*BLUE ICE/99-199: .6X TO 1.5X BASIC INSERTS
36 Connor McDavid R0 150.00 400.00

2015-16 Fleer Showcase Flair Materials Premium

36 Connor McDavid AU/35 1200.00 3000.00

2015-16 Fleer Showcase Metal Universe

MU1 Connor McDavid 40.00 100.00
MU2 Max Domi 2.00 5.00
MU3 Joonas Donskoi 1.00 2.50
MU4 Robby Fabbri 1.25 3.00
MU5 Sam Bennett 3.00 8.00
MU6 Nikolaj Ehlers 2.00 5.00
MU7 Noah Hanifin 1.50 4.00
MU8 Dylan Larkin 3.00 8.00
MU9 Artemi Panarin 4.00 10.00
MU10 Jared McCann 1.25 3.00
MU11 Oscar Lindberg 1.00 2.50
MU12 Mikko Rantanen 5.00 12.00
MU13 Nicolas Petan 1.00 2.50
MU14 Mattias Janmark 1.00 2.50
MU15 Daniel Sprong 1.25 3.00
MU16 Nikolay Goldobin 1.00 2.50
MU17 Nick Shore .60 1.50
MU18 Zachary Fucale .75 2.00
MU19 Radek Faksa 1.00 2.50
MU20 Jack Eichel 4.00 10.00
MU21 Nick Ritchie 1.00 2.50
MU22 Colin Miller .75 2.00
MU23 Sergei Plotnikov .60 1.50
MU24 Chandler Stephenson 1.25 3.00
MU25 Colton Parayko 1.50 4.00
MU26 Sergei Kalinin .60 1.50
MU27 Hunter Shinkaruk 1.00 2.50
MU28 Connor Brickley .75 2.00
MU29 Brock McGinn 1.00 2.50
MU30 Jake Virtanen 1.25 3.00

2015-16 Fleer Showcase Metal Universe Precious Metal Gems Blue

*BLUE/50 2X TO 5X BASIC INSERTS
MU1 Connor McDavid 2500.00 6000.00
MU8 Dylan Larkin 30.00 80.00
MU9 Artemi Panarin 30.00 80.00
MU22 Colin Miller 10.00 25.00

2015-16 Fleer Showcase Metal Universe Precious Metal Gems Red

MU1 Connor McDavid 1500.00 4000.00
MU5 Sam Bennett 12.00 30.00
MU8 Dylan Larkin 25.00 50.00

2015-16 Fleer Showcase SkyBox Premium Prospects

S1 Jack Eichel 5.00 12.00
S2 Joonas Donskoi 1.25 3.00
S3 Noah Hanifin 2.00 5.00
S4 Malcolm Subban 2.00 5.00
S5 Max Domi 2.50 6.00
S6 Nikolaj Ehlers 2.50 6.00
S7 Mikko Rantanen 6.00 15.00
S8 Artemi Panarin 5.00 12.00
S9 Dylan Larkin 4.00 10.00
S10 Nicolas Petan 1.25 3.00
S11 Daniel Sprong 1.50 4.00
S12 Jared McCann 1.50 4.00
S13 Mattias Janmark 1.25 3.00
S14 Jake Virtanen 1.50 4.00
S15 Nikolay Goldobin 1.25 3.00
S16 Juuse Saros 3.00 8.00
S17 Linus Ullmark 2.50 6.00
S18 Connor Hellebuyck 5.00 12.00
S19 Robby Fabbri 1.50 4.00
S20 Connor McDavid 125.00 300.00
S21 Sam Bennett 4.00 10.00
S22 Colton Parayko 2.00 5.00
S23 Kevin Fiala 1.50 4.00
S24 Hunter Shinkaruk 1.25 3.00
S25 Garret Sparks 1.25 3.00
S26 Mike Condon 1.25 3.00
S27 Frank Vatrano 1.50 4.00
S28 Oscar Lindberg 1.25 3.00
S29 Colin Miller 1.00 2.50
S30 Nick Ritchie 1.25 3.00

2015-16 Fleer Showcase SkyBox Premium Prospects Star Rubies

*RUBIES: 1.5X TO 4X BASIC INSERTS
S20 Connor McDavid 250.00 600.00

2015-16 Fleer Showcase Ultra Rookies

U1 Connor McDavid 125.00 300.00
U2 Jack Eichel 8.00 20.00
U3 Noah Hanifin 3.00 8.00
U4 Dylan Larkin 6.00 15.00
U5 Artemi Panarin 8.00 20.00
U6 Max Domi 4.00 10.00
U7 Nikolaj Ehlers 4.00 10.00
U8 Mattias Janmark 2.00 5.00
U9 Robby Fabbri 2.50 6.00
U10 Joonas Donskoi 2.00 5.00
U11 Nicolas Petan 2.00 5.00
U12 Mike Condon 2.00 5.00
U13 Daniel Sprong 2.50 6.00
U14 Jared McCann 2.50 6.00
U15 Juuse Saros 5.00 12.00
U16 Ben Hutton 2.00 5.00
U17 Jake Virtanen 2.50 6.00
U18 Jaccob Slavin 3.00 8.00
U19 Colton Parayko 3.00 8.00
U20 Sam Bennett 6.00 15.00
U21 Oscar Lindberg 2.00 5.00
U22 Connor Brickley 1.50 4.00
U23 Frank Vatrano 2.50 6.00
U24 Sergei Plotnikov 1.25 3.00
U25 Nick Ritchie 2.00 5.00
U26 Mikko Rantanen 10.00 25.00
U27 Nick Cousins 2.00 5.00
U28 Hunter Shinkaruk 2.00 5.00
U29 Garret Sparks 2.00 5.00
U30 Gustav Olofsson 2.00 5.00

2015-16 Fleer Showcase Ultra Rookies Violet Medallion

*VIOLET/25: .8X TO 5X BASIC INSERTS
U2 Jack Eichel 100.00 200.00
U4 Dylan Larkin 60.00 150.00
U5 Artemi Panarin 50.00 125.00
U23 Frank Vatrano 20.00 50.00

2016-17 Fleer Showcase

1 Sidney Crosby 1.50 4.00
2 Anze Kopitar .60 1.50
3 Ryan Getzlaf .40 1.00
4 Daniel Sedin .50 1.25
5 Alexander Ovechkin 1.50 4.00
6 Shayne Gostisbehere .40 1.00
7 Henrik Zetterberg .50 1.25
8 Frederik Andersen .50 1.25
9 P.K. Subban .50 1.25
10 Rick Nash .40 1.00
11 Jordan Eberle .40 1.00
12 Frans Nielsen .25 .60
13 Corey Crawford .50 1.25
14 Shea Weber .30 .75
15 John Tavares .60 1.50
16 Joe Thornton .60 1.50
17 Patrice Bergeron .50 1.25
18 Evgeni Malkin .75 2.00
19 Claude Giroux .40 1.00
20 Vladimir Tarasenko .50 1.25
21 Ryan O'Reilly .40 1.00
22 Seth Jones .40 1.00
23 Jonathan Drouin .30 .75
24 Loui Eriksson .25 .60
25 Tyler Seguin .50 1.25
26 Gabriel Landeskog .50 1.25
27 Roman Josi .40 1.00
28 Kris Letang .50 1.25
29 T.J. Oshie .40 1.00
30 Max Pacioretty .40 1.00
31 Jonathan Quick .50 1.25
32 Brandon Saad .30 .75
33 Nazem Kadri .50 1.25
34 Johnny Gaudreau .60 1.50
35 Joe Pavelski .50 1.25
36 Teuvo Teravainen .40 1.00
37 Jonathan Toews .60 1.50
38 Oliver Ekman-Larsson .40 1.00
39 Andrew Ladd .25 .60
40 Derek Stepan .25 .60
41 Logan Couture .50 1.25
42 Henrik Sedin .50 1.25
43 Zemgus Girgensons .30 .75
44 Jaromir Jagr 1.25 3.00
45 John Gibson .40 1.00
46 Jarome Iginla .50 1.25
47 David Backes .25 .60
48 Braden Holtby .50 1.25
49 Connor McDavid 2.00 5.00
50 Steven Stamkos .75 2.00
51 Carey Price .75 2.00
52 Ondrej Palat .30 .75
53 Marian Hossa .40 1.00
54 Jeff Skinner .50 1.25
55 Jakub Voracek .30 .75
56 Mark Stone .50 1.25
57 Robby Fabbri .25 .60
58 Aaron Ekblad .50 1.25
59 Ryan Suter .30 .75
60 Sean Monahan .25 .60
61 Brendan Gallagher .40 1.00
62 Drew Doughty .50 1.25
63 Jaroslav Halak .40 1.00
64 Patrick Kane .75 2.00
65 Corey Perry .60 1.50
66 Cory Schneider .40 1.00
67 James van Riemsdyk .30 .75
68 Kevin Shattenkirk .25 .60
69 Andrei Vasilevskiy .60 1.50
70 Matt Duchene .40 1.00
71 Henrik Lundqvist 1.00 2.50
72 Jack Eichel .60 1.50
73 Pekka Rinne .40 1.00
74 Ryan Johansen .30 .75
75 Max Domi .40 1.00
76 Zach Parise .40 1.00
77 Patric Hornqvist .25 .60
78 Erik Karlsson .50 1.25
79 Nicklas Backstrom .40 1.00
80 Brad Marchand .75 2.00
81 Jamie Benn .40 1.00
82 Mark Giordano .40 1.00
83 Leon Draisaitl 1.25 3.00
84 Taylor Hall .40 1.00
85 Nikita Kucherov .75 2.00
86 Gustav Nyquist .25 .60
87 Nathan MacKinnon 1.50 4.00
88 Jonathan Marchessault .50 1.25
89 Kyle Palmieri .30 .75
90 Dustin Byfuglien .40 1.00
91 Phil Kessel .40 1.00
92 Mike Hoffman .25 .60
93 Patrick Sharp .30 .75
94 Aleksander Barkov .60 1.50
95 Mats Zuccarello .40 1.00
96 Blake Wheeler .40 1.00
97 Artemi Panarin .75 2.00
98 Evgeny Kuznetsov .50 1.25
99 Martin Jones .30 .75
100 Brent Burns .40 1.00
101 Mozik RC/Pietila RC Auvitu RC/Lappin RC 3.00 8.00
102 Kase RC/Cramarossa RC/Dowling RC/Smith RC 3.00 8.00
103 Kuraly RC/Lyubimov RC/Archibald RC/Hrivik RC 10.00 25.00
104 Tanev RC/Nelson RC Benning RC/Johnston RC 4.00 10.00
105 Coreau RC/Dell RC/Mcintyre RC/Wedgewood RC 5.00 12.00
106 Johnston RC/Hyman RC/Stecher RC/Robinson RC 8.00 20.00
107 Lernout RC/Hanley RC/Czarnik RC/Acciari RC 5.00 12.00
108 McFarland RC/Malgin RC/Regner RC/Harper RC 5.00 12.00
109 Carrier RC/Catenacci RC/Nutivaara RC/Sedlak RC 3.00 8.00
110 Gravel RC/O'Gara RC/Hathaway RC/Kosmachuk RC 4.00 10.00
111 Brandon Carlo RC 5.00 12.00
112 A.J. Greer RC 3.00 8.00
113 Michal Kempny RC 3.00 8.00
114 Martin Frk RC 4.00 10.00
115 Gustav Forsling RC 6.00 15.00
116 Zach Sanford RC 3.00 8.00
117 Tyler Bertuzzi RC 5.00 12.00
118 Tobias Lindberg RC 5.00 12.00
119 Nick Baptiste RC 3.00 8.00
120 Jacob Larsson RC 5.00 12.00
121 Frederick Gaudreau RC 4.00 10.00
122 Joseph LaBate RC 4.00 10.00
123 Jake Guentzel RC 10.00 25.00
124 Drake Caggiula RC 3.00 8.00
125 Cristoval Nieves RC 4.00 10.00
126 Steven Santini RC 2.50 6.00
127 Tristan Jarry AU/499 RC 8.00 20.00
128 Spencer Martin RC 4.00 10.00
129 Zack Mitchell RC 3.00 8.00
130 Cole Schneider RC 3.00 8.00
131 Nick Paul RC 4.00 10.00
132 Nic Dowd RC 2.50 6.00
133 Frederik Gauthier RC 2.50 6.00
134 Stephen Johns RC 2.50 6.00
135 Mark Jankowski RC 2.50 6.00
136 Nick Sorensen RC 3.00 8.00
137 Daniel O' Regan RC 3.00 8.00
138 Alan Quine RC 3.00 8.00
139 Blake Speers RC 3.00 8.00
140 Nikita Zaitsev RC 3.00 8.00
141 Sonny Milano AU/499 RC 5.00 12.00
142 Justin Bailey AU/499 RC 4.00 10.00
143 Ryan Pulock AU/499 RC 4.00 10.00
144 Charlie Lindgren AU/499 RC 6.00 15.00
145 Brendan Leipsic AU/499 RC 3.00 8.00
146 Nikita Soshnikov AU/499 RC 2.50 6.00
147 Kasperi Kapanen AU/499 RC 6.00 15.00
148 Oliver Kylington AU/499 RC 3.00 8.00
149 Connor Brown AU/499 RC 6.00 15.00
150 Oskar Sundqvist AU/499 RC 4.00 10.00
151 Jason Dickinson AU/499 RC 3.00 8.00
152 Hudson Fasching AU/499 RC 4.00 10.00
153 Michael Matheson AU/499 RC 4.00 10.00
154 Miles Wood AU/499 RC 3.00 8.00
155 Daniel Altshuller AU/499 RC 3.00 8.00
156 Oliver Bjorkstrand AU/499 RC 5.00 12.00
157 Josh Morrissey AU/499 RC 10.00 25.00
158 Pontus Aberg AU/499 RC 5.00 12.00
159 Ivan Provorov AU/499 RC 6.00 15.00
160 Jimmy Vesey AU/499 RC 6.00 15.00
161 Kyle Connor AU/499 RC 12.00 30.00
162 Christian Dvorak AU/499 RC 5.00 12.00
163 Sebastian Aho AU/499 RC 12.00 30.00
164 Nick Schmaltz AU/499 RC 5.00 12.00
165 Zach Werenski AU/499 RC 12.00 30.00
166 Mathew Barzal AU/499 RC 12.00 30.00
167 Thomas Chabot AU/499 RC 8.00 20.00
168 Jakob Chychrun AU/499 RC 8.00 20.00
169 Joel Eriksson Ek AU/499 RC 6.00 15.00
170 Brayden Point AU/499 RC 20.00 50.00
171 Tyler Motte AU/499 RC 4.00 10.00
172 Pavel Buchnevich AU/499 RC 6.00 15.00
173 Anthony Beauvillier AU/499 RC 4.00 10.00
174 Lawson Crouse AU/499 RC 3.00 8.00
175 Kevin Labanc AU/499 RC 4.00 10.00
176 Anthony DeAngelo AU/499 RC 3.00 8.00
177 Mikhail Sergachev AU/499 RC 6.00 15.00
178 Danton Heinen AU/499 RC 3.00 8.00
179 Julius Honka AU/499 RC 4.00 10.00
180 Artturi Lehkonen AU/499 RC 5.00 12.00
181 Patrik Laine AU/299 RC 30.00 80.00
182 Matthew Tkachuk AU/299 RC 30.00 80.00
183 Jesse Puljujarvi AU/299 RC 8.00 20.00
184 Travis Konecny AU/299 RC 8.00 20.00
185 William Nylander AU/299 RC 25.00 60.00
186 Anthony Mantha AU/299 RC 10.00 25.00
187 Mitch Marner AU/99 RC 150.00 400.00
188 Pavel Zacha AU/299 RC 6.00 15.00
189 Dylan Strome AU/299 RC 10.00 25.00
190 Auston Matthews AU/99 RC 200.00 300.00
191 Brendan Perlini AU/499 RC 4.00 10.00
192 Brendan Guhle AU/499 RC 4.00 10.00
193 John Quenneville AU/499 RC 4.00 10.00
194 Timo Meier AU/499 RC 8.00 20.00
195 Nikita Tryamkin AU/499 RC 3.00 8.00
196 Thatcher Demko AU/499 RC 25.00 60.00
197 Jakub Vrana AU/499 RC 5.00 12.00
198 Brandon Montour AU/499 RC 10.00 25.00
199 Sergey Tolchinsky AU/499 RC 3.00 8.00
200 Blidh RC/Grzelcyk RC/Burgdoerfer RC/Kasdorf RC 6.00 15.00
201 Alves RC/Ryan RC/Nakladal RC/Carrick RC 3.00 8.00
202 Henley RC/Elson RC/Kukan RC/Jensen RC 6.00 15.00
203 Simpson RC/Ellis RC/Cannone RC/Liambas RC 3.00 8.00
204 Englund RC/Harpur RC/Sieloff RC/De Leo RC 3.00 8.00
205 Friesen RC/Megan RC/Rodin RC/Garteig RC 4.00 10.00
206 Erne RC/Wilcox RC/Peca RC/Richard RC 4.00 10.00
207 Johansson RC/Will RC/Halverson RC/Treutle RC 3.00 8.00

2016-17 Fleer Showcase Red Glow

*VETS: 1.25X TO 3X BASIC CARDS
*ROOKIES/25-49: .6X TO 1.5X BASIC CARDS
79 Nicklas Backstrom 1.25 3.00
98 Evgeny Kuznetsov 1.50 4.00
183 Jesse Puljujarvi AU/25 80.00 150.00
184 Travis Konecny AU/25 25.00 60.00
186 Anthony Mantha AU/25 30.00 80.00

2016-17 Fleer Showcase White Hot

*VETS/25: 2.5X TO 6X BASIC CARDS
*ROOKIES/15: .75X TO 2X BASIC CARDS
79 Nicklas Backstrom 2.50 6.00
98 Evgeny Kuznetsov 3.00 8.00
159 Ivan Provorov AU/15 60.00 120.00

2016-17 Fleer Showcase E-X2017

1 Connor McDavid 5.00 12.00
2 Sidney Crosby 4.00 10.00
3 Wayne Gretzky 6.00 15.00
4 Bobby Orr 4.00 10.00
5 Steven Stamkos 2.00 5.00
6 Patrick Kane 2.00 5.00
7 Henrik Lundqvist 2.50 6.00
8 Alexander Ovechkin 4.00 10.00
9 Matt Duchene 1.00 2.50
10 Carey Price 2.00 5.00
11 Anze Kopitar 1.50 4.00
12 John Tavares 1.50 4.00
13 Johnny Gaudreau 1.50 4.00
14 Jamie Benn 1.00 2.50
15 Ryan Getzlaf 1.00 2.50
16 Joe Pavelski 1.25 3.00
17 Dylan Larkin 1.25 3.00
18 Brad Marchand 2.00 5.00
19 Jonathan Toews 1.50 4.00
20 Vladimir Tarasenko 1.25 3.00
21 Patrick Roy 2.50 6.00
22 Tyler Motte 1.00 2.50
23 Sebastian Aho 3.00 8.00
24 Nick Schmaltz 1.25 3.00
25 Zach Werenski 3.00 8.00
26 Anthony Mantha 2.00 5.00
27 Pavel Zacha 1.50 4.00
28 Artturi Lehkonen 1.25 3.00
29 Ivan Provorov 1.50 4.00
30 Mathew Barzal 3.00 8.00
31 Travis Konecny 2.00 5.00
32 Christian Dvorak 1.25 3.00
33 Mikhail Sergachev 1.50 4.00
34 Matthew Tkachuk 4.00 10.00
35 Kyle Connor 3.00 8.00
36 Jimmy Vesey 1.50 4.00
37 Jesse Puljujarvi 2.00 5.00
38 Dylan Strome 2.50 6.00
39 Mitch Marner 3.00 8.00
40 William Nylander 4.00 10.00
41 Patrik Laine 8.00 20.00
42 Auston Matthews 12.00 30.00

2016-17 Fleer Showcase E-X2017 Essential Credentials Future

1 Connor McDavid/42 400.00 100.00
3 Wayne Gretzky/40 250.00 600.00

2016-17 Fleer Showcase Flair

1 Sidney Crosby R1 6.00 15.00
2 Carey Price R1 3.00 8.00
3 Patrick Kane R1 3.00 8.00
4 Joe Pavelski R1 2.00 5.00
5 Mario Lemieux R1 6.00 15.00
6 Jonathan Quick R1 2.00 5.00
7 Alexander Ovechkin R1 6.00 15.00
8 Jamie Benn R1 1.50 4.00
9 Claude Giroux R1 1.50 4.00
10 Patrick Roy R1 4.00 10.00
11 Connor McDavid R1 8.00 20.00
12 Mark Messier R1 3.00 8.00
13 Henrik Lundqvist R1 4.00 10.00
14 Jack Eichel R1 2.50 6.00
15 Bobby Orr R1 6.00 15.00
16 Dylan Larkin R1 2.00 5.00
17 Vladimir Tarasenko R1 2.00 5.00
18 John Tavares R1 2.50 6.00
19 Johnny Gaudreau R1 2.50 6.00
20 Wayne Gretzky R1 10.00 25.00
21 Auston Matthews R0 10.00 25.00
22 Kyle Connor R0 5.00 12.00
23 Mikhail Sergachev R0 2.50 6.00
24 Travis Konecny R0 3.00 8.00
25 William Nylander R0 6.00 15.00
26 Christian Dvorak R0 2.00 5.00
27 Joel Eriksson Ek R0 2.50 6.00
28 Artturi Lehkonen R0 2.00 5.00
29 Pavel Buchnevich R0 2.50 6.00
30 Jesse Puljujarvi R0 4.00 10.00
31 Zach Werenski R0 5.00 12.00
32 Tyler Motte R0 1.50 4.00
33 Pavel Zacha R0 2.50 6.00
34 Anthony Mantha R0 3.00 8.00
35 Mathew Barzal R0 6.00 15.00
36 Nick Schmaltz R0 2.00 5.00
37 Ivan Provorov R0 2.50 6.00
38 Brayden Point R0 4.00 10.00
39 Jakob Chychrun R0 3.00 8.00
40 Jimmy Vesey R0 2.50 6.00
41 Sebastian Aho R0 5.00 12.00
42 Matthew Tkachuk R0 6.00 15.00
43 Lawson Crouse R0 1.25 3.00
44 Anthony Beauvillier R0 1.50 4.00
45 Mitch Marner R0 5.00 12.00
46 Thomas Chabot R0 3.00 8.00
47 Brandon Carlo R0 2.50 6.00
48 Dylan Strome R0 4.00 10.00
49 Connor Brown R0 2.50 6.00
50 Patrik Laine R0 4.00 10.00

2016-17 Fleer Showcase Flair Blue Ice

*R1/99: .75X TO 2X BASIC INSERTS
*R0/199: .75X TO 2X BASIC INSERTS
21 Auston Matthews R0 30.00 80.00
50 Patrik Laine R0 20.00 50.00

2016-17 Fleer Showcase Flair Hot Gloves

HG1 Patrick Roy 3.00 8.00
HG2 Henrik Lundqvist 3.00 8.00
HG3 Jonathan Quick 1.50 4.00
HG4 Pekka Rinne 1.25 3.00
HG5 Martin Brodeur 3.00 8.00
HG6 Cory Schneider 1.25 3.00
HG7 Corey Crawford 1.50 4.00
HG8 Braden Holtby 1.50 4.00
HG9 Matt Murray 2.00 5.00
HG10 Carey Price 2.50 6.00

2016-17 Fleer Showcase Hot Prospects Autograph Patches

141 Sonny Milano/135 10.00 25.00
142 Justin Bailey/135 8.00 20.00
143 Ryan Pulock/135 8.00 20.00
144 Charlie Lindgren/135 12.00 30.00
145 Brendan Leipsic/135 6.00 15.00
146 Nikita Soshnikov/135 5.00 12.00
147 Kasperi Kapanen/135 12.00 30.00
148 Oliver Kylington/135 6.00 15.00
149 Connor Brown/135 12.00 30.00
150 Oskar Sundqvist/135 8.00 20.00
151 Jason Dickinson/135 6.00 15.00
152 Hudson Fasching/135 8.00 20.00
153 Michael Matheson/135 8.00 20.00
154 Miles Wood/135 6.00 15.00
155 Daniel Altshuller/135 6.00 15.00
156 Oliver Bjorkstrand/135 10.00 25.00
157 Josh Morrissey/135 20.00 50.00
158 Pontus Aberg/135 10.00 25.00
159 Ivan Provorov/135 12.00 30.00
160 Jimmy Vesey/135 12.00 30.00
161 Kyle Connor/135 25.00 60.00
162 Christian Dvorak/135 10.00 25.00
163 Sebastian Aho/135 25.00 60.00
164 Nick Schmaltz/135 10.00 25.00
165 Zach Werenski/135 25.00 60.00
166 Mathew Barzal/135 25.00 60.00
167 Thomas Chabot/135 15.00 40.00
168 Jakob Chychrun/135 15.00 40.00
169 Joel Eriksson Ek/135 12.00 30.00
170 Brayden Point/135 20.00 50.00
171 Tyler Motte/135 8.00 20.00
172 Pavel Buchnevich/135 12.00 30.00
173 Anthony Beauvillier/135 8.00 20.00
174 Lawson Crouse/135 6.00 15.00
175 Kevin Labanc/135 8.00 20.00
176 Anthony DeAngelo/135 6.00 15.00
177 Mikhail Sergachev/135 12.00 30.00
179 Julius Honka/135 8.00 20.00
181 Patrik Laine/85 30.00 80.00
182 Matthew Tkachuk/85 50.00 125.00
183 Jesse Puljujarvi/85 25.00 60.00
184 Travis Konecny/85 25.00 60.00
185 William Nylander/85 50.00 125.00
186 Anthony Mantha/85 25.00 60.00
188 Pavel Zacha/85 20.00 50.00
189 Dylan Strome/85 30.00 80.00
190 Auston Matthews/35 300.00 500.00

2016-17 Fleer Showcase Metal Universe

MU1 Connor McDavid 5.00 12.00
MU2 Sidney Crosby 4.00 10.00
MU3 Carey Price 2.00 5.00
MU4 Steven Stamkos 2.00 5.00
MU5 P.K. Subban 1.25 3.00
MU6 Shea Weber .75 2.00
MU7 Taylor Hall 1.00 2.50
MU8 Henrik Lundqvist 2.50 6.00
MU9 Dylan Larkin 1.25 3.00
MU10 Patrick Kane 2.00 5.00
MU11 John Tavares 1.50 4.00
MU12 Brent Burns 1.00 2.50
MU13 Jack Eichel 1.50 4.00
MU14 Jamie Benn 1.00 2.50
MU15 Drew Doughty 1.25 3.00
MU16 Patrice Bergeron 1.25 3.00
MU17 Johnny Gaudreau 1.50 4.00
MU18 Vladimir Tarasenko 1.25 3.00
MU19 Jaromir Jagr 3.00 8.00
MU20 Alexander Ovechkin 4.00 10.00
MU21 Matthew Tkachuk 4.00 10.00
MU22 Anthony Mantha 2.00 5.00
MU23 Christian Dvorak 1.25 3.00
MU24 Mathew Barzal 3.00 8.00
MU25 Mitch Marner 3.00 8.00
MU26 Kyle Connor 3.00 8.00
MU27 Mikhail Sergachev 1.50 4.00
MU28 Pavel Buchnevich 1.50 4.00
MU29 Artturi Lehkonen 1.25 3.00
MU30 William Nylander 4.00 10.00
MU31 Travis Konecny 2.00 5.00
MU32 Jesse Puljujarvi 2.00 5.00
MU33 Sebastian Aho 3.00 8.00
MU34 Anthony Beauvillier 1.00 2.50
MU35 Dylan Strome 2.50 6.00
MU36 Tyler Motte 1.00 2.50
MU37 Pavel Zacha 1.50 4.00
MU38 Connor Brown 1.50 4.00
MU39 Lawson Crouse .75 2.00
MU40 Patrik Laine 2.50 6.00
MU41 Ivan Provorov 1.50 4.00
MU42 Nick Schmaltz 1.25 3.00
MU43 Brayden Point 2.50 6.00
MU44 Zach Werenski 3.00 8.00
MU45 Jimmy Vesey 1.50 4.00
MU46 Jakob Chychrun 2.00 5.00
MU47 Joel Eriksson Ek 1.50 4.00
MU48 Brandon Carlo 1.50 4.00
MU49 Thomas Chabot 2.00 5.00
MU50 Auston Matthews 6.00 15.00

2016-17 Fleer Showcase Metal Universe Planet Metal

PM1 Alexander Ovechkin 5.00 12.00
PM2 Steven Stamkos 2.50 6.00
PM3 P.K. Subban 1.50 4.00
PM4 Jaromir Jagr 4.00 10.00
PM5 Jonathan Toews 2.00 5.00
PM6 Wayne Simmonds 1.50 4.00
PM7 Erik Karlsson 1.50 4.00
PM8 Artemi Panarin 2.50 6.00
PM9 Drew Doughty 1.50 4.00
PM10 Jamie Benn 1.25 3.00
PM11 Patrice Bergeron 1.50 4.00
PM12 Brent Burns 1.25 3.00
PM13 John Tavares 2.00 5.00
PM14 Shea Weber 1.00 2.50
PM15 Sidney Crosby 5.00 12.00

2016-17 Fleer Showcase Metal Universe Precious Metal Gems Blue

*BLUE/50: 2X TO 5X BASIC INSERTS
MU1 Connor McDavid 20.00 50.00
MU50 Auston Matthews 60.00 150.00

2016-17 Fleer Showcase Metal Universe Precious Metal Gems Red

*RED/150: 1X TO 2.5X BASIC INSERTS
MU1 Connor McDavid 15.00 40.00
MU40 Patrik Laine 30.00 80.00
MU50 Auston Matthews 30.00 80.00

2016-17 Fleer Showcase SkyBox Premium Prospects
S1 Patrik Laine 5.00 12.00
S2 Travis Konecny 4.00 10.00
S3 Matthew Tkachuk 8.00 20.00
S4 Jimmy Vesey 3.00 8.00
S5 Jesse Puljujarvi 4.00 10.00
S6 Christian Dvorak 2.50 6.00
S7 Sebastian Aho 6.00 15.00
S8 Zach Werenski 6.00 15.00
S9 Mathew Barzal 6.00 15.00
S10 Dylan Strome 5.00 12.00
S11 Kyle Connor 6.00 15.00
S12 Anthony Mantha 4.00 10.00
S13 Nick Schmaltz 2.50 6.00
S14 Ivan Provorov 3.00 8.00
S15 Pavel Zacha 3.00 8.00
S16 Tyler Motte 2.00 5.00
S17 Artturi Lehkonen 2.50 6.00
S18 Mikhail Sergachev 3.00 8.00
S19 Lawson Crouse 1.50 4.00
S20 William Nylander 8.00 20.00
S21 Brandon Carlo 3.00 8.00
S22 Jake Guentzel 15.00 40.00
S23 Pavel Buchnevich 3.00 8.00
S24 Julius Honka 2.00 5.00
S25 Mitch Marner 6.00 15.00
S26 Anthony DeAngelo 1.50 4.00
S27 Jakob Chychrun 4.00 10.00
S28 Denis Malgin 1.50 4.00
S29 Connor Brown 3.00 8.00
S30 Auston Matthews 12.00 30.00

2016-17 Fleer Showcase '92-93 Ultra Buybacks Autographs
80 Paul Coffey 12.00 30.00
83 Wayne Gretzky 200.00 300.00
85 Jari Kurri 10.00 25.00
139 Mark Messier 30.00 80.00
177 Owen Nolan 10.00 25.00

2016-17 Fleer Showcase Ultra Rookies Platinum Medallion
*PLATINUM/99: .6X TO 1.5X BASIC INSERTS
U1 Auston Matthews 40.00 100.00
U30 Patrik Laine 25.00 60.00

2016-17 Fleer Showcase Ultra Rookies Violet Medallion
U25 Mitch Marner 60.00 150.00
U30 Patrik Laine 90.00 150.00

2002-03 Fleer Throwbacks
1 Terry O'Reilly .20 .50
2 Barry Beck .12 .30
3 Bobby Clarke .30 .75
4 Mike Foligno .12 .30
5 Danny Gare .12 .30
6 Clark Gillies .20 .50
7 Bernie Federko .15 .40
8 Dale Hunter .15 .40
9 Kris King .12 .30
10 Ted Lindsay .25 .60
11 Tie Domi .15 .40
12 Rob Ramage .12 .30
13 Jim Schoenfeld .12 .30
14 Steve Smith .12 .30
15 Harold Snepsts .12 .30
16 Rod Langway .15 .40
17 Denis Potvin .20 .50
18 John Bucyk .20 .50
19 Dirk Graham .12 .30
20 Lanny McDonald .15 .40
21 Stan Smyl .12 .30
22 Andre Dupont .12 .30
23 Todd Ewen .12 .30
24 George McPhee .12 .30
25 Paul Baxter .12 .30
26 Keith Magnuson .12 .30
27 Kevin Kaminski .12 .30
28 Mike Peluso .12 .30
29 Dave Semenko .15 .40
30 David Maley .12 .30
31 Jeff Deukeboom .12 .30
32 Dave Brown .12 .30
33 Troy Crowder .12 .30
34 Bobby Hull .40 1.00
35 Dan Maloney .12 .30
36 Jimmy Mann .12 .30
37 Rudy Poeschek .12 .30
38 John Wensink .12 .30
39 Kim Clackson .12 .30
40 Jay Wells .12 .30
41 Glen Cochrane RC .20 .50
42 Alan May .12 .30
43 Willi Plett .12 .30
44 Kevin McClelland .12 .30
45 Jim Cummins .12 .30
46 Basil McRae .12 .30
47 Ron Delorme .12 .30
48 John Ferguson .12 .30
49 Gord Donnelly .12 .30
50 Nick Kypreos .15 .40
51 Larry Playfair .12 .30
52 Marty McSorley .15 .40
53 Tim Hunter .12 .30
54 Billy Smith .20 .50
55 Laurie Boschman .12 .30
56 Wayne Cashman .15 .40
57 Link Gaetz .12 .30
58 Darin Kimble .12 .30
59 Bob Nystrom .15 .40
60 Ronnie Stern .12 .30
61 Ken Baumgartner .12 .30
62 Ken Linseman .15 .40
63 Kelly Chase .12 .30
64 Bob Gassoff .12 .30
65 Joey Kocur .12 .30
66 Chris Nilan .12 .30
67 Dave Schultz .20 .50
68 Tony Twist .15 .40
69 Enrico Ciccone .12 .30
70 Jay Miller .12 .30
71 Phil Russell .12 .30
72 Bryan Watson .12 .30
73 Paul Holmgren .15 .40
74 Garth Butcher .12 .30
75 Al Iafrate .15 .40
76 Barclay Plager .12 .30
77 Brent Severyn .12 .30
78 Ron Hextall .20 .50
79 Shane Churla .12 .30
80 Dino Ciccarelli .20 .50
81 Cam Neely .20 .50
82 Ulf Samuelsson .12 .30
83 Mick Vukota .12 .30
84 Garry Howatt .12 .30
85 Gary Rissling RC .20 .50
86 Behn Wilson .12 .30
87 Jack Carlson RC .25 .60
88 Bob Bassen .12 .30
89 Curt Brackenbury .12 .30
90 Mario Roberge .12 .30
91 Serge Roberge RC .20 .50
92 Bob Probert 2.00 5.00

2002-03 Fleer Throwbacks Gold
*GOLD: 2X TO 5X BASIC CARDS

2002-03 Fleer Throwbacks Platinum
*PLATINUM/50: 6X TO 15X BASE HI

2002-03 Fleer Throwbacks Autographs
1 Terry O'Reilly 12.00 30.00
2 Bobby Clarke 20.00 50.00
3 Clark Gillies 12.00 30.00
4 Dale Hunter 10.00 25.00
5 Ted Lindsay 15.00 40.00
6 Tie Domi 10.00 25.00
7 Jim Schoenfeld 8.00 20.00
8 Denis Potvin 12.00 30.00
9 Todd Ewen 8.00 20.00
10 Kevin Kaminski 8.00 20.00
11 Bob Probert 12.00 30.00
12 Dave Brown 8.00 20.00
13 Bobby Hull 25.00 60.00
14 Basil McRae 8.00 20.00
15 Larry Playfair 8.00 20.00
16 Marty McSorley 10.00 25.00
17 Billy Smith 12.00 30.00
18 Bob Nystrom 10.00 25.00
19 Ken Baumgartner 8.00 20.00
20 Kelly Chase 8.00 20.00
21 Joey Kocur 8.00 20.00
22 Dave Schultz 12.00 30.00
23 Tony Twist 10.00 25.00

2002-03 Fleer Throwbacks Drop the Gloves
1 Bob Probert 30.00 80.00
2 Ron Hextall 20.00 50.00
3 Tony Twist 8.00 20.00
4 Marty McSorley 8.00 20.00
5 Jim Cummins 8.00 20.00

2002-03 Fleer Throwbacks Scraps
1 Basil McRae 5.00 12.00
2 Enrico Ciccone 5.00 12.00
3 Bob Bassen 6.00 15.00
4 Joey Kocur 6.00 15.00
5 Clark Gillies 5.00 12.00
6 Marty McSorley 5.00 12.00
7 Tony Twist 5.00 12.00
8 Dale Hunter 5.00 12.00

2002-03 Fleer Throwbacks Tie Downs
1 Basil McRae 6.00 15.00
2 Enrico Ciccone 6.00 15.00
3 Bob Bassen 6.00 15.00
4 Joey Kocur 6.00 15.00
5 Clark Gillies 10.00 25.00
6 Marty McSorley 8.00 20.00
7 Tony Twist 8.00 20.00
8 Dale Hunter 8.00 20.00

2002-03 Fleer Throwbacks Squaring Off
COMPLETE SET (9) 15.00 30.00
1 B.Probert/J.Kocur 2.50 6.00
2 D.Schultz/C.Gillies 2.00 5.00
3 C.Neely/U.Samuelsson 2.00 5.00
4 T.O'Reilly/J.Schoenfeld 1.50 4.00
5 B.Beck/D.Potvin 1.50 4.00
6 B.Clarke/D.Hunter 1.50 4.00
7 T.Twist/M.McSorley 2.50 6.00
8 D.Brown/D.Schultz 2.50 6.00
9 R.Hextall/B.Smith 2.00 5.00

2002-03 Fleer Throwbacks Squaring Off Memorabilia
1 B.Probert J/J.Kocur S 8.00 20.00
2 D.Schultz J/C.Gillies J 6.00 15.00
3 C.Neely J/U.Samuelsson J 8.00 20.00
4 T.O'Reilly J/J.Schoenfeld J 6.00 15.00
5 B.Beck J/D.Potvin J 6.00 15.00
6 B.Clarke S/D.Hunter J 6.00 15.00
7 T.Twist J/M.McSorley J 8.00 20.00
8 D.Brown J/D.Schultz J 8.00 20.00

2002-03 Fleer Throwbacks Stickwork
1 Kelly Chase 1.50 4.00
2 Dale Hunter 2.00 5.00
3 Curt Brackenbury 1.50 4.00
4 Todd Ewen 1.50 4.00
5 Jim Cummins 1.50 4.00
6 Rudy Poeschek 1.50 4.00
7 Jay Wells 1.50 4.00
8 Enrico Ciccone 1.50 4.00
9 Marty McSorley 2.00 5.00
10 Bobby Hull 5.00 12.00
11 Cam Neely 2.50 6.00
12 Bobby Clarke 4.00 10.00
13 Bob Probert 2.50 6.00

1994 Fleury Hockey Tips
COMPLETE SET (14) 2.00 5.00
COMMON CARD (1-14) .20 .50

1970-71 Flyers Postcards
COMPLETE SET (12) 20.00 40.00
1 Barry Ashbee 3.00 6.00
2 Gary Dornhoefer 3.00 6.00
3 Warren Elliott
Frank Leurs 1.00 2.00
4 Doug Favell 3.00 6.00
5 Earl Heiskala 1.50 3.00
6 Larry Hillman 2.50 5.00
7 Andre Lacroix 2.50 5.00
8 Lew Morrison 1.50 3.00
9 Simon Nolet 2.00 4.00
10 Garry Peters 1.50 3.00
11 Vic Stasiuk CO 1.50 3.00
12 George Swarbrick 1.50 3.00

1972 Flyers Mighty Milk
COMPLETE SET (8) 87.50 175.00
1 Serge Bernier 7.50 15.00
2 Bobby Clarke 40.00 80.00
3 Gary Dornhoefer 10.00 20.00
4 Doug Favell 15.00 30.00
5 Jean-Guy Gendron 7.50 15.00
7 Bill Lesuk 7.50 15.00
8 Ed Van Impe 10.00 20.00

1973-74 Flyers Linnett
COMPLETE SET (1-18) 40.00 80.00
1 Barry Ashbee 1.50 3.00
2 Bill Barber 5.00 10.00
3 Tom Bladon 1.50 3.00
4 Bob Clarke 5.00 10.00
5 Bill Clement 3.00 6.00
6 Terry Crisp 2.50 5.00
7 Bill Flett 2.00 4.00
8 Bob Kelly 1.50 3.00
9 Orest Kindrachuk 1.50 3.00
10 Ross Lonsberry 1.50 3.00
11 Rick Macleish 2.00 4.00
12 Simon Nolet 2.00 4.00
13 Bernard Parent 5.00 10.00
14 Don Saleski 1.50 3.00
15 Dave Schultz 3.00 6.00
16 Ed Van Impe 1.50 3.00
17 Jimmy Watson 2.00 4.00
18 Joe Watson 2.00 4.00

1983-84 Flyers J.C. Penney
COMPLETE SET (22) 14.00 35.00
1 Ray Allison .40 1.00
2 Bill Barber .75 2.00
3 Frank Bathe .40 1.00
4 Lindsay Carson .40 1.00
5 Bobby Clarke 2.00 5.00
6 Glen Cochrane .40 1.00
7 Doug Crossman .60 1.50
8 Miroslav Dvorak .40 1.00
9 Thomas Eriksson .40 1.00
10 Bob Froese .60 1.50
11 Randy Holt .40 1.00
12 Mark Howe .75 2.00
13 Tim Kerr .75 2.00
14 Pelle Lindbergh 6.00 15.00
15 Brad Marsh .60 1.50
16 Brad McCrimmon .60 1.50
17 Dave Poulin .60 1.50
18 Brian Propp .75 2.00
19 Ilkka Sinisalo .60 1.50
20 Darryl Sittler 1.50 4.00
21 Rich Sutter .40 1.00
22 Ron Sutter .40 1.00

1985-86 Flyers Postcards
COMPLETE SET (31) 15.00 30.00
1 Bill Barber .40 1.00
2 Dave Brown .30 .75
3 Lindsay Carson .20 .50
4 Bob Clarke .75 2.00
5 Murray Craven .20 .50
6 Pat Croce .08 .25
7 Doug Crossman .20 .50
8 Per-Erik Eklund .20 .50
9 Thomas Eriksson .20 .50
10 Bob Froese .30 .75
11 Len Hachborn .08 .25
12 Paul Holmgren .20 .50
13 Ed Hospodar .20 .50
14 Mark Howe .30 .75
15 Mike Keenan .40 1.00
16 Tim Kerr .30 .75
17 Pelle Lindbergh 6.00 15.00
18 Brad Marsh .20 .50
19 Brad McCrimmon .30 .75
20 E.J. McGuire CO .08 .25
21 Bernie Parent CO .40 1.00
22 Joe Paterson .08 .25
23 Dave Poulin .20 .50
24 Brian Propp .40 1.00
25 Ilkka Sinisalo .20 .50
26 Derrick Smith .20 .50
27 Rich Sutter .20 .50
28 Ron Sutter .20 .50
29 Rick Tocchet 2.50 6.00
30 Peter Zezel 1.00 2.50
31 Team Photo .75 2.00

1986-87 Flyers Postcards
COMPLETE SET (29) 10.00 25.00
1 Bill Barber CO .40 1.00
2 Dave Brown .30 .75
3 Lindsay Carson .20 .50
4 Murray Craven .20 .50
5 Pat Croce TR .08 .25
6 Doug Crossman .20 .50
7 Jean-Jacques Daigneault .20 .50
8 Pelle Eklund .30 .75
9 Ron Hextall 1.50 4.00
10 Paul Holmgren CO .20 .50
11 Ed Hospodar .20 .50
12 Mark Howe .60 1.50
13 Mike Keenan CO .40 1.00
14 Tim Kerr .60 1.50
15 Brad Marsh .20 .50
16 Brad McCrimmon .30 .75
17 E.J. McGuire CO .30 .75
18 Scott Mellanby .60 1.50
19 Bernie Parent CO .40 1.00
20 Dave Poulin .30 .75
21 Brian Propp .40 1.00
22 Glenn Resch .40 1.00
23 Ilkka Sinisalo .20 .50
24 Derrick Smith .20 .50
25 Daryl Stanley .20 .50
26 Ron Sutter .20 .50
27 Rick Tocchet 2.00 5.00
28 Peter Zezel .60 1.50
29 Team Photo .75 2.00

1989-90 Flyers Postcards
COMPLETE SET (29) 8.00 20.00
1 Keith Acton .20 .50
2 Craig Berube .20 .50
3 Mike Bullard .20 .50
4 Terry Carkner .20 .50
5 Jeff Chychrun .20 .50
6 Bob Clarke VP/GM .75 2.00
7 Murray Craven .20 .50
8 Mike Eaves ACO .08 .25
9 Pelle Eklund .30 .75
10 Ron Hextall .75 2.00
11 Paul Holmgren CO .20 .50
12 Mark Howe .40 1.00
13 Kerry Huffman .20 .50
14 Tim Kerr .40 1.00
15 Scott Mellanby .40 1.00
16 Gord Murphy .20 .50
17 Andy Murray ACO .08 .25
18 Pete Peeters .40 1.00
19 Dave Poulin .40 1.00
20 Brian Propp .40 1.00
21 Kjell Samuelsson .40 1.00
22 Ilkka Sinisalo .20 .50
23 Derrick Smith .20 .50
24 Doug Sulliman .20 .50
25 Ron Sutter .20 .50
26 Rick Tocchet .75 2.00
27 Jay Wells .20 .50
28 Ken Wregget .75 2.00
29 Team Photo .75 2.00

1990-91 Flyers Postcards
COMPLETE SET (26) 6.00 15.00
1 Keith Acton .30 .75
2 Murray Baron .20 .50
3 Craig Berube .20 .50
4 Terry Carkner .20 .50
5 Jeff Chychrun .20 .50
6 Murray Craven .30 .75
7 Pelle Eklund .30 .75
8 Ron Hextall .60 1.50
9 Tony Horacek .20 .50
10 Martin Hostak .20 .50
11 Mark Howe .40 1.00
12 Kerry Huffman .20 .50
13 Tim Kerr .40 1.00
14 Dale Kushner .20 .50
15 Norman Lacombe .20 .50
16 Jiri Latal .20 .50
17 Scott Mellanby .40 1.00
18 Gord Murphy .20 .50
19 Pete Peeters .30 .75
20 Mike Ricci .60 1.50
21 Kjell Samuelsson .30 .75
22 Derrick Smith .20 .50
23 Ron Sutter .20 .50
24 Rick Tocchet .75 2.00
25 Ken Wregget .40 1.00
26 Team Photo .75 2.00

1991-92 Flyers J.C. Penney
COMPLETE SET (26) 6.00 15.00
1 Keith Acton .30 .75
2 Rod Brind'Amour .60 1.50
3 Dave Brown .30 .75
4 Terry Carkner .20 .50
5 Kimbi Daniels .20 .50
6 Kevin Dineen .40 1.00
7 Steve Duchesne .30 .75
8 Pelle Eklund .20 .50
9 Corey Foster .20 .50
10 Ron Hextall .60 1.50
11 Tony Horacek .20 .50
12 Mark Howe .40 1.00
13 Kerry Huffman .20 .50
14 Brad Jones .20 .50
15 Steve Kasper UER
(Misspelled Kaspar
on front) .20 .50
16 Dan Kordic .20 .50
17 Jiri Latal .20 .50
18 Andrei Lomakin .20 .50
19 Gord Murphy .20 .50
20 Mark Pederson .20 .50
21 Dan Quinn .20 .50
22 Mike Ricci .40 1.00
23 Kjell Samuelsson .25 .60
24 Rick Tocchet .60 1.50
25 Ken Wregget .40 1.00
26 Team Photo .60 1.50

1992-93 Flyers J.C. Penney
COMPLETE SET (23) 8.00 20.00
1 Keith Acton .25 .60
2 Stephane Beauregard .25 .60
3 Brian Benning .20 .50
4 Rod Brind'Amour .60 1.50
5 Claude Boivin .20 .50
6 Dave Brown .30 .75
7 Terry Carkner .20 .50
8 Shawn Cronin .20 .50
9 Kevin Dineen .30 .75
10 Pelle Eklund .20 .50
11 Doug Evans .20 .50
12 Brent Fedyk .20 .50
13 Garry Galley .30 .75
14 Gord Hynes .20 .50
15 Eric Lindros 4.00 10.00
16 Andrei Lomakin .20 .50
17 Ryan McGill .20 .50
18 Ric Nattress .20 .50
19 Greg Paslawski .20 .50
20 Mark Recchi .75 2.00
21 Dominic Roussel .30 .75
22 Dimitri Yushkevich .20 .50
23 Team Photo .60 1.50

1992-93 Flyers Upper Deck Sheets
COMPLETE SET (44) 100.00 250.00
1 Quebec Nordiques
Sept. 19& 1992 (4&500)
Kevin Di 2.00 5.00
2 New Jersey Devils
Sept. 24& 1992 (4&500)
Brian B 1.25 3.00
3 Washington Capitals
Oct. 3& 1992 (4&500)
Mark Re 3.00 8.00
4 New Jersey Devils
Oct. 9& 1992 (7&500)
Keith Act 1.50 4.00
5 New York Islanders
Oct. 15& 1992 (4&500)
Rod Bri 3.00 8.00
6 Winnipeg Jets
Oct. 18& 1992 (4&500)
Dave Brown 1.50 4.00
7 Vancouver Canucks
Oct. 22& 1992 (4&500)
Dominic 2.00 5.00
8 Montreal Canadiens
Oct. 24& 1992 (4&500)
Gord Hy 1.25 3.00
9 St. Louis Blues
Nov. 7& 1992 (4&500)
Claude Boiv 1.25 3.00
10 New York Islanders
Nov. 12& 1992 (4&500)
Dimitri 1.25 3.00
11 Ottawa Senators
Nov. 15& 1992 (5&500)
Eric Lindr 15.00 40.00
12 New York Rangers
Nov. 19& 1992 (4&500)
Steve Kas 1.50 4.00
13A Buffalo Sabres
Nov. 22& 1992
(4&500)/1992-93 Tea 5.00 12.00
13B Buffalo Sabres
Nov. 22& 1992/1992-93
Team Pictur 4.00 10.00
14 New York Islanders
Nov. 27& 1992 (5&500)
Greg Pa 1.25 3.00
15 Quebec Nordiques
Dec. 3& 1992 (4&500)
Terry Cark 1.50 4.00
16 Boston Bruins
Dec. 6& 1992 (4&500)
Shawn Cronin 1.25 3.00
17 Washington Capitals
Dec. 12& 1992 (4&500)
Brent 1.25 3.00
18 Pittsburgh Penguins
Dec. 17& 1992 (4&500)
Garry 1.50 4.00
19 Chicago Blackhawks
Dec. 19& 1992 (5&000)
Andrei 1.25 3.00
20 Pittsburgh Penguins
Dec. 23& 1992 (5&500)
Bill a 2.00 5.00
21 Washington Capitals
Jan. 7& 1993 (4&500)
Stephan 1.50 4.00
22 New York Rangers
Jan. 9& 1993 (6&000)
Mark Recch 3.00 8.00
23 Edmonton Oilers
Jan. 10& 1993 (5&000)
Ryan McGil 1.25 3.00
24 Calgary Flames
Jan. 14& 1993 (6&500)
Doug Evans 1.25 3.00
25 Detroit Red Wings
Jan. 17& 1993 (5&000)
The Capt 2.00 5.00
26 Boston Bruins
Jan. 21& 1993 (5&000)
Ric Nattress 1.25 3.00
27 Hartford Whalers
Jan. 24& 1993 (5&000)
Rod Brind 3.00 8.00
28 Buffalo Sabres
Jan. 26& 1993 (5&000)
Tommy Soder 2.00 5.00
29 Quebec Nordiques
Jan. 28& 1993 (5&000)
Pelle Ekl 1.50 4.00
30 Ottawa Senators
Feb. 9& 1993 (5&000)
Dave Brown 1.50 4.00
31 Montreal Canadiens
Feb. 11& 1993 (5&500)
The Roo 10.00 25.00
32 New Jersey Devils
Feb. 14& 1993 (5&000)
Josef Be 1.25 3.00
33 New Jersey Devils
Feb. 25& 1993 (6&000)
Greg Pas 1.25 3.00
34 New York Islanders
Feb. 27& 1993 (5&000)
The Coa 1.50 4.00
35 Pittsburgh Penguins
Mar. 2& 1993 (5&000)
Keith A 1.50 4.00
36 Washington Capitals
Mar. 11& 1993 (5&500)
NHL Al 3.00 8.00
37A Los Angeles Kings
Mar. 13& 1993 (5&500)
Garry Ga 1.50 4.00
37B Los Angeles Kings
Make-up Game/1992-93 Team Pict 3.00 8.00
38 Minnesota North Stars
Mar. 16& 1993 (5&000)
Terr 1.50 4.00
39 New Jersey Devils
Mar. 21& 1993 (5&000)
Dominic 2.00 5.00
40 San Jose Sharks
Mar. 25& 1993 (5&000)
Greg Hawgo 1.25 3.00
41 Tampa Bay Lightning
Apr. 3& 1993 (5&500)
Viaches 1.25 3.00
42 Toronto Maple Leafs
Apr. 4& 1993 (6&000)
Crazy 8 10.00 25.00
43 Washington Capitals
Apr. 8& 1993 (5&500)
Europea 2.00 5.00
44 New York Rangers
Apr. 12& 1993 (5&500)
Hockey Ha 4.00 10.00

1993-94 Flyers J.C. Penney
COMPLETE SET (24) 8.00 20.00
1 Josef Beranek .30 .75
2 Claude Boivin .20 .50
3 Jason Bowen .20 .50
4 Rod Brind'Amour .60 1.50
5 Slava Butsayev .20 .50
6 Dave Brown .30 .75
7 Al Conroy .20 .50
8 Kevin Dineen .30 .75
9 Pelle Eklund .20 .50
10 Brent Fedyk .20 .50
11 Jeff Finley .20 .50
12 Garry Galley .30 .75
13 Eric Lindros 3.00 8.00
14 Stewart Malgunas .20 .50
15 Ryan McGill .20 .50
16 Rob Ramage .20 .50
17 Mark Recchi .75 2.00
18 Mikael Renberg .60 1.50
19 Dominic Roussel .30 .75
20 Yves Racine .20 .50
21 Tommy Soderstrom .30 .75
22 Dave Tippett .20 .50
23 Dimitri Yuskevich .20 .50
NNO Team Photo .40 1.00

1993-94 Flyers Lineup Sheets
COMPLETE SET (43) 50.00 125.00
1 Josef Beranek 1.00 2.50
2 Claude Boivin 1.00 2.50
3 Jason Bowen 1.00 2.50
4 Rod Brind'Amour 2.00 5.00
5 Rod Brind'Amour 2.00 5.00
6 Dave Brown 2.00 5.00
7 Slava Butsayev 1.00 2.50
8 Terry Carkner 1.00 2.50
9 Al Conroy 1.00 2.50
10 Kevin Dineen 1.00 2.50
11 Kevin Dineen 1.00 2.50
12 Pelle Eklund 1.00 2.50
13 Andre Faust 1.00 2.50
14 Brent Fedyk 1.00 2.50
15 Brent Fedyk 1.00 2.50
16 Jeff Finley 1.00 2.50
17 Garry Galley 1.00 2.50
18 Greg Hawgood 1.00 2.50
19 Tim Kerr 2.00 5.00
20 Mark Lamb 1.00 2.50
21 Eric Lindros 4.00 10.00
22 Eric Lindros 4.00 10.00
23 Eric Lindros 4.00 10.00
24 Stewart Malgunas 1.00 2.50
25 Ryan McGill 1.00 2.50
26 Yves Racine 1.00 2.50
27 Rob Ramage 1.00 2.50
28 Mark Recchi 2.00 5.00
29 Mark Recchi 2.00 5.00
30 Mikael Renberg 1.00 2.50
31 Dominic Roussel 1.50 4.00
32 Dominic Roussel 1.50 4.00
33 Dave Tippett 1.00 2.50
34 Dmitri Yushkevich 1.00 2.50
35 Dmitri Yushkevich 1.00 2.50
36 Rob Zettler 1.00 2.50
37 The Coaches 1.00 2.50
38 Team Photo 1.00 2.50
39 Team Photo 1.00 2.50
40 Renberg, Bowen, Malgunas 1.00 2.50
41 The Captains 2.00 5.00
42 Recchi, Lindros, Galley 2.00 5.00
43 Flyers and their Fans 1.00 2.50

1996-97 Flyers Postcards
COMPLETE SET (24) 6.00 15.00
1 Team Photo .20 .50
2 Rod Brind'Amour .30 .75
3 Paul Coffey .40 1.00
4 Scott Daniels .08 .25
5 Eric Desjardins .15 .40
6 John Druce .08 .25
7 Karl Dykhuis .08 .25
8 Pat Falloon .08 .25
9 Dale Hawerchuk .30 .75
10 Ron Hextall .30 .75
11 Trent Klatt .08 .25
12 Dan Kordic .08 .25
13 Daniel Lacroix .08 .25
14 John LeClair .75 2.00
15 Eric Lindros 2.00 5.00
16 Janne Niinimaa .60 1.50
17 Joel Otto .08 .25
18 Shjon Podein .08 .25
19 Mikael Renberg .30 .75
20 Kjell Samuelsson .08 .25
21 Garth Snow .20 .50
22 Petr Svoboda .08 .25
23 Chris Therien .08 .25
24 Dainius Zubrus .75 2.00

1997 Flyers Phone Cards
COMPLETE SET (4) 3.00 8.00
1 Alexandre Daigle .40 1.00
2 Chris Gratton .40 1.00
3 John LeClair 1.25 3.00
4 Eric Lindros 2.00 5.00

1998-99 Flyers Postcards
COMPLETE SET (24) 5.00 12.00
1 Dave Babych .20 .50
2 Rod Brind'Amour .30 .75
3 Marc Bureau .20 .50
4 Alexandre Daigle .20 .50
5 Eric Desjardins .20 .50
6 Colin Forbes .20 .50
7 Ron Hextall .30 .75
8 Jody Hull .20 .50
9 Keith Jones .20 .50
10 John LeClair .60 1.50
11 Eric Lindros 1.25 3.00
12 Dan McGillis .20 .50
13 Luke Richardson .20 .50
14 Dmitri Tertyshny .20 .50
15 Chris Therien .20 .50
16 John Vanbiesbrouck .30 .75
17 Roman Vopat .20 .50
18 Valeri Zelepukin .20 .50
19 Dainius Zubrus .40 1.00
20 Bill Barber .20 .50
21 Broadcasters .08 .25
22 Coaches .08 .25
23 Philadelphia Flyers .08 .25
24 Philadelphia Phantoms .08 .25

2001-02 Flyers Postcards
COMPLETE SET (30) 10.00 25.00
1 Brian Boucher 1.00 2.50
2 Donald Brashear .30 .75
3 Roman Cechmanek .40 1.00
4 Eric Desjardins .20 .50
5 Jiri Dopita .40 1.00
6 Todd Fedoruk .30 .75
7 Ruslan Fedotenko .30 .75
8 Simon Gagne 1.25 3.00
9 Kim Johnsson .20 .50
10 Kent Manderville .20 .50
11 John LeClair .75 2.00
12 Chris McAllister .20 .50
13 Dam McGillis .20 .50
14 Marty Murray .20 .50
15 Keith Primeau .40 1.00
16 Paul Ranheim .20 .50
17 Mark Recchi .40 1.00
18 Luke Richardson .20 .50
19 Jeremy Roenick .75 2.00
20 Chris Therien .20 .50
21 Rick Tocchet .30 .75
22 Eric Weinrich .20 .50
23 Justin Williams .40 1.00
24 Flyers Team Photo .40 1.00
25 Bill Barber
Mike Stothers
E.J. McGuire .10 .25
26 Broadcasters .04 .10
27 Bob Clarke GM .30 .75
28 Ron Hextall ACO .30 .75
29 Phantoms Team Photo .20 .50
30 Phlex MASCOT .10 .25

2002-03 Flyers Postcards
COMPLETE SET (24) 8.00 20.00
1 Eric Weinrich .30 .75
2 Kim Johnsson .30 .75
3 Mark Recchi .40 1.00
4 John LeClair .40 1.00
5 Simon Gagne .60 1.50
6 Justin Williams .30 .75
7 Paul Ranheim .30 .75
8 Radovan Somik .30 .75
9 Chris McAllister .30 .75
10 Keith Primeau .40 1.00
11 Chris Therien .30 .75
12 Michal Handzus .30 .75
13 Todd Fedoruk .40 1.00
14 Roman Cechmanek .40 1.00
15 Dennis Seidenberg .30 .75
16 Eric Desjardins .30 .75
17 Marty Murray .30 .75
18 Robert Esche .40 1.00
19 Pavel Brendl .30 .75
20 Donald Brashear .30 .75
21 Jeremy Roenick .75 2.00
22 The Coaches .10 .25
23 Team Card .20 .50
24 Philadelphia Phantoms .20 .50

2003-04 Flyers Program Inserts
1 Jeremy Roenick 2.00 5.00
2 Joni Pitkanen 1.25 3.00
3 Tony Amonte 1.50 4.00
4 Robert Esche 1.50 4.00
5 Danny Markov 1.25 3.00
6 Keith Primeau 1.50 4.00

2003-04 Flyers Postcards
COMPLETE SET (24) 8.00 20.00
1 Tony Amonte .40 1.00
2 Donald Brashear .40 1.00
3 Mike Comrie .40 1.00
4 Eric Desjardins .20 .50
5 Robert Esche .40 1.00
6 Todd Fedoruk .40 1.00
7 Simon Gagne .40 1.00
8 Jeff Hackett .30 .75
9 Michal Handzus .20 .50
10 Kim Johnsson .20 .50
11 Sami Kapanen .20 .50
12 Claude Lapointe .20 .50
13 John LeClair .40 1.00
14 Danny Markov .20 .50
15 Joni Pitkanen .40 1.00
16 Keith Primeau .40 1.00
17 Marcus Ragnarsson .20 .50
18 Mark Recchi .40 1.00
19 Jeremy Roenick .75 2.00
20 Radovan Somik .20 .50
21 Chris Therien .20 .50
22 Jim Vandermeer .20 .50
23 Eric Weinrich .20 .50
24 Coaches .10 .25

2005-06 Flyers Team Issue
COMPLETE SET (25) 8.00 15.00
1 Philadelphia Flyers CL .01 .01
2 Donald Brashear .30 .75
3 Jeff Carter 2.00 5.00
4 Eric Desjardins .20 .50
5 Robert Esche .30 .75
6 Peter Forsberg .75 2.00
7 Simon Gagne .40 1.00
8 Michal Handzus .20 .50
9 Derian Hatcher .20 .50
10 Kim Johnsson .20 .50
11 Sami Kapanen .20 .50
12 Mike Knuble .20 .50
13 Antero Niittymaki .75 2.00
14 Joni Pitkanen .40 1.00
15 Keith Primeau .20 .50
16 Branko Radivojevic .20 .50
17 Mike Rathje .20 .50
18 Mike Richards .40 1.00
19 Brian Savage .20 .50
20 Dennis Seidenberg .20 .50
21 Patrick Sharp .20 .50
22 Jonathan Sim .20 .50
23 Turner Stevenson .20 .50
24 Chris Therien .20 .50
25 R.J. Umberger .40 1.00

2006-07 Flyers Postcards

COMPLETE SET (23) 10.00 25.00
1 Derian Hatcher .40 1.00
2 Mike Rathje .40 1.00
3 Randy Jones .40 1.00
4 Geoff Sanderson .40 1.00
5 Scottie Upshall .40 1.00
6 Simon Gagne .75 2.00
7 Jeff Carter .75 2.00
8 Mike Richards .75 2.00
9 Kyle Calder .40 1.00
10 R.J. Umberger .40 1.00
11 Mike Knuble .40 1.00
12 Denis Gauthier .40 1.00
13 Sami Kapanen .40 1.00
14 Dmitry Afanasenkov .40 1.00
15 Todd Fedoruk .75 2.00
16 Antero Niittymaki .60 1.50
17 Robert Esche .60 1.50
18 Joni Pitkanen .40 1.00
19 Alexandre Picard .40 1.00
20 Michael Leighton .60 1.50
21 Ben Eager .40 1.00
22 Mike York .40 1.00
23 Alexei Zhitnik .40 1.00

1936 Frank Coffey Olympics

NNO Ice Hockey 15.00 30.00
NNO Field Hockey 15.00 30.00

1971-72 Frito-Lay

COMPLETE SET (10) 50.00 100.00
1 Yvan Cournoyer 4.00 8.00
2 Ken Dryden 25.00 50.00
3 Frank Mahovlich 5.00 10.00
4 Henri Richard 5.00 10.00
5 J.C. Tremblay 2.00 4.00
6 Bobby Baun 2.00 4.00
7 Ron Ellis 2.00 4.00
8 Paul Henderson 3.00 6.00
9 Jacques Plante 10.00 20.00
10 Norm Ullman 3.00 6.00

1988-89 Frito-Lay Stickers

COMPLETE SET (42) 12.00 30.00
1 Mario Lemieux 66 2.50 6.00
2 Bryan Trottier 19 .20 .50
3 Steve Yzerman 19 1.50 4.00
4 Bernie Federko 24 .15 .40
5 Brian Bellows 23 .15 .40
6 Denis Savard 18 .20 .50
7 Neal Broten 7 .15 .40
8 Doug Gilmour 9 .60 1.50
9 Dale Hawerchuk 10 .20 .50
10 Luc Robitaille 20 .60 1.50
11 Ed Olczyk 16 .08 .25
12 Andrew McBain 20 .08 .25
13 Mike Gartner 11 .20 .50
14 Pat LaFontaine 16 .40 1.00
15 Scott Stevens 3 .20 .50
16 Ray Bourque 77 .75 2.00
17 Cam Neely 8 .60 1.50
18 Mike Foligno 17 .08 .25
19 Tom Barrasso 30 .20 .50
20 Ron Francis 10 .30 .75
21 Peter Stastny 26 .20 .50
22 Michel Goulet 16 .20 .50
23 Bernie Nicholls 9 .20 .50
24 Paul Coffey 77 .60 1.50
25 Mats Naslund 26 .15 .40
26 Glenn Anderson 9 .20 .50
27 Dave Poulin 20 .08 .25
28 Kevin Dineen 11 .08 .25
29 Wendel Clark 17 .30 .75
30 James Patrick 3 .08 .25
31 Al MacInnis 2 .30 .75
32 Troy Murray 19 .08 .25
33 Kirk Muller 9 .20 .50
34 Marcel Dionne 16 .20 .50
35 Mark Messier 11 .75 2.00
36 Joe Nieuwendyk 25 .60 1.50
37 Ron Hextall 27 .30 .75
38 Sean Burke 1 .20 .50
39 Barry Pederson 7 .08 .25
40 Stephane Richer 44 .20 .50
41 Bob Probert 24 .75 2.00
42 Tony Tanti 9 .08 .25
NNO Set Poster 1.25 3.00

1996-97 Frosted Flakes Masks

COMPLETE SET (7) 8.00 20.00
1 Felix Potvin 1.25 3.00
2 Curtis Joseph 2.00 5.00
3 Montreal Canadiens 1.25 3.00
4 Ottawa Senators 1.25 3.00
5 Calgary Flames 1.25 3.00
6 Vancouver Canucks 1.25 3.00
7 Tony the Tiger 1.25 3.00

1991-92 Future Trends Canada '72 Promos

COMPLETE SET (3) 8.00 20.00
1 The Goal
The Scoreboard
Paul Henderson 3.00 8.00
2 The Leader
Phil Esposito 4.00 10.00
3 The Challenge/The Kid
Vladislav Tretiak 3.00 8.00

1991-92 Future Trends Canada '72

COMPLETE SET (101) 10.00 25.00
1 In The Beginning .15 .40
2 The Backyard Rink .08 .20
3 It Didn't Take Long .08 .20
4 The Patriarch
Anatoli Tarasov .15 .40
5 More Hours a Day
Vladislav Tretiak .75 2.00
6 Coming Out Party .15 .40
7 Never In Doubt .08 .20
8 Team Canada .30 .75
9 Pat Stapleton .08 .20
10 Vsevolod Bobrov .08 .20
11 Vladislav Tretiak .75 2.00
12 Faceoff
Game 1, Montreal (9/2/72) .08 .20
13 30 Seconds
Game 1, Montreal (9/2/72) .15 .40
14 Yevgeny Zimin .08 .20
15 Bill White .08 .20
16 7-3, Game 1 Statistics .08 .20
17 Don Awrey .08 .20
18 Mickey Redmond .15 .40
19 Alexander Gusev .15 .40
20 Alexander Maltsev .30 .75
21 Rod Seiling .08 .20
22 Dale Tallon .08 .20
23 Coming Back
Game 2, Toronto (9/4/72) .08 .20
24 Unforgettable
Game 2 Statistics .08 .20
25 Wayne Cashman .15 .40
26 Frank Mahovlich .30 .75
27 Peter Mahovlich .08 .20
28 Vyacheslav Solodukhin
Alexander Sidelnikov .15 .40
29 Yuri Shatalov .15 .40
30 Brothers
Frank Mahovlich
Peter Mahovlich .15 .40
31 The Goalies .75 2.00
32 Alexander Bodunov .08 .20
33 All Even
Game 3 Statistics .08 .20
34 Yuri Blinov .08 .20
35 Jocelyn Guevremont .08 .20
36 Vic Hadfield .08 .20
37 Yuri Lebedev .08 .20
38 Yevgeny Poladiev
Vyacheslav Starshinov .15 .40
39 Disaster
Game 4 Statistics .08 .20
40 Address to The Nation
Phil Esposito .30 .75
41 Victor Kuzkin .08 .20
42 Vladimir Lutchenko .30 .75
43 Boris Mikhailov .40 1.00
44 Grace Under Pressure
Game 5, Moscow (9/22/72) .08 .20
45 Afraid to Lose .08 .20
46 Ready To Win
Game 5 Statistics .08 .20
47 Vladimir Vikulov .08 .20
48 Red Berenson .08 .20
49 Richard Martin .08 .20
50 Alexander Martynyuk .08 .20
51 Gilbert Perreault .30 .75
52 Vladimir Petrov .40 1.00
53 Serge Savard .15 .40
54 Vladimir Shadrin .08 .20
55 Ready To Win
Game 5 Statistics .08 .20
56 One Step Back
Game 6 Statistics .08 .20
57 Bobby Clarke .40 1.00
58 Valeri Kharlamov .75 2.00
59 Alexander Volchkov .15 .40
60 Standing Guard .15 .40
61 Stan Mikita .40 1.00
62 One More To Go
Game 7 Statistics
Moscow (9/26/72) .08 .20
63 The Winner .08 .20
64 The Fans Go Wild .08 .20
65 Alexander Ragulin .15 .40
66 Jean Ratelle .15 .40
67 Gennady Tsygankov .15 .40
68 Valeri Vasiliev .40 1.00
69 International Dialogue .08 .20
70 Series Stars
Phil Esposito
Alexander Yakushev .40 1.00
71 Series Stars
Paul Henderson
Vladislav Tretiak .40 1.00
72 No Solitudes
Game 8& Moscow (9/28/72)
The Telegrams .08 .20
73 2-2, Game 8, Moscow (9/28/72) .08 .20
74 Rod Gilbert .15 .40
75 Yevgeny Mishakov .15 .40
76 Ron Ellis .08 .20
77 5-4 score .08 .20
78 Different Games
Game 8, Moscow (9/28/72)
Interlude .08 .20
79 Bill Goldsworthy .08 .20
80 The Huddle .08 .20
81 The Moment 1.00 2.50
82 Yvan Cournoyer .30 .75
83 Yuri Liapkin .08 .20
84 Phil Esposito .40 1.00
85 Ken Dryden .75 2.00
86 Peace
Game 8 Statistics .08 .20
87 Gary Bergman .08 .20
88 Brian Glennie .08 .20
89 Dennis Hull .08 .20
90 Vyacheslav Anisin .08 .20
91 Marcel Dionne .30 .75
92 Guy Lapointe .15 .40
93 Ed Johnston .15 .40
94 Harry Sinden GM .08 .20
95 Brad Park .30 .75
96 Tony Esposito .40 1.00
97 Alexander Yakushev .60 1.50
98 Paul Henderson .75 2.00
99 J.P. Parise .08 .20
100 Valeri Kharlamov
Alex Kharlamov on back .75 2.00
101 Checklist .15 .40

1992 Future Trends '76 Canada Cup

COMPLETE SET (100) 8.00 20.00
102 Phil Esposito
Sergeant .20 .50
103 Vladislav Tretiak
Soviet Ambassador
Retrospective .30 .75
104 Bobby Orr
Impossible .40 1.00
105 Paul Henderson
The Goal .05 .15
106 Alexander Yakushev .15 .40
107 Bobby Hull .30 .75
108 Valeri Kharlamov
Soviet .40 1.00
109 Gerry Cheevers
Vladislav Tretiak .20 .50
110 Bobby Hull
Vladislav Tretiak
What If Series .30 .75
111 Soviet on-ice workout .02 .10
112 Czech on-ice workout .01 .05
113 Finn on-ice workout .01 .05
114 Swedes take the ice .01 .05
115 USA on-ice workout .02 .10
116 Darryl Sittler .08 .25
117 Serge Savard .05 .15
118 Team Finland .01 .05
119 Team Sweden .01 .05
120 Team Czechoslavakia .01 .05
121 Soviets .05 .15
122 Team USA .05 .15
123 Team Canada .05 .15
124 The Opening Barrage .01 .05
125 Richard Martin
Canada Cup .01 .05
126 Bobby Orr .40 1.00
127 Sweden vs. USA
Power Play .01 .05
128 Ivan Hlinka .01 .05
129 CSSR 5 - CCCP 3
Canada Cup .01 .05
130 Helmut Balderis
Canada Cup .05 .15
131 Peter Stastny
Canada Cu .07 .20
132 Valeri Vasiliev
Canada Cup .10 .25
133 Out of Contention
Canada Cup .01 .05
134 Standing Alone
Canada Cup .01 .05
135 The Miracle On Ice .01 .05
136 Josef Augusta
Canada Cup .01 .05
137 A Soviet Rout
Canada Cup .01 .05
138 Viktor Zhluktov
Canada Cup .02 .10
139 Bobby Hull
Phil Esposito
Marcel Dionne .20 .50
140 Bob Gainey .05 .15
141 Anders Hedberg
Canada Cup .05 .15
142 Bobby Hull .30 .75
143 Ulf Nilsson .05 .15
144 Sergei Kapustin
Canada Cup .05 .15
145 Borje Salming
Canada Cup .05 .15
146 Well Enough To Win
Canada Cup .01 .05
147 Biggest Upset
Canada Cup .01 .05
148 Matti Hagman .01 .05
149 Unbeatable .01 .05
150 Boris Alexandrov
Canada .05 .15
151 A Goal Tending Duel
Can .02 .10
152 Vladimir Dzurilla
Canad .02 .10
153 Phil Esposito
Canada Cup .20 .50
154 Rogatien Vachon
Canada Cup .05 .15
155 Milan Novy .01 .05
156 Vladimir Martinec
Canada Cup .02 .10
157 Good For Hockey
Canada Cup .01 .05
158 Bill Nyrop .01 .05
159 Pride .01 .05
160 Another Summit
Canada Cup .01 .05
161 Alexander Maltsev
Canada Cup .15 .40
162 Gilbert Perreault
Canada Cup .08 .25
163 Vladislav Tretiak .40 1.00
164 Vladimir Vikulov
Canada Cup .02 .10
165 Canada Cup Final
Game 1 .01 .05
166 Not There Yet
Canada Cup .01 .05
167 Fast and Furious
Canada Cup .01 .05
168 4 - 3/Canada Cup/4 - 4 .01 .05
169 Bill Barber .05 .15
170 The Grapevine
Canada Cup .02 .10
171 Guy Lapointe .05 .15
172 Reggie Leach .01 .05
173 Sittler's Goal
Canada Cup .08 .25
174 Lanny McDonald
Canada Cup .08 .25
175 Darryl Sittler
Canada Cup .08 .25
176 The Canada Cup
Canada Cup .05 .15
177 Bobby Clarke .08 .25
178 Last Time for No. 9
Canada Cup .08 .25
179 Marcel Dionne
Canada Cup .08 .25
180 Peter Mahovlich
Canada Cup .01 .05
181 Denis Potvin .08 .25
182 Larry Robinson
Canada Cup .08 .25
183 Steve Shutt .05 .15
184 Bobby Orr
Tournament MVP .40 1.00
185 Rogatien Vachon
MVP .05 .15
186 Milan Novy
MVP -- CSSR .02 .10
187 Matti Hagman
MVP -- Finland .01 .05
188 Borje Salming
MVP -- Sweden .05 .15
189 Robbie Ftorek
MVP -- US .01 .05
190 Alexander Maltsev
MVP .15 .40
191 Canada Final Series .01 .05
192 Canada Series Totals
Canada Cup .01 .05
193 CSSR Final Series
Total .01 .05
194 CSSR Series Totals
Canada Cup .01 .05
195 Rogatien Vachon AS
Canada Cup .05 .15
196 Bobby Orr AS .40 1.00
197 Borje Salming AS
Canada .05 .15
198 Milan Novy AS
Canada Cup .01 .05
199 Darryl Sittler AS
Canada Cup .05 .15
200 Alexander Maltsev AS
Canada Cup .15 .40
201 Canada Cup Checklist .02 .10
NNO Checklist Sheet 8-1/2x11
artist rendition .75 2.00

1992 Future Trends Promo Sheet

1 Team USA Sheet 1.50 4.00

1997 Gatorade Stickers

COMPLETE SET (6) 8.00 20.00
PAN1 Daniel Alfredsson
Vincent Damphousse
Bill Guerin
Jarome Iginla .40 1.00
PAN3 Alexander Mogilny
Jose Theodore
Ron Tugnutt
Doug Weight .60 1.50
PAN4 Joe Nieuwendyk
Chris Pronger
Mark Recchi
Luc Robitaille .60 1.50
PAN5 Tie Domi
Grant Fuhr
Jaromir Jagr
Paul Kariya 2.00 5.00
PAN6 Patrick Roy
Joe Sakic
Teemu Selanne
Mats Sundin 4.00 10.00

2006-07 Gatorade

COMPLETE SET (91) 60.00 100.00
1 Miikka Kiprusoff 1.50 4.00
2 Dion Phaneuf 2.00 5.00
3 Jarome Iginla 2.00 5.00
4 Alex Tanguay 1.25 3.00
5 Daymond Langkow .75 2.00
6 Matthew Lombardi .75 2.00
7 Chuck Kobasew .40 1.00
8 Kristian Huselius .40 1.00
9 Roman Hamrlik .40 1.00
10 Stephane Yelle .40 1.00
11 Tony Amonte .40 1.00
12 Robyn Regehr .40 1.00
13 Jeff Friesen .40 1.00
14 Marcus Nilson .40 1.00
15 Andrew Ference .40 1.00
16 Petr Sykora .40 1.00
17 Ales Hemsky 1.25 3.00
18 Joffrey Lupul .75 2.00
19 Dwayne Roloson .75 2.00
20 Ryan Smyth 1.25 3.00
21 Jarret Stoll .75 2.00
22 Patrick Thoresen .75 2.00
23 Raffi Torres .75 2.00
24 Fernando Pisani .75 2.00
25 Shawn Horcoff .75 2.00
26 Marc-Andre Bergeron .40 1.00
27 Jason Smith .40 1.00
28 Ladislav Smid .40 1.00
29 Steve Staios .40 1.00
30 Jussi Markkanen .60 1.50
31 Saku Koivu 2.00 5.00
32 Chris Higgins .75 2.00
33 Sheldon Souray .40 1.00
34 Andrei Markov .40 1.00
35 Michael Ryder .75 2.00
36 Cristobal Huet 1.50 4.00
37 David Aebischer .75 2.00
38 Alex Kovalev .40 1.00
39 Mike Johnson .40 1.00
40 Alexander Perezhogin .40 1.00
41 Guillaume Latendresse 2.00 5.00
42 Radek Bonk .40 1.00
43 Sergei Samsonov .75 2.00
44 Tomas Plekanec .75 2.00
45 Michael Komisarek .75 2.00
46 Jason Spezza 1.25 3.00
47 Dany Heatley 1.50 4.00
48 Joe Corvo .40 1.00
49 Daniel Alfredsson 1.25 3.00
50 Martin Gerber .75 2.00
51 Ray Emery 1.25 3.00
52 Antoine Vermette .40 1.00
53 Patrick Eaves .75 2.00
54 Dean McAmmond .40 1.00
55 Mike Fisher .75 2.00
56 Chris Neil .75 2.00
57 Wade Redden .75 2.00
58 Chris Phillips .75 2.00
59 Andrej Meszaros .75 2.00
60 Chris Kelly .40 1.00
61 Mats Sundin 1.25 3.00
62 Alexander Steen 1.25 3.00
63 Darcy Tucker 1.25 3.00
64 Kyle Wellwood .75 2.00
65 Andrew Raycroft .75 2.00
66 Bryan McCabe .75 2.00
67 Tomas Kaberle .75 2.00
68 Jeff O'Neill .40 1.00
69 Alexei Ponikarovsky .40 1.00
70 Ian White .40 1.00
71 Michael Peca .75 2.00
72 Chad Kilger .40 1.00
73 Hal Gill .40 1.00
74 Matt Stajan .75 2.00
75 Pavel Kubina .40 1.00
76 Markus Naslund .75 2.00
77 Roberto Luongo 2.00 5.00
78 Daniel Sedin .75 2.00
79 Henrik Sedin .75 2.00
80 Brendan Morrison .40 1.00
81 Sami Salo .40 1.00
82 Jan Bulis .40 1.00
83 Taylor Pyatt .40 1.00
84 Mattias Ohlund .40 1.00
85 Lukas Krajicek .40 1.00
86 Trevor Linden 1.25 3.00
87 Ryan Kesler .40 1.00
88 Matt Cooke .40 1.00
89 Willie Mitchell .40 1.00
90 Kevin Bieksa .75 2.00
91 Sidney Crosby SP 25.00 60.00

1967-68 General Mills

COMPLETE SET (5) 500.00 1000.00
1 Jean Beliveau 75.00 150.00
2 Gordie Howe 150.00 300.00
3 Harry Howell 40.00 80.00
4 Stan Mikita 62.50 125.00
5 Bobby Orr 250.00 500.00

1991-92 Gillette

COMPLETE SET (48) 10.00 25.00
1 Luc Robitaille .20 .50
2 Esa Tikkanen .20 .50
3 Pat Falloon .05 .15
4 Theo Fleury .30 .75
5 Trevor Linden .20 .50
6 Rob Blake .20 .50
7 Al MacInnis .20 .50
8 Bob Essensa .20 .50
9 Bill Ranford .20 .50
10 Pavel Bure .75 2.00
11 Wendel Clark .20 .50
12 Sergei Fedorov .60 1.50
13 Jeremy Roenick .30 .75
14 Brett Hull .40 1.00
15 Mike Modano .40 1.00
16 Chris Chelios .30 .75
17 Dave Ellett .05 .15
18 Ed Belfour .30 .75
19 Grant Fuhr .20 .50
20 Martin Lapointe .05 .15
21 Kirk Muller .08 .25
22 Joe Sakic .60 1.50
23 Pat LaFontaine .20 .50
24 Pat Verbeek .20 .50
25 Owen Nolan .20 .50
26 Ray Bourque .40 1.00
27 Eric Desjardins .08 .25
28 Patrick Roy 1.50 4.00
29 Andy Moog .20 .50
30 Valeri Kamensky .20 .50
31 Mark Messier .40 1.00
32 Mike Ricci .20 .50
33 Mario Lemieux 1.50 4.00
34 Jaromir Jagr 1.00 2.50
35 Pierre Turgeon .20 .50
36 Kevin Hatcher .05 .15
37 Paul Coffey .30 .75
38 Chris Terreri .08 .25
39 Mike Richter .30 .75
40 Kevin Todd .05 .15
NNO Patrick Checklist .02 .10
NNO Norris Checklist .02 .10
NNO Adams Trivia .02 .10
NNO Patrick Trivia .02 .10
NNO Smythe Checklist .02 .10
NNO Adams Checklist .02 .10
NNO Smythe Trivia .02 .10
NNO Norris Trivia .02 .10

2001-02 Greats of the Game

COMPLETE SET (89) 15.00 30.00
1 Gordie Howe .75 2.00
2 Glenn Hall .25 .60
3 Jean Beliveau .30 .75
4 Bob Nystrom .20 .50
5 Phil Esposito .40 1.00
6 Dennis Maruk .20 .50
7 Bobby Hull .50 1.25
8 Guy Lafleur .30 .75
9 Gilbert Perreault .25 .60
10 John Davidson .25 .60
11 Peter Stastny .25 .60
12 Steve Shutt .25 .60
13 Henri Richard .30 .75
14 Johnny Bower .25 .60
15 Barry Beck .20 .50
16 Marcel Dionne .30 .75
17 Billy Smith .25 .60
18 Dale Hunter .20 .50
19 Tony Esposito .40 1.00
20 Guy Lapointe .20 .50
21 Ed Giacomin .25 .60
22 Denis Savard .25 .60
23 Rod Gilbert .30 .75
24 Steve Larmer .20 .50
25 Yvan Cournoyer .25 .60
26 Ulf Nilsson .20 .50
27 Jean Ratelle .20 .50
28 Dino Ciccarelli .25 .60
29 Bryan Trottier .25 .60
30 Tim Horton .25 .60
31 Stan Mikita .40 1.00
32 Glenn Anderson .20 .50
33 Bobby Clarke .40 1.00
34 Wendel Clark .40 1.00
35 Reggie Leach .20 .50
36 Terry Sawchuk .40 1.00
37 Bernie Geoffrion .30 .75
38 Bill Barber .25 .60
39 Tiger Williams .15 .40
40 Alex Delvecchio .25 .60
41 Bernie Parent .30 .75
42 Paul Henderson .20 .50
43 Norm Ullman .25 .60
44 Larry Robinson .25 .60
45 Dave Schultz .25 .60
46 John Ogrodnick .15 .40
47 Rick MacLeish .20 .50
48 Richard Brodeur .25 .60
49 Rick Martin .20 .50
50 Bobby Smith .20 .50
51 Denis Potvin .20 .50
52 Darryl Sittler .30 .75
53 Lanny McDonald .20 .50
54 Brian Bellows .20 .50
55 Frank Mahovlich .25 .60
56 Cam Neely .25 .60
57 Grant Fuhr .40 1.00
58 Harry Howell .20 .50
59 Michel Goulet .20 .50
60 Gerry Cheevers .25 .60
61 Dave Taylor .20 .50
62 Clark Gillies .25 .60
63 Bernie Federko .20 .50
64 Chico Resch .20 .50
65 Andy Bathgate .30 .75
66 Jacques Lemaire .20 .50
67 Ken Hodge .20 .50
68 Rogie Vachon .25 .60
69 Brian Sutter .25 .60
70 Rick Middleton .20 .50
71 Neal Broten .20 .50
72 Mike Bossy .25 .60
73 Borje Salming .25 .60
74 Ted Lindsay .25 .60
75 Mike Gartner .30 .75
76 John Bucyk .25 .60
77 Brad Park .20 .50
78 Red Kelly .25 .60
79 Joe Mullen .20 .50
80 Terry O'Reilly .20 .50
81 Mario Lemieux 1.00 2.50
82 Butch Goring .20 .50
83 Mike Liut .15 .40
84 Marcel Pronovost .20 .50
85 Serge Savard .25 .60
86 Jari Kurri .25 .60
87 Rick Kehoe .25 .60
88 Gump Worsley .30 .75
89 Kent Nilsson .20 .50

2001-02 Greats of the Game Retro Collection

COMPLETE SET (13) 15.00 30.00
1 Gordie Howe 2.50 6.00
2 Jean Beliveau 1.00 2.50
3 Phil Esposito 1.25 3.00
4 Bobby Hull 1.25 3.00
5 Guy LaFleur 1.00 2.50
6 Peter Stastny .60 1.50
7 Henri Richard .60 1.50
8 Marcel Dionne .75 2.00
9 Bryan Trottier .60 1.50
10 Bobby Clarke .75 2.00
11 Terry Sawchuk 1.25 3.00
12 Mario Lemieux 3.00 8.00
13 Tony Esposito 1.00 2.50

2001-02 Greats of the Game Autographs

1 Gordie Howe SP 200.00 500.00
2 Glenn Hall SP 25.00 60.00
3 Jean Beliveau SP 60.00 125.00
4 Bob Nystrom 8.00 20.00
5 Phil Esposito SP 50.00 125.00
6 Dennis Maruk 8.00 20.00
7 Bobby Hull SP 60.00 150.00
8 Guy Lafleur SP 60.00 150.00
9 Gilbert Perreault 20.00 50.00
10 John Davidson 8.00 20.00
11 Peter Stastny SP 40.00 80.00
12 Steve Shutt 8.00 20.00
13 Henri Richard SP 30.00 80.00
14 Johnny Bower 12.00 30.00
15 Barry Beck 6.00 15.00
16 Marcel Dionne SP 20.00 50.00
17 Billy Smith 8.00 20.00
18 Dale Hunter 8.00 20.00
19 Tony Esposito 15.00 40.00
20 Guy LaPointe 12.00 30.00
21 Ed Giacomin 10.00 25.00
22 Denis Savard 8.00 20.00
23 Rod Gilbert 25.00 60.00
24 Steve Larmer 10.00 25.00
25 Yvan Cournoyer 10.00 25.00
26 Ulf Nilsson 8.00 20.00
27 Jean Ratelle 15.00 40.00
28 Dino Ciccarelli 10.00 25.00
29 Bryan Trottier SP 15.00 40.00
31 Stan Mikita SP 40.00 100.00
32 Glenn Anderson 8.00 20.00
33 Bobby Clarke SP 30.00 60.00
34 Wendel Clark 15.00 40.00
35 Reggie Leach 8.00 20.00
37 Bernie Geoffrion 30.00 80.00
38 Bill Barber 4.00 10.00
39 Tiger Williams 12.00 30.00
40 Alex Delvecchio SP 15.00 40.00
41 Bernie Parent 10.00 25.00
42 Paul Henderson SP 60.00 150.00
43 Norm Ullman 8.00 20.00
44 Larry Robinson 8.00 20.00
45 Dave Schultz 8.00 20.00
46 John Ogrodnick 8.00 20.00
47 Rick MacLeish 8.00 20.00
48 Richard Brodeur 8.00 20.00
49 Rick Martin 25.00 60.00
50 Bobby Smith 4.00 10.00
51 Denis Potvin 10.00 25.00
52 Darryl Sittler 8.00 20.00
53 Lanny McDonald 8.00 20.00
54 Brian Bellows 10.00 25.00
55 Frank Mahovlich 12.00 30.00
56 Cam Neely SP 25.00 60.00
57 Grant Fuhr 10.00 25.00
58 Harry Howell 25.00 60.00
59 Michel Goulet 8.00 20.00
60 Gerry Cheevers 15.00 40.00
61 Dave Taylor 8.00 20.00
62 Clark Gillies 8.00 20.00
63 Bernie Federko 8.00 20.00
64 Chico Resch 15.00 30.00
65 Andy Bathgate 8.00 20.00
66 Jacques Lemaire 8.00 20.00
67 Ken Hodge 8.00 20.00
68 Rogie Vachon 8.00 20.00
69 Brian Sutter 8.00 20.00
70 Rick Middleton 8.00 20.00
71 Neal Broten 8.00 20.00
72 Mike Bossy SP 60.00 150.00
73 Borje Salming 12.00 30.00
74 Ted Lindsay SP 25.00 60.00
75 Mike Gartner SP 15.00 40.00
76 John Bucyk 10.00 25.00
77 Brad Park 8.00 20.00
78 Red Kelly 8.00 20.00
79 Joe Mullen 8.00 20.00
80 Terry O'Reilly 8.00 20.00
81 Mario Lemieux 80.00 200.00
82 Butch Goring 8.00 20.00
83 Mike Liut 10.00 25.00
84 Marcel Pronovost 8.00 20.00
85 Serge Savard 8.00 20.00
86 Jari Kurri 10.00 25.00
87 Rick Kehoe 8.00 20.00
89 Kent Nilsson 8.00 20.00
NNO Rod Langway 8.00 20.00

2001-02 Greats of the Game Board Certified

1 Mike Bossy 5.00 12.00
2 Guy LaFleur 4.00 10.00
3 Mario Lemieux 8.00 20.00
4 Cam Neely 4.00 10.00
5 Peter Stastny 3.00 8.00

2001-02 Greats of the Game Jerseys

1 Dino Ciccarelli 6.00 15.00
2 Tony Esposito 6.00 15.00
3 Michel Goulet 6.00 15.00
4 Guy Lafleur 10.00 25.00
5 Larry Robinson 8.00 20.00
6 Borje Salming 6.00 15.00
7 Glen Sather 6.00 15.00
8 Denis Savard 6.00 15.00
9 Patrick Roy 15.00 40.00

2001-02 Greats of the Game Sticks

1 Marcel Dionne 10.00 25.00
2 Phil Esposito 12.50 30.00
3 Tony Esposito 10.00 25.00
4 Gordie Howe 12.50 30.00
5 Bobby Hull 12.50 30.00
6 Cam Neely 10.00 25.00
7 Willie O'Ree 8.00 20.00
8 Brad Park 10.00 25.00
9 Henri Richard 10.00 25.00
10 Terry Sawchuk 20.00 50.00
11 Darryl Sittler 10.00 25.00
12 Patrick Roy 12.50 30.00

1983 Hall of Fame Postcards

COMPLETE SET (240) 140.00 350.00
A1 Sid Abel .75 2.00
A2 Punch Broadbent .40 1.00
A3 Clarence Campbell .40 1.00
A4 Neil Colville .40 1.00
A5 Charlie Conacher 1.25 3.00
A6 Red Dutton .40 1.00
A7 Foster Hewitt 1.25 3.00
A8 Fred Hume .40 1.00
A9 Mickey Ion .40 1.00
A10 Ernest Johnson .40 1.00
A11 Bill Mosienko .40 1.00
A12 Maurice Richard 6.00 15.00
A13 Barney Stanley .40 1.00
A14 Lord Stanley .75 2.00
A15 Cyclone Taylor 1.00 2.50
A16 Tiny Thompson 1.25 3.00
B1 Dan Bain .40 1.00
B2 Hobey Baker .75 2.00
B3 Frank Calder .40 1.00
B4 Frank Foyston .40 1.00
B5 James Hendy .40 1.00
B6 Gordie Howe 6.00 15.00
B7 Harry Lumley 1.25 3.00
B8 Reg Noble .40 1.00
B9 Frank Patrick .40 1.00
B10 Harvey Pulford .40 1.00
B11 Ken Reardon .60 1.50
B12 Bullet Joe Simpson .60 1.50
B13 Conn Smythe .75 2.00
B14 Red Storey .40 1.00
B15 Lloyd Turner .40 1.00
B16 Georges Vezina 3.00 8.00
C1 Jean Beliveau 3.00 8.00
C2 Max Bentley .60 1.50
C3 King Clancy 1.25 3.00
C4 Babe Dye .40 1.00
C5 Ebbie Goodfellow .40 1.00
C6 Charles Hay .40 1.00
C7 Percy Lesueur .60 1.50
C8 Tommy Lockhart .40 1.00
C9 Jack Marshall .40 1.00
C10 Lester Patrick .75 2.00
C11 Bill Quackenbush .60 1.50
C12 Frank Selke .60 1.50
C13 Cooper Smeaton .40 1.00
C14 Hooley Smith .40 1.00
C15 Capt.J.T.Sutherland .40 1.00
C16 Fred Whitcroft .40 1.00
D1 Charles F. Adams .40 1.00
D2 Russell Bowie .40 1.00
D3 Frank Fredrickson .40 1.00
D4 H.L. Gilmour .40 1.00
D5 Ching Johnson .60 1.50
D6 Tom Johnson .60 1.50
D7 Aurel Joliat 1.50 4.00
D8 Duke Keats .40 1.00
D9 Red Kelly 1.25 3.00
D10 Frank McGee .40 1.00
D11 James D. Norris .60 1.50
D12 Philip D. Ross .40 1.00
D13 Terry Sawchuk 3.00 8.00
D14 Babe Siebert .60 1.50
D15 Anatoli V. Tarasov .60 1.50
D16 Roy Worters .75 2.00
E1 T. Franklin Ahearn .40 1.00
E2 Harold E. Ballard .75 2.00
E3 Billy Burch .40 1.00
E4 Bill Chadwick .40 1.00
E5 Sprague Cleghorn .75 2.00
E6 Rusty Crawford .40 1.00

E7 Alex Delvecchio 1.25 3.00
E8 George S. Dudley .40 1.00
E9 Ted Kennedy .75 2.00
E10 Newsy Lalonde 1.00 2.50
E11 Billy McGimsie .40 1.00
E12 Frank Nighbor .60 1.50
E13 Bobby Orr 6.00 15.00
E14 Sen. Donat Raymond .40 1.00
E15 Art Ross 1.00 2.50
E16 Jack Walker .40 1.00
F1 Doug Bentley .60 1.50
F2 Walter A. Brown .40 1.00
F3 Dit Clapper 1.00 2.50
F4 Hap Day .40 1.00
F5 Frank Dilio .40 1.00
F6 Bobby Hewitson .40 1.00
F7 Harry Howell .40 1.00
F8 Paul Loicq .40 1.00
F9 Sylvio Mantha .60 1.50
F10 Jacques Plante 3.00 8.00
F11 George Richardson .40 1.00
F12 Nels Stewart .75 2.00
F13 Hod Stuart .40 1.00
F14 Harry Trihey .40 1.00
F15 Marty Walsh .40 1.00
F16 Arthur M. Wirtz .40 1.00
G1 Toe Blake 1.25 3.00
G2 Frank Boucher .60 1.50
G3 Turk Broda 1.50 4.00
G4 Harry Cameron .40 1.00
G5 Leo Dandurand .40 1.00
G6 Joe Hall .40 1.00
G7 George Hay .40 1.00
G8 William A. Hewitt .40 1.00
G9 Bouse Hutton .40 1.00
G10 Dick Irvin .75 2.00
G11 Henri Richard 1.25 3.00
G12 John Ross Robertson .40 1.00
G13 Frank D. Smith .40 1.00
G14 Allan Stanley .40 1.00
G15 Norm Ullman .40 1.00
G16 Harry Watson .40 1.00
H1 Clint Benedict 1.25 3.00
H2 Dickie Boon .40 1.00
H3 Gordie Drillon .60 1.50
H4 Bill Gadsby .40 1.00
H5 Rod Gilbert .40 1.00
H6 Moose Goheen .40 1.00
H7 Tommy Gorman .40 1.00
H8 Glenn Hall 1.25 3.00
H9 Red Horner .40 1.00
H10 Gen.J.R.Kilpatrick .40 1.00
H11 Robert Lebel .40 1.00
H12 Howie Morenz 3.00 8.00
H13 Fred Scanlan .40 1.00
H14 Tommy Smith .40 1.00
H15 Fred C. Waghorne .40 1.00
H16 Cooney Weiland .75 2.00
I1 Weston Adams .40 1.00
I2 Sir Montagu Allan .40 1.00
I3 Frank Brimsek 1.25 3.00
I4 Angus Campbell .40 1.00
I5 Bill Cook .75 2.00
I6 Tom Dunderdale .40 1.00
I7 Emile Francis .40 1.00
I8 Charlie Gardiner .60 1.50
I9 Elmer Lach .60 1.50
I10 Frank Mahovlich 1.25 3.00
I11 Didier Pitre .40 1.00
I12 Joe Primeau 1.25 3.00
I13 Frank Rankin .40 1.00
I14 Ernie Russell .40 1.00
I15 Thayer Tutt .40 1.00
I16 Harry Westwick .40 1.00
J1 Jack Adams .40 1.00
J2 Bunny Ahearne .40 1.00
J3 J.P. Bickell .40 1.00
J4 Johnny Ducyk .00 1.50
J5 Art Coulter .40 1.00
J6 C.G. Drinkwater .40 1.00
J7 George Hainsworth 1.25 3.00
J8 Tim Horton 2.00 5.00
J9 Maj. F. McLaughlin .40 1.00
J10 Dickie Moore .75 2.00
J11 Pierre Pilote .40 1.00
J12 Claude C. Robinson .40 1.00
J13 Sweeney Schriner .40 1.00
J14 Oliver Seibert .40 1.00
J15 Alfred Smith .40 1.00
J16 Phat Wilson .60 1.50
K1 Yvan Cournoyer .60 1.50
K2 Scotty Davidson .40 1.00
K3 Cy Denneny .60 1.50
K4 Bill Durnan 1.00 2.50
K5 Shorty Green .40 1.00
K6 Riley Hern .40 1.00
K7 Bryan Hextall Sr. .40 1.00
K8 Bill Jennings .40 1.00
K9 Gordon W. Juckes .40 1.00
K10 Paddy Moran .60 1.50
K11 James Norris .40 1.00
K12 Harry Oliver .40 1.00
K13 Sam Pollock .40 1.00
K14 Marcel Pronovost .40 1.00
K15 Jack Ruttan .40 1.00
K16 Earl Seibert .40 1.00
L1 Buck Boucher .40 1.00
L2 George V. Brown .40 1.00
L3 Arthur F. Farrell .40 1.00
L4 Herb Gardiner .40 1.00
L5 Si Griffis .40 1.00
L6 Hap Holmes .40 1.00
L7 Harry Hyland .40 1.00
L8 Tommy Ivan .40 1.00
L9 Jack Laviolette .40 1.00
L10 Ted Lindsay 1.25 3.00
L11 Francis Nelson .40 1.00
L12 William M. Northey .40 1.00
L13 Babe Pratt .40 1.00
L14 Chuck Rayner .75 2.00
L15 Milt Rodden .40 1.00
L16 Milt Schmidt 1.00 2.50
M1 Butch Bouchard .60 1.50
M2 Jack Butterfield .40 1.00
M3 Joseph Cattarinich .40 1.00
M4 Alex Connell .75 2.00
M5 Bill Cowley .60 1.50
M6 Chaucer Elliott .40 1.00
M7 James Gardner .40 1.00
M8 Boom Boom Geoffrion 1.50 4.00
M9 Tom Hooper .40 1.00
M10 Syd Howe .40 1.00
M11 Harvey(Busher)Jackson .60 1.50
M12 Al Leader .40 1.00
M13 Steamer Maxwell .40 1.00
M14 Blair Russell .40 1.00
M15 William W. Wirtz .40 1.00
M16 Gump Worsley 1.25 3.00
N1 George Armstrong .75 2.00
N2 Ace Bailey 1.25 3.00
N3 Jack Darragh .40 1.00
N4 Ken Dryden 3.00 8.00
N5 Eddie Gerard .40 1.00
N6 Jack Gibson .40 1.00
N7 Hugh Lehman .40 1.00
N8 Mickey MacKay .40 1.00
N9 Joe Malone 1.25 3.00
N10 Bruce A. Norris .40 1.00
N11 J. Ambrose O'Brien .40 1.00
N12 Lynn Patrick .60 1.50
N13 Tommy Phillips .40 1.00
N14 Allan W. Pickard .40 1.00
N15 Jack Stewart .40 1.00
N16 Frank Udvari .40 1.00
O1 Syl Apps .75 2.00
O2 John G. Ashley .40 1.00
O3 Marty Barry .40 1.00
O4 Andy Bathgate .60 1.50
O5 Johnny Bower 1.25 3.00
O6 Frank Buckland .40 1.00
O7 Jimmy Dunn .40 1.00
O8 Michael Grant .40 1.00
O9 Doug Harvey 1.25 3.00
O10 George McNamara .40 1.00
O11 Stan Mikita 1.25 3.00
O12 Sen.H.de M. Molson .40 1.00
O13 Gordon Roberts .40 1.00
O14 Eddie Shore 3.00 8.00
O15 Bruce Stuart .40 1.00
O16 Carl P. Voss .40 1.00
NNO Binder .40 1.00

1985-87 Hall of Fame

COMPLETE SET (261) 40.00 100.00
1 Maurice Richard 3.00 8.00
2 Sid Abel .30 .75
3 Punch Broadbent .15 .40
4 Clarence S. Campbell .15 .40
5 Neil Colville .15 .40
6 Charlie Conacher .40 1.00
7 Red Dutton .15 .40
8 Foster W. Hewitt .40 1.00
9 Mickey Ion .15 .40
10 Ernest Johnson .15 .40
11 Bill Mosienko .15 .40
12 Russell Stanley .15 .40
13 Lord Stanley .30 .75
14 Cyclone Taylor .30 .75
15 Tiny Thompson .30 .75
16 Gordie Howe 3.00 8.00
17 Hobey Baker .30 .75
18 Frank Calder .15 .40
19 Jim Hendy .15 .40
20 Frank Foyston .15 .40
21 Harry Lumley .40 1.00
22 Reg Noble .15 .40
23 Frank A. Patrick .15 .40
24 Harvey Pulford .15 .40
25 Ken Reardon .20 .50
26 Bullet Joe Simpson .20 .50
27 Conn Smythe .30 .75
28 Red Storey .15 .40
29 Lloyd Turner .15 .40
30 Georges Vezina 1.00 2.50
31 Jean Beliveau 1.00 2.50
32 Max Bentley .20 .50
33 King Clancy .40 1.00
34 Babe Dye .15 .40
35 Ebbie Goodfellow .15 .40
36 Charles Hay .15 .40
37 Percy Lesueur .20 .50
38 Tommy Lockhart .15 .40
39 Jack Marshall .15 .40
40 Lester Patrick .30 .75
41 Frank Selke .20 .50
42 J. Cooper Smeaton .15 .40
43 Hooley Smith .15 .40
44 Capt.J.T. Sutherland .15 .40
45 Fred Whitcroft .15 .40
46 Terry Sawchuk 1.50 4.00
47 Charles F. Adams .15 .40
48 Russell Bowie .15 .40
49 Frank Frederickson .15 .40
50 Billy Gilmour .15 .40
51 Ching Johnson .20 .50
52 Tom Johnson .30 .75
53 Aurel Joliat .60 1.50
54 Duke Keats .15 .40
55 Red Kelly .40 1.00
56 Frank McGee .15 .40
57 James D. Norris .15 .40
58 Philip D. Ross .15 .40
59 Babe Siebert .20 .50
60 Roy Worters .30 .75
61 Bobby Orr 3.00 8.00
62 T. Franklin Ahearn .15 .40
63 Harold E. Ballard .30 .75
64 Billy Burch .15 .40
65 Bill Chadwick .15 .40
66 Sprague Cleghorn .30 .75
67 Rusty Crawford .15 .40
68 George S. Dudley .15 .40
69 Teeder Kennedy .30 .75
70 Newsy Lalonde .40 1.00
71 Billy McGimsie .15 .40
72 Frank Nighbor .20 .50
73 Sen. Donat Raymond .15 .40
74 Art Ross .40 1.00
75 Jack Walker .15 .40
76 Jacques Plante 1.50 4.00
77 Doug Bentley .20 .50
78 Walter A. Brown .15 .40
79 Dit Clapper .40 1.00
80 Hap Day .15 .40
81 Frank Dilio .15 .40
82 Bobby Hewitson .15 .40
83 Harry Howell .15 .40
84 Sylvio Mantha .20 .50
85 George Richardson .15 .40
86 Nels Stewart .30 .75
87 Hod Stuart .15 .40
88 Harry Trihey .15 .40
89 Marty Walsh .15 .40
90 Arthur M. Wirtz .15 .40
91 Henri Richard .60 1.50
92 Toe Blake .40 1.00
93 Frank Boucher .20 .50
94 Turk Broda .60 1.50
95 Harry Cameron .15 .40
96 Leo J.V. Dandurand .15 .40
97 Joe Hall .15 .40
98 George W. Hay .15 .40
99 William A. Hewitt .15 .40
100 Bouse Hutton .15 .40
101 Dick Irvin .20 .50
102 John Ross Robertson .15 .40
103 Frank D. Smith .15 .40
104 Norm Ullman .15 .40
105 Moose Watson .15 .40
106 Howie Morenz 1.00 2.50
107 Clint Benedict .40 1.00
108 Dickie Boon .15 .40
109 Gordon Drillon .20 .50
110 Bill Gadsby .15 .40
111 Rod Gilbert .15 .40
112 Moose Goheen .15 .40
113 Tommy Gorman .15 .40
114 Glenn Hall .40 1.00
115 Red Horner .15 .40
116 Gen.J.R. Kilpatrick .15 .40
117 Robert Lebel .15 .40
118 Fred Scanlan .15 .40
119 Fred C. Waghorne .15 .40
120 Cooney Weiland .30 .75
121 Frank Mahovlich .40 1.00
122 Weston Adams Sr. .15 .40
123 Sir Montagu Allan .15 .40
124 Frank Brimsek .40 1.00
125 Angus D. Campbell .15 .40
126 Bill Cook .30 .75
127 Tom Dunderdale .15 .40
128 Chuck Gardiner .15 .40
129 Elmer Lach .20 .50
130 Didier Pitre .15 .40
131 Joe Primeau .40 1.00
132 Frank Rankin .15 .40
133 Ernie Russell .15 .40
134 W. Thayer Tutt .15 .40
135 Harry Westwick .15 .40
136 Yvan Cournoyer .20 .50
137 Scotty Davidson .15 .40
138 Cy Denneny .20 .50
139 Bill Durnan .40 1.00
140 Shorty Green .15 .40
141 Bryan Hextall Sr. .15 .40
142 Bill Jennings .15 .40
143 Gordon W. Juckes .15 .40
144 Paddy Moran .20 .50
145 James Norris .15 .40
146 Harold Oliver .15 .40
147 Sam Pollock .15 .40
148 Marcel Pronovost .15 .40
149 Jack Ruttan .15 .40
150 Earl W. Seibert .15 .40
151 Ted Lindsay .40 1.00
152 George V. Brown .15 .40
153 Arthur F. Farrell .15 .40
154 Herb Gardiner .15 .40
155 Si Griffis .15 .40
156 Hap Holmes .15 .40
157 Harry Hyland .15 .40
158 Tommy Ivan .15 .40
159 Jack Laviolette .15 .40
160 Francis Nelson .15 .40
161 William M. Northey .15 .40
162 Babe Pratt .15 .40
163 Chuck Rayner .30 .75
164 Mike Rodden .15 .40
165 Milt Schmidt .40 1.00
166 Boom Boom Geoffrion .60 1.50
167 Jack Butterfield .15 .40
168 Joseph Cattarinich .15 .40
169 Alex Connell .30 .75
170 Bill Cowley .20 .50
171 Chaucer Eliott .15 .40
172 James Gardner .15 .40
173 Tom Hooper .15 .40
174 Syd Howe .15 .40
175 Harvey(Busher) Jackson .20 .50
176 Al Leader .15 .40
177 Steamer Maxwell .15 .40
178 Blair Russell .15 .40
179 William W. Wirtz .15 .40
180 Gump Worsley .40 1.00
181 Johnny Bucyk .20 .50
182 Jack Adams .15 .40
183 Bunny Ahearne .15 .40
184 J.P. Bickell .15 .40
185 Art Coulter .15 .40
186 C.G. Drinkwater .15 .40
187 George Hainsworth .40 1.00
188 Tim Horton 1.00 2.50
189 Maj.F. McLaughlin .15 .40
190 Dickie Moore .30 .75
191 Pierre Pilote .15 .40
192 Claude C. Robinson .15 .40
193 Oliver L. Seibert .15 .40
194 Alfred E. Smith .15 .40
195 Phat Wilson .15 .40
196 Ken Dryden 1.50 4.00
197 George Armstrong .30 .75
198 Ace Bailey .40 1.00
199 Jack Darragh .15 .40
200 Eddie Gerard .15 .40
201 Jack Gibson .15 .40
202 Hugh Lehman .15 .40
203 Mickey MacKay .15 .40
204 Joe Malone .30 .75
205 Bruce A. Norris .15 .40
206 J.Ambrose O'Brien .15 .40
207 Lynn Patrick .20 .50
208 Tommy Phillips .15 .40
209 Allan W. Pickard .15 .40
210 Jack Stewart .15 .40
211 Johnny Bower .40 1.00
212 Syl Apps .30 .75
213 John G. Ashley .15 .40
214 Marty Barry .15 .40
215 Andy Bathgate .20 .50
216 Frank Buckland .15 .40
217 Jimmy Dunn .15 .40
218 Michael Grant .15 .40
219 Doug Harvey .40 1.00
220 George McNamara .15 .40
221 Sen.H.deM. Molson .15 .40
222 Gordon Roberts .15 .40
223 Eddie Shore 1.00 2.50
224 Bruce Stuart .15 .40
225 Carl P. Voss .15 .40
226 Stan Mikita .40 1.00
227 Dan Bain .15 .40
228 Butch Bouchard .20 .50
229 Buck Boucher .15 .40
230 Alex Delvecchio .40 1.00
231 Emile P. Francis .15 .40
232 Riley Hern .15 .40
233 Fred J. Hume .15 .40
234 Paul Loicq .15 .40
235 Bill Quackenbush .20 .50
236 Sweeney Schriner .15 .40
237 Tommy Smith .15 .40
238 Allan Stanley .15 .40
239 Anatoli V. Tarasov .20 .50
240 Frank Udvari .15 .40
241 Harry Sinden .30 .75
242 Bobby Hull 1.50 4.00
243 Punch Imlach .25 .60
244 Phil Esposito .75 2.00
245 Jacques Lemaire .30 .75
246 Bernie Parent .40 1.00
247 Rudy Pilous .25 .60
248 Bert Olmstead .25 .60
249 Jean Ratelle .40 1.00
250 Gerry Cheevers .40 1.00
251 William Hanley .25 .60
252 Leo Boivin .25 .60
253 Jake Milford .25 .60
254 John Mariucci .25 .60
255 Dave Keon .40 1.00
256 Serge Savard .25 .60
257 John A. Ziegler Jr. .25 .60
258 Bobby Clarke .60 1.50
259 Ed Giacomin .40 1.00
260 Jacques Laperriere .25 .60
261 Matt Pavelich .25 .60

1992-96 Hall of Fame Legends

COMPLETE SET (90) 60.00 150.00
1 Harry Lumley 2.00 5.00
2 Conn Smythe CO 1.50 4.00
3 Maurice Richard 6.00 15.00
4 Bobby Orr 8.00 20.00
5 Bernie Geoffrion 2.50 6.00
6 Hobey Baker 2.00 5.00
7 Phil Esposito 2.50 6.00
8 King Clancy 2.50 6.00
9 Gordie Howe 6.00 15.00
10 Emile Francis 1.50 4.00
11 Jacques Plante 3.00 8.00
12 Sid Abel 1.50 4.00
13 Foster Hewitt 2.00 5.00
14 Charlie Conacher 2.00 5.00
15 Stan Mikita 2.50 6.00
16 Bobby Clarke 2.00 5.00
17 Norm Ullman 1.50 4.00
18 Lord Stanley of Preston 2.00 5.00
19 Ted Lindsay 2.00 5.00
20 Duke Keats 1.50 4.00
21 Jack Adams 1.50 4.00
22 Bill Mosienko 1.50 4.00
23 Johnny Bower 2.00 5.00
24 Tim Horton 3.00 8.00
25 Punch Imlach 1.50 4.00
26 Georges Vezina 4.00 10.00
27 Earl Seibert 1.50 4.00
28 Bryan Hextall Sr. 1.50 4.00
29 Babe Pratt 1.50 4.00
30 Gump Worsley 2.00 5.00
31 Ed Giacomin 2.00 5.00
32 Ace Bailey 2.00 5.00
33 Harry Sinden 1.50 4.00
34 Lanny McDonald 2.00 5.00
35 Tommy Ivan 1.50 4.00
36 Frank Calder 1.50 4.00

1994 Hall of Fame Tickets

COMPLETE SET (12) 18.00 45.00
1 Stanley Cup 1.50 4.00
2 O'Brien Trophy 1.25 3.00
3 Dan Bain Artifacts 1.25 3.00
4 Art Ross Artifacts 1.50 4.00
5 Artifacts of Irvine (Ac 1.50 4.00
6 Artifacts of Clint Bene 2.00 5.00
7 Artifacts of Howie More 3.00 8.00
8 Artifacts of Roy (Shrim 1.50 4.00
9 Artifacts of Andy Bathg 1.25 3.00
10 Artifacts of Jacques Pl 3.00 8.00
11 Artifacts of Terry Sawc 3.00 8.00
12 Artifacts of Milt Schmi 1.50 4.00

1998 Hall of Fame Medallions

COMPLETE SET (2) 6.00 15.00
1 Michel Goulet 3.00 8.00
2 Peter Stastny 4.00 8.00

1914 Happy Christmas Postcard

NNO Happy Christmas 10.00 20.00

1999 Hasbro Starting Lineup Cards

COMPLETE SET (17) 10.00 25.00
1 Mike Dunham .40 1.00
2 Peter Forsberg .60 1.50
3 Wayne Gretzky 2.00 5.00
4 Jeff Hackett .60 1.50
5 Dominik Hasek .60 1.50
6 Jaromir Jagr .60 1.50
7 Curtis Joseph .75 2.00
8 Paul Kariya .60 1.50
9 Nikolai Khabibulin .40 1.00
10 Olaf Kolzig .40 1.00
11 Nicklas Lidstrom .75 2.00
12 Eric Lindros .60 1.50
13 Mike Modano .40 1.00
14 Keith Primeau .40 1.00
15 Chris Pronger .40 1.00
16 Sergei Samsonov .75 2.00
17 Steve Yzerman 1.25 3.00

1975-76 HCA Steel City Vacuum

COMPLETE SET (22) 5.00 10.00
1 Mike Buchko .25 .50
2 Pino Caterini .25 .50
3 Rich Chittley .25 .50
4 S. Hutchings .25 .50
5 Jim Italiano .25 .50
6 Scott Kyle .25 .50
7 Stan Malecki .25 .50
8 Mike McHugh .25 .50
9 Jeff Ninham .25 .50
10 Brad Roberts .25 .50
11 Chris Roberts .25 .50
12 Bruce Shipley .25 .50
13 G. Stevenson .25 .50
14 Keith Taylor .25 .50
15 Mark Tonaj .25 .50
16 F. Warwick .25 .50
17 Pat Windsor .25 .50
18 Bill Zenette .25 .50
19 Fred LeBlanc PR .13 .25
20 John Taylor VP .13 .25
21 Management .13 .25
22 Ange Savelli CO .50 1.00

1975-76 Heroes Stand-Ups

COMPLETE SET (31) 125.00 250.00
1 Gerry Cheevers 6.00 12.00
2 Terry O'Reilly 3.00 6.00
3 Bobby Orr 25.00 50.00
4 Brad Park 4.00 8.00
5 Jean Ratelle 4.00 8.00
6 Andre Savard 2.50 5.00
7 Gregg Sheppard 2.50 5.00
8 Yvan Cournoyer 4.00 8.00
9 Guy Lafleur 10.00 20.00
10 Jacques Lemaire 4.00 8.00
11 Peter Mahovlich 2.50 5.00
12 Doug Risebrough 2.50 5.00
13 Larry Robinson 6.00 12.00
14 Billy Harris 2.50 5.00
15 Gerry Hart 2.50 5.00
16 Denis Potvin 6.00 12.00
17 Glenn Resch 4.00 8.00
18 Bryan Trottier 6.00 12.00
19 Ed Westfall 2.50 5.00
20 Bill Barber 4.00 8.00
21 Bobby Clarke 6.00 12.00
22 Reggie Leach 2.50 5.00
23 Rick MacLeish 2.50 5.00
24 Bernie Parent 6.00 12.00
25 Dave Schultz 4.00 8.00
26 Lanny McDonald 4.00 8.00
27 Borje Salming 3.00 6.00
28 Darryl Sittler 4.00 8.00
29 Wayne Thomas 3.00 6.00
30 Errol Thompson 2.50 5.00
31 Tiger Williams 4.00 8.00

1992-93 High Liner Stanley Cup

COMPLETE SET (28) 16.00 40.00
1 Montreal AAA .40 1.00
2 Winnipeg Victorias .40 1.00
3 Montreal Victorias .40 1.00
4 Montreal Shamrocks .40 1.00
5 Ottawa Silver Seven .40 1.00
6 Kenora Thistles .40 1.00
7 Montreal Wanderers 1.00 2.50
8 Quebec Bulldogs .40 1.00
9 Toronto Blueshirts 1.00 2.50
10 Vancouver Millionaires 1.00 2.50
11 Seattle Metropolitans 1.00 2.50
12 Toronto Arenas 1.00 2.50
13 Toronto St. Patricks 1.00 2.50
14 Victoria Cougars .40 1.00
15 Ottawa Senators .40 1.00
16 Montreal Maroons 1.00 2.50
17 New York Rangers .40 1.00
18 Detroit Red Wings 1.25 3.00
19 Montreal Canadiens 1.50 4.00
20 Chicago Blackhawks .40 1.00
21 Toronto Maple Leafs 1.25 3.00
22 Boston Bruins 1.25 3.00
23 Philadelphia Flyers .40 1.00
24 New York Islanders .40 1.00
25 Edmonton Oilers 2.00 5.00
26 Calgary Flames .40 1.00
27 Pittsburgh Penguins 1.00 2.50
28 Checklist Card .40 1.00

1993-94 High Liner Greatest Goalies

COMPLETE SET (15) 8.00 20.00
1 Patrick Roy 3.00 8.00
2 Ed Belfour .60 1.50
3 Grant Fuhr .40 1.00
4 Ron Hextall .40 1.00
5 John Vanbiesbrouck New .40 1.00
6 Tom Barrasso .40 1.00
7 Bernie Parent .40 1.00
8 Tony Esposito .60 1.50
9 Johnny Bower .60 1.50
10 Jacques Plante 1.00 2.50
11 Terry Sawchuk 1.00 2.50
12 Bill Durnan .40 1.00
13 Felix Potvin Toronto Ma .75 2.00
14 The Evolution of the Goalie Mask 1.00 2.50
15 Vezina Trophy Checklist .40 1.00

1992 High-5 Previews

P1 Ray Bourque 1.25 3.00
P2 Brett Hull 1.25 3.00
P3 Wayne Gretzky 5.00 12.00
P4 Mark Messier 1.50 4.00
P5 Mario Lemieux 3.00 8.00
P6 Ed Belfour DP .75 2.00
P6A Ed Belfour AU/1500 5.00 12.00

1997 Highland Mint Legends Mint-Cards

1 Gordie Howe 95 S/1000 175.00 250.00
2 Gordie Howe 95 B/5000 20.00 50.00
3 Bobby Orr 95 S/1000 150.00 225.00
4 Bobby Orr 95 B/5000 20.00 50.00

1997 Highland Mint Magnum Series Medallions

1 Colorado Avalanche S/250 150.00 200.00
2 Colorado Avalanche B/1000 25.00 50.00

1997 Highland Mint Mint-Cards Pinnacle/Score

1 Martin Brodeur 95 S/250 150.00 225.00
2 Martin Brodeur 95 B/1500 25.00 60.00
3 Alexandre Daigle 94 S/250 150.00 200.00
4 Alexandre Daigle 94 B/1500 20.00 50.00
5 Jaromir Jagr 94 S/500 150.00 200.00
6 Jaromir Jagr 94 B/2500 25.00 60.00
7 Paul Kariya 94 S/250 150.00 225.00
8 Paul Kariya 94 B/1500 25.00 60.00
9 Pat LaFontaine 93 S/250 150.00 225.00
10 Pat LaFontaine 93 B/1500 20.00 50.00
11 Cam Neely 95 S/250 150.00 225.00
12 Cam Neely 95 B/1500 20.00 50.00
13 Jeremy Roenick 94 S/500 150.00 225.00
14 Jeremy Roenick 94 B/2500 20.00 50.00

1997 Highland Mint Mint-Cards Topps

1 Ray Bourque 80 S/128 150.00 250.00
2 Ray Bourque 80 B/634 25.00 60.00
3 Pavel Bure 92 S/414 150.00 225.00
4 Pavel Bure 92 B/1519 20.00 50.00
5 Sergei Fedorov 91 S/208 150.00 250.00
6 Sergei Fedorov 91 B/914 25.00 60.00
7 Doug Gilmour 85 S/101 150.00 250.00
8 Doug Gilmour 85 B/461 20.00 50.00
9 Wayne Gretzky 79 S/1000 200.00 350.00
10 Wayne Gretzky 79 B/5000 40.00 100.00
11 Bobby Hull 95 S/500 150.00 225.00
12 Bobby Hull 95 B/2500 20.00 50.00
13 Brett Hull 88 S/500 150.00 225.00
14 Brett Hull 88 B/1202 20.00 50.00
15 Mario Lemieux 85 S/999 200.00 350.00
16 Mario Lemieux 85 B/3557 25.00 60.00
17 Eric Lindros 92 S/694 150.00 250.00
18 Eric Lindros 92 B/2668 25.00 60.00
19 Mark Messier 84 S/280 150.00 225.00
20 Mark Messier 84 B/1034 20.00 50.00
21 Felix Potvin 92 S/210 150.00 225.00
22 Felix Potvin 92 B/902 20.00 50.00
23 Patrick Roy 86 S/500 150.00 250.00
24 Patrick Roy 86 B/1986 25.00 60.00
25 Teemu Selanne 92 S/131 150.00 225.00
26 Teemu Selanne 92 B/537 20.00 50.00
27 Steve Yzerman 84 S/233 150.00 225.00
28 Steve Yzerman 84 B/926 30.00 60.00

1997 Highland Mint Mint-Coins

1 Ray Bourque S/5000 35.00 50.00
2 Pavel Bure S/5000 35.00 50.00
3 Sergei Fedorov S/5000 35.00 50.00
4 Brett Hull S/5000 35.00 50.00
5 Jaromir Jagr S/5000 35.00 50.00
6 Mario Lemieux Gold Sig./1000 35.00 60.00
7 Mario Lemieux S/5000 35.00 50.00
8 Mario Lemieux B/25000 5.00 12.00
9 Eric Lindros Gold Sig./1000 35.00 60.00
10 Eric Lindros S/5000 35.00 50.00
11 Bobby Orr S/5000 35.00 50.00
12 B.Orr R.Bourque S/500 35.00 50.00
13 Chris Osgood S/5000 35.00 50.00
14 Patrick Roy S/5000 35.00 50.00
15 Teemu Selanne S/5000 35.00 50.00
16 John Vanbiesbrouck S/5000 35.00 50.00
17 Steve Yzerman S/5000 35.00 50.00

1997 Highland Mint Sandblast Mint-Cards

1 Mario Lemieux 96 S/250 175.00 250.00
2 Mario Lemieux 96 B/1500 25.00 60.00

1994 Hockey Wit

COMPLETE SET (108) 8.00 20.00
1 Mike Richter New York R .07 .20
2 Tony Amonte .07 .20
3 Patrick Roy Montreal Ca 1.25 3.00
4 Craig Janney .02 .10
5 Adam Oates Boston Bruin .07 .20
6 Geoff Sanderson .07 .20
7 Pavel Bure .60 1.50
8 Steve Duchesne .02 .10
9 Gordie Howe .75 2.00
10 Brad Park .07 .20
11 Brian Bellows .02 .10
12 Chris Chelios Chicago B .20 .50
13 Bill Barber .07 .20
14 Gump Worsley .07 .20
15 The Stanley Cup .07 .20
16 Maurice Richard .20 .50
17 Kevin Hatcher .02 .10
18 Ed Belfour Chicago Blac .20 .50
19 Kirk Muller .07 .20
20 Kevin Stevens Pittsburg .07 .20
21 Dave Taylor .02 .10
22 Dale Hawerchuk .08 .25
23 Jean Beliveau .08 .25
24 Rogatien Vachon .07 .20
25 Tom Barrasso .07 .20
26 Rod Langway .02 .10
27 Pierre Turgeon .08 .25
28 Derek King .02 .10
29 Brendan Shanahan St. Lo .40 1.00
30 Darren Turcotte .02 .10
31 Chris Terreri .02 .10
32 Tony Granato .02 .10
33 Michel Goulet .02 .10
34 Felix Potvin .15 .40
35 Curtis Joseph St. Louis .30 .75
36 Cam Neely .08 .25
37 Borje Salming .07 .20
38 Denis Savard .07 .20
39 Stan Mikita Chicago Bla .08 .25
40 Grant Fuhr .07 .20
41 Gary Suter .02 .10
42 Serge Savard .02 .10
43 Steve Larmer .07 .20
44 Bryan Trottier .08 .25
45 Mike Vernon Calgary Fla .07 .20
46 Paul Coffey Detroit Red .08 .25
47 Bernie Federko .02 .10
48 Larry Murphy .07 .20
49 Scotty Bowman CO .08 .25
50 Glenn Anderson .02 .10
51 Mats Sundin Quebec Nord .20 .50
52 Henri Richard .08 .25
53 Ron Francis Pittsburgh .08 .25
54 Scott Niedermayer .07 .20
55 Teemu Selanne Winnipeg .40 1.00
56 Frank Mahovlich .08 .25
57 Owen Nolan Quebec Nordi .07 .20
58 Rick Tocchet Pittsburgh .07 .20
59 Rod Brind'Amour Philade .07 .20
60 Mike Modano .08 .25
61 Doug Gilmour Toronto Ma .08 .25
62 Jimmy Carson .02 .10
63 Mike Keane .02 .10
64 Bernie Nicholls .07 .20
65 Scott Stevens .07 .20
66 Mario Lemieux Pittsburg 1.25 3.00
67 Keith Primeau Detroit R .08 .25
68 Bobby Carpenter .02 .10
69 Sergei Fedorov Detroit .40 1.00
70 Peter Stastny .07 .20
71 Brian Leetch New York R .08 .25
72 Vincent Damphousse .07 .20
73 Darryl Sitter .07 .20
74 Al Iafrate .07 .20
75 Alexander Mogilny .07 .20
76 Bill Ranford Edmonton O .08 .25
77 Ray Bourque Boston .30 .75
78 Joey Mullen Pittsburgh .02 .10
79 Mike Ricci .07 .20
80 Bobby Clarke .08 .25
81 Gerry Cheevers .07 .20
82 Joe Nieuwendyk .07 .20
83 Terry Sawchuk Detroit R .08 .25
84 Ray Ferraro .02 .10
85 Lanny McDonald .07 .20
86 Adam Graves .07 .20
87 Tomas Sandstrom

Los Ang .02 .10
88 Eric Lindros
Philadelph .60 1.50
89 Jari Kurri .08 .25
90 Al MacInnis .07 .20
91 Alexandre Daigle
Ottawa .02 .10
92 Larry Robinson .08 .25
93 Kelly Hrudey .07 .20
94 Theo Fleury
Calgary .08 .25
95 Billy Smith .07 .20
96 Luc Robitaille
Los Ange .08 .25
97 Brett Hull
St. Louis Bl .30 .75
98 Pat Falloon .07 .20
99 Wayne Gretzky
Los Angel 1.50 4.00
100 Joe Sakic
Quebec Nordiq .40 1.00
101 Phil Housley .07 .20
102 Mark Messier .20 .50
103 Jeremy Roenick .08 .25
104 Mark Recchi
Philadelphi .08 .25
105 Pat LaFontaine
Buffalo .08 .25
106 Trevor Linden
Vancouver .07 .20
107 Jaromir Jagr
Pittsburgh .75 2.00
108 Steve Yzerman
Detroit R .75 2.00

1996-97 Hockey Greats Coins

COMPLETE SET (25) 30.00 75.00
*GOLD PLATED: 6X TO 15X SILVER
*GOLD CHELIOS: 1.5X TO 4X SILVER
1 Ed Belfour .40 1.00
2 Ray Bourque .50 1.25
3 Pavel Bure .60 1.50
4 Chris Chelios 5.00 12.00
5 Vincent Damphousse .30 .75
6 Sergei Fedorov .75 2.00
7 Theo Fleury .40 1.00
8 Doug Gilmour .40 1.00
9 Wayne Gretzky 2.50 6.00
10 Brett Hull .50 1.25
11 Jaromir Jagr .75 2.00
12 Paul Kariya .60 1.50
13 Mario Lemieux 1.50 4.00
14 Eric Lindros .75 2.00
15 Mark Messier .50 1.25
16 Alexander Mogilny .30 .75
17 Jeremy Roenick .40 1.00
18 Patrick Roy 1.50 4.00
19 Joe Sakic .60 1.50
20 Steve Yzerman 1.00 2.50
21 Sergei Berezin .20 .50
22 Jim Campbell .20 .50
23 Jarome Iginla .40 1.00
24 Rem Murray .20 .50
25 David Wilkie .20 .50
NNO Album 1.50 4.00

1924-25 Holland Creameries

COMPLETE SET (10) 1000.00 1500.00
1 Wally Fridfinson 60.00 150.00
2 Harold McMunn 60.00 150.00
3 Art Somers 60.00 150.00
4 Frank Woodall 60.00 150.00
5 Frank Frederickson 125.00 300.00
6 Bobby Benson 60.00 150.00
7 Harry Neal 60.00 150.00
8 Wally Byron 60.00 150.00
9 Connie Neil SP 300.00 500.00
10 J. Austman 60.00 150.00

2005-06 Hot Prospects

COMPLETE SET w/o SPs (100) 8.00 20.00
1 Joffrey Lupul .20 .50
2 Jean-Sebastien Giguere .30 .75
3 Teemu Selanne .60 1.50
4 Marian Hossa .30 .75
5 Ilya Kovalchuk .30 .75
6 Kari Lehtonen .25 .60
7 Patrice Bergeron .40 1.00
8 Brian Leetch .25 .60
9 Andrew Raycroft .25 .60
10 Glen Murray .25 .60
11 Ryan Miller .30 .75
12 Chris Drury .25 .60
13 Tim Connolly .20 .50
14 Jarome Iginla .40 1.00
15 Miikka Kiprusoff .30 .75
16 Mark Recchi .40 1.00
17 Eric Staal .40 1.00
18 Martin Gerber .25 .60
19 Doug Weight .30 .75
20 Erik Cole .20 .50
21 Nikolai Khabibulin .30 .75
22 Tuomo Ruutu .30 .75
23 Joe Sakic .60 1.50
24 Marek Svatos .25 .60
25 Milan Hejduk .25 .60
26 Alex Tanguay .30 .75
27 Jose Theodore .30 .75
28 Sergei Fedorov .50 1.25
29 Rick Nash .30 .75
30 Mike Modano .50 1.25
31 Marty Turco .30 .75
32 Brenden Morrow .25 .60
33 Steve Yzerman .75 2.00
34 Brendan Shanahan .30 .75
35 Pavel Datsyuk .50 1.25
36 Henrik Zetterberg .40 1.00
37 Nicklas Lidstrom .30 .75
38 Chris Pronger .30 .75
39 Shawn Horcoff .20 .50
40 Ryan Smyth .25 .60
41 Ales Hemsky .25 .60
42 Olli Jokinen .30 .75
43 Roberto Luongo .50 1.25
44 Nathan Horton .30 .75
45 Alexander Frolov .20 .50
46 Luc Robitaille .30 .75
47 Pavol Demitra .40 1.00
48 Jeremy Roenick .50 1.25
49 Marian Gaborik .30 .75
50 Manny Fernandez .20 .50
51 David Aebischer .25 .60
52 Saku Koivu .30 .75
53 Michael Ryder .25 .60
54 Mike Ribeiro .20 .50
55 Paul Kariya .30 .75
56 Tomas Vokoun .25 .60
57 Steve Sullivan .20 .50
58 Martin Brodeur .75 2.00
59 Patrik Elias .30 .75
60 Brian Gionta .20 .50
61 Scott Gomez .25 .60
62 Alexei Yashin .25 .60
63 Rick DiPietro .25 .60
64 Miroslav Satan .25 .60
65 Jaromir Jagr 1.00 2.50
66 Martin Straka .20 .50
67 Jason Spezza .30 .75
68 Dominik Hasek .50 1.25
69 Daniel Alfredsson .30 .75
70 Dany Heatley .25 .60
71 Peter Forsberg .60 1.50
72 Simon Gagne .30 .75
73 Keith Primeau .25 .60
74 Antero Niittymaki .25 .60
75 Curtis Joseph .40 1.00
76 Shane Doan .25 .60
77 Ladislav Nagy .20 .50
78 Mario Lemieux 1.25 3.00
79 Marc-Andre Fleury .60 1.50
80 Sergei Gonchar .20 .50
81 Ryan Malone .20 .50
82 Joe Thornton .50 1.25
83 Patrick Marleau .30 .75
84 Evgeni Nabokov .25 .60
85 Jonathan Cheechoo .25 .60
86 Barret Jackman .20 .50
87 Keith Tkachuk .30 .75
88 Vincent Lecavalier .30 .75
89 Brad Richards .30 .75
90 Vaclav Prospal .20 .50
91 Martin St. Louis .30 .75
92 Mats Sundin .30 .75
93 Ed Belfour .30 .75
94 Bryan McCabe .20 .50
95 Eric Lindros .50 1.25
96 Markus Naslund .30 .75
97 Alexander Auld .20 .50
98 Todd Bertuzzi .30 .75
99 Brendan Morrison .20 .50
100 Olaf Kolzig .30 .75
101 Dustin Penner RC 3.00 8.00
102 Zenon Konopka RC 2.00 5.00
103 Michael Wall RC 2.50 6.00
104 Brian Eklund RC 2.50 6.00
105 Jay Leach RC 2.50 6.00
106 Eric Healey RC 2.50 6.00
107 Ben Guite RC 2.50 6.00
108 Nathan Paetsch RC 2.50 6.00
109 Jiri Novotny RC 2.50 6.00
110 Richie Regehr RC 2.00 5.00
111 Mark Giordano RC 4.00 10.00
112 Chad Larose RC 2.00 5.00
113 Keith Aucoin RC 2.00 5.00
114 David Gove RC 2.50 6.00
115 Cam Barker RC 2.50 6.00
116 Corey Crawford RC 10.00 20.00
117 Martin St. Pierre RC 2.00 5.00
118 Mark Cullen RC 2.50 6.00
119 James Wisniewski RC 2.50 6.00
120 Vitaly Kolesnik RC 2.50 6.00
121 Steven Goertzen RC 2.00 5.00
122 Joakim Lindstrom RC 2.00 5.00
123 Andrew Penner RC 2.50 6.00
124 Geoff Platt RC 2.50 6.00
125 Junior Lessard RC 2.00 5.00
126 Vojtech Polak RC 2.00 5.00
127 Kyle Brodziak RC 2.00 5.00
128 Matt Greene RC 2.00 5.00
129 Danny Syvret RC 2.00 5.00
130 Adam Hauser RC 2.50 6.00
131 J-F Jacques RC 2.00 5.00
132 Mathieu Roy RC 3.00 8.00
133 Petr Taticek RC 2.50 6.00
134 Greg Jacina RC 2.00 5.00
135 Rob Globke RC 2.00 5.00
136 Yanick Lehoux RC 3.00 8.00
137 Petr Kanko RC 2.50 6.00
138 Jeff Giuliano RC 2.50 6.00
139 Matt Ryan RC 2.50 6.00
140 Connor James RC 2.50 6.00
141 Richard Petiot RC 2.50 6.00
142 J-P Cote RC 2.00 5.00
143 Mark Streit RC 2.00 5.00
144 Jonathan Ferland RC 2.50 6.00
145 Kevin Klein RC 2.00 5.00
146 Pekka Rinne RC 5.00 12.00
147 Greg Zanon RC 2.50 6.00
148 Jason Ryznar RC 2.00 5.00
149 Cam Janssen RC 2.50 6.00
150 Bruno Gervais RC 2.00 5.00
151 Kevin Colley RC 2.50 6.00
152 Petr Prucha RC 3.00 8.00
153 Brandon Bochenski RC 3.00 8.00
154 Brian McGrattan RC 2.00 5.00
155 Stefan Ruzicka RC 2.00 5.00
156 Wade Skolney RC 2.00 5.00
157 Ryan Ready RC 2.50 6.00
158 Josh Gratton RC 2.50 6.00
159 Alexandre Picard RC 2.00 5.00
160 Matt Jones RC 2.00 5.00
161 Colby Armstrong RC 3.00 8.00
162 Doug Murray RC 2.00 5.00
163 Grant Stevenson RC 2.00 5.00
164 Dennis Wideman RC 2.00 5.00
165 Andy Roach RC 2.00 5.00
166 Colin Hemingway RC 2.00 5.00
167 Chris Beckford-Tseu RC 2.50 6.00
168 Jon DiSalvatore RC 2.50 6.00
169 Mike Glumac RC 2.50 6.00
170 Gerald Coleman RC 2.00 5.00
171 Nick Tarnasky RC 2.00 5.00
172 Paul Ranger RC 2.00 5.00
173 Darren Reid RC 2.00 5.00
174 Doug O'Brien RC 2.00 5.00
175 Chris Holt RC 2.00 5.00
176 Jay Harrison RC 2.50 6.00
177 Staffan Kronwall RC 2.00 5.00
178 Tomas Mojzis RC 2.00 5.00
179 Rob McVicar RC 2.50 6.00
180 Rick Rypien RC 4.00 10.00
181 Alexandre Burrows RC 4.00 10.00
182 Prestin Ryan RC 1.50 4.00
183 Mike Green RC 4.00 10.00
184 David Steckel RC 2.50 6.00
185 Joey Tenute RC 2.50 6.00
186 Louis Robitaille RC 2.00 5.00
187 Jim Slater AU RC 4.00 10.00
188 Adam Berkhoel AU RC 4.00 10.00
189 Jordan Sigalet AU RC 3.00 8.00
190 Ben Walter AU RC 3.00 8.00
191 Chris Thorburn AU RC 4.00 10.00
192 Niklas Nordgren AU RC 5.00 12.00
193 Danny Richmond AU RC 3.00 8.00
194 Rene Bourque AU RC 5.00 12.00
195 Duncan Keith AU RC 15.00 40.00
196 Jaroslav Balastik AU RC 3.00 8.00
197 Ole-Kristian Tollefsen AU RC 4.00 10.00
198 Alexandre Picard AU RC 3.00 8.00
199 Brett Lebda AU RC 3.00 8.00
200 Kyle Quincey AU RC 4.00 10.00
201 George Parros AU RC 3.00 8.00
202 Matt Foy AU RC 3.00 8.00
203 Derek Boogaard AU RC 8.00 20.00
204 Maxim Lapierre AU RC 5.00 12.00
205 Chris Campoli AU RC 3.00 8.00
206 Ryan Hollweg AU RC 3.00 8.00
207 Patrick Eaves AU RC 5.00 12.00
208 Christoph Schubert AU RC 3.00 8.00
209 Erik Christensen AU RC 3.00 8.00
210 Dimitri Patzold AU RC 3.00 8.00
211 Josh Gorges AU RC 4.00 10.00
212 Ryane Clowe AU RC 6.00 15.00
213 Jay McClement AU RC 3.00 8.00
214 Lee Stempniak AU RC 5.00 12.00
215 Kevin Dallman AU RC 4.00 10.00
216 Andrew Wozniewski AU RC 4.00 10.00
217 C.Perry JSY AU RC 12.00 30.00
218 R.Getzlaf JSY AU RC 15.00 40.00
219 B.Coburn JSY AU RC 8.00 20.00
220 Andrew Alberts JSY AU RC 5.00 12.00
221 H.Toivonen JSY AU RC 8.00 20.00
222 Milan Jurcina JSY AU RC 6.00 15.00
223 Daniel Paille JSY AU RC 8.00 20.00
224 T.Vanek JSY AU RC 15.00 40.00
225 Eric Nystrom JSY AU RC 6.00 15.00
226 A.Ladd JSY AU RC 10.00 25.00
227 Cam Ward JSY AU RC 12.00 30.00
228 K.Nastiuk JSY AU RC 5.00 12.00
229 B.Seabrook JSY AU RC 15.00 40.00
230 Brad Richardson JSY AU RC 8.00 20.00
231 P.Budaj JSY AU RC 10.00 25.00
232 W.Wolski JSY AU RC 6.00 15.00
233 G.Brule JSY AU RC 12.00 30.00
234 J.Jokinen JSY AU RC 8.00 20.00
235 J.Howard JSY AU RC 20.00 50.00
236 Johan Franzen JSY AU RC 12.00 30.00
238 Brad Winchester JSY AU RC 8.00 20.00
239 A.Stewart JSY AU RC 6.00 15.00
240 R.Olesz JSY AU RC 6.00 15.00
241 Jeff Tambellini JSY AU RC 5.00 12.00
242 M.Koivu JSY AU RC 10.00 25.00
243 A.Perezhogin JSY AU RC 6.00 15.00
244 A.Kostitsyn JSY AU RC 15.00 40.00
245 Y.Danis JSY AU RC 6.00 15.00
246 Raitis Ivanans JSY AU RC 5.00 12.00
247 Ryan Suter JSY AU RC 10.00 25.00
248 Barry Tallackson JSY AU RC 6.00 15.00
249 Z.Parise JSY AU RC 25.00 50.00
250 Jeremy Colliton JSY AU RC 5.00 12.00
251 Petteri Nokelainen JSY AU RC 5.00 12.00
252 Robert Nilsson JSY AU RC 8.00 20.00
253 A.Montoya JSY AU RC 8.00 20.00
254 H.Lundqvist JSY AU RC 60.00 150.00
255 A.Meszaros JSY AU RC 6.00 15.00
256 Ben Eager JSY AU RC 6.00 15.00
257 Jeff Carter JSY AU RC 12.00 30.00
258 M.Richards JSY AU RC 15.00 40.00
259 R.J. Umberger JSY AU RC 8.00 20.00
260 D.LeNeveu JSY AU RC 10.00 25.00
261 Keith Ballard JSY AU RC 6.00 15.00
262 Maxime Talbot JSY AU RC 8.00 20.00
263 Ryan Whitney JSY AU RC 8.00 20.00
264 Steve Bernier AU RC 8.00 20.00
265 Jeff Hoggan JSY AU RC 5.00 12.00
266 Jeff Woywitka JSY AU RC 5.00 12.00
267 Timo Helbling JSY AU RC 5.00 12.00
268 E.Artyukhin JSY AU RC 6.00 15.00
269 Ryan Craig JSY AU RC 5.00 12.00
270 A.Steen JSY AU RC 15.00 40.00
271 Kevin Bieksa JSY AU RC 12.00 30.00
272 Jakub Klepis JSY AU RC 5.00 12.00
273 T.Fleischmann JSY AU RC 8.00 20.00
274 D.Phaneuf JSY AU RC 25.00 60.00
275 A. Ovechkin JSY AU RC 1000.00 2500.00
276 S. Crosby JSY AU RC 350.00 600.00

2005-06 Hot Prospects Hot Materials

HMAA Andrew Alberts 1.50 4.00
HMAH Adam Hall 1.50 4.00
HMAK Andrei Kostitsyn 3.00 8.00
HMAL Andrew Ladd 3.00 8.00
HMAM Andrej Meszaros 2.00 5.00
HMAO Alexander Ovechkin 80.00 200.00
HMAP Alexander Perezhogin 2.00 5.00
HMAS Anthony Stewart 2.00 5.00
HMBC Braydon Coburn 2.50 6.00
HMBE Ben Eager 2.00 5.00
HMBG Bill Guerin 2.50 6.00
HMBI Kevin Bieksa 4.00 10.00
HMBR Brad Richardson 2.50 6.00
HMBS Brent Seabrook 5.00 12.00
HMBT Barry Tallackson 2.00 5.00
HMBW Brad Winchester 2.50 6.00
HMCA Carlo Colaiacovo 1.50 4.00
HMCC Chris Campoli 1.50 4.00
HMCO Jeremy Colliton 1.50 4.00
HMCP Corey Perry 8.00 20.00
HMCS Christoph Schubert 1.50 4.00
HMCT Chris Thorburn 2.00 5.00
HMCW Cam Ward 4.00 10.00
HMDB Derek Boogaard 4.00 10.00
HMDH Dan Hamhuis 2.00 5.00
HMDK Duncan Keith 5.00 12.00
HMDL David Legwand 2.00 5.00
HMDP Dimitri Patzold 1.50 4.00
HMDR Danny Richmond 1.50 4.00
HMEA Evgeny Artyukhin 2.00 5.00
HMEC Erik Christensen 1.50 4.00
HMEN Eric Nystrom 2.00 5.00
HMFP Fernando Pisani 1.50 4.00
HMGB Gilbert Brule 2.50 6.00
HMGP George Parros 1.50 4.00
HMHL Henrik Lundqvist 12.00 30.00
HMHT Hannu Toivonen 2.50 6.00
HMJB Jaroslav Balastik 1.50 4.00
HMJC Jeff Carter 4.00 10.00
HMJF Johan Franzen 4.00 10.00
HMJH Jim Howard 6.00 15.00
HMJJ Jussi Jokinen 2.50 6.00
HMJK Jakub Klepis 1.50 4.00
HMJS Jim Slater 2.00 5.00
HMJT Jeff Tambellini 1.50 4.00
HMJW Jeff Woywitka 1.50 4.00
HMKB Keith Ballard 2.00 5.00
HMKD Kevin Dallman 2.00 5.00
HMKI Jason King 1.50 4.00
HMKN Kevin Nastiuk 1.50 4.00
HMKQ Kyle Quincey 2.00 5.00
HMLE David Leneveu 2.00 5.00
HMLS Lee Stempniak 2.50 6.00
HMMC Mike Cammalleri 2.50 6.00
HMMF Matt Foy 1.50 4.00
HMMG Martin Gerber 2.00 5.00
HMMJ Milan Jurcina 2.00 5.00
HMMK Mikko Koivu 3.00 8.00
HMML Maxim Lapierre 2.50 6.00
HMMO Al Montoya 2.50 6.00
HMMR Mike Richards 5.00 12.00
HMMT Maxime Talbot 2.50 6.00
HMNN Niklas Nordgren 2.50 6.00
HMOT Ole-Kristian Tollefsen 2.00 5.00
HMPA Daniel Paille 2.50 6.00
HMPB Peter Budaj 3.00 8.00
HMPH Dion Phaneuf 4.00 10.00
HMPN Petteri Nokelainen 1.50 4.00
HMPS Patrik Stefan 1.50 4.00
HMRC Ryan Craig 1.50 4.00
HMRG Ryan Getzlaf 6.00 15.00
HMRI Raitis Ivanans 1.50 4.00
HMRN Robert Nilsson 2.50 6.00
HMRO Rostislav Olesz 2.00 5.00
HMRS Ryan Suter 3.00 8.00
HMRU R.J. Umberger 2.50 6.00
HMRW Ryan Whitney 2.50 6.00
HMSA Philippe Sauve 2.00 5.00
HMSB Steve Bernier 2.50 6.00
HMSC Sidney Crosby 40.00 100.00
HMSI Jordan Sigalet 1.50 4.00
HMST Alexander Steen 4.00 10.00
HMTF Tomas Fleischmann 2.50 6.00
HMTH Timo Helbling 1.50 4.00
HMTV Thomas Vanek 5.00 12.00
HMVF Valtteri Filppula 3.00 8.00
HMWI Brendan Witt 1.50 4.00
HMWW Wojtek Wolski 2.00 5.00
HMYD Yann Danis 2.00 5.00
HMZP Zach Parise 6.00 15.00

2005-06 Hot Prospects Red Hot

*VETS 1-100: 5X TO 12X BASIC CARDS
*ROOKIES 101-186: .8X TO 2X RC/1999
*ROOKIE AU 187-216: .8X TO 2X AU RC
*RK.JSY AU: .6X TO 1.5X JSY AU/349
*RK.JSY AU: .5X TO 1.2X JSY AU/199
275 A. Ovechkin JSY AU 1200.00 3000.00
276 Sidney Crosby JSY AU 350.00 500.00

2006-07 Hot Prospects

COMP.SET w/o SPs (100) 12.00 30.00
1 Chris Pronger .30 .75
2 Jean-Sebastien Giguere .30 .75
3 Teemu Selanne .60 1.50
4 Ilya Kovalchuk .30 .75
5 Marian Hossa .30 .75
6 Kari Lehtonen .25 .60
7 Patrice Bergeron .40 1.00
8 Hannu Toivonen .25 .60
9 Zdeno Chara .30 .75
10 Brad Boyes .20 .50
11 Ryan Miller .30 .75
12 Thomas Vanek .25 .60
13 Daniel Briere .30 .75
14 Maxim Afinogenov .20 .50
15 Jarome Iginla .40 1.00
16 Dion Phaneuf .25 .60
17 Alex Tanguay .20 .50
18 Miikka Kiprusoff .30 .75
19 Eric Staal .40 1.00
20 Cam Ward .30 .75
21 Rod Brind`Amour .30 .75
22 Tuomo Ruutu .30 .75
23 Nikolai Khabibulin .30 .75
24 Martin Havlat .20 .50
25 Joe Sakic .60 1.50
26 Jose Theodore .30 .75
27 Milan Hejduk .25 .60
28 Marek Svatos .20 .50
29 Rick Nash .30 .75
30 Sergei Fedorov .50 1.25
31 Pascal LeClaire .25 .60
32 Nikolai Zherdev .20 .50
33 Mike Modano .50 1.25
34 Eric Lindros .50 1.25
35 Marty Turco .30 .75
36 Pavel Datsyuk .50 1.25
37 Dominik Hasek .50 1.25
38 Nicklas Lidstrom .30 .75
39 Henrik Zetterberg .40 1.00
40 Ryan Smyth .25 .60
41 Ales Hemsky .25 .60
42 Dwayne Roloson .25 .60
43 Ed Belfour .30 .75
44 Todd Bertuzzi .30 .75
45 Olli Jokinen .30 .75
46 Rob Blake .30 .75
47 Alexander Frolov .20 .50
48 Marian Gaborik .30 .75
49 Manny Fernandez .20 .50
50 Pavol Demitra .40 1.00
51 Saku Koivu .30 .75
52 Cristobal Huet .25 .60
53 Michael Ryder .20 .50
54 David Aebischer .25 .60
55 Paul Kariya .30 .75
56 Tomas Vokoun .25 .60
57 Martin Brodeur .75 2.00
58 Patrik Elias .30 .75
59 Brian Gionta .20 .50
60 Rick DiPietro .25 .60
61 Alexei Yashin .25 .60
62 Miroslav Satan .25 .60
63 Jaromir Jagr 1.00 2.50
64 Brendan Shanahan .30 .75
65 Henrik Lundqvist .75 2.00
66 Daniel Alfredsson .30 .75
67 Jason Spezza .30 .75
68 Dany Heatley .25 .60
69 Martin Gerber .25 .60
70 Peter Forsberg .60 1.50
71 Simon Gagne .30 .75
72 Jeff Carter .25 .60
73 Antero Niittymaki .25 .60
74 Shane Doan .25 .60
75 Jeremy Roenick .50 1.25
76 Curtis Joseph .40 1.00
77 Sidney Crosby 1.25 3.00
78 Marc-Andre Fleury .60 1.50
79 Mark Recchi .40 1.00
80 Doug Weight .30 .75
81 Manny Legace .25 .60
82 Keith Tkachuk .30 .75
83 Joe Thornton .50 1.25
84 Jonathan Cheechoo .25 .60
85 Patrick Marleau .30 .75
86 Vesa Toskala .25 .60
87 Vincent Lecavalier .30 .75
88 Brad Richards .30 .75
89 Martin St. Louis .30 .75
90 Mats Sundin .30 .75
91 Andrew Raycroft .25 .60
92 Alexander Steen .20 .50
93 Darcy Tucker .25 .60
94 Roberto Luongo .50 1.25
95 Markus Naslund .30 .75
96 Daniel Sedin .40 1.00
97 Henrik Sedin .40 1.00
98 Alexander Ovechkin 1.25 3.00
99 Olaf Kolzig .30 .75
100 Alexander Semin .30 .75
101 Ryan Shannon JSY AU RC 6.00 15.00
102 Shane O'Brien JSY AU RC 6.00 15.00
103 Yan Stastny JSY AU RC 6.00 15.00
104 Mark Stuart JSY AU RC 6.00 15.00
105 D.Stafford JSY AU RC/199 12.50 30.00
106 Dustin Boyd JSY AU RC 6.00 15.00
107 Dustin Byfuglien JSY AU RC 15.00 40.00
108 Paul Stastny JSY AU RC 10.00 25.00
109 Fredrik Norrena JSY AU RC 6.00 15.00
110 Filip Novak JSY AU RC 6.00 15.00
111 Loui Eriksson JSY AU RC 12.00 30.00
112 Tomas Kopecky JSY AU RC 8.00 20.00
113 M-A Pouliot JSY AU RC 6.00 15.00
114 Ladislav Smid JSY AU RC 6.00 15.00
115 Patrick Thoresen JSY AU RC 6.00 15.00
116 Patrick O'Sullivan JSY AU RC 10.00 25.00
117 Anze Kopitar JSY AU RC 15.00 40.00
118 Pushkarev JSY AU RC 8.00 20.00
119 G. Latendresse JSY AU RC 10.00 25.00
120 Shea Weber JSY AU RC 15.00 40.00
121 A. Radulov JSY AU RC 12.00 30.00
122 Travis Zajac JSY AU RC 12.00 30.00
123 Jarkko Immonen JSY AU RC 8.00 20.00
124 Nigel Dawes JSY AU RC 6.00 15.00
125 Ryan Potulny JSY AU RC 6.00 15.00
126 Benoit Pouliot JSY AU RC 8.00 20.00
127 Keith Yandle JSY AU RC 15.00 40.00
128 Noah Welch JSY AU RC 6.00 15.00
129 Kristopher Letang JSY AU RC 25.00 60.00
130 Michel Ouellet JSY AU RC 8.00 20.00
131 Matt Carle JSY AU RC 6.00 15.00
132 M-E Vlasic JSY AU RC 10.00 25.00
133 Marek Schwarz JSY AU RC 10.00 25.00
134 Roman Polak JSY AU RC 8.00 20.00
135 Ben Ondrus JSY AU RC 6.00 15.00
136 Brendan Bell JSY AU RC 6.00 15.00
137 Ian White JSY AU RC 8.00 20.00
138 Jeremy Williams JSY AU RC 6.00 15.00
139 Eric Fehr JSY AU RC 10.00 25.00
140 J. Staal JSY AU RC/199 12.00 30.00
141 P. Kessel JSY AU RC/199 30.00 80.00
142 E. Malkin JSY AU RC/199 100.00 200.00
143 David McKee RC 2.50 6.00
144 Mike Brown RC 2.50 6.00
145 Matt Lashoff RC 2.50 6.00
146 Nate Thompson RC 2.50 6.00
147 Mike Card RC 2.50 6.00
148 Adam Dennis RC 2.50 6.00
149 Michael Funk RC 2.50 6.00
150 Michael Ryan RC 2.50 6.00
151 Brandon Prust RC 2.50 6.00
152 Adam Burish RC 4.00 10.00
153 Michael Blunden RC 2.50 6.00
154 Dave Bolland RC 4.00 10.00
155 Stefan Liv RC 2.50 6.00
156 Alexei Mikhnov RC 2.50 6.00
157 Jan Hejda RC 2.50 6.00
158 Jeff Drouin-Deslauriers RC 2.50 6.00
159 Drew Larman RC 2.50 6.00
160 Janis Sprukts RC 2.50 6.00
161 David Booth RC 3.00 8.00
162 Peter Harrold RC 2.50 6.00
163 Benoit Pouliot RC 3.00 8.00
164 Niklas Backstrom RC 5.00 12.00
165 Miroslav Kopriva RC 2.50 6.00
166 Mikko Lehtonen RC 3.00 8.00
167 John Oduya RC 4.00 10.00
168 Alex Brooks RC 2.50 6.00
169 Kelly Guard RC 3.00 8.00
170 Martin Houle RC 3.00 8.00
171 Jussi Timonen RC 3.00 8.00
172 Lars Jonsson RC 2.50 6.00
173 Triston Grant RC 2.50 6.00
174 Bill Thomas RC 2.50 6.00
175 Patrick Fischer RC 2.50 6.00
176 Joe Pavelski RC 12.00 30.00
177 D.J. King RC 2.50 6.00
178 Blair Jones RC 2.50 6.00
179 Jean-Francois Racine RC 3.00 8.00
180 Nathan McIver RC 2.50 6.00
181 Alexander Edler RC 4.00 10.00
182 Luc Bourdon RC 4.00 10.00
183 Patrick Coulombe RC 2.50 6.00
184 Jesse Schultz RC 2.50 6.00
185 Kyle Cumiskey RC 3.00 8.00
186 David Backes RC 10.00 25.00
187 Mikhail Grabovski RC 5.00 12.00
188 Daren Machesney RC 2.50 6.00
189 Enver Lisin RC 2.50 6.00
190 Tim Brent RC 3.00 8.00
191 Blake Comeau RC 4.00 10.00
192 Barry Brust RC 3.00 8.00
193 Karri Ramo RC 2.50 6.00
194 Kris Newbury RC 2.50 6.00
195 Kamil Kreps RC 2.50 6.00
196 Derek Meech RC 2.50 6.00
197 Andrej Sekera RC 3.00 8.00
198 Clarke MacArthur RC 3.00 8.00
199 Josh Hennessy RC 2.50 6.00
200 Niklas Grossman RC 4.00 10.00
201 Joel Perrault RC 2.50 6.00
202 Troy Brouwer RC 3.00 8.00

2006-07 Hot Prospects Red Hot

*1-100: 8X TO 20X BASE
*101-142: .5X TO 1.2X BASE
*143-184 NON-AU: .6X TO 1.5X BASE
*143-184 AU: .8X TO 2X BASE

2006-07 Hot Prospects Hot Materials

*RED HOT/100: .6X TO 1.5X BASIC JSY
*RED HOT/100: .5X TO 1.2X BASIC JSY SP
HMAE David Aebischer 2.50 6.00
HMAK Anze Kopitar 8.00 20.00
HMAO Alexander Ovechkin SP 10.00 25.00
HMAS Alexander Steen SP 2.50 6.00
HMBB Brandon Bochenski 2.00 5.00
HMBE Brendan Bell 2.00 5.00
HMBM Brenden Morrow 2.50 6.00
HMBO Ben Ondrus 2.00 5.00
HMBR Brad Boyes 2.00 5.00
HMBS Brendan Shanahan 4.00 10.00
HMBT Billy Thompson 2.00 5.00
HMCD Chris Drury 2.50 6.00
HMCJ Curtis Joseph 4.00 10.00
HMCP Corey Perry 5.00 12.00
HMCS Curtis Sanford 2.50 6.00
HMCW Cam Ward 3.00 8.00
HMDA Daniel Alfredsson 3.00 8.00
HMDH Dominik Hasek SP 6.00 15.00
HMDP Dion Phaneuf 2.50 6.00
HMDS Drew Stafford 2.50 6.00
HMEB Ed Belfour 3.00 8.00
HMEF Eric Fehr 2.50 6.00
HMEM Evgeni Malkin 8.00 20.00
HMES Eric Staal 4.00 10.00
HMGL Guillaume Latendresse 2.50 6.00
HMGM Glen Murray 2.50 6.00
HMGR Gary Roberts 2.00 5.00
HMHA Martin Havlat 2.00 5.00
HMHE Dany Heatley SP 3.00 8.00
HMHJ Milan Hejduk 2.50 6.00
HMHS Henrik Sedin 4.00 10.00
HMHT Hannu Toivonen 2.50 6.00
HMIG Jarome Iginla 4.00 10.00
HMIK Ilya Kovalchuk 3.00 8.00
HMIW Ian White 2.50 6.00
HMJB Jay Bouwmeester 2.00 5.00
HMJC Jeff Carter 2.50 6.00
HMJD J.P. Dumont 2.00 5.00
HMJI Jarkko Immonen 2.50 6.00
HMJJ Jaromir Jagr 10.00 25.00
HMJL Jere Lehtinen 2.00 5.00
HMJP Joni Pitkanen 2.00 5.00
HMJS Jarret Stoll 2.50 6.00
HMJT Joe Thornton 5.00 12.00
HMKL Kristopher Letang 6.00 15.00
HMKP Konstantin Pushkarev 2.50 6.00
HMKY Keith Yandle 4.00 10.00
HMLB Luc Bourdon 2.50 6.00
HMLE Loui Eriksson 3.00 8.00
HMLS Ladislav Smid 2.00 5.00
HMLU Joffrey Lupul 2.00 5.00
HMMB Martin Brodeur 8.00 20.00
HMMC Matt Carle 2.00 5.00
HMMG Marian Gaborik 3.00 8.00
HMMH Marian Hossa 3.00 8.00
HMMI Mike Grier 2.00 5.00
HMML Mario Lemieux 12.00 30.00
HMMM Mike Modano 5.00 12.00
HMMN Markus Naslund 3.00 8.00
HMMP Marc-Antoine Pouliot 2.00 5.00
HMMR Mark Recchi 4.00 10.00
HMMS Mark Stuart 2.00 5.00
HMMV Marc-Edouard Vlasic 3.00 8.00
HMND Nigel Dawes 2.00 5.00
HMNL Nicklas Lidstrom 3.00 8.00
HMNW Noah Welch 2.00 5.00
HMOK Olaf Kolzig 3.00 8.00
HMOS Patrick O'Sullivan 3.00 8.00
HMPA Patrick Thoresen 2.00 5.00
HMPB Patrice Bergeron 4.00 10.00
HMPE Michael Peca 2.50 6.00
HMPF Peter Forsberg 6.00 15.00
HMPK Phil Kessel 5.00 12.00
HMPM Patrick Marleau 3.00 8.00
HMPR Patrick Roy 8.00 20.00
HMPS Paul Stastny 4.00 10.00
HMPT Pierre Turgeon 2.50 6.00
HMRE Robert Esche 2.50 6.00
HMRI Brad Richards 3.00 8.00
HMRL Roberto Luongo 5.00 12.00
HMRN Rick Nash 3.00 8.00
HMRY Michael Ryder 2.00 5.00
HMSA Joe Sakic 6.00 15.00
HMSC Sidney Crosby SP 15.00 40.00
HMSD Shane Doan 2.50 6.00
HMSK Saku Koivu 3.00 8.00
HMSO Shane O'Brien 2.00 5.00
HMSP Jason Spezza 3.00 8.00
HMSS Sergei Samsonov 2.50 6.00
HMST Jordan Staal 4.00 10.00
HMSU Mats Sundin 3.00 8.00
HMSW Shea Weber 4.00 10.00
HMTH Tomas Holmstrom 2.50 6.00
HMTP Tom Poti 2.00 5.00
HMTS Teemu Selanne 6.00 15.00
HMTT Tim Thomas 3.00 8.00
HMTV Tomas Vokoun 2.50 6.00
HMTZ Travis Zajac 4.00 10.00
HMZC Zdeno Chara 3.00 8.00

2006-07 Hot Prospects Hotagraphs

HAF Alexander Frolov 5.00 12.00
HAK Anze Kopitar 25.00 60.00
HAR Andrew Raycroft 6.00 15.00
HBB Brendan Bell 5.00 12.00
HBE Patrice Bergeron 10.00 25.00
HBI Martin Biron 6.00 15.00
HBM Brenden Morrow 6.00 15.00
HBO Ben Ondrus 5.00 12.00
HBP Benoit Pouliot 6.00 15.00
HBR Brad Boyes 5.00 12.00
HBT Barry Tallackson 5.00 12.00
HCA Mike Cammalleri 5.00 12.00
HCH Chris Higgins 5.00 12.00
HCK Chris Kunitz 8.00 20.00
HCP Chris Phillips 5.00 12.00
HDA David Aebischer 6.00 15.00
HDK Duncan Keith 6.00 15.00
HDL David Leneveu 6.00 15.00
HDR Dwayne Roloson 6.00 15.00
HEF Eric Fehr 8.00 20.00
HEM Evgeni Malkin 30.00 60.00
HES Eric Staal 10.00 25.00
HFL Marc-Andre Fleury 15.00 40.00
HFN Filip Novak 5.00 12.00
HFP Fernando Pisani 5.00 12.00
HGB Gilbert Brule 6.00 15.00
HGL Guillaume Latendresse 8.00 20.00
HHA Martin Havlat 5.00 12.00
HHO Tomas Holmstrom 6.00 15.00
HHU Cristobal Huet 6.00 15.00
HIG Jarome Iginla 10.00 25.00
HIK Ilya Kovalchuk 8.00 20.00
HIW Ian White 6.00 15.00
HJB Jaroslav Balastik 5.00 12.00
HJC Jeff Carter 6.00 15.00
HJI Jarkko Immonen 6.00 15.00
HJL John-Michael Liles 5.00 12.00
HJO Jonathan Cheechoo 6.00 15.00
HJP Joni Pitkanen 5.00 12.00
HJS Jarret Stoll 6.00 15.00
HJT Joe Thornton 12.00 30.00
HJW Jeremy Williams 5.00 12.00
HKB Keith Ballard 5.00 12.00
HKC Kyle Calder 5.00 12.00
HKE Kevin Bieksa 6.00 15.00
HKL Kari Lehtonen 6.00 15.00
HKO Chuck Kobasew 5.00 12.00
HLE Loui Eriksson 10.00 25.00
HLN Ladislav Nagy 5.00 12.00
HLS Ladislav Smid 5.00 12.00
HMA Mark Stuart 5.00 12.00
HMB Martin Brodeur EXCH 20.00 50.00
HMC Matt Carle 5.00 12.00
HMF Matt Foy 5.00 12.00
HMH Marcel Hossa 5.00 12.00
HMI Michal Handzus 6.00 15.00
HMM Masi Marjamaki 5.00 12.00
HMO Michel Ouellet 6.00 15.00
HMP Marc-Antoine Pouliot 5.00 12.00
HMR Michael Ryder 5.00 12.00
HMS Marek Svatos 5.00 12.00
HMV Mike Van Ryn 5.00 12.00
HND Nigel Dawes 5.00 12.00
HNW Noah Welch 5.00 12.00
HNZ Nikolai Zherdev 5.00 12.00
HOT Ole-Kristian Tollefsen 5.00 12.00
HPA Patrik Elias 8.00 20.00
HPB Pierre-Marc Bouchard 8.00 20.00
HPE Michael Peca 6.00 15.00
HPK Phil Kessel EXCH 15.00 40.00
HPM Paul Mara 5.00 12.00
HPO Patrick O'Sullivan 8.00 20.00
HPP Petr Prucha 6.00 15.00
HPR Paul Ranger 5.00 12.00
HPS Paul Stastny 12.00 30.00
HRA Alexander Radulov 10.00 25.00
HRB Keith Yandle 12.00 30.00
HRE Robert Esche 6.00 15.00
HRK Rostislav Klesla 5.00 12.00
HRL Roberto Luongo 12.00 30.00
HRM Ryan Malone 5.00 12.00
HRP Roman Polak 6.00 15.00
HRS Ryan Shannon 5.00 12.00
HRY Ryan Potulny 5.00 12.00
HSC Sidney Crosby 75.00 150.00
HSG Scott Gomez 6.00 15.00
HSO Shane O'Brien 5.00 12.00
HST Jordan Staal 12.00 30.00
HSW Shea Weber 12.00 30.00
HTH Trent Hunter 5.00 12.00
HTK Tomas Kopecky 6.00 15.00
HTZ Travis Zajac 10.00 25.00
HVF Valtteri Filppula 5.00 12.00
HVL Vincent Lecavalier 8.00 20.00
HYS Yan Stastny 5.00 12.00
HZC Zdeno Chara 8.00 20.00

2007-08 Hot Prospects

COMP.SET w/o SP's (100) 15.00 40.00
1 Ales Hemsky .25 .60
2 Alex Tanguay .25 .60
3 Alexander Frolov .20 .50
4 Alexander Ovechkin 1.25 3.00
5 Alexander Radulov .30 .75
6 Alexander Semin .30 .75
7 Alexander Steen .20 .50
8 Anze Kopitar .50 1.25
9 Bill Guerin .30 .75
10 Brad Richards .30 .75
11 Brendan Shanahan .30 .75
12 Brian Gionta .20 .50
13 Cam Ward .30 .75
14 Chris Drury .25 .60
15 Chris Mason .25 .60
16 Corey Perry .50 1.25
17 Cristobal Huet .25 .60
18 Daniel Alfredsson .30 .75
19 Daniel Briere .30 .75
20 Daniel Sedin .40 1.00

Card	Low	High
21 Dany Heatley	.25	.60
22 Darcy Tucker	.25	.60
23 David Vyborny	.20	.50
24 Dion Phaneuf	.25	.60
25 Dominik Hasek	.50	1.25
26 Doug Weight	.30	.75
27 Drew Stafford	.20	.50
28 Dwayne Roloson	.25	.60
29 Eric Staal	.40	1.00
30 Evgeni Malkin	.60	1.50
31 Guillaume Latendresse	.25	.60
32 Henrik Lundqvist	.75	2.00
33 Henrik Sedin	.40	1.00
34 Henrik Zetterberg	.40	1.00
35 Ilya Kovalchuk	.30	.75
36 Jarome Iginla	.40	1.00
37 Jaromir Jagr	1.00	2.50
38 Jason Spezza	.30	.75
39 Jean-Sebastien Giguere	.30	.75
40 Jeff Carter	.25	.60
41 Joe Sakic	.60	1.50
42 Joe Thornton	.50	1.25
43 Jonathan Cheechoo	.25	.60
44 Joni Pitkanen	.20	.50
45 Jordan Staal	.25	.60
46 Justin Williams	.25	.60
47 Kari Lehtonen	.25	.60
48 Keith Tkachuk	.30	.75
49 Marc Savard	.20	.50
50 Marc-Andre Fleury	.60	1.50
51 Marian Gaborik	.30	.75
52 Marian Hossa	.30	.75
53 Markus Naslund	.30	.75
54 Martin Brodeur	.75	2.00
55 Tuomo Ruutu	.30	.75
56 Martin St. Louis	.30	.75
57 Marty Turco	.30	.75
58 Mats Sundin	.30	.75
59 Michael Ryder	.20	.50
60 Miikka Kiprusoff	.30	.75
61 Mike Modano	.50	1.25
62 Mike Ribeiro	.20	.50
63 Mikko Koivu	.25	.60
64 Milan Hejduk	.25	.60
65 Miroslav Satan	.25	.60
66 Nathan Horton	.30	.75
67 Nicklas Lidstrom	.30	.75
68 Niklas Backstrom	.30	.75
69 Nikolai Khabibulin	.30	.75
70 Olaf Kolzig	.30	.75
71 Olli Jokinen	.25	.60
72 Patrice Bergeron	.40	1.00
73 Patrick Marleau	.30	.75
74 Patrik Elias	.30	.75
75 Paul Kariya	.30	.75
76 Paul Stastny	.25	.60
77 Pavel Datsyuk	.50	1.25
78 Phil Kessel	.30	.75
79 Ray Emery	.25	.60
80 Rick DiPietro	.25	.60
81 Rick Nash	.30	.75
82 Rob Blake	.30	.75
83 Roberto Luongo	.50	1.25
84 Ryan Getzlaf	.30	.75
85 Ryan Miller	.30	.75
86 Ryan Smyth	.25	.60
87 Saku Koivu	.30	.75
88 Chris Pronger	.30	.75
89 Sergei Fedorov	.50	1.25
90 Sergei Samsonov	.25	.60
91 Shane Doan	.25	.60
92 Sidney Crosby	1.25	3.00
93 Simon Gagne	.30	.75
94 Steve Bernier	.20	.50
95 Jason Arnott	.25	.60
96 Thomas Vanek	.25	.60
97 Tomas Vokoun	.25	.60
98 Vesa Toskala	.25	.60
99 Vincent Lecavalier	.30	.75
100 Zach Parise	.30	.75
101 Alexander Ovechkin HC	6.00	15.00
102 Alexander Radulov HC	1.50	4.00
103 Alexander Semin HC	1.50	4.00
104 Anze Kopitar HC	2.50	6.00
105 Bobby Orr HC	6.00	15.00
106 Brendan Shanahan HC	1.50	4.00
107 Cam Ward HC	1.50	4.00
108 Daniel Briere HC	1.50	4.00
109 Dany Heatley HC	1.25	3.00
110 Dominik Hasek HC	2.50	6.00
111 Dwayne Roloson HC	1.25	3.00
112 Eric Staal HC	2.00	5.00
113 Evgeni Malkin HC	3.00	8.00
114 Gordie Howe HC	5.00	12.00
115 Henrik Lundqvist HC	4.00	10.00
116 Henrik Zetterberg HC	2.00	5.00
117 Ilya Kovalchuk HC	1.50	4.00
118 Jarome Iginla HC	2.00	5.00
119 Jaromir Jagr HC	5.00	12.00
120 Jason Spezza HC	1.50	4.00
121 Jean-Sebastien Giguere HC	1.50	4.00
122 Joe Sakic HC	3.00	8.00
123 Joe Thornton HC	2.50	6.00
124 Jonathan Cheechoo HC	1.25	3.00
125 Kari Lehtonen HC	1.25	3.00
126 Marc-Andre Fleury HC	3.00	8.00
127 Marian Gaborik HC	1.50	4.00
128 Marian Hossa HC	1.50	4.00
129 Mario Lemieux HC	6.00	15.00
130 Mark Messier HC	3.00	8.00
131 Markus Naslund HC	1.50	4.00
132 Martin Brodeur HC	4.00	10.00
133 Martin Havlat HC	1.50	4.00
134 Martin St. Louis HC	1.50	4.00
135 Marty Turco HC	1.50	4.00
136 Mats Sundin HC	1.50	4.00
137 Michael Ryder HC	1.00	2.50
138 Miikka Kiprusoff HC	1.50	4.00
139 Mike Modano HC	2.50	6.00
140 Nicklas Lidstrom HC	1.50	4.00
141 Patrice Bergeron HC	2.00	5.00
142 Patrick Marleau HC	1.50	4.00
143 Paul Kariya HC	1.50	4.00
144 Paul Stastny HC	1.25	3.00
145 Phil Kessel HC	1.50	4.00
146 Rick DiPietro HC	1.25	3.00
147 Rick Nash HC	1.50	4.00
148 Roberto Luongo HC	2.50	6.00
149 Ryan Getzlaf HC	1.50	4.00
150 Ryan Miller HC	1.50	4.00
151 Saku Koivu HC	1.50	4.00
152 Scott Niedermayer HC	1.50	4.00
153 Shane Doan HC	1.25	3.00
154 Sidney Crosby HC	6.00	15.00
155 Simon Gagne HC	1.50	4.00
156 Thomas Vanek HC	1.25	3.00
157 Tomas Vokoun HC	1.25	3.00
158 Vincent Lecavalier HC	1.50	4.00
159 Mark Recchi HC	2.00	5.00
160 Zach Parise HC	1.50	4.00
161 Mike Weber RC	2.50	6.00
162 Tyler Kennedy RC	2.50	6.00
163 Bryan Young RC	2.50	6.00
164 Cal Clutterbuck RC	4.00	10.00
165 Curtis Glencross RC	4.00	10.00
166 Daniel Carcillo RC	3.00	8.00
167 Magnus Johansson RC	2.50	6.00
168 Marc Methot RC	2.50	6.00
169 David Clarkson RC	2.50	6.00
170 Drew Fata RC	2.50	6.00
171 Duncan Milroy RC	2.50	6.00
172 Tobias Enstrom RC	4.00	10.00
173 Chris Bourque RC	3.00	8.00
174 Jeff Finger RC	2.50	6.00
175 Jeff Schultz RC	3.00	8.00
176 Joel Lundqvist RC	2.50	6.00
177 John Zeiler RC	2.50	6.00
178 Cory Murphy RC	2.50	6.00
179 Kent Huskins RC	2.50	6.00
180 Mark Fraser RC	2.50	6.00
181 Mark Mancari RC	2.50	6.00
182 Martin Lojek RC	2.50	6.00
183 Matt Keetley RC	2.50	6.00
184 Steve Wagner RC	2.50	6.00
185 Nathan Guenin RC	3.00	8.00
186 Ryan Carter RC	2.50	6.00
187 Petteri Wirtanen RC	2.50	6.00
188 Rod Pelley RC	2.50	6.00
189 David Moss RC	4.00	10.00
190 Matt Ellis RC	3.00	8.00
191 Sebastien Bisaillon RC	2.50	6.00
192 Daniel Winnik RC	3.00	8.00
193 Craig Weller RC	2.50	6.00
194 Tomas Plihal RC	2.50	6.00
195 Riley Cote RC	3.00	8.00
196 Brady Murray RC	2.50	6.00
197 Tomas Popperle RC	2.50	6.00
198 Tom Gilbert RC	3.00	8.00
199 Denis Tolpeko RC	2.50	6.00
200 Zach Stortini RC	2.50	6.00
201 B Ryan JSY AU RC	25.00	50.00
202 S Gagner JSY AU RC	6.00	15.00
203 N Bergfors JSY AU RC	6.00	15.00
204 J Bernier JSY AU RC	12.00	30.00
205 Bryan Little JSY AU RC	10.00	25.00
206 Kris Russell JSY AU RC	10.00	25.00
207 M Niskanen JSY AU RC	10.00	25.00
208 A Cogliano JSY AU RC	8.00	20.00
209 Nick Foligno JSY AU RC	12.00	30.00
210 B Sterling JSY AU RC	6.00	15.00
211 M Hanzal JSY AU RC	8.00	20.00
212 J Hlinka JSY AU RC	8.00	20.00
213 Matt Smaby JSY AU RC	6.00	15.00
214 Petr Kalus JSY AU RC	6.00	15.00
215 A Greene JSY AU RC	8.00	20.00
216 Frans Nielsen JSY AU RC	10.00	25.00
217 R Schremp JSY AU RC	8.00	20.00
218 J Sheppard JSY AU RC	6.00	15.00
219 K Chipchura JSY AU RC	8.00	20.00
220 R Parent JSY AU RC	6.00	15.00
221 D Krejci JSY AU RC	20.00	50.00
222 L Tukonen JSY AU RC	6.00	15.00
223 T Rask JSY AU RC	20.00	50.00
224 M Raymond JSY AU RC	10.00	25.00
225 B Dubinsky JSY AU RC	12.00	30.00
226 C McElhinney JSY AU RC	10.00	25.00
227 B Elliott JSY AU RC	12.00	30.00
228 Drew Miller JSY AU RC	8.00	20.00
229 R Callahan JSY AU RC	15.00	30.00
230 O Pavelec JSY AU RC	12.00	30.00
231 V Koistinen JSY AU RC	6.00	15.00
232 T Mitchell JSY AU RC	8.00	20.00
233 D Perron JSY AU RC	12.00	30.00
234 J Sigalet JSY AU RC	6.00	15.00
235 J Hansen JSY AU RC	8.00	20.00
236 J Halak JSY AU RC	15.00	40.00
237 D Setoguchi JSY AU RC	10.00	25.00
238 Milan Lucic JSY AU RC	25.00	60.00
239 L Kaspar JSY AU RC	6.00	15.00
240 T Weiman JSY AU RC	8.00	20.00
241 T Stephan JSY AU RC	8.00	20.00
242 D Girardi JSY AU RC	8.00	20.00
243 S Meyer JSY AU RC	8.00	20.00
244 Jared Boll JSY AU RC	8.00	20.00
245 Jiri Tlusty JSY AU RC	10.00	25.00
246 J Hiller JSY AU RC	12.00	30.00
247 T.J. Hensick JSY AU RC	8.00	20.00
248 A Stralman JSY AU RC	6.00	15.00
249 J Toews JSY AU/199 RC	80.00	200.00
250 C Price JSY AU/199 RC	60.00	150.00
251 P Mueller JSY AU/199 RC	12.00	30.00
252 P Kane JSY AU/199 RC	125.00	300.00
253 M Staal JSY AU/199 RC	15.00	40.00
254 N Backstrom JSY AU/199 RC	30.00	80.00
255 E Johnson JSY AU/199 RC	12.00	30.00
256 J Johnson JSY AU/199 RC	12.00	30.00

2007-08 Hot Prospects Red Hot

Card	Low	High
COMMON CARD (1-100)	4.00	10.00
SEMISTARS JSY	5.00	12.00
UNL.STARS JSY	6.00	15.00

*101-160 HC/100: .5X TO 1.2X BASIC HC
*161-200 PP/100: .5X TO 1.2X BASIC PP
*201-248 PP JSY AU/25: .5X TO 1.2X
*249-256 PP JSY AU/25: .6X TO 1.5X

Card	Low	High
4 Alexander Ovechkin JSY	25.00	60.00
8 Anze Kopitar JSY	10.00	25.00
21 Dany Heatley JSY	5.00	12.00
25 Dominik Hasek JSY	10.00	25.00
30 Evgeni Malkin JSY	15.00	40.00
32 Henrik Lundqvist JSY	15.00	40.00
34 Henrik Zetterberg JSY	8.00	20.00
36 Jarome Iginla JSY	8.00	20.00
37 Jaromir Jagr JSY	20.00	50.00
41 Joe Sakic JSY	12.00	30.00
42 Joe Thornton JSY	10.00	25.00
51 Marian Gaborik JSY	6.00	15.00
54 Martin Brodeur JSY	15.00	40.00
67 Nicklas Lidstrom JSY	6.00	15.00
83 Roberto Luongo JSY	10.00	25.00
84 Ryan Getzlaf JSY	6.00	15.00
92 Sidney Crosby JSY	25.00	60.00
96 Thomas Vanek JSY	5.00	12.00
100 Zach Parise JSY	6.00	15.00
249 Jonathan Toews JSY AU	125.00	250.00
250 Carey Price JSY AU	80.00	200.00
252 Patrick Kane JSY AU	150.00	400.00

2007-08 Hot Prospects Hot Materials

Card	Low	High
HMAG Andy Greene	4.00	10.00
HMAK Alex Kovalev	4.00	10.00
HMAM Andrej Meszaros	3.00	8.00
HMAO Alexander Ovechkin	20.00	50.00
HMAR Alexander Radulov	5.00	12.00
HMAS Alexander Steen	3.00	8.00
HMBB Brad Boyes	3.00	8.00
HMBD Brandon Dubinsky	6.00	15.00
HMBE Bryan Berard	3.00	8.00
HMBG Bill Guerin	5.00	12.00
HMBJ Barret Jackman	3.00	8.00
HMBL Brendan Bell	3.00	8.00
HMBM Brendan Morrison	3.00	8.00
HMBO Brandon Bochenski	3.00	8.00
HMBR Brenden Morrow	4.00	10.00
HMBS Brad Stuart	3.00	8.00
HMCA Matt Carle	3.00	8.00
HMCH Jonathan Cheechoo	4.00	10.00
HMCK Chuck Kobasew	3.00	8.00
HMCM Mike Cammalleri	4.00	10.00
HMCS Curtis Sanford	4.00	10.00
HMCW Cam Ward	5.00	12.00
HMDA David Aebischer	4.00	10.00
HMDB Dustin Brown	5.00	12.00
HMDH Dany Heatley	4.00	10.00
HMDK David Krejci	10.00	25.00
HMDL David Legwand	4.00	10.00
HMDM Drew Miller	4.00	10.00
HMDO Dominik Hasek	8.00	20.00
HMDP Daniel Paille	3.00	8.00
HMDR Dwayne Roloson	4.00	10.00
HMDU Duncan Keith	4.00	10.00
HMDW Doug Weight	5.00	12.00
HMEC Erik Cole	3.00	8.00
HMES Eric Staal	6.00	15.00
HMFN Frans Nielsen	5.00	12.00
HMGB Gilbert Brule	4.00	10.00
HMGE Martin Gerber	4.00	10.00
HMGI Brian Gionta	3.00	8.00
HMHA Jannik Hansen	4.00	10.00
HMHS Henrik Sedin	6.00	15.00
HMIK Ilya Kovalchuk	5.00	12.00
HMIW Ian White	3.00	8.00
HMJA Jaromir Jagr	15.00	40.00
HMJB Jay Bouwmeester	3.00	8.00
HMJC Jeff Carter	4.00	10.00
HMJH Jaroslav Halak	10.00	25.00
HMJI Jarome Iginla	6.00	15.00
HMJJ Jack Johnson	4.00	10.00
HMJL Jere Lehtinen	3.00	8.00
HMJO Jussi Jokinen	3.00	8.00
HMJP Joni Pitkanen	3.00	8.00
HMJS Jonathan Sigalet	3.00	8.00
HMJT Joe Thornton	8.00	20.00
HMJW Justin Williams	4.00	10.00
HMKE Phil Kessel	5.00	12.00
HMKL Kari Lehtonen	4.00	10.00
HMKT Keith Tkachuk	5.00	12.00
HMLE Jordan Leopold	3.00	8.00
HMLT Lauri Tukonen	3.00	8.00
HMLU Joffrey Lupul	3.00	8.00
HMMA Marc Savard	3.00	8.00
HMMB Martin Brodeur	12.00	30.00
HMMC Bryan McCabe	3.00	8.00
HMMF Manny Fernandez	3.00	8.00
HMMG Marian Gaborik	5.00	12.00
HMMH Marian Hossa	5.00	12.00
HMMI Milan Michalek	3.00	8.00
HMMK Mikko Koivu	4.00	10.00
HMMM Marc Methot	3.00	8.00
HMMN Markus Naslund	5.00	12.00
HMMO Mike Modano	8.00	20.00
HMMR Mike Richards	4.00	10.00
HMMS Matt Stajan	3.00	8.00
HMMT Marty Turco	5.00	12.00
HMNH Nathan Horton	5.00	12.00
HMNL Nicklas Lidstrom	5.00	12.00
HMPB Patrice Bergeron	6.00	15.00
HMPF Peter Forsberg	10.00	25.00
HMPK Petr Kalus	3.00	8.00
HMPL Pascal Leclaire	4.00	10.00
HMRA Andrew Raycroft	4.00	10.00
HMRC Ryan Callahan	6.00	15.00
HMRE Mark Recchi	6.00	15.00
HMRP Ryan Parent	3.00	8.00
HMRS Rob Schremp	4.00	10.00
HMRY Michael Ryder	3.00	8.00
HMSA Joe Sakic	10.00	25.00
HMSB Steve Bernier	3.00	8.00
HMSC Sidney Crosby	12.00	30.00
HMSE Brent Seabrook	3.00	8.00
HMSH Brendan Shanahan	5.00	12.00
HMSL Martin St. Louis	5.00	12.00
HMSM Ryan Smyth	4.00	10.00
HMSP Jason Spezza	5.00	12.00
HMST Jarret Stoll	4.00	10.00
HMSV Marek Svatos	3.00	8.00
HMTR Tuomo Ruutu	5.00	12.00
HMVL Vincent Lecavalier	5.00	12.00

2007-08 Hot Prospects Hot Materials Red Hot

*RED HOT: .5X TO 1.2X HOT MATERIALS

1995-96 Hoyle Eastern Playing Cards

Card	Low	High
COMPLETE SET (54)	8.00	20.00
1 Eric Lindros	.20	.50
2 Peter Bondra	.20	.50
3 Radek Bonk	.08	.25
4 Ray Bourque	.40	1.00
5 Brian Bradley	.08	.25
6 Rod Brind'Amour	.20	.50
7 Martin Brodeur	.75	2.00
8 Wendel Clark	.40	1.00
9 Alexandre Daigle	.08	.25
10 Vincent Damphousse	.08	.25
11 Ray Ferraro	.08	.25
12 Stephane Fiset	.20	.50
13 Peter Forsberg	.60	1.50
14 Joe Sakic	.75	2.00
15 Mikael Renberg	.08	.25
16 Stephane Richer	.08	.25
17 Mike Richter	.40	1.00
18 Luc Robitaille	.40	1.00
19 Geoff Sanderson	.08	.25
20 Bryan Smolinski	.08	.25
21 Kevin Stevens	.08	.25
22 Scott Stevens	.08	.25
23 Steve Thomas	.08	.25
24 Darren Turcotte	.08	.25
25 John Vanbiesbrouck	.20	.50
26 New Jersey Devils Cup Winners	.08	.25
27 Patrick Roy	1.25	3.00
28 Chris Gratton	.08	.25
29 Adam Graves	.08	.25
30 Dominik Hasek	.60	1.50
31 Ron Hextall	.40	1.00
32 Jaromir Jagr	.60	1.50
33 Joe Juneau	.08	.25
34 Dimitri Khristich	.08	.25
35 Petr Klima	.08	.25
36 Bob Kudelski	.08	.25
37 Scott Lachance	.08	.25
38 Pat Lafontaine	.08	.25
39 John Leclair	.08	.25
40 Mark Messier	.40	1.00
41 Brian Leetch	.20	.50
42 Alexander Mogilny	.20	.50
43 Kirk Muller	.08	.25
44 Cam Neely	.40	1.00
45 Rob Niedermayer	.08	.25
46 Scott Niedermayer	.20	.50
47 Owen Nolan	.08	.25
48 Adam Oates	.08	.25
49 Michal Pivonka	.08	.25
50 Derek Plante	.08	.25
51 Chris Pronger	.20	.50
52 Mark Recchi	.20	.50
53 Sergei Zubov	.08	.25
54 Alexei Yashin	.08	.25

1995-96 Hoyle Western Playing Cards

Card	Low	High
COMPLETE SET (54)	8.00	20.00
1 Jeremy Roenick	.40	1.00
2 Dave Andreychuk	.08	.25
3 Jason Arnott	.08	.25
4 Ed Belfour	.40	1.00
5 Rob Blake	.20	.50
6 Jeff Brown	.08	.25
7 Patrick Carnback	.08	.25
8 Chris Chelois	.30	.75
9 Tim Cheveldae	.20	.50
10 Paul Coffey	.30	.75
11 Shayne Corson	.08	.25
12 Geoff Courtnall	.08	.25
13 Russ Courtnall	.08	.25
14 Wayne Gretzky	2.00	5.00
15 Joe Sacco	.08	.25
16 Denis Savard	.20	.50
17 Teemu Selanne	.40	1.00
18 Brendan Shanahan	.40	1.00
19 Ray Sheppard	.08	.25
20 Mats Sundin	.40	1.00
21 Esa Tikkanen	.08	.25
22 German Titov	.08	.25
23 Keith Tkachuk	.20	.50
24 Rick Tocchet	.08	.25
25 Doug Weight	.08	.25
26 Detroit Red Wings Team Photo	.08	.25
27 Sergei Fedorov	.40	1.00
28 Ulf Dahlen	.08	.25
29 Pat Falloon	.08	.25
30 Theoren Fleury	.20	.50
31 Doug Gilmour	.40	1.00
32 Todd Harvey	.08	.25
33 Kevin Hatcher	.08	.25
34 Guy Hebert	.20	.50
35 Phil Housley	.08	.25
36 Brett Hull	.60	1.50
37 Arturs Irbe	.20	.50
38 Curtis Joseph	.40	1.00
39 Paul Kariya	.40	1.00
40 Pavel Bure	.30	.75
41 Jari Kurri	.30	.75
42 Igor Larionov	.08	.25
43 Nicklas Lidstrom	.20	.50
44 Trevor Linden	.40	1.00
45 Marty McSorley	.08	.25
46 Mike Modano	.40	1.00
47 Bernie Nicholls	.08	.25
48 Joe Nieuwendyk	.20	.50
49 David Oliver	.08	.25
50 Felix Potvin	.40	1.00
51 Bill Ranford	.20	.50
52 Gary Roberts	.08	.25
53 Steve Yzerman	1.25	3.00
54 Alexei Zhamnov	.08	.25

1975-76 Houston Aeros WHA

Card	Low	High
COMPLETE SET (19)	40.00	80.00
1 Ron Grahame	2.00	4.00
2 Larry Hale	1.00	2.00
3 Murray Hall	1.50	3.00
4 Gordie Howe	15.00	30.00
5 Mark Howe	5.00	10.00
6 Marty Howe	4.00	8.00
7 Andre Hinse	1.00	2.00
8 Frank Hughes	1.00	2.00
9 Glen Irwin	1.00	2.00
10 Gord Labossiere	1.50	3.00
11 Don Larway	1.00	2.00
12 Larry Lund	1.50	3.00
13 Paul Popeil	1.50	3.00
14 Rich Preston	1.50	3.00
15 Terry Ruskowski	1.50	3.00
16 Wayne Rutledge	2.00	4.00
17 John Schella	1.00	2.00
18 Ted Taylor	1.00	2.00
19 John Tonelli	5.00	10.00

1992-93 Humpty Dumpty I

Card	Low	High
COMPLETE SET (26)	8.00	20.00
1 Ray Bourque	.40	1.00
2 Rod Brind'Amour	.20	.50
3 Chris Chelios	.30	.75
4 Wendel Clark Toronto Ma	.20	.50
5 Gilbert Dionne	.08	.25
6 Pat Falloon San Jose Sh	.15	.40
7 Ray Ferraro	.15	.40
8 Theo Fleury	.30	.75
9 Grant Fuhr	.20	.50
10 Wayne Gretzky Los Angel	2.00	5.00
11 Kevin Hatcher	.08	.25
12 Valeri Kamensky	.20	.50
13 Mike Keane	.08	.25
14 Brian Leetch New York R	.30	.75
15 Kirk McLean Vancouver C	.20	.50
16 Alexander Mogilny Buffa	.25	.60
17 Troy Murray	.08	.25
18 Patrick Roy Montreal Ca	1.50	4.00
19 Joe Sakic Quebec Nordiq	.60	1.50
20 Brendan Shanahan	.60	1.50
21 Kevin Stevens	.15	.40
22 Scott Stevens	.20	.50
23 Mark Tinordi	.08	.25
24 Steve Yzerman	1.00	2.50
25 Zarley Zalapski	.08	.25
26 Checklist	.20	.50

1992-93 Humpty Dumpty II

Card	Low	High
COMPLETE SET (26)	8.00	20.00
1 Drake Berehowsky	.08	.25
2 Shayne Corson Edmonton	.15	.40
3 Russ Courtnall	.15	.40
4 Dave Ellett	.08	.25
5 Sergei Fedorov Detroit	.60	1.50
6 Dave Gagner	.15	.40
7 Doug Gilmour Toronto Ma	.30	.75
8 Phil Housley	.15	.40
9 Brett Hull St. Louis Bl	.40	1.00
10 Jaromir Jagr Pittsburgh	1.00	2.50
11 Pat LaFontaine Buffalo	.20	.50
12 Mario Lemieux	1.50	4.00
13 Trevor Linden Vancouver	.15	.40
14 Al MacInnis	.20	.50
15 Mark Messier New York R	.40	1.00
16 Cam Neely	.30	.75
17 Owen Nolan Quebec Nordi	.20	.50
18 Bill Ranford	.20	.50
19 Luc Robitaille	.25	.60
20 Jeremy Roenick	.30	.75
21 Mats Sundin	.30	.75
22 Chris Terreri	.15	.40
23 Steve Thomas	.15	.40
24 Pat Verbeek	.15	.40
25 Neil Wilkinson	.08	.25
26 Checklist	.20	.50

1997-98 Hurricanes Team Issue

Card	Low	High
COMPLETE SET (28)	4.80	12.00
1 Jeff Brown	.08	.25
2 Sean Burke	.40	1.00
3 Adam Burt	.08	.25
4 Steve Chiasson	.08	.25
5 Enrico Ciccone	.08	.25
6 Kevin Dineen	.10	.30
7 Nelson Emerson	.10	.30
8 Martin Gelinas	.10	.30
9 Stu Grimson	.10	.30
10 Steve Halko	.08	.25
11 Kevin Haller	.08	.25
12 Sean Hill	.08	.25
13 Sami Kapanen	1.25	3.00
14 Trevor Kidd	.40	1.00
15 Robert Kron	.10	.30
16 Steve Leach	.08	.25
17 Curtis Leschyshyn	.08	.25
18 Kent Manderville	.08	.25
19 Jeff O'Neill	.08	.25
20 Nolan Pratt	.08	.25
21 Keith Primeau	.60	1.50
22 Paul Ranheim	.08	.25
23 Steven Rice	.10	.30
24 Gary Roberts	.10	.30
25 Geoff Sanderson	.20	.50
26 Glen Wesley	.10	.30
27 Paul Maurice Tom Webster Randy Ladouceur CO	.07	.20
28 Stormy the Mascot	.02	.10

1998-99 Hurricanes Team Issue

Card	Low	High
COMPLETE SET (25)	12.00	30.00
1 Arturs Irbe	.75	2.00
2 Glen Wesley	.40	1.00
3 Steve Chiasson	.40	1.00
4 Nolan Pratt	.40	1.00
5 Marek Malik	.40	1.00
6 Adam Burt	.40	1.00
7 Curtis Leschyshyn	.40	1.00
8 Gary Roberts	.40	1.00
9 Kevin Dineen	.40	1.00
10 Bates Battaglia	.60	1.50
11 Steven Halko	.40	1.00
12 Byron Ritchie	.40	1.00
13 Ron Francis	1.25	3.00
14 Sean Hill	.40	1.00
15 Martin Gelinas	.40	1.00
16 Sami Kapanen	.75	2.00
17 Ray Sheppard	.40	1.00
18 Paul Ranheim	.40	1.00
19 Dave Karpa	.40	1.00
20 Trevor Kidd	.60	1.50
21 Kent Manderville	.40	1.00
22 Mike Rucinski	.40	1.00
23 Keith Primeau	.60	1.50
24 Jeff O'Neill	.75	2.00
25 Stormy MASCOT	.08	.25

1999-00 Hurricanes Team Issue

Card	Low	High
COMPLETE SET (21)	6.00	15.00
1 Arturs Irbe	.60	1.50
2 Glen Wesley	.40	1.00
3 Nolan Pratt	.40	1.00
4 Marek Malik	.40	1.00
5 Curtis Leschyshyn	.40	1.00
6 Gary Roberts	.40	1.00
7 Bates Battaglia	.40	1.00
8 Steve Halko	.40	1.00
9 Tommy Westlund	.40	1.00
10 Jeff Daniels	.40	1.00
11 Robert Kron	.40	1.00
12 Ron Francis	.60	1.50
13 Sean Hill	.40	1.00
14 Martin Gelinas	.40	1.00
15 Sami Kapanen	.40	1.00
16 Rod Brind'Amour	.60	1.50
17 Dave Karpa	.40	1.00
18 Andrei Kovalenko	.40	1.00
19 Paul Coffey	.60	1.50
20 Jeff O'Neill	.40	1.00
21 Randy Ladouceur Kevin McCarthy Paul Maurice	.40	1.00

2002-03 Hurricanes Postcards

Card	Low	High
COMPLETE SET		
1 Rod Brind'Amour	.60	1.50
2 Erik Cole	.60	1.50
3 Ron Francis	.60	1.50
4 Arturs Irbe	.75	2.00
5 Jeff O'Neill	.40	1.00
6 Kevin Weekes	.60	1.50
7 Glen Wesley	.40	1.00

2003-04 Hurricanes Postcards

Card	Low	High
COMPLETE SET (24)	10.00	25.00
1 Craig Adams	.30	.75
2 Kevyn Adams	.30	.75
3 Ryan Bayda	.30	.75
4 Bob Boughner	.30	.75
5 Jesse Boulerice	.30	.75
6 Pavel Brendl	.30	.75
7 Rod Brind'Amour	.60	1.50
8 Erik Cole	.40	1.00
9 Ron Francis	.60	1.50
10 Bret Hedican	.30	.75
11 Sean Hill	.30	.75
12 Kevin McCarthy	.30	.75
13 Marty Murray	.30	.75
14 Jeff O'Neill	.40	1.00
15 Eric Staal	2.00	5.00
16 Bruno St. Jacques	.30	.75
17 Jamie Storr	.40	1.00
18 Jaroslav Svoboda	.30	.75
19 Josef Vasicek	.30	.75
20 Radim Vrbata	.30	.75
21 Niclas Wallin	.30	.75
22 Aaron Ward	.30	.75
23 Kevin Weekes	.40	1.00
24 Glen Wesley	.30	.75

2006-07 Hurricanes Postcards

Card	Low	High
COMPLETE SET (28)	15.00	25.00
1 Logo Card	.10	.25
2 Craig Adams	.40	1.00
3 Kevyn Adams	.40	1.00
4 Anton Babchuk	.40	1.00
5 Eric Belanger	.40	1.00
6 Rod Brind'Amour	.75	2.00
7 Erik Colo	1.00	2.50
8 Mike Commodore	.40	1.00
9 Jeff Daniels ACO	.10	.25
10 Tim Gleason	.40	1.00
11 John Grahame	.60	1.50
12 Bret Hedican	.40	1.00
13 Andrew Hutchinson	.40	1.00
14 Frantisek Kaberle	.40	1.00
15 Andrew Ladd	.40	1.00
16 Chad Larose	.40	1.00
17 Peter Laviolette CO	.20	.50
18 Trevor Letowski	.40	1.00
19 Kevin McCarthy ACO	.10	.25
20 Eric Staal	1.25	3.00
21 Cory Stillman	.40	1.00
22 David Tanabe	.40	1.00
23 Scott Walker	.40	1.00
24 Niclas Wallin	.40	1.00
25 Cam Ward	.75	2.00
26 Glen Wesley	.40	1.00
27 Ray Whitney	.40	1.00
28 Justin Williams	.75	2.00

1991 Impel U.S. Olympic Hall of Fame

Card	Low	High
COMPLETE SET (90)	6.00	15.00
66 1980 U.S. Hockey Team Moment of Victory	.20	.50
67 1980 U.S. Hockey Team Aggressive blocking	.12	.30
68 Dave Christian Buzz Schneider	.12	.30
69 1980 U.S. Hockey Team Victory Celebration	.20	.50
71 1980 U.S. Hockey Team Gold-medal victory	.20	.50
72 Herb Brooks CO	.12	.30

1927 Imperial Tobacco

Card	Low	High
NNO Montreal Victorias	25.00	50.00

1929 Imperial Tobacco

Card	Low	High
NNO Ice Hockey	20.00	40.00

2010-11 ITG 100 Years of Card Collecting

Card	Low	High
1 Georges Vezina BTP	3.00	8.00
2 Eddie Shore HP	2.00	5.00
3 Charlie Conacher HP	2.00	5.00
4 Ron Francis D	3.00	8.00
5 Bill Barilko HP	1.50	4.00
6 Doug Harvey CW	2.50	6.00
7 Howie Morenz HP	2.00	5.00
8 Luc Robitaille D	2.50	6.00
9 Bobby Hull CW	5.00	12.00
10 Daniel Sedin CW	3.00	8.00
11 Peter Forsberg CW	5.00	12.00
12 Borje Salming CW	2.50	6.00
13 Teemu Selanne CW	5.00	12.00
14 Dave Keon HP	2.50	6.00
15 Cyclone Taylor HP	2.50	6.00
16 Brett Hull CW	5.00	12.00
17 Valeri Kharlamov CW	1.50	4.00
18 Hobey Baker HP	2.00	5.00
19 Ted Lindsay HP	2.50	6.00
20 Vladislav Tretiak BTP	2.00	5.00
21 Mario Lemieux D	10.00	25.00
22 Mike Bossy D	2.50	6.00
23 Red Kelly HP	2.50	6.00
24 Steven Stamkos CW	5.00	12.00
25 Felix Potvin BTP	4.00	10.00
26 Lester Patrick HP	2.50	6.00
27 Darryl Sittler CW	3.00	8.00
28 Gump Worsley BTP	2.50	6.00
29 George Hainsworth BTP	2.50	6.00
30 Martin Brodeur BTP	6.00	15.00
31 Pelle Lindbergh D	2.00	5.00
32 Denis Potvin D	2.50	6.00
33 Patrick Roy BTP	6.00	15.00
34 Charlie Gardiner BTP	2.00	5.00
35 Tony Esposito BTP	2.50	6.00
36 Newsy Lalonde HP	2.00	5.00
37 Turk Broda BTP	2.50	6.00
38 Aurel Joliat HP	2.50	6.00
39 Sid Abel HP	2.00	5.00
40 Sid Abel CW	2.00	5.00
41 Igor Larionov CW	2.50	6.00
42 Maurice Richard HP	5.00	12.00
43 Bobby Bauer HP	2.50	6.00
44 Teeder Kennedy HP	2.50	6.00
45 Woody Dumart HP	1.50	4.00
46 Carey Price BTP	5.00	12.00
47 Chris Chelios D	2.50	6.00
48 Paul Coffey D	2.50	6.00
49 Syl Apps HP	3.00	8.00
50 Bill Durnan BTP	2.50	6.00
51 Terry Sawchuk BTP	3.00	8.00
52 Milt Schmidt HP	2.00	5.00
53 Elmer Lach HP	2.00	5.00
54 Marcel Dionne D	3.00	8.00
55 Johnny Bucyk D	2.50	6.00
56 Henri Richard HP	2.50	6.00
57 Miikka Kiprusoff BTP	2.50	6.00
58 Frank Mahovlich CW	2.50	6.00
59 Stan Mikita D	3.00	8.00
60 Jean Beliveau D	2.50	6.00
61 Glenn Hall BTP	2.50	6.00
62 Vincent Lecavalier CW	2.50	6.00
63 Phil Esposito D	4.00	10.00
64 Ron Hextall BTP	2.50	6.00
65 Gerry Cheevers BTP	2.50	6.00
66 Bernie Parent BTP	3.00	8.00
67 Johnny Bower BTP	2.50	6.00
68 Jaromir Jagr CW	8.00	20.00
69 Toe Blake HP	1.50	4.00
70 Gilbert Perreault D	2.50	6.00
71 Ilya Kovalchuk CW	2.50	6.00
72 Guy Lafleur D	3.00	8.00
73 Larry Robinson D	2.50	6.00
74 Tim Horton HP	2.50	6.00
75 Bobby Clarke CW	4.00	10.00
76 Bryan Trottier D	2.50	6.00
77 Raymond Bourque D	4.00	10.00
78 Ed Giacomin BTP	4.00	10.00
79 Bernie Geoffrion HP	2.00	5.00
80 Peter Stastny D	2.00	5.00
81 Grant Fuhr BTP	4.00	10.00
82 Marian Gaborik CW	2.50	6.00
83 Jacques Plante BTP	3.00	8.00
84 Pat LaFontaine D	2.50	6.00
85 Patrick Roy BTP	6.00	15.00
86 Jari Kurri D	2.50	6.00
87 Joe Sakic CW	5.00	12.00
88 Mike Modano CW	5.00	12.00
89 Lanny McDonald D	2.50	6.00
90 Henrik Sedin CW	3.00	8.00
91 Sergei Fedorov CW	4.00	10.00
92 Nicklas Lidstrom CW	2.50	6.00
93 Doug Gilmour D	3.00	8.00
94 Cam Neely D	2.50	6.00
95 Pavel Bure CW	2.50	6.00
96 Roberto Luongo BTP	4.00	10.00
97 Joe Thornton CW	4.00	10.00
98 Wendel Clark D	4.00	10.00
99 Tim Thomas BTP	2.50	6.00
100A Steve Yzerman BTP	6.00	15.00
100B Steve Yzerman D	6.00	15.00

2003-04 ITG Action

Card	Low	High
COMP.SET w/o SP's (600)	30.00	80.00
1 Joe Thornton	.40	1.00
2 Dany Heatley	.20	.50
3 Ales Kotalik	.15	.40
4 Steve Montador	.15	.40
5 Dan Bylsma	.15	.40
6 Andrew Ference	.15	.40
7 Andy Hilbert	.15	.40
8 Andy McDonald	.20	.50
9 Bob Boughner	.15	.40
10 Brad Tapper	.15	.40
11 Brian Campbell	.20	.50
12 Brian Rolston	.20	.50
13 Daniel Tjarnqvist	.15	.40
14 Glen Murray	.20	.50
15 Byron Dafoe	.20	.50
16 Bryan Berard	.20	.50
17 Alexei Zhitnik	.20	.50
18 Craig Conroy	.15	.40
19 Curtis Brown	.15	.40
20 Dan McGillis	.15	.40
21 Dan Snyder	.15	.40
22 Daniel Briere	.25	.60
23 Chris Clark	.15	.40
24 Frantisek Kaberle	.15	.40
25 Adam Oates	.25	.60
26 Denis Gauthier	.15	.40
27 Dimitri Kalinin	.15	.40
28 Martin Lapointe	.20	.50
29 Keith Carney	.15	.40
30 Garnet Exelby	.15	.40
31 Dean McAmmond	.15	.40

32 Hal Gill .15 .40
33 Henrik Tallinder .15 .40
34 Ilya Kovalchuk .25 .60
35 Ivan Huml .15 .40
36 J-P Dumont .15 .40
37 Alexei Smirnov .15 .40
38 Jarome Iginla .30 .75
39 Jason Krog .15 .40
40 Jay McKee .15 .40
41 Jean-Sebastien Giguere .25 .60
42 Krzysztof Oliwa .15 .40
43 Jeff Odgers .15 .40
44 Jochen Hecht .15 .40
45 Joe DiPenta RC .20 .50
46 Adam Mair .15 .40
47 Jonathan Girard .15 .40
48 Jordan Leopold .15 .40
49 Andrew Raycroft .20 .50
50 Kamil Piros .15 .40
51 Eric Boulton .15 .40
52 Kurt Sauer .15 .40
53 Lubos Bartecko .15 .40
54 Marc Chouinard .15 .40
55 Marc Savard .15 .40
56 Martin Biron .20 .50
57 Martin Gelinas .15 .40
58 Martin Gerber .15 .40
59 Chuck Kobasew .15 .40
60 Martin Samuelsson .20 .50
61 Jamie McLennan .15 .40
62 Mika Noronen .15 .40
63 Mike Knuble .15 .40
64 Mike Leclerc .15 .40
65 Pasi Nurminen .20 .50
66 Miroslav Satan .20 .50
67 Nick Boynton .15 .40
68 Niclas Havelid .15 .40
69 Oleg Saprykin .15 .40
70 Milan Bartovic RC .20 .50
71 P.J. Stock .15 .40
72 Roman Turek .20 .50
73 Patrik Stefan .15 .40
74 Maxim Afinogenov .15 .40
75 Petr Sykora .20 .50
76 Rick Mrozik RC .15 .40
77 Rob Niedermayer .20 .50
78 Robyn Regehr .15 .40
79 P.J. Axelsson .15 .40
80 Ruslan Salei .15 .40
81 Ryan Miller .25 .60
82 Sandis Ozolinsh .15 .40
83 Blake Sloan .20 .50
84 Tim Connolly .15 .40
85 Shaone Morrisonn .15 .40
86 Shawn McEachern .15 .40
87 Shean Donovan .15 .40
88 Simon Gamache .15 .40
89 Stanislav Chistov .15 .40
90 Stephane Yelle .15 .40
91 Steve Rucchin .15 .40
92 Steve Shields .20 .50
93 Steve Thomas .15 .40
94 Taylor Pyatt .15 .40
95 Yannick Tremblay .15 .40
96 Toni Lydman .15 .40
97 Tony Hrkac .15 .40
98 Vitali Vishnevsky .15 .40
99 Slava Kozlov .20 .50
100 Sergei Samsonov .20 .50
101 Riku Hahl .15 .40
102 Tyler Wright .15 .40
103 Tyler Arnason .15 .40
104 Tomas Kurka .15 .40
105 Theo Fleury .30 .75
106 Stu Barnes .15 .40
107 Steve Sullivan .15 .40
108 Paul Kariya .25 .60
109 Steve Poapst .15 .40
110 Steve Ott .15 .40
111 Steve McCarthy .15 .40
112 Sergei Zubov .20 .50
113 Serge Aubin .15 .40
114 Niko Kapanen .15 .40
115 Pascal Leclaire .15 .40
116 Patrick Roy .60 1.50
117 Pavel Brendl .15 .40
118 Peter Forsberg .50 1.25
119 Philippe Boucher .15 .40
120 Radim Vrbata .15 .40
121 Ray Whitney .20 .50
122 Richard Matvichuk .15 .40
123 Rick Nash .25 .60
124 Sami Helenius .15 .40
125 Rob Blake .25 .60
126 Rob DiMaio .15 .40
127 Rod Brind'Amour .25 .60
128 Chris McAllister .15 .40
129 Ron Tugnutt .20 .50
130 Rostislav Klesla .15 .40
131 Ryan Bayda .15 .40
132 Ryan VandenBussche .15 .40
133 Ron Francis .30 .75
134 Charlie Stephens .15 .40
135 Scott Young .15 .40
136 Sean Hill .15 .40
137 Sean Pronger .15 .40
138 Nathan Dempsey .15 .40
139 Jason Bacashihua .15 .40
140 Jason Strudwick .15 .40
141 Jeff O'Neill .15 .40
142 Jere Lehtinen .20 .50
143 Alexander Karpovtsev .15 .40
144 Jody Shelley .15 .40
145 Alex Tanguay .20 .50
146 John Erskine .15 .40
147 Jon Klemm .15 .40
148 Josef Vasicek .15 .40
149 Kent McDonell RC .20 .50
150 Kevyn Adams .15 .40
151 Kyle Calder .15 .40
152 Lasse Pirjeta .15 .40
153 Manny Malhotra .15 .40
154 Marc Denis .20 .50
155 Mark Bell .15 .40
156 Martin Skoula .15 .40
157 Marty Turco .25 .60
158 Matt Davidson .15 .40
159 Michael Leighton .15 .40
160 Kevin Weekes .20 .50
161 Luke Richardson .15 .40
162 Mike Keane .20 .50
163 Mike Modano .40 1.00
164 Scott Lachance .15 .40
165 Mike Zigomanis .15 .40
166 Milan Hejduk .20 .50
167 Jason Arnott .20 .50
168 Jaroslav Svoboda .15 .40
169 Jaroslav Spacek .15 .40
170 Aaron Ward .15 .40
171 Alexei Zhamnov .20 .50
172 Teemu Selanne .50 1.25
173 Jan Hlavac .15 .40
174 Duvie Westcott .15 .40
175 Erik Cole .15 .40
176 Philippe Sauve .20 .50
177 Eric Daze .20 .50
178 Derrick Walser .15 .40
179 Aaron Downey .15 .40
180 Derek Morris .15 .40
181 David Vyborny .15 .40
182 Craig Andersson .25 .60
183 Patrick DesRochers .15 .40
184 David Aebischer .20 .50
185 Stephane Robidas .20 .50
186 Dan Hinote .15 .40
187 Craig Adams .15 .40
188 Burke Henry .15 .40
189 Bret Hedican .15 .40
190 Brenden Morrow .20 .50
191 Brad DeFauw .15 .40
192 Bill Guerin .25 .60
193 Bates Battaglia .15 .40
194 Andrew Cassels .15 .40
195 Adam Foote .15 .40
196 Geoff Sanderson .15 .40
197 Jocelyn Thibault .20 .50
198 Joe Sakic .50 1.25
199 Espen Knutsen .15 .40
200 Igor Radulov .15 .40
201 Jason Smith .15 .40
202 Dominik Hasek .40 1.00
203 Sean Avery .15 .40
204 Steve Staios .15 .40
205 Kirk Maltby .15 .40
206 Denis Shvidki .15 .40
207 Sergei Fedorov .40 1.00
208 Sergei Zholtok .15 .40
209 Shawn Horcoff .15 .40
210 Stephen Weiss .15 .40
211 Steve Yzerman .60 1.50
212 Brad Chartrand .15 .40
213 Brad Isbister .15 .40
214 Valeri Bure .15 .40
215 Brendan Shanahan .25 .60
216 Ryan Smyth .20 .50
217 Chris Chelios .25 .60
218 Cliff Ronning .15 .40
219 Curtis Joseph .30 .75
220 Darcy Hordichuk .15 .40
221 Darren McCarty .15 .40
222 Eric Brewer .15 .40
223 Derek Armstrong .15 .40
224 Dwayne Roloson .20 .50
225 Eric Belanger .15 .40
226 Brett Hull .50 1.25
227 Joe Corvo .15 .40
228 Ethan Moreau .15 .40
229 Felix Potvin .40 1.00
230 Fernando Pisani .15 .40
231 Filip Kuba .15 .40
232 Georges Laraque .20 .50
233 Henrik Zetterberg .30 .75
234 Ian Laperriere .15 .40
235 Igor Larionov .25 .60
236 Mattias Norstrom .15 .40
237 Ivan Novoseltsev .15 .40
238 Jamie Storr .20 .50
239 Jani Hurme .15 .40
240 Jani Rita .15 .40
241 Willie Mitchell .15 .40
242 Jaroslav Bednar .15 .40
243 Jaroslav Modry .15 .40
244 Lubomir Sekeras .15 .40
245 Lubomir Visnovsky .15 .40
246 Manny Fernandez .15 .40
247 Jared Aulin .15 .40
248 Marcus Nilson .15 .40
249 Ales Hemsky .25 .60
250 Igor Ulanov .15 .40
251 Alexei Semenov .15 .40
252 Mathieu Schneider .15 .40
253 Matt Cullen .15 .40
254 Andrew Brunette .15 .40
255 Viktor Kozlov .15 .40
256 Mike Comrie .20 .50
257 Brad Bombardir .15 .40
258 Scott Ferguson .15 .40
259 Tomas Holmstrom .20 .50
260 Tomas Zizka .15 .40
261 Manny Legace .15 .40
262 Jon Sim .15 .40
263 Wes Walz .15 .40
264 Jay Bouwmeester .15 .40
265 Zigmund Palffy .25 .60
266 Andreas Lilja .15 .40
267 Pascal Dupuis .15 .40
268 Alexander Frolov .20 .50
269 Tommy Salo .20 .50
270 Antti Laaksonen .15 .40
271 Mike Cammalleri .25 .60
272 Bill Muckalt .15 .40
273 Mike York .15 .40
274 Nick Schultz .15 .40
275 Nicklas Lidstrom .25 .60
276 Andrei Zyuzin .15 .40
277 Adam Deadmarsh .15 .40
278 Olli Jokinen .25 .60
279 Pavel Datsyuk .40 1.00
280 Jason Chimera .15 .40
281 Kristian Huselius .15 .40
282 Jarret Stoll .15 .40
283 Jason Allison .20 .50
284 Richard Park .15 .40
285 Marty Reasoner .15 .40
286 Mathieu Biron .20 .50
287 Jason Woolley .15 .40
288 Pavel Trnka .15 .40
289 Jim Dowd .15 .40
290 Kris Draper .15 .40
291 Peter Worrell .15 .40
292 P-M Bouchard .25 .60
293 Radek Dvorak .20 .50
294 Matt Johnson .15 .40
295 Aaron Miller .15 .40
296 Mathieu Dandenault .15 .40
297 Marian Gaborik .25 .60
298 Roberto Luongo .40 1.00
299 Jason Williams .15 .40
300 Niklas Hagman .15 .40
301 Jamie Langenbrunner .20 .50
302 Greg Johnson .15 .40
303 Alexei Kovalev .20 .50
304 Ron Hainsey .15 .40
305 Ari Ahonen .15 .40
306 Mark Parrish .15 .40
307 Andrei Markov .25 .60
308 Jason York .15 .40
309 Jason Wiemer .15 .40
310 Mark Messier .50 1.25
311 Joe Juneau .15 .40
312 Colin White .15 .40
313 Mike Dunham .20 .50
314 Brian Finley .15 .40
315 Jeff Friesen .15 .40
316 Boris Mironov .15 .40
317 Brian Rafalski .20 .50
318 Chad Kilger .15 .40
319 Arron Asham .15 .40
320 Corey Schwab .20 .50
321 Craig Rivet .15 .40
322 Dale Purinton .15 .40
323 John Madden .15 .40
324 Bill Houlder .15 .40
325 Denis Arkhipov .15 .40
326 Bobby Holik .15 .40
327 Jay Pandolfo .15 .40
328 Adam Hall .15 .40
329 Adrian Aucoin .15 .40
330 Michael Rupp .15 .40
331 Donald Audette .15 .40
332 Brian Gionta .15 .40
333 Jan Bulis .15 .40
334 Jamie Lundmark .15 .40
335 Jason Ward .15 .40
336 Anson Carter .20 .50
337 Grant Marshall .15 .40
338 Garth Snow .20 .50
339 Eric Lindros .40 1.00
340 Dusan Salficky RC .20 .50
341 Darius Kasparaitis .15 .40
342 Patrik Elias .25 .60
343 David Legwand .20 .50
344 Brian Leetch .20 .50
345 Jason Blake .15 .40
346 Kimmo Timonen .15 .40
347 Dan Blackburn .20 .50
348 Jose Theodore .25 .60
349 Justin Mapletoft .15 .40
350 Vernon Fiddler .15 .40
351 Ken Daneyko .20 .50
352 Martin Erat .15 .40
353 Janne Niinimaa .15 .40
354 Marcel Hossa .15 .40
355 Scott Niedermayer .25 .60
356 Petr Nedved .15 .40
357 Martin Brodeur .60 1.50
358 Rick DiPietro .20 .50
359 Mathieu Garon .15 .40
360 Vladimir Malakhov .15 .40
361 Mike Ribeiro .15 .40
362 Michael Peca .20 .50
363 Andreas Dackell .15 .40
364 Scott Stevens .25 .60
365 Dave Scatchard .15 .40
366 Mike Richter .25 .60
367 Niklas Sundstrom .15 .40
368 Oleg Petrov .15 .40
369 Alexei Yashin .20 .50
370 Darren Haydar .15 .40
371 Patrice Brisebois .15 .40
372 Scott Walker .15 .40
373 Pavel Bure .25 .60
374 Yanic Perreault .15 .40
375 Vladimir Orszagh .15 .40
376 Kenny Jonsson .15 .40
377 Vitali Yachmenev .15 .40
378 Turner Stevenson .15 .40
379 Trent Hunter .15 .40
380 Tomas Vokoun .20 .50
381 Tom Poti .15 .40
382 Shawn Bates .15 .40
383 Sergei Brylin .15 .40
384 Scottie Upshall .20 .50
385 Mattias Weinhandl .15 .40
386 Joe Nieuwendyk .20 .50
387 Mike Komisarek .15 .40
388 Matthew Barnaby .15 .40
389 Scott Gomez .20 .50
390 Sandy McCarthy .15 .40
391 Saku Koivu .25 .60
392 Ronald Petrovicky .15 .40
393 Scott Hartnell .15 .40
394 Roman Hamrlik .15 .40
395 Andreas Johansson .15 .40
396 Richard Zednik .15 .40
397 Rem Murray .15 .40
398 Randy Robitaille .15 .40
399 Randy McKay .15 .40
400 Oleg Kvasha .15 .40
401 Steve McKenna .15 .40
402 Radoslav Suchy .15 .40
403 Wayne Primeau .15 .40
404 Wade Redden .15 .40
405 Vincent Damphousse .20 .50
406 Sebastien Caron .20 .50
407 Vaclav Varada .15 .40
408 Tony Amonte .20 .50
409 Tomas Surovy .15 .40
410 Sami Kapanen .15 .40
411 Mike Ricci .15 .40
412 Alexei Morozov .15 .40
413 Miroslav Zalesak .15 .40
414 Mark Recchi .30 .75
415 Patrick Marleau .25 .60
416 Robert Esche .15 .40
417 Brooks Orpik .15 .40
418 Ville Nieminen .15 .40
419 Mike Rathje .15 .40
420 Michal Rozsival .15 .40
421 Todd Harvey .15 .40
422 Zdeno Chara .25 .60
423 Scott Hannan .15 .40
424 Rob Ray .15 .40
425 Zac Bierk .15 .40
426 Vesa Toskala .15 .40
427 Todd White .15 .40
428 Eric Meloche .15 .40
429 Niko Dimitrakos .15 .40
430 Patrick Lalime .20 .50
431 Simon Gagne .25 .60
432 Sean Burke .15 .40
433 John LeClair .25 .60
434 Petr Schastlivy .15 .40
435 Scott Thornton .20 .50
436 Radek Bonk .20 .50
437 Rico Fata .15 .40
438 Mike Johnson .15 .40
439 Mike Fisher .15 .40
440 Radovan Somik .15 .40
441 Peter Schaefer .15 .40
442 Michal Handzus .20 .50
443 Landon Wilson .15 .40
444 Jonathan Cheechoo .20 .50
445 Mario Lemieux 1.00 2.50
446 Martin Havlat .25 .60
447 Mark Smith .15 .40
448 Kris Beech .15 .40
449 Keith Primeau .20 .50
450 Marian Hossa .25 .60
451 Marcus Ragnarsson .15 .40
452 Martin Straka .15 .40
453 Kim Johnsson .15 .40
454 Milan Kraft .15 .40
455 Martin Prusek .15 .40
456 Krys Kolanos .15 .40
457 Kyle McLaren .15 .40
458 Ladislav Nagy .15 .40
459 Claude Lapointe .15 .40
460 Magnus Arvedson .15 .40
461 Marco Sturm .15 .40
462 Karel Rachunek .15 .40
463 Justin Williams .20 .50
464 Evgeni Nabokov .20 .50
465 Mathias Johansson .15 .40
466 Eric Desjardins .20 .50
467 Daniel Alfredsson .25 .60
468 Chris Therien .15 .40
469 Jeremy Roenick .40 1.00
470 Jeff Taffe .15 .40
471 Johan Hedberg .20 .50
472 Dimitri Yushkevich .15 .40
473 Shane Doan .20 .50
474 Paul Mara .15 .40
475 Eric Weinrich .15 .40
476 Jim Fahey .15 .40
477 Konstantin Koltsov .15 .40
478 Jason Jaspers .15 .40
479 Jason Spezza .25 .60
480 J-S Aubin .15 .40
481 Deron Quint .15 .40
482 Dennis Seidenberg .15 .40
483 Daymond Langkow .15 .40
484 Kelly Buchberger .20 .50
485 Michal Sivek .15 .40
486 Donald Brashear .15 .40
487 Chris Phillips .15 .40
488 Chris Gratton .15 .40
489 Bryan Smolinski .15 .40
490 Guillaume Lefebvre .15 .40
491 Brian Savage .15 .40
492 Alyn McCauley .15 .40
493 Andrei Nazarov .15 .40
494 Anton Volchenkov .15 .40
495 Brad Ference .15 .40
496 Brad Stuart .15 .40
497 Branko Radivojevic .15 .40
498 Brian Boucher .20 .50
499 Dick Tarnstrom .15 .40
500 Adam Graves .20 .50
501 Al MacInnis .30 .75
502 Scott Mellanby .15 .40
503 Matt Stajan RC .25 .60
504 Andre Roy .15 .40
505 Alexander Mogilny .20 .50
506 Barret Jackman .15 .40
507 Nik Antropov .20 .50
508 Ben Clymer .15 .40
509 Maxime Ouellet .20 .50
510 Trevor Kidd .15 .40
511 Brad Richards .25 .60
512 Todd Bertuzzi .25 .60
513 Wade Belak .15 .40
514 Brian Sutherby .15 .40
515 Fedor Fedorov .15 .40
516 Cory Sarich .15 .40
517 Brent Sopel .15 .40
518 Chris Pronger .25 .60
519 Brendan Morrison .20 .50
520 Sebastien Charpentier .15 .40
521 Alexander Svitov .15 .40
522 Calle Johansson .15 .40
523 Bryan McCabe .15 .40
524 Bryan Allen .15 .40
525 Bryce Salvador .15 .40
526 Dainius Zubrus .15 .40
527 Dallas Drake .15 .40
528 Dan Boyle .15 .40
529 Dan Cloutier .20 .50
530 Ken Klee .15 .40
531 Keith Tkachuk .25 .60
532 Brandon Reid .20 .50
533 Sergei Berezin .15 .40
534 Alex Auld .15 .40
535 Jaromir Jagr .75 2.00
536 Markus Naslund .25 .60
537 Jamal Mayers .15 .40
538 Ivan Ciernik .15 .40
539 Marek Malik .15 .40
540 Karel Pilar .15 .40
541 Fredrik Modin .15 .40
542 Gary Roberts .15 .40
543 Eric Boguniecki .15 .40
544 Henrik Sedin .30 .75
545 Ed Belfour .25 .60
546 Doug Weight .25 .60
547 Carlo Colaiacovo .15 .40
548 Peter Sejna RC .20 .50
549 Michael Nylander .15 .40
550 Daniel Sedin .30 .75
551 Kip Miller .15 .40
552 Robert Reichel .15 .40
553 Olaf Kolzig .25 .60
554 Reed Low .15 .40
555 Mikael Renberg .15 .40
556 Mike Grier .15 .40
557 Owen Nolan .25 .60
558 Nikolai Khabibulin .25 .60
559 Brad May .15 .40
560 Nikita Alexeev .15 .40
561 Sami Salo .15 .40
562 Martin St. Louis .25 .60
563 Brendan Witt .15 .40
564 Martin Rucinsky .15 .40
565 Mattias Ohlund .15 .40
566 Doug Gilmour .30 .75
567 Matt Cooke .15 .40
568 Dave Andreychuk .25 .60
569 Robert Lang .15 .40
570 Alexander Khavanov .15 .40
571 Tie Domi .20 .50
572 Ruslan Fedotenko .15 .40
573 Robert Svehla .15 .40
574 Tim Taylor .15 .40
575 Brent Johnson .20 .50
576 Brad Lukowich .15 .40
577 Sergei Gonchar .15 .40
578 Sheldon Keefe .15 .40
579 Steve Eminger .15 .40
580 Tomas Kaberle .15 .40
581 Steve Konowalchuk .15 .40
582 Chris Osgood .25 .60
583 Trevor Linden .25 .60
584 Travis Green .15 .40
585 Steve Martins .15 .40
586 John Grahame .15 .40
587 Darcy Tucker .20 .50
588 Jassen Cullimore .15 .40
589 Peter Bondra .25 .60
590 Pavol Demitra .30 .75
591 Nolan Pratt .15 .40
592 Jeff Halpern .15 .40
593 Vincent Lecavalier .25 .60
594 Petr Cajanek .15 .40
595 Chris Dingman .15 .40
596 Artem Chubarov .15 .40
597 Curtis Sanford .15 .40
598 Ed Jovanovski .20 .50
599 Mats Sundin .25 .60
600 Jarkko Ruutu .15 .40
601 Marc-Andre Fleury RC/321 20.00 50.00
602 Eric Staal RC/340 15.00 40.00
603 Tuomo Ruutu RC/299 5.00 12.00
604 Joni Pitkanen RC/316 5.00 12.00
605 Dustin Brown RC/287 8.00 20.00
606 Alexander Semin RC/291 10.00 25.00
607 Boyd Gordon RC/268 4.00 10.00
608 Pavel Vorobiev RC/203 4.00 10.00
609 Dan Hamhuis RC/286 4.00 10.00
610 Marek Zidlicky RC/308 3.00 8.00
611 Brent Burns RC/270 10.00 25.00
612 Cody McCormick RC/271 4.00 10.00
613 Antoine Vermette RC/280 6.00 15.00
614 Sean Bergenheim RC/291 4.00 10.00
615 Ryan Malone RC/310 6.00 15.00
616 Peter Sarno RC/284 3.00 8.00
617 Nathan Horton XRC/301 8.00 20.00
618 Joffrey Lupul XRC/306 8.00 20.00
619 Jordin Tootoo XRC/302 6.00 15.00
620 Patrice Bergeron XRC/299 15.00 40.00
621 Jiri Hudler XRC/291 8.00 20.00
622 Chris Higgins XRC/297 6.00 15.00
623 Maxim Kondratiev XRC/293 3.00 8.00
624 Brent Krahn XRC/283 3.00 8.00
625 Cover Card Checklist .15 .40
626 Kari Lehtonen XRC 2.00 5.00
627 Dan Fritsche XRC .50 1.25
628 Tim Gleason XRC .60 1.50
629 Derek Roy XRC .75 2.00
630 Matthew Lombardi XRC .60 1.50
631 John-Michael Liles XRC .60 1.50
632 Brian Leetch .40 1.00
633 Michael Ryder .40 1.00
634 Karl Stewart XRC .50 1.25
635 Jed Ortmeyer XRC .50 1.25
636 Dominic Moore XRC .50 1.25
637 Andrew Allen XRC .50 1.25
638 Ryan Kesler XRC 2.00 5.00
639 Tony Salmelainen XRC .50 1.25
640 Mikhail Yakubov XRC .50 1.25
641 Nathan Robinson XRC .50 1.25
642 Chris Simon .30 .75
643 Jeff Hamilton XRC .50 1.25
644 Nikolai Zherdev XRC 1.00 2.50
645 Steve Sullivan .30 .75
646 Niklas Kronwall XRC 1.00 2.50
647 Joey MacDonald XRC .60 1.50
648 Antero Niittymaki XRC 1.25 3.00
649 Noah Clarke XRC .50 1.25
650 Tim Jackman XRC .60 1.50
651 Timofei Shishkanov XRC .50 1.25
652 Marek Svatos XRC 1.00 2.50
653 Sergei Fedorov .75 2.00
654 Aleksander Suglobov XRC .50 1.25
655 Darryl Bootland XRC .60 1.50
656 Andrew Peters XRC .60 1.50
657 Anton Babchuk XRC .50 1.25
658 Kyle Wellwood XRC .75 2.00
659 Chris Kunitz XRC 1.00 2.50
660 Jozef Balej XRC .50 1.25
661 Christian Ehrhoff XRC .60 1.50
662 Dan Ellis XRC .60 1.50
663 Robert Lang .30 .75
664 Thomas Pihlman XRC .60 1.50
665 Andy Chiodo XRC .50 1.25
666 Adam Munro XRC .50 1.25
667 Denis Grebeshkov XRC .50 1.25
668 Matt Underhill XRC .50 1.25
669 Brad Boyes XRC .75 2.00
670 Paul Martin XRC .60 1.50
671 Matthew Yeats XRC .50 1.25
672 Alexei Zhamnov .40 1.00
673 Wade Dubielewicz XRC .50 1.25
674 Miikka Kiprusoff .50 1.25

2003-04 ITG Action Center of Attention

COMPLETE SET (10) 20.00 40.00
CA1 Mario Lemieux 4.00 10.00
CA2 Steve Yzerman 6.00 15.00
CA3 Joe Sakic 2.50 6.00
CA4 Peter Forsberg 2.50 6.00
CA5 Todd Bertuzzi 1.25 3.00
CA6 Joe Thornton 1.50 4.00
CA7 Sergei Fedorov 1.50 4.00
CA8 Mike Modano 1.50 4.00
CA9 Jason Spezza 2.00 5.00
CA10 Mats Sundin 1.25 3.00

2003-04 ITG Action First Time All-Star

COMPLETE SET (10) 8.00 15.00
FT1 Marian Gaborik 2.00 5.00
FT2 Dany Heatley 1.25 3.00
FT3 Marty Turco .75 2.00
FT4 Todd Bertuzzi .75 2.00
FT5 Olli Jokinen .75 2.00
FT6 Vincent Lecavalier .75 2.00
FT7 Patrick Lalime .75 2.00
FT8 Glen Murray .75 2.00
FT9 Martin St-Louis .75 2.00
FT10 Jocelyn Thibault .75 2.00

2003-04 ITG Action Highlight Reel

COMPLETE SET (12) 20.00 40.00
HR1 Jean-Sebastien Giguere .75 2.00
HR2 Patrick Roy 2.50 6.00
HR3 Martin Brodeur 2.50 6.00
HR4 Mario Lemieux 4.00 10.00
HR5 Dany Heatley .75 2.00
HR6 Joe Sakic 1.50 4.00
HR7 Joe Nieuwendyk .75 2.00
HR8 Jaromir Jagr 1.25 3.00
HR9 Brett Hull .75 2.00
HR10 Rick Nash 1.00 2.50
HR11 Marty Turco .75 2.00
HR12 Marian Gaborik 1.25 3.00

2003-04 ITG Action Homeboys

COMPLETE SET (14) 15.00 30.00
HB1 M.Naslund/P.Forsberg 1.25 3.00
HB2 R.Francis/M.Turco .75 2.00
HB3 Z.Chara/M.Gaborik .75 2.00
HB4 M.Comrie/S.Niedermayer .75 2.00
HB5 M.Messier/J.Iginla .75 2.00
HB6 D.Gilmour/K.Muller .75 2.00
HB7 E.Lindros/J.Thornton 1.00 2.50
HB8 N.Khabibulin/A.Yashin .75 2.00
HB9 J.Hurme/S.Koivu .75 2.00
HB10 M.Brodeur/M.Lemieux 4.00 10.00
HB11 B.Battaglia/C.Chelios .75 2.00
HB12 S.Weiss/A.Carter .75 2.00
HB13 J-S Giguere/R.Luongo 1.00 2.50
HB14 P.Bure/S.Samsonov .75 2.00

2003-04 ITG Action Jerseys

M1 Nik Antropov 4.00 10.00
M2 Jason Arnott 4.00 10.00
M3 Jared Aulin 4.00 10.00
M4 Mark Bell 4.00 10.00
M5 Bryan Berard 4.00 10.00
M6 Martin Biron 4.00 10.00
M7 Radek Bonk 4.00 10.00
M8 Nick Boynton 4.00 10.00
M9 Donald Brashear 6.00 15.00
M10 Eric Brewer 4.00 10.00
M11 Sergei Brylin 4.00 10.00
M12 Mike Cammalleri 4.00 10.00
M13 Dan Cloutier 4.00 10.00
M14 Carlo Colaiacovo 4.00 10.00
M15 Tim Connolly 4.00 10.00
M16 Byron Dafoe 4.00 10.00
M17 Adam Deadmarsh 4.00 10.00
M18 Shane Doan 4.00 10.00
M19 Tie Domi 4.00 10.00
M20 J-P Dumont 4.00 10.00
M21 Robert Esche 4.00 10.00
M22 Mike Fisher 4.00 10.00
M23 Adam Foote 4.00 10.00
M24 Martin Gerber 6.00 15.00
M25 Scott Gomez 4.00 10.00
M26 John Grahame 6.00 15.00
M27 Jeff Hackett 6.00 15.00
M28 Ron Hainsey 4.00 10.00
M29 Scott Hartnell 4.00 10.00
M30 Derian Hatcher 4.00 10.00
M31 Bobby Holik 4.00 10.00
M32 Marcel Hossa 4.00 10.00
M33 Ivan Huml 4.00 10.00
M34 Barret Jackman 6.00 15.00
M35 Brent Johnson 6.00 15.00
M36 Ed Jovanovski 6.00 15.00
M37 Tomas Kaberle 4.00 10.00
M38 Niko Kapanen 4.00 10.00
M39 Sami Kapanen 4.00 10.00
M40 Darius Kasparaitis 4.00 10.00
M41 Rostislav Klesla 4.00 10.00
M42 Chuck Kobasew 4.00 10.00
M43 Vyacheslav Kozlov 4.00 10.00
M44 Georges Laraque 6.00 15.00
M45 Igor Larionov 6.00 15.00
M46 Manny Legace 4.00 10.00
M47 David Legwand 4.00 10.00
M48 Jordan Leopold 4.00 10.00
M49 Trevor Linden 4.00 10.00
M50 John Madden 4.00 10.00
M51 Patrick Marleau 6.00 15.00
M52 Aleksey Morozov 4.00 10.00
M53 Derek Morris 4.00 10.00
M54 Brendan Morrison 6.00 15.00
M55 Brenden Morrow 6.00 15.00
M56 Rob Niedermayer 4.00 10.00
M57 Scott Niedermayer 4.00 10.00
M58 Joe Nieuwendyk 6.00 15.00
M59 Mika Noronen 4.00 10.00
M60 Pasi Nurminen 4.00 10.00
M61 Sandis Ozolinsh 4.00 10.00
M62 Yanic Perreault 4.00 10.00
M63 Chris Phillips 4.00 10.00
M64 Tom Poti 4.00 10.00
M65 Keith Primeau 4.00 10.00
M66 Branko Radivojevic 4.00 10.00
M67 Brian Rafalski 4.00 10.00
M68 Wade Redden 4.00 10.00
M69 Brandon Reid 4.00 10.00
M70 Steven Reinprecht 4.00 10.00
M71 Mike Richter 8.00 20.00
M72 Brian Rolston 4.00 10.00
M73 Miroslav Satan 4.00 10.00
M74 Kevin Sawyer 4.00 10.00
M75 Nick Schultz 4.00 10.00
M76 Daniel Sedin 6.00 15.00
M77 Henrik Sedin 6.00 15.00
M78 Alexei Smirnov 4.00 10.00
M79 Ryan Smyth 4.00 10.00
M80 Garth Snow 4.00 10.00
M81 Radovan Somik 4.00 10.00
M82 Martin Straka 4.00 10.00
M83 Alexander Svitov 4.00 10.00
M84 Darryl Sydor 4.00 10.00
M85 Roman Turek 6.00 15.00
M86 Pierre Turgeon 4.00 10.00
M87 Scottie Upshall 4.00 10.00
M88 Anton Volchenkov 4.00 10.00
M89 Peter Worrell 4.00 10.00
M90 Scott Young 5.00 10.00
M91 David Aebischer 6.00 15.00
M92 Jason Allison 6.00 15.00
M93 Tyler Arnason 6.00 15.00
M94 Dan Blackburn 6.00 15.00
M95 Daniel Briere 6.00 15.00
M96 Sean Burke 6.00 15.00
M97 Roman Cechmanek 6.00 15.00
M98 Erik Cole 6.00 15.00
M99 Vincent Damphousse 6.00 15.00
M100 Pavol Demitra 6.00 15.00
M101 Marc Denis 6.00 15.00
M102 Chris Drury 6.00 15.00
M103 Mike Dunham 6.00 15.00
M104 Manny Fernandez 6.00 15.00
M105 Simon Gagne 10.00 25.00
M106 Mathieu Garon 6.00 15.00
M107 Sergei Gonchar 6.00 15.00
M108 Johan Hedberg 6.00 15.00
M109 Ales Hemsky 6.00 15.00
M110 Kristian Huselius 6.00 15.00
M111 Jamie Langenbrunner 6.00 15.00
M112 Felix Potvin 12.00 30.00
M113 Brad Richards 6.00 15.00
M114 Dwayne Roloson 10.00 25.00
M115 Patrik Stefan 6.00 15.00
M116 Scott Stevens 6.00 15.00
M117 Alex Tanguay 6.00 15.00
M118 Kevin Weekes 6.00 15.00
M119 Stephen Weiss 6.00 15.00
M120 Sergei Zubov 6.00 15.00
M121 Daniel Alfredsson 8.00 20.00
M122 Tony Amonte 8.00 20.00
M123 Peter Bondra 8.00 20.00
M124 Chris Chelios 10.00 25.00
M125 Stanislav Chistov 8.00 20.00
M126 Pavel Datsyuk 12.00 30.00
M127 Eric Daze 8.00 20.00
M128 Patrik Elias 8.00 20.00
M129 Alexander Frolov 8.00 20.00
M130 Doug Gilmour 8.00 20.00
M131 Martin Havlat 8.00 20.00
M132 Olli Jokinen 8.00 20.00
M133 Nikolai Khabibulin 10.00 25.00
M134 Olaf Kolzig 8.00 20.00
M135 Patrick Lalime 8.00 20.00
M136 Vincent Lecavalier 10.00 25.00
M137 Ryan Miller 8.00 20.00
M138 Glen Murray 8.00 20.00
M139 Evgeni Nabokov 8.00 20.00
M140 Adam Oates 8.00 20.00
M141 Zigmund Palffy 8.00 20.00
M142 Mike Peca 8.00 20.00
M143 Chris Pronger 8.00 20.00
M144 Mark Recchi 8.00 20.00
M145 Gary Roberts 8.00 20.00
M146 Tommy Salo 8.00 20.00
M147 Martin St-Louis 8.00 20.00
M148 Keith Tkachuk 10.00 25.00
M149 Doug Weight 8.00 20.00
M150 Alexei Yashin 8.00 20.00
M151 Ed Belfour 12.00 30.00
M152 Todd Bertuzzi 12.00 30.00
M153 Rob Blake 10.00 25.00
M154 Jay Bouwmeester 10.00 25.00
M155 Mike Comrie 10.00 25.00
M156 Rick DiPietro 10.00 25.00
M157 Ron Francis 10.00 25.00
M158 Bill Guerin 10.00 25.00
M159 Milan Hejduk 12.00 30.00
M160 Marian Hossa 12.00 30.00
M161 Jarome Iginla 15.00 40.00
M162 Saku Koivu 12.00 30.00
M163 John LeClair 12.00 30.00
M164 Brian Leetch 10.00 25.00
M165 Eric Lindros 12.00 30.00
M166 Roberto Luongo 12.00 30.00
M167 Al MacInnis 10.00 25.00
M168 Mark Messier 15.00 40.00
M169 Alexander Mogilny 10.00 25.00
M170 Rick Nash 12.00 30.00
M171 Markus Naslund 12.00 30.00
M172 Owen Nolan 10.00 25.00
M173 Luc Robitaille 10.00 25.00
M174 Jeremy Roenick 15.00 40.00
M175 Sergei Samsonov 12.00 30.00
M176 Brendan Shanahan 12.00 30.00
M177 Jason Spezza 12.00 30.00
M178 Mats Sundin 12.00 30.00
M179 Jocelyn Thibault 10.00 25.00
M180 Marty Turco 10.00 20.00
M181 Martin Brodeur 30.00 80.00
M182 Pavel Bure 12.50 30.00
M183 Sergei Fedorov 20.00 50.00
M184 Peter Forsberg 15.00 40.00
M185 Marian Gaborik 15.00 40.00

M186 Jean-Sebastien Giguere 12.50 30.00
M187 Dany Heatley 12.50 30.00
M188 Brett Hull 20.00 50.00
M189 Jaromir Jagr 20.00 50.00
M190 Paul Kariya 12.50 30.00
M191 Ilya Kovalchuk 20.00 50.00
M192 Mario Lemieux 30.00 80.00
M193 Nicklas Lidstrom 12.50 30.00
M194 Mike Modano 15.00 40.00
M195 Patrick Roy 25.00 60.00
M196 Joe Sakic 25.00 60.00
M197 Dominik Hasek 15.00 40.00
M198 Jose Theodore 15.00 40.00
M199 Joe Thornton 15.00 40.00
M200 Steve Yzerman 30.00 80.00
M221 Gig/Chistv/Kriya/Sykra 15.00 40.00
M222 Brdur/Elias/Stens/Maddn 15.00 40.00
M223 Belfr/Sndin/Mgilny/Noln 25.00 50.00
M224 LeClr/Rnick/Amnte/Ggne 30.00 80.00
M225 Berrd/Smsnv/Thrntn/Mrry 20.00 50.00
M226 Hull/Yze/Hasek/Fedrv 40.00 80.00
M227 Roy/Frsbrg/Sakic/Hduk 40.00 100.00
M228 Turco/Mdno/Guerin/Mrrow 20.00 50.00
M229 Blckbrn/Bure/Mess/Lndros 25.00 60.00
M230 Lalime/Hssa/Spzza/Hvlat 25.00 60.00
M231 Thiblt/Daze/Sllvn/Arnson 15.00 40.00
M232 Miller/Satn/Afingnv/Briere 20.00 50.00
M233 Salo/Comrie/Smith/Laraque 20.00 50.00
M234 Heat/Kvlchuk/Dfoe/Stfan 20.00 50.00
M235 Osgd/Jkmn/Prngr/McInns 20.00 50.00
M236 Klzig/Jagr/Bndra/Emnger 15.00 40.00
M237 Lmieux/Hdbrg/Strka/Mrzv 30.00 80.00
M238 Clotier/Brtzzi/Nslnd/Jovo 15.00 40.00
M239 Vkun/Hartnll/Lgwnd/Upshll 20.00 50.00
M240 Theodre/Koivu/Garn/Hnsy 25.00 60.00
M241 J-S Giguere 10.00 25.00
M242 Dany Heatley 12.00 30.00
M243 Joe Thornton 12.00 30.00
M244 Miroslav Satan 10.00 25.00
M245 Jarome Iginla 15.00 40.00
M246 Ron Francis 10.00 25.00
M247 Jocelyn Thibault 10.00 25.00
M248 Patrick Roy 20.00 50.00
M249 Rick Nash 12.00 30.00
M250 Mike Modano 12.00 30.00
M251 Steve Yzerman 40.00 80.00
M252 Mike Comrie 10.00 25.00
M253 Roberto Luongo 15.00 40.00
M254 Zigmund Palffy 10.00 25.00
M255 Marian Gaborik 15.00 40.00
M256 Jose Theodore 15.00 40.00
M257 David Legwand 10.00 25.00
M258 Martin Brodeur 20.00 50.00
M259 Alexei Yashin 10.00 25.00
M260 Pavel Bure 12.00 30.00
M261 Marian Hossa 12.00 30.00
M262 Jeremy Roenick 12.00 30.00
M263 Sean Burke 10.00 25.00
M264 Mario Lemieux 30.00 80.00
M265 Chris Pronger 10.00 25.00
M266 Evgeni Nabokov 10.00 25.00
M267 Vincent Lecavalier 12.00 30.00
M268 Mats Sundin 12.00 30.00
M269 Markus Naslund 10.00 25.00
M270 Jaromir Jagr 12.00 30.00

2003-04 ITG Action League Leaders

COMPLETE SET (10) 12.50 25.00
L1 P.Forsberg/M.Hejduk 2.50 5.00
L2 Milan Hejduk .60 1.50
L3 Peter Forsberg 1.50 4.00
L4 Peter Forsberg 1.50 4.00
L5 Marty Turco .60 1.50
L6 Henrik Zetterberg .75 2.00
L7 Martin Brodeur 1.50 4.00
L8 Martin Brodeur 1.50 4.00
L9 Markus Naslund .60 1.50
L10 Dany Heatley .75 2.00

2003-04 ITG Action Oh Canada

COMPLETE SET 25.00 50.00
OC1 Mario Lemieux 4.00 10.00
OC2 Patrick Roy 3.00 8.00
OC3 Steve Yzerman 3.00 8.00
OC4 Martin Brodeur 2.50 6.00
OC5 Paul Kariya .75 2.00
OC6 Joe Sakic 2.00 5.00
OC7 Mark Messier .75 2.00
OC8 Jean-Sebastien Giguere .75 2.00
OC9 Jason Spezza 1.25 3.00
OC10 Dany Heatley 1.00 2.50
OC11 Curtis Joseph .75 2.00
OC12 Ed Belfour .75 2.00
OC13 Brendan Shanahan .75 2.00
OC14 Joe Thornton 1.00 2.50

2003-04 ITG Action Trophy Winners

TW1 Peter Forsberg 2.50 6.00
TW2 Martin Brodeur 3.00 8.00
TW3 Nicklas Lidstrom 1.50 4.00
TW4 Barret Jackman 1.50 4.00
TW5 Markus Naslund 1.50 4.00
TW6 Peter Forsberg 2.50 6.00

2004 ITG NHL All-Star FANtasy All-Star History Jerseys

SB42 Jeremy Roenick 12.50 30.00
SB43 Jaromir Jagr 12.50 30.00
SB44 Luc Robitaille 12.50 30.00
SB45 Joe Sakic 15.00 40.00
SB46 Eric Lindros 12.50 30.00
SB47 Paul Kariya 15.00 40.00
SB48 Mike Modano 12.50 30.00
SB49 Peter Forsberg 20.00 50.00
SB50 Pavel Bure 12.50 30.00
SB51 Milan Hejduk 12.50 30.00
SB52 Mats Sundin 12.50 30.00
SB53 Marian Gaborik 15.00 40.00
SB54 Ilya Kovalchuk 12.50 30.00

2004 ITG All-Star FANtasy Hall Minnesota

COMPLETE SET (10) 75.00 125.00
1 Mike Gartner 4.00 10.00
2 Derian Hatcher 4.00 10.00
3 Mike Modano 12.00 30.00
4 Jordan Leopold 4.00 10.00
5 Manny Fernandez 6.00 15.00
6 Dwayne Roloson 6.00 15.00
7 Marian Gaborik 20.00 50.00
8 Pierre-Marc Bouchard 6.00 15.00
9 Gump Worsley 12.00 30.00
10 Dino Ciccarelli 4.00 10.00

2008-09 ITG Bleu Blanc et Rouge

1 Alex Tanguay 6.00 15.00
2 Bernie Geoffrion 6.00 15.00
3 Bobby Rousseau 8.00 20.00
4 Bobby Smith 6.00 15.00
5 Carey Price 20.00 50.00
6 Charlie Hodge 8.00 20.00
7 Chris Chelios 10.00 25.00
8 Denis Savard 10.00 25.00
9 Dick Duff 8.00 20.00
10 Dickie Moore 8.00 20.00
11 Dollard St. Laurent 6.00 15.00
12 Doug Gilmour 15.00 40.00
13 Doug Harvey 10.00 25.00
14 Frank Mahovlich 10.00 25.00
15 Guillaume Latendresse 6.00 15.00
16 Gump Worsley 8.00 20.00
17 Guy Carbonneau 10.00 25.00
18 Guy Lafleur 12.00 30.00
19 Guy Lapointe 8.00 20.00
20 Henri Richard 12.00 30.00
21 J.C. Tremblay 6.00 15.00
22 Jacques Laperriere 8.00 20.00
23 Jacques Lemaire 8.00 20.00
24 Jacques Plante 15.00 40.00
25 Jean Beliveau 10.00 25.00
26 Jean Guy Talbot 8.00 20.00
27 Cristobal Huet 8.00 20.00
28 Larry Robinson 10.00 25.00
29 Mats Naslund 6.00 15.00
30 Patrick Roy 25.00 60.00
31 Pete Mahovlich 12.00 30.00
32 Phil Goyette 6.00 15.00
33 Ralph Backstrom 6.00 15.00
34 Rogie Vachon 12.00 30.00
35 Saku Koivu 10.00 25.00
36 Serge Savard 15.00 40.00
37 Stephane Richer 8.00 20.00
38 Steve Shutt 12.00 30.00
39 Terry Harper 6.00 15.00
40 Yvan Cournoyer 10.00 25.00

2008-09 ITG Bleu Blanc et Rouge Autographs

AAT Alex Tanguay/19 12.00 30.00
ABR Bobby Rousseau/40 10.00 25.00
ABS Bobby Smith/40 8.00 20.00
ABSA Brian Savage/25 12.00 30.00
ACC Chris Chelios/25 20.00 50.00
ACH Charlie Hodge/40 10.00 25.00
ACHU Cristobal Huet/25 15.00 40.00
ACP1 Carey Price/25 30.00 80.00
ACP2 Carey Price/25 30.00 80.00
ADD Dick Duff/40 10.00 25.00
ADG Doug Gilmour/40 15.00 40.00
ADM1 Dickie Moore/40 10.00 25.00
ADM2 Dickie Moore/25 15.00 40.00
AEB Emile Bouchard/40 15.00 40.00
AEL1 Elmer Lach/40 10.00 25.00
AEL2 Elmer Lach/40 10.00 25.00
AGC Guy Carbonneau/40 12.00 30.00
AGL1 Guy Lafleur/19 20.00 50.00
AGL2 Guy Lafleur/19 20.00 50.00
AGLA Guy Lapointe/40 10.00 25.00
AGLAT G.Latendresse/25 12.00 30.00
AHR1 Henri Richard/19 25.00 60.00
AHR2 Henri Richard/19 25.00 60.00
AJB1 Jean Beliveau/19 25.00 60.00
AJB2 Jean Beliveau/19 25.00 60.00
AJGT1 Jean Guy Talbot/25 15.00 40.00
AJGT2 Jean Guy Talbot/25 15.00 40.00
AJL1 Jacques Laperriere/40 25.00 60.00
AJL2 Jacques Laperriere/25 30.00 80.00
AJLE Jacques Lemaire/40 15.00 40.00
ALR1 Larry Robinson/25 20.00 50.00
ALR2 Larry Robinson/25 20.00 50.00
AMD Mathieu Dandenault/40 12.00 30.00
AMN Mats Naslund/40 8.00 20.00
AMT Marc Tardif/40 12.00 30.00
AMTR Mario Tremblay/40 15.00 40.00
APG1 Phil Goyette/25 15.00 40.00
APG2 Phil Goyette/25 15.00 40.00
APM Pete Mahovlich/40 15.00 40.00
APR1 Patrick Roy/19 50.00 125.00
APR2 Patrick Roy/19 50.00 125.00
ARV Rogie Vachon/25 25.00 60.00
ARW Ryan Walter/40 8.00 20.00
ASD Denis Savard/40 12.00 30.00
ASK1 Saku Koivu/19 20.00 50.00
ASK2 Saku Koivu/19 20.00 50.00
ASQ Stephane Quintal/25 12.00 30.00
ASR Stephane Richer/40 10.00 25.00
ASS1 Serge Savard/25 25.00 60.00
ASS2 Serge Savard/25 25.00 60.00
ASSH1 Steve Shutt/25 20.00 50.00
ASSH2 Steve Shutt/25 20.00 50.00
AYC1 Yvan Cournoyer/40 12.00 30.00
AYC2 Yvan Cournoyer/25 20.00 50.00
AYL Yvon Lambert/40 12.00 30.00

2008-09 ITG Bleu Blanc et Rouge Vintage

1 Armand Mondou 6.00 15.00
2 Aurel Joliat 10.00 25.00
3 Babe Siebert 8.00 20.00
4 Albert Leduc 8.00 20.00
5 Bill Boucher 6.00 15.00
6 Bill Durnan 10.00 25.00
7 Cecil Hart 6.00 15.00
8 Didier Pitre 6.00 15.00
9 Elmer Lach 8.00 20.00
10 Pit Lepine 12.00 30.00
11 George Hainsworth 12.00 30.00
12 Georges Vezina 15.00 40.00
13 Herb Gardiner 6.00 15.00
14 Howie Morenz 6.00 15.00
15 Jack Laviolette 8.00 20.00
16 Joe Malone 8.00 20.00
17 Johnny Gagnon 6.00 15.00
18 Lorne Chabot 8.00 20.00
19 Maurice Richard 20.00 50.00
20 Newsy Lalonde 8.00 20.00
21 Paul Haynes 6.00 15.00
22 Sprague Cleghorn 15.00 40.00
23 Sylvio Mantha 8.00 20.00
24 Toe Blake 6.00 15.00
25 Wilf Cude 12.00 30.00

2011-12 ITG Broad Street Boys

1 Andre Lacroix EY .75 2.00
2 Bernie Parent EY 1.50 4.00
3 Bill Sutherland EY .75 2.00
4 Brit Selby EY .75 2.00
5 Doug Favell EY 1.25 3.00
6 Ed Van Impe EY 1.00 2.50
7 Forbes Kennedy EY .75 2.00
8 Gary Dornhoefer EY .75 2.00
9 Joe Watson EY .75 2.00
10 Larry Zeidel EY .75 2.00
11 Leon Rochefort EY .75 2.00
12 Lou Angotti EY .75 2.00
13 Pat Hannigan EY .75 2.00
14 Simon Nolet EY 1.00 2.50
15 Andre Dupont BSB .75 2.00
16 Bernie Parent BSB 1.50 4.00
17 Bill Barber BSB 1.25 3.00
18 Bill Clement BSB 1.00 2.50
19 Bob Dailey BSB .75 2.00
20 Bob Kelly BSB .75 2.00
21 Bobby Clarke BSB 2.00 5.00
22 Bobby Taylor BSB .75 2.00
23 Dave Schultz BSB 1.25 3.00
24 Don Saleski BSB .75 2.00
25 Jack McIlhargey BSB 1.00 2.50
26 Jim Watson BSB 1.00 2.50
27 Larry Goodenough BSB .75 2.00
28 Orest Kindrachuk BSB .75 2.00
29 Paul Holmgren BSB 1.00 2.50
30 Reggie Leach BSB 1.00 2.50
31 Rick MacLeish BSB 1.00 2.50
32 Ross Lonsberry BSB .75 2.00
33 Simon Nolet BSB 1.00 2.50
34 Terry Crisp BSB .75 2.00
35 Tom Bladon BSB .75 2.00
36 Wayne Stephenson BSB .75 2.00
37 Dave Brown TT .75 2.00
38 Brad Marsh TT .75 2.00
39 Brian Propp TT 1.00 2.50
40 Darryl Sittler TT 1.50 4.00
41 Dave Poulin TT .75 2.00
42 Ken Linseman TT 1.25 3.00
43 Mark Howe TT 1.25 3.00
44 Mel Bridgman TT .75 2.00
45 Mike Keenan TT 1.00 2.50
46 Murray Craven TT .75 2.00
47 Pelle Lindbergh TT 1.00 2.50
48 Phil Myre TT 1.00 2.50
49 Rich Sutter TT 1.00 2.50
50 Ron Hextall TT 1.25 3.00
51 Ron Sutter TT 1.00 2.50
52 Tim Kerr TT .75 2.00
53 Bob Froese TT 1.00 2.50
54 Pete Peeters TT 1.00 2.50
55 Chico Resch TT 1.25 3.00
56 Craig Berube C90 .75 2.00
57 Dale Hawerchuk C90 1.50 4.00
58 Eric Desjardins C90 1.00 2.50
59 Eric Lindros C90 2.00 5.00
60 John LeClair C90 1.25 3.00
61 John Vanbiesbrouck C90 1.25 3.00
62 Chris Therien C90 1.00 2.50
63 Kjell Samuelsson C90 .75 2.00
64 Mark Recchi C90 1.50 4.00
65 Paul Coffey C90 1.25 3.00
66 Rod Brind'Amour C90 1.25 3.00
67 Sandy McCarthy C90 1.00 2.50
68 Scott Mellanby C90 1.00 2.50
69 Antero Niittymaki NM 1.00 2.50
70 Brian Boucher NM 1.00 2.50
71 Dan Carcillo NM .75 2.00
72 Donald Brashear NM 1.00 2.50
73 Jeff Carter NM 1.00 2.50
74 Jeremy Roenick NM 2.00 5.00
75 Joffrey Lupul NM .75 2.00
76 Keith Primeau NM 1.00 2.50
77 Mike Richards NM 1.00 2.50
78 Peter Forsberg NM 2.50 6.00
79 Ray Emery NM 1.00 2.50
80 Roman Cechmanek NM 1.25 3.00
81 Tony Amonte NM 1.00 2.50
82 Erik Gustafsson TC 1.00 2.50
83 Matt Carle TC 1.00 2.50
84 Braydon Coburn TC .75 2.00
85 Sean Couturier TC 2.00 5.00
86 Maxime Talbot TC .75 2.00
87 Brayden Schenn TC 1.25 3.00
88 Chris Pronger TC 1.25 3.00
89 Claude Giroux TC 1.25 3.00
90 Daniel Briere TC 1.25 3.00
91 Ilya Bryzgalov TC 1.25 3.00
92 James van Riemsdyk TC 1.25 3.00
93 Jaromir Jagr TC 4.00 10.00
94 Matt Read TC .75 2.00
95 Sergei Bobrovsky TC 2.00 5.00
96 Tom Sestito TC .75 2.00
97 Zac Rinaldo TC 1.00 2.50
98 First Cup GM/B.Clarke/B.Parent 2.00 5.00
99 Second Cup GM/Clarke/Parent 2.00 5.00
100 1976 Red Army Game GM 2.00 5.00

2011-12 ITG Broad Street Boys Gold

GOLD/50: 1.5X TO 4X BASIC CARDS

2011-12 ITG Broad Street Boys Autographs

AAD Andre Dupont 5.00 12.00
AAL Andre Lacroix 5.00 12.00
AAN Antero Niittymaki 6.00 15.00
ABB Bill Barber 8.00 20.00
ABC Bill Clement 6.00 15.00
ABCL Bobby Clarke SP 40.00 80.00
ABCO Braydon Coburn SP 40.00 80.00
ABD Bob Dailey 5.00 12.00
ABF Bob Froese 6.00 15.00
ABK Bob Kelly 5.00 12.00
ABM Brad Marsh 5.00 12.00
ABP Bernie Parent SP 40.00 80.00
ABPR Brian Propp 8.00 20.00
ABS Brit Selby 5.00 12.00
ABSU Bill Sutherland 6.00 15.00
ABT Bobby Taylor 8.00 20.00
ACB Craig Berube 5.00 12.00
ACG Claude Giroux SP 30.00 60.00
ACP Chris Pronger SP 30.00 60.00
ACT Chris Therien 6.00 15.00
ADB Daniel Briere SP 20.00 50.00
ADBR Dave Brown 5.00 12.00
ADC Dan Carcillo 5.00 12.00
ADF Doug Favell SP 30.00 80.00
ADH Dale Hawerchuk SP 25.00 50.00
ADL1 Dave Leonardi 5.00 12.00
ADL2 Dave Leonardi 5.00 12.00
ADL3 Dave Leonardi 6.00 15.00
ADP Dave Poulin 5.00 12.00
ADS Dave Schultz 6.00 15.00
ADSA Don Saleski 6.00 15.00
ADSI Darryl Sittler SP 75.00 150.00
AED Eric Desjardins 6.00 15.00
AEL Eric Lindros SP 60.00 100.00
AEVA Ed Van Impe 6.00 15.00
AFK Forbes Kennedy 6.00 15.00
AGD Gary Dornhoefer 5.00 12.00
AGR Glenn Resch 8.00 20.00
AIB Ilya Bryzgalov SP 25.00 50.00
AJJ Jaromir Jagr SP 40.00 80.00
AJL Joffrey Lupul 5.00 12.00
AJLE John LeClair SP 25.00 60.00
AJM Jack McIlhargey 6.00 15.00
AJR Jeremy Roenick SP 40.00 80.00
AJV John Vanbiesbrouck 15.00 30.00
AJW Joe Watson 5.00 12.00
AJWA Jim Watson 6.00 15.00
AKL Ken Linseman 8.00 20.00
AKP Keith Primeau 6.00 15.00
AKS Kjell Samuelsson 6.00 15.00
ALA Lou Angotti 5.00 12.00
ALG Larry Goodenough 5.00 12.00
ALR Leon Rochefort 5.00 12.00
ALZ Larry Zeidel 6.00 15.00
AMB Mel Bridgman 5.00 12.00
AMC Murray Craven 5.00 12.00
AMH Mark Howe SP 20.00 40.00
AMK Mike Keenan 8.00 20.00
AML Michael Leighton 6.00 15.00
AMLA Mark Laforest 5.00 12.00
AMR Mark Recchi 15.00 30.00
AMRE Matt Read SP 20.00 50.00
AOK Orest Kindrachuk 6.00 15.00
APC Paul Coffey SP 60.00 120.00
APF Peter Forsberg SP 75.00 125.00
APH Paul Holmgren 6.00 15.00
APM Phil Myre 6.00 15.00
APP Pete Peeters 8.00 20.00
ARB Rod Brind'Amour 12.50 25.00
ARH Ron Hextall SP 25.00 50.00
ARL Reggie Leach 6.00 15.00
ARLO Ross Lonsberry 6.00 15.00
ARM Rick MacLeish 8.00 20.00
ARS Rich Sutter 6.00 15.00
ARST Rick St. Croix 5.00 12.00
ARSU Ron Sutter 6.00 15.00
ASB Sean Burke SP 75.00 135.00
ASBO Sergei Bobrovsky 12.00 30.00
ASC Sean Couturier SP 60.00 100.00
ASD Steve Downie 6.00 15.00
ASM Sandy McCarthy 6.00 15.00
ASME Scott Mellanby 6.00 15.00
ASN Simon Nolet 6.00 15.00
ASP Shjon Podein 5.00 12.00
ATA Tony Amonte 6.00 15.00
ATC Terry Crisp 5.00 12.00
ATK Tim Kerr 8.00 20.00
AUS Ulf Samuelsson 8.00 20.00

2011-12 ITG Broad Street Boys Brotherly Love Dual Jerseys

CBL01 J.Watson/J.Watson 15.00 40.00
CBL02 R.Sutter/R.Sutter 10.00 25.00

2011-12 ITG Broad Street Boys Game-Used Jerseys

M01 Tony Amonte/120* 5.00 12.00
M02 Blair Betts/120* 5.00 12.00
M03 Sergei Bobrovsky/120* 10.00 25.00
M04 Brian Boucher/120* 5.00 12.00
M05 Donald Brashear/120* 5.00 12.00
M06 Mel Bridgman/120* 5.00 12.00
M07 Daniel Briere/120* 6.00 15.00
M08 Rod Brind'Amour/120* 6.00 15.00
M09 Dave Brown/120* 4.00 10.00
M10 Ilya Bryzgalov/120* 6.00 15.00
M11 Dan Carcillo/120* 4.00 10.00
M12 Jeff Carter/120* 5.00 12.00
M13 Braydon Coburn/120* 4.00 10.00
M14 Eric Desjardins/120* 6.00 15.00
M15 Ray Emery/120* 6.00 15.00
M16 Peter Forsberg/120* 12.00 30.00
M17 Nicklas Grossman/120* 6.00 15.00
M18 Ron Hextall/120* 6.00 15.00
M19 Mark Howe/120* 6.00 15.00
M20 Pavel Kubina/120* 4.00 10.00
M21 Mark LaForest/120* 4.00 10.00
M22 Reggie Leach/120* 6.00 15.00
M23 John LeClair/120* 8.00 20.00
M24 Andreas Lilja/120* 4.00 10.00
M25 Eric Lindros/120* 6.00 15.00
M26 Phil Myre/120* 5.00 12.00
M27 Keith Primeau/120* 5.00 12.00
M28 Brian Propp/120* 5.00 12.00
M29 Mark Recchi/120* 6.00 15.00
M30 Chico Resch/120* 6.00 15.00
M31 Zac Rinaldo/120* 5.00 12.00
M32 Jeremy Roenick/120* 10.00 25.00
M33 Jody Shelley/120* 5.00 12.00
M34 Darryl Sittler/120* 8.00 20.00
M35 P.J. Stock/120* 5.00 12.00
M36 Rich Sutter/120* 5.00 12.00
M37 Ron Sutter/120* 5.00 12.00
M38 John Vanbiesbrouck/120* 10.00 25.00
M39 Bill Barber/40* 10.00 25.00
M40 Bobby Clarke/40* 20.00 50.00
M41 Rick MacLeish/40* 10.00 25.00
M42 Claude Giroux/40* 20.00 40.00
M43 Bernie Parent/15* 40.00 80.00
M44 Dave Schultz/15* 100.00 200.00

2011-12 ITG Broad Street Boys Goaltenders Jerseys

G01 Sergei Bobrovsky/50* 12.00 30.00
G02 Brian Boucher/50* 6.00 15.00
G03 Ilya Bryzgalov/50* 8.00 20.00
G04 Roman Cechmanek/50* 10.00 25.00
G05 Ray Emery/50* 6.00 15.00
G06 Robert Esche/50* 6.00 15.00
G07 Ron Hextall/50* 8.00 20.00
G08 Chico Resch/50* 8.00 20.00
G09 Michael Leighton/50* 6.00 15.00
G10 Phil Myre/50* 6.00 15.00
G11 Antero Niittymaki/50* 6.00 15.00
G12 John Vanbiesbrouck/50* 10.00 25.00

2011-12 ITG Broad Street Boys Quad Memorabilia

QM01 Rnick/Amnte/Lndrs/Leclr 25.00 60.00
QM02 Briere/Bryzg/Girx/Coburn 15.00 40.00
QM03 Brshr/Brwn/Brb/McCrth 12.00 30.00
QM04 Saleski/Drnh/Lch/Brdg 15.00 40.00
QM05 Clrke/Barbr/McLsh/Lch 15.00 40.00
QM06 Hextl/Prnt/Bryzg/Vanbs 20.00 50.00

2011-12 ITG Broad Street Boys Raised To The Rafters Jerseys

RTR01 Bernie Parent 40.00 80.00
RTR02 Bill Barber 20.00 50.00
RTR03 Bobby Clarke 30.00 80.00
RTR04 Mark Howe 20.00 50.00

2011-12 ITG Broad Street Boys Starting Line-Up Six Jerseys

SL01 Prn/Wts/Wts/Clk/Brb/McLs 60.00 120.00
SL02 Vnb/Dsj/Sml/Lnd/Lclr/Rec 50.00 100.00

2011-12 ITG Broad Street Boys Tough Materials Triples

TM01 Brash/Brube/Brwn/120* 8.00 20.00
TM02 Carcillo/Kane/Shlly/120* 8.00 20.00
TM03 Hxtll/Lndrs/McCrthy/120* 15.00 40.00
TM04 Clrke/Salski/Schultz/19* 60.00 120.00

2011-12 ITG Canada vs The World Autographs

AAH Anders Hedberg 5.00 12.00
AAI Arturs Irbe 8.00 20.00
AAJ Angela James 5.00 12.00
AAL Adam Larsson 6.00 15.00
AAM Al MacInnis 8.00 20.00
AAMA Alexander Maltsev 10.00 25.00
AAN Antti Niemi 5.00 12.00
AAO Alexander Ovechkin 40.00 100.00
AAS Alexander Semin 6.00 15.00
AAY Alexander Yakushev SP 20.00 50.00
ABBA Bill Barber 6.00 15.00
ABC Bobby Clarke SP 20.00 50.00
ABH Bobby Hull 20.00 50.00
ABHU Brett Hull SP 20.00 50.00
ABL Brian Leetch 5.00 12.00
ABM Boris Mikhailov 30.00 60.00
ABMO Brendan Morrow SP 8.00 20.00
ABP Brad Park 5.00 12.00
ABPR Brian Propp 5.00 12.00
ABR Bobby Ryan 5.00 12.00
ABRA Bill Ranford 6.00 15.00
ABS Borje Salming 6.00 15.00
ABSM Billy Smith 8.00 20.00
ABSMI Bobby Smith 5.00 12.00
ACC Chris Chelios 6.00 15.00
ACG Clark Gillies SP 8.00 20.00
ACH Craig Hartsburg 4.00 10.00
ACHO Cody Hodgson 12.50 30.00
ACJ Curtis Joseph 8.00 20.00
ACL Charline Labonte SP 15.00 40.00
ACN Chris Nilan 4.00 10.00
ACP Carey Price 12.00 30.00
ADG Doug Gilmour 12.00 30.00
ADGA Danny Gare 5.00 12.00
ADH Dominik Hasek 12.00 30.00
ADHA Dale Hawerchuk 5.00 12.00
ADHE Darren Helm 4.00 10.00
ADK Duncan Keith 8.00 20.00
ADP Denis Potvin 6.00 15.00
ADS Darryl Sittler 8.00 20.00
ADSE Daniel Sedin SP 25.00 60.00
ADW Doug Wilson 5.00 12.00
AEL Eric Lindros 40.00 80.00
AES Eric Staal 8.00 20.00
AET Esa Tikkanen 5.00 12.00
AGA Glenn Anderson 5.00 12.00
AGC Gerry Cheevers 6.00 15.00
AGF Grant Fuhr SP 25.00 60.00
AGL Guy Lafleur 8.00 20.00
AGLA Guy Lapointe 6.00 15.00
AGP Gilbert Perreault 6.00 15.00
AHS Henrik Sedin SP 30.00 60.00
AIK Ilya Kovalchuk 8.00 20.00
AIL Igor Larionov SP 15.00 40.00
AJA Jake Allen 10.00 25.00
AJC Jim Craig 15.00 40.00
AJH Jaroslav Halak SP 12.00 30.00
AJHI Jonas Hiller SP 12.00 30.00
AJJ Jaromir Jagr 40.00 80.00
AJK Jari Kurri 6.00 15.00
AJL John LeClair 6.00 15.00
AJM Jacob Markstrom 6.00 15.00
AJMU Joe Mullen 5.00 12.00
AJN Joe Nieuwendyk SP 8.00 20.00
AJPP J-P Parise 4.00 10.00
AJR Jeremy Roenick 12.00 30.00
AJS Joe Sakic 20.00 50.00
AJT Joe Thornton SP 10.00 25.00
AJV John Vanbiesbrouck 6.00 15.00
AKD Kevin Dineen 5.00 12.00
AKN Kent Nilsson SP 6.00 15.00
AKT Keith Tkachuk 6.00 15.00
AKTU Kyle Turris 5.00 12.00
ALC Logan Couture 8.00 20.00
ALMU Larry Murphy 5.00 12.00
ALR Luc Robitaille 10.00 25.00
ALRO Larry Robinson 6.00 15.00
AMB Mike Bossy 8.00 20.00
AMBR Martin Brodeur SP 20.00 50.00
AMD Marcel Dionne SP 15.00 40.00
AMF Marc-Andre Fleury SP 12.00 30.00
AMG Michel Goulet 5.00 12.00
AMGA Marian Gaborik 6.00 15.00
AMGAR Mike Gartner 12.00 30.00
AMGR Mike Green 5.00 12.00
AMH Mark Howe 6.00 15.00
AMH Matt Halischuk 4.00 10.00
AMK Mikko Koivu 5.00 12.00
AML Mario Lemieux SP 50.00 100.00
AMLI Mike Liut SP 15.00 40.00
AMLU Milan Lucic 6.00 15.00
AMM Mike Modano 10.00 25.00
AMM Mark Messier SP 40.00 80.00
AMN Mats Naslund 4.00 10.00
AMR Manon Rheaume 15.00 40.00
AMRI Mike Richter SP 25.00 60.00
AMS Marian Stastny 6.00 15.00
AMSL Martin St. Louis 6.00 15.00
AMW Mark Wells 4.00 10.00
ANB Niklas Backstrom 8.00 20.00
ANBR Neal Broten SP 6.00 15.00
ANL Nicklas Lidstrom 8.00 20.00
AOE Oliver Ekman-Larsson 6.00 15.00
APB Pavel Bure SP 15.00 40.00
APC Paul Coffey 8.00 20.00
APE Phil Esposito 10.00 25.00
APF Peter Forsberg 20.00 50.00
APH Phil Housley 5.00 12.00
APHE Paul Henderson 12.00 30.00
APL Pat LaFontaine 6.00 15.00
APM Patrick Marleau 8.00 20.00
APR Patrick Roy SP 60.00 120.00
APS Pat Stapleton 4.00 10.00
APST Peter Stastny 10.00 25.00
ARB Raymond Bourque SP 15.00 40.00
ARG Ryan Getzlaf 6.00 15.00
ARH Ron Hextall 6.00 15.00
ARL Rod Langway SP 6.00 15.00
ARLU Roberto Luongo 10.00 25.00
ARM Rick Middleton 10.00 25.00
ARN Rick Nash SP 20.00 50.00
ARV Rogie Vachon 8.00 20.00
ASB Sean Burke 6.00 15.00
ASK Saku Koivu SP 40.00 80.00
ASL Steve Larmer 5.00 12.00
ASM Stan Mikita 10.00 25.00
ASN Scott Niedermayer 6.00 15.00
ASS Steve Shutt 10.00 25.00
ASSA Serge Savard 6.00 15.00
ASSM Sami Jo Small 5.00 12.00
ASST Steven Stamkos 15.00 40.00
ASV Semyon Varlamov 12.00 30.00
ASW Shea Weber SP 12.00 30.00
ASY Steve Yzerman SP 50.00 100.00
ATA Tony Amonte 6.00 15.00
ATB Tom Barrasso 6.00 15.00
ATE Tony Esposito SP 10.00 25.00
ATE2 Tony Esposito SP 10.00 25.00
ATF Theoren Fleury 15.00 40.00
ATG Tony Granato 4.00 10.00
ATH Thomas Hickey 5.00 12.00
ATL Trevor Linden 15.00 40.00
ATR Tuukka Rask SP 15.00 30.00
ATS Teemu Selanne 12.00 30.00
ATST Thomas Steen 4.00 10.00
ATT Tim Thomas 10.00 25.00
ATV Tomas Vokoun 8.00 20.00
AUN Ulf Nilsson 5.00 12.00
AUS Ulf Samuelsson 6.00 15.00
AVK Vladimir Krutov 12.00 30.00
AVL Vincent Lecavalier SP 10.00 25.00
AVT Vladislav Tretiak SP 50.00 100.00
AVTA Vladimir Tarasenko 50.00 100.00
AVV Valeri Vasiliev 10.00 25.00
AYC Yvan Cournoyer 6.00 15.00
AZB Zach Boychuk 4.00 10.00
AZC Zdeno Chara 8.00 20.00
AZP Zigmund Palffy 6.00 15.00

2011-12 ITG Canada vs The World Canada's Best Silver

CB01 Lngo/Brodr/Roy/Joseph 30.00 60.00
CB02 Price/Ward/Fleury/Pogge 30.00 60.00
CB03 Stmk/Lecv/Thrntn/St.L 30.00 60.00
CB04 Sakic/Yzer/Bike/Nieuw 25.00 50.00
CB05 Lind/Flry/Hwrchk/MacInn 30.00 60.00
CB06 Sittlr/Espos/Perrlt/Bossy 25.00 50.00

2011-12 ITG Canada vs The World Canadian Cloth Black

*SILVER/30: .6X TO 1.5X BLACK/120
CCM01 Alex Auld 3.00 8.00
CCM02 Jonathan Bernier 3.00 8.00
CCM03 Dino Ciccarelli 4.00 10.00
CCM04 Martin Brodeur 10.00 25.00
CCM05 Angela James 3.00 8.00
CCM06 Devan Dubnyk 3.00 8.00
CCM07 Theoren Fleury 12.00 30.00
CCM08 Sami Jo Small 3.00 8.00
CCM09 Danny Gare 3.00 8.00
CCM10 Michel Goulet 3.00 8.00
CCM11 Dale Hawerchuk 5.00 12.00
CCM12 Curtis Joseph 5.00 12.00
CCM13 Vincent Lecavalier 4.00 10.00
CCM14 Kristopher Letang 12.00 30.00
CCM15 Eric Lindros 6.00 15.00
CCM16 Roberto Luongo 6.00 15.00
CCM17 Al MacInnis 5.00 12.00
CCM18 Patrick Marleau 4.00 10.00
CCM19 Joe Nieuwendyk 3.00 8.00
CCM20 Ron Francis 3.00 8.00
CCM21 Joe Sakic 8.00 20.00
CCM22 Darryl Sittler 5.00 12.00
CCM23 Steve Shutt 4.00 10.00
CCM24 Martin St. Louis 4.00 10.00
CCM25 Marc Staal 3.00 8.00
CCM26 Garry Unger 5.00 12.00
CCM27 Joe Thornton 6.00 15.00
CCM28 Kim St-Pierre 4.00 10.00
CCM29 Cam Ward 4.00 10.00
CCM30 Darren Helm 2.50 6.00
CCM31 Kyle Turris 2.50 6.00
CCM32 Patrice Bergeron 5.00 12.00
CCM33 Logan Couture 5.00 12.00
CCM34 Zach Boychuk 2.50 6.00
CCM35 Marcel Dionne 5.00 12.00

2011-12 ITG Canada vs The World Global Greats Silver

GG01 Mark Messier 8.00 20.00
GG02 Raymond Bourque 6.00 15.00
GG03 Steve Yzerman 10.00 25.00
GG04 Paul Coffey 4.00 10.00
GG05 Theoren Fleury 15.00 40.00
GG06 Mario Lemieux 15.00 40.00
GG07 Joe Sakic 8.00 20.00
GG08 Rick Nash 4.00 10.00
GG09 Scott Niedermayer 4.00 10.00
GG10 Jaromir Jagr 8.00 20.00
GG11 Dominik Hasek 6.00 15.00
GG12 Teemu Selanne 8.00 20.00
GG13 Jari Kurri 4.00 10.00
GG14 Saku Koivu 4.00 10.00
GG15 Mike Richter 4.00 10.00
GG16 Brett Hull 8.00 20.00
GG17 Keith Tkachuk 4.00 10.00
GG18 Jeremy Roenick 8.00 20.00
GG19 Ryan Miller 4.00 10.00
GG20 Tim Thomas 5.00 12.00
GG21 Henrik Sedin 5.00 12.00
GG22 Daniel Sedin 5.00 12.00
GG23 Borje Salming 4.00 10.00
GG24 Henrik Lundqvist 10.00 25.00
GG25 Peter Forsberg 8.00 20.00
GG26 Alexander Ovechkin 15.00 40.00
GG27 Ilya Kovalchuk 4.00 10.00
GG28 Pavel Bure 4.00 10.00
GG29 Vladislav Tretiak 12.00 30.00
GG30 Marian Gaborik 4.00 10.00

2011-12 ITG Canada vs The World Great Moments

COMPLETE SET (15) 15.00 40.00
GM01 Phil Esposito 1.50 4.00
GM02 Paul Henderson .75 2.00
GM03 Darryl Sittler 1.25 3.00
GM04 Jim Craig 1.50 4.00
GM05 Vladislav Tretiak .75 2.00
GM06 Larry Robinson 1.00 2.50
GM07 Mario Lemieux 4.00 10.00
GM08 Bill Ranford 1.00 2.50
GM09 Peter Forsberg 2.00 5.00
GM10 Mike Richter 1.00 2.50
GM11 Dominik Hasek 1.50 4.00
GM12 Martin Brodeur 2.50 6.00
GM13 Joe Sakic 2.00 5.00
GM14 Henrik Lundqvist 2.50 6.00
GM15 Roberto Luongo 1.50 4.00

2011-12 ITG Canada vs The World International Goalies Silver

IG01 Niklas Backstrom 8.00 20.00
IG02 Robin Lehner 4.00 10.00
IG03 Ilya Bryzgalov 5.00 12.00
IG04 Tim Thomas 10.00 25.00
IG05 Philipp Grubauer 5.00 12.00
IG06 Mikael Tellqvist 4.00 10.00
IG07 Nikolai Khabibulin 4.00 10.00
IG08 Olaf Kolzig 5.00 12.00
IG09 Roman Turek 4.00 10.00
IG10 Tommy Salo 4.00 10.00
IG11 Roman Cechmanek 5.00 12.00
IG12 Jacob Markstrom 5.00 12.00
IG13 Jonas Gustavsson 5.00 12.00
IG14 Tuukka Rask 6.00 15.00
IG15 Mike Richter 8.00 20.00
IG16 Vladimir Myshkin 5.00 12.00
IG17 Sergei Mylnikov 5.00 12.00
IG18 Vladimir Dzurilla 5.00 12.00
IG19 Pelle Lindbergh 30.00 80.00
IG20 Vladislav Tretiak 25.00 50.00

2011-12 ITG Canada vs The World International Materials Black

*SILVER/30: .6X TO 1.5X BLACK/120
IM01 Adam Larsson 4.00 10.00
IM02 Philipp Grubauer 5.00 12.00
IM03 Alexander Maltsev 5.00 12.00
IM04 Vladimir Myshkin 4.00 10.00
IM05 Sergei Mylnikov 4.00 10.00
IM06 Ulf Nilsson 3.00 8.00
IM07 Pavel Bure 12.00 30.00
IM08 Peter Forsberg 8.00 20.00
IM09 Tony Amonte 3.00 8.00
IM10 Nicklas Lidstrom 2.50 6.00
IM11 Mike Modano 6.00 15.00
IM12 Alexander Semin 4.00 10.00
IM13 Nikolai Khabibulin 3.00 8.00
IM14 Alexander Mogilny 3.00 8.00
IM15 Chris Chelios 4.00 10.00
IM16 Niklas Backstrom 6.00 15.00
IM17 Kyle Okposo 2.50 6.00
IM18 Oliver Ekman-Larsson 4.00 10.00
IM19 Brian Leetch 3.00 8.00
IM20 Teemu Selanne 6.00 15.00
IM21 Mikko Koivu 3.00 8.00
IM22 Saku Koivu 4.00 10.00
IM23 Ulf Samuelsson 4.00 10.00
IM24 Ilya Bryzgalov 4.00 10.00
IM25 Jaromir Jagr 10.00 25.00
IM26 Mats Sundin 4.00 10.00
IM27 Zigmund Palffy 4.00 10.00
IM28 Pat LaFontaine 4.00 10.00
IM29 Tuukka Rask 5.00 12.00
IM30 Jacob Markstrom 4.00 10.00
IM31 Robin Lehner 3.00 8.00
IM32 Keith Tkachuk 3.00 8.00
IM33 Olaf Kolzig 4.00 10.00
IM34 Mats Naslund 2.50 6.00
IM35 Brett Hull 8.00 20.00
IM37 Alexander Ovechkin 60.00 120.00
IM39 Jari Kurri 20.00 50.00
IM41 Mike Richter 20.00 50.00
IM43 Boris Mikhailov 30.00 60.00
IM45 Pelle Lindbergh 25.00 60.00

2011-12 ITG Canada vs The World International Showdown Rivals Silver

ISR01 Hndr/Dryd/Khrlv/Trtk 60.00 120.00
ISR02 Hull/Hwe/Yaksh/Mikhv 25.00 60.00
ISR03 Sittlr/Orr/Ststny/Dzurilla 25.00 60.00
ISR04 Laflr/Gret/Krutov/Tretiak 40.00 100.00
ISR05 Mess/Bossy/Nslnd/Loob 25.00 60.00
ISR06 Lem/Gret/Mylnikv/Larnv 40.00 100.00
ISR07 Ranfrd/Lind/Hull/Rnick 30.00 80.00
ISR08 Gret/Joseph/Rich/Leetch 40.00 100.00
ISR09 Bourque/Roy/Hasek/Jagr 30.00 80.00

ISR10 Lem/Brodr/Rchtr/Chelios 25.00 60.00
ISR11 Sak/Brodr/Kiprsf/Koivu 25.00 60.00
ISR12 Weber/Lngo/Miller/Kane 20.00 50.00

2011-12 ITG Canada vs The World International Showdown Teammates Silver

IST01 Hend/Crnyer/Clrke/Dryden 50.00 100.00
IST03 Sittlr/Bo.Hull/Vachon/Orr 25.00 60.00
IST04 Lafleur/Bossy/Trott/Grtzky 30.00 80.00
IST05 Mess/Yzrman/Robin/Bssy 30.00 80.00
IST06 Lemx/Fuhr/Hawer/Gretz 30.00 80.00
IST07 Rnfrd/Mess/Fleury/Lindrs 25.00 60.00
IST08 Shan/Coffy/Lindrs/Josph 25.00 60.00
IST09 Bourq/Lindrs/Gretz/Roy 50.00 100.00
IST10 Lem/Sakc/Yzrmn/Brodr 25.00 60.00
IST11 Sakc/Lecav/Lem/Brodr 25.00 60.00
IST12 Webr/Ignla/Toews/Lngo 20.00 50.00

2011-12 ITG Canada vs The World My Country My Team Silver

MCMT01 Peter Stastny 5.00 12.00
MCMT02 Teemu Selanne 15.00 40.00
MCMT03 Borje Salming 6.00 15.00
MCMT04 Nicklas Lidstrom 4.00 10.00
MCMT05 Mike Richter 6.00 15.00
MCMT06 Pavel Bure 6.00 15.00
MCMT07 Brian Leetch 5.00 12.00
MCMT08 Jaromir Jagr 10.00 25.00
MCMT09 Alexander Ovechkin 10.00 25.00
MCMT10 Mats Sundin 6.00 15.00
MCMT11 Theoren Fleury 10.00 25.00
MCMT12 Eric Lindros 10.00 25.00
MCMT13 Joe Sakic 12.00 30.00
MCMT14 Carey Price 12.00 30.00
MCMT15 Phil Esposito 10.00 25.00
MCMT16 Mario Lemieux 25.00 60.00
MCMT17 Joe Thornton 8.00 20.00
MCMT18 Martin Brodeur 15.00 40.00
MCMT19 Roberto Luongo 10.00 25.00
MCMT20 Marc-Andre Fleury 12.00 30.00
MCMT21 Martin St. Louis 6.00 15.00

2011-12 ITG Canada vs The World Protecting Canada's Crease

COMPLETE SET (10) 12.00 30.00
PCC01 M.Liut/B.Smith 1.00 2.50
PCC02 G.Fuhr/R.Hextall 1.50 4.00
PCC03 B.Ranford/E.Belfour 1.00 2.50
PCC04 P.Roy/C.Joseph 2.50 6.00
PCC05 M.Brodeur/C.Joseph 2.50 6.00
PCC06 C.Labonte/K.St-Pierre 2.00 5.00
PCC07 C.Price/L.Irving 2.00 5.00
PCC08 C.Ward/D.Roloson 1.00 2.50
PCC09 R.Luongo/M.Brodeur 2.50 6.00
PCC10 J.Reimer/J.Bernier 1.00 2.50

2011-12 ITG Canada vs The World Roots of International Hockey

COMPLETE SET (10) 8.00 20.00
RIH01 Frank Frederickson .75 2.00
RIH02 Harry Watson .75 2.00
RIH03 Anatoli Tarasov 1.00 2.50
RIH04 Harry Sinden .60 1.50
RIH05 Bunny Ahearne 1.00 2.50
RIH06 Jack McCartan 1.00 2.50
RIH07 Tumba Johansson 1.00 2.50
RIH08 Valeri Kharlamov .75 2.00
RIH09 Alexander Ragulin 1.00 2.50
RIH10 Borje Salming 1.00 2.50

2011-12 ITG Canada vs The World Summit Series

COMPLETE SET (10) 10.00 25.00
SS01 Paul Henderson .75 2.00
SS02 Bobby Clarke 1.50 4.00
SS03 Phil Esposito 1.50 4.00
SS04 Yvan Cournoyer 1.00 2.50
SS05 Frank Mahovlich 1.00 2.50
SS06 Brad Park .75 2.00
SS07 Valeri Kharlamov .75 2.00
SS08 Boris Mikhailov 1.50 4.00
SS09 Alexander Yakushev 2.00 5.00
SS10 Vladislav Tretiak .75 2.00

2011-12 ITG Canada vs The World Triple Gold Silver

TG01 Peter Forsberg 10.00 25.00
TG02 Igor Larionov 8.00 20.00
TG03 Joe Sakic 10.00 25.00
TG04 Eric Staal 6.00 15.00
TG05 Nicklas Lidstrom 3.00 8.00
TG06 Scott Niedermayer 5.00 12.00
TG07 Mats Naslund 3.00 8.00
TG08 Hakan Loob 6.00 15.00
TG09 Patrice Bergeron 6.00 15.00
TG10 Jaromir Jagr 10.00 25.00

2011-12 ITG Canada vs The World World Junior Grads Silver

WJG01 Joe Sakic 8.00 20.00
WJG02 Eric Lindros 6.00 15.00
WJG03 Mario Lemieux 15.00 40.00
WJG04 Joe Thornton 6.00 15.00
WJG05 Roberto Luongo 6.00 15.00
WJG06 Marc-Andre Fleury 8.00 20.00
WJG07 Carey Price 8.00 20.00
WJG08 Vincent Lecavalier 4.00 10.00
WJG09 Jason Spezza 4.00 10.00
WJG10 Brad Marchand 8.00 20.00
WJG11 Kyle Turris 2.50 6.00
WJG12 Eric Staal 5.00 12.00
WJG13 Justin Pogge 2.50 6.00
WJG14 Kristopher Letang 5.00 12.00
WJG15 Patrice Bergeron 5.00 12.00
WJG16 Jay Bouwmeester 2.50 6.00
WJG17 Esa Tikkanen 6.00 15.00
WJG18 Saku Koivu 4.00 10.00
WJG19 Oliver Ekman-Larsson 4.00 10.00
WJG20 Peter Forsberg 8.00 20.00
WJG21 Nicklas Lidstrom 2.50 6.00
WJG22 Jaromir Jagr 10.00 25.00
WJG23 Keith Tkachuk 4.00 10.00
WJG24 Chris Chelios 4.00 10.00
WJG25 Mike Modano 6.00 15.00
WJG26 Brian Leetch 3.00 8.00
WJG27 Alexander Semin 4.00 10.00
WJG28 Alexander Ovechkin 15.00 40.00
WJG29 Nikolai Khabibulin 3.00 8.00
WJG30 Pavel Bure 12.00 30.00

2011-12 ITG Canada vs The World World's Best Silver

WB01 Rchtr/Mlr/Brrso/Vanbies 20.00 50.00
WB02 Lids/Frsbrg/Nslnd/Slmg 20.00 50.00
WB03 Koiv/Slne/Kurri/Tikk 30.00 80.00
WB04 Ovech/Bre/Fdrv/Mlkn 40.00 100.00
WB05 Khrlmv/Trtk/Mikh/Yak 25.00 60.00
WB06 Hull/LaFont/Mod/Ltch 20.00 50.00

2011-12 ITG Captain-C

COMPLETE SET (100) 100.00 175.00
1 Al MacInnis 2.00 5.00
2 Alex Delvecchio 1.50 4.00
3 Alexander Ovechkin 6.00 15.00
4 Andrew Ladd 1.00 2.50
5 Andy Bathgate 1.50 4.00
6 Bill Durnan 1.50 4.00
7 Bob Baun 1.50 4.00
8 Bobby Clarke 2.50 6.00
9 Brad Park 1.25 3.00
10 Brenden Morrow 1.25 3.00
11 Brett Hull 3.00 8.00
12 Brian Leetch 1.25 3.00
13 Butch Bouchard 1.25 3.00
14 Charlie Conacher 1.25 3.00
15 Chris Chelios 1.50 4.00
16 Clark Gillies 1.50 4.00
17 Dale Hawerchuk 2.00 5.00
18 Dale Hunter 1.25 3.00
19 Danny Gare 1.25 3.00
20 Darryl Sittler 2.00 5.00
21 Dave Keon 1.50 4.00
22 David Backes 1.00 2.50
23 Denis Potvin 1.50 4.00
24 Denis Savard 1.50 4.00
25 Dit Clapper 1.00 2.50
26 Doug Gilmour 2.00 5.00
27 Doug Harvey 1.50 4.00
28 Mats Sundin 1.50 4.00
29 Eric Lindros 2.50 6.00
30 Eric Staal 2.00 5.00
31 Fern Flaman 1.00 2.50
32 Garry Unger 2.00 5.00
33 George Hainsworth 1.50 4.00
34 Gilbert Perreault 1.50 4.00
35 Guy Carbonneau 1.50 4.00
36 Dion Phaneuf 1.25 3.00
37 Henri Richard 1.50 4.00
38 Henrik Sedin 2.00 5.00
39 Jaromir Jagr 5.00 12.00
40 Jean Beliveau 1.50 4.00
41 Joe Nieuwendyk 1.25 3.00
42 Joe Sakic 3.00 8.00
43 Joe Thornton 2.50 6.00
44 Johnny Bucyk 1.50 4.00
45 Keith Tkachuk 1.50 4.00
46 King Clancy 1.25 3.00
47 Kirk Muller 1.25 3.00
48 Lanny McDonald 1.50 4.00
49 Luc Robitaille 1.50 4.00
50 Mario Lemieux 6.00 15.00
51 Mark Messier 3.00 8.00
52 Maurice Richard 3.00 8.00
53 Mikko Koivu 1.25 3.00
54 Milt Schmidt 1.25 3.00
55 Gordie Howe 5.00 12.00
56 Newsy Lalonde 1.25 3.00
57 Nicklas Lidstrom 1.00 2.50
58 Pat LaFontaine 1.50 4.00
59 Pat Verbeek 1.00 2.50
60 Patrick Marleau 1.50 4.00
61 Pavel Bure 1.50 4.00
62 Peter Stastny 1.25 3.00
63 Phil Esposito 2.50 6.00
64 Pierre Pilote 1.00 2.50
65 Ray Bourque 2.50 6.00
66 Red Dutton 1.00 2.50
67 Red Kelly 1.50 4.00
68 Rick Nash 1.50 4.00
69 Rick Vaive 1.25 3.00
70 Mike Modano 2.50 6.00
71 Roberto Luongo 2.50 6.00
72 Rod Langway 1.25 3.00
73 Ron Francis 2.00 5.00
74 Ron Greschner 1.25 3.00
75 Ryan Getzlaf 1.50 4.00
76 Saku Koivu 1.50 4.00
77 Scott Niedermayer 1.50 4.00
78 Serge Savard 1.50 4.00
79 Shea Weber 1.25 3.00
80 Sid Abel 1.25 3.00
81 Sprague Cleghorn 1.25 3.00
82 Stan Mikita 2.00 5.00
83 Steve Yzerman 4.00 10.00
84 Sweeney Schriner 1.00 2.50
85 Syl Apps 1.25 3.00
86 Ted Kennedy 1.50 4.00
87 Ted Lindsay 1.50 4.00
88 Teemu Selanne 3.00 8.00
89 Terry O'Reilly 1.25 3.00
90 Terry Ruskowski 1.25 3.00
91 Theoren Fleury 2.50 6.00
92 Toe Blake 1.00 2.50
93 Tony Amonte 1.25 3.00
94 Trevor Linden 1.50 4.00
95 Vincent Lecavalier 1.50 4.00
96 Wayne Cashman 1.00 2.50
97 Wendel Clark 2.50 6.00
98 Yvan Cournoyer 1.50 4.00
99 Zach Parise 1.50 4.00
100 Zdeno Chara 1.50 4.00

2011-12 ITG Captain-C Gold

*GOLD/50: .6X TO 1.5X BASIC CARDS

2011-12 ITG Captain-C Autographs Silver

AAA Al Arbour 5.00 12.00
AAB Andy Bathgate 5.00 12.00
AAD Alex Delvecchio 6.00 15.00
AAM Al MacInnis SP 15.00 30.00
AAO Alexander Ovechkin SP 40.00 80.00
ABB Bill Barber 6.00 15.00
ABBA Bob Baun 4.00 10.00
ABBE Brian Bellows 4.00 10.00
ABBK Barry Beck 3.00 8.00
ABC Bobby Clarke SP 20.00 40.00
ABF Bernie Federko 4.00 10.00
ABG Bill Gadsby 8.00 20.00
ABH Brett Hull SP 30.00 60.00
ABL Brian Leetch 8.00 20.00
ABM Brad Marsh 3.00 8.00
ABMO Brenden Morrow 4.00 10.00
ABP Brad Park 6.00 15.00
ACC Chris Chelios SP 8.00 20.00
ACG Clark Gillies 5.00 12.00
ACH Craig Hartsburg 3.00 8.00
ACP Chris Pronger SP 8.00 20.00
ADG Danny Gare 4.00 10.00
ADGI Doug Gilmour 10.00 25.00
ADH Dale Hawerchuk 6.00 15.00
ADHU Dale Hunter 4.00 10.00
ADK Dave Keon SP 20.00 50.00
ADL Don Lever 8.00 20.00
ADP Denis Potvin 5.00 12.00
ADPH Dion Phaneuf 8.00 20.00
ADS Denis Savard 5.00 12.00
ADSI Darryl Sittler 8.00 20.00
ADT Dave Taylor 4.00 10.00
AEL Eric Lindros SP 40.00 100.00
AES Eric Staal 6.00 15.00
AEV Ed Van Impe 4.00 10.00
AFF Fern Flaman 8.00 20.00
AGB Garth Butcher 3.00 8.00
AGC Guy Carbonneau 6.00 15.00
AGH Gordie Howe SP 50.00 100.00
AGP Gilbert Perreault 8.00 20.00
AGU Garry Unger 6.00 15.00
AHH Harry Howell 4.00 10.00
AHR Henri Richard 10.00 25.00
AHS Henrik Sedin SP 15.00 30.00
AJB Jean Beliveau SP 40.00 80.00
AJBU Johnny Bucyk 6.00 15.00
AJJ Jaromir Jagr SP 30.00 60.00
AJN Joe Nieuwendyk SP 8.00 20.00
AJS Joe Sakic SP 25.00 50.00
AJT Joe Thornton SP 10.00 25.00
AKM Kirk Muller 4.00 10.00
AKT Keith Tkachuk 5.00 12.00
ALM Lanny McDonald 6.00 15.00
ALR Luc Robitaille SP 15.00 30.00
AMD Marcel Dionne 6.00 15.00
AMK Mikko Koivu SP 8.00 20.00
AML Mario Lemieux SP 40.00 80.00
AMM Mark Messier SP 40.00 80.00
AMMO Mike Modano 8.00 20.00
AMR Maurice Richard SP 150.00 300.00
AMS Milt Schmidt SP 6.00 15.00
AMS Mats Sundin SP 50.00 100.00
ANL Nicklas Lidstrom SP 25.00 50.00
APB Pavel Bure SP 25.00 50.00
APE Phil Esposito 10.00 25.00
APL Pat Lafontaine 12.50 25.00
APM Patrick Marleau 6.00 15.00
APP Pierre Pilote 6.00 15.00
APS Peter Stastny 8.00 20.00
ARB Ray Bourque SP 20.00 40.00
ARBL Rob Blake 5.00 12.00
ARK Red Kelly SP 12.00 30.00
ARL Rod Langway 4.00 10.00
ARLA Reed Larson 3.00 8.00
ARLU Roberto Luongo 10.00 25.00
ARM Rick Middleton 8.00 20.00
ARN Rick Nash SP 8.00 20.00
ARV Rick Vaive 10.00 25.00
ASK Saku Koivu SP 20.00 40.00
ASM Stan Mikita SP 10.00 25.00
ASN Scott Niedermayer 5.00 12.00
ASS Serge Savard 6.00 15.00
ASW Shea Weber SP 10.00 25.00
ASY Steve Yzerman SP 40.00 80.00
ATA Tony Amonte 6.00 15.00
ATF Theoren Fleury SP 20.00 40.00
ATK Ted Kennedy SP 30.00 60.00
ATL Trevor Linden 10.00 25.00
ATLI Ted Lindsay 8.00 20.00
ATLY Tom Lysiak 3.00 8.00
ATO Terry O'Reilly 6.00 15.00
ATR Terry Ruskowski 4.00 10.00
ATS Teemu Selanne SP 20.00 40.00
ATST Thomas Steen 3.00 8.00
AVH Vic Hadfield 4.00 10.00
AVL Vincent Lecavalier SP 10.00 25.00
AWC Wayne Cashman 5.00 12.00
AWCL Wendel Clark 12.50 25.00
AYC Yvan Cournoyer 6.00 15.00
AZC Zdeno Chara SP 10.00 25.00

2011-12 ITG Captain-C Franchise Captains Jerseys Silver

FC01 Bucyk/Schmdt/O'Rlly 25.00 50.00
FC02 Chara/Thrntn/Brque 15.00 30.00
FC03 Fleury/Nieuw/McDnld 15.00 40.00
FC04 Mikita/Chelios/Amonte 15.00 30.00
FC05 Lindsay/Delvec/Howe 20.00 40.00
FC06 Lidstrm/Dnne/Yzerman 20.00 40.00
FC07 Hwrchk/Steen/Tkchk 12.00 30.00
FC08 Taylor/Robitlle/Brown 6.00 15.00
FC10 Koivu/Keane/Muller 20.00 40.00
FC11 Carbon/Savrd/Crnyr 15.00 30.00
FC12 Richrd/Beliv/Harvy 60.00 120.00
FC13 Leetch/Messier/Jagr 15.00 30.00
FC14 P.Espo/Park/Hadfield 8.00 20.00
FC15 Frsbrg/Primeau/Lindrs 20.00 40.00
FC16 Barber/Clarke/Toccht 25.00 50.00
FC17 Lemieux/Jagr/Francis 15.00 40.00
FC18 MacInns/Ungr/Arbour 25.00 50.00
FC19 Sundin/Gilmour/Clark/9* 20.00 40.00

2011-12 ITG Captain-C Jerseys Silver

M01 Al MacInnis 4.00 10.00
M02 Alexander Ovechkin 20.00 50.00
M03 Brenden Morrow 4.00 10.00
M04 Brett Hull 10.00 25.00
M05 Brian Bellows 4.00 10.00
M06 Brian Leetch 5.00 12.00
M07 Chris Chelios 5.00 12.00
M08 Chris Pronger 5.00 12.00
M09 Craig Hartsburg 3.00 8.00
M10 Dale Hawerchuk 5.00 12.00
M11 Dale Hunter 4.00 10.00
M12 Dave Taylor 4.00 10.00
M13 Denis Savard 5.00 12.00
M14 Dion Phaneuf 4.00 10.00
M15 Mats Sundin 5.00 12.00
M16 Dustin Brown 5.00 12.00
M17 Eric Lindros 6.00 15.00
M18 Eric Staal 6.00 15.00
M19 Gilbert Perreault 5.00 12.00
M20 Guy Carbonneau 5.00 12.00
M21 Henrik Sedin 6.00 15.00
M22 Jaromir Jagr 6.00 15.00
M23 Jaromir Jagr 6.00 15.00
M24 Joe Nieuwendyk 4.00 10.00
M25 Joe Sakic 10.00 25.00
M26 Joe Sakic 10.00 25.00
M27 Joe Thornton 8.00 20.00
M28 Joe Thornton 8.00 20.00
M29 Keith Tkachuk 5.00 12.00
M30 Kirk Muller 5.00 12.00
M31 Lanny McDonald 5.00 12.00
M32 Luc Robitaille 5.00 12.00
M33 Mario Lemieux 20.00 50.00
M34 Mark Messier 10.00 25.00
M35 Mark Messier 10.00 25.00
M36 Mark Messier 10.00 25.00
M37 Mike Modano 8.00 20.00
M38 Mikko Koivu 4.00 10.00
M39 Nicklas Lidstrom 3.00 8.00
M40 Pat LaFontaine 5.00 12.00
M41 Patrick Marleau 5.00 12.00
M42 Pavel Bure 6.00 15.00
M43 Peter Stastny 4.00 10.00
M44 Ray Bourque 8.00 20.00
M45 Rick Nash 5.00 12.00
M46 Roberto Luongo 8.00 20.00
M47 Rod Langway 4.00 10.00
M48 Ryan Getzlaf 5.00 12.00
M49 Saku Koivu 5.00 12.00
M50 Scott Niedermayer 5.00 12.00
M51 Shea Weber 5.00 12.00
M52 Steve Yzerman 12.00 30.00
M53 Teemu Selanne 10.00 25.00
M54 Theoren Fleury 6.00 15.00
M55 Tony Amonte 4.00 10.00
M56 Trevor Linden 6.00 15.00
M57 Vincent Lecavalier 5.00 12.00
M58 Wendel Clark 5.00 12.00
M59 Zach Parise 5.00 12.00
M60 Zdeno Chara 5.00 12.00

2011-12 ITG Captain-C Junior Captains Jerseys Silver

JC01 Karl Alzner 4.00 10.00
JC02 Tyson Barrie 4.00 10.00
JC03 Jonathon Blum 5.00 12.00
JC04 Ryan Callahan 4.00 10.00
JC05 Landon Ferraro 4.00 10.00
JC06 Cody Eakin 8.00 20.00
JC07 Ryan Ellis 5.00 12.00
JC08 Cory Emmerton 5.00 12.00
JC09 Colton Sissons 4.00 10.00
JC10 Thomas Hickey 4.00 10.00
JC11 Cody Hodgson 6.00 15.00
JC12 Boone Jenner 6.00 15.00
JC13 Zack Kassian 6.00 15.00
JC14 Bryan Little 6.00 15.00
JC15 Greg McKegg 5.00 12.00
JC16 Mark Pysyk 4.00 10.00
JC17 Ryan Murray 8.00 20.00
JC18 Ryan O'Marra 4.00 10.00
JC19 Patrick O'Sullivan 4.00 10.00
JC20 Marc-Antoine Pouliot 5.00 12.00
JC21 Brayden Schenn 5.00 12.00
JC22 Duncan Siemens 5.00 12.00
JC23 Chris Stewart 4.00 10.00
JC24 Chris Terry 5.00 12.00

2011-12 ITG Captain-C Stick and Jersey Silver

SJ01 Alexander Ovechkin 20.00 50.00
SJ02 Al MacInnis 10.00 25.00
SJ03 Chris Chelios 8.00 20.00
SJ04 Mike Modano 12.00 30.00
SJ05 Denis Potvin 8.00 20.00
SJ06 Dale Hawerchuk 10.00 25.00
SJ07 Doug Gilmour 12.00 30.00
SJ08 Eric Lindros 12.00 30.00
SJ09 Gilbert Perreault 8.00 20.00
SJ10 Jaromir Jagr 15.00 40.00
SJ11 Joe Sakic 15.00 40.00
SJ12 Joe Thornton 12.00 30.00
SJ13 Keith Tkachuk 8.00 20.00
SJ14 Mario Lemieux 25.00 50.00
SJ15 Mark Messier 20.00 40.00
SJ16 Nicklas Lidstrom 10.00 25.00
SJ17 Dale Hunter 6.00 15.00
SJ18 Pavel Bure 12.00 30.00
SJ19 Ray Bourque 12.00 30.00
SJ20 Eric Staal 10.00 25.00
SJ21 Ryan Getzlaf 8.00 20.00
SJ22 Luc Robitaille 12.00 30.00
SJ23 Pat LaFontaine 10.00 25.00
SJ24 Steve Yzerman 20.00 50.00
SJ25 Teemu Selanne 12.00 30.00
SJ26 Theoren Fleury 15.00 40.00
SJ27 Tony Amonte 6.00 15.00
SJ28 Trevor Linden 12.00 30.00
SJ29 Vincent Lecavalier 8.00 20.00
SJ30 Mats Sundin 10.00 25.00

2010-11 ITG Decades 1980s All-Stars Jerseys Silver

AS01 Dion/Laflr/Robnsn/Espo 10.00 25.00
AS02 Liut/Simmer/Bossy/Potvin 20.00 50.00
AS03 Smith/Bourq/Bossy/Mess 15.00 40.00
AS04 Lang/Bourq/Mess/Peetrs 15.00 40.00
AS05 Barras/Goult/Bourq/Bossy 20.00 50.00
AS06 Lindbrg/Bourq/Coffy/Kurri 12.00 30.00
AS07 Vanbies/Goult/Bossy/Coffy 15.00 40.00
AS08 Hextall/Bourq/Kurri/Goult 12.00 30.00
AS09 Fuhr/Robit/Mario/Bourq 30.00 80.00
AS10 Roy/Mario/Coffy/Robit 30.00 80.00

2010-11 ITG Decades 1980s Autographs

AAA Al Arbour 5.00 12.00
AAB Allan Bester 5.00 12.00
AAH Anders Hedberg 5.00 12.00
AAM Andy Moog 6.00 15.00
AAMA Al MacInnis 8.00 20.00
AAS Anton Stastny 6.00 15.00
ABA Brent Ashton 4.00 10.00
ABB Bill Barber 5.00 12.00
ABBA Bill Baker USA 12.00 30.00
ABBA2 Bill Baker MTL 8.00 20.00
ABBE Brian Bellows 5.00 12.00
ABBK Barry Beck 4.00 10.00
ABD Bill Derlago 5.00 12.00
ABF Bernie Federko 5.00 12.00
ABH Bobby Hull 15.00 40.00
ABM Brad Marsh 5.00 12.00
ABN Bernie Nicholls 5.00 12.00
ABNY Bob Nystrom 4.00 10.00
ABOS Bobby Smith 5.00 12.00
ABP Brad Park 5.00 12.00
ABPE Barry Pederson 4.00 10.00
ABPR Brian Propp 6.00 15.00
ABS Buzz Schneider USA 15.00 30.00
ABSA Borje Salming 8.00 20.00
ABSK Brian Skrudland 6.00 15.00
ABSM Billy Smith 6.00 15.00
ABST Blaine Stoughton 5.00 12.00
ABSU Bob Suter 8.00 20.00
ABSV Bob Sauve 6.00 15.00
ABT Bryan Trottier 6.00 15.00
ACC Chris Chelios 8.00 20.00
ACGA Guy Carbonneau 6.00 15.00
ACH Craig Hartsburg 4.00 10.00
ACN Cam Neely 6.00 15.00
ACR Chico Resch 6.00 15.00
ACS Charlie Simmer 4.00 10.00
ADB Don Beaupre 5.00 12.00
ADBA Dave Babych 6.00 15.00
ADBO Dan Bouchard 8.00 20.00
ADC Dave Christian USA 12.00 30.00
ADC Dino Ciccarelli 8.00 20.00
ADC2 Dave Christian WIN 8.00 20.00
ADG Doug Gilmour 15.00 40.00
ADGA Danny Gare 6.00 15.00
ADH Dale Hawerchuk 10.00 25.00
ADHU Dale Hunter 5.00 12.00
ADK Dave Keon SP 20.00 50.00
ADL Don Lever 8.00 20.00
ADM Dennis Maruk 5.00 12.00
ADP Denis Potvin 6.00 15.00
ADPA Darren Pang 8.00 20.00
ADS Dave Silk USA 25.00 50.00
ADS2 Dave Silk NYR 6.00 15.00
ADSA Denis Savard 6.00 15.00
ADSE Dave Semenko 6.00 15.00
ADSI Darryl Sittler 12.00 30.00
ADT Dave Taylor 6.00 15.00
ADW Doug Wilson 5.00 12.00
AES Eric Strobel 8.00 20.00
AET Esa Tikkanen 6.00 15.00
AGA Glenn Anderson 6.00 15.00
AGC Gerry Cheevers 8.00 20.00
AGF Grant Fuhr 10.00 25.00
AGL Guy Lafleur 20.00 50.00
AGLE Gary Leeman 5.00 12.00
AGM Greg Millen 5.00 12.00
AGP Gilbert Perreault 6.00 15.00
AGS Gary Suter 4.00 10.00
AHS Harold Snepsts 6.00 15.00
AIL Igor Larionov 15.00 30.00
AJC Jim Craig USA 15.00 40.00
AJC2 Jim Craig BOS 10.00 25.00
AJG John Garrett 6.00 15.00
AJH John Harrington USA 10.00 25.00
AJK Jari Kurri 10.00 25.00
AJM Joe Mullen CAL 5.00 12.00
AJM2 Joe Mullen USA 6.00 15.00
AJO Jack O'Callahan USA 20.00 40.00
AJO2 Jack O'Callahan CHI 10.00 25.00
AJOG John Ogrodnick 5.00 12.00
AJR Jeremy Roenick SP 15.00 40.00
AJS Joe Sakic 40.00 80.00
AJV John Vanbiesbrouck 12.00 30.00
AKB Kelly Buchberger 4.00 10.00
AKD Kevin Dineen 6.00 15.00
AKH Kelly Hrudey 5.00 12.00
AKM Ken Morrow USA 25.00 50.00
AKM2 Ken Morrow NYI 6.00 15.00
AKMC Kirk McLean 8.00 20.00
AKMU Kirk Muller 4.00 10.00
AKN Kent Nilsson 4.00 10.00
ALM Lanny McDonald 6.00 15.00
ALMU Larry Murphy 6.00 15.00
ALR Larry Robinson 6.00 15.00
ALRO Luc Robitaille 8.00 20.00
AMB Mike Bossy 10.00 25.00
AMBA Murray Bannerman 6.00 15.00
AMBU Mike Bullard 5.00 12.00
AMD Marcel Dionne 8.00 20.00
AME Mike Eruzione 25.00 50.00
AMG Michel Goulet QUE 8.00 20.00
AMG2 Michel Goulet CAN 8.00 20.00
AMGA Mike Gartner 8.00 20.00
AMH Mark Hunter 5.00 12.00
AMHO Mark Howe 6.00 15.00
AMJ Mark Johnson USA 30.00 60.00
AMJ2 Mark Johnson HART 5.00 12.00
AML Mario Lemieux SP 75.00 150.00
AMLI Mike Liut 4.00 10.00
AMLU Morris Lukowich 4.00 10.00
AMM Mark Messier EDM SP 40.00 80.00
AMM2 Mark Messier CAN SP 90.00 150.00
AMN Mats Naslund 8.00 20.00
AMP Mark Pavelich USA 25.00 50.00
AMP2 Mark Pavelich NYR 8.00 20.00
AMR Mike Ramsey BUF 6.00 15.00
AMR2 Mike Ramsey USA 40.00 80.00
AMRO Mike Rogers 4.00 10.00
AMST Marian Stastny 8.00 20.00
AMV Mike Vernon 5.00 12.00
AMW Mark Wells 10.00 25.00
ANB Neal Broten USA 30.00 60.00
ANB2 Neal Broten MIN 8.00 20.00
APC Paul Coffey SP 15.00 30.00
APE Phil Esposito SP 8.00 20.00
APH Phil Housley 6.00 15.00
APL Pat LaFontaine 10.00 25.00
APP Pete Peeters 6.00 15.00
APR Patrick Roy SP 50.00 100.00
APRE Pokey Reddick 5.00 12.00
APRH Paul Reinhart 4.00 10.00
APRI Pat Riggin 4.00 10.00
APS Peter Stastny 10.00 25.00
APV Phil Verchota 12.00 30.00
APVE Pat Verbeek 5.00 12.00
ARB Raymond Bourque SP 30.00 60.00
ARBR Richard Brodeur 6.00 15.00
ARC Randy Carlyle 5.00 12.00
ARF Ron Francis 12.00 30.00
ARG Ron Greschner 4.00 10.00
ARH Ron Hextall 6.00 15.00
ARK Rick Kehoe 5.00 12.00
ARL Rod Langway 5.00 12.00
ARLA Reed Larson 4.00 10.00
ARLO Ron Low 6.00 15.00
ARM Rob McClanahan USA 15.00 30.00
ARM2 Rob McClanahan BUF 6.00 15.00
ARMI Rick Middleton 6.00 15.00
ARV Rick Vaive 5.00 12.00
ARW Rick Wamsley 8.00 20.00
ASC Steve Christoff 10.00 25.00
ASJ Steve Janaszak 10.00 25.00
ASK Steve Kasper 4.00 10.00
ASP Steve Payne 4.00 10.00
ASPE Steve Penney 8.00 20.00
ASS Steve Shutt 10.00 25.00
ASY Steve Yzerman SP 25.00 60.00
ATB Tom Barrasso 8.00 20.00
ATE Tony Esposito SP 20.00 50.00
ATK Tim Kerr 4.00 10.00
ATL Tom Lysiak 4.00 10.00
ATLI Trevor Linden 12.00 30.00
ATS Thomas Steen 4.00 10.00
ATT Tony Tanti 5.00 12.00
ATW Tiger Williams 4.00 10.00
AVK Vladimir Krutov 20.00 50.00
AVT Vladislav Tretiak SP 75.00 135.00
AWC Wendel Clark 10.00 25.00
AWP Willi Plett 5.00 12.00
AWW Wally Weir 5.00 12.00

2010-11 ITG Decades 1980s Battle of Alberta

COMPLETE SET (5) 8.00 20.00
BA01 M.Vernon/G.Fuhr 3.00 8.00
BA02 L.McDonald/M.Messier 4.00 10.00
BA03 H.Loob/J.Kurri 2.00 5.00
BA04 P.Reinhart/P.Coffey 2.00 5.00
BA05 J.Mullen/G.Anderson 1.50 4.00

2010-11 ITG Decades 1980s Battle of New York

COMPLETE SET (5) 8.00 20.00
BNY01 D.Potvin/B.Beck 2.00 5.00
BNY02 B.Smith/J.Vanbiesbrouck 2.00 5.00
BNY03 M.Bossy/A.Hedberg 2.00 5.00
BNY04 K.Morrow/R.Greschner 1.50 4.00
BNY05 B.Trottier/P.Esposito 3.00 8.00

2010-11 ITG Decades 1980s Battle of Quebec

COMPLETE SET (5) 10.00 25.00
BQ01 P.Stastny/G.Lafleur 2.50 6.00
BQ02 M.Goulet/S.Shutt 2.00 5.00
BQ03 D.Bouchard/P.Roy 5.00 12.00
BQ04 D.Hunter/L.Robinson 2.00 5.00
BQ05 J.Sakic/C.Chelios 4.00 10.00

2010-11 ITG Decades 1980s Between The Pipes Jerseys Black

SILVER/30: .5X TO 1.2X BLACK/100*
BTPJ01 Patrick Roy 12.00 30.00
BTPJ02 Billy Smith 5.00 12.00
BTPJ03 Tony Esposito 6.00 15.00
BTPJ04 Grant Fuhr 8.00 20.00
BTPJ05 Tom Barrasso 8.00 20.00
BTPJ06 John Vanbiesbrouck 5.00 12.00
BTPJ07 Allan Bester 4.00 10.00
BTPJ08 Richard Brodeur 5.00 12.00
BTPJ09 Darren Pang 5.00 12.00
BTPJ10 Pokey Reddick 10.00 25.00
BTPJ11 Ron Hextall 5.00 12.00
BTPJ12 Pelle Lindbergh/29* 15.00 40.00
BTPJ13 Mike Palmateer 5.00 12.00
BTPJ14 Don Beaupre 4.00 10.00
BTPJ15 Andy Moog 6.00 15.00
BTPJ16 Pat Riggin 3.00 8.00
BTPJ17 Ed Belfour 6.00 15.00
BTPJ18 Mike Vernon 6.00 15.00
BTPJ19 Dan Bouchard 8.00 20.00
BTPJ20 Bill Ranford 5.00 12.00

2010-11 ITG Decades 1980s Canada's Best

COMPLETE SET (5) 10.00 25.00
CB01 Mark Messier 4.00 10.00
CB02 Paul Coffey 2.00 5.00
CB03 Guy Lafleur 2.50 6.00
CB04 Grant Fuhr 3.00 8.00
CB05 Mario Lemieux 8.00 20.00

2010-11 ITG Decades 1980s Decades Rookies

DR01 Andy Moog 2.00 5.00
DR02 Bernie Nicholls 2.00 5.00
DR03 Brian Bellows 2.00 5.00
DR04 Brian Propp 2.50 6.00
DR05 Cam Neely 2.50 6.00
DR06 Dale Hawerchuk 2.50 6.00
DR07 Darren Pang 2.50 6.00
DR08 Denis Savard 2.00 5.00
DR09 Dino Ciccarelli 2.50 6.00
DR10 Don Beaupre 2.00 5.00
DR11 Doug Gilmour 3.00 8.00
DR12 Gary Suter 1.50 4.00
DR13 Glenn Anderson 2.00 5.00
DR14 Grant Fuhr 4.00 10.00
DR15 Guy Carbonneau 2.50 6.00
DR16 Jari Kurri 2.00 5.00
DR17 Jeremy Roenick 4.00 10.00
DR18 Joe Mullen 2.00 5.00
DR19 Joe Nieuwendyk 1.50 4.00
DR20 Joe Sakic 5.00 12.00
DR21 John Vanbiesbrouck 2.50 6.00
DR22 Kelly Hrudey 2.00 5.00
DR23 Kirk McLean 2.50 6.00
DR24 Kirk Muller 1.50 4.00
DR25 Larry Murphy 2.00 5.00
DR26 Luc Robitaille 2.00 5.00
DR27 Mario Lemieux 8.00 20.00
DR28 Mats Naslund 1.50 4.00
DR29 Mike Vernon 2.00 5.00
DR30 Neal Broten 2.00 5.00
DR31 Pat LaFontaine 2.50 6.00
DR32 Pat Verbeek 1.50 4.00
DR33 Patrick Roy 6.00 15.00
DR34 Paul Coffey 2.00 5.00
DR35 Pelle Lindbergh 2.00 5.00
DR36 Peter Stastny 1.50 4.00
DR37 Phil Housley 2.50 6.00
DR38 Raymond Bourque 4.00 10.00
DR39 Ron Francis 2.50 6.00
DR40 Ron Hextall 2.00 5.00
DR41 Steve Penney 2.50 6.00
DR42 Steve Yzerman 6.00 15.00
DR43 Thomas Steen 1.50 4.00
DR44 Tom Barrasso 2.00 5.00
DR45 Wendel Clark 4.00 10.00

2010-11 ITG Decades 1980s Edmonton Dynasty

COMPLETE SET (5) 8.00 20.00
ED01 Mark Messier 4.00 10.00
ED02 Grant Fuhr 3.00 8.00
ED03 Glenn Anderson 1.50 4.00
ED04 Paul Coffey 2.00 5.00
ED05 Jari Kurri 2.00 5.00

2010-11 ITG Decades 1980s For Your Country Jerseys Black

SILVER/30: .5X TO 1.2X BLACK/90*
01 Bossy/Perr/Bourq/Goulet 10.00 25.00
02 Laflr/Yzer/Hawer/Robnsn 15.00 40.00
03 Dion/Ststny/Coffy/Mario 15.00 40.00
04 Messr/Gilmr/Potvin/Fuhr 12.00 30.00
05 Mullen/Espo/Chelios/Brrs 12.00 30.00
06 Housley/Vnbs/LaFnt/Lang 12.00 30.00
07 Slmng/Nslnd/Lndbrg/Loob 15.00 40.00
08 Tretk/Krutv/Larnv/Mshkn 25.00 60.00

2010-11 ITG Decades 1980s Franchise Jerseys Silver

F01 Bourq/Neely/Moog/Mddltn 20.00 50.00
F02 Perrlt/Barrso/Hsley/Gare 15.00 40.00
F03 MacInn/Loob/Vern/McDnld 10.00 25.00
F04 T.Espo/Savard/Belfr/Rnick 25.00 60.00
F05 Yzerman/Sittlr/Gilbrt/Larsn 15.00 40.00
F06 Fuhr/Messier/Coffey/Kurri 25.00 60.00
F07 Keon/Francis/Howe/Babych 15.00 40.00
F08 Dionne/Robit/Hrudey/Nichls 15.00 40.00
F09 Bellws/Harts/Ciccr/Payne 15.00 40.00
F10 Carbn/Rbnsn/Lafleur/Roy 20.00 50.00
F11 Smith/Trottier/Bossy/Potvin 15.00 40.00
F12 P.Espo/Vanbs/Dione/Ltch 12.00 30.00
F13 Lindb/Clarke/Propp/Hextall 15.00 40.00
F14 Lemieux/Coffy/Barrso/Carly 30.00 80.00
F15 Ststny/Bchrd/Sakic/Goulet 15.00 40.00
F16 Fedrko/Gilmr/Mullen/Liut 25.00 60.00
F17 Vaive/Salming/Bestr/Sittl 15.00 40.00
F18 Brodr/Willms/Snpsts/Tanti 12.00 30.00
F19 Riggin/Hntr/Grtnr/Lngwy 12.00 30.00
F20 Hwrchk/Hull/Redd/Carly 20.00 50.00

2010-11 ITG Decades 1980s Game Used Jerseys Black

SILVER/30: .5X TO 1.2X BLACK/120*
M01 Al MacInnis 6.00 15.00
M02 Allan Bester 4.00 10.00
M03 Bernie Federko 4.00 10.00
M04 Bernie Nicholls 4.00 10.00
M05 Bill Barber 4.00 10.00
M06 Billy Smith 5.00 12.00
M07 Bob Nystrom 3.00 8.00
M08 Tony Tanti 4.00 10.00
M09 Bobby Clarke 8.00 20.00
M10 Borje Salming 5.00 12.00
M11 Brian Bellows 4.00 10.00
M12 Brian Propp 5.00 12.00
M13 Brian Skrudland 5.00 12.00
M14 Bryan Trottier 5.00 12.00
M15 Cam Neely 5.00 12.00
M16 Chris Chelios 5.00 12.00
M17 Craig Hartsburg 3.00 8.00
M18 Dale Hunter 6.00 15.00
M19 Dan Bouchard 6.00 15.00
M20 Dave Babych 5.00 12.00
M21 Darryl Sittler 6.00 15.00
M22 Dale Hawerchuk 6.00 15.00
M23 Denis Potvin 5.00 12.00
M24 Denis Savard 5.00 12.00
M25 Dino Ciccarelli 5.00 12.00
M26 Wendel Clark 8.00 20.00
M27 Gary Leeman 4.00 10.00
M28 Gary Suter 3.00 8.00
M29 Gilbert Perreault/30* 5.00 12.00
M30 Glenn Anderson 4.00 10.00
M31 Grant Fuhr/30* 8.00 20.00
M32 Guy Carbonneau 5.00 12.00
M33 Harold Snepsts 5.00 12.00
M34 Jari Kurri/30* 6.00 15.00
M35 Jeremy Roenick 8.00 20.00
M36 Joe Mullen 8.00 20.00
M37 John Vanbiesbrouck 8.00 20.00
M38 Lanny McDonald 5.00 12.00
M39 Larry Robinson 5.00 12.00
M40 Luc Robitaille 5.00 12.00
M41 Marcel Dionne 8.00 20.00
M42 Mats Naslund 8.00 20.00
M43 Mike Bossy 5.00 12.00
M44 Mike Gartner 10.00 25.00
M45 Mike Modano 8.00 20.00
M46 Neal Broten 4.00 10.00
M47 Pat LaFontaine 5.00 12.00
M48 Pat Riggin 3.00 8.00
M49 Paul Reinhart 3.00 8.00
M50 Peter Stastny 4.00 10.00
M51 Anders Hedberg 4.00 10.00
M52 Randy Carlyle 4.00 10.00
M53 Raymond Bourque 8.00 20.00
M54 Richard Brodeur 5.00 12.00
M55 Rick Middleton 5.00 12.00
M56 Rick Vaive 4.00 10.00
M57 Rod Langway 4.00 10.00
M58 Ron Hextall 5.00 12.00
M59 Steve Payne 3.00 8.00
M60 Steve Shutt 5.00 12.00
M61 Tiger Williams 3.00 8.00

M62 Trevor Linden 10.00 25.00
M63 Doug Gilmour/30* 12.00 30.00
M64 Brad Park/30* 4.00 10.00
M65 Reed Larson 3.00 8.00
M66 Guy Lafleur 10.00 25.00
M67 Joe Sakic 10.00 25.00
M68 Mario Lemieux 20.00 50.00
M69 Mark Messier/30* 10.00 25.00
M70 Patrick Roy/30* 12.00 30.00
M71 Phil Esposito/30* 8.00 20.00
M72 Paul Coffey 8.00 20.00
M73 Steve Yzerman 12.00 30.00
M74 Tony Esposito/30* 6.00 15.00
M75 Dave Keon/30* 5.00 12.00

2010-11 ITG Decades 1980s Great Moments

COMPLETE SET (5) 10.00 25.00
GM01 Mike Bossy 2.00 5.00
GM02 Jim Craig 1.50 4.00
GM03 Mark Messier 4.00 10.00
GM04 Bob Nystrom 1.25 3.00
GM05 Mario Lemieux 8.00 20.00

2010-11 ITG Decades 1980s Long Island Dynasty

COMPLETE SET (5) 6.00 15.00
LID01 Denis Potvin 2.00 5.00
LID02 Mike Bossy 2.00 5.00
LID03 Bryan Trottier 2.00 5.00
LID04 Billy Smith 2.00 5.00
LID05 Clark Gillies 2.00 5.00

2010-11 ITG Decades 1980s Memorable Masks

COMPLETE SET (10) 20.00 50.00
MM01 Grant Fuhr 4.00 10.00
MM02 Andy Moog 2.50 6.00
MM03 Mike Liut 1.50 4.00
MM04 Tom Barrasso 2.50 6.00
MM05 Bunny Larocque 2.00 5.00
MM06 Pelle Lindbergh 2.00 5.00
MM07 Michel Dion 2.00 5.00
MM08 Allan Bester 2.00 5.00
MM09 Patrick Roy 6.00 15.00
MM10 Murray Bannerman 2.50 6.00

2010-11 ITG Decades 1980s Rivalries Jerseys Silver

R01 Fuhr/Messr/McDon/Nieu 15.00 40.00
R02 Kurri/Coffey/Trottier/Gillies 25.00 60.00
R03 Chelios/Roy/Mcln/Vernon 20.00 50.00
R04 Vanbies/Dnne/Ptvin/Smith 20.00 50.00
R05 Naslnd/Carbon/Bchrd/Stst 15.00 40.00
R06 Laflr/Robn/Middle/Brque 15.00 40.00
R07 Vaive/Slmng/T.Esp/Svrd 20.00 50.00
R08 Clark/Bester/Fedrko/Gilm 20.00 50.00
R09 Andrsn/Fuhr/Hext/Propp 12.00 30.00
R10 Langwy/Riggn/Sittlr/Clrke 12.00 30.00
R11 Perrlt/Gare/Shutt/Lafleur 15.00 40.00
R12 Bossy/Mess/Tretk/Krutv 12.00 30.00

2010-11 ITG Decades 1980s Rookie Game Used Jerseys Silver

RJ01 Raymond Bourque 10.00 25.00
RJ02 Paul Coffey 10.00 25.00
RJ03 Denis Savard 6.00 15.00
RJ04 Jari Kurri 8.00 20.00
RJ05 Ron Francis 15.00 40.00
RJ06 Dale Hawerchuk 8.00 20.00
RJ07 Grant Fuhr 10.00 25.00
RJ08 Doug Gilmour 12.00 30.00
RJ09 Tom Barrasso 6.00 15.00
RJ10 Steve Yzerman 15.00 40.00
RJ11 Chris Chelios 6.00 15.00
RJ12 Pat LaFontaine 8.00 20.00
RJ13 Mario Lemieux 25.00 60.00
RJ14 Patrick Roy 15.00 40.00
RJ15 Wendel Clark 10.00 25.00
RJ16 Ron Hextall 6.00 15.00
RJ17 Luc Robitaille 10.00 25.00
RJ18 Joe Nieuwendyk 5.00 12.00
RJ19 Brian Leetch 10.00 25.00
RJ20 Joe Sakic 15.00 40.00

2010-11 ITG Decades 1980s Stanley Cup Clashes Jerseys Silver

CC01 Nystrom/Trottier/Clrke/Barbr 15.00 40.00
CC03 Bossy/Trottier/Brodeur/Will 25.00 60.00
CC04 Smith/Potvin/Andrsn/Kurri 15.00 40.00
CC05 Fuhr/Messier/Gillies/LaFont 15.00 40.00
CC06 Kurri/Coffey/Propp/Lind 20.00 50.00
CC07 Roy/Naslnd/Mulln/Vern 20.00 50.00
CC08 Messier/Andrsn/Hext/Propp 15.00 40.00
CC09 Tikkan/Fuhr/Moog/Brque 60.00 120.00
CC10 Macln/McDon/Rbinsn/Roy 20.00 50.00

2010-11 ITG Decades 1980s Trophy Winners Jerseys Black

SILVER/20-30: .5X TO 1.2X BLACK/50-100*
TWJ01 Raymond Bourque 8.00 20.00
TWJ02 Bryan Trottier 5.00 12.00
TWJ03 Larry Robinson 5.00 12.00
TWJ04 Peter Stastny 4.00 10.00
TWJ05 Dale Hawerchuk 8.00 20.00
TWJ06 Billy Smith 5.00 12.00
TWJ07 Mike Bossy 5.00 12.00
TWJ08 Mike Bossy 5.00 12.00
TWJ09 Mario Lemieux 20.00 50.00
TWJ10 Billy Smith 5.00 12.00
TWJ11 Rod Langway 4.00 10.00
TWJ12 Tom Barrasso 5.00 12.00
TWJ13 Tom Barrasso 5.00 12.00
TWJ14 Mark Messier 10.00 25.00
TWJ15 Mario Lemieux 20.00 50.00
TWJ16 Pelle Lindbergh/50* 12.00 30.00
TWJ17 Paul Coffey 5.00 12.00
TWJ18 Gary Suter 3.00 8.00
TWJ19 John Vanbiesbrouck 8.00 20.00
TWJ20 Patrick Roy 12.00 30.00
TWJ21 Paul Coffey 5.00 12.00
TWJ22 Luc Robitaille 6.00 15.00
TWJ23 Ron Hextall 5.00 12.00
TWJ24 Ron Hextall 5.00 12.00
TWJ25 Joe Nieuwendyk 4.00 10.00
TWJ26 Grant Fuhr/50* 8.00 20.00
TWJ27 Raymond Bourque 8.00 20.00
TWJ28 Brian Leetch 4.00 10.00
TWJ29 Patrick Roy 12.50 30.00
TWJ30 Al MacInnis/50* 8.00 20.00

2013-14 ITG Decades 1990s

1 Brett Hull INTL 2.50 6.00
2 Al MacInnis INTL 1.50 4.00
3 Bill Ranford INTL 1.25 3.00
4 Borje Salming INTL 1.25 3.00
5 Pat LaFontaine INTL 1.25 3.00
6 Dale Hawerchuk INTL 1.50 4.00
7 Dominik Hasek INTL 2.00 5.00
8 Ed Belfour INTL 1.25 3.00
9 Eric Lindros INTL 2.00 5.00
10 Jari Kurri INTL 1.25 3.00
11 Jaromir Jagr INTL 4.00 10.00
12 Paul Coffey INTL 1.25 3.00
13 Luc Robitaille INTL 1.25 3.00
14 Mark Messier INTL 2.50 6.00
15 Mats Naslund INTL .75 2.00
16 Mats Sundin INTL 1.25 3.00
17 Mike Modano INTL 2.00 5.00
18 Mike Richter INTL 1.25 3.00
19 Nicklas Lidstrom INTL 1.25 3.00
20 Sergei Fedorov INTL 2.00 5.00
21 Teemu Selanne INTL 2.50 6.00
22 Teppo Numminen INTL .75 2.00
23 Theoren Fleury INTL 1.50 4.00
24 Tony Granato INTL .75 2.00
25 Adam Oates 1.25 3.00
26 Al Iafrate 1.00 2.50
27 Al MacInnis 1.50 4.00
28 Andy Moog 1.25 3.00
29 Arturs Irbe 1.00 2.50
30 Bernie Nicholls 1.00 2.50
31 Bill Ranford 1.25 3.00
32 Bob Boughner .75 2.00
33 Bob Essensa 1.25 3.00
34 Bob Sweeney .75 2.00
35 Bobby Holik .75 2.00
36 Brad May .75 2.00
37 Brian Skrudland .75 2.00
38 Byron Dafoe 1.00 2.50
39 Cam Neely 1.25 3.00
40 Chris Chelios 1.25 3.00
41 Chris Terreri .75 2.00
42 Claude Lemieux 1.00 2.50
43 Craig Billington .75 2.00
44 Curtis Joseph 1.50 4.00
45 Damian Rhodes .75 2.00
46 Dan Cloutier 1.00 2.50
47 Dave Andreychuk 1.25 3.00
48 Dave Ellett .75 2.00
49 Denis Savard 1.25 3.00
50 Dominik Hasek 2.00 5.00
51 Don Beaupre .75 2.00
52 Doug Gilmour 1.50 4.00
53 Doug Weight 1.25 3.00
54 Ed Belfour 1.25 3.00
55 Eric Lindros 2.00 5.00
56 Felix Potvin 2.00 5.00
57 Garth Snow 1.00 2.50
58 Gary Roberts .75 2.00
59 Gary Suter .75 2.00
60 Gilbert Dionne 1.00 2.50
61 Gino Odjick .75 2.00
62 Gordie Howe 4.00 10.00
63 Grant Fuhr 2.00 5.00
64 Greg Johnson .75 2.00
65 Guy Carbonneau 1.25 3.00
66 Guy Hebert 1.00 2.50
67 Igor Larionov 1.25 3.00
68 Jaromir Jagr 4.00 10.00
69 Jason Woolley .75 2.00
70 Jeff Odgers .75 2.00
71 Jeremy Roenick 2.00 5.00
72 Jim Carey 1.00 2.50
73 Jim Cummins .75 2.00
74 Joe Mullen 1.00 2.50
75 Joe Nieuwendyk 1.00 2.50
76 Joe Sakic 2.50 6.00
77 Joe Thornton 2.00 5.00
78 Joel Otto .75 2.00
79 John Cullen .75 2.00
80 John Druce .75 2.00
81 John LeClair 1.25 3.00
82 John Vanbiesbrouck 1.25 3.00
83 Keith Tkachuk 1.25 3.00
84 Kelly Buchberger .75 2.00
85 Kelly Chase .75 2.00
86 Kelly Hrudey 1.00 2.50
87 Ken Hodge, Jr. .75 2.00
88 Kevin Stevens 1.00 2.50
89 Kirk McLean 1.00 2.50
90 Kirk Muller 1.00 2.50
91 Kris Draper 1.00 2.50
92 Kris King .75 2.00
93 Kyle McLaren .75 2.00
94 Larry Murphy 1.00 2.50
95 Louie DeBrusk .75 2.00
96 Luc Robitaille 1.25 3.00
97 Lyle Odelein .75 2.00
98 Mario Lemieux 5.00 12.00
99 Mariusz Czerkawski .75 2.00
100 Mark Howe 1.25 3.00
101 Mark Messier 2.50 6.00
102 Marty McSorley 1.00 2.50
103 Mats Sundin 1.25 3.00
104 Brett Hull 2.50 6.00
105 Michael Peca 1.00 2.50
106 Mike Gartner 1.50 4.00
107 Mike Modano 2.00 5.00
108 Mike Richter 1.25 3.00
109 Nicklas Lidstrom 1.25 3.00
110 Nikolai Borschevsky .75 2.00
111 Nikolai Khabibulin 1.25 3.00
112 Olaf Kolzig 1.25 3.00
113 Owen Nolan 1.25 3.00
114 Pat Elynuik .75 2.00
115 Patrick Marleau 1.25 3.00
116 Patrick Roy 3.00 8.00
117 Paul Laus .75 2.00
118 Pavel Bure 1.25 3.00
119 Peter Bondra 1.25 3.00
120 Peter Forsberg 2.50 6.00
121 Peter Sidorkiewicz .75 2.00
122 Phil Housley 1.00 2.50
123 Ray Ferraro .75 2.00
124 Raymond Bourque 2.00 5.00
125 Rob Ray .75 2.00
126 Ron Francis 1.50 4.00
127 Ron Hextall 1.25 3.00
128 Ron Tugnutt 1.00 2.50
129 Russ Courtnall 1.00 2.50
130 Ryan VandenBussche 1.00 2.50
131 Sean Burke .75 2.00
132 Sergei Fedorov 2.00 5.00
133 Sergei Samsonov 1.00 2.50
134 Shayne Corson 1.00 2.50
135 Stephane Richer .75 2.00
136 Steve Smith .75 2.00
137 Steve Thomas .75 2.00
138 Steve Yzerman 3.00 8.00
139 Stu Grimson .75 2.00
140 Teemu Selanne 2.50 6.00
141 Teppo Numminen .75 2.00
142 Theoren Fleury 1.50 4.00
143 Tie Domi 1.00 2.50
144 Tim Cheveldae 1.25 3.00
145 Tony Amonte 1.00 2.50
146 Tony Granato .75 2.00
147 Trevor Linden 1.25 3.00
148 Vincent Damphousse 1.00 2.50
149 Mark Recchi 1.50 4.00
150 Warren Rychel .75 2.00
151 Wendel Clark 2.00 5.00
152 Wendell Young .75 2.00
153 Adam Graves 1.00 2.50
154 Geoff Courtnall .75 2.00
155 Guy Lafleur 1.50 4.00
156 Doug MacLean DC .75 2.00
157 Jacques Lemaire DC 1.00 2.50
158 Mike Keenan DC 1.00 2.50
159 Pat Quinn DC 1.25 3.00
160 Scotty Bowman DC 1.25 3.00
161 Ted Nolan DC 1.00 2.50
162 Mario Lemieux DYN 5.00 12.00
163 Jaromir Jagr DYN 4.00 10.00
164 Bryan Trottier DYN 1.25 3.00
165 Kevin Stevens DYN 1.00 2.50
166 Joe Mullen DYN 1.00 2.50
167 Steve Yzerman DYN 3.00 8.00
168 Nicklas Lidstrom DYN 1.25 3.00
169 Igor Larionov DYN 1.25 3.00
170 Darren McCarty DYN 1.00 2.50
171 Sergei Fedorov DYN 2.00 5.00
172 Eric Lindros FRP 2.00 5.00
173 Jaromir Jagr FRP 4.00 10.00
174 Joe Thornton FRP 2.00 5.00
175 Keith Tkachuk FRP 1.25 3.00
176 Owen Nolan FRP 1.25 3.00
177 Patrick Marleau FRP 1.25 3.00
178 Peter Forsberg FRP 2.50 6.00
179 Roberto Luongo FRP 2.00 5.00
180 Scott Niedermayer FRP 1.25 3.00
181 B.Probert/T.Domi ENF 1.25 3.00
182 P.Roy/C.Osgood ENF 3.00 8.00
183 J.Kocur/K.Bchbrgr ENF .75 2.00
184 K.Chase/C.Berube ENF .75 2.00
185 J.Odgers/G.Odjick ENF .75 2.00
186 C.Lemieux/D.McCarty ENF 1.00 2.50
187 F.Potvin/R.Hextall ENF 2.00 5.00
188 S.Grimson/B.Probert ENF 1.25 3.00
189 R.Ray/T.Domi ENF 1.00 2.50
190 M.McSorley/W.Clark ENF 2.00 5.00
191 B.Ranford/R.Bourque CC 2.00 5.00
192 M.Lemieux/M.Modano CC 5.00 12.00
193 R.Francis/J.Roenick CC 2.00 5.00
194 P.Roy/L.Robitaille CC 3.00 8.00
195 P.Bure/M.Richter CC 1.25 3.00
196 C.Lemieux/N.Lidstrom CC 1.25 3.00
197 J.Sakic/J.Vnbsbrck CC 2.50 6.00
198 M.Vernon/E.Lindros CC 2.00 5.00
199 S.Yzrmn/A.Oates CC 3.00 8.00
200 B.Hull/D.Hasek CC 2.50 6.00

2013-14 ITG Decades 1990s Gold

GOLD/30: .6X TO 1.5X BASIC CARDS
187 F.Potvin/R.Hextall ENF 3.00 8.00

2013-14 ITG Decades 1990s All Stars Quad Jerseys Black

SILVER/30: .5X TO 1.2X BLACK/95*
AS01 McInns/Jsph/Rnck/Brque 4.00 10.00
AS02 Fdrv/Lmeux/Ptvn/Chlios 10.00 25.00
AS03 Hsek/Nlan/Flry/Yzrmn 6.00 15.00
AS04 Lndrs/Skic/Khbbln/Jagr 8.00 20.00
AS05 Ldstrm/Sndin/Tkchk/Mdno 4.00 10.00
AS06 Slnne/Irbe/Rcchi/Roy 6.00 15.00
AS07 Hull/Mssier/Blfr/Osgd 5.00 12.00
AS08 Bure/LeClr/Ndrmyr/Frsbrg 5.00 12.00

2013-14 ITG Decades 1990s Autographs

AAI Arturs Irbe 6.00 15.00
AAI Al Iafrate 6.00 15.00
AAM Al MacInnis 10.00 25.00
AAMO Andy Moog 8.00 20.00
AAO Adam Oates 8.00 20.00
ABB Bob Boughner 5.00 12.00
ABD Byron Dafoe 6.00 15.00
ABE Bob Essensa 8.00 20.00
ABH Brett Hull SP 15.00 40.00
ABHAO B.Hull/A.Oates SP 15.00 40.00
ABHO Bobby Holik 5.00 12.00
ABL Brian Leetch SP 6.00 15.00
ABM Brad May 5.00 12.00
ABN Bernie Nicholls 6.00 15.00
ABR Bill Ranford 8.00 20.00
ABS Bob Sweeney 5.00 12.00
ABS Brian Skrudland 5.00 12.00
ACB Craig Billington 5.00 12.00
ACC Chris Chelios SP 8.00 20.00
ACJ Curtis Joseph 10.00 25.00
ACL Claude Lemieux 6.00 15.00
ACN Cam Neely SP 15.00 40.00
ACT Chris Terreri 5.00 12.00
ADA Dave Andreychuk 8.00 20.00
ADB Don Beaupre 5.00 12.00
ADC Dan Cloutier 6.00 15.00
ADE Dave Ellett 5.00 12.00
ADG Doug Gilmour 10.00 25.00
ADGWC D.Gilmour/W.Clark SP 12.00 30.00
ADH Dominik Hasek SP 30.00 80.00
ADM Doug MacLean 5.00 12.00
ADR Damian Rhodes 5.00 12.00
ADS Denis Savard 8.00 20.00
ADW Doug Weight 8.00 20.00
AEB Ed Belfour SP 8.00 20.00
AED Eric Desjardins 6.00 15.00
AFP Felix Potvin 12.00 30.00
AGC Guy Carbonneau 8.00 20.00
AGCO Geoff Courtnall 5.00 12.00
AGD Gilbert Dionne 6.00 15.00
AGF Grant Fuhr 12.00 30.00
AGH Gordie Howe SP 100.00 250.00
AGHE Guy Hebert 6.00 15.00
AGJ Greg Johnson 5.00 12.00
AGO Gino Odjick 5.00 12.00
AGR Gary Roberts 5.00 12.00
AGS Garth Snow 6.00 15.00
AGSU Gary Suter 5.00 12.00
AIL Igor Larionov 8.00 20.00
AJC Jim Carey 6.00 15.00
AJCU John Cullen 5.00 12.00
AJCUM Jim Cummins 5.00 12.00
AJD John Druce 5.00 12.00
AJD Jacques Demers 6.00 15.00
AJJ Jaromir Jagr SP 60.00 150.00
AJL Jacques Lemaire 6.00 15.00
AJL John LeClair 8.00 20.00
AJM Joe Mullen 6.00 15.00
AJN Joe Nieuwendyk 6.00 15.00
AJO Jeff Odgers 5.00 12.00
AJOT Joel Otto 5.00 12.00
AJR Jeremy Roenick 12.00 30.00
AJS Joe Sakic SP 30.00 80.00
AJSPF J.Sakic/P.Forsberg SP 30.00 80.00
AJT Joe Thornton SP 12.00 30.00
AJV John Vanbiesbrouck 8.00 20.00
AJW Jason Woolley 5.00 12.00
AKB Kelly Buchberger 5.00 12.00
AKC Kelly Chase 5.00 12.00
AKD Kris Draper 6.00 15.00
AKH Kelly Hrudey 6.00 15.00
AKHJR Ken Hodge, Jr. 5.00 12.00
AKK Kris King 5.00 12.00
AKM Kyle McLaren 5.00 12.00
AKM Kirk Muller 6.00 15.00
AKS Kevin Stevens 6.00 15.00
AKT Keith Tkachuk 8.00 20.00
ALD Louis DeBrusk 5.00 12.00
ALM Larry Murphy 6.00 15.00
ALO Lyle Odelein 5.00 12.00
ALR Luc Robitaille 8.00 20.00
AMC Mariusz Czerkawski 5.00 12.00
AMG Mike Gartner 10.00 25.00
AMH Mark Howe 8.00 20.00
AMK Mike Keenan 6.00 15.00
AML Mario Lemieux SP 100.00 200.00
AMM Mike Modano SP 12.00 30.00
AMMC Marty McSorley 6.00 15.00
AMMC Kirk McLean 6.00 15.00
AMME Mark Messier SP 25.00 60.00
AMP Michael Peca 6.00 15.00
AMR Mike Richter 8.00 20.00
AMRE Mark Recchi SP 15.00 40.00
AMS1 Mats Sundin SP 25.00 60.00
AMS2 Mats Sundin SP 40.00 100.00
ANB Nikolai Borschevsky 5.00 12.00
ANK Nikolai Khabibulin 8.00 20.00
ANL Nicklas Lidstrom SP 15.00 40.00
AOK Olaf Kolzig 8.00 20.00
AON Owen Nolan 8.00 20.00
APB Pavel Bure SP 40.00 100.00
APBO Peter Bondra 8.00 20.00
APE Pat Elynuik 5.00 12.00
APF Peter Forsberg SP 30.00 80.00
APH Phil Housley 6.00 15.00
APLA Paul Laus 5.00 12.00
APM Patrick Marleau 8.00 20.00
APQ Pat Quinn 8.00 20.00
APR Patrick Roy SP 60.00 150.00
APS Peter Sidorkiewicz 5.00 12.00
ARB Raymond Bourque SP 15.00 40.00
ARC Russ Courtnall 6.00 15.00
ARF Ron Francis 10.00 25.00
ARFE Ray Ferraro 5.00 12.00
ARH Ron Hextall 8.00 20.00
ARR Rob Ray 5.00 12.00
ART Ron Tugnutt 6.00 15.00
ARV Ryan VandenBussche 6.00 15.00
ASB Scotty Bowman 8.00 20.00
ASB Sean Burke 5.00 12.00
ASC Shayne Corson 6.00 15.00
ASF Sergei Fedorov SP 20.00 50.00
ASG Stu Grimson 5.00 12.00
ASR Stephane Richer 5.00 12.00
ASS Sergei Samsonov 6.00 15.00
ASSM Steve Smith 5.00 12.00
AST Steve Thomas 5.00 12.00
ASY Steve Yzerman 20.00 50.00
ATA Tony Amonte 6.00 15.00
ATB Tom Barrasso SP 8.00 20.00
ATC Tim Cheveldae 8.00 20.00
ATD Tie Domi 6.00 15.00
ATF Theoren Fleury 10.00 25.00
ATG Tony Granato 5.00 12.00
ATL Trevor Linden 8.00 20.00
ATN Ted Nolan 6.00 15.00
ATNU Teppo Numminen 5.00 12.00
ATS Teemu Selanne 15.00 40.00
AVD Vincent Damphousse 6.00 15.00
AVL Vincent Lecavalier SP 12.00 30.00
AWC Wendel Clark SP 15.00 40.00
AWR Warren Rychel 5.00 12.00
AWY Wendell Young 5.00 12.00
EEL Eric Lindros SP 20.00 50.00

2013-14 ITG Decades 1990s Between the Pipes Jerseys Black

SILVER/30: .6X TO 1.5X BLACK/80*
BTPJ01 Arturs Irbe 3.00 8.00
BTPJ02 Chris Osgood 4.00 10.00
BTPJ03 Curtis Joseph 5.00 12.00
BTPJ04 Dominik Hasek 6.00 15.00
BTPJ05 Felix Potvin 6.00 15.00
BTPJ06 John Vanbiesbrouck 4.00 10.00
BTPJ07 Mike Richter 4.00 10.00
BTPJ08 Nikolai Khabibulin 4.00 10.00
BTPJ09 Olaf Kolzig 4.00 10.00
BTPJ10 Patrick Roy 10.00 25.00
BTPJ11 Ron Hextall 4.00 10.00
BTPJ12 Tom Barrasso 4.00 10.00

2013-14 ITG Decades 1990s Cup Clashes Quad Jerseys Black

SILVER/30: .5X TO 1.2X BLACK/80*
CC01 Msser/Fhr/Neely/Brque 8.00 20.00
CC02 Lmeux/Brrsso/Mdno/Bllws 15.00 40.00
CC03 Lmeux/Frncs /Rnck/Blfr 15.00 40.00
CC04 Roy/Mller/Rbtlle/Kurri 10.00 25.00
CC05 Rchtr/Msser/Bure/Lnden 8.00 20.00
CC06 Hlik/Ndrmyr/Cccrlli/Fdrv 6.00 15.00
CC07 Roy/Skic/Vnbsbrck/Laus 10.00 25.00
CC08 Yzrmn/Vrnon/LeClr/Lndrs 10.00 25.00
CC09 Yzrmn/Ldstrm/Klzg/Bndra 10.00 25.00
CC10 Hull/Blfr/Hsek/Peca 8.00 20.00

2013-14 ITG Decades 1990s Entire Decade Jerseys Black

SILVER/30: .6X TO 1.5X BLACK JSY/87*
ED01 Olaf Kolzig 2.50 6.00
ED02 Steve Yzerman 6.00 15.00
ED03 Tom Barrasso 2.50 6.00
ED04 Rob Ray 1.50 4.00
ED05 Mike Richter 2.50 6.00
ED06 Raymond Bourque 4.00 10.00
ED07 Mike Modano 4.00 10.00
ED08 Joe Sakic 5.00 12.00

2013-14 ITG Decades 1990s European Influence Dual Jerseys Black

SILVER/30: .6X TO 1.5X BLACK.80*
EI01 J.Jagr/N.Khabibulin 10.00 25.00
EI02 D.Hasek/A.Irbe 5.00 12.00
EI03 M.Sundin/S.Fedorov 5.00 12.00
EI04 O.Kolzig/T.Selanne 6.00 15.00
EI05 T.Holmstrom/P.Bure 3.00 8.00
EI06 N.Lidstrom/P.Forsberg 6.00 15.00

2013-14 ITG Decades 1990s For Your Country Quad Jerseys Black

SILVER/30: .5X TO 1.2X BLACK/85*
FYCJ01 Lndrs/Skic/Cffy/Yzrmn 8.00 20.00
FYCJ02 Roy/Brque/Mssr/Flry 8.00 20.00
FYCJ03 Rchtr/Rnck/Hull/Mdno 6.00 15.00
FYCJ04 Fdrv/Lrnov/Bure/Khbbln 5.00 12.00
FYCJ05 Ldstrm/Frsbrg/Sndn/Nslnd 6.00 15.00
FYCJ06 Nmmnen/Slnne/Krri/Tkknn 6.00 15.00

2013-14 ITG Decades 1990s Franchises Quad Jerseys Black

SILVER/30: .5X TO 1.2X BLACK/95*
F01 Brque/Neely/Thrntn/Oates 5.00 12.00
F02 Flry/Vrnon/McInns/Nwndk 4.00 10.00
F03 Blfr/Rnck/Glet/Chlios 5.00 12.00
F04 Yzrmn/Ldstrm/Osgd/Vrnon 8.00 20.00
F05 Mssr/Jsph/Wght/Rnfrd 6.00 15.00
F06 Rbtlle/Hrdy/Krri/McSrly 3.00 8.00
F07 Mdno/Blfr/Nuwndk/Hull 6.00 15.00
F08 Roy/Mller/Crbnnu/Crsn 8.00 20.00
F09 Lmeux/Brrsso/Frncs/Jagr 12.00 30.00
F10 Roy/Frsbrg/Skic/Odgrs 8.00 20.00
F11 Hull/Jsph/Chse/McInns 6.00 15.00
F12 Ptvn/Glmr/Clrk/Sndn 5.00 12.00
F13 Bure/Lndn/Mssr/Odjck 6.00 15.00
F14 Slnne/Tkchk/Khbbln/Chvlde 6.00 15.00

2013-14 ITG Decades 1990s Game Used Jerseys Black

SILVER/30: .6X TO 1.5X BLACK/84*
M01 Adam Oates 3.00 8.00
M02 Bernie Nicholls 2.50 6.00
M03 Brett Hull 6.00 15.00
M04 Cam Neely 3.00 8.00
M05 Chris Chelios 3.00 8.00
M06 Curtis Joseph 4.00 10.00
M07 Dominik Hasek 5.00 12.00
M08 Doug Gilmour 4.00 10.00
M09 Ed Belfour 3.00 8.00
M10 Eric Lindros 5.00 12.00
M11 Felix Potvin 5.00 12.00
M12 Jaromir Jagr 10.00 25.00
M13 Jeremy Roenick 5.00 12.00
M14 Joe Nieuwendyk 2.50 6.00
M15 Joe Sakic 6.00 15.00
M16 Joe Thornton 5.00 12.00
M17 John LeClair 3.00 8.00
M18 John Vanbiesbrouck 3.00 8.00
M19 Keith Tkachuk 3.00 8.00
M20 Larry Murphy 2.50 6.00
M21 Luc Robitaille 3.00 8.00
M22 Mario Lemieux 12.00 30.00
M23 Mark Messier 6.00 15.00
M24 Mats Sundin 3.00 8.00
M25 Michael Peca 2.50 6.00
M26 Mike Modano 5.00 12.00
M27 Mike Richter 3.00 8.00
M28 Nicklas Lidstrom 3.00 8.00
M29 Olaf Kolzig 3.00 8.00
M30 Patrick Roy 8.00 20.00
M31 Pavel Bure 3.00 8.00
M32 Peter Bondra 3.00 8.00
M33 Peter Forsberg 6.00 15.00
M34 Raymond Bourque 5.00 12.00
M35 Ron Francis 4.00 10.00
M36 Ron Hextall 3.00 8.00
M37 Sergei Fedorov 5.00 12.00
M38 Sergei Samsonov 2.50 6.00
M39 Steve Yzerman 8.00 20.00
M40 Teemu Selanne 6.00 15.00
M41 Teppo Numminen 2.00 5.00
M42 Theoren Fleury 4.00 10.00
M43 Tie Domi 2.50 6.00
M44 Trevor Linden 3.00 8.00
M45 Wendel Clark 5.00 12.00

2013-14 ITG Decades 1990s Masks

DM01 Andy Moog 2.50 6.00
DM02 Arturs Irbe 2.00 5.00
DM03 Bill Ranford 2.50 6.00
DM04 Bob Essensa 2.50 6.00
DM05 Brian Hayward 2.00 5.00
DM06 Curtis Joseph 3.00 8.00
DM07 Ed Belfour 2.50 6.00
DM08 Felix Potvin 4.00 10.00
DM09 Grant Fuhr 4.00 10.00
DM10 Guy Hebert 2.00 5.00
DM11 Jim Carey 2.00 5.00
DM12 John Vanbiesbrouck 2.50 6.00
DM13 Kelly Hrudey 2.00 5.00
DM14 Kirk McLean 2.00 5.00
DM15 Mike Richter 2.50 6.00
DM16 Mike Vernon 2.00 5.00
DM17 Patrick Roy 6.00 15.00
DM18 Patrick Roy 6.00 15.00
DM19 Ron Hextall 2.50 6.00
DM20 Ron Tugnutt 2.00 5.00
DM21 Sean Burke 1.50 4.00
DM22 Tom Barrasso 2.50 6.00

2013-14 ITG Decades 1990s Rivalries Quad Jerseys Black

SILVER/30: .5X TO 1.2X BLACK/95*
R1 Rnfrd/Mssr/Flry/McInns 6.00 15.00
R2 Skc/Roy/Yzrmn/Osgd 8.00 20.00
R3 Skrdlnd/Crbnnau/Nly/Brque 5.00 12.00
R4 Hsek/Ray/Domi/Jsph 5.00 12.00
R5 Chlos/Rnck/Ldstrm/Yzrmn 8.00 20.00
R6 Hull/Jsph/Glmr/Ptvn 6.00 15.00
R7 Mller/Roy/Skic/Nlan 8.00 20.00
R8 Lmeux/Jagr/Mssr/Rchtr 12.00 30.00

2013-14 ITG Decades 1990s Rookie and Retired Dual Jerseys Black

SILVER/30: .5X TO 1.2X BLACK/80*
RRDM01 M.Sundin/G.Lafleur 4.00 10.00
RRDM02 E.Lindros/R.Langway 5.00 12.00
RRDM03 C.Osgood/M.Goulet 3.00 8.00
RRDM04 D.McCarty/D.Taylor 2.50 6.00
RRDM05 N.Khabibulin/T.Steen 3.00 8.00
RRDM06 T.Holmstrom/D.Savard 3.00 8.00

2013-14 ITG Decades 1990s Rookies

DR01 Curtis Joseph 1.50 4.00
DR02 Mats Sundin 1.25 3.00
DR03 Owen Nolan 1.25 3.00
DR04 Sergei Fedorov 2.00 5.00
DR05 Jaromir Jagr 4.00 10.00
DR06 Peter Bondra 1.25 3.00
DR07 Dominik Hasek 2.00 5.00
DR08 John LeClair 1.25 3.00
DR09 Tony Amonte 1.00 2.50
DR10 Nicklas Lidstrom 1.25 3.00
DR11 Scott Niedermayer 1.25 3.00
DR12 Pavel Bure 1.25 3.00
DR13 Arturs Irbe 1.00 2.50
DR14 Felix Potvin 2.00 5.00
DR15 Keith Tkachuk 1.25 3.00
DR16 Eric Lindros 2.00 5.00
DR17 Teemu Selanne 2.50 6.00
DR18 Chris Osgood 1.25 3.00
DR19 Peter Forsberg 2.50 6.00
DR20 Tomas Holmstrom .75 2.00
DR21 Sergei Samsonov 1.00 2.50
DR22 Joe Thornton 2.00 5.00
DR23 Roberto Luongo 2.00 5.00

2013-14 ITG Decades 1990s Trophy Winners Jerseys Black

SILVER/30: .6X TO 1.5X BLACK/80*
TW01 Dominik Hasek 5.00 12.00
TW02 Ed Belfour 3.00 8.00
TW03 Steve Yzerman 8.00 20.00
TW04 Jaromir Jagr 10.00 25.00
TW05 Joe Sakic 6.00 15.00
TW06 Mario Lemieux 12.00 30.00
TW07 Mark Messier 6.00 15.00
TW08 Patrick Roy 8.00 20.00
TW09 Pavel Bure 3.00 8.00
TW10 Eric Lindros 5.00 12.00
TW11 Teemu Selanne 6.00 15.00
TW12 Sergei Fedorov 5.00 12.00

2012-13 ITG Draft Prospects

1 Adam Erne 1.25 3.00
2 Aleksander Barkov 5.00 12.00
3 Alexander Wennberg 1.25 3.00
4 Anthony Duclair 2.00 5.00
5 Anthony Mantha 2.00 5.00
6 Bo Horvat 2.50 6.00
7 Brody Silk .75 2.00
8 Connor Rankin .75 2.00
9 Curtis Lazar 1.25 3.00
10 Darnell Nurse 1.50 4.00
11 Dillon Heatherington 1.25 3.00
12 Elias Lindholm 3.00 8.00
13 Eric Comrie 1.25 3.00
14 Eric Roy 1.25 3.00
15 Frederik Gauthier 2.00 5.00
16 Hunter Shinkaruk 2.00 5.00
17 Jackson Whistle .75 2.00
18 Jacob de la Rose 1.50 4.00
19 Jason Dickinson 1.00 2.50
20 Jonathan Drouin 4.00 10.00
21 Jordan Subban 1.50 4.00
22 Josh Morrissey 1.25 3.00
23 Justin Bailey 1.00 2.50
24 Kerby Rychel 1.25 3.00
25 Madison Bowey .75 2.00
26 Max Domi 2.50 6.00
27 Morgan Klimchuk 1.25 3.00
28 Nathan MacKinnon 4.00 10.00
29 Nicolas Petan 1.25 3.00
30 Nicholas Baptiste 1.00 2.50
31 Nick Sorensen 1.25 3.00
32 Nikita Zadorov .75 2.00
33 Rasmus Ristolainen 2.00 5.00
34 Robert Hagg 2.00 5.00
35 Ryan Hartman 1.25 3.00
36 Ryan Kujawinski 1.00 2.50
37 Ryan Pulock 1.50 4.00
38 Samuel Morin .75 2.00
39 Sean Monahan 2.50 6.00
40 Sergey Tolchinsky .75 2.00
41 Seth Jones 2.50 6.00
42 Shea Theodore 1.50 4.00
43 Spencer Martin 1.00 2.50
44 Stephen Harper 1.50 4.00
45 Tristan Jarry 1.25 3.00
46 Valentin Zykov 1.50 4.00
47 William Carrier 1.25 3.00
48 Zachary Fucale 1.50 4.00
49 Mirco Mueller 1.50 4.00
50 Chris Bigras 1.00 2.50
51 Marc-Olivier Roy 1.25 3.00
52 Mitchell Wheaton 1.00 2.50
53 Zach Nastasiuk 1.25 3.00
54 Gabryel Paquin-Boudreau 1.00 2.50
55 Philippe Desrosiers 1.00 2.50
56 Jimmy Lodge 1.25 3.00
57 Oliver Bjorkstrand 1.00 2.50
58 Laurent Dauphin .75 2.00
59 Michael Giugovaz .75 2.00
60 Aaron Ekblad FDP 4.00 10.00
61 Alexis Pepin FDP 1.00 2.50
62 Anthony DeAngelo FDP 1.00 2.50
63 Blake Clarke FDP 1.25 3.00
64 Brandon Robinson FDP 1.00 2.50
65 Brayden Point FDP 2.00 5.00
66 Brycen Martin FDP 1.25 3.00
67 Daniel Audette FDP 1.50 4.00
68 Eric Cornel FDP 1.00 2.50
69 Haydn Fleury FDP 1.25 3.00
70 Ivan Barbashev FDP 1.25 3.00
71 Jake Virtanen FDP 1.50 4.00
72 Jared McCann FDP 1.50 4.00
73 Jordan Thomson FDP 1.00 2.50
74 Josh Ho-Sang FDP 1.50 4.00
75 Leon Draisaitl FDP 3.00 8.00
76 Matt Mistele FDP 1.00 2.50
77 Michael Dal Colle FDP 1.00 2.50
78 Nick Ritchie FDP 1.25 3.00
79 Nikolay Goldobin FDP 1.25 3.00
80 Robby Fabbri FDP 1.00 2.50
81 Roland McKeown FDP 1.00 2.50
82 Sam Bennett FDP 3.00 8.00
83 Sam Reinhart FDP 4.00 10.00
84 Connor McDavid FDP 12.50 25.00
85 Travis Konecny FDP 2.50 6.00
86 Dylan Strome FDP 3.00 8.00
87 Sean Day FDP 2.50 6.00
88 Tyler Benson FDP 3.00 8.00
89 Sam Steel FDP 2.50 6.00
90 Alexander Ovechkin FRP 5.00 12.00
91 Bobby Smith FRP 1.00 2.50
92 Brad Park FRP 1.00 2.50
93 Brian Bellows FRP 1.00 2.50
94 Cam Neely FRP 1.25 3.00
95 Carey Price FRP 2.50 6.00
96 Al MacInnis FRP 1.50 4.00
97 Dale Hawerchuk FRP 1.50 4.00
98 Daniel Sedin FRP 1.50 4.00
99 Darryl Sittler FRP 1.50 4.00
100 Denis Savard FRP 1.25 3.00
101 Eric Lindros FRP 2.00 5.00
102 Evgeni Malkin FRP 2.50 6.00
103 Gary Roberts FRP .75 2.00
104 Gilbert Perreault FRP 1.25 3.00
105 Grant Fuhr FRP 2.00 5.00
106 Guy Lafleur FRP 1.50 4.00
107 Henrik Sedin FRP 1.50 4.00
108 Jaromir Jagr FRP 4.00 10.00
109 Jeremy Roenick FRP 2.00 5.00
111 Joe Sakic FRP 2.50 6.00
112 Joe Thornton FRP 2.00 5.00
113 Kari Lehtonen FRP 1.00 2.50
114 Keith Primeau FRP 1.00 2.50
116 Kirk Muller FRP 1.00 2.50
117 Lanny McDonald FRP 1.25 3.00
118 Larry Murphy FRP 1.00 2.50
119 Marc-Andre Fleury FRP 2.50 6.00
120 Marcel Dionne FRP 1.50 4.00
121 Marian Gaborik FRP 1.25 3.00
122 Mario Lemieux FRP 5.00 12.00
123 Mats Sundin FRP 2.00 5.00
124 Mike Bossy FRP 1.25 3.00
125 Mike Gartner FRP 1.50 4.00
126 Mike Modano FRP 2.00 5.00
127 Niklas Kronwall FRP 1.00 2.50
128 Olaf Kolzig FRP 1.25 3.00
129 Owen Nolan FRP 1.25 3.00
130 Pat LaFontaine FRP 1.25 3.00
131 Patrick Marleau FRP 1.25 3.00
132 Paul Coffey FRP 1.25 3.00
133 Peter Forsberg FRP 2.50 6.00
134 Raymond Bourque FRP 2.00 5.00
136 Roberto Luongo FRP 2.00 5.00
138 Ron Francis FRP 1.50 4.00
139 Scott Niedermayer FRP 1.25 3.00
140 Semyon Varlamov FRP 1.25 3.00
141 Steve Yzerman FRP 3.00 8.00
142 Teemu Selanne FRP 2.50 6.00
143 Trevor Linden FRP 1.25 3.00
144 Vincent Damphousse FRP 1.00 2.50
145 Wendel Clark FRP 2.00 5.00
146 Mark Scheifele FRP 2.00 5.00
147 Ryan Strome FRP 1.50 4.00
148 Ryan Murphy FRP 1.25 3.00
149 Phillip Danault FRP 1.25 3.00
150 Malcolm Subban FRP 1.50 4.00
151 Morgan Rielly FRP 1.50 4.00
152 Ryan Murray FRP 1.50 4.00
153 Griffin Reinhart FRP 1.25 3.00
154 Mathew Dumba FRP .75 2.00
155 Derrick Pouliot FRP 1.50 4.00
156 Peter Bondra DS 1.25 3.00
157 Jari Kurri DS 1.25 3.00
158 Sergei Fedorov DS 2.00 5.00
159 Jonathan Quick DS 1.50 4.00
160 Nicklas Lidstrom DS 1.25 3.00
161 Mark Messier DS 2.50 6.00
162 Mark Recchi DS 1.50 4.00
163 Theoren Fleury DS 1.50 4.00
164 Patrick Roy DS 3.00 8.00
165 Henrik Lundqvist DS 3.00 8.00
166 Luc Robitaille DS 1.25 3.00
167 Doug Gilmour DS 1.50 4.00
168 Brett Hull DS 2.50 6.00
169 Dominik Hasek DS 2.00 5.00
170 Pavel Bure DS 1.25 3.00
171 Ilya Bryzgalov DS 1.25 3.00
172 Bernie Nicholls DS 1.00 2.50
173 Shea Weber DS 1.00 2.50
174 Tony Amonte DS 1.00 2.50
175 Ron Hextall DS 1.25 3.00
176 Evgeni Nabokov DS 1.00 2.50
177 Glenn Anderson DS 1.00 2.50
178 Igor Larionov DS 1.25 3.00
179 Tomas Holmstrom DS .75 2.00
180 Joe Nieuwendyk DS 1.00 2.50

2012-13 ITG Draft Prospects Emerald

EMERALD/50: .5X TO 1.2X BASIC CARDS

2012-13 ITG Draft Prospects Autographs

GOLD/20: .6X TO 1.5X BASIC AU
GOLD/20: .5X TO 1.2X BASIC AU SP
AAB Aleksander Barkov 20.00 40.00
AAB2 Aleksander Barkov 20.00 40.00
AAD Anthony Duclair 8.00 20.00
AAD2 Anthony Duclair 8.00 20.00
AAE Aaron Ekblad 12.00 30.00
AAE2 Aaron Ekblad 12.00 30.00
AAER Adam Erne 5.00 12.00
AAER2 Adam Erne 5.00 12.00
AAM Anthony Mantha 8.00 20.00
AAM2 Anthony Mantha 8.00 20.00
AAW Alexander Wennberg 5.00 12.00
AAW2 Alexander Wennberg 5.00 12.00
ABH Bo Horvat 10.00 25.00
ABH2 Bo Horvat 10.00 25.00
ABS Brody Silk 3.00 8.00
ABS2 Brody Silk 3.00 8.00
ACL Curtis Lazar 5.00 12.00
ACL2 Curtis Lazar 5.00 12.00
ACM Connor McDavid 100.00 175.00
ACM2 Connor McDavid 100.00 175.00
ACR Connor Rankin 3.00 8.00
ACR2 Connor Rankin 3.00 8.00
ADH Dillon Heatherington 5.00 12.00
ADH2 Dillon Heatherington 5.00 12.00
ADN Darnell Nurse 6.00 15.00
ADN2 Darnell Nurse 6.00 15.00
ADS Dylan Strome 10.00 25.00
ADS2 Dylan Strome 10.00 25.00
AEC Eric Comrie 5.00 12.00
AEC2 Eric Comrie 5.00 12.00
AEL Elias Lindholm 6.00 15.00
AEL2 Elias Lindholm 6.00 15.00
AER Eric Roy 5.00 12.00
AER2 Eric Roy 5.00 12.00
AFG Frederik Gauthier 8.00 20.00
AFG2 Frederik Gauthier 8.00 20.00
AHS Hunter Shinkaruk 6.00 15.00
AHS2 Hunter Shinkaruk 6.00 15.00
AJB Justin Bailey 4.00 10.00
AJB2 Justin Bailey 4.00 10.00
AJD Jonathan Drouin SP 30.00 80.00
AJD2 Jonathan Drouin SP 30.00 80.00
AJDI Jason Dickinson 4.00 10.00
AJDI2 Jason Dickinson 4.00 10.00
AJDLR Jacob de la Rose 8.00 20.00
AJDLR2 Jacob de la Rose 8.00 20.00
AJG Jeremy Gregoire 4.00 10.00
AJG2 Jeremy Gregoire 4.00 10.00
AJM Josh Morrissey 5.00 12.00
AJM2 Josh Morrissey 5.00 12.00
AJS Jordan Subban 6.00 15.00
AJS2 Jordan Subban 5.00 12.00
AJW Jackson Whistle 3.00 8.00
AJW2 Jackson Whistle 3.00 8.00
AKR Kerby Rychel 5.00 12.00
AKR2 Kerby Rychel 5.00 12.00
AMB Madison Bowey 3.00 8.00
AMB2 Madison Bowey 3.00 8.00
AMD Max Domi 10.00 25.00
AMD2 Max Domi 10.00 25.00
AMG Morgan Klimchuk 5.00 12.00
AMG2 Morgan Klimchuk 5.00 12.00
AMM Mirco Mueller 6.00 15.00
AMM2 Mirco Mueller 6.00 15.00
ANB Nicholas Baptiste 4.00 10.00
ANB2 Nicholas Baptiste 4.00 10.00
ANM Nathan MacKinnon SP 30.00 80.00
ANM2 Nathan MacKinnon SP 30.00 80.00
ANP Nicolas Petan 5.00 12.00
ANP2 Nicolas Petan 5.00 12.00
ANS Nick Sorensen 5.00 12.00
ANS2 Nick Sorensen 5.00 12.00
ANZ Nikita Zadorov 3.00 8.00
ANZ2 Nikita Zadorov 3.00 8.00
ARH Robert Hagg 8.00 20.00
ARH2 Robert Hagg 8.00 20.00
ARHA Ryan Hartman 5.00 12.00
ARHA2 Ryan Hartman 5.00 12.00
ARK Ryan Kujawinski 4.00 10.00
ARK2 Ryan Kujawinski 4.00 10.00
ARP Ryan Pulock 6.00 15.00
ARP2 Ryan Pulock 5.00 12.00
ARR Rasmus Ristolainen 8.00 20.00
ARR2 Rasmus Ristolainen 8.00 20.00
ASD Sean Day 12.00 30.00
ASD2 Sean Day 12.00 30.00
ASH Stephen Harper 6.00 15.00
ASH2 Stephen Harper 6.00 15.00
ASJ Seth Jones SP 30.00 60.00
ASJ2 Seth Jones SP 30.00 60.00
ASM Spencer Martin 4.00 10.00
ASM2 Spencer Martin 4.00 10.00
ASMO Samuel Morin 3.00 8.00
ASMO2 Samuel Morin 3.00 8.00
ASMON Sean Monahan 8.00 20.00
ASMON2 Sean Monahan 8.00 20.00
ASS Sam Steel 10.00 25.00
ASS2 Sam Steel 10.00 25.00
AST Shea Theodore 6.00 15.00
AST2 Shea Theodore 6.00 15.00
ATB Tyler Benson 12.00 30.00
ATB2 Tyler Benson 12.00 30.00
ATJ Tristan Jarry 5.00 12.00
ATJ2 Tristan Jarry 5.00 12.00
ATK Travis Konecny 10.00 25.00
ATK2 Travis Konecny 10.00 25.00
AVZ Valentin Zykov 8.00 20.00
AVZ2 Valentin Zykov 8.00 20.00
AWC William Carrier 5.00 12.00
AWC2 William Carrier 5.00 12.00
AZF Zachary Fucale 15.00 40.00
AZF2 Zachary Fucale 15.00 40.00

2012-13 ITG Draft Prospects Country of Origin Jerseys

COO01 Seth Jones 6.00 15.00
COO02 Nathan MacKinnon 10.00 25.00
COO03 Jonathan Drouin 6.00 15.00
COO04 Robert Hagg 5.00 12.00
COO05 Valentin Zykov 4.00 10.00
COO06 Nikita Zadorov 2.00 5.00
COO07 Sergey Tolchinsky 3.00 8.00
COO08 Aleksander Barkov 12.00 30.00

2012-13 ITG Draft Prospects Draft Year Jerseys

DY01 Connor McDavid 15.00 40.00
DY02 Jake Virtanen 6.00 15.00
DY03 Robert Hagg 6.00 15.00
DY04 Hunter Shinkaruk 8.00 20.00
DY05 Curtis Lazar 5.00 12.00
DY06 Morgan Klimchuk 5.00 12.00
DY07 Nikita Zadorov 3.00 8.00
DY08 Darnell Nurse 6.00 15.00
DY09 Justin Bailey 4.00 10.00
DY10 Seth Jones 12.00 30.00
DY11 Nathan MacKinnon 12.00 30.00
DY12 Jonathan Drouin 10.00 25.00
DY13 Jacob de la Rose 6.00 15.00
DY14 Aleksander Barkov 10.00 25.00
DY15 Carey Price 10.00 25.00
DY16 Jonathan Quick 6.00 15.00
DY17 Alexander Ovechkin 20.00 50.00
DY18 Evgeni Malkin 10.00 25.00
DY19 Marc-Andre Fleury 10.00 25.00
DY20 Jimmy Howard 6.00 15.00
DY21 Daniel Sedin 6.00 15.00
DY22 Henrik Sedin 6.00 15.00
DY23 Joe Thornton 8.00 20.00
DY24 Roberto Luongo 8.00 20.00
DY25 Peter Forsberg 6.00 15.00
DY26 Eric Lindros 8.00 20.00
DY27 Felix Potvin 8.00 20.00
DY28 Jaromir Jagr 15.00 40.00
DY29 Jeremy Roenick 6.00 15.00
DY30 Mike Modano 8.00 20.00
DY31 Mario Lemieux 20.00 50.00
DY32 Patrick Roy 12.00 30.00
DY33 Steve Yzerman 15.00 40.00
DY34 Cam Neely 6.00 15.00

2012-13 ITG Draft Prospects Future Prospects Jerseys

FPM01 Jake Virtanen 5.00 12.00
FPM02 Connor McDavid 15.00 40.00
FPM03 Dylan Strome 8.00 20.00
FPM04 Travis Konecny 8.00 20.00
FPM05 Nick Ritchie 4.00 10.00
FPM06 Josh Ho-Sang 5.00 12.00
FPM07 Daniel Audette 5.00 12.00
FPM08 Sam Reinhart 12.00 30.00
FPM09 Roland McKeown 3.00 8.00
FPM10 Storm Phaneuf 3.00 8.00

2012-13 ITG Draft Prospects Jerseys

M01 Adam Erne 4.00 10.00
M02 Anthony Duclair 6.00 15.00
M03 Anthony Mantha 8.00 20.00
M04 Bo Horvat 8.00 20.00
M05 Curtis Lazar 4.00 10.00
M06 Darnell Nurse 5.00 12.00
M07 Eric Comrie 4.00 10.00
M08 Frederik Gauthier 6.00 15.00
M09 Hunter Shinkaruk 6.00 15.00
M10 Jacob de la Rose 5.00 12.00
M11 Philippe Desrosiers 3.00 8.00
M12 Jason Dickinson 3.00 8.00
M13 Aleksander Barkov 15.00 40.00
M14 Jonathan Drouin 8.00 20.00
M15 Jordan Subban 5.00 12.00
M16 Josh Morrissey 4.00 10.00
M17 Justin Bailey 3.00 8.00
M18 Kerby Rychel 4.00 10.00
M19 Max Domi 8.00 20.00
M20 Morgan Klimchuk 4.00 10.00
M21 Nathan MacKinnon 12.00 30.00
M22 Nicolas Petan 4.00 10.00
M23 Nikita Zadorov 2.50 6.00
M24 Robert Hagg 6.00 15.00
M25 Ryan Kujawinski 3.00 8.00
M26 Ryan Pulock 5.00 12.00
M27 Samuel Morin 2.50 6.00
M28 Sean Monahan 8.00 20.00
M29 Seth Jones 10.00 25.00
M30 Spencer Martin 3.00 8.00
M31 Stephen Harper 5.00 12.00
M32 Tristan Jarry 4.00 10.00
M33 Valentin Zykov 5.00 12.00
M34 William Carrier 4.00 10.00
M35 Zachary Fucale 5.00 12.00

2012-13 ITG Draft Prospects Past and Future Jerseys

PF01 Lindros/MacKinnon 12.00 30.00
PF02 Kurri/Barkov 15.00 40.00
PF03 Roenick/Jones 8.00 20.00
PF04 Joseph/Desrosiers 5.00 12.00
PF05 Lemieux/MacKinnon 15.00 40.00
PF06 Bossy/McDavid 15.00 40.00
PF07 Modano/Erne 5.00 12.00
PF08 Nolan/Shinkaruk 6.00 15.00
PF09 Forsberg/Hagg 6.00 15.00
PF10 Niedermayer/Jones 10.00 25.00
PF11 Yzerman/Drouin 12.00 30.00
PF12 Roy/Fucale 12.00 30.00

2012-13 ITG Draft Prospects Past Present and Future Jerseys

PPF01 Bure/Ovechkin/Tolchinsky 12.00 30.00
PPF02 Forsberg/Sedin/de la Rose 10.00 25.00
PPF03 Larionov/Malkin/Zadorov 12.00 30.00
PPF04 Hasek/Lundqvist/Comrie 10.00 25.00
PPF05 Kurri/Lehtonen/Barkov 25.00 60.00
PPF06 Fedorov/Malkin/Zykov 15.00 40.00
PPF07 Roenick/Kesler/Jones 12.00 30.00
PPF08 Yzerman/Giroux/McDavid 20.00 50.00
PPF09 Lemieux/Thornton/MacKin 15.00 40.00
PPF10 Sundin/Sedin/Hagg 10.00 25.00
PPF11 Roy/Price/Fucale 15.00 40.00
PPF12 Messier/Thornton/Drouin 12.00 30.00

2012-13 ITG Draft Prospects Present and Future Jerseys

PAF01 Ovechkin/Zykov 8.00 20.00
PAF02 Price/Fucale 10.00 25.00
PAF03 Sedin/Hagg 6.00 15.00
PAF04 Malkin/Zadorov 8.00 20.00
PAF05 H.Sedin/J.de la Rs 12.00 30.00
PAF06 Lehtonen/Barkov 15.00 40.00
PAF07 Fleury/Comrie 6.00 10.00
PAF08 Thornton/MacKinnon 12.00 30.00
PAF09 Jagr/Gauthier 10.00 25.00
PAF10 Marleau/Monahan 8.00 20.00
PAF11 Giroux/Drouin 8.00 20.00
PAF12 Luongo/Martin 6.00 15.00

2012-13 ITG Draft Prospects Teammates Jerseys

TM01 Roy/Pulock 6.00 15.00
TM02 MacKinnon/Drouin 15.00 40.00
TM03 Fucale/Drouin 8.00 20.00
TM04 MacKinnon/Fucale 12.00 30.00
TM05 Horvat/Zadorov 8.00 20.00
TM06 Domi/Horvat 8.00 20.00
TM07 Zadorov/Domi 8.00 20.00
TM08 Jones/Petan 10.00 25.00
TM09 Duclair/Erne 6.00 15.00
TM10 Lazar/Jarry 4.00 10.00
TM11 Nurse/Tolchinsky 6.00 15.00
TM12 Morin/Gauthier 6.00 15.00

2014-15 ITG Draft Prospects

*BRONZE/25: .6X TO 1.5X BASIC CARDS
1 Sam Bennett 3.00 8.00
2 Leon Draisaitl 6.00 15.00
3 Aaron Ekblad 2.50 6.00
4 Sam Reinhart 5.00 12.00
5 Michael Dal Colle 1.50 4.00
6 Haydn Fleury 1.25 3.00
7 Nick Ritchie 1.25 3.00
8 Brendan Perlini 2.00 5.00
9 Jake Virtanen 1.50 4.00
10 Anthony DeAngelo 1.00 2.50
11 Jared McCann 1.50 4.00
12 Ivan Barbashev 1.25 3.00
13 Julius Honka 1.00 2.50
14 Nikolay Goldobin 1.25 3.00
15 Roland McKeown 1.25 3.00
16 Josh Ho-Sang 1.50 4.00
17 Brycen Martin 1.25 3.00
18 Nikolaj Ehlers 2.50 6.00
19 Eric Cornel 1.00 2.50
20 Nikita Scherbak 1.25 3.00
21 Robby Fabbri 1.00 2.50
22 Chase De Leo 1.00 2.50
23 Aaron Haydon 1.00 2.50
24 Connor Chatham 1.25 3.00
25 Conner Bleackley 1.25 3.00
26 Ryan MacInnis 1.00 2.50
27 John Quenneville 1.00 2.50
28 Vaclav Karabacek .75 2.00
29 Alex Peters .75 2.00
30 Michael Bunting 1.50 4.00
31 Brendan Lemieux 1.25 3.00
32 Reid Gardiner .75 2.00
33 Jayce Hawryluk .75 2.00
34 Spencer Watson 1.25 3.00
35 Dylan Sadowy .75 2.00
36 Nicolas Aube-Kubel .75 2.00
37 Brett Pollock 1.25 3.00
38 Blake Siebenaler 1.00 2.50
39 Hunter Smith .75 2.00
40 Julien Nantel .75 2.00
41 Richard Nejezchleb .75 2.00
42 Nick Magyar .75 2.00
43 Brayden Point 1.50 4.00
44 Brett Lernout .75 2.00
45 Travis Sanheim 1.25 3.00
46 Jaden Lindo .75 2.00
47 Brandon Robinson 1.00 2.50
48 Alexis Pepin 1.00 2.50
49 Clark Bishop .75 2.00
50 Matt Mistele 1.00 2.50
51 Reid Duke .75 2.00
52 Brandon Prophet .75 2.00
53 Olivier LeBlanc 1.00 2.50
54 Blake Clarke 1.00 2.50
55 Matthew Mancina .75 2.00
56 Alex Nedeljkovic 1.25 3.00
57 Brent Moran 1.00 2.50
58 Mason McDonald 1.25 3.00
59 Ty Edmonds 1.25 3.00
60 Julio Billia 1.00 2.50
61 Brandon Halverson 1.25 3.00
62 Kasperi Kapanen 2.00 5.00
63 William Nylander 4.00 10.00
64 Adrian Kempe 1.25 3.00
65 David Pastrnak 8.00 20.00
66 Jakub Vrana 1.50 4.00
67 Anton Karlsson .75 2.00
68 Marcus Pettersson 1.00 2.50
69 Adam Ollas Mattsson 1.00 2.50
70 Julius Bergman 1.00 2.50
71 Connor McDavid 6.00 15.00
72 Mathew Barzal 2.50 6.00
73 Dylan Strome 2.50 6.00
74 Jeremy Roy .75 2.00
75 Travis Konecny 2.50 6.00
76 Nicolas Roy 1.25 3.00
77 Ryan Pilon .75 2.00
78 Nathan Noel .75 2.00
79 Mitchell Marner 4.00 10.00
80 Daniel Sprong 2.00 5.00
81 Bobby Clarke 2.00 5.00
82 Gilbert Perreault 1.25 3.00
83 Guy Lafleur 1.50 4.00
84 Denis Potvin 1.25 3.00
85 Mike Bossy 1.25 3.00
86 Raymond Bourque 2.00 5.00
87 Mark Messier 2.50 6.00
88 Steve Yzerman 3.00 8.00
89 Vladislav Tretiak 1.00 2.50
90 Mario Lemieux 5.00 12.00
91 Patrick Roy 3.00 8.00
92 Joe Sakic 2.50 6.00
93 Teemu Selanne 2.50 6.00
94 Pavel Bure 1.25 3.00
95 Nicklas Lidstrom 1.25 3.00
96 Jaromir Jagr 3.00 8.00
97 Eric Lindros 2.00 5.00
98 Joe Thornton 2.00 5.00
99 Marc-Andre Fleury 2.50 6.00
100 Carey Price 2.50 6.00

2014-15 ITG Draft Prospects Autographs

GOLD/20: .8X TO 2X BASIC AUTO
AAD1 Anthony DeAngelo 3.00 8.00
AAD2 Anthony DeAngelo 3.00 8.00
AAE1 Aaron Ekblad 10.00 25.00
AAE2 Aaron Ekblad 10.00 25.00
AAK1 Adrian Kempe 4.00 10.00
AAK2 Adrian Kempe 4.00 10.00
AAKA1 Anton Karlsson 2.50 6.00
AAKA2 Anton Karlsson 2.50 6.00
AAM1 Aleksandar Mikulovich 4.00 10.00
AAM2 Aleksandar Mikulovich 4.00 10.00
AAO1 Adam Ollas Mattsson 3.00 8.00
AAO2 Adam Ollas Mattsson 3.00 8.00
AAP1 Alexis Pepin 3.00 8.00
AAP2 Alexis Pepin 3.00 8.00
AAPR1 Alexander Protapovich 2.50 6.00
AAPR2 Alexander Protapovich 2.50 6.00
ABC1 Blake Clarke 3.00 8.00
ABC2 Blake Clarke 3.00 8.00
ABM1 Brent Moran 3.00 8.00
ABM2 Brent Moran 3.00 8.00
ABMA1 Brycen Martin 4.00 10.00
ABMA2 Brycen Martin 4.00 10.00
ABP1 Brandon Prophet 2.50 6.00
ABP2 Brandon Prophet 2.50 6.00
ABPE1 Brendan Perlini 6.00 15.00
ABPE2 Brendan Perlini 6.00 15.00
ABPO1 Brayden Point 5.00 12.00
ABPO2 Brayden Point 5.00 12.00
ABR1 Brandon Robinson 3.00 8.00
ABR2 Brandon Robinson 3.00 8.00
ACB1 Clark Bishop 2.50 6.00
ACB2 Clark Bishop 2.50 6.00
ADP1 David Pastrnak 20.00 50.00
ADP2 David Pastrnak 20.00 50.00
AEC1 Eric Cornel 3.00 8.00
AEC2 Eric Cornel 3.00 8.00
AHF1 Haydn Fleury 4.00 10.00
AHF2 Haydn Fleury 4.00 10.00
AIB1 Ivan Barbashev 4.00 10.00
AIB2 Ivan Barbashev 4.00 10.00
AJB1 Julius Bergman 3.00 8.00
AJB2 Julius Bergman 3.00 8.00
AJL1 Jaden Lindo 2.50 6.00
AJL2 Jaden Lindo 2.50 6.00
AJM1 Jared McCann 5.00 12.00
AJM2 Jared McCann 5.00 12.00
AJV1 Jake Virtanen 5.00 12.00
AJV2 Jake Virtanen 5.00 12.00
AJVR1 Jakub Vrana 5.00 12.00
AJVR2 Jakub Vrana 5.00 12.00
AKK1 Kasperi Kapanen 6.00 15.00
AKK2 Kasperi Kapanen 6.00 15.00
ALD1 Leon Draisaitl 20.00 50.00
ALD2 Leon Draisaitl 20.00 50.00
AMD1 Michael Dal Colle 5.00 12.00
AMD2 Michael Dal Colle 5.00 12.00
AML1 Maxim Lazarev 2.50 6.00
AML2 Maxim Lazarev 2.50 6.00
AMM1 Matt Mistele 3.00 8.00
AMM2 Matt Mistele 3.00 8.00
AMP1 Marcus Pettersson 3.00 8.00
AMP2 Marcus Pettersson 3.00 8.00
ANA1 Nicolas Aube-Kubel 2.50 6.00
ANA2 Nicolas Aube-Kubel 2.50 6.00
ANE1 Nikolaj Ehlers 8.00 20.00
ANE2 Nikolaj Ehlers 8.00 20.00
ANG1 Nikolay Goldobin 4.00 10.00
ANG2 Nikolay Goldobin 4.00 10.00
ANR1 Nick Ritchie 4.00 10.00
ANR2 Nick Ritchie 4.00 10.00
AOL1 Olivier LeBlanc 3.00 8.00
AOL2 Olivier LeBlanc 3.00 8.00
ARD1 Reid Duke 2.50 6.00
ARD2 Reid Duke 2.50 6.00
ARF1 Robby Fabbri 3.00 8.00
ARF2 Robby Fabbri 3.00 8.00
ARM1 Ryan MacInnis 3.00 8.00
ARM2 Ryan MacInnis 3.00 8.00
ARMC1 Roland McKeown 4.00 10.00
ARMC2 Roland McKeown 4.00 10.00
ASB1 Sam Bennett 10.00 25.00
ASB2 Sam Bennett 10.00 25.00
ASR1 Sam Reinhart 15.00 40.00
ASR2 Sam Reinhart 15.00 40.00
ASW1 Spencer Watson 4.00 10.00
ASW2 Spencer Watson 4.00 10.00
AWN1 William Nylander 12.00 30.00
AWN2 William Nylander 12.00 30.00
DPACM1 Connor McDavid/50 80.00 200.00
DPACM2 Connor McDavid/50 80.00 200.00
PA9 Dylan Strome 8.00 20.00
PA31 Travis Konecny 8.00 20.00

2014-15 ITG Draft Prospects Draft Class Dual Jerseys Blue

DC21 C.Neely/S.Yzerman 8.00 20.00
DC22 P.Roy/M.Lemieux 12.00 30.00
DC23 O.Nolan/J.Jagr 10.00 25.00
DC24 J.Howard/M.Fleury 6.00 15.00
DC25 J.Drouin/N.Zadorov 6.00 15.00
DC26 J.Roenick/M.Modano 5.00 12.00
DC27 S.Bennett/S.Reinhart 12.00 30.00
DC28 F.Gauthier/B.Horvat 8.00 20.00

2014-15 ITG Draft Prospects Draft Dream Team Jerseys Blue

*BRONZE/30: .5X TO 1.2X BLUE/55
DT1 Carey Price 6.00 15.00
DT2 Claude Giroux 3.00 8.00
DT3 Corey Crawford 4.00 10.00
DT4 Dominik Hasek 5.00 12.00
DT5 Eric Lindros 5.00 12.00
DT6 Igor Larionov 3.00 8.00
DT7 Jari Kurri 3.00 8.00
DT8 Jeremy Roenick 5.00 12.00
DT9 Jimmy Howard 4.00 10.00
DT10 Joe Sakic 6.00 15.00
DT11 Joe Thornton 5.00 12.00
DT12 Mario Lemieux 12.00 30.00
DT13 Mark Messier 6.00 15.00
DT14 Mats Sundin 3.00 8.00
DT15 Mike Bossy 3.00 8.00
DT17 Patrick Marleau 3.00 8.00
DT18 Patrick Roy 8.00 20.00
DT19 Pavel Bure 3.00 8.00
DT20 Peter Forsberg 6.00 15.00
DT21 Sergei Fedorov 5.00 12.00
DT22 Steve Yzerman 8.00 20.00

2014-15 ITG Draft Prospects Dream Trios Jerseys Blue

D31 Roy/Howard/Crawford 8.00 20.00
D33 Modano/Roenick/Howard 5.00 12.00
D34 Price/Roy/Hasek 8.00 20.00
D35 Thornton/Giroux/Lemieux 12.00 30.00
D37 Forsberg/Sundin/Lidstrom 6.00 15.00
D38 Yzerman/Lemieux/Messier 20.00 50.00

2014-15 ITG Draft Prospects Future Prospects Jerseys Blue

*BRONZE/45: .5X TO 1.2X BLUE
FP1 Connor McDavid 12.00 30.00
FP2 Dylan Strome 5.00 12.00
FP3 Mathew Barzal 5.00 12.00
FP4 Travis Konecny 5.00 12.00

2014-15 ITG Draft Prospects Go Big Or Go Home Jerseys Blue

BIG1 Aaron Ekblad 8.00 20.00
BIG2 Brendan Perlini 5.00 12.00
BIG4 Leon Draisaitl 15.00 40.00
BIG5 Mario Lemieux 12.00 30.00
BIG6 Mark Messier 6.00 15.00
BIG7 Patrick Roy 8.00 20.00
BIG9 Sam Reinhart 12.00 30.00
BIG10 Steve Yzerman 8.00 20.00

2014-15 ITG Draft Prospects Jerseys Blue

*BRONZE/45: .5X TO 1.2X BLUE/75
PGU1 Aaron Ekblad 8.00 20.00
PGU2 Alex Nedeljkovic 3.00 8.00
PGU3 Anthony DeAngelo 2.50 6.00
PGU4 Blake Clarke 2.50 6.00
PGU5 Brendan Perlini 5.00 12.00
PGU6 Brycen Martin 3.00 8.00
PGU7 Chase De Leo 2.50 6.00
PGU8 Daniel Audette 3.00 8.00
PGU9 Dominic Turgeon 3.00 8.00
PGU10 Eric Cornel 2.50 6.00
PGU11 Haydn Fleury 3.00 8.00
PGU12 Ivan Barbashev 3.00 8.00
PGU13 Jaden Lindo 2.00 5.00
PGU14 Jared McCann 4.00 10.00
PGU15 Josh Ho-Sang 4.00 10.00
PGU16 Julius Bergman 2.50 6.00
PGU17 Leon Draisaitl 15.00 40.00
PGU18 Marcus Pettersson 2.50 6.00
PGU19 Matt Mistele 2.50 6.00
PGU20 Michael Dal Colle 4.00 10.00
PGU21 Nick Ritchie 3.00 8.00
PGU22 Nikolay Goldobin 3.00 8.00
PGU23 Nikolaj Ehlers 6.00 15.00
PGU24 Olivier LeBlanc 2.50 6.00
PGU25 Robby Fabbri 2.50 6.00
PGU26 Roland McKeown 3.00 8.00
PGU27 Sam Bennett 8.00 20.00
PGU28 Sam Reinhart 12.00 30.00
PGU29 Tyson Baillie 2.50 6.00
PGU30 William Nylander 10.00 25.00

2014-15 ITG Draft Prospects Pride of a Nation Jerseys Blue

*BRONZE/40: .5X TO 1.2X BLUE/70
PN1 Ivan Barbashev 3.00 8.00
PN2 Jack Glover 2.00 5.00
PN3 Julius Bergman 2.50 6.00
PN4 Julius Honka 2.50 6.00
PN5 Leon Draisaitl 15.00 40.00
PN6 Marcus Pettersson 2.50 6.00
PN7 Nikolay Goldobin 3.00 8.00
PN8 Dylan Larkin 10.00 25.00
PN9 Sam Bennett 8.00 20.00
PN10 Sam Reinhart 12.00 30.00

2011-12 ITG Enforcers

1 Wens/Millr/O'Rlly/Jnthn 1.25 3.00
2 Will/McGill/Clark/Domi 2.00 5.00
3 Kord/Niln/Odel/Crsn 1.00 2.50
4 Fotiu/Beck/King/Domi 1.00 2.50
5 Lind/Gall/Prbrt/Kocr 1.25 3.00
6 Cicc/Mnsn/Grim/Prbrt 1.25 3.00
7 Rychl/Wlls/McSrl/Mil 1.25 3.00
8 Schltz/Klly/Brbe/Brsh 1.25 3.00
9 Ray/May/Barn/Petrs 1.00 2.50
10 Snep/Will/Butch/Odjick .75 2.00
11 Sem/McSr/Buch/Lara 1.00 2.50
12 Paie/Hntr/Weir/Twist 1.00 2.50
13 Gtz/Odgrs/Mrch/McSr 1.00 2.50
14 Nystrm/Gill/Piln/Knpka 1.25 3.00
15 Ewn/Grim/Pros/Knpka 1.00 2.50
16 McCrt/Brbe/Olwa/Phnf 1.00 2.50
17 Laus/Wor/Thmp/Belak 1.00 2.50
18 Twst/McR/Chase/Low .75 2.00
19 Dave Schultz RH 1.25 3.00
20 Tiger Williams RH .75 2.00
21 Brad MayÂ•RH .75 2.00
22 D.Brashear RH/Z.Chara 1.25 3.00
23 Kelly Buchberger RH .75 2.00
24 Steve PayneÂ•RH .75 2.00
25 Chris Nilan RH .75 2.00
26 Chris Nilan RH .75 2.00
27 Dale Hunter RH 1.00 2.50
28 Dave Schultz RH 1.25 3.00
29 Brashear/Laraque TOTT 1.00 2.50
30 Z.Chara/D.Koci TOTT 1.25 3.00
31 R.Cote/S.Thornton TOTT .75 2.00
32 D.Schultz/T.Williams TOTT 1.25 3.00
33 R.Horner/E.Shore TOTT 1.00 2.50
34 W.Clark/M.McSorley TOTT 2.00 5.00
35 M.Richard/H.Laycoe TOTT 2.50 6.00
36 Watson/V.Hadfield TOTT 1.00 2.50
37 T.Domi/B.Probert TOTT 1.25 3.00
38 B.May/J.Wells TOTT .75 2.00
39 J.Miller/C.Nilan TOTT 1.25 3.00
40 McSorley/Probert TOTT 1.25 3.00
41 D.Brashear/R.Ray TOTT 1.00 2.50
42 Mirasty/J.Yablonski TOTT 1.25 3.00
43 T.Ewen/S.Churla TOTT .75 2.00
44 D.Schultz/C.Gillies TOTT 1.25 3.00
45 D.Hunter/M.Hunter TOTT 1.00 2.50
46 L.Gaetz/G.Odjick TOTT 1.00 2.50
47 Kocur/Buchberger TOTT .75 2.00
48 J.Kordic/B.McRae TOTT .75 2.00
49 T.Williams/T.O'Reilly TOTT 1.00 2.50
50 Odelein/M.Barnaby TOTT .75 2.00
51 Grimson/B.Probert TOTT 1.25 3.00
52 R.Ray/T.Domi TOTT 1.00 2.50
53 G.Laraque/B.Probert BB 1.25 3.00
54 C.Berube/C.Tamer BB .75 2.00
55 C.Berube/J.Cummins BB .75 2.00
56 D.Kordic/C.Berube BB .75 2.00
57 T.Domi/B.Probert BB 1.25 3.00
58 Brashear/McSorley BB 1.00 2.50
59 Brashear/Z.Chara BB 1.25 3.00
60 D.Brashear/C.Orr BB 1.00 2.50
61 D.Brashear/G.Parros BB 1.00 2.50
62 B.Probert/McSorley BB 1.25 3.00
63 W.Clark/M.McSorley BB 2.00 5.00
64 Brashear/B.Probert BB 1.25 3.00
65 L.Odelein/T.Domi BB 1.00 2.50
66 Gillies/S.Brookbank BB .75 2.00
67 Grimson/M.Barnaby BB .75 2.00
68 K.King/L.Odelein BB .75 2.00
69 K.King/W.Rychel BB .75 2.00
70 D.Koci/W.Belak BB 1.00 2.50
71 J.Kocur/S.Grimson BB .75 2.00
72 D.Lambert/C.Berube BB .75 2.00
73 Laraque/Brashear BB 1.00 2.50
74 G.Laraque/R.Ray BB 1.00 2.50
75 McCarthy/Probert BB 1.25 3.00
76 T.Domi/B.McRae BB 1.00 2.50
77 B.McRae/G.Odjick BB .75 2.00
78 J.Mirasty/R.Hand BB 1.25 3.00
79 G.Odjick/L.Gaetz BB 1.00 2.50
80 B.Probert/W.Clark BB 2.00 5.00
81 A.Peters/R.Emery BB 1.00 2.50
82 B.Probert/T.Domi BB 1.25 3.00
83 R.Ray/J.Odgers BB .75 2.00
84 D.Manson/W.Rychel BB .75 2.00
85 D.Schultz/D.Rolfe BB 1.25 3.00
86 Semenko/L.Playfair BB .75 2.00
87 W.Rychel/T.Twist BB .75 2.00
88 P.Worrell/E.Lindros BB 2.00 5.00
89 T.Twist/B.Probert BB 1.25 3.00
90 J.Cummins/T.Twist BB .75 2.00

2011-12 ITG Enforcers Autographs

AAD Andre Dupont 4.00 10.00
AAP Andrew Peters 5.00 12.00
ABB Barry Beck 4.00 10.00
ABBO Bob Boughner 4.00 10.00
ABG Bill Goldthorpe 5.00 12.00
ABK Bob Kelly 4.00 10.00
ABMAR Bryan Marchment 5.00 12.00
ABMAY Brad May 4.00 10.00
ABMCG Bob McGill 4.00 10.00
ABMCR Basil McRae 4.00 10.00
ABN Bob Nystrom 4.00 10.00
ABP Bob Probert 250.00 400.00
ABW Bryan Watson 4.00 10.00
ACBE Craig Berube 4.00 10.00
ACB Curt Brackenbury 4.00 10.00
ACG Clark Gillies 40.00 100.00
ACN Chris Nilan 4.00 10.00
ADB Dave Brown 4.00 10.00
ADBRA Donald Brashear 40.00 100.00
ADC Dan Carcillo 4.00 10.00
ADL Denny Lambert 4.00 10.00
ADM Dan Maloney 4.00 10.00
ADMAN Dave Manson 4.00 10.00
ADS Dave Schultz 8.00 20.00
ADSE Dave Semenko 8.00 20.00
ADT Darcy Tucker 5.00 12.00
AEC Enrico Ciccone 4.00 10.00
AEV Ed Van Impe 5.00 12.00
AFB Frank Bialowas 4.00 10.00
AGB Garth Butcher 4.00 10.00
AGG Gerard Gallant 5.00 12.00
AGL Georges Laraque 5.00 12.00
AGO Gino Odjick 4.00 10.00
AHS Harold Snepsts 4.00 10.00
AJC Jim Cummins 4.00 10.00
AJK Joey Kocur 4.00 10.00
AJKY Jim Kyte 4.00 10.00
AJM Jon Mirasty 6.00 15.00
AJMA Jimmy Mann 4.00 10.00
AJMC Jim McKenzie 4.00 10.00
AJMCI Jack McIlhargey 5.00 12.00
AJMI Jay Miller 6.00 15.00
AJO Jeff Odgers 4.00 10.00
AJT Jordin Tootoo 5.00 12.00
AJW John Wensink 4.00 10.00
AJWA Joe Watson 4.00 10.00
AJWE Jay Wells 4.00 10.00
AKB Kelly Buchberger 4.00 10.00
AKC Kelly Chase 4.00 10.00
AKK Kris King 4.00 10.00
ALB Laurie Boschman 4.00 10.00
ALF Lou Fontinato 5.00 12.00
ALG Link Gaetz 5.00 12.00
ALO Lyle Odelein 4.00 10.00
AMB Matthew Barnaby 4.00 10.00
AMM Marty McSorley 5.00 12.00
ANF Nick Fotiu 5.00 12.00
APH Paul Holmgren 5.00 12.00
APL Paul Laus 4.00 10.00
APR Phil Russell 4.00 10.00
APW Peter Worrell 4.00 10.00
ARL Reed Low 4.00 10.00
ARP Rich Pilon 4.00 10.00
ARR Rob Ray 4.00 10.00
ASC Shayne Corson 5.00 12.00
ASCH Shane Churla 4.00 10.00
ASG Stu Grimson 4.00 10.00
ASJ Stan Jonathan 4.00 10.00
ASM Sandy McCarthy 5.00 12.00
ATD Tie Domi 15.00 40.00
ATE Todd Ewen 4.00 10.00
ATG Trevor Gillies 4.00 10.00
ATL Tom Lysiak 4.00 10.00
ATO Terry O'Reilly 8.00 20.00
ATP Theo Peckham 4.00 10.00
ATR Terry Ruskowski 5.00 12.00
ATT Tony Twist 4.00 10.00
ATW Tiger Williams 12.00 30.00
AWB Wade Belak 25.00 60.00
AWC Wendel Clark 80.00 200.00
AWP Wilf Paiement 8.00 20.00
AWPL Willi Plett 5.00 12.00
AWR Warren Rychel 4.00 10.00
AWW Wally Weir 4.00 10.00
AZK Zenon Konopka 5.00 12.00

2011-12 ITG Enforcers Combatants Jersey Duals

C01 W.Clark/M.McSorley 10.00 25.00
C02 D.Schultz/T.O'Reilly 6.00 15.00
C03 J.Odgers/D.Manson 4.00 10.00
C04 J.Miller/J.Kocur 6.00 15.00
C05 T.Domi/M.Barnaby 5.00 12.00
C06 W.Belak/D.Brashear 5.00 12.00
C07 P.Laus/C.Berube 4.00 10.00
C08 J.Kocur/D.Manson 4.00 10.00
C09 D.Maloney/T.Williams 4.00 10.00
C10 M.Barnaby/L.Odelein 4.00 10.00
C11 A.Peters/W.Belak 5.00 12.00
C12 Z.Chara/P.Worrell 6.00 15.00
C13 B.Probert/W.Clark 10.00 25.00
C14 C.Berube/T.Domi 5.00 12.00
C15 T.Ewen/S.Churla 4.00 10.00
C16 R.Ray/T.Domi 5.00 12.00
C17 T.Twist/B.Probert 6.00 15.00
C18 B.May/G.Laraque 5.00 12.00
C19 D.Brashear/C.Orr 5.00 12.00
C20 G.Laraque/W.Belak 5.00 12.00
C21 S.Grimson/J.Cummins 4.00 10.00
C22 T.Williams/T.O'Reilly 5.00 12.00
C23 L.Odelein/D.Lambert 4.00 10.00
C24 C.Gillies/D.Schultz 6.00 15.00
C25 J.Odgers/T.Domi 5.00 12.00
C27 H.Snepsts/D.Schultz 6.00 15.00
C28 S.Grimson/B.Probert 6.00 15.00
C29 B.McRae/D.Manson 4.00 10.00
C30 D.Brashear/M.McSorley 5.00 12.00
C31 S.Grimson/E.Ciccone 4.00 10.00
C32 B.McRae/T.Ewen 4.00 10.00
C33 P.Laus/R.Ray 4.00 10.00
C34 D.Hunter/T.O'Reilly 5.00 12.00
C35 K.Oliwa/T.Domi 5.00 12.00
C36 C.Orr/A.Peters 5.00 12.00
C37 G.Odjick/S.Grimson 4.00 10.00
C38 P.Worrell/D.Bonvie 4.00 10.00
C39 K.Chase/C.Berube 4.00 10.00
C40 F.Bialowas/T.Twist 4.00 10.00

2011-12 ITG Enforcers Instigator Jerseys

I01 Matthew Barnaby 2.00 5.00
I02 Barry Beck 2.00 5.00
I03 Wade Belak 2.50 6.00
I04 Craig BerubeÂ• 2.00 5.00
I05 Frank Bialowas 2.00 5.00
I06 Dennis Bonvie 2.00 5.00
I07 Donald Brashear 2.50 6.00
I08 Sheldon Brookbank 2.00 5.00
I09 Dan Carcillo 2.00 5.00
I10 Matt Carkner 2.50 6.00
I11 Zdeno Chara 3.00 8.00
I12 Kelly Chase 2.00 5.00
I13 Shane Churla 5.00 12.00
I14 Enrico Ciccone 2.00 5.00
I15 Wendel Clark 5.00 12.00
I16 Shayne Corson 2.50 6.00
I17 Jim Cummins 2.00 5.00
I18 Tie Domi 2.50 6.00
I19 Steve Downie 2.00 5.00
I20 Todd Ewen 2.00 5.00
I21 Gerard Gallant 2.50 6.00
I22 Clark Gillies 3.00 8.00
I23 Bill Goldthorpe 2.50 6.00
I24 Stu Grimson 2.00 5.00
I25 Dale Hunter 2.50 6.00
I26 Boyd Kane 2.00 5.00
I27 Darius Kasparaitis 2.50 6.00
I28 Joey Kocur 2.00 5.00
I29 Jim Kyte 2.00 5.00
I30 Denny Lambert 2.00 5.00
I31 Georges Laraque 2.50 6.00
I32 Paul Laus 2.00 5.00
I33 Dan Maloney 2.00 5.00
I34 Dave Manson 2.00 5.00
I35 Brad May 2.00 5.00
I36 Cody McCormick 2.00 5.00
I37 Basil McRae 2.00 5.00
I38 Marty McSorley 2.50 6.00
I39 Jay Miller 3.00 8.00
I40 Tyson Nash 2.00 5.00
I41 Bob Nystrom 2.00 5.00
I42 Terry O'Reilly 2.50 6.00
I43 Lyle Odelein 2.00 5.00
I44 Jeff Odgers 2.00 5.00
I45 Gino Odjick 2.00 5.00
I46 Krzysztof Oliwa 2.00 5.00
I47 Colton Orr 2.00 5.00
I48 Theo Peckham 2.00 5.00
I49 Andrew Peters 2.50 6.00
I50 Dion Phaneuf 2.50 6.00
I51 Bob Probert 3.00 8.00
I52 Rob Ray 2.00 5.00
I53 Dave Schultz 3.00 8.00
I54 Harold Snepsts 2.00 5.00
I55 Jordin Tootoo 2.50 6.00
I56 Darcy Tucker 2.50 6.00
I57 Tony Twist 2.00 5.00
I58 Pat Verbeek 2.00 5.00
I59 Tiger Williams 2.00 5.00
I60 Peter Worrell 2.00 5.00

2011-12 ITG Enforcers Tough Franchise Jersey Quads

TF01 Snps/Will/Odjick/Brshr 20.00 50.00
TF02 Will/Clark/Belk/Phnf 25.00 60.00
TF04 Ray/Brnby/May/Ptrs 20.00 50.00
TF05 Lndsy/Prbrt/Gllnt/Kcur 25.00 60.00
TF06 Chse/McR/Twst/Nsh 40.00 80.00
TF07 Mik/Mnsn/Grmsn/Prbrt 25.00 60.00
TF08 Cshm/O'Rlly/Jnth/Chra 20.00 50.00
TF10 Schltz/Brbe/Brshr/Crclo 12.00 30.00
TF11 Mssr/Crsn/Lrque/Pckhm 40.00 100.00
TF12 Hntr/Odgrs/Cmns/McCrm 15.00 40.00

2013-14 ITG Enforcers

91 F.Potvin/R.Hextall CC 2.00 5.00
92 P.Myre/G.Hanlon CC 1.00 2.50
93 C.Joseph/T.Cheveldae CC 1.50 4.00
94 O.Kolzig/B.Dafoe CC 1.25 3.00
95 T.Salo/D.Cloutier CC 1.00 2.50
96 P.Roy/M.Vernon CC 3.00 8.00
97 C.Osgood/P.Roy CC 3.00 8.00
98 S.Burke/M.LaForest CC .75 2.00
99 B.Parent/E.Giacomin CC 1.50 4.00
100 Tiger Williams PIM .75 2.00
101 Dale Hunter PIM 1.00 2.50
102 Tie Domi PIM 1.00 2.50
103 Marty McSorley PIM 1.00 2.50
104 Bob Probert PIM 1.25 3.00

105 Rob Ray PIM .75 2.00
106 Craig Berube PIM .75 2.00
107 Tim Hunter PIM .75 2.00
108 Chris Nilan PIM .75 2.00
109 Dave Schultz LL 1.25 3.00
110 Paul Baxter LL 1.00 2.50
111 Mike Peluso LL .75 2.00
112 Marty McSorley LL 1.00 2.50
113 Bob Probert LL 1.25 3.00
114 Joe Kocur LL .75 2.00
115 Tim Hunter LL .75 2.00
116 Gino Odjick LL .75 2.00
117 Maurice Richard LL 2.50 6.00
118 B.Probert/J.Kocur TT 1.25 3.00
119 R.Ray/M.Hartman TT .75 2.00
120 L.DeBrusk/D.Bonvie TT .75 2.00
121 T.Williams/C.Fraser TT .75 2.00
122 G.Howatt/B.Nystrom TT .75 2.00
123 T.Hunter/J.Otto TT .75 2.00
124 M.Peluso/C.Russell TT .75 2.00
125 J.Dorey/F.Kennedy TT .75 2.00
126 K.McClelland/M.McSorley TT 1.00 2.50
127 B.Witt/K.Kaminski TT 1.00 2.50
128 D.Schultz/D.Saleski TT 1.25 3.00
129 T.Horton/B.Baun TT 1.25 3.00
130 E.Shore/L.Hitchman TT 1.00 2.50
131 S.Cleghorn/O.Cleghorn TT 1.00 2.50
132 G.Howe/T.Lindsay TT 4.00 10.00
133 D.Vial/P.Laus TOTT .75 2.00
134 Dingman/VandnBshe TOTT 1.00 2.50
135 B.May/D.McCarty TOTT 1.00 2.50
136 B.Probert/C.Coxe TOTT 1.25 3.00
137 M.McSorley/M.Messier TOTT 2.50 6.00
138 T.Domi/C.Russell TOTT .75 2.00
139 G.Odjick/K.Buchberger TOTT .75 2.00
140 G.Howe/L.Fontinato TOTT 4.00 10.00
141 M.Vukota/M.Peluso TOTT .75 2.00
142 J.Caufield/J.Chychrun TOTT .75 2.00
143 T.Mallette/K.Chase TOTT .75 2.00
144 A.Roy/T.Domi TOTT 1.00 2.50
145 S.Brown/J.Cummins TOTT .75 2.00
146 D.Bonvie/R.Ray TOTT .75 2.00
147 L.McDonald/D.Polonich TOTT 1.25 3.00
148 G.Howatt/D.Schultz TOTT 1.25 3.00
149 C.Fraser/T.O'Reilly TOTT 1.00 2.50
150 J.McIlhargey/K.Walker TOTT .75 2.00
151 T.Williams/M.Bridgman TOTT .75 2.00
152 C.Neely/D.Semenko TOTT 1.25 3.00
153 J.Shelley/S.Parker TOTT .75 2.00
154 T.Hunter/M.McSorley TOTT 1.00 2.50
155 R.Stern/S.Corson TOTT 1.00 2.50
156 K.Daneyko/C.Berube TOTT .75 2.00
157 M.Peluso/T.Domi BB 1.00 2.50
158 K.Belanger/S.Brown BB .75 2.00
159 D.Bonvie/D.Langdon BB .75 2.00
160 J.Chychrun/B.Probert BB 1.25 3.00
161 L.DeBrusk/G.Odjick BB .75 2.00
162 J.Cummins/P.Kruse BB .75 2.00
163 D.McCarty/C.Lemieux BB 1.00 2.50
164 A.Downey/T.Fedoruk BB .75 2.00
165 D.Kimble/J.Kordic BB .75 2.00
166 T.Hunter/J.Kordic BB .75 2.00
167 M.McSorley/S.Grimson BB 1.00 2.50
168 P.Kruse/D.McCarty BB 1.00 2.50
169 G.Odjick/D.Langdon BB .75 2.00
170 B.Probert/K.Chase BB 1.25 3.00
171 R.Ray/G.Dwyer BB .75 2.00
172 T.Ewen/P.Kruse BB .75 2.00
173 K.Daneyko/R.Ray BB .75 2.00
174 R.VndnBssche/J.Shelley BB 1.00 2.50
175 D.Vial/M.Vukota BB .75 2.00
176 B.Witt/L.Laperriere BB .75 2.00
177 L.DeBrusk/T.Ewen BB .75 2.00
178 P.Kruse/D.Langdon BB .75 2.00
179 T.Domi/R.Stern BB 1.00 2.50
180 B.Probert/S.Grimson BB 1.25 3.00

2013-14 ITG Enforcers Autographs

AAD Aaron Downey 3.00 8.00
AAN Andrei Nazarov 3.00 8.00
AAR Andre Roy 3.00 8.00
ABH Bob Halkidis 3.00 8.00
ABM Brantt Myhres 3.00 8.00
ABS Brent Severyn 3.00 8.00
ABW Brendan Witt 3.00 8.00
ACC Cam Connor 3.00 8.00
ACCO Craig Coxe 3.00 8.00
ACD Chris Dingman 3.00 8.00
ACF Curt Fraser 3.00 8.00
ACN Cam Neely 25.00 60.00
ACR Cam Russell 3.00 8.00
ACS Chris Simon 3.00 8.00
ADB Dennis Bonvie 3.00 8.00
ADH Dave Hanson 5.00 12.00
ADK Darin Kimble 3.00 8.00
ADL Darren Langdon 3.00 8.00
ADM Darren McCarty 4.00 10.00
ADP Dennis Polonich 3.00 8.00
ADV Dennis Vial 3.00 8.00
AFK Forbes Kennedy 3.00 8.00
AGC Glen Cochrane 3.00 8.00
AGD Gordie Dwyer 3.00 8.00
AGH Garry Howatt 3.00 8.00
AGHO Gordie Howe 200.00 300.00
AIL Ian Laperriere 3.00 8.00
AJC Jay Caufield 3.00 8.00
AJCH Jeff Chychrun 3.00 8.00
AJD Jim Dorey 3.00 8.00
AJN Jim Nill 3.00 8.00
AJR Jeremy Roenick 60.00 150.00
AJS Jim Sandlak 3.00 8.00
AJSH Jody Shelley 3.00 8.00
AKB Ken Belanger 3.00 8.00
AKC Kim Clackson 3.00 8.00
AKD Ken Daneyko 3.00 8.00
AKK Kevin Kaminski 4.00 10.00
AKM Kevin McClelland 3.00 8.00
AKW Kurt Walker 3.00 8.00
ALB Lyndon Byers 3.00 8.00
ALD Louie DeBrusk 3.00 8.00
ALP Larry Playfair 3.00 8.00
AMH Mike Hartman 3.00 8.00
AMP Mike Peluso 3.00 8.00
AMV Mick Vukota 3.00 8.00
APB Paul Baxter 4.00 10.00
APK Paul Kruse 3.00 8.00
ARS Ron Stern 3.00 8.00
ART Rocky Thompson 3.00 8.00
ARV Ryan VandenBussche 4.00 10.00
ASB Sean Brown 4.00 10.00
ASC Steve Carlson 4.00 10.00
ASH Sami Helenius 3.00 8.00
ASP Scott Parker 3.00 8.00
AST Scott Thornton 3.00 8.00
ATF Todd Fedoruk 3.00 8.00
ATH Tim Hunter 3.00 8.00
ATL Ted Lindsay 15.00 40.00
ATM Troy Mallette 3.00 8.00

2013-14 ITG Enforcers Between the Pipes Battles Jersey Duals

BTPB01 C.Joseph/T.Cheveldae 8.00 20.00
BTPB02 P.Roy/C.Osgood 15.00 40.00
BTPB03 P.Roy/M.Vernon 15.00 40.00
BTPB04 O.Kolzig/B.Dafoe 6.00 15.00
BTPB05 F.Potvin/R.Hextall 10.00 25.00
BTPB06 D.Cloutier/T.Salo 5.00 12.00

2013-14 ITG Enforcers Combatants Jersey Duals

C01 K.Belanger/B.May 4.00 10.00
C02 D.Bonvie/R.VndnBssche 5.00 12.00
C03 J.Caufield/G.Odjick 4.00 10.00
C04 J.Chychrun/W.Clark 10.00 25.00
C05 G.Cochrane/R.Larson 4.00 10.00
C06 C.Coxe/B.Probert 6.00 15.00
C07 C.Dingman/R.VndnBssche 5.00 12.00
C08 A.Downey/P.Worrell 4.00 10.00
C09 T.Hunter/M.McSorley 5.00 12.00
C10 D.Langdon/S.McCarthy 4.00 10.00
C11 I.Laperriere/K.Tkachuk 6.00 15.00
C12 T.Mallette/P.Laus 4.00 10.00
C13 D.McCarty/C.Lemieux 5.00 12.00
C14 S.Parker/B.Probert 6.00 15.00
C15 C.Simon/R.Ray 4.00 10.00
C16 A.Roy/T.Domi 5.00 12.00
C17 B.Severyn/M.Vukota 4.00 10.00
C18 C.Simon/D.McCarty 5.00 12.00
C19 S.Thornton/P.Laus 4.00 10.00
C20 R.VndnBssche/S.Brown 5.00 12.00
C21 R.Ray/M.Vukota 4.00 10.00
C22 K.Walker/S.Jonathan 4.00 10.00
C23 B.Witt/J.Thornton 10.00 25.00
C24 B.Probert/C.Dingman 6.00 15.00
C25 S.Brown/B.May 4.00 10.00
C26 T.Fedoruk/A.Downey 4.00 10.00
C27 D.Brown/T.Hunter 4.00 10.00
C28 B.Nystrom/M.Bridgman 4.00 10.00
C29 D.Langdon/C.Simon 4.00 10.00
C30 T.O'Reilly/D.Maloney 5.00 12.00
C31 K.Daneyko/C.Berube 4.00 10.00
C32 J.Chychrun/G.Odjick 4.00 10.00
C33 M.McSorley/M.Messier 12.00 30.00
C34 K.Daneyko/K.Primeau 5.00 12.00
C35 S.Brown/K.Belanger 4.00 10.00
C36 M.Vukota/K.Daneyko 4.00 10.00
C37 M.Bridgman/T.Williams 4.00 10.00
C38 A.Roy/C.Simon 4.00 10.00

2013-14 ITG Enforcers Instigator Jerseys

PATCH/20: 1X TO 2.5X BASIC JSY/150*
IM01 Ken Belanger 2.00 5.00
IM02 Dennis Bonvie 2.00 5.00
IM03 Jay Caufield 2.00 5.00
IM04 Jeff Chychrun 2.00 5.00
IM05 Glen Cochrane 2.00 5.00
IM06 Chris Simon 2.00 5.00
IM07 Chris Dingman 2.00 5.00
IM08 Aaron Downey 2.00 5.00
IM09 Todd Fedoruk 2.00 5.00
IM10 Tim Hunter 2.00 5.00
IM11 Darren Langdon 2.00 5.00
IM12 Ian Laperriere 2.00 5.00
IM13 Troy Mallette 2.00 5.00
IM14 Darren McCarty 2.50 6.00
IM15 Scott Parker 2.00 5.00
IM16 Brantt Myhres 2.00 5.00
IM17 Andre Roy 2.00 5.00
IM18 Brent Severyn 2.00 5.00
IM19 Scott Thornton 2.00 5.00
IM20 Rocky Thompson 2.00 5.00
IM21 Ryan VandenBussche 2.50 6.00
IM22 Mick Vukota 2.00 5.00
IM23 Kurt Walker 2.00 5.00
IM24 Brendan Witt 2.00 5.00

2013-14 ITG Enforcers Pugilistic Puck Stoppers Jerseys

PATCH/20: 1.5X TO 4X BASIC JSY/150*
PPSM01 Tom Barrasso 5.00 12.00
PPSM02 Dan Cloutier 4.00 10.00
PPSM03 Byron Dafoe 4.00 10.00
PPSM04 Ray Emery 4.00 10.00
PPSM05 Ron Hextall 5.00 12.00
PPSM06 Curtis Joseph 6.00 15.00
PPSM07 Olaf Kolzig 5.00 12.00
PPSM08 Chris Osgood 5.00 12.00
PPSM09 Felix Potvin 8.00 20.00
PPSM10 Patrick Roy 12.00 30.00
PPSM11 Garth Snow 4.00 10.00
PPSM12 Mike Vernon 4.00 10.00

2013-14 ITG Enforcers Tough Franchise Jerseys Quad

TF01 Cshm/O'Rly/Nly/Blngr 8.00 20.00
TF02 Gare/Wlley/Ray/May 5.00 12.00
TF03 Brdgm/Brwn/Shlly/Fdrk 5.00 12.00
TF04 Hnter/Rbrts/Fleury/Phnf 6.00 15.00
TF05 Prbrt/Rnck/Rsll/VndBs 12.00 30.00
TF06 Chls/Prbrt/Kcur/McCrty 8.00 20.00
TF07 Dngm/Odgr/Cmns/Prkr 5.00 12.00
TF08 Smth/Gilies/Nystrm/Vkta 8.00 20.00
TF09 Chych/McSrl/Bck/Mlny 6.00 15.00
TF10 Svryn/Wrll/Laus/Thmps 5.00 12.00

2010-11 ITG Enshrined

1 Ace Bailey 2.00 5.00
2 Al Arbour 2.50 6.00
3 Al MacInnis 4.00 10.00
4 Alex Connell 2.50 6.00
5 Alex Delvecchio 3.00 8.00
6 Allan Stanley 3.00 8.00
7 Andy Bathgate 3.00 8.00
8 Angela James 3.00 8.00
9 Art Ross 2.00 5.00
10 Aurel Joliat 3.00 8.00
11 Babe Dye 2.00 5.00
12 Babe Pratt 2.00 5.00
13 Babe Siebert 2.50 6.00
14 Bernie Federko 2.50 6.00
15 Bernie Geoffrion 2.50 6.00
16 Bernie Parent 4.00 10.00
17 Bert Olmstead 2.50 6.00
18 Bill Barber 2.50 6.00
19 Bill Cook 2.00 5.00
20 Bill Cowley 2.00 5.00
21 Bill Durnan 3.00 8.00
22 Bill Gadsby 3.00 8.00
23 Bill Mosienko 2.50 6.00
24 Bill Quackenbush 2.50 6.00
25 Billy Burch 2.50 6.00
26 Billy Smith 3.00 8.00
27 Bob Johnson 2.00 5.00
28 Bob Pulford 2.50 6.00
29 Bobby Bauer 3.00 8.00
30 Bobby Clarke 5.00 12.00
31 Bobby Hull 6.00 15.00
32 Borje Salming 3.00 8.00
33 Brad Park 3.00 8.00
34 Brian Leetch 2.50 6.00
35 Bryan Hextall 2.50 6.00
36 Bryan Trottier 3.00 8.00
37 Bun Cook 3.00 8.00
38 Busher Jackson 2.50 6.00
39 Cam Neely 3.00 8.00
40 Cammi Granato 3.00 8.00
41 Carl Voss 3.00 8.00
42 Charlie Conacher 2.50 6.00
43 Charlie Gardiner 2.50 6.00
44 Ching Johnson 2.00 5.00
45 Chuck Rayner 3.00 8.00
46 Clarence Campbell 2.00 5.00
47 Clark Gillies 3.00 8.00
48 Clint Benedict 2.50 6.00
49 Clint Smith 2.00 5.00
50 Conn Smythe 2.50 6.00
51 Cooney Weiland 2.50 6.00
52 Cy Denneny 2.50 6.00
53 Cyclone Taylor 3.00 8.00
54 Dale Hawerchuk 4.00 10.00
55 Darryl Sittler 4.00 10.00
56 Dave Keon 3.00 8.00
57 Denis Potvin 3.00 8.00
58 Denis Savard 3.00 8.00
59 Dick Duff 2.00 5.00
60 Dick Irvin 2.50 6.00
61 Dickie Moore 2.50 6.00
62 Didier Pitre 2.50 6.00
63 Dino Ciccarelli 2.50 6.00
64 Dit Clapper 2.50 6.00
65 Doug Bentley 2.50 6.00
66 Doug Harvey 3.00 8.00
67 Earl Seibert 2.50 6.00
68 Ebbie Goodfellow 2.50 6.00
69 Ed Giacomin 5.00 12.00
70 Eddie Shore 2.50 6.00
71 Edgar Laprade 2.50 6.00
72 Elmer Lach 2.50 6.00
73 Emile Bouchard 3.00 8.00
74 Emile Francis 2.00 5.00
75 Fern Flaman 4.00 10.00
76 Foster Hewitt 2.50 6.00
77 Frank Boucher 2.00 5.00
78 Frank Brimsek 2.00 5.00
79 Frank Calder 2.00 5.00
80 Frank Fredrickson 2.50 6.00
81 Frank Mahovlich 3.00 8.00
82 Frank McGee 3.00 8.00
83 Frank Nighbor 2.50 6.00
84 Frank Patrick 2.00 5.00
85 Frank Selke 2.50 6.00
86 George Hainsworth 3.00 8.00
87 Georges Vezina 4.00 10.00
88 Gerry Cheevers 3.00 8.00
89 Gilbert Perreault 3.00 8.00
90 Glenn Anderson 2.50 6.00
91 Glenn Hall 3.00 8.00
92 Gordie Drillon 2.50 6.00
93 Grant Fuhr 5.00 12.00
94 Gump Worsley 3.00 8.00
95 Guy Lafleur 4.00 10.00
96 Guy Lapointe 2.50 6.00
97 Hap Day 2.50 6.00
98 Hap Holmes 2.50 6.00
99 Harold Ballard 2.00 5.00
100 Harry Howell 2.50 6.00
101 Harry Lumley 3.00 8.00
102 Harry Oliver 2.50 6.00
103 Harry Sinden 2.00 5.00
104 Harry Watson 2.50 6.00
105 Henri Richard 3.00 8.00
106 Herb Brooks 2.50 6.00
107 Hobey Baker 2.50 6.00
108 Hooley Smith 2.50 6.00
109 Howie Morenz 2.50 6.00
110 Igor Larionov 3.00 8.00
111 Jack Adams 3.00 8.00
112 Jack Darragh 3.00 8.00
113 Jack Stewart 2.00 5.00
114 Jacques Laperriere 2.50 6.00
115 Jacques Lemaire 2.50 6.00
116 Jacques Plante 4.00 10.00
117 Jari Kurri 3.00 8.00
118 Jean Beliveau 3.00 8.00
119 Jean Ratelle 2.50 6.00
120 Joe Hall 2.00 5.00
121 Joe Malone 2.50 6.00
122 Joe Mullen 2.00 5.00
123 Joe Primeau 2.50 6.00
124 Joe Simpson 2.00 5.00
125 Johnny Bower 3.00 8.00
126 Johnny Bucyk 3.00 8.00
127 Ken Reardon 2.50 6.00
128 King Clancy 2.50 6.00
129 Lanny McDonald 2.50 6.00
130 Larry Murphy 2.50 6.00
131 Larry Robinson 2.50 6.00
132 Lester Patrick 2.50 6.00
133 Lionel Conacher 2.50 6.00
134 Lord Stanley 3.00 8.00
135 Luc Robitaille 3.00 8.00
136 Lynn Patrick 2.00 5.00
137 Marcel Dionne 4.00 10.00
138 Marcel Pronovost 3.00 8.00
139 Mario Lemieux 12.00 30.00
140 Mark Messier 6.00 15.00
141 Maurice Richard 6.00 15.00
142 Max Bentley 2.00 5.00
143 Michel Goulet 2.50 6.00
144 Mike Bossy 3.00 8.00
145 Mike Gartner 4.00 10.00
146 Milt Schmidt 2.50 6.00
147 Moose Goheen 2.00 5.00
148 Neil Colville 2.00 5.00
149 Nels Stewart 2.00 5.00
150 Newsy Lalonde 2.50 6.00
151 Norm Ullman 3.00 8.00
152 Paddy Moran 2.50 6.00
153 Pat LaFontaine 3.00 8.00
154 Patrick Roy 8.00 20.00
155 Paul Coffey 3.00 8.00
156 Percy LeSueur 2.50 6.00
157 Peter Stastny 2.50 6.00
158 Phil Esposito 5.00 12.00
159 Pierre Pilote 2.50 6.00
160 Punch Broadbent 2.00 5.00
161 Punch Imlach 2.00 5.00
162 Raymond Bourque 5.00 12.00
163 Red Dutton 2.00 5.00
164 Red Horner 2.50 6.00
165 Red Kelly 3.00 8.00
166 Red Storey 2.00 5.00
167 Rod Gilbert 3.00 8.00
168 Rod Langway 2.50 6.00
169 Roger Neilson 2.00 5.00
170 Ron Francis 4.00 10.00
171 Roy Conacher 3.00 8.00
172 Roy Worters 3.00 8.00
173 Rudy Pilous 3.00 8.00
174 Sam Pollock 2.00 5.00
175 Scotty Bowman 3.00 8.00
176 Serge Savard 3.00 8.00
177 Sid Abel 2.50 6.00
178 Sprague Cleghorn 2.50 6.00
179 Stan Mikita 4.00 10.00
180 Steve Shutt 3.00 8.00
181 Steve Yzerman 8.00 20.00
182 Sweeney Schriner 2.00 5.00
183 Syd Howe 2.00 5.00
184 Syl Apps 4.00 10.00
185 Sylvio Mantha 2.00 5.00
186 Ted Kennedy 3.00 8.00
187 Ted Lindsay 3.00 8.00
188 Terry Sawchuk 4.00 10.00
189 Tim Horton 3.00 8.00
190 Tiny Thompson 3.00 8.00
191 Toe Blake 2.50 6.00
192 Tom Johnson 2.50 6.00
193 Tommy Ivan 2.50 6.00
194 Tony Esposito 3.00 8.00
195 Turk Broda 3.00 8.00
196 Valeri Kharlamov 2.00 5.00
197 Vladislav Tretiak 2.50 6.00
198 Wilfred Green 2.00 5.00
199 Woody Dumart 2.00 5.00
200 Yvan Cournoyer 3.00 8.00

2010-11 ITG Enshrined Autographs Silver

AAA Al Arbour 10.00 25.00
AAB Andy Bathgate 12.00 30.00
AAD Alex Delvecchio 12.00 30.00
AAJ Angela James 12.00 30.00
AAM Al MacInnis 15.00 40.00
AAS Allan Stanley 12.00 30.00
ABB Bill Barber 10.00 25.00
ABF Bernie Federko 10.00 25.00
ABG Bill Gadsby 12.00 30.00
ABH Bobby Hull 15.00 40.00
ABL Brian Leetch 10.00 25.00
ABO Bert Olmstead 15.00 40.00
ABP Bernie Parent 15.00 40.00
ABPA Brad Park/48* 10.00 25.00
ABPU Bob Pulford/48* 10.00 25.00
ABS Billy Smith 8.00 20.00
ABSA Borje Salming 12.00 30.00
ABT Bryan Trottier 12.00 30.00
ACG Clark Gillies 12.00 30.00
ACGR Cammi Granato 10.00 25.00
ACN Cam Neely 12.00 30.00
ADC Dino Ciccarelli 12.00 30.00
ADD Dick Duff 10.00 25.00
ADH Dale Hawerchuk 15.00 40.00
ADK Dave Keon 12.00 30.00
ADM Dickie Moore 12.50 30.00
ADP Denis Potvin 12.00 30.00
ADS Darryl Sittler 15.00 40.00
ADSA Denis Savard 12.00 30.00
AEB Emile Bouchard 12.00 30.00
AEF Emile Francis 15.00 40.00
AEG Ed Giacomin 12.00 30.00
AEL Elmer Lach 15.00 40.00
AELA Edgar Laprade 10.00 25.00
AFF Fern Flaman/48* 15.00 40.00
AFM Frank Mahovlich 12.00 30.00
AGA Glenn Anderson 15.00 40.00
AGC Gerry Cheevers 12.00 30.00
AGF Grant Fuhr 20.00 50.00
AGH Glenn Hall 12.00 30.00
AGL Guy Lafleur 15.00 40.00
AGLA Guy Lapointe 10.00 25.00
AGP Gilbert Perreault 12.00 30.00
AHH Harry Howell 10.00 25.00
AHR Henri Richard 12.00 30.00
AHS Harry Sinden 8.00 20.00
AIL Igor Larionov 25.00 60.00
AJB Jean Beliveau 40.00 80.00
AJBO Johnny Bower 15.00 40.00
AJBU John Bucyk 8.00 20.00
AJK Jari Kurri 12.00 30.00
AJL Jacques Laperriere 15.00 40.00
AJLE Jacques Lemaire 10.00 25.00
AJM Joe Mullen 10.00 25.00
ALM Lanny McDonald 12.00 30.00
ALMU Larry Murphy 12.00 30.00
ALR Larry Robinson 12.00 30.00
ALRO Luc Robitaille 15.00 40.00
AMB Mike Bossy 12.00 30.00
AMD Marcel Dionne 15.00 40.00
AMG Michel Goulet 10.00 25.00
AMGA Mike Gartner 15.00 40.00
AML Mario Lemieux 60.00 120.00
AMM Mark Messier 40.00 80.00
AMP Marcel Pronovost 12.00 30.00
AMS Milt Schmidt 10.00 25.00
ANU Norm Ullman 12.00 30.00
APC Paul Coffey 12.00 30.00
APE Phil Esposito 20.00 50.00
APL Pat Lafontaine 12.00 30.00
APP Pierre Pilote 10.00 25.00
APR Patrick Roy 30.00 80.00
APS Peter Stastny 10.00 25.00
ARB Raymond Bourque 20.00 50.00
ARF Ron Francis 12.00 30.00
ARG Rod Gilbert/48* 12.00 30.00
ARK Red Kelly 12.00 30.00
ARL Rod Langway/48* 10.00 25.00
ASB Scotty Bowman 12.00 30.00
ASM Stan Mikita 15.00 40.00
ASS Steve Shutt 15.00 40.00
ASSA Serge Savard 12.00 30.00
ASY Steve Yzerman 25.00 60.00
ATE Tony Esposito 15.00 40.00
ATL Ted Lindsay 12.00 30.00
AVT Vladislav Tretiak 15.00 40.00
AYC Yvan Cournoyer 12.00 30.00

2015-16 ITG Enshrined

C001 A.Delvecchio/T.Horton 6.00 15.00
C002 B.Parent/P.Esposito 10.00 25.00
C003 B.Barber/G.Perreault 6.00 15.00
C004 B.Hull/S.Mikita 12.00 30.00
C006 C.Chelios/B.Shanahan 6.00 15.00
C007 D.Hasek/P.Forsberg 12.00 30.00
C008 D.Gilmour/E.Belfour 8.00 20.00
C009 E.Giacomin/B.Clarke 10.00 25.00
C010 G.Fuhr/P.LaFontaine 10.00 25.00
C014 J.Ratelle/G.Cheevers 6.00 15.00
C015 J.Sakic/P.Bure 12.00 30.00
C016 L.Robitaille/B.Leetch 6.00 15.00
C017 M.Dionne/L.McDonald 8.00 20.00
C018 M.Messier/S.Stevens 12.00 30.00
C020 M.Bossy/D.Potvin 6.00 15.00
C021 R.Bourque/P.Coffey 10.00 25.00
C022 R.Blake/M.Modano 10.00 25.00
C023 R.Langway/C.Gillies 6.00 15.00
C024 S.Yzerman/B.Hull 15.00 40.00
C025 T.Esposito/G.Lafleur 8.00 20.00

2015-16 ITG Enshrined Eight All Star Seasons Silver

E8S01 Bur/Roy/Skc/Fdv/Lmx/Brq/Blk/Fbg 25.00 60.00
E8S02 Fdv/Lmx/Lds/Hsk/Shn/Blk/Roy/Chl 25.00 60.00
E8S03 Gtz/Chl/Fbg/Hsk/Mod/Roy/Skc/Bur 40.00 100.00
E8S04 Gtz/Hul/Roy/Fdv/Brq/Bur/Msr/Blk 40.00 100.00
E8S05 Hsl/Msr/Yzm/Stv/Mod/Bur/Snd/Shn 15.00 40.00
E8S06 Lmx/Fdv/Blf/Hul/Msr/Fbg/Chl/Shn 25.00 60.00
E8S07 Mod/Prng/Snd/Rbtl/Lds/Mcn/Hsk/Shn 10.00 25.00

2015-16 ITG Enshrined Eight Silver

E801 Blk/Fbg/Hsk/Mod/Fdv/Hsl/Lds/Prng/35 12.00 30.00
E803 Frn/Mcn/Msr/Stv/Hul/Yzm/Ltch/Rbtl/35 15.00 40.00
E804 Grt/Mrp/Oat/LFnt/Hwck/Frn/Cic/Mln/40 8.00 20.00
E805 Hul/Fdv/Skc/Lds/Mod/Bur/Chl/Glm/40 12.00 30.00
E806 Lflr/Clk/Esp/Bsy/Dio/Slm/Sht/Glb/20 10.00 25.00
E807 Lnv/Fdv/Lds/Yzm/How/Lnd/Hul/Shn/20 20.00 50.00
E808 Lmx/Gtz/Roy/Yzm/Msr/Fdv/Brq/Hsk/40 40.00 100.00
E809 Orr/Nly/Esp/Shr/Oat/Brq/Cby/Rrn/20 25.00 60.00
E810 Pro/Hsl/Mcn/Brq/Chl/Stv/Ltch/Blk/35 8.00 20.00
E811 Rch/How/Orr/Hrv/Saw/Hrt/Gtz/Esp/20 40.00 100.00

2015-16 ITG Enshrined Exhibits Silver

EE01 Bobby Clarke/20 10.00 25.00
EE02 Brett Hull/25 12.00 30.00
EE03 Doug Gilmour/25 8.00 20.00
EE05 Grant Fuhr/20 10.00 25.00
EE06 Marcel Dionne/20 8.00 20.00
EE07 Mats Sundin/25 6.00 15.00
EE09 Pavel Bure/25 6.00 15.00
EE12 Mario Lemieux/25 25.00 60.00
EE13 Patrick Roy/25 15.00 40.00
EE15 Wayne Gretzky/20 40.00 100.00

2015-16 ITG Enshrined Hall Patch Silver

HP01 Adam Oates/20 6.00 15.00
HP03 Brendan Shanahan/20 6.00 15.00
HP04 Brett Hull/20 12.00 30.00
HP05 Brian Leetch/20 5.00 12.00
HP11 Dominik Hasek/20 10.00 25.00
HP19 Luc Robitaille/20 6.00 15.00
HP21 Mario Lemieux/20 25.00 60.00
HP23 Mike Bossy/20 6.00 15.00
HP24 Mike Modano/20 10.00 25.00
HP25 Nicklas Lidstrom/20 6.00 15.00
HP27 Patrick Roy/20 15.00 40.00
HP28 Pavel Bure/20 6.00 15.00
HP31 Raymond Bourque/20 10.00 25.00
HP32 Rob Blake/20 6.00 15.00
HP34 Sergei Fedorov/20 10.00 25.00
HP36 Steve Yzerman/20 15.00 40.00

2015-16 ITG Enshrined Mount Rushmore Silver

MR04 Grtzk/Fhr/Cffy/Mssr/20 40.00 100.00
MR05 Grtzk/Roy/Lmx/Brq/30 40.00 100.00
MR06 How/Yzrmn/Swchk/Lids/25 20.00 50.00
MR09 Ndrmyr/Lids/Skc/Prngr/35 12.00 30.00
MR10 Orr/Dion/Lflr/Hll/25 25.00 60.00
MR13 Prnt/Clrk/Brbr/Lndbrg/25 10.00 25.00
MR18 Sndn/Kndy/Hrtn/Salm/20 6.00 15.00
MR19 Lmx/Grtzk/Yzrmn/Roy/30 40.00 100.00

2015-16 ITG Enshrined Retired Numbers Silver

RN02 Bernie Parent/25 8.00 20.00
RN03 Bill Barber/25 5.00 12.00
RN04 Billy Smith/40 6.00 15.00
RN05 Bobby Clarke/25 10.00 25.00
RN06 Bobby Hull/20 12.00 30.00
RN08 Brett Hull/35 12.00 30.00
RN09 Cam Neely/30 6.00 15.00
RN10 Denis Potvin/25 6.00 15.00
RN11 Denis Savard/20 6.00 15.00
RN14 Gilbert Perreault/25 6.00 15.00
RN16 Grant Fuhr/25 10.00 25.00
RN18 Joe Sakic/40 12.00 30.00
RN20 Lanny McDonald/25 6.00 15.00
RN21 Luc Robitaille/35 6.00 15.00
RN22 Marcel Dionne/20 8.00 20.00
RN23 Mario Lemieux/40 25.00 60.00
RN25 Mike Bossy/40 6.00 15.00
RN26 Pat LaFontaine/35 6.00 15.00
RN27 Patrick Roy/40 15.00 40.00
RN28 Patrick Roy/35 15.00 40.00
RN29 Phil Esposito/20 10.00 25.00
RN30 Raymond Bourque/35 10.00 25.00
RN31 Scott Stevens/40 5.00 12.00
RN32 Stan Mikita/20 8.00 20.00
RN33 Steve Yzerman/35 15.00 40.00
RN34 Ted Lindsay/20 6.00 15.00
RN36 Tony Esposito/25 6.00 15.00

2015-16 ITG Enshrined Signature Showcase Silver

SSBH1 Bobby Hull/35 12.00 30.00
SSBH2 Brett Hull/35 12.00 30.00
SSCG1 Clark Gillies/35 6.00 15.00
SSDG1 Doug Gilmour/35 8.00 20.00
SSEB1 Ed Belfour/35 6.00 15.00
SSEG1 Ed Giacomin/35 6.00 15.00
SSGC1 Gerry Cheevers/35 6.00 15.00
SSGL1 Guy Lafleur/35 8.00 20.00
SSIL1 Igor Larionov/35 6.00 15.00
SSMD1 Marcel Dionne/35 8.00 20.00
SSML1 Mario Lemieux/25 25.00 60.00
SSNL1 Nicklas Lidstrom/35 6.00 15.00
SSPB1 Pavel Bure/35 6.00 15.00
SSPH1 Phil Housley/35 5.00 12.00
SSPR1 Patrick Roy/25 15.00 40.00
SSRB1 Raymond Bourque/35 10.00 25.00

2015-16 ITG Enshrined Silverware Seasons Silver

SS01 Esp/Orr/Delv/Clrk/Esp/Prnt/20 25.00 60.00
SS02 Grtzk/Lmx/Brq/Belf/Hull/Glbrt/25 40.00 100.00
SS03 Grtzk/Lmx/Cffy/Roy/Hwe/Bsy/25 40.00 100.00
SS04 Lflr/Bsy/Esp/Ptvn/Rob/Gny/20 10.00 25.00
SS05 Stvn/Nly/Hsk/Brq/Fdrv/Grtzk/35 40.00 100.00

2015-16 ITG Enshrined Silverware Silver

SW01 Bernie Parent/30 8.00 20.00
SW03 Brett Hull/45 12.00 30.00
SW04 Dale Hawerchuk/35 8.00 20.00
SW05 Dominik Hasek/45 10.00 25.00
SW06 Ed Belfour/45 6.00 15.00
SW08 Glenn Hall/20 6.00 15.00
SW10 Guy Lafleur/30 8.00 20.00
SW12 Joe Nieuwendyk/45 5.00 12.00
SW13 Joe Sakic/45 12.00 30.00
SW14 Luc Robitaille/45 6.00 15.00
SW15 Mario Lemieux/45 25.00 60.00
SW17 Nicklas Lidstrom/45 6.00 15.00
SW18 Patrick Roy/45 15.00 40.00
SW19 Pavel Bure/45 6.00 15.00
SW20 Raymond Bourque/45 10.00 25.00
SW22 Sergei Fedorov/45 10.00 25.00
SW24 Steve Yzerman/45 15.00 40.00
SW27 Wayne Gretzky/25 40.00 100.00

2010-11 ITG Fall Expo Team ITG VIP

ITG1 Antti Niemi 1.25 3.00
ITG2 Bobby Clarke 2.50 6.00
ITG3 Bobby Hull 3.00 8.00
ITG4 Borje Salming 1.50 4.00
ITG5 Cam Neely 1.50 4.00
ITG6 Daniel Sedin 2.00 5.00
ITG7 Darryl Sittler 2.00 5.00
ITG8 Dave Keon 1.50 4.00
ITG9 Denis Potvin 1.50 4.00
ITG10 Doug Gilmour 2.00 5.00
ITG11 Doug Harvey 1.50 4.00
ITG12 Guy LaFleur 2.00 5.00
ITG13 Henrik Sedin 2.00 5.00
ITG14 Jacques Plante 2.00 5.00
ITG15 Jari Kurri 1.50 4.00
ITG16 Jaromir Jagr 5.00 12.00
ITG17 Jean Beliveau 1.50 4.00
ITG18 Joe Sakic 3.00 8.00
ITG19 Joe Thornton 2.50 6.00
ITG20 Mario Lemieux 6.00 15.00
ITG21 Mark Messier 3.00 8.00
ITG22 Martin Brodeur 4.00 10.00
ITG23 Martin St. Louis 1.50 4.00
ITG24 Maurice Richard 2.00 5.00
ITG25 Mike Bossy 1.50 4.00
ITG26 Mike Modano 2.50 6.00
ITG27 Nicklas Lidstrom 1.50 4.00
ITG28 Patrick Roy 4.00 10.00
ITG29 Paul Coffey 1.50 4.00
ITG30 Pavel Bure 1.50 4.00
ITG31 Phil Esposito 2.50 6.00
ITG32 Raymond Bourque 2.50 6.00
ITG33 Rick Nash 1.50 4.00
ITG34 Roberto Luongo 2.50 6.00
ITG35 Scott Niedermayer 1.50 4.00
ITG36 Steve Yzerman 4.00 10.00
ITG37 Steven Stamkos 3.00 8.00
ITG38 Ted Lindsay 1.50 4.00
ITG39 Teemu Selanne 3.00 8.00
ITG40 Terry Sawchuk 2.00 5.00
ITG41 Tim Horton 1.50 4.00
ITG42 Tyler Seguin 4.00 10.00
ITG43 Valeri Kharlamov 1.00 2.50
ITG44 Vincent Lecavalier 1.50 4.00
ITG45 Vladislav Tretiak 1.25 3.00

2012-13 ITG Forever Rivals

1 Georges Vezina 2.00 5.00
2 Joe Malone 1.25 3.00
3 Newsy Lalonde 1.50 4.00
4 Aurel Joliat 2.00 5.00
5 George Hainsworth 2.00 5.00
6 Howie Morenz 1.50 4.00
7 Bill Durnan 2.00 5.00
8 Elmer Lach 1.50 4.00
9 Maurice Richard 4.00 10.00
10 Toe Blake 1.25 3.00
11 Bernie Geoffrion 1.50 4.00
12 Butch Bouchard 1.50 4.00
13 Dickie Moore 1.50 4.00
14 Doug Harvey 2.00 5.00
15 Jacques Plante 2.50 6.00
16 Jean Beliveau 2.00 5.00
17 Jean-Guy Talbot 1.50 4.00
18 Tom Johnson 1.50 4.00
19 Bobby Rousseau 1.50 4.00
20 Charlie Hodge 1.50 4.00
21 Claude Provost 1.25 3.00
22 Gump Worsley 2.00 5.00
23 Henri Richard 2.00 5.00
24 J.C. Tremblay 1.25 3.00
25 Jacques Laperriere 1.50 4.00
26 Ralph Backstrom 1.25 3.00
27 Rogie Vachon 2.50 6.00
28 Bunny Larocque 1.50 4.00
29 Guy Lafleur 2.50 6.00
30 Guy Lapointe 1.50 4.00
31 Jacques Lemaire 1.50 4.00
32 Larry Robinson 2.00 5.00
33 Serge Savard 2.00 5.00
34 Steve Shutt 1.50 4.00
35 Bobby Smith 2.00 5.00
36 Chris Chelios 2.00 5.00
37 Guy Carbonneau 2.00 5.00
38 Mats Naslund 1.25 3.00
39 Patrick Roy 5.00 12.00
40 Denis Savard 2.00 5.00
41 John LeClair 2.00 5.00
42 Kirk Muller 1.50 4.00
43 Mark Recchi 2.50 6.00
44 Jose Theodore 2.00 5.00
45 Saku Koivu 2.00 5.00
46 Brian Gionta 1.25 3.00
47 Josh Gorges 1.50 4.00
48 Lars Eller 1.25 3.00
49 Carey Price 4.00 10.00
50 P.K. Subban 2.50 6.00
51 Hap Day 1.50 4.00
52 Ace Bailey 1.25 3.00
53 Busher Jackson 1.50 4.00
54 Charlie Conacher 1.50 4.00
55 Joe Primeau 1.50 4.00
56 King Clancy 1.50 4.00
57 Wally Stanowski 1.50 4.00
58 Red Horner 1.50 4.00
59 Bill Barilko 1.50 4.00
60 Bob Davidson 1.50 4.00
61 Howie Meeker 2.00 5.00
62 Max Bentley 1.25 3.00
63 Syl Apps 1.50 4.00
64 Ted Kennedy 2.00 5.00
65 Turk Broda 2.00 5.00
66 Bob Pulford 1.50 4.00
67 Dick Duff 1.50 4.00
68 Harry Lumley 2.00 5.00
69 Tim Horton 2.00 5.00
70 Bob Baun 2.00 5.00
71 Dave Keon 2.00 5.00
72 Bob Nevin 1.25 3.00
73 Frank Mahovlich 2.00 5.00
74 Johnny Bower 2.00 5.00
75 Red Kelly 2.00 5.00
76 Terry Sawchuk 2.00 5.00
77 Borje Salming 2.00 5.00
78 Darryl Sittler 2.50 6.00
79 Lanny McDonald 2.00 5.00
80 Mike Palmateer 2.00 5.00
81 Paul Henderson 1.50 4.00
82 Ron Ellis 1.25 3.00
83 Tiger Williams 1.25 3.00
84 Gary Leeman 1.50 4.00
85 Rick Vaive 1.50 4.00
86 Dave Andreychuk 2.00 5.00
87 Doug Gilmour 2.50 6.00
88 Felix Potvin 4.00 10.00
89 Glenn Anderson 1.50 4.00
90 Mats Sundin 3.00 8.00
91 Wendel Clark 3.00 8.00
92 Curtis Joseph 2.50 6.00
93 Darcy Tucker 1.50 4.00
94 Ed Belfour 2.00 5.00
95 Tie Domi 1.50 4.00
96 Joffrey Lupul 1.25 3.00
97 Jake Gardiner 1.25 3.00
98 Dion Phaneuf 1.50 4.00
99 James Reimer 2.00 5.00
100 Mikhail Grabovski 1.25 3.00

2012-13 ITG Forever Rivals Gold

GOLD/30: 1X TO 2.5X BASIC CARDS

2012-13 ITG Forever Rivals Autographs

AAB Andy Bathgate 8.00 20.00
AABE Allan Bester 6.00 15.00
AAM Ab McDonald 6.00 15.00
ABB Butch Bouchard 20.00 40.00
ABBA Bob Baun 8.00 20.00
ABD Bill Derlago 5.00 12.00
ABE Brian Engblom 8.00 20.00
ABG Brian Glennie 6.00 15.00
ABN Bob Nevin 5.00 12.00
ABO Bert Olmstead 8.00 20.00
ABP Bernie Parent 12.00 30.00
ABPU Bob Pulford SP 30.00 60.00
ABR Bobby Rousseau 6.00 15.00
ABS Bobby Smith 6.00 15.00
ABSA Borje Salming 8.00 20.00
ABSE Brit Selby 6.00 15.00
ABSK Brian Skrudland 8.00 20.00
ACC Chris Chelios SP 20.00 50.00
ACH Charlie Hodge 6.00 15.00
ACJ Curtis Joseph 10.00 25.00
ACL Claude Lemieux 6.00 15.00

ACN Chris Nilan 6.00 15.00
ACP Carey Price SP 25.00 60.00
ADA Dave Andreychuk 8.00 20.00
ADD Dick Duff SP 12.00 30.00
ADD2 Dick Duff SP 12.00 30.00
ADDA Dan Daoust 6.00 15.00
ADE Dave Ellett 5.00 12.00
ADG Doug Gilmour SP 60.00 125.00
ADJ Doug Jarvis 6.00 15.00
ADK Dave Keon SP 40.00 80.00
ADM Dickie Moore 8.00 20.00
ADMA Don Marshall 5.00 12.00
ADMAL Dan Maloney 6.00 15.00
ADP Dion Phaneuf 6.00 15.00
ADSA Denis Savard 8.00 20.00
ADSI Darryl Sittler 12.00 30.00
ADT1 Darcy Tucker 6.00 15.00
ADT2 Darcy Tucker 6.00 15.00
AEB Ed Belfour 10.00 25.00
AEC Ed Chadwick 6.00 15.00
AED Eric Desjardins 6.00 15.00
AEL Elmer Lach 15.00 30.00
AES Eddie Shack 8.00 20.00
AET Errol Thompson 5.00 12.00
AFM Fleming MacKell 6.00 15.00
AFMA Frank Mahovlich SP 30.00 60.00
AFP Felix Potvin 15.00 40.00
AGC Guy Carbonneau 8.00 20.00
AGD Gilbert Dionne 8.00 20.00
AGL Guy Lafleur SP 100.00 200.00
AGLA Guy Lapointe 6.00 15.00
AGLE Gary Leeman 6.00 15.00
AGR Gary Roberts SP 20.00 40.00
AGT Greg Terrion 5.00 12.00
AHM Howie Meeker 8.00 20.00
AHR Henri Richard 15.00 30.00
AIT Ian Turnbull 5.00 12.00
AJA John Anderson 5.00 12.00
AJB Jean Beliveau SP 100.00 175.00
AJBO Johnny Bower SP 30.00 60.00
AJC Jiri Crha 8.00 20.00
AJD Jim Dorey 5.00 12.00
AJGT Jean-Guy Talbot 8.00 20.00
AJL Jacques Lemaire 6.00 15.00
AJLA Jacques Laperriere 6.00 15.00
AJLE John LeClair 8.00 20.00
AJM Jim McKenny 5.00 12.00
AJP Jim Pappin 5.00 12.00
AJR Jim Roberts 6.00 15.00
AKK Kris King 5.00 12.00
AKM Kirk Muller 6.00 15.00
ALB Laurie Boschman 5.00 12.00
ALM Lanny McDonald SP 30.00 60.00
ALO Lyle Odelein 6.00 15.00
ALR Larry Robinson 8.00 20.00
AMF Miroslav Frycer 5.00 12.00
AMG Mike Gartner SP 20.00 40.00
AMK Mike Keane 6.00 15.00
AMM Mike McPhee 5.00 12.00
AMN Mats Naslund 6.00 15.00
AMP Marcel Pronovost 8.00 20.00
AMPA Mike Palmateer SP 15.00 40.00
AMS Mats Sundin SP 40.00 80.00
ANB Nikolai Borschevsky 8.00 20.00
ANU Norm Ullman 8.00 20.00
APG Phil Goyette 6.00 15.00
APH Paul Henderson 8.00 20.00
APM Pete Mahovlich 8.00 20.00
APR Patrick Roy SP 100.00 200.00
ARB Ralph Backstrom 8.00 20.00
ARC Russ Courtnall 6.00 15.00
ARC2 Russ Courtnall 6.00 15.00
ARE Ron Ellis 6.00 15.00
ARK Red Kelly SP 25.00 50.00
ARL Rod Langway 6.00 15.00
ARS Richard Sevigny 8.00 20.00
ARST Rick St. Croix 6.00 15.00
ARV Rogie Vachon 10.00 25.00
ARVA Rick Vaive 6.00 15.00
ARW Ryan Walter 5.00 12.00
ARWA Rick Wamsley 8.00 20.00
ASB Scotty Bowman 12.00 30.00
ASC1 Shayne Corson 6.00 15.00
ASC2 Shayne Corson 6.00 15.00
ASP Steve Penney 8.00 20.00
ASR Stephane Richer 6.00 15.00
ASS Serge Savard 8.00 20.00
ASSH Steve Shutt 6.00 15.00
AST Steve Thomas 5.00 12.00
ATD Tie Domi 10.00 25.00
ATE Tony Esposito SP 40.00 80.00
ATG Todd Gill 5.00 12.00
ATL Trevor Linden 8.00 20.00
ATS Tod Sloan 8.00 20.00
ATW Tiger Williams 5.00 12.00
AVD1 Vincent Damphousse SP 30.00 60.00
AVD2 Vincent Damphousse SP 30.00 60.00
AWC Wendel Clark SP 30.00 60.00
AWP Wilf Paiement 6.00 15.00
AWS Wally Stanowski 8.00 20.00
AYC Yvan Cournoyer 8.00 20.00
AYL Yvon Lambert 8.00 20.00

2012-13 ITG Forever Rivals Autographs Dual

DABSLR B.Salming/L.Robinson 50.00 100.00
DADGKM D.Gilmour/K.Muller 100.00 200.00
DADKJB D.Keon/J.Beliveau 100.00 200.00

2012-13 ITG Forever Rivals Between The Pipes Jerseys Dual

BTPD01 F.Potvin/P.Roy/85 15.00 30.00
BTPD02 C.Joseph/J.Theodore/85 8.00 20.00
BTPD03 V.Toskala/J.Halak/85 6.00 15.00
BTPD04 A.Bester/P.Roy/85 15.00 40.00
BTPD05 J.Reimer/C.Price/85 12.00 30.00
BTPD06 A.Raycroft/C.Huet/85 5.00 12.00
BTPD07 E.Belfour/J.Hackett/85 6.00 15.00

2012-13 ITG Forever Rivals Between The Pipes Memorabilia Blue/Red

SILVER/30: .5X TO 1.2X BLUE-RED/130*
BTP01 Felix Potvin/130* 8.00 20.00
BTP02 James Reimer/130* 5.00 12.00
BTP03 Curtis Joseph/130* 6.00 15.00
BTP04 Ed Belfour/130* 5.00 12.00
BTP05 Grant Fuhr/130* 8.00 20.00
BTP06 Mike Palmateer/130* 5.00 12.00
BTP07 Vesa Toskala/130* 5.00 12.00
BTP08 Patrick Roy/130* 12.00 30.00
BTP09 Carey Price/130* 10.00 25.00
BTP10 Jaroslav Halak/130* 5.00 12.00
BTP11 Cristobal Huet/130* 4.00 10.00
BTP12 Jose Theodore/130* 5.00 12.00
BTP13 Jeff Hackett/130* 4.00 10.00
BTP14 Doug Soetaert/130* 4.00 10.00

2012-13 ITG Forever Rivals Cup Winners Jerseys Silver

CW01 Patrick Roy/85* 10.00 25.00
CW02 Guy Lafleur/85* 10.00 25.00
CW03 Kirk Muller/85* 5.00 12.00
CW04 Mike Keane/85* 5.00 12.00
CW05 Guy Carbonneau/85* 6.00 15.00
CW06 Guy Lapointe/85* 8.00 20.00
CW07 Bob Baun/85* 8.00 20.00
CW08 Mats Naslund/85* 4.00 10.00
CW09 Larry Robinson/85* 6.00 15.00
CW10 Yvan Cournoyer/85* 6.00 15.00
CW11 Denis Savard/85* 6.00 15.00
CW12 Harry Watson/85* 8.00 20.00

2012-13 ITG Forever Rivals Double Agents

DAG01 Darcy Tucker 1.50 4.00
DAG02 Dick Duff 1.50 4.00
DAG03 Shayne Corson 1.50 4.00
DAG04 Doug Gilmour 2.50 6.00
DAG05 Frank Mahovlich 2.00 5.00
DAG06 Jacques Plante 2.50 6.00
DAG07 Kirk Muller 1.50 4.00
DAG08 Lorne Chabot 1.50 4.00

2012-13 ITG Forever Rivals Dual Rivals Jerseys Silver

R01 D.Gilmour/K.Muller/85 8.00 20.00
R02 B.Salming/L.Robinson/85 6.00 15.00
R03 L.McDonald/S.Shutt/85 6.00 15.00
R04 R.Vaive/B.Smith/85 6.00 15.00
R05 F.Potvin/P.Roy/85 15.00 40.00
R06 J.Gustavsson/C.Price/85 12.00 30.00
R07 W.Clark/G.Carbonneau/85 8.00 20.00
R08 M.Sundin/S.Koivu/85 8.00 20.00
R09 D.Phaneuf/P.Subban/85 8.00 20.00
R10 T.Domi/S.Corson/85 5.00 12.00
R11 G.Leeman/M.Naslund/85 5.00 12.00
R12 M.Gartner/M.Recchi/85 8.00 20.00

2012-13 ITG Forever Rivals Game Used Jerseys Blue/Red

SILVER/30: .6X TO 1.5X BLUE-RED/130*
M01 Ed Belfour/130* 5.00 12.00
M02 Wendel Clark/130* 5.00 12.00
M03 Dion Phaneuf/130* 4.00 10.00
M04 Tie Domi/130* 4.00 10.00
M05 Mike Gartner/130* 6.00 15.00
M06 Doug Gilmour/130* 6.00 15.00
M07 Curtis Joseph/130* 6.00 15.00
M08 Nikolai Kulemin/130* 3.00 8.00
M09 Gary Leeman/130* 4.00 10.00
M10 Brian Leetch/130* 4.00 10.00
M11 Mikhail Grabovski/130* 3.00 8.00
M12 Larry Murphy/130* 4.00 10.00
M13 Clarke MacArthur/130* 3.00 8.00
M14 Mike Palmateer/130* 5.00 12.00
M15 Felix Potvin/130* 8.00 20.00
M16 James Reimer/130* 5.00 12.00
M17 Grant Fuhr/130* 8.00 20.00
M18 Borje Salming/130* 5.00 12.00
M19 Alexander Mogilny/130* 5.00 12.00
M20 Matt Stajan/130* 3.00 8.00
M21 Mats Sundin/130* 8.00 20.00
M22 Steve Thomas/130* 3.00 8.00
M23 Darcy Tucker/130* 4.00 10.00
M24 Rick Vaive/130* 4.00 10.00
M25 Nik Antropov/130* 4.00 10.00
M26 Brian Bellows/130* 4.00 10.00
M27 Guy Carbonneau/130* 5.00 12.00
M28 Chris Chelios/130* 5.00 12.00
M29 Shayne Corson/130* 4.00 10.00
M30 Patrick Roy/130* 12.00 30.00
M31 Gilbert Dionne/130* 5.00 12.00
M32 Lars Eller/130* 3.00 8.00
M33 Doug Gilmour/130* 6.00 15.00
M34 Jeff Hackett/130* 4.00 10.00
M35 Brian Savage/130* 4.00 10.00
M36 Saku Koivu/130* 5.00 12.00
M37 Guy Lafleur/130* 6.00 15.00
M38 Claude Lemieux/130* 4.00 10.00
M39 Patrick Poulin/130* 3.00 8.00
M40 Michael Ryder/130* 3.00 8.00
M41 Trevor Linden/130* 5.00 12.00
M42 Mats Naslund/130* 3.00 8.00
M43 Mark Recchi/130* 5.00 12.00
M44 Larry Robinson/130* 5.00 12.00
M45 Jose Theodore/130* 5.00 12.00
M46 Carey Price/130* 10.00 25.00
M47 Chris Higgins/130* 3.00 8.00
M48 Bobby Smith/130* 4.00 10.00
M49 P.K. Subban/130* 6.00 15.00
M50 Denis Savard/130* 5.00 12.00
M51 Darryl Sittler/20* 10.00 25.00
M52 Tiger Williams/20* 8.00 20.00
M53 Lanny McDonald/20* 10.00 25.00
M54 Bob Baun/20* 8.00 20.00
M55 Terry Sawchuk/20* 12.00 30.00
M56 Steve Shutt/20* 6.00 15.00
M57 Serge Savard/20* 8.00 20.00
M58 Jacques Laperriere/20* 6.00 15.00
M59 Henri Richard/20* 10.00 25.00
M60 Jean Beliveau/20* 15.00 40.00

2012-13 ITG Forever Rivals Greatest Moments

GM01 Maurice Richard 4.00 10.00
GM02 Turk Broda 2.00 5.00
GM03 Bill Barilko 1.50 4.00
GM04 Bernie Geoffrion 1.50 4.00
GM05 Rogie Vachon 2.50 6.00
GM06 Curtis Joseph 2.50 6.00

2012-13 ITG Forever Rivals Immortals

I01 Georges Vezina 2.00 5.00
I02 Howie Morenz 1.50 4.00
I03 Aurel Joliat 2.00 5.00
I04 Newsy Lalonde 1.50 4.00
I05 King Clancy 1.50 4.00
I06 Joe Primeau 1.25 3.00
I07 Busher Jackson 1.50 4.00
I08 Charlie Conacher 1.50 4.00

2012-13 ITG Forever Rivals Net Rivals

NR01 J.Bower/J.Plante 2.50 6.00
NR02 M.Palmateer/B.Larocque 2.00 5.00
NR03 T.Broda/B.Durnan 2.00 5.00
NR04 J.Reimer/C.Price 4.00 10.00
NR05 E.Belfour/C.Huet 2.00 5.00
NR06 C.Joseph/J.Theodore 2.50 6.00
NR07 H.Lumley/G.McNeil 2.00 5.00
NR08 F.Potvin/P.Roy 5.00 12.00

2012-13 ITG Forever Rivals Playoff Matchups

PM01 D.Keon/R.Vachon 2.50 6.00
PM02 J.Beliveau/R.Kelly 2.00 5.00
PM03 F.Mahovlich/C.Hodge 2.00 5.00
PM04 J.Plante/T.Horton 2.50 6.00
PM05 D.Moore/J.Bower 2.00 5.00
PM06 B.Barilko/G.McNeil 1.50 4.00
PM07 T.Kennedy/B.Durnan 2.00 5.00
PM08 F.McCool/M.Richard 4.00 10.00

2012-13 ITG Forever Rivals Post Season Battles Quad Jerseys Silver

PSB01 Lemre/Shtt/Slmng/Sittlr/85 10.00 25.00
PSB02 Lafl/Rbn/McDn/Plmtr/85 12.00 30.00
PSB03 Vchn/Blv/Swchk/Keon/85 15.00 40.00

2012-13 ITG Forever Rivals Quad Memorabilia Silver

QM01 Grbvsk/Phnf/Plek/Sbbn 12.00 30.00
QM02 Reimer/Gustv/Prce/Hlk 12.00 30.00
QM03 Josph/Belfr/Hcktt/Thdre 12.00 30.00
QM04 Gilmour/Potvn/Roy/Mull 25.00 60.00
QM05 Sundn/Grtnr/Rcchi/Kvu 12.00 30.00
QM06 Lmn/Bstr/Corsn/Chelios 12.00 30.00
QM07 Vaive/Clrk/Rbin/Nslnd 12.00 30.00
QM08 Palmtr/Will/Lemre/Crnyr 12.00 30.00
QM09 Sittlr/Slmng/Laflr/Shutt 15.00 40.00

2012-13 ITG Forever Rivals Rivalry

RI01 Fleming Mackell 1.25 3.00
RI02 Johnny Bower 2.00 5.00
RI03 Frank Mahovlich 2.00 5.00
RI04 Dave Keon 2.00 5.00
RI05 Gerry McNeil 1.25 3.00
RI06 Yvan Cournoyer 2.00 5.00
RI07 Jean Beliveau 2.00 5.00

2012-13 ITG Forever Rivals Trophy Winners Memorabilia Silver

TW01 Patrick Roy/85* 15.00 40.00
TW02 Chris Chelios/85* 6.00 15.00
TW03 Doug Gilmour/85* 8.00 20.00
TW04 Guy Lafleur/85* 8.00 20.00
TW05 Mats Naslund/85* 4.00 10.00
TW06 Saku Koivu/85* 6.00 15.00
TW07 Larry Robinson/85* 6.00 15.00
TW08 Jose Theodore/85* 6.00 15.00

2004-05 ITG Franchises Canadian

COMPLETE SET (150) 25.00 60.00
1 Dan Bouchard .20 .50
2 Phil Housley .20 .50
3 Reggie Lemelin .15 .40
4 Hakan Loob .15 .40
5 Jamie Macoun .20 .50
6 Kent Nilsson .20 .50
7 Joel Otto .20 .50
8 Jim Peplinski .20 .50
9 Paul Ranheim .20 .50
10 Mark Hunter .20 .50
11 Doug Gilmour .30 .75
12 Joe Mullen .20 .50
13 Lanny McDonald .20 .50
14 Paul Reinhart .20 .50
15 Gary Suter .15 .40
16 Guy Chouinard .20 .50
17 Grant Fuhr .40 1.00
18 Bernie Nicholls .20 .50
19 Andy Moog .25 .60
20 Esa Tikkanen .20 .50
21 Dave Semenko .20 .50
22 Mark Napier .20 .50
23 Bill Ranford .20 .50
24 Paul Coffey .25 .60
25 Glenn Anderson .20 .50
26 Kent Nilsson .20 .50
27 Jari Kurri .25 .60
28 Randy Gregg .15 .40
29 Charlie Huddy .20 .50
30 Dave Hunter .20 .50
31 Mike Krushelnyski .20 .50
32 Ed Mio .20 .50
33 Garry Unger .20 .50
34 Lee Fogolin .20 .50
35 Billy Burch .20 .50
36 Goldie Prodgers .20 .50
37 Rocket Richard .50 1.25
38 Henri Richard .25 .60
39 Jean Beliveau .30 .75
40 Jacques Plante .30 .75
41 Doug Harvey .25 .60
42 Howie Morenz .20 .50
43 Bernie Geoffrion .25 .60
44 Georges Vezina .30 .75
45 Gump Worsley .25 .60
46 Rogie Vachon .25 .60
47 John Ferguson .20 .50
48 Guy Lafleur .30 .75
49 Dickie Moore .15 .40
50 Larry Robinson .25 .60
51 Serge Savard .25 .60
52 Yvan Cournoyer .25 .60
53 Toe Blake .25 .60
54 Butch Bouchard .20 .50
55 Steve Shutt .20 .50
56 Jacques Lemaire .20 .50
57 Frank Mahovlich .25 .60
58 Georges Hainsworth .20 .50
59 Patrick Roy .60 1.50
60 Guy Lapointe .20 .50
61 Elmer Lach .20 .50
62 Jacques Laperriere .20 .50
63 Aurel Joliat .20 .50
64 Bill Durnan .20 .50
65 Nels Stewart .20 .50
66 Clint Benedict .20 .50
67 Hooley Smith .20 .50
68 Art Ross .20 .50
69 Cy Denneny .20 .50
70 Frank Finnigan .20 .50
71 Joe Malone .20 .50
72 Harry Mummery RC .20 .50
73 Andre Savard .20 .50
74 Marian Stastny .20 .50
75 Marc Tardif .20 .50
76 Peter Stastny .20 .50
77 Dan Bouchard .20 .50
78 Michel Goulet .15 .40
79 Dale Hunter .20 .50
80 Real Cloutier .15 .40
81 Robbie Ftorek .20 .50
82 Mike Hough .20 .50
83 Anton Stastny .20 .50
84 Jack Adams .20 .50
85 Reg Noble .20 .50
86 Ken Randall .20 .50
87 Red Kelly .25 .60
88 Teeder Kennedy .25 .60
89 Frank Mahovlich .25 .60
90 Dick Duff .20 .50
91 Bob Pulford .20 .50
92 Ace Bailey .20 .50
93 Sid Smith .20 .50
94 Johnny Bower .25 .60
95 Bob Nevin .20 .50
96 Bob Baun .25 .60
97 Jim McKenny .20 .50
98 Mike Palmateer .20 .50
99 Frank McCool RC .20 .50
100 Lanny McDonald .20 .50
101 Tiger Williams .15 .40
102 Darryl Sittler .30 .75
103 Borje Salming .25 .60
104 Ian Turnbull .15 .40
105 King Clancy .20 .50
106 Joe Primeau .20 .50
107 Turk Broda .20 .50
108 Howie Meeker .20 .50
109 Rick Vaive .20 .50
110 Tim Horton .25 .60
111 Wendel Clark .40 1.00
112 Doug Gilmour .30 .75
113 Bill Barilko .20 .50
114 Red Horner .20 .50
115 Babe Dye .20 .50
116 Hap Day .20 .50
117 Tiger Williams .15 .40
118 Harold Snepsts .15 .40
119 Richard Brodeur .20 .50
120 Stan Smyl .20 .50
121 Cam Neely .25 .60
122 Dennis Kearns .20 .50
123 Brian Bradley .20 .50
124 Jack McIlhargey .20 .50
125 Andre Boudrias .20 .50
126 Gary Smith .20 .50
127 Gino Odjick .15 .40
128 Kirk McLean .20 .50
129 Darcy Rota .20 .50
130 Garth Butcher .20 .50
131 Ron Delorme .20 .50
132 Thomas Gradin .20 .50
133 Dale Tallon .20 .50
134 Don Lever .20 .50
135 Bobby Hull .50 1.25
136 Laurie Boschman .20 .50
137 Bob Essensa .20 .50
138 Jimmy Mann .20 .50
139 Randy Carlyle .20 .50
140 Dale Hawerchuck .30 .75
141 Thomas Steen .25 .60
142 Darrin Shannon .20 .50
143 Doug Smail .20 .50
144 Mario Marois .20 .50
145 Morris Lukowich .20 .50
146 Jim Kyte .20 .50
147 Dave Ellet .20 .50
148 Dave Babych .20 .50
149 Tim Watters .20 .50
150 Paul MacLean .20 .50

2004-05 ITG Franchises Canadian Autographs

AM2 Andy Moog 8.00 20.00
AS2 Allan Stanley 5.00 12.00
BB2 Bobby Baun 8.00 20.00
BG Bernie Geoffrion 8.00 20.00
BH2 Bobby Hull SP 25.00 60.00
BN2 Bob Nevin 6.00 15.00
BR Bill Ranford 6.00 15.00
BS Borje Salming SP 8.00 20.00
CN2 Cam Neely SP 8.00 20.00
DB2 Dan Bouchard 6.00 15.00
DB3 Dan Bouchard 6.00 15.00
DD Dick Duff 6.00 15.00
DG2 Doug Gilmour 15.00 40.00
DK Dennis Kearns 6.00 15.00
DM2 Dickie Moore 5.00 12.00
DS2 Darryl Sittler SP 15.00 40.00
EL Elmer Lach SP 6.00 15.00
EM Ed Mio 6.00 15.00
FM2 Frank Mahovlich SP 8.00 20.00
FM3 Frank Mahovlich SP 8.00 20.00
GA Glenn Anderson 6.00 15.00
GB Garth Butcher 6.00 15.00
GF Grant Fuhr SP 20.00 50.00
GL Guy Lafleur SP 20.00 50.00
GO Gino Odjick 5.00 12.00
GS Gary Suter 5.00 12.00
GU2 Garry Unger 6.00 15.00
GW3 Gump Worsley 8.00 20.00
HM Howie Meeker 6.00 15.00
HR Henri Richard SP 8.00 20.00
HS Harold Snepsts 5.00 12.00
IT Ian Turnbull 5.00 12.00
JB Johnny Bower 8.00 20.00
JF John Ferguson 6.00 15.00
JK Jari Kurri SP 8.00 20.00
JL Jacques Laperriere 6.00 15.00
KN Kent Nilsson 6.00 15.00
LF Lee Fogolin 6.00 15.00
LM2 Lanny McDonald SP 6.00 15.00
LM3 Lanny McDonald SP 6.00 15.00
MG2 Michel Goulet 5.00 12.00
MM Mario Marois 6.00 15.00
MN Mark Napier 6.00 15.00
MP Mike Palmateer 6.00 15.00
MT Marc Tardiff 6.00 15.00
PC1 Paul Coffey SP 8.00 20.00
PH2 Phil Housley 6.00 15.00
PR2 Patrick Roy 100.00 200.00
RC2 Randy Carlyle 6.00 15.00
RD Ron Delorme 6.00 15.00
RV2 Rogie Vachon 8.00 20.00
TG Thomas Gradin 6.00 15.00
TK Teeder Kennedy 8.00 20.00
TW1 Tiger Williams 5.00 12.00
TW2 Tiger Williams SP 5.00 12.00
YC Yvan Cournoyer 8.00 20.00
ABO Andre Boudrias 6.00 15.00
ASV Andre Savard 6.00 15.00
BBO Butch Bouchard 6.00 15.00
BES Bob Essensa 6.00 15.00
BPL Bob Pulford 6.00 15.00
CHU Charlie Huddy 6.00 15.00
DBB Dave Babych 6.00 15.00
DEL Dave Ellett 6.00 15.00
DHA Dale Hawerchuk 10.00 25.00
DHU2 Dale Hunter 6.00 15.00
DLV Don Lever 6.00 15.00
DRO Darcy Rota 6.00 15.00
DSE Dave Semenko 6.00 15.00
DSH Darrin Shannon 6.00 15.00
DSM Doug Smail 6.00 15.00
DTL Dale Tallon 6.00 15.00
DVH Dave Hunter 6.00 15.00
GCH Guy Chouinard 6.00 15.00
GLP Guy Lapointe 6.00 15.00
JBE Jean Beliveau SP 40.00 100.00
JKY Jim Kyte 6.00 15.00
JLE Jacques Lemaire 6.00 15.00
JMC Jamie Macoun 6.00 15.00
JMI0 Jack McIlhargey 6.00 15.00
JMK Jim McKenny 6.00 15.00
JMN Jimmy Mann 6.00 15.00
JOT Joel Otto 6.00 15.00
JPE Jim Peplinski 6.00 15.00
KML Kirk McLean 6.00 15.00
LBH Laurie Boschman 6.00 15.00
MKR Mike Krushelnyski 6.00 15.00
MLU Morris Lukowich 6.00 15.00
MST Marian Stastny 6.00 15.00
PML Paul MacLean 6.00 15.00
PRA Paul Ranheim 6.00 15.00
PRE Paul Reinhart 6.00 15.00
RBR Richard Brodeur 6.00 15.00
RCL Real Cloutier 5.00 12.00
RFT Robbie Ftorek 6.00 15.00
RGR Randy Gregg 5.00 12.00
RHO Red Horner SP 6.00 15.00
RLM Reggie Lemelin 5.00 12.00
RVA Rick Vaive 6.00 15.00
SSH Steve Shutt 6.00 15.00
SSM Stan Smyl 6.00 15.00
SSV Serge Savard 8.00 20.00
TWA Tim Watters 6.00 15.00
WCL2 Wendel Clark 12.00 30.00

2004-05 ITG Franchises Canadian Barn Burners

GOLD/20: .5X TO 1.2X MEM/50*
BB1 Lanny McDonald 4.00 10.00
BB2 Darryl Sittler 6.00 15.00
BB3 Jean Beliveau 6.00 15.00
BB4 Rick Vaive 4.00 10.00
BB5 Paul Coffey 5.00 12.00
BB6 Henri Richard 5.00 12.00
BB7 Jacques Plante 6.00 15.00
BB8 Rocket Richard 10.00 25.00

2004-05 ITG Franchises Canadian Boxtoppers

TH1 Calgary Flames Original 2.00 5.00
TH2 Calgary Flames Horse 2.00 5.00
TH3 Calgary Flames 2.00 5.00
TH4 Edmonton Oilers Original 2.00 5.00
TH5 Edmonton Oilers 2.00 5.00
TH6 Edmonton Oilers 25th Ann. 2.00 5.00
TH7 Hamilton Tigers 2.00 5.00
TH8 Montreal Canadiens 2.00 5.00
TH9 Montreal Maroons 2.00 5.00
TH10 Montreal Wanderers 2.00 5.00
TH11 Ottawa Senators Original 2.00 5.00
TH12 Ottawa Senators 2.00 5.00
TH13 Quebec Bulldogs 2.00 5.00
TH14 Quebec Nordiques 2.00 5.00
TH15 Toronto Arenas 2.00 5.00
TH16 Toronto Maple Leafs Original 2.00 5.00
TH17 Toronto Maple Leafs 1950s 2.00 5.00
TH18 Toronto Maple Leafs 1960s 2.00 5.00
TH19 Toronto Maple Leafs 2.00 5.00
TH20 Toronto St. Patricks 2.00 5.00
TH21 Vancouver Canucks original 2.00 5.00
TH22 Vancouver Canucks 1980s 2.00 5.00
TH23 Vancouver Canucks 2.00 5.00
TH24 Winnipeg Jets 1980s 2.00 5.00
TH25 Winnipeg Jets 1990s 2.00 5.00

2004-05 ITG Franchises Canadian Double Memorabilia

GOLD/20: .5X TO 1.2X DUAL/60*
DM1 George Hainsworth 4.00 10.00
DM2 Jean Beliveau 6.00 15.00
DM3 Johnny Bower 5.00 12.00
DM4 Georges Vezina 6.00 15.00
DM5 Patrick Roy 12.00 30.00
DM6 Aurel Joliat 4.00 10.00
DM7 Jacques Plante 6.00 15.00
DM8 Howie Morenz 4.00 10.00
DM9 Gump Worsley 5.00 12.00
DM10 Guy Lafleur 6.00 15.00
DM11 Wendel Clark 8.00 20.00
DM12 Grant Fuhr 8.00 20.00
DM13 Bernie Geoffrion 5.00 12.00
DM14 Tim Horton 5.00 12.00
DM15 Frank Mahovlich 5.00 12.00
DM16 Joe Mullen 4.00 10.00
DM17 Henri Richard 5.00 12.00
DM18 Jari Kurri 5.00 12.00
DM19 Glenn Anderson 4.00 10.00
DM20 Paul Coffey 5.00 12.00
DM21 Phil Housley 4.00 10.00
DM22 Doug Gilmour 6.00 15.00

2004-05 ITG Franchises Canadian Forever Rivals

FR1 J.Bower/J.Plante 12.00 30.00
FR2 R.Kelly/J.Beliveau 12.00 30.00
FR3 G.Fuhr/M.Vernon 15.00 40.00
FR4 B.Salming/G.Lafleur 12.00 30.00
FR5 P.Coffey/J.Mullen 10.00 25.00
FR6 J.Kurri/H.Loob 10.00 25.00
FR7 D.Sittler/L.Robinson 12.00 30.00
FR8 W.Clark/P.Roy 25.00 60.00
FR9 T.Horton/H.Richard 10.00 25.00
FR10 L.McDonald/S.Shutt 8.00 20.00

2004-05 ITG Franchises Canadian Goalie Gear

GOLD/20: .5X TO 1.2X GEAR/70*
GG1 Bill Durnan 15.00 40.00
GG2 Johnny Bower 15.00 40.00
GG3 Patrick Roy 25.00 60.00
GG4 Grant Fuhr 15.00 40.00
GG5 Jacques Plante 25.00 60.00
GG6 Gump Worsley 15.00 40.00
GG7 Mike Vernon 15.00 40.00
GG8 Dan Bouchard 10.00 25.00
GG9 Bill Ranford 10.00 25.00
GG10 Richard Brodeur 10.00 25.00

2004-05 ITG Franchises Canadian Memorabilia

GOLD/20: .5X TO 1.2X BASIC MEM/70*
SM1 Jacques Plante 20.00 50.00
SM2 Henri Richard 10.00 25.00
SM3 Jean Beliveau 15.00 40.00
SM4 Larry Robinson 8.00 20.00
SM5 Patrick Roy 15.00 40.00
SM6 Paul Coffey 10.00 25.00
SM7 Grant Fuhr 10.00 25.00
SM8 Yvan Cournoyer 8.00 20.00
SM9 Lanny McDonald 8.00 20.00
SM10 Guy Lapointe 8.00 20.00
SM11 Serge Savard 8.00 20.00
SM12 Gump Worsley 10.00 25.00
SM13 Guy Lafleur 12.00 30.00
SM14 Borje Salming 10.00 25.00
SM15 Joe Mullen 8.00 20.00
SM17 Steve Shutt 8.00 20.00
SM18 Wendel Clark 10.00 25.00
SM19 Frank Mahovlich 10.00 25.00
SM21 John Ferguson 8.00 20.00
SM22 Richard Brodeur 8.00 20.00
SM23 Tim Horton 20.00 50.00
SM24 Jari Kurri 10.00 25.00
SM25 Jacques Laperriere 8.00 20.00
SM26 Newsy Lalonde 25.00 60.00
SM27 Phil Housley 8.00 20.00
SM28 Bernie Geoffrion 10.00 25.00
SM29 Aurel Joliat 20.00 50.00
SM30 Doug Gilmour 10.00 25.00
SM31 Rick Vaive 8.00 20.00
SM32 Hakan Loob 8.00 20.00

2004-05 ITG Franchises Canadian Original Sticks

GOLD/20: .6X TO 1.5X STICK/70*
OS1 Jean Beliveau 15.00 40.00
OS2 Paul Coffey 8.00 20.00
OS3 Guy Lafleur 12.50 30.00
OS4 Lanny McDonald 10.00 25.00
OS5 Guy Lapointe 6.00 15.00
OS6 Larry Robinson 6.00 15.00
OS7 Steve Shutt 6.00 15.00
OS8 Patrick Roy 15.00 40.00
OS9 Rogie Vachon 12.00 30.00
OS10 Denis Savard 10.00 25.00
OS11 Jacques Plante 15.00 40.00
OS12 Dale Hawerchuk 8.00 20.00
OS13 Phil Housley 6.00 15.00
OS14 Doug Gilmour 12.00 30.00
OS15 Jari Kurri 10.00 25.00
OS16 Glenn Anderson 6.00 15.00

2004-05 ITG Franchises Canadian Teammates

GOLD/20: .5X TO 1.2X TEAMMATE/60*
TM1 G.Hainsworth/A.Joliat 25.00 60.00
TM2 G.Anderson/J.Kurri 15.00 40.00
TM3 M.Vernon/P.Housley 12.50 30.00
TM4 J.Beliveau/J.Plante 20.00 50.00
TM5 L.McDonald/D.Sittler 12.50 30.00
TM6 G.Fuhr/P.Coffey 15.00 40.00
TM7 G.Lapointe/L.Robinson 12.50 30.00
TM8 P.Roy/D.Savard 25.00 60.00
TM9 H.Richard/G.Worsley 20.00 50.00
TM10 D.Gilmour/W.Clark 12.50 30.00

2004-05 ITG Franchises Canadian Triple Memorabilia

TM1 Patrick Roy 75.00 135.00
TM2 Maurice Richard 75.00 150.00
TM3 Guy Lafleur 50.00 100.00
TM4 Jacques Plante 40.00 80.00
TM5 Aurel Joliat 90.00 150.00
TM9 Johnny Bower 30.00 80.00
TM10 Wendel Clark 25.00 60.00

2004-05 ITG Franchises Canadian Trophy Winners

GOLD/20: .5X TO 1.2X BASIC MEM/70*
TW1 Guy Lafleur 12.50 30.00
TW2 Jacques Plante 25.00 50.00
TW3 Gump Worsley 12.50 30.00
TW4 Patrick Roy 20.00 50.00
TW5 Larry Robinson 8.00 20.00
TW6 Paul Coffey 12.50 30.00
TW7 Bill Ranford 8.00 20.00
TW8 Jean Beliveau 15.00 40.00
TW9 Doug Gilmour 12.50 30.00
TW10 Henri Richard 12.50 30.00

2004-05 ITG Franchises Update

COMPLETE SET (50) 20.00 40.00
451 Jari Kurri .40 1.00
452 Bill Quackenbush .20 .50
453 Jean Ratelle .40 1.00
454 Lionel Hitchman .20 .50
455 Terry Sawchuk .60 1.50
456 Grant Fuhr .40 1.00
457 Bill Clement .20 .50
458 Paul Coffey .40 1.00
459 Dick Irvin .20 .50
460 Pierre Pilote .40 1.00
461 Mike Karakas .20 .50
462 Tom Lysiak .20 .50
463 Andy Moog .30 .75
464 Marcel Dionne .40 1.00
465 Borje Salming .30 .75
466 Johnny Bucyk .40 1.00
467 Norm Smith .20 .50
468 Marty McSorley .20 .50
469 Dave Keon .20 .50
470 Rick MacLeish .20 .50
471 Steve Shutt .20 .50
472 Billy Smith .30 .75
473 Neal Broten .20 .50
474 Guy Carbonneau .30 .75
475 Peter Mahovlich .20 .50
476 Tony Esposito .40 1.00
477 Rod Langway .20 .50
478 Newsy Lalonde .50 1.25
479 Pat Verbeek .20 .50
480 Joe Simpson .20 .50
481 Wendel Clark .30 .75
482 Marcel Dionne .40 1.00
483 Frank Boucher .20 .50
484 Johnny Bower .40 1.00
485 Don Beaupre .20 .50
486 Brad Marsh .20 .50
487 Darryl Sittler .40 1.00
488 Barry Ashbee .20 .50
489 Michel Briere 8.00 20.00
490 Guy Lafleur .50 1.25
491 Brian Sutter .20 .50
492 Denis Savard .40 1.00
493 Terry Sawchuk .60 1.50
494 Syl Apps .20 .50
495 Marcel Pronovost .30 .75
496 Dave Keon .20 .50
497 Garth Boesch .20 .50
498 Rick Vaive .20 .50
499 Dino Ciccarelli .20 .50
500 Serge Savard .40 1.00

2004-05 ITG Franchises Update Autographs

AA Al Arbour 8.00 20.00
CK Cliff Koroll 8.00 20.00
DC2 Dino Ciccarelli 8.00 20.00
ET Esa Tikkanen 6.00 15.00
HL Hakan Loob 5.00 12.00
JG John Garrett 8.00 20.00
KW Ken Wregget 8.00 20.00
PF Pat Falloon 8.00 20.00
PV1 Pat Verbeek SP 8.00 20.00
TR Tom Reid 8.00 20.00
TS Thomas Steen 8.00 20.00
ALX Andre Lacroix 8.00 20.00
DKN1 Dave Keon Har. SP 8.00 20.00
DKN2 Dave Keon TML SP 8.00 20.00
JPA Jim Pappin 8.00 20.00
MBU Mike Bullard 8.00 20.00
PBR Pat Price 8.00 20.00
RBA Ralph Backstrom 8.00 20.00
RLY Rick Ley 8.00 20.00

2004-05 ITG Franchises Update Double Memorabilia

GOLD/20: .5X TO 1.2X BASIC MEM/60*
UDM1 Pat Lafontaine 15.00 40.00
UDM2 Bill Durnan 20.00 50.00
UDM3 Frank Brimsek 15.00 40.00
UDM4 Billy Smith 12.50 30.00

2004-05 ITG Franchises Update Goalie Gear

GOLD/20: .5X TO 1.2X MEM/60*
UGG1 Jacques Plante 25.00 50.00
UGG2 Terry Sawchuk 25.00 50.00
UGG3 Mike Richter 12.50 30.00
UGG4 John Vanbiesbrouck 12.50 30.00

2004-05 ITG Franchises Update Memorabilia

GOLD/20: .6X TO 1.5X BASIC MEM/70*
USM1 Patrick Roy 15.00 40.00
USM2 Mario Lemieux 12.00 30.00
USM3 Steve Yzerman 12.00 30.00
USM4 Frank Brimsek 10.00 25.00
USM5 Gary Dornhoefer 8.00 20.00
USM6 Rick MacLeish 8.00 20.00
USM7 Pelle Lindbergh 15.00 40.00
USM8 Marcel Dionne 8.00 20.00

2004-05 ITG Franchises Update Original Sticks

GOLD/20: .5X TO 1.2X BASIC MEM/70*
UOS1 Doug Harvey 20.00 50.00
UOS2 Dave Keon 12.00 30.00
UOS3 Bill Durnan 10.00 25.00
UOS4 Terry Sawchuk 25.00 60.00
UOS5 Wayne Cashman 8.00 20.00
UOS6 Phil Esposito 15.00 40.00
UOS7 Mark Howe 10.00 25.00
UOS8 Clark Gillies 8.00 20.00
UOS9 Howie Morenz 25.00 60.00
UOS10 Bob Davidson 8.00 20.00

2004-05 ITG Franchises Update Teammates

GOLD/20: .5X TO 1.2X TEAMMATE/60*
UTM1 G.Gilbert/G.Cheevers 12.00 30.00
UTM2 M.Dionne/C.Simmer 10.00 25.00
UTM3 D.Keon/R.Kelly 12.00 30.00

2004-05 ITG Franchises Update Trophy Winners

COMPLETE SET (4)
GOLD/20: .5X TO 1.2X BASIC MEM/70*
UTW1 Mario Lemieux 15.00 40.00
UTW2 Steve Yzerman 12.50 30.00

UTW3 Dave Keon 10.00 25.00
UTW4 John Vanbiesbrouck 8.00 20.00

2004-05 ITG Franchises US East

COMPLETE SET (150) 25.00 50.00
301 Tom Lysiak .15 .40
302 Bob MacMillan .15 .40
303 Guy Chouinard .20 .50
304 Pat Quinn .20 .50
305 Eric Vail .20 .50
306 Dan Bouchard .20 .50
307 Curt Bennett .15 .40
308 Phil Myre .15 .40
309 Milt Schmidt .15 .40
310 Woody Dumart .20 .50
311 Gerry Cheevers .25 .60
312 Brad Park .20 .50
313 Jacques Plante .30 .75
314 Johnny Bucyk .25 .60
315 Terry O'Reilly .20 .50
316 Derek Sanderson .25 .60
317 Phil Esposito .40 1.00
318 Wayne Cashman .15 .40
319 Frank Brimsek .15 .40
320 Wayne Carleton .15 .40
321 Gilles Gilbert .20 .50
322 Bronco Horvath .15 .40
323 Eddie Shore .15 .40
324 Bill Cowley .15 .40
325 Don Marcotte .15 .40
326 Cam Neely .25 .60
327 Ray Bourque .40 1.00
328 Andy Moog .25 .60
329 Pete Peeters .15 .40
330 Bobby Bauer .15 .40
331 Tiny Thompson .15 .40
332 Don Awrey .15 .40
333 Rogie Vachon .25 .60
334 Dit Clapper .15 .40
335 Rick Middleton .15 .40
336 Chuck Rayner .15 .40
337 Mel Hill .15 .40
338 Rick Martin .15 .40
339 Pat LaFontaine .15 .40
340 Sean McKenna RC .15 .40
341 Gilbert Perreault .25 .60
342 Mike Foligno .15 .40
343 Don Edwards .15 .40
344 Danny Gare .15 .40
345 Phil Housley .20 .50
346 Larry Playfair .15 .40
347 Don Luce .15 .40
348 Tim Horton .25 .60
349 Roger Crozier .15 .40
350 John Vanbiesbrouck .25 .60
351 Mike Hough .20 .50
352 Bobby Hull .50 1.25
353 Dave Babych .20 .50
354 Tiger Williams .15 .40
355 Mark Howe .25 .60
356 Mike Liut .15 .40
357 Chico Resch .15 .40
358 Bob Carpenter .20 .50
359 Doug Gilmour .30 .75
360 Chris Terreri .15 .40
361 Kirk Muller .15 .40
362 John MacLean .15 .40
363 Don Lever .20 .50
364 Bruce Driver .15 .40
365 Red Dutton .15 .40
366 Ching Johnson .15 .40
367 Roy Worters .15 .40
368 Sweeney Schriner .15 .40
369 Mike Bossy .25 .60
370 Billy Smith .20 .50
371 Denis Potvin .25 .60
372 Butch Goring .15 .40
373 Clark Gillies .25 .60
374 Bryan Trottier .25 .60
375 Chico Resch .15 .40
376 Pat LaFontaine .15 .40
377 Garry Howatt .15 .40
378 Bob Bourne .15 .40
379 Bob Nystrom .15 .40
380 J.P. Parise .15 .40
381 Edgar Laprade .15 .40
382 Nick Fotiu .15 .40
383 Rod Gilbert .15 .40
384 Ed Giacomin .25 .60
385 Brad Park .20 .50
386 Jean Ratelle .20 .50
387 John Davidson .15 .40
388 Barry Beck .15 .40
389 Gump Worsley .25 .60
390 Ron Duguay .20 .50
391 Andy Bathgate .25 .60
392 Harry Howell .15 .40
393 Phil Esposito .40 1.00
394 Bob Nevin .20 .50
395 Bill Cook .15 .40
396 Allan Stanley .15 .40
397 Bernie Geoffrion .25 .60
398 Red Garrett RC .15 .40
399 Don Marshall .15 .40
400 Ron Greschner .15 .40
401 Mike Richter .25 .60
402 Doug Harvey .25 .60
403 Don Murdoch .15 .40
404 Red Sullivan .15 .40
405 Camille Henry .15 .40
406 Terry Sawchuk .30 .75
407 Fred Shero .15 .40
408 Red Berenson .15 .40
409 Jim Neilson .15 .40
410 Vic Hadfield .15 .40
411 Bobby Clarke .40 1.00
412 Dave Schultz .20 .50
413 Joe Watson .15 .40
414 Bernie Parent .30 .75
415 Ron Hextall .25 .60
416 Reggie Leach .20 .50
417 Bill Barber .20 .50
418 Gary Dornhoefer .15 .40
419 Don Saleski .15 .40
420 Bill Clement .15 .40
421 Orest Kindrachuk .15 .40
422 Pelle Lindbergh .20 .50
423 Bobby Taylor .20 .50
424 Mark Howe .25 .60
425 Tom Bladon .20 .50
426 Doug Favell .20 .50
427 Mel Bridgman .20 .50
428 Andre Dupont .20 .50
429 Bob Kelly .15 .40
430 Tim Kerr .15 .40
431 Brad Marsh .15 .40
432 Brian Propp .20 .50
433 Rick MacLeish .20 .50
434 Paul Holmgren .20 .50
435 Keith Acton .20 .50
436 Syd Howe .20 .50
437 Brian Bradley .20 .50
438 Wendel Clark .40 1.00
439 Dino Ciccarelli .25 .60
440 Daren Puppa .20 .50
441 Larry Murphy .20 .50
442 Bob Mason RC .20 .50
443 Yvon Labre .20 .50
444 Dennis Maruk .20 .50
445 Dale Hunter .20 .50
446 Al Iafrate .20 .50
447 Rod Langway .20 .50
448 Ryan Walter .20 .50
449 Mike Palmateer .20 .50
450 Don Beaupre .20 .50

2004-05 ITG Franchises US East Autographs

AIA Al Iafrate 5.00 12.00
AADU Andre Dupont 6.00 15.00
AAB Andy Bathgate 8.00 20.00
AAM1 Andy Moog 10.00 25.00
ABBK1 Barry Beck 5.00 12.00
ABPA Bernie Parent 20.00 50.00
ABBA Bill Barber 10.00 25.00
ABCL Bill Clement 8.00 20.00
ABSM Billy Smith 12.00 30.00
ABBN Bob Bourne 5.00 12.00
ABK Bob Kelly 8.00 20.00
ABMM Bob MacMillan 5.00 12.00
ABMS Bob Mason 5.00 12.00
ABN1 Bob Nevin 10.00 25.00
ABNY Bob Nystrom 6.00 15.00
ABCA Bobby Carpenter 5.00 12.00
ABC Bobby Clarke 15.00 40.00
ABTA Bobby Taylor 6.00 15.00
ABM Brad Marsh 5.00 12.00
ABP1 Brad Park BOS SP 20.00 50.00
ABP2 Brad Park NYR SP 15.00 40.00
ABBR Brian Bradley 5.00 12.00
ABPR Brian Propp 8.00 20.00
ABHV Bronco Horvath 10.00 25.00
ABDR Bruce Driver 5.00 12.00
ABT Bryan Trottier 12.00 30.00
ABGO2 Butch Goring 5.00 12.00
ACN1 Cam Neely SP 25.00 60.00
ACR2 Chico Resch 10.00 25.00
ACR3 Chico Resch 10.00 25.00
ACT Chris Terreri 5.00 12.00
ACG Clark Gillies 8.00 20.00
ACBN Curt Bennett 5.00 12.00
ADHU1 Dale Hunter 5.00 12.00
ADB1 Dan Bouchard 10.00 25.00
ADGA Danny Gare 8.00 20.00
ADPU Daren Puppa 5.00 12.00
ADSC1 Dave Schultz 10.00 25.00
ADP Denis Potvin 8.00 20.00
ADMK1 Dennis Maruk 6.00 15.00
ADSA1 Derek Sanderson 10.00 25.00
ADC1 Dino Ciccarelli SP 10.00 25.00
ADA Don Awrey 6.00 15.00
ADBR Don Beaupre 5.00 12.00
ADE Don Edwards 8.00 20.00
ADLU Don Luce 8.00 20.00
ADMA Don Marcotte 5.00 12.00
ADMR Don Marshall 5.00 12.00
ADMU Don Murdoch 8.00 20.00
ADOS Don Saleski 6.00 15.00
ADF1 Doug Favell 6.00 15.00
AEG1 Ed Giacomin 15.00 40.00
AEV Eric Vail 5.00 12.00
AGHO Garry Howatt 5.00 12.00
AGD Gary Dornhoefer 6.00 15.00
AGC Gerry Cheevers SP 15.00 40.00
AGP Gilbert Perreault 12.00 30.00
AGG Gilles Gilbert 10.00 25.00
AHH Harry Howell 5.00 12.00
AJR Jean Ratelle 8.00 20.00
AJN Jim Neilson 5.00 12.00
AJW1 Joe Watson 5.00 12.00
AJD John Davidson 8.00 20.00
AJMA John MacLean 5.00 12.00
AJV John Vanbiesbrouck 8.00 20.00
AJBU Johnny Bucyk 8.00 20.00
AKM2 Kirk Muller 6.00 15.00
ALMU2 Larry Murphy 10.00 25.00
ALP Larry Playfair 5.00 12.00
ALA Lou Angotti 8.00 20.00
AMH Mark Howe 6.00 15.00
AMBO Mike Bossy 10.00 25.00
AMF Mike Foligno 8.00 20.00
AMHO Mike Hough 5.00 12.00
ANF Nick Fotiu 6.00 15.00
AOK Orest Kindrachuk 6.00 15.00
APL1 Pat LaFontaine BUF SP 40.00 80.00
APL2 Pat LaFontaine NYI SP 40.00 80.00
APQ Pat Quinn 8.00 20.00
APV2 Pat Verbeek 6.00 15.00
APC2 Paul Coffey SP 25.00 60.00
APHO Paul Holmgren 5.00 12.00
APPE1 Pete Peeters 8.00 20.00
APPE2 Pete Peeters 8.00 20.00
APE1 Phil Esposito BOS SP 25.00 60.00
APE2 Phil Esposito NYR SP 20.00 50.00
APH1 Phil Housley 20.00 40.00
APMY Phil Myre 8.00 20.00
ARB1 Ray Bourque SP 75.00 125.00
ARSU Red Sullivan 6.00 15.00
ARL Reggie Leach 10.00 25.00
ARM Rick MacLeish 8.00 20.00
ARMA Rick Martin 8.00 20.00
ARMI Rick Middleton 8.00 20.00
ARGI Rod Gilbert 12.00 30.00
ARLN Rod Langway 6.00 15.00
ARDU Ron Duguay 6.00 15.00
ARG Ron Greschner 5.00 12.00
ARH Ron Hextall 12.50 30.00
ARW Ryan Walter 6.00 15.00
ASMK Sean McKenna 5.00 12.00
ATO Terry O'Reilly 8.00 20.00
ATKR Tim Kerr 5.00 12.00
ATBL Tom Bladon 8.00 20.00
ATLY Tom Lysiak 5.00 12.00
AWCA Wayne Carleton 6.00 15.00
AWC Wayne Cashman 6.00 15.00
AWCL Wendel Clark SP 20.00 50.00
AYL Yvon Labre 5.00 12.00

2004-05 ITG Franchises US East Barn Burners

GOLD/20: .6X TO 1.5X BASIC JSY/50*
EBB1 Jean Ratelle 8.00 20.00
EBB2 Mike Bossy 10.00 25.00
EBB3 Denis Potvin 8.00 20.00
EBB4 Gerry Cheevers 12.50 30.00
EBB5 Reggie Leach 8.00 20.00
EBB6 Ray Bourque 15.00 40.00
EBB7 Billy Smith 8.00 20.00
EBB8 Cam Neely 20.00 50.00
EBB9 Pat LaFontaine 15.00 40.00
EBB10 Mike Richter 10.00 25.00

2004-05 ITG Franchises US East Boxtoppers

COMPLETE SET (25) 60.00 150.00
TH51 Atlanta Flames 4.00 10.00
TH52 Atlanta Thrashers 3.00 8.00
TH53 Atlanta Thrashers Alt 3.00 8.00
TH54 Boston Bruins Orig 4.00 10.00
TH55 Boston Bruins 3.00 8.00
TH56 Boston Bruins Alt 3.00 8.00
TH57 Brooklyn Americans 6.00 15.00
TH58 Buffalo Sabres Orig 3.00 8.00
TH59 Buffalo Sabres 3.00 8.00
TH60 Carolina Hurricanes 3.00 8.00
TH61 Florida Panthers 3.00 8.00
TH62 Hartford Whalers 4.00 10.00
TH63 Nashville Predators 3.00 8.00
TH64 Nashville Predators Alt 3.00 8.00
TH65 New Jersey Devils 3.00 8.00
TH66 New York Americans 6.00 15.00
TH67 New York Islanders 3.00 8.00
TH68 New York Islanders Fish 3.00 8.00
TH69 New York Rangers 3.00 8.00
TH70 New York Rangers Liberty 4.00 10.00
TH71 Philadelphia Flyers 3.00 8.00
TH72 Philadelphia Quakers 6.00 15.00
TH73 Tampa Bay Lightning 3.00 8.00
TH74 Washington Capitals Orig 3.00 8.00
TH75 Washington Capitals 3.00 8.00

2004-05 ITG Franchises US East Double Memorabilia

GOLD/20: .6X TO 1.5X MEM/60*
EDM1 Eddie Shore 12.00 30.00
EDM2 Bobby Clarke 12.50 30.00
EDM3 Gerry Cheevers 15.00 40.00
EDM4 Cam Neely 25.00 60.00
EDM5 Bernie Parent 20.00 50.00
EDM6 Tiny Thompson 20.00 50.00
EDM7 Ray Bourque 15.00 40.00
EDM8 Ron Hextall 30.00 80.00
EDM9 Ed Giacomin 15.00 40.00
EDM10 Gilles Gilbert 10.00 25.00
EDM11 Bryan Trottier 10.00 25.00
EDM12 Mike Bossy 10.00 25.00
EDM13 Gilbert Perreault 15.00 40.00
EDM14 Denis Potvin 10.00 25.00
EDM15 Bill Barber 10.00 25.00
EDM16 Terry O'Reilly 8.00 20.00
EDM17 Reggie Leach 10.00 25.00
EDM18 Bob Nystrom 10.00 25.00
EDM19 Pelle Lindbergh 25.00 60.00
EDM20 Phil Esposito 20.00 50.00
EDM21 Rick Middleton 10.00 25.00
EDM22 Mike Richter 12.50 30.00

2004-05 ITG Franchises US East Forever Rivals

GOLD/20: .5X TO 1.2X MEM/50*
EFR1 P.Esposito/B.Park 15.00 40.00
EFR2 M.Bossy/R.Middleton 12.50 30.00
EFR3 G.Perreault/B. Clarke 12.50 30.00
EFR4 C.Neely/P.LaFontaine 12.50 20.00
EFR5 G.Cheevers/B.Parent 30.00 60.00
EFR6 R.Bourque/D.Potvin 15.00 40.00

2004-05 ITG Franchises US East Goalie Gear

GOLD/20: .5X TO 1.2X GEAR/60*
EGG1 Gerry Cheevers 12.50 30.00
EGG2 Billy Smith 12.50 30.00
EGG3 Tiny Thompson 15.00 40.00
EGG4 Bernie Parent 15.00 40.00
EGG5 Pelle Lindbergh 20.00 50.00
EGG6 Ed Giacomin 20.00 50.00
EGG7 Andy Moog 12.50 30.00
EGG8 Gilles Gilbert 12.50 30.00

2004-05 ITG Franchises US East Memorabilia

GOLD/20: .5X TO 1.2X BASIC MEM/70*
ESM1 Eddie Shore 12.50 30.00
ESM2 Bobby Clarke 8.00 20.00
ESM3 Ray Bourque 12.50 30.00
ESM4 Reggie Leach 8.00 20.00
ESM5 Gerry Cheevers 12.50 30.00
ESM6 Ron Hextall 15.00 40.00
ESM7 Paul Coffey 10.00 25.00
ESM8 Cam Neely 15.00 40.00
ESM9 Gilbert Perreault 10.00 25.00
ESM10 Brad Park 8.00 20.00
ESM11 Billy Smith 8.00 20.00
ESM12 Dave Schultz 12.50 30.00
ESM13 Denis Potvin 8.00 20.00
ESM14 Bill Barber 6.00 15.00
ESM15 Tiny Thompson 12.50 30.00
ESM16 Mike Bossy 8.00 20.00
ESM17 Bryan Trottier 8.00 20.00
ESM18 Gilles Gilbert 10.00 25.00
ESM19 Phil Esposito 15.00 40.00
ESM20 Roy Worters 12.50 30.00
ESM21 Ed Giacomin 15.00 40.00
ESM22 Terry O'Reilly 8.00 20.00
ESM23 Rick Middleton 8.00 20.00
ESM24 Doug Gilmour 8.00 20.00
ESM25 Dale Hawerchuk 12.50 30.00
ESM26 Kirk McLean 8.00 20.00
ESM27 Andy Moog 10.00 25.00
ESM28 Bob Nystrom 6.00 15.00
ESM29 Bernie Parent 12.00 30.00
ESM30 Jean Ratelle 8.00 20.00
ESM31 Pat Verbeek 6.00 15.00
ESM32 John Vanbiesbrouck 10.00 25.00
ESM33 Pat LaFontaine 12.00 30.00
ESM34 Mike Richter 10.00 25.00

2004-05 ITG Franchises US East Original Sticks

GOLD/20: .6X TO 1.5X STICK/70*
EOS1 Cam Neely 10.00 25.00
EOS2 Larry Murphy 8.00 20.00
EOS3 Bobby Clarke 8.00 20.00
EOS4 Ron Duguay 6.00 15.00
EOS5 Phil Esposito 12.50 30.00
EOS6 Vic Hadfield 6.00 15.00
EOS7 Reggie Leach 6.00 15.00
EOS8 Pelle Lindbergh 20.00 50.00
EOS9 Ray Bourque 12.50 30.00
EOS10 Bob Nystrom 6.00 15.00
EOS11 Terry O'Reilly 6.00 15.00
EOS12 Denis Potvin 6.00 15.00
EOS13 Bill Barber 8.00 20.00
EOS14 Ed Giacomin 15.00 40.00
EOS15 Ron Hextall 15.00 40.00
EOS16 Bernie Parent 12.50 30.00
EOS17 Gerry Cheevers 10.00 25.00
EOS18 Johnny Bucyk 8.00 20.00
EOS19 Rick Middleton 8.00 20.00
EOS20 John Davidson 6.00 15.00

2004-05 ITG Franchises US East Teammates

GOLD/20: .6X TO 1.5X BASIC JSY/60
ETM1 E.Shore/T.Thompson 25.00 60.00
ETM2 M.Bossy/B.Trottier 15.00 40.00
ETM3 B.Clarke/B.Barber 12.50 30.00
ETM4 R.Bourque/C.Neely 20.00 50.00
ETM5 B.Park/R.Middleton 12.50 30.00
ETM6 R.Leach/D.Schultz 15.00 40.00
ETM7 B.Nystrom/D.Potvin 12.50 30.00
ETM8 G.Cheevers/T.O'Reilly 12.50 30.00

2004-05 ITG Franchises US East Triple Memorabilia

ETM1 Gerry Cheevers 30.00 80.00
ETM3 Eddie Shore 40.00 80.00
ETM4 Ray Bourque 40.00 100.00
ETM5 Cam Neely 40.00 100.00
ETM6 Ron Hextall 40.00 80.00
ETM7 Ed Giacomin 40.00 80.00

2004-05 ITG Franchises US East Trophy Winners

ETW1 Eddie Shore 15.00 40.00
ETW2 Bobby Clarke 8.00 20.00
ETW3 Mike Bossy 8.00 20.00
ETW4 Bryan Trottier 8.00 20.00
ETW5 Ray Bourque 15.00 40.00
ETW6 Reggie Leach 8.00 20.00
ETW7 Ron Hextall 20.00 50.00
ETW8 Denis Potvin 8.00 20.00
ETW9 Bernie Parent 12.00 30.00
ETW10 Pelle Lindbergh 15.00 40.00

2004-05 ITG Franchises US West

COMPLETE SET (150) 20.00 40.00
151 Guy Hebert .30 .75
152 Wayne Carleton .20 .50
153 Gary Sabourin .20 .50
154 Gilles Meloche .30 .75
155 Gary Smith .30 .75
156 Bob Stewart .20 .50
157 Reggie Leach .20 .50
158 Glenn Hall .40 1.00
159 Bobby Hull .60 1.50
160 Dennis Hull .30 .75
161 Stan Mikita .50 1.25
162 Bill White .20 .50
163 Tony Esposito .50 1.25
164 Pat Stapleton .20 .50
165 Elmer Vasko .20 .50
166 Bill Mosienko .40 1.00
167 Michel Goulet .30 .75
168 Dirk Graham .20 .50
169 Doug Bentley .20 .50
170 Max Bentley .20 .50
171 Phil Esposito .75 2.00
172 Charlie Gardiner .30 .75
173 Lou Angotti .20 .50
174 Denis Savard .40 1.00
175 Murray Bannerman .30 .75
176 Cliff Koroll .20 .50
177 Johnny Gottselig .20 .50
178 Al MacAdam .20 .50
179 Dennis Maruk .20 .50
180 Greg Smith .20 .50
181 Dave Gardner .20 .50
182 Gilles Meloche .20 .50
183 Patrick Roy .75 2.00
184 Ray Bourque .60 1.50
185 Barry Beck .20 .50
186 Chico Resch .30 .75
187 Joe Watson .20 .50
188 Wilf Paiement .20 .50
189 Doug Favell .20 .50
190 Lanny McDonald .30 .75
191 Bob MacMillan .20 .50
192 Jack Valiquette .20 .50
193 Guy Carbonneau .30 .75
194 Kirk Muller .20 .50
195 Neal Broten .20 .50
196 Craig Ludwig .20 .50
197 Frank Foyston .50 1.25
198 Carson Cooper .20 .50
199 Ebbie Goodfellow .30 .75
200 Herb Lewis .20 .50
201 Frank Mahovlich .40 1.00
202 Peter Mahovlich .20 .50
203 Ted Lindsay .40 1.00
204 Red Kelly .40 1.00
205 Ed Giacomin .30 .75
206 Roger Crozier .30 .75
207 Henry Boucha .20 .50
208 Reed Larson .20 .50
209 Vladimir Konstantinov .20 .50
210 Steve Yzerman .75 2.00
211 Glenn Hall .40 1.00
212 Sid Abel .40 1.00
213 Terry Sawchuk .50 1.25
214 Alex Delvecchio .40 1.00
215 Mud Bruneteau .20 .50
216 Mark Howe .20 .50
217 Harry Lumley .30 .75
218 Bruce MacGregor .20 .50
219 Jack Stewart .20 .50
220 Darryl Sittler .40 1.00
221 John Ogrodnick .20 .50
222 Norm Ullman .20 .50
223 Alex Faulkner .20 .50
224 Marcel Pronovost .30 .75
225 Joe Kocur .20 .50
226 Wilf Paiement .20 .50
227 Denis Herron .30 .75
228 Henry Boucha .20 .50
229 Gary Croteau .20 .50
230 Marcel Dionne .40 1.00
231 Charlie Simmer .20 .50
232 Dave Taylor .20 .50
233 Terry Sawchuk .50 1.25
234 Grant Fuhr .40 1.00
235 Rogie Vachon .40 1.00
236 Mike Murphy .20 .50
237 Bob Pulford .30 .75
238 Butch Goring .30 .75
239 Larry Robinson .30 .75
240 Jari Kurri .40 1.00
241 Bernie Nicholls .20 .50
242 Larry Murphy .20 .50
243 Bill Masterton RC 1.25 3.00
244 Bobby Smith .20 .50
245 J.P. Parise .20 .50
246 Gump Worsley .40 1.00
247 Cesare Maniago .30 .75
248 Keith Acton .20 .50
249 Fred Barrett .20 .50
250 Brian Bellows .20 .50
251 Don Beaupre .20 .50
252 Dino Ciccarelli .30 .75
253 Lou Nanne .20 .50
254 Dave Gagner .20 .50
255 Bill Goldsworthy .20 .50
256 Danny Grant .20 .50
257 Craig Hartsburg .20 .50
258 Basil McRae .20 .50
259 Bob Baun .30 .75
260 Bill Hicke .20 .50
261 Carol Vadnais .20 .50
262 Ted Hampson .20 .50
263 Charlie Hodge .20 .50
264 Kent Dougs .20 .50
265 Harry Howell .20 .50
266 Darrin Shannon .20 .50
267 Mario Lemieux 1.00 2.50
268 Greg Malone .20 .50
269 Rick Kehoe .20 .50
270 Les Binkley .30 .75
271 Randy Carlyle .20 .50
272 Lowell MacDonald .20 .50
273 Paul Coffey .40 1.00
274 Kevin Stevens .20 .50
275 Syl Apps Jr. .20 .50
276 Dave Schultz .20 .50
277 Pierre Larouche .20 .50
278 Tim Horton .40 1.00
279 Mike Bullard .20 .50
280 Lionel Conacher .20 .50
281 Odie Cleghorn .20 .50
282 Roy Worters .30 .75
283 Red Berenson .20 .50
284 Mark Hunter .20 .50
285 Glenn Hall .40 1.00
286 Dickie Moore .40 1.00
287 Derek Sanderson .20 .50
288 Wayne Babych .20 .50
289 Bernie Federko .30 .75
290 Doug Harvey .30 .75
291 Jacques Plante .50 1.25
292 Garry Unger .20 .50
293 Doug Gilmour .30 .75
294 Joe Mullen .30 .75
295 Mike Liut .30 .75
296 Frank Finnigan .20 .50
297 Syd Howe .20 .50
298 Brian Hayward .20 .50
299 Kelly Kisio .20 .50
300 Pat Falloon .20 .50

2004-05 ITG Franchises US West Autographs

AAMA Al MacAdam 8.00 20.00
AAD Alex Delvecchio SP 20.00 50.00
AAF Alex Faulkner 15.00 40.00
ABBK2 Barry Beck 5.00 12.00
ABMC Basil McRae 5.00 12.00
ABF Bernie Federko 8.00 20.00
ABNI Bernie Nicholls 5.00 12.00
ABHI Bill Hicke 5.00 12.00
ABW Bill White 5.00 12.00
ABST Bob Stewart 5.00 12.00
ABB1 Bobby Baun 12.00 30.00
ABH1 Bobby Hull SP 40.00 80.00
ABSH Bobby Smith 6.00 15.00
ABBE Brian Bellows 5.00 12.00
ABHA Brian Hayward 6.00 15.00
ABMG Bruce MacGregor 5.00 12.00
ABGO1 Butch Goring 6.00 15.00
ACV Carol Vadnais 8.00 20.00
ACM Cesare Maniago 8.00 20.00
ACH Charlie Hodge 8.00 20.00
ACS Charlie Simmer 5.00 12.00
ACR1 Chico Resch 8.00 20.00
ACHA Craig Hartsburg 5.00 12.00
ACLU Craig Ludwig 5.00 12.00
ADGR Danny Grant 5.00 12.00
ADS1 Darryl Sittler 20.00 50.00
ADGG Dave Gagner 5.00 12.00
ADVG Dave Gardner 6.00 15.00
ADTA Dave Taylor 6.00 15.00
ADHE Denis Herron 5.00 12.00
ADSV Denis Savard 15.00 40.00
ADH Dennis Hull 10.00 25.00
ADMK2 Dennis Maruk 8.00 20.00
ADM1 Dickie Moore 15.00 40.00
ADGH Dirk Graham 5.00 12.00
ADF1 Doug Favell 5.00 12.00
ADG1 Doug Gilmour SP 20.00 50.00
AEG2 Ed Giacomin SP 30.00 80.00
AFM1 Frank Mahovlich SP 30.00 80.00
AFB Fred Barrett 5.00 12.00
AGU Garry Unger 5.00 12.00
AGCR Gary Croteau 5.00 12.00
AGSB Gary Sabourin 5.00 12.00
AGAS Gary Smith 12.00 30.00
AGME1 Gilles Meloche 8.00 20.00
AGME2 Gilles Meloche 8.00 20.00
AGH3 Glenn Hall SP 15.00 40.00
AGH2 Glenn Hall SP 20.00 50.00
AGH1 Glenn Hall SP 20.00 50.00
AGMA Greg Malone 5.00 12.00
AGRS Greg Smith 5.00 12.00
AGCA Guy Carbonneau 5.00 12.00
AGHE Guy Hebert 10.00 25.00
AHB Henry Boucha 8.00 20.00
AJPP J.P. Parise 6.00 15.00
AJVA Jack Valiquette 5.00 12.00
AJM2 Joe Mullen 10.00 25.00
AJKO Joey Kocur 6.00 15.00
AJOG John Ogrodnick 5.00 12.00
AKA Keith Acton 5.00 12.00
AKK Kelly Kisio 5.00 12.00
AKD Kent Douglas 5.00 12.00
AKS Kevin Stevens 8.00 20.00
AKM1 Kirk Muller 8.00 20.00
ALM1 Lanny McDonald SP 20.00 50.00
ALMU1 Larry Murphy 8.00 20.00
ALR1 Larry Robinson 12.00 30.00
ALB Les Binkley 10.00 25.00
ALN Lou Nanne 5.00 12.00
ALMD Lowell MacDonald 8.00 20.00
AMD Marcel Dionne SP 15.00 40.00
AMPR Marcel Pronovost 10.00 25.00
AMLE Mario Lemieux 75.00 150.00
AMHU Mark Hunter 8.00 20.00
AMG1 Michel Goulet 8.00 20.00
AML Mike Liut 8.00 20.00
AMIM Mike Murphy 5.00 12.00
AMBN Murray Bannerman 10.00 25.00
ANB Neal Broten 5.00 12.00
ANU Norm Ullman 6.00 15.00
APS Pat Stapleton 10.00 25.00
APR1 Patrick Roy SP 100.00 200.00
APC3 Paul Coffey SP 40.00 100.00
APE3 Phil Esposito SP 30.00 80.00
APLA Pierre Larouche 5.00 12.00
ARC1 Randy Carlyle 8.00 20.00
ARB2 Ray Bourque SP 40.00 80.00
ARBE Red Berenson 6.00 15.00
ARK Red Kelly 15.00 40.00
ARLA Reed Larson 5.00 12.00
ARKE Rick Kehoe 5.00 12.00
ARV1 Rogie Vachon 15.00 30.00
ASM Stan Mikita SP 15.00 40.00
ASY Steve Yzerman SP 75.00 150.00
ASA Syl Apps Jr 6.00 15.00
ATHA Ted Hampson 5.00 12.00
ATL Ted Lindsay SP 20.00 40.00
ATE Tony Esposito SP 25.00 50.00
AWB Wayne Babych 8.00 20.00
AWP1 Wilf Paiement 5.00 12.00
AWP2 Wilf Paiement 8.00 20.00

2004-05 ITG Franchises US West Barn Burners

GOLD/20: .5X TO 1.2X BASIC JSY/70*
WBB1 Mario Lemieux 20.00 50.00
WBB2 Bill Mosienko 10.00 25.00
WBB3 Ray Bourque 15.00 40.00
WBB4 Garry Unger 10.00 25.00
WBB5 Patrick Roy 15.00 40.00
WBB6 Marcel Dionne 10.00 25.00
WBB7 Ted Lindsay 12.50 30.00
WBB8 Bobby Hull 12.50 30.00
WBB9 Steve Yzerman 15.00 40.00
WBB10 Glenn Hall 12.50 30.00

2004-05 ITG Franchises US West Boxtoppers

COMPLETE SET (25) 60.00 150.00
TH26 Mighty Ducks of Anaheim 3.00 8.00
TH27 California Golden Seals 4.00 10.00
TH28 Chicago Blackhawks/1930's 4.00 10.00
TH29 Chicago Blackhawks 3.00 8.00
TH30 Cleveland Barons 4.00 10.00
TH31 Colorado Avalanche 3.00 8.00
TH32 Colorado Rockies 6.00 15.00
TH33 Columbus Blue Jackets 3.00 8.00
TH34 Dallas Stars 3.00 8.00
TH35 Detroit Cougars 5.00 12.00
TH36 Detroit Falcons 6.00 15.00
TH37 Detroit Red Wings 3.00 8.00
TH38 Kansas City Scouts 4.00 10.00
TH39 LA Kings Original 3.00 8.00
TH40 Los Angeles Kings 3.00 8.00
TH41 Minnesota North Stars 3.00 8.00
TH42 Minnesota Wild 3.00 8.00
TH43 Oakland Seals 4.00 10.00
TH44 Phoenix Coyotes 3.00 8.00
TH45 Pittsburgh Penguins Original 3.00 8.00
TH46 Pittsburgh Penguins 3.00 8.00
TH47 Pittsburgh Pirates 3.00 8.00
TH48 St. Louis Blues 3.00 8.00
TH49 St. Louis Eagles 5.00 12.00
TH50 San Jose Sharks 3.00 8.00

2004-05 ITG Franchises US West Double Memorabilia

GOLD/20: .5X TO 1.2X BASIC JSY/60*
WDM1 Bill Mosienko 15.00 40.00
WDM2 Harry Lumley 15.00 40.00
WDM3 Dino Ciccarelli 12.50 30.00
WDM4 Marcel Dionne 12.50 30.00
WDM5 Frank Brimsek 10.00 25.00
WDM6 Patrick Roy 20.00 50.00
WDM7 Ray Bourque 12.50 30.00
WDM8 Glenn Hall 15.00 40.00
WDM9 Jari Kurri 12.50 30.00
WDM10 Mario Lemieux 25.00 60.00
WDM11 Stan Mikita 12.50 30.00
WDM12 Bobby Hull 12.50 30.00
WDM13 Steve Yzerman 20.00 50.00
WDM14 Tony Esposito 12.50 30.00
WDM15 Terry Sawchuk 25.00 60.00
WDM16 Norm Ullman 12.50 30.00
WDM17 Garry Unger 12.50 30.00
WDM18 Michel Goulet 10.00 25.00
WDM19 Roger Crozier 10.00 25.00

2004-05 ITG Franchises US West Forever Rivals

GOLD/20: .5X TO 1.2X DUAL/50*
WFR1 P.Roy/S.Yzerman 25.00 60.00
WFR2 B.Mosienko/S.Abel 12.50 30.00
WFR3 T.Lindsay/H.Lumley 15.00 40.00
WFR4 A.Delvecchio/S.Mikita 20.00 50.00
WFR5 B.Hull/T.Sawchuk 25.00 60.00

2004-05 ITG Franchises US West Goalie Gear

GOLD/20: .5X TO 1.2X GEAR/60*
WGG1 Roger Crozier 10.00 25.00
WGG2 Tony Esposito 12.50 30.00
WGG3 Charlie Gardiner 10.00 25.00
WGG4 Patrick Roy 15.00 40.00
WGG5 Frank Brimsek 12.50 30.00
WGG6 Glenn Hall 12.50 30.00

2004-05 ITG Franchises US West Memorabilia

WSM1 Bill Mosienko 10.00 25.00
WSM2 Roger Crozier 8.00 20.00
WSM3 Ted Lindsay 12.00 30.00
WSM4 Harry Lumley 10.00 25.00
WSM5 Dino Ciccarelli 8.00 20.00
WSM6 Alex Delvecchio 8.00 20.00
WSM7 Marcel Dionne 8.00 20.00
WSM8 Frank Brimsek 10.00 25.00
WSM9 Patrick Roy 15.00 40.00
WSM10 Ray Bourque 12.50 30.00
WSM11 Charlie Gardiner 12.00 30.00
WSM12 Glenn Hall 10.00 25.00
WSM13 Jari Kurri 12.50 30.00
WSM14 Mario Lemieux 12.50 30.00
WSM15 Stan Mikita 8.00 20.00
WSM16 Sid Abel 8.00 20.00
WSM17 Bobby Hull 12.50 30.00
WSM18 Craig Hartsburg 8.00 20.00
WSM19 Paul Coffey 12.50 30.00
WSM20 Grant Fuhr 10.00 25.00
WSM21 Steve Yzerman 12.50 30.00
WSM22 Tony Esposito 10.00 25.00
WSM23 Bill Gadsby 8.00 20.00
WSM24 Michel Goulet 8.00 20.00
WSM25 Dennis Hull 8.00 20.00
WSM26 Terry Sawchuk 15.00 40.00
WSM27 Norm Ullman 8.00 20.00
WSM28 Steve Yzerman 12.50 30.00
WSM29 Patrick Roy 12.00 30.00
WSM30 Mario Lemieux 15.00 40.00
WSM31 Garry Unger 8.00 20.00
WSM32 Larry Murphy 8.00 20.00
WSM33 Mike Vernon 12.50 30.00

2004-05 ITG Franchises US West Original Sticks

GOLD/20: .5X TO 1.2X STICK/70*
WOS1 Patrick Roy 15.00 40.00
WOS2 Harry Lumley 10.00 25.00
WOS3 Steve Yzerman 12.50 30.00
WOS4 Glenn Hall 8.00 20.00
WOS5 Jari Kurri 10.00 25.00
WOS6 Garry Unger 6.00 15.00
WOS7 Stan Mikita 6.00 15.00
WOS8 Ray Bourque 12.50 30.00
WOS9 Roger Crozier 6.00 15.00
WOS10 Marcel Dionne 6.00 15.00
WOS11 Tony Esposito 8.00 20.00
WOS12 Denis Savard 6.00 15.00
WOS13 Mario Lemieux 15.00 40.00
WOS14 Cesare Maniago 6.00 15.00
WOS15 Charlie Simmer 6.00 15.00

2004-05 ITG Franchises US West Teammates

GOLD/20: .5X TO 1.2X TEAMMATE/60*
WTM1 S.Abel/T.Lindsay 20.00 50.00
WTM2 S.Mikita/B.Hull 15.00 40.00
WTM3 G.Unger/G.Hall 12.50 30.00
WTM4 P.Roy/R.Bourque 20.00 50.00
WTM5 M.Lemieux/P.Coffey 20.00 50.00
WTM6 B.Gadsby/N.Ullman 12.50 30.00
WTM7 M.Goulet/D.Savard 12.50 30.00
WTM8 S.Yzerman/D.Ciccarelli 20.00 50.00
WTM9 T.Esposito/D.Hull 12.50 30.00
WTM10 T.Sawchuk/A.Delvecchio 20.00 50.00

2004-05 ITG Franchises US West Triple Memorabilia

WTM1 Roger Crozier 25.00 50.00
WTM3 Marcel Dionne 30.00 60.00
WTM4 Patrick Roy 60.00 120.00
WTM5 Ray Bourque 30.00 60.00
WTM6 Glenn Hall 40.00 80.00
WTM7 Steve Yzerman 50.00 100.00
WTM8 Mario Lemieux 60.00 120.00
WTM9 Stan Mikita 40.00 80.00
WTM10 Tony Esposito 30.00 60.00

2004-05 ITG Franchises US West Trophy Winners

GOLD/20: .5X TO 1.2X JSY/70*
WTW1 Stan Mikita 8.00 20.00
WTW2 Mario Lemieux 12.50 30.00
WTW3 Bobby Hull 10.00 25.00
WTW4 Ted Lindsay 10.00 25.00
WTW5 Marcel Dionne 8.00 20.00
WTW6 Roger Crozier 8.00 20.00
WTW7 Glenn Hall 10.00 25.00
WTW8 Patrick Roy 15.00 40.00
WTW9 Steve Yzerman 12.50 30.00
WTW10 Charlie Gardiner 8.00 20.00

2006 ITG Going For Gold Women's National Team

COMPLETE SET (25) 4.00 10.00
1 Charline Labonte .40 1.00
2 Kim St. Pierre .40 1.00
3 Gillian Ferrari .20 .50
4 Becky Kellar .20 .50

5 Carla MacLeod .20 .50
6 Caroline Ouellette .20 .50
7 Cheryl Pounder .20 .50
8 Colleen Sostorics .20 .50
9 Meghan Agosta .20 .50
10 Gillian Apps .20 .50
11 Jennifer Botterill .20 .50
12 Cassie Campbell .40 1.00
13 Danielle Goyette .20 .50
14 Jayna Hefford .40 1.00
15 Gina Kingsbury .20 .50
16 Cherie Piper .20 .50
17 Vicky Sunohara .20 .50
18 Sarah Vaillancourt .20 .50
19 Katie Weatherston .20 .50
20 Hayley Wickenheiser .75 2.00
21 Sami Jo Small .40 1.00
22 Delaney Collins .20 .50
23 France St. Louis .20 .50
24 Stacy Wilson .20 .50
25 Checklist .02 .10

2006 ITG Going For Gold Women's National Team Autographs

AA Meghan Agosta 10.00 25.00
AAP Gillian Apps 15.00 40.00
AB Jennifer Botterill 10.00 25.00
AC Cassie Campbell 25.00 60.00
ACO Delaney Collins 10.00 25.00
AF Gillian Ferrari 10.00 25.00
AG Danielle Goyette 10.00 25.00
AH Jayna Hefford 15.00 40.00
AK Becky Kellar 10.00 25.00
AKI Gina Kingsbury 10.00 25.00
AL Charline Labonte 15.00 40.00
AM Carla MacLeod 10.00 25.00
AO Caroline Ouellette 10.00 25.00
AP Cherie Piper 10.00 25.00
APO Cheryl Pounder 10.00 25.00
AS Colleen Sostorics 10.00 25.00
ASM Sami Jo Small 15.00 40.00
AST Kim St. Pierre 15.00 40.00
ASTL France St. Louis 10.00 25.00
ASU Vicky Sunohara 10.00 25.00
AV Sarah Vaillancourt 10.00 25.00
AW Katie Weatherston 10.00 25.00
AWI Hayley Wickenheiser 25.00 60.00
AWIL Stacy Wilson 10.00 25.00

2006 ITG Going For Gold Women's National Team Jerseys

GUJ01 Charline Labonte 15.00 40.00
GUJ02 Kim St. Pierre 12.00 30.00
GUJ03 Gillian Ferrari 10.00 25.00
GUJ04 Becky Kellar 10.00 25.00
GUJ05 Carla MacLeod 10.00 25.00
GUJ06 Caroline Ouellette 10.00 25.00
GUJ07 Cheryl Pounder 10.00 25.00
GUJ08 Colleen Sostorics 10.00 25.00
GUJ09 Meghan Agosta 10.00 25.00
GUJ10 Gillian Apps 10.00 25.00
GUJ11 Jennifer Botterill 10.00 25.00
GUJ12 Cassie Campbell 20.00 50.00
GUJ13 Danielle Goyette 10.00 25.00
GUJ14 Jayna Hefford 15.00 40.00
GUJ15 Gina Kingsbury 10.00 25.00
GUJ16 Cherie Piper 10.00 25.00
GUJ17 Vicky Sunohara 10.00 25.00
GUJ18 Sarah Vaillancourt 10.00 25.00
GUJ19 Katie Weatherston 10.00 25.00
GUJ20 Hayley Wickenheiser 15.00 40.00
GUJ21 Sami Jo Small 15.00 40.00
GUJ22 Delaney Collins 10.00 25.00

2007 ITG Going For Gold World Juniors

COMPLETE SET (30) 10.00 25.00
1 Carey Price 2.00 5.00
2 Leland Irving .40 1.00
3 Karl Alzner .30 .75
4 Ryan Parent .20 .50
5 Kristopher Letang .30 .75
6 Luc Bourdon .30 .75
7 Kris Russell .20 .50
8 Marc Staal .30 .75
9 Cody Franson .20 .50
10 Steve Downie .40 1.00
11 Andrew Cogliano .30 .75
12 Marc-Andre ClichÃ© .20 .50
13 Kenndal McArdle .20 .50
14 Darren Helm .30 .75
15 Brad Marchand .20 .50
16 James Neal .30 .75
17 Bryan Little .30 .75
18 Daniel Bertram .20 .50
19 Ryan O'Marra .20 .50
20 Tom Pyatt .20 .50
21 Jonathan Toews 1.25 3.00
22 Sam Gagner .75 2.00
23 Eric Lindros .40 1.00
24 Roberto Luongo .60 1.50
25 Jason Spezza .40 1.00
26 Dion Phaneuf .40 1.00
27 Marc-Andre Fleury .60 1.50
28 Joe Thornton .60 1.50
29 Justin Pogge .40 1.00
30 Checklist .02 .10

2007 ITG Going For Gold World Juniors Autographs

1 Carey Price 40.00 80.00
2 Leland Irving 15.00 40.00
3 Karl Alzner 10.00 25.00
4 Ryan Parent 10.00 25.00
5 Kristopher Letang 10.00 25.00
6 Luc Bourdon 10.00 25.00
7 Kris Russell 8.00 20.00
8 Marc Staal 8.00 20.00
9 Cody Franson 6.00 15.00
10 Steve Downie 12.00 30.00
11 Andrew Cogliano 8.00 20.00
12 Marc-Andre Cliche 6.00 15.00
13 Kenndal McArdle 8.00 20.00
14 Darren Helm 8.00 20.00
15 Brad Marchand 6.00 15.00
16 James Neal 8.00 20.00
17 Bryan Little 8.00 20.00
18 Daniel Bertram 6.00 15.00
19 Ryan O'Marra 6.00 15.00
20 Tom Pyatt 6.00 15.00
21 Jonathan Toews 20.00 50.00
22 Sam Gagner 20.00 50.00
23 Eric Lindros 10.00 25.00
24 Roberto Luongo 15.00 40.00
25 Jason Spezza 10.00 25.00
26 Dion Phaneuf 10.00 25.00
27 Marc-Andre Fleury 15.00 40.00
28 Joe Thornton 12.00 30.00
29 Justin Pogge 12.00 30.00

2007 ITG Going For Gold World Juniors Emblems

GUE1 Carey Price 30.00 80.00
GUE2 Leland Irving 25.00 60.00
GUE3 Karl Alzner 20.00 50.00
GUE4 Ryan Parent 20.00 50.00
GUE5 Kristopher Letang 15.00 40.00
GUE6 Luc Bourdon 20.00 50.00
GUE7 Kris Russell 20.00 50.00
GUE8 Marc Staal 15.00 40.00
GUE9 Cody Franson 15.00 40.00
GUE10 Steve Downie 25.00 60.00
GUE11 Andrew Cogliano 25.00 60.00
GUE12 Marc-Andre Cliche 15.00 40.00
GUE13 Kenndal McArdle 15.00 40.00
GUE14 Darren Helm 15.00 40.00
GUE15 Brad Marchand 15.00 40.00
GUE16 James Neal 25.00 50.00
GUE17 Bryan Little 15.00 40.00
GUE18 Daniel Bertram 15.00 40.00
GUE19 Ryan O'Marra 15.00 40.00
GUE20 Tom Pyatt 15.00 40.00
GUE21 Jonathan Toews 30.00 80.00
GUE22 Sam Gagner 25.00 60.00

2007 ITG Going For Gold World Juniors Jerseys

GUJ1 Carey Price 20.00 50.00
GUJ2 Leland Irving 12.00 30.00
GUJ3 Karl Alzner 10.00 25.00
GUJ4 Ryan Parent 8.00 20.00
GUJ5 Kristopher Letang 8.00 20.00
GUJ6 Luc Bourdon 10.00 25.00
GUJ7 Kris Russell 8.00 20.00
GUJ8 Marc Staal 8.00 20.00
GUJ9 Cody Franson 8.00 20.00
GUJ10 Steve Downie 10.00 25.00
GUJ11 Andrew Cogliano 10.00 25.00
GUJ12 Marc-Andre Cliche 8.00 20.00
GUJ13 Kenndal McArdle 8.00 20.00
GUJ14 Darren Helm 8.00 20.00
GUJ15 Brad Marchand 8.00 20.00
GUJ16 James Neal 10.00 25.00
GUJ17 Bryan Little 10.00 25.00
GUJ18 Daniel Bertram 8.00 20.00
GUJ19 Ryan O'Marra 8.00 20.00
GUJ20 Tom Pyatt 8.00 20.00
GUJ21 Jonathan Toews 12.00 30.00
GUJ22 Sam Gagner 12.00 30.00

2007 ITG Going For Gold World Juniors Numbers

GUN1 Carey Price 30.00 80.00
GUN2 Leland Irving 25.00 60.00
GUN3 Karl Alzner 20.00 50.00
GUN4 Ryan Parent 20.00 50.00
GUN5 Kristopher Letang 15.00 40.00
GUN6 Luc Bourdon 20.00 50.00
GUN7 Kris Russell 20.00 50.00
GUN8 Marc Staal 15.00 40.00
GUN9 Cody Franson 15.00 40.00
GUN10 Steve Downie 25.00 60.00
GUN11 Andrew Cogliano 20.00 50.00
GUN12 Marc-Andre Cliche 15.00 40.00
GUN13 Kenndal McArdle 15.00 40.00
GUN14 Darren Helm 15.00 40.00
GUN15 Brad Marchand 15.00 40.00
GUN16 James Neal 25.00 50.00
GUN17 Bryan Little 15.00 40.00
GUN18 Daniel Bertram 15.00 40.00
GUN19 Ryan O'Marra 15.00 40.00
GUN20 Tom Pyatt 15.00 40.00
GUN21 Jonathan Toews 30.00 80.00
GUN22 Sam Gagner 25.00 60.00

2004-05 ITG Heroes and Prospects

1 Cory Pecker .15 .40
2 Hannu Toivonen .25 .60
3 Duncan Keith .25 .60
4 Jiri Novotny .15 .40
5 Carlo Colaiacovo .15 .40
6 Igor Knyazev .15 .40
7 Pascal Leclaire .20 .50
8 Brad Boyes .25 .60
9 Duncan Milroy .15 .40
10 Jeff Woywitka .15 .40
11 Peter Budaj .25 .60
12 Timofei Shishkanov .15 .40
13 Brandon Nolan .15 .40
14 Denis Grebeshkov .15 .40
15 Danny Groulx .15 .40
16 Martin Kariya .25 .60
17 Greg Watson .15 .40
18 Tomas Kopecky .15 .40
19 Petr Taticek .15 .40
20 Filip Novak .15 .40
21 Matt Foy .15 .40
22 Adam Hauser .15 .40
23 Yanick Lehoux .15 .40
24 Kari Lehtonen .30 .75
25 Marcel Goc .25 .60
26 Scottie Upshall .15 .40
27 David LeNeveu .20 .50
28 Kiel McLeod .15 .40
29 Jean-Marc Pelletier .20 .50
30 Colby Armstrong .20 .50
31 Adrian Foster .15 .40
32 Victor Uchevatov .15 .40
33 Jay McClement .15 .40
34 Marc-Andre Fleury .50 1.25
35 Kirill Koltsov .15 .40
36 Alexandre Giroux .15 .40
37 Rastislav Stana .15 .40
38 Ryan Miller .25 .60
39 Mike Glumac .15 .40
40 Chris Kunitz .30 .75
41 Martin Podlesak .15 .40
42 Michel Ouellet .25 .60
43 Ryan Kesler .25 .60
44 Garrett Stafford .15 .40
45 Ray Emery .25 .60
46 Fedor Tyutin .15 .40
47 Jozef Balej .15 .40
48 Antero Niittymaki .15 .40
49 Tom Lawson .15 .40
50 Grant Stevenson .15 .40
51 Adam Berti .15 .40
52 Alexandre Picard .25 .60
53 Andrew Ladd .25 .60
54 Anthony Stewart .20 .50
55 Bobby Ryan .30 .75
56 Boris Valabik .15 .40
57 Braydon Coburn .20 .50
58 Brent Seabrook .20 .50
59 Bryan Bickell .20 .50
60 Bryan Little .25 .60
61 Cam Barker .25 .60
62 Cam Ward .25 .60
63 Chris Campoli .15 .40
64 Corey Locke .15 .40
65 Corey Perry .60 1.50
66 Andy Rogers .15 .40
67 Daniel Paille .20 .50
68 David Bolland .20 .50
69 David Shantz .20 .50
70 Dennis Wideman .15 .40
71 Devan Dubnyk .40 1.00
72 Dion Phaneuf .60 1.50
73 Doug O'Brien .15 .40
74 Eric Fehr .20 .50
75 Eric Himelfarb .15 .40
76 Gilbert Brule .25 .60
77 James Wisniewski .15 .40
78 Jeff Carter .50 1.25
79 Jeff Drouin-Deslauriers .20 .50
80 Jeff Glass .20 .50
81 Jeff Schultz .15 .40
82 Josh Gorges .15 .40
83 Julien Ellis-Plante .20 .50
84 Justin Peters .15 .40
85 Kelly Guard .20 .50
86 Kevin Klein .15 .40
87 Kyle Chipchura .25 .60
88 Liam Reddox .15 .40
89 Marc Staal .25 .60
90 Marc-Antoine Pouliot .20 .50
91 Martin Houle .20 .50
92 Martin St. Pierre .15 .40
93 Matt Lashoff .20 .50
94 Maxime Daigneault .20 .50
95 Mike Green .15 .40
96 Mike Richards .25 .60
97 Paulo Colaiacovo .20 .50
98 Patrick O'Sullivan .25 .60
99 Philippe Roberge .15 .40
100 Robbie Schremp .25 .60
101 Ryan Garlock .15 .40
102 Ryan Getzlaf .40 1.00
103 Shawn Belle .20 .50
104 Sidney Crosby 5.00 12.00
105 Stefan Ruzicka .20 .50
106 Steve Bernier .20 .50
107 Tim Brent .15 .40
108 Tomas Fleischmann .15 .40
109 Vaclav Meidl .15 .40
110 Wojtek Wolski .25 .60
111 Stephen Weiss .15 .40
112 Fredrik Sjostrom .15 .40
113 Alexander Svitov .15 .40
114 Anton Babchuk .15 .40
115 Jason Spezza .25 .60
116 Alexander Ovechkin 3.00 8.00
117 Alexander Ovechkin 3.00 8.00
118 Alexander Ovechkin 3.00 8.00
119 Alexander Ovechkin 3.00 8.00
120 Marc-Andre Fleury .50 1.25
121 Marc-Andre Fleury .50 1.25
122 Marc-Andre Fleury .50 1.25
123 Tim Horton .25 .60
124 Frank Mahovlich .25 .60
125 Gilbert Perreault .25 .60
126 Ed Giacomin .25 .60
127 Jean Ratelle .20 .50
128 Marcel Dionne .30 .75
129 Milt Schmidt .15 .40
130 Phil Esposito .40 1.00
131 Bernie Parent .30 .75
132 Serge Savard .25 .60
133 Stan Mikita .30 .75
134 Tony Esposito .25 .60
135 Vic Hadfield .15 .40
136 Wayne Cashman .15 .40
137 Yvan Cournoyer .25 .60
138 Johnny Bower .25 .60
139 Bill Barber .20 .50
140 Bobby Hull .50 1.25
141 Denis Potvin .25 .60
142 Gerry Cheevers .25 .60
143 Guy Lafleur .30 .75
144 Larry Robinson .25 .60
145 Rogie Vachon .25 .60
146 Steve Shutt .20 .50
147 Ted Lindsay .25 .60
148 Red Kelly .25 .60
149 Wendel Clark .40 1.00
150 Ray Bourque .40 1.00
151 Cam Neely .25 .60
152 Glenn Hall .25 .60
153 Jean Beliveau .30 .75
154 Grant Fuhr .40 1.00
155 Andy Bathgate .25 .60
156 Gump Worsley .25 .60
157 Henri Richard .25 .60
158 Mike Bossy .25 .60
159 Johnny Bucyk .25 .60
160 Elmer Lach .20 .50
161 Vladislav Tretiak .20 .50
162 Lanny McDonald .20 .50
163 Guy Lapointe .20 .50
164 Jacques Plante .30 .75
165 Terry Sawchuk .30 .75
166 Rocket Richard .50 1.25
167 Doug Harvey .25 .60
168 Howie Morenz .20 .50
169 Bill Barilko .20 .50
170 Brad Park .20 .50
171 Bobby Orr 1.00 2.50
172 Mario Lemieux 1.00 2.50
173 Paul Coffey .25 .60
174 Patrick Roy .60 1.50
175 Bobby Clarke .40 1.00
176 Georges Vezina .30 .75
177 Alex Delvecchio .25 .60
178 Toe Blake .25 .60
179 Sid Abel .25 .60
180 Woody Dumart .20 .50
181 Jason King .15 .40
182 Yann Danis .20 .50
183 Zach Parise .40 1.00
184 Dan Hamhuis .20 .50
185 Thomas Vanek .60 1.50
186 Mikko Koivu .25 .60
187 Ryan Whitney .20 .50
188 Jakub Klepis .15 .40
189 Ben Eager .15 .40
190 Kyle Wellwood .20 .50
191 Jiri Hudler .25 .60
192 Aaron Voros .15 .40
193 Eric Staal .30 .75
194 Jay Bouwmeester .15 .40
195 Patrice Bergeron .30 .75
196 Peter Sarno .15 .40
197 Mike Cammalleri .20 .50
198 Derek Roy .15 .40
199 R.J. Umberger .20 .50
200 Junior Lessard .15 .40
201 Rene Vydareny .15 .40
202 Alexander Ovechkin 3.00 8.00
203 Dylan Hunter .15 .40
204 Alexandre Vincent .20 .50
205 Kevin Nastiuk .20 .50
206 Evan McGrath .15 .40
207 Alex Bourret .15 .40
208 Andrej Meszaros .15 .40
209 Benoit Pouliot .15 .40
210 Dany Roussin .15 .40
211 Jeremy Colliton .15 .40
212 Danny Syvret .15 .40
213 Jonathan Boutin .20 .50
214 Ryan Stone .20 .50
215 Jordan Staal .75 2.00
216 Marek Zagrapan .15 .40
217 Clarke MacArthur .20 .50
218 John Hughes .15 .40
219 Alexander Radulov .40 1.00
220 Colin Fraser .15 .40
221 Jakub Petruzalek .15 .40
222 Sidney Crosby 8.00 20.00
223 Nigel Dawes .20 .50
224 Luc Bourdon .30 .75
225 Devin Setoguchi .20 .50
226 Carey Price 5.00 12.00
227 Daren Machesney .20 .50
228 Corey Crawford .60 1.50
229 Marek Schwarz .20 .50
230 Gerald Coleman .20 .50
NNO Roy/AO/Sid/Fleury CL 2.00 5.00

2004-05 ITG Heroes and Prospects Aspiring

1 M. Lemieux/S.Crosby 30.00 80.00
2 M.Lemieux/A.Ovechkin 25.00 60.00
3 P.Roy/M.Fleury 25.00 60.00
4 P.Roy/K.Lehtonen 25.00 60.00
5 R.Bourque/D.Phaneuf 15.00 40.00
6 C.Neely/A.Ovechkin 10.00 25.00
7 M.Bossy/M.Richards 12.00 30.00
8 F.Mahovlich/O'Sullivan 15.00 40.00
9 P.Esposito/B.Boyes 12.00 30.00
10 G.Fuhr/D.Dubnyk 15.00 40.00
11 B.Clarke/J.Carter 12.00 30.00
12 J.Plante/J.Ellis-Plante 12.00 30.00
13 G.Perreault/S.Crosby 25.00 60.00
14 S.Mikita/C.Perry 10.00 25.00
15 J.Beliveau/C.Locke 12.00 30.00
16 Cheevers/D.LeNeveu 12.00 30.00

2004-05 ITG Heroes and Prospects Autographs

AB Adam Berti 4.00 10.00
AD Alex Delvecchio 10.00 25.00
AF Adrian Foster 4.00 10.00
AG Alexandre Giroux 4.00 10.00
AH Adam Hauser 4.00 10.00
AL Andrew Ladd 8.00 20.00
AO1 Alexander Ovechkin 200.00 500.00
AO2 Alexander Ovechkin 200.00 500.00
AO3 Alexander Ovechkin 200.00 500.00
AO4 Alexander Ovechkin 200.00 500.00
AP Alexandre Picard 8.00 20.00
AR Andy Rogers 4.00 10.00
AS Anthony Stewart 8.00 20.00
BB Brad Boyes 4.00 10.00
BC Braydon Coburn 8.00 20.00
BH Bobby Hull 25.00 60.00
BL Bryan Little 6.00 15.00
BN Brandon Nolan 4.00 10.00
BO Bobby Orr 60.00 120.00
BP Bernie Parent 10.00 25.00
BR Bobby Ryan 10.00 25.00
BS Brent Seabrook 6.00 15.00
BV Boris Valabik 4.00 10.00
CA Colby Armstrong 8.00 20.00
CB Cam Barker 8.00 20.00
CC Carlo Colaiacovo 4.00 10.00
CK Chris Kunitz 8.00 20.00
CL Corey Locke 4.00 10.00
CN Cam Neely 12.00 30.00
CP Cory Pecker 4.00 10.00
CW Cam Ward 10.00 25.00
DB David Bolland 8.00 20.00
DD Devan Dubnyk 6.00 15.00
DG Denis Grebeshkov 4.00 10.00
DK Duncan Keith 6.00 15.00
DL David LeNeveu 4.00 10.00
DM Duncan Milroy 4.00 10.00
DO Doug O'Brien 4.00 10.00
DP Daniel Paille 4.00 10.00
DS David Shantz 4.00 10.00
DW Dennis Wideman 4.00 10.00
EF Eric Fehr 8.00 20.00
EG Ed Giacomin 15.00 40.00
EH Eric Himelfarb 6.00 15.00
EL Elmer Lach 10.00 25.00
FM Frank Mahovlich 8.00 20.00
FN Filip Novak 4.00 10.00
FS Fredrik Sjostrom 4.00 10.00
FT Fedor Tyutin 6.00 15.00
GB Gilbert Brule 10.00 25.00
GC Gerry Cheevers 8.00 20.00
GF Grant Fuhr 10.00 25.00
GH Glenn Hall 10.00 25.00
GL Guy Lafleur 10.00 25.00
GP Gilbert Perreault 10.00 25.00
GS Garrett Stafford 6.00 15.00
GW Greg Watson 4.00 10.00
HR Henri Richard 10.00 25.00
HT Hannu Toivonen 6.00 15.00
JB Jozef Balej 6.00 15.00
JC Jeff Carter 20.00 50.00
JD Jeff Drouin-Deslauriers 6.00 15.00
JE Julien Ellis-Plante 6.00 15.00
JG Jeff Glass 8.00 20.00
JM Jay McClement 4.00 10.00
JN Jiri Novotny 4.00 10.00
JP Jean-Marc Pelletier 4.00 10.00
JR Jean Ratelle 8.00 20.00
JS Jeff Schultz 4.00 10.00
JW Jeff Woywitka 6.00 15.00
KC Kyle Chipchura 8.00 20.00
KG Kelly Guard 4.00 10.00
KM Kiel McLeod 4.00 10.00
LM Lanny McDonald 8.00 20.00
LR Liam Reddox 4.00 10.00
LW Lorne Worsley 10.00 25.00
MC Marcel Goc 8.00 20.00
MF1 Marc-Andre Fleury 12.00 30.00
MF2 Marc-Andre Fleury 12.00 30.00
MF3 Marc-Andre Fleury 12.00 30.00
MF4 Marc-Andre Fleury 12.00 30.00
MH Martin Houle 6.00 15.00
MK Martin Kariya 8.00 20.00
ML Matt Lashoff 4.00 10.00
MO Michel Ouellet 6.00 15.00
MP Martin Podlesak 4.00 10.00
MR Mike Richards 15.00 40.00
MS Marc Staal 12.00 30.00
PB Peter Budaj 4.00 10.00
PC Paulo Colaiacovo 4.00 10.00
PE Phil Esposito 12.50 30.00
PL Pascal Leclaire 4.00 10.00
PO Patrick O'Sullivan 10.00 25.00
PR Philippe Roberge 4.00 10.00
PT Petr Taticek 4.00 10.00
RB Ray Bourque 15.00 40.00
RE Ray Emery 5.00 12.00
RG Ryan Garlock 4.00 10.00
RK Ryan Kesler 4.00 10.00
RM Ryan Miller 10.00 25.00
RV Rogie Vachon 8.00 20.00
SB Shawn Belle 6.00 15.00
SC Sidney Crosby 150.00 300.00
SM Stan Mikita 12.00 30.00
SR Stefan Ruzicka 4.00 10.00
SS Serge Savard 10.00 25.00
SU Scottie Upshall 4.00 10.00
TB Tim Brent 4.00 10.00
TE Tony Esposito 15.00 40.00
TF Tomas Fleischmann 4.00 10.00
TK Tomas Kopecky 4.00 10.00
TL Tom Lawson 4.00 10.00
TS Timofei Shishkanov 4.00 10.00
VH Vic Hadfield 8.00 20.00
VM Vaclav Meidl 4.00 10.00
VT Vladislav Tretiak 15.00 40.00
VU Victor Uchevatov 4.00 10.00
WC Wayne Cashman 8.00 20.00
WW Wojtek Wolski 12.00 30.00
YC Yvan Cournoyer 10.00 25.00
YL Yanick Lehoux 4.00 10.00
ABA Andy Bathgate 8.00 20.00
BBA Bill Barber 6.00 15.00
BBI Bryan Bickell 6.00 15.00
BCL Bobby Clarke 12.00 30.00
BPA Brad Park 6.00 15.00
CCA Chris Campoli 4.00 10.00
CPE Corey Perry 15.00 40.00
DGR Danny Groulx 4.00 10.00
DPH Dion Phaneuf 20.00 50.00
DPO Denis Potvin 10.00 25.00
GLA Guy Lapointe 8.00 20.00
GST Grant Stevenson 4.00 10.00
JBE Jean Beliveau 25.00 50.00
JBO Johnny Bower 10.00 25.00
JBU Johnny Bucyk 6.00 15.00
JGO Josh Gorges 4.00 10.00
JPE Justin Peters 6.00 15.00
JWI James Wisniewski 4.00 10.00
KKL Kevin Klein 4.00 10.00
LRO Larry Robinson 8.00 20.00
MBO Mike Bossy 6.00 15.00
MDI Marcel Dionne 10.00 25.00
MFO Matt Foy 4.00 10.00
MGL Mike Glumac 4.00 10.00
MGR Mike Green 4.00 10.00
MLE Mario Lemieux 30.00 80.00
MPO Marc-Antoine Pouliot 8.00 20.00
MSC Milt Schmidt 8.00 20.00
MSP Martin St. Pierre 4.00 10.00
PCO Paul Coffey 10.00 25.00
PRO Patrick Roy 30.00 80.00
RGE Ryan Getzlaf 20.00 50.00
RKE Red Kelly 6.00 15.00
RSC Robbie Schremp 10.00 25.00
SBE Steve Bernier 8.00 20.00
SSH Steve Shutt 8.00 20.00
TLI Ted Lindsay 8.00 20.00
WCL Wendel Clark 10.00 25.00
UJBW Jay Bouwmeester 6.00 15.00
UPBE Patrice Bergeron 10.00 25.00
UPSR Peter Sarno 6.00 15.00
UMCA Mike Cammalleri 4.00 10.00
UMKO Mikko Koivu 6.00 15.00
UAN Antero Niittymaki 10.00 25.00
UDH Dan Hamhuis 4.00 10.00
UDR Derek Roy 6.00 15.00
UES Eric Staal 10.00 25.00
UJH Jiri Hudler 8.00 20.00
UKW Kyle Wellwood 10.00 25.00
UMD Maxime Daigneault 4.00 10.00
URS Rastislav Stana 6.00 15.00
URV Rene Vydareny 4.00 10.00
URW Ryan Whitney 4.00 10.00
SC2 Sidney Crosby 150.00 350.00
USW Stephen Weiss 4.00 10.00
UTV Thomas Vanek 15.00 40.00
UZP Zach Parise 15.00 40.00
ABAB Anton Babchuk 4.00 10.00

2004-05 ITG Heroes and Prospects Combos

COMMON CARD (1-14) 6.00 15.00
1 M.Fleury/K.Lehtonen 25.00 60.00
2 S.Crosby/M.Ouellet 75.00 200.00
3 D.Dubnyk/R.Miller 10.00 25.00
4 R.Getzlaf/B.Boyes 25.00 60.00
5 B.Seabrook/G.Stafford 6.00 15.00
6 D.Bolland/K.McLeod 6.00 15.00
7 M.Pouliot/T.Kopecky 8.00 20.00
8 C.Perry/S.Upshall 15.00 40.00
9 J.Ellis-Plante/P.Leclaire 12.50 30.00
10 J.Carter/R.Emery 12.50 30.00
11 P.O'Sullivan/R.Kesler 12.50 30.00
12 M.Richards/M.Green 15.00 40.00
13 K.Chipchura/D.Phaneuf 12.50 30.00
14 B.Coburn/C.Colaiacovo 15.00 40.00
15 S.Crosby/A.Ovechkin Jsys/90 150.00 300.00

2004-05 ITG Heroes and Prospects Gloves

1 Sidney Crosby 60.00 150.00

2004-05 ITG Heroes and Prospects Hero Memorabilia

1 Tony Esposito 8.00 20.00
2 Stan Mikita 8.00 20.00
3 Gump Worsley 10.00 25.00
4 Ray Bourque 12.50 30.00
5 Phil Esposito 15.00 40.00
6 Patrick Roy 40.00 100.00
7 Mike Bossy 15.00 40.00
8 Marcel Dionne 8.00 20.00
9 Larry Robinson 8.00 20.00
10 Johnny Bower 12.50 30.00
11 Jean Beliveau 25.00 60.00
12 Jacques Plante 25.00 60.00
13 Henri Richard 8.00 20.00
14 Mario Lemieux 25.00 60.00
15 Gilbert Perreault 12.50 30.00
16 Gerry Cheevers 12.00 30.00
17 Ed Giacomin 15.00 40.00
18 Denis Potvin 8.00 20.00
19 Cam Neely 30.00 80.00
21 Alex Delvecchio 15.00 40.00
22 Rogie Vachon 15.00 40.00
23 Serge Savard 15.00 40.00
24 Guy Lapointe 12.50 30.00
25 Bill Barber 12.50 30.00
27 Ted Lindsay 25.00 60.00
28 Paul Coffey 15.00 40.00
30 Bobby Orr 40.00 100.00

2004-05 ITG Heroes and Prospects Jerseys

1-58 EMBLEM/30: .6X TO 1.5X JSY/90*
59-66 EMBLEM/20: .8X TO 2X JSY
1-58 NUMBERS/25: .8X TO 2X JSY/90*

1 Jiri Novotny 4.00 10.00
2 Marc-Andre Fleury 15.00 40.00
3 Corey Perry 15.00 40.00
4 Jeff Carter 15.00 40.00
5 Kari Lehtonen 15.00 40.00
6 David LeNeveu 5.00 12.00
7 Colby Armstrong 5.00 12.00
8 Adrian Foster 4.00 10.00
9 Ryan Miller 10.00 25.00
10 Grant Stevenson 4.00 10.00
11 Garrett Stafford 4.00 10.00
12 Michel Ouellet 6.00 15.00
13 Ray Emery 6.00 15.00
14 Fedor Tyutin 4.00 10.00
15 Brad Boyes 6.00 15.00
16 Marc-Andre Fleury 15.00 40.00
17 Eric Healey 6.00 15.00
18 Devan Dubnyk 6.00 15.00
19 Alexandre Picard 6.00 15.00
20 Patrick O'Sullivan 6.00 15.00
21 Corey Locke 5.00 12.00
22 Kyle Chipchura 6.00 15.00
23 Jean-Marc Pelletier 5.00 12.00
24 Mike Richards 12.00 30.00
25 Michael Ryder 6.00 15.00
26 Carlo Colaiacovo 4.00 10.00
27 Garth Murray 4.00 10.00
28 John Pohl 4.00 10.00
29 Mark Popovic 4.00 10.00
30 Trent Hunter 5.00 12.00
31 Ron Hainsey 4.00 10.00
32 Tony Salmelainen 4.00 10.00
33 Jason Spezza 10.00 25.00
34 Fedor Fedorov 6.00 15.00
35 Denis Shvidki 4.00 10.00
36 Andrew Hutchinson 4.00 10.00
37 Denis Grebeshkov 4.00 10.00
38 Julien Vauclair 5.00 12.00
39 Brandon Reid 4.00 10.00
40 Kiel McLeod 4.00 10.00
41 Chris Kunitz 6.00 15.00
42 Timofei Shishkanov 4.00 10.00
43 Peter Budaj 6.00 15.00
44 Danny Groulx 4.00 10.00
45 Brent Seabrook 12.50 30.00
46 Dion Phaneuf 15.00 40.00
47 Eric Fehr 6.00 15.00
48 Yanick Lehoux 4.00 10.00
49 Ryan Getzlaf 15.00 40.00
50 Matt Foy 4.00 10.00
51 Marc-Antoine Pouliot 6.00 15.00
52 Tomas Kopecky 5.00 12.00
53 David Bolland 6.00 15.00
54 Wojtek Wolski 6.00 15.00
55 Sidney Crosby 50.00 100.00
56 Anthony Stewart 6.00 15.00
57 Alexander Ovechkin 25.00 60.00
58 Scottie Upshall 6.00 15.00
59 Alexander Ovechkin 25.00 60.00
60 Sidney Crosby 40.00 80.00
61 Patrice Bergeron 8.00 20.00
62 Robbie Schremp 6.00 15.00
63 Ryan Whitney 5.00 12.00
64 Danny Syvret 5.00 12.00
65 Dany Roussin 4.00 10.00
66 Wojtek Wolski 6.00 15.00

2004-05 ITG Heroes and Prospects National Pride

1 Sidney Crosby 100.00 200.00
2 Jeff Carter 20.00 50.00
3 Jason Spezza 15.00 40.00
4 Alexander Ovechkin 40.00 100.00
5 Marc-Andre Fleury 25.00 60.00
6 Mike Richards 15.00 40.00
7 Kari Lehtonen 25.00 60.00
8 Patrick O'Sullivan 15.00 40.00

2004-05 ITG Heroes and Prospects Net Prospects

1 Kari Lehtonen 15.00 40.00
2 Marc-Andre Fleury 15.00 40.00
3 Andrew Raycroft 12.00 30.00
4 Rick DiPietro 6.00 15.00
5 Ilja Bryzgalov 6.00 15.00
6 Antero Niittymaki 12.00 30.00
7 Ryan Miller 12.00 30.00
8 Jason Bacashihua 10.00 25.00
9 Rastislav Stana 6.00 15.00
10 Philippe Sauve 6.00 15.00
11 Ray Emery 10.00 25.00
12 Ari Ahonen 6.00 15.00
13 Alex Auld 10.00 25.00
14 David LeNeveu 10.00 25.00
15 Neil Little 6.00 15.00
16 Tim Thomas 8.00 20.00
17 Devan Dubnyk 10.00 25.00
18 Jean-Marc Pelletier 6.00 15.00
19 Mathieu Garon 10.00 25.00
20 Marc-Andre Fleury 15.00 40.00
21 Michael Garnett 6.00 15.00
22 Sebastien Centomo 6.00 15.00
23 Peter Budaj 8.00 20.00
24 Sebastien Charpentier 6.00 15.00
25 Martin Prusek 6.00 15.00
26 Pascal Leclaire 10.00 25.00
27 Mikael Tellqvist 10.00 25.00
28 Reinhard Divis 6.00 15.00
29 Phil Osaer 6.00 15.00
30 Maxime Ouellet 6.00 15.00
31 Mika Noronen 6.00 15.00
32 Julien Ellis-Plante 10.00 25.00

2004-05 ITG Heroes and Prospects Top Prospects

1 Wojtek Wolski 1.25 3.00
2 David Shantz .75 2.00
3 Adam Berti .75 2.00
4 Cam Barker 1.25 3.00
5 Dave Bolland .75 2.00
6 Jeff Schultz .75 2.00
7 Alexandre Picard 1.25 3.00
8 Julien Ellis-Plante .75 2.00
9 Vaclav Meidl .75 2.00
10 Eric Fehr .75 2.00
11 Robbie Schremp 1.25 3.00
12 Andrew Ladd 1.25 3.00
13 Devan Dubnyk .75 2.00
14 Boris Valabik .75 2.00
15 Justin Peters .75 2.00
16 Mike Green .75 2.00
17 Bryan Bickell 1.25 3.00
18 Marc-Andre Fleury 2.00 5.00
19 Anthony Stewart 1.25 3.00
20 Ryan Getzlaf 1.25 3.00

2005-06 ITG Heroes and Prospects

1 Martin Brodeur .75 2.00
2 Bobby Hull .60 1.50
3 Glenn Hall .30 .75
4 Harry Howell .20 .50
5 Doug Gilmour .40 1.00
6 Phil Esposito .50 1.25
7 Red Kelly .30 .75
8 Cam Neely .30 .75
9 Jean Beliveau .30 .75
10 Johnny Bower .30 .75
11 Milt Schmidt .20 .50
12 Jose Theodore .30 .75
13 Ray Bourque .50 1.25
14 Dave Keon .30 .75
15 Henri Richard .25 .60
16 Marcel Dionne .40 1.00
17 Paul Henderson .25 .60
18 Wendel Clark .50 1.25
19 Steve Yzerman .75 2.00
20 Vladislav Tretiak .25 .60
21 Brett Hull .60 1.50
22 Mike Bossy .30 .75
23 Tony Esposito .30 .75
24 Bobby Clarke .50 1.25
25 Brian Leetch .25 .60
26 Guy Lafleur .40 1.00
27 Grant Fuhr .50 1.25
28 Pat LaFontaine .30 .75
29 Jean Ratelle .20 .50
30 Bernie Parent .40 1.00
31 Ed Giacomin .20 .50
32 Darryl Sittler .40 1.00
33 Patrick Roy .75 2.00
34 Dino Ciccarelli .20 .50
35 Frank Mahovlich .30 .75
36 Stan Mikita .40 1.00
37 Neal Broten .20 .50
38 Ted Lindsay .20 .50
39 Derek Sanderson .30 .75
40 Mario Lemieux 1.25 3.00
41 Cam Ward .50 1.25
42 Brandon Bochenski .30 .75
43 Steve Ott .20 .50
44 Kevin Bieksa .50 1.25
45 Ryane Clowe .40 1.00
46 Jason Spezza .30 .75
47 Adam Hauser .25 .60
48 Derek Roy .20 .50
49 R.J. Umberger .30 .75
50 Alex Auld .20 .50
51 Joey MacDonald .20 .50

52 Denis Hamel .25 .60
53 Yann Danis .25 .60
54 Brent Burns .30 .75
55 Josh Harding .20 .50
56 Jason LaBarbera .25 .60
57 Antero Niittymaki .25 .60
58 Mike Egener .20 .50
59 Thomas Vanek .60 1.50
60 Rene Bourque .30 .75
61 Brad Boyes .25 .60
62 Kari Lehtonen .25 .60
63 Jeff Carter .50 1.25
64 Ryan Kesler .30 .75
65 Cam Barker .25 .60
66 Ray Emery .30 .75
67 Michel Ouellet .25 .60
68 Andrew Hutchinson .20 .50
69 Mike Richards .60 1.50
70 Yanick Lehoux .30 .75
71 Lawrence Nycholat .20 .50
72 Jay Bouwmeester .20 .50
73 Ryan Whitney .30 .75
74 Zach Parise .75 2.00
75 Jordin Tootoo .30 .75
76 Joni Pitkanen .20 .50
77 Chris Bourque .50 1.25
78 Mikko Koivu .40 1.00
79 Eric Nystrom .25 .60
80 Mathieu Garon .25 .60
81 Patrice Bergeron .40 1.00
82 Eric Staal .40 1.00
83 Dustin Brown .30 .75
84 Marc-Andre Fleury .60 1.50
85 Marek Svatos .25 .60
86 Steve Eminger .20 .50
87 Andy Hilbert .25 .60
88 Chris Campoli .20 .50
89 Pascal Leclaire .25 .60
90 Anton Volchenkov .20 .50
91 Corey Locke .20 .50
92 Ryan Miller .30 .75
93 Mike Cammalleri .30 .75
94 Simon Gamache .20 .50
95 Chuck Kobasew .20 .50
96 Christian Ehrhoff .20 .50
97 Hannu Toivonen .30 .75
98 Mike Zigomanis .20 .50
99 Niklas Kronwall .20 .50
100 Patrick Sharp .30 .75
101 Ryan Suter .40 1.00
102 Michael Leighton .20 .50
103 Denis Grebeshkov .20 .50
104 Dan Hamhuis .25 .60
105 Sidney Crosby 2.00 5.00
106 Alexander Svitov .20 .50
107 Al Montoya .30 .75
108 Carlo Colaiacovo .20 .50
109 Alexander Ovechkin 10.00 25.00
110 Evgeni Malkin 1.25 3.00
111 John Tavares .75 2.00
112 Bobby Ryan .30 .75
113 Steve Downie .20 .50
114 Adam McQuaid .20 .50
115 Robbie Schremp .30 .75
116 Jordan Staal .20 .50
117 Matt Lashoff .20 .50
118 Ryan O'Marra .20 .50
119 James Neal .20 .50
120 Bryan Little .30 .75
121 David Bolland .30 .75
122 Evan McGrath .20 .50
123 Kevin Lalande .20 .50
124 Radek Smolenak .20 .50
125 Marc Staal .40 1.00
126 Michael Blunden .20 .50
127 Tom Pyatt .20 .50
128 Daren Machesney .20 .50
129 Evan Brophey .20 .50
130 Jakub Kindl .20 .50
131 Ryan Parent .20 .50
132 Daniel Ryder .20 .50
133 Matt Pelech .20 .50
134 Benoit Pouliot .20 .50
135 Derick Brassard .20 .50
136 Brad Marchand 1.00 2.50
137 Alexander Radulov .30 .75
138 Marc-Andre Cliche .20 .50
139 Luc Bourdon .50 1.25
140 David Krejci .20 .50
141 Marek Zagrapan .25 .60
142 Chad Denny .20 .50
143 James Sheppard .20 .50
144 Jean-Philippe Levasseur .20 .50
145 Alex Bourret .20 .50
146 Kristopher Letang .40 1.00
147 Pier-Olivier Pelletier .20 .50
148 Jean-Philippe Paquet .20 .50
149 Marc-Edouard Vlasic .20 .50
150 Nicolas Blanchard .20 .50
151 Guillaume Latendresse .20 .50
152 Jonathan Bernier .20 .50
153 Oskars Bartulis .20 .50
154 Corey Perry 1.00 2.50
155 Alexandre Vincent .20 .50
156 Marc-Andre Gragnani .20 .50
157 Carey Price 1.25 3.00
158 Brett Sutter .20 .50
159 Angelo Esposito .20 .50
160 Devin Setoguchi .30 .75
161 Shea Weber .30 .75
162 Tyler Plante .20 .50
163 Kris Russell .25 .60
164 Gilbert Brule .30 .75
165 Brendan Mikkelson .20 .50
166 Dustin Kohn .20 .50
167 Chris Durand .20 .50
168 Kristofer Westblom .20 .50
169 Blair Jones .20 .50
170 Raymond Macias .20 .50
171 Michael Sauer .20 .50
172 Brodie Dupont .20 .50
173 Ben Maxwell .20 .50
174 Kenndal McArdle .20 .50
175 Matt Kassian .20 .50
176 J.D. Watt .20 .50
177 Scott Jackson .20 .50
178 Devan Dubnyk .40 1.00
179 Tyler Mosienko .20 .50
180 Cody Bass .20 .50
181 Martin Brodeur .75 2.00
182 Ray Bourque .50 1.25
183 Steve Yzerman .75 2.00
184 Dany Heatley .25 .60
185 Herb Carnegie .20 .50
186 Jim Craig .25 .60
187 Gilbert Perreault .30 .75
188 Ron Hextall .30 .75
189 Gerry Cheevers .30 .75
190 Yvan Cournoyer .30 .75
191 Larry Robinson .25 .60
192 Borje Salming .30 .75
193 Ted Kennedy .30 .75
194 Rod Gilbert .30 .75
195 Patrick Roy .75 2.00
196 Mario Lemieux 1.25 3.00
197 Eric Lindros .50 1.25
198 Ilya Kovalchuk .30 .75
199 Tod Sloan .20 .50
200 Mark Howe .20 .50
201 Erik Westrum .20 .50
202 Chris Madden .20 .50
203 Alexandre Picard .20 .50
204 Jeff Tambellini .20 .50
205 Marc-Antoine Pouliot .25 .60
206 Brian Finley .20 .50
207 Sean Bergenheim .20 .50
208 Ryan Shannon .20 .50
209 Clarke MacArthur .20 .50
210 Nicklas Bergfors .20 .50
211 Noah Welch .20 .50
212 Mark Hartigan .20 .50
213 Dan DaSilva .20 .50
214 Eric Fehr .25 .60
215 Shawn Belle .20 .50
216 Joey Tenute .25 .60
217 Maxime Ouellet .60 1.50
218 Yan Stastny .25 .60
219 Petr Taticek .25 .60
220 Ladislav Smid .20 .50
221 Curtis Sanford .25 .60
222 Erik Christensen .20 .50
223 Tyler Redenbach .20 .50
224 Roman Voloshenko .20 .50
225 Dustin Penner .30 .75
226 Rejean Beauchemin .25 .60
227 Martin St. Pierre .20 .50
228 Tim Gleason .20 .50
229 Brent Krahn .25 .60
230 Jason Pominville .20 .50
231 Andrei Kostitsyn .40 1.00
232 Steve Gainey .20 .50
233 Pekka Rinne .50 1.25
234 Nigel Dawes .20 .50
235 Braydon Coburn .30 .75
236 Corey Crawford 1.00 2.50
237 Ryan Stone .20 .50
238 Jeremy Colliton .20 .50
239 Ron Hainsey .20 .50
240 Nolan Schaefer .20 .50
241 Jason Bacashihua .40 1.00
242 Geoff Platt .25 .60
243 Chad Larose .20 .50
244 Drew MacIntyre .20 .50
245 Peter Sejna .20 .50
246 Ryan Vesce .20 .50
247 Brian Pothier .20 .50
248 Colin Murphy .20 .50
249 Curtis McElhinney .20 .50
250 Mike Glumac .25 .60
251 Lauri Tukonen .20 .50
252 Nathan Marsters .20 .50
253 Matt Ellison .20 .50
254 Kurtis Foster .20 .50
255 Jean-Francois Jacques .20 .50
256 Dmitri Patzold .20 .50
257 John Pohl .20 .50
258 Alexander Perezhogin .25 .60
259 Nathan Paetsch .25 .60
260 Kelly Guard .20 .50
261 Andrew Wozniewski .25 .60
262 Tomi Maki .20 .50
263 Tomas Plekanec .20 .50
264 Noah Clarke .20 .50
265 Steve Bernier .30 .75
266 Gerald Coleman .20 .50
267 Jiri Hudler .20 .50
268 Daniel Carcillo .20 .50
269 Bruno Gervais .20 .50
270 Dany Sabourin .20 .50
271 Junior Lessard .20 .50
272 Thomas Pock .20 .50
273 Andy Chiodo .20 .50
274 Vitaly Kolesnik .25 .60
275 Patrick Eaves .30 .75
276 Petr Prucha .30 .75
277 Henrik Lundqvist 1.50 4.00
278 Evgeni Malkin 1.25 3.00
279 Alexander Ovechkin 10.00 25.00
280 Nick Foligno .20 .50
281 Chris Stewart .20 .50
282 Ryan MacDonald .20 .50
283 Liam Reddox .20 .50
284 Tyler Kennedy .20 .50
285 Dylan Hunter .20 .50
286 Bob Sanguinetti .20 .50
287 Dan LaCosta .20 .50
288 Derek Joslin .20 .50
289 Ryan Daniels .20 .50
290 Sergei Kostitsyn .40 1.00
291 Jonathan D'Aversa .20 .50
292 Cory Emmerton .20 .50
293 Dan Turple .20 .50
294 John de Gray .20 .50
295 Bobby Hughes .20 .50
296 Rafael Rotter .20 .50
297 Justin Garay .20 .50
298 Marek Horsky .20 .50
299 Joe Ryan .20 .50
300 Ondrej Pavelec .20 .50
301 Olivier LaBondresse .20 .50
302 Maxime Boisclair .20 .50
303 Mathieu Roy .30 .75
304 Ryan Hillier .20 .50
305 Stanislav Lascek .20 .50
306 Julien Ellis .50 1.25
307 Mathiew Carle .20 .50
308 Alex Grant .20 .50
309 David Desharnais .20 .50
310 Bryce Swan .20 .50
311 Jeff Schultz .20 .50
312 Zach Hamill .20 .50
313 A.J. Thelen .20 .50
314 Brandon Sutter .30 .75
315 Brady Calla .20 .50
316 Troy Brouwer .20 .50
317 Mark Fistric .20 .50
318 Codey Burki .20 .50
319 Kevin Armstrong .20 .50
320 Michael Funk .20 .50
321 Ty Wishart .20 .50
322 Dustin Boyd .20 .50
323 Peter Mueller .20 .50
324 Wacey Rabbit .20 .50
325 Andy Rogers .20 .50
326 Leland Irving .20 .50
327 Logan Stephenson .20 .50
328 Kyle Chipchura .20 .50
329 Ryan White .20 .50
330 Blake Comeau .30 .75
331 Justin Pogge .25 .60
332 Corey Perry 1.00 2.50
333 Ryan Getzlaf .75 2.00
334 Dion Phaneuf .50 1.25
335 Cam Ward .50 1.25
336 Mike Richards .60 1.50
337 Sidney Crosby 2.00 5.00
338 Mario Lemieux 1.25 3.00
339 Guy Lafleur .40 1.00
340 Jeff Carter .50 1.25
341 Eric Lindros .50 1.25
342 Jose Theodore .30 .75
343 Mike Cammalleri .30 .75
344 Jason Spezza .30 .75
345 Patrick Roy .75 2.00
346 Brett Hull .60 1.50
347 Ron Hextall .30 .75
348 Kari Lehtonen .25 .60
349 Keith Ballard .25 .60
350 Greg Hogeboom .20 .50
351 Hugh Jessiman .20 .50
352 Chris Beckford-Tseu .25 .60
353 Mike Brodeur .20 .50
354 Andy Franck .20 .50
355 Brett Jaeger .20 .50
356 D'Arcy McConvey .20 .50
357 Chris Durno .20 .50
358 Rosario Ruggeri .20 .50
359 Garett Bembridge .20 .50
360 Mike Morrison .20 .50
361 Sidney Crosby 2.00 5.00
362 Alexander Ovechkin 10.00 25.00
363 Marek Svatos .25 .60
364 Mike Richards .60 1.50
365 Jeff Carter .50 1.25
366 Eric Nystrom .25 .60
367 Evgeni Malkin 1.25 3.00
368 Ray Emery .30 .75
369 Thomas Vanek .60 1.50
370 Eric Staal .40 1.00
371 John Tavares .75 2.00
372 Bobby Ryan .30 .75
373 Angelo Esposito .20 .50
374 Al Montoya .30 .75
375 Patrick O'Sullivan .30 .75
376 Dion Phaneuf .50 1.25
377 Corey Perry 1.00 2.50
378 Henrik Lundqvist 1.50 4.00
379 Andrew Ladd .40 1.00
380 Wojtek Wolski .25 .60
381 Staffan Kronwall .20 .50
382 Ben Walter .20 .50
383 Jamie Holden .20 .50
384 Danny Richmond .20 .50
385 Tomas Fleischmann .30 .75
386 Alexandre Picard .20 .50
387 Jeff Glass .20 .50
388 Josh Hennessy .20 .50
389 Brad Winchester .30 .75
390 Richie Regehr .20 .50
391 Alexandre Burrows .40 1.00
392 Robert Nilsson .30 .75
393 Mark Stuart .20 .50
394 Filip Novak .20 .50
395 Stefan Ruzicka .20 .50
396 Loui Eriksson .20 .50
397 Jay McClement .20 .50
398 Ryan Callahan .20 .50
399 Ben Shutron .20 .50
400 Logan Couture .20 .50
401 Adam Dennis .20 .50
402 Justin Donati .20 .50
403 Luch Aquino .20 .50
404 John Armstrong .20 .50
405 Matt Beleskey .20 .50
406 Jamie McGinn .20 .50
407 Matthew Corrente .20 .50
408 Theo Peckham .20 .50
409 Mike Weber .20 .50
410 Cal Clutterbuck .20 .50
411 Jean-Christophe Blanchard .20 .50
412 Francois Bouchard .20 .50
413 Claude Giroux .30 .75
414 Ilya Ejov .20 .50
415 Benjamin Breault .20 .50
416 Keith Yandle .20 .50
417 Ivan Vishnevskiy .20 .50
418 Ondrej Fiala .20 .50
419 Michael Grabner .20 .50
420 Riley Holzapfel .20 .50
421 Lukas Bohunicky .20 .50
422 Tysen Dowzak .20 .50
423 Colton Yellow Horn .20 .50
424 Dustin Slade .20 .50
425 Bud Holloway .20 .50
426 David Ruzicka .20 .50
427 Marek Schwarz .20 .50
428 Michael Frolik .25 .60
429 Cristobal Huet .25 .60
430 Ray Emery .30 .75

2005-06 ITG Heroes and Prospects AHL Grads

AG1 Jason Spezza 6.00 15.00
AG2 Brett Hull 6.00 15.00
AG3 Patrick Roy 15.00 40.00
AG4 Kari Lehtonen 8.00 20.00
AG5 Keith Ballard 3.00 8.00
AG6 Jose Theodore 6.00 15.00
AG7 Ron Hextall 6.00 15.00
AG8 Mike Cammalleri 4.00 10.00
AG9 Cam Ward 8.00 20.00

2005-06 ITG Heroes and Prospects Aspiring

ASP1 P.Roy/C.Price 15.00 40.00
ASP2 M.Lemieux/E.Malkin 15.00 40.00
ASP3 D.Keon/P.O'Sullivan 4.00 10.00
ASP4 B.Mosienko/T.Mosienko 2.50 6.00
ASP5 P.Coffey/J.Pitkanen 4.00 10.00
ASP6 C.Neely/P.Bergeron 5.00 12.00
ASP7 M.Bossy/R.Schremp 4.00 10.00
ASP8 P.LaFontaine/B.Ryan 4.00 10.00
ASP9 R.Bourque/S.Weber 6.00 15.00
ASP10 B.Parent/A.Niittymaki 5.00 12.00
ASP11 M.Dionne/D.Brown 5.00 12.00
ASP12 B.Clarke/J.Carter 6.00 15.00
ASP13 G.Lafleur/G.Latendresse 5.00 12.00
ASP14 J.Beliveau/P.Bouchard 4.00 10.00
ASP15 D.Sittler/E.Staal 5.00 12.00
ASP16 B.Hull/J.Spezza 8.00 20.00
ASP17 S.Yzerman/B.Pouliot 10.00 25.00
ASP18 M.Brodeur/M.Fleury 10.00 25.00
ASP19 M.Lemieux/S.Crosby 25.00 60.00
ASP20 M.Lemieux/A.Ovechkin 100.00 125.00

2005-06 ITG Heroes and Prospects Autographs

AAA Alex Auld 6.00 15.00
AAB Alex Bourret 5.00 12.00
AAH Adam Hauser 5.00 12.00
AAHI Andy Hilbert 4.00 10.00
AAHU Andrew Hutchinson 4.00 10.00
AAM Al Montoya 10.00 25.00
AAMQ Adam McQuaid 4.00 10.00
AAN Antero Niittymaki 8.00 20.00
AAO Alexander Ovechkin SP 200.00 500.00
AAR Alexander Radulov 12.00 30.00
AAS Alexander Svitov 4.00 10.00
AAV Anton Volchenkov 4.00 10.00
AAVI Alexandre Vincent 4.00 10.00
ABB Brad Boyes 4.00 10.00
ABBO Brandon Bochenski 5.00 12.00
ABBU Brent Burns 5.00 12.00
ABCL Bobby Clarke SP 12.50 30.00
ABD Brodie Dupont 4.00 10.00
ABJ Blair Jones 4.00 10.00
ABL Brian Leetch SP 10.00 25.00
ABLI Bryan Little 8.00 20.00
ABMA Brad Marchand 6.00 15.00
ABMI Brendan Mikkelson 4.00 10.00
ABMX Ben Maxwell 4.00 10.00
ABOH Bobby Hull SP 15.00 40.00
ABP Benoit Pouliot 6.00 15.00
ABPA Bernie Parent 12.50 30.00
ABR Bobby Ryan SP 12.00 30.00
ABRH Brett Hull SP 15.00 40.00
ABS Brett Sutter 5.00 12.00
ACB Cam Barker 6.00 15.00
ACBA Cody Bass 6.00 15.00
ACBQ Chris Bourque SP 8.00 20.00
ACC Chris Campoli 4.00 10.00
ACCO Carlo Colaiacovo 4.00 10.00
ACD Chad Denny 4.00 10.00
ACDU Chris Durand 4.00 10.00
ACEO Christian Ehrhoff 4.00 10.00
ACK Chuck Kobasew 4.00 10.00
ACL Corey Locke 4.00 10.00
ACN Cam Neely SP 10.00 25.00
ACP Carey Price 40.00 80.00
ACPE Corey Perry 10.00 25.00
ACW Cam Ward 15.00 40.00
ADB David Bolland 6.00 15.00
ADBN Dustin Brown 8.00 20.00
ADBR Derick Brassard 8.00 20.00
ADC Dino Ciccarelli 4.00 10.00
ADD Devan Dubnyk 8.00 20.00
ADG Denis Grebeshkov 4.00 10.00
ADGI Doug Gilmour 6.00 15.00
ADH Denis Hamel 4.00 10.00
ADHA Dan Hamhuis 5.00 12.00
ADK Dave Keon SP 20.00 50.00
ADKO Dustin Kohn 5.00 12.00
ADKR David Krejci 8.00 20.00
ADMA Daren Machesney 4.00 10.00
ADR Daniel Ryder 4.00 10.00
ADRY Derek Roy 6.00 15.00
ADS Darryl Sittler SP 8.00 20.00
ADSA Derek Sanderson 6.00 15.00
ADSE Devin Setoguchi 6.00 15.00
AEB Evan Brophey 4.00 10.00
AEG Ed Giacomin 12.00 30.00
AEM Evan McGrath 4.00 10.00
AEMA Evgeni Malkin SP 60.00 120.00
AEN Eric Nystrom 4.00 10.00
AES Eric Staal 12.00 30.00
AFM Frank Mahovlich 8.00 20.00
AGB Gilbert Brule 10.00 25.00
AGF Grant Fuhr 8.00 20.00
AGH Glenn Hall 10.00 25.00
AGL Guillaume Latendresse 8.00 20.00
AGLF Guy Lafleur 8.00 20.00
AHH Harry Howell 5.00 12.00
AHR Henri Richard 10.00 25.00
AHT Hannu Toivonen 8.00 20.00
AJB Jean Beliveau 25.00 50.00
AJBE Jonathan Bernier 10.00 25.00
AJBO Jay Bouwmeester SP 8.00 20.00
AJBW Johnny Bower 8.00 20.00
AJC Jeff Carter 15.00 40.00
AJDW J.D. Watt 4.00 10.00
AJH Josh Harding 8.00 20.00
AJK Jakub Kindl 4.00 10.00
AJLB Jason LaBarbera 4.00 10.00
AJM Joey MacDonald 12.50 25.00
AJN James Neal 10.00 25.00
AJPI Joni Pitkanen 4.00 10.00
AJPL Jean-Philippe Levasseur 4.00 10.00
AJPP Jean-Philippe Paquet 4.00 10.00
AJR Jean Ratelle 8.00 20.00
AJSH James Sheppard 6.00 15.00
AJST Jordan Staal 30.00 80.00
AJT John Tavares SP 60.00 120.00
AJTH Jose Theodore SP 20.00 40.00
AJTO Jordin Tootoo 8.00 20.00
AKBI Kevin Bieksa 6.00 15.00
AKLA Kevin Lalande 4.00 10.00
AKLT Kristopher Letang 8.00 20.00
AKMC Kenndal McArdle 5.00 12.00
AKR Kris Russell 5.00 12.00
AKW Kristofer Westblom 4.00 10.00
ALB Luc Bourdon 8.00 20.00
ALN Lawrence Nycholat 4.00 10.00
AMAC Marc-Andre Cliche 4.00 10.00
AMAF Marc-Andre Fleury 10.00 25.00
AMAG Marc-Andre Gragnani 4.00 10.00
AMB Martin Brodeur SP 15.00 40.00
AMBL Michael Blunden 5.00 12.00
AMBO Mike Bossy 6.00 15.00
AMC Mike Cammalleri 5.00 12.00
AMD Marcel Dionne 6.00 15.00
AME Mike Egener 4.00 10.00
AMEV Marc-Edouard Vlasic 8.00 20.00
AMG Mathieu Garon 6.00 15.00
AMK Mikko Koivu 8.00 20.00
AMKA Matt Kassian 4.00 10.00
AML Mario Lemieux SP 30.00 80.00
AMLF Matt Lashoff 5.00 12.00
AMLN Michael Leighton 5.00 12.00
AMO Michel Ouellet 6.00 15.00
AMP Matt Pelech 4.00 10.00
AMR Mike Richards 10.00 25.00
AMSH Milt Schmidt 6.00 15.00
AMSR Michael Sauer 4.00 10.00
AMST Marc Staal 10.00 25.00
AMSV Marek Svatos 8.00 20.00
AMZ Marek Zagrapan 4.00 10.00
AMZI Mike Zigomanis 4.00 10.00
ANB Neal Broten 8.00 20.00
ANBL Nicolas Blanchard 4.00 10.00
AOB Oksars Bartulis 4.00 10.00
APBR Patrice Bergeron 10.00 25.00
APE Phil Esposito SP 10.00 25.00
APH Paul Henderson 6.00 15.00
APL Pascal Leclaire 5.00 12.00
APLF Pat LaFontaine 8.00 20.00
APOP Pier-Olivier Pelletier 4.00 10.00
APR Patrick Roy SP 30.00 80.00
APS Patrick Sharp 10.00 25.00
ARB Ray Bourque SP 15.00 40.00
ARBQ Rene Bourque 4.00 10.00
ARC Ryane Clowe 8.00 20.00
ARE Ray Emery 6.00 15.00
ARJU R.J. Umberger 5.00 12.00
ARK Red Kelly 6.00 15.00
ARKS Ryan Kesler 6.00 15.00
ARM Raymond Macias 4.00 10.00
ARMI Ryan Miller 12.50 30.00
ARO Ryan O'Marra 5.00 12.00
ARP Ryan Parent 5.00 12.00
ARS Radek Smolenak 6.00 15.00
ARSC Robbie Schremp 8.00 20.00
ARSU Ryan Suter 8.00 20.00
ASC Sidney Crosby SP 75.00 200.00
ASD Steve Downie 10.00 25.00
ASE Steve Eminger 6.00 15.00
ASG Simon Gamache 4.00 10.00
ASJ Scott Jackson 4.00 10.00
ASM Stan Mikita 10.00 25.00
ASO Steve Ott 5.00 12.00
ASW Shea Weber 6.00 15.00
ASY Steve Yzerman SP 30.00 80.00
ATE Tony Esposito 8.00 20.00
ATL Ted Lindsay 6.00 15.00
ATM Tyler Mosienko 4.00 10.00
ATP Tom Pyatt 4.00 10.00
ATPL Tyler Plante 4.00 10.00
ATV Thomas Vanek 15.00 30.00
AVT Vladislav Tretiak SP 15.00 40.00
AWC Wendel Clark 10.00 25.00
AYD Yann Danis 6.00 15.00
AYL Yanick Lehoux 4.00 10.00
AZP Zach Parise 8.00 20.00
DACR Jeff Carter
Mike Richards 15.00 30.00
DASY Eric Staal
Steve Yzerman 40.00 80.00

2005-06 ITG Heroes and Prospects Autographs Series II

AAC Andy Chiodo 6.00 15.00
AAE2 Angelo Esposito SP 60.00 150.00
AAF Andy Franck 4.00 10.00
AAG Alex Grant 6.00 15.00
AAJT A.J. Thelen 4.00 10.00
AAK Andrei Kostitsyn 8.00 20.00
AAL Andrew Ladd SP 8.00 20.00
AAM2 Al Montoya SP 6.00 15.00
AAO2 Alexander Ovechkin SP 200.00 500.00
AAO3 Alexander Ovechkin SP 200.00 500.00
AAP Alexandre Picard 6.00 15.00
AAPR Alexander Perezhogin 8.00 20.00
AARG Andy Rogers 4.00 10.00
AAW Andrew Wozniewski 4.00 10.00
ABC Braydon Coburn 6.00 15.00
ABCA Brady Calla 4.00 10.00
ABCO Blake Comeau 5.00 12.00
ABF Brian Finley 4.00 10.00
ABG Bruno Gervais 4.00 10.00
ABH Bobby Hughes 4.00 10.00
ABJG Brett Jaeger 4.00 10.00
ABJS Borje Salming 10.00 25.00
ABK Brent Krahn 6.00 15.00
ABPO Brian Pothier 4.00 10.00
ABR2 Bobby Ryan SP 12.00 30.00
ABRH2 Brett Hull SP 12.00 30.00
ABSG Bob Sanguinetti 10.00 25.00
ABSU Brandon Sutter 8.00 20.00
ABSW Bryce Swan 4.00 10.00
ACBK Codey Burki 4.00 10.00
ACCR Corey Crawford 8.00 20.00
ACDR Chris Durno 4.00 10.00
ACEM Cory Emmerton 4.00 10.00
ACLR Chad Larose 4.00 10.00
ACM Clarke MacArthur 4.00 10.00
ACMD Chris Madden 4.00 10.00
ACME Curtis McElhinney 4.00 10.00
ACMU Colin Murphy 4.00 10.00
ACP2 Corey Perry SP 8.00 20.00
ACP3 Corey Perry SP 10.00 25.00
ACS Chris Stewart 5.00 12.00
ACSA Curtis Sanford 6.00 15.00
ACW2 Cam Ward SP 10.00 25.00
ADBO Dustin Boyd 6.00 15.00
ADCA Daniel Carcillo 4.00 10.00
ADDE David Desharnais 6.00 15.00
ADDS Dan DaSilva 4.00 10.00
ADHE Dany Heatley SP 10.00 25.00
ADHU Dylan Hunter 5.00 12.00
ADJ Derek Joslin 4.00 10.00
ADL Dan LaCosta 4.00 10.00
ADMC D'Arcy McConvey 4.00 10.00
ADMI Drew MacIntyre 4.00 10.00
ADP Dion Phaneuf SP 20.00 40.00
ADP2 Dion Phaneuf SP 20.00 50.00
ADPE Dustin Penner 6.00 15.00
ADPZ Dmitri Patzold 5.00 12.00
ADSB Dany Sabourin 4.00 10.00
ADT Dan Turple 4.00 10.00
AEF Eric Fehr 6.00 15.00
AEL Eric Lindros SP 15.00 40.00
AEL2 Eric Lindros SP 12.00 30.00
AEMA2 Evgeni Malkin SP 40.00 100.00
AEMA3 Evgeni Malkin SP 40.00 100.00
AEN2 Eric Nystrom SP 5.00 12.00
AES2 Eric Staal SP 15.00 40.00
AEW Erik Westrum 4.00 10.00
AGBE Garrett Bembridge 4.00 10.00
AGC Gerry Cheevers 10.00 25.00
AGCL Gerald Coleman 5.00 12.00
AGHO Greg Hogeboom 4.00 10.00
AGLF2 Guy Lafleur SP 10.00 25.00
AGP Gilbert Perreault 10.00 25.00
AGPL Geoff Platt 4.00 10.00
AHC Herb Carnegie 20.00 50.00
AHJ Hugh Jessiman 4.00 10.00
AHL Henrik Lundqvist SP 25.00 60.00
AHL2 Henrik Lundqvist SP 30.00 80.00
AIK Ilya Kovalchuk SP 12.00 30.00
AJBC Jason Bacashihua 6.00 15.00
AJC2 Jeff Carter SP 12.00 30.00
AJC3 Jeff Carter SP 12.00 30.00
AJCO Jeremy Colliton 6.00 15.00
AJCR Jim Craig 8.00 20.00
AJD John de Gray 4.00 10.00
AJDA Jonathan D'Aversa 4.00 10.00
AJE Julien Ellis-Plante 6.00 15.00
AJFJ Jean-Francois Jacques 4.00 10.00
AJG Justin Garay 6.00 15.00
AJHU Jiri Hudler 6.00 15.00
AJL Junior Lessard 6.00 15.00
AJOP John Pohl 6.00 15.00
AJPG Justin Pogge 20.00 50.00
AJPO Jason Pominville 8.00 20.00
AJRY Joe Ryan 4.00 10.00
AJSC Jeff Schultz 4.00 10.00
AJT2 John Tavares SP 90.00 150.00
AJTA Jeff Tambellini 6.00 15.00
AJTE Joey Tenute 4.00 10.00
AJTH2 Jose Theodore SP 8.00 20.00
AKA Kevin Armstrong 4.00 10.00
AKB Keith Ballard SP 5.00 12.00
AKC Kyle Chipchura 6.00 15.00
AKF Kurtis Foster 4.00 10.00
AKG Kelly Guard 5.00 12.00
AKL2 Kari Lehtonen SP 12.00 30.00
ALI Leland Irving 8.00 20.00
ALR Larry Robinson 6.00 15.00
ALRD Liam Reddox 4.00 10.00
ALS Ladislav Smid 4.00 10.00
ALST Logan Stephenson 4.00 10.00
ALT Lauri Tukonen 4.00 10.00
AMAP Marc-Antoine Pouliot 6.00 15.00
AMB2 Martin Brodeur 40.00 80.00
AMBR Mike Brodeur SP 6.00 15.00
AMC2 Mike Cammalleri SP 5.00 12.00
AMCL Mathieu Carle 4.00 10.00
AMEL Matt Ellison 4.00 10.00
AMFI Mark Fistric 4.00 10.00
AMFU Michael Funk 4.00 10.00
AMGL Mike Glumac 4.00 10.00
AMH Mark Howe 10.00 25.00
AMHA Mark Hartigan 6.00 15.00
AMHO Marek Horsky 4.00 10.00
AML2 Mario Lemieux SP 40.00 80.00
AML3 Mario Lemieux SP 40.00 80.00
AMM Mike Morrison 6.00 15.00
AMR2 Mike Richards SP 10.00 25.00
AMR3 Mike Richards SP 10.00 25.00
AMRY Mathieu Roy 6.00 15.00
AMSP Martin St. Pierre 4.00 10.00
AMSV2 Marek Svatos SP 5.00 12.00
AMXB Maxime Boisclair 6.00 15.00
AMXO Maxime Ouellet 4.00 10.00
ANBG Nicklas Bergfors 6.00 15.00
ANC Noah Clarke 4.00 10.00
AND Nigel Dawes 5.00 12.00
ANF Nick Foligno 5.00 12.00
ANM Nathan Marsters 4.00 10.00
ANP Nathan Paetsch 4.00 10.00
ANS Nolan Schaefer 4.00 10.00
ANW Noah Welch 6.00 15.00
AOL Olivier Latendresse 6.00 15.00
AOP Ondrej Pavelec 6.00 15.00
APM Peter Mueller 10.00 25.00
APOS Patrick O'Sullivan SP 8.00 20.00
APP Petr Prucha SP 10.00 25.00
APR2 Patrick Roy SP 40.00 100.00
APR3 Patrick Roy SP 40.00 80.00
APRI Pekka Rinne 8.00 20.00
APSJ Peter Sejna 4.00 10.00
APT Petr Taticek 4.00 10.00
ARB2 Ray Bourque SP 25.00 60.00
ARBE Rejean Beauchemin 5.00 12.00
ARD Ryan Daniels 4.00 10.00
ARE2 Ray Emery SP 6.00 15.00
ARG Ryan Getzlaf SP 10.00 25.00
ARGI Rod Gilbert 8.00 20.00
ARH Ron Hextall 20.00 50.00
ARH2 Ron Hextall SP 20.00 50.00
ARHA Ron Hainsey 6.00 15.00
ARHI Ryan Hillier 4.00 10.00
ARMC Ryan MacDonald 5.00 12.00
ARR Rosario Ruggeri 4.00 10.00
ARRO Rafael Rotter 4.00 10.00
ARSH Ryan Shannon 4.00 10.00
ARST Ryan Stone 4.00 10.00
ARV Roman Voloshenko 6.00 15.00
ARVE Ryan Vesce 4.00 10.00
ARWH Ryan White 4.00 10.00
ASB Sean Bergenheim 4.00 10.00
ASBE Shawn Belle 4.00 10.00
ASBR Steve Bernier 8.00 20.00
ASC2 Sidney Crosby SP 75.00 150.00
ASC3 Sidney Crosby SP 75.00 150.00
ASGA Steve Gainey 4.00 10.00
ASKO Sergei Kostitsyn 6.00 15.00
ASL Stanislav Lascek 4.00 10.00
ASY2 Steve Yzerman SP 40.00 80.00
ATB Troy Brouwer 4.00 10.00
ATG Tim Gleason 4.00 10.00
ATK Tyler Kennedy 4.00 10.00
ATKE Ted Kennedy 8.00 20.00
ATMK Tomi Maki 4.00 10.00
ATPC Tomas Plekanec 4.00 10.00
ATPK Thomas Pock 4.00 10.00
ATR Tyler Redenbach 4.00 10.00
ATS Tod Sloan 4.00 10.00
ATV2 Thomas Vanek SP 12.00 30.00
ATW Ty Wishart 4.00 10.00
AVK Vitaly Kolesnik 5.00 12.00
AWR Wacey Rabbit 6.00 15.00
AYC Yvan Cournoyer 8.00 20.00
AYS Yan Stastny 4.00 10.00
AZH Zach Hamill 6.00 15.00

2005-06 ITG Heroes and Prospects Autographs Update

AAE Angelo Esposito SP 75.00 150.00
AFB Francois Bouchard 3.00 8.00
AFN Filip Novak 3.00 8.00
AMF Michael Frolik SP 20.00 50.00
AOF Ondrej Fiala 3.00 8.00
ARN Robert Nilsson 4.00 10.00
ASK Staffan Kronwall 3.00 8.00
ATD Tysen Dowzak 3.00 8.00
ATF Tomas Fleischmann 4.00 10.00
ABSH Ben Shutron 3.00 8.00
ACBT Chris Beckford-Tseu 12.00 30.00
ACHT Cristobal Huet SP 15.00 40.00
ADRI Danny Richmond 3.00 8.00
AJGL Jeff Glass 5.00 12.00
AJHO Jamie Holden 3.00 8.00
AMCO Matthew Corrente 4.00 10.00
AMKS Mark Stuart 4.00 10.00
AMSZ Marek Schwarz SP 15.00 30.00
ARE3 Ray Emery SP 6.00 15.00
ARRG Richie Regehr 3.00 8.00
DAET J.Tavares/A.Esposito 125.00 250.00

2005-06 ITG Heroes and Prospects CHL Grads

CG1 Marc Antoine Pouliot 6.00 15.00
CG2 Gilbert Brule 10.00 25.00
CG3 Jeff Carter 12.00 30.00
CG4 Mike Richards 6.00 15.00
CG5 Mario Lemieux 15.00 40.00
CG6 Patrick Roy 15.00 40.00
CG7 Steve Yzerman 15.00 40.00
CG8 Guy Lafleur 10.00 25.00
CG9 Dion Phaneuf 15.00 40.00
CG10 Ryan Getzlaf 10.00 25.00
CG11 Corey Perry 8.00 20.00
CG12 Ray Bourque 10.00 25.00
CG13 Grant Fuhr 10.00 25.00
CG14 Martin Brodeur 12.00 30.00
CG15 Eric Fehr 6.00 15.00
CG16 Sidney Crosby 25.00 60.00

2005-06 ITG Heroes and Prospects Future Teammates

FT1 P.Bouchard/M.Koivu 10.00 25.00
FT2 J.Pitkanen/A.Niittymaki 10.00 25.00
FT3 C.Perry/R.Getzlaf 15.00 40.00
FT4 M.Fleury/M.Lemieux 50.00 125.00
FT5 J.Spezza/B.Bochenski 20.00 50.00
FT6 C.Ward/E.Staal 20.00 50.00
FT7 D.Keon/F.Mahovlich 20.00 50.00
FT8 P.Roy/R.Bourque 25.00 60.00
FT9 P.LaFontaine/G.Fuhr 15.00 40.00
FT10 P.Bergeron/B.Boyes 15.00 40.00
FT11 R.Bourque/C.Neely 20.00 50.00
FT12 B.Hull/G.Hall 20.00 50.00
FT13 S.Crosby/E.Malkin 40.00 100.00
FT14 A.Ovechkin/E.Fehr 50.00 120.00

2005-06 ITG Heroes and Prospects He Shoots He Scores Prizes

1 S.Crosby/M.Lemieux 60.00 120.00
2 G.Latendresse/G.Lafleur 8.00 20.00
3 K.Lehtonen/M.Brodeur 15.00 40.00
4 D.Phaneuf/R.Bourque 10.00 25.00
5 J.Theodore/P.Roy 15.00 40.00
6 E.Malkin/A.Ovechkin 50.00 120.00
7 B.Pouliot/S.Yzerman 15.00 40.00
8 A.Ovechkin/M.Lemieux 50.00 120.00
9 J.Bouwmeester/B.Leetch 8.00 20.00
10 C.Price/J.Theodore 25.00 60.00
11 E.Malkin/M.Lemieux 25.00 60.00
12 T.Mosienko/B.Mosienko 5.00 12.00
13 E.Staal/M.Staal 12.00 30.00
14 Br.Hull/Bo.Hull 15.00 40.00
15 D.Syvret/D.Fritsche 5.00 12.00
16 C.Perry/D.Bolland 20.00 50.00
17 K.Westblom/B.Comeau 8.00 20.00
18 B.Ryan/R.Getzlaf 15.00 40.00
19 K.Lehtonen/A.Ovechkin 50.00 120.00
20 P.Bergeron/B.Boyes 8.00 20.00
21 D.Roy/R.Miller 8.00 20.00
22 B.Krahn/D.Phaneuf 10.00 25.00
23 C.Ward/E.Staal 10.00 25.00
24 B.Seabrook/P.Vorobiev 12.00 30.00
25 W.Wolski/M.Svatos 5.00 12.00
26 P.Leclaire/D.Fritsche 6.00 15.00
27 M.Pouliot/R.Schremp 8.00 20.00
28 J.Bouwmeester/A.Stewart 6.00 15.00
29 J.LaBarbera/M.Cammalleri 8.00 20.00
30 M.Koivu/P.O'Sullivan 8.00 20.00
31 K.Chipchura/G.Latendresse 5.00 12.00
32 S.Upshall/D.Hamhuis 6.00 15.00
33 B.Bochenski/J.Spezza 8.00 20.00
34 A.Niittymaki/J.Pitkanen 6.00 15.00

35 J.Carter/M.Richards 12.00 30.00
36 S.Crosby/E.Malkin 75.00 150.00
37 M.Fleury/R.Whitney 12.00 30.00
38 S.Crosby/C.Colaiacovo 40.00 100.00
39 R.Kesler/A.Auld 6.00 15.00
40 A.Ovechkin/E.Fehr 50.00 120.00
41 A.Ovechkin/A.Radulov 50.00 120.00
42 M.Lemieux/E.Malkin 25.00 60.00
43 S.Yzerman/J.Tavares 15.00 40.00
44 P.Roy/A.Esposito 15.00 40.00
45 M.Messier/S.Downie 12.00 30.00
46 F.Mahovlich/B.Pouliot 8.00 20.00
47 M.Brodeur/C.Price 25.00 60.00
48 J.Jagr/M.Frolik 20.00 50.00
49 T.Sawchuk/L.Irving 10.00 25.00
50 M.Richard/J.Tavares 15.00 40.00
51 A.Ovechkin/D.Phaneuf 50.00 120.00
52 M.Lemieux/J.Staal 25.00 60.00
53 S.Yzerman/P.O'Sullivan 15.00 40.00
54 P.Roy/C.Crawford 20.00 50.00
55 M.Messier/P.Mueller 10.00 25.00
56 T.Horton/M.Staal 8.00 20.00
57 M.Brodeur/M.Schwarz 15.00 40.00
58 J.Jagr/J.Tlusty 12.00 30.00
59 B.Hull/R.Getzlaf 15.00 40.00
60 J.Bower/J.Pogge 6.00 15.00

2005-06 ITG Heroes and Prospects Hero Memorabilia

HM1 Mario Lemieux 20.00 50.00
HM2 Ray Bourque 10.00 25.00
HM3 Cam Neely 6.00 15.00
HM4 Doug Gilmour 6.00 15.00
HM5 Wendel Clark 6.00 15.00
HM6 Stan Mikita 6.00 15.00
HM7 Pat LaFontaine 6.00 15.00
HM8 Patrick Roy 20.00 50.00
HM9 Dino Ciccarelli 6.00 15.00
HM10 Ed Giacomin 12.50 30.00
HM11 Vladislav Tretiak 15.00 40.00
HM12 Brad Park 6.00 15.00
HM13 Brett Hull 8.00 20.00
HM14 Brian Leetch 6.00 15.00
HM15 Martin Brodeur 20.00 50.00
HM16 Steve Yzerman 12.50 30.00
HM17 Jose Theodore 8.00 20.00
HM18 Bobby Hull 10.00 25.00
HM19 Jean Beliveau 15.00 40.00
HM20 Guy Lafleur 10.00 25.00
HM21 Frank Mahovlich 8.00 20.00
HM22 Grant Fuhr 12.00 30.00
HM23 Glenn Hall 6.00 15.00
HM24 Gerry Cheevers 15.00 40.00
HM25 Marcel Dionne 6.00 15.00
HM26 Phil Esposito 12.50 30.00
HM27 Valeri Kharlamov 15.00 40.00
HM28 Tony Esposito 8.00 20.00
HM29 Bobby Clarke 10.00 25.00
HM30 Eddie Shore 8.00 20.00
HM31 Bernie Parent 10.00 25.00
HM32 Mike Bossy 12.50 30.00
HM33 Jean Ratelle 15.00 40.00
HM34 Gump Worsley 12.00 30.00
HM35 Darryl Sittler 8.00 20.00
HM36 Jacques Plante 20.00 50.00
HM37 Steve Shutt 8.00 20.00
HM38 Ted Lindsay 8.00 20.00
HM39 Red Kelly 8.00 20.00
HM40 Johnny Bower 12.50 30.00
HM41 Dave Keon 15.00 40.00
HM42 Borje Salming 15.00 40.00
HM43 Lanny McDonald 6.00 15.00
HM44 Rod Gilbert 6.00 15.00
HM45 Eric Lindros 6.00 15.00
HM46 Ilya Kovalchuk 10.00 25.00
HM47 Dany Heatley 10.00 25.00
HM48 George Hainsworth 25.00 60.00
HM49 Bill Barber 6.00 15.00
HM50 Serge Savard 6.00 15.00
HM51 Guy Lapointe 6.00 15.00
HM52 Yvan Cournoyer 6.00 15.00
HM53 Denis Potvin 10.00 25.00
HM54 Larry Robinson 6.00 15.00
HM55 Rogie Vachon 6.00 15.00
HM56 Mark Howe 6.00 15.00

2005-06 ITG Heroes and Prospects Hero Memorabilia Dual

HDM1 Bill Mosienko 8.00 20.00
HDM2 Brett Hull 15.00 40.00
HDM3 Wendel Clark 12.50 30.00
HDM4 Patrick Roy 20.00 50.00
HDM5 Ray Bourque 15.00 40.00
HDM6 Cam Neely 10.00 25.00
HDM7 Doug Gilmour 8.00 20.00
HDM8 Steve Yzerman 25.00 60.00
HDM9 Brian Leetch 10.00 25.00
HDM10 Grant Fuhr 15.00 40.00
HDM11 Jose Theodore 10.00 25.00
HDM12 Guy Lafleur 10.00 25.00
HDM13 Dave Keon 8.00 20.00
HDM14 Mario Lemieux 25.00 60.00
HDM15 Bobby Hull 12.50 30.00
HDM16 Stan Mikita 8.00 20.00
HDM17 Ron Hextall 12.50 30.00

2005-06 ITG Heroes and Prospects Jerseys

EMBLEMS/30: .8X TO 2X JSY/100*
NUMBERS/30: .8X TO 2X JSY/100*
NUMBERS/15: 1X TO 2.5X JSY/100*
GUJ1 Bobby Ryan 6.00 15.00
GUJ2 Brian Sutherby 4.00 10.00
GUJ3 Jay Bouwmeester 4.00 10.00
GUJ4 Denis Hamel 5.00 12.00
GUJ5 Andy Hilbert 5.00 12.00
GUJ6 Mike Cammalleri 6.00 15.00
GUJ7 Mikko Koivu 8.00 20.00
GUJ8 Boyd Gordon 4.00 10.00
GUJ9 Brad Boyes 5.00 12.00
GUJ10 Ryan Kesler 6.00 15.00
GUJ11 Joni Pitkanen 4.00 10.00
GUJ12 Pascal Leclaire 5.00 12.00
GUJ13 Derek Roy 4.00 10.00
GUJ14 Ryan Whitney 6.00 15.00
GUJ15 Jason Spezza 6.00 15.00
GUJ16 Eric Staal 8.00 20.00
GUJ17 Dustin Brown 6.00 15.00
GUJ18 Chuck Kobasew 4.00 10.00
GUJ19 Ray Emery 6.00 15.00
GUJ20 Jason LaBarbera 5.00 12.00
GUJ21 Michel Ouellet 5.00 12.00
GUJ22 Antero Niittymaki 5.00 12.00
GUJ23 Cam Ward 10.00 25.00
GUJ24 Marc-Andre Fleury 10.00 25.00
GUJ25 Devin Setoguchi 6.00 15.00
GUJ26 Shea Weber 6.00 15.00
GUJ27 Chris Durand 4.00 10.00
GUJ28 Guillaume Latendresse 6.00 15.00
GUJ29 Brandon Bochenski 6.00 15.00
GUJ30 Pavel Vorobiev 4.00 10.00
GUJ31 P-M Bouchard 6.00 15.00
GUJ32 Patrice Bergeron 8.00 20.00
GUJ33 Kenndal McArdle 4.00 10.00
GUJ34 Patrick O'Sullivan 6.00 15.00
GUJ35 Marek Zagrapan 5.00 12.00
GUJ36 Carey Price 25.00 60.00
GUJ37 Corey Crawford 8.00 20.00
GUJ38 Rob Schremp 6.00 15.00
GUJ39 Lee Goren 4.00 10.00
GUJ40 Tyler Mosienko 4.00 10.00
GUJ41 Brent Burns 6.00 15.00
GUJ42 Travis Roche 4.00 10.00
GUJ43 Kristofer Westblom 4.00 10.00
GUJ44 Lawrence Nycholat 4.00 10.00
GUJ45 Wojtek Wolski 5.00 12.00
GUJ46 Mathieu Garon 5.00 12.00
GUJ47 Adam Munro 4.00 10.00
GUJ48 Blake Comeau 6.00 15.00
GUJ49 Evgeni Malkin 25.00 60.00
GUJ50 Benoit Pouliot 4.00 10.00
GUJ51 Gerald Coleman 4.00 10.00
GUJ52 Marc Staal 8.00 20.00
GUJ53 Sidney Crosby 50.00 80.00
GUJ54 Alexander Ovechkin 50.00 125.00
GUJ55 Al Montoya 6.00 15.00
GUJ56 Gilbert Brule 6.00 15.00
GUJ57 David Bolland 6.00 15.00
GUJ58 Zach Parise 15.00 40.00
GUJ59 Mike Richards 12.00 30.00
GUJ60 Jeff Carter 12.00 30.00
GUJ61 Jeff Tambellini 4.00 10.00
GUJ62 Chris Campoli 4.00 10.00
GUJ63 Shawn Belle 4.00 10.00
GUJ64 Chris Bourque 10.00 25.00
GUJ65 John Tavares 25.00 50.00
GUJ66 Tim Thomas 6.00 15.00
GUJ67 Justin Pogge 5.00 12.00
GUJ68 Bryan Little 6.00 15.00
GUJ69 Patrick Eaves 6.00 15.00
GUJ70 Brett Sutter 4.00 10.00
GUJ71 Yan Stastny 5.00 12.00
GUJ72 Gerald Coleman 4.00 10.00
GUJ73 Rejean Beauchemin 5.00 12.00
GUJ74 Chris Beckford-Tseu 5.00 12.00
GUJ75 Luc Bourdon 10.00 25.00
GUJ76 Matt Ellison 4.00 10.00
GUJ77 Brian Pothier 4.00 10.00
GUJ78 Alexandre Vincent 4.00 10.00
GUJ79 Corey Perry 20.00 50.00
GUJ80 Anthony Stewart 5.00 12.00
GUJ81 Ryan Getzlaf 15.00 40.00
GUJ82 Eric Fehr 5.00 12.00
GUJ83 Keith Ballard 5.00 12.00
GUJ84 Marc-Antoine Pouliot 5.00 12.00
GUJ85 Julien Ellis 10.00 25.00
GUJ86 Dany Roussin 4.00 10.00
GUJ87 Eric Nystrom 5.00 12.00
GUJ88 Brent Krahn 5.00 12.00
GUJ89 Evgeni Malkin 25.00 60.00
GUJ90 Sidney Crosby 50.00 80.00
GUJ91 Alexander Ovechkin 50.00 125.00
GUJ92 Maxime Ouellet 12.00 30.00
GUJ93 Carlo Colaiacovo 4.00 10.00
GUJ94 Henrik Lundqvist 12.00 30.00
GUJ95 Alexander Perezhogin 5.00 12.00
GUJ96 Sean Bergenheim 4.00 10.00
GUJ97 Kari Lehtonen 5.00 12.00
GUJ98 Jason Bacashihua 8.00 20.00
GUJ99 Jordin Tootoo 6.00 15.00
GUJ100 Marek Svatos 5.00 12.00
GUJ101 Dennis Wideman 4.00 10.00
GUJ102 Colby Armstrong 6.00 15.00
GUJ103 Mike Brodeur 4.00 10.00
GUJ104 Matt Foy 4.00 10.00
GUJ105 Grant Stevenson 4.00 10.00
GUJ106 Ari Ahonen 5.00 12.00
GUJ107 Andrew Ladd 8.00 20.00
GUJ108 Adam Hauser 5.00 12.00
GUJ109 Dion Phaneuf 12.00 30.00
GUJ110 Jeff Schultz 4.00 10.00
GUJ111 Petr Prucha 6.00 15.00
GUJ112 Alexander Mogilny 5.00 12.00
GUJ113 Devan Dubnyk 8.00 20.00
GUJ114 Thomas Vanek 12.00 30.00
GUJ115 Carey Price 25.00 60.00
GUJ116 Tom Pyatt 4.00 10.00

2005-06 ITG Heroes and Prospects Making the Bigs

MTB1 Jose Theodore 8.00 20.00
MTB2 Jason Spezza 10.00 25.00
MTB3 P-M Bouchard 5.00 12.00
MTB4 Brian Sutherby 4.00 10.00
MTB5 Eric Staal 10.00 25.00
MTB6 Boyd Gordon 4.00 10.00
MTB7 Alexander Ovechkin 40.00 100.00
MTB8 Ray Emery 6.00 15.00
MTB9 Derek Roy 8.00 20.00
MTB10 Maxime Ouellet 5.00 12.00
MTB11 Dustin Brown 5.00 12.00
MTB12 Scottie Upshall 4.00 10.00
MTB13 Guillaume Latendresse 6.00 15.00
MTB14 Mike Richards 6.00 15.00
MTB15 Jeff Carter 12.00 30.00
MTB16 Gerald Coleman 4.00 10.00

2005-06 ITG Heroes and Prospects Measuring Up

COMMON CARD (MU1-MU20) 15.00 30.00
MU1 C.Ward/P.Roy 15.00 30.00
MU2 J.LaBarbera/P.Roy 15.00 30.00
MU3 J.Ellis-Plante/P.Roy 15.00 30.00
MU4 J.Bacashihua/P.Roy 15.00 30.00
MU5 A.Auld/P.Roy 15.00 30.00
MU6 S.Clemmensen/P.Roy 15.00 30.00
MU7 M.Ouellet/P.Roy 20.00 40.00
MU8 B.Krahn/P.Roy 15.00 30.00
MU9 H.Lundqvist/P.Roy 20.00 50.00
MU10 R.Miller/P.Roy 20.00 50.00
MU11 A.Niittymaki/P.Roy 20.00 40.00
MU12 M.Fleury/P.Roy 20.00 40.00
MU13 G.Coleman/P.Roy 15.00 30.00
MU14 D.Dubnyk/P.Roy 15.00 30.00
MU15 R.Beauchemin/P.Roy 15.00 30.00
MU16 K.Guard/P.Roy 15.00 30.00
MU17 C.Price/P.Roy 25.00 50.00
MU18 A.Montoya/P.Roy 20.00 40.00
MU19 J.Pogge/P.Roy 20.00 40.00
MU20 K.Lehtonen/P.Roy 20.00 40.00

2005-06 ITG Heroes and Prospects Memorial Cup

COMPLETE SET (13) 8.00 20.00
COMMON CARD (MC1-MC13) 1.00 2.50
MC1 Danny Syvret 1.00 2.50
MC2 Robbie Schremp 2.00 5.00
MC3 Dylan Hunter 1.00 2.50
MC4 Corey Perry 2.00 5.00
MC5 Dan Fritsche 1.00 2.50
MC6 David Bolland 1.00 2.50
MC7 Adam Dennis 1.00 2.50
MC8 Gerald Coleman 1.00 2.50
MC9 Brandon Prust 1.00 2.50
MC10 Bryan Rodney 1.00 2.50
MC11 Drew Larman 1.00 2.50
MC12 Josh Beaulieu 1.00 2.50
MC13 Marc Methot 1.00 2.50

2005-06 ITG Heroes and Prospects National Pride

NPR1 Kari Lehtonen 6.00 15.00
NPR2 Marc-Andre Fleury 8.00 20.00
NPR3 Dany Roussin 4.00 10.00
NPR4 Jason Spezza 8.00 20.00
NPR5 Jay Bouwmeester 4.00 10.00
NPR6 Dion Phaneuf 15.00 40.00
NPR7 P-M Bouchard 4.00 10.00
NPR8 Mikko Koivu 4.00 10.00
NPR9 Mike Cammalleri 4.00 10.00
NPR10 Evgeni Malkin 25.00 60.00
NPR11 Sidney Crosby 40.00 100.00
NPR12 Alexander Ovechkin 60.00 150.00
NPR17 Martin Brodeur 15.00 40.00
NPR22 Pelle Lindbergh 15.00 40.00
NPR23 Phil Esposito 8.00 20.00
NPR24 Lanny McDonald 4.00 10.00
NPR25 Dany Heatley 8.00 20.00
NPR26 Borje Salming 6.00 15.00
NPR27 Eric Lindros 8.00 20.00
NPR28 Gilbert Perreault 6.00 15.00
NPR29 Gerry Cheevers 8.00 20.00
NPR30 Larry Robinson 6.00 15.00
NPR31 Ilya Kovalchuk 12.00 30.00
NPR32 Justin Pogge 15.00 40.00
NPR33 Alexander Ovechkin 60.00 150.00
NPR34 Bobby Ryan 8.00 20.00
NPR35 Evgeni Malkin 20.00 50.00
NPR36 Sidney Crosby 40.00 100.00
NPR37 Corey Perry 8.00 20.00
NPR38 Jeff Carter 10.00 25.00
NPR39 Mike Richards 6.00 15.00
NPR40 Al Montoya 6.00 15.00
NPR41 Anthony Stewart 4.00 10.00

2005-06 ITG Heroes and Prospects Net Prospects

COMMON CARD (NP1-NP21) 4.00 10.00
SEMISTARS 6.00 15.00
NP1 Kari Lehtonen 6.00 15.00
NP2 Marc-Andre Fleury 8.00 20.00
NP3 Antero Niittymaki 6.00 15.00
NP4 Adam Hauser 4.00 10.00
NP5 Mathieu Garon 4.00 10.00
NP6 Pascal Leclaire 4.00 10.00
NP7 Ray Emery 6.00 15.00
NP8 Adam Munro 4.00 10.00
NP9 Cam Ward 8.00 20.00
NP10 Jason LaBarbera 4.00 10.00
NP11 Ryan Miller 8.00 20.00
NP12 Brent Krahn 4.00 10.00
NP13 Alex Auld 5.00 12.00
NP14 Devan Dubnyk 4.00 10.00
NP15 Carey Price 12.00 30.00
NP16 Kyle Moir 4.00 10.00
NP17 Corey Crawford 8.00 20.00
NP18 Kevin Nastiuk 4.00 10.00
NP19 Jonathan Boutin 4.00 10.00
NP20 Gerald Coleman 4.00 10.00
NP21 Kristofer Westblom 4.00 10.00

2005-06 ITG Heroes and Prospects Net Prospects Dual

COMMON CARD (NPD1-NPD10) 6.00 15.00
NPD1 M.Ouellet/A.Auld 8.00 20.00
NPD2 A.Hauser/J.LaBarbera 6.00 15.00
NPD3 A.Niittymaki/R.Beauchemin 8.00 20.00
NPD4 K.Westblom/G.Coleman 6.00 15.00
NPD5 A.Montoya/P.Leclaire 12.00 30.00
NPD6 B.Krahn/C.Ward 6.00 15.00
NPD7 K.Lehtonen/M.Fleury 20.00 50.00
NPD8 D.Dubnyk/J.Pogge 15.00 40.00
NPD9 C.Beckford-Tseu/Mi.Brodeur 6.00 15.00
NPD10 C.Price/J.Ellis-Plante 10.00 25.00

2005-06 ITG Heroes and Prospects Oh Canada

OC1 Liam Reddox 8.00 20.00
OC2 Julien Ellis-Plante 8.00 20.00
OC3 Cody Bass 8.00 20.00
OC4 Derick Brassard 8.00 20.00
OC5 Ryan O'Marra 8.00 20.00
OC6 Kristopher Letang 10.00 25.00
OC7 David Bolland 8.00 20.00
OC8 Benoit Pouliot 10.00 25.00
OC9 Blake Comeau 8.00 20.00
OC10 Ryan Parent 8.00 20.00
OC11 Dustin Boyd 8.00 20.00
OC12 Steve Downie 8.00 20.00
OC13 Kyle Chipchura 8.00 20.00
OC14 Justin Peters 8.00 20.00
OC15 Dustin Kohn 8.00 20.00
OC16 Justin Keller 8.00 20.00
OC17 Dan LaCosta 8.00 20.00

2005-06 ITG Heroes and Prospects Shooting Stars

COMPLETE SET (12) 8.00 15.00
AS1 Jason LaBarbera .60 1.50
AS2 Lawrence Nycholat .40 1.00
AS3 Dennis Wideman .40 1.00
AS4 Jason Spezza .75 2.00
AS5 Mike Cammalleri .75 2.00
AS6 Michel Ouellet .60 1.50
AS7 Kari Lehtonen 2.00 5.00
AS8 Niklas Kronwall .75 2.00
AS9 Joni Pitkanen .60 1.50
AS10 Zach Parise 1.00 2.50
AS11 Andy Hilbert .40 1.00
AS12 Dustin Brown 1.00 2.50

2005-06 ITG Heroes and Prospects Team Cherry

TC1 Ty Wishart 2.00 5.00
TC2 Mike Weber 2.00 5.00
TC3 Chris Stewart 2.00 5.00
TC4 Joe Ryan 2.00 5.00
TC5 Theo Peckham 2.00 5.00
TC6 Peter Mueller 2.50 6.00
TC7 Jamie McGinn 2.00 5.00
TC8 Ben Maxwell 2.00 5.00
TC9 Bobby Hughes 2.00 5.00
TC10 Ryan Hillier 2.00 5.00
TC11 Nick Foligno 2.00 5.00
TC12 John de Gray 2.00 5.00
TC13 Cal Clutterbuck 2.50 6.00
TC14 Mathieu Carle 2.00 5.00
TC15 Brady Calla 2.00 5.00
TC16 Derick Brassard 2.50 6.00
TC17 Francois Bouchard 2.00 5.00
TC18 Jonathan Bernier 4.00 10.00
TC19 Matt Beleskey 2.00 5.00
TC20 Kevin Armstrong 2.00 5.00

2005-06 ITG Heroes and Prospects Team Orr

TO1 John Armstrong 2.00 5.00
TO2 Lukas Bohunicky 2.00 5.00
TO3 Benjamin Breault 2.00 5.00
TO4 Codey Burki 2.00 5.00
TO5 Matthew Corrente 2.00 5.00
TO6 Ryan Daniels 2.00 5.00
TO7 Tysen Dowzak 2.00 5.00
TO8 Cory Emmerton 2.00 5.00
TO9 Ondrej Fiala 2.00 5.00
TO10 Claude Giroux 4.00 10.00
TO11 Michael Grabner 3.00 8.00
TO12 Riley Holzapfel 2.00 5.00
TO13 Leland Irving 2.50 6.00
TO14 Bryan Little 3.00 8.00
TO15 Bob Sanguinetti 2.00 5.00
TO16 James Sheppard 2.00 5.00
TO17 Ben Shutron 2.00 5.00
TO18 Jordan Staal 3.00 8.00
TO19 Ivan Vishnevskiy 2.00 5.00
TO20 Ryan White 2.00 5.00

2006-07 ITG Heroes and Prospects

COMPLETE SET (200) 25.00 60.00
COMP.SET (150) 12.50 30.00
COMP.UPDATE SET (50) 12.50 30.00
1 Elmer Lach .20 .50
2 Milt Schmidt .25 .60
3 Brian Leetch .20 .50
4 Peter Stastny .20 .50
5 Mark Messier .50 1.25
6 Willie O'Ree .30 .75
7 Bryan Trottier .25 .60
8 Jaromir Jagr .75 2.00
9 Mario Lemieux 1.00 2.50
10 Luc Robitaille .25 .60
11 Dick Duff .20 .50
12 Ron Francis .30 .75
13 Guy Lafleur .30 .75
14 Patrick Roy .60 1.50
15 Martin Brodeur .60 1.50
16 Tim Thomas .25 .60
17 Cristobal Huet .20 .50
18 Jeff Carter .20 .50
19 Marc-Andre Fleury .50 1.25
20 Billy Smith .25 .60
21 Johnny Bower .25 .60
22 Antero Niittymaki .20 .50
23 Brad Boyes .15 .40
24 Sidney Crosby 1.00 2.50
25 Cam Ward .25 .60
26 Kyle Wellwood .20 .50
27 Jason Spezza .25 .60
28 Wendel Clark .40 1.00
29 Denis Potvin .25 .60
30 Bobby Clarke .40 1.00
31 Tony Voce .15 .40
32 Martin Houle .20 .50
33 Brendan Bell .15 .40
34 Eric Fehr .25 .60
35 Carsen Germyn .15 .40
36 Yann Danis .20 .50
37 Roman Voloshenko .15 .40
38 Tomas Kopecky .20 .50
39 Ben Ondrus .15 .40
40 Nathan Marsters .15 .40
41 Marc-Antoine Pouliot .15 .40
42 Konstantin Pushkarev .20 .50
43 Ian White .20 .50
44 Jeremy Williams .15 .40
45 Noah Welch .15 .40
46 Rick Rypien .40 1.00
47 Lauri Tukonen .15 .40
48 Danny Syvret .15 .40
49 Mark Giordano .25 .60
50 Andrew Penner .20 .50
51 Aleksander Suglobov .15 .40
52 David LeNeveu .20 .50
53 Doug O'Brien .15 .40
54 Martin St. Pierre .15 .40
55 Dan Fritsche .15 .40
56 Connor James .15 .40
57 Dustin Penner .20 .50
58 Ryan Vesce .15 .40
59 Colby Genoway .15 .40
60 Ben Walter .15 .40
61 Richie Regehr .15 .40
62 Trevor Gillies .15 .40
63 Mark Hartigan .15 .40
64 Garett Bembridge .15 .40
65 Ladislav Smid .15 .40
66 Braydon Coburn .15 .40
67 Jeremy Colliton .15 .40
68 Nathan Paetsch .15 .40
69 Pavel Vorobiev .15 .40
70 Matt Jones .15 .40
71 Corey Locke .15 .40
72 Corey Crawford .25 .60
73 Erik Westrum .15 .40
74 Patrick O'Sullivan .25 .60
75 Jeff Tambellini .15 .40
76 Al Montoya .25 .60
77 Matthew Spiller .15 .40
78 Nigel Dawes .15 .40
79 Ryan Shannon .15 .40
80 Steven Stamkos 2.00 5.00
81 Angelo Esposito .30 .75
82 John Tavares 2.00 5.00
83 Jordan Staal .40 1.00
84 Derick Brassard .15 .40
85 Peter Mueller .25 .60
86 Bryan Little .15 .40
87 James Sheppard .15 .40
88 Cory Emmerton .20 .50
89 Bob Sanguinetti .20 .50
90 Ondrej Fiala .15 .40
91 Logan Couture .40 1.00
92 Ty Wishart .15 .40
93 Ryan Hillier .15 .40
94 Jared Staal .25 .60
95 Bobby Hughes .15 .40
96 Brady Calla .15 .40
97 Joe Ryan .15 .40
98 Ivan Vishnevskiy .20 .50
99 Gilbert Brule .20 .50
100 Bud Holloway .15 .40
101 Ben Maxwell .25 .60
102 Matt Beleskey .25 .60
103 John Armstrong .15 .40
104 Michael Grabner .25 .60
105 Oskar Osala .15 .40
106 Jamie McGinn .20 .50
107 Luke Lynes .15 .40
108 Drew Doughty .50 1.25
109 Alex Bourret .15 .40
110 Chris Stewart .20 .50
111 Jonathan Bernier .50 1.25
112 Leland Irving .30 .75
113 Claude Giroux .75 2.00
114 Ryan Daniels .20 .50
115 Nick Foligno .20 .50
116 Matthew Corrente .15 .40
117 Francois Bouchard .20 .50
118 Brandon Sutter .25 .60
119 Michael Del Zotto .25 .60
120 Sergei Kostitsyn .20 .50
121 Corey Syvret .15 .40
122 Steve Downie .15 .40
123 Brett Sutter .15 .40
124 Shawn Matthias .20 .50
125 Alexander Radulov .30 .75
126 Guillaume Latendresse .25 .60
127 Ryan White .20 .50
128 Luc Bourdon .25 .60
129 Colton Gillies .20 .50
130 Marc Staal .25 .60
131 Anze Kopitar .75 2.00
132 Jiri Tlusty .25 .60
133 Yuri Alexandrov .15 .40
134 Tuukka Rask .60 1.50
135 Evgeni Malkin 1.00 2.50
136 Phil Kessel .50 1.25
137 Alexander Vasyunov .15 .40
138 Michael Frolik .20 .50
139 John Tavares 1.00 2.50
140 Justin Pogge .20 .50
141 Jonathan Bernier .50 1.25
142 Brandon Sutter .25 .60
143 Luc Bourdon .40 1.00
144 Steve Downie .15 .40
145 Kristopher Letang .60 1.50
146 Ryan Parent .25 .60
147 Sidney Crosby 1.00 2.50
148 Marc Staal .25 .60
149 Guillaume Latendresse .25 .60
150 Tom Pyatt .15 .40
151 Joe Pavelski .75 2.00
152 Chris Harrington .15 .40
153 Bill Thomas .15 .40
154 Loui Eriksson .30 .75
155 Benoit Pouliot .20 .50
156 Eric Nystrom .15 .40
157 Bryan Bickell .30 .75
158 Nicklas Bergfors .25 .60
159 Hugh Jessiman .15 .40
160 Jiri Hudler .25 .60
161 Alexander Radulov .30 .75
162 Mike Green .20 .50
163 Staffan Kronwall .15 .40
164 Drew Miller .20 .50
165 Brett Sterling .15 .40
166 Jeff Taffe .15 .40
167 Geoff Platt .15 .40
168 Blake Comeau .25 .60
169 Ryan Carter .15 .40
170 Drew Stafford .25 .60
171 Petr Kalus .15 .40
172 Josh Hennessy .15 .40
173 Rob Schremp .20 .50
174 Janis Sprukts .15 .40
175 Patrick Kane 2.50 6.00
176 Bobby Ryan .25 .60
177 Devin Setoguchi .25 .60
178 Michael Frolik .20 .50
179 Brodie Dupont .15 .40
180 Tom Pyatt .15 .40
181 Kenndal McArdle .15 .40
182 Michael Caruso .15 .40
183 James Neal .40 1.00
184 Ben Shutron .15 .40
185 Marc-Andre Cliche .15 .40
186 Felix Schutz .15 .40
187 Cody Bass .15 .40
188 Dustin Kohn .15 .40
189 Marc-Edouard Vlasic .25 .60
190 Dan Ryder .15 .40
191 Mathieu Carle .15 .40
192 Justin Azevedo .15 .40
193 Kristopher Letang .60 1.50
194 Kris Russell .20 .50
195 Patrick McNeill .15 .40
196 Marc-Andre Gragnani .15 .40
197 Cody Franson .20 .50
198 Cal Clutterbuck .20 .50
199 Jakub Voracek .60 1.50
200 Sam Gagner .30 .75

2006-07 ITG Heroes and Prospects AHL All-Star Emblems

AE01 Jeff Tambellini 6.00 15.00
AE02 Martin St. Pierre 6.00 15.00
AE03 Jiri Hudler 10.00 25.00
AE04 John Pohl 8.00 20.00
AE05 Yann Danis 8.00 20.00
AE06 Patrick O'Sullivan 10.00 25.00
AE07 Denis Hamel 8.00 20.00
AE08 Keith Ballard 6.00 15.00
AE09 Denis Shvidki 8.00 20.00
AE10 Rick DiPietro 8.00 20.00
AE11 Phillipe Sauve 8.00 20.00
AE12 Kyle Wellwood 8.00 20.00

2006-07 ITG Heroes and Prospects AHL All-Star Jerseys

AJ01 Jeff Tambellini 2.50 6.00
AJ02 Martin St. Pierre 3.00 8.00
AJ03 Jiri Hudler 4.00 10.00
AJ04 John Pohl 3.00 8.00
AJ05 Yann Danis 3.00 8.00
AJ06 Patrick O'Sullivan 4.00 10.00
AJ07 Denis Hamel 3.00 8.00
AJ08 Keith Ballard 2.50 6.00
AJ09 Denis Shvidki 3.00 8.00
AJ10 Rick DiPietro 3.00 8.00
AJ11 Phillipe Sauve 3.00 8.00
AJ12 Kyle Wellwood 3.00 8.00

2006-07 ITG Heroes and Prospects AHL All-Star Numbers

AN01 Jeff Tambellini 6.00 15.00
AN02 Martin St. Pierre 6.00 15.00
AN03 Jiri Hudler 10.00 25.00
AN04 John Pohl 8.00 20.00
AN05 Yann Danis 8.00 20.00
AN06 Patrick O'Sullivan 10.00 25.00
AN07 Denis Hamel 8.00 20.00
AN08 Keith Ballard 6.00 15.00
AN09 Denis Shvidki 8.00 20.00
AN10 Rick DiPietro 8.00 20.00
AN11 Phillipe Sauve 8.00 20.00
AN12 Kyle Wellwood 8.00 20.00

2006-07 ITG Heroes and Prospects AHL Shooting Stars

AS01 Pekka Rinne .50 1.25
AS02 Sven Butenschon .30 .75
AS03 Noah Welch .30 .75
AS04 Jiri Hudler .50 1.25
AS05 John Pohl .40 1.00
AS06 Erik Westrum .30 .75
AS07 Wade Flaherty .30 .75
AS08 Nathan Paetsch .30 .75
AS09 John Slaney .30 .75
AS10 Jimmy Roy .30 .75
AS11 Kirby Law .30 .75
AS12 Eric Fehr .50 1.25

2006-07 ITG Heroes and Prospects Autographs

AAB Alex Bourret 3.00 8.00
AAE Angelo Esposito 6.00 15.00
AAK Anze Kopitar 15.00 40.00
AAN Antero Niittymaki 4.00 10.00
AAP Andrew Penner 4.00 10.00
AAR Alexander Radulov 6.00 15.00
AAS Aleksander Suglobov 3.00 8.00
AAV Alexander Vasyunov 3.00 8.00
ABB Brendan Bell 3.00 8.00
ABC Bobby Clarke 8.00 20.00
ABD Brodie Dupont 3.00 8.00
ABH Bobby Hughes 3.00 8.00
ABL Brian Leetch 4.00 10.00
ABM Ben Maxwell 5.00 12.00
ABO Ben Ondrus 3.00 8.00
ABP Benoit Pouliot 4.00 10.00
ABR Bobby Ryan 5.00 12.00
ABT Bill Thomas 3.00 8.00
ABW Ben Walter 3.00 8.00
ACB Cody Bass 3.00 8.00
ACC Corey Crawford 5.00 12.00
ACE Cory Emmerton 4.00 10.00
ACF Cody Franson 4.00 10.00
ACG Carsen Germyn 3.00 8.00
ACH Cristobal Huet 4.00 10.00
ACJ Connor James 3.00 8.00
ACL Corey Locke 3.00 8.00
ACS Chris Stewart 4.00 10.00
ACW Cam Ward 5.00 12.00
ADB Derick Brassard 3.00 8.00
ADD Dick Duff 4.00 10.00
ADF Dan Fritsche 3.00 8.00
ADK Dustin Kohn 3.00 8.00
ADL David LeNeveu 4.00 10.00
ADM Drew Miller 4.00 10.00
ADO Doug O'Brien 3.00 8.00
ADP Denis Potvin 5.00 12.00
ADR Dan Ryder 3.00 8.00
ADS Drew Stafford 5.00 12.00
AEF Eric Fehr 5.00 12.00
AEL Elmer Lach 4.00 10.00
AEM Evgeni Malkin 20.00 50.00
AEN Eric Nystrom 3.00 8.00
AEW Erik Westrum 3.00 8.00
AFB Francois Bouchard 4.00 10.00
AFS Felix Schutz 3.00 8.00
AGB Garett Bembridge 3.00 8.00
AGP Geoff Platt 3.00 8.00
AHJ Hugh Jessiman 3.00 8.00
AIV Ivan Vishnevskiy 4.00 10.00
AIW Ian White 4.00 10.00
AJA John Armstrong 3.00 8.00
AJC Jeremy Colliton 3.00 8.00
AJH Jiri Hudler 5.00 12.00
AJJ Jaromir Jagr 15.00 40.00
AJM Jamie McGinn 4.00 10.00
AJN James Neal 8.00 20.00
AJP Justin Pogge 4.00 10.00
AJR Joe Ryan 3.00 8.00
AJS Jason Spezza 5.00 12.00
AJV Jakub Voracek 12.00 30.00
AJW Jeremy Williams 3.00 8.00
AKL Kristopher Letang 12.00 30.00
AKM Kenndal McArdle 3.00 8.00
AKP Konstantin Pushkarev 4.00 10.00
AKR Kris Russell 4.00 10.00
AKW Kyle Wellwood 4.00 10.00
ALC Logan Couture 8.00 20.00
ALE Loui Eriksson 6.00 15.00
ALI Leland Irving 6.00 15.00
ALL Luke Lynes 3.00 8.00
ALR Luc Robitaille 5.00 12.00
ALS Ladislav Smid 3.00 8.00
ALT Lauri Tukonen 3.00 8.00
AMB Martin Brodeur 12.00 30.00
AMC Matthew Corrente 3.00 8.00
AMF Michael Frolik 4.00 10.00
AMG Mike Green 4.00 10.00
AMH Martin Houle 4.00 10.00
AMJ Matt Jones 3.00 8.00
AML Mario Lemieux 20.00 50.00
AMM Mark Messier 10.00 25.00
ANB Nicklas Bergfors 5.00 12.00
AND Nigel Dawes 3.00 8.00
ANF Nick Foligno 4.00 10.00
ANM Nathan Marsters 3.00 8.00
ANP Nathan Paetsch 3.00 8.00
ANW Noah Welch 3.00 8.00
AOF Ondrej Fiala 3.00 8.00
AOO Oskar Osala 3.00 8.00
APK Phil Kessel 10.00 25.00
APM Peter Mueller 5.00 12.00
APR Patrick Roy 12.00 30.00
APS Peter Stastny 4.00 10.00
APV Pavel Vorobiev 3.00 8.00
ARC Ryan Carter 3.00 8.00
ARF Ron Francis 6.00 15.00
ARH Ryan Hillier 3.00 8.00
ARP Ryan Parent 5.00 12.00
ARR Rick Rypien 8.00 20.00
ARS Ryan Shannon 3.00 8.00
ARV Roman Voloshenko 3.00 8.00
ARW Ryan White 4.00 10.00
ASG Sam Gagner 6.00 15.00
ASK Sergei Kostitsyn 4.00 10.00
ASM Shawn Matthias 4.00 10.00
ASS Steven Stamkos 25.00 60.00
ATG Trevor Gillies 3.00 8.00
ATK Tomas Kopecky 4.00 10.00
ATP Tom Pyatt 3.00 8.00
ATR Tuukka Rask 12.00 30.00
ATT Tim Thomas 5.00 12.00
ATV Tony Voce 3.00 8.00
ATW Ty Wishart 3.00 8.00
AWC Wendel Clark 8.00 20.00
AWO Willie O'Ree 6.00 15.00
AYA Yuri Alexandrov 3.00 8.00
AYD Yann Danis 4.00 10.00
AAMO Al Montoya 5.00 12.00
AAR2 Alexander Radulov 6.00 15.00
ABBI Bryan Bickell 6.00 15.00
ABBO Brad Boyes 3.00 8.00
ABCA Brady Calla 3.00 8.00
ABCM Blake Comeau 5.00 12.00
ABCO Braydon Coburn 3.00 8.00
ABHO Bud Holloway 3.00 8.00
ABLI Bryan Little 3.00 8.00
ABRS Brett Sutter 3.00 8.00
ABS1 Brandon Sutter 5.00 12.00
ABS2 Brandon Sutter 5.00 12.00
ABSA Bob Sanguinetti 4.00 10.00
ABSH Ben Shutron 3.00 8.00
ABSM Billy Smith 5.00 12.00
ABST Brett Sterling 3.00 8.00
ABTR Bryan Trottier 5.00 12.00
ACCL Cal Clutterbuck 4.00 10.00
ACGE Colby Genoway 3.00 8.00
ACGI Colton Gillies 4.00 10.00
ACGR Claude Giroux 15.00 40.00
ACHA Chris Harrington 3.00 8.00
ACSV Corey Syvret 3.00 8.00
ADDO Drew Doughty 10.00 25.00
ADPE Dustin Penner 4.00 10.00
ADSE Devin Setoguchi 5.00 12.00
ADSV Danny Syvret 3.00 8.00
AGBR Gilbert Brule 4.00 10.00
AGLF Guy Lafleur 6.00 15.00
AJAS Jared Staal 5.00 12.00
AJAZ Justin Azevedo 3.00 8.00
AJB1 Jonathan Bernier 10.00 25.00
AJB2 Jonathan Bernier 10.00 25.00
AJBO Johnny Bower 5.00 12.00
AJCA Jeff Carter 4.00 10.00
AJHE Josh Hennessy 3.00 8.00
AJPV Joe Pavelski 15.00 40.00
AJSH James Sheppard 3.00 8.00
AJSP Janis Sprukts 3.00 8.00
AJST Jordan Staal 8.00 20.00
AJT1 John Tavares 20.00 50.00
AJT2 John Tavares 20.00 50.00
AJTA Jeff Tambellini 3.00 8.00
AJTF Jeff Taffe 3.00 8.00
AJTL Jiri Tlusty 5.00 12.00
AKL2 Kristopher Letang 12.00 30.00
ALB1 Luc Bourdon 5.00 12.00
ALB2 Luc Bourdon 5.00 12.00
AMAC Marc-Andre Cliche 3.00 8.00
AMAF Marc-Andre Fleury 10.00 25.00
AMAG Marc-Andre Gragnani 3.00 8.00
AMAP Marc-Antoine Pouliot 3.00 8.00
AMBL Matt Beleskey 5.00 12.00
AMCA Michael Caruso 3.00 8.00
AMCR Mathieu Carle 3.00 8.00
AMDZ Michael Del Zotto 5.00 12.00
AMEV Marc-Edouard Vlasic 5.00 12.00
AMF2 Michael Frolik 4.00 10.00
AMGI Mark Giordano 5.00 12.00
AMGR Michael Grabner 5.00 12.00
AMHA Mark Hartigan 3.00 8.00
AMS1 Marc Staal 5.00 12.00
AMS2 Marc Staal 5.00 12.00

AMSC Milt Schmidt 5.00 12.00
AMSP Matthew Spiller 3.00 8.00
AMST Martin St. Pierre 3.00 8.00
APKA Petr Kalus 3.00 8.00
APKN Patrick Kane 40.00 100.00
APMC Patrick McNeill 3.00 8.00
APOS Patrick O'Sullivan 5.00 12.00
ARDA Ryan Daniels 4.00 10.00
ARRG Richie Regehr 3.00 8.00
ARSC Rob Schremp 4.00 10.00
ARVE Ryan Vesce 3.00 8.00
ASC1 Sidney Crosby 60.00 150.00
ASC2 Sidney Crosby 60.00 150.00
ASD1 Steve Downie 3.00 8.00
ASD2 Steve Downie 3.00 8.00
ASKR Staffan Kronwall 3.00 8.00
ATP2 Tom Pyatt 3.00 8.00

2006-07 ITG Heroes and Prospects Calder Cup Champions

CC01 Frederic Cassivi .60 1.50
CC02 Tomas Fleischmann .50 1.25
CC03 Mike Green .60 1.50
CC04 Kris Beech .50 1.25
CC05 Brooks Laich .50 1.25
CC06 Graham Mink .50 1.25
CC07 Boyd Gordon .50 1.25
CC08 Dave Steckel .50 1.25
CC09 Lawrence Nycholat .50 1.25
CC10 Boyd Kane .50 1.25
CC11 Joey Tenute .50 1.25
CC12 Jeff Schultz .50 1.25
CC13 Eric Fehr .75 2.00

2006-07 ITG Heroes and Prospects CHL Top Prospects

TP01 Ben Shutron 1.50 4.00
TP02 Claude Giroux 8.00 20.00
TP03 Francois Bouchard 2.00 5.00
TP04 Ivan Visnevskiy 2.00 5.00
TP05 Corey Perry 4.00 10.00
TP06 Mike Richards 3.00 8.00
TP07 Bob Sanguinetti 2.00 5.00
TP08 Derick Brassard 1.50 4.00
TP09 James Sheppard 1.50 4.00
TP10 Jonathan Bernier 5.00 12.00
TP11 Jordan Staal 4.00 10.00
TP12 Matthew Corrente 1.50 4.00
TP13 Ryan Daniels 2.00 5.00
TP14 Tysen Dowzak 1.50 4.00
TP15 Ben Maxwell 2.50 6.00
TP16 Carey Price 10.00 25.00
TP17 Eric Fehr 2.50 6.00
TP18 Julien Ellis 2.00 5.00
TP19 Eric Staal 3.00 8.00

2006-07 ITG Heroes and Prospects Class of 2006

COMMON CARD .50 1.25
SEMISTARS .60 1.50
UNLISTED STARS .75 2.00
CL01 Jordan Staal 1.25 3.00
CL02 Phil Kessel 1.50 4.00
CL03 Derick Brassard .50 1.25
CL04 Peter Mueller .75 2.00
CL05 James Sheppard .50 1.25
CL06 Michael Frolik .60 1.50
CL07 Jonathan Bernier 1.50 4.00
CL08 Bryan Little .50 1.25
CL09 Michael Grabner .75 2.00
CL10 Ty Wishart .50 1.25
CL11 Chris Stewart .60 1.50
CL12 Bob Sanguinetti .60 1.50
CL13 Claude Giroux 2.50 6.00

2006-07 ITG Heroes and Prospects Double Memorabilia

DM01 Jordan Staal 8.00 20.00
DM02 Mario Lemieux 20.00 50.00
DM03 Sidney Crosby 20.00 50.00
DM04 Martin Brodeur 12.00 30.00
DM05 Patrick Roy 12.00 30.00
DM06 Mark Messier 10.00 25.00
DM07 Joe Sakic 10.00 25.00
DM08 John Tavares 20.00 50.00
DM09 Roberto Luongo 8.00 20.00
DM10 Sam Gagner 6.00 15.00

2006-07 ITG Heroes and Prospects Emblems

GUE01 Marek Schwarz 6.00 15.00
GUE02 David Ruzicka 4.00 10.00
GUE03 Jimmy Howard 10.00 25.00
GUE04 Daniel Girardi 4.00 10.00
GUE05 Mike Green 5.00 12.00
GUE06 Nigel Dawes 4.00 10.00
GUE07 Curtis McElhinney 5.00 12.00
GUE08 Mike Smith 10.00 25.00
GUE09 Corey Locke 4.00 10.00
GUE10 Yann Danis 5.00 12.00
GUE11 Tomi Maki 4.00 10.00
GUE12 Erik Christensen 5.00 12.00
GUE13 Maxime Talbot 4.00 10.00
GUE14 Tony Voce 4.00 10.00
GUE15 Josh Harding 6.00 15.00
GUE16 Ian White 5.00 12.00
GUE17 Jarkko Immonen 5.00 12.00
GUE18 Ryan Getzlaf 6.00 15.00
GUE19 Jeremy Colliton 4.00 10.00
GUE20 Fernando Pisani 4.00 10.00
GUE21 Noah Welch 4.00 10.00
GUE22 Billy Thompson 4.00 10.00
GUE23 Staffan Kronwall 4.00 10.00
GUE24 Darryl Bootland 4.00 10.00
GUE25 Dustin Penner 5.00 12.00
GUE26 Paul Ranger 4.00 10.00
GUE27 Alexandre Picard 4.00 10.00
GUE28 Daniel Paille 5.00 12.00
GUE29 Andy Rogers 4.00 10.00
GUE30 Tysen Dowzak 4.00 10.00
GUE31 Jamie McGinn 5.00 12.00
GUE32 Ryan Callahan 6.00 15.00
GUE33 Angelo Esposito 8.00 20.00
GUE34 John Tavares 25.00 60.00
GUE35 Tim Thomas 6.00 15.00
GUE36 Bud Holloway 4.00 10.00
GUE37 Kevin Lalande 5.00 12.00
GUE38 Leland Irving 8.00 20.00
GUE39 Peter Mueller 6.00 15.00
GUE40 Marc Staal 6.00 15.00
GUE41 Benoit Pouliot 5.00 12.00
GUE42 Wojtek Wolski 5.00 12.00
GUE43 Bryan Little 4.00 10.00
GUE44 Ben Shutron 4.00 10.00
GUE45 Ryan O'Marra 4.00 10.00
GUE46 Adam Perry 4.00 10.00
GUE47 James Sheppard 4.00 10.00
GUE48 Nicholas Drazenovic 4.00 10.00
GUE49 Bobby Ryan 6.00 15.00
GUE50 Tyler Plante 5.00 12.00
GUE51 Matt Corrente 4.00 10.00
GUE52 Ondrej Fiala 4.00 10.00
GUE53 J-S Aubin 5.00 12.00
GUE54 Ryan Vesce 4.00 10.00
GUE55 Petr Taticek 4.00 10.00
GUE56 Ben Walter 4.00 10.00
GUE57 Andrew Penner 5.00 12.00
GUE58 Francois Beauchemin 4.00 10.00
GUE59 Cristobal Huet 5.00 12.00
GUE60 Jay Bouwmeester 4.00 10.00
GUE61 Phil Kessel 12.00 30.00
GUE62 Petr Kalus 4.00 10.00
GUE63 Drew Stafford 6.00 15.00
GUE64 Alexander Radulov 8.00 20.00
GUE65 Jiri Hudler 6.00 15.00
GUE66 Cory Emmerton 5.00 12.00
GUE67 Loui Eriksson 8.00 20.00
GUE68 Bobby Ryan 6.00 15.00
GUE69 Jakub Voracek 15.00 40.00
GUE70 Sam Gagner 8.00 20.00
GUE71 Michael Grabner 6.00 15.00
GUE72 Rob Schremp 5.00 12.00
GUE73 Cal Clutterbuck 5.00 12.00

2006-07 ITG Heroes and Prospects He Shoots He Scores Points

1 Acadie-Bathurst Titan .40 1.00
2 Albany River Rats .40 1.00
3 Baie-Comeau Drakkar .40 1.00
4 Barrie Colts .40 1.00
5 Belleville Bulls .40 1.00
6 Binghamton Senators .40 1.00
7 Brampton Battalion .40 1.00
8 Brandon Wheat Kings .40 1.00
9 Bridgeport Sound Tigers .40 1.00
10 Calgary Hitmen .40 1.00
11 Cape Breton Screaming Eagles .40 1.00
12 Chicago Wolves .40 1.00
13 Chicoutimi Sagueneens .40 1.00
14 Cleveland Barons .40 1.00
15 Drummondville Voltigeurs .40 1.00
16 Erie Otters .40 1.00
17 Everett Silvertips .40 1.00
18 Gatineau Olympiques .40 1.00
19 Grand Rapids Griffins .40 1.00
20 Guelph Storm .40 1.00
21 Halifax Mooseheads .40 1.00
22 Hamilton Bulldogs .40 1.00
23 Hartford Wolf Pack .40 1.00
24 Hershey Bears .40 1.00
25 Houston Aeros .40 1.00
26 Iowa Stars .40 1.00
27 Kamloops Blazers .40 1.00
28 Kelowna Rockets .40 1.00
29 Kingston Frontenacs .40 1.00
30 Kitchener Rangers .40 1.00
31 Kootenay Ice .40 1.00
32 Lethbridge Hurricanes .40 1.00
33 Lewiston Maineiacs .40 1.00
34 London Knights .40 1.00
35 Lowell Lock Monsters .40 1.00
36 Manchester Monarchs .40 1.00
37 Manitoba Moose .40 1.00
38 Medicine Hat Tigers .40 1.00
39 Milwaukee Admirals .40 1.00
40 Mississauga Icedogs .40 1.00
41 Moncton Wildcats .40 1.00
42 Moose Jaw Warriors .40 1.00
43 Norfolk Admirals .40 1.00
44 Omaha Ak-Sar-Ben Knights .40 1.00
45 Oshawa Generals .40 1.00
46 Ottawa 67s .40 1.00
47 Owen Sound Attack .40 1.00
48 Pei Rocket .40 1.00
49 Peoria Reivermen .40 1.00
50 Peterborough Petes .40 1.00
51 Philadelphia Phantoms .40 1.00
52 Plymouth Whalers .40 1.00
53 Portland Pirates .40 1.00
54 Portland Winterhawks .40 1.00
55 Prince Albert Raiders .40 1.00
56 Prince George Cougars .40 1.00
57 Providence Bruins .40 1.00
58 Quebec Remparts .40 1.00
59 Red Deer Rebels .40 1.00
60 Regina Pats .40 1.00
61 Rimouski Oceanic .40 1.00
62 Rochester Americans .40 1.00
63 Rouyn-Noranda Huskies .40 1.00
64 Saginaw Spirit .40 1.00
65 San Antonio Rampage .40 1.00
66 Sarnia Sting .40 1.00
67 Saskatoon Blades .40 1.00
68 Sault Ste. Marie Greyhounds .40 1.00
69 Seattle Thunderbirds .40 1.00
70 Shawinigan Cataractes .40 1.00
71 Spokane Chiefs .40 1.00
72 Springfield Falcons .40 1.00
73 St. Michael's Majors .40 1.00
74 Sudbury Wolves .40 1.00
75 Swift Current Broncos .40 1.00
76 Syracuse Crunch .40 1.00
77 Toronto Marlies .40 1.00
78 Tri-City Americans .40 1.00
79 Val-D'or Foreurs .40 1.00
80 Vancouver Giants .40 1.00
81 Victoriaville Tigres .40 1.00
82 Wilkes-Barre/Scranton Penguins .40 1.00
83 Windsor Spitfires .40 1.00
84 In The Game Logo .40 1.00
85 AHL Logo .40 1.00
86 CHL Logo .40 1.00
87 LHJMQ Logo .40 1.00
88 OHL Logo .40 1.00
89 PHPA Logo .40 1.00
90 WHL Logo .40 1.00

2006-07 ITG Heroes and Prospects He Shoots He Scores Prizes

HSHS01 A.Ovechkin/P.Kessel 20.00 50.00
HSHS02 M.Brodeur/L.Irving 12.00 30.00
HSHS03 S.Yzerman/A.Esposito 12.00 30.00
HSHS04 J.Jagr/M.Frolik 15.00 40.00
HSHS05 M.Lemieux/E.Malkin 20.00 50.00
HSHS06 T.Sawchuk/J.Howard 8.00 20.00
HSHS07 M.Messier/J.Tavares 20.00 50.00
HSHS08 B.Leetch/M.Staal 5.00 12.00
HSHS09 M.Richard/D.Brassard 10.00 25.00
HSHS10 R.Francis/E.Staal 6.00 15.00
HSHS11 T.Horton/D.Phaneuf 6.00 15.00
HSHS12 D.Gilmour/S.Downie 6.00 15.00
HSHS13 P.LaFontaine/P.Mueller 5.00 12.00
HSHS14 J.Bower/J.Pogge 5.00 12.00
HSHS15 B.Hull/J.Spezza 10.00 25.00
HSHS16 C.Neely/M.Richards 5.00 12.00
HSHS17 I.Kovalchuk/A.Ovechkin 20.00 50.00
HSHS18 H.Morenz/G.Latendresse 5.00 12.00
HSHS19 D.Keon/K.Wellwood 5.00 12.00
HSHS20 S.Yzerman/M.Grabner 12.00 30.00
HSHS21 F.Mahovlich/P.Kessel 10.00 25.00
HSHS22 P.Roy/C.Huet 12.00 30.00
HSHS23 B.Barilko/M.Staal 5.00 12.00
HSHS24 M.Brodeur/J.Bernier 12.00 30.00
HSHS25 R.Bourque/W.Wolski 8.00 20.00
HSHS26 M.Messier/R.Schremp 10.00 25.00
HSHS27 G.Fuhr/L.Irving 8.00 20.00
HSHS28 J.Jagr/J.Tlusty 15.00 40.00
HSHS29 J.Beliveau/A.Esposito 6.00 15.00
HSHS30 T.Sawchuk/R.Miller 6.00 15.00
HSHS31 G.Cheevers/H.Toivonen 5.00 12.00
HSHS32 J.Plante/C.Huet 5.00 12.00
HSHS33 E.Lindros/J.Tavares 20.00 50.00
HSHS34 S.Yzerman/J.Sheppard 12.00 30.00
HSHS35 B.Hull/A.Ovechkin 20.00 50.00
HSHS36 P.Roy/C.Price 20.00 50.00
HSHS37 M.Messier/E.Malkin 20.00 50.00
HSHS38 M.Brodeur/C.Ward 12.00 30.00
HSHS39 T.Lindsay/B.Ryan 5.00 12.00
HSHS40 G.Lafleur/G.Latendresse 6.00 15.00

2006-07 ITG Heroes and Prospects Heroes Memorabilia

HM01 Luc Robitaille 6.00 15.00
HM02 Billy Smith 6.00 15.00
HM03 Steve Yzerman 15.00 40.00
HM04 Ron Francis 8.00 20.00
HM05 Martin Brodeur 15.00 40.00
HM06 Patrick Roy 15.00 40.00
HM07 Jaromir Jagr 20.00 50.00
HM08 Mark Messier 12.00 30.00
HM09 Brian Leetch 5.00 12.00
HM10 Dave Keon 6.00 15.00
HM11 Milt Schmidt 6.00 15.00
HM12 Jacques Plante 6.00 15.00
HM13 Bobby Hull 12.00 30.00
HM14 Frank Mahovlich 6.00 15.00
HM15 Jean Beliveau 6.00 15.00
HM16 Red Kelly 6.00 15.00
HM17 Stan Mikita 8.00 20.00
HM18 Tim Horton 8.00 20.00
HM19 Terry Sawchuk 8.00 20.00
HM20 Johnny Bower 6.00 15.00
HM21 Joe Sakic 12.00 30.00
HM22 Ed Belfour 6.00 15.00
HM23 Joe Thornton 10.00 25.00
HM24 Roberto Luongo 10.00 25.00
HM25 Nicklas Lidstrom 6.00 15.00
HM26 Manny Fernandez 4.00 10.00

2006-07 ITG Heroes and Prospects Jerseys

GUJ01 Marek Schwarz 4.00 10.00
GUJ02 David Ruzicka 2.50 6.00
GUJ03 Jimmy Howard 6.00 15.00
GUJ04 Daniel Girardi 2.50 6.00
GUJ05 Mike Green 3.00 8.00
GUJ06 Nigel Dawes 2.50 6.00
GUJ07 Curtis McElhinney 3.00 8.00
GUJ08 Mike Smith 6.00 15.00
GUJ09 Corey Locke 2.50 6.00
GUJ10 Yann Danis 3.00 8.00
GUJ11 Tomi Maki 2.50 6.00
GUJ12 Erik Christensen 3.00 8.00
GUJ13 Maxime Talbot 2.50 6.00
GUJ14 Tony Voce 2.50 6.00
GUJ15 Josh Harding 4.00 10.00
GUJ16 Ian White 3.00 8.00
GUJ17 Jarkko Immonen 3.00 8.00
GUJ18 Ryan Getzlaf 4.00 10.00
GUJ19 Jeremy Colliton 2.50 6.00
GUJ20 Fernando Pisani 2.50 6.00
GUJ21 Noah Welch 2.50 6.00
GUJ22 Billy Thompson 2.50 6.00
GUJ23 Staffan Kronwall 2.50 6.00
GUJ24 Darryl Bootland 2.50 6.00
GUJ25 Dustin Penner 3.00 8.00
GUJ26 Paul Ranger 2.50 6.00
GUJ27 Alexandre Picard 2.50 6.00
GUJ28 Daniel Paille 3.00 8.00
GUJ29 Andy Rogers 2.50 6.00
GUJ30 Tysen Dowzak 2.50 6.00
GUJ31 Jamie McGinn 3.00 8.00
GUJ32 Ryan Callahan 4.00 10.00
GUJ33 Angelo Esposito 5.00 12.00
GUJ34 John Tavares 15.00 40.00
GUJ35 Tim Thomas 4.00 10.00
GUJ36 Bud Holloway 2.50 6.00
GUJ37 Kevin Lalande 3.00 8.00
GUJ38 Leland Irving 5.00 12.00
GUJ39 Peter Mueller 4.00 10.00
GUJ40 Marc Staal 4.00 10.00
GUJ41 Benoit Pouliot 3.00 8.00
GUJ42 Wojtek Wolski 3.00 8.00
GUJ43 Bryan Little 2.50 6.00
GUJ44 Ben Shutron 2.50 6.00
GUJ45 Ryan O'Marra 2.50 6.00
GUJ46 Adam Perry 2.50 6.00
GUJ47 James Sheppard 2.50 6.00
GUJ48 Nicholas Drazenovic 2.50 6.00
GUJ49 Bobby Ryan 4.00 10.00
GUJ50 Tyler Plante 3.00 8.00
GUJ51 Matt Corrente 2.50 6.00
GUJ52 Ondrej Fiala 2.50 6.00
GUJ53 J-S Aubin 3.00 8.00
GUJ54 Ryan Vesce 2.50 6.00
GUJ55 Petr Taticek 2.50 6.00
GUJ56 Ben Walter 2.50 6.00
GUJ57 Andrew Penner 3.00 8.00
GUJ58 Francois Beauchemin 2.50 6.00
GUJ59 Cristobal Huet 3.00 8.00
GUJ60 Jay Bouwmeester 2.50 6.00
GUJ61 Phil Kessel 8.00 20.00
GUJ62 Petr Kalus 2.50 6.00
GUJ63 Drew Stafford 4.00 10.00
GUJ64 Alexander Radulov 5.00 12.00
GUJ65 Jiri Hudler 4.00 10.00
GUJ66 Cory Emmerton 3.00 8.00
GUJ67 Loui Eriksson 5.00 12.00
GUJ68 Bobby Ryan 4.00 10.00
GUJ69 Jakub Voracek 10.00 25.00
GUJ70 Sam Gagner 5.00 12.00
GUJ71 Michael Grabner 4.00 10.00
GUJ72 Rob Schremp 3.00 8.00
GUJ73 Cal Clutterbuck 3.00 8.00

2006-07 ITG Heroes and Prospects Making The Bigs

MTB01 Wojtek Wolski 3.00 8.00
MTB02 Tim Gleason 2.50 6.00
MTB03 Cam Ward 4.00 10.00
MTB04 Ryan Miller 4.00 10.00
MTB05 Mike Glumac 3.00 8.00
MTB06 Pascal Leclaire 3.00 8.00
MTB07 Ryan Getzlaf 4.00 10.00
MTB08 Eric Nystrom 2.50 6.00
MTB09 Ray Emery 3.00 8.00
MTB10 Eric Staal 5.00 12.00
MTB11 Marc-Antoine Pouliot 2.50 6.00
MTB12 Alexander Ovechkin 15.00 40.00

2006-07 ITG Heroes and Prospects Memorial Cup Champions

MC01 Cedrick Desjardins .50 1.25
MC02 Joe Ryan .50 1.25
MC03 Brent Aubin .50 1.25
MC04 Jordan LaVallee .50 1.25
MC05 Andrew Andricopoulos .50 1.25
MC06 Marc-Edouard Vlasic .75 2.00
MC07 Mathieu Melanson .50 1.25
MC08 Michal Sersen .50 1.25
MC09 Angelo Esposito 1.00 2.50
MC10 Maxime Lacroix .50 1.25
MC11 Alexander Radulov 1.00 2.50
MC12 Patrick Roy 2.00 5.00

2006-07 ITG Heroes and Prospects National Pride

NP01 Logan Stephenson 2.50 6.00
NP02 Sidney Crosby 15.00 40.00
NP03 Frederik Cabana 2.50 6.00
NP04 Alex Bourret 2.50 6.00
NP05 Tom Pyatt 2.50 6.00
NP06 Marc-Andre Gragnani 2.50 6.00
NP07 Olivier Latendresse 2.50 6.00
NP08 Marc Staal 4.00 10.00
NP09 Tyler Kennedy 2.50 6.00
NP10 Stephane Goulet 2.50 6.00
NP11 Devin Setoguchi 4.00 10.00
NP12 Benoit Pouliot 3.00 8.00
NP13 Jeff Schultz 2.50 6.00
NP14 Wacey Rabbit 2.50 6.00
NP15 Patrick McNeill 2.50 6.00
NP16 Steve Downie 2.50 6.00
NP17 Blake Comeau 4.00 10.00
NP18 Dustin Boyd 2.50 6.00
NP19 Kyle Chipchura 2.50 6.00
NP20 Carey Price 15.00 40.00
NP21 Marc Staal 4.00 10.00
NP22 Sam Gagner 5.00 12.00
NP23 Steve Downie 2.50 6.00

2006-07 ITG Heroes and Prospects Net Prospects

NPR01 Leland Irving 5.00 12.00
NPR02 Marek Schwarz 4.00 10.00
NPR03 Jimmy Howard 6.00 15.00
NPR04 Cam Ward 4.00 10.00
NPR05 Cristobal Huet 3.00 8.00
NPR06 Ryan Miller 4.00 10.00
NPR07 Ray Emery 3.00 8.00
NPR08 Justin Pogge 3.00 8.00
NPR09 Carey Price 15.00 40.00
NPR10 Jonathan Bernier 8.00 20.00
NPR11 Hannu Toivonen 3.00 8.00
NPR12 Thomas McCollum 4.00 10.00
NPR13 Justin Pogge 3.00 8.00
NPR14 Mike Smith 6.00 15.00

2006-07 ITG Heroes and Prospects Numbers

GUN01 Marek Schwarz 6.00 15.00
GUN02 David Ruzicka 4.00 10.00
GUN03 Jimmy Howard 10.00 25.00
GUN04 Daniel Girardi 4.00 10.00
GUN05 Mike Green 5.00 12.00
GUN06 Nigel Dawes 4.00 10.00
GUN07 Curtis McElhinney 5.00 12.00
GUN08 Mike Smith 10.00 25.00
GUN09 Corey Locke 4.00 10.00
GUN10 Yann Danis 5.00 12.00
GUN11 Tomi Maki 4.00 10.00
GUN12 Erik Christensen 5.00 12.00
GUN13 Maxime Talbot 4.00 10.00
GUN14 Tony Voce 4.00 10.00
GUN15 Josh Harding 6.00 15.00
GUN16 Ian White 5.00 12.00
GUN17 Jarkko Immonen 5.00 12.00
GUN18 Ryan Getzlaf 6.00 15.00
GUN19 Jeremy Colliton 4.00 10.00
GUN20 Fernando Pisani 4.00 10.00
GUN21 Noah Welch 4.00 10.00
GUN22 Billy Thompson 4.00 10.00
GUN23 Staffan Kronwall 4.00 10.00
GUN24 Darryl Bootland 4.00 10.00
GUN25 Dustin Penner 5.00 12.00
GUN26 Paul Ranger 4.00 10.00
GUN27 Alexandre Picard 4.00 10.00
GUN28 Daniel Paille 5.00 12.00
GUN29 Andy Rogers 4.00 10.00
GUN30 Tysen Dowzak 4.00 10.00
GUN31 Jamie McGinn 5.00 12.00
GUN32 Ryan Callahan 6.00 15.00
GUN33 Angelo Esposito 8.00 20.00
GUN34 John Tavares 25.00 60.00
GUN35 Tim Thomas 6.00 15.00
GUN36 Bud Holloway 4.00 10.00
GUN37 Kevin Lalande 5.00 12.00
GUN38 Leland Irving 8.00 20.00
GUN39 Peter Mueller 6.00 15.00
GUN40 Marc Staal 6.00 15.00
GUN41 Benoit Pouliot 5.00 12.00
GUN42 Wojtek Wolski 5.00 12.00
GUN43 Bryan Little 4.00 10.00
GUN44 Ben Shutron 4.00 10.00
GUN45 Ryan O'Marra 4.00 10.00
GUN46 Adam Perry 4.00 10.00
GUN47 James Sheppard 4.00 10.00
GUN48 Nicholas Drazenovic 4.00 10.00
GUN49 Bobby Ryan 6.00 15.00
GUN50 Tyler Plante 5.00 12.00
GUN51 Matt Corrente 4.00 10.00
GUN52 Ondrej Fiala 4.00 10.00
GUN53 J-S Aubin 5.00 12.00
GUN54 Ryan Vesce 4.00 10.00
GUN55 Petr Taticek 4.00 10.00
GUN56 Ben Walter 4.00 10.00
GUN57 Andrew Penner 5.00 12.00
GUN58 Francois Beauchemin 4.00 10.00
GUN59 Cristobal Huet 5.00 12.00
GUN60 Jay Bouwmeester 4.00 10.00
GUN61 Phil Kessel 12.00 30.00
GUN62 Petr Kalus 4.00 10.00
GUN63 Drew Stafford 6.00 15.00
GUN64 Alexander Radulov 8.00 20.00
GUN65 Jiri Hudler 6.00 15.00
GUN66 Cory Emmerton 5.00 12.00
GUN67 Loui Eriksson 8.00 20.00
GUN68 Bobby Ryan 6.00 15.00
GUN69 Jakub Voracek 15.00 40.00
GUN70 Sam Gagner 8.00 20.00
GUN71 Michael Grabner 6.00 15.00
GUN72 Rob Schremp 5.00 12.00
GUN73 Cal Clutterbuck 5.00 12.00

2006-07 ITG Heroes and Prospects Sticks and Jerseys

SJ01 Eric Staal 5.00 12.00
SJ02 John Tavares 15.00 40.00
SJ03 Patrice Bergeron 5.00 12.00
SJ04 Alexander Ovechkin 15.00 40.00
SJ05 Peter Mueller 4.00 10.00
SJ06 Brady Calla 2.50 6.00
SJ07 Leland Irving 5.00 12.00
SJ08 Ondrej Fiala 2.50 6.00
SJ09 Ryan Miller 4.00 10.00
SJ10 Sidney Crosby 15.00 40.00
SJ11 Antero Niittymaki 3.00 8.00
SJ12 Jason Spezza 4.00 10.00
SJ13 Petr Prucha 3.00 8.00
SJ14 Henrik Lundqvist 10.00 25.00
SJ15 Al Montoya 4.00 10.00
SJ16 Dion Phaneuf 3.00 8.00
SJ17 Marek Svatos 2.50 6.00
SJ18 Hannu Toivonen 3.00 8.00
SJ19 Ray Emery 3.00 8.00
SJ20 Brad Boyes 2.50 6.00

2006-07 ITG Heroes and Prospects Triple Memorabilia

TM01 Messier/Fuhr/Kurri 8.00 20.00
TM02 Roy/Brodeur/Parent 10.00 25.00
TM03 Ovech/Malkin/Koval 15.00 40.00
TM04 Crosby/Malkin/Lemieux 15.00 40.00
TM05 Irving/Price/Pogge 15.00 40.00
TM06 Latend/Radulov/Bourdon 5.00 12.00
TM07 Perry/Ryan/Getzlaf 6.00 15.00
TM08 Staal/Staal/Staal 6.00 15.00
TM09 Radulov/Stafford/Pouliot 5.00 12.00
TM10 Sakic/Thornton/Jagr 12.00 30.00
TM11 Esposito/Gagner/Alzner 5.00 12.00
TM12 Belfour/Luongo/Fernandez 6.00 15.00

2007-08 ITG Heroes and Prospects

COMP.SET w/o SP's (100) 10.00 25.00
COMP.UPDATE SET (50) 10.00 25.00
1 Joe Sakic .50 1.25
2 Ed Belfour .25 .60
3 Mike Modano .40 1.00
4 Vincent Lecavalier .25 .60
5 Chris Pronger .25 .60
6 Jean-Sebastien Giguere .25 .60
7 Dominik Hasek .40 1.00
8 Roberto Luongo .40 1.00
9 Joe Thornton .40 1.00
10 Keith Tkachuk .25 .60
11 Dave Keon .25 .60
12 Alexei Cherepanov .30 .75
13 Tuukka Rask .60 1.50
14 Ilya Zubov .20 .50
15 Simeon Varlamov .50 1.25
16 Jack Skille .20 .50
17 Adam Dennis .20 .50
18 Ryan Callahan .30 .75
19 Justin Pogge .20 .50
20 Nathan Oystrick .15 .40
21 Benoit Pouliot .15 .40
22 Andrew Ebbett .15 .40
23 Matt Moulson .25 .60
24 Bobby Ryan .40 1.00
25 Cal Clutterbuck .25 .60
26 Matt D'Agostini .15 .40
27 Kyle Wilson .15 .40
28 Keith Yandle .15 .40
29 Bob Sanguinetti .15 .40
30 T.J. Kemp .15 .40
31 Cal O'Reilly .30 .75
32 Marek Zagrapan .15 .40
33 Jannik Hansen .20 .50
34 Danny Irmen .15 .40
35 Marek Schwarz .25 .60
36 Alex Bourret .20 .50
37 David Krejci .50 1.25
38 Brett Sterling .15 .40
39 Tobias Stephan .20 .50
40 Mikhail Grabovski .15 .40
41 Carey Price 1.00 2.50
42 Tyler Weiman .20 .50
43 Rich Peverley .15 .40
44 Jordan Caron .15 .40
45 Claude Giroux .75 2.00
46 T.J. Brennan .20 .50
47 Francois Bouchard .15 .40
48 Maxime Tanguay .15 .40
49 Antoine Lafleur .20 .50
50 Yann Sauve .25 .60
51 Jonathan Bernier .30 .75
52 Olivier Fortier .15 .40
53 Jean-Simon Allard .15 .40
54 Brad Marchand .75 2.00
55 Alex Grant .15 .40
56 Kevin Armstrong .15 .40
57 Colten Teubert .25 .60
58 Jusso Puustinen .20 .50
59 Riley Holzapfel .20 .50
60 Codey Burki .15 .40
61 Milan Lucic .60 1.50
62 Luke Schenn .30 .75
63 Dana Tyrell .20 .50
64 Kyle Beach .25 .60
65 Zach Boychuk .25 .60
66 Mark Santorelli .15 .40
67 Justin McCrae .15 .40
68 Ryan White .20 .50
69 Cass Mappin .15 .40
70 Leland Irving .25 .60
71 Scott Jackson .15 .40
72 Jesse Dudas .15 .40
73 Graham Potuer .15 .40
74 John Tavares 1.00 2.50
75 Matt Caria .15 .40
76 Josh Godfrey .15 .40
77 P.K. Subban 1.25 3.00
78 Jamie McGinn .20 .50
79 Cody Hodgson .50 1.25
80 Steve Mason .50 1.25
81 Drew Doughty .50 1.25
82 Cory Emmerton .20 .50
83 Ryan O'Reilly .40 1.00
84 Dale Mitchell .15 .40
85 Steven Stamkos 1.00 2.50
86 Thomas McCollum .25 .60
87 Matt Duchene .40 1.00
88 Michael Del Zotto .25 .60
89 Alex Pietrangelo .40 1.00
90 Zack Torquato .15 .40
91 J.Staal/T.Cann .20 .50
92 D.Sittler/S.Gagner .30 .75
93 A.Delvecchio/J.Tavares 1.00 2.50
94 G.Lafleur/A.Esposito .30 .75
95 D.Potvin/L.Couture .25 .60
96 J.Thornton/J.Tlusty .40 1.00
97 J.Sakic/K.Moir .50 1.25
98 W.Clark/C.Gillies .40 1.00
99 R.Luongo/B.Marchand .75 2.00
100 V.Lecavalier/J.Caron .25 .60
101 Thomas Hickey TP JSY 10.00 25.00
102 Logan MacMillan TP JSY 5.00 12.00
103 Akim Aliu TP JSY 10.00 25.00
104 Linden Rowat TP JSY 8.00 20.00
105 Zach Hamill TP JSY 6.00 15.00
106 Nick Ross TP JSY 5.00 12.00
107 Jakub Voracek TP JSY 8.00 20.00
108 Ruslan Bashkirov TP JSY 5.00 12.00
109 John Negrin TP JSY 6.00 15.00
110 Sam Gagner TP JSY 10.00 25.00
111 Stefan Legein TP JSY 5.00 12.00
112 Jeremy Smith TP JSY 8.00 20.00
113 Nick Palmieri TP JSY 5.00 12.00
114 David Skokan TP JSY 5.00 12.00
115 Logan Couture TP JSY 8.00 20.00
116 Drayson Bowman TP JSY 5.00 12.00
117 Alex Plante TP JSY 5.00 12.00
118 Eric Doyle TP JSY 5.00 12.00
119 Keaton Ellerby TP JSY 0.00 15.00
120 Brandon Sutter TP JSY 8.00 20.00
121 Trevor Cann TP JSY 6.00 15.00
122 Keven Veilleux TP JSY 6.00 15.00
123 Karl Alzner TP JSY 5.00 12.00
124 Michal Repik TP JSY 10.00 25.00
125 Angelo Esposito TP JSY 10.00 25.00
126 Taylor Ellington TP JSY 5.00 12.00
127 Brett MacLean TP JSY 5.00 12.00
128 Tyson Sexsmith TP JSY 6.00 15.00
129 Mark Katic TP JSY 5.00 12.00
130 Jonathon Blum TP JSY 8.00 20.00
131 Bryan Cameron TP JSY 5.00 12.00
132 Colton Gillies TP JSY 8.00 20.00
133 Brett Sonne TP JSY 5.00 12.00
134 David Stich TP JSY 5.00 12.00
135 Patrick Kane TP JSY 12.00 30.00
136 Kevin Marshall TP JSY 5.00 12.00
137 Oscar Moller TP JSY 6.00 15.00
138 Maxim Gratchev TP JSY 5.00 12.00
139 Carey Price TP JSY 12.00 30.00
140 Jordan Staal TP JSY 6.00 15.00
141 Kyle Okposo .50 1.25
142 Teddy Purcell .50 1.25
143 Alex Goligoski .50 1.25
144 T.J. Hensick .30 .75
145 Brian Lee .50 1.25
146 Derick Brassard .25 .60
147 Darryl Boyce .40 1.00
148 Jonathan Matsumoto .25 .60
149 John Curry .40 1.00
150 Alexander Nikulin .25 .60
151 Cody Franson .50 1.25
152 Chris Stewart .30 .75
153 Jaroslav Halak .75 2.00
154 Kyle Greentree .25 .60
155 Jerome Samson .30 .75
156 Brian Boyle .50 1.25
157 Julian Talbot .25 .60
158 Devin Setoguchi .40 1.00
159 Michael Grabner .30 .75
160 Steve Downie .30 .75
161 Chris Doyle .40 1.00
162 Mikhail Stefanovich .25 .60
163 Joel Champagne .40 1.00
164 Maxime Sauve .40 1.00
165 Kelsey Tessier .30 .75
166 Philippe Cornet .25 .60
167 Tomas Knotek .25 .60
168 Nicolas Deschamps .40 1.00
169 Jordan Eberle .75 2.00
170 Chet Pickard .30 .75
171 Mitch Wahl .40 1.00
172 Colby Robak .25 .60
173 James Wright .40 1.00
174 Tyler Ennis .25 .60
175 Geordie Wudrick .25 .60
176 Kruise Reddick .25 .60
177 Mitch Fadden .40 1.00
178 Tyler Myers .40 1.00
179 Luca Sbisa .25 .60
180 Shawn Matthias .25 .60
181 Patrick Maroon .40 1.00
182 Zach Bogosian .60 1.50
183 Mikkel Boedker .50 1.25
184 Jared Staal .40 1.00
185 Luca Caputi .40 1.00
186 Jamie Arniel .30 .75
187 Taylor Hall 1.25 3.00
188 Josh Bailey .25 .60
189 Tyler Cuma .25 .60
190 Philip McRae .30 .75

2007-08 ITG Heroes and Prospects Autographs

AAA Akim Aliu 6.00 15.00
AAC Alexei Cherepanov 15.00 30.00
AAD Adam Dennis 4.00 10.00
AAE Angelo Esposito 6.00 15.00
AAEB Andrew Ebbett 3.00 8.00
AAG Alex Grant 3.00 8.00
AAL Antoine Lafleur 4.00 10.00
AAO Alexander Ovechkin 30.00 80.00
AAP Alex Pietrangelo 8.00 20.00
ABB Brian Boyle 6.00 15.00
ABC Blake Comeau 3.00 8.00
ABLI Bryan Little 4.00 10.00
ABM Brad Marchand 15.00 40.00
ABP Benoit Pouliot 3.00 8.00
ABR Bobby Ryan 8.00 20.00
ABS Brandon Sutter 5.00 12.00
ABST Brett Sterling 3.00 8.00
ACB Codey Burki 3.00 8.00
ACC Cal Clutterbuck 5.00 12.00
ACD Chris Doyle 5.00 12.00
ACE Cory Emmerton 4.00 10.00
ACF Cody Franson 6.00 15.00
ACG Claude Giroux 15.00 40.00
ACH Cody Hodgson 12.00 30.00
ACM Curtis McElhinney 5.00 12.00
ACMA Cass Mappin 3.00 8.00
ACO Cal O'Reilly 6.00 15.00
ACP Chris Pronger 8.00 20.00
ACPR Carey Price 25.00 60.00
ACS Chris Stewart 10.00 25.00
ACT Colten Teubert 5.00 12.00
ADB Derick Brassard 3.00 8.00
ADB Darryl Boyce 5.00 12.00
ADD Drew Doughty 10.00 25.00
ADI Danny Irmen 3.00 8.00
ADK Dave Keon 10.00 25.00
ADM Dale Mitchell 3.00 8.00
ADS Drew Stafford 3.00 8.00
ADS Devin Setoguchi 5.00 12.00
ADT Dana Tyrell 4.00 10.00
AFB Francois Bouchard 3.00 8.00
AGP Graham Potuer 3.00 8.00
AGW Geordie Wudrick 3.00 8.00
AJB Josh Bailey 15.00 40.00
AJB Jonathan Bernier 15.00 40.00
AJC Joel Champagne 5.00 12.00
AJC Jordan Caron 3.00 8.00
AJD Jeff Deslauriers 4.00 10.00
AJDU Jesse Dudas 3.00 8.00
AJE Jordan Eberle 30.00 60.00
AJG Josh Godfrey 3.00 8.00
AJH Jaroslav Halak 10.00 25.00
AJHA Jannik Hansen 4.00 10.00
AJM Jamie McGinn 4.00 10.00
AJM Jonathan Matsumoto 3.00 8.00
AJMC Justin McCrae 3.00 8.00
AJOS Joe Sakic 40.00 80.00
AJP Justin Pogge 4.00 10.00
AJPU Jusso Puustinen 4.00 10.00
AJPV Joe Pavelski 6.00 15.00
AJS Jerome Samson 4.00 10.00
AJS Jordan Sigalet 4.00 10.00
AJSA Jean-Simon Allard 3.00 8.00
AJSH James Sheppard 3.00 8.00
AJSK Jack Skille 4.00 10.00
AJSM Jeremy Smith 5.00 12.00
AJST Jordan Staal 4.00 10.00
AJT John Tavares 20.00 50.00
AJTH Joe Thornton 8.00 20.00
AKA Kevin Armstrong 3.00 8.00
AKAL Karl Alzner 3.00 8.00
AKB Kyle Beach 5.00 12.00
AKO Kyle Okposo 15.00 40.00
AKT Kelsey Tessier 4.00 10.00
AKT Keith Tkachuk 5.00 12.00
AKW Kyle Wilson 3.00 8.00
AKY Keith Yandle 3.00 8.00
ALI Leland Irving 5.00 12.00
ALR Linden Rowat 5.00 12.00
ALS Luke Schenn 6.00 15.00
AMB Mikael Boedker 6.00 15.00
AMC Matt Caria 3.00 8.00
AMD Matt Duchene 10.00 25.00
AMDA Matt D'Agostini 3.00 8.00
AMDZ Michael Del Zotto 10.00 25.00
AMF Mitch Fadden 5.00 12.00
AMG Mikhail Grabovski 3.00 8.00
AMM Matt Moulson 5.00 12.00
AMMO Mike Modano 8.00 20.00
AMN Michal Neuvirth 6.00 15.00
AMS Marek Schwarz 5.00 12.00
AMT Maxime Tanguay 3.00 8.00
AMW Mitch Wahl 5.00 12.00
AMZ Marek Zagrapan 3.00 8.00
AND Nicolas Deschamps 5.00 12.00
AOF Olivier Fortier 3.00 8.00
APD Peter Delmas 3.00 8.00
APK Patrick Kane 25.00 60.00
APKS P.K. Subban 12.50 30.00
APMU Peter Mueller 4.00 10.00
APO Patrick O'Sullivan 4.00 10.00
ARC Ryan Callahan 8.00 20.00
ARH Riley Holzapfel 4.00 10.00

ARL Roberto Luongo 15.00 40.00
ARO Ryan O'Reilly 8.00 20.00
ARP Rich Peverley 3.00 8.00
ARS Rob Schremp 4.00 10.00
ARW Ryan White 4.00 10.00
ASD Steve Downie 4.00 10.00
ASG Sam Gagner 6.00 15.00
ASJ Scott Jackson 3.00 8.00
ASM Shawn Matthias 3.00 8.00
ASM Shawn Matthias 3.00 8.00
ASMA Steve Mason 10.00 25.00
ASMU Scott Munroe 3.00 8.00
ASS Steven Stamkos 20.00 50.00
ATC Trevor Cann 4.00 10.00
ATH Thomas Hickey 6.00 15.00
ATJB T.J. Brennan 4.00 10.00
ATJK T.J. Kemp 3.00 8.00
ATK Tomas Knotek 3.00 8.00
ATM Thomas McCollum 5.00 12.00
ATP Teddy Purcell 5.00 12.00
ATR Tuukka Rask 12.00 30.00
ATS Tobias Stephan 4.00 10.00
ATSE Tyson Sexsmith 4.00 10.00
AVL Vincent Lecavalier 5.00 12.00
AYS Yann Sauve 5.00 12.00
AZB Zach Bogosian 15.00 40.00
AZB Zach Boychuk 5.00 12.00
AZT Zack Torquato 3.00 8.00

2007-08 ITG Heroes and Prospects Calder Cup Champions

COMPLETE SET (9) 5.00 12.00
CC01 Corey Locke .60 1.50
CC02 Kyle Chipchura 1.00 2.50
CC03 Dan Jancevski .60 1.50
CC04 Matt D'Agostini .60 1.50
CC05 Maxime Lapierre .60 1.50
CC06 Mikhail Grabovski .60 1.50
CC07 Ajay Baines .60 1.50
CC08 Andre Benoit 1.00 2.50
CC09 Carey Price 4.00 10.00

2007-08 ITG Heroes and Prospects Canada and Russia Challenge

CR01 Logan Couture 6.00 15.00
CR02 John Tavares 25.00 60.00
CR03 Drew Doughty 12.00 30.00
CR04 Sam Gagner 8.00 20.00
CR05 Bryan Little 5.00 12.00
CR06 Steve Mason 12.00 30.00
CR07 Chris Stewart 5.00 12.00
CR08 Francois Bouchard 4.00 10.00
CR09 Jean-Philippe Levasseur 4.00 10.00
CR10 Angelo Esposito 8.00 20.00
CR11 Claude Giroux 20.00 50.00
CR12 Yann Sauve 6.00 15.00
CR13 Brad Marchand 20.00 50.00
CR14 Karl Alzner 4.00 10.00
CR15 Keaton Ellerby 5.00 12.00
CR16 Colton Gillies 6.00 15.00
CR17 Zach Hamill 5.00 12.00
CR18 Carey Price 25.00 60.00
CR19 Kris Russell 6.00 15.00
CR20 Brandon Sutter 6.00 15.00

2007-08 ITG Heroes and Prospects Double Memorabilia

DM01 P.Kane/S.Gagner 20.00 50.00
DM02 B.Sutter/B.Sutter 15.00 30.00
DM03 J.Tavares/S.Stamkos 25.00 60.00
DM04 A.Esposito/C.Giroux 15.00 40.00
DM05 B.Ryan/B.Pouliot 20.00 40.00
DM06 J.Pogge/C.Price 20.00 50.00

2007-08 ITG Heroes and Prospects Gloves Are Off

GO01 Patrick Kane 20.00 50.00
GO02 Angelo Esposito 12.00 30.00
GO03 Keaton Ellerby 8.00 20.00
GO04 Drew Doughty 20.00 50.00
GO05 Luc Bourdon 10.00 25.00
GO06 Marc Staal 10.00 25.00
GO07 Karl Alzner 6.00 15.00
GO08 Jordan Staal 8.00 20.00
GO09 James Sheppard 6.00 15.00
GO10 Sam Gagner 12.00 30.00
GO11 Bryan Little 8.00 20.00
GO12 Peter Mueller 8.00 20.00
GO13 Devin Setoguchi 10.00 25.00
GO14 Zach Hamill 8.00 20.00
GO15 Benoit Pouliot 6.00 15.00
GO16 Steve Downie 8.00 20.00

2007-08 ITG Heroes and Prospects Heroes Memorabilia

HM01 Chris Pronger 8.00 20.00
HM02 Vincent Lecavalier 8.00 20.00
HM03 Roberto Luongo 12.00 30.00
HM04 Dominik Hasek 12.00 30.00
HM05 Joe Thornton 12.00 30.00
HM06 Dany Heatley 6.00 15.00
HM07 Joe Sakic 15.00 40.00
HM08 Mike Modano 12.00 30.00
HM09 Ilya Kovalchuk 8.00 20.00
HM10 Dave Keon 8.00 20.00
HM11 Peter Forsberg 15.00 40.00
HM12 Mats Sundin 8.00 20.00

2007-08 ITG Heroes and Prospects Jerseys

*EMBLEMS/30: .8X TO 2X JERSEY/130
GUJ01 Alexei Cherepanov 6.00 15.00
GUJ02 Tuukka Rask 8.00 20.00
GUJ03 Jack Skille 4.00 10.00
GUJ04 John Tavares 15.00 40.00
GUJ05 Karl Alzner 3.00 8.00
GUJ06 Brandon Sutter 5.00 12.00
GUJ07 Angelo Esposito 6.00 15.00
GUJ08 Zach Hamill 4.00 10.00
GUJ09 Marc Staal 5.00 12.00
GUJ10 Sam Gagner 6.00 15.00
GUJ11 Leland Irving 5.00 12.00
GUJ12 Steve Downie 4.00 10.00
GUJ13 Peter Mueller 4.00 10.00
GUJ14 Thomas McCollum 5.00 12.00
GUJ15 Luc Bourdon 5.00 12.00
GUJ16 Cal Clutterbuck 5.00 12.00
GUJ17 Keaton Ellerby 4.00 10.00
GUJ18 Patrick Kane 20.00 50.00
GUJ19 Bryan Cameron 3.00 8.00
GUJ20 Claude Giroux 10.00 25.00
GUJ21 Drew Doughty 10.00 25.00
GUJ22 Michael Del Zotto 5.00 12.00
GUJ23 Trevor Cann 4.00 10.00
GUJ24 Michael Frolik 4.00 10.00
GUJ25 Trevor Lewis 5.00 12.00
GUJ26 James Sheppard 3.00 8.00
GUJ27 Steven Stamkos 10.00 25.00
GUJ28 Alexander Radulov 5.00 12.00
GUJ29 Marc-Antoine Pouliot 3.00 8.00
GUJ30 Ryan Callahan 6.00 15.00
GUJ31 Cody Bass 3.00 8.00
GUJ32 Benoit Pouliot 3.00 8.00
GUJ33 Rob Schremp 4.00 10.00
GUJ34 Marek Schwarz 5.00 12.00
GUJ35 Andrew Ebbett 3.00 8.00
GUJ36 Justin Pogge 4.00 10.00
GUJ37 Drew Stafford 3.00 8.00
GUJ38 Carey Price 12.00 30.00
GUJ39 Jiri Tlusty 5.00 12.00
GUJ40 Jeff Glass 4.00 10.00
GUJ41 Adam Dennis 4.00 10.00
GUJ42 Tobias Stephan 4.00 10.00
GUJ43 Josh Hennessy 3.00 8.00
GUJ44 Nigel Dawes 3.00 8.00
GUJ45 Loui Eriksson 3.00 8.00
GUJ46 Martin Houle 3.00 8.00
GUJ47 Jon Filewich 3.00 8.00
GUJ48 Jimmy Howard 8.00 20.00
GUJ49 Keith Aucoin 3.00 8.00
GUJ50 Bryan Little 4.00 10.00
GUJ51 Kevin Klein 3.00 8.00
GUJ52 Tyler Weiman 4.00 10.00
GUJ53 Stefan Legein 3.00 8.00
GUJ54 Michael Grabner 4.00 10.00
GUJ55 Thomas Hickey 6.00 15.00
GUJ56 David LeNeveu 4.00 10.00
GUJ57 Keith Yandle 3.00 8.00
GUJ58 Mikhail Grabovski 3.00 8.00
GUJ59 David Krejci 10.00 25.00
GUJ60 Jonathan Bernier 6.00 15.00
GUJ61 Kyle Okposo 8.00 20.00
GUJ62 Alex Pietrangelo 10.00 25.00
GUJ63 Luke Schenn 8.00 20.00
GUJ64 Jonas Hiller 8.00 20.00
GUJ65 Steve Mason 12.00 30.00
GUJ66 Devin Setoguchi 6.00 15.00
GUJ67 Brett MacLean 4.00 10.00
GUJ68 Zach Bogosian 10.00 25.00
GUJ69 Cody Hodgson 12.00 30.00

2007-08 ITG Heroes and Prospects John Tavares Firsts

COMPLETE SET (9) 25.00 60.00
COMMON CARD 4.00 10.00
JT01 John Tavares First Overall 4.00 10.00
JT02 John Tavares First Game 4.00 10.00
JT03 John Tavares First Goal 4.00 10.00
JT04 John Tavares First Multi-Point Game 4.00 10.00
JT05 John Tavares First Assist 4.00 10.00
JT06 John Tavares First Hat Trick 4.00 10.00
JT07 John Tavares First ADT Canada Russia Challenge 4.00 10.00
JT08 John Tavares First OHL All-Star Classic 4.00 10.00
JT09 John Tavares First Playoff Game 4.00 10.00

2007-08 ITG Heroes and Prospects Memorial Cup Champions

COMPLETE SET (9) 8.00 20.00
MC01 Spencer Machacek 1.50 4.00
MC02 Kenndal McArdle 1.50 4.00
MC03 Michal Repik 3.00 8.00
MC04 Milan Lucic 6.00 15.00
MC05 Brendan Mikkelson 1.50 4.00
MC06 Cody Franson 3.00 8.00
MC07 Jonathon Blum 2.50 6.00
MC08 A.J. Thelen 2.00 5.00
MC09 Tyson Sexsmith 2.00 5.00

2007-08 ITG Heroes and Prospects My Country My Team

MCT01 John Tavares 15.00 40.00
MCT02 Marc Staal 6.00 15.00
MCT03 Ty Wishart 4.00 10.00
MCT04 Ryan O'Marra 4.00 10.00
MCT05 Angelo Esposito 8.00 20.00
MCT06 Bryan Little 5.00 12.00
MCT08 Carey Price 25.00 60.00
MCT09 Joe Sakic 12.00 30.00
MCT10 Martin Brodeur 15.00 40.00

2007-08 ITG Heroes and Prospects Net Prospects

NP01 Carey Price 25.00 60.00
NP02 Adam Dennis 5.00 12.00
NP03 Justin Pogge 5.00 12.00
NP04 Tobias Stephan 5.00 12.00
NP05 Jeremy Smith 6.00 15.00
NP06 Thomas McCollum 6.00 15.00
NP07 Steve Mason 12.00 30.00
NP08 Trevor Cann 5.00 12.00
NP09 Tyson Sexsmith 5.00 12.00
NP10 Jonathan Bernier 8.00 20.00
NP11 Leland Irving 6.00 15.00
NP12 Tuukka Rask 15.00 40.00
NP14 Chet Pickard 6.00 15.00

2007-08 ITG Heroes and Prospects Numbers

GUN01 Alexei Cherepanov 20.00 50.00
GUN02 Tuukka Rask 40.00 100.00
GUN03 Jack Skille 12.00 30.00
GUN04 John Tavares 50.00 120.00
GUN05 Karl Alzner 10.00 25.00
GUN06 Brandon Sutter 15.00 40.00
GUN07 Angelo Esposito 20.00 50.00
GUN08 Zach Hamill 12.00 30.00
GUN09 Marc Staal 15.00 40.00
GUN10 Sam Gagner 20.00 50.00
GUN11 Leland Irving 15.00 40.00
GUN12 Steve Downie 12.00 30.00
GUN13 Peter Mueller 12.00 30.00
GUN14 Thomas McCollum 12.00 30.00
GUN15 Luc Bourdon 15.00 40.00
GUN16 Cal Clutterbuck 15.00 40.00
GUN17 Keaton Ellerby 12.00 30.00
GUN18 Patrick Kane 60.00 150.00
GUN19 Bryan Cameron 10.00 25.00
GUN20 Claude Giroux 40.00 100.00
GUN21 Drew Doughty 15.00 40.00
GUN22 Michael Del Zotto 15.00 40.00
GUN23 Trevor Cann 12.00 30.00
GUN24 Michael Frolik 12.00 30.00
GUN25 Trevor Lewis 15.00 40.00
GUN26 James Sheppard 10.00 25.00
GUN27 Steven Stamkos 60.00 150.00
GUN28 Alexander Radulov 15.00 40.00
GUN29 Marc-Antoine Pouliot 10.00 25.00
GUN30 Ryan Callahan 15.00 40.00
GUN31 Cody Bass 10.00 25.00
GUN32 Benoit Pouliot 10.00 25.00
GUN33 Rob Schremp 12.00 30.00
GUN34 Marek Schwarz 15.00 40.00
GUN35 Andrew Ebbett 10.00 25.00
GUN36 Justin Pogge 12.00 30.00
GUN37 Drew Stafford 10.00 25.00
GUN38 Carey Price 60.00 150.00
GUN39 Jiri Tlusty 15.00 40.00
GUN40 Jeff Glass 12.00 30.00
GUN41 Adam Dennis 12.00 30.00
GUN42 Tobias Stephan 12.00 30.00
GUN43 Josh Hennessy 10.00 25.00
GUN44 Nigel Dawes 10.00 25.00
GUN45 Loui Eriksson 10.00 25.00
GUN46 Martin Houle 10.00 25.00
GUN47 Jon Filewich 10.00 25.00
GUN48 Jimmy Howard 25.00 60.00
GUN49 Keith Aucoin 10.00 25.00
GUN50 Bryan Little 12.00 30.00
GUN51 Kevin Klein 10.00 25.00
GUN52 Tyler Weiman 12.00 30.00
GUN53 Stefan Legein 10.00 25.00
GUN54 Michael Grabner 12.00 30.00
GUN55 Thomas Hickey 20.00 50.00
GUN56 David LeNeveu 12.00 30.00
GUN57 Keith Yandle 10.00 25.00
GUN58 Mikhail Grabovski 10.00 25.00
GUN59 David Krejci 30.00 80.00
GUN60 Jonathan Bernier 15.00 40.00
GUN62 Alex Pietrangelo 15.00 40.00
GUN64 Jonas Hiller 20.00 50.00
GUN66 Devin Setoguchi 15.00 40.00
GUN67 Brett MacLean 10.00 25.00
GUN68 Zach Bogosian 25.00 60.00

2007-08 ITG Heroes and Prospects Triple Memorabilia

TM01 Montoya/Pogge/Price 30.00 80.00
TM02 Alzner/Sutter/Gillies 15.00 30.00
TM03 Tavar/Dougty/Stamk 50.00 80.00
TM04 Vorack/Espo/Shep 25.00 50.00
TM05 Staffd/O'Sulli/Radulv 25.00 50.00
TM06 Staal/Staal/Staal 30.00 60.00

2008-09 ITG Heroes and Prospects

1 Mats Sundin .20 .50
2 Peter Forsberg .40 1.00
3 Pavel Datsyuk .30 .75
4 Ryan Getzlaf .20 .50
5 Alexander Ovechkin .75 2.00
6 Teemu Selanne .40 1.00
7 Chris Osgood .20 .50
8 Fabian Brunnstrom .15 .40
9 Ville Leino .25 .60
10 Victor Hedman .50 1.25
11 Alex Goligoski .25 .60
12 Alexander Nikulin .12 .30
13 Benoit Pouliot .12 .30
14 Blake Comeau .12 .30
15 Brendan Mikkelson .12 .30
16 Brian Boyle .15 .40
17 Brian Lee .15 .40
18 Bryan Little .15 .40
19 Chris Collins .12 .30
20 Chris Stewart .20 .50
21 Cody Franson .15 .40
22 Darren Helm .20 .50
23 Derick Brassard .20 .50
24 Devin Setoguchi .15 .40
25 Jack Skille .15 .40
26 Max Pacioretty .40 1.00
27 Jiri Tlusty .12 .30
28 Julian Talbot .12 .30
29 Kyle Greentree .20 .50
30 Kyle Okposo .25 .60
31 Marc-Andre Gragnani .15 .40
32 Michael Grabner .20 .50
33 Mike Santorelli .15 .40
34 Nick Foligno .20 .50
35 Rob Schremp .15 .40
36 Ryan Parent .12 .30
37 Sergei Kostitsyn .12 .30
38 Justin Pogge .15 .40
39 Teddy Purcell .15 .40
40 Vladimir Mihalik .12 .30
41 Alex Pietrangelo .30 .75
42 Brett MacLean .12 .30
43 Cody Hodgson .50 1.25
44 Drew Doughty .50 1.25
45 Greg Nemisz .12 .30
46 Jamie Arniel .15 .40
47 Jared Staal .30 .75
48 John Tavares .60 1.50
49 Joshua Bailey .25 .60
50 Justin Azevedo .12 .30
51 Matt Duchene .40 1.00
52 John McFarland .12 .30
53 Michael Del Zotto .15 .40
54 Mikkel Boedker .25 .60
55 P.K. Subban .40 1.00
56 John Carlson .20 .50
57 Ryan O'Reilly .25 .60
58 Taylor Hall .60 1.50
59 Steven Stamkos .75 2.00
60 Tyler Cuma .12 .30
61 Zach Bogosian .25 .60
62 Brandon Sutter .20 .50
63 Brayden Schenn .40 1.00
64 Colton Gillies .15 .40
65 Drayson Bowman .25 .60
66 Geordie Wudrick .12 .30
67 Jared Cowen .20 .50
68 Jonathon Blum .20 .50
69 Jordan Eberle .40 1.00
70 Jyri Niemi .12 .30
71 Karl Alzner .12 .30
72 Keaton Ellerby .15 .40
73 Kyle Beach .20 .50
74 Luke Schenn .25 .60
75 Landon Ferraro .12 .30
76 Mitch Wahl .12 .30
77 Nick Ross .12 .30
78 Oscar Moller .15 .40
79 T.J. Galiardi .15 .40
80 Thomas Hickey .25 .60
81 Tyler Ennis .12 .30
82 Zach Hamill .12 .30
83 Zach Boychuk .20 .50
84 Angelo Esposito .30 .75
85 Claude Giroux .40 1.00
86 Danick Paquette .12 .30
87 Francois Bouchard .12 .30
88 Philippe Cornet .12 .30
89 Jakub Voracek .40 1.00
90 Joel Champagne .12 .30
91 Kelsey Tessier .12 .30
92 Keven Veilleux .12 .30
93 Logan MacMillan .12 .30
94 Marco Scandella .12 .30
95 Mathieu Perreault .25 .60
96 Mikhail Stefanovich .12 .30
97 Nicolas Deschamps .20 .50
98 Patrice Cormier .15 .40
99 Stefan Chaput .12 .30
100 Yann Sauve .20 .50
101 Nikita Filatov .20 .50
102 Chris Minard .20 .50
103 Justin Abdelkader .30 .75
104 Oskar Osala .20 .50
105 David Desharnais .40 1.00
106 Mattias Karlsson .12 .30
107 Brad Marchand .60 1.50
108 Bob Sanguinetti .15 .40
109 Chad Kolarik .12 .30
110 Simeon Varlamov .40 1.00
111 Luca Caputi .20 .50
112 Michal Repik .20 .50
113 Mark Dekanich .12 .30
114 Zack Smith .15 .40
115 Jeff Frazee .15 .40
116 Tim Kennedy .20 .50
117 Patrick Maroon .20 .50
118 Ben Maxwell .20 .50
119 Viatcheslav Voynov .20 .50
120 Nathan Gerbe .20 .50
121 Simon Despres .20 .50
122 Andrej Nestrasil .20 .50
123 Charles-Olivier Roussel .20 .50
124 Christopher DiDomenico .20 .50
125 David Gilbert .12 .30
126 Dmitry Kulikov .20 .50
127 Jordan Caron .20 .50
128 Olivier Roy .20 .50
129 Keith Aulie .12 .30
130 Colten Teubert .20 .50
131 Carter Ashton .20 .50
132 Brett Sonne .12 .30
133 Tyler Myers .20 .50
134 Scott Glennie .20 .50
135 Levko Koper .20 .50
136 Cody Eakin .20 .50
137 Jamie Benn .40 1.00
138 Stefan Elliott .20 .50
139 Jimmy Bubnick .12 .30
140 Evander Kane .40 1.00
141 Peter Holland .15 .40
142 Evgeny Grachev .20 .50
143 Edward Pasquale .20 .50
144 Stefan Della Rovere .20 .50
145 Nazem Kadri .40 1.00
146 Zack Kassian .20 .50
147 Calvin de Haan .15 .40
148 Michael Latta .20 .50
149 Ryan Ellis .20 .50
150 John Tavares .60 1.50

2008-09 ITG Heroes and Prospects ADT Canada/Russia Challenge Jerseys

CRJ01 John Tavares 15.00 40.00
CRJ02 Alex Pietrangelo 8.00 20.00
CRJ05 Luke Schenn 6.00 15.00
CRJ07 Steve Mason 8.00 20.00
CRJ09 Thomas Hickey 6.00 15.00

2008-09 ITG Heroes and Prospects Autographs

AAE Angelo Esposito 10.00 25.00
AAN Alexander Nikulin 4.00 10.00
AANE Andrej Nestrasil 6.00 15.00
AAO Alexander Ovechkin SP 40.00 80.00
AAP Alex Pietrangelo 10.00 25.00
ABB Brian Boyle 5.00 12.00
ABLE Brian Lee 5.00 12.00
ABLI Bryan Little 5.00 12.00
ABMA Brett MacLean 4.00 10.00
ABMAR Brad Marchand 20.00 50.00
ABMAR2 Brad Marchand 20.00 50.00
ABMAX Ben Maxwell 6.00 15.00
ABMI Brendan Mikkelson 4.00 10.00
ABP Benoit Pouliot 4.00 10.00
ABR Bobby Ryan 5.00 12.00
ABS Bob Sanguinetti 5.00 12.00
ABSC Brayden Schenn 12.00 30.00
ABSU Brandon Sutter 6.00 15.00
ACA Carter Ashton 6.00 15.00
ACD Chris Doyle 5.00 12.00
ACDH Calvin de Haan 5.00 12.00
ACE Cody Eakin 6.00 15.00
ACF Cody Franson 5.00 12.00
ACG Claude Giroux 20.00 50.00
ACH Cody Hodgson 12.00 30.00
ACO Chris Osgood SP 12.00 30.00
ACR Charles-Olivier Roussel 6.00 15.00
ACS Chris Stewart 6.00 15.00
ADB Derick Brassard 6.00 15.00
ADD Drew Doughty 10.00 25.00
ADG David Gilbert 4.00 10.00
ADH Darren Helm 6.00 15.00
ADK Dmitry Kulikov 6.00 15.00
ADS Devin Setoguchi 5.00 12.00
AEK Evander Kane 12.00 30.00
AEP Edward Pasquale 6.00 15.00
AFB Fabian Brunnstrom SP 5.00 12.00
AGB Gilbert Brule 4.00 10.00
AGW Geordie Wudrick 4.00 10.00
AIV Ivan Vishnevskiy 4.00 10.00
AJAR Jamie Arniel 5.00 12.00
AJAZ Justin Azevedo 4.00 10.00
AJBA Joshua Bailey 8.00 20.00
AJBL Jonathon Blum 6.00 15.00
AJBU Jimmy Bubnick 4.00 10.00
AJCA Jordan Caron 6.00 15.00
AJCH Joel Champagne 4.00 10.00
AJCO Jared Cowen 6.00 15.00
AJE Jordan Eberle 20.00 50.00
AJM Jonathan Matsumoto 4.00 10.00
AJN James Neal 8.00 20.00
AJN Jyri Niemi 4.00 10.00
AJSA Jerome Samson 4.00 10.00
AJST Jared Staal 10.00 25.00
AJT Jiri Tlusty 4.00 10.00
AJTAV John Tavares 30.00 60.00
AJTAV2 John Tavares 30.00 60.00
AJTAV3 John Tavares 25.00 60.00
AJV Jakub Voracek 8.00 20.00
AKA Karl Alzner 4.00 10.00
AKE Keaton Ellerby 5.00 12.00
AKL Kristopher Letang 8.00 20.00
AKO Kyle Okposo 8.00 20.00
AKT Kelsey Tessier 4.00 10.00
AKV Keven Veilleux 4.00 10.00
ALC Luca Caputi 6.00 15.00
ALC Logan Couture 12.00 30.00
ALC2 Luca Caputi 6.00 15.00
ALK Levko Koper 6.00 15.00
ALM Logan MacMillan 4.00 10.00
AMAG Marc-Andre Gragnani 5.00 12.00
AMB Mikkel Boedker 8.00 20.00
AMD Matt Duchene 12.00 30.00
AMDZ Michael Del Zotto 5.00 12.00
AMFA Mitch Fadden 4.00 10.00
AMFR Michael Frolik 6.00 15.00
AMG Michael Grabner 6.00 15.00
AML Matt Lashoff 4.00 10.00
AMLA Michael Latta 6.00 15.00
AMO Oscar Moller 5.00 12.00
AMR Michal Repik 6.00 15.00
AMSA Mark Santorelli 4.00 10.00
AMSU Mats Sundin SP 20.00 50.00
AMW Mitch Wahl 4.00 10.00
AND Nicolas Deschamps 6.00 15.00
ANK Nazem Kadri 15.00 30.00
ANR Nick Ross 4.00 10.00
AOR Olivier Roy 6.00 15.00
APD Pavel Datsyuk SP 15.00 40.00
APF Peter Forsberg SP 25.00 60.00
APH Peter Holland 5.00 12.00
APKS P.K. Subban 12.00 30.00
ARE Ryan Ellis 6.00 15.00
ARG Ryan Getzlaf SP 15.00 40.00
ARP Ryan Parent 4.00 10.00
ARS Rob Schremp 5.00 12.00
ASD Simon Despres 6.00 15.00
ASE Stefan Elliott 6.00 15.00
ASG Scott Glennie 6.00 15.00
ASMA Spencer Machacek 4.00 10.00
ASMAT Shawn Matthias 6.00 15.00
ASST Steven Stamkos 25.00 60.00
ASV Simeon Varlamov 12.00 30.00
ATE Tyler Ennis 4.00 10.00
ATH Thomas Hickey 8.00 20.00
ATH Taylor Hall 40.00 80.00
ATP Teddy Purcell 5.00 12.00
ATS Teemu Selanne SP 25.00 50.00
ATW Ty Wishart 5.00 12.00
AVH Victor Hedman 30.00 80.00
AVL Ville Leino 8.00 20.00
AYS Yann Sauve 6.00 15.00
AZBOG Zach Bogosian 8.00 20.00
AZBOY Zack Boychuk 6.00 15.00
AZH Zach Hamill 4.00 10.00
AZK Zack Kassian 15.00 30.00

2008-09 ITG Heroes and Prospects Autographs Team Canada

4 P.K. Subban 15.00 30.00
9 Cody Hodgson 20.00 40.00

2008-09 ITG Heroes and Prospects Calder Cup Winners

COMPLETE SET (13) 20.00 50.00
1 Jason Krog 5.00 12.00
2 Darren Haydar 2.50 6.00
3 Joel Kwiatkowski 2.50 6.00
4 Brian Fahey 2.50 6.00
5 Steve Martins 2.50 6.00
6 Brett Sterling 3.00 8.00
7 Jesse Shultz 2.50 6.00
8 Joe Motzko 2.50 6.00
9 Nathan Oystrick 4.00 10.00
10 Jordan LaVallee 4.00 10.00
11 Boris Valabik 4.00 10.00
12 Bryan Little 3.00 8.00
13 Ondrej Pavelec 5.00 12.00

2008-09 ITG Heroes and Prospects Draft Picks

COMPLETE SET (20) 15.00 40.00
DP1 Steven Stamkos 4.00 10.00
DP2 Drew Doughty 2.50 6.00
DP3 Zach Bogosian 1.25 3.00
DP4 Alex Pietrangelo 1.50 4.00
DP5 Luke Schenn 1.25 3.00
DP6 Mikkel Boedker 1.25 3.00
DP7 Joshua Bailey 1.25 3.00
DP8 Cody Hodgson 2.50 6.00
DP9 Kyle Beach 1.00 2.50
DP10 Tyler Myers 1.00 2.50
DP11 Zach Boychuk 1.00 2.50
DP12 Chet Pickard 1.00 2.50
DP13 Michael Del Zotto .75 2.00
DP14 Jordan Eberle 2.00 5.00
DP15 Tyler Ennis .60 1.50
DP16 Thomas McCollum 1.00 2.50
DP17 Philip McRae .75 2.00
DP18 Nicolas Deschamps 1.00 2.50
DP19 Mitch Wahl .60 1.50
DP20 Jared Staal 1.50 4.00

2008-09 ITG Heroes and Prospects Hero and Prospect Memorabilia

HP01 P.Roy/C.Price 60.00 120.00
HP02 A.Ovechkin/S.Kostitsyn 15.00 40.00
HP03 M.Brodeur/J.Bernier 15.00 40.00
HP04 J.Jagr/J.Tlusty 12.00 30.00
HP05 M.Lemieux/M.Gragnani 50.00 100.00
HP06 C.Neely/J.Tavares 20.00 50.00
HP07 V.Lecavalier/S.Stamkos 20.00 50.00
HP08 M.Gaborik/J.Voracek 25.00 60.00
HP09 B.Clarke/S.Downie 12.00 30.00
HP10 J.Sakic/K.Alzner 20.00 50.00

2008-09 ITG Heroes and Prospects Heroes Memorabilia

HM01 Mats Sundin 8.00 20.00
HM02 Peter Forsberg 15.00 40.00
HM03 Pavel Datsyuk 12.00 30.00
HM04 Ryan Getzlaf 8.00 20.00
HM05 Alexander Ovechkin 30.00 80.00
HM06 Teemu Selanne 15.00 40.00
HM07 Chris Osgood 8.00 20.00

2008-09 ITG Heroes and Prospects Jerseys

GUJ01 Bryan Little 4.00 10.00
GUJ02 Blake Comeau 3.00 8.00
GUJ03 Benoit Pouliot 3.00 8.00
GUJ04 Matt Duchene 10.00 25.00
GUJ05 Chris Collins 3.00 8.00
GUJ06 Chris Stewart 5.00 12.00
GUJ07 Nick Foligno 5.00 12.00
GUJ08 Brian Lee 4.00 10.00
GUJ09 Stephen Dixon 4.00 10.00
GUJ10 Cody Hodgson 12.00 30.00
GUJ11 Joshua Bailey 6.00 15.00
GUJ12 Michael Del Zotto 4.00 10.00
GUJ13 Steven Stamkos 15.00 40.00
GUJ14 Brandon Sutter 5.00 12.00
GUJ15 Colton Gillies 4.00 10.00
GUJ16 Keaton Ellerby 4.00 10.00
GUJ17 Karl Alzner 3.00 8.00
GUJ18 Jakub Voracek 8.00 20.00
GUJ19 Logan MacMillan 3.00 8.00
GUJ20 Carey Price 10.00 25.00
GUJ21 P.K. Subban 10.00 25.00
GUJ22 Patrick Maroon 5.00 12.00
GUJ23 Keven Veilleux 3.00 8.00
GUJ24 Mark Katic 3.00 8.00
GUJ25 Kyle DeCoste 4.00 10.00
GUJ26 John Tavares 15.00 40.00
GUJ27 Mikhail Grabovski 8.00 20.00
GUJ28 Marc Staal 3.00 8.00
GUJ29 Marc-Andre Gragnani 4.00 10.00
GUJ30 Bobby Hughes 3.00 8.00
GUJ31 Alexander Nikulin 3.00 8.00
GUJ32 Brendan Mikkelson 3.00 8.00
GUJ33 Cody Franson 4.00 10.00
GUJ34 Devin Setoguchi 4.00 10.00
GUJ35 Gilbert Brule 3.00 8.00
GUJ36 James Neal 10.00 25.00
GUJ37 Jerome Samson 3.00 8.00
GUJ38 Jiri Tlusty 3.00 8.00
GUJ39 Julian Talbot 3.00 8.00
GUJ40 Kristopher Letang 6.00 15.00
GUJ41 Kyle Greentree 5.00 12.00
GUJ42 Matt Lashoff 3.00 8.00
GUJ43 Mike Santorelli 4.00 10.00
GUJ44 Sergei Kostitsyn 3.00 8.00
GUJ45 Vladimir Mihalik 3.00 8.00

2008-09 ITG Heroes and Prospects Jerseys Autographs

JAAN Alexander Nikulin 6.00 15.00
JABB Brian Boyle 8.00 20.00
JABC Blake Comeau 6.00 15.00
JABL Brian Lee 8.00 20.00
JACC Chris Collins 6.00 15.00
JACF Cody Franson 8.00 20.00
JACS Chris Stewart 10.00 25.00
JADD Drew Doughty 25.00 60.00
JADP Dustin Penner 8.00 20.00
JADS Devin Setoguchi 8.00 20.00
JAGB Gilbert Brule 6.00 15.00
JAJH Jonas Hiller 8.00 20.00
JAJN James Neal 20.00 50.00
JAJP Justin Pogge 8.00 20.00
JAJS Jack Skille 8.00 20.00
JAJSA Jerome Samson 6.00 15.00
JAJT John Tavares 40.00 80.00
JAJTL Jiri Tlusty 6.00 15.00
JAJV Jakub Voracek 20.00 50.00
JAKA Karl Alzner 6.00 15.00
JAKE Keaton Ellerby 8.00 20.00
JAKL Kristopher Letang 30.00 60.00
JAKO Kyle Okposo 12.00 30.00
JALM Logan MacMillan 6.00 15.00
JAMD Michael Del Zotto 8.00 20.00
JAMG Marc-Andre Gragnani 8.00 20.00
JAML Matt Lashoff 6.00 15.00
JAMS Marc Staal 6.00 15.00
JAPS P.K. Subban 25.00 50.00
JASG Sam Gagner 6.00 15.00
JASK Sergei Kostitsyn 6.00 15.00
JASS Steven Stamkos 60.00 120.00

2008-09 ITG Heroes and Prospects Memorial Cup Winners

COMPLETE SET (12) 15.00 40.00
1 Mitch Wahl 2.50 6.00
2 Chris Bruton 2.50 6.00
3 Jared Cowen 4.00 10.00
4 Levko Koper 4.00 10.00
5 Dustin Tokarski 4.00 10.00
6 Drayson Bowman 5.00 12.00
7 Justin Falk 4.00 10.00
8 Trevor Glass 2.50 6.00
9 Ondrej Roman 2.50 6.00
10 Judd Blackwater 2.50 6.00
11 Justin McCrae 2.50 6.00
12 Jared Spurgeon 4.00 10.00

2008-09 ITG Heroes and Prospects Prospect Combos Memorabilia

PC01 K.Letang/J.Tavares 15.00 40.00
PC02 J.Neal/S.Stamkos 15.00 40.00
PC03 M.Lashoff/D.Doughty 12.00 30.00
PC04 J.Pogge/S.Mason 12.00 30.00
PC05 M.Gragnani/M.Del Zotto 10.00 25.00
PC06 G.Brule/B.Sutter 6.00 15.00
PC07 C.Franson/P.Subban 12.00 30.00
PC08 J.Tlusty/L.Schenn 10.00 25.00
PC09 S.Kostitsyn/A.Plante 6.00 15.00
PC10 A.Nikulin/M.Boedker 6.00 15.00

2008-09 ITG Heroes and Prospects Top Prospects Jerseys

TPJ01 Akim Aliu 4.00 10.00
TPJ02 Trevor Cann 5.00 12.00
TPJ03 Keaton Ellerby 5.00 12.00
TPJ04 Angelo Esposito 10.00 25.00
TPJ05 Sam Gagner 4.00 10.00
TPJ06 Zach Hamill 4.00 10.00
TPJ09 Brandon Sutter 6.00 15.00
TPJ10 Jakub Voracek 10.00 25.00
TPJ11 Jonathon Blum 6.00 15.00
TPJ12 Alex Pietrangelo 10.00 25.00
TPJ13 Jared Staal 10.00 25.00
TPJ14 Joshua Bailey 8.00 20.00
TPJ15 Michael Del Zotto 5.00 12.00
TPJ17 Logan MacMillan 4.00 10.00
TPJ18 Colton Gillies 5.00 12.00
TPJ19 Zach Boychuk 6.00 15.00
TPJ20 Zach Bogosian 8.00 20.00

2009-10 ITG Heroes and Prospects

COMPLETE SET (200) 20.00 50.00
COMP.SERIES 1 (150) 15.00 40.00
COMP.UPDATE SET (52) 12.00 30.00
1 Elmer Lach .20 .50
2 Ted Lindsay .20 .50
3 Larry Kwong .60 1.50
4 Ted Kennedy .25 .60
5 Oliver Ekman-Larsson .30 .75
6 Jacob Josefson .20 .50
7 Dmitry Kulikov .25 .60
8 Mikkel Boedker .15 .40
9 Kevin Bieksa .20 .50
10 Jay Bouwmeester .15 .40
11 Mike Cammalleri .20 .50
12 David Backes .15 .40
13 Kyle Okposo .15 .40
14 Kristopher Letang .30 .75
15 Ryan Getzlaf .25 .60
16 Eric Staal .30 .75
17 Jason Spezza .25 .60
18 Maxime Talbot .15 .40
19 Devin Setoguchi .20 .50
20 Jason Pominville .15 .40
21 Zach Parise .25 .60
22 Matt Stajan .15 .40
23 Shea Weber .20 .50
24 Jhonas Enroth .30 .75
25 Mattias Karlsson .15 .40
26 Yannick Weber .25 .60
27 Justin Abdelkader .20 .50
28 Ben Maxwell .20 .50
29 Shawn Matthias .25 .60
30 Bobby Sanguinetti .15 .40
31 Michal Neuvirth .40 1.00
32 Brad Marchand 1.00 2.50
33 Brandon Sutter .15 .40
34 Maxsim Mayorov .20 .50
35 Nathan Gerbe .20 .50
36 Karl Alzner .15 .40
37 Artem Anisimov .15 .40
38 Justin Azevedo .15 .40
39 Nathan Lawson .20 .50
40 Matt Beaudoin .15 .40
41 Jonathan Bernier .20 .50
42 Kevin Porter .15 .40
43 David Desharnais .50 1.25
44 Zack Smith .15 .40
45 Chad Kolarik .15 .40
46 Cory Schneider .25 .60
47 Byron Bitz .20 .50
48 Tim Kennedy .20 .50
49 Tuukka Rask .30 .75
50 Patrick Maroon .15 .40
51 Kyle Turris .25 .60
52 Cody Franson .25 .60
53 Luca Caputi .25 .60
54 Mikko Lehtonen .40 1.00
55 Nikita Filatov .20 .50
56 Max Pacioretty .25 .60
57 Michal Repik .20 .50
58 Spencer Machacek .25 .60
59 Angelo Esposito .20 .50
60 Andrei Loktionov .30 .75
61 Jonathon Blum .25 .60
62 Christian Hanson .25 .60
63 Viktor Stalberg .25 .60
64 P.K. Subban .75 2.00
65 Thomas Hickey .15 .40
66 Tyler Ennis .30 .75
67 Zach Boychuk .20 .50
68 Lars Eller .25 .60
69 Brayden Schenn .50 1.25
70 Scott Glennie .20 .50
71 Jared Cowen .25 .60
72 Evander Kane .50 1.25
73 Matt Duchene .50 1.25
74 Peter Holland .20 .50
75 Zack Kassian .25 .60
76 Calvin de Haan .20 .50
77 Ryan Ellis .25 .60
78 Nazem Kadri .50 1.25
79 Ryan O'Reilly .50 1.25
80 Matthew Hackett .30 .75
81 Tyler Seguin .75 2.00
82 Shawn Lalonde .20 .50
83 Taylor Beck .20 .50
84 Michael Latta .25 .60
85 Taylor Doherty .15 .40
86 John McFarland .25 .60
87 Ryan Spooner .25 .60

88 Tyler Toffoli .50 1.25
89 Erik Gudbranson .25 .60
90 Cody Hodgson .50 1.25
91 Jesse Blacker .20 .50
92 Ethan Werek .15 .40
93 Edward Pasquale .25 .60
94 Joey Hishon .25 .60
95 Taylor Hall .75 2.00
96 Cam Fowler .30 .75
97 Cameron Gaunce .20 .50
98 Ryan Bourque .25 .60
99 Jake Allen .40 1.00
100 Simon Despres .25 .60
101 Brandon Gormley .30 .75
102 Nicolas Deschamps .25 .60
103 Marco Scandella .15 .40
104 Benjamin Casavant .15 .40
105 Charles-Olivier Roussel .25 .60
106 Luke Adam .25 .60
107 Kirill Kabanov .30 .75
108 Peter Delmas .20 .50
109 Mathieu Brodeur .20 .50
110 Jordan Caron .25 .60
111 Dave Labrecque .15 .40
112 Olivier Roy .25 .60
113 Eric Gelinas .30 .75
114 Chris Doyle .15 .40
115 Kelsey Tessier .15 .40
116 Philippe Paradis .25 .60
117 Nicolas Deslauriers .15 .40
118 Gleason Fournier .15 .40
119 Andrej Nestrasil .20 .50
120 Louis Domingue .30 .75
121 Ryan Howse .15 .40
122 Brayden McNabb .25 .60
123 Quinton Howden .25 .60
124 Carter Ashton .25 .60
125 Jimmy Bubnick .15 .40
126 Stefan Elliott .25 .60
127 Nathan Lieuwen .30 .75
128 Tyson Barrie .15 .40
129 Landon Ferraro .15 .40
130 Jordan Eberle .50 1.25
131 Travis Hamonic .15 .40
132 Martin Jones .40 1.00
133 Calvin Pickard .40 1.00
134 Adam Morrison .20 .50
135 Brandon McMillan .15 .40
136 Brandon Kozun .25 .60
137 Brett Ponich .15 .40
138 Colby Robak .15 .40
139 Brett Connolly .25 .60
140 Cody Eakin .25 .60
141 Stanislav Galiev .30 .75
142 Daniel Catenacci .20 .50
143 Brandon Maxwell .20 .50
144 Matt Puempel .25 .60
145 Ivan Telegin .15 .40
146 Olivier Archambault .20 .50
147 Brent Andrews .15 .40
148 Alexander Burmistrov .25 .60
149 Ryan Nugent-Hopkins .75 2.00
150 Shane McColgan .25 .60
151 Logan Couture .50 1.25
152 Jamie McBain .25 .60
153 Sergei Shirokov .15 .40
154 Evgeny Dadonov .25 .60
155 John Carlson .50 1.25
156 Brad Thiessen .25 .60
157 Tyler Bozak .40 1.00
158 Anton Khudobin .40 1.00
159 Mikael Backlund .40 1.00
160 Chris Terry .25 .60
161 Tomas Tatar .50 1.25
162 Dustin Tokarski .25 .60
163 Ryan Stoa .20 .50
164 Nick Palmieri .25 .60
165 Travis Moran .25 .60
166 Benn Ferriero .25 .60
167 Corey Elkins .25 .60
168 Matt Taormina .25 .60
169 Philipp Grubauer .30 .75
170 Ryan Martindale .25 .60
171 Jeff Skinner .40 1.00
172 Jacob Muzzin .25 .60
173 Austin Watson .40 1.00
174 Adam Henrique .50 1.25
175 Brock Beukeboom .25 .60
176 Devante Smith-Pelly .30 .75
177 Alex Pietrangelo .20 .50
178 Boone Jenner .25 .60
179 Stephen Silas .25 .60
180 Greg Nemisz .20 .50
181 Sean Couturier .50 1.25
182 Gabriel Bourque .25 .60
183 Michael Bournival .25 .60
184 Jakub Culek .25 .60
185 Gabriel Levesque .25 .60
186 Michael Kirkpatrick .15 .40
187 Maxime Clermont .20 .50
188 Jerome Gauthier-Leduc .25 .60
189 Petr Straka .15 .40
190 Nino Niederreiter .25 .60
191 Dylan McIlrath .20 .50
192 Ryan Johansen .40 1.00
193 Alexander Petrovic .25 .60
194 Emerson Etem .25 .60
195 Troy Rutkowski .25 .60
196 Jordan Weal .15 .40
197 Luca Sbisa .25 .60
198 Mark Pysyk .20 .50
199 Vladimir Tarasenko .60 1.50
200 Jacob Markstrom .50 1.25

2009-10 ITG Heroes and Prospects AHL All Star Legends

COMPLETE SET (20) 40.00 100.00
AS01 Tuukka Rask 3.00 8.00
AS02 Bobby Ryan 2.00 5.00
AS03 Drew Stafford 1.50 4.00
AS04 Dustin Byfuglien 2.50 6.00
AS05 Jaroslav Halak 2.50 6.00
AS06 Pekka Rinne 2.50 6.00
AS07 Mike Keane 2.00 5.00
AS08 Patrick O'Sullivan 2.00 5.00
AS09 Zach Parise 2.50 6.00
AS10 Jason Spezza 2.50 6.00
AS11 Mikko Koivu 2.50 6.00
AS12 Ryan Miller 2.50 6.00
AS13 Jay Bouwmeester 1.50 4.00
AS14 Mike Cammalleri 2.00 5.00
AS15 Eric Staal 3.00 8.00
AS16 Patrice Bergeron 3.00 8.00
AS17 Brad Boyes 1.50 4.00
AS18 Miikka Kiprusoff 2.50 6.00
AS19 Kari Lehtonen 2.00 5.00
AS20 Jason LaBarbera 2.00 5.00

2009-10 ITG Heroes and Prospects AHL Grad Jerseys

AG01 Blake Comeau 2.00 5.00
AG02 Corey Perry 5.00 12.00
AG03 David Krejci 3.00 8.00
AG04 Devin Setoguchi 2.50 6.00
AG05 Jay Bouwmeester 2.00 5.00
AG06 Jeff Carter 2.50 6.00
AG07 Kari Lehtonen 2.50 6.00
AG08 Kyle Okposo 2.00 5.00
AG09 Carey Price 6.00 15.00
AG10 Marc-Andre Fleury 6.00 15.00
AG11 Mike Green 2.50 6.00
AG12 Pascal Leclaire 3.00 8.00
AG13 Ryan Callahan 2.00 5.00
AG14 Ryan Getzlaf 3.00 8.00
AG15 Ryan Miller 3.00 8.00
AG16 Tim Thomas 3.00 8.00
AG17 Jaroslav Halak 3.00 8.00
AG18 Claude Giroux 3.00 8.00
AG19 Loui Eriksson 2.00 5.00
AG20 Bobby Ryan 2.50 6.00
AG21 Tuuka Rask 4.00 10.00

2009-10 ITG Heroes and Prospects Autographs

AAB Alex Bourret 3.00 8.00
AAE Angelo Esposito 4.00 10.00
AAL Andrei Loktionov 6.00 15.00
AAN Andrej Nestrasil 4.00 10.00
ABA Brent Andrews 3.00 8.00
ABB Byron Bitz 4.00 10.00
ABC2 Brett Connolly 5.00 12.00
ABC Brett Connolly 5.00 12.00
ABG Brandon Gormley 6.00 15.00
ABG2 Brandon Gomley 6.00 15.00
ABH Bobby Hull 15.00 40.00
ABK Brandon Kozun 5.00 12.00
ABM Brad Marchand 20.00 50.00
ABMA Brandon Maxwell 4.00 10.00
ABMC Brandon McMillan 3.00 8.00
ABP Benoit Pouliot 3.00 8.00
ABR2 Bobby Ryan 4.00 10.00
ABS Bobby Sanguinetti 3.00 8.00
ABSC Brayden Schenn 10.00 25.00
ABSU Brandon Sutter 3.00 8.00
ACA Carter Ashton 5.00 12.00
ACC Cal Clutterbuck 3.00 8.00
ACDH Calvin de Haan 4.00 10.00
ACF Cody Franson 5.00 12.00
ACF2 Cam Fowler 6.00 15.00
ACFO Cam Fowler 6.00 15.00
ACG2 Colton Gillies 5.00 12.00
ACG Claude Giroux 5.00 12.00
ACGA Cameron Gaunce 4.00 10.00
ACH Christian Hanson 5.00 12.00
ACK Chuck Kobasew 3.00 8.00
ACR Charles-Olivier Roussel 5.00 12.00
ACRO Colby Robak 3.00 8.00
ACS Cory Schneider 5.00 12.00
ADB2 Derick Brassard 3.00 8.00
ADC Daniel Catenacci 4.00 10.00
ADK Dmitry Kulikov 5.00 12.00
ADP2 Dustin Penner 3.00 8.00
ADS2 Drew Stafford 3.00 8.00
ADS Devin Setoguchi 4.00 10.00
AEG2 Erik Gudbranson 5.00 12.00
AFG Erik Gudbranson 5.00 12.00
AEK Evander Kane 10.00 25.00
AEL Elmer Lach 4.00 10.00
AES Eric Staal 6.00 15.00
AEW Ethan Werek 3.00 8.00
AGB Gilbert Brule 6.00 15.00
AIL Igor Larionov 5.00 12.00
AIT Ivan Telegin 3.00 8.00
AJA Justin Azevedo 3.00 8.00
AJAL Jake Allen 8.00 20.00
AJB Jonathan Bernier 4.00 10.00
AJBE Jean Beliveau 5.00 12.00
AJBL Jonathon Blum 5.00 12.00
AJBU Jimmy Bubnick 3.00 8.00
AJC Jeff Carter 4.00 10.00
AJCA Jordan Caron 5.00 12.00
AJCO Jared Cowen 5.00 12.00
AJD2 Jacob DeSerres 10.00 25.00
AJE Jordan Eberle 10.00 25.00
AJH Joey Hishon 5.00 12.00
AJJ Jacob Josefson 4.00 10.00
AJM John McFarland 5.00 12.00
AJM2 Jacob Markstrom 10.00 25.00
AJS2 Jared Staal 4.00 10.00
AKA Karl Alzner 3.00 8.00
AKM Kenndal McArdle 4.00 10.00
AKO Kyle Okposo 3.00 8.00
AKT Kyle Turris 5.00 12.00
AKV Keven Veilleux 3.00 8.00
ALA Luke Adam 5.00 12.00
ALC Luca Caputi 5.00 12.00
ALCO Logan Couture 10.00 25.00
ALD Louis Domingue 6.00 15.00
ALE2 Loui Eriksson 3.00 8.00
ALE Lars Eller 5.00 12.00
ALF Landon Ferraro 3.00 8.00
ALK Larry Kwong 12.00 30.00
AMB Mikkel Boedker 3.00 8.00
AMBE Matt Beaudoin 3.00 8.00
AMC Mike Cammalleri 4.00 10.00
AMD Matt Duchene 10.00 25.00
AMF2 Marcus Foligno 6.00 15.00
AMH2 Matt Halischuk 4.00 10.00
AMH Matthew Hackett 6.00 15.00
AMJ Martin Jones 8.00 20.00
AML Michael Latta 5.00 12.00
AMM Maxsim Mayorov 4.00 10.00
AMN Michal Neuvirth 8.00 20.00
AMP Max Pacioretty 5.00 12.00
AMPU Matt Puempel 5.00 12.00
AMR Michal Repik 4.00 10.00
AMS Marco Scandella 3.00 8.00
AMW Mike Weber 3.00 8.00
ANB2 Nicklas Bergfors 5.00 12.00
AND Nicolas Deschamps 5.00 12.00
ANK Nazem Kadri 10.00 25.00
ANL Nathan Lawson 4.00 10.00
ANP Nick Petrecki 4.00 10.00
AOA Olivier Archambault 4.00 10.00
AOEL Oliver Ekman-Larsson 6.00 15.00
AOM2 Oscar Moller 3.00 8.00
AOR Olivier Roy 5.00 12.00
APH Peter Holland 4.00 10.00
APO2 Patrick O'Sullivan 4.00 10.00
APP Philippe Paradis 5.00 12.00
APS2 P.K. Subban 15.00 40.00
AQH Quinton Howden 5.00 12.00
AQH2 Quinton Howden 5.00 12.00
ARB Raphael Bussieres 3.00 8.00
ARG Ryan Getzlaf 5.00 12.00
ARNH Ryan Nugent-Hopkins 15.00 40.00
ARO Ryan O'Reilly 10.00 25.00
ARS Ryan Spooner 5.00 12.00
ASD Simon Despres 5.00 12.00
ASE Stefan Elliott 5.00 12.00
ASG Scott Glennie 4.00 10.00
ASGA Stanislav Galiev 6.00 15.00
ASL Shawn Lalonde 4.00 10.00
ASM Spencer Machacek 5.00 12.00
ASMA Shawn Matthias 5.00 12.00
ASMC Shane McColgan 5.00 12.00
ASV2 Simeon Varlamov 5.00 12.00
ATB Tyler Bozak 8.00 20.00
ATBA Tyson Barrie 3.00 8.00
ATBE Taylor Beck 4.00 10.00
ATD Taylor Doherty 3.00 8.00
ATE Tyler Ennis 6.00 15.00
ATH2 Taylor Hall 15.00 40.00
ATH Thomas Hickey 3.00 8.00
ATHA Taylor Hall 15.00 40.00
ATHS2 T.Hall/T.Seguin 15.00 40.00
ATK Ted Kennedy 5.00 12.00
ATL Ted Lindsay 4.00 10.00
ATP Tom Pyatt 5.00 12.00
ATS2 Tyler Seguin 15.00 40.00
ATS Tyler Seguin 15.00 40.00
ATT Tyler Toffoli 10.00 25.00
ATW Tyler Weiman 5.00 12.00
AVS Viktor Stalberg 5.00 12.00
AVT2 Vladimir Tarasenko 25.00 60.00
AVT2 Vladimir Tarasenko 25.00 60.00
AYW Yannick Weber 5.00 12.00
AZK Zack Kassian 5.00 12.00
AZP Zach Parise 5.00 12.00

2009-10 ITG Heroes and Prospects Calder Cup Winners

COMPLETE SET (18) 50.00 100.00
CC01 Michal Neuvirth 5.00 12.00
CC02 Alexandre Giroux 4.00 10.00
CC03 Keith Aucoin 4.00 10.00
CC04 Chris Bourque 3.00 8.00
CC05 Graham Mink 3.00 8.00
CC06 Staffan Kronwall 2.50 6.00
CC07 Andrew Gordon 2.50 6.00
CC08 Oskar Osala 3.00 8.00
CC09 Mathieu Perreault 4.00 10.00
CC10 Karl Alzner 2.00 5.00
CC11 Francois Bouchard 3.00 8.00
CC12 John Carlson 6.00 15.00
CC13 Tyler Sloan 3.00 8.00
CC14 Kyle Wilson 2.00 5.00
CC15 Bryan Helmer 4.00 10.00
CC16 Steve Pinizzotto 2.50 6.00
CC17 Quintin Lang 2.50 6.00
CC18 Jay Beagle 4.00 10.00

2009-10 ITG Heroes and Prospects Class of 2010

COMPLETE SET (15)
C01A Taylor Hall 10.00 25.00
C02 Kirill Kabanov 4.00 10.00
C03 John McFarland 3.00 8.00
C04A Cam Fowler 4.00 10.00
C05A Tyler Seguin 10.00 25.00
C06A Joey Hishon 3.00 8.00
C07A Erik Gudbranson 3.00 8.00
C08A Brett Connolly 3.00 8.00
C09A Brandon Gormley 4.00 10.00
C10 Stanislav Galiev 5.00 12.00
C11A Quinton Howden 3.00 8.00
C12A Jeffery Skinner 5.00 12.00
C13A Mark Pysyk 2.50 6.00
C14A Alexander Burmistrov 3.00 8.00
C15A Vladimir Tarasenko 12.00 30.00

2009-10 ITG Heroes and Prospects Enforcers

COMPLETE SET (10) 30.00 60.00
E01 Matt Clackson 4.00 10.00
E02 Jeremy Yablonski 5.00 12.00
E03 Justin Soryal 4.00 10.00
E04 Trevor Gillies 4.00 10.00
E05 Kip Brennan 4.00 10.00
E06 Wade Brookbank 3.00 8.00
E07 Tim Spencer 3.00 8.00
E08 Brodie Dupont 3.00 8.00
E09 Jesse Boulerice 5.00 12.00
E10 Brett Henley 4.00 10.00

2009-10 ITG Heroes and Prospects Game Used Jerseys

M01 Leland Irving 4.00 10.00
M02 Brandon Sutter 2.50 6.00
M03 Brian Lee 4.00 10.00
M04 Cody Hodgson 8.00 20.00
M05 Matt Duchene 8.00 20.00
M06 Brayden Schenn 8.00 20.00
M07 Scott Glennie 3.00 8.00
M08 Mark Katic 2.50 6.00
M09 Michael Latta 4.00 10.00
M10 Peter Holland 3.00 8.00
M11 Sergei Kostitsyn 2.50 6.00
M12 Karl Alzner 2.50 6.00
M13 Tyler Myers 6.00 15.00
M14 Tyson Barrie 2.50 6.00
M15 Phillippe Paradis 4.00 10.00
M16 Chris Stewart 3.00 8.00
M17 Jonathan Bernier 3.00 8.00
M18 James Neal 2.50 6.00
M19 Chet Pickard 5.00 12.00
M20 Jonathon Blum 4.00 10.00
M21 Calvin de Haan 3.00 8.00
M22 Joey Hishon 4.00 10.00
M23 Ben Duffy 3.00 8.00
M24 Zack Kassian 4.00 10.00
M25 Tyler Seguin 12.00 30.00
M26 Riley Boychuk 4.00 10.00
M27 Brett Connolly 4.00 10.00
M28 Mikhail Stefanovich 2.50 6.00
M29 Alex Petrovic 2.50 6.00
M30 Landon Ferraro 2.50 6.00
M31 Jordan Weal 2.50 6.00
M32 Partrice Cormier 4.00 10.00
M33 Carter Ashton 4.00 10.00
M34 Michal Repik 3.00 8.00
M35 Andrej Nestrasil 3.00 8.00
M36 Stefan Elliott 4.00 10.00
M37 Jared Cowen 4.00 10.00
M38 Jared Staal 3.00 8.00
M39 Cody Eakin 4.00 10.00
M40 Brandon Gormley 5.00 12.00
M41 Evander Kane 8.00 20.00
M42 Keven Veilleux 2.50 6.00
M43 Ryan Ellis 4.00 10.00
M44 Taylor Hall 12.00 30.00
M45 Erik Gudbranson 4.00 10.00
M46 P.K. Subban 12.00 30.00
M47 Mikkel Boedker 2.50 6.00
M48 Jeff Skinner 6.00 15.00
M49 Cam Fowler 5.00 12.00
M50 Ryan Nugent-Hopkins 12.00 30.00
M51 Vladimir Tarasenko 10.00 25.00
M52 Jacob Markstrom 8.00 20.00
M53 Alexander Burmistrov 4.00 10.00

2009-10 ITG Heroes and Prospects Game Used Jerseys Silver

*SINGLES: .5X TO 1.2X BASIC INSERTS

2009-10 ITG Heroes and Prospects Gloves Are Off

GA001 Angelo Esposito 5.00 12.00
GA002 Bob Sanguinetti 4.00 10.00
GA003 Cody Hodgson 12.00 30.00
GA004 Bryan Little 6.00 15.00
GA005 Devin Setoguchi 5.00 12.00
GA006 Karl Alzner 4.00 10.00
GA007 Zach Hamill 6.00 15.00
GA008 Marc-Andre Gragnani 5.00 12.00

2009-10 ITG Heroes and Prospects Hero and Prospect Jerseys

HP01 Roy/Price 8.00 20.00
HP02 Brodeur/Bernier 8.00 20.00
HP03 Kovalchuk/Esposito 3.00 8.00
HP04 Lemieux/Hall 12.00 30.00
HP05 Neely/Lucic 3.00 8.00
HP06 Kiprusoff/Irving 3.00 8.00
HP07 Sakic/Duchene 6.00 15.00
HP08 Robinson/Subban 10.00 25.00
HP09 Hall/Messier 10.00 25.00
HP10 Seguin/Yzerman 10.00 25.00

2009-10 ITG Heroes and Prospects Memorial Cup Winners

MC01 Taylor Hall 5.00 12.00
MC02 Greg Nemisz 1.25 3.00
MC03 Scott Timmins 2.50 6.00
MC04 Dale Mitchell 2.50 6.00
MC05 Ryan Ellis 1.50 4.00
MC06 Jesse Blacker 1.25 3.00
MC07 Andrei Loktionov 2.00 5.00
MC08 Rob Kwiet 1.00 2.50
MC09 Eric Wellwood 2.00 5.00
MC10 Ben Shutron 1.25 3.00
MC11 Lane MacDermid 1.50 4.00
MC12 Adam Henrique 3.00 8.00
MC13 Justin Shugg 1.00 2.50
MC14 Mark Cundari 2.50 6.00
MC15 Andrew Engelage 3.00 8.00
MC16 Harry Young 2.50 6.00
MC17 Conor O'Donnell 1.25 3.00
MC18 Austin Watson 2.50 6.00

2009-10 ITG Heroes and Prospects Prospect Combos Jerseys

PC01 Ellis/Subban 10.00 25.00
PC02 Kane/Esposito 6.00 15.00
PC03 Hodgson/Couture 6.00 15.00
PC04 Schenn/Boychuk 6.00 15.00
PC05 Hall/Marchand 12.00 30.00
PC06 Roy/Bernier 3.00 8.00
PC07 de Haan/Hickey 2.50 6.00
PC08 Allen/McCollum 5.00 12.00
PC09 Nugent-Hopkins/Sutter 10.00 25.00
PC10 Kadri/Stewart 6.00 15.00
PC11 Gudbranson/Alzner 3.00 8.00
PC12 Skinner/Boychuk 5.00 12.00

2009-10 ITG Heroes and Prospects Real Heroes

RH01 Woody Dumart 2.50 6.00
RH02 Milt Schmidt 3.00 8.00
RH03 Gordie Drillon 4.00 10.00
RH04 Ken Reardon 4.00 10.00
RH05 Sid Abel 4.00 10.00
RH06 Turk Broda 4.00 10.00
RH07 Hobey Baker 3.00 8.00
RH08 Frank Brimsek 3.00 8.00
RH10 Conn Smythe 4.00 10.00
RH11 Red Garrett 2.50 6.00
RH12 Joe Turner 2.50 6.00
RH13 Bobby Bauer 5.00 12.00
RH14 Frank McGee 4.00 10.00
RH15 Howie Meeker 4.00 10.00
RH16 Johnny Bower 4.00 10.00
RH17 Frank Frederickson 2.50 6.00
RH18 Bob Carse 3.00 8.00
RH19 Alex Shibicky 4.00 10.00
RH20 Lynn Patrick 6.00 15.00
RH21 Max Bentley 2.50 6.00
RH22 Neil Colville 2.50 6.00
RH23 Chuck Rayner 3.00 8.00
RH24 Roy Conacher 4.00 10.00

2009-10 ITG Heroes and Prospects Subway Series Jerseys

*SILVER/30: .4X TO 1X BASIC JSY
CRM34 Karl Alzner 2.50 6.00
CRM35 P.K. Subban 12.00 30.00
CRM36 Brandon Sutter 2.50 6.00
SSM01 Jake Allen 6.00 15.00
SSM02 Maxime Clermont 3.00 8.00
SSM03 Louis Domingue 5.00 12.00
SSM04 Olivier Roy 4.00 10.00
SSM05 Simon Despres 4.00 10.00
SSM06 Brandon Gormley 5.00 12.00
SSM07 Charles-Olivier Roussel 4.00 10.00
SSM09 Jordan Caron 4.00 10.00
SSM10 Patrice Cormier 4.00 10.00
SSM11 Michael Kirkpatrick 2.50 6.00
SSM12 Philippe Paradis 4.00 10.00
SSM13 Taylor Hall 12.00 30.00
SSM14 Nazem Kadri 8.00 20.00
SSM15 Peter Holland 3.00 8.00
SSM16 Jeff Skinner 6.00 15.00
SSM17 Michael Hutchinson 5.00 12.00
SSM18 Erik Gudbranson 4.00 10.00
SSM19 Stefan Della Rovere 4.00 10.00
SSM20 Tyler Toffoli 8.00 20.00
SSM21 Colten Teubert 4.00 10.00
SSM22 Zack Kassian 4.00 10.00
SSM23 Scott Glennie 3.00 8.00
SSM24 Brayden Schenn 8.00 20.00
SSM26 Linden Vey 3.00 8.00
SSM27 Jordan Eberle 8.00 20.00
SSM29 Mark Pysyk 3.00 8.00
SSM30 Jared Cowen 4.00 10.00
SSM31 Martin Jones 6.00 15.00
SSM32 Calvin Pickard 6.00 15.00
SSM33 Brett Ponich 2.50 6.00

2009-10 ITG Heroes and Prospects Top Prospects Game Used Jerseys

JM01 Bobby Hughes 4.00 10.00
JM02 Brayden Schenn 10.00 25.00
JM03 Calvin de Haan 5.00 12.00
JM04 Carter Ashton 6.00 15.00
JM05 Chet Pickard 8.00 20.00
JM06 Chris Stewart 5.00 12.00
JM07 Colten Teubert 6.00 15.00
JM08 Corey Perry 10.00 25.00
JM09 Dmitry Kulikov 6.00 15.00
JM10 Ethan Werek 4.00 10.00
JM11 Evander Kane 12.00 30.00
JM12 Greg Nemisz 5.00 12.00
JM13 Jamie Arniel 5.00 12.00
JM14 Jared Cowen 6.00 15.00
JM15 Jared Staal 5.00 12.00
JM16 Jimmy Bubnick 4.00 10.00
JM17 Jordan Caron 6.00 15.00
JM18 Jordan Eberle 12.00 30.00
JM19 Landon Ferraro 4.00 10.00
JM20 Luca Sbisa 6.00 15.00
JM21 Marcus Foligno 8.00 20.00
JM22 Matt Duchene 20.00 50.00
JM23 Maxime Sauve 6.00 15.00
JM24 Nazem Kadri 12.00 30.00
JM25 Nicholas Deschamps 6.00 15.00
JM26 Olivier Roy 6.00 15.00
JM27 Peter Delmas 5.00 12.00
JM28 Ryan Ellis 6.00 15.00
JM29 Ryan Getzlaf 6.00 15.00
JM30 Scott Glennie 5.00 12.00
JM31 Simon Despres 6.00 15.00
JM32 Stefan Elliott 6.00 15.00
JM33 Thomas McCollum 6.00 15.00
JM34 Tyler Cuma 4.00 10.00
JM35 Zach Boychuk 5.00 12.00
JM36 Zack Kassian 6.00 15.00

2009-10 ITG Heroes and Prospects Top Prospects Game Used Jerseys Silver

*SINGLES: .5X TO 1.2X BASIC INSERTS
JM09 Dmitry Kulikov 8.00 20.00

2010-11 ITG Heroes and Prospects

COMPLETE SET (200) 20.00 50.00
COMP.SERIES 1 (150) 15.00 40.00
COMP.UPDATE (50) 10.00 25.00
1 D.Sedin/H.Sedin HH .30 .75
2 Pavel Bure HH .25 .60
3 Steve Yzerman HH .60 1.50
4 Roberto Luongo HH .40 1.00
5 Steven Stamkos HH .50 1.25
6 Pelle Lindbergh HH .20 .50
7 Rick Nash HH .25 .60
8 Adam Larsson .40 1.00
9 Victor Rask .15 .40
10 Sergei Bobrovsky .75 2.00
11 Tyler Seguin .60 1.50
12 J.P. Anderson .25 .60
13 Greg McKegg .25 .60
14 Ryan Murphy .30 .75
15 Richard Panik .20 .50
16 Tyler Toffoli .50 1.25
17 Freddie Hamilton .25 .60
18 Erik Gudbranson .25 .60
19 Michael Curtis .15 .40
20 Matt Puempel .25 .60
21 Boone Jenner .25 .60
22 Taylor Beck .20 .50
23 Jack Campbell .25 .60
24 Austin Watson .25 .60
25 Jarred Tinordi .25 .60
26 Joey Hishon .25 .60
27 Philipp Grubauer .30 .75
28 Ryan Spooner .25 .60
29 Christian Thomas .20 .50
30 Taylor Doherty .15 .40
31 Brock Beukeboom .15 .40
32 Mark Visentin .25 .60
33 Devante Smith-Pelly .30 .75
34 John McFarland .20 .50
35 Ryan Ellis .25 .60
36 Gabriel Landeskog .50 1.25
37 Peter Holland .20 .50
38 Philip Danault .25 .60
39 Tomas Jurco .40 1.00
40 Kirill Kabanov .20 .50
41 Maxime Clermont .20 .50
42 Gabriel Beaupre .15 .40
43 Jerome Gauthier-Leduc .15 .40
44 Michael Bournival .20 .50
45 Ryan Bourque .25 .60
46 Nathan Beaulieu .15 .40
47 Jakub Culek .15 .40
48 Brandon Gormley .25 .60
49 Robin Gusse .25 .60
50 Louis-Marc Aubry .15 .40
51 Stanislav Galiev .25 .60
52 Michael Chaput .15 .40
53 Jonathan Huberdeau .50 1.25
54 Gleason Fournier .15 .40
55 Olivier Archambault .20 .50
56 Louis Domingue .25 .60
57 Louis Leblanc .30 .75
58 Zack Phillips .25 .60
59 Petr Straka .15 .40
60 Olivier Roy .25 .60
61 Sean Couturier .50 1.25
62 Ryan Johansen .40 1.00
63 Michael St. Croix .15 .40
64 Curtis Hamilton .20 .50
65 Brett Connolly .25 .60
66 Calvin Pickard .25 .60
67 Joey Leach .15 .40
68 Jordan Weal .15 .40
69 Dylan McIlrath .20 .50
70 Alexander Petrovic .15 .40
71 Quinton Howden .20 .50
72 Emerson Etem .25 .60
73 Brendan Shinnimin .15 .40
74 Ryan Nugent-Hopkins .75 2.00
75 Brad Ross .20 .50
76 Kevin Sundher .15 .40
77 Matt MacKenzie .15 .40
78 Tyler Bunz .20 .50
79 Shane McColgan .20 .50
80 Taylor Aronson .15 .40
81 Mark Pysyk .15 .40
82 Kent Simpson .20 .50
83 Nino Niederreiter .30 .75
84 Scott Glennie .20 .50
85 Craig Cunningham .15 .40
86 Brendan Ranford .25 .60
87 David Musil .20 .50
88 Ryan Murray .30 .75
89 Tobias Rieder .25 .60
90 Brandon Saad .30 .75
91 Alex Galchenyuk .75 2.00
92 Brendan Gaunce .25 .60
93 Max Iafrate .25 .60
94 Nail Yakupov 1.00 2.50
95 Nick Ebert .20 .50
96 Luca Ciampini .25 .60
97 Martin Frk .20 .50
98 Tomas Filippi .15 .40
99 Derrick Pouliot .30 .75
100 David Toews .20 .50
101 P.K. Subban .60 1.50
102 Andrei Loktionov .20 .50
103 Tomas Tatar .50 1.25
104 Chris Terry .20 .50
105 Anton Khudobin .25 .60
106 Jonathon Blum .25 .60
107 Dana Tyrell .20 .50
108 Ryan Stoa .15 .40
109 Thomas Hickey .15 .40
110 Mikael Backlund .20 .50
111 Evgeny Grachev .20 .50
112 Kyle Turris .20 .50
113 Braden Holtby .30 .75
114 Erik Karlsson .30 .75
115 Tyler Ennis .15 .40
116 Tyler Bozak .15 .40
117 Travis Morin .15 .40
118 John Carlson .25 .60
119 Alex Stalock .20 .50
120 Brett Sonne .15 .40
121 Dustin Tokarski .20 .50
122 Sergei Shirokov .20 .50
123 Corey Elkins .15 .40
124 Evgeny Dadonov .25 .60
125 Christian Hanson .15 .40
126 Brad Thiessen .25 .60
127 Logan Couture .30 .75
128 Chet Pickard .20 .50
129 Nick Palmieri .20 .50
130 Benn Ferriero .15 .40
131 Chad Johnson .20 .50
132 Zach Boychuk .20 .50
133 Colton Sceviour .15 .40
134 Jamie Arniel .20 .50
135 Lars Eller .15 .40
136 Eric Tangradi .20 .50
137 John Moore .20 .50
138 Ryan McDonagh .50 1.25
139 Jordan Schroeder .25 .60
140 Blake Geoffrion .25 .60
141 Jussi Rynnas .25 .60
142 Kevin Shattenkirk .40 1.00
143 Luke Adam .20 .50
144 Jared Staal .20 .50
145 Joe Colborne .25 .60
146 Cody Hodgson .50 1.25
147 Linus Omark .25 .60
148 Kyle Beach .25 .60
149 Nazem Kadri .60 1.50
150 Mattias Tedenby .20 .50
151 Mark Olver .20 .50
152 Zac Dalpe .25 .60
153 Bill Sweatt .20 .50
154 Tomas Kubalik .20 .50
155 Colin Greening .30 .75
156 Rhett Rakhshani .20 .50
157 Bobby Butler .20 .50
158 Teemu Hartikainen .25 .60
159 Erik Gustafsson .25 .60
160 Adam Henrique .50 1.25
161 Mats Zuccarello .40 1.00
162 Kyle Palmieri .40 1.00
163 Brandon Kozun .25 .60
164 Nick Leddy .25 .60
165 Gabriel Bourque .25 .60
166 Jake Allen .40 1.00
167 Linus Klasen .20 .50
168 Jacob Markstrom .50 1.25
169 Ryan Strome .30 .75
170 Shane Prince .15 .40
171 Garrett Wilson .20 .50
172 Ryan Martindale .20 .50
173 Maxim Kitsyn .20 .50
174 Nicklas Jensen .25 .60
175 Jordan Binnington .40 1.00
176 Richard Rakell .25 .60
177 Mark Scheifele .50 1.25
178 Vladislav Namestnikov .40 1.00
179 Dougie Hamilton .50 1.25
180 Alexander Khokhlachev .30 .75
181 Christopher Gibson .30 .75
182 David Honzik .20 .50
183 Xavier Ouellet .15 .40
184 Maximilien Le Sieur .20 .50
185 Ryan Tesink .25 .60
186 Logan Shaw .20 .50
187 Scott Oke .20 .50
188 Linden Vey .20 .50
189 Ty Rattie .25 .60
190 Sven Bartschi .25 .60
191 Joel Edmundson .20 .50
192 Griffin Reinhart .25 .60
193 Mark McNeill .20 .50
194 Joe Morrow .40 1.00
195 Duncan Siemens .15 .40
196 Colin Jacobs .20 .50
197 Reece Scarlett .20 .50
198 Morgan Rielly .30 .75
199 Eric Lindros .40 1.00
200 Theoren Fleury .40 1.00

2010-11 ITG Heroes and Prospects AHL 75th Anniversary

AHLA01 Bill Sweeney 2.00 5.00
AHLA02 Billy Smith 2.50 6.00
AHLA03 Brett Hull 5.00 12.00
AHLA04 Bruce Boudreau 2.50 6.00
AHLA05 Carey Price 5.00 12.00
AHLA06 Doug Harvey 2.50 6.00
AHLA07 Eddie Shore 2.00 5.00
AHLA08 Emile Francis 1.50 4.00
AHLA09 Frank Mathers 2.00 5.00
AHLA10 Fred Glover 2.00 5.00
AHLA11 Gerry Cheevers 4.00 10.00
AHLA12 Gil Mayer 2.00 5.00
AHLA13 Jason Spezza 2.50 6.00
AHLA14 Jim Anderson 2.00 5.00
AHLA15 Jody Gage 2.00 5.00
AHLA16 John Paddock 2.00 5.00
AHLA17 John Slaney 2.00 5.00
AHLA18 Johnny Bower 2.50 6.00
AHLA19 Kent Douglas 2.00 5.00
AHLA20 Larry Robinson 2.50 6.00
AHLA21 Les Cunningham 2.00 5.00
AHLA22 Lou Trudel 2.00 5.00
AHLA23 Marcel Paille 2.00 5.00
AHLA24 Martin Brodeur 5.00 12.00
AHLA25 Mike Nykoluk 2.00 5.00
AHLA26 Milt Schmidt 2.00 5.00
AHLA27 Noel Price 2.00 5.00
AHLA28 Patrick Roy 6.00 15.00
AHLA29 Paul Gardner 2.00 5.00
AHLA30 Pelle Lindbergh 2.00 5.00
AHLA31 Steve Kraftcheck 2.00 5.00
AHLA32 Terry Sawchuk 3.00 8.00
AHLA33 Mitch Lamoureux 2.00 5.00
AHLA34 Willie Marshall 2.00 5.00
AHLA35 Zdeno Chara 2.50 6.00

2010-11 ITG Heroes and Prospects AHL 75th Anniversary Autographs

AHLAABB Bruce Boudreau 10.00 25.00
AHLAAGC Gerry Cheevers 5.00 12.00
AHLAAGM Gil Mayer 8.00 20.00
AHLAAJP John Paddock 8.00 20.00
AHLAAJS Jason Spezza 10.00 25.00
AHLAAMK Mike Nykoluk 10.00 25.00
AHLAAML Mitch Lamoureux 12.00 30.00
AHLAAMS Milt Schmidt 6.00 15.00
AHLAANP Noel Price 12.00 30.00
AHLAAPG Paul Gardner 6.00 15.00
AHLAAWM Willie Marshall 6.00 15.00

2010-11 ITG Heroes and Prospects Autographs

AAA Akim Aliu 6.00 15.00
AAK Anton Khudobin 5.00 12.00
AAL Andrei Loktionov SP 6.00 15.00
AALA Adam Larsson SP 20.00 40.00
AALA2 Adam Larsson SP 20.00 40.00
AALD Andrew Ladd 3.00 8.00
AAN Andrej Nestrasil 5.00 12.00
AAS Alex Stalock 4.00 10.00
AAW Austin Watson 5.00 12.00
ABA Brent Andrews SP 8.00 20.00
ABB Brock Beukeboom 3.00 8.00
ABC Brett Connolly 5.00 12.00
ABF Benn Ferriero 5.00 12.00
ABG Brendan Gaunce 5.00 12.00
ABGE Blake Geoffrion 5.00 12.00
ABGO Brandon Gormley 5.00 12.00
ABH Braden Holtby 8.00 20.00
ABJ Boone Jenner 5.00 12.00
ABK Brandon Kozun SP 8.00 20.00
ABM Brayden McNabb 8.00 20.00
ABR Bobby Ryan 4.00 10.00
ABS Brett Sonne 3.00 8.00
ABSC Brayden Schenn SP 15.00 40.00
ABT Brad Thiessen 5.00 12.00
ACB Cody Bass 4.00 10.00
ACD Cedrick Desjardins 5.00 12.00
ACDO Chris Doyle 4.00 10.00
ACE Corey Elkins 3.00 8.00
ACEA Cody Eakin 5.00 12.00
ACH Christian Hanson 3.00 8.00
ACHO Cody Hodgson 10.00 25.00
ACJ Chad Johnson 4.00 10.00
ACOR Charles-Olivier Roussel 3.00 8.00
ACP Calvin Pickard 5.00 12.00
ACPR Carey Price SP 15.00 40.00
ACR Chad Rau 3.00 8.00
ACS Colton Sceviour 3.00 8.00
ACT Chris Terry 4.00 10.00

ADC Daniel Catenacci 5.00 12.00
ADD David Desharnais 10.00 25.00
ADG David Gilbert 4.00 10.00
ADM David Musil 4.00 10.00
ADO Dylan Olsen 6.00 15.00
ADP Derrick Pouliot 6.00 15.00
ADT David Toews 6.00 15.00
ADTO Dustin Tokarski 4.00 10.00
ADTY Dana Tyrell 4.00 10.00
AED Evgeny Dadonov 5.00 12.00
AEE Emerson Etem 8.00 20.00
AEG Evgeny Grachev 4.00 10.00
AEGE Eric Gelinas 6.00 15.00
AEGU Erik Gudbranson 5.00 12.00
AET Eric Tangradi 4.00 10.00
AGL Gabriel Landeskog 15.00 40.00
AGL2 Gabriel Landeskog SP 30.00 60.00
AIB Igor Bobkov 10.00 25.00
AIT Ivan Telegin SP 6.00 15.00
AJA J.P. Anderson 5.00 12.00
AJAR Jamie Arniel 4.00 10.00
AJB Jonathon Blum 5.00 12.00
AJBA Johan Backlund 4.00 10.00
AJBE Jonathan Bernier 4.00 10.00
AJBU Jimmy Bubnick 3.00 8.00
AJC Jack Campbell 15.00 40.00
AJCA Jordan Caron SP 8.00 20.00
AJCH Joel Champagne 5.00 12.00
AJCO Joe Colborne 6.00 15.00
AJCU Jakub Culek 3.00 8.00
AJE Jhonas Enroth 5.00 12.00
AJF Jeff Frazee 6.00 15.00
AJH Jonathan Huberdeau 20.00 40.00
AJL Jacob Lagace 5.00 12.00
AJMA Jacob Markstrom SP 15.00 40.00
AJMF John McFarland SP 6.00 15.00
AJS Jared Staal SP 6.00 15.00
AJSC Jordan Schroeder 5.00 12.00
AJT Jarred Tinordi 5.00 12.00
AJZ Jeff Zatkoff 5.00 12.00
AKB Kyle Beach 5.00 12.00
AKE Keaton Ellerby 3.00 8.00
AKS Kent Simpson 4.00 10.00
AKSE Keith Seabrook 3.00 8.00
AKT Kyle Turris 4.00 10.00
ALA Luke Adam SP 6.00 15.00
ALC Luca Ciampini 8.00 20.00
ALCA Luca Caputi 4.00 10.00
ALCO Logan Couture 8.00 20.00
ALCO2 Logan Couture 6.00 15.00
ALD Louis Domingue 5.00 12.00
ALE Lars Eller 3.00 8.00
ALER Loui Eriksson 5.00 12.00
ALF Landon Ferraro 3.00 8.00
ALI Leland Irving 5.00 12.00
ALK Levko Koper 3.00 8.00
ALL Louis Leblanc 12.00 30.00
AMBE Matt Beleskey 4.00 10.00
AMC Matt Climie 4.00 10.00
AMCL Maxime Clermont 4.00 10.00
AMDZ Michael Del Zotto 5.00 12.00
AMF Martin Frk 10.00 25.00
AMFO Marcus Foligno SP 10.00 25.00
AMH Matt Halischuk 4.00 10.00
AMI Max Iafrate 5.00 12.00
AMK Mark Katic 3.00 8.00
AMKO Mikko Koivu SP 8.00 20.00
AMLA Michael Latta 5.00 12.00
AMM Mike Murphy 5.00 12.00
AMP Mark Pysyk 3.00 8.00
AMPU Matt Puempel 10.00 25.00
AMV Mark Visentin 5.00 12.00
ANE Nick Ebert 4.00 10.00
ANK Nazem Kadri 12.00 30.00
ANN Nino Niederreiter 6.00 15.00
AOA Olivier Archambault SP 6.00 15.00
AOEL Oliver Ekman-Larsson 6.00 15.00
AOR Olivier Roy 5.00 12.00
APB Pavel Bure SP 25.00 50.00
APBE Patrice Bergeron 6.00 15.00
APP Philippe Paradis 3.00 8.00
APS Petr Straka 3.00 8.00
AQH Quinton Howden 4.00 10.00
ARG Robin Gusse 5.00 12.00
ARJ Ryan Johansen 8.00 20.00
ARLU Roberto Luongo SP 25.00 50.00
ARM Ryan Murray 10.00 25.00
ARMC Ryan McDonagh 6.00 15.00
ARN Ryan Nugent-Hopkins 15.00 40.00
ARN2 Ryan Nugent-Hopkins SP 30.00 60.00
ARNA Rick Nash SP 15.00 40.00
ARO Ryan O'Marra 3.00 8.00
ARS Ryan Stoa 3.00 8.00
ASB Sergei Bobrovsky 6.00 15.00
ASC Sean Couturier 15.00 40.00
ASC2 Sean Couturier SP 20.00 50.00
ASD Simon Despres 5.00 12.00
ASG Stanislav Galiev 10.00 25.00
ASM Shane McColgan 4.00 10.00
ASS Steven Stamkos SP 15.00 40.00
ATB Tyler Bunz 5.00 12.00
ATBA Tyson Barrie 3.00 8.00
ATBE Taylor Beck 4.00 10.00
ATBO Tyler Bozak SP 5.00 12.00
ATBR T.J. Brennan 4.00 10.00
ATD Taylor Doherty 3.00 8.00
ATF Theoren Fleury SP 40.00 80.00
ATH Thomas Hickey 3.00 8.00
ATJ Tomas Jurco 8.00 20.00
ATM Travis Morin 3.00 8.00
ATMC Thomas McCollum 5.00 12.00
ATT Tyson Teichmann 4.00 10.00
ATTA Tomas Tatar 10.00 25.00
ATTH Tim Thomas SP 25.00 50.00
ATTO Tyler Toffoli 10.00 25.00
AVR Victor Rask 4.00 10.00
AVT Vladimir Tarasenko 50.00 100.00
AYA Yuri Alexandrov 4.00 10.00
AZB Zach Boychuk 4.00 10.00
AZC Zdeno Chara SP 15.00 30.00
AZH Zach Hamill SP 6.00 15.00
AZP Zack Phillips 5.00 12.00

2010-11 ITG Heroes and Prospects Calder Cup Champions

CC01 Alexandre Giroux 6.00 15.00
CC02 Chris Bourque 3.00 8.00
CC03 Keith Aucoin 4.00 10.00
CC04 Andrew Gordon 6.00 15.00
CC05 Mathieu Perreault 2.00 5.00
CC06 Kyle Wilson 3.00 8.00
CC07 Francois Bouchard 3.00 8.00
CC08 Karl Alzner 2.00 5.00
CC09 John Carlson 3.00 8.00
CC10 Patrick McNeill 2.50 6.00
CC11 Bryan Helmer 5.00 12.00
CC12 Jay Beagle 6.00 15.00
CC13 Steve Pinizzotto 4.00 10.00
CC14 Braden Holtby 4.00 10.00
CC15 Michal Neuvirth 2.50 6.00

2010-11 ITG Heroes and Prospects Draft Star Jerseys Black

SILVER/19: .5X TO 1.2X BLACK/40*
DS01 Ryan Nugent-Hopkins 20.00 50.00
DS02 Gabriel Landeskog 12.00 30.00
DS03 Jonathan Huberdeau 12.00 30.00
DS04 Sean Couturier 12.00 30.00
DS05 Dougie Hamilton 12.00 30.00
DS06 Nathan Beaulieu 4.00 10.00
DS07 Sven Bartschi 6.00 15.00
DS08 Ryan Murphy 8.00 20.00

2010-11 ITG Heroes and Prospects Game Used Jerseys Black

SILVER/30-40: .5X TO 1.2X BLACK
M01 Blake Geoffrion 5.00 12.00
M02 Brandon Gormley 5.00 12.00
M03 Brayden Schenn 10.00 25.00
M04 Brendan Shinnimin 3.00 8.00
M05 Brett Connolly 5.00 12.00
M06 Brock Beukeboom 3.00 8.00
M07 Chet Pickard 4.00 10.00
M08 Chris Terry 4.00 10.00
M09 Cody Eakin 5.00 12.00
M10 Cody Hodgson 10.00 25.00
M11 Cory Schneider 8.00 20.00
M12 Drayson Bowman 4.00 10.00
M13 Ethan Werek 5.00 12.00
M14 Greg McKegg 5.00 12.00
M15 Jake Allen 8.00 20.00
M16 Jamie Arniel 4.00 10.00
M17 Jared Cowen 4.00 10.00
M18 Jean-Francois Berube 5.00 12.00
M19 Joe Colborne 6.00 15.00
M20 Joey Hishon 5.00 12.00
M21 John Carlson 10.00 25.00
M22 John McFarland 4.00 10.00
M23 Jordan Binnington 8.00 20.00
M24 Jordan Weal 3.00 8.00
M25 Kevin Shattenkirk 8.00 20.00
M26 Kyle Turris 4.00 10.00
M27 Landon Ferraro 3.00 8.00
M28 Lars Eller 3.00 8.00
M29 Logan Couture 8.00 20.00
M30 Matt Puempel 5.00 12.00
M31 Michael St. Croix 3.00 8.00
M32 Nathan Beaulieu 3.00 8.00
M33 Nazem Kadri 10.00 25.00
M34 Oliver Ekman-Larsson 6.00 15.00
M35 Oscar Moller 4.00 10.00
M36 P.K. Subban 12.00 30.00
M37 Petr Straka 3.00 8.00
M38 Philipp Grubauer 6.00 15.00
M39 Riley Boychuk 3.00 8.00
M40 Ryan Ellis 5.00 12.00
M41 Ryan Nugent-Hopkins 12.00 30.00
M42 Ryan Stoa 3.00 8.00
M43 Scott Glennie 4.00 10.00
M44 Sean Couturier 12.00 30.00
M45 Stanislav Galiev 5.00 12.00
M46 Taylor Doherty 3.00 8.00
M47 Thomas Hickey 3.00 8.00
M48 Tomas Jurco 6.00 15.00
M49 Tyler Ennis 3.00 8.00
M50 Tyler Seguin 12.00 30.00
M51 Vladimir Tarasenko 15.00 40.00
M52 Zach Boychuk 4.00 10.00
M53 Zach Hamill 4.00 10.00
M54 Zack Kassian 5.00 12.00
M55 Robin Lehner/100 8.00 20.00
M56 Boone Jenner/100 5.00 12.00
M57 Luke Adam/100 4.00 10.00
M58 Louis Leblanc/100 6.00 15.00
M59 Nathan Lieuwen/100 4.00 10.00
M60 Ryan Murray/100 6.00 15.00
M61 Matt Calvert/100 6.00 15.00
M62 Sergei Bobrovsky/100 15.00 40.00
M63 Michael Del Zotto/100 4.00 10.00
M64 Jordan Caron/100 5.00 12.00

2010-11 ITG Heroes and Prospects He Shoots He Scores Prizes

HSHS01 Brodeur/Luongo/Roy 15.00 40.00
HSHS02 Dionne/Schenn/Robitle 12.00 30.00
HSHS03 Couture/Ennis/Eller 8.00 20.00
HSHS04 Gilmour/Kadri/Sittler 15.00 40.00
HSHS05 Bure/Tarsnko/Fedorov 12.00 30.00
HSHS06 Jurco/Huberd/Beaulieu 12.00 30.00
HSHS07 Sedin/Landeskog/Sedin 12.00 30.00
HSHS08 Lecvlr/Yzerman/Stamkos 15.00 40.00
HSHS09 Subban/LeBlanc/Eller 15.00 40.00
HSHS10 Roy/Roy/Domingue 15.00 40.00
HSHS11 Saad/Bourque/Hamilton 12.00 30.00
HSHS12 Kadri/Reimer/Colborne 15.00 40.00
HSHS13 Lapointe/Subban/Robnsn 15.00 40.00
HSHS14 RNH/Stamkos/Couturier 20.00 50.00
HSHS15 Ennis/Kassian/Adam 6.00 15.00
HSHS16 Kurri/Messier/Fuhr 12.00 30.00
HSHS17 Johansen/Neely/Niedrtr 10.00 25.00
HSHS18 Geoffrion/Pickard/Ellis 6.00 15.00
HSHS19 Bure/Hodgson/Sedin 12.00 30.00
HSHS20 Lndbrgh/Bobrvsky/Prent 20.00 50.00
HSHS21 Markstrom/Holtby/Allen 12.00 30.00
HSHS22 Rask/Esposito/Caron 10.00 25.00
HSHS23 Lemieux/Lafleur/Beliveau 25.00 60.00
HSHS24 Couturier/RNH/Landeskog 20.00 50.00
HSHS25 Nash/Kadri/Ciccarelli 15.00 40.00
HSHS26 Murphy/Coffey/Landeskog 12.00 30.00
HSHS27 Ellis/Connolly/Schenn 12.00 30.00
HSHS28 Hishon/Sakic/Shattenkirk 12.00 30.00
HSHS29 Selanne/Etem/Getzlaf 12.00 30.00
HSHS30 Gormley/Chara/Gudbrnsn 6.00 15.00

2010-11 ITG Heroes and Prospects Hero and Prospect Jerseys Silver

HP01 V.Tarasenko/P.Bure 15.00 40.00
HP02 T.Seguin/M.Lemieux 25.00 60.00
HP03 P.Subban/S.Savard 15.00 40.00
HP04 N.Kadri/S.Stamkos 15.00 40.00
HP05 O.Roy/R.Luongo 10.00 25.00
HP06 J.Bernier/M.Brodeur 15.00 40.00
HP07 B.Connolly/S.Yzerman 15.00 40.00
HP08 L.Couture/J.Thornton 10.00 25.00
HP09 J.Allen/P.Roy 15.00 40.00
HP10 B.Schenn/L.Robitaille 12.00 30.00
HP11 G.Landeskog/P.Forsberg 12.00 30.00
HP12 R.Nugent-Hopkins/M.Messier 25.00 50.00
HP13 D.Hamilton/Z.Chara 12.00 30.00
HP14 S.Couturier/E.Lindros 10.00 25.00
HP15 R.Murphy/P.Coffey 8.00 20.00

2010-11 ITG Heroes and Prospects Heroes Game Used Jerseys Silver

HM01 Daniel Sedin 15.00 40.00
HM02 Patrick Roy 15.00 40.00
HM03 Rick Nash 10.00 25.00
HM04 Steven Stamkos 12.00 30.00
HM05 Henrik Sedin 15.00 40.00
HM07 Pavel Bure 12.50 30.00
HM08 Steve Yzerman 15.00 40.00
HM09 Roberto Luongo 10.00 25.00
HM10 Vladislav Tretiak 20.00 50.00
HM12 Theoren Fleury 25.00 50.00
HM13 Tim Thomas 6.00 15.00

2010-11 ITG Heroes and Prospects Memorial Cup Champions

MC01 Taylor Hall 10.00 25.00
MC02 Adam Henrique 6.00 15.00
MC03 Justin Shugg 4.00 10.00
MC04 Dale Mitchell 3.00 8.00
MC05 Cam Fowler 4.00 10.00
MC06 Eric Wellwood 3.00 8.00
MC07 Zack Kassian 5.00 12.00
MC08 Scott Timmins 3.00 8.00
MC09 Greg Nemisz 2.50 6.00
MC10 Ryan Ellis 3.00 8.00
MC11 Kenny Ryan 2.50 6.00
MC12 Mark Cundari 2.50 6.00
MC13 Marc Cantin 2.50 6.00
MC14 Stephen Johnston 2.50 6.00
MC15 Philipp Grubauer 4.00 10.00

2010-11 ITG Heroes and Prospects National Pride Jerseys Black

SILVER/30: .5X TO 1.2X JSY BLK/80*
NATP01 Andrej Nestrasil 5.00 12.00
NATP03 Lars Eller 3.00 8.00
NATP04 Jacob Markstrom 10.00 25.00
NATP05 John Carlson 10.00 25.00
NATP06 Nazem Kadri 8.00 20.00
NATP07 Nino Niederreiter 6.00 15.00
NATP08 P.K. Subban 12.00 30.00
NATP09 Philipp Grubauer 6.00 15.00
NATP10 Vladimir Tarasenko 15.00 40.00

2010-11 ITG Heroes and Prospects Net Prospects Jerseys Black

SILVER/20: .6X TO 1.5X BLACK/80*
NPM01 Jake Allen 8.00 20.00
NPM02 Calvin Pickard 5.00 12.00
NPM03 Olivier Roy 5.00 12.00
NPM04 Louis Domingue 6.00 15.00
NPM05 Mark Visentin 5.00 12.00
NPM06 Chet Pickard 4.00 10.00
NPM07 Cory Schneider 8.00 20.00
NPM08 Braden Holtby 8.00 20.00
NPM09 Philipp Grubauer 6.00 15.00
NPM10 Jacob Markstrom 10.00 25.00

2010-11 ITG Heroes and Prospects Prospect Trios Silver

PT1 Subban/LeBlanc/Eller 25.00 60.00
PT2 Hopkins/Couturier/Puempel 15.00 40.00
PT3 Kadri/Cowen/Glennie 12.00 30.00
PT4 Markstrm/Ellerby/Gudbrans 20.00 50.00
PT5 Seguin/Hamill/Colbourne 25.00 60.00

2010-11 ITG Heroes and Prospects Subway Series Jumbo Jerseys Black

*SILVER/30: .5X TO 1.2X JUMBO JSY BLK
CRM31 Chris Stewart 4.00 10.00
CRM32 Steven Stamkos 8.00 20.00
CRM35 Logan Couture 6.00 15.00
SSM01 Scott Stajcer 4.00 10.00
SSM02 Scott Wedgewood 4.00 10.00
SSM03 J.P. Anderson 5.00 12.00
SSM04 Mark Visentin 5.00 12.00
SSM05 Christian Thomas 4.00 10.00
SSM06 Boone Jenner 5.00 12.00
SSM07 Matt Puempel 5.00 12.00
SSM08 Taylor Doherty 3.00 8.00
SSM09 Devante Smith-Pelly 6.00 15.00
SSM10 Greg McKegg 5.00 12.00
SSM11 Jean-Francois Berube 5.00 12.00
SSM12 Brandon Gormley 5.00 12.00
SSM13 Jonathan Huberdeau 10.00 25.00
SSM14 Sean Couturier 12.00 30.00
SSM15 Louis Leblanc 8.00 20.00
SSM16 Zack Phillips 5.00 12.00
SSM17 Michael Bournival 4.00 10.00
SSM18 Xavier Ouellet 3.00 8.00
SSM19 Nathan Beaulieu 3.00 8.00
SSM20 Olivier Roy 5.00 12.00
SSM21 Quinton Howden 4.00 10.00
SSM22 Ryan Murray 8.00 20.00
SSM23 Kent Simpson 4.00 10.00
SSM24 Calvin Pickard 5.00 12.00
SSM25 Ty Rattie 5.00 12.00
SSM26 Ryan Nugent-Hopkins 6.00 15.00
SSM27 Curtis Hamilton 4.00 10.00
SSM28 Ryan Johansen 6.00 15.00
SSM29 Brad Ross 4.00 10.00
SSM30 Dougie Hamilton 10.00 25.00
SSM34 Tyler Seguin 10.00 25.00

2010-11 ITG Heroes and Prospects Top Prospects Game Used Jerseys Black

SILVER/30: .5X TO 1.2X JSY BLK/100*
JM01 Alexander Petrovic 3.00 8.00
JM02 Brock Beukeboom 3.00 8.00
JM03 Alex Hutchings 3.00 8.00
JM04 Cody Eakin 5.00 12.00
JM05 Michael Latta 5.00 12.00
JM06 Philippe Paradis 3.00 8.00
JM07 Emerson Etem 5.00 12.00
JM08 Levko Koper 3.00 8.00
JM09 John McFarland 4.00 10.00
JM10 Louis Domingue 5.00 12.00
JM11 Mark Pysyk 3.00 8.00
JM12 Mark Visentin 5.00 12.00
JM13 Maxime Clermont 4.00 10.00
JM14 Nino Niederreiter 6.00 15.00
JM15 Michael Bournival 4.00 10.00
JM16 Peter Holland 4.00 10.00
JM17 Taylor Beck 4.00 10.00
JM18 Quinton Howden 4.00 10.00
JM19 Ryan Spooner 5.00 12.00
JM20 Scott Stajcer 4.00 10.00
JM21 Stanislav Galiev 5.00 12.00
JM22 Stephen Silas 4.00 10.00
JM23 Taylor Doherty 3.00 8.00
JM24 Troy Rutkowski 3.00 8.00
JM25 Tyler Seguin 15.00 40.00
JM26 Tyler Toffoli 10.00 25.00

2011-12 ITG Heroes and Prospects

COMP.SERIES 1 (200) 20.00 50.00
1 Brad Park HH .20 .50
2 Cam Neely HH .25 .60
3 Henri Richard HH .25 .60
4 Mike Gartner HH .30 .75
5 Red Kelly HH .25 .60
6 Teemu Selanne HH .50 1.25
7 Tony Amonte HH .20 .50
8 Adam Larsson INT .25 .60
9 Mika Zibanejad INT .60 1.50
10 Vladimir Tarasenko INT .60 1.50
11 Alex Galchenyuk CP .75 2.00
12 Alexander Khokhlachev CP .30 .75
13 Boone Jenner CP .25 .60
14 Brandon Saad CP .40 1.00
15 Brendan Gaunce CP .20 .50
16 Brett Ritchie CP .20 .50
17 Dougie Hamilton CP .50 1.25
18 Jarrod Maidens CP .25 .60
19 Jordan Binnington CP .40 1.00
20 Malcolm Subban CP .40 1.00
21 Mark Scheifele CP .75 2.00
22 Matia Marcantuoni CP .20 .50
23 Matt Murray CP .30 .75
24 Matt Puempel CP .25 .60
25 Mathew Campagna CP .20 .50
26 Max Iafrate CP .25 .60
27 Nail Yakupov CP .75 2.00
28 Nick Cousins CP .15 .40
29 Nick Ebert CP .15 .40
30 Nicklas Jensen CP .25 .60
31 Rickard Rakell CP .25 .60
32 Ryan Murphy CP .25 .60
33 Ryan Spooner CP .25 .60
34 Ryan Strome CP .30 .75
35 Shane Prince CP .15 .40
36 Scott Harrington CP .25 .60
37 Scott Laughton CP .25 .60
38 Slater Koekkoek CP .15 .40
39 Stefan Noesen CP .15 .40
40 Stuart Percy CP .25 .60
41 Vladislav Namestnikov CP .40 1.00
42 Alexandre Grenier CP .20 .50
43 Andrew Ryan CP .20 .50
44 Charles Hudon CP .25 .60
45 Christopher Gibson CP .25 .60
46 David Honzik CP .25 .60
47 Domenic Graham CP .20 .50
48 Dominic Poulin CP .20 .50
49 Jean-Gabriel Pageau CP .25 .60
50 Jeremie Fraser CP .15 .40
51 Jonathan Huberdeau CP .50 1.25
52 Jonathan Racine CP .20 .50
53 Logan Shaw CP .20 .50
54 Luca Ciampini CP .25 .60
55 Martin Frk CP .25 .60
56 Nathan Beaulieu CP .15 .40
57 Olivier Archambault CP .20 .50
58 Phillip Danault CP .25 .60
59 Ryan Tesink CP .25 .60
60 Scott Oke CP .20 .50
61 Sean Couturier CP .40 1.00
62 Tomas Jurco CP .30 .75
63 Xavier Ouellet CP .25 .60
64 Zach O'Brien CP .20 .50
65 Zack Phillips CP .25 .60
66 Adam Lowry CP .25 .60
67 Brendan Ranford CP .20 .50
68 Colin Jacobs CP .20 .50
69 Colton Sissons CP .20 .50
70 David Musil CP .20 .50
71 Derrick Pouliot CP .30 .75
72 Duncan Siemens CP .15 .40
73 Griffin Reinhart CP .25 .60
74 Joe Morrow CP .30 .75
75 Joel Edmundson CP .20 .50
76 Kale Kessy CP .15 .40
77 Keegan Lowe CP .20 .50
78 Keith Hamilton CP .20 .50
79 Laurent Brossoit CP .25 .60
80 Mark McNeill CP .20 .50
81 Mathew Dumba CP .15 .40
82 Morgan Rielly CP .30 .75
83 Ryan Murray CP .30 .75
84 Sven Baertschi CP .25 .60
85 Troy Bourke CP .15 .40
86 Ty Rattie CP .25 .60
87 Ty Rimmer CP .20 .50
88 Tyler Wotherspoon CP .25 .60
89 Zachary Yuen CP .20 .50
90 Aaron Ekblad CR .60 1.50
91 Alex Forsberg CR .30 .75
92 Curtis Lazar CR .25 .60
93 Daniel Altshuller CR .25 .60
94 Denis Kamaev CR .25 .60
95 Dominik Volek CR .25 .60
96 Eric Comrie CR .20 .50
97 Jamie Oleksiak CR .20 .50
98 Jordan Subban CR .40 1.00
99 Max Domi CR .50 1.25
100 Mikhail Grigorenko CR .60 1.50
101 Nathan MacKinnon CR 3.00 8.00
102 Olli Maatta CR .50 1.25
103 Adam Henrique AP .40 1.00
104 Ben Scrivens AP .20 .50
105 Bill Sweatt AP .20 .50
106 Blake Geoffrion AP .20 .50
107 Brandon Kozun AP .20 .50
108 Brandon Pirri AP .20 .50
109 Brendan Smith AP .20 .50
110 Casey Wellman AP .20 .50
111 Colin Greening AP .20 .50
112 David Savard AP .20 .50
113 Erik Gustafsson AP .25 .60
114 Gabriel Bourque AP .20 .50
115 Gabriel Dumont AP .20 .50
116 Greg Nemisz AP .20 .50
117 Jake Allen AP .40 1.00
118 Joe Colborne AP .20 .50
119 John Moore AP .20 .50
120 Jordan Caron AP .25 .60
121 Keven Veilleux AP .15 .40
122 Kyle Palmieri AP .20 .50
123 Luke Adam AP .20 .50
124 Mark Olver AP .15 .40
125 Martin Jones AP .40 1.00
126 Maxime Sauve AP .25 .60
127 Mike Murphy AP .20 .50
128 Nazem Kadri AP .30 .75
129 Rhett Rakhshani AP .20 .50
130 Richard Bachman AP .20 .50
131 Robin Lehner AP .20 .50
132 Ryan Thang AP .15 .40
133 Tomas Kubalik AP .20 .50
134 Zac Dalpe AP .15 .40
135 Andy Miele AR .20 .50
136 Blake Kessel AR .20 .50
137 Brayden Schenn AR .25 .60
138 Calvin de Haan AR .20 .50
139 Cam Atkinson AR .50 1.25
140 Carl Klingberg AR .20 .50
141 Carter Ashton AR .25 .60
142 Cody Eakin AR .30 .75
143 Harri Sateri AR .20 .50
144 Justin Faulk AR .30 .75
145 Landon Ferraro AR .15 .40
146 Nathan Moon AR .15 .40
147 Ryan Ellis AR .20 .50
148 Stefan Elliott AR .20 .50
149 Taylor Beck AR .15 .40
150 Zack Kassian AR .25 .60
151 David Backes AG .15 .40
152 Patrice Bergeron AG .30 .75
153 Jay Bouwmeester AG .15 .40
154 Dustin Brown AG .25 .60
155 Mike Cammalleri AG .20 .50
156 Loui Eriksson AG .15 .40
157 Claude Giroux AG .25 .60
158 Michael Grabner AG .20 .50
159 Mikhail Grabovski AG .15 .40
160 Jaroslav Halak AG .25 .60
161 Jimmy Howard AG .30 .75
162 Ryan Kesler AG .25 .60
163 Mikko Koivu AG .20 .50
164 Kari Lehtonen AG .20 .50
165 Ryan Miller AG .25 .60
166 Kyle Okposo AG .15 .40
167 Zach Parise AG .25 .60
168 Jason Pominville AG .15 .40
169 Tuukka Rask AG .30 .75
170 Chris Stewart AG .20 .50
171 Cory Schneider AG .25 .60
172 Eric Staal AG .30 .75
173 Joey Crabb AG .15 .40
174 Thomas Vanek AG .20 .50
175 Semyon Varlamov AG .25 .60
176 Pekka Rinne AG .25 .60
177 Ryan Callahan CG .15 .40
178 Corey Crawford CG .30 .75
179 Logan Couture CG .30 .75
180 Tyler Ennis CG .15 .40
181 Marc-Andre Fleury CG .50 1.25
182 Ryan Getzlaf CG .25 .60
183 Cody Hodgson CG .75 2.00
184 David Krejci CG .25 .60
185 Bryan Little CG .25 .60
186 Brad Marchand CG .50 1.25
187 Corey Perry CG .40 1.00
188 Carey Price CG .50 1.25
189 Bobby Ryan CG .20 .50
190 Devin Setoguchi CG .20 .50
191 Jason Spezza CG .25 .60
192 Dion Phaneuf CG .20 .50
193 P.K. Subban CG .30 .75
194 Cam Ward CG .25 .60
195 Shea Weber CG .20 .50
196 Jonathan Bernier CG .20 .50
197 Luc Bourdon TRIB .50 1.25
198 Rick Rypien TRIB .40 1.00
199 Derek Boogaard TRIB .30 .75
200 Wade Belak TRIB .40 1.00
201 Jason Akeson .40 1.00
202 Matt Donovan .30 .75
204 Gustav Nyquist 1.00 2.50
205 Louis Leblanc .40 1.00
206 Justin Fontaine .30 .75
207 Linden Vey .40 1.00
208 Cory Conacher .60 1.50
209 Tyler Johnson 1.00 2.50
210 Cade Fairchild .30 .75
211 Carter Camper .30 .75
212 Andrew Shaw 1.00 2.50
213 Edward Pasquale .40 1.00
214 Peter Holland .40 1.00
215 Matt Fraser .50 1.25
216 Tanner Pearson .50 1.25
217 Daniil Zharkov .30 .75
218 Matt Finn .30 .75
219 Scott Kosmachuk .30 .75
220 Radek Faksa .75 2.00
221 Cody Ceci .40 1.00
222 Sean Monahan 1.25 3.00
223 Gemel Smith .60 1.50
224 Tom Wilson .75 2.00
225 J.T. Miller .50 1.25
226 Kerby Rychel .30 .75
227 Brady Vail .30 .75
228 Mark Stone 1.00 2.50
229 Henrik Samuelsson .30 .75
230 Tim Bozon .30 .75
231 Damon Severson .50 1.25
232 Sam Reinhart 1.50 4.00
233 Emerson Etem .40 1.00
234 Hunter Shinkaruk .60 1.50
235 Mike Winther .30 .75
236 Chandler Stephenson .30 .75
237 Lukas Sutter .60 1.50
238 Dalton Thrower .30 .75
239 Branden Troock .30 .75
240 Raphael Bussieres .50 1.25
241 Christopher Clapperton .30 .75
242 Jeremy Gregoire .30 .75
243 Tomas Hyka .60 1.50
244 Zachary Fucale 1.00 2.50
245 Anthony Duclair .75 2.00
246 Adam Erne .60 1.50
247 Francis Beauvillier .30 .75
248 Dillon Fournier .30 .75
249 Charlie Coyle .50 1.25
250 Brandon Whitney .75 2.00

2011-12 ITG Heroes and Prospects Autographs

AAE Aaron Ekblad 20.00 40.00
AAEN Andreas Engqvist 4.00 10.00
AAG Alex Galchenyuk 25.00 50.00
AAH Adam Henrique 8.00 20.00
AAK Alexander Khokhlachev 8.00 20.00
AAL Adam Larsson 10.00 25.00
AALO Adam Lowry 5.00 12.00
AAM Andy Miele 4.00 10.00
AAR Andrew Ryan 4.00 10.00
ABF Brian Foster UPD 5.00 12.00
ABG Brendan Gaunce 4.00 10.00
ABGE Blake Geoffrion 4.00 10.00
ABJ Boone Jenner 5.00 12.00
ABK Brandon Kozun 4.00 10.00
ABKE Blake Kessel 4.00 10.00
ABM Brad Marchand SP 8.00 20.00
ABP Brad Park SP 8.00 20.00
ABR Brett Ritchie 4.00 10.00
ABRA Brendan Ranford SP 10.00 25.00
ABRY Bobby Ryan SP 5.00 12.00
ABS Brandon Saad 8.00 20.00
ABSC Ben Scrivens 4.00 10.00
ABSW Bill Sweatt 4.00 10.00
ACA Cam Atkinson 10.00 25.00
ACB Chris Bourque UPD SP 6.00 15.00
ACD Calvin de Haan 4.00 10.00
ACG Colin Greening 4.00 10.00
ACGI Christopher Gibson 5.00 12.00
ACGIR Claude Giroux SP 5.00 30.00
ACH Charles Hudon 5.00 12.00
ACHO Cody Hodgson SP 25.00 50.00
ACK Carl Klingberg 4.00 10.00
ACN Cam Neely SP 10.00 25.00
ACPR Carey Price SP 12.00 30.00
ACS Colton Sissons 4.00 10.00
ACW Casey Wellman 4.00 10.00
ADG Domenic Graham 4.00 10.00
ADH Dougie Hamilton 12.00 30.00
ADHO David Honzik 5.00 12.00
ADM David Musil 4.00 10.00
ADP Dominic Poulin 4.00 10.00
ADPH Dion Phaneuf SP 8.00 20.00
ADPO Derrick Pouliot 6.00 15.00
ADS David Savard 4.00 10.00
ADSI Duncan Siemens SP 4.00 10.00
AEP Edward Pasquale UPD SP 5.00 12.00
AGB Gabriel Bourque 4.00 10.00
AGD Gabriel Dumont 4.00 10.00
AGH Gordie Howe 60.00 100.00
AGN Greg Nemisz 4.00 10.00
AGR Griffin Reinhart SP 6.00 15.00
AHR Henri Richard SP 10.00 25.00
AHS Harri Sateri UPD 4.00 10.00
AIB Igor Bobkov UPD SP 6.00 15.00
AJA J.P. Anderson UPD SP 5.00 12.00
AJB Jordan Binnington 8.00 20.00
AJC Joey Crabb 3.00 8.00
AJE Joel Edmundson 4.00 10.00
AJF Jeremie Fraser 3.00 8.00
AJH Jonathan Huberdeau 12.00 30.00
AJHO Jimmy Howard SP 12.50 25.00
AJL Jacob Lagace UPD 4.00 10.00
AJM John Moore 4.00 10.00
AJMA Jarrod Maidens 5.00 12.00
AJMO Joe Morrow 6.00 15.00
AJP Jean-Gabriel Pageau 5.00 12.00
AJR Jonathan Racine SP 5.00 12.00
AJS Jordan Schroeder UPD SP 6.00 15.00
AKH Keith Hamilton SP 6.00 15.00
AKL Keegan Lowe 4.00 10.00
ALB Laurent Brossoit 5.00 12.00
ALBO Luc Bourdon TRIB 25.00 60.00
ALC Luca Ciampini 5.00 12.00
ALE Loui Eriksson SP 6.00 15.00
ALF Landon Ferraro 3.00 8.00
ALL Louis Leblanc UPD 8.00 20.00
ALS Logan Shaw 4.00 10.00
AMC Mathew Campagna 4.00 10.00
AMCA Mike Cammalleri SP 5.00 12.00
AMD Mathew Dumba SP 4.00 10.00
AMDO Max Domi 12.00 30.00
AMF Martin Frk 5.00 12.00
AMG Mike Gartner SP 25.00 50.00
AMGR Mikhail Grigorenko 25.00 50.00
AMGRA Michael Grabner SP 8.00 20.00
AMGRAB Mikhail Grabovski SP 12.50 30.00
AMH Michael Houser UPD SP 5.00 12.00
AMI Max Iafrate 5.00 12.00
AMJ Martin Jones SP 10.00 25.00
AMM Matia Marcantuoni 4.00 10.00
AMMC Mark McNeill 4.00 10.00
AMMU Matt Murray SP 8.00 20.00
AMMUR Mike Murphy SP 5.00 12.00
AMO Mark Olver 3.00 8.00
AMP Matt Puempel 5.00 12.00
AMR Morgan Rielly 8.00 20.00
AMS Malcolm Subban SP 10.00 25.00
AMSC Mark Scheifele 8.00 20.00
AMZ Mika Zibanejad SP 8.00 20.00
ANB Nathan Beaulieu 3.00 8.00
ANE Nick Ebert 3.00 8.00
ANJ Nicklas Jensen 5.00 12.00
ANM Nathan MacKinnon 25.00 60.00
ANMO Nathan Moon 3.00 8.00
ANN Nino Niederreiter UPD 3.00 8.00
ANY Nail Yakupov 20.00 50.00
AOM Olli Maatta 15.00 30.00
APB Patrice Bergeron SP 20.00 40.00
APD Phillip Danault 5.00 12.00
APM Patrick Maroon UPD 4.00 10.00
ARC Ryan Callahan SP 8.00 20.00
ARE Ryan Ellis SP 8.00 20.00
ARK Red Kelly SP 8.00 20.00
ARKE Ryan Kesler SP 20.00 40.00
ARM Ryan Murphy 5.00 12.00
ARMU Ryan Murray SP 8.00 20.00
ARR Rickard Rakell 5.00 12.00
ARST Ryan Strome 8.00 20.00
ART Ryan Tesink 5.00 12.00
ASB Sven Baertschi 10.00 25.00
ASC Sean Couturier 8.00 20.00
ASD Simon Despres UPD SP 8.00 20.00
ASK Slater Koekkoek 3.00 8.00
ASL Scott Laughton 5.00 12.00
ASM Shane McColgan UPD 5.00 12.00
ASN Stefan Noesen 5.00 12.00
ASO Scott Oke 4.00 10.00
ASP Stuart Percy 5.00 12.00
ASV Semyon Varlamov SP 12.00 30.00
ATA Tony Amonte SP 8.00 20.00
ATB Troy Bourke 3.00 8.00
ATJ Tomas Jurco 6.00 15.00
ATK Tomas Kubalik 4.00 10.00
ATR Ty Rattie 5.00 12.00
ATRI Ty Rimmer SP 5.00 12.00
ATS Teemu Selanne SP 20.00 40.00
ATV Thomas Vanek SP 10.00 25.00
ATW Tyler Wotherspoon 5.00 12.00
AVN Vladislav Namestnikov 8.00 20.00
AVR Victor Rask UPD 5.00 12.00
AVT Vladimir Tarasenko 40.00 100.00
AWB Wade Belak TRIB 15.00 40.00
AXO Xavier Ouellet 5.00 12.00
AZB Zach Boychuk UPD 3.00 8.00
AZD Zac Dalpe 3.00 8.00
AZK Zack Kassian 10.00 25.00
AZO Zach O'Brien 4.00 10.00
AZP Zack Phillips UPD 5.00 12.00
AAG2 Alex Galchenyuk UPD 25.00 50.00
ABG2 Brendan Gaunce UPD 4.00 10.00
ABMC Brayden McNabb UPD 4.00 10.00
ACS2 Colton Sissons UPD 4.00 10.00
AGR2 Griffin Reinhart UPD SP 6.00 15.00
AJCA Jack Campbell UPD SP 6.00 15.00
AMD2 Mathew Dumba UPD 3.00 8.00
AMF2 Martin Frk UPD SP 6.00 15.00
AMR2 Morgan Rielly UPD SP 10.00 25.00
AMS2 Malcolm Subban UPD 10.00 25.00
ANY2 Nail Yakupov UPD 40.00 80.00
AOM2 Olli Maatta UPD SP 15.00 30.00
ARBU Raphael Bussieres UPD SP 6.00 15.00
ASK2 Slater Koekkoek UPD SP 4.00 10.00
ATBE Tyler Beskorowany UPD SP 4.00 10.00
ATBR T.J. Brennan UPD SP 5.00 12.00
ATSE Tyson Sexsmith UPD SP 5.00 12.00
AALOK Andrei Loktionov UPD 4.00 10.00
ADPO2 Derrick Pouliot UPD 6.00 15.00
AMGR2 Mikhail Grigorenko UPD 15.00 40.00
ARMU2 Ryan Murray UPD 6.00 15.00

2011-12 ITG Heroes and Prospects Calder Cup Champions

COMPLETE SET (10) 15.00 30.00
CC01 Robin Lehner 1.50 4.00
CC02 Colin Greening 1.50 4.00
CC03 Ryan Potulny 1.25 3.00
CC04 Ryan Keller 1.25 3.00
CC05 Kaspars Daugavins 1.25 3.00
CC06 Zack Smith 1.25 3.00
CC07 Erik Condra 1.50 4.00
CC08 Bobby Butler 1.50 4.00
CC09 Andre Benoit 2.00 5.00
CC10 Corey Locke 1.50 4.00

2011-12 ITG Heroes and Prospects Class of 2012

C01 Nail Yakupov 8.00 20.00
C02 Mathew Dumba 12.00 30.00
C03 Morgan Rielly 6.00 15.00
C04 Alex Galchenyuk 10.00 25.00
C05 Mikhail Grigorenko 6.00 15.00
C06 Griffin Reinhart 6.00 15.00
C07 Ryan Murray 6.00 15.00
C08 Radek Faksa 5.00 12.00
C09 Martin Frk 4.00 10.00
C10 Derrick Pouliot 5.00 12.00

2011-12 ITG Heroes and Prospects Draft Day Stars Memorabilia Black

SILVER/20: .6X TO 1.5X BLACK/60*
DDSJ01 Nail Yakupov 10.00 25.00
DDSJ02 Ryan Murray 6.00 15.00
DDSJ03 Alex Galchenyuk 15.00 40.00
DDSJ04 Griffin Reinhart 5.00 12.00
DDSJ05 Morgan Rielly 6.00 15.00
DDSJ06 Mathew Dumba 3.00 8.00
DDSJ07 Derrick Pouliot 6.00 15.00
DDSJ08 Slater Koekkoek 3.00 8.00

2011-12 ITG Heroes and Prospects Dual Jerseys Silver

DJ01 N.Kadri/J.Colborne 12.00 30.00
DJ02 G.Reinhart/R.Murray 12.00 30.00
DJ03 N.MacKinnon/L.Ciampini 20.00 40.00
DJ04 S.Wedgewood/M.Visentin 5.00 12.00
DJ05 R.Murphy/M.Marcantuoni 5.00 12.00
DJ06 T.Rattie/S.Bartschi 10.00 25.00
DJ07 F.Hamilton/D.Hamilton 8.00 20.00
DJ08 L.Leblanc/P.Subban 15.00 40.00
DJ09 R.Ellis/B.Geoffrion 12.00 30.00

DJ10 J.Allen/J.Markstrom 8.00 20.00
DJ11 S.Couturier/B.Schenn 12.00 30.00
DJ12 S.Percy/J.Anderson 5.00 12.00
DJ13 J.Huberdeau/N.Beaulieu 15.00 30.00
DJ14 B.Jenner/N.Jensen 5.00 12.00
DJ15 A.Galchenyuk/N.Yakupov 20.00 50.00
DJ16 L.Brossoit/G.Reinhart 6.00 15.00
DJ17 Z.Kassian/C.Hodgson 8.00 20.00

2011-12 ITG Heroes and Prospects Family Ties

FT01 Reinhart/Reinhart
Reinhart/Reinhart 6.00 15.00
FT02 Geoffrion/Geoffrion/Morenz 2.50 6.00
FT03 Subban/Subban/Subban 3.00 8.00
FT04 Bourque/Bourque/Bourque 2.00 5.00
FT05 T.Domi/M.Domi 4.00 10.00
FT06 B.Ashton/C.Ashton 2.00 5.00
FT07 S.Burke/B.Burke 1.25 3.00
FT08 P.Roy/F.Roy 3.00 8.00

2011-12 ITG Heroes and Prospects Game Used Jerseys Black

*GOLD/10: .8X TO 2X BASIC JSY
*SILVER/30: .5X TO 1.2X BASIC JSY
M01 Zach Boychuk 3.00 8.00
M02 Matt Kassian 3.00 8.00
M03 Aaron Boogaard 4.00 10.00
M04 Dustin Boyd 4.00 10.00
M05 Alex Bourret 4.00 10.00
M06 Alexander Vasyunov 5.00 12.00
M07 Teddy Purcell 3.00 8.00
M08 Devan Dubnyk 4.00 10.00
M09 Ben Bishop 4.00 10.00
M10 Kyle Chipchura 3.00 8.00
M11 Mike MooreÂ• 3.00 8.00
M12 Joe Colborne 6.00 15.00
M13 Cal O'Reilly 3.00 8.00
M14 Kevin Shattenkirk 3.00 8.00
M15 Jeremie Fraser 3.00 8.00
M16 Logan Shaw 4.00 10.00
M17 Charles Hudon 5.00 12.00
M18 Dominic Poulin 4.00 10.00
M19 Sean Couturier 8.00 20.00
M20 Griffin Reinhart 5.00 12.00
M21 Keegan Lowe 4.00 10.00
M22 Laurent Brossoit 5.00 12.00
M23 Michael St. Croix 4.00 10.00
M24 Ryan Murray 6.00 15.00
M25 Richard Panik 5.00 12.00
M26 Anthony Terenzio 3.00 8.00
M27 Luca Ciampini 5.00 12.00
M28 Brendan Ranford 4.00 10.00
M29 Colton Sissons 4.00 10.00
M30 Matia Marcantuoni 4.00 10.00
M31 Scott Harrington 5.00 12.00
M32 Max Domi 8.00 20.00
M33 Stuart Percy 5.00 12.00
M34 Morgan Rielly 6.00 15.00
M35 Sean Aschim 3.00 8.00
M36 Boone Jenner 5.00 12.00
M37 Nicklas Jensen 5.00 12.00
M38 Slater Koekkoek 3.00 8.00
M39 Mark McNeill 4.00 10.00
M40 Troy Bourke 3.00 8.00
M41 Ty Rimmer 4.00 10.00
M42 Alex Galchenyuk 8.00 20.00
M43 Scott Oke 4.00 10.00
M44 Ryan Tesink 5.00 12.00
M45 Zack Phillips 5.00 12.00
M46 Zack Kassian 6.00 15.00
M47 Mac Engel 3.00 8.00
M48 Adam Lowry 5.00 12.00
M49 David Musil 4.00 10.00
M50 Nail Yakupov 12.00 30.00
M51 Ryan Kujawinski 4.00 10.00
M52 Scott Glennie 4.00 10.00
M53 Brody Silk 4.00 10.00
M54 Cody Ceci 3.00 8.00
M55 Mikhail Grigorenko 10.00 25.00
M56 Radek Faksa 6.00 15.00

2011-12 ITG Heroes and Prospects He Shoots He Scores Prizes

HSHS01 Nail Yakupov 25.00 60.00
HSHS02 R.Strome/Niederreiter 10.00 25.00
HSHS03 Sean Couturier 12.00 30.00
HSHS04 J.Blum/R.Ellis 6.00 15.00
HSHS05 Jonathan Huberdeau 15.00 40.00
HSHS06 R.Lehner/B.Bishop 6.00 15.00
HSHS07 Dougie Hamilton 15.00 40.00
HSHS08 B.Schenn/S.Couturier 12.00 30.00
HSHS09 Charles Hudon 8.00 20.00
HSHS10 N.Yakupov/Galchenyuk 25.00 60.00
HSHS11 Louis Leblanc 6.00 15.00
HSHS12 D.Hamilton/F.Hamilton 15.00 40.00
HSHS13 Ryan Murray 10.00 25.00
HSHS14 M.Domi/N.MacKinnon 30.00 60.00
HSHS15 Sven Baertschi 8.00 20.00
HSHS16 R.Faksa/R.Murphy 12.00 30.00
HSHS17 Mikhail Grigorenko 20.00 50.00
HSHS18 N.Kadri/J.Reimer 10.00 25.00
HSHS19 Matt Dumba 5.00 12.00
HSHS20 M.Visentin/Wedgewood 8.00 20.00
HSHS21 Nathan MacKinnon 30.00 60.00
HSHS22 Grigorenko/N.Yakupov 25.00 60.00
HSHS23 Max Domi 15.00 40.00
HSHS24 M.Dumba/R.Murray 10.00 25.00
HSHS25 Griffin Reinhart 8.00 20.00
HSHS26 S.Bartschi/G.Nemisz 8.00 20.00
HSHS27 Robin Lehner 6.00 15.00
HSHS28 L.Leblanc/N.Beaulieu 6.00 15.00
HSHS29 Alex Galchenyuk 25.00 60.00
HSHS30 J.Binnington/S.Stajcer 6.00 15.00

2011-12 ITG Heroes and Prospects Hero and Prospect Jerseys Silver

HP01 S.Weber/R.Ellis 20.00 50.00
HP02 B.Clarke/S.Couturier 8.00 20.00
HP03 R.Bourque/D.Hamilton 12.00 30.00
HP04 G.Hall/J.Allen 10.00 25.00
HP05 G.Lafleur/L.Leblanc 15.00 40.00
HP06 E.Lindros/B.Schenn 12.00 30.00
HP07 T.Domi/M.Domi 12.00 30.00
HP08 P.Coffey/G.Reinhart 6.00 15.00
HP09 N.Lidstrom/A.Larsson 8.00 20.00
HP10 A.Ovechkin/N.Yakupov 15.00 40.00

2011-12 ITG Heroes and Prospects Heroes Memorabilia Silver

HM01 Brett Hull 10.00 25.00
HM02 Cam Neely 5.00 12.00
HM03 Eric Lindros 8.00 20.00
HM04 Mike Gartner 6.00 15.00
HM05 Pavel Bure 10.00 25.00
HM06 Shea Weber 6.00 15.00
HM07 Teemu Selanne 8.00 20.00
HM08 Theoren Fleury 12.00 30.00
HM10 Trevor Linden 10.00 25.00
HM11 Mats Sundin 10.00 25.00
HM12 Joe Sakic 20.00 50.00
HM13 Pavel Bure 10.00 25.00
HM14 Adam Oates 10.00 25.00

2011-12 ITG Heroes and Prospects Memorial Cup Champions

COMPLETE SET (10) 20.00 40.00
MC01 Jonathan Huberdeau 4.00 10.00
MC02 Michael Kirkpatrick 2.00 5.00
MC03 Stanislav Galiev 2.00 5.00
MC04 Tomas Jurco 2.50 6.00
MC05 Ryan Tesink 2.00 5.00
MC06 Simon Despres 1.50 4.00
MC07 Zack Phillips 2.00 5.00
MC08 Kevin Gagne 1.50 4.00
MC09 Jacob DeSerres 2.00 5.00
MC10 Nathan Beaulieu 1.25 3.00

2011-12 ITG Heroes and Prospects Moving All the Way Up Dual Jerseys Silver

MAU01 Marc-Andre Fleury 10.00 25.00
MAU02 Ryan Getzlaf 6.00 15.00
MAU03 Mikko Koivu 4.00 10.00
MAU04 Ryan Miller 5.00 12.00
MAU05 Rick Nash 10.00 25.00
MAU06 Corey Perry 8.00 20.00
MAU07 Carey Price 10.00 25.00
MAU08 Jason Spezza 5.00 12.00
MAU09 Shea Weber 6.00 15.00
MAU10 Alexander Ovechkin 20.00 50.00

2011-12 ITG Heroes and Prospects Moving Up Dual Jerseys Silver

MU01 Robin Lehner 5.00 12.00
MU02 Devan Dubnyk 6.00 15.00
MU03 Zach Boychuk 4.00 10.00
MU04 Thomas Hickey 5.00 12.00
MU05 Patrick O'Sullivan 4.00 10.00

2011-12 ITG Heroes and Prospects National Pride Jerseys Silver

NAT03 Sven Bartschi 8.00 20.00
NAT04 Alex Galchenyuk 10.00 25.00
NAT05 Emerson Etem 10.00 25.00
NAT06 Christopher Gibson 6.00 15.00
NAT07 Nicklas Jensen 6.00 15.00
NAT08 David Musil 5.00 12.00
NAT09 Jonathan Huberdeau 12.00 30.00
NAT10 Brendan Gallagher 15.00 40.00

2011-12 ITG Heroes and Prospects Net Prospects Jerseys Silver

NP01 Kevin Bailie 6.00 15.00
NP02 Jacob Markstrom 6.00 15.00
NP03 Martin Jones 8.00 20.00
NP05 Christopher Gibson 6.00 15.00
NP06 Scott Wedgewood 6.00 15.00
NP07 Mark Visentin 5.00 12.00
NP08 Louis Domingue 4.00 10.00
NP10 Calvin Pickard 6.00 15.00

2011-12 ITG Heroes and Prospects Prospects Trios Jerseys Silver

PT01 Machck/Holzpfel/Cormier 8.00 20.00
PT02 Tarasenko/Rattie/Allen 20.00 50.00
PT03 Larssn/Clermnt/Wedgewd 8.00 20.00
PT04 Colborne/Kadri/Percy 10.00 25.00
PT05 Hamilton/Caron/Spooner 8.00 20.00
PT06 Lehner/Pageau/Puempel 12.00 30.00
PT07 Huber/Markstrom/Howden 12.00 30.00
PT08 Jones/Hickey/Toffoli 6.00 15.00
PT09 Ellis/Geoffrio/Pickard 10.00 25.00
PT10 Adam/Kassian/EnrothÂ• 8.00 20.00

2011-12 ITG Heroes and Prospects Quad Jerseys Silver

*PATCH SILVER/19: 1X TO 2.5X SLVR JSY/80
QJ01 Rnhrt/Lwe/St.Crx/Brss 12.00 30.00
QJ02 Mrph/Mrks/Allen/Jnes 12.00 30.00
QJ03 Strme/Hmiltn's/Visnt 12.00 30.00
QJ04 Huber/Phill/Beaul/Jrco 12.00 30.00
QJ05 Kadri/Adm/Carn/Geof 10.00 25.00
QJ06 Schn/Ashtn/Kassn/Vey 8.00 20.00
QJ07 Mrry/Rielly/Dmba/Rein 12.00 30.00
QJ08 Hmltn/Mrphy/Lrsn/Smns 12.00 30.00
QJ09 Rattie/Brts/Mrrw/Wthr 15.00 40.00
QJ10 Listn/Hnzik/Gbsn/Binn 10.00 25.00

2011-12 ITG Heroes and Prospects Subway Series Jerseys Black

*GOLD/10: .8X TO 2X BASIC JSY
*SILVER/30: .5X TO 1.2X BASIC JSY
SSM01 Matthew Bissonnette 3.00 8.00
SSM02 Daniel Catenacci 4.00 10.00
SSM03 Andrew D'Agostini 4.00 10.00
SSM04 Yannick Dube 5.00 12.00
SSM05 Mathew Dumba 5.00 12.00
SSM06 Brendan Gallagher 12.00 30.00
SSM07 Tyler Graovac 5.00 12.00
SSM08 Philippe Halley 4.00 10.00
SSM09 Freddie Hamilton 5.00 12.00
SSM10 Quinton Howden 4.00 10.00
SSM11 Charles Hudon 5.00 12.00
SSM12 Maxime Lagace 5.00 12.00
SSM13 Lucas Lessio 4.00 10.00
SSM14 Adam Lowry 5.00 12.00
SSM15 Nathan MacKinnon 20.00 40.00
SSM16 Joe Morrow 6.00 15.00
SSM17 Zach O'Brien 4.00 10.00
SSM18 Jean-Gabriel Pageau 5.00 12.00
SSM19 Tanner Pearson 5.00 12.00
SSM20 Stuart Percy 4.00 10.00
SSM21 Brett Ritchie 4.00 10.00
SSM22 Ryan Spooner 5.00 12.00
SSM23 Ryan Strome 5.00 12.00
SSM24 Kevin Sundher 4.00 10.00
SSM25 Sean Couturier 6.00 15.00

2011-12 ITG Heroes and Prospects Subway Series Trios Jerseys Silver

SST01 Dumba/Gallagher/Morrow 8.00 20.00
SST02 MacKin/Hudon/Pagu 10.00 25.00
SST03 Pearson/Strome/Catenci 8.00 20.00
SST04 Wdgewd/Andrsn/Visentin 6.00 15.00
SST05 Roy/Stajcer/Pickard 5.00 12.00
SST06 Coutur/Grmly/Beaul 10.00 25.00
SST07 Bourn/Hubr/Leblanc 15.00 40.00
SST08 Dohrty/Hamilt/Pmpl 15.00 40.00
SST09 Howdn/Murry/Ratt 15.00 40.00
SST10 Jenner/McKg/Thoms 6.00 15.00
SST11 Allen/Domingue/Jones 10.00 25.00
SST12 Vey/Glennie/Pysyk 8.00 20.00
SST13 Kadri/Kassn/Schenn 12.00 30.00
SST14 Cormier/Carn/Desprs 12.00 30.00
SST16 Ellis/Subban/Matthias 12.00 30.00
SST17 Sexsmith/Irving/Hickey 8.00 20.00
SST18 Alzner/Mrchnd/Del Zot 10.00 25.00
SST19 Stewart/Setoguchi/Little 6.00 15.00
SST20 Price/Giroux/Helm 10.00 25.00

2011-12 ITG Heroes and Prospects Top Prospects Jerseys Black

*GOLD/10: .8X TO 2X BASIC JSY
*SILVER/30: .5X TO 1.2X BASIC JSY
TPM01 Sven Bartschi 5.00 12.00
TPM02 Myles Bell 4.00 10.00
TPM03 Jordan Binnington 8.00 20.00
TPM04 Sean Couturier 6.00 15.00
TPM05 Christopher Gibson 5.00 12.00
TPM06 Dougie Hamilton 10.00 25.00
TPM07 David Honzik 5.00 12.00
TPM08 Colin Jacobs 4.00 10.00
TPM09 Tomas Jurco 6.00 15.00
TPM10 Lucas Lessio 4.00 10.00
TPM11 Liam Liston 3.00 8.00
TPM12 Shane McColgan 5.00 12.00
TPM13 Ryan Murphy 5.00 12.00
TPM14 David Musil 4.00 10.00
TPM15 Vladislav Namestnikov 8.00 20.00
TPM16 Matt Puempel 5.00 12.00
TPM17 Ty Rattie 5.00 12.00
TPM18 Brandon Saad 6.00 15.00
TPM19 Duncan Siemens 3.00 8.00
TPM20 Ryan Strome 6.00 15.00

2011-12 ITG Heroes and Prospects Tough Customers

TC01 Joel Rechlicz 1.50 4.00
TC02 Zack FitzGerald 1.25 3.00
TC03 Garnet Exelby 1.25 3.00
TC04 Matt Clackson 1.50 4.00
TC05 Pierre-Luc Letourneau-Leblond 1.50 4.00
TC06 Zac Rinaldo 1.50 4.00
TC07 Francis Lessard 1.25 3.00

2012-13 ITG Heroes and Prospects

COMP.SET w/o SPs (150) 15.00 40.00
1 Adam Oates H .25 .60
2 Al MacInnis H .30 .75
3 Chris Chelios H .25 .60
4 Doug Gilmour H .30 .75
6 Eric Lindros H .40 1.00
6 Evgeni Malkin H .50 1.25
7 Gilbert Perreault H .25 .60
8 Gordie Howe H .75 2.00
9 Grant Fuhr H .40 1.00
10 Guy Lafleur H .30 .75
11 Henri Richard H .25 .60
12 Jari Kurri H .25 .60
13 Jean Beliveau H .25 .60
14 Jeremy Roenick H .40 1.00
15 Joe Sakic H .50 1.25
16 Keith Tkachuk H .25 .60
17 Mario Lemieux H 1.00 2.50
18 Mark Recchi H .30 .75
19 Mats Sundin H .40 1.00
20 Nicklas Lidstrom H .25 .60
21 Patrick Roy H .60 1.50
22 Pavel Bure H .25 .60
23 Peter Forsberg H .50 1.25
24 Phil Esposito H .40 1.00
25 Scott Niedermayer H .25 .60
26 Sergei Fedorov H .40 1.00
27 Steve Yzerman H .60 1.50
28 Theoren Fleury H .30 .75
29 Tony Esposito H .25 .60
30 Trevor Linden H .25 .60
31 Connor McDavid CHL 4.00 10.00
32 Roland McKeown CHL .20 .50
33 Sam Bennett CHL .60 1.50
34 Michael Dal Colle CHL .20 .50
35 Dominik Kubalik CHL .25 .60
36 Josh Ho-Sang CHL .30 .75
37 Stefan Matteau CHL .25 .60
38 Laurent Dauphin CHL .15 .40
39 Ivan Barbashev CHL .25 .60
40 Alexis Pepin CHL .20 .50
41 Anthony DeLuca CHL .25 .60
42 Frederik Gauthier CHL .40 1.00
43 Dylan Labbe CHL .15 .40
44 Daniel Audette CHL .30 .75
45 Jake Virtanen CHL .30 .75
46 Miles Koules CHL .15 .40
47 Brayden Point CHL .40 1.00
48 Oliver Bjorkstrand CHL .20 .50
49 Eetu Laurikainen CHL .25 .60
50 Patrik Polivka CHL .25 .60
51 Aaron Ekblad OHL .60 1.50
52 Mark Scheifele OHL .40 1.00
53 Brendan Gaunce OHL .20 .50
54 Daniil Zharkov OHL .15 .40
55 Malcolm Subban OHL .30 .75
56 Dylan Blujus OHL .15 .40
57 Oscar Dansk OHL .30 .75
58 Garret Sparks OHL .25 .60
59 Matt Finn OHL .25 .60
60 Scott Kosmachuk OHL .15 .40
61 Matt Puempel OHL .25 .60
62 Radek Faksa OHL .30 .75
63 Ryan Murphy OHL .25 .60
64 Olli Maatta OHL .40 1.00
65 Seth Griffith OHL .15 .40
66 Stuart Percy OHL .25 .60
67 Brett Ritchie OHL .20 .50
68 Dougie Hamilton OHL .75 2.00
69 Ryan Strome OHL .30 .75
70 Boone Jenner OHL .25 .60
71 Scott Laughton OHL .25 .60
72 Cody Ceci OHL .20 .50
73 Tyler Graovac OHL .15 .40
74 Gemel Smith OHL .25 .60
75 Nick Ritchie OHL .25 .60
76 Slater Koekkoek OHL .15 .40
77 Rickard Rakell OHL .25 .60
78 Stefan Noesen OHL .15 .40
79 Tom Wilson OHL .50 1.25
80 Vincent Trocheck OHL .30 .75
81 Alex Galchenyuk OHL 1.00 2.50
82 Anthony DeAngelo OHL .20 .50
83 Matt Murray OHL .25 .60
84 Ryan Sproul OHL .25 .60
85 Joshua Leivo OHL .20 .50
86 Brady Vail OHL .15 .40
87 Zach Oâ•™Brien QMJHL .20 .50
88 Christophe Lalancette QMJHL .15 .40
89 Raphael Bussieres QMJHL .25 .60
90 Christopher Clapperton QMJHL .15 .40
91 Xavier Ouellet QMJHL .25 .60
92 Charles Hudon QMJHL .25 .60
93 Olivier Archambault QMJHL .20 .50
94 Tomas Hyka QMJHL .25 .60
95 Konrad Abeltshauser QMJHL .15 .40
96 Luca Ciampini QMJHL .25 .60
97 Martin Frk QMJHL .25 .60
98 James Melindy QMJHL .15 .40
99 Jonathan Racine QMJHL .20 .50
100 Mikhail Grigorenko QMJHL .75 2.00
101 Logan Shaw QMJHL .20 .50
102 Ryan Culkin QMJHL .20 .50
103 Francois Brassard QMJHL .15 .40
104 Scott Oke QMJHL .20 .50
105 Francis Beauvillier QMJHL .15 .40
106 Jean-Sebastien Dea QMJHL .25 .60
107 Dillon Fournier QMJHL .15 .40
108 Jonathan Huberdeau QMJHL .60 1.50
109 Ryan Tesink QMJHL .25 .60
110 Stephen MacAulay QMJHL .20 .50
111 Anton Zlobin QMJHL .20 .50
112 Francois Tremblay QMJHL .20 .50
113 Phillip Danault QMJHL .25 .60
114 Brandon Whitney QMJHL .25 .60
115 Chris Driedger WHL .20 .50
116 Griffin Reinhart WHL .25 .60
117 Henrik Samuelsson WHL .20 .50
118 Laurent Brossoit WHL .25 .60
119 Michael St. Croix WHL .15 .40
120 Mitchell Moroz WHL .20 .50
121 Ryan Murray WHL .30 .75
122 Brendan Ranford WHL .20 .50
123 Tim Bozon WHL .40 1.00
124 Colton Sissons WHL .20 .50
125 Damon Severson WHL .20 .50
126 Myles Bell WHL .15 .40
127 Sam Reinhart WHL .75 2.00
128 Jayden Hart WHL .15 .40
129 Morgan Rielly WHL .30 .75
130 Derrick Pouliot WHL .30 .75
131 Nicolas Petan WHL .25 .60
132 Troy Rutkowski WHL .15 .40
133 Ty Rattie WHL .25 .60
134 Mark McNeill WHL .25 .60
135 Colin Jacobs WHL .15 .40
136 Troy Bourke WHL .16 .10
137 Mathew Dumba WHL .15 .40
138 Chandler Stephenson WHL .15 .40
139 Andrey Makarov WHL .25 .60
140 Dalton Thrower WHL .15 .40
141 Lukas Sutter WHL .25 .60
142 Shane McColgan WHL .15 .40
143 Branden Troock WHL .15 .40
144 Liam Stewart WHL .20 .50
145 Adam Lowry WHL .25 .60
146 Coda Gordon WHL .15 .40
147 Zachary Yuen WHL .20 .50
148 David Musil WHL .20 .50
149 Marek Tvrdon WHL .15 .40
150 Keegan Kanzig WHL .15 .40
151 Nathan MacKinnon C13 10.00 25.00
152 Sean Monahan C13 6.00 15.00
153 Seth Jones C13 6.00 15.00
154 Ryan Kujawinski C13 2.50 6.00
155 Kerby Rychel C13 3.00 8.00
156 Eric Roy C13 3.00 8.00
157 Darnell Nurse C13 4.00 10.00
158 Morgan Klimchuk C13 3.00 8.00
159 Nick Baptiste C13 2.50 6.00
160 Jeremy Gregoire C13 2.50 6.00
161 Ryan Pulock C13 4.00 10.00
162 Zachary Fucale C13 4.00 10.00
163 Adam Erne C13 3.00 8.00
164 Curtis Lazar C13 3.00 8.00
165 Hunter Shinkaruk C13 5.00 12.00
166 Anthony Duclair C13 5.00 12.00
167 Jonathan Drouin C13 6.00 15.00
168 Nick Sorensen C13 3.00 8.00
169 Josh Morrissey C13 3.00 8.00
170 Eric Comrie C13 3.00 8.00
171 Bo Horvat C13 6.00 15.00
172 Madison Bowey C13 2.00 5.00
173 Alex Forsberg C13 3.00 8.00
174 Max Domi C13 6.00 15.00
175 William Carrier C13 3.00 8.00
176 Jordan Subban C13 4.00 10.00
177 Anthony Mantha C13 5.00 12.00
178 Connor Rankin C13 2.50 6.00
179 Shea Theodore C13 4.00 10.00
180 Jason Dickinson C13 2.50 6.00
181 Spencer Martin C13 2.50 6.00
182 Greg Chase C13 2.50 6.00
183 Jamal Watson C13 2.50 6.00
184 Stephen Harper C13 4.00 10.00
185 Zach Nastasiuk C13 3.00 8.00
186 Nikita Zadorov C13 2.00 5.00
187 Brody Silk C13 2.50 6.00
188 Carter Hansen C13 2.50 6.00
189 Brian Williams C13 2.50 6.00
190 Chris Bigras C13 2.50 6.00
191 Matt Murphy C13 3.00 8.00
192 Nikolas Brouillard C13 4.00 10.00
193 Ryan Hartman C13 3.00 8.00
194 Matt Needham C13 4.00 10.00
195 Samuel Morin C13 2.00 5.00
196 Jay Merkley C13 2.50 6.00
197 Justin Bailey C13 2.50 6.00
198 Martin Reway C13 2.50 6.00
199 Sergey Tolchinsky C13 2.50 6.00

2012-13 ITG Heroes and Prospects Autographs

AAD Anthony DeLuca 5.00 12.00
AADU Anthony Duclair 8.00 20.00
AAE Aaron Ekblad 12.00 30.00
AAER Adam Erne 5.00 12.00
AAF Alex Forsberg SP 6.00 15.00
AAG Alex Galchenyuk 25.00 50.00
AAL Adam Lowry 5.00 12.00
AAM Anthony Mantha SP 10.00 25.00
AAMA Andrey Makarov SP 6.00 15.00
AAO Adam Oates Hero SP 15.00 30.00
AAP Alexis Pepin 4.00 10.00
AAZ Anton Zlobin 4.00 10.00
ABG Brendan Gaunce 4.00 10.00
ABH Bo Horvat 8.00 20.00
ABW Brandon Whitney SP 6.00 15.00
ACB Clark Bishop 3.00 8.00
ACC Cody Ceci 4.00 10.00
ACCH Chris Chelios Hero SP 8.00 20.00
ACD Chris Driedger SP 5.00 12.00
ACG Christopher Gibson SP 6.00 15.00
ACH Charles Hudon 5.00 12.00
ACJ Colin Jacobs 3.00 8.00
ACL Curtis Lazar SP 6.00 15.00
ACM Connor McDavid SP 100.00 175.00
ACR Connor Rankin 3.00 8.00
ACS Chandler Stephenson 3.00 8.00
ACSI Colton Sissons 4.00 10.00
ADA Daniel Audette 6.00 15.00
ADAL Daniel Altshuller SP 5.00 12.00
ADB Dakota Odgers 4.00 10.00
ADG Doug Gilmour Hero SP 20.00 40.00
ADH Dougie Hamilton 8.00 20.00
ADN Darnell Nurse 10.00 25.00
ADP Derrick Pouliot 6.00 15.00
AEC Eric Comrie SP 6.00 15.00
AEL Eetu Laurikainen SP 6.00 15.00
AER Eric Roy 8.00 20.00
AFG Frederik Gauthier 12.00 30.00
AFT Francois Tremblay SP 5.00 12.00
AGH Gordie Howe Hero SP 60.00 120.00
AGL Guy Lafleur Hero SP 20.00 40.00
AGP Gilbert Perreault Hero SP 20.00 40.00
AGR Griffin Reinhart 5.00 12.00
AHR Henri Richard Hero SP 15.00 30.00
AHS Henrik Samuelsson 4.00 10.00
AHSH Hunter Shinkaruk 10.00 25.00
AJA J.P. Anderson SP 5.00 12.00
AJB Justin Bailey 4.00 10.00
AJBE Jean Beliveau Hero SP 20.00 50.00
AJBI Jordan Binnington SP 10.00 25.00
AJD Jason Dickinson SP 5.00 12.00
AJDR Jonathan Drouin SP 25.00 60.00
AJG Jeremy Gregoire 4.00 10.00
AJGI John Gibson SP 12.50 25.00
AJH Josh Ho-Sang 6.00 15.00
AJHU Jonathan Huberdeau 12.00 30.00
AJK Jari Kurri Hero SP 15.00 30.00
AJM Josh Morrissey 5.00 12.00
AJP Jake Paterson SP 8.00 20.00
AJR Jeremy Roenick Hero SP 15.00 40.00
AJS Jordan Subban 6.00 15.00
AJ3A Joe Sakic Hero SP 25.00 50.00
AJV Jake Virtanen 6.00 15.00
AKA Konrad Abeltshauser 3.00 8.00
AKB Kevin Bailie SP 6.00 15.00
AKK Kale Kessy 3.00 8.00
AKR Kerby Rychel 5.00 12.00
AKT Keith Tkachuk Hero SP 10.00 25.00
ALB Laurent Brossoit SP 6.00 15.00
ALS Liam Stewart 4.00 10.00
AMB Madison Bowey 3.00 8.00
AMD Mathew Dumba 3.00 8.00
AMDO Max Domi 10.00 25.00
AMF Martin Frk 5.00 12.00
AMFI Matt Finn 5.00 12.00
AMG Mikhail Grigorenko 10.00 25.00
AMK Morgan Klimchuk 5.00 12.00
AMM Mitchell Moroz 4.00 10.00
AMMU Matt Murray 5.00 12.00
AMR Morgan Reilly 6.00 15.00
AMRE Mark Recchi Hero SP 15.00 30.00
AMS Mark Scheifele 8.00 20.00
AMST Michael St. Croix 3.00 8.00
AMSU Malcolm Subban SP 10.00 25.00
ANB Nick Baptiste 4.00 10.00
ANL Nicklas Lidstrom Hero SP 25.00 50.00
ANM Nathan MacKinnon SP 40.00 80.00
ANP Nicolas Petan 5.00 12.00
ANR Nick Ritchie 5.00 12.00
ANS Nick Sorensen 5.00 12.00
ANY Nail Yakupov 15.00 40.00
ANZ Nikita Zadorov 3.00 8.00
AOD Oscar Dansk SP 8.00 20.00
AOM Olli Maatta 20.00 40.00
APB Pavel Bure Hero SP 25.00 50.00
APD Phillip Danault 5.00 12.00
APE Phil Esposito Hero SP 20.00 40.00
APF Peter Forsberg Hero SP 25.00 50.00
APP Patrik Polivka SP 6.00 15.00
ARB Raphael Bussieres 5.00 12.00
ARC Ryan Culkin 4.00 10.00
ARF Radek Faksa 6.00 15.00
ARG Robin Gusse SP 5.00 12.00
ARH Ryan Hartman 5.00 12.00
ARK Ryan Kujawinski 4.00 10.00
ARM Roland McKeown 4.00 10.00
ARM Ryan Murray 6.00 15.00
ARMU Ryan Murphy SP 6.00 15.00
ARP Ryan Pulock 6.00 15.00
ARS Ryan Strome 6.00 15.00
ASG Seth Griffith 3.00 8.00
ASJ Seth Jones SP 12.00 30.00
ASK Slater Koekkoek 3.00 8.00
ASL Scott Laughton 5.00 12.00
ASM Sean Monahan 10.00 25.00
ASMA Stefan Matteau 5.00 12.00
ASMAR Spencer Martin SP 5.00 12.00
ASN Scott Niedermayer Hero SP 20.00 40.00
ASR Sam Reinhart SP 25.00 50.00
AST Shea Theodore 6.00 15.00
ASTO Sergey Tolchinsky 3.00 8.00
ASY Steve Yzerman Hero SP 30.00 60.00
ATB Tim Bozon 8.00 20.00
ATF Theoren Fleury Hero SP 20.00 40.00
ATW Tom Wilson 10.00 25.00
AVT Vincent Trocheck 6.00 15.00
AWC William Carrier 5.00 12.00
AZF Zachary Fucale SP 20.00 40.00
AZO Zach O'Brien 4.00 10.00

2012-13 ITG Heroes and Prospects Dual Jerseys

DJ01 Subban/Gaunce 8.00 20.00
DJ02 Galchenyk/Yakupov 30.00 60.00
DJ03 Strome/D.Hamilton 12.00 30.00
DJ04 R.Faksa/R.Murphy 8.00 20.00
DJ05 McKeown/Kujawnsk 5.00 12.00
DJ06 Jenner/Altshuller 6.00 15.00
DJ07 Ranford/Bozon 10.00 25.00
DJ08 Reinhart/Brossoit 6.00 15.00
DJ09 McDavid/Reinhart 15.00 40.00
DJ10 Bourke/Forsberg 6.00 15.00
DJ11 Huberdeau/Tesink 15.00 40.00
DJ12 Murphy/Mantha 10.00 25.00
DJ13 DeLuca/Gauthier 10.00 25.00
DJ14 Shaw/Grigorenko 12.00 30.00
DJ15 MacKinnon/Drouin 20.00 50.00

2012-13 ITG Heroes and Prospects Hero and Prospect Jerseys

HP01 D.Potvin/Reinhart 8.00 20.00
HP02 B.Salming/M.Rielly 10.00 25.00
HP03 E.Lindros/B.Jenner 12.00 30.00
HP04 Lemieux/MacKinn 25.00 50.00
HP05 C.Price/E.Comrie 15.00 40.00
HP06 P.Bure/Yakupov 20.00 50.00
HP07 J.Jagr/R.Faksa 12.00 30.00
HP08 Bourque/Hamilton 12.00 30.00
HP09 Perreault/Grigornk 15.00 40.00

2012-13 ITG Heroes and Prospects Heroes Memorabilia

HM01 Al MacInnis 15.00 40.00
HM02 Patrick Roy 20.00 50.00
HM04 Theoren Fleury 15.00 40.00
HM05 Sergei Fedorov 15.00 40.00
HM06 Pavel Bure 12.00 30.00
HM07 Joe Sakic 15.00 40.00
HM08 Mario Lemieux 20.00 50.00
HM09 Scott Niedermayer 12.00 30.00

2012-13 ITG Heroes and Prospects Net Prospects Memorabilia

N01 Laurent Brossoit 5.00 12.00
N02 Ty Rimmer 4.00 10.00
N03 Cole Cheveldave 4.00 10.00
N04 Jordan Binnington 8.00 20.00
N05 Kevin Bailie 5.00 12.00
N06 J.P. Anderson 4.00 10.00
N07 Robin Gusse 4.00 10.00
N08 Malcolm Subban 6.00 15.00
N09 Zach Fucale 6.00 15.00

2012-13 ITG Heroes and Prospects Prospects Trios Jerseys

PT01 Fucal/MacKin/Drn 25.00 60.00
PT02 Koekko/Ritch/Gioqvz 8.00 20.00
PT03 Ranford/Bozn/Chevldv 12.00 30.00
PT04 Cooke/Baillie/Sissons 6.00 15.00
PT05 Huberd/Shaw/Hodgs 20.00 50.00
PT06 Poult/Murry/Marcantni 10.00 25.00
PT07 Galchenyk/Hudn/Bozn 25.00 60.00
PT08 Scheifl/Suttr/Lowry 12.00 30.00
PT09 Rielly/Finn/Percy 10.00 25.00

2012-13 ITG Heroes and Prospects He Shoots He Scores Points

AG1 Alex Galchenyuk 1.00 2.50
AM1 Anthony Mantha .50 1.25
CM1 Connor McDavid 1.25 3.00
HS1 Hunter Shinkaruk .50 1.25
MG1 Mikhail Grigorenko .60 1.50
MS1 Malcolm Subban .40 1.00
NM1 Nathan MacKinnon 1.00 2.50
RM1 Ryan Murray .40 1.00
SJ1 Seth Jones .60 1.50
MSC1 Mark Scheifele .50 1.25

2012-13 ITG Heroes and Prostpects He Shoots He Scores Prizes

HSHS01 Nathan MacKinnon 25.00 60.00
HSHS02 Stefan Matteau AU 15.00 40.00
HSHS03 Griffin Reinhart 8.00 20.00
HSHS04 Connor McDavid AU 175.00 300.00
HSHS05 Jonathan Drouin 15.00 40.00
HSHS06 Sam Reinhart AU 40.00 100.00
HSHS07 Adam Erne 8.00 20.00
HSHS08 Hunter Shinkaruk AU 20.00 50.00
HSHS-09 Morgan Rielly 10.00 25.00
HSHS10 Sean Monahan AU 30.00 60.00
HSHS11 Malcolm Subban 10.00 25.00
HSHS12 Ryan Murphy AU 12.00 30.00
HSHS13 Mark Scheifele 12.00 30.00
HSHS14 Seth Jones AU 25.00 60.00
HSHS15 Mathew Dumba 5.00 12.00
HSHS16 Nathan MacKinnon AU 60.00 120.00
HSHS17 Stefan Matteau 8.00 20.00
HSHS18 Griffin Reinhart AU 12.00 30.00
HSHS19 Connor McDavid 30.00 60.00
HSHS20 Jonathan Drouin AU 60.00 120.00
HSHS21 Sam Reinhart 25.00 60.00
HSHS22 Adam Erne AU 12.00 30.00
HSHS23 Hunter Shinkaruk 12.00 30.00
HSHS24 Morgan Rielly AU 15.00 40.00
HSHS25 Sean Monahan 20.00 40.00
HSHS26 Malcolm Subban AU 15.00 40.00
HSHS27 Ryan Murphy 8.00 20.00
HSHS28 Mark Scheifele AU 25.00 50.00
HSHS29 Seth Jones 15.00 40.00
HSHS30 Mathew Dumba AU 8.00 20.00

2012-13 ITG Heroes and Prospects Jersey

*PATCH/25: .8X TO 2X JERSEY/120
*SILVER/30: .5X TO 1.2X JERSEY/120
M01 Daniel Altshuller 4.00 10.00
M02 Daniel Audette 6.00 15.00
M03 Justin Bailey 4.00 10.00
M04 Tyson Baillie 4.00 10.00
M05 Tim Bozon 8.00 20.00
M06 William Carrier 6.00 15.00
M07 Cole Cheveldave 5.00 12.00
M08 Jordon Cooke 4.00 10.00
M09 Anthony DeLuca 5.00 12.00
M10 Jason Dickinson 4.00 10.00
M11 Radek Faksa 8.00 20.00
M12 Alex Forsberg 5.00 12.00
M13 Frederik Gauthier 8.00 20.00
M14 John Gibson 8.00 20.00
M15 Sam Reinhart 15.00 40.00
M16 Jeremy Gregoire 4.00 10.00
M17 Stefan Matteau 5.00 12.00
M18 Ryan Hartman 5.00 12.00
M19 Josh Ho-Sang 6.00 15.00
M20 Anthony Mantha 8.00 20.00
M21 Roland McKeown 4.00 10.00
M22 Samuel Morin 3.00 8.00
M23 Xavier Ouellet 5.00 12.00
M24 Nick Ritchie 5.00 12.00
M25 Kerby Rychel 5.00 12.00
M26 Hunter Shinkaruk 6.00 15.00
M27 Garret Sparks 5.00 12.00
M28 Lukas Sutter 5.00 12.00
M29 Sergey Tolchinsky 3.00 8.00
M30 Jake Virtanen 6.00 15.00
M31 Matt Murray 5.00 12.00
M32 Stuart Percy 5.00 12.00
M33 Nick Baptiste 4.00 10.00
M34 Max Domi 6.00 15.00
M35 Scott Harrington 3.00 8.00
M36 Adam Lowry 5.00 12.00
M37 Matia Marcantuoni 3.00 8.00
M38 Mark McNeill 5.00 12.00
M39 Brendan Ranford 4.00 10.00
M40 Morgan Rielly 5.00 12.00
M41 Colton Sissons 4.00 10.00
M42 Tyler Wotherspoon 4.00 10.00
M43 Michael Giugovaz 3.00 8.00
M44 Robin Gusse 4.00 10.00
M45 Connor McDavid 20.00 50.00

2012-13 ITG Heroes and Prospects Jersey Autographs

MAAF Alex Forsberg 12.00 30.00
MAAG Alex Galchenyuk 50.00 80.00
MAAL Adam Lowry 12.00 30.00
MABG Brendan Gaunce 10.00 25.00
MACC Cody Ceci 10.00 25.00
MACH Charles Hudon 12.00 30.00
MACM Connor McDavid 125.00 200.00
MACS Colton Sissons 10.00 25.00
MADH Dougie Hamilton 20.00 50.00
MAJD Jason Dickinson 10.00 25.00
MAJH Josh Ho-Sang 15.00 40.00
MAJV Jake Virtanen 15.00 40.00
MAMD Max Domi 15.00 40.00
MAMF Martin Frk 15.00 40.00
MAMG Mikhail Grigorenko 20.00 50.00
MAMR Morgan Rielly 12.00 30.00
MANM Nathan MacKinnon 40.00 100.00
MANY Nail Yakupov 25.00 60.00
MARF Radek Faksa 15.00 40.00
MARK Ryan Kujawinski 8.00 20.00
MARMU Ryan Murphy 15.00 40.00
MARS Ryan Strome 12.00 30.00
MASK Slater Koekkoek 8.00 20.00
MATB Tim Bozon 30.00 60.00

2012-13 ITG Heroes and Prospects Jersey Quads Silver

QJ01 MacKinn/Drn/Fucl/Frk 25.00 60.00
QJ02 Puempl/Faks/Murph/Bail 10.00 25.00
QJ03 Low/Brosst/St.Crx/Rein 8.00 20.00
QJ04 Lazr/Domi/Shinkrk/Mon 15.00 40.00
QJ05 Lipn/Chevld/Bozn/Rnfrd 12.00 30.00
QJ06 Subbn/Binnt/Sprk/Andrs 12.00 30.00
QJ07 Galchyk/Yaku/Murry/Rein 25.00 60.00
QJ08 Manth/MacKin/DeLc/Gth 25.00 60.00
QJ09 Reinhrt/Murry/Riel/Dumb 10.00 25.00

2012-13 ITG Heroes and Prospects Memorial Cup

COMPLETE SET (15) 10.00 25.00
MC01 Brossoir/Poudrier 1.00 2.50
MC02Â•R.Tesink/S.Griffith 1.00 2.50
MC03Â•Girard/Athanas 1.25 3.00
MC04Â•Huberdeau/Samuels 2.50 6.00
MC05Â•B.Horvat/K.Lowe 2.00 5.00
MC06Â•Arseneau/MacAuly 1.25 3.00
MC07Â•Veilleux/Reinhart 1.00 2.50
MC08Â•Le Sieur/Gagne .75 2.00
MC09 A.Zlobin/M.Domi 2.00 5.00
MC10 Vincent Arseneau 1.25 3.00
MC11 Yannick Veilleux .75 2.00
MC12 Maximilien Le Sieur .75 2.00
MC13 Anton Zlobin .75 2.00
MC14 Loik Poudrier .75 2.00
MC15 Gabriel Girard 1.00 2.50

2012-13 ITG Heroes and Prospects Subway Series

COMPLETE SET (15) 15.00 40.00
SSS01 Zachary Fucale 1.25 3.00
SSS02 Anthony Mantha 1.50 4.00
SSS03 Jonathan Huberdeau 2.50 6.00
SSS04 Nathan MacKinnon 3.00 8.00
SSS05 Jean-Sebastien Dea 1.00 2.50
SSS06 Jordan Binnington 1.50 4.00
SSS07 Connor McDavid 6.00 15.00
SSS08 Ryan Strome 1.25 3.00

SSS09 Dougie Hamilton 2.00 5.00
SSS10 Mark Scheifele 1.50 4.00
SSS11 Morgan Rielly 1.25 3.00
SSS12 Sam Reinhart 3.00 8.00
SSS13 Hunter Shinkaruk 1.50 4.00
SSS14 Mark McNeill 1.00 2.50
SSS15 Nail Yakupov 3.00 8.00

2012-13 ITG Heroes and Prospects Subway Super Series Jersey

*PATCH/25: .8X TO 2X BASIC JSY/120
*SILVER/30: .5X TO 1.2X BASIC JSY/120
SSM01 Cody Ceci 4.00 10.00
SSM02 Dougie Hamilton 10.00 25.00
SSM03 Jake Paterson 6.00 15.00
SSM04 Joshua Leivo 4.00 10.00
SSM05 Kerby Rychel 5.00 12.00
SSM06 Malcolm Subban 6.00 15.00
SSM07 Mark Scheifele 8.00 20.00
SSM08 Matt Finn 5.00 12.00
SSM09 Max Domi 6.00 15.00
SSM10 Ryan Murphy 5.00 12.00
SSM11 Scott Harrington 3.00 8.00
SSM12 Scott Laughton 5.00 12.00
SSM13 Sean Monahan 10.00 25.00
SSM14 Seth Griffith 3.00 8.00
SSM15 Slater Koekkoek 3.00 8.00
SSM16 Tom Wilson 10.00 25.00
SSM17 Anthony Mantha 8.00 20.00
SSM18 Christopher Clapperton 3.00 8.00
SSM19 James Melindy 3.00 8.00
SSM20 Jean-Sebastien Dea 5.00 12.00
SSM21 Jonathan Drouin 10.00 25.00
SSM22 Jonathan Huberdeau 12.00 30.00
SSM23 Matt Murphy 5.00 12.00
SSM24 Nathan MacKinnon 15.00 40.00
SSM25 Stephen Hodges 4.00 10.00
SSM26 Phillip Danault 5.00 12.00
SSM27 William Carrier 6.00 15.00
SSM28 Zachary Fucale 6.00 15.00
SSM29 Graham Black 3.00 8.00
SSM30 Ty Rattie 5.00 12.00
SSM31 Derrick Pouliot 6.00 15.00
SSM32 J.C. Lipon 4.00 10.00
SSM33 Sam Reinhart 6.00 15.00
SSM34 Michael St. Croix 3.00 8.00
SSM35 Mathew Dumba 3.00 8.00
SSM36 Griffin Reinhart 5.00 12.00
SSM37 Morgan Rielly 5.00 12.00
SSM38 Duncan Siemens 3.00 8.00
SSM39 Ryan Pulock 6.00 15.00
SSM40 Curtis Lazar 5.00 12.00
SSM41 Eric Comrie 5.00 12.00
SSM42 Ryan Murray 6.00 15.00
SSM43 Hunter Shinkaruk 6.00 15.00
SSM44 Mark McNeill 5.00 12.00
SSM45 Laurent Brossoit 5.00 12.00

2012-13 ITG Heroes and Prospects Subway Super Series Jersey Autographs

SSMAAM A.Mantha QMJHL 20.00 50.00
SSMACC Cody Ceci OHL 10.00 25.00
SSMACL Curtis Lazar WHL 12.00 30.00
SSMADH Dougie Hamilton OHL 15.00 40.00
SSMADP Derrick Pouliot WHL 15.00 40.00
SSMAGR Griffin Reinhart WHL 12.00 30.00
SSMAHS Hunter Shinkaruk WHL 15.00 40.00
SSMAJD J.Drouin QMJHL 60.00 125.00
SSMAJH J.Huberdeau QMJHL 15.00 40.00
SSMAMD Max Domi OHL 15.00 40.00
SSMAMDU Mathew Dumba WHL 10.00 25.00
SSMAMF Matt Finn OHL 10.00 25.00
SSMAMR Morgan Rielly WHL 15.00 40.00
SSMAMS Mark Scheifele OHL 12.00 30.00
SSMANM N.MacKinnon QMJHL 50.00 100.00
SSMAPD Phillip Danault QMJHL 12.00 30.00
SSMARM Ryan Murphy OHL 15.00 40.00
SSMARP Ryan Pulock WHL 15.00 40.00
SSMASG Seth Griffith OHL 15.00 40.00
SSMASK Slater Koekkoek OHL 8.00 20.00
SSMASL Scott Laughton OHL 12.00 30.00
SSMASM Sean Monahan OHL 25.00 50.00
SSMASR Sam Reinhart WHL 15.00 40.00
SSMATW Tom Wilson OHL 25.00 60.00

2012-13 ITG Heroes and Prospects Subway Super Series Trios Jerseys

SST01 Ceci/Hamilton/Finn 15.00 40.00
SST02 Subban/Percy/Patrsn 10.00 25.00
SST03 Rychel/Domi/Monahn 15.00 40.00
SST04 Carrier/Murph/Fucal 10.00 25.00
SST05 Drouin/Manth/MacKinn 25.00 50.00
SST06 DanaultÂ◆Dea/Huberd 12.00 30.00
SST07 Reinhart/Shinkrk/Lazr 25.00 60.00
SST08 Dumba/Rielly/Murray 10.00 25.00
SST09 Brosst/St.Croix/Reinhrt 8.00 20.00
SST10 Murph/Harrngtn/Koek 8.00 20.00
SST11 Rattie/Pouliot/McNeill 10.00 25.00
SST12 Strom/Ritchie/Graovc 10.00 25.00

2012-13 ITG Heroes and Prospects Top Prospects

COMPLETE SET (15) 10.00 25.00
TOP01 Tom Wilson 2.50 6.00
TOP02 Brendan Gaunce 1.00 2.50
TOP03 Tim Bozon 2.00 5.00
TOP04 Scott Laughton 1.25 3.00
TOP05 Mathew Dumba .75 2.00
TOP06 Ryan Murray 1.50 4.00
TOP07 Matt Murray .75 2.00
TOP08 Griffin Reinhart 1.25 3.00
TOP09 Branden Troock .75 2.00
TOP10 Colton Sissons 1.00 2.50
TOP11 Mikhail Grigorenko 2.50 6.00
TOP12 Derrick Pouliot 1.50 4.00
TOP13 Tomas Hyka 1.25 3.00
TOP14 Radek Faksa 1.50 4.00
TOP15 Chris Driedger 1.00 2.50

2012-13 ITG Heroes and Prospects Top Prospects Jerseys

TP01 Mathew Dumba 4.00 10.00
TP02 Radek Faksa 8.00 20.00
TP03 Martin Frk 6.00 15.00
TP04 Brendan Gaunce 5.00 12.00
TP05 Mikhail Grigorenko 15.00 40.00
TP06 Ryan Murray 8.00 20.00
TP07 Derrick Pouliot 8.00 20.00
TP08 Griffin Reinhart 6.00 15.00
TP09 Gemel Smith 6.00 15.00
TP10 Jordan Binnington 10.00 25.00
TP11 Dougie Hamilton 15.00 40.00
TP12 Ryan Murphy 6.00 15.00
TP13 Matt Puempel 6.00 15.00
TP14 Ty Rattie 6.00 15.00
TP15 Ryan Strome 8.00 20.00

2013-14 ITG Heroes and Prospects

COMP.SET w/o SP's (150) 15.00 40.00
1 Zach Hall OHL .15 .40
2 Brendan Gaunce OHL .20 .50
3 Jordan Subban OHL .25 .60
4 Remi Elie OHL .15 .40
5 Connor McDavid OHL 3.00 8.00
6 Jason Dickinson OHL .20 .50
7 Matt Finn OHL .25 .60
8 Scott Kosmachuk OHL .15 .40
9 Tyler Bertuzzi OHL .25 .60
10 Justin Bailey OHL .20 .50
11 Radek Faksa OHL .25 .60
12 Anthony Stolarz OHL .30 .75
13 Bo Horvat OHL .50 1.25
14 Max Domi OHL .50 1.25
15 Michael McCarron OHL .25 .60
16 Ryan Rupert OHL .15 .40
17 Spencer Martin OHL .25 .60
18 Trevor Carrick OHL .15 .40
19 Cole Cassels OHL .15 .40
20 Scott Laughton OHL .30 .75
21 Sean Monahan OHL .40 1.00
22 Chris Bigras OHL .20 .50
23 Gemel Smith OHL .25 .60
24 Zach Nastasiuk OHL .25 .60
25 Ryan Hartman OHL .25 .60
26 Jake Paterson OHL .25 .60
27 Jimmy Lodge OHL .25 .60
28 Darnell Nurse OHL .30 .75
29 Connor Crisp OHL .15 .40
30 Nicholas Baptiste OHL .20 .50
31 Kerby Rychel OHL .25 .60
32 Slater Koekkoek OHL .15 .40
33 Eric Roy WHL .25 .60
34 Ryan Pulock WHL .25 .60
35 Greg Chase WHL .20 .50
36 Curtis Lazar WHL .25 .60
37 Griffin Reinhart WHL .25 .60
38 Henrik Samuelsson WHL .20 .50
39 Tristan Jarry WHL .25 .60
40 Mirco Mueller WHL .25 .60
41 Tim Bozon WHL .30 .75
42 Jordon Cooke WHL .15 .40
43 Madison Bowey WHL .15 .40
44 Mitchell Wheaton WHL .20 .50
45 Curtis Valk WHL .15 .40
46 Hunter Shinkaruk WHL .30 .75
47 Brendan Burke WHL .15 .40
48 Brendan Leipsic WHL .20 .50
49 Derrick Pouliot WHL .30 .75
50 Nicolas Petan WHL .25 .60
51 Oliver Bjorkstrand WHL .20 .50
52 Cole Cheveldave WHL .25 .60
53 Josh Morrissey WHL .25 .60
54 Patrik Bartosak WHL .15 .40
55 Morgan Klimchuk WHL .20 .50
56 Shea Theodore WHL .30 .75
57 Mitch Holmberg WHL .15 .40
58 Dillon Heatherington WHL .25 .60
59 Eetu Laurikainen WHL .25 .60
60 Eric Comrie WHL .20 .50
61 Keegan Kanzig WHL .15 .40
62 Ryan Pilon WHL .15 .40
63 G.Paquin-Boudreau QMJHL .20 .50
64 Jeremy Gregoire QMJHL .25 .60
65 Valentin Zykov QMJHL .25 .60
66 C.Clapperton QMJHL .15 .40
67 Etienne Marcoux QMJHL .15 .40
68 Marc-Olivier Roy QMJHL .25 .60
69 William Carrier QMJHL .25 .60
70 Yan Pavel Laplante QMJHL .15 .40
71 Charles Hudon QMJHL .25 .60
72 Laurent Dauphin QMJHL .15 .40
73 C.Lalancette QMJHL .15 .40
74 Nikolas Brouillard QMJHL .25 .60
75 Emile Poirier QMJHL .25 .60
76 Martin Reway QMJHL .50 1.25
77 Jonathan Drouin QMJHL .50 1.25
78 MacKenzie Weegar QMJHL .15 .40
79 Zachary Fucale QMJHL .30 .75
80 Adam Erne QMJHL .25 .60
81 Anthony Duclair QMJHL .40 1.00
82 Francois Brassard QMJHL .15 .40
83 Nick Sorensen QMJHL .20 .50
84 Frederik Gauthier QMJHL .25 .60
85 Philippe Desrosiers QMJHL .20 .50
86 Samuel Morin QMJHL .15 .40
87 Alexandre Belanger QMJHL .20 .50
88 Jean-Sebastien Dea QMJHL .25 .60
89 Anthony Mantha QMJHL .40 1.00
90 Brandon Whitney QMJHL .25 .60
91 Rihards Bukarts WHL .15 .40
92 Daniel Sprong QMJHL .30 .75
93 Nicolas Roy QMJHL .20 .50
94 Sergei Boikov QMJHL .15 .40
95 Andre Burakovsky OHL .60 1.50
96 Dylan Strome OHL .50 1.25
97 Ivan Nikolishin WHL .15 .40
98 Anthony Brodeur QMJHL .30 .75
99 Ty Edmonds WHL .25 .60
100 Mitchell Marner OHL .60 1.50
101 Sean Day OHL .40 1.00
102 Alex Lintuniemi OHL .15 .40
103 Travis Konecny OHL .50 1.25
104 Matt Spencer OHL .15 .40
105 Adam Musil WHL .20 .50
106 Mathew Barzal WHL .50 1.25
107 Anthony Beauvillier QMJHL .25 .60
108 Nikita Yazkov OHL .15 .40
109 Dmitri Osipov WHL .15 .40
110 Ty Ronning WHL .15 .40
111 Marcus Pettersson IP .20 .50
112 Adam Ollas Mattsson IP .20 .50
113 Aleksandar Mikulovich IP .25 .60
114 Alexander Protapovich IP .25 .60
115 Alexander Wennberg IP .25 .60
116 Elias Lindholm IP .60 1.50
117 Jacob de la Rose IP .25 .60
118 Aleksander Barkov IP .75 2.00
119 Rasmus Ristolainen IP .40 1.00
120 Robert Hagg IP .30 .75
121 Tomas Hertl IP .50 1.25
122 Borje Salming H .25 .60
123 Brett Hull H .50 1.25
124 Brian Leetch H .20 .50
125 Carey Price H .50 1.25
126 Claude Giroux H .25 .60
127 Darryl Sittler H .30 .75
128 Dave Andreychuk H .25 .60
129 Dave Keon H .25 .60
130 Denis Savard H .25 .60
131 Dominik Hasek H .40 1.00
132 Felix Potvin H .40 1.00
133 Frank Mahovlich H .25 .60
134 Georges Vezina H .25 .60
135 Igor Larionov H .25 .60
136 Joe Nieuwendyk H .20 .50
137 John LeClair H .25 .60
138 Kelly Hrudey H .20 .50
139 Luc Robitaille H .25 .60
140 Marian Gaborik H .25 .60
141 Mike Modano H .40 1.00
142 Mike Richter H .25 .60
143 Owen Nolan H .25 .60
144 Pat LaFontaine H .25 .60
145 Peter Bondra H .25 .60
146 Ron Francis H .30 .75
147 Ron Hextall H .25 .60
148 Sergei Samsonov H .20 .50
149 Tom Barrasso H .25 .60
150 Vladislav Tretiak H .20 .50
151 Mason McDonald C14 2.00 5.00
152 Aaron Ekblad C14 5.00 12.00
153 Brendan Lemieux C14 2.00 5.00
154 Nikita Scherbak C14 2.00 5.00
155 Jayce Hawryluk C14 1.25 3.00
156 Jake Virtanen C14 2.50 6.00
157 Alex Bureau C14 1.50 4.00
158 Alexis Pepin C14 1.50 4.00
159 Tyler Sandhu C14 2.00 5.00
160 Robby Fabbri C14 1.50 4.00
161 Nikolaj Ehlers C14 4.00 10.00
162 Ryan Falkenham C14 2.00 5.00
163 Rourke Chartier C14 1.50 4.00
164 Tyson Baillie C14 1.50 4.00
165 Roland McKeown C14 2.00 5.00
166 Sam Bennett C14 5.00 12.00
167 Spencer Watson C14 2.00 5.00
168 Ryan MacInnis C14 1.50 4.00
169 Luke Philp C14 1.50 4.00
170 Sam Reinhart C14 6.00 15.00
171 Ivan Barbashev C14 2.00 5.00
172 Brayden Point C14 3.00 8.00
173 Justin Paulic C14 2.00 5.00
174 Aaron Haydon C14 1.50 4.00
175 Brendan Perlini C14 3.00 8.00
176 Blake Clarke C14 1.50 4.00
177 Brandon Robinson C14 1.50 4.00
178 Michael Dal Colle C14 2.50 6.00
179 Jacob Middleton C14 1.50 4.00
180 Nick Ritchie C14 2.00 5.00
181 Alex Nedeljkovic C14 2.00 5.00
182 Matt Mistele C14 1.50 4.00
183 Chase De Leo C14 1.50 4.00
184 Dominic Turgeon C14 2.00 5.00
185 Leon Draisaitl C14 5.00 12.00
186 Duncan MacIntyre C14 1.50 4.00
187 Conner Bleackley C14 2.00 5.00
188 Haydn Fleury C14 2.00 5.00
189 Nikita Serebryakov C14 2.00 5.00
190 Anthony DeAngelo C14 1.50 4.00
191 Nikolay Goldobin C14 2.00 5.00
192 Jared McCann C14 2.50 6.00
193 Daniel Audette C14 2.00 5.00
194 Brycen Martin C14 2.00 5.00
195 Nicolas Aube-Kubel C14 1.25 3.00
196 Josh Ho-Sang C14 2.50 6.00
197 Julius Honka C14 1.50 4.00
198 Julius Bergman C14 1.50 4.00
199 William Nylander C14 6.00 15.00

2013-14 ITG Heroes and Prospects Autographs

AAB Anthony Brodeur 15.00 30.00
AABI Antoine Bibeau 2.50 6.00
AAD Anthony DeAngelo 3.00 8.00
AAE Aaron Ekblad 8.00 20.00
AAER Adam Erne 4.00 10.00
AAF Alex Forsberg 4.00 10.00
AAM Anthony Mantha 10.00 25.00
AAMI Aleksandar Mikulovich 4.00 10.00
AAO Adam Ollas Mattsson 3.00 8.00
AAP Alexis Pepin 3.00 8.00
AAPR Alexander Protapovich 4.00 10.00
ABC Blake Clarke 3.00 8.00
ABG Brendan Gaunce 3.00 8.00
ABH Bo Horvat 8.00 20.00
ABHU Brett Hull SP 15.00 30.00
ABL Brian Leetch SP 8.00 20.00
ABM Brent Moran 3.00 8.00
ABMA Brycen Martin 4.00 10.00
ABP Brayden Point 6.00 15.00
ABPR Brandon Prophet 2.50 6.00
ABR Brandon Robinson 3.00 8.00
ABS Brody Silk 2.50 6.00
ACB Clark Bishop 2.50 6.00
ACG Claude Giroux SP 8.00 20.00
ACL Curtis Lazar 6.00 15.00
ACM Connor McDavid 90.00 150.00
ACR Connor Rankin 3.00 8.00
ADA Daniel Audette 4.00 10.00
ADAN Dave Andreychuk SP 10.00 25.00
ADM Duncan MacIntyre 3.00 8.00
ADN Darnell Nurse 5.00 12.00
ADO Dakota Odgers 3.00 8.00
ADS Dylan Strome 8.00 20.00
ADT Dominic Turgeon 4.00 10.00
AEC Eric Comrie 3.00 8.00
AEP Emile Poirier 4.00 10.00
AER Eric Roy 4.00 10.00
AFG Frederik Gauthier 4.00 10.00
AFM Frank Mahovlich SP 10.00 25.00
AHF Haydn Fleury 4.00 10.00
AHS Hunter Shinkaruk 5.00 12.00
AIB Ivan Barbashev 4.00 10.00
AIL Igor Larionov SP 10.00 25.00
AJB Julius Bergman 3.00 8.00
AJBA Justin Bailey 3.00 8.00
AJD Jonathan Drouin 15.00 30.00
AJG Jeremy Gregoire 4.00 10.00
AJH Jayce Hawryluk 2.50 6.00
AJHS Josh Ho-Sang 8.00 20.00
AJL Jaden Lindo 2.50 6.00
AJM Josh Morrissey 4.00 10.00
AJMC Jared McCann 5.00 12.00
AJN Joe Nieuwendyk SP 8.00 20.00
AJS Jordan Subban SP 5.00 12.00
AJV Jake Virtanen 5.00 12.00
AKR Kerby Rychel 4.00 10.00
ALD Leon Draisaitl 15.00 40.00
ALS Liam Stewart 2.50 6.00
AMB Mathew Barzal 20.00 50.00
AMBO Madison Bowey 2.50 6.00
AMD Mathew Dumba 2.50 6.00
AMDC Michael Dal Colle 5.00 12.00
AMG Marian Gaborik 6.00 15.00
AMGI Michael Giugovaz SP 5.00 12.00
AMI Max Iafrate 3.00 8.00
AMK Morgan Klimchuk 3.00 8.00
AML Maxim Lazarev 2.50 6.00
AMM Matt Mistele 3.00 8.00
AMMO Mike Modano SP 15.00 40.00
AMMU Mirco Mueller 4.00 10.00
AMP Marcus Pettersson 3.00 8.00
ANA Nicolas Aube-Kubel 2.50 6.00
ANB Nicholas Baptiste 3.00 8.00
ANE Nikolaj Ehlers 8.00 20.00
ANG Nikolay Goldobin 4.00 10.00
ANR Nicolas Roy 3.00 8.00
ANRI Nick Ritchie 4.00 10.00
ANS Nick Sorensen 3.00 8.00
AOL Olivier Leblanc 3.00 8.00
APB Peter Bondra SP 15.00 40.00
APL Payton Lee 3.00 8.00
ARC Rourke Chartier 3.00 8.00
ARD Reid Duke 2.50 6.00
ARF Robby Fabbri 3.00 8.00
ARFR Ron Francis SP 12.00 30.00
ARH Ryan Hartman 4.00 10.00
ARK Ryan Kujawinski 3.00 8.00
ARM Roland McKeown 4.00 10.00
ARMA Ryan MacInnis 3.00 8.00
ARP Ryan Pulock 4.00 10.00
ARR Rasmus Ristolainen 6.00 15.00
ASB Sam Bennett 10.00 25.00
ASD Sean Day 6.00 15.00
ASM Samuel Morin 2.50 6.00
ASMA Spencer Martin 4.00 10.00
ASMO Sean Monahan 6.00 15.00
ASP Storm Phaneuf 2.50 6.00
ASR Sam Reinhart 10.00 25.00
AST Shea Theodore 5.00 12.00
ASTO Sergey Tolchinsky 3.00 8.00
ASW Spencer Watson 4.00 10.00
ATB Tim Bozon 5.00 12.00
ATH Tomas Hertl 12.50 25.00
ATJ Tristan Jarry 4.00 10.00
ATK Travis Konecny 8.00 20.00
AWC William Carrier 5.00 12.00
AWN William Nylander 12.00 30.00

2013-14 ITG Heroes and Prospects AutoThreads

ATJC Jared Cowen/25 8.00 20.00
ATMD Matt Duchene/25 12.00 30.00
ATTS Tyler Seguin/25 12.00 30.00
ATJT1 John Tavares/15 20.00 50.00
ATJT2 John Tavares/25 20.00 50.00

2013-14 ITG Heroes and Prospects Canadiana

CAE Aaron Ekblad 12.00 30.00
CAM Anthony Mantha 8.00 20.00
CAP Adam Pelech 5.00 12.00
CBH Bo Horvat 10.00 25.00
CCB Chris Bigras 4.00 10.00
CCH Charles Hudon 5.00 12.00
CCL Curtis Lazar 5.00 12.00
CCM Connor McDavid 40.00 100.00
CDP Derrick Pouliot 6.00 15.00
CFGA Frederik Gauthier 5.00 12.00
CGR Griffin Reinhart 5.00 12.00
CJA Josh Anderson 6.00 15.00
CJD Jonathan Drouin 10.00 25.00
CJM Josh Morrissey 5.00 12.00
CJP Jake Paterson 5.00 12.00
CKR Kerby Rychel 5.00 12.00
CMD Mathew Dumba 3.00 8.00
CNP Nicolas Petan 5.00 12.00
CSL Scott Laughton 6.00 15.00
CSR Sam Reinhart 15.00 40.00
CTL Taylor Leier 8.00 20.00
CZF Zachary Fucale 6.00 15.00

2013-14 ITG Heroes and Prospects Dual Autographs

FSDABBSB B.Burke/S.Burke 10.00 25.00
FSDAGRPR G.Reinhart/P.Reinhrt 12.00 30.00
FSDASRPR S.Reinhart/P.Reinhrt 25.00 60.00
FSDAWNMN W.Nylander/M.Nylndr 15.00 40.00

2013-14 ITG Heroes and Prospects Dual Jerseys Silver

DJ01 Aaron Ekblad 12.00 30.00
DJ02 Bo Horvat 10.00 25.00
DJ03 Connor McDavid 20.00 50.00
DJ04 Curtis Lazar 5.00 12.00
DJ05 Frederik Gauthier 5.00 12.00
DJ06 Jonathan Drouin 10.00 25.00
DJ07 Max Domi 10.00 25.00
DJ08 Sam Reinhart 15.00 40.00
DJ09 Sean Monahan 10.00 25.00

2013-14 ITG Heroes and Prospects He Shoots He Scores Points

AM1 Anthony Mantha C .50 1.25
CM1 Connor McDavid C 1.25 3.00
DN1 Darnell Nurse C .40 1.00
FG1 Frederik Gauthier C .30 .75
HF1 Haydn Fleury C .30 .75
JD1 Jonathan Drouin C .60 1.50
LD1 Leon Draisaitl C .75 2.00
MB1 Matthew Barzal C .60 1.50
NP1 Nicolas Petan C .30 .75
SR1 Sam Reinhart C 1.00 2.50
WN1 William Nylander C 1.00 2.50

2013-14 ITG Heroes and Prospects Hero and Prospect Jerseys Silver

HP01 B.Leetch/G.Reinhart 5.00 12.00
HP02 C.Price/E.Comrie 10.00 25.00
HP03 J.Kurri/A.Barkov 15.00 40.00
HP04 C.Giroux/S.Laughton 6.00 15.00
HP05 B.Salming/R.Hagg 6.00 15.00
HP06 P.Roy/Z.Fucale 12.00 30.00
HP07 M.Lemieux/C.McDavid 20.00 50.00
HP08 T.Barrasso/M.Murray 5.00 12.00
HP09 B.Hull/S.Monahan 10.00 25.00

2013-14 ITG Heroes and Prospects Jersey Autographs Silver

MAAE Aaron Ekblad 25.00 60.00
MAAM Anthony Mantha 15.00 40.00
MAAP Alexis Pepin 8.00 20.00
MACL Curtis Lazar 10.00 25.00
MACM Connor McDavid 125.00 200.00
MADA Daniel Audette 10.00 25.00
MAEC Eric Comrie 8.00 20.00
MAEP Emile Poirier 10.00 25.00
MAFG Frederik Gauthier 10.00 25.00
MAHS Hunter Shinkaruk 12.00 30.00
MAIB Ivan Barbashev 10.00 25.00
MAJB Justin Bailey 8.00 20.00
MAJG Jeremy Gregoire 10.00 25.00
MAJH Josh Ho-Sang 12.00 30.00
MAJM Jared McCann 12.00 30.00
MAKR Kerby Rychel 10.00 25.00
MAMD Max Domi 20.00 50.00
MANB Nicholas Baptiste 8.00 20.00
MANR Nick Ritchie 10.00 25.00
MAOL Olivier Leblanc 8.00 20.00
MAPD Philippe Desrosiers 8.00 20.00
MASM Samuel Morin 6.00 15.00
MATJ Tristan Jarry 8.00 20.00
MAWC William Carrier 10.00 25.00

2013-14 ITG Heroes and Prospects Jersey Quads Silver

QJ01 McDvd/Rnhrt/Lmeux/Lflr 25.00 50.00
QJ02 Rose/Brkv/Krri/Sndin 12.00 30.00
QJ03 Pliot/Mrry/Mlkn/Fleury 12.00 30.00
QJ04 Shnkrk/Hrvt/Sdin/Sdin 12.00 30.00
QJ05 Mnhn/Prier/McInns/Fleury 12.00 30.00
QJ06 Mntha/Ptrsn/Yzrmn/Osgd 15.00 40.00
QJ07 Mrin/Hagg/Clrke/Lndros 10.00 25.00
QJ08 Mrtn/Brke/Roy/Sakic 15.00 40.00
QJ09 Rose/Fcle/Nslnd/Roy 15.00 40.00

2013-14 ITG Heroes and Prospects Jersey

PATCH/30: .8X TO 2X BASIC JSY
SILVER/30: .5X TO 1.2X BASIC JSY
M01 Aaron Ekblad 10.00 25.00
M02 Frederik Gauthier 4.00 10.00
M03 Jared McCann 5.00 12.00
M04 Emile Poirier 4.00 10.00
M05 Curtis Lazar 4.00 10.00
M06 Daniel Audette 4.00 10.00
M07 Leon Draisaitl 10.00 25.00
M08 Jake Virtanen 5.00 12.00
M09 Sam Reinhart 12.00 30.00
M10 Rourke Chartier 4.00 10.00
M11 Niki Petti 3.00 8.00
M12 Alexis Pepin 3.00 8.00
M13 Matt Mistele 3.00 8.00
M14 Connor McDavid 15.00 40.00
M15 Olivier Leblanc 3.00 8.00
M16 Ivan Barbashev 4.00 10.00
M17 Conor Garland 3.00 8.00
M18 Sam Bennett 10.00 25.00
M19 Sean Day 6.00 15.00
M20 Nikolay Goldobin 4.00 10.00
M21 Matt Fonteyne 3.00 8.00
M22 Colby Cave 4.00 10.00
M23 Noah Juulesen 3.00 8.00
M24 Bo Horvat 8.00 20.00
M25 Mathew Barzal 8.00 20.00
M26 Anthony Duclair 6.00 15.00
M27 Nick Sorensen 3.00 8.00
M28 Robby Fabbri 3.00 8.00
M29 Ryan Hartman 4.00 10.00
M30 Eric Cornel 3.00 8.00

2013-14 ITG Heroes and Prospects Prospects Trios Jerseys Silver

PT01 McDvd/Rnhrt/Ekbld 25.00 60.00
PT02 Audtte/Ppin/Brbshv 6.00 15.00
PT03 Chvldve/Jarry/Cmrie 6.00 15.00
PT04 Prier/Grgre/Crrier 6.00 15.00
PT05 Altshllr/Mrry/Ggvaz 6.00 15.00
PT06 Shnkrk/Vrtnen/Lazar 8.00 20.00
PT07 Mntha/Gthier/Drouin 12.00 30.00
PT08 Domi/Rychl/Hrtman 12.00 30.00
PT09 Rnhart/Ekbld/Adette 20.00 50.00

2013-14 ITG Heroes and Prospects Subway Series Jersey Autographs Silver

SSMAAD Anthony Duclair 10.00 25.00
SSMAAE Aaron Ekblad 15.00 40.00
SSMAAM Anthony Mantha 10.00 25.00
SSMABG Brendan Gaunce 5.00 12.00
SSMABH Bo Horvat 12.00 30.00
SSMACM Connor McDavid 100.00 250.00
SSMADA Daniel Audette 6.00 15.00
SSMADN Darnell Nurse 8.00 20.00
SSMAEC Eric Comrie 5.00 12.00
SSMAEP Emile Poirier 6.00 15.00
SSMAFG Frederik Gauthier 6.00 15.00
SSMAJD Jonathan Drouin 12.00 30.00
SSMAJG Jeremy Gregoire 6.00 15.00
SSMAJM Josh Morrissey 6.00 15.00
SSMAMB Madison Bowey 4.00 10.00
SSMAMD Max Domi 12.00 30.00
SSMAMK Morgan Klimchuk 5.00 12.00
SSMANP Nicolas Petan 6.00 15.00
SSMASB Sam Bennett 15.00 40.00
SSMASL Scott Laughton 8.00 20.00
SSMASM Samuel Morin 4.00 10.00
SSMASR Sam Reinhart 20.00 50.00
SSMAWC William Carrier 6.00 15.00
SSMAZF Zachary Fucale 8.00 20.00

2013-14 ITG Heroes and Prospects Subway Series Jersey

PATCH/30: .8X TO 2X BASIC JSY
SILVER/30: .5X TO 1.2X BASIC JSY
SSM01 Anthony DeLuca 3.00 8.00
SSM02 Jonathan Drouin 5.00 12.00
SSM03 Anthony Duclair 6.00 15.00
SSM04 Dillon Fournier 3.00 8.00
SSM05 Frederik Gauthier 4.00 10.00
SSM06 Samuel Morin 2.50 6.00
SSM07 Emile Poirier 4.00 10.00
SSM08 Chris Bigras 3.00 8.00
SSM09 Aaron Ekblad 10.00 25.00
SSM10 Brendan Gaunce 3.00 8.00
SSM11 Bo Horvat 8.00 20.00
SSM12 Connor McDavid 15.00 40.00
SSM13 Matt Murray 4.00 10.00
SSM14 Darnell Nurse 5.00 12.00
SSM15 Sam Bennett 10.00 25.00
SSM16 Sam Reinhart 12.00 30.00
SSM17 Nicolas Petan 4.00 10.00
SSM18 Eric Comrie 3.00 8.00
SSM19 Morgan Klimchuk 3.00 8.00
SSM20 Josh Morrissey 4.00 10.00
SSM21 Madison Bowey 2.50 6.00
SSM22 Brendan Leipsic 3.00 8.00
SSM23 Jaedon Descheneau 2.50 6.00
SSM24 Jujhar Khaira 3.00 8.00
SSM25 Tristan Jarry 4.00 10.00
SSM26 Carter Verhaeghe 5.00 12.00
SSM27 Nicholas Baptiste 3.00 8.00
SSM28 Sebastien Auger 3.00 8.00
SSM29 Jeremy Gregoire 4.00 10.00
SSM30 Daniel Audette 4.00 10.00

2013-14 ITG Heroes and Prospects Tenth Anniversary Jersey

AP11 Carey Price/20* 12.00 30.00
AP12 Eric Staal/20* 8.00 20.00
AP13 Claude Giroux/20* 6.00 15.00
AP14 Taylor Hall/20* 6.00 15.00
AP15 Marc-Andre Fleury/20* 12.00 30.00
AP16 Tuukka Rask/20* 8.00 20.00
AP17 Phil Kessel/20* 6.00 15.00
AP18 Kari Lehtonen/20* 5.00 12.00
AP19 Shea Weber/20* 5.00 12.00
AP20 Alex Galchenyuk/20* 15.00 40.00
AP21 Alex Pietrangelo/30* 4.00 10.00
AP22 Ryan Miller/30* 5.00 12.00
AP23 Anze Kopitar/30* 8.00 20.00
AP24 Sean Monahan/30* 5.00 12.00
AP25 Dion Phaneuf/30* 4.00 10.00
AP26 Patrice Bergeron/30* 6.00 15.00
AP27 Ryan Nugent-Hopkins/30* 6.00 15.00
AP28 Nail Yakupov/30* 8.00 20.00
AP29 Nathan MacKinnon/30* 12.00 30.00
AP30 Seth Jones/30* 5.00 12.00
AP31 Pekka Rinne/40* 5.00 12.00
AP32 Connor McDavid/40* 25.00 50.00
AP33 Aleksander Barkov/40* 6.00 15.00
AP34 Malcolm Subban/40* 5.00 12.00
AP35 Hunter Shinkaruk/40* 6.00 15.00
AP36 Brendan Gallagher/40* 8.00 20.00
AP37 Matt Duchene/40* 5.00 12.00
AP38 Jimmy Howard/40* 6.00 15.00
AP39 Sergei Bobrovsky/40* 8.00 20.00
AP40 Thomas Vanek/40* 4.00 10.00
AP41 Loui Eriksson/50* 3.00 8.00
AP42 Mike Richards/50* 6.00 15.00
AP43 Jonathan Huberdeau/50* 5.00 12.00
AP44 Mikko Koivu/50* 4.00 10.00
AP45 Jaroslav Halak/50* 5.00 12.00
AP46 Jason Spezza/50* 5.00 12.00
AP47 Tyler Seguin/50* 6.00 15.00
AP48 Ryan Kesler/50* 5.00 12.00
AP49 Sam Reinhart/50* 15.00 40.00
AP50 Lars Eller/50* 3.00 8.00
AP51 Mark Scheifele/60* 6.00 15.00
AP52 Cody Hodgson/60* 2.50 6.00
AP53 Jonathan Drouin/60* 8.00 20.00
AP54 Drew Doughty/60* 5.00 12.00
AP55 Morgan Rielly/60* 5.00 12.00
AP56 Darnell Nurse/60* 5.00 12.00
AP57 Sam Gagner/60* 2.50 6.00
AP58 Jeff Carter/60* 3.00 8.00
AP59 Dougie Hamilton/60* 6.00 15.00
AP60 Ondrej Pavelec/60* 4.00 10.00
AP61 Vladimir Tarasenko/70* 6.00 15.00
AP62 Bobby Ryan/70* 3.00 8.00
AP63 Logan Couture/70* 5.00 12.00
AP64 James Neal/70* 2.50 6.00
AP65 Ryan Getzlaf/70* 4.00 10.00
AP66 Nazem Kadri/70* 5.00 12.00
AP67 Brent Seabrook/70* 2.50 6.00
AP68 Jordan Staal/70* 3.00 8.00
AP69 Aaron Ekblad/70* 10.00 25.00
AP70 Mikhail Grigorenko/70* 2.50 6.00
AP71 Sean Couturier/80* 3.00 8.00
AP72 Corey Crawford/80* 5.00 12.00
AP73 Gabriel Landeskog/80* 5.00 12.00
AP74 Max Domi/80* 8.00 20.00
AP75 Braden Holtby/80* 5.00 12.00
AP76 Evander Kane/80* 4.00 10.00
AP77 Jakub Voracek/80* 3.00 8.00
AP78 Chris Kunitz/80* 4.00 10.00
AP79 David Bolland/80* 2.50 6.00
AP80 Dustin Brown/80* 4.00 10.00
AP81 Oliver Ekman-Larsson/90* 4.00 10.00
AP82 Milan Lucic/90* 4.00 10.00
AP83 Jordan Eberle/90* 4.00 10.00
AP84 Zachary Fucale/90* 5.00 12.00
AP85 Ryan Strome/90* 6.00 15.00
AP86 Boone Jenner/90* 8.00 20.00
AP87 Brandon Saad/90* 3.00 8.00
AP88 Kris Letang/90* 5.00 12.00
AP89 Brad Marchand/90* 8.00 20.00
AP90 Jonathan Bernier/90* 3.00 8.00
AP91 Jeff Skinner/100* 5.00 12.00
AP92 David Krejci/100* 4.00 10.00
AP93 Mathew Dumba/100* 2.50 6.00
AP94 Cam Ward/100* 4.00 10.00
AP95 Semyon Varlamov/100* 4.00 10.00
AP96 Mikhail Grabovski/100* 2.50 6.00
AP97 Mike Green/100* 3.00 8.00
AP98 Ryan Murray/100* 6.00 15.00
AP99 Cory Schneider/100* 4.00 10.00
AP100 Ryan Callahan/100* 2.50 6.00

2013-14 ITG Heroes and Prospects Tenth Anniversary Tribute

T01 Valentin Zykov 2.00 5.00
T02 Aaron Ekblad 5.00 12.00
T03 Brendan Gaunce 1.50 4.00
T04 Marc-Olivier Roy 2.00 5.00
T05 Jake Virtanen 2.50 6.00
T06 Alexis Pepin 1.50 4.00
T07 Laurent Dauphin 1.25 3.00
T08 Nicolas Roy 1.50 4.00
T09 Curtis Lazar 2.00 5.00
T10 Griffin Reinhart 2.00 5.00
T11 Tristan Jarry 2.00 5.00
T12 Connor McDavid 8.00 20.00
T13 Andre Burakovsky 5.00 12.00
T14 Aleksander Barkov 6.00 15.00
T15 Emile Poirier 2.00 5.00
T16 Jonathan Drouin 4.00 10.00
T17 Nikolaj Ehlers 4.00 10.00
T18 Madison Bowey 1.25 3.00
T19 Spencer Watson 2.00 5.00
T20 Radek Faksa 2.00 5.00
T21 Sam Reinhart 6.00 15.00
T22 Max Domi 4.00 10.00
T23 Bo Horvat 4.00 10.00
T24 Hunter Shinkaruk 2.50 6.00
T25 Spencer Martin 2.00 5.00
T26 Sean Day 3.00 8.00
T27 Ivan Barbashev 2.00 5.00
T28 Scott Laughton 2.50 6.00
T29 Michael Dal Colle 2.50 6.00
T30 Sean Monahan 3.00 8.00
T31 Travis Konecny 4.00 10.00
T32 Ryan Hartman 2.00 5.00
T33 Nicolas Petan 2.00 5.00
T34 Josh Morrissey 2.00 5.00
T35 Haydn Fleury 2.00 5.00
T36 Morgan Klimchuk 1.50 4.00
T37 Frederik Gauthier 2.00 5.00
T38 Darnell Nurse 2.50 6.00
T39 Shea Theodore 2.50 6.00
T40 Mathew Barzal 4.00 10.00
T41 Daniel Audette 2.00 5.00
T42 William Nylander 6.00 15.00
T43 Eric Comrie 1.50 4.00
T44 Anthony Mantha 3.00 8.00
T45 Kerby Rychel 2.00 5.00

2013-14 ITG Heroes and Prospects Top Prospects Jersey Autographs Silver

TPMAAD Anthony Duclair 15.00 40.00
TPMABG Brendan Gaunce 8.00 20.00
TPMABH Bo Horvat 20.00 50.00
TPMACL Curtis Lazar 10.00 25.00
TPMADN Darnell Nurse 8.00 20.00
TPMADP Derrick Pouliot 12.00 30.00
TPMAER Eric Roy 10.00 25.00
TPMAFG Frederik Gauthier 10.00 25.00
TPMAJD Jonathan Drouin 40.00 80.00
TPMAJM Josh Morrissey 10.00 25.00
TPMAJS Jordan Subban 10.00 25.00
TPMAMD Max Domi 20.00 40.00
TPMAMK Morgan Klimchuk 8.00 20.00
TPMANP Nicolas Petan 10.00 25.00
TPMANS Nick Sorensen 8.00 20.00
TPMARF Radek Faksa 10.00 25.00
TPMARH Ryan Hartman 10.00 25.00
TPMASM Sean Monahan 12.00 30.00
TPMAST Shea Theodore 12.00 30.00
TPMATJ Tristan Jarry 10.00 25.00
TPMAZF Zachary Fucale 12.00 30.00
TPMASMA Spencer Martin 10.00 25.00

2013-14 ITG Heroes and Prospects Top Prospects Jersey

PATCH/30: .8X TO 2X BASIC JSY
SILVER/30: .5X TO 1.2X BASIC JSY
TPM01 Oliver Bjorkstrand 3.00 8.00
TPM02 Laurent Dauphin 2.50 6.00
TPM03 Max Domi 8.00 20.00
TPM04 Jonathan Drouin 8.00 20.00
TPM05 Anthony Duclair 6.00 15.00
TPM06 Adam Erne 4.00 10.00
TPM07 Radek Faksa 4.00 10.00
TPM08 Zachary Fucale 5.00 12.00
TPM09 Brendan Gaunce 3.00 8.00
TPM10 Frederik Gauthier 4.00 10.00
TPM11 Stephen Harper 2.50 6.00
TPM12 Ryan Hartman 4.00 10.00
TPM13 Bo Horvat 8.00 20.00
TPM14 Tristan Jarry 4.00 10.00
TPM15 Morgan Klimchuk 3.00 8.00
TPM16 Curtis Lazar 4.00 10.00
TPM17 Spencer Martin 4.00 10.00
TPM18 Sean Monahan 6.00 15.00
TPM19 Josh Morrissey 4.00 10.00
TPM20 Darnell Nurse 5.00 12.00
TPM21 Nicolas Petan 4.00 10.00
TPM22 Derrick Pouliot 5.00 12.00
TPM23 Griffin Reinhart 4.00 10.00
TPM24 Eric Roy 4.00 10.00
TPM25 Gemel Smith 4.00 10.00
TPM26 Nick Sorensen 3.00 8.00
TPM27 Jordan Subban 4.00 10.00
TPM28 Shea Theodore 5.00 12.00
TPM29 Nikita Zadorov 2.50 6.00
TPM30 Valentin Zykov 4.00 10.00

2013-14 ITG Heroes and Prospects Top Prospects Trios Jerseys Silver

TPT01 Domi/Hrpr/Hrvat 8.00 20.00
TPT02 Dphin/Drouin/Erne 6.00 15.00
TPT03 Bjrkst/Klmchk/Lzar 6.00 15.00
TPT04 Hrtmn/Ptan/Mnhn 15.00 40.00
TPT05 Dclair/Gthier/Zykv 10.00 25.00
TPT06 Thdore/Sbban/Pliot 8.00 20.00
TPT07 Rnhart/Nrse/Mrrssy 8.00 20.00

TPT08 Mrtn/Jrry/Fcale 8.00 20.00
TPT09 Fksa/Gnce/Smith 6.00 15.00

2014-15 ITG Heroes and Prospects Prospect Autographs

*EXPO.EMERALD: .4X TO 1X BASIC INSERTS
*GOLD/30: .6X TO 1.5X BASIC AU/80
1 Adam Mascherin/50 5.00 12.00
2 Adam Musil/80 5.00 12.00
3 Alex Forsberg/80 4.00 10.00
4 Alexandre Carrier/50 5.00 12.00
5 Andrew Picco/80 4.00 10.00
6 Anthony Beauvillier/80 5.00 12.00
7 Beck Malenstyn/50 4.00 10.00
8 Blake Speers/80 5.00 12.00
9 Brandon Saigeon/50 5.00 12.00
10 Brendan Guhle/80 4.00 10.00
11 Brett Howden/50 4.00 10.00
12 Brett McKenzie/50 5.00 12.00
13 Cameron Askew/80 5.00 12.00
14 Chaz Reddekopp/80 4.00 10.00
15 Cliff Pu/80 4.00 10.00
16 Cole Johnson/80 5.00 12.00
17 Connor Hobbs/80 4.00 10.00
18 Connor Ingram/80 5.00 12.00
19 Connor McDavid/50 100.00 250.00
20 Daniel Sprong/50 10.00 25.00
21 Dante Salituro/50 6.00 15.00
22 Davis Koch/80 8.00 20.00
23 Dylan Strome/50 12.00 30.00
24 Evan Fitzpatrick/80 8.00 20.00
25 Evan Sarthou/80 4.00 10.00
26 Evgeny Svechnikov/50 8.00 20.00
27 Frederic Allard/80 4.00 10.00
28 Gabriel Gagne/80 5.00 12.00
29 Giorgio Estephan/80 4.00 10.00
30 Glenn Gawdin/80 5.00 12.00
31 Graham Knott/80 5.00 12.00
32 Ivan Provorov/50 10.00 25.00
33 Jaeger White/80 4.00 10.00
34 Jakob Chychrun/50 12.00 30.00
35 Jakub Zboril/50 5.00 12.00
36 Jansen Harkins/50 6.00 15.00
37 Jason Bell/80 12.00 30.00
38 Jeremiah Addison/80 4.00 10.00
39 Jeremy Roy/50 4.00 10.00
40 Jonathan Ang/80 5.00 12.00
41 Jordan Hollett/80 8.00 20.00
42 Josh Anderson/80 6.00 15.00
43 Julien Gauthier/50 4.00 10.00
44 Justin Almeida/80 4.00 10.00
45 Kaden Elder/80 4.00 10.00
46 Kale Clague/50 6.00 15.00
47 Keoni Texeira/80 4.00 10.00
48 Kody McDonald/80 4.00 10.00
49 Kyle Capobianco/80 4.00 10.00
50 Lawson Crouse/50 6.00 15.00
51 Logan Brown/80 5.00 12.00
52 Loik Leveille/80 4.00 10.00
53 Luke Green/80 4.00 10.00
54 Mackenzie Blackwood/50 8.00 20.00
55 Mathew Barzal/50 12.00 30.00
56 Matt Spencer/50 8.00 20.00
57 Matteo Gennaro/80 4.00 10.00
58 Matthew Kreis/80 5.00 12.00
59 Maxime Fortier/80 4.00 10.00
60 Medric Mercier/80 4.00 10.00
61 Michael McLeod/50 5.00 12.00
62 Mitchell Marner/50 20.00 50.00
63 Mitchell Stephens/80 4.00 10.00
64 Nathan Noel/50 4.00 10.00
65 Nick Merkley/50 10.00 25.00
66 Nicolas Meloche/50 5.00 12.00
67 Nicolas Roy/50 6.00 15.00
68 Nikita Korostelev/50 8.00 20.00
69 Nolan Kneen/80 5.00 12.00
70 Nolan Patrick/80 10.00 25.00
71 Parker Wotherspoon/80 4.00 10.00
72 Pascal Laberge/80 6.00 15.00
73 Paul Bittner/50 8.00 20.00
74 Pavel Karnaukhov/80 6.00 15.00
75 Pavel Zacha/50 10.00 25.00
76 Pierre-Luc Dubois/80 10.00 25.00
77 Quinn Benjafield/80 5.00 12.00
78 Ryan Gropp/80 6.00 15.00
79 Ryan Kubic/80 6.00 15.00
80 Ryan Pilon/80 4.00 10.00
81 Sam Steel/50 6.00 15.00
82 Samuel Girard/80 5.00 12.00
83 Simon Stransky/80 4.00 10.00
84 Tanner Kaspick/80 4.00 10.00
85 Thomas Schemitsch/80 4.00 10.00
86 Timo Meier/80 12.00 30.00
87 Travis Barron/80 4.00 10.00
88 Travis Konecny/50 12.00 30.00
89 Ty Ronning/50 5.00 12.00
90 Tyler Benson/50 12.00 30.00
91 Tyler Soy/80 4.00 10.00
92 Vince Dunn/50 6.00 15.00
93 Will Bitten/50 6.00 15.00

2014-15 ITG Heroes and Prospects All-Star Heroes Jerseys

*EXPO.EMERALD: .4X TO 1X BASIC INSERTS
ASH01 Jaromir Jagr 10.00 25.00
ASH02 Mario Lemieux 12.00 30.00
ASH03 Nicklas Lidstrom 3.00 8.00
ASH04 Patrick Roy 8.00 20.00
ASH05 Sergei Fedorov 5.00 12.00
ASH06 Steve Yzerman 8.00 20.00
ASH07 Wayne Gretzky 20.00 50.00

2014-15 ITG Heroes and Prospects Hero and Prospect Jerseys

*EXPO.EMERALD: .4X TO 1X BASIC INSERTS
HPJ01 C.McDavid/W.Gretzky 60.00 150.00
HPJ02 J.Roy/R.Bourque 3.00 8.00
HPJ03 L.Crouse/M.Lemieux 20.00 50.00
HPJ04 M.Barzal/S.Yzerman 12.00 30.00
HPJ05 P.Roy/M.Blackwood 12.00 30.00
HPJ06 P.Bittner/M.Modano 8.00 20.00
HPJ07 P.Zacha/J.Jagr 15.00 40.00
HPJ08 P.Zacha/S.Fedorov 8.00 20.00
HPJ09 T.Konecny/J.Sakic 10.00 25.00

2014-15 ITG Heroes and Prospects Hero Autographs

1 Bill Gadsby 8.00 20.00
2 Bobby Hull 15.00 40.00
3 Brett Hull 15.00 40.00
4 Gerry Cheevers 8.00 20.00
5 Grant Fuhr 12.00 30.00
6 Harry Howell 6.00 15.00
7 Henri Richard 8.00 20.00
8 Jacques Lemaire 6.00 15.00
9 Jaromir Jagr 25.00 60.00
10 Joe Thornton 12.00 30.00
11 Johnny Bucyk 8.00 20.00
12 Paul Coffey 8.00 20.00
13 Raymond Bourque 12.00 30.00
14 Sergei Fedorov 12.00 30.00
15 Vladislav Tretiak 6.00 15.00
16 Wendel Clark 12.00 30.00

2014-15 ITG Heroes and Prospects Jersey

*EXPO.EMERALD: .4X TO 1X BASIC INSERTS
*PATCH/20: .8X TO 2X JSY/60
AM1 Adam Mascherin 2.50 6.00
CMD Connor McDavid 15.00 40.00
DS1 Daniel Sprong 5.00 12.00
DS2 Dylan Strome 6.00 15.00
GG1 Glenn Gawdin 2.50 6.00
JC1 Jakob Chychrun 6.00 15.00
JH1 Jansen Harkins 3.00 8.00
JR1 Jeremy Roy 2.00 5.00
LC1 Lawson Crouse 3.00 8.00
MB1 Mackenzie Blackwood 4.00 10.00
MB3 Mathew Barzal 6.00 15.00
MM3 Mitchell Marner 10.00 25.00
MS1 Matt Spencer 4.00 10.00
NM1 Nick Merkley 5.00 12.00
NM2 Nicolas Meloche 2.50 6.00
NR1 Nicolas Roy 3.00 8.00
SS1 Sam Steel 3.00 8.00
TB3 Tyler Benson 6.00 15.00
TK2 Travis Konecny 6.00 15.00

2014-15 ITG Heroes and Prospects Prospect Trio Jerseys

P301 Benson/Day/Chychrun 8.00 20.00
P302 Bittner/Barzal/Harkins 8.00 20.00
P303 Blackwood/Zacha/McDavid 20.00 50.00
P304 Domi/McDavid/Crouse 20.00 50.00
P305 McDavid/Barzal/Marner 20.00 50.00
P306 McDavid/Strome/Crouse 20.00 50.00
P307 McDavid/Virtanen/Comrie 20.00 50.00
P308 Meloche/Roy/McDavid 20.00 50.00
P309 Merkley/Konecny/Bittner 8.00 20.00
P310 Trenin/Svechnikov/McDavid 20.00 50.00

2014-15 ITG Heroes and Prospects Subway Series Jerseys

*PATCH/20: .6X TO 1.5X JSY/60
SSJ01 Alexandre Alain 2.50 6.00
SSJ02 Alexandre Carrier 2.50 6.00
SSJ03 Anthony Beauvillier 2.50 6.00
SSJ04 Brayden Point 4.00 10.00
SSJ05 Brendan Lemieux 3.00 8.00
SSJ06 Carter Verhaeghe 4.00 10.00
SSJ07 Conner Bleackley 3.00 8.00
SSJ09 Eric Comrie 3.00 8.00
SSJ10 Greg Chase 2.00 5.00
SSJ11 Guillaume Brisebois 3.00 8.00
SSJ12 Haydn Fleury 3.00 8.00
SSJ13 Jake Virtanen 4.00 10.00
SSJ14 Jason Dickinson 2.50 6.00
SSJ15 Jayce Hawryluk 2.00 5.00
SSJ17 John Quenneville 2.50 6.00
SSJ18 Josh Ho-Sang 4.00 10.00
SSJ19 Julien Pelletier 2.50 6.00
SSJ20 Mackenzie Blackwood 4.00 10.00
SSJ21 Max Domi 5.00 12.00
SSJ22 Nicolas Aube-Kubel 2.00 5.00
SSJ23 Nicolas Meloche 2.50 6.00
SSJ24 Nicolas Roy 3.00 8.00
SSJ25 Philippe Desrosiers 2.50 6.00
SSJ26 Spencer Martin 4.00 10.00
SSJ27 Travis Sanheim 3.00 8.00
SSJ28 Tristan Jarry 3.00 8.00
SSJ29 Tyler Bertuzzi 3.00 8.00
SSJ30 Zach Nastasiuk 2.50 6.00

2014-15 ITG Heroes and Prospects Top Prospects Jersey

*PATCH/20: .6X TO 1.5X JSY/60
TPJ01 Adam Musil 2.50 6.00
TPJ02 Connor McDavid 15.00 40.00
TPJ03 Daniel Sprong 5.00 12.00
TPJ04 Dennis Yan 2.50 6.00
TPJ05 Dylan Strome 6.00 15.00
TPJ06 Evgeny Svechnikov 4.00 10.00
TPJ07 Filip Chlapik 2.50 6.00
TPJ08 Jeremy Roy 2.00 5.00
TPJ09 Lawson Crouse 3.00 8.00
TPJ10 Matt Spencer 4.00 10.00
TPJ11 Mitchell Marner 10.00 25.00
TPJ12 Nick Merkley 5.00 12.00
TPJ13 Paul Bittner 4.00 10.00
TPJ14 Travis Konecny 6.00 15.00
TPJ15 Yakov Trenin 2.50 6.00

2015-16 ITG Heroes and Prospects Prospect Autographs

PSAC1 Alexander Chmelevski 5.00 12.00
PSAD1 Alex DeBrincat 6.00 15.00
PSAD2 Arnaud Durandeau 4.00 10.00
PSAM1 Antoine Morand 4.00 10.00
PSAP1 Austin Pratt 4.00 10.00
PSAR1 Anthony Richard 5.00 12.00
PSBC1 Brett Crossley 4.00 10.00
PSBD1 Brett Davis 6.00 15.00
PSBG1 Brady Gilmour 6.00 15.00
PSBH1 Brett Howden 4.00 10.00
PSBJ1 Ben Jones 4.00 10.00
PSBM1 Beck Malenstyn 6.00 15.00
PSCB2 Connor Bunnaman 4.00 10.00
PSCG1 Conor Garland 4.00 10.00
PSCH1 Carter Hart 10.00 25.00
PSCH2 Cameron Hebig 5.00 12.00
PSCP1 Christopher Paquette 4.00 10.00
PSDB1 Dereck Baribeau 4.00 10.00
PSDD1 Dillon Dube 6.00 15.00
PSDL1 David Levin 6.00 15.00
PSDS1 Dmitry Sokolov 6.00 15.00
PSDS1 Dylan Sadowy 6.00 15.00
PSDT1 Dmytro Timashov 6.00 15.00
PSDW1 Dylan Wells 4.00 10.00
PSDZ1 Dmitry Zhukenov 4.00 10.00
PSEB1 Egor Babenko 4.00 10.00
PSEC2 Evan Cormier 5.00 12.00
PSGS1 Gabriel Sylvestre 4.00 10.00
PSGS2 Givani Smith 4.00 10.00
PSGV1 Gabriel Vilardi 6.00 15.00
PSHD1 Hayden Davis 4.00 10.00
PSJA1 Josh Anderson 12.00 30.00
PSJB1 Jake Bean 6.00 15.00
PSJB2 Jordy Bellerive 4.00 10.00
PSJC1 Jakob Chychrun 8.00 20.00
PSJD1 Jared Dmytriw 4.00 10.00
PSJE1 Jack Eichel 25.00 60.00
PSJG1 Julien Gauthier 8.00 20.00
PSJK1 Jake Kryski 4.00 10.00
PSJK2 Jordan Kyrou 6.00 15.00
PSJM1 Josh Mahura 4.00 10.00
PSJP1 Jesse Puljujarvi 12.00 30.00
PSJV1 Joe Veleno 6.00 15.00
PSJV2 Juuso Valimaki 4.00 10.00
PSJW1 Jaeger White 4.00 10.00
PSJW2 Jeff De Wit 4.00 10.00
PSKA1 Kristian Afanasyev 4.00 10.00
PSKC1 Kale Clague 6.00 15.00
PSKM2 Keaton Middleton 4.00 10.00
PSKY2 Keanu Yamamoto 5.00 12.00
PSLB1 Logan Brown 10.00 25.00
PSLC1 Louis-Filip Cote 4.00 10.00
PSLJ1 Lucas Johansen 4.00 10.00
PSLM1 Liam Murphy 4.00 10.00
PSLT1 Lucas Thierus 4.00 10.00
PSMB1 Matt Barberis 5.00 12.00
PSMB1 Mitchell Balmas 4.00 10.00
PSMC1 Maxime Comtois 8.00 20.00
PSMD1 Martins Dzierkals 4.00 10.00
PSMJ1 Max Jones 6.00 15.00
PSML1 Max Lajoie 6.00 15.00
PSMM1 Michael McLeod 6.00 15.00
PSMS1 Mathieu Sevigny 4.00 10.00
PSMS2 Michael Spacek 4.00 10.00
PSMS3 Mikhail Sergachev 8.00 20.00
PSMT1 Matthew Tkachuk 20.00 50.00
PSNB1 Nathan Bastian 6.00 15.00
PSNC1 Noah Carroll 5.00 12.00
PSNK1 Nolan Kneen 4.00 10.00
PSNP1 Nolan Patrick 12.00 30.00
PSNV1 Nolan Volcan 4.00 10.00
PSOT1 Owen Tippett 4.00 10.00
PSPB1 Patrick Bajkov 4.00 10.00
PSPD1 Pierre-Luc Dubois 10.00 25.00
PSPH1 Peyton Hoyt 4.00 10.00
PSPL1 Pascal Laberge 5.00 12.00
PSRB1 Radovan Bondra 4.00 10.00
PSRK1 Ryan Kubic 4.00 10.00
PSSB1 Shawn Boudrias 4.00 10.00
PSSG1 Samuel Girard 5.00 12.00
PSSM1 Stelio Mattheos 6.00 15.00
PSSS1 Sam Steel 8.00 20.00
PSSS2 Simon Stransky 6.00 15.00
PSSS3 Stuart Skinner 8.00 20.00
PSTB1 Travis Barron 4.00 10.00
PSTB2 Tyler Benson 8.00 20.00
PSTF1 Tye Felhaber 4.00 10.00
PSTK1 Tanner Kaspick 4.00 10.00
PSTP1 Tyler Parsons 4.00 10.00
PSTR1 Taylor Raddysh 6.00 15.00
PSTR2 Ty Ronning 4.00 10.00
PSTT1 Troy Timpano 4.00 10.00
PSVK1 Vladimir Kuznetsov 4.00 10.00
PSVM1 Victor Mete 5.00 12.00
PSVS1 Vili Saarijarvi 4.00 10.00
PSWB1 Will Bitten 4.00 10.00
PSZG1 Zach Gallant 4.00 10.00
PSZS1 Zach Sawchenko 4.00 10.00
PSZS2 Zachary Senyshyn 4.00 10.00
PSAN1 Alexander Nylander 10.00 25.00

2015-16 ITG Heroes and Prospects Canada Russia Series Jerseys

CR01 Anthony Beauvillier 4.00 10.00
CR02 Brendan Guhle 3.00 8.00
CR03 Carter Hart 8.00 20.00
CR04 Clark Bishop 5.00 12.00
CR05 Dylan Strome 10.00 25.00
CR06 Jansen Harkins 5.00 12.00
CR07 Julien Gauthier 6.00 15.00
CR08 Julien Nantel 5.00 12.00
CR09 Kale Clague 5.00 12.00
CR10 Lawson Crouse 5.00 12.00
CR11 Mathew Barzal 12.00 30.00
CR12 Maxime Fortier 3.00 8.00
CR13 Michael McLeod 5.00 12.00
CR14 Michael McNiven 5.00 12.00
CR15 Mitchell Marner 15.00 40.00
CR16 Nathan Bastian 5.00 12.00
CR17 Nick Merkley 6.00 15.00
CR18 Noah Juulsen 5.00 12.00
CR19 Nolan Patrick 10.00 25.00
CR20 Pierre-Luc Dubois 8.00 20.00
CR21 Ryan Gropp 5.00 12.00
CR22 Samuel Girard 4.00 10.00
CR23 Samuel Montembeault 5.00 12.00
CR24 Thomas Chabot 5.00 12.00
CR25 Victor Mete 4.00 10.00
CR26 Will Bitten 3.00 8.00

2015-16 ITG Heroes and Prospects Canada Russia Series Patches

CRP01 Anthony Beauvillier 5.00 12.00
CRP02 Brendan Guhle 4.00 10.00
CRP03 Carter Hart 10.00 25.00
CRP04 Clark Bishop 6.00 15.00
CRP05 Dylan Strome 12.00 30.00
CRP06 Jansen Harkins 6.00 15.00
CRP07 Julien Gauthier 8.00 20.00
CRP08 Julien Nantel 6.00 15.00
CRP09 Kale Clague 6.00 15.00
CRP10 Lawson Crouse 6.00 15.00
CRP11 Mathew Barzal 15.00 40.00
CRP12 Maxime Fortier 4.00 10.00
CRP13 Michael McLeod 6.00 15.00
CRP14 Michael McNiven 6.00 15.00
CRP15 Mitchell Marner 15.00 40.00
CRP16 Nathan Bastian 6.00 15.00
CRP17 Nick Merkley 8.00 20.00
CRP18 Noah Juulsen 6.00 15.00
CRP19 Nolan Patrick 20.00 50.00
CRP20 Pierre-Luc Dubois 10.00 25.00
CRP21 Ryan Gropp 6.00 15.00
CRP22 Samuel Girard 5.00 12.00
CRP23 Samuel Montembeault 6.00 15.00
CRP24 Thomas Chabot 6.00 15.00
CRP25 Victor Mete 5.00 12.00
CRP26 Will Bitten 4.00 10.00

2015-16 ITG Heroes and Prospects Draft Prospect Autographs

DPAD1 Alex DeBrincat 10.00 25.00
DPJB1 Jake Bean 10.00 25.00
DPJC1 Jakob Chychrun 12.00 30.00
DPJG1 Julien Gauthier 12.00 30.00
DPJP1 Jesse Puljujarvi 20.00 50.00
DPMJ1 Max Jones 10.00 25.00
DPMS1 Mikhail Sergachev 12.00 30.00
DPMT1 Matthew Tkachuk 30.00 80.00
DPPD1 Pierre-Luc Dubois 15.00 40.00
DPVA1 Vitalii Abramov 12.00 30.00

2015-16 ITG Heroes and Prospects Hero and Prospect Jerseys

HPJ01 D.Gilmour/B.Gilmour/30 5.00 12.00
HPJ02 J.Brodeur/M.Brodeur/30 10.00 25.00
HPJ03 J.Veleno/W.Gretzky/20 25.00 60.00
HPJ04 K.Tkachuk/M.Tkachuk/30 12.00 30.00
HPJ05 N.Patrick/E.Lindros/30 8.00 20.00
HPJ06 V.Abramov/P.Bure/30 5.00 12.00
HPJ07 X.Potvin/F.Potvin/30 6.00 15.00

2015-16 ITG Heroes and Prospects Hero Autographs

HABB1 Bill Barber/30 8.00 20.00
HABS1 Billy Smith/20 10.00 25.00
HAGL1 Guy Lafleur/25 12.00 30.00
HAIL1 Igor Larionov/25 10.00 25.00
HAMB1 Martin Brodeur/20 25.00 60.00
HAMD1 Marcel Dionne/30 12.00 30.00
HAME1 Mike Eruzione/30 8.00 20.00
HAOK1 Olaf Kolzig/30 10.00 25.00
HAPB1 Pavel Bure/25 10.00 25.00
HAPS1 Peter Stastny/30 8.00 20.00
HATE1 Tony Esposito/20 10.00 25.00

2015-16 ITG Heroes and Prospects Hero Eight Jerseys

H801 Larkin/Eichel/McDavid/Domi/Bennett
Reinhart/Duclair/Ehlers 30.00 80.00
H802 Roy/Gretzky/Lemieux/Messier/Bourque
Fedorov/Hull/Yzerman 30.00 80.00
H803 Selanne/Kariya/Fedorov
Getzlaf/Niedermayer
Niedermayer/Oates/Pronger 30.00 80.00

2015-16 ITG Heroes and Prospects Jersey Autographs

AGBD1 Brett Davis/20 10.00 25.00
AGDT1 Dmytro Timashov/20 10.00 25.00
AGJB1 Jake Bean/20 10.00 25.00
AGJE1 Jack Eichel/25 40.00 100.00
AGJE2 Jack Eichel/20 40.00 100.00
AGJV1 Joe Veleno/25 10.00 25.00
AGMJ1 Max Jones/15 10.00 25.00
AGSM1 Stelio Mattheos/15 10.00 25.00
AGVA1 Vitalii Abramov/15 12.00 30.00

2015-16 ITG Heroes and Prospects Jerseys

GU01 Alex DeBrincat 5.00 12.00
GU02 Alexander Chmelevski 4.00 10.00
GU03 Alexander Nylander 8.00 20.00
GU04 Beck Malenstyn 5.00 12.00
GU05 Brady Gilmour 5.00 12.00
GU06 David Levin 5.00 12.00
GU07 Dillon Dube 6.00 12.00
GU08 Dmitry Sokolov 5.00 12.00
GU09 Dmytro Timashov 5.00 12.00
GU10 Dylan Sadowy 5.00 12.00
GU11 Dylan Strome 10.00 25.00
GU12 Gabriel Vilardi 5.00 12.00
GU13 Jack Eichel 20.00 50.00
GU14 Jakob Chychrun 6.00 15.00
GU15 Joe Veleno 5.00 12.00
GU16 Jordan Kyrou 5.00 12.00
GU17 Julien Gauthier 6.00 15.00
GU18 Juuso Valimaki 3.00 8.00
GU19 Matthew Tkachuk 15.00 40.00
GU20 Max Jones 5.00 12.00
GU21 Max Lajoie 5.00 12.00
GU22 Maxime Comtois 6.00 15.00
GU23 Nolan Patrick 10.00 25.00
GU24 Sam Steel 6.00 15.00
GU25 Simon Stransky 5.00 12.00
GU26 Stelio Mattheos 5.00 12.00
GU27 Taylor Raddysh 5.00 12.00
GU28 Vitalii Abramov 6.00 15.00

2015-16 ITG Heroes and Prospects Metal Autographs

BMJE1 Jack Eichel 25.00 60.00
BMJP1 Jesse Puljujarvi 20.00 50.00
BMJV1 Joe Veleno 20.00 50.00

2015-16 ITG Heroes and Prospects Patches

GUP01 Alex DeBrincat 8.00 20.00
GUP02 Alexander Chmelevski 6.00 15.00
GUP03 Alexander Nylander 12.00 30.00
GUP04 Beck Malenstyn 8.00 20.00
GUP05 Brady Gilmour 8.00 20.00
GUP06 David Levin 8.00 20.00
GUP07 Dillon Dube 8.00 20.00
GUP08 Dmitry Sokolov 8.00 20.00
GUP09 Dmytro Timashov 8.00 20.00
GUP10 Dylan Sadowy 8.00 20.00
GUP11 Dylan Strome 15.00 40.00
GUP12 Gabriel Vilardi 8.00 20.00
GUP13 Jack Eichel 30.00 80.00
GUP14 Jakob Chychrun 10.00 25.00
GUP15 Joe Veleno 8.00 20.00
GUP16 Jordan Kyrou 8.00 20.00
GUP17 Julien Gauthier 10.00 25.00
GUP18 Juuso Valimaki 5.00 12.00
GUP19 Matthew Tkachuk 25.00 60.00
GUP20 Max Jones 8.00 20.00
GUP21 Max Lajoie 8.00 20.00
GUP22 Maxime Comtois 10.00 25.00
GUP23 Nolan Patrick 15.00 40.00
GUP24 Sam Steel 10.00 25.00
GUP25 Simon Stransky 8.00 20.00
GUP26 Stelio Mattheos 8.00 20.00
GUP27 Taylor Raddysh 8.00 20.00
GUP28 Vitalii Abramov 10.00 25.00

2015-16 ITG Heroes and Prospects Prospect Eight Jerseys

P801 DeBrincat/Strome/Raddysh
Vilardi/McLeod/Nylander
Gilmour/Chychrun 15.00 40.00
P802 Patrick/Malenstyn/Bean
Steel/Benson/Stransky
Valimaki/Mahura 15.00 40.00
P803 Abramov/Veleno/Comtois
Timashov/Gauthier/Morand
Girard/Sylvestre 10.00 25.00
P804 Blackwood/Cormier/Papirny
McDonald/Potvin/Brodeur
Dumont-Bouchard/Smith 10.00 25.00
P805 Patrick/DeBrincat/Levin/Abramov/Benson
Tkachuk/Bean/Gauthier 25.00 60.00

2015-16 ITG Heroes and Prospects Rare Materials Signatures

RMBS1 Borje Salming/15 10.00 25.00
RMGL1 Guy Lafleur/15 12.00 30.00
RMJE1 Jack Eichel/15 40.00 100.00
RMJT1 Jose Theodore/15 10.00 25.00
RMJV1 Joe Veleno/20 10.00 25.00
RMMC1 Maxime Comtois/15 12.00 30.00
RMPB1 Pavel Bure/15 10.00 25.00
RMTS1 Teemu Selanne/15 20.00 50.00

2015-16 ITG Heroes and Prospects Top Prospects Jerseys

TP01 Alex DeBrincat 5.00 12.00
TP02 Alexander Nylander 8.00 20.00
TP03 Brett Howden 3.00 8.00
TP04 Carter Hart 8.00 20.00
TP05 Evan Fitzpatrick 6.00 15.00
TP06 Jake Bean 5.00 12.00
TP07 Jordan Kyrou 5.00 12.00
TP08 Julien Gauthier 6.00 15.00
TP09 Logan Brown 8.00 20.00
TP10 Matthew Tkachuk 15.00 40.00
TP11 Max Jones 5.00 12.00
TP12 Michael McLeod 5.00 12.00
TP13 Mikhail Sergachev 6.00 15.00
TP14 Olli Juolevi 5.00 12.00
TP15 Pierre-Luc Dubois 8.00 20.00
TP16 Simon Stransky 5.00 12.00
TP17 Taylor Raddysh 5.00 12.00
TP18 Vitalii Abramov 6.00 15.00

2015-16 ITG Heroes and Prospects Top Prospects Patches

TPP01 Alex DeBrincat 8.00 20.00
TPP02 Alexander Nylander 12.00 30.00
TPP03 Brett Howden 5.00 12.00
TPP04 Carter Hart 12.00 30.00
TPP05 Evan Fitzpatrick 10.00 25.00
TPP06 Jake Bean 8.00 20.00
TPP07 Jordan Kyrou 8.00 20.00
TPP08 Julien Gauthier 10.00 25.00
TPP09 Logan Brown 12.00 30.00
TPP10 Matthew Tkachuk 25.00 60.00
TPP11 Max Jones 8.00 20.00
TPP12 Michael McLeod 8.00 20.00
TPP13 Mikhail Sergachev 10.00 25.00
TPP14 Olli Juolevi 8.00 20.00
TPP15 Pierre-Luc Dubois 12.00 30.00
TPP16 Simon Stransky 8.00 20.00
TPP17 Taylor Raddysh 8.00 20.00
TPP18 Vitalii Abramov 10.00 25.00

2015-16 ITG Heroes and Prospects Trinity Signatures

JE Jack Eichel 30.00 80.00

2016-17 ITG Heroes and Prospects Prospect Autographs

*PALTINUM: .5X TO 1.25X BASIC CARDS
PAAC1 Alexander Chmelevski 4.00 10.00
PAAD1 Alex DeBrincat 8.00 20.00
PAAH1 Aleksi Heponiemi 6.00 15.00
PAAM1 Adam McMaster 5.00 12.00
PAAM2 Antoine Morand 4.00 10.00
PAAMD Anderson MacDonald 4.00 10.00
PAAR1 Adam Ruzicka 6.00 15.00
PABG1 Benoit-Olivier Groulx 4.00 10.00
PABG2 Brady Gilmour 4.00 10.00
PABK1 Boris Katchouk 8.00 20.00
PABM1 Beck Malenstyn SP 4.00 10.00
PACB1 Connor Bunnaman SP 4.00 10.00
PACF1 Cal Foote 8.00 20.00
PACG1 Cody Glass 6.00 15.00
PACH1 Carter Hart 6.00 15.00
PACR1 Connor Roberts 4.00 10.00
PADA1 Danil Antropov 6.00 15.00
PADB1 Dennis Busby 6.00 15.00
PADG1 Damien Giroux 4.00 10.00
PADS1 Dylan Strome 10.00 25.00
PADV1 Daniil Vertiy 8.00 20.00
PAGF1 Gabriel Fortier 8.00 20.00
PAGS1 Givani Smith SP 4.00 10.00
PAGV1 Gabriel Vilardi 4.00 10.00
PAHD1 Hayden Davis 4.00 10.00
PAIL1 Ivan Lodnia 10.00 25.00
PAIS1 Ian Scott 8.00 20.00
PAJAD Jaret Anderson-Dolan 8.00 20.00
PAJB1 Jordy Bellerive 4.00 10.00
PAJD1 Jared Dmytriw 4.00 10.00
PAJDW Jeff De Wit 4.00 10.00
PAJK1 Jordan Kyrou 4.00 10.00
PAJL1 Jake Leschyshyn SP 4.00 10.00
PAJM1 Josh Mahura SP 3.00 8.00
PAJP1 Jacob Paquette 4.00 10.00
PAJR1 Jason Robertson 12.00 30.00
PAJV1 Joe Veleno 12.00 30.00
PAJV2 Juuso Valimaki 4.00 10.00
PAJW1 Jaeger White 4.00 10.00
PAKC1 Kale Clague 4.00 10.00
PAKK1 Klim Kostin SP 8.00 20.00
PAKV1 Kristian Vesalainen 10.00 25.00
PAKY1 Kailer Yamamoto 6.00 15.00
PAKY2 Keanu Yamamoto SP 8.00 20.00
PALJ1 Lucas Johansen 4.00 10.00
PALM1 Liam Murphy 4.00 10.00
PALT1 Lucas Thierus 4.00 10.00
PAMB1 Mitchell Balmas SP 4.00 10.00
PAMC1 Maxime Comtois 5.00 12.00
PAMD1 Michael DiPietro 8.00 20.00
PAML1 Max Lajoie SP 4.00 10.00
PAMM1 Michael McLeod 4.00 10.00
PAMR1 Michael Rasmussen 8.00 20.00
PAMS1 Mathieu Sevigny SP 4.00 10.00
PAMS2 Matthew Strome 4.00 10.00
PAMS3 Michael Spacek 4.00 10.00
PANB1 Nathan Bastian SP 4.00 10.00
PAND1 Nathan Dunkley 5.00 12.00
PANH1 Nick Henry 4.00 10.00
PANH2 Nicolas Hague 3.00 8.00
PANH3 Nico Hischier 15.00 40.00
PANJ1 Noah Juulsen 4.00 10.00
PANM1 Nick Merkley 8.00 20.00
PANP1 Nikita Popugaev 4.00 10.00
PANP2 Nolan Patrick 25.00 60.00
PANS1 Nick Suzuki 8.00 20.00
PANV1 Nolan Volcan 4.00 10.00
PAOR1 Olivier Rodrigue 4.00 10.00
PAOT1 Owen Tippett 4.00 10.00
PAPB1 Patrick Bajkov SP 4.00 10.00
PAPL1 Pascal Laberge SP 3.00 8.00
PARM1 Ryan McLeod 4.00 10.00
PARM2 Ryan Merkley 8.00 20.00
PASE1 Shawn Element 4.00 10.00
PASG1 Samuel Girard SP 3.00 8.00
PASS1 Stuart Skinner 5.00 12.00
PATB1 Travis Barron SP 2.50 6.00
PATD1 Ty Dellandrea 4.00 10.00
PATF1 Tye Felhaber SP 4.00 10.00
PATK1 Tanner Kaspick SP 4.00 10.00
PATP1 Tyler Parsons SP 4.00 10.00
PATR1 Taylor Raddysh SP 4.00 10.00
PATR2 Ty Ronning SP 4.00 10.00
PATS1 Ty Smith 6.00 15.00
PATT1 Troy Timpano SP 4.00 10.00
PAVA1 Vitalii Abramov SP 4.00 10.00
PAVM1 Victor Mete 3.00 8.00
PAVS1 Vili Saarijarvi SP 4.00 10.00
PAWB1 Will Bitten SP 3.00 8.00
PAZS1 Zach Sawchenko SP 4.00 10.00
PAZS2 Zachary Senyshyn 4.00 10.00

2016-17 ITG Heroes and Prospects Heroes Eight Memorabilia

*PLATINUM/20: .4X TO 1X BASIC INSERTS
H801 Gretzky/Lemieux/Bourque/Hull/Messier
Yzerman/Roy/Fedorov 40.00 100.00
H802 Hall/Kane/Burns/Draisaitl/Subban
Tavares/MacKinnon/Stamkos 25.00 60.00
H803 Brodeur/Nabokov/Luongo
Turco/Kolzig/Khabibulin
Theodore/Vokoun 15.00 40.00
H804 Thornton/Iginla/Lecavalier
St. Louis/Kovalchuk/Kovalev
Hossa/Alfredsson 10.00 25.00
H805 Belfour/Vanbiesbrouck/Richter/Joseph
Hasek/Vernon/Potvin/Burke 10.00 25.00
H806 Coffey/Bourque/Murphy
Housley/Reinhart/MacInnis
Potvin/Babych 8.00 20.00
H807 Fuhr/Beaupre/Smith/Riggin/Moog
Barrasso/Resch/Meloche 10.00 25.00
H808 Orr/Sittler/Unger/Lafleur/Esposito
Dionne/Cashman/Redmond 25.00 60.00

2016-17 ITG Heroes and Prospects Heroes Memorabilia

*PLATINUM: .8X TO 2X BASIC INSERTS
HM01 Adam Oates 3.00 8.00
HM02 Alexander Mogilny 3.00 8.00
HM03 Alexander Ovechkin 12.00 30.00
HM04 Arturs Irbe 2.50 6.00
HM05 Brian Leetch 2.50 6.00
HM06 Bryan Berard 3.00 8.00
HM07 Carey Price 6.00 15.00
HM08 Chris Chelios 3.00 8.00
HM09 Chris Osgood 3.00 8.00
HM10 Chris Pronger 3.00 8.00
HM11 Curtis Joseph 4.00 10.00
HM12 Daniel Alfredsson 3.00 8.00
HM13 Dany Heatley 2.50 6.00
HM14 Darryl Sydor 3.00 8.00
HM15 Doug Weight 3.00 8.00
HM16 Gary Sargent 3.00 8.00
HM17 Guy Lafleur 4.00 10.00
HM18 Henrik Lundqvist 8.00 20.00
HM19 Jack Eichel 5.00 12.00
HM20 Jaromir Jagr 10.00 25.00
HM21 Jason Arnott 3.00 8.00
HM22 Jeremy Roenick 5.00 12.00
HM23 Joe Nieuwendyk 2.50 6.00
HM24 Joe Sakic 6.00 15.00
HM25 Joe Thornton 5.00 12.00
HM26 John LeClair 3.00 8.00
HM27 Markus Naslund 3.00 8.00
HM28 Martin Brodeur 8.00 20.00
HM29 Mats Sundin 3.00 8.00
HM30 Mike Modano 5.00 12.00
HM31 Milan Hejduk 3.00 8.00
HM32 Nicklas Lidstrom 3.00 8.00
HM33 Owen Nolan 3.00 8.00
HM34 Patrick Roy 8.00 20.00
HM35 Paul Kariya 3.00 8.00
HM36 Pavel Bure 3.00 8.00
HM37 Peter Forsberg 6.00 15.00
HM38 Pierre Turgeon 2.50 6.00
HM39 Raymond Bourque 5.00 12.00
HM40 Rick Nash 3.00 8.00
HM41 Scott Niedermayer 3.00 8.00
HM42 Sergei Fedorov 5.00 12.00
HM43 Steve Larmer 3.00 8.00
HM44 Steve Shutt 3.00 8.00
HM45 Teemu Selanne 6.00 15.00
HM46 Trevor Linden 3.00 8.00
HM47 Vincent Damphousse 3.00 8.00
HM48 Wayne Gretzky SP 20.00 50.00
HM49 Zdeno Chara 3.00 8.00

2016-17 ITG Heroes and Prospects International Ice Autographs

*PLATINUM: .6X TO 1.5X BASIC INSERTS
IIAD1 Alex DeBrincat 10.00 25.00
IIAH1 Aleksi Heponiemi 8.00 20.00
IIAR1 Adam Ruzicka 8.00 20.00
IIBG1 Brady Gilmour 5.00 12.00
IIBK1 Boris Katchouk 10.00 25.00
IIBOG Benoit-Olivier Groulx 5.00 12.00
IICH1 Carter Hart 8.00 20.00
IIDS1 Dylan Strome SP 12.00 30.00
IIDV1 Daniil Vertiy 10.00 25.00
IIJB1 Jordy Bellerive 5.00 12.00
IIJE1 Jack Eichel 8.00 20.00
IIJV1 Joe Veleno 15.00 40.00
IIJV2 Juuso Valimaki 5.00 12.00
IIKC1 Kale Clague 5.00 12.00
IIKK1 Klim Kostin SP 10.00 25.00
IIKV1 Kristian Vesalainen 12.00 30.00
IINH1 Nico Hischier SP 20.00 50.00
IINP1 Nikita Popugaev 5.00 12.00
IINP2 Nolan Patrick 30.00 80.00
IISS1 Stuart Skinner 6.00 15.00

2016-17 ITG Heroes and Prospects Reflections Memorabilia

*PLATINUM: .5X TO 1.25X BASIC INSERTS
R01 W.Gretzky/C.McDavid 20.00 50.00
R02 G.Howe/M.Howe 10.00 25.00
R03 J.Eichel/M.Modano 5.00 12.00
R04 P.Roy/C.Price 8.00 20.00
R05 J.Kurri/T.Selanne 6.00 15.00
R06 P.Esposito/M.Lemieux 12.00 30.00
R07 S.Fedorov/A.Ovechkin 12.00 30.00
R08 G.Lafleur/S.Crosby 12.00 30.00
R09 D.Doughty/S.Stevens 4.00 10.00
R10 P.Kane/P.LaFontaine 6.00 15.00
R11 P.Bure/E.Malkin 6.00 15.00
R12 P.Turgeon/T.Seguin 4.00 10.00
R13 S.Patrick/N.Patrick 20.00 50.00
R14 B.Burns/K.Hatcher 3.00 8.00
R15 P.Kane/M.Marner 10.00 25.00
R16 T.Sawchuk/P.Roy 8.00 20.00

2016-17 ITG Heroes and Prospects Stars of the OHL Autographs

*PLATINUM: .4X TO 1X BASIC INSERTS
S001 DeBrincat/Suzuki/Strome 15.00 40.00
S002 McLeod/Vilardi/Lodnia SP 15.00 40.00

2016-17 ITG Heroes and Prospects Stars of the QMJHL Autographs

*PLATINUM: .4X TO 1X BASIC INSERTS
S001 Hischier/Comtois
MacDonald SP 15.00 40.00

2016-17 ITG Heroes and Prospects Stars of the WHL Autographs

*PLATINUM: .4X TO 1X BASIC INSERTS
S001 Henry/Heponiemi/Popugaev 15.00 40.00

2016-17 ITG Heroes and Prospects The Eichel Tower Autographs

*PLATINUM: .4X TO 1X BASIC INSERTS
*RED/25: .4X TO 1.25X BASIC INSERTS
ETJE1 Jack Eichel 8.00 20.00
ETJE2 Jack Eichel 8.00 20.00
ETJE3 Jack Eichel 8.00 20.00
ETJE4 Jack Eichel 8.00 20.00

2012-13 ITG History Of Hockey Great Moments Memorabilia Silver

81 Roy breaks Sawchuk Mark 30.00 60.00
82 Finally Sakic/Bourque 50.00 125.00
83 Esposito Shatters Record 30.00 80.00
84 Ovechkin scores on back 30.00 60.00
85 First Rookie to Score 50 40.00 100.00
86 Canada Wins 2002 Games 30.00 60.00
87 Ten Point Game 30.00 60.00
88 Esposito First To 100 Points 30.00 60.00
89 Flyers win 35 straight-Parent 30.00 60.00
90 Esposito's 1972 Speech 40.00 80.00
91 Captain Returns-Koivu 30.00 60.00
92 Hextall scores a goal 30.00 60.00
93 Controverisal Cup Winner 40.00 80.00
94 The Fog Game-Parent 25.00 60.00
95 First Cup Since 55 Yzerman 25.00 60.00
96 Eddie Returns to MSG 20.00 50.00
97 Lafleur's Comeback 15.00 40.00
98 US Wins First World Cup 20.00 50.00
99 Rookie Scoring T.Selanne 40.00 80.00
100 The China Wall-Bower 15.00 40.00
101 Clarke Wins First Hart 40.00 100.00
102 Lemieux Scores Five Ways 50.00 100.00
103 Lindros Plays Canada Cup 40.00 100.00
104 Clarke's Big Break 40.00 100.00
105 Longest Undefeated Streak 20.00 50.00
106 Baun Scores on Broken leg 12.00 30.00
107 Nolan Calls Shot AS Game 15.00 40.00
108 Hasek Lead Czech Gold 40.00 100.00
109 Lemieux Returns 40.00 80.00
110 Pelle Lindbergh Death 30.00 80.00
111 Roy's Last Game 40.00 80.00
112 Canada Cup Winner-Sittler 30.00 80.00
113 First Heritage Classic-Messier 50.00 125.00
114 Greatest Tie 30.00 60.00
115 Passing The Torch 30.00 60.00
116 Four Straight Cups-Bossy 25.00 60.00
117 Lemieux leads Pens Cup 40.00 80.00
118 LaFontaine overtime winner 25.00 60.00
119 Hull signs contract with Jets 15.00 40.00
120 Russian Invasion 30.00 80.00
121 48 Goals by Defenseman 25.00 60.00
122 Richter beats Bure 15.00 40.00
123 Rangers End 54-Year Drought 20.00 50.00
124 Gold Medal Save-Salo 20.00 50.00

125 Gold Medal Goal-Forsberg 50.00 125.00
126 Saying Goodbye-Tkachuk 15.00 40.00
127 The Save-McLean 20.00 50.00
128 50 Goals in 49 Games-Neely 15.00 40.00
129 Howe Family In Houston 25.00 60.00
130 Final Game Maple Leaf Gardens 40.00 100.00
131 87 Canada Cup-Gretzky 40.00 80.00
132 Canada Wins 04 World Cup 40.00 80.00
133 First Goalie to Score 25.00 60.00
134 Roy wins cup rookie year 50.00 100.00
135 Thomas Bruins to Cup 15.00 40.00
136 McDonald Scores Winner 25.00 60.00
137 Oilers Win Cup-Messier 50.00 125.00
138 First Overall-M.Lemieux 25.00 60.00
139 Neilson Surrenders 15.00 40.00
140 Calgary's First Stanley Cup 25.00 60.00
141 Back-To-Back Playoff MVP 30.00 80.00
142 Dionne Scores 40, 10X 15.00 40.00
143 Esposito Sets Rookie Record 20.00 50.00
144 Miracle on Ice-Jim Craig 40.00 100.00

2006-07 ITG International Ice

1 Vladislav Tretiak 1.00 2.50
2 Bobby Hull 2.50 6.00
3 Bobby Clarke 2.00 5.00
4 Raymond Bourque 2.00 5.00
5 Paul Coffey 1.25 3.00
6 Pat LaFontaine 1.25 3.00
7 Brett Hull 2.50 6.00
8 Steve Yzerman 3.00 8.00
9 Marek Schwarz 1.25 3.00
10 Sidney Crosby 5.00 12.00
11 Gerry Cheevers 1.25 3.00
12 Phil Esposito 2.00 5.00
13 Marcel Dionne 1.50 4.00
14 Grant Fuhr 2.00 5.00
15 Jaromir Jagr 4.00 10.00
16 Antero Niittymaki 1.00 2.50
17 Mario Lemieux 5.00 12.00
18 Henrik Lundqvist 3.00 8.00
19 Alexander Yakushev 1.00 2.50
20 Michel Goulet 1.00 2.50
21 Paul Coffey 1.25 3.00
22 Darryl Sittler 1.50 4.00
23 Stan Mikita 1.50 4.00
24 Borje Salming 1.25 3.00
25 Vladislav Tretiak 1.00 2.50
26 Steve Yzerman 3.00 8.00
27 Dale Hawerchuk 1.50 4.00
28 Martin Brodeur 3.00 8.00
29 Ilya Bryzgalov 1.25 3.00
30 Bobby Ryan 1.25 3.00
31 Tony Esposito 1.25 3.00
32 Jari Kurri 1.25 3.00
33 Larry Robinson 1.25 3.00
34 Doug Gilmour 1.50 4.00
35 Mike Richter 1.25 3.00
36 Brett Hull 2.50 6.00
37 Michael Frolik 1.00 2.50
38 Cristobal Huet 1.00 2.50
39 Phil Esposito 2.00 5.00
40 Valeri Vasilyev .75 2.00
41 Borje Salming 1.25 3.00
42 Glenn Anderson 1.00 2.50
43 Raymond Bourque 2.00 5.00
44 Luc Robitaille 1.25 3.00
45 Pat LaFontaine 1.25 3.00
46 Petr Prucha 1.00 2.50
47 Steve Shutt 1.25 3.00
48 Larry Robinson 1.25 3.00
49 Mats Naslund .75 2.00
50 Dale Hawerchuk 1.50 4.00
51 Pat LaFontaine 1.25 3.00
52 Jaromir Jagr 4.00 10.00
53 John Tavares 5.00 12.00
54 Tuukka Rask 3.00 8.00
55 Anders Hedberg .75 2.00
56 John Vanbiesbrouck 1.25 3.00
57 Larry Murphy 1.00 2.50
58 Jari Kurri 1.25 3.00
59 Alexander Ovechkin 5.00 12.00
60 Mike Bossy 1.25 3.00
61 Valeri Kharlamov 1.25 3.00
62 Rick Ley .75 2.00
63 Guy Lafleur 1.50 4.00
64 Tony Esposito 1.25 3.00
65 Kent Nilsson .75 2.00
66 Paul Coffey 1.25 3.00
67 Bill Ranford 1.25 3.00
68 Nicklas Lidstrom 1.25 3.00
69 Evgeni Malkin 5.00 12.00
70 Alexander Radulov 1.50 4.00
71 Borje Salming 1.25 3.00
72 Michel Goulet 1.00 2.50
73 Thomas Steen .75 2.00
74 Denis Potvin 1.25 3.00
75 Larry Robinson 1.25 3.00
76 Mark Howe 1.25 3.00
77 Wayne Cashman .75 2.00
78 Marcel Dionne 1.50 4.00
79 Neal Broten .75 2.00
80 Grant Fuhr 2.00 5.00
81 Jari Kurri 1.25 3.00
82 Brian Leetch 1.00 2.50
83 Jim Craig .75 2.00
84 Al Montoya 1.25 3.00
85 Mark Messier 2.50 6.00
86 Esa Tikkanen .75 2.00
87 Glenn Anderson 1.00 2.50
88 Brian Bellows 1.00 2.50
89 Ulf Nilsson .75 2.00
90 Gilbert Perreault 1.25 3.00
91 Peter Mahovlich 1.25 3.00
92 Peter Stastny 1.00 2.50
93 Igor Larionov 1.25 3.00
94 Mark Messier 2.50 6.00
95 Vladimir Krutov .75 2.00
96 Mats Naslund .75 2.00
97 Mike Richter 1.25 3.00
98 Martin Brodeur 3.00 8.00
99 Justin Pogge 1.00 2.50
100 Paul Coffey 1.25 3.00
101 Paul Henderson 1.00 2.50
102 Mark Messier 2.50 6.00
103 Gilbert Perreault 1.25 3.00
104 Pelle Lindbergh 1.00 2.50
105 Bill Barber 1.00 2.50
106 Andre Lacroix .75 2.00
107 J.P. Parise .75 2.00
108 Brad Park 1.00 2.50
109 Alex Auld .75 2.00
110 Phil Kessel 2.50 6.00
111 Yan Stastny .75 2.00
112 Steve Larmer .75 2.00
113 Mats Naslund .75 2.00
114 Rod Langway 1.00 2.50
115 Peter Stastny 1.00 2.50
116 Bryan Trottier 1.25 3.00
117 Bobby Hull 2.50 6.00
118 Frank Mahovlich 1.25 3.00
119 Guy Lapointe 1.00 2.50
120 Danny Gare .75 2.00
121 Guy Lafleur 1.50 4.00
122 Rick Middleton 1.00 2.50
123 Larry Murphy 1.00 2.50
124 Jeff Glass 1.00 2.50
125 Chris Chelios 1.25 3.00
126 Ryan Malone .75 2.00
127 Marc-Andre Fleury 2.50 6.00
128 Patrick Roy 3.00 8.00
129 Paul Henderson 1.00 2.50
130 Marcel Dionne 1.50 4.00
131 Serge Savard 1.25 3.00
132 Gilbert Perreault 1.25 3.00
133 Raymond Bourque 2.00 5.00
134 Phil Housley 1.00 2.50
135 Rogie Vachon 1.50 4.00
136 Vladimir Myshkin .75 2.00
137 Bobby Clarke 2.00 5.00
138 Robbie Schremp 1.00 2.50
139 Peter Mahovlich 1.25 3.00
140 Mike Bossy 1.25 3.00
141 Esa Tikkanen .75 2.00
142 Chris Chelios 1.25 3.00
143 Serge Savard 1.25 3.00
144 Lanny McDonald 1.25 3.00
145 Ilya Kovalchuk 1.25 3.00
146 Jason Spezza 1.25 3.00
147 Ryan Miller 1.25 3.00
148 Denis Potvin 1.25 3.00
149 Peter Mueller 1.25 3.00
150 Yvan Cournoyer 1.25 3.00
151 Ladislav Smid .75 2.00
152 Chris Bourque .75 2.00
153 Ralph Backstrom .75 2.00
154 Henrik Zetterberg 1.50 4.00
155 Angelo Esposito 1.50 4.00
156 Alexei Kasatonov .75 2.00
157 Ed Olczyk .75 2.00
158 Mark Messier 2.50 6.00
159 Andrei Markov 1.25 3.00
160 A.Ovechkin/E.Malkin 3.00 8.00

2006-07 ITG International Ice Autographs

AAA Alex Auld 5.00 12.00
AAE Angelo Esposito SP 10.00 25.00
AAH Anders Hedberg 5.00 12.00
AAK Alexei Kasatonov 5.00 12.00
AAL Andre Lacroix 5.00 12.00
AAM Al Montoya 8.00 20.00
AAMK Andrei Markov 8.00 20.00
AAN Antero Niittymaki 6.00 15.00
AAO Alexander Ovechkin SP 80.00 200.00
AAR Alexander Radulov SP 10.00 25.00
AAY Alexander Yakushev 6.00 15.00
ABB Brian Bellows 6.00 15.00
ABBR Bill Barber 6.00 15.00
ABC Bobby Clarke 12.00 30.00
ABC2 Bobby Clarke 12.00 30.00
ABH Bobby Hull SP 15.00 40.00
ABH2 Bobby Hull SP 15.00 40.00
ABHU Brett Hull SP 30.00 80.00
ABHU2 Brett Hull SP 30.00 80.00
ABL Brian Leetch SP 6.00 15.00
ABP Brad Park 6.00 15.00
ABR Bill Ranford 8.00 20.00
ABRY Bobby Ryan 8.00 20.00
ABS Borje Salming 8.00 20.00
ABS2 Borje Salming 8.00 20.00
ABS3 Borje Salming 8.00 20.00
ABT Bryan Trottier 8.00 20.00
ACB Chris Bourque 5.00 12.00
ACC Chris Chelios 8.00 20.00
ACC2 Chris Chelios 8.00 20.00
ACH Cristobal Huet 6.00 15.00
ADG Doug Gilmour 10.00 25.00
ADGR Danny Gare 5.00 12.00
ADH Dale Hawerchuk 10.00 25.00
ADH2 Dale Hawerchuk 10.00 25.00
ADP Denis Potvin 8.00 20.00
ADP2 Denis Potvin 8.00 20.00
ADS Darryl Sittler 10.00 25.00
AEM Evgeni Malkin SP 60.00 150.00
AEO Ed Olczyk 5.00 12.00
AET Esa Tikkanen 5.00 12.00
AET2 Esa Tikkanen 5.00 12.00
AFM Frank Mahovlich SP 8.00 20.00
AGA Glenn Anderson 6.00 15.00
AGA2 Glenn Anderson 6.00 15.00
AGC Gerry Cheevers 8.00 20.00
AGF Grant Fuhr 12.00 30.00
AGF2 Grant Fuhr 12.00 30.00
AGL Guy Lafleur 10.00 25.00
AGL2 Guy Lafleur 10.00 25.00
AGLP Guy Lapointe 6.00 15.00
AGP Gilbert Perreault 8.00 20.00
AGP2 Gilbert Perreault 8.00 20.00
AGP3 Gilbert Perreault 8.00 20.00
AHL Henrik Lundqvist 20.00 50.00
AHZ Henrik Zetterberg SP 10.00 25.00
AIB Ilya Bryzgalov 8.00 20.00
AIK Ilya Kovalchuk SP 8.00 20.00
AIL Igor Larionov 8.00 20.00
AJC Jim Craig 5.00 12.00
AJG Jeff Glass 6.00 15.00
AJJ Jaromir Jagr SP 50.00 125.00
AJJ2 Jaromir Jagr SP 50.00 125.00
AJK Jari Kurri 8.00 20.00
AJK2 Jari Kurri 8.00 20.00
AJK3 Jari Kurri 8.00 20.00
AJP Justin Pogge 6.00 15.00
AJPP J.P. Parise 5.00 12.00
AJS Jason Spezza SP 8.00 20.00
AJT John Tavares SP 30.00 80.00
AJV John Vanbiesbrouck 8.00 20.00
AKN Kent Nilsson 5.00 12.00
ALM Larry Murphy 6.00 15.00
ALM2 Larry Murphy 6.00 15.00
ALMC Lanny McDonald 8.00 20.00
ALR Larry Robinson 8.00 20.00
ALR2 Larry Robinson 8.00 20.00
ALR3 Larry Robinson 8.00 20.00
ALRO Luc Robitaille SP 8.00 20.00
ALS Ladislav Smid 5.00 12.00
AMAF Marc-Andre Fleury 15.00 40.00
AMB Martin Brodeur SP 30.00 80.00
AMB2 Martin Brodeur SP 30.00 80.00
AMBO Mike Bossy 8.00 20.00
AMBO2 Mike Bossy 8.00 20.00
AMD Marcel Dionne 10.00 25.00
AMD2 Marcel Dionne 10.00 25.00
AMD3 Marcel Dionne 10.00 25.00
AMF Michael Frolik 6.00 15.00
AMG Michel Goulet 6.00 15.00
AMG2 Michel Goulet 6.00 15.00
AMH Mark Howe 8.00 20.00
AML Mario Lemieux SP 60.00 150.00
AMM Mark Messier SP 15.00 40.00
AMM2 Mark Messier SP 15.00 40.00
AMM3 Mark Messier SP 15.00 40.00
AMM4 Mark Messier SP 15.00 40.00
AMN Mats Naslund 5.00 12.00
AMN2 Mats Naslund 5.00 12.00
AMN3 Mats Naslund 5.00 12.00
AMS Marek Schwarz 8.00 20.00
ANB Neal Broten 5.00 12.00
ANL Nicklas Lidstrom SP 8.00 20.00
APC Paul Coffey SP 8.00 20.00
APC2 Paul Coffey SP 8.00 20.00
APC3 Paul Coffey SP 8.00 20.00
APC4 Paul Coffey SP 8.00 20.00
APE Phil Esposito SP 12.00 30.00
APE2 Phil Esposito SP 12.00 30.00
APH Paul Henderson 6.00 15.00
APH2 Paul Henderson 6.00 15.00
APHO Phil Housley 6.00 15.00
APK Phil Kessel 15.00 40.00
APL Pat LaFontaine SP 8.00 20.00
APL2 Pat LaFontaine SP 8.00 20.00
APL3 Pat LaFontaine SP 8.00 20.00
APM Peter Mahovlich 8.00 20.00
APM2 Peter Mahovlich 8.00 20.00
APMU Peter Mueller 8.00 20.00
APP Petr Prucha 6.00 15.00
APR Patrick Roy 30.00 80.00
APS Peter Stastny 6.00 15.00
APS2 Peter Stastny 6.00 15.00
ARB Raymond Bourque SP 12.00 30.00
ARB2 Raymond Bourque SP 12.00 30.00
ARB3 Raymond Bourque SP 12.00 30.00
ARBA Ralph Backstrom 5.00 12.00
ARL Rick Ley 5.00 12.00
ARLW Rod Langway 6.00 15.00
ARM Rick Middleton 6.00 15.00
ARMI Ryan Miller 8.00 20.00
ARML Ryan Malone 5.00 12.00
ARS Robbie Schremp 6.00 15.00
ARV Rogie Vachon 10.00 25.00
ASC Sidney Crosby SP 60.00 150.00
ASL Steve Larmer 5.00 12.00
ASM Stan Mikita 10.00 25.00
ASS Steve Shutt 8.00 20.00
ASSV Serge Savard 8.00 20.00
ASSV2 Serge Savard 8.00 20.00
ASY Steve Yzerman SP 30.00 80.00
ASY2 Steve Yzerman SP 30.00 80.00
ATE Tony Esposito SP 8.00 20.00
ATE2 Tony Esposito SP 8.00 20.00
ATR Tuukka Rask 20.00 50.00
ATS Thomas Steen 5.00 12.00
AUN Ulf Nilsson 5.00 12.00
AVK Vladimir Krutov 5.00 12.00
AVM Vladimir Myshkin 5.00 12.00
AVT Vladislav Tretiak 6.00 15.00
AVT2 Vladislav Tretiak 6.00 15.00
AVV Valeri Vasilyev 5.00 12.00
AWC Wayne Cashman 5.00 12.00
AYC Yvan Cournoyer 8.00 20.00
AYS Yan Stastny 5.00 12.00

2006-07 ITG International Ice Best of the Best

BB01 Vladislav Tretiak 4.00 10.00
BB02 Brian Leetch 4.00 10.00
BB03 Paul Coffey 5.00 12.00
BB04 Mark Messier 10.00 25.00
BB05 Valeri Kharlamov 5.00 12.00
BB06 Mario Lemieux 20.00 50.00
BB07 Martin Brodeur 12.00 30.00
BB08 Raymond Bourque 8.00 20.00
BB09 Nicklas Lidstrom 5.00 12.00
BB10 Phil Esposito 8.00 20.00
BB11 Jaromir Jagr 15.00 40.00
BB12 Bobby Hull 10.00 25.00

2006-07 ITG International Ice Canadian Dream Team

DT01 Bobby Hull 10.00 25.00
DT02 Mark Messier 10.00 25.00
DT03 Martin Brodeur 12.00 30.00
DT04 Bobby Clarke 8.00 20.00
DT05 Phil Esposito 8.00 20.00
DT06 Darryl Sittler 6.00 15.00
DT07 Raymond Bourque 8.00 20.00
DT08 Mario Lemieux 20.00 50.00
DT09 Grant Fuhr 8.00 20.00
DT10 Paul Coffey 5.00 12.00
DT11 Sidney Crosby 20.00 50.00
DT12 John Tavares 20.00 50.00

2006-07 ITG International Ice Double Memorabilia

DM01 Eric Lindros 12.00 30.00
DM02 Patrick Roy 20.00 50.00
DM03 Martin Brodeur 20.00 50.00
DM04 Alexander Ovechkin 30.00 80.00
DM05 Sidney Crosby 30.00 80.00
DM06 Mario Lemieux 30.00 80.00

2006-07 ITG International Ice Goaltending Glory

GG01 Tony Esposito 4.00 10.00
GG02 Grant Fuhr 6.00 15.00
GG03 Martin Brodeur 10.00 25.00
GG04 Justin Pogge 3.00 8.00
GG05 Henrik Lundqvist 10.00 25.00
GG06 Mike Richter 4.00 10.00
GG07 Pelle Lindbergh 3.00 8.00
GG08 Vladimir Dzurilla 2.50 6.00
GG09 Jonathan Bernier 8.00 20.00
GG10 Rogie Vachon 5.00 12.00
GG11 Bill Ranford 4.00 10.00
GG12 Antero Niittymaki 3.00 8.00
GG13 Cristobal Huet 3.00 8.00
GG14 John Vanbiesbrouck 4.00 10.00
GG15 Vladislav Tretiak 3.00 8.00
GG16 Vladimir Myshkin 2.50 6.00
GG17 Ilya Bryzgalov 4.00 10.00
GG18 Al Montoya 4.00 10.00
GG19 Gerry Cheevers 4.00 10.00
GG20 Sergei Mylnikov 3.00 8.00
GG21 Patrick Roy 10.00 25.00
GG22 Miikka Kiprusoff 4.00 10.00

2006-07 ITG International Ice Greatest Moments

GM01 Russian Upset 2.50 6.00
GM02 Esposito's Speech 5.00 12.00
GM03 Cournoyer's Assist 3.00 8.00
GM04 Hull Gets His Chance 6.00 15.00
GM05 Sittler's Goal 4.00 10.00
GM06 Swapping Sweaters 6.00 15.00
GM07 1984 Comeback 6.00 15.00
GM08 Lemieux's Big Moment 12.00 30.00
GM09 American Victory 3.00 8.00
GM10 WJC Gold/Crosby 12.00 30.00

2006-07 ITG International Ice Hockey Passport

HP01 Jaromir Jagr 12.00 30.00
HP02 Vladislav Tretiak 3.00 8.00
HP03 Valeri Kharlamov 4.00 10.00
HP04 Bobby Hull 8.00 20.00
HP05 Martin Brodeur 10.00 25.00
HP06 Borje Salming 4.00 10.00
HP07 Jari Kurri 4.00 10.00
HP08 Mark Messier 8.00 20.00
HP09 Brett Hull 8.00 20.00
HP10 Mario Lemieux 15.00 40.00
HP11 Henrik Lundqvist 10.00 25.00
HP12 Sidney Crosby 15.00 40.00

2006-07 ITG International Ice International Rivals

IR01 T.Esposito/V.Tretiak 5.00 12.00
IR02 A.Maltsev/P.Esposito 8.00 20.00
IR03 F.Mahovlich/A.Yakushev 5.00 12.00
IR04 V.Kharlamov/G.Cheevers 5.00 12.00
IR05 D.Sittler/V.Dzurilla 6.00 15.00
IR06 P.Stastny/B.Hull 10.00 25.00
IR07 G.Fuhr/S.Mylnikov 8.00 20.00
IR08 R.Bourque/M.Naslund 8.00 20.00
IR09 M.Bossy/J.Kurri 5.00 12.00
IR10 G.LaFleur/B.Salming 6.00 15.00
IR11 V.Krutov/M.Lemieux 20.00 50.00
IR12 S.Yzerman/P.LaFontaine 12.00 30.00
IR13 M.Goulet/V.Myshkin 4.00 10.00
IR14 P.LaFontaine/B.Ranford 5.00 12.00
IR15 J.Jagr/I.Larionov 15.00 40.00
IR16 M.Messier/B.Hull 10.00 25.00
IR17 M.Brodeur/M.Richter 12.00 30.00
IR18 S.Crosby/A.Montoya 20.00 50.00
IR19 E.Malkin/J.Pogge 20.00 50.00
IR20 P.Coffey/C.Chelios 5.00 12.00

2006-07 ITG International Ice Jerseys

GUJ01 Brett Hull 6.00 15.00
GUJ02 Alexander Yakushev 2.50 6.00
GUJ03 Vladimir Krutov 2.00 5.00
GUJ04 Vladislav Tretiak 2.50 6.00
GUJ05 Valeri Kharlamov 3.00 8.00
GUJ06 Nicklas Lidstrom 3.00 8.00
GUJ07 Vladimir Myshkin 2.00 5.00
GUJ08 Michel Goulet 2.50 6.00
GUJ09 Jason Spezza 3.00 8.00
GUJ10 Jay Bouwmeester 2.00 5.00
GUJ11 John Tavares 12.00 30.00
GUJ12 Martin Brodeur 8.00 20.00
GUJ13 Sidney Crosby 12.00 30.00
GUJ14 Dale Hawerchuk 4.00 10.00
GUJ15 Steve Yzerman 8.00 20.00
GUJ16 Mike Bossy 3.00 8.00
GUJ17 Patrice Bergeron 4.00 10.00
GUJ18 Sergei Mylnikov 2.50 6.00
GUJ19 Mario Lemieux 12.00 30.00
GUJ20 Gilbert Perreault 3.00 8.00
GUJ21 Phil Esposito 5.00 12.00
GUJ22 Ilya Bryzgalov 3.00 8.00
GUJ23 Jaromir Jagr 10.00 25.00
GUJ24 Vladimir Dzurilla 2.00 5.00
GUJ25 Borje Salming 3.00 8.00
GUJ26 Mats Naslund 2.00 5.00
GUJ27 Brian Leetch 2.50 6.00
GUJ28 Pat LaFontaine 3.00 8.00
GUJ29 Jari Kurri 3.00 8.00
GUJ30 Peter Stastny 2.50 6.00
GUJ31 Danny Gare 2.00 5.00
GUJ33 Bobby Clarke 5.00 12.00
GUJ34 Marcel Dionne 4.00 10.00
GUJ35 Darryl Sittler 4.00 10.00
GUJ36 Eric Lindros 5.00 12.00
GUJ37 Boris Mikhailov 2.50 6.00
GUJ38 Patrick Roy 8.00 20.00
GUJ39 Chris Chelios 3.00 8.00
GUJ40 Ilya Kovalchuk 3.00 8.00

2006-07 ITG International Ice My Country My Team

MC1 Chris Chelios 5.00 12.00
MC2 Jaromir Jagr 15.00 40.00
MC3 Steve Yzerman 12.00 30.00
MC4 Brett Hull 10.00 25.00
MC5 Pat LaFontaine 5.00 12.00
MC7 Steve Shutt 5.00 12.00
MC8 Gilbert Perreault 5.00 12.00
MC9 Michel Goulet 4.00 10.00
MC10 Patrick Roy 12.00 30.00
MC11 Jason Spezza 5.00 12.00
MC12 Jay Bouwmeester 3.00 8.00
MC13 Mike Bossy 5.00 12.00
MC14 Phil Esposito 8.00 20.00
MC15 Mario Lemieux 20.00 50.00
MC16 Mats Naslund 3.00 8.00
MC17 Borje Salming 5.00 12.00
MC18 Jari Kurri 5.00 12.00
MC19 Dale Hawerchuk 6.00 15.00
MC20 Bobby Clarke 8.00 20.00
MC21 Eric Lindros 8.00 20.00
MC22 Ilya Bryzgalov 5.00 12.00
MC23 Marcel Dionne 6.00 15.00
MC24 Darryl Sittler 6.00 15.00
MC25 John Tavares 20.00 50.00
MC26 Martin Brodeur 12.00 30.00

2006-07 ITG International Ice Passing The Torch

PTT1 T.Esposito/G.Fuhr 8.00 20.00
PTT2 G.Fuhr/M.Brodeur 12.00 30.00
PTT3 M.Brodeur/J.Pogge 12.00 30.00
PTT4 M.Richter/A.Montoya 5.00 12.00
PTT5 S.Mylnikov/I.Bryzgalov 5.00 12.00
PTT6 M.Kiprusoff/A.Niittymaki 5.00 12.00
PTT7 V.Dzurilla/M.Schwarz 5.00 12.00
PTT8 V.Tretiak/V.Myshkin 4.00 10.00
PTT9 P.Esposito/M.Messier 10.00 25.00
PTT10 M.Lemieux/S.Crosby 20.00 50.00
PTT11 P.Statsny/J.Jagr 15.00 40.00
PTT12 V.Kharlamov/I.Kovalchuk 5.00 12.00
PTT13 A.Yakushev/E.Malkin 20.00 50.00
PTT14 B.Salming/N.Lidstrom 5.00 12.00
PTT15 I.Larionov/A.Ovechkin 20.00 50.00
PTT16 J.Jagr/M.Frolik 15.00 40.00

2006-07 ITG International Ice Stick and Jersey

SJ01 Mario Lemieux 20.00 50.00
SJ02 Mark Messier 10.00 25.00
SJ03 Raymond Bourque 8.00 20.00
SJ04 Steve Yzerman 12.00 30.00
SJ05 Brian Leetch 4.00 10.00
SJ06 Sidney Crosby 20.00 50.00
SJ07 Alexander Ovechkin 20.00 50.00
SJ08 Patrick Roy 12.00 30.00
SJ09 Henrik Lundqvist 12.00 30.00
SJ10 Eric Lindros 8.00 20.00
SJ11 Peter Stastny 4.00 10.00
SJ12 Mike Richter 5.00 12.00
SJ13 Bobby Clarke 8.00 20.00
SJ14 Phil Esposito 8.00 20.00
SJ15 Brett Hull 10.00 25.00
SJ16 Jaromir Jagr 15.00 40.00
SJ17 Jason Spezza 5.00 12.00
SJ18 Jari Kurri 5.00 12.00
SJ19 Martin Brodeur 12.00 30.00
SJ20 Guy Lafleur 6.00 15.00
SJ21 Gilbert Perreault 5.00 12.00
SJ22 Igor Larionov 5.00 12.00
SJ23 Vladimir Krutov 3.00 8.00
SJ24 Chris Chelios 5.00 12.00
SJ25 Henrik Zetterberg 6.00 15.00
SJ26 Nicklas Lidstrom 5.00 12.00
SJ27 Marcel Dionne 6.00 15.00
SJ28 Cristobal Huet 4.00 10.00

2006-07 ITG International Ice Teammates

IT01 P.Esposito/T.Esposito 8.00 20.00
IT02 M.Lemieux/M.Messier 20.00 50.00
IT03 D.Sittler/L.McDonald 6.00 15.00
IT04 M.Dionne/G.Perreault 6.00 15.00
IT05 M.Bossy/G.Lafleur 6.00 15.00
IT06 R.Bourque/R.Middleton 8.00 20.00
IT07 S.Yzerman/P.Coffey 12.00 30.00
IT08 E.Lindros/M.Messier 10.00 25.00
IT09 M.Lemieux/M.Brodeur 20.00 50.00
IT10 S.Crosby/D.Phaneuf 20.00 50.00
IT11 G.Cheevers/B.Hull 10.00 25.00
IT12 M.Richter/B.Leetch 5.00 12.00
IT13 B.Hull/C.Chelios 10.00 25.00
IT14 J.Vanbiesbrouck/P.LaFontaine 5.00 12.00
IT15 M.Naslund/B.Salming 5.00 12.00
IT16 N.Lidstrom/H.Lundqvist 12.00 30.00
IT17 I.Larionov/V.Krutov 5.00 12.00
IT18 V.Tretiak/A.Yakushev 4.00 10.00
IT19 V.Kharlamov/A.Maltsev 5.00 12.00
IT20 P.Stastny/V.Dzurilla 4.00 10.00
IT21 A.Ovechkin/E.Malkin 20.00 50.00
IT22 F.Mahovlich/P.Mahovlich 5.00 12.00

2014-15 ITG Leaf Metal

*BLUE: .6X TO 1.5X BASIC CARDS
HB1 Hanson Brothers 30.00 80.00
BAAB1 Anthony Beauvillier 3.00 8.00
BAAC1 Alexandre Carrier 3.00 8.00
BAAF1 Alex Forsberg 2.50 6.00
BAAM1 Adam Mascherin 3.00 8.00
BAAM2 Adam Musil 3.00 8.00
BAAP1 Andrew Picco 2.50 6.00
BABG2 Brendan Guhle 2.50 6.00
BABH3 Brett Howden 2.50 6.00
BABM1 Beck Malenstyn 2.50 6.00
BABM2 Brett McKenzie 3.00 8.00
BABS1 Blake Speers 3.00 8.00
BABS2 Brandon Saigeon 3.00 8.00
BACA1 Cameron Askew 3.00 8.00
BACH1 Connor Hobbs 2.50 6.00
BACI1 Connor Ingram 3.00 8.00
BACJ1 Cole Johnson 3.00 8.00
BACMD Connor McDavid 100.00 200.00
BACP1 Cliff Pu 2.50 6.00
BACR1 Chaz Reddekopp 2.50 6.00
BADK1 Davis Koch 5.00 12.00
BADS1 Daniel Sprong 6.00 15.00
BADS2 Dante Salituro 4.00 10.00
BADS3 Dylan Strome 8.00 20.00
BAEF1 Evan Fitzpatrick 5.00 12.00
BAES1 Evan Sarthou 2.50 6.00
BAES2 Evgeny Svechnikov 5.00 12.00
BAFA1 Frederic Allard 2.50 6.00
BAGE1 Giorgio Estephan 2.50 6.00
BAGG1 Gabriel Gagne 3.00 8.00
BAGG2 Glenn Gawdin 3.00 8.00
BAGK1 Graham Knott 3.00 8.00
BAIP1 Ivan Provorov 6.00 15.00
BAJA1 Jeremiah Addison 2.50 6.00
BAJA2 Jonathan Ang 3.00 8.00
BAJA3 Josh Anderson 4.00 10.00
BAJB3 Jason Bell 8.00 20.00
BAJC1 Jakob Chychrun 8.00 20.00
BAJG1 Julien Gauthier 2.50 6.00
BAJH1 Jansen Harkins 4.00 10.00
BAJH2 Jordan Hollett 5.00 12.00
BAJR1 Jeremy Roy 2.50 6.00
BAJW1 Jaeger White 2.50 6.00
BAJZ1 Jakub Zboril 3.00 8.00
BAKC1 Kale Clague 4.00 10.00
BAKC2 Kyle Capobianco 2.50 6.00
BAKE1 Kaden Elder 2.50 6.00
BAKM1 Kody McDonald 2.50 6.00
BAKT1 Keoni Texeira 2.50 6.00
BALB1 Logan Brown 3.00 8.00
BALC1 Lawson Crouse 4.00 10.00
BALG1 Luke Green 2.50 6.00
BALL1 Loik Leveille 2.50 6.00
BAMB1 Mackenzie Blackwood 5.00 12.00
BAMB2 Mathew Barzal 10.00 25.00
BAMF1 Maxime Fortier 2.50 6.00
BAMG1 Matteo Gennaro 2.50 6.00
BAMK1 Matthew Kreis 3.00 8.00
BAMM2 Medric Mercier 2.50 6.00
BAMM3 Michael McLeod 3.00 8.00
BAMM4 Mitchell Marner 15.00 40.00
BAMS1 Matt Spencer 5.00 12.00
BAMS2 Mitchell Stephens 2.50 6.00
BANK1 Nikita Korostelev 5.00 12.00
BANK2 Nolan Kneen 3.00 8.00
BANM1 Nick Merkley 6.00 15.00
BANM2 Nicolas Meloche 3.00 8.00
BANN1 Nathan Noel 2.50 6.00
BANP1 Nolan Patrick 6.00 15.00
BANR2 Nicolas Roy 4.00 10.00
BAPB1 Paul Bittner 5.00 12.00
BAPD1 Pierre-Luc Dubois 6.00 15.00
BAPK1 Pavel Karnaukhov 4.00 10.00
BAPL1 Pascal Laberge 4.00 10.00
BAPW1 Parker Wotherspoon 2.50 6.00
BAPZ1 Pavel Zacha 6.00 15.00
BAQB1 Quinn Benjafield 3.00 8.00
BARG2 Ryan Gropp 4.00 10.00
BARK2 Ryan Kubic 4.00 10.00
BARP1 Ryan Pilon 2.50 6.00
BASG1 Samuel Girard 3.00 8.00
BASS1 Simon Stransky 2.50 6.00
BASS2 Sam Steel 4.00 10.00
BATB1 Travis Barron 2.50 6.00
BATB2 Tyler Benson 8.00 20.00
BATK1 Tanner Kaspick 2.50 6.00
BATK2 Travis Konecny 8.00 20.00
BATM1 Timo Meier 8.00 20.00
BATR1 Ty Ronning 3.00 8.00
BATS1 Thomas Schemitsch 2.50 6.00
BATS2 Tyler Soy 2.50 6.00
BAVD1 Vince Dunn 4.00 10.00
BAWB1 Will Bitten 4.00 10.00

2014-15 ITG Leaf Metal Canadian Pride

CPBP1 Brad Park 5.00 12.00
CPEG1 Ed Giacomin 6.00 15.00
CPJB2 Johnny Bucyk 6.00 15.00
CPJS1 Joe Sakic 12.00 30.00
CPMAF Marc-Andre Fleury 12.00 30.00
CPPC1 Paul Coffey 6.00 15.00
CPPE1 Phil Esposito 10.00 25.00
CPRB1 Raymond Bourque 10.00 25.00
CPWC1 Wendel Clark 10.00 25.00

2014-15 ITG Leaf Metal ETA 2015 Die Cut

ETABM2 Brett McKenzie 4.00 10.00
ETACH1 Connor Hobbs 3.00 8.00
ETADS1 Daniel Sprong 8.00 20.00
ETADS3 Dylan Strome 10.00 25.00
ETAGG1 Gabriel Gagne 4.00 10.00
ETAGK1 Graham Knott 4.00 10.00
ETAJR1 Jeremy Roy 3.00 8.00
ETALC1 Lawson Crouse 5.00 12.00
ETAMB1 Mackenzie Blackwood 6.00 15.00
ETAMB2 Mathew Barzal 10.00 25.00
ETAMM4 Mitchell Marner 15.00 40.00
ETAMS1 Matt Spencer 6.00 15.00
ETANM1 Nick Merkley 8.00 20.00
ETANM2 Nicolas Meloche 4.00 10.00
ETANR2 Nicolas Roy 5.00 12.00
ETAPB1 Paul Bittner 6.00 15.00
ETARG2 Ryan Gropp 5.00 12.00
ETATK2 Travis Konecny 10.00 25.00
ETATS1 Thomas Schemitsch 3.00 8.00

2014-15 ITG Leaf Metal Heroes

MHAD1 Alex Delvecchio 10.00 25.00
MHBG1 Bill Gadsby 10.00 25.00
MHBH1 Bobby Hull 20.00 50.00
MHBH2 Brett Hull 20.00 50.00
MHBP1 Brad Park 8.00 20.00
MHBT1 Bryan Trottier 10.00 25.00
MHCC1 Chris Chelios 10.00 25.00
MHEG1 Ed Giacomin 10.00 25.00
MHGC1 Gerry Cheevers 10.00 25.00
MHGF1 Grant Fuhr 15.00 40.00
MHHH1 Harry Howell 8.00 20.00
MHHR1 Henri Richard 10.00 25.00
MHJB1 Johnny Bower 10.00 25.00
MHJB2 Johnny Bucyk 10.00 25.00
MHJJ1 Jaromir Jagr 30.00 80.00
MHJL1 Jacques Lemaire 8.00 20.00
MHJS1 Joe Sakic 20.00 50.00
MHML1 Mario Lemieux 40.00 100.00
MHMM1 Mike Modano 15.00 40.00
MHNU1 Norm Ullman 10.00 25.00
MHPC1 Paul Coffey 10.00 25.00
MHPE1 Phil Esposito 15.00 40.00
MHPR1 Patrick Roy 25.00 60.00
MHRB1 Raymond Bourque 15.00 40.00
MHRK1 Red Kelly 10.00 25.00
MHSS1 Serge Savard 10.00 25.00
MHSY1 Steve Yzerman 25.00 60.00
MHTL1 Ted Lindsay 10.00 25.00
MHVT1 Vladislav Tretiak 8.00 20.00
MHWC1 Wendel Clark 15.00 40.00
MHYC1 Yvan Cournoyer 10.00 25.00

2014-15 ITG Leaf Metal Star is Born Die Cut

SIBDS1 Daniel Sprong 8.00 20.00
SIBDS3 Dylan Strome 10.00 25.00
SIBJR1 Jeremy Roy 3.00 8.00
SIBLC1 Lawson Crouse 5.00 12.00
SIBMB2 Mathew Barzal 10.00 25.00
SIBMM4 Mitchell Marner 15.00 40.00
SIBMS1 Matt Spencer 6.00 15.00
SIBNR2 Nicolas Roy 5.00 12.00
SIBTK2 Travis Konecny 10.00 25.00

2014-15 ITG Leaf Metal Team Effort Dual

TE1 M.Blackwood/M.Kreis 6.00 15.00
TE2 K.Clague/R.Pilon 5.00 12.00
TE3 J.Bell/P.L.Dubois 10.00 25.00
TE4 C.Reddekopp/T.Soy 3.00 8.00
TE5 P.Wotherspoon/E.Sarthou 3.00 8.00
TE6 G.Gawdin/C.Johnson 4.00 10.00
TE7 A.Beauvillier/S.Girard 4.00 10.00
TE8 B.Speers/M.Mercier 4.00 10.00
TE9 J.Chychrun/N.Korostelev 10.00 25.00
TE10 L.Green/N.Noel 3.00 8.00
TE11 J.Addison/M.Stephens 3.00 8.00
TE12 J.Hollett/S.Steel 6.00 15.00
TE13 J.Harkins/A.Forsberg 5.00 12.00
TE14 K.McDonald/J.Anderson 5.00 12.00
TE16 D.Salituro/T.Barron 5.00 12.00
TE18 G.Estephan/J.White 3.00 8.00
TE19 M.Fortier/T.Meier 10.00 25.00
TE20 A.Carrier/P.Laberge 4.00 10.00
TE21 N.Kneen/Q.Benjafield 4.00 10.00
TE22 L.Leveille/E.Svechnikov 6.00 15.00

2015-16 Leaf Metal

BAAC1 Alexander Chmelevski 5.00 12.00
BAAD1 Alex DeBrincat 6.00 15.00
BAAD2 Arnaud Durandeau 4.00 10.00
BAAM1 Antoine Morand 4.00 10.00
BAAN1 Alexander Nylander 10.00 25.00
BAAP1 Austin Pratt 4.00 10.00
BAAR1 Anthony Richard 5.00 12.00
BABC1 Brett Crossley 4.00 10.00
BABD1 Brett Davis 6.00 15.00
BABG1 Brady Gilmour 6.00 15.00
BABH1 Brett Howden 4.00 10.00
BABJ1 Ben Jones 4.00 10.00
BABM1 Beck Malenstyn 6.00 15.00
BACB1 Connor Bunnaman 4.00 10.00
BACG1 Conor Garland 4.00 10.00
BACH1 Carter Hart 10.00 25.00
BACP1 Christopher Paquette 4.00 10.00
BADB1 Dereck Baribeau 4.00 10.00
BADD1 Dillon Dube 6.00 15.00
BADL1 David Levin 6.00 15.00
BADS1 Dmitry Sokolov 6.00 15.00
BADS2 Dylan Sadowy 6.00 15.00
BADT1 Dmytro Timashov 6.00 15.00
BADW1 Dylan Wells 4.00 10.00
BADZ1 Dmitry Zhukenov 4.00 10.00
BAEB1 Egor Babenko 4.00 10.00
BAEC2 Evan Cormier 5.00 12.00
BAGS1 Gabriel Sylvestre 4.00 10.00
BAGS2 Givani Smith 4.00 10.00
BAGV1 Gabriel Vilardi 6.00 15.00
BAHD1 Hayden Davis 4.00 10.00
BAJA1 Josh Anderson 12.00 30.00
BAJB1 Jake Bean 6.00 15.00
BAJB2 Jordy Bellerive 4.00 10.00
BAJC1 Jakob Chychrun 8.00 20.00
BAJD1 Jared Dmytriw 4.00 10.00
BAJD2 Jeff De Wit 4.00 10.00
BAJE1 Jack Eichel 25.00 60.00
BAJG1 Julien Gauthier 8.00 20.00
BAJK1 Jordan Kyrou 6.00 15.00
BAJK2 Jake Kryski 4.00 10.00
BAJM1 Josh Mahura 4.00 10.00
BAJP1 Jesse Puljujarvi 12.00 30.00
BAJV1 Joe Veleno 6.00 15.00
BAJV2 Juuso Valimaki 4.00 10.00
BAJW1 Jaeger White 4.00 10.00
BAKA1 Kristian Afanasyev 4.00 10.00
BAKC1 Kale Clague 6.00 15.00
BAKM1 Keaton Middleton 4.00 10.00
BALB1 Logan Brown 10.00 25.00
BALC1 Louis-Filip Cote 4.00 10.00
BALJ1 Lucas Johansen 4.00 10.00
BALM1 Liam Murphy 4.00 10.00
BALT1 Lucas Thierus 4.00 10.00
BAMB1 Mitchell Balmas 4.00 10.00
BAMC1 Maxime Comtois 8.00 20.00
BAMD1 Martins Dzierkals 4.00 10.00
BAMJ1 Max Jones 6.00 15.00
BAML1 Max Lajoie 6.00 15.00
BAMM1 Michael McLeod 6.00 15.00
BAMS1 Mikhail Sergachev 8.00 20.00
BAMS2 Mathieu Sevigny 4.00 10.00
BAMS3 Michael Spacek 4.00 10.00
BAMT1 Matthew Tkachuk 20.00 50.00
BANB1 Nathan Bastien 4.00 10.00
BANC1 Noah Carroll 4.00 10.00
BANK1 Nolan Kneen 4.00 10.00
BANP1 Nolan Patrick 12.00 30.00
BANV1 Nolan Volcan 4.00 10.00
BAOT1 Owen Tippett 4.00 10.00
BAPB1 Patrick Bajkov 4.00 10.00
BAPD1 Pierre-Luc Dubois 10.00 25.00
BAPH1 Peyton Hoyt 4.00 10.00
BAPL1 Pascal Laberge 5.00 12.00
BARB1 Radovan Bondra 4.00 10.00
BARK1 Ryan Kubic 4.00 10.00
BASB1 Shawn Boudrias 4.00 10.00
BASG1 Samuel Girard 5.00 12.00
BASM1 Stelio Mattheos 6.00 15.00
BASS1 Stuart Skinner 8.00 20.00
BASS2 Sam Steel 8.00 20.00
BASS3 Simon Stransky 6.00 15.00
BATB1 Travis Barron 4.00 10.00
BATB2 Tyler Benson 8.00 20.00
BATF1 Tye Felhaber 4.00 10.00
BATK1 Tanner Kaspick 4.00 10.00
BATP1 Tyler Parsons 4.00 10.00
BATR1 Taylor Raddysh 6.00 15.00
BATR2 Ty Ronning 4.00 10.00
BATT1 Troy Timpano 4.00 10.00
BAVA1 Vitalii Abramov 8.00 20.00
BAVK1 Vladimir Kuznetsov 4.00 10.00
BAVM1 Victor Mete 5.00 12.00
BAVS1 Vili Saarijarvi 4.00 10.00
BAWB1 Will Bitten 4.00 10.00
BAZG1 Zach Gallant 4.00 10.00
BAZS1 Zachary Senyshyn 4.00 10.00
BAZS2 Zach Sawchenko 4.00 10.00

2015-16 Leaf Metal ETA The Show

TSAD1 Alex DeBrincat 8.00 20.00
TSGV1 Gabriel Vilardi 8.00 20.00
TSJC1 Jakob Chychrun 10.00 25.00
TSJP1 Jesse Puljujarvi 15.00 40.00
TSJV1 Juuso Valimaki 5.00 12.00
TSJV2 Joe Veleno 8.00 20.00
TSKT1 Matthew Tkachuk 25.00 60.00
TSKY1 Brady Gilmour 8.00 20.00
TSLB1 Logan Brown 12.00 30.00
TSMM1 Michael McLeod 8.00 20.00
TSMS1 Mikhail Sergachev 10.00 25.00
TSNP1 Nolan Patrick 15.00 40.00
TSOT1 Owen Tippett 5.00 12.00
TSPD1 Pierre-Luc Dubois 12.00 30.00
TSTB1 Tyler Benson 10.00 25.00
TSVA1 Vitalii Abramov 10.00 25.00

2015-16 Leaf Metal Immortals

MIBS1 Borje Salming 8.00 20.00
MIDM1 Dickie Moore 6.00 15.00
MIEF1 Emile Francis 6.00 15.00
MIGF1 Grant Fuhr 12.00 30.00
MIGH1 Glenn Hall 8.00 20.00
MIJB1 Johnny Bower 8.00 20.00
MIMB1 Martin Brodeur 25.00 60.00
MIMS1 Milt Schmidt 8.00 20.00
MIPH1 Phil Housley 6.00 15.00
MIPR1 Patrick Roy 25.00 60.00

2015-16 Leaf Metal Light the Lamp

LTLAD1 Alex DeBrincat 8.00 20.00
LTLAN1 Alexander Nylander 12.00 30.00
LTLJE1 Jack Eichel 30.00 80.00
LTLJG1 Julien Gauthier 10.00 25.00
LTLJP1 Jesse Puljujarvi 15.00 40.00
LTLNP1 Nolan Patrick 15.00 40.00

2015-16 Leaf Metal Pride of a Nation

PNBS1 Borje Salming 8.00 20.00
PNEL1 Eric Lindros 12.00 30.00
PNGL1 Guy Lafleur 10.00 25.00
PNIL1 Igor Larionov 8.00 20.00
PNJE1 Jack Eichel 30.00 80.00
PNJP1 Jesse Puljujarvi 15.00 40.00
PNJV1 Joe Veleno 8.00 20.00
PNMB1 Martin Brodeur 20.00 50.00
PNME1 Mike Eruzione 6.00 15.00
PNOK1 Olaf Kolzig 8.00 20.00
PNPB1 Pavel Bure 8.00 20.00
PNPH1 Paul Henderson 8.00 20.00
PNPS1 Peter Stastny 6.00 15.00
PNTB1 Tom Barrasso 8.00 20.00
PNTS1 Teemu Selanne 15.00 40.00
PNVT1 Vladislav Tretiak 6.00 15.00

2015-16 Leaf Metal Team Miracle

TMBS1 Buzz Schneider 15.00 40.00
TMCP1 Craig Patrick 15.00 40.00
TMDC1 Dave Christian 12.00 30.00
TMDS1 Dave Silk 15.00 40.00
TMES1 Eric Strobel 25.00 60.00
TMJC1 Jim Craig 25.00 60.00
TMJH1 John Harrington 20.00 50.00
TMJO1 Jack Oâ•™Callahan 20.00 50.00
TMKM1 Ken Morrow 12.00 30.00
TMME1 Mike Eruzione 15.00 40.00
TMMJ1 Mark Johnson 15.00 40.00
TMMR1 Mike Ramsey 20.00 50.00
TMMW1 Mark Wells 15.00 40.00
TMNB1 Neal Broten 15.00 40.00
TMPV1 Phil Verchota 20.00 50.00
TMRM1 Rob McClanahan 15.00 40.00
TMSJ1 Steve Janaszak 20.00 50.00

2015-16 Leaf Metal The Naturals

TNAD1 Alex DeBrincat 8.00 20.00
TNAN1 Alexander Nylander 12.00 30.00
TNBG1 Brady Gilmour 8.00 20.00
TNDL1 David Levin 8.00 20.00
TNEB1 Egor Babenko 5.00 12.00
TNGV1 Gabriel Vilardi 8.00 20.00
TNJB1 Jake Bean 8.00 20.00
TNJC1 Jakob Chychrun 10.00 25.00
TNJE1 Jack Eichel 30.00 80.00
TNJP1 Jesse Puljujarvi 15.00 40.00
TNJV1 Joe Veleno 8.00 20.00
TNMC1 Maxime Comtois 10.00 25.00
TNMJ1 Max Jones 8.00 20.00
TNMT1 Matthew Tkachuk 25.00 60.00
TNNP1 Nolan Patrick 15.00 40.00
TNSM1 Stelio Mattheos 8.00 20.00

2016-17 Leaf Metal

BAAD1 Alex DeBrincat 8.00 20.00
BAAD2 Arnaud Durandeau 4.00 10.00
BAAH1 Aleksi Heponiemi 6.00 15.00
BAAM1 Adam McMaster 5.00 12.00
BAAM2 Anderson MacDonald 4.00 10.00
BAAM3 Antoine Morand 4.00 10.00
BAAP1 Austin Pratt 4.00 10.00
BAAR1 Adam Ruzicka 6.00 15.00
BABC1 Brett Crossley 5.00 12.00
BABD2 Brett Davis 4.00 10.00
BABG1 Benoit-Olivier Groulx 4.00 10.00
BABG2 Brady Gilmour 4.00 10.00
BABH1 Brett Howden 2.50 6.00
BABJ1 Ben Jones 4.00 10.00
BABK1 Boris Katchouk 8.00 20.00
BACF1 Cal Foote 8.00 20.00
BACG1 Cody Glass 6.00 15.00
BACH1 Cameron Hebig 4.00 10.00
BACH2 Carter Hart 6.00 15.00
BACP1 Christopher Paquette 4.00 10.00
BACR1 Connor Roberts 6.00 15.00
BADA1 Danil Antropov 6.00 15.00
BADB1 Dennis Busby 6.00 15.00
BADB2 Dereck Baribeau 4.00 10.00
BADD1 Dillon Dube 4.00 10.00
BADG1 Damien Giroux 4.00 10.00
BADS1 Dmitry Sokolov 10.00 25.00
BADS3 Dylan Strome 10.00 25.00
BADV1 Daniil Vertiy 8.00 20.00
BADW1 Dylan Wells 4.00 10.00
BADZ1 Dmitry Zhukenov 4.00 10.00
BAEB1 Egor Babenko 4.00 10.00
BAGF1 Gabriel Fortier 8.00 20.00
BAGS1 Gabriel Sylvestre 4.00 10.00
BAGV1 Gabriel Vilardi 4.00 10.00
BAIL1 Ivan Lodnia 10.00 25.00
BAIS1 Ian Scott 8.00 20.00
BAJAD Jaret Anderson-Dolan 8.00 20.00
BAJB1 Jordy Bellerive 4.00 10.00
BAJE1 Jack Eichel 6.00 15.00
BAJE2 Jack Eichel 6.00 15.00
BAJE3 Jack Eichel 6.00 15.00
BAJK1 Jake Kryski 3.00 8.00
BAJL1 Jake Leschyshyn 4.00 10.00
BAJP1 Jacob Paquette 4.00 10.00
BAJR1 Jason Robertson 12.00 30.00
BAJV1 Joe Veleno 12.00 30.00
BAJV2 Joe Veleno 12.00 30.00
BAJV3 Juuso Valimaki 4.00 10.00
BAKK1 Klim Kostin 8.00 20.00
BAKM1 Keaton Middleton 4.00 10.00
BAKV1 Kristian Vesalainen 10.00 25.00
BAKY1 Kailer Yamamoto 6.00 15.00
BAKY2 Keanu Yamamoto 8.00 20.00
BALC1 Louis-Filip Cote 4.00 10.00
BAMB1 Matt Barberis 4.00 10.00
BAMC1 Maxime Comtois 5.00 12.00
BAMD1 Michael DiPietro 8.00 20.00
BAMM1 Michael McLeod 4.00 10.00
BAMR1 Michael Rasmussen 8.00 20.00
BAMS1 Matthew Strome 4.00 10.00
BANC1 Noah Carroll 4.00 10.00
BAND1 Nathan Dunkley 5.00 12.00
BANH1 Nico Hischier 30.00 80.00
BANH2 Nicolas Hague 3.00 8.00
BANH3 Nick Henry 4.00 10.00
BANJ1 Noah Juulsen 4.00 10.00
BANK1 Nolan Kneen 4.00 10.00
BANM1 Nick Merkley 8.00 20.00
BANP1 Nikita Popugaev 4.00 10.00
BANP2 Nolan Patrick 25.00 60.00
BANP4 Nolan Patrick 25.00 60.00
BANS1 Nick Suzuki 8.00 20.00
BAOR1 Olivier Rodrigue 4.00 10.00
BAOT1 Owen Tippett 4.00 10.00
BAPH1 Peyton Hoyt 4.00 10.00
BARK1 Ryan Kubic 4.00 10.00
BARM1 Ryan McLeod 4.00 10.00
BARM2 Ryan Merkley 8.00 20.00
BASB1 Shawn Boudrias 4.00 10.00
BASE1 Shawn Element 4.00 10.00
BASM1 Stelio Mattheos 4.00 10.00
BASS1 Stuart Skinner 5.00 12.00
BATD1 Ty Dellandrea 4.00 10.00
BATS1 Ty Smith 6.00 15.00
BAVK1 Vladimir Kuznetsov 4.00 10.00
BAZG1 Zach Gallant 4.00 10.00

2016-17 Leaf Metal Draft Class

DCBG1 Benoit-Olivier Groulx 5.00 12.00
DCCG1 Cody Glass 8.00 20.00
DCDB1 Dennis Busby 8.00 20.00
DCGV1 Gabriel Vilardi 5.00 12.00
DCJR1 Jason Robertson 15.00 40.00
DCJV1 Joe Veleno 15.00 40.00
DCMC2 Maxime Comtois 6.00 15.00
DCNH1 Nico Hischier 20.00 50.00
DCNP2 Nolan Patrick 30.00 80.00
DCRM1 Ryan Merkley 10.00 25.00

2016-17 Leaf Metal National Pride

NPAK1 Alexei Kasatonov 6.00 15.00
NPAO1 Adam Oates 6.00 15.00
NPCC2 Chris Chelios 6.00 15.00
NPGF1 Grant Fuhr 10.00 25.00
NPJE1 Jack Eichel 10.00 25.00
NPJLC John LeClair 6.00 15.00
NPJR3 Jeremy Roenick 10.00 25.00
NPMN1 Mats Naslund 4.00 10.00
NPNL1 Nicklas Lidstrom 6.00 15.00
NPNP3 Nolan Patrick 40.00 100.00

2016-17 Leaf Metal Vision Quest

VQAM1 Antoine Morand 5.00 12.00
VQCF1 Cal Foote 10.00 25.00
VQGV2 Gabriel Vilardi 5.00 12.00
VQJE2 Jack Eichel 8.00 20.00
VQJL1 Jake Leschyshyn 5.00 12.00
VQJV2 Joe Veleno 15.00 40.00
VQJV3 Juuso Valimaki 5.00 12.00
VQKK1 Klim Kostin 10.00 25.00
VQKY1 Kailer Yamamoto 8.00 20.00
VQMC1 Maxime Comtois 6.00 15.00
VQMR1 Michael Rasmussen 10.00 25.00
VQMS1 Matthew Strome 5.00 12.00
VQNP4 Nolan Patrick 30.00 80.00
VQOT1 Owen Tippett 5.00 12.00
VQRB1 Radovan Bondra 5.00 12.00
VQSS1 Stuart Skinner 6.00 15.00

2016-17 Leaf Metal Winters Future

WFAM2 Antoine Morand 5.00 12.00
WFCF2 Cal Foote 10.00 25.00
WFCG2 Cody Glass 8.00 20.00
WFDV1 Daniil Vertiy 10.00 25.00
WFIL1 Ivan Lodnia 12.00 30.00
WFIS1 Ian Scott 10.00 25.00
WFJE3 Jack Eichel 8.00 20.00
WFJR2 Jason Robertson 15.00 40.00
WFJV4 Joe Veleno 15.00 40.00
WFKK2 Klim Kostin 10.00 25.00
WFKV1 Kristian Vesalainen 12.00 30.00
WFKY2 Kailer Yamamoto 8.00 20.00
WFMR2 Michael Rasmussen 10.00 25.00
WFMS2 Matthew Strome 5.00 12.00
WFNH2 Nico Hischier 20.00 50.00
WFNP1 Nikita Popugaev 5.00 12.00
WFNP5 Nolan Patrick 30.00 80.00
WFNS1 Nick Suzuki 10.00 25.00
WFOT2 Owen Tippett 5.00 12.00
WFRM1 Ryan McLeod 5.00 12.00
WFSS2 Stuart Skinner 6.00 15.00

2013-14 ITG Lord Stanley's Mug

COMPLETE SET (100) 75.00 150.00
1 Sid Abel 1.25 3.00
2 Glenn Anderson 1.25 3.00
3 Syl Apps 1.25 3.00
4 Bill Barber 1.50 4.00
5 Bill Barilko 1.25 3.00
6 Tom Barrasso 1.50 4.00
7 Bob Baun 1.50 4.00
8 Ed Belfour 1.50 4.00
9 Jean Beliveau 2.50 6.00
10 Clint Benedict 1.25 3.00
11 Toe Blake 1.00 2.50
12 Mike Bossy 1.50 4.00
13 Frank Boucher 1.00 2.50
14 Raymond Bourque 2.50 6.00
15 Johnny Bower 1.50 4.00
16 Frank Brimsek 1.25 3.00
17 Turk Broda 1.50 4.00
18 Guy Carbonneau 1.50 4.00
19 Gerry Cheevers 1.50 4.00
20 Chris Chelios 1.50 4.00
21 King Clancy 1.25 3.00
22 Dit Clapper 1.00 2.50
23 Bobby Clarke 2.50 6.00
24 Paul Coffey 1.50 4.00
25 Charlie Conacher 1.25 3.00
26 Yvan Cournoyer 1.50 4.00
27 Corey Crawford 2.00 5.00
28 Alex Delvecchio 1.50 4.00
29 Cy Denneny 1.00 2.50
30 Bill Durnan 1.50 4.00
31 Phil Esposito 2.50 6.00
32 Peter Forsberg 3.00 8.00
33 Grant Fuhr 2.50 6.00
34 Charlie Gardiner 1.25 3.00
35 Bernie Geoffrion 1.25 3.00
36 Glenn Hall 1.50 4.00
37 Doug Harvey 1.25 3.00
38 Dominik Hasek 2.50 6.00
39 Tim Horton 1.50 4.00
40 Gordie Howe 5.00 12.00
41 Bobby Hull 3.00 8.00
42 Brett Hull 3.00 8.00
43 Jaromir Jagr 3.00 8.00
44 Aurel Joliat 1.50 4.00
45 Red Kelly 1.50 4.00
46 Ted Kennedy 1.50 4.00
47 Dave Keon 1.50 4.00
48 Jari Kurri 1.50 4.00
49 Elmer Lach 1.25 3.00
50 Guy Lafleur 2.00 5.00
51 Newsy Lalonde 1.25 3.00
52 Guy Lapointe 1.25 3.00
53 Igor Larionov 1.50 4.00
54 Jacques Lemaire 1.25 3.00
55 Mario Lemieux 6.00 15.00
56 Nicklas Lidstrom 2.00 5.00
57 Ted Lindsay 1.50 4.00
58 Al MacInnis 2.00 5.00
59 Rick MacLeish 1.25 3.00
60 Frank Mahovlich 1.50 4.00
61 Lanny McDonald 1.50 4.00
62 Howie Meeker 1.50 4.00
63 Mark Messier 3.00 8.00
64 Stan Mikita 2.00 5.00
65 Mike Modano 2.50 6.00
66 Dickie Moore 1.25 3.00
67 Howie Morenz 1.25 3.00
68 Antti Niemi 1.25 3.00
69 Joe Nieuwendyk 1.25 3.00
70 Frank Nighbor 1.25 3.00
71 Bob Nystrom 1.00 2.50
72 Chris Osgood 1.50 4.00
73 Bernie Parent 2.00 5.00
74 Lester Patrick 1.50 4.00
75 Jacques Plante 2.00 5.00
76 Denis Potvin 1.50 4.00
77 Mark Recchi 2.00 5.00
78 Henri Richard 1.50 4.00
79 Maurice Richard 3.00 8.00
80 Larry Robinson 1.50 4.00
81 Art Ross 1.00 2.50
82 Patrick Roy 5.00 12.00
83 Joe Sakic 3.00 8.00
84 Serge Savard 1.50 4.00
85 Terry Sawchuk 1.50 4.00
86 Milt Schmidt 1.25 3.00
87 Dave Schultz 1.50 4.00
88 Teemu Selanne 2.50 6.00
89 Eddie Shore 1.25 3.00
90 Billy Smith 1.50 4.00
91 Martin St. Louis 1.50 4.00
92 Nels Stewart 1.00 2.50
93 Cyclone Taylor 1.50 4.00
94 Tiny Thompson 1.50 4.00
95 J.C. Tremblay 1.00 2.50
96 Bryan Trottier 1.50 4.00
97 Rogie Vachon 2.00 5.00
98 Georges Vezina 1.50 4.00
99 Gump Worsley 1.50 4.00
100 Steve Yzerman 4.00 10.00

2013-14 ITG Lord Stanley's Mug Autographs

AAM Al MacInnis 10.00 25.00
ABH Bobby Hull 15.00 30.00
AMF Marc-Andre Fleury 15.00 40.00
ARL Reggie Leach 6.00 15.00
ASM Stan Mikita 12.00 30.00
AAD1 Alex Delvecchio 10.00 25.00
AAD2 Alex Delvecchio 10.00 25.00
AAD3 Alex Delvecchio 10.00 25.00
ABB1 Bob Baun 8.00 20.00
ABB2 Bob Baun 8.00 20.00
ABB3 Bob Baun 8.00 20.00
ABB4 Bob Baun 8.00 20.00
ABBA1 Bill Barber 8.00 20.00
ABBA2 Bill Barber 8.00 20.00
ABC1 Bobby Clarke 12.00 30.00
ABC2 Bobby Clarke 12.00 30.00
ABN1 Bob Nystrom 6.00 15.00
ABN2 Bob Nystrom 6.00 15.00
ABN3 Bob Nystrom 6.00 15.00
ABN4 Bob Nystrom 6.00 15.00
ABP1 Bernie Parent 10.00 25.00
ABP2 Bernie Parent 10.00 25.00
ABS1 Billy Smith 8.00 20.00
ABS2 Billy Smith 8.00 20.00
ABS3 Billy Smith 8.00 20.00
ABS4 Billy Smith 8.00 20.00
ABT1 Bryan Trottier 8.00 20.00
ABT2 Bryan Trottier 8.00 20.00
ABT3 Bryan Trottier 8.00 20.00
ABT4 Bryan Trottier 8.00 20.00
ABT5 Bryan Trottier 8.00 20.00
ABT6 Bryan Trottier 8.00 20.00
ACC1 Chris Chelios 10.00 25.00
ACC2 Chris Chelios 10.00 25.00
ACC3 Chris Chelios 10.00 25.00
ACCR Corey Crawford 10.00 25.00
ACH1 Charlie Hodge 10.00 25.00
ACH2 Charlie Hodge 10.00 25.00
ACH3 Charlie Hodge 10.00 25.00
ACH4 Charlie Hodge 10.00 25.00
ACH5 Charlie Hodge 10.00 25.00
ACH6 Charlie Hodge 10.00 25.00
ACO1 Chris Osgood 8.00 20.00
ACO2 Chris Osgood 8.00 20.00
ACO3 Chris Osgood 8.00 20.00
ADD1 Dick Duff 8.00 20.00
ADD2 Dick Duff 8.00 20.00
ADD3 Dick Duff 8.00 20.00
ADD4 Dick Duff 8.00 20.00
ADD5 Dick Duff 8.00 20.00
ADD6 Dick Duff 8.00 20.00
ADH1 Dominik Hasek 20.00 50.00
ADH2 Dominik Hasek 20.00 50.00
ADK1 Dave Keon 12.00 30.00
ADK2 Dave Keon 12.00 30.00
ADK3 Dave Keon 12.00 30.00
ADK4 Dave Keon 12.00 30.00
ADM1 Dickie Moore 6.00 15.00
ADM2 Dickie Moore 6.00 15.00
ADM3 Dickie Moore 6.00 15.00
ADM4 Dickie Moore 6.00 15.00
ADM5 Dickie Moore 6.00 15.00
ADM6 Dickie Moore 6.00 15.00
ADMC1 Darren McCarty 6.00 15.00
ADMC2 Darren McCarty 6.00 15.00
ADMC3 Darren McCarty 6.00 15.00
ADMC4 Darren McCarty 6.00 15.00
ADP1 Denis Potvin 8.00 20.00
ADP2 Denis Potvin 8.00 20.00
ADP3 Denis Potvin 8.00 20.00
ADP4 Denis Potvin 8.00 20.00
ADS1 Dave Schultz 8.00 20.00
ADS2 Dave Schultz 8.00 20.00
ADSA1 Derek Sanderson 8.00 20.00
ADSA2 Derek Sanderson 8.00 20.00
AEL1 Elmer Lach 12.00 30.00
AEL2 Elmer Lach 12.00 30.00
AEL3 Elmer Lach 12.00 30.00
AFM1 Frank Mahovlich 12.00 30.00
AFM2 Frank Mahovlich 12.00 30.00
AFM3 Frank Mahovlich 12.00 30.00
AFM4 Frank Mahovlich 12.00 30.00
AFM5 Frank Mahovlich 12.00 30.00
AFM6 Frank Mahovlich 12.00 30.00
AGA1 Glenn Anderson 6.00 15.00
AGA2 Glenn Anderson 6.00 15.00
AGA3 Glenn Anderson 6.00 15.00
AGA4 Glenn Anderson 6.00 15.00
AGA5 Glenn Anderson 6.00 15.00
AGA6 Glenn Anderson 6.00 15.00
AGC1 Gerry Cheevers 10.00 25.00
AGC2 Gerry Cheevers 10.00 25.00
AGCA1 Guy Carbonneau 8.00 20.00
AGCA2 Guy Carbonneau 8.00 20.00
AGCA3 Guy Carbonneau 8.00 20.00
AGF1 Grant Fuhr 12.00 30.00
AGF2 Grant Fuhr 12.00 30.00
AGF3 Grant Fuhr 12.00 30.00
AGF4 Grant Fuhr 12.00 30.00
AGF5 Grant Fuhr 12.00 30.00
AGH1 Gordie Howe 50.00 120.00
AGH2 Gordie Howe 50.00 120.00
AGH3 Gordie Howe 50.00 120.00
AGH4 Gordie Howe 50.00 120.00
AGHA Glenn Hall 10.00 25.00
AGL1 Guy Lafleur 10.00 25.00
AGL2 Guy Lafleur 10.00 25.00
AGL3 Guy Lafleur 10.00 25.00
AGL4 Guy Lafleur 10.00 25.00
AGL5 Guy Lafleur 10.00 25.00
AGLA1 Guy Lapointe 6.00 15.00
AGLA2 Guy Lapointe 6.00 15.00
AGLA3 Guy Lapointe 6.00 15.00
AGLA4 Guy Lapointe 6.00 15.00
AGLA5 Guy Lapointe 6.00 15.00
AGLA6 Guy Lapointe 6.00 15.00
AHM1 Howie Meeker 6.00 15.00
AHM2 Howie Meeker 6.00 15.00
AHM3 Howie Meeker 6.00 15.00
AHM4 Howie Meeker 6.00 15.00
AHR1 Henri Richard 12.00 30.00
AHR2 Henri Richard 12.00 30.00
AHR3 Henri Richard 12.00 30.00
AHR4 Henri Richard 12.00 30.00
AHR5 Henri Richard 12.00 30.00
AHR6 Henri Richard 12.00 30.00
AHR7 Henri Richard 12.00 30.00
AHR8 Henri Richard 12.00 30.00
AHR9 Henri Richard 12.00 30.00
AHR10 Henri Richard 12.00 30.00
AHR11 Henri Richard 12.00 30.00
AIL1 Igor Larionov 8.00 20.00
AIL2 Igor Larionov 8.00 20.00
AIL3 Igor Larionov 8.00 20.00
AJB1 Jean Beliveau 30.00 80.00
AJB2 Jean Beliveau 30.00 80.00
AJB3 Jean Beliveau 30.00 80.00
AJB4 Jean Beliveau 30.00 80.00
AJB5 Jean Beliveau 30.00 80.00
AJB6 Jean Beliveau 30.00 80.00
AJB7 Jean Beliveau 30.00 80.00
AJB8 Jean Beliveau 30.00 80.00
AJB9 Jean Beliveau 30.00 80.00
AJB10 Jean Beliveau 30.00 80.00
AJBO1 Johnny Bower 8.00 20.00
AJBO2 Johnny Bower 8.00 20.00
AJBO3 Johnny Bower 8.00 20.00
AJBO4 Johnny Bower 8.00 20.00
AJBU1 Johnny Bucyk 8.00 20.00
AJBU2 Johnny Bucyk 8.00 20.00
AJJ1 Jaromir Jagr 30.00 80.00
AJJ2 Jaromir Jagr 30.00 80.00
AJK1 Jari Kurri 8.00 20.00
AJK2 Jari Kurri 8.00 20.00
AJK3 Jari Kurri 8.00 20.00
AJK4 Jari Kurri 8.00 20.00
AJK5 Jari Kurri 8.00 20.00
AJKO1 Joe Kocur 6.00 15.00
AJKO2 Joe Kocur 6.00 15.00
AJKO3 Joe Kocur 6.00 15.00
AJL1 Jacques Lemaire 6.00 15.00
AJL2 Jacques Lemaire 6.00 15.00
AJL3 Jacques Lemaire 6.00 15.00
AJL4 Jacques Lemaire 6.00 15.00
AJL5 Jacques Lemaire 6.00 15.00
AJL6 Jacques Lemaire 6.00 15.00
AJL7 Jacques Lemaire 6.00 15.00
AJL8 Jacques Lemaire 6.00 15.00
AJLA1 Jacques Laperriere 6.00 15.00
AJLA2 Jacques Laperriere 6.00 15.00
AJLA3 Jacques Laperriere 6.00 15.00
AJLA4 Jacques Laperriere 6.00 15.00
AJLA5 Jacques Laperriere 6.00 15.00
AJLA6 Jacques Laperriere 6.00 15.00
AJN1 Joe Nieuwendyk 6.00 15.00
AJN2 Joe Nieuwendyk 6.00 15.00
AJN3 Joe Nieuwendyk 6.00 15.00
AJS1 Joe Sakic 15.00 40.00
AJS2 Joe Sakic 15.00 40.00
AJW1 Joe Watson 5.00 12.00
AJW1 Joe Watson 5.00 12.00
AJW2 Joe Watson 5.00 12.00
AJWA1 Jim Watson 6.00 15.00
AJWA2 Jim Watson 6.00 15.00
ALM1 Larry Murphy 6.00 15.00
ALM2 Larry Murphy 6.00 15.00
ALM3 Larry Murphy 6.00 15.00
ALM4 Larry Murphy 6.00 15.00
ALMC Lanny McDonald 8.00 20.00
ALRO1 Larry Robinson 8.00 20.00
ALRO2 Larry Robinson 8.00 20.00
ALRO3 Larry Robinson 8.00 20.00
ALRO4 Larry Robinson 8.00 20.00
ALRO5 Larry Robinson 8.00 20.00
ALRO6 Larry Robinson 8.00 20.00
AMB1 Mike Bossy 12.00 30.00
AMB2 Mike Bossy 12.00 30.00
AMB3 Mike Bossy 12.00 30.00
AMB4 Mike Bossy 12.00 30.00
AML1 Mario Lemieux 60.00 100.00
AML2 Mario Lemieux 60.00 100.00
AMM1 Mark Messier 20.00 50.00
AMM2 Mark Messier 20.00 50.00
AMM3 Mark Messier 20.00 50.00
AMM4 Mark Messier 20.00 50.00
AMM5 Mark Messier 20.00 50.00
AMM6 Mark Messier 20.00 50.00
AMMC1 Marty McSorley 6.00 15.00
AMMC2 Marty McSorley 6.00 15.00
AMR1 Mark Recchi 12.00 30.00
AMR2 Mark Recchi 12.00 30.00
AMR3 Mark Recchi 12.00 30.00
AMS1 Milt Schmidt 8.00 20.00
AMS2 Milt Schmidt 8.00 20.00
AMST Martin St. Louis 8.00 20.00
ANL1 Nicklas Lidstrom 12.00 30.00
ANL2 Nicklas Lidstrom 12.00 30.00
ANL3 Nicklas Lidstrom 12.00 30.00
ANL4 Nicklas Lidstrom 12.00 30.00
APC1 Paul Coffey 8.00 20.00
APC2 Paul Coffey 8.00 20.00
APC3 Paul Coffey 8.00 20.00
APC4 Paul Coffey 8.00 20.00
APE1 Phil Esposito 10.00 25.00
APE2 Phil Esposito 10.00 25.00
APF1 Peter Forsberg 15.00 40.00
APF2 Peter Forsberg 15.00 40.00
APR1 Patrick Roy 25.00 50.00
APR2 Patrick Roy 25.00 50.00
APR3 Patrick Roy 25.00 50.00
APR4 Patrick Roy 25.00 50.00
ARB1 Ralph Backstrom 5.00 12.00
ARB2 Ralph Backstrom 5.00 12.00
ARB3 Ralph Backstrom 5.00 12.00
ARB4 Ralph Backstrom 5.00 12.00
ARB5 Ralph Backstrom 5.00 12.00
ARB6 Ralph Backstrom 5.00 12.00
ARBO Raymond Bourque 12.00 30.00
ARK1 Red Kelly 8.00 20.00
ARK2 Red Kelly 8.00 20.00
ARK3 Red Kelly 8.00 20.00
ARK4 Red Kelly 8.00 20.00
ARK5 Red Kelly 8.00 20.00
ARK6 Red Kelly 8.00 20.00
ARK7 Red Kelly 8.00 20.00
ARK8 Red Kelly 8.00 20.00
ARM1 Rick MacLeish 8.00 20.00
ARM2 Rick MacLeish 8.00 20.00
ARV1 Rogie Vachon 10.00 25.00
ARV2 Rogie Vachon 10.00 25.00
ARV3 Rogie Vachon 10.00 25.00
ASN1 Scott Niedermayer 8.00 20.00
ASN2 Scott Niedermayer 8.00 20.00
ASN3 Scott Niedermayer 8.00 20.00
ASN4 Scott Niedermayer 8.00 20.00
ASS1 Steve Shutt 6.00 15.00
ASS2 Steve Shutt 6.00 15.00
ASS3 Steve Shutt 6.00 15.00
ASS4 Steve Shutt 6.00 15.00
ASS5 Steve Shutt 6.00 15.00
ASY1 Steve Yzerman 40.00 80.00
ASY2 Steve Yzerman 40.00 80.00
ASY3 Steve Yzerman 40.00 80.00
ATB1 Tom Barrasso 8.00 20.00
ATB2 Tom Barrasso 8.00 20.00
ATL1 Ted Lindsay 8.00 20.00
ATL2 Ted Lindsay 8.00 20.00
ATL3 Ted Lindsay 8.00 20.00
ATL4 Ted Lindsay 8.00 20.00
AWC1 Wayne Cashman 6.00 15.00
AWC2 Wayne Cashman 6.00 15.00
AYC1 Yvan Cournoyer 8.00 20.00
AYC2 Yvan Cournoyer 8.00 20.00
AYC3 Yvan Cournoyer 8.00 20.00
AYC4 Yvan Cournoyer 8.00 20.00
AYC5 Yvan Cournoyer 8.00 20.00
AYC6 Yvan Cournoyer 8.00 20.00
AYC7 Yvan Cournoyer 8.00 20.00
AYC8 Yvan Cournoyer 8.00 20.00
AYC9 Yvan Cournoyer 8.00 20.00
AYC10 Yvan Cournoyer 8.00 20.00

2013-14 ITG Lord Stanley's Mug Back to Back Cup Jerseys

BBC01 Johnny Bower/20* 6.00 15.00
BBC02 Bob Baun/20* 5.00 12.00
BBC03 Serge Savard/20* 5.00 12.00
BBC04 Jacques Lemaire/20* 4.00 10.00
BBC05 Bobby Clarke/20* 8.00 20.00
BBC06 Bernie Parent/20* 6.00 15.00
BBC07 Rick MacLeish/20* 4.00 10.00
BBC08 Guy Lafleur/20* 6.00 15.00
BBC09 Steve Shutt/20* 4.00 10.00
BBC10 Larry Robinson/20* 5.00 12.00
BBC11 Mike Bossy/20* 5.00 12.00
BBC12 Denis Potvin/20* 5.00 12.00
BBC13 Mark Messier/20* 10.00 25.00
BBC14 Grant Fuhr/20* 8.00 20.00
BBC15 Glenn Anderson/20* 4.00 10.00
BBC16 Mario Lemieux/20* 20.00 50.00
BBC17 Jaromir Jagr/20* 15.00 40.00
BBC18 Steve Yzerman/20* 12.00 30.00
BBC19 Nicklas Lidstrom/20* 5.00 12.00
BBC20 Sergei Fedorov/20* 8.00 20.00

2013-14 ITG Lord Stanley's Mug Cup Holders Jerseys

CH01 C.Osgood/N.Lidstrom/80* 3.00 8.00
CH02 T.Selanne/S.Ndrmyer/80* 6.00 15.00
CH03 N.Khbbln/M.St.Louis/80* 3.00 8.00
CH04 C.Chelios/D.Hasek/80* 5.00 12.00
CH05 J.Sakic/P.Roy/80* 8.00 20.00
CH06 B.Hull/M.Modano/80* 6.00 15.00
CH07 S.Yzerman/N.Lidstrom/80* 8.00 20.00
CH08 S.Fedorov/I.Larionov/80* 5.00 12.00
CH09 P.Forsberg/P.Roy/80* 8.00 20.00
CH10 M.Richter/M.Messier/80* 6.00 15.00
CH11 K.Muller/P.Roy/80* 8.00 20.00
CH12 M.Lemieux/T.Brrsso/80* 12.00 30.00
CH13 P.Coffey/J.Jagr/80* 10.00 25.00
CH14 M.Messier/J.Kurri/80* 6.00 15.00
CH15 M.Vernon/J.Nwndyk/80* 2.50 6.00
CH16 M.Messier/G.Anderson/80* 6.00 15.00
CH17 C.Chelios/G.Crbnneau/80* 3.00 8.00
CH18 D.Potvin/B.Smith/80* 3.00 8.00
CH19 B.Nystrom/B.Trttier/80* 3.00 8.00
CH20 G.Lafleur/S.Shutt/80* 4.00 10.00
CH21 S.Savard/L.Robinson/80* 3.00 8.00
CH22 B.Clarke/R.MacLeish/80* 5.00 12.00
CH23 G.Drnhfer/B.Barber/80* 3.00 8.00
CH24 P.Esposito/W.Cashman/80* 5.00 12.00
CH25 J.Lprrere/J.Beliveau/80* 3.00 8.00
CH26 J.Bucyk/G.Cheevers/80* 3.00 8.00
CH33 Osgd/Ldstrm/Chlios/50* 3.00 8.00
CH34 Nwndyk/Dnkyo/Brdeur/50* 8.00 20.00
CH35 Hsek/Fdrv/Rbtlle/50* 5.00 12.00
CH36 Yzrmn/Ldstrm/Hull/50* 8.00 20.00
CH37 Skic/Roy/Brque/50* 8.00 20.00
CH38 Hull/Mdno/Blfr/50* 6.00 15.00
CH39 Yzrmn/Ldstrm/Fdrv/50* 8.00 20.00
CH40 Yzrmn/Lrnv/McCrty/50* 8.00 20.00
CH41 Frsbrg/Ry/Skic/50* 8.00 20.00
CH42 Svrd/Roy/Mller/50* 8.00 20.00
CH43 Lmux/Brrsso/Frncs/50* 12.00 30.00
CH44 Lmx/Jagr/Cffy/50* 12.00 30.00
CH45 Mssr/Krri/Rnfrd/50* 6.00 15.00
CH46 Flry/McInns/Nwndyk/50* 4.00 10.00
CH47 Andrsn/Fhr/Grtzky/50* 20.00 50.00
CH48 Roy/Crbnnu/Nslnd/50* 8.00 20.00
CH49 Ptvn/Smth/Nystrm/50* 3.00 8.00
CH50 Lflr/Svrd/Shtt/50* 4.00 10.00
CH51 Clrke/Prnt/Brbr/50* 5.00 12.00
CH52 Mhvlch/Crnyer/Lflr/50* 4.00 10.00

2013-14 ITG Lord Stanley's Mug Cup Records Jerseys

CR01 Jean Beliveau/80* 3.00 8.00
CR02 Mike Bossy/80* 3.00 8.00
CR03 Chris Chelios/80* 3.00 8.00
CR04 Dino Ciccarelli/80* 3.00 8.00
CR05 Paul Coffey/80* 3.00 8.00
CR06 Wayne Gretzky/80* 20.00 50.00
CR07 Brett Hull/80* 6.00 15.00
CR08 Bryan Trottier/80* 3.00 8.00
CR09 Reggie Leach/80* 2.50 6.00
CR10 Mario Lemieux/80* 12.00 30.00
CR11 Mark Messier/80* 6.00 15.00
CR13 Larry Robinson/80* 3.00 8.00
CR15 Patrick Roy/80* 8.00 20.00
CR16 Joe Sakic/80* 6.00 15.00

2013-14 ITG Lord Stanley's Mug Cup Rivals Jerseys

CRI01 C.Crawford/T.Rask/80* 5.00 12.00
CRI02 M.A.Fleury/C.Osgood/80* 8.00 20.00
CRI03 N.Lidstrom/R.Francis/80* 5.00 12.00
CRI04 B.Hull/D.Hasek/80* 8.00 20.00
CRI05 S.Fedorov/P.Bondra/80* 6.00 15.00
CRI06 S.Yzerman/E.Lindros/80* 10.00 25.00
CRI07 P.Roy/J.Vnbsbrck/80* 10.00 25.00
CRI08 M.Messier/T.Linden/80* 8.00 20.00
CRI09 D.Savard/L.Robitaille/80* 4.00 10.00
CRI10 J.Jagr/J.Roenick/80* 12.00 30.00
CRI11 M.Lemieux/M.Modano/80* 15.00 40.00
CRI12 B.Ranford/A.Moog/80* 3.00 8.00
CRI13 L.McDonald/P.Roy/80* 10.00 25.00
CRI14 G.Fuhr/R.Hextall/80* 6.00 15.00
CRI15 M.Messier/D.Potvin/80* 8.00 20.00
CRI16 B.Smith/T.Williams/80* 4.00 10.00
CRI17 J.Lemaire/P.Esposito/80* 6.00 15.00
CRI18 G.Lafleur/T.O'Reilly/80* 5.00 12.00
CRI25 Ldstrm/Lrnv/Frncs/Irbe/40* 5.00 12.00
CRI26 Hll/Nwndyk/Hsk/Pca/40* 8.00 20.00
CRI27 Yzrmn/Osgd/Bndra/Klzg/40* 10.00 25.00
CRI28 Vrnn/McCrty/Lndrs/LClr/40* 6.00 15.00
CRI29 Mssr/Rchtr/Lndn/Bure/40* 8.00 20.00
CRI30 Lmx/Brrsso/Rnck/Blfr/40* 15.00 40.00
CRI31 Rnfrd/Krri/Brque/Nly/40* 6.00 15.00
CRI32 McDnld/Vrnn/Roy/Nslnd/40* 10.00 25.00

2013-14 ITG Lord Stanley's Mug Cup Winning Goals Jerseys

CWG01 Patrice Bergeron/80* 5.00 12.00
CWG02 Henrik Zetterberg/80* 5.00 12.00
CWG03 Brendan Shanahan/80* 4.00 10.00
CWG04 Jason Arnott/80* 3.00 8.00
CWG05 Brett Hull/80* 8.00 20.00
CWG06 Darren McCarty/80* 3.00 8.00
CWG07 Mark Messier/80* 8.00 20.00
CWG08 Kirk Muller/80* 3.00 8.00
CWG09 Ron Francis/80* 5.00 12.00
CWG10 Ulf Samuelsson/80* 4.00 10.00
CWG11 Wayne Gretzky/80* 25.00 60.00
CWG12 Jari Kurri/80* 4.00 10.00
CWG13 Bobby Smith/80* 3.00 8.00
CWG14 Paul Coffey/80* 4.00 10.00
CWG15 Mike Bossy/80* 4.00 10.00
CWG16 Bob Nystrom/80* 2.50 6.00
CWG17 Jacques Lemaire/80* 3.00 8.00
CWG18 Guy Lafleur/80* 5.00 12.00
CWG19 Rick MacLeish/80* 3.00 8.00
CWG20 Yvan Cournoyer/80* 4.00 10.00

2013-14 ITG Lord Stanley's Mug History

HLSM01 Lord Stanley 1.50 4.00
HLSM02 Dan Bain 1.50 4.00
HLSM03 Frank McGee 1.50 4.00
HLSM04 Art Ross 1.00 2.50
HLSM05 Joe Malone 1.00 2.50
HLSM06 Cyclone Taylor 1.50 4.00
HLSM07 Georges Vezina 1.50 4.00
HLSM08 Hap Holmes 1.25 3.00
HLSM09 Frank Nighbor 1.25 3.00
HLSM10 Aurel Joliat 1.50 4.00
HLSM11 Clint Benedict 1.25 3.00
HLSM12 Lester Patrick 1.50 4.00
HLSM13 Eddie Shore 1.25 3.00
HLSM14 Howie Morenz 1.25 3.00
HLSM15 Charlie Conacher 1.25 3.00
HLSM16 Charlie Gardiner 1.25 3.00
HLSM17 Syd Howe 1.00 2.50
HLSM18 Frank Brimsek 1.25 3.00
HLSM19 Turk Broda 1.50 4.00
HLSM20 Toe Blake 1.00 2.50
HLSM21 Ted Kennedy 1.50 4.00
HLSM22 Bill Barilko 1.25 3.00
HLSM23 Terry Sawchuk 1.50 4.00
HLSM24 Gordie Howe 5.00 12.00
HLSM25 Maurice Richard 3.00 8.00
HLSM26 Glenn Hall 1.50 4.00
HLSM27 Dave Keon 1.50 4.00
HLSM28 Jean Beliveau 1.50 4.00
HLSM29 Yvan Cournoyer 1.50 4.00
HLSM30 Phil Esposito 2.50 6.00
HLSM31 Bobby Clarke 2.50 6.00
HLSM32 Guy Lafleur 2.00 5.00
HLSM33 Billy Smith 1.50 4.00
HLSM34 Jari Kurri 1.50 4.00
HLSM35 Patrick Roy 4.00 10.00
HLSM36 Lanny McDonald 1.50 4.00
HLSM37 Mario Lemieux 6.00 15.00
HLSM38 Mark Messier 3.00 8.00
HLSM39 Steve Yzerman 4.00 10.00
HLSM40 Joe Sakic 3.00 8.00
HLSM41 Brett Hull 3.00 8.00
HLSM42 Teemu Selanne 3.00 8.00
HLSM43 Nicklas Lidstrom 1.50 4.00
HLSM44 Marc-Andre Fleury 3.00 8.00
HLSM45 Corey Crawford 2.00 5.00

2013-14 ITG Lord Stanley's Mug Hoisting the Cup Jerseys

HTC01 Mario Lemieux/60* 12.00 30.00
HTC02 Nicklas Lidstrom/60* 3.00 8.00
HTC03 Martin St. Louis/60* 3.00 8.00
HTC04 Corey Crawford/60* 4.00 10.00
HTC05 Joe Sakic/60* 6.00 15.00
HTC06 Bob Nystrom/60* 2.00 5.00
HTC08 Bryan Trottier/60* 3.00 8.00
HTC09 Peter Forsberg/60* 6.00 15.00
HTC10 Raymond Bourque/60* 5.00 12.00
HTC11 Al MacInnis/60* 4.00 10.00
HTC12 Tom Barrasso/60* 3.00 8.00
HTC13 Mark Messier/60* 6.00 15.00
HTC14 Mark Messier/60* 6.00 15.00
HTC15 Jimmy Howard/60* 4.00 10.00
HTC16 Mike Modano/60* 5.00 12.00
HTC17 Bill Ranford/60* 3.00 8.00
HTC18 Mike Richter/60* 3.00 8.00
HTC19 Ed Belfour/60* 3.00 8.00
HTC20 Lanny McDonald/60* 3.00 8.00
HTC21 Jean Beliveau/60* 3.00 8.00
HTC22 Mike Bossy/60* 3.00 8.00
HTC23 Teemu Selanne/60* 6.00 15.00
HTC24 Chris Chelios/60* 3.00 8.00
HTC25 Antti Niemi/60* 2.50 6.00
HTC26 Steve Yzerman/60* 8.00 20.00
HTC27 Patrick Roy/60* 8.00 20.00
HTC28 Patrick Roy/60* 8.00 20.00
HTC29 Chris Osgood/60* 3.00 8.00
HTC30 Dominik Hasek/60* 5.00 12.00

2013-14 ITG Lord Stanley's Mug Mug Shots Jerseys

MS01 Mario Lemieux 12.00 30.00
MS02 Mark Messier 6.00 15.00
MS03 Steve Yzerman 8.00 20.00
MS04 Nicklas Lidstrom 3.00 8.00
MS05 Patrick Roy 8.00 20.00
MS06 Patrick Roy 8.00 20.00
MS07 Grant Fuhr 5.00 12.00
MS08 Mike Bossy 3.00 8.00
MS09 Chris Osgood 3.00 8.00
MS10 Bryan Trottier 3.00 8.00
MS11 Jaromir Jagr 10.00 25.00
MS12 Marc-Andre Fleury 6.00 15.00
MS13 Corey Crawford 4.00 10.00
MS14 Peter Forsberg 6.00 15.00
MS15 Brett Hull 6.00 15.00
MS16 Mike Modano 5.00 12.00
MS17 Ed Belfour 3.00 8.00
MS18 Joe Sakic 6.00 15.00
MS19 Larry Robinson 3.00 8.00
MS20 Mike Richter 3.00 8.00

2012-13 ITG Motown Madness

1 Sid Abel 1.25 3.00
2 Jack Adams 1.00 2.50
3 Larry Aurie 1.25 3.00
4 Doug Barkley 1.00 2.50
5 John Barrett 1.00 2.50
6 Hank Bassen 1.25 3.00
7 Andy Bathgate 1.50 4.00
8 Bobby Baun 1.50 4.00
9 Red Berenson 1.25 3.00
10 Gary Bergman 1.00 2.50
11 Henry Boucha 1.00 2.50
12 Scotty Bowman 1.50 4.00
13 Rick Bowness 1.00 2.50
14 Mud Bruneteau 1.00 2.50
15 Johnny Bucyk 1.50 4.00
16 Shawn Burr 1.25 3.00

17 Jimmy Carson 1.00 2.50
18 Joe Carveth 1.00 2.50
19 Chris Chelios 1.50 4.00
20 Tim Cheveldae 1.50 4.00
21 Dino Ciccarelli 1.50 4.00
22 Wendel Clark 2.50 6.00
23 Paul Coffey 1.50 4.00
24 Carson Cooper 1.00 2.50
25 Roger Crozier 1.25 3.00
26 Billy Dea 1.00 2.50
27 Alex Delvecchio 1.50 4.00
28 Bill Dineen 1.00 2.50
29 Connie Dion 1.25 3.00
30 Marcel Dionne 2.00 5.00
31 Kris Draper 1.25 3.00
32 Ron Duguay 1.25 3.00
33 Art Duncan 1.00 2.50
34 Hap Emms 1.25 3.00
35 Bob Essensa 1.50 4.00
36 Bernie Federko 1.25 3.00
37 Sergei Fedorov 2.50 6.00
38 Guyle Fielder 1.00 2.50
39 Mike Foligno 1.25 3.00
40 Val Fonteyne 1.00 2.50
41 Frank Foyston 1.00 2.50
42 Frank Fredrickson 1.00 2.50
43 Bill Gadsby 1.50 4.00
44 Gerard Gallant 1.00 2.50
45 Danny Gare 1.00 2.50
46 Ed Giacomin 1.50 4.00
47 Gilles Gilbert 1.25 3.00
48 Warren Godfrey 1.00 2.50
49 Pete Goegan 1.00 2.50
50 Bob Goldham 1.00 2.50
51 Ebbie Goodfellow 1.00 2.50
52 Danny Grant 1.00 2.50
53 Don Grosso 1.00 2.50
54 Glenn Hall 1.50 4.00
55 Glen Hanlon 1.25 3.00
56 Ron Harris 1.00 2.50
57 Dominik Hasek 2.50 6.00
58 George Hay 1.25 3.00
59 Darren Helm 1.00 2.50
60 Paul Henderson 1.25 3.00
61 Dennis Hextall 1.00 2.50
62 Flash Hollett 1.00 2.50
63 Hap Holmes 1.00 2.50
64 Jimmy Howard 2.00 5.00
65 Gordie Howe 5.00 12.00
66 Mark Howe 1.50 4.00
67 Syd Howe 1.00 2.50
68 Stu Grimson 1.00 2.50
69 Brett Hull 2.00 5.00
70 Larry Jeffrey 1.00 2.50
71 Greg Johnson 1.00 2.50
72 Curtis Joseph 2.00 5.00
73 Duke Keats 1.00 2.50
74 Red Kelly 1.50 4.00
75 Forbes Kennedy 1.25 3.00
76 Kelly Kisio 1.00 2.50
77 Joe Kocur 1.50 4.00
78 Niklas Kronwall 1.25 3.00
79 Martin Lapointe 1.00 2.50
80 Igor Larionov 1.50 4.00
81 Reed Larson 1.00 2.50
82 Reggie Leach 1.25 3.00
83 Manny Legace 1.25 3.00
84 Tony Leswick 1.00 2.50
85 Herbie Lewis 1.00 2.50
86 Nick Libett 1.00 2.50
87 Nicklas Lidstrom 2.00 5.00
88 Ted Lindsay 2.00 5.00
89 Harry Lumley 1.50 4.00
90 Len Lunde 1.00 2.50
91 Parker MacDonald 1.00 2.50
92 Bruce MacGregor 1.00 2.50
93 Rick MacLeish 2.50 6.00
94 Frank Mahovlich 1.50 4.00
95 Peter Mahovlich 1.50 4.00
96 Dan Maloney 1.25 3.00
97 Darren McCarty 1.50 4.00
98 Dale McCourt 1.25 3.00
99 Corrado Micalef 1.00 2.50
100 Mike Modano 2.50 6.00
101 Johnny Mowers 1.00 2.50
102 Joe Murphy 1.00 2.50
103 Larry Murphy 2.00 5.00
104 Jim Nill 1.00 2.50
105 Ted Nolan 1.50 4.00
106 Adam Oates 1.50 4.00
107 Gerry Odrowski 1.00 2.50
108 John Ogrodnick 1.00 2.50
109 Jimmy Orlando 1.00 2.50
110 Chris Osgood 2.00 5.00
111 Brad Park 1.25 3.00
112 Bud Poile 1.00 2.50
113 Dennis Polonich 1.00 2.50
114 Dean Prentice 1.00 2.50
115 Keith Primeau 1.25 3.00
116 Bob Probert 2.50 6.00
117 Marcel Pronovost 1.50 4.00
118 Metro Prystai 1.25 3.00
119 Bill Quackenbush 1.25 3.00
120 Dutch Reibel 1.00 2.50
121 Leo Reise 1.25 3.00
122 Dennis Riggin 2.00 5.00
123 Luc Robitaille 1.50 4.00
124 Borje Salming 1.50 4.00
125 Terry Sawchuk 2.00 5.00
126 Ray Sheppard 1.00 2.50
127 Darryl Sittler 2.00 5.00
128 Brad Smith 1.00 2.50
129 Floyd Smith 1.25 3.00
130 Greg Smith 1.00 2.50
131 Harold Snepsts 1.00 2.50
132 Vic Stasiuk 1.00 2.50
133 Greg Stefan 1.25 3.00
134 Jack Stewart 1.25 3.00
135 Errol Thompson 1.00 2.50
136 Tiny Thompson 1.50 4.00
137 Norm Ullman 1.50 4.00
138 Garry Unger 1.00 2.50
139 Rogie Vachon 2.00 5.00
140 Mike Vernon 1.25 3.00
141 Carl Voss 1.00 2.50
142 Bryan Watson 1.00 2.50
143 Harry Watson 1.25 3.00
144 Tiger Williams 1.50 4.00
145 Paul Woods 1.00 2.50
146 Jason Woolley 1.00 2.50
147 Howie Young 1.25 3.00
148 Warren Young 1.00 2.50
149 Steve Yzerman 4.00 10.00
150 Rick Zombo 1.00 2.50

2012-13 ITG Motown Madness Autographs

AAB Andy Bathgate 5.00 12.00
AAO Adam Oates 6.00 15.00
ABB Bobby Baun 6.00 15.00
ABD Bill Dineen 4.00 10.00
ABDE Billy Dea 4.00 10.00
ABE Bob Essensa 6.00 15.00
ABF Bernie Federko 5.00 12.00
ABG Bill Gadsby SP 15.00 30.00
ABH Brett Hull SP 30.00 60.00
ABM Bruce MacGregor 4.00 10.00
ABP Brad Park SP 15.00 30.00
ABPR Bob Probert SP 100.00 200.00
ABR Bill Ranford SP 15.00 40.00
ABS Brad Smith 4.00 10.00
ABSA Borje Salming SP 25.00 50.00
ABW Bryan Watson 4.00 10.00
ACC Chris Chelios 12.50 25.00
ACD Connie Dion 5.00 12.00
ACJ Curtis Joseph SP 20.00 40.00
ACM Corrado Micalef 4.00 10.00
ACO Chris Osgood SP 20.00 40.00
ADB Doug Barkley 4.00 10.00
ADBR Damien Brunner 60.00 120.00
ADC Dino Ciccarelli SP 15.00 40.00
ADG Danny Gare 4.00 10.00
ADGR Danny Grant 4.00 10.00
ADH Dennis Hextall 4.00 10.00
ADHA Dominik Hasek SP 30.00 60.00
ADHE Darren Helm 4.00 10.00
ADM Dale McCourt 5.00 12.00
ADMA Dan Maloney 5.00 12.00
ADMC Darren McCarty 6.00 15.00
ADP Dean Prentice 4.00 10.00
ADPO Dennis Polonich 4.00 10.00
ADR Dennis Riggin 8.00 20.00
AEG Ed Giacomin 8.00 20.00
AEM Ed Mio 6.00 15.00
AET Errol Thompson 4.00 10.00
AFK Forbes Kennedy 5.00 12.00
AFM Frank Mahovlich SP 15.00 40.00
AFS Floyd Smith 5.00 12.00
AGF Guyle Fielder 4.00 10.00
AGG Gilles Gilbert 8.00 20.00
AGGA Gerard Gallant 4.00 10.00
AGH Glen Hanlon 5.00 12.00
AGHA Glenn Hall SP 20.00 40.00
AGHO Gordie Howe SP 75.00 135.00
AGJ Greg Johnson 4.00 10.00
AGO Gerry Odrowski 4.00 10.00
AGS Greg Stefan 5.00 12.00
AGSM Greg Smith 4.00 10.00
AGU Garry Unger 4.00 10.00
AHB Henry Boucha 4.00 10.00
AHS Harold Snepsts 5.00 12.00
AIL Igor Larionov 12.50 25.00
AJA Joakim Andersson 5.00 12.00
AJB John Barrett 4.00 10.00
AJBU Johnny Bucyk SP 15.00 40.00
AJC Jimmy Carson 4.00 10.00
AJH Jimmy Howard 8.00 20.00
AJK Joe Kocur 6.00 15.00
AJM Joe Murphy 4.00 10.00
AJN Jim Nill 4.00 10.00
AJO John Ogrodnick 4.00 10.00
AJT Jordin Tootoo 8.00 20.00
AJW Jason Woolley 4.00 10.00
AKD Kris Draper 6.00 15.00
AKK Kelly Kisio 4.00 10.00
AKP Keith Primeau 5.00 12.00
ALJ Larry Jeffrey 4.00 10.00
ALM Larry Murphy 5.00 12.00
ALR Leo Reise 5.00 12.00
ALRO Luc Robitaille SP 15.00 40.00
AMD Marcel Dionne SP 20.00 50.00
AMF Mike Foligno 5.00 12.00
AMH Mark Howe 8.00 20.00
AML Manny Legace 5.00 12.00
AMLA Martin Lapointe 4.00 10.00
AMM Mike Modano SP 25.00 50.00
AMP Metro Prystai 5.00 12.00
AMPR Marcel Pronovost 6.00 15.00
AMV Mike Vernon SP 60.00 100.00
ANK Niklas Kronwall 5.00 12.00
ANL Nick Libett 4.00 10.00
ANLI Nicklas Lidstrom SP 50.00 100.00
ANU Norm Ullman 6.00 15.00
APC Paul Coffey SP 25.00 50.00
APH Paul Henderson SP 25.00 50.00
APM Parker MacDonald 4.00 10.00
APMA Peter Mahovlich SP 12.00 30.00
APW Paul Woods 4.00 10.00
ARB Red Berenson 5.00 12.00
ARBO Rick Bowness 4.00 10.00
ARD Ron Duguay 5.00 12.00
ARH Ron Harris 4.00 10.00
ARK Red Kelly SP 20.00 40.00
ARL Reed Larson 4.00 10.00
ARLE Reggie Leach 5.00 12.00
ARLO Ron Low 5.00 12.00
ARM Rick MacLeish SP 25.00 50.00
ARS Ray Sheppard 4.00 10.00
ARV Rogie Vachon SP 30.00 60.00
ARZ Rick Zombo 4.00 10.00
ASB Scotty Bowman 15.00 30.00
ASBU Shawn Burr 5.00 12.00
ASF Sergei Fedorov SP 90.00 150.00
ASG Stu Grimson 4.00 10.00
ASY Steve Yzerman SP 90.00 150.00
ATC Tim Cheveldae 6.00 15.00
ATH Tomas Holmstrom 6.00 15.00
ATL Ted Lindsay 8.00 20.00
ATN Ted Nolan 6.00 15.00
ATW Tiger Williams 6.00 15.00
AVF Val Fonteyne 4.00 10.00
AVS Vic Stasiuk 4.00 10.00
AWY Warren Young 4.00 10.00

2012-13 ITG Motown Madness Battle For The Cup Jerseys

BC1 Osgd/Lids/Fleury/Malkn/30* 25.00 60.00
BC2 Hsk/Yzr/Lds/Irb/Brn/Frns/30* 50.00 100.00
BC3 Hask/Yzer/Irbe/Brind/30 30.00 80.00
BC4 Yzr/Lar/Lds/Hnt/Klz/Ots/30* 25.00 60.00
BC5 Yzer/Lids/Ots/Kolzg/30* 30.00 80.00
BC6 Yzr/Vrn/Kcr/Lnd/Lclr/Hx/30* 20.00 50.00
BC7 Yzer/Vern/Lindrs//Hex/30* 30.00 80.00

2012-13 ITG Motown Madness Equipment Room Memorabilia

EQ1 Sergei Fedorov/60* 12.00 30.00
EQ2 Chris Osgood/60* 8.00 20.00
EQ3 Steve Yzerman/60* 15.00 40.00
EQ4 Manny Legace/60* 5.00 12.00
EQ5 Nicklas Lidstrom/60* 8.00 20.00
EQ6 Chris Chelios/60* 6.00 15.00

2012-13 ITG Motown Madness Game Used Jersey

M1 Steve Yzerman/140* 12.00 30.00
M2 Sergei Fedorov/140* 10.00 25.00
M3 Shawn Burr/140* 4.00 10.00
M4 Mike Foligno/140* 4.00 10.00
M5 Bob Probert/140* 8.00 20.00
M6 Jimmy Carson/140* 3.00 8.00
M7 Brad Marsh/140* 4.00 10.00
M8 Jim Nill/140* 3.00 8.00
M9 Bill Ranford/140* 5.00 12.00
M10 Dominik Hasek/140* 8.00 20.00
M11 Martin Lapointe/140* 3.00 8.00
M12 Manny Legace/140* 4.00 10.00
M13 Nicklas Lidstrom/140* 5.00 12.00
M14 Chris Osgood/140* 5.00 12.00
M15 Joe Kocur/140* 5.00 12.00
M16 Dino Ciccarelli/140* 5.00 12.00
M17 Darren Helm/140* 3.00 8.00
M18 Curtis Joseph/140* 6.00 15.00
M19 Igor Larionov/140* 6.00 15.00
M20 Reed Larson/140* 3.00 8.00
M21 Darren McCarty/140* 5.00 12.00
M22 Larry Murphy/140* 4.00 10.00
M23 Keith Primeau/140* 4.00 10.00
M24 Greg Stefan/140* 4.00 10.00
M25 Mike Vernon/140* 4.00 10.00
M26 Jason Woolley/140* 3.00 8.00
M27 Chris Chelios/140* 5.00 12.00
M28 Darryl Sittler/140* 6.00 15.00
M29 Kris Draper/140* 4.00 10.00
M30 Tomas Holmstrom/140* 4.00 10.00
M31 Danny Gare/140* 3.00 8.00
M32 Niklas Kronwall/140* 4.00 10.00
M33 Dennis Hextall/140* 4.00 10.00
M34 Gerard Gallant/140* 3.00 8.00
M35 Tim Cheveldae/140* 5.00 12.00
M36 Brett Hull/140* 10.00 25.00

2012-13 ITG Motown Madness Games To Remember Jerseys

GTR1 Yzer/Fed/Sakic/Roy/19* 60.00 120.00
GTR2 Lids/Yzer/Francs/Brind/19* 60.00 120.00
GTR3 Vern/Fed/Roy/Sakic/19* 60.00 120.00
GTR4 Howe/Sawc/Beliv/Rich/19* 50.00 125.00
GTR6 Yzer/Vern/Lindrs/Hxtl/19* 60.00 120.00
GTR7 Yzer/Os/Fed/Kolz/Huntr/19* 60.00 120.00
GTR8 Hull/Robit/Roy/Sakic/19* 50.00 100.00

2012-13 ITG Motown Madness Goaltenders Memorabilia

G1 Jimmy Howard/60* 8.00 20.00
G2 Curtis Joseph/60* 8.00 20.00
G3 Chris Osgood/60* 6.00 15.00
G4 Greg Stefan/60* 5.00 12.00
G5 Mike Vernon/60* 6.00 15.00
G6 Dominik Hasek/60* 10.00 25.00
G7 Manny Legace/60* 5.00 12.00
G8 Tim Cheveldae/60* 8.00 20.00

2012-13 ITG Motown Madness Jersey Quads

MQ1 Howrd/Hsk/Vern/Jsph 12.00 30.00
MQ2 Lids/Cheli/Murph/Osgd 15.00 40.00
MQ3 Prob/Kocr/McCrt/Drapr 20.00 50.00
MQ4 Yzer/Delvc/Howe/Lids 30.00 80.00
MQ5 Larion/Fedr/Hull/Robt 25.00 50.00
MQ6 Lrsn/Yzer/Stefn/Gare 15.00 40.00

2012-13 ITG Motown Madness Patch of Honor

PH1 Sergei Fedorov 10.00 25.00
PH2 Chris Osgood 6.00 15.00
PH3 Mike Vernon 8.00 20.00
PH4 Steve Yzerman 15.00 40.00
PH5 Joe Kocur 6.00 15.00
PH6 Darren McCarty 6.00 15.00
PH7 Larry Murphy 5.00 12.00
PH8 Chris Chelios 6.00 15.00
PH9 Dominik Hasek 10.00 25.00
PH10 Brett Hull 8.00 20.00
PH11 Luc Robitaille 6.00 15.00
PH12 Kris Draper 5.00 12.00
PH13 Ed Giacomin 5.00 12.00
PH14 Dennis Hextall 4.00 10.00
PH15 Nick Libett 4.00 10.00
PH16 Bryan Watson 4.00 10.00
PH17 Danny Gare 4.00 10.00
PH18 Frank Mahovlich 6.00 15.00
PH19 Alex Delvecchio 6.00 15.00
PH20 Marcel Dionne 5.00 12.00
PH21 Bill Gadsby 6.00 15.00
PH22 Glenn Hall 5.00 12.00
PH23 Red Kelly 6.00 15.00
PH24 Reed Larson 4.00 10.00
PH25 John Ogrodnick 4.00 10.00
PH26 Marcel Pronovost 6.00 15.00
PH27 Terry Sawchuk 8.00 20.00
PH28 Dale McCourt 5.00 12.00
PH29 Norm Ullman 6.00 15.00
PH30 Jimmy Howard 8.00 20.00
PH31 Igor Larionov 6.00 15.00
PH32 Nicklas Lidstrom 8.00 20.00
PH33 Sid Abel 5.00 12.00
PH34 Jack Adams 4.00 10.00
PH35 Gordie Howe 10.00 25.00
PH36 Syd Howe 4.00 10.00
PH37 Ted Lindsay 6.00 15.00
PH38 Harry Lumley 6.00 15.00
PH39 Jack Stewart 5.00 12.00
PH40 Tiny Thompson 6.00 15.00
PH41 Gerard Gallant 4.00 10.00
PH42 Dino Ciccarelli 6.00 15.00
PH43 Adam Oates 5.00 12.00
PH44 Keith Primeau 5.00 12.00
PH45 Bob Probert 8.00 20.00

2012-13 ITG Motown Madness Starting Lineup Jerseys

SL1 Os/Lds/Chl/Hl/Fd/Yz/19* 60.00 120.00

2012-13 ITG Motown Madness Teammates Jerseys

TM1 Yzerman/Lidstrom/110* 15.00 40.00
TM2 Osgood/Hasek/110* 10.00 25.00
TM3 Hull/Larionov/110* 8.00 20.00
TM4 Draper/McCarty/110* 6.00 15.00
TM5 Joseph/Legacy/110* 8.00 20.00
TM6 Robitaille/Fedorov/110* 10.00 25.00
TM7 Chelios/Lidstrom/110* 6.00 15.00
TM8 Lapointe/Primeau/110* 5.00 12.00
TM9 Vernon/Osgood/110* 6.00 15.00
TM10 Draper/Kocur/110* 8.00 20.00
TM11 Fedorov/Larionov/110* 8.00 20.00
TM12 Hull/Robitaille/110* 8.00 20.00
TM13 Murphy/Lidstrom/110* 6.00 15.00
TM14 Yzerman/Gallant/110* 10.00 25.00
TM15 Ciccarelli/Premeau/110* 6.00 15.00
TM16 Probert/Kocur/110* 10.00 25.00
TM17 Sittler/Yzerman/110* 10.00 25.00
TM18 Larson/Stefan/110* 5.00 12.00
TM19 Gare/Sittler/110* 8.00 20.00
TM20 Maloney/Giacomin/110* 5.00 12.00

2012-13 ITG Motown Madness Tough Materials

TM1 Bob Probert/140* 8.00 20.00
TM2 Chris Chelios/140* 5.00 12.00
TM3 Darren McCarty/140* 5.00 12.00
TM4 Reed Larson/140* 3.00 8.00
TM5 Dan Maloney/140* 4.00 10.00
TM6 Joe Kocur/140* 5.00 12.00
TM7 Shawn Burr/140* 4.00 10.00
TM8 Gerard Gallant/140* 3.00 8.00

2007-08 ITG O Canada

COMPLETE SET (100) 10.00 25.00
1 Alex Grant .15 .40
2 Angelo Esposito .30 .75
3 Braden Holtby .60 1.50
4 Brandon Sutter .25 .60
5 Colton Gillies .25 .60
6 Dion Knelsen .15 .40
7 Drew Doughty .50 1.25
8 Eric Doyle .15 .40
9 Jamie Arniel .20 .50
10 John Negrin .20 .50
11 Kyle Turris .75 2.00
12 Logan Couture .25 .60
13 Luke Schenn .30 .75
14 Mark Katic .15 .40
15 Olivier Fortier .15 .40
16 Steven Stamkos 1.00 2.50
17 Trevor Cann .20 .50
18 Yann Sauve .25 .60
19 Yves Bastien .15 .40
20 Zachary Boychuk .25 .60
21 Zack Torquato .15 .40
22 Carla MacLeod .25 .60
23 Caroline Ouellette .25 .60
24 Charline Labonte .40 1.00
25 Cheryl Pounder .25 .60
26 Colleen Sostorics .25 .60
27 Danielle Goyette .20 .50
28 Delaney Collins .25 .60
29 Gillian Apps .30 .75
30 Gillian Ferrari .25 .60
31 Gina Kingsbury .25 .60
32 Hayley Wickenheiser .60 1.50
33 Jayna Hefford .30 .75
34 Jennifer Botterill .25 .60
35 Katie Weatherston .25 .60
36 Kelly Bechard .25 .60
37 Kim St. Pierre .75 2.00
38 Meghan Agosta .30 .75
39 Sarah Vaillancourt .25 .60
40 Tessa Bonhomme .25 .60
41 Vicky Sunohara .20 .50
42 Karl Alzner .15 .40
43 Daniel Bertram .15 .40
44 Luc Bourdon .25 .60
45 Marc-Andre ClichÃ© .15 .40
46 Andrew Cogliano .20 .50
47 Steve Downie .20 .50
48 Cody Franson .30 .75
49 Sam Gagner .30 .75
50 Darren Helm .25 .60
51 Leland Irving .25 .60
52 Kristopher Letang .30 .75
53 Bryan Little .20 .50
54 Brad Marchand .75 2.00
55 Kenndal McArdle .15 .40
56 James Neal .40 1.00
57 Ryan O'Marra .15 .40
58 Ryan Parent .15 .40
59 Carey Price 1.00 2.50
60 Tom Pyatt .30 .75
61 Kris Russell .25 .60
62 Marc Staal .25 .60
63 Jonathan Toews 1.00 2.50
64 Martin Brodeur .60 1.50
65 Marc-Andre Fleury .50 1.25
66 Vincent Lecavalier .25 .60
67 Chris Pronger .25 .60
68 Eric Lindros .40 1.00
69 Roberto Luongo .40 1.00
70 Dion Phaneuf .20 .50
71 Justin Pogge .20 .50
72 Joe Sakic .50 1.25
73 Jason Spezza .25 .60
74 Patrick Roy .60 1.50
75 Jordan Staal .20 .50
76 Joe Thornton .40 1.00
77 Dany Heatley .20 .50
78 Steve Yzerman .60 1.50
79 Cassie Campbell .25 .60
80 Manon Rheaume .60 1.50
81 A.Esposito/S.Stamkos 1.00 2.50
82 D.Goyette/V.Sunohara .20 .50
83 H.Wickenheiser/J.Botterill .60 1.50
84 K.Alzner/M.Staal .25 .60
85 S.Downie/J.Toews 1.00 2.50
86 C.Price/L.Irving 1.00 2.50
87 K.Letang/L.Bourdon .30 .75
88 S.Gagner/B.Little .30 .75
89 C.Labonte/K.St. Pierre .75 2.00
90 C.Campbell/M.Rheaume .60 1.50
91 Jaromir Jagr .75 2.00
92 Henrik Zetterberg .30 .75
93 Alexei Cherepanov .30 .75
94 Dominik Hasek .40 1.00
95 Mike Modano .40 1.00
96 Bill Guerin .25 .60
97 Alexander Ovechkin 1.00 2.50
98 Vladislav Tretiak .20 .50
99 Chris Chelios .25 .60
100 Jari Kurri .25 .60

2007-08 ITG O Canada Autographs

AAC Andrew Cogliano 5.00 12.00
AACH Alexei Cherepanov SP 20.00 50.00
AAE Angelo Esposito 8.00 20.00
AAG Alex Grant 4.00 10.00
AAO Alexander Ovechkin SP 30.00 80.00
ABG Bill Guerin SP 6.00 15.00
ABH Braden Holtby 15.00 40.00
ABL Bryan Little 5.00 12.00
ABM Brad Marchand 20.00 50.00
ABS Brandon Sutter 6.00 15.00
ACC Cassie Campbell 6.00 15.00
ACF Cody Franson 8.00 20.00
ACG Colton Gillies 6.00 15.00
ACL Charline Labonte 10.00 25.00
ACM Carla MacLeod 6.00 15.00
ACO Caroline Ouellette 6.00 15.00
ACP Carey Price 25.00 60.00
ACPD Cheryl Pounder 6.00 15.00
ACPR Chris Pronger SP 6.00 15.00
ACS Colleen Sostorics 6.00 15.00
ADB Daniel Bertram 4.00 10.00
ADC Delaney Collins 6.00 15.00
ADD Drew Doughty 12.00 30.00
ADG Danielle Goyette 5.00 12.00
ADH Darren Helm 6.00 15.00
ADHA Dominik Hasek SP 20.00 50.00
ADK Dion Knelsen 4.00 10.00
ADP Dion Phaneuf SP 5.00 12.00
AED Eric Doyle 4.00 10.00
AGA Gillian Apps 8.00 20.00
AGF Gillian Ferrari 6.00 15.00
AGK Gina Kingsbury 6.00 15.00
AHW Hayley Wickenheiser 15.00 40.00
AJA Jamie Arniel 5.00 12.00
AJB Jennifer Botterill 6.00 15.00
AJH Jayna Hefford 8.00 20.00
AJJ Jaromir Jagr SP 30.00 80.00
AJK Jari Kurri SP 6.00 15.00
AJN James Neal 10.00 25.00
AJNE John Negrin 5.00 12.00
AJP Justin Pogge SP 5.00 12.00
AJS Joe Sakic SP 25.00 60.00
AJSP Jason Spezza SP 6.00 15.00
AJST Jordan Staal SP 5.00 12.00
AJT Jonathan Toews 25.00 60.00
AJTA John Tavares SP 25.00 60.00
AJTH Joe Thornton SP 10.00 25.00
AKA Karl Alzner 4.00 10.00
AKB Kelly Bechard 6.00 15.00
AKL Kristopher Letang 8.00 20.00
AKMA Kenndal McArdle 4.00 10.00
AKR Kris Russell 6.00 15.00
AKS Kim St. Pierre 20.00 50.00
AKT Kyle Turris 20.00 50.00
AKW Katie Weatherston 6.00 15.00
ALB Luc Bourdon 6.00 15.00
ALC Logan Couture 6.00 15.00
ALI Leland Irving 6.00 15.00
ALS Luke Schenn 8.00 20.00
AMAC Marc-Andre Cliche 4.00 10.00
AMAC Meghan Agosta 8.00 20.00
AMAF Marc-Andre Fleury SP 15.00 40.00
AMB Martin Brodeur SP 40.00 100.00
AMK Mark Katic 4.00 10.00
AMM Mike Modano SP 10.00 25.00
AMR Manon Rheaume 15.00 40.00
AMS Marc Staal 6.00 15.00
AOF Olivier Fortier 4.00 10.00
ARL Roberto Luongo SP 40.00 100.00
ARO Ryan O'Marra 4.00 10.00
ARP Ryan Parent 4.00 10.00
ASD Steve Downie 5.00 12.00
ASG Sam Gagner 8.00 20.00
ASS Steven Stamkos 25.00 60.00
ASV Sarah Vaillancourt 6.00 15.00
ASY Steve Yzerman SP 30.00 80.00
ATB Tessa Bonhomme 6.00 15.00
ATC Trevor Cann 5.00 12.00
ATP Tom Pyatt 8.00 20.00
AVL Vincent Lecavalier SP 6.00 15.00
AVS Vicky Sunohara 5.00 12.00
AVT Vladislav Tretiak SP 20.00 50.00
AYB Yves Bastien 4.00 10.00
AYS Yann Sauve 6.00 15.00
AZB Zachary Boychuk 6.00 15.00
AZT Zack Torquato 4.00 10.00

2007-08 ITG O Canada Dual Jerseys

DJ01 C.Labonte/K.St. Pierre 8.00 20.00
DJ02 V.Sunohara/D.Goyette 2.00 5.00
DJ03 Wickenheiser/Botterill 6.00 15.00
DJ04 J.Hefford/C.Ouellette 3.00 8.00
DJ05 C.Labonte/C.Price 10.00 25.00
DJ06 K.Turris/C.Gillies 8.00 20.00
DJ07 A.Esposito/L.Couture 3.00 8.00
DJ08 S.Stamkos/B.Sutter 10.00 25.00
DJ09 D.Doughty/Y.Sauve 5.00 12.00
DJ10 T.Cann/B.Holtby 6.00 15.00
DJ11 J.Toews/D.Bertram 10.00 25.00
DJ12 S.Gagner/S.Downie 3.00 8.00
DJ13 K.Alzner/L.Bourdon 2.50 6.00
DJ14 K.Letang/K.Russell 3.00 8.00
DJ15 C.Price/L.Irving 10.00 25.00
DJ16 D.Goyette/S.Downie 2.00 5.00
DJ17 V.Sunohara/S.Stamkos 10.00 25.00
DJ18 J.Botterill/J.Toews 10.00 25.00
DJ19 Wickenheiser/Turris 8.00 20.00

2007-08 ITG O Canada Formidable Foes Jerseys

FF01 D.Hasek/P.Roy 15.00 40.00
FF02 J.Jagr/J.Sakic 20.00 50.00
FF03 K.Lehtonen/D.Roloson 5.00 12.00
FF04 K.Tkachuk/E.Lindros 10.00 25.00
FF05 Modano/Lecavalier 10.00 25.00
FF06 C.Chelios/C.Pronger 6.00 15.00
FF07 H.Zetterberg/J.Thornton 10.00 25.00
FF08 M.Richter/M.Brodeur 15.00 40.00
FF09 A.Ovechkin/D.Phaneuf 25.00 60.00
FF10 V.Tretiak/P.Henderson 20.00 50.00
FF11 V.Kharlamov/B.Clarke 10.00 25.00
FF12 B.Salming/L.Robinson 6.00 15.00
FF13 J.Kurri/M.Bossy 6.00 15.00
FF14 B.Hull/S.Yzerman 12.00 30.00
FF15 P.Housley/R.Bourque 10.00 25.00
FF16 P.Stastny/G.Lafleur 8.00 20.00
FF17 B.Leetch/P.Coffey 6.00 15.00
FF18 LaFontaine/Robitaille 8.00 20.00
FF19 A.Yakushev/P.Esposito 10.00 25.00
FF20 M.Naslund/M.Goulet 4.00 10.00

2007-08 ITG O Canada International Goalies Jerseys

IG01 Mike Richter 6.00 15.00
IG02 Vladislav Tretiak 12.00 30.00
IG03 Cristobal Huet 5.00 12.00
IG04 Dominik Hasek 10.00 25.00
IG05 Tom Barrasso 6.00 15.00
IG06 Tony Esposito 6.00 15.00
IG07 John Vanbiesbrouck 8.00 20.00
IG08 Vladimir Dzurilla 6.00 15.00
IG09 Tuukka Rask 15.00 40.00
IG10 Kari Lehtonen 5.00 12.00

2007-08 ITG O Canada Jerseys

EMBLEMS/20: .8X TO 2X JSY/100*
GUJ01 Alex Grant 2.50 6.00
GUJ02 Angelo Esposito 5.00 12.00
GUJ03 Braden Holtby 10.00 25.00
GUJ04 Brandon Sutter 4.00 10.00
GUJ05 Colton Gillies 4.00 10.00
GUJ06 Dion Knelsen 2.50 6.00
GUJ07 Drew Doughty 8.00 20.00
GUJ08 Eric Doyle 2.50 6.00
GUJ09 Jamie Arniel 3.00 8.00
GUJ10 John Negrin 3.00 8.00
GUJ11 Keven Veilleux 3.00 8.00
GUJ12 Kyle Turris 12.00 30.00
GUJ13 Logan Couture 4.00 10.00
GUJ14 Luke Schenn 5.00 12.00
GUJ15 Mark Katic 2.50 6.00
GUJ16 Olivier Fortier 2.50 6.00
GUJ17 Steven Stamkos 15.00 40.00
GUJ18 Trevor Cann 3.00 8.00
GUJ19 Yann Sauve 4.00 10.00
GUJ20 Yves Bastien 2.50 6.00
GUJ21 Zachary Boychuk 4.00 10.00
GUJ22 Zack Torquato 2.50 6.00
GUJ23 Carla MacLeod 4.00 10.00
GUJ24 Caroline Ouellette 4.00 10.00
GUJ25 Charline Labonte 6.00 15.00
GUJ26 Cheryl Pounder 4.00 10.00
GUJ27 Colleen Sostorics 4.00 10.00
GUJ28 Danielle Goyette 3.00 8.00
GUJ29 Delaney Collins 4.00 10.00
GUJ30 Gillian Apps 5.00 12.00
GUJ31 Gillian Ferrari 4.00 10.00
GUJ32 Gina Kingsbury 4.00 10.00
GUJ33 Hayley Wickenheiser 10.00 25.00
GUJ34 Jayna Hefford 5.00 12.00
GUJ35 Jennifer Botterill 4.00 10.00
GUJ36 Katie Weatherston 4.00 10.00
GUJ37 Kelly Bechard 4.00 10.00
GUJ38 Kim St. Pierre 12.00 30.00
GUJ39 Meghan Agosta 5.00 12.00
GUJ40 Sarah Vaillancourt 4.00 10.00
GUJ41 Tessa Bonhomme 4.00 10.00
GUJ42 Vicky Sunohara 3.00 8.00
GUJ43 Karl Alzner 2.50 6.00
GUJ44 Daniel Bertram 2.50 6.00
GUJ45 Luc Bourdon 4.00 10.00
GUJ46 Marc-Andre ClichÃ© 2.50 6.00
GUJ47 Andrew Cogliano 3.00 8.00
GUJ48 Steve Downie 3.00 8.00
GUJ49 Cody Franson 5.00 12.00
GUJ50 Sam Gagner 5.00 12.00
GUJ51 Darren Helm 4.00 10.00
GUJ52 Leland Irving 4.00 10.00
GUJ53 Kristopher Letang 5.00 12.00
GUJ54 Bryan Little 3.00 8.00
GUJ55 Brad Marchand 12.00 30.00
GUJ56 Kenndal McArdle 2.50 6.00
GUJ57 James Neal 6.00 15.00
GUJ58 Ryan O'Marra 2.50 6.00
GUJ59 Ryan Parent 2.50 6.00
GUJ60 Carey Price 15.00 40.00
GUJ61 Tom Pyatt 5.00 12.00
GUJ62 Kris Russell 4.00 10.00
GUJ63 Marc Staal 4.00 10.00
GUJ64 Jonathan Toews 12.00 30.00
GUJ65 Cassie Campbell 4.00 10.00
GUJ66 Vincent Lecavalier 6.00 15.00
GUJ67 Roberto Luongo 6.00 15.00
GUJ68 John Tavares 10.00 25.00
GUJ69 Joe Thornton 6.00 15.00
GUJ70 Jason Spezza 4.00 10.00
GUJ71 Joe Sakic 8.00 20.00
GUJ73 Dany Heatley 3.00 8.00
GUJ74 Eric Lindros 6.00 15.00
GUJ75 Chris Pronger 4.00 10.00
GUJ77 Steve Yzerman 10.00 25.00
GUJ78 Martin Brodeur 10.00 25.00
GUJ79 Marc-Andre Fleury 8.00 20.00
GUJ80 Dion Phaneuf 3.00 8.00

2005 ITG Passing the Torch

COMPLETE SET (25) 8.00 20.00
1 Checklist .40 1.00
2 Martin Brodeur
Rookie Season .40 1.00
3 Martin Brodeur
Calder Trophy .40 1.00
4 Martin Brodeur
First Stanley Cup .40 1.00
5 Martin Brodeur
First Vezina Trophy .40 1.00
6 Martin Brodeur
First NHL All-Star Game .40 1.00
7 Martin Brodeur/400th Career Win .40 1.00
8 Martin Brodeur/50th Career Shutout .40 1.00
9 Martin Brodeur
Winning Streak .40 1.00
10 Martin Brodeur
International Experience .40 1.00
11 Martin Brodeur
Patrick Roy NHL Dreams .40 1.00
12 Martin Brodeur
Patrick Roy Immediate Impact .40 1.00
13 Martin Brodeur
Patrick Roy First Cup .40 1.00
14 Martin Brodeur
Patrick Roy Best of the Best .40 1.00
15 Martin Brodeur
Patrick Roy Among the Stars .40 1.00
16 Martin Brodeur
Patrick Roy Passing the Torch .40 1.00
17 Patrick Roy
Rookie Season .40 1.00
18 Patrick Roy
First Stanley Cup and Conn Smythe Trophy .40 1.00
19 Patrick Roy
First NHL All-Star Game .40 1.00
20 Patrick Roy
First Vezina Trophy .40 1.00
21 Patrick Roy
Traded to Colorado .40 1.00
22 Patrick Roy
First Stanley Cup in Colorado .40 1.00
23 Patrick Roy
Most Career Playoff Wins .40 1.00
24 Patrick Roy
Most Career Wins .40 1.00
25 Patrick Roy
Retirement .40 1.00

2005 ITG Passing the Torch Memorabilia

PTT1 Martin Brodeur NJ 12.00 30.00
PTT2 Martin Brodeur AS 12.00 30.00
PTT3 Martin Brodeur AS 12.00 30.00
PTT4 Martin Brodeur AS 12.00 30.00
PTT5 Martin Brodeur Pad 12.00 30.00
PTT6 Martin Brodeur Stk 12.00 30.00
PTT7 Patrick Roy MTL 12.00 30.00
PTT8 Patrick Roy COL 12.00 30.00
PTT9 Patrick Roy AS 12.00 30.00
PTT10 Patrick Roy AS 12.00 30.00
PTT11 Patrick Roy AS 12.00 30.00
PTT12 Patrick Roy Glove 12.00 30.00
PTT13 Patrick Roy Pad 12.00 30.00
PTT14 Patrick Roy Stk 12.00 30.00
PTT15 M.Brodeur
P.Roy MTL J/J 15.00 40.00
PTT16 M.Brodeur
P.Roy AVS J/J 15.00 40.00
PTT17 M.Brodeur
P.Roy AS J/J 15.00 40.00
PTT18 M.Brodeur
P.Roy Dual Pad 15.00 40.00
PTT19 M.Brodeur
P.Roy S/S 15.00 40.00
PTT20 Martin Brodeur Jsy/Stk 15.00 40.00
PTT21 Patrick Roy Jsy/Stk MTL 15.00 40.00
PTT22 Patrick Roy Jsy/Stk COL 15.00 40.00
PTT25 M.Brodeur NUM/30 40.00 100.00
PTT27 P.Roy NUM MTL/33 50.00 125.00
PTT28 P.Roy EMB MTL/30 50.00 125.00
PTT29 P.Roy NUM COL/33 40.00 100.00
PTT30 P.Roy EMB COL/30 40.00 100.00

2005-06 ITG Sidney Crosby Series

COMPLETE SET (25) 15.00 40.00
COMMON CARD (1-25) 1.00 2.50
COMMON GOLD/87* 8.00 20.00

2005-06 ITG Sidney Crosby Series Autographs

COMMON AUTO/35* 75.00 150.00

2005-06 ITG Sidney Crosby Series Memorabilia

SCM1 S.Crosby
M.Lemieux Jsys/87* 75.00 200.00
SCM5 S.Crosby/M.Fleury Jsys/87* 60.00 150.00
SCM9 S.Crosby/E.Malkin Jsys/87* 75.00 200.00
SCM11 Sidney Crosby Jsy/87* 40.00 100.00
SCM12 Sidney Crosby Jsy/87* 40.00 100.00
SCM13 Sidney Crosby Jsy/Stk/87* 50.00 125.00
SCM14 Sidney Crosby Jsy/Stk/87* 50.00 125.00
SCM18 Sidney Crosby
Triple Mem/87* 100.00 200.00
SCM19 Sidney Crosby Jsy/Glve/87* 60.00150.00
SCM20 Sidney Crosby Dual Jsy/87* 50.00125.00

2005-06 ITG Sidney Crosby Series Signed Memorabilia

CAM1 Sidney Crosby Jsy 200.00 400.00
CAM2 Sidney Crosby Jsy 200.00 400.00
CAM3 Sidney Crosby Glove 200.00 400.00
CAM4 Sidney Crosby Stk 200.00 400.00

2013-14 ITG Stickwork Game Used Sticks Silver

GUS01 Al MacInnis 12.00 30.00
GUS02 Alexander Ovechkin 40.00 100.00
GUS03 Aleksander Barkov 30.00 80.00
GUS04 Anders Hedberg 6.00 15.00
GUS05 Andrew Ladd 6.00 15.00
GUS06 Bernie Nicholls 8.00 20.00
GUS07 Bob Gainey 10.00 25.00
GUS08 Bob Probert 10.00 25.00
GUS09 Bobby Orr 40.00 100.00
GUS10 Brad Richards 10.00 25.00
GUS11 Brayden Schenn 10.00 25.00
GUS12 Brendan Gallagher 25.00 60.00
GUS13 Brian Bellows 8.00 20.00
GUS14 Brian Leetch 8.00 20.00
GUS15 Bryan Trottier 10.00 25.00
GUS16 Chris Chelios 10.00 25.00
GUS17 Chris Pronger 10.00 25.00
GUS18 Dale Hawerchuk 12.00 30.00
GUS19 David Clarkson 6.00 15.00
GUS20 David Krejci 10.00 25.00
GUS21 Denis Savard 10.00 25.00

GUS22 Denis Potvin 10.00 25.00
GUS23 Zach Parise 10.00 25.00
GUS24 Dion Phaneuf 8.00 20.00
GUS25 Doug Gilmour 12.00 30.00
GUS26 Dougie Hamilton 15.00 40.00
GUS27 Drew Doughty 12.00 30.00
GUS28 Dustin Brown 8.00 20.00
GUS29 Dustin Byfuglien 10.00 25.00
GUS30 Evgeni Malkin 20.00 50.00
GUS31 Gabriel Landeskog 12.00 30.00
GUS32 George Armstrong 10.00 25.00
GUS33 Gilbert Perreault 10.00 25.00
GUS34 Guy Carbonneau 10.00 25.00
GUS35 Guy Lafleur 12.00 30.00
GUS36 Ilya Kovalchuk 10.00 25.00
GUS37 James Van Riemsdyk 8.00 20.00
GUS38 Jari Kurri 10.00 25.00
GUS39 Jason Pominville 6.00 15.00
GUS40 Jason Spezza 10.00 25.00
GUS41 Jeff Carter 8.00 20.00
GUS42 Jeff Skinner 12.00 30.00
GUS43 Jeremy Roenick 15.00 40.00
GUS44 Joe Mullen 8.00 20.00
GUS45 Joe Sakic 20.00 50.00
GUS46 Joffrey Lupul 6.00 15.00
GUS47 John LeClair 10.00 25.00
GUS48 Jonathan Huberdeau 25.00 60.00
GUS49 Kyle Turris 6.00 15.00
GUS50 Larry Robinson 10.00 25.00
GUS51 Lars Eller 6.00 15.00
GUS52 Luc Robitaille 10.00 25.00
GUS53 Marc Staal 6.00 15.00
GUS54 Marcel Dionne 12.00 30.00
GUS55 Marian Gaborik 10.00 25.00
GUS56 Marian Hossa 10.00 25.00
GUS57 Mario Lemieux 40.00 100.00
GUS58 Mark Messier 20.00 50.00
GUS59 Mark Recchi 12.00 30.00
GUS60 Mark Scheifele 15.00 40.00
GUS61 Mathew Dumba 6.00 15.00
GUS62 Mats Sundin 10.00 25.00
GUS63 Sidney Crosby 40.00 100.00
GUS64 Mike Bossy 10.00 25.00
GUS65 Mike Gartner 12.00 30.00
GUS66 Mike Modano 15.00 40.00
GUS67 Mike Richards 8.00 20.00
GUS68 Mikko Koivu 8.00 20.00
GUS69 Nazem Kadri 12.00 30.00
GUS70 Niklas Kronwall 8.00 20.00
GUS71 Patrice Bergeron 12.00 30.00
GUS72 Paul Coffey 10.00 25.00
GUS73 Peter Stastny 8.00 20.00
GUS74 Phil Kessel 10.00 25.00
GUS75 Raymond Bourque 15.00 40.00
GUS76 Rick Nash 10.00 25.00
GUS77 Rob Blake 10.00 25.00
GUS78 Rod Langway 8.00 20.00
GUS79 Ron Francis 12.00 30.00
GUS80 Ryan Callahan 6.00 15.00
GUS81 Ryan O'Reilly 10.00 25.00
GUS82 Ryan Suter 8.00 20.00
GUS83 Saku Koivu 10.00 25.00
GUS84 Sean Couturier 8.00 20.00
GUS85 Sergei Fedorov 15.00 40.00
GUS86 Sergei Samsonov 8.00 20.00
GUS87 Steve Yzerman 25.00 60.00
GUS88 Steven Stamkos 20.00 50.00
GUS89 Teemu Selanne 20.00 50.00
GUS90 Terry O'Reilly 8.00 20.00
GUS91 Theoren Fleury 12.00 30.00
GUS92 Tony Amonte 8.00 20.00
GUS93 Trevor Linden 10.00 25.00
GUS94 Tyler Bozak 6.00 15.00
GUS95 Vincent Damphousse 8.00 20.00
GUS96 Wayne Gretzky 60.00 150.00

2015-16 ITG Stickwork Complete Stick Silver

CS02 Curtis Joseph/25 12.00 30.00
CS03 Gordie Howe/15 30.00 80.00
CS05 Marcel Dionne/30 10.00 25.00
CS06 Mario Lemieux/40 20.00 50.00
CS07 Maurice Richard/35 30.00 60.00
CS08 Patrick Roy/40 15.00 40.00
CS09 Paul Coffey/25 10.00 25.00
CS10 Phil Esposito/25 15.00 40.00
CS11 Raymond Bourque/25 15.00 40.00
CS12 Sergei Fedorov/25 12.00 30.00
CS13 Wayne Gretzky/35 20.00 80.00
CS14 Yvan Cournoyer/20 10.00 25.00

2015-16 ITG Stickwork Face Off Silver

FO01 J.Roenick/S.Fedorov/30 12.00 30.00
FO04 N.Ullman/Y.Cournoyer/40 8.00 20.00
FO05 P.Mahovlich/G.Howe/40 25.00 60.00
FO06 S.Fedorov/M.Modano/25 12.00 30.00
FO07 W.Gretzky/M.Lemieux/40 30.00 80.00
FO08 W.Gretzky/R.Francis/15 40.00 80.00
FO09 W.Gretzky/S.Fedorov/40 30.00 80.00

2015-16 ITG Stickwork Game Used Goalie Paddles Silver

GGP01 Andy Moog/25 12.00 30.00
GGP02 Ben Bishop/30 8.00 20.00
GGP03 Bernie Parent/40 12.00 30.00
GGP04 Carey Price/25 25.00 60.00
GGP05 Charlie Hodge/25 10.00 25.00
GGP06 Chris Osgood/25 12.00 30.00
GGP07 Curtis Joseph/40 12.00 30.00
GGP08 Ed Giacomin/15 12.00 30.00
GGP09 Felix Potvin/40 15.00 40.00
GGP10 Grant Fuhr/30 15.00 40.00
GGP11 Gump Worsley/24 12.00 30.00
GGP12 Harry Lumley/15 15.00 40.00
GGP13 Henrik Lundqvist/30 25.00 60.00
GGP14 Jacques Plante/15 15.00 40.00
GGP15 Jim Carey/30 8.00 20.00
GGP16 Jim Rutherford/20 10.00 25.00
GGP17 Jimmy Howard/30 12.00 30.00
GGP18 John Vanbiesbrouck/30 10.00 25.00
GGP20 Marc-Andre Fleury/20 25.00 60.00
GGP21 Miikka Kiprusoff/30 15.00 40.00
GGP22 Mike Richter/18 12.00 30.00
GGP23 Niklas Backstrom/26 10.00 25.00
GGP24 Nikolai Khabibulin/30 10.00 25.00
GGP25 Olaf Kolzig/30 10.00 25.00
GGP26 Patrick Roy/40 30.00 60.00
GGP27 Sean Burke/30 12.00 30.00
GGP28 Terry Sawchuk/18 15.00 40.00
GGP29 Tom Barrasso/25 12.00 30.00
GGP30 Tuukka Rask/30 12.00 30.00
GGP31 Vladislav Tretiak/40 8.00 20.00

2015-16 ITG Stickwork Game Used Goalie Sticks Silver

GGS03 Bernie Parent/25 12.00 30.00
GGS04 Carey Price/20 20.00 50.00
GGS05 Charlie Hodge/30 6.00 15.00
GGS07 Curtis Joseph/35 10.00 25.00
GGS08 Ed Giacomin/19 10.00 25.00
GGS09 Felix Potvin/30 12.00 30.00
GGS10 Grant Fuhr/35 12.00 30.00
GGS11 Gump Worsley/15 10.00 25.00
GGS13 Henrik Lundqvist/20 25.00 60.00
GGS17 Jimmy Howard/15 12.00 30.00
GGS23 Niklas Backstrom/14 8.00 20.00
GGS26 Patrick Roy/25 25.00 60.00
GGS27 Sean Burke/14 6.00 15.00
GGS29 Tom Barrasso/14 10.00 25.00
GGS31 Vladislav Tretiak/18 8.00 20.00

2015-16 ITG Stickwork Game Used Sticks Silver

GUS01 Adam Oates/19 15.00 40.00
GUS02 Al MacInnis/40 10.00 25.00
GUS03 Alexander Mogilny/25 12.00 30.00
GUS04 Alexander Ovechkin/30 15.00 40.00
GUS12 Brett Hull/40 15.00 40.00
GUS13 Brian Bellows/40 6.00 15.00
GUS15 Chris Chelios/26 10.00 25.00
GUS16 Chris Pronger/40 8.00 20.00
GUS17 Claude Lemieux/40 6.00 15.00
GUS18 Daniel Alfredsson/25 10.00 25.00
GUS19 Dave Andreychuk/40 8.00 20.00
GUS23 Eric Lindros/30 15.00 40.00
GUS28 Gordie Howe/40 40.00 80.00
GUS31 Jari Kurri/23 10.00 25.00
GUS33 Jeremy Roenick/39 12.00 30.00
GUS34 Joe Kocur/25 12.00 30.00
GUS35 Joe Thornton/28 15.00 40.00
GUS36 Keith Tkachuk/25 12.00 30.00
GUS41 Luc Robitaille/38 8.00 20.00
GUS42 Luke Schenn/30 8.00 20.00
GUS43 Marcel Dionne/40 12.00 30.00
GUS45 Mario Lemieux/40 20.00 50.00
GUS46 Mark Messier/40 10.00 25.00
GUS48 Mats Naslund/25 6.00 15.00
GUS50 Maurice Richard/40 30.00 60.00
GUS52 Mike Gartner/17 12.00 30.00
GUS54 Mike Ricci/27 6.00 15.00
GUS55 Norm Ullman/35 8.00 20.00
GUS56 Paul Coffey/29 10.00 25.00
GUS58 Phil Housley/18 8.00 20.00
GUS61 Raymond Bourque/35 12.00 30.00
GUS63 Rick Nash/34 8.00 20.00
GUS66 Ron Duguay/23 12.00 30.00
GUS67 Serge Savard/40 8.00 20.00
GUS68 Sergei Fedorov/40 12.00 30.00
GUS71 Steve Yzerman/27 25.00 50.00
GUS78 Wayne Gretzky/40 30.00 80.00
GUS79 Yvan Cournoyer/40 8.00 20.00

2015-16 ITG Stickwork Hockey History Assist Leaders Silver

HHA02 Al MacInnis/40 10.00 25.00
HHA04 Gordie Howe/40 25.00 60.00
HHA06 Joe Thornton/30 12.00 30.00
HHA07 Larry Murphy/40 8.00 20.00
HHA08 Marcel Dionne/40 10.00 25.00
HHA09 Mario Lemieux/40 20.00 50.00
HHA10 Mark Messier/15 12.00 30.00
HHA11 Mark Recchi/25 12.00 30.00
HHA13 Paul Coffey/40 8.00 20.00
HHA14 Phil Esposito/40 12.00 30.00
HHA15 Phil Housley/40 6.00 15.00
HHA16 Raymond Bourque/40 12.00 30.00
HHA20 Wayne Gretzky/40 30.00 80.00

2015-16 ITG Stickwork Hockey History Goal Leaders Silver

HHG02 Brendan Shanahan/16 10.00 25.00
HHG04 Dave Andreychuk/40 8.00 20.00
HHG06 Gordie Howe/40 25.00 60.00
HHG11 Luc Robitaille/40 8.00 20.00
HHG12 Marcel Dionne/40 10.00 25.00
HHG13 Mario Lemieux/40 20.00 50.00
HHG14 Mark Messier/25 12.00 30.00
HHG15 Maurice Richard/35 30.00 60.00
HHG16 Mike Gartner/35 10.00 25.00
HHG17 Phil Esposito/40 12.00 30.00
HHG20 Wayne Gretzky/40 30.00 80.00

2015-16 ITG Stickwork Stick Rack Dual Silver

SR201 A.Mogilny/T.Linden/25 12.00 30.00
SR202 A.Ovechkin/S.Fedorov/35 15.00 40.00
SR204 B.Bishop/T.Rask/17 12.00 30.00
SR206 B.Mosienko/S.Mikita/30 10.00 25.00
SR210 B.Orr/W.Gretzky/40 40.00 80.00
SR211 B.Shanahan/H.Zetterberg/19 12.00 30.00
SR212 C.Neely/R.Bourque/35 12.00 30.00
SR213 C.Chelios/A.MacInnis/40 10.00 25.00
SR214 C.Chelios/S.Savard/40 8.00 20.00
SR215 C.Pronger/A.MacInnis/35 10.00 25.00
SR217 C.Joseph/F.Potvin/40 12.00 30.00
SR218 C.Joseph/G.Fuhr/40 12.00 30.00
SR219 D.Savard/C.Chelios/30 8.00 20.00
SR220 D.Doughty/R.Blake/30 10.00 25.00
SR221 E.Malkin/A.Ovechkin/30 30.00 80.00
SR224 J.Kurri/G.Anderson/30 8.00 20.00
SR225 J.Spezza/I.Kovalchuk/30 8.00 20.00
SR226 J.Skinner/S.Stamkos/30 15.00 40.00
SR228 J.Kocur/M.Messier/35 15.00 30.00
SR229 K.Tkachuk/J.Roenick/30 12.00 30.00
SR230 K.Hodge/P.Esposito/40 12.00 30.00
SR231 M.Dionne/S.Fedorov/40 12.00 30.00
SR232 M.Gaborik/D.Ciccarelli/30 8.00 20.00
SR233 M.Backstrom/G.Landeskog/25 8.00 20.00
SR234 M.Naslund/B.Bellows/40 6.00 15.00
SR239 N.Ullman/R.Kelly/40 10.00 25.00
SR241 P.Stastny/P.Stastny/30 6.00 15.00
SR242 P.Turgeon/D.Andreychuk/25 10.00 25.00
SR244 R.Langway/L.Robinson/30 8.00 20.00
SR245 S.Savard/Y.Cournoyer/40 8.00 20.00
SR246 S.Gagne/R.Nash/35 8.00 20.00
SR247 W.Gretzky/G.Howe/35 40.00 80.00
SR248 W.Gretzky/M.Richard/35 30.00 80.00

2015-16 ITG Stickwork Stick Rack Quad Silver

SR403 Dion/Rbtl/Cffy/Grtzk/40 50.00 125.00
SR404 Dion/Trttr/Espo/Lflr/15 15.00 40.00
SR405 Espo/Mkta/Rchrd/Gflrn/15 15.00 40.00
SR406 Fdrv/Yzrmn/Hull/Ldstrm/20 25.00 50.00
SR407 Gny/Shtt/Llr/Svrd/15 12.00 30.00
SR409 Grtzk/Lemx/Fdrv/Rnck/25 40.00 100.00
SR410 Hsly/McInn/Brq/Ptvn/15 15.00 40.00
SR411 Hsly/McInn/Mrphy/Brq/40 12.00 30.00
SR413 Kur/Grtzk/Mssr/Fhr/35 50.00 125.00
SR414 Lndrs/Fdrv/Mssr/Rnck/35 15.00 40.00
SR416 Mlln/Mglny/Bllws/Flry/20 12.00 30.00
SR417 Oat/Lndn/Rnck/Nslnd/15 15.00 40.00
SR418 Ovchkn/Stmks/Nsh/Kvlchk/15 25.00 50.00
SR419 Prnt/Ptvn/Jsph/Trtk/40 12.00 30.00
SR421 Prngr/McInn/Chls/Hsly/35 10.00 25.00
SR423 Roy/Fhr/Ptvn/Jsph/40 20.00 50.00
SR424 Roy/Trtk/Prnt/Fhr/40 20.00 50.00
SR425 Svrd/Chls/Nslnd/Bllws/40 8.00 20.00
SR426 Svrd/Shtt/Crnyr/Lflr/15 12.00 30.00

2015-16 ITG Stickwork Stick Rack Triple Silver

SR301 Anderson/Kurri/Coffey/25 10.00 25.00
SR303 Byfuglien/Bergeron/Suter/30 10.00 25.00
SR305 Carter/Parise/Phaneuf/30 8.00 20.00
SR306 Chelios/MacInnis/Coffey/40 10.00 25.00
SR307 Chelios/Pronger/Housley/35 8.00 20.00
SR308 Dionne/Esposito/Mikita/30 12.00 30.00
SR309 Gretzky/Esposito
Cournoyer/40 30.00 80.00
SR310 Gretzky/Howe/Richard/40 40.00 80.00
SR311 Gretzky/Messier/Lindros/30 30.00 80.00
SR313 Housley/MacInnis/Bourque/40 12.00 30.00
SR314 Howe/Kelly/Ullman/40 25.00 60.00
SR315 Joseph/Potvin/Parent/40 12.00 30.00
SR316 Kurri/Gretzky/Dionne/40 30.00 80.00
SR319 Langway/Potvin/Savard/25 15.00 40.00
SR320 Lemieux/Gretzky/Richard/40 40.00 80.00
SR321 Lidstrom/Fedorov/Yzerman/25 25.00 60.00
SR324 Murphy/MacInnis/Housley/40 10.00 25.00
SR325 Orr/Hodge/Esposito/40 30.00 80.00
SR326 Parise/Skinner/Spezza/25 12.00 30.00
SR329 Savard/Naslund/Cournoyer/40 8.00 20.00
SR330 Ullman/Richard/Howe/40 25.00 50.00
SR332 Zetterberg/Nash/Malkin/25 20.00 50.00

2015-16 ITG Stickwork Tape Job Silver

TJ03 Guy Lafleur/30 10.00 25.00
TJ05 Marcel Dionne/20 12.00 30.00
TJ06 Mario Lemieux/40 20.00 50.00
TJ07 Mark Messier/40 10.00 25.00
TJ08 Patrick Roy/40 20.00 50.00
TJ09 Saku Koivu/15 20.00 40.00
TJ10 Trevor Linden/30 8.00 20.00
TJ11 Wayne Gretzky/20 50.00 100.00

2015-16 ITG Stickwork Tape to Tape Silver

TT03 M.Messier/W.Gretzky/15 30.00 80.00
TT04 N.Lidstrom/S.Fedorov/25 15.00 40.00
TT05 P.Roy/G.Fuhr/30 15.00 40.00
TT06 S.Yzerman/S.Fedorov/35 20.00 40.00
TT08 W.Gretzky/M.Lemieux/20 40.00 100.00
TT09 Y.Cournoyer/G.Lafleur/18 12.00 30.00

2016-17 ITG Stickwork 100 Greatest of All Time

GAT01 Adam Oates/25 6.00 15.00
GAT02 Al MacInnis/25 8.00 20.00
GAT03 Alex Delvecchio/25 6.00 15.00
GAT04 Alexander Ovechkin/25 25.00 60.00
GAT05 Andy Bathgate/25 6.00 15.00
GAT06 Bob Gainey/25 6.00 15.00
GAT07 Bobby Clarke/25 10.00 25.00
GAT08 Bobby Hull/25 12.00 30.00
GAT09 Bobby Orr/25 25.00 60.00
GAT10 Borje Salming/25 6.00 15.00
GAT11 Brad Park/25 6.00 15.00
GAT12 Brendan Shanahan/25 6.00 15.00
GAT13 Chris Chelios/25 6.00 15.00
GAT14 Darryl Sittler/25 8.00 20.00
GAT15 Dave Keon/25 6.00 15.00
GAT16 Denis Potvin/25 6.00 15.00
GAT17 Denis Savard/25 6.00 15.00
GAT18 Eddie Shore/25 6.00 15.00
GAT19 Eric Lindros/25 10.00 25.00
GAT20 Frank Mahovlich/25 6.00 15.00
GAT21 Gilbert Perreault/25 6.00 15.00
GAT22 Gordie Howe/25 20.00 50.00
GAT23 Grant Fuhr/25 10.00 25.00
GAT24 Guy Lafleur/25 8.00 20.00
GAT25 Henri Richard/25 6.00 15.00
GAT26 Jacques Plante/25 10.00 25.00
GAT27 Jari Kurri/25 6.00 15.00
GAT28 Jaromir Jagr/25 20.00 50.00
GAT29 Jean Beliveau/25 6.00 15.00
GAT30 Jean Ratelle/25 6.00 15.00
GAT31 Joe Nieuwendyk/25 5.00 12.00
GAT32 Joe Sakic/25 12.00 30.00
GAT33 Johnny Bower/20 6.00 15.00
GAT34 Johnny Bucyk/25 6.00 15.00
GAT35 Ken Dryden/25 12.00 30.00
GAT36 King Clancy/20 5.00 12.00
GAT37 Larry Robinson/25 6.00 15.00
GAT38 Luc Robitaille/25 6.00 15.00
GAT39 Marcel Dionne/25 8.00 20.00
GAT40 Mario Lemieux/25 25.00 60.00
GAT41 Mark Messier/25 12.00 30.00
GAT42 Martin Brodeur/25 15.00 40.00
GAT43 Mats Sundin/25 6.00 15.00
GAT44 Maurice Richard/25 12.00 30.00
GAT45 Mike Bossy/25 6.00 15.00
GAT46 Mike Gartner/25 8.00 20.00
GAT47 Mike Modano/25 10.00 25.00
GAT48 Milt Schmidt/25 6.00 15.00
GAT49 Pat LaFontaine/25 6.00 15.00
GAT50 Patrick Roy/25 15.00 40.00
GAT51 Paul Coffey/25 6.00 15.00
GAT52 Peter Forsberg/25 8.00 20.00
GAT53 Peter Stastny/25 5.00 12.00
GAT54 Phil Esposito/25 10.00 25.00
GAT55 Raymond Bourque/25 12.00 30.00
GAT56 Red Kelly/25 6.00 15.00
GAT57 Ron Francis/25 8.00 20.00
GAT58 Scott Stevens/25 5.00 12.00
GAT59 Serge Savard/25 6.00 15.00
GAT60 Sergei Fedorov/25 10.00 25.00
GAT61 Sid Abel/25 6.00 15.00
GAT62 Sidney Crosby/25 25.00 60.00
GAT63 Stan Mikita/25 8.00 20.00
GAT64 Steve Yzerman/25 15.00 40.00
GAT65 Ted Kennedy/20 6.00 15.00
GAT66 Ted Lindsay/20 6.00 15.00
GAT67 Teemu Selanne/25 12.00 30.00
GAT68 Tim Horton/25 12.00 30.00
GAT69 Wayne Gretzky/25 40.00 100.00
GAT70 Yvan Cournoyer/25 6.00 15.00

2016-17 ITG Stickwork Award Season

AS01 Shore/Abel/Richard/Howe/Kennedy
Beliveau/Bathgate/Geoffrion 20.00 50.00
AS02 Hull/Esposito/Orr/Mikita/Clarke
Lafleur/Trottier/Gretzky 40.00 100.00
AS03 Keon/Hull/Mikita/Bucyk/Ratelle
Perreault/Goring/Dionne 12.00 30.00
AS04 Lumley/Plante/Worsley/Barrasso
Vanbiesbrouck/Hextall/Fuhr/Roy 15.00 40.00
AS05 Stewart/Worsley/Mahovlich/Keon
Rousseau/Laperriere/Orr
Sanderson 25.00 60.00
AS06 Perreault/Potvin/Trottier/Bossy
Smith/Bourque/Hawerchuk/Stastny 8.00 20.00
AS07 Larmer/Lemieux/Robitaille
Nieuwendyk/Makarov/Selanne
Brodeur/Forsberg 25.00 60.00
AS08 Lindsay/Howe/Beliveau/Hull
Mikita/Esposito/Orr/Lafleur 25.00 60.00
AS09 Beliveau/Keon/Orr/Cournoyer/Leach
Lafleur/Robinson/Gainey 25.00 60.00
AS10 Trottier/Goring/Bossy/Messier/Gretzky
Lemieux/Sakic/Yzerman 40.00 100.00
AS11 Laperriere/Orr/Potvin/Robinson/Carlyle
Langway/Coffey/Bourque 25.00 60.00
AS12 Ratelle/Clarke/Richard/Gilbert/Goring
McDonald/Park/Lemieux 25.00 60.00

2016-17 ITG Stickwork Decade Leaders

DL01 Mikita/Howe/Hull/Ullman 20.00 50.00
DL02 Mikita/Howe/Beliveau/Richard 20.00 50.00
DL03 Hull/Mahovlich/Howe/Mikita 20.00 50.00
DL04 Howe/Lindsay/Richard/Beliveau 20.00 50.00
DL05 Howe/Lindsay
Beliveau/Bathgate 20.00 50.00

2016-17 ITG Stickwork Enshrined Eight

EE01 Hull/Beliveau/Richard/Howe/Orr
Keon/Ullman/Abel 25.00 60.00
EE02 Bower/Plante/Lumley/Worsley/Dryden
Cheevers/Roy/Fuhr 15.00 40.00
EE03 Harris/Pronovost/Orr/Lapointe/Savard
Salming/Stanley/Bourque 25.00 60.00

2016-17 ITG Stickwork Enshrined Eight Franchise

E8F01 Bower/Stanley/Salming/Sittler/McDonald
Keon/Horton/Kennedy 20.00 50.00
E8F02 Beliveau/Dryden/Cournoyer
Laperriere/Plante/Richard
Robinson/Shutt 20.00 50.00
E8F03 Gainey/Lafleur/Chelios/Lapointe
Roy/Langway/Savard/Mahovlich 25.00 60.00
E8F04 Abel/Hull/Mikita/Esposito/Orr
Goulet/Savard/Chelios 40.00 100.00
E8F05 Bucyk/Cheevers/Esposito/Neely
Oates/Orr/Park/Bourque 40.00 100.00
E8F06 Howe/Lindsay/Yzerman/Abel/Pronovost
Ullman/Shanahan/Larionov 30.00 80.00
E8F07 Gretzky/Coffey/Messier/Fuhr/Anderson
Kurri/Oates/Ullman 60.00 150.00
E8F08 Gretzky/Dionne/Kurri/Coffey/Robinson
Robitaille/Fuhr/Murphy 60.00 150.00
E8F09 Lemieux/Murphy/Francis
Coffey/Horton/Mullen
Robitaille/Bathgate 40.00 100.00
E8F10 Messier/Gartner
Esposito/Stanley/Bathgate
Ratelle/Park/Lafleur 20.00 50.00

2016-17 ITG Stickwork Enshrined Goalie Sticks

EGS01 Dominik Hasek/19 10.00 25.00
EGS02 Gerry Cheevers/22 6.00 15.00
EGS03 Grant Fuhr/22 10.00 25.00
EGS07 Patrick Roy/25 15.00 40.00
EGS08 Vladislav Tretiak/22 5.00 12.00

2016-17 ITG Stickwork Enshrined Sticks

ES01 Adam Oates/19 6.00 15.00
ES03 Bobby Hull/25 12.00 30.00
ES04 Bobby Orr/17 25.00 60.00
ES05 Cam Neely/22 3.00 8.00
ES06 Chris Pronger/19 6.00 15.00
ES07 Denis Savard/17 6.00 15.00
ES08 Gordie Howe/17 20.00 50.00
ES09 Guy Lafleur/25 8.00 20.00
ES10 Henri Richard/17 6.00 15.00
ES11 Jacques Laperriere/17 5.00 12.00
ES12 Jean Beliveau/17 6.00 15.00
ES14 Mario Lemieux/25 25.00 60.00
ES15 Maurice Richard/22 12.00 30.00
ES16 Phil Esposito/22 10.00 25.00
ES19 Sergei Fedorov/25 10.00 25.00
ES20 Stan Mikita/22 8.00 20.00
ES21 Tim Horton/17 12.00 30.00
ES22 Wayne Gretzky/22 40.00 100.00

2016-17 ITG Stickwork Game Used Goalie Sticks

GGS01 Andy Moog/25 8.00 20.00
GGS02 Bruce Gamble/22 8.00 20.00
GGS03 Charlie Hodge/22 8.00 20.00
GGS04 Curtis Joseph/17 10.00 25.00
GGS05 Dan Bouchard/22 8.00 20.00
GGS06 Eddie Johnston/25 8.00 20.00
GGS07 John Vanbiesbrouck/25 8.00 20.00
GGS08 Kirk McLean/22 8.00 20.00
GGS09 Manon Rheaume/22 20.00 50.00
GGS10 Martin Brodeur/25 20.00 50.00
GGS12 Mike Vernon/22 6.00 15.00

2016-17 ITG Stickwork Game Used Sticks

GS01 Al Iafrate/19 8.00 20.00
GS02 Alexander Ovechkin/17 30.00 80.00
GS03 Brent Sutter/17 8.00 20.00
GS04 Brian Sutter/17 8.00 20.00
GS05 Claude Lemieux/19 8.00 20.00
GS06 Claude Provost/17 8.00 20.00
GS07 Craig Hartsburg/19 8.00 20.00
GS10 Garry Unger/17 8.00 20.00
GS11 Gary Leeman/17 8.00 20.00
GS12 Jeremy Roenick/22 12.00 30.00
GS13 Ken Linseman/20 8.00 20.00
GS14 Kirk Muller/18 8.00 20.00
GS15 Marc Tardif/19 8.00 20.00
GS16 Mark Messier/17 15.00 40.00
GS17 Owen Nolan/17 8.00 20.00
GS18 Paul Kariya/17 8.00 20.00
GS19 Pete Mahovlich/22 8.00 20.00
GS20 Peter Forsberg/22 15.00 40.00
GS21 Petr Nedved/21 8.00 20.00
GS22 Rod Brind'Amour/19 8.00 20.00
GS23 Sidney Crosby/25 30.00 80.00
GS25 Steve Larmer/16 8.00 20.00
GS27 Vincent Damphousse/19 8.00 20.00

2016-17 ITG Stickwork Stick Rack 4

SR01 Hull/Esposito/Dionne/Lafleur 15.00 40.00
SR02 Orr/Shore/Bourque/Park 30.00 80.00
SR03 Salming/Sittler/Keon/Horton 15.00 40.00
SR04 Larionov/Fedorov
Makarov/Krutov 12.00 30.00
SR05 Richard/Richard
Mahovlich/Mahovlich 15.00 40.00
SR06 Roy/Richter/Joseph
Vanbiesbrouck 20.00 50.00
SR07 Lindros/Lemieux/Jagr/Messier 30.00 80.00
SR08 Mikita/Hull/Bucyk/Orr 30.00 80.00

2016-17 ITG Stickwork Stick Save

SS01 Curtis Joseph 8.00 20.00
SS02 Grant Fuhr 10.00 25.00
SS03 Harry Lumley 6.00 15.00
SS04 Jacques Plante 10.00 25.00
SS05 John Vanbiesbrouck 6.00 15.00
SS06 Johnny Bower 6.00 15.00
SS07 Manon Rheaume 15.00 40.00
SS08 Martin Brodeur 15.00 40.00
SS09 Mike Richter 6.00 15.00
SS10 Patrick Roy 15.00 40.00
SS11 Tom Barrasso 6.00 15.00
SS12 Vladislav Tretiak 5.00 12.00

2016-17 ITG Stickwork Tape to Twine

TT01 Howe/Mahovlich/Richard
Lindsay/Mikita/Hull
Horton/Beliveau/25 30.00 80.00
TT02 Messier/Kurri/Hull
Yzerman/Robitaille/Hawerchuk
Modano/Oates/25 25.00 60.00
TT03 Savard/Lafleur/Gainey
Bucyk/Trottier/Richard
Hull/Park/25 20.00 50.00
TT04 Bathgate/Richard/Beliveau
Stewart/Howe/Lindsay
Delvecchio/Keon/20 30.00 80.00

2016-17 ITG Stickwork Vintage Stick Rack 4

VSR01 Howe/Beliveau
Mahovlich/Richard/25 40.00 100.00
VSR02 Plante/Bower
Lumley/Worsley/25 15.00 40.00
VSR04 Howe/Lindsay
Pronovost/Delvecchio/25 15.00 40.00
VSR05 Barilko/Stanley
Kennedy/Armstrong/25 10.00 25.00
VSR06 Ullman/Keon/Horton/Baun/25 20.00 50.00

2007-08 ITG Superlative Autographs Silver

AAO Alexander Ovechkin 50.00 125.00
ABC Bobby Clarke 20.00 40.00
ABH Brett Hull 20.00 50.00
ABL Brian Leetch 8.00 20.00
ABOH Bobby Hull 20.00 50.00
ABP Bernie Parent 12.00 30.00
ACC Chris Chelios 20.00 40.00
ACN Cam Neely 10.00 25.00
ACO Chris Osgood 12.50 30.00
ACP Chris Pronger 12.00 30.00
ADH Dany Heatley 8.00 20.00
ADH Dominik Hasek 20.00 40.00
ADK Dave Keon 15.00 30.00
ADP Denis Potvin 10.00 25.00
AEG Ed Giacomin 10.00 25.00
AFM Frank Mahovlich 15.00 30.00
AGF Grant Fuhr 15.00 40.00
AGH Glenn Hall 12.00 30.00
AGL Guy Lafleur 20.00 40.00
AHR Henri Richard 12.00 30.00
AIK Ilya Kovalchuk 10.00 25.00
AJB Jean Beliveau 25.00 50.00
AJBO Johnny Bower 15.00 30.00
AJJ Jaromir Jagr 25.00 50.00
AJSG Jean-Sebastien Giguere 8.00 20.00
AJSK Joe Sakic 25.00 60.00
AJT Joe Thornton 10.00 25.00
AMB Martin Brodeur 30.00 60.00
AMD Marcel Dionne 8.00 20.00
AMG Marian Gaborik 10.00 25.00
AML Mario Lemieux 50.00 100.00
AMM Mike Modano 15.00 40.00
AMS Milt Schmidt 10.00 25.00
AMSL Martin St-Louis 10.00 25.00
AMT Marty Turco 8.00 20.00
ANL Nicklas Lidstrom 15.00 30.00
APC Paul Coffey 10.00 25.00
APD Pavel Datsyuk 20.00 40.00
APE Phil Esposito 20.00 40.00
APR Patrick Roy 50.00 100.00
ARB Raymond Bourque 20.00 40.00
ARE Ray Emery 8.00 20.00
ARK Red Kelly 10.00 25.00
ARL Roberto Luongo 12.00 30.00
ASM Stan Mikita 15.00 40.00
ATE Tony Esposito 10.00 25.00
ATL Ted Lindsay 12.50 30.00
AVL Vincent Lecavalier 12.50 30.00
AVT Vladislav Tretiak 20.00 40.00
AJSN Scott Niedermayer 10.00 25.00

2007-08 ITG Superlative Jerseys Autographs Silver

AJAO Alexander Ovechkin 40.00 100.00
AJBC Bobby Clarke 20.00 50.00
AJBH Brett Hull 25.00 60.00
AJBL Brian Leetch 10.00 25.00
AJBOH Bobby Hull 15.00 40.00
AJBP Bernie Parent 15.00 40.00
AJCC Chris Chelios 12.50 30.00
AJCN Cam Neely 12.00 30.00
AJCO Chris Osgood 12.50 30.00
AJCP Chris Pronger 12.00 30.00
AJDH Dany Heatley 12.50 30.00
AJDH Dominik Hasek 15.00 40.00
AJDK Dave Keon 15.00 40.00
AJDP Denis Potvin 12.00 30.00
AJEG Ed Giacomin 12.00 30.00
AJFM Frank Mahovlich 15.00 40.00
AJGF Grant Fuhr 12.50 30.00
AJGH Glenn Hall 15.00 40.00
AJGL Guy Lafleur 25.00 50.00
AJHR Henri Richard 20.00 50.00
AJIK Ilya Kovalchuk 10.00 25.00
AJJB Jean Beliveau 25.00 60.00
AJJBO Johnny Bower 15.00 30.00
AJJJ Jaromir Jagr 25.00 60.00
AJJSG Jean-Sebastien Giguere 15.00 40.00
AJJSK Joe Sakic 20.00 50.00
AJJT Joe Thornton 15.00 40.00
AJMB Martin Brodeur 30.00 80.00
AJMD Marcel Dionne 15.00 40.00
AJMG Marian Gaborik 12.00 30.00
AJML Mario Lemieux 60.00 120.00
AJMM Mike Modano 20.00 50.00
AJMS Milt Schmidt 15.00 40.00
AJMSL Martin St-Louis 12.00 30.00
AJMT Marty Turco 12.00 30.00
AJNL Nicklas Lidstrom 15.00 40.00
AJPC Paul Coffey 12.00 30.00
AJPD Pavel Datsyuk 15.00 40.00
AJPE Phil Esposito 15.00 40.00
AJPR Patrick Roy 30.00 80.00
AJRB Raymond Bourque 25.00 60.00
AJRE Ray Emery 10.00 25.00
AJRK Red Kelly 10.00 25.00
AJRL Roberto Luongo 15.00 40.00
AJSM Stan Mikita 12.50 30.00
AJSN Scott Niedermayer 10.00 25.00
AJTE Tony Esposito 12.00 30.00
AJTL Ted Lindsay 12.50 30.00
AJVL Vincent Lecavalier 12.00 30.00
AJVT Vladislav Tretiak 25.00 60.00

2007-08 ITG Superlative Jerseys Silver

GUJ01 Jean Beliveau 12.00 30.00
GUJ02 Raymond Bourque BOS 15.00 40.00
GUJ03 Raymond Bourque COL 15.00 40.00
GUJ04 Martin Brodeur 25.00 50.00
GUJ05 Gerry Cheevers 10.00 25.00
GUJ06 Chris Chelios 10.00 25.00
GUJ07 Alexei Cherepanov 15.00 40.00
GUJ08 Bobby Clarke 15.00 40.00
GUJ09 Paul Coffey 10.00 25.00
GUJ10 Marcel Dionne 10.00 25.00
GUJ11 Ray Emery 8.00 20.00
GUJ12 Angelo Esposito 12.00 30.00
GUJ13 Phil Esposito 15.00 40.00
GUJ14 Tony Esposito 10.00 25.00
GUJ15 Grant Fuhr 12.00 30.00
GUJ16 Jaromir Jagr Pittsburgh 30.00 80.00
GUJ17 Ed Giacomin 10.00 25.00
GUJ18 Glenn Hall 10.00 25.00
GUJ19 Dominik Hasek 15.00 40.00
GUJ21 Bobby Hull 20.00 50.00
GUJ22 Brett Hull Dallas 20.00 50.00
GUJ23 Brett Hull Detroit 20.00 50.00
GUJ24 Jaromir Jagr New York 30.00 80.00
GUJ25 Dave Keon 10.00 25.00
GUJ26 Ilya Kovalchuk 10.00 25.00
GUJ27 Guy Lafleur 15.00 40.00
GUJ28 Pat LaFontaine 8.00 20.00
GUJ29 Vincent Lecavalier 10.00 25.00
GUJ30 Brian Leetch 8.00 20.00
GUJ31 Joe Thornton San Jose 12.00 30.00
GUJ32 Ted Lindsay 10.00 25.00
GUJ33 Roberto Luongo Vancouver 15.00 40.00
GUJ34 Roberto Luongo Florida 15.00 40.00
GUJ35 Frank Mahovlich 10.00 25.00
GUJ36 Stan Mikita 12.00 30.00
GUJ37 Mike Modano 15.00 40.00
GUJ38 Cam Neely 10.00 25.00
GUJ39 Alexander Ovechkin 30.00 80.00
GUJ40 Denis Potvin 10.00 25.00
GUJ41 Felix Potvin 20.00 50.00
GUJ42 Carey Price 30.00 60.00
GUJ43 Chris Pronger 10.00 25.00
GUJ44 Tuukka Rask 25.00 60.00
GUJ45 Henri Richard 12.00 30.00
GUJ46 Maurice Richard 50.00 100.00
GUJ47 Patrick Roy Montreal 25.00 60.00
GUJ48 Patrick Roy Colorado 25.00 60.00
GUJ49 Joe Sakic 15.00 40.00
GUJ50 Milt Schmidt 8.00 20.00
GUJ51 Jari Kurri 20.00 50.00
GUJ52 John Tavares 30.00 60.00
GUJ53 Joe Thornton Boston 20.00 50.00
GUJ54 Vladislav Tretiak 15.00 40.00
GUJ55 Marty Turco 10.00 25.00
GUJ56 Mario Lemieux 25.00 60.00
GUJ57 Pavel Datsyuk 15.00 40.00
GUJ58 Mats Sundin 10.00 25.00
GUJ59 Steven Stamkos 25.00 60.00
GUJ60 Ed Belfour 12.00 30.00
GUJ61 Markus Naslund 10.00 25.00
GUJ62 Paul Stastny 8.00 20.00
GUJ63 Doug Gilmour 12.00 30.00
GUJ64 Marc Staal 8.00 20.00
GUJ65 Sam Gagner 8.00 20.00
GUJ66 Jordan Staal 8.00 20.00
GUJ67 Bill Barber 6.00 15.00
GUJ68 Martin St. Louis 10.00 25.00
GUJ69 Scott Niedermayer 10.00 25.00
GUJ70 Lanny McDonald 12.00 30.00
GUJ71 Borje Salming 10.00 25.00
GUJ72 Darryl Sittler 12.00 30.00
GUJ73 Marian Gaborik 10.00 25.00
GUJ74 Jean-Sebastien Giguere 10.00 25.00
GUJ75 Paul Kariya 10.00 25.00

2007-08 ITG Superlative Patches Silver

SP01 Alexander Ovechkin 30.00 60.00
SP02 Alexei Cherepanov 15.00 40.00
SP03 Angelo Esposito 15.00 40.00
SP04 Bobby Clarke 15.00 40.00
SP05 Bobby Hull 25.00 60.00
SP06 Borje Salming 15.00 40.00
SP07 Brett Hull Dallas 15.00 40.00
SP08 Brett Hull Detroit 15.00 40.00
SP09 Brian Leetch 10.00 25.00
SP10 Cam Neely 15.00 40.00
SP11 Carey Price 25.00 50.00
SP12 Chris Chelios 12.00 30.00
SP13 Chris Osgood 15.00 40.00
SP14 Chris Pronger 12.00 30.00
SP15 Dany Heatley 10.00 25.00
SP16 Darryl Sittler 15.00 40.00
SP17 Dave Keon 12.00 30.00
SP18 Denis Potvin 15.00 40.00
SP19 Dominik Hasek 15.00 40.00
SP20 Doug Gilmour 10.00 25.00
SP21 Ed Belfour 12.00 30.00
SP22 Felix Potvin 20.00 50.00
SP23 Frank Mahovlich 15.00 40.00
SP25 Guy Lafleur 20.00 50.00
SP26 Henri Richard 20.00 50.00
SP27 Ilya Kovalchuk 12.00 30.00
SP28 Jari Kurri 12.00 30.00
SP29 Jaromir Jagr Pittsburgh 30.00 60.00
SP30 Jaromir Jagr New York 30.00 60.00
SP31 Jean Beliveau 15.00 40.00
SP32 Joe Sakic 20.00 50.00
SP33 Joe Thornton San Jose 15.00 40.00
SP34 Joe Thornton Boston 20.00 50.00
SP35 John Tavares 20.00 50.00
SP36 Jordan Staal 10.00 25.00
SP37 Jean-Sebastien Giguere 15.00 40.00
SP38 Lanny McDonald 12.00 30.00
SP39 Marc Staal 12.00 30.00
SP40 Marcel Dionne 10.00 25.00
SP41 Marian Gaborik 12.00 30.00
SP42 Mario Lemieux 30.00 60.00
SP43 Markus Naslund 10.00 25.00
SP44 Martin Brodeur 30.00 60.00
SP45 Martin St. Louis 12.00 30.00
SP46 Marty Turco 12.00 30.00
SP47 Mats Sundin 20.00 50.00
SP48 Mike Modano 20.00 50.00
SP49 Milt Schmidt 15.00 40.00
SP50 Pat LaFontaine 20.00 50.00
SP51 Patrick Roy MONT 40.00 80.00
SP52 Patrick Roy COL 40.00 80.00
SP53 Paul Coffey 12.00 30.00
SP54 Paul Stastny 10.00 25.00
SP55 Pavel Datsyuk 15.00 40.00
SP56 Phil Esposito 20.00 50.00
SP57 Ray Emery 10.00 25.00
SP58 Ray Bourque BOS 15.00 40.00
SP59 Ray Bourque COL 15.00 40.00
SP60 R. Luongo VAN 20.00 50.00
SP61 R. Luongo FLA 15.00 40.00
SP62 Sam Gagner 12.00 30.00
SP63 Scott Niedermayer 10.00 25.00
SP64 Stan Mikita 12.00 30.00
SP65 Vladislav Tretiak 30.00 60.00
SP66 Steven Stamkos 40.00 80.00
SP67 Tony Esposito 12.00 30.00
SP68 Tuukka Rask 40.00 80.00
SP69 Vincent Lecavalier 12.00 30.00
SP70 Larry Robinson 15.00 40.00
SP71 Grant Fuhr Edmonton 20.00 50.00
SP72 Gilbert Perreault 12.00 30.00
SP73 Jean Ratelle 15.00 40.00
SP74 Peter Forsberg 15.00 40.00
SP75 Paul Kariya 12.00 30.00

2007-08 ITG Superlative Prospects Jerseys Autographs Silver

SPAB Alex Bourret 8.00 20.00
SPACO Andrew Cogliano 15.00 40.00
SPAE Angelo Esposito 15.00 40.00
SPAP Alex Pietrangelo 15.00 40.00
SPAS Alexander Semin 15.00 40.00
SPBB Brian Boyle 12.00 30.00
SPBL Bryan Little 12.00 30.00
SPBLE Brian Lee 10.00 25.00
SPBM Brett MacLean 10.00 25.00
SPBS Brandon Sutter 12.00 30.00
SPCF Cody Franson 10.00 25.00
SPCG Colton Gillies 10.00 25.00
SPCGI Claude Giroux 25.00 60.00
SPCPR Carey Price 50.00 100.00
SPDD Drew Doughty 20.00 50.00
SPDP Dustin Penner 12.00 30.00
SPDS Devin Setoguchi 12.00 30.00
SPGB Gilbert Brule 15.00 40.00
SPJBL Jonathon Blum 12.00 30.00
SPJH Jonas Hiller 10.00 25.00
SPJS Jordan Staal 15.00 40.00
SPJSK Jack Skille 12.00 30.00
SPJT John Tavares 60.00 120.00
SPJTL Jiri Tlusty 15.00 40.00
SPKA Karl Alzner 15.00 40.00
SPKE Keaton Ellerby 10.00 25.00
SPKM Kenndal McArdle 8.00 20.00
SPKR Kris Russell 10.00 25.00
SPLB Luc Bourdon 12.00 30.00
SPLC Logan Couture 15.00 40.00
SPLI Leland Irving 10.00 25.00
SPMC Matthew Corrente 8.00 20.00
SPMDZ Michael Del Zotto 15.00 40.00
SPMF Michael Frolik 8.00 20.00
SPMG Michael Grabner 10.00 25.00
SPML Matt Lashoff 8.00 20.00
SPMS Marc Staal 15.00 40.00
SPOM Oscar Moller 12.00 30.00
SPPM Peter Mueller 12.00 30.00
SPPS Paul Stastny 15.00 40.00

2007-08 ITG Superlative Prospects Jerseys Autographs Silver

SPRP Ryan Parent 15.00 40.00
SPSD Steve Downie 12.00 30.00
SPSG Sam Gagner 15.00 40.00
SPSM Steve Mason 15.00 40.00
SPSS Steven Stamkos 40.00 100.00
SPTH Thomas Hickey 12.00 30.00
SPTM Thomas McCollum 10.00 25.00
SPTP Tom Pyatt 8.00 20.00
SPTR Tuukka Rask 15.00 40.00
SPTW Ty Wishart 8.00 20.00

2009-10 ITG Superlative Autographs

AAK Anze Kopitar 12.00 30.00
AAO Alexander Ovechkin 30.00 80.00
AAS Alexander Semin 8.00 20.00
ACC Chris Chelios 8.00 20.00
ACP Carey Price 15.00 40.00
ADB Daniel Briere 8.00 20.00
ADG Doug Gilmour 10.00 25.00
ADH Dominik Hasek 12.00 30.00
AEN Evgeni Nabokov 6.00 15.00
AGL Guy Lafleur 10.00 25.00
AIK Ilya Kovalchuk 8.00 20.00
AJB Jean Beliveau 20.00 50.00
AJJ Jaromir Jagr 25.00 60.00
AJS Joe Sakic 15.00 40.00
AJT Joe Thornton 12.00 30.00
ALR Larry Robinson 8.00 20.00
AMB Martin Brodeur 20.00 50.00
AMG Mike Green 6.00 15.00
AMGA Marian Gaborik 8.00 20.00
AMK Mikko Koivu 8.00 20.00
AML Mario Lemieux 30.00 80.00
AMM Mike Modano 12.00 30.00
AMS Martin St. Louis 8.00 20.00
ANL Nicklas Lidstrom 5.00 12.00
APM Patrick Marleau 8.00 20.00
APR Patrick Roy 20.00 50.00
APRO Patrick Roy 20.00 50.00
ARB Rob Blake 8.00 20.00
ARBO Ray Bourque 12.00 30.00
ARG Ryan Getzlaf 8.00 20.00
ARL Roberto Luongo 12.00 30.00
ASF Sergei Fedorov 12.00 30.00
ASK Saku Koivu 8.00 20.00
ASN Scott Niedermayer 8.00 20.00
ATS Teemu Selanne 15.00 40.00
ATT Tim Thomas 8.00 20.00

2009-10 ITG Superlative Game Used Jerseys Silver

*PATCH SLVR/30: .5X TO 1.2X BASIC JSY
GUJ01 Alexander Ovechkin/40 15.00 40.00
GUJ02 John Tavares 20.00 50.00
GUJ03 Corey Perry 12.00 30.00
GUJ04 Jean-Sebastien Giguere 15.00 40.00
GUJ05 Ryan Getzlaf 8.00 20.00
GUJ06 Scott Niedermayer 8.00 20.00
GUJ07 Teemu Selanne 15.00 40.00
GUJ08 Ilya Kovalchuk 8.00 20.00
GUJ09 Kari Lehtonen 6.00 15.00
GUJ10 Ray Bourque 10.00 25.00
GUJ11 Milan Lucic 6.00 15.00
GUJ12 Tim Thomas 8.00 20.00
GUJ13 Gilbert Perreault 8.00 20.00
GUJ14 Ryan Miller 15.00 40.00
GUJ15 Miikka Kiprusoff 8.00 20.00
GUJ16 Cam Ward 8.00 20.00
GUJ17 Chris Chelios 8.00 20.00
GUJ18 Denis Savard 8.00 20.00
GUJ19 Ray Bourque 12.00 30.00
GUJ20 Joe Sakic 15.00 40.00
GUJ21 Patrick Roy 15.00 40.00
GUJ22 Rob Blake 8.00 20.00
GUJ23 Brenden Morrow 6.00 15.00
GUJ24 Brett Hull 12.00 30.00
GUJ25 Ed Belfour 8.00 20.00
GUJ26 Marty Turco 8.00 20.00
GUJ27 Mike Modano 12.00 30.00
GUJ28 Dominik Hasek 12.00 30.00
GUJ29 Nicklas Lidstrom 5.00 12.00
GUJ30 Sergei Fedorov 12.00 30.00
GUJ31 Nazem Kadri 15.00 40.00
GUJ32 Anze Kopitar 12.00 30.00
GUJ33 Luc Robitaille 8.00 20.00
GUJ34 Marcel Dionne 10.00 25.00
GUJ35 Rob Blake 8.00 20.00
GUJ36 Marian Gaborik 8.00 20.00
GUJ37 Carey Price 15.00 40.00
GUJ38 Eric Staal 10.00 25.00
GUJ39 Mats Sundin 8.00 20.00
GUJ40 Patrick Roy 15.00 40.00
GUJ41 Saku Koivu 8.00 20.00
GUJ42 Martin Brodeur 15.00 40.00
GUJ43 Scott Niedermayer 8.00 20.00
GUJ44 Ilya Kovalchuk 8.00 20.00
GUJ45 Marian Gaborik 8.00 20.00
GUJ46 Dominik Hasek 12.00 30.00
GUJ47 Dale Hawerchuk 10.00 25.00
GUJ48 Daniel Briere 8.00 20.00
GUJ49 Jaromir Jagr 25.00 60.00
GUJ50 Marc-Andre Fleury 12.00 30.00
GUJ51 Mario Lemieux 15.00 40.00
GUJ52 Tyler Seguin 15.00 40.00
GUJ53 Patrick Marleau 8.00 20.00
GUJ54 Doug Gilmour 10.00 25.00
GUJ55 Martin St. Louis 8.00 20.00
GUJ56 Mike Green 6.00 15.00
GUJ57 Alexander Semin 8.00 20.00
GUJ58 Jaromir Jagr 25.00 60.00
GUJ59 Taylor Hall 15.00 40.00
GUJ60 Teemu Selanne 15.00 40.00

2009-10 ITG Superlative Game Used Patches Silver

*PATCH SLVR/30: .5X TO 1.2X BASIC JSY
SP02 John Tavares 30.00 80.00

2009-10 ITG Superlative Jerseys Autographs Silver

AJAK Anze Kopitar 12.00 30.00
AJAO Alexander Ovechkin 40.00 80.00
AJAS Alexander Semin 12.00 30.00
AJCC Chris Chelios 15.00 40.00
AJCP Carey Price 20.00 50.00
AJDB Daniel Briere 12.00 30.00
AJDG Doug Gilmour 12.00 30.00
AJDH Dominik Hasek 15.00 40.00
AJEN Evgeni Nabokov 10.00 25.00
AJGL Guy Lafleur 20.00 50.00
AJIK Ilya Kovalchuk 15.00 40.00
AJJB Jean Beliveau 20.00 50.00
AJJJ Jaromir Jagr 25.00 60.00
AJJS Joe Sakic 25.00 60.00
AJJT Joe Thornton 15.00 40.00
AJLR Larry Robinson 10.00 25.00
AJMB Martin Brodeur 25.00 60.00
AJMG Mike Green 10.00 25.00
AJMGA2 Marian Gaborik 12.00 30.00
AJMGA Marian Gaborik 15.00 40.00
AJMK Mikko Koivu 12.00 30.00
AJML Mario Lemieux 40.00 80.00
AJMM Mike Modano 15.00 40.00
AJMS Martin St. Louis 10.00 25.00
AJNL Nicklas Lidstrom 15.00 40.00
AJPM Patrick Marleau 12.00 30.00
AJPR Patrick Roy 30.00 80.00
AJPRO Patrick Roy 30.00 80.00
AJRBO Ray Bourque 20.00 50.00
AJRG Ryan Getzlaf 10.00 25.00
AJRL Roberto Luongo 20.00 50.00
AJSF Sergei Fedorov 15.00 40.00
AJSK Saku Koivu 15.00 40.00
AJSN Scott Niedermayer 10.00 25.00
AJTS Teemu Selanne 15.00 40.00
AJTT Tim Thomas 15.00 40.00

2009-10 ITG Superlative Prospect Autographs Silver

PABS Brayden Schenn 12.00 30.00
PACH Cody Hodgson 12.00 30.00
PACP Chet Pickard 8.00 20.00
PADH Darren Helm 6.00 15.00
PADT Dana Tyrell 6.00 15.00
PAEK Evander Kane 12.00 30.00
PAFB Fabian Brunnstrom 5.00 12.00
PAJC Jared Cowen 6.00 15.00
PAJE Jordan Eberle 25.00 60.00
PAJT John Tavares 25.00 60.00
PAKA Karl Alzner 4.00 10.00
PAMB Mikkel Boedker 4.00 10.00
PAMD Matt Duchene 12.00 30.00
PANK Nazem Kadri 15.00 40.00
PARN Ryan Nugent-Hopkins 30.00 80.00
PASV Semyon Varlamov 6.00 15.00
PATH Taylor Hall 25.00 60.00
PATS Tyler Seguin 40.00 80.00
PAVH Victor Hedman 15.00 40.00
PAZB Zach Boychuk 5.00 12.00
PATHI Thomas Hickey 4.00 10.00

2009-10 ITG Superlative Prospect Jerseys Autographs Silver

PAJBS Brayden Schenn 20.00 50.00
PAJCH Cody Hodgson 30.00 60.00
PAJCP Chet Pickard 12.00 30.00
PAJDH Darren Helm 12.00 30.00
PAJDT Dana Tyrell 10.00 25.00
PAJEK Evander Kane 15.00 40.00
PAJFB Fabian Brunnstrom 10.00 25.00
PAJJC Jared Cowen 10.00 25.00
PAJJE Jordan Eberle 40.00 80.00
PAJJT John Tavares 60.00 120.00
PAJKA Karl Alzner 10.00 25.00
PAJMB Mikkel Boedker 10.00 25.00
PAJMD Matt Duchene 30.00 60.00
PAJNK Nazem Kadri 30.00 60.00
PAJSV Semyon Varlamov 25.00 60.00
PAJTH Taylor Hall 40.00 100.00
PAJTS Tyler Seguin 30.00 80.00
PAJVH Victor Hedman 12.00 30.00
PAJZB Zach Boychuk 12.00 30.00
PAJRNH Ryan Nugent-Hopkins 50.00 100.00
PAJTHI Thomas Hickey 20.00 50.00

2008-09 ITG Superlative Franchise Vintage Blue

1 Syl Apps 12.00 30.00
2 Ace Bailey 6.00 15.00
3 Bill Barilko 5.00 12.00
4 Max Bentley 5.00 12.00
5 Hugh Bolton 6.00 15.00
6 Turk Broda 8.00 20.00
7 Lorne Chabot 6.00 15.00
8 King Clancy 8.00 20.00
9 Charlie Conacher 6.00 15.00
10 Baldy Cotton 5.00 12.00
11 Bob Davidson 6.00 15.00
12 Hap Day 8.00 20.00
13 Gordie Drillon 5.00 12.00
14 Bob Goldham 5.00 12.00
15 George Hainsworth 10.00 25.00
16 Reg Hamilton 5.00 12.00
17 Red Horner 5.00 12.00
18 Busher Jackson 6.00 15.00
19 Ted Kennedy 8.00 20.00
20 Harry Lumley 5.00 12.00
21 Frank McCool 6.00 15.00
22 Howie Meeker 8.00 20.00
23 Nick Metz 5.00 12.00
24 Babe Pratt 5.00 12.00
25 Joe Primeau 6.00 15.00
26 Al Rollins 5.00 12.00
27 Sweeney Schriner 5.00 12.00
28 Tod Sloan 8.00 20.00
29 Sid Smith 5.00 12.00
30 Conn Smythe 6.00 15.00
31 Gaye Stewart 5.00 12.00
32 Harry Watson 5.00 12.00

2008-09 ITG Superlative Franchise Autograph Plus Jersey

APAB Allan Bester 10.00 25.00
APBB Bob Baun 12.00 30.00
APBS Borje Salming 12.00 30.00
APDG Doug Gilmour 15.00 40.00
APDK Dave Keon 12.00 30.00
APDS Darryl Sittler 15.00 40.00
APDT Darcy Tucker 10.00 25.00
APDW Dave Williams 8.00 20.00
APEB Ed Belfour 12.00 30.00
APFM Frank Mahovlich 12.00 30.00
APFP Felix Potvin 20.00 50.00
APGF Grant Fuhr 20.00 50.00
APGL Gary Leeman 10.00 25.00
APGR Gary Roberts 8.00 20.00
APJB Johnny Bower 12.00 30.00
APJN Joe Nieuwendyk 10.00 25.00
APLM Lanny McDonald 12.00 30.00
APMG Mikael Grabovski 8.00 20.00
APMP Mike Palmateer 12.00 30.00
APNK Nikoalai Kulemin 12.00 30.00
APRK Red Kelly 12.00 30.00
APRV Rick Vaive 8.00 20.00
APSC Shayne Corson 10.00 25.00
APST Steve Thomas 8.00 20.00
APTD Tie Domi 10.00 25.00
APTG Todd Gill 8.00 20.00
APWC Wendel Clark 20.00 50.00

2008-09 ITG Superlative Franchise Autographs

AAB Allan Bester/40* 8.00 20.00
ABP Bernie Parent/40* 12.00 30.00
ADD Dick Duff/40* 8.00 20.00
AEB Ed Belfour/19* 10.00 25.00
AGG Gerry Cheevers/40* 10.00 25.00
AJN Joe Nieuwendyk/40* 8.00 20.00
AMG Mikhail Grabovski/40* 6.00 15.00
ANK Nikolai Kulemin/40* 10.00 25.00
APH Paul Henderson/40* 8.00 20.00
ARC Russ Courtnall/19* 6.00 15.00
ARK Red Kelly/40* 10.00 25.00
ARV Rick Vaive/40* 6.00 15.00
ATS Tod Sloan/40* 10.00 25.00
AAA1 Al Arbour/40* 8.00 20.00
AAA2 Al Arbour/40* 8.00 20.00
AAS1 Allan Stanley/40* 10.00 25.00
AAS2 Allan Stanley/40* 10.00 25.00
ABB1 Bob Baun/40* 10.00 25.00
ABB2 Bob Baun/40* 10.00 25.00
ABO1 Bert Olmstead/19* 8.00 20.00
ABO2 Bert Olmstead/19* 8.00 20.00
ABPU Bob Pulford/40* 8.00 20.00
ABS1 Borje Salming/19* 10.00 25.00
ABS2 Borje Salming/19* 10.00 25.00
ADG1 Doug Gilmour/19* 12.00 30.00
ADG2 Doug Gilmour/19* 12.00 30.00
ADK1 Dave Keon/19* 10.00 25.00
ADK2 Dave Keon/19* 10.00 25.00
ADS1 Darryl Sittler/19* 12.00 30.00
ADS2 Darryl Sittler/19* 12.00 30.00
ADT1 Darcy Tucker/19* 8.00 20.00
ADT2 Darcy Tucker/19* 8.00 20.00
ADW1 Dave Williams/40* 6.00 15.00
ADW2 Dave Williams/40* 6.00 15.00
AES1 Eddie Shack/40* 10.00 25.00
AES2 Eddie Shack/40* 10.00 25.00
AFM1 Frank Mahovlich/19* 10.00 25.00
AFM2 Frank Mahovlich/19* 10.00 25.00
AFP1 Felix Potvin/19* 15.00 40.00
AFP2 Felix Potvin/19* 15.00 40.00
AGF1 Grant Fuhr/19* 15.00 40.00
AGF2 Grant Fuhr/19* 15.00 40.00
AGR1 Gary Roberts/40* 6.00 15.00
AGR2 Gary Roberts/40* 6.00 15.00
AHM1 Howie Meeker/19* 10.00 25.00
AHM2 Howie Meeker/19* 10.00 25.00
AIT1 Ian Turnbull/40* 6.00 15.00
AIT2 Ian Turnbull/40* 6.00 15.00
AJB1 Johnny Bower/19* 10.00 25.00
AJB2 Johnny Bower/19* 10.00 25.00
ALM1 Lanny McDonald/19* 10.00 25.00
ALM2 Lanny McDonald/19* 10.00 25.00
AMPA Mike Palmateer/40* 10.00 25.00
ANU1 Norm Ullman/19* 10.00 25.00
ANU2 Norm Ullman/19* 10.00 25.00
APQ1 Pat Quinn/40* 10.00 25.00
ARE1 Ron Ellis/40* 6.00 15.00
ARE2 Ron Ellis/40* 6.00 15.00
ASC1 Shayne Corson/40* 8.00 20.00
ASC2 Shayne Corson/40* 8.00 20.00
ATD1 Tie Domi/35* 8.00 20.00
ATD2 Tie Domi/35* 8.00 20.00
AWC1 Wendel Clark/19* 15.00 40.00
AWC2 Wendel Clark/19* 15.00 40.00
AABA1 Andy Bathgate/40* 10.00 25.00
AABA2 Andy Bathgate/40* 10.00 25.00

2008-09 ITG Superlative Franchise Double Autographs

DABB J.Bower/E.Belfour 12.00 30.00
DAEH R.Ellis/P.Henderson 12.00 30.00
DAGC D.Gilmour/W.Clark 20.00 50.00
DAMK F.Mahovlich/R.Kelly 12.00 30.00
DAMS H.Meeker/T.Sloan 12.00 30.00
DASB A.Stanley/B.Baun 12.00 30.00
DASC D.Sittler/W.Clark 15.00 40.00
DASM D.Sittler/L.McDonald 15.00 40.00
DAST B.Salming/I.Turnbull 12.00 30.00
DAWD D.Williams/T.Domi 10.00 25.00

2008-09 ITG Superlative Franchise Famous Fabrics 500 Goal Scorers

GS03 Lanny McDonald 6.00 15.00
GS04 Mike Gartner 8.00 20.00

2008-09 ITG Superlative Franchise Patch Blue

1 Allan Bester/25* 8.00 20.00
2 Allan Stanley/25* 10.00 25.00
3 Andy Bathgate/25* 10.00 25.00
4 Bob Baun/25* 10.00 25.00
5 Bob Pulford/25* 8.00 20.00
6 Borje Salming/25* 10.00 25.00
7 Brian Glennie/25* 10.00 25.00
8 Darcy Tucker/25* 8.00 20.00
9 Darryl Sittler/25* 12.00 30.00
10 Dave Tiger Williams/25* 6.00 15.00
11 Dave Keon/25* 10.00 25.00
12 Dick Duff/25* 8.00 20.00
13 Doug Gilmour/25* 12.00 30.00
14 Ed Belfour/25* 10.00 25.00
15 Eddie Shack/25* 10.00 25.00
16 Errol Thompson/25* 6.00 15.00
17 Felix Potvin/25* 15.00 40.00
18 Frank Mahovlich/25* 10.00 25.00
19 Gary Leeman/25* 8.00 20.00
20 Gary Roberts/25* 6.00 15.00
21 Grant Fuhr/25* 15.00 40.00
22 Ian Turnbull/25* 6.00 15.00
23 Jacques Plante/25* 15.00 40.00
24 Johnny Bower/25* 10.00 25.00
25 Lanny McDonald/25* 10.00 25.00
26 Marcel Pronovost/25* 10.00 25.00
27 Mats Sundin/25* 10.00 25.00
28 Mikhail Grabovski/25* 6.00 15.00
29 Mike Palmateer/25* 10.00 25.00
30 Joe Nieuwendyk/25* 8.00 20.00
31 Nikolai Kulemin/25* 10.00 25.00
32 Norm Ullman/25* 10.00 25.00
33 Paul Henderson/25* 8.00 20.00
34 Red Kelly/25* 10.00 25.00
35 Rick Vaive/25* 6.00 15.00
36 Ron Ellis/25* 6.00 15.00
37 Bert Olmstead/25* 8.00 20.00
38 Russ Courtnall/25* 6.00 15.00
39 Shayne Corson/25* 8.00 20.00
40 Steve Thomas/25* 6.00 15.00
41 Terry Sawchuk/30* 12.00 30.00
42 Tie Domi/30* 8.00 20.00
43 Tim Horton/30* 20.00 50.00
44 Vesa Toskala/30* 12.00 30.00
45 Wendel Clark/30* 15.00 40.00

2008-09 ITG Superlative Franchise Triple Autographs

TABFF Bester/Favell/Fuhr 25.00 60.00
TABPP Bower/Palmateer/Potvin 25.00 60.00
TABUP Baun/Ullman/Pronovost 15.00 40.00
TACLC Clark/Leeman/Courtnall 25.00 60.00
TADMK Duff/Mahovlich/Kelly 15.00 40.00
TAEGH Ellis/Glennie/Henderson 15.00 40.00
TALDH Ley/Dorey/Henderson 12.00 30.00
TALTG Leeman/Thomas/Gill 12.00 30.00
TAMPS Meeker/Pulford/Sloan 15.00 40.00
TAOSM Olmstead/Sloan/Mahovlich 15.00 40.00
TAOUP Olmstead/Ullman/Pulford 15.00 40.00
TAPGC Potvin/Gilmour/Clark 25.00 60.00
TAQAK Quinn/Arbour/Kelly 15.00 40.00
TASBQ Stanley/Baun/Quinn 15.00 40.00
TASMW Sittler/McDonald/Williams 10.00 25.00
TASTM Salming/Turnbull/McKenny 15.00 40.00
TAVSC Vaive/Sittler/Clark 25.00 60.00
TAWDS Williams/Domi/Shack 15.00 40.00

2012-13 ITG Superlative Autographs Silver

AAM Al MacInnis/40 12.00 30.00
ADK Dave Keon/30 10.00 25.00
AJQ Jonathan Quick/40 12.00 30.00
AJR Jeremy Roenick/40 15.00 40.00
AJS Joe Sakic/20 30.00 80.00
AML Mario Lemieux/20 60.00 150.00
AMM Mark Messier/20 30.00 80.00
APB Pavel Bure/20 15.00 40.00
APR Patrick Roy MON/20 40.00 100.00
ARB Raymond Bourque/30 15.00 40.00
ASN Scott Niedermayer/20 15.00 40.00
ASW Shea Weber/40 8.00 20.00
ASY Steve Yzerman/30 40.00 80.00
ATF Theoren Fleury/40 12.00 30.00
ATL Trevor Linden/40 12.50 30.00
AVT Vladislav Tretiak/20 12.00 30.00
AAO2 A.Ovechkin WAS/20 25.00 50.00
AAO3 A.Ovechkin KHL/20 30.00 60.00
ABH1 Brett Hull DAL/40 12.50 30.00
ABH2 Brett Hull/40 12.50 30.00
ABHU Bobby Hull/30 30.00 80.00
AGH1 Gordie Howe D/15 40.00 100.00
AGH2 Gordie Howe H/15 40.00 100.00
AGH3 Gordie Howe/15 40.00 100.00
AGHA Glenn Hall/30 10.00 25.00
AJJ1 Jaromir Jagr PHI/20 30.00 60.00
AJJ2 Jaromir Jagr WAS/20 30.00 60.00
AJJ3 Jaromir Jagr PIT/20 30.00 60.00
AMME Mark Messier/20 30.00 80.00
AMSL Martin St. Louis/40 10.00 25.00
APRO Patrick Roy COL/20 30.00 60.00

2012-13 ITG Superlative Jerseys Autographs Silver

AJAM Al MacInnis 15.00 40.00
AJAO Alexander Ovechkin 30.00 80.00
AJDK Dave Keon 12.00 30.00
AJJQ Jonathan Quick 25.00 60.00
AJJR Jeremy Roenick 15.00 40.00
AJJS Joe Sakic 40.00 100.00
AJLR Luc Robitaille 12.00 30.00
AJML Mario Lemieux 40.00 80.00
AJMM Mark Messier 40.00 100.00
AJRB Raymond Bourque 20.00 50.00
AJRK Ryan Kesler 20.00 50.00
AJSW Shea Weber 15.00 40.00
AJSY Steve Yzerman 40.00 80.00
AJTF Theoren Fleury 15.00 40.00
AJTL Trevor Linden 20.00 50.00
AJVT Vladislav Tretiak 15.00 40.00
AJBH1 Brett Hull 25.00 50.00
AJBH2 Brett Hull 25.00 50.00
AJBHU Bobby Hull 25.00 60.00
AJGH1 Gordie Howe 60.00 120.00
AJGH2 Gordie Howe 60.00 120.00
AJGH3 Gordie Howe 60.00 120.00
AJGHA Glenn Hall 12.00 30.00
AJJJ1 Jaromir Jagr 15.00 40.00
AJJJ2 Jaromir Jagr 15.00 40.00
AJJJ3 Jaromir Jagr 15.00 40.00
AJMME Mark Messier 40.00 100.00
AJMSL Martin St. Louis 12.00 30.00
AJPB1 Pavel Bure 20.00 50.00
AJPB2 Pavel Bure 20.00 50.00
AJPR1 Patrick Roy 30.00 80.00
AJPR2 Patrick Roy 50.00 100.00

2012-13 ITG Superlative Jerseys Silver

GUJ01 Adam Oates/30 8.00 20.00
GUJ02 Alexander Ovechkin/30 30.00 80.00
GUJ03 Brett Hull/30 15.00 40.00
GUJ04 Carey Price/30 15.00 40.00
GUJ05 Claude Giroux/30 8.00 20.00
GUJ06 Corey Perry/30 12.00 30.00
GUJ07 Curtis Joseph/30 10.00 25.00
GUJ08 Daniel Sedin/30 10.00 25.00
GUJ09 Denis Potvin/30 8.00 20.00
GUJ10 Doug Gilmour/30 10.00 25.00
GUJ11 Ed Belfour/30 8.00 20.00
GUJ12 Eric Lindros/30 12.00 30.00
GUJ13 Henrik Lundqvist/30 8.00 20.00
GUJ14 Henrik Sedin/30 10.00 25.00
GUJ15 Jaromir Jagr/30 25.00 60.00
GUJ16 Jeremy Roenick/30 12.00 30.00
GUJ17 Joe Sakic/30 15.00 40.00
GUJ18 Joe Thornton/30 12.00 30.00
GUJ19 Mario Lemieux/30 12.00 30.00
GUJ20 Mats Sundin/30 12.00 30.00
GUJ21 Mike Bossy/30 8.00 20.00
GUJ22 Nicklas Lidstrom/30 8.00 20.00
GUJ23 Patrick Roy/30 20.00 50.00
GUJ24 Patrick Roy/30 20.00 50.00
GUJ25 Pavel Bure/30 12.00 30.00
GUJ26 Peter Forsberg/30 15.00 40.00
GUJ27 Raymond Bourque/30 12.00 30.00
GUJ28 Roberto Luongo/30 12.00 30.00
GUJ29 Theoren Fleury/30 10.00 25.00
GUJ30 Trevor Linden/30 8.00 20.00

2012-13 ITG Superlative Prospect Autographs Silver

PAAG Alex Galchenyuk 60.00 100.00
PABD Brenden Dillon 5.00 12.00
PACC Cody Ceci 5.00 12.00
PAIS Ian Schultz 5.00 12.00
PAMC Matt Calvert 4.00 10.00
PAMM Matt Murray 6.00 15.00
PANB Nick Baptiste 5.00 12.00
PANY Nail Yakupov 30.00 60.00
PARK Ryan Kujawinski 5.00 12.00
PASC Sean Couturier 8.00 20.00
PATH Thomas Hickey 12.00 30.00

2012-13 ITG Superlative Prospect Jerseys Autographs Silver

PAJAG Alex Galchenyuk 80.00 150.00
PAJCC Cody Ceci 6.00 15.00
PAJDT Dana Tyrell 5.00 12.00
PAJIS Ian Schultz 6.00 15.00
PAJMC Matt Calvert 5.00 12.00
PAJMM Matt Murray 8.00 20.00
PAJNB Nick Baptiste 6.00 15.00
PAJNY Nail Yakupov 30.00 80.00
PAJRM Ryan Murphy 15.00 40.00
PAJSC Sean Couturier 6.00 15.00
PAJSG Scott Glennie 6.00 15.00
PAJTH Thomas Hickey 5.00 12.00

2013-14 ITG Superlative The First Six Jerseys

GUJ01 Borje Salming/20* 8.00 20.00
GUJ02 Mats Sundin/20* 8.00 20.00
GUJ03 Doug Gilmour/20* 10.00 25.00
GUJ04 Wendel Clark/20* 12.00 30.00
GUJ05 Curtis Joseph/20* 10.00 25.00
GUJ06 Felix Potvin/20* 12.00 30.00
GUJ07 Darryl Sittler/20* 12.00 30.00
GUJ08 Bob Baun/20* 8.00 20.00
GUJ09 Pavel Bure/20* 15.00 30.00
GUJ10 Marian Gaborik/20* 8.00 20.00
GUJ11 Henrik Lundqvist/20* 8.00 20.00
GUJ12 Brian Leetch/20* 6.00 15.00
GUJ13 Mike Richter/20* 8.00 20.00
GUJ14 John Vanbiesbrouck/20* 12.00 30.00
GUJ15 Carey Price/20* 10.00 25.00
GUJ16 Guy Lafleur/20* 10.00 25.00
GUJ17 Patrick Roy/20* 20.00 50.00
GUJ18 Guy Lapointe/20* 6.00 15.00
GUJ19 Mark Recchi/20* 10.00 25.00
GUJ20 Jacques Lemaire/20* 6.00 15.00
GUJ21 Larry Robinson/20* 8.00 20.00
GUJ22 Steve Yzerman/20* 25.00 50.00
GUJ23 Dominik Hasek/20* 12.00 30.00
GUJ24 Jimmy Howard/20* 10.00 25.00
GUJ25 Niklas Kronwall/20* 8.00 20.00
GUJ26 Chris Osgood/20* 8.00 20.00
GUJ27 Bob Probert/20* 8.00 20.00
GUJ28 Nicklas Lidstrom/20* 10.00 25.00
GUJ29 Tony Amonte/20* 6.00 15.00
GUJ30 Jeremy Roenick/20* 12.00 30.00
GUJ31 Corey Crawford/20* 10.00 25.00
GUJ32 Denis Savard/20* 8.00 20.00
GUJ33 Ed Belfour/20* 8.00 20.00
GUJ34 Chris Chelios/20* 8.00 20.00
GUJ35 Cam Neely/20* 8.00 20.00
GUJ36 Joe Thornton/20* 12.00 30.00
GUJ37 Raymond Bourque/20* 12.00 30.00
GUJ38 Tuukka Rask/20* 10.00 25.00
GUJ39 Sergei Samsonov/20* 8.00 20.00
GUJ40 Andy Moog/20* 8.00 20.00

2013-14 ITG Superlative The First Six Autographs

AU+MEM/20: .5X TO 1.2X AU/20*
JSY AU/20: .5X TO 1.2X AU/20*
AAD Alex Delvecchio 12.00 30.00
AAO Adam Oates 20.00 40.00
ABB Bob Baun 12.00 30.00
ABH Brett Hull 20.00 40.00
ABHU Bobby Hull 20.00 50.00
ABL Brian Leetch 10.00 25.00
ABP Brad Park 10.00 25.00
ABS Borje Salming 20.00 40.00
ACC1 Chris Chelios 12.00 30.00
ACCR Corey Crawford 15.00 40.00
ACJ Curtis Joseph 15.00 40.00
ACN Cam Neely 12.00 30.00
ACO Chris Osgood 12.00 30.00
ACP Carey Price 12.00 30.00
ADG Doug Gilmour 15.00 40.00
ADH Dominik Hasek 15.00 40.00
ADK Dave Keon 12.00 30.00
ADP Dion Phaneuf 10.00 25.00
ADS Darryl Sittler 15.00 40.00
AEB Ed Belfour 12.00 30.00
AEG Ed Giacomin 12.00 30.00
AEL Elmer Lach 12.00 30.00
AFM Frank Mahovlich 12.00 30.00
AFP Felix Potvin 15.00 40.00
AGC Gerry Cheevers 12.00 30.00
AGH Glenn Hall 12.00 30.00
AGH Gordie Howe 50.00 100.00
AGL Guy Lafleur 15.00 40.00
AGLA Guy Lapointe 10.00 25.00
AHR Henri Richard 12.00 30.00
AJB Jean Beliveau 15.00 40.00
AJBO Johnny Bower 25.00 50.00
AJBU Johnny Bucyk 12.00 30.00
AJH Jimmy Howard 15.00 40.00
AJR Jeremy Roenick 20.00 50.00
AJV John Vanbiesbrouck 12.00 30.00
ALM Lanny McDonald 12.00 30.00
ALR Larry Robinson 12.00 30.00
AMM Mark Messier 25.00 60.00
AMR Mike Richter 12.00 30.00
AMS Milt Schmidt 10.00 25.00
ANL Nicklas Lidstrom 20.00 40.00
APE1 Phil Esposito 20.00 50.00
APE2 Phil Esposito 20.00 50.00
ARB Raymond Bourque 20.00 50.00
ARG Rod Gilbert 12.00 30.00
ARK Red Kelly 12.00 30.00
ARV Rogie Vachon 15.00 40.00
ASM Stan Mikita 15.00 40.00
ASS Serge Savard 12.00 30.00
ASSA Sergei Samsonov 10.00 25.00
ASY Steve Yzerman 30.00 60.00
ATA Tony Amonte 10.00 25.00
ATE Tony Esposito 12.00 30.00
ATL Ted Lindsay 12.00 30.00
ATO Terry O'Reilly 10.00 25.00
ATR Tuukka Rask 15.00 40.00
AVH Vic Hadfield 10.00 25.00
AWC Wendel Clark 12.00 30.00
AWCA Wayne Cashman 10.00 25.00

2013-14 ITG Superlative The First Six Captain C

CC02 Cnchr/Sttlr/Sndin 25.00 50.00
CC03 Hdfld/Park/Mssier 30.00 80.00
CC04 Espsto/Ltch/Jagr 25.00 50.00
CC05 LInde/Hnswrth/Crnneau 40.00 80.00
CC06 Rchrd/Blveau/Rchrd 60.00 120.00
CC07 Lndsy/Yzrmn/Ldstrm 40.00 100.00
CC08 Howe/Dlvcchio/Dnne 50.00 125.00
CC09 Grdner/Stpltn/Svrd 15.00 40.00
CC10 Mkta/Chlios/Amnte 20.00 50.00
CC11 Schmdt/Bcyk/Cshmn 15.00 40.00
CC12 O'Rlly/Brque/Thrntn 25.00 60.00

2013-14 ITG Superlative The First Six Cup Final Jerseys Six

FL01 Bqe/Mta/Hw/Lfr/Gbt/Sdn 40.00 80.00
FL02 Esp/Hll/Yzm/Lfr/Jgr/Vve 30.00 80.00
FL03 Esp/Svd/Yzn/Lf/Jgr/Glmr 40.00 80.00
FL04 Byk/Hl/Hwe/Rc/Glb/Sdn 50.00 100.00
FL05 Bqe/Lmr/Yz/Cny/Glr/Sdn 40.00 80.00
FL06 Esp/Mkt/Yzm/Lfr/Glrt/Sdn 40.00 80.00
FL07 Chv/Esp/Osg/Ry/Vbk/Plt 40.00 80.00
FL08 Bqe/Mkt/Yzm/Lfr/Lch/Sg 40.00 100.00
FL09 Thm/Esp/Sch/Hns/Gn/Bd 50.00 100.00
FL10 Thm/Esp/Sch/Pln/Rct/Bd 40.00 80.00
FL11 Esp/Hl/Yzm/Lfr/Jgr/Sttlr 50.00 100.00
FL12 Esp/Rnk/Fdv/Lfr/Msr/Sn 40.00 80.00

2013-14 ITG Superlative The First Six Cup Final Quad Jerseys

1 Lfr/Lmre/Epsto/Hbrg/19* 25.00 60.00
2 Rbsn/Svrd/Mdltn/Byk/19* 15.00 40.00
3 Shtt/Lfr/Prk/O'Rly/19* 20.00 50.00
4 Svrd/Lpte/Prk/Mdltn/19* 15.00 40.00
5 Rbsn/Lfr/O'Rly/Gbrt/19* 20.00 50.00
6 Lpte/Lre/Epsto/Wte/19* 15.00 40.00
7 Crnr/Mhvch/Hll/Mkta/19* 20.00 50.00
8 Epsto/Chvrs/Gbrt/Gmn/19* 25.00 60.00
9 Cshmn/Bck/Prk/Hfld/19* 15.00 40.00
10 Mvlch/Blvau/Mkta/Sttn/19* 25.00 60.00
11 Rcrd/Crnr/Epsto/Hll/19* 20.00 50.00
12 Hrtn/Bwr/Blvau/Rhrd/19* 25.00 60.00
13 Keon/Swck/Vchn/Cnyr/19* 20.00 50.00
14 Rchrd/Lprre/Ulmn/Czr/19* 15.00 40.00
15 Blvau/Wsly/Hll/Mkta/19* 40.00 80.00
16 Baun/Hrtn/Hwe/Ulmn/19* 50.00 125.00
17 Bwr/Mvlh/Swck/Dvco/19* 25.00 50.00
18 Keon/Klly/Hall/Mkta/19* 20.00 50.00

2013-14 ITG Superlative The First Six Draft Highlights Triple Jerseys

DH01 Sttlr/McDnld/Plmteer 20.00 50.00
DH02 Bstr/Clrk/Ptvn 25.00 60.00
DH03 Park/Vnbsbrck/Rchtr 15.00 40.00
DH04 Ltch/Cltier/Lndqvst 40.00 100.00
DH05 Lflr/Rbnsn/Shutt 20.00 50.00
DH06 Nslnd/Chlios/Roy 20.00 50.00
DH07 Dnne/Fdrov/Ldstrm 25.00 60.00
DH08 Yzrmn/Osgd/Hwrd 30.00 60.00
DH09 Lrmr/Svrd/Rnick 25.00 50.00
DH10 Hsek/Mnsn/Crwfrd 15.00 40.00
DH11 O'Rlly/Jnthn/Brque 25.00 60.00
DH12 Leach/Smsnv/Thrntn 25.00 60.00

2013-14 ITG Superlative The First Six Enshrined Triple Jerseys

E01 Wtsn/Keon/Sndin 15.00 40.00
E02 Hrtn/Sttlr/Glmour 20.00 50.00
E03 Gcmn/Park/Dnne 30.00 80.00
E04 Glbrt/Mssier/Bure 20.00 50.00
E05 Rchrd/Lfleur/Roy 40.00 80.00
E06 Jliat/Plnte/Blveau 60.00 120.00
E07 Lndsy/Ullmn/Yzrmn 25.00 60.00
E08 Howe/Dlvcchio/Hull 40.00 80.00
E09 Hall/Espsto/Blfour 15.00 40.00
E10 Msnko/Hull/Mkita 25.00 60.00
E11 Schmdt/Espsto/Neely 25.00 60.00
E12 Shre/Chvers/Brque 25.00 60.00

2013-14 ITG Superlative The First Six Franchises Jerseys Six

F01 Crfd/Hrd/Phn/Lnq/Rsk/Prc 30.00 60.00
F02 Ant/Hsk/Sdn/Ldrs/Thrt/Rch 40.00 80.00
F03 Rnk/Lstm/Glmr/Msr/Brq/Ry 40.00 80.00
F05 Blfr/Prbrt/Clrk/Lflr/Moog/Rbn 30.00 60.00
F06 Mta/Dlc/McDd/Esp/Byk/Lflr 40.00 80.00
F07 Esp/Dne/Stlr/Glbt/Esp/Lmre 30.00 80.00
F08 Hll/Hwe/Bwr/Hfld/Chvr/Blv 40.00 80.00
F09 Hll/Ullm/Keon/Gcm/Prnt/Plnt 40.00 80.00
F10 Mko/Sch/Mlc/Rynr/Sch/Rcrd 40.00 80.00
F11 Lmly/Ldsy/Knd/Wrl/Clpr/Hrv 50.00 100.00
F12 Bmsk/Thp/Cnch/Frn/Shr/Jlt 40.00 80.00

2013-14 ITG Superlative The First Six Memorable Moments Jerseys

MM01 King Clancy 40.00 80.00
MM02 Johnny Bower 12.00 30.00
MM03 Darryl Sittler 20.00 50.00
MM04 Ed Giacomin 12.00 30.00
MM05 Mike Richter 10.00 25.00
MM06 Mark Messier 10.00 25.00
MM07 Maurice Richard 30.00 60.00
MM08 Jacques Plante 12.00 30.00
MM09 Jean Beliveau 20.00 50.00
MM10 Ted Lindsay 12.00 30.00
MM11 Gordie Howe 20.00 50.00
MM12 Steve Yzerman 12.00 30.00
MM13 Bill Mosienko 12.00 30.00
MM14 Stan Mikita 10.00 25.00
MM15 Tony Esposito 8.00 20.00
MM16 Eddie Shore 15.00 40.00
MM17 Phil Esposito 12.00 30.00
MM18 Cam Neely 8.00 20.00

2013-14 ITG Superlative The First Six Raised to the Rafters Triple Jerseys

RTR01 Bwer/Clncy/Glmour 50.00 120.00
RTR02 Cnchr/Hrtn/Sttler 25.00 60.00
RTR03 Mhvlch/Slmng/Sndin 20.00 50.00
RTR04 Gcmin/Mssr/Rchtr 20.00 50.00
RTR05 Blveau/Lflr/Rbnsn 40.00 80.00
RTR06 Plnte/Rchrd/Roy 60.00 120.00
RTR07 Hrvy/Rchrd/Svrd 15.00 40.00
RTR08 Howe/Lndsy/Yzrmn 30.00 60.00
RTR09 Hull/Mkta/Svrd 30.00 80.00
RTR10 Hall/Espsto/Hull 25.00 60.00
RTR11 Brque/Espsto/Neely 25.00 60.00
RTR12 Shre/O'Rlly/Bcyk 20.00 50.00

2013-14 ITG Superlative The First Six Rivalry Quad Jerseys

R01 Roy/Mllr/Ptvn/Glmr/19* 25.00 60.00
R02 Clk/Lmn/Prbt/Yzmn/19* 40.00 100.00
R03 Rbsn/Crnu/Lflr/Dne/19* 20.00 50.00
R04 Chs/Bfr/Chde/Lstm/19* 15.00 40.00
R05 Jsph/Sdn/Rctr/Bre/19* 20.00 50.00
R06 Ltch/Mssr/Nly/Otes/19* 20.00 50.00
R07 Clk/Ptn/McCty/Osgd/19* 25.00 60.00
R08 Roy/Chls/Brqe/Moog/19* 20.00 50.00
R09 Svrd/Epsto/Bstr/Slng/19* 15.00 40.00
R10 Prk/Brqe/Rbsn/Svrd/19* 12.00 30.00
R11 Shtt/Lflr/McDnld/Sttlr/19* 20.00 50.00
R12 Yzmn/Fdrv/Msr/Ldrs/19* 30.00 60.00
R13 Epsto/Chvs/Gcmn/Hfld/19* 25.00 60.00
R14 Lprre/Blvau/Hrtn/Keon/19* 30.00 60.00
R15 Chmn/Bcyk/Rcrd/Crnyr/19* 25.00 50.00
R16 Dnne/Dlvcio/Epsto/Mkta/19* 20.00 50.00
R17 Vchn/Hdge/Swck/Bwr/19* 20.00 50.00
R19 Espsto/Glbrt/Lflr/Rbnsn/19* 25.00 60.00
R20 Hwe/Lndsy/Rcrd/Blvau/19* 60.00 120.00
R21 Hull/Hall/Plnte/Moore/19* 25.00 60.00
R22 Dlvcio/Ulmn/Kon/Kly/19* 15.00 40.00

2013-14 ITG Superlative The First Six Trophy Case Jerseys

TC01 Frank Mahovlich/19* 10.00 25.00
TC02 Dave Keon/19* 8.00 20.00
TC03 Doug Gilmour/19* 10.00 25.00
TC04 Red Kelly/19* 8.00 20.00
TC05 Dave Keon/19* 8.00 20.00
TC06 Ted Kennedy/19* 8.00 20.00
TC07 Johnny Bower/19* 8.00 20.00
TC08 Terry Sawchuk/19* 12.00 30.00
TC09 Mark Messier/19* 15.00 40.00
TC10 Brian Leetch/19* 6.00 15.00
TC11 Rod Gilbert/19* 12.00 30.00
TC12 John Vanbiesbrouck/19* 15.00 40.00
TC13 Jaromir Jagr/19* 25.00 60.00
TC14 Mark Messier/19* 12.00 30.00
TC15 Phil Esposito/19* 12.00 30.00
TC16 Henrik Lundqvist/19* 8.00 20.00
TC17 Guy Lafleur/19* 10.00 25.00
TC18 Larry Robinson/19* 8.00 20.00
TC19 Patrick Roy/19* 20.00 50.00
TC20 Chris Chelios/19* 8.00 20.00
TC21 Mats Naslund/19* 5.00 12.00
TC22 Jacques Plante/19* 12.00 30.00
TC23 Jean Beliveau/19* 15.00 40.00
TC24 Maurice Richard/19* 30.00 80.00
TC25 Steve Yzerman/19* 20.00 50.00
TC26 Sergei Fedorov/19* 10.00 25.00
TC27 Roger Crozier/19* 10.00 25.00
TC28 Nicklas Lidstrom/19* 10.00 25.00
TC29 Alex Delvecchio/19* 10.00 25.00
TC30 Marcel Dionne/19* 10.00 25.00
TC31 Steve Yzerman/19* 20.00 50.00
TC32 Dominik Hasek/19* 12.00 30.00
TC33 Bobby Hull/19* 15.00 40.00
TC34 Stan Mikita/19* 10.00 25.00
TC35 Tony Esposito/19* 8.00 20.00
TC36 Ed Belfour/19* 8.00 20.00
TC37 Steve Larmer/19* 10.00 25.00
TC38 Chris Chelios/19* 8.00 20.00
TC39 Corey Crawford/19* 10.00 25.00
TC40 Stan Mikita/19* 10.00 25.00
TC41 Joe Thornton/19* 12.00 30.00
TC42 Cam Neely/19* 8.00 20.00
TC43 Phil Esposito/19* 12.00 30.00
TC44 Raymond Bourque/19* 12.00 30.00
TC45 Phil Esposito/19* 12.00 30.00
TC46 Johnny Bucyk/19* 8.00 20.00
TC47 Andy Moog/19* 8.00 20.00
TC48 Sergei Samsonov/19* 6.00 15.00

2015-16 ITG Superlative Famous Fabrics 1000 Point Club Silver

TPC01 Adam Oates/25 6.00 15.00
TPC02 Alexander Mogilny/25 5.00 12.00
TPC03 Bobby Clarke/25 10.00 25.00
TPC04 Bobby Hull/25 12.00 30.00
TPC05 Bobby Smith/25 5.00 12.00
TPC06 Brendan Shanahan/25 6.00 15.00
TPC07 Darryl Sittler/25 8.00 20.00
TPC08 Denis Potvin/25 6.00 15.00
TPC09 Dino Ciccarelli/25 6.00 15.00
TPC10 Gilbert Perreault/25 6.00 15.00
TPC12 Guy Lafleur/25 8.00 20.00
TPC13 Jaromir Jagr/25 20.00 50.00
TPC14 Jean Ratelle/25 5.00 12.00
TPC15 Jeremy Roenick/25 10.00 25.00
TPC16 Joe Mullen/25 5.00 12.00
TPC17 Joe Nieuwendyk/25 5.00 12.00
TPC18 Joe Sakic/25 12.00 30.00
TPC19 Marcel Dionne/25 8.00 20.00
TPC20 Michel Goulet/25 5.00 12.00
TPC21 Mike Modano/25 10.00 25.00
TPC22 Paul Coffey/25 6.00 15.00
TPC23 Peter Stastny/25 5.00 12.00
TPC25 Ron Francis/25 8.00 20.00

TPC26 Sergei Fedorov/25 10.00 25.00
TPC27 Stan Mikita/25 8.00 20.00
TPC28 Teemu Selanne/25 12.00 30.00
TPC29 Theoren Fleury/25 8.00 20.00

2015-16 ITG Superlative Famous Fabrics Four Silver

F403 Roy/Josph/Blfr/Hask/20 15.00 40.00

2015-16 ITG Superlative Famous Fabrics Record Book Silver

RB07 Mario Lemieux/25 25.00 60.00
RB09 Patrick Roy/25 15.00 40.00
RB10 Raymond Bourque/25 10.00 25.00
RB11 Teemu Selanne/25 12.00 30.00

2015-16 ITG Superlative Immortals Autographs Silver

TIAD1 Alex Delvecchio/25 10.00 25.00
TIBG1 Bill Gadsby/25 10.00 25.00
TIBH1 Bobby Hull/20 20.00 50.00
TIBH2 Brett Hull/20 20.00 50.00
TIGH1 Glenn Hall/20 10.00 25.00
TIJB1 Johnny Bower/25 10.00 25.00
TIJB2 Johnny Bucyk/25 10.00 25.00
TIML1 Mario Lemieux/20 40.00 100.00
TIMM1 Mike Modano/25 15.00 40.00
TINL1 Nicklas Lidstrom/25 10.00 25.00
TINU1 Norm Ullman/25 10.00 25.00
TIPE1 Phil Esposito/20 EXCH 15.00 40.00
TIPR1 Patrick Roy/20 25.00 60.00
TIRB1 Raymond Bourque/25 15.00 40.00
TISF1 Sergei Fedorov/25 EXCH 15.00 40.00
TISY1 Steve Yzerman/20 25.00 60.00
TITE1 Tony Esposito/20 10.00 25.00
TITL1 Ted Lindsay/25 10.00 25.00
TIVT1 Vladislav Tretiak/20 8.00 20.00

2015-16 ITG Superlative International Ice Autographs

IIBH1 Bobby Hull 15.00 40.00
IIBH2 Brett Hull 15.00 40.00
IIEL1 Eric Lindros 12.00 30.00
IIJS1 Joe Sakic 15.00 40.00
IIML1 Mario Lemieux 30.00 80.00
IIMM1 Mike Modano 12.00 30.00
IINL1 Nicklas Lidstrom 8.00 20.00
IIPR1 Patrick Roy 20.00 50.00
IISF1 Sergei Fedorov EXCH 12.00 30.00
IISY1 Steve Yzerman 20.00 50.00
IITS1 Teemu Selanne EXCH 15.00 40.00
IIVT1 Vladislav Tretiak 6.00 15.00

2015-16 ITG Superlative Jumbo Numbers Silver

SN02 Brett Hull/25 15.00 40.00
SN04 Eric Lindros/25 10.00 25.00
SN08 Mario Lemieux/25 25.00 60.00
SN09 Martin Brodeur/25 15.00 40.00
SN11 Patrick Roy/25 15.00 40.00
SN13 Raymond Bourque/25 10.00 25.00
SN14 Steve Yzerman/25 15.00 40.00

2015-16 ITG Superlative Signature Memorabilia Silver

SSMBB1 Brian Bellows/30 8.00 20.00
SSMBH1 Brett Hull/20 20.00 50.00
SSMBP1 Bernie Parent/20 12.00 30.00
SSMCJ1 Curtis Joseph/30 12.00 30.00
SSMDG1 Doug Gilmour/20 12.00 30.00
SSMEL1 Eric Lindros/30 15.00 40.00
SSMFP1 Felix Potvin/20 15.00 40.00
SSMGC1 Gerry Cheevers/20 10.00 25.00
SSMGF1 Grant Fuhr/20 15.00 40.00
SSMGH1 Glenn Hall/25 10.00 25.00
SSMJLC John LeClair/25 10.00 25.00
SSMJS1 Joe Sakic/20 20.00 50.00
SSMJV1 John Vanbiesbrouck/20 10.00 25.00
SSMML1 Mario Lemieux/20 40.00 100.00
SSMMM1 Mike Modano/30 15.00 40.00
SSMNL1 Nicklas Lidstrom/20 10.00 25.00
SSMPE1 Phil Esposito/25 15.00 40.00
SSMPLF Pat LaFontaine/25 10.00 25.00
SSMPR1 Patrick Roy/25 25.00 60.00
SSMRB1 Raymond Bourque/30 15.00 40.00
SSMRL1 Reggie Leach/25 8.00 20.00
SSMSF1 Sergei Fedorov/30 EXCH 15.00 40.00
SSMSY1 Steve Yzerman/20 25.00 60.00
SSMTE1 Tony Esposito/20 10.00 25.00
SSMTL1 Ted Lindsay/30 10.00 25.00
SSMTL2 Trevor Linden/20 10.00 25.00
SSMVT1 Vladislav Tretiak Pads/20 8.00 20.00

2015-16 ITG Superlative Signatures Silver

SIGBB1 Brian Bellows/35 8.00 20.00
SIGBG1 Bill Gadsby/35 10.00 25.00
SIGBH1 Bobby Hull/30 20.00 50.00
SIGBH2 Brett Hull/30 20.00 50.00
SIGBP1 Bernie Parent/35 12.00 30.00
SIGBT1 Bryan Trottier/30 10.00 25.00
SIGCJ1 Curtis Joseph/35 12.00 30.00
SIGDM1 Dickie Moore/30 8.00 20.00
SIGEL1 Eric Lindros/35 15.00 40.00
SIGFP1 Felix Potvin/25 15.00 40.00
SIGGC1 Gerry Cheevers/30 10.00 25.00
SIGGF1 Grant Fuhr/30 EXCH 15.00 40.00
SIGGH1 Glenn Hall/25 10.00 25.00
SIGJB1 Johnny Bower/35 EXCH 10.00 25.00
SIGJB2 Johnny Bucyk/35 10.00 25.00
SIGJE1 Jack Eichel/25 150.00 250.00
SIGJLC John LeClair/35 10.00 25.00
SIGJS1 Joe Sakic/25 20.00 50.00
SIGKH1 Ken Hodge/35 8.00 20.00
SIGML1 Mario Lemieux/25 40.00 100.00
SIGMM1 Mike Modano/35 15.00 40.00
SIGMN1 Mats Naslund/35 6.00 15.00
SIGNL1 Nicklas Lidstrom/30 10.00 25.00
SIGNU1 Norm Ullman/35 10.00 25.00
SIGPE1 Phil Esposito/30 EXCH 15.00 40.00
SIGPF1 Peter Forsberg/20 EXCH 20.00 50.00
SIGPL1 Pat LaFontaine/30 10.00 25.00
SIGPR1 Patrick Roy/25 25.00 60.00
SIGRB1 Raymond Bourque/30 15.00 40.00
SIGRL1 Reggie Leach/35 8.00 20.00
SIGSF1 Sergei Fedorov/30 EXCH 15.00 40.00
SIGTE1 Tony Esposito/30 10.00 25.00
SIGTL1 Trevor Linden/35 10.00 25.00
SIGTS1 Teemu Selanne/30 EXCH 20.00 50.00
SIGVT1 Vladislav Tretiak/25 8.00 20.00

2015-16 ITG Superlative Sticks Silver

SS10 Raymond Bourque/20 10.00 25.00

2015-16 ITG Superlative Swatch Jerseys Silver

SSP02 Theoren Fleury/30 8.00 20.00
SSP03 Teemu Selanne/30 12.00 30.00
SSP04 Ted Lindsay/25 6.00 15.00
SSP05 Ron Francis/25 8.00 20.00
SSP06 Phil Esposito/25 10.00 25.00
SSP07 Patrick Roy/30 15.00 40.00
SSP09 Mario Lemieux/30 25.00 60.00
SSP10 Marc-Andre Fleury/30 12.00 30.00
SSP11 John LeClair/25 6.00 15.00
SSP12 Joe Sakic/30 12.00 30.00
SSP14 Jaromir Jagr/30 20.00 50.00
SSP15 Grant Fuhr/25 10.00 25.00
SSP17 Ed Giacomin/25 6.00 15.00
SSP18 Doug Gilmour/25 8.00 20.00
SSP19 Bobby Hull/25 12.00 30.00

2017-18 ITG Superlative Signatures Spectrum Magenta

SSAD1 Alex Delvecchio 10.00 25.00
SSBH1 Bobby Hull 20.00 50.00
SSBP1 Bernie Parent 12.00 30.00
SSBS1 Billy Smith 10.00 25.00
SSDH1 Dale Hawerchuk 12.00 30.00
SSJB1 Johnny Bower 10.00 25.00
SSJS1 Joe Sakic 20.00 50.00
SSJV1 Joe Veleno 10.00 25.00
SSLM1 Larry Murphy 8.00 20.00
SSLMD Lanny McDonald 10.00 25.00
SSMG1 Mike Gartner 12.00 30.00
SSML1 Mario Lemieux 40.00 100.00
SSMR1 Manon Rheaume 25.00 60.00
SSNH1 Nico Hischier 30.00 80.00
SSNP1 Nolan Patrick EXCH 20.00 50.00
SSPB1 Pavel Bure 10.00 25.00
SSPE1 Phil Esposito 15.00 40.00
SSPS1 Peter Stastny 8.00 20.00
SSPT1 Pierre Turgeon 8.00 20.00
SSRB1 Raymond Bourque 15.00 40.00
SSSS1 Serge Savard 10.00 25.00
SSSS2 Steve Shutt 10.00 25.00
SSTE1 Tony Esposito 10.00 25.00
SSTL1 Ted Lindsay 10.00 25.00
SSYC1 Yvan Cournoyer 10.00 25.00

2017-18 ITG Superlative Blades of Steel Spectrum Magenta

BS01 Al MacInnis/25 6.00 15.00
BS02 Alexander Ovechkin/19 20.00 50.00
BS03 Brendan Shanahan/25 5.00 12.00
BS04 Dany Heatley/25 4.00 10.00
BS05 Darryl Sittler/19 6.00 15.00
BS06 Dave Keon/19 5.00 12.00
BS07 Denis Potvin/25 5.00 12.00
BS08 Doug Gilmour/19 6.00 15.00
BS09 Gilbert Perreault/19 5.00 12.00
BS10 Henrik Zetterberg/19 6.00 15.00
BS11 Jarome Iginla/25 6.00 15.00
BS12 John LeClair/25 5.00 12.00
BS13 Johnny Bucyk/19 5.00 12.00
BS14 Keith Tkachuk/25 5.00 12.00
BS15 Luc Robitaille/19 5.00 12.00
BS16 Mario Lemieux/25 20.00 50.00
BS17 Pavel Datsyuk/25 8.00 20.00
BS18 Rick Nash/25 5.00 12.00
BS19 Scott Gomez/19 5.00 12.00
BS20 Stan Mikita/19 6.00 15.00
BS21 Tim Horton/25 5.00 12.00
BS22 Vincent Lecavalier/25 5.00 12.00
BS23 Willie Oâ•™Ree/25 6.00 15.00

2017-18 ITG Superlative Careers Spectrum Magenta

C01 Bobby Orr 20.00 50.00
C02 Brendan Shanahan 5.00 12.00
C03 Brett Hull 10.00 25.00
C04 Brian Leetch 4.00 10.00
C05 Carey Price 10.00 25.00
C06 Chris Chelios 5.00 12.00
C07 Darryl Sittler 6.00 15.00
C08 Gordie Howe 15.00 40.00
C09 Guy Lafleur 6.00 15.00
C10 Jaromir Jagr 15.00 40.00
C11 Joe Sakic 10.00 25.00
C12 Larry Murphy 4.00 10.00
C13 Mario Lemieux 20.00 50.00
C14 Martin Brodeur 12.00 30.00
C15 Mats Sundin 5.00 12.00
C16 Mike Modano 8.00 20.00
C17 Nikolai Khabibulin 5.00 12.00
C18 Patrick Roy 12.00 30.00
C19 Pavel Bure 5.00 12.00
C20 Phil Esposito 8.00 20.00
C21 Pierre Turgeon 4.00 10.00
C22 Raymond Bourque 8.00 20.00
C23 Sergei Fedorov 8.00 20.00
C24 Teemu Selanne 10.00 25.00
C25 Wayne Gretzky 30.00 80.00

2017-18 ITG Superlative Debut Spectrum Magenta

SD01 Dave Andreychuk
Phil Housley
Brian Bellows
Scott Stevens 5.00 12.00
SD02 Martin Brodeur
Pavel Bure
Nicklas Lidstrom
Scott Niedermayer 12.00 30.00
SD03 Phil Esposito
Yvan Cournoyer
John Ferguson
Roger Crozier 8.00 20.00
SD04 Doug Gilmour
Kelly Hrudey
Chris Chelios
Claude Lemieux 6.00 15.00
SD05 Wayne Gretzky
Mark Messier
Raymond Bourque
Mike Gartner 30.00 80.00
SD06 Brett Hull
Adam Oates
Wendel Clark
Gary Suter 10.00 25.00
SD07 Jaromir Jagr
Sergei Fedorov
Dominik Hasek
Mats Sundin 15.00 40.00
SD08 Curtis Joseph
Rob Blake
Alexander Mogilny
Igor Larionov 6.00 15.00
SD09 Paul Kariya
Peter Forsberg
Tommy Salo
Nikolai Khabibulin 10.00 25.00
SD10 Guy Lafleur
Billy Smith
Marcel Dionne
Rick Martin 6.00 15.00
SD11 Mario Lemieux
Patrick Roy
Ulf Samuelsson
Kevin Hatcher 20.00 50.00
SD12 Pelle Lindbergh
Dale Hawerchuk
Ron Francis
Grant Fuhr 8.00 20.00
SD13 Eric Lindros
Teemu Selanne
Sandis Ozolinsh
Alexei Zhamnov 10.00 25.00
SD14 Mike Modano
Joe Sakic
Jeremy Roenick
Mike Richter 10.00 25.00
SD15 Larry Murphy
Paul Coffey
Peter Stastny
Denis Savard 5.00 12.00
SD16 Bobby Orr
Carol Vadnais
Serge Savard
Rogie Vachon 20.00 50.00
SD17 Gilbert Perreault
Gilles Meloche
Darryl Sittler
Reggie Leach 6.00 15.00
SD18 Denis Potvin
John Davidson
Borje Salming
Lanny McDonald 5.00 12.00
SD19 Larry Robinson
Steve Shutt
Bob Nystrom
Bill Barber 5.00 12.00
SD20 Bobby Rousseau
Rod Gilbert
Jean Ratelle
Dave Keon 5.00 12.00
SD21 Derek Sanderson
Ed Giacomin
Bernie Parent
Pete Mahovlich 6.00 15.00
SD22 Brendan Shanahan
Brian Leetch
Pierre Turgeon
Kevin Stevens 5.00 12.00
SD23 Steve Yzerman
Tom Barrasso
Cam Neely
Pat LaFontaine 12.00 30.00

2017-18 ITG Superlative League Leaders Spectrum Magenta

LL01 Peter Bondra
Ron Francis
Eric Lindros/25 8.00 20.00
LL03 Pavel Bure
Mark Recchi
Jaromir Jagr/25 15.00 40.00
LL04 Crosby/McDavid/Holtby/25 25.00 60.00
LL05 Phil Esposito
Bobby Orr
Bernie Parent/20 20.00 50.00
LL06 Wayne Gretzky
Mario Lemieux
Grant Fuhr/25 30.00 80.00
LL07 Wayne Gretzky
Mario Lemieux
Brett Hull/25 30.00 80.00
LL11 Reggie Leach
Bobby Clarke
Phil Esposito/25 8.00 20.00
LL12 Teemu Selanne
Jaromir Jagr
Martin Brodeur/25 15.00 40.00
LL13 Steve Shutt
Guy Lafleur
Ken Dryden/20 6.00 15.00
LL14 Keith Tkachuk
Mario Lemieux
Patrick Roy/25 20.00 50.00

2017-18 ITG Superlative Retired Numbers Multi Spectrum Magenta

RNM01 Bill Barber
Paul Coffey
Tim Horton
Ted Lindsay
Phil Esposito 8.00 20.00
RNM02 Andy Bathgate
Gordie Howe
Mike Modano
Lanny McDonald
Bobby Hull 15.00 40.00
RNM03 Pavel Bure
Guy Lafleur
George Armstrong
Alex Delvecchio
Ron Francis 6.00 15.00
RNM04 Bobby Clarke
Marcel Dionne
Pat LaFontaine
Trevor Linden
Brett Hull 10.00 25.00
RNM07 Markus Naslund
Larry Robinson
Joe Sakic
Bryan Trottier
Steve Yzerman 12.00 30.00
RNM10 Brian Sutter
Daniel Alfredsson
Mark Messier
Mike Gartner
Gilbert Perreault 10.00 25.00

2017-18 ITG Superlative Rookie Spectrum Magenta

SRNH1 Nico Hischier 25.00 60.00
SRNP1 Nolan Patrick EXCH 15.00 20.00

2017-18 ITG Superlative Seasons Spectrum Magenta

SE01 Jean Beliveau
Alex Delvecchio
Andy Bathgate
Tom Johnson
Jacques Plante
Doug Harvey 5.00 12.00
SE02 Phil Esposito
Bobby Orr
Gordie Howe
Stan Mikita
Gump Worsley
Derek Sanderson 20.00 50.00
SE03 Wayne Gretzky
Mike Bossy
Marcel Dionne
Randy Carlyle
Butch Goring
Peter Stastny 30.00 80.00
SE04 Gordie Howe
Doug Harvey
Jean Beliveau
Jacques Plante
Ted Lindsay
Glenn Hall 15.00 40.00
SE05 Gordie Howe
Stan Mikita
Tim Horton
Phil Goyette
Dave Keon
Glenn Hall 15.00 40.00
SE06 Jaromir Jagr
Teemu Selanne
Paul Kariya
Joe Sakic
Nicklas Lidstrom
Dominik Hasek 15.00 40.00
SE07 Hakan Loob
Patrick Roy
Wayne Gretzky
Grant Fuhr
Mario Lemieux
Raymond Bourque 30.00 80.00
SE08 McDavid/Crosby/Kane
Holtby/Burns/Draisaitl 25.00 60.00
SE09 Stan Mikita
Jean Beliveau
Bobby Hull
Terry Sawchuk
Norm Ullman
Roger Crozier 10.00 25.00
SE11 Bobby Orr
Phil Esposito
Bill White
Vic Hadfield
Jean Ratelle
Rod Gilbert 20.00 50.00
SE12 Bobby Orr
Denis Potvin
Bernie Parent
Guy Lafleur
Bobby Clarke
Marcel Dionne 20.00 50.00
SE13 Thornton/Jagr/Ovechkin
Alfredsson/Chara/Kiprusoff 20.00 50.00

2017-18 ITG Superlative Super Teams Spectrum Magenta

ST01 Wayne Gretzky
Mark Messier
Jari Kurri
Grant Fuhr
Paul Coffey
Glenn Anderson/25 30.00 80.00
ST02 Mario Lemieux
Jaromir Jagr
Larry Murphy
Ron Francis
Joe Mullen
Tom Barrasso/25 20.00 50.00
ST03 Guy Lafleur
Steve Shutt
Serge Savard
Larry Robinson
Ken Dryden
Guy Lapointe/20 6.00 15.00
ST04 Sergei Fedorov
Steve Yzerman
Nicklas Lidstrom
Igor Larionov
Chris Osgood
Larry Murphy/25 12.00 30.00
ST05 Bryan Trottier
Denis Potvin
Mike Bossy
Billy Smith
Clark Gillies
Butch Goring/25 5.00 12.00
ST06 Bobby Orr
Phil Esposito
Wayne Cashman
Gerry Cheevers
Johnny Bucyk
Ken Hodge/20 20.00 50.00
ST09 Adam Graves
Mark Messier
Alexei Kovalev
Brian Leetch
Sergei Zubov
Mike Richter/25 10.00 25.00
ST10 Hakan Loob
Joe Mullen
Doug Gilmour
Al MacInnis
Joe Nieuwendyk
Mike Vernon/25 6.00 15.00
ST11 Patrick Roy
Joe Sakic
Rob Blake
Peter Forsberg
Milan Hejduk
Raymond Bourque/25 12.00 30.00
ST12 Brett Hull
Mike Modano
Joe Nieuwendyk
Sergei Zubov
Darryl Sydor
Ed Belfour/25 10.00 25.00
ST13 Rick MacLeish
Bobby Clarke
Bill Barber
Reggie Leach
Joe Watson
Bernie Parent/25 8.00 20.00
ST15 Kane/Toews/Crawford
Hossa/Saad/Seabrook 10.00 25.00

2003-04 ITG Toronto Fall Expo Forever Rivals

FR1 M.Sundin
S.Koivu 6.00 15.00
FR2 D.Gilmour
P.Roy 8.00 20.00
FR3 W.Clark
C.Chelios 6.00 15.00
FR4 R.Vaive
G.Lafleur 8.00 20.00
FR5 L.McDonald
L.Robinson 6.00 15.00
FR6 D.Sittler
Y.Cournoyer 6.00 15.00
FR7 J.Bower
J.Plante 8.00 20.00
FR8 T.Horton
D.Harvey 6.00 15.00
FR9 T.Kennedy
M.Richard 6.00 15.00
FR10 G.Hainsworth
H.Morenz 6.00 15.00

2003-04 ITG Toronto Fall Expo Jerseys

FE1 Pavel Datsyuk 12.00 30.00
FE2 Vincent Lecavalier 12.00 30.00
FE3 Jay Bouwmeester 10.00 25.00
FE4 Saku Koivu 12.00 30.00
FE5 Roberto Luongo 12.00 30.00
FE6 Rick Nash 12.00 30.00
FE7 Owen Nolan 10.00 25.00
FE8 Brendan Shanahan 12.00 30.00
FE9 Jason Spezza 10.00 25.00
FE10 Mats Sundin 12.00 30.00
FE11 Marty Turco 10.00 25.00
FE12 Henrik Zetterberg 12.00 30.00
FE13 Nicklas Lidstrom 12.00 30.00
FE14 Pavel Bure 12.00 30.00
FE15 Jose Theodore 12.00 30.00
FE16 Joe Thornton 15.00 40.00
FE17 Jaromir Jagr 15.00 40.00
FE18 Ilya Kovalchuk 15.00 40.00
FE19 Mike Modano 15.00 40.00
FE20 Brett Hull 15.00 40.00

2003-04 ITG Toronto Spring Expo Class of 2004

1 E.Staal
T.Ruutu 6.00 15.00
2 M.Fleury
M.Lombardi 8.00 20.00
3 R.Malone
J.Lupul 6.00 15.00
4 M.Stajan
D.Brown 6.00 15.00
5 P.Bergeron
J.Hudler 6.00 15.00
6 F.Tyutin
A.Babchuk 6.00 15.00
7 D.Roy
N.Zherdev 8.00 20.00
8 N.Horton
J.Tootoo 6.00 15.00
9 J.Pitkanen
D.Hamhuis 6.00 15.00
10 K.Lehtonen
A.Munro 10.00 25.00

2006-07 ITG Toronto Spring Expo Maple Leafs Forever

1 Charlie Conacher 8.00 20.00
2 Hap Day 8.00 20.00
3 Joe Primeau 8.00 20.00
4 Johnny Bower 8.00 20.00
5 Tim Horton 10.00 25.00
6 Dave Keon 8.00 20.00
7 Dave Keon 8.00 20.00
8 Terry Sawchuk 10.00 25.00
9 Red Kelly 8.00 20.00
10 Frank Mahovlich 8.00 20.00
11 Lanny McDonald 8.00 20.00
12 Darryl Sittler 10.00 25.00
13 Borje Salming 8.00 20.00
14 Borje Salming 8.00 20.00
15 Tiger Williams 5.00 12.00
16 Darryl Sittler 10.00 25.00
17 Wendel Clark 12.00 30.00
18 Wendel Clark 12.00 30.00
19 Rick Vaive 8.00 20.00
20 Doug Gilmour 10.00 25.00
21 Felix Potvin 12.00 30.00
22 Felix Potvin 12.00 30.00
23 Ed Belfour 8.00 20.00
24 Ed Belfour 8.00 20.00
25 Brian Leetch 6.00 15.00

2014-15 ITG Toronto Spring Expo Beliveau Tribute

JB Jean Beliveau 3.00 8.00

2005-06 ITG Tough Customers

BG Bill Goldthorpe .20 .50
BM Basil McRae .20 .50
BP Bob Probert .40 1.00
CN Cam Neely .40 1.00
DB Donald Brashear .20 .50
DH Dale Hunter .20 .50
DM Dan Maloney .20 .50
DS Dave Schultz .20 .50
ES Eddie Shack .20 .50
FB Frank Bialowas .20 .50
GO Gino Odjick .20 .50
JF John Ferguson .20 .50
JK Joey Kocur .20 .50
JM Jimmy Mann .20 .50
KC Kelly Chase .20 .50
LF Lou Fontinato .20 .50
LG Link Gaetz .20 .50
SG Stu Grimson .20 .50
SJ Stan Jonathan .20 .50
TL Ted Lindsay .20 .50
TO Terry O'Reilly .30 .75
TW Tiger Williams .20 .50
WC Wendel Clark .60 1.50
CNI Chris Nilan .20 .50
DSE Dave Semenko .20 .50

2005-06 ITG Tough Customers Autographs

BG Bill Goldthorpe 5.00 12.00
BM Basil McRae 5.00 12.00
BP Bob Probert 8.00 20.00
CN Chris Nilan 5.00 12.00
DB Donald Brashear 5.00 12.00
DH Dale Hunter 5.00 12.00
DM Dan Maloney 5.00 12.00
DS Dave Schultz 5.00 12.00
ES Eddie Shack 5.00 12.00
FB Frank Bialowas 5.00 12.00
GO Gino Odjick 5.00 12.00
JK Joey Kocur 5.00 12.00
JM Jimmy Mann 5.00 12.00
KC Kelly Chase 5.00 12.00
LF Lou Fontinato 5.00 12.00
LG Link Gaetz 5.00 12.00
SG Stu Grimson 5.00 12.00
SJ Stan Jonathan 5.00 12.00
TL Ted Lindsay 5.00 12.00
TO Terry O'Reilly 6.00 15.00
TW Tiger Williams 5.00 12.00
WC Wendel Clark 12.00 30.00

2005-06 ITG Tough Customers Double Memorabilia

BP Bob Probert 10.00 25.00
CN Cam Neely 12.00 30.00
DB Donald Brashear 8.00 20.00
SG Stu Grimson 8.00 20.00
TO Terry O'Reilly 12.00 30.00
WC Wendel Clark 12.00 30.00

2005-06 ITG Tough Customers Famous Battles Autographs

BB Donald Brashear
Frank Bialowas 5.00 12.00
GP Stu Grimson
Bob Probert 8.00 20.00
HN Dale Hunter
Chris Nilan 5.00 12.00
PC Bob Probert
Wendel Clark 12.00 30.00
SO Dave Schultz
Terry O'Reilly 6.00 15.00
WS Tiger Williams
Dave Schultz 5.00 12.00

2005-06 ITG Tough Customers Jerseys

BG Bill Goldthorpe 2.00 5.00
BP Bob Probert 3.00 8.00
DB Donald Brashear 2.00 5.00
DM Dan Maloney 2.00 5.00
DS Dave Schultz 2.00 5.00
FB Frank Bialowas 2.00 5.00
GO Gino Odjick 2.00 5.00
JF John Ferguson 2.00 5.00
KC Kelly Chase 2.00 5.00
SG Stu Grimson 2.00 5.00
SJ Stan Jonathan 2.00 5.00
TO Terry O'Reilly 2.50 6.00
TW Tiger Williams 2.00 5.00
WC Wendel Clark 5.00 12.00

2005-06 ITG Tough Customers Signed Memorabilia

BG Bill Goldthorpe 8.00 20.00
BP Bob Probert 12.00 30.00
CN Cam Neely 12.00 30.00
DB Donald Brashear 8.00 20.00
DM Dan Maloney 8.00 20.00
DS Dave Schultz 8.00 20.00
FB Frank Bialowas 8.00 20.00
GO Gino Odjick 8.00 20.00
KC Kelly Chase 8.00 20.00
SG Stu Grimson 8.00 20.00
TW Tiger Williams 8.00 20.00
WC Wendel Clark 20.00 50.00

2005-06 ITG Tough Customers Stickwork

BP Bob Probert 5.00 12.00
CN Cam Neely 5.00 12.00
DH Dale Hunter 3.00 8.00
DS Dave Semenko 3.00 8.00
SG Stu Grimson 3.00 8.00
SJ Stan Jonathan 3.00 8.00
CNI Chris Nilan 3.00 8.00

2004-05 ITG Ultimate Memorabilia

1 Bun Cook 6.00 15.00
2 Doug Harvey 6.00 15.00
3 Butch Bouchard 6.00 15.00
4 Bill Barilko 20.00 50.00
5 Jean Ratelle 10.00 25.00
6 Phil Esposito 12.00 30.00
7 Ted Lindsay 10.00 25.00
8 Gordie Drillon 6.00 15.00
9 Johnny Bucyk 6.00 15.00
10 Bobby Hull 12.00 30.00
11 Ted Lindsay 10.00 25.00
12 Bill Gadsby 6.00 15.00
13 Busher Jackson 6.00 15.00
14 Aurel Joliat 12.00 30.00
15 John Davidson 12.00 30.00
16 Billy Smith 10.00 25.00
17 Bill Cook 12.00 30.00
18 Bill Cowley 10.00 25.00
19 Babe Pratt 10.00 25.00
20 Ed Giacomin 10.00 25.00
21 Neil Colville 6.00 15.00
22 Foster Hewitt 10.00 25.00
23 Georges Vezina 20.00 50.00
24 King Clancy 10.00 25.00
25 Red Dutton 6.00 15.00
26 Cyclone Taylor 30.00 80.00
27 Dale Hawerchuk 6.00 15.00
28 Norm Ullman 10.00 25.00
29 Harry Howell 12.00 30.00
30 Stan Mikita 12.00 30.00
31 Borje Salming 10.00 25.00
32 Ching Johnson 12.00 30.00
33 Harry Lumley 12.00 30.00
34 Bernie Geoffrion 12.00 30.00
35 Ted Kennedy 12.00 30.00
36 Howie Morenz 12.00 30.00
37 Ace Bailey 12.00 30.00
38 Bill Ranford 6.00 15.00
39 Charlie Gardiner 10.00 25.00
40 Rod Gilbert 10.00 25.00
41 Syl Apps 10.00 25.00
42 Ed Giacomin 10.00 25.00
43 Norm Ullman 10.00 25.00
44 Guy Lafleur 12.00 30.00
45 Andy Bathgate 10.00 25.00
46 Max Bentley 10.00 25.00
47 Steve Shutt 10.00 25.00
48 Bobby Hull 12.00 30.00
49 Denis Potvin 10.00 25.00
50 Dit Clapper 10.00 25.00
51 Phil Esposito 12.00 30.00
52 Hap Day 10.00 25.00
53 Henri Richard 12.00 30.00
54 Bernie Geoffrion 12.00 30.00
55 Marcel Pronovost 10.00 25.00
56 Bill Gadsby 6.00 15.00
57 Jean-Guy Talbot 6.00 15.00
58 Pelle Lindbergh 12.00 30.00
59 Marcel Dionne 10.00 25.00
60 Allan Stanley 10.00 25.00
61 Frank Brimsek 12.00 30.00
62 Alex Delvecchio 12.00 30.00
63 Chuck Rayner 10.00 25.00
64 Frank Brimsek 12.00 30.00
65 Ebbie Goodfellow 10.00 25.00
66 Newsy Lalonde 12.00 30.00
67 Jean Ratelle 10.00 25.00
68 Bryan Hextall 6.00 15.00
69 Bobby Bauer 6.00 15.00
70 Red Horner 12.00 30.00
71 Lord Stanley 6.00 15.00
72 Phil Esposito 12.00 30.00
73 Jacques Laperriere 10.00 25.00
74 Ken Wharram 6.00 15.00
75 Dickie Moore 10.00 25.00
76 Harry Lumley 12.00 30.00
77 Charlie Conacher 10.00 25.00
78 Elmer Lach 10.00 25.00
79 Terry Sawchuk 12.00 30.00
80 George Hainsworth 12.00 30.00
81 Red Kelly 12.00 30.00
82 Joe Primeau 12.00 30.00
83 Eddie Shore 12.00 30.00
84 Pierre Pilote 10.00 25.00
85 Lester Patrick 10.00 25.00
86 Ken Reardon 10.00 25.00
87 Bobby Baun 10.00 25.00
88 Jack Stewart 10.00 25.00
89 Doug Gilmour 12.00 30.00
90 Frank Boucher 6.00 15.00
91 Red Kelly 12.00 30.00
92 Joe Mullen 6.00 15.00
93 John Ferguson 12.00 30.00
94 Allan Stanley 10.00 25.00
95 Bill Mosienko 10.00 25.00
96 Milt Schmidt 12.00 30.00
97 Sweeney Schriner 10.00 25.00
98 Marcel Dionne 10.00 25.00
99 Bill Durnan 12.00 30.00
100 Babe Siebert 10.00 25.00
101 Brad Park 10.00 25.00
102 Cam Neely 12.00 30.00
103 Derek Sanderson 12.00 30.00
104 Gerry Cheevers 12.00 30.00
105 Milt Schmidt 12.00 30.00
106 Ray Bourque 12.00 30.00
107 Terry O'Reilly 10.00 25.00
108 Tiny Thompson 12.00 30.00
109 Wayne Cashman 10.00 25.00
110 Woody Dumart 10.00 25.00
111 Terry Sawchuk 12.00 30.00
112 Gilbert Perreault 12.00 30.00
113 Grant Fuhr 12.00 30.00
114 Pat LaFontaine 6.00 15.00
115 Rick Martin 6.00 15.00
116 Roger Crozier 12.00 30.00
117 Lanny McDonald 12.00 30.00
118 Denis Savard 12.00 30.00
119 Doug Bentley 10.00 25.00
120 Glenn Hall 12.00 30.00
121 Roy Conacher 10.00 25.00
122 Tony Esposito 12.00 30.00
123 Howie Morenz 12.00 30.00
124 Patrick Roy 30.00 80.00
125 Ray Bourque 12.00 30.00
126 Brad Park 10.00 25.00
127 Darryl Sittler 12.00 30.00
128 Dino Ciccarelli 6.00 15.00
129 Glenn Hall 12.00 30.00
130 Paul Coffey 10.00 25.00
131 Roger Crozier 12.00 30.00
132 Tiny Thompson 12.00 30.00
133 Sid Abel 10.00 25.00
134 Steve Yzerman 20.00 50.00
135 Syd Howe 10.00 25.00
136 Frank Mahovlich 12.00 30.00
137 Vladimir Konstantinov 12.00 30.00
138 Sid Abel 10.00 25.00
139 Grant Fuhr 12.00 30.00
140 Jari Kurri 10.00 25.00
141 Paul Coffey 10.00 25.00
142 Jari Kurri 10.00 25.00
143 Larry Robinson 10.00 25.00
144 Rogie Vachon 10.00 25.00

145 Dino Ciccarelli 6.00 15.00
146 Gump Worsley 12.00 30.00
147 Denis Savard 12.00 30.00
148 Frank Mahovlich 12.00 30.00
149 Gump Worsley 12.00 30.00
150 Guy Lapointe 6.00 15.00
151 Jacques Lemaire 10.00 25.00
152 Jacques Plante 12.00 30.00
153 Jean Beliveau 12.00 30.00
154 Larry Robinson 10.00 25.00
155 Maurice Richard 25.00 60.00
156 Patrick Roy 30.00 80.00
157 Rogie Vachon 10.00 25.00
158 Serge Savard 10.00 25.00
159 Toe Blake 10.00 25.00
160 Toe Blake 10.00 25.00
161 Lionel Conacher 10.00 25.00
162 Art Ross 10.00 25.00
163 Lady Byng 10.00 25.00
164 Roy Worters 10.00 25.00
165 Al Arbour 6.00 15.00
166 Bryan Trottier 10.00 25.00
167 Clark Gillies 10.00 25.00
168 Mike Bossy 12.00 30.00
169 Brad Park 10.00 25.00
170 Gump Worsley 12.00 30.00
171 Guy Lafleur 12.00 30.00
172 Vic Hadfield 10.00 25.00
173 Jacques Plante 12.00 30.00
174 Bernie Parent 12.00 30.00
175 Bill Barber 6.00 15.00
176 Bobby Clarke 12.00 30.00
177 Fred Shero 6.00 15.00
178 Bryan Trottier 10.00 25.00
179 Larry Murphy 6.00 15.00
180 Mario Lemieux 30.00 80.00
181 Paul Coffey 10.00 25.00
182 Hobey Baker 6.00 15.00
183 Guy Lafleur 12.00 30.00
184 Michel Goulet 6.00 15.00
185 Glenn Hall 12.00 30.00
186 Jack Adams 10.00 25.00
187 Al Arbour 6.00 15.00
188 Andy Bathgate 10.00 25.00
189 Darryl Sittler 12.00 30.00
190 Frank Mahovlich 12.00 30.00
191 Jacques Plante 12.00 30.00
192 Johnny Bower 10.00 25.00
193 Lanny McDonald 12.00 30.00
194 Terry Sawchuk 12.00 30.00
195 Tim Horton 12.00 30.00
196 Turk Broda 6.00 15.00
197 Wendel Clark 12.00 30.00
198 Valeri Kharlamov 12.00 30.00
199 Cam Neely 12.00 30.00
200 Roger Neilson 6.00 15.00

2004-05 ITG Ultimate Memorabilia Art Ross Trophy

1 Mario Lemieux 25.00 60.00
2 Jean Beliveau 15.00 40.00
3 Bobby Hull 15.00 40.00
4 Stan Mikita 12.50 30.00
5 Bryan Trottier 12.50 30.00
6 Phil Esposito 12.50 30.00
7 Ted Lindsay 12.50 30.00
8 Guy Lafleur 20.00 50.00

2004-05 ITG Ultimate Memorabilia Autographs

1 Henri Richard 20.00 50.00
2 Larry Robinson 20.00 50.00
3 Marcel Dionne 20.00 50.00
4 Ray Bourque COL 20.00 50.00
5 Guy Lapointe 15.00 40.00
6 Cam Neely 20.00 50.00
7 Patrick Roy COL 50.00 125.00
8 Ray Bourque BOS 25.00 60.00
9 Ed Giacomin 20.00 50.00
10 Wendel Clark 25.00 60.00
11 Stan Mikita 20.00 50.00
12 Alex Delvecchio 20.00 50.00
13 Marcel Pronovost 15.00 40.00
14 Paul Coffey 15.00 40.00
15 Patrick Roy MTL 60.00 150.00
16 Glenn Hall 20.00 50.00
17 Cam Neely 15.00 40.00
18 Marcel Dionne 15.00 40.00
19 Joe Mullen 15.00 40.00
20 Phil Esposito 25.00 60.00
21 Denis Savard 15.00 40.00
22 Glenn Hall 15.00 40.00
23 Tony Esposito 25.00 60.00
24 Bobby Hull 30.00 80.00
25 Phil Esposito 20.00 50.00
26 Jean Beliveau 40.00 80.00
27 Bobby Hull 25.00 60.00
28 Steve Yzerman 50.00 100.00
29 Terry O'Reilly 15.00 40.00
30 Denis Potvin 20.00 50.00
31 Harry Howell 20.00 50.00
32 Dino Ciccarelli 15.00 40.00
33 Gilbert Perreault 20.00 50.00
34 Mark Howe 15.00 40.00
35 Bobby Clarke 20.00 50.00
36 Brad Park NYR 20.00 50.00
37 Ron Hextall 30.00 80.00
38 Jean Ratelle 15.00 40.00
39 John Bucyk 15.00 40.00
40 Bernie Parent 25.00 60.00
41 Billy Smith 15.00 40.00
42 Brad Park BOS 20.00 50.00
43 Bryan Trottier 15.00 40.00
44 Mike Bossy 25.00 60.00
45 Bill Barber 15.00 40.00
46 Gerry Cheevers 25.00 60.00
47 Pat LaFontaine 15.00 40.00
48 Johnny Bower 20.00 50.00
49 Doug Gilmour 25.00 60.00
50 Glenn Anderson 20.00 50.00
51 Bill Gadsby 15.00 40.00
52 Pierre Pilote 20.00 50.00
53 Grant Fuhr 20.00 50.00
54 Mario Lemieux 60.00 125.00
55 Butch Bouchard 15.00 40.00
56 Chuck Rayner 25.00 60.00
57 Elmer Lach 20.00 50.00
58 Frank Brimsek 50.00 100.00
59 Harry Lumley 25.00 60.00
60 Harry Watson 50.00 100.00
61 Howie Meeker 15.00 40.00
62 Rocket Richard 150.00 300.00
63 Milt Schmidt 15.00 40.00
64 Red Horner 75.00 150.00
65 Red Kelly 20.00 50.00
66 Sid Abel 30.00 80.00
67 Ted Kennedy 30.00 80.00
68 Ted Lindsay 20.00 50.00
69 Woody Dumart 25.00 60.00

2004-05 ITG Ultimate Memorabilia Blades of Steel

1 Bill Barilko 60.00 150.00
2 Rocket Richard 75.00 200.00
3 Cyclone Taylor 100.00 250.00
4 Jacques Plante 40.00 100.00
5 Hap Day 30.00 80.00
6 Elmer Lach 25.00 60.00
7 Eddie Shore 50.00 125.00
8 Nels Stewart 25.00 60.00
9 Tim Horton 30.00 80.00
10 Toe Blake 30.00 80.00
11 Busher Jackson 30.00 80.00
12 Jean Beliveau 40.00 100.00
13 Mario Lemieux 30.00 80.00
14 Clint Benedict 30.00 80.00
15 Joe Primeau 25.00 60.00
16 Paddy Moran 30.00 80.00
17 Dit Clapper 40.00 100.00

2004-05 ITG Ultimate Memorabilia Broad Street Bullies Jerseys

1 Bobby Clarke 25.00 60.00
2 Bill Barber 15.00 40.00
3 Bernie Parent 20.00 50.00
4 Dave Schultz 25.00 60.00
5 Rick MacLeish 15.00 40.00
6 Reggie Leach 15.00 40.00
7 Gary Dornhoefer 15.00 40.00
8 Joe Watson 15.00 40.00

2004-05 ITG Ultimate Memorabilia Calder Trophy

1 Mario Lemieux 30.00 80.00
2 Mike Bossy 15.00 40.00
3 Bryan Trottier 12.50 30.00
4 Gilbert Perreault 20.00 50.00
5 Terry Sawchuk 25.00 60.00
6 Glenn Hall 12.50 30.00
7 Ray Bourque 15.00 40.00
8 Denis Potvin 10.00 25.00

2004-05 ITG Ultimate Memorabilia Changing the Game

1 Phil Esposito 12.50 30.00
2 Patrick Roy 40.00 100.00
3 Mario Lemieux 40.00 100.00
4 Ted Lindsay 12.50 30.00
5 Bobby Hull 15.00 40.00
6 Jacques Plante 30.00 80.00
7 Rocket Richard 40.00 100.00
8 Borje Salming 15.00 40.00
9 Steve Yzerman 25.00 60.00
10 Howie Morenz 30.00 80.00
11 Eddie Shore 30.00 80.00
12 Doug Harvey 15.00 40.00

2004-05 ITG Ultimate Memorabilia Conn Smythe Trophy

1 Jean Beliveau 15.00 40.00
2 Patrick Roy 40.00 100.00
3 Steve Yzerman 30.00 80.00
4 Mario Lemieux 40.00 100.00
5 Mike Bossy 12.50 30.00
6 Bryan Trottier 12.50 30.00
7 Glenn Hall 12.50 30.00
8 Guy Lafleur 20.00 50.00

2004-05 ITG Ultimate Memorabilia Country of Origin

1 Pelle Lindbergh 40.00 80.00
2 Gilbert Perreault 20.00 50.00
3 Bobby Hull 20.00 50.00
4 Mario Lemieux 60.00 120.00
5 Jari Kurri 20.00 50.00
6 Valeri Kharlamov 25.00 60.00
7 Steve Yzerman 40.00 100.00
8 Patrick Roy 40.00 100.00
9 Mike Bossy 15.00 40.00
10 Phil Esposito 20.00 50.00
11 Joe Mullen 15.00 40.00
12 Lanny McDonald 15.00 40.00
13 Ray Bourque 20.00 50.00
14 Tony Esposito 20.00 50.00
15 Yvan Cournoyer 15.00 40.00
16 Denis Potvin 15.00 40.00
17 Bobby Clarke 15.00 40.00
18 Paul Coffey 15.00 40.00
19 Larry Robinson 15.00 40.00
20 Guy Lafleur 25.00 60.00

2004-05 ITG Ultimate Memorabilia Gloves are Off

1 Ray Bourque 15.00 40.00
2 Cam Neely 25.00 60.00
3 Steve Yzerman 30.00 80.00
4 Mario Lemieux 40.00 100.00
5 Patrick Roy 40.00 100.00
6 Dale Hawerchuk 25.00 60.00
7 Pelle Lindbergh 30.00 80.00
8 Charlie Conacher 25.00 60.00

2004-05 ITG Ultimate Memorabilia Hart Trophy

1 Mario Lemieux 40.00 100.00
2 Rocket Richard 40.00 100.00
3 Jacques Plante 20.00 50.00
4 Stan Mikita 12.50 30.00
5 Guy Lafleur 15.00 40.00
6 Bobby Hull 20.00 50.00
7 Phil Esposito 12.50 30.00
8 Howie Morenz 30.00 80.00

2004-05 ITG Ultimate Memorabilia Heroes Mario Lemieux

1 Rookie Season 30.00 80.00
2 Five Goals, Five Ways 30.00 80.00
3 First Cup 30.00 80.00
4 M.Lemieux
P.Coffey 25.00 60.00
5 M.Lemieux
L.Murphy 25.00 60.00
6 M.Lemieux
B.Trottier 30.00 80.00
7 All-Star Career 30.00 80.00
8 International Play AU 75.00 150.00
9 Short-Handed Goals AU 75.00 150.00
10 Points in Playoff Game AU 75.00 150.00

2004-05 ITG Ultimate Memorabilia Heroes Patrick Roy

1 Rookie Season 30.00 80.00
2 First Conn Smythe Trophy 30.00 80.00
3 First Cup 30.00 80.00
4 P.Roy/L.Robinson 30.00 80.00
5 P.Roy/R.Bourque 30.00 80.00
6 All-Star Career 30.00 80.00
7 International Play 30.00 80.00

2004-05 ITG Ultimate Memorabilia Heroes Steve Yzerman

1 Rookie Season 25.00 60.00
2 First Cup 25.00 60.00
3 Team Points Record 25.00 60.00
4 S.Yzerman/D.Sittler 25.00 60.00
5 S.Yzerman/P.Coffey 25.00 60.00
6 S.Yzerman/D.Ciccarelli 25.00 60.00
7 All-Star Career 25.00 60.00
8 International Play 25.00 60.00
9 Youngest All-Star AU 75.00 150.00
10 Longest Captaincy AU 75.00 150.00

2004-05 ITG Ultimate Memorabilia Jerseys

1 Ray Bourque 15.00 40.00
2 Patrick Roy 40.00 100.00
3 Aurel Joliat 30.00 80.00
4 Paul Coffey 15.00 40.00
5 George Hainsworth 20.00 50.00
6 Mario Lemieux 30.00 80.00
7 Red Kelly 15.00 40.00
8 Terry Sawchuk 25.00 60.00
9 Jean Beliveau 20.00 50.00
10 Rocket Richard 50.00 100.00
11 Steve Yzerman 25.00 60.00
12 Roy Worters 20.00 50.00
13 Frank Brimsek 12.50 30.00
14 Phil Esposito 12.50 30.00
15 Norm Ullman 12.50 30.00
16 Sid Abel 12.50 30.00
17 Ted Lindsay 12.50 30.00

2004-05 ITG Ultimate Memorabilia Jersey Autographs

1 Larry Robinson 12.00 30.00
2 Steve Yzerman 50.00 120.00
3 Jean Beliveau 50.00 100.00
4 Bill Barber 12.00 30.00
5 Paul Coffey 15.00 40.00
6 Guy Lapointe 15.00 40.00
7 Pat LaFontaine 15.00 40.00
8 Guy Lafleur 30.00 80.00
9 Dino Ciccarelli 15.00 40.00
10 Jari Kurri 25.00 60.00
11 Bobby Hull 40.00 80.00
12 Dale Hawerchuk 12.00 30.00
13 Bernie Parent 25.00 60.00
14 Patrick Roy COL 75.00 150.00
15 Gerry Cheevers 15.00 40.00
16 Brad Park 20.00 50.00
17 Gilbert Perreault 15.00 40.00
18 Joe Mullen 12.00 30.00
19 Terry O'Reilly 15.00 40.00
20 Cam Neely 25.00 60.00
21 Patrick Roy MTL 100.00 200.00
22 Mike Bossy 12.00 30.00
23 Jacques Laperriere 12.00 30.00
24 Marcel Dionne 12.00 30.00
25 Yvan Cournoyer 12.00 30.00
26 Grant Fuhr 25.00 60.00
27 Ed Giacomin 20.00 50.00
28 Johnny Bower 25.00 60.00
29 Jean Ratelle 12.00 30.00
30 Ted Lindsay 20.00 50.00
31 Mario Lemieux 75.00 150.00
32 Frank Mahovlich 25.00 60.00
33 Denis Potvin 20.00 50.00
34 Stan Mikita 20.00 50.00
35 Billy Smith 12.00 30.00
36 Red Kelly 20.00 50.00
37 Lanny McDonald 15.00 40.00
38 Phil Esposito 25.00 60.00
39 Darryl Sittler 25.00 60.00
40 Denis Savard 20.00 50.00
41 John Ferguson 12.00 30.00
42 Tony Esposito 25.00 60.00
43 Wendel Clark 25.00 60.00
44 Doug Gilmour 25.00 60.00
45 Glenn Anderson/33 12.00 30.00
46 Bobby Clarke 20.00 50.00
47 Henri Richard 15.00 40.00
48 Johnny Bucyk 15.00 40.00
49 Michel Goulet 12.00 30.00
50 Ray Bourque 40.00 80.00
51 Alex Delvecchio 15.00 40.00
52 Gump Worsley 20.00 50.00
53 Bryan Trottier 12.00 30.00

2004-05 ITG Ultimate Memorabilia Jersey and Sticks

1 Doug Harvey 15.00 40.00
2 Denis Potvin 12.50 30.00
3 Ray Bourque 20.00 50.00
4 Paul Coffey 20.00 50.00
5 Brad Park 12.50 30.00
6 Mike Bossy 15.00 40.00
7 Jean Beliveau 20.00 50.00
8 Steve Yzerman 30.00 80.00
9 Phil Esposito 20.00 50.00
10 Marcel Dionne 12.50 30.00
11 Bobby Hull 20.00 50.00
12 Doug Gilmour 25.00 60.00
13 Mario Lemieux 40.00 100.00
14 Guy Lafleur 25.00 60.00
15 Cam Neely 25.00 60.00
16 Patrick Roy 40.00 100.00
17 Grant Fuhr 20.00 50.00
18 Johnny Bower 20.00 50.00
19 Jacques Plante 30.00 80.00
20 Harry Lumley 12.50 30.00

2004-05 ITG Ultimate Memorabilia Nicknames

1 Stan Mikita 25.00 60.00
2 Rocket Richard 60.00 120.00
3 Toe Blake 30.00 80.00
4 Jacques Plante 25.00 60.00
5 Mario Lemieux 60.00 120.00
6 Terry Sawchuk 30.00 80.00
7 Steve Yzerman 25.00 60.00
8 Glenn Hall 15.00 40.00
9 Larry Robinson 15.00 40.00
10 Bernie Geoffrion Glv 20.00 40.00
11 Henri Richard 15.00 40.00
12 Jean Beliveau 20.00 50.00
13 Johnny Bower 25.00 60.00
15 Doug Gilmour 25.00 60.00
16 Ace Bailey 30.00 80.00
17 Nels Stewart 30.00 80.00
18 Tony Esposito 20.00 50.00
19 Frank Mahovlich 15.00 40.00
20 Gump Worsley 25.00 60.00
22 Frank Brimsek 25.00 60.00
23 Ted Lindsay 15.00 40.00
24 Gerry Cheevers 50.00 100.00
25 Patrick Roy 50.00 100.00
26 Cyclone Taylor 250.00 350.00
27 Howie Morenz 50.00 100.00
28 Bobby Hull 20.00 50.00
29 Guy Lafleur 25.00 60.00
30 Georges Vezina 125.00 200.00

2004-05 ITG Ultimate Memorabilia Norris Trophy

1 Ray Bourque 25.00 60.00
2 Larry Robinson 15.00 40.00
3 Doug Harvey 15.00 40.00
4 Jacques Laperriere 10.00 25.00
5 Paul Coffey 15.00 40.00
6 Denis Potvin 10.00 25.00

2004-05 ITG Ultimate Memorabilia Raised to the Rafters

1 Patrick Roy 40.00 100.00
2 Jacques Plante 30.00 80.00
3 Ray Bourque 20.00 50.00
4 Johnny Bower 20.00 50.00
5 Doug Harvey 20.00 50.00
6 Stan Mikita 20.00 50.00
7 Bobby Hull 20.00 50.00
8 Jean Beliveau 25.00 60.00
9 Bobby Clarke 25.00 60.00
10 Jari Kurri 25.00 60.00

2004-05 ITG Ultimate Memorabilia Retro Teammates

1 Bourq/Neely/Middle/Moog 50.00 100.00
2 Rich/Rich/Harvey/Plante 100.00 200.00
3 Mik/Hull/Hall/Hull 60.00 120.00
4 Sittler/McD/Salm/Williams 40.00 100.00
5 Trott/Boss/Pot/Smith 25.00 60.00
6 Abel/Delv/Lndsy/Sawchuk 60.00 120.00
7 Shore/Thomp/Stewrt/Clap 75.00 150.00
8 Coffey/Fuhr/Ander/Kurri 60.00 120.00
9 Lafleur/Shutt/Robin/Savrd 100.00 200.00
10 Bailey/Day/Clancy/Prim 100.00 200.00
11 Barb/Parent/Clarke/Leach 75.00 150.00
12 Ratelle/Giac/Park/Gilbert 40.00 100.00
13 Bucyk/Espo/Cheev/Cash 40.00 100.00
14 O'Reilly/Park/Bourq/Gilb 60.00 120.00
15 Beliveau/Worsly/Courn/Lap 60.00 120.00

2004-05 ITG Ultimate Memorabilia Seams Unbelievable

1 Mario Lemieux 40.00 100.00
2 Steve Yzerman 25.00 60.00
3 Patrick Roy 50.00 125.00
4 Mike Bossy 15.00 40.00
5 Bryan Trottier 15.00 40.00
6 Charlie Gardiner 25.00 60.00
7 Rocket Richard 75.00 200.00
8 Darryl Sittler 20.00 50.00
9 Ray Bourque 25.00 60.00
10 Roy Worters 25.00 60.00

2004-05 ITG Ultimate Memorabilia Stick Autographs

1 Michel Goulet 12.50 30.00
2 Mike Bossy 12.50 30.00
3 Cam Neely 25.00 60.00
4 Phil Esposito 25.00 60.00
5 Ray Bourque 25.00 60.00
6 Dale Hawerchuk 12.50 30.00
7 Tony Esposito 20.00 50.00
8 Mario Lemieux 60.00 150.00
9 Guy Lapointe 12.50 30.00
10 Marcel Dionne 12.50 30.00
11 Henri Richard 15.00 40.00
12 Larry Robinson 12.50 30.00
13 Gerry Cheevers 20.00 50.00
14 Bobby Hull 30.00 80.00
15 Bryan Trottier 12.50 30.00
16 Dino Ciccarelli 12.50 30.00
17 Gump Worsley 30.00 80.00
18 Guy Lafleur 25.00 60.00
19 Johnny Bower 25.00 60.00
20 Pat LaFontaine 12.50 30.00
21 Steve Yzerman 50.00 125.00
22 Terry O'Reilly 12.50 30.00
23 Bernie Geoffrion/30 30.00 80.00
24 Bill Barber/30 12.50 30.00
25 Bobby Clarke/30 25.00 60.00
26 Frank Mahovlich/30 25.00 60.00
27 Gilbert Perreault/30 25.00 60.00
28 Johnny Bucyk/30 20.00 50.00
29 Paul Coffey/30 25.00 60.00
30 Stan Mikita/30 25.00 60.00
31 Jean Beliveau/30 50.00 100.00
32 Jari Kurri 20.00 50.00
33 Bernie Parent 20.00 50.00
34 Alex Delvecchio 20.00 50.00
35 John Ferguson 12.50 30.00
36 Joe Mullen 12.50 30.00
37 Brad Park 20.00 50.00
38 Wendel Clark 20.00 50.00
39 Doug Gilmour 20.00 50.00
40 Yvan Cournoyer 12.50 30.00
41 Billy Smith 12.50 30.00
42 Ed Giacomin 12.50 30.00
43 Denis Savard/30 20.00 50.00
44 Grant Fuhr/30 30.00 80.00
45 Darryl Sittler/30 25.00 60.00

2004-05 ITG Ultimate Memorabilia Triple Threads

1 Savard/Lapointe/Laperriere 20.00 50.00
2 Park/Potvin/Robinson 20.00 50.00
3 Worsley/Bower/Lumley 25.00 60.00
4 Brimsek/Hains/Worters 30.00 80.00
5 Crozier/Cheevers/T.Esposito 25.00 60.00
6 Bourque/Coffey/Housley 30.00 80.00
7 R.Brodeur/B.Smith/Parent 20.00 50.00
8 P.Esposito/Dionne/Clarke 30.00 80.00
9 Kurri/Bossy/Neely 30.00 80.00
10 Williams/Schultz/Ferguson 25.00 50.00
11 Lemieux/Yzer/Gilmour 50.00 125.00
12 Sittler/Trottier/Lafleur 25.00 60.00
13 Beliv/Richard/Mahov 30.00 80.00

2004-05 ITG Ultimate Memorabilia Vezina Trophy

1 Jacques Plante 25.00 60.00
2 Terry Sawchuk 25.00 60.00
3 Pelle Lindbergh 40.00 100.00
4 George Hainsworth 25.00 60.00
5 Bernie Parent 30.00 80.00
6 Patrick Roy 40.00 100.00
7 Grant Fuhr 25.00 60.00
8 Tony Esposito 25.00 60.00

2005-06 ITG Ultimate Memorabilia Level 2

1 Alex Delvecchio 6.00 15.00
2 Alexander Ovechkin 25.00 60.00
3 Alexander Yakushev 6.00 15.00
4 Antero Niittymaki 6.00 15.00
5 Aurel Joliat 6.00 15.00
6 Bernie Geoffrion 8.00 20.00
7 Bernie Parent 6.00 15.00
8 Bill Barilko 12.00 30.00
9 Bill Durnan 6.00 15.00
10 Billy Smith 6.00 15.00
11 Bobby Clarke 8.00 20.00
12 Bobby Hull 10.00 25.00
13 Borje Salming 6.00 15.00
14 Brett Hull 8.00 20.00
15 Brian Leetch 5.00 12.00
16 Cam Neely 6.00 15.00
17 Charlie Conacher 6.00 15.00
18 Charlie Gardiner 5.00 12.00
19 Corey Perry 6.00 15.00
20 Cyclone Taylor 20.00 50.00
21 Dany Heatley 6.00 15.00
22 Darryl Sittler 5.00 12.00
23 Dave Keon 8.00 20.00
24 Denis Potvin 6.00 15.00
25 Dion Phaneuf 8.00 20.00
26 Dit Clapper 6.00 15.00
27 Doug Gilmour 6.00 15.00
28 Doug Harvey 6.00 15.00
29 Ed Giacomin 6.00 15.00
30 Eddie Shack 6.00 15.00
31 Eddie Shore 6.00 15.00
32 Elmer Lach 6.00 15.00
33 Eric Lindros 10.00 25.00
34 Evgeni Malkin 20.00 50.00
35 Frank Brimsek 6.00 15.00
36 Frank Mahovlich 6.00 15.00
37 Frank McGee 6.00 15.00
38 Frank Nighbor 6.00 15.00
39 George Hainsworth 6.00 15.00
40 Georges Vezina 12.00 30.00
41 Gerry Cheevers 6.00 15.00
42 Gilbert Perreault 6.00 15.00
43 Glenn Hall 6.00 15.00
44 Grant Fuhr 6.00 15.00
45 Gump Worsley 6.00 15.00
46 Guy Lafleur 6.00 15.00
47 Henri Richard 6.00 15.00
48 Henrik Lundqvist 8.00 20.00
49 Howie Meeker 5.00 12.00
50 Howie Morenz 8.00 20.00
51 Ilya Kovalchuk 6.00 15.00
52 Jacques Plante 8.00 20.00
53 Jari Kurri 8.00 20.00
54 Jean Beliveau 6.00 15.00
55 Jim Craig 6.00 15.00
56 Joe Malone 6.00 15.00
57 Johnny Bower 4.00 10.00
58 Johnny Bucyk 4.00 10.00
59 Jose Theodore 6.00 15.00
60 King Clancy 6.00 15.00
61 Lanny McDonald 6.00 15.00
62 Larry Robinson 6.00 15.00
63 Lester Patrick 4.00 10.00
64 Lionel Conacher 6.00 15.00
65 Lord Stanley 5.00 12.00
66 Marcel Dionne 5.00 12.00
67 Mario Lemieux 12.00 30.00
68 Martin Brodeur 10.00 25.00
69 Maurice Richard 8.00 20.00
70 Mike Bossy 6.00 15.00
71 Mike Richards 6.00 15.00
72 Milt Schmidt 4.00 10.00
73 Nels Stewart 6.00 15.00
74 Newsy Lalonde 6.00 15.00
75 Pat LaFontaine 5.00 12.00
76 Patrick Roy 12.00 30.00
77 Paul Coffey 6.00 15.00
78 Paul Henderson 5.00 12.00
79 Pelle Lindbergh 8.00 20.00
80 Petr Prucha 6.00 15.00
81 Phil Esposito 6.00 15.00
82 Raymond Bourque 8.00 20.00
83 Red Kelly 4.00 10.00
84 Rogie Vachon 4.00 10.00
85 Ron Hextall 6.00 15.00
86 Sid Abel 6.00 15.00
87 Sidney Crosby 40.00 100.00
88 Stan Mikita 6.00 15.00
89 Steve Yzerman 10.00 25.00
90 Ted Kennedy 6.00 15.00
91 Ted Lindsay 6.00 15.00
92 Terry Sawchuk 8.00 20.00
93 Tim Horton 8.00 20.00
94 Tiny Thompson 6.00 15.00
95 Toe Blake 6.00 15.00
96 Tony Esposito 6.00 15.00
97 Turk Broda 6.00 15.00
98 Valeri Kharlamov 6.00 15.00
99 Vladislav Tretiak 8.00 20.00
100 Yvan Cournoyer 5.00 12.00

2005-06 ITG Ultimate Memorabilia Level 3

*LEVEL 3/40: .4X TO 1X LEVEL 2/45

2005-06 ITG Ultimate Memorabilia Level 4

*LEVEL 2/30: .5X TO 1.2X LEVEL 2/45

2005-06 ITG Ultimate Memorabilia Blades of Steel

1 Alexander Ovechkin 50.00 120.00
2 Mario Lemieux 30.00 80.00
3 Ray Bourque 20.00 50.00
4 Joe Primeau 25.00 50.00
5 Elmer Lach 15.00 40.00
6 Jack Adams 30.00 80.00
7 Nels Stewart 20.00 50.00
8 Tim Horton 25.00 60.00
9 Toe Blake 20.00 50.00
10 Frank Nighbor 20.00 50.00
11 Aurel Joliat 40.00 100.00
12 Dit Clapper 20.00 50.00
13 Eddie Shore 20.00 50.00
14 Jean Beliveau 40.00 80.00
15 Georges Vezina 90.00 150.00
16 Jacques Plante 20.00 50.00
17 Cyclone Taylor 450.00 600.00
18 Clint Benedict 25.00 60.00
19 Maurice Richard 30.00 80.00
20 Bill Barilko 40.00 80.00

2005-06 ITG Ultimate Memorabilia Double Autos

1 D.Phaneuf/B.Leetch 30.00 60.00
2 P.Roy/A.Esposito 50.00 125.00
3 P.Esposito/G.Cheevers 25.00 50.00
4 P.Henderson/V.Tretiak 30.00 60.00
5 A.Niittymaki/B.Parent 15.00 40.00
6 M.Brodeur/P.Roy 75.00 200.00
7 D.Keon/T.Kennedy 30.00 60.00
8 M.Lemieux/J.Beliveau 75.00 125.00
9 Lundqvist/Giacomin 30.00 60.00
10 S.Yzerman/T.Lindsay 40.00 80.00
11 B.Salming/L.Robinson 20.00 40.00
12 A.Ovechkin/E.Malkin 125.00 300.00
13 G.Hall/T.Esposito 25.00 50.00
14 M.Lemieux/R.Francis 75.00 125.00
15 T.Esposito/P.Esposito 25.00 50.00
16 M.Schmidt/E.Lach 20.00 40.00
17 C.Huet/P.Roy 50.00 125.00
18 P.Coffey/G.Fuhr 25.00 50.00
19 D.Heatley/I.Kovalchuk 20.00 40.00
20 Cournoyer/Henderson 30.00 60.00

2005-06 ITG Ultimate Memorabilia Double Memorabilia

1 Martin Brodeur 12.00 30.00
2 Eric Lindros 8.00 20.00
3 Vladislav Tretiak 4.00 10.00
4 Patrick Roy 12.00 30.00
5 Guy Lafleur 6.00 15.00
6 Stan Mikita 6.00 15.00
7 Brett Hull 10.00 25.00
8 Cam Neely 5.00 12.00
9 Marcel Dionne 6.00 15.00
10 Bernie Parent 6.00 15.00
11 Borje Salming 5.00 12.00
12 Jose Theodore 5.00 12.00
13 Dave Keon 5.00 12.00
14 Paul Coffey 5.00 12.00
15 Raymond Bourque 8.00 20.00
16 Steve Yzerman 12.00 30.00
17 Mario Lemieux 20.00 50.00
18 Jacques Plante 8.00 20.00
19 Eddie Shore 5.00 12.00
20 Bobby Hull 10.00 25.00
21 Bobby Clarke 8.00 20.00
22 Grant Fuhr 8.00 20.00
23 Sidney Crosby 30.00 80.00
24 Alexander Ovechkin 60.00 150.00
25 Tony Esposito 5.00 12.00

2005-06 ITG Ultimate Memorabilia Double Memorabilia Autos

1 Ovechkin/Malkin 125.00 300.00
2 Brodeur/Roy 40.00 100.00
3 P. Esposito/Cheevers 25.00 60.00
4 Phaneuf/Leetch 25.00 60.00
5 Lundqvist/Giacomin 80.00 200.00
6 Yzerman/Lindsay 40.00 100.00
7 Keon/Kennedy 15.00 40.00
8 Lemieux/Beliveau 60.00 150.00
9 Niittymaki/Parent 20.00 50.00
10 Esposito/Esposito 25.00 60.00
11 Coffey/Fuhr 25.00 60.00
12 Hall/T.Esposito 15.00 40.00
13 LaFontaine/Perreault 15.00 40.00
14 Sittler/McDonald 20.00 50.00
15 Mahovlich/Richard 15.00 40.00
16 Hextall/Parent 20.00 50.00
17 Hull/Mikita 30.00 80.00
18 Tretiak/Cournoyer 15.00 40.00
19 Gilmour/Clark 25.00 60.00
20 Bossy/Lafleur 20.00 50.00

2005-06 ITG Ultimate Memorabilia First Overall Jerseys

1 Gilbert Perreault 20.00 40.00
2 Guy Lafleur 20.00 40.00
3 Denis Potvin 20.00 40.00
4 Dale Hawerchuk 20.00 40.00
5 Mario Lemieux 40.00 80.00
6 Wendel Clark 20.00 40.00
7 Marc-Andre Fleury 20.00 50.00
8 Alexander Ovechkin 50.00 120.00
9 Sidney Crosby 75.00 150.00

2005-06 ITG Ultimate Memorabilia First Rounders Jerseys

1 Mario/Perr/Guy/Hawer 50.00 100.00
2 Fleury/Mario/Crosby/Malk 100.00 200.00
3 Fuhr/Leetch/Yzerm/Savard 40.00 80.00
4 Dionne/Lafleur/Bossy/Sittler 40.00 80.00
5 Brodr/Lehtn/Montya/Fleury 40.00 80.00
6 Mario/Crosby/Malkin/AO 50.00 120.00
7 Neely/Phaneuf/Getzlaf/Ward 40.00 80.00
8 Brque/Leetch/Phnf/Pitkanen 40.00 80.00
9 Bourq/Goul/Hawer/Mario 40.00 80.00
10 Yzer/AO/Perry/Rich 40.00 100.00

2005-06 ITG Ultimate Memorabilia Future Stars Autographs

1 Marc-Andre Fleury 15.00 40.00
2 Henrik Lundqvist 20.00 50.00
3 Marek Svatos 8.00 20.00
4 Ray Emery 10.00 25.00
5 Cam Ward 15.00 40.00
6 Sidney Crosby 100.00 175.00
7 Alexander Ovechkin 400.00 1000.00
8 Evgeni Malkin 60.00 125.00
9 Cristobal Huet 12.00 30.00
10 Thomas Vanek 15.00 40.00
11 Al Montoya 8.00 20.00
12 Dion Phaneuf 20.00 50.00
13 Ryan Getzlaf 12.00 30.00
14 Marek Schwarz 8.00 20.00
15 David Ruzicka 8.00 20.00
16 Jason LaBarbera 8.00 20.00
17 Mike Richards 15.00 40.00
18 Petr Prucha 12.00 30.00
19 Angelo Esposito 20.00 50.00
20 Michael Frolik 12.00 30.00
21 Eric Nystrom 8.00 20.00
22 Antero Niittymaki 12.00 30.00

2005-06 ITG Ultimate Memorabilia Future Stars Jerseys

1 Marc-Andre Fleury 30.00 60.00
2 Henrik Lundqvist 20.00 50.00
3 Marek Svatos 20.00 40.00
4 Ray Emery 20.00 40.00
5 Cam Ward 25.00 50.00
6 Sidney Crosby 60.00 150.00
7 Alexander Ovechkin 50.00 120.00
8 Evgeni Malkin 30.00 80.00
9 Antero Niittymaki 20.00 40.00
10 Thomas Vanek 20.00 40.00
12 Dion Phaneuf 30.00 60.00
13 Ryan Getzlaf 20.00 40.00
14 Corey Perry 20.00 40.00
15 Marek Schwarz 10.00 25.00
16 David Ruzicka 10.00 25.00
17 Jason LaBarbera 10.00 25.00
18 Mike Richards 20.00 40.00
19 Petr Prucha 25.00 50.00

2005-06 ITG Ultimate Memorabilia Future Stars Memorabilia Autographs

1 Marc-Andre Fleury 15.00 40.00
2 Henrik Lundqvist 30.00 60.00
3 Marek Svatos 10.00 25.00
4 Ray Emery 10.00 25.00
5 Cam Ward 12.00 30.00
6 Sidney Crosby 125.00 200.00
7 Alexander Ovechkin 125.00 300.00
8 Evgeni Malkin 75.00 200.00
9 Antero Niittymaki 12.00 30.00
10 Thomas Vanek 25.00 50.00
11 Al Montoya 10.00 25.00
12 Dion Phaneuf 20.00 50.00
13 Ryan Getzlaf 12.00 30.00
14 Marek Schwarz 10.00 25.00
15 David Ruzicka 10.00 25.00
16 Jason LaBarbera 10.00 25.00
17 Mike Richards 12.00 30.00
18 Petr Prucha 12.00 30.00

2005-06 ITG Ultimate Memorabilia Gloves Are Off

1 Sidney Crosby 60.00 125.00
2 Alexander Ovechkin 50.00 125.00
3 Mario Lemieux 40.00 80.00
4 Paul Coffey 20.00 40.00
5 Maurice Richard 50.00 100.00
6 Steve Yzerman 30.00 60.00
7 Raymond Bourque 25.00 50.00
8 Patrick Roy 40.00 80.00
9 Cam Neely 25.00 50.00
10 Brett Hull 25.00 50.00
11 King Clancy 20.00 40.00
12 Glenn Hall 20.00 40.00
13 Jacques Plante 30.00 60.00
14 Ace Bailey 20.00 40.00
15 Charlie Conacher 20.00 40.00
16 Bill Durnan 20.00 40.00
17 Stan Mikita 20.00 40.00
18 Eddie Shore 25.00 50.00
19 Howie Morenz 40.00 80.00
20 Aurel Joliat 20.00 40.00

2005-06 ITG Ultimate Memorabilia Goalie Gear

1 Bernie Parent 20.00 50.00
2 Bill Durnan 20.00 50.00
3 Billy Smith 20.00 50.00
4 Ed Giacomin 20.00 50.00
5 Frank Brimsek 20.00 50.00
6 George Hainsworth 25.00 60.00

7 Gerry Cheevers 20.00 50.00
8 Glenn Hall 15.00 40.00
9 Gump Worsley 20.00 50.00
10 Harry Lumley 15.00 50.00
11 Jacques Plante 40.00 80.00
12 Johnny Bower 20.00 50.00
13 Martin Brodeur 25.00 60.00
14 Patrick Roy MON 50.00 100.00
15 Patrick Roy COL 30.00 80.00
16 Pelle Lindbergh 25.00 60.00
17 Jose Theodore 15.00 40.00
18 Ron Hextall 15.00 40.00
19 Tiny Thompson 20.00 50.00
20 Tony Esposito 20.00 50.00

2005-06 ITG Ultimate Memorabilia Jersey Autos

1 Martin Brodeur 40.00 80.00
2 Marcel Dionne 12.00 30.00
3 Bobby Clarke 20.00 40.00
4 Phil Esposito 20.00 40.00
5 Tony Esposito 20.00 40.00
6 Ed Giacomin 20.00 40.00
7 Rod Gilbert 12.00 30.00
8 Doug Gilmour 12.00 30.00
9 Glenn Hall 15.00 40.00
10 Dany Heatley 20.00 40.00
11 Bobby Hull 25.00 50.00
13 Dave Keon 25.00 50.00
14 Ilya Kovalchuk 20.00 50.00
15 Guy Lafleur 20.00 40.00
16 Brian Leetch 12.00 30.00
17 Mario Lemieux 50.00 100.00
18 Eric Lindros 20.00 40.00
19 Frank Mahovlich 20.00 40.00
20 Stan Mikita 20.00 40.00
21 Jean Beliveau 25.00 50.00
22 Gilbert Perreault 20.00 40.00
23 Henri Richard 20.00 40.00
24 Larry Robinson 12.00 30.00
25 Patrick Roy 50.00 100.00
26 Borje Salming 20.00 40.00
27 Jose Theodore 25.00 50.00
28 Vladislav Tretiak 40.00 80.00
29 Gump Worsley 20.00 40.00
30 Steve Yzerman 40.00 100.00
31 Wendel Clark 20.00 40.00
32 Brad Park 12.00 30.00
33 Denis Potvin 12.00 30.00
34 Lanny McDonald 12.00 30.00
35 Terry O'Reilly 12.00 30.00
36 Alexander Ovechkin 125.00 300.00
37 Sidney Crosby 125.00 200.00
38 Henrik Lundqvist 25.00 60.00
39 Marek Svatos 20.00 40.00
40 Antero Niittymaki 20.00 40.00

2005-06 ITG Ultimate Memorabilia Jerseys

1 Alexander Ovechkin 50.00 120.00
2 Bernie Parent 6.00 15.00
3 Bobby Clarke 8.00 20.00
4 Bobby Hull 10.00 25.00
5 Brett Hull 10.00 25.00
6 Brian Leetch 4.00 10.00
7 Bryan Trottier 5.00 12.00
8 Cam Neely 5.00 12.00
9 Darryl Sittler 6.00 15.00
10 Dave Keon 5.00 12.00
11 Denis Potvin 5.00 12.00
12 Doug Gilmour 6.00 15.00
13 Evgeni Malkin 20.00 50.00
14 Frank Mahovlich 5.00 12.00
15 Gilbert Perreault 5.00 12.00
16 Guy Lafleur 6.00 15.00
17 Henri Richard 4.00 10.00
18 Jacques Plante 8.00 20.00
19 Jari Kurri 5.00 12.00
20 Jean Beliveau 5.00 12.00
21 Jose Theodore 5.00 12.00
22 Lanny McDonald 5.00 12.00
23 Marcel Dionne 6.00 16.00
24 Mario Lemieux 20.00 50.00
25 Martin Brodeur 12.00 30.00
26 Mike Bossy 5.00 12.00
27 Pat LaFontaine 5.00 12.00
28 Patrick Roy 12.00 30.00
29 Paul Coffey 5.00 12.00
30 Phil Esposito 8.00 20.00
31 Raymond Bourque 8.00 20.00
32 Rod Gilbert 5.00 12.00
33 Ron Hextall 5.00 12.00
34 Sidney Crosby 30.00 80.00
35 Stan Mikita 6.00 15.00
36 Steve Yzerman 12.00 30.00
37 Terry Sawchuk 8.00 20.00
38 Tony Esposito 5.00 12.00
39 Wendel Clark 8.00 20.00

2005-06 ITG Ultimate Memorabilia Passing the Torch Jerseys

COMMON CARD 30.00 60.00
1 Rocket/Mario/Sid 150.00 250.00
2 Plante/Roy/Theo 90.00 150.00
3 Kharlamov/Krutov/AO 50.00 120.00
4 Sawchuk/Fuhr/Brod 60.00 100.00
5 Tiny/Cheesy/Gilbert 40.00 80.00
6 Shore/Park/Bourque 60.00 100.00
7 Bower/Cheesy/Roy 75.00 125.00
8 Harvey/Savard/Robin 30.00 60.00
9 Worters/Giaco/Richt 30.00 60.00
10 Lindsay/Delv/Yzer 60.00 100.00
11 Mosien/Mikita/Sav 30.00 80.00
12 Hull/Hull/Hull 40.00 80.00
13 Joliat/Beliveau/Guy 60.00 100.00
14 Gardiner/Hall/TonyO 40.00 80.00
15 Parent/Pelle/Hexy 50.00 100.00
16 Horton/Borje/Leetch 20.00 50.00
17 Fergie/Schultz/Probt 40.00 80.00
18 Roy/Brodeur/Fleury 50.00 125.00
19 Keon/Trots/Gilmour 30.00 60.00
20 Perreault/LaF/ Vanek 30.00 60.00

2005-06 ITG Ultimate Memorabilia R.O.Y. Autos

1 Brian Leetch 20.00 40.00
2 Denis Potvin 15.00 30.00
3 Thomas Vanek 20.00 40.00
4 Cam Ward 20.00 40.00
5 Dion Phaneuf 30.00 60.00
6 Sidney Crosby 125.00 250.00
7 Mike Richards 15.00 30.00
8 Henrik Lundqvist 25.00 50.00
9 Petr Prucha 10.00 25.00
10 Jason LaBarbera 10.00 25.00
11 Dany Heatley 20.00 40.00
12 Dave Keon 25.00 50.00
13 Tony Esposito 20.00 40.00
14 Martin Brodeur 40.00 80.00
15 Marek Svatos 10.00 25.00
16 Gilbert Perreault 15.00 30.00
17 Raymond Bourque 25.00 50.00
18 Mario Lemieux 60.00 125.00
19 Antero Niittymaki 15.00 30.00
20 Alexander Ovechkin 125.00 300.00

2005-06 ITG Ultimate Memorabilia R.O.Y. Jerseys

1 Dave Keon 6.00 15.00
2 Tony Esposito 6.00 15.00
3 Gilbert Perreault 6.00 15.00
4 Raymond Bourque 10.00 25.00
5 Mario Lemieux 25.00 60.00
6 Brian Leetch 5.00 12.00
7 Martin Brodeur 15.00 40.00
8 Dany Heatley 5.00 12.00
9 Alexander Ovechkin 50.00 120.00
10 Sidney Crosby 25.00 60.00
11 Henrik Lundqvist 30.00 80.00
12 Dion Phaneuf 10.00 25.00
13 Petr Prucha 6.00 15.00
14 Marek Svatos 5.00 12.00
15 Thomas Vanek 12.00 30.00

2005-06 ITG Ultimate Memorabilia Raised to the Rafters

1 Mario Lemieux 60.00 150.00
2 Henri Richard 12.00 30.00
3 Grant Fuhr 25.00 60.00
4 Bobby Clarke 25.00 60.00
5 Darryl Sittler 20.00 50.00
6 Mike Bossy 12.00 30.00
7 Pat LaFontaine 15.00 40.00
8 Gilbert Perreault 15.00 40.00
9 Bernie Parent 20.00 50.00
10 Denis Potvin 15.00 40.00
11 Alex Delvecchio 15.00 40.00
12 Yvan Cournoyer 15.00 40.00
13 Lanny McDonald 15.00 40.00
14 Tim Horton 20.00 50.00
15 Patrick Roy 40.00 100.00
16 Raymond Bourque 25.00 60.00
17 Cam Neely 15.00 40.00
18 Stan Mikita 20.00 50.00
19 Bobby Hull 30.00 80.00
20 Jean Beliveau 15.00 40.00

2005-06 ITG Ultimate Memorabilia Record Breakers Jerseys

2 Bobby Hull
Phil Esposito 12.00 30.00
6 Patrick Roy
Martin Brodeur 20.00 50.00
9 Jari Kurri
Brett Hull 15.00 40.00
13 Grant Fuhr
Patrick Roy 20.00 50.00
17 Nels Stewart
Maurice Richard 30.00 60.00
19 Dave Schultz
Tiger Williams 20.00 50.00

2005-06 ITG Ultimate Memorabilia Retro Teammates Jerseys

COMPLETE SET (30)
1 Bossy/Trottier 15.00 30.00
2 Shore/Thompson 20.00 40.00
3 Smith/Potvin 20.00 40.00
4 Lindsay/Abel 15.00 30.00
5 Coffey/Lemieux 30.00 75.00
6 Kurri/Fuhr 25.00 50.00
7 Hainsworth/Joliat 25.00 50.00
8 Clarke/Parent 20.00 40.00
9 Sittler/Salming 15.00 30.00
10 Beliveau/Mahovlich 20.00 40.00
11 Gilmour/Clark 20.00 40.00
12 H.Richard/F.Mahovlich 20.00 40.00
13 Lafleur/Cournoyer 20.00 40.00
14 Roy/Robinson 30.00 60.00
15 Beliveau/Harvey 20.00 50.00
16 Shutt/Lafleur 20.00 40.00
17 Cheevers/O'Reilly 15.00 30.00
18 Roy/Bourque 30.00 60.00
19 Neely/Bourque 20.00 50.00
21 Ratelle/Giacomin 15.00 30.00
23 Esposito/Savard 15.00 30.00
24 Delvecchio/Ullman 15.00 30.00
25 Ciccarelli/Yzerman 20.00 50.00
26 Goulet/Savard 15.00 30.00
28 Mosienko/Lumley 15.00 30.00
29 Richter/Leetch 15.00 30.00
30 Kharlamov/Tretiak 15.00 40.00

2005-06 ITG Ultimate Memorabilia Stick Autographs

1 Jean Beliveau 25.00 50.00
2 Raymond Bourque 15.00 40.00
3 Martin Brodeur 40.00 80.00
4 Marcel Dionne 15.00 30.00
5 Phil Esposito 20.00 40.00
6 Grant Fuhr 15.00 40.00
7 Gerry Cheevers 15.00 40.00
8 Glenn Hall 20.00 40.00
9 Dany Heatley 20.00 40.00
10 Ron Francis 25.00 50.00
11 Red Kelly 25.00 50.00
12 Dave Keon 20.00 40.00
13 Ilya Kovalchuk 25.00 50.00
14 Vladimir Krutov 20.00 40.00
15 Guy Lafleur 15.00 40.00
16 Brian Leetch 15.00 30.00
17 Mario Lemieux 50.00 100.00
18 Eric Lindros 20.00 40.00
19 Petr Prucha 20.00 40.00
20 Cam Neely 15.00 40.00
21 Bernie Parent 15.00 30.00
22 Gilbert Perreault 20.00 40.00
23 Jose Theodore 15.00 40.00
24 Gump Worsley 20.00 40.00
25 Steve Yzerman 40.00 80.00
26 Marek Svatos 20.00 40.00
27 Paul Coffey 15.00 30.00
28 Bill Barber 15.00 30.00
29 Marc-Andre Fleury 25.00 50.00
30 Alexander Ovechkin 125.00 300.00
31 Sidney Crosby 125.00 250.00
32 Ed Giacomin 20.00 40.00
33 Antero Niittymaki 20.00 40.00
34 Frank Mahovlich 20.00 40.00
35 Patrick Roy 50.00 100.00
36 Wendel Clark 15.00 30.00
37 Denis Potvin 15.00 30.00
38 Doug Gilmour 20.00 40.00
39 Lanny McDonald 20.00 40.00
40 Stan Mikita 15.00 30.00

2005-06 ITG Ultimate Memorabilia Sticks and Jerseys

1 Mario Lemieux 20.00 50.00
2 Steve Yzerman 12.00 30.00
3 Ilya Kovalchuk 5.00 12.00
4 Phil Esposito 8.00 20.00
5 Eric Lindros 8.00 20.00
6 Alexander Ovechkin 50.00 120.00
7 Sidney Crosby 30.00 80.00
8 Doug Harvey 5.00 12.00
9 Dany Heatley 4.00 10.00
10 Jean Beliveau 5.00 12.00
11 Guy Lafleur 6.00 15.00
12 Pat LaFontaine 5.00 12.00
13 Jari Kurri 5.00 12.00
14 Red Kelly 5.00 12.00
15 Lanny McDonald 5.00 12.00
16 Cam Neely 5.00 12.00
17 Mark Howe 3.00 8.00
18 Paul Coffey 5.00 12.00
19 Denis Potvin 5.00 12.00
20 Steve Shutt 5.00 12.00
21 Gump Worsley 4.00 10.00
22 Roger Crozier 4.00 10.00
23 Ed Giacomin 3.00 8.00
24 Grant Fuhr 8.00 20.00
25 Marc-Andre Fleury 10.00 25.00
26 Tony Esposito 5.00 12.00
27 Patrick Roy 12.00 30.00
28 Martin Brodeur 12.00 30.00
29 Ron Hextall 5.00 12.00
30 Jacques Plante 8.00 20.00

2005-06 ITG Ultimate Memorabilia Three Stars of the Game Jerseys

1 Shore/Tiny/ Joliat 6.00 15.00
2 Harvey/Kennedy/Durnan 6.00 15.00
3 Brimsek/Mosienko/Abel 6.00 15.00
4 Plante/Lind/H.Richard 10.00 25.00
5 Geoff/Moore/Horton 8.00 20.00
6 Big M/Bob. Hull/Kelly 12.00 30.00
7 Delvec/Keon/Ullman 6.00 15.00
8 Gump/Beliveau/Bower 6.00 15.00
9 Crozier/Hall/Mikita 8.00 20.00
10 Ratelle/Giaco/Bucyk 6.00 15.00
11 Lafleur/Shutt/Cheev 8.00 20.00
12 Terry O/Tony O/Park 6.00 15.00
13 Sittler/Savard/Courn 8.00 20.00
14 Espo/Nystrom/Gilbert 10.00 25.00
15 Perreault/Clarke/Leach 10.00 25.00
16 Smith/Anderson/Trottier 6.00 15.00
17 Kurri/Lanny/Fuhr 10.00 25.00
18 Roy/Robinson/Middle. 15.00 40.00
19 Tiger/Dionne/R. Brod 8.00 20.00
20 Potvin/Verbeek/Bossy 6.00 15.00
21 Salming/Savard/Vaive 6.00 15.00
22 Yzer./Gilmour/Clark 15.00 40.00
23 Richter/McL./Leetch 5.00 12.00
24 Bourque/Brodeur/Roy 15.00 40.00
25 Dion/Sid/Ovechkin 50.00 120.00

2005-06 ITG Ultimate Memorabilia Triple Threads Jerseys

1 A.O./Crosby/Malkin 80.00 200.00
2 Brodeur/Roy/Fleury 60.00 100.00
3 Yzerman/Mario/Cam 50.00 100.00
4 Smith/Hextall/Fuhr 25.00 60.00
5 Bourque/Robin/Potvin 25.00 60.00
6 Bob Hull/Big M/Ullman 25.00 60.00
7 H.Richard/Keon/Mikita 20.00 50.00
8 Bower/Hall/Plante 40.00 80.00
9 Parent/Cheev/T.Espo 40.00 80.00
10 Lafleur/Dionne/Perr 25.00 60.00

2005-06 ITG Ultimate Memorabilia Ultimate Autos

1 Steve Yzerman 25.00 60.00
2 Gump Worsley 20.00 40.00
3 Valeri Vasilyev 15.00 30.00
4 Vladislav Tretiak 25.00 50.00
5 Darryl Sittler 15.00 30.00
6 Tod Sloan 10.00 25.00
7 Milt Schmidt 15.00 30.00
8 Borje Salming 20.00 40.00
9 Patrick Roy 40.00 100.00
10 Larry Robinson 10.00 25.00
11 Henri Richard 15.00 30.00
12 Jean Ratelle 10.00 25.00
13 Gilbert Perreault 15.00 30.00
14 Bernie Parent 20.00 40.00
15 Cam Neely 20.00 40.00
16 Stan Mikita 15.00 30.00
17 Frank Mahovlich 15.00 30.00
19 Eric Lindros 20.00 40.00
20 Mario Lemieux 40.00 100.00
21 Brian Leetch 10.00 25.00
22 Pat LaFontaine 15.00 30.00
23 Guy Lafleur 20.00 40.00
24 Elmer Lach 20.00 40.00
25 Vladimir Krutov 12.50 30.00
26 Alexander Yakushev 20.00 40.00
27 Dave Keon 20.00 40.00
28 Ted Kennedy 10.00 25.00
29 Red Kelly 10.00 25.00
30 Brett Hull 10.00 25.00
31 Bobby Hull 12.00 30.00
32 Paul Henderson 10.00 25.00
33 Dany Heatley 15.00 30.00
34 Glenn Hall 15.00 30.00
35 Doug Gilmour 20.00 40.00
36 Rod Gilbert 10.00 25.00
37 Ed Giacomin 10.00 25.00
38 Grant Fuhr 25.00 50.00
39 Tony Esposito 15.00 30.00
40 Phil Esposito 15.00 30.00
41 Bobby Clarke 15.00 30.00
42 Marcel Dionne 10.00 25.00
43 Paul Coffey 20.00 40.00
44 Jim Craig 15.00 40.00
45 Yvan Cournoyer 15.00 30.00
46 Gerry Cheevers 20.00 40.00
47 Martin Brodeur 30.00 80.00
48 Raymond Bourque 20.00 40.00
49 Mike Bossy 15.00 30.00
50 Jean Beliveau 20.00 50.00

2005-06 ITG Ultimate Memorabilia Ultimate Hero Double Jerseys

1 Terry Sawchuk 8.00 20.00
2 Maurice Richard 10.00 25.00
3 Jacques Plante 8.00 20.00
4 Dave Keon 5.00 12.00
5 Mario Lemieux 20.00 50.00
6 Patrick Roy 12.00 30.00
7 Martin Brodeur 12.00 30.00
8 Steve Yzerman 12.00 30.00

2005-06 ITG Ultimate Memorabilia Ultimate Hero Single Jerseys

1 Terry Sawchuk 8.00 20.00
2 Maurice Richard 10.00 25.00
3 Jacques Plante 8.00 20.00
4 Dave Keon 5.00 12.00
5 Mario Lemieux 20.00 50.00
6 Patrick Roy 12.00 30.00
7 Martin Brodeur 12.00 30.00
8 Steve Yzerman 12.00 30.00

2005-06 ITG Ultimate Memorabilia Ultimate Hero Triple Jerseys

3 Jacques Plante 25.00 60.00
8 Steve Yzerman 30.00 80.00

2005-06 ITG Ultimate Memorabilia Vintage Lumber

1 Howie Morenz 50.00 100.00
2 Georges Vezina 60.00 125.00
3 Jacques Plante 30.00 80.00
4 Henri Richard 15.00 40.00
5 Maurice Richard 50.00 100.00
6 Terry Sawchuk 60.00 120.00
7 Bernie Geoffrion 15.00 40.00
8 Joe Primeau 15.00 40.00
9 Red Kelly 15.00 40.00
10 Doug Harvey 15.00 40.00
11 Stan Mikita 20.00 50.00
12 Johnny Bucyk 15.00 40.00
13 Glenn Hall 20.00 50.00
14 Bill Durnan 15.00 40.00
15 Jean Beliveau 20.00 50.00
16 Bobby Hull 40.00 100.00
17 Harry Lumley 20.00 50.00
18 Ed Giacomin 15.00 40.00
19 Dave Keon 25.00 60.00
20 Alex Delvecchio 15.00 40.00
21 Turk Broda 15.00 40.00
22 Tim Horton 25.00 60.00
23 Bob Davidson 12.00 30.00
24 Frank Mahovlich 15.00 40.00
25 Phil Esposito 15.00 40.00
26 Emile Francis 15.00 40.00
27 King Clancy 25.00 60.00
28 Bill Barilko 40.00 80.00
29 Gump Worsley 15.00 40.00
30 Roger Crozier 12.00 30.00

2006-07 ITG Ultimate Memorabilia

1 Ace Bailey 1.50 4.00
2 Al Montoya 2.00 5.00
3 Alex Connell 1.50 4.00
4 Alex Delvecchio 2.00 5.00
5 Alexander Ovechkin 8.00 20.00
6 Anders Hedberg 1.25 3.00
7 Angelo Esposito 2.50 6.00
8 Antero Niittymaki 1.50 4.00
9 Art Ross 2.00 5.00
10 Aurel Joliat 2.00 5.00
11 Babe Pratt 2.00 5.00
12 Bernie Geoffrion 2.00 5.00
13 Bernie Parent 2.50 6.00
14 Bill Barber 1.50 4.00
15 Bill Barilko 2.00 5.00
16 Bill Durnan 2.00 5.00
17 Bobby Clarke 3.00 8.00
18 Bobby Hull 4.00 10.00
19 Borje Salming 2.00 5.00
20 Brad Park 1.50 4.00
21 Brett Hull 4.00 10.00
22 Brian Leetch 1.50 4.00
23 Bryan Trottier 2.00 5.00
24 Butch Bouchard 1.50 4.00
25 Cam Neely 2.00 5.00
26 Cam Ward 2.00 5.00
27 Charlie Conacher 2.00 5.00
28 Charlie Gardiner 2.00 5.00
29 Ching Johnson 2.00 5.00
30 Chris Chelios 2.00 5.00
31 Clarence Campbell 2.00 5.00
32 Conn Smythe 2.00 5.00
33 Cristobal Huet 1.50 4.00
34 Cyclone Taylor 2.00 5.00
35 Dany Heatley 1.50 4.00
36 Darryl Sittler 2.50 6.00
37 Dave Keon 2.00 5.00
38 Dave Schultz 1.50 4.00
39 Denis Potvin 2.00 5.00
40 Dion Phaneuf 1.50 4.00
41 Dominik Hasek 3.00 8.00
42 Doug Gilmour 2.50 6.00
43 Ed Belfour 2.00 5.00
44 Ed Giacomin 3.00 8.00
45 Ed Olczyk 1.25 3.00
46 Eddie Shore 2.00 5.00
47 Eric Staal 2.50 6.00
48 Evgeni Malkin 8.00 20.00
49 Foster Hewitt 2.00 5.00
50 Frank Calder 2.00 5.00
51 Frank Mahovlich 2.00 5.00
52 George Hainsworth 2.00 5.00
53 Georges Vezina 3.00 8.00
54 Gerry Cheevers 2.00 5.00
55 Gilbert Brule 1.50 4.00
56 Gilbert Perreault 2.00 5.00
57 Glenn Hall 2.00 5.00
58 Grant Fuhr 3.00 8.00
59 Gump Worsley 2.00 5.00
60 Guy Lafleur 2.50 6.00
61 Guy Lapointe 1.50 4.00
62 Hap Day 2.00 5.00
63 Henri Richard 2.00 5.00
64 Henrik Lundqvist 5.00 12.00
65 Henrik Zetterberg 2.50 6.00
66 Herb Carnegie 2.00 5.00
67 Hobey Baker 2.00 5.00
68 Howie Morenz 2.00 5.00
69 Igor Larionov 2.00 5.00
70 Jack Adams 2.00 5.00
71 Jacques Plante 2.00 5.00
72 Jari Kurri 2.00 5.00
73 Jaromir Jagr 6.00 15.00
74 Jason Spezza 2.00 5.00
75 Jean Beliveau 2.00 5.00
76 Jean Ratelle 2.00 5.00
77 Joe Malone 2.00 5.00
78 Joe Sakic 4.00 10.00
79 Joe Thornton 3.00 8.00
80 John Bucyk 2.00 5.00
81 John Tavares 8.00 20.00
82 Johnny Bower 2.00 5.00
83 Jordan Staal 3.00 8.00
84 Kari Lehtonen 1.50 4.00
85 Lady Byng 2.00 5.00
86 Lanny McDonald 2.00 5.00
87 Larry Robinson 2.00 5.00
88 Lester Patrick 2.00 5.00
89 Lionel Conacher 2.00 5.00
90 Ilya Kovalchuk 2.00 5.00
91 Lord Stanley 2.00 5.00
92 Luc Robitaille 2.00 5.00
93 Lynn Patrick 2.00 5.00
94 Marc-Andre Fleury 4.00 10.00
95 Marcel Dionne 2.50 6.00
96 Mario Lemieux 8.00 20.00
97 Mark Messier 4.00 10.00
98 Martin Brodeur 5.00 12.00
99 Marty Turco 2.00 5.00
100 Mats Naslund 1.25 3.00
101 Maurice Richard 4.00 10.00
102 Max Bentley 2.00 5.00
103 Michel Goulet 1.50 4.00
104 Mike Bossy 2.00 5.00
105 Mike Modano 3.00 8.00
106 Milt Schmidt 2.00 5.00
107 Newsy Lalonde 2.00 5.00
108 Nicklas Lidstrom 2.00 5.00
109 Pat LaFontaine 2.00 5.00
110 Patrick Roy Colorado 5.00 12.00
111 Patrick Roy Montreal 5.00 12.00
112 Paul Coffey 2.00 5.00
113 Paul Henderson 1.50 4.00
114 Pelle Lindbergh 1.50 4.00
115 Peter Stastny 1.50 4.00
116 Phil Esposito 3.00 8.00
117 Phil Kessel 4.00 10.00
118 Punch Imlach 2.00 5.00
119 Raymond Bourque 3.00 8.00
120 Red Kelly 2.00 5.00
121 Roberto Luongo 3.00 8.00
122 Rod Gilbert 1.50 4.00
123 Rogie Vachon 2.50 6.00
124 Ron Francis 2.50 6.00
125 Ron Hextall 2.00 5.00
126 Ryan Miller 2.00 5.00
127 Scotty Bowman 2.00 5.00
128 Serge Savard 2.00 5.00
129 Sid Abel 2.00 5.00
130 Stan Mikita 2.50 6.00
131 Steve Shutt 2.00 5.00
132 Steve Yzerman 5.00 12.00
133 Syl Apps 2.00 5.00
134 Ted Kennedy 2.00 5.00
135 Ted Lindsay 2.00 5.00
136 Terry Sawchuk 2.50 6.00
137 Tiger Williams 1.25 3.00
138 Tim Horton 2.50 6.00
139 Tiny Thompson 2.00 5.00
140 Toe Blake 2.00 5.00
141 Tom Barrasso 2.00 5.00
142 Tommy Ivan 2.00 5.00
143 Tony Esposito 2.00 5.00
144 Turk Broda 2.00 5.00
145 Ulf Nilsson 1.25 3.00
146 Valeri Kharlamov 2.00 5.00
147 Vladislav Tretiak 1.50 4.00
148 Wendel Clark 3.00 8.00
149 Willie O'Ree 2.50 6.00
150 Yvan Cournoyer 2.00 5.00

2006-07 ITG Ultimate Memorabilia Autographs

1 Bill Barber 6.00 15.00
2 Jean Beliveau 8.00 20.00
3 Martin Brodeur 20.00 50.00
4 Chris Chelios 8.00 20.00
5 Wendel Clark 12.00 30.00
6 Paul Coffey 8.00 20.00
7 Bobby Clarke 12.00 30.00
8 Alex Delvecchio 8.00 20.00
9 Marcel Dionne 10.00 25.00
10 Angelo Esposito 10.00 25.00
11 Phil Esposito 12.00 30.00
12 Tony Esposito 8.00 20.00
13 Doug Gilmour 10.00 25.00
14 Michel Goulet 6.00 15.00
15 Glenn Hall 8.00 20.00
16 Bobby Hull 15.00 40.00
17 Brett Hull 15.00 40.00
18 Jaromir Jagr 25.00 60.00
19 Dave Keon 8.00 20.00
20 Jari Kurri 8.00 20.00
21 Guy Lafleur 10.00 25.00
22 Pat LaFontaine 8.00 20.00
23 Lanny McDonald 8.00 20.00
24 Ted Lindsay 8.00 20.00
25 Mark Messier 15.00 40.00
26 Stan Mikita 10.00 25.00
27 Cam Neely 8.00 20.00
28 Brad Park 6.00 15.00
29 Gilbert Perreault 8.00 20.00
30 Larry Robinson 8.00 20.00
31 Darryl Sittler 10.00 25.00
32 Vladislav Tretiak 6.00 15.00
33 Bryan Trottier 8.00 20.00
34 Rogie Vachon 10.00 25.00
35 Gump Worsley 8.00 20.00
36 Denis Potvin 8.00 20.00
37 Ray Emery 6.00 15.00
38 Marc-Andre Fleury 15.00 40.00
39 Dominik Hasek 12.00 30.00
40 Dany Heatley 6.00 15.00
41 Cristobal Huet 6.00 15.00
42 Ilya Kovalchuk 8.00 20.00
43 Brian Leetch 6.00 15.00
44 Kari Lehtonen 6.00 15.00
45 Nicklas Lidstrom 8.00 20.00
46 Henrik Lundqvist 20.00 50.00
47 Roberto Luongo 12.00 30.00
48 Frank Mahovlich 8.00 20.00
49 Mike Modano 12.00 30.00
50 Alexander Ovechkin 80.00 200.00
51 Dion Phaneuf 6.00 15.00
52 Petr Prucha 6.00 15.00
53 Henri Richard 8.00 20.00
54 Patrick Roy 20.00 50.00
55 Joe Sakic 15.00 40.00
56 Eric Staal 10.00 25.00
57 John Tavares 30.00 80.00
58 Joe Thornton 12.00 30.00
59 Marty Turco 8.00 20.00
60 Cam Ward 8.00 20.00
61 Steve Yzerman 20.00 50.00
62 Henrik Zetterberg 10.00 25.00
63 Ed Belfour 8.00 20.00
64 Ryan Miller 8.00 20.00
65 Boris Mikhailov 6.00 15.00
66 Bernie Parent 10.00 25.00
67 Paul Henderson 6.00 15.00
68 Felix Potvin 12.00 30.00
69 Jason Spezza 8.00 20.00
70 Vincent Lecavalier 8.00 20.00
71 Thomas Vanek 6.00 15.00
72 Maurice Richard/30 15.00 40.00

2006-07 ITG Ultimate Memorabilia Autographs Dual

1 J.Jagr/M.Lemieux 40.00 100.00
2 S.Yzerman/T.Lindsay 25.00 60.00
3 M.Brodeur/P.Roy 25.00 60.00
4 E.Staal/J.Staal 15.00 40.00
5 P.Kessel/P.Esposito 20.00 50.00
6 N.Lidstrom/H.Zetterberg 12.00 30.00
7 A.Ovechkin/J.Thornton 40.00 100.00
8 M.Messier/J.Tavares 40.00 100.00
9 V.Tretiak/P.Henderson 8.00 20.00
10 M.Modano/D.Gilmour 15.00 40.00
11 I.Kovalchuk/K.Lehtonen 10.00 25.00
12 R.Luongo/D.Hasek 15.00 40.00

2006-07 ITG Ultimate Memorabilia Blades of Steel

1 Elmer Lach 5.00 12.00
2 Aurel Joliat 6.00 15.00
3 Busher Jackson 6.00 15.00
4 Clint Benedict 6.00 15.00
5 Darryl Sittler 8.00 20.00
6 Dave Keon 6.00 15.00
7 Dit Clapper 4.00 10.00
8 Doug Gilmour 8.00 20.00
9 Eddie Shore 6.00 15.00
10 Jaromir Jagr 20.00 50.00
11 Frank Nighbor 6.00 15.00
12 Frank Patrick 6.00 15.00
13 Gilbert Perreault 6.00 15.00
14 Hap Day 6.00 15.00
15 Henrik Zetterberg 8.00 20.00
16 Jack Adams 6.00 15.00
17 Jacques Plante 6.00 15.00
18 Jean Beliveau 6.00 15.00
19 Joe Thornton 10.00 25.00
20 Johnny Bucyk 6.00 15.00
21 Keith Tkachuk 6.00 15.00
22 King Clancy 5.00 12.00
23 Luc Robitaille 6.00 15.00
24 Mario Lemieux 25.00 60.00
25 Nels Stewart 6.00 15.00
26 Paddy Moran 6.00 15.00
27 Paul Coffey 6.00 15.00
28 Phil Esposito 10.00 25.00
29 Stan Mikita 8.00 20.00
30 Tim Horton 8.00 20.00

2006-07 ITG Ultimate Memorabilia Bloodlines

1 Stastny/Stastny/Stastny 10.00 25.00
2 Staal/Staal/Staal 10.00 25.00
3 R.Bourque/C.Bourque 10.00 25.00
4 F.Mahovlich/P.Mahovlich 6.00 15.00
5 M.Richard/H.Richard 12.00 30.00
6 P.Esposito/T.Esposito 10.00 25.00
7 Hull/Hull/Hull 12.00 30.00

2006-07 ITG Ultimate Memorabilia Bowman Factor

1 Glenn Hall 6.00 15.00
2 Frank Mahovlich 6.00 15.00
3 Yvan Cournoyer 6.00 15.00
4 Guy Lafleur 8.00 20.00
5 Steve Shutt 6.00 15.00
6 Larry Robinson 6.00 15.00
7 Henri Richard 6.00 15.00
8 Serge Savard 6.00 15.00
9 Gilbert Perreault 6.00 15.00
10 Danny Gare 4.00 10.00
11 Ron Francis 8.00 20.00
12 Paul Coffey 6.00 15.00
13 Jaromir Jagr 20.00 50.00
14 Mario Lemieux 25.00 60.00
15 Brett Hull 12.00 30.00
16 Steve Yzerman 15.00 40.00

2006-07 ITG Ultimate Memorabilia Bowman Factor Autos

1 S.Bowman/G.Hall 12.00 30.00
2 S.Bowman/F.Mahovlich 12.00 30.00
3 S.Bowman/Y.Cournoyer 12.00 30.00
4 S.Bowman/G.Lafleur 15.00 40.00
5 S.Bowman/L.Robinson 12.00 30.00
6 S.Bowman/H.Richard 12.00 30.00
7 S.Bowman/S.Savard 12.00 30.00
8 S.Bowman/G.Perreault 12.00 30.00
9 S.Bowman/R.Francis 15.00 40.00
10 S.Bowman/P.Coffey 12.00 30.00
11 S.Bowman/J.Jagr 40.00 100.00
12 S.Bowman/M.Lemieux 50.00 125.00
13 S.Bowman/B.Hull 25.00 60.00
14 S.Bowman/S.Yzerman 30.00 80.00

2006-07 ITG Ultimate Memorabilia Boys Will Be Boys

1 Brett Hull 12.00 30.00
2 Frank Mahovlich 6.00 15.00
3 Guy Lafleur 8.00 20.00
4 Howie Morenz 6.00 15.00
5 Jean Beliveau 6.00 15.00
6 Larry Robinson 6.00 15.00
7 Mario Lemieux 25.00 60.00
8 Glenn Hall 6.00 15.00
9 Norm Ullman 6.00 15.00
10 Dave Keon 6.00 15.00
11 Alex Delvecchio 6.00 15.00
12 Ed Giacomin 10.00 25.00
13 Rod Gilbert 5.00 12.00
14 Steve Shutt 6.00 15.00
15 Guy Lapointe 5.00 12.00
16 Serge Savard 6.00 15.00
17 Billy Smith 6.00 15.00
18 Denis Potvin 6.00 15.00
19 Mike Bossy 6.00 15.00
20 Bryan Trottier 6.00 15.00
21 Peter Stastny 5.00 12.00
22 Red Kelly 6.00 15.00
23 Bobby Hull 12.00 30.00
24 Brad Park 5.00 12.00
25 Bobby Clarke 10.00 25.00
26 Marcel Dionne 8.00 20.00
27 Vladislav Tretiak 5.00 12.00
28 Ed Belfour 6.00 15.00

2006-07 ITG Ultimate Memorabilia Double Memorabilia

1 Mark Messier 12.00 30.00
2 Patrick Roy 15.00 40.00
3 Martin Brodeur 15.00 40.00
4 Mike Modano 10.00 25.00
5 Steve Yzerman 15.00 40.00
6 John Tavares 25.00 60.00
7 Joe Thornton 10.00 25.00
8 Bobby Hull 12.00 30.00
9 Alexander Ovechkin 25.00 60.00
10 Jean Beliveau 6.00 15.00
11 Tim Horton 8.00 20.00
12 Dave Keon 6.00 15.00
13 Aurel Joliat 6.00 15.00
14 Brett Hull 12.00 30.00
15 Chris Chelios 6.00 15.00
16 Dominik Hasek 10.00 25.00
17 Borje Salming 6.00 15.00
18 Cam Neely 6.00 15.00
19 Joe Sakic 12.00 30.00
20 Ed Belfour 6.00 15.00
21 Raymond Bourque 10.00 25.00
22 Vladislav Tretiak 5.00 12.00
23 Guy Lafleur 8.00 20.00
24 Mario Lemieux 25.00 60.00
25 Henrik Zetterberg 8.00 20.00
26 Jacques Plante 6.00 15.00
27 Doug Harvey 6.00 15.00
28 Jordan Staal 10.00 25.00
29 Eddie Shore 6.00 15.00
30 Stan Mikita 8.00 20.00

2006-07 ITG Ultimate Memorabilia Double Memorabilia Autographs

1 E.Staal/J.Staal 15.00 40.00
2 R.Emery/D.Heatley 8.00 20.00
3 G.Lafleur/M.Dionne 12.00 30.00
4 J.Jagr/M.Lemieux 40.00 100.00
5 M.Brodeur/P.Roy 25.00 60.00
6 S.Yzerman/D.Gilmour 25.00 60.00
7 J.Thornton/P.Esposito 15.00 40.00
8 A.Ovechkin/I.Kovalchuk 80.00 200.00
9 J.Tavares/M.Messier 40.00 100.00
10 D.Phaneuf/N.Lidstrom 10.00 25.00
11 B.Hull/M.Modano 20.00 50.00
12 R.Luongo/C.Price 40.00 100.00

2006-07 ITG Ultimate Memorabilia First Round Picks

1 Evgeni Malkin 25.00 60.00
2 Alexander Ovechkin 25.00 60.00
3 Ilya Kovalchuk 6.00 15.00
4 Jaromir Jagr 20.00 50.00
5 Joe Thornton 10.00 25.00
6 Carey Price 25.00 60.00
7 Marc-Andre Fleury 12.00 30.00
8 Eric Staal 8.00 20.00
9 Kari Lehtonen 5.00 12.00
10 Anze Kopitar 20.00 50.00
11 Guy Lafleur 8.00 20.00
12 Marcel Dionne 8.00 20.00
13 Mike Bossy 6.00 15.00
14 Paul Coffey 6.00 15.00
15 Ron Francis 8.00 20.00
16 Pat LaFontaine 6.00 15.00
17 Steve Yzerman 15.00 40.00
18 Wendel Clark 10.00 25.00
19 Martin Brodeur 15.00 40.00
20 Joe Sakic 12.00 30.00
21 Mike Modano 10.00 25.00
22 Marc Staal 6.00 15.00
23 Vincent Lecavalier 6.00 15.00
24 Gilbert Perreault 6.00 15.00

25 Jordan Staal 10.00 25.00
26 Jason Spezza 6.00 15.00
27 Roberto Luongo 10.00 25.00
28 Brian Leetch 5.00 12.00
29 Mario Lemieux 25.00 60.00
30 Raymond Bourque 10.00 25.00

2006-07 ITG Ultimate Memorabilia Future Star

1 Angelo Esposito 8.00 20.00
2 John Tavares 25.00 60.00
3 Evgeni Malkin 25.00 60.00
4 Wojtek Wolski 5.00 12.00
5 Marek Schwarz 6.00 15.00
6 Carey Price 25.00 60.00
7 Anze Kopitar 20.00 50.00
8 Jordan Staal 10.00 25.00
9 Gilbert Brule 5.00 12.00
10 Phil Kessel 12.00 30.00
11 Peter Mueller 6.00 15.00
12 Bobby Ryan 6.00 15.00
13 Rob Schremp 5.00 12.00
14 Paul Stastny 10.00 25.00
15 Dustin Penner 5.00 12.00
16 Bryan Little 4.00 10.00
17 Derick Brassard 4.00 10.00
18 Justin Pogge 5.00 12.00
19 Alexander Radulov 8.00 20.00
20 Al Montoya 6.00 15.00
21 Ryan Getzlaf 6.00 15.00
22 Marc Staal 6.00 15.00
23 Alexei Cherepanov 5.00 12.00
24 Ryan Callahan 6.00 15.00
25 Jack Skille 5.00 12.00

2006-07 ITG Ultimate Memorabilia Future Star Autographs

1 Phil Kessel/40* 12.00 30.00
2 Peter Mueller/40* 10.00 25.00
3 Bobby Ryan/40* 12.00 30.00
4 Rob Schremp/40* 8.00 20.00
5 Paul Stastny/40* 15.00 30.00
6 Dustin Penner/40* 8.00 20.00
7 Bryan Little/40* 10.00 25.00
8 Derick Brassard/40* 15.00 30.00
9 Justin Pogge/40* 12.00 30.00
10 Jeff Glass/40* 8.00 20.00
11 Ryan Getzlaf/40* 15.00 40.00
12 Jack Skille/40* 8.00 20.00
13 Ryan Callahan/40* 8.00 20.00
14 Alexei Cherepanov/40* 40.00 80.00
15 Angelo Esposito/30* 30.00 60.00
16 John Tavares/30* 60.00 120.00
17 Alexander Radulov/30* 12.00 30.00
18 Wojtek Wolski/30* 10.00 25.00
19 Marek Schwarz/30* 8.00 20.00
20 Carey Price/30* 50.00 100.00
21 Anze Kopitar/30* 20.00 40.00
22 Jordan Staal/30* 30.00 60.00
23 Gilbert Brule/30* 15.00 30.00
24 Michael Frolik/30* 8.00 20.00
25 Jonathan Toews/40* 50.00 100.00

2006-07 ITG Ultimate Memorabilia Future Star Patches Autographs

1 Phil Kessel 30.00 60.00
2 Peter Mueller 25.00 60.00
3 Bobby Ryan 20.00 50.00
4 Rob Schremp 15.00 40.00
5 Paul Stastny 20.00 50.00
6 Dustin Penner 15.00 40.00
7 Bryan Little 12.00 30.00
8 Derick Brassard 15.00 40.00
9 Justin Pogge 15.00 40.00
10 Jeff Glass 12.00 30.00
11 Al Montoya 12.00 30.00
12 Jack Skille 12.00 30.00
13 Ryan Callahan 15.00 40.00
14 Alexei Cherepanov 40.00 80.00
15 Angelo Esposito 20.00 50.00
16 John Tavares 60.00 120.00
17 Hannu Toivonen 15.00 40.00
18 Wojtek Wolski 12.00 30.00
19 Marek Schwarz 12.00 30.00
20 Carey Price 40.00 80.00
21 Anze Kopitar 30.00 80.00
22 Jordan Staal 30.00 60.00
23 Gilbert Brule 15.00 40.00
24 Michael Frolik 15.00 40.00
25 Benoit Pouliot 15.00 40.00
26 Jonathan Toews 60.00 120.00

2006-07 ITG Ultimate Memorabilia Gloves Are Off

1 Alexander Ovechkin 30.00 60.00
2 Bobby Clarke 20.00 40.00
3 Brett Hull 15.00 40.00
4 Bryan Trottier 12.00 30.00
5 Cam Neely 15.00 40.00
6 Charlie Conacher 20.00 50.00
7 Dale Hawerchuk 12.00 30.00
8 Dominik Hasek 20.00 40.00
9 Eddie Shore 20.00 50.00
10 Eric Lindros 15.00 40.00
11 Jacques Plante 20.00 50.00
12 Joe Sakic 25.00 50.00
13 Joe Thornton 15.00 40.00
14 Mario Lemieux 30.00 80.00
15 Martin Brodeur 20.00 50.00
16 Pat LaFontaine 10.00 25.00
17 Patrick Roy 30.00 80.00
18 Raymond Bourque 15.00 40.00
19 Stan Mikita 10.00 25.00
20 Steve Yzerman 25.00 60.00

2006-07 ITG Ultimate Memorabilia Going For Gold

1 Alexander Ovechkin 15.00 40.00
2 Mike Modano 10.00 25.00
3 Bobby Clarke 10.00 25.00
4 Brett Hull 12.00 30.00
5 Brian Leetch 8.00 20.00
6 Cristobal Huet 10.00 25.00
7 Eric Staal 10.00 25.00
8 Evgeni Malkin 20.00 50.00
9 Henrik Lundqvist 15.00 30.00
10 Henrik Zetterberg 12.00 30.00
11 Ilya Kovalchuk 12.00 30.00
12 Jari Kurri 20.00 40.00
13 Jaromir Jagr 20.00 40.00
14 Jason Spezza 10.00 25.00
15 Joe Thornton 15.00 30.00
16 Alexei Cherepanov 12.00 30.00
17 Mario Lemieux 20.00 50.00
18 Mark Messier 20.00 40.00
19 Martin Brodeur 20.00 40.00
20 Nicklas Lidstrom 12.00 30.00
21 Phil Esposito 12.00 30.00
22 Raymond Bourque 15.00 30.00
23 Steve Yzerman 15.00 40.00
24 Valeri Kharlamov 15.00 40.00
25 Vladislav Tretiak 20.00 40.00
26 Dominik Hasek 12.00 30.00
27 Keith Tkachuk 8.00 20.00
28 Vincent Lecavalier 12.00 30.00
29 Joe Sakic 15.00 40.00
30 John Tavares 20.00 50.00

2006-07 ITG Ultimate Memorabilia Jerseys

1 Evgeni Malkin 20.00 50.00
2 Joe Thornton 10.00 25.00
3 Brett Hull 15.00 40.00
4 Chris Chelios 10.00 25.00
5 Patrick Roy 20.00 50.00
6 Alexander Ovechkin 15.00 40.00
7 Dominik Hasek 12.00 30.00
8 Joe Sakic 15.00 40.00
9 Mark Messier 15.00 40.00
10 Steve Yzerman 15.00 40.00
11 Jean Beliveau 12.00 30.00
12 Milt Schmidt 10.00 25.00
13 Martin Brodeur 15.00 40.00
14 Jaromir Jagr 15.00 40.00
15 Ed Belfour 10.00 25.00
16 Mario Lemieux 20.00 50.00
17 Borje Salming 10.00 25.00
18 Bobby Hull 10.00 25.00
19 Doug Gilmour 10.00 25.00
20 Guy Lafleur 10.00 25.00
21 Dave Keon 10.00 25.00
22 Jason Spezza 10.00 25.00
23 Nicklas Lidstrom 10.00 25.00
24 Eric Staal 10.00 25.00
25 Luc Robitaille 10.00 25.00
26 John Tavares 25.00 60.00
27 Vincent Lecavalier 10.00 25.00

2006-07 ITG Ultimate Memorabilia Jerseys and Emblems

1 Evgeni Malkin 40.00 80.00
2 Joe Thornton 30.00 60.00
3 Patrick Roy 50.00 100.00
5 Martin Brodeur 30.00 60.00
6 Alexander Ovechkin 25.00 60.00
7 Mark Messier 30.00 60.00
8 Joe Sakic 30.00 60.00
9 Brian Leetch 30.00 60.00
10 Jean Beliveau 30.00 60.00
11 Mario Lemieux 50.00 100.00
12 Dominik Hasek 25.00 50.00
13 Dave Keon 25.00 50.00
14 Ilya Kovalchuk 25.00 50.00
15 Bobby Hull 30.00 60.00
16 Steve Yzerman 40.00 80.00
17 Jaromir Jagr 30.00 60.00
18 Nicklas Lidstrom 25.00 50.00
19 John Tavares 75.00 125.00
20 Jordan Staal 30.00 60.00
21 Vincent Lecavalier 15.00 40.00

2006-07 ITG Ultimate Memorabilia Jerseys Autographs

1 Tom Barrasso 12.00 30.00
2 Glenn Hall 15.00 40.00
3 Chris Chelios 15.00 40.00
4 Martin Brodeur 40.00 80.00
5 Gerry Cheevers 15.00 40.00
6 Dominik Hasek 25.00 60.00
7 Bobby Clarke 15.00 40.00
8 Paul Coffey 15.00 40.00
9 Yvan Cournoyer 12.00 30.00
10 Ron Hextall 12.00 30.00
11 Marcel Dionne 12.00 30.00
12 Ray Emery 10.00 25.00
13 Angelo Esposito 25.00 50.00
14 Phil Esposito 15.00 40.00
15 Cristobal Huet 10.00 25.00
16 Manny Fernandez 8.00 20.00
17 Ron Francis 12.00 30.00
18 Grant Fuhr 12.00 30.00
19 Ed Giacomin 12.00 30.00
20 Doug Gilmour 12.00 30.00
21 Jean Beliveau 20.00 50.00
22 Wendel Clark 15.00 40.00
23 Alex Delvecchio 10.00 30.00
24 Brett Hull 12.00 30.00
25 Jaromir Jagr 25.00 60.00
26 Dave Keon 12.00 30.00
27 Ilya Kovalchuk 15.00 40.00
28 Jari Kurri 15.00 40.00
29 Guy Lafleur 25.00 60.00
30 Pat LaFontaine 12.00 30.00
31 Brian Leetch 12.00 30.00
32 Kari Lehtonen 12.00 30.00
33 Nicklas Lidstrom 15.00 40.00
34 Henrik Lundqvist 15.00 40.00
35 Roberto Luongo 15.00 40.00
36 Frank Mahovlich 12.00 30.00
37 Lanny McDonald 8.00 20.00
38 Mark Messier 50.00 100.00
39 Stan Mikita 20.00 50.00
40 Mike Modano 15.00 40.00
41 Cam Neely 15.00 40.00
42 Alexander Ovechkin 50.00 125.00
43 Brad Park 12.00 30.00
44 Gilbert Perreault 12.00 30.00
45 Dion Phaneuf 15.00 40.00
46 Denis Potvin 12.00 30.00
47 Petr Prucha 8.00 20.00
48 Jean Ratelle 12.00 30.00
49 Larry Robinson 12.00 30.00
50 Luc Robitaille 25.00 60.00
51 Patrick Roy 40.00 100.00
52 Joe Sakic 30.00 80.00
53 Darryl Sittler 12.00 30.00
54 Jason Spezza 12.00 30.00
55 Eric Staal 12.00 30.00
56 Marek Svatos 8.00 20.00
57 John Tavares 25.00 60.00
58 Joe Thornton 20.00 50.00
59 Vladislav Tretiak 25.00 60.00
60 Bryan Trottier 12.00 30.00
61 Marty Turco 12.00 30.00
62 Rogie Vachon 12.00 30.00
63 Cam Ward 12.00 30.00
64 Steve Yzerman 40.00 80.00
65 Henrik Zetterberg 20.00 40.00
66 Felix Potvin 20.00 50.00
67 Vincent Lecavalier 15.00 40.00
68 Keith Tkachuk 12.00 30.00
69 Thomas Vanek 15.00 40.00

2006-07 ITG Ultimate Memorabilia Journey Jersey

1 Raymond Bourque 15.00 40.00
2 Patrick Roy 25.00 60.00
3 Dave Keon 12.00 30.00
4 Dany Heatley 12.00 30.00
5 Joe Sakic 15.00 40.00
6 Ed Giacomin 12.00 30.00
7 Eric Lindros 12.00 30.00
8 Brian Leetch 12.00 30.00
9 Jaromir Jagr 15.00 40.00
10 Ron Francis 12.00 30.00
11 Ed Belfour 12.00 30.00
12 Doug Gilmour 12.00 30.00
13 Mark Messier 15.00 40.00
14 Brett Hull 12.00 30.00
15 Luc Robitaille 12.00 30.00
16 Dominik Hasek 15.00 40.00
17 Paul Coffey 12.00 30.00
18 Felix Potvin 20.00 50.00

2006-07 ITG Ultimate Memorabilia Legendary Captains

2 Dave Keon 12.00 30.00
3 Jean Beliveau 15.00 40.00
4 Steve Yzerman 15.00 40.00
5 Mario Lemieux 15.00 40.00
6 Mark Messier 15.00 40.00
7 Bobby Clarke 12.00 30.00
8 Raymond Bourque 12.00 30.00
9 Darryl Sittler 12.00 30.00
10 Phil Esposito 12.00 30.00
11 Henri Richard 12.00 30.00
12 Gilbert Perreault 12.00 30.00
13 Joe Sakic 15.00 40.00
14 Mike Modano 12.00 30.00
16 Milt Schmidt 12.00 30.00

2006-07 ITG Ultimate Memorabilia Passing The Torch

1 J.Beliveau/G.Lafleur 20.00 50.00
2 D.Keon/D.Sittler 20.00 50.00
3 M.Dionne/L.Robitaille 20.00 50.00
4 J.Plante/P.Roy 20.00 50.00
5 S.Yzerman/N.Lidstrom 20.00 50.00
6 E.Shore/R.Bourque 12.00 30.00
7 T.Horton/B.Salming 25.00 60.00
8 B.Parent/R.Hextall 15.00 40.00
9 B.Clarke/M.Messier 12.00 30.00
10 M.Schmidt/J.Thornton 12.00 30.00
12 B.Hull/B.Hull 15.00 40.00
13 E.Belfour/M.Turco 12.00 30.00
14 M.Lemieux/J.Jagr 30.00 60.00
15 D.Hasek/R.Miller 20.00 50.00
16 G.Hall/T.Esposito 15.00 40.00
17 V.Kharlamov/A.Ovechkin 15.00 40.00
18 I.Kovalchuk/E.Malkin 20.00 50.00
19 E.Lindros/J.Tavares 20.00 50.00
20 E.Giacomin/M.Richter 12.00 30.00

2006-07 ITG Ultimate Memorabilia R.O.Y. Autographs

COMMON CARDS 10.00 25.00
SEMISTARS 12.00 30.00
UNLISTED STARS 15.00 40.00
1 Anze Kopitar 30.00 60.00
2 Gilbert Brule 20.00 40.00
3 Phil Kessel 25.00 50.00
4 Alexander Radulov 25.00 50.00
5 Wojtek Wolski 20.00 40.00
6 Jordan Staal 10.00 25.00
7 Dustin Penner 10.00 25.00
8 Paul Stastny 30.00 60.00
9 Evgeni Malkin 50.00 100.00
10 Alexander Ovechkin 60.00 150.00
11 Dany Heatley 12.00 30.00
13 Ed Belfour 15.00 40.00
15 Luc Robitaille 15.00 40.00
16 Mario Lemieux 40.00 80.00
17 Tony Esposito 20.00 40.00
18 Dave Keon 20.00 40.00
19 Glenn Hall 20.00 40.00
20 Gump Worsley 25.00 50.00

2006-07 ITG Ultimate Memorabilia R.O.Y. Jerseys

COMMON CARDS 10.00 25.00
SEMISTARS 12.00 30.00
UNLISTED STARS 15.00 40.00
1 Anze Kopitar 20.00 40.00
2 Gilbert Brule 10.00 25.00
3 Phil Kessel 12.00 30.00
4 Alexander Radulov 12.00 30.00
5 Wojtek Wolski 12.00 30.00
7 Dustin Penner 10.00 25.00
8 Paul Stastny 12.00 30.00
9 Evgeni Malkin 25.00 60.00
10 Alexander Ovechkin 20.00 50.00
11 Dany Heatley 10.00 25.00
12 Martin Brodeur 15.00 40.00
13 Ed Belfour 10.00 25.00
14 Brian Leetch 10.00 25.00
15 Luc Robitaille 10.00 25.00
16 Mario Lemieux 25.00 60.00
17 Tony Esposito 12.00 30.00
18 Dave Keon 15.00 40.00
19 Glenn Hall 12.00 30.00
20 Gump Worsley 15.00 40.00

2006-07 ITG Ultimate Memorabilia Raised to the Rafters

1 Pat LaFontaine 5.00 12.00
2 Mark Messier 10.00 25.00
3 Yvan Cournoyer 5.00 12.00
4 Bernie Geoffrion 5.00 12.00
5 Paul Coffey 5.00 12.00
6 Luc Robitaille 5.00 12.00
7 Ron Francis 6.00 15.00
8 Milt Schmidt 5.00 12.00
9 Brett Hull 10.00 25.00
10 Steve Yzerman 12.00 30.00
11 Mario Lemieux 20.00 50.00
12 Bobby Hull 10.00 25.00

2006-07 ITG Ultimate Memorabilia Retro Teammates

1 Morenz/Joliat/Hains 50.00 100.00
2 Thomp/Schmidt/Shore 30.00 60.00
4 Plante/Richard/Harvey 50.00 100.00
5 Bower/Keon/Horton 50.00 100.00
6 Beliv/Gump/Richard 40.00 80.00
7 Mikita/Hall/Hull 20.00 50.00
8 Delv/Crozier/Ullman 15.00 40.00
9 Gilbert/Ratelle/Giac 30.00 60.00
10 Cheev/Bucyk/Espo 25.00 60.00
11 Kharla/Tretiak/Yakus 50.00 100.00
12 Lafleur/Courn/Shutt 20.00 50.00
13 Clarke/Parent/Barber 30.00 80.00
14 Sittler/Salm/Lanny 20.00 50.00
15 Bossy/Trot/Potvin 30.00 60.00
16 Mess/Coffey/Kurri 50.00 100.00
17 Richard/Lach/Blake 75.00 150.00
18 Roy/Chelios/Robin 40.00 80.00
19 Bourq/Moog/Neely 30.00 60.00
20 Messier/Fuhr/Ander 40.00 80.00
21 Mario/Francis/Jagr 50.00 100.00
22 Gilm/Clark/Potvin 30.00 60.00
23 Mess/Leetch/Richt 30.00 80.00
24 Yzer/Hasek/Larion 40.00 80.00
25 Hull/Yzer/Lidstrom 40.00 80.00

2006-07 ITG Ultimate Memorabilia Ring Leaders

1 Henri Richard 15.00 40.00
2 Jean Beliveau 12.00 30.00
3 Steve Yzerman 20.00 50.00
4 Jaromir Jagr 15.00 40.00
5 Mario Lemieux 20.00 50.00
6 Mark Messier 15.00 40.00
7 Martin Brodeur 15.00 40.00
8 Larry Robinson 10.00 25.00
9 Dave Keon 12.00 30.00
10 Guy Lafleur 12.00 30.00
11 Jari Kurri 10.00 25.00
12 Red Kelly 12.00 30.00
13 Frank Mahovlich 10.00 25.00
14 Johnny Bower 12.00 30.00
15 Serge Savard 10.00 25.00
16 Patrick Roy 20.00 50.00
17 Paul Coffey 10.00 25.00
18 Yvan Cournoyer 12.00 30.00

2006-07 ITG Ultimate Memorabilia Sensational Season

UNLISTED STARS 12.00 30.00
1 Phil Esposito 12.00 30.00
2 Mario Lemieux 20.00 50.00
3 Stan Mikita 12.00 30.00
4 George Hainsworth 15.00 40.00
5 Maurice Richard 30.00 80.00
6 Paul Coffey 12.00 30.00
7 John Tavares 30.00 80.00
8 Tony Esposito 12.00 30.00
9 Martin Brodeur 15.00 40.00
10 Mike Bossy 12.00 30.00
11 Brett Hull 15.00 40.00

2006-07 ITG Ultimate Memorabilia Stick Rack

1 Lafleur/Beliv/Courn 60.00 125.00
2 Harv/Richard/Plante 60.00 125.00
3 Big M/Keon/Bower 50.00 100.00
4 Roy/Plante/Huet 50.00 100.00
5 Hull/Yzerm/Ciccar 50.00 100.00
6 Bucyk/Espo/Cheev 30.00 80.00
7 Harvey/Kelly/Horton 30.00 80.00
8 Mario/Francis/Trots 60.00 125.00
9 Keon/Sitt/Gilmour 60.00 125.00
10 Robin/Savard/Lap 30.00 80.00
11 Sawchuk/Kelly/Delv 30.00 80.00
12 Hull/Mikita/Hall 30.00 80.00
13 Roy/Bourque/Svatos 30.00 80.00
14 Gump/Giaco/Lundq 60.00 125.00
15 Clarke/Barber/Leach 30.00 80.00
16 Mario/Beliv/Richard 90.00 150.00
17 Staal/Ovech/Dion 50.00 100.00
18 Stastny Brothers 25.00 60.00
19 Durnan/Broda/Lum 30.00 80.00
22 Sittler/Lanny/Williams 30.00 80.00
23 Parent/Hextall/Niitty 30.00 80.00
24 Bossy/Trottier/Potvin 60.00 100.00
25 Gump/Giac/Richter 30.00 80.00
26 Kurri/Anderson/Fuhr 40.00 100.00
27 Bourque/Leetch/Coff 30.00 80.00
28 Clancy/Prim/Barilko 75.00 125.00

2006-07 ITG Ultimate Memorabilia Sticks and Jerseys

COMMON CARDS 10.00 25.00
UNLISTED STARS 12.00 30.00
SEMISTARS 10.00 25.00
1 Patrick Roy 30.00 60.00
2 Dave Keon 12.50 30.00
3 Steve Yzerman 25.00 50.00
4 Martin Brodeur 15.00 30.00
5 Ray Emery 10.00 25.00
6 Ron Francis 10.00 25.00
7 Dominik Hasek 15.00 40.00
8 Eric Staal 15.00 40.00
9 Peter Stastny 12.50 30.00
10 Roberto Luongo 20.00 50.00
11 Bernie Parent 12.50 30.00
12 Vincent Lecavalier 12.50 30.00
13 Rogie Vachon 15.00 40.00
14 Gilbert Perreault 12.50 30.00
15 Mario Lemieux 30.00 60.00

2006-07 ITG Ultimate Memorabilia Sticks Autographs

1 Marcel Dionne 10.00 25.00
2 Manny Fernandez 5.00 12.00
3 Bobby Clarke 12.00 30.00
4 Ed Belfour 8.00 20.00
5 Guy Lafleur 10.00 25.00
6 Jari Kurri 8.00 20.00
7 Cam Neely 8.00 20.00
8 Mark Messier 15.00 40.00
9 Roberto Luongo 12.00 30.00
10 Henrik Lundqvist 20.00 50.00
11 Nicklas Lidstrom 8.00 20.00
12 Pat LaFontaine 8.00 20.00
13 Dave Keon 8.00 20.00
14 Paul Coffey 8.00 20.00
15 Petr Prucha 6.00 15.00
16 Luc Robitaille 8.00 20.00
17 Phil Esposito 12.00 30.00
18 Doug Gilmour 10.00 25.00
19 Glenn Hall 8.00 20.00
20 Brett Hull 15.00 40.00
21 Mike Modano 15.00 40.00
22 Alexander Ovechkin 30.00 80.00
23 Brad Park 6.00 15.00
24 Dion Phaneuf 6.00 15.00
25 Patrick Roy 20.00 50.00
26 Joe Sakic 15.00 40.00
27 Darryl Sittler 10.00 25.00
28 Eric Staal 10.00 25.00
29 John Tavares 30.00 80.00
30 Steve Yzerman 20.00 50.00
31 Felix Potvin 12.00 30.00
32 Vincent Lecavalier 8.00 20.00

2006-07 ITG Ultimate Memorabilia Triple Thread Jerseys

1 Malkin/Kovalchuk/Ovechkin 30.00 80.00
2 Perreault/Clarke/Lafleur 25.00 50.00
4 Luongo/Brodeur/Hasek 30.00 80.00
5 Roy/Potvin/Belfour 40.00 100.00
6 Chelios/Leetch/Lidstrom 25.00 60.00
7 Keon/Beliveau/Hull 20.00 50.00
8 Lindsay/Richard/Schmidt 40.00 100.00
9 Gilmour/Neely/Tkachuk 20.00 50.00
10 Sawchuk/Plante/Bower 40.00 80.00
11 Giacomin/Cheevers/Parent 40.00 80.00
12 Tavares/Esposito/Mueller 50.00 125.00
13 Staal/Spezza/Phaneuf 15.00 40.00
14 Radulov/Kopitar/Staal 30.00 80.00
15 Robitaille/Hull/Lindros 30.00 60.00
16 Sakic/Thornton/Jagr 30.00 80.00

2006-07 ITG Ultimate Memorabilia Ultimate Hero Single Jerseys

1 Maurice Richard 30.00 80.00
2 Terry Sawchuk 15.00 40.00
3 Patrick Roy 25.00 60.00
4 Steve Yzerman 20.00 50.00
5 Mark Messier 15.00 40.00
6 Mario Lemieux 20.00 50.00

2006-07 ITG Ultimate Memorabilia Ultimate Hero Double Jerseys

1 Maurice Richard 30.00 80.00
2 Terry Sawchuk 15.00 40.00
3 Patrick Roy 25.00 60.00
4 Steve Yzerman 20.00 50.00
5 Mark Messier 15.00 40.00
6 Mario Lemieux 25.00 60.00

2006-07 ITG Ultimate Memorabilia Ultimate Hero Triple Jerseys

1 Maurice Richard 40.00 100.00
2 Terry Sawchuk 25.00 50.00
3 Patrick Roy 30.00 80.00
4 Steve Yzerman 30.00 60.00
5 Mark Messier 25.00 50.00
6 Mario Lemieux 40.00 80.00

2007-08 ITG Ultimate Memorabilia

1 Alexander Ovechkin 15.00 40.00
2 Gilbert Perreault 4.00 10.00
3 Martin Brodeur 10.00 25.00
4 Dave Keon 4.00 10.00
5 Joe Sakic 6.00 15.00
6 Patrick Roy 10.00 25.00
7 Eddie Shore 4.00 10.00
8 Ilya Kovalchuk 4.00 10.00
9 Luc Robitaille 4.00 10.00
10 Bernie Parent 5.00 12.00
11 Glenn Hall 4.00 10.00
12 Maurice Richard 8.00 20.00
13 Cyclone Taylor 4.00 10.00
14 Bobby Hull 8.00 20.00
15 Dany Heatley 3.00 8.00
16 Georges Vezina 4.00 10.00
17 Dominik Hasek 6.00 15.00
18 Brett Hull 6.00 15.00
19 Phil Esposito 6.00 15.00
20 Guy Lafleur 5.00 12.00
21 Brian Leetch 3.00 8.00
22 Ted Lindsay 4.00 10.00
23 Frank Mahovlich 4.00 10.00
24 Johnny Bower 4.00 10.00
25 Larry Robinson 4.00 10.00
26 Jaromir Jagr 12.00 30.00
27 Jean Beliveau 5.00 12.00
28 Turk Broda 4.00 10.00
29 Tony Esposito 4.00 10.00
30 Markus Naslund 4.00 10.00
31 Henri Richard 6.00 15.00
32 Terry Sawchuk 5.00 12.00
33 Howie Morenz 3.00 8.00
34 Patrick Roy 10.00 25.00
35 Marian Gaborik 4.00 10.00
36 Chris Osgood 4.00 10.00
37 Jacques Plante 6.00 15.00
38 Pelle Lindbergh 3.00 8.00
39 Red Kelly 3.00 8.00
40 Peter Forsberg 8.00 20.00
41 Mike Modano 6.00 15.00
42 Pat LaFontaine 4.00 10.00
43 Syl Apps 3.00 8.00
44 Ron Hextall 4.00 10.00
45 Stan Mikita 5.00 12.00
46 Tim Horton 4.00 10.00
47 Roberto Luongo 6.00 15.00
48 Pavel Datsyuk 6.00 15.00
49 Mats Sundin 4.00 10.00
50 Nicklas Lidstrom 4.00 10.00
51 Alex Delvecchio 4.00 10.00
52 Bill Durnan 4.00 10.00
53 Bobby Clarke 6.00 15.00
54 Borje Salming 4.00 10.00
55 Brad Park 2.50 6.00
56 Cam Neely 4.00 10.00
57 Chris Chelios 4.00 10.00
58 Darryl Sittler 5.00 12.00
59 Denis Potvin 4.00 10.00
60 Doug Gilmour 5.00 12.00
61 Drew Doughty 10.00 25.00
62 Ed Belfour 4.00 10.00
63 Ed Giacomin 4.00 10.00
64 George Hainsworth 4.00 10.00
65 Gerry Cheevers 4.00 10.00
66 Grant Fuhr 6.00 15.00
67 Gump Worsley 5.00 12.00
68 Guy Lapointe 3.00 8.00
69 Jari Kurri 4.00 10.00
70 Jean Ratelle 3.00 8.00
71 Joe Thornton 6.00 15.00
72 John Tavares 10.00 25.00
73 Lanny McDonald 4.00 10.00
74 Lord Stanley 4.00 10.00
75 Mario Lemieux 15.00 40.00
76 Marcel Dionne 5.00 12.00
77 Marty Turco 4.00 10.00
78 Michel Goulet 3.00 8.00
79 Mike Bossy 4.00 10.00
80 Milt Schmidt 3.00 8.00
81 Paul Coffey 4.00 10.00
82 Paul Stastny 3.00 8.00
83 Peter Stastny 3.00 8.00
84 Raymond Bourque 6.00 15.00
85 Elmer Lach 3.00 8.00
86 Rogie Vachon 5.00 12.00
87 Ron Francis 5.00 12.00
88 Sam Gagner 5.00 12.00
89 Scott Niedermayer 4.00 10.00
90 Sid Abel 2.50 6.00
91 Steven Stamkos 15.00 40.00
92 Ted Kennedy 4.00 10.00
93 Roy Worters 4.00 10.00
94 Toe Blake 2.50 6.00
95 Valeri Kharlamov 4.00 10.00
96 Victor Hedman 10.00 25.00
97 Vincent Lecavalier 4.00 10.00
98 Vladislav Tretiak 3.00 8.00
99 Wendel Clark 6.00 15.00
100 Yvan Cournoyer 4.00 10.00

2007-08 ITG Ultimate Memorabilia Autographs

1 Alexander Ovechkin 60.00 150.00
2 Bobby Clarke 12.00 30.00
3 Bobby Hull 15.00 40.00
5 Cam Neely 8.00 20.00
6 Chris Chelios 8.00 20.00
7 Chris Osgood 8.00 20.00
8 Dominik Hasek 12.00 30.00
9 Glenn Hall 8.00 20.00
10 Gump Worsley 10.00 25.00
11 Guy Lafleur 10.00 25.00
12 Henri Richard 12.00 30.00
13 Ilya Kovalchuk 8.00 20.00
14 Jaromir Jagr 25.00 60.00
15 Jean Beliveau 25.00 50.00
16 Joe Sakic 15.00 40.00
17 Joe Thornton 12.00 30.00
18 John Tavares 20.00 50.00
19 Johnny Bower 8.00 20.00
20 Jean-Sebastien Giguere 12.00 30.00
21 Luc Robitaille 8.00 20.00
22 Marian Gaborik 12.00 30.00
23 Marcel Dionne 10.00 25.00
24 Mario Lemieux 30.00 80.00
25 Martin Brodeur 25.00 60.00
26 Martin St. Louis 8.00 20.00
27 Marty Turco 8.00 20.00
28 Mats Sundin 8.00 20.00
29 Mike Modano 12.00 30.00
30 Nicklas Lidstrom 12.00 30.00
31 Patrick Roy 40.00 80.00
32 Pavel Datsyuk 12.00 30.00
33 Peter Forsberg 15.00 40.00
34 Phil Esposito 12.00 30.00
35 Roberto Luongo 12.00 30.00
36 Ron Francis 10.00 25.00
37 Scott Niedermayer 8.00 20.00
38 Stan Mikita 10.00 25.00
39 Steven Stamkos 15.00 40.00
40 Ted Lindsay 8.00 20.00
41 Tony Esposito 12.00 30.00
42 Vincent Lecavalier 8.00 20.00
43 Vladislav Tretiak 15.00 40.00
44 Elmer Lach 6.00 15.00
45 Dave Keon 6.00 15.00
46 Milt Schmidt 6.00 15.00
47 Ted Kennedy 8.00 20.00

2007-08 ITG Ultimate Memorabilia Autos Dual

1 Ovechkin/Kovalchuk 60.00 150.00
2 D.Keon/D.Sittler 20.00 50.00
3 B.Hull/B.Hull 30.00 80.00
4 S.Niedermayer/C.Pronger 15.00 40.00
5 T.Esposito/P.Esposito 25.00 60.00
6 M.Lemieux/J.Jagr 60.00 150.00
7 J.Tavares/S.Stamkos 60.00 150.00
8 J.Thornton/M.Schmidt 25.00 60.00
9 M.Brodeur/P.Roy 40.00 100.00
10 Lecavalier/M.St. Louis 15.00 40.00
11 R.Luongo/J.Giguere 25.00 60.00
12 D.Hasek/C.Osgood 25.00 60.00
13 J.Beliveau/G.Lafleur 20.00 50.00
14 B.Leetch/R.Bourque 25.00 60.00
15 M.Sundin/M.Naslund 15.00 40.00
16 E.Giacomin/G.Cheevers 15.00 40.00
17 P.Forsberg/J.Sakic 30.00 80.00
18 C.Chelios/N.Lidstrom 15.00 40.00
19 B.Clarke/B.Parent 25.00 60.00
20 M.Gaborik/P.Datsyuk 25.00 60.00
21 R.Francis/L.Robitaille 20.00 50.00
22 F.Mahovlich/J.Bower 15.00 40.00
23 P.Stastny/P.Stastny 12.00 30.00

2007-08 ITG Ultimate Memorabilia Battle of Alberta

1 McDonald/Kurri 15.00 40.00
2 B.Hull/G.Anderson 12.00 30.00
3 M.Vernon/G.Fuhr 25.00 60.00
4 Nieuwendyk/Coffey 15.00 40.00
5 P.Housley/B.Ranford 15.00 40.00

2007-08 ITG Ultimate Memorabilia Battle of Quebec

1 M.Sundin/P.Roy 30.00 80.00
2 D.Bouchard/G.Lafleur 25.00 60.00
3 M.Goulet/L.Robinson 12.00 30.00
4 P.Stastny/S.Shutt 10.00 25.00
5 J.Sakic/P.Roy 30.00 80.00

2007-08 ITG Ultimate Memorabilia Blades of Steel

1 Dave Keon 12.00 30.00
2 Jaromir Jagr 40.00 100.00
3 Dany Heatley 10.00 25.00
4 Gerry Cheevers 12.00 30.00
5 Doug Gilmour 15.00 40.00
6 Phil Esposito 20.00 50.00
7 Pavel Datsyuk 20.00 50.00
8 Gilbert Perreault 12.00 30.00
9 Luc Robitaille 12.00 30.00
10 Mario Lemieux 50.00 125.00
11 Paul Coffey 12.00 30.00
12 Alexander Ovechkin 50.00 125.00
13 Darryl Sittler 15.00 40.00
14 Marcel Dionne 15.00 40.00
15 Joe Thornton 20.00 50.00
16 Jacques Plante 20.00 50.00
17 Jean Beliveau 15.00 40.00
18 Maurice Richard 25.00 60.00
19 Tim Horton 12.00 30.00
20 Stan Mikita 15.00 40.00

2007-08 ITG Ultimate Memorabilia Country Wide

1 Jaromir Jagr 15.00 40.00
2 Jari Kurri 5.00 12.00
3 Roberto Luongo 8.00 20.00
4 Vincent Lecavalier 5.00 12.00
5 Brett Hull 10.00 25.00
6 Michel Goulet 4.00 10.00
7 Marcel Dionne 6.00 15.00
8 Bobby Clarke 8.00 20.00
9 Chris Chelios 5.00 12.00
10 Gilbert Perreault 5.00 12.00
11 Chris Pronger 5.00 12.00
12 Mats Naslund 3.00 8.00
13 Mike Richter 5.00 12.00
14 Joe Sakic 10.00 25.00
15 Borje Salming 5.00 12.00
16 Mats Sundin 5.00 12.00
17 Joe Thornton 8.00 20.00
18 Brian Leetch 4.00 10.00
19 Mike Modano 8.00 20.00
20 Nicklas Lidstrom 5.00 12.00
21 Mario Lemieux 20.00 50.00
22 Alexander Ovechkin 20.00 50.00
23 Patrick Roy 12.00 30.00
24 Kyle Okposo 6.00 15.00
25 John Tavares 20.00 50.00
26 Steven Stamkos 20.00 50.00
27 Sam Gagner 6.00 15.00
28 Martin Brodeur 12.00 30.00
29 Dany Heatley 4.00 10.00
30 Peter Forsberg 10.00 25.00
31 Pelle Lindbergh 4.00 10.00

2007-08 ITG Ultimate Memorabilia Double Memorabilia Autos

1 Ovechkin/Kovalchuk 60.00 150.00
2 D.Keon/D.Sittler 20.00 50.00
3 B.Hull/B.Hull 30.00 80.00
4 Niedermayer/Pronger 15.00 40.00
5 T.Esposito/P.Esposito 25.00 60.00
6 M.Lemieux/J.Jagr 60.00 150.00
7 J.Tavares/S.Stamkos 60.00 150.00
8 J.Thornton/M.Schmidt 25.00 60.00
9 M.Brodeur/P.Roy 40.00 100.00
10 Lecavalier/M.St. Louis 15.00 40.00
11 R.Luongo/J.Giguere 25.00 60.00
12 D.Hasek/C.Osgood 25.00 60.00
13 J.Beliveau/G.Lafleur 20.00 50.00
14 B.Leetch/R.Bourque 25.00 60.00
15 M.Sundin/M.Naslund 15.00 40.00
16 E.Giacomin/G.Cheevers 15.00 40.00
17 P.Forsberg/J.Sakic 30.00 80.00
18 C.Chelios/N.Lidstrom 15.00 40.00
19 B.Clarke/B.Parent 25.00 60.00
20 M.Gaborik/P.Datsyuk 25.00 60.00
21 R.Francis/L.Robitaille 20.00 50.00
22 F.Mahovlich/J.Bower 15.00 40.00
23 P.Stastny/P.Stastny 12.00 30.00

2007-08 ITG Ultimate Memorabilia First Rounders

1 John Tavares 20.00 50.00
2 Victor Hedman 12.00 30.00
3 Steven Stamkos 20.00 50.00
4 Drew Doughty 10.00 25.00
5 Alex Pietrangelo 8.00 20.00
6 Luke Schenn 6.00 15.00
7 Karl Alzner 3.00 8.00
8 Sam Gagner 6.00 15.00
9 Peter Mueller 4.00 10.00
10 Kyle Okposo 6.00 15.00
11 Bryan Little 4.00 10.00
12 Carey Price 20.00 50.00
13 Alexander Ovechkin 20.00 50.00
14 Alexander Semin 5.00 12.00
15 Ilya Kovalchuk 5.00 12.00
16 Dany Heatley 4.00 10.00
17 Marian Gaborik 5.00 12.00
18 Vincent Lecavalier 5.00 12.00
19 Joe Thornton 8.00 20.00
20 Roberto Luongo 8.00 20.00
21 Scott Niedermayer 5.00 12.00

22 Peter Forsberg 10.00 25.00
23 Jaromir Jagr 15.00 40.00
24 Martin Brodeur 12.00 30.00
25 Mats Sundin 5.00 12.00
26 Mike Modano 8.00 20.00
27 Joe Sakic 10.00 25.00
28 Brian Leetch 4.00 10.00
29 Wendel Clark 8.00 20.00
30 Mario Lemieux 20.00 50.00
31 Raymond Bourque 8.00 20.00
32 Denis Potvin 5.00 12.00
33 Guy Lafleur 6.00 15.00
34 Gilbert Perreault 5.00 12.00
35 Darryl Sittler 6.00 15.00

2007-08 ITG Ultimate Memorabilia Franchises

1 Sundin/Gilmour/Potvin 20.00 50.00
2 Keon/Mahov/Horton 12.00 30.00
3 Beliveau/Harvey/Plante 20.00 50.00
4 Lafleur/Robinsn/Savard 15.00 40.00
5 Delvecchio/Abel/Lindsay 12.00 30.00
6 Datsyk/Lidstrm/Osgd 20.00 50.00
7 Lumley/Mosienko/Gadsby 12.00 30.00
8 Chelios/Belfour/Goulet 12.00 30.00
9 Giacomin/Park/Ratelle 12.00 30.00
10 Richter/Leetch/Vanbies 12.00 30.00
11 Shore/Thompson/Brimsk 12.00 30.00
12 Neely/Moog/Bourque 20.00 50.00
13 Forsberg/Roy/Sakic 30.00 80.00
14 Fuhr/Kurri/Anderson 20.00 50.00
15 Modano/Hull/Turco 25.00 60.00
16 Potvin/Smith/Bossy 12.00 30.00
17 Parent/Barber/Clarke 20.00 50.00
18 Lemieux/Jagr/Francis 50.00 125.00
19 Giguere/Hiller/Nieder 15.00 40.00
20 Lecav/St.L/Stamks 50.00 125.00
21 Sittler/McDonald/Salming 15.00 40.00

2007-08 ITG Ultimate Memorabilia Future Star Autos

1 John Tavares 40.00 100.00
2 Ryan Parent 15.00 40.00
3 Ryan O'Marra 6.00 15.00
4 Logan Couture 10.00 25.00
5 Jonas Hiller 12.00 30.00
6 Alex Pietrangelo 15.00 40.00
7 Steve Mason 20.00 50.00
8 Andrew Cogliano 8.00 20.00
9 Leland Irving 15.00 40.00
10 Tuukka Rask 25.00 60.00
11 Kyle Okposo 8.00 20.00
12 Karl Alzner 6.00 15.00
13 Steven Stamkos 40.00 100.00
14 Steve Downie 8.00 20.00
15 Sam Gagner 12.00 30.00
16 Peter Mueller 8.00 20.00
17 Paul Stastny 8.00 20.00
18 Michael Frolik 8.00 20.00
19 Michael Del Zotto 10.00 25.00
20 Marc Staal 10.00 25.00
21 Jordan Staal 8.00 20.00
22 Jiri Tlusty 10.00 25.00
23 Jack Skille 8.00 20.00
24 Drew Doughty 20.00 50.00
25 Devin Setoguchi 10.00 25.00
26 Carey Price 60.00 120.00
27 Bryan Little 8.00 20.00
28 Angelo Esposito 12.00 30.00
29 Alexei Cherepanov 12.00 30.00
30 Brandon Sutter 10.00 25.00
31 Victor Hedman 15.00 40.00

2007-08 ITG Ultimate Memorabilia Gloves Are Off

1 Joe Sakic 20.00 50.00
2 Joe Thornton 15.00 40.00
3 Alexander Ovechkin 40.00 100.00
4 Stan Mikita 12.00 30.00
5 Raymond Bourque 15.00 40.00
6 Pat LaFontaine 10.00 25.00
7 Martin Brodeur 25.00 60.00
8 Mario Lemieux 40.00 100.00
9 Eddie Shore 10.00 25.00
10 Dominik Hasek 15.00 40.00
11 Cam Neely 10.00 25.00
12 Brett Hull 20.00 50.00
13 Bobby Clarke 15.00 40.00
14 Patrick Roy 25.00 60.00
15 Sam Gagner 12.00 30.00
16 Bill Durnan 10.00 25.00
17 Paul Coffey 10.00 25.00
18 Mats Sundin 10.00 25.00
19 Drew Doughty 20.00 50.00
20 Charlie Conacher 8.00 20.00

2007-08 ITG Ultimate Memorabilia Jerseys

1 Alexander Ovechkin 20.00 50.00
2 Bobby Hull 20.00 50.00
3 Borje Salming 10.00 25.00
4 Brett Hull 10.00 25.00
5 Carey Price 12.00 30.00
6 Chris Osgood 10.00 25.00
7 Dave Keon 20.00 50.00
8 Dominik Hasek 15.00 40.00
9 Glenn Hall 10.00 25.00
10 Guy Lafleur 12.00 30.00
11 Ilya Kovalchuk 10.00 25.00
12 Jean Beliveau 12.00 30.00
13 Joe Sakic 20.00 50.00
14 Joe Thornton 10.00 25.00
15 John Tavares 40.00 100.00
16 Marian Gaborik 10.00 25.00
17 Mario Lemieux 40.00 100.00
18 Martin Brodeur 25.00 60.00
19 Marty Turco 10.00 25.00
20 Mats Sundin 10.00 25.00
21 Maurice Richard 25.00 60.00
22 Mike Modano 15.00 40.00
23 Patrick Roy 25.00 60.00
24 Pavel Datsyuk 15.00 40.00
25 Peter Forsberg 20.00 50.00
26 Roberto Luongo 15.00 40.00
27 Scott Niedermayer 8.00 20.00
28 Steven Stamkos 40.00 100.00
29 Vincent Lecavalier 10.00 25.00
30 Vladislav Tretiak 15.00 30.00
31 Victor Hedman 25.00 60.00
32 Joe Nieuwendyk 8.00 20.00

2007-08 ITG Ultimate Memorabilia Jerseys Autographs

1 Alexander Ovechkin 60.00 150.00
2 Bobby Clarke 25.00 60.00
3 Bobby Hull 30.00 80.00
4 Brett Hull 30.00 80.00
5 Cam Neely 15.00 40.00
6 Chris Chelios 15.00 40.00
7 Chris Osgood 15.00 40.00
8 Dominik Hasek 25.00 60.00
9 Ed Giacomin 15.00 40.00
10 Glenn Hall 15.00 40.00
11 Guy Lafleur 25.00 60.00
12 Ilya Kovalchuk 15.00 40.00
13 Jaromir Jagr 50.00 120.00
14 Jean Beliveau 20.00 50.00
15 Joe Sakic 30.00 80.00
16 Joe Thornton 25.00 60.00
17 John Tavares 25.00 60.00
18 Jean-Sebastien Giguere 15.00 40.00
19 Luc Robitaille 15.00 40.00
20 Marian Gaborik 15.00 40.00
21 Marcel Dionne 20.00 50.00
22 Mario Lemieux 60.00 120.00
23 Martin Brodeur 40.00 80.00
24 Martin St. Louis 15.00 40.00
25 Marty Turco 15.00 40.00
26 Mats Sundin 15.00 40.00
27 Mike Modano 25.00 60.00
28 Nicklas Lidstrom 15.00 40.00
29 Patrick Roy 40.00 100.00
30 Paul Stastny 12.00 30.00
31 Pavel Datsyuk 25.00 60.00
32 Peter Forsberg 30.00 80.00
33 Phil Esposito 25.00 60.00
34 Roberto Luongo 25.00 60.00
35 Ron Francis 20.00 50.00
36 Scott Niedermayer 15.00 40.00
37 Stan Mikita 15.00 40.00
38 Steven Stamkos 60.00 150.00
39 Tony Esposito 15.00 30.00
40 Vincent Lecavalier 15.00 40.00
41 Vladislav Tretiak 20.00 50.00
42 Joe Nieuwendyk 12.00 30.00
43 Victor Hedman 40.00 100.00
44 Brian Leetch 12.00 30.00
45 Bernie Parent 20.00 50.00
46 Frank Mahovlich 15.00 40.00
47 Pat LaFontaine 15.00 40.00
48 Red Kelly 15.00 40.00
49 Doug Gilmour 20.00 50.00
50 Alex Delvecchio 15.00 40.00

2007-08 ITG Ultimate Memorabilia Journey Jersey

1 Mats Sundin 20.00 50.00
2 Ed Belfour 20.00 50.00
3 Raymond Bourque 30.00 80.00
4 Martin Brodeur 30.00 80.00
5 Chris Chelios 20.00 50.00
6 Paul Coffey 20.00 50.00
7 Peter Forsberg 40.00 100.00
9 Brett Hull 40.00 100.00
10 Jaromir Jagr 60.00 150.00
11 Brian Leetch 15.00 40.00
12 Mario Lemieux 80.00 200.00
13 Nicklas Lidstrom 20.00 50.00
14 Felix Potvin 30.00 80.00
15 Luc Robitaille 20.00 50.00
16 Patrick Roy 50.00 125.00
17 Dany Heatley 15.00 40.00
18 Joe Thornton 30.00 80.00
19 Mike Modano 30.00 80.00
20 Joe Sakic 40.00 100.00

2007-08 ITG Ultimate Memorabilia Net Average

1 R.Worters/T.Thompson 20.00 50.00
3 Marty Turco 10.00 25.00
4 Patrick Roy 25.00 60.00
5 Dominik Hasek 15.00 40.00
6 Bernie Parent 12.00 30.00
7 Tony Esposito 10.00 25.00
8 Frank Brimsek 10.00 25.00

2007-08 ITG Ultimate Memorabilia Net Wins

1 P.Roy/M.Brodeur 40.00 100.00
2 Richter/Vanbiesbrouck 15.00 40.00
3 B.Parent/R.Hextall 20.00 50.00
4 Ed Belfour 10.00 25.00
6 Jacques Plante 15.00 40.00
7 Tony Esposito 10.00 25.00
8 Glenn Hall 10.00 25.00
9 Grant Fuhr 15.00 40.00
10 Dominik Hasek 15.00 40.00
12 Billy Smith 10.00 25.00

2007-08 ITG Ultimate Memorabilia Net Zero

2 G.Hall/T.Esposito 12.00 30.00
3 J.Plante/P.Roy 30.00 80.00
4 George Hainsworth 15.00 40.00
5 Tiny Thompson 20.00 50.00
6 Dominik Hasek 20.00 50.00
7 Ed Belfour 12.00 30.00
8 Harry Lumley 12.00 30.00
9 Roy Worters 15.00 40.00
10 Bernie Parent 15.00 40.00
11 Ed Giacomin 12.00 30.00
12 Rogie Vachon 15.00 40.00

2007-08 ITG Ultimate Memorabilia New Millennium First Rounders Autographs

1 Alexei Cherepanov 25.00 50.00
2 Angelo Esposito 15.00 40.00
3 Bryan Little 10.00 25.00
4 Carey Price 40.00 80.00
5 Devin Setoguchi 12.00 30.00
6 Jack Skille 10.00 25.00
7 Jiri Tlusty 12.00 30.00
8 Jordan Staal 10.00 25.00
9 Marc Staal 12.00 30.00
10 Michael Del Zotto 10.00 25.00
11 Michael Frolik 10.00 25.00
12 Peter Mueller 10.00 25.00
13 Sam Gagner 15.00 40.00
14 Steve Downie 10.00 25.00
15 Karl Alzner 8.00 20.00
16 Kyle Okposo 15.00 40.00
17 Tuukka Rask 30.00 80.00
18 Leland Irving 12.00 30.00
19 Andrew Cogliano 10.00 25.00
20 Logan Couture 12.00 30.00
21 Ryan O'Marra 8.00 20.00
22 Ryan Parent 8.00 20.00
23 Brandon Sutter 12.00 30.00
24 Thomas Hickey 15.00 40.00
25 Benoit Pouliot 8.00 20.00
26 Jonathon Blum 12.00 30.00
27 Alex Pietrangelo 20.00 50.00
28 Steven Stamkos 40.00 80.00
29 Drew Doughty 25.00 60.00
30 John Tavares 40.00 80.00
31 Victor Hedman 30.00 80.00

2007-08 ITG Ultimate Memorabilia Past Present and Future

1 Keon/Sundin/Schenn 6.00 15.00
2 Harvey/Nieder/Doughty 10.00 25.00
3 Beliveau/Lecav/Giroux 15.00 40.00
4 Hall/Luongo/Mason 10.00 25.00
5 Lafleur/Gaborik/Tavares 20.00 50.00
6 Lemieux/Thorntn/Gagner 20.00 50.00
7 Richard/St. Louis/Brule 10.00 25.00
8 Fuhr/Brodeur/Irving 12.00 30.00
9 Clarke/Heatley/Cogliano 8.00 20.00
10 Larionov/Ovech/Chere 20.00 50.00
11 Roy/Sakic/Budaj 12.00 30.00
12 Potvin/Pronger/Del Zotto 5.00 12.00
13 Salming/Chelios/Hickey 6.00 15.00
14 Richter/Modano/Okposo 8.00 20.00
15 Lindsay/Datsyuk/McCollum 8.00 20.00
16 Sawchuk/Turco/Hiller 6.00 15.00
17 Lindbergh/Giguere/Rask 12.00 30.00
18 Stastny/Jagr/Tlusty 15.00 40.00
19 Horton/Lidstrom/Pietrangelo 8.00 20.00
20 Naslund/Forsberg/Hedmn 12.00 30.00
21 Tretiak/Osgood/Price 20.00 50.00

2007-08 ITG Ultimate Memorabilia Raised to the Rafters

1 Glenn Hall 10.00 25.00
2 Brian Leetch 8.00 20.00
3 Tony Esposito 10.00 25.00
4 Guy Lafleur 12.00 30.00
5 Larry Robinson 10.00 25.00
6 Johnny Bucyk 10.00 25.00

2007-08 ITG Ultimate Memorabilia Retro Teammates

1 T.Thompson/E.Shore 12.00 30.00
2 S.Abel/A.Delvecchio 12.00 30.00
3 R.Bourque/C.Neely 20.00 50.00
4 P.Coffey/R.Francis 15.00 40.00
5 J.Sakic/M.Sundin 25.00 60.00
6 Hasek/LaFontaine 20.00 50.00
7 Anderson/Fuhr 20.00 50.00
8 E.Belfour/C.Chelios 12.00 30.00
9 Beliveau/J.Plante 15.00 40.00
10 M.Bossy/D.Potvin 12.00 30.00
11 B.Clarke/P.Lindbergh 20.00 50.00
12 B.Barber/B.Parent 15.00 40.00
13 D.Keon/Mahovlich 12.00 30.00
14 G.Lafleur/Cournoyer 15.00 40.00
15 R.Gilbert/E.Giacomin 12.00 30.00
16 T.Esposito/S.Mikita 15.00 40.00
17 G.Hall/B.Hull 25.00 60.00
18 G.Hainsworth/A.Joliat 20.00 50.00
19 T.Horton/J.Bower 12.00 30.00
20 B.Hull/L.McDonald 25.00 60.00
21 M.Lemieux/J.Jagr 50.00 125.00
22 Richter/Vanbiesbrouck 12.00 30.00
23 B.Mosienko/H.Lumley 12.00 30.00
24 B.Park/J.Ratelle 10.00 25.00
25 P.Roy/P.Forsberg 30.00 80.00
26 Lapointe/Robinson 12.00 30.00
27 B.Leetch/L.Robitaille 12.00 30.00
28 D.Gilmour/F.Potvin 20.00 50.00
29 B.Salming/D.Sittler 15.00 40.00
30 V.Tretiak/V.Kharlamov 10.00 25.00

2007-08 ITG Ultimate Memorabilia St. Patrick's Legacy

1 Patrick Roy Montreal Jersey 10.00 25.00
2 Patrick Roy Colorado Jersey 10.00 25.00
3 Patrick Roy Dual Jersey 12.00 30.00
4 Patrick Roy Montreal Pad 15.00 40.00
5 Patrick Roy Colorado Pad 15.00 40.00
6 Patrick Roy Dual Pad 20.00 50.00
7 Patrick Roy Montreal Glove 15.00 40.00
8 Patrick Roy Colorado Glove 15.00 40.00
9 Patrick Roy Dual Glove 20.00 50.00

2007-08 ITG Ultimate Memorabilia Stick Rack

1 Martin Brodeur 40.00 100.00
2 Felix Potvin 25.00 60.00
3 Pat LaFontaine 15.00 40.00
4 Mike Richter 20.00 50.00
5 Cam Neely 15.00 40.00
6 Joe Sakic 30.00 80.00
7 Jaromir Jagr 50.00 125.00
8 Vincent Lecavalier 15.00 40.00
9 Rogie Vachon 20.00 50.00
10 Grant Fuhr 25.00 60.00
11 Mario Lemieux 60.00 150.00
12 Alexander Ovechkin 40.00 100.00
13 Peter Stastny 15.00 40.00
14 Peter Forsberg 30.00 80.00
15 Martin St. Louis 15.00 40.00
16 Joe Thornton 25.00 60.00
17 Tony Esposito 15.00 40.00
18 Dominik Hasek 25.00 60.00
19 Chris Osgood 15.00 40.00
20 Luc Robitaille 15.00 40.00
21 Guy Lafleur 30.00 80.00
22 Phil Housley 12.00 30.00
23 Dale Hawerchuk 20.00 50.00
24 Michel Goulet 12.00 30.00
25 Ron Francis 20.00 50.00

2007-08 ITG Ultimate Memorabilia Sticks Autos

1 Alexander Ovechkin 40.00 100.00
2 Marcel Dionne 12.00 30.00
3 Cam Neely 10.00 25.00
4 Chris Chelios 10.00 25.00
5 Dominik Hasek 15.00 40.00
6 Guy Lafleur 12.00 30.00
7 Jaromir Jagr 30.00 80.00
8 Joe Sakic 20.00 50.00
9 Joe Thornton 15.00 40.00
10 Jean-Sebastien Giguere 10.00 25.00
11 Luc Robitaille 10.00 25.00
12 Mario Lemieux 40.00 100.00
13 Martin Brodeur 25.00 60.00
14 Martin St. Louis 10.00 25.00
15 Marty Turco 10.00 25.00
16 Mike Modano 15.00 40.00
17 Tony Esposito 10.00 25.00
18 Mats Sundin 10.00 25.00
19 Pavel Datsyuk 15.00 40.00
20 Peter Forsberg 20.00 50.00
21 Roberto Luongo 15.00 40.00
22 Ron Francis 12.00 30.00
23 Scott Niedermayer 10.00 25.00
24 Stan Mikita 12.00 30.00
25 Vincent Lecavalier 10.00 25.00

2007-08 ITG Ultimate Memorabilia Vintage Lumber

13 Chuck Rayner 12.00 30.00
14 Ed Giacomin 12.00 30.00
15 Stan Mikita 12.00 30.00
16 Joe Primeau 30.00 60.00
17 Johnny Bucyk 12.00 30.00
18 Roger Crozier 12.00 30.00
19 Norm Ullman 12.00 30.00
20 Harry Lumley 12.00 30.00

2008-09 ITG Ultimate Memorabilia

1 Alex Delvecchio/30* 8.00 20.00
2 Alexander Ovechkin/30* 30.00 80.00
3 Denis Potvin/30* 8.00 20.00
4 Dominik Hasek/30* 12.00 30.00
5 Georges Vezina/30* 12.00 30.00
6 Gump Worsley/30* 6.00 15.00
7 Howie Morenz/30* 5.00 12.00
8 Joe Thornton/30* 12.00 30.00
9 Mario Lemieux/30* 30.00 80.00
10 Mario Lemieux/30* 30.00 80.00
11 Marty Turco/30* 8.00 20.00
12 Mike Modano/30* 12.00 30.00
13 Raymond Bourque/30* 12.00 30.00
14 Ted Lindsay/30* 8.00 20.00
15 Terry Sawchuk/30* 12.00 30.00
16 Brett Hull/50* 15.00 40.00
17 Chris Osgood/50* 6.00 15.00
18 Henri Richard/50* 8.00 20.00
19 Martin Brodeur/50* 15.00 40.00
20 Maurice Richard/50* 12.00 30.00
21 Maurice Richard/50* 12.00 30.00
22 Maurice Richard/50* 12.00 30.00
23 Maurice Richard/50* 12.00 30.00
24 Maurice Richard/50* 12.00 30.00
25 Maurice Richard/50* 12.00 30.00
26 Maurice Richard/50* 12.00 30.00
27 Maurice Richard/50* 12.00 30.00
28 Maurice Richard/50* 12.00 30.00
29 Maurice Richard/50* 12.00 30.00
30 Mikko Koivu/50* 5.00 12.00
31 Alexander Ovechkin/90* 25.00 60.00
32 Bill Barilko/90* 4.00 10.00
33 Borje Salming/90* 6.00 15.00
34 Cam Neely/90* 6.00 15.00
35 Carey Price/90* 12.00 30.00
36 Chris Chelios/90* 10.00 25.00
37 Chris Chelios/90* 12.00 30.00
38 Chris Osgood/90* 6.00 15.00
39 Darryl Sittler/90* 8.00 20.00
40 Dave Keon/90* 6.00 15.00
41 Dominik Hasek/90* 10.00 25.00
42 Doug Gilmour/90* 8.00 20.00
43 Ed Belfour/90* 6.00 15.00
44 Elmer Lach/90* 5.00 12.00
45 Evgeni Nabokov/90* 5.00 12.00
46 Frank Mahovlich/90* 6.00 15.00
47 Grant Fuhr/90* 10.00 25.00
48 Grant Fuhr/90* 10.00 25.00
49 Guy Lafleur/90* 8.00 20.00
50 Jacques Plante 10.00 25.00
51 Jari Kurri/90* 6.00 15.00
52 Jaromir Jagr/90* 10.00 25.00
53 Jaromir Jagr/90* 10.00 25.00
54 Jean Beliveau/90* 6.00 15.00
55 Joe Sakic/90* 12.00 30.00
56 Joe Sakic/90* 12.00 30.00
57 Joe Sakic/90* 12.00 30.00
58 Joe Thornton/90* 10.00 25.00
59 Johnny Bower/90* 6.00 15.00
60 John Tavares/90* 20.00 50.00
61 Lanny McDonald/90* 8.00 20.00
62 Larry Robinson/90* 6.00 15.00
63 Mario Lemieux/90* 25.00 60.00
64 Martin Brodeur/90* 15.00 40.00
65 Martin Brodeur/90* 15.00 40.00
66 Martin St. Louis/90* 6.00 15.00
67 Mats Sundin/90* 6.00 15.00
68 Mike Modano/90* 10.00 25.00
69 Nicklas Lidstrom/90* 12.50 30.00
70 Nicklas Lidstrom/90* 12.50 30.00
71 Pat LaFontaine/90* 6.00 15.00
72 Pat LaFontaine/90* 6.00 15.00
73 Patrick Roy/90* 15.00 40.00
74 Patrick Roy/90* 15.00 40.00
75 Patrick Roy/90* 15.00 40.00
76 Patrick Roy/90* 15.00 40.00
77 Phil Esposito/90* 10.00 25.00
78 Red Kelly/90* 6.00 15.00
79 Rob Blake/90* 6.00 15.00
80 Roberto Luongo/90* 10.00 25.00
81 Saku Koivu/90* 6.00 15.00
82 Scott Niedermayer/90* 6.00 15.00
83 Sergei Fedorov/90* 10.00 25.00
84 Syl Apps/90* 10.00 25.00
85 Ted Kennedy/90* 6.00 15.00
86 Tim Horton/90* 12.00 30.00
87 Tim Horton/90* 12.00 30.00
88 Tim Thomas/90* 6.00 15.00
89 Tony Esposito/90* 6.00 15.00
90 Turk Broda/90* 6.00 15.00

2008-09 ITG Ultimate Memorabilia Autographs

1 Alexander Ovechkin 40.00 100.00
2 Alexander Semin 10.00 25.00
3 Anze Kopitar 15.00 40.00
4 Carey Price 20.00 50.00
5 Chris Chelios 10.00 25.00
6 Miikka Kiprusoff 10.00 25.00
7 Evgeni Nabokov 8.00 20.00
8 Joe Thornton 15.00 40.00
9 Martin St. Louis 10.00 25.00
10 Marty Turco 10.00 25.00
11 Mike Green 8.00 20.00
12 Mike Modano 15.00 40.00
13 Mikko Koivu 8.00 20.00
14 Niklas Backstrom 10.00 25.00
15 Nicklas Lidstrom 10.00 25.00
16 Pavel Datsyuk 15.00 40.00
17 Roberto Luongo 15.00 40.00
18 Ryan Getzlaf 10.00 25.00
19 Scott Niedermayer 10.00 25.00
20 Sergei Fedorov 15.00 40.00
21 Teemu Selanne 20.00 50.00
22 Rob Blake 10.00 25.00
23 Saku Koivu 10.00 25.00
24 Jaromir Jagr 30.00 80.00
25 Marian Gaborik 10.00 25.00
26 Martin Brodeur 25.00 60.00
27 Daniel Briere 10.00 25.00
28 Ilya Kovalchuk 10.00 25.00
29 Patrick Marleau 10.00 25.00
30 Mats Sundin 10.00 25.00

2008-09 ITG Ultimate Memorabilia AutoMates

1 Ovechkin/Semin 50.00 125.00
2 Niedermayer/Selanne 25.00 60.00
3 Ovechkin/Green 50.00 125.00
4 Tavares/Kadri 40.00 100.00
5 Nabokov/Marleau 12.00 30.00
6 Datsyuk/Helm 20.00 50.00
7.Alzner/Varlamov 25.00 60.00
8 Koivu/Backstrom 12.00 30.00
9 Blake/Thornton 20.00 50.00
10 Price/Koivu 25.00 60.00
11 Turco/Modano 20.00 50.00
12 Chelios/Lidstrom 12.00 30.00
13 Stastny/Sakic 25.00 60.00
14 Luongo/Sundin 20.00 50.00
15 Giguere/Getzlaf 12.00 30.00
16 Thomas/Fernandez 12.00 30.00
17 Fedorov/Lidstrom 20.00 50.00
18 Henderson/Esposito 20.00 50.00
19 Yakushev/Mikhailov 15.00 40.00
20 Parent/Sanderson 15.00 40.00
21 Kane/Boychuk 25.00 60.00
22 Hickey/Eberle 25.00 60.00
23 Jagr/Lemieux 50.00 125.00
24 Duchene/Hodgson 30.00 80.00
25 Brodeur/Luongo 30.00 80.00
26 Esposito/Cheevers 20.00 50.00
27 Hasek/Hull 30.00 80.00
28 Richard/Lafleur 15.00 40.00
29 Hull/Mikita 25.00 60.00
30 Sittler/Salming 15.00 40.00

2008-09 ITG Ultimate Memorabilia Blades of Steel

1 Alexander Ovechkin 20.00 50.00
2 Ryan Getzlaf 8.00 20.00
3 Gilbert Perreault 6.00 15.00
4 Phil Esposito 15.00 40.00
5 Marcel Dionne 8.00 20.00
6 Joe Thornton 10.00 25.00
7 Jacques Plante 12.00 30.00
8 Stan Mikita 8.00 20.00
9 Johnny Bucyk 6.00 15.00
10 Mario Lemieux 25.00 60.00
11 Pavel Datsyuk 12.00 30.00
12 Jaromir Jagr 12.00 30.00

2008-09 ITG Ultimate Memorabilia Cityscapes

1 Clarke/Schmidt 12.00 30.00
2 Gilbert/Namath 8.00 20.00
3 Br.Hull/Warner 20.00 50.00
4 Sakic/Roy 20.00 50.00
5 Lemieux/Jagr 30.00 80.00
6 P.Esposito/Jackson 12.00 30.00
7 Hull/Rodman 15.00 40.00
8 Park/Pele 6.00 15.00
9 Beliveau/Carter 8.00 20.00
10 St. Louis/Sapp 8.00 20.00

2008-09 ITG Ultimate Memorabilia Cornerstones

1 Kharl/Tretiak/Datsyuk/Ovech 30.00 80.00
2 Thmp/Brimsc/Cheev/Thmas 8.00 20.00
3 Hainsworth/Plante/Roy/Price 15.00 40.00
4 Broda/Bower/Potvin/Toskala 12.00 30.00
5 Clarke/Parent/Lindbgh/Briere 12.00 30.00
6 Morenz/Richard/Lafleur/Koivu 8.00 20.00
7 Esposito/Sittler/Lemieux/Sakic 15.00 40.00
8 Salm/Naslnd/Lidstrm/Hedman 20.00 50.00
9 Esposito/Vachon/Fuhr/Brodeur 20.00 50.00
10 Lindsy/Delvch/Dionne/Datsyk 12.00 30.00
11 Luong/Thrnton/Price/Tavares 25.00 60.00
12 Sawchk/Dionne/Blake/Kopitr 12.00 30.00

2008-09 ITG Ultimate Memorabilia Decade Dominance

1 Gbk/Thn/Dts/Lds/Lng/Ovi 30.00 80.00
2 Brd/Lmx/Jgr/Ry/Snd/Skc 20.00 50.00
3 Ry/Smt/Nly/Clk/Brq/Lmx 30.00 80.00
4 Lfl/Str/Esp/Clk/Trk/Slm 12.00 30.00
5 Rch/Kn/Glb/Bwr/Hll/Mkt 15.00 40.00
6 Rch/Lnd/Blv/Plt/Swc/Abl 15.00 40.00

2008-09 ITG Ultimate Memorabilia Franchises

1 Ovechkin/Semin/Varlamov 20.00 50.00
2 Clarke/MacLeish/Parent 15.00 30.00
3 Hull/Mikita/White 15.00 30.00
4 Park/Hadfield/Tkaczuk 15.00 30.00
5 Hull/Nieuwendyk/McDonald 15.00 30.00
6 Sittler/McDonald/Salming 15.00 30.00
7 Mahovlich/Kelly/Sawchuk 25.00 50.00
9 Bucyk/Cheevers/Esposito 15.00 30.00
10 L.Robinson/S.Savard/Lapointe 15.00 30.00
11 Brodeur/Nieuwndyk/S.Niedrmyr 15.00 30.00
12 Sundin/W.Clark/Gilmour 20.00 40.00
13 M.Richard/Beliveau/H.Richard 20.00 50.00
14 Modano/Turco/Brunnstrom 10.00 25.00
15 Roy/Chelios/Naslund 20.00 40.00
17 Selanne/S.Niedermayer/Hiller 20.00 40.00
18 Thomas/Lucic/Fernandez 12.00 30.00

2008-09 ITG Ultimate Memorabilia From Russia with Love

1 Alexander Ovechkin 15.00 40.00
2 Vladislav Tretiak 20.00 50.00
4 Evgeni Nabokov 15.00 40.00
5 Valeri Kharlamov 20.00 50.00
6 Alexander Semin 15.00 40.00
7 Alexander Yakushev 15.00 40.00
9 Sergei Fedorov 15.00 40.00
10 Nikolai Kulemin 15.00 40.00
11 Simeon Varlamov 15.00 40.00
12 Ilya Kovalchuk 15.00 40.00

2008-09 ITG Ultimate Memorabilia Future Stars Autographs

1 Simeon Varlamov 25.00 50.00
5 Dana Tyrell 6.00 15.00
6 Darren Helm 6.00 15.00
7 Scott Glennie 12.00 30.00
8 Evander Kane 12.00 30.00
9 Fabian Brunnstrom 6.00 15.00
10 Thomas Hickey 6.00 15.00
11 John Tavares 50.00 100.00
12 Taylor Hall 30.00 80.00
13 Jordan Eberle 25.00 50.00
16 Matt Duchene 15.00 40.00
17 Mikkel Boedker 6.00 15.00
18 Milan Lucic 15.00 40.00
19 Nazem Kadri 15.00 40.00
20 Oliver Ekman-Larsson 15.00 40.00
21 Ryan Ellis 15.00 40.00
22 Dustin Tokarski 12.00 30.00
23 Jonas Hiller 10.00 25.00
24 Jared Cowen 5.00 12.00
25 Victor Hedman 12.00 30.00
27 Mikhail Grabovski 15.00 40.00
28 Brayden Schenn 12.00 30.00
29 Paul Stastny 10.00 25.00
30 Cody Hodgson 25.00 50.00

2008-09 ITG Ultimate Memorabilia Future Stars Jerseys Autographs

1 Simeon Varlamov 20.00 50.00
2 Nikolai Kulemin 10.00 25.00
3 Chet Pickard 10.00 25.00
4 Zach Boychuk 10.00 25.00
5 Dana Tyrell 10.00 25.00
6 Darren Helm 10.00 25.00
7 Scott Glennie 10.00 25.00
8 Evander Kane 20.00 50.00
9 Fabian Brunnstrom 8.00 20.00
10 Thomas Hickey 12.00 30.00
11 John Tavares 75.00 125.00
12 Taylor Hall 20.00 50.00
13 Jordan Eberle 20.00 50.00
14 Azne Kopitar 15.00 40.00
15 Guillaume Latendresse 6.00 15.00
16 Matt Duchene 20.00 50.00
17 Mikkel Boedker 12.00 30.00
18 Milan Lucic 15.00 40.00
19 Nazem Kadri 20.00 50.00
20 Ryan Ellis 10.00 25.00
21 Dustin Tokarski 10.00 25.00
22 Jonas Hiller 8.00 20.00
23 Jared Cowen 10.00 25.00
24 Victor Hedman 25.00 60.00
25 Carter Ashton 10.00 25.00
26 Mikhail Grabovski 6.00 15.00
27 Brayden Schenn 20.00 50.00
28 Paul Stastny 8.00 20.00
29 Cody Hodgson 25.00 60.00
30 Karl Alzner/15 6.00 15.00

2008-09 ITG Ultimate Memorabilia Future Stars Patches Autographs

1 Oliver Ekman-Larsson 12.00 30.00
2 Simeon Varlamov 20.00 50.00
3 Nikolai Kulemin 10.00 25.00
4 Chet Pickard 10.00 25.00
5 Zach Boychuk 10.00 25.00
6 Dana Tyrell 10.00 25.00
7 Darren Helm 10.00 25.00
8 Scott Glennie 10.00 25.00
9 Evander Kane 20.00 50.00
10 Fabian Brunnstrom 8.00 20.00
11 Thomas Hickey 12.00 30.00
12 John Tavares 30.00 80.00
13 Taylor Hall 30.00 80.00
14 Jordan Eberle 20.00 50.00
15 Karl Alzner 6.00 15.00
16 Guillaume Latendresse 6.00 15.00
17 Matt Duchene 20.00 50.00
18 Mikkel Boedker 12.00 30.00
19 Milan Lucic 15.00 40.00
20 Nazem Kadri 20.00 50.00
21 Ryan Ellis 10.00 25.00
22 Dustin Tokarski 10.00 25.00
23 Jonas Hiller 8.00 20.00
24 Jared Cowen 10.00 25.00
25 Victor Hedman 25.00 60.00
26 Carter Ashton 10.00 25.00
27 Mikhail Grabovski 6.00 15.00
28 Brayden Schenn 20.00 50.00
29 Paul Stastny 8.00 20.00
30 Cody Hodgson 25.00 60.00
31 Anze Kopitar 15.00 40.00

2008-09 ITG Ultimate Memorabilia Gloves are Off

1 Alexander Ovechkin 25.00 60.00
2 Bobby Clarke 10.00 25.00
3 Ryan Getzlaf 6.00 15.00
4 Dominik Hasek 10.00 25.00
5 Ed Belfour 6.00 15.00
6 Evgeni Nabokov 5.00 12.00
7 Joe Sakic 12.00 30.00
8 Joe Thornton 10.00 25.00
9 John Tavares 20.00 50.00
10 Marian Gaborik 6.00 15.00
11 Mario Lemieux 25.00 60.00
12 Martin Brodeur 15.00 40.00
13 Patrick Roy Canadiens 15.00 40.00
14 Patrick Roy Avs 15.00 40.00
15 Raymond Bourque 10.00 25.00
16 Rob Blake 6.00 15.00
17 Chris Chelios 6.00 15.00
18 Scott Niedermayer 6.00 15.00
19 Sergei Fedorov 10.00 25.00
20 Stan Mikita 8.00 20.00

2008-09 ITG Ultimate Memorabilia Hometown Heroes

1 Alexander Ovechkin 25.00 60.00
2 Joe Sakic 12.00 30.00
3 Joe Thornton 10.00 25.00
4 John Tavares 20.00 50.00
5 Martin Brodeur 15.00 40.00
6 Patrick Roy 15.00 40.00
7 Bobby Clarke 10.00 25.00
8 Borje Salming 6.00 15.00
9 Mario Lemieux 25.00 60.00
10 Guy Lafleur 8.00 20.00
11 Teemu Selanne 10.00 25.00
12 Jaromir Jagr 12.00 30.00
13 Miikka Kiprusoff 6.00 15.00
14 Raymond Bourque 10.00 25.00
15 Roberto Luongo 10.00 25.00
16 Dominik Hasek 10.00 25.00
17 Ryan Getzlaf 6.00 15.00
18 Mike Modano 10.00 25.00

2008-09 ITG Ultimate Memorabilia Journey Jersey

1 Mats Sundin 10.00 25.00
2 Joe Sakic 12.00 30.00
3 Raymond Bourque 10.00 25.00
4 Patrick Roy 15.00 40.00
5 Joe Thornton 10.00 25.00
6 Roberto Luongo 10.00 25.00

2008-09 ITG Ultimate Memorabilia Legends Autographs

1 Jean Beliveau 25.00 50.00
2 Raymond Bourque 15.00 40.00
3 Johnny Bower 8.00 20.00
4 Gerry Cheevers 8.00 20.00
5 Wendel Clark 8.00 20.00
6 Bobby Clarke 12.00 30.00
7 Yvan Cournoyer 8.00 20.00
8 Marcel Dionne 10.00 25.00
9 Phil Esposito 12.00 30.00
10 Tony Esposito 8.00 20.00
11 Grant Fuhr 12.00 30.00
12 Glenn Hall 12.00 30.00
13 Dominik Hasek 12.00 30.00
14 Bobby Hull 15.00 40.00
15 Doug Gilmour 10.00 25.00
16 Brett Hull 15.00 40.00
17 Dave Keon 8.00 20.00
18 Derek Sanderson 10.00 25.00
19 Elmer Lach 6.00 15.00
20 Guy Lafleur 10.00 25.00
21 Ted Lindsay 15.00 30.00
22 Lanny McDonald 8.00 20.00
23 Stan Mikita 10.00 25.00
24 Boris Mikhailov 10.00 25.00
25 Alexander Yakushev 25.00 50.00
26 Joe Sakic 25.00 50.00
27 Henri Richard 25.00 50.00
28 Vladislav Tretiak 20.00 40.00
29 Mario Lemieux 40.00 80.00
30 Joe Nieuwendyk 8.00 20.00

2008-09 ITG Ultimate Memorabilia Numerology

1 Alexander Ovechkin 25.00 60.00
2 Mario Lemieux 25.00 60.00
3 Joe Sakic 12.00 30.00
4 Martin Brodeur 15.00 40.00
5 Patrick Roy 15.00 40.00
6 Pavel Datsyuk 10.00 25.00
7 Nicklas Lidstrom 6.00 15.00
8 John Tavares 20.00 50.00
9 Mats Sundin 6.00 15.00
10 Raymond Bourque 10.00 25.00
11 Jaromir Jagr 20.00 50.00
12 Frank Brimsek 5.00 12.00
13 Mike Modano 10.00 25.00
14 Carey Price 12.00 30.00
15 Vladislav Tretiak 5.00 12.00
16 Bobby Hull 12.00 30.00
17 Stan Mikita 8.00 20.00
18 Dominik Hasek 10.00 25.00
19 Ed Belfour 6.00 15.00
20 Brett Hull 15.00 40.00
21 Doug Harvey 6.00 15.00
22 Miikka Kiprusoff 6.00 15.00
23 Ilya Kovalchuk 6.00 15.00
24 Ryan Getzlaf 6.00 15.00

2008-09 ITG Ultimate Memorabilia Past Present and Future

1 Slmng/Ldstrm/Hedmn 12.00 30.00
2 Hull/Turco/Glennie 12.00 30.00
3 Neely/Thomas/Lucic 12.00 30.00
4 Sittler/Grabovski/Kadri 25.00 50.00
5 Gilmour/Tskla/Kulemin 8.00 20.00
6 Fuhr/Luongo/Price 12.00 30.00
7 Nwndyk/Modno/Brnstrm 10.00 25.00
8 Sakic/Stastny/Duchene 12.00 30.00
9 Dionne/Kopitar/Schenn 12.00 30.00
10 Dionne/Datsyuk/Helm 8.00 20.00
11 Lemx/Thorntn/Tavars 25.00 60.00
12 Kolzig/Ovech/Varlamov 25.00 60.00
13 Roy/Brodeur/Pickard 15.00 40.00
14 Brque/Ndrmayer/Cowen 12.00 30.00
15 Blake/Kopitar/Hickey 10.00 25.00
16 Vachon/Brdeur/Tokrski 25.00 50.00
17 Fedorov/Getzlaf/Hiller 10.00 25.00
18 Tretiak/Nabkv/Varlamv 15.00 40.00

2008-09 ITG Ultimate Memorabilia Retro Teammates
1 Bernie Parent / Bobby Clarke 15.00 40.00
2 Bobby Hull / Glenn Hall 20.00 50.00
3 Brad Park / Rod Gilbert 10.00 25.00
4 Darryl Sittler / Lanny McDonald 12.00 30.00
5 Dave Keon / Frank Mahovlich 10.00 25.00
6 Felix Potvin / Wendel Clark 15.00 40.00
7 Gilbert Perreault / Rick Martin 10.00 25.00
8 Guy Lafleur / Steve Shutt 12.00 30.00
9 Jacques Plante / Henri Richard 15.00 40.00
10 Jean Beliveau / Maurice Richard 20.00 50.00
11 Joe Sakic / Patrick Roy 20.00 50.00
12 Mario Lemieux / Jaromir Jagr 40.00 100.00
13 Phil Esposito / Johnny Bucyk 15.00 40.00
14 Stan Mikita / Tony Esposito 12.00 30.00
15 Ted Lindsay / Alex Delvecchio 10.00 25.00
16 Terry Sawchuk / Johnny Bower 20.00 40.00
17 Tim Horton / Red Kelly 10.00 25.00
18 Valeri Kharlamov / Vladislav Tretiak 10.00 25.00

2008-09 ITG Ultimate Memorabilia Stick Autographs
1 Mike Modano 20.00 50.00
2 Pavel Datsyuk 20.00 50.00
3 Jean-Sebastien Giguere 12.00 30.00
4 Alexander Ovechkin 50.00 125.00
5 John Tavares 40.00 100.00
6 Ryan Getzlaf 12.00 30.00
7 Doug Gilmour 15.00 40.00
8 Brett Hull 30.00 80.00
9 Jaromir Jagr 40.00 100.00
10 Guy Lafleur 15.00 40.00
11 Chris Chelios 12.00 30.00
12 Nicklas Lidstrom 12.00 30.00
13 Joe Nieuwendyk 10.00 25.00
14 Joe Sakic 25.00 60.00
15 Borje Salming 12.00 30.00
16 Derek Sanderson 12.00 30.00
17 Teemu Selanne 25.00 60.00
18 Alexander Semin 12.00 30.00
19 Darryl Sittler 15.00 40.00
20 Mats Sundin 12.00 30.00
21 Marian Gaborik 12.00 30.00
22 Joe Thornton 20.00 50.00
23 Dominik Hasek 20.00 50.00
24 Evgeni Nabokov 10.00 25.00
25 Sergei Fedorov 20.00 50.00
26 Patrick Roy 30.00 80.00
27 Martin Brodeur 30.00 80.00
28 Daniel Briere 12.00 30.00
29 Roberto Luongo 20.00 50.00
30 Carey Price 25.00 60.00

2008-09 ITG Ultimate Memorabilia Stick Rack
1 Alexander Ovechkin 50.00 125.00
2 Chris Chelios 12.00 30.00
3 Marian Gaborik 12.00 30.00
4 Nicklas Lidstrom 15.00 40.00
5 Joe Thornton 20.00 50.00
6 Pavel Datsyuk 15.00 40.00
7 Dominik Hasek 20.00 50.00
8 Ryan Getzlaf 15.00 40.00
9 John Tavares 20.00 50.00
10 Evegeni Nabokov 10.00 25.00
11 Joe Sakic 25.00 60.00
12 Teemu Selanne 30.00 60.00
13 Jaromir Jagr 30.00 60.00
14 Martin Brodeur 40.00 80.00
15 Patrick Roy 30.00 60.00
16 Roberto Luongo 20.00 50.00
17 Mike Modano 25.00 50.00
18 Milan Lucic 20.00 50.00

2008-09 ITG Ultimate Memorabilia Trophy Winners
1 Alexander Ovechkin 25.00 60.00
2 Alexander Ovechkin 25.00 60.00
3 Mario Lemieux 25.00 60.00
4 Sergei Fedorov 10.00 25.00
5 Alexander Ovechkin 25.00 60.00
6 Pavel Datsyuk 10.00 25.00
7 Nicklas Lidstrom 6.00 15.00
8 Alexander Ovechkin 25.00 60.00
9 Alexander Ovechkin 25.00 60.00
10 Martin Brodeur 15.00 40.00
11 Jaromir Jagr 12.00 30.00
12 Martin Brodeur 15.00 40.00
13 Patrick Roy 15.00 40.00
14 Doug Gilmour 8.00 20.00
15 Joe Sakic 12.00 30.00
16 Joe Sakic 12.00 30.00
17 Raymond Bourque 10.00 25.00
18 Mario Lemieux 25.00 60.00
19 Ilya Kovalchuk 6.00 15.00
20 Patrick Roy 15.00 40.00

2008-09 ITG Ultimate Memorabilia Ultimate Defensemen
1 Scott Niedermayer/Nicklas LidstromChris Chelios/Borje SalmingLarry Robinson 15.0040.00

2008-09 ITG Ultimate Memorabilia Ultimate Draft Pick Autographs
COMMON TAVARES/19* 30.00 60.00
COMMON TVRES/OVECH/19* 100.00 200.00

2008-09 ITG Ultimate Memorabilia Ultimate Forwards
1 Ovn/Thn/Skc/Hll/Abl/Jol 25.00 60.00
2 Tvr/Snd/Dne/Kn/Rch/Sch 40.00 80.00
3 Dat/Lmx/Esp/Lfl/Blv/Mrn 12.00 30.00

2008-09 ITG Ultimate Memorabilia Ultimate Goalies
2 Nbv/Hsk/Roy/Prt/Esp/Saw 30.00 80.00

2008-09 ITG Ultimate Memorabilia Ultimate Players Dual Swatch
TRIPLE/19: .4X TO 1X DUAL/19*
QUAD/19: .5X TO 1.2X DUAL/19*
FIVE/19: .6X TO 1.5X DUAL/19*
1 Alexander Ovechkin 20.00 50.00
2 John Tavares 10.00 25.00
3 Roberto Luongo 10.00 25.00
4 Nicklas Lidstrom 8.00 20.00
5 Mario Lemieux 25.00 60.00
6 Martin Brodeur 15.00 40.00
7 Patrick Roy 15.00 40.00
8 Joe Sakic 12.00 30.00
9 Jaromir Jagr 12.00 30.00

2008-09 ITG Ultimate Memorabilia Jerseys
1 Alexander Ovechkin 25.00 60.00
2 Joe Sakic 12.00 30.00
3 John Tavares 10.00 25.00
4 Ryan Getzlaf 6.00 15.00
5 Martin Brodeur 15.00 40.00
6 Patrick Roy 15.00 40.00
7 Mario Lemieux 25.00 60.00
8 Raymond Bourque 10.00 25.00
9 Mike Modano 10.00 25.00
10 Miikka Kiprusoff 6.00 15.00
11 Milan Lucic 10.00 25.00
12 Pavel Datsyuk 10.00 25.00

2010-11 ITG Ultimate Memorabilia
1 Georges Vezina 8.00 20.00
2 Eddie Shore 5.00 12.00
3 Charlie Conacher 5.00 12.00
4 Ron Francis 8.00 20.00
5 Bill Barilko 4.00 10.00
6 Doug Harvey 6.00 15.00
7 Howie Morenz 5.00 12.00
8 Luc Robitaille 6.00 15.00
9 Bobby Hull 12.00 30.00
10 Daniel Sedin 10.00 25.00
11 Peter Forsberg 12.00 30.00
12 Borje Salming 6.00 15.00
13 Teemu Selanne 15.00 40.00
14 Dave Keon 6.00 15.00
15 Cyclone Taylor 6.00 15.00
16 Brett Hull 12.00 30.00
17 Valeri Kharlamov 4.00 10.00
18 Hobey Baker 5.00 12.00
19 Ted Lindsay 6.00 15.00
20 Vladislav Tretiak 5.00 12.00
21 Mario Lemieux 25.00 60.00
22 Mike Bossy 6.00 15.00
23 Red Kelly 6.00 15.00
24 Steven Stamkos 10.00 25.00
25 Felix Potvin 10.00 25.00
26 Lester Patrick 6.00 15.00
27 Darryl Sittler 8.00 20.00
28 Gump Worsley 6.00 15.00
29 George Hainsworth 6.00 15.00
30 Martin Brodeur 12.00 30.00
31 Pelle Lindbergh 5.00 12.00
32 Denis Potvin 6.00 15.00
33 Patrick Roy COL 12.00 30.00
34 Charlie Gardiner 5.00 12.00
35 Tony Esposito 6.00 15.00
36 Newsy Lalonde 5.00 12.00
37 Turk Broda 6.00 15.00
38 Aurel Joliat 6.00 15.00
39 Dominik Hasek 10.00 25.00
40 Sid Abel 5.00 12.00
41 Igor Larionov 6.00 15.00
42 Maurice Richard 12.00 30.00
43 Bobby Bauer 6.00 15.00
44 Ted Kennedy 6.00 15.00
45 Woody Dumart 4.00 10.00
46 Carey Price 10.00 25.00
47 Chris Chelios 6.00 15.00
48 Paul Coffey 6.00 15.00
49 Syl Apps 8.00 20.00
50 Bill Durnan 6.00 15.00
51 Terry Sawchuk 8.00 20.00
52 Milt Schmidt 5.00 12.00
53 Elmer Lach 5.00 12.00
54 Marcel Dionne 8.00 20.00
55 Johnny Bucyk 6.00 15.00
56 Henri Richard 6.00 15.00
57 Miikka Kiprusoff 8.00 20.00
58 Frank Mahovlich 6.00 15.00
59 Stan Mikita 8.00 20.00
60 Jean Beliveau 6.00 15.00
61 Glenn Hall 6.00 15.00
62 Vincent Lecavalier 8.00 20.00
63 Phil Esposito 10.00 25.00
64 Ron Hextall 6.00 15.00
65 Gerry Cheevers 6.00 15.00
66 Bernie Parent 8.00 20.00
67 Johnny Bower 6.00 15.00
68 Jaromir Jagr 20.00 50.00
69 Toe Blake 4.00 10.00
70 Gilbert Perreault 6.00 15.00
71 Ilya Kovalchuk 8.00 20.00
72 Guy Lafleur 8.00 20.00
73 Larry Robinson 6.00 15.00
74 Tim Horton 6.00 15.00
75 Bobby Clarke 10.00 25.00
76 Bryan Trottier 6.00 15.00
77 Raymond Bourque 10.00 25.00
78 Ed Giacomin 10.00 25.00
79 Bernie Geoffrion 5.00 12.00
80 Peter Stastny 5.00 12.00
81 Grant Fuhr 10.00 25.00
82 Marian Gaborik 8.00 20.00
83 Jacques Plante 8.00 20.00
84 Pat LaFontaine 6.00 15.00
85 Patrick Roy MTL 12.00 30.00
86 Jari Kurri 6.00 15.00
87 Joe Sakic 12.00 30.00
88 Mike Modano 12.00 30.00
89 Lanny McDonald 6.00 15.00
90 Henrik Sedin 10.00 25.00
91 Sergei Fedorov 10.00 25.00
92 Nicklas Lidstrom 8.00 20.00
93 Doug Gilmour 8.00 20.00
94 Cam Neely 6.00 15.00
95 Tyler Seguin 8.00 20.00
96 Roberto Luongo 12.00 30.00
97 Joe Thornton 12.00 30.00
98 Wendel Clark 10.00 25.00
99 Tim Thomas 8.00 20.00
100 Steve Yzerman 20.00 50.00

2010-11 ITG Ultimate Memorabilia 500 Goal Combos
1 M.Richard/G.Hall 20.00 50.00
2 G.Howe/G.Worsley 30.00 80.00
3 B.Hull/E.Giacomin 25.00 50.00
4 J.Beliveau/G.Gilbert 15.00 30.00
5 S.Mikita/C.Maniago 12.00 30.00
6 G.Lafleur/C.Resch 12.00 30.00
7 D.Ciccarelli/K.Hrudy 10.00 25.00
8 M.Lemieux/T.Soderstrom 40.00 100.00
9 M.Messier/R.Tabaracci 20.00 30.00
10 S.Yzerman/P.Roy 25.00 60.00
11 D.Hawerchuk/F.Potvin 15.00 40.00
12 B.Hull/S.Fiset 20.00 50.00
13 J.Mullen/P.Roy 20.00 50.00
14 D.Andreychuk/B.Ranford 10.00 25.00
15 L.Robitaille/D.Roloson 10.00 25.00
16 P.Verbeek/F.Brathwaite 8.00 20.00
17 R.Francis/B.Dafoe 15.00 40.00
18 B.Shanahan/P.Roy 25.00 60.00
19 J.Sakic/D.Cloutier 20.00 50.00
20 J.Nieuwendyk/K.Weekes 8.00 20.00
21 J.Jagr/J.Grahame 15.00 40.00
22 P.Turgeon/V.Toskala 8.00 20.00
23 M.Sundin/M.Kiprusoff 25.00 50.00
24 T.Selanne/J.Theodore 15.00 40.00
25 P.Bondra/J.Aubin 10.00 25.00
26 M.Recchi/M.Turco 12.00 30.00
27 M.Modano/A.Niittymaki 15.00 40.00
28 J.Roenick/A.Auld 15.00 40.00

2010-11 ITG Ultimate Memorabilia Autographs
1 Rick Nash 12.00 30.00
2 Carey Price 20.00 50.00
3 Martin Brodeur 20.00 50.00
6 Niklas Backstrom 12.00 30.00
8 Roberto Luongo 12.00 30.00
10 Teemu Selanne 12.00 30.00
13 Martin St. Louis 10.00 25.00
14 Miikka Kiprusoff 8.00 20.00
17 Jimmy Howard 12.00 30.00
18 Zdeno Chara 12.00 30.00
19 Steven Stamkos 20.00 40.00
20 Daniel Sedin 12.00 30.00
22 Ilya Kovalchuk 8.00 20.00
23 Brenden Morrow 10.00 25.00
26 Mike Modano 12.00 30.00
27 Marty Turco 10.00 25.00

2010-11 ITG Ultimate Memorabilia Autographs Duals
1 Mahovlich/Kelly 40.00 80.00
2 Salming/Clark 15.00 40.00
3 R.Brodeur/Luongo 20.00 40.00
4 Stamkos/Nash 40.00 80.00
5 Beliveau/Lafleur 30.00 60.00
6 Yzerman/Hull 40.00 80.00
7 Fuhr/Messier 30.00 60.00
10 P.Esposito/Bucyk 20.00 50.00
11 Lecavalier/St. Louis 12.00 30.00
13 Bure/Neely 15.00 40.00
14 Hull/Mikita 25.00 50.00
15 M.Brodeur/Kovalchuk 40.00 80.00
16 Clark/Sittler 20.00 40.00
17 Gaborik/Jagr 30.00 60.00
18 Price/Roy 50.00 100.00
19 Niedermayer/Selanne 20.00 50.00
20 D.Sedin/H.Sedin 20.00 40.00
21 Bure/Larionov 20.00 50.00
22 Lindsay/Lach 15.00 40.00
23 Niemi/Keith 15.00 40.00
24 Hull/Hall 25.00 50.00

2010-11 ITG Ultimate Memorabilia AutoMates
1 Lach/Beliveau 40.00 80.00
2 Keon/Bower 20.00 40.00
3 Sittler/McDonald 20.00 40.00
5 M.Koivu/Gaborik 20.00 40.00
6 Yzerman/Robitaille 40.00 80.00
8 Lidstrom/Salming 30.00 60.00
10 P.Esposito/T.Esposito 25.00 50.00
12 Keith/Niedermayer 20.00 40.00
13 Trottier/Smith 25.00 50.00
14 Hull/Hall 25.00 50.00
16 Clarke/Schultz 25.00 50.00
17 Gilmour/Clark 30.00 60.00
18 Neely/Bourque 30.00 60.00
19 Lafleur/Richard 30.00 60.00
20 Mahovlich/Olmstead 25.00 50.00

2010-11 ITG Ultimate Memorabilia Brotherly Love
1 P.Bure/V.Bure 10.00 25.00
2 M.Dionne/G.Dionne 12.00 30.00
3 P.Esposito/T.Esposito 15.00 40.00
4 M.Hossa/M.Hossa 10.00 25.00
5 B.Hull/D.Hull 12.00 30.00
6 S.Koivu/M.Koivu 10.00 25.00
7 F.Mahovlich/P.Mahovlich 10.00 25.00
8 S.Niedermayer/R.Niedermayer 10.00 25.00
9 R.Sutter/R.Sutter 8.00 20.00
10 K.Primeau/W.Primeau 8.00 20.00
11 M.Richard/H.Richard 20.00 50.00
12 S.Fedorov/F.Fedorov 15.00 40.00
13 H.Sedin/D.Sedin 12.00 30.00
14 E.Staal/M.Staal 12.00 30.00
15 J.Staal/J.Staal 8.00 20.00
16 P.Stastny/A.Stastny 10.00 25.00

2010-11 ITG Ultimate Memorabilia Country of Origin
2 M.Messier/S.Yzerman 20.00 50.00
4 M.Brodeur/J.Thornton 15.00 40.00
5 J.Jagr/D.Hasek 20.00 40.00
6 P.Stastny/M.Gaborik 12.00 30.00
7 M.Modano/B.Hull 15.00 40.00
8 P.LaFontaine/C.Chelios 12.00 30.00
9 R.Miller/Z.Parise 15.00 30.00
11 M.Kiprusoff/S.Koivu 20.00 40.00
12 I.Kovalchuk/E.Malkin 15.00 40.00
13 P.Bure/S.Fedorov 20.00 50.00
14 V.Tretiak/V.Kharlamov 30.00 80.00
15 N.Lidstrom/P.Forsberg 20.00 40.00
16 P.Lindbergh/M.Naslund 10.00 25.00

2010-11 ITG Ultimate Memorabilia Days Gone By
1 Lanny McDonald 10.00 25.00
2 Roy Worters 15.00 40.00
3 Keith Tkachuk 10.00 25.00
4 Dave Keon 10.00 25.00
5 Mike Modano 15.00 40.00
6 Mats Sundin 10.00 25.00
7 Joe Sakic 20.00 50.00
8 Michel Goulet 8.00 20.00
9 Bobby Hull 20.00 50.00
10 Teemu Selanne 20.00 50.00

2010-11 ITG Ultimate Memorabilia Decades
2 Shore/Joliat/Mornz/Hnswrth 75.00 135.00
3 Wortrs/Clncy/Cnchr/Baily 60.00 120.00
4 Richrd/Schmdt/Abel/Durnn 60.00 120.00
5 Mosnko/Hrvy/Swchk/Plante 40.00 80.00
6 Hull/Beliveau/Mahovlich/Hall 40.00 80.00
7 Esposito/Sittler/Laflr/Clrk 25.00 60.00
8 Messr/Bossy/Dionne/Mario 40.00 80.00
9 Fuhr/Roy/Bourque/Potvin 40.00 80.00
10 Brodeur/Hasek/Belfour/Roy 40.00 80.00
11 Yzerman/Sakic/Jagr/Mario 40.00 80.00
12 Brodeur/Thrntn/Lecavl/Kvlchk 25.00 60.00

2010-11 ITG Ultimate Memorabilia European Influence
1 Evgeni Malkin 15.00 40.00
2 Ilya Kovalchuk 8.00 20.00
3 Igor Larionov 8.00 20.00
4 Sergei Fedorov 12.00 30.00
5 Peter Forsberg 15.00 40.00
6 Borje Salming 8.00 20.00
7 Mats Naslund 5.00 12.00
8 Pelle Lindbergh 6.00 15.00
9 Nicklas Lidstrom 8.00 20.00
10 Jari Kurri 8.00 20.00
11 Esa Tikkanen 8.00 20.00
12 Teemu Selanne 15.00 40.00
13 Saku Koivu 8.00 20.00
14 Miikka Kiprusoff 8.00 20.00
15 Peter Stastny 6.00 15.00
16 Jaromir Jagr 25.00 60.00
17 Dominik Hasek 12.00 30.00
18 Marian Gaborik 6.00 15.00

2010-11 ITG Ultimate Memorabilia Father's Day
1 T.Lindsay/B.Lindsay 10.00 25.00
2 J.Grahame/R.Grahame 10.00 25.00
3 R.Hextall/B.Hextall Jr. 10.00 25.00
4 B.Hull/B.Hull 20.00 50.00
5 E.Nystrom/B.Nystrom 8.00 20.00
6 Z.Parise/J.Parise 10.00 25.00
7 C.Bourque/R.Bourque 10.00 25.00
8 Y.Stastny/P.Stastny 8.00 20.00

2010-11 ITG Ultimate Memorabilia Future Stars Autographs
2 Jacob Markstrom 20.00 50.00
3 Oliver Ekman-Larsson 12.00 30.00
5 Mikkel Boedker 6.00 15.00
6 Colton Gillies 6.00 15.00
7 Cody Hodgson 30.00 60.00
8 Brayden Schenn 20.00 40.00
9 Ryan Nugent-Hopkins 30.00 80.00
10 Kyle Turris 8.00 20.00
13 Jared Cowen 8.00 20.00
14 Lars Eller 6.00 15.00
15 Oscar Moller 8.00 20.00
16 Dana Tyrell 8.00 20.00
17 Karl Alzner 6.00 15.00
18 Tyler Bozak 6.00 15.00
19 Michal Neuvirth 8.00 20.00
20 P.K. Subban 25.00 60.00
21 Vladimir Tarasenko 40.00 80.00
22 Ryan Murray 12.00 30.00
23 Antti Niemi 8.00 20.00

2010-11 ITG Ultimate Memorabilia Future Stars Jerseys Autographs
PATCH/19: .4X TO 1X JSY/24*
2 Nazem Kadri 25.00 60.00
3 Vladimir Tarasenko 75.00 150.00
4 Jacob Markstrom 20.00 50.00
6 Zach Boychuk 8.00 20.00
7 Mikkel Boedker 6.00 15.00
8 Colton Gillies 6.00 15.00
9 Cody Hodgson 30.00 60.00
10 Brayden Schenn 20.00 50.00
11 Ryan Nugent-Hopkins 30.00 80.00
12 Kyle Turris 10.00 25.00
13 Scott Glennie 8.00 20.00
15 Jared Cowen 8.00 20.00
17 Oscar Moller 10.00 25.00
18 Dana Tyrell 8.00 20.00
19 Ryan Murray 12.00 30.00
20 Antti Niemi 8.00 20.00

2010-11 ITG Ultimate Memorabilia Goalies Autographs
1 Martin Brodeur 40.00 80.00
2 Jean-Sebastien Giguere 12.00 30.00
3 Roberto Luongo 15.00 40.00
6 Jonathan Quick 30.00 60.00
8 Semyon Varlamov 20.00 40.00
9 Niklas Backstrom 15.00 40.00
10 Jonas Hiller 10.00 25.00

2010-11 ITG Ultimate Memorabilia Goalies Legends Autographs
1 Patrick Roy 50.00 100.00
2 Glenn Hall 12.00 30.00
4 Tony Esposito 12.00 30.00
5 Gump Worsley 15.00 40.00
6 Bernie Parent 12.00 30.00
7 Ed Giacomin 12.00 30.00
8 Gerry Cheevers 20.00 40.00
9 Vladislav Tretiak 15.00 40.00
10 Dominik Hasek 15.00 40.00

2010-11 ITG Ultimate Memorabilia Goalies Legends Memorabilia Autographs
2 Glenn Hall 12.00 30.00
3 Billy Smith 12.00 30.00
5 Gump Worsley 15.00 40.00
6 Bernie Parent 12.00 30.00
7 Ed Giacomin 25.00 50.00
8 Gerry Cheevers 15.00 40.00
9 Vladislav Tretiak 30.00 60.00
10 Dominik Hasek 25.00 50.00

2010-11 ITG Ultimate Memorabilia Goalies Memorabilia Autographs
1 Martin Brodeur 30.00 60.00
2 Jean-Sebastien Giguere 10.00 25.00
3 Roberto Luongo 40.00 80.00
4 Evgeni Nabokov 8.00 20.00
5 Carey Price 25.00 50.00
6 Jonathan Quick 30.00 60.00
7 Tim Thomas 15.00 40.00
8 Semyon Varlamov 10.00 25.00

2010-11 ITG Ultimate Memorabilia Hall of Famer Autographs
1 Mario Lemieux 50.00 100.00
4 Johnny Bucyk 25.00 50.00
9 Bernie Parent 25.00 50.00
12 Borje Salming 15.00 40.00
13 Glenn Anderson 12.00 30.00
14 Milt Schmidt 15.00 40.00
16 Henri Richard 15.00 40.00
17 Denis Potvin 12.00 30.00
19 Cam Neely 15.00 40.00
20 Ted Lindsay 15.00 40.00
22 Pat Lafontaine 15.00 40.00
23 Guy Lafleur 20.00 50.00
24 Elmer Lach 12.00 30.00
25 Jari Kurri 15.00 40.00
26 Dave Keon 15.00 40.00
27 Phil Esposito 25.00 60.00
28 Marcel Dionne 20.00 50.00
29 Alex Delvecchio 15.00 40.00
30 Paul Coffey 15.00 40.00
31 Ron Francis 12.00 30.00
32 Grant Fuhr 25.00 60.00
33 Jean Beliveau 25.00 50.00
34 Gilbert Perreault 15.00 40.00
35 Luc Robitaille 15.00 40.00
36 Yvan Cournoyer 15.00 40.00
37 Scotty Bowman 15.00 40.00
38 Bert Olmstead 15.00 40.00
39 Brett Hull 30.00 80.00
40 Brad Park 12.00 30.00
43 Igor Larionov 12.00 30.00
44 Serge Savard 15.00 40.00
46 Dick Duff 12.00 30.00
47 Lanny McDonald 10.00 25.00
48 Steve Yzerman 30.00 60.00

2010-11 ITG Ultimate Memorabilia Legends Autographs
1 Doug Gilmour 15.00 40.00
2 Sergei Fedorov 12.00 30.00
3 Jaromir Jagr 25.00 50.00
4 Joe Sakic 25.00 60.00
5 Mats Sundin 25.00 50.00
7 Dominik Hasek 30.00 60.00
8 Joe Nieuwendyk 10.00 25.00
9 Rob Blake 12.00 30.00
10 Chris Chelios 10.00 25.00
11 Scott Niedermayer 12.00 30.00
12 Keith Tkachuk 12.00 30.00
13 Wendel Clark 15.00 40.00
15 Richard Brodeur 12.00 30.00
16 Tod Sloan 10.00 25.00
17 Lou Fontinato 10.00 25.00
18 Pavel Bure 25.00 50.00
21 Peter Forsberg 15.00 40.00

2010-11 ITG Ultimate Memorabilia Les Capitaines
7 Jean Beliveau 12.00 30.00
8 Henri Richard 10.00 25.00
9 Yvan Cournoyer 10.00 25.00
10 Serge Savard 10.00 25.00
11 Bob Gainey 10.00 25.00
12 Guy Carbonneau 10.00 25.00
13 Chris Chelios 10.00 25.00
14 Kirk Muller 6.00 15.00
15 Pierre Turgeon 8.00 20.00
16 Vincent Damphousse 8.00 20.00
17 Saku Koivu 10.00 25.00
18 Brian Gionta 6.00 15.00

2010-11 ITG Ultimate Memorabilia Memorabilia Autographs Duals
COMMON CARD 20.00 40.00
1 Richard/Beliveau 30.00 60.00
2 Keon/Clark 25.00 50.00
3 Brodeur/Luongo 30.00 60.00
4 Thornton/Nash 25.00 50.00
5 Gilbert/Lafleur 30.00 60.00
6 Yzerman/Hull 40.00 80.00
7 Fuhr/Messier 30.00 60.00
8 Lidstrom/Bourque 30.00 60.00
9 Tretiak/Nabokov 30.00 60.00
10 P.Esposito/Bucyk 30.00 60.00
12 Giguere/Bower 20.00 40.00
13 Bure/Neely 25.00 50.00
14 Hull/Mikita 25.00 50.00
15 M.Brodeur/Kovalchuk 30.00 60.00
16 Clarke/Sittler 25.00 50.00
17 Gaborik/Jagr 25.00 50.00
18 Price/Roy 75.00 125.00
19 Niedermayer/Selanne 30.00 60.00

2010-11 ITG Ultimate Memorabilia Pads and Gloves
1 Carey Price 20.00 50.00
2 Olaf Kolzig 10.00 25.00
3 Michael Leighton 8.00 20.00
4 Marc-Andre Fleury 20.00 50.00
5 Ilya Bryzgalov 8.00 20.00
6 Cam Ward 10.00 25.00
7 Dominik Hasek 15.00 40.00
8 Niklas Backstrom 10.00 25.00
9 Gerry Cheevers 10.00 25.00
10 Marty Turco 10.00 25.00
11 Vladislav Tretiak 8.00 20.00
12 Patrick Roy 25.00 60.00
13 Chris Osgood 10.00 25.00
14 Nikolai Khabibulin 8.00 20.00
15 Ed Belfour 10.00 25.00
16 Curtis Joseph 12.00 30.00
17 Martin Brodeur 25.00 60.00
18 Ron Hextall 10.00 25.00
19 Grant Fuhr 15.00 40.00
20 Rick DiPietro 8.00 20.00
21 Tim Thomas 10.00 25.00

2010-11 ITG Ultimate Memorabilia Past Present Future
1 Sittler/Giguere/Kadri 25.00 60.00
2 Perreault/Stamkos/RNH 40.00 80.00
3 Sakic/Thornton/Schenn 20.00 50.00
4 Cheevers/Thomas/Rask 12.00 30.00
5 Yzerman/Lidstrom/Helm 25.00 60.00
6 Messier/Sedin/Hodgson 20.00 50.00
7 Neely/Lucic/Seguin 30.00 80.00
8 Niedermyr/Selanne/Fowler 20.00 50.00
9 Hasek/Osgood/Howard 15.00 40.00
10 Kharlmv/Kvlchk/Tarsnko 25.00 60.00
11 Nieuwendyk/Mrrw/Glenn 8.00 20.00
12 Roy/Miller/Markstrom 25.00 60.00

2010-11 ITG Ultimate Memorabilia Stick and Jersey Autographs
1 Steve Yzerman 50.00 100.00
2 Ryan Getzlaf 30.00 60.00
5 Mark Messier 30.00 60.00
6 Guy Lafleur 25.00 50.00
7 Vincent Lecavalier 12.00 30.00
8 Mats Sundin 15.00 40.00
9 Jean Beliveau 50.00 100.00
10 Rob Blake 12.00 30.00
11 Raymond Bourque 30.00 60.00
12 Wendel Clark 15.00 40.00
14 Marian Gaborik 15.00 40.00
15 Ilya Kovalchuk 25.00 50.00
18 Scott Niedermayer 10.00 25.00
20 Martin Brodeur 30.00 60.00

2010-11 ITG Ultimate Memorabilia Stick Work
1 Peter Forsberg 40.00 100.00
2 Brad Richards 20.00 50.00
3 Eric Staal 25.00 60.00
4 Zdeno Chara 20.00 50.00
5 Miikka Kiprusoff 20.00 50.00
6 Ryan Miller 20.00 50.00
7 Johan Franzen 15.00 40.00
8 Tyler Bozak 12.00 30.00
9 Jaromir Jagr 60.00 150.00
10 Jarome Iginla 25.00 60.00
11 Chris Pronger 20.00 50.00
12 Evgeni Malkin 40.00 100.00
13 Trevor Linden 20.00 50.00
14 Simon Gagne 20.00 50.00
15 Pavel Bure 20.00 50.00
16 Ed Jovanovski 12.00 30.00
17 Jack Johnson 12.00 30.00
18 Joe Sakic 20.00 50.00
19 Steven Stamkos 40.00 100.00
20 Benoit Pouliot 12.00 30.00
21 Ryan Suter 15.00 40.00
22 Joe Thornton 30.00 80.00
23 Tyler Seguin 50.00 100.00
24 Kyle Okposo 12.00 30.00
25 Mike Richter 20.00 50.00
26 Alexander Ovechkin 80.00 200.00
27 Jonathan Toews 30.00 80.00
28 Patrick Kane 40.00 100.00
29 Phil Kessel 20.00 50.00
30 Ilya Kovalchuk 20.00 50.00

2010-11 ITG Ultimate Memorabilia Ultimate All-Stars
1 Teemu Selanne 10.00 25.00
2 Jaromir Jagr 25.00 60.00
3 Joe Thornton 12.00 30.00
4 Mario Lemieux 30.00 80.00
5 Rob Blake 8.00 20.00
6 Nicklas Lidstrom 8.00 20.00
7 Patrick Roy 20.00 50.00
8 Dominik Hasek 12.00 30.00
9 Sergei Fedorov 10.00 25.00
10 Joe Sakic 15.00 40.00
11 Peter Forsberg 15.00 40.00
12 Pavel Bure 8.00 20.00
13 Chris Chelios 8.00 20.00
14 Paul Coffey 8.00 20.00
15 Evgeni Nabokov 6.00 15.00
16 Martin Brodeur 20.00 50.00
17 Steve Yzerman 20.00 50.00
18 Mats Sundin 8.00 20.00
19 Mike Modano 12.00 30.00
20 Mark Messier 15.00 40.00
21 Raymond Bourque 12.00 30.00
22 Scott Niedermayer 8.00 20.00
23 Felix Potvin 12.00 30.00
24 Chris Osgood 8.00 20.00

2010-11 ITG Ultimate Memorabilia Ultimate Rivalry
2 Richrd/Plnte/Howe/Sawchuk 30.00 60.00
3 Beliv/Worsly/Mahvlich/Keon 30.00 60.00
4 Richrd/Fergsn/Baun/Swchk 15.00 40.00
5 P.Espo/Drydn/Trtiak/Khrlm 30.00 60.00
6 Lemre/Cournyr/P.Espo/Orr 40.00 80.00
7 Laflr/Gainey/Mddltn/Chvrs 30.00 60.00
9 Grtzky/Coffy/Bossy/Smith 60.00 120.00
10 Kurri/Andrsn/Mclnn/Loob 15.00 40.00
11 Mess/Fuhr/McDnld/Vern 25.00 60.00
12 Nslnd/Roy/Bchrd/Ststny 25.00 60.00
15 Sndin/Domi/Alfrdsn/Hossa 25.00 50.00
16 Crsby/Mlkin/Ovech/Green 40.00 80.00

2010-11 ITG Ultimate Memorabilia When There Were Six
1 Boston 6 40.00 80.00
2 Chicago 6 40.00 80.00
3 Detroit 6 40.00 80.00
5 Toronto 6 40.00 80.00
6 Montreal 6 75.00 150.00

2011-12 ITG Ultimate Memorabilia
1 Tony Amonte/63* 5.00 12.00
2 Hobey Baker/62* 5.00 12.00
3 Bill Barilko/62* 4.00 10.00
4 Jean Beliveau/62* 8.00 20.00
5 Mike Bossy/63* 6.00 15.00
6 Raymond Bourque/63* 10.00 25.00
7 Johnny Bower/62* 6.00 15.00
8 Turk Broda/63* 6.00 15.00
9 Pavel Bure/63* 6.00 15.00
10 Chris Chelios/62* 6.00 15.00
11 Wendel Clark/63* 10.00 25.00
12 Bobby Clarke/62* 5.00 12.00
13 Paul Coffey/63* 5.00 12.00
14 Marcel Dionne/62* 8.00 20.00
15 Phil Esposito/63* 10.00 25.00
16 Tony Esposito/63* 6.00 15.00
17 Theoren Fleury/63* 8.00 20.00
18 Peter Forsberg/63* 12.00 30.00
19 Ron Francis/63* 8.00 20.00
20 Grant Fuhr/62* 6.00 15.00
21 Bernie Geoffrion/62* 5.00 12.00
22 Ryan Getzlaf/63* 6.00 15.00
23 Ed Giacomin/62* 6.00 15.00
24 Doug Gilmour/62* 8.00 20.00
25 George Hainsworth/62* 6.00 15.00
26 Glenn Hall/62* 6.00 15.00
27 Doug Harvey/62* 6.00 15.00
28 Dominik Hasek/62* 10.00 25.00
29 Ron Hextall/63* 6.00 15.00
30 Tim Horton/63* 8.00 20.00
31 Mark Howe/62* 6.00 15.00
32 Bobby Hull/62* 12.00 30.00
33 Brett Hull/62* 12.00 30.00
34 Jaromir Jagr/62* 20.00 50.00
35 Aurel Joliat/62* 6.00 15.00
36 Curtis Joseph/62* 8.00 20.00
37 Dave Keon/62* 6.00 15.00
38 Valeri Kharlamov/63* 5.00 12.00
39 Ilya Kovalchuk/62* 6.00 15.00
40 Jari Kurri/62* 6.00 15.00
41 Elmer Lach/62* 5.00 12.00
42 Guy Lafleur/62* 8.00 20.00
43 Pat LaFontaine/63* 6.00 15.00
44 Newsy Lalonde/63* 5.00 12.00
45 Igor Larionov/62* 6.00 15.00
46 Vincent Lecavalier/63* 6.00 15.00
47 John LeClair/62* 6.00 15.00
48 Mario Lemieux/62* 25.00 60.00
49 Nicklas Lidstrom/63* 4.00 10.00
50 Pelle Lindbergh/63* 5.00 12.00
51 Trevor Linden/63* 6.00 15.00
52 Eric Lindros/62* 10.00 25.00
53 Ted Lindsay/63* 6.00 15.00
54 Henrik Lundqvist/62* 15.00 40.00
55 Roberto Luongo/63* 8.00 20.00
56 Al MacInnis/62* 8.00 20.00
57 Frank Mahovlich/62* 6.00 15.00
58 Patrick Marleau/63* 6.00 15.00
59 Mark Messier/63* 12.00 30.00
60 Mike Modano/63* 10.00 25.00
61 Howie Morenz/62* 5.00 12.00
62 Rick Nash/63* 6.00 15.00
63 Cam Neely/62* 6.00 15.00
64 Antti Niemi/62* 5.00 12.00
65 Chris Osgood/62* 6.00 15.00
66 Alexander Ovechkin/62* 15.00 40.00
67 Bernie Parent/62* 8.00 20.00
68 Gilbert Perreault/62* 6.00 15.00
69 Jacques Plante/62* 6.00 15.00
70 Denis Potvin/62* 6.00 15.00
71 Felix Potvin/62* 6.00 15.00
72 Carey Price/62* 10.00 25.00
73 Henri Richard/62* 6.00 15.00
74 Maurice Richard/63* 12.00 30.00
75 Mike Richter/63* 6.00 15.00
76 Larry Robinson/62* 6.00 15.00
77 Luc Robitaille/62* 6.00 15.00
78 Jeremy Roenick/62* 10.00 25.00
79 Patrick Roy/63* 12.00 30.00
80 Joe Sakic/62* 12.00 30.00
81 Borje Salming/62* 6.00 15.00
82 Terry Sawchuk/63* 6.00 15.00
83 Milt Schmidt/63* 6.00 15.00
84 Daniel Sedin/62* 8.00 20.00
85 Henrik Sedin/62* 8.00 20.00
86 Teemu Selanne/63* 12.00 30.00
87 Darryl Sittler/62* 8.00 20.00
88 Eric Staal/62* 8.00 20.00
89 Steven Stamkos/63* 10.00 25.00
90 Cyclone Taylor/62* 8.00 20.00
91 Tim Thomas/63* 6.00 15.00
92 Joe Thornton/62* 10.00 25.00
93 Keith Tkachuk/62* 6.00 15.00
94 Vladislav Tretiak/63* 5.00 12.00
95 Mike Vernon/63* 5.00 12.00
96 Georges Vezina/62* 6.00 15.00
97 Cam Ward/62* 6.00 15.00
98 Shea Weber/63* 5.00 12.00
99 Gump Worsley/62* 6.00 15.00
100 Steve Yzerman/63* 12.00 30.00

2011-12 ITG Ultimate Memorabilia 600 Goal Combo Memorabilia
1 D.Andreychuk/C.Schwab 12.00 30.00
2 D.Ciccarelli/C.Osgood 12.00 30.00
3 M.Dionne/Lemelin 12.00 30.00
4 P.Esposito/C.Maniago 15.00 40.00
5 M.Gartner/C.Terreri 15.00 40.00
6 W.Gretzky/G.Stefan 30.00 80.00
7 G.Howe/G.Worsley 20.00 50.00
8 Bo.Hull/G.Cheevers 20.00 50.00

9 Br.Hull/G.Hebert 30.00 80.00
10 J.Jagr/J.Holmqvist 15.00 40.00
11 J.Kurri/S.Fiset 15.00 40.00
12 Mario Lemieux 15.00 40.00
13 M.Messier/K.McLean 20.00 50.00
14 L.Robitaille/JS Giguere 12.00 30.00
15 Joe Sakic 15.00 40.00
16 B.Shanahan/O.Kolzig 15.00 40.00
17 T.Selanne/C.Anderson 15.00 40.00
18 S.Yzerman/T.Salo 20.00 40.00

2011-12 ITG Ultimate Memorabilia All-Stars Memorabilia

1 Raymond Bourque 15.00 40.00
2 Pavel Bure 10.00 25.00
4 Theoren Fleury 12.00 30.00
5 Peter Forsberg 10.00 25.00
6 Dominik Hasek 15.00 40.00
7 Brett Hull 12.00 30.00
8 Jaromir Jagr 15.00 40.00
9 Curtis Joseph 10.00 25.00
10 Brian Leetch 12.00 30.00
11 Mario Lemieux 15.00 40.00
12 Nicklas Lidstrom 12.00 30.00
13 Eric Lindros 12.00 30.00
15 Patrick Roy 20.00 50.00
16 Steve Yzerman 15.00 40.00

2011-12 ITG Ultimate Memorabilia Autographs

2 Ilya Bryzgalov 15.00 40.00
3 Zdeno Chara 12.00 30.00
4 Marian Gaborik 12.00 30.00
5 Ryan Getzlaf 12.00 30.00
6 Claude Giroux 15.00 40.00
8 Jimmy Howard 15.00 30.00
9 Jaromir Jagr 40.00 80.00
10 Ryan Kesler 8.00 20.00
11 Mikko Koivu 6.00 15.00
12 Saku Koivu 8.00 20.00
13 Ilya Kovalchuk 12.00 30.00
14 Vincent Lecavalier 12.00 30.00
16 Henrik Lundqvist 40.00 80.00
17 Roberto Luongo 12.00 30.00
19 Brenden Morrow 6.00 15.00
20 Rick Nash 8.00 20.00
21 Antti Niemi 8.00 20.00
22 Alexander Ovechkin 50.00 100.00
23 Carey Price 25.00 50.00
24 Dwayne Roloson 6.00 15.00
25 Daniel Sedin 10.00 25.00
26 Henrik Sedin 10.00 25.00
27 Teemu Selanne 12.00 30.00
28 Alexander Semin 8.00 20.00
29 Martin St. Louis 8.00 20.00
30 Eric Staal 10.00 25.00
31 Steven Stamkos 30.00 60.00
32 Joe Thornton 12.00 30.00
33 Semyon Varlamov 8.00 20.00
34 Tomas Vokoun 6.00 15.00
35 Shea Weber 6.00 15.00

2011-12 ITG Ultimate Memorabilia Blue and White Captains Memorabilia

1 Wendel Clark/24* 15.00 40.00
3 Doug Gilmour/24* 12.00 30.00
6 Darryl Sittler/24* 10.00 25.00
7 Mats Sundin/24* 10.00 25.00
8 Rick Vaive/24* 10.00 25.00

2011-12 ITG Ultimate Memorabilia Country of Origin Memorabilia

1 C.Chelios/B.Leetch 15.00 40.00
2 P.Forsberg/M.Sundin 12.00 30.00
3 M.Gaborik/J.Halak 15.00 40.00
4 D.Hasek/J.Jagr 20.00 50.00
5 B.Hull/M.Modano 10.00 25.00
6 V.Kharlamov/A.Yakushev 15.00 40.00
7 J.Kurri/T.Selanne 15.00 40.00
8 M.Lemieux/J.Sakic 20.00 50.00
9 P.Lindbergh/H.Lundqvist 25.00 60.00
10 M.Messier/S.Yzerman 20.00 50.00
11 A.Ovechkin/I.Kovalchuk 30.00 80.00
12 B.Salming/N.Lidstrom 15.00 40.00

2011-12 ITG Ultimate Memorabilia Cup Finals Memorabilia

2 Bss/Smth/Trt/Wllm/Brd/Snps 20.00 50.00
3 Clrk/Prnt/Mclsh/Prlt/Mrt/Crzr 20.00 50.00
4 Crny/Mvl/Lpn/Esp/Stp/Mkt 20.00 50.00
5 Flry/Mac/Vrn/Roy/Nsld/Rbi 20.00 50.00
6 Fhr/Esa/Ands/Moog/Brg/Nly 20.00 50.00
8 Hort/Keon/Mvl/Rgl/Bli/Rich 25.00 60.00
9 Jari/Mss/Coff/Trot/LaFnt/Gill 25.00 60.00
10 Guy/Lmr/Rbi/Chvr/Mdlt/Park 25.00 60.00
11 Ltch/Mss/Rctr/Kirk/Lnd/Bre 30.00 80.00
12 Mrio/Jgr/Brso/Chls/Rnck/Gul 30.00 80.00
13 Sak/Roy/Brg/Mgl/Ndrm/Nwn 25.00 60.00
14 Tmu/Ndrm/Gig/Emry/Spz/Grb 20.00 50.00
15 Thm/Chr/Brgn/Lngo/Sdin/Sdin 25.00 60.00
16 Yzer/Ldst/Vrn/Lndr/LeCl/Hex 20.00 50.00

2011-12 ITG Ultimate Memorabilia Days Gone By Memorabilia

2 Bossy/O'Reilly/Dionne/Shutt 15.00 40.00
5 Br.Hull/Sakic/Lemieux/Neely 25.00 60.00
6 Messr/Goulet/Yzerm/Gilmr 15.00 40.00
7 McDonld/Brdr/Sttsny/Brque 12.00 30.00
8 Park/T.Esp/Potvn/H.Richrd 15.00 40.00
9 M.Richd/Delvc/Bucyk/Bo.Hll 15.00 40.00
10 Roenick/Leetch/Bure/Nieder 15.00 40.00
11 Roy/Hawrchk/Ciccarl/Hextll 20.00 50.00
12 Sawchuk/Hall/Giaco/Vachn 20.00 50.00

2011-12 ITG Ultimate Memorabilia Draft Day Memorabilia

1 MA Fleury/J.Halak 15.00 40.00
2 M.Gaborik/H.Lundqvist 15.00 40.00
3 D.Hawerchuk/J.Vanbiesbrouck 20.00 50.00
6 M.Lemieux/L.Robitaille 20.00 50.00
7 A.Ovechkin/P.Rinne 15.00 40.00
9 D.Savard/J.Kurri 8.00 20.00
10 H.Sedin/R.Miller 12.00 30.00
11 M.Sundin/P.Bure 12.00 30.00
12 S.Yzerman/D.Hasek 15.00 40.00

2011-12 ITG Ultimate Memorabilia Dynamic Duos Memorabilia

1 B.Barber/B.Clarke 12.00 30.00
2 P.Bure/T.Linden 15.00 40.00
3 D.Gilmour/W.Clark 20.00 50.00
4 Bo.Hull/S.Mikita 12.00 30.00
5 G.Lafleur/Y.Cournoyer 12.00 30.00
6 J.LeClair/E.Lindros 12.00 30.00
7 M.Lemieux/J.Jagr 20.00 50.00
8 M.Messier/B.Leetch 12.00 30.00
9 A.Ovechkin/A.Semin 20.00 50.00
10 D.Sittler/L.McDonald 10.00 25.00

2011-12 ITG Ultimate Memorabilia Entire Career Memorabilia

1 Jean Beliveau 15.00 40.00
2 Mike Bossy 8.00 20.00
3 Bobby Clarke 8.00 20.00
4 Alex Delvecchio 8.00 20.00
5 Rod Gilbert 8.00 20.00
6 Mario Lemieux 15.00 40.00
7 Stan Mikita 8.00 20.00
9 Denis Potvin 8.00 20.00
10 Henri Richard 12.00 30.00
11 Mike Richter 8.00 20.00
12 Steve Yzerman 15.00 40.00

2011-12 ITG Ultimate Memorabilia Franchise Favorites Memorabilia

1 Delv/Yzer/Lids/Osgd 20.00 50.00
2 Giac/Ltch/Msr/Lund 15.00 40.00
3 Glet/Stast/Bchrd/Skic 15.00 40.00
4 Hall/Br.Hll/Jsph/Mcln 15.00 40.00
5 Bo.Hll/Hwrch/Crly/Slne 15.00 40.00
6 Keon/Sitt/Slm/Sndin 15.00 40.00
7 Mrnz/M.Rich/Roy/Prce 50.00 100.00
8 Mosi/Bo.Hll/T.Esp/Svrd 15.00 40.00
9 Prnt/Clrke/Hxtll/Lndros 25.00 60.00
10 Swchk/Vchn/Dnne/Rbit 20.00 50.00

2011-12 ITG Ultimate Memorabilia Future Star Autograph Jerseys

*PATCH/19: .5X TO 1.2X BASIC JSY AU/30
1 Jake Allen 15.00 40.00
2 Sven Bartschi 10.00 25.00
3 Jonathan Bernier 8.00 20.00
4 Sergei Bobrovsky 15.00 40.00
5 Zach Boychuk 6.00 15.00
6 Jordan Caron 10.00 25.00
7 Logan Couture 12.00 30.00
8 Sean Couturier 15.00 40.00
9 Michael Del Zotto 10.00 25.00
10 Taylor Doherty 8.00 20.00
11 Oliver Ekman-Larsson 10.00 25.00
12 Lars Eller 6.00 15.00
13 Blake Geoffrion 8.00 20.00
14 Colton Gillies 6.00 15.00
15 Dougie Hamilton 12.00 30.00
16 Thomas Hickey 8.00 20.00
17 Cody Hodgson 20.00 50.00
18 Nazem Kadri 12.00 30.00
19 Adam Larsson 10.00 25.00
20 Ryan Murray 15.00 40.00
21 Greg Nemisz 12.00 30.00
22 Stuart Percy 10.00 25.00
23 Matt Puempel 10.00 25.00
24 Griffin Reinhart 12.00 30.00
25 Duncan Siemens 6.00 15.00
26 Kyle Turris 8.00 20.00
27 Dana Tyrell 6.00 15.00
28 Tyler Wotherspoon 10.00 25.00

2011-12 ITG Ultimate Memorabilia Future Star Autographs

1 Jake Allen 12.00 30.00
2 Sven Bartschi 8.00 20.00
3 Jonathan Bernier 6.00 15.00
4 Sergei Bobrovsky 12.00 30.00
5 Zach Boychuk 5.00 12.00
6 Jordan Caron 8.00 20.00
7 Logan Couture 10.00 25.00
8 Sean Couturier 12.00 30.00
9 Taylor Doherty 6.00 15.00
10 Oliver Ekman-Larsson 8.00 20.00
11 Lars Eller 5.00 12.00
12 Blake Geoffrion 6.00 15.00
13 Colton Gillies 5.00 12.00
14 Dougie Hamilton 10.00 25.00
15 Thomas Hickey 6.00 15.00
16 Cody Hodgson 25.00 50.00
17 Nazem Kadri 10.00 25.00
18 Adam Larsson 8.00 20.00
19 Ryan Murray 12.00 30.00
20 Greg Nemisz 6.00 15.00
21 Stuart Percy 8.00 20.00
22 Matt Puempel 8.00 20.00
23 Griffin Reinhart 8.00 20.00
24 Duncan Siemens 5.00 12.00
25 Kyle Turris 6.00 15.00
26 Dana Tyrell 5.00 12.00
27 Tyler Wotherspoon 8.00 20.00
28 Mika Zibanejad 20.00 50.00

2011-12 ITG Ultimate Memorabilia Gloves Are Off Memorabilia

1 Bobby Clarke 15.00 40.00
2 Marian Gaborik 8.00 20.00
3 Ryan Getzlaf 8.00 20.00
4 Brett Hull 12.00 30.00
5 Denis Potvin 8.00 20.00
6 Luc Robitaille 8.00 20.00
7 Joe Thornton 8.00 20.00
8 Bryan Trottier 8.00 20.00

2011-12 ITG Ultimate Memorabilia Goalie Autograph Jerseys

1 Niklas Backstrom 12.00 30.00
2 Marc-Andre Fleury 25.00 60.00
3 Jaroslav Halak 12.00 30.00
4 Henrik Lundqvist 30.00 80.00
5 Roberto Luongo 20.00 50.00
6 Antti Niemi 10.00 25.00
7 Chris Osgood 12.00 30.00
8 Carey Price 25.00 60.00
9 Jonathan Quick 25.00 50.00
10 Tim Thomas 25.00 60.00

2011-12 ITG Ultimate Memorabilia Goalie Autograph Memorabilia

1 Craig Anderson 12.00 30.00
2 Niklas Backstrom 12.00 30.00
3 Marc-Andre Fleury 25.00 60.00
4 Nikolai Khabibulin 15.00 40.00
5 Henrik Lundqvist 30.00 80.00
6 Roberto Luongo 20.00 50.00
7 Chris Osgood 12.00 30.00
8 Carey Price 25.00 60.00
9 Tim Thomas 30.00 60.00
10 Tomas Vokoun 10.00 25.00

2011-12 ITG Ultimate Memorabilia Goalie Generations Memorabilia

1 T.Esp/Vachn/Tretiak 15.00 40.00
2 Giac/Sawchk/Chvers 10.00 25.00
3 Hall/Crozier/Sawchuk 12.00 30.00
4 Hall/Worsley/Sawchuk 25.00 50.00
5 Hasek/Kolzig/Potvin 25.00 60.00
6 Moog/Brodeur/Lind 25.00 60.00
7 Osgood/Vanbies/Irbe 25.00 60.00
8 Parent/Meloche/Smith 15.00 40.00
9 Plante/Lumly/Sawchk 15.00 40.00
10 Richter/Roy/Joseph 25.00 60.00
11 Roy/Vernon/Barasso 25.00 60.00

2011-12 ITG Ultimate Memorabilia Goalie Legend Autograph Jerseys

1 Tony Esposito 15.00 40.00
2 Ed Giacomin 12.00 30.00
3 Glenn Hall 15.00 40.00
4 Dominik Hasek 15.00 40.00
5 Arturs Irbe 12.00 30.00
6 Curtis Joseph 15.00 40.00
7 Bernie Parent 15.00 40.00
8 Patrick Roy 40.00 80.00
9 Billy Smith 12.00 30.00
10 Mike Vernon 10.00 25.00

2011-12 ITG Ultimate Memorabilia Goalie Legend Autograph Memorabilia

1 Sean Burke 10.00 25.00
2 Tony Esposito 15.00 40.00
3 Dominik Hasek 15.00 40.00
4 Ron Hextall 12.00 30.00
5 Arturs Irbe 12.00 30.00
6 Curtis Joseph 15.00 40.00
7 Bernie Parent 15.00 40.00
8 Patrick Roy 40.00 80.00
9 Vladislav Tretiak 25.00 50.00
10 Mike Vernon 10.00 25.00

2011-12 ITG Ultimate Memorabilia Goalie Legend Autographs

1 Gerry Cheevers 10.00 25.00
2 Tony Esposito 12.00 30.00
3 Grant Fuhr 15.00 40.00
4 Ed Giacomin 12.00 30.00
5 Glenn Hall 10.00 25.00
6 Dominik Hasek 12.00 30.00
7 Curtis Joseph 12.00 30.00
8 Bernie Parent 12.00 30.00
9 Patrick Roy 30.00 60.00
10 Billy Smith 10.00 25.00

2011-12 ITG Ultimate Memorabilia Hall of Famer Autographs

1 Glenn Anderson/15* 8.00 20.00
3 Andy Bathgate/15* 12.00 30.00
6 Raymond Bourque/15* 25.00 50.00
7 Johnny Bower/15* 20.00 40.00
8 Scotty Bowman/15* 12.00 30.00
9 Gerry Cheevers/15* 12.00 30.00
10 Dino Ciccarelli/15* 10.00 25.00
11 Paul Coffey/15* 15.00 40.00
12 Yvan Cournoyer/15* 12.00 30.00
13 Marcel Dionne/15* 15.00 40.00
15 Phil Esposito/15* 25.00 50.00
16 Tony Esposito/15* 12.00 30.00
17 Grant Fuhr/15* 15.00 40.00
19 Mike Gartner/15* 12.00 30.00
20 Ed Giacomin/15* 12.00 30.00
21 Glenn Hall/15* 12.00 30.00
22 Dale Hawerchuk/15* 15.00 40.00
23 Harry Howell/15* 10.00 25.00
24 Bobby Hull/15* 30.00 60.00
25 Brett Hull/15* 30.00 60.00
26 Red Kelly/15* 10.00 25.00
28 Jari Kurri/15* 15.00 40.00
29 Elmer Lach/15* 10.00 25.00
30 Guy Lafleur/15* 20.00 40.00
31 Pat Lafontaine/15* 10.00 25.00
32 Rod Langway/15* 10.00 25.00
35 Brian Leetch/15* 10.00 25.00
40 Stan Mikita/15* 12.00 30.00
41 Dickie Moore/15* 12.00 30.00
42 Cam Neely/15* 15.00 40.00
44 Bernie Parent/15* 12.00 30.00
45 Brad Park/15* 8.00 20.00
46 Gilbert Perreault/15* 12.00 30.00
47 Pierre Pilote/15* 12.00 30.00
48 Denis Potvin/15* 10.00 25.00
50 Luc Robitaille/15* 25.00 50.00
51 Patrick Roy/15* 40.00 80.00
52 Borje Salming/15* 10.00 25.00
53 Serge Savard/15* 10.00 25.00
54 Milt Schmidt/15* 12.00 30.00
55 Darryl Sittler/15* 10.00 25.00
56 Billy Smith/15* 10.00 25.00
57 Vladislav Tretiak/15* 30.00 60.00
58 Norm Ullman/15* 10.00 25.00

2011-12 ITG Ultimate Memorabilia Idols Memorabilia

1 J.Beliveau/G.Lafleur 12.00 30.00
2 D.Bouchard/P.Roy 20.00 50.00
4 G.Fuhr/R.Luongo 12.00 30.00
5 Kharlamov/Ovechkin 25.00 60.00
6 J.Kurri/T.Selanne 12.00 30.00
7 G.Lafleur/M.Lemieux 20.00 50.00
8 LaFontaine/Thornton 12.00 30.00
9 L.McDonald/T.Linden 12.00 30.00
10 M.Messier/T.Amonte 10.00 25.00
11 M.Messier/E.Lindros 15.00 40.00
12 M.Naslund/M.Sundin 12.00 30.00
14 J.Plante/B.Parent 12.00 30.00
16 P.Roy/D.Cloutier 20.00 50.00
17 B.Salming/N.Lidstrom 12.00 30.00
18 M.Sundin/R.Nash 12.00 30.00
19 B.Trottier/S.Yzerman 15.00 40.00
20 S.Yzerman/S.Stamkos 15.00 40.00

2011-12 ITG Ultimate Memorabilia Journey Jersey Memorabilia

1 Chris Chelios 8.00 20.00
2 Theoren Fleury 10.00 25.00
3 Peter Forsberg 15.00 40.00
4 Michel Goulet 6.00 15.00
5 Bobby Hull 12.00 30.00
6 Dave Keon 8.00 20.00
7 Ilya Kovalchuk 8.00 20.00
8 Roberto Luongo 10.00 25.00
9 Al MacInnis 6.00 15.00
10 Scott Niedermayer 6.00 15.00
11 Teemu Selanne 12.50 30.00
12 Darryl Sittler 10.00 25.00
13 Joe Thornton 12.00 30.00
14 Keith Tkachuk 8.00 20.00
15 Rogie Vachon 10.00 25.00
16 John Vanbiesbrouck 10.00 25.00

2011-12 ITG Ultimate Memorabilia Lord Stanley's Mug Memorabilia

1 Anderson/Fuhr/Messier/24* 15.00 40.00
2 Chara/Thomas/Bergeron/24* 15.00 40.00
3 Cheevers/Bucyk/Esposito/24* 15.00 40.00
4 Clarke/Barber/Parent/24* 15.00 40.00
5 Fleury/McDnld/MacInnis/24* 15.00 40.00
7 Hasek/Larionov/Hull/24* 20.00 50.00
8 Jagr/Lemieux/Francis/24* 25.00 60.00
9 Kurri/Coffey/Messier/24* 15.00 40.00
10 Lecav/St.Louis/Khabib/24* 20.00 50.00
11 Messier/Richter/Leetch/24* 12.00 30.00
12 Osgood/Lidstrom/Chelios/24* 15.00 40.00
14 Potvin/Bossy/Trottier/24* 12.00 30.00
15 Robinson/Roy/Naslund/24* 20.00 50.00
16 Roy/Bourque/Sakic/24* 20.00 50.00
17 Roy/Carbonneau/Savard/24* 20.00 50.00
19 Selanne/Nieder/Getzlaf/24* 20.00 50.00
20 Yzerman/Vernon/Fedor/24* 20.00 50.00

2011-12 ITG Ultimate Memorabilia Number 11 Memorabilia

1 Daniel Alfredsson 8.00 20.00
2 Tony Amonte 6.00 15.00
3 Mike Gartner 10.00 25.00
4 Saku Koivu 12.00 30.00
5 Anze Kopitar 10.00 25.00
6 Gary Leeman 6.00 15.00
7 Mark Messier 15.00 40.00
8 Kirk Muller 6.00 15.00
9 Ulf Nilsson 6.00 15.00
10 Mark Recchi 8.00 20.00
11 Jordan Staal 6.00 15.00

2011-12 ITG Ultimate Memorabilia Past Present Future Memorabilia

1 Bourq/Chara/Hamltn 15.00 40.00
2 Bure/Ovech/Trsnk 30.00 80.00
3 Franc/Staal/Bychk 12.00 30.00
4 Joseph/Halak/Allen 12.00 30.00
5 Irbe/Ward/Murphy 20.00 50.00
6 Lind/Lund/Markstrm 15.00 40.00
7 Linden/Sedin/Hdgsn 15.00 40.00
8 McDnld/Grabv/Kdri 12.00 30.00
10 Slmng/Lids/E-Larssn 12.00 30.00
11 Selne/Thrntn/Cture 15.00 40.00
12 Vachn/Quick/Bernr 12.00 30.00

2011-12 ITG Ultimate Memorabilia Plus Minus Memorabilia

1 Bobby Clarke 8.00 20.00
2 Theoren Fleury 10.00 25.00
3 Ron Francis 8.00 20.00
4 Mark Howe 6.00 15.00
5 Guy Lafleur 10.00 25.00
6 Mario Lemieux 15.00 40.00
7 Larry Robinson 8.00 20.00
8 Martin St. Louis 6.00 15.00
9 Joe Sakic 8.00 20.00
10 Bryan Trottier 8.00 20.00

2011-12 ITG Ultimate Memorabilia The Boys Are Back Memorabilia

1 Hawerchuk/Little 10.00 25.00
2 Bo.Hull/B.Maxwell 8.00 20.00
3 Khabibulin/Mason 10.00 25.00
4 T.Selanne/A.Ladd 12.00 30.00
5 Carlyle/Selanne/Steen 15.00 40.00
6 Bo.Hll/Hawer/Tkchk 12.00 30.00
7 Khabi/Tkchk/Bo.Hull 15.00 40.00
8 Veisor/Rdick/Khab 12.00 30.00
9 Crly/Bo.Hll/Selne/Kyte 15.00 40.00
10 Hawr/Tkchk/Stn/Khbi 12.00 30.00
11 Khbi/Crlyle/Hnsy/Masn 12.00 30.00
12 Selne/Tkchk/Ldd/Ltle 15.00 40.00

2011-12 ITG Ultimate Memorabilia Ultimate Rivalry Memorabilia

2 Bli/Crn/Lma/Kn/Hrt/Mho/19* 20.00 50.00
3 Glt/Sts/Hntr/Ns/Crb/Ry/19* 30.00 80.00
4 Hal/Hul/Mkt/Crz/Ulm/Dlv/19* 15.00 40.00
5 Hed/Esp/Nls/Bss/Trt/Pot/19* 15.00 40.00
8 Rct/Mss/Ltc/Hx/LCl/Lind/19* 25.00 60.00
9 Ry/Frs/Skc/Yzr/Osg/Lids/19* 50.00 120.00
12 Stm/Lcv/StL/Hrt/Ws/Bw/19* 15.00 40.00

2012-13 ITG Ultimate Memorabilia

1 Dave Andreychuk 5.00 12.00
2 Ed Belfour 5.00 12.00
3 Jean Beliveau 5.00 12.00
4 Peter Bondra 5.00 12.00
5 Mike Bossy 5.00 12.00
6 Raymond Bourque 8.00 20.00
7 Johnny Bower 5.00 12.00
8 Turk Broda 5.00 12.00
9 Pavel Bure 5.00 12.00
10 Gerry Cheevers 5.00 12.00
11 Chris Chelios 5.00 12.00
12 Wendel Clark 8.00 20.00
13 Bobby Clarke 8.00 20.00
14 Paul Coffey 5.00 12.00
15 Marcel Dionne 6.00 15.00
16 Jonathan Drouin 10.00 25.00
17 Phil Esposito 8.00 20.00
18 Tony Esposito 5.00 12.00
19 Sergei Fedorov 6.00 15.00
20 Marc-Andre Fleury 10.00 25.00
21 Theoren Fleury 6.00 15.00
22 Peter Forsberg 10.00 25.00
23 Grant Fuhr 6.00 15.00
24 Marian Gaborik 5.00 12.00
25 Doug Gilmour 6.00 15.00
26 Claude Giroux 6.00 15.00
27 Glenn Hall 5.00 12.00
28 Doug Harvey 5.00 12.00
29 Dominik Hasek 8.00 20.00
30 Dale Hawerchuk 6.00 15.00
31 Jimmy Howard 6.00 15.00
32 Gordie Howe 15.00 40.00
33 Bobby Hull 10.00 25.00
34 Brett Hull 10.00 25.00
35 Jaromir Jagr 10.00 25.00
36 Seth Jones 6.00 15.00
37 Curtis Joseph 6.00 15.00
38 Red Kelly 5.00 12.00
39 Dave Keon 5.00 12.00
40 Valeri Kharlamov 4.00 10.00
41 Jari Kurri 5.00 12.00
42 Elmer Lach 4.00 10.00
43 Guy Lafleur 6.00 15.00
44 Pat LaFontaine 5.00 12.00
45 Mario Lemieux 20.00 50.00
46 Nicklas Lidstrom 5.00 12.00
47 Pelle Lindbergh 4.00 10.00
48 Trevor Linden 5.00 12.00
49 Eric Lindros 6.00 15.00
50 Ted Lindsay 5.00 12.00
51 Henrik Lundqvist 12.00 30.00
52 Roberto Luongo 8.00 20.00
53 Al MacInnis 5.00 12.00
54 Nathan MacKinnon 8.00 20.00
55 Frank Mahovlich 5.00 12.00
56 Evgeni Malkin 10.00 25.00
57 Lanny McDonald 5.00 12.00
58 Mark Messier 10.00 25.00
59 Stan Mikita 6.00 15.00
60 Mike Modano 8.00 20.00
61 Sean Monahan 6.00 15.00
62 Howie Morenz 4.00 10.00
63 Cam Neely 5.00 12.00
64 Scott Niedermayer 5.00 12.00
65 Owen Nolan 5.00 12.00
66 Adam Oates 5.00 12.00
67 Chris Osgood 5.00 12.00
68 Alexander Ovechkin 10.00 25.00
69 Bernie Parent 6.00 15.00
70 Gilbert Perreault 5.00 12.00
71 Jacques Plante 6.00 15.00
72 Felix Potvin 8.00 20.00
73 Carey Price 10.00 25.00
74 Jonathan Quick 6.00 15.00
75 Mark Recchi 5.00 12.00
76 Henri Richard 5.00 12.00
77 Maurice Richard 10.00 25.00
78 Larry Robinson 5.00 12.00
79 Luc Robitaille 5.00 12.00
80 Jeremy Roenick 8.00 20.00
81 Patrick Roy 8.00 20.00
82 Patrick Roy 8.00 20.00
83 Joe Sakic 10.00 25.00
84 Borje Salming 6.00 15.00
85 Denis Savard 5.00 12.00
86 Terry Sawchuk 5.00 12.00
87 Daniel Sedin 5.00 12.00
88 Henrik Sedin 6.00 15.00
89 Teemu Selanne 8.00 20.00
90 Eddie Shore 4.00 10.00
91 Darryl Sittler 6.00 15.00
92 Martin St. Louis 6.00 15.00
93 Peter Stastny 4.00 10.00
94 Mats Sundin 8.00 20.00
95 Joe Thornton 8.00 20.00
96 Keith Tkachuk 6.00 15.00
97 Vladislav Tretiak 4.00 10.00
98 Steve Yzerman 10.00 25.00

2012-13 ITG Ultimate Memorabilia Silver

SILVER/30: .5X TO 1.2X BASIC CARD

2012-13 ITG Ultimate Memorabilia 500 Goal Scorer Stick Rack

2 Bondra/Recchi/Modano/24* 25.00 60.00
4 Ciccarelli/Lemieux/Messier/24* 50.00 100.00
5 Gartner/Goulet/Kurri/24* 30.00 60.00
6 Gretzky/McDonald/Trottier/24* 50.00 100.00
7 Lafleur/Bossy/Perreault/24* 30.00 60.00
8 Mullen/Andreychu/Robitaille/24* 30.00 60.00
10 Roenick/Tkachuk/Iginla/24* 30.00 80.00
11 Sakic/Nieuwendyk/Jagr/24* 30.00 80.00
12 Turgeon/Sundin/Selanne/24* 25.00 60.00
13 Verbeek/Francis/Shanahan/24* 40.00 80.00
14 Yzerman/Hawerchuk/Hull/24* 50.00 100.00

2012-13 ITG Ultimate Memorabilia All-Star Player Memorabilia

1 Tony Amonte 8.00 20.00
2 Raymond Bourque 15.00 40.00
3 Pavel Bure 15.00 40.00
4 Chris Chelios 10.00 25.00
5 Sergei Fedorov 15.00 40.00
6 Theoren Fleury 12.00 30.00
7 Peter Forsberg 20.00 50.00
8 Dominik Hasek 15.00 40.00
9 Jaromir Jagr 30.00 80.00
10 John LeClair 10.00 25.00
11 Mario Lemieux 30.00 60.00
12 Nicklas Lidstrom 10.00 25.00
13 Eric Lindros 15.00 40.00
14 Al MacInnis 12.00 30.00
15 Mark Messier 12.00 30.00
16 Mike Modano 15.00 40.00
17 Jeremy Roenick 20.00 40.00
18 Patrick Roy 25.00 60.00
19 Teemu Selanne 15.00 40.00
20 Mats Sundin 12.00 30.00

2012-13 ITG Ultimate Memorabilia All-Star Year Memorabilia

1 Amonte/Bourque/Bure 15.00 40.00
2 Belfour/Forsberg/Lindros 25.00 60.00
3 Bondra/Hasek/Fleury 12.00 30.00
4 Bure/Fleury/LeClair 15.00 40.00
5 Chelios/Hull/Messier 25.00 60.00
6 Coffey/Sundin/Yzerman 30.00 80.00
7 Fedorov/Fleury/Forsberg 15.00 40.00
8 Fedorov/Hasek/Jagr 40.00 100.00
9 Fedorov/Irbe/MacInnis 25.00 60.00
10 Fedorov/LeClair/Osgood 15.00 40.00
11 Forsberg/Hasek/Lindros 25.00 60.00
12 Gaborik/Jagr/Khabibulin 15.00 40.00
13 Hasek/Khabibulin/Roy 30.00 80.00
14 Hasek/Lemieux/Lidstrom 50.00 125.00
15 Hasek/Selanne/Bondra 12.00 30.00
16 Hasek/Roy/Belfour 20.00 50.00
17 Hebert/Nolan/Bourque 12.00 30.00
18 Hull/Joseph/Roenick 25.00 60.00
19 Irbe/Lidstrom/Modano 15.00 40.00
20 Jagr/Joseph/Kolzig 15.00 40.00
21 Khabibulin/Jagr/Chelios 40.00 100.00
22 Khabibulin/Lemieux/Nolan 15.00 40.00
23 Khabibulin/Robitaille/Selanne 15.00 40.00
24 LeClair/Lindros/MacInnis 15.00 40.00
25 LeClair/Niedermayer/Belfour 12.00 30.00
26 Lemieux/Jagr/Potvin 20.00 50.00
27 Lidstrom/Roy/Selanne 30.00 80.00
28 Lindros/Forsberg/MacInnis 25.00 50.00
29 Messier/Housley/Amonte 25.00 60.00
30 Messier/Modano/Nolan 25.00 60.00
31 Messier/Modano/Sakic 25.00 60.00
32 Messier/Recchi/Bourque 25.00 60.00
33 Nabokov/Roy/Sakic 20.00 40.00
34 Recchi/Richter/Roenick 15.00 40.00
35 Roy/Bourque/Bure 30.00 60.00
36 Roy/Selanne/Bure 25.00 60.00
37 Sundin/Tkachuk/Amonte 12.00 30.00
38 Sundin/Yzerman/Bure 25.00 60.00
39 Roy/Selanne/Lidstrom 30.00 60.00
40 Thornton/Burke/Chelios 20.00 50.00

2012-13 ITG Ultimate Memorabilia Autograph Jerseys

1 Marian Gaborik 12.00 30.00
2 Claude Giroux 12.00 30.00
3 Jaromir Jagr 30.00 60.00
4 Ryan Kesler 12.00 30.00
5 Henrik Lundqvist 30.00 60.00
6 Evgeni Malkin 25.00 50.00
7 Patrick Marleau 12.00 30.00
8 Alexander Ovechkin 30.00 80.00
9 Jonathan Quick 25.00 60.00
10 Daniel Sedin 12.00 30.00
11 Henrik Sedin 12.00 30.00
12 Teemu Selanne 25.00 60.00
13 Martin St. Louis 12.00 30.00
14 Joe Thornton 20.00 50.00
15 Jakub Voracek 10.00 25.00
16 Shea Weber 10.00 25.00

2012-13 ITG Ultimate Memorabilia Autographs

1 Marian Gaborik 10.00 25.00
2 Claude Giroux 10.00 25.00
3 Jaromir Jagr 25.00 50.00
4 Ryan Kesler 10.00 25.00
5 Henrik Lundqvist 25.00 60.00
6 Evgeni Malkin 20.00 50.00
7 Patrick Marleau 10.00 25.00
8 Alexander Ovechkin 25.00 60.00
9 Jonathan Quick 20.00 50.00
10 Daniel Sedin 10.00 25.00
11 Henrik Sedin 10.00 25.00
12 Teemu Selanne 15.00 40.00
13 Martin St. Louis 10.00 25.00
14 Joe Thornton 15.00 40.00
15 Jakub Voracek 8.00 20.00
16 Shea Weber 8.00 20.00

2012-13 ITG Ultimate Memorabilia Country of Origin Memorabilia

1 Bondra/Gaborik/Stastny 25.00 60.00
2 Bure/Fedorov/Khabibulin 25.00 60.00
3 Esposito/Sittler/Bossy 20.00 50.00
4 Hasek/Jagr/Holik 40.00 100.00
5 Kharlmv/Mikhailv/Tretiak 30.00 80.00
6 Kurri/Selanne/Tikkanen 30.00 80.00
7 Lemieux/Sakic/Yzerman 20.00 50.00
8 Lundqvist/Sedin/Sedin 30.00 80.00
9 Modano/Hull/Richter 25.00 60.00
10 Naslund/Salming/Loob 15.00 40.00
11 Ovechkin/Malkn/Larionv 30.00 60.00
12 Price/Luongo/Fuhr 25.00 60.00
15 Vanbies/Howard/Tkachk 15.00 40.00

2012-13 ITG Ultimate Memorabilia Cup Finals Memorabilia

1 Blveau/Plnte/Hwe/Dlvc/24 50.00 100.00
2 Clrke/Prnt/P.Espo/Bcyk/24 20.00 50.00
3 Crnyr/Mhvlch/T.Espo/Mikt/24 20.00 50.00
4 Fleury/Mlkn/Osgd/Ldstrm/24 20.00 50.00
5 Fuhr/Coffey/Lind/Propp/24 25.00 60.00
6 Hull/Belfour/Hasek/Ray/24 30.00 80.00
7 Hull/Hasek/Irbe/Francis/24 30.00 60.00
9 Lemx/Jgr/Belfr/Roenick/24 15.00 40.00
10 Mess/Rchtr/McLn/Bure/24 25.00 60.00
11 Potvn/Smth/Andrsn/Krri/24 15.00 40.00
12 Ranfrd/Mess/Nly/Moog/24 20.00 50.00
13 Rbnsn/Lafir/Chvers/Park/24 20.00 50.00
14 Roy/Carbon/McDon/Vrnn/24 25.00 60.00

2012-13 ITG Ultimate Memorabilia Days Gone By

1 Chelios/Nchlls/Vernon/Lemx 50.00 125.00
2 Esposito/Howe/Horton/Plante 40.00 80.00
3 Fedorov/Hasek/Messier/Bure 20.00 50.00
4 Hawerchuk/Smith/Vaive/Ciccarelli 15.00 40.00
5 Hull/MacLsh/Courn/Espo 20.00 50.00
6 Mikita/Hdge/Blveau/Baun 12.00 30.00
7 Richrd/Mahvlch/Harvey/Hall 15.00 40.00
8 Sittler/Leach/Potvin/Park 15.00 40.00
9 Trottier/Lafleur/Dnne/P.Espo 20.00 50.00
10 Vanbies/Coffey/Roy/Clark 15.00 40.00

2012-13 ITG Ultimate Memorabilia Decades Memorabilia

1 Bsy/Lem/Msr/Brq/Cfy/Fhr/24* 80.00 200.00
2 Chv/Hal/Crz/Vch/Gia/Bwr/24* 25.00 60.00
3 Clrk/Sit/Hul/Slm/Prk/Esp/24* 40.00 100.00
4 Esp/Ll/Dio/Rbn/Ptv/Prt/24* 30.00 80.00
5 Jgr/Yzr/Rnk/Mcl/Chl/Ry/24* 60.00 150.00
6 Lml/Hwe/Pln/Hrt/Hul/Rch/24* 60.00 120.00
7 McK/Drn/Shk/Mn/Jns/Fcl/24* 30.00 80.00
8 McD/Trt/Kri/Ptv/Lng/Hxt/24* 20.00 50.00
10 Rbt/Bre/Lmx/Lds/Brq/Hk/24* 40.00 80.00

2012-13 ITG Ultimate Memorabilia Draft Day Memorabilia

1 Clarke/Saleski/Gilbert 15.00 40.00
2 Francis/Hawerchuk/MacInnis 15.00 40.00
3 Hextall/Bellows/Gilmour 20.00 50.00
4 Kurri/Coffey/Savard 15.00 40.00
5 Lafleur/Dionne/Robinson 12.00 30.00
6 MacKinnon/Drouin/Jones 30.00 80.00
7 McDonald/Potvin/Middleton 10.00 30.00
8 Messier/Bourque/Gartner 25.00 60.00
9 Modano/Linden/Selanne 15.00 40.00
10 Niedermayer/Lindros/Forsberg 15.00 40.00
11 Nieuwendyk/Clark/Burke 20.00 50.00
12 Nolan/Jagr/Tkachuk 40.00 100.00
13 Perreault/Sittler/MacLeish 15.00 40.00
14 Roy/Lemieux/Hull 50.00 125.00
15 Sakic/Fleury/LeClair 15.00 40.00
16 Shutt/Barber/Nystrom 10.00 25.00
17 Sundin/Lidstrom/Bure 20.00 50.00
18 Thornton/Marleau/Luongo 20.00 50.00
19 Trottier/Williams/Gillies 12.00 30.00
20 Yzerman/LaFontaine/Barrasso 30.00 80.00

2012-13 ITG Ultimate Memorabilia Dynamic Duos Memorabilia

1 M.Bossy/B.Trottier 10.00 25.00
2 B.Hull/S.Mikita 12.00 30.00
3 G.Lafleur/S.Shutt 10.00 25.00
4 C.Neely/A.Oates 10.00 25.00
5 B.Probert/J.Kocur 15.00 40.00
6 H.Sedin/D.Sedin 12.00 30.00
7 D.Sittler/L.McDonald 12.00 30.00
8 P.Stastny/M.Goulet 10.00 25.00
9 J.Thornton/P.Marleau 15.00 40.00
10 K.Tkachuk/T.Selanne 12.00 30.00

2012-13 ITG Ultimate Memorabilia Enforcers Memorabilia

1 D.Brown/C.Nilan 6.00 15.00
2 K.Chase/C.Berube 6.00 15.00
3 W.Clark/M.McSorley 15.00 40.00
4 T.Domi/R.Ray 8.00 20.00
5 S.Grimson/B.Probert 12.00 30.00
6 R.Hextall/F.Potvin 15.00 40.00
7 D.Hunter/C.Nilan 8.00 20.00
8 D.McCarty/C.Lemieux 10.00 25.00
9 M.McSorley/M.Messier 20.00 50.00
10 G.Odjick/J.Odgers 6.00 15.00
11 T.O'Reilly/D.Schultz 10.00 25.00
12 B.Probert/T.Domi 12.00 30.00
13 R.Ray/P.Laus 6.00 15.00
14 P.Roy/M.Vernon 25.00 60.00
15 T.Williams/T.O'Reilly 8.00 20.00

2012-13 ITG Ultimate Memorabilia Enshrined Autograph Jerseys

1 Jean Beliveau 30.00 60.00
2 Mike Bossy 15.00 40.00
3 Raymond Bourque 25.00 50.00
4 Pavel Bure 30.00 60.00
5 Bobby Clarke 25.00 50.00
6 Phil Esposito 15.00 40.00
7 Ron Francis 15.00 40.00
8 Mike Gartner 25.00 50.00
9 Ed Giacomin 15.00 40.00
10 Doug Gilmour 30.00 60.00
11 Dale Hawerchuk 15.00 40.00
12 Gordie Howe 60.00 100.00
13 Bobby Hull 25.00 50.00
14 Dave Keon 12.00 30.00
15 Jari Kurri 12.00 30.00
16 Guy Lafleur 20.00 50.00
17 Jacques Laperriere 10.00 25.00
18 Igor Larionov 30.00 60.00
19 Mario Lemieux 60.00 120.00
20 Lanny McDonald 12.00 30.00
21 Mark Messier 30.00 60.00
22 Stan Mikita 12.00 30.00
23 Joe Mullen 10.00 25.00
24 Cam Neely 15.00 40.00
25 Gilbert Perreault 12.00 30.00
26 Henri Richard 12.00 30.00
27 Luc Robitaille 15.00 40.00
28 Joe Sakic 30.00 60.00
29 Borje Salming 15.00 40.00
30 Serge Savard 12.00 30.00
31 Milt Schmidt 15.00 40.00
32 Darryl Sittler 15.00 40.00
33 Mats Sundin 30.00 60.00
34 Vladislav Tretiak 30.00 60.00
35 Steve Yzerman 40.00 80.00

2012-13 ITG Ultimate Memorabilia Enshrined Autographs

1 Jean Beliveau 25.00 50.00
2 Mike Bossy 12.00 30.00
3 Raymond Bourque 15.00 40.00
4 Pavel Bure 20.00 40.00
5 Bobby Clarke 12.00 30.00
6 Phil Esposito 12.00 30.00
7 Ron Francis 12.00 30.00
8 Mike Gartner 15.00 40.00
9 Ed Giacomin 12.00 30.00
10 Doug Gilmour 15.00 40.00
11 Dale Hawerchuk 12.00 30.00
12 Gordie Howe 50.00 100.00
13 Bobby Hull 15.00 40.00
14 Dave Keon 10.00 25.00
15 Jari Kurri 15.00 30.00
16 Guy Lafleur 15.00 30.00
17 Jacques Laperriere 8.00 20.00
18 Igor Larionov 20.00 40.00
19 Mario Lemieux 50.00 100.00
20 Lanny McDonald 10.00 25.00
21 Mark Messier 25.00 50.00
22 Stan Mikita 12.00 30.00
23 Joe Mullen 8.00 20.00
24 Cam Neely 12.00 30.00
25 Gilbert Perreault 20.00 40.00
26 Henri Richard 10.00 25.00
27 Luc Robitaille 12.00 30.00
28 Joe Sakic 25.00 50.00
29 Borje Salming 10.00 25.00
30 Serge Savard 10.00 25.00
31 Milt Schmidt 12.00 30.00
32 Darryl Sittler 12.00 30.00
33 Mats Sundin 25.00 50.00
34 Vladislav Tretiak 25.00 50.00
35 Steve Yzerman 30.00 60.00

2012-13 ITG Ultimate Memorabilia Entire Career Memorabilia

1 Jean Beliveau 10.00 25.00
2 Mike Bossy 10.00 25.00
3 Bobby Clarke 15.00 40.00
4 Ted Kennedy 10.00 25.00
5 Mario Lemieux 15.00 40.00
6 Nicklas Lidstrom 10.00 25.00
7 Stan Mikita 12.00 30.00
8 Denis Potvin 10.00 25.00
9 Henri Richard 10.00 25.00
10 Maurice Richard 10.00 25.00
11 Milt Schmidt 8.00 20.00
12 Steve Yzerman 15.00 40.00

2012-13 ITG Ultimate Memorabilia Franchise Captains Memorabilia

1 Arbour/Unger/Hull/MacInnis 25.00 60.00
2 Clrke/Lndrs/Prnu/Frsberg 15.00 40.00
3 Howe/Delv/Yzrmn/Lidstrm 30.00 80.00
4 Keon/Sittler/Clark/Sundin 25.00 60.00
5 Lalnde/Rchrd/Bliv/Svrd 30.00 60.00
6 Lngwy/Hntr/Oates/Ovech 15.00 40.00
7 Lemieux/Coffey/FrancisÂ•Jagr 25.00 60.00
8 Linden/Messier/Luongo/Sedin 15.00 40.00
9 Rchrd/Courn/CarbonMuller 30.00 60.00
10 Schmdt/Brque/Bcyk/O'Reil 20.00 50.00

2012-13 ITG Ultimate Memorabilia Franchise Favorites Memorabilia

1 Clarke/Lindros/Parent/Lindb 40.00 80.00
2 Dionne/Taylor/Robit/Quick 15.00 40.00
3 Howe/Yzrmn/Prbert/Lidstrom 40.00 100.00
4 Kurri/Messier/Coffey/Ranford 20.00 50.00
5 Lemieux/Jagr/Malkin/Fleury 50.00 125.00
6 McDonald/MacInnis/Fleury/Vernon 15.00 40.00
7 Mikita/Esposito/Savard/Roenick 15.00 40.00
8 Richard/Lafleur/Roy/Price 40.00 80.00
9 Schmidt/Bucyk/P.Espo/Neely 15.00 40.00
10 Sittler/Clark/Gilmour/Sundin 15.00 40.00

2012-13 ITG Ultimate Memorabilia From Russia With Love Ovechkin Autographs

COMMON OVECHKIN AU/19* 40.00 80.00

2012-13 ITG Ultimate Memorabilia Future Star Autograph Jerseys

PATCH/24: .5X TO 1.2X BASIC JSY AU
1 Justin Bailey 10.00 25.00
2 Aleksander Barkov 40.00 80.00
3 Ben Bishop 12.00 30.00
4 William Carrier 12.00 30.00
5 Cody Ceci 10.00 25.00
6 Eric Comrie 8.00 20.00
7 Jason Dickinson 10.00 25.00
8 Max Domi 15.00 40.00
9 Jonathan Drouin 50.00 100.00
10 Anthony Duclair 20.00 50.00
11 Adam Erne 12.00 30.00
12 Zachary Fucale 15.00 40.00
13 Alex Galchenyuk 25.00 60.00
14 Frederik Gauthier 20.00 50.00
15 Stephen Harper 15.00 40.00
16 Bo Horvat 25.00 60.00
17 Seth Jones 20.00 50.00
18 Morgan Klimchuk 12.00 30.00
19 Ryan Kujawinski 10.00 25.00
20 Curtis Lazar 12.00 30.00
21 Nathan MacKinnon 50.00 100.00
22 Anthony Mantha 20.00 50.00
23 Spencer Martin 10.00 25.00
24 Connor McDavid 175.00 300.00
25 Sean Monahan 20.00 50.00
26 Josh Morrissey 12.00 30.00
27 Ryan Murphy 12.00 30.00
28 Matt Murray 12.00 30.00
29 Darnell Nurse 15.00 40.00
30 Nicolas Petan 12.00 30.00
31 Ryan Pulock 15.00 40.00
32 Eric Roy 12.00 30.00
33 Kerby Rychel 12.00 30.00
34 Hunter Shinkaruk 25.00 60.00
35 Nick Sorensen 12.00 30.00
36 Jordan Subban 15.00 40.00
37 Shea Theodore 15.00 40.00
38 Jake Virtanen 15.00 40.00
39 Nail Yakupov 40.00 80.00
40 Nikita Zadorov 8.00 20.00

2012-13 ITG Ultimate Memorabilia Future Star Autographs

1 Justin Bailey 8.00 20.00
2 Aleksander Barkov 40.00 100.00
3 Ben Bishop 10.00 25.00
4 William Carrier 10.00 25.00
5 Cody Ceci 8.00 20.00
6 Eric Comrie 10.00 25.00
7 Jason Dickinson 8.00 20.00
8 Max Domi 20.00 50.00
9 Jonathan Drouin 40.00 100.00
10 Anthony Duclair 15.00 40.00
11 Adam Erne 10.00 25.00
12 Zachary Fucale 12.00 30.00
13 Alex Galchenyuk 30.00 80.00
14 Frederik Gauthier 15.00 40.00
15 Stephen Harper 12.00 30.00
16 Bo Horvat 15.00 40.00
17 Seth Jones 25.00 60.00
18 Morgan Klimchuk 10.00 25.00
19 Ryan Kujawinski 8.00 20.00
20 Curtis Lazar 10.00 25.00
21 Nathan MacKinnon 40.00 80.00
22 Anthony Mantha 15.00 40.00
23 Spencer Martin 8.00 20.00
24 Connor McDavid 175.00 300.00
25 Sean Monahan 25.00 50.00
26 Josh Morrissey 10.00 25.00
27 Ryan Murphy 10.00 25.00
28 Matt Murray 10.00 25.00
29 Darnell Nurse 12.00 30.00
30 Nicolas Petan 10.00 25.00
31 Ryan Pulock 12.00 30.00
32 Eric Roy 10.00 25.00
33 Kerby Rychel 10.00 25.00
34 Hunter Shinkaruk 15.00 40.00
35 Nick Sorensen 10.00 25.00
36 Jordan Subban 12.00 30.00
37 Shea Theodore 12.00 30.00
38 Jake Virtanen 12.00 30.00
39 Nail Yakupov 40.00 80.00
40 Nikita Zadorov 6.00 15.00

2012-13 ITG Ultimate Memorabilia Gloves Are Off Memorabilia

1 Raymond Bourque 15.00 40.00
2 Brett Hull 20.00 50.00
3 John LeClair 10.00 25.00
4 Mario Lemieux 40.00 100.00
5 Eric Lindros 15.00 40.00
6 Cam Neely 12.00 30.00
7 Joe Sakic 20.00 50.00
8 Eddie Shore 12.00 30.00
9 Doug Weight 10.00 25.00
10 Steve Yzerman 15.00 40.00

2012-13 ITG Ultimate Memorabilia Goalie Autograph Jerseys

1 Ilya Bryzgalov 12.00 30.00
2 Corey Crawford 20.00 40.00
3 Rick DiPietro 10.00 25.00
4 Brian Elliott 10.00 25.00
5 Ray Emery 10.00 25.00
6 Marc-Andre Fleury 25.00 60.00
7 Jonas Hiller 10.00 25.00
8 Jimmy Howard 15.00 40.00
9 Nikolai Khabibulin 15.00 40.00
10 Kari Lehtonen 10.00 25.00
11 Henrik Lundqvist 25.00 50.00
12 Roberto Luongo 12.00 30.00
13 Evgeni Nabakov 25.00 60.00
14 Antti Niemi 10.00 25.00
15 Ondrej Pavelec 20.00 50.00
16 Carey Price 25.00 50.00
17 Jonathan Quick 25.00 60.00
18 Semyon Varlamov 12.00 30.00

2012-13 ITG Ultimate Memorabilia Goalie Autographs

1 Ilya Bryzgalov 10.00 25.00
2 Corey Crawford 12.00 30.00
3 Rick DiPietro 8.00 20.00
4 Brian Elliott 8.00 20.00
5 Ray Emery 8.00 20.00
6 Marc-Andre Fleury 12.00 30.00
7 Jonas Hiller 8.00 20.00
8 Jimmy Howard 12.00 30.00
9 Nikolai Khabibulin 12.00 30.00
10 Kari Lehtonen 8.00 20.00
11 Henrik Lundqvist 15.00 40.00
12 Roberto Luongo 12.00 30.00
13 Evgeni Nabakov 20.00 50.00
14 Antti Niemi 8.00 20.00
15 Ondrej Pavelec 15.00 40.00
16 Carey Price 20.00 40.00
17 Jonathan Quick 25.00 50.00
18 Semyon Varlamov 10.00 25.00

2012-13 ITG Ultimate Memorabilia Goalie Generations Memorabilia

1 Brodeur/Cloutier/Luongo 20.00 50.00
2 Esposito/Belfour/Crawford 15.00 40.00
3 Giacomin/Richter/Lundqvist 30.00 80.00
4 Hall/Joseph/Elliott 15.00 40.00
5 Hebert/Bryzgalov/Hiller 12.00 30.00
6 Parent/Hextall/Bryzgalov 15.00 40.00
7 Plante/Roy/Price 30.00 80.00
8 Sawchuk/Osgood/Howard 20.00 50.00
9 Smith/Snow/DiPietro 12.00 30.00
10 Vachon/Hrudey/Quick 15.00 40.00
11 Vernon/Nabokov/Niemi 10.00 25.00

2012-13 ITG Ultimate Memorabilia Goalie Legend Autograph Jerseys

1 Johnny Bower 12.00 30.00
2 Sean Burke 8.00 20.00
3 Gerry Cheevers 12.00 30.00
4 Tony Esposito 15.00 40.00
5 Grant Fuhr 20.00 40.00
6 Ed Giacomin 12.00 30.00
7 Glenn Hall 15.00 40.00
8 Dominik Hasek 15.00 40.00
9 Ron Hextall 40.00 80.00
10 Arturs Irbe 40.00 80.00
11 Curtis Joseph 15.00 40.00
12 Olaf Kolzig 20.00 50.00
13 Chris Osgood 12.00 30.00
14 Bernie Parent 25.00 50.00
15 Felix Potvin 20.00 50.00
16 Bill Ranford 20.00 40.00
17 Mike Richter 20.00 40.00
18 Patrick Roy 40.00 80.00
19 Vladislav Tretiak 30.00 60.00
20 John Vanbiesbrouck 30.00 60.00

2012-13 ITG Ultimate Memorabilia Goalie Legend Autographs

1 Johnny Bower 10.00 25.00
2 Sean Burke 6.00 15.00
3 Gerry Cheevers 10.00 25.00
4 Tony Esposito 12.00 30.00
5 Grant Fuhr 12.00 30.00
6 Ed Giacomin 10.00 25.00
7 Glenn Hall 12.00 30.00
8 Dominik Hasek 12.00 30.00
9 Ron Hextall 12.00 30.00
10 Arturs Irbe 25.00 60.00
11 Curtis Joseph 12.00 30.00
12 Olaf Kolzig 15.00 40.00
13 Chris Osgood 10.00 25.00
14 Bernie Parent 20.00 40.00
15 Felix Potvin 25.00 50.00
16 Bill Ranford 15.00 30.00
17 Mike Richter 12.00 30.00
18 Patrick Roy 30.00 60.00
19 Vladislav Tretiak 25.00 50.00
20 John Vanbiesbrouck 20.00 40.00

2012-13 ITG Ultimate Memorabilia History of the Franchise In the Net Memorabilia

1 Bower/Potvin/Joseph/Belfour 25.00 60.00
2 Brimsek/Chvers/Moog/Dafoe 20.00 50.00
3 Hall/T.Espo/Belfr/Crawford 20.00 50.00
4 Plante/Vachon/Roy/Price 40.00 100.00
5 Sawchk/Osgd/Vernn/Howrd 20.00 50.00
6 Sawchk/Vachn/Hrudey/Quick 20.00 50.00

2012-13 ITG Ultimate Memorabilia Journey Jersey Memorabilia

1 Raymond Bourque 15.00 40.00
2 Pavel Bure 15.00 40.00
3 Marcel Dionne 12.00 30.00
4 Michel Goulet 8.00 20.00
5 Gordie Howe 25.00 60.00
6 Brett Hull 20.00 50.00
7 Jaromir Jagr 30.00 80.00
8 Guy Lafleur 12.00 30.00
9 Lanny McDonald 10.00 25.00
10 Mark Messier 20.00 50.00
11 Jeremy Roenick 15.00 40.00
12 Patrick Roy 25.00 60.00
13 Joe Sakic 20.00 50.00
14 Darryl Sittler 12.00 30.00
15 Mats Sundin 15.00 40.00

2012-13 ITG Ultimate Memorabilia Nicknames Jerseys

1 Ed Belfour 10.00 25.00
2 Gerry Cheevers 10.00 25.00
3 Tony Esposito 10.00 25.00
4 Peter Forsberg 20.00 50.00
5 Doug Gilmour 12.00 30.00
6 Glenn Hall 10.00 25.00
7 Gordie Howe 30.00 80.00
8 Bobby Hull 20.00 50.00
9 Brett Hull 20.00 50.00
10 Curtis Joseph 12.00 30.00
11 Guy Lafleur 12.00 30.00
12 Mario Lemieux 15.00 40.00
13 Trevor Linden 10.00 25.00
14 Mark Messier 20.00 50.00
15 Alexander Ovechkin 40.00 100.00
16 Felix Potvin 15.00 40.00
17 Jeremy Roenick 15.00 40.00
18 Teemu Selanne 20.00 50.00
19 Keith Tkachuk 10.00 25.00
20 Steve Yzerman 25.00 60.00

2012-13 ITG Ultimate Memorabilia Number 12 Memorabilia

1 Peter Bondra 12.00 30.00
2 Yvan Cournoyer 10.00 25.00
3 Gary Dornhoefer 6.00 15.00
4 Simon Gagne 10.00 25.00
5 Bill Guerin 10.00 25.00
6 Jarome Iginla 12.00 30.00
7 Hakan Loob 8.00 20.00
8 Patrick Marleau 10.00 25.00
9 Adam Oates 10.00 25.00
10 Eric Staal 12.00 30.00
11 Pat Stapleton 6.00 15.00
12 Pat Verbeek 8.00 20.00

2012-13 ITG Ultimate Memorabilia Overtime Heroes Jerseys

1 Pavel Bure 10.00 25.00
2 Theoren Fleury 12.00 30.00
3 Brett Hull 20.00 50.00
4 Pat LaFontaine 10.00 25.00
5 Brad May 6.00 15.00
6 Lanny McDonald 10.00 25.00
7 Bob Nystrom 6.00 15.00
8 Keith Primeau 8.00 20.00
9 Henri Richard 10.00 25.00
10 Henrik Sedin 12.00 30.00
11 Steve Yzerman 15.00 40.00

2012-13 ITG Ultimate Memorabilia To the Hall Autograph Jerseys

1 Tony Amonte 10.00 25.00
2 Dave Andreychuk 12.00 30.00
3 Peter Bondra 25.00 50.00
4 Chris Chelios 12.00 30.00
5 Wendel Clark 15.00 40.00
6 Vincent Damphousse 20.00 40.00
7 Sergei Fedorov 25.00 60.00
8 Theoren Fleury 20.00 40.00
9 Peter Forsberg 25.00 50.00
10 Danny Gare 8.00 20.00
11 Anders Hedberg 10.00 25.00
12 Phil Housley 10.00 25.00
13 Vladimir Krutov 40.00 80.00
14 Steve Larmer 20.00 50.00
15 John LeClair 25.00 50.00
16 Claude Lemieux 10.00 25.00
17 Nicklas Lidstrom 25.00 50.00
18 Trevor Linden 15.00 40.00
19 Eric Lindros 30.00 60.00
20 Mike Modano 15.00 40.00
21 Markus Naslund 15.00 40.00
22 Bernie Nicholls 15.00 40.00
23 Scott Niedermayer 12.00 30.00
24 Ulf Nilsson 8.00 20.00
25 Owen Nolan 12.00 30.00
26 Mark Recchi 15.00 40.00
27 Gary Roberts 20.00 40.00
28 Jeremy Roenick 30.00 60.00
29 Keith Tkachuk 15.00 40.00

2012-13 ITG Ultimate Memorabilia To the Hall Autographs

1 Tony Amonte 8.00 20.00
2 Dave Andreychuk 8.00 20.00
3 Peter Bondra 15.00 40.00
4 Chris Chelios 10.00 25.00
5 Wendel Clark 12.00 30.00
6 Vincent Damphousse 10.00 25.00
7 Sergei Fedorov 20.00 50.00
8 Theoren Fleury 20.00 40.00
9 Peter Forsberg 15.00 40.00
11 Anders Hedberg 8.00 20.00
12 Phil Housley 8.00 20.00
13 Vladimir Krutov 30.00 60.00
14 Steve Larmer 15.00 40.00
15 John LeClair 15.00 40.00
16 Claude Lemieux 8.00 20.00
17 Nicklas Lidstrom 15.00 40.00
18 Trevor Linden 12.00 30.00
19 Eric Lindros 25.00 50.00
20 Mike Modano 12.00 30.00
21 Markus Naslund 12.00 30.00
22 Bernie Nicholls 12.00 30.00
23 Scott Niedermayer 10.00 25.00
24 Ulf Nilsson 6.00 15.00
25 Owen Nolan 10.00 25.00
26 Mark Recchi 12.00 30.00
27 Gary Roberts 10.00 25.00
28 Jeremy Roenick 15.00 30.00
29 Keith Tkachuk 12.00 30.00

2012-13 ITG Ultimate Memorabilia To the Hall Memorabilia

1 Chris Chelios 10.00 25.00
2 Sergei Fedorov 15.00 40.00
3 Theoren Fleury 12.00 30.00
4 Dominik Hasek 10.00 25.00
5 Phil Housley 8.00 20.00
6 Jaromir Jagr 30.00 80.00
7 Curtis Joseph 12.00 30.00
8 Nicklas Lidstrom 10.00 25.00
9 Eric Lindros 12.00 30.00
10 Mike Modano 15.00 40.00
11 Scott Niedermayer 10.00 25.00
12 Chris Osgood 10.00 25.00
13 Jeremy Roenick 15.00 40.00
14 Teemu Selanne 20.00 50.00
15 Keith Tkachuk 10.00 25.00
16 Rogie Vachon 8.00 20.00

2012-13 ITG Ultimate Memorabilia Triple Gold Club Jerseys

1 Peter Forsberg 20.00 50.00
2 Jaromir Jagr 30.00 80.00
3 Niklas Kronwall 8.00 20.00
4 Igor Larionov 10.00 25.00
5 Nicklas Lidstrom 12.00 30.00
6 Hakan Loob 8.00 20.00
7 Mats Naslund 6.00 15.00
8 Scott Niedermayer 6.00 15.00
9 Joe Sakic 20.00 50.00

2012-13 ITG Ultimate Memorabilia Ultimate Legacy Memorabilia Toronto Spring Expo

CKR Chvlde/Khbbln/Rddck 12.00 30.00
EPS Espsto/Prbrt/Svrd 15.00 40.00
FSH Fdrv/Slnne/Hllr 15.00 40.00
GDL Gbrk/Dnne/Lndqvst 12.00 30.00
LBC Lch/Brbr/Clrke 20.00 40.00
MCF Mssr/Cffy/Fhr 20.00 50.00
PRP Prce/Ry/Plnte 50.00 100.00

2012-13 ITG Ultimate Memorabilia Ultimate Rivalry Memorabilia

1 Crb/Rbn/Ry/Glt/Hnt/Sty 25.00 60.00
2 Hdf/Prk/Gia/Smt/Nys/Ptv 20.00 50.00
3 Lfl/Sht/Lmr/Slm/McD/Stlr 15.00 40.00
4 Lnd/LeC/Hxt/Lmx/Jgr/Frn 30.00 60.00
5 Mcl/McD/Mln/Fhr/Msr/Kur 40.00 100.00
6 Nly/Brq/Mg/Ry/Lmx/Nsl 25.00 60.00
7 O'R/Esp/Byk/McL/Clr/Prt 20.00 50.00
8 Rnk/Chl/Blf/Chv/Lds/Fdv 25.00 60.00
9 Skc/Ry/Lmx/Yzr/Vrn/McC 30.00 80.00
10 Yzr/Prb/Fdv/Glm/Clrk/Ptv 50.00 125.00

2012-13 ITG Ultimate Memorabilia Vintage Dual Jerseys

1 B.Baun/T.Sawchuk 12.00 30.00
2 J.Beliveau/S.Mikita 15.00 40.00
3 J.Bower/T.Sawchuk 12.00 30.00
4 B.Clarke/D.Sittler 20.00 50.00
5 M.Dionne/G.Lafleur 15.00 40.00
6 T.Horton/D.Harvey 12.00 30.00
7 G.Howe/G.Howe 20.00 50.00
8 B.Parent/R.Vachon 15.00 40.00
9 D.Potvin/L.Robinson 12.00 30.00
10 M.Richard/G.Howe 40.00 80.00
11 V.Tretiak/V.Kharlamov 30.00 60.00
12 R.Worters/G.Hainsworth 20.00 50.00

2014-15 ITG Ultimate Memorabilia

*SILVER/20: .5X TO 1.2X BASIC CARDS/50
1 Aaron Ekblad 10.00 25.00
2 Art Ross 3.00 8.00
3 Bobby Hull 10.00 25.00
4 Bryan Trottier 5.00 12.00
5 Cam Neely 5.00 12.00
6 Carey Price 10.00 25.00
7 Chris Chelios 5.00 12.00
8 Dominik Hasek 8.00 20.00
9 Ed Belfour 5.00 12.00
10 Georges Vezina 5.00 12.00
11 Gordie Howe 15.00 40.00
12 Guy Lafleur 6.00 15.00
13 Hap Day 4.00 10.00
14 Henri Richard 5.00 12.00
15 Hobey Baker 4.00 10.00
16 Howie Morenz 4.00 10.00
17 Jacques Plante 6.00 15.00
18 Jean Beliveau 8.00 20.00
19 Joe Sakic 10.00 25.00
20 King Clancy 4.00 10.00
21 Lady Byng 3.00 8.00
22 Larry Robinson 5.00 12.00
23 Leon Draisaitl 25.00 60.00
24 Lester Patrick 5.00 12.00
25 Lord Stanley 5.00 12.00
26 Marc-Andre Fleury 10.00 25.00
27 Mario Lemieux 20.00 50.00
28 Mark Messier 10.00 25.00
29 Martin St. Louis 5.00 12.00
30 Mats Sundin 5.00 12.00
31 Maurice Richard 8.00 20.00
32 Michael Dal Colle 6.00 15.00
33 Mike Eruzione 4.00 10.00
34 Mike Modano 8.00 20.00
35 Mike Richter 5.00 12.00
36 Patrick Roy 12.00 30.00
37 Paul Coffey 5.00 12.00
38 Pelle Lindbergh 4.00 10.00
39 Peter Forsberg 10.00 25.00
40 Raymond Bourque 8.00 20.00
41 Sam Bennett 12.00 30.00
42 Sam Reinhart 20.00 50.00
43 Scott Niedermayer 5.00 12.00
44 Sid Abel 4.00 10.00
45 Steve Yzerman 12.00 30.00
46 Ted Lindsay 5.00 12.00
47 Terry Sawchuk 5.00 12.00
48 Tim Horton 5.00 12.00
49 Tony Esposito 5.00 12.00
50 Vladislav Tretiak 4.00 10.00

2014-15 ITG Ultimate Memorabilia Artistic Moments Autographs

AMAD1 Alex Delvecchio/25 6.00 15.00
AMBH1 Bobby Hull/25 12.00 30.00
AMCC1 Chris Chelios/25 6.00 15.00
AMEB1 Ed Belfour/25 10.00 25.00
AMHR1 Henri Richard/25 6.00 15.00
AMJB1 Jean Beliveau/25 6.00 15.00
AMMM2 Mike Modano/25 10.00 25.00
AMPE1 Phil Esposito/25 10.00 25.00
AMRB1 Raymond Bourque/25 10.00 25.00
AMVT1 Vladislav Tretiak/25 5.00 12.00

2014-15 ITG Ultimate Memorabilia Cup Heroes Jerseys

CH1 Bryan Trottier 4.00 10.00
CH2 Chris Chelios 4.00 10.00
CH3 Dave Keon 4.00 10.00
CH4 Dominik Hasek 6.00 15.00
CH5 Gordie Howe 12.00 30.00
CH6 Guy Lafleur 5.00 12.00
CH7 Guy Lapointe 3.00 8.00
CH8 Jacques Lemaire 3.00 8.00
CH9 Jari Kurri 4.00 10.00
CH10 Joe Sakic 8.00 20.00
CH11 Mario Lemieux 15.00 40.00
CH12 Mark Messier 8.00 20.00
CH13 Maurice Richard 8.00 20.00
CH14 Mike Bossy 4.00 10.00
CH15 Mike Modano 6.00 15.00
CH16 Mike Richter 4.00 10.00
CH17 Patrick Roy 10.00 25.00
CH18 Paul Coffey 4.00 10.00
CH19 Phil Esposito 6.00 15.00
CH20 Steve Yzerman 10.00 25.00

2014-15 ITG Ultimate Memorabilia Dynamic Duos Autographs

DD13 R.Bourque/C.Chelios/25 15.00 40.00
DD14 R.Kelly/J.Bower/25 15.00 40.00
DD17 T.Esposito/P.Esposito/25 15.00 40.00

2014-15 ITG Ultimate Memorabilia Enshrined Autographs

EAAD1 Alex Delvecchio/25 10.00 25.00
EABH1 Bobby Hull/25 20.00 50.00
EABS1 Billy Smith/19 10.00 25.00
EABT1 Bryan Trottier/25 10.00 25.00
EACC1 Chris Chelios/25 10.00 25.00
EAGL1 Guy Lapointe/25 8.00 20.00
EAJB1 Johnny Bower/25 10.00 25.00
EAJB2 Johnny Bucyk/25 10.00 25.00
EAMB1 Mike Bossy/17 10.00 25.00
EAMS1 Milt Schmidt/16 8.00 20.00
EAPE1 Phil Esposito/25 15.00 40.00
EARK1 Red Kelly/25 10.00 25.00
EATE1 Tony Esposito/25 10.00 25.00
EATL1 Ted Lindsay/25 10.00 25.00
EAVT1 Vladislav Tretiak/25 8.00 20.00

2014-15 ITG Ultimate Memorabilia Future Star Autograph Jerseys

FSRMI Ryan MacInnis/25 5.00 12.00

2014-15 ITG Ultimate Memorabilia Future Star Autographs

FSAP1 Alexis Pepin/25 4.00 10.00
FSCB1 Clark Bishop/25 3.00 8.00
FSHF1 Haydn Fleury/25 5.00 12.00
FSJL1 Jaden Lindo/25 3.00 8.00
FSJV1 Jake Virtanen/25 6.00 15.00
FSMM1 Matt Mistele/25 4.00 10.00
FSNR1 Nick Ritchie/25 5.00 12.00
FSOLB Olivier LeBlanc/25 4.00 10.00
FSSB1 Sam Bennett/25 12.00 30.00
FSSR1 Sam Reinhart/17 20.00 50.00

2014-15 ITG Ultimate Memorabilia Hall Bound Jerseys

HB1 Chris Osgood 3.00 8.00
HB2 Dominik Hasek 5.00 12.00
HB3 Teemu Selanne 6.00 15.00
HB4 Jaromir Jagr 10.00 25.00
HB5 Jeremy Roenick 5.00 12.00
HB6 Mike Modano 5.00 12.00
HB7 Mike Richter 3.00 8.00
HB8 Nicklas Lidstrom 3.00 8.00
HB9 Peter Forsberg 6.00 15.00
HB10 Sergei Fedorov 5.00 12.00

2014-15 ITG Ultimate Memorabilia Hall Bound Patches

HB1 Chris Osgood 4.00 10.00
HB2 Dominik Hasek 6.00 15.00
HB3 Teemu Selanne 8.00 20.00
HB4 Jaromir Jagr 12.00 30.00
HB5 Jeremy Roenick 6.00 15.00
HB6 Mike Modano 6.00 15.00
HB7 Mike Richter 4.00 10.00
HB8 Nicklas Lidstrom 4.00 10.00
HB9 Peter Forsberg 8.00 20.00
HB10 Sergei Fedorov 6.00 15.00

2014-15 ITG Ultimate Memorabilia Legendary Sweaters Jerseys

LSBH1 Bobby Hull 8.00 20.00
LSGH1 Gordie Howe 12.00 30.00
LSGL1 Guy Lafleur 5.00 12.00
LSML1 Mario Lemieux 15.00 40.00
LSMM1 Mark Messier 8.00 20.00
LSPR1 Patrick Roy 10.00 25.00
LSRB1 Raymond Bourque 6.00 15.00
LSSY1 Steve Yzerman 10.00 25.00
LSTL1 Ted Lindsay 4.00 10.00
LSVT1 Vladislav Tretiak 3.00 8.00

2014-15 ITG Ultimate Memorabilia Super Swatch Jerseys

SS1 Bobby Hull 6.00 15.00
SS2 Gordie Howe 10.00 25.00
SS3 Joe Sakic 6.00 15.00
SS4 Joe Thornton 5.00 12.00
SS5 Mario Lemieux 12.00 30.00
SS6 Mark Messier 6.00 15.00
SS7 Mats Sundin 3.00 8.00
SS8 Patrick Roy 8.00 20.00
SS9 Raymond Bourque 5.00 12.00
SS10 Stan Mikita 4.00 10.00
SS11 Steve Shutt 2.50 6.00
SS12 Steve Yzerman 8.00 20.00
SS13 Steve Yzerman 8.00 20.00
SS14 Teemu Selanne 6.00 15.00

2014-15 ITG Ultimate Memorabilia Ultimate Autograph Jerseys

UAMSL Martin St. Louis/15 10.00 25.00

2014-15 ITG Ultimate Memorabilia Ultimate Autographs

UAAD1 Alex Delvecchio/25 10.00 25.00
UAAE1 Aaron Ekblad/25 15.00 40.00
UACP1 Carey Price/18 20.00 50.00
UAEL1 Eddie Lack/20 8.00 20.00
UAJJ1 Jaromir Jagr/25 30.00 80.00
UAMAF Marc-Andre Fleury/25 20.00 50.00
UASR1 Sam Reinhart/15 30.00 80.00

2014-15 ITG Ultimate Memorabilia Ultimate Journey Jerseys

UJBH1 Brett Hull 6.00 15.00
UJCC1 Chris Chelios 3.00 8.00
UJEB1 Ed Belfour 3.00 8.00
UJGF1 Guy Lafleur 4.00 10.00
UJJJ1 Jaromir Jagr 10.00 25.00
UJJT1 Joe Thornton 5.00 12.00
UJMM1 Mark Messier 6.00 15.00
UJPC1 Paul Coffey 3.00 8.00
UJPF1 Peter Forsberg 6.00 15.00
UJPR1 Patrick Roy 8.00 20.00
UJRB1 Raymond Bourque 5.00 12.00
UJTS1 Teemu Selanne 6.00 15.00

2002-03 ITG Used

1 Adam Oates 2.00 5.00
2 Paul Kariya 2.00 5.00
3 Petr Sykora 1.50 4.00
4 Dany Heatley 1.50 4.00
5 Ilya Kovalchuk 2.50 6.00
6 Jeff O'Neill 1.25 3.00
7 Joe Thornton 3.00 8.00
8 Sergei Samsonov 1.50 4.00
9 Jarome Iginla 2.50 6.00
10 Ron Francis 2.50 6.00
11 Jocelyn Thibault 1.50 4.00
12 Alex Tanguay 1.50 4.00
13 Joe Sakic 4.00 10.00
14 Milan Hejduk 1.50 4.00
15 Patrick Roy 5.00 12.00
16 Peter Forsberg 4.00 10.00
17 Rob Blake 2.00 5.00
18 Rostislav Klesla 1.25 3.00
19 Brett Hull 4.00 10.00
20 Marty Turco 2.00 5.00
21 Mike Modano 3.00 8.00
22 Bill Guerin 2.00 5.00
23 Brendan Shanahan 2.00 5.00
24 Chris Chelios 2.00 5.00
25 Curtis Joseph 2.50 6.00
26 Luc Robitaille 2.00 5.00
27 Nicklas Lidstrom 2.00 5.00
28 Pavel Datsyuk 3.00 8.00
29 Sergei Fedorov 3.00 8.00
30 Steve Yzerman 5.00 12.00
31 Mike Comrie 2.00 5.00
32 Erik Cole 1.25 3.00
33 Kristian Huselius 1.25 3.00
34 Roberto Luongo 3.00 8.00
35 Felix Potvin 3.00 8.00
36 Jason Allison 1.50 4.00
37 Zigmund Palffy 2.00 5.00
38 Marian Gaborik 2.00 5.00
39 Jose Theodore 2.00 5.00
40 Saku Koivu 2.00 5.00
41 Martin Brodeur 5.00 12.00
42 Patrik Elias 2.00 5.00
43 Scott Gomez 1.50 4.00
44 Alexei Yashin 1.50 4.00
45 Chris Osgood 2.00 5.00
46 Rick DiPietro 1.50 4.00
47 Brian Leetch 1.50 4.00
48 Eric Lindros 3.00 8.00
49 Mark Messier 4.00 10.00
50 Mike Richter 2.00 5.00
51 Pavel Bure 2.00 5.00
52 Daniel Alfredsson 2.00 5.00
53 Marian Hossa 2.00 5.00
54 Martin Havlat 1.50 4.00
55 Jeremy Roenick 3.00 8.00
56 John LeClair 2.00 5.00
57 Mark Recchi 2.50 6.00
58 Simon Gagne 2.00 5.00
59 Nikolai Khabibulin 2.00 5.00
60 Sean Burke 1.25 3.00
61 Johan Hedberg 2.00 5.00
62 Mario Lemieux 8.00 20.00
63 Evgeni Nabokov 1.50 4.00
64 Owen Nolan 2.00 5.00
65 Teemu Selanne 4.00 10.00
66 Al MacInnis 2.50 6.00
67 Chris Pronger 2.00 5.00
68 Doug Weight 2.00 5.00
69 Keith Tkachuk 2.00 5.00
70 Vincent Lecavalier 2.00 5.00
71 Ed Belfour 2.00 5.00
72 Mats Sundin 2.00 5.00
73 Daniel Sedin 2.50 6.00
74 Henrik Sedin 2.50 6.00
75 Markus Naslund 2.00 5.00
76 Todd Bertuzzi 2.00 5.00
77 Jaromir Jagr 6.00 15.00
78 Olaf Kolzig 2.00 5.00
79 Peter Bondra 2.00 5.00
80 Tony Amonte 1.50 4.00
81 P-M Bouchard RC 4.00 10.00
82 Rick Nash RC 15.00 40.00
83 Dennis Seidenberg RC 4.00 10.00
84 Jay Bouwmeester RC 8.00 20.00
85 Stanislav Chistov RC 2.50 6.00
86 Tom Koivisto RC 2.50 6.00
87 Ivan Majesky RC 2.50 6.00
88 Chuck Kobasew RC 3.00 8.00
89 Ales Hemsky RC 10.00 25.00
90 Radovan Somik RC 2.50 6.00
91 Dmitri Bykov RC 2.50 6.00
92 Ryan Miller RC 15.00 40.00
93 Ron Hainsey RC 2.50 6.00
94 Anton Volchenkov RC 2.50 6.00
95 Dick Tarnstrom RC 2.50 6.00
96 Scottie Upshall RC 3.00 8.00
97 Jordan Leopold RC 4.00 10.00
98 Carlo Colaiacovo RC 4.00 10.00
99 Levente Szuper RC 4.00 10.00
100 Lynn Loyns RC 2.50 6.00
101 Adam Oates 2.00 5.00
102 Paul Kariya 2.00 5.00
103 Petr Sykora 1.50 4.00
104 Dany Heatley 1.50 4.00
105 Ilya Kovalchuk 2.50 6.00
106 Jeff O'Neill 1.25 3.00
107 Joe Thornton 3.00 8.00
108 Sergei Samsonov 1.50 4.00
109 Jarome Iginla 2.50 6.00
110 Ron Francis 2.50 6.00
111 Jocelyn Thibault 1.50 4.00
112 Alex Tanguay 1.50 4.00
113 Joe Sakic 4.00 10.00
114 Milan Hejduk 1.50 4.00
115 Patrick Roy 5.00 12.00
116 Peter Forsberg 4.00 10.00
117 Rob Blake 2.00 5.00
118 Rostislav Klesla 1.25 3.00
119 Brett Hull 4.00 10.00
120 Marty Turco 2.00 5.00
121 Mike Modano 3.00 8.00
122 Bill Guerin 2.00 5.00
123 Brendan Shanahan 2.00 5.00
124 Chris Chelios 2.00 5.00
125 Curtis Joseph 2.50 6.00
126 Luc Robitaille 2.00 5.00
127 Nicklas Lidstrom 2.00 5.00
128 Pavel Datsyuk 3.00 8.00
129 Sergei Fedorov 3.00 8.00
130 Steve Yzerman 5.00 12.00
131 Mike Comrie 2.00 5.00
132 Erik Cole 1.25 3.00
133 Kristian Huselius 1.25 3.00
134 Roberto Luongo 3.00 8.00
135 Felix Potvin 3.00 8.00
136 Jason Allison 1.50 4.00
137 Zigmund Palffy 2.00 5.00
138 Marian Gaborik 2.00 5.00
139 Jose Theodore 2.00 5.00
140 Saku Koivu 2.00 5.00
141 Martin Brodeur 5.00 12.00
142 Patrik Elias 2.00 5.00
143 Scott Gomez 1.50 4.00
144 Alexei Yashin 1.50 4.00
145 Chris Osgood 2.00 5.00
146 Rick DiPietro 1.50 4.00
147 Brian Leetch 1.50 4.00
148 Eric Lindros 3.00 8.00
149 Mark Messier 4.00 10.00
150 Mike Richter 2.00 5.00
151 Pavel Bure 2.00 5.00

152 Daniel Alfredsson 2.00 5.00
153 Marian Hossa 2.00 5.00
154 Martin Havlat 1.50 4.00
155 Jeremy Roenick 3.00 8.00
156 John LeClair 2.00 5.00
157 Mark Recchi 2.50 6.00
158 Simon Gagne 2.00 5.00
159 Nikolai Khabibulin 2.00 5.00
160 Sean Burke 1.25 3.00
161 Johan Hedberg 2.00 5.00
162 Mario Lemieux 8.00 20.00
163 Evgeni Nabokov 1.50 4.00
164 Owen Nolan 2.00 5.00
165 Teemu Selanne 4.00 10.00
166 Al MacInnis 2.50 6.00
167 Chris Pronger 2.00 5.00
168 Doug Weight 2.00 5.00
169 Keith Tkachuk 2.00 5.00
170 Vincent Lecavalier 2.00 5.00
171 Ed Belfour 2.00 5.00
172 Mats Sundin 2.00 5.00
173 Daniel Sedin 2.50 6.00
174 Henrik Sedin 2.50 6.00
175 Markus Naslund 2.00 5.00
176 Todd Bertuzzi 2.00 5.00
177 Jaromir Jagr 6.00 15.00
178 Olaf Kolzig 2.00 5.00
179 Peter Bondra 2.00 5.00
180 Tony Amonte 1.50 4.00
181 Shaone Morrisonn RC 4.00 10.00
182 Kari Haakana RC 4.00 10.00
183 Ray Emery RC 10.00 25.00
184 Mike Cammalleri RC 12.00 30.00
185 Ari Ahonen RC 4.00 10.00
186 Martin Gerber RC 6.00 15.00
187 Adam Hall RC 4.00 10.00
188 Lasse Pirjeta RC 4.00 10.00
189 Stephane Veilleux RC 4.00 10.00
190 Jeff Taffe RC 4.00 10.00
191 Mikael Tellqvist RC 4.00 10.00
192 Alexander Frolov RC 10.00 25.00
193 Steve Eminger RC 4.00 10.00
194 Shawn Thornton RC 5.00 12.00
195 Alexander Svitov RC 4.00 10.00
196 Alexei Smirnov RC 5.00 12.00
197 Curtis Sanford RC 6.00 15.00
198 Henrik Zetterberg RC 50.00 100.00
199 Eric Godard RC 4.00 10.00
200 Jason Spezza RC 40.00 80.00

2002-03 ITG Used Calder Jerseys

C1 Jason Spezza 20.00 50.00
C2 Rick Nash 20.00 50.00
C3 Jay Bouwmeester 10.00 20.00
C4 Stephen Weiss 8.00 20.00
C5 Chuck Kobasew 6.00 15.00
C6 Ales Hemsky 8.00 20.00
C7 Alexander Svitov 6.00 15.00
C8 Ron Hainsey 6.00 15.00
C9 Jordan Leopold 6.00 15.00
C10 Stanislav Chistov 6.00 15.00
C11 Alexei Smirnov 6.00 15.00
C12 Ryan Miller 12.00 30.00
C13 Dennis Seidenberg 6.00 15.00
C14 Adam Hall 6.00 15.00
C15 Niko Kapanen 6.00 15.00
C16 Alexander Frolov 8.00 20.00
C17 Anton Volchenkov 6.00 15.00
C18 Radovan Somik 6.00 15.00
C19 Ivan Huml 6.00 15.00
C20 Mike Cammalleri 8.00 20.00

2002-03 ITG Used Franchise Players Jerseys

FR1 Paul Kariya 8.00 20.00
FR2 Ilya Kovalchuk 10.00 25.00
FR3 Joe Thornton 12.50 30.00
FR4 Miroslav Satan 8.00 20.00
FR5 Jarome Iginla 10.00 25.00
FR6 Jeff O'Neill 8.00 20.00
FR7 Eric Daze 8.00 20.00
F8 Patrick Roy 18.00 40.00
FR9 Rostislav Klesla 8.00 20.00
FR10 Mike Modano 8.00 20.00
FR11 Steve Yzerman 18.00 40.00
FR12 Mike Comrie 5.00 15.00
FR13 Roberto Luongo 10.00 25.00
FR14 Zigmund Palffy 5.00 15.00
FR15 Marian Gaborik 10.00 25.00
FR16 Jose Theodore 10.00 25.00
FR17 Scott Hartnell 5.00 15.00
FR18 Martin Brodeur 18.00 40.00
FR19 Alexei Yashin 5.00 15.00
FR20 Pavel Bure 8.00 20.00
FR21 Marian Hossa 8.00 20.00
FR22 Simon Gagne 10.00 25.00
FR23 Daniel Briere 5.00 15.00
FR24 Mario Lemieux 20.00 50.00
FR25 Chris Pronger 5.00 15.00
FR26 Owen Nolan 5.00 15.00
FR27 Nikolai Khabibulin 5.00 15.00
FR28 Mats Sundin 8.00 20.00
FR29 Markus Naslund 5.00 15.00
FR30 Jaromir Jagr 10.00 25.00

2002-03 ITG Used Goalie Pad and Jersey

GP1 Jose Theodore 15.00 40.00
GP2 Patrick Roy 40.00 100.00
GP3 Martin Brodeur 30.00 80.00
GP4 Jocelyn Thibault 10.00 25.00
GP5 Mike Dunham 10.00 25.00
GP6 Ed Belfour 15.00 40.00
GP7 J-S Aubin 10.00 25.00
GP8 Dan Cloutier 10.00 25.00
GP9 Roman Turek 10.00 25.00
GP10 Chris Osgood 12.00 30.00
GP11 Marty Turco 10.00 25.00
GP12 Roman Cechmanek 10.00 25.00
GP13 Sean Burke 10.00 25.00
GP14 Tomas Vokoun 10.00 25.00
GP15 Gerry Cheevers 12.00 30.00
GP16 Bernie Parent 10.00 25.00
GP17 Brian Boucher 10.00 25.00
GP18 Jeff Hackett 10.00 25.00
GP19 Ron Hextall 12.00 30.00
GP20 Terry Sawchuk 50.00 125.00

2002-03 ITG Used International Experience Jerseys

IE1 Mario Lemieux 20.00 50.00
IE2 Jaromir Jagr 15.00 40.00
IE3 Mats Sundin 12.50 30.00
IE4 Steve Yzerman 25.00 60.00
IE5 Nicklas Lidstrom 12.50 30.00
IE6 Mike Modano 12.50 30.00
IE7 Peter Forsberg 15.00 40.00
IE8 Zigmund Palffy 10.00 25.00
IE9 Olaf Kolzig 12.50 30.00
IE10 Teemu Selanne 12.50 30.00
IE11 Bill Guerin 10.00 25.00
IE12 Alexander Mogilny 10.00 25.00
IE13 Alexei Yashin 10.00 25.00
IE14 Saku Koivu 10.00 25.00
IE15 Bobby Holik 10.00 25.00
IE16 Tony Amonte 10.00 25.00
IE17 Joe Sakic 15.00 40.00
IE18 Chris Chelios 10.00 25.00
IE19 Curtis Joseph 10.00 25.00
IE20 Martin Brodeur 20.00 50.00
IE21 Radek Bonk 10.00 25.00
IE22 Brian Leetch 12.50 30.00
IE23 Darius Kasparaitis 10.00 25.00
IE24 Tommy Salo 10.00 25.00
IE25 Roman Turek 10.00 25.00
IE26 Johan Hedberg 10.00 25.00
IE27 Roman Cechmanek 10.00 25.00
IE28 Nikolai Khabibulin 10.00 25.00

2002-03 ITG Used Jerseys

GUJ1 Mario Lemieux 15.00 40.00
GUJ2 Steve Yzerman 15.00 40.00
GUJ3 Peter Forsberg 12.50 30.00
GUJ4 Patrick Roy 15.00 40.00
GUJ5 Jarome Iginla 10.00 25.00
GUJ6 Pavel Bure 8.00 20.00
GUJ7 Jaromir Jagr 8.00 20.00
GUJ8 Eric Lindros 8.00 20.00
GUJ9 Paul Kariya 8.00 20.00
GUJ10 Ilya Kovalchuk 10.00 25.00
GUJ11 Mike Modano 10.00 25.00
GUJ12 Joe Thornton 10.00 25.00
GUJ13 Jose Theodore 8.00 20.00
GUJ14 Jeremy Roenick 10.00 25.00
GUJ15 Martin Brodeur 15.00 40.00
GUJ16 Mats Sundin 8.00 20.00
GUJ17 Mark Messier 8.00 20.00
GUJ18 Alexei Yashin 8.00 20.00
GUJ19 Marian Gaborik 12.50 30.00
GUJ20 Brendan Shanahan 8.00 20.00
GUJ21 Owen Nolan 8.00 20.00
GUJ22 Joe Sakic 12.50 30.00
GUJ23 Daniel Alfredsson 8.00 20.00
GUJ24 Teemu Selanne 8.00 20.00
GUJ25 Nicklas Lidstrom 8.00 20.00
GUJ26 John LeClair 8.00 20.00
GUJ27 Keith Tkachuk 8.00 20.00
GUJ28 Brian Leetch 8.00 20.00
GUJ29 Milan Hejduk 8.00 20.00
GUJ30 Dany Heatley 8.00 20.00
GUJ31 Sergei Samsonov 8.00 20.00
GUJ32 Todd Bertuzzi 8.00 20.00
GUJ33 Markus Naslund 8.00 20.00
GUJ34 Chris Chelios 8.00 20.00
GUJ35 Rob Blake 8.00 20.00
GUJ36 Sergei Fedorov 10.00 25.00
GUJ37 Al MacInnis 8.00 20.00
GUJ38 Luc Robitaille 8.00 20.00
GUJ39 Eric Daze 8.00 20.00
GUJ40 Ron Francis 8.00 20.00
GUJ41 Alexander Mogilny 8.00 20.00
GUJ42 Chris Pronger 8.00 20.00
GUJ43 Doug Weight 8.00 20.00
GUJ44 Zigmund Palffy 8.00 20.00
GUJ45 Peter Bondra 8.00 20.00
GUJ46 Mike Comrie 8.00 20.00
GUJ47 Mark Recchi 8.00 20.00
GUJ48 Marian Hossa 8.00 20.00
GUJ49 Saku Koivu 8.00 20.00
GUJ50 Pierre Turgeon 8.00 20.00

2002-03 ITG Used Jersey and Stick

*STK/JSY: .5X TO 1.25X BASIC JERSEY

2002-03 ITG Used Magnificent Inserts

MI1 2000-01 Jersey 30.00 80.00
MI2 1985-86 Jersey 30.00 80.00
MI3 2002 All-Star Jersey 30.00 80.00
MI4 1987 Canada Cup Jersey 30.00 80.00
MI5 Dual Jersey 50.00 125.00

2002-03 ITG Used Teammates Jerseys

T1 M.Lemieux/A.Kovalev 25.00 60.00
T2 P.Forsberg/P.Roy 15.00 40.00
T3 J.Thornton/S.Samsonov 12.50 30.00
T4 P.Bure/E.Lindros 10.00 25.00
T5 S.Yzerman/C.Chelios 25.00 60.00
T6 S.Koivu/J.Theodore 12.50 30.00
T7 I.Kovalchuk/D.Heatley 15.00 40.00
T8 C.Pronger/K.Tkachuk 10.00 25.00
T9 N.Lidstrom/B.Shanahan 12.50 30.00
T10 R.Blake/J.Sakic 12.50 30.00
T11 B.Leetch/M.Messier 12.50 30.00
T12 M.Sundin/A.Mogilny 12.50 30.00
T13 M.Modano/M.Turco 12.50 30.00
T14 M.Brodeur/S.Niedermayer 20.00 50.00
T15 S.Gagne/J.LeClair 12.50 30.00
T16 O.Nolan/T.Selanne 12.50 30.00
T17 Z.Palffy/F.Potvin 12.50 30.00
T18 J.Jagr/O.Kolzig 12.50 30.00
T19 M.Naslund/T.Bertuzzi 10.00 25.00
T20 S.Fedorov/B.Hull 15.00 40.00

2002-03 ITG Used Triple Memorabilia

TM1 Joe Thornton 20.00 50.00
TM2 Mario Lemieux 50.00 125.00
TM3 Mats Sundin 12.00 30.00
TM4 Jarome Iginla 15.00 40.00
TM5 Nicklas Lidstrom 12.00 30.00
TM6 John LeClair 12.00 30.00
TM7 Chris Chelios 12.00 30.00
TM8 Joe Sakic 25.00 60.00
TM9 Eric Lindros 12.00 30.00
TM10 Al MacInnis 12.00 30.00
TM11 Sergei Fedorov 20.00 50.00
TM12 Sergei Samsonov 10.00 25.00
TM13 Simon Gagne 12.00 30.00
TM14 Doug Weight 8.00 20.00
TM15 Alexei Yashin 8.00 20.00
TM16 Scott Niedermayer 8.00 20.00
TM17 Steve Yzerman 40.00 100.00
TM18 Rob Blake 10.00 25.00
TM19 Brett Hull 20.00 50.00
TM20 Adam Deadmarsh 10.00 25.00

2002-03 ITG Used Vintage Memorabilia

VM1 Newsy Lalonde 30.00 80.00
VM2 Jacques Plante 30.00 80.00
VM3 Roy Worters 30.00 80.00
VM4 Tiny Thompson 12.50 30.00
VM5 Ace Bailey 40.00 100.00
VM6 Jean Beliveau 25.00 60.00
VM7 Maurice Richard 40.00 100.00
VM8 Red Kelly 20.00 50.00
VM9 Harry Lumley 20.00 50.00
VM10 Eddie Shore 20.00 50.00
VM11 Alex Delvecchio 12.50 30.00
VM12 Bill Mosienko 12.50 30.00
VM13 Tim Horton 30.00 80.00
VM14 Doug Harvey 12.50 30.00
VM15 Johnny Bower 12.50 30.00
VM16 George Hainsworth 20.00 50.00
VM17 Bill Durnan 12.50 30.00
VM18 Terry Sawchuk 30.00 80.00
VM19 Frank Brimsek 12.50 30.00
VM20 King Clancy 50.00 125.00

2003-04 ITG Used Signature Series

COMMON ROOKIE/390 3.00 8.00
ROOKIE SEMISTARS/390 4.00 10.00
ROOKIE UNL.STARS/390 5.00 12.00
1 Rick Nash 1.50 4.00
2 Tomas Vokoun 1.25 3.00
3 Alexander Frolov 1.25 3.00
4 Eric Brewer 1.00 2.50
5 Pavel Datsyuk 2.50 6.00
6 Bill Guerin 1.50 4.00
7 Rob Blake 1.50 4.00
8 Rostislav Klesla 1.00 2.50
9 Ron Francis 2.00 5.00
10 Glen Murray 1.25 3.00
11 Chris Drury 1.25 3.00
12 Alexei Yashin 1.25 3.00
13 Teemu Selanne 3.00 8.00
14 Henrik Zetterberg 2.00 5.00
15 Olli Jokinen 1.50 4.00
16 Marian Gaborik 1.50 4.00
17 Patrik Elias 1.50 4.00
18 Alex Kovalev 1.50 4.00
19 Simon Gagne 1.50 4.00
20 Martin St. Louis 1.50 4.00
21 Chris Pronger 1.50 4.00
22 Jeremy Roenick 2.50 6.00
23 Manny Fernandez 1.00 2.50
24 Zigmund Palffy 1.50 4.00
25 Erik Cole 1.00 2.50
26 Sergei Samsonov 1.25 3.00
27 Niko Kapanen 1.00 2.50
28 Ales Hemsky 1.50 4.00
29 Eric Daze 1.25 3.00
30 Vincent Lecavalier 1.50 4.00
31 Shane Doan 1.25 3.00
32 Marian Hossa 1.50 4.00
33 Scott Stevens 1.50 4.00
34 Roberto Luongo 2.50 6.00
35 Joe Thornton 2.50 6.00
36 Marc Denis 1.25 3.00
37 Marty Turco 1.50 4.00
38 Daniel Alfredsson 1.50 4.00
39 Ryan Smyth 1.25 3.00
40 Miroslav Satan 1.25 3.00
41 Nicklas Lidstrom 1.50 4.00
42 Chuck Kobasew 1.00 2.50
43 Mark Recchi 2.00 5.00
44 Rick DiPietro 1.25 3.00
45 Nikolai Khabibulin 1.50 4.00
46 Keith Tkachuk 1.50 4.00
47 Jason Spezza 1.50 4.00
48 Felix Potvin 2.50 6.00
49 Patrick Lalime 1.25 3.00
50 Milan Hejduk 1.25 3.00
51 Sergei Fedorov 2.50 6.00
52 Ed Jovanovski 1.25 3.00
53 Jarome Iginla 2.00 5.00
54 Jocelyn Thibault 1.25 3.00
55 Brian Leetch 1.25 3.00
56 Michael Ryder 1.25 3.00
57 Jay Bouwmeester 1.00 2.50
58 Saku Koivu 1.50 4.00
59 Jose Theodore 1.50 4.00
60 Anson Carter 1.25 3.00
61 John LeClair 1.25 3.00
62 Sean Burke 1.00 2.50
63 Markus Naslund 1.25 3.00
64 Olaf Kolzig 1.25 3.00
65 Peter Bondra 1.50 4.00
66 Doug Weight 1.50 4.00
67 Sergei Gonchar 1.00 2.50
68 Dwayne Roloson 1.25 3.00
69 Roman Cechmanek 1.25 3.00
70 David Legwand 1.25 3.00
71 Mike Peca 1.25 3.00
72 Mike Dunham 1.25 3.00
73 Dany Heatley 1.25 3.00
74 Chris Osgood 1.50 4.00
75 Tommy Salo 1.25 3.00
76 David Aebischer 1.25 3.00
77 Jeff O'Neill 1.00 2.50
78 Tyler Arnason 1.00 2.50
79 Roman Turek 1.25 3.00
80 Ryan Miller 1.50 4.00
81 Pasi Nurminen 1.25 3.00
82 Kevin Weekes 1.25 3.00
83 Byron Dafoe 1.25 3.00
84 Ray Whitney 1.25 3.00
85 Al MacInnis 2.00 5.00
86 Adam Oates 1.50 4.00
87 Vincent Damphousse 1.25 3.00
88 Evgeni Nabokov 1.25 3.00
89 Daymond Langkow 1.00 2.50
90 Todd Bertuzzi 1.50 4.00
91 Dan Cloutier 1.25 3.00
92 Aleksey Morozov 1.00 2.50
93 Tony Amonte 1.25 3.00
94 Brett Hull 3.00 8.00
95 Martin Biron 1.25 3.00
96 Ilya Kovalchuk 1.50 4.00
97 Andrew Raycroft 1.25 3.00
98 Curtis Joseph 2.00 5.00
99 Peter Forsberg 3.00 8.00
100 Joe Sakic 3.00 8.00
101 Steve Yzerman 8.00 20.00
102 Brendan Shanahan 3.00 8.00
103 Owen Nolan 3.00 8.00
104 Mike Modano 5.00 12.00
105 Dominik Hasek 5.00 12.00
106 Martin Brodeur 8.00 20.00
107 Eric Lindros 5.00 12.00
108 Jaromir Jagr 10.00 25.00
109 Mats Sundin 3.00 8.00
110 Mario Lemieux 12.00 30.00
111 Jean Beliveau 6.00 15.00
112 Frank Mahovlich 5.00 12.00
113 Ted Lindsay 3.00 8.00
114 Red Kelly 3.00 8.00
115 Bobby Orr 10.00 25.00
116 Ray Bourque 5.00 12.00
117 Patrick Roy 10.00 20.00
118 Guy Lafleur 4.00 10.00
119 Ted Kennedy 3.00 8.00
120 Phil Esposito 5.00 12.00
121 Tuomo Ruutu AU RC 10.00 25.00
122 Chris Higgins AU RC 12.00 30.00
123 Antoine Vermette AU RC 12.00 30.00
124 David Hale AU RC 6.00 15.00
125 Pavel Vorobiev AU RC 8.00 20.00
126 Antti Miettinen AU RC 10.00 25.00
127 Patrice Bergeron AU RC 30.00 60.00
128 Nathan Horton AU RC 15.00 40.00
129 Tim Gleason AU RC 8.00 20.00
130 Matthew Lombardi AU RC 8.00 20.00
131 Paul Martin AU RC 8.00 20.00
132 Marek Zidlicky AU RC 6.00 15.00
133 Joni Pitkanen AU RC 10.00 25.00
134 Marc-Andre Fleury AU RC 25.00 60.00
135 Jordin Tootoo AU RC 15.00 40.00
136 Eric Staal AU RC 20.00 40.00
137 Fredrik Sjostrom AU RC 10.00 25.00
138 Dustin Brown AU RC 20.00 50.00
139 Jiri Hudler AU RC 15.00 40.00
140 Derek Roy AU RC 10.00 25.00
141 Ryan Malone AU RC 12.00 30.00
142 Chris Kunitz AU RC 12.00 30.00
143 Jozef Balej AU RC 6.00 15.00
144 Boyd Gordon AU RC 8.00 20.00
145 Alexander Semin AU RC 15.00 40.00
146 Dan Fritsche AU RC 6.00 15.00
147 Brent Burns AU RC 20.00 50.00
148 Milan Michalek AU RC 12.00 30.00
149 Matt Stajan AU RC 10.00 25.00
150 Nikolai Zherdev AU RC 12.00 30.00
151 Darryl Bootland RC 4.00 10.00
152 Kari Lehtonen RC 12.00 30.00
153 Noah Clarke RC 3.00 8.00
154 Sean Bergenheim RC 4.00 10.00
155 Niklas Kronwall RC 6.00 15.00
156 Matt Murley RC 4.00 10.00
157 Mark Popovic RC 4.00 10.00
158 John-Michael Liles RC 4.00 10.00
159 Brent Krahn RC 3.00 8.00
160 Sergei Zinovjev RC 3.00 8.00
161 Trevor Daley RC 5.00 12.00
162 Matt Ellison RC 3.00 8.00
163 Timofei Shishkanov RC 3.00 8.00
164 John Pohl RC 3.00 8.00
165 Adam Munro RC 3.00 8.00
166 Rostislav Stana RC 5.00 12.00
167 Peter Sejna RC 4.00 10.00
168 Jed Ortmeyer RC 4.00 10.00
169 Aleksander Suglobov RC 3.00 8.00
170 Seamus Kotyk RC 3.00 8.00
171 Andy Chiodo RC 3.00 8.00
172 Ryan Kesler RC 10.00 25.00
173 Mikhail Yakubov RC 3.00 8.00
174 Nathan Robinson RC 3.00 8.00
175 Tom Preissing RC 4.00 10.00
176 Jeff Hamilton RC 3.00 8.00
177 Dan Hamhuis RC 4.00 10.00
178 Antero Niittymaki RC 8.00 20.00
179 Joffrey Lupul RC 8.00 20.00
180 Garth Murray RC 4.00 10.00
181 Denis Grebeshkov RC 3.00 8.00
182 Dan Ellis RC 4.00 10.00
183 Tomas Plekanec RC 10.00 25.00
184 Tuomas Pihlman RC 4.00 10.00
185 Nolan Schaefer RC 3.00 8.00
186 Joey MacDonald RC 4.00 10.00
187 Carl Corazzini RC 3.00 8.00
188 Mike Smith RC 10.00 25.00
189 Anton Babchuk RC 3.00 8.00
190 Kyle Wellwood RC 5.00 12.00
191 Marek Svatos RC 6.00 15.00
192 Ryan Barnes RC 3.00 8.00
193 Fedor Tyutin RC 3.00 8.00
194 Dominic Moore RC 3.00 8.00
195 Colton Orr RC 4.00 10.00
196 Andrew Peters RC 4.00 10.00
197 Wade Brookbank RC 4.00 10.00
198 Cody McCormick RC 4.00 10.00
199 Michal Barinka RC 3.00 8.00
200 Mikhail Kuleshov RC 3.00 8.00

2003-04 ITG Used Signature Series Gold

1-100 VETS/50: 1.5X TO 4X BASIC CARDS
101-120 RETIRED/50: .8X TO 2X BASIC CARDS
*151-200 ROOKIE/50: .5X TO 1.2X BASIC RC

2003-04 ITG Used Signature Series Autographs

151A Darryl Bootland/25* 30.00 80.00
152A Kari Lehtonen/25* 20.00 50.00
AC1 Anson Carter NYR 6.00 15.00
AC2 Anson Carter LA/20* 6.00 15.00
AF Alexander Frolov 6.00 15.00
AH Ales Hemsky 8.00 20.00
AK1 Alex Kovalev NYR 6.00 15.00
AK2 Alexei Kovalev MON/20* 6.00 15.00
AM Alexei Morozov 5.00 12.00
AO Adam Oates 8.00 20.00
AR Andrew Raycroft 6.00 15.00
AY Alexei Yashin 6.00 15.00
BD Byron Dafoe 6.00 15.00
BG Bill Guerin 8.00 20.00
BJ Barret Jackman 5.00 12.00
BL Brian Leetch/100* 6.00 15.00
CD Chris Drury 6.00 15.00
CJ Curtis Joseph 10.00 25.00
CK Chuck Kobasew 5.00 12.00
CO Chris Osgood 8.00 20.00
CP Chris Pronger 8.00 20.00
DA Daniel Alfredsson 8.00 20.00
DC Dan Cloutier 6.00 15.00
DL David Legwand 6.00 15.00
DR Dwayne Roloson 6.00 15.00
DW Doug Weight 8.00 20.00
EB Eric Brewer 5.00 12.00
EC Erik Cole 5.00 12.00
ED Eric Daze 6.00 15.00
EJ Ed Jovanovski 6.00 15.00
EN Evgeni Nabokov 6.00 15.00
FP Felix Potvin 12.00 30.00
GM Glen Murray 6.00 15.00
HZ Henrik Zetterberg 10.00 25.00
IK Ilya Kovalchuk 8.00 20.00
JH Jeff Hackett 6.00 15.00
JI Jarome Iginla 10.00 25.00
JL John LeClair 8.00 20.00
JO Jeff O'Neill 5.00 12.00
JR Jeremy Roenick 12.00 30.00
JS Jason Spezza 8.00 20.00
JT Joe Thornton 12.00 30.00
KT Keith Tkachuk 8.00 20.00
KW Kevin Weekes 6.00 15.00
MD Marc Denis 6.00 15.00
MF Manny Fernandez 5.00 12.00
MG Marian Gaborik 8.00 20.00
MH Marian Hossa 8.00 20.00
MN Markus Naslund 8.00 20.00
MP Mike Peca 6.00 15.00
MR Mark Recchi 10.00 25.00
MS Martin St. Louis 8.00 20.00
MT Marty Turco 8.00 20.00
NK Niko Kapanen 5.00 12.00
NL Nicklas Lidstrom 8.00 20.00
OJ Olli Jokinen 8.00 20.00
OK Olaf Kolzig 8.00 20.00
PB1 Peter Bondra WAS 8.00 20.00
PB2 Peter Bondra OTT/20* 8.00 20.00
PD Pavel Datsyuk 12.00 30.00
PE Patrik Elias 8.00 20.00
PF Peter Forsberg 15.00 40.00
PL Patrick Lalime 6.00 15.00
PN Pasi Nurminen 6.00 15.00
PS Petr Sykora 6.00 15.00
RB Rob Blake 8.00 20.00
RC Roman Cechmanek 6.00 15.00
RD Rick DiPietro 6.00 15.00
RF1 Ron Francis CAR 10.00 25.00
RF2 Ron Francis TOR/20* 10.00 25.00
RK1 Rostislav Klesla 5.00 12.00
RL Roberto Luongo 12.00 30.00
RM Ryan Miller 8.00 20.00
RN Rick Nash/195* 8.00 20.00
RS Ryan Smyth 6.00 15.00
RT Roman Turek 6.00 15.00
RW Ray Whitney 6.00 15.00
SB1 Sean Burke PHX 5.00 12.00
SB2 Sean Burke PHI/20* 5.00 12.00
SD Shane Doan 6.00 15.00
SF Sergei Fedorov 12.00 30.00
SG Simon Gagne 8.00 20.00
SK Saku Koivu 8.00 20.00
SS Sergei Samsonov 6.00 15.00
TA Tyler Arnason 5.00 12.00
TB Todd Bertuzzi 8.00 20.00
TS Teemu Selanne 15.00 40.00
TV Tomas Vokoun 6.00 15.00
VD Vincent Damphousse 6.00 15.00
VL Vincent Lecavalier 8.00 20.00
ZP Zigmund Palffy 6.00 15.00
AMA Al MacInnis 10.00 25.00
BHU Brett Hull 15.00 40.00
DAE David Aebischer 6.00 15.00
DHE Dany Heatley 6.00 15.00
DLA Daymond Langkow 5.00 12.00
JBO Jay Bouwmeester 5.00 12.00
JHE Johan Hedberg 6.00 15.00
JSA Joe Sakic 15.00 40.00
JTH Jocelyn Thibault 6.00 15.00
MBI Martin Biron 6.00 15.00
MDU Mike Dunham 6.00 15.00
MHE Milan Hejduk 6.00 15.00
MRY Michael Ryder 6.00 15.00
MSA Miroslav Satan 6.00 15.00
NKH Nikolai Khabibulin 8.00 20.00
SG01 Sergei Gonchar WAS 5.00 12.00
SG02 Sergei Gonchar BOS/20* 5.00 12.00
SST Scott Stevens 8.00 20.00
TAM Tony Amonte 6.00 15.00
TSA1 Tommy Salo EDM 6.00 15.00
TSA2 Tommy Salo COL/20* 6.00 15.00
JTHE Jose Theodore 8.00 20.00
BS Brendan Shanahan/70* 8.00 20.00
DH Dominik Hasek/70* 12.00 30.00
EL Eric Lindros/70* 12.00 30.00
JJ Jaromir Jagr/70* 25.00 60.00
MB Martin Brodeur/70* 20.00 50.00
ML Mario Lemieux/70* 50.00 125.00
MM Mike Modano/70* 12.00 30.00
ON Owen Nolan/70* 8.00 20.00
SY Steve Yzerman/70* 20.00 50.00
MSU Mats Sundin/70* 8.00 20.00
BO Bobby Orr/50* 100.00 200.00
FM Frank Mahovlich/50* 8.00 20.00
GL Guy Lafleur/50* 10.00 25.00
JB Jean Beliveau/50* 10.00 25.00
PE Phil Esposito/50* 12.00 30.00
PR Patrick Roy/50* 20.00 50.00
RK Red Kelly/50* 8.00 20.00
TK Ted Kennedy/50* 8.00 20.00
TL Ted Lindsay/50* 8.00 20.00
RBO Ray Bourque/50* 12.00 30.00

2003-04 ITG Used Signature Series Autographs Gold

134 Marc-Andre Fleury 50.00 125.00
136 Eric Staal 40.00 100.00

2003-04 ITG Used Signature Series Franchise Jerseys

1 Sergei Fedorov 10.00 25.00
2 Ilya Kovalchuk 10.00 25.00
3 Joe Thornton 10.00 25.00
4 Miroslav Satan 6.00 15.00
5 Jarome Iginla 10.00 25.00
6 Jeff O'Neill 6.00 15.00
7 Tyler Arnason 6.00 15.00
8 Peter Forsberg 10.00 25.00
9 Rick Nash 8.00 20.00
10 Mike Modano 10.00 25.00
11 Steve Yzerman 20.00 50.00
12 Ryan Smyth 6.00 15.00
13 Roberto Luongo 10.00 25.00
14 Zigmund Palffy 8.00 20.00
15 Marian Gaborik 12.50 30.00
16 Jose Theodore 10.00 25.00
17 Tomas Vokoun 6.00 15.00
18 Martin Brodeur 20.00 50.00
19 Eric Lindros 8.00 20.00
20 Rick DiPietro 8.00 20.00
21 Marian Hossa 8.00 20.00
22 Jeremy Roenick 10.00 25.00
23 Shane Doan 6.00 15.00
24 Mario Lemieux 20.00 50.00
25 Evgeni Nabokov 8.00 20.00
26 Chris Pronger 8.00 20.00
27 Vincent Lecavalier 8.00 20.00
28 Mats Sundin 8.00 20.00
29 Markus Naslund 8.00 20.00
30 Olaf Kolzig 8.00 20.00

2003-04 ITG Used Signature Series Game-Day Jerseys

1 Mats Sundin 10.00 25.00
2 Mike Modano 10.00 25.00
3 Steve Yzerman 25.00 60.00
4 Mario Lemieux 15.00 40.00
5 Ray Bourque 15.00 40.00
6 Patrick Roy 20.00 50.00
7 Martin Brodeur 15.00 40.00
8 Peter Forsberg 12.00 30.00
9 John LeClair 10.00 25.00
10 Brendan Shanahan 10.00 25.00
11 Joe Sakic 15.00 40.00

2003-04 ITG Used Signature Series Goalie Gear

1 Martin Brodeur/60* 25.00 60.00
2 Roberto Luongo/50* 12.50 30.00
3 Sean Burke/50* 8.00 20.00
4 Rick DiPietro/50* 8.00 20.00
5 Nikolai Khabibulin/60* 10.00 25.00
6 Marty Turco/60* 10.00 25.00
7 Jose Theodore/50* 10.00 25.00
9 Jocelyn Thibault/60* 10.00 25.00
10 Tomas Vokoun/60* 8.00 20.00
11 Olaf Kolzig/60* 8.00 20.00
12 Felix Potvin/60* 15.00 40.00
13 Roman Cechmanek/60* 8.00 20.00
14 Roman Turek/60* 8.00 20.00
15 Evgeni Nabokov/60* 8.00 20.00
16 Tommy Salo/60* 6.00 15.00
17 Mike Dunham/60* 6.00 15.00
18 Jeff Hackett/60* 6.00 15.00
19 Chris Osgood/60* 8.00 20.00
20 Byron Dafoe/60* 5.00 12.00
21 David Aebischer/50* 10.00 25.00
25 Bernie Parent/60* 20.00 50.00
26 Patrick Lalime/60* 8.00 20.00
27 Dan Cloutier/60* 8.00 20.00
28 Jean-Sebastien Giguere/60* 8.00 20.00
31 Vladislav Tretiak/60* 30.00 80.00
32 Frank Brimsek/20* 20.00 40.00
33 Andrew Raycroft/50* 10.00 25.00
34 Ed Belfour/60* 10.00 25.00
35 Harry Lumley/30* 20.00 40.00
36 Roger Crozier/40* 12.50 30.00

2003-04 ITG Used Signature Series International Experience Jerseys

1 Martin Brodeur 15.00 40.00
2 Mario Lemieux 20.00 50.00
3 Steve Yzerman 15.00 40.00
4 Joe Sakic 12.50 30.00
5 Curtis Joseph 10.00 25.00
6 Jarome Iginla 10.00 25.00
7 Jason Spezza 8.00 20.00
8 Barret Jackman 6.00 15.00
9 Joe Nieuwendyk 6.00 15.00
10 Rob Blake 6.00 15.00
11 Paul Kariya 8.00 20.00
12 Ed Jovanovski 6.00 15.00
13 Chris Pronger 6.00 15.00
14 Dany Heatley 10.00 25.00
15 Jaromir Jagr 8.00 20.00
16 Teemu Selanne 8.00 20.00
17 Saku Koivu 6.00 15.00
18 Vladislav Tretiak 20.00 50.00
19 Alexander Mogilny 6.00 15.00
20 Alexei Yashin 6.00 15.00
21 Nikolai Khabibulin 8.00 20.00
22 Zigmund Palffy 6.00 15.00
23 Nicklas Lidstrom 8.00 20.00
24 Peter Forsberg 15.00 40.00
25 Mats Sundin 8.00 20.00
26 Mike Modano 8.00 20.00
27 Bill Guerin 6.00 15.00
28 Brian Leetch 6.00 15.00
29 Chris Chelios 8.00 20.00
30 Tony Amonte 6.00 15.00

2003-04 ITG Used Signature Series Jerseys

*JSY/STK/80: .5X TO 1.2X JSY
1 Alex Kovalev 4.00 10.00
2 Alexei Yashin 4.00 10.00
3 Bill Guerin 4.00 10.00
4 Bobby Orr 40.00 100.00
5 Brett Hull 6.00 15.00
6 Chris Pronger 4.00 10.00
7 Dominik Hasek 10.00 25.00
8 Eric Lindros 8.00 20.00
9 Felix Potvin 10.00 25.00
10 Henrik Zetterberg 8.00 20.00
11 Ilya Kovalchuk 10.00 25.00
12 Jarome Iginla 10.00 25.00
13 Jaromir Jagr 10.00 25.00
14 Jason Spezza 6.00 15.00
15 Jeremy Roenick 10.00 25.00
16 Joe Sakic 12.00 30.00
17 Joe Thornton 10.00 25.00
18 John LeClair 4.00 10.00
19 Jose Theodore 10.00 25.00
20 Keith Tkachuk 8.00 20.00
21 Marc-Andre Fleury 12.00 30.00
22 Marian Gaborik 10.00 25.00
23 Marian Hossa 8.00 20.00
24 Mario Lemieux 25.00 60.00
25 Martin Brodeur 15.00 40.00
26 Marty Turco 6.00 15.00
27 Mats Sundin 8.00 20.00
28 Mike Modano 10.00 25.00
29 Milan Hejduk 10.00 25.00
30 Nicklas Lidstrom 8.00 20.00
31 Nikolai Khabibulin 8.00 20.00
32 Olaf Kolzig 8.00 20.00
33 Patrick Roy 20.00 50.00
34 Pavel Datsyuk 10.00 25.00
35 Peter Forsberg 10.00 25.00
36 Ray Bourque 10.00 25.00
37 Rick Dipietro 6.00 15.00
38 Rick Nash 10.00 25.00
39 Rob Blake 4.00 10.00
40 Roberto Luongo 10.00 25.00
41 Roman Cechmanek 4.00 10.00
42 Ron Francis 4.00 10.00
43 Steve Yzerman 15.00 40.00
44 Teemu Selanne 8.00 20.00
45 Vincent Lecavalier 8.00 20.00
46 Zigmund Palffy 6.00 15.00
47 Markus Naslund 8.00 20.00
48 Todd Bertuzzi 8.00 20.00
49 Jean-Sebastien Giguere 6.00 15.00
50 Sergei Fedorov 10.00 25.00
51 Kari Lehtonen 12.00 30.00

2003-04 ITG Used Signature Series Norris Trophy

1 Nicklas Lidstrom 12.50 30.00
2 Chris Pronger 8.00 20.00
3 Al MacInnis 8.00 20.00
4 Rob Blake 8.00 20.00
5 Chris Chelios 8.00 20.00
6 Chris Chelios 8.00 20.00
7 Bobby Orr 40.00 80.00
8 Doug Harvey 12.50 30.00
9 Ray Bourque 15.00 40.00
10 Brian Leetch 8.00 20.00
11 Larry Robinson 8.00 20.00
12 Denis Potvin 8.00 20.00
13 Jacques Laperriere 8.00 20.00

2003-04 ITG Used Signature Series Oh Canada

1 Curtis Joseph 10.00 25.00
2 Martin Brodeur 20.00 50.00
3 Ed Jovanovski 8.00 20.00
4 Scott Niedermayer 8.00 20.00
5 Al MacInnis 8.00 20.00
6 Rob Blake 8.00 20.00
7 Eric Brewer 8.00 20.00
8 Owen Nolan 8.00 20.00
9 Eric Lindros 10.00 25.00
10 Paul Kariya 8.00 20.00
11 Steve Yzerman 20.00 50.00
12 Mike Peca 8.00 20.00
13 Brendan Shanahan 15.00 40.00
14 Ryan Smyth 8.00 20.00
15 Joe Nieuwendyk 8.00 20.00
16 Jarome Iginla 12.50 30.00

2003-04 ITG Used Signature Series Retrospectives

1A Patrick Roy 15.00 40.00
1B Patrick Roy 15.00 40.00
1C Patrick Roy 15.00 40.00
1D Patrick Roy 15.00 40.00
1E Patrick Roy 15.00 40.00
1F Patrick Roy 15.00 40.00
2A Jaromir Jagr 10.00 25.00
2B Jaromir Jagr 10.00 25.00
2C Jaromir Jagr 10.00 25.00
2D Jaromir Jagr 10.00 25.00
2E Jaromir Jagr 10.00 25.00
2F Jaromir Jagr 10.00 25.00
3A Brett Hull 10.00 25.00
3B Brett Hull 10.00 25.00
3C Brett Hull 10.00 25.00
3D Brett Hull 10.00 25.00
3E Brett Hull 10.00 25.00
3F Brett Hull 10.00 25.00
4A Mario Lemieux 15.00 40.00
4B Mario Lemieux 15.00 40.00
4C Mario Lemieux 15.00 40.00
4D Mario Lemieux 15.00 40.00
4E Mario Lemieux 15.00 40.00
4F Mario Lemieux 15.00 40.00
5A Mats Sundin 8.00 20.00
5B Mats Sundin 8.00 20.00
5C Mats Sundin 8.00 20.00
5D Mats Sundin 8.00 20.00
5E Mats Sundin 8.00 20.00
5F Mats Sundin 8.00 20.00
6A Curtis Joseph 8.00 20.00
6B Curtis Joseph PAD 12.00 30.00
6C Curtis Joseph 8.00 20.00
6D Curtis Joseph 8.00 20.00
6E Curtis Joseph 8.00 20.00
6F Curtis Joseph 8.00 20.00
7A Paul Kariya 8.00 20.00
7B Paul Kariya 8.00 20.00
7C Paul Kariya 8.00 20.00
7D Paul Kariya 8.00 20.00
7E Paul Kariya 8.00 20.00
7F Paul Kariya 8.00 20.00
8A Pavel Bure 8.00 20.00
8B Pavel Bure 8.00 20.00
8C Pavel Bure 8.00 20.00
8D Pavel Bure 8.00 20.00

8E Pavel Bure 8.00 20.00
8F Pavel Bure 8.00 20.00
9A Ed Belfour 8.00 20.00
9B Ed Belfour 8.00 20.00
9C Ed Belfour 8.00 20.00
9D Ed Belfour 8.00 20.00
9E Ed Belfour 8.00 20.00
9F Ed Belfour 8.00 20.00
10A Mark Messier 10.00 25.00
10B Mark Messier 10.00 25.00
10C Mark Messier 10.00 25.00
10D Mark Messier 10.00 25.00
10E Mark Messier 10.00 25.00
10F Mark Messier 10.00 25.00
11A Martin Brodeur 15.00 40.00
11B Martin Brodeur 15.00 40.00
11C Martin Brodeur 15.00 40.00
11D Martin Brodeur 15.00 40.00
11E Martin Brodeur 15.00 40.00
11F Martin Brodeur 15.00 40.00
12A Dominik Hasek 10.00 25.00
12B Dominik Hasek 10.00 25.00
12C Dominik Hasek STK 10.00 25.00
12D Dominik Hasek 10.00 25.00
12E Dominik Hasek 10.00 25.00
12F Dominik Hasek 10.00 25.00
13A Steve Yzerman 15.00 40.00
13B Steve Yzerman 15.00 40.00
13C Steve Yzerman 15.00 40.00
13D Steve Yzerman 15.00 40.00
13E Steve Yzerman 15.00 40.00
13F Steve Yzerman 15.00 40.00
14A Brian Leetch 8.00 20.00
14B Brian Leetch 8.00 20.00
14C Brian Leetch 8.00 20.00
14D Brian Leetch 8.00 20.00
14E Brian Leetch 8.00 20.00
14F Brian Leetch 8.00 20.00

2003-04 ITG Used Signature Series Teammates

1 P.Kariya/T.Selanne 10.00 25.00
2 M.Recchi/J.LeClair 10.00 25.00
3 J.Spezza/M.Hossa 10.00 25.00
4 B.Hull/H. Zetterberg 15.00 40.00
5 T.Bertuzzi/M.Naslund 10.00 25.00
6 T.Amonte/J.Roenick 10.00 25.00
7 J.Sakic/P.Forsberg 12.00 30.00
8 D. Weight/K.Tkachuk 10.00 25.00
9 M.Lemieux/M.Fleury 25.00 60.00
10 E.Lindros/A.Kovalev 10.00 25.00
11 R.Luongo/J.Bouwmeester 10.00 25.00
12 M.Messier/B.Leetch 10.00 25.00
13 S.Yzerman/D.Hasek 15.00 40.00
14 J.Giguere/S.Fedorov 10.00 25.00
15 M.Sundin/E.Belfour 10.00 25.00
16 M.Brodeur/S.Stevens 15.00 40.00
17 J.Thornton/G.Murray 10.00 25.00
18 R.Bourque/C. Neely 15.00 40.00
19 M.Modano/M.Turco 10.00 25.00
20 P.Roy/R.Blake 12.00 30.00

2003-04 ITG Used Signature Series Triple Memorabilia

1 Henrik Zetterberg/30 30.00 80.00
2 Mats Sundin/15 40.00 100.00
3 Ray Bourque/20 30.00 60.00
4 Bobby Orr/20 125.00 200.00
5 Eddie Shore/15 50.00 100.00
6 Stan Mikita/25 15.00 40.00
7 Pavel Datsyuk/35 30.00 80.00
8 Aurel Joliat/20 30.00 60.00
9 Marty Turco/50 12.50 30.00
10 Martin Brodeur/40 50.00 125.00
11 Jocelyn Thibault/50 12.50 30.00
12 Sean Burke/50 12.50 30.00
13 Gerry Cheevers/45 25.00 60.00
14 Jean-Sebastien Giguere/30 12.50 30.00
15 Milan Hejduk/40 12.50 30.00
16 Jarome Iginla/40 20.00 50.00
17 Olaf Kolzig/45 12.50 30.00
18 Eric Lindros/35 20.00 50.00
19 Evgeni Nabokov/35 12.50 30.00
20 Mario Lemieux/45 40.00 100.00
21 Cam Neely/40 20.00 50.00
22 Bernie Parent/45 30.00 80.00
23 Jacques Plante/35 50.00 125.00
24 Patrick Roy/20 25.00 60.00
25 Joe Sakic/35 25.00 60.00
26 Joe Thornton/35 15.00 40.00
27 Keith Tkachuk/35 20.00 50.00
28 Alexei Yashin/40 12.50 30.00
29 Andrew Raycroft/45 15.00 40.00
30 David Aebischer/50 12.50 30.00

2003-04 ITG Used Signature Series Vintage Memorabilia

1 Bobby Orr/25 75.00 150.00
2 Ray Bourque/25 30.00 80.00
3 Phil Esposito/25 15.00 40.00
4 Tony Esposito/25 15.00 40.00
5 Ted Lindsay/25 15.00 40.00
6 Bobby Hull/25 40.00 80.00
7 Jean Beliveau/25 25.00 60.00
8 Ted Kennedy/25 15.00 40.00
9 Ed Giacomin/25 25.00 60.00
10 Red Kelly/40 20.00 50.00
11 Borje Salming/45 20.00 50.00
12 Bernie Parent/45 15.00 40.00
13 Gerry Cheevers/45 15.00 40.00
14 Guy Lafleur/25 20.00 50.00
15 Henri Richard/25 15.00 40.00
16 Bill Gadsby/45 15.00 40.00
17 Gump Worsley/25 25.00 60.00
18 Stan Mikita/45 15.00 40.00
19 Mike Bossy/45 15.00 40.00
20 Marcel Dionne/45 15.00 40.00
21 Aurel Joliat/50 20.00 50.00
22 Tiny Thompson/50 15.00 40.00
23 George Hainsworth/45 25.00 60.00
24 Eddie Shore/45 20.00 50.00
25 Tim Horton/45 25.00 60.00
26 Bill Mosienko/45 15.00 40.00
27 Chuck Gardiner/45 20.00 50.00
28 Doug Harvey/45 15.00 40.00
29 Rocket Richard/25 40.00 80.00
30 Jacques Plante/45 25.00 60.00

2003-04 ITG Used Signature Series Vintage Memorabilia Autographs

*AUTO: .75X TO 2X BASIC INSERTS

2013-14 ITG Used Jerseys Silver

GUJ01 Pavel Bure 6.00 15.00
GUJ02 Corey Crawford 6.00 15.00
GUJ03 Marc-Andre Fleury 10.00 25.00
GUJ04 Mario Lemieux 20.00 50.00
GUJ05 Claude Giroux 5.00 12.00
GUJ06 Jimmy Howard 6.00 15.00
GUJ07 Jaromir Jagr 15.00 40.00
GUJ08 Nicklas Lidstrom 5.00 12.00
GUJ09 Trevor Linden 5.00 12.00
GUJ10 Eric Lindros 8.00 20.00
GUJ11 Henrik Lundqvist 12.00 30.00
GUJ12 Roberto Luongo 10.00 25.00
GUJ13 Patrick Marleau 5.00 12.00
GUJ14 Cam Neely 5.00 12.00
GUJ15 Dion Phaneuf 4.00 10.00
GUJ16 Carey Price 10.00 25.00
GUJ17 Tuukka Rask 6.00 15.00
GUJ18 Joe Sakic 10.00 25.00
GUJ19 Daniel Sedin 6.00 15.00
GUJ20 Henrik Sedin 6.00 15.00
GUJ21 Teemu Selanne 8.00 20.00
GUJ22 Patrick Roy 12.00 30.00
GUJ23 Mats Sundin 5.00 12.00
GUJ24 Joe Thornton 8.00 20.00

2013-14 ITG Used Captain C Silver

CC01 Steve Yzerman 15.00 40.00
CC02 Brian Leetch 5.00 12.00
CC03 Mario Lemieux 25.00 60.00
CC04 Pavel Bure 6.00 15.00
CC05 Raymond Bourque 10.00 25.00
CC06 Mark Messier 12.00 30.00
CC07 Wendel Clark 10.00 25.00
CC08 Mike Modano 5.00 12.00
CC09 Theoren Fleury 8.00 20.00
CC10 Trevor Linden 6.00 15.00
CC11 Joe Thornton 10.00 25.00
CC12 Nicklas Lidstrom 6.00 15.00
CC13 Jaromir Jagr 20.00 50.00
CC14 Martin St. Louis 6.00 15.00
CC15 Dale Hawerchuk 8.00 20.00
CC16 Eric Lindros 10.00 25.00
CC17 Mats Sundin 6.00 15.00
CC18 Chris Chelios 6.00 15.00
CC19 Joe Sakic 12.00 30.00
CC20 Dion Phaneuf 5.00 12.00

2013-14 ITG Used Captain C Quad Jerseys Silver

QCC01 Bcyk/O'Rlly/Thrntn/Brqe 12.00 30.00
QCC02 Mkta/Chls/Amnte/Svrd 10.00 25.00
QCC03 Ldstm/Dlvch/Hwe/Yzrm 25.00 50.00
QCC04 Sndin/Clrk/Glmr/Phnf 12.00 30.00
QCC05 Svrd/Chls/Blvu/Crbnu 15.00 40.00
QCC06 Clrke/Lndrs/Frsbrg/Grx 15.00 40.00
QCC07 Jagr/Espsto/Mssr/Ltch 25.00 60.00
QCC08 Lndn/Mssr/Lngo/Nslnd 15.00 40.00
QCC09 Nln/Dmphe/Mrlu/Thrntn 10.00 25.00

2013-14 ITG Used Classic Scraps Dual Memorabilia Silver

CS01 T.Domi/B.Probert 6.00 15.00
CS02 P.Roy/C.Osgood 8.00 20.00
CS03 D.McCarty/C.Lemieux 6.00 15.00
CS04 T.Williams/T.O'Reilly 5.00 12.00
CS05 C.Chelios/R.Hextall 6.00 15.00
CS06 K.Daneyko/M.Vukota 4.00 10.00
CS07 D.Langdon/G.Odjick 4.00 10.00
CS08 D.Hunter/T.O'Reilly 5.00 12.00
CS09 C.Simon/T.Domi 4.00 10.00
CS10 P.Roy/M.Vernon 8.00 20.00
CS11 M.McSorley/M.Messier 8.00 20.00
CS12 B.Probert/W.Clark 6.00 15.00
CS13 P.Laus/R.Ray 5.00 12.00
CS14 D.Maloney/T.Williams 5.00 12.00
CS15 C.Neely/W.Clark 6.00 15.00
CS16 F.Potvin/R.Hextall 8.00 20.00
CS17 D.McCarty/C.Simon 4.00 10.00
CS18 R.Ray/T.Domi 4.00 10.00
CS19 B.Probert/C.Coxe 5.00 12.00
CS20 W.Clark/M.McSorley 8.00 20.00

2013-14 ITG Used Cup Battles Quad Jerseys Silver

CB01 Hsk/Lrnv/Frncs/Irbe 10.00 25.00
CB02 Brqe/Skic/Hlk/Ndrmyr 12.00 30.00
CB03 Hll/Blfr/Hsk/Peca 10.00 25.00
CB04 Yzrmn/Ldstrm/Bndra/Ots 10.00 25.00
CB05 Fdrv/McCrty/Lndrs/LClr 15.00 40.00
CB06 Roy/Frsbrg/Vnbsbrk/Laus 10.00 25.00
CB07 Mssr/Rchtr/Lndn/Bre 8.00 20.00
CB08 Mllr/Roy/Rbtlle/McSrly 10.00 25.00
CB09 Lmux/Brrsso/Rnck/Chls 25.00 60.00
CB10 Rnfrd/Krri/Brqe/Nly 12.00 30.00
CB11 McDn/Mclns/Crbn/Rbns 8.00 20.00
CB12 Cffy/Andrsn/Hxtll/Prpp 8.00 20.00
CB13 Roy/Nslnd/Mlln/Vrnn 10.00 25.00
CB14 Mssr/Fhr/Ptvn/LFntne 8.00 20.00
CB15 Bssy/Smth/Bodr/Wllms 8.00 20.00
CB16 Trttr/Nystrm/Brbr/McLsh 6.00 15.00
CB17 Rbnsn/Lmre/Mdltn/Chv 6.00 15.00
CB18 Lflr/Shtt/Lch/Drnhfr 8.00 20.00
CB19 Clrke/Brbr/Espsto/Bcyk 8.00 20.00
CB20 Crnyr/Lmre/Hll/Espsto 6.00 15.00

2013-14 ITG Used Decades Triple Jerseys Silver

D01 Rnhrt/Ekbld/McDvd 20.00 50.00
D02 Thrntn/Grx/St.Louis 8.00 20.00
D03 Prce/Lndqvst/Flry 12.00 30.00
D04 Jgr/Frsbrg/Ndrmyr 20.00 50.00
D05 Lmux/Nuwndk/Skic 25.00 60.00
D06 Roy/Sndn/Blfr 10.00 25.00
D07 Mssr/Flry/Ldstrm 8.00 20.00
D08 Fdrv/Lndrs/Oates 15.00 40.00
D09 Lmux/Cffy/Hsk 10.00 25.00
D10 Rnck/Hull/Bure 8.00 20.00
D11 Yzrmn/Jgr/Skic 20.00 50.00
D12 Krri/Slnne/Brque 10.00 25.00
D13 Fhr/Brrsso/Roy 15.00 40.00
D14 Dnne/Trttr/Hwrchk 8.00 20.00
D15 Lmux/Yzrmn/Roy 25.00 60.00
D16 Mssr/Svrd/McDnld 8.00 20.00
D17 Brque/Ststny/Bssy 12.00 30.00
D18 Espsto/Prrlt/Ptvin 12.00 30.00
D19 Lflr/Howe/Slmng 20.00 50.00
D20 Clrke/Dnne/Park 10.00 25.00
D21 Rbnsn/Sttler/Hull 12.00 30.00
D22 Espsto/Chvrs/Prnt 10.00 25.00

2013-14 ITG Used Enshrined Classmates Jerseys Silver

EC01 J.Sakic/A.Oates 10.00 25.00
EC02 P.Bure/M.Sundin 10.00 25.00
EC03 E.Belfour/M.Howe 6.00 15.00
EC04 D.Gilmour/J.Nieuwndyk 6.00 15.00
EC05 B.Hull/S.Yzerman 12.00 30.00
EC06 L.Robitaille/B.Leetch 5.00 12.00
EC07 R.Francis/M.Messier 10.00 25.00
EC08 C.Neely/V.Kharlamov 6.00 15.00
EC09 R.Bourque/P.Coffey 8.00 20.00
EC10 G.Fuhr/P.LaFontaine 8.00 20.00
EC11 D.Hawerchuk/J.Kurri 6.00 15.00
EC12 M.Lemieux/B.Trottier 20.00 50.00
EC13 S.Shutt/B.Smith 5.00 12.00
EC14 M.Dionne/L.McDonald 6.00 15.00
EC15 M.Bossy/D.Potvin 6.00 15.00
EC16 T.Esposito/G.Lafleur 8.00 20.00
EC17 D.Sittler/V.Tretiak 10.00 25.00
EC18 B.Clarke/E.Giacomin 12.00 30.00
EC19 S.Savard/D.Keon 8.00 20.00
EC20 Espsto/Prnt/Mkta 10.00 25.00
EC22 G.Howe/J.Beliveau 25.00 60.00

2013-14 ITG Used Forever Rivals Quad Jerseys Silver

FR01 Mhvlch/Hrtn/Blvu/Rchrd 15.00 40.00
FR02 Fhr/Mssr/Smth/Bssy 10.00 25.00
FR03 Sttlr/Slmng/Trttr/Ptvn 10.00 25.00
FR04 McDnld/Mclnns/Mssr/Cffy 15.00 40.00
FR05 Roy/Chls/Moog/Brque 12.00 30.00
FR06 Ststny/Glet/Crbnnu/Nslnd 12.00 30.00
FR07 Shtt/Lflr/Mddltn/O'Rlly 10.00 25.00
FR08 Roy/Frsbrg/Osgd/McCrty 12.00 30.00
FR09 Bssy/Nystrm/Hdbrg/Espsto 12.00 30.00

2013-14 ITG Used Game Used All Star Quad Jerseys Silver

ASQJ01 Brqe/Roy/Mssr/Rcchi 12.00 30.00
ASQJ02 Hull/Fdrv/Bure/Slnne 20.00 50.00
ASQJ03 Lndrs/Ptvn/Osgd/Lmux 15.00 40.00
ASQJ04 Nln/Cffy/Hsk/Sndn 10.00 25.00
ASQJ05 Frsbrg/Mssr/LClr/Ndrmyr 20.00 50.00
ASQJ06 Rbtlle/Irbe/Bndra/Tkchk 12.00 30.00
ASQJ07 Bre/Sndn/Mclnns/Rcchi 12.00 30.00
ASQJ08 Jsph/Yzrmn/Lndrs/Mdno 15.00 40.00
ASQJ09 Brqe/Flry/Skc/Roy 15.00 40.00
ASQJ10 Roy/Dmphsse/Brke/Hsk 12.00 30.00
ASQJ11 Lmux/Fdrv/Chls/Thrntn 15.00 40.00
ASQJ12 Roy/Slnne/Jgr/Ldstrm 15.00 40.00

2013-14 ITG Used Game Used Quad Jerseys Silver

QJ01 Hull/Yzrmn/Skc/Jagr 20.00 50.00
QJ02 Lndqvst/Sndn/Ldstrm/Slmng 10.00 25.00
QJ03 Thrntn/St.Ls/Grx/Slnne 8.00 20.00
QJ04 Flry/Lngo/Prce/Crwfrd 12.00 30.00
QJ05 Lndrs/Ots/Hull/Lmux 25.00 60.00
QJ06 Fdrv/Nly/Glmr/Rnck 10.00 25.00
QJ07 Mssr/Brque/Skc/Yzrmn 15.00 40.00
QJ08 Hsk/Blfr/Jsph/Roy 15.00 40.00
QJ09 Prbrt/Ray/McSrly/Clrk 10.00 25.00
QJ10 Bre/Jagr/Frsbrg/Slnne 20.00 50.00
QJ11 Ndrmyr/Brqe/Ltch/Ldstrm 10.00 25.00
QJ12 McDvd/Rnhrt/Ekbld/Nylndr 25.00 60.00

2013-14 ITG Used Game Used Stick and Memorabilia Silver

GUSM01 Mario Lemieux 30.00 80.00
GUSM02 Raymond Bourque 12.00 30.00
GUSM03 Mark Messier 15.00 40.00
GUSM04 Steve Yzerman 12.00 30.00
GUSM05 Patrick Roy 20.00 50.00
GUSM06 Joe Sakic 15.00 40.00
GUSM07 Brett Hull 10.00 25.00
GUSM08 Mats Sundin 10.00 25.00
GUSM10 Joe Thornton 12.00 30.00
GUSM11 Jeremy Roenick 12.00 30.00
GUSM12 Ron Francis 10.00 25.00

2013-14 ITG Used Goalie Gear Silver

GG01 Ed Belfour 10.00 25.00
GG02 Sean Burke 10.00 25.00
GG03 Dan Cloutier 8.00 20.00
GG04 Grant Fuhr 15.00 40.00
GG05 Dominik Hasek 15.00 40.00
GG06 Ron Hextall 20.00 50.00
GG07 Curtis Joseph 12.00 30.00
GG08 Chris Osgood 8.00 20.00
GG09 Carey Price 20.00 50.00
GG10 Patrick Roy 25.00 60.00
GG11 Patrick Roy 25.00 60.00
GG12 Patrick Lalime 10.00 25.00
GG13 Marty Turco 10.00 25.00
GG14 Henrik Lundqvist 15.00 40.00
GG15 Kelly Hrudey 10.00 25.00
GG16 Semyon Varlamov 15.00 40.00

2013-14 ITG Used Guarding the Net Triple Jerseys Silver

GTN01 Dfoe/Moog/Rsk 12.00 30.00
GTN02 Brrsso/Fhr/Hsek 15.00 40.00
GTN03 Espsto/Blfr/Crwfrd 12.00 30.00
GTN04 Osgd/Jsph/Hwrd 12.00 30.00
GTN05 Osgd/Slo/Nbkv 10.00 25.00
GTN06 Vnbsbrk/Rchtr/Lndqvst 10.00 25.00
GTN07 Bpre/Emry/Hsk 10.00 25.00
GTN08 Hxtll/Vnbsbrk/Emry 12.00 30.00
GTN09 Brrsso/Hdbrg/Flry 20.00 50.00
GTN10 Brdr/Cltr/Lngo 10.00 25.00
GTN11 Ptvn/Jsph/Blfr 15.00 40.00
GTN12 Vchn/Roy/Price 25.00 60.00
GTN13 Brrsso/Vnbsbrk/Rchtr 10.00 25.00
GTN14 Lngo/Price/Flry 20.00 50.00

2013-14 ITG Used International Influence Quad Jerseys Silver

II01 Sndn/Ldstrm/Lndqvst/Slmng 12.00 30.00
II02 Bre/Lrnv/Fdrv/Nbkv 15.00 40.00
II03 Krri/Nmi/Slnne/Rask 15.00 40.00
II04 Hll/Chls/Rnck/Vnbsbrk 10.00 25.00
II05 Lmux/Hwrchk/Yzrmn/Lndrs 30.00 80.00
II06 Skc/Thrntn/Flry/St.Ls 15.00 40.00
II07 Roy/Flry/Prce/Lngo 20.00 50.00
II08 Jgr/Hsk/Hlik/Trek 25.00 60.00

2013-14 ITG Used Kick Save Silver

KS01 Patrick Roy 15.00 40.00
KS02 Dominik Hasek 15.00 40.00
KS03 Carey Price 20.00 50.00
KS04 Ed Belfour 10.00 25.00
KS05 Marty Turco 10.00 25.00
KS06 Curtis Joseph 12.00 30.00

2013-14 ITG Used On the Move Jerseys Silver

OTM01 Roberto Luongo 8.00 20.00
OTM02 Eric Lindros 8.00 20.00
OTM03 Dion Phaneuf 4.00 10.00
OTM04 Pavel Bure 6.00 15.00
OTM05 Lanny McDonald 5.00 12.00
OTM06 Felix Potvin 8.00 20.00
OTM07 Marcel Dionne 6.00 15.00
OTM08 Darryl Sittler 6.00 15.00
OTM09 Al MacInnis 6.00 15.00
OTM10 Patrick Roy 12.00 30.00
OTM11 Jaromir Jagr 15.00 40.00
OTM12 Raymond Bourque 8.00 20.00
OTM13 Curtis Joseph 6.00 15.00
OTM14 Teemu Selanne 6.00 15.00
OTM15 Jeremy Roenick 8.00 20.00
OTM16 Dominik Hasek 8.00 20.00
OTM17 Tony Amonte 4.00 10.00
OTM18 Brett Hull 10.00 25.00
OTM19 Mark Messier 10.00 25.00
OTM20 Keith Tkachuk 5.00 12.00
OTM21 Brian Leetch 4.00 10.00
OTM22 Paul Coffey 5.00 12.00
OTM23 Mats Sundin 5.00 12.00
OTM24 Peter Forsberg 10.00 25.00

2013-14 ITG Used Past Present and Future Jerseys Silver

PPF01 Glmr/Grx/Bnntt 6.00 15.00
PPF02 Rbtlle/Mrleau/Dl Clle 6.00 15.00
PPF03 Ststny/Slnne/Drstl 15.00 40.00
PPF04 Ptvn/Phnf/Ekbld 8.00 20.00
PPF05 Flry/Flry/Flry 8.00 20.00
PPF06 Lflr/Grx/Gthr 8.00 20.00
PPF07 Rnck/Crwfrd/Hrtmn 10.00 25.00
PPF08 Lndn/Sdin/Hrvt 12.00 30.00
PPF09 Lmx/Thrntn/McDvd 25.00 60.00
PPF10 Ndrmyr/Phnf/McKwn 6.00 15.00
PPF11 Sndn/Sdn/Nylndr 6.00 15.00
PPF12 Hwrchk/Pvlc/Ptn 8.00 20.00
PPF13 Skc/St.Louis/Rnhrt 8.00 20.00
PPF14 Yzrmn/Slnne/Rtche 15.00 40.00
PPF15 Nly/Thrntn/Rychl 10.00 25.00
PPF16 Bssy/Vrck/Vrtnn 8.00 20.00

2013-14 ITG Used Prospect Game Used Jerseys Silver

PJ01 Sam Bennett 8.00 20.00
PJ02 Eric Cornel 3.00 8.00
PJ03 Michael Dal Colle 4.00 10.00
PJ04 Sean Day 5.00 12.00
PJ05 Anthony DeAngelo 3.00 8.00
PJ06 Leon Draisaitl 8.00 20.00
PJ07 Nikolaj Ehlers 6.00 15.00
PJ08 Aaron Ekblad 8.00 20.00
PJ09 Robby Fabbri 3.00 8.00
PJ10 Haydn Fleury 3.00 8.00
PJ11 Frederik Gauthier 3.00 8.00
PJ12 Nikolay Goldobin 3.00 8.00
PJ13 Ryan Hartman 3.00 8.00
PJ14 Bo Horvat 6.00 15.00
PJ15 Connor McDavid 12.00 30.00
PJ16 Roland McKeown 3.00 8.00
PJ17 Matt Mistele 3.00 8.00
PJ18 William Nylander 10.00 25.00
PJ19 Brendan Perlini 5.00 12.00
PJ20 Nicolas Petan 3.00 8.00
PJ21 Sam Reinhart 10.00 25.00
PJ22 Nick Ritchie 3.00 8.00
PJ23 Kerby Rychel 3.00 8.00
PJ24 Jake Virtanen 4.00 10.00

2013-14 ITG Used Quad Franchise Jerseys Silver

QF01 Hntr/Grtnr/Bndra/Klzg 12.00 30.00
QF02 Ltch/Mssr/Rchtr/Lndqvst 10.00 25.00
QF03 Yzrmn/Ldstrm/Fdrv/Hwrd 12.00 30.00
QF04 Mssr/Fhr/Krri/Wght 12.00 30.00
QF05 Nslnd/Bre/Lndn/Lngo 10.00 25.00
QF06 Clrke/Lndros/Hxtll/Grx 15.00 40.00
QF07 Prce/Lflr/Blvu/Roy 25.00 60.00
QF08 Flry/Mclnns/Nwndk/McDnld 12.00 30.00
QF09 Clrk/Glmr/Sndn/Phnf 15.00 40.00
QF10 Bssy/Ptvn/Pca/Nbkv 10.00 25.00
QF11 Fdrko/Hull/Mclnns/Tkchk 20.00 50.00
QF12 Mdno/Blfr/Nwndyk/Hll 20.00 50.00
QF13 Lmux/Jgr/Frncs/Flry 12.00 30.00
QF14 Roy/Skc/Frsbrg/Vrlmv 12.00 30.00
QF15 Slnne/Fdrv/Ndrmyr/Hllr 15.00 40.00
QF16 Nly/Thrntn/Rsk/Brque 15.00 40.00
QF17 Blfr/Amnte/Rnck/Crwfrd 15.00 40.00
QF18 Nbkv/Nln/Thrntn/Nmi 15.00 40.00

2013-14 ITG Used Stat Leaders Triple Jerseys Silver

SL01 Grtzky/Howe/Hull 40.00 100.00
SL02 Grtzky/Frncs/Mssr 40.00 100.00
SL03 Grtzky/Mssr/Howe 40.00 100.00
SL04 Grtzky/Jagr/Dionne 40.00 100.00
SL05 Andrchk/Hull/Slnne 10.00 25.00
SL06 Grtzky/Mssr/Yzrmn 40.00 100.00
SL07 Brque/Dnne/Mclnns 10.00 25.00
SL08 Brdr/Roy/Blfr 15.00 40.00
SL09 Brdr/Roy/Jsph 15.00 40.00
SL10 Grtzky/Mssr/Krri 40.00 100.00
SL11 Grtzky/Mssr/Brqe 40.00 100.00
SL12 Grtzky/Mssr/Kurri 40.00 100.00
SL13 Chls/Ldstrm/Roy 10.00 25.00
SL14 Roy/Brdr/Fuhr 15.00 40.00
SL15 Brdr/Roy/Jsph 15.00 40.00

2013-14 ITG Used Teammates Jerseys Silver

TM01 H.Sedin/D.Sedin 8.00 20.00
TM02 W.Clark/D.Gilmour 10.00 25.00
TM03 J.Thornton/P.Marleau 10.00 25.00
TM04 J.Sakic/P.Forsberg 8.00 20.00
TM05 B.Hull/A.MacInnis 10.00 25.00
TM06 T.Selanne/J.Hiller 10.00 25.00
TM07 C.Giroux/J.Voracek 6.00 15.00
TM08 P.Coffey/M.Messier 12.00 30.00
TM09 B.Nicholls/L.Robitaille 6.00 15.00
TM10 J.Jagr/M.Lemieux 25.00 60.00
TM11 M.Recchi/E.Lindros 10.00 25.00
TM12 M.Messier/M.Richter 8.00 20.00
TM13 P.Bure/T.Linden 6.00 15.00
TM14 E.Belfour/J.Roenick 10.00 25.00
TM15 C.Chelios/L.Robinson 6.00 15.00
TM16 O.Nolan/M.Sundin 6.00 15.00
TM17 M.Richard/J.Beliveau 15.00 40.00
TM18 D.Sittler/L.McDonald 12.00 30.00
TM19 G.Howe/N.Ullman 15.00 40.00
TM20 P.Roy/G.Carbonneau 12.00 30.00
TM21 R.Bourque/C.Neely 12.00 30.00
TM22 B.Hull/S.Mikita 20.00 50.00
TM23 P.Esposito/W.Cashman 15.00 40.00
TM24 G.Lafleur/J.Lemaire 12.00 30.00
TM25 H.Watson/T.Horton 10.00 25.00
TM26 T.Selanne/K.Tkachuk 20.00 50.00
TM27 S.Yzerman/S.Fedorov 25.00 60.00
TM28 P.Lindbergh/M.Naslund 12.00 30.00

2015-16 ITG Used Jerseys Silver

GUJAD1 Alex Delvecchio/25 5.00 12.00
GUJBH1 Brett Hull/40 10.00 25.00
GUJBH2 Brett Hull/45 10.00 25.00
GUJCJ1 Curtis Joseph/45 6.00 15.00
GUJCMD Connor McDavid/45 80.00 200.00
GUJDS1 Darryl Sittler/25 6.00 15.00
GUJEL1 Eric Lindros/35 8.00 20.00
GUJFP1 Felix Potvin/45 8.00 20.00
GUJGL1 Guy Lafleur/25 6.00 15.00
GUJJLC John LeClair/40 5.00 12.00
GUJJR1 Jeremy Roenick/45 8.00 20.00
GUJJV1 John Vanbiesbrouck/45 5.00 12.00
GUJLR1 Larry Robinson/25 5.00 12.00
GUJMD1 Marcel Dionne/25 6.00 15.00
GUJML1 Mario Lemieux/35 20.00 50.00
GUJMM1 Mark Messier/45 10.00 25.00
GUJMM2 Mike Modano/45 8.00 20.00
GUJNM1 Nathan MacKinnon/45 20.00 50.00
GUJNY1 Nail Yakupov/45 3.00 8.00
GUJPE1 Phil Esposito/25 8.00 20.00
GUJPR1 Patrick Roy/40 12.00 30.00
GUJPR2 Patrick Roy/45 12.00 30.00
GUJRB1 Raymond Bourque/45 8.00 20.00
GUJRNH Ryan Nugent-Hopkins/45 6.00 15.00
GUJSY1 Steve Yzerman/45 12.00 30.00
GUJTH1 Taylor Hall/40 5.00 12.00
GUJTS1 Teemu Selanne/45 10.00 25.00
GUJVT1 Vladimir Tarasenko/45 6.00 15.00
GUJWG1 Wayne Gretzky/25 30.00 80.00

2015-16 ITG Used 4 Your Country Jerseys Silver

*GOLD/25: .6X TO 1.5X SILVER/40
4YC01 Clrke/Bssy/Sht/Epsto 6.00 15.00
4YC02 Lmx/Skc/Yzrmn/Frncs 15.00 40.00
4YC03 Jsph/Lndrs/Thrtn/Lngo 6.00 15.00
4YC04 Dnne/Sttlr/Sht/Clrke 6.00 15.00
4YC05 Slne/Korsff/Kvu/Krri 8.00 20.00
4YC06 Mdno/Rchtr/LaFntne/Hll 8.00 20.00
4YC07 Brso/Tkchk/Chls/Ltch 4.00 10.00
4YC08 Trtk/Krtv/Mkhlv/Ykshv 4.00 10.00
4YC09 Lndbrgh/Sndn/Frsbrg/Ldstrm 15.00 40.00
4YC10 Slmng/Ldstrm/Frsbrg/Sndn 8.00 20.00

2015-16 ITG Used 50 in 50 Cut Autographs Silver

MR1 Maurice Richard 100.00 200.00

2015-16 ITG Used Dynasty Collection Jerseys Silver

DCGA1 Glenn Anderson/45 3.00 8.00
DCGF1 Grant Fuhr/40 6.00 15.00
DCGL1 Guy Lafleur/35 5.00 12.00
DCGL2 Guy Lapointe/30 3.00 8.00
DCJK1 Jari Kurri/45 4.00 10.00
DCLR1 Larry Robinson/45 4.00 10.00
DCMM1 Mark Messier/45 8.00 20.00
DCSS1 Steve Shutt/45 3.00 8.00
DCYC1 Yvan Cournoyer/30 4.00 10.00

2015-16 ITG Used Dynasty Duo Jerseys Silver

DCD02 M.Bossy/B.Trottier/35 6.00 15.00
DCD03 J.Kurri/G.Anderson/35 6.00 15.00
DCD07 S.Shutt/L.Robinson/25 6.00 15.00
DCD10 P.Coffey/G.Fuhr/35 10.00 25.00

2015-16 ITG Used Fantasy Team 8's Jerseys Silver

FT801 Gtz/Lx/Ry/Brq/Lds Hk/Hl/Fd/30 40.00 100.00
FT803 MD/Dn/MK/Tr/Hl RNH/Lz/Yk/45 100.00 250.00
FT804 Th/Sc/Fg/Sln Lds/Flr/Crd/Pr/45 12.00 30.00
FT805 Lf/Cs/Brd/Pe/Rb/Ch/Yz/Kn/35 25.00 60.00
FT806 Ms/Blv/Pt/Pc/Cf/Hr/Lc/Trt/25 12.00 30.00
FT807 Wr/Ln/Lnd/Ly/Pt/Nd/Slm/Jr/35 20.00 50.00
FT808 Ry/Blf/By/Md/Brq Cf/Clr/Dn/40 15.00 40.00

2015-16 ITG Used Hat Trick Jerseys Silver

HT02 Hll/Dnne/Espsto/45 12.00 30.00
HT03 Hll/Slnne/Lndrs/45 12.00 30.00
HT04 Mdno/Clrk/LClr/45 10.00 25.00
HT05 Yzrmn/Lmx/Hll/45 25.00 60.00
HT06 Krri/Andrsn/Bssy/25 8.00 20.00
HT07 Crsby/Ovchkn/Mlkn/45 25.00 60.00
HT08 Jgr/Skc/Rnck/40 20.00 50.00

2015-16 ITG Used Jersey Autographs Silver

GUABB1 Brian Bellows/40 8.00 20.00
GUABG1 Bill Gadsby/45 10.00 25.00
GUABH1 Bobby Hull/20 20.00 50.00
GUABH2 Brett Hull/40 20.00 50.00
GUABP1 Bernie Parent/40 12.00 30.00
GUACJ1 Curtis Joseph/30 12.00 30.00
GUAEG1 Ed Giacomin/40 10.00 25.00
GUAEL1 Eric Lindros/40 15.00 40.00
GUAJJ1 Jaromir Jagr/30 30.00 80.00
GUAJT1 Jose Theodore/40 10.00 25.00
GUAMD1 Marcel Dionne/30 12.00 30.00
GUAMM2 Mike Modano/30 15.00 40.00
GUANL1 Nicklas Lidstrom/40 10.00 25.00
GUAPR1 Patrick Roy/20 25.00 60.00
GUARB1 Raymond Bourque/30 15.00 40.00
GUASF1 Sergei Fedorov/20 15.00 40.00
GUATB1 Tom Barrasso/45 10.00 25.00
GUATL1 Ted Lindsay/45 10.00 25.00
GUATL2 Trevor Linden/40 10.00 25.00

2015-16 ITG Used Jerseys Dual Silver

*GOLD: .6X TO 1.5X BASIC INSERTS
GU2J01 C.McDavid/RNH/60 100.00 250.00
GU2J02 C.McDavid/T.Hall/60 100.00 250.00
GU2J03 McDavid/Yakupov/60 100.00 250.00
GU2J04 McDavid/S.Crosby/60 100.00 250.00
GU2J05 Gretzky/McDavid/25 100.00 250.00
GU2J06 Lemieux/Yzerman/50 25.00 60.00
GU2J07 J.Roenick/B.Hull/60 12.00 30.00
GU2J08 B.Hull/M.Modano/60 12.00 30.00
GU2J09 G.Howe/Gretzky/20 40.00 100.00
GU2J10 Lafleur/J.Beliveau/20 8.00 20.00
GU2J11 S.Fedorov/J.Jagr/50 20.00 50.00
GU2J12 D.Harvey/G.Howe/20 20.00 50.00
GU2J13 B.Salming/D.Sittler/35 8.00 20.00
GU2J14 Barrasso/M.Fleury/50 12.00 30.00
GU2J15 P.Esposito/Lafleur/40 10.00 25.00
GU2J16 Messier/G.Lafleur/45 12.00 30.00
GU2J17 Gretzky/G.Lafleur/25 40.00 100.00
GU2J18 Bourque/C.Neely/50 10.00 25.00
GU2J19 Fedorov/Selanne/50 12.00 30.00
GU2J20 B.Hull/T.Selanne/20 12.00 30.00
GU2J21 B.Trottier/M.Bossy/45 6.00 15.00
GU2J22 G.Hall/T.Esposito/25 6.00 15.00
GU2J23 Giacomin/Cheevers/20 6.00 15.00
GU2J24 Lemieux/E.Lindros/45 25.00 60.00
GU2J25 Lidstrom/S.Fedorov/55 10.00 25.00

2015-16 ITG Used Jerseys Quad Silver

*GOLD: 1X TO 2.5X SILVER/40-55
GU4J01 McDvd/RNH/Ykpv/Hall/55 40.00 100.00
GU4J02 Hll/Lndn/Nslnd/Rnck/55 5.00 12.00
GU4J03 Roy/Jsph/Hsk/Rchtr/40 6.00 15.00
GU4J04 Mssr/Yzrmn/Lmx/Fdrv/40 10.00 25.00
GU4J05 Ldstrm/Yzrmn/Fdrv/Hll/40 6.00 15.00
GU4J06 Clrk/Kn/Sttlr/Slmng/20 4.00 10.00
GU4J07 Rbnsn/Ry/Lflr/Sht/20 6.00 15.00
GU4J08 LClr/Lndrs/Rnck/Vnbs/45 4.00 10.00
GU4J09 McDv/Crsby/Ovch/Stmk/45 40.00 100.00

2015-16 ITG Used Jerseys Trios Silver

*GOLD: .5X TO 1.2X SILVER
GU3J01 Grtzky/Lflr/Mssr/25 30.00 80.00
GU3J02 McDvid/RNH/Ykpv/55 80.00 200.00
GU3J03 McDvd/Crsby/Ovch/55 80.00 200.00
GU3J04 Fdrv/Yzrmn/Ldstrm/40 12.00 30.00
GU3J07 Ovchkn/Mlkn/Gtzlf/40 20.00 50.00
GU3J08 Kn/Sttlr/Slmng/35 6.00 15.00
GU3J09 Thrntn/Frsbrg/Skc/45 10.00 25.00
GU3J10 Hll/Mdno/LClr/50 10.00 25.00
GU3J11 Swchk/Vchn/Dnne/25 6.00 15.00
GU3J12 Grtzky/Rbtlle/Krri/20 50.00 125.00
GU3J13 Trsnko/Mlkn/Ovch/45 20.00 50.00
GU3J14 Brrsso/Ptvn/Jsph/45 8.00 20.00
GU3J15 Lndn/Hll/Mdno/45 10.00 25.00
GU3J16 Lndrs/Lndn/Skc/45 10.00 25.00
GU3J17 Bssy/Slnne/Lmx/30 20.00 50.00
GU3J18 Ldstrm/Brqe/Rbnsn/30 8.00 20.00

2015-16 ITG Used Locker Room Collection Jerseys Silver

LRDH1 Dominik Hasek/20 20.00 50.00
LRRB1 Raymond Bourque/20 10.00 25.00

2015-16 ITG Used Maximum Memorabilia Silver

*GOLD/20-25: .5X TO 1.2X SILVER
MMAMI Al MacInnis/50 5.00 12.00
MMBH2 Brett Hull/45 8.00 20.00
MMBS1 Brendan Shanahan/45 4.00 10.00
MMCL1 Curtis Lazar/50 2.50 6.00
MMCMD1 Connor McDavid/50 60.00 150.00
MMCMD2 Connor McDavid/50 60.00 150.00
MMDH2 Dale Hawerchuk/50 5.00 12.00
MMHL1 Henrik Lundqvist/50 10.00 25.00
MMJD1 Jonathan Drouin/50 3.00 8.00
MMJH1 Jeff Hackett/50 3.00 8.00
MMJI1 Jarome Iginla/50 5.00 12.00
MMJJ1 Jaromir Jagr/40 12.00 30.00
MMJR1 Jeremy Roenick/50 6.00 15.00
MMJT1 Jose Theodore/40 4.00 10.00
MMLR2 Luc Robitaille/50 4.00 10.00
MMMAF Marc-Andre Fleury/45 8.00 20.00
MMMG1 Marian Gaborik/50 4.00 10.00
MMMH1 Milan Hejduk/50 3.00 8.00
MMMK1 Miikka Kiprusoff/50 4.00 10.00
MMML1 Mario Lemieux/45 15.00 40.00
MMMM1 Mark Messier/40 8.00 20.00
MMMN1 Markus Naslund/50 4.00 10.00
MMMT1 Marty Turco/50 4.00 10.00
MMNK1 Nikolai Khabibulin/50 4.00 10.00
MMNM1 Nathan MacKinnon/50 15.00 40.00
MMPB1 Pavel Bure/50 4.00 10.00
MMPK1 Patrick Kane/50 8.00 20.00
MMPR1 Patrick Roy/45 10.00 25.00
MMRB2 Rob Blake/50 4.00 10.00
MMRL1 Roberto Luongo/50 6.00 15.00
MMRNH1 Ryan Nugent-Hopkins/50 5.00 12.00
MMRNH2 Ryan Nugent-Hopkins/50 5.00 12.00
MMSC1 Sidney Crosby/45 15.00 40.00
MMTH1 Taylor Hall/45 4.00 10.00
MMTV1 Tomas Vokoun/50 3.00 8.00

2015-16 ITG Used Stack The Pads Silver

SPBP1 Bernie Parent/20 8.00 20.00
SPCJ1 Curtis Joseph/20 8.00 20.00
SPCP1 Carey Price/25 12.00 30.00
SPDH1 Dominik Hasek/20 10.00 25.00
SPGF1 Grant Fuhr/20 10.00 25.00
SPJT1 Jose Theodore/20 6.00 15.00
SPJV1 John Vanbiesbrouck/20 6.00 15.00
SPPR1 Patrick Roy/20 15.00 40.00

2015-16 ITG Used Team 8's Jerseys Silver

T801 Yz/Ld/Hw/Sw/Ly/Hl/Fd/Ch/25 30.00 80.00
T802 Ry/Bv/Pn/Hy/Lr/Rc/St/Rc/25 25.00 60.00
T803 Gz/Ms/Fr/Kr/An/Cy/Lw/Rn/20 60.00 150.00
T804 Hl/Mk/Es/Hl/Ch/Ms/Rn/Br/20 20.00 50.00
T805 Hn/Br/Sr/Kn/Sm/Cl/Mh/Cn/20 12.00 30.00
T806 Bq/Tn/Cs/Sr/Es/Nl/Bk/Pk/20 15.00 40.00
T807 Ln/Pt/Ck/Vb/LC/Rk/Hx/Lh/30 15.00 40.00
T808 Lx/Br/Mk/Cy/Rb/Fr/Fy/Jr/35 40.00 100.00

2015-16 ITG Used Vintage Memorabilia Silver

VMJP1 Jacques Plante/20 8.00 20.00
VMTS2 Terry Sawchuk/20 6.00 15.00

2015-16 ITG Used Vintage Memorabilia Dual Silver

VM201 G.Howe/M.Richard/25 25.00 60.00
VM204 T.Sawchuk/J.Plante/25 10.00 25.00
VM206 P.Lindbergh/B.Parent/30 10.00 25.00
VM208 P.Esposito/B.Hull/25 15.00 40.00
VM210 G.Worsley/E.Giacomin/20 8.00 20.00
VM216 B.Geoffrion/J.Beliveau/25 8.00 20.00

2016-17 ITG Used Jerseys

GU02 Bobby Baun/20 5.00 12.00
GU03 Brett Hull/45 10.00 25.00
GU04 Curtis Joseph/45 6.00 15.00
GU05 Dave Keon/25 5.00 12.00
GU06 Gerry Cheevers/25 5.00 12.00
GU07 Grant Fuhr/45 8.00 20.00
GU08 Jacques Laperriere/25 4.00 10.00
GU09 Jeremy Roenick/45 8.00 20.00
GU10 Joe Sakic/45 10.00 25.00
GU11 Joe Thornton/45 8.00 20.00
GU12 John Vanbiesbrouck/45 5.00 12.00
GU13 Lanny McDonald/45 5.00 12.00
GU14 Larry Murphy/45 4.00 10.00
GU15 Marian Gaborik/45 5.00 12.00
GU16 Mario Lemieux/45 20.00 50.00
GU17 Matt Murray/45 8.00 20.00
GU18 P.K. Subban/45 6.00 15.00
GU19 Patrick Roy/45 12.00 30.00
GU20 Paul Coffey/45 5.00 12.00
GU21 Paul Kariya/45 5.00 12.00
GU22 Peter Forsberg/45 10.00 25.00
GU23 Peter Stastny/20 4.00 10.00
GU24 Pierre Turgeon/45 4.00 10.00
GU25 Rick Martin/20 5.00 12.00
GU26 Rick Nash/45 5.00 12.00
GU27 Ryan Nugent-Hopkins/45 6.00 15.00
GU28 Sergei Fedorov/45 8.00 20.00
GU29 Steve Shutt/25 5.00 12.00
GU30 Steven Stamkos/45 10.00 25.00
GU31 Teemu Selanne/45 10.00 25.00
GU32 Wayne Gretzky/25 30.00 80.00

2016-17 ITG Used Autographs

GUABB1 Bill Barber/30 10.00 25.00
GUABH1 Bobby Hull/30 20.00 50.00
GUABH2 Brett Hull/30 20.00 50.00
GUAGF1 Grant Fuhr/30 15.00 40.00
GUAGL1 Guy Lafleur/30 12.00 30.00
GUAJS1 Joe Sakic/30 20.00 50.00
GUAJT1 Jose Theodore/30 10.00 25.00
GUAPB1 Pavel Bure/30 10.00 25.00
GUAPC1 Paul Coffey/30 10.00 25.00
GUAPF1 Peter Forsberg/30 20.00 50.00
GUATL1 Trevor Linden/30 10.00 25.00
GUATS1 Teemu Selanne/30 20.00 50.00
GUAVT1 Vladislav Tretiak/30 8.00 20.00
GUAWC1 Wendel Clark/30 15.00 40.00

2016-17 ITG Used Countrymen Memorabilia

C01 Yzerman/Sakic/Brodeur Thornton/Lemieux/Joseph Francis/Lindros 20.00 50.00
C02 Bossy/Shutt/Esposito Sittler/Perreault/Clarke Dionne/Goulet 8.00 20.00
C03 Crosby/Price/Fleury Luongo/Toews/Doughty Stamkos/Tavares 20.00 50.00
C04 Koivu/Selanne/Koivu Nittymaki/Kurri/Tikkanen Kiprusoff/Backstrom 10.00 25.00
C05 Samuelsson/Sundin/Lindbergh Lidstrom/Forsberg/Zetterberg Salming/Naslund 10.00 25.00
C06 Hull/Tkachuk/Leetch Richter/Modano LaFontaine/Barrasso/Chelios 10.00 25.00
C07 Yakushev/Mikhailov Kharlamov/Maltsev/Myshkin Krutov/Mylnikov/Tretiak 4.00 10.00

2016-17 ITG Used Fantasy Team 8's Memorabilia

FT801 Gretzky/Howe/Plante/Harvey Lemieux/Richard/Orr/Roy/30 40.00 100.00
FT802 Hull/Cheevers/Clarke/Lidstrom/Lafleur Esposito/Parent/Dionne/35 12.00 30.00
FT803 Delvecchio/Robinson Esposito/Keon/Laperriere/Sittler Giacomin/Shutt/35 8.00 20.00
FT804 Sakic/Ovechkin/Kane/Sundin/Hasek Price/Chelios/Pronger/35 25.00 60.00
FT805 Gretzky/Lindsay/Potvin Lemieux/Tretiak/Brodeur Salming/Howe/35 40.00 100.00
FT806 Selanne/Bure/Lidstrom/Leetch Roy/Brodeur/Messier Fedorov/35 15.00 40.00
FT807 Sawchuk/Parent/McDonald Sittler/Esposito/Robinson Bourque/Bossy/25 10.00 25.00
FT808 Tkachuk/Turgeon/Modano Roenick/Richter/Pronger Belfour/Niedermayer/35 10.00 25.00
FT809 Dionne/Lemieux/MacInnis Bourque/Fuhr/Price Selanne/Tkachuk/35 25.00 60.00
FT810 Yzerman/Esposito Cheevers/Roy/Robinson Neely/Pronger/Hull/35 15.00 40.00

2016-17 ITG Used International Showdown Memorabilia
IS01 Chelios/Hull/Modano LaFontaine/Mikhailov/Krutov Yakushev/Kharlamov 10.00 25.00
IS02 Lemieux/Esposito/Shutt Bossy/Hull/Richter LaFontaine/Modano 20.00 50.00
IS03 Selanne/Koivu/Tikkanen/Kurri Sundin/Lindbergh Forsberg/Lidstrom 10.00 25.00
IS04 Bure/Ovechkin/Mogilny Malkin/Sittler/Yzerman Clarke/Sakic 20.00 50.00
IS05 Tretiak/Kharlamov Mikhailov/Krutov/Jagr Holik/Dzurilla/Stastny 15.00 40.00

2016-17 ITG Used Legends of Chicago Stadium Relics
LCS01 Bobby Hull 12.00 30.00
LCS02 Bobby Orr 25.00 60.00
LCS03 Glenn Hall 6.00 15.00
LCS04 Phil Esposito 10.00 25.00
LCS05 Pierre Pilote 6.00 15.00
LCS06 Stan Mikita 8.00 20.00
LCS07 Tony Esposito 6.00 15.00

2016-17 ITG Used Legends of Olympia Stadium Relics
LOS01 Alex Delvecchio 6.00 15.00
LOS02 Bill Gadsby 6.00 15.00
LOS03 Gordie Howe 20.00 50.00
LOS04 Harry Lumley 6.00 15.00
LOS05 Marcel Pronovost 6.00 15.00
LOS06 Norm Ullman 6.00 15.00
LOS07 Red Kelly 6.00 15.00
LOS08 Sid Abel 6.00 15.00
LOS09 Ted Lindsay 6.00 15.00
LOS10 Terry Sawchuk 6.00 15.00

2016-17 ITG Used Legendary Starting Six Memorabilia
LS601 Gretzky/Lemieux/Chelios Roy/Pronger/Hull/30 25.00 60.00
LS602 Howe/Orr/Gretzky/Ovechkin Hasek/Stevens/25 25.00 60.00
LS603 Lemieux/Sakic/Lidstrom/Roy Lafleur/Housley/30 15.00 40.00
LS604 Mikita/Bure/Lidstrom/Hasek Chelios/Fedorov/30 6.00 15.00
LS605 Savard/Lafleur/Hall/Niedermayer Lidstrom/Lemieux/30 15.00 40.00

2016-17 ITG Used Quad Jerseys
GQ01 Baun/Plante/Salming/Keon/30 8.00 20.00
GQ02 Esposito/Hall Belfour/Crawford/35 6.00 15.00
GQ03 Fedorov/Bure/Mogilny Ovechkin/35 20.00 50.00
GQ04 Gretzky/Lemieux Lafleur/Esposito/35 30.00 80.00
GQ05 Howe/Delvecchio Lindsay/Fedorov/35 15.00 40.00
GQ06 Kariya/Sakic/Forsberg/Hull/35 10.00 25.00
GQ07 Kariya/Selanne/Getzlaf/Perry/35 10.0025.00
GQ08 MacInnis/Coffey Murphy/Chelios/35 6.00 15.00
GQ09 Nugent-Hopkins/Hall/MacKinnon/Drouin/35 20.00 50.00
GQ10 Vokoun/Vernon Nabokov/Khabibulin/35 4.00 10.00

2016-17 ITG Used Quad Patches
GQP01 Baun/Plante/Salming/Keon/30 8.00 20.00
GQP02 Esposito/Hall Belfour/Crawford/35 6.00 15.00
GQP03 Fedorov/Bure Mogilny/Ovechkin/35 20.00 50.00
GQP04 Gretzky/Lemieux Lafleur/Esposito/35 30.00 80.00
GQP05 Howe/Delvecchio Lindsay/Fedorov/35 15.00 40.00
GQP06 Kariya/Sakic/Forsberg/Hull/35 10.0025.00
GQP07 Kariya/Selanne Getzlaf/Perry/35 10.00 25.00
GQP08 MacInnis/Coffey Murphy/Chelios/35 6.00 15.00
GQP09 Nugent-Hopkins/Hall/MacKinnon/Drouin/35 20.00 50.00
GQP10 Vokoun/Vernon Nabokov/Khabibulin/35 4.00 10.00

2016-17 ITG Used Super Swatch
SS01 Alexander Ovechkin 20.00 50.00
SS02 Alexei Kovalev 4.00 10.00
SS03 Arturs Irbe 4.00 10.00
SS04 Bill Guerin 5.00 12.00
SS05 Brendan Shanahan 5.00 12.00
SS06 Brett Hull 10.00 25.00
SS07 Brian Leetch 4.00 10.00
SS08 Carey Price 10.00 25.00
SS09 Chris Chelios 5.00 12.00
SS10 Chris Pronger 5.00 12.00
SS11 Corey Crawford 6.00 15.00
SS12 Daniel Alfredsson 5.00 12.00
SS13 Drew Doughty 6.00 15.00
SS14 Ed Belfour 5.00 12.00
SS15 Ed Jovanovski 5.00 12.00
SS16 Gabriel Landeskog 6.00 15.00
SS17 Ilya Kovalchuk 5.00 12.00
SS18 Jarome Iginla 6.00 15.00
SS19 Jaromir Jagr 15.00 40.00
SS20 Jeff Friesen 5.00 12.00
SS21 Jeremy Roenick 8.00 20.00
SS22 Joe Sakic 10.00 25.00
SS23 John LeClair 5.00 12.00
SS24 John Tavares 8.00 20.00
SS25 Marian Hossa 5.00 12.00
SS26 Martin Brodeur 12.00 30.00
SS27 Mats Sundin 5.00 12.00
SS28 Nathan MacKinnon 20.00 50.00
SS29 P.K. Subban 6.00 15.00
SS30 Pavol Demitra 6.00 15.00
SS31 Peter Forsberg 10.00 25.00
SS32 Rob Blake 5.00 12.00
SS33 Ryan Getzlaf 5.00 12.00
SS34 Sandis Ozolinsh 3.00 8.00
SS35 Simon Gagne 5.00 12.00
SS36 Steven Stamkos 10.00 25.00
SS37 Taylor Hall 5.00 12.00
SS38 Teemu Selanne 10.00 25.00
SS39 Tie Domi 4.00 10.00
SS40 Tommy Salo 5.00 12.00
SS41 Tony Amonte 4.00 10.00
SS42 Vincent Lecavalier 5.00 12.00

2016-17 ITG Used Triple Jerseys
GT01 Arbour/Bossy/Potvin/30 5.00 12.00
GT02 Esposito/Hall/Crawford/45 6.00 15.00
GT03 Giacomin/Richter/Lundqvist/45 12.0030.00
GT04 Gilmour/Modano/Hull/45 10.00 25.00
GT05 Gretzky/Lemieux/Howe/30 30.00 80.00
GT06 Hall/MacKinnon/Tavares/45 20.00 50.00
GT07 Kane/Nash/Tavares/45 10.00 25.00
GT08 Khabibulin/Kolzig/Nabokov/45 5.00 12.00
GT09 Landeskog/Nugent-Hopkins/Hall/45 6.00 15.00
GT10 Laperriere/Shutt/Lafleur/25 6.00 15.00
GT11 Lecavalier/Stamkos/Drouin/45 10.00 25.00
GT12 Lemieux/Hull/Sakic/45 20.00 50.00
GT13 Plante/Potvin/Joseph/25 8.00 20.00
GT14 Quick/Crawford/Price/45 10.00 25.00
GT15 Turco/Vokoun/Luongo/45 8.00 20.00

2017 ITG Used Autographs
GUAAK1 Alexei Kovalev/25 8.00 20.00
GUAAM1 Andy Moog/25 10.00 25.00
GUAAO1 Adam Oates/25 10.00 25.00
GUABL1 Brian Leetch/25 8.00 20.00
GUACO1 Chris Osgood/25 10.00 25.00
GUAEB1 Ed Belfour/25 12.00 30.00
GUAGF1 Grant Fuhr/25 20.00 50.00
GUAJK1 Joe Kocur/25 10.00 25.00
GUAJR1 Jeremy Roenick/25 15.00 40.00
GUAMR1 Manon Rheaume/25 80.00 150.00
GUANH1 Nico Hischier/40 30.00 80.00
GUANU1 Norm Ullman/25 10.00 25.00

2017 ITG Used Draft History Materials
DH01 Turgeon/Shanahan/Sakic Richardson/LeClair/Desjardins 15.00 40.00
DH02 Clark/Burke/Richter/Nieuwendyk Ranford/Larionov 12.00 30.00
DH03 Lemieux/Roberts/Roy Robitaille/Hull/Muller 30.00 80.00
DH04 LaFontaine/Yzerman/Neely Barrasso/Hasek/Fetisov 15.00 40.00
DH05 Bellows/Stevens/Housley Andreychuk/Leeman/Gilmour 8.00 20.00
DH06 Hawerchuk/Francis/Fuhr/MacInnis Chelios/Vanbiesbrouck 15.00 40.00
DH07 Savard/Babych/Murphy Coffey/Kurri/Sutter 6.00 15.00
DH08 Gartner/Bourque/Goulet/Messier Foligno/Anderson 15.00 40.00
DH09 Gillies/Valiquette/Maloney Trottier/Howe/Williams 8.00 20.00
DH10 Potvin/McDonald/Gainey Middleton/Davidson/Savard 8.00 20.00
DH11 Lafleur/Dionne/Martin/O'Reilly Robinson/Garrett 10.00 25.00
DH12 Perreault/Leach/Sittler/Maloney Smith/Meloche 10.00 25.00
DH13 Modano/Linden/Roenick Brind'Amour/Selanne/Blake 12.00 30.00
DH14 Sundin/Guerin/Holik/Kolzig Lidstrom/Fedorov 12.00 30.00

2017 ITG Used Jerseys
GU01 Al Secord 3.00 8.00
GU02 Alexander Ovechkin 12.00 30.00
GU03 Alexei Zhitnik 3.00 8.00
GU04 Bill Guerin 3.00 8.00
GU05 Bobby Holik 3.00 8.00
GU06 Boris Mironov 3.00 8.00
GU07 Brett Hull 6.00 15.00
GU08 Brian Leetch 2.50 6.00
GU09 Bryan Berard 3.00 8.00
GU10 Chris Drury 3.00 8.00
GU11 Chris Osgood 3.00 8.00
GU12 Chris Pronger 3.00 8.00
GU13 Dan Maloney 3.00 8.00
GU14 Darryl Sittler 4.00 10.00
GU15 Dave Maloney 3.00 8.00
GU16 Dick Redmond 3.00 8.00
GU17 Doug Jarrett 3.00 8.00
GU18 Evgeni Nabokov 3.00 8.00
GU19 Gary Dornhoefer 2.00 5.00
GU20 Gary Suter 3.00 8.00
GU21 Gilles Meloche 3.00 8.00
GU22 Jaromir Jagr 12.00 30.00
GU23 Jason Arnott 3.00 8.00
GU24 Jim Rutherford 3.00 8.00
GU25 Kevin Hatcher 3.00 8.00
GU26 Larry Murphy 2.50 6.00
GU27 Manon Rheaume 8.00 20.00
GU28 Mark Messier 6.00 15.00
GU29 Mike Gartner 4.00 10.00
GU30 Mike Peca 3.00 8.00
GU31 Nazem Kadri 3.00 8.00
GU32 Patrick Marleau 3.00 8.00
GU33 Patrick Roy 8.00 20.00
GU34 Pavel Bure 3.00 8.00
GU35 Pavel Datsyuk 5.00 12.00
GU36 Peter Forsberg 5.00 12.00
GU37 Rick Nash 3.00 8.00
GU38 Roman Cechmanek 3.00 8.00
GU39 Sandis Ozolinsh 3.00 8.00
GU40 Sergei Fedorov 5.00 12.00
GU41 Steve Larmer 3.00 8.00
GU42 Steve Mason 3.00 8.00
GU43 Teemu Selanne 5.00 12.00
GU44 Trevor Kidd 3.00 8.00
GU45 Vincent Damphousse 2.50 6.00
GU46 Zdeno Chara 3.00 8.00
GU47 Zigmund Palffy 3.00 8.00

2017 ITG Used Le Forum de Montreal Seats
LFM01 Aurele Joliat 6.00 15.00
LFM02 Bernie Geoffrion 6.00 15.00
LFM03 Bert Olmstead 6.00 15.00
LFM04 Bill Durnan 6.00 15.00
LFM05 Claude Provost 6.00 15.00
LFM06 Dickie Moore 6.00 15.00
LFM07 Doug Harvey 6.00 15.00
LFM08 Elmer Lach 5.00 12.00
LFM09 George Hainsworth 6.00 15.00
LFM10 Guy Lafleur 8.00 20.00
LFM11 Howie Morenz 6.00 15.00
LFM12 Jacques Plante 6.00 15.00
LFM13 Jean Beliveau 6.00 15.00
LFM14 Maurice Richard 12.00 30.00
LFM15 Toe Blake 6.00 15.00
LFM16 Tom Johnson 6.00 15.00

2017 ITG Used Putting on the Foil Materials
PF01 Barry Beck/15 6.00 15.00
PF02 Bob Probert/30 8.00 20.00
PF03 Craig Berube/30 6.00 15.00
PF04 Dave Manson/30 6.00 15.00
PF05 Donald Brashear/30 6.00 15.00
PF06 Dave Brown/30 5.00 12.00
PF07 Georges Laraque/30 6.00 15.00
PF08 Terry O'Reilly/30 6.00 15.00
PF09 Tie Domi/30 6.00 15.00
PF10 Tiger Williams/30 5.00 12.00

2017 ITG Used Quad Jerseys
GU401 Jarrett/White/Mikita/Redmond 5.00 12.00
GU402 Unger/Clarke/Tkaczuk/Sittler 8.00 20.00
GU403 Riggin/Beaupre Lemelin/Meloche 5.00 12.00
GU404 Ranford/Resch Bouchard/Vernon 5.00 12.00
GU405 Rutherford/Myre Davidson/Meloche 5.00 12.00
GU406 Brind'Amour/Andreychuk Recchi/Damphousse 5.00 12.00
GU407 Hatcher/Chelios Richardson/Desjardins 5.00 12.00
GU408 Lowe/Babych/Murphy/Carlyle 4.00 10.00
GU409 Cashman/Lafleur Tkaczuk/Mahovlich 6.00 15.00

2017 ITG Used Team Eights Materials
T801 Esposito/Orr/Bourque Cheevers/O'Ree/Neely Middleton/Sanderson/20 30.00 80.00
T802 Delvecchio/Crozier/Howe Lindsay/Ullman/Giacomin Sawchuk/Rutherford/30 25.00 60.00
T803 Yzerman/Shanahan Lidstrom/Osgood/Hull/Hasek Fedorov/Chelios/30 15.00 40.00
T804 Maloney/Gretzky/Robitaille Blake/Dionne/Palffy Sargent/Vachon/30 50.00 125.00
T805 Maloney/Rousseau/Ratelle Gilbert/Dionne/Lafleur Tkaczuk/Giacomin/30 10.00 25.00
T806 Lacroix/Clarke/MacLeish Barber/Watson/Watson Parent/Leach/30 12.00 30.00
T807 Unger/Picard/Huck McDonald/Hall/Johnston Federko/Arbour/30 8.00 20.00
T808 Broten/Modano/Bellows Ciccarelli/Hartsburg/Musil Beaupre/Payne/30 12.00 30.00
T809 Baun/Keon/Vaive/McDonald Sittler/Salming Williams/Valiquette/30 10.00 25.00
T810 Martin/Perreault/LaFontaine Robert/Hasek/Zhitnik Fuhr/Mogilny/30 15.00 40.00
T811 Bure/Brodeur/Snepsts Tanti/Linden/Sedin Sedin/Naslund/30 10.00 25.00
T812 Ovechkin/Bure/Malkin Khabibulin/Mogilny/Bryzgalov Kasparaitis/Yashin/30 30.00 80.00
T813 Bossy/Gillies/Smith/Potvin Trottier/LaFontaine Tavares/Nystrom/30 12.00 30.00
T814 Hull/Tkachuk/Chelios Barrasso/Amonte/Guerin Leetch/Modano/30 15.00 40.00
T815 Goulet/Shutt/Ciccarelli Hawerchuk/Perreault Unger/Sittler/Clarke/30 12.00 30.00
T816 Lemieux/Yzerman/Lindros Joseph/Sakic/Brodeur Thornton/Francis/30 30.00 80.00
T817 Fleury/Burns/Toews/Price Doughty/Carter/Spezza Bouwmeester/30 12.00 30.00
T818 Gretzky/Lemieux/Howe Jagr/Roy/Brodeur Yzerman/Bourque/30 50.00 125.00
T819 Orr/Clarke/Cheevers/Dionne Lafleur/Esposito/Perreault Sittler/30 30.00 80.00
T820 Plante/Howe/Ullman/Hall Mikita/Giacomin/Keon/Hull/20 25.00 60.00
T821 White/Redmond/Jarrett/Mikita Hull/Goulet/Savard/Larmer/30 15.00 40.00

2017 ITG Used Triple Jerseys
GU301 Howe/Gretzky/Orr 40.00 100.00
GU302 Bure/Ovechkin/Fedorov 25.00 60.00
GU303 Fleury/Mason/Crawford 10.00 25.00
GU304 Hasek/Roy/Brodeur 15.00 40.00
GU305 Joseph/Potvin/Khabibulin 10.00 25.00
GU306 Kariya/Lindros/Hull 12.00 30.00
GU307 Messier/Gartner/Vaive 12.00 30.00
GU308 Housley/Murphy/MacInnis 6.00 15.00
GU309 Turgeon/Oates/Sakic 12.00 30.00
GU310 Mikita/Howe/Keon 20.00 50.00
GU311 Iginla/St./Vincent 8.00 20.00
GU312 Payne/Musil/Hartsburg 6.00 15.00
GU313 Salo/Khabibulin/Turek 6.00 15.00
GU314 Suter/Roberts/MacInnis 6.00 15.00
GU315 Redmond/Sargent/Jarrett 6.00 15.00
GU316 Inness/Johnston/Davidson 5.00 12.00
GU317 Snow/Shields/Osgood 6.00 15.00
GU318 Sargent/Blake/Doughty 8.00 20.00
GU319 Vokoun/Nabokov/Khabibulin 6.00 15.00
GU320 Carlyle/Babych/Reinhart 5.00 12.00
GU321 Mikita/McDonald/Keon 6.00 15.00

2017-18 ITG Used All Time Gr8s Memorabilia
AT801 Bourque/Housley/MacInnis/Coffey Chelios/Stevens/Blake/Lidstrom 8.00 20.00
AT802 Gretzky/Lemieux/Sakic/Hull Turgeon/Modano/Fedorov/Bure 40.00 100.00
AT803 Howe/Lemieux/Harvey/Plante Gretzky/Horton/Gadsby/Roy 40.00 100.00
AT804 Hull/Roenick/Turgeon/Lidstrom Kariya/Selanne/Jagr/Lindros 20.00 50.00
AT805 Kharlamov/Krutov/Maltsev Tretiak/Mikhailov/Mylnikov Myshkin/Yakushev 6.00 15.00
AT806 McDavid/Ovechkin Stamkos/Crosby/Malkin Tavares/Kane/MacKinnon 30.00 80.00
AT807 Mikita/Howe/Hull/Ullman Beliveau/Delvecchio Mahovlich/Keon 20.00 50.00
AT808 Orr/Potvin/Park/Salming/Robinson Savard/Redmond/White 25.00 60.00
AT809 Roy/Brodeur/Potvin/Joseph Hasek/Belfour/Richter/Fuhr 15.00 40.00
AT810 Thornton/Alfredsson/Lecavalier St. Louis/Hossa/Iginla Hejduk/Marleau 10.00 25.00
AT811 Unger/Esposito/Dionne Clarke/Perreault/Sittler Mahovlich/Martin 10.00 25.00
AT812 Vachon/Dryden/Parent Cheevers/Smith/Giacomin Esposito/Johnston 8.00 20.00

2020-21 ITG Used Memorabilia Autographs
GUABH1 Bobby Hull/40 25.00 60.00
GUABH2 Brett Hull/35 20.00 50.00
GUABR1 Bill Ranford/35 8.00 20.00
GUABS1 Borje Salming/20 10.00 25.00
GUABT1 Bryan Trottier/35 10.00 25.00
GUACC1 Chris Chelios/35 10.00 25.00
GUACL1 Claude Lemieux/40 10.00 25.00
GUADP1 Denis Potvin/35 10.00 25.00
GUAEL1 Eric Lindros/30 15.00 40.00
GUAFP1 Felix Potvin/25 15.00 40.00
GUAGC1 Gerry Cheevers/30 15.00 40.00
GUAGF1 Grant Fuhr/35 15.00 40.00
GUAGL1 Guy Lafleur/20 25.00 60.00
GUAJK1 Jari Kurri/35 12.00 30.00
GUAJR1 Jeremy Roenick/35 15.00 40.00
GUAKP1 Keith Primeau/40 8.00 20.00
GUALR1 Luc Robitaille/40 10.00 25.00
GUAMD1 Marcel Dionne/30 12.00 30.00
GUAMM1 Mike Modano/20 15.00 40.00
GUAOP1 Oleg Petrov/40 6.00 15.00
GUASL1 Stephan Lebeau/40 6.00 15.00
GUAWO1 Willie O'Ree/35 50.00 125.00

2020-21 ITG Used 4 Your Country Memorabilia
4YC01 Gre/Mes/Fra/Sak 25.00 60.00
4YC02 How/Oat/Esp/Tro 12.00 30.00
4YC03 Lem/Dio/Cof/Gil 15.00 40.00
4YC04 Hul/Cro/Laf/Haw 15.00 40.00
4YC05 Has/Eli/Hej/Ham 6.00 15.00
4YC06 Jag/Bon/Vok/Hol 12.00 30.00
4YC07 Sel/Jok/Koi/Kip 8.00 20.00
4YC08 Kur/Ras/Koi/Num 5.00 12.00
4YC09 Dra/Kol/Sei/Gri 12.00 30.00
4YC10 Sun/Alf/Sed/Sed 8.00 20.00
4YC11 Lid/Zet/For/Nas 8.00 20.00
4YC12 Sal/Nas/Loo/Hed 10.00 25.00
4YC13 Lin/Lun/Sal/Hed 10.00 25.00
4YC14 Hul/Kan/Roe/Tka 8.00 20.00
4YC15 Mod/LaF/Hou/Lee 6.00 15.00
4YC16 Che/Mul/Gue/LeC 4.00 10.00
4YC17 Van/Bar/Ric/Mil 4.00 10.00

2020-21 ITG Used A Year to Remember Memorabilia
AYR01 Bobby Hull/35 15.00 40.00
AYR02 Bobby Orr/35 25.00 60.00
AYR03 Brett Hull/35 12.00 30.00
AYR04 Cam Neely/35 6.00 15.00
AYR05 Dave Keon/35 6.00 15.00
AYR06 Denis Potvin/35 6.00 15.00
AYR07 Doug Gilmour/35 8.00 20.00
AYR08 Eric Lindros/35 10.00 25.00
AYR09 Gordie Howe/35 20.00 50.00
AYR10 Jacques Plante/30 6.00 15.00
AYR11 Jaromir Jagr/35 20.00 50.00
AYR12 Joe Sakic/35 12.00 30.00
AYR13 Marcel Dionne/35 8.00 20.00
AYR14 Mario Lemieux/35 25.00 60.00
AYR15 Mats Sundin/35 6.00 15.00
AYR17 Pat LaFontaine/35 6.00 15.00
AYR18 Paul Coffey/35 6.00 15.00
AYR19 Pavel Bure/35 25.00 60.00
AYR20 Raymond Bourque/35 10.00 25.00
AYR21 Stan Mikita/35 6.00 15.00
AYR22 Terry Sawchuk/35 6.00 15.00
AYR23 Wayne Gretzky/35 40.00 100.00
AYR24 Wendel Clark/35 10.00 25.00

2020-21 ITG Used Center Pieces Memorabilia
CP01 Bobby Clarke/35 6.00 15.00
CP02 Bryan Trottier/35 4.00 10.00
CP03 Connor McDavid/35 20.00 50.00
CP04 Eric Lindros/35 6.00 15.00
CP05 Jean Beliveau/25 4.00 10.00
CP06 Joe Sakic/35 8.00 20.00
CP07 Marcel Dionne/35 5.00 12.00
CP08 Mario Lemieux/35 15.00 40.00
CP09 Mark Messier/35 8.00 20.00
CP10 Pat LaFontaine/35 4.00 10.00
CP11 Peter Forsberg/35 8.00 20.00
CP12 Peter Stastny/35 3.00 8.00
CP13 Phil Esposito/35 6.00 15.00
CP14 Ron Francis/35 5.00 12.00
CP15 Sergei Fedorov/35 6.00 15.00
CP16 Sidney Crosby/35 15.00 40.00
CP17 Stan Mikita/25 4.00 10.00
CP18 Steve Yzerman/35 10.00 25.00
CP19 Wayne Gretzky/35 25.00 60.00

2020-21 ITG Used Dual Memorabilia Autographs
GUDA01 J.Kurri/G.Fuhr/20 20.00 50.00
GUDA02 B.Trottier/D.Potvin/20 8.00 20.00
GUDA04 C.Chelios/J.Roenick/20 20.00 50.00
GUDA06 L.Robitaille/B.Hull/25 20.00 50.00

2020-21 ITG Used Gear
ITGUG01 Alex Pietrangelo/30 5.00 12.00
ITGUG02 Bernie Parent/30 15.00 40.00
ITGUG03 Billy Smith/30 6.00 15.00
ITGUG04 Bobby Orr/25 25.00 60.00
ITGUG05 Curtis Joseph/30 12.00 30.00
ITGUG06 Dominik Hasek/30 10.00 25.00
ITGUG07 Eric Lindros/30 10.00 25.00
ITGUG08 Felix Potvin/30 10.00 25.00
ITGUG09 Gerry Cheevers/30 15.00 40.00
ITGUG10 Gilles Gilbert/30 5.00 12.00
ITGUG11 Gordie Howe/25 20.00 50.00
ITGUG12 Grant Fuhr/30 10.00 25.00
ITGUG13 Jaromir Jagr/30 12.00 30.00
ITGUG14 Joe Thornton/30 10.00 25.00
ITGUG15 John Vanbiesbrouck/30 10.00 25.00
ITGUG16 Jordan Binnington/30 10.00 25.00
ITGUG17 Marian Hossa/30 8.00 20.00
ITGUG18 Mario Lemieux/30 25.00 60.00
ITGUG19 Martin Brodeur/30 15.00 40.00
ITGUG20 Martin St. Louis/30 6.00 15.00
ITGUG21 Mats Sundin/30 10.00 25.00
ITGUG22 Nathan MacKinnon/30 10.00 25.00
ITGUG23 Patrick Roy/30 15.00 40.00
ITGUG24 Paul Coffey/30 6.00 15.00
ITGUG25 Paul Kariya/30 6.00 15.00
ITGUG26 Pelle Lindbergh/30 15.00 40.00
ITGUG27 Ron Hextall/30 8.00 20.00
ITGUG28 Sandis Ozolinsh/30 4.00 10.00
ITGUG29 Terry Sawchuk/30 6.00 15.00
ITGUG30 Tony Amonte/30 5.00 12.00
ITGUG31 Vladislav Tretiak/30 12.00 30.00
ITGUG32 Wayne Gretzky/30 30.00 80.00

2020-21 ITG Used Hockey Redraft Memorabilia
HR01 Cof/Kur/Sav/Mur/Nic/Lar 8.00 20.00
HR02 Bou/Mes/Gar/Gou/Lin/And 15.00 40.00
HR03 Tro/Gil/How/Lar/Gar/Sim 8.00 20.00
HR04 Laf/Dio/Rob/Mar/O'R/Gar 10.00 25.00
HR05 Per/Sit/Smi/Lea/Mel/Mac 10.00 25.00
HR06 Ste/Hou/Gil/And/Hex/Bel 10.00 25.00
HR07 Has/Yze/Nee/LaF/Bar/Lem 20.00 50.00
HR08 Lem/Roy/Hul/Rob/Mul/Rob 12.00 30.00
HR09 Sak/Sha/Tur/LeC/Fle/Des 15.00 40.00
HR10 Sel/Mod/Bla/Rec/Roe/Mog 15.00 40.00
HR11 Lid/Sun/Fed/Bur/Gue/Kol 20.00 50.00
HR12 Bro/Jag/Zub/Nol/Tka/Pot 12.00 30.00
HR13 For/Lin/Nie/Osg/Ozo/Nas 15.00 40.00
HR14 Pro/Kar/Koi/Dem/Arn/Thi 8.00 20.00

2020-21 ITG Used Once in a Generation Memorabilia Autographs
OGBH1 Bobby Hull/30 15.00 40.00
OGDP1 Denis Potvin/30 6.00 15.00
OGEL1 Eric Lindros/20 10.00 25.00
OGLR1 Luc Robitaille/30 6.00 15.00
OGMB1 Mike Bossy/20 6.00 15.00

2020-21 ITG Used Passing the Baton Memorabilia
PTB01 G.Howe/W.Gretzky/25 30.00 80.00
PTB02 M.Lemieux/S.Crosby/25 20.00 50.00
PTB03 B.Orr/R.Bourque/30 20.00 50.00
PTB04 D.Hawerchuk/T.Selanne/30 10.00 25.00
PTB05 T.Horton/B.Salming/30 8.00 20.00
PTB06 B.Parent/R.Hextall/30 6.00 15.00
PTB07 J.Plante/K.Dryden/25 5.00 12.00
PTB08 P.Roy/C.Price/30 12.00 30.00
PTB09 P.Lindbergh/R.Hextall/30 5.00 12.00
PTB10 J.Jagr/E.Malkin/30 15.00 40.00
PTB11 D.Savard/J.Roenick/30 8.00 20.00
PTB12 P.Esposito/C.Neely/30 8.00 20.00
PTB13 S.Mikita/P.Stastny/25 5.00 12.00
PTB14 J.Jagr/M.Hossa/30 15.00 40.00
PTB15 L.Robitaille/A.Kopitar/30 8.00 20.00
PTB16 G.Howe/S.Yzerman/25 16.00 40.00
PTB17 M.Naslund/H.Sedin/30 6.00 15.00
PTB18 P.Kariya/R.Getzlaf/30 5.00 12.00
PTB19 P.Lindbergh/H.Lundqvist/30 12.00 30.00

2020-21 ITG Used Ring Leaders Memorabilia
RL03 Bryan Trottier/30 4.00 10.00
RL07 Glenn Anderson/25 3.00 8.00
RL08 Guy Lafleur/30 5.00 12.00
RL11 Jacques Laperriere/25 3.00 8.00
RL12 Jacques Lemaire/25 3.00 8.00
RL14 Jari Kurri/25 4.00 10.00
RL17 Kevin Lowe/25 4.00 10.00
RL18 Larry Robinson/30 4.00 10.00
RL19 Mark Messier/30 8.00 20.00
RL22 Serge Savard/25 4.00 10.00
RL23 Yvan Cournoyer/25 4.00 10.00

2020-21 ITG Used Super Swatch Signatures
SSSBG1 Bill Guerin/30 10.00 25.00
SSSBH1 Bobby Hull/20 25.00 60.00
SSSBH2 Brett Hull/25 20.00 50.00
SSSBT1 Bryan Trottier/20 10.00 25.00
SSSCC1 Chris Chelios/20 10.00 25.00
SSSCL1 Claude Lemieux/30 10.00 25.00
SSSGF1 Grant Fuhr/20 15.00 40.00
SSSJR1 Jeremy Roenick/20 15.00 40.00
SSSLR1 Luc Robitaille/20 10.00 25.00

2020-21 ITG Used The Champions Club Memorabilia Autographs
CC05 J.Kurri/M.Krushelnyski/20 15.00 40.00

2020-21 ITG Used Timeworn 2 Memorabilia
T201 G.Howe B.Hull 6.00 15.00

2020-21 ITG Used Triple Memorabilia
TM04 Jag/Hul/Sak/20 15.00 40.00
TM05 Lem/Bur/Mes/20 20.00 50.00
TM06 How/Fed/Yze/20 15.00 40.00
TM08 Has/Par/Che/20 8.00 20.00
TM09 How/Ric/Mik/20 15.00 40.00
TM10 Bel/How/Olm/20 15.00 40.00
TM12 Gil/Fuh/Par/20 8.00 20.00
TM13 Tho/Igi/Alf/20 8.00 20.00
TM14 Has/Bro/Bel/20 12.00 30.00
TM15 Keo/Del/Hul/20 12.00 30.00

2020-21 ITG Used Triple Memorabilia Autographs
GUTA04 Kurri/Hull/Bossy/20 30.00 80.00

2003-04 ITG VIP Brightest Stars
1 Mario Lemieux 25.00 60.00
2 Marian Gaborik 20.00 50.00
3 Dany Heatley 15.00 40.00
4 Ilya Kovalchuk 15.00 40.00
5 Jason Spezza 20.00 50.00
6 Dominik Hasek 20.00 50.00
7 Peter Forsberg 25.00 60.00
8 Steve Yzerman 20.00 50.00
9 Martin Brodeur 25.00 60.00
10 Patrick Roy 25.00 60.00

2003-04 ITG VIP Collages
1 Mario Lemieux 10.00 25.00
2 Martin Brodeur 8.00 20.00
3 Steve Yzerman 8.00 20.00
4 Patrick Roy 8.00 20.00
5 Paul Kariya 3.00 8.00
6 Peter Forsberg 6.00 15.00
7 Joe Sakic 6.00 15.00
8 Marian Gaborik 6.00 15.00
9 Mark Messier 5.00 12.00
10 Ilya Kovalchuk 5.00 12.00
11 Mike Modano 5.00 12.00
12 Brett Hull 5.00 12.00
13 Jean-Sebastien Giguere 2.00 5.00
14 Joe Thornton 5.00 12.00
15 Pavel Bure 2.00 5.00
16 Dany Heatley 5.00 12.00
17 Rick Nash 4.00 10.00
18 Henrik Zetterberg 4.00 10.00
19 Dominik Hasek 6.00 15.00
20 Jose Theodore 4.00 10.00
21 Jason Spezza 5.00 12.00
22 Ed Belfour 3.00 8.00
23 Nicklas Lidstrom 3.00 8.00
24 Roberto Luongo 4.00 10.00
25 Tony Esposito 4.00 10.00
26 Ted Lindsay 3.00 8.00
27 Bobby Hull 6.00 15.00
28 Jacques Plante 4.00 10.00
29 Phil Esposito 2.00 5.00
30 Turk Broda 2.00 5.00
31 Georges Vezina 4.00 12.00
32 Terry Sawchuk 4.00 10.00
33 Rocket Richard 5.00 12.00
34 Jean Beliveau 3.00 8.00
35 Doug Harvey 2.00 5.00

2003-04 ITG VIP Collage Autographs
1 Mario Lemieux 50.00 125.00
2 Martin Brodeur/20 50.00 125.00
3 Steve Yzerman/20 50.00 125.00
6 Peter Forsberg 30.00 80.00
7 Joe Sakic 25.00 60.00
10 Ilya Kovalchuk 20.00 50.00
12 Brett Hull 20.00 50.00
14 Joe Thornton 20.00 50.00
17 Rick Nash 20.00 50.00
18 Henrik Zetterberg 25.00 60.00
19 Dominik Hasek/20 25.00 60.00
23 Nicklas Lidstrom 15.00 40.00
24 Roberto Luongo 15.00 40.00
25 Tony Esposito 20.00 50.00
26 Ted Lindsay 12.50 30.00
27 Bobby Hull 15.00 40.00
29 Phil Esposito 12.50 30.00
34 Jean Beliveau 20.00 50.00

2003-04 ITG VIP International Experience
1 Mario Lemieux 30.00 80.00
2 Jay Bouwmeester 12.50 30.00
3 Jason Spezza 20.00 50.00
4 Mike Modano 12.50 30.00
5 Joe Sakic 25.00 60.00
6 Nicklas Lidstrom 12.50 30.00
7 Peter Forsberg 16.00 40.00
8 Mats Sundin 12.50 30.00
9 Jaromir Jagr 20.00 50.00
10 Steve Yzerman 15.00 40.00
11 Dany Heatley 12.50 30.00
12 Martin Brodeur 20.00 50.00

2003-04 ITG VIP Jerseys
1 Joe Thornton 12.50 30.00
2 Mario Lemieux 25.00 60.00
3 Mats Sundin 8.00 20.00
4 Pavel Bure 8.00 20.00
5 Dany Heatley 15.00 40.00
6 Joe Sakic 25.00 60.00
7 Rick Nash 15.00 40.00
8 Nicklas Lidstrom 8.00 20.00
9 Markus Naslund 8.00 20.00
10 Patrick Roy 25.00 60.00
11 Peter Forsberg 20.00 50.00
12 Dominik Hasek 15.00 40.00
13 Henrik Zetterberg 15.00 40.00
14 Mike Modano 12.50 30.00
15 Jay Bouwmeester 12.50 30.00
16 Ilya Kovalchuk 12.50 30.00
17 Marian Gaborik 15.00 40.00
18 Brett Hull 12.50 30.00
19 Martin Brodeur 25.00 60.00
20 Milan Hejduk 8.00 20.00
21 Steve Yzerman 25.00 60.00
22 Jeremy Roenick 12.50 30.00
23 Jean-Sebastien Giguere 6.00 15.00
24 Brendan Shanahan 8.00 20.00
25 Todd Bertuzzi 8.00 20.00
26 Jarome Iginla 12.50 30.00
27 Al MacInnis 6.00 15.00
28 Saku Koivu 8.00 20.00
29 Jason Spezza 20.00 50.00
30 Ed Belfour 8.00 20.00

2003-04 ITG VIP Making the Bigs
1 Jay Bouwmeester 15.00 40.00
2 Rick Nash 25.00 60.00
3 Scottie Upshall 12.50 30.00
4 Jason Spezza 20.00 50.00
5 Ron Hainsey 12.50 30.00
6 Barret Jackman 12.50 30.00
7 Dany Heatley 15.00 40.00
8 Dan Blackburn 12.50 30.00

2003-04 ITG VIP MVP
8 Bobby Hull/50 20.00 50.00
9 Stan Mikita/50 15.00 40.00
10 Phil Esposito/50 12.00 30.00
11 Bobby Clarke/50 12.50 30.00
12 Dominik Hasek/50 15.00 40.00
13 Roger Crozier/50 15.00 40.00
14 Glenn Hall/40 20.00 50.00
15 Bernie Parent/50 20.00 50.00
16 Mike Bossy/50 12.50 30.00
17 Patrick Roy/50 30.00 80.00
18 Patrick Roy/50 30.00 80.00
19 Steve Yzerman/50 25.00 60.00
20 Jean-Sebastien Giguere/50 12.50 30.00
21 Bryan Trottier/50 12.50 30.00
22 Jean Beliveau/50 25.00 60.00
23 Guy Lafleur/50 15.00 40.00
24 Mark Messier/50 15.00 40.00
25 Mario Lemieux/50 20.00 50.00
26 Joe Sakic/50 20.00 50.00

2003-04 ITG VIP Netminders
1 Martin Brodeur 15.00 40.00
2 Roberto Luongo 12.50 30.00
3 Ed Belfour 10.00 25.00
4 Patrick Roy 20.00 50.00
5 Marty Turco 10.00 25.00
6 Jean-Sebastien Giguere 10.00 25.00
7 Olaf Kolzig 10.00 25.00
8 Patrick Lalime 10.00 25.00
9 Dan Blackburn 15.00 40.00
10 Rick DiPietro 10.00 25.00
11 Ryan Miller 12.50 30.00
12 Jose Theodore 12.50 30.00

2003-04 ITG VIP Sophomores
1 Rick Nash 15.00 40.00
2 Jay Bouwmeester 6.00 15.00
3 Barret Jackman 15.00 40.00
4 Henrik Zetterberg 15.00 40.00
5 Ryan Miller 12.50 30.00
6 Stanistov Chistov 6.00 15.00
7 Jason Spezza 15.00 40.00
8 Alexander Frolov 6.00 15.00

2003-04 ITG VIP Vintage Memorabilia
9 Ted Lindsay/30 20.00 50.00
11 Tim Horton/30 20.00 50.00
12 Jacques Plante/30 30.00 80.00
14 Doug Harvey/30 12.50 30.00
16 Harry Lumley/30 15.00 40.00
17 Tony Esposito/30 12.50 30.00
18 Jean Beliveau/30 30.00 80.00
19 Frank Mahovlich/30 20.00 50.00
20 Glenn Hall/30 20.00 50.00
21 Bobby Hull/30 30.00 80.00
22 Stan Mikita/30 15.00 40.00

2009-10 ITG 1972 The Year In Hockey Blank Backs
BLANK BACK/72: 1.5X TO 4X BASIC CARDS

2009-10 ITG 1972 The Year In Hockey Autographs
AAB Andre Boudrias 6.00 15.00
AAD Alex Delvecchio SP 20.00 50.00
AAG Alexander Gusev 12.00 30.00
AAH Al Hamilton 5.00 12.00
AAL Andre Lacroix 6.00 15.00
AAM Al McDonough 5.00 12.00
AAW Alton White 5.00 12.00
AAY Alexander Yakushev 15.00 40.00
ABB Bill Barber SP 6.00 15.00
ABC Bobby Clarke SP 15.00 40.00
ABG Butch Goring 8.00 20.00
ABH Bryan Hextall 6.00 15.00
ABL Bob Leiter 5.00 12.00
ABM Bob MacMillan 5.00 12.00
ABN Bob Nystrom 5.00 12.00
ABP Brad Park SP 12.00 30.00
ABS Bobby Schmautz 5.00 12.00
ARW Bill White 5.00 12.00
ACB Curt Bennett 5.00 12.00
ACM Cesare Maniago 6.00 15.00
ADA Don Awrey 5.00 12.00
ADB Dan Bouchard 6.00 15.00
ADF Doug Favell 8.00 20.00
ADG Danny Grant 10.00 25.00
ADH Denis Herron 6.00 15.00
ADJ Doug Jarrett 5.00 12.00
ADK Dave Keon SP 12.00 30.00
ADL Don Lever 12.00 30.00
ADS Dallas Smith 10.00 25.00
ADT Dale Tallon Summit 8.00 20.00
ADW Dunc Wilson 8.00 20.00
AEG Ed Giacomin SP 15.00 40.00
AEJ Eddie Johnston 12.00 30.00
AES Eddie Shack 8.00 20.00
AEW Ernie Wakely 6.00 15.00
AFM Frank Mahovlich SP 25.00 60.00
AGC Gerry Cheevers 8.00 20.00
AGD Gerry Desjardins 6.00 15.00
AGE Gary Edwards 5.00 12.00
AGG Gilles Gratton 8.00 20.00
AGJ Gary Jarrett 6.00 15.00
AGL Guy Lafleur SP 15.00 40.00
AGM Gilles Meloche 8.00 20.00
AGO Gerry Odrowski 5.00 12.00
AGP Gilbert Perreault SP 8.00 20.00
AGS Gary Sabourin 6.00 15.00
AGU Garry Unger 5.00 12.00
AGV Gilles Villemure 10.00 25.00
AHH Harry Howell 6.00 15.00
AHS Harry Sinden Summit 15.00 40.00
AJB Johnny Bucyk 8.00 20.00
AJD Joe Daley 5.00 12.00
AJE Jack Egers 5.00 12.00
AJJ Joey Johnston 5.00 12.00
AJL Jacques Lemaire 12.00 30.00
AJN Jack Norris 5.00 12.00
AJS Jim Schoenfeld 5.00 12.00
AJW Joe Watson 5.00 12.00
AKB Ken Brown 6.00 15.00
AKH Ken Hodge 6.00 15.00
ALB Les Binkley 8.00 20.00
ALL Larry Lund 5.00 12.00
ALM Lowell MacDonald 5.00 12.00
ALP Larry Pleau 5.00 12.00

ALR Larry Robinson 8.00 20.00
AMA Mike Antonovich 6.00 15.00
AMC Mike Curran 6.00 15.00
AMD Marcel Dionne SP 20.00 50.00
ANF Norm Ferguson 5.00 12.00
ANL Nick Libett 6.00 15.00
ANP Noel Picard 5.00 12.00
ANU Norm Ullman 8.00 20.00
APE Phil Esposito 12.00 30.00
APH Paul Henderson 10.00 25.00
APM Phil Myre 5.00 12.00
APP Poul Popiel 6.00 15.00
APQ Pat Quinn 8.00 20.00
APS Pat Stapleton 6.00 15.00
ARB Richard Brodeur 8.00 20.00
ARE Ron Ellis SP 12.00 30.00
ARG Rod Gilbert SP 12.00 30.00
ARH Rejean Houle SP 12.00 30.00
ARK Rick Kehoe 6.00 15.00
ARL Rick Ley 5.00 12.00
ARM Rick Martin 8.00 20.00
ARP Rosaire Paiement 5.00 12.00
ARR Rene Robert 8.00 20.00
ARS Rod Seiling 6.00 15.00
ARV Rogie Vachon 10.00 25.00
ARW Ron Ward 5.00 12.00
ASA Syl Apps Jr. 8.00 20.00
ASB Serge Bernier 5.00 12.00
ASM Stan Mikita SP 20.00 50.00
ASS Serge Savard SP 20.00 5.00
ASW Stan Weir 5.00 12.00
ATE Tony Esposito SP 8.00 20.00
ATH Ted Hampson 6.00 15.00
ATO Terry O'Reilly 6.00 15.00
ATT Ted Taylor 5.00 12.00
ATW Tom Webster 5.00 12.00
AVF Val Fonteyne 6.00 15.00
AVH Vic Hadfield 6.00 15.00
AVP Vladimir Petrov 15.00 40.00
AVS Vladimir Shadrin 12.00 30.00
AVT Vladislav Tretiak 30.00 80.00
AVV Valeri Vasiliev 12.00 30.00
AWC Wayne Cashman 6.00 15.00
AWM Walt McKechnie 6.00 15.00
AWT Walt Tkaczuk 6.00 15.00
AYC Yvan Cournoyer SP 8.00 20.00
AAMC Ab McDonald 6.00 15.00
ABC2 Bobby Clarke Summit SP 25.00 60.00
ABCR Bart Crashley 5.00 12.00
ABGL Brian Glennie 8.00 20.00
ABHU Bobby Hull SP 15.00 40.00
ABMI Boris Mikhailov 15.00 40.00
ABP2 Brad Park Summit SP 15.00 40.00
ABPA Bernie Parent SP 30.00 80.00
ABSC Bob Sicinski 5.00 12.00
ABSM Billy Smith 8.00 20.00
ABW2 Bill White Summit 5.00 12.00
ACBO Christian Bordeleau 8.00 20.00
ADA2 Don Awrey Summit 5.00 12.00
ADHE Dennis Hextall 5.00 12.00
ADHU Dennis Hull 10.00 25.00
ADSA Derek Sanderson Phil.SP 30.00 80.00
ADSC Dave Schultz 8.00 20.00
ADSI Darryl Sittler SP 10.00 25.00
AEWE Ed Westfall 6.00 15.00
AFM2 Frank Mahovlich Summit SP 25.00 60.00
AGDO Gary Dornhoefer 5.00 12.00
AGLA Guy Lapointe SP 15.00 40.00
AGP2 Gilbert Perreault Summit SP 15.00 40.00
AGPI Gerry Pinder 5.00 12.00
AGVE Gary Veneruzzo 6.00 15.00
AJDO Jim Dorey 5.00 12.00
AJGG Jean-Guy Gendron 6.00 15.00
AJLO Jim Lorentz 6.00 15.00
AJMC Jim McKenny 5.00 12.00
AJPP J.P. Parise 8.00 20.00
ALMA Larry Mavety 5.00 12.00
AMD2 Marcel Dionne Summit SP 30.00 80.00
APE2 Phil Esposito Summit 25.00 60.00
APH2 Paul Henderson Summit 15.00 40.00
APMA Pete Mahovlich 25.00 60.00
APS2 Pat Stapleton Summit 15.00 40.00
ARBE Red Berenson 15.00 40.00
ARE2 Ron Ellis Summit SP 20.00 50.00
ARG2 Rod Gilbert Summit SP 10.00 25.00
ARMA Rick MacLeish 6.00 15.00
ARSM Rick Smith 6.00 15.00
ASM2 Stan Mikita Summit SP 25.00 60.00
ASS2 Serge Savard Summit SP 25.00 60.00
ASSH Steve Shutt 8.00 20.00
ATE2 Tony Esposito Summit SP 20.00 50.00
AVH2 Vic Hadfield Summit 8.00 20.00
AWC2 Wayne Cashman Summit 6.00 15.00
AWCA Wayne Carleton 5.00 12.00
AWCO Wayne Connelly 5.00 12.00
AYC2 Yvan Cournoyer Summit SP 12.00 30.00
ABGL2 Brian Glennie Summit 8.00 20.00
ADHU2 Dennis Hull Summit 10.00 25.00
ADSAN Derek Sanderson Bos.SP 8.00 20.00
AGLA2 Guy Lapointe Summit SP 25.00 60.00
AGLAB Gord Labossiere 5.00 12.00
AJMCK John McKenzie 12.00 30.00
AJMCL Jimmy McLeod 5.00 12.00
AJPP2 J.P. Parise Summit 8.00 20.00
APMA2 Pete Mahovlich Summit 10.00 25.00
ARBE2 Red Berenson Summit 15.00 40.00

2003-04 ITG VIP Rookie Debut

1 Tuomo Ruutu/114* 4.00 10.00
2 Joffrey Lupul/101* 5.00 12.00
3 Brent Burns/71* 5.00 12.00
4 David Hale/65* 4.00 10.00
5 Paul Martin/52* 4.00 10.00
6 Patrice Bergeron/166* 8.00 20.00
7 Travis Moen/64* 5.00 12.00
8 Lasse Kukkonen/58* 4.00 10.00
9 Christoph Brandner/62* 5.00 12.00
10 Garrett Burnett/48* 4.00 10.00
11 Antti Miettinen/59* 5.00 12.00
12 Antoine Vermette/50* 4.00 10.00
13 Andrew Peters/63* 4.00 10.00
14 Joni Pitkanen/81* 5.00 12.00
15 Sean Bergenheim/54* 5.00 12.00
16 Boyd Gordon/53* 4.00 10.00
17 Dan Fritsche/54* 6.00 15.00
18 Eric Staal/165* 12.50 30.00
19 Nathan Horton/102* 6.00 15.00
20 Dustin Brown/65 6.00 15.00
21 Tim Gleason/58* 4.00 10.00
22 Esa Pirnes/54* 4.00 10.00
23 Wade Brookbank/51* 4.00 10.00
24 Dan Hamhuis/56* 5.00 12.00
25 Jordin Tootoo/156* 8.00 20.00
26 Marek Zidlicky/61* 5.00 12.00
27 Christian Ehrhoff/54* 4.00 10.00
28 Milan Michalek/58* 12.00 30.00
29 Matthew Lombardi/70* 4.00 10.00
30 John-Michael Liles/56* 4.00 10.00
31 Marek Svatos/53* 4.00 10.00
32 Marc-Andre Fleury/580* 6.00 15.00
33 Martin Strbak/66* 4.00 10.00
34 Ryan Malone/84* 8.00 20.00
35 Matt Murley/74* 4.00 10.00
36 Matthew Spiller/62* 4.00 10.00
37 Chris Higgins/67* 10.00 25.00
38 Maxim Kondratiev/62* 4.00 10.00
39 Tom Preissing/58* 4.00 10.00
40 Cody McCormick/37* 4.00 10.00
41 Pavel Vorobiev/30* 4.00 10.00
42 Alexander Semin/47* 10.00 25.00
43 Brent Krahn/32* 4.00 10.00
44 Jiri Hudler/122* 5.00 12.00
45 Boyd Kane/38* 4.00 10.00
46 Gregory Campbell/36* 4.00 10.00
47 Andrew Hutchinson/36* 4.00 10.00
48 Mike Stuart/24* 4.00 10.00
49 Sergei Zinovjev/45* 4.00 10.00
50 Trevor Daley/34* 4.00 10.00
51 Julien Vauclair/32* 4.00 10.00
52 Alan Rourke/33* 4.00 10.00
53 Tony Salmelainen/34* 4.00 10.00
54 John Pohl/36* 4.00 10.00
55 Dominic Moore/42* 4.00 10.00
56 Peter Sarno/34* 4.00 10.00
57 Rastislav Stana/66* 4.00 10.00
58 Karl Stewart/58* 4.00 10.00
59 Darryl Bootland/43* 4.00 10.00
60 Pat Rissmiller/35* 4.00 10.00
61 Jed Ortmeyer/42* 4.00 10.00
62 Nathan Smith/31* 4.00 10.00
63 Grant McNeill/31* 4.00 10.00
64 Seamus Kotyk/39* 4.00 10.00
65 Phil Osaer/35* 4.00 10.00
66 Ryan Kesler/62* 4.00 10.00
67 Libor Pivko/39* 4.00 10.00
68 Mikhail Yakubov/33* 4.00 10.00
69 Nathan Robinson/35* 4.00 10.00
70 Fredrik Sjostrom/37* 4.00 10.00
71 Tony Martensson/43* 4.00 10.00
72 Aaron Johnson/48* 4.00 10.00
73 Jeff Hamilton/47* 4.00 10.00
74 Nikolai Zherdev/255* 15.00 40.00
75 Gavin Morgan/53* 4.00 10.00
76 Patrick Leahy/50* 4.00 10.00
77 Jeff MacMillan/47* 4.00 10.00
78 Antero Niittymaki/90* 8.00 20.00
79 Niklas Kronwall/77* 12.50 30.00
80 Joey MacDonald/56* 4.00 10.00
81 Doug Doull/59* 12.50 30.00
82 Dwayne Zinger/50* 4.00 10.00
83 Jason MacDonald/47* 4.00 10.00
84 Rob Skrlac/39* 4.00 10.00
85 Derek Roy/88* 12.50 30.00
86 Ryan Barnes/39* 4.00 10.00
87 Noah Clarke/48* 12.50 30.00
88 Steve McLaren/54* 4.00 10.00
89 Tim Jackman/32* 6.00 15.00
90 Timofei Shishkanov/39* 8.00 20.00
91 Jason Pominville/40* 8.00 20.00
92 Mikko Luoma/36* 4.00 10.00
93 Jeremy Yablonski/39* 4.00 10.00
94 Tomas Plekanec/37* 10.00 25.00
95 Tuomas Pihlman/36* 4.00 10.00
96 Darcy Verot/55* 4.00 10.00
97 Mark Popovic/38* 4.00 10.00
98 Doug Lynch/36* 4.00 10.00
99 Aleksander Suglobov/31* 4.00 10.00
100 Nolan Schaefer/35* 4.00 10.00
101 Colton Orr/54* 4.00 10.00
102 Mike Smith/64* 5.00 12.00
103 Anton Babchuk/37* 4.00 10.00
104 Kyle Wellwood/41* 4.00 10.00
105 Jamie Pollock/36* 4.00 10.00
106 Carl Corazzini/49* 4.00 10.00
107 Zbynek Michalek/31* 4.00 10.00
108 Chris Kunitz/27* 4.00 10.00
109 Lawrence Nycholat/37* 6.00 15.00
110 Jozef Balej/56* 8.00 20.00
111 Mike Bishai/33* 4.00 10.00
112 Garth Murray/39* 4.00 10.00
113 Matt Ellison/29* 4.00 10.00
114 Joe Motzko/36* 4.00 10.00
115 Graham Mink/54* 4.00 10.00
116 Brooks Laich/46* 4.00 10.00
117 Mike Green/27* 4.00 10.00
118 Dan Ellis/37* 4.00 10.00
119 Robert Scuderi/37* 4.00 10.00
120 Fedor Tyutin/50* 4.00 10.00
121 Michael Morrison/37* 4.00 10.00
122 Cory Larose/38* 4.00 10.00
123 Andy Chiodo/62* 4.00 10.00
124 Adam Munro/43* 4.00 10.00
125 Mikhail Kuleshov/76* 4.00 10.00
126 Matt Keith/31* 4.00 10.00
127 Denis Grebeshkov/32* 4.00 10.00
128 Quintin Laing/16* 4.00 10.00
129 Benoit Dusablon/23* 4.00 10.00
130 Matt Underhill/27* 4.00 10.00
131 Fred Meyer/20* 4.00 10.00
132 Randy Jones/23* 4.00 10.00
133 Brad Boyes/67* 12.50 30.00
134 Erik Westrum/16* 4.00 10.00
135 Bryce Lampman/23* 4.00 10.00
136 Goran Bezina/32* 4.00 10.00
137 Owen Fussey/48* 4.00 10.00
138 Josh Olson/14* 4.00 10.00
139 Michal Barinka/21* 4.00 10.00
140 Kari Lehtonen/526* 15.00 40.00
141 Matt Hussey/28* 4.00 10.00
142 Mike Stutzel/18* 4.00 10.00
143 Roman Tvrdon/34* 4.00 10.00
144 Matthew Yeats/50* 4.00 10.00
145 Thomas Pock/40* 4.00 10.00
146 Wade Dubielewicz/59* 4.00 10.00
147 Greg Mauldin/34* 4.00 10.00
148 Mike Pandolfo/32* 4.00 10.00
149 Eric Perrin/48* 4.00 10.00

2009-10 ITG 1972 The Year In Hockey

COMPLETE SET (200) 20.00 50.00
1 Phil Esposito .50 1.25
2 Johnny Bucyk .30 .75
3 Ken Hodge .25 .60
4 Wayne Cashman .25 .60
5 Terry O'Reilly .25 .60
6 Don Awrey .20 .50
7 Dallas Smith .40 1.00
8 Jacques Plante .50 1.25
9 Eddie Johnston .50 1.25
10 Jacques Lemaire .25 .60
11 Frank Mahovlich .30 .75
12 Yvan Cournoyer .30 .75
13 Guy Lafleur .40 1.00
14 Guy Lapointe .25 .60
15 Rejean Houle .20 .50
16 Serge Savard .40 1.00
17 Larry Robinson .30 .75
18 Michel Plasse .20 .50
19 Steve Shutt .30 .75
20 Darryl Sittler .40 1.00
21 Rick Kehoe .20 .50
22 Dave Keon .30 .75
23 Norm Ullman .30 .75
24 Ron Ellis .20 .50
25 Paul Henderson .40 1.00
26 Brian Glennie .20 .50
27 Gerry Desjardins .25 .60
28 Ed Westfall .25 .60
29 Bob Nystrom .20 .50
30 Billy Smith .30 .75
31 Gilles Villemure .40 1.00
32 Rod Gilbert .40 1.00
33 Walt Tkaczuk .25 .60
34 Vic Hadfield .25 .60
35 Brad Park .25 .60
36 Rod Seiling .25 .60
37 Ed Giacomin .40 1.00
38 Red Berenson .60 1.50
39 Marcel Dionne .40 1.00
40 Alex Delvecchio .30 .75
41 Nick Libett .20 .50
42 Roy Edwards .20 .50
43 Rene Robert .30 .75
44 Gilbert Perreault .30 .75
45 Rick Martin .20 .50
46 Jim Lorentz .25 .60
47 Tim Horton .30 .75
48 Roger Crozier .20 .50
49 Jim Schoenfeld .20 .50
50 Bobby Schmautz .20 .50
51 Andre Boudrias .25 .60
52 Don Lever .50 1.25
53 Dunc Wilson .30 .75
54 Doug Jarrett .20 .50
55 Bill White .20 .50
56 Dennis Hull .40 1.00
57 Pit Martin .20 .50
58 Stan Mikita .40 1.00
59 Pat Stapleton .25 .60
60 Tony Esposito .30 .75
61 Keith Magnuson .20 .50
62 Garry Unger .20 .50
63 Jack Egers .25 .60
64 Noel Picard .20 .50
65 Gary Sabourin .25 .60
66 Phil Myre .25 .60
67 Dan Bouchard .25 .60
68 Pat Quinn .20 .50
69 Bob Leiter .30 .75
70 Curt Bennett .20 .50
71 Bobby Clarke .50 1.25
72 Rick MacLeish .20 .50
73 Gary Dornhoefer .20 .50
74 Bill Flett .20 .50
75 Bill Barber .25 .60
76 Joe Watson .20 .50
77 Dave Schultz .30 .75
78 Doug Favell .30 .75
79 Serge Bernier .20 .50
80 Rogie Vachon .40 1.00
81 Gary Edwards .20 .50
82 Butch Goring .30 .75
83 Harry Howell .25 .60
84 Bill Goldsworthy .20 .50
85 Dennis Hextall .20 .50
86 J.P. Parise .20 .50
87 Gump Worsley .50 1.25
88 Danny Grant .40 1.00
89 Cesare Maniago .25 .60
90 Eddie Shack .30 .75
91 Brian Hextall .25 .60
92 Syl Apps Jr. .20 .50
93 Lowell MacDonald .20 .50
94 Al McDonough .20 .50
95 Denis Herron .25 .60
96 Walt McKechnie .25 .60
97 Stan Weir .20 .50
98 Joey Johnston .20 .50
99 Gilles Meloche .20 .50
100 Checklist .25 .60
101 Rick Smith .25 .60
102 Wayne Rutledge .25 .60
103 Poul Popiel .20 .50
104 Larry Lund .20 .50
105 Ted Taylor .20 .50
106 Gord Labossiere .20 .50
107 Andre Lacroix .20 .50
108 Bernie Parent .40 1.00
109 Derek Sanderson .30 .75
110 John McKenzie .50 1.25
111 Rosaire Paiement .20 .50
112 Bob Sicinski .20 .50
113 Jim McLeod .20 .50
114 Larry Mavety .20 .50
115 Gary Jarrett .20 .50
116 Gerry Pinder .20 .50
117 Gerry Cheevers .25 .60
118 Paul Shmyr .20 .50
119 Wayne Connelly .20 .50
120 Ted Hampson .20 .50
121 Mike Antonovich .25 .60
122 Mike Curran .25 .60
123 Bob MacMillan .20 .50
124 Bobby Hull .60 1.50
125 Joe Daley .20 .50
126 Ernie Wakely .25 .60
127 Chris Bordeleau .30 .75
128 Ab McDonald .25 .60
129 Wayne Carleton .30 .75
130 Gilles Gratton .30 .75
131 Les Binkley .30 .75
132 J.C. Tremblay .20 .50
133 Richard Brodeur .30 .75
134 Jean-Guy Gendron .25 .60
135 Ken Brown .20 .50
136 Val Fonteyne .25 .60
137 Al Hamilton .20 .50
138 Jack Norris .20 .50
139 Bill Hicke .20 .50
140 Ron Ward .20 .50
141 Norm Ferguson .20 .50
142 Kent Douglas .20 .50
143 Alton White .20 .50
144 Gary Veneruzzo .25 .60
145 Bart Crashley .20 .50
146 Gerry Odrowski .20 .50
147 Tom Webster .20 .50
148 Larry Pleau .20 .50
149 Jim Dorey .20 .50
150 Al Smith .20 .50
151 Rick Ley .20 .50
152 Don Awrey .20 .50
153 Red Berenson .60 1.50
154 Gary Bergman .20 .50
155 Wayne Cashman .25 .60
156 Bobby Clarke .50 1.25
157 Yvan Cournoyer .30 .75
158 Ron Ellis .20 .50
159 Phil Esposito .50 1.25
160 Tony Esposito .30 .75
161 Rod Gilbert .40 1.00
162 Vic Hadfield .25 .60
163 Paul Henderson .40 1.00
164 Dennis Hull .40 1.00
165 Valeri Kharlamov .20 .50
166 Guy Lapointe .25 .60
167 Frank Mahovlich .30 .75
168 Pete Mahovlich .40 1.00
169 Alexander Maltsev .20 .50
170 Bill Goldsworthy .20 .50
171 Boris Mikhailov .60 1.50
172 Stan Mikita .40 1.00
173 J.P. Parise .30 .75
174 Brad Park .25 .60
175 Gilbert Perreault .30 .75
176 Vladimir Petrov .60 1.50
177 Alexander Ragulin .20 .50
178 Eddie Johnston .50 1.25
179 Serge Savard .40 1.00
180 Rod Seiling .25 .60
181 Pat Stapleton .25 .60
182 Dale Tallon .30 .75
183 Vladislav Tretiak .25 .60
184 Valeri Vasiliev .50 1.25
185 Vladimir Shadrin .50 1.25
186 Bill White .20 .50
187 Alexander Yakushev .60 1.50
188 Harry Sinden .20 .50
189 Vsevolod Bobrov .20 .50
190 V.Kharlamov/B.Clarke .50 1.25
191 T.Esposito/V.Tretiak .30 .75
192 P.Henderson/V.Tretiak .40 1.00
193 B.Mikhailov/P.Esposito .60 1.50
194 V.Petrov/T.Esposito .60 1.50
195 G.Bergman/A.Yakushev .60 1.50
196 B.White/B.Mikhailov .60 1.50
197 P.Henderson/Yakushev .60 1.50
198 Paul Henderson .40 1.00
199 Vladislav Tretiak .25 .60
200 Checklist .20 .50

2009-10 ITG 1972 The Year In Hockey Coaches

C01 Scotty Bowman 1.50 4.00
C02 Tom Johnson 1.25 3.00
C03 Emile Francis 1.00 2.50
C04 Phil Goyette 1.00 2.50
C05 Billy Reay 1.00 2.50
C06 Fred Shero 1.00 2.50
C07 Al Arbour 1.25 3.00
C08 Bob Pulford 1.25 3.00
C09 Red Kelly 1.50 4.00
C10 Bernie Geoffrion 1.00 2.50

2009-10 ITG 1972 The Year In Hockey Forever Linked

FL01 Paul Henderson/Vladislav Tretiak 3.00 8.00
FL02 Bobby Hull/Gerry Cheevers 5.00 12.00
FL03 Bobby Clarke/Valeri Kharlamov 4.00 10.00
FL04 Jean Beliveau/Guy Lafleur 3.00 8.00

2009-10 ITG 1972 The Year In Hockey Game Used Jersey Black

SILVER/30: .5X TO 1.2X BASIC JSY
M01 Bill Barber 4.00 10.00
M02 Johnny Bucyk 5.00 12.00
M03 Alexander Yakushev 10.00 25.00
M04 Bobby Clarke 8.00 20.00
M05 Yvan Cournoyer 5.00 12.00
M06 Alex Delvecchio 5.00 12.00
M07 Marcel Dionne 6.00 15.00
M08 Gary Dornhoefer 3.00 8.00
M09 Phil Esposito 8.00 20.00
M10 Tony Esposito 5.00 12.00
M11 Ed Giacomin 6.00 15.00
M12 Rod Gilbert 6.00 15.00
M13 Vladislav Tretiak 6.00 15.00
M14 Pete Mahovlich 6.00 15.00
M15 Rejean Houle 3.00 8.00
M16 Bobby Hull 10.00 25.00
M17 Dennis Hull 6.00 15.00
M18 Boris Mikhailov 10.00 25.00
M19 Dave Keon 5.00 12.00
M20 Guy Lafleur 6.00 15.00
M21 Guy Lapointe 4.00 10.00
M22 Jacques Lemaire 4.00 10.00
M23 Rick MacLeish 4.00 10.00
M24 Henri Richard 12.00 30.00
M25 Rick Martin 5.00 12.00
M26 Stan Mikita 6.00 15.00
M27 Bob Nystrom 3.00 8.00
M28 Terry O'Reilly 4.00 10.00
M29 Brad Park 4.00 10.00
M30 Gilbert Perreault 6.00 15.00
M31 Vic Hadfield 4.00 10.00
M32 Valeri Kharlamov 3.00 8.00
M33 Larry Robinson 5.00 12.00
M34 Phil Myre 3.00 8.00
M35 Serge Savard 6.00 15.00
M36 Dave Schultz 5.00 12.00
M37 Steve Shutt 5.00 12.00
M38 Darryl Sittler 6.00 15.00
M39 Billy Smith 5.00 12.00
M40 Pat Stapleton 4.00 10.00
M41 Walt Tkaczuk 4.00 10.00
M42 Garry Unger 3.00 8.00
M43 Rogie Vachon 6.00 15.00
M44 Joe Watson 3.00 8.00
M45 Bill White 3.00 8.00

2009-10 ITG 1972 The Year In Hockey Great Moments

COMPLETE SET (8) 10.00 25.00
COMMON CARD .75 2.00
SEMISTARS 1.00 2.50
UNLISTED STARS 1.25 3.00
GM01 Gerry Cheevers 1.25 3.00
GM02 Johnny Bucyk 1.25 3.00
GM03 Bobby Hull 2.50 6.00
GM04 Vladislav Tretiak 1.00 2.50
GM05 Phil Esposito 2.00 5.00
GM06 Paul Henderson 1.50 4.00
GM07 Billy Smith 1.25 3.00
GM08 Les Binkley 1.25 3.00

2009-10 ITG 1972 The Year In Hockey Masked Men

COMPLETE SET (10) 15.00 40.00
MM01 Doug Favell 2.50 6.00
MM02 Gerry Cheevers 2.50 6.00
MM03 Rogie Vachon 3.00 8.00
MM04 Ed Giacomin 3.00 8.00
MM05 Gilles Villemure 3.00 8.00
MM06 Tony Esposito 2.50 6.00
MM07 Jacques Plante 4.00 10.00
MM08 Cesare Maniago 2.00 5.00
MM09 Bernie Parent 3.00 8.00
MM10 Ken Brown 1.50 4.00

2009-10 ITG 1972 The Year In Hockey Past and Present

PP01 Guy Lafleur/Carey Price 10.00 25.00
PP02 T.Esposito/Martin Brodeur 12.00 30.00
PP03 M.Dionne/Pavel Datsyuk 8.00 20.00
PP04 Bobby Clarke/Daniel Briere 8.00 20.00
PP05 Delvecchio/N.Lidstrom 5.00 12.00
PP06 Goldsworthy/Mike Modano 8.00 20.00
PP07 D.Wilson/Roberto Luongo 8.00 20.00
PP08 J.Plante/Vesa Toskala 8.00 20.00
PP09 G.Cheevers/Tim Thomas 5.00 12.00
PP10 Ed Westfall/John Tavares 15.00 40.00

2009-10 ITG 1972 The Year In Hockey Rookies

COMPLETE SET (8) 8.00 20.00
R01 Dan Bouchard/Jim Schoenfeld 1.00 2.50
R02 Denis Herron/Billy Smith 1.25 3.00
R03 Bill Barber/Dave Schultz 1.25 3.00
R04 Steve Shutt/Terry O'Reilly 1.25 3.00
R05 Bob Nystrom/Richard Brodeur 1.25 3.00
R06 Larry Robinson/Gilles Gratton 1.25 3.00
R07 Bob MacMillan/Bob Sicinski .75 2.00
R08 Don Lever/Mike Antonovich 2.00 5.00

1979-80 Islanders Transparencies

COMPLETE SET (22) 20.00 40.00
1 Mike Bossy 7.50 15.00
2 Bob Bourne .38 .75
3 Clark Gillies .38 .75
4 Billy Harris .38 .75
5 Lorne Henning .38 .75
6 Anders Kallur .38 .75
7 Mike Kaszycki .38 .75
8 Dave Langevin .38 .75
9 Dave Lewis .38 .75
10 Bob Lorimer .38 .75
11 Wayne Merrick .38 .75
12 Bob Nystrom 1.00 2.00
13 Stefan Persson .38 .75
14 Denis Potvin 1.00 2.00
15 Jean Potvin .38 .75
16 Garry Howatt .38 .75
17 Glenn Resch 2.50 5.00
18 Bill Smith 2.50 5.00
19 Steven Tambellini .38 .75
20 John Tonelli .75 1.50
21 Bryan Trottier 2.00 4.00
22 Header Card .38 .75

1983-84 Islanders Team Issue

COMPLETE SET (19) 12.00 30.00
1 Mike Bossy 2.00 5.00
2 Bob Bourne .40 1.00
3 Billy Carroll .40 1.00
4 Clark Gillies .75 2.00
5 Mats Hallin .40 1.00
6 Kelly Hrudey 1.50 4.00
7 Tomas Jonsson .40 1.00
8 Dave Langevin .40 1.00
9 Roland Melanson .60 1.50
10 Wayne Merrick .40 1.00
11 Ken Morrow .60 1.50
12 Bob Nystrom .60 1.50
13 Denis Potvin 1.50 4.00
14 Billy Smith 1.50 4.00
15 Brent Sutter .75 2.00
16 Duane Sutter .60 1.50
17 John Tonelli .75 2.00
18 Bryan Trottier 1.50 4.00
19 Team Photo .75 2.00

1984 Islanders News

COMPLETE SET (38) 10.00 25.00
1 Checklist Card .20 .50
2 Mike Bossy 1.50 4.00
3 Bob Bourne .20 .50
4 Billy Carroll .20 .50
5 Greg Gilbert .20 .50
6 Clark Gillies .50 1.25
7 Butch Goring .40 1.00
8 Mats Hallin .20 .50
9 Anders Kallur .20 .50
10 Wayne Merrick .20 .50
11 Bob Nystrom .30 .75
12 Brent Sutter .50 1.25
13 Duane Sutter .40 1.00
14 John Tonelli .50 1.25
15 Bryan Trottier 1.25 3.00
16 Tomas Jonsson .20 .50
17 Gordie Lane .20 .50
18 Dave Langevin .20 .50
19 Ken Morrow .40 1.00
20 Stefan Persson .20 .50
21 Denis Potvin 1.00 2.50
22 Roland Melanson .30 .75
23 Billy Smith .75 2.00
24 Cup Number 1 .20 .50
25 Cup Number 2 .20 .50
26 Cup Number 3 .20 .50
27 Lorne Henning CO .20 .50
28 Bill Torrey GM .20 .50
29 Al Arbour CO .40 1.00
30 Waske-Pickard Two Trainers .08 .25
31 1979-80 Team Photo .40 1.00
32 1980-81 Team Photo .40 1.00
33 1981-82 Team Photo .40 1.00
34 1982-83 Team Photo .40 1.00
35 Mike Bossy '82 Conn Smythe Winner .75 2.00
36 Billy Smith '83 Conn Smythe Winner .50 1.25
37 Bryan Trottier '80 Conn Smythe Winner .60 1.50
38 Butch Goring '81 Conn Smythe Winner .30 .75

1985 Islanders News

COMPLETE SET (37) 12.00 30.00
1 Checklist Card .20 .50
2 Mike Bossy 1.50 4.00
3 Bob Bourne .20 .50
4 Pat Flatley .30 .75
5 Greg Gilbert .20 .50
6 Clark Gillies .40 1.00
7 Mats Hallin .20 .50
8 Anders Kallur .20 .50
9 Alan Kerr .20 .50
10 Roger Kortko .20 .50
11 Pat LaFontaine 3.00 8.00
12 Bob Nystrom .30 .75
13 Brent Sutter .40 1.00
14 Duane Sutter .30 .75
15 John Tonelli .40 1.00
16 Bryan Trottier 1.25 3.00
17 Paul Boutilier .20 .50
18 Gerald Diduck .20 .50
19 Gord Dineen .20 .50
20 Tomas Jonsson .30 .75
21 Gordie Lane .20 .50
22 Dave Langevin .20 .50
23 Ken Morrow .30 .75
24 Stefan Persson .20 .50
25 Denis Potvin 1.00 2.50
26 Kelly Hrudey 1.25 3.00
27 Billy Smith .75 2.00
28 Bill Torrey GM/P .30 .75
29 Al Arbour CO .40 1.00
30 Brian Kilrea CO .08 .25
31 Pickard Smith Two Trainers .08 .25
32 Mike Bossy Milestone-400 Goals .75 2.00
33 Denis Potvin Milestone-600 Assists .60 1.50
34 Billy Smith Milestone-500 Games .40 1.00
35 Bryan Trottier Milestone-1000 Points .60 1.50
36 1984-85 Team .40 1.00
37 Wales Champs .30 .75

1985 Islanders News Trottier

COMPLETE SET (33) 10.00 25.00
1 Penalty box .40 1.00
2 Swift Current Broncos .40 1.00
3 Three goals in first game at Nassau Coliseum .20 .50
4 All-Star game .30 .75
5 Four goals vs. Atlanta .20 .50
6 Ross and Hart Trophies .30 .75
7 Street hockey equipment .20 .50
8 Bearing down on the draw against Maruk .30 .75
9 Pleading with referee .20 .50
10 Trottier Rangers action .20 .50
11 Trottier Holmgren action .30 .75
12 Trottier Canadiens action .30 .75
13 1980 Boston playoff .30 .75
14 1980 Final Game vs. Flyers .30 .75
15 NHL Awards Luncheon .20 .50
16 Trottier Rangers action .30 .75
17 Watching action in resting area .20 .50
18 Warm-up time .20 .50
19 Debating with referee .20 .50
20 1981 Playoff with Oilers .30 .75
21 Trottier Gretzky action 4.00 10.00
22 Trottier North Stars action .30 .75
23 Congratulating Don Beaupre .30 .75
24 Second Stanley Cup Championship .20 .50
25 Trottier Sutter celebrate .30 .75
26 Trottier psyching himself .20 .50
27 Trottier Devils action .30 .75
28 1983 All-Star .30 .75
29 Bryan Trottier Wayne Gretzky 3.00 8.00
30 Fourth Stanley Cup Championship .20 .50
31 Bryan Trottier Denis Potvin .60 1.50
32 Bryan Trottier Mike Bossy .75 2.00
33 1984 Canada Cup Series .40 1.00

1986-87 Islanders Team Issue

COMPLETE SET (30) 10.00 25.00
1 Alan Kerr .20 .50
2 Ari Haanpaa .20 .50
3 Bill Smith 1.25 3.00
4 Bob Nystrom .30 .75
5 Bob Bassen .20 .50
6 Brad Lauer .20 .50
7 Brent Sutter .60 1.50
8 Brian Curran .20 .50
9 Bryan Trottier .60 1.50
10 Trainers .08 .25
11 Dale Henry .20 .50
12 Denis Potvin 1.25 3.00
13 Duane Sutter .30 .75
14 Gerald Diduck .20 .50
15 Gord Dineen .20 .50
16 Greg Gilbert .20 .50
17 Islander Emblem .02 .10
18 Kelly Hrudey .75 2.00
19 Ken Leiter .20 .50
20 Ken Morrow .30 .75
21 Mike Bossy 1.25 3.00
22 Mikko Makela .20 .50
23 Pat Lafontaine .75 2.00
24 Patrick Flatley .20 .50
25 Randy Boyd .20 .50
26 Richard Kromm .20 .50
27 Roger Kortko .20 .50
28 Steve Konroyd .20 .50
29 Terry Simpson CO .08 .25
30 Tomas Jonsson .20 .50

1989-90 Islanders Team Issue

COMPLETE SET (22) 4.80 12.00
1 Al Arbour CO .30 .75
2 Dean Chynoweth .20 .50
3 Dave Chyzowski .20 .50
4 Doug Crossman .20 .50
5 Gerald Diduck .20 .50
6 Tom Fitzgerald .20 .50
7 Mark Fitzpatrick .60 1.50
8 Patrick Flatley .30 .75
9 Glenn Healy .40 1.00
10 Alan Kerr .20 .50
11 Pat LaFontaine 1.00 2.50
12 Mikko Makela .20 .50
13 Don Maloney .20 .50
14 Jeff Norton .20 .50
15 Gary Nylund .20 .50
16 Rich Pilon .20 .50
17 Brent Sutter .30 .75
18 Gilles Thibaudeau .20 .50
19 Bryan Trottier .75 2.00
20 David Volek .20 .50
21 Mick Vukota .20 .50
22 Randy Wood .20 .50

1993-94 Islanders Chemical Bank Alumni

COMPLETE SET (10) 3.00 8.00
1 Title Card .08 .25
2 Mike Bossy .75 2.00
3 Clark Gillies .30 .75
4 Gerry Hart .20 .50
5 Wayne Merrick .20 .50
6 Bob Nystrom .30 .75
7 Denis Potvin .60 1.50
8 Bill Smith .60 1.50
9 John Tonelli .30 .75
10 Eddie Westfall .20 .50

1996-97 Islander Postcards

COMPLETE SET (23) 6.00 15.00
1 Niclas Andersson .20 .50
2 Derek Armstrong .20 .50
3 Todd Bertuzzi .30 .75
4 Eric Fichaud .75 2.00
5 Travis Green .20 .50
6 Doug Houda .20 .50
7 Brent Hughes .30 .75
8 Kenny Jonsson .30 .75
9 Derek King .30 .75
10 Paul Kruse .20 .50
11 Claude Lapointe .20 .50
12 Scott Lachance .20 .50
13 Bryan McCabe .20 .50
14 Marty McInnis .20 .50
15 Mike Milbury .20 .50
16 Zigmund Palffy 1.25 3.00
17 Dan Plante .20 .50
18 Rich Pilon .20 .50
19 Tommy Salo .60 1.50
20 Bryan Smolinski .30 .75
21 Dennis Vaske .20 .50
22 Mick Vukota .20 .50
23 Randy Wood .20 .50

1998-99 Islanders Power Play

COMPLETE SET (4) 2.50 6.00
NYI1 Trevor Linden .75 2.00
NYI2 Bryan Smolinski .40 1.00
NYI3 Mike Watt .20 .50
NYI4 Zigmund Palffy 2.00 5.00

1993-94 Jell-O Punch Outs

COMPLETE SET (8) 3.00 8.00
1 Pavel Bure Kirk McLean .50 1.25
2 Doug Gilmour Felix Potvin .50 1.25
3 Wayne Gretzky Kelly Hrudey .75 2.00
4 Mario Lemieux Tom Barrasso .60 1.50
5 Eric Lindros Dominic Roussel .50 1.25
6 Kirk Muller Patrick Roy .60 1.50

7 Joe Nieuwendyk
Mike Vernon .40 1.00
8 Joe Sakic
Stephane Fiset .40 1.00
AD Mario Lemieux Ad Display 4.00 10.00

1997-98 Jell-O Pinnacle Juniors To Pros

COMPLETE SET (12)
1 Wayne Gretzky 2.00 5.00
2 Paul Kariya 1.00 2.50
3 Eric Lindros .40 1.00
4 Mark Messier .40 1.00
5 Patrick Roy 1.50 4.00
6 Joe Sakic .75 2.00
7 Chris Chelios .40 1.00
8 Sergei Fedorov .75 2.00
9 Jaromir Jagr .75 2.00
10 Saku Koivu .40 1.00
11 Zigmund Palffy .40 1.00
12 Mats Sundin .40 1.00

1998 Jell-O Spoons

COMPLETE SET (8) 6.00 15.00
1 Rod Brind'Amour .25 .60
2 Theo Fleury .30 .75
3 Wayne Gretzky 1.50 4.00
4 Curtis Joseph .30 .75
5 Paul Kariya 1.00 2.50
6 Eric Lindros .75 2.00
7 Patrick Roy 1.25 3.00
8 Joe Sakic .60 1.50

1999-00 Jell-O Partners of Power

COMPLETE SET (6) 6.00 15.00
1 S.Stevens
M.Brodeur .75 2.00
2 J.Jagr
T.Barrasso .40 1.00
3 E.Lindros
J.Vanbiesbrouck .60 1.50
4 M.Peca
D.Hasek .40 1.00
5 R.Bourque
B.Dafoe .75 2.00
6 M.Sundin
C.Joseph .40 1.00
7 D.Hatcher
E.Belfour .30 .75
8 D.Weight
T.Salo .20 .50
9 J.Sakic
P.Roy 2.00 5.00
10 S.Yzerman
C.Osgood 1.25 3.00
11 P.Kariya
G.Hebert .75 2.00
12 O.Nolan
M.Vernon .20 .50

1999-00 Jell-O Pudding Super Skills

COMPLETE SET (6) 1.50 4.00
1 Peter Bondra .30 .75
2 Ray Bourque .60 1.50
3 John LeClair .40 1.00
4 Al MacInnis .30 .75
5 Mike Modano .40 1.00
6 Jeremy Roenick .30 .75

2000-01 Jell-O NHL Tattoos

COMPLETE SET (32) 8.00 20.00
COMMON DUAL TEAM (1-30) .80 2.00
COMMON NHL LOGO (31-32) .20 .50

1978-79 Jets Postcards

COMPLETE SET (23) 12.50 25.00
1 Mike Amodeo .38 .75
2 Scott Campbell .38 .75
3 Kim Clackson .50 1.00
4 Joe Daley 1.00 2.00
5 John Gray .38 .75
6 Ted Green 1.00 2.00
7 Robert Guindon .38 .75
8 Glenn Hicks .38 .75
9 Larry Hillman .38 .75
10 Bill Lesuk .50 1.00
11 Willy Lindstrom .75 1.50
12 Barry Long .38 .75
13 Morris Lukowich .75 1.50
14 Paul MacKinnon .38 .75
15 Markus Mattsson .75 1.50
16 Lyle Moffat .38 .75
17 Kent Nilsson 2.50 5.00
18 Rich Preston .50 1.00
19 Terry Ruskowski 1.25 2.50
20 Lars-Erik Sjoberg 1.25 2.50
21 Peter Sullivan .38 .75
22 Paul Terbenche .38 .75
23 Steve West .38 .75

1979-80 Jets Postcards

COMPLETE SET (28) 12.50 25.00
1 Mike Amodeo .38 .75
2 Al Cameron .38 .75
3 Scott Campbell .38 .75
4 Wayne Dillon .38 .75
5 Jude Drouin .38 .75
6 John Ferguson GM .50 1.00
7 Hilliard Graves .38 .75
8 Pierre Hamel .38 .75
9 Dave Hoyda .38 .75
10 Bobby Hull 4.00 8.00
11 Bill Lesuk .38 .75
12 Willy Lindstrom .75 1.50
13 Morris Lukowich .75 1.50
14 Jimmy Mann .75 1.50
15 Peter Marsh .50 1.00
16 Gord McTavish .38 .75
17 Tom McVie CO .38 .75
18 Barry Melrose 1.50 3.00
19 Lyle Moffat .38 .75
20 Craig Norwich .38 .75
21 Lars-Erik Sjoberg 1.25 2.50
22 Gary Smith .50 1.00
23 Gordon Smith .38 .75
24 Lorne Stamler .38 .75
25 Peter Sullivan .38 .75
26 Bill Sutherland ACO .25 .50
27 Ron Wilson .50 1.00
28 Title Card .25 .50

1980-81 Jets Postcards

COMPLETE SET (24) 10.00 20.00
1 David Babych 1.00 2.50
2 Al Cameron .40 1.00
3 Scott Campbell .40 1.00
4 Dave Chartier .40 1.00
5 Dave Christian .40 1.00
6 Jude Drouin .40 1.00
7 Norm Dupont .40 1.00
8 Dan Geoffrion .40 1.00
9 Pierre Hamel .40 1.00
10 Barry Legge .40 1.00
11 Willy Lindstrom .60 1.50
12 Barry Long .60 1.50
13 Morris Lukowich .40 1.00
14 Kris Manery .40 1.00
15 Jimmy Mann .60 1.50
16 Moe Mantha .60 1.50
17 Markus Mattsson .60 1.50
18 Richard Mulhern .40 1.00
19 Doug Smail .60 1.50
20 Don Spring .40 1.00
21 Anders Steen .40 1.00
22 Pete Sullivan .40 1.00
23 Tim Trimper .40 1.00
24 Ron Wilson .60 1.50

1981-82 Jets Postcards

COMPLETE SET (24) 12.00 30.00
1 Scott Arniel .40 1.00
2 Dave Babych .60 1.50
3 Dave Christian .60 1.50
4 Lucien Deblois .40 1.00
5 Normand Dupont .30 .75
6 Dale Hawerchuk 4.00 10.00
7 Larry Hopkins .30 .75
8 Craig Levie .30 .75
9 Willy Lindstrom .40 1.00
10 Morris Lukowich .40 1.00
11 Bengt Lundholm .30 .75
12 Paul MacLean .60 1.50
13 Jimmy Mann .40 1.00
14 Bryan Maxwell .30 .75
15 Serge Savard .50 1.25
16 Doug Smail .60 1.50
17 Doug Soetaert .60 1.50
18 Don Spring .30 .75
19 Ed Staniowski .30 .75
20 Thomas Steen .75 2.00
21 Bill Sutherland CO .30 .75
22 Tim Trimper .30 .75
23 Tom Watt CO .30 .75
24 Tim Watters .30 .75

1982-83 Jets Postcards

COMPLETE SET (28) 10.00 25.00
1 Scott Arniel .30 .75
2 Dave Babych .40 1.00
3 Jerry Butler .20 .50
4 Wade Campbell .20 .50
5 Dave Christian .40 1.00
6 Lucien DeBlois .30 .75
7 Norm Dupont .20 .50
8 Dale Hawerchuk
(Sitting holding trophy) 3.00 8.00
9 Dale Hawerchuk 3.00 8.00
10 Jim Kyte .20 .50
11 Craig Levie .20 .50
12 Willy Lindstrom .30 .75
13 Morris Lukowich .20 .50
14 Bengt Lundholm .30 .75
15 Paul MacLean .30 .75
16 Jimmy Mann .20 .50
17 Bryan Maxwell .20 .50
18 Brian Mullen .20 .50
19 Serge Savard .40 1.00
20 Doug Smail .40 1.00
21 Doug Soetaert .30 .75
22 Don Spring .20 .50
23 Ed Staniowcki .20 .50
24 Thomas Steen .60 1.50
25 Bill Sutherland ACO .20 .50
26 Tom Watt CO .20 .50
27 Tim Watters .20 .50
28 Team Photo .20 .50

1983-84 Jets Postcards

COMPLETE SET (25) 6.00 15.00
1 Scott Arniel .20 .50
2 Dave Babych .30 .75
3 Laurie Boschman .20 .50
4 Wade Campbell .20 .50
5 Lucien DeBlois .30 .75
6 John Ferguson VP/GM .30 .75
7 John Gibson .20 .50
8 Dale Hawerchuk 1.50 4.00
9 Brian Hayward .40 1.00
10 Jim Kyte .30 .75
11 Barry Long CO .20 .50
12 Morris Lukowich .20 .50
13 Bengt Lundholm .20 .50
14 Paul MacLean .30 .75
15 Jimmy Mann .20 .50
16 Moe Mantha .20 .50
17 Andrew McBain .20 .50
18 Brian Mullen .20 .50
19 Robert Picard .20 .50
20 Doug Smail .30 .75
21 Doug Soetaert .30 .75
22 Thomas Steen .40 1.00
23 Tim Watters .20 .50
24 Ron Wilson .20 .50
25 Tim Young .20 .50

1993-94 Jets Readers Club

COMPLETE SET (23) 6.00 15.00
1 Stu Barnes .20 .50
2 Sergei Bautin .08 .25
3 Stephane Beauregard .20 .50
4 Arto Blomsten .20 .50
5 Luciano Borsato .08 .25
6 Tie Domi .60 1.50
7 Mike Eagles .08 .25
8 Nelson Emerson .20 .50
9 Bryan Erickson .08 .25
10 Bob Essensa .20 .50
11 Yan Kaminsky .08 .25
12 Dean Kennedy .08 .25
13 Boris Mironov .08 .25
14 Teppo Numminen .40 1.00
15 Fredrik Olausson .40 1.00
16 Stephane Quintal .08 .25
17 Teemu Selanne 2.00 5.00
18 Darrin Shannon .08 .25
19 Thomas Steen .08 .25
20 Keith Tkachuk .20 .50
21 Igor Ulanov .08 .25
22 Paul Ysebaert .08 .25
23 Alexei Zhamnov .20 .50

1984-85 Jets Police

COMPLETE SET (24) 3.00 8.00
1 Scott Arniel 11 .08 .25
2 Dave Babych 44 .30 .75
3 Marc Behrend 29 .20 .50
4 Laurie Boschman 16 .20 .50
5 Randy Carlyle 8 .30 .75
6 Dave Ellett 2 .40 1.00
7 John Ferguson VP/GM .30 .75
8 Dale Hawerchuk 10 .75 2.00
9 Brian Hayward 1 .40 1.00
10 Jim Kyte 6 .08 .25
11 Morris Lukowich 12 .20 .50
12 Bengt Lundholm 22 .08 .25
13 Paul MacLean 15 .30 .75
14 Andrew McBain 20 .08 .25
15 Brian Mullen 19 .20 .50
16 Robert Picard 3 .08 .25
17 Paul Pooley 23 .08 .25
18 Doug Smail 9 .30 .75
19 Thomas Steen 25 .50 1.25
20 Perry Turnbull 27 .08 .25
21 Tim Watters 7 .08 .25
22 Ron Wilson 24 .08 .25
23 Assistant Coaches
Bill Sutherland
Barry Long
Rick Bowness .08 .25
24 Team Photo .30 .75

1985-86 Jets Police

COMPLETE SET (24) 3.00 8.00
1 Scott Arniel 11 .08 .25
2 Laurie Boschman 16 .20 .50
3 Dan Bouchard 35 .20 .50
4 Randy Carlyle 8 .30 .75
5 Dave Ellett 2 .40 1.00
6 John Ferguson VP/GM .20 .50
7 Dale Hawerchuk 10 .75 2.00
8 Brian Hayward 1 .40 1.00
9 Jim Kyte 6 .08 .25
10 Paul MacLean 15 .30 .75
11 Mario Marois 22 .08 .25
12 Andrew McBain 20 .08 .25
13 Anssi Melametsa 14 .08 .25
14 Brian Mullen 19 .20 .50
15 Ray Neufeld 28 .08 .25
16 Jim Nill 17 .08 .25
17 Dave Silk 34 .08 .25
18 Doug Smail 9 .30 .75
19 Thomas Steen 25 .50 1.25
20 Perry Turnbull 27 .08 .25
21 Tim Watters 7 .20 .50
22 Ron Wilson 24 .20 .50
23 Assistant Coaches
Bill Sutherland
Barry Long
Rick Bowness .08 .25
24 Team Photo .20 .50

1985-86 Jets Silverwood Dairy

COMPLETE SET (6) 24.00 60.00
1 Laurie Boschman 4.00 10.00
2 Randy Carlyle 5.00 12.00
3 Dave Ellett 5.00 12.00
4 Dale Hawerchuk 10.00 25.00
5 Paul MacLean 4.00 10.00
6 Brian Mullen 5.00 12.00

1986-87 Jets Postcards

COMPLETE SET (26) 8.00 20.00
1 Brad Berry .30 .75
2 Laurie Boschman .40 1.00
3 Rick Bowness ACO
Dan Maloney CO
Bill Sutherland ACO .20 .50
4 Randy Carlyle .75 2.00
5 Bill Derlago .40 1.00
6 Dave Ellett .60 1.50
7 John Ferguson GM .40 1.00
8 Gilles Hamel .30 .75
9 Dale Hawerchuk 1.50 4.00
10 Hannu Jarvenpaa .30 .75
11 Jim Kyte .30 .75
12 Paul MacLean .40 1.00
13 Mario Marois .30 .75
14 Andrew McBain .30 .75
15 Brian Mullen .40 1.00
16 Ray Neufeld .30 .75
17 Jim Nill .30 .75
18 Fredrik Olausson .60 1.50
19 Steve Penney .40 1.00
20 Eldon Reddick .40 1.00
21 Doug Smail .40 1.00
22 Thomas Steen .60 1.50
23 Perry Turnbull .30 .75
24 Tim Watters .30 .75
25 Ron Wilson .30 .75
26 Team Photo .75 2.00

1987-88 Jets Postcards

COMPLETE SET (24) 4.80 12.00
1 Brad Berry .20 .50
2 Daniel Berthiaume .40 1.00
3 Laurie Boschman .20 .50
4 Randy Carlyle .30 .75
5 Iain Duncan .20 .50
6 Dave Ellett .30 .75
7 Pat Elynuik .20 .50
8 Gilles Hamel .20 .50
9 Dale Hawerchuk .60 1.50
10 Hannu Jarvenpaa .20 .50
11 Jim Kyte .20 .50
12 Paul MacLean .30 .75
13 Mario Marois .20 .50
14 Andrew McBain .20 .50
15 Ray Neufeld .20 .50
16 Fredrik Olausson .40 1.00
17 Eldon Reddick .40 1.00
18 Steve Rooney .30 .75
19 Doug Smail .30 .75
20 Thomas Steen .40 1.00
21 Peter Taglianetti .20 .50
22 Tim Watters .20 .50
23 Ron Wilson .20 .50
24 Team Photo .40 1.00

1988-89 Jets Police

COMPLETE SET (24) 3.00 8.00
1 Brent Ashton 7 .08 .25
2 Laurie Boschman 16 .20 .50
3 Randy Carlyle 8 .30 .75
4 Alain Chevrier 31 .20 .50
5 Iain Duncan 19 .08 .25
6 Dave Ellett 2 .30 .75
7 Pat Elynuik 34 .08 .25
8 Randy Gilhen 39 .08 .25
9 Dale Hawerchuk 10 .60 1.50
10 Dave Hunter 12 .08 .25
11 Hannu Jarvenpaa 23 .08 .25
12 Jim Kyte 6 .08 .25
13 Dan Maloney CO .08 .25
14 Mario Marois 22 .08 .25
15 Andrew McBain 20 .08 .25
16 Ray Neufeld 28 .08 .25
17 Teppo Numminen 27 .30 .75
18 Fredrik Olausson 4 .20 .50
19 Eldon Reddick 33 .20 .50
20 Doug Smail 9 .20 .50
21 Thomas Steen 25 .30 .75
22 Peter Taglianetti 32 .08 .25
23 Assistant Coaches
Bill Sutherland
Bruce Southern
Rick St.Croix .08 .25
24 Team Photo .30 .75

1988-89 Jets Postcards

COMPLETE SET (24) 8.00 15.00
1 Brent Ashton .20 .50
2 Mascot .02 .10
3 Daniel Berthiaume .40 1.00
4 Laurie Boschman .20 .50
5 Randy Carlyle .30 .75
6 Iain Duncan .20 .50
7 Dave Ellett .30 .75
8 Pat Elynuik .20 .50
9 Paul Fenton .20 .50
10 Randy Gilhen .20 .50
11 Dale Hawerchuk .75 2.00
12 Hannu Jarvenpaa .20 .50
13 Brad Jones .20 .50
14 Jim Kyte .20 .50
15 Dan Maloney CO .08 .25
16 Andrew McBain .20 .50
17 Teppo Numminen .75 2.00
18 Fredrik Olausson .30 .75
19 Eldon Reddick .40 1.00
20 Doug Smail .30 .75
21 Thomas Steen .40 1.00
22 Coaches .08 .25
23 Peter Taglianetti .20 .50
24 Team Photo .40 1.00

1989-90 Jets Safeway

COMPLETE SET (30) 4.80 12.00
1 Brent Ashton 7 .20 .50
2 Stu Barnes 14 .30 .75
3 Brad Berry 29 .20 .50
4 Daniel Berthiaume 30 .30 .75
5 Laurie Boschman 16 .20 .50
6 Randy Carlyle 8 .30 .75
7 Shawn Cronin 44 .20 .50
8 Randy Cunneyworth 18 .20 .50
9 Gord Donnelly 34 .20 .50
10 Tom Draper 37 .30 .75
11 Iain Duncan 19 .20 .50
12 Dave Ellett 2 .30 .75
13 Pat Elynuik 15 .20 .50
14 Bob Essensa 35 .30 .75
15 Paul Fenton 11 .20 .50
16 Dale Hawerchuk 10 .60 1.50
17 Brent Hughes 46 .20 .50
18 Mark Kumpel 21 .20 .50
19 Moe Mantha 22 .20 .50
20 Dave McLlwain 20 .20 .50
21 Brian McReynolds 26 .20 .50
22 Teppo Numminen 27 .30 .75
23 Fredrik Olausson 4 .30 .75
24 Greg Paslawski 28 .20 .50
25 Doug Smail 12 .30 .75
26 Thomas Steen 25 .30 .75
27 Peter Taglianetti 32 .20 .50
28 Benny 00 (Mascot) .08 .25
29 Coaches Card
Alpo Suhonen
Bob Murdoch
Clare Drake .08 .25
30 Team Photo .40 1.00

1990-91 Jets IGA

COMPLETE SET (35) 4.00 10.00
1 Scott Arniel .15 .40
2 Brent Ashton .15 .40
3 Don Barber .15 .40
4 Stephane Beauregard .20 .50
5 Randy Carlyle .30 .75
6 Danton Cole .15 .40
7 Shawn Cronin .15 .40
8 Gord Donnelly .15 .40
9 Clare Drake CO .08 .25
10 Kris Draper .40 1.00
11 Iain Duncan .15 .40
12 Pat Elynuik .15 .40
13 Bob Essensa .20 .50
14 Doug Evans .15 .40
15 Phil Housley .40 1.00
16 Sergei Kharin .15 .40
17 Mark Kumpel .15 .40
18 Guy Larose .15 .40
19 Paul MacDermid .15 .40
20 Moe Mantha .15 .40
21 Brian Marchment .20 .50
22 Dave McLlwain .15 .40
23 Bob Murdoch CO .08 .25
24 Teppo Numminen .30 .75
25 Fredrik Olausson .20 .50
26 Ed Olczyk .20 .50
27 Mark Osborne .15 .40
28 Greg Paslawski .15 .40
29 Terry Simpson CO .08 .25
30 Thomas Steen .30 .75
31 Phil Sykes .15 .40
32 Rick Tabaracci .25 .60
33 Simon Wheeldon .15 .40
34 Benny (Mascot) .08 .25
35 Team Photo .40 1.00

1991 Jets Panini Team Stickers

COMPLETE SET (32) 1.00 2.50
1 Scott Arniel .02 .10
2 Brent Ashton .02 .10
3 Stephane Beauregard .02 .10
4 Randy Carlyle .02 .10
5 Danton Cole .01 .05
6 Shawn Cronin .02 .10
7 Gord Donnelly .01 .05
8 Kris Draper .05 .15
9 Dave Ellett .02 .10
10 Pat Elynuik .01 .05
11 Doug Evans .01 .05
12 Paul Fenton .01 .05
13 Phil Housley .08 .25
14 Mark Kumpel .01 .05
15 Paul MacDermid .01 .05
16 Moe Mantha .01 .05
17 Dave McLlwain .01 .05
18 Teppo Numminen .05 .15
19 Fredrik Olausson .02 .10
20 Greg Paslawski .01 .05
21 Doug Smail .01 .05
22 Thomas Steen .02 .10
23 Phil Sykes .01 .05
24 Rick Tabaracci .05 .15
A Team Logo
Left Side .01 .05
B Team Logo
Right Side .01 .05
C Jets in Action
Upper Left Corner .01 .05
D Jets in Action
Lower Left Corner .01 .05
E Jets in Action
Upper Right Corner .01 .05
F Jets in Action
Lower Right Corner .01 .05
G Paul Fenton .01 .05
H Phil Housley .08 .25

1991-92 Jets IGA

COMPLETE SET (35) 4.00 10.00
1 Stu Barnes .20 .50
2 Stephane Beauregard .20 .50
3 Luciano Borsato .15 .40
4 Randy Carlyle .20 .50
5 Danton Cole .15 .40
6 Shawn Cronin .15 .40
7 Burton Cummings .20 .50
8 Mike Eagles .15 .40
9 Pat Elynuik .15 .40
10 Bryan Erickson .15 .40
11 Bob Essensa .20 .50
12 Doug Evans .15 .40
13 Mike Hartman .15 .40
14 Phil Housley .30 .75
15 Dean Kennedy .15 .40
16 Paul MacDermid .15 .40
17 Moe Mantha .15 .40
18 Rob Murray .15 .40
19 Troy Murray .15 .40
20 Teppo Numminen .20 .50
21 Fredrik Olausson .20 .50
22 Ed Olczyk .15 .40
23 Mark Osborne .15 .40
24 John Paddock CO .08 .25
25 Kent Paynter .15 .40
26 Dave Prior .15 .40
27 Russ Romaniuk .15 .40
28 Darrin Shannon .20 .50
29 Terry Simpson CO .08 .25
30 Thomas Steen .20 .50
31 Phil Sykes .15 .40
32 Rick Tabaracci .20 .50
33 Glen Williamson CO .08 .25
34 Benny (Mascot) .08 .25
35 Team Photo UER
(Incorrectly
marked 1990-91) .30 .75

1993-94 Jets Ruffles

COMPLETE SET (29) 6.00 15.00
1 Stu Barnes .30 .75
2 Sergei Bautin .15 .40
3 Stephane Beauregard .20 .50
4 Benny (Mascot) .08 .25
5 Zinetula Bilyaletdinov ACO .08 .25
6 Arto Blomsten .15 .40
7 Luciano Borsato .15 .40
8 Tie Domi .40 1.00
9 Mike Eagles .15 .40
10 Nelson Emerson .30 .75
11 Bryan Erickson .15 .40
12 Bob Essensa .20 .50
13 Yan Kaminsky .15 .40
14 Dean Kennedy .15 .40
15 Kris King .15 .40
16 Boris Mironov .25 .60
17 Andy Murray ACO .08 .25
18 Teppo Numminen .25 .60
19 Fredrik Olausson .15 .40
20 John Paddock CO .08 .25
21 Stephane Quintal .15 .40
22 Teemu Selanne 2.00 5.00
23 Darrin Shannon .15 .40
24 Thomas Steen .30 .75
25 Keith Tkachuk 1.00 2.50
26 Igor Ulanov .15 .40
27 Paul Ysebaert .15 .40
28 Alexei Zhamnov .40 1.00
29 Team Picture .20 .50

1995-96 Jets Readers Club

COMPLETE SET (12) 3.00 8.00
1 Tim Cheveldae .20 .50
2 Dallas Drake .08 .25
3 Mike Eastwood .08 .25
4 Nikolai Khabibulin .40 1.00
5 Kris King .20 .50
6 Igor Korolev .08 .25
7 Dave Manson .08 .25
8 Teppo Numminen .20 .50
9 Teemu Selanne 1.25 3.00
10 Darrin Shannon .08 .25
11 Keith Tkachuk .60 1.50
12 Alexei Zhamnov .40 1.00

1995-96 Jets Team Issue

COMPLETE SET (26) 6.00 15.00
1 Title Card .08 .25
2 Benny (Mascot) .02 .10
3 Tim Cheveldae .30 .75
4 Coaches .08 .25
5 Shane Doan .30 .75
6 Jason Doig .20 .50
7 Dallas Drake .20 .50
8 Mike Eastwood .20 .50
9 Randy Gilhen .20 .50
10 Nikolai Khabibulin .40 1.00
11 Kris King .20 .50
12 Igor Korolev .20 .50
13 Stewart Malgunas .20 .50
14 Dave Manson .20 .50
15 Jim McKenzie .20 .50
16 Teppo Numminen .30 .75
17 Eddie Olczyk .20 .50
18 Deron Quint .20 .50
19 Ed Ronan .20 .50
20 Teemu Selanne 1.50 4.00
21 Darrin Shannon .20 .50
22 Darryl Shannon .20 .50
23 Mike Stapleton .20 .50
24 Keith Tkachuk .75 2.00
25 Darren Turcotte .20 .50
26 Alexei Zhamnov .30 .75

2011-12 Jets Upper Deck Return to Winnipeg

COMPLETE SET (15) 25.00 50.00
1 Alexander Burmistrov 4.00 10.00
2 Andrew Ladd 2.00 5.00
3 Blake Wheeler 3.00 8.00
4 Bryan Little 3.00 8.00
5 Carl Klingberg 2.50 6.00
6 Chris Mason 2.50 6.00
7 Dustin Byfuglien 3.00 8.00
8 Mark Scheifele 4.00 10.00
9 Evander Kane 6.00 15.00
10 Jim Slater 2.00 5.00
11 Nik Antropov 2.50 6.00
12 Ondrej Pavelec 3.00 8.00
13 Patrice Cormier 2.00 5.00
14 Tobias Enstrom 2.00 5.00
15 Zach Bogosian 2.50 6.00
NNO Checklist 1.50 3.00

1992 Jofa/Koho

COMPLETE SET (6) 4.80 12.00
1 Theo Fleury
Jofa .75 2.00
2 Jari Kurri
Koho .40 1.00
3 Mario Lemieux
Koho 2.00 5.00
4 Eric Lindros
Titan 1.50 4.00
5 Denis Savard
Canadien .40 1.00
6 Mats Sundin
Jofa .60 1.50

1997-98 Katch

COMPLETE SET (168) 100.00 100.00
COMP.GOLD SET (168) 2500.00 4000.00
*GOLD: 7.5X TO 15X HI COLUMN
COMP.SILVER SET (168) 1000.00 600.00
*SILVER: 3X TO 6X HI COLUMN
1 Guy Hebert .40 1.00
2 Paul Kariya 2.50 5.00
3 Espen Knutsen .10 .30
4 Tomas Sandstrom .10 .30
5 Teemu Selanne 1.00 2.50
6 Scott Young .10 .30
7 Per Johan Axelsson .10 .30
8 Ray Bourque .60 1.50
9 Jim Carey .40 1.00
10 Ted Donato .10 .30
11 Dimitri Khristich .40 1.00
12 Sergei Samsonov .50 1.25
13 Matthew Barnaby .40 1.00
14 Jason Dawe .10 .30
15 Dominik Hasek 1.00 2.50
16 Mike Peca .40 1.00
17 Rob Ray .40 1.00
18 Alexei Zhitnik .10 .30
19 Andrew Cassels .10 .30
20 Theo Fleury .50 1.25
21 Jarome Iginla .40 1.00
22 Sandy McCarthy .10 .30
23 Tyler Moss .10 .30
24 Cory Stillman .10 .30
25 Sean Burke .40 1.00
26 Kevin Dineen .10 .30
27 Stu Grimson .40 1.00
28 Steven Rice .10 .30
29 Keith Primeau .40 1.00
30 Geoff Sanderson .40 1.00
31 Tony Amonte .40 1.00
32 Chris Chelios .50 1.25
33 Daniel Cleary .10 .30
34 Jeff Hackett .40 1.00
35 Ethan Moreau .10 .30
36 Bob Probert .10 .30
37 Adam Deadmarsh .40 1.00
38 Peter Forsberg 1.25 3.00
39 Claude Lemieux .40 1.00
40 Sandis Ozolinsh .40 1.00
41 Patrick Roy 3.00 6.00
42 Joe Sakic 1.00 2.50
43 Ed Belfour .50 1.25
44 Derian Hatcher .10 .30
45 Jere Lehtinen .40 1.00
46 Mike Modano .60 1.50
47 Joe Nieuwendyk .40 1.00
48 Darryl Sydor .40 1.00
49 Sergei Fedorov 1.00 2.50
50 Vyacheslav Kozlov .40 1.00
51 Darren McCarty .40 1.00
52 Chris Osgood .50 1.25
53 Brendan Shanahan .75 2.00
54 Steve Yzerman 1.50 4.00
55 Jason Arnott .40 1.00
56 Boyd Devereaux .10 .30
57 Curtis Joseph .60 1.50
58 Andrei Kovalenko .10 .30
59 Ryan Smyth .40 1.00
60 Doug Weight .40 1.00
61 Ed Jovanovski .10 .30
62 Scott Mellanby .10 .30
63 David Nemirovsky .10 .30
64 Rob Niedermayer .10 .30
65 Ray Sheppard .40 1.00
66 John Vanbiesbrouck .50 1.25
67 Aki Berg .10 .30
68 Rob Blake .10 .30
69 Stephane Fiset .40 1.00
70 Donald MacLean .10 .30
71 Yanic Perreault .10 .30
72 Luc Robitaille .40 1.00
73 Valeri Bure .40 1.00
74 Vincent Damphousse .40 1.00
75 Saku Koivu .50 1.25
76 Vladimir Malakhov .10 .30
77 Mark Recchi .40 1.00
78 Jocelyn Thibault .40 1.00
79 Martin Brodeur .75 2.00
80 Patrik Elias .40 1.00
81 Doug Gilmour .50 1.25
82 Bill Guerin .40 1.00
83 Scott Niedermayer .10 .30
84 Scott Stevens .40 1.00
85 Bryan Berard .10 .30
86 Eric Fichaud .40 1.00
87 Travis Green .10 .30
88 Kenny Jonsson .10 .30
89 Bryan McCabe .10 .30
90 Zigmund Palffy .50 1.25
91 Adam Graves .40 1.00
92 Wayne Gretzky 4.00 8.00
93 Pat LaFontaine .40 1.00
94 Brian Leetch .50 1.25
95 Mike Richter .50 1.25
96 Kevin Stevens .10 .30
97 Daniel Alfredsson .40 1.00
98 Alexandre Daigle .10 .30
99 Chris Phillips .10 .30
100 Wade Redden .10 .30
101 Damian Rhodes .10 .30
102 Alexei Yashin .40 1.00
103 Paul Coffey .50 1.25
104 Chris Gratton .10 .30
105 Ron Hextall .40 1.00
106 John LeClair .75 2.00
107 Eric Lindros 1.25 3.00
108 Dainius Zubrus .10 .30
109 Mike Gartner .40 1.00
110 Brad Isbister .10 .30
111 Nikolai Khabibulin .40 1.00
112 Jeremy Roenick .50 1.25
113 Keith Tkachuk .50 1.25
114 Oleg Tverdovsky .10 .30
115 Tom Barrasso .40 1.00
116 Ron Francis .40 1.00
117 Kevin Hatcher .40 1.00
118 Jaromir Jagr 1.50 4.00
119 Alexei Morozov .10 .30
120 Petr Nedved .40 1.00
121 Patrick Marleau .40 1.00
122 Marty McSorley .10 .30
123 Bernie Nicholls .10 .30
124 Owen Nolan .40 1.00
125 Marco Sturm .40 1.00
126 Mike Vernon .40 1.00
127 Jim Campbell .40 1.00
128 Grant Fuhr .40 1.00
129 Brett Hull .60 1.50
130 Al MacInnis .40 1.00
131 Pierre Turgeon .40 1.00
132 Tony Twist .40 1.00
133 Brian Bradley .10 .30
134 Dino Ciccarelli .10 .30
135 Roman Hamrlik .10 .30
136 Daymond Langkow .10 .30
137 Daren Puppa .10 .30
138 Mikael Renberg .10 .30
139 Wendel Clark .10 .30
140 Tie Domi .40 1.00
141 Alyn McCauley .10 .30
142 Felix Potvin .40 1.00
143 Mathieu Schneider .10 .30
144 Mats Sundin .50 1.25
145 Pavel Bure 1.25 3.00
146 Trevor Linden .40 1.00
147 Kirk McLean .40 1.00
148 Mark Messier .60 1.50
149 Alexander Mogilny .40 1.00
150 Mattias Ohlund .40 1.00
151 Peter Bondra .50 1.25
152 Joe Juneau .10 .30
153 Adam Oates .40 1.00
154 Bill Ranford .40 1.00
155 Jaroslav Svejkovsky .10 .30
156 Richard Zednik .10 .30
157 Wayne Gretzky TL 1.50 4.00
158 Eric Lindros TL .60 1.50
159 Paul Kariya TL 1.00 2.50
160 Patrick Roy TL 1.25 3.00
161 Steve Yzerman TL .75 2.00
162 Jaromir Jagr TL .75 2.00
163 Brett Hull TL .30 .75
164 Joe Thornton .50 1.25
165 Vaclav Prospal .40 1.00
166 Mike Johnson .40 1.00
167 Eric Messier .40 1.00
168 Jan Bulis .40 1.00

1972 Kellogg's Iron-On Transfers
COMPLETE SET (6) 150.00 300.00
1 Ron Ellis 12.50 25.00
2 Phil Esposito 37.50 75.00
3 Rod Gilbert 20.00 40.00
4 Bobby Hull 62.50 125.00
5 Frank Mahovlich 20.00 40.00
6 Stan Mikita 25.00 50.00

1984-85 Kellogg's Accordion Discs
COMPLETE SET (8) 12.00 30.00
1 Dino Ciccarelli
Mike Bossy
Richard Brodeur
Michel Goulet
Jari Kurri
Paul Reinhart 2.50 6.00
2 Reed Larson
Marcel Dionne
Peter Statsny
Paul MacLean
Doug Risebrough
Larry Robinson 1.50 4.00
3A Stanley Cup
Gilbert Perreault
Rick Middleton
Bob Gainey
Kevin Lowe
Borje Salming 2.00 5.00
3B Stanley Cup
Gilbert Perreault
Rick Middleton
Guy Lafleur
Kevin Lowe
Borje Salming 2.00 5.00
4 Bernie Federko
Ron Francis
Stan Smyl
Mike Gartner
Dave Babych
Lanny McDonald 2.00 5.00
5A Barry Beck
Rick Kehoe
Dale Hawerchuk
John Anderson
Mario Tremblay
Paul Coffey 1.50 4.00
5B Barry Beck
Denis Herron
Dale Hawerchuk
Dan Daoust
Mario Tremblay
Paul Coffey 1.50 4.00
6 Thomas Gradin
Dale Hunter
Doug Wilson
Darryl Sittler
Glenn Resch
Rick Vaive 1.50 4.00
7 Tracy Austin
Tennis
Olga Korbut
Gymnastics
Kathy Kreiner
Alpine Skiing
Angela Taylor
Track and Field
Anne Ottenbrite
Swimming
Paul Martini
Skating
Barbara Underhill
Skating 1.25 3.00
8 Tatiana Kolpakova
Long Jump
Kay Thompson
Skating
Kornelia Ender
Swimming
Melanie Smith
Equestrian
Nadia Comaneci
Gymnastics
Carling Bassett
Tennis 1.25 3.00

1992 Kellogg's All-Star Posters
COMPLETE SET (3) 2.00 5.00
1 Campbell Conf. All-Stars .75 2.00
2 Wales Conf. All-Stars .75 2.00
3 Snap, Crackle, Pop .40 1.00

1992 Kellogg's Trophies
COMPLETE SET (11) 8.00 20.00
1 Stanley Cup 1.25 3.00
2 Presidents' Trophy .75 2.00
3 Hart Memorial Trophy .75 2.00
4 Conn Smythe Trophy .75 2.00
5 Vezina Trophy .75 2.00
6 James Norris Memorial
T .75 2.00
7 Calder Memorial Trophy .75 2.00
8 Frank J. Selke Trophy .75 2.00
9 Lady Byng Memorial
Trop .75 2.00
10 Art Ross Trophy .75 2.00
11 Jack Adams Trophy .75 2.00

1992-93 Kellogg's Posters
COMPLETE SET 16.00 40.00
1 Mario Lemieux 8.00 20.00
2 Mark Messier 2.00 5.00
3 Luc Robitaille 1.25 3.00
4 Patrick Roy 6.00 15.00
5 Cornelius Rooster
Mascot 1.25 3.00

1995-96 Kellogg's Donruss
COMPLETE SET (6) 12.00 30.00
1 Mario Lemieux
The Fiver 3.00 8.00
2 Mario Lemieux
The Cup 3.00 8.00
3 Mario Lemieux
The 500th 3.00 8.00
4 Mario Lemieux
The Comeback 3.00 8.00
5 Brett Hull/ 1.25 3.00
6 Brett Hull
The MVP 1.25 3.00

1993 Kenner Starting Lineup Cards
COMPLETE SET (12) 40.00 100.00
1 Ed Belfour 8.00 20.00
2 Ray Bourque 1.00 2.50
3 Grant Fuhr 10.00 25.00
4 Brett Hull .75 2.00
5 Jaromir Jagr 1.25 3.00
6 Pat LaFontaine 1.00 2.50
7 Mario Lemieux 1.50 4.00
8 Eric Lindros 1.00 2.50
9 Mark Messier 1.00 2.50
10 Jeremy Roenick .75 2.00
11 Patrick Roy 2.00 5.00
12 Steve Yzerman 2.00 5.00

1994 Kenner Starting Lineup Cards
COMPLETE SET (21) 32.00 80.00
1 Tom Barrasso .75 2.00
2 Ray Bourque .75 2.00
3 Pavel Bure 1.00 2.50
4 Sergei Fedorov 1.00 2.50
5 Grant Fuhr 1.25 3.00
6 Doug Gilmour .60 1.50
7 Brett Hull .60 1.50
8 Arturs Irbe .60 1.50
9 Jaromir Jagr .60 1.50
10 Pat Lafontaine .60 1.50
11 Brian Leetch .60 1.50
12 Mario Lemieux 1.00 2.50
13 Eric Lindros .75 2.00
14 Mark Messier .60 1.50
15 Alexander Mogilny .60 1.50
16 Adam Oates .60 1.50
17 Mike Richter .75 2.00
18 Luc Robitaille .75 2.00
19 Jeremy Roenick .50 1.25
20 Teemu Selanne 1.00 2.50
21 Steve Yzerman 1.50 4.00

1995 Kenner Starting Lineup Cards
COMPLETE SET (21) 24.00 60.00
1 Tom Barrasso .60 1.50
2 Rob Blake .60 1.50
3 Martin Brodeur 1.50 4.00
4 Pavel Bure .60 1.50
5 Chris Chelios .75 2.00
6 Bob Corkum .30 .75
7 Sergei Fedorov .60 1.50
8 Theo Fleury .60 1.50
9 Adam Graves .30 .75
10 Dominik Hasek 1.25 3.00
11 Brett Hull .60 1.50
12 Arturs Irbe .40 1.00
13 Mike Modano .75 2.00
14 Kirk Muller .40 1.00
15 Cam Neely .60 1.50
16 Sandis Ozolinsh .60 1.50
17 Felix Potvin .75 2.00
18 Luc Robitaille .60 1.50
19 Brendan Shanahan 1.00 2.50
20 Scott Stevens .30 .75
21 Pierre Turgeon .75 2.00

1996 Kenner Starting Lineup Cards
COMPLETE SET (24) 24.00 60.00
1 Tom Barrasso .60 1.50
2 Brian Bradley .30 .75
3 Jim Carey .75 2.00
4 Paul Coffey .75 2.00
5 Sergei Fedorov .60 1.50
6 Ron Francis .75 2.00
7 Dominik Hasek .60 1.50
8 Paul Kariya 1.00 2.50
9 Pat Lafontaine .60 1.50
10 John LeClair .75 2.00
11 Brian Leetch .40 1.00
12 Eric Lindros .60 1.50
13 Al MacInnis .60 1.50
14 Scott Mellanby .30 .75
15 Mark Messier .60 1.50
16 Mike Modano .40 1.00
17 Adam Oates .40 1.00
18 Mikael Renberg .30 .75
19 Stephane Richer .30 .75
20 Jeremy Roenick .50 1.25
21 Patrick Roy 1.25 3.00
22 Joe Sakic 1.50 4.00
23 Brendan Shanahan .75 2.00
24 Mats Sundin .75 2.00

1997 Kenner Starting Lineup Cards
COMPLETE SET (20) 16.00 40.00
1 Daniel Alfredsson .30 .75
2 Jason Arnott .40 1.00
3 Peter Bondra .60 1.50
4 Martin Brodeur 1.00 2.50
5 Paul Coffey .50 1.25
6 Chris Chelios .60 1.50
7 Peter Forsberg 1.00 2.50
8 Wayne Gretzky 2.50 6.00
9 Ron Hextall .75 2.00
10 Jaromir Jagr .60 1.50
11 Patrick Lalime .60 1.50
12 Eric Lindros .60 1.50
13 Mark Messier .60 1.50
14 Chris Osgood .75 2.00
15 Sandis Ozolinsh .40 1.00
16 Zigmund Palffy .50 1.25
17 Daren Puppa .50 1.25
18 Mark Recchi .60 1.50
19 Teemu Selanne .60 1.50
20 Keith Tkachuk .60 1.50
21 John Vanbiesbrouck .60 1.50

1998 Kenner Starting Lineup Cards
COMPLETE SET (34) 20.00 50.00
1 Tony Amonte .40 1.00
2 Bryan Berard .30 .75
3 Ed Belfour .75 2.00
4 Peter Bondra .30 .75
5 Martin Brodeur 1.00 2.50
6 Jim Campbell .30 .75
7 Vincent Damphousse .30 .75
8 Theo Fleury .40 1.00
9 Grant Fuhr .60 1.50
10 Doug Gilmour .40 1.00
11 Wayne Gretzky 2.00 5.00
12 Wayne Gretzky Cup 2.00 5.00
13 Dominik Hasek .75 2.00
14 Jaromir Jagr .60 1.50
15 Paul Kariya .60 1.50
16 Trevor Kidd .40 1.00
17 Nikolai Khabibulin .40 1.00
18 Olaf Kolzig .40 1.00
19 Brian Leetch .40 1.00
20 Eric Lindros .60 1.50
21 Kirk McLean .40 1.00
22 Mark Messier .60 1.50
23 Rob Neidermayer .30 .75
24 Chris Osgood .60 1.50
25 Felix Potvin .60 1.50
26 Daren Puppa .30 .75
27 Jeremy Roenick .60 1.50
28 Patrick Roy 1.25 3.00
29 Joe Sakic Cup .75 2.00
30 Brendan Shanahan .60 1.50
31 Joe Thornton .75 2.00
32 John Vanbiesbrouck .40 1.00
33 Alexei Yashin .40 1.00
34 Steve Yzerman Cup 1.25 3.00

1980-81 Kings Card Night
COMPLETE SET (14) 10.00 20.00
1 Marcel Dionne 4.00 8.00
2 Glenn Goldup .30 .75
3 Doug Halward .30 .75
4 Billy Harris .40 1.00
5 Steve Jensen .40 1.00
6 Jerry Korab .30 .75
7 Mario Lessard .60 1.50
8 Dave Lewis .40 1.00
9 Mike Murphy .30 .75
10 Rob Palmer .30 .75
11 Charlie Simmer .75 2.00
12 Dave Taylor 1.25 3.00
13 Garry Unger .60 1.50
14 Jay Wells .40 1.00

1984-85 Kings Smokey
COMPLETE SET (23) 8.00 20.00
1 Russ Anderson .20 .50
2 Marcel Dionne 2.00 5.00
3 Brian Engblom .30 .75
4 Daryl Evans .20 .50
5 Jim Fox .30 .75
6 Garry Galley .60 1.50
7 Anders Hakansson .20 .50
8 Mark Hardy .20 .50
9 Bob Janecyk .30 .75
10 John Paul Kelly .20 .50
11 Brian MacLellan .20 .50
12 Bernie Nicholls 1.00 2.50
13 Craig Redmond .20 .50
14 Terry Ruskowski .30 .75
15 Doug Smith .20 .50
16 Dave Taylor .75 2.00
17 Jay Wells .20 .50
18 Darren Eliot .30 .75
19 Rick Lapointe .20 .50
20 Bob Miller .20 .50
21 Steve Seguin .20 .50
22 Phil Sykes .20 .50
23 Pat Quinn CO .20 .50

1986-87 Kings 20th Anniversary Team Issue
COMPLETE SET (23) 10.00 25.00
1 Bob Bourne .08 .25
2 Jimmy Carson .75 2.00
3 Steve Duchesne .75 2.00
4 Darren Eliot .08 .25
5 Bryan Erickson .08 .25
6 Jim Fox .08 .25
7 Garry Galley .40 1.00
8 Paul Guay .08 .25
9 Mark Hardy .08 .25
10 Bob Janecyk .30 .75
11 Dean Kennedy .08 .25
12 Grant Ledyard .20 .50
13 Morris Lukowich .08 .25
14 Sean McKenna .08 .25
15 Roland Melanson .30 .75
16 Bernie Nicholls .75 2.00
17 Joe Paterson .08 .25
18 Larry Playfair .08 .25
19 Luc Robitaille 5.00 12.00
20 Phil Sykes .08 .25
21 Dave Taylor .30 .75
22 Jay Wells .08 .25
23 Tiger Williams .30 .75

1988-89 Kings Smokey
COMPLETE SET (25) 12.00 30.00
1 Mike Allison .20 .50
2 Ken Baumgartner .30 .75
3 Bob Carpenter .20 .50
4 Doug Crossman .20 .50
5 Dale DeGray .20 .50
6 Steve Duchesne .60 1.50
7 Ron Duguay .30 .75
8 Mark Fitzpatrick .40 1.00
9 Jim Fox .20 .50
10 Robbie Ftorek CO .20 .50
11 Wayne Gretzky 6.00 15.00
12 Gilles Hamel .20 .50
13 Glenn Healy .40 1.00
14 Mike Krushelnyski .20 .50
15 Tom Laidlaw .20 .50
16 Bryan Maxwell CO .08 .25
17 Wayne McBean .20 .50
18 Marty McSorley 1.25 3.00
19 Bernie Nicholls .60 1.50
20 Cap Raeder CO .08 .25
21 Luc Robitaille 1.50 4.00
22 Dave Taylor .60 1.50
23 John Tonelli .30 .75
24 Tim Watters .20 .50
25 Title Card
(Checklist on back) .20 .50

1989-90 Kings Smokey
COMPLETE SET (24) 10.00 25.00
1 Wayne Gretzky 5.00 12.00
2 Tim Watters .20 .50
3 Mikael Lindholm .20 .50
4 Mike Allison .20 .50
5 Steve Kasper .20 .50
6 Dave Taylor .40 1.00
7 Larry Robinson .75 2.00
8 Luc Robitaille 1.25 3.00
9 Barry Beck .30 .75
10 Keith Crowder .20 .50
11 Petr Prajsler .20 .50
12 Mike Krushelnyski .20 .50
13 John Tonelli .30 .75
14 Steve Duchesne .40 1.00
15 Jay Miller .20 .50
16 Kelly Hrudey .60 1.50
17 Marty McSorley .75 2.00
18 Mario Gosselin .30 .75
19 Craig Duncanson .20 .50
20 Bob Kudelski .20 .50
21 Brian Benning .20 .50
22 Mikko Makela .20 .50
23 Tom Laidlaw .20 .50
24 Checklist Card .20 .50

1989-90 Kings Smokey Gretzky 8x10
NNO Wayne Gretzky 6.00 15.00

1990-91 Kings Smokey
COMPLETE SET (25) 6.00 15.00
1 Wayne Gretzky 3.00 8.00
2 Brian Benning .08 .25
3 Rob Blake .40 1.00
4 Tim Watters .08 .25
5 Todd Elik .08 .25
6 Tomas Sandstrom .20 .50
7 Steve Kasper .08 .25
8 Dave Taylor .40 1.00
9 Larry Robinson .40 1.00
10 Luc Robitaille .60 1.50
11 Tony Granato .20 .50
12 Tom Laidlaw .08 .25
13 Francois Breault .08 .25
14 John Tonelli .20 .50
15 Steve Duchesne .20 .50
16 Jay Miller .08 .25
17 Kelly Hrudey .60 1.50
18 Marty McSorley .40 1.00
19 Daniel Berthiaume .20 .50
20 Bob Kudelski .08 .25
21 Brad Jones .08 .25
22 John McIntyre .08 .25
23 Rod Buskas .08 .25
24 Kingston (Mascot)
(Checklist on back) .02 .10
NNO RC Cola Challenge .02 .10

1991-92 Kings Upper Deck Season Ticket
NNO Los Angeles Kings
Season Ticket Holders/25th Ann 40.00 100.00

1992-93 Kings Upper Deck Season Ticket
NNO Los Angeles Kings
Season Ticket Holders 30.00 75.00

1993 Kings Forum
8 Rogie Vachon .40 1.00
9 Marcel Dionne .40 1.00
10 Wayne Gretzky 4.00 10.00

1993-94 Kings Upper Deck Season Ticket
NNO Los Angeles Kings
Season Ticket Holders 20.00 50.00

1994-95 Kings Upper Deck Season Ticket
NNO Los Angeles Kings
Wayne Gretzky 10.00 25.00

1998-99 Kings LA Times Coins
COMPLETE SET (6) 12.00 30.00
1 Rob Blake .75 2.00
2 Marcel Dionne 4.00 10.00
3 Larry Robinson 2.50 6.00
4 Luc Robitaille 4.00 10.00
5 Dave Taylor .75 2.00
6 Rogie Vachon 1.50 4.00

1999 Kings AAA Magnets
COMPLETE SET (2) 1.50 4.00
1 Luc Robitaille 1.25 3.00
2 Ziggy Palffy .75 2.00

2002-03 Kings Game Sheets
COMPLETE SET (40) 30.00 75.00
1 Bryan Smolinski
Wetzel's Pretzels 1.00 2.50
2 Bryan Smolinski
Wilshire Grand 1.00 2.50
3 Dmitry Yushkevich
Wetzel's Pretzels 1.00 2.50
4 Dmitry Yushkevich
Wilshire Grand 1.00 2.50
5 Craig Johnson
Wetzel's Pretzels 1.00 2.50
6 Craig Johnson
Wilshire Grand 1.00 2.50
7 Jaroslav Modry
Wetzel's Pretzels 1.00 2.50
8 Jaroslav Modry
Wilshire Grand 1.00 2.50
9 Eric Belanger
Wetzel's Pretzels 1.00 2.50
10 Eric Belanger
Wilshire Grand 1.00 2.50
11 Erik Rasmussen
Wetzel's Pretzels 1.00 2.50
12 Erik Rasmussen
Wilshire Grand 1.00 2.50
13 Ian Laperriere
Wetzel's Pretzels 1.00 2.50
14 Ian Laperriere
Wilshire Grand 1.00 2.50
15 Felix Potvin
Wetzel's Pretzels 2.00 5.00
16 Felix Potvin
Wilshire Grand 2.00 5.00
17 Brad Chartrand
Wetzel's Pretzels 1.00 2.50
18 Brad Chartrand
Wilshire Grand 1.00 2.50
19 Mathieu Schneider
Wetzel's Pretzels 1.00 2.50
20 Mathieu Schneider
Wilshire Grand 1.00 2.50
21 Mikko Eloranta
Wetzel's Pretzels 1.00 2.50
22 Mikko Eloranta
Wilshire Grand 1.00 2.50
23 Jason Allison
Wetzel's Pretzels 1.25 3.00
24 Jason Allison
Wilshire Grand 1.25 3.00
25 Mattias Norstrom
Wetzel's Pretzels 1.00 2.50
26 Mattias Norstrom
Wilshire Grand 1.00 2.50
27 Jamie Storr
Wetzel's Pretzels 1.00 2.50
28 Jamie Storr
Wilshire Grand 1.00 2.50
29 Lubomir Visnovsky
Wetzel's Pretzels 1.00 2.50
30 Lubomir Visnovsky
Wilshire Grand 1.00 2.50
31 Aaron Miller
Wetzel's Pretzels 1.00 2.50
32 Aaron Miller
Wilshire Grand 1.00 2.50
33 Alexander Frolov
Wetzel's Pretzels 1.50 4.00
34 Alexander Frolov
Wilshire Grand 1.50 4.00
35 Zigmund Palffy
Wetzel's Pretzels 1.50 4.00
36 Zigmund Palffy
Wilshire Grand 1.50 4.00
37 Adam Deadmarsh
Wetzel's Pretzels 1.00 2.50
38 Adam Deadmarsh
Wilshire Grand 1.00 2.50
39 Derek Armstrong
Wetzel's Pretzels 1.00 2.50
40 Derek Armstrong
Wilshire Grand 1.00 2.50

2002-03 Kings Team Issue
COMPLETE SET
1 Adam Deadmarsh 1.00 2.50
2 Ziggy Palffy 1.00 2.50
3 Mattias Norstrom .75 2.00
4 Felix Potvin .75 2.00
5 Bryan Smolinski .75 2.00
6 Jason Allison .75 2.00
7 Aaron Miller .75 2.00

2005-06 Kings Team Issue
COMPLETE SET (15) 5.00 10.00
1 Header Card .02 .10
2 Luc Robitaille .75 2.00
3 Jeremy Roenick .75 2.00
4 Derek Armstrong .20 .50
5 Craig Conroy .20 .50
6 Alexander Frolov .40 1.00
7 Mathieu Garon .40 1.00
8 Joe Corvo .20 .50
9 Lubomir Visnovsky .20 .50
10 Aaron Miller .20 .50
11 Mattias Norstrom .20 .50
12 Eric Belanger .20 .50
13 Dustin Brown .40 1.00
14 Michael Cammalleri .40 1.00
15 Pavol Demitra .20 .50

1994 Kollectorfest
COMPLETE SET (5) 4.00 10.00
1 Woody Dumart 1.25 3.00
2 Dutch Hiller .75 2.00
3 Milt Schmidt 2.00 5.00
4 Title Card
Kollectorfest '94 .20 .50
5 Title Card
Oktoberfest 1994 .20 .50

1986-87 Kraft Drawings
COMPLETE SET (81) 40.00 100.00
COMPLETE FACT.SET (81) 50.00 125.00
1 Glenn Anderson .40 1.00
2 Brent Ashton .20 .50
3 Laurie Boschman .20 .50
4 Richard Brodeur .30 .75
5 Guy Carbonneau .30 .75
6 Randy Carlyle .30 .75
7 Chris Chelios 1.25 3.00
8 Wendel Clark 4.00 10.00
9 Glen Cochrane .20 .50
10 Paul Coffey 1.25 3.00
11 Alain Cote .20 .50
12 Russ Courtnall .40 1.00
13 Kjell Dahlin .20 .50
14 Dan Daoust .20 .50
15 Bill Derlago .20 .50
16 Tom Fergus .20 .50
17 Grant Fuhr 1.50 4.00
18 Bob Gainey .40 1.00
19 Gaston Gingras .20 .50
20 Mario Gosselin .30 .75
21 Michel Goulet .40 1.00
22 Rick Green .20 .50
23 Wayne Gretzky 15.00 40.00
24 Doug Halward .20 .50
25 Dale Hawerchuk .60 1.50
26 Brian Hayward .30 .75
27 Dale Hunter .40 1.00
28 Mike Krushelnyski .20 .50
29 Jari Kurri 1.25 3.00
30 Mike Lalor .20 .50
31 Gary Leeman .20 .50
32 Rejean Lemelin .40 1.00
33 Claude Lemieux 2.00 5.00
34 Doug Lidster .20 .50
35 Hakan Loob .40 1.00
36 Kevin Lowe .40 1.00
37 Craig Ludwig .20 .50
38 Paul MacLean .20 .50
39 Clint Malarchuk .40 1.00
40 Mario Marois .20 .50
41 Lanny McDonald .40 1.00
42 Mike McPhee .30 .75
43 Mark Messier 4.00 10.00
44 Randy Moller .20 .50
45 Sergio Momesso .20 .50
46 Andy Moog 1.00 2.50
47 Brian Mullen .20 .50
48 Joe Mullen .40 1.00
49 Mark Napier .20 .50
50 Mats Naslund .40 1.00
51 Chris Nilan .40 1.00
52 Barry Pederson .30 .75
53 Steve Penney .30 .75
54 Jim Peplinski .20 .50
55 Brent Peterson .20 .50
56 Pat Price .20 .50
57 Paul Reinhart .20 .50
58 Stephane Richer .60 1.50
59 Doug Risebrough .20 .50
60 Larry Robinson .40 1.00
61 Patrick Roy 15.00 40.00
62 Borje Salming .40 1.00
63 Petri Skriko .20 .50
64 Brian Skrudland .30 .75
65 Bobby Smith .30 .75
66 Stan Smyl UER
(Misspelled Syml
on card front) .30 .75
67 Anton Stastny .20 .50
68 Peter Stastny .40 1.00
69 Thomas Steen .30 .75
70 Patrik Sundstrom .20 .50
71 Gary Suter .60 1.50
72 Petr Svoboda .30 .75
73 Tony Tanti .20 .50
74 Greg Terrion .20 .50
75 Steve Thomas .75 2.00
76 Perry Turnbull .20 .50
77 Rick Vaive .40 1.00
78 Mike Vernon 1.50 4.00
79 Ryan Walter .20 .50
80 Carey Wilson .20 .50
81 Ken Wregget .60 1.50
ALB Album 10.00 25.00

1989-90 Kraft
COMPLETE SET (64) 40.00 100.00
COMPLETE FACT.SET (64) 50.00 125.00
1 Doug Gilmour .75 2.00
2 Theo Fleury 1.50 4.00
3 Al MacInnis .40 1.00
4 Sergei Makarov .30 .75
5 Joe Nieuwendyk .40 1.00
6 Joel Otto .20 .50
7 Colin Patterson .20 .50
8 Sergei Priakin .20 .50
9 Paul Ranheim .20 .50
10 Glenn Anderson .40 1.00
11 Grant Fuhr .60 1.50
12 Charlie Huddy .20 .50
13 Jari Kurri .75 2.00
14 Kevin Lowe .20 .50
15 Mark Messier 1.25 3.00
16 Craig Simpson .20 .50
17 Steve Smith .20 .50
18 Esa Tikkanen .40 1.00
19 Guy Carbonneau .30 .75
20 Chris Chelios .75 2.00
21 Shayne Corson .40 1.00
22 Russ Courtnall .30 .75
23 Mats Naslund .30 .75
24 Stephane Richer .30 .75
25 Patrick Roy 2.50 6.00
26 Bobby Smith .30 .75
27 Petr Svoboda .20 .50
28 Jeff Brown .20 .50
29 Paul Gillis .20 .50
30 Michel Goulet .30 .75
31 Guy Lafleur .75 2.00
32 Joe Sakic 2.00 5.00
33 Peter Stastny .30 .75
34 Wendel Clark .60 1.50
35 Vincent Damphousse .40 1.00
36 Gary Leeman .20 .50
37 Daniel Marois .20 .50
38 Ed Olczyk .20 .50
39 Rob Ramage .20 .50
40 Vladimir Krutov .20 .50
41 Igor Larionov .40 1.00
42 Trevor Linden .40 1.00
43 Kirk McLean .40 1.00
44 Paul Reinhart .20 .50
45 Tony Tanti .20 .50
46 Brent Ashton .20 .50
47 Randy Carlyle .20 .50
48 Randy Cunneyworth .20 .50
49 Dave Ellett .20 .50
50 Dale Hawerchuk .40 1.00
51 Fredrik Olausson .20 .50
52 Ray Bourque AS .75 2.00
53 Sean Burke AS .40 1.00
54 Paul Coffey AS .75 2.00
55 Mario Lemieux AS 2.50 6.00
56 Cam Neely AS .75 2.00
57 Rick Tocchet AS .40 1.00
58 Steve Duchesne AS .20 .50
59 Wayne Gretzky AS 4.00 10.00
60 Joe Mullen AS .40 1.00
61 Gary Suter AS .20 .50
62 Mike Vernon AS .40 1.00
63 Steve Yzerman AS 2.00 5.00
64 Checklist Card .20 .50
xx Album 10.00 25.00

1989-90 Kraft All-Stars Stickers
COMPLETE SET (6) 8.00 20.00
1 Mike McPhee
Paul Reinhart .40 1.00
2 Wayne Gretzky
Rick Tocchet 5.00 12.00
3 Paul Coffey
Steve Yzerman 2.50 6.00
4 Mike Vernon
Ray Bourque 1.25 3.00
5 Jari Kurri
Mario Lemieux 3.00 8.00
6 Kevin Lowe
Sean Burke .40 1.00

1990-91 Kraft
COMPLETE SET (115) 30.00 80.00
COMPLETE FACT.SET (115) 30.00 80.00
1 Dave Babych .20 .50
2 Brian Bellows .30 .75
3 Ray Bourque .60 1.50
4 Sean Burke .40 1.00
5 Jimmy Carson .20 .50
6 Chris Chelios .60 1.50
7 Dino Ciccarelli .30 .75
8 Paul Coffey .60 1.50
9 Geoff Courtnall .30 .75
10 Doug Crossman .20 .50
11 Kevin Dineen .20 .50
12 Pat Elynuik .20 .50
13 Ron Francis .40 1.00
14 Gerard Gallant .20 .50
15 Wayne Gretzky 4.00 10.00
16 Dale Hawerchuk .40 1.00
17 Ron Hextall .40 1.00
18 Phil Housley .30 .75
19 Mark Howe .30 .75
20 Brett Hull .75 2.00
21 Al Iafrate .25 .60
22 Guy Lafleur .60 1.50
23 Pat LaFontaine .40 1.00
24 Rod Langway .20 .50
25 Igor Larionov .40 1.00
26 Steve Larmer .30 .75
27 Gary Leeman .20 .50
28 Brian Leetch .60 1.50
29 Mario Lemieux 3.00 8.00
30 Trevor Linden .40 1.00
31 Mike Liut .25 .60
32 Mark Messier .75 2.00
33 Al MacInnis .30 .75
34 Mike Modano .75 2.00
35 Andy Moog .40 1.00
36 Joe Mullen .30 .75
37 Kirk Muller .30 .75
38 Petr Nedved .50 1.25
39 Cam Neely .60 1.50
40 Bernie Nicholls .30 .75
41 Joe Nieuwendyk .30 .75
42 Mats Sundin .60 1.50
43 Daren Puppa .30 .75
44 Rob Ramage .20 .50
45 Bill Ranford .40 1.00
46 Stephane Richer .30 .75
47 Larry Robinson .40 1.00
48 Luc Robitaille .40 1.00
49 Patrick Roy 3.00 8.00
50 Joe Sakic 1.25 3.00
51 Denis Savard .40 1.00
52 Craig Simpson .20 .50
53 Bobby Smith .25 .60
54 Peter Stastny .40 1.00
55 Thomas Steen .20 .50
56 Scott Stevens .30 .75
57 Brent Sutter .20 .50
58 Rick Tocchet .40 1.00
59 Pierre Turgeon .40 1.00
60 John Vanbiesbrouck .60 1.50
61 Mike Vernon .40 1.00
62 Doug Wilson .30 .75
63 Steve Yzerman 2.00 5.00
64 Checklist Card .20 .50
65 Steve Duchesne AS .20 .50
66 Wayne Gretzky AS 2.50 6.00
67 Brett Hull AS .50 1.25
68 Jari Kurri AS .40 1.00
69 Mike Gartner AS .30 .75
70 Kirk McLean AS .30 .75
71 Mark Messier AS .50 1.25
72 Joe Mullen AS .25 .60
73 Bernie Nicholls AS .25 .60
74 Joe Nieuwendyk AS .30 .75
75 Luc Robitaille AS .30 .75
76 Mike Vernon AS .30 .75
77 Doug Wilson AS .20 .50
78 Steve Yzerman AS 1.25 3.00
79 Joe Sakic AS .75 2.00
80 Ray Bourque AS .50 1.25
81 Chris Chelios AS .50 1.25
82 Paul Coffey AS .50 1.25
83 Ron Francis AS .40 1.00
84 Cam Neely AS .40 1.00
85 Phil Housley AS .25 .60
86 Pat LaFontaine AS .40 1.00
87 Mario Lemieux AS 2.00 5.00
88 Kirk Muller AS .25 .60
89 Stephane Richer AS .25 .60
90 Patrick Roy AS 2.00 5.00
91 Pierre Turgeon AS .40 1.00
92 Boston Bruins .25 .60
93 Buffalo Sabres .20 .50
94 Calgary Flames .20 .50
95 Chicago Blackhawks .25 .60
96 Detroit Red Wings .25 .60
97 Edmonton Oilers .20 .50
98 Hartford Whalers .20 .50
99 Los Angeles Kings .25 .60
100 Minnesota North Stars .20 .50
101 Montreal Canadiens .25 .60
102 New Jersey Devils .20 .50
103 New York Islanders .20 .50
104 New York Rangers .25 .60
105 Philadelphia Flyers .20 .50
106 Pittsburgh Penguins .20 .50
107 Quebec Nordiques .20 .50
108 St. Louis Blues .20 .50
109 Toronto Maple Leafs .25 .60
110 Vancouver Canucks .20 .50
111 Washington Capitals .20 .50
112 Winnipeg Jets .20 .50
113 Unnumbered Checklist .08 .25
114 Unnumbered Checklist .08 .25
115 Unnumbered Checklist .08 .25
xx Album 10.00 25.00

1991-92 Kraft
COMPLETE SET (92) 30.00 80.00
COMPLETE FACT.SET (92) 40.00 100.00
1 Mario Lemieux 3.00 8.00
2 Mark Recchi .40 1.00
3 Jaromir Jagr 3.00 8.00
4 Mats Sundin .75 2.00
5 Adam Oates .60 1.50
6 Great Moments
Canadien Dynasty
Maurice Richard
Jacques Plante .60 1.50
7 Brendan Shanahan 1.50 4.00
8 Pat Falloon .20 .50
9 Grant Fuhr .40 1.00
10 Gary Leeman .20 .50
11 Petr Nedved .50 1.25
12 Kirk Muller .30 .75
13 Theo Fleury .75 2.00
14 Dino Ciccarelli .25 .60
15 Geoff Courtnall .20 .50
16 Mark Messier 1.00 2.50
17 Ken Hodge Jr. .20 .50
18 Chris Chelios .75 2.00
19 Mike Vernon .30 .75
20 Kevin Hatcher .25 .60
21 Stephane Richer .20 .50
22 Mark Tinordi .20 .50
23 Pat Verbeek .25 .60
24 John Cullen .20 .50
25 Pat LaFontaine .40 1.00
26 Stephan Lebeau .20 .50
27 Mike Gartner .30 .75
28 Great Moments
Last Leaf Dynasty
Bobby Baun .30 .75
29 Shayne Corson .25 .60
30 Trevor Linden .40 1.00
31 Craig Janney .25 .60
32 Al MacInnis .30 .75
33 Phil Housley .25 .60
34 Doug Wilson .20 .50
35 Tony Granato .20 .50
36 Dale Hawerchuk .30 .75
37 Bill Durnan
Turk Broda .75 2.00
38 Brian Bellows .20 .50
39 Great Moments
Number 23 with number 23
Bob Gainey .30 .75
40 Great Moments
A Night to Remember
Darryl Sittler .30 .75
41 Joe Sakic 1.50 4.00
42 Wendel Clark .40 1.00
43 Brent Sutter .20 .50
44 Bill Ranford .30 .75
45 Rick Tocchet .25 .60
46 Paul Ysebaert .20 .50
47 Adam Creighton .20 .50
48 Mike Modano .75 2.00
49 Russ Courtnall .20 .50
50 Great Moments
Evolution of Stanley Cup
Syl Apps .20 .50
51 Sergei Fedorov 1.25 3.00
52 Mike Ricci .25 .60
53 Scott Stevens .25 .60
54 Great Moments
The Ultimate Expansion
Bobby Clarke .40 1.00
55 Owen Nolan .30 .75
56 Jeremy Roenick .60 1.50
57 Ray Bourque .75 2.00
58 Gerard Gallant .20 .50
59 Andy Moog .40 1.00
60 Alexander Mogilny .50 1.25
61 Great Moments
Islander Tradition
Denis Potvin .20 .50
62 Ed Olczyk .20 .50
63 Tomas Sandstrom .20 .50
64 Checklist .20 .50
65 Wayne Gretzky
Maurice Richard 4.00 10.00
66 Brett Hull
Guy Lafleur .75 2.00
67 Jari Kurri
Bobby Clarke .40 1.00
68 Steve Yzerman
Jean Beliveau 2.00 5.00
69 Steve Larmer
Pat Stapleton .30 .75
70 Luc Robitaille
Ted Lindsay .60 1.50
71 Larry Murphy
Doug Harvey .40 1.00
72 Denis Potvin
Gary Suter .30 .75
73 Brian Leetch
Harry Howell .75 2.00
74 Paul Coffey
Bill Gadsby .75 2.00
75 Jon Casey
Terry Sawchuk .60 1.50
76 Patrick Roy
Jacques Plante 3.00 8.00
77 Denis Savard
Serge Savard .40 1.00
78 Doug Gilmour
Bob Baun .60 1.50
79 Guy Carbonneau
Yvan Cournoyer .30 .75
80 Gilbert Perreault
Larry Robinson .40 1.00
81 Red Kelly
Craig Simpson .30 .75
82 Bobby Smith
Rod Gilbert .30 .75
83 Syl Apps
Peter Stastny .30 .75
84 BoomBoom Geoffrion
Vincent Damphousse .60 1.50
85 Marcel Dionne
Steve Smith .30 .75
86 Tim Horton
Kevin Dineen .75 2.00
87 Michel Goulet
Frank Mahovlich .40 1.00
88 Mike Richter
Henri Richard .60 1.50
89 Boston Bruins logo
New York Rangers logo
Original Six/(Unnumbered) .20 .50
90 Montreal Canadiens logo
Toronto Maple Leafs logo
Original Six/(Unnumbered) .20 .50
91 Chicago Blackhawks logo
Detroit Red Wings logo
Original Six/(Unnumbered) .20 .50
92 Stanley Cup
(Unnumbered) .40 1.00
ALB Album 10.00 25.00

1992-93 Kraft
COMPLETE SET (48) 28.00 70.00
COMPLETE FACT.SET (48) 34.00 85.00
1 Boston Bruins .60 1.50
2 Buffalo Sabres .40 1.00
3 Calgary Flames .40 1.00
4 Chicago Blackhawks .60 1.50
5 Detroit Red Wings .60 1.50
6 Edmonton Oilers .40 1.00
7 Hartford Whalers .40 1.00
8 Los Angeles Kings .60 1.50
9 Minnesota North Stars .40 1.00
10 Montreal Canadiens .60 1.50
11 New Jersey Devils .40 1.00
12 New York Islanders .40 1.00
13 New York Rangers .60 1.50
14 Ottawa Senators .40 1.00
15 Philadelphia Flyers .40 1.00
16 Pittsburgh Penguins .60 1.50
17 Quebec Nordiques .40 1.00
18 San Jose Sharks .40 1.00
19 St. Louis Blues .40 1.00
20 Tampa Bay Lightning .40 1.00
21 Toronto Maple Leafs .60 1.50
22 Vancouver Canucks .40 1.00
23 Washington Capitals .40 1.00
24 Winnipeg Jets .40 1.00
25 Tom Barrasso
Wendell Young .40 1.00
26 Don Beaupre
Bob Essensa .40 1.00
27 Jon Casey
Dominic Roussel .40 1.00
28 Tim Cheveldae
Sean Burke .40 1.00
29 Jeff Hackett
Kirk McLean .60 1.50
30 Dominik Hasek
Chris Terreri 1.25 3.00
31 Ron Hextall
Curtis Joseph .75 2.00
32 Andy Moog
Mark Fitzpatrick .60 1.50
33 Bill Ranford
Kelly Hrudey .60 1.50
34 Patrick Roy
John Vanbiesbrouck 4.00 10.00
35 Peter Sidorkiewicz
Grant Fuhr .60 1.50
36 Mike Vernon
Ed Belfour .75 2.00
37 Ray Bourque AS .60 1.50
38 Chris Chelios AS .60 1.50
39 Paul Coffey AS .60 1.50
40 Wayne Gretzky AS 3.00 8.00
41 Brett Hull AS .75 2.00
42 Jaromir Jagr AS 1.50 4.00
43 Mario Lemieux AS 2.00 5.00
44 Trevor Linden AS .30 .75
45 Mark Messier AS .75 2.00
46 Jeremy Roenick AS .60 1.50
47 Patrick Roy AS 2.00 5.00
48 Steve Yzerman AS 1.25 3.00
ALB Album 6.00 15.00

1993-94 Kraft
COMPLETE SET (72) 30.00 80.00
COMPLETE FACT.SET (72) 40.00 100.00
1 Ed Belfour .60 1.50
2 Brian Bradley .20 .50
3 Pavel Bure .75 2.00
4 Paul Coffey .40 1.00
5 Russ Courtnall .20 .50
6 Alexandre Daigle .30 .75
7 Pat Falloon .20 .50
8 Theo Fleury .40 1.00
9 Doug Gilmour .40 1.00
10 Adam Graves .30 .75
11 Stu Grimson .20 .50
12 Al Iafrate .20 .50
13 Jaromir Jagr 1.25 3.00
14 Joe Juneau .30 .75
15 Eric Lindros 1.25 3.00
16 Alexander Mogilny .60 1.50
17 Kirk Muller .20 .50
18 Bill Ranford .30 .75
19 Mike Ricci .20 .50
20 Luc Robitaille .40 1.00
21 Geoff Sanderson .25 .60
22 Teemu Selanne 1.00 2.50
23 Brendan Shanahan 1.00 2.50
24 Pierre Turgeon .40 1.00
25 John Vanbiesbrouck .75 2.00
26 Valeri Zelepukin .20 .50
27 Al Arbour CO .75 2.00
28 Bob Berry CO .75 2.00
29 R.Bourque/P.Flatley 1.25 3.00
30 Scott Bowman CO 1.25 3.00
31 Pat Burns CO .75 2.00
32 Jacques Demers CO .75 2.00
33 K.Dineen/K.Hatcher .75 2.00
34 W.Gretzky/W.Clark 3.00 8.00
35 B.Hull/B.Shaw 1.25 3.00
36 Eddie Johnston CO .75 2.00
37 D.Kennedy/D.Savard .75 2.00
38 Dave King CO .75 2.00
39 P.LaFontaine/P.Verbeek 1.00 2.50
40 M.Lalor/M.Tinordi .75 2.00
41 T.Linden/T.Loney .50 1.25
42 Barry Melrose CO .75 2.00
43 M.Messier/M.Lemieux 3.00 8.00
44 John Muckler CO .75 2.00
45 J.Nieuwendyk/J.Sakic 1.00 2.50
46 Pierre Page CO .75 2.00
47 J.Roenick/G.Carbonneau 1.25 3.00
48 B.Skrudland/C.MacTavish .75 2.00
49 S.Stevens/S.Yzerman 1.50 4.00
50 Tom Barrasso .20 .50
51 Pavel Bure .75 2.00
52 Stephane Fiset .30 .75
53 Doug Gilmour .40 1.00
54 Wayne Gretzky 2.50 6.00
55 Kelly Hrudey .20 .50
56 Mario Lemieux 1.50 4.00
57 Eric Lindros 1.25 3.00
58 Kirk McLean .20 .50
59 Kirk Muller .20 .50
60 Joe Nieuwendyk .20 .50
61 Felix Potvin .40 1.00
63 Dominic Roussel .20 .50
64 Patrick Roy 1.50 4.00
65 Joe Sakic 1.00 2.50
66 Mike Vernon .20 .50
67 Jason Arnott .40 1.00
68 Rob Niedermayer .60 1.50
69 Chris Pronger .30 .75
70 Chris Chelios .30 .75
71 Mario Lemieux 1.50 4.00
72 Patrick Roy 1.50 4.00
ALB Album 10.00 25.00

1993-94 Kraft Recipes
COMPLETE SET (8) 2.00 5.00
1 Vincent Damphousse .30 .75
2 Bob Essensa .20 .50
3 Doug Gilmour .50 1.25
4 Trevor Linden .30 .75
5 Al MacInnis .30 .75
6 Bill Ranford .30 .75
7 Mike Ricci .20 .50
8 Brad Shaw .20 .50

1994-95 Kraft
COMPLETE SET (72) 40.00 100.00
1 Dave Andreychuk .20 .50
2 Chris Chelios .60 1.50
3 Wendel Clark .25 .60
4 Theo Fleury .60 1.50
5 Wayne Gretzky 2.00 5.00
6 Breyt Hull .75 2.00
7 Al Iafrate .20 .50
8 Jaromir Jagr 2.00 5.00
9 Kirk Muller .20 .50
10 Pat LaFontaine .30 .75
11 Mark Recchi .30 .75
12 Gary Roberts .20 .50
13 Mats Sundin .60 1.50
14 Steve Yzerman 2.00 5.00
15 Jason Arnott .30 .75
16 Vincent Damphousse .20 .50
17 Doug Gilmour .60 1.50
18 Craig Janney .20 .50
19 Joe Juneau .20 .50
20 Trevor Linden .20 .50
21 Eric Lindros 2.00 5.00
22 Mark Messier .75 2.00
23 Mike Modano .75 2.00
24 Alexander Mogilny .40 1.00
25 Adam Oates .25 .60
26 Robert Reichel .20 .50
27 Jeremy Roenick .40 1.00
28 Joe Sakic 1.25 3.00
29 Keith Tkachuk .60 1.50
30 Alexei Yashin .50 1.25
31 Tom Barrasso .20 .50
32 Don Beaupre .20 .50
33 Ed Belfour .60 1.50
34 Craig Billington .20 .50
35 Martin Brodeur 1.50 4.00
36 Sean Burke .20 .50
37 Tim Cheveldae .20 .50
38 Stephane Fiset .30 .75
39 Dominik Hasek 1.25 3.00
40 Guy Hebert .20 .50
41 Ron Hextall .30 .75
42 Kelly Hrudey .20 .50
43 Arthurs Irbe .00 .20 .50
44 Curtis Joseph .75 2.00
45 Trevor Kidd .30 .75
46 Kirk McLean .30 .75
47 Jamie McLennan .20 .50
48 Andy Moog .40 1.00
49 Felix Potvin .60 1.50
50 Daren Puppa .30 .75
51 Bill Ranford .30 .75
52 Mike Richter .60 1.50
53 Vincent Riendeau .20 .50
54 Patrick Roy 3.00 8.00
55 John Vanbiesbrouck .60 1.50
56 Mike Vernon .30 .75
57 Ray Bourque .75 2.00
58 Martin Brodeur 1.50 4.00
59 Sergei Fedorov 1.25 3.00
60 Dominik Hasek 1.25 3.00
61 Jacques Lemaire .40 1.00
62 Adam Graves .40 1.00
63 Wayne Gretzky 4.00 10.00
64 Brian Leetch .60 1.50
65 Cam Neely .60 1.50
66 New York Rangers Champs 1.25 3.00
67 Ray Bourque .75 2.00
68 Pavel Bure 1.50 4.00
69 Sergei Fedorov 1.25 3.00
70 Dominik Hasek 1.25 3.00
71 Brendan Shanahan 1.25 3.00
72 Scott Stevens .40 1.00
NNO Collector's Album 10.00 25.00

1994-95 Kraft Goalie Masks
COMPLETE SET (8) 8.00 20.00
1 Ed Belfour 1.25 3.00
2 Guy Hebert .60 1.50
3 Curtis Joseph 1.25 3.00
4 Andy Moog .75 2.00
5 Felix Potvin .75 2.00
6 Vincent Riendeau .75 2.00
7 Patrick Roy 3.00 8.00
8 John Vanbiesbrouck .75 2.00

1995-96 Kraft
COMPLETE SET (79) 30.00 80.00
1 Sergei Fedorov .75 2.00
2 Jason Arnott .20 .50
3 Teemu Selanne .75 2.00
4 Pierre Turgeon .25 .60
5 Joe Juneau .15 .40
6 Scott Stevens .25 .60
7 Cam Neely .20 .50
8 Mario Lemieux 1.50 4.00
9 Wendel Clark .20 .50
10 Alexandre Daigle .15 .40
11 Peter Forsberg 1.00 2.50
12 Trevor Linden .20 .50
13 Phil Housley .15 .40
14 Doug Gilmour .30 .75
15 Sean Burke .25 .60
16 Dominik Hasek .75 2.00
17 Patrick Roy 1.50 4.00
18 Kirk McLean .20 .50
19 Blaine Lacher .15 .40
20 Jim Carey .20 .50
21 Martin Brodeur 1.00 2.50
22 Mike Richter .30 .75
23 Felix Potvin .30 .75
24 Trevor Kidd .20 .50
25 Ed Belfour .30 .75
26 Stephane Fiset .20 .50
27 Ron Hextall .20 .50
28 Grant Fuhr .20 .50
29 Daren Puppa .20 .50
30 Andy Moog .20 .50
31 Mike Vernon .20 .50
32 John Vanbiesbrouck .40 1.00
33 Bill Ranford .25 .60
34 Tommy Soderstrom .20 .50
35 Tom Barrasso .20 .50
36 Kelly Hrudey .20 .50
37 Guy Hebert .25 .60
38 Arturs Irbe .20 .50
39 Tim Cheveldae .20 .50
40 Don Beaupre .20 .50
41 Eric Lindros 1.25 3.00
42 Jaromir Jagr 1.25 3.00
43 Paul Coffey .30 .75
44 Chris Chelios .30 .75
45 Dominik Hasek .75 2.00
46 John LeClair .60 1.50
47 Alexei Zhamnov .15 .40
48 Keith Tkachuk .40 1.00
49 Theo Fleury .30 .75
50 Larry Murphy .15 .40
51 Ray Bourque .75 2.00
52 Ed Belfour .40 1.00
53 Wayne Gretzky 2.00 5.00
54 Adam Oates .25 .60
55 Paul Kariya 1.25 3.00
56 Alexander Mogilny .25 .60
57 Dave Gagner .15 .40
58 Theo Fleury .30 .75
59 Jesse Belanger .15 .40
60 Joe Sakic .75 2.00
61 Peter Bondra .30 .75
62 Andrew Cassels .15 .40
63 Alexandre Daigle .15 .40
64 Paul Coffey .30 .75
65 Ulf Dahlen .15 .40
66 Brett Hull .40 1.00
67 Bernie Nicholls .15 .40
68 Doug Weight .25 .60
69 Brian Bradley .15 .40
70 Mark Messier .50 1.25
71 Stephane Richer .15 .40
72 Eric Lindros 1.25 3.00
73 Mark Recchi .25 .60
74 Ray Ferraro .15 .40
75 Mats Sundin .30 .75
76 Alexei Zhamnov .15 .40
77 Pavel Bure 1.00 2.50
78 Jaromir Jagr 1.00 2.50
79 Claude Lemieux 10.00 25.00
NNO Binder 4.00 10.00

1996-97 Kraft Upper Deck
COMPLETE SET (72) 40.00 100.00
1 Brian Leetch .40 1.00
2 Keith Tkachuk .60 1.50
3 Geoff Sanderson .30 .75
4 Owen Nolan .30 .75
5 Saku Koivu .60 1.50
6 Adam Oates .30 .75
7 Mats Sundin .40 1.00
8 Theo Fleury .30 .75
9 Zigmund Palffy .40 1.00
10 Alexei Yashin .30 .75
11 Brett Hull .40 1.00
12 Michal Pivonka .20 .50
13 Joe Nieuwendyk .30 .75
14 Martin Brodeur .75 2.00
15 Ed Belfour .40 1.00
16 Guy Hebert .30 .75
17 Patrick Roy 1.50 4.00
18 Dominik Hasek .75 2.00
19 John Vanbiesbrouck .60 1.50
20 Yanic Perreault .20 .50
21 Doug Weight .30 .75
22 Mario Lemieux 1.50 4.00
23 Eric Lindros 1.00 2.50
24 Alexander Mogilny .40 1.00
25 Sergei Fedorov .75 2.00
26 Daren Puppa .30 .75
27 Chris Chelios .40 1.00
28 Mario Lemieux 1.50 4.00
29 Paul Kariya 1.25 3.00
30 Ray Bourque .40 1.00
31 Chris Osgood .40 1.00
32 Jaromir Jagr 1.25 3.00
33 Rob Blake
Paul Kariya
Kevin Dineen
Peter Bondra 1.50 4.00
34 Ray Bourque
Adam Graves
Randy Cunneyworth
Pat L 1.00 2.50
35 Al MacInnis
Trevor Linden
Kris King
Mike Modano 1.00 2.50
36 Paul Ysebaert
Owen Nolan
Theo Fleury
Kelly Buch 1.00 2.50
37 Vince Damphousse
Doug Gilmour
Mario Lemieux
Eri 2.00 5.00
38 Ziggy Palffy
Scott Stevens
Steve Yzerman
Chris 1.50 4.00
39 Brian Skrudland
Joe Sakic 1.50 4.00
40 Scott Bowman CO .40 1.00
41 Marc Crawford .30 .75
42 Chris Chelios .40 1.00
43 Paul Kariya 1.25 3.00
44 Ron Francis .30 .75
45 Daniel Alfredsson .30 .75
46 Adam Oates .30 .75
47 Joe Sakic .75 2.00
48 Peter Forsberg 1.00 2.50
49 Jarome Iginla .30 .75
50 Jim Carey .30 .75
51 C.Osgood
M.Vernon .40 1.00
52 Mike Richter .40 1.00
53 Jocelyn Thibault .30 .75
54 Mario Lemieux 1.50 4.00
55 Ed Jovanovski .30 .75
56 Mario Lemieux 1.50 4.00
57 J.LeClair
B.Shanahan
J.Jagr 1.25 3.00
58 Eric Lindros 1.00 2.50
59 Sergei Fedorov .75 2.00
60 T.Selanne
Wild Wing 1.25 3.00
61 F.Potvin
Carlton the Bear .40 1.00
62 M.McSorley
S.J. Sharkie .30 .75
63 R.Niedermayer
Stanley C. Panther .30 .75
64 D.Gagner
Harvey the Hound .20 .50
65 Theo Fleury .75 2.00
66 Saku Koivu 1.25 3.00
67 Mario Lemieux 4.00 10.00
68 Eric Lindros 2.00 5.00
69 Alexander Mogilny .60 1.50
70 Mats Sundin 1.00 2.50
71 Doug Weight .60 1.50
72 Alexei Yashin .60 1.50

1997-98 Kraft Pinnacle
COMPLETE SET (26)
1 Vincent Damphousse .30 .75
2 Theo Fleury .40 1.00
3 Ron Francis .40 1.00
4 Wayne Gretzky 2.50 6.00
5 Paul Kariya .60 1.50
6 Eric Lindros 1.00 2.50
7 Mark Messier 1.00 2.50
8 Adam Oates .30 .75
9 Steve Yzerman 2.00 5.00
10 Jaromir Jagr 1.00 2.50
11 Saku Koivu .40 1.00
12 Teemu Selanne .75 2.00
13 Uwe Krupp .30 .75
14 Sergei Fedorov 1.00 2.50
15 Alexei Yashin .30 .75
16 Peter Bondra .30 .75
17 Zigmund Palffy .30 .75
18 Jozef Stumpel .30 .75
19 Peter Forsberg 1.00 2.50
20 Mikael Renberg .30 .75
21 Mats Sundin .40 1.00
22 Brett Hull .75 2.00
23 John LeClair .30 .75
24 Mike Modano 1.00 2.50
25 Keith Tkachuk .40 1.00
26 Doug Weight .30 .75

1997-98 Kraft Pinnacle 3-D World's Best
COMPLETE SET (8) 2.50 6.00
1 Doug Weight .25 .60
2 Mats Sundin .30 .75
3 Alexei Yashin .25 .60
4 Saku Koivu .30 .75
5 Theo Fleury .30 .75
6 Mark Messier .40 1.00
7 Vincent Damphousse .30 .75
8 Paul Kariya 1.25 3.00

1997-98 Kraft Team Canada
COMPLETE SET (12) 8.00 20.00
1 Ray Bourque
Shayne Corson .75 2.00
2 Martin Brodeur
Joe Sakic 1.25 3.00
3 Marc Crawford
Eric Lindros .40 1.00
4 Eric Desjardins
Adam Foote .40 1.00
5 Theoren Fleury
Al MacInnis .40 1.00
6 Curtis Joseph
Patrick Roy 2.00 5.00
7 Paul Kariya
Rod Brind'Amour .75 2.00
8 Trevor Linden
Keith Primeau .75 2.00
9 Joe Nieuwendyk
Rob Blake .40 1.00
10 Scott Stevens
Rob Zamuner .40 1.00
11 Brendan Shanahan
Wayne Gretzky 2.50 6.00
12 Steve Yzerman
Chris Pronger 1.25 3.00

1998-99 Kraft Dinners Zoomer Stickers
COMPLETE SET 8.00 20.00
1 Atlanta Thrashers 1.50 4.00
2 Columbus Blue Jackets 1.50 4.00
3 Los Angeles Kings 1.50 4.00
4 Minnesota Wild 1.50 4.00
5 Nashville Predators 1.50 4.00

1998-99 Kraft Fearless Forwards
COMPLETE SET (13) 6.00 15.00
1 Peter Bondra .40 1.00
2 Pavel Bure .75 2.00
3 Vincent Damphousse .40 1.00
4 Jaromir Jagr 1.25 3.00
5 Paul Kariya .75 2.00
6 John Leclair .40 1.00
7 Claude Lemieux .40 1.00
8 Mike Modano .75 2.00
9 Brendan Shanahan .75 2.00
10 Cory Stillman .40 1.00
11 Mats Sundin .75 2.00
12 Doug Weight .40 1.00
13 Alexei Yashin .40 1.00

1998-99 Kraft Peanut Butter
COMPLETE SET (8) 4.00 10.00
1 Rob Blake
Larry Murphy .75 2.00
2 Brian Leetch
Robert Svehla .75 2.00
3 Patrice Brisebois
Scott Niedermayer .75 2.00
4 Vladimir Malakhov
Darryl Sydor .40 1.00
5 Al MacInnis
Alexei Zhitnik .40 1.00
6 Ray Bourque
Boris Mironov 1.25 3.00
7 Mathieu Schneider
Nicklas Lidstrom 1.25 3.00
8 Teppo Numminen
Chris Chelios .75 2.00

1999-00 Kraft Dinner
COMPLETE SET (15) 4.80 12.00
1 Shayne Corson .20 .50
2 Jaromir Jagr .60 1.50
3 Curtis Joseph .40 1.00
4 Paul Kariya .75 2.00
5 Saku Koivu .30 .75
6 Mike Modano .40 1.00
7 Eric Lindros .60 1.50
8 Mattias Ohlund .20 .50
9 Chris Pronger .20 .50
10 Joe Sakic .60 1.50
11 Brendan Shanahan .40 1.00
12 Scott Stevens .20 .50
13 Mats Sundin .30 .75
14 Alexei Yashin .20 .50
15 Steve Yzerman 1.25 3.00

1999-00 Upper Deck Kraft Dinner The Great One
COMPLETE SET (4) 6.00 15.00
COMMON GRETZKY 1.50 4.00

1999-00 Kraft Face Off Rivals
COMPLETE SET (6) 4.00 10.00
1 Mats Sundin
Stu Barnes .75 2.00
2 Theoren Fleury
Joe Nieuwendyk .75 2.00
3 Pierre Turgeon
Guy Carbonneau .75 2.00
4 Yanic Perreault
Curtis Brown .40 1.00
5 Steve Yzerman
Claude Lemieux 1.25 3.00
6 Mike Modano
Mike Eastwood .75 2.00

1999-00 Kraft Peanut Butter
COMPLETE SET (11) 6.00 15.00
1 Ray Bourque .75 2.00
2 Martin Brodeur .75 2.00
3 Peter Forsberg .75 2.00
4 Dominik Hasek .60 1.50
5 Jaromir Jagr .75 2.00
6 Paul Kariya 1.25 3.00
7 Nicklas Lidstrom .40 1.00
8 Al MacInnis .20 .50
9 Teppo Numminen .20 .50
10 Teemu Selanne .60 1.50
11 Brendan Shanahan .60 1.50

1999-00 Kraft Overtime Winners
COMPLETE SET (6) 2.50 6.00
1 Brett Hull .75 2.00
2 Garry Valk .08 .25
3 Mike Modano .75 2.00
4 Pierre Turgeon .40 1.00
5 Jaromir Jagr 1.25 3.00
6 Milan Hejduk .40 1.00

1999-00 Kraft Stanley Cup Moments
COMPLETE SET (15) 2.00 5.00
1 Mark Messier 1.25 3.00
2 Eric Desjardins .20 .50
3 Brett Hull 1.25 3.00
4 Claude Lemieux .20 .50
5 Michael Peca .20 .50
6 Bill Ranford .40 1.00

1999-00 Kraft Whiz Kid
COMPLETE SET (8) 1.50 4.00
1 Milan Hejduk .40 1.00
2 Marian Hossa .40 1.00
3 Jan Hrdina .08 .25
4 Tomas Kaberle .08 .25
5 Chris Drury .40 1.00
6 Daniil Markov .08 .25
7 Erik Rasmussen .08 .25
8 Brendan Morrison .40 1.00

2000-01 Kraft
COMPLETE SET (30) 40.00 100.00
1 Jaromir Jagr 5.00 12.00
2 Markus Naslund 1.20 3.00
3 Luc Robitaille 1.20 3.00
4 Scott Stevens .40 1.00
5 Mike Modano 2.50 6.00
6 Doug Weight 1.20 3.00
7 Peter Bondra 1.25 3.00
8 Paul Kariya 5.00 12.00
9 Radek Bonk .40 1.00
10 John LeClair 2.00 5.00
11 Sandis Ozolinsh .40 1.00
12 Steve Yzerman 10.00 25.00
13 Joe Thornton 2.00 5.00
14 Valeri Bure .40 1.00
15 Pavel Bure 2.50 6.00
16 Cliff Ronning .40 1.00
17 Dominik Hasek 2.50 6.00
18 Vincent Lecavalier 1.20 3.00
19 Andrew Brunette .40 1.00
20 Chris Pronger 1.20 3.00
21 Owen Nolan 1.20 3.00
22 Joe Sakic 4.00 10.00
23 Jeremy Roenick 2.50 6.00
24 Tony Amonte 1.50 4.00
25 Mariusz Czerkawski .40 1.00
26 Trevor Linden 1.50 4.00
27 Mats Sundin 2.00 5.00
28 Mark Messier 3.00 8.00
29 Ron Tugnutt 2.00 5.00
30 Scott Pellerin 2.00 5.00

2003-04 Kraft
COMPLETE SET (10) 8.00 15.00
1 Ed Belfour 1.25 3.00
2 Anson Carter .40 1.00
3 Paul Kariya .75 2.00
4 Trevor Linden .40 1.00
5 Vincent Lecavalier .75 2.00
6 Al MacInnis .40 1.00
7 Mike Ribeiro .40 1.00
8 Ryan Smyth .40 1.00
9 Joe Thornton 1.25 3.00
10 Jordin Tootoo .75 2.00

1979-80 Lakers/Kings Alta-Dena
COMPLETE SET (8) 10.00 20.00
5 Marcel Dionne 3.00 6.00
6 Butch Goring .50 1.00
7 Mike Murphy .50 1.00
8 Dave Taylor 1.50 3.00

1927-28 La Patrie
COMPLETE SET (21) 1250.00 2500.00
1 Sylvio Mantha 50.00 100.00
2 Art Gagne 30.00 60.00
3 Leo Lafrance 30.00 60.00
4 Aurel Joliat 150.00 300.00
5 Pit Lepine 40.00 80.00
6 Gizzy Hart 30.00 60.00
7 Wildor Larochelle 40.00 80.00
8 Georges Hainsworth 100.00 200.00
9 Herb Gardiner 40.00 80.00
10 Albert Leduc 40.00 80.00
11 Marty Burke 40.00 80.00
12 Charlie Langlois 30.00 60.00
13 Leonard Gaudreault 30.00 60.00
14 Howie Morenz 350.00 700.00
15 Cecil M. Hart 40.00 80.00
16 Leo Dandurand 30.00 60.00
17 Newsy Lalonde 150.00 300.00
18 Didier Pitre 30.00 60.00
19 Jack Laviolette 50.00 100.00
20 Georges Patterson 30.00 60.00
21 Georges Vezina 250.00 500.00

1927-28 La Presse Photos
1 Howie Morenz 200.00 300.00
2 Aurel Joliat 125.00 200.00
3 Sylvio Mantha 50.00 100.00
4 Pit Lepine 50.00 100.00
5 George Hainsworth 125.00 200.00
6 Art Gagne 50.00 100.00
7 Herb Gardiner 50.00 100.00
8 Art Gagne 50.00 100.00
9 Herb Gardiner 50.00 100.00
10 Albert Leduc 50.00 100.00
11 Wildor Larochelle 50.00 100.00
12 Leonard Gaudreault 50.00 100.00
13 Gizzy Hart 50.00 100.00
14 Charlie Langlois 50.00 100.00
15 Georges Vezina 200.00 300.00
16 Cattarinich
Hart
Dandurand
Letourmeau 60.00 150.00
17 Eddie Shore 150.00 250.00
18 Lionel Conacher 125.00 200.00
19 Red Porter 50.00 100.00
20 George Patterson 50.00 100.00

1928-29 La Presse Photos
COMPLETE SET (14) 400.00 800.00
1 Clint Benedict 50.00 100.00
2 Frank Boucher 37.50 75.00
3 George Boucher 37.50 75.00
4 Lucien Brunet 10.00 20.00
5 Marty Burke 37.50 75.00
6 Bun Cook 50.00 100.00
7 Hap Day 37.50 75.00
8 Red Dutton 37.50 75.00
9 Georges Mantha 50.00 100.00
10 Armand Mondou 37.50 75.00
11 Bill Phillips 37.50 75.00
12 Babe Siebert 50.00 100.00
13 Nels Stewart 62.50 125.00
14 Jimmy Ward 37.50 75.00

1993 Leaf Chicago National
1 Mario Lemieux 5.00 12.00

1993-94 Leaf
1 Mario Lemieux .60 1.50
2 Curtis Joseph .20 .50
3 Steve Leach .10 .25
4 Vincent Damphousse .12 .30
5 Murray Craven .10 .25
6 Pat Elynuik .10 .25
7 Bill Guerin .15 .40
8 Zarley Zalapski .10 .25
9 Rob Gaudreau RC .15 .40
10 Pavel Bure .15 .40
11 Brad Shaw .10 .25
12 Pat LaFontaine .15 .40
13 Teemu Selanne .30 .75
14 Trent Klatt .10 .25
15 Kevin Todd .10 .25
16 Larry Murphy .12 .30
17 Tony Amonte .12 .30
18 Dino Ciccarelli .12 .30

19 Doug Bodger .10 .25
20 Luc Robitaille .15 .40
21 John Tucker .10 .25
22 Todd Gill .10 .25
23 Mike Ricci .10 .25
24 Evgeny Davydov .10 .25
25 Pierre Turgeon .12 .30
26 Rod Brind'Amour .12 .30
27 Jeremy Roenick .25 .60
28 Joel Otto .10 .25
29 Jeff Brown .10 .25
30 Brendan Shanahan .15 .40
31 Jiri Slegr .10 .25
32 Vladimir Malakhov .10 .25
33 Patrick Roy .40 1.00
34 Kevin Hatcher .10 .25
35 Alexander Semak .10 .25
36 Gary Roberts .10 .25
37 Tommy Soderstrom .12 .30
38 Bob Essensa .12 .30
39 Kelly Hrudey .12 .30
40 Shawn Chambers .10 .25
41 Glenn Anderson .12 .30
42 Owen Nolan .15 .40
43 Patrick Flatley .10 .25
44 Ray Sheppard .12 .30
45 Darren Turcotte .10 .25
46 Shayne Corson .12 .30
47 Brad May .12 .30
48 Bob Kudelski .10 .25
49 Pat Falloon .10 .25
50 Andrew Cassels .10 .25
51 Chris Chelios .15 .40
52 Sylvain Cote .10 .25
53 Mathieu Schneider .10 .25
54 Ted Donato .10 .25
55 Kirk McLean .12 .30
56 Bruce Driver .10 .25
57 Uwe Krupp .10 .25
58 Brent Fedyk .10 .25
59 Robert Reichel .10 .25
60 Scott Stevens .15 .40
61 Phil Housley .12 .30
62 Ed Belfour .15 .40
63 Dave Andreychuk .15 .40
64 Claude Lapointe .10 .25
65 Russ Courtnall .10 .25
66 Grant Fuhr .25 .60
67 Paul Coffey .15 .40
68 Bill Ranford .12 .30
69 Kevin Stevens .12 .30
70 Brian Leetch .12 .30
71 Dale Hawerchuk .20 .50
72 Geoff Courtnall .10 .25
73 Sandis Ozolinsh .10 .25
74 Sylvain Turgeon .10 .25
75 Nelson Emerson .10 .25
76 Brian Bellows .12 .30
77 Geoff Sanderson .12 .30
78 Petr Nedved .10 .25
79 Peter Bondra .15 .40
80 Scott Niedermayer .15 .40
81 Steve Thomas .10 .25
82 Dimitri Yushkevich .10 .25
83 Mike Vernon .12 .30
84 Alexei Zhamnov .12 .30
85 Adam Creighton .10 .25
86 Dave Ellett .10 .25
87 Joe Sakic .30 .75
88 Mike Craig .10 .25
89 Nicklas Lidstrom .15 .40
90 Ed Olczyk .10 .25
91 Alexander Mogilny .12 .30
92 Ulf Samuelsson .10 .25
93 Doug Gilmour .20 .50
94 Michael Nylander .10 .25
95 Steve Smith .10 .25
96 Igor Korolev .10 .25
97 Dixon Ward .10 .25
98 John LeClair .15 .40
99 Cam Neely .15 .40
100 Patrick Roy Cup Champs .40 1.00
101 Darius Kasparaitis .10 .25
102 Mike Ridley .10 .25
103 Josef Beranek .10 .25
104 Valeri Zelepukin .10 .25
105 Keith Tkachuk .15 .40
106 Tomas Sandstrom .10 .25
107 Peter Zezel .10 .25
108 Scott Young .10 .25
109 Rick Tocchet .12 .30
110 Teemu Selanne CL .30 .75
111 Steve Chiasson .10 .25
112 Doug Zmolek .10 .25
113 Patrick Poulin .10 .25
114 Stephane Matteau .10 .25
115 Yves Racine .10 .25
116 Steve Heinze .10 .25
117 Gilbert Dionne .10 .25
118 Dale Hunter .10 .25
119 Derek King .10 .25
120 Garry Galley .10 .25
121 Ray Ferraro .10 .25
122 Andrei Kovalenko .10 .25
123 Alexei Zhitnik .10 .25
124 Fredrik Olausson .10 .25
125 Claude Lemieux .10 .25
126 Joe Nieuwendyk .12 .30
127 Travis Green .10 .25
128 Dave Gagner .12 .30
129 Sergei Fedorov .25 .60
130 Adam Graves .10 .25
131 Petr Svoboda .10 .25
132 Sean Burke .10 .25
133 Johan Garpenlov .10 .25
134 Jamie Baker .10 .25
135 Teppo Numminen .10 .25
136 Mats Sundin .15 .40
137 Nikolai Borschevsky .10 .25
138 Stephane Richer .12 .30
139 Scott Lachance .10 .25
140 Gary Suter .10 .25
141 Al Iafrate .10 .25
142 Brent Sutter .10 .25
143 Dmitri Kvartalnov .10 .25
144 Pat Verbeek .10 .25
145 Ed Courtenay .10 .25
146 Mark Tinordi .10 .25
147 Alexei Kovalev .12 .30
148 Dallas Drake RC .15 .40
149 Jimmy Carson .10 .25
150 Florida Panthers .05 .15
151 Roman Hamrlik .10 .25
152 Martin Rucinsky .10 .25
153 Calle Johansson .10 .25
154 Theo Fleury .10 .25
155 Benoit Hogue .10 .25
156 Kevin Dineen .10 .25
157 Jody Hull .10 .25
158 Mark Messier .30 .75
159 Dave Manson .10 .25
160 Chris Kontos .10 .25
161 Ron Francis .20 .50
162 Steve Yzerman .40 1.00
163 Igor Kravchuk .10 .25
164 Sergei Zubov .12 .30
165 Thomas Steen .10 .25
166 Wendel Clark .25 .60
167 Scott Pellerin RC .15 .40
168 Dimitri Khristich .10 .25
169 Bernie Nicholls .12 .30
170 Paul Ranheim .10 .25
171 Robert Kron .10 .25
172 Rob Blake .12 .30
173 Rob Zamuner .10 .25
174 Rob Pearson .10 .25
175 Ed Belfour CL .15 .40
176 Steve Duchesne .10 .25
177 Pelle Eklund .10 .25
178 Michal Pivonka .10 .25
179 Joe Murphy .10 .25
180 Al MacInnis .20 .50
181 Craig Janney .12 .30
182 Kirk Muller .10 .25
183 Cliff Ronning .10 .25
184 Doug Weight .12 .30
185 Mike Richter .15 .40
186 Bob Probert .15 .40
187 Robert Petrovicky .10 .25
188 Richard Smehlik .10 .25
189 Norm Maciver .10 .25
190 Stephan Lebeau .10 .25
191 Patrice Brisebois .10 .25
192 Kevin Miller .10 .25
193 Trevor Linden .15 .40
194 Darrin Shannon .10 .25
195 Tim Cheveldae .12 .30
196 Tom Barrasso .12 .30
197 Zdeno Ciger .10 .25
198 Ulf Dahlen .10 .25
199 Arturs Irbe .10 .25
200 Anaheim Mighty Ducks .05 .15
201 Tony Granato .10 .25
202 Mike Modano .25 .60
203 Eric Desjardins .12 .30
204 Bryan Smolinski .10 .25
205 Mark Recchi .20 .50
206 Darryl Sydor .10 .25
207 Valeri Kamensky .12 .30
208 Kelly Kisio .10 .25
209 Brian Bradley .10 .25
210 Mario Lemieux CL .60 1.50
211 Yuri Khmylev .10 .25
212 Derian Hatcher .10 .25
213 Mike Gartner .20 .50
214 Mike Needham UER .10 .25
215 Ray Bourque .25 .60
216 Tie Domi .12 .30
217 Shawn McEachern .10 .25
218 Joe Juneau .10 .25
219 Greg Adams .10 .25
220 Martin Straka .10 .25
221 Tom Fitzgerald .10 .25
222 Gary Shuchuk .10 .25
223 Kevin Haller .10 .25
224 Bryan Marchment .10 .25
225 Louie DeBrusk .10 .25
226 Randy Wood .10 .25
227 Bobby Holik .10 .25
228 Troy Mallette .10 .25
229 Adam Foote .10 .25
230 Bob Rouse .10 .25
231 Jyrki Lumme .10 .25
232 James Patrick .10 .25
233 Eric Lindros .25 .60
234 Joe Reekie .10 .25
235 Adam Oates .15 .40
236 Frank Musil .10 .25
237 Vladimir Konstantinov .12 .30
238 Dave Lowry .10 .25
239 Garth Butcher .10 .25
240 Jari Kurri .15 .40
241 Rick Tabaracci .10 .25
242 Sergei Bautin .10 .25
243 Scott Scissons .10 .25
244 Dominic Roussel .12 .30
245 John Cullen .10 .25
246 Sheldon Kennedy .10 .25
247 Mike Hough .10 .25
248 Paul DiPietro .10 .25
249 David Shaw .10 .25
250 Sergio Momesso .10 .25
251 Jeff Daniels .10 .25
252 Sergei Nemchinov .10 .25
253 Kris King .10 .25
254 Kelly Miller .10 .25
255 Brett Hull .30 .75
256 Dominik Hasek .25 .60
257 Chris Pronger .15 .40
258 Derek Plante RC .15 .40
259 Mark Howe .15 .40
260 Oleg Petrov .10 .25
261 Ronnie Stern .10 .25
262 Scott Mellanby .12 .30
263 Warren Rychel .10 .25
264 John MacLean .12 .30
265 Radek Hamr RC .15 .40
266 Greg Hawgood .10 .25
267 Sylvain Lefebvre .10 .25
268 Glen Wesley .10 .25
269 Joe Cirella .10 .25
270 Dirk Graham .10 .25
271 Eric Weinrich .10 .25
272 Donald Audette .10 .25
273 Jason Woolley .10 .25
274 Kjell Samuelsson .10 .25
275 Ron Sutter .10 .25
276 Keith Primeau .10 .25
277 Ron Tugnutt .12 .30
278 Jesse Belanger .10 .25
279 Mike Keane .10 .25
280 Adam Burt .10 .25
281 Don Sweeney .10 .25
282 Mike Donnelly .10 .25
283 Lyle Odelein .10 .25
284 Gord Murphy .10 .25
285 Mikael Andersson .10 .25
286 Bret Hedican .10 .25
287 Bill Berg .10 .25
288 Esa Tikkanen .10 .25
289 Markus Naslund .15 .40
290 Checklist .05 .15
291 Kerry Huffman .10 .25
292 Dana Murzyn .10 .25
293 Rob Niedermayer .12 .30
294 Andre Racicot .10 .25
295 Ken Sutton .10 .25
296 Shawn Burr .10 .25
297 Scott Pearson .10 .25
298 Joby Messier RC .15 .40
299 Darrin Madeley RC .15 .40
300 Joe Mullen .12 .30
301 Stephane Fiset .12 .30
302 Geoff Smith .10 .25
303 Slava Kozlov .12 .30
304 Wayne Gretzky 1.00 2.50
305 Curtis Leschyshyn .10 .25
306 Mike Sillinger .10 .25
307 Vyacheslav Butsayev .10 .25
308 Mark Lamb .10 .25
309 German Titov RC .15 .40
310 Gerard Gallant .10 .25
311 Alexandre Daigle .10 .25
312 Jim Hrivnak .10 .25
313 Corey Hirsch .12 .30
314 Craig Berube .10 .25
315 Bill Houlder .10 .25
316 Ron Wilson .10 .25
317 Glen Murray .12 .30
318 Bryan Trottier .15 .40
319 Jeff Hackett .10 .25
320 Brad Dalgarno .10 .25
321 Petr Klima .10 .25
322 Jon Casey .12 .30
323 Mikael Renberg .15 .40
324 Jimmy Waite .12 .30
325 Brian Skrudland .10 .25
326 Vitali Prokhorov .10 .25
327 Glenn Healy .12 .30
328 Brian Benning .10 .25
329 Tony Hrkac .10 .25
330 Stu Grimson .10 .25
331 Chris Gratton .12 .30
332 Dave Poulin .10 .25
333 Jarrod Skalde .10 .25
334 Christian Ruuttu .10 .25
335 Mark Fitzpatrick .10 .25
336 Martin Lapointe .10 .25
337 Cam Stewart RC .15 .40
338 Anatoli Semenov .10 .25
339 Gaetan Duchesne .10 .25
340 Checklist .05 .15
341 Ron Hextall .15 .40
342 Mikhail Tatarinov .10 .25
343 Danny Lorenz .10 .25
344 Craig Simpson .10 .25
345 Martin Brodeur .40 1.00
346 Jaromir Jagr .50 1.25
347 Tyler Wright .10 .25
348 Greg Gilbert .10 .25
349 Dave Tippett .10 .25
350 Stu Barnes .10 .25
351 Daniel Lacroix RC .10 .25
352 Marty McSorley .10 .25
353 Sean Hill .10 .25
354 Craig Billington .12 .30
355 Donald Dufresne .10 .25
356 Guy Hebert .12 .30
357 Neil Wilkinson .10 .25
358 Sandy McCarthy .10 .25
359 Aaron Ward RC .15 .40
360 Scott Thomas RC .10 .25
361 Corey Millen .10 .25
362 Matthew Barnaby .12 .30
363 Benoit Brunet .10 .25
364 Boris Mironov .10 .25
365 Doug Lidster .10 .25
366 Pavol Demitra .20 .50
367 Damian Rhodes RC .15 .40
368 Shawn Antoski .10 .25
369 Andy Moog .15 .40
370 Greg Johnson .10 .25
371 John Vanbiesbrouck .15 .40
372 Denis Savard .15 .40
373 Michel Goulet .10 .25
374 Dave Taylor .10 .25
375 Enrico Ciccone .10 .25
376 Sergei Zholtok .10 .25
377 Bob Errey .10 .25
378 Doug Brown .10 .25
379 Bill McDougall RC .10 .25
380 Pat Conacher .10 .25
381 Alexei Kasatonov .10 .25
382 Jason Arnott RC .30 .75
383 Jarkko Varvio .10 .25
384 Sergei Makarov .10 .25
385 Trevor Kidd .12 .30
386 Alexei Yashin .15 .40
387 Gerald Diduck .10 .25
388 Paul Ysebaert .10 .25
389 Jason Smith RC .12 .30
390 Jeff Norton .10 .25
391 Igor Larionov .10 .25
392 Pierre Sevigny .10 .25
393 Wes Walz .10 .25
394 Grant Ledyard .10 .25
395 Brad McCrimmon .10 .25
396 Martin Gelinas .10 .25
397 Paul Cavallini .10 .25
398 Brian Noonan .10 .25
399 Mike Lalor .10 .25
400 Dimitri Filimonov .10 .25
401 Andrei Lomakin .10 .25
402 Steve Junker RC .10 .25
403 Daren Puppa .10 .25
404 Jozef Stumpel .10 .25
405 Jeff Shantz RC .10 .25
406 Terry Yake .10 .25
407 Mike Peluso .10 .25
408 Vitali Karamnov .10 .25
409 Felix Potvin .30 .75
410 Steven King .10 .25
411 Roman Oksiuta RC .15 .40
412 Mark Greig .10 .25
413 Wayne McBean .10 .25
414 Nick Kypreos .10 .25
415 Dominic Lavoie .10 .25
416 Chris Simon RC .15 .40
417 Peter Popovic RC .15 .40
418 Gino Odjick .10 .25
419 Mike Rathje .10 .25
420 Keith Acton .10 .25
421 Bob Carpenter .12 .30
422 Steven Finn .10 .25
423 Ian Herbers RC .10 .25
424 Ted Drury .10 .25
425 Sergei Petrenko .10 .25
426 Mattias Norstrom RC .15 .40
427 Todd Ewen .10 .25
428 Jocelyn Thibault RC .15 .40
429 Robert Burakovsky RC .15 .40
430 Chris Terreri .12 .30
431 Michal Sykora RC .15 .40
432 Craig Ludwig .10 .25
433 Vesa Viitakoski RC .15 .40
434 Sergei Krivokrasov .10 .25
435 Darren McCarty RC .25 .60
436 Dean McAmmond .10 .25
437 J.J. Daigneault .10 .25
438 Vladimir Ruzicka .10 .25
439 Vlastimil Kroupa RC .15 .40
440 Checklist .05 .15

1993-94 Leaf Freshman Phenoms

COMPLETE SET (10) 4.00 10.00
1 Alexandre Daigle .20 .50
2 Chris Pronger 1.00 2.50
3 Chris Gratton .20 .50
4 Markus Naslund 1.00 2.50
5 Mikael Renberg .20 .50
6 Rob Niedermayer .20 .50
7 Jason Arnott .60 1.50
8 Jarkko Varvio .20 .50
9 Alexei Yashin .20 .50
10 Jocelyn Thibault .60 1.50

1993-94 Leaf Gold All-Stars

COMPLETE SET (10) 20.00 50.00
COMP.SERIES 1 (5) 10.00 25.00
COMP.SERIES 2 (5) 10.00 25.00
1 M.Lemieux/P.LaFontaine 4.00 10.00
2 C.Chelios/L.Murphy 1.25 3.00
3 B.Hull/T.Selanne 2.00 5.00
4 K.Stevens/Andreychuk 1.25 3.00
5 P.Roy/T.Barrasso 6.00 15.00
6 W.Gretzky/D.Gilmour 6.00 15.00
7 R.Bourque/P.Coffey 2.50 6.00
8 A.Mogilny/P.Bure 1.25 3.00
9 L.Robitaille/Shanahan 1.25 3.00
10 E.Belfour/F.Potvin 1.25 3.00

1993-94 Leaf Gold Rookies

COMPLETE SET (15) 5.00 12.00
1 Teemu Selanne .60 1.50
2 Joe Juneau .20 .50
3 Eric Lindros .75 2.00
4 Felix Potvin .75 2.00
5 Alexei Zhamnov .20 .50
6 Andrei Kovalenko .20 .50
7 Shawn McEachern .20 .50
8 Alexei Zhitnik .20 .50
9 Vladimir Malakhov .20 .50
10 Patrick Poulin .20 .50
11 Keith Tkachuk .40 1.00
12 Tommy Soderstrom .20 .50
13 Darius Kasparaitis .20 .50
14 Scott Niedermayer .20 .50
15 Darryl Sydor .20 .50

1993-94 Leaf Hat Trick Artists

COMPLETE SET (10) 8.00 20.00
COMP.SERIES 1 (5) 5.00 12.00
COMP.SERIES 2 (5) 3.00 8.00
1 M.Lemieux Title Card 2.00 5.00
2 Alexander Mogilny .40 1.00
3 Teemu Selanne .75 2.00
4 Mario Lemieux 2.00 5.00
5 Pierre Turgeon .40 1.00
6 Kevin Dineen .20 .50
7 Eric Lindros .75 2.00
8 Adam Oates .40 1.00
9 Kevin Stevens .20 .50
10 Steve Yzerman 2.00 5.00

1993-94 Leaf Mario Lemieux

COMPLETE SET (10) 8.00 20.00
COMP.SERIES 1 (5) 4.00 10.00
COMP.SERIES 2 (5) 4.00 10.00
COMMON LEMIEUX (1-10) 1.00 2.50
NNO Mario Lemieux AU/2000 60.00 120.00

1993-94 Leaf Painted Warriors

COMPLETE SET (10) 6.00 15.00
COMP.SERIES 1 (5) 4.00 10.00
COMP.SERIES 2 (5) 2.00 5.00
1 Felix Potvin .75 2.00
2 Curtis Joseph .60 1.50
3 Kirk McLean .30 .75
4 Patrick Roy 3.00 8.00
5 Grant Fuhr .40 1.00
6 Ed Belfour .60 1.50
7 Mike Vernon .30 .75
8 John Vanbiesbrouck .30 .75
9 Tom Barrasso UER .30 .75
10 Bill Ranford .30 .75

1993-94 Leaf Studio Signature

COMPLETE SET (10) 12.00 30.00
COMP.SERIES 1 (5) 10.00 20.00
COMP.SERIES 2 (5) 6.00 15.00
1 Doug Gilmour .40 1.00
2 Pat Falloon .40 1.00
3 Pat LaFontaine .75 2.00
4 Wayne Gretzky 5.00 12.00
5 Steve Yzerman 3.00 8.00
6 Patrick Roy 2.50 6.00
7 Jeremy Roenick 1.00 2.50
8 Brett Hull .75 2.00
9 Alexandre Daigle .25 .60
10 Eric Lindros .60 1.50

1994-95 Leaf

1 Mario Lemieux .60 1.50
2 Tony Amonte .12 .30
3 Steve Duchesne .10 .25
4 Glen Murray .12 .30
5 John LeClair .15 .40
6 Glen Wesley .10 .25
7 Chris Chelios .15 .40
8 Alexei Zhitnik .10 .25
9 Mike Modano .25 .60
10 Pavel Bure .15 .40
11 Mark Messier .30 .75
12 Rob Blake .15 .40
13 Tony Twist .10 .25
14 Glenn Anderson .12 .30
15 Keith Redmond .12 .30
16 Brett Hull .30 .75
17 Valeri Zelepukin .10 .25
18 Mike Richter .15 .40
19 Alexei Yashin .15 .40
20 Luc Robitaille .15 .40
21 Tim Sweeney .10 .25
22 Ted Drury .10 .25
23 Guy Carbonneau .10 .25
24 Stephane Richer .12 .30
25 Ulf Dahlen .10 .25
26 Fred Brathwaite .10 .25
27 Darius Kasparaitis .10 .25
28 Kris Draper .10 .25
29 Alexander Godynyuk .10 .25
30 Brent Sutter .12 .30
31 Josef Beranek .10 .25
32 Stephane Matteau .10 .25
33 Derek Plante .10 .25
34 Vesa Viitakoski .12 .30
35 Dave Ellett .10 .25
36 Martin Straka .10 .25
37 Dimitri Yushkevich .10 .25
38 John Tucker .10 .25
39 Rob Gaudreau .10 .25
40 Doug Weight .12 .30
41 Patrick Roy .40 1.00
42 Brian Bradley .10 .25
43 Bob Beers .10 .25
44 Dino Ciccarelli .12 .30
45 Dean Evason .10 .25
46 Ron Tugnutt .12 .30
47 Andy Moog .15 .40
48 Jason Dawe .10 .25
49 Ted Donato .10 .25
50 Ron Hextall .15 .40
51 Derek Armstrong RC .10 .25
52 Craig Janney .12 .30
53 Geoff Courtnall .10 .25
54 Mikael Renberg .12 .30
55 Theo Fleury .15 .40
56 Martin Brodeur .40 1.00
57 Mattias Norstrom .10 .25
58 David Sacco .10 .25
59 Jeff Reese .10 .25
60 Bill Ranford .12 .30
61 Dan Quinn .12 .30
62 Joe Juneau .10 .25
63 Jeremy Roenick .25 .60
64 Donald Audette .10 .25
65 Zdeno Ciger .10 .25
66 Cliff Ronning .10 .25
67 Steve Thomas .10 .25
68 Norm Maciver .10 .25
69 Vincent Damphousse .12 .30
70 John Vanbiesbrouck .15 .40
71 Andrei Kovalenko .10 .25
72 Dave Andreychuk .15 .40
73 Stu Barnes .10 .25
74 Jamie McLennan .12 .30
75 Rudy Poeschek .10 .25
76 Ken Wregget .12 .30
77 Ray Bourque .25 .60
78 Grant Fuhr .25 .60
79 Paul Cavallini .10 .25
80 Nelson Emerson .10 .25
81 Tim Cheveldae .12 .30
82 Mariusz Czerkawski RC .15 .40
83 Pat Peake .10 .25
84 Craig Billington .12 .30
85 Sean Burke .12 .30
86 Chris Gratton .10 .25
87 Andrei Trefilov .10 .25
88 Terry Yake .10 .25
89 Mark Recchi .20 .50
90 Igor Korolev .10 .25
91 Mark Tinordi .10 .25
92 Alexei Kovalev .12 .30
93 Bob Essensa .10 .25
94 Keith Tkachuk .15 .40
95 Pat Falloon .10 .25
96 John Slaney .10 .25
97 Alexei Zhamnov .12 .30
98 Jeff Norton .10 .25
99 Doug Gilmour .20 .50
100 Rick Tocchet .12 .30
101 Robert Kron .10 .25
102 Patrik Carnback .10 .25
103 Tom Barrasso .12 .30
104 Jari Kurri .12 .30
105 Iain Fraser .10 .25
106 Mike Donnelly .10 .25
107 Ray Sheppard .12 .30
108 Scott Young .10 .25
109 Kirk McLean .12 .30
110 Checklist .05 .15
111 Sergei Zubov .12 .30
112 Ivan Droppa .10 .25
113 Brendan Shanahan .15 .40
114 Michal Pivonka .10 .25
115 Pavol Demitra .20 .50
116 Doug Brown .10 .25
117 Valeri Kamensky .12 .30
118 Alexander Karpovtsev .10 .25
119 Alexandre Daigle .10 .25
120 Dominik Hasek .25 .60
121 Murray Craven .10 .25
122 Michal Sykora .10 .25
123 Aris Brimanis RC .10 .25
124 Benoit Hogue .10 .25
125 Arto Blomsten .12 .30
126 Russ Courtnall .10 .25
127 Bryan Marchment .12 .30
128 Jeff Hackett .10 .25
129 Kevin Miller .10 .25
130 Bryan Smolinski .10 .25
131 John Druce .12 .30
132 Roman Hamrlik .10 .25
133 Jason Arnott .12 .30
134 Chris Terreri .12 .30
135 Mike Gartner .20 .50
136 Darryl Sydor .10 .25
137 Lyle Odelein .12 .30
138 Martin Gelinas .10 .25
139 Mike Rathje .10 .25
140 Sylvain Cote .10 .25
141 Nicklas Lidstrom .15 .40
142 Guy Hebert .12 .30
143 Jozef Stumpel .10 .25
144 Owen Nolan .15 .40
145 Jesse Belanger .10 .25
146 Bill Guerin .15 .40
147 Mike Stapleton .12 .30
148 Steve Yzerman .40 1.00
149 Michael Nylander .12 .30
150 Rod Brind'Amour .12 .30
151 Jaromir Jagr .50 1.25
152 Darcy Wakaluk .12 .30
153 Sergei Nemchinov .10 .25
154 Wes Walz .10 .25
155 Sergei Fedorov .25 .60
156 Dan Laperriere .10 .25
157 Marty McInnis .10 .25
158 Chris Joseph .10 .25
159 Matt Martin .10 .25
160 Checklist .05 .15
161 Denis Tsygurov RC .15 .40
162 Stephan Lebeau .10 .25
163 Kirk Muller .10 .25
164 Shayne Corson .12 .30
165 Joe Sakic .30 .75
166 Denis Savard .15 .40
167 Kevin Dineen .10 .25
168 Paul Coffey .15 .40
169 Sandis Ozolinsh .10 .25
170 Stewart Malgunas .10 .25
171 Petr Klima .10 .25
172 Pat Verbeek .12 .30
173 Yan Kaminsky .10 .25
174 Marty McSorley .12 .30
175 Arturs Irbe .12 .30
176 Peter Popovic .10 .25
177 Brian Skrudland .10 .25
178 John Lilley .10 .25
179 Boris Mironov .10 .25
180 Garth Snow .10 .25
181 Alexei Kudashov .10 .25
182 Scott Mellanby .12 .30
183 Dale Hunter .10 .25
184 Tommy Soderstrom .12 .30
185 Claude Lemieux .15 .40
186 Felix Potvin .25 .60
187 Corey Millen .10 .25
188 Derek King .10 .25
189 Kelly Hrudey .12 .30
190 Dimitri Khristich .10 .25
191 Sylvain Turgeon .10 .25
192 John Gruden RC .10 .25
193 Mike Peca .12 .30
194 Vladimir Malakhov .10 .25
195 Mathieu Schneider .10 .25
196 Jeff Shantz .10 .25
197 Darren McCarty .15 .40
198 Craig Simpson .10 .25
199 Jarkko Varvio .15 .40
200 Gino Odjick .10 .25
201 Martin Lapointe .10 .25
202 Paul Ysebaert .10 .25
203 Mike McPhee .10 .25
204 John MacLean .12 .30
205 Ulf Samuelsson .10 .25
206 Garry Valk .10 .25
207 Tomas Sandstrom .10 .25
208 Curtis Joseph .20 .50
209 Mikhail Shtalenkov RC .10 .25
210 Darren Turcotte .10 .25
211 Markus Naslund .15 .40
212 Al Iafrate .10 .25
213 Jim Storm .12 .30
214 Dan Plante RC .10 .25
215 Brad May .10 .25
216 Nathan Lafayette .10 .25
217 Brian Noonan .10 .25
218 Brent Hughes .10 .25
219 Geoff Sanderson .12 .30
220 Checklist .05 .15
221 Eric Weinrich .10 .25
222 Greg Adams .10 .25
223 Dominic Roussel .12 .30
224 Daren Puppa .12 .30
225 Rob Niedermayer .12 .30
226 Todd Elik .10 .25
227 Donald Brashear RC .12 .30
228 Joe Nieuwendyk .12 .30
229 Tony Granato .10 .25
230 Kirk Maltby .10 .25
231 Jocelyn Thibault .12 .30
232 Shawn McEachern .10 .25
233 Teppo Numminen .10 .25
234 Johan Garpenlov .10 .25
235 Ron Francis .20 .50
236 Slava Kozlov .12 .30
237 Scott Niedermayer .15 .40
238 Sergei Krivokrasov .10 .25
239 Dave Manson .10 .25
240 Mike Ricci .10 .25
241 Chad Penney .10 .25
242 Calle Johansson .10 .25
243 Robert Reichel .10 .25
244 Igor Kravchuk .10 .25
245 Jason Smith .12 .30
246 Neal Broten .12 .30
247 Jeff Brown .10 .25
248 Jason Bowen .10 .25
249 Larry Murphy .12 .30
250 Gord Murphy .10 .25
251 Darrin Shannon .10 .25
252 Bobby Holik .10 .25
253 Zigmund Palffy .12 .30
254 Dmitri Mironov .10 .25
255 Adam Graves .10 .25
256 Alexander Mogilny .12 .30
257 Steve Smith .10 .25
258 Jim Montgomery .10 .25
259 Danton Cole .10 .25
260 Dave McLlwain .10 .25
261 German Titov .10 .25
262 Tom Chorske .10 .25
263 Grant Ledyard .10 .25
264 Garry Galley .10 .25
265 Vlastimil Kroupa .10 .25
266 Keith Primeau .12 .30
267 Cam Neely .15 .40
268 Chris Pronger .15 .40
269 Richard Matvichuk .10 .25
270 Steve Larmer .12 .30
271 James Patrick .10 .25
272 Joel Otto .10 .25
273 Todd Nelson .10 .25
274 Joe Sacco .10 .25
275 Jason York RC .10 .25
276 Andrew Cassels .10 .25
277 Peter Bondra .15 .40
278 Pat LaFontaine .15 .40
279 Nikolai Borschevsky .10 .25
280 Dave Mackey .10 .25
281 Cam Stewart .10 .25
282 Sergei Makarov .10 .25
283 Byron Dafoe RC .50 1.25
284 Joe Murphy .10 .25
285 Matthew Barnaby .12 .30
286 Derian Hatcher .10 .25
287 Jyrki Lumme .10 .25
288 Travis Green .12 .30
289 Milos Holan .10 .25
290 Ed Patterson .10 .25
291 Randy Burridge .10 .25
292 Brian Savage .10 .25
293 Stephane Quintal .10 .25
294 Zarley Zalapski .10 .25
295 Vitali Prokhorov .10 .25
296 Ed Belfour .15 .40
297 Yuri Khmylev .10 .25
298 Dean McAmmond .10 .25
299 Bob Corkum .10 .25
300 Darrin Madeley .10 .25
301 Brian Bellows .12 .30
302 Andrei Lomakin .10 .25
303 Anatoli Semenov .10 .25
304 Claude Lapointe .10 .25
305 Adam Oates .15 .40
306 Richard Smehlik .10 .25
307 Jim Dowd .10 .25
308 Mark Fitzpatrick .12 .30
309 Pierre Sevigny .10 .25
310 Glenn Healy .12 .30
311 Igor Larionov .10 .25
312 Aaron Ward .10 .25
313 Dale Hawerchuk .20 .50
314 Bob Kudelski .10 .25
315 Chris Osgood .25 .60
316 Trent Klatt .10 .25
317 Gary Suter .10 .25
318 Tie Domi .12 .30
319 Dave Gagner .12 .30
320 Kevin Smyth .10 .25
321 Philippe Bozon .12 .30
322 Trevor Kidd .12 .30
323 Warren Rychel .10 .25
324 Steven Rice .10 .25
325 Patrice Brisebois .10 .25
326 Gary Roberts .10 .25
327 Fredrik Olausson .10 .25
328 Andrei Nazarov .10 .25
329 Stephane Fiset .12 .30
330 Checklist .05 .15
331 Fred Knipscheer .10 .25
332 Shawn Chambers .10 .25
333 Kelly Buchberger .10 .25
334 Ray Ferraro .10 .25
335 Dirk Graham .10 .25
336 Ken Daneyko .10 .25
337 Mark Lamb .10 .25
338 Shaun Van Allen .10 .25
339 Chris Simon .10 .25
340 Brent Gilchrist .10 .25
341 Greg Gilbert .10 .25
342 Brent Severyn .10 .25
343 Craig Berube .10 .25
344 Randy Moller .10 .25
345 Wayne Gretzky 1.00 2.50
346 Shawn Anderson .10 .25
347 Mikael Andersson .10 .25
348 Jim Montgomery .10 .25
349 Scott Pearson .10 .25
350 Kevin Todd .10 .25
351 Ron Sutter .10 .25
352 Paul Kruse RC .10 .25
353 Doug Lidster .10 .25
354 Oleg Petrov .10 .25
355 Greg Johnson .10 .25
356 Kevin Stevens .12 .30
357 Doug Bodger .10 .25
358 Troy Mallette .10 .25
359 Keith Carney .10 .25
360 Petr Nedved .12 .30
361 Mark Janssens .10 .25
362 Teemu Selanne .30 .75
363 Scott Stevens .15 .40
364 Shane Churla .10 .25
365 John McIntyre .10 .25
366 Geoff Smith .10 .25
367 Pierre Turgeon .12 .30
368 Shawn Burr .10 .25
369 Kevin Hatcher .10 .25
370 Paul Ranheim .10 .25
371 Kevin Haller .10 .25

372 Scott Lachance .10 .25
373 Craig Muni .10 .25
374 Mike Ridley .10 .25
375 Joby Messier .10 .25
376 Thomas Steen .10 .25
377 Bruce Driver .10 .25
378 Mike Eastwood .10 .25
379 Brian Benning .10 .25
380 Dallas Drake .10 .25
381 Patrick Flatley .10 .25
382 Cam Russell .10 .25
383 Bobby Dollas .10 .25
384 Marc Bergevin .10 .25
385 Joe Mullen .12 .30
386 Chris Dahlquist .10 .25
387 Robert Petrovicky .10 .25
388 Yves Racine .10 .25
389 Adam Bennett .10 .25
390 Patrick Poulin .10 .25
391 Vladimir Konstantinov .12 .30
392 Frank Kucera .10 .25
393 Petr Svoboda .10 .25
394 Mike Sillinger .10 .25
395 Kris King .10 .25
396 Kelly Chase .10 .25
397 Peter Douris .10 .25
398 Bob Errey .10 .25
399 Ronnie Stern .10 .25
400 Randy McKay .10 .25
401 Benoit Brunet .10 .25
402 Gerald Diduck .10 .25
403 Brian Leetch .12 .30
404 Steve Heinze .10 .25
405 Jimmy Waite .10 .25
406 Nick Kypreos .10 .25
407 J.J. Daigneault .10 .25
408 Alexei Gusarov .12 .30
409 Paul Broten .10 .25
410 Drake Berehowsky .10 .25
411 Sandy McCarthy .10 .25
412 John Cullen .10 .25
413 Dan Quinn .12 .30
414 Dave Lowry .10 .25
415 Eric Lindros .25 .60
416 Igor Ulanov .10 .25
417 Bob Sweeney .10 .25
418 Jamie Macoun .10 .25
419 Brian Mullen .10 .25
420 Steve Leach .10 .25
421 Jamie Baker .10 .25
422 Uwe Krupp .10 .25
423 Steve Konowalchuk .10 .25
424 Craig Ludwig .10 .25
425 Bret Hedican .10 .25
426 Steve Dubinsky .10 .25
427 Rob Zamuner .10 .25
428 Dave Brown .10 .25
429 Robert Lang .10 .25
430 Dave Babych .10 .25
431 Scott Thornton .10 .25
432 Dave Archibald .10 .25
433 Eric Desjardins .12 .30
434 Jim Cummins .10 .25
435 Troy Loney .10 .25
436 Bob Carpenter .12 .30
437 Joe Reekie .10 .25
438 Mike Krushelnyski .10 .25
439 Jeff Odgers .10 .25
440 Checklist .05 .15
441 Brian Rolston .10 .25
442 Adam Deadmarsh .12 .30
443 Eric Fichaud RC .15 .40
444 Michel Petit .10 .25
445 Brett Lindros .10 .25
446 Pat Jablonski .10 .25
447 Janne Laukkanen .12 .30
448 Ray Whitney .10 .25
449 Tom Kurvers .10 .25
450 Phil Housley .12 .30
451 Viktor Kozlov .10 .25
452 Aaron Gavey .10 .25
453 Doug Zmolek .10 .25
454 Tony Twist .12 .30
455 Paul Kariya .15 .40
456 Vladislav Boulin RC .15 .40
457 Kevin Brown RC .15 .40
458 David Wilkie .12 .30
459 Jamie Pushor .12 .30
460 Glen Wesley .10 .25
461 Al MacInnis .20 .50
462 Bernie Nicholls .12 .30
463 Luc Robitaille .15 .40
464 Mike Vernon .12 .30
465 Alex Cherbayev .12 .30
466 Garth Butcher .10 .25
467 Todd Harvey .10 .25
468 Viktor Gordiouk .12 .30
469 Pat Neaton .12 .30
470 Jason Muzzatti .12 .30
471 Valeri Bure .10 .25
472 Kenny Jonsson .10 .25
473 Alexei Kasatonov .10 .25
474 Rick Tocchet .12 .30
475 Peter Forsberg .30 .75
476 Sean Hill .10 .25
477 Steven Rice .10 .25
478 David Roberts .10 .25
479 Justin Hocking RC .10 .25
480 Chris Therien .10 .25
481 Cale Hulse RC .12 .30
482 Jeff Friesen .10 .25
483 Brandon Convery .10 .25
484 Ian Laperriere RC .15 .40
485 Brent Grieve RC .10 .25
486 Valeri Karpov RC .10 .25
487 Steve Chiasson .10 .25
488 Jassen Cullimore .10 .25
489 Jason Wiemer RC .10 .25
490 Checklist .05 .15
491 Len Barrie .10 .25
492 Turner Stevenson .10 .25
493 Kelly Kisio .10 .25
494 Dwayne Norris .10 .25
495 Ron Hextall .15 .40
496 Jaroslav Modry .10 .25
497 Todd Gill .10 .25
498 Ken Sutton .10 .25
499 Sergio Momesso .15 .40
500 Dean Kennedy .10 .25
501 David Reid .10 .25
502 Jocelyn Lemieux .10 .25
503 Mark Osborne .10 .25
504 Mike Hough .10 .25
505 Todd Marchant .10 .25
506 Keith Jones .10 .25
507 Sylvain Lefebvre .10 .25
508 Sergei Zholtok .10 .25
509 Jay More .10 .25
510 Mike Craig .10 .25
511 Jason Allison .12 .30
512 Jim Paek .10 .25
513 Chris Tamer RC .10 .25
514 Craig MacTavish .10 .25
515 Mikko Makela .10 .25
516 Tom Fitzgerald .10 .25
517 Brent Fedyk .10 .25
518 Don Sweeney .10 .25
519 Kelly Miller .10 .25
520 Jiri Slegr .10 .25
521 Wayne Presley .10 .25
522 Mark Greig .10 .25
523 Doug Houda .10 .25
524 Kay Whitmore .10 .25
525 Craig Ferguson RC .10 .25
526 Kent Manderville .10 .25
527 Trevor Linden .15 .40
528 Jeff Beukeboom .10 .25
529 Adam Foote .10 .25
530 Mats Sundin .15 .40
531 Shjon Podein .10 .25
532 Louie DeBrusk .10 .25
533 Peter Zezel .10 .25
534 Greg Hawgood .10 .25
535 Pat Elynuik .10 .25
536 Mike Ramsey .10 .25
537 Bob Beers .10 .25
538 David Williams .10 .25
539 Philippe Boucher .10 .25
540 Rob Brown .10 .25
541 Marc Potvin .10 .25
542 Wendel Clark .25 .60
543 Alexander Semak .10 .25
544 Randy Wood .10 .25
545 Frank Musil .10 .25
546 Mike Peluso .10 .25
547 Gaetan Duchesne .10 .25
548 Curtis Leschyshyn .10 .25
549 Rob DiMaio .10 .25
550 Checklist .05 .15

1994-95 Leaf Crease Patrol

COMPLETE SET (10) 3.00 8.00
1 Patrick Roy 1.25 3.00
2 Ed Belfour .25 .60
3 Curtis Joseph .30 .75
4 Felix Potvin .30 .75
5 John Vanbiesbrouck .20 .50
6 Dominik Hasek .60 1.50
7 Kirk McLean .10 .30
8 Mike Richter .25 .60
9 Martin Brodeur .75 2.00
10 Bill Ranford .10 .30

1994-95 Leaf Fire on Ice

COMPLETE SET (12) 10.00 25.00
1 Sergei Fedorov 1.00 2.50
2 Jeremy Roenick .75 2.00
3 Pavel Bure .60 1.50
4 Wayne Gretzky 4.00 10.00
5 Doug Gilmour .30 .75
6 Eric Lindros .60 1.50
7 Joe Juneau .30 .75
8 Paul Coffey .60 1.50
9 Mario Lemieux 3.00 8.00
10 Alexander Mogilny .30 .75
11 Mike Gartner .30 .75
12 Teemu Selanne .60 1.50

1994-95 Leaf Gold Rookies

COMPLETE SET (15) 10.00 25.00
1 Martin Brodeur 3.00 8.00
2 Jason Arnott .75 2.00
3 Alexei Yashin .75 2.00
4 Chris Gratton .75 2.00
5 Alexandre Daigle .75 2.00
6 Mikael Renberg .75 2.00
7 Rob Niedermayer .75 2.00
8 Boris Mironov .75 2.00
9 Chris Pronger 1.25 3.00
10 Chris Osgood 1.25 3.00
11 Derek Plante .75 2.00
12 Pat Peake .75 2.00
13 Jason Allison .75 2.00
14 Bryan Smolinski .75 2.00
15 Jocelyn Thibault .75 2.00

1994-95 Leaf Gold Stars

COMPLETE SET (15) 60.00 150.00
1 S.Fedorov/W.Gretzky 15.00 30.00
2 D.Gilmour/J.Roenick 5.00 12.00
3 P.Roy/M.Richter 12.00 30.00
4 B.Hull/P.Bure 5.00 12.00
5 M.Messier/A.Yashin 5.00 12.00
6 R.Bourque/B.Leetch 5.00 12.00
7 C.Joseph/E.Belfour 5.00 12.00
8 M.Brodeur/D.Hasek 8.00 20.00
9 C.Neely/M.Renberg 4.00 10.00
10 M.Modano/J.Arnott 4.00 10.00
11 E.Lindros/M.Lemieux 8.00 20.00
12 S.Stevens/R.Blake 4.00 10.00
13 F.Potvin/J.Vanbiesbrouck 6.00 15.00
14 A.Oates/P.Lafontaine 4.00 10.00
15 J.Jagr/M.Recchi 4.00 10.00

1994-95 Leaf Leaf Limited Inserts

COMPLETE SET (28) 20.00 50.00
1 Guy Hebert .20 .50
2 Adam Oates .40 1.00
3 Dominik Hasek 1.00 2.50
4 Robert Reichel .20 .50
5 Jeremy Roenick .75 2.00
6 Mike Modano 1.00 2.50
7 Sergei Fedorov .75 2.00
8 Jason Arnott .20 .50
9 John Vanbiesbrouck .40 1.00
10 Chris Pronger .40 1.00
11 Wayne Gretzky 5.00 12.00
12 Patrick Roy 3.00 8.00
13 Martin Brodeur 2.00 5.00
14 Pierre Turgeon .20 .50
15 Mark Messier 1.00 2.50
16 Alexei Yashin .20 .50
17 Eric Lindros .75 2.00
18 Mario Lemieux 4.00 10.00
19 Joe Sakic 1.25 3.00
20 Brendan Shanahan .75 2.00
21 Arturs Irbe .20 .50
22 Chris Gratton .20 .50
23 Doug Gilmour .40 1.00
24 Pavel Bure .75 2.00
25 Joe Juneau .20 .50
26 Teemu Selanne .75 2.00
27 Paul Kariya .75 2.00
28 Peter Forsberg 2.00 5.00

1994-95 Leaf Phenoms

COMPLETE SET (10) 10.00 25.00
1 Jamie Storr .60 1.50
2 Brett Lindros 1.25 3.00
3 Peter Forsberg 5.00 12.00
4 Jason Wiemer .40 1.00
5 Paul Kariya 1.25 3.00
6 Oleg Tverdovsky .60 1.50
7 Eric Fichaud .60 1.50
8 Viktor Kozlov .40 1.00
9 Jeff Friesen .40 1.00
10 Valeri Karpov .40 1.00

1994-95 Leaf Limited

1 Mario Lemieux .75 2.00
2 Brett Hull .40 1.00
3 Ed Belfour .20 .50
4 Brian Rolston .15 .40
5 Garry Galley .12 .30
6 Steve Thomas .12 .30
7 Kevin Brown RC .20 .50
8 Doug Gilmour .25 .60
9 Bill Ranford .15 .40
10 Wayne Gretzky 1.25 3.00
11 Rob Niedermayer .15 .40
12 Larry Murphy .15 .40
13 Glen Wesley .12 .30
14 Pat Falloon .12 .30
15 Jocelyn Thibault .15 .40
16 Felix Potvin .30 .75
17 Mike Richter .20 .50
18 Jeff Brown .12 .30
19 Jesse Belanger .12 .30
20 Benoit Hogue .12 .30
21 Viktor Kozlov .12 .30
22 Chris Pronger .20 .50
23 Kirk McLean .15 .40
24 Oleg Tverdovsky .15 .40
25 Derian Hatcher .12 .30
26 Ray Sheppard .15 .40
27 Pat Verbeek .15 .40
28 Patrick Roy .50 1.25
29 Mariusz Czerkawski RC .20 .50
30 Ron Francis .25 .60
31 Wendel Clark .30 .75
32 Rob Blake .20 .50
33 Brian Leetch .15 .40
34 Dave Andreychuk .20 .50
35 Russ Courtnall .12 .30
36 Alexander Mogilny .15 .40
37 Kirk Muller .12 .30
38 Joe Juneau .12 .30
39 Robert Reichel .12 .30
40 Scott Niedermayer .20 .50
41 Owen Nolan .20 .50
42 Mats Sundin .20 .50
43 Sandis Ozolinsh .12 .30
44 Derek Plante .12 .30
45 Eric Fichaud RC .20 .50
46 Kevin Stevens .15 .40
47 Igor Larionov .12 .30
48 Mikael Renberg .15 .40
49 Cam Neely .20 .50
50 Brett Lindros .12 .30
51 Valeri Karpov RC .12 .30
52 Pierre Turgeon .15 .40
53 Doug Weight .15 .40
54 Geoff Sanderson .15 .40
55 Slava Kozlov .15 .40
56 Chris Gratton .12 .30
57 Bryan Smolinski .12 .30
58 Eric Lindros .30 .75
59 Alexei Kovalev .15 .40
60 Mike Modano .30 .75
61 Jeremy Roenick .60 1.50
62 Martin Straka .15 .40
63 Pat LaFontaine .20 .50
64 Vlastimil Kroupa .12 .30
65 Sergei Zubov .12 .30
66 Jason Arnott .15 .40
67 Petr Nedved .15 .40
68 Teemu Selanne .40 1.00
69 Geoff Courtnall .12 .30
70 Martin Brodeur .50 1.25
71 Mark Recchi .25 .60
72 John Vanbiesbrouck .25 .60
73 Adam Graves .12 .30
74 Arturs Irbe .15 .40
75 Paul Coffey .20 .50
76 Ulf Dahlen .12 .30
77 Phil Housley .15 .40
78 Rod Brind'Amour .15 .40
79 Al MacInnis .25 .60
80 Alexei Yashin .20 .50
81 Sergei Fedorov .30 .75
82 Joe Nieuwendyk .15 .40
83 Chris Chelios .25 .60
84 Ray Bourque .20 .50
85 Scott Stevens .20 .50
86 Jaromir Jagr .60 1.50
87 Alexandre Daigle .12 .30
88 Luc Robitaille .20 .50
89 Mark Messier .40 1.00
90 Vincent Damphousse .15 .40
91 Craig Janney .15 .40
92 John MacLean .20 .50
93 Steve Duchesne .12 .30
94 Dale Hawerchuk .25 .60
95 Curtis Joseph .25 .60
96 Chris Osgood .30 .75
97 Brendan Shanahan .20 .50
98 Jason Allison .15 .40
99 Theo Fleury .20 .50
100 Pavel Bure .20 .50
101 Mathieu Schneider .12 .30
102 Dominik Hasek .30 .75
103 Scott Mellanby .15 .40
104 Adam Oates .20 .50
105 Jari Kurri .15 .40
106 Joe Sakic .40 1.00
107 Paul Kariya .20 .50
108 Keith Tkachuk .20 .50
109 Daren Puppa .15 .40
110 Keith Primeau .15 .40
111 Alexei Zhitnik .15 .40
112 Trevor Linden .20 .50
113 Alexei Zhamnov .15 .40
114 Gary Roberts .12 .30
115 Kenny Jonsson .12 .30
116 Peter Forsberg .40 1.00
117 Rick Tocchet .15 .40
118 Aaron Gavey .12 .30
119 Jason Wiemer RC .12 .30
120 Steve Yzerman .50 1.25

1994-95 Leaf Limited Gold

COMPLETE SET (10) 40.00 100.00
1 Mario Lemieux 10.00 25.00
2 Brett Hull 5.00 12.00
3 Doug Gilmour 2.50 6.00
4 Eric Lindros 6.00 15.00
5 Paul Kariya 5.00 12.00
6 Jaromir Jagr 5.00 12.00
7 Wayne Gretzky 20.00 50.00
8 Jeremy Roenick 5.00 12.00
9 Sergei Fedorov 5.00 12.00
10 Pavel Bure 4.00 10.00

1994-95 Leaf Limited World Juniors Canada

COMPLETE SET (10) 30.00 60.00
1 Nolan Baumgartner 2.00 5.00
2 Eric Daze 2.00 5.00
3 Jeff Friesen 3.00 8.00
4 Todd Harvey 2.00 5.00
5 Ed Jovanovski 3.00 8.00
6 Jeff O'Neill 2.00 5.00
7 Wade Redden 4.00 10.00
8 Jamie Rivers 2.00 5.00
9 Ryan Smyth 6.00 15.00
10 Jamie Storr 2.00 5.00

1994-95 Leaf Limited World Juniors USA

COMPLETE SET (10) 20.00 40.00
1 Bryan Berard 2.00 5.00
2 Doug Bonner 2.00 5.00
3 Jason Bonsignore 2.00 5.00
4 Adam Deadmarsh 2.00 5.00
5 Rory Fitzpatrick 2.00 5.00
6 Sean Haggerty 2.00 5.00
7 Jamie Langenbrunner 4.00 8.00
8 Jeff Mitchell 2.00 5.00
9 Richard Park 2.00 5.00
10 Deron Quint 2.00 5.00

1995-96 Leaf

1 Mario Lemieux .60 1.50
2 Todd Harvey .10 .25
3 Blaine Lacher .12 .30
4 Alexei Zhitnik .10 .25
5 Cory Stillman .10 .25
6 Murray Craven .10 .25
7 Mike Kennedy .12 .30
8 Mike Vernon .12 .30
9 David Oliver .10 .25
10 Magnus Svensson RC .12 .30
11 Andrei Nikolishin .10 .25
12 Jamie Storr .12 .30
13 David Roberts .10 .25
14 Chris McAlpine RC .12 .30
15 Brett Lindros .12 .30
16 Pat Verbeek .12 .30
17 Tony Amonte .12 .30
18 Chris Therien .10 .25
19 Ken Wregget .12 .30
20 Peter Forsberg .30 .75
21 Jeff Friesen .12 .30
22 Patrice Tardif .12 .30
23 Jason Wiemer .12 .30
24 Kenny Jonsson .15 .40
25 Jassen Cullimore .10 .25
26 Sergei Gonchar .10 .25
27 Nikolai Khabibulin .10 .25
28 Oleg Tverdovsky .15 .40
29 Rick Tocchet .12 .30
30 Garry Galley .10 .25
31 German Titov .10 .25
32 Sergei Krivokrasov .10 .25
33 Sylvain Turgeon .10 .25
34 Sergei Fedorov .25 .60
35 Ralph Intranuovo .10 .25
36 Stu Barnes .10 .25
37 Mike Gartner .20 .50
38 Kevin Brown .12 .30
39 Valeri Bure .10 .25
40 Sergei Brylin .15 .40
41 Kirk Muller .12 .30
42 Mike Richter .15 .40
43 Stanislav Neckar .10 .25
44 Patrik Juhlin .10 .25
45 Ron Francis .20 .50
46 Janne Laukkanen .10 .25
47 Shean Donovan .10 .25
48 Igor Korolev .10 .25
49 Alexander Selivanov .12 .30
50 Frantisek Kucera .10 .25
51 Russ Courtnall .12 .30
52 Don Beaupre .12 .30
53 Michal Grosek .10 .25
54 Steve Rucchin .12 .30
55 Mariusz Czerkawski .10 .25
56 Dominik Hasek .25 .60
57 Trent Klatt .10 .25
58 Sergio Momesso .10 .25
59 Mark Lawrence .10 .25
60 Steve Yzerman .40 1.00
61 Todd Marchant .10 .25
62 Jesse Belanger .10 .25
63 Sean Burke .10 .25
64 Matt Johnson .12 .30
65 Mark Recchi .20 .50
66 Martin Brodeur .40 1.00
67 Mathieu Schneider .10 .25
68 Mark Messier .30 .75
69 Radim Bicanek .12 .30
70 Eric Desjardins .12 .30
71 Jaromir Jagr .50 1.25
72 Adam Deadmarsh .10 .25
73 Viktor Kozlov .12 .30
74 Jeff Norton .10 .25
75 Brantt Myhres RC .10 .25
76 Darby Hendrickson .10 .25
77 Roman Oksiuta .10 .25
78 Jim Carey .12 .30
79 Keith Tkachuk .15 .40
80 Valeri Karpov .10 .25
81 Adam Oates .15 .40
82 Eric Lindros .25 .60
83 Trevor Kidd .12 .30
84 Bernie Nicholls .12 .30
85 Craig Conroy RC .12 .30
86 Bill Ranford .12 .30
87 Scott Mellanby .12 .30
88 Geoff Sanderson .10 .25
89 Wayne Gretzky 1.00 2.50
90 Pierre Turgeon .12 .30
91 Stephane Richer .12 .30
92 Chris Marinucci RC .12 .30
93 Brian Leetch .12 .30
94 Steve Larouche .10 .25
95 John LeClair .15 .40
96 Dmitri Mironov .10 .25
97 Jocelyn Thibault .12 .30
98 Craig Janney .10 .25
99 Ian Laperriere .10 .25
100 Dino Ciccarelli .12 .30
101 Todd Warriner .12 .30
102 Kirk McLean .12 .30
103 Jason Allison .12 .30
104 Alexei Zhamnov .15 .40
105 Keith Jones .10 .25
106 Ray Bourque .25 .60
107 John Druce .10 .25
108 Scott Walker RC .10 .25
109 Joe Murphy .10 .25
110 Checklist (1-110) .05 .15
111 Philippe DeRouville .10 .25
112 Greg Adams .10 .25
113 Cam Neely .15 .40
114 Mike Peca .12 .30
115 Theo Fleury .20 .50
116 Jeremy Roenick .25 .60
117 Kevin Hatcher .12 .30
118 Ray Sheppard .12 .30
119 Jason Arnott .12 .30
120 Mark Fitzpatrick .12 .30
121 Brendan Shanahan .15 .40
122 Jari Kurri .15 .40
123 Shayne Corson .12 .30
124 Scott Stevens .15 .40
125 Steve Thomas .12 .30
126 Sergei Zubov .12 .30
127 Denis Savard .15 .40
128 Mikael Renberg .12 .30
129 Luc Robitaille .15 .40
130 Andrei Kovalenko .10 .25
131 Andrei Nazarov .10 .25
132 Denis Chasse .10 .25
133 Chris Gratton .10 .25
134 Benoit Hogue .12 .30
135 Pavel Bure .15 .40
136 Peter Bondra .15 .40
137 Teemu Selanne .30 .75
138 Darren Van Impe RC .10 .25
139 Dimitri Khristich .10 .25
140 Pat LaFontaine .15 .40
141 Phil Housley .15 .40
142 Chris Chelios .15 .40
143 Steve Duchesne .10 .25
144 Paul Coffey .15 .40
145 Doug Weight .15 .40
146 Gord Murphy .10 .25
147 Andrew Cassels .15 .40
148 Rob Blake .12 .30
149 Vladimir Malakhov .12 .30
150 Scott Niedermayer .15 .40
151 Patrick Flatley .10 .25
152 Adam Graves .12 .30
153 Alexei Yashin .12 .30
154 Rod Brind'Amour .15 .40
155 Joe Mullen .10 .25
156 Mike Ricci .12 .30
157 Ulf Dahlen .10 .25
158 Dave Manson .10 .25
159 Brian Bradley .10 .25
160 Felix Potvin .25 .60
161 Trevor Linden .15 .40
162 Michal Pivonka .10 .25
163 Nelson Emerson .10 .25
164 Joe Sacco .10 .25
165 Todd Elik .10 .25
166 Derek Plante .10 .25
167 Mike Sullivan .10 .25
168 Randy Wood .10 .25
169 Manny Fernandez .12 .30
170 Keith Primeau .15 .40
171 Marko Tuomainen .10 .25
172 John Vanbiesbrouck .15 .40
173 Darren Turcotte .10 .25
174 Tony Granato .10 .25
175 Brian Savage .10 .25
176 John MacLean .12 .30
177 Tommy Salo RC .25 .60
178 Steve Larmer .12 .30
179 Alexandre Daigle .12 .30
180 Petr Svoboda .10 .25
181 John Cullen .10 .25
182 Joe Sakic .30 .75
183 Sandis Ozolinsh .10 .25
184 Dale Hawerchuk .20 .50
185 Paul Ysebaert .10 .25
186 Larry Murphy .12 .30
187 Alexander Mogilny .12 .30
188 Joe Juneau .10 .25
189 Craig Martin RC .10 .25
190 Jason Marshall .10 .25
191 Don Sweeney .10 .25
192 Ron Hextall .15 .40
193 Steve Chiasson .10 .25
194 Steve Smith .10 .25
195 Lyle Odelein .10 .25
196 Ryan Smyth .12 .30
197 Rob Niedermayer .12 .30
198 Steven Rice .12 .30
199 Darryl Sydor .12 .30
200 Patrick Roy .40 1.00
201 Bill Guerin .15 .40
202 Scott Lachance .10 .25
203 Alexei Kovalev .12 .30
204 Ronnie Stern .10 .25
205 Kevin Dineen .12 .30
206 Ulf Samuelsson .10 .25
207 Wendel Clark .25 .60
208 Ray Whitney .12 .30
209 Brett Hull .30 .75
210 Slava Kozlov .12 .30
211 Doug Gilmour .20 .50
212 Mike Ridley .10 .25
213 Mike Torchia .10 .25
214 Tavis Hansen RC .10 .25
215 Dale Hunter .12 .30
216 Kevin Stevens .12 .30
217 Mike Donnelly .10 .25
218 Sylvain Cote .10 .25
219 Gary Suter .10 .25
220 Checklist (111-120) .05 .15
221 Richard Park .15 .40
222 Dave Gagner .10 .25
223 Jozef Stumpel .10 .25
224 Brad May .10 .25
225 Zarley Zalapski .10 .25
226 Eric Daze .30 .75
227 Mike Modano .25 .60
228 Nicklas Lidstrom .15 .40
229 Jason Bonsignore .10 .25
230 Robert Svehla RC .10 .25
231 Glen Wesley .10 .25
232 Jozef Beranek .10 .25
233 Geoff Courtnall .10 .25
234 Shawn Chambers .10 .25
235 Darius Kasparaitis .10 .25
236 Sergei Nemchinov .10 .25
237 Patrick Poulin .10 .25
238 Anatoli Semenov .12 .30
239 Bryan Smolinski .10 .25
240 Owen Nolan .15 .40
241 Pat Falloon .10 .25
242 Chris Pronger .15 .40
243 Daren Puppa .12 .30
244 Mats Sundin .15 .40
245 Jeff Brown .10 .25
246 Jeff Nelson .10 .25
247 Teppo Numminen .10 .25
248 Shaun Van Allen .10 .25
249 Yanic Perreault .15 .40
250 Brian Holzinger RC .30 .75
251 Paul Kruse .10 .25
252 Jeff Shantz .10 .25
253 Martin Straka .10 .25
254 Chris Osgood .15 .40
255 Joaquin Gage RC .12 .30
256 Dave Lowry .10 .25
257 Robert Kron .10 .25
258 Dan Quinn .10 .25
259 David Wilkie .10 .25
260 Valeri Zelepukin .10 .25
261 Derek King .12 .30
262 Darren Langdon RC .30 .75
263 Radek Bonk .12 .30
264 Karl Dykhuis .10 .25
265 Tomas Sandstrom .10 .25
266 Uwe Krupp .10 .25
267 Arturs Irbe .12 .30
268 Dallas Drake .10 .25
269 John Tucker .10 .25
270 Dave Andreychuk .10 .25
271 Guy Hebert .12 .30
272 Sandy Moger RC .10 .25
273 Craig Johnson .10 .25
274 Donald Audette .12 .30
275 Cory Cross .10 .25
276 Richard Smehlik .10 .25
277 Gary Roberts .12 .30
278 Todd Gill .10 .25
279 Derian Hatcher .10 .25
280 Slava Fetisov .10 .25
281 Curtis Joseph .20 .50
282 Johan Garpenlov .10 .25
283 Vladimir Konstantinov .12 .30
284 Ray Ferraro .10 .25
285 Turner Stevenson .10 .25
286 Neal Broten .10 .25
287 Jason Wiemer RC .12 .30
288 Mattias Norstrom .12 .30
289 Michel Picard .10 .25
290 Brent Fedyk .10 .25
291 Dimitri Yushkevich .10 .25
292 Sylvain Lefebvre .10 .25
293 Sergei Makarov .10 .25
294 Brian Rolston .10 .25
295 Roman Hamrlik .12 .30
296 Mark Wotton RC .10 .25
297 Alek Stojanov RC .10 .25
298 Calle Johansson .10 .25
299 Mike Eastwood .10 .25
300 Bob Corkum .10 .25
301 Petr Nedved .12 .30
302 Vincent Damphousse .12 .30
303 Brett Harkins RC .10 .25
304 Paul Kariya .25 .60
305 Joe Nieuwendyk .12 .30
306 Dennis Bonvie RC .10 .25
307 Jason Woolley .10 .25
308 Jimmy Carson .10 .25
309 Marty McSorley .12 .30
310 Craig Rivet RC .12 .30
311 Claude Lemieux .15 .40
312 Al MacInnis .20 .50
313 Gerald Diduck .10 .25
314 Randy McKay .10 .25
315 Bob Errey .10 .25
316 Rusty Fitzgerald RC .10 .25
317 Scott Young .10 .25
318 Igor Larionov .10 .25
319 Esa Tikkanen .10 .25
320 Darren McCarty .10 .25
321 Petr Klima .10 .25
322 Jon Rohloff .10 .25
323 Steve Konowalchuk .12 .30
324 Milos Holan .10 .25
325 Checklist (221-330) .05 .15
326 Ted Donato .10 .25
327 Grant Marshall .10 .25
328 Jyrki Lumme .10 .25
329 Ed Belfour .12 .30
330 Checklist (inserts) .05 .15
NNO M.Lemieux Redemption 6.00 15.00

1995-96 Leaf Fire On Ice

COMPLETE SET (12) 10.00 20.00
1 Pavel Bure .60 1.50
2 Eric Lindros .60 1.50
3 Alexei Zhamnov .30 .75
4 Paul Coffey .60 1.50
5 Theo Fleury .20 .50
6 Peter Forsberg 1.50 4.00
7 Sergei Fedorov .75 2.00
8 Mats Sundin .60 1.50
9 Brett Hull .75 2.00
10 Wayne Gretzky 5.00 12.00
11 Paul Kariya .60 1.50
12 Mikael Renberg .30 .75

1995-96 Leaf Freeze Frame

COMPLETE SET (8) 10.00 25.00
1 Jim Carey 1.00 2.50
2 Pierre Turgeon 1.00 2.50
3 Mikael Renberg 1.00 2.50
4 Jaromir Jagr 1.50 4.00
5 Alexei Zhamnov 1.00 2.50
6 New Jersey Devils 1.00 2.50
7 Mario Lemieux 4.00 10.00
8 A.Mogilny
P.Bure 2.00 5.00

1995-96 Leaf Gold Stars

COMPLETE SET (6) 10.00 20.00
1 D.Hasek
J.Carey 2.50 6.00
2 P.Coffey
C.Chelios 1.50 4.00
3 R.Bourque
B.Leetch 1.50 4.00
4 E.Lindros
A.Zhamnov 2.00 5.00
5 J.Jagr
T.Fleury 2.50 6.00
6 B.Hull
M.Renberg 1.50 4.00

1995-96 Leaf Lemieux's Best

COMPLETE SET (10) 20.00 40.00
COMMON CARD (1-10) 3.00 6.00

1995-96 Leaf Road To The Cup

COMPLETE SET (10) 5.00 10.00
1 Ray Whitney .30 .75
2 Martin Brodeur 1.50 4.00
3 Jaromir Jagr 1.00 2.50
4 Eric Lindros .60 1.50
5 Paul Coffey .60 1.50
6 Chris Chelios .60 1.50
7 Neal Broten .30 .75
8 Slava Kozlov .30 .75
9 Scott Niedermayer .30 .75
10 Claude Lemieux .30 .75

1995-96 Leaf Studio Rookies

COMPLETE SET (20) 15.00 30.00
1 Jim Carey 1.00 2.50
2 Peter Forsberg 2.50 6.00
3 Paul Kariya 1.50 4.00
4 David Oliver .75 2.00
5 Blaine Lacher 1.00 2.50
6 Oleg Tverdovsky .75 2.00
7 Jeff Friesen .75 2.00
8 Todd Marchant 1.00 2.50
9 Todd Harvey 1.00 2.50
10 Ian Laperriere .75 2.00
11 Eric Daze 1.00 2.50
12 Jason Bonsignore .75 2.00
13 Jamie Storr 1.00 2.50
14 Brian Holzinger 1.50 4.00
15 Brian Savage .75 2.00
16 Roman Oksiuta .75 2.00
17 Mariusz Czerkawski .75 2.00
18 Sergei Krivokrasov .75 2.00
19 Jason Wiemer .75 2.00
20 Radek Bonk .75 2.00

1996-97 Leaf

1 Sergei Fedorov .30 .75
2 Bill Ranford .15 .40
3 Oleg Tverdovsky .15 .40
4 Brad May .12 .30
5 Chris Pronger .20 .50
6 Martin Brodeur .50 1.25
7 Yanic Perreault .12 .30
8 Garry Galley .12 .30
9 Shawn McEachern .12 .30
10 Brian Bellows .15 .40
11 Ron Francis .25 .60
12 Mike Modano .30 .75
13 Steve Yzerman .50 1.25
14 Joe Mullen .15 .40
15 Pavel Bure .20 .50
16 Dino Ciccarelli .20 .50
17 Claude Lemieux .12 .30
18 Stephane Richer .15 .40
19 Dominik Hasek .30 .75
20 Adam Graves .12 .30
21 Joe Juneau .12 .30
22 Rob Niedermayer .15 .40
23 Zigmund Palffy .20 .50
24 Dave Andreychuk .20 .50
25 Steve Thomas .12 .30
26 Tom Barrasso .15 .40
27 Eric Desjardins .15 .40
28 Curtis Joseph .25 .60
29 Russ Courtnall .12 .30
30 Stu Barnes .12 .30
31 Mark Tinordi .12 .30

32 Gary Suter .12 .30
33 Greg Johnson .12 .30
34 Joe Nieuwendyk .15 .40
35 Norm Maciver .12 .30
36 Craig Janney .15 .40
37 Mark Recchi .25 .60
38 Patrick Roy .50 1.25
39 Petr Klima .12 .30
40 Ken Wregget .15 .40
41 Rod Brind'Amour .20 .50
42 Slava Fetisov .12 .30
43 Kirk McLean .15 .40
44 Pat LaFontaine .20 .50
45 Brett Hull .40 1.00
46 Chris Chelios .20 .50
47 Damian Rhodes .15 .40
48 Kevin Hatcher .12 .30
49 Uwe Krupp .12 .30
50 Bernie Nicholls .15 .40
51 Tommy Soderstrom .15 .40
52 Teemu Selanne .40 1.00
53 Mats Sundin .20 .50
54 Jeff Hackett .15 .40
55 Ulf Dahlen .12 .30
56 Dale Hunter .15 .40
57 Robert Kron .12 .30
58 Brian Bradley .12 .30
59 Pat Verbeek .12 .30
60 Kenny Jonsson .12 .30
61 Theo Fleury .40 1.00
62 Alexander Selivanov .12 .30
63 Nikolai Khabibulin .15 .40
64 Grant Fuhr .30 .75
65 Phil Housley .15 .40
66 Bill Lindsay .12 .30
67 Trevor Kidd .12 .30
68 Jim Carey .20 .50
69 Brian Skrudland .12 .30
70 Todd Krygier .12 .30
71 Petr Nedved .15 .40
72 Kirk Muller .12 .30
73 Daren Puppa .15 .40
74 Doug Gilmour .25 .60
75 Nicklas Lidstrom .25 .60
76 Zdeno Ciger .12 .30
77 Robert Svehla .12 .30
78 Andrew Cassels .12 .30
79 Vincent Damphousse .12 .30
80 Alexandre Daigle .12 .30
81 Tomas Sandstrom .12 .30
82 Brent Fedyk .12 .30
83 John LeClair .20 .50
84 Mario Lemieux .75 2.00
85 Sean Burke .12 .30
86 Cam Neely .20 .50
87 Jeff Friesen .12 .30
88 Guy Hebert .15 .40
89 Jon Casey .15 .40
90 Rick Tocchet .15 .40
91 Mike Gartner .25 .60
92 Tony Amonte .15 .40
93 Jason Dawe .12 .30
94 Chris Terreri .15 .40
95 Zarley Zalapski .12 .30
96 Martin Rucinsky .12 .30
97 Garth Snow .15 .40
98 Sylvain Lefebvre .12 .30
99 Andy Moog .20 .50
100 Larry Murphy .15 .40
101 Alexei Yashin .15 .40
102 Pat Falloon .12 .30
103 Greg Adams .12 .30
104 Igor Larionov .20 .50
105 Geoff Sanderson .15 .40
106 Jaromir Jagr .60 1.50
107 Alexei Zhamnov .15 .40
108 Mikael Renberg .15 .40
109 Kelly Hrudey .15 .40
110 Vladimir Konstantinov .15 .40
111 Brian Savage .12 .30
112 Adam Oates .20 .50
113 Teppo Numminen .12 .30
114 Ray Sheppard .15 .40
115 Michael Nylander .12 .30
116 Jozef Stumpel .12 .30
117 Ed Olczyk .12 .30
118 Roman Hamrlik .12 .30
119 Kris Draper .12 .30
120 Chris Gratton .15 .40
121 Randy Burridge .12 .30
122 Ray Bourque .30 .75
123 Jyrki Lumme .12 .30
124 Dale Hawerchuk .25 .60
125 Dave Lowry .12 .30
126 Curtis Leschyshyn .12 .30
127 Martin Gelinas .12 .30
128 Owen Nolan .20 .50
129 Radek Bonk .12 .30
130 Sergei Zubov .15 .40
131 Travis Green .15 .40
132 Scott Mellanby .15 .40
133 Keith Tkachuk .20 .50
134 Luc Robitaille .20 .50
135 Alexei Kovalev .15 .40
136 Doug Weight .20 .50
137 Benoit Hogue .12 .30
138 Cory Stillman .12 .30
139 Joe Sakic .40 1.00
140 Wayne Gretzky 1.25 3.00
141 Mike Ricci .12 .30
142 Kyle McLaren .12 .30
143 Deron Quint .12 .30
144 Ville Peltonen .12 .30
145 Todd Harvey .12 .30
146 Brendan Shanahan .20 .50
147 Mike Vernon .15 .40
148 Eric Lindros .30 .75
149 Rick Tabaracci .15 .40
150 Stephane Yelle .12 .30
151 Chris Osgood .20 .50
152 Corey Hirsch .15 .40
153 Todd Marchant .12 .30
154 Keith Primeau .15 .40
155 Alexei Zhitnik .12 .30
156 Felix Potvin .30 .75
157 Vitali Yachmenev .12 .30
158 Geoff Courtnall .12 .30
159 Peter Forsberg .40 1.00
160 Radek Dvorak .15 .40
161 Bryan McCabe .12 .30
162 Alexander Mogilny .15 .40
163 Shayne Corson .15 .40
164 Paul Coffey .20 .50
165 Brian Leetch .15 .40
166 Wendel Clark .30 .75
167 Aaron Gavey .12 .30
168 Dimitri Khristich .12 .30
169 Grant Marshall .12 .30
170 Valeri Kamensky .15 .40
171 Ryan Smyth .15 .40
172 Niklas Sundstrom .12 .30
173 Cliff Ronning .12 .30
174 Al MacInnis .25 .60
175 Scott Stevens .20 .50
176 Paul Kariya .20 .50
177 Rob Blake .20 .50
178 Mike Richter .20 .50
179 Jason Arnott .15 .40
180 Mark Messier .40 1.00
181 Scott Young .12 .30
182 Jocelyn Thibault .15 .40
183 Marcus Ragnarsson .12 .30
184 Darren Turcotte .12 .30
185 Joe Murphy .12 .30
186 Pierre Turgeon .15 .40
187 Trevor Linden .20 .50
188 Stephane Fiset .15 .40
189 Miroslav Satan .12 .30
190 Mathieu Schneider .12 .30
191 Jeremy Roenick .30 .75
192 Craig MacTavish .12 .30
193 John Vanbiesbrouck .20 .50
194 Ron Hextall .20 .50
195 John MacLean .15 .40
196 Vyacheslav Kozlov .15 .40
197 Sandis Ozolinsh .12 .30
198 Scott Niedermayer .12 .30
199 Ed Belfour .20 .50
200 Peter Bondra .20 .50
201 Jere Lehtinen .12 .30
202 Eric Daze .15 .40
203 Chad Kilger .12 .30
204 Saku Koivu .20 .50
205 Todd Bertuzzi .20 .50
206 Petr Sykora .12 .30
207 Valeri Bure .12 .30
208 Ed Jovanovski .15 .40
209 Jeff O'Neill .12 .30
210 Daniel Alfredsson .20 .50
211 Bryan Dafoe .15 .40
212 Brian Holzinger .12 .30
213 Martin Biron RC .25 .60
214 Anders Eriksson .12 .30
215 Landon Wilson .12 .30
216 Alexei Yegorov RC .20 .50
217 Jan Caloun RC .20 .50
218 David Sacco .12 .30
219 David Nemirovsky .12 .30
220 Anders Myrvold .12 .30
221 Tommy Salo .15 .40
222 Jan Vopat .12 .30
223 Steve Staios RC .20 .50
224 Patrick Labrecque .12 .30
225 Jamie Langenbrunner .12 .30
226 Denis Pederson .12 .30
227 Marek Malik .12 .30
228 Geoff Sarjeant .12 .30
229 Chris Ferraro .12 .30
230 Zdenek Nedved .12 .30
231 Wayne Primeau .12 .30
232 Daymond Langkow .15 .40
233 Marko Kiprusoff .12 .30
234 Niklas Sundblad .12 .30
235 Jamie Ram RC .20 .50
236 Jamie Rivers .12 .30
237 Steve Washburn RC .20 .50
238 Teemu Selanne CL .40 1.00
239 Steve Yzerman CL .50 1.25
240 Eric Lindros CL .30 .75

1996-97 Leaf Press Proofs

*VETS: 8X TO 20X BASIC CARDS
*ROOKIES: 4X TO 10X

1996-97 Leaf Fire On Ice

COMPLETE SET (15) 25.00 50.00
1 Mario Lemieux 6.00 15.00
2 Alexander Mogilny 1.25 3.00
3 Joe Sakic 5.00 12.00
4 Paul Kariya 2.00 5.00
5 Wayne Gretzky 12.50 30.00
6 Doug Weight 1.00 2.50
7 Zigmund Palffy 1.00 2.50
8 Eric Lindros 6.00 15.00
9 Teemu Selanne 1.50 4.00
10 Doug Gilmour 1.50 4.00
11 Jeremy Roenick 3.00 8.00
12 Steve Yzerman 6.00 15.00
13 Ed Jovanovski 1.00 2.50
14 Mike Modano 2.50 6.00
15 Mark Messier 3.00 8.00

1996-97 Leaf Gold Rookies

COMPLETE SET (10) 10.00 25.00
1 Ethan Moreau .75 2.00
2 Kevin Hodson .75 2.00
3 Jose Theodore 2.50 6.00
4 Peter Ferraro .75 2.00
5 Ralph Intranuovo .75 2.00
6 Nolan Baumgartner .75 2.00
7 Brandon Convery .75 2.00
8 Darcy Tucker 1.50 4.00
9 Eric Fichaud .75 2.00
10 Steve Sullivan 1.50 4.00

1996-97 Leaf Leather And Laces Promos

COMPLETE SET (20) 40.00 100.00
*PROMOS: .5X TO 1.2X BASIC INSERTS

1996-97 Leaf Leather And Laces

COMPLETE SET (20) 50.00 100.00
1 Joe Sakic 5.00 12.00
2 Keith Tkachuk 1.50 4.00
3 Brett Hull 3.00 8.00
4 Paul Coffey 2.00 5.00
5 Jaromir Jagr 4.00 10.00
6 Peter Forsberg 2.50 6.00
7 Zigmund Palffy 1.25 3.00
8 Wayne Gretzky 10.00 25.00
9 Pavel Bure 2.50 6.00
10 Eric Lindros 2.50 6.00
11 Alexander Mogilny 1.25 3.00
12 Trevor Linden 2.00 5.00
13 Jeremy Roenick 3.00 8.00
14 Doug Gilmour 2.00 5.00
15 Mike Modano 2.50 6.00
16 Sergei Fedorov 3.00 8.00
17 Brendan Shanahan 2.50 6.00
18 Pierre Turgeon 1.50 4.00
19 Ed Jovanovski 1.25 3.00
20 Saku Koivu 2.00 5.00

1996-97 Leaf Shut Down

COMPLETE SET (15) 50.00 100.00
1 Patrick Roy 10.00 25.00
2 John Vanbiesbrouck 4.00 10.00
3 Jocelyn Thibault 2.00 5.00
4 Ed Belfour 4.00 10.00
5 Curtis Joseph 4.00 10.00
6 Martin Brodeur 8.00 20.00
7 Damian Rhodes 1.50 4.00
8 Felix Potvin 6.00 15.00
9 Nikolai Khabibulin 3.00 8.00
10 Jim Carey 2.00 5.00
11 Mike Richter 3.00 8.00
12 Corey Hirsch 1.50 4.00
13 Chris Osgood 3.00 8.00
14 Ron Hextall 4.00 10.00
15 Daren Puppa 2.00 5.00

1996-97 Leaf Sweaters Away

COMPLETE SET (15) 40.00 100.00
*HOME/1000: .8X TO 2X AWAY/5000
1 Mario Lemieux 10.00 25.00
2 Patrick Roy 10.00 25.00
3 Eric Lindros 5.00 12.00
4 John Vanbiesbrouck 3.00 8.00
5 Paul Kariya 4.00 10.00
6 Martin Brodeur 6.00 15.00
7 Eric Daze 2.50 6.00
8 Mark Messier 4.00 10.00
9 Jim Carey 2.50 6.00
10 Brendan Shanahan 4.00 10.00
11 Sergei Fedorov 4.00 10.00
12 Brett Hull 4.00 10.00
13 Pavel Bure 4.00 10.00
14 Daniel Alfredsson 3.00 8.00
15 Saku Koivu 3.00 8.00

1996-97 Leaf The Best Of

COMPLETE SET (9) 20.00 50.00
1 Jaromir Jagr 6.00 15.00
2 Eric Daze 2.00 5.00
3 Eric Lindros 3.00 8.00
4 Chris Osgood 3.00 8.00
5 Keith Tkachuk 3.00 8.00
6 Nikolai Khabibulin 3.00 8.00
7 Doug Weight 2.00 5.00
8 Peter Forsberg 6.00 15.00
9 Jocelyn Thibault 2.00 5.00

1997-98 Leaf

1 Eric Lindros .30 .75
2 Dominik Hasek .30 .75
3 Peter Forsberg .40 1.00
4 Steve Yzerman .50 1.25
5 John Vanbiesbrouck .20 .50
6 Paul Kariya .20 .50
7 Martin Brodeur .50 1.25
8 Wayne Gretzky 1.25 3.00
9 Mark Messier .40 1.00
10 Jaromir Jagr .60 1.50
11 Brett Hull .40 1.00
12 Brendan Shanahan .20 .50
13 Ray Bourque .30 .75
14 Jarome Iginla .25 .60
15 Mike Modano .30 .75
16 Curtis Joseph .25 .60
17 Ed Jovanovski .12 .30
18 Teemu Selanne .40 1.00
19 Saku Koivu .20 .50
20 Eric Fichaud .15 .40
21 Paul Coffey .20 .50
22 Jeremy Roenick .30 .75
23 Owen Nolan .20 .50
24 Felix Potvin .30 .75
25 Alexander Mogilny .15 .40
26 Alexandre Daigle .12 .30
27 Chris Gratton .12 .30
28 Geoff Sanderson .15 .40
29 Dimitri Khristich .15 .40
30 Bryan Berard .12 .30
31 Vyacheslav Kozlov .15 .40
32 Jeff Hackett .12 .30
33 Bill Ranford .15 .40
34 Pat LaFontaine .20 .50
35 Joe Sakic .40 1.00
36 Niklas Sundstrom .15 .40
37 Martin Gelinas .12 .30
38 Mikael Renberg .15 .40
39 Trevor Linden .20 .50
40 Jozef Stumpel .12 .30
41 Joe Thornton CL (1-46) .30 .75
42 Jocelyn Thibault .15 .40
43 Pierre Turgeon .15 .40
44 Ron Francis .25 .60
45 Damian Rhodes .15 .40
46 Jamie Langenbrunner .15 .40
47 Chris Osgood .20 .50
48 Vaclav Varada .12 .30
49 Ryan Smyth .15 .40
50 Daren Puppa .15 .40
51 Petr Nedved .20 .50
52 Ron Hextall .20 .50
53 Joe Juneau .12 .30
54 Jim Campbell .12 .30
55 Zigmund Palffy .12 .30
56 Roman Turek .15 .40
57 Adam Deadmarsh .12 .30
58 Rob Niedermayer .12 .30
59 Alexei Yashin .15 .40
60 Pavel Bure .20 .50
61 Jason Arnott .15 .40
62 Nikolai Khabibulin .20 .50
63 Sean Burke .12 .30
64 Chris Chelios .20 .50
65 Mike Ricci .12 .30
66 Sergei Berezin .15 .40
67 Jaroslav Svejkovsky CL .15 .40
68 Brian Savage .12 .30
69 Roman Vopat .15 .40
70 Mike Richter .20 .50
71 Jim Carey .12 .30
72 Guy Hebert .15 .40
73 Keith Tkachuk .20 .50
74 Kirk McLean .15 .40
75 Janne Niinimaa .15 .40
76 Roman Hamrlik .12 .30
77 Darcy Tucker .20 .50
78 Pat Verbeek .15 .40
79 Hnat Domenichelli .15 .40
80 Doug Gilmour .25 .60
81 Mike Grier .15 .40
82 Ken Wregget .12 .30
83 Dino Ciccarelli .20 .50
84 Steve Sullivan .15 .40
85 Anson Carter .12 .30
86 Steve Shields RC .20 .50
87 Ed Belfour .20 .50
88 Darren McCarty .15 .40
89 Adam Graves .12 .30
90 Chris Pronger .20 .50
91 Peter Bondra .20 .50
92 Oleg Tverdovsky .15 .40
93 Stephane Fiset .15 .40
94 Mike Vernon .15 .40
95 Scott Lachance .15 .40
96 Corey Schwab .15 .40
97 Eric Daze .12 .30
98 Jere Lehtinen .15 .40
99 Donald Audette .15 .40
100 John LeClair .20 .50
101 Steve Rucchin .15 .40
102 Jeff Friesen .15 .40
103 Daymond Langkow .12 .30
104 Mike Dunham .15 .40
105 Marc Denis CL .20 .50
106 Andrew Cassels .12 .30
107 Mike Peca .15 .40
108 Joe Nieuwendyk .15 .40
109 Vincent Damphousse .15 .40
110 Scott Mellanby .15 .40
111 Patrick Lalime .15 .40
112 Derek Plante .15 .40
113 Wade Redden .12 .30
114 Marcel Cousineau .15 .40
115 Ray Sheppard .15 .40
116 Dave Andreychuk .20 .50
117 Brian Leetch .15 .40
118 Sandis Ozolinsh .12 .30
119 Keith Primeau .15 .40
120 Brian Holzinger .15 .40
121 Luc Robitaille .20 .50
122 Jose Theodore .20 .50
123 Grant Fuhr .30 .75
124 Dainius Zubrus .15 .40
125 Rod Brind'Amour .20 .50
126 Trevor Kidd .12 .30
127 Mark Recchi .25 .60
128 Patrick Roy .50 1.25
129 Kevin Hatcher .12 .30
130 Adam Oates .20 .50
131 Doug Weight .20 .50
132 Vaclav Prospal RC .15 .40
133 Harry York .15 .40
134 Todd Bertuzzi .20 .50
135 Sergei Fedorov .30 .75
136 Theo Fleury .25 .60
137 Chad Kilger .15 .40
138 Jamie Storr .15 .40
139 Tony Amonte .15 .40
140 Rem Murray .12 .30
141 Chris O'Sullivan .15 .40
142 Mats Sundin .20 .50
143 Ethan Moreau .12 .30
144 Derian Hatcher .15 .40
145 Daniel Alfredsson .20 .50
146 Corey Hirsch .15 .40
147 Landon Wilson .12 .30
148 Marc Denis GLR .20 .50
149 Boyd Devereaux GLR .15 .40
150 Joe Thornton GLR .30 .75
151 Sergei Samsonov GLR .15 .40
152 Alyn McCauley GLR .15 .40
153 Erik Rasmussen GLR .15 .40
154 Patrick Marleau GLR .20 .50
155 Olli Jokinen GLR RC .25 .60
156 Chris Phillips GLR .15 .40
157 Tomas Vokoun GLR RC .20 .50
158 Chris Dingman RC GLR .20 .50
159 Daniel Cleary GLR .15 .40
160 Juha Lind GLR RC .20 .50
161 Jean-Yves Leroux RC GLR .20 .50
162 Brad Isbister GLR .15 .40
163 Vadim Sharifijanov GLR .15 .40
164 Alexei Morozov GLR .15 .40
165 Vaclav Prospal GLR .15 .40
166 Vaclav Varada GLR .12 .30
167 Jaroslav Svejkovsky GLR .15 .40
168 Eric Lindros GM .30 .75
169 Dominik Hasek GM .30 .75
170 Peter Forsberg GM .40 1.00
171 Steve Yzerman GM .50 1.25
172 John Vanbiesbrouck GM .20 .50
173 Paul Kariya GM .20 .50
174 Martin Brodeur GM .50 1.25
175 Wayne Gretzky GM 1.25 3.00
176 Mark Messier GM .40 1.00
177 Jaromir Jagr GM .60 1.50
178 Brett Hull GM .40 1.00
179 Brendan Shanahan GM .20 .50
180 Jarome Iginla GM .25 .60
181 Mike Modano GM .30 .75
182 Teemu Selanne GM .40 1.00
183 Bryan Berard GM .12 .30
184 Ryan Smyth GM .15 .40
185 Keith Tkachuk GM .20 .50
186 Dainius Zubrus GM .15 .40
187 Patrick Roy GM .50 1.25
188 Trevor Linden DIL .20 .50
189 Trevor Linden DIL .20 .50
190 Trevor Linden DIL .20 .50
191 Trevor Linden DIL .20 .50
192 Trevor Linden DIL .20 .50
193 Trevor Linden DIL .20 .50
194 Trevor Linden DIL .20 .50
195 Trevor Linden DIL .20 .50
196 Trevor Linden DIL .20 .50
197 Trevor Linden DIL .20 .50
198 Chris Phillips CL .15 .40
199 Sergei Samsonov CL .15 .40
200 Daniel Cleary CL .15 .40
P5 Felix Potvin PROMO .60 1.50
P6 Martin Brodeur PROMO 3.00 8.00
P10 Jim Carey PROMO .50 1.25
NNO Trevor Linden AU/500 15.00 30.00

1997-98 Leaf Fractal Matrix

1 Eric Lindros GX/50* 15.00 40.00
2 Dominik Hasek GZ/350* 12.00 30.00
3 Peter Forsberg GZ/350* 8.00 20.00
4 Steve Yzerman GZ/350* 10.00 25.00
5 John Vanbiesbrouck GZ/350* 6.00 15.00
6 Paul Kariya GX/50* 20.00 50.00
7 Martin Brodeur GZ/350* 10.00 25.00
8 Wayne Gretzky GX/50* 60.00 150.00
9 Mark Messier GY/250* 5.00 12.00
10 Jaromir Jagr GZ/350* 8.00 20.00
11 Brett Hull GY/250* 6.00 15.00
12 Brendan Shanahan GZ/350* 6.00 15.00
13 Ray Bourque GY/250* 10.00 25.00
14 Jarome Iginla GY/250* 6.00 15.00
15 Mike Modano GY/250* 6.00 15.00
16 Curtis Joseph GY/250* 5.00 12.00
17 Ed Jovanovski SX/500* 2.50 6.00
18 Teemu Selanne GZ/350* 6.00 15.00
19 Saku Koivu GY/250* 5.00 12.00
20 Eric Fichaud SZ/800* 2.00 5.00
21 Paul Coffey SX/500* 3.00 8.00
22 Jeremy Roenick SX/500* 3.00 8.00
23 Owen Nolan BX/1400* 1.00 2.50
24 Felix Potvin GY/250* 8.00 20.00
25 Alexander Mogilny SZ/800* 2.50 6.00
26 Alexandre Daigle SX/500* 2.50 6.00
27 Chris Gratton SX/500* 2.00 5.00
28 Geoff Sanderson SX/500* 2.50 6.00
29 Dimitri Khristich SX/500* 2.00 5.00
30 Bryan Berard GY/250* 3.00 8.00
31 Vyacheslav Kozlov BX/1400* .75 2.00
32 Jeff Hackett BY/1600* .75 2.00
33 Bill Ranford BY/1600* .75 2.00
34 Pat LaFontaine SY/700* 2.50 6.00
35 Joe Sakic GY/250* 12.00 30.00
36 Niklas Sundstrom BX/1400* .75 2.00
37 Martin Gelinas BX/1400* .75 2.00
38 Mikael Renberg BX/1400* .75 2.00
39 Trevor Linden BX/1400* 1.25 3.00
40 Jozef Stumpel BY/1600* .75 2.00
41 Joe Thornton CL SZ/800* 4.00 10.00
42 Jocelyn Thibault GY/250* 4.00 10.00
43 Pierre Turgeon BX/1400* 1.00 2.50
44 Ron Francis BX/1400* 1.25 3.00
45 Damian Rhodes SY/700* 2.00 5.00
46 Jamie Langenbrunner SY/700* 2.50 6.00
47 Chris Osgood SZ/800* 3.00 8.00
48 Vaclav Varada SX/500* 2.00 5.00
49 Ryan Smyth GZ/350* 3.00 8.00
50 Darren Puppa BX/1400* .75 2.00
51 Petr Nedved BX/1400* .75 2.00
52 Ron Hextall BX/1400* 1.25 3.00
53 Joe Juneau BX/1400* .75 2.00
54 Jim Campbell SY/700* 2.00 5.00
55 Zigmund Palffy SZ/800* 2.50 6.00
56 Roman Turek BX/1400* .75 2.00
57 Adam Deadmarsh GY/250* 3.00 8.00
58 Rob Niedermayer BX/1400* 1.00 2.50
59 Alexei Yashin GY/250* 4.00 10.00
60 Pavel Bure GY/250* 5.00 12.00
61 Jason Arnott GY/250* 4.00 10.00
62 Nikolai Khabibulin SY/700* 2.50 6.00
63 Sean Burke SY/700* 2.50 6.00
64 Chris Chelios SX/500* 2.50 6.00
65 Mike Ricci BX/1400* 1.00 2.50
66 Sergei Berezin SY/700* 2.00 5.00
67 Jaroslav Svejkovsky GY CL/250* 3.00 8.00
68 Brian Savage BX/1400* .75 2.00
69 Roman Vopat BX/1400* .75 2.00
70 Mike Richter SX/500* 3.00 8.00
71 Jim Carey SY/700* 2.50 6.00
72 Guy Hebert BY/1600* 1.00 2.50
73 Keith Tkachuk GY/250* 5.00 12.00
74 Kirk McLean BX/1400* 1.00 2.50
75 Janne Niinimaa SY/700* 2.00 5.00
76 Roman Hamrlik SY/700* 2.50 6.00
77 Darcy Tucker SY/700* 2.00 5.00
78 Pat Verbeek BX/1400* .75 2.00
79 Hnat Domenichelli BX/1400* .75 2.00
80 Doug Gilmour SY/700* 3.00 8.00
81 Mike Grier GY/250* 3.00 8.00
82 Ken Wregget BX/1400* .75 2.00
83 Dino Ciccarelli BX/1400* 1.00 2.50
84 Steve Sullivan BX/1400* .75 2.00
85 Anson Carter SX/500* 2.00 5.00
86 Steve Shields BY/1600* .75 2.00
87 Ed Belfour SY/700* 3.00 8.00
88 Darren McCarty BX/1400* .75 2.00
89 Adam Graves BX/1400* .75 2.00
90 Chris Pronger BX/1400* 1.00 2.50
91 Peter Bondra SY/700* 2.50 6.00
92 Oleg Tverdovsky SY/700* 2.00 5.00
93 Stephane Fiset BX/1400* .75 2.00
94 Mike Vernon BY/1600* 1.25 3.00
95 Scott Lachance BX/1400* .75 2.00
96 Corey Schwab BX/1400* .75 2.00
97 Eric Daze BY/1600* .75 2.00
98 Jere Lehtinen BX/1400* 1.00 2.50
99 Donald Audette BX/1400* .75 2.00
100 John LeClair GY/250* 5.00 12.00
101 Steve Rucchin BX/1400* .75 2.00
102 Jeff Friesen SX/500* 2.00 5.00
103 Daymond Langkow SX/500* 2.00 5.00
104 Mike Dunham SY/700* 2.00 5.00
105 Marc Denis
BZ CL (93-138)/1700* .75 2.00
106 Andrew Cassels BX/1400* .75 2.00
107 Mike Peca BX/1400* 1.00 2.50
108 Joe Nieuwendyk BX/1400* 1.25 3.00
109 Vincent Damphousse BX/1400* 1.00 2.50
110 Scott Mellanby BX/1400* .75 2.00
111 Patrick Lalime BX/1400* .75 2.00
112 Derek Plante SY/700* 2.00 5.00
113 Wade Redden SY/700* 2.00 5.00
114 Marcel Cousineau BY/1600* .75 2.00
115 Ray Sheppard BX/1400* .75 2.00
116 Dave Andreychuk BX/1400* 1.00 2.50
117 Brian Leetch GY/250* 5.00 12.00
118 Sandis Ozolinsh BY/1600* .75 2.00
119 Keith Primeau BX/1400* 1.00 2.50
120 Brian Holzinger BX/1400* .75 2.00
121 Luc Robitaille BX/1400* 1.00 2.50
122 Jose Theodore SX/500* 2.50 6.00
123 Grant Fuhr SY/700* 3.00 8.00
124 Dainius Zubrus GY/250* 3.00 8.00
125 Rod Brind'Amour BX/1400* 1.00 2.50
126 Trevor Kidd SY/700* 2.00 5.00
127 Mark Recchi BX/1400* 1.00 2.50
128 Patrick Roy GY/250* 20.00 50.00
129 Kevin Hatcher BX/1400* .75 2.00
130 Adam Oates SY/700* 3.00 8.00
131 Doug Weight SX/500* 2.50 6.00
132 Vaclav Prospal SX/500* 2.00 5.00
133 Harry York SY/700* 2.00 5.00
134 Todd Bertuzzi BX/1400* .75 2.00
135 Sergei Fedorov GY/250* 12.00 30.00
136 Theo Fleury SX/500* 3.00 8.00
137 Chad Kilger BY/1600* .75 2.00
138 Jamie Storr SX/500* 2.00 5.00
139 Tony Amonte BY/1600* .75 2.00
140 Rem Murray BY/1600* .75 2.00
141 Chris O'Sullivan BX/1400* .75 2.00
142 Mats Sundin SZ/800* 3.00 8.00
143 Ethan Moreau SZ/800* 2.00 5.00
144 Derian Hatcher SY/700* 2.50 6.00
145 Daniel Alfredsson SY/700* 2.50 6.00
146 Corey Hirsch BX/1400* .75 2.00
147 Landon Wilson BX/1400* .75 2.00
148 Marc Denis GLR GY/250* 3.00 8.00
149 Boyd Devereaux GLR BZ/1700* .75 2.00
150 Joe Thornton GLR GX/50* 25.00 50.00
151 Sergei Samsonov GLR GZ/350* 6.00 15.00
152 Alyn McCauley GLR SZ/800* 2.00 5.00
153 Erik Rasmussen GLR SZ/800* 2.00 5.00
154 Patrick Marleau GLR SX/500* 2.50 6.00
155 Olli Jokinen GLR BX/1400* 2.50 6.00
156 Chris Phillips GLR GY/250* 3.00 8.00
157 Tomas Vokoun GLR BX/1400* 1.00 2.50
158 Chris Dingman GLR SZ/800* 2.00 5.00
159 Daniel Cleary GLR GY/250* 3.00 8.00
160 Juha Lind GLR BX/1400* .75 2.00
161 Jean-Yves Leroux GLR BY/1600* .75 2.00
162 Brad Isbister GLR SY/700* 2.00 5.00
163 Vadim Sharifijanov GLR BX/1400* .75 2.00
164 Alexei Morozov GLR SX/500* 2.00 5.00
165 Vaclav Prospal GLR BX/1400* .75 2.00
166 Vaclav Varada GLR BY/1600* .75 2.00
167 Jaro. Svejkovsky GLR BZ/1700* .75 2.00
168 Eric Lindros GM SY/700* 4.00 10.00
169 Dominik Hasek GM BY/1600* 2.50 6.00
170 Peter Forsberg GM BY/1600* 3.00 8.00
171 Steve Yzerman GM SY/700* 10.00 25.00
172 J.Vanbiesbrouck GM BX/1400* 1.50 4.00
173 Paul Kariya GM SY/700* 5.00 12.00
174 Martin Brodeur GM BZ/1700* 3.00 8.00
175 Wayne Gretzky GM SY/700* 15.00 40.00
176 Mark Messier GM BX/1400* 1.25 3.00
177 Jaromir Jagr GM BZ/1700* 2.00 5.00
178 Brett Hull GM BX/1400* 2.00 5.00
179 Brendan Shanahan GM BY/1600* 1.25 3.00
180 Jarome Iginla GM BX/1400* 1.50 4.00
181 Mike Modano GM BY/1600* 2.00 5.00
182 Teemu Selanne GM BY/1600* 1.25 3.00
183 Bryan Berard GM BY/1600* .75 2.00
184 Ryan Smyth GM SY/700* 2.50 6.00
185 Keith Tkachuk GM BX/1400* 1.25 3.00
186 Dainius Zubrus GM BX/1400* .75 2.00
187 Patrick Roy GM BX/1400* 6.00 15.00
188 Trevor Linden BX/1400* 1.00 2.50
189 Trevor Linden BX/1400* 1.00 2.50
190 Trevor Linden BX/1400* 1.00 2.50
191 Trevor Linden BX/1400* 1.00 2.50
192 Trevor Linden BX/1400* 1.00 2.50
193 Trevor Linden BX/1400* 1.00 2.50
194 Trevor Linden BX/1400* 1.00 2.50
195 Trevor Linden BX/1400* 1.00 2.50
196 Trevor Linden BX/1400* 1.00 2.50
197 Trevor Linden BX/1400* 1.00 2.50
198 Chris Phillips BX CL/1400* .75 2.00
199 Sergei Samsonov BX CL/1400* 1.00 2.50
200 Daniel Cleary BX CL/1400* .75 2.00

1997-98 Leaf Fractal Matrix Die Cuts

BX/400: 1X TO 2.5X BX/1400*
BY/200: 2X TO 5X BY/1600*
BZ/100: 3X TO 8X BZ/1700*
SX/400: .4X TO 1X SX/500*
SY/200: 1X TO 2.5X SY/700*
SZ/100: 1.2X TO 3X SZ/800*
GX/400: .15X TO .4X GX/50*
GY/200: .4X TO 1X GY/250*
GZ/100: .6X TO 1.5X GZ/350*

1997-98 Leaf Banner Season

COMPLETE SET (24) 30.00 80.00
1 Paul Kariya 1.50 4.00
2 Eric Lindros 1.50 4.00
3 Wayne Gretzky 10.00 25.00
4 Jaromir Jagr 2.50 6.00
5 Steve Yzerman 8.00 20.00
6 Brendan Shanahan 1.50 4.00
7 John LeClair 1.50 4.00
8 Teemu Selanne 1.50 4.00
9 Mike Modano 2.50 6.00
10 Ryan Smyth 1.25 3.00
11 Brett Hull 2.00 5.00
12 Zigmund Palffy 1.25 3.00
13 Peter Forsberg 4.00 10.00
14 Keith Tkachuk 1.50 4.00
15 Saku Koivu 1.50 4.00
16 Sergei Fedorov 2.50 6.00
17 Brian Leetch 1.50 4.00
18 Bryan Berard .50 1.25
19 Mats Sundin 1.50 4.00
20 Jarome Iginla 2.00 5.00
21 Sergei Berezin .50 1.25
22 Dainius Zubrus 1.50 4.00
23 Mike Grier .50 1.25
24 Joe Sakic 3.00 8.00

1997-98 Leaf Fire On Ice

COMPLETE SET (16) 75.00 150.00
1 Wayne Gretzky 12.00 30.00
2 Eric Lindros 4.00 10.00
3 Jaromir Jagr 4.00 10.00
4 Steve Yzerman 8.00 25.00
5 Brendan Shanahan 2.50 20.00
6 Mike Modano 5.00 12.00
7 Joe Sakic 6.00 15.00
8 Pavel Bure 3.00 8.00
9 Ryan Smyth 2.00 5.00
10 Teemu Selanne 2.50 6.00
11 Mark Messier 2.50 6.00
12 Peter Forsberg 6.00 15.00
13 Dainius Zubrus 2.50 6.00
14 Joe Thornton 12.00 30.00
15 Sergei Samsonov 12.00 30.00
16 Paul Kariya 2.50 6.00

1997-98 Leaf Lindros Collection

1 E.Lindros Home Jersey 30.00 60.00
2 E.Lindros Away Jersey 30.00 60.00
3 E.Lindros Stick 25.00 60.00
4 E.Lindros Glove 25.00 60.00
5 E.Lindros Stirrups 25.00 60.00

1997-98 Leaf Pipe Dreams

COMPLETE SET (16) 50.00 100.00
*PROMOS: .3X TO .8X BASIC INSERTS
1 Dominik Hasek 8.00 20.00
2 John Vanbiesbrouck 3.00 8.00
3 Patrick Roy 12.00 30.00
4 Curtis Joseph 3.00 8.00
5 Felix Potvin 4.00 10.00
6 Martin Brodeur 10.00 25.00
7 Guy Hebert 1.50 4.00
8 Mike Richter 3.00 8.00
9 Jose Theodore 5.00 12.00
10 Jim Carey 1.50 4.00
11 Damian Rhodes 1.50 4.00
12 Jocelyn Thibault 1.50 4.00
13 Nikolai Khabibulin 3.00 8.00
14 Chris Osgood 3.00 8.00
15 Eric Fichaud 1.50 4.00
16 Mike Dunham 1.50 4.00

2017-18 Leaf '90 Leaf Autographs Magenta

BAAK1 Alexei Kovalev/30 8.00 20.00
BABB1 Brian Bellows/30 10.00 25.00
BADA1 Donald Audette/30 8.00 20.00
BAJK1 Joe Kocur/30 10.00 25.00
BAJR1 Jeremy Roenick/25 15.00 40.00
BAJS1 Joe Sakic/20 20.00 50.00
BAMN1 Mats Naslund/30 6.00 15.00
BAMR1 Manon Rheaume/20 25.00 60.00

2017-18 Leaf '90 Memorabilia

*RED/20-25: .6X TO 1.5X BASIC INSERTS
BM01 Adam Oates 3.00 8.00
BM02 Al MacInnis 4.00 10.00
BM03 Alexander Mogilny 2.50 6.00
BM04 Andy Moog 3.00 8.00
BM05 Brett Hull 6.00 15.00
BM06 Brian Bellows 3.00 8.00
BM07 Brian Leetch 2.50 6.00
BM08 Chris Chelios 3.00 8.00
BM09 Curtis Joseph 4.00 10.00
BM10 Dale Hawerchuk 4.00 10.00
BM11 Dominik Hasek 5.00 12.00
BM12 Doug Gilmour 4.00 10.00
BM13 Ed Belfour 4.00 10.00
BM14 Eric Lindros 5.00 12.00
BM15 Felix Potvin 5.00 12.00
BM16 Jaromir Jagr 10.00 25.00
BM17 Jeremy Roenick 5.00 12.00
BM18 Joe Sakic 6.00 15.00
BM19 John Vanbiesbrouck 3.00 8.00
BM20 Larry Murphy 2.50 6.00
BM21 Luc Robitaille 3.00 8.00
BM22 Manon Rheaume 8.00 20.00
BM23 Mario Lemieux 12.00 30.00
BM24 Mark Messier 6.00 15.00
BM25 Mike Gartner 4.00 10.00
BM26 Mike Modano 5.00 12.00
BM27 Mike Richter 3.00 8.00
BM28 Paul Coffey 3.00 8.00
BM29 Paul Kariya 3.00 8.00
BM30 Phil Housley 2.50 6.00
BM31 Pierre Turgeon 2.50 6.00
BM32 Raymond Bourque 5.00 12.00
BM33 Ron Francis 4.00 10.00
BM34 Sergei Fedorov 5.00 12.00
BM35 Steve Yzerman 8.00 20.00
BM36 Tom Barrasso 2.50 6.00
BM37 Wayne Gretzky 20.00 50.00
BM38 Wayne Gretzky 20.00 50.00
BM39 Wayne Gretzky 20.00 50.00

2016 Leaf Clear

*BLUE/25: .8X TO 2X BASIC CARDS

2016 Leaf Sports Heroes Gold

*GOLD/15-25: .6X TO 1.5X BASIC AU

2017-18 Leaf Gold All Stars Memorabilia Magenta

GLAS01 F.Potvin/C.Osgood/25 8.00 20.00
GLAS02 E.Belfour/M.Brodeur/25 12.00 30.00
GLAS03 S.Fedorov/A.Mogilny/25 8.00 20.00
GLAS04 B.Hull/P.Kariya/25 10.00 25.00
GLAS05 M.Lemieux/J.Jagr/25 20.00 50.00
GLAS06 M.Messier/B.Leetch/25 10.00 25.00
GLAS07 E.Lindros/J.LeClair/25 8.00 20.00
GLAS09 A.Irbe/C.Joseph/25 6.00 15.00
GLAS10 P.Bure/S.Fedorov/25 8.00 20.00
GLAS11 R.Bourque/B.Leetch/25 4.00 10.00
GLAS12 N.Khabibulin/D.Hasek/25 8.00 20.00
GLAS13 D.Alfredsson/P.Forsberg/25 10.00 25.00
GLAS15 M.Messier/M.Modano/25 10.00 25.00
GLAS16 P.Roy/E.Belfour/25 12.00 30.00
GLAS17 L.Robitaille/J.Roenick/25 8.00 20.00
GLAS18 T.Selanne/J.Jagr/25 15.00 40.00
GLAS19 A.MacInnis/C.Pronger/25 6.00 15.00
GLAS20 T.Fleury/T.Amonte/25 4.00 10.00
GLAS21 M.Sundin/M.Naslund/25 5.00 12.00
GLAS22 P.Roy/G.Hebert/25 12.00 30.00

GLAS23 P.Kariya/T.Selanne/25 10.00 25.00
GLAS24 R.Bourque/P.Coffey/25 5.00 12.00
GLAS25 S.Yzerman/M.Sundin/25 12.00 30.00
GLAS26 P.Bure/P.Bondra/25 5.00 12.00

2017-18 Leaf Gold Leaf Legends

*WAVE/25: 1X TO 2.5X BASIC INSERTS
GLL01 Bobby Clarke 1.50 4.00
GLL02 Bobby Hull 2.00 5.00
GLL03 Borje Salming 1.00 2.50
GLL04 Brett Hull 2.00 5.00
GLL05 Cyclone Taylor .75 2.00
GLL06 Dave Keon 1.00 2.50
GLL07 Eddie Shore 1.00 2.50
GLL08 Eric Lindros 1.50 4.00
GLL09 Georges Vezina .75 2.00
GLL10 Gordie Howe 3.00 8.00
GLL11 Guy Lafleur 1.25 3.00
GLL12 Howie Morenz 1.00 2.50
GLL13 Jacques Plante 1.00 2.50
GLL14 Jean Beliveau 1.00 2.50
GLL15 Joe Sakic 2.00 5.00
GLL16 Mario Lemieux 4.00 10.00
GLL17 Martin Brodeur 2.50 6.00
GLL18 Maurice Richard 2.00 5.00
GLL19 Mike Bossy 1.00 2.50
GLL20 Pavel Bure 1.00 2.50
GLL21 Pelle Lindbergh .75 2.00
GLL22 Phil Esposito 1.50 4.00
GLL23 Pierre Turgeon .75 2.00
GLL24 Raymond Bourque 1.50 4.00
GLL25 Sergei Fedorov 1.50 4.00
GLL26 Stan Mikita 1.25 3.00
GLL27 Teemu Selanne 2.00 5.00
GLL28 Terry Sawchuk .75 2.00
GLL29 Tim Horton 1.00 2.50
GLL30 Vladislav Tretiak .75 2.00
GLL31 Jari Kurri 1.00 2.50
GLL32 Grant Fuhr 1.50 4.00
GLL33 Larry Robinson 1.00 2.50
GLL34 Bryan Trottier 1.00 2.50
GLL35 Bernie Parent 1.25 3.00
GLL36 Gerry Cheevers 1.00 2.50
GLL37 Darryl Sittler 1.25 3.00
GLL38 Mike Modano 1.50 4.00
GLL39 Frank Mahovlich 1.00 2.50
GLL40 Luc Robitaille 1.00 2.50

2017-18 Leaf Stickwork Stick Rack Quad

SR401 Beliveau/Mahovlich/Howe/Keon 30.00 80.00
SR402 Hull/Mikita/Clarke/Orr 40.00 100.00
SR403 Gretzky/Lemieux/Messier/Sakic 60.00 150.00
SR404 Roy/Brodeur/Fuhr/Potvin 25.00 60.00
SR405 Clarke/Dionne/Hull/Esposito 20.00 50.00
SR406 Orr/Salming/Potvin/Horton 40.00 100.00
SR407 Tretiak/Roy/Dryden/Brodeur 25.00 60.00
SR408 Gretzky/Beliveau/Lemieux/Howe 60.00 150.00
SR409 Gretzky/Messier/Coffey/Lowe 60.00150.00
SR410 Howe/Beliveau/Hull/Mahovlich 30.0080.00
SR411 Mahovlich/Geoffrion/Howe/Beliveau 30.00 80.00
SR412 Richard/Beliveau/Laperriere/Lafleur 12.00 30.00
SR413 Roy/Brodeur/Vanbiesbrouck/Potvin 25.00 60.00
SR414 Mahovlich/Larouche/Gainey/Houle 10.00 25.00
SR415 Khabibulin/Kolzig/Thibault/Vernon 10.00 25.00
SR416 Cheevers/Parent/Dryden/Plante 12.00 30.00
SR417 Vachon/Parent/Cheevers/Gilbert 12.00 30.00
SR418 Beliveau/Moore/Olmstead/Harvey 10.00 25.00

2017-18 Leaf Stickwork Stick Rack Triple

SR301 Mahovlich/Howe/Hull/17 25.00 60.00
SR302 Beliveau/Gretzky/Howe/17 50.00 125.00
SR303 Plante/Roy/Dryden/17 20.00 50.00
SR306 Brodeur/Roy/Potvin/17 20.00 50.00
SR307 Cheevers/Parent/Tretiak/17 10.00 25.00
SR309 Maruk/Gartner/Stevens/17 10.00 25.00
SR310 Ciccarelli/Payne/Broten/17 8.00 20.00
SR311 Dionne/Taylor/Simmer/17 10.00 25.00
SR312 Potvin/Trottier/Nystrom/17 8.00 20.00
SR313 Krushelnyski/Kurri/Gretzky/17 50.00 125.00

2017-18 Leaf Stickwork Sticks and Stones

SS01 Al Secord 8.00 20.00
SS02 Bob Probert 8.00 20.00
SS03 Bobby Clarke 12.00 30.00
SS04 Cam Neely 8.00 20.00
SS05 Chris Chelios 8.00 20.00
SS06 Clark Gillies 8.00 20.00
SS07 Dino Ciccarelli 8.00 20.00
SS08 Gino Odjick 5.00 12.00
SS09 Gordie Howe 25.00 60.00

2017-18 Leaf Stickwork Super Sticks

SSY01 Geoffrion/Beliveau/Moore/Delvecchio/Olmstead/Ullman/Harvey/Hall 10.00 25.00
SSY02 Mahovlich/Plante/Moore/Harvey/Geoffrion/Beliveau/Olmstead/Lindsay 10.00 25.00
SSY03 Orr/Hull/Howe/Mahovlich/Beliveau/Keon/Mikita/Plante 40.00 100.00
SSY04 Orr/Horton/Laperriere/Baun/White/Jarrett/Vadnais/Stanley 40.00 100.00
SSY05 Esposito/Orr/Clarke/Lafleur/Dryden/Parent/Pronovost/Mahovlich 40.00 100.00
SSY06 Vadnais/Drouin/Esposito/Clarke/Unger/Tkaczuk/Potvin/Lacroix 15.00 40.00
SSY07 Parent/Vachon/Cheevers/Dryden/Clarke/Esposito/Dionne/Orr 40.00 100.00
SSY08 Gretzky/Lemieux/Goulet/Messier/Hawerchuk/Trottier/Kurri/Gartner 60.00 150.00
SSY09 Murphy/Bourque/Babych/Lowe/Salming/Reinhart/Stevens/Coffey 10.00 25.00
SSY10 Murphy/Sundin/Chelios/Fedorov/Modano/Oates/Robitaille/Sakic 20.00 50.00
SSY11 Roy/Belfour/Joseph/Vanbiesbrouck/Fuhr/Brodeur/Potvin/Richter 25.00 60.00

2017-18 Leaf Stickwork Titans of Timber

TOT01 Orr/Hull/Keon/Beliveau/Mahovlich/Mikita 40.00 100.00
TOT02 Gretzky/Lemieux/Messier/Robitaille/Fedorov/Lindros 60.00 150.00
TOT03 Howe/Horton/Beliveau/Mahovlich/Laperriere/Armstrong 30.00 80.00
TOT04 Lafleur/Hull/Richard/Orr/Howe/Horton 40.00 100.00
TOT05 LaFontaine/Federko/Gainey/Trottier/Potvin/Goulet 10.00 25.00
TOT06 Roy/Brodeur/Potvin/Vanbiesbrouck/Richter/Joseph 25.00 60.00
TOT07 Geoffrion/Harvey/Mahovlich/Mikita/Delvecchio/Beliveau 12.00 30.00

2014-15 Leaf Acetate Toronto Spring Expo

COMPLETE SET (4) 4.00 10.00
CMD Connor McDavid 2.50 6.00
DS1 Dylan Strome 1.00 2.50
MB1 Mathew Barzal .75 2.00
MM1 Mitchell Marner .60 1.50

2015-16 Leaf Genesis Jersey Autographs

AMCH1 Cameron Hebig/25 6.00 15.00
AMJE1 Jack Eichel/25 30.00 80.00
AMJL1 Jake Leschyshyn/20 6.00 15.00
AMJV1 Joe Veleno/25 8.00 20.00
AMJV2 Juuso Valimaki/20 5.00 12.00
AMTR1 Taylor Raddysh/20 8.00 20.00

2015-16 Leaf Genesis Epic Materials

*EMERALD: .4X TO 1X BASIC INSERTS
EMAB1 Anthony Dumont-Bouchard/50 5.0012.00
EMAC1 Alexander Chmelevski/25 5.00 12.00
EMAD1 Alex DeBrincat/25 6.00 15.00
EMAK1 Austen Keating/50 5.00 12.00
EMAM1 Antoine Morand/50 4.00 10.00
EMAN1 Alexander Nylander/25 10.00 25.00
EMBC1 Brett Crossley/50 4.00 10.00
EMBD1 Brett Davis/50 6.00 15.00
EMBG1 Brady Gilmour/25 6.00 15.00
EMBJ1 Ben Jones/50 4.00 10.00
EMBM1 Beck Malenstyn/25 6.00 15.00
EMCB1 Connor Bunnaman/50 4.00 10.00
EMCH1 Cameron Hebig/50 5.00 12.00
EMDB1 Dereck Baribeau/50 4.00 10.00
EMDD1 Dillon Dube/25 6.00 15.00
EMDL1 David Levin/25 8.00 20.00
EMDS1 Dante Salituro/50 4.00 10.00
EMDS2 Deven Sideroff/50 6.00 15.00
EMDS3 Dmitry Sokolov/25 6.00 15.00
EMDS4 Dylan Sadowy/25 6.00 15.00
EMDS5 Dylan Strome/25 12.00 30.00
EMDT1 Dmytro Timashov/50 6.00 15.00
EMDZ1 Dmitry Zhukenov/50 6.00 15.00
EMEB1 Egor Babenko/50 4.00 10.00
EMEC1 Evan Cormier/50 5.00 12.00
EMGG1 Gabriel Gagne/50 5.00 12.00
EMGS1 Gabriel Sylvestre/50 4.00 10.00
EMGS2 Givani Smith/50 4.00 10.00
EMGV1 Gabriel Vilardi/25 6.00 15.00
EMHD1 Hayden Davis/50 4.00 10.00
EMJB1 Jake Bean/50 6.00 15.00
EMJC1 Jakob Chychrun/25 8.00 20.00
EMJE1 Jack Eichel/25 25.00 60.00
EMJG1 Julien Gauthier/25 8.00 20.00
EMJK1 Jake Kryski/50 4.00 10.00
EMJK2 Jordan Kyrou/25 6.00 15.00
EMJL1 Jake Leschyshyn/50 4.00 10.00
EMJM1 Josh Mahura/50 4.00 10.00
EMJP1 Jordan Papirny/50 5.00 12.00
EMJS1 Jake Smith/50 6.00 15.00
EMJV1 Joe Veleno/25 6.00 15.00
EMJV2 Juuso Valimaki/50 4.00 10.00
EMJZ1 Jakub Zboril/50 6.00 15.00
EMKA1 Kristian Afanasyev/50 4.00 10.00
EMKY1 Keanu Yamamoto/50 4.00 10.00
EMMB1 Mackenzie Blackwood/50 8.00 20.00
EMMB2 Mitchell Balmas/50 4.00 10.00
EMMC1 Maxime Comtois/25 8.00 20.00
EMMD1 Martins Dzierkals/25 4.00 10.00
EMMJ1 Max Jones/25 6.00 15.00
EMML1 Max Lajoie/25 6.00 15.00
EMMMD Mason McDonald/50 5.00 12.00
EMMML Michael McLeod/50 6.00 15.00
EMMR1 Michael Rasmussen/50 6.00 15.00
EMMS1 Michael Spacek/50 4.00 10.00
EMMT1 Matthew Tkachuk/25 20.00 50.00
EMNJ1 Noah Juulsen/50 6.00 15.00
EMNP1 Nolan Patrick/25 12.00 30.00
EMNS1 Nick Suzuki/50 12.00 30.00
EMPB1 Patrick Bajkov/50 4.00 10.00
EMRB1 Radovan Bondra/50 4.00 10.00
EMSG1 Samuel Girard/50 5.00 12.00
EMSM1 Stelio Mattheos/25 8.00 20.00
EMSS1 Sam Steel/25 8.00 20.00
EMSS2 Simon Stransky/25 6.00 15.00
EMTB1 Travis Barron/50 4.00 10.00
EMTB2 Tyler Benson/50 8.00 20.00
EMTC1 Travis Child/50 4.00 10.00
EMTR1 Taylor Raddysh/25 8.00 20.00
EMVA1 Vitalii Abramov/25 8.00 20.00
EMXP1 Xavier Potvin/50 4.00 10.00

2015-16 Leaf Genesis Epic Materials Patch

EMPAB1 Anthony Dumont-Bouchard/20 5.00 12.00
EMPAK1 Austen Keating/20 5.00 12.00
EMPAM1 Antoine Morand/20 4.00 10.00
EMPBC1 Brett Crossley/20 4.00 10.00
EMPBD1 Brett Davis/20 6.00 15.00
EMPBJ1 Ben Jones/20 4.00 10.00
EMPCB1 Connor Bunnaman/20 4.00 10.00
EMPDB1 Dereck Baribeau/20 4.00 10.00
EMPDS1 Dante Salituro/20 4.00 10.00
EMPDS2 Deven Sideroff/20 4.00 10.00
EMPDT1 Dmytro Timashov/20 6.00 15.00
EMPDZ1 Dmitry Zhukenov/20 6.00 15.00
EMPEB1 Egor Babenko/20 4.00 10.00
EMPEC1 Evan Cormier/20 5.00 12.00
EMPGG1 Gabriel Gagne/20 5.00 12.00
EMPGS1 Gabriel Sylvestre/20 4.00 10.00
EMPGS2 Givani Smith/20 4.00 10.00
EMPHD1 Hayden Davis/20 4.00 10.00
EMPJB1 Jake Bean/20 6.00 15.00
EMPJK1 Jake Kryski/20 4.00 10.00
EMPJL1 Jake Leschyshyn/20 5.00 12.00
EMPJM1 Josh Mahura/20 4.00 10.00
EMPJP1 Jordan Papirny/20 5.00 12.00
EMPJS1 Jake Smith/20 5.00 12.00
EMPJV2 Juuso Valimaki/20 4.00 10.00
EMPJZ1 Jakub Zboril/20 6.00 15.00
EMPKA1 Kristian Afanasyev/20 4.00 10.00
EMPKY1 Keanu Yamamoto/20 5.00 12.00
EMPMB1 Mackenzie Blackwood/20 8.00 20.00
EMPMB2 Mitchell Balmas/20 4.00 10.00
EMPMMD Mason McDonald/20 5.00 12.00
EMPMML Michael McLeod/20 6.00 15.00
EMPMR1 Michael Rasmussen/20 4.00 10.00
EMPMS1 Michael Spacek/20 4.00 10.00
EMPNJ1 Noah Juulsen/20 6.00 15.00
EMPNS1 Nick Suzuki/20 12.00 30.00
EMPPB1 Patrick Bajkov/20 4.00 10.00
EMPRB1 Radovan Bondra/20 4.00 10.00
EMPSG1 Samuel Girard/20 5.00 12.00
EMPTB1 Travis Barron/20 4.00 10.00
EMPTB2 Tyler Benson/20 8.00 20.00
EMPTC1 Travis Child/20 4.00 10.00
EMPTR1 Taylor Raddysh/20 6.00 15.00
EMPXP1 Xavier Potvin/20 4.00 10.00

2015-16 Leaf Genesis New Dawn Autographs

*EMERALD: .4X TO 1X BASIC INSERTS
NDAC1 Alexander Chmelevski 6.00 15.00
NDAD1 Alex DeBrincat 8.00 20.00
NDAD2 Arnaud Durandeau 5.00 12.00
NDAM1 Antoine Morand 5.00 12.00
NDAN1 Alexander Nylander 12.00 30.00
NDAP1 Austin Pratt 5.00 12.00
NDAR1 Anthony Richard 6.00 15.00
NDBC1 Brett Crossley 5.00 12.00
NDBD1 Brett Davis 8.00 20.00
NDBG1 Brady Gilmour 8.00 20.00
NDBH1 Brett Howden 5.00 12.00
NDBJ1 Ben Jones 5.00 12.00
NDBM1 Beck Malenstyn 8.00 20.00
NDCB1 Connor Bunnaman 5.00 12.00
NDCG1 Conor Garland 5.00 12.00
NDCH1 Cameron Hebig 6.00 15.00
NDCH2 Carter Hart 12.00 30.00
NDCP1 Christopher Paquette 5.00 12.00
NDDB1 Dereck Baribeau 5.00 12.00
NDDD1 Dillon Dube 8.00 20.00
NDDL1 David Levin 8.00 20.00
NDDS1 Dmitry Sokolov 8.00 20.00
NDDS2 Dylan Sadowy 8.00 20.00
NDDT1 Dmytro Timashov 8.00 20.00
NDDW1 Dylan Wells 5.00 12.00
NDDZ1 Dmitry Zhukenov 8.00 20.00
NDEB1 Egor Babenko 5.00 12.00
NDEC1 Evan Cormier 6.00 15.00
NDGS1 Gabriel Sylvestre 5.00 12.00
NDGS2 Givani Smith 5.00 12.00
NDGV1 Gabriel Vilardi 8.00 20.00
NDHD1 Hayden Davis 5.00 12.00
NDJA1 Josh Anderson 15.00 40.00
NDJB1 Jake Bean 8.00 20.00
NDJB2 Jordy Bellerive 5.00 12.00
NDJC1 Jakob Chychrun 10.00 25.00
NDJD1 Jared Dmytriw 5.00 12.00
NDJE1 Jack Eichel 30.00 80.00
NDJG1 Julien Gauthier 10.00 25.00
NDJK1 Jake Kryski 5.00 12.00
NDJK2 Jordan Kyrou 8.00 20.00
NDJM1 Josh Mahura 5.00 12.00
NDJP1 Jesse Puljujarvi 15.00 40.00
NDJV1 Joe Veleno 8.00 20.00
NDJV2 Juuso Valimaki 5.00 12.00
NDJW1 Jaeger White 5.00 12.00
NDJW2 Jeff De Wit 5.00 12.00
NDKA1 Kristian Afanasyev 5.00 12.00
NDKC1 Kale Clague 8.00 20.00
NDKM1 Keaton Middleton 5.00 12.00
NDKY1 Keanu Yamamoto 6.00 15.00
NDLB1 Logan Brown 12.00 30.00
NDLC1 Louis-Filip Cote 5.00 12.00
NDLJ1 Lucas Johansen 5.00 12.00
NDLM1 Liam Murphy 5.00 12.00
NDLT1 Lucas Thierus 5.00 12.00
NDMB1 Matt Barberis 6.00 15.00
NDMB2 Mitchell Balmas 5.00 12.00
NDMC1 Maxime Comtois 10.00 25.00
NDMD1 Martins Dzierkals 5.00 12.00
NDMJ1 Max Jones 8.00 20.00
NDML1 Max Lajoie 8.00 20.00
NDMM1 Michael McLeod 8.00 20.00
NDMS1 Mathieu Sevigny 5.00 12.00
NDMS2 Michael Spacek 5.00 12.00
NDMS3 Mikhail Sergachev 10.00 25.00
NDMT1 Matthew Tkachuk 25.00 60.00
NDNB1 Nathan Bastian 8.00 20.00
NDNC1 Noah Carroll 6.00 15.00
NDNK1 Nolan Kneen 5.00 12.00
NDNP1 Nolan Patrick 15.00 40.00
NDNV1 Nolan Volcan 5.00 12.00
NDPB1 Patrick Bajkov 5.00 12.00
NDPD1 Pierre-Luc Dubois 12.00 30.00
NDPH1 Peyton Hoyt 5.00 12.00
NDPL1 Pascal Laberge 6.00 15.00
NDRB1 Radovan Bondra 5.00 12.00
NDRK1 Ryan Kubic 5.00 12.00
NDSB1 Shawn Boudrias 5.00 12.00
NDSG1 Samuel Girard 6.00 15.00
NDSM1 Stelio Mattheos 8.00 20.00
NDSS1 Sam Steel 10.00 25.00
NDSS2 Stuart Skinner 10.00 25.00
NDSS3 Simon Stransky 8.00 20.00
NDTB1 Travis Barron 5.00 12.00
NDTB2 Tyler Benson 10.00 25.00
NDTF1 Tyler Felhaber 5.00 12.00
NDTK1 Tanner Kaspick 5.00 12.00
NDTP1 Tyler Parsons 5.00 12.00
NDTR1 Taylor Raddysh 8.00 20.00
NDTR2 Ty Ronning 5.00 12.00
NDTT1 Tyler Timpano 5.00 12.00
NDVA1 Vitalii Abramov 10.00 25.00
NDVK1 Vladimir Kuznetsov 5.00 12.00
NDVM1 Victor Mete 6.00 15.00
NDVS1 Vili Saarijarvi 5.00 12.00
NDWB1 Will Bitten 5.00 12.00
NDZG1 Zach Gallant 5.00 12.00
NDZS1 Zach Senchenko 5.00 12.00
NDZS2 Zachary Senyshyn 5.00 12.00

2015-16 Leaf Genesis Signs of Nobility

SNBB2 Bill Barber/20 8.00 20.00
SNBH1 Bobby Hull/20 20.00 50.00
SNBT1 Bryan Trottier/20 10.00 25.00
SNDM1 Dickie Moore/20 8.00 20.00
SNEG1 Ed Giacomin/20 10.00 25.00
SNGC1 Gerry Cheevers/20 10.00 25.00
SNGF1 Grant Fuhr/20 15.00 40.00
SNGL1 Guy Lafleur/20 12.00 30.00
SNJB2 Johnny Bower/20 10.00 25.00
SNJB3 Johnny Bucyk/20 10.00 25.00
SNJS1 Joe Sakic/20 20.00 50.00
SNME1 Mike Eruzione/20 8.00 20.00
SNMS1 Milt Schmidt/20 10.00 25.00
SNNL2 Nicklas Lidstrom/20 10.00 25.00
SNPC1 Paul Coffey/20 10.00 25.00
SNPP1 Pierre Pilote/20 10.00 25.00
SNRK1 Red Kelly/20 10.00 25.00
SNTE1 Tony Esposito/20 10.00 25.00
SNTL1 Ted Lindsay/20 10.00 25.00
SNVT1 Vladislav Tretiak/20 8.00 20.00

2015-16 Leaf L'Anti Expo

COMPLETE SET (1) 3.00 8.00
LAEJE1 Jack Eichel 3.00 8.00

1995-96 Leaf Limited

1 Mario Lemieux .75 2.00
2 Peter Forsberg .40 1.00
3 Geoff Courtnall .12 .30
4 Vincent Damphousse .15 .40
5 Jason Allison .15 .40
6 Theo Fleury .25 .60
7 Shane Doan RC .60 1.50
8 Chris Gratton .12 .30
9 Paul Kariya .20 .50
10 Radek Dvorak RC .25 .60
11 Adam Graves .15 .40
12 Donald Audette .15 .40
13 Craig Janney .12 .30
14 Sean Burke .12 .30
15 Ed Belfour .20 .50
16 Ray Bourque .30 .75
17 Pavel Bure .20 .50
18 Martin Brodeur .50 1.25
19 Todd Bertuzzi RC .25 .60
20 Aki Berg RC .12 .30
21 Dave Andreychuk .20 .50
22 Jason Arnott .15 .40
23 Ron Francis .25 .60
24 Paul Coffey .20 .50
25 Daniel Alfredsson RC 1.00 2.50
26 Todd Harvey .12 .30
27 Claude Lemieux .20 .50
28 Brett Hull .40 1.00
29 Felix Potvin .30 .75
30 Peter Bondra .20 .50
31 Trevor Kidd .15 .40
32 Igor Korolev .12 .30
33 Roman Hamrlik .12 .30
34 Chad Kilger RC .20 .50
35 Rob Niedermayer .15 .40
36 Richard Park .20 .50
37 Mathieu Dandenault .40 1.00
38 Alexandre Daigle .12 .30
39 Jere Lehtinen .15 .40
40 Chris Chelios .20 .50
41 Blaine Lacher .15 .40
42 Trevor Linden .20 .50
43 Scott Niedermayer .20 .50
44 Teemu Selanne .40 1.00
45 Daymond Langkow RC .20 .50
46 Oleg Tverdovsky .20 .50
47 John Vanbiesbrouck .20 .50
48 Alexei Kovalev .15 .40
49 Sergei Fedorov .30 .75
50 Alexei Yashin .15 .40
51 Mike Modano .30 .75
52 Sandis Ozolinsh .12 .30
53 Ian Laperriere .12 .30
54 Mark Recchi .25 .60
55 Jim Carey .15 .40
56 Joe Nieuwendyk .15 .40
57 Keith Tkachuk .20 .50
58 Daren Puppa .15 .40
59 Jason Bonsignore .12 .30
60 Tomas Sandstrom .12 .30
61 Chris Osgood .20 .50
62 Jeff Friesen .12 .30
63 Jeff O'Neill .20 .50
64 Joe Sakic .40 1.00
65 Eric Daze .40 1.00
66 Patrick Roy .50 1.25
67 Kirk McLean .15 .40
68 Stephane Richer .15 .40
69 Rod Brind'Amour .20 .50
70 Wendel Clark .30 .75
71 Rob Blake .15 .40
72 Doug Gilmour .20 .50
73 Jaromir Jagr .60 1.50
74 Sergei Zubov .15 .40
75 Mark Messier .40 1.00
76 Dominik Hasek .30 .75
77 Viktor Kozlov .25 .60
78 Marcus Ragnarsson RC .25 .60
79 Jocelyn Thibault .15 .40
80 Jeremy Roenick .30 .75
81 Cam Neely .20 .50
82 Brian Savage .12 .30
83 Alexander Mogilny .15 .40
84 Steve Thomas .15 .40
85 John LeClair .20 .50
86 Brett Lindros .12 .30
87 Wayne Gretzky 1.25 3.00
88 Kenny Jonsson .20 .50
89 David Oliver .12 .30
90 Brian Leetch .15 .40
91 Luc Robitaille .15 .40
92 Keith Primeau .15 .40
93 Owen Nolan .20 .50
94 Brendan Shanahan .20 .50
95 Al MacInnis .25 .60
96 Kevin Stevens .15 .40
97 Larry Murphy .15 .40
98 Joe Juneau .12 .30
99 Eric Lindros .30 .75
100 Travis Green .15 .40
101 Jamie Storr .15 .40
102 Pierre Turgeon .15 .40
103 Bill Ranford .15 .40
104 Niklas Sundstrom .20 .50
105 Steve Yzerman .50 1.25
106 Ray Sheppard .15 .40
107 Chris Pronger .20 .50
108 Adam Oates .20 .50
109 Mike Gartner .25 .60
110 Doug Weight .20 .50
111 Jason Dawe .12 .30
112 Rick Tocchet .15 .40
113 Pat LaFontaine .20 .50
114 Scott Mellanby .15 .40
115 Vitali Yachmenev .20 .50
116 Alexei Zhamnov .20 .50
117 Brendan Witt .20 .50
118 Saku Koivu .20 .50
119 Mikael Renberg .15 .40
120 Mats Sundin .20 .50

1995-96 Leaf Limited Rookie Phenoms

COMPLETE SET (10) 5.00 12.00
1 Marcus Ragnarsson .20 .50
2 Daniel Alfredsson 2.00 5.00
3 Chad Kilger .20 .50
4 Niklas Sundstrom .20 .50
5 Vitali Yachmenev .20 .50
6 Eric Daze .40 1.00
7 Radek Dvorak .20 .50
8 Jeff O'Neill .20 .50
9 Saku Koivu 2.00 5.00
10 Todd Bertuzzi 1.00 2.50

1995-96 Leaf Limited Stars of the Game

COMPLETE SET (12) 20.00 40.00
1 Mario Lemieux 5.00 12.00
2 Eric Lindros .60 1.50
3 Wayne Gretzky 4.00 10.00
4 Peter Forsberg 2.50 6.00
5 Paul Kariya .60 1.50
6 Alexander Mogilny .30 .75
7 Teemu Selanne .60 1.50
8 Jaromir Jagr 1.50 4.00
9 Mats Sundin .60 1.50
10 Brett Hull 1.25 3.00
11 Sergei Fedorov 1.25 3.00
12 Jeremy Roenick .75 2.00

1995-96 Leaf Limited Stick Side

COMPLETE SET (8) 30.00 60.00
1 Jim Carey 5.00 12.00
2 Martin Brodeur 6.00 15.00
3 Felix Potvin 4.00 10.00
4 Patrick Roy 8.00 20.00
5 Dominik Hasek 3.00 8.00
6 John Vanbiesbrouck 6.00 15.00
7 Ron Hextall 5.00 12.00
8 Ed Belfour 2.00 5.00

1996-97 Leaf Limited

COMPLETE SET (90) 15.00 40.00
1 Chris Chelios .30 .75
2 Brendan Shanahan .30 .75
3 Keith Tkachuk .30 .75
4 Roman Hamrlik .20 .50
5 Adam Oates .30 .75
6 Chris Osgood .30 .75
7 Wayne Gretzky 2.50 6.00
8 Alexander Mogilny .25 .60
9 Patrick Roy 2.00 5.00
10 Saku Koivu .30 .75
11 Jaromir Jagr 1.00 2.50
12 Wendel Clark .50 1.25
13 Mike Modano .50 1.25
14 Ed Jovanovski .25 .60
15 John LeClair .30 .75
16 Jim Carey .30 .75
17 Paul Kariya .30 .75
18 Paul Coffey .30 .75
19 Todd Bertuzzi .30 .75
20 Owen Nolan .30 .75
21 Dominik Hasek .50 1.25
22 Bill Ranford .25 .60
23 Scott Stevens .25 .60
24 Brett Hull .60 1.50
25 Trevor Kidd .20 .50
26 Slava Fetisov .20 .50
27 Luc Robitaille .20 .50
28 Mats Sundin .20 .50
29 Peter Forsberg .60 1.50
30 John Vanbiesbrouck .20 .50
31 Alexei Yashin .25 .60
32 Pavel Bure .20 .50
33 Pat Verbeek .20 .50
34 Vitali Yachmenev .20 .50
35 Ron Hextall .20 .50
36 Michal Pivonka .20 .50
37 Eric Daze .25 .60
38 Pierre Turgeon .20 .50
39 Petr Nedved .20 .50
40 Steve Yzerman .75 2.00
41 Mike Richter .30 .75
42 Marcus Ragnarsson .20 .50
43 Jason Arnott .25 .60
44 Jocelyn Thibault .25 .60
45 Alexander Selivanov .20 .50
46 Claude Lemieux .20 .50
47 Eric Lindros .50 1.25
48 Grant Fuhr .50 1.25
49 Ray Bourque .50 1.25
50 Scott Mellanby .25 .60
51 Craig Janney .25 .60
52 Ron Francis .40 1.00
53 Ed Belfour .30 .75
54 Petr Sykora .30 .75
55 Damian Rhodes .25 .60
56 Joe Sakic .60 1.50
57 Zigmund Palffy .30 .75
58 Daren Puppa .25 .60
59 Pat LaFontaine .25 .60
60 Nikolai Khabibulin .25 .60
61 Sergei Fedorov .50 1.25
62 Valeri Bure .20 .50
63 Peter Bondra .30 .75
64 Teemu Selanne .60 1.50
65 Mark Messier .60 1.50
66 Shayne Corson .25 .60
67 Theo Fleury .60 1.50
68 Jeff O'Neill .20 .50
69 Eric Fichaud .25 .60
70 Doug Gilmour .40 1.00
71 Doug Weight .30 .75
72 Stephane Fiset .25 .60
73 Daniel Alfredsson .30 .75
74 Trevor Linden .30 .75
75 Joe Nieuwendyk .25 .60
76 Brian Bradley .20 .50
77 Jere Lehtinen .20 .50
78 Rob Niedermayer .25 .60
79 Mikael Renberg .25 .60
80 Felix Potvin .50 1.25
81 Valeri Kamensky .25 .60
82 Brian Leetch .25 .60
83 Jeff Friesen .20 .50
84 Vincent Damphousse .25 .60
85 Mario Lemieux 1.25 3.00
86 Jeremy Roenick .50 1.25
87 Martin Brodeur .75 2.00
88 Vyacheslav Kozlov .20 .50
89 Corey Hirsch .25 .60
90 Curtis Joseph .40 1.00
NNO Eric Lindros CL Jumbo .50 1.25

1996-97 Leaf Limited Gold

*SINGLES: 2.5X TO 6X BASIC CARDS

1996-97 Leaf Limited Bash The Boards Promos

COMPLETE SET (10) 40.00 100.00
*PROMOS: .6X TO 1.5X BASIC INSERTS 4.00 10.00

1996-97 Leaf Limited Bash The Boards

COMPLETE SET (10) 25.00 60.00
*LIMITED EDIT: 1.5X TO 4X BASIC INSERTS
1 Eric Lindros 4.00 10.00
2 Mark Messier 4.00 10.00
3 Owen Nolan 2.00 5.00
4 Doug Gilmour 4.00 10.00
5 Keith Tkachuk 4.00 10.00
6 Claude Lemieux 2.00 5.00
7 Ed Jovanovski 2.00 5.00
8 Peter Forsberg 6.00 15.00
9 Brendan Shanahan 4.00 10.00
10 Eric Daze 2.00 5.00

1996-97 Leaf Limited Rookies

COMPLETE SET (10) 25.00 50.00
1 Ethan Moreau .75 2.00
2 Jarome Iginla 4.00 10.00
3 Bryan Berard .75 2.00
4 Hnat Domenichelli .75 2.00
5 Wade Redden 1.25 3.00
6 Dainius Zubrus 1.25 3.00
7 Sergei Berezin .75 2.00
8 Jamie Langenbrunner 1.25 3.00
9 Tomas Holmstrom 2.00 5.00
10 Jonas Hoglund .75 2.00

1996-97 Leaf Limited Stubble

COMPLETE SET (20) 75.00 150.00
1 Patrick Roy 10.00 25.00
2 Eric Lindros 6.00 15.00
3 Wayne Gretzky 12.50 30.00
4 Paul Coffey 1.50 4.00
5 Jim Carey 1.50 4.00
6 Ed Belfour 3.00 8.00
7 Mario Lemieux 10.00 25.00
8 Mike Modano 3.00 8.00
9 Todd Bertuzzi 1.50 4.00
10 Pavel Bure 3.00 8.00
11 Martin Brodeur 6.00 15.00
12 Petr Nedved 1.50 4.00
13 Alexander Mogilny 1.50 4.00
14 Steve Yzerman 10.00 25.00
15 Brett Hull 3.00 8.00
16 Joe Sakic 4.00 10.00
17 Scott Mellanby 1.50 4.00
18 Trevor Linden 2.00 5.00
19 Rob Niedermayer 1.50 4.00
20 Wendel Clark 3.00 8.00

2019-20 Leaf Lumber Kings Game Used Lumber

GUL01 Alexander Ovechkin/20 30.00 80.00
GUL13 Gino Odjick/20 8.00 20.00
GUL20 Jaromir Jagr/30 20.00 50.00
GUL26 Mario Lemieux/30 20.00 50.00
GUL27 Mark Messier/30 10.00 25.00
GUL32 Patrice Bergeron/20 12.00 30.00
GUL34 Peter Forsberg/18 10.00 25.00
GUL42 Steve Yzerman/30 30.00 80.00

2019-20 Leaf Lumber Kings Fantastick Four

*PURPLE: .5X TO 1.25X BASIC
F401 Lemieux/Crosby/Malkin/Jagr/25 30.0080.00
F402 McDavid/Ovechkin/Crosby/Malkin/25 40.00 100.00
F403 Howe/Yzerman/Fedorov/Delvecchio/30 25.00 60.00
F404 Plante/Sawchuk/Dryden/Esposito/35 15.00 40.00
F405 Brodeur/Roy/Fuhr/Belfour/35 20.00 50.00
F406 LaFontaine/Gartner/Hawerchuk/Goulet/35 10.00 25.00
F407 Lafleur/Shutt/Lapointe/Savard/35 10.00 25.00
F408 Lindbergh/Fuhr/Barrasso/Resch/35 12.00 30.00
F409 Bourque/Coffey/Savard/Leetch/35 8.00 20.00

2019-20 Leaf Lumber Kings Game Used Goalie Lumber

*PURPLE: .5X TO 1.25X BASIC
GUGL01 Curtis Joseph/15 12.00 30.00
GUGL02 Ed Belfour/35 10.00 25.00
GUGL03 Gary Edwards/30 6.00 15.00
GUGL04 Gerry Cheevers/15 10.00 25.00
GUGL05 Gilles Gilbert/17 8.00 20.00
GUGL06 Glenn Hall/21 10.00 25.00
GUGL07 Glenn Resch/35 10.00 25.00
GUGL08 Grant Fuhr/35 15.00 40.00
GUGL09 Jacques Plante/30 10.00 25.00
GUGL10 Jocelyn Thibault/35 8.00 20.00
GUGL11 Jose Theodore/35 10.00 25.00
GUGL12 Ken Dryden/35 20.00 50.00
GUGL13 Martin Brodeur/35 25.00 60.00
GUGL14 Nikolai Khabibulin/35 10.00 25.00
GUGL15 Patrick Lalime/22 8.00 20.00
GUGL16 Pelle Lindbergh/30 8.00 20.00
GUGL17 Richard Brodeur/35 10.00 25.00
GUGL18 Roberto Luongo/30 15.00 40.00
GUGL19 Rogie Vachon/30 10.00 25.00
GUGL20 Roman Cechmanek/20 10.00 25.00
GUGL21 Terry Sawchuk/30 10.00 25.00
GUGL22 Tom Barrasso/30 8.00 20.00
GUGL23 Tony Esposito/30 10.00 25.00

2019-20 Leaf Lumber Kings Hat Trick Heroes

HTH01 Bobby Hull/35 6.00 15.00
HTH02 Glenn Anderson/25 4.00 10.00
HTH03 Gordie Howe/25 12.00 30.00
HTH04 Guy Lafleur/25 6.00 15.00
HTH05 Jari Kurri/25 5.00 12.00
HTH06 Jean Beliveau/25 6.00 15.00
HTH07 Marcel Dionne/25 6.00 15.00
HTH08 Mario Lemieux/35 12.00 30.00
HTH09 Mark Messier/35 10.00 25.00
HTH10 Mike Bossy/25 5.00 12.00
HTH11 Phil Esposito/25 8.00 20.00
HTH12 Stan Mikita/25 8.00 20.00
HTH13 Steve Yzerman/35 12.00 30.00
HTH14 Wayne Gretzky/25 25.00 60.00

2019-20 Leaf Lumber Kings Sensational Stix

SS01 Orr/Howe/Lemieux/Beliveau/Hull/Harvey/35 20.00 50.00
SS02 Plante/Sawchuk/Brodeur/Dryden/Esposito/Roy/35 12.00 30.00
SS03 Clarke/Hull/Cournoyer/Mikita/Esposito/Richard/30 12.00 30.00
SS04 Lemieux/Lindros/LaFontaine/Yzerman/Fedorov/Messier/35 20.00 50.00
SS05 Mahovlich/Mikita/Hull/Beliveau/Ullman/Olmstead/25 12.00 30.00

2019-20 Leaf Lumber Kings Six Sticks of Dynamite

SSD01 Hull/Howe/Mikita/Orr/Lemieux/Mahovlich/30 15.00 40.00
SSD02 Jagr/Fedorov/Lemieux/Yzerman/Messier/Kurri/35 15.00 40.00
SSD03 Lemieux/Beliveau/Howe/Mantle/Williams/Maris/20 15.00 40.00
SSD04 Richard/Cournoyer/Gainey/Lafleur/Shutt/Savard/35 6.00 15.00
SSD05 Clarke/Lafleur/Esposito/Hull/Orr/Hodge/30 15.00 40.00
SSD06 Gretzky/Lemieux/Hull/Griffey Jr./Mays/Jeter/30 25.00 60.00
SSD07 Moore/Mahovlich/Olmstead/Beliveau/Geoffrion/Harvey/30 10.00 25.00
SSD08 Gretzky/Lemieux/Yzerman/Hull/Beliveau/Howe/25 25.00 60.00

2019-20 Leaf Lumber Kings Stick Save Six

SSS01 Sawchuk/Plante/Dryden/Roy/Brodeur/Esposito/35 12.00 30.00
SSS02 Fuhr/Barrasso/Belfour/Potvin/Lindbergh/Vanbiesbrouck/35 20.00 50.00
SSS03 Hall/Parent/Cheevers/Esposito/Vachon/Gilbert/30 12.00 30.00
SSS04 Theodore/Belfour/Kolzig/Barrasso/Resch/Vernon/30 20.00 50.00
SSS05 Lalime/Cechmanek/Khabibulin/Luongo/Thibault/Burke/30 12.00 30.00
SSS06 Roy/Brodeur/Belfour/Fuhr/Joseph/Potvin/35 20.00 50.00

2019-20 Leaf Lumber Kings Sunrise and Sunset

SAS01 Barrasso/Chelios/Yzerman/Loob/Lapointe/Esposito/Clarke/Barber/30 12.00 30.00
SAS02 Francis/Fuhr/Lindbergh/Vanbiesbrouck/Vachon/Keon/Pronovost/Martin/30 8.00 20.00
SAS03 Bourque/Messier/Lowe/Gartner/Mikita/Howe/Hull/Cheevers/25 15.00 40.00
SAS04 Secord/Smith/Payne/Langway/Orr/Lemaire/Dryden/Cournoyer/25 20.00 50.00
SAS05 Shanahan/Stevens/Turgeon/Tugnutt/Potvin/Brodeur/Gillies/Middleton/25 20.00 50.00
SAS06 Belfour/Linden/Recchi/Richter/Loob/McDonald/Gainey/Dionne/30 8.00 20.00
SAS07 Salming/Potvin/Resch/McDonald/Horton/Delvecchio/Mahovlich/Laperriere/25 15.0040.00
SAS08 Perreault/Dryden/MacLeish/Leach/Hall/Hodge/Beliveau/Bathgate/30 10.00 25.00

2019-20 Leaf Lumber Kings Tale of the Tape

TT02 M.Lemieux/M.Messier 20.00 50.00
TT05 G.Howe/W.Gretzky 30.00 80.00
TT08 M.Brodeur/E.Belfour 10.00 25.00

2019-20 Leaf Lumber Kings Team Twigs

TT601 Clarke/Parent/Leach/Dupont/Lacroix/MacLeish/30 15.00 40.00
TT602 Esposito/Orr/Cheevers/Hodge/Gilbert/Bucyk/35 15.00 40.00
TT603 Gilbert/Ratelle/Messier/Vadnais/Esposito/Park/30 8.00 20.00
TT604 Howe/Delvecchio/Ullman/Yzerman/Fedorov/Sawchuk/25 15.00 40.00
TT605 Hull/Mikita/Esposito/Hall/Savard/Goulet/35 15.00 40.00
TT606 Dionne/Taylor/Simmer/Robitaille/Vachon/Blake/30 12.00 30.00
TT607 Beliveau/Plante/Olmstead/Harvey/Moore/Geoffrion/25 15.00 40.00
TT608 Savard/Cournoyer/Richard/Dryden/Lafleur/Mahovlich/35 12.00 30.00
TT609 Mahovlich/Sundin/Sittler/Salming/Keon/Potvin/30 20.00 50.00

TT610 Lemieux/Jagr/Barrasso Pronovost/Stevens/Crosby/30 20.00 50.00
TT611 Gretzky/Fuhr/Messier/Coffey Lowe/Kurri/25 20.00 50.00

2019-20 Leaf Lumber Kings The Champions Club

TCC02 Hull/Howe/Ullman/Esposito/Clarke Parent/Mahovlich/Delvecchio/30 15.00 40.00
TCC03 Cournoyer/Savard/Lafleur Lemaire/Lapointe/Dryden Robinson/Gainey/30 15.00 40.00
TCC04 Lemieux/Jagr/Fedorov/Hull/Messier Coffey/Kurri/Bourque/17 20.00 50.00
TCC05 Brodeur/Roy/Belfour/Barrasso Fuhr/Vachon/Hall/Vernon/30 20.00 50.00
TCC06 Potvin/Orr/Lapointe/Bourque/Harvey Coffey/Chelios/Savard/30 12.00 30.00
TCC07 Howe/Yzerman/Fedorov Delvecchio/Sawchuk/Chelios Larionov/Robitaille/30 15.00 40.00
TCC08 Lemieux/Jagr/Francis/Coffey/Barrasso Recchi/Murphy/Stevens/30 20.00 50.00
TCC09 Mahovlich/Mahovlich Cournoyer/Lemaire/Lapointe Savard/Houle/Dryden/30 15.00 40.00

2019-20 Leaf Lumber Kings Twig Sigs

TSAD1 Andre Dupont/35 6.00 15.00
TSAK1 Alexei Kasatonov/35 10.00 25.00
TSAO1 Adam Oates/35 10.00 25.00
TSBH1 Bobby Hull/35 25.00 60.00
TSBH2 Brett Hull/35 20.00 50.00
TSCC1 Chris Chelios/30 10.00 25.00
TSCJ1 Curtis Joseph/30 12.00 30.00
TSDD1 Dick Duff/35 8.00 20.00
TSDM1 Dickie Moore/35 10.00 25.00
TSDP1 Denis Potvin/35 10.00 25.00
TSEL1 Eric Lindros/30 15.00 40.00
TSFM1 Frank Mahovlich/25 10.00 25.00
TSGF1 Grant Fuhr/35 15.00 40.00
TSGH1 Glenn Hall/25 10.00 25.00
TSGL1 Guy Lafleur/35 12.00 30.00
TSGR1 Glenn Resch/35 10.00 25.00
TSJLC John LeClair/35 10.00 25.00
TSLR1 Luc Robitaille/35 10.00 25.00
TSMB1 Mike Bossy/20 10.00 25.00
TSMD1 Marcel Dionne/30 12.00 30.00
TSMK1 Mike Krushelnyski/35 8.00 20.00
TSMR1 Manon Rheaume/35 30.00 80.00
TSPC1 Paul Coffey/20 10.00 25.00
TSPE1 Phil Esposito/35 15.00 40.00
TSPS1 Peter Stastny/35 8.00 20.00
TSRH1 Roman Hamrlik/35 6.00 15.00
TSRL1 Rod Langway/35 8.00 20.00
TSSF1 Sergei Fedorov/20 30.00 80.00

2016-17 Leaf Masked Men Goalie Graphs

GGRAM1 Andy Moog/25 6.00 15.00
GGRBP1 Bernie Parent/25 8.00 20.00
GGRCJ1 Curtis Joseph/25 8.00 20.00
GGRCO1 Chris Osgood/25 6.00 15.00
GGREG1 Ed Giacomin/25 5.00 12.00
GGRFP1 Felix Potvin/25 10.00 25.00
GGRGC1 Gerry Cheevers/25 6.00 15.00
GGRGF1 Grant Fuhr/25 10.00 25.00
GGRGH1 Glenn Hall/25 6.00 15.00
GGRJB1 Johnny Bower/25 6.00 15.00
GGRJT1 Jose Theodore/25 6.00 15.00
GGRKM1 Kirk McLean/25 6.00 15.00
GGRMR1 Mike Richter/20 6.00 15.00
GGRTB1 Tom Barrasso/20 6.00 15.00
GGRVT1 Vladislav Tretiak/25 5.00 12.00

2016-17 Leaf Masked Men Goalie Legacy

GL01 Brimsek/Cheevers/Thomas Rask/Dafoe/Moog/20 8.00 20.00
GL02 Broda/Potvin/Joseph/Plante Fuhr/Belfour/20 10.00 25.00
GL03 Esposito/Crawford/Hall/Belfour Hackett/Thibault/20 8.00 20.00
GL04 Hasek/Brodeur/Roy/Cechmanek Turco/Kiprusoff/20 15.00 40.00
GL05 Hextall/Vanbiesbrouck/Cechmanek Parent/Lindbergh/Mason/20 8.00 20.00
GL06 Kiprusoff/Vernon/Lemelin/Kidd Turek/Brathwaite/20 5.00 12.00
GL07 Niemi/Nabokov/Vernon/Irbe Shields/Toskala/20 5.00 12.00
GL08 Parent/Cheevers/Giacomin/Hall Esposito/Smith/20 8.00 20.00
GL09 Price/Crawford/Lundqvist Luongo/Rask/Quick/20 15.00 40.00
GL10 Quick/Vachon/Hrudey Storr/Potvin/Fiset/20 10.00 25.00
GL11 Roy/Brodeur/Potvin/Joseph Vanbiesbrouck/Barrasso/20 15.00 40.00
GL13 Sawchuk/Osgood/Howard/Hasek Giacomin/Cheveldae/20 10.00 25.00
GL14 Smith/DiPietro/Nabokov/Hrudey Salo/Resch/20 6.00 15.00

2016-17 Leaf Masked Men Goals Against

GA03 M.Brodeur/D.Hasek/25 15.00 40.00
GA04 M.Richter/F.Potvin/25 10.00 25.00
GA05 O.Kolzig/C.Osgood/25 6.00 15.00
GA06 P.Roy/E.Belfour/25 15.00 40.00
GA07 P.Roy/R.Hextall/25 15.00 40.00

2016-17 Leaf Masked Men Jumbo Pads

JP01 Carey Price/20 12.00 30.00
JP02 Curtis Joseph/25 8.00 20.00
JP03 Dan Cloutier/25 5.00 12.00
JP05 Grant Fuhr/25 10.00 25.00
JP06 Henrik Lundqvist/25 15.00 40.00
JP07 Jeff Hackett/25 5.00 12.00
JP08 Jocelyn Thibault/25 5.00 12.00
JP09 Kelly Hrudey/25 5.00 12.00
JP10 Marty Turco/25 5.00 12.00
JP11 Miikka Kiprusoff/25 5.00 12.00
JP12 Niklas Backstrom/25 5.00 12.00
JP13 Nikolai Khabibulin/25 5.00 12.00
JP14 Rick DiPietro/25 5.00 12.00
JP15 Roman Cechmanek/25 5.00 12.00
JP16 Roman Turek/25 5.00 12.00
JP17 Sean Burke/25 5.00 12.00
JP18 Steve Shields/25 5.00 12.00
JP19 Tim Thomas/25 6.00 15.00

2016-17 Leaf Masked Men Signature Goalies

SG01 Andy Moog/25 10.00 25.00
SG02 Bernie Parent/25 12.00 30.00
SG03 Curtis Joseph/25 12.00 30.00
SG04 Felix Potvin/25 15.00 40.00
SG06 Glenn Hall/20 10.00 25.00
SG07 Grant Fuhr/25 15.00 40.00
SG08 Jose Theodore/25 10.00 25.00
SG09 Kirk McLean/25 10.00 25.00
SG10 Martin Brodeur/20 25.00 60.00
SG11 Olaf Kolzig/16 10.00 25.00
SG13 Tom Barrasso/20 10.00 25.00

2016-17 Leaf Masked Men Stack The Pads

SP01 Bernie Parent/20 8.00 20.00
SP02 Carey Price/25 12.00 30.00
SP03 Curtis Joseph/25 8.00 20.00
SP04 Dominik Hasek/20 10.00 25.00
SP06 Grant Fuhr/25 10.00 25.00
SP07 Henrik Lundqvist/25 15.00 40.00
SP09 Jocelyn Thibault/25 5.00 12.00
SP11 Jose Theodore/20 6.00 15.00
SP12 Kelly Hrudey/20 5.00 12.00
SP14 Marty Turco/25 5.00 12.00
SP15 Miikka Kiprusoff/20 5.00 12.00
SP16 Mike Vernon/25 5.00 12.00
SP17 Nikolai Khabibulin/25 5.00 12.00
SP18 Patrick Lalime/20 5.00 12.00
SP19 Patrick Roy/25 15.00 40.00
SP21 Roman Turek/20 5.00 12.00
SP22 Ron Tugnutt/25 5.00 12.00
SP23 Sean Burke/20 5.00 12.00
SP24 Tomas Vokoun/20 5.00 12.00

2016-17 Leaf Masked Men Vezina Winner

VWBH1 Braden Holtby/20 8.00 20.00
VWBS1 Billy Smith/20 6.00 15.00
VWCP1 Carey Price/20 12.00 30.00
VWDH1 Dominik Hasek/20 10.00 25.00
VWEB1 Ed Belfour/20 6.00 15.00
VWGF1 Grant Fuhr/20 10.00 25.00
VWHL2 Henrik Lundqvist/20 15.00 40.00
VWJT1 Jose Theodore/20 6.00 15.00
VWJV1 John Vanbiesbrouck/20 6.00 15.00
VWMB1 Martin Brodeur/20 15.00 40.00
VWMK1 Miikka Kiprusoff/20 5.00 12.00
VWOK1 Olaf Kolzig/20 6.00 15.00
VWPL1 Pelle Lindbergh/20 5.00 12.00
VWPR1 Patrick Roy/20 15.00 40.00
VWRH1 Ron Hextall/20 6.00 15.00
VWRM1 Ryan Miller/20 6.00 15.00
VWTB1 Tom Barrasso/20 6.00 15.00
VWTT1 Tim Thomas/20 6.00 15.00

1996-97 Leaf Preferred

COMPLETE SET (150) 12.00 30.00
1 Patrick Roy .75 2.00
2 Alexander Mogilny .25 .60
3 Bill Ranford .25 .60
4 Jeremy Roenick .50 1.25
5 Travis Green .25 .60
6 Owen Nolan .30 .75
7 Paul Kariya .30 .75
8 Pat Verbeek .20 .50
9 Jeff O'Neill .20 .50
10 Nikolai Khabibulin .25 .60
11 Pat LaFontaine .30 .75
12 Rob Niedermayer .25 .60
13 Luc Robitaille .30 .75
14 Mats Sundin .30 .75
15 Cory Stillman .20 .50
16 Ray Ferraro .20 .50
17 Alexei Yashin .25 .60
18 Brian Bradley .20 .50
19 Chris Chelios .30 .75
20 Jason Arnott .25 .60
21 Petr Sykora .20 .50
22 Jaromir Jagr 1.00 2.50
23 Jim Carey .30 .75
24 Claude Lemieux .20 .50
25 Vincent Damphousse .25 .60
26 Shayne Corson .25 .60
27 Joe Nieuwendyk .25 .60
28 Kenny Jonsson .20 .50
29 Peter Bondra .30 .75
30 Ed Belfour .30 .75
31 Brendan Shanahan .30 .75
32 Eric Desjardins .25 .60
33 Corey Hirsch .25 .60
34 Slava Fetisov .20 .50
35 Craig Janney .25 .60
36 Felix Potvin .50 1.25
37 Joe Sakic .60 1.50
38 Scott Stevens .30 .75
39 Kelly Hrudey .25 .60
40 Adam Oates .30 .75
41 John Vanbiesbrouck .30 .75
42 Brian Leetch .25 .60
43 Alexander Selivanov .20 .50
44 Mike Modano .50 1.25
45 Saku Koivu .30 .75
46 Tom Barrasso .25 .60
47 Jere Lehtinen .20 .50
48 Daniel Alfredsson .30 .75
49 Joe Juneau .20 .50
50 Chris Osgood .30 .75
51 Dave Andreychuk .30 .75
52 Marcus Ragnarsson .20 .50
53 Valeri Kamensky .25 .60
54 Doug Weight .30 .75
55 Mike Richter .30 .75
56 Teemu Selanne .60 1.50
57 Stephane Fiset .25 .60
58 Mikael Renberg .25 .60
59 Trevor Linden .30 .75
60 Bernie Nicholls .25 .60
61 Eric Daze .25 .60
62 Ron Francis .40 1.00
63 Sergei Zubov .25 .60
64 Rod Brind'Amour .30 .75
65 Sergei Fedorov .50 1.25
66 Mark Messier .60 1.50
67 Theo Fleury .60 1.50
68 Ed Jovanovski .25 .60
69 Daren Puppa .25 .60
70 Pierre Turgeon .25 .60
71 Oleg Tverdovsky .25 .60
72 Ryan Smyth .25 .60
73 Jocelyn Thibault .25 .60
74 Brendan Witt .20 .50
75 Igor Larionov .30 .75
76 Stephane Richer .25 .60
77 Ron Hextall .30 .75
78 Mike Ricci .20 .50
79 Dimitri Khristich .20 .50
80 Derian Hatcher .20 .50
81 Martin Brodeur .75 2.00
82 Petr Nedved .25 .60
83 Ray Bourque .50 1.25
84 Keith Primeau .25 .60
85 Sean Burke .20 .50
86 Geoff Sanderson .25 .60
87 Wendel Clark .50 1.25
88 Valeri Bure .20 .50
89 Keith Tkachuk .30 .75
90 Roman Hamrlik .20 .50
91 Dominik Hasek .50 1.25
92 Ray Sheppard .25 .60
93 Todd Bertuzzi .30 .75
94 Pavel Bure .30 .75
95 Alexei Zhamnov .25 .60
96 Alexei Kovalev .25 .60
97 Jeff Friesen .20 .50
98 Scott Young .20 .50
99 Vitali Yachmenev .20 .50
100 Michal Pivonka .20 .50
101 Paul Coffey .30 .75
102 Steve Yzerman .75 2.00
103 Zigmund Palffy .30 .75
104 Doug Gilmour .40 1.00
105 John LeClair .30 .75
106 Brett Hull .60 1.50
107 Yanic Perreault .20 .50
108 Bill Guerin .30 .75
109 Damian Rhodes .25 .60
110 Peter Forsberg .60 1.50
111 Scott Mellanby .25 .60
112 Wayne Gretzky 2.00 5.00
113 Mario Lemieux 1.25 3.00
114 Todd Harvey .20 .50
115 Mark Recchi .40 1.00
116 Trevor Kidd .20 .50
117 Eric Lindros .50 1.25
118 Jarome Iginla .40 1.00
119 Eric Fichaud .25 .60
120 Mattias Timander RC .30 .75
121 Hnat Domenichelli .20 .50
122 Chris O'Sullivan .20 .50
123 Sergei Berezin RC .50 1.25
124 Jonas Hoglund .20 .50
125 Anders Eriksson .20 .50
126 Corey Schwab .25 .60
127 Janne Niinimaa .30 .75
128 Dainius Zubrus RC .40 1.00
129 Bryan Berard .30 .75
130 Wade Redden .20 .50
131 Wayne Primeau .20 .50
132 Brandon Convery .20 .50
133 Richard Zednik RC .40 1.00
134 Darcy Tucker .20 .50
135 Christian Dube .20 .50
136 Rem Murray RC .30 .75
137 Kevin Hodson RC .30 .75
138 Steve Washburn RC .30 .75
139 Ethan Moreau RC .30 .75
140 Daymond Langkow .25 .60
141 Terry Ryan RC .30 .75
142 Curtis Brown .20 .50
143 Steve Sullivan RC .25 .60
144 Jamie Langenbrunner .20 .50
145 Daniel Goneau RC .30 .75
146 Anson Carter .25 .60
147 Jim Campbell .20 .50
148 Keith Tkachuk CL (1-76) .30 .75
149 Eric Daze CL (77-150) .25 .60
150 Mike Modano CL (inserts) .50 1.25

1996-97 Leaf Preferred Press Proofs

*VETS: 15X TO 40X BASIC CARDS
*ROOKIES: 6X TO 15X

1996-97 Leaf Preferred Steel

*GOLDS: 2X TO 5X SILVER
1 Sergei Fedorov 1.50 4.00
2 Martin Brodeur 2.50 6.00
3 Corey Hirsch .60 1.50
4 Ray Bourque 1.50 4.00
5 Saku Koivu 1.00 2.50
6 Ron Francis .60 1.50
7 Chris Chelios 1.00 2.50
8 Scott Mellanby .60 1.50
9 Ron Hextall .60 1.50
10 Doug Gilmour .60 1.50
11 Joe Sakic 2.00 5.00
12 Petr Sykora .40 1.00
13 Marcus Ragnarsson .40 1.00
14 Pat Verbeek .40 1.00
15 Stephane Fiset .60 1.50
16 Alexei Yashin .40 1.00
17 Daren Puppa .60 1.50
18 Eric Lindros 1.00 2.50
19 Jason Arnott .40 1.00
20 Todd Bertuzzi 1.00 2.50
21 Jim Carey 1.00 2.50
22 Pat LaFontaine 1.00 2.50
23 Brian Leetch 1.00 2.50
24 Trevor Linden .60 1.50
25 Eric Daze .60 1.50
26 Pierre Turgeon .60 1.50
27 Tom Barrasso .60 1.50
28 Mike Modano 1.50 4.00
29 Brendan Shanahan 1.00 2.50
30 Nikolai Khabibulin .60 1.50
31 Claude Lemieux .40 1.00
32 Zigmund Palffy .60 1.50
33 Mats Sundin 1.00 2.50
34 Paul Kariya 1.00 2.50
35 Daniel Alfredsson .60 1.50
36 Patrick Roy 5.00 12.00
37 Jaromir Jagr 1.50 4.00
38 Vyacheslav Kozlov .40 1.00
39 John LeClair 1.00 2.50
40 Bill Ranford .60 1.50
41 Vitali Yachmenev .40 1.00
42 Mark Messier 1.00 2.50
43 Valeri Bure .40 1.00
44 Roman Hamrlik .60 1.50
45 Joe Nieuwendyk .40 1.00
46 Mike Richter 1.00 2.50
47 Theo Fleury .40 1.00
48 Wendel Clark .60 1.50
49 Doug Weight .60 1.50
50 Damian Rhodes .60 1.50
51 Alexander Mogilny .60 1.50
52 Dominik Hasek 2.00 5.00
53 Eric Fichaud .60 1.50
54 Adam Oates .60 1.50
55 Jocelyn Thibault 1.00 2.50
56 Petr Nedved .40 1.00
57 Mike Vernon .60 1.50
58 Mikael Renberg .60 1.50
59 Valeri Kamensky .40 1.00
60 Peter Forsberg 2.50 6.00
61 Rob Niedermayer .40 1.00
62 Owen Nolan .60 1.50
63 Jere Lehtinen .40 1.00
77 Eric Lindros promo .40 1.00

1996-97 Leaf Preferred Masked Marauders

COMPLETE SET (12) 30.00 80.00
1 Jim Carey 2.00 5.00
2 Martin Brodeur 6.00 15.00
3 John Vanbiesbrouck 3.00 8.00
4 Patrick Roy 10.00 25.00
5 Felix Potvin 4.00 10.00
6 Chris Osgood 3.00 8.00
7 Dominik Hasek 5.00 12.00
8 Jocelyn Thibault 2.00 5.00
9 Nikolai Khabibulin 3.00 8.00
10 Curtis Joseph 3.00 8.00
11 Mike Richter 3.00 8.00
12 Ed Belfour 4.00 10.00

1996-97 Leaf Preferred Steel Power

COMPLETE SET (12) 15.00 40.00
1 Joe Sakic 3.00 8.00
2 Mario Lemieux 5.00 12.00
3 Pavel Bure 2.00 5.00
4 Mark Messier 1.50 3.00
5 Wayne Gretzky 6.00 15.00
6 Peter Forsberg 2.50 6.00
7 Sergei Fedorov 2.50 6.00
8 Jaromir Jagr 3.00 8.00
9 Brett Hull 2.00 5.00
10 Teemu Selanne 1.50 3.00
11 Paul Kariya 1.50 3.00
12 Eric Lindros 2.50 6.00

1996-97 Leaf Preferred Vanity Plates

COMPLETE SET (14) 25.00 60.00
*GOLD: .8X TO 2X SILVER
1 Wayne Gretzky 6.00 15.00
2 John Vanbiesbrouck 2.50 6.00
3 Chris Osgood 2.50 6.00
4 Steve Yzerman 2.50 6.00
5 Brett Hull 2.00 5.00
6 Mario Lemieux 4.00 10.00
7 Eric Lindros 1.50 4.00
8 Ed Jovanovski .75 2.00
9 Pavel Bure 2.50 6.00
10 Felix Potvin 1.50 4.00
11 Teemu Selanne 2.00 5.00
12 Keith Tkachuk 1.00 2.50
13 Curtis Joseph 1.25 3.00
14 Ed Belfour 1.00 2.50

2015-16 Leaf Signature Series Prospects Autographs

*GRAY: .4X TO 1X BASIC INSERTS
*RED: .5X TO 1.2X BASIC INSERTS
SPAB1 Anthony Beauvillier/44* 5.00 12.00
SPAC1 Alexandre Carrier/109* 4.00 10.00
SPAF1 Alex Forsberg/99* 4.00 10.00
SPAM1 Adam Mascherin/120* 4.00 10.00
SPAM2 Adam Musil/42* 5.00 12.00
SPAP1 Andrew Picco/109* 4.00 10.00
SPBG1 Brendan Guhle/99* 4.00 10.00
SPBH1 Brett Howden/87* 4.00 10.00
SPBM1 Beck Malenstyn/149* 6.00 15.00
SPBM2 Brett McKenzie/99* 4.00 10.00
SPBS1 Blake Speers/49* 4.00 10.00
SPBS2 Brandon Saigeon/149* 5.00 12.00
SPCA1 Cameron Askew/74* 4.00 10.00
SPCH1 Connor Hobbs/36* 4.00 10.00
SPCI1 Connor Ingram/99* 5.00 12.00
SPCJ1 Cole Johnson/87* 8.00 20.00
SPCP1 Cliff Pu/69* 4.00 10.00
SPCR1 Chaz Reddekopp/84* 4.00 10.00
SPDK1 Davis Koch/69* 4.00 10.00
SPDS1 Daniel Sprong/59* 8.00 20.00
SPDS2 Dante Salituro/109* 4.00 10.00
SPDS3 Dylan Strome/41* 12.00 30.00
SPEF1 Evan Fitzpatrick/106* 8.00 20.00
SPES1 Evan Sarthou/89* 4.00 10.00
SPES2 Evgeny Svechnikov/86* 8.00 20.00
SPFA1 Frederic Allard/111* 4.00 10.00
SPGE1 Giorgio Estephan/86* 4.00 10.00
SPGG1 Gabriel Gagne/81* 5.00 12.00
SPGG2 Glenn Gawdin/86* 5.00 12.00
SPGK1 Graham Knott/49* 4.00 10.00
SPIP1 Ivan Provorov/135* 10.00 25.00
SPJA1 Jeremiah Addison/81* 4.00 10.00
SPJA2 Jonathan Ang/99* 4.00 10.00
SPJA3 Josh Anderson/88* 12.00 30.00
SPJA4 Justin Almeida/180* 4.00 10.00
SPJB1 Jason Bell/89* 4.00 10.00
SPJC1 Jakob Chychrun/100* 8.00 20.00
SPJG1 Julien Gauthier/85* 8.00 20.00
SPJH1 Jansen Harkins/86* 6.00 15.00
SPJH2 Jordan Hollett/80* 8.00 20.00
SPJR1 Jeremy Roy/53* 4.00 10.00
SPJW1 Jaeger White/49* 4.00 10.00
SPJZ1 Jakub Zboril/159* 6.00 15.00
SPKC1 Kale Clague/114* 6.00 15.00
SPKC2 Kyle Capobianco/104* 4.00 10.00
SPKE1 Kaden Elder/104* 4.00 10.00
SPKM1 Kody McDonald/83* 5.00 12.00
SPKT1 Keoni Texeira/104* 4.00 10.00
SPLB1 Logan Brown/103* 10.00 25.00
SPLC1 Lawson Crouse/29* 6.00 15.00
SPLG1 Luke Green/84* 4.00 10.00
SPLL1 Loik Leveille/84* 4.00 10.00
SPMB1 Mackenzie Blackwood/66* 8.00 20.00
SPMB2 Mathew Barzal/41* 15.00 40.00
SPMF1 Maxime Fortier/44* 4.00 10.00
SPMG1 Matteo Gennaro/85* 4.00 10.00
SPMK1 Matthew Kreis/87* 4.00 10.00
SPMM1 Medric Mercier/84* 5.00 12.00
SPMM2 Michael McLeod/147* 6.00 15.00
SPMM3 Mitchell Marner/26* 20.00 50.00
SPMS1 Matt Spencer/67* 4.00 10.00
SPMS2 Mitchell Stephens/44* 4.00 10.00
SPNK1 Nikita Korostelev/114* 4.00 10.00
SPNK2 Nolan Kneen/86* 4.00 10.00
SPNM1 Nick Merkley/76* 8.00 20.00
SPNM2 Nicolas Meloche/100* 5.00 12.00
SPNN1 Nathan Noel/112* 4.00 10.00
SPNP1 Nolan Patrick/109* 12.00 30.00
SPNR1 Nicolas Roy/52* 4.00 10.00
SPPB1 Paul Bittner/100* 4.00 10.00
SPPD1 Pierre-Luc Dubois/84* 10.00 25.00
SPPK1 Pavel Karnaukhov/104* 4.00 10.00
SPPL1 Pascal Laberge/84* 5.00 12.00
SPPW1 Parker Wotherspoon/44* 4.00 10.00
SPPZ1 Pavel Zacha/115* 6.00 15.00
SPRG1 Ryan Gropp/36* 6.00 15.00
SPRK1 Ryan Kubic/103* 4.00 10.00
SPRP1 Ryan Pilon/84* 4.00 10.00
SPSG1 Samuel Girard/89* 5.00 12.00
SPSS1 Sam Steel/80* 8.00 20.00
SPSS2 Simon Stransky/104* 6.00 15.00
SPTB1 Travis Barron/84* 4.00 10.00
SPTB2 Tyler Benson/135* 8.00 20.00
SPTK1 Tanner Kaspick/104* 4.00 10.00
SPTK2 Travis Konecny/63* 12.00 30.00
SPTM1 Timo Meier/82* 6.00 15.00
SPTR1 Ty Ronning/154* 4.00 10.00
SPTS1 Thomas Schemitsch/51* 4.00 10.00
SPTS2 Tyler Soy/85* 4.00 10.00
SPVD1 Vince Dunn/87* 6.00 15.00
SPWB1 Will Bitten/86* 4.00 10.00

2015-16 Leaf Signature Series '90 Leaf Tribute Autographs

LTBH1 Brett Hull/25 15.00 40.00
LTJLC John LeClair/25 8.00 20.00
LTMM1 Mike Modano/25 12.00 30.00
LTPF1 Peter Forsberg/25 15.00 40.00
LTPR1 Patrick Roy/25 20.00 50.00
LTSF1 Sergei Fedorov/25 12.00 30.00
LTWC1 Wendel Clark/25 12.00 30.00

2015-16 Leaf Signature Series Captains Autographs

*GRAY/20-25: .4X TO 1X BASIC CARDS
SCAD1 Alex Delvecchio/30 8.00 20.00
SCRB1 Raymond Bourque/61 12.00 30.00
SCRK1 Red Kelly/60 8.00 20.00
SCSS1 Serge Savard/125 8.00 20.00
SCTL1 Ted Lindsay/90 8.00 20.00
SCYC1 Yvan Cournoyer/25 8.00 20.00

2015-16 Leaf Signature Series Champions Autographs

*GRAY: .4X TO 1X BASIC INSERTS
SCHBH2 Bobby Hull/30 15.00 40.00
SCHBP1 Bernie Parent/140 10.00 25.00
SCHBT1 Bryan Trottier/45 8.00 20.00
SCHCC1 Corey Crawford/72 10.00 25.00
SCHGA1 Glenn Anderson/85 6.00 15.00
SCHGF1 Grant Fuhr/60 12.00 30.00
SCHGL1 Guy Lapointe/56 6.00 15.00
SCHHR1 Henri Richard/104 8.00 20.00
SCHJL1 Jacques Lemaire/50 6.00 15.00
SCHPR1 Patrick Roy/20 20.00 50.00
SCHSF1 Sergei Fedorov/50 12.00 30.00
SCHTL1 Ted Lindsay/90 8.00 20.00
SCHYC1 Yvan Cournoyer35 8.00 20.00

2015-16 Leaf Signature Series Decades Autographs

*GRAY: .4X TO 1X BASIC INSERTS
SDBG1 Bill Gadsby/170* 8.00 20.00
SDBP2 Brad Park/92* 6.00 15.00
SDCC1 Corey Crawford/60* 10.00 25.00
SDEG1 Ed Giacomin/169* 8.00 20.00
SDGA1 Glenn Anderson/65* 6.00 15.00
SDGL1 Guy Lapointe/56* 6.00 15.00
SDHH1 Harry Howell/170* 6.00 15.00
SDJB1 Johnny Bower/60* 8.00 20.00
SDJH2 Jimmy Howard/151* 10.00 25.00
SDJL1 Jacques Lemaire/50* 6.00 15.00
SDJLC John LeClair/122* 8.00 20.00
SDMAF Marc-Andre Fleury/32* 15.00 40.00
SDMD1 Marcel Dionne/175* 10.00 25.00
SDNU1 Norm Ullman/170* 8.00 20.00
SDPF1 Peter Forsberg/30* 15.00 40.00
SDRB1 Raymond Bourque/69* 12.00 30.00
SDRK1 Red Kelly/51* 8.00 20.00
SDTL1 Ted Lindsay/90* 8.00 20.00
SDYC1 Yvan Cournoyer/25* 8.00 20.00

2015-16 Leaf Signature Series Dual MVP Autographs

MVP21 B.Hull/B.Hull 20.00 50.00
MVP24 P.Forsberg/J.Thornton 20.00 50.00

2015-16 Leaf Signature Series Dynasty Autographs

*GRAY: .4X TO 1X BASIC CARDS
SDYAD1 Alex Delvecchio/30* 8.00 20.00
SDYBT1 Bryan Trottier/50* 6.00 15.00
SDYGA1 Glenn Anderson/76* 6.00 15.00
SDYGF1 Grant Fuhr/59* 12.00 30.00
SDYGL1 Guy Lapointe/40* 6.00 15.00
SDYHR1 Henri Richard/100* 8.00 20.00
SDYJB1 Johnny Bower/36* 8.00 20.00
SDYJL1 Jacques Lemaire/40* 6.00 15.00
SDYRK1 Red Kelly/40* 8.00 20.00
SDYSS1 Serge Savard/99* 8.00 20.00
SDYTL1 Ted Lindsay/80* 8.00 20.00
SDYYC1 Yvan Cournoyer/34* 8.00 20.00

2015-16 Leaf Signature Series Fourever Legends Autographs

FL2 Gdsby/Dlvcchio/Ullmn/Lndsy/20 15.0040.00
FL3 Gcmn/Chvrs/Bwr/Fhr/25 25.00 60.00
FL5 Rchrd/Crnyr/Lpnte/Lmre/20 15.00 40.00

2015-16 Leaf Signature Series Miracle Team Autographs

M80BS1 Bob Suter 12.00 30.00
M80BS2 Buzz Schneider 10.00 25.00
M80DC1 Dave Christian 8.00 20.00
M80DS1 Dave Silk 10.00 25.00
M80ES1 Eric Strobel 15.00 40.00
M80JC1 Jim Craig 15.00 40.00
M80JH1 John Harrington 12.00 30.00
M80JO1 Jack O'Callahan 12.00 30.00
M80KM1 Ken Morrow 8.00 20.00
M80ME1 Mike Eruzione 10.00 25.00
M80MP1 Mark Pavelich 10.00 25.00
M80MR1 Mike Ramsey 12.00 30.00
M80MW1 Mark Wells 10.00 25.00
M80PV1 Phil Verchota 12.00 30.00
M80RM1 Rob McClanahan 10.00 25.00
M80SJ1 Steve Janaszak 12.00 30.00

2015-16 Leaf Signature Series MVP Autographs

MVPBH2 Bobby Hull 15.00 40.00
MVPBT1 Bryan Trottier 8.00 20.00
MVPPF1 Peter Forsberg 15.00 40.00
MVPSF1 Sergei Fedorov 12.00 30.00

2015-16 Leaf Signature Series Signature Prospect Jersey Autographs

PAJAB1 Anthony Beauvillier/30* 5.00 12.00
PAJAM1 Adam Musil/30* 5.00 12.00
PAJBH1 Brett Howden/30* 4.00 10.00
PAJBS1 Blake Speers/30* 4.00 10.00
PAJCA1 Cameron Askew/30* 4.00 10.00
PAJCH1 Connor Hobbs/30* 4.00 10.00
PAJCP1 Cliff Pu/30* 4.00 10.00
PAJDK1 Davis Koch/30* 4.00 10.00
PAJGK1 Graham Knott/30* 4.00 10.00
PAJJG1 Julien Gauthier/30* 8.00 20.00
PAJJW1 Jaeger White/30* 4.00 10.00
PAJMF1 Maxime Fortier/30* 4.00 10.00
PAJMG1 Matteo Gennaro/30* 4.00 10.00
PAJMS1 Mitchell Stephens/30* 4.00 10.00
PAJPW1 Parker Wotherspoon/30* 4.00 10.00
PAJRG1 Ryan Gropp/30* 6.00 15.00
PAJTS1 Thomas Schemitsch/30* 4.00 10.00
PAJVD1 Vince Dunn/30* 6.00 15.00
PAJWB1 Will Bitten/30* 4.00 10.00

1997-98 Leaf International

COMPLETE SET (150) 30.00 60.00
1 Eric Lindros .25 .60
2 Dominik Hasek .50 1.25
3 Peter Forsberg .60 1.50
4 Steve Yzerman 1.25 3.00
5 John Vanbiesbrouck .20 .50
6 Paul Kariya .25 .60
7 Martin Brodeur .60 1.50
8 Wayne Gretzky 1.50 4.00
9 Mark Messier .25 .60
10 Jaromir Jagr .40 1.00
11 Brett Hull .30 .75
12 Brendan Shanahan .25 .60
13 Ray Bourque .40 1.00
14 Jarome Iginla .30 .75
15 Mike Modano .40 1.00
16 Curtis Joseph .25 .60
17 Ed Jovanovski .20 .50
18 Teemu Selanne .25 .60
19 Saku Koivu .25 .60
20 Eric Fichaud .20 .50
21 Paul Coffey .25 .60
22 Jeremy Roenick .30 .75
23 Owen Nolan .20 .50
24 Felix Potvin .25 .60
25 Alexander Mogilny .20 .50
26 Alexandre Daigle .10 .30
27 Chris Gratton .20 .50
28 Geoff Sanderson .20 .50
29 Dimitri Khristich .10 .30
30 Bryan Berard .10 .30
31 Vyacheslav Kozlov .10 .30
32 Jeff Hackett .20 .50
33 Bill Ranford .20 .50
34 Pat LaFontaine .25 .60
35 Joe Sakic .50 1.25
36 Niklas Sundstrom .10 .30
37 Martin Gelinas .10 .30
38 Mikael Renberg .10 .30
39 Trevor Linden .20 .50
40 Jozef Stumpel .20 .50
41 Joe Thornton CL .10 .30
42 Jocelyn Thibault .20 .50
43 Pierre Turgeon .20 .50
44 Ron Francis .20 .50
45 Damian Rhodes .20 .50
46 Jamie Langenbrunner .10 .30
47 Chris Osgood .20 .50
48 Vaclav Varada .20 .50
49 Ryan Smyth .20 .50
50 Daren Puppa .20 .50
51 Petr Nedved .20 .50
52 Ron Hextall .20 .50
53 Joe Juneau .20 .50
54 Jim Campbell .10 .30
55 Zigmund Palffy .20 .50
56 Roman Turek .20 .50
57 Adam Deadmarsh .10 .30
58 Rob Niedermayer .20 .50
59 Alexei Yashin .10 .30
60 Pavel Bure .25 .60
61 Jason Arnott .10 .30
62 Nikolai Khabibulin .20 .50
63 Sean Burke .20 .50
64 Chris Chelios .25 .60
65 Mike Ricci .20 .50
66 Sergei Berezin .10 .30
67 Jaroslav Svejkovsky CL .10 .30
68 Brian Savage .10 .30
69 Roman Vopat .10 .30
70 Mike Richter .25 .60
71 Jim Carey .20 .50
72 Guy Hebert .20 .50
73 Keith Tkachuk .25 .60
74 Kirk McLean .20 .50
75 Janne Niinimaa .20 .50
76 Roman Hamrlik .10 .30
77 Darcy Tucker .10 .30
78 Pat Verbeek .10 .30
79 Hnat Domenichelli .10 .30
80 Doug Gilmour .20 .50
81 Mike Grier .10 .30
82 Ken Wregget .10 .30
83 Dino Ciccarelli .10 .30
84 Steve Sullivan .10 .30
85 Anson Carter .20 .50
86 Steve Shields RC .40 1.00
87 Ed Belfour .25 .60
88 Darren McCarty .10 .30
89 Adam Graves .10 .30
90 Chris Pronger .20 .50
91 Peter Bondra .20 .50
92 Oleg Tverdovsky .10 .30
93 Stephane Fiset .20 .50
94 Mike Vernon .20 .50
95 Scott Lachance .10 .30
96 Corey Schwab .10 .30
97 Eric Daze .20 .50
98 Jere Lehtinen .10 .30
99 Donald Audette .10 .30
100 John LeClair .25 .60
101 Steve Rucchin .10 .30
102 Jeff Friesen .10 .30
103 Daymond Langkow .20 .50
104 Mike Dunham .20 .50
105 Marc Denis CL .10 .30
106 Andrew Cassels .10 .30
107 Mike Peca .10 .30
108 Joe Nieuwendyk .20 .50
109 Vincent Damphousse .10 .30
110 Scott Mellanby .10 .30
111 Patrick Lalime .20 .50
112 Derek Plante .10 .30
113 Wade Redden .10 .30
114 Marcel Cousineau .20 .50
115 Ray Sheppard .10 .30
116 Dave Andreychuk .10 .30
117 Brian Leetch .25 .60
118 Sandis Ozolinsh .10 .30
119 Keith Primeau .10 .30
120 Brian Holzinger .10 .30
121 Luc Robitaille .20 .50
122 Jose Theodore .30 .75
123 Grant Fuhr .20 .50
124 Dainius Zubrus .25 .60
125 Rod Brind'Amour .20 .50
126 Trevor Kidd .20 .50
127 Mark Recchi .20 .50
128 Patrick Roy 1.00 2.50
129 Kevin Hatcher .10 .30
130 Adam Oates .20 .50
131 Doug Weight .20 .50
132 Vaclav Prospal RC .25 .60
133 Harry York .10 .30
134 Todd Bertuzzi .25 .60
135 Sergei Fedorov .40 1.00
136 Theo Fleury .10 .30
137 Chad Kilger .10 .30
138 Jamie Storr .20 .50
139 Tony Amonte .20 .50
140 Rem Murray .10 .30
141 Chris O'Sullivan .10 .30
142 Mats Sundin .25 .60
143 Ethan Moreau .10 .30
144 Derian Hatcher .10 .30
145 Daniel Alfredsson .20 .50
146 Corey Hirsch .20 .50
147 Landon Wilson .10 .30
148 Chris Phillips CL .10 .30
149 Sergei Samsonov CL (149,150 inserts) .10 .30
150 Daniel Cleary CL .10 .30

1997-98 Leaf International Universal Ice

*VETS: 4X TO 10X BASIC CARDS
*ROOKIES: 2X TO 5X BASIC CARDS

2015-16 Leaf Toronto Fall Expo Jack Eichel Patches

PJE1 Jack Eichel Patch Slvr/99 40.00 100.00
PJE2 Jack Eichel Patch Blue/35 40.00 100.00
APJE1 Jack Eichel JSY AU Slvr/25 40.00 100.00

2015-16 Leaf Ultimate Signatures

USBB1 Brian Bellows/30 6.00 15.00
USBG1 Bill Gadsby/35 8.00 20.00
USBH1 Bobby Hull/30 15.00 40.00
USBH2 Brett Hull/30 15.00 40.00
USCJ1 Curtis Joseph/30 10.00 25.00
USDM1 Dickie Moore/45 6.00 15.00
USEF1 Emile Francis/30 6.00 15.00
USEG1 Ed Giacomin/45 8.00 20.00
USEL2 Eric Lindros/25 12.00 30.00
USFP1 Felix Potvin/35 12.00 30.00
USGH1 Glenn Hall/25 8.00 20.00
USJB2 Johnny Bower/45 8.00 20.00
USJB3 Johnny Bucyk/35 8.00 20.00
USJE1 Jack Eichel/45 30.00 80.00
USJP1 Jesse Puljujarvi/45 15.00 40.00
USJT1 Jose Theodore/45 8.00 20.00
USJV1 John Vanbiesbrouck/40 8.00 20.00
USKH1 Ken Hodge/45 6.00 15.00
USMB1 Martin Brodeur/30 20.00 50.00
USMD1 Marcel Dionne/40 10.00 25.00
USML1 Mario Lemieux/25 30.00 80.00
USMN1 Mats Naslund/45 5.00 12.00
USNL1 Nicklas Lidstrom/25 8.00 20.00
USPH1 Phil Housley/30 6.00 15.00
USPL1 Pat LaFontaine/30 8.00 20.00
USPP1 Pierre Pilote/35 8.00 20.00
USPR1 Patrick Roy/25 20.00 50.00
USRD1 Ron Duguay/20 6.00 15.00
USRK1 Red Kelly/45 8.00 20.00
USRL1 Reggie Leach/45 6.00 15.00
USSB1 Scotty Bowman/25 12.00 30.00
USSL1 Steve Larmer/45 6.00 15.00
USTE1 Tony Esposito/35 8.00 20.00
USTL2 Trevor Linden/30 8.00 20.00

USTS1 Teemu Selanne/25 15.00 40.00
USVT1 Vladislav Tretiak/35 6.00 15.00
USWC1 Wendel Clark/40 12.00 30.00

2015-16 Leaf Ultimate Autograph Memorabilia

AMBH1 Bobby Hull/30 15.00 40.00
AMEB1 Ed Belfour/35 8.00 20.00
AMGH1 Glenn Hall/30 8.00 20.00
AMJE1 Jack Eichel/45 30.00 80.00
AMML1 Mario Lemieux/30 30.00 80.00
AMOK1 Olaf Kolzig/40 8.00 20.00
AMPH1 Phil Housley/40 6.00 15.00
AMPL1 Pat LaFontaine/40 8.00 20.00
AMPR1 Patrick Roy/30 20.00 50.00
AMRL1 Reggie Leach/30 6.00 15.00

2015-16 Leaf Ultimate Dual Signatures

DS01 C.Joseph/F.Potvin/20 15.00 40.00
DS02 E.Lindros/R.Leach/25 15.00 40.00
DS03 J.Eichel/P.LaFontaine/20 40.00 100.00
DS04 J.Puljujarvi/J.Eichel/25 40.00 100.00
DS05 J.Kocur/W.Clark/20 15.00 40.00
DS06 J.Bower/C.Joseph/20 12.00 30.00
DS07 J.Bucyk/K.Hodge/25 10.00 25.00
DS09 M.Naslund/B.Bellows/25 8.00 20.00
DS11 P.LaFontaine/B.Hull/20 20.00 50.00
DS13 P.Housley/P.LaFontaine/25 10.00 25.00
DS14 P.Pilote/B.Hull/25 20.00 50.00
DS15 R.Kelly/B.Gadsby/25 10.00 25.00

2015-16 Leaf Ultimate Dual Ultimate Memorabilia

UD01 B.Clarke/R.Leach/20 4.00 10.00
UD02 C.Joseph/F.Potvin/35 4.00 10.00
UD04 J.Eichel/M.Lemieux/25 10.00 25.00
UD05 M.Lemieux/W.Gretzky/20 15.00 40.00
UD06 M.Sundin/W.Clark/35 4.00 10.00
UD07 M.Bossy/W.Gretzky/20 15.00 40.00
UD08 O.Kolzig/J.Theodore/30 4.00 10.00
UD09 P.LaFontaine/J.Eichel/35 10.00 25.00
UD10 P.Roy/D.Hasek/35 6.00 15.00
UD11 P.Roy/M.Brodeur/30 6.00 15.00
UD12 P.Kariya/T.Selanne/30 5.00 12.00
UD13 P.Bure/T.Linden/35 2.50 6.00
UD14 R.Gilbert/P.Esposito/20 6.00 15.00
UD15 S.Mikita/B.Hull/20 5.00 12.00
UD16 T.Selanne/J.Sakic/25 5.00 12.00
UD17 T.Esposito/P.Esposito/20 4.00 10.00

2015-16 Leaf Ultimate Enforcers Jerseys

UE01 Bob Probert 3.00 8.00
UE02 Clark Gillies 3.00 8.00
UE03 Darren McCarty 3.00 8.00
UE04 Dave Schultz 3.00 8.00
UE05 Gino Odjick 2.00 5.00
UE06 Marty McSorley 2.50 6.00
UE07 Matthew Barnaby 2.00 5.00
UE08 Stu Grimson 3.00 8.00
UE09 Tie Domi 3.00 8.00
UE10 Tiger Williams 2.00 5.00
UE11 Tony Twist 3.00 8.00

2015-16 Leaf Ultimate Honoured Members Autographs

HMAD1 Alex Delvecchio/25 8.00 20.00
HMBG1 Bill Gadsby/25 8.00 20.00
HMBH1 Bobby Hull/25 15.00 40.00
HMBP1 Bernie Parent/25 10.00 25.00
HMDM1 Dickie Moore/25 6.00 15.00
HMEF1 Emile Francis/25 6.00 15.00
HMEG1 Ed Giacomin/25 8.00 20.00
HMGC1 Gerry Cheevers/25 8.00 20.00
HMGH1 Glenn Hall/20 8.00 20.00
HMJB2 Johnny Bower/25 8.00 20.00
HMJB3 Johnny Bucyk/25 8.00 20.00
HMMD1 Marcel Dionne/25 10.00 25.00
HMML1 Mario Lomioux/25 30.00 80.00
HMMM1 Mike Modano/25 12.00 30.00
HMMS1 Milt Schmidt/20 8.00 20.00
HMNL1 Nicklas Lidstrom/20 8.00 20.00
HMPH1 Phil Housley/25 6.00 15.00
HMPL1 Pat LaFontaine/25 8.00 20.00
HMPP1 Pierre Pilote/25 8.00 20.00
HMPR1 Patrick Roy/25 20.00 50.00
HMRK1 Red Kelly/25 8.00 20.00
HMSB1 Scotty Bowman/25 12.00 30.00

2015-16 Leaf Ultimate Journey Jerseys

UJ04 Curtis Joseph/20 12.00 30.00
UJ06 Felix Potvin/20 15.00 40.00
UJ08 Jeremy Roenick/20 15.00 40.00
UJ12 Patrick Roy/20 25.00 60.00
UJ13 Paul Kariya/20 10.00 25.00
UJ14 Pavel Bure/20 10.00 25.00
UJ15 Peter Forsberg/20 20.00 50.00
UJ18 Sergei Fedorov/20 15.00 40.00
UJ19 Teemu Selanne/20 20.00 50.00

2015-16 Leaf Ultimate Time Capsule Signatures

TCBH1 Bobby Hull/40 15.00 40.00
TCBP1 Bernie Parent/35 10.00 25.00
TCDM1 Dickie Moore/40 6.00 15.00
TCEL2 Eric Lindros/30 12.00 30.00
TCJB2 Johnny Bower/40 8.00 20.00
TCJE1 Jack Eichel/40 30.00 80.00
TCJE2 Jack Eichel/25 30.00 80.00
TCJP1 Jesse Puljujarvi/40 15.00 40.00
TCMD1 Marcel Dionne/40 10.00 25.00
TCML1 Mario Lemieux/20 30.00 80.00
TCMS1 Milt Schmidt/25 8.00 20.00
TCPH1 Phil Housley/40 6.00 15.00
TCPL1 Pat LaFontaine/25 8.00 20.00
TCPR1 Patrick Roy/25 20.00 50.00
TCRK1 Red Kelly/40 8.00 20.00
TCSB1 Scotty Bowman/25 12.00 30.00
TCTS1 Teemu Selanne/25 15.00 40.00

2015-16 Leaf Ultimate Triple Signatures

TS02 Delvecchio/Kelly/Lindsay/20 20.00 50.00
TS03 Eichel/LaFontaine/Modano/20 75.00 150.00

2015-16 Leaf Ultimate Triple Ultimate Memorabilia

UT01 Barber/Clarke/Leach/30 10.00 25.00
UT02 Bourque/Lidstrom/Coffey/30 6.00 15.00
UT03 Eichel/Modano/LaFontaine/30 25.00 60.00
UT04 Fedorov/Bure/Mogilny/30 10.00 25.00
UT05 Fuhr/Potvin/Joseph/35 10.00 25.00
UT06 Gilbert/Lafleur/Esposito/30 10.00 25.00
UT07 Lemieux/Lindros/Eichel/30 25.00 60.00
UT08 Lidstrom/Shanahan/Fedorov/30 10.00 25.00
UT09 Naslund/Bellows/Koivu/35 6.00 15.00
UT10 Orr/Gretzky/Howe/12 40.00 100.00
UT11 Roy/Joseph/Belfour/30 15.00 40.00

2016-17 Leaf Ultimate Quad Memorabilia

UQ01 Gretzky/Lemieux
Esposito/Howe/25 40.00 100.00
UQ02 Hull/Roenick/Lemieux/Sakic/25 25.00 60.00
UQ03 Hawerchuk/Sakic
Robitaille/Oates/25 12.00 30.00
UQ04 Chelios/Blake
Lidstrom/Pronger/25 6.00 15.00
UQ05 Kariya/Selanne
Jagr/Fedorov/25 20.00 50.00
UQ06 Modano/Shanahan
Sundin/Bure/25 10.00 25.00
UQ07 Howe/Delvecchio
Sawchuk/Lindsay/25 20.00 50.00
UQ08 Ovechkin/Bure
Fedorov/Mogilny/25 25.00 60.00
UQ09 Tavares/Hall/Nugent-
Hopkins/Stamkos/25 12.00 30.00
UQ10 Goulet/Stastny
Gretzky/Savard/25 40.00 100.00
UQ11 Housley/Murphy
Potvin/Bourque/25 6.00 15.00
UQ12 Arbour/Potvin/Smith/Bossy/25 6.00 15.00
UQ13 Lafleur/Esposito
Clarke/Dionne/25 10.00 25.00
UQ14 Taylor/Ciccarelli
Francis/Mullen/25 8.00 20.00
UQ15 Roy/Moog/Barrasso/Smith/25 15.00 40.00

2016-17 Leaf Ultimate Signature Memorabilia

SMBS1 Borje Salming/20 6.00 15.00
SMDH1 Dale Hawerchuk/20 8.00 20.00
SMDS1 Denis Savard/20 6.00 15.00
SMJE1 Jack Eichel/20 10.00 25.00
SMJM1 Joe Mullen/20 5.00 12.00
SMLM1 Larry Murphy/20 5.00 12.00
SMLR1 Larry Robinson/20 6.00 15.00
SMLR2 Luc Robitaille/20 6.00 15.00
SMMB1 Martin Brodeur/20 15.00 40.00
SMMG1 Michel Goulet/20 6.00 15.00
SMMR1 Mike Richter/20 6.00 15.00
SMRB1 Raymond Bourque/20 10.00 25.00
SMRL1 Rod Langway/20 5.00 12.00
SMSS1 Serge Savard/20 6.00 15.00
SMSS2 Steve Shutt/20 6.00 15.00
SMTB1 Tom Barrasso/20 6.00 15.00
SMTE1 Tony Esposito/20 6.00 15.00

2016-17 Leaf Ultimate Triple Memorabilia

UT01 Howe/Ullman/Lindsay 20.00 50.00
UT02 Roy/Plante/Sawchuk 15.00 40.00
UT03 McDavid/Crosby/Stamkos 30.00 80.00
UT04 Jagr/Lemieux/Malkin 25.00 60.00
UT05 McDavid/Eichel/Larkin 30.00 80.00
UT06 Gretzky/Bossy/Esposito 40.00 100.00
UT07 Ovechkin/Fedorov/Malkin 25.00 60.00
UT08 Beliveau/Joliat/Harvey 6.00 15.00
UT09 Dionne/Esposito/Clarke 10.00 25.00
UT10 Orr/Salming/Robinson 25.00 60.00
UT11 Mikita/Hull/Esposito 12.00 30.00

2017-18 Leaf Ultimate Compatriots Relics

UC02 Brodeur/Francis/Lindros
Lemieux/Yzerman/Sakic 25.00 60.00
UC03 Bure/Mogilny/Yashin/Khabibulin
Kasparaitis/Bryzgalov 6.00 15.00
UC04 Chelios/Hull/Leetch/Amonte
Barrasso/Guerin 12.00 30.00
UC05 Dzurilla/Cechmanek/Bonk
Holik/Turek/Stastny 6.00 15.00
UC06 Lindbergh/Lidstrom/Salming
Salo/Forsberg/Naslund 12.00 30.00
UC07 Perreault/Clarke/Esposito
Shutt/Sittler/Dionne 10.00 25.00
UC08 Tretiak/Mikhailov/Kharlamov
Mylnikov/Yakushev/Krutov 6.00 15.00

2017-18 Leaf Ultimate Dual Signatures

US201 B.Hull/A.Oates/15 25.00 40.00
US206 N.Patrick/N.Hischier/25 25.00 60.00
US207 P.Esposito/M.Schmidt/12 15.00 40.00
US208 P.Pilote/B.Gadsby/12 15.00 40.00
US209 V.Tretiak/T.Esposito/12 15.00 40.00

1971-72 Letraset Action Replays

COMPLETE SET (24) 100.00 200.00
1 Rogatien Vachon
Dave Keon
Gilles Marotte 5.00 10.00
2 Ken Dryden
Chico Maki
Jacques Laperriere 10.00 20.00
3 Gary Dornhoefer
Roger Crozier
Tracy Pratt 4.00 8.00
4 Walt Tkaczuk
Gump Worsley
Vic Hadfield 4.00 8.00
5 Dallas Smith
Bobby Orr
Walt McKechnie 17.50 35.00
6 Ab McDonald
Gary Sabourin
Garry Unger 4.00 8.00
7 Jim Rutherford
Orland Kurtenbach
Bob Woytovich 4.00 8.00
8 Gerry Cheevers
Frank Mahovlich
Don Awrey 6.00 12.00
9 Tim Ecclestone
Bob Baun
Jacques Plante 5.00 10.00
10 Stan Mikita
Ed Giacomin
Jim Pappin 6.00 12.00
11 Doug Favell
Danny Grant
Ed Van Impe 4.00 8.00
12 Ernie Wakely
Barclay Plager
Gary Croteau 4.00 8.00
13 Bryan Hextall
Tony Esposito
Pat Stapleton 5.00 10.00
14 Jean Ratelle
Rod Gilbert
Jim Roberts 5.00 10.00
15 Jacques Lemaire
Henri Richard
Yvan Cournoyer 6.00 12.00
16 George Gardiner
Dennis Hull
Lou Angotti 4.00 8.00
17 Ed Johnston
Norm Ullman
Bobby Orr 17.50 35.00
18 Gilles Meloche
Wayne Carleton
Dick Redmond 4.00 8.00
19 Al Smith
Gary Bergman
Stan Gilbertson 4.00 8.00
20 Dunc Wilson
Brad Park
Dale Tallon 4.00 8.00
21 Jude Drouin
Doug Favell
Barry Ashbee 4.00 8.00
22 Ron Ellis
Ken Dryden
Paul Henderson 10.00 20.00
23 Gary Edwards
Jean Pronovost
Ron Shock 4.00 8.00
24 Cesare Maniago
Chris Bordeleau
Ted Harris 4.00 8.00

1980 Liberty Matchbooks

NNO Ray Bourque 10.00 20.00

1992-93 Lightning Sheraton

COMPLETE SET (28) 8.00 20.00
1 Mikael Andersson .20 .50
2 Bob Beers .20 .50
3 J.C. Bergeron .30 .75
4 Marc Bergevin .20 .50
5 Tim Bergland .20 .50
6 Brian Bradley .60 1.50
7 Marc Bureau .20 .50
8 Wayne Cashman CO .20 .50
9 Shawn Chambers .20 .50
10 Danton Cole .20 .50
11 Adam Creighton .30 .75
12 Terry Crisp CO .20 .50
13 Rob DiMaio .30 .75
14 Phil Esposito GM .75 2.00
15 Tony Esposito DIR .60 1.50
16 Roman Hamrlik .75 2.00
17 Pat Jablonski .30 .75
18 Steve Kasper .20 .50
19 Chris Kontos .20 .50
20 Steve Maltais .20 .50
21 Joe Reekie .20 .50
22 Thunderbug (Mascot) .08 .25
23 John Tucker .30 .75
24 Wendell Young .30 .75
25 Rob Zamuner .30 .75
26 Title card .20 .50
27 Inaugural season card .08 .25
28 Sheraton logo card .08 .25

1993-94 Lightning Kash n'Karry

COMPLETE SET (6) 3.00 8.00
1 Brian Bradley .75 2.00
2 Shawn Chambers .40 1.00
3 Chris Gratton .75 2.00
4 Adam Creighton .40 1.00
5 Rob DiMaio .40 1.00
6 Wendell Young .60 1.50

1993-94 Lightning Season in Review

COMPLETE SET (28) 6.00 15.00
1 Mikael Andersson .20 .50
2 Marc Bergevin .20 .50
3 Brian Bradley .30 .75
4 Marc Bureau .20 .50
5 Wayne Cashman ACO .20 .50
6 Shawn Chambers .20 .50
7 Enrico Ciccone .20 .50
8 Danton Cole .20 .50
9 Adam Creighton .20 .50
10 Terry Crisp CO .20 .50
11 Jim Cummins .20 .50
12 Pat Elynuik .20 .50
13 Phil Esposito GM .60 1.50
14 Tony Esposito DIR .40 1.00
15 Gerard Gallant .20 .50
16 Danny Gare ACO .08 .25
17 Chris Gratton .60 1.50
18 Roman Hamrlik .60 1.50
19 Chris Joseph .20 .50
20 Petr Klima .20 .50
21 Chris LiPuma .20 .50
22 Rudy Poeschek .30 .75
23 Daren Puppa .60 1.50
24 Denis Savard .40 1.00
25 Thunderbug MASCOT .08 .25
26 John Tucker .20 .50
27 Wendell Young .25 .60
28 Rob Zamuner .20 .50

1994-95 Lightning Health Plan

COMPLETE SET (2) 2.50 6.00
1 Daren Puppa 1.50 4.00
2 Chris Gratton 1.25 3.00

1994-95 Lightning Photo Album

COMPLETE SET (29) 4.80 12.00
1 Mikael Andersson .15 .40
2 J.C. Bergeron .20 .50
3 Marc Bergevin .15 .40
4 Brian Bradley .30 .75
5 Marc Bureau .15 .40
6 Wayne Cashman ACO .15 .40
7 Eric Charron .15 .40
8 Enrico Ciccone .20 .50
9 Terry Crisp CO .15 .40
10 Cory Cross .15 .40
11 Phil Esposito PRES/GM .40 1.00
12 Tony Esposito DIR .20 .50
13 Danny Gare ACO .15 .40
14 Chris Gratton .30 .75
15 Bob Halkidis .15 .40
16 Roman Hamrlik .40 1.00
17 Ben Hankinson .15 .40
18 Petr Klima .15 .40
19 Brantt Myhres .15 .40
20 Adrien Plavsic .15 .40
21 Rudy Poeschek .20 .50
22 Daren Puppa .50 1.25
23 Alexander Selivanov .40 1.00
24 Alexander Semak .15 .40
25 John Tucker .20 .50
26 Jason Wiemer .30 .75
27 Paul Ysebaert .15 .40
28 Rob Zamuner .15 .40
29 Team Photo .40 1.00

1994-95 Lightning Postcards

COMPLETE SET (20) 8.00 20.00
1 Mikael Andersson .30 .75
2 Brian Bradley .40 1.00
3 Shawn Burr .30 .75
4 Terry Crisp .20 .50
5 Cory Cross .30 .75
6 John Cullen .30 .75
7 Phil Esposito .75 2.00
8 Tony Esposito .75 2.00
9 Chris Gratton .40 1.00
10 Roman Hamrlik .40 1.00
11 Bill Houlder .30 .75
12 Daymond Langkow .75 2.00
13 Brantt Myhres .30 .75
14 Daren Puppa .40 1.00
15 Chris Reichart .30 .75
16 Alexander Selivanov .30 .75
17 David Shaw .30 .75
18 Jason Wiemer .30 .75
19 Paul Ysebaert .30 .75
20 Rob Zamuner .30 .75

1995-96 Lightning Team Issue

COMPLETE SET (21) 8.00 20.00
1 Mikael Andersson .40 1.00
2 Brian Bellows .40 1.00
3 J.C. Bergeron .50 1.25
4 Brian Bradley .50 1.25
5 Shawn Burr .40 1.00
6 Enrico Ciccone .40 1.00
7 Cory Cross .40 1.00
8 John Cullen .40 1.00
9 Aaron Gavey .40 1.00
10 Chris Gratton .60 1.50
11 Roman Hamrlik .50 1.25
12 Bill Houlder .40 1.00
13 Petr Klima .40 1.00
14 Rudy Poeschek .40 1.00
15 Daren Puppa .50 1.25
16 Alexander Selivanov .40 1.00
17 David Shaw .40 1.00
18 John Tucker .40 1.00
19 Jason Wiemer .40 1.00
20 Paul Ysebaert .40 1.00
21 Rob Zamuner .40 1.00

2002-03 Lightning Team Issue

COMPLETE SET
1 Nikita Alexeev .40 1.00
2 Dave Andreychuk .75 2.00
3 Dan Boyle .75 2.00
4 Chris Dingman .40 1.00
5 Nikolai Khabibulin .75 2.00
6 Pavel Kubina .40 1.00
7 Vincent Lecavalier 2.00 5.00
8 Brad Lukowich .40 1.00
9 Fredrik Modin .40 1.00
10 Brad Richards 1.25 3.00
11 Andre Roy .40 1.00
12 Martin St-Louis .75 2.00

2003-04 Lightning Team Issue

COMPLETE SET (36) 15.00 30.00
1 Cover Card .02 .10
2 Team Card .02 .10
3 John Tortorella CO .20 .50
4 Craig Ramsay ACO .20 .50
5 Jeff Reese ACO .20 .50
6 Nigel Kirwan ACO .20 .50
7 Paul Kennedy ANN .20 .50
8 Rick Peckham ANN .20 .50
9 Phil Esposito ANN .75 2.00
10 Vincent Lecavalier 2.00 5.00
11 Jassen Cullimore .40 1.00
12 Ben Clymer .40 1.00
13 Martin Cibak .40 1.00
14 Eric Perrin .75 2.00
15 Brian Bradley Alumni .40 1.00
16 Chris Dingman .40 1.00
17 Pavel Kubina .40 1.00
18 John Tucker Alumni .40 1.00
19 Alexander Svitov .40 1.00
20 Ruslan Fedotenko .40 1.00
21 Brad Richards 1.50 4.00
22 Cory Sarich .40 1.00
23 Dan Boyle .40 1.00
24 Shane Willis .40 1.00
25 Dave Andreychuk .40 1.00
26 Martin St. Louis 1.25 3.00
27 Tim Taylor .40 1.00
28 Sheldon Keefe .40 1.00
29 Dmitry Afanasenkov .40 1.00
30 Fredrik Modin .40 1.00
31 Nikolai Khabibulin .75 2.00
32 Andre Roy .75 2.00
33 Brad Lukowich .40 1.00
34 Nolan Pratt .40 1.00
35 Cory Stillman .40 1.00
36 Daren Puppa Alumni .40 1.00

2005-06 Lightning Team Issue

1 John Tortorella CO .40 1.00
2 Craig Ramsay ACO .40 1.00
3 Jeff Reese ACO .40 1.00
4 Vincent Lecavalier 2.00 5.00
5 Darryl Sydor .75 2.00
6 Chris Dingman .75 2.00
7 Vaclav Prospal .75 2.00
8 Dan Boyle .75 2.00
9 Martin St. Louis 1.25 3.00
10 Tim Taylor .75 2.00
11 Nolan Pratt .75 2.00

2006-07 Lightning Postcards

COMPLETE SET (23) 15.00 30.00
1 Logo Card .10 .25
2 Dmitry Afanasenkov .40 1.00
3 Nikita Alexeev .40 1.00
4 Dan Boyle .40 1.00
5 Ryan Craig .40 1.00
6 Marc Denis .60 1.50
7 Ruslan Fedotenko .40 1.00
8 Doug Janik .40 1.00
9 Johan Holmqvist .75 2.00
10 Andreas Karlsson .40 1.00
11 Filip Kuba .40 1.00
12 Vincent Lecavalier 2.00 5.00
13 Eric Perrin .40 1.00
14 Nolan Pratt .40 1.00
15 Vaclav Prospal .40 1.00
16 Paul Ranger .40 1.00
17 Brad Richards 1.25 3.00
18 Luke Richardson .40 1.00
19 Andre Roy .40 1.00
20 Cory Sarich .40 1.00
21 Martin St. Louis 1.25 3.00
22 Nick Tarnasky .40 1.00
23 Tim Taylor .40 1.00

2010-11 Limited

1 Ryan Miller 2.00 5.00
2 Henrik Sedin 2.50 6.00
3 Alex Ovechkin 8.00 20.00
4 Shane Doan 1.50 4.00
5 Phil Kessel 2.00 5.00
6 Marty Turco 2.00 5.00
7 Sidney Crosby 8.00 20.00
8 Daniel Sedin 2.50 6.00
9 Teemu Selanne 4.00 10.00
10 Kyle Okposo 1.25 3.00
11 Martin Brodeur 5.00 12.00
12 Nicklas Backstrom 2.00 5.00
13 Patrick Marleau 2.00 5.00
14 Sam Gagner 1.25 3.00
15 Tomas Vokoun 1.50 4.00
16 Jonathan Bernier 1.50 4.00
17 Steven Stamkos 4.00 10.00
18 Zach Parise 2.00 5.00
19 Claude Giroux 2.00 5.00
20 Erik Johnson 1.25 3.00
21 Roberto Luongo 3.00 8.00
22 Joe Thornton 3.00 8.00
23 Henrik Zetterberg 2.50 6.00
24 Dion Phaneuf 1.50 4.00
25 Marc Savard 1.25 3.00
26 Carey Price 4.00 10.00
27 Brad Richards 2.00 5.00
28 Marian Hossa 2.00 5.00
29 Dany Heatley 1.50 4.00
30 Chris Mason 1.50 4.00
31 Tuukka Rask 2.50 6.00
32 Evgeni Malkin 4.00 10.00
33 James Neal 1.25 3.00
34 Simon Gagne 2.00 5.00
35 Mike Modano 3.00 8.00
36 Ilya Bryzgalov 1.50 4.00
37 Pavel Datsyuk 3.00 8.00
38 Thomas Vanek 1.50 4.00
39 Marian Gaborik 2.00 5.00
40 Brent Burns 2.00 5.00
41 Jaroslav Halak 2.00 5.00
42 Paul Stastny 1.50 4.00
43 Michael Cammalleri 2.00 5.00
44 Ilya Kovalchuk 2.00 5.00
45 Nikolai Khabibulin 1.50 4.00
46 Anze Kopitar 3.00 8.00
47 Dustin Byfuglien 2.00 5.00
48 Daniel Alfredsson 2.00 5.00
49 Sergei Gonchar 1.25 3.00
50 Wojtek Wolski 1.25 3.00
51 Henrik Lundqvist 5.00 12.00
52 Eric Staal 2.50 6.00
53 Drew Doughty 2.50 6.00
54 Andrei Markov 2.00 5.00
55 Duncan Keith 1.50 4.00
56 Jonas Gustavsson 2.50 6.00
57 Vincent Lecavalier 2.00 5.00
58 Nicklas Lidstrom 2.00 5.00
59 Brandon Sutter 1.25 3.00
60 Zdeno Chara 2.00 5.00
61 Marc-Andre Fleury 4.00 10.00
62 Ryan Getzlaf 2.00 5.00
63 Alexander Frolov 1.25 3.00
64 Steve Mason 1.50 4.00
65 Ales Hemsky 1.50 4.00
66 Niklas Backstrom 2.00 5.00
67 Jonathan Toews 3.00 8.00
68 Rick Nash 2.00 5.00
69 Tomas Plekanec 1.25 3.00
70 Loui Eriksson 1.25 3.00
71 Jimmy Howard 2.50 6.00
72 Mike Richards 1.50 4.00
73 Jarome Iginla 2.50 6.00
74 Pekka Rinne 2.00 5.00
75 Mikko Koivu 2.00 5.00
76 Craig Anderson 2.00 5.00
77 Jeff Carter 1.50 4.00
78 Tyler Myers 1.25 3.00
79 Ryan Kesler 2.00 5.00
80 Mike Green 1.50 4.00
81 Miikka Kiprusoff 2.00 5.00
82 Jason Spezza 2.00 5.00
83 Shea Weber 1.50 4.00
84 Chris Pronger 2.00 5.00
85 Antti Niemi 1.50 4.00
86 Semyon Varlamov 2.00 5.00
87 Matt Duchene 2.00 5.00
88 Nathan Horton 1.50 4.00
89 Guillaume Latendresse 1.50 4.00
90 Stephen Weiss 1.50 4.00
91 Cam Ward 2.00 5.00
92 John Tavares 3.00 8.00
93 Patrick Kane 4.00 10.00
94 Wayne Simmonds 2.50 6.00
95 Jordan Staal 1.50 4.00
96 Michael Leighton 1.50 4.00
97 T.J. Oshie 2.00 5.00
98 Corey Perry 3.00 8.00
99 Tyler Bozak 1.25 3.00
100 Erik Karlsson 2.50 6.00
101 Kari Lehtonen 1.50 4.00
102 Joe Pavelski 2.50 6.00
103 Andrei Loktionov 1.50 4.00
104 Scott Gomez 1.50 4.00
105 Nikolay Zherdev 1.25 3.00
106 Nikita Filatov 1.25 3.00
107 Patrik Elias 2.00 5.00
108 Peter Mueller 1.50 4.00
109 Saku Koivu 2.00 5.00
110 Milan Lucic 2.00 5.00
111 Troy Brouwer 1.25 3.00
112 Ville Leino 1.50 4.00
113 Zach Bogosian 1.50 4.00
114 Bobby Ryan 1.50 4.00
115 Colton Orr 1.25 3.00
116 Dan Hamhuis 1.50 4.00
117 Dan Ellis 1.50 4.00
118 Tim Connolly 1.25 3.00
119 Travis Zajac 1.25 3.00
120 Dwayne Roloson 1.50 4.00
121 Milan Hejduk 1.50 4.00
122 Brian Elliott 1.50 4.00
123 Mike Comrie 1.25 3.00
124 Niclas Bergfors 1.50 4.00
125 Matthew Lombardi 1.25 3.00
126 Mario Lemieux L 6.00 15.00
127 Trevor Linden L 1.50 4.00
129 Terry O'Reilly L 1.25 3.00
130 Luc Robitaille L 1.50 4.00
131 Denis Savard L 1.50 4.00
132 Doug Gilmour L 2.00 5.00
133 Brad Park L 1.25 3.00
134 Felix Potvin L 2.50 6.00
135 Eric Lindros L 2.50 6.00
136 Jim Craig L 1.25 3.00
137 Darryl Sittler L 2.00 5.00
138 Bobby Rousseau L 1.25 3.00
139 Tony Esposito L 1.50 4.00
140 Normand Leveille L 1.00 2.50
141 Tom Barrasso L 1.50 4.00
142 Curtis Joseph L 2.00 5.00
143 Gilbert Perreault L 1.50 4.00
144 Dan Bouchard L 1.25 3.00
145 Guy Lafleur L 2.00 5.00
146 Ken Linseman L 1.50 4.00
147 Ed Belfour L 1.50 4.00
148 Jean Beliveau L 1.50 4.00
149 Simon Nolet L 1.25 3.00
150 Dale Hawerchuk L 2.00 5.00
151 Brian Leetch L 1.25 3.00
152 Cam Neely L 1.50 4.00
153 Glenn Hall L 1.50 4.00
154 Ron Hextall L 1.50 4.00
155 Joe Sakic L 3.00 8.00
156 Phil Esposito L 2.50 6.00
157 Yvan Cournoyer L 1.50 4.00
158 Patrick Roy L 4.00 10.00
159 Gerry Cheevers L 1.50 4.00
160 Al Arbour L 1.25 3.00
161 Joe Nieuwendyk L 1.25 3.00
162 Mike Bossy L 1.50 4.00
163 Johnny Bucyk L 1.50 4.00
164 Brett Hull L 3.00 8.00
165 Bobby Hull L 3.00 8.00
166 Ray Bourque L 2.50 6.00
167 Rogie Vachon L 2.00 5.00
168 Reggie Lemelin L 1.00 2.50
169 Richard Brodeur L 1.50 4.00
170 Rick Middleton L 1.50 4.00
171 Peter Stastny L 1.25 3.00
172 Stan Mikita L 2.00 5.00
173 Henri Richard L 1.50 4.00
174 Brendan Shanahan L 1.50 4.00
175 Steve Yzerman L 4.00 10.00
176 P.K. Subban AU RC 25.00 50.00
177 Eric Tangradi AU RC 6.00 15.00
178 Kevin Shattenkirk AU RC 12.00 30.00
179 Brandon Yip AU RC 6.00 15.00
180 Jamie McBain AU RC 6.00 15.00
181 Jared Cowen AU RC 6.00 15.00
182 Brandon Pirri AU RC 6.00 15.00
183 Jonas Holos AU RC 6.00 15.00
184 Zac Dalpe AU RC 8.00 20.00
185 Justin Mercier AU RC 6.00 15.00
186 Brayden Irwin AU RC 6.00 15.00
187 Nick Bonino AU RC 8.00 20.00
188 John McCarthy AU RC 6.00 15.00
189 Philip Larsen AU RC 6.00 15.00
190 Bobby Butler AU RC 6.00 15.00
191 Henrik Karlsson AU RC 6.00 15.00
192 Casey Wellman AU RC 6.00 15.00
193 Tommy Wingels AU RC 6.00 15.00
194 Robin Lehner AU RC 12.00 30.00
195 Marcus Johansson AU RC 10.00 25.00
196 Maxim Noreau AU RC 5.00 12.00
197 Nick Palmieri AU RC 6.00 15.00
198 Dustin Tokarski AU RC 6.00 15.00
199 Cam Fowler AU RC 15.00 40.00
200 Jake Muzzin AU RC 15.00 40.00
201 Justin Falk AU RC 5.00 12.00
202 Matt Taormina AU RC 6.00 15.00
203 Dana Tyrell AU RC 6.00 15.00
204 Sergei Bobrovsky AU RC 25.00 60.00
205 Mark Olver AU RC 6.00 15.00
206 T.J. Brodie AU RC 6.00 15.00
207 Tyler Seguin AU RC 15.00 40.00
208 Nazem Kadri AU RC 15.00 40.00
209 Jordan Eberle AU RC 15.00 40.00
210 Magnus Paajarvi AU RC 8.00 20.00
211 Nino Niederreiter AU RC 10.00 25.00
212 Jordan Caron AU RC 8.00 20.00
213 Derek Stepan AU RC 8.00 20.00
214 Luke Adam AU RC 6.00 15.00
215 Nick Leddy AU RC 8.00 20.00
216 Alexander Burmistrov AU RC 6.00 15.00
217 Zach Hamill AU RC 6.00 15.00
218 Nick Johnson AU RC 5.00 12.00
219 Oliver Ekman-Larsson AU RC 10.00 25.00
220 Kyle Clifford AU RC 8.00 20.00
221 Brayden Schenn AU RC 15.00 40.00
222 Anders Lindback AU RC 6.00 15.00
223 Taylor Hall AU RC 30.00 80.00
224 Steve Carlson AU 12.00 30.00
225 Dave Hanson AU 12.00 30.00

2010-11 Limited Silver Spotlight

*1-125 SILVER/49: .8X TO 2X BASIC CARDS
*126-175 SILVER LEG/49: .8X TO 2X BASE
*176-224 ROOKIE AU: .5X TO 1.2X AU RC
12 Nicklas Backstrom 4.00 10.00
74 Pekka Rinne 4.00 10.00
183 Jonas Holos AU/50 15.00 40.00
223 Taylor Hall AU/50 60.00 120.00

2010-11 Limited Back To The Future

1 D.Savard/J.Toews 3.00 8.00
2 C.Joseph/J.Gustavsson 2.50 6.00
3 C.Neely/T.Seguin 5.00 12.00
4 B.Leetch/D.Doughty 4.00 10.00
5 B.Clarke/M.Richards 4.00 10.00
6 T.Esposito/M.Turco 2.00 5.00
7 J.Iginla/T.Hall 4.00 10.00
8 P.Stastny/P.Stastny 1.50 4.00
9 R.Bourque/Z.Chara 3.00 8.00
10 P.Roy/C.Price 8.00 20.00
11 D.Maruk/A.Ovechkin 8.00 20.00
12 J.Beliveau/V.Lecavalier 2.00 5.00
13 J.Craig/R.Miller 2.00 5.00
14 M.Lemieux/E.Malkin 8.00 20.00
15 T.Barrasso/M.Fleury 4.00 10.00
16 B.Park/M.Staal 1.50 4.00
17 G.Cheevers/T.Thomas 2.00 5.00
18 D.Ciccarelli/A.Semin 2.00 5.00
19 B.Trottier/J.Tavares 3.00 8.00
20 C.Hodge/C.Schneider 2.00 5.00
21 D.Bouchard/C.Anderson 2.00 5.00
22 R.Vachon/J.Bernier 2.50 6.00
23 Y.Cournoyer/M.Paajarvi 2.00 5.00
24 P.LaFontaine/D.Roy 2.00 5.00
25 G.Hall/J.Halak 8.00 20.00

2010-11 Limited Back To The Future Signatures

1 D.Savard/J.Toews 40.00 100.00
2 Joseph/Gustavsson 15.00 30.00
3 C.Neely/T.Seguin 30.00 80.00
4 B.Leetch/D.Doughty 15.00 40.00
5 B.Clarke/M.Richards 15.00 40.00
6 T.Esposito/M.Turco 15.00 40.00
7 J.Iginla/T.Hall EX 40.00 100.00
8 Stastny/Stastny 10.00 25.00
9 R.Bourque/Z.Chara 20.00 50.00
10 P.Roy/C.Price 60.00 120.00
11 D.Maruk/A.Ovechkin EX 40.00 100.00
12 J.Beliveau/V.Lecavalier 25.00 60.00
13 J.Craig/R.Miller 15.00 40.00
14 M.Lemieux/E.Malkin 75.00 150.00
15 T.Barrasso/M.Fleury 40.00 80.00
16 Park/Staal 10.00 25.00
17 Cheevers/T.Thomas 12.00 30.00
18 Ciccarelli/Semin 12.00 30.00
19 B.Trottier/J.Tavares 20.00 50.00
20 Hodge/Schneider 12.00 30.00
21 Bouchard/Anderson EX 20.00 50.00
22 R.Vachon/J.Bernier 15.00 40.00
23 Y.Cournoyer/M.Paajarvi 30.00 80.00
24 P.LaFontaine/D.Roy EX 25.00 60.00
25 G.Hall/J.Halak 12.00 30.00

2010-11 Limited Banner Season

*GOLD/24: 1X TO 2.5X BASIC
*SILVER/49: .6X TO 1.5X BASIC
1 Alex Ovechkin 8.00 20.00
2 Anze Kopitar 3.00 8.00
3 Cam Ward 2.00 5.00
4 Corey Perry 3.00 8.00
5 Craig Anderson 2.00 5.00
6 Daniel Alfredsson 2.00 5.00
7 Drew Doughty 2.50 6.00
8 Evgeni Malkin 4.00 10.00
9 Henrik Sedin 2.50 6.00
10 Ilya Kovalchuk 2.00 5.00
11 Jarome Iginla 2.50 6.00
12 Jason Spezza 2.00 5.00
13 Jonathan Quick 2.50 6.00
14 Marc-Andre Fleury 4.00 10.00
15 Martin Brodeur 5.00 12.00
16 Martin St. Louis 2.00 5.00
17 Nicklas Lidstrom 2.00 5.00
18 Rick Nash 2.00 5.00
19 Teemu Selanne 4.00 10.00
20 Tim Thomas 2.00 5.00

2010-11 Limited Banner Season Materials

2 Anze Kopitar 8.00 20.00
4 Corey Perry 8.00 20.00
5 Craig Anderson 5.00 12.00
6 Daniel Alfredsson 5.00 12.00
7 Drew Doughty/49 6.00 15.00
8 Evgeni Malkin 6.00 15.00
9 Henrik Sedin 6.00 15.00
10 Ilya Kovalchuk 5.00 12.00
11 Jarome Iginla 6.00 15.00
12 Jason Spezza 5.00 12.00
13 Jonathan Quick/50 6.00 15.00
14 Marc-Andre Fleury 10.00 25.00
15 Martin Brodeur 6.00 15.00
16 Martin St. Louis/50 5.00 12.00
17 Nicklas Lidstrom/50 5.00 12.00
18 Rick Nash/25 6.00 15.00
19 Teemu Selanne 10.00 25.00

2010-11 Limited Banner Season Materials Prime

*PRIME/25: .8X TO 2X BASIC JSY
1 Alex Ovechkin 15.00 40.00
20 Tim Thomas 12.00 30.00

2010-11 Limited Banner Season Materials Signatures

2 Anze Kopitar 20.00 50.00
4 Corey Perry 20.00 50.00
6 Daniel Alfredsson 12.00 30.00
7 Drew Doughty 15.00 40.00
8 Evgeni Malkin 25.00 60.00
9 Henrik Sedin 15.00 40.00

10 Ilya Kovalchuk 12.00 30.00
11 Jarome Iginla 15.00 40.00
12 Jason Spezza 10.00 25.00
13 Jonathan Quick/25 30.00 60.00
14 Marc-Andre Fleury 25.00 60.00
15 Martin Brodeur 30.00 80.00
16 Martin St. Louis 12.00 30.00
17 Nicklas Lidstrom 12.00 30.00
18 Rick Nash 12.00 30.00
19 Teemu Selanne 25.00 60.00
20 Tim Thomas 25.00 50.00

2010-11 Limited Banner Season Materials Signatures Prime

*PRIME/25: .5X TO 1.2X MAT.SIG
1 Alex Ovechkin 50.00 125.00
14 Marc-Andre Fleury 25.00 60.00
18 Rick Nash 25.00 60.00

2010-11 Limited Banner Season Signatures

1 Alex Ovechkin 30.00 80.00
2 Anze Kopitar 12.00 30.00
3 Cam Ward 8.00 20.00
4 Corey Perry 12.00 30.00
5 Craig Anderson 8.00 20.00
7 Drew Doughty 10.00 25.00
8 Evgeni Malkin 20.00 50.00
9 Henrik Sedin 10.00 25.00
11 Jarome Iginla 10.00 25.00
12 Jason Spezza EXCH 8.00 20.00
13 Jonathan Quick 12.00 30.00
14 Marc-Andre Fleury 15.00 40.00
15 Martin Brodeur 25.00 60.00
17 Nicklas Lidstrom 12.00 30.00
18 Rick Nash 12.00 30.00
19 Teemu Selanne 12.00 30.00
20 Tim Thomas 12.00 30.00

2010-11 Limited Brothers In Arms

1 J.Hiller/C.McElhinney 4.00 10.00
3 T.Rask/T.Thomas 6.00 15.00
8 C.Anderson/P.Budaj 5.00 12.00
11 C.Mason/O.Pavelec 5.00 12.00
12 J.Deslauriers/N.Khabibulin 4.00 10.00
15 R.Luongo/C.Schneider 8.00 20.00
24 J.Gustavsson/J.Giguere 6.00 15.00

2010-11 Limited Jumbo Materials

1 Teemu Selanne/40 6.00 15.00
2 Tyler Seguin 12.00 30.00
4 Jarome Iginla 5.00 12.00
5 Eric Staal 5.00 12.00
8 Matt Duchene 4.00 10.00
9 James Neal 2.50 6.00
10 Pavel Datsyuk 6.00 15.00
11 Taylor Hall 8.00 20.00
12 Jordan Eberle 8.00 20.00
14 Niklas Backstrom/49 4.00 10.00
15 Carey Price 8.00 20.00
16 Marian Gaborik 4.00 10.00
17 Daniel Alfredsson 4.00 10.00
18 Jeff Carter 5.00 12.00
19 Sidney Crosby 8.00 20.00
20 Patrick Roy 10.00 25.00
21 Steven Stamkos 12.00 30.00
22 Mario Lemieux 15.00 40.00
23 Henrik Sedin 5.00 12.00
24 Phil Kessel 4.00 10.00

2010-11 Limited Jumbo Materials Jersey Numbers

1 Teemu Selanne/35 10.00 25.00
2 Tyler Seguin 20.00 50.00
4 Jarome Iginla 6.00 15.00
8 Matt Duchene/49 8.00 20.00
9 James Neal 4.00 10.00
10 Pavel Datsyuk 8.00 20.00
11 Taylor Hall 15.00 40.00
12 Jordan Eberle 12.00 30.00
14 Niklas Backstrom 5.00 12.00
15 Carey Price 10.00 25.00
16 Marian Gaborik 5.00 12.00
17 Daniel Alfredsson 5.00 12.00
18 Jeff Carter 4.00 10.00
19 Sidney Crosby 10.00 25.00
20 Patrick Roy 12.00 30.00
21 Steven Stamkos/25 15.00 40.00
22 Mario Lemieux 20.00 50.00
23 Henrik Sedin 6.00 15.00
24 Phil Kessel 5.00 12.00

2010-11 Limited Jumbo Materials Jersey Numbers Signatures

2 Tyler Seguin 25.00 60.00
3 Ryan Miller 10.00 25.00
4 Jarome Iginla 10.00 25.00
8 Matt Duchene/30 12.00 30.00
9 James Neal 8.00 20.00
10 Pavel Datsyuk 20.00 50.00
11 Taylor Hall 40.00 100.00
12 Jordan Eberle 30.00 80.00
14 Niklas Backstrom 8.00 20.00
16 Marian Gaborik 12.00 30.00
17 Daniel Alfredsson 12.00 30.00
18 Jeff Carter/50 10.00 25.00
19 Sidney Crosby 75.00 150.00
20 Patrick Roy 30.00 80.00
21 Steven Stamkos 25.00 60.00
23 Henrik Sedin 8.00 20.00
24 Phil Kessel 12.00 30.00

2010-11 Limited Jumbo Materials Signatures

1 Teemu Selanne 15.00 40.00
2 Tyler Seguin 15.00 40.00
4 Jarome Iginla 12.00 30.00
7 Patrick Kane/30 25.00 60.00
8 Matt Duchene 10.00 25.00
9 James Neal 6.00 15.00
10 Pavel Datsyuk 15.00 40.00
11 Taylor Hall 40.00 100.00
12 Jordan Eberle 20.00 50.00
13 Drew Doughty/22 15.00 40.00
14 Niklas Backstrom 10.00 25.00
15 Carey Price 20.00 50.00
16 Marian Gaborik 10.00 25.00
18 Jeff Carter 8.00 20.00
19 Sidney Crosby 75.00 150.00
20 Patrick Roy 50.00 100.00
21 Steven Stamkos 20.00 50.00
22 Mario Lemieux 40.00 100.00
23 Henrik Sedin 12.00 30.00
24 Phil Kessel 10.00 25.00

2010-11 Limited Material Monikers

4 Brad Richards 12.00 30.00
5 Chris Pronger 12.00 30.00
6 Claude Giroux 12.00 30.00
7 Corey Perry 20.00 50.00
8 Daniel Alfredsson 12.00 30.00
9 Daniel Sedin 15.00 40.00
10 Dany Heatley 10.00 25.00
12 Derek Roy 8.00 20.00
13 Dion Phaneuf 10.00 25.00
15 Dustin Penner 10.00 25.00
18 Erik Karlsson 15.00 40.00
19 Evgeni Malkin 25.00 60.00
20 Henrik Lundqvist 30.00 80.00
21 Henrik Sedin 15.00 40.00
22 Ilya Bryzgalov 10.00 25.00
23 Ilya Kovalchuk 20.00 40.00
25 Jeff Carter 15.00 40.00
26 Joe Thornton 15.00 40.00
27 John Tavares 20.00 50.00
30 Marian Gaborik 12.00 30.00
31 Martin Brodeur 30.00 80.00
32 Martin St. Louis 12.00 30.00
34 Michael Frolik 8.00 20.00
38 Pavel Datsyuk 20.00 50.00
39 Paul Stastny 10.00 25.00
41 Phil Kessel 12.00 30.00
42 Rick Nash 12.00 30.00
43 Ryan Miller 12.00 30.00
44 Semyon Varlamov 12.00 30.00
45 Sidney Crosby 100.00 200.00
46 Steven Stamkos 25.00 60.00
47 Tomas Vokoun 10.00 25.00
48 Tyler Bozak 8.00 20.00
50 Zach Parise 12.00 30.00

2010-11 Limited Monikers Gold

1 Ryan Miller 8.00 20.00
4 Shane Doan 6.00 15.00
5 Phil Kessel/25 8.00 20.00
8 Daniel Sedin 10.00 25.00
13 Patrick Marleau 8.00 20.00
14 Sam Gagner/25 5.00 12.00
15 Tomas Vokoun 6.00 15.00
16 Jonathan Bernier 6.00 15.00
17 Steven Stamkos 20.00 50.00
18 Zach Parise 10.00 25.00
19 Claude Giroux 8.00 20.00
22 Joe Thornton 12.00 30.00
26 Carey Price 15.00 40.00
27 Brad Richards 8.00 20.00
28 Marian Hossa 8.00 20.00
33 James Neal 5.00 12.00
34 Simon Gagne 8.00 20.00
35 Mike Modano 12.00 30.00
36 Ilya Bryzgalov 6.00 15.00
37 Pavel Datsyuk 12.00 30.00
38 Thomas Vanek 6.00 15.00
39 Marian Gaborik/25 8.00 20.00
41 Jaroslav Halak 15.00 40.00
42 Paul Stastny 12.00 30.00
43 Michael Cammalleri 8.00 20.00
46 Anze Kopitar 12.00 30.00
47 Dustin Byfuglien 10.00 25.00
50 Wojtek Wolski 5.00 12.00
51 Henrik Lundqvist 20.00 50.00
52 Eric Staal/25 10.00 25.00
53 Drew Doughty 10.00 25.00
56 Jonas Gustavsson 10.00 25.00
57 Vincent Lecavalier 8.00 20.00
59 Brandon Sutter 5.00 12.00
61 Marc-Andre Fleury 15.00 40.00
62 Ryan Getzlaf 8.00 20.00
64 Steve Mason 6.00 15.00
65 Ales Hemsky/25 12.00 30.00
66 Niklas Backstrom 8.00 20.00
68 Rick Nash 8.00 20.00
71 Jimmy Howard 10.00 25.00
72 Mike Richards 6.00 15.00
74 Pekka Rinne 8.00 20.00
76 Craig Anderson/25 8.00 20.00
77 Jeff Carter 6.00 15.00
78 Tyler Myers 5.00 12.00
79 Ryan Kesler 10.00 25.00
83 Shea Weber 6.00 15.00
84 Chris Pronger 8.00 20.00
86 Semyon Varlamov 15.00 40.00
89 Guillaume Latendresse/25 6.00 15.00
90 Stephen Weiss 6.00 15.00
91 Cam Ward 8.00 20.00
92 John Tavares 12.00 30.00
93 Patrick Kane/25 15.00 40.00
94 Wayne Simmonds 10.00 25.00
95 Jordan Staal 6.00 15.00
96 Michael Leighton 6.00 15.00
97 T.J. Oshie 8.00 20.00
98 Corey Perry/25 12.00 30.00
99 Tyler Bozak 5.00 12.00
100 Erik Karlsson 12.00 30.00
101 Kari Lehtonen 6.00 15.00
102 Joe Pavelski 10.00 25.00
104 Scott Gomez 6.00 15.00
113 Zach Bogosian 6.00 15.00
114 Bobby Ryan 6.00 15.00
115 Colton Orr 15.00 40.00
116 Joe Thornton 6.00 15.00
122 Brian Elliott 6.00 15.00
132 Doug Gilmour/25 10.00 25.00
133 Brad Park/25 6.00 15.00
134 Felix Potvin/25 12.00 30.00
135 Eric Lindros/25 30.00 60.00
136 Jim Craig/25 8.00 20.00
137 Darryl Sittler/25 8.00 20.00
138 Bobby Rousseau/25 6.00 15.00
140 Normand Leveille/25 5.00 12.00
142 Curtis Joseph/25 25.00 60.00
144 Dan Bouchard/25 6.00 15.00
145 Guy Lafleur/25 20.00 50.00
147 Ed Belfour/25 20.00 40.00
148 Jean Beliveau/25 50.00 100.00
149 Simon Nolet/25 15.00 30.00
150 Dale Hawerchuk/25 10.00 25.00
151 Brian Leetch/25 6.00 15.00
152 Cam Neely/25 8.00 20.00
154 Ron Hextall/25 15.00 40.00
155 Joe Sakic/25 15.00 40.00
156 Phil Esposito/25 12.00 30.00
157 Yvan Cournoyer/25 12.00 30.00
158 Patrick Roy/25 60.00 120.00
159 Gerry Cheevers/25 25.00 60.00
160 Al Arbour/25 6.00 15.00
161 Joe Nieuwendyk/25 6.00 15.00
162 Mike Bossy/25 8.00 20.00
163 Johnny Bucyk/25 EXCH 8.00 20.00
166 Ray Bourque/25 12.00 30.00
167 Rogie Vachon/25 10.00 25.00
168 Reggie Lemelin/25 12.00 30.00
169 Richard Brodeur/25 8.00 20.00
170 Rick Middleton/25 8.00 20.00
171 Peter Stastny/25 25.00 60.00
173 Henri Richard/25 12.00 30.00

2010-11 Limited Retired Numbers

*GOLD/24: 1X TO 2.5X BASIC INSERTS
*SILVER/49: .6X TO 1.5X BASIC INSERTS
1 Ray Bourque 3.00 8.00
2 Joe Sakic 4.00 10.00
3 Marcel Dionne 2.50 6.00
4 Johnny Bucyk 2.00 5.00
5 Brett Hull 4.00 10.00
6 Patrick Roy 5.00 12.00
7 Mario Lemieux 8.00 20.00
8 Bobby Clarke 3.00 8.00
9 Elmer Lach 1.50 4.00
10 Ed Giacomin 3.00 8.00
11 Glenn Hall 2.00 5.00
12 Dale Hawerchuk 2.50 6.00
13 Guy Lafleur 2.50 6.00
15 Trevor Linden 2.00 5.00
16 Henri Richard 2.00 5.00
17 Luc Robitaille 2.00 5.00
18 Denis Savard 2.00 5.00
19 Steve Yzerman 5.00 12.00
20 Lanny McDonald 2.00 5.00

2010-11 Limited Retired Numbers Materials

1 Ray Bourque 8.00 20.00
2 Joe Sakic 10.00 25.00
3 Marcel Dionne 5.00 12.00
4 Johnny Bucyk 5.00 12.00
6 Patrick Roy 12.00 30.00
7 Mario Lemieux 20.00 50.00
17 Luc Robitaille 5.00 12.00
18 Denis Savard 5.00 12.00

2010-11 Limited Retired Numbers Materials Signatures

1 Ray Bourque 20.00 50.00
2 Joe Sakic 20.00 50.00
3 Marcel Dionne 15.00 40.00
4 Johnny Bucyk 12.00 30.00
6 Patrick Roy 40.00 100.00
7 Mario Lemieux 50.00 100.00
17 Luc Robitaille 12.00 30.00
18 Denis Savard 12.00 30.00

2010-11 Limited Retired Numbers Signatures

1 Ray Bourque/25 25.00 50.00
2 Joe Sakic/25 20.00 50.00
3 Marcel Dionne 10.00 25.00
4 Johnny Bucyk 10.00 25.00
5 Brett Hull 15.00 40.00
6 Patrick Roy/25 30.00 80.00
7 Mario Lemieux/25 50.00 100.00
8 Bobby Clarke 10.00 25.00
9 Elmer Lach 12.00 30.00
10 Ed Giacomin 12.00 30.00
11 Glenn Hall 10.00 25.00
12 Dale Hawerchuk 10.00 25.00
13 Guy Lafleur 12.00 30.00
15 Trevor Linden 20.00 50.00
16 Henri Richard 12.00 30.00
17 Luc Robitaille/24 12.00 30.00
18 Denis Savard/24 10.00 25.00
20 Lanny McDonald 8.00 20.00

2010-11 Limited Select Signatures

1 Normand Leveille 5.00 12.00
2 Brendan Shanahan/49 40.00 80.00
3 Joe Sakic/49 20.00 50.00
4 Mario Lemieux/49 40.00 100.00
5 Steve Yzerman/49 40.00 100.00
6 Glenn Hall 8.00 20.00
7 Manon Rheaume 20.00 50.00
8 Brad Park 6.00 15.00
9 Brett Hull/49 15.00 40.00
10 Al Arbour/94 6.00 15.00
11 Bobby Rousseau 6.00 15.00

2010-11 Limited Threads

*PRIME/25: .8X TO 2X BASIC THREADS
1 Ryan Miller/99 4.00 10.00
2 Henrik Sedin 5.00 12.00
4 Shane Doan 3.00 8.00
5 Phil Kessel 4.00 10.00
7 Sidney Crosby 15.00 40.00
8 Daniel Sedin/99 5.00 12.00
9 Teemu Selanne/99 8.00 20.00
10 Kyle Okposo 2.50 6.00
11 Martin Brodeur 10.00 25.00
12 Nicklas Backstrom/15 8.00 20.00
13 Patrick Marleau 4.00 10.00
14 Sam Gagner/99 2.50 6.00
15 Tomas Vokoun 3.00 8.00
17 Steven Stamkos 6.00 15.00
18 Zach Parise/99 4.00 10.00
19 Claude Giroux/25 4.00 10.00
21 Roberto Luongo 6.00 15.00
22 Joe Thornton 6.00 15.00
23 Henrik Zetterberg 5.00 12.00
24 Dion Phaneuf 3.00 8.00
26 Carey Price 8.00 20.00
27 Brad Richards 4.00 10.00
28 Marian Hossa 4.00 10.00
29 Dany Heatley 3.00 8.00
31 Tuukka Rask 5.00 12.00
32 Evgeni Malkin 8.00 20.00
33 James Neal 2.50 6.00
36 Ilya Bryzgalov 3.00 8.00
37 Pavel Datsyuk 6.00 15.00
39 Marian Gaborik 4.00 10.00
42 Paul Stastny 3.00 8.00
44 Ilya Kovalchuk 4.00 10.00
45 Nikolai Khabibulin/99 3.00 8.00
46 Anze Kopitar 6.00 15.00
48 Daniel Alfredsson 4.00 10.00
51 Henrik Lundqvist 10.00 25.00
52 Eric Staal/99 5.00 12.00
53 Drew Doughty/99 5.00 12.00
55 Duncan Keith 3.00 8.00
56 Jonas Gustavsson 5.00 12.00
57 Vincent Lecavalier 4.00 10.00
58 Nicklas Lidstrom/99 4.00 10.00
60 Zdeno Chara 4.00 10.00
61 Marc-Andre Fleury 8.00 20.00
62 Ryan Getzlaf 4.00 10.00
64 Steve Mason 3.00 8.00
65 Ales Hemsky 3.00 8.00
66 Niklas Backstrom 4.00 10.00
67 Jonathan Toews/85 6.00 15.00
68 Rick Nash/99 4.00 10.00
69 Tomas Plekanec 2.50 6.00
70 Loui Eriksson 2.50 6.00
73 Jarome Iginla 5.00 12.00
74 Pekka Rinne 4.00 10.00
76 Craig Anderson 4.00 10.00
77 Jeff Carter 3.00 8.00
79 Ryan Kesler 4.00 10.00
80 Mike Green 3.00 8.00
81 Miikka Kiprusoff 4.00 10.00
82 Jason Spezza 4.00 10.00
83 Shea Weber 3.00 8.00
84 Chris Pronger 4.00 10.00
86 Semyon Varlamov 4.00 10.00
87 Matt Duchene/99 4.00 10.00
90 Stephen Weiss 3.00 8.00
92 John Tavares 6.00 15.00
94 Wayne Simmonds 5.00 12.00
95 Jordan Staal 3.00 8.00
98 Corey Perry 6.00 15.00
99 Tyler Bozak/99 2.50 6.00
100 Erik Karlsson 5.00 12.00
101 Kari Lehtonen 3.00 8.00
102 Joe Pavelski 5.00 12.00
104 Scott Gomez/25 3.00 8.00
108 Peter Mueller 3.00 8.00
110 Milan Lucic 4.00 10.00
113 Zach Bogosian 3.00 8.00
115 Colton Orr 2.50 6.00
119 Travis Zajac 2.50 6.00
121 Milan Hejduk 3.00 8.00
122 Brian Elliott 3.00 8.00
124 Niclas Bergfors 3.00 8.00

2010-11 Limited Trios

*SILVER/25: .6X TO 1.5X BASIC TRIOS
BTS Richards/Thornton/Sedin 3.00 8.00
DSB Doughty/Subban/Bogosian 5.00 12.00
HTS Hall/Tavares/Stamkos 4.00 10.00
IPM Iginla/Perry/Miller 3.00 8.00
KNP Kane/Nash/Perry 4.00 10.00
KPZ Kovalchuk/Parise/Zajac 2.00 5.00
KSO Kovalchuk/Stamkos/Ovechkin 8.00 20.00
ODM Ovechkin/Datsyuk/Malkin 8.00 20.00
RBG Roy/Bernier/Gustavsson 5.00 12.00
SSS Staal/Staal/Staal 2.50 6.00

2010-11 Limited Trios Materials Prime

HTS Hall/Tavares/Stamkos 20.00 50.00
IPM Iginla/Perry/Miller 15.00 40.00
KNP Kane/Nash/Perry 20.00 50.00
KPZ Koval/Parise/Zajac 12.00 30.00
KSO Koval/Stamks/Ovech 15.00 40.00
ODM Ovech/Datsyk/Malkn 20.00 50.00
RTS Richrds/Thrntn/Sedin 15.00 40.00
SSS Staal/Staal/Staal 15.00 40.00

2010-11 Limited Trios Signatures

DSB Dougty/Subbn/Bogos 30.00 80.00
HTS Hall/Tavars/Stamks 100.00 200.00
KNP Kane/Nash/Perry 25.00 60.00
KPZ Koval/Parise/Zajac 15.00 40.00
KSO Koval/Stamks/Ovech 60.00 120.00
RBG Roy/Bernier/Gustavssn 30.00 80.00
SSS Staal/Staal/Staal 20.00 50.00

2010-11 Limited Vintage Pucks

1 Curtis Joseph 40.00 80.00
2 Saku Koivu 15.00 40.00
4 Luc Robitaille 12.00 30.00
5 Brett Hull 25.00 60.00
8 Martin Brodeur 30.00 80.00
10 Trevor Linden 25.00 60.00
12 Eric Lindros 20.00 50.00

2011-12 Limited

1 Brett Hull 4.00 10.00
2 Patrick Roy 5.00 12.00
3 Mark Messier 4.00 10.00
4 Dale Hunter 1.50 4.00
5 Trevor Linden 2.50 6.00
6 Wendel Clark 3.00 8.00
7 Cam Neely 2.00 5.00
8 Tony Esposito 2.00 5.00
9 Brendan Shanahan 2.00 5.00
10 Adam Graves 1.50 4.00
11 Brad Park 1.50 4.00
12 Eric Lindros 2.50 6.00
13 Dennis Maruk 1.50 4.00
14 Joe Mullen 1.50 4.00
15 Joe Nieuwendyk 1.50 4.00
16 Darryl Sittler 2.50 6.00
17 Dale Tallon 1.25 3.00
18 Milt Schmidt 1.50 4.00
19 Jean Beliveau 2.00 5.00
20 Charlie Simmer 1.25 3.00
21 Yvan Cournoyer 2.00 5.00
22 Steve Yzerman 5.00 12.00
23 Ron Francis 2.50 6.00
24 Brett Hull 4.00 10.00
25 Patrick Roy 5.00 12.00
26 Mark Messier 4.00 10.00
27 Dale Hunter 1.50 4.00
28 Trevor Linden 2.50 6.00
29 Wendel Clark 3.00 8.00
30 Cam Neely 2.00 5.00
31 Tony Esposito 2.00 5.00
32 Brendan Shanahan 2.00 5.00
33 Adam Graves 1.50 4.00
34 Brad Park 1.50 4.00
35 John Davidson 1.50 4.00
36 Eric Lindros 2.50 6.00
37 Pat Verbeek 1.25 3.00
38 Jeremy Roenick 3.00 8.00
39 Johnny Bower 2.00 5.00
40 Luc Robitaille 2.00 5.00
41 Mario Lemieux 8.00 20.00
42 Bobby Clarke 3.00 8.00
43 Bernie Parent 2.50 6.00
44 Bernie Nicholls 1.50 4.00
45 Ray Bourque 3.00 8.00
46 Charlie Simmer 1.25 3.00
47 Gary Simmons 2.00 5.00
48 John Davidson 1.50 4.00
49 Ed Belfour 2.00 5.00
50 Denis Savard 2.00 5.00
51 Daniel Sedin 2.50 6.00
52 Martin St. Louis 2.00 5.00
53 Corey Perry 3.00 8.00
54 Henrik Sedin 2.50 6.00
55 Steven Stamkos 4.00 10.00
56 Jarome Iginla 2.50 6.00
57 Alex Ovechkin 8.00 20.00
58 Teemu Selanne 4.00 10.00
59 Henrik Zetterberg 2.50 6.00
60 Brad Richards 2.00 5.00
61 Eric Staal 2.50 6.00
62 Jonathan Toews 3.00 8.00
63 Claude Giroux 2.00 5.00
64 Ryan Getzlaf 2.00 5.00
65 Ryan Kesler 2.00 5.00
66 Patrick Marleau 2.00 5.00
67 Thomas Vanek 1.50 4.00
68 Patrick Kane 4.00 10.00
69 Loui Eriksson 1.25 3.00
70 Anze Kopitar 3.00 8.00
71 Bobby Ryan 1.50 4.00
72 Patrick Sharp 2.00 5.00
73 Mike Ribeiro 1.25 3.00
74 Joe Thornton 3.00 8.00
75 Jay Bouwmeester 1.25 3.00
76 Danny Briere 2.00 5.00
77 Lubomir Visnovsky 1.25 3.00
78 John Tavares 3.00 8.00
79 Matt Duchene 2.00 5.00
80 Jeff Carter 1.50 4.00
81 Rick Nash 2.00 5.00
82 Sidney Crosby 8.00 20.00
83 Mike Richards 1.50 4.00
84 Joe Pavelski 2.50 6.00
85 Nicklas Backstrom 2.00 5.00
86 Phil Kessel 2.00 5.00
87 Dany Heatley 1.50 4.00
88 Jeff Skinner 2.50 6.00
89 David Backes 1.25 3.00
90 Milan Lucic 2.00 5.00
91 Ryane Clowe 1.25 3.00
92 Brent Burns 2.00 5.00
93 Clarke MacArthur 1.25 3.00
94 Mattias Tedenby 1.25 3.00
95 Mikko Koivu 1.50 4.00
96 Nicklas Lidstrom 2.50 6.00
97 David Krejci 2.00 5.00
98 Ilya Kovalchuk 2.00 5.00
99 Shane Doan 1.50 4.00
100 Andrew Ladd 1.25 3.00
101 Pavel Datsyuk 3.00 8.00
102 Keith Yandle 1.25 3.00
103 Mikhail Grabovski 1.25 3.00
104 Nikolai Kulemin 1.25 3.00
105 Dustin Brown 2.00 5.00
106 Marian Hossa 2.00 5.00
107 R.J. Umberger 1.25 3.00
108 Tomas Plekanec 1.25 3.00
109 Patrice Bergeron 2.50 6.00
110 Paul Stastny 1.50 4.00
111 Ryan Callahan 1.25 3.00
112 Jason Spezza 2.00 5.00
113 Tuomo Ruutu 1.50 4.00
114 Ray Whitney 1.50 4.00
115 Brenden Morrow 1.50 4.00
116 Logan Couture 2.50 6.00
117 Ryan O'Reilly 2.00 5.00
118 Jamie Benn 2.00 5.00
119 Johan Franzen 1.50 4.00
120 Brad Boyes 1.25 3.00
121 Alexander Semin 2.00 5.00
122 Vincent Lecavalier 2.00 5.00
123 Brandon Dubinsky 1.25 3.00
124 Olli Jokinen 1.50 4.00
125 Matt Moulson 1.25 3.00
126 Tyler Seguin 2.50 6.00
127 Tyler Myers 1.25 3.00
128 Drew Stafford 1.25 3.00
129 Jean-Sebastien Giguere 2.00 5.00
130 Erik Johnson 1.25 3.00
131 Valtteri Filppula 1.25 3.00
132 Jack Johnson 1.25 3.00
133 Pierre-Marc Bouchard 2.00 5.00
134 Michael Cammalleri 1.50 4.00
135 Michael Grabner 1.50 4.00
136 Zach Parise 2.00 5.00
137 Marian Gaborik 2.00 5.00
138 Daniel Alfredsson 2.00 5.00
139 Nikita Filatov 1.25 3.00
140 Jaromir Jagr 3.00 8.00
141 Brayden Schenn 2.00 5.00
142 Evgeni Malkin 4.00 10.00
143 Jordan Staal 1.50 4.00
144 Jordan Eberle 2.00 5.00
145 Victor Hedman 2.50 6.00
146 Luke Schenn 2.00 5.00
147 Mason Raymond 1.25 3.00
148 Mike Green 1.50 4.00
149 Alexander Burmistrov 1.50 4.00
150 Evander Kane 2.00 5.00
151 Nik Antropov 1.50 4.00
152 Dustin Byfuglien 2.00 5.00
153 Brooks Laich 1.25 3.00
154 Alexandre Burrows 1.25 3.00
155 Nazem Kadri 2.50 6.00
156 Dion Phaneuf 1.50 4.00
157 Chris Stewart 1.50 4.00
158 T.J. Oshie 2.00 5.00
159 Kris Letang 2.50 6.00
160 Martin Hanzal 1.25 3.00
161 Chris Pronger 2.00 5.00
162 James van Riemsdyk 1.50 4.00
163 Erik Karlsson 2.50 6.00
164 Derek Stepan 1.25 3.00
165 Kyle Okposo 1.25 3.00
166 Mattias Tedenby 1.25 3.00
167 Brian Gionta 1.25 3.00
168 P.K. Subban 2.50 6.00
169 Devin Setoguchi 1.50 4.00
170 Simon Gagne 2.00 5.00
171 Derick Brassard 1.25 3.00
172 Duncan Keith 1.50 4.00
173 Curtis Glencross 1.25 3.00
174 Tyler Ennis 1.25 3.00
175 Zdeno Chara 2.00 5.00
176 Roberto Luongo 6.00 15.00
177 Carey Price 8.00 20.00
178 Cam Ward 4.00 10.00
179 Miikka Kiprusoff 4.00 10.00
180 Jimmy Howard 5.00 12.00
181 Henrik Lundqvist 10.00 25.00
182 Marc-Andre Fleury 8.00 20.00
183 Ilya Bryzgalov 4.00 10.00
184 Tim Thomas 4.00 10.00
185 Jonathan Quick 5.00 12.00
186 Antti Niemi 3.00 8.00
187 Kari Lehtonen 3.00 8.00
188 Ryan Miller 4.00 10.00
189 Pekka Rinne 4.00 10.00
190 Corey Crawford 5.00 12.00
191 Jaroslav Halak 4.00 10.00
192 Jonas Hiller 3.00 8.00
193 Dwayne Roloson 3.00 8.00
194 Steve Mason 3.00 8.00
195 Martin Brodeur 10.00 25.00
196 Tomas Vokoun 3.00 8.00
197 Niklas Backstrom 4.00 10.00
198 Ondrej Pavelec 4.00 10.00
199 James Reimer 4.00 10.00
200 Jose Theodore 4.00 10.00
201 Joe Colborne AU/299 RC 5.00 12.00
202 Cody Hodgson AU/299 RC 8.00 20.00
203 Adam Henrique AU/299 RC 12.00 30.00
204 Marcus Kruger AU/299 RC 8.00 20.00
205 Blake Geoffrion AU/299 RC 5.00 12.00
206 Aaron Palushaj AU/299 RC 5.00 12.00
207 Greg Nemisz AU/299 RC 5.00 12.00
208 Carl Klingberg AU/299 RC 5.00 12.00
209 John Moore AU/299 RC 5.00 12.00
210 Jake Gardiner AU/299 RC 8.00 20.00
211 Tim Erixon AU/299 RC 5.00 12.00
212 D.Smith-Pelly AU/299 RC 6.00 15.00
213 G.Landeskog AU/299 RC 15.00 40.00
214 Ryan Johansen AU/299 RC 15.00 40.00
215 Nugent-Hopkins AU/299 RC 20.00 50.00
216 Adam Larsson AU/299 RC 6.00 15.00
217 Sean Couturier AU/299 RC 10.00 25.00
218 Matt Frattin AU/299 RC 5.00 12.00
219 Mark Scheifele AU/299 RC 20.00 50.00
220 Brett Connolly AU/299 RC 5.00 12.00
221 Mika Zibanejad AU/299 RC 15.00 40.00
222 Brandon Saad AU/299 RC 10.00 25.00
223 Roman Horak AU/299 RC 5.00 12.00
224 Ben Scrivens AU/299 RC 5.00 12.00
225 Jonathon Blum AU/299 RC 5.00 12.00
226 Tomas Vincour AU/299 RC 5.00 12.00
227 Matt Read AU/299 RC 6.00 15.00
228 Justin Faulk AU/299 RC 8.00 20.00
229 Joe Vitale AU/291 RC 5.00 12.00
230 S.Da Costa AU/299 RC 5.00 12.00
231 Craig Smith AU/299 RC 6.00 15.00
232 Anton Lander AU/299 RC 5.00 12.00
233 Gudbranson AU/299 RC 6.00 15.00
234 Zac Rinaldo AU/299 RC 5.00 12.00
235 Patrick Wiercioch AU/299 RC 5.00 12.00
236 Lance Bouma AU/299 RC 5.00 12.00
237 Brett Bulmer AU/299 RC 5.00 12.00
238 T.Hartikainen AU/299 RC 5.00 12.00
239 Alexei Emelin AU/299 RC 5.00 12.00
240 Erik Condra AU/299 RC 5.00 12.00
241 Marcus Foligno AU/299 RC 8.00 20.00
242 Ryan Ellis AU/299 RC 5.00 12.00
243 Zack Kassian AU/299 RC 6.00 15.00
244 Cody Eakin AU/299 RC 8.00 20.00
245 David Rundblad AU/299 RC 5.00 12.00
246 Brendan Smith AU/299 RC 5.00 12.00
247 Brad Malone AU/299 RC 5.00 12.00
248 Brayden McNabb AU/299 RC 5.00 12.00
249 Carl Hagelin AU/598 RC 8.00 20.00
250 Colin Greening AU/299 RC 5.00 12.00
251 David Savard AU/299 RC 5.00 12.00
252 Stefan Elliott AU/299 RC 5.00 12.00
253 Dmitry Orlov AU/299 RC 12.00 30.00
254 Dylan Olsen AU/299 RC 6.00 15.00
255 Gustav Nyquist AU/299 RC 12.00 30.00
256 Harry Zolnierczyk AU/299 RC 5.00 12.00
257 Jimmy Hayes AU/299 RC 6.00 15.00
258 Leland Irving AU/299 RC 5.00 12.00
259 Louis Leblanc AU/299 RC 5.00 12.00
260 Simon Despres AU/299 RC 5.00 12.00
261 Anders Nilsson AU/299 RC 5.00 12.00
262 Calvin de Haan AU/299 RC 5.00 12.00
263 Peter Holland AU/299 RC 5.00 12.00
264 Eddie Lack AU/299 RC 5.00 12.00

2011-12 Limited Gold Spotlight

*LEGENDS 1-50: 1X TO 2.5X BASIC CARDS
*VETS 51-175: 1X TO 2.5X BASIC CARDS
*GOALIES 176-200: .5X TO 1.2X BASIC CARDS
85 Nicklas Backstrom 5.00 12.00
190 Corey Crawford 6.00 15.00

2011-12 Limited Ruby Spotlight

*LEGENDS 1-50: .8X TO 2X BASIC CARDS
*VETS 51-175: .8X TO 2X BASIC CARDS
*GOALIES 176-200: .4X TO 1X BASIC CARDS
85 Nicklas Backstrom 4.00 10.00
190 Corey Crawford 5.00 12.00

2011-12 Limited Silver Spotlight

*ROOKIE AU/49-50: .5X TO 1.2X BASIC AU/299
202 Cody Hodgson AU 20.00 50.00
215 Ryan Nugent-Hopkins AU 80.00 200.00

2011-12 Limited Back To The Future Signatures

1 H.Lundqvist/J.Davidson 25.00 50.00
2 C.Giroux/T.Kerr 25.00 50.00
3 Marchand/K.Linseman 15.00 40.00
4 S.Stamkos/S.Yzerman 40.00 100.00
6 J.Tavares/P.LaFontaine 30.00 60.00
8 J.Colborne/D.Gilmour 25.00 50.00
9 J.Toews/J.Roenick 50.00 100.00
12 J.Quick/K.Hrudey 40.00 80.00
14 T.Vanek/LaFontaine 20.00 50.00
15 Luongo/R.Brodeur 20.00 50.00
16 T.Seguin/M.Schmidt 50.00 100.00
17 Z.Parise/Niedermayer 25.00 60.00
18 A.Ovechkin/M.Messier 60.00 120.00
19 E.Kane/B.Hull 30.00 60.00
21 L.Schenn/W.Clark 25.00 50.00
22 C.Perry/B.Shanahan 25.00 60.00
23 M.Fleury/P.Roy 50.00 100.00
24 M.Duchene/J.Sakic 20.00 40.00
25 Ovechkin/M.Lemieux 100.00 200.00

2011-12 Limited Banner Season

*GOLD/25: 1X TO 2.5X BASIC INSERT/199
*SILVER/49: .6X TO 1.5X BASIC INSERT/199
1 Corey Perry 3.00 8.00
2 Daniel Sedin 2.50 6.00
3 Martin St. Louis 2.00 5.00
4 Ryan Kesler 2.00 5.00
5 Steven Stamkos 4.00 10.00
6 Tim Thomas 2.00 5.00
7 Corey Crawford 2.50 6.00
8 Loui Eriksson 1.25 3.00
9 Pavel Datsyuk 3.00 8.00
10 Roberto Luongo 3.00 8.00
11 Jonathan Toews 3.00 8.00
12 Pekka Rinne 2.00 5.00
13 Taylor Hall 2.00 5.00
14 Carey Price 4.00 10.00
15 Nicklas Lidstrom 1.25 3.00
16 Keith Yandle 1.25 3.00
17 Dustin Byfuglien 2.00 5.00
18 Zdeno Chara 2.00 5.00
19 Jordan Eberle 2.00 5.00
20 Jeff Skinner 2.50 6.00
21 Jarome Iginla 2.50 6.00
22 Henrik Lundqvist 5.00 12.00
23 Cam Ward 2.00 5.00
24 Claude Giroux 2.00 5.00
25 Brad Marchand 4.00 10.00

2011-12 Limited Banner Season Materials

*PRIME/50: .6X TO 1.5X BASIC JSY/99
*PRIME/25: .8X TO 2X BASIC JSY/99
1 Corey Perry 8.00 20.00
2 Daniel Sedin 6.00 15.00
3 Martin St. Louis 5.00 12.00
4 Ryan Kesler 5.00 12.00
5 Steven Stamkos 6.00 15.00
6 Tim Thomas 5.00 12.00
7 Corey Crawford 6.00 15.00
8 Loui Eriksson 3.00 8.00
9 Pavel Datsyuk 8.00 20.00
10 Roberto Luongo 8.00 20.00
11 Jonathan Toews 8.00 20.00
12 Pekka Rinne 5.00 12.00
13 Taylor Hall 5.00 12.00
14 Carey Price 10.00 25.00
15 Nicklas Lidstrom 6.00 15.00
16 Keith Yandle 3.00 8.00
17 Dustin Byfuglien 5.00 12.00
18 Zdeno Chara 5.00 12.00
19 Jordan Eberle 5.00 12.00
20 Jeff Skinner 5.00 12.00
21 Jarome Iginla 4.00 10.00
22 Henrik Lundqvist 12.00 30.00
23 Cam Ward 5.00 12.00
24 Claude Giroux 5.00 12.00
25 Brad Marchand 10.00 25.00

2011-12 Limited Banner Season Materials Signatures

*PRIME/15: .6X TO 1.5X JSY AU/24-25
2 Daniel Sedin 15.00 40.00
3 Martin St. Louis 12.00 30.00
4 Ryan Kesler 12.00 30.00
5 Steven Stamkos 30.00 60.00
6 Tim Thomas 12.00 30.00
8 Loui Eriksson 8.00 20.00
9 Pavel Datsyuk 15.00 40.00
10 Roberto Luongo 20.00 50.00
12 Pekka Rinne 12.00 30.00
13 Taylor Hall 25.00 50.00
14 Carey Price/24 30.00 60.00
15 Nicklas Lidstrom 20.00 40.00
16 Keith Yandle 8.00 20.00
17 Dustin Byfuglien 12.00 30.00
18 Zdeno Chara 15.00 40.00
21 Jarome Iginla 15.00 40.00
22 Henrik Lundqvist 15.00 40.00
24 Claude Giroux 20.00 40.00
25 Brad Marchand 10.00 25.00

2011-12 Limited Banner Season Signatures

1 Corey Perry 15.00 40.00
2 Daniel Sedin 12.00 30.00
3 Martin St. Louis 10.00 25.00
4 Ryan Kesler 10.00 25.00
5 Steven Stamkos 20.00 40.00
6 Tim Thomas 30.00 60.00
8 Loui Eriksson 6.00 15.00
9 Pavel Datsyuk 15.00 40.00
10 Roberto Luongo 15.00 40.00
12 Pekka Rinne 12.00 30.00
13 Taylor Hall 10.00 25.00
14 Carey Price/24 20.00 50.00
15 Nicklas Lidstrom 6.00 15.00
17 Dustin Byfuglien 10.00 25.00
18 Zdeno Chara 12.00 30.00
21 Jarome Iginla 12.00 30.00
22 Henrik Lundqvist 20.00 40.00
23 Cam Ward 10.00 25.00
24 Claude Giroux 20.00 40.00
25 Brad Marchand 20.00 50.00

2011-12 Limited Brothers In Arms Materials

*PRIME/25: .8X TO 2X BASIC DUAL/199
*PRIME/25: .6X TO 1.5X BASIC DUAL/99

Card	Low	High
1 T.Thomas/T.Rask/199	8.00	20.00
2 M.Kiprusoff/H.Karlsson/199	6.00	15.00
3 K.Lehtonen/A.Raycroft/199	5.00	12.00
4 N.Khabibulin/D.Dubnyk/199	5.00	12.00
5 J.Quick/J.Bernier/199	8.00	20.00
6 M.Brodeur/J.Hedberg/199	10.00	25.00
7 J.Halak/B.Elliott/199	6.00	15.00
8 J.Reimer/J.Gustavsson/199	6.00	15.00
9 C.Anderson/R.Lehner/199	6.00	15.00
10 M.Fleury/B.Johnson/199	5.00	12.00
11 O.Pavelec/C.Mason/199	8.00	20.00
12 H.Lundqvist/M.Biron/199	15.00	40.00
13 T.Vokoun/M.Neuvirth/199	5.00	12.00
14 J.Theodore/J.Markstrom/199	6.00	15.00
15 R.Luongo/C.Schneider/199	10.00	25.00
16 P.Rinne/A.Lindback/199	6.00	15.00
17 R.Miller/J.Enroth/99	8.00	20.00
18 E.Belfour/M.Turco/99	6.00	15.00
19 R.Luongo/M.Brodeur/99	10.00	25.00
20 R.Miller/T.Thomas/99	8.00	20.00

2011-12 Limited Crease Cleaners

*GOLD/25: 1X TO 2.5X BASIC INSERT/199
*SILVER/49: .6X TO 1.5X BASIC INSERT/199

Card	Low	High
1 Tim Thomas	2.50	6.00
2 Cam Ward	2.50	6.00
3 Carey Price	5.00	12.00
4 Jaroslav Halak	2.50	6.00
5 Jonathan Quick	2.50	6.00
6 Martin Brodeur	6.00	15.00
7 Jimmy Howard	3.00	8.00
8 Kari Lehtonen	2.00	5.00
9 Pekka Rinne	2.50	6.00
10 Jonas Hiller	2.00	5.00
11 Craig Anderson	2.50	6.00
12 Niklas Backstrom	2.50	6.00
13 Jonathan Bernier	2.00	5.00
14 Nikolai Khabibulin	2.00	5.00
15 Robin Lehner	2.00	5.00
16 Corey Crawford	3.00	8.00
17 Ryan Miller	2.50	6.00
18 Ondrej Pavelec	2.50	6.00
19 Ilya Bryzgalov	2.50	6.00
20 Steve Mason	2.00	5.00

2011-12 Limited Crease Cleaners Materials

*PRIME/25: .8X TO 2X BASIC JSY/99

Card	Low	High
1 Tim Thomas	5.00	12.00
2 Cam Ward	5.00	12.00
3 Carey Price	10.00	25.00
4 Jaroslav Halak	5.00	12.00
5 Jonathan Quick	6.00	15.00
6 Martin Brodeur	8.00	20.00
7 Jimmy Howard	6.00	15.00
8 Kari Lehtonen	4.00	10.00
9 Pekka Rinne	5.00	12.00
10 Jonas Hiller	4.00	10.00
11 Craig Anderson	5.00	12.00
12 Niklas Backstrom	5.00	12.00
13 Jonathan Bernier	4.00	10.00
14 Nikolai Khabibulin	4.00	10.00
15 Robin Lehner	6.00	15.00
16 Corey Crawford	6.00	15.00
17 Ryan Miller	5.00	12.00
18 Ondrej Pavelec	6.00	15.00
19 Ilya Bryzgalov	5.00	12.00
20 Steve Mason	4.00	10.00

2011-12 Limited Crease Cleaners Materials Patches Signatures

Card	Low	High
2 Cam Ward/15	12.00	30.00
3 Carey Price/15	40.00	80.00
4 Jaroslav Halak/15	15.00	40.00
9 Pekka Rinne/15	12.00	30.00
11 Craig Anderson/15	12.00	30.00
12 Niklas Backstrom/15	15.00	40.00
13 Jonathan Bernier/15	20.00	50.00
17 Ryan Miller/15	30.00	60.00

2011-12 Limited Crease Cleaners Signatures

Card	Low	High
1 Tim Thomas/49	25.00	50.00
2 Cam Ward/99	12.00	30.00
3 Carey Price/48	20.00	40.00
4 Jaroslav Halak/99	8.00	20.00
5 Jonathan Quick/99	15.00	40.00
7 Jimmy Howard/99	12.00	30.00
8 Kari Lehtonen/99	8.00	20.00
9 Pekka Rinne/99	10.00	25.00
10 Jonas Hiller/91	6.00	15.00
11 Craig Anderson/99	8.00	20.00
12 Niklas Backstrom/99	8.00	20.00
13 Jonathan Bernier/99	10.00	25.00
14 Nikolai Khabibulin/99	6.00	15.00
15 Robin Lehner/99	8.00	20.00
17 Ryan Miller/99	8.00	20.00
18 Ondrej Pavelec/99	10.00	25.00
20 Steve Mason/99	6.00	15.00

2011-12 Limited Freshmen Jumbo Materials Draft Position

*DRAFT PRIME/25: .8X TO 2X DRAFT JSY/99
*BASIC JUMBO/199: .25X TO .6X DRFT JSY/99
*BASIC PRIME/50: .5X TO 1.2X DRFT JSY/99
*BASIC PRIME/50: .25X TO .6X DRFT JSY/25
*BASIC PRIME/25: .8X TO 2X DRFT JSY/99

Card	Low	High
1 Cody Hodgson/25	20.00	50.00
2 Joe Colborne/99	4.00	10.00
3 Gabriel Landeskog/99	10.00	25.00
4 Ryan Nugent-Hopkins/99	30.00	80.00
5 Mika Zibanejad/99	12.00	30.00
6 Brett Connolly/99	4.00	10.00
7 Ryan Johansen/99	12.00	30.00
8 Sean Couturier/99	8.00	20.00
9 Erik Gudbranson/99	5.00	12.00
10 Adam Henrique/99	10.00	25.00

2011-12 Limited Freshmen Jumbo Materials Draft Position Signatures

*BASIC JSY AU/99: .4X TO 1X AU/99

Card	Low	High
1 Cody Hodgson/25	30.00	80.00
2 Joe Colborne/99	15.00	40.00
3 G.Landeskog/99	20.00	50.00
4 Ryan Nugent-Hopkins/99	50.00	120.00
5 Mika Zibanejad/99	25.00	60.00
6 Brett Connolly/99	8.00	20.00
7 Ryan Johansen/99	25.00	60.00
8 Sean Couturier/99	15.00	40.00
9 Erik Gudbranson/99	10.00	25.00
10 Adam Henrique/99	12.00	30.00

2011-12 Limited Game Pucks Signatures

Card	Low	High
1 Mario Lemieux/20	50.00	100.00
3 Jaromir Jagr/20	50.00	125.00
4 Steve Yzerman/20	40.00	80.00
5 Curtis Joseph/20	40.00	80.00
6 Bill Ranford/20	20.00	50.00
7 Mark Messier/20	25.00	60.00
8 Eric Lindros/25	30.00	60.00
9 Trevor Linden/20	40.00	80.00
11 Nicklas Lidstrom/20	25.00	60.00
12 Patrick Kane/20	30.00	80.00
13 Taylor Hall/20	20.00	50.00
14 Matt Duchene/20	15.00	40.00
16 Ryan Miller/20	15.00	40.00
18 Jamie Benn/20	15.00	40.00
20 Roberto Luongo/20	30.00	60.00

2011-12 Limited Jumbo Materials

*JUMBO PRIME/50: .6X TO 1.5X JUMBO/99
*JUMBO PRIME/25: .8X TO 2X JUMBO/99
*JSY NUMBER/49: .5X TO 1.2X JUMBO/99
*JSY NUMBER/25: .6X TO 1.5X JUMBO/99
*JSY # PRIME/10: 1.2X TO 3X JUMBO/99

Card	Low	High
1 Alex Ovechkin	10.00	25.00
2 Rick Nash	5.00	12.00
3 Corey Perry	8.00	20.00
4 Claude Giroux	5.00	12.00
5 Sidney Crosby	12.00	30.00
6 Joe Thornton	8.00	20.00
7 Patrick Marleau	5.00	12.00
8 Ryan Kesler	6.00	15.00
9 Saku Koivu	5.00	12.00
10 Anze Kopitar	8.00	20.00
11 Tyler Myers	3.00	8.00
12 Matt Duchene	5.00	12.00
13 Jeff Skinner	6.00	15.00
14 James van Riemsdyk	3.00	8.00
15 Bobby Ryan	4.00	10.00
16 Jimmy Howard	6.00	15.00
17 Brad Marchand	10.00	25.00
18 Loui Eriksson	3.00	8.00
19 Taylor Hall	8.00	20.00
20 Marian Gaborik	5.00	12.00
21 Henrik Lundqvist	12.00	30.00
22 Antti Niemi	4.00	10.00
23 Alexander Semin	4.00	10.00
24 Ryane Clowe	3.00	8.00
25 Paul Stastny	4.00	10.00
26 Brenden Morrow	4.00	10.00
27 Ryan Getzlaf	5.00	12.00
28 Pavel Datsyuk	8.00	20.00
29 Jonathan Bernier	4.00	10.00
30 Chris Pronger	5.00	12.00
31 David Backes	5.00	12.00
32 Evgeni Malkin	8.00	20.00
33 Vincent Lecavalier	5.00	12.00
34 Martin Brodeur	12.00	30.00
35 Evander Kane	5.00	12.00
36 Daniel Alfredsson	5.00	12.00
37 Mark Letestu	4.00	10.00
38 Rene Bourque	3.00	8.00
39 P.K. Subban	6.00	15.00
40 Tim Thomas	5.00	12.00

2011-12 Limited Jumbo Materials Jersey Numbers Signatures

Card	Low	High
1 Alex Ovechkin/25	40.00	100.00
3 Corey Perry/25	20.00	50.00
4 Claude Giroux/25	20.00	50.00
6 Joe Thornton/25	16.00	40.00
7 Patrick Marleau/25	12.50	30.00
8 Ryan Kesler/25	25.00	50.00
9 Saku Koivu/25	20.00	40.00
11 Tyler Myers/25	8.00	20.00
13 Jeff Skinner/25	25.00	50.00
14 James van Riemsdyk/25	10.00	25.00
18 Loui Eriksson/25	8.00	20.00
21 Henrik Lundqvist/25	15.00	30.00
22 Antti Niemi/25	10.00	25.00
23 Alexander Semin/25	12.00	30.00
26 Brenden Morrow/25	10.00	25.00
28 Pavel Datsyuk/25	20.00	40.00
29 Jonathan Bernier/25	10.00	25.00
30 Chris Pronger/25	12.00	30.00
31 David Backes/25	8.00	20.00
32 Evgeni Malkin/25	30.00	60.00
33 Vincent Lecavalier/25	12.00	30.00
35 Evander Kane/25	25.00	50.00
38 Rene Bourque/25	8.00	20.00

2011-12 Limited Jumbo Materials Prime Signatures

*PRME AU/25: .5X TO 1.2X JSY # AU/25

Card	Low	High
10 Anze Kopitar/25	25.00	60.00
21 Henrik Lundqvist/25	20.00	50.00
34 Martin Brodeur/25	50.00	100.00

2011-12 Limited Materials

Card	Low	High
1 Brett Hull/99	10.00	25.00
2 Patrick Roy/99	12.00	30.00
6 Wendel Clark/99	6.00	15.00
7 Cam Neely/99	5.00	12.00
9 Brendan Shanahan/99	5.00	12.00
10 Adam Graves/99	4.00	10.00
12 Eric Lindros/99	6.00	15.00
14 Joe Mullen/99	4.00	10.00
15 Joe Nieuwendyk/99	4.00	10.00
16 Darryl Sittler/99	6.00	15.00
21 Yvan Cournoyer/99	5.00	12.00
22 Steve Yzerman/99	8.00	20.00
24 Brett Hull/99	10.00	25.00
25 Patrick Roy/99	12.00	30.00
26 Mark Messier/99	10.00	25.00
30 Cam Neely/99	5.00	12.00
32 Brendan Shanahan/99	5.00	12.00
36 Eric Lindros/99	6.00	15.00
37 Pat Verbeek/99	3.00	8.00
40 Luc Robitaille/99	5.00	12.00
42 Bobby Clarke/99	6.00	15.00
44 Bernie Nicholls/99	4.00	10.00
46 Charlie Simmer/99	3.00	8.00
51 Daniel Sedin/99	6.00	15.00
52 Martin St. Louis/25	6.00	15.00
53 Corey Perry/99	8.00	20.00
54 Henrik Sedin/99	6.00	15.00
55 Steven Stamkos/99	6.00	15.00
56 Jarome Iginla/99	6.00	15.00
57 Alex Ovechkin/99	5.00	12.00
58 Teemu Selanne/99	10.00	25.00
59 Henrik Zetterberg/99	6.00	15.00
60 Brad Richards/99	5.00	12.00
61 Eric Staal/99	6.00	15.00
62 Jonathan Toews/25	10.00	25.00
63 Claude Giroux/99	5.00	12.00
64 Ryan Getzlaf/99	5.00	12.00
65 Ryan Kesler/99	5.00	12.00
66 Patrick Marleau/99	5.00	12.00
67 Thomas Vanek/99	4.00	10.00
68 Patrick Kane/25	8.00	20.00
69 Loui Eriksson/99	3.00	8.00
70 Anze Kopitar/99	8.00	20.00
71 Bobby Ryan/99	4.00	10.00
72 Patrick Sharp/99	5.00	12.00
74 Joe Thornton/99	5.00	12.00
76 Danny Briere/99	5.00	12.00
78 John Tavares/25	6.00	15.00
79 Matt Duchene/99	5.00	12.00
80 Jeff Carter/99	4.00	10.00
81 Rick Nash/99	5.00	12.00
82 Sidney Crosby/99	10.00	25.00
83 Mike Richards/99	4.00	10.00
84 Joe Pavelski/99	6.00	15.00
85 Nicklas Backstrom/99	5.00	12.00
86 Phil Kessel/25	6.00	15.00
87 Dany Heatley/99	4.00	10.00
88 Jeff Skinner/99	6.00	15.00
90 Milan Lucic/99	5.00	12.00
91 Ryane Clowe/99	3.00	8.00
92 Brent Burns/99	5.00	12.00
94 Mattias Tedenby/99	3.00	8.00
95 Mikko Koivu/99	4.00	10.00
96 Nicklas Lidstrom/25	4.00	10.00
97 David Krejci/99	5.00	12.00
98 Ilya Kovalchuk/99	5.00	12.00
99 Shane Doan/99	4.00	10.00
100 Andrew Ladd/99	3.00	8.00
101 Pavel Datsyuk/99	8.00	20.00
102 Keith Yandle/99	3.00	8.00
103 Mikhail Grabovski/99	3.00	8.00
104 Nikolai Kulemin/99	3.00	8.00
105 Dustin Brown/99	5.00	12.00
106 Marian Hossa/99	5.00	12.00
108 Tomas Plekanec/99	3.00	8.00
109 Patrice Bergeron/99	6.00	15.00
110 Paul Stastny/99	4.00	10.00
112 Jason Spezza/99	5.00	12.00
115 Brenden Morrow/99	4.00	10.00
116 Logan Couture/99	6.00	15.00
118 Jamie Benn/99	5.00	12.00
119 Johan Franzen/99	4.00	10.00
121 Alexander Semin/99	5.00	12.00
122 Vincent Lecavalier/99	5.00	12.00
123 Brandon Dubinsky /99	3.00	8.00
125 Matt Moulson/99	3.00	8.00
126 Tyler Seguin/99	6.00	15.00
127 Tyler Myers/99	3.00	8.00
129 Jean-Sebastien Giguere/99	5.00	12.00
130 Erik Johnson/99	3.00	8.00
131 Valtteri Filppula/99	3.00	8.00
134 Michael Cammalleri/99	4.00	10.00
136 Zach Parise/25	6.00	15.00
137 Marian Gaborik/99	5.00	12.00
138 Daniel Alfredsson/99	5.00	12.00
142 Evgeni Malkin/99	0.00	20.00
143 Jordan Staal/99	4.00	10.00
144 Jordan Eberle/25	6.00	15.00
145 Victor Hedman/99	5.00	12.00
146 Luke Schenn/99	5.00	12.00
148 Mike Green/99	4.00	10.00
149 Alexander Burmistrov/99	4.00	10.00
150 Evander Kane/99	5.00	12.00
152 Dustin Byfuglien/99	5.00	12.00
153 Eric Fehr/99	3.00	8.00
154 Alexandre Burrows/99	3.00	8.00
155 Nazem Kadri/99	6.00	15.00
156 Dion Phaneuf/99	4.00	10.00
159 Kris Letang/99	6.00	15.00
161 Chris Pronger/99	5.00	12.00
162 James van Riemsdyk/99	4.00	10.00
163 Erik Karlsson/99	5.00	12.00
164 Derek Stepan/99	3.00	8.00
165 Kyle Okposo/99	3.00	8.00
166 Mattias Tedenby/99	3.00	8.00
168 P.K. Subban/99	6.00	15.00
169 Devin Setoguchi/99	4.00	10.00
171 Derick Brassard/99	3.00	8.00
173 Curtis Glencross/99	3.00	8.00
174 Tyler Ennis/99	3.00	8.00
175 Zdeno Chara/99	5.00	12.00
176 Roberto Luongo/99	8.00	20.00
177 Carey Price/99	10.00	25.00
179 Miikka Kiprusoff/99	5.00	12.00
180 Jimmy Howard/99	6.00	15.00
181 Henrik Lundqvist/99	12.00	30.00
182 Marc-Andre Fleury/99	10.00	25.00
183 Ilya Bryzgalov/99	5.00	12.00
184 Tim Thomas/99	5.00	12.00
185 Jonathan Quick/99	6.00	15.00
186 Antti Niemi/99	4.00	10.00
187 Kari Lehtonen/99	4.00	10.00
188 Ryan Miller/99	5.00	12.00
189 Pekka Rinne/99	5.00	12.00
192 Jonas Hiller/99	4.00	10.00
195 Martin Brodeur/99	6.00	15.00
196 Tomas Vokoun/99	4.00	10.00
197 Niklas Backstrom/99	5.00	12.00
198 Ondrej Pavelec/99	8.00	20.00
199 James Reimer/99	5.00	12.00
200 Jose Theodore/99	5.00	12.00

2011-12 Limited Materials Prime

Card	Low	High
COMMON CARD/15-25	6.00	15.00
SEMISTARS/15-25	8.00	20.00
UNL.STARS/15-25	10.00	25.00
1 Brett Hull/25	20.00	50.00
2 Patrick Roy/25	25.00	60.00
6 Wendel Clark/25	12.00	30.00
7 Cam Neely/25	10.00	25.00
9 Brendan Shanahan/25	10.00	25.00
22 Steve Yzerman/25	15.00	40.00
25 Patrick Roy/25	25.00	60.00
26 Mark Messier/25	20.00	50.00
30 Cam Neely/25	10.00	25.00
32 Brendan Shanahan/25	10.00	25.00
36 Eric Lindros/25	12.00	30.00
42 Bobby Clarke/25	12.00	30.00
54 Henrik Sedin/25	12.00	30.00
55 Steven Stamkos/25	12.00	30.00
57 Alex Ovechkin/25	12.00	30.00
59 Henrik Zetterberg/25	12.00	30.00
62 Jonathan Toews/25	15.00	40.00
63 Claude Giroux/25	10.00	25.00
65 Ryan Kesler/25	10.00	25.00
68 Patrick Kane/25	20.00	50.00
78 John Tavares/25	12.00	30.00
82 Sidney Crosby/25	20.00	50.00
85 Nicklas Backstrom/25	10.00	25.00
88 Jeff Skinner/25	12.00	30.00
117 Ryan O'Reilly/25	10.00	25.00
126 Tyler Seguin/25	12.00	30.00
127 Tyler Myers/25	6.00	15.00
129 Jean-Sebastien Giguere/25	12.00	30.00
140 Jaromir Jagr/25	30.00	80.00
142 Evgeni Malkin/25	15.00	40.00
145 Victor Hedman/25	12.00	30.00
146 Luke Schenn/25	10.00	25.00
158 T.J. Oshie/20	10.00	25.00
168 P.K. Subban/15	12.00	30.00
176 Roberto Luongo/25	15.00	40.00
177 Carey Price/25	20.00	50.00
181 Henrik Lundqvist/25	25.00	60.00
190 Corey Crawford/25	12.00	30.00

2011-12 Limited Men of Mayhem Signatures

Card	Low	High
1 Wendel Clark/199	10.00	25.00
3 Al Secord/199	8.00	20.00
7 Dale Hunter/99	8.00	20.00
8 Jody Shelley/199	8.00	20.00
9 Brendan Shanahan/49	15.00	40.00
10 Pat Verbeek/199	8.00	20.00

2011-12 Limited Monikers Gold

Card	Low	High
2 Patrick Roy/25	40.00	80.00
3 Mark Messier/25	20.00	50.00
5 Trevor Linden/19	25.00	60.00
6 Wendel Clark/25	15.00	40.00
7 Cam Neely/25	15.00	40.00
8 Tony Esposito/25	15.00	40.00
10 Adam Graves/25	10.00	25.00
11 Brad Park/25	8.00	20.00
12 Eric Lindros/25	30.00	60.00
14 Joe Mullen/25	8.00	20.00
16 Darryl Sittler/25	12.00	30.00
17 Dale Tallon/25	6.00	15.00
18 Milt Schmidt/25	8.00	20.00
19 Jean Beliveau/25	30.00	60.00
20 Charlie Simmer/25	6.00	15.00
22 Steve Yzerman/25	40.00	80.00
25 Patrick Roy/25	40.00	80.00
29 Wendel Clark/25	15.00	40.00
30 Cam Neely/25	25.00	50.00
31 Tony Esposito/25	15.00	40.00
33 Adam Graves/25	10.00	25.00
34 Brad Park/25	8.00	20.00
36 Eric Lindros/25	40.00	80.00
37 Pat Verbeek/25	15.00	40.00
38 Jeremy Roenick/25	30.00	60.00
39 Johnny Bower/25	15.00	40.00
40 Luc Robitaille/25	12.00	30.00
42 Bobby Clarke/25	12.00	30.00
43 Bernie Parent/25	20.00	40.00
44 Bernie Nicholls/25	8.00	20.00
46 Charlie Simmer/25	6.00	15.00
47 Gary Simmons/25	15.00	40.00
51 Daniel Sedin/25	10.00	25.00
52 Martin St. Louis/25	8.00	20.00
53 Corey Perry/25	12.00	30.00
54 Henrik Sedin/25	10.00	25.00
55 Steven Stamkos/25	15.00	40.00
56 Jarome Iginla/25	10.00	25.00
57 Alex Ovechkin/25	40.00	100.00
60 Brad Richards/25	20.00	40.00
61 Eric Staal/25	10.00	25.00
63 Claude Giroux/25	20.00	40.00
65 Ryan Kesler/25	10.00	25.00
66 Patrick Marleau/25	10.00	25.00
68 Patrick Kane/25	25.00	50.00
70 Anze Kopitar/25	12.00	30.00
71 Bobby Ryan/25	10.00	25.00
74 Joe Thornton/25	12.00	30.00
75 Jay Bouwmeester/25	5.00	12.00
76 Danny Briere/25	8.00	20.00
78 John Tavares/25	20.00	40.00
79 Matt Duchene/25	12.00	30.00
80 Jeff Carter/25	6.00	15.00
84 Joe Pavelski/25	10.00	25.00
86 Phil Kessel/25	10.00	25.00
87 Dany Heatley/25	10.00	25.00
88 Jeff Skinner/25	20.00	40.00
89 David Backes/25	8.00	20.00
92 Brent Burns/25	8.00	20.00
94 Mattias Tedenby/25	5.00	12.00
96 Nicklas Lidstrom/25	25.00	50.00
99 Shane Doan/25	6.00	15.00
100 Andrew Ladd/25	8.00	20.00
101 Pavel Datsyuk/25	15.00	40.00
102 Keith Yandle/25	5.00	12.00
104 Nikolai Kulemin/25	5.00	12.00
105 Dustin Brown/25	8.00	20.00
106 Marian Hossa/25	12.00	30.00
110 Paul Stastny/25	20.00	40.00
113 Tuomo Ruutu/25	8.00	20.00
115 Brenden Morrow/25	10.00	25.00
116 Logan Couture/25	10.00	25.00
117 Ryan O'Reilly/25	15.00	40.00
119 Johan Franzen/25	8.00	20.00
120 Brad Boyes/25	5.00	12.00
121 Alexander Semin/25	8.00	20.00
122 Vincent Lecavalier/25	8.00	20.00
125 Matt Moulson/25	5.00	12.00
127 Tyler Myers/25	5.00	12.00
129 Jean-Sebastien Giguere/25	10.00	25.00
130 Erik Johnson/25	5.00	12.00
131 Valtteri Filppula/25	12.00	30.00
134 Michael Cammalleri/25	8.00	20.00
136 Zach Parise/25	8.00	20.00
137 Marian Gaborik/25	10.00	25.00
140 Jaromir Jagr/25	40.00	80.00
141 Brayden Schenn/25	10.00	25.00
142 Evgeni Malkin/25	25.00	50.00
146 Luke Schenn/25	8.00	20.00
149 Alexander Burmistrov/25	6.00	15.00
150 Evander Kane/25	12.00	30.00
151 Nik Antropov/25	12.00	30.00
154 Alexandre Burrows/25	12.00	30.00
155 Nazem Kadri/22	12.00	30.00
156 Dion Phaneuf/25	12.00	30.00
157 Chris Stewart/25	6.00	15.00
158 T.J. Oshie/25	12.00	30.00
161 Chris Pronger/25	10.00	25.00
162 James van Riemsdyk/25	6.00	15.00
163 Erik Karlsson/25	15.00	40.00
164 Derek Stepan/25	12.00	30.00
165 Kyle Okposo/25	5.00	12.00
166 Mattias Tedenby/25	5.00	12.00
167 Brian Gionta/25	5.00	12.00
170 Simon Gagne/25	8.00	20.00
173 Curtis Glencross/25	8.00	20.00
174 Tyler Ennis/25	5.00	12.00
176 Roberto Luongo/25	15.00	40.00
178 Cam Ward/25	8.00	20.00
180 Jimmy Howard/25	12.00	30.00
181 Henrik Lundqvist/25	25.00	50.00
182 Marc-Andre Fleury/25	12.00	30.00
183 Ilya Bryzgalov/25	10.00	25.00
185 Jonathan Quick/25	30.00	60.00
186 Antti Niemi/25	10.00	25.00
187 Kari Lehtonen/25	6.00	15.00
188 Ryan Miller/25	8.00	20.00
191 Jaroslav Halak/25	8.00	20.00
192 Jonas Hiller/25	10.00	25.00
193 Dwayne Roloson/25	8.00	20.00
194 Steve Mason/25	8.00	20.00
196 Tomas Vokoun/25	6.00	15.00
197 Niklas Backstrom/25	10.00	25.00
199 James Reimer/25	15.00	40.00
200 Jose Theodore/25	8.00	20.00

2011-12 Limited Net Presence Memorabilia

Card	Low	High
1 C.Price/P.Kane/99	15.00	40.00
2 C.Price/S.Stamkos/99	15.00	40.00
3 C.Price/P.Kessel/99	15.00	40.00
4 C.Price/N.Lidstrom/99	20.00	50.00
5 C.Price/A.Kopitar/25	40.00	100.00
6 T.Thomas/A.Ovechkin/99	60.00	150.00
7 T.Thomas/E.Staal/25	25.00	60.00
8 T.Thomas/R.Nash/99	15.00	40.00
9 T.Thomas/C.Perry/99	25.00	60.00
10 C.Ward/T.Hall/99	15.00	40.00
11 C.Ward/M.Duchene/25	20.00	50.00
12 C.Ward/J.Toews/98	20.00	50.00
13 C.Ward/H.Sedin/25	15.00	40.00
14 J.Hiller/A.Ovechkin/99	12.00	30.00
15 J.Hiller/J.Skinner/25	25.00	60.00
16 J.Hiller/P.Subban/25	25.00	60.00
18 H.Lundqvist/B.Richards/99	15.00	40.00
19 H.Lundqvist/M.St. Louis/25	50.00	125.00
20 H.Lundqvist/P.Kane/99	20.00	50.00
21 H.Lundqvist/D.Stepan/25	20.00	50.00
22 M.Fleury/D.Sedin/49	20.00	50.00
23 M.Fleury/C.Giroux/99	12.00	30.00
25 M.Fleury/K.Letang/49	25.00	60.00

2011-12 Limited Retired Numbers

*GOLD/25: .8X TO 2X BASIC INSERT/199
*SILVER/49: .5X TO 1.2X BASIC INSERT/199

Card	Low	High
1 Johnny Bucyk	3.00	8.00
2 Mark Messier	6.00	15.00
3 Steve Yzerman	8.00	20.00
4 Cam Neely	3.00	8.00
5 Bobby Clarke	5.00	12.00
6 Luc Robitaille	3.00	8.00
7 Stan Mikita	4.00	10.00
8 Patrick Roy	8.00	20.00
9 Ron Francis	4.00	10.00
10 Bryan Trottier	3.00	8.00

2011-12 Limited Retired Numbers Materials

*PRIME/25: .8X TO 2X BASIC JSY/99

Card	Low	High
1 Johnny Bucyk	5.00	12.00
2 Mark Messier	10.00	25.00
3 Steve Yzerman	15.00	40.00
4 Cam Neely	5.00	12.00
5 Bobby Clarke	8.00	20.00
6 Luc Robitaille	5.00	12.00
7 Stan Mikita	6.00	15.00
8 Patrick Roy	10.00	25.00
9 Ron Francis	6.00	15.00
10 Bryan Trottier	5.00	12.00

2011-12 Limited Retired Numbers Materials Signatures

Card	Low	High
1 Johnny Bucyk	15.00	40.00
2 Mark Messier	25.00	50.00
3 Steve Yzerman	50.00	100.00
4 Cam Neely	25.00	50.00
5 Bobby Clarke	30.00	60.00
7 Stan Mikita	15.00	40.00
8 Patrick Roy	50.00	100.00
9 Ron Francis	15.00	40.00
10 Bryan Trottier	12.00	30.00

2011-12 Limited Retired Numbers Signatures

Card	Low	High
1 Johnny Bucyk/25	20.00	40.00
2 Mark Messier/25	30.00	60.00
3 Steve Yzerman/25	40.00	80.00
4 Cam Neely/25	15.00	40.00
5 Bobby Clarke/25	30.00	60.00
6 Luc Robitaille/25	15.00	40.00
7 Stan Mikita/25	15.00	30.00
8 Patrick Roy/25	30.00	60.00
9 Ron Francis/25	12.00	30.00
10 Bryan Trottier/25	30.00	60.00

2011-12 Limited Select Signatures

Card	Low	High
1 Ron Francis/49	12.00	30.00
3 Stan Mikita/97	12.00	30.00
4 Scott Niedermayer/25	15.00	40.00
5 Patrick Roy/25	40.00	80.00
6 Pat LaFontaine/99	10.00	25.00
7 Milt Schmidt/99	8.00	20.00
8 Mike Bossy/97	8.00	20.00
9 Johnny Bower/99	12.00	30.00
10 Jean Beliveau/99	25.00	50.00
11 Eric Lindros/49	25.00	50.00
12 Ray Bourque/99	12.00	30.00
13 Doug Gilmour/99	12.00	30.00
14 Mark Messier/25	30.00	60.00
15 Cam Neely/99	12.00	30.00
16 Dale Hawerchuk/99	8.00	20.00
17 Curtis Joseph/99	10.00	25.00
19 Jim Craig/99	10.00	25.00
20 Doug Wilson/99	6.00	15.00
21 Felix Potvin/99	15.00	40.00
22 Gilbert Perreault/99	8.00	20.00
24 Luc Robitaille/49	10.00	25.00
25 Wendel Clark/25	15.00	40.00

2011-12 Limited Stanley Cup Signatures

Card	Low	High
AL Andrew Ladd/99	8.00	20.00
AN Antti Niemi/99	10.00	25.00
BG Brian Gionta/99	8.00	20.00
BH Brett Hull/23	30.00	80.00
BM Brad Marchand/99	12.00	30.00
BR Brad Richards/25	15.00	30.00
BS Brendan Shanahan/25	20.00	40.00
CP Chris Pronger/99	12.00	30.00
CW Cam Ward/99	10.00	25.00
DB Dustin Byfuglien/25	15.00	30.00
DG Doug Gilmour/99	12.00	30.00
EM Evgeni Malkin/99	40.00	80.00
ES Eric Staal/99	8.00	20.00
GF Grant Fuhr/99	10.00	25.00
JB Jean Beliveau/99	30.00	80.00
JBO Johnny Bower/79	20.00	40.00
JF Johan Franzen/99	8.00	20.00
JN Joe Nieuwendyk/98	8.00	20.00
JS Joe Sakic/25	40.00	100.00
JSG Jean-Sebastien Giguere/100	12.00	30.00
JST Jordan Staal/99	12.00	30.00
JT J.Toews/25 EXCH	30.00	80.00
KL Kris Letang/99	15.00	40.00
MB Martin Brodeur/25	50.00	100.00
MF Marc-Andre Fleury/99	15.00	40.00
MM Mark Messier/25	25.00	60.00
MS Martin St. Louis/99	10.00	25.00
NK Nikolai Khabibulin/99	8.00	20.00
NL Nicklas Lidstrom/99	25.00	50.00
PB Patrice Bergeron/25	30.00	60.00
PK Patrick Kane/99	30.00	80.00
RB Ray Bourque/49	25.00	50.00
RG Ryan Getzlaf/99	10.00	25.00
SC Sidney Crosby/25	100.00	175.00
SG Scott Gomez/99	8.00	20.00
SN Scott Niedermayer/99	10.00	25.00
TT Tim Thomas/25	50.00	100.00
VL Vincent Lecavalier/25	15.00	30.00

2011-12 Limited Stanley Cup Winners

Card	Low	High
AL Andrew Ladd	2.50	6.00
AN Antti Niemi	3.00	8.00
BG Brian Gionta	2.50	6.00
BH Brett Hull	8.00	20.00
BM Brad Marchand	8.00	20.00
BR Brad Richards	4.00	10.00
BS Brendan Shanahan	4.00	10.00
CP Corey Perry	6.00	15.00
CPR Chris Pronger	4.00	10.00
CW Cam Ward	4.00	10.00
DB Dustin Byfuglien	4.00	10.00
DG Doug Gilmour	5.00	12.00
EM Evgeni Malkin	0.00	20.00
ES Eric Staal	5.00	12.00
GF Grant Fuhr	6.00	15.00
HR Henri Richard	4.00	10.00
JB Jean Beliveau	4.00	10.00
JBO Johnny Bower	4.00	10.00
JF Johan Franzen	3.00	8.00
JN Joe Nieuwendyk	3.00	8.00
JS Joe Sakic	8.00	20.00
JSG Jean-Sebastien Giguere	4.00	10.00
JST Jordan Staal	3.00	8.00
JT Jonathan Toews	6.00	15.00
KL Kris Letang	5.00	12.00
MB Martin Brodeur	6.00	15.00
MF Marc-Andre Fleury	8.00	20.00
MM Mark Messier	8.00	20.00
MS Milt Schmidt	3.00	8.00
MSL Martin St. Louis	4.00	10.00
MT Max Talbot	2.50	6.00
NK Nikolai Khabibulin	3.00	8.00
NL Nicklas Lidstrom	5.00	12.00
PB Patrice Bergeron	6.00	15.00
PD Pavel Datsyuk	6.00	15.00
PK Patrick Kane	8.00	20.00
PR Patrick Roy	10.00	25.00
PS Patrick Sharp	4.00	10.00
RB Ray Bourque	6.00	15.00
RG Ryan Getzlaf	4.00	10.00
SC Sidney Crosby	10.00	25.00
SG Scott Gomez	3.00	8.00
SN Scott Niedermayer	4.00	10.00
ST Shawn Thornton	6.00	15.00
SY Steve Yzerman	10.00	25.00
TH Tomas Holmstrom	2.50	6.00
TS Tyler Seguin	5.00	12.00
TT Tim Thomas	8.00	20.00
VL Vincent Lecavalier	4.00	10.00
YC Yvan Cournoyer	6.00	15.00

2011-12 Limited Team Trademarks

*GOLD/25: 1X TO 2.5X BASIC INSERT/199
*SILVER/49: .6X TO 1.5X BASIC INSERT/199

Card	Low	High
1 Taylor Hall	2.00	5.00
2 Nicklas Lidstrom	1.25	3.00
3 Dustin Byfuglien	2.00	5.00
4 Tyler Seguin	2.50	6.00
5 Daniel Sedin	2.50	6.00
6 Joe Thornton	3.00	8.00
7 Anze Kopitar	3.00	8.00
8 Jarome Iginla	2.50	6.00
9 Luke Schenn	2.00	5.00
10 Ryan Miller	2.00	5.00
11 Rick Nash	2.00	5.00
12 Matt Duchene	2.00	5.00
13 Jamie Benn	2.00	5.00
14 Jaroslav Halak	2.00	5.00
15 Jeff Skinner	2.50	6.00
16 Sidney Crosby	8.00	20.00
17 Henrik Lundqvist	5.00	12.00
18 John Tavares	3.00	8.00
19 Claude Giroux	2.00	5.00
20 Zach Parise	2.00	5.00

2011-12 Limited Team Trademarks Materials

*PRIME/25: .8X TO 2X BASIC JSY/99

Card	Low	High
1 Taylor Hall	5.00	12.00
2 Nicklas Lidstrom	6.00	15.00
3 Dustin Byfuglien	5.00	12.00
4 Tyler Seguin	6.00	15.00
5 Daniel Sedin	6.00	15.00
6 Joe Thornton	8.00	20.00
7 Anze Kopitar	8.00	20.00
8 Jarome Iginla	6.00	15.00
9 Luke Schenn	5.00	12.00
10 Ryan Miller	5.00	12.00
11 Rick Nash	5.00	12.00
12 Matt Duchene	5.00	12.00
13 Jamie Benn	5.00	12.00
14 Jaroslav Halak	5.00	12.00
15 Jeff Skinner	6.00	15.00
16 Sidney Crosby	12.00	30.00
17 Henrik Lundqvist	5.00	12.00
18 John Tavares	6.00	15.00
19 Claude Giroux	5.00	12.00
20 Zach Parise	6.00	15.00

2011-12 Limited Team Trademarks Materials Prime Signatures

Card	Low	High
1 Taylor Hall/25	20.00	50.00
3 Dustin Byfuglien/15	15.00	40.00
5 Daniel Sedin/25	12.00	30.00
6 Joe Thornton/25	12.00	30.00
8 Jarome Iginla/25	12.00	30.00
9 Luke Schenn/25	10.00	25.00
10 Ryan Miller/25	10.00	25.00
11 Rick Nash/25	20.00	50.00
12 Matt Duchene/25	10.00	25.00
13 Jamie Benn/25	10.00	25.00
14 Jaroslav Halak/25	10.00	25.00
16 Sidney Crosby/25	75.00	150.00
17 Henrik Lundqvist/25	15.00	40.00
18 John Tavares/25	15.00	40.00
19 Claude Giroux/25	25.00	50.00

2011-12 Limited Team Trademarks Materials Signatures

Card	Low	High
1 Taylor Hall/49	12.00	30.00
2 Nicklas Lidstrom/49	20.00	50.00
3 Dustin Byfuglien/49	10.00	25.00
5 Daniel Sedin/49	10.00	25.00
6 Joe Thornton/49	10.00	25.00
9 Luke Schenn/49	8.00	20.00
10 Ryan Miller/19	10.00	25.00
11 Rick Nash/49	8.00	20.00
12 Matt Duchene/49	8.00	20.00
13 Jamie Benn/49	8.00	20.00
14 Jaroslav Halak/49	10.00	25.00
17 Henrik Lundqvist/49	12.00	30.00
18 John Tavares/49	15.00	30.00
19 Claude Giroux/49	20.00	40.00
20 Zach Parise/49	8.00	20.00

2011-12 Limited Team Trademarks Signatures

Card	Low	High
1 Taylor Hall/99	20.00	50.00
2 Nicklas Lidstrom/99	12.00	30.00
3 Dustin Byfuglien/99	8.00	20.00
5 Daniel Sedin/99	10.00	25.00
6 Joe Thornton/49	10.00	25.00
8 Jarome Iginla/99	10.00	25.00
9 Luke Schenn/99	8.00	20.00
10 Ryan Miller/99	10.00	25.00
11 Rick Nash/99	8.00	20.00
12 Matt Duchene/99	8.00	20.00
13 Jamie Benn/99	6.00	15.00
14 Jaroslav Halak/99	12.00	30.00
17 Henrik Lundqvist/99	12.00	30.00
18 John Tavares/99	12.00	30.00
19 Claude Giroux/49	15.00	40.00
20 Zach Parise/99	8.00	20.00

2011-12 Limited Trios Materials

*PRIME/25: .8X TO 2X BASIC TRIO/99

Card	Low	High
1 Giroux/Lindros/Clarke	12.00	30.00
2 Reimer/Joseph/Fuhr	12.00	30.00
3 Hall/Eberle/Omark	10.00	25.00
4 Bergeron/Lucic/Seguin	10.00	25.00
5 Perry/Getzlaf/Ryan	12.00	30.00
6 DiPietro/Hamonic/Tavares	8.00	20.00
7 Ovechkin/Backstrom/Neuvirth	30.00	80.00
8 Kessel/Grabovski/Kulemin	8.00	20.00
9 Thornton/Pavelski/Marleau	12.00	30.00
10 Backstrom/Clutterbuck/Koivu	8.00	20.00
11 Zetterberg/Datsyuk/Franzen	12.00	30.00
12 Toews/Sharp/Hossa	8.00	20.00
13 Myers/Ennis/Roy	8.00	20.00
14 Lecavalier/St. Louis/Purcell	8.00	20.00
15 Alfredsson/Spezza/Butler	8.00	20.00
16 Staal/Malkin/Fleury	8.00	20.00
17 Brodeur/Luongo/Fleury	12.00	30.00
18 Clark/Neely/Tocchet	12.00	30.00
19 Shanahan/Verbeek/Francis	10.00	25.00
20 Lemieux/Yzerman/Sakic	12.00	30.00

2012-13 Limited

Card	Low	High
COMMON CAPTAIN (151-180)	1.50	4.00
1 Steven Stamkos	4.00	10.00
2 Marcus Johansson	1.50	4.00
3 Ryan Johansen	1.50	4.00
4 Jason Spezza	2.00	5.00
5 Jake Gardiner	1.25	3.00
6 James Neal	1.25	3.00
7 Claude Giroux	2.00	5.00
8 Craig Anderson	2.00	5.00
9 Ed Jovanovski	1.25	3.00
10 Nicklas Backstrom	2.00	5.00
11 Duncan Keith	1.50	4.00

12 Cam Ward 2.00 5.00
13 Zach Parise 2.00 5.00
14 Logan Couture 2.50 6.00
15 Zack Kassian 1.25 3.00
16 Patrik Elias 2.00 5.00
17 John Tavares 3.00 8.00
18 Dennis Wideman 1.25 3.00
19 Andy McDonald 1.50 4.00
20 Ryan Whitney 1.25 3.00
21 Jussi Jokinen 1.25 3.00
22 Adam Henrique 1.50 4.00
23 Scott Clemmensen 1.50 4.00
24 Jaromir Jagr 6.00 15.00
25 Brendan Smith 1.25 3.00
26 Jordan Eberle 2.00 5.00
27 Jonathan Quick 2.50 6.00
28 Daniel Sedin 2.50 6.00
29 Taylor Hall 2.00 5.00
30 Jimmy Howard 2.50 6.00
31 Devante Smith-Pelly 1.50 4.00
32 Tim Gleason 1.25 3.00
33 Brett Connolly 1.25 3.00
34 Loui Eriksson 1.25 3.00
35 Henrik Lundqvist 5.00 12.00
36 Carey Price 4.00 10.00
37 Anze Kopitar 3.00 8.00
38 Patrick Kane 4.00 10.00
39 Tuukka Rask 2.50 6.00
40 Dan Boyle 1.25 3.00
41 David Perron 1.50 4.00
42 Ryan Miller 2.00 5.00
43 Brian Campbell 1.25 3.00
44 Jack Johnson 1.25 3.00
45 Bobby Ryan 1.50 4.00
46 Adam Larsson 2.00 5.00
47 Carl Hagelin 1.25 3.00
48 Kyle Okposo 1.25 3.00
49 Brian Elliott 1.50 4.00
50 Evander Kane 2.00 5.00
51 Kris Versteeg 1.25 3.00
52 Derek Dorsett 1.25 3.00
53 Colin Greening 1.25 3.00
54 Stephen Weiss 1.50 4.00
55 Steve Downie 1.25 3.00
56 Sean Couturier 1.50 4.00
57 Mike Smith 2.00 5.00
58 Ryan Suter 1.50 4.00
59 Steve Mason 1.50 4.00
60 Semyon Varlamov 2.00 5.00
61 Corey Crawford 2.50 6.00
62 Drew Doughty 2.50 6.00
63 Joffrey Lupul 1.25 3.00
64 Cal Clutterbuck 1.25 3.00
65 Alexander Burmistrov 1.50 4.00
66 Nazem Kadri 2.50 6.00
67 Ryan Kesler 2.00 5.00
68 Ray Whitney 1.50 4.00
69 T.J. Oshie 2.00 5.00
70 David Krejci 2.00 5.00
71 Miikka Kiprusoff 2.00 5.00
72 Cam Fowler 2.00 5.00
73 Michael Grabner 1.50 4.00
74 Matt Duchene 2.00 5.00
75 Mikael Backlund 1.50 4.00
76 Mike Fisher 1.25 3.00
77 Patrice Bergeron 2.50 6.00
78 Chris Neil 1.25 3.00
79 Kari Lehtonen 1.50 4.00
80 Jay Bouwmeester 1.25 3.00
81 Braden Holtby 2.50 6.00
82 Ryan Nugent-Hopkins 2.50 6.00
83 Mike Richards 1.50 4.00
84 Jeff Skinner 2.50 6.00
85 Alex Tanguay 1.50 4.00
86 Jonas Gustavsson 2.00 5.00
87 Marian Gaborik 2.00 5.00
88 Pekka Rinne 2.00 5.00
89 Devin Setoguchi 1.50 4.00
90 Marcus Kruger 1.25 3.00
91 Martin Erat 1.25 3.00
92 Steve Ott 1.25 3.00
93 Martin Havlat 1.50 4.00
94 Martin Hanzal 1.25 3.00
95 Niklas Backstrom 1.50 4.00
96 Martin St. Louis 2.00 5.00
97 Alex Goligoski 1.25 3.00
98 Jeff Carter 1.50 4.00
99 Louis Leblanc 1.25 3.00
100 Devan Dubnyk 1.50 4.00
101 Jiri Hudler 1.50 4.00
102 Danny Briere 2.00 5.00
103 Erik Karlsson 2.50 6.00
104 Tyler Seguin 2.50 6.00
105 Cody Hodgson 1.25 3.00
106 Ilya Bryzgalov 2.00 5.00
107 Marc-Andre Fleury 4.00 10.00
108 Brad Richards 2.00 5.00
109 Cody Eakin 1.25 3.00
110 Erik Johnson 1.25 3.00
111 Ondrej Pavelec 2.00 5.00
112 Marcus Foligno 1.50 4.00
113 Pavel Datsyuk 3.00 8.00
114 Phil Kessel 2.00 5.00
115 Keith Yandle 1.25 3.00
116 Lars Eller 1.25 3.00
117 Corey Perry 3.00 8.00
118 Oliver Ekman-Larsson 2.00 5.00
119 Marc Staal 1.25 3.00
120 Rick Nash 2.00 5.00
121 Jamie Benn 2.00 5.00
122 Craig Smith 1.25 3.00
123 Jonas Hiller 1.50 4.00
124 Tuomo Ruutu 1.50 4.00
125 Jordan Staal 1.50 4.00
126 Dustin Byfuglien 2.00 5.00
127 Cory Schneider 2.00 5.00
128 Antti Niemi 1.50 4.00
129 Michael Cammalleri 1.50 4.00
130 Gabriel Landeskog 2.50 6.00
131 Milan Lucic 2.00 5.00
132 Alex Pietrangelo 1.50 4.00
133 Al Montoya 1.25 3.00
134 Matt Cullen 1.25 3.00
135 Victor Hedman 2.50 6.00
136 Max Pacioretty 2.00 5.00
137 Henrik Zetterberg 2.50 6.00
138 Patrick Marleau 2.00 5.00
139 Nathan Gerbe 1.25 3.00
140 Blake Wheeler 2.00 5.00
141 Mathieu Garon 1.50 4.00
142 Martin Brodeur 5.00 12.00
143 Dany Heatley 1.50 4.00
144 Kris Letang 2.50 6.00
145 Patrick Sharp 2.00 5.00
146 P.K. Subban 2.50 6.00
147 Kevin Bieksa 1.50 4.00
148 Tyler Myers 1.25 3.00
149 Matt Moulson 1.25 3.00
150 Evgeni Malkin 4.00 10.00
151 Ryan Getzlaf/199 C 2.50 6.00
152 Zdeno Chara/199 C 2.50 6.00
153 Jason Pominville/199 C 1.50 4.00
154 Jarome Iginla/199 C 3.00 8.00
155 Eric Staal/199 C 3.00 8.00
156 Jonathan Toews/199 C 4.00 10.00
157 Milan Hejduk/199 C 2.00 5.00
158 R.J. Umberger/199 C 1.50 4.00
159 Brenden Morrow/199 C 2.00 5.00
160 Nicklas Lidstrom/199 C 2.50 6.00
161 Shawn Horcoff/199 C 1.50 4.00
162 Ed Jovanovski/199 C 1.50 4.00
163 Dustin Brown/199 C 2.50 6.00
164 Mikko Koivu/199 C 2.00 5.00
165 Brian Gionta/199 C 1.50 4.00
166 Shea Weber/199 C 2.00 5.00
167 Ilya Kovalchuk/199 C 2.50 6.00
168 Mark Streit/199 C 1.50 4.00
169 Ryan Callahan/199 C 1.50 4.00
170 Daniel Alfredsson/199 C 2.50 6.00
171 Chris Pronger/199 C 2.50 6.00
172 Shane Doan/199 C 2.00 5.00
173 Sidney Crosby/199 C 5.00 12.00
174 David Backes/199 C 1.50 4.00
175 Joe Thornton/199 C 4.00 10.00
176 Vincent Lecavalier/199 C 2.50 6.00
177 Dion Phaneuf/199 C 2.00 5.00
178 Henrik Sedin/199 C 3.00 8.00
179 Alex Ovechkin/199 C 10.00 25.00
180 Andrew Ladd/199 C 1.50 4.00
181 Mark Messier/99 C 8.00 20.00
182 Eric Lindros/99 C 6.00 15.00
183 Steve Yzerman/99 C 10.00 25.00
184 Joe Sakic/99 C 8.00 20.00
185 Jean Beliveau/99 C 4.00 10.00
186 Bobby Clarke/99 C 6.00 15.00
187 Trevor Linden/99 C 5.00 12.00
188 Ray Bourque/99 C 6.00 15.00
189 Pat LaFontaine/99 C 4.00 10.00
190 Doug Gilmour/99 C 5.00 12.00
191 Lanny McDonald/99 C 4.00 10.00
192 Brett Hull/99 C 8.00 20.00
193 Mike Modano/99 C 6.00 15.00
194 Yvan Cournoyer/99 C 4.00 10.00
195 Mario Lemieux/99 C 15.00 40.00
196 Ron Francis/99 C 5.00 12.00
197 Luc Robitaille/99 C 4.00 10.00
198 Johnny Bucyk/99 C 4.00 10.00
199 Dale Hawerchuk/99 C 5.00 12.00
200 Gordie Howe/99 C 12.00 30.00
201 Aaron Ness AU/499 RC 3.00 8.00
202 J.T. Brown AU/499 RC 4.00 10.00
203 Brandon Bollig AU/499 RC 6.00 15.00
204 Brandon Manning AU/499 RC 4.00 10.00
205 Brenden Dillon AU/499 RC 4.00 10.00
206A C.Ashton AU/499 RC TOR 3.00 8.00
206B C.Ashton AU/499 RC TB 3.00 8.00
207 Carter Camper AU/299 RC 3.00 8.00
208 Casey Cizikas AU/499 RC 4.00 10.00
209 Chay Genoway AU/499 RC 3.00 8.00
210 Chet Pickard AU/499 RC 4.00 10.00
211 Cody Goloubef AU/499 RC 3.00 8.00
212 Colby Robak AU/499 RC 3.00 8.00
213 Dalton Prout AU/499 RC 3.00 8.00
214 Jake Allen AU/499 RC 10.00 25.00
215 Jakob Silfverberg AU/499 RC 5.00 12.00
216 Jordan Nolan AU/499 RC 3.00 8.00
217 Jussi Rynnas AU/499 RC 3.00 8.00
218 Kris Foucault AU/499 RC 3.00 8.00
219 Mat Clark AU/499 RC 4.00 10.00
220 Matt Donovan AU/499 RC 4.00 10.00
221 Max Sauve AU/299 RC 3.00 8.00
222 Tyson Sexsmith AU/499 RC 3.00 8.00
223 Michael Stone AU/499 RC 4.00 10.00
224 Mike Connolly AU/499 RC 4.00 10.00
225 Philippe Cornet AU/499 RC 4.00 10.00
226 Robert Mayer AU/499 RC 5.00 12.00
227 Scott Glennie AU/499 RC 4.00 10.00
228 Reilly Smith AU/499 RC 10.00 25.00
229 Tyler Cuma AU/299 RC 3.00 8.00
230 Tyson Barrie AU/499 RC 10.00 25.00
231 Chris Kreider AU/499 RC 12.00 30.00
232 Sven Baertschi AU/499 RC 6.00 15.00
233 Jaden Schwartz AU/499 RC 8.00 20.00
234 Riley Sheahan AU/499 RC 5.00 12.00
235 Andrew Joudrey AU/299 RC 4.00 10.00
236 Ryan Garbutt AU/299 RC 3.00 8.00
237 Travis Turnbull AU/499 RC 3.00 8.00
238 Ryan Hamilton AU/499 RC 6.00 15.00
239 Shawn Hunwick AU/299 RC 3.00 8.00
240 Gabriel Dumont AU/499 RC 4.00 10.00
241 Akim Aliu AU/499 RC 4.00 10.00
242 Jeremy Welsh AU/499 RC 4.00 10.00

2012-13 Limited Back To The Future

BTFAG C.Ashton/D.Gilmour 4.00 10.00
BTFBN D.Brown/B.Nicholls 3.00 8.00
BTFDD A.Delvecchio/P.Datsyuk 5.00 12.00
BTFEJ L.Eriksson/J.Jagr 5.00 12.00
BTFFL M.Foligno/P.LaFontaine 3.00 8.00
BTFGE E.Lindros/G.Landeskog 5.00 12.00
BTFHN A.Henrique/J.Nieuwendyk 2.50 6.00
BTFIB J.Iginla/S.Baertschi 8.00 20.00
BTFJA C.Joseph/J.Allen 6.00 15.00
BTFLC R.Leach/S.Couturier 2.50 6.00
BTFLK T.Linden/Z.Kassian 3.00 8.00
BTFLL L.Leblanc/G.Lafleur 4.00 10.00
BTFLS N.Lidstrom/B.Smith 3.00 8.00
BTFMG M.Modano/S.Glennie 5.00 12.00
BTFMK M.Messier/C.Kreider 8.00 20.00
BTFMP A.MacInnis/A.Pietrangelo 4.00 10.00
BTFPD D.Potvin/C.de Haan 3.00 8.00
BTFPR C.Pickard/P.Rinne 6.00 15.00
BTFPR F.Potvin/J.Rynnas 5.00 12.00
BTFQB J.Quick/M.Brodeur 8.00 20.00
BTFRH B.Richards/C.Hagelin 3.00 8.00
BTFRK M.Read/T.Kerr 4.00 10.00
BTFSB M.St. Louis/J.Brown 3.00 8.00
BTFSR A.Shaw/J.Roenick 5.00 12.00
BTFSS B.Shanahan/J.Schwartz 6.00 15.00

2012-13 Limited Back To The Future Signatures

BTFAG C.Ashton/D.Gilmour 20.00 50.00
BTFBN D.Brown/B.Nicholls 25.00 50.00
BTFDD A.Delvecchio/P.Datsyuk 25.00 50.00
BTFEJ L.Eriksson/J.Jagr 40.00 80.00
BTFFL M.Foligno/P.LaFontaine 10.00 25.00
BTFGE E.Lindros/G.Landeskog 50.00 100.00
BTFHN A.Henrique/J.Nieuwendyk 12.00 30.00
BTFIB J.Iginla/S.Baertschi 30.00 60.00
BTFJA C.Joseph/J.Allen 30.00 80.00
BTFLC R.Leach/S.Couturier 12.00 30.00
BTFLK Linden/Kassian 2.00 50.00
BTFLL L.Leblanc/G.Lafleur 15.00 40.00
BTFLS N.Lidstrom/B.Smith 15.00 40.00
BTFMG M.Modano/S.Glennie 15.00 40.00
BTFMK M.Messier/C.Kreider 25.00 50.00
BTFMP A.MacInnis/A.Pietrangelo 20.00 50.00
BTFPD D.Potvin/C.de Haan 15.00 40.00
BTFPR C.Pickard/P.Rinne 20.00 50.00
BTFQB J.Quick/M.Brodeur 20.00 50.00
BTFRH B.Richards/C.Hagelin 15.00 40.00
BTFRK M.Read/T.Kerr 12.00 30.00
BTFSB M.St. Louis/J.Brown 12.00 30.00
BTFSR A.Shaw/J.Roenick 40.00 80.00
BTFSS B.Shanahan/J.Schwartz 25.00 60.00

2012-13 Limited Board Members

*DIECUT/25: 2X TO 5X BASIC INS
1 Alex Ovechkin 10.00 25.00
2 Eric Lindros 4.00 10.00
3 Dustin Brown 2.50 6.00
4 David Backes 1.50 4.00
5 Cam Neely 2.50 6.00
6 Dion Phaneuf 2.00 5.00
7 Shea Weber 2.00 5.00
8 Zdeno Chara 2.50 6.00
9 Duncan Keith 2.00 5.00
10 Ryan Kesler 2.50 6.00
11 Mike Richards 2.00 5.00
12 Scott Hartnell 3.00 8.00
13 Dustin Byfuglien 2.50 6.00
14 Drew Doughty 3.00 8.00
15 Milan Lucic 2.50 6.00
16 P.K. Subban 3.00 8.00
17 Ryan Getzlaf 2.50 6.00
18 Paul Bissonnette 1.50 4.00
19 Ryan Callahan 1.50 4.00
20 Steve Ott 1.50 4.00
21 Shane Doan 2.00 5.00
22 Gabriel Landeskog 3.00 8.00
23 Steven Stamkos 5.00 12.00
24 Sidney Crosby 4.00 10.00
25 Jarome Iginla 3.00 8.00
26 Henrik Zetterberg 3.00 8.00
27 Zach Parise 2.50 6.00
28 Alex Pietrangelo 2.00 5.00
29 Erik Gudbranson 1.50 4.00
30 Claude Giroux 5.00 12.00
31 Jordan Eberle 2.50 6.00
32 Chris Kreider 5.00 12.00
33 Jaden Schwartz 5.00 12.00
34 Sven Baertschi 6.00 15.00
35 Jeff Skinner 3.00 8.00
36 Ryan Nugent-Hopkins 3.00 8.00
37 John Tavares 4.00 10.00
38 Mario Lemieux 6.00 15.00
39 Mark Messier 5.00 12.00
40 Brendan Shanahan 2.50 6.00
41 Brett Hull 5.00 12.00
42 Doug Gilmour 3.00 8.00
43 Cody Hodgson 1.50 4.00
44 Andrew Ladd 1.50 4.00
45 Zack Kassian 1.50 4.00
46 Erik Karlsson 3.00 8.00
47 Keith Primeau 2.50 6.00
48 Jeremy Roenick 4.00 10.00
49 Steve Downie 1.50 4.00
50 Victor Hedman 3.00 8.00

2012-13 Limited Crease Cleaners Materials

*PRIME/25: .8X TO 2X BASIC JSY/99
1 Chet Pickard/99 4.00 10.00
2 Jake Allen/99 10.00 25.00
3 Patrick Roy/99 12.00 30.00
4 Tuukka Rask/99 6.00 15.00
5 Pekka Rinne/99 5.00 12.00
6 Jimmy Howard/99 6.00 15.00
7 Cory Schneider/99 5.00 12.00
8 Jonathan Quick/99 6.00 15.00
9 Martin Brodeur/99 12.00 30.00
10 Jonas Hiller/99 4.00 10.00
11 Henrik Lundqvist/99 12.00 30.00
12 Jhonas Enroth/99 5.00 12.00
13 Kari Lehtonen/99 4.00 10.00
14 Carey Price/99 10.00 25.00
15 Ron Hextall/99 8.00 20.00
16 Felix Potvin/99 6.00 15.00
17 Johan Hedberg/99 8.00 20.00
18 Grant Fuhr/99 8.00 20.00
19 Niklas Backstrom/99 4.00 10.00
20 Ryan Miller/99 5.00 12.00
21 Mike Smith/25 8.00 20.00
22 Roberto Luongo/99 8.00 20.00
23 Craig Anderson/99 5.00 12.00
24 Tomas Vokoun/99 4.00 10.00
25 Jaroslav Halak/99 5.00 12.00
26 Braden Holtby/99 6.00 15.00
27 Marc-Andre Fleury/99 10.00 25.00
28 Brian Elliott/99 4.00 10.00
29 Ondrej Pavelec/99 5.00 12.00
30 Miikka Kiprusoff/99 5.00 12.00
32 Jonathan Bernier/99 4.00 10.00
33 Ilya Bryzgalov/99 5.00 12.00
34 Nikolai Khabibulin/99 5.00 12.00
35 Evgeni Nabokov/99 4.00 10.00
36 Antti Niemi/99 4.00 10.00
37 James Reimer/99 5.00 12.00
38 Scott Clemmensen/99 4.00 10.00
39 Curtis Joseph/99 6.00 15.00
40 Bernie Parent/99 8.00 20.00

2012-13 Limited Duels Silver

LD1A Claude Giroux 4.00 10.00
LD1B Sidney Crosby 15.00 40.00
LD2A Dustin Brown 4.00 10.00
LD2B Shane Doan 3.00 8.00
LD3A Henrik Lundqvist 10.00 25.00
LD3B Martin Brodeur 10.00 25.00
LD4A Mike Smith 4.00 10.00
LD4B Jonathan Quick 5.00 12.00
LD5A Evgeni Malkin 8.00 20.00
LD5B Sean Couturier 3.00 8.00
LD6A Alex Ovechkin 6.00 15.00
LD6B Marian Gaborik 4.00 10.00
LD7A Ryan Kesler 4.00 10.00
LD7B Mike Richards 3.00 8.00
LD8A Loui Eriksson 2.50 6.00
LD8B Pavel Datsyuk 10.00 25.00
LD9A Ryan Nugent-Hopkins 5.00 12.00
LD9B Gabriel Landeskog 5.00 12.00
LD10A Carey Price 8.00 20.00
LD10B Tim Thomas 4.00 10.00
LD11A Dion Phaneuf 3.00 8.00
LD11B Tyler Myers 2.50 6.00
LD12A Brad Marchand 6.00 15.00
LD12B P.K. Subban 5.00 12.00
LD13A Adam Henrique 3.00 8.00
LD13B Chris Kreider 10.00 25.00
LD14A David Backes 2.50 6.00
LD14B Jonathan Toews 6.00 15.00
LD15A Steven Stamkos 8.00 20.00
LD15B James Neal 2.50 6.00
LD16A Corey Perry 6.00 15.00
LD16B Patrick Kane 8.00 20.00
LD17A John Tavares 6.00 15.00
LD17B Matt Duchene 4.00 10.00
LD18A Tyler Seguin 5.00 12.00
LD18B Taylor Hall 4.00 10.00
LD19A Scott Glennie 3.00 8.00
LD19B Jaden Schwartz 8.00 20.00
LD20A Jake Allen 8.00 20.00
LD20B Chet Pickard 3.00 8.00
LD21A Brendan Shanahan 4.00 10.00
LD21B Patrick Roy 10.00 25.00
LD22A Eric Lindros 6.00 15.00
LD22B Mark Messier 8.00 20.00
LD23A Joe Sakic 8.00 20.00
LD23B Steve Yzerman 15.00 40.00
LD24A Guy Lafleur 5.00 12.00
LD24B Bobby Clarke 6.00 15.00
LD25A Gordie Howe 12.00 30.00
LD25B Johnny Bower 4.00 10.00

2012-13 Limited Freshman Dual Jumbo Materials

FDAR C.Ashton/J.Rynnas 10.00 25.00
FDBB S.Baertschi/T.Barrie 8.00 20.00
FDKS C.Kreider/J.Silfverberg 8.00 20.00
FDPG C.Pickard/S.Glennie 6.00 15.00
FDSA J.Schwartz/J.Allen 8.00 20.00

2012-13 Limited Freshman Jumbo Materials

*PRIME/49: .6X TO 1.5X JSY/149-199
FJCA Carter Ashton/199 2.00 5.00
FJCK Chris Kreider/199 8.00 20.00
FJCP Chet Pickard/199 2.50 6.00
FJJA Jake Allen/199 6.00 15.00
FJJB J.T. Brown/199 2.50 6.00
FJJR Jussi Rynnas/199 2.00 5.00
FJJS Jakob Silfverberg/199 4.00 10.00
FJJS Jaden Schwartz/199 6.00 15.00
FJRS Reilly Smith/199 6.00 15.00
FJSB Sven Baertschi/149 3.00 8.00
FJSG Scott Glennie/199 2.50 6.00
FJTB Tyson Barrie/199 6.00 15.00

2012-13 Limited Freshman Jumbo Materials Signatures

FJCA Carter Ashton 5.00 12.00
FJCK Chris Kreider 15.00 40.00
FJJA Jake Allen 12.00 30.00
FJJB J.T. Brown 5.00 12.00
FJJR Jussi Rynnas 8.00 20.00
FJJS Jakob Silfverberg 12.00 30.00
FJJS Jaden Schwartz 8.00 20.00
FJRS Reilly Smith 12.00 30.00
FJSB Sven Baertschi 6.00 15.00
FJSG Scott Glennie 5.00 12.00
FJTB Tyson Barrie 12.00 30.00

2012-13 Limited Game Pucks

GPAO Alex Ovechkin 20.00 50.00
GPBR Bobby Ryan 6.00 15.00
GPCG Claude Giroux 8.00 20.00
GPDB Dustin Brown 8.00 20.00
GPEM Evgeni Malkin 15.00 40.00
GPJA John Tavares 12.00 30.00
GPJO Joe Thornton 12.00 30.00
GPLE Loui Eriksson 5.00 12.00
GPMA Marc Staal 5.00 12.00
GPMB Martin Brodeur 20.00 50.00
GPMG Marian Gaborik 8.00 20.00
GPMS Mike Smith 8.00 20.00
GPOP Ondrej Pavelec 8.00 20.00
GPPD Pavel Datsyuk 10.00 25.00
GPRK Ryan Kesler 10.00 25.00
GPRM Ryan Miller 10.00 25.00
GPSS Steven Stamkos 15.00 40.00
GPSW Shea Weber 6.00 15.00
GPTS Tyler Seguin 10.00 25.00

2012-13 Limited Gold

*1-150 GOLD/25: 1X TO 2.5X BASIC CARDS
*151-180 GOLD/25: 1X TO 2.5X BASIC C/199
*181-200 GOLD/25: .6X TO 1.5X BASIC C/99
*201-233 GOLD AU/25: .8X TO 2X AU RC
10 Nicklas Backstrom 5.00 12.00
61 Corey Crawford 6.00 15.00

2012-13 Limited Jumbo Materials

*PRIME/49: .6X TO 1.5X JUM.JSY/50-99
*PRIME/25: .8X TO 2X JUM.JSY/50-99
JJAB Alexander Burmistrov/99 4.00 10.00
JJAL Adam Larsson/99 5.00 12.00
JJAN Antti Niemi/99 4.00 10.00
JJAO Alex Ovechkin/99 20.00 50.00
JJAX Alexandre Burrows/99 3.00 8.00
JJBL Bryan Little/99 5.00 12.00
JJCG Claude Giroux/99 5.00 12.00
JJCH Carl Hagelin/99 3.00 8.00
JJCN Chris Neil/99 3.00 8.00
JJCO Corey Perry/99 8.00 20.00
JJCP Carey Price/99 10.00 25.00
JJDG Dan Girardi/99 3.00 8.00
JJDP David Perron/99 4.00 10.00
JJDS Devin Setoguchi/75 4.00 10.00
JJEL Eric Lindros/99 8.00 20.00
JJGL Gabriel Landeskog/50 6.00 15.00
JJHL Henrik Lundqvist/99 12.00 30.00
JJJA John Tavares/99 8.00 20.00
JJJC Jeff Carter/99 4.00 10.00
JJJE Jordan Eberle/99 5.00 12.00
JJJG Josh Gorges/99 4.00 10.00
JJJH Joe Thornton/99 8.00 20.00
JJJN James Neal/99 3.00 8.00
JJJO Joe Nieuwendyk/99 4.00 10.00
JJJP Jason Pominville/99 3.00 8.00
JJJQ Jonathan Quick/99 6.00 15.00
JJJS Jordan Staal/99 4.00 10.00
JJJT Jonathan Toews/99 8.00 20.00
JJJV James van Riemsdyk/99 4.00 10.00
JJKL Kari Lehtonen/99 4.00 10.00
JJKP Keith Primeau/99 4.00 10.00
JJLE Loui Eriksson/99 3.00 8.00
JJMF Marc-Andre Fleury/99 10.00 25.00
JJMG Marian Gaborik/99 5.00 12.00
JJMH Martin Hanzal/99 3.00 8.00
JJMI Mikhail Grabovski/99 3.00 8.00
JJMK Miikka Kiprusoff/99 5.00 12.00
JJMR Matt Read/99 4.00 10.00
JJMS Mike Smith/25 15.00 30.00
JJNG Nathan Gerbe/99 3.00 8.00
JJNL Nicklas Lidstrom/99 5.00 12.00
JJPD Pavel Datsyuk/99 8.00 20.00
JJPS P.K. Subban/99 6.00 15.00
JJRF Ron Francis/99 6.00 15.00
JJRL Robin Lehner/99 4.00 10.00
JJRN Ryan Nugent-Hopkins/99 6.00 15.00
JJRS Ryan Suter/99 4.00 10.00
JJSC Sidney Crosby/99 10.00 25.00
JJSG Sam Gagner/99 3.00 8.00
JJSK Saku Koivu/99 5.00 12.00
JJSM Scott Clemmensen/99 4.00 10.00
JJSW Shea Weber/99 4.00 10.00
JJSY Steve Yzerman/99 12.00 30.00
JJTS Tyler Seguin/99 6.00 15.00

2012-13 Limited Jumbo Materials Signatures

JJAB Alexander Burmistrov/49 6.00 15.00
JJAL Adam Larsson/49 EXCH 8.00 20.00
JJAN Antti Niemi/49 6.00 15.00
JJCG Claude Giroux/49 8.00 20.00
JJCH Carl Hagelin/49 5.00 12.00
JJCN Chris Neil/49 5.00 12.00
JJCO Corey Perry/49 10.00 25.00
JJCP Carey Price/49 15.00 40.00
JJGL Gabriel Landeskog/49 10.00 25.00
JJJA John Tavares/49 15.00 40.00
JJJE Jordan Eberle/49 8.00 20.00
JJJH Joe Thornton/49 8.00 20.00
JJJN James Neal/49 12.00 30.00
JJJO Joe Nieuwendyk/49 6.00 15.00
JJJQ Jonathan Quick/49 25.00 60.00
JJJS Jordan Staal/49 EXCH 10.00 25.00
JJJT Jonathan Toews/49 25.00 50.00
JJJV James van Riemsdyk/49 6.00 15.00
JJKL Kari Lehtonen/49 6.00 15.00
JJKP Keith Primeau/49 6.00 15.00
JJLE Loui Eriksson/49 5.00 12.00
JJMF Marc-Andre Fleury/49 15.00 40.00
JJMG Marian Gaborik/49 8.00 20.00
JJMI Mikhail Grabovski/49 5.00 12.00
JJNG Nathan Gerbe/49 5.00 12.00
JJNL Nicklas Lidstrom/49 12.00 30.00
JJPD Pavel Datsyuk/49 15.00 40.00
JJPS P.K. Subban/49 12.00 30.00
JJRF Ron Francis/49 10.00 25.00
JJRL Robin Lehner/49 6.00 15.00
JJRN Ryan Nugent-Hopkins/49 15.00 40.00
JJSG Sam Gagner/49 5.00 12.00
JJSK Saku Koivu/49 8.00 20.00
JJSW Shea Weber/49 8.00 20.00
JJTS Tyler Seguin/49 15.00 40.00

2012-13 Limited Materials

*PRIME/25: .6X TO 1.5X JSY/75-99
*PRIME/25: .8X TO 1.2X JSY/49-50
LJAA Artem Anisimov/99 2.50 6.00
LJAB Alexander Burmistrov/99 3.00 8.00
LJAG Adam Graves/99 3.00 8.00
LJAK Andrei Kostitsyn/99 3.00 8.00
LJAN Antti Niemi/99 3.00 8.00
LJAT Alex Tanguay/99 3.00 8.00
LJAV Antoine Vermette/99 2.50 6.00
LJAZ Anze Kopitar/99 6.00 15.00
LJBD Brandon Dubinsky/99 2.50 6.00
LJBE Brian Boyle/99 2.50 6.00
LJBG Brian Gionta/99 2.50 6.00
LJBH Brett Hull/99 8.00 20.00
LJBL Bryan Little/99 4.00 10.00
LJBO Dan Boyle/99 2.50 6.00
LJBP Brandon Prust/99 2.50 6.00
LJBR Danny Briere/99 4.00 10.00
LJBS Brad Boyes/99 2.50 6.00
LJCC Chris Chelios/99 4.00 10.00
LJCG Curtis Glencross/99 2.50 6.00
LJCL Scott Clemmensen/99 3.00 8.00
LJCO Sean Couturier/99 3.00 8.00
LJCS Chris Stewart/99 3.00 8.00
LJCW Cam Ward/49 5.00 12.00
LJDA Daniel Alfredsson/99 4.00 10.00
LJDD Devan Dubnyk/99 3.00 8.00
LJDE Simon Despres/99 3.00 8.00
LJDG Dan Girardi/99 2.50 6.00
LJDK Dmitry Kulikov/99 2.50 6.00
LJDP David Perron/99 3.00 8.00
LJDT Dana Tyrell/99 2.50 6.00
LJEB Jordan Eberle/99 4.00 10.00
LJEK Erik Karlsson/99 5.00 12.00
LJEL Eric Lindros/99 6.00 15.00
LJEN Jhonas Enroth/99 4.00 10.00
LJES Eric Staal/50 6.00 15.00
LJGF Grant Fuhr/99 6.00 15.00
LJGI Mikhail Grabovski/99 2.50 6.00
LJGL Gabriel Landeskog/99 5.00 12.00
LJGN Mike Green/99 3.00 8.00
LJGP George Parros/99 3.00 8.00
LJHA Martin Hanzal/99 2.50 6.00
LJHO Marian Hossa/99 4.00 10.00
LJHZ Henrik Zetterberg/99 5.00 12.00
LJJC Jeff Carter/99 3.00 8.00
LJJH Johan Hedberg/99 3.00 8.00
LJJL Jamie Langenbrunner/99 2.50 6.00
LJJM Joe Mullen/99 3.00 8.00
LJJN James Neal/99 2.50 6.00
LJJS Jarret Stoll/99 3.00 8.00
LJJV James van Riemsdyk/99 3.00 8.00
LJKL Kari Lehtonen/99 3.00 8.00
LJKO Niklas Kronwall/99 3.00 8.00
LJKP Keith Primeau/99 3.00 8.00
LJKR David Krejci/99 4.00 10.00
LJKS Kevin Shattenkirk/99 2.50 6.00
LJKU Nikolai Kulemin/99 2.50 6.00
LJLA Adam Larsson/99 4.00 10.00
LJLC Logan Couture/99 5.00 12.00
LJLE Loui Eriksson/99 2.50 6.00
LJLI Anders Lindback/49 3.00 8.00
LJLS Luca Sbisa/99 3.00 8.00
LJMA Martin Brodeur/99 10.00 25.00
LJMC Michael Cammalleri/99 3.00 8.00
LJMD Michael Del Zotto/99 2.50 6.00
LJMF Marc-Andre Fleury/99 8.00 20.00
LJMI Mikkel Boedker/99 2.50 6.00
LJMR Matt Read/99 3.00 8.00
LJMS Al MacInnis/99 5.00 12.00
LJMZ Alec Martinez/99 3.00 8.00
LJNC Nicklas Backstrom/99 4.00 10.00
LJNG Nathan Gerbe/99 2.50 6.00
LJNH Ryan Nugent-Hopkins/99 5.00 12.00
LJNK Niklas Backstrom/75 3.00 8.00
LJNO Nick Bonino/99 2.50 6.00
LJPB Paul Bissonnette/99 2.50 6.00
LJPC Paul Coffey/99 4.00 10.00
LJPM Peter Mueller/99 2.50 6.00
LJPR Pekka Rinne/99 4.00 10.00
LJPS Patrick Sharp/99 4.00 10.00
LJRN Rick Nash/99 4.00 10.00
LJRS Ryan Smyth/99 3.00 8.00
LJSA Joe Sakic/99 8.00 20.00
LJSC Sidney Crosby/99 10.00 25.00
LJSD Shane Doan/99 3.00 8.00
LJSG Sam Gagner/99 2.50 6.00
LJSH Scott Hartnell/99 2.50 6.00
LJSM Derek Smith/99 2.50 6.00
LJSP Jason Spezza/99 4.00 10.00
LJST Paul Stastny/99 3.00 8.00
LJSU Ryan Suter/99 3.00 8.00
LJSV Denis Savard/99 4.00 10.00
LJTA John Tavares/99 6.00 15.00
LJTB Tyler Bozak/99 2.50 6.00
LJTE Tyler Ennis/99 2.50 6.00
LJTH Joe Thornton/99 6.00 15.00
LJTO Jonathan Toews/99 10.00 25.00
LJTR Tuukka Rask/99 5.00 12.00
LJTS Teemu Selanne/99 8.00 20.00
LJTZ Travis Zajac/99 2.50 6.00
LJZC Zdeno Chara/99 4.00 10.00

2012-13 Limited Materials Signatures

LJAO Alex Ovechkin/25 30.00 60.00
LJBA Bernie Parent/25 20.00 50.00
LJBB Brent Burns/25 12.00 30.00
LJBH Brett Hull/25 20.00 50.00
LJBN Brayden Schenn/25 12.00 30.00
LJCA Craig Anderson/25 12.00 30.00
LJCC Chris Chelios/25 12.00 30.00
LJCH Carl Hagelin/25 8.00 20.00
LJCP Chris Pronger/25 12.00 30.00
LJDB David Backes/25 8.00 20.00
LJDD Devan Dubnyk/25 10.00 25.00
LJDU Dustin Brown/25 12.00 30.00
LJEM Evgeni Malkin/25 30.00 60.00
LJES Eric Staal/25 15.00 40.00
LJHS Henrik Sedin/25 15.00 40.00
LJJB Jamie Benn/25 12.00 30.00
LJJJ Jaromir Jagr/25 30.00 60.00
LJJN James Neal/25 8.00 20.00
LJJT Jordin Tootoo/25 10.00 25.00
LJKG Kris Letang/25 15.00 40.00
LJLE Loui Eriksson/25 8.00 20.00
LJMS Al MacInnis/25 15.00 40.00
LJMT Martin St. Louis/25 12.00 30.00
LJMU Matt Duchene/25 12.00 30.00
LJMY Mason Raymond/25 8.00 20.00
LJNI Nikolai Khabibulin/25 12.00 30.00
LJPC Paul Coffey/25 20.00 40.00
LJPD Pavel Datsyuk/25 20.00 40.00
LJRK Ryan Kesler/25 12.00 30.00
LJSA Joe Sakic/25 20.00 40.00

2012-13 Limited Monikers

*GOLD/25: .5X TO 1.2X MONIKER/99
MAB Alexander Burmistrov/99 8.00 20.00
MAO Alex Ovechkin/99 40.00 80.00
MAP Alex Pietrangelo/99 8.00 20.00
MBH Bobby Hull/25 40.00 80.00
MBR Bobby Ryan/99 8.00 20.00
MBS Brendan Shanahan/25 30.00 60.00
MCA Craig Anderson/99 10.00 25.00
MCG Claude Giroux/99 20.00 50.00
MCP Carey Price/99 20.00 50.00
MCP Chris Pronger/99 10.00 25.00
MCS Cory Schneider/99 10.00 25.00
MDD Drew Doughty/99 15.00 30.00
MEL Eric Lindros/25 30.00 60.00
MEM Evgeni Malkin/99 20.00 50.00
MES Eric Staal/99 12.00 30.00
MGH Gordie Howe/25 100.00 200.00
MJH Joe Thornton/99 15.00 40.00
MJI Jarome Iginla/99 12.00 30.00
MJQ Jonathan Quick/99 20.00 40.00
MJS Joe Sakic/25 20.00 50.00
MJT Jonathan Toews/99 25.00 50.00
MKY Keith Yandle/99 6.00 15.00
MLC Logan Couture/99 12.00 30.00
MLE Loui Eriksson/99 6.00 15.00
MMB Martin Brodeur/49 25.00 60.00
MMF Marc-Andre Fleury/99 20.00 50.00
MMG Marian Gaborik/49 10.00 25.00
MMG Patrick Kane/99 20.00 50.00
MMM Matt Moulson/99 6.00 15.00
MMM Mark Messier/25 25.00 60.00
MMS Martin St. Louis/99 10.00 25.00
MPB Patrice Bergeron/99 40.00 100.00
MPD Pavel Datsyuk/99 12.00 30.00
MPE Corey Perry/99 15.00 40.00
MPK Phil Kessel/99 10.00 25.00
MPR Patrick Roy/25 60.00 120.00
MPRI Pekka Rinne/99 10.00 25.00
MRB Ray Bourque/25 30.00 80.00
MRF Ron Francis/25 15.00 40.00
MRK Ryan Kesler/99 10.00 25.00
MRM Ryan Miller/99 10.00 25.00
MSG Sam Gagner/99 6.00 15.00
MSY Steve Yzerman/25 50.00 120.00
MVL Vincent Lecavalier/99 10.00 25.00
MZP Zach Parise/99 10.00 25.00

2012-13 Limited Monikers Silver

*SILVER/49: .5X TO 1.2X MNKR/99
*SILVER/25: .6X TO 1.5X MNKR/49-99
*SILVER/15: .4X TO 1X MNKR/25
MAO Alex Ovechkin/25 50.00 100.00
MEL Eric Lindros/15 40.00 80.00
MPB Patrice Bergeron/49 80.00 200.00

2012-13 Limited Net Assets

NABCKY B.Campbell/K.Yandle 6.00 15.00
NACGPK C.Giroux/P.Kane 20.00 50.00
NACPSH C.Perry/S.Hartnell 15.00 40.00
NADSHS D.Sedin/H.Sedin 15.00 40.00
NADWCP C.Price/D.Wideman 10.00 25.00
NAEMJT E.Malkin/J.Tavares 20.00 50.00
NAHLJH H.Lundqvist/J.Howard 25.00 60.00
NAJBAE A.Edler/J.Benn 10.00 25.00
NAJILO J.Iginla/L.Couture 15.00 40.00
NAJLDA D.Alfredsson/J.Lupul 8.00 20.00
NAJQTT J.Quick/T.Thomas 25.00 50.00
NAJSJE J.Spezza/J.Eberle 10.00 25.00
NAKTKL K.Timonen/K.Letang 10.00 25.00
NAMGDG D.Girardi/M.Gaborik 10.00 25.00
NAMMBE B.Elliott/M.Michalek 8.00 20.00
NAPDSS P.Datsyuk/S.Stamkos 20.00 50.00
NAPKJN J.Neal/P.Kessel 15.00 40.00
NARSEK E.Karlsson/R.Suter 10.00 25.00
NATSJP J.Pominville/T.Seguin 10.00 25.00
NAZCSH S.Weber/Z.Chara 10.00 25.00

2012-13 Limited Net Crashers

NCCG Claude Giroux/50 10.00 25.00
NCCH Cody Hodgson/50 6.00 15.00
NCDP Dion Phaneuf/50 8.00 20.00
NCEM Evgeni Malkin/40 20.00 50.00
NCHS Henrik Sedin/50 12.00 30.00
NCJI Jarome Iginla/50 12.00 30.00
NCJN James Neal/50 6.00 15.00
NCJT John Tavares/25 15.00 40.00
NCKT Kimmo Timonen/50 6.00 15.00
NCMR Matt Read/50 8.00 20.00
NCPD Pavel Datsyuk/50 15.00 40.00
NCPK Phil Kessel/50 10.00 25.00
NCRD Raphael Diaz/50 6.00 15.00
NCRJ Ryan Johansen/50 8.00 20.00
NCSS Steven Stamkos/25 20.00 50.00
NCZC Zdeno Chara/50 10.00 25.00
NCCGR Colin Greening/50 6.00 15.00
NCCSM Craig Smith/50 6.00 15.00
NCDAL Daniel Alfredsson/50 10.00 25.00
NCGAB Marian Gaborik/50 8.00 20.00
NCHAG Carl Hagelin/50 6.00 15.00
NCJFA Justin Faulk/50 8.00 20.00
NCJPO Jason Pominville/50 6.00 15.00
NCKAN Patrick Kane/50 20.00 50.00
NCLAN Gabriel Landeskog/50 12.00 30.00
NCRSU Ryan Suter/50 8.00 20.00
NCSCO Sean Couturier/50 8.00 20.00
NCSED Daniel Sedin/50 12.00 30.00
NCSHA Scott Hartnell/50 6.00 15.00
NCSPE Jason Spezza/50 10.00 25.00

2012-13 Limited Rookie Redemption

1 Etem/Rakell/Lind/Fasth 5.00 12.00
2 Hamit/Spner/Soderbrg 8.00 20.00
3 Grigor/Girgns/Pysyk/Risto 8.00 20.00
4 Monahan/Street 5.00 12.00
5 Lindholm/Staal/Murphy 5.00 12.00
6 Nordstrom/LeBlanc 5.00 12.00
7 MacKinnon/Pickard 8.00 20.00
8 Jenner/Murray 5.00 12.00
9 Nich/Chson/Rssl/Cmpbll 4.00 10.00
10 Lashoff/DeKey/Mrazek 8.00 20.00
11 Yakupov/Schultz 8.00 20.00
12 Barkv/Hber/Howden 8.00 20.00
13 Toffoli/Pearson 8.00 20.00
14 Grnlnd/Cyle/Dmba/Brdin 5.00 12.00
15 Galch/Gllghr/Blieu/Tinrdi 8.00 20.00
16 Forsberg/Jones 5.00 12.00
17 Brunner/Matteau 4.00 10.00
18 Nelson/Hickey 6.00 15.00
19 Miller/Fast 4.00 10.00
20 Conacher/Pageau 4.00 10.00
21 Laughton/McGinn 4.00 10.00
22 Brown/Lessio 3.00 8.00
23 Bennett/Maatta 6.00 15.00
24 Vladimir Tarasenko 6.00 15.00
25 Hertl/Nieto/Irwin 6.00 15.00
26 Killrn/Pank/Palat/Gudas 5.00 12.00
27 Morgan Rielly 5.00 12.00
28 Jensen/Schroeder 4.00 10.00
29 Carrick/Wilson 8.00 20.00
30 Peluso/Trouba 5.00 12.00

2012-13 Limited Silver

*1-150 SILVER/49: .5X TO 1.2X BASIC CARD
*151-180 SILVER/49: .6X TO 1.5X BASIC C/199
*181-200 SILVER/49: .4X TO 1X BASIC C/99
*201-233 SLVR AU/49: .5X TO 1.2X AU RC
10 Nicklas Backstrom 2.50 6.00
61 Corey Crawford 3.00 8.00

2012-13 Limited Stanley Cup Winners

SC1 Gordie Howe 15.00 40.00
SC2 Bernie Parent 5.00 12.00
SC3 Phil Esposito 8.00 20.00
SC4 Bryan Trottier 5.00 12.00
SC5 Paul Coffey 5.00 12.00
SC6 Ed Belfour 5.00 12.00
SC7 John LeClair 5.00 12.00
SC8 Mike Bossy 5.00 12.00
SC9 Red Kelly 5.00 12.00
SC10 Dave Schultz 5.00 12.00

SC11 Jaromir Jagr 15.00 40.00
SC12 Larry Robinson 5.00 12.00
SC13 Dan Boyle 3.00 8.00
SC14 Denis Potvin 5.00 12.00
SC15 Bill Barber 4.00 10.00
SC16 Dave Andreychuk 5.00 12.00
SC17 Guy Lafleur 6.00 15.00
SC18 Patrick Roy 10.00 20.00
SC19 Johnny Bucyk 5.00 12.00
SC20 Mike Modano 8.00 20.00
SC21 Jamie Langenbrunner 3.00 8.00
SC23 Lanny McDonald 5.00 12.00
SC24 Gerry Cheevers 5.00 12.00
SC25 Al MacInnis 6.00 15.00
SC26 Stan Mikita 6.00 15.00
SC27 Alex Tanguay 4.00 10.00
SC28 Bobby Clarke 6.00 15.00
SC29 Joe Nieuwendyk 4.00 10.00
SC30 Bobby Hull 10.00 25.00
SC31 Ron Francis 6.00 15.00
SC32 Brett Hull 10.00 25.00
SC33 Adam Graves 4.00 10.00
SC34 Teemu Selanne 10.00 25.00
SC35 Jonathan Quick 8.00 20.00
SC36 Dustin Brown 5.00 12.00
SC37 Anze Kopitar 8.00 20.00
SC38 Jeff Carter 4.00 10.00
SC39 Drew Doughty 6.00 15.00
SC40 Simon Gagne 5.00 12.00
SC41 Derian Hatcher 3.00 8.00
SC42 Mark Messier 10.00 25.00
SC43 Clark Gillies 5.00 12.00
SC46 Mike Richter 5.00 12.00
SC47 Grant Fuhr 6.00 15.00
SC48 Igor Larionov 5.00 12.00
SC49 Luc Robitaille 5.00 12.00
SC50 Alex Delvecchio 6.00 15.00

2012-13 Limited Stanley Cup Winners Signatures

SC1 Gordie Howe/25 60.00 150.00
SC2 Bernie Parent/99 20.00 50.00
SC3 Phil Esposito/99 15.00 40.00
SC4 Bryan Trottier/99 10.00 25.00
SC5 Paul Coffey/99 10.00 25.00
SC6 Ed Belfour/99 10.00 25.00
SC7 John LeClair/99 15.00 30.00
SC8 Mike Bossy/99 10.00 25.00
SC9 Red Kelly/99 10.00 25.00
SC10 Dave Schultz/99 10.00 25.00
SC11 Jaromir Jagr/50 30.00 60.00
SC12 Larry Robinson/99 10.00 25.00
SC13 Dan Boyle/99 8.00 20.00
SC14 Denis Potvin/99 10.00 25.00
SC15 Bill Barber/99 8.00 20.00
SC16 Dave Andreychuk/99 10.00 25.00
SC17 Guy Lafleur/99 15.00 40.00
SC18 Patrick Roy/50 100.00 200.00
SC19 Johnny Bucyk/99 15.00 40.00
SC20 Mike Modano/99 15.00 40.00
SC23 Lanny McDonald/99 8.00 20.00
SC24 Gerry Cheevers/99 10.00 25.00
SC25 Al MacInnis/99 10.00 25.00
SC26 Stan Mikita/99 15.00 30.00
SC28 Bobby Clarke/99 15.00 40.00
SC29 Joe Nieuwendyk/99 10.00 25.00
SC30 Bobby Hull/50 20.00 50.00
SC31 Ron Francis/50 15.00 30.00
SC32 Brett Hull/50 20.00 50.00
SC33 Adam Graves/99 8.00 20.00
SC34 Teemu Selanne/99 20.00 50.00
SC35 Jonathan Quick/99 20.00 40.00
SC36 Dustin Brown/99 12.00 30.00
SC37 Anze Kopitar/99 20.00 50.00
SC39 Drew Doughty/99 15.00 40.00
SC41 Derian Hatcher/99 10.00 25.00
SC42 Mark Messier/50 25.00 60.00
SC43 Clark Gillies/99 10.00 25.00
SC46 Mike Richter/99 15.00 30.00
SC47 Grant Fuhr/99 15.00 30.00
SC48 Igor Larionov/99 12.00 30.00
SC49 Luc Robitaille/99 10.00 25.00
SC50 Alex Delvecchio/25 25.00 50.00

2012-13 Limited Travels Dual Jerseys

*PRIME/49: .6X TO 1.5X DUAL JSY/199
TDAB Alexander Burmistrov 4.00 10.00
TDAC Andrew Cogliano 3.00 8.00
TDAN Antti Niemi 4.00 10.00
TDBR Brad Richards 5.00 12.00
TDCA Craig Anderson 5.00 12.00
TDEJ Erik Johnson 3.00 8.00
TDGL Guy Lafleur 6.00 15.00
TDIB Ilya Bryzgalov 5.00 12.00
TDJH Jaroslav Halak 5.00 12.00
TDJL Jamie Langenbrunner 3.00 8.00
TDJM Joe Mullen 4.00 10.00
TDJN James Neal 3.00 8.00
TDJR Jeremy Roenick 8.00 20.00
TDJS Joe Sakic 5.00 12.00
TDJV Jakub Voracek 4.00 10.00
TDKP Keith Primeau 4.00 10.00
TDLR Luc Robitaille 5.00 12.00
TDMF Mike Fisher 3.00 8.00
TDMH Marian Hossa 5.00 12.00
TDMR Mike Richards 4.00 10.00
TDNH Nathan Horton 5.00 12.00
TDNK Nikolai Khabibulin 5.00 12.00
TDOP Ondrej Pavelec 5.00 12.00
TDPR Patrick Roy 10.00 25.00
TDRB Ray Bourque 8.00 20.00
TDSV Semyon Varlamov 5.00 12.00
TDTS Teemu Selanne 8.00 20.00

2012-13 Limited Travels Triple Jerseys

*PRIME/25: .6X TO 1.5X TRIPLE/99
TTBET Brian Elliott 5.00 12.00
TTBSH Brendan Shanahan 6.00 15.00
TTGF Grant Fuhr 10.00 25.00
TTHUL Brett Hull 12.00 30.00
TTJAG Jaromir Jagr 12.00 30.00
TTJN Joe Nieuwendyk 5.00 12.00
TTPC Paul Coffey 6.00 15.00
TTRF Ron Francis 8.00 20.00

2012-13 Limited Trophy Winners

TW1 Corey Perry 5.00 12.00
TW2 Henrik Sedin 4.00 10.00
TW3 Alex Ovechkin 12.00 30.00
TW4 Sidney Crosby 12.00 30.00
TW5 Eric Lindros 4.00 10.00
TW6 Joe Sakic 6.00 15.00
TW7 Gabriel Landeskog 4.00 10.00
TW8 Patrick Kane 6.00 15.00
TW9 Ed Belfour 3.00 8.00
TW10 Brian Leetch 2.50 6.00
TW11 Luc Robitaille 3.00 8.00
TW12 Tim Thomas 3.00 8.00
TW13 Ryan Miller 3.00 8.00
TW14 Martin Brodeur 8.00 20.00
TW15 Patrick Roy 8.00 20.00
TW16 Ron Hextall 3.00 8.00
TW17 Evgeni Malkin 6.00 15.00
TW18 Daniel Sedin 4.00 10.00
TW19 Joe Thornton 5.00 12.00
TW20 Martin St. Louis 3.00 8.00
TW21 Jarome Iginla 4.00 10.00
TW22 Nicklas Lidstrom 3.00 8.00
TW23 Scott Niedermayer 3.00 8.00
TW24 Chris Pronger 3.00 8.00
TW25 Ray Bourque 5.00 12.00
TW26 Denis Potvin 3.00 8.00
TW27 Ryan Kesler 3.00 8.00
TW28 Pavel Datsyuk 5.00 12.00
TW29 Steve Yzerman 8.00 20.00
TW30 Ron Francis 4.00 10.00
TW31 Bobby Clarke 5.00 12.00
TW32 Steven Stamkos 6.00 15.00
TW33 Vincent Lecavalier 3.00 8.00
TW34 Milan Hejduk 2.50 6.00
TW35 Brad Richards 3.00 8.00
TW36 Joe Sakic 6.00 15.00
TW37 Brett Hull 6.00 15.00
TW38 Mike Bossy 3.00 8.00
TW39 Rick Middleton 2.50 6.00
TW40 Jonathan Toews 5.00 12.00
TW41 Jean-Sebastien Giguere 3.00 8.00
TW42 Mario Lemieux 12.00 30.00
TW43 Bernie Parent 4.00 10.00
TW44 Guy Lafleur 4.00 10.00
TW45 Mark Messier 6.00 15.00
TW46 Jonathan Quick 4.00 10.00
TW47 Phil Kessel 3.00 8.00
TW48 Cam Neely 3.00 8.00
TW49 Charlie Simmer 2.00 5.00
TW50 Jeff Skinner 4.00 10.00

2012-13 Limited Trophy Winners Signatures

TW1 Corey Perry/99 15.00 40.00
TW2 Henrik Sedin/99 12.50 30.00
TW3 Alex Ovechkin/50 25.00 60.00
TW4 Sidney Crosby/25 60.00 120.00
TW5 Eric Lindros/99 20.00 50.00
TW6 Joe Sakic/50 25.00 60.00
TW7 Gabriel Landeskog/99 12.00 30.00
TW8 Patrick Kane/99 20.00 50.00
TW9 Ed Belfour/50 20.00 40.00
TW10 Brian Leetch/99 8.00 20.00
TW11 Luc Robitaille/99 10.00 25.00
TW12 Tim Thomas/99 20.00 40.00
TW13 Ryan Miller/99 10.00 25.00
TW14 Martin Brodeur/50 40.00 80.00
TW15 Patrick Roy/50 50.00 120.00
TW16 Ron Hextall/99 15.00 40.00
TW17 Evgeni Malkin/99 20.00 40.00
TW18 Daniel Sedin/99 12.50 30.00
TW19 Joe Thornton/99 12.00 30.00
TW20 Martin St. Louis/99 10.00 25.00
TW21 Jarome Iginla/50 12.00 30.00
TW22 Nicklas Lidstrom/99 15.00 40.00
TW23 Scott Niedermayer/99 10.00 25.00
TW24 Chris Pronger/99 10.00 25.00
TW25 Ray Bourque/99 20.00 50.00
TW26 Denis Potvin/99 10.00 25.00
TW27 Ryan Kesler/99 10.00 25.00
TW28 Pavel Datsyuk/99 12.00 30.00
TW29 Steve Yzerman/25 60.00 120.00
TW30 Ron Francis/50 15.00 40.00
TW31 Bobby Clarke/99 20.00 40.00
TW33 Vincent Lecavalier/99 10.00 25.00
TW34 Milan Hejduk/99 8.00 20.00
TW35 Brad Richards/99 10.00 25.00
TW36 Joe Sakic/50 20.00 50.00
TW37 Brett Hull/50 20.00 50.00
TW38 Mike Bossy/99 10.00 25.00
TW39 Rick Middleton/99 8.00 20.00
TW40 Jonathan Toews/99 25.00 50.00
TW41 Jean-Sebastien Giguere/99 12.00 30.00
TW42 Mario Lemieux/25 60.00 120.00
TW43 Bernie Parent/99 15.00 40.00
TW44 Guy Lafleur/99 12.00 30.00
TW45 Mark Messier/25 30.00 80.00
TW46 Jonathan Quick/99 20.00 50.00
TW47 Phil Kessel/99 15.00 40.00
TW48 Cam Neely/99 15.00 40.00
TW49 Charlie Simmer/99 6.00 15.00
TW50 Jeff Skinner/99 12.00 30.00

1974-75 Lipton Soup

COMPLETE SET (51) 175.00 350.00
1 Norm Ullman 4.00 8.00
2 Gilbert Perreault 4.00 8.00
3 Darryl Sittler 6.00 12.00
4 Jean-Paul Parise 2.00 4.00
5 Garry Unger 2.00 4.00
6 Ron Ellis 2.50 5.00
7 Rogatien Vachon 5.00 10.00
8 Bobby Orr 50.00 100.00
9 Wayne Cashman 2.50 5.00
10 Brad Park 3.00 6.00
11 Serge Savard 2.50 5.00
12 Walt Tkaczuk 2.00 4.00
13 Yvan Cournoyer 4.00 8.00
14 Andre Boudrias 1.50 3.00
15 Gary Smith 2.50 5.00
16 Guy Lapointe 2.00 4.00
17 Dennis Hull 2.50 5.00
18 Bernie Parent 5.00 10.00
19 Ken Dryden 25.00 50.00
20 Rick MacLeish 2.50 5.00
21 Bobby Clarke 7.50 15.00
22 Dale Tallon 2.00 4.00
23 Jim McKenny 1.50 3.00
24 Rene Robert 2.50 5.00
25 Red Berenson 2.00 4.00
26 Ed Giacomin 5.00 10.00
27 Cesare Maniago 3.00 6.00
28 Ken Hodge 2.50 5.00
29 Gregg Sheppard 1.50 3.00
30 Dave Schultz 5.00 10.00
31 Bill Barber 4.00 8.00
32 Henry Boucha 2.00 4.00
33 Richard Martin 2.50 5.00
34 Steve Vickers 2.00 4.00
35 Billy Harris 1.50 3.00
36 Jim Pappin 1.50 3.00
37 Pit Martin 1.50 3.00
38 Jacques Lemaire 4.00 8.00
39 Peter Mahovlich 2.50 5.00
40 Rod Gilbert 4.00 8.00
41A Borje Salming (Horizontal pose) 6.00 12.00
41B Borje Salming (Vertical pose) 6.00 12.00
42 Pete Stemkowski 1.50 3.00
43 Ron Schock 1.50 3.00
44 Dan Bouchard 3.00 6.00
45 Tony Esposito 6.00 12.00
46 Craig Patrick 2.00 4.00
47 Ed Westfall 1.50 3.00
48 Jocelyn Guevremont 1.50 3.00
49 Syl Apps 2.00 4.00
50 Dave Keon 4.00 8.00

1972-73 Los Angeles Sharks WHA

COMPLETE SET (19) 20.00 40.00
1 Mike Byers 1.25 2.50
2 Bart Crashley 2.00 4.00
3 George Gardner 1.25 2.50
4 Russ Gillow 1.25 2.50
5 Tom Gilmore 1.25 2.50
6 Earl Heiskala 1.25 2.50
7 J.P. LeBlanc 1.50 3.00
8 Ralph McSweyn 1.25 2.50
9 Ted McCaskill 1.25 2.50
10 Jim Niekamp 1.25 2.50
11 Gerry Odrowski 1.50 3.00
12 Tom Serviss 1.25 2.50
13 Peter Slater 1.25 2.50
14 Steve Sutherland 1.25 2.50
15 Joe Szura 1.50 3.00
16 Gary Veneruzzo 1.25 2.50
17 Jim Watson 1.25 2.50
18 Alton White 1.25 2.50
19 Bill Young 1.25 2.50

1998 Lunchables Goalie Greats Rounds

COMPLETE SET (8) 4.00 10.00
1 Ed Belfour .30 .75
2 Martin Brodeur .75 2.00
3 Dominik Hasek .60 1.50
4 Olaf Kolzig .25 .60
5 Chris Osgood .30 .75
6 Damian Rhodes .25 .60
7 Mike Richter .30 .75
8 Patrick Roy 1.50 4.00

1998 Lunchables Goalie Greats Squares

COMPLETE SET (8) 4.00 10.00
1 Ed Belfour .30 .75
2 Martin Brodeur .75 2.00
3 Dominik Hasek .60 1.50
4 Olaf Kolzig .25 .60
5 Chris Osgood .30 .75
6 Damian Rhodes .25 .60
7 Mike Richter .30 .75
8 Patrick Roy 1.50 4.00

2010-11 Luxury Suite

1 Ryan Getzlaf JSY 3.00 8.00
2 Corey Perry JSY 5.00 12.00
3 Dustin Byfuglien JSY 3.00 8.00
4 Evander Kane JSY 3.00 8.00
5 Tim Thomas JSY 5.00 12.00
6 Patrice Bergeron JSY 4.00 10.00
7 Milan Lucic JSY 3.00 8.00
8 Ryan Miller JSY 3.00 8.00
9 Thomas Vanek JSY 2.50 6.00
10 Tyler Myers JSY 2.00 5.00
11 Miikka Kiprusoff JSY 3.00 8.00
12 Jarome Iginla JSY 4.00 10.00
13 Eric Staal JSY 4.00 10.00
14 Cam Ward JSY 3.00 8.00
15 Patrick Kane JSY 8.00 20.00
16 Jonathan Toews JSY 8.00 20.00
17 Marian Hossa JSY 3.00 8.00
18 Paul Stastny JSY 2.50 6.00
19 Matt Duchene JSY 3.00 8.00
20 Steve Mason JSY/100 4.00 10.00
21 Rick Nash JSY 3.00 8.00
22 Brad Richards JSY 3.00 8.00
23 Steve Ott JSY/525 2.00 5.00
24 Henrik Zetterberg JSY 5.00 12.00
25 Nicklas Lidstrom JSY 3.00 8.00
26 Pavel Datsyuk JSY 6.00 15.00
27 Ales Hemsky JSY 2.50 6.00
28 Sam Gagner JSY 2.00 5.00
29 Tomas Vokoun JSY 2.50 6.00
30 Michael Frolik JSY 2.00 5.00
31 Anze Kopitar JSY 5.00 12.00
32 Drew Doughty JSY 4.00 10.00
33 Jonathan Bernier JSY 2.50 6.00
34 Niklas Backstrom JSY 3.00 8.00
35 Cal Clutterbuck JSY 2.00 5.00
36 Mikko Koivu JSY 3.00 8.00
37 Carey Price JSY 8.00 20.00
38 Scott Gomez JSY/525 2.50 6.00
39 Tomas Plekanec JSY 2.00 5.00
40 Ilya Kovalchuk JSY 3.00 8.00
41 Martin Brodeur JSY 8.00 20.00
42 Zach Parise JSY 3.00 8.00
43 John Tavares JSY 6.00 15.00
44 Kyle Okposo JSY 2.00 5.00
45 Sean Avery JSY 2.50 6.00
46 Marian Gaborik JSY 3.00 8.00
47 Henrik Lundqvist JSY 5.00 12.00
48 Daniel Alfredsson JSY 3.00 8.00
49 Jason Spezza JSY 3.00 8.00
50 Chris Pronger JSY 3.00 8.00
51 Jeff Carter JSY 2.50 6.00
52 Claude Giroux JSY 3.00 8.00
53 Ilya Bryzgalov JSY 2.50 6.00
54 Shane Doan JSY 2.50 6.00
55 Jordan Staal JSY 2.50 6.00
56 Sidney Crosby JSY 10.00 25.00
57 Marc-Andre Fleury JSY 6.00 15.00
58 Evgeni Malkin JSY 6.00 15.00
59 Dany Heatley JSY/525 2.50 6.00
60 Joe Thornton JSY 5.00 12.00
62 Jaroslav Halak JSY 3.00 8.00
63 T.J. Oshie JSY 3.00 8.00
64 Vincent Lecavalier JSY 3.00 8.00
65 Mike Smith JSY 3.00 8.00
66 Steven Stamkos JSY 6.00 15.00
67 Phil Kessel JSY 3.00 8.00
68 Jonas Gustavsson JSY 4.00 10.00
69 Luke Schenn JSY 5.00 12.00
70 Roberto Luongo JSY 6.00 15.00
71 Henrik Sedin JSY 5.00 12.00
72 Daniel Sedin JSY 4.00 10.00
73 Alex Ovechkin JSY 8.00 20.00
74 Nicklas Backstrom JSY 3.00 8.00
75 Alexander Semin JSY 3.00 8.00
76 S.Koivu JSY/B.Ryan JSY 3.00 8.00
77 N.Bergfors JSY/B.Little JSY 3.00 8.00
78 M.Recchi JSY/N.Horton JSY 4.00 10.00
79 R.Bourque JSY/A.Tanguay JSY 2.00 5.00
80 P.Budaj JSY/C.Anderson JSY 3.00 8.00
81 M.Hejduk JSY/M.Duchene JSY 3.00 8.00
82 S.Ott JSY/K.Barch JSY 2.00 5.00
83 T.Holmstrom JSY/J.Franzen JSY 2.50 6.00
84 N.Khabibulin JSY/D.Dubnyk JSY 2.50 6.00
85 R.Smyth JSY/D.Brown JSY 3.00 8.00
86 M.Cammalleri JSY/A.Kostitsyn JSY 3.00 8.00
87 S.Weber JSY/P.Rinne JSY 3.00 8.00
88 P.Hornqvist JSY/M.Erat JSY 2.00 5.00
89 M.Staal JSY/A.Anisimov JSY 2.00 5.00
90 N.Foligno JSY/C.Neil JSY 2.50 6.00
91 S.Hartnell JSY/V.Leino JSY 2.50 6.00
92 K.Letang JSY/M.Talbot JSY 6.00 15.00
94 R.Malone JSY/M.St. Louis JSY 3.00 8.00
95 D.Phaneuf JSY/L.Schenn JSY 6.00 15.00
96 M.Grabovski JSY/N.Kulemin JSY 2.00 5.00
97 M.Raymond JSY/R.Kesler JSY 3.00 8.00
98 A.Burrows JSY/M.Samuelsson JSY 2.00 5.00
99 M.Green JSY/S.Varlamov JSY 3.00 8.00
100 B.Laich JSY/E.Fehr JSY 2.00 5.00
101 Brad Park AU 5.00 12.00
102 Dale Hawerchuk AU 8.00 20.00
103 Darren Pang AU 6.00 15.00
104 Denis Savard AU 6.00 15.00
105 Derek Sanderson AU 8.00 20.00
106 Doug Gilmour AU 8.00 20.00
107 Jeremy Roenick AU 10.00 25.00
108 Johnny Bower AU 15.00 40.00
109 Johnny Bucyk AU 6.00 15.00
110 Keith Primeau AU 5.00 12.00
111 Ken Hodge AU 5.00 12.00
112 Marcel Dionne AU 8.00 20.00
113 Richard Brodeur AU 6.00 15.00
114 Rick Middleton AU 6.00 15.00
115 Rogie Vachon AU 8.00 20.00
116 Simon Nolet AU 5.00 12.00
117 Terry O'Reilly AU 8.00 20.00
118 Doug Wilson AU 5.00 12.00
119 Jean Ratelle AU EXCH 5.00 12.00
120 Guy Chouinard AU 5.00 12.00
121 Dirk Graham AU 5.00 12.00
122 Tim Kerr AU 8.00 20.00
123 Dale Hunter AU EXCH 5.00 12.00
124 Rick Kehoe AU 5.00 12.00
125 Al Secord AU 6.00 15.00
126 Cam Fowler JSY AU/199 RC 15.00 40.00
127 Tomas Tatar JSY AU/199 RC 15.00 40.00
128 Tyler Seguin JSY AU/199 RC 20.00 50.00
129 Jeff Skinner JSY AU/199 RC 10.00 25.00
130 Shattenkirk JSY AU/199 RC 10.00 25.00
131 Jordan Eberle JSY AU/199 RC 15.00 40.00
132 Taylor Hall JSY AU/199 RC 25.00 60.00
133 M.Paajarvi JSY AU/199 RC 8.00 20.00
134 M.Tedenby JSY AU/199 RC 6.00 15.00
135 Derek Stepan JSY AU/199 RC 8.00 20.00
136 Jordan Caron JSY AU/299 RC 8.00 20.00
137 R.McDonagh JSY AU/299 RC 8.00 20.00
138 Linus Omark JSY AU/199 RC 8.00 20.00
139 B.Schenn JSY AU/299 RC 15.00 40.00
140 A.Burmistrov JSY AU/199 RC 8.00 20.00
141 J.Markstrom JSY AU/299 RC 15.00 40.00
142 N.Niederreiter JSY AU/299 RC 10.00 25.00
143 M.Zuccarello JSY AU/299 RC 15.00 40.00
144 Ekman-Larsson JSY AU/299 RC 15.00 40.00
145 Nazem Kadri JSY AU/299 RC 10.00 25.00
146 Brandon McMillan AU RC 2.50 6.00
147 Nick Bonino AU RC 3.00 8.00
148 Jeremy Morin AU RC 2.50 6.00
149 Zach Hamill AU RC 2.50 6.00
150 Steven Kampfer AU RC 4.00 10.00
151 Zac Dalpe AU RC 3.00 8.00
152 Brandon Pirri AU RC 2.50 6.00
153 Nick Leddy AU RC 3.00 8.00
154 Brandon Yip AU RC 2.50 6.00
155 Justin Mercier AU RC 2.50 6.00
156 Kyle Clifford AU RC 3.00 8.00
157 Casey Wellman AU RC 2.50 6.00
158 Robin Lehner AU RC 5.00 12.00
159 A.Vasyunov AU RC 2.50 6.00
160 Brad Mills AU RC 2.50 6.00
161 Nick Palmieri AU RC 2.50 6.00
162 Anders Lindback AU RC 2.50 6.00
163 Travis Hamonic AU RC 3.00 8.00
164 P.K. Subban AU RC 15.00 40.00
165 Nick Spaling AU RC 2.50 6.00
166 Jared Cowen AU RC 2.50 6.00
167 Sergei Bobrovsky AU RC 6.00 15.00
168 Eric Tangradi AU RC 2.50 6.00
169 Nick Johnson AU RC 2.00 5.00
170 Ian Cole AU RC 2.50 6.00
171 Stefan Della Rovere AU RC 2.50 6.00
172 Dana Tyrell AU RC 2.50 6.00
173 Dustin Tokarski AU RC 2.50 6.00
174 Brayden Irwin AU RC 2.50 6.00
175 M.Johansson AU RC 4.00 10.00
176 Kyle Palmieri RC 5.00 12.00
177 Patrice Cormier RC 3.00 8.00
178 Jamie Arniel RC 2.50 6.00
179 Luke Adam RC 2.50 6.00
180 T.J. Brodie RC 2.50 6.00
181 Henrik Karlsson RC 2.50 6.00
182 Jon Matsumoto RC 2.50 6.00
183 Jamie McBain RC 2.50 6.00
184 Evan Brophey RC 2.50 6.00
185 Rob Klinkhammer RC 2.50 6.00
186 Ben Smith RC 3.00 8.00
187 Mark Olver RC 2.50 6.00
188 Jonas Holos RC 2.50 6.00
189 Nick Holden RC 2.50 6.00
190 Richard Bachman RC 3.00 8.00
191 Nathan Lawson RC 2.50 6.00
192 Joe Callahan RC 3.00 8.00
193 Evgeny Dadonov RC 3.00 8.00
194 Jake Muzzin RC 6.00 15.00
195 Dwight King RC 2.50 6.00
196 Matt Kassian RC 2.50 6.00
197 Jared Spurgeon RC 6.00 15.00
198 Justin Falk RC 2.00 5.00
199 Linus Klasen RC 2.50 6.00
200 Mark Dekanich RC 2.50 6.00
201 Trevor Gillies RC 2.50 6.00
202 Alex Urbom RC 2.50 6.00
203 Jacob Josefson RC 2.50 6.00
204 Olivier Magnan RC 2.50 6.00
205 Stephen Gionta RC 3.00 8.00
206 Mark Fayne RC 2.50 6.00
207 Matt Taormina RC 2.50 6.00
208 Mark Flood RC 2.00 5.00
209 Evgeny Grachev RC 2.50 6.00
210 Dale Weise RC 3.00 8.00
211 Derek Smith RC 2.50 6.00
212 Eric Wellwood RC 3.00 8.00
213 Alexander Pechurskiy RC 3.00 8.00
214 Aaron Volpatti RC 3.00 8.00
215 Mike Moore RC 2.50 6.00
216 Justin Braun RC 2.50 6.00
217 John McCarthy RC 2.50 6.00
218 Ryan Reaves RC 3.00 8.00
219 Nikita Nikitin RC 2.50 6.00
220 Nicholas Drazenovic RC 3.00 8.00
221 Adam Cracknell RC 2.50 6.00
222 Johan Harju RC 2.50 6.00
223 Keith Aulie RC 2.50 6.00
224 Korbinian Holzer RC 2.50 6.00
225 Brian Fahey RC 2.50 6.00
226 Matt Bartkowski RC 3.00 8.00
227 Grant Clitsome RC 2.50 6.00
228 Matt Calvert RC 4.00 10.00
229 Jan Mursak RC 5.00 12.00
230 Rhett Rakhshani RC 2.50 6.00
231 Jeff Petry RC 5.00 12.00
232 Chris Tanev RC 6.00 15.00
233 Kevin Poulin RC 3.00 8.00
234 Jim O'Brien RC 3.00 8.00
235 Brandon Mashinter RC 3.00 8.00
236 Brett MacLean RC 3.00 8.00
237 Tommy Wingels RC 2.50 6.00
238 Cedrick Desjardins RC 3.00 8.00
239 Marcel Mueller RC 3.00 8.00
240 Jeff Frazee RC 4.00 10.00
241 Paul Byron RC 3.00 8.00
242 Colby Cohen RC 2.50 6.00
243 Andrew Desjardins RC 2.50 6.00
244 Andreas Engqvist RC 4.00 10.00
245 Chris Mueller RC 2.50 6.00
246 Chad Kolarik RC 2.50 6.00
247 Marco Scandella RC 2.50 6.00
248 Alex Stalock RC 2.50 6.00
249 Cory Emmerton RC 3.00 8.00
250 Brodie Dupont RC 3.00 8.00

2010-11 Luxury Suite Jersey Numbers Sticks

1 Ryan Getzlaf 4.00 10.00
5 Tim Thomas 6.00 15.00
6 Patrice Bergeron 6.00 15.00
7 Milan Lucic 4.00 10.00
9 Thomas Vanek 3.00 8.00
11 Miikka Kiprusoff 4.00 10.00
12 Jarome Iginla 5.00 12.00
14 Cam Ward/25 6.00 15.00
16 Jonathan Toews 12.00 30.00
17 Marian Hossa/25 6.00 15.00
18 Paul Stastny 3.00 8.00
21 Rick Nash/25 4.00 10.00
23 Steve Ott 2.50 6.00
24 Henrik Zetterberg 5.00 12.00
25 Nicklas Lidstrom/25 6.00 15.00
26 Pavel Datsyuk 10.00 25.00
27 Ales Hemsky 3.00 8.00
28 Sam Gagner/25 6.00 15.00
29 Tomas Vokoun 3.00 8.00
30 Michael Frolik 2.50 6.00
33 Jonathan Bernier 8.00 20.00
35 Cal Clutterbuck 2.50 6.00
36 Mikko Koivu 4.00 10.00
37 Carey Price 12.00 30.00
38 Scott Gomez 3.00 8.00
39 Tomas Plekanec 2.50 6.00
40 Ilya Kovalchuk 4.00 10.00
41 Martin Brodeur 10.00 25.00
43 John Tavares/25 6.00 15.00
44 Kyle Okposo 2.50 6.00
45 Sean Avery 3.00 8.00
46 Marian Gaborik 4.00 10.00
47 Henrik Lundqvist 10.00 25.00
48 Daniel Alfredsson/20 6.00 15.00
49 Jason Spezza 4.00 10.00
50 Chris Pronger 4.00 10.00
51 Jeff Carter 3.00 8.00
53 Ilya Bryzgalov 3.00 8.00
54 Shane Doan 3.00 8.00
55 Jordan Staal 3.00 8.00
56 Sidney Crosby 15.00 40.00
57 Marc-Andre Fleury 8.00 20.00
58 Evgeni Malkin 8.00 20.00
59 Dany Heatley 3.00 8.00
60 Joe Thornton 6.00 15.00
62 Jaroslav Halak 4.00 10.00
64 Vincent Lecavalier 4.00 10.00
65 Mike Smith 4.00 10.00
67 Phil Kessel 4.00 10.00
70 Roberto Luongo 6.00 15.00
71 Henrik Sedin 5.00 12.00
72 Daniel Sedin 5.00 12.00
73 Alex Ovechkin 15.00 40.00
74 Nicklas Backstrom 4.00 10.00

2010-11 Luxury Suite Jerseys Prime

1 Ryan Getzlaf 6.00 15.00
2 Corey Perry 10.00 25.00
3 Dustin Byfuglien/125 6.00 15.00
4 Evander Kane 6.00 15.00
5 Tim Thomas 10.00 25.00
6 Patrice Bergeron 8.00 20.00
7 Milan Lucic 6.00 15.00
8 Ryan Miller 6.00 15.00
9 Thomas Vanek 5.00 12.00
10 Tyler Myers 4.00 10.00
11 Miikka Kiprusoff 6.00 15.00
12 Jarome Iginla 8.00 20.00
13 Eric Staal 8.00 20.00
14 Cam Ward 6.00 15.00
15 Patrick Kane 12.00 30.00
16 Jonathan Toews 10.00 25.00
17 Marian Hossa 6.00 15.00
18 Paul Stastny 5.00 12.00
19 Matt Duchene 6.00 15.00
20 Steve Mason/50 5.00 12.00
21 Rick Nash 6.00 15.00
22 Brad Richards 6.00 15.00
23 Steve Ott 4.00 10.00
24 Henrik Zetterberg 8.00 20.00
25 Nicklas Lidstrom 6.00 15.00
26 Pavel Datsyuk 10.00 25.00
27 Ales Hemsky 5.00 12.00
28 Sam Gagner 4.00 10.00
29 Tomas Vokoun 5.00 12.00
30 Michael Frolik 4.00 10.00
31 Anze Kopitar 10.00 25.00
32 Drew Doughty 8.00 20.00
33 Jonathan Bernier 5.00 12.00
34 Niklas Backstrom 6.00 15.00
35 Cal Clutterbuck 4.00 10.00
36 Mikko Koivu 6.00 15.00
37 Carey Price 15.00 40.00
38 Scott Gomez 5.00 12.00
39 Tomas Plekanec 8.00 20.00
40 Ilya Kovalchuk 6.00 15.00
41 Martin Brodeur 10.00 25.00
42 Zach Parise 6.00 15.00
43 John Tavares 8.00 20.00
44 Kyle Okposo 4.00 10.00
45 Sean Avery 5.00 12.00
46 Marian Gaborik 6.00 15.00
47 Henrik Lundqvist 8.00 20.00
48 Daniel Alfredsson 6.00 15.00
49 Jason Spezza 6.00 15.00
50 Chris Pronger 6.00 15.00
51 Jeff Carter 5.00 12.00
52 Claude Giroux 6.00 15.00
53 Ilya Bryzgalov 5.00 12.00
54 Shane Doan 5.00 12.00
55 Jordan Staal 8.00 20.00
56 Sidney Crosby 25.00 60.00
57 Marc-Andre Fleury 8.00 20.00
58 Evgeni Malkin 8.00 20.00
60 Joe Thornton 8.00 20.00
62 Jaroslav Halak 6.00 15.00
63 T.J. Oshie 6.00 15.00
64 Vincent Lecavalier 6.00 15.00
65 Mike Smith 6.00 15.00
66 Steven Stamkos 10.00 25.00
67 Phil Kessel 6.00 15.00
68 Jonas Gustavsson 8.00 20.00
69 Luke Schenn 8.00 20.00
70 Roberto Luongo/100 8.00 20.00
71 Henrik Sedin 8.00 20.00
72 Daniel Sedin 8.00 20.00
73 Alex Ovechkin 10.00 25.00
74 Nicklas Backstrom 6.00 15.00
75 Alexander Semin 6.00 15.00
76 B.Ryan/S.Koivu 12.00 30.00
77 N.Bergfors/B.Little 8.00 20.00
78 M.Recchi/N.Horton 10.00 25.00
79 R.Bourque/A.Tanguay 5.00 12.00
80 C.Anderson/P.Budaj 8.00 20.00
81 M.Duchene/M.Hejduk 8.00 20.00
83 T.Holmstrom/J.Franzen 8.00 20.00
85 D.Brown/R.Smyth 8.00 20.00
86 A.Kostitsyn/M.Cammalleri 8.00 20.00
87 S.Weber/P.Rinne 8.00 20.00
88 M.Erat/P.Hornqvist 5.00 12.00
90 N.Foligno/C.Neil 6.00 15.00
91 S.Hartnell/V.Leino 8.00 20.00
92 K.Letang/M.Talbot 12.00 30.00
94 R.Malone/M.St. Louis 8.00 20.00
95 D.Phaneuf/L.Schenn 8.00 20.00
96 M.Grabovski/N.Kulemin 8.00 20.00
97 M.Raymond/R.Kesler 10.00 25.00
98 A.Burrows/M.Samuelsson 5.00 12.00
99 M.Green/S.Varlamov 12.00 30.00
100 B.Laich/E.Fehr 5.00 12.00

2010-11 Luxury Suite Jerseys Sticks

*JSY #/STCK/50: .6X TO 1.5X JSY/STCK/100
*JSY #/STCK/15-25: .8X TO 2X JSY/STCK/100
*JSY #/STCK/50: .5X TO 1.2X JSY/STCK/25
1 Ryan Getzlaf 6.00 15.00
5 Tim Thomas 10.00 25.00
6 Patrice Bergeron 8.00 20.00
7 Milan Lucic 6.00 15.00
9 Thomas Vanek 5.00 12.00
11 Miikka Kiprusoff 6.00 15.00
12 Jarome Iginla 8.00 20.00
14 Cam Ward 6.00 15.00
16 Jonathan Toews/25 12.00 30.00
17 Marian Hossa 6.00 15.00
18 Paul Stastny 5.00 12.00
21 Rick Nash 12.00 30.00
22 Brad Richards 6.00 15.00
23 Steve Ott 4.00 10.00
24 Henrik Zetterberg 8.00 20.00
25 Nicklas Lidstrom 6.00 15.00
26 Pavel Datsyuk 10.00 25.00
27 Ales Hemsky 5.00 12.00
28 Sam Gagner 4.00 10.00
29 Tomas Vokoun 5.00 12.00
30 Michael Frolik 4.00 10.00
33 Jonathan Bernier/50 5.00 12.00
35 Cal Clutterbuck 4.00 10.00
36 Mikko Koivu 6.00 15.00
37 Carey Price 12.00 30.00
38 Scott Gomez 5.00 12.00
39 Tomas Plekanec 4.00 10.00
40 Ilya Kovalchuk 6.00 15.00
41 Martin Brodeur 15.00 40.00
43 John Tavares 10.00 25.00
44 Kyle Okposo 4.00 10.00
45 Sean Avery 5.00 12.00
46 Marian Gaborik 6.00 15.00
47 Henrik Lundqvist 15.00 40.00
48 Daniel Alfredsson 6.00 15.00
49 Jason Spezza 6.00 15.00
50 Chris Pronger 6.00 15.00
51 Jeff Carter 5.00 12.00
53 Ilya Bryzgalov 5.00 12.00
54 Shane Doan 5.00 12.00
55 Jordan Staal 5.00 12.00
56 Sidney Crosby 25.00 60.00
57 Marc-Andre Fleury 12.00 30.00
58 Evgeni Malkin 12.00 30.00
59 Dany Heatley 5.00 12.00
60 Joe Thornton 10.00 25.00
62 Jaroslav Halak 6.00 15.00
64 Vincent Lecavalier 6.00 15.00
65 Mike Smith 6.00 15.00
67 Phil Kessel 8.00 20.00
70 Roberto Luongo 10.00 25.00
71 Henrik Sedin 8.00 20.00
72 Daniel Sedin 8.00 20.00
73 Alex Ovechkin/25 30.00 80.00
74 Nicklas Backstrom 6.00 15.00

2010-11 Luxury Suite Prime Patches

*PATCH/20: .6X TO 1.5X PRIME/50-150
59 Dany Heatley 8.00 20.00
74 Nicklas Backstrom 10.00 25.00

2011-12 Luxury Suite

1 Ryan Getzlaf JSY STK 5.00 12.00
2 Blake Wheeler JSY STK 6.00 15.00
3 David Krejci JSY STK 6.00 15.00
4 Nathan Gerbe JSY STK 3.00 8.00
5 Henrik Lundqvist JSY STK 8.00 20.00
6 Saku Koivu JSY STK 5.00 12.00
7 Dion Phaneuf JSY STK 4.00 10.00
8 David Legwand JSY STK 4.00 10.00
9 Andrei Markov JSY STK 3.00 8.00
10 Derek Stepan JSY STK 3.00 8.00
11 Ilya Kovalchuk JSY STK 6.00 15.00
12 Jonas Hiller JSY STK 8.00 20.00
13 Jason Spezza JSY STK 5.00 12.00
14 Mats Zuccarello JSY STK 5.00 12.00
15 Brandon Dubinsky JSY STK 3.00 8.00
16 Alex Ovechkin JSY STK 20.00 50.00
17 Patrick Sharp JSY STK 10.00 25.00
18 Chris Pronger JSY STK 5.00 12.00
19 Shawn Thornton JSY STK 6.00 15.00
20 Ryan Callahan JSY STK 6.00 15.00
21 Pavel Datsyuk JSY STK 8.00 20.00
22 Jaromir Jagr JSY STK 10.00 25.00
23 Joe Thornton JSY STK 8.00 20.00
24 Zdeno Chara JSY STK 5.00 12.00
25 Tomas Plekanec JSY STK 3.00 8.00
26 Marc Staal JSY STK 3.00 8.00
27 Jarome Iginla JSY STK 8.00 20.00
28 Scott Gomez JSY STK 4.00 10.00
29 Carey Price JSY STK 12.00 30.00
30 Simon Gagne JSY STK 6.00 15.00
31 Semyon Varlamov JSY STK 6.00 15.00
32 Tuukka Rask JSY STK 8.00 20.00
33 Marian Gaborik JSY STK 5.00 12.00
34 Milan Hejduk JSY STK 4.00 10.00
35 Michael Del Zotto JSY STK 3.00 8.00
36 Curtis Joseph JSY STK 6.00 15.00
37 Ron Francis JSY STK 8.00 20.00
38 Ray Bourque JSY STK 8.00 20.00
39 Brian Leetch JSY STK 4.00 10.00
40 Tom Barrasso JSY STK 6.00 15.00
41 Adam Henrique JSY AU RC 25.00 60.00
42 Adam Larsson JSY AU RC 20.00 50.00
43 Blake Geoffrion JSY AU RC 12.00 30.00
44 Brandon Saad JSY AU RC 25.00 60.00
45 Brendan Smith JSY AU RC 15.00 40.00
46 Brett Connolly JSY AU RC 12.00 30.00
47 Carl Hagelin JSY AU RC 12.00 30.00
48 Cody Eakin JSY AU RC 20.00 50.00
49 Cody Hodgson JSY AU RC 12.00 30.00
50 Craig Smith JSY AU RC 10.00 25.00
51 David Rundblad JSY AU RC 10.00 25.00
52 D.Smith-Pelly JSY AU RC 10.00 25.00
53 G.Landeskog JSY AU RC 12.00 30.00
54 G.Nyquist JSY AU RC 25.00 50.00
55 J.Gardiner JSY AU RC 20.00 50.00
56 Joe Colborne JSY AU RC 20.00 50.00
57 Brett Bulmer JSY AU RC 12.00 30.00
58 L.Leblanc JSY AU RC 15.00 40.00
59 M.Scheifele JSY AU RC 15.00 40.00
60 C.de Haan JSY AU RC 12.00 30.00
61 H.Zolnierczyk JSY AU RC 12.00 30.00
62 Nugent-Hopkins JSY AU RC 60.00 120.00
63 Ryan Johansen JSY AU RC 40.00 100.00
64 Sean Couturier JSY AU RC 12.00 30.00
65 Simon Despres JSY AU RC 20.00 50.00
66 Tim Erixon JSY AU RC 10.00 25.00
67 Zack Kassian JSY AU RC 20.00 50.00
68 Aaron Palushaj JSY AU RC 8.00 20.00
69 Gudbranson JSY AU RC 12.00 30.00
70 Justin Faulk JSY AU RC 10.00 25.00

2012-13 Luxury Suite

1 Adam Henrique STK 4.00 10.00
2 Adam Graves STK 6.00 15.00
3 Alex Ovechkin STK 10.00 25.00
4 Bernie Parent STK SP 8.00 20.00
5 Bobby Hull STK 15.00 40.00
6 Bobby Ryan STK 4.00 10.00
7 Brad Richards STK 5.00 12.00
8 Brayden Schenn STK 5.00 12.00
9 Brett Hull STK 10.00 25.00
10 Carey Price STK 10.00 25.00
11 Curtis Joseph STK 6.00 15.00
12 Daniel Sedin STK 6.00 15.00
13 Doug Gilmour STK 10.00 25.00
14 Ed Belfour STK 8.00 20.00
15 Rick Nash STK 5.00 12.00
16 Felix Potvin STK 8.00 20.00

17 Gordie Howe STK SP 20.00 50.00
18 James van Riemsdyk STK 6.00 15.00
19 Jarome Iginla STK 6.00 15.00
20 Jaroslav Halak STK 5.00 12.00
21 John Tavares STK 8.00 20.00
22 Dale Hawerchuk STK 6.00 15.00
23 Luc Robitaille STK 5.00 12.00
24 Patrik Elias STK 8.00 20.00
25 Joe Mullen STK 4.00 10.00
26 Mario Lemieux STK 6.00 15.00
27 Mark Messier STK 15.00 40.00
28 Martin Brodeur STK 12.00 30.00
29 Martin St. Louis STK 5.00 12.00
30 Michael Del Zotto STK 3.00 8.00
31 Shane Doan STK 4.00 10.00
32 Nicklas Lidstrom STK 6.00 15.00
33 Patrick Marleau STK 5.00 12.00
34 Patrick Roy STK 10.00 25.00
35 Pavel Datsyuk STK 8.00 20.00
36 Roberto Luongo STK 8.00 20.00
37 Rogie Vachon STK 10.00 25.00
38 Saku Koivu STK 8.00 20.00
39 Sean Couturier STK 6.00 15.00
40 Jaromir Jagr STK 15.00 40.00
41 Stan Mikita STK 10.00 25.00
42 Steve Yzerman STK 12.00 30.00
43 Tim Thomas STK 5.00 12.00
44 Vincent Lecavalier STK 5.00 12.00
45 Bobby Clarke STK 12.00 30.00
46 Denis Potvin STK 8.00 20.00
47 Lanny McDonald STK 6.00 15.00
48 Ray Bourque STK 8.00 20.00
49 Guy Lafleur STK 10.00 25.00
50 Adam Oates STK 6.00 15.00
51 Rick Middleton STK 6.00 15.00
52 Cam Ward STK 5.00 12.00
53 Mat Clark JSY AU RC 6.00 15.00
54 Carter Camper JSY AU RC 5.00 12.00
55 Lane MacDermid JSY AU RC 6.00 15.00
56 Max Sauve JSY AU RC 5.00 12.00
57 Torey Krug JSY AU RC 20.00 50.00
58 Michael Hutchinson JSY AU RC 10.00 25.00
59 Travis Turnbull JSY AU RC 5.00 12.00
60 Akim Aliu JSY AU RC 6.00 15.00
61 Jeremy Welsh JSY AU RC 6.00 15.00
62 Brandon Bollig JSY AU RC 5.00 12.00
63 Tyson Barrie JSY AU RC 12.00 30.00
64 Mike Connolly JSY AU RC 6.00 15.00
65 Andrew Joudrey JSY AU RC 6.00 15.00
66 Shawn Hunwick JSY AU RC 5.00 12.00
67 Cody Goloubef JSY AU RC 5.00 12.00
68 Dalton Prout JSY AU RC 5.00 12.00
69 Ryan Garbutt JSY AU RC 5.00 12.00
70 Reilly Smith JSY AU RC 12.00 30.00
71 Scott Glennie JSY AU RC 6.00 15.00
72 Brenden Dillon JSY AU RC 6.00 15.00
73 Riley Sheahan JSY AU RC 8.00 20.00
74 Philippe Cornet JSY AU RC 6.00 15.00
75 Colby Robak JSY AU RC 5.00 12.00
76 Jordan Nolan JSY AU RC 5.00 12.00
77 Kris Foucault JSY AU RC 5.00 12.00
78 Tyler Cuma JSY AU RC 5.00 12.00
79 Chay Genoway JSY AU RC 5.00 12.00
80 Jason Zucker JSY AU RC 8.00 20.00
81 Robert Mayer JSY AU RC 8.00 20.00
82 Gabriel Dumont JSY AU RC 10.00 25.00
83 Chet Pickard JSY AU RC 6.00 15.00
84 Aaron Ness JSY AU RC 5.00 12.00
85 Casey Cizikas JSY AU RC 6.00 15.00
86 Matt Donovan JSY AU RC 6.00 15.00
87 Matt Watkins JSY AU RC 5.00 12.00
88 Jakob Silfverberg JSY AU RC 15.00 30.00
89 Mark Stone JSY AU RC 20.00 50.00
90 Brandon Manning JSY AU RC 6.00 15.00
91 Michael Stone JSY AU RC 8.00 20.00
92 Tyson Sexsmith JSY AU RC 5.00 12.00
93 Jake Allen JSY AU RC 15.00 40.00
94 J.T. Brown JSY AU RC 6.00 15.00
95 Carter Ashton JSY AU RC 5.00 12.00
96 Ryan Hamilton JSY AU RC 5.00 12.00
97 Jussi Rynnas JSY AU RC 20.00 50.00
98 Chris Kreider JSY AU RC 15.00 40.00
99 Sven Baertschi JSY AU RC 8.00 20.00
100 Jaden Schwartz JSY AU RC 12.00 30.00

2012-13 Luxury Suite Autographs Gold

*53-97 RK.JSY AU/25: .6X TO 1.5X JSY AU/99

2013-14 Luxury Suite

1 Gordie Howe STK/100 12.00 30.00
2 Patrick Roy STK/199 12.00 30.00
3 Dave Andreychuk STK/199 5.00 12.00
4 Mike Richter STK/199 5.00 12.00
5 Marty Turco STK/199 5.00 12.00
6 Paul Coffey STK/199 5.00 12.00
7 Michel Goulet STK/199 4.00 10.00
8 Pierre Turgeon STK/199 4.00 10.00
9 Jonathan Toews STK/199 8.00 20.00
10 Evgeni Malkin STK/199 10.00 25.00
11 Dale Hawerchuk STK/199 6.00 15.00
12 Mark Streit STK/199 3.00 8.00
13 Paul Stastny STK/199 4.00 10.00
14 Adam Graves STK/199 4.00 10.00
15 Alex Delvecchio STK/199 5.00 12.00
16 Bobby Hull STK/199 8.00 20.00
17 Brenden Morrow STK/199 4.00 10.00
18 Curtis Joseph STK/199 6.00 15.00
19 Dale Hawerchuk STK/199 6.00 15.00
20 Dany Heatley STK/199 4.00 10.00
21 Denis Potvin STK/199 6.00 15.00
22 Doug Gilmour STK/199 6.00 15.00
23 Gerry Cheevers STK/199 5.00 12.00
24 Grant Fuhr STK/199 8.00 20.00
25 Henrik Zetterberg STK/199 6.00 15.00
26 Jimmy Howard STK/199 6.00 15.00
27 Joe Nieuwendyk STK/199 4.00 10.00
28 J.Vanbiesbrouck STK/199 6.00 15.00
29 Johnny Bower STK/199 8.00 20.00
30 Jordan Staal STK/199 4.00 10.00
31 Marc Staal STK/199 3.00 8.00
32 Marian Gaborik STK/199 6.00 15.00
33 Mario Lemieux STK/199 15.00 40.00
34 Mark Messier STK/199 10.00 25.00
35 Mikhail Grabovski STK/199 6.00 15.00
36 Nicklas Lidstrom STK/199 5.00 12.00
37 Paul Coffey STK/199 6.00 15.00
38 Phil Esposito STK/199 8.00 20.00
39 Ray Bourque STK/199 8.00 20.00
40 Roberto Luongo STK/199 8.00 20.00
41 Ron Francis STK/199 6.00 15.00
42 Ryan Callahan STK/199 3.00 8.00
43 Sheldon Souray STK/199 3.00 8.00
44 Steve Yzerman STK/199 12.00 30.00
45 Tony Esposito STK/199 5.00 12.00
46 Valtteri Filppula STK/199 3.00 8.00
47 Vincent Lecavalier STK/199 5.00 12.00
48 Zach Parise STK/199 5.00 12.00
49 Andrei Markov STK/199 3.00 8.00
50 Andrew Shaw STK/199 3.00 8.00
51 T.Selanne JSY STK/99 8.00 20.00
52 Jason Spezza JSY STK/99 8.00 20.00
53 Corey Perry JSY STK/99 10.00 25.00
54 Adam Larsson JSY STK/99 6.00 15.00
55 P.Bergeron JSY STK/99 8.00 20.00
56 Ryan Getzlaf JSY STK/99 6.00 15.00
57 Steve Ott JSY STK/99 4.00 10.00
58 Joe Pavelski JSY STK/99 8.00 20.00
59 Sam Gagner JSY STK/75 5.00 12.00
60 Marian Gaborik JSY STK/99 6.00 15.00
61 Max Pacioretty JSY STK/99 6.00 15.00
62 Stan Mikita JSY STK/99 8.00 20.00
63 B.Dubinsky JSY STK/99 4.00 10.00
64 Alex Ovechkin JSY STK/99 12.00 30.00
65 S.Stamkos JSY STK/99 12.00 30.00
66 Alex Goligoski JSY STK/99 4.00 10.00
67 Alex Tanguay JSY STK/99 4.00 10.00
68 Brad Richards JSY STK/99 6.00 15.00
69 Brendan Shanahan JSY STK/99 6.00 15.00
70 Brian Leetch JSY STK/99 5.00 12.00
71 Bryan Little JSY STK/99 6.00 15.00
72 Carey Price JSY STK/99 12.00 30.00
73 Cam Neely JSY STK/99 6.00 15.00
74 Derek Stepan JSY STK/99 4.00 10.00
75 Devan Dubnyk JSY STK/99 5.00 12.00
76 Kari Lehtonen JSY STK/99 5.00 12.00
77 Evgeni Malkin JSY STK/99 12.00 30.00
78 Gordie Howe STK/25 25.00 60.00
79 H.Lundqvist JSY STK/99 15.00 40.00
80 Henrik Sedin JSY STK/99 6.00 15.00
81 Jacob Josefson JSY STK/99 4.00 10.00
82 Jaromir Jagr JSY STK/99 15.00 40.00
83 Jaroslav Halak JSY STK/99 8.00 20.00
84 Jeff Carter JSY STK/99 5.00 12.00
85 Joe Sakic JSY STK/99 12.00 30.00
86 Joe Thornton JSY STK/99 10.00 25.00
87 Jonas Hiller JSY STK/99 4.00 10.00
88 Kris Versteeg JSY STK/99 4.00 10.00
89 Loui Eriksson JSY STK/99 4.00 10.00
90 Marc-Andre Fleury JSY/99 12.00 30.00
91 Martin St. Louis JSY STK/99 6.00 15.00
92 Martin Brodeur JSY STK/99 6.00 15.00
93 Pavel Datsyuk JSY STK/99 10.00 25.00
94 Rob Blake JSY STK/99 6.00 15.00
95 Ryan McDonagh JSY STK/99 4.00 10.00
96 Saku Koivu JSY STK/99 6.00 15.00
97 Sidney Crosby JSY STK/25 30.00 60.00
98 Tomas Plekanec JSY STK/99 4.00 10.00
99 Tyler Seguin JSY STK/99 8.00 20.00
100 Wayne Simmonds JSY STK/99 8.00 20.00
101 Nail Yakupov JSY AU RC 15.00 40.00
102 N.MacKinnon JSY AU RC 25.00 60.00
103 Ryan Murray JSY AU RC 12.00 30.00
104 A.Barkov JSY AU RC 25.00 60.00
105 A.Galchenyuk JSY AU RC 15.00 40.00
106 Seth Jones JSY AU RC 15.00 40.00
107 Morgan Rielly JSY AU RC 12.00 30.00
108 Elias Lindholm JSY AU RC 20.00 50.00
109 H.Lindholm JSY AU RC 12.00 30.00
110 Sean Monahan JSY AU RC 15.00 40.00
111 Matt Dumba JSY AU RC 5.00 12.00
113 Jacob Trouba JSY AU RC 12.00 30.00
114 V.Nichushkin JSY AU RC 15.00 40.00
115 Filip Forsberg JSY AU RC 25.00 60.00
116 M.Grigorenko JSY AU RC 5.00 12.00
117 Z.Girgensons JSY AU RC 12.00 30.00
118 Nikita Zadorov JSY AU RC 5.00 12.00
119 Tom Wilson JSY AU RC 15.00 40.00
120 Tomas Hertl JSY AU RC 15.00 40.00
121 Scott Laughton JSY AU RC 10.00 25.00
122 Olli Maatta JSY AU RC 15.00 40.00
123 Stefan Matteau JSY AU RC 6.00 15.00
124 Tanner Pearson JSY AU RC 8.00 20.00
125 Marek Mazanec JSY AU RC 8.00 20.00
126 Dougie Hamilton JSY AU RC 12.00 30.00
129 Jamie Oleksiak JSY AU RC 6.00 15.00
131 Nathan Beaulieu JSY AU RC 5.00 12.00
132 Nicklas Jensen JSY AU RC 6.00 15.00
133 Rickard Rakell JSY AU RC 8.00 20.00
134 Boone Jenner JSY AU RC 15.00 40.00
135 Magnus Hellberg JSY AU RC 8.00 20.00
136 Dmitrij Jaskin JSY AU RC 8.00 20.00
137 Matt Nieto JSY AU RC 6.00 15.00
138 Xavier Ouellet JSY AU RC 8.00 20.00
139 Lucas Lessio JSY AU RC 5.00 12.00
141 Michael Raffl JSY AU RC 6.00 15.00
142 Frank Corrado JSY AU RC 5.00 12.00
143 Jamie Devane JSY AU RC 6.00 15.00
144 Mikael Granlund JSY AU RC 12.00 30.00
145 V.Tarasenko JSY AU RC 20.00 50.00
146 Austin Watson JSY AU RC 6.00 15.00
147 Nick Bjugstad JSY AU RC 8.00 20.00
148 Beau Bennett JSY AU RC 8.00 20.00
150 Mark Pysyk JSY AU RC 6.00 15.00
151 Quinton Howden JSY AU RC 5.00 12.00
153 Emerson Etem JSY AU RC 6.00 15.00
154 Brock Nelson JSY AU RC 12.00 30.00
155 Martin Jones JSY AU RC 10.00 25.00
156 Reto Berra JSY AU RC 6.00 15.00
157 Jon Merrill JSY AU RC 6.00 15.00
158 Christian Thomas JSY AU RC 5.00 12.00
159 Ryan Spooner JSY AU RC 6.00 15.00
160 Tyler Toffoli JSY AU RC 12.00 30.00
161 Calvin Pickard JSY AU RC 8.00 20.00
162 Johan Larsson JSY AU RC 8.00 20.00
163 Max Reinhart JSY AU RC 6.00 15.00
164 Michael Bournival JSY AU RC 6.00 15.00
165 Joakim Nordstrom JSY AU RC 5.00 12.00
166 B.Gallagher JSY AU RC 15.00 40.00
167 Jesper Fast JSY AU RC 6.00 15.00
168 F.Andersen JSY AU RC 15.00 40.00
169 Viktor Fasth JSY AU RC 6.00 15.00
170 Carl Soderberg JSY AU RC 6.00 15.00
171 Jared Staal JSY AU RC 5.00 12.00
172 Connor Murphy JSY AU RC 5.00 12.00
173 Antoine Roussel JSY AU RC 6.00 15.00
174 Jack Campbell JSY AU RC 15.00 40.00
175 Alex Chiasson JSY AU RC 6.00 15.00
176 Petr Mrazek JSY AU RC 12.00 30.00
177 Kevin Connauton JSY AU RC 5.00 12.00
178 Mark Arcobello JSY AU RC 6.00 15.00
179 J.Huberdeau JSY AU RC 15.00 40.00
180 Drew Shore JSY AU RC 5.00 12.00
181 Thomas Hickey JSY AU RC 5.00 12.00
182 Cory Conacher JSY AU RC 4.00 10.00
183 Matt Irwin JSY AU RC 5.00 12.00
184 Alex Killorn JSY AU RC 10.00 25.00
186 Philipp Grubauer JSY AU RC 15.00 40.00
187 Zach Redmond JSY AU RC 5.00 12.00
188 Dylan McIlrath JSY AU RC 4.00 10.00
189 Tomas Jurco JSY AU RC 8.00 20.00
190 Sami Vatanen JSY AU RC 6.00 15.00
191 John Gibson JSY AU RC 15.00 40.00
192 D.DeKeyser JSY AU RC 8.00 20.00
193 Michael Caruso JSY AU RC 4.00 10.00
194 Tye McGinn JSY AU RC 6.00 15.00
195 Michael Kostka JSY AU RC 5.00 12.00
196 Edward Pasquale JSY AU RC 4.00 10.00
197 Darcy Kuemper JSY AU RC 12.00 30.00
198 Justin Schultz JSY AU RC 6.00 15.00
199 Chris Brown JSY AU RC 4.00 10.00
200 Ryan Strome JSY AU RC 10.00 25.00

2013-14 Luxury Suite Rookie Autographs Prime

*PRIME/25: .5X TO 1.2X BASIC INSERTS
102 Nathan MacKinnon 30.00 80.00
105 Alex Galchenyuk 30.00 60.00

1973-74 Mac's Milk

COMPLETE SET (30) 75.00 150.00
1 Gary Bergman 1.50 3.00
2 Johnny Bucyk 2.50 5.00
3 Wayne Cashman 2.00 4.00
4 Bobby Clarke 7.50 15.00
5 Yvan Cournoyer 3.00 6.00
6 Ron Ellis 1.50 3.00
7 Rod Gilbert 2.50 5.00
8 Brian Glennie 1.50 3.00
9 Paul Henderson 2.50 5.00
10 Ed Johnston 2.50 5.00
11 Rick Kehoe 1.50 3.00
12 Orland Kurtenbach 1.50 3.00
13 Guy Lapointe 2.50 5.00
14 Jacques Lemaire 2.50 5.00
15 Frank Mahovlich 5.00 10.00
16 Pete Mahovlich 2.50 5.00
17 Richard Martin 2.00 4.00
18 Jim McKenny 1.50 3.00
19 Bobby Orr 20.00 40.00
20 Jean-Paul Parise 1.50 3.00
21 Brad Park 4.00 8.00
22 Jacques Plante 7.50 15.00
23 Jean Ratelle 2.50 5.00
24 Mickey Redmond 2.50 5.00
25 Serge Savard 2.50 5.00
26 Darryl Sittler 5.00 10.00
27 Pat Stapleton 1.50 3.00
28 Dale Tallon 1.50 3.00
29 Norm Ullman 2.50 5.00
30 Bill White 2.00 4.00

1996 Maggers

COMPLETE SET (108) 90.00 180.00
1 Jason Arnott .50 1.25
2 Tom Barrasso .50 1.25
3 Ed Belfour .60 1.50
4 Peter Bondra .60 1.50
5 Ray Bourque 1.25 3.00
6 Martin Brodeur 1.50 4.00
7 Benoit Brunet .40 1.00
8 Pavel Bure 1.50 4.00
9 Sean Burke .50 1.25
10 Jim Carey .50 1.25
11 Chris Chelios .60 1.50
12 Steve Chiasson .40 1.00
13 Dino Ciccarelli .40 1.00
14 Zdeno Ciger .40 1.00
15 Wendel Clark .40 1.00
16 Paul Coffey .50 1.25
17 Shayne Corson .40 1.00
18 Alexandre Daigle .40 1.00
19 Vincent Damphousse .50 1.25
20 Eric Daze .40 1.00
21 Tie Domi .50 1.25
22 Sergei Fedorov 1.25 3.00
23 Eric Fichaud .40 1.00
24 Theo Fleury .60 1.50
25 Peter Forsberg 1.50 4.00
26 Ron Francis .50 1.25
27 Grant Fuhr .50 1.25
28 Doug Gilmour .60 1.50
29 Sergei Gonchar .40 1.00
30 Tony Granato .40 1.00
31 Adam Graves .50 1.25
32 Wayne Gretzky 4.00 10.00
33 Alexei Gusarov .40 1.00
34 Derian Hatcher .40 1.00
35 Dale Hawerchuk .40 1.00
36 Guy Hebert .50 1.25
37 Ron Hextall .40 1.00
38 Corey Hirsch .40 1.00
39 Phil Housley .40 1.00
40 Kelly Hrudey .40 1.00
41 Brett Hull .75 2.00
42 Jaromir Jagr 1.50 4.00
43 Ed Jovanovski .50 1.25
44 Joe Juneau .40 1.00
45 Valeri Kamensky .50 1.25
46 Paul Kariya 2.00 5.00
47 Trevor Kidd .50 1.25
48 Petr Klima .40 1.00
49 Saku Koivu .50 1.25
50 Andrei Kovalenko .40 1.00
51 Vyacheslav Kozlov .40 1.00
52 Igor Larionov .40 1.00
53 John LeClair .75 2.00
54 Brian Leetch .50 1.25
55 Claude Lemieux .50 1.25
56 Mario Lemieux 4.00 10.00
57 Trevor Linden .50 1.25
58 Eric Lindros 1.00 2.50
59 Al MacInnis .50 1.25
60 Mark Messier .75 2.00
61 Mike Modano 1.00 2.50
62 Alexander Mogilny .50 1.25
63 Andy Moog .50 1.25
64 Joe Murphy .40 1.00
65 Petr Nedved .40 1.00
66 Cam Neely .50 1.25
67 Bernie Nicholls .40 1.00
68 Joe Nieuwendyk .50 1.25
69 Owen Nolan .50 1.25
70 Adam Oates .50 1.25
71 Jeff Odgers .40 1.00
72 Chris Osgood .75 2.00
73 Sandis Ozolinsh .50 1.25
74 Zigmund Palffy .60 1.50
75 Yanic Perreault .40 1.00
76 Michal Pivonka .40 1.00
77 Felix Potvin .60 1.50
78 Keith Primeau .50 1.25
79 Chris Pronger .40 1.00
80 Daren Puppa .40 1.00
81 Bill Ranford .40 1.00
82 Mikael Renberg .40 1.00
83 Mike Ricci .40 1.00
84 Mike Richter .60 1.50
85 Gary Roberts .40 1.00
86 Luc Robitaille .60 1.50
87 Jeremy Roenick .60 1.50
88 Patrick Roy 3.00 8.00
89 Joe Sakic 1.25 3.00
90 Tomas Sandstrom .40 1.00
91 Denis Savard .40 1.00
92 Teemu Selanne 1.25 3.00
93 Brendan Shanahan 1.00 2.50
94 Kevin Stevens .40 1.00
95 Scott Stevens .40 1.00
96 Mats Sundin .60 1.50
97 Gary Suter .40 1.00
98 Chris Terreri .50 1.25
99 Jocelyn Thibault .50 1.25
100 Esa Tikkanen .40 1.00
101 German Titov .40 1.00
102 Rick Tocchet .40 1.00
103 Pierre Turgeon .50 1.25
104 John Vanbiesbrouck .60 1.50
105 Pat Verbeek .50 1.25
106 Mike Vernon .50 1.25
107 Alexei Yashin .50 1.25
108 Steve Yzerman 2.50 6.00

1963-64 Maple Leafs Team Issue

COMPLETE SET (22) 62.50 125.00
1 Bob Baun (Posed) 2.50 5.00
2 Bob Baun (Posed in white uniform& position not listed) 2.50 5.00
3 Carl Brewer (White uniform) 2.50 5.00
4 Carl Brewer (Dark uniform) 2.50 5.00
5 Kent Douglas 1.50 3.00
6 Dick Duff 2.00 4.00
7 Ron Ellis 2.00 4.00
8 Billy Harris (Portrait) 1.50 3.00
9 Billy Harris (Action) 1.50 3.00
10 Larry Hillman 1.50 3.00
11 Red Kelly 4.00 8.00
12 Dave Keon (No number) 7.50 15.00
13 Dave Keon (Number 14) 7.50 15.00
14 Frank Mahovlich (Dark uniform) 7.50 15.00
15 Frank Mahovlich (Dark uniform with added line NHL All-Star) 7.50 15.00
16 Don McKenney 1.50 3.00
17 Dickie Moore 4.00 8.00
18 Bob Nevin 2.00 4.00
19 Bert Olmstead 2.50 5.00
20 Eddie Shack 5.00 10.00
21 Don Simmons 2.00 4.00
22 Allan Stanley 3.00 6.00

1965-66 Maple Leafs White Border

COMPLETE SET (17) 30.00 60.00
1 George Armstrong 4.00 8.00
2 Bob Baun 2.00 4.00
3 Johnny Bower 4.00 8.00
4 John Brenneman 1.50 3.00
5 Brian Conacher 1.50 3.00
6 Ron Ellis (Portrait) 2.00 4.00
7 Ron Ellis (Full length; name in print) 2.00 4.00
8 Larry Hillman 1.50 3.00
9 Larry Jeffrey 1.50 3.00
10 Bruce Gamble 2.00 4.00
11 Red Kelly 4.00 8.00
12 Dave Keon 5.00 10.00
13 Orland Kurtenbach 2.00 4.00
14 Jim Pappin 1.50 3.00
15 Marcel Pronovost 3.00 6.00
16 Eddie Shack 4.00 8.00
17 Allan Stanley 3.00 6.00

1966-67 Maple Leafs Hockey Talks

COMPLETE SET (10) 300.00 600.00
1 George Armstrong 30.00 60.00
2 Johnny Bower 40.00 80.00
3 Dave Keon 30.00 60.00
4 Frank Mahovlich 30.00 60.00
5 Tim Horton 30.00 60.00
6 Bob Pulford 40.00 80.00
7 Brit Selby 25.00 50.00
8 Eddie Shack 30.00 60.00
9 Ron Ellis 30.00 60.00
10 Punch Imlach 30.00 60.00
NNO Hockey Caravan Envelope 15.00 30.00

1968-69 Maple Leafs White Border

COMPLETE SET (11) 20.00 40.00
1 Johnny Bower 4.00 8.00
2 Jim Dorey 1.50 3.00
3 Paul Henderson 2.00 4.00
4 Tim Horton 5.00 10.00
5 Rick Ley 1.50 3.00
6 Murray Oliver 1.50 3.00
7 Mike Pelyk 1.50 3.00
8 Pierre Pilote 3.00 6.00
9 Darryl Sly 1.50 3.00
10 Floyd Smith 1.50 3.00
11 Bill Sutherland 1.50 3.00

1969-70 Maple Leafs White Border Glossy

COMPLETE SET (40) 75.00 150.00
1 George Armstrong 3.00 6.00
2 Johnny Bower 4.00 8.00
3 Wayne Carleton 1.00 2.00
4 King Clancy 3.00 6.00
5 Terry Clancy 1.00 2.00
6 Brian Conacher 1.00 2.00
7 Marv Edwards 1.50 3.00
8 Ron Ellis (Number 6) 1.50 3.00
9 Ron Ellis (Number 8) 1.50 3.00
10 Ron Ellis (No number) 1.50 3.00
11 Bruce Gamble (Front view) 1.50 3.00
12 Bruce Gamble (Side view) 1.50 3.00
13 Brian Glennie (Portrait) 1.50 3.00
14 Brian Glennie (Full length) 1.50 3.00
15 Jim Harrison 1.00 2.00
16 Larry Hillman 1.00 2.00
17 Tim Horton 5.00 10.00
18 Dave Keon (A on sweater) 3.00 6.00
19 Dave Keon (C on sweater) 3.00 6.00
20 Rick Ley 1.50 3.00
21 Frank Mahovlich 5.00 10.00
22 Jim McKenny 1.00 2.00
23 Larry Mickey 1.00 2.00
24 Murray Oliver 1.00 2.00
25 Jim Pappin 1.00 2.00
26 Mike Pelyk 1.00 2.00
27 Marcel Pronovost 2.00 4.00
28 Bob Pulford (Number on gloves) 2.50 5.00
29 Bob Pulford (No number on gloves) 2.50 5.00
30 Pat Quinn 2.00 4.00
31 Brit Selby 1.00 2.00
32 Al Smith 1.00 2.00
33 Floyd Smith 1.00 2.00
34 Allan Stanley 2.50 5.00
35 Norm Ullman 2.50 5.00
36 Mike Walton (Stick touching border) 1.50 3.00
37 Mike Walton (Stick away from border) 1.50 3.00
38 Ron Ward 1.00 2.00
39 Team Photo 1966-67 3.00 6.00
40 Punch Imlach and King Clancy 3.00 6.00

1969-70 Maple Leafs White Border Matte

COMPLETE SET (6) 10.00 20.00
1 Brian Glennie 1.50 3.00
2 Dave Keon 4.00 8.00
3 Bill MacMillan 1.25 2.50
4 Larry McIntyre 1.25 2.50
5 Brian Spencer 2.50 5.00
6 Norm Ullman 3.00 6.00

1970-71 Maple Leafs Postcards

COMPLETE SET (15) 25.00 50.00
1 Jim Dorey 1.00 2.00
2 Ron Ellis 1.50 3.00
3 Bruce Gamble 1.50 3.00
4 Jim Harrison 1.00 2.00
5 Paul Henderson 1.50 3.00
6 Rick Ley 1.25 2.50
7 Bob Liddington 1.00 2.00
8 Jim McKenny 1.00 2.00
9 Garry Monahan 1.00 2.00
10 Mike Pelyk 1.00 2.00
11 Jacques Plante 6.00 12.00
12 Brad Selwood 1.00 2.00
13 Darryl Sittler 12.50 25.00
14 Guy Trottier 1.00 2.00
15 Mike Walton 1.50 3.00

1971-72 Maple Leafs Postcards

COMPLETE SET (21) 25.00 50.00
1 Bob Baun 1.50 3.00
2 Jim Dorey 1.00 2.00
3 Denis Dupere 1.00 2.00
4 Ron Ellis 1.50 3.00
5 Brian Glennie 1.00 2.00
6 Jim Harrison 1.00 2.00
7 Paul Henderson 1.50 3.00
8 Dave Keon 2.50 5.00
9 Rick Ley 1.00 2.00
10 Billy MacMillan 1.00 2.00
11 Don Marshall 1.00 2.00
12 Jim McKenny 1.00 2.00
13 Garry Monahan 1.00 2.00
14 Bernie Parent 4.00 8.00
15 Mike Pelyk 1.00 2.00
16 Jacques Plante 4.00 8.00
17 Brad Selwood 1.00 2.00
18 Darryl Sittler 5.00 10.00
19 Brian Spencer 1.50 3.00
20 Guy Trottier 1.00 2.00
21 Norm Ullman 2.00 4.00

1972-73 Maple Leafs Postcards

COMPLETE SET (30) 40.00 80.00
1 Bob Baun 1.25 2.50
2 Terry Clancy .75 1.50
3 Denis Dupere .75 1.50
4 Ron Ellis (Dark print) 1.25 2.50
5 Ron Ellis (Light print) 1.25 2.50
6 George Ferguson .75 1.50
7 Brian Glennie (Autograph touches stick) .75 1.50
8 Brian Glennie (Autograph away from stick) .75 1.50
9 John Grisdale .75 1.50
10 Paul Henderson (Light print) 1.25 2.50
11 Paul Henderson (Dark print) 1.25 2.50
12 Pierre Jarry .75 1.50
13 Rick Kehoe 1.25 2.50
14 Dave Keon (Autograph touches skate) 2.50 5.00
15 Dave Keon (Autograph away from skate) 2.50 5.00
16 Ron Low 1.25 2.50
17 Joe Lundrigan .75 1.50
18 Larry McIntyre .75 1.50
19 Jim McKenny (Blue tinge) .75 1.50
20 Jim McKenny (Red tinge) .75 1.50
21 Garry Monahan .75 1.50
22 Randy Osburn .75 1.50
23 Mike Pelyk .75 1.50
24 Jacques Plante (Autograph through tape) 5.00 10.00
25 Jacques Plante (Autograph under tape) 5.00 10.00
26 Darryl Sittler (Autograph over stick) 5.00 10.00
27 Darryl Sittler (Autograph away from stick) 5.00 10.00
28 Errol Thompson .75 1.50
29 Norm Ullman (Best Wishes above blueline) 2.00 4.00
30 Norm Ullman (Best Wishes across blueline) 2.00 4.00

1973-74 Maple Leafs Postcards

COMPLETE SET (29) 45.00 90.00
1 Johnny Bower 2.50 5.00
2 Willie Brossart .75 1.50
3 Denis Dupere .75 1.50
4 Ron Ellis 1.25 2.50
5 Doug Favell (Standing) 1.50 3.00
6 Doug Favell (Bending) 1.50 3.00
7 Brian Glennie .75 1.50
8 Jim Gregory .75 1.50
9 Inge Hammarstrom .75 1.50
10 Paul Henderson 1.25 2.50
11 Eddie Johnston 1.50 3.00
12 Rick Kehoe (Same as 1972-73 set) 1.50 3.00
13 Rick Kehoe (Bending) 1.50 3.00
14 Rick Kehoe (Standing) 1.50 3.00
15 Red Kelly 3.00 6.00
16 Dave Keon 3.00 6.00
17 Lanny McDonald 6.00 12.00
18 Jim McKenny .75 1.50
19 Garry Monahan .75 1.50
20 Bob Neely .75 1.50
21 Mike Pelyk .75 1.50
22 Borje Salming 4.00 8.00
23 Eddie Shack 3.00 6.00
24 Darryl Sittler (Bending) 3.00 6.00
25 Darryl Sittler (Standing) 3.00 6.00
26 Errol Thompson .75 1.50
27 Ian Turnbull .75 1.50
28 Norm Ullman 1.75 3.50
29 Dunc Wilson 1.25 2.50

1974-75 Maple Leafs Postcards

COMPLETE SET (27) 25.00 50.00
1 Claire Alexander .75 1.50
2 Dave Dunn .75 1.50
3 Ron Ellis 1.00 2.00
4 George Ferguson (Bending) .75 1.50
5 George Ferguson (Standing) .75 1.50
6 Bill Flett (Front view) .75 1.50
7 Bill Flett (Side view) .75 1.50
8 Brian Glennie .75 1.50
9 Inge Hammarstrom .75 1.50
10 Dave Keon (Bending) 2.00 4.00
11 Dave Keon (Standing) 2.00 4.00
12 Lanny McDonald 3.00 6.00
13 Jim McKenny .75 1.50
14 Gord McRae .75 1.50
15 Lyle Moffat .75 1.50
16 Bob Neely .75 1.50
17 Gary Sabourin .75 1.50
18 Borje Salming 2.00 4.00
19 Rod Seiling .75 1.50
20 Eddie Shack 2.00 4.00
21 Darryl Sittler 2.00 4.00
22 Blaine Stoughton 1.00 2.00
23 Errol Thompson .75 1.50
24 Ian Turnbull 1.00 2.00
25 Norm Ullman 1.50 3.00
26 Tiger Williams 2.00 4.00
27 Dunc Wilson 1.00 2.00

1975-76 Maple Leafs Postcards

COMPLETE SET (30) 25.00 50.00
1 Claire Alexander .75 1.50
2 Don Ashby (Bending) .75 1.50
3 Don Ashby (Standing) .75 1.50
4 Pat Boutette .75 1.50
5 Dave Dunn .75 1.50
6 Doug Favell 1.00 2.00
7 George Ferguson .75 1.50
8 Brian Glennie .75 1.50
9 Inge Hammarstrom (Bending) .75 1.50
10 Inge Hammarstrom (Standing) .75 1.50
11 Greg Hubick .75 1.50
12 Lanny McDonald 2.50 5.00
13 Jim McKenny .75 1.50
14 Gord McRae .75 1.50
15 Bob Neely .75 1.50
16 Borje Salming (Side view) 2.00 4.00
17 Borje Salming (Front view) 2.00 4.00
18 Rod Seiling .75 1.50
19 Darryl Sittler (Bending) 2.00 4.00
20 Darryl Sittler (Standing) 2.50 5.00
21 Blaine Stoughton 1.00 2.00
22 Wayne Thomas (Crouching) 1.25 2.50
23 Wayne Thomas (Standing) 1.25 2.50
24 Errol Thompson .75 1.50
25 Ian Turnbull (Bending) 1.00 2.00
26 Ian Turnbull (Standing) 1.00 2.00
27 Stan Weir .75 1.50
28 Tiger Williams Bending 1.25 2.50
29 Tiger Williams Standing 1.25 2.50
30 Maple Leaf Gardens (Painting) 1.00 2.00

1976-77 Maple Leafs Postcards

COMPLETE SET (24) 20.00 40.00
1 Claire Alexander .63 1.25
2 Don Ashby .63 1.25
3 Pat Boutette .63 1.25
4 Randy Carlyle 1.50 3.00
5 George Ferguson .63 1.25
6 Scott Garland .63 1.25
7 Brian Glennie .63 1.25
8 Inge Hammarstrom .63 1.25
9 Lanny McDonald 2.00 4.00
10 Jim McKenny .63 1.25
11 Gord McRae .63 1.25
12 Bob Neely .63 1.25
13 Mike Palmateer 2.00 4.00
14 Mike Pelyk .63 1.25
15 Borje Salming 1.50 3.00
16 Darryl Sittler 2.00 4.00
17 Wayne Thomas 1.00 2.00
18 Errol Thompson .63 1.25
19 Ian Turnbull .75 1.50
20 Ian Turnbull .75 1.50
21 Jack Valiquette .63 1.25
22 Kurt Walker .63 1.25
23 Stan Weir .63 1.25
24 Tiger Williams 2.00 4.00

1977-78 Maple Leafs Postcards

COMPLETE SET (19) 12.50 25.00
1 Pat Boutette .50 1.00
2 Randy Carlyle 1.00 2.00
3 Ron Ellis .75 1.50
4 George Ferguson .50 1.00
5 Brian Glennie .50 1.00
6 Inge Hammarstrom .50 1.00
7 Trevor Johansen .50 1.00
8 Jimmy Jones .50 1.00
9 Lanny McDonald 2.00 4.00
10 Jim McKenny .50 1.00
11 Gord McRae .50 1.00
12 Mike Palmateer 1.50 3.00
13 Borje Salming 1.50 3.00
14 Darryl Sittler 2.00 4.00
15 Errol Thompson .50 1.00
16 Ian Turnbull .50 1.00
17 Jack Valiquette .50 1.00
18 Kurt Walker .50 1.00
19 Tiger Williams 1.50 3.00

1978-79 Maple Leafs Postcards

COMPLETE SET (25) 15.00 30.00
1 John Anderson .75 1.50
2 Bruce Boudreau 1.50 4.00
3 Pat Boutette .50 1.00
4 Pat Boutette .50 1.00
5 Dave Burrows .50 1.00
6 Jerry Butler .50 1.00
7 Ron Ellis .75 1.50
8 Paul Harrison .50 1.00
9 Dave Hutchison .50 1.00
10 Trevor Johansen .50 1.00
11 Jimmy Jones .50 1.00
12 Dan Maloney .75 1.50
13 Lanny McDonald 2.00 4.00
14 Walt McKechnie .50 1.00
15 Garry Monahan .50 1.00
16 Roger Neilson 1.00 2.00
17 Mike Palmateer 1.25 2.50
18 Borje Salming 1.25 2.50
19 Darryl Sittler 2.00 4.00
20 Lorne Stamler .50 1.00
21 Ian Turnbull .50 1.00
22 Tiger Williams 1.25 2.50
23 Ron Wilson .50 1.00
24 H.Ballard/K.Clancy 1.00 2.00
25 Team Photo 1.25 2.50

1979-80 Maple Leafs Postcards

COMPLETE SET (34) 20.00 40.00
1 John Anderson .50 1.00
2 Harold Ballard .75 1.50
3 Laurie Boschman .50 1.00
4 Pat Boutette .38 .75
5 Carl Brewer .75 1.50
6 Dave Burrows .38 .75
7 Jerry Butler .38 .75
8 Jiri Crha .75 1.50
9 Ron Ellis .50 1.00
10 Paul Gardner .38 .75
11 Paul Harrison .38 .75

12 Greg Hotham .38 .75
13 Dave Hutchison .38 .75
14 Punch Imlach CO 1.00 2.00
15 Jimmy Jones .38 .75
16 Mark Kirton .38 .75
17 Dan Maloney .38 .75
18 Terry Martin .50 1.00
19 Lanny McDonald 2.00 4.00
20 Walt McKechnie .38 .75
21 Mike Palmateer 1.00 2.00
22 Mike Palmateer (Autograph at different angle) 1.00 2.00
23 Joel Quenneville .50 1.00
24 Rocky Saganiuk .38 .75
25 Borje Salming (Autograph touches blue panel) 1.25 2.50
26 Borje Salming (Autograph away from blue panel) 1.25 2.50
27 Darryl Sittler (Autograph closer to blue panel) 2.00 4.00
28 Darryl Sittler 2.00 4.00
29 Floyd Smith .38 .75
30 Bob Stephenson (Action shot taken at rink; borderless; no facsimile autograph; black print on back) .50 1.00
31 Ian Turnbull .38 .75
32 Tiger Williams 1.00 2.00
33 Ron Wilson .38 .75
34 Faceoff with Cardinal .63 1.25

1980-81 Maple Leafs Postcards

COMPLETE SET (28) 12.50 25.00
1 John Anderson .40 1.00
2 Harold Ballard .60 1.50
3 Laurie Boschman (Portrait) .40 1.00
4 Laurie Boschman (Action) .40 1.00
5 Johnny Bower 1.25 3.00
6 King Clancy .75 2.00
7 Jiri Crha .60 1.50
8 Joe Crozier CO .30 .75
9 Bill Derlago .40 1.00
10 Dick Duff .40 1.00
11 Vitezslav Duris .30 .75
12 Dave Farrish .30 .75
13 Stewart Gavin .40 1.00
14 Paul Harrison .30 .75
15 Pat Hickey .30 .75
16 Mark Kirton .30 .75
17 Terry Martin .30 .75
18 Gerry McNamara .30 .75
19 Wilf Paiement .40 1.00
20 Robert Picard .30 .75
21 Curt Ridley .30 .75
22 Rocky Saganiuk .30 .75
23 Borje Salming .75 2.00
24 Dave Shand .30 .75
25 Darryl Sittler (Portrait) 1.50 4.00
26 Darryl Sittler (Action) 1.50 4.00
27 Ian Turnbull .30 .75
28 Rick Vaive .60 1.50

1981-82 Maple Leafs Postcards

COMPLETE SET (26) 10.00 25.00
1 John Anderson .40 1.00
2 Harold Ballard (Painting) .75 2.00
3 Jim Benning .30 .75
4 Fred Boimistruck .30 .75
5 Laurie Boschman .30 .75
6 Bill Derlago .40 1.00
7 Stewart Gavin .40 1.00
8 Bunny Larocque .60 1.50
9 Don Luce .30 .75
10 Dan Maloney .30 .75
11 Bob Manno .30 .75
12 Paul Marshall .30 .75
13 Terry Martin .30 .75
14 Bob McGill .30 .75
15 Barry Melrose .60 1.50
16 Mike Nykoluk CO .30 .75
17 Wilf Paiement .40 1.00
18 Rene Robert .40 1.00
19 Rocky Saganiuk .30 .75
20 Borje Salming .75 2.00
21 Darryl Sittler 1.50 4.00
22 Vincent Tremblay .30 .75
23 Rick Vaive .60 1.50
24 Gary Yaremchuk .30 .75
25 Ron Zanussi .30 .75
26 Frank J. Selke and Harold Ballard .60 1.50

1982-83 Maple Leafs Postcards

COMPLETE SET (37) 10.00 25.00
1 Russ Adam .30 .75
2 John Anderson .40 1.00
3 Normand Aubin .30 .75
4 Jim Benning .30 .75
5 Fred Boimistruck .30 .75
6 Serge Boisvert .30 .75
7 Dan Daoust .30 .75
8 Bill Derlago (Autograph 1 8 from border) .40 1.00
9 Bill Derlago (Autograph 1 4 from border) .40 1.00
10 Vitezslav Duris .30 .75
11 Miroslav Frycer (Autograph touching skate blade) .30 .75
12 Miroslav Frycer (Autograph away from skate blade .30 .75
13 Stewart Gavin .40 1.00
14 Gaston Gingras (Dark background) .30 .75
15 Gaston Gingras (Light background) .30 .75
16 Billy Harris .30 .75
17 Paul Higgins .30 .75
18 Peter Ihnacak .30 .75
19 Jim Korn .30 .75
20 Bunny Larocque (Bunny touching stick) .40 1.00
21 Bunny Larocque (Bunny touching goalie pad) .40 1.00
22 Dan Maloney .40 1.00
23 Terry Martin .30 .75
24 Bob McGill .30 .75
25 Frank Nigro .30 .75
26 Mike Nykoluk CO .30 .75
27 Gary Nylund .30 .75
28 Mike Palmateer .75 2.00
29 Walt Poddubny .40 1.00
30 Borje Salming (Autograph 1 8 from skate) .75 2.00
31 Borje Salming (Autograph 1 4 from skate) .75 2.00
32 Rick St. Croix .40 1.00
33 Greg Terrion (Dark background) .30 .75
34 Greg Terrion (Light background) .30 .75
35 Vincent Tremblay .30 .75
36 Rick Vaive (Autograph touching blade) .50 1.25
37 Rick Vaive (Autograph touching toe of skate) .50 1.25

1983-84 Maple Leafs Postcards

COMPLETE SET (26) 8.00 20.00
1 John Anderson .40 1.00
2 Jim Benning .30 .75
3 Dan Daoust .30 .75
4 Bill Derlago .40 1.00
5 Dave Farrish .30 .75
6 Miroslav Frycer .30 .75
7 Stewart Gavin .40 1.00
8 Gaston Gingras .30 .75
9 Pat Graham .30 .75
10 Billy Harris .30 .75
11 Peter Ihnacak .30 .75
12 Jim Korn .30 .75
13 Gary Leeman .40 1.00
14 Dan Maloney .30 .75
15 Terry Martin .30 .75
16 Basil McRae .40 1.00
17 Frank Nigro .30 .75
18 Mike Nykoluk CO .30 .75
19 Gary Nylund .30 .75
20 Mike Palmateer .60 1.50
21 Walt Poddubny .40 1.00
22 Borje Salming .75 2.00
23 Bill Stewart .30 .75
24 Rick St. Croix .40 1.00
25 Greg Terrion .30 .75
26 Rick Vaive .50 1.25

1984-85 Maple Leafs Postcards

COMPLETE SET (25) 10.00 25.00
1 John Anderson .40 1.00
2 Jim Benning .30 .75
3 Allan Bester .50 1.25
4 John Brophy CO .40 1.00
5 Jeff Brubaker .30 .75
6 Russ Courtnall 1.25 3.00
7 Dan Daoust .30 .75
8 Bill Derlago .30 .75
9 Miroslav Frycer .30 .75
10 Stewart Gavin .40 1.00
11 Al Iafrate 1.50 4.00
12 Peter Ihnacak .30 .75
13 Jeff Jackson .30 .75
14 Jim Korn .30 .75
15 Gary Leeman .40 1.00
16 Dan Maloney CO .30 .75
17 Bob McGill .30 .75
18 Gary Nylund .30 .75
19 Walt Poddubny .40 1.00
20 Bill Root .30 .75
21 Borje Salming .75 2.00
22 Bill Stewart .30 .75
23 Greg Terrion .30 .75
24 Rick Vaive .50 1.25
25 Ken Wregget 1.00 2.50

1985-86 Maple Leafs Postcards

COMPLETE SET (35) 12.00 30.00
1 Harold Ballard PRES .40 1.00
2 Jim Benning .30 .75
3 Tim Bernhardt .40 1.00
4 Johnny Bower ACO .60 1.50
5 Jeff Brubaker .30 .75
6 Wendel Clark 4.00 10.00
7 Russ Courtnall (Dark uniform) .75 2.00
8 Russ Courtnall (Light uniform) .75 2.00
9 Dan Daoust .30 .75
10 Don Edwards .60 1.50
11 Tom Fergus .30 .75
12 Miroslav Frycer .30 .75
13 Dan Hodgson .30 .75
14 Al Iafrate 1.25 3.00
15 Miroslav Ihnacak .30 .75
16 Peter Ihnacak .30 .75
17 Jim Korn .30 .75
18 Chris Kotsopoulos .30 .75
19 Gary Leeman .30 .75
20 Brad Maxwell (Dark uniform) .40 1.00
21 Brad Maxwell (Light uniform) .40 1.00
22 Bob McGill .30 .75
23 Gary Nylund .30 .75
24 Walt Poddubny .40 1.00
25 Bill Root .30 .75
26 Borje Salming .75 2.00
27 Marian Stastny .30 .75
28 Greg Terrion .30 .75
29 Steve Thomas 1.00 2.50
30 Rick Vaive (Taking slapshot) .40 1.00
31 Rick Vaive (Light uniform) .40 1.00
32 Blake Wesley .30 .75
33 Ken Wregget .60 1.50
34 Team Photo (5 1/2 by 8 1/2) 1.25 3.00
35 John Bower SPECIAL .30 .75

1986-87 Maple Leafs Postcards

COMPLETE SET (22) 10.00 25.00
1 Mike Allison .30 .75
2 Harold Ballard PR .60 1.50
3 Tim Bernhardt .40 1.00
4 Wendel Clark 2.00 5.00
5 Russ Courtnall .75 2.00
6 Vincent Damphousse 2.00 5.00
7 Jerome Dupont .30 .75
8 Tom Fergus .30 .75
9 Miroslav Frycer .30 .75
10 Todd Gill .30 .75
11 Al Iafrate 1.25 3.00
12 Peter Ihnacak .30 .75
13 Jeff Jackson .30 .75
14 Terry Johnson .30 .75
15 Chris Kotsopoulos .30 .75
16 Gary Leeman .30 .75
17 Borje Salming .75 2.00
18 Brad Smith .40 1.00
19 Greg Terrion .30 .75
20 Steve Thomas .60 1.50
21 Rick Vaive .40 1.00
22 Ken Wregget 1.00 2.50

1987-88 Maple Leafs PLAY

COMPLETE SET (30) 8.00 20.00
1 N.Laverne Shipley (Police Chief) .02 .10
2 Tom Gosnell (Mayor) .02 .10
3 Sponsor's Card Kellogg Salada .02 .10
4 Harold E. Ballard PR .20 .50
5 D. Almond (Police Superintendent) .02 .10
6 Wendel Clark 17 2.00 5.00
7 Tom Fergus 19 .30 .75
8 Borje Salming 21 .60 1.50
9 Ed Olczyk 16 .30 .75
10 Gary Leeman 11 .30 .75
11 Rick Lanz 4 .20 .50
12 Allan Bester 30 .30 .75
13 Todd Gill 23 .30 .75
14 Al Secord 20 .30 .75
15 Miroslav Frycer 14 .20 .50
16 Chris Kotsopoulos 26 .20 .50
17 Vincent Damphousse 10 1.50 4.00
18 Mike Allison 8 .20 .50
19 Al Iafrate 33 .75 2.00
20 Dan Daoust 24 .20 .50
21 Greg Terrion 7 .20 .50
22 Brad Smith 29 .30 .75
23 Mark Osborne 12 .20 .50
24 Peter Ihnacak 18 .20 .50
25 Dale Degray 3 .20 .50
26 Dave Semenko 27 .30 .75
27 Luke Richardson 2 .30 .75
28 John Brophy CO .20 .50
29 Ken Wregget 31 .60 1.50
30 Russ Courtnall 9 .40 1.00

1987-88 Maple Leafs Postcards

COMPLETE SET (21) 8.00 20.00
1 Allan Bester .30 .75
2 Wendel Clark 2.00 5.00
3 Russ Courtnall .40 1.00
4 Vincent Damphousse 1.50 4.00
5 Dan Daoust .20 .50
6 Tom Fergus .30 .75
7 Miroslav Frycer .20 .50
8 Todd Gill .30 .75
9 Al Iafrate .75 2.00
10 Peter Ihnacak .20 .50
11 Chris Kotsopoulos .20 .50
12 Rick Lanz .20 .50
13 Gary Leeman .30 .75
14 Ed Olczyk .30 .75
15 Mark Osborne .20 .50
16 Luke Richardson .30 .75
17 Borje Salming .60 1.50
18 Al Secord .30 .75
19 Dave Semenko .30 .75
20 Ken Wregget .60 1.50
21 Team Photo .75 2.00

1987-88 Maple Leafs Postcards Oversized

COMPLETE SET (21) 8.00 20.00
1 Allan Bester .30 .75
2 Wendel Clark 2.00 5.00
3 Russ Courtnall .40 1.00
4 Vincent Damphousse 1.50 4.00
5 Dan Daoust .20 .50
6 Tom Fergus .30 .75
7 Miroslav Frycer .20 .50
8 Todd Gill .30 .75
9 Al Iafrate .75 2.00
10 Peter Ihnacak .20 .50
11 Chris Kotsopoulos .20 .50
12 Rick Lanz .20 .50
13 Gary Leeman .30 .75
14 Ed Olczyk .30 .75
15 Mark Osborne .20 .50
16 Luke Richardson .30 .75
17 Borje Salming .60 1.50
18 Al Secord .30 .75
19 Dave Semenko .30 .75
20 Ken Wregget .60 1.50
21 Team Photo .75 2.00

1988-89 Maple Leafs PLAY

COMPLETE SET (30) 4.80 12.00
1 Rules and Tips .08 .25
2 Wendel Clark 17 .75 2.00
3 Tom Fergus 19 .20 .50
4 D. Almond (Superintendent) .08 .25
5 Borje Salming 21 .60 1.50
6 Ed Olczyk 16 .20 .50
7 Sponsor's Card Kellogg Canada .08 .25
8 Gary Leeman 11 .20 .50
9 Rick Lanz 4 .20 .50
10 N.LaVerne Shipley (Chief of Police) .08 .25
11 Allan Bester 30 .30 .75
12 Todd Gill 23 .20 .50
13 Harold E. Ballard PR .40 1.00
14 Al Secord 20 .30 .75
15 Daniel Marois 32 .20 .50
16 Chris Kotsopoulos 26 .20 .50
17 Vincent Damphousse 10 .75 2.00
18 Craig Laughlin 14 .20 .50
19 Al Iafrate 33 .40 1.00
20 Dan Daoust 24 .20 .50
21 Derek Laxdal 35 .20 .50
22 Darren Veitch 25 .20 .50
23 Mark Osborne 12 .20 .50
24 David Reid 34 .30 .75
25 Brad Marsh 3 .30 .75
26 Brian Curran 28 .20 .50
27 Sean McKenna 8 .20 .50
28 John Brophy CO .20 .50
29 Ken Wregget 31 .40 1.00
30 Russ Courtnall 9 .40 1.00

1990-91 Maple Leafs Postcards

COMPLETE SET (21) 4.80 12.00
1 Aaron Broten .20 .50
2 Vincent Damphousse .60 1.50
3 Dave Ellett .20 .50
4 Paul Fenton .20 .50
5 Tom Fergus .20 .50
6 Lou Franceschetti .30 .75
7 Al Iafrate .30 .75
8 Peter Ing .30 .75
9 Mike Krushelnyski .30 .75
10 Tom Kurvers .20 .50
11 Gary Leeman .30 .75
12 Kevin Maguire .30 .75
13 Brad Marsh .30 .75
14 Scott Pearson .20 .50
15 Michel Petit .20 .50
16 Rob Ramage .20 .50
17 Dave Reid .20 .50
18 Luke Richardson .20 .50
19 Joe Sacco .20 .50
20 Doug Shedden .20 .50
21 Scott Thornton .20 .50

1991 Maple Leafs Panini Team Stickers

COMPLETE SET (32) 1.25 3.00
1 Drake Berehowsky .01 .05
2 Allan Bester .02 .10
3 Wendel Clark .20 .50
4 Brian Curran .01 .05
5 Vincent Damphousse .20 .50
6 Lou Franceschetti .01 .05
7 Todd Gill .01 .05
8 Dave Hannan .01 .05
9 Al Iafrate .02 .10
10 Peter Ing .02 .10
11 Tom Kurvers .01 .05
12 Gary Leeman .01 .05
13 Kevin Maguire .01 .05
14 Daniel Marois .01 .05
15 Brad Marsh .02 .10
16 John McIntyre .01 .05
17 Ed Olczyk .01 .05
18 Mark Osborne .01 .05
19 Scott Pearson .01 .05
20 Rob Ramage .02 .10
21 Jeff Reese .02 .10
22 Dave Reid .02 .10
23 Luke Richardson .01 .05
24 Maple Leafs in Action .01 .05
A Team Logo Left Side .01 .05
B Team Logo Right Side .01 .05
C Maple Leafs in Action Upper Left Corner Al Iafrate Dave Reid .01 .05
D Maple Leafs in Action Lower Left Corner Al Iafrate Dave Reid .01 .05
E Maple Leafs in Action Upper Right Corner Al Iafrate Dave Reid .01 .05
F Maple Leafs in Action Lower Right Corner Al Iafrate Dave Reid .01 .05
G Al Iafrate Ken Wregget .05 .15
H Gary Leeman John Kordic .08 .25

1991-92 Maple Leafs PLAY

COMPLETE SET (30) 6.00 15.00
1 Glenn Anderson .40 1.00
2 Craig Berube .20 .50
3 Brian Bradley .20 .50
4 Mike Bullard .20 .50
5 Rob Cimetta .20 .50
6 Wendel Clark .75 2.00
7 Bryan Cousineau .20 .50
8 Lucien Deblois .20 .50
9 Dave Ellett .20 .50
10 Tom Fergus .20 .50
11 Cliff Fletcher .08 .25
12 Mike Foligno .20 .50
13 Grant Fuhr .75 2.00
14 Todd Gill .20 .50
15 Alexander Godynyuk .20 .50
16 Bob Halkidis .20 .50
17 Dave Hannan .20 .50
19 Mike Krushelnyski .20 .50
20 Lanny the Police Dog .02 .10
21 Gary Leeman .30 .75
22 Claude Loiselle .20 .50
23 Daniel Marois .20 .50
24 Rob Pearson .20 .50
25 Michel Petit .20 .50
26 Jeff Reese .25 .60
27 Bob Rouse .20 .50
28 Darryl Shannon .20 .50
29 Tom Watt .08 .25
30 Peter Zezel .20 .50

1992-93 Maple Leafs Kodak

COMPLETE SET (22) 8.00 20.00
1 Glenn Anderson .30 .75
2 Dave Andreychuk .30 .75
3 Dave Andreychuk In front of the net .30 .75
4 Ken Baumgartner .20 .50
5 Drake Berehowsky .20 .50
6 Bill Berg .20 .50
7 Nikolai Borschevsky .20 .50
8 Wendel Clark .75 2.00
9 John Cullen .20 .50
10 Mike Eastwood .20 .50
11 Dave Ellett .20 .50
12 Doug Gilmour .75 2.00
13 Sylvain Lefebvre .20 .50
14 Jamie Macoun .20 .50
15 Kent Manderville .20 .50
16 Dave McIlwain .20 .50
17 Dmitri Mironov .20 .50
18 Mark Osborne .20 .50
19 Rob Pearson .20 .50
20 Felix Potvin 1.25 3.00
21 Bob Rouse .20 .50
22 Peter Zezel .20 .50
23 Mike Foligno .20 .50
24 Grant Fuhr .60 1.50
25 Todd Gill .20 .50
26 Mike Krushelnyski .30 .75
27 Guy Larose .20 .50
28 Bob McGill .20 .50
29 Dave McLLwain .20 .50
30 Daren Puppa .30 .75
31 Joe Sacco .20 .50
32 Darryl Shannon .20 .50
33 Rick Wamsley .30 .75

1993-94 Maple Leafs Score Black's

COMPLETE SET (24) 12.00 30.00
1 Wendel Clark 1.50 4.00
2 Doug Gilmour 2.00 5.00
3 Glenn Anderson .60 1.50
4 Peter Zezel .30 .75
5 Bob Rouse .20 .50
6 Rob Pearson .20 .50
7 Mark Osborne .20 .50
8 Dmitri Mironov .40 1.00
9 Dave McLlwain .20 .50
10 Kent Manderville .20 .50
11 Jamie Macoun .20 .50
12 Sylvain Lefebvre .30 .75
13 Dave Andreychuk .75 2.00
14 Drake Berehowsky .20 .50
15 Bill Berg .20 .50
16 John Cullen .30 .75
17 Ken Baumgartner .30 .75
18 Nikolai Borschevsky .30 .75
19 Mike Eastwood .20 .50
20 Dave Ellett .20 .50
21 Mike Foligno .30 .75
22 Todd Gill .20 .50
23 Mike Krushelnyski .20 .50
24 Felix Potvin 3.00 8.00
NNO Album 2.00 5.00

1994-95 Maple Leafs Gangsters

COMPLETE SET (17) 4.80 12.00
1 Dave Andreychuk .40 1.00
2 Ken Baumgartner .20 .50
3 Bill Borg .20 .50
4 Nikolai Borschevsky .20 .50
5 Mike Eastwood .20 .50
6 Dave Ellett .20 .50
7 Mike Gartner .40 1.00
8 Todd Gill .20 .50
9 Doug Gilmour .75 2.00
10 Alexei Kudashov .20 .50
11 Jamie Macoun .20 .50
12 Kent Manderville .20 .50
13 Dmitri Mironov .20 .50
14 Mark Osborne .20 .50
15 Felix Potvin .75 2.00
16 Damian Rhodes .40 1.00
17 Title Card .08 .25

1994-95 Maple Leafs Kodak

COMPLETE SET (30) 6.00 15.00
1 Dave Andreychuk .40 1.00
2 Ken Baumgartner .20 .50
3 Drake Berehowsky .20 .50
4 Bill Berg .20 .50
5 Nikolai Borschevsky .20 .50
6 Pat Burns .08 .25
7 Garth Butcher .20 .50
8 Mike Craig .20 .50
9 Paul Dipietro .08 .25
10 Tie Domi .30 .75
11 Mike Gartner .40 1.00
12 Todd Gill .20 .50
13 Doug Gilmour .75 2.00
14 David Harlock .20 .50
15 Benoit Hogue .20 .50
16 Grant Jennings .08 .25
17 Kenny Jonsson .30 .75
18 Jamie Macoun .20 .50
19 Terry Martin .08 .25
20 Dmitri Mironov .20 .50
21 Felix Potvin 1.25 3.00
22 Damian Rhodes .40 1.00
23 Mike Ridley .20 .50
24 Warren Rychel .20 .50
25 Mats Sundin .75 2.00
26 Rich Sutter .08 .25
27 Dixon Ward .20 .50
28 Todd Warriner .20 .50
29 Randy Wood .20 .50
30 Terry Yake .08 .25

1994-95 Maple Leafs Pin-up Posters

COMPLETE SET (30) 6.00 15.00
1 Mats Sundin .75 2.00
2 Doug Gilmour .75 2.00
3 Dave Ellett .20 .50
4 Mike Eastland .20 .50
5 Garth Butcher .20 .50
6 Nikolai Borschevsky .20 .50
7 Kenny Jonsson .30 .75
8 Todd Gill .20 .50
9 Bill Berg .20 .50
10 Jamie Macoun .20 .50
11 Damian Rhodes .30 .75
12 Mike Ridley .20 .50
13 Terry Yake .08 .25
14 Felix Potvin 1.25 3.00
15 Warren Rychel .08 .25
16 Randy Wood .08 .25
17 Kent Manderville .20 .50
18 Dave Andreychuk .30 .75
19 Ken Baumgartner .20 .50
20 Dmitri Mironov .20 .50
21 Mike Craig .20 .50
21A Mike Gartner .30 .75
23 Matt Martin .20 .50
24 Tie Domi .40 1.00
25 Paul DiPietro .08 .25
26 Rich Sutter .08 .25
27 Grant Jennings .08 .25
28 Benoit Hogue .20 .50
29 Darby Hendrickson .20 .50
30 Pat Burns CL .08 .25

1994-95 Maple Leafs Postcards

COMPLETE SET (4) 3.00 8.00
1 Dave Andreychuk Todd Gill Doug Gilmour Jamie Ma 1.00 2.50
2 Garth Butcher Doug Gilmour Felix Potvin Mats Su 1.25 3.00
3 Dmitri Mironov Mike Ridley Mats Sundin .60 1.50
4 Felix Potvin 1.00 2.50

1995-96 Maple Leafs Postcards

COMPLETE SET (6) 3.00 8.00
1 Dave Andreychuk Doug Gilmour 1.00 2.50
2 Tie Domi Gary Suter .50 1.25
3 Felix Potvin Kenny Jonsson Mike Ricci Claude Lapointe 1.25 3.00
4 Mats Sundin Tommy Salo .60 1.50
5 Cover Card .40 1.00
6 Becker's Coupon .40 1.00

1996-97 Maple Leafs Postcards

COMPLETE SET (4) 2.50 6.00
1 Sundin/Clark/Gilmour .75 2.00
2 Potvin/Lemieux 1.25 3.00
3 Wendel Clark .75 2.00
4 Domi/Berezin .40 1.00

1997-98 Maple Leafs Postcards

COMPLETE SET 4.00 10.00
1 Mats Sundin 1.00 2.50
2 Felix Potvin 1.00 2.50
3 Wendel Clark 1.00 2.50
4 Tie Domi Sergei Berezin 1.00 2.50

1999-00 Maple Leafs Pizza Pizza

COMPLETE SET (20) 4.80 12.00
1 Dimitri Khristich .20 .50
2 Jonas Hoglund .20 .50
3 Tomas Kaberle .20 .50
4 Garry Valk .20 .50
5 Curtis Joseph AS 1.25 3.00
6 Danny Markov .20 .50
7 Bryan Berard .20 .50
8 Kevyn Adams .20 .50
9 Alexander Karpovtsev .20 .50
10 Steve Thomas .20 .50
11 Alyn McCauley .20 .50
12 Tie Domi .60 1.50
13 Nikolai Antropov .40 1.00
14 Sergei Berezin .20 .50
15 Alexander Karpovtsev AS .20 .50
16 Igor Korolev .20 .50
17 Darcy Tucker .30 .75
18 Glenn Healy .30 .75
19 Yanic Perreault .20 .50
20 Mats Sundin AS .60 1.50

2000-01 Maple Leafs Pizza Pizza

COMPLETE SET (20) 4.00 10.00
1 Dmitri Khristich .20 .50
2 Jonas Hoglund .20 .50
3 Tomas Kaberle .20 .50
4 Garry Valk .20 .50
5 Curtis Joseph 1.00 2.50
6 Danil Markov .20 .50
7 Bryan Berard .20 .50
8 Kevyn Adams .20 .50
9 Alexander Karpovtsev .20 .50
10 Steve Thomas .20 .50
11 Alyn McCauley .20 .50
12 Tie Domi .60 1.50
13 Nikolai Antropov .40 1.00
14 Sergei Berezin .20 .50
15 Dmitri Yushkevich .20 .50
16 Igor Korolev .20 .50
17 Darcy Tucker .20 .50
18 Glenn Healy .20 .50
19 Yanic Perreault .20 .50
20 Mats Sundin .75 2.00

2002-03 Maple Leafs Platinum Collection

COMPLETE SET (120) 30.00 80.00
1 Wade Belak .20 .50
2 Ed Belfour 1.25 3.00
3 Aki Berg .20 .50
4 Shayne Corson .30 .75
5 Tie Domi .75 2.00
6 Tom Fitzgerald .20 .50
7 Travis Green .20 .50
8 Jonas Hoglund .20 .50
9 Tomas Kaberle .20 .50
10 Trevor Kidd .30 .75
11 Jyrki Lumme .20 .50
12 Bryan McCabe .20 .50
13 Alyn McCauley .20 .50
14 Alexander Mogilny .30 .75
15 Robert Reichel .20 .50
16 Mikael Renberg .20 .50
17 Gary Roberts .30 .75
18 Mats Sundin .75 2.00
19 Robert Svehla .20 .50
20 Darcy Tucker .30 .75
21 Nik Antropov .30 .75
22 Karel Pilar .20 .50
23 Richard Jackman .20 .50
24 Carlo Colaiacovo .30 .75
25 Dave Andreychuk .30 .75
26 Andy Bathgate .30 .75
27 Wendel Clark .75 2.00
28 Bill Derlago .20 .50
29 Todd Gill .20 .50
30 Doug Gilmour .75 2.00
31 Billy Harris .20 .50
32 Curtis Joseph 1.25 3.00
33 Bob Nevin .20 .50
34 Felix Potvin 1.25 3.00
35 Eddie Shack .40 1.00
36 Sid Smith .20 .50
37 Ron Stewart .20 .50
38 Ian Turnbull .30 .75
39 Tiger Williams .75 2.00
40 Syl Apps .40 1.00
41 George Armstrong .40 1.00
42 Ace Bailey .75 2.00
43 Max Bentley .30 .75
44 Johnny Bower .75 2.00
45 Turk Broda .75 2.00
46 King Clancy .75 2.00
47 Charlie Conacher .40 1.00
48 Hap Day .30 .75
49 Gordie Drillon .30 .75
50 Babe Dye .30 .75
51 Mike Gartner .30 .75
52 Red Horner .30 .75
53 Tim Horton 1.25 3.00
54 Busher Jackson .30 .75
55 Red Kelly .30 .75
56 Ted Kennedy .40 1.00
57 Harry Lumley .40 1.00
58 Frank Mahovlich .40 1.00
59 Lanny McDonald .30 .75
60 Babe Pratt .30 .75
61 Joe Primeau .30 .75
62 Marcel Pronovost .30 .75
63 Bob Pulford .40 1.00
64 Borje Salming .40 1.00
65 Terry Sawchuk 1.25 3.00
66 Sweeney Schriner .30 .75
67 Darryl Sittler .40 1.00
68 Allan Stanley .30 .75
69 Norm Ullman .30 .75
70 Harry Watson .30 .75
71 Bobby Baun .30 .75
72 Ron Ellis .30 .75
73 Pat Quinn .30 .75
74 Rick Vaive .30 .75
75 Paul Henderson .30 .75
76 Red Kelly .30 .75
77 Frank Mahovlich .40 1.00
78 Lanny McDonald .30 .75
79 Jim McKenny .20 .50
80 Mike Palmateer .40 1.00
81 John Anderson .20 .50
82 Laurie Boschman .20 .50
83 Randy Carlyle .20 .50
84 Wendel Clark .75 2.00
85 Ron Ellis .20 .50
86 Jim McKenny .20 .50
87 Gary Nylund .20 .50
88 Mike Palmateer .40 1.00
89 Joel Quenneville .20 .50
90 Borje Salming .40 1.00
91 Brit Selby .20 .50
92 Darryl Sittler .40 1.00
93 MLG Opening Night .20 .50
94 MLG Closing Night .20 .50
95 AAC Opening Night .20 .50
96 Bill Barilko The Goal .40 1.00
97 1991-92 St. Pats .20 .50
98 1st NHL All-Star Game .20 .50
99 50th NHL All-Star Game .20 .50
100 Tim Horton 1.25 3.00
101 Darryl Sittler/10 Point Night .40 1.00
102 Gordie Drillon Art Ross Trophy .30 .75
103 Ted Kennedy Hart Memorial Trophy .40 1.00
104 Sid Smith Lady Byng Trophy .20 .50
105 Terry Sawchuk Johnny Bower Vezina Trophy 1.25 3.00
106 Harry Lumley Bickell Memorial Trophy .40 1.00
107 Curtis Joseph King Clancy Memorial Trophy 1.25 3.00
108 Borje Salming Molson Cup .40 1.00
109 Doug Gilmour Selke Trophy .75 2.00
110 Pat Burns Jack Adams Trophy .30 .75
111 Gus Bodnar Calder Trophy .30 .75
112 1931-32 Stanley Cup Winners .30 .75
113 1941-42 Stanley Cup Winners .30 .75
114 1946-47 Stanley Cup Winners .30 .75
115 1948-49 Stanley Cup Winners .30 .75
116 1961-62 Stanley Cup Winners .30 .75
117 1962-63 Stanley Cup Winners .30 .75
118 1963-64 Stanley Cup Winners .30 .75
119 1966-67 Stanley Cup Winners .30 .75
120 Checklist .04 .10

2002-03 Maple Leafs Team Issue
COMPLETE SET 8.00 20.00
1 Nik Antropov .40 1.00
2 Ed Belfour 1.25 3.00
3 Tie Domi .75 2.00
4 Tom Fitzgerald .40 1.00
5 Travis Green .40 1.00
6 Tomas Kaberle .40 1.00
7 Trevor Kidd .60 1.50
8 Alexander Mogilny .60 1.50
9 Robert Reichel .40 1.00
10 Mikael Renberg .40 1.00
11 Mats Sundin 1.25 3.00
12 Robert Svehla .40 1.00
13 Mikael Tellqvist .75 2.00
14 Darcy Tucker .60 1.50

2007 Maple Leafs 1967 Commemorative
COMPLETE SET (30) 10.00 25.00
1 Bob Baun .20 .50
2 Johnny Bower .40 1.00
3 John Brenneman .10 .25
4 Wayne Carleton .20 .50
5 Brian Conacher .20 .50
6 Kent Douglas .20 .50
7 Ron Ellis .20 .50
8 Aut Erickson .20 .50
9 Bob Haggert .20 .50
10 Larry Hillman .20 .50
11 Tim Horton .75 2.00
12 Larry Jeffrey .20 .50
13 Red Kelly .20 .50
14 Dave Keon .75 2.00
15 Frank Mahovlich .40 1.00
16 Frank Mahovlich Red Kelly .40 1.00
17 Milan Marcetta .20 .50
18 Jim McKenny .20 .50
19 Jim Pappin .20 .50
20 Marcel Pronovost .20 .50
21 Bob Pulford .20 .50
22 Terry Sawchuk .75 2.00
23 Brit Selby .20 .50
24 Eddie Shack .40 1.00
25 Allan Stanley .20 .50
26 Pete Stemkowski .20 .50
27 Mike Walton .20 .50
28 Group Photo .10 .25
29 Victory Parade .10 .25
30 Johnny Bower CL .20 .50

2007 Maple Leafs 1967 Commemorative Autographs
ABB1 Bob Baun 12.00 30.00
ABB2 Bob Baun 12.00 30.00
ABC1 Brian Conacher 6.00 15.00
ABC2 Brian Conacher 6.00 15.00
ABP1 Bob Pulford 12.00 30.00
ABP2 Bob Pulford 12.00 30.00
AES1 Eddie Shack 15.00 40.00
AES2 Eddie Shack 15.00 40.00
AJB1 Johnny Bower 15.00 40.00
AJB2 Johnny Bower 15.00 40.00
ALJ1 Larry Jeffrey 6.00 15.00
ALJ2 Larry Jeffrey 6.00 15.00
ARE1 Ron Ellis 12.00 30.00
ARE2 Ron Ellis 12.00 30.00
ARK1 Red Kelly 12.00 30.00
ARK2 Red Kelly 12.00 30.00

2007 Maple Leafs 1967 Commemorative Box Topper
ML67 Group Photo .40 1.00

2007 Maple Leafs 1967 Commemorative Jerseys
JES Eddie Shack 6.00 15.00
JJB Johnny Bower 8.00 20.00

2007 Maple Leafs 1967 Commemorative Sticks
SDK Dave Keon 30.00 80.00
SFM Frank Mahovlich 30.00 80.00

2003 Marc-Andre Fleury Stadium Giveaways
COMPLETE SET (4) 15.00 35.00
COMMON CARD (1-4) 4.00 10.00

2004 MasterCard Priceless Moments
COMPLETE SET (10) 20.00
1 Scotty Bowman 2002 Stanley Cup 1.25 3.00
2 Mark Messier 1994 Stanley Cup 1.50 4.00
3 Bobby Baun 1964 Stanley Cup 1.25 3.00
4 Bobby Orr 1970 Stanley Cup 4.00 10.00
5 Bob Nystrom 1980 Stanley Cup 1.25 3.00
6 Jari Kurri 1984 Stanley Cup 1.50 4.00
7 Martin Brodeur 2003 Stanley Cup 3.00 8.00
8 Lanny McDonald 1989 Stanley Cup 1.25 3.00
9 Mario Lemieux Larry Murphy 1991 Stanley Cup 5.00 12.00
10 Ray Bourque 2001 Stanley Cup 2.00 5.00

1982-83 McDonald's Stickers
COMPLETE SET (36) 15.00 40.00
1 Dan Bouchard .20 .50
2 Richard Brodeur .25 .60
3 Gilles Meloche .20 .50
4 Billy Smith .40 1.00
5 Rick Wamsley .20 .50
6 Mike Bossy .75 2.00
7 Dino Ciccarelli .30 .75
8 Guy Lafleur .75 2.00
9 Rick Middleton .30 .75
10 Marian Stastny .15 .40
11 Bill Barber .25 .60
12 Bob Gainey .40 1.00
13 Clark Gillies .20 .50
14 Michel Goulet .30 .75
15 Mark Messier 3.00 8.00
16 Billy Smith AS .75 2.00
17 Larry Robinson AS 1.00 2.50
18 Denis Potvin AS .75 2.00
19 Michel Goulet AS .75 2.00
20 Wayne Gretzky AS 8.00 20.00
21 Mike Bossy AS 2.50 6.00
22 Wayne Gretzky 6.00 15.00
23 Denis Savard .30 .75
24 Peter Stastny .30 .75
25 Bryan Trottier .40 1.00
26 Doug Wickenheiser .15 .40
27 Barry Beck .15 .40
28 Ray Bourque 1.25 3.00
29 Brian Engblom .15 .40
30 Craig Hartsburg .20 .50
31 Mark Howe .40 1.00
32 Rod Langway .20 .50
33 Denis Potvin .30 .75
34 Larry Robinson .40 1.00
35 Normand Rochefort .15 .40
36 Doug Wilson .25 .60
NNO Album 2.00 5.00

1991-92 McDonald's Upper Deck
COMPLETE SET (31) 6.00 15.00
1 Cam Neely .20 .50
2 Rick Tocchet .15 .40
3 Kevin Stevens .15 .40
4 Mark Recchi .25 .60
5 Joe Sakic .60 1.50
6 Pat LaFontaine .20 .50
7 Darren Turcotte .15 .40
8 Patrick Roy .50 1.25
9 Andy Moog .20 .50
10 Ray Bourque .30 .75
11 Paul Coffey .20 .50
12 Brian Leetch .15 .40
13 Brett Hull .40 1.00
14 Luc Robitaille .20 .50
15 Steve Larmer .15 .40
16 Vincent Damphousse .15 .40
17 Wayne Gretzky 1.25 3.00
18 Theo Fleury .15 .40
19 Steve Yzerman .60 1.50
20 Mike Vernon .15 .40
21 Bill Ranford .15 .40
22 Chris Chelios .20 .50
23 Al MacInnis .25 .60
24 Scott Stevens .20 .50
25 Checklist .12 .30
H1 Wayne Gretzky 1.25 3.00
H2 Chris Chelios .20 .50
H3 Ray Bourque .30 .75
H4 Brett Hull .40 1.00
H5 Cam Neely .20 .50
H6 Patrick Roy .50 1.25

1992-93 McDonald's Upper Deck Iron-Ons
COMPLETE SET (26) 16.00 40.00
1 Boston Bruins .75 2.00
2 Buffalo Sabres .75 2.00
3 Calgary Flames .75 2.00
4 Chicago Blackhawks .75 2.00
5 Minnesota North Stars .75 2.00
6 Detroit Red Wings .75 2.00
7 Edmonton Oilers .75 2.00
8 Hartford Whalers .75 2.00
9 Los Angeles Kings .75 2.00
10 Montreal Canadiens .75 2.00
11 New Jersey Devils .75 2.00
12 New York Islanders .75 2.00
13 New York Rangers .75 2.00
14 Ottawa Senators .75 2.00
15 Philadelphia Flyers .75 2.00
16 Pittsburgh Penguins .75 2.00
17 Quebec Nordiques .75 2.00
18 St. Louis Blues .75 2.00
19 San Jose Sharks .75 2.00
20 Tampa Bay Lightning .75 2.00
21 Toronto Maple Leafs .75 2.00
22 Vancouver Canucks .75 2.00
23 Washington Capitals .75 2.00
24 Winnipeg Jets .75 2.00
25 All-Stars Logo .75 2.00
26 44th NHL All-Star Game 2.00 5.00

1992-93 McDonald's Upper Deck
1 Ed Belfour .20 .50
2 Brian Bellows .15 .40
3 Chris Chelios .20 .50
4 Vincent Damphousse .15 .40
5 Dave Ellett .12 .30
6 Sergei Fedorov .30 .75
7 Theo Fleury .30 .75
8 Phil Housley .15 .40
9 Trevor Linden .20 .50
10 Al MacInnis .25 .60
11 Adam Oates .20 .50
12 Luc Robitaille .20 .50
13 Jeremy Roenick .30 .75
14 Steve Yzerman .50 1.25
15 Don Beaupre .15 .40
16 Rod Brind'Amour .12 .30
17 Paul Coffey .20 .50
18 John Cullen .12 .30
19 Kevin Hatcher .12 .30
20 Jaromir Jagr .40 1.00
21 Mario Lemieux .75 2.00
22 Alexander Mogilny .15 .40
23 Kirk Muller .12 .30
24 Owen Nolan .20 .50
25 Mike Richter .20 .50
26 Joe Sakic .40 1.00
27 Scott Stevens .20 .50
H1 Mark Messier HOLO .60 1.50
H2 Brett Hull HOLO 1.00 2.50
H3 Kevin Stevens HOLO .50 1.25
H4 Brian Leetch HOLO .60 1.50
H5 Ray Bourque HOLO 1.50 4.00
H6 Patrick Roy HOLO 1.50 4.00
NNO Checklist UER SP .75 2.00

1993-94 McDonald's Upper Deck
COMPLETE SET (34) 6.00 15.00
1 Brian Bradley .08 .25
2 Pavel Bure .50 1.25
3 Jon Casey .08 .25
4 Paul Coffey .25 .60
5 Doug Gilmour .25 .60
6 Phil Housley .08 .25
7 Brett Hull .40 1.00
8 Jari Kurri .08 .25
9 Dave Manson .08 .25
10 Mike Modano .40 1.00
11 Gary Roberts .08 .25
12 Jeremy Roenick .25 .60
13 Steve Yzerman .60 1.50
14 Steve Duchesne .08 .25
15 Mike Gartner .08 .25
16 Al Iafrate .08 .25
17 Jaromir Jagr .60 1.50
18 Pat LaFontaine .15 .40
19 Alexander Mogilny .15 .40
20A Kirk Muller ERR .08 .25
20B Kirk Muller COR .08 .25
21 Adam Oates .15 .40
22 Mark Recchi .15 .40
23 Patrick Roy 1.25 3.00
23L Patrick Roy jumbo 5.00 12.00
24 Joe Sakic .60 1.50
25 Kevin Stevens .08 .25
26 Scott Stevens .08 .25
27 Pierre Turgeon .15 .40
H1 Mario Lemieux 2.00 5.00
H2 Teemu Selanne .75 2.00
H3 Luc Robitaille .25 .60
H4 Ray Bourque .25 .60
H5 Chris Chelios .25 .60
H6 Ed Belfour .40 1.00
NNO Checklist SP 1.00 2.50

1994-95 McDonald's Upper Deck
COMPLETE SET (40) 10.00 25.00
McD1 Joe Sakic .60 1.50
McD2 Adam Graves .08 .25
McD3 Alexei Yashin .08 .25
McD4 Patrick Roy 1.50 4.00
McD5 Ray Bourque .40 1.00
McD6 Brian Leetch .25 .60
McD7 Scott Stevens .08 .25
McD8 Alexander Mogilny .15 .40
McD9 Eric Lindros .75 2.00
McD10 Jaromir Jagr 1.00 2.50
McD11 Sandis Ozonlish .08 .25
McD12 Sergei Fedorov .60 1.50
McD13 Brett Hull .40 1.00
McD14 Felix Potvin .15 .40
McD15 Al MacInnis .08 .25
McD16 Chris Chelios .25 .60
McD17 Rob Blake .08 .25
McD18 Dave Andreychuk .08 .25
McD19 Paul Coffey .25 .60
McD20 Jeremy Roenick .25 .60
McD21 Joe Nieuwendyk .15 .40
McD22 Cam Neely .15 .40
McD23 Pavel Bure .75 2.00
McD24 Wendel Clark .15 .40
McD25 Teemu Selanne .60 1.50
McD26 Pierre Turgeon .15 .40
McD27 Alexei Zhamnov .08 .25
McD28 Doug Gilmour .25 .60
McD29 Vincent Damphousse .08 .25
McD30 Brendan Shanahan .50 1.25
McD31 Peter Forsberg 1.00 2.50
McD32 Paul Kariya 1.25 3.00
McD33 Viktor Kozlov .08 .25
McD34 Brett Lindros .08 .25
McD35 Martin Brodeur .75 2.00
McD36 Alexandre Daigle .08 .25
McD37 Jason Arnott .15 .40
McD38 Alexei Kovalev .08 .25
McD39 Mikael Renberg .25 .60
NNO Mike Richter CL .25 .60

1995-96 McDonald's Pinnacle
COMPLETE SET (41) 10.00 25.00
MCD1 Jaromir Jagr .75 2.00
MCD2 Eric Lindros .60 1.50
MCD3 Alexei Zhamnov .08 .25
MCD4 Paul Coffey .25 .60
MCD5 Mark Messier .30 .75
MCD6 Brett Hull .30 .75
MCD7 Peter Forsberg .60 1.50
MCD8 Pavel Bure .60 1.50
MCD9 Doug Gilmour .25 .60
MCD10 Owen Nolan .25 .60
MCD11 Paul Kariya 1.00 2.50
MCD12 Joe Nieuwendyk .15 .40
MCD13 Pierre Turgeon .15 .40
MCD14 Jason Arnott .15 .40
MCD15 Mario Lemieux 1.25 3.00
MCD16 Jeremy Roenick .25 .60
MCD17 Sergei Fedorov .40 1.00
MCD18 Mats Sundin .25 .60
MCD19 Teemu Selanne .40 1.00
MCD20 John LeClair .40 1.00
MCD21 Alexander Mogilny .25 .60
MCD22 Mikael Renberg .08 .25
MCD23 Chris Chelios .25 .60
MCD24 Mark Recchi .15 .40
MCD25 Patrick Roy 1.25 3.00
MCD26 Felix Potvin .08 .25
MCD27 Martin Brodeur .60 1.50
MCD28 Dominik Hasek .40 1.00
MCD29 Ed Belfour .25 .60
MCD30 Kirk McLean .15 .40
MCD31 Jeff Friesen .15 .40
MCD32 Todd Harvey .08 .25
MCD33 Brett Lindros .08 .25
MCD34 Valeri Bure .15 .40
MCD35 Oleg Tverdovsky .08 .25
MCD36 Kenny Jonsson .08 .25
MCD37 Mariusz Czerkawski .08 .25
MCD38 Alexandre Daigle .08 .25
MCD39 Saku Koivu .25 .60
MCD40 Jim Carey .15 .40
NNO Joe Sakic CL .25 .60

1996-97 McDonald's Pinnacle
COMPLETE SET (40) 15.00 30.00
1 Paul Coffey .10 .30
2 Teemu Selanne .40 1.00
3 Eric Daze .08 .25
4 John LeClair .40 1.00
5 Saku Koivu .30 .75
6 Ed Jovanovski .25 .60
7 Chris Osgood .30 .75
8 Chris Chelios .10 .30
9 Daniel Alfredsson .08 .25
10 Joe Sakic .50 1.25
11 Alexander Mogilny .08 .25
12 Jeremy Roenick .10 .30
13 Keith Tkachuk .30 .75
14 Doug Gilmour .10 .30
15 Theo Fleury .25 .60
16 Doug Weight .08 .25
17 Steve Yzerman .60 1.50
18 Zigmund Palffy .25 .60
19 Pierre Turgeon .08 .25
20 Brian Leetch .10 .30
21 Mario Lemieux SP 2.00 5.00
22 Mark Messier SP .60 1.50
23 Jaromir Jagr SP 1.25 3.00
24 Brett Hull SP .60 1.50
25 Eric Lindros SP 1.25 3.00
26 Sergei Fedorov SP .75 2.00
27 Pavel Bure SP 1.00 2.50
28 Peter Forsberg SP 1.00 2.50
29 Paul Kariya SP 1.50 4.00
30 Patrick Roy SP 2.00 5.00
31 Ray Bourque SP .50 1.25
32 Jim Carey .20 .50
33 Martin Brodeur .60 1.50
34 Trevor Kidd .15 .40
35 John Vanbiesbrouck .50 1.25
36 Jocelyn Thibault .20 .50
37 Ed Belfour .25 .60
38 Felix Potvin .25 .60
39 Damian Rhodes .15 .40
40 Curtis Joseph .30 .75
NNO Checklist .01 .05

1997 McDonald's Team Canada Coins
COMPLETE SET (10) 10.00 25.00
1 Rod Brind'Amour Trevor Linden .75 2.00
2 Rob Blake Al MacInnis .75 2.00
3 Martin Brodeur Curtis Joseph 1.25 3.00
4 Ray Bourque Chris Pronger 1.25 3.00
5 Shayne Corson Brendan Shanahan .75 2.00
6 Eric DesJardins Adam Foote .75 2.00
7 Theoren Fleury Paul Kariya .75 2.00
8 Wayne Gretzky Joe Sakic 1.50 4.00
9 Eric Lindros Joe Nieuwendyk .75 2.00
10 Keith Primeau Steve Yzerman 1.25 3.00
11 Patrick Roy Olympic Games Logo 1.25 3.00
12 Scott Stevens Rob Zamuner .75 2.00

1997-98 McDonald's Upper Deck
COMPLETE SET (40) 12.50 25.00
1 Wayne Gretzky 2.50 6.00
2 Theo Fleury .25 .60
3 Pavel Bure .60 1.50
4 Saku Koivu .25 .60
5 Joe Sakic .50 1.25
6 Wade Redden .08 .25
7 Keith Tkachuk .30 .75
8 Eric Lindros .75 2.00
9 Paul Kariya 1.00 2.50
10 Bryan Berard .15 .40
11 Teemu Selanne .50 1.25
12 Jarome Iginla .15 .40
13 Mats Sundin .25 .60
14 Brendan Shanahan .50 1.25
15 Peter Forsberg .60 1.50
16 Brett Hull .30 .75
17 Ray Bourque .25 .60
18 Doug Weight .15 .40
19 Steve Yzerman .75 2.00
20 Jaromir Jagr .75 2.00
21 Vincent Damphousse .15 .40
22 Trevor Linden .15 .40
23 Patrick Roy 1.25 3.00
24 John Vanbiesbrouck .25 .60
25 Martin Brodeur .60 1.50
26 Dominik Hasek .50 1.25
27 Curtis Joseph .30 .75
28 Andy Moog .15 .40
29 Mike Richter .25 .60
30 Damian Rhodes .15 .40
31 Felix Potvin .25 .60
32 Chris Osgood .25 .60
33 Joe Thornton .40 1.00
34 Patrick Marleau .40 1.00
35 Jaroslav Svejkovsky .15 .40
36 Daniel Cleary .15 .40
37 Chris Phillips .08 .25
38 Alexei Morozov .15 .40
39 Vaclav Prospal .25 .60
40 Sergei Samsonov .40 1.00

1997-98 McDonald's Upper Deck Game Film
COMPLETE SET (10) 25.00 60.00
1 Wayne Gretzky 10.00 25.00
2 Alexander Mogilny 1.50 4.00
3 Steve Yzerman 6.00 15.00
4 Eric Lindros 2.00 5.00
5 Patrick Roy 8.00 20.00
6 Paul Kariya 6.00 15.00
7 Ray Bourque 2.50 6.00
8 Saku Koivu 2.00 5.00
9 Theo Fleury 1.50 4.00
10 Mats Sundin 2.50 6.00

1998-99 McDonald's Upper Deck
COMPLETE SET (28) 7.50 15.00
1 Wayne Gretzky 2.00 5.00
2 Theo Fleury .20 .50
3 Joe Sakic .60 1.50
4 Saku Koivu .20 .50
5 Brendan Shanahan .40 1.00
6 Steve Yzerman 1.25 3.00
7 Peter Forsberg .60 1.50
8 Paul Kariya .75 2.00
9 Alexei Yashin .15 .40
10 Eric Lindros .60 1.50
11 Jaromir Jagr .60 1.50
12 Mats Sundin .20 .50
13 Sergei Samsonov .20 .50
14 Pavel Bure .60 1.50
15 Patrick Roy 1.25 3.00
16 Dominik Hasek .40 1.00
17 Martin Brodeur .60 1.50
18 Curtis Joseph .40 1.00
19 Jocelyn Thibault .20 .50
20 Chris Osgood .20 .50
21 Ed Belfour .20 .50
22 Mattias Ohlund .15 .40
23 Marian Hossa .20 .50
24 Brendan Morrison .15 .40
25 Jason Botterill .15 .40
26 Cameron Mann .15 .40
27 Daniel Briere .20 .50
28 Terry Ryan .15 .40
NNO Wayne Gretzky JUMBO 83-84 Stanley Cup 8.00 20.00
NNO Wayne Gretzky JSY/198 300.00 800.00
NNO Wayne Gretzky JSY AU/99 1250.00 3000.00

1998-99 McDonald's Upper Deck Gretzky's Moments
COMPLETE SET (10) 25.00 30.00
COMMON CARD (1-10) 1.50 4.00

1998-99 McDonald's Upper Deck Gretzky's Teammates
COMPLETE SET (13) 2.00 5.00
T1 Walter Gretzky .50 1.25
T2 Gordie Howe .75 2.00
T3 Marty McSorley .10 .30
T4 Brian Leetch .20 .50
T5 Brett Hull .30 .75
T6 Esa Tikkanen .10 .30
T7 Grant Fuhr .20 .50
T8 Mike Richter .20 .50
T9 Jari Kurri .20 .50
T10 Paul Coffey .20 .50
T11 Rob Blake .20 .50
T12 Mario Lemieux .75 2.00
T13 Luc Robitaille .20 .50

1999-00 McDonald's Upper Deck Gretzky Performance for the Record
COMPLETE SET (24) 12.00 30.00
COMMON RECORD (1-15) .75 2.00
COMMON CHECKLIST (C1-C9) .60 1.50

1999-00 McDonald's Upper Deck
COMPLETE SET (35) 8.00 20.00
MCD1 Paul Kariya .50 1.25
MCD1R Paul Kariya .50 1.25
MCD2 Eric Lindros .20 .50
MCD2R Eric Lindros .20 .50
MCD3 Dominik Hasek .40 1.00
MCD3R Dominik Hasek .40 1.00
MCD4 Steve Yzerman 1.00 2.50
MCD4R Steve Yzerman 1.00 2.50
MCD5 Jarome Iginla .20 .50
MCD5R Jarome Iginla .20 .50
MCD6 Jaromir Jagr .30 .75
MCD6R Jaromir Jagr .30 .75
MCD7 Brett Hull .25 .60
MCD7R Brett Hull .25 .60
MCD8 Ed Belfour .20 .50
MCD8R Ed Belfour .20 .50
MCD9 Mats Sundin .20 .50
MCD9R Mats Sundin .20 .50
MCD10 Peter Forsberg .50 1.25
MCD10R Peter Forsberg .50 1.25
MCD11 Doug Weight .20 .50
MCD11R Doug Weight .20 .50
MCD12 Curtis Joseph .20 .50
MCD12R Curtis Joseph .20 .50
MCD13 Michael Peca .20 .50
MCD13R Michael Peca .20 .50
MCD14 Saku Koivu .20 .50
MCD14R Saku Koivu .20 .50
MCD15 Patrick Roy .75 2.00
MCD15R Patrick Roy .75 2.00
MCD16 Jose Theodore .20 .50
MCD17 David Legwand .20 .50
MCD18 Chris Drury .20 .50
MCD19 Milan Hejduk .20 .50
MCD20 Marian Hossa .20 .50
NNO Wayne Gretzky 5 x 7 4.00 10.00

1999-00 McDonald's Upper Deck Game Jerseys
GJCP Chris Pronger 15.00 40.00
GJDS Darryl Sydor 12.00 30.00
GJEL Eric Lindros 50.00 100.00
GJGF Grant Fuhr 30.00 80.00
GJJJ Jaromir Jagr 30.00 80.00
GJMM Mike Modano 15.00 40.00
GJPB Peter Bondra 15.00 40.00
GJPF Peter Forsberg 30.00 80.00
GJSS Scott Stevens 15.00 4.00
GJTA Tony Amonte 15.00 40.00
GJWG Wayne Gretzky/99 600.00 1000.00
GJWG Wayne Gretzky AU 750.00 2000.00

1999-00 McDonald's Upper Deck Signatures
AY Alexei Yashin 15.00 40.00
BH Brett Hull 30.00 80.00
CJ Curtis Joseph 30.00 80.00
CO Chris Osgood 15.00 40.00
EB Ed Belfour 25.00 50.00
GF Grant Fuhr 15.00 40.00
JL John LeClair 15.00 40.00
JT Jose Theodore 15.00 40.00
LR Luc Robitaille 15.00 40.00
RB Ray Bourque 40.00 100.00
SK Saku Koivu 15.00 40.00
ST Steve Thomas 15.00 40.00
SY Steve Yzerman 80.00 150.00
TA Tony Amonte 15.00 40.00
TD Tie Domi 30.00 80.00

1999-00 McDonald's Upper Deck The Great Career
COMPLETE SET (5) 4.00 10.00
COMMON CARD .75 2.00

2000-01 McDonald's Pacific
COMPLETE SET (36) 6.00 15.00
1 Paul Kariya .20 .50
2 Teemu Selanne .40 1.00
3 Patrik Stefan .15 .40
4 Joe Thornton .30 .75
5 Dominik Hasek .30 .75
6 Valeri Bure .15 .40
7 Ray Bourque .30 .75
8 Peter Forsberg .40 1.00
9 Patrick Roy .50 1.25
10 Joe Sakic .40 1.00
11 Brett Hull .40 1.00
12 Mike Modano .30 .75
13 Chris Osgood .20 .50
14 Brendan Shanahan .20 .50
15 Steve Yzerman .50 1.25
16 Doug Weight .20 .50
17 Pavel Bure .20 .50
18 Jeff Hackett .12 .30
19 Saku Koivu .20 .50
20 Martin Brodeur .50 1.25
21 Scott Gomez .15 .40
22 Scott Stevens .20 .50
23 Marian Hossa .20 .50
24 Brian Boucher .15 .40
25 John LeClair .20 .50
26 Eric Lindros .30 .75
27 Jaromir Jagr .60 1.50
28 Chris Pronger .20 .50
29 Roman Turek .15 .40
30 Vincent Lecavalier .20 .50
31 Nikolai Antropov .15 .40
32 Curtis Joseph .25 .60
33 Mats Sundin .20 .50
34 Mattias Ohlund .12 .30
35 Felix Potvin .30 .75
36 Olaf Kolzig .20 .50

2000-01 McDonald's Pacific Blue
COMPLETE SET (36) 15.00 40.00
*BLUE: 2X TO 5X BASIC CARDS

2000-01 McDonald's Pacific Checklists
COMPLETE SET (9) 1.50 3.00
1 Valeri Bure .10 .25
2 Doug Weight .15 .40
3 Jeff Hackett .15 .40
4 Saku Koivu .20 .50
5 Marian Hossa .20 .50
6 Curtis Joseph .20 .50
7 Mats Sundin .20 .50
8 Mattias Ohlund .10 .25
9 Felix Potvin .20 .50

2000-01 McDonald's Pacific Dial-A-Stats
COMPLETE SET (6) 7.50 15.00
1 Paul Kariya 2.50 6.00
2 Steve Yzerman 5.00 12.00
3 Pavel Bure 1.00 2.50
4 Eric Lindros 1.00 2.50
5 Jaromir Jagr 1.50 4.00
6 Mats Sundin 1.00 2.50

2000-01 McDonald's Pacific Glove Side Net Fusions
COMPLETE SET (6) 8.00 20.00
1 Dominik Hasek 2.00 5.00
2 Patrick Roy 5.00 12.00
3 Chris Osgood 1.00 2.50
4 Martin Brodeur 2.50 6.00
5 Brian Boucher 1.00 2.50
6 Curtis Joseph 1.00 2.50

2000-01 McDonald's Pacific Gold Crown Die Cuts
COMPLETE SET (6) 4.00 8.00
1 Patrik Stefan .60 1.50
2 Alex Tanguay .60 1.50
3 David Legwand .60 1.50
4 Scott Gomez .60 1.50
5 Tim Connolly .60 1.50
6 Vincent Lecavalier .60 1.50

2000-01 McDonald's Pacific Game Jerseys
1 Teemu Selanne 12.00 30.00
2 Peter Forsberg 12.00 30.00
3 Patrick Roy 25.00 60.00
4 Mike Modano 12.00 30.00
5 Steve Yzerman 15.00 40.00
6 Pavel Bure 12.00 30.00
7 Martin Brodeur 15.00 40.00
8 Eric Lindros 20.00 50.00
9 Jaromir Jagr 25.00 60.00
10 Mats Sundin 15.00 40.00

2001-02 McDonald's Pacific
COMPLETE SET (42) 12.50 25.00
1 Paul Kariya .25 .60
2 Joe Thornton .40 1.00
3 Jarome Iginla .30 .75
4 Ray Bourque .40 1.00
5 Peter Forsberg .50 1.25
6 Patrick Roy SP 1.25 3.00
7 Joe Sakic .50 1.25
8 Ed Belfour SP .50 1.25
9 Brett Hull .50 1.25
10 Mike Modano .40 1.00
11 Sergei Fedorov .40 1.00
12 Dominik Hasek SP .75 2.00
13 Chris Osgood SP .50 1.25
14 Brendan Shanahan .25 .60
15 Steve Yzerman .60 1.50
16 Tommy Salo SP .40 1.00
17 Ryan Smyth .20 .50
18 Pavel Bure .25 .60
19 Felix Potvin SP .75 2.00
20 Marian Gaborik .25 .60
21 Saku Koivu .25 .60
22 Jose Theodore SP .50 1.25
23 Jason Arnott .20 .50
24 Martin Brodeur SP 1.25 3.00
25 Rick DiPietro SP .40 1.00
26 Marian Hossa .25 .60
27 Patrick Lalime SP .40 1.00
28 Roman Cechmanek SP .40 1.00
29 John LeClair .25 .60
30 Johan Hedberg SP .40 1.00
31 Mario Lemieux SP 2.00 5.00
32 Fred Brathwaite SP .40 1.00
33 Chris Pronger .25 .60
34 Doug Weight .25 .60
35 Evgeni Nabokov SP .40 1.00
36 Teemu Selanne .50 1.25
37 Vincent Lecavalier .25 .60
38 Curtis Joseph SP .60 1.50
39 Mats Sundin .25 .60
40 Dan Cloutier SP .40 1.00
41 Markus Naslund .25 .60
42 Jaromir Jagr SP 1.50 4.00

2001-02 McDonald's Pacific Cosmic Force
COMPLETE SET (6) 15.00 30.00
1 Pavel Bure 2.00 5.00
2 Mario Lemieux 5.00 12.00
3 Doug Weight 1.50 4.00
4 Teemu Selanne 2.00 5.00
5 Mats Sundin 2.00 5.00
6 Jaromir Jagr 2.00 5.00

2001-02 McDonald's Pacific Future Legends
COMPLETE SET (6) 15.00 30.00
1 Mike Comrie 2.00 5.00
2 Rick DiPietro 2.00 5.00
3 Martin Havlat 2.00 5.00
4 Evgeni Nabokov 2.00 5.00
5 Daniel Sedin 2.50 6.00
6 Henrik Sedin 2.50 6.00

2001-02 McDonald's Pacific Glove-Side Net-Fusion
COMPLETE SET (6) 12.00 30.00
1 Patrick Roy 4.00 10.00
2 Tommy Salo 2.00 5.00
3 Jose Theodore 2.50 6.00
4 Martin Brodeur 3.00 8.00
5 Johan Hedberg 2.50 6.00
6 Curtis Joseph 2.00 5.00

2001-02 McDonald's Pacific Hockey Greats
COMPLETE SET (6) 15.00 30.00
1 Ray Bourque 3.00 8.00
2 Joe Sakic 3.00 8.00
3 Brett Hull 2.50 6.00
4 Dominik Hasek 3.00 8.00
5 Steve Yzerman 5.00 12.00
6 Mark Messier 2.00 5.00

2001-02 McDonald's Pacific Hometown Pride
COMPLETE SET (10) 5.00 10.00
1 J.Friesen/W.Redden .40 1.00
2 P.Kariya/B.Morrison .40 1.00
3 S.Pellerin/D.Sweeney .40 1.00
4 M.Comrie/J.Iginla .40 1.00
5 B.Richards/G.Sanderson .40 1.00
6 E.Belfour/T.Fleury .60 1.50
7 L.Robitaille/V.Lecavalier .40 1.00
8 D.Cleary/H.Druken .40 1.00
9 A.MacInnis/C.White .40 1.00
10 G.Roberts/S.Thomas .40 1.00

2001-02 McDonald's Pacific Jersey Patches Silver
1 Jarome Iginla/238 30.00 80.00
2 Peter Forsberg/229 30.00 80.00
3 Patrick Roy/217 30.00 80.00
4 Joe Sakic/231 20.00 50.00
5 Ed Belfour/230 20.00 50.00
6 Brett Hull/234 25.00 60.00
7 Mike Modano/241 25.00 60.00
8 Joe Nieuwendyk/225 15.00 40.00
9 Dominik Hasek/211 30.00 80.00
10 Brendan Shanahan/236 25.00 60.00
11 Steve Yzerman/231 40.00 80.00
12 Saku Koivu/239 25.00 60.00
13 Theo Fleury/236 25.00 60.00
14 Daniel Alfredsson/239 15.00 40.00
15 Mario Lemieux/184 50.00 120.00
16 Teemu Selanne/242 30.00 80.00
17 Vincent Lecavalier/246 15.00 40.00
18 Curtis Joseph/219 25.00 60.00
19 Mats Sundin/237 30.00 80.00
20 Jaromir Jagr/182 40.00 100.00

2001-02 McDonald's Pacific Jersey Patches Gold
3 Patrick Roy/33 200.00 400.00
8 Joe Nieuwendyk/25 150.00 300.00
9 Dominik Hasek/39 150.00 300.00
15 Mario Lemieux/66 200.00 400.00
20 Jaromir Jagr/68 150.00 300.00

2002-03 McDonald's Pacific
COMPLETE SET (42) 12.50 30.00
COMP.SET w/CL's (52) 15.00 40.00
COMP.MASTER SET (76) 40.00 100.00
1 Paul Kariya .30 .75
2 Dany Heatley .25 .60
3 Ilya Kovalchuk .40 1.00
4 Joe Thornton .50 1.25
5 Jarome Iginla .40 1.00
6 Derek Morris .20 .50
7 Roman Turek .30 .75
8 Peter Forsberg .60 1.50
9 Patrick Roy .75 2.00
10 Joe Sakic .60 1.50
11 Dominik Hasek .50 1.25
12 Brendan Shanahan .30 .75
13 Steve Yzerman .75 2.00
14 Anson Carter .25 .60
15 Mike Comrie .30 .75
16 Ryan Smyth .25 .60
17 Roberto Luongo .50 1.25
18 Jason Allison .25 .60
19 Marian Gaborik .30 .75
20 Doug Gilmour .40 1.00
21 Saku Koivu .30 .75

22 Jose Theodore .30 .75
23 Martin Brodeur .75 2.00
24 Michael Peca .25 .60
25 Alexei Yashin .25 .60
26 Pavel Bure .30 .75
27 Eric Lindros .50 1.25
28 Daniel Alfredsson .30 .75
29 Marian Hossa .30 .75
30 Patrick Lalime .25 .60
31 Simon Gagne .30 .75
32 Mario Lemieux 1.25 3.00
33 Chris Pronger .30 .75
34 Evgeni Nabokov .25 .60
35 Teemu Selanne .60 1.50
36 Curtis Joseph .40 1.00
37 Gary Roberts .20 .50
38 Mats Sundin .30 .75
39 Todd Bertuzzi .30 .75
40 Brendan Morrison .25 .60
41 Markus Naslund .30 .75
42 Jaromir Jagr 1.00 2.50

2002-03 McDonald's Pacific Atomic

COMPLETE SET (6)
1 Paul Kariya 1.50 4.00
2 Ron Francis 1.50 4.00
3 Brett Hull 2.00 5.00
4 Steve Yzerman 5.00 12.00
5 Mats Sundin 1.50 4.00
6 Jaromir Jagr 1.50 4.00

2002-03 McDonald's Pacific Clear Advantage

COMPLETE SET (6) 12.50 30.00
1 Dany Heatley 2.50 6.00
2 Ilya Kovalchuk 4.00 10.00
3 Jarome Iginla 3.00 8.00
4 Mike Comrie 3.00 8.00
5 Martin Havlat 2.00 5.00
6 Todd Bertuzzi 2.00 5.00

2002-03 McDonald's Pacific Cup Contenders Die-Cuts

COMPLETE SET (6) 15.00 30.00
1 Joe Thornton 2.50 6.00
2 Patrick Roy 5.00 12.00
3 Sergei Fedorov 2.50 6.00
4 Saku Koivu 2.00 5.00
5 Daniel Alfredsson 1.50 4.00
6 Mats Sundin 1.50 4.00

2002-03 McDonald's Pacific Glove Side Net-Fusions

COMPLETE SET (6) 12.00 30.00
1 Patrick Roy 4.00 10.00
2 Dominik Hasek 2.50 6.00
3 Tommy Salo 2.00 5.00
4 Jose Theodore 2.50 6.00
5 Patrick Lalime 2.50 6.00
6 Evgeni Nabokov 2.00 5.00

2002-03 McDonald's Pacific Jersey Patches Silver

1 Dany Heatley/235 50.00 100.00
2 Ilya Kovalchuk/233 50.00 100.00
3 Ron Francis/240 50.00 100.00
4 Joe Sakic/231 60.00 120.00
5 Dominik Hasek/211 60.00 120.00
6 Mike Comrie/161 50.00 100.00
7 Yanic Perreault/156 40.00 80.00
8 Jose Theodore/190 40.00 80.00
9 Martin Brodeur/220 60.00 120.00
10 Pavel Bure/241 60.00 120.00
11 Eric Lindros/162 50.00 100.00
12 Daniel Alfredsson/239 25.00 60.00
13 Adam Oates/173 40.00 80.00
14 Mario Lemieux/184 75.00 150.00
15 Chris Pronger/206 60.00 120.00
16 Curtis Joseph/219 50.00 100.00
17 Alexander Mogilny/161 40.00 80.00
18 Gary Roberts/243 40.00 80.00
19 Markus Naslund/231 40.00 80.00
20 Jaromir Jagr/182 60.00 120.00

2002-03 McDonald's Pacific Jersey Patches Gold

5 Dominik Hasek/39 125.00 250.00
6 Mike Comrie/89 150.00 300.00
9 Martin Brodeur/30 150.00 300.00
11 Eric Lindros/88 125.00 250.00
13 Adam Oates/77 75.00 150.00
14 Mario Lemieux/66 200.00 400.00
15 Chris Pronger/44 75.00 150.00
16 Curtis Joseph/31 125.00 250.00
17 Alexander Mogilny/89 60.00 120.00
20 Jaromir Jagr/68 150.00 300.00

2002-03 McDonald's Pacific Salt Lake Gold

COMPLETE SET (10) 5.00 10.00
1 M.Brodeur
C.Joseph
E.Belfour .40 1.00
2 A.Foote
R.Blake
S.Niedermayer .25 .60
3 E.Jovanovski
C.Pronger
A.MacInnis .25 .60
4 R.Smyth
E.Brewer .25 .60
5 B.Shanahan
S.Yzerman 1.25 3.00
6 E.Lindros
T.Fleury .30 .75
7 P.Kariya
J.Nieuwendyk .25 .60
8 J.Iginla
O.Nolan .25 .60
9 J.Sakic
M.Peca .25 .60
10 M.Lemieux
S.Gagne 1.25 3.00

2003-04 McDonald's Pacific

COMP.SET w/o SP's (55) 12.00 25.00
COMP.SET w/CL's (65) 15.00 30.00
COMP.MASTER SET (89) 50.00 100.00
1 Jean-Sebastien Giguere .25 .60
2 Dany Heatley .40 1.00
3 Ilya Kovalchuk .40 1.00
4 Joe Thornton .50 1.25
5 Martin Biron .25 .60
6 Chris Drury .25 .60
7 Jarome Iginla .40 1.00
8 Chuck Kobasew .12 .30
9 Jocelyn Thibault .25 .60
10 Peter Forsberg .60 1.50
11 Milan Hejduk .30 .75
12 Paul Kariya .30 .75
13 Joe Sakic .60 1.50
14 Rick Nash .40 1.00
15 Mike Modano .50 1.25
16 Marty Turco .25 .60
17 Sergei Fedorov .40 1.00
18 Curtis Joseph .30 .75
19 Steve Yzerman 1.25 3.00
20 Henrik Zetterberg .40 .75
21 Mike Comrie .25 .60
22 Georges Laraque .12 .30
23 Ryan Smyth .12 .30
24 Jay Bouwmeester .12 .30
25 Roberto Luongo .40 1.00
26 Marian Gaborik .50 1.25
27 Marcel Hossa .30 .75
28 Saku Koivu .30 .75
29 Jose Theodore .40 1.00
30 Martin Brodeur 1.00 2.50
31 Scott Stevens .25 .60
32 Michael Peca .12 .30
33 Eric Lindros .30 .75
34 Mark Messier .30 .75
35 Daniel Alfredsson .25 .60
36 Marian Hossa .30 .75
37 Patrick Lalime .25 .60
38 Simon Gagne .30 .75
39 Jeremy Roenick .40 1.00
40 Sean Burke .25 .60
41 Mario Lemieux 2.00 4.00
42 Barret Jackman .25 .60
43 Peter Sejna .30 .75
44 Vincent Lecavalier .30 .75
45 Martin St. Louis .25 .60
46 Ed Belfour .30 .75
47 Tie Domi .25 .60
48 Owen Nolan .25 .60
49 Matt Stajan .30 .75
50 Mats Sundin .30 .75
51 Todd Bertuzzi .30 .75
52 Ed Jovanovski .25 .60
53 Brendan Morrison .25 .60
54 Markus Naslund .30 .75
55 Jaromir Jagr .50 1.25
56 Eric Staal AU 175.00 300.00
57 Tuomo Ruutu AU 100.00 200.00
58 Nathan Horton AU 100.00 200.00
59 Chris Higgins AU 75.00 150.00
60 Jordin Tootoo AU 100.00 200.00
61 Marc-Andre Fleury AU 80.00 200.00

2003-04 McDonald's Pacific Canadian Pride

COMPLETE SET (6) 12.00 25.00
1 Dany Heatley 1.50 4.00
2 Joe Thornton 2.00 5.00
3 Rick Nash 2.00 5.00
4 Jay Bouwmeester 1.25 3.00
5 Jason Spezza 2.00 5.00
6 Vincent Lecavalier 1.25 3.00

2003-04 McDonald's Pacific Etched in Time

COMPLETE SET (6) 12.00 25.00
1 Joe Sakic 2.50 6.00
2 Brett Hull 1.50 4.00
3 Steve Yzerman 4.00 10.00
4 Mark Messier 1.50 4.00
5 Mario Lemieux 5.00 12.00
6 Jaromir Jagr 2.50 6.00

2003-04 McDonald's Pacific Hockey Roots Checklists

COMPLETE SET (10) 3.00 6.00
1 Dany Heatley .25 .60
2 Joe Thornton .25 .60
3 Jarome Iginla .30 .75
4 Rob Blake .30 .75
5 Paul Kariya .25 .60
6 Rick Nash .25 .60
7 Jeff Friesen .25 .60
8 Vincent Lecavalier .30 .75
9 Brad Richards .30 .75
10 Gary Roberts .25 .60

2003-04 McDonald's Pacific Patches Silver

UNLISTED STARS 40.00 100.00
COMMON CARD (1-25) 40.00 100.00
1 Paul Kariya 40.00 100.00
2 Dany Heatley 40.00 100.00
3 Joe Thornton 60.00 120.00
4 Jarome Iginla 40.00 100.00
5 Peter Forsberg 40.00 100.00
6 Ilya Kovalchuk 50.00 125.00
7 Joe Sakic 60.00 120.00
8 Mike Modano 40.00 100.00
9 Marty Turco 40.00 100.00
10 Brendan Shanahan 40.00 100.00
11 Steve Yzerman 60.00 120.00
12 Mike Comrie 40.00 100.00
13 Ryan Smyth 40.00 100.00
14 Saku Koivu 40.00 100.00
15 Jose Theodore 40.00 100.00
16 Martin Brodeur 60.00 150.00
17 Marian Hossa 40.00 100.00
18 Patrick Lalime 40.00 100.00
19 Jason Spezza 60.00 120.00
20 Mario Lemieux 60.00 120.00
21 Vincent Lecavalier 40.00 100.00
22 Ed Belfour 60.00 120.00
23 Mats Sundin 40.00 100.00
24 Todd Bertuzzi 40.00 100.00
25 Markus Naslund 40.00 100.00

2003-04 McDonald's Pacific Patches Gold

*GOLD: 1X TO 2X SILVER JSY

2003-04 McDonald's Pacific Patches and Sticks

COMMON CARD (1-25) 60.00 150.00
UNLISTED STARS 100.00 200.00
*PATCH/STK: .8X TO 2X BASE JSY
1 Paul Kariya 125.00 250.00
2 Dany Heatley 125.00 250.00
3 Joe Thornton 150.00 400.00
4 Jarome Iginla 150.00 400.00
5 Peter Forsberg 125.00 250.00
6 Ilya Kovalchuk 125.00 250.00
7 Joe Sakic 150.00 400.00
8 Mike Modano 100.00 200.00
9 Marty Turco 100.00 200.00
10 Brendan Shanahan 100.00 200.00
11 Steve Yzerman 150.00 400.00
12 Mike Comrie 60.00 150.00
13 Ryan Smyth 100.00 200.00
14 Saku Koivu 100.00 200.00
15 Jose Theodore 125.00 250.00
16 Martin Brodeur 200.00 400.00
17 Marian Hossa 125.00 250.00
18 Patrick Lalime 100.00 200.00
19 Jason Spezza 150.00 400.00
20 Mario Lemieux 250.00 500.00
21 Vincent Lecavalier 125.00 250.00
22 Ed Belfour 150.00 300.00
23 Mats Sundin 100.00 200.00
24 Todd Bertuzzi 125.00 250.00
25 Markus Naslund 125.00 250.00

2003-04 McDonald's Pacific Net Fusions

COMPLETE SET (6) 10.00 20.00
1 Jean-Sebastien Giguere 1.25 3.00
2 Curtis Joseph 1.50 4.00
3 Roberto Luongo 1.50 4.00
4 Jose Theodore 1.50 4.00
5 Martin Brodeur 2.00 5.00
6 Ed Belfour 1.50 4.00

2003-04 McDonald's Pacific Saturday Night Rivals

COMPLETE SET (1-6) 8.00 15.00
UNLISTED STARS 2.00 5.00
1 J.Iginla/M.Comrie 1.50 4.00
2 T.Bertuzzi/R.Smyth 1.50 4.00
3 B.Morrison/C.Conroy 1.25 3.00
4 M.Sundin/S.Koivu 2.00 5.00
5 P.Lalime/E.Belfour 2.00 5.00
6 Mar.Hossa/Marc.Hossa 2.00 5.00

2005-06 McDonald's Upper Deck

COMPLETE SET (51) 15.00 40.00
1 Jay Bouwmeester .25 .60
2 Eric Lindros .60 1.50
3 Sergei Fedorov .60 1.50
4 Vincent Lecavalier .40 1.00
5 Miikka Kiprusoff .40 1.00
6 Scott Niedermayer .40 1.00
7 Chris Pronger .40 1.00
8 Joe Thornton .60 1.50
9 Rick Nash .40 1.00
10 Saku Koivu .40 1.00
11 Wade Redden .25 .60
12 Mats Sundin .40 1.00
13 Jason Smith .25 .60
14 Tuomo Ruutu .40 1.00
15 Olaf Kolzig .40 1.00
16 Simon Gagne .40 1.00
17 Brendan Shanahan .40 1.00
18 Jean-Sebastien Giguere .40 1.00
19 Roberto Luongo .60 1.50
20 Michael Ryder .30 .75
21 Ed Jovanovski .30 .75
22 Daniel Briere .40 1.00
23 Jarome Iginla .50 1.25
24 Joe Sakic .75 2.00
25 Dany Heatley .30 .75
26 Steve Yzerman 1.00 2.50
27 Mike Ribeiro .25 .60
28 Mario Lemieux 1.50 4.00
29 Brendan Morrison .25 .60
30 Brad Richards .40 1.00
31 Luc Robitaille .40 1.00
32 Daniel Alfredsson .40 1.00
33 Andrew Raycroft .30 .75
34 Eric Staal .50 1.25
35 Jose Theodore .40 1.00
36 Jaromir Jagr 1.25 3.00
37 Jeremy Roenick .60 1.50
38 Martin St. Louis .40 1.00
39 Ed Belfour .40 1.00
40 Mike Modano .60 1.50
41 Marian Hossa .40 1.00
42 Ilya Kovalchuk .40 1.00
43 Jonathan Cheechoo .30 .75
44 Ryan Smyth .30 .75
45 Peter Forsberg .75 2.00
46 Shean Donovan .25 .60
47 Marian Gaborik .40 1.00
48 Martin Brodeur 1.00 2.50
49 Bryan McCabe .25 .60
50 Markus Naslund .40 1.00
51 Sidney Crosby 8.00 20.00

2005-06 McDonald's Upper Deck Autographs

COMMON CARD
MA1 Wayne Gretzky 500.00 1200.00
MA2 Markus Naslund 50.00 125.00
MA3 Joe Thornton 100.00 200.00
MA4 Dominik Hasek 100.00 200.00
MA5 Jarome Iginla 125.00 250.00
MA6 Martin Brodeur 250.00 400.00
MA7 Rick Nash 125.00 250.00
MA8 Jose Theodore 150.00 300.00
MA9 Mats Sundin 150.00 300.00

2005-06 McDonald's Upper Deck Chasing the Cup

CC1 Simon Gagne 30.00 60.00
CC2 Jose Theodore 40.00 80.00
CC3 Jarome Iginla 40.00 80.00
CC4 Markus Naslund 40.00 80.00
CC5 Jason Spezza 50.00 100.00
CC6 Mats Sundin 50.00 100.00
CC7 Joe Thornton 60.00 120.00
CC8 Ilya Kovalchuk 50.00 100.00

2005-06 McDonald's Upper Deck CHL Graduates

COMPLETE SET (6) 2.00 4.00
CG1 Joe Sakic .50 1.25
CG2 Jarome Iginla .30 .75
CG3 Wade Redden .25 .60
CG4 Vincent Lecavalier .25 .60
CG5 Joe Thornton .40 1.00
CG6 Rick Nash .30 .75

2005-06 McDonald's Upper Deck Goalie Factory

COMPLETE SET (15) 20.00 50.00
GF1 Dominik Hasek 3.00 8.00
GF2 Roberto Luongo 2.50 6.00
GF3 Martin Brodeur 4.00 10.00
GF4 Marty Turco 2.00 5.00
GF5 Miikka Kiprusoff 2.00 5.00
GF6 Jean-Sebastien Giguere 2.00 5.00
GF7 Tomas Vokoun 2.00 5.00
GF8 Dan Cloutier 2.00 5.00
GF9 Jose Theodore 2.00 5.00
GF10 Nikolai Khabibulin 2.00 5.00
GF11 Marc-Andre Fleury 2.50 6.00
GF12 Kari Lehtonen 2.00 5.00
GF13 Ed Belfour 2.00 5.00
GF14 Curtis Joseph 2.00 5.00
GF15 Andrew Raycroft 2.00 5.00

2005-06 McDonald's Upper Deck Goalie Gear

MG1 Marc-Andre Fleury 125.00 250.00
MG2 Jocelyn Thibault 60.00 150.00
MG3 Roberto Luongo 75.00 200.00
MG4 Rick DiPietro 60.00 150.00
MG5 Olaf Kolzig 100.00 200.00
MG6 Jose Theodore 75.00 150.00
MG7 Andrew Raycroft 60.00 150.00
MG8 Marty Turco 60.00 150.00
MG9 Dominik Hasek 125.00 250.00
MG10 Ed Belfour 125.00 250.00
MG11 Chris Osgood 60.00 150.00
MG12 Curtis Joseph 40.00 100.00

2005-06 McDonald's Upper Deck Jerseys

MJ1 Mario Lemieux 125.00 250.00
MJ2 Joe Thornton 75.00 200.00
MJ3 Mats Sundin 60.00 150.00
MJ4 Markus Naslund 60.00 150.00
MJ5 Dany Heatley 60.00 150.00
MJ6 Martin Brodeur 150.00 300.00
MJ7 Steve Yzerman 150.00 300.00
MJ8 Saku Koivu 60.00 150.00
MJ9 Jose Theodore 75.00 150.00
MJ10 Ed Belfour 100.00 200.00
MJ11 Jarome Iginla 125.00 250.00
MJ12 Jason Spezza 75.00 150.00
MJ13 Martin Havlat 40.00 100.00
MJ14 Sergei Fedorov 75.00 150.00
MJ15 Jeremy Roenick 50.00 120.00

2005-06 McDonald's Upper Deck Next Generation

COMPLETE SET (15) 20.00 50.00
NG1 Andrew Raycroft 2.50 6.00
NG2 Rick Nash 3.00 8.00
NG3 Marc-Andre Fleury 3.00 8.00
NG4 Nikolai Zherdev 2.00 5.00
NG5 Tuomo Ruutu 2.00 5.00
NG6 Jonathan Cheechoo 2.50 6.00
NG7 Kari Lehtonen 2.50 6.00
NG8 Jason Spezza 3.00 8.00
NG9 Alexander Frolov 2.00 5.00
NG10 Stephen Weiss 2.50 6.00
NG11 Patrice Bergeron 2.50 6.00
NG12 Derek Roy 2.00 5.00
NG13 Eric Staal 3.00 8.00
NG14 Michael Ryder 2.50 6.00
NG15 Matthew Lombardi 2.00 5.00

2005-06 McDonald's Upper Deck Superstar Spotlight

COMPLETE SET (10) 30.00 60.00
COMMON CARD (SS1-SS10) 1.50 4.00
SS1 Mario Lemieux 6.00 15.00
SS2 Joe Thornton 2.50 6.00
SS3 Mats Sundin 1.50 4.00
SS4 Jarome Iginla 2.00 5.00
SS5 Martin Brodeur 5.00 12.00
SS6 Jose Theodore 2.00 5.00
SS7 Martin St. Louis 1.50 4.00
SS8 Joe Sakic 3.00 8.00
SS9 Steve Yzerman 5.00 12.00
SS10 Vincent Lecavalier 1.50 4.00

2005-06 McDonald's Upper Deck Top Scorers

COMPLETE SET (15) 100.00 175.00
TS1 Wayne Gretzky 15.00 40.00
TS2 Martin St. Louis 4.00 10.00
TS3 Joe Sakic 8.00 25.00
TS4 Mario Lemieux 10.00 25.00
TS5 Peter Forsberg 8.00 20.00
TS6 Steve Yzerman 12.00 30.00
TS7 Mike Modano 8.00 20.00
TS8 Mike Ribeiro 4.00 10.00
TS9 Mats Sundin 6.00 15.00
TS10 Markus Naslund 6.00 15.00
TS11 Jarome Iginla 8.00 20.00
TS12 Daniel Alfredsson 6.00 15.00
TS13 Ilya Kovalchuk 6.00 15.00
TS14 Rick Nash 8.00 20.00
TS15 Joe Thornton 8.00 20.00

2006-07 McDonald's Upper Deck

COMPLETE SET (56) 15.00 40.00
1 Teemu Selanne 1.00 2.50
2 Ilya Kovalchuk .50 1.25
3 Patrice Bergeron .60 1.50
4 Ryan Miller .50 1.25
5 Jarome Iginla .60 1.50
6 Miikka Kiprusoff .50 1.25
7 Dion Phaneuf .40 1.00
8 Eric Staal .60 1.50
9 Nikolai Khabibulin .50 1.25
10 Joe Sakic 1.00 2.50
11 Milan Hejduk .40 1.00
12 Rick Nash .50 1.25
13 Mike Modano .75 2.00
14 Marty Turco .50 1.25
15 Steve Yzerman 1.25 3.00
16 Brendan Shanahan .50 1.25
17 Jarret Stoll .40 1.00
18 Ales Hemsky .40 1.00
19 Ryan Smyth .40 1.00
20 Jay Bouwmeester .30 .75
21 Alexander Frolov .30 .75
22 Marian Gaborik .50 1.25
23 Saku Koivu .50 1.25
24 Michael Ryder .30 .75
25 Mike Ribeiro .30 .75
26 Paul Kariya .50 1.25
27 Martin Brodeur 1.25 3.00
28 Miroslav Satan .40 1.00
29 Jaromir Jagr 1.50 4.00
30 Henrik Lundqvist 1.25 3.00
31 Jason Spezza .50 1.25
32 Dany Heatley .40 1.00
33 Daniel Alfredsson .50 1.25
34 Peter Forsberg 1.00 2.50
35 Simon Gagne .50 1.25
36 Shane Doan .40 1.00
37 Marc-Andre Fleury 1.00 2.50
38 Joe Thornton .75 2.00
39 Jonathan Cheechoo .50 1.25
40 Keith Tkachuk .50 1.25
41 Brad Richards .50 1.25
42 Martin St. Louis .50 1.25
43 Vincent Lecavalier .50 1.25
44 Darcy Tucker .40 1.00
45 Mats Sundin .50 1.25
46 Alexander Steen .30 .75
47 Markus Naslund .50 1.25
48 Ed Jovanovski .40 1.00
49 Brendan Morrison .30 .75
50 Alexander Ovechkin 2.00 5.00
51 Saku Koivu CL .75 2.00
52 Mats Sundin CL .75 2.00
53 Jarome Iginla CL 1.00 2.50
54 Markus Naslund CL .75 2.00
55 Daniel Alfredsson CL .75 2.00
56 Jason Smith CL .50 1.25

2006-07 McDonald's Upper Deck Autographs

AAH Ales Hemsky 125.00 250.00
AAT Alex Tanguay 75.00 150.00
ABM Bryan McCabe 75.00 150.00
ADP Dion Phaneuf 100.00 175.00
AES Eric Staal 100.00 200.00
AHL Henrik Lundqvist 125.00 250.00
AHZ Henrik Zetterberg 125.00 250.00
AIK Ilya Kovalchuk 125.00 300.00
AJC Jonathan Cheechoo 100.00 200.00
AJI Jarome Iginla 125.00 250.00
AKD Kris Draper 100.00 175.00
ALR Luc Robitaille 100.00 200.00
AMF Marc-Andre Fleury 125.00 250.00
AMK Miikka Kiprusoff 100.00 200.00
AMN Markus Naslund 100.00 200.00
AMP Michael Peca 75.00 150.00
AMR Michael Ryder 75.00 150.00
AMT Marty Turco 60.00 125.00
APB Patrice Bergeron 75.00 150.00
APM Patrick Marleau 75.00 150.00
ARL Roberto Luongo 150.00 250.00
ARM Ryan Miller 125.00 225.00
ARN Rick Nash 125.00 225.00
ARS Ryan Smyth 100.00 200.00
ASH Shawn Horcoff 75.00 150.00

2006-07 McDonald's Upper Deck Clear Cut Winners

COMPLETE SET (10) 300.00 400.00
CC1 Joe Sakic 20.00 50.00
CC2 Jarome Iginla 20.00 50.00
CC3 Rick Nash 15.00 40.00
CC4 Eric Staal 15.00 40.00
CC5 Saku Koivu 20.00 50.00
CC6 Martin Brodeur 20.00 50.00
CC7 Dany Heatley 15.00 40.00
CC8 Joe Thornton 15.00 40.00
CC9 Mats Sundin 15.00 40.00
CC10 Ryan Smyth 15.00 40.00

2006-07 McDonald's Upper Deck Hardware Heroes

COMPLETE SET (10) 15.00 40.00
HH1 Joe Thornton 5.00 12.00
HH2 Alexander Ovechkin 6.00 15.00
HH3 Nicklas Lidstrom 2.50 6.00
HH4 Martin Brodeur 5.00 12.00
HH5 Cam Ward 3.00 8.00
HH6 Miikka Kiprusoff 4.00 10.00
HH7 Jonathan Cheechoo 2.50 6.00
HH8 Eric Staal 3.00 8.00
HH9 Ryan Smyth 3.00 8.00
HH10 Rod Brind'Amour 2.50 6.00

2006-07 McDonald's Upper Deck Hot Gloves

COMPLETE SET (10) 20.00 50.00
HG1 Martin Brodeur 5.00 12.00
HG2 Dominik Hasek 5.00 12.00
HG3 Dwayne Roloson 2.50 6.00
HG4 Miikka Kiprusoff 5.00 12.00
HG5 Cristobal Huet 2.50 6.00
HG6 Jean-Sebastien Giguere 3.00 8.00
HG7 Roberto Luongo 3.00 8.00
HG8 Marty Turco 2.50 6.00
HG9 Marc-Andre Fleury 4.00 10.00
HG10 Henrik Lundqvist 4.00 10.00

2006-07 McDonald's Upper Deck Jerseys

JAH Ales Hemsky 30.00 80.00
JAO Alexander Ovechkin 75.00 150.00
JAT Alex Tanguay 30.00 80.00
JBS Brendan Shanahan 50.00 120.00
JCP Chris Pronger 30.00 80.00
JDH Dany Heatley 50.00 120.00
JDT Darcy Tucker 25.00 60.00
JES Eric Staal 30.00 80.00
JHZ Henrik Zetterberg 75.00 150.00
JIK Ilya Kovalchuk 50.00 120.00
JJG Jean-Sebastien Giguere 40.00 100.00
JJI Jarome Iginla 50.00 120.00
JJJ Jaromir Jagr 50.00 120.00
JJS Joe Sakic 50.00 120.00
JJT Joe Thornton 40.00 100.00
JMB Martin Brodeur 60.00 150.00
JMK Miikka Kiprusoff 40.00 100.00
JMN Markus Naslund 40.00 100.00
JMR Michael Ryder 25.00 60.00
JMS Mats Sundin 40.00 100.00
JMT Marty Turco 30.00 80.00
JPB Patrice Bergeron 40.00 100.00
JPF Peter Forsberg 30.00 80.00
JPK Paul Kariya 40.00 100.00
JRL Roberto Luongo 30.00 80.00
JRN Rick Nash 40.00 100.00
JSC Brad Richards 50.00 120.00
JSK Saku Koivu 40.00 100.00
JSP Jason Spezza 30.00 80.00
JVL Vincent Lecavalier 50.00 100.00

2006-07 McDonald's Upper Deck Rookie Review

COMPLETE SET (15) 10.00 25.00
RR1 Kyle Wellwood 1.50 4.00
RR2 Alexander Ovechkin 5.00 12.00
RR3 Henrik Lundqvist 2.50 6.00
RR4 Dion Phaneuf 2.50 6.00
RR5 Alexander Steen 1.50 4.00
RR6 Thomas Vanek 2.00 5.00
RR7 Corey Perry 2.00 5.00
RR8 Andrej Meszaros 1.50 4.00
RR9 Jeff Carter 2.00 5.00
RR10 Patrick Eaves 1.50 4.00
RR11 Ryan Miller 2.00 5.00
RR12 Marek Svatos 1.50 4.00
RR13 Brad Boyes 1.50 4.00
RR14 Chris Higgins 2.00 5.00
RR15 Cam Ward 2.00 5.00

2007-08 McDonald's Upper Deck

COMPLETE SET (50) 10.00 25.00
1 Alexander Ovechkin 2.00 5.00
2 Markus Naslund .50 1.25
3 Roberto Luongo .75 2.00
4 Daniel Sedin .60 1.50
5 Mats Sundin .50 1.25
6 Bryan McCabe .30 .75
7 Darcy Tucker .40 1.00
8 Vincent Lecavalier .50 1.25
9 Martin St. Louis .50 1.25
10 Doug Weight .50 1.25
11 Joe Thornton .75 2.00
12 Jonathan Cheechoo .40 1.00
13 Marc-Andre Fleury 1.00 2.50
14 Jordan Staal .40 1.00
15 Evgeni Malkin 1.00 2.50
16 Shane Doan .40 1.00
17 Simon Gagne .50 1.25
18 Dany Heatley .40 1.00
19 Ray Emery .40 1.00
20 Jason Spezza .50 1.25
21 Jaromir Jagr 1.50 4.00
22 Henrik Lundqvist 1.25 3.00
23 Rick DiPietro .40 1.00
24 Martin Brodeur 1.25 3.00
25 Alexander Radulov .50 1.25
26 Saku Koivu .50 1.25
27 Guillaume Latendresse .40 1.00
28 Cristobal Huet .40 1.00
29 Marian Gaborik .75 2.00
30 Anze Kopitar .75 2.00
31 Nathan Horton .50 1.25
32 Ales Hemsky .40 1.00
33 Dwayne Roloson .40 1.00
34 Rob Schremp RC .40 1.00
35 Nicklas Lidstrom .50 1.25
36 Henrik Zetterberg .60 1.50
37 Pavel Datsyuk .75 2.00
38 Marty Turco .50 1.25
39 Rick Nash .50 1.25
40 Joe Sakic 1.00 2.50
41 Martin Havlat .50 1.25
42 Eric Staal .60 1.50
43 Jarome Iginla .60 1.50
44 Miikka Kiprusoff .50 1.25
45 Dion Phaneuf .40 1.00
46 Thomas Vanek .40 1.00
47 Ryan Miller .50 1.25
48 Patrice Bergeron .60 1.50
49 Marian Hossa .50 1.25
50 Scott Niedermayer .50 1.25

2007-08 McDonald's Upper Deck Autographs

MAAH Ales Hemsky 80.00 200.00
MAAR Andrew Raycroft 80.00 200.00
MAAS Alexander Steen 60.00 150.00
MAAT Alex Tanguay 80.00 200.00
MABM Brendan Morrison 60.00 150.00
MACH Chris Higgins 60.00 150.00
MACW Cam Ward 100.00 250.00
MADB Daniel Briere 100.00 200.00
MADH Dany Heatley 150.00 300.00
MADR Dwayne Roloson 80.00 200.00
MAEC Erik Cole 60.00 150.00
MAEM Evgeni Malkin 150.00 300.00
MAES Eric Staal 120.00 250.00
MAGL Guillaume Latendresse 80.00 200.00
MAHC Cristobal Huet 80.00 200.00
MAJC Jonathan Cheechoo 80.00 200.00
MAJI Jarome Iginla 125.00 300.00
MAJS Jarret Stoll 80.00 200.00
MAKL Kari Lehtonen 80.00 200.00
MAMF Marc-Andre Fleury 150.00 300.00
MAMR Michael Ryder 60.00 150.00
MAMT Marty Turco 40.00 100.00
MAPM Patrick Marleau 100.00 250.00
MAPS Paul Stastny 80.00 200.00
MARL Roberto Luongo 150.00 300.00
MARN Rick Nash 100.00 250.00
MASK Saku Koivu 100.00 250.00
MAST Jordan Staal 150.00 300.00
MATV Thomas Vanek 80.00 200.00
MAWR Wade Redden 60.00 150.00

2007-08 McDonald's Upper Deck In the Crease

COMPLETE SET (6) 10.00 25.00
ICDH Dominik Hasek 3.00 8.00
ICMB Martin Brodeur 5.00 12.00
ICMF Marc-Andre Fleury 4.00 10.00
ICMK Miikka Kiprusoff 2.00 5.00
ICRL Roberto Luongo 3.00 8.00
ICRM Ryan Miller 2.00 5.00

2007-08 McDonald's Upper Deck Jerseys

MJAH Ales Hemsky 25.00 60.00
MJAO Alexander Ovechkin 75.00 150.00
MJAR Andrew Raycroft 25.00 60.00
MJAT Alex Tanguay 25.00 60.00
MJBS Brendan Shanahan 30.00 80.00
MJCH Cristobal Huet 25.00 60.00
MJDH Dany Heatley 25.00 60.00
MJDR Dwayne Roloson 25.00 60.00
MJEM Evgeni Malkin 100.00 200.00
MJES Eric Staal 40.00 100.00
MJIK Ilya Kovalchuk 30.00 80.00
MJJC Jonathan Cheechoo 25.00 60.00
MJJI Jarome Iginla 40.00 100.00
MJJS Joe Sakic 60.00 150.00
MJJT Joe Thornton 30.00 80.00
MJMB Martin Brodeur 40.00 100.00
MJMK Miikka Kiprusoff 30.00 80.00
MJMN Markus Naslund 30.00 80.00
MJMR Michael Ryder 20.00 50.00
MJMS Martin St. Louis 30.00 80.00
MJMT Marty Turco 30.00 80.00
MJPB Patrice Bergeron 40.00 100.00
MJPK Paul Kariya 30.00 80.00
MJRL Roberto Luongo 50.00 125.00
MJRN Rick Nash 30.00 80.00
MJSG Simon Gagne 30.00 80.00
MJSK Saku Koivu 30.00 80.00
MJSP Jason Spezza 30.00 80.00
MJSU Mats Sundin 30.00 80.00
MJVL Vincent Lecavalier 30.00 80.00

2007-08 McDonald's Upper Deck Pride of Canada

COMPLETE SET (6) 8.00 20.00
PC1 Joe Sakic 3.00 8.00
PC2 Rick Nash 1.50 4.00
PC3 Joe Thornton 2.50 6.00
PC4 Vincent Lecavalier 1.50 4.00
PC5 Eric Staal 2.00 5.00
PC6 Jarome Iginla 2.00 5.00

2007-08 McDonald's Upper Deck Season in Review

COMPLETE SET (6) 10.00 25.00
SR1 Evgeni Malkin 3.00 8.00
SR2 Mats Sundin 1.50 4.00
SR3 Mike Modano 2.00 5.00
SR4 Martin Brodeur 4.00 10.00
SR5 Roberto Luongo 2.50 6.00
SR6 Joe Sakic 3.00 8.00

2007-08 McDonald's Upper Deck Superstar Spotlight

COMPLETE SET (10) 15.00 40.00
SS1 Ray Emery 1.25 3.00
SS2 Joe Sakic 3.00 8.00
SS3 Alexander Ovechkin 6.00 15.00
SS4 Dany Heatley 1.25 3.00
SS5 Martin St. Louis 1.50 4.00
SS6 Jaromir Jagr 5.00 12.00
SS7 Jarome Iginla 2.00 5.00
SS8 Joe Thornton 2.50 6.00
SS9 Vincent Lecavalier 1.50 4.00
SS10 Teemu Selanne 3.00 8.00

2007-08 McDonald's Upper Deck Three Stars Checklists

COMPLETE SET (6) 1.00 2.50
CL1 Koivu/Ryder/Huet .20 .50
CL2 Sundin/Tucker/McCabe .20 .50
CL3 Spezza/Heatley/Emery .20 .50
CL4 Horcoff/Roloson/Hemsky .15 .40
CL5 Iginla/Kiprusoff/Phaneuf .25 .60
CL6 Naslund/Luongo/Sedin .30 .75

2008-09 McDonald's Upper Deck

COMPLETE SET (50) 8.00 20.00
1 Ryan Getzlaf .50 1.25
2 Teemu Selanne 1.00 2.50
3 Ilya Kovalchuk .50 1.25
4 Patrice Bergeron .60 1.50
5 Ryan Miller .50 1.25
6 Jarome Iginla .60 1.50
7 Miikka Kiprusoff .50 1.25
8 Dion Phaneuf .40 1.00
9 Eric Staal .60 1.50
10 Patrick Kane 1.00 2.50
11 Jonathan Toews .75 2.00
12 Paul Stastny .40 1.00
13 Peter Forsberg 1.00 2.50
14 Joe Sakic 1.00 2.50
15 Rick Nash .50 1.25
16 Marty Turco .50 1.25
17 Mike Modano .75 2.00
18 Henrik Zetterberg .60 1.50
19 Chris Osgood .50 1.25
20 Nicklas Lidstrom .50 1.25
21 Sam Gagner .30 .75
22 Ales Hemsky .40 1.00
23 Andrew Cogliano .30 .75
24 Anze Kopitar .75 2.00
25 Marian Gaborik .50 1.25
26 Carey Price 1.00 2.50
27 Saku Koivu .50 1.25
28 Alex Kovalev .40 1.00
29 Martin Brodeur 1.25 3.00
30 Rick DiPietro .40 1.00
31 Marc Staal .30 .75
32 Henrik Lundqvist 1.25 3.00
33 Dany Heatley .40 1.00
34 Daniel Alfredsson .50 1.25
35 Jason Spezza .50 1.25
36 Simon Gagne .50 1.25
37 Shane Doan .40 1.00
38 Jordan Staal .40 1.00
39 Evgeni Malkin 1.00 2.50
40 Marc-Andre Fleury 1.00 2.50
41 Joe Thornton .75 2.00
42 Paul Kariya .50 1.25
43 Vincent Lecavalier .50 1.25
44 Martin St. Louis .50 1.25
45 Mats Sundin .50 1.25
46 Vesa Toskala .60 1.50
47 Tomas Kaberle .30 .75

48 Roberto Luongo .75 2.00
49 Markus Naslund .50 1.25
50 Alexander Ovechkin 2.00 5.00

2008-09 McDonald's Upper Deck Gold

*GOLD: 10X TO 25X BASE

2008-09 McDonald's Upper Deck Autographs

AAC Andrew Cogliano 150.00 250.00
AAK Anze Kopitar 150.00 250.00
AAO Alexander Ovechkin 175.00 300.00
ADH Dany Heatley 125.00 200.00
AES Eric Staal 100.00 175.00
AHZ Henrik Zetterberg 250.00 400.00
AJT Jonathan Toews 200.00 350.00
AKE Phil Kessel 75.00 150.00
AMS Martin St. Louis 175.00 300.00
AMT Marty Turco 30.00 60.00
ANF Nick Foligno 125.00 200.00
APS Paul Stastny 150.00 250.00
ARM Ryan Miller 75.00 150.00
ASG Sam Gagner 100.00 200.00
ASK Saku Koivu 200.00 350.00
ATH Joe Thornton 100.00 200.00

2008-09 McDonald's Upper Deck Canadian Goalie Checklist

COMPLETE SET (6) 5.00 12.00
CLCGY Miikka Kiprusoff 1.00 2.50
CLEDM Mathieu Garon .75 2.00
CLMTL Carey Price 2.00 5.00
CLOTT Martin Gerber .75 2.00
CLTOR Vesa Toskala 1.25 3.00
CLVAN Roberto Luongo 1.50 4.00

2008-09 McDonald's Upper Deck Clear Path to Greatness

COMPLETE SET (14) 250.00 500.00
CP1 Joe Sakic 20.00 50.00
CP2 Alexander Ovechkin 15.00 40.00
CP3 Vincent Lecavalier 10.00 25.00
CP4 Dany Heatley 8.00 20.00
CP5 Ilya Kovalchuk 10.00 25.00
CP6 Joe Thornton 15.00 40.00
CP7 Jaromir Jagr 30.00 80.00
CP8 Martin Brodeur 15.00 40.00
CP9 Henrik Zetterberg 12.00 30.00
CP10 Markus Naslund 10.00 25.00
CP11 Mats Sundin 10.00 25.00
CP12 Jarome Iginla 12.00 30.00
CP13 Mike Modano 15.00 40.00
CP14 Evgeni Malkin 20.00 40.00

2008-09 McDonald's Upper Deck Jerseys

JAO Alexander Ovechkin 60.00 150.00
JBS Brendan Shanahan 15.00 40.00
JDA Daniel Alfredsson 15.00 40.00
JDH Dany Heatley 12.00 30.00
JDS Daniel Sedin 20.00 50.00
JEM Evgeni Malkin 30.00 80.00
JES Eric Staal 20.00 50.00
JGA Simon Gagne 15.00 40.00
JHZ Henrik Zetterberg 20.00 50.00
JIK Ilya Kovalchuk 15.00 40.00
JJI Jarome Iginla 20.00 50.00
JJJ Jaromir Jagr 50.00 120.00
JJS Joe Sakic 30.00 80.00
JJT Joe Thornton 25.00 60.00
JKA Patrick Kane 30.00 80.00
JMB Martin Brodeur 40.00 100.00
JMG Marian Gaborik 15.00 40.00
JMK Miikka Kiprusoff 15.00 40.00
JMM Mike Modano 25.00 60.00
JMS Mats Sundin 15.00 40.00
JNL Nicklas Lidstrom 15.00 40.00
JPF Peter Forsberg 30.00 80.00
JPK Paul Kariya 15.00 40.00
JRG Ryan Getzlaf 15.00 40.00
JRL Roberto Luongo 25.00 60.00
JRM Ryan Miller 15.00 40.00
JRN Rick Nash 15.00 40.00
JSG Sam Gagner 10.00 25.00
JSK Saku Koivu 15.00 40.00
JVL Vincent Lecavalier 15.00 40.00

2008-09 McDonald's Upper Deck Profiles

COMPLETE SET (10) 15.00 40.00
PRO1 Roberto Luongo 5.00 12.00
PRO2 Mats Sundin 3.00 8.00
PRO3 Jarome Iginla 4.00 10.00
PRO4 Dany Heatley 2.50 6.00
PRO5 Saku Koivu 3.00 8.00
PRO6 Vincent Lecavalier 3.00 8.00
PRO7 Martin Brodeur 8.00 20.00
PRO8 Alexander Ovechkin 12.00 30.00
PRO9 Nicklas Lidstrom 3.00 8.00
PRO10 Joe Thornton 5.00 12.00

2008-09 McDonald's Upper Deck Speed Skaters

COMPLETE SET (10) 30.00 60.00
SS1 Martin St. Louis 4.00 10.00
SS2 Paul Kariya 4.00 10.00
SS3 Teemu Selanne 8.00 20.00
SS4 Marian Hossa 4.00 10.00
SS5 Jaromir Jagr 12.00 30.00
SS6 Marian Gaborik 4.00 10.00
SS7 Simon Gagne 4.00 10.00
SS8 Ilya Kovalchuk 4.00 10.00
SS9 Alexander Ovechkin 15.00 40.00
SS10 Scott Niedermayer 4.00 10.00

2008-09 McDonald's Upper Deck Superstar Spotlight

COMPLETE SET (14) 20.00 50.00
IS1 Carey Price 4.00 10.00
IS2 Vincent Lecavalier 2.00 5.00
IS3 Jonathan Toews 3.00 8.00
IS4 Vesa Toskala 2.50 6.00
IS5 Miikka Kiprusoff 2.00 5.00
IS6 Joe Thornton 3.00 8.00
IS7 Pavel Datsyuk 3.00 8.00
IS8 Evgeni Malkin 4.00 10.00
IS9 Roberto Luongo 3.00 8.00
IS10 Jarome Iginla 2.50 6.00
IS11 Daniel Alfredsson 2.00 5.00
IS12 Jaromir Jagr 6.00 15.00
IS13 Alexander Ovechkin 8.00 20.00
IS14 Martin Brodeur 5.00 12.00

2009-10 McDonald's Upper Deck

COMPLETE SET (50) 8.00 20.00
1 Ryan Getzlaf .40 1.00
2 Ilya Kovalchuk .40 1.00
3 Tim Thomas .40 1.00
4 Marc Savard .25 .60
5 Thomas Vanek .30 .75
6 Ryan Miller .40 1.00
7 Jarome Iginla .50 1.25
8 Miikka Kiprusoff .40 1.00
9 Dion Phaneuf .30 .75
10 Eric Staal .50 1.25
11 Jonathan Toews .60 1.50
12 Patrick Kane .75 2.00
13 Paul Stastny .30 .75
14 Rick Nash .40 1.00
15 Steve Mason .30 .75
16 Marty Turco .40 1.00
17 Henrik Zetterberg .50 1.25
18 Pavel Datsyuk .60 1.50
19 Andrew Cogliano .25 .60
20 Sheldon Souray .25 .60
21 Ales Hemsky .30 .75
22 Drew Doughty .50 1.25
23 Niklas Backstrom .40 1.00
24 Carey Price .75 2.00
25 Andrei Markov .40 1.00
26 Saku Koivu .40 1.00
27 Shea Weber .30 .75
28 Martin Brodeur 1.00 2.50
29 Zach Parise .40 1.00
30 Rick DiPietro .30 .75
31 Henrik Lundqvist 1.00 2.50
32 Dany Heatley .30 .75
33 Jason Spezza .40 1.00
34 Daniel Alfredsson .40 1.00
35 Jeff Carter .30 .75
36 Mike Richards .30 .75
37 Shane Doan .30 .75
38 Evgeni Malkin .75 2.00
39 Marc-Andre Fleury .75 2.00
40 Joe Thornton .60 1.50
41 Patrick Marleau .40 1.00
42 Paul Kariya .40 1.00
43 Steven Stamkos .75 2.00
44 Vincent Lecavalier .40 1.00
45 Matt Stajan .25 .60
46 Luke Schenn .40 1.00
47 Ryan Kesler .40 1.00
48 Roberto Luongo .60 1.50
49 Alexander Ovechkin 1.50 4.00
50 Mike Green .30 .75

2009-10 McDonald's Upper Deck Checklists

COMPLETE SET (6) 2.50 6.00
CL1 Patrick Roy 1.00 2.50
CL2 Jarome Iginla .50 1.25
CL3 Roberto Luongo .60 1.50
CL4 Grant Fuhr .60 1.50
CL5 Jason Spezza .40 1.00
CL6 Doug Gilmour .50 1.25

2009-10 McDonald's Upper Deck Goaltending Greats

COMPLETE SET (6) 8.00 20.00
GG1 Carey Price 2.00 5.00
GG2 Roberto Luongo 1.50 4.00
GG3 Miikka Kiprusoff 1.00 2.50
GG4 Steve Mason .75 2.00
GG5 Marc-Andre Fleury 2.00 5.00
GG6 Martin Brodeur 2.50 6.00

2009-10 McDonald's Upper Deck Horizons

COMPLETE SET (14) 20.00 50.00
H1 Tim Thomas 2.00 5.00
H2 Jarome Iginla 2.50 6.00
H3 Jonathan Toews 3.00 8.00
H4 Henrik Zetterberg 2.50 6.00
H5 Andrew Cogliano 1.25 3.00
H6 Carey Price 4.00 10.00
H7 Henrik Lundqvist 5.00 12.00
H8 Dany Heatley 1.50 4.00
H9 Luke Schenn 2.00 5.00
H10 Roberto Luongo 3.00 8.00
H11 Drew Doughty 2.50 6.00
H12 Marty Turco 2.00 5.00
H13 Evgeni Malkin 4.00 10.00
H14 Alexander Ovechkin 8.00 20.00

2009-10 McDonald's Upper Deck In the Spotlight

COMPLETE SET (10) 100.00 200.00
IS1 Alexander Ovechkin 20.00 50.00
IS2 Evgeni Malkin 8.00 20.00
IS3 Joe Thornton 8.00 20.00
IS4 Jarome Iginla 6.00 15.00
IS5 Ilya Kovalchuk 6.00 15.00
IS6 Carey Price 10.00 25.00
IS7 Martin Brodeur 12.00 30.00
IS8 Steven Stamkos 10.00 25.00
IS9 Jonathan Toews 8.00 20.00
IS10 Vincent Lecavalier 5.00 12.00

2009-10 McDonald's Upper Deck Pride of Canada

COMPLETE SET (14) 75.00 150.00
PC1 Dany Heatley 5.00 12.00
PC2 Vincent Lecavalier 6.00 15.00
PC3 Jarome Iginla 8.00 20.00
PC4 Rick Nash 6.00 15.00
PC5 Mike Richards 5.00 12.00
PC6 Joe Thornton 10.00 25.00
PC7 Ryan Getzlaf 6.00 15.00
PC8 Mike Green 5.00 12.00
PC9 Jeff Carter 5.00 12.00
PC10 Jonathan Toews 10.00 25.00
PC11 Dion Phaneuf 5.00 12.00
PC12 Chris Pronger 6.00 15.00
PC13 Martin Brodeur 15.00 40.00
PC14 Roberto Luongo 10.00 25.00

2011-12 McDonald's Upper Deck Canadiens

COMPLETE SET (25)
*GOLD: 20X TO 50X BASIC CARDS
1 Alexei Emelin .30 .75
2 Andrei Kostitsyn .30 .75
3 Andrei Markov .25 .60
4 Brian Gionta .25 .60
5 Carey Price .75 2.00
6 Chris Campoli .25 .60
7 David Desharnais .25 .60
8 Erik Cole .25 .60
9 Hal Gill .25 .60
10 Tomas Kaberle .25 .60
11 Josh Gorges .25 .60
12 Lars Eller .25 .60
13 Max Pacioretty .40 1.00
14 Michael Cammalleri .30 .75
15 P.K. Subban .50 1.25
16 Peter Budaj .30 .75
17 Petteri Nokelainen .25 .60
18 Raphael Diaz .30 .75
19 Ryan White .25 .60
20 Scott Gomez .30 .75
21 Tomas Plekanec .25 .60
22 Travis Moen .25 .60
23 Yannick Weber .25 .60
24 Mathieu Darche .30 .75
25 Youppi mascot .25 .60

1906 McGill Men at Hockey Postcard

NNO McGill Men at Hockey Montreal 60.00 120.00

1995-96 Metal

1 Guy Hebert .12 .30
2 Paul Kariya .15 .40
3 Todd Krygier .10 .25
4 Steve Rucchin .12 .30
5 Oleg Tverdovsky .15 .40
6 Ray Bourque .25 .60
7 Blaine Lacher .12 .30
8 Shawn McEachern .10 .25
9 Cam Neely .15 .40
10 Adam Oates .15 .40
11 Kevin Stevens .12 .30
12 Donald Audette .12 .30
13 Randy Burridge .10 .25
14 Jason Dawe .10 .25
15 Dominik Hasek .25 .60
16 Pat LaFontaine .15 .40
17 Alexei Zhitnik .10 .25
18 Theo Fleury .20 .50
19 Phil Housley .12 .30
20 Trevor Kidd .12 .30
21 Joe Nieuwendyk .12 .30
22 Michael Nylander .10 .25
23 Ed Belfour .12 .30
24 Chris Chelios .15 .40
25 Joe Murphy .10 .25
26 Bernie Nicholls .12 .30
27 Patrick Poulin .10 .25
28 Jeremy Roenick .25 .60
29 Gary Suter .10 .25
30 Adam Deadmarsh .10 .25
31 Stephane Fiset .12 .30
32 Peter Forsberg .30 .75
33 Valeri Kamensky .12 .30
34 Claude Lemieux .15 .40
35 Sandis Ozolinsh .10 .25
36 Joe Sakic .30 .75
37 Greg Adams .10 .25
38 Dave Gagner .10 .25
39 Todd Harvey .10 .25
40 Derian Hatcher .12 .30
41 Kevin Hatcher .12 .30
42 Mike Modano .25 .60
43 Andy Moog .15 .40
44 Paul Coffey .15 .40
45 Sergei Fedorov .25 .60
46 Vladimir Konstantinov .12 .30
47 Slava Kozlov .12 .30
48 Nicklas Lidstrom .15 .40
49 Chris Osgood .15 .40
50 Keith Primeau .12 .30
51 Steve Yzerman .40 1.00
52 Jason Arnott .12 .30
53 Zdeno Ciger .12 .30
54 Todd Marchant .10 .25
55 David Oliver .10 .25
56 Bill Ranford .12 .30
57 Doug Weight .15 .40
58 Stu Barnes .10 .25
59 Jody Hull .10 .25
60 Scott Mellanby .12 .30
61 Rob Niedermayer .12 .30
62 John Vanbiesbrouck .15 .40
63 Sean Burke .10 .25
64 Andrew Cassels .10 .25
65 Nelson Emerson .10 .25
66 Geoff Sanderson .10 .25
67 Brendan Shanahan .15 .40
68 Glen Wesley .10 .25
69 Rob Blake .12 .30
70 Tony Granato .10 .25
71 Wayne Gretzky 1.00 2.50
72 Dimitri Khristich .10 .25
73 Yanic Perreault .10 .25
74 Rick Tocchet .12 .30
75 Benoit Brunet .10 .25
76 Vincent Damphousse .12 .30
77 Mark Recchi .20 .50
78 Patrick Roy .40 1.00
79 Brian Savage .10 .25
80 Pierre Turgeon .12 .30
81 Martin Brodeur .40 1.00
82 Neal Broten .12 .30
83 John MacLean .12 .30
84 Scott Niedermayer .15 .40
85 Scott Stevens .12 .30
86 Stephane Richer .15 .40
87 Esa Tikkanen .12 .30
88 Steve Thomas .10 .25
89 Wendel Clark .25 .60
90 Travis Green .12 .30
91 Kirk Muller .12 .30
92 Zigmund Palffy .15 .40
93 Mathieu Schneider .10 .25
94 Ray Ferraro .10 .25
95 Alexei Kovalev .12 .30
96 Brian Leetch .12 .30
97 Mark Messier .30 .75
98 Mike Richter .15 .40
99 Luc Robitaille .15 .40
100 Ulf Samuelsson .10 .25
101 Pat Verbeek .12 .30
102 Radek Bonk .10 .25
103 Don Beaupre .12 .30
104 Alexandre Daigle .10 .25
105 Steve Duchesne .10 .25
106 Dan Quinn .12 .30
107 Martin Straka .10 .25
108 Rod Brind'Amour .15 .40
109 Eric Desjardins .12 .30
110 Ron Hextall .15 .40
111 John LeClair .15 .40
112 Eric Lindros .25 .60
113 Mikael Renberg .12 .30
114 Chris Therien .10 .25
115 Tom Barrasso .12 .30
116 Ron Francis .20 .50
117 Jaromir Jagr .50 1.25
118 Mario Lemieux .60 1.50
119 Tomas Sandstrom .12 .30
120 Bryan Smolinski .10 .25
121 Sergei Zubov .12 .30
122 Shayne Corson .12 .30
123 Grant Fuhr .25 .60
124 Dale Hawerchuk .20 .50
125 Brett Hull .30 .75
126 Al MacInnis .20 .50
127 Chris Pronger .15 .40
128 Ulf Dahlen .10 .25
129 Jeff Friesen .10 .25
130 Arturs Irbe .12 .30
131 Craig Janney .10 .25
132 Andrei Nazarov .12 .30
133 Owen Nolan .15 .40
134 Ray Sheppard .12 .30
135 Brian Bradley .12 .30
136 Chris Gratton .10 .25
137 Roman Hamrlik .10 .25
138 Petr Klima .10 .25
139 Daren Puppa .12 .30
140 Alexander Selivanov .12 .30
141 Dave Andreychuk .15 .40
142 Mike Gartner .20 .50
143 Doug Gilmour .20 .50
144 Kenny Jonsson .15 .40
145 Larry Murphy .12 .30
146 Felix Potvin .25 .60
147 Mats Sundin .15 .40
148 Jeff Brown .12 .30
149 Pavel Bure .15 .40
150 Russ Courtnall .10 .25
151 Trevor Linden .15 .40
152 Kirk McLean .12 .30
153 Alexander Mogilny .12 .30
154 Roman Oksiuta .10 .25
155 Mike Ridley .10 .25
156 Peter Bondra .15 .40
157 Jim Carey .12 .30
158 Sylvain Cote .10 .25
159 Sergei Gonchar .10 .25
160 Keith Jones .12 .30
161 Joe Juneau .10 .25
162 Nikolai Khabibulin .12 .30
163 Igor Korolev .10 .25
164 Teppo Numminen .10 .25
165 Teemu Selanne .30 .75
166 Keith Tkachuk .15 .40
167 Darren Turcotte .10 .25
168 Alexei Zhamnov .15 .40
169 Daniel Alfredsson RC .75 2.00
170 Aki Berg RC .15 .40
171 Todd Bertuzzi RC .20 .50
172 Jason Bonsignore .10 .25
173 Byron Dafoe .12 .30
174 Eric Daze .30 .75
175 Shane Doan RC .50 1.25
176 Radek Dvorak RC .20 .50
177 Brian Holzinger RC .30 .75
178 Ed Jovanovski .15 .40
179 Chad Kilger RC .15 .40
180 Saku Koivu .15 .40
181 Darren Langdon RC .30 .75
182 Daymond Langkow RC .15 .40
183 Jere Lehtinen .12 .30
184 Kyle McLaren RC .10 .25
185 Marty Murray .15 .40
186 Jeff O'Neill .15 .40
187 Richard Park .15 .40
188 Deron Quint .12 .30
189 Marcus Ragnarsson RC .20 .50
190 Miroslav Satan RC .20 .50
191 Tommy Salo RC .25 .60
192 Jamie Storr .12 .30
193 Niklas Sundstrom .15 .40
194 Robert Svehla RC .10 .25
195 Denis Pederson .40 1.00
196 Antti Tormanen RC .10 .25
197 Brendan Witt .15 .40
198 Vitali Yachmenev .15 .40
199 Checklist (1-114) .05 .15
200 Checklist (115-200 inserts) UER .05 .15
NNO Joe Sakic EXCH .75 2.00
NNO Joe Sakic Coin Card 8.00 20.00

1995-96 Metal Heavy Metal

COMPLETE SET (12) 15.00 40.00
1 Pavel Bure 1.25 3.00
2 Sergei Fedorov 1.25 3.00
3 Theo Fleury .60 1.50
4 Wayne Gretzky 8.00 20.00
5 Brett Hull 1.25 3.00
6 Jaromir Jagr 2.00 5.00
7 Paul Kariya 1.25 3.00
8 Brian Leetch .60 1.50
9 Mario Lemieux 6.00 15.00
10 Mike Modano 2.00 5.00
11 Adam Oates .60 1.50
12 Joe Sakic 3.00 8.00

1995-96 Metal International Steel

COMPLETE SET (24) 15.00 30.00
1 Pavel Bure .60 1.50
2 Chris Chelios .40 1.00
3 Sergei Fedorov .75 2.00
4 Peter Forsberg 1.25 3.00
5 Wayne Gretzky 2.50 6.00
6 Roman Hamrlik .20 .50
7 Dominik Hasek 1.25 3.00
8 Brett Hull .75 2.00
9 Jaromir Jagr 1.00 2.50
10 Saku Koivu .60 1.50
11 Pat LaFontaine .40 1.00
12 Brian Leetch .40 1.00
13 Jere Lehtinen .40 1.00
14 Mario Lemieux 2.00 5.00
15 Alexander Mogilny .40 1.00
16 Mikael Renberg .20 .50
17 Jeremy Roenick .60 1.50
18 Joe Sakic 1.25 3.00
19 Teemu Selanne .60 1.50
20 Mats Sundin .60 1.50
21 Niklas Sundstrom .20 .50
22 Vitali Yachmenev .20 .50
23 Alexei Zhamnov .20 .50
24 Sergei Zubov .20 .50

1995-96 Metal Iron Warriors

COMPLETE SET (15) 20.00 40.00
1 Jason Arnott .60 1.50
2 Ed Belfour 1.25 3.00
3 Theo Fleury .60 1.50
4 Ron Francis .75 2.00
5 John LeClair .75 2.00
6 Claude Lemieux .60 1.50
7 Eric Lindros 2.00 5.00
8 Mark Messier 2.00 5.00
9 Cam Neely 2.00 5.00
10 Keith Primeau .60 1.50
11 Kevin Stevens .60 1.50
12 Scott Stevens .60 1.50
13 Brendan Shanahan 2.00 5.00
14 Keith Tkachuk 1.25 3.00
15 Rick Tocchet .75 2.00

1995-96 Metal Promo Panel

COMPLETE SHEET .75 2.00
1 Felix Potvin .40 1.00
2 Jeremy Roenick .30 .75
3 Theo Fleury .20 .50
4 Richard Park .08 .25
PAN Uncut Panel Felix Potvin Jeremy Roenick Theo Fleury Richard Park .75 2.00

1995-96 Metal Winners

COMPLETE SET (9) 8.00 20.00
1 Peter Forsberg 4.00 10.00
2 Saku Koivu 2.00 5.00
3 Alexei Kovalev .40 1.00
4 Eric Lindros 2.00 5.00
5 Alexander Mogilny .75 2.00
6 Tommy Salo .75 2.00
7 Brian Savage .40 1.00
8 Sergei Zubov .40 1.00
9 Alexei Zhamnov .40 1.00

1996-97 Metal Universe

1 Guy Hebert .12 .30
2 Paul Kariya .15 .40
3 Jari Kurri .15 .40
4 Roman Oksiuta .10 .25
5 Steve Rucchin .10 .25
6 Teemu Selanne .30 .75
7 Ray Bourque .25 .60
8 Kyle McLaren .10 .25
9 Adam Oates .15 .40
10 Bill Ranford .12 .30
11 Rick Tocchet .12 .30
12 Donald Audette .10 .25
13 Jason Dawe .10 .25
14 Dominik Hasek .25 .60
15 Pat LaFontaine .15 .40
16 Derek Plante .10 .25
17 Wayne Primeau .10 .25
18 Theo Fleury .30 .75
19 Dave Gagner .15 .40
20 Trevor Kidd .10 .25
21 James Patrick .10 .25
22 Robert Reichel .10 .25
23 German Titov .10 .25
24 Tony Amonte .12 .30
25 Ed Belfour .15 .40
26 Chris Chelios .15 .40
27 Eric Daze .12 .30
28 Gary Suter .10 .25
29 Alexei Zhamnov .12 .30
30 Adam Deadmarsh .10 .25
31 Adam Foote .10 .25
32 Peter Forsberg .30 .75
33 Valeri Kamensky .12 .30
34 Uwe Krupp .10 .25
35 Claude Lemieux .10 .25
36 Sandis Ozolinsh .10 .25
37 Patrick Roy .40 1.00
38 Joe Sakic .30 .75
39 Derian Hatcher .10 .25
40 Mike Modano .25 .60
41 Andy Moog .15 .40
42 Joe Nieuwendyk .12 .30
43 Pat Verbeek .10 .25
44 Sergei Zubov .12 .30
45 Sergei Fedorov .25 .60
46 Vladimir Konstantinov .12 .30
47 Slava Kozlov .10 .25
48 Nicklas Lidstrom .20 .50
49 Chris Osgood .15 .40
50 Brendan Shanahan .15 .40
51 Steve Yzerman .40 1.00
52 Jason Arnott .12 .30
53 Curtis Joseph .20 .50
54 Andrei Kovalenko .10 .25
55 Miroslav Satan .10 .25
56 Doug Weight .15 .40
57 Radek Dvorak .12 .30
58 Per Gustafsson RC .15 .40
59 Ed Jovanovski .12 .30
60 Scott Mellanby .12 .30
61 Rob Niedermayer .12 .30
62 Ray Sheppard .12 .30
63 Robert Svehla .10 .25
64 John Vanbiesbrouck .15 .40
65 Jeff Brown .10 .25
66 Sean Burke .10 .25
67 Paul Coffey .15 .40
68 Nelson Emerson .10 .25
69 Jeff O'Neill .10 .25
70 Keith Primeau .12 .30
71 Geoff Sanderson .12 .30
72 Aki Berg .10 .25
73 Rob Blake .15 .40
74 Stephane Fiset .12 .30
75 Dimitri Khristich .10 .25
76 Petr Klima .10 .25
77 Ed Olczyk .10 .25
78 Vitali Yachmenev .10 .25
79 Vincent Damphousse .12 .30
80 Saku Koivu .15 .40
81 Mark Recchi .20 .50
82 Stephane Richer .12 .30
83 Jocelyn Thibault .12 .30
84 Pierre Turgeon .12 .30
85 Dave Andreychuk .15 .40
86 Martin Brodeur .40 1.00
87 Scott Niedermayer .15 .40
88 Scott Stevens .15 .40
89 Petr Sykora .10 .25
90 Steve Thomas .10 .25
91 Todd Bertuzzi .15 .40
92 Travis Green .12 .30
93 Kenny Jonsson .10 .25
94 Bryan McCabe .10 .25
95 Zigmund Palffy .15 .40
96 Wayne Gretzky 1.00 2.50
97 Alexei Kovalev .12 .30
98 Brian Leetch .12 .30
99 Mark Messier .30 .75
100 Mike Richter .15 .40
101 Luc Robitaille .15 .40
102 Niklas Sundstrom .10 .25
103 Daniel Alfredsson .15 .40
104 Radek Bonk .10 .25
105 Alexandre Daigle .10 .25
106 Steve Duchesne .10 .25
107 Damian Rhodes .12 .30
108 Alexei Yashin .12 .30
109 Rod Brind'Amour .15 .40
110 Eric Desjardins .12 .30
111 Dale Hawerchuk .20 .50
112 Ron Hextall .15 .40
113 John LeClair .15 .40
114 Eric Lindros .25 .60
115 Mikael Renberg .12 .30
116 Mike Gartner .20 .50
117 Craig Janney .12 .30
118 Nikolai Khabibulin .12 .30
119 Dave Manson .10 .25
120 Teppo Numminen .10 .25
121 Jeremy Roenick .25 .60
122 Keith Tkachuk .15 .40
123 Oleg Tverdovsky .12 .30
124 Tom Barrasso .12 .30
125 Ron Francis .20 .50
126 Kevin Hatcher .10 .25
127 Jaromir Jagr .50 1.25
128 Mario Lemieux .60 1.50
129 Petr Nedved .12 .30
130 Shayne Corson .12 .30
131 Grant Fuhr .25 .60
132 Brett Hull .30 .75
133 Al MacInnis .20 .50
134 Joe Murphy .10 .25
135 Chris Pronger .15 .40
136 Kelly Hrudey .12 .30
137 Al Iafrate .10 .25
138 Bernie Nicholls .12 .30
139 Owen Nolan .15 .40
140 Marcus Ragnarsson .10 .25
141 Darren Turcotte .10 .25
142 Brian Bradley .10 .25
143 Dino Ciccarelli .15 .40
144 Chris Gratton .12 .30
145 Roman Hamrlik .10 .25
146 Daren Puppa .12 .30
147 Alexander Selivanov .10 .25
148 Wendel Clark .25 .60
149 Doug Gilmour .20 .50
150 Kirk Muller .10 .25
151 Larry Murphy .12 .30
152 Felix Potvin .25 .60
153 Mathieu Schneider .10 .25
154 Mats Sundin .15 .40
155 Pavel Bure .15 .40
156 Russ Courtnall .10 .25
157 Trevor Linden .15 .40
158 Kirk McLean .12 .30
159 Alexander Mogilny .12 .30
160 Esa Tikkanen .10 .25
161 Peter Bondra .15 .40
162 Jim Carey .15 .40
163 Sergei Gonchar .10 .25
164 Phil Housley .12 .30
165 Calle Johansson .12 .30
166 Joe Juneau .10 .25
167 Michal Pivonka .10 .25
168 Brendan Witt .10 .25
169 Nolan Baumgartner .10 .25
170 Bryan Berard .15 .40
171 Sergei Berezin RC .25 .60
172 Curtis Brown .10 .25
173 Jan Caloun RC .15 .40
174 Andreas Dackell RC .15 .40
175 Hnat Domenichelli .10 .25
176 Christian Dube .10 .25
177 Anders Eriksson .10 .25
178 Peter Ferraro .10 .25
179 Eric Fichaud .12 .30
180 Daniel Goneau RC .15 .40
181 Mike Grier RC .20 .50
182 Jarome Iginla .20 .50
183 Steve Kelly RC .12 .30
184 Jamie Langenbrunner .10 .25
185 Daymond Langkow .12 .30
186 Jay McKee RC .10 .25
187 Ethan Moreau RC .15 .40
188 Rem Murray RC .15 .40
189 Janne Niinimaa .15 .40
190 Wade Redden .10 .25
191 Ruslan Salei RC .15 .40
192 Jamie Storr .10 .25
193 Darren Van Impe .10 .25
194 Roman Vopat .10 .25
195 David Wilkie .10 .25
196 Landon Wilson .10 .25
197 Richard Zednik RC .20 .50
198 Dainius Zubrus RC .20 .50
199 Checklist (1-118) .05 .15
200 Checklist (119-200 inserts) .05 .15

1996-97 Metal Universe Armor Plate

COMPLETE SET (12) 30.00 80.00
*SUPER POWER: 2X TO 5X BASIC INSERTS
1 Ed Belfour 3.00 8.00
2 Martin Brodeur 8.00 20.00
3 Jim Carey 2.00 5.00
4 Dominik Hasek 6.00 15.00
5 Ron Hextall 2.50 6.00
6 Chris Osgood 3.00 8.00
7 Felix Potvin 6.00 15.00
8 Daren Puppa 2.00 5.00
9 Damian Rhodes 2.00 5.00
10 Mike Richter 3.00 8.00
11 Patrick Roy 12.00 30.00
12 John Vanbiesbrouck 3.00 8.00

1996-97 Metal Universe Cool Steel

COMPLETE SET (12) 25.00 50.00
*SUPER POWER: 1.5X TO 4X BASIC INSERTS
1 Chris Chelios 2.00 5.00
2 Peter Forsberg 3.00 8.00
3 Ron Francis 1.50 4.00
4 Dominik Hasek 4.00 10.00
5 Ed Jovanovski 1.50 4.00
6 Vladimir Konstantinov 1.50 4.00
7 Eric Lindros 3.00 10.00
8 Mark Messier 2.50 6.00
9 Patrick Roy 10.00 25.00
10 Brendan Shanahan 2.00 5.00
11 Keith Tkachuk 2.00 5.00
12 John Vanbiesbrouck 1.50 4.00

1996-97 Metal Universe Ice Carvings

COMPLETE SET (12) 30.00 60.00
*SUPER POWER: 1.5X TO 4X BASIC INSERTS
1 Martin Brodeur 6.00 15.00
2 Pavel Bure 4.00 10.00
3 Jim Carey 2.00 5.00
4 Paul Coffey 4.00 10.00
5 Sergei Fedorov 3.00 8.00
6 Jaromir Jagr 3.00 8.00
7 Paul Kariya 4.00 10.00
8 Pat LaFontaine 2.00 5.00
9 Brian Leetch 4.00 10.00
10 Mario Lemieux 10.00 25.00
11 Alexander Mogilny 2.00 5.00
12 Joe Sakic 4.00 10.00

1996-97 Metal Universe Lethal Weapons

COMPLETE SET (20) 20.00 50.00
*SUPER POWER: 1.5X TO 4X BASIC INSERTS
1 Peter Bondra 1.00 2.50
2 Pavel Bure 1.50 4.00
3 Sergei Fedorov 1.50 4.00
4 Peter Forsberg 2.50 6.00
5 Ron Francis 1.50 4.00
6 Wayne Gretzky 6.00 15.00
7 Brett Hull 1.25 3.00
8 Jaromir Jagr 1.50 4.00
9 Paul Kariya 1.50 4.00
10 John LeClair 1.50 4.00
11 Mario Lemieux 5.00 12.00
12 Eric Lindros 2.00 5.00
13 Mark Messier 1.50 4.00
14 Alexander Mogilny 1.00 2.50
15 Adam Oates 1.00 2.50
16 Joe Sakic 2.50 6.00
17 Teemu Selanne 1.50 4.00
18 Brendan Shanahan 1.50 4.00
19 Keith Tkachuk 1.50 4.00
20 Doug Weight 1.50 4.00

2020-21 Metal Universe

1 Mathew Barzal .60 1.50
2 Anze Kopitar .75 2.00
3 Seth Jones .50 1.25
4 Elias Pettersson .75 2.00
5 Colton Parayko .40 1.00
6 Mats Zuccarello .50 1.25
7 Brady Tkachuk .75 2.00
8 Alex Ovechkin 2.00 5.00
9 Jack Eichel .75 2.00
10 Artemi Panarin 1.00 2.50
11 Jonathan Huberdeau .60 1.50
12 Alex DeBrincat .60 1.50
13 Johnny Gaudreau .75 2.00
14 Jamie Benn .50 1.25
15 Dylan Larkin .60 1.50
16 Mitch Marner .75 2.00
17 Niklas Hjalmarsson .30 .75
18 Andrei Svechnikov .60 1.50
19 Matthew Tkachuk 1.00 2.50
20 Sebastian Aho .75 2.00
21 Jack Hughes 1.25 3.00
22 James van Riemsdyk .40 1.00
23 Brock Boeser .60 1.50
24 Phillip Danault .50 1.25
25 John Tavares .75 2.00
26 Blake Wheeler .50 1.25
27 Shea Theodore .60 1.50
28 Claude Giroux .50 1.25
29 Leon Draisaitl 1.50 4.00
30 Rasmus Dahlin .60 1.50
31 Carey Price 1.00 2.50
32 Elvis Merzlikins .50 1.25
33 Joe Pavelski .60 1.50
34 Auston Matthews 2.00 5.00
35 Quinn Hughes 1.25 3.00

36 John Gibson .50 1.25
37 Connor Hellebuyck 1.00 2.50
38 Patrice Bergeron .60 1.50
39 Keith Yandle .30 .75
40 Tuukka Rask .60 1.50
41 Jonathan Drouin .40 1.00
42 Mackenzie Blackwood .50 1.25
43 Jonathan Marchessault .60 1.50
44 Travis Konecny .50 1.25
45 Matt Dumba .30 .75
46 Philipp Grubauer .50 1.25
47 Zach Werenski .75 2.00
48 Tomas Hertl .50 1.25
49 John Klingberg .50 1.25
50 Jordan Binnington .75 2.00
51 Jake Guentzel .75 2.00
52 Andrei Vasilevskiy .75 2.00
53 Sergei Bobrovsky .75 2.00
54 Brayden Schenn .50 1.25
55 Mark Scheifele .75 2.00
56 Dominik Kubalik .50 1.25
57 Igor Shesterkin 1.00 2.50
58 Thomas Chabot .50 1.25
59 Roman Josi .50 1.25
60 Cale Makar 1.25 3.00
61 Mark Stone .60 1.50
62 Ryan Dzingel .40 1.00
63 Brad Marchand 1.00 2.50
64 Brayden Point .60 1.50
65 Anders Lee .40 1.00
66 Devan Dubnyk .40 1.00
67 Rickard Rakell .40 1.00
68 Teuvo Teravainen .50 1.25
69 Miro Heiskanen .60 1.50
70 Sean Monahan .30 .75
71 Evgeni Malkin 1.00 2.50
72 Drew Doughty .60 1.50
73 Patrick Kane 1.00 2.50
74 John Carlson .50 1.25
75 Tom Wilson .50 1.25
76 Anthony Mantha .40 1.00
77 Jonathan Toews .75 2.00
78 Pekka Rinne .50 1.25
79 Carter Hart .50 1.25
80 Josh Bailey .40 1.00
81 Kyle Connor .75 2.00
82 Aleksander Barkov .75 2.00
83 Matt Murray .50 1.25
84 Eric Staal .50 1.25
85 Brent Burns .50 1.25
86 Nikita Kucherov 1.00 2.50
87 Sidney Crosby 2.00 5.00
88 David Pastrnak 1.25 3.00
89 Jesperi Kotkaniemi .50 1.25
90 Ryan O'Reilly .50 1.25
91 Steven Stamkos 1.00 2.50
92 Nathan MacKinnon 2.00 5.00
93 Mika Zibanejad .60 1.50
94 Bo Horvat .60 1.50
95 Jean-Gabriel Pageau .30 .75
96 Mikko Rantanen 1.25 3.00
97 Connor McDavid 2.50 6.00
98 Evander Kane .50 1.25
99 Clayton Keller .60 1.50
100 Nico Hischier .75 2.00
101 Jason Robertson RC 3.00 8.00
102 Alexander Alexeyev RC 1.00 2.50
103 Alexander Barabanov RC 1.25 3.00
104 Nicolas Beaudin RC 1.25 3.00
105 Logan Stanley RC 1.25 3.00
106 Keegan Kolesar RC 1.00 2.50
107 Nick Robertson RC 2.00 5.00
108 Vitek Vanecek RC 2.00 5.00
109 Morgan Geekie RC 1.25 3.00
110 Kevin Lankinen RC 2.00 5.00
111 Tyler Benson RC 1.25 3.00
112 Ty Dellandrea RC 1.25 3.00
113 Mikey Anderson RC 1.25 3.00
114 Gabe Vilardi RC 2.00 5.00
115 Liam Foudy RC 1.25 3.00
116 Brandon Hagel RC 1.50 4.00
117 Alexander True RC 1.00 2.50
118 Pierre-Olivier Joseph RC 1.25 3.00
119 Victor Soderstrom RC 1.00 2.50
120 Bowen Byram RC 2.50 6.00
121 Calvin Thurkauf RC 1.00 2.50
122 Matiss Kivlenieks RC 1.50 4.00
123 Joel Kiviranta RC 1.25 3.00
124 Philipp Kurashev RC 1.50 4.00
125 Kirill Kaprizov RC 5.00 12.00
126 Michael DiPietro RC 1.50 4.00
127 Josh Norris RC 2.00 5.00
128 Kieffer Bellows RC 1.00 2.50
129 Martin Kaut RC 1.25 3.00
130 Peyton Krebs RC 2.00 5.00
131 Jake Evans RC 1.25 3.00
132 Mathias Brome RC 1.00 2.50
133 Philip Broberg RC 1.25 3.00
134 Nikolai Knyzhov RC 1.00 2.50
135 Timothy Liljegren RC 1.25 3.00
136 Olli Juolevi RC 1.25 3.00
137 Alexander Romanov RC 1.50 4.00
138 Connor McMichael RC 2.00 5.00
139 Ian Mitchell RC 1.00 2.50
140 Tim Stutzle RC 2.50 6.00
141 Ilya Sorokin RC 3.00 8.00
142 Nils Hoglander RC 1.25 3.00
143 Thomas Harley RC 2.00 5.00
144 Yegor Sharangovich RC 2.00 5.00
145 Dylan Cozens RC 2.00 5.00
146 Cal Foote RC 1.50 4.00
147 Pius Suter RC 1.50 4.00
148 K'Andre Miller RC 2.50 6.00
149 Ty Smith RC 2.00 5.00
150 Alexis Lafreniere RC 4.00 10.00
151 Shea Weber SKILL .50 1.25
152 Mathew Barzal SKILL .60 1.50
153 Jordan Binnington SKILL .75 2.00
154 Patrick Kane SKILL 1.00 2.50
155 Jaccob Slavin SKILL .40 1.00
156 Kris Letang AS .60 1.50
157 Anze Kopitar AS .75 2.00
158 David Pastrnak AS 1.25 3.00
159 Braden Holtby AS .60 1.50
160 Patrick Kane AS 1.00 2.50
161 David Perron AS .40 1.00
162 Nathan MacKinnon AS 2.00 5.00
163 Leon Draisaitl AS 1.50 4.00
164 Mitch Marner AS .75 2.00
165 Jack Eichel AS .75 2.00
166 Tristan Jarry AS .50 1.25
167 Elias Pettersson AS .75 2.00
168 Travis Konecny AS .50 1.25
169 Matthew Tkachuk AS 1.00 2.50
170 Quinn Hughes AS 1.25 3.00
171 Jaccob Slavin AS .40 1.00
172 Tyler Bertuzzi AS .40 1.00
173 Mathew Barzal AS .60 1.50
174 Alex Pietrangelo AS .40 1.00
175 Mark Scheifele AS .75 2.00
176 Tomas Hertl AS .50 1.25
177 Seth Jones AS .50 1.25
178 Ryan O'Reilly AS .50 1.25
179 Andrei Vasilevskiy AS .75 2.00
180 Connor Hellebuyck AS 1.00 2.50
181 Roman Josi AS .50 1.25
182 Frederik Andersen AS .60 1.50
183 Brady Tkachuk AS .75 2.00
184 Tyler Seguin AS .60 1.50
185 Shea Weber AS .50 1.25
186 Victor Hedman AS .60 1.50
187 Jacob Markstrom AS .50 1.25
188 John Carlson AS .50 1.25
189 Jonathan Huberdeau AS .60 1.50
190 Mark Giordano AS .50 1.25
191 Eric Staal AS .50 1.25
192 Connor McDavid AS 2.50 6.00
193 Nico Hischier AS .75 2.00
194 David Rittich AS .40 1.00
195 Jordan Binnington AS .75 2.00
196 Chris Kreider AS .60 1.50
197 Max Pacioretty AS .50 1.25
198 T.J. Oshie AS .50 1.25
199 Anthony Duclair AS .40 1.00
200 David Pastrnak AS MVP 1.25 3.00

2020-21 Metal Universe Blue Spectrum

*BLUE: .75X TO 2X BASIC
*BLUE.RC: .6X TO 1.5X BASIC
125 Kirill Kaprizov 15.00 40.00
140 Tim Stutzle 12.00 30.00
150 Alexis Lafreniere 15.00 40.00

2020-21 Metal Universe Precious Metal Gems Red

*RED: 8X TO 20X BASIC
*RED.RC: 4X TO 10X BASIC
8 Alex Ovechkin 125.00 300.00
31 Carey Price 40.00 100.00
34 Auston Matthews 80.00 200.00
52 Andrei Vasilevskiy 30.00 80.00
60 Cale Makar 60.00 150.00
87 Sidney Crosby 150.00 400.00
92 Nathan MacKinnon 125.00 300.00
97 Connor McDavid 250.00 600.00
101 Jason Robertson 80.00 200.00
108 Vitek Vanecek 12.00 30.00
120 Bowen Byram 60.00 150.00
125 Kirill Kaprizov 200.00 500.00
141 Ilya Sorokin 50.00 125.00
150 Alexis Lafreniere 200.00 500.00
162 Nathan MacKinnon AS 125.00 300.00
192 Connor McDavid AS 250.00 600.00

2020-21 Metal Universe Purple Spectrum

*PURPLE: 1.25X TO 3X BASIC
*PURPLE.RC: 1X TO 2.5X BASIC
125 Kirill Kaprizov 50.00 125.00
140 Tim Stutzle 25.00 60.00
150 Alexis Lafreniere 40.00 100.00

2020-21 Metal Universe Silver

*SILVER: 5X TO 12X BASIC
*SILVER.RC: 1.5X TO 4X BASIC
4 Elias Pettersson AU B 20.00 50.00
9 Jack Eichel AU B 25.00 60.00
21 Jack Hughes AU B 30.00 80.00
50 Jordan Binnington AU D 40.00 100.00
52 Andrei Vasilevskiy AU D 20.00 50.00
60 Cale Makar AU C 30.00 80.00
69 Miro Heiskanen AU F 20.00 50.00
73 Patrick Kane AU B 30.00 80.00
79 Carter Hart AU E 20.00 50.00
97 Connor McDavid AU A 1500.00 4000.00
100 Nico Hischier AU B 40.00 100.00
101 Jason Robertson AU/299 20.00 50.00
120 Bowen Byram AU/99 30.00 80.00
125 Kirill Kaprizov AU/99 150.00 400.00
127 Josh Norris AU/199 15.00 40.00
131 Jake Evans AU/399 10.00 25.00
136 Olli Juolevi AU/299 8.00 20.00
137 Alexander Romanov AU/99 25.00 60.00
138 Connor McMichael AU/199 25.00 60.00
140 Tim Stutzle AU/99 80.00 200.00
141 Ilya Sorokin AU/199 50.00 125.00
142 Nils Hoglander AU/199 25.00 60.00
144 Yegor Sharangovich AU/299 25.00 60.00
153 Jordan Binnington SKILL AU C 40.00 100.00
154 Patrick Kane SKILL AU B 30.00 80.00
160 Patrick Kane AS AU B 30.00 80.00
165 Jack Eichel AS AU B 25.00 60.00
167 Elias Pettersson AS AU B 20.00 50.00
179 Andrei Vasilevskiy AS AU C 20.00 50.00
192 Connor McDavid AS AU A 1500.00 4000.00
193 Nico Hischier AS AU C 40.00 100.00
195 Jordan Binnington AS AU C 40.00 100.00

2020-21 Metal Universe '97-98 Retro

R1 Sidney Crosby 4.00 10.00
R2 Patrick Kane 2.00 5.00
R3 Roman Josi 1.00 2.50
R4 Andrei Vasilevskiy 1.50 4.00
R5 Jack Eichel 1.50 4.00
R6 Nikita Kucherov 2.00 5.00
R7 Leon Draisaitl 3.00 8.00
R8 Drew Doughty 1.25 3.00
R9 Elias Pettersson 1.50 4.00
R10 Steven Stamkos 2.00 5.00
R11 Mitch Marner 1.50 4.00
R12 Carey Price 2.00 5.00
R13 Evgeni Malkin 2.00 5.00
R14 Mikko Rantanen 2.50 6.00
R15 David Pastrnak 2.50 6.00
R16 Mark Stone 1.25 3.00
R17 Nathan MacKinnon 4.00 10.00
R18 Mark Scheifele 1.50 4.00
R19 Artemi Panarin 2.00 5.00
R20 Ryan O'Reilly 1.00 2.50
R21 Tyler Seguin 1.25 3.00
R22 Sebastian Aho 1.50 4.00
R23 Carter Hart 1.00 2.50
R24 Alex Ovechkin 4.00 10.00
R25 Mathew Barzal 1.25 3.00
R26 Brad Marchand 2.00 5.00
R27 Johnny Gaudreau 1.50 4.00
R28 Auston Matthews 4.00 10.00
R29 Erik Karlsson 1.25 3.00
R30 Connor McDavid 5.00 12.00
R31 Timothy Liljegren 1.25 3.00
R32 Gabe Vilardi 2.00 5.00
R33 Josh Norris 2.00 5.00
R34 Kieffer Bellows 1.00 2.50
R35 Liam Foudy 1.25 3.00
R36 Nick Robertson 2.00 5.00
R37 Jason Robertson 3.00 8.00
R38 Tyler Benson 1.25 3.00
R39 Peyton Krebs 2.00 5.00
R40 Bowen Byram 2.50 6.00
R41 Ty Dellandrea 1.25 3.00
R42 Vitali Kravtsov 2.50 6.00
R43 Connor McMichael 2.00 5.00
R44 Kirill Kaprizov 12.00 30.00
R45 Alexander Romanov 1.50 4.00
R46 Dylan Cozens 2.00 5.00
R47 Nils Hoglander 1.25 3.00
R48 Ilya Sorokin 3.00 8.00
R49 Tim Stutzle 2.50 6.00
R50 Alexis Lafreniere 4.00 10.00

2020-21 Metal Universe '97-98 Retro Precious Metal Gems Red

*RED: 4X TO 10X BASIC
R1 Sidney Crosby 250.00 600.00
R2 Patrick Kane 80.00 200.00
R4 Andrei Vasilevskiy 30.00 80.00
R6 Nikita Kucherov 30.00 80.00
R7 Leon Draisaitl 100.00 250.00
R9 Elias Pettersson 60.00 150.00
R11 Mitch Marner 80.00 200.00
R12 Carey Price 60.00 150.00
R13 Evgeni Malkin 60.00 150.00
R15 David Pastrnak 30.00 80.00
R17 Nathan MacKinnon 60.00 150.00
R18 Mark Scheifele 20.00 50.00
R20 Ryan O'Reilly 12.00 30.00
R22 Sebastian Aho 30.00 80.00
R23 Carter Hart 30.00 80.00
R24 Alex Ovechkin 200.00 500.00
R28 Auston Matthews 150.00 400.00
R30 Connor McDavid 800.00 2000.00
R32 Gabe Vilardi 25.00 60.00
R37 Jason Robertson 125.00 300.00
R44 Kirill Kaprizov 250.00 600.00
R46 Dylan Cozens 60.00 150.00
R47 Nils Hoglander 50.00 125.00

2020-21 Metal Universe '97-98 Retro Purple Spectrum

*PURPLE: 2.5X TO 6X BASIC
R50 Alexis Lafreniere 25.00 60.00

2020-21 Metal Universe Alloyance

AL1 S.Crosby/E.Malkin 4.00 10.00
AL2 A.Barkov/J.Huberdeau 1.50 4.00
AL3 A.Ovechkin/N.Backstrom 4.00 10.00
AL4 A.Lee/M.Barzal 1.25 3.00
AL5 A.Matthews/M.Marner 4.00 10.00
AL6 E.Pettersson/B.Boeser 1.50 4.00
AL7 B.Gallagher/T.Tatar 1.00 2.50
AL8 J.Eichel/T.Hall 1.50 4.00
AL9 L.Draisaitl/C.McDavid 5.00 12.00
AL10 M.Scheifele/K.Connor 1.50 4.00
AL11 M.Pacioretty/M.Stone 1.25 3.00
AL12 M.Zibanejad/A.Panarin 2.00 5.00
AL13 M.Rantanen/N.MacKinnon 4.00 10.00
AL14 P.Bergeron/D.Pastrnak 2.50 6.00
AL15 P.Kane/A.DeBrincat 2.00 5.00
AL16 C.Atkinson/P.Laine 1.25 3.00
AL17 R.O'Reilly/V.Tarasenko 1.25 3.00
AL18 S.Aho/A.Svechnikov 1.50 4.00
AL19 S.Stamkos/N.Kucherov 2.00 5.00
AL20 Z.Parise/R.Suter 1.00 2.50

2020-21 Metal Universe ALON

A1 Connor McDavid 15.00 40.00
A2 Brent Burns 2.00 5.00
A3 Andrei Vasilevskiy 3.00 8.00
A4 Sidney Crosby 12.00 30.00
A5 Drew Doughty 2.50 6.00
A6 Brady Tkachuk 3.00 8.00
A7 Alex Ovechkin 8.00 20.00
A8 Carey Price 4.00 10.00
A9 John Tavares 3.00 8.00
A10 Matthew Tkachuk 4.00 10.00
A11 Jordan Binnington 3.00 8.00
A12 Clayton Keller 2.50 6.00
A13 Nathan MacKinnon 8.00 20.00
A14 Max Pacioretty 2.00 5.00
A15 Kyle Connor 3.00 8.00
A16 Artemi Panarin 4.00 10.00
A17 Miro Heiskanen 2.50 6.00
A18 Andrei Svechnikov 2.50 6.00
A19 Carter Hart 2.00 5.00
A20 Zach Werenski 3.00 8.00
A21 David Pastrnak 5.00 12.00
A22 Jack Eichel 3.00 8.00
A23 Brock Boeser 2.50 6.00
A24 Nico Hischier 3.00 8.00
A25 John Gibson 2.00 5.00
A26 Bowen Byram 5.00 12.00
A27 Peyton Krebs 4.00 10.00
A28 Nick Robertson 4.00 10.00
A29 Tim Stutzle 5.00 12.00
A30 Alexis Lafreniere 8.00 20.00

2020-21 Metal Universe Championship Hardware

CH1 Victor Hedman 4.00 10.00
CH2 Nikita Kucherov 6.00 15.00
CH3 Sidney Crosby 12.00 30.00
CH4 Ryan Getzlaf 3.00 8.00
CH5 Jonathan Quick 4.00 10.00
CH6 Dustin Brown 3.00 8.00
CH8 Nicklas Backstrom 3.00 8.00
CH9 Zdeno Chara 3.00 8.00
CH10 Alex Ovechkin 12.00 30.00
CH11 Evgeni Malkin 6.00 15.00
CH12 Alex Pietrangelo 2.50 6.00
CH13 Kris Letang 4.00 10.00
CH14 Jonathan Toews 5.00 12.00
CH15 Duncan Keith 2.50 6.00
CH16 Evgeny Kuznetsov 4.00 10.00
CH17 Ryan O'Reilly 3.00 8.00
CH18 Anze Kopitar 5.00 12.00
CH19 Jordan Binnington 5.00 12.00
CH20 Patrick Kane 6.00 15.00

2020-21 Metal Universe Intimidation Nation

IN1 Igor Shesterkin 2.50 6.00
IN2 Ilya Samsonov 1.25 3.00
IN3 Tristan Jarry 1.25 3.00
IN4 Matt Murray 1.25 3.00
IN5 Mackenzie Blackwood 1.25 3.00
IN6 Carey Price 2.50 6.00
IN7 Philipp Grubauer 1.25 3.00
IN8 Ben Bishop 1.00 2.50
IN9 Pekka Rinne 1.25 3.00
IN10 Sergei Bobrovsky 2.00 5.00
IN11 Jonathan Quick 1.50 4.00
IN12 Petr Mrazek 1.25 3.00
IN13 Martin Jones 1.00 2.50
IN14 Carter Hart 1.25 3.00
IN15 Braden Holtby 1.50 4.00
IN16 Jacob Markstrom 1.25 3.00
IN17 Tuukka Rask 1.50 4.00
IN18 Jonathan Bernier 1.00 2.50
IN19 Linus Ullmark 1.25 3.00
IN20 Frederik Andersen 1.50 4.00
IN21 Malcolm Subban 1.00 2.50
IN22 Elvis Merzlikins 1.25 3.00
IN23 Robin Lehner 1.00 2.50
IN24 Andrei Vasilevskiy 2.00 5.00
IN25 Semyon Varlamov 1.25 3.00
IN26 Mikko Koskinen .75 2.00
IN27 Connor Hellebuyck 2.50 6.00
IN28 Marc-Andre Fleury 2.50 6.00
IN29 Darcy Kuemper 1.25 3.00
IN30 John Gibson 1.25 3.00
IN31 Jordan Binnington 2.00 5.00
IN32 Alex Stalock .75 2.00

2020-21 Metal Universe Intimidation Nation Autographs Gold

IN2 Ilya Samsonov C 30.00 80.00
IN4 Matt Murray B 30.00 80.00
IN6 Carey Price A 125.00 300.00
IN7 Philipp Grubauer C 30.00 80.00
IN10 Sergei Bobrovsky A 50.00 125.00
IN11 Jonathan Quick A 40.00 100.00
IN14 Carter Hart B 80.00 200.00
IN22 Elvis Merzlikins C 30.00 80.00
IN30 John Gibson C 30.00 80.00
IN31 Jordan Binnington C 80.00 200.00

2020-21 Metal Universe Jambalaya

10F20 Connor McDavid 1200.00 3000.00
20F20 Auston Matthews 300.00 800.00
40F20 Mika Zibanejad 60.00 150.00
50F20 John Carlson 50.00 125.00
60F20 Jonathan Huberdeau 60.00 150.00
70F20 Ryan O'Reilly 50.00 125.00
80F20 Pierre-Luc Dubois 40.00 100.00
90F20 Jonathan Toews 150.00 400.00
100F20 Nikita Kucherov 150.00 400.00
110F20 Mark Stone 60.00 150.00
120F20 Tuukka Rask 60.00 150.00
130F20 Nathan MacKinnon 200.00 500.00
140F20 Sidney Crosby 600.00 1500.00
150F20 Mitch Marner 80.00 200.00
160F20 Tyler Seguin 60.00 150.00
170F20 Roman Josi 50.00 125.00
180F20 Blake Wheeler 50.00 125.00
190F20 Mathew Barzal 60.00 150.00
200F20 Alexis Lafreniere 200.00 500.00

2020-21 Metal Universe Net Deposits

ND1 Kirill Kaprizov 4.00 10.00
ND2 Dylan Cozens 1.50 4.00
ND3 Nick Robertson 1.50 4.00
ND4 Nils Hoglander 1.00 2.50
ND5 Alexander Romanov 1.25 3.00
ND6 Bowen Byram 2.00 5.00
ND7 Alexis Lafreniere 3.00 8.00
ND8 Tim Stutzle 2.00 5.00
ND9 Sebastian Aho 1.25 3.00
ND10 Aleksander Barkov 1.25 3.00
ND11 Nathan MacKinnon 3.00 8.00
ND12 Alex DeBrincat 1.00 2.50
ND13 Jake Guentzel 1.25 3.00
ND14 Alex Ovechkin 3.00 8.00
ND15 Elias Pettersson 1.25 3.00
ND16 Andrei Svechnikov 1.00 2.50
ND17 David Pastrnak 2.00 5.00
ND18 Brad Marchand 1.50 4.00
ND19 Connor McDavid 4.00 10.00
ND20 Mark Scheifele 1.25 3.00
ND21 Auston Matthews 3.00 8.00
ND22 Max Pacioretty .75 2.00
ND23 Sidney Crosby 3.00 8.00
ND24 Tomas Hertl .75 2.00

2020-21 Metal Universe Net Deposits Gold

ND1 Kirill Kaprizov 200.00 500.00
ND7 Alexis Lafreniere 80.00 200.00
ND14 Alex Ovechkin 80.00 200.00
ND19 Connor McDavid 250.00 600.00

2020-21 Metal Universe Net Deposits Autographs Gold

ND1 Kirill Kaprizov A 200.00 500.00
ND3 Nick Robertson C 20.00 50.00
ND4 Nils Hoglander C 20.00 50.00
ND5 Alexander Romanov C 25.00 60.00
ND7 Alexis Lafreniere A 300.00 800.00
ND8 Tim Stutzle B 40.00 100.00
ND10 Aleksander Barkov D 25.00 60.00
ND13 Jake Guentzel D 25.00 60.00
ND15 Elias Pettersson B 40.00 100.00
ND16 Andrei Svechnikov C 20.00 50.00
ND18 Brad Marchand B 30.00 80.00
ND19 Connor McDavid A 300.00 800.00
ND20 Mark Scheifele C 25.00 60.00
ND22 Max Pacioretty D 15.00 40.00
ND24 Tomas Hertl D 15.00 40.00

2020-21 Metal Universe Platinum Portraits

PP1 Aleksander Barkov 120.00 300.00
PP4 Elias Pettersson 125.00 300.00
PP5 Jack Eichel 120.00 300.00
PP6 Patrick Kane 150.00 400.00
PP7 Nathan MacKinnon 300.00 800.00
PP8 Steven Stamkos 150.00 400.00
PP9 Marc-Andre Fleury 150.00 400.00
PP10 Sidney Crosby 400.00 1000.00
PP11 Sebastian Aho 125.00 300.00
PP12 Patrice Bergeron 100.00 250.00
PP13 Alexis Lafreniere 300.00 800.00
PP15 Claude Giroux 80.00 200.00
PP16 Mark Scheifele 125.00 300.00
PP17 Artemi Panarin 125.00 300.00
PP18 Auston Matthews 400.00 1000.00
PP19 Johnny Gaudreau 40.00 100.00
PP20 Connor McDavid 1000.00 2500.00
PP21 Dylan Larkin 100.00 250.00
PP23 Vladimir Tarasenko 30.00 80.00

2020-21 Metal Universe Skybox Premium Prospects

*SAPPHIRES: .75X TO 2X BASIC
PP1 Alexis Lafreniere 4.00 10.00
PP2 Jason Robertson 3.00 8.00
PP3 Liam Foudy 1.25 3.00
PP4 Martin Kaut 1.25 3.00
PP5 Timothy Liljegren 1.25 3.00
PP6 Gabe Vilardi 2.00 5.00
PP7 Tyler Benson 1.25 3.00
PP8 Michael DiPietro 1.50 4.00
PP9 Morgan Geekie 1.25 3.00
PP10 Mikey Anderson 1.25 3.00
PP11 Jake Evans 1.25 3.00
PP12 Kieffer Bellows 1.00 2.50
PP13 Alexander True 1.00 2.50
PP14 Peyton Krebs 2.00 5.00
PP15 Olli Juolevi 1.25 3.00
PP16 Nicolas Beaudin 1.25 3.00
PP17 Alec Regula .75 2.00
PP18 Alexander Alexeyev 1.00 2.50
PP19 Matiss Kivlenieks 1.50 4.00
PP20 Bowen Byram 2.50 6.00
PP21 Ty Dellandrea 1.25 3.00
PP22 Jake Oettinger 3.00 8.00
PP23 Vitek Vanecek 2.00 5.00
PP24 Pierre-Olivier Joseph 1.25 3.00
PP25 Steven Lorentz 1.00 2.50
PP26 Josh Norris 2.00 5.00
PP27 Victor Soderstrom 1.00 2.50
PP28 Shane Bowers 1.00 2.50
PP29 Connor Ingram 1.00 2.50
PP30 Egor Korshkov .75 2.00
PP31 Lucas Carlsson 1.00 2.50
PP32 Dylan Coghlan 1.25 3.00
PP33 Jani Hakanpaa .75 2.00
PP34 Gustav Lindstrom 1.00 2.50
PP35 Nick Robertson 2.00 5.00
PP36 Brandon Hagel 1.50 4.00
PP37 Kirill Kaprizov 5.00 12.00
PP38 Maxim Letunov 1.00 2.50
PP39 Alexander Romanov 1.50 4.00
PP40 Jonas Johansson 1.25 3.00
PP41 Dylan Cozens 2.00 5.00
PP42 Calvin Thurkauf 1.00 2.50
PP43 Connor McMichael 2.00 5.00
PP44 Anthony Angello 1.00 2.50
PP45 Nils Hoglander 1.25 3.00
PP46 Gage Quinney .75 2.00
PP47 Ilya Sorokin 3.00 8.00
PP48 Keegan Kolesar 1.00 2.50
PP49 Philippe Maillet 1.00 2.50
PP50 Tim Stutzle 2.50 6.00

2020-21 Metal Universe Skybox Premium Prospects '97-98 Retro Star Autographs Rubies

PP1 Alexis Lafreniere A 125.00 300.00
PP2 Jason Robertson C 40.00 100.00
PP3 Liam Foudy E 6.00 15.00
PP4 Martin Kaut E 6.00 15.00
PP5 Timothy Liljegren D 6.00 15.00
PP6 Gabe Vilardi C 10.00 25.00
PP7 Tyler Benson F 6.00 15.00
PP9 Morgan Geekie F 6.00 15.00
PP10 Mikey Anderson E 6.00 15.00
PP11 Jake Evans F 12.00 30.00
PP12 Kieffer Bellows E 5.00 12.00
PP13 Alexander True F 5.00 12.00
PP14 Peyton Krebs D 10.00 25.00
PP15 Olli Juolevi D 6.00 15.00
PP16 Nicolas Beaudin D 6.00 15.00
PP17 Alec Regula E 4.00 10.00
PP18 Alexander Alexeyev F 5.00 12.00
PP21 Ty Dellandrea F 6.00 15.00
PP22 Jake Oettinger F 15.00 40.00
PP23 Vitek Vanecek F 10.00 25.00
PP24 Pierre-Olivier Joseph F 6.00 15.00
PP25 Steven Lorentz F 5.00 12.00
PP26 Josh Norris E 20.00 50.00
PP27 Victor Soderstrom D 5.00 12.00
PP28 Shane Bowers E 5.00 12.00
PP29 Connor Ingram B 5.00 12.00
PP31 Lucas Carlsson F 5.00 12.00
PP32 Dylan Coghlan D 6.00 15.00
PP33 Jani Hakanpaa E 4.00 10.00
PP34 Gustav Lindstrom F 5.00 12.00
PP35 Nick Robertson C 12.00 30.00
PP36 Brandon Hagel F 8.00 20.00
PP37 Kirill Kaprizov C 250.00 600.00
PP38 Maxim Letunov E 5.00 12.00
PP39 Alexander Romanov D 30.00 80.00
PP40 Jonas Johansson E 6.00 15.00
PP42 Calvin Thurkauf F 5.00 12.00
PP43 Connor McMichael D 25.00 60.00
PP44 Anthony Angello E 5.00 12.00
PP45 Nils Hoglander D 6.00 15.00
PP46 Gage Quinney F 4.00 10.00
PP47 Ilya Sorokin D 40.00 100.00
PP49 Philippe Maillet E 5.00 12.00
PP50 Tim Stutzle D 30.00 80.00

2021-22 Metal Universe

1 Connor McDavid 2.50 6.00
2 Jonathan Marchessault .60 1.50
3 Miro Heiskanen .60 1.50
4 John Gibson .50 1.25
5 Mitch Marner .75 2.00
6 Niklas Hjalmarsson .30 .75
7 Dougie Hamilton .40 1.00
8 Teuvo Teravainen .50 1.25
9 Nikolaj Ehlers .50 1.25
10 Patrick Kane 1.00 2.50
11 Sebastian Aho .75 2.00
12 Nick Suzuki 1.00 2.50
13 Anze Kopitar .75 2.00
14 Sean Monahan .30 .75
15 Brad Marchand 1.00 2.50
16 Nico Hischier .75 2.00
17 Alex DeBrincat .60 1.50
18 Jakub Vrana .40 1.00
19 Matthew Tkachuk 1.00 2.50
20 Leon Draisaitl 1.50 4.00
21 Matt Dumba .40 1.00
22 Jonathan Huberdeau .60 1.50
23 Josh Bailey .40 1.00
24 John Klingberg .50 1.25
25 Auston Matthews 2.00 5.00
26 Roman Josi .50 1.25
27 Kirill Kaprizov 1.50 4.00
28 Jack Hughes 1.25 3.00
29 Ilya Sorokin .75 2.00
30 Mark Scheifele .75 2.00
31 Brady Tkachuk .75 2.00
32 Aleksander Barkov .75 2.00
33 Alexis Lafreniere .75 2.00
34 Mark Giordano .50 1.25
35 Adam Fox .60 1.50
36 Jakub Voracek .40 1.00
37 Pius Suter .40 1.00
38 Rasmus Dahlin .60 1.50
39 Tim Stutzle .60 1.50
40 Andrei Vasilevskiy .75 2.00
41 Yanni Gourde .40 1.00
42 Evgeni Malkin 1.00 2.50
43 Victor Olofsson .50 1.25
44 Elvis Merzlikins .50 1.25
45 Cale Makar 1.25 3.00
46 Ryan Getzlaf .50 1.25
47 Carter Hart .50 1.25
48 James van Riemsdyk .40 1.00
49 Quinn Hughes 1.25 3.00
50 Alex Ovechkin 2.00 5.00
51 John Tavares .75 2.00
52 Pierre-Luc Dubois .40 1.00
53 Brock Boeser .60 1.50
54 Shea Theodore .60 1.50
55 David Pastrnak 1.25 3.00
56 Colton Parayko .40 1.00
57 Tom Wilson .50 1.25
58 Phillip Danault .50 1.25
59 Erik Karlsson .60 1.50
60 Carey Price 1.00 2.50
61 Max Pacioretty .50 1.25
62 Brent Burns .50 1.25
63 Ryan O'Reilly .50 1.25
64 William Karlsson .60 1.50
65 Artemi Panarin 1.00 2.50
66 Ryan Nugent-Hopkins .60 1.50
67 Clayton Keller .60 1.50
68 Cam Atkinson .50 1.25
69 Tomas Hertl .50 1.25
70 Nikita Kucherov 1.00 2.50
71 Jonathan Toews .75 2.00
72 Johnny Gaudreau .75 2.00
73 Anders Lee .40 1.00
74 Jake Guentzel .75 2.00
75 Nathan MacKinnon 2.00 5.00
76 Patrice Bergeron .60 1.50
77 Elias Pettersson .75 2.00
78 Tyler Toffoli .50 1.25
79 Steven Stamkos 1.00 2.50
80 Mark Stone .60 1.50
81 Filip Forsberg .75 2.00
82 Brendan Gallagher .50 1.25
83 Nicklas Backstrom .50 1.25
84 Igor Shesterkin 1.00 2.50
85 Connor Hellebuyck 1.00 2.50
86 Nick Foligno .30 .75
87 Jeff Petry .50 1.25
88 Tyler Seguin .60 1.50
89 Brayden Point .60 1.50
90 Marc-Andre Fleury 1.00 2.50
91 Drew Doughty .60 1.50
92 Duncan Keith .40 1.00
93 Mikko Rantanen 1.25 3.00
94 Claude Giroux .50 1.25
95 Dylan Larkin .60 1.50
96 David Perron .40 1.00
97 Jordan Eberle .50 1.25
98 Tyler Bertuzzi .40 1.00
99 Philipp Grubauer .50 1.25
100 Sidney Crosby 2.00 5.00
101 Connor McDavid AJ 2.50 6.00
102 Kevin Fiala AJ .40 1.00
103 Kirill Kaprizov AJ 1.50 4.00
104 Connor Hellebuyck AJ 1.00 2.50
105 Matthew Tkachuk AJ 1.00 2.50
106 John Gibson AJ .50 1.25
107 Phillip Danault AJ .50 1.25
108 Tristan Jarry AJ .50 1.25
109 Aleksander Barkov AJ .75 2.00
110 Sebastian Aho AJ .75 2.00
111 Quinn Hughes AJ 1.25 3.00
112 Cale Makar AJ 1.25 3.00
113 Brent Burns AJ .50 1.25
114 Luke Kunin AJ .30 .75
115 Brady Tkachuk AJ .75 2.00
116 Joe Pavelski AJ .60 1.50
117 Yanni Gourde AJ .40 1.00
118 Ryan Suter AJ .40 1.00
119 Josh Bailey AJ .40 1.00
120 Auston Matthews AJ 2.00 5.00
121 Nico Hischier AJ .75 2.00
122 Vladislav Namestnikov AJ .30 .75
123 Keith Yandle AJ .30 .75
124 Mark Scheifele AJ .75 2.00
125 Alex Ovechkin AJ 2.00 5.00
126 Brock Boeser AJ .60 1.50
127 Robin Lehner AJ .40 1.00
128 Ryan O'Reilly AJ .50 1.25
129 Roman Josi AJ .50 1.25
130 Nathan MacKinnon AJ 2.00 5.00
131 Andrei Vasilevskiy AJ .75 2.00
132 Jean-Gabriel Pageau AJ .30 .75
133 Elvis Merzlikins AJ .50 1.25
134 Anthony Mantha AJ .40 1.00
135 Patrick Kane AJ 1.00 2.50
136 Elias Lindholm AJ .50 1.25
137 Nick Suzuki AJ 1.00 2.50
138 Jonathan Huberdeau AJ .60 1.50
139 Alexis Lafreniere AJ .75 2.00
140 Leon Draisaitl AJ 1.50 4.00
141 Noah Hanifin AJ .50 1.25
142 Alex Tuch AJ .50 1.25
143 Jamie Benn AJ .50 1.25
144 Adam Fox AJ .60 1.50
145 Carey Price AJ 1.00 2.50
146 Mark Giordano AJ .50 1.25
147 Brad Marchand AJ 1.00 2.50
148 Victor Olofsson AJ .50 1.25
149 Drake Batherson AJ .50 1.25
150 Sidney Crosby AJ 2.00 5.00
151 Quinton Byfield RC 2.50 6.00
152 Wade Allison RC 1.00 2.50
153 Grigori Denisenko RC 1.25 3.00
154 Mason McTavish RC 2.00 5.00
155 Jamie Drysdale RC 1.50 4.00
156 Seth Jarvis RC 2.50 6.00
157 Shane Pinto RC 1.50 4.00
158 Ukko-Pekka Luukkonen RC 1.50 4.00
159 Filip Gustavsson RC 2.00 5.00
160 Spencer Knight RC 2.00 5.00
161 Cole Sillinger RC 1.50 4.00
162 Calen Addison RC 1.00 2.50
163 Jacob Bernard-Docker RC 1.00 2.50
164 Wyatt Kalynuk RC 1.00 2.50
165 William Eklund RC 2.50 6.00
166 Matthew Phillips RC 1.00 2.50
167 David Farrance RC 1.00 2.50
168 Morgan Barron RC .75 2.00
169 Taylor Raddysh RC 1.50 4.00
170 Jeremy Swayman RC 3.00 8.00
171 Scott Perunovich RC 1.00 2.50
172 Tanner Jeannot RC 1.00 2.50
173 Rasmus Kupari RC 1.00 2.50
174 Vasily Podkolzin RC 1.25 3.00
175 Trevor Zegras RC 2.00 5.00
176 Adam Beckman RC 1.00 2.50
177 Joe Veleno RC 1.25 3.00
178 Ross Colton RC 1.25 3.00
179 Sampo Ranta RC 1.00 2.50
180 Alex Newhook RC 1.50 4.00
181 Hendrix Lapierre RC 1.00 2.50
182 Cam York RC 1.00 2.50
183 Cole Perfetti RC 2.00 5.00
184 Nico Daws RC 1.50 4.00
185 Philip Tomasino RC 1.25 3.00
186 John-Jason Peterka RC 2.00 5.00
187 Anton Lundell RC 2.00 5.00
188 Dawson Mercer RC 2.50 6.00
189 Nils Lundkvist RC 1.00 2.50
190 Lucas Raymond RC 3.00 8.00
191 Alexander Holtz RC 1.50 4.00
192 Alex Turcotte RC 1.25 3.00
193 Kole Lind RC 1.25 3.00
194 Lassi Thomson RC 1.00 2.50
195 Moritz Seider RC 2.50 6.00
196 Alex Barre-Boulet RC 1.00 2.50
197 Jonathan Dahlen RC 1.00 2.50
198 Jake Neighbours RC 2.00 5.00
199 Ryan Merkley RC 1.25 3.00
200 Cole Caufield RC 4.00 10.00

2021-22 Metal Universe Blue Spectrum

*BLUE: .75X TO 2X BASIC
*BLUE.RC: .6X TO 1.5X BASIC

2021-22 Metal Universe Precious Metal Gems Red

*RED: 12X TO 30X BASIC
*RED.RC: 6X TO 15X BASIC
1 Connor McDavid 150.00 400.00

2021-22 Metal Universe Purple Spectrum

*PURPLE: 1.25X TO 3X BASIC
*PURPLE.RC: 1X TO 2.5X BASIC

2021-22 Metal Universe Silver

*VETS: 5X TO 12X BASIC
*ROOKIES: 2.5X TO 6X BASIC
25 Auston Matthews AU A 125.00 300.00
39 Tim Stutzle AU E 25.00 60.00
100 Sidney Crosby AU A 200.00 500.00
120 Auston Matthews AJ AU A 125.00 300.00
150 Sidney Crosby AJ AU A 200.00 500.00
151 Quinton Byfield AU/99 25.00 60.00
160 Spencer Knight AU/99 25.00 60.00
170 Jeremy Swayman AU/199 40.00 100.00
175 Trevor Zegras AU/99 125.00 300.00
190 Lucas Raymond AU/99 40.00 100.00
195 Moritz Seider AU/99 80.00 200.00
200 Cole Caufield AU/99 200.00 500.00

2021-22 Metal Universe '97-98 Retro Rookies

*PURPLE/199: 2.5X TO 6X BASIC
R1 Cole Caufield 4.00 10.00
R2 Morgan Barron .75 2.00
R3 Mason McTavish 2.00 5.00
R4 Cole Sillinger 1.50 4.00
R5 Jeremy Swayman 3.00 8.00
R6 Yegor Chinakhov 1.50 4.00
R7 Joe Veleno 1.25 3.00
R8 Calen Addison 1.00 2.50
R9 William Eklund 2.50 6.00
R10 Jamie Drysdale 1.50 4.00
R11 Ross Colton 1.25 3.00
R12 David Farrance 1.00 2.50
R13 Filip Gustavsson 2.00 5.00
R14 Taylor Raddysh 1.50 4.00

R15 Rasmus Kupari 1.00 2.50
R16 Scott Perunovich 1.00 2.50
R17 Alex Barre-Boulet 1.00 2.50
R18 Vasily Podkolzin 1.25 3.00
R19 Hendrix Lapierre 1.00 2.50
R20 Alex Newhook 1.50 4.00
R21 Adam Beckman 1.00 2.50
R22 Cam York 1.00 2.50
R23 Zac Jones 1.25 3.00
R24 Cole Perfetti 2.00 5.00
R25 Trevor Zegras 3.00 8.00
R26 Nico Daws 1.50 4.00
R27 Philip Tomasino 1.25 3.00
R28 Kole Lind 1.25 3.00
R29 Grigori Denisenko 1.25 3.00
R30 Spencer Knight 2.00 5.00
R31 Wade Allison 1.00 2.50
R32 Robin Salo 1.00 2.50
R33 Sampo Ranta 1.00 2.50
R34 Shane Pinto 1.50 4.00
R35 Anton Lundell 2.00 5.00
R36 Dawson Mercer 2.50 6.00
R37 Jacob Bernard-Docker 1.00 2.50
R38 Nils Lundkvist 1.00 2.50
R39 Alexander Holtz 1.50 4.00
R40 Lucas Raymond 3.00 8.00
R41 Seth Jarvis 2.50 6.00
R42 Wyatt Kalynuk 1.00 2.50
R43 Alex Turcotte 1.25 3.00
R44 Lassi Thomson 1.00 2.50
R45 Moritz Seider 2.50 6.00
R46 Jonathan Dahlen 1.00 2.50
R47 Ukko-Pekka Luukkonen 1.50 4.00
R48 Ryan Merkley 1.25 3.00
R49 Jake Neighbours 2.00 5.00
R50 Quinton Byfield 2.50 6.00

2021-22 Metal Universe '97-98 Retro Rookies Precious Metal Gems Red

*RED/100: 4X TO 10X BASIC
R5 Jeremy Swayman 100.00 250.00
R10 Jamie Drysdale 80.00 200.00
R24 Cole Perfetti 80.00 200.00
R30 Spencer Knight 100.00 250.00
R35 Anton Lundell 60.00 150.00
R36 Dawson Mercer 40.00 100.00
R45 Moritz Seider 150.00 400.00

2021-22 Metal Universe Amped Up

AU1 Connor McDavid 2.50 6.00
AU2 Evgeni Malkin 1.00 2.50
AU3 Patrick Kane 1.00 2.50
AU4 Mark Stone .60 1.50
AU5 Carey Price 1.00 2.50
AU6 Nikita Kucherov 1.00 2.50
AU8 Kirill Kaprizov 1.50 4.00
AU9 Aleksander Barkov .75 2.00
AU10 Nathan MacKinnon 2.00 5.00
AU11 Sebastian Aho .75 2.00
AU12 Artemi Panarin 1.00 2.50
AU13 Alex Newhook .75 2.00
AU14 Lucas Raymond 1.50 4.00
AU15 Brad Marchand 1.00 2.50
AU16 Spencer Knight 1.00 2.50
AU17 Moritz Seider 1.25 3.00
AU18 Mitch Marner .75 2.00
AU19 Quinton Byfield 1.25 3.00
AU20 Auston Matthews 2.00 5.00
AU21 Alexander Holtz .75 2.00
AU22 Quinn Hughes 1.25 3.00
AU23 Vasily Podkolzin .60 1.50
AU24 Mark Scheifele .75 2.00
AU25 Trevor Zegras 1.00 2.50
AU26 Alex Ovechkin 2.00 5.00
AU27 William Eklund 1.25 3.00
AU28 Andrei Vasilevskiy .75 2.00
AU29 Cole Caufield 2.00 5.00
AU30 Sidney Crosby 2.00 5.00

2021-22 Metal Universe Big Man on Ice

BM1 Sidney Crosby 4.00 10.00
BM2 Aleksander Barkov 1.50 4.00
BM3 Alexis Lafreniere 1.50 4.00
BM4 Roman Josi 1.00 2.50
BM5 Mark Stone 1.25 3.00
BM6 Johnny Gaudreau 1.50 4.00
BM7 Dylan Larkin 1.25 3.00
BM8 Ryan Getzlaf 1.00 2.50
BM9 Brad Marchand 2.00 5.00
BM10 Nathan MacKinnon 4.00 10.00
BM11 Clayton Keller 1.25 3.00
BM12 Patrick Kane 2.00 5.00
BM13 Sebastian Aho 1.50 4.00
BM14 Anze Kopitar 1.50 4.00
BM15 Mark Giordano 1.00 2.50
BM16 Quinn Hughes 2.50 6.00
BM17 Mathew Barzal 1.25 3.00
BM18 Jack Hughes 2.50 6.00
BM19 Kirill Kaprizov 3.00 8.00
BM20 Auston Matthews 4.00 10.00
BM21 Ryan O'Reilly 1.00 2.50
BM22 Brent Burns 1.00 2.50
BM23 Artemi Panarin 2.00 5.00
BM24 Mark Scheifele 1.50 4.00
BM25 Alex Ovechkin 4.00 10.00
BM26 Claude Giroux 1.00 2.50
BM27 Steven Stamkos 2.00 5.00
BM28 David Pastrnak 2.50 6.00
BM29 Mitch Marner 1.50 4.00
BM30 Tyler Seguin 1.25 3.00
BM31 Andrei Vasilevskiy 1.50 4.00
BM32 Leon Draisaitl 3.00 8.00
BM33 Nikita Kucherov 2.00 5.00
BM34 Evgeni Malkin 2.00 5.00
BM35 Carey Price 2.00 5.00
BM36 Mikko Rantanen 2.50 6.00
BM37 Nicklas Backstrom 1.00 2.50
BM38 Nick Suzuki 2.00 5.00
BM39 Brady Tkachuk 1.50 4.00
BM40 Connor McDavid 5.00 12.00

2021-22 Metal Universe Big Man on Ice Gold

*GOLD/96: 4X TO 10X BASIC
BM1 Sidney Crosby 80.00 200.00
BM19 Kirill Kaprizov 60.00 150.00
BM20 Auston Matthews 60.00 150.00
BM25 Alex Ovechkin 80.00 200.00
BM40 Connor McDavid 125.00 300.00

2021-22 Metal Universe Championship Galaxy

CG1 Sidney Crosby 2.00 5.00
CG2 Brayden Point .60 1.50
CG3 Anze Kopitar .75 2.00
CG4 Tom Wilson .50 1.25
CG5 Brad Marchand 1.00 2.50
CG6 Jake Guentzel .75 2.00
CG7 Andrei Vasilevskiy .75 2.00
CG8 Colton Parayko .40 1.00
CG9 Evgeni Malkin 1.00 2.50
CG10 Patrick Kane 1.00 2.50
CG11 Jonathan Toews .75 2.00
CG12 David Perron .40 1.00
CG13 Drew Doughty .60 1.50
CG14 Nicklas Backstrom .50 1.25
CG15 Steven Stamkos 1.00 2.50
CG16 Nikita Kucherov 1.00 2.50
CG17 Ryan O'Reilly .50 1.25
CG18 Patrice Bergeron .60 1.50
CG19 Tyler Toffoli .50 1.25
CG20 Alex Ovechkin 2.00 5.00

2021-22 Metal Universe Championship Galaxy Gold

*GOLD/97: 6X TO 15X BASIC
CG20 Alex Ovechkin 50.00 125.00

2021-22 Metal Universe Championship Galaxy Autographs

CG3 Anze Kopitar C 15.00 40.00
CG4 Tom Wilson D 10.00 25.00
CG5 Brad Marchand C 20.00 50.00
CG7 Andrei Vasilevskiy B 15.00 40.00
CG8 Colton Parayko D 8.00 20.00
CG10 Patrick Kane A 100.00 250.00
CG11 Jonathan Toews B 15.00 40.00
CG12 David Perron D 8.00 20.00
CG17 Ryan O'Reilly C 10.00 25.00

2021-22 Metal Universe Ice Carvings

IC1 Connor McDavid 5.00 12.00
IC2 Mark Scheifele 1.50 4.00
IC3 Leon Draisaitl 3.00 8.00
IC4 Brad Marchand 2.00 5.00
IC5 Nathan MacKinnon 4.00 10.00
IC6 Artemi Panarin 2.00 5.00
IC7 Alexis Lafreniere 1.50 4.00
IC8 Mark Stone 1.25 3.00
IC9 Patrick Kane 2.00 5.00
IC10 Carey Price 2.00 5.00
IC11 Kirill Kaprizov 3.00 8.00
IC12 Aleksander Barkov 1.50 4.00
IC13 Mitch Marner 1.50 4.00
IC14 Andrei Vasilevskiy 1.50 4.00
IC15 Alex Ovechkin 4.00 10.00
IC16 Trevor Zegras 6.00 15.00
IC17 Sebastian Aho 1.50 4.00
IC18 Johnny Gaudreau 1.50 4.00
IC19 Lucas Raymond 3.00 8.00
IC20 Cole Caufield 20.00 50.00
IC21 Moritz Seider 2.50 6.00
IC22 Alexander Holtz 1.50 4.00
IC23 Jeremy Swayman 3.00 8.00
IC24 Spencer Knight 2.00 5.00
IC25 Sidney Crosby 4.00 10.00
IC26 Vasily Podkolzin 1.25 3.00
IC27 William Eklund 2.50 6.00
IC28 Alex Newhook 1.50 4.00
IC29 Quinton Byfield 2.50 6.00
IC30 Auston Matthews 4.00 10.00

2021-22 Metal Universe Ice Carvings Spectrum

*SPECTRUM/25: 2.5X TO 6X BASIC
IC1 Connor McDavid 80.00 200.00
IC20 Cole Caufield 30.00 80.00
IC25 Sidney Crosby 60.00 150.00
IC30 Auston Matthews 80.00 200.00

2021-22 Metal Universe Jambalaya

1 Sidney Crosby 200.00 500.00
2 Artemi Panarin 100.00 250.00
3 Patrick Kane 100.00 250.00
4 Mitch Marner 80.00 200.00
5 Auston Matthews 400.00 1000.00
6 Carey Price 100.00 250.00
7 Nathan MacKinnon 200.00 500.00
8 Mark Scheifele 80.00 200.00
9 Leon Draisaitl 150.00 400.00
10 Alex Ovechkin 300.00 800.00
11 Kirill Kaprizov 200.00 500.00
12 Brad Marchand 100.00 250.00
13 Jack Eichel 80.00 200.00
14 Anze Kopitar 80.00 200.00
15 Cole Caufield 300.00 800.00
16 Aleksander Barkov 80.00 200.00
17 Quinn Hughes 125.00 300.00
18 Andrei Vasilevskiy 80.00 200.00
19 Lucas Raymond 200.00 500.00
20 Connor McDavid 400.00 1000.00

2021-22 Metal Universe Metal-X

MX1 Connor McDavid 60.00 150.00
MX2 Adam Fox 10.00 25.00
MX3 Cale Makar 20.00 50.00
MX4 Anze Kopitar 12.00 30.00
MX5 Mathew Barzal 10.00 25.00
MX6 John Tavares 12.00 30.00
MX7 Kirill Kaprizov 25.00 60.00
MX8 Steven Stamkos 15.00 40.00
MX9 Quinn Hughes 20.00 50.00
MX10 Brady Tkachuk 12.00 30.00
MX11 Mitch Marner 12.00 30.00
MX12 Sebastian Aho 12.00 30.00
MX13 Claude Giroux 8.00 20.00
MX14 David Pastrnak 20.00 50.00
MX15 Mark Stone 10.00 25.00
MX16 Evgeni Malkin 20.00 50.00
MX17 Nikita Kucherov 15.00 40.00
MX18 Alexis Lafreniere 15.00 40.00
MX19 Jonathan Huberdeau 10.00 25.00
MX20 Leon Draisaitl 25.00 60.00
MX21 Connor Hellebuyck 15.00 40.00
MX22 Brad Marchand 15.00 40.00
MX23 Mikko Rantanen 20.00 50.00
MX24 Matt Duchene 8.00 20.00
MX25 Nathan MacKinnon 30.00 80.00
MX26 Jack Hughes 20.00 50.00
MX27 Carter Hart 8.00 20.00
MX28 Ryan O'Reilly 8.00 20.00
MX29 Alex DeBrincat 10.00 25.00
MX30 Mark Scheifele 12.00 30.00
MX31 Jack Eichel 12.00 30.00
MX32 Johnny Gaudreau 12.00 30.00
MX33 Dylan Larkin 10.00 25.00
MX34 Andrei Vasilevskiy 12.00 30.00
MX35 Mark Giordano 8.00 20.00
MX36 Nicklas Backstrom 8.00 20.00
MX37 Carey Price 15.00 40.00
MX38 Tyler Seguin 10.00 25.00
MX39 Jonathan Toews 12.00 30.00
MX40 Auston Matthews 60.00 150.00
MX41 Brent Burns 8.00 20.00
MX42 Nazem Kadri 10.00 25.00
MX43 Jamie Benn 8.00 20.00
MX44 Roman Josi 8.00 20.00
MX45 Kyle Connor 12.00 30.00
MX46 Nick Suzuki 15.00 40.00
MX47 Moritz Seider 20.00 50.00
MX48 Dawson Mercer 20.00 50.00
MX49 Vasily Podkolzin 10.00 25.00
MX50 Alex Ovechkin 60.00 150.00
MX51 Trevor Zegras 60.00 150.00
MX52 Grigori Denisenko 10.00 25.00
MX53 Spencer Knight 15.00 40.00
MX54 Jeremy Swayman 25.00 60.00
MX55 Aleksander Barkov 12.00 30.00
MX56 Alexander Holtz 12.00 30.00
MX57 Jamie Drysdale 12.00 30.00
MX58 Alex Newhook 12.00 30.00
MX59 Anton Lundell 15.00 40.00
MX60 Cole Caufield 80.00 200.00
MX61 Cole Perfetti 15.00 40.00
MX62 Joe Veleno 10.00 25.00
MX63 Shane Pinto 12.00 30.00
MX64 William Eklund 20.00 50.00
MX65 Artemi Panarin 15.00 40.00
MX66 Seth Jarvis 20.00 50.00
MX67 Mason McTavish 15.00 40.00
MX68 Lucas Raymond 25.00 60.00
MX69 Quinton Byfield 20.00 50.00
MX70 Sidney Crosby 50.00 125.00

2021-22 Metal Universe Neon Icon

NI1 Connor McDavid 5.00 12.00
NI2 Claude Giroux 1.00 2.50
NI3 Quinn Hughes 2.50 6.00
NI4 Matthew Tkachuk 2.00 5.00
NI5 Auston Matthews 4.00 10.00
NI6 Andrei Vasilevskiy 1.50 4.00
NI7 Nathan MacKinnon 4.00 10.00
NI8 Mark Stone 1.25 3.00
NI9 Ryan O'Reilly 1.00 2.50
NI10 Alex Ovechkin 4.00 10.00
NI11 Carey Price 2.00 5.00
NI12 Aleksander Barkov 1.50 4.00
NI13 Mathew Barzal 1.25 3.00
NI14 Artemi Panarin 2.00 5.00
NI15 Brady Tkachuk 1.50 4.00
NI16 Patrick Kane 2.00 5.00
NI17 Mark Scheifele 1.50 4.00
NI18 Mark Giordano 1.00 2.50
NI19 Brad Marchand 2.00 5.00
NI20 Sidney Crosby 4.00 10.00

2021-22 Metal Universe Neon Icon Autographs

NI1 Connor McDavid B 250.00 600.00
NI4 Matthew Tkachuk B 30.00 80.00
NI5 Auston Matthews B 150.00 400.00
NI6 Andrei Vasilevskiy D 60.00 150.00
NI8 Mark Stone C 50.00 125.00
NI9 Ryan O'Reilly C 15.00 40.00
NI11 Carey Price B 80.00 200.00
NI12 Aleksander Barkov C 60.00 150.00
NI15 Brady Tkachuk B 60.00 150.00
NI16 Patrick Kane A 80.00 200.00
NI17 Mark Scheifele B 60.00 150.00
NI19 Brad Marchand C 25.00 60.00
NI20 Sidney Crosby A 150.00 400.00

2021-22 Metal Universe Pitter Patter

*GOLD/99: 1.5X TO 4X BASIC
PP1 Ryan Reaves 1.25 3.00
PP2 Zack MacEwen 1.00 2.50
PP3 Marcus Foligno 1.25 3.00
PP4 Ben Chiarot 1.00 2.50
PP5 Milan Lucic 1.25 3.00
PP6 Radko Gudas 1.00 2.50
PP7 Matt Martin 1.00 2.50
PP8 John Hayden 1.00 2.50
PP9 Givani Smith 1.00 2.50
PP10 Jamie Oleksiak 1.25 3.00
PP11 Austin Watson 1.00 2.50
PP12 Nicolas Deslauriers 1.00 2.50
PP13 Brenden Dillon 1.00 2.50
PP14 Nick Ritchie 1.00 2.50
PP15 Zack Kassian 1.00 2.50
PP16 Brendan Smith 1.00 2.50
PP17 Tom Wilson 1.50 4.00
PP18 Kyle Clifford 1.00 2.50
PP19 Kurtis MacDermid 1.00 2.50
PP20 Zdeno Chara 1.50 4.00

2021-22 Metal Universe Planet Metal

*GOLD: .75X TO 2X BASIC
PM1 Sidney Crosby 3.00 8.00
PM2 Sebastian Aho 1.00 2.50
PM3 Patrick Kane 1.50 4.00
PM4 Quinton Byfield 2.00 5.00
PM5 Nathan MacKinnon 3.00 8.00
PM6 Lucas Raymond 2.50 6.00
PM7 Andrei Vasilevskiy 1.00 2.50
PM8 Kirill Kaprizov 2.50 6.00
PM9 Mitch Marner 1.25 3.00
PM10 Alex Ovechkin 3.00 8.00
PM11 Mark Stone 1.00 2.50
PM13 Trevor Zegras 1.50 4.00
PM14 Alexis Lafreniere 1.25 3.00
PM15 Carey Price 1.50 4.00
PM16 Moritz Seider 2.00 5.00
PM17 Mark Giordano .75 2.00
PM18 Brad Marchand 1.50 4.00
PM19 Mikko Rantanen 2.00 5.00
PM20 Auston Matthews 3.00 8.00
PM21 Nikita Kucherov 1.50 4.00
PM22 Leon Draisaitl 2.50 6.00
PM23 Aleksander Barkov 1.25 3.00
PM24 Cole Caufield 3.00 8.00
PM25 Connor McDavid 4.00 10.00

2021-22 Metal Universe Skybox Metal Picks

*SPECTRUM/25: 8X TO 20X BASIC
P1 Connor McDavid 2.50 6.00
P2 Patrick Kane 1.00 2.50
P3 Brad Marchand 1.00 2.50
P4 Mark Scheifele .75 2.00
P5 Nathan MacKinnon 2.00 5.00
P6 Artemi Panarin 1.00 2.50
P7 Carey Price 1.00 2.50
P8 Mark Stone .60 1.50
P10 Alex Ovechkin 2.00 5.00
P11 Lucas Raymond 1.50 4.00
P12 Leon Draisaitl 1.50 4.00
P13 Moritz Seider 1.25 3.00
P14 Trevor Zegras 1.00 2.50
P15 Auston Matthews 2.00 5.00
P16 Quinton Byfield 1.25 3.00
P17 Mikko Rantanen 1.25 3.00
P18 Mitch Marner .75 2.00
P19 Cole Caufield 2.00 5.00
P20 Sidney Crosby 2.00 5.00

2021-22 Metal Universe Skybox Premium Prospects

*SAPPHIRE: .5X TO 1.2X BASIC
PP1 Cole Caufield 4.00 10.00
PP2 Mason McTavish 2.00 5.00
PP3 Alex Barre-Boulet 1.00 2.50
PP4 Spencer Knight 2.00 5.00
PP5 Lucas Raymond 3.00 8.00
PP6 Seth Jarvis 2.50 6.00
PP7 Joe Veleno 1.25 3.00
PP8 Cole Sillinger 1.50 4.00
PP9 Sampo Ranta 1.00 2.50
PP10 Jeremy Swayman 3.00 8.00
PP11 Yegor Chinakhov 1.50 4.00
PP12 Wyatt Kalynuk 1.00 2.50
PP13 Wade Allison 1.00 2.50
PP14 Cam York 1.00 2.50
PP15 Ukko-Pekka Luukkonen 1.50 4.00
PP16 William Eklund 2.50 6.00
PP17 Taylor Raddysh 1.50 4.00
PP18 Jacob Bernard-Docker 1.00 2.50
PP19 Scott Perunovich 1.00 2.50
PP20 Jamie Drysdale 1.50 4.00
PP21 Vasily Podkolzin 1.25 3.00
PP22 David Farrance 1.00 2.50
PP23 Hendrix Lapierre 1.00 2.50
PP24 Adam Beckman 1.00 2.50
PP25 Trevor Zegras 2.00 5.00
PP26 Cole Perfetti 2.00 5.00
PP27 Filip Gustavsson 2.00 5.00
PP28 Shane Pinto 1.50 4.00
PP29 Nico Daws 1.50 4.00
PP30 Alex Newhook 1.50 4.00
PP31 Philip Tomasino 1.25 3.00
PP32 Morgan Barron .75 2.00
PP33 Robin Salo 1.00 2.50
PP34 Calen Addison 1.00 2.50
PP35 Anton Lundell 2.00 5.00
PP36 Dawson Mercer 2.50 6.00
PP37 Rasmus Kupari 1.00 2.50
PP38 Zac Jones 1.25 3.00
PP39 Nils Lundkvist 1.00 2.50
PP40 Moritz Seider 2.50 6.00
PP41 Alexander Holtz 1.50 4.00
PP42 Kole Lind 1.25 3.00
PP43 Egor Sokolov 1.00 2.50
PP44 Lassi Thomson 1.00 2.50
PP45 Ross Colton 1.25 3.00
PP46 Jonathan Dahlen 1.00 2.50
PP47 Ryan Merkley 1.25 3.00
PP48 Grigori Denisenko 1.25 3.00
PP49 Jake Neighbours 2.00 5.00
PP50 Quinton Byfield 2.50 6.00

2021-22 Metal Universe Skybox Premium Prospects Star Rubies

*RUBIES/50: 3X TO 8X BASIC
PP1 Cole Caufield 60.00 150.00
PP25 Trevor Zegras 60.00 150.00

2021-22 Metal Universe Skybox Premium Prospects '98-99 Retro Star Rubies

PP1 Cole Caufield 150.00 400.00
PP2 Mason McTavish 20.00 50.00
PP3 Alex Barre-Boulet 10.00 25.00
PP4 Spencer Knight 20.00 50.00
PP5 Lucas Raymond 30.00 80.00
PP6 Seth Jarvis 25.00 60.00
PP7 Joe Veleno 12.00 30.00
PP8 Cole Sillinger 15.00 40.00
PP9 Sampo Ranta 10.00 25.00
PP10 Jeremy Swayman 30.00 80.00
PP11 Yegor Chinakhov 15.00 40.00
PP12 Wyatt Kalynuk 10.00 25.00
PP13 Wade Allison 10.00 25.00
PP14 Cam York 10.00 25.00
PP15 Ukko-Pekka Luukkonen 15.00 40.00
PP16 William Eklund 25.00 60.00
PP17 Taylor Raddysh 15.00 40.00
PP18 Jacob Bernard-Docker 10.00 25.00
PP19 Scott Perunovich 10.00 25.00
PP20 Jamie Drysdale 15.00 40.00
PP21 Vasily Podkolzin 12.00 30.00
PP22 David Farrance 10.00 25.00
PP23 Hendrix Lapierre 10.00 25.00
PP24 Adam Beckman 10.00 25.00
PP25 Trevor Zegras 20.00 50.00
PP26 Cole Perfetti 20.00 50.00
PP27 Filip Gustavsson 20.00 50.00
PP28 Shane Pinto 15.00 40.00
PP29 Nico Daws 15.00 40.00
PP30 Alex Newhook 15.00 40.00
PP31 Philip Tomasino 12.00 30.00
PP32 Morgan Barron 8.00 20.00
PP33 Robin Salo 10.00 25.00
PP34 Calen Addison 10.00 25.00
PP35 Anton Lundell 20.00 50.00
PP36 Dawson Mercer 25.00 60.00
PP37 Rasmus Kupari 10.00 25.00
PP38 Zac Jones 12.00 30.00
PP39 Nils Lundkvist 10.00 25.00
PP40 Moritz Seider 25.00 60.00
PP41 Alexander Holtz 15.00 40.00
PP42 Kole Lind 12.00 30.00
PP43 Egor Sokolov 10.00 25.00
PP44 Lassi Thomson 10.00 25.00
PP45 Ross Colton 12.00 30.00
PP46 Jonathan Dahlen 10.00 25.00
PP47 Ryan Merkley 12.00 30.00
PP48 Grigori Denisenko 12.00 30.00
PP49 Jake Neighbours 20.00 50.00
PP50 Quinton Byfield 25.00 60.00

2021-22 Metal Universe Skybox Premium Prospects Star Autographs Sapphires

PP1 Cole Caufield A 100.00 250.00
PP2 Mason McTavish B 15.00 40.00
PP4 Spencer Knight C 40.00 100.00
PP7 Joe Veleno D 10.00 25.00
PP8 Cole Sillinger C 12.00 30.00
PP9 Sampo Ranta D 8.00 20.00
PP10 Jeremy Swayman B 25.00 60.00
PP12 Wyatt Kalynuk D 8.00 20.00
PP13 Wade Allison D 8.00 20.00
PP15 Ukko-Pekka Luukkonen D 12.00 30.00
PP16 William Eklund B 20.00 50.00
PP17 Taylor Raddysh D 12.00 30.00
PP18 Jacob Bernard-Docker D 8.00 20.00
PP19 Scott Perunovich C 8.00 20.00
PP20 Jamie Drysdale C 12.00 30.00
PP21 Vasily Podkolzin C 10.00 25.00
PP23 Hendrix Lapierre D 8.00 20.00
PP24 Adam Beckman D 8.00 20.00
PP25 Trevor Zegras B 80.00 200.00
PP26 Cole Perfetti B 15.00 40.00
PP27 Filip Gustavsson D 15.00 40.00
PP28 Shane Pinto D 12.00 30.00
PP31 Philip Tomasino C 10.00 25.00
PP32 Morgan Barron D 6.00 15.00
PP33 Robin Salo D 8.00 20.00
PP34 Calen Addison D 8.00 20.00
PP36 Dawson Mercer B 20.00 50.00
PP37 Rasmus Kupari D 8.00 20.00
PP38 Zac Jones D 10.00 25.00
PP39 Nils Lundkvist C 8.00 20.00
PP40 Moritz Seider B 80.00 200.00
PP41 Alexander Holtz B 12.00 30.00
PP42 Kole Lind D 10.00 25.00
PP43 Egor Sokolov D 8.00 20.00
PP44 Lassi Thomson C 8.00 20.00
PP45 Ross Colton D 10.00 25.00
PP46 Jonathan Dahlen D 8.00 20.00
PP47 Ryan Merkley C 10.00 25.00
PP48 Grigori Denisenko D 10.00 25.00
PP49 Jake Neighbours D 15.00 40.00
PP50 Quinton Byfield B 20.00 50.00

2021-22 Metal Universe The Cheddar

*GOLD/50: 2.5X TO 6X BASIC
TC1 Connor McDavid 2.50 6.00
TC2 Mikko Rantanen 1.25 3.00
TC3 Aleksander Barkov .75 2.00
TC4 Cole Caufield 2.00 5.00
TC5 Leon Draisaitl 1.50 4.00
TC6 Max Pacioretty .50 1.25
TC7 Kirill Kaprizov 1.50 4.00
TC8 Joe Pavelski .60 1.50
TC9 Patrick Kane 1.00 2.50
TC11 Lucas Raymond 1.50 4.00
TC12 Brad Marchand 1.00 2.50
TC13 Ryan O'Reilly .50 1.25
TC14 Sebastian Aho .75 2.00
TC15 Alex DeBrincat .60 1.50
TC16 Moritz Seider 1.25 3.00
TC17 Mika Zibanejad .60 1.50
TC18 Tyler Toffoli .50 1.25
TC19 Trevor Zegras 1.00 2.50
TC20 Auston Matthews 2.00 5.00
TC21 Alexander Holtz .75 2.00
TC22 Kyle Connor .75 2.00
TC23 Quinton Byfield 1.25 3.00
TC24 Vasily Podkolzin .60 1.50
TC25 Alex Ovechkin 2.00 5.00
TC26 Spencer Knight 1.00 2.50
TC27 Mikko Rantanen 1.25 3.00
TC28 Alex Newhook .75 2.00
TC29 William Eklund 1.25 3.00
TC30 Sidney Crosby 2.00 5.00

2022-23 Metal Universe

1 Steven Stamkos 1.00 2.50
2 Bo Horvat .60 1.50
3 Brent Burns .50 1.25
4 Mats Zuccarello .50 1.25
5 Quinn Hughes 1.25 3.00
6 Brock Nelson .50 1.25
7 Mark Scheifele .75 2.00
8 Alexis Lafreniere .75 2.00
9 Mikko Rantanen 1.25 3.00
10 Tyler Toffoli .50 1.25
11 Dougie Hamilton .40 1.00
12 Kris Letang .60 1.50
13 Teuvo Teravainen .50 1.25
14 Anders Lee .40 1.00
15 Michael Bunting .50 1.25
16 Cole Sillinger .40 1.00
17 Aaron Ekblad .60 1.50
18 Elias Lindholm .50 1.25
19 Mika Zibanejad .60 1.50
20 Marcus Foligno .40 1.00
21 Quinton Byfield .60 1.50
22 Yanni Gourde .40 1.00
23 Seth Jones .50 1.25
24 Torey Krug .40 1.00
25 Cole Perfetti .50 1.25
26 Logan Thompson .60 1.50
27 K'Andre Miller .40 1.00
28 Phil Kessel .50 1.25
29 Carter Hart .50 1.25
30 Clayton Keller .60 1.50
31 Brayden Point .60 1.50
32 Zach Werenski .75 2.00
33 Joe Pavelski .60 1.50
34 Nikolaj Ehlers .50 1.25
35 John Tavares .75 2.00
36 David Perron .40 1.00
37 Sean Monahan .30 .75
38 Sean Durzi .30 .75
39 Marc-Andre Fleury 1.00 2.50
40 Josh Norris .50 1.25
41 Evgeni Malkin 1.00 2.50
42 Jonathan Marchessault .60 1.50
43 Mason McTavish .50 1.25
44 Kirby Dach .50 1.25
45 Tage Thompson .60 1.50
46 Oliver Bjorkstrand .40 1.00
47 Rasmus Dahlin .60 1.50
48 Connor Hellebuyck 1.00 2.50
49 William Nylander 1.00 2.50
50 Victor Hedman .60 1.50
51 Brad Marchand 1.00 2.50
52 Carey Price 1.00 2.50
53 Martin Necas .75 2.00
54 Matt Duchene .50 1.25
55 Charlie McAvoy .60 1.50
56 Nick Schmaltz .40 1.00
57 J.T. Miller .60 1.50
58 Taylor Hall .50 1.25
59 Boone Jenner .50 1.25
60 Nico Hischier .75 2.00
61 Troy Terry .40 1.00
62 Jonathan Quick .60 1.50
63 Victor Olofsson .50 1.25
64 Gabriel Landeskog .60 1.50
65 Jack Campbell .50 1.25
66 Jesse Puljujarvi .50 1.25
67 Cam Atkinson .50 1.25
68 Juuse Saros .60 1.50
69 Claude Giroux .50 1.25
70 Miro Heiskanen .60 1.50
71 Tim Stutzle .60 1.50
72 Jacob Markstrom .50 1.25
73 Jesper Bratt .50 1.25
74 Dylan Cozens .50 1.25
75 John Gibson .50 1.25
76 Jared McCann .40 1.00
77 Morgan Rielly .50 1.25
78 Ryan Nugent-Hopkins .60 1.50
79 Sergei Bobrovsky .75 2.00
80 Adam Fox .60 1.50
81 Shayne Gostisbehere .50 1.25
82 David Krejci .50 1.25
83 Dylan Larkin .60 1.50
84 Tomas Hertl .50 1.25
85 Noah Dobson .60 1.50
86 Ryan O'Reilly .50 1.25
87 Nicklas Backstrom .50 1.25
88 Seth Jarvis .60 1.50
89 Jamie Benn .50 1.25
90 Robert Thomas .50 1.25
91 Max Domi .50 1.25
92 Filip Forsberg .75 2.00
93 Dylan Strome .60 1.50
94 Bowen Byram .60 1.50
95 John Carlson .50 1.25
96 Gabe Vilardi .50 1.25
97 Brock Boeser .60 1.50
98 Joel Eriksson Ek .40 1.00
99 Erik Karlsson .60 1.50
100 Tyler Seguin .60 1.50
101 Connor McDavid 2.50 6.00
102 Mitch Marner .75 2.00
103 Nikita Kucherov .75 2.00
104 Cole Caufield 1.00 2.50
105 Sidney Crosby 2.00 5.00
106 Brady Tkachuk .75 2.00
107 Patrik Laine .60 1.50
108 Nazem Kadri .60 1.50
109 Mark Stone .60 1.50
110 Andrei Svechnikov .60 1.50
111 Trevor Zegras .50 1.25
112 Jonathan Huberdeau .60 1.50
113 Leon Draisaitl 1.50 4.00
114 Patrice Bergeron .60 1.50
115 Johnny Gaudreau .75 2.00
116 Patrick Kane 1.00 2.50
117 James van Riemsdyk .40 1.00
118 Timo Meier .50 1.25
119 Andrei Vasilevskiy .75 2.00
120 Kyle Connor .75 2.00
121 Lucas Raymond .75 2.00
122 Jake Guentzel .75 2.00
123 Roman Josi .50 1.25
124 Nick Suzuki 1.00 2.50
125 Cale Makar 1.25 3.00
126 Jordan Eberle .50 1.25
127 Jack Hughes 1.25 3.00
128 Jason Robertson .75 2.00
129 Anze Kopitar .75 2.00
130 Jonathan Toews .75 2.00
131 Sebastian Aho .75 2.00
132 Igor Shesterkin 1.00 2.50
133 Alex Ovechkin 2.00 5.00
134 Aleksander Barkov .75 2.00
135 Kirill Kaprizov 1.50 4.00
136 Elias Pettersson .75 2.00
137 Mathew Barzal .60 1.50
138 Jack Eichel .75 2.00
139 Artemi Panarin 1.00 2.50
140 Auston Matthews 2.00 5.00
141 Nathan MacKinnon 2.00 5.00
142 David Pastrnak 1.25 3.00
143 Jake Oettinger .75 2.00
144 Alex DeBrincat .60 1.50
145 Ilya Sorokin .75 2.00
146 Jordan Kyrou .50 1.25
147 Kevin Fiala .40 1.00
148 Matthew Tkachuk 1.00 2.50
149 Vladimir Tarasenko .60 1.50
150 Moritz Seider .60 1.50
151 Juraj Slafkovsky RC 5.00 12.00
152 Shane Wright RC 2.50 6.00
153 Matt Boldy RC 3.00 8.00
154 Matty Beniers RC 2.50 6.00
155 Owen Power RC 2.00 5.00
156 Wyatt Johnston RC 4.00 10.00
157 Jack Quinn RC 1.50 4.00
158 Marco Rossi RC 2.50 6.00
159 Jacob Perreault RC 1.00 2.50
160 Kent Johnson RC 2.00 5.00
161 Lukas Dostal RC 2.00 5.00
162 Matias Maccelli RC 1.50 4.00
163 Jack McBain RC .75 2.00
164 Jake Sanderson RC 2.50 6.00
165 Brayden Tracey RC .75 2.00
166 Elmer Soderblom RC 2.00 5.00
167 Jordan Harris RC 1.25 3.00
168 Braden Schneider RC 1.50 4.00
169 Mads Sogaard RC 1.25 3.00
170 Isaac Ratcliffe RC 1.00 2.50
171 Pyotr Kochetkov RC 2.00 5.00
172 Pavol Regenda RC 1.00 2.50
173 Samuel Fagemo RC .75 2.00
174 Nick Blankenburg RC .75 2.00
175 Dylan Samberg RC 1.00 2.50
176 Hunter Drew RC 1.00 2.50
177 Trey Fix-Wolansky RC 1.00 2.50
178 Chase Pearson RC .75 2.00
179 Jordan Spence RC 1.00 2.50
180 Mark Kastelic RC .75 2.00
181 Michael Eyssimont RC 1.00 2.50
182 Nick Abruzzese RC 1.00 2.50
183 Kaiden Guhle RC 2.00 5.00
184 Arber Xhekaj RC 2.00 5.00
185 Jakub Lauko RC 1.25 3.00
186 Ronnie Attard RC 1.00 2.50
187 Jacob Moverare RC .75 2.00
188 Kirill Marchenko RC 2.50 6.00
189 Jonatan Berggren RC 1.50 4.00
190 David Jiricek RC 2.00 5.00
191 Ben Meyers RC 1.00 2.50
192 Noah Cates RC 1.00 2.50
193 Kaedan Korczak RC .75 2.00
194 Nils Aman RC 1.00 2.50
195 Brandt Clarke RC 2.00 5.00
196 Thomas Bordeleau RC 1.00 2.50
197 Dylan Holloway RC 2.00 5.00
198 Lukas Reichel RC 2.00 5.00
199 Dylan Guenther RC 2.50 6.00
200 Andrei Kuzmenko RC 2.00 5.00

2022-23 Metal Universe Blue Spectrum FX

*BLUE: .75X TO 2X BASIC
*BLUE RC: .6X TO 1.5X BASIC

2022-23 Metal Universe Precious Metal Gems Red

*PMG RED: 12X TO 30X BASIC
*PMG RED RC: 6X TO 15X BASIC
101 Connor McDavid/90* 150.00 400.00
104 Cole Caufield/90* 60.00 150.00
127 Jack Hughes/90* 60.00 150.00
151 Juraj Slafkovsky/90* 100.00 250.00
156 Wyatt Johnston/90* 80.00 200.00

2022-23 Metal Universe Purple Spectrum FX

*PURPLE: 1.25X TO 3X BASIC
*PURPLE RC: 1X TO 2.5X BASIC

2022-23 Metal Universe Silver FX

*SILVER: 5X TO 12X BASIC
*SILVER RC: 3X TO 8X BASIC
12 Kris Letang AU C 15.00 40.00
45 Tage Thompson AU E 15.00 40.00
151 Juraj Slafkovsky AU/199 60.00 150.00
153 Matt Boldy AU/199 30.00 80.00
160 Kent Johnson AU/199 30.00 80.00

2022-23 Metal Universe '13 Retro

RT1 Connor McDavid 80.00 200.00
RT2 Aleksander Barkov 25.00 60.00
RT3 Kirill Kaprizov 60.00 150.00
RT4 Andrei Vasilevskiy 25.00 60.00
RT5 Alex Ovechkin 60.00 150.00
RT6 Artemi Panarin 30.00 80.00
RT7 Roman Josi 15.00 40.00
RT8 David Pastrnak 40.00 100.00
RT9 Mitch Marner 30.00 80.00
RT10 Auston Matthews 60.00 150.00
RT11 Brad Marchand 30.00 80.00
RT12 Leon Draisaitl 50.00 125.00
RT13 Steven Stamkos 30.00 80.00
RT14 Kyle Connor 25.00 60.00
RT15 Nathan MacKinnon 60.00 150.00
RT16 Sergei Bobrovsky 25.00 60.00
RT17 Cale Makar 80.00 200.00
RT18 Patrick Kane 30.00 80.00
RT19 Dylan Larkin 20.00 50.00
RT20 Sidney Crosby 60.00 150.00

2022-23 Metal Universe '98-99 Retro

*PURPLE/199: 2.5X TO 6X BASIC
R1 Juraj Slafkovsky 5.00 12.00
R2 Shane Wright 2.50 6.00
R3 Matt Boldy 3.00 8.00
R4 Matty Beniers 2.50 6.00
R5 Owen Power 2.00 5.00
R6 Wyatt Johnston 4.00 10.00
R7 Jack Quinn 1.50 4.00
R8 Marco Rossi 2.50 6.00
R9 Jacob Perreault 1.00 2.50
R10 Kent Johnson 2.00 5.00
R11 Lukas Dostal 2.00 5.00
R12 Matias Maccelli 1.50 4.00
R13 Jack McBain .75 2.00
R14 Jake Sanderson 2.50 6.00
R15 Brayden Tracey .75 2.00
R16 Elmer Soderblom 2.00 5.00
R17 Jordan Harris 1.25 3.00
R18 Braden Schneider 1.50 4.00
R19 Mads Sogaard 1.25 3.00
R20 Isaac Ratcliffe 1.00 2.50
R21 Pyotr Kochetkov 2.00 5.00
R22 Pavol Regenda 1.00 2.50
R23 Samuel Fagemo .75 2.00
R24 Nick Blankenburg .75 2.00
R25 Dylan Samberg 1.00 2.50
R26 Hunter Drew 1.00 2.50
R27 Trey Fix-Wolansky 1.00 2.50
R28 Chase Pearson .75 2.00

R29 Jordan Spence 1.00 2.50
R30 Mark Kastelic .75 2.00
R31 Michael Eyssimont 1.00 2.50
R32 Nick Abruzzese 1.00 2.50
R33 Kaiden Guhle 2.00 5.00
R34 Arber Xhekaj 2.00 5.00
R35 Jakub Lauko 1.25 3.00
R36 Ronnie Attard 1.00 2.50
R37 Jacob Moverare .75 2.00
R38 Mitchell Chaffee .75 2.00
R39 Brandon Biro 1.50 4.00
R40 Brayden Pachal .75 2.00
R41 Ben Meyers 1.00 2.50
R42 Noah Cates 1.00 2.50
R43 Kaedan Korczak .75 2.00
R44 Nils Aman 1.00 2.50
R45 Brandt Clarke 2.00 5.00
R46 Thomas Bordeleau 1.00 2.50
R47 Dylan Holloway 2.00 5.00
R48 Lukas Reichel 2.00 5.00
R49 Dylan Guenther 2.50 6.00
R50 Andrei Kuzmenko 2.00 5.00

2022-23 Metal Universe '98-99 Retro Precious Metal Gems Red

*PMG RED: 5X TO 12X BASIC
R3 Matt Boldy/90* 40.00 100.00
R14 Jake Sanderson/90* 60.00 150.00
R24 Nick Blankenburg/90* 30.00 80.00
R48 Lukas Reichel/90* 40.00 100.00

2022-23 Metal Universe '98-99 SkyBox Premium Prospects Autographs

SR1 Juraj Slafkovsky B 60.00 150.00
SR2 Shane Wright B 30.00 80.00
SR3 Matt Boldy B 40.00 100.00
SR5 Owen Power B 25.00 60.00
SR6 Wyatt Johnston C 50.00 125.00
SR7 Jack Quinn C 20.00 50.00
SR8 Marco Rossi A 30.00 80.00
SR9 Jacob Perreault E 12.00 30.00
SR10 Kent Johnson C 25.00 60.00
SR11 Lukas Dostal D 25.00 60.00
SR12 Matias Maccelli D 20.00 50.00
SR13 Jack McBain E 12.00 30.00
SR14 Jake Sanderson D 30.00 80.00
SR15 Brayden Tracey E 10.00 25.00
SR17 Jordan Harris E 15.00 40.00
SR18 Braden Schneider D 20.00 50.00
SR19 Mads Sogaard E 15.00 40.00
SR20 Isaac Ratcliffe E 12.00 30.00
SR21 Pyotr Kochetkov D 25.00 60.00
SR23 Samuel Fagemo C 10.00 25.00
SR25 Dylan Samberg E 12.00 30.00
SR27 Trey Fix-Wolansky D 12.00 30.00
SR28 Chase Pearson E 10.00 25.00
SR30 Mark Kastelic E 10.00 25.00
SR31 Michael Eyssimont E 12.00 30.00
SR32 Nick Abruzzese E 12.00 30.00
SR33 Kaiden Guhle E 25.00 60.00
SR34 Arber Xhekaj D 25.00 60.00
SR35 Jakub Lauko E 15.00 40.00
SR36 Ronnie Attard E 12.00 30.00
SR37 Jacob Moverare D 10.00 25.00
SR41 Ben Meyers D 12.00 30.00
SR42 Noah Cates D 12.00 30.00
SR43 Kaedan Korczak D 10.00 25.00
SR44 Nils Aman E 12.00 30.00
SR45 Brandt Clarke D 25.00 60.00
SR47 Dylan Holloway C 25.00 60.00
SR48 Lukas Reichel D 25.00 60.00
SR49 Dylan Guenther C 30.00 80.00
SR50 Andrei Kuzmenko C 25.00 60.00

2022-23 Metal Universe '98-99 SkyBox Premium Prospects Star Rubies

SR1 Juraj Slafkovsky 50.00 125.00
SR2 Shane Wright 25.00 60.00
SR3 Matt Boldy 30.00 80.00
SR4 Matty Beniers 25.00 60.00
SR5 Owen Power 20.00 50.00
SR6 Wyatt Johnston 40.00 100.00
SR7 Jack Quinn 15.00 40.00
SR8 Marco Rossi 25.00 60.00
SR9 Jacob Perreault 10.00 25.00
SR10 Kent Johnson 20.00 50.00
SR11 Lukas Dostal 20.00 50.00
SR12 Matias Maccelli 15.00 40.00
SR13 Jack McBain 10.00 25.00
SR14 Jake Sanderson 25.00 60.00
SR15 Brayden Tracey 8.00 20.00
SR16 Elmer Soderblom 20.00 50.00
SR17 Jordan Harris 12.00 30.00
SR18 Braden Schneider 15.00 40.00
SR19 Mads Sogaard 12.00 30.00
SR20 Isaac Ratcliffe 10.00 25.00
SR21 Pyotr Kochetkov 20.00 50.00
SR22 Pavol Regenda 20.00 50.00
SR23 Samuel Fagemo 8.00 20.00
SR24 Kirill Marchenko 25.00 60.00
SR25 Dylan Samberg 10.00 25.00
SR26 David Jiricek 20.00 50.00
SR27 Trey Fix-Wolansky 10.00 25.00
SR28 Chase Pearson 8.00 20.00
SR29 Jordan Spence 10.00 25.00
SR30 Mark Kastelic 8.00 20.00
SR31 Michael Eyssimont 10.00 25.00
SR32 Nick Abruzzese 10.00 25.00
SR33 Kaiden Guhle 20.00 50.00
SR34 Arber Xhekaj 20.00 50.00
SR35 Jakub Lauko 12.00 30.00
SR36 Ronnie Attard 10.00 25.00
SR37 Jacob Moverare 8.00 20.00
SR38 Mitchell Chaffee 8.00 20.00
SR39 Brandon Biro 15.00 40.00
SR40 Brayden Pachal 8.00 20.00
SR41 Ben Meyers 10.00 25.00
SR42 Noah Cates 10.00 25.00
SR43 Kaedan Korczak 8.00 20.00
SR44 Nils Aman 10.00 25.00
SR45 Brandt Clarke 20.00 50.00
SR46 Thomas Bordeleau 10.00 25.00
SR47 Dylan Holloway 20.00 50.00
SR48 Lukas Reichel 20.00 50.00
SR49 Dylan Guenther 25.00 60.00
SR50 Andrei Kuzmenko 20.00 50.00

2022-23 Metal Universe All Starring

*GOLD/50: .75X TO 2X BASIC
AS1 Connor McDavid 20.00 50.00
AS2 Auston Matthews 15.00 40.00
AS3 Jack Hughes 10.00 25.00
AS4 Tom Wilson 4.00 10.00
AS5 Nazem Kadri 5.00 12.00
AS6 Claude Giroux 4.00 10.00
AS7 Adam Pelech 2.50 6.00
AS8 Clayton Keller 5.00 12.00
AS9 Johnny Gaudreau 6.00 15.00
AS10 Jordan Kyrou 4.00 10.00
AS11 John Gibson 4.00 10.00
AS12 Joe Pavelski 5.00 12.00
AS13 Jonathan Huberdeau 5.00 12.00
AS14 Thatcher Demko 5.00 12.00
AS15 Roman Josi 4.00 10.00
AS16 Patrice Bergeron 5.00 12.00
AS17 Cale Makar 10.00 25.00
AS18 Frederik Andersen 5.00 12.00
AS19 Juuse Saros 5.00 12.00
AS20 Tristan Jarry 4.00 10.00
AS21 Evgeny Kuznetsov 5.00 12.00
AS22 Cam Talbot 4.00 10.00
AS23 Jack Campbell 4.00 10.00
AS24 Zach Werenski 6.00 15.00
AS25 Dylan Larkin 5.00 12.00
AS26 Trevor Zegras 4.00 10.00
AS27 Leon Draisaitl 12.00 30.00
AS28 Jake Guentzel 6.00 15.00
AS29 Jordan Eberle 4.00 10.00
AS30 Alex Pietrangelo 3.00 8.00
AS31 Sebastian Aho 6.00 15.00
AS32 Timo Meier 4.00 10.00
AS33 Nick Suzuki 8.00 20.00
AS34 Mark Stone 5.00 12.00
AS35 Adrian Kempe 4.00 10.00
AS36 Kyle Connor 6.00 15.00
AS37 Troy Terry 3.00 8.00
AS38 Alex DeBrincat 5.00 12.00
AS39 Brady Tkachuk 6.00 15.00
AS40 Kirill Kaprizov 12.00 30.00
AS41 Rasmus Dahlin 5.00 12.00
AS42 Jonathan Marchessault 5.00 12.00
AS43 Andrei Vasilevskiy 6.00 15.00
AS44 Chris Kreider 5.00 12.00
AS45 Victor Hedman 5.00 12.00
AS46 Mika Zibanejad 5.00 12.00
AS47 Adam Fox 5.00 12.00
AS48 Steven Stamkos 8.00 20.00

2022-23 Metal Universe Aspects

A1 Aleksander Barkov 1.50 4.00
A2 Roman Josi 1.00 2.50
A3 Sidney Crosby 4.00 10.00
A4 Nazem Kadri 1.25 3.00
A5 Nathan MacKinnon 4.00 10.00
A6 Tim Stutzle 1.25 3.00
A7 Sebastian Aho 1.50 4.00
A8 Trevor Zegras 1.00 2.50
A9 Leon Draisaitl 3.00 8.00
A10 Johnny Gaudreau 1.50 4.00
A11 Robert Thomas 1.00 2.50
A12 Kirill Kaprizov 3.00 8.00
A13 David Pastrnak 2.50 6.00
A15 Cale Makar 2.50 6.00
A16 Anze Kopitar 1.50 4.00
A17 Auston Matthews 4.00 10.00
A18 Connor McDavid 5.00 12.00
A19 Cole Caufield 2.00 5.00
A20 Mitch Marner 1.50 4.00
A21 Juraj Slafkovsky 5.00 12.00
A22 Owen Power 2.00 5.00
A23 Matty Beniers 2.50 6.00
A24 Jake Sanderson 2.50 6.00
A25 Kent Johnson 2.00 5.00
A26 Jack Quinn 1.50 4.00
A27 Matt Boldy 3.00 8.00
A28 Dylan Holloway 2.00 5.00
A29 Wyatt Johnston 4.00 10.00
A30 Shane Wright 2.50 6.00

2022-23 Metal Universe Aspects Gold

*GOLD/49: 2.5X TO 6X BASIC
A29 Wyatt Johnston 30.00 80.00

2022-23 Metal Universe Bottle Rockets

BR1 Alex Ovechkin 4.00 10.00
BR2 Gabriel Landeskog 1.25 3.00
BR3 Jordan Kyrou 1.00 2.50
BR4 Anders Lee .75 2.00
BR5 John Tavares 1.50 4.00
BR6 Jack Eichel 1.50 4.00
BR7 Jonathan Huberdeau 1.25 3.00
BR8 Johnny Gaudreau 1.50 4.00
BR9 Aleksander Barkov 1.50 4.00
BR10 Brock Boeser 1.25 3.00
BR11 Jake Guentzel 1.50 4.00
BR12 Trevor Zegras 1.00 2.50
BR13 Andrei Svechnikov 1.25 3.00
BR15 Sebastian Aho 1.50 4.00
BR16 Brady Tkachuk 1.50 4.00
BR17 Nick Suzuki 2.00 5.00
BR18 Kirill Kaprizov 3.00 8.00
BR19 Mason McTavish 1.00 2.50
BR20 Mark Stone 1.25 3.00
BR21 Logan Couture 1.25 3.00
BR22 Clayton Keller 1.25 3.00
BR23 Taylor Hall 1.00 2.50
BR24 Jason Robertson 1.50 4.00
BR25 Kyle Connor 1.50 4.00
BR26 Oliver Bjorkstrand .75 2.00
BR27 Tyler Bertuzzi .75 2.00
BR28 Kevin Fiala .75 2.00
BR29 Yanni Gourde .75 2.00
BR30 Elias Pettersson 1.50 4.00

2022-23 Metal Universe Bottle Rockets Gold

*GOLD/35: 1.5X TO 4X BASIC
BR1 Alex Ovechkin 25.00 60.00

2022-23 Metal Universe Cache

*GOLD/50: 2.5X TO 6X BASIC
C1 Connor McDavid 8.00 20.00
C2 Roman Josi 1.50 4.00
C3 Kirill Kaprizov 5.00 12.00
C4 Quinn Hughes 4.00 10.00
C5 Matty Beniers 4.00 10.00
C6 Elias Pettersson 2.50 6.00
C7 Jack Quinn 2.50 6.00
C8 Wyatt Johnston 6.00 15.00
C9 Moritz Seider 2.00 5.00
C10 Patrick Kane 3.00 8.00
C11 Dylan Holloway 3.00 8.00
C12 Aleksander Barkov 2.50 6.00
C13 Brad Marchand 3.00 8.00
C14 Matt Boldy 5.00 12.00
C15 Anze Kopitar 2.50 6.00
C16 Jonathan Huberdeau 2.00 5.00
C17 Mitch Marner 2.50 6.00
C18 Connor Hellebuyck 3.00 8.00
C19 Nick Suzuki 3.00 8.00
C20 Auston Matthews 6.00 15.00
C21 Jordan Kyrou 1.50 4.00
C22 Kent Johnson 3.00 8.00
C23 Jack Hughes 4.00 10.00
C24 Andrei Vasilevskiy 2.50 6.00
C25 Nathan MacKinnon 6.00 15.00
C26 Sebastian Aho 2.50 6.00
C27 Matthew Tkachuk 3.00 8.00
C28 Jack Eichel 2.50 6.00
C29 Cole Caufield 3.00 8.00
C30 Cale Makar 4.00 10.00
C31 Nazem Kadri 2.00 5.00
C32 Leon Draisaitl 5.00 12.00
C33 David Pastrnak 4.00 10.00
C34 Tim Stutzle 2.00 5.00
C35 Juraj Slafkovsky 8.00 20.00
C36 Trevor Zegras 1.50 4.00
C37 Clayton Keller 2.00 5.00
C38 Shane Wright 4.00 10.00
C39 Mathew Barzal 2.00 5.00
C40 Alex Ovechkin 6.00 15.00
C42 Steven Stamkos 3.00 8.00
C43 Jake Sanderson 4.00 10.00
C44 Timo Meier 1.50 4.00
C45 Patrik Laine 2.00 5.00
C46 Cam Atkinson 1.50 4.00
C47 Owen Power 3.00 8.00
C48 Artemi Panarin 3.00 8.00
C49 Jake Oettinger 2.50 6.00
C50 Sidney Crosby 6.00 15.00

2022-23 Metal Universe Flash the Glove

*GOLD/99: 2X TO 5X BASIC
FL1 Andrei Vasilevskiy 1.50 4.00
FL2 Igor Shesterkin 2.00 5.00
FL3 Jake Oettinger 1.50 4.00
FL4 Jacob Markstrom 1.00 2.50
FL5 Ilya Sorokin 1.00 2.50
FL6 Tristan Jarry 1.00 2.50
FL7 Connor Hellebuyck 2.00 5.00
FL8 Juuse Saros 1.25 3.00
FL9 Frederik Andersen 1.25 3.00
FL10 Jack Campbell 1.00 2.50
FL11 Darcy Kuemper 1.00 2.50
FL12 Sergei Bobrovsky 1.50 4.00
FL13 Jordan Binnington 1.50 4.00
FL14 Alexandar Georgiev 1.00 2.50
FL15 Thatcher Demko 1.25 3.00
FL16 Logan Thompson 1.25 3.00
FL17 Marc-Andre Fleury 2.00 5.00
FL18 Jeremy Swayman 1.50 4.00
FL19 Ville Husso .60 1.50
FL20 Elvis Merzlikins 1.00 2.50
FL21 John Gibson 1.00 2.50
FL22 Ilya Samsonov 1.00 2.50
FL23 Cam Talbot 1.00 2.50
FL24 Carter Hart 1.00 2.50
FL25 Linus Ullmark 1.00 2.50
FL26 Matt Murray 1.00 2.50
FL28 Pavel Francouz .75 2.00
FL29 Jonathan Quick 1.25 3.00
FL30 Jake Allen 1.00 2.50
FL31 Petr Mrazek .75 2.00
FL32 Vitek Vanecek 1.00 2.50
FL33 Alex Nedeljkovic .75 2.00
FL34 Philipp Grubauer 1.00 2.50
FL35 Cal Petersen .60 1.50
FL36 Karel Vejmelka .60 1.50
FL37 Carey Price 2.00 5.00
FL38 Mads Sogaard 1.25 3.00
FL39 Lukas Dostal 2.00 5.00
FL40 Pyotr Kochetkov 2.00 5.00

2022-23 Metal Universe Flash the Glove Autographs

FL1 Andrei Vasilevskiy B 25.00 60.00
FL2 Igor Shesterkin B 30.00 80.00
FL3 Jake Oettinger B 25.00 60.00
FL6 Tristan Jarry C 15.00 40.00
FL7 Connor Hellebuyck A 30.00 80.00
FL8 Juuse Saros C 20.00 50.00
FL10 Jack Campbell B 15.00 40.00
FL11 Darcy Kuemper A 15.00 40.00
FL15 Thatcher Demko C 20.00 50.00
FL16 Logan Thompson A 20.00 50.00
FL17 Marc-Andre Fleury B 30.00 80.00
FL18 Jeremy Swayman D 25.00 60.00
FL19 Ville Husso C 10.00 25.00
FL20 Elvis Merzlikins C 15.00 40.00
FL21 John Gibson D 15.00 40.00
FL24 Carter Hart C 15.00 40.00
FL28 Pavel Francouz D 12.00 30.00
FL30 Jake Allen D 15.00 40.00
FL32 Vitek Vanecek D 15.00 40.00
FL33 Alex Nedeljkovic D 12.00 30.00
FL34 Philipp Grubauer D 15.00 40.00
FL37 Carey Price B 30.00 80.00
FL38 Mads Sogaard D 20.00 50.00
FL39 Lukas Dostal D 30.00 80.00
FL40 Pyotr Kochetkov D 30.00 80.00

2022-23 Metal Universe Hardware

*GOLD/25: .75X TO 2X BASIC
HW1 Nathan MacKinnon 40.00 100.00
HW2 Cale Makar 25.00 60.00
HW3 Gabriel Landeskog 12.00 30.00
HW4 Nazem Kadri 12.00 30.00
HW5 Mikko Rantanen 25.00 60.00
HW6 Darcy Kuemper 10.00 25.00
HW7 Artturi Lehkonen 8.00 20.00
HW8 Valeri Nichushkin 10.00 25.00
HW9 Devon Toews 8.00 20.00
HW10 Bowen Byram 12.00 30.00

2022-23 Metal Universe Hot Numbers

HN1 Connor McDavid 150.00 400.00
HN2 Patrice Bergeron 40.00 100.00
HN3 Andrei Svechnikov 40.00 100.00
HN4 Mika Zibanejad 40.00 100.00
HN5 Jake Oettinger 50.00 125.00
HN6 Alex Ovechkin 125.00 300.00
HN7 Matthew Tkachuk 60.00 150.00
HN8 Kyle Connor 50.00 120.00
HN9 Clayton Keller 40.00 100.00
HN10 Jack Eichel 50.00 120.00
HN11 Patrik Laine 40.00 100.00
HN12 Jack Hughes 80.00 200.00
HN13 Kirill Kaprizov 100.00 250.00
HN14 Andrei Vasilevskiy 50.00 125.00
HN15 Moritz Seider 40.00 100.00
HN16 Roman Josi 30.00 80.00
HN17 Jonathan Toews 50.00 125.00
HN18 Vladimir Tarasenko 40.00 100.00
HN19 Adam Fox 40.00 100.00
HN20 Rasmus Dahlin 40.00 100.00
HN21 Andre Burakovsky 20.00 50.00
HN22 Mikko Rantanen 80.00 200.00
HN23 Kevin Fiala 25.00 60.00
HN24 Trevor Zegras 30.00 80.00
HN25 Brady Tkachuk 50.00 125.00
HN26 Mitch Marner 50.00 125.00
HN27 Bo Horvat 40.00 100.00
HN28 Nazem Kadri 40.00 100.00
HN29 Mathew Barzal 40.00 100.00
HN30 Erik Karlsson 40.00 100.00
HN31 Cole Caufield 60.00 150.00
HN32 David Pastrnak 80.00 200.00
HN33 Leon Draisaitl 100.00 250.00
HN34 Carter Hart 30.00 80.00
HN35 Sidney Crosby 125.00 300.00

2022-23 Metal Universe Hot Shots

1OF20HS Sidney Crosby 40.00 100.00
2OF20HS Connor McDavid 60.00 150.00
3OF20HS Cole Caufield 30.00 80.00
4OF20HS Auston Matthews 40.00 100.00
5OF20HS Artemi Panarin 30.00 80.00
6OF20HS Nikita Kucherov 15.00 40.00
7OF20HS Jack Eichel 25.00 60.00
8OF20HS Aleksander Barkov 25.00 60.00
9OF20HS Jason Robertson 25.00 60.00
10OF20HS Nathan MacKinnon 25.00 60.00
11OF20HS Leon Draisaitl 50.00 125.00
12OF20HS Shane Wright 25.00 60.00
13OF20HS Tage Thompson 20.00 50.00
14OF20HS Patrice Bergeron 20.00 50.00
15OF20HS Elias Pettersson 25.00 60.00
16OF20HS Alex Ovechkin 60.00 150.00
17OF20HS Nazem Kadri 20.00 50.00
18OF20HS Matt Boldy 50.00 125.00
19OF20HS Johnny Gaudreau 25.00 60.00
20OF20HS Tim Stutzle 20.00 50.00

2022-23 Metal Universe Jambalaya

1 Connor McDavid 100.00 250.00
2 Nick Suzuki 40.00 100.00
3 Auston Matthews 80.00 200.00
4 Elias Pettersson 30.00 80.00
5 Cale Makar 50.00 125.00
6 Matthew Tkachuk 40.00 100.00
7 David Pastrnak 50.00 125.00
8 Steven Stamkos 40.00 100.00
9 Moritz Seider 25.00 60.00
10 Patrik Laine 25.00 60.00
11 Mitch Marner 30.00 80.00
12 Igor Shesterkin 40.00 100.00
13 Kyle Connor 30.00 80.00
14 Alex DeBrincat 25.00 60.00
15 Nathan MacKinnon 80.00 200.00
16 Kirill Kaprizov 60.00 150.00
17 Alex Ovechkin 80.00 200.00
18 Leon Draisaitl 60.00 150.00
19 Jonathan Huberdeau 25.00 60.00
20 Sidney Crosby 80.00 200.00

2022-23 Metal Universe Jarring

*GOLD/50: 3X TO 8X BASIC
JR1 Auston Matthews 6.00 15.00
JR2 Jack Eichel 2.50 6.00
JR3 Vladimir Tarasenko 2.00 5.00
JR4 Rasmus Dahlin 2.00 5.00
JR5 Tom Wilson 1.50 4.00
JR6 Mattias Ekholm 1.25 3.00
JR7 Victor Hedman 2.00 5.00
JR8 Tage Thompson 2.00 5.00
JR9 Jacob Slavin 1.25 3.00
JR10 Darnell Nurse 1.25 3.00
JR11 Andrei Kuzmenko 3.00 8.00
JR12 Kris Letang 2.00 5.00
JR13 Shea Theodore 2.00 5.00
JR14 Sam Reinhart 3.00 8.00
JR15 Morgan Rielly 1.50 4.00
JR16 J.T. Miller 2.00 5.00
JR17 Brent Burns 1.50 4.00
JR18 K'Andre Miller 1.25 3.00
JR19 Clayton Keller 2.00 5.00
JR20 Connor McDavid 8.00 20.00
JR21 Bryan Rust 1.50 4.00
JR22 Kent Johnson 3.00 8.00
JR23 Anders Lee 1.25 3.00
JR24 Mason McTavish 3.00 8.00
JR25 Jack Quinn 2.50 6.00
JR26 Brock Nelson 1.50 4.00
JR27 Brandon Hagel 1.25 3.00
JR28 Taylor Hall 1.50 4.00
JR29 Blake Coleman 1.25 3.00
JR30 Yegor Sharangovich 1.50 4.00
JR31 Bo Horvat 2.00 5.00
JR32 Kirby Dach 1.50 4.00

2022-23 Metal Universe Linchpins

1OF20LP Connor McDavid 100.00 250.00
2OF20LP Sidney Crosby 40.00 100.00
3OF20LP Kirill Kaprizov 30.00 80.00
4OF20LP Trevor Zegras 10.00 25.00
5OF20LP Juraj Slafkovsky 50.00 125.00
6OF20LP Igor Shesterkin 20.00 50.00
7OF20LP Owen Power 20.00 50.00
8OF20LP Alex Ovechkin 80.00 200.00
9OF20LP Kyle Connor 15.00 40.00
10OF20LP Jonathan Huberdeau 12.00 30.00
11OF20LP David Pastrnak 25.00 60.00
12OF20LP Patrick Kane 20.00 50.00
13OF20LP Moritz Seider 30.00 80.00
14OF20LP Matty Beniers 25.00 60.00
15OF20LP Cale Makar 25.00 60.00
16OF20LP Jack Hughes 25.00 60.00
17OF20LP Brady Tkachuk 15.00 40.00
18OF20LP Andrei Vasilevskiy 15.00 40.00
19OF20LP Matthew Tkachuk 20.00 50.00
20OF20LP Auston Matthews 40.00 100.00

2022-23 Metal Universe Metal Ore

*GOLD/50: 2X TO 5X BASIC
MO1 Brayden Point 1.50 4.00
MO2 Jason Robertson 2.00 5.00
MO3 Tage Thompson 1.50 4.00
MO4 Juuse Saros 1.50 4.00
MO5 Jonathan Marchessault 1.50 4.00
MO6 Kevin Fiala 1.00 2.50
MO7 Brent Burns 1.25 3.00
MO8 Tomas Hertl 1.25 3.00
MO9 Aleksander Barkov 2.00 5.00
MO10 Gabriel Landeskog 1.50 4.00
MO11 Jonathan Huberdeau 1.50 4.00
MO12 Evgeny Kuznetsov 1.50 4.00
MO13 Morgan Rielly 1.25 3.00
MO14 Drake Batherson 1.25 3.00
MO15 Tyler Toffoli 1.25 3.00
MO16 Robert Thomas 1.25 3.00
MO17 James van Riemsdyk 1.00 2.50
MO18 Cam Atkinson 1.25 3.00
MO19 Gabe Vilardi 1.25 3.00
MO20 Bo Horvat 1.50 4.00

2022-23 Metal Universe Metal X

MX1 Nathan MacKinnon 20.00 50.00
MX2 Cole Perfetti 5.00 12.00
MX3 Alex Tuch 5.00 12.00
MX4 Bo Horvat 6.00 15.00
MX5 Kirill Kaprizov 15.00 40.00
MX6 Sebastian Aho 8.00 20.00
MX7 Roman Josi 5.00 12.00
MX8 Cole Caufield 10.00 25.00
MX9 David Perron 4.00 10.00
MX10 Miro Heiskanen 6.00 15.00
MX11 Chris Kreider 6.00 15.00
MX12 Charlie McAvoy 6.00 15.00
MX13 Ilya Sorokin 8.00 20.00
MX14 Ryan O'Reilly 5.00 12.00
MX15 Brock Boeser 6.00 15.00
MX16 Tage Thompson 6.00 15.00
MX17 Dougie Hamilton 4.00 10.00
MX18 Phil Kessel 5.00 12.00
MX19 Erik Karlsson 6.00 15.00
MX20 Jake Guentzel 8.00 20.00
MX21 Alex DeBrincat 6.00 15.00
MX22 Cale Makar 12.00 30.00
MX23 William Nylander 10.00 25.00
MX24 Oliver Bjorkstrand 4.00 10.00
MX25 Andrei Svechnikov 6.00 15.00
MX26 Nazem Kadri 6.00 15.00
MX27 Nikita Kucherov 10.00 25.00
MX28 Noah Dobson 6.00 15.00
MX29 Mason McTavish 5.00 12.00
MX30 Aaron Ekblad 6.00 15.00
MX31 Artemi Panarin 10.00 25.00
MX32 Dylan Larkin 6.00 15.00
MX33 Mitch Marner 8.00 20.00
MX34 Kevin Fiala 4.00 10.00
MX35 Dylan Strome 6.00 15.00
MX36 Jonathan Toews 8.00 20.00
MX37 Aleksander Barkov 8.00 20.00
MX38 Evgeni Malkin 10.00 25.00
MX39 Jason Robertson 8.00 20.00
MX40 Filip Forsberg 8.00 20.00
MX41 Trevor Zegras 5.00 12.00
MX42 Claude Giroux 5.00 12.00
MX43 Nick Suzuki 10.00 25.00
MX44 Brad Marchand 10.00 25.00
MX45 Patrik Laine 6.00 15.00
MX46 Mikko Rantanen 12.00 30.00
MX47 Elias Lindholm 5.00 12.00
MX48 Jesper Bratt 5.00 12.00
MX49 Morgan Rielly 5.00 12.00
MX50 Auston Matthews 20.00 50.00
MX51 Jakob Chychrun 5.00 12.00
MX52 Adrian Kempe 5.00 12.00
MX53 Timo Meier 5.00 12.00
MX54 Shea Theodore 6.00 15.00
MX55 Leon Draisaitl 15.00 40.00
MX56 Mathew Barzal 6.00 15.00
MX57 Sidney Crosby 20.00 50.00
MX58 Patrick Kane 10.00 25.00
MX59 Victor Hedman 6.00 15.00
MX60 Connor McDavid 25.00 60.00
MX61 Juraj Slafkovsky 25.00 60.00
MX62 Shane Wright 12.00 30.00
MX63 Owen Power 10.00 25.00
MX64 Matt Boldy 15.00 40.00
MX65 Matty Beniers 12.00 30.00
MX66 Jack Quinn 8.00 20.00
MX67 Marco Rossi 12.00 30.00
MX68 Andrei Kuzmenko 10.00 25.00
MX69 Kent Johnson 10.00 25.00
MX70 Wyatt Johnston 20.00 50.00

2022-23 Metal Universe Palladium

*GOLD/25: 2X TO 5X BASIC
P1 Auston Matthews 8.00 20.00
P2 Cale Makar 5.00 12.00
P3 David Pastrnak 5.00 12.00
P4 Igor Shesterkin 4.00 10.00
P5 Nick Suzuki 4.00 10.00
P6 Roman Josi 2.00 5.00
P7 Jack Hughes 5.00 12.00
P8 Sidney Crosby 8.00 20.00
P9 Connor McDavid 10.00 25.00
P10 Patrick Kane 4.00 10.00
P11 Jason Robertson 3.00 8.00
P12 Andrei Svechnikov 2.50 6.00
P13 Andrei Vasilevskiy 3.00 8.00
P14 Carter Hart 2.00 5.00
P15 Kirill Kaprizov 6.00 15.00
P16 Leon Draisaitl 6.00 15.00
P17 Nathan MacKinnon 8.00 20.00
P18 Mitch Marner 3.00 8.00
P19 Matthew Tkachuk 4.00 10.00
P20 Claude Giroux 2.00 5.00
P21 Trevor Zegras 2.00 5.00
P22 Anze Kopitar 3.00 8.00
P23 Quinn Hughes 5.00 12.00
P24 Logan Thompson 2.50 6.00
P25 Moritz Seider 2.50 6.00
P26 Juraj Slafkovsky 10.00 25.00
P27 Jack Quinn 3.00 8.00
P28 Owen Power 4.00 10.00
P29 Jake Sanderson 5.00 12.00
P30 Kent Johnson 4.00 10.00

2022-23 Metal Universe Skybox Premium Prospects

*BLUE: .8X TO 2X BASIC
*STAR RUBIES/50: 3X TO 8X BASIC
PP1 Juraj Slafkovsky 5.00 12.00
PP2 Shane Wright 2.50 6.00
PP3 Matt Boldy 3.00 8.00
PP4 Matty Beniers 2.50 6.00
PP5 Owen Power 2.00 5.00
PP6 Wyatt Johnston 4.00 10.00
PP7 Jack Quinn 1.50 4.00
PP8 Marco Rossi 2.50 6.00
PP9 Jacob Perreault 1.00 2.50
PP10 Kent Johnson 2.00 5.00
PP11 Lukas Dostal 2.00 5.00
PP12 Matias Maccelli 1.50 4.00
PP13 Jack McBain 1.00 2.50
PP14 Jake Sanderson 2.50 6.00
PP15 Brayden Tracey .75 2.00
PP16 Elmer Soderblom 2.00 5.00
PP17 Jordan Harris 1.25 3.00
PP18 Braden Schneider 1.50 4.00
PP19 Mads Sogaard 1.25 3.00
PP20 Isaac Ratcliffe 1.00 2.50
PP21 Pyotr Kochetkov 2.00 5.00
PP22 Pavol Regenda 1.00 2.50
PP23 Samuel Fagemo .75 2.00
PP24 Nick Blankenburg .75 2.00
PP25 Dylan Samberg 1.00 2.50
PP26 Hunter Drew 1.00 2.50
PP27 Trey Fix-Wolansky 1.00 2.50
PP28 Jonatan Berggren 1.50 4.00
PP29 Jordan Spence 1.00 2.50
PP30 Mark Kastelic .75 2.00
PP31 Michael Eyssimont 1.00 2.50
PP32 Nick Abruzzese 1.00 2.50
PP33 Kaiden Guhle 2.00 5.00
PP34 Arber Xhekaj 2.00 5.00
PP35 Jakub Lauko 1.25 3.00
PP36 Ronnie Attard 1.00 2.50
PP37 Kirill Marchenko 2.50 6.00
PP38 Mitchell Chaffee .75 2.00
PP39 Brandon Biro 1.50 4.00
PP40 Brayden Pachal .75 2.00
PP41 Ben Meyers 1.00 2.50
PP42 Noah Cates 1.00 2.50
PP43 Kaedan Korczak .75 2.00
PP44 Nils Aman 1.00 2.50
PP45 Brandt Clarke 2.00 5.00
PP46 Thomas Bordeleau 1.00 2.50
PP47 Dylan Holloway 2.00 5.00
PP48 Lukas Reichel 2.00 5.00
PP49 Dylan Guenther 2.50 6.00
PP50 Andrei Kuzmenko 2.00 5.00

2022-23 Metal Universe Tetrad

TR1 Mitch Marner 10.00 25.00
TR2 Jack Eichel 10.00 25.00
TR3 Patrice Bergeron 8.00 20.00
TR4 Jeff Skinner 6.00 15.00
TR5 Filip Forsberg 10.00 25.00
TR6 Auston Matthews 25.00 60.00
TR7 Brock Nelson 6.00 15.00
TR8 Tyler Bertuzzi 5.00 12.00
TR9 Leon Draisaitl 20.00 50.00
TR10 David Pastrnak 25.00 60.00
TR11 John Tavares 10.00 25.00
TR12 Blake Wheeler 6.00 15.00
TR13 Anze Kopitar 10.00 25.00
TR14 Evander Kane 6.00 15.00
TR15 Alex Ovechkin 25.00 60.00
TR16 Max Pacioretty 6.00 15.00
TR17 Tyler Seguin 8.00 20.00
TR18 Tomas Hertl 6.00 15.00
TR19 Sam Bennett 10.00 25.00
TR20 Connor McDavid 30.00 80.00

2022-23 Metal Universe The House

TH1 Connor McDavid 8.00 20.00
TH2 Nathan MacKinnon 6.00 15.00
TH3 Sidney Crosby 6.00 15.00
TH4 Jack Eichel 2.50 6.00
TH5 Jack Hughes 4.00 10.00
TH6 Patrice Bergeron 2.50 6.00
TH7 Nick Suzuki 3.00 8.00
TH8 Mathew Barzal 2.00 5.00
TH9 Leon Draisaitl 5.00 12.00
TH10 Sebastian Aho 2.50 6.00
TH11 Tomas Hertl 1.50 4.00
TH12 J.T. Miller 2.00 5.00
TH13 Aleksander Barkov 2.50 6.00
TH14 Robert Thomas 1.50 4.00
TH15 Elias Lindholm 1.50 4.00
TH16 Dylan Larkin 2.00 5.00
TH17 Clayton Keller 2.00 5.00
TH18 Steven Stamkos 3.00 8.00
TH19 Auston Matthews 6.00 15.00
TH20 Mika Zibanejad 2.00 5.00
TH21 Anze Kopitar 2.50 6.00
TH22 Josh Norris 1.50 4.00
TH23 Tage Thompson 2.00 5.00
TH24 Sean Couturier 1.25 3.00
TH25 Trevor Zegras 1.50 4.00
TH26 Wyatt Johnston 6.00 15.00
TH27 Marco Rossi 4.00 10.00
TH28 Shane Wright 4.00 10.00
TH29 Matty Beniers 4.00 10.00
TH30 Lukas Reichel 3.00 8.00

2022-23 Metal Universe The House Gold Spectrum

*GOLD/50: 2X TO 5X BASIC
TH1 Connor McDavid 80.00 200.00

2023-24 Metal Universe

1 Steven Stamkos 1.00 2.50
2 Bowen Byram .60 1.50
3 Lucas Raymond .75 2.00
4 Mark Stone .60 1.50
5 Filip Gustavsson .50 1.25
6 Torey Krug .40 1.00
7 Shea Theodore .60 1.50
8 Jake Oettinger .75 2.00
9 Tristan Jarry .50 1.25
10 Pavel Buchnevich .40 1.00
11 Tomas Hertl .50 1.25
12 Karel Vejmelka .30 .75
13 Marcus Foligno .40 1.00
14 J.T. Miller .60 1.50
15 Brandon Montour .60 1.50
16 Mattias Ekholm .40 1.00
17 Seth Jones .50 1.25
18 William Eklund .60 1.50
19 Jaccob Slavin .40 1.00
20 Logan Thompson .60 1.50
21 Jacob Markstrom .50 1.25
22 Philipp Grubauer .50 1.25
23 John Gibson .50 1.25
24 Seth Jarvis .60 1.50
25 Brandon Hagel .40 1.00
26 Colton Parayko .40 1.00
27 Nico Hischier .75 2.00
28 Filip Forsberg .75 2.00
29 Robert Thomas .50 1.25
30 Zach Werenski .75 2.00
31 MacKenzie Weegar .40 1.00
32 Joe Pavelski .60 1.50
33 Ryan O'Reilly .50 1.25
34 Chandler Stephenson .40 1.00
35 Wyatt Johnston 1.00 2.50
36 Pavel Zacha .40 1.00
37 Cole Perfetti .50 1.25
38 Jake Sanderson .60 1.50
39 Anders Lee .40 1.00
40 Juraj Slafkovsky 1.00 2.50
41 Mario Ferraro .30 .75
42 Tom Wilson .50 1.25
43 Stuart Skinner .60 1.50
44 Ryan Strome .50 1.25
45 John Tavares .75 2.00
46 Alexandar Georgiev .50 1.25
47 Kent Johnson .50 1.25
48 Patrik Laine .60 1.50
49 Owen Power .50 1.25
50 Nick Suzuki 1.00 2.50
51 Nazem Kadri .60 1.50
52 Frederik Andersen .50 1.25
53 Dylan Larkin .60 1.50
54 Josh Morrissey .60 1.50
55 Andrei Svechnikov .60 1.50
56 Nicklas Backstrom .50 1.25
57 Shane Wright .60 1.50
58 Morgan Frost .40 1.00
59 Mika Zibanejad .60 1.50
60 Dawson Mercer .60 1.50
61 Andrei Kuzmenko .50 1.25
62 Timo Meier .50 1.25
63 Tyler Bertuzzi .40 1.00
64 Zach Hyman .75 2.00
65 Bo Horvat .60 1.50
66 Victor Hedman .60 1.50
67 Dylan Guenther .60 1.50
68 Darcy Kuemper .50 1.25
69 JJ Peterka .50 1.25
70 Noah Cates .30 .75
71 Claude Giroux .50 1.25
72 Dylan Cozens .50 1.25
73 Alex Newhook .40 1.00
74 Marc-Andre Fleury 1.00 2.50
75 Jared McCann .40 1.00
76 J.T. Compher .30 .75
77 Anthony Beauvillier .30 .75
78 Kevin Fiala .40 1.00
79 Josh Norris .50 1.25
80 Alexis Lafreniere .75 2.00
81 Sergei Bobrovsky .75 2.00
82 Nick Schmaltz .40 1.00
83 Linus Ullmark .50 1.25
84 K'Andre Miller .40 1.00
85 Evan Bouchard .60 1.50
86 Charlie McAvoy .60 1.50
87 Anton Lundell .50 1.25
88 Taylor Raddysh .40 1.00
89 Mason McTavish .60 1.50
90 Pierre-Luc Dubois .40 1.00
91 Kyle Connor .75 2.00
92 Noah Dobson .60 1.50
93 Taylor Hall .50 1.25
94 Kirby Dach .50 1.25
95 Quinton Byfield .60 1.50
96 Vladimir Tarasenko .60 1.50
97 Jonathan Marchessault .60 1.50
98 Carter Hart .60 1.50
99 Jake Guentzel .75 2.00
100 Troy Terry .40 1.00
101 Connor McDavid 2.50 6.00
102 Juuse Saros .60 1.50
103 Jordan Kyrou .60 1.50
104 Sidney Crosby 2.00 5.00
105 Tage Thompson .60 1.50
106 Clayton Keller .60 1.50
107 Ilya Sorokin .75 2.00
108 Auston Matthews 2.00 5.00
109 Ryan Nugent-Hopkins .60 1.50
110 Aleksander Barkov .75 2.00
111 Brady Tkachuk .75 2.00
112 Igor Shesterkin 1.00 2.50
113 Brayden Point .60 1.50
114 Rasmus Dahlin .60 1.50
115 Miro Heiskanen .60 1.50
116 Jonathan Huberdeau .60 1.50
117 Sebastian Aho .75 2.00
118 Matthew Tkachuk 1.00 2.50
119 Roman Josi .50 1.25
120 Brent Burns .50 1.25
121 Mikko Rantanen 1.25 3.00

122 Andrei Vasilevskiy .75 2.00
123 Alex Ovechkin 2.00 5.00
124 Brad Marchand 1.00 2.50
125 Cale Makar 1.25 3.00
126 Leon Draisaitl 1.50 4.00
127 Tim Stutzle .60 1.50
128 Jack Hughes 1.25 3.00
129 William Nylander 1.00 2.50
130 Mathew Barzal .60 1.50
131 Matty Beniers .60 1.50
132 Trevor Zegras .50 1.25
133 Jason Robertson .75 2.00
134 Moritz Seider .60 1.50
135 Cole Caufield 1.00 2.50
136 Erik Karlsson .60 1.50
137 David Pastrnak 1.25 3.00
138 Nathan MacKinnon 2.00 5.00
139 Johnny Gaudreau .75 2.00
140 Anze Kopitar .75 2.00
141 Kirill Kaprizov 1.50 4.00
142 Artemi Panarin 1.00 2.50
143 Connor Hellebuyck 1.00 2.50
144 Evgeni Malkin 1.00 2.50
145 Quinn Hughes 1.25 3.00
146 Nikita Kucherov 1.00 2.50
147 Mitch Marner .75 2.00
148 Jack Eichel .75 2.00
149 Elias Pettersson .75 2.00
150 Adam Fox .60 1.50
151 Leo Carlsson RC 3.00 8.00
152 Adam Fantilli RC 3.00 8.00
153 Marco Kasper RC 2.50 6.00
154 Tyson Foerster RC 2.00 5.00
155 Matthew Knies RC 4.00 10.00
156 Jakob Pelletier RC 1.25 3.00
157 Owen Beck RC 1.50 4.00
158 Sean Farrell RC 1.00 2.50
159 Luke Evangelista RC 1.50 4.00
160 Matthew Coronato RC 1.50 4.00
161 Will Cuylle RC 1.50 4.00
162 Ridly Greig RC 1.50 4.00
163 Tye Kartye RC 1.50 4.00
164 Adam Ginning RC 1.00 2.50
165 Fraser Minten RC 2.00 5.00
166 Danil Gushchin RC 1.00 2.50
167 David Gust RC 1.00 2.50
168 Connor Zary RC 2.00 5.00
169 Raphael Lavoie RC 1.00 2.50
170 John Beecher RC 2.00 5.00
171 Matthew Poitras RC 2.00 5.00
172 Matt Savoie RC 2.00 5.00
173 Matt Murray RC 1.00 2.50
174 Ivan Miroshnichenko RC 1.50 4.00
175 Stanislav Svozil RC .75 2.00
176 Vincent Iorio RC 1.00 2.50
177 William Dufour RC .75 2.00
178 Kevin Korchinski RC 1.50 4.00
179 Arnaud Durandeau RC 1.00 2.50
180 Justin Sourdif RC 1.00 2.50
181 Brock Faber RC 2.50 6.00
182 Samuel Bolduc RC 1.00 2.50
183 Leevi Merilainen RC 1.00 2.50
184 Jonathan Gruden RC 1.00 2.50
185 Matthew Kessel RC .75 2.00
186 Aidan McDonough RC .75 2.00
187 Jiri Patera RC 1.50 4.00
188 Vincent Desharnais RC 1.25 3.00
189 Jackson LaCombe RC 1.00 2.50
190 Pavel Mintyukov RC 1.50 4.00
191 Zach Benson RC 1.50 4.00
192 Mackie Samoskevich RC 1.50 4.00
193 Dustin Wolf RC 3.00 8.00
194 Devon Levi RC 2.50 6.00
195 Logan Cooley RC 3.00 8.00
196 Yaroslav Askarov RC 2.50 6.00
197 Simon Edvinsson RC 2.00 5.00
198 Connor Bedard RC 8.00 20.00
199 Luke Hughes RC 3.00 8.00
200 Simon Nemec RC 2.00 5.00

2023-24 Metal Universe Blue Spectrum FX

*BLUE: .8X TO 2X BASIC
*BLUE RC: .6X TO 1.5X BASIC

2023-24 Metal Universe Precious Metal Gems Red

*PMG RED/100: 10X TO 25X BASIC
*PMG RED RC/100: 5X TO 12X BASIC
152 Adam Fantilli 80.00 200.00
198 Connor Bedard 600.00 1500.00

2023-24 Metal Universe Purple Spectrum FX

*PURPLE: 1.2X TO 3X BASIC
*PURPLE RC: 1X TO 2.5X BASIC

2023-24 Metal Universe '08-09 Rookie Retro Autographs

R2 Matthew Poitras 15.00 40.00
R4 Logan Cooley 25.00 60.00
R5 Simon Edvinsson 15.00 40.00
R6 Matthew Knies 30.00 80.00
R7 Tyson Foerster 15.00 40.00
R8 Matthew Coronato 12.00 30.00
R9 Luke Philp 8.00 20.00
R10 Jackson LaCombe 8.00 20.00
R11 Tye Kartye 12.00 30.00
R12 Raphael Lavoie 8.00 20.00
R13 Connor Zary 15.00 40.00
R14 Leevi Merilainen 8.00 20.00
R15 Devon Levi 20.00 50.00
R17 Jonathan Gruden 8.00 20.00
R18 Arnaud Durandeau 8.00 20.00
R19 William Dufour 6.00 15.00
R20 Mackie Samoskevich 12.00 30.00
R22 Leo Carlsson SP 40.00 100.00
R23 Kevin Korchinski 12.00 30.00
R25 Aidan McDonough 6.00 15.00
R26 Vincent Iorio 8.00 20.00
R27 Matthew Kessel 6.00 15.00
R28 Luke Hughes SP 40.00 100.00
R29 Fraser Minten 15.00 40.00
R30 John Beecher 15.00 40.00
R31 Jiri Patera 12.00 30.00
R32 Will Cuylle 12.00 30.00
R33 Lukas Rousek 6.00 15.00
R35 Owen Beck 12.00 30.00
R37 Stanislav Svozil 6.00 15.00
R38 Marco Kasper 20.00 50.00
R39 Dustin Wolf 25.00 60.00
R40 Pavel Mintyukov 12.00 30.00
R41 Jakob Pelletier 10.00 25.00
R43 Danil Gushchin 8.00 20.00
R44 Justin Sourdif 8.00 20.00
R45 Vincent Desharnais 10.00 25.00
R46 Alex Laferriere 12.00 30.00
R47 Simon Nemec 15.00 40.00
R49 Yaroslav Askarov 20.00 50.00
R50 Zach Benson 12.00 30.00

2023-24 Metal Universe '08-09 Rookie Retros

*PURPLE/199: 2X TO 5X BASIC
R1 Connor Bedard 10.00 25.00
R2 Matthew Poitras 2.00 5.00
R3 Adam Fantilli 3.00 8.00
R4 Logan Cooley 3.00 8.00
R5 Simon Edvinsson 2.00 5.00
R6 Matthew Knies 4.00 10.00
R7 Tyson Foerster 2.00 5.00
R8 Matthew Coronato 1.50 4.00
R9 Luke Philp 1.00 2.50
R10 Jackson LaCombe 1.00 2.50
R11 Tye Kartye 1.50 4.00
R12 Raphael Lavoie 1.00 2.50
R13 Connor Zary 2.00 5.00
R14 Leevi Merilainen 1.00 2.50
R15 Devon Levi 2.50 6.00
R16 Emil Andrae 1.00 2.50
R17 Jonathan Gruden 1.00 2.50
R18 Arnaud Durandeau 1.00 2.50
R19 William Dufour .75 2.00
R20 Mackie Samoskevich 1.50 4.00
R21 Brock Faber 2.50 6.00
R22 Leo Carlsson 3.00 8.00
R23 Kevin Korchinski 1.50 4.00
R24 Sean Farrell 1.00 2.50
R25 Aidan McDonough .75 2.00
R26 Vincent Iorio 1.00 2.50
R27 Matthew Kessel .75 2.00
R28 Luke Hughes 3.00 8.00
R29 Fraser Minten 2.00 5.00
R30 John Beecher 2.00 5.00
R31 Jiri Patera 1.50 4.00
R32 Will Cuylle 1.50 4.00
R33 Lukas Rousek .75 2.00
R34 Ridly Greig 1.50 4.00
R35 Owen Beck 1.50 4.00
R37 Stanislav Svozil .75 2.00
R38 Marco Kasper 2.50 6.00
R39 Dustin Wolf 3.00 8.00
R40 Pavel Mintyukov 1.50 4.00
R41 Jakob Pelletier 1.25 3.00
R42 Matt Savoie 2.00 5.00
R43 Danil Gushchin 1.00 2.50
R44 Justin Sourdif 1.00 2.50
R45 Vincent Desharnais 1.25 3.00
R46 Alex Laferriere 1.50 4.00
R46 Matt Murray 1.00 2.50
R47 Simon Nemec 2.00 5.00
R48 Luke Evangelista 1.50 4.00
R49 Yaroslav Askarov 2.50 6.00
R50 Zach Benson 1.50 4.00

2023-24 Metal Universe '08-09 Rookie Retros Precious Metal Gems Red

RED/90: 3X TO 8X BASIC
R1 Connor Bedard/90* 300.00 800.00
R3 Adam Fantilli/90* 40.00 100.00
R4 Logan Cooley/90* 40.00 100.00
R21 Brock Faber/90* 40.00 100.00
R22 Leo Carlsson/90* 40.00 100.00
R28 Luke Hughes/90* 40.00 100.00

2023-24 Metal Universe '13 Retros

*BLUE/50: 2X TO 5X BASIC
RT1 Auston Matthews 25.00 60.00
RT2 Jason Robertson 10.00 25.00
RT3 Kirill Kaprizov 20.00 50.00
RT4 Matthew Tkachuk 12.00 30.00
RT5 Igor Shesterkin 12.00 30.00
RT6 Alex Ovechkin 25.00 60.00
RT7 Ilya Sorokin 10.00 25.00
RT8 Nikita Kucherov 12.00 30.00
RT9 Trevor Zegras 6.00 15.00
RT10 Connor McDavid 30.00 80.00
RT11 Nathan MacKinnon 25.00 60.00
RT12 Tim Stutzle 8.00 20.00
RT13 Matty Beniers 8.00 20.00
RT14 David Pastrnak 15.00 40.00
RT15 Connor Bedard 150.00 400.00
RT16 Sidney Crosby 25.00 60.00
RT17 Luke Hughes 20.00 50.00
RT18 Jack Eichel 10.00 25.00
RT19 Jack Hughes 15.00 40.00
RT20 Cole Caufield 12.00 30.00

2023-24 Metal Universe '13 Retros Precious Metal Gems Red

RED/90: 1.2X TO 3X BASIC
RT10 Connor McDavid/90* 150.00 400.00
RT15 Connor Bedard/90* 600.00 1500.00

2023-24 Metal Universe '90 Skybox Metal Retros

1 Connor McDavid 60.00 150.00
2 Mitch Marner 10.00 25.00
3 Artemi Panarin 12.00 30.00
4 Nathan MacKinnon 25.00 60.00
5 Logan Cooley 20.00 50.00
6 Connor Bedard 250.00 600.00
7 Nikita Kucherov 12.00 30.00
8 Brad Marchand 12.00 30.00
9 Ilya Sorokin 10.00 25.00
10 Jack Hughes 15.00 40.00
11 Alex Ovechkin 25.00 60.00
12 Igor Shesterkin 12.00 30.00
13 Matthew Tkachuk 12.00 30.00
14 Alex Pietrangelo 5.00 12.00
15 Jason Robertson 10.00 25.00
16 Adam Fantilli 20.00 50.00
17 Luke Hughes 20.00 50.00
18 Trevor Zegras 6.00 15.00
19 Tim Stutzle 8.00 20.00
20 Cale Makar 15.00 40.00
21 Travis Konecny 6.00 15.00
22 Cole Caufield 12.00 30.00
23 Auston Matthews 25.00 60.00
24 Leon Draisaitl 20.00 50.00
25 David Pastrnak 15.00 40.00
26 Leo Carlsson 20.00 50.00
27 Andrei Vasilevskiy 10.00 25.00
28 Anze Kopitar 10.00 25.00
29 Marc-Andre Fleury 12.00 30.00
30 Sidney Crosby 40.00 100.00

2023-24 Metal Universe '97-98 Rookie Retros Precious Metal Gems Red

MR1 Adam Fantilli/90* 80.00 200.00
MR2 Luke Hughes/90* 80.00 200.00
MR3 Simon Edvinsson/90* 40.00 100.00
MR4 Connor Bedard/90* 1500.00 4000.00
MR5 Yaroslav Askarov/90* 50.00 125.00
MR6 Marco Kasper/90* 50.00 125.00
MR7 Matthew Knies/90* 80.00 200.00
MR8 Dustin Wolf/90* 60.00 150.00
MR9 Devon Levi/90* 50.00 125.00
MR10 Logan Cooley/90* 80.00 2000.00

2023-24 Metal Universe 9.461e KM

LY1 Connor Bedard 20.00 50.00
LY2 Juraj Slafkovsky 3.00 8.00
LY3 Matty Beniers 2.00 5.00
LY4 Logan Cooley 5.00 12.00
LY5 Owen Power 1.50 4.00
LY6 Noah Cates 1.00 2.50
LY7 Matthew Knies 6.00 15.00
LY8 Jake Sanderson 2.00 5.00
LY9 Matt Boldy 2.50 6.00
LY10 Luke Evangelista 2.50 6.00
LY11 Brandt Clarke 1.50 4.00
LY12 Lukas Dostal 1.50 4.00
LY13 Brock Faber 4.00 10.00
LY14 Pavel Mintyukov 2.50 6.00
LY15 Kent Johnson 1.50 4.00
LY16 Nick Perbix 1.00 2.50
LY17 Dylan Guenther 2.00 5.00
LY18 William Eklund 2.00 5.00
LY19 Leo Carlsson 5.00 12.00
LY20 Marco Rossi 2.00 5.00
LY21 Marco Kasper 4.00 10.00
LY22 Shane Wright 2.00 5.00
LY23 Wyatt Johnston 3.00 8.00
LY24 Adam Fantilli 5.00 12.00
LY25 Elias Pettersson 2.50 6.00

2023-24 Metal Universe 9.461e KM Gold

*GOLD/99: .5X TO 1.2X BASIC
LY1 Connor Bedard 60.00 150.00

2023-24 Metal Universe 9.461e KM Autographs

LY2 Juraj Slafkovsky 30.00 80.00
LY3 Matty Beniers 20.00 50.00
LY4 Logan Cooley 80.00 200.00
LY5 Owen Power 15.00 40.00
LY6 Noah Cates 10.00 25.00
LY7 Matthew Knies 60.00 150.00
LY9 Matt Boldy 25.00 60.00
LY11 Brandt Clarke 15.00 40.00
LY12 Lukas Dostal 40.00 100.00
LY14 Pavel Mintyukov 25.00 60.00
LY15 Kent Johnson 15.00 40.00
LY18 William Eklund 20.00 50.00
LY19 Leo Carlsson 50.00 125.00
LY20 Marco Rossi 20.00 50.00
LY21 Marco Kasper 40.00 100.00
LY22 Shane Wright 20.00 50.00
LY23 Wyatt Johnston 30.00 80.00

2023-24 Metal Universe Autographs Silver

*BLUE/50: .5X TO 1.2X SILVER
2 Bowen Byram SP 8.00 20.00
4 Mark Stone 8.00 20.00
5 Filip Gustavsson 6.00 15.00
6 Torey Krug 5.00 12.00
7 Shea Theodore 8.00 20.00
8 Jake Oettinger SP 10.00 25.00
9 Tristan Jarry SP 6.00 15.00
11 Tomas Hertl 6.00 15.00
12 Karel Vejmelka 4.00 10.00
15 Brandon Montour 8.00 20.00
18 William Eklund 8.00 20.00
19 Jaccob Slavin 5.00 12.00
20 Logan Thompson 8.00 20.00
21 Jacob Markstrom 6.00 15.00
22 Philipp Grubauer 6.00 15.00
23 John Gibson SP 6.00 15.00
24 Seth Jarvis 8.00 20.00
26 Colton Parayko 5.00 12.00
27 Nico Hischier 10.00 25.00
32 Joe Pavelski 8.00 20.00
34 Chandler Stephenson 5.00 12.00
35 Wyatt Johnston 12.00 30.00
36 Pavel Zacha 5.00 12.00
37 Cole Perfetti 6.00 15.00
38 Jake Sanderson 8.00 20.00
39 Anders Lee 5.00 12.00
40 Juraj Slafkovsky SP 12.00 30.00
41 Mario Ferraro 4.00 10.00
42 Tom Wilson 6.00 15.00
43 Stuart Skinner 8.00 20.00
45 John Tavares SP 10.00 25.00
47 Kent Johnson 6.00 15.00
49 Owen Power 6.00 15.00
50 Nick Suzuki SP 12.00 30.00
54 Josh Morrissey 8.00 20.00
55 Andrei Svechnikov SP 8.00 20.00
57 Shane Wright 8.00 20.00
58 Morgan Frost 5.00 12.00
60 Dawson Mercer 8.00 20.00
61 Andrei Kuzmenko SP 6.00 15.00
62 Timo Meier 6.00 15.00
63 Tyler Bertuzzi 5.00 12.00
65 Bo Horvat 8.00 20.00
67 Dylan Guenther SP 8.00 20.00
69 JJ Peterka 6.00 15.00
70 Noah Cates 4.00 10.00
72 Dylan Cozens 6.00 15.00
73 Alex Newhook SP 5.00 12.00
74 Marc-Andre Fleury SP 12.00 30.00
75 Jared McCann 5.00 12.00
76 J.T. Compher SP 4.00 10.00
77 Anthony Beauvillier 4.00 10.00
80 Alexis Lafreniere SP 10.00 25.00
82 Nick Schmaltz SP 5.00 12.00
84 K'Andre Miller 5.00 12.00
85 Evan Bouchard SP 8.00 20.00
87 Anton Lundell SP 6.00 15.00
88 Taylor Raddysh 5.00 12.00
89 Mason McTavish 6.00 15.00
90 Pierre-Luc Dubois 5.00 12.00
92 Noah Dobson 8.00 20.00
93 Taylor Hall 6.00 15.00
95 Quinton Byfield 8.00 20.00
97 Jonathan Marchessault SP 8.00 20.00
99 Jake Guentzel 10.00 25.00
101 Connor McDavid SP 60.00 150.00
102 Juuse Saros 8.00 20.00
104 Sidney Crosby SP 25.00 60.00
105 Tage Thompson 8.00 20.00
108 Auston Matthews SP 25.00 60.00
110 Aleksander Barkov 10.00 25.00
111 Brady Tkachuk 10.00 25.00
112 Igor Shesterkin SP 12.00 30.00
115 Miro Heiskanen SP 8.00 20.00
116 Jonathan Huberdeau 8.00 20.00
119 Roman Josi 6.00 15.00
120 Brent Burns 6.00 15.00
121 Mikko Rantanen 15.00 40.00
122 Andrei Vasilevskiy SP 10.00 25.00
123 Alex Ovechkin SP 60.00
124 Brad Marchand SP 12.00 30.00
125 Cale Makar SP 15.00 40.00
126 Leon Draisaitl SP 20.00 50.00
127 Tim Stutzle 8.00 20.00
131 Matty Beniers 8.00 20.00
140 Anze Kopitar SP 10.00 25.00
141 Kirill Kaprizov SP 20.00 50.00
143 Connor Hellebuyck 12.00 30.00
145 Quinn Hughes SP 15.00 40.00
147 Mitch Marner SP 10.00 25.00
148 Jack Eichel SP 10.00 25.00
151 Leo Carlsson/399 25.00 60.00
153 Marco Kasper/399 20.00 50.00
154 Tyson Foerster/399 15.00 40.00
155 Matthew Knies/399 30.00 80.00
158 Sean Farrell/399 8.00 20.00
160 Matthew Coronato/399 12.00 30.00
161 Will Cuylle/399 12.00 30.00
162 Ridly Greig/399 12.00 30.00
163 Tye Kartye/399 12.00 30.00
164 Adam Ginning/399 8.00 20.00
165 Fraser Minten/399 15.00 40.00
166 Danil Gushchin/399 8.00 20.00
168 Connor Zary/399 15.00 40.00
169 Raphael Lavoie/399 8.00 20.00
170 John Beecher/399 15.00 40.00
171 Matthew Poitras/399 15.00 40.00
172 Matt Savoie/399 15.00 40.00
173 Matt Murray/399 8.00 20.00
174 Ivan Miroshnichenko/399 12.00 30.00
175 Stanislav Svozil/399 6.00 15.00
177 William Dufour/399 6.00 15.00
178 Kevin Korchinski/399 12.00 30.00
179 Arnaud Durandeau/399 8.00 20.00
180 Justin Sourdif/399 8.00 20.00
182 Samuel Bolduc/399 8.00 20.00
182 Leevi Merilainen/399 8.00 20.00
184 Jonathan Gruden/399 8.00 20.00
185 Matthew Kessel/399 6.00 15.00
186 Aidan McDonough/399 6.00 15.00
187 Jiri Patera/399 12.00 30.00
188 Vincent Desharnais/399 10.00 25.00
189 Jackson LaCombe/399 8.00 20.00
190 Pavel Mintyukov/399 12.00 30.00
191 Zach Benson/399 12.00 30.00
192 Mackie Samoskevich/399 12.00 30.00
193 Dustin Wolf/199 25.00 60.00
194 Devon Levi/399 20.00 50.00
195 Logan Cooley/199 25.00 60.00
196 Yaroslav Askarov/199 20.00 50.00
197 Simon Edvinsson/199 15.00 40.00
198 Connor Bedard/199 300.00 800.00
199 Luke Hughes/199 25.00 60.00
200 Simon Nemec/199 15.00 40.00

2023-24 Metal Universe Constellations

*SPECTRUM/199: .6X TO 1.5X BASIC
*GOLD/99: .8X TO 2X BASIC
CN1 Brady Tkachuk 1.50 4.00
CN2 Evgeny Kuznetsov 1.25 3.00
CN3 Jonathan Huberdeau 1.25 3.00
CN4 Tyler Bertuzzi .75 2.00
CN5 Charlie McAvoy 1.25 3.00
CN6 Dylan Guenther 1.25 3.00
CN7 Seth Jarvis 1.25 3.00
CN8 Marc-Andre Fleury 2.00 5.00
CN9 Dylan Larkin 1.25 3.00
CN10 Kirill Marchenko 1.25 3.00
CN11 Roope Hintz 1.25 3.00
CN12 Ryan Nugent-Hopkins 1.25 3.00
CN13 Andrei Kuzmenko 1.00 2.50
CN14 Ross Colton .75 2.00
CN15 Troy Terry .75 2.00
CN16 Morgan Frost .75 2.00
CN17 Arber Xhekaj 1.00 2.50
CN18 K'Andre Miller .75 2.00
CN19 Thomas Novak .60 1.50
CN20 Jesper Bratt 1.00 2.50
CN21 Peyton Krebs .75 2.00
CN22 Mathew Barzal 1.25 3.00
CN23 Anton Lundell 1.00 2.50
CN24 Tomas Hertl 1.00 2.50
CN25 Jared McCann .75 2.00
CN26 Brayden Schenn 1.00 2.50
CN27 William Eklund 1.25 3.00
CN28 Anze Kopitar 1.50 4.00
CN29 Josh Morrissey 1.25 3.00
CN30 Bryan Rust 1.00 2.50
CN31 Quinn Hughes 2.50 6.00
CN32 Jack Eichel 1.50 4.00

2023-24 Metal Universe Constellations Autographs

CN3 Jonathan Huberdeau 10.00 25.00
CN7 Seth Jarvis 10.00 25.00
CN8 Marc-Andre Fleury SP 15.00 40.00
CN10 Kirill Marchenko 10.00 25.00
CN13 Andrei Kuzmenko 8.00 20.00
CN14 Ross Colton 6.00 15.00
CN16 Morgan Frost 6.00 15.00
CN17 Arber Xhekaj 8.00 20.00
CN18 K'Andre Miller 6.00 15.00
CN19 Thomas Novak 5.00 12.00
CN21 Peyton Krebs 6.00 15.00
CN24 Tomas Hertl 8.00 20.00
CN25 Jared McCann 6.00 15.00
CN26 Brayden Schenn 8.00 20.00
CN27 William Eklund 10.00 25.00
CN29 Josh Morrissey 10.00 25.00
CN30 Bryan Rust 8.00 20.00
CN31 Quinn Hughes SP 20.00 50.00
CN32 Jack Eichel SP 12.00 30.00

2023-24 Metal Universe Energetic Explosions

EE1 Connor McDavid 5.00 12.00
EE2 Brent Burns 1.00 2.50
EE3 Josh Norris 1.00 2.50
EE4 Mark Scheifele 1.50 4.00
EE5 Andrei Svechnikov 1.25 3.00
EE6 Timo Meier 1.00 2.50
EE7 Jordan Eberle 1.00 2.50
EE8 Leo Carlsson 3.00 8.00
EE9 Kirby Dach 1.00 2.50
EE10 Brayden Point 1.25 3.00
EE11 Dylan Cozens 1.00 2.50
EE12 Mark Stone 1.25 3.00
EE13 Sidney Crosby 4.00 10.00
EE14 Matty Beniers 1.25 3.00
EE15 Connor Bedard 6.00 15.00
EE16 Leon Draisaitl 3.00 8.00
EE17 Brandt Clarke 1.00 2.50
EE18 Alex Ovechkin 4.00 10.00
EE19 Matthew Tkachuk 2.00 5.00
EE20 Cole Perfetti 1.00 2.50
EE21 Tom Wilson 1.00 2.50
EE22 Robert Thomas 1.00 2.50
EE23 K'Andre Miller .75 2.00

2023-24 Metal Universe Energetic Explosions Gold

*GOLD/99: 1.2X TO 3X BASIC
EE15 Connor Bedard 100.00 250.00

2023-24 Metal Universe Energetic Explosions Spectrum

*SPECTRUM/199: .6X TO 1.5X BASIC
EE15 Connor Bedard 50.00 125.00

2023-24 Metal Universe Energetic Explosions Autographs

EE2 Brent Burns 8.00 20.00
EE4 Mark Scheifele SP 12.00 30.00
EE6 Timo Meier 8.00 20.00
EE7 Jordan Eberle 8.00 20.00
EE8 Leo Carlsson SP 25.00 60.00
EE11 Dylan Cozens 8.00 20.00
EE12 Mark Stone 25.00 60.00
EE14 Matty Beniers 10.00 25.00
EE16 Leon Draisaitl SP 25.00 60.00
EE20 Cole Perfetti 8.00 20.00
EE21 Tom Wilson 8.00 20.00
EE23 K'Andre Miller 6.00 15.00

2023-24 Metal Universe Goose Eggs

GE1 John Gibson 10.00 25.00
GE2 Ilya Sorokin 15.00 40.00
GE3 Alexandar Georgiev 10.00 25.00
GE4 Jake Oettinger 15.00 40.00
GE5 Jeremy Swayman 40.00 100.00
GE6 Connor Hellebuyck 20.00 50.00
GE7 Andrei Vasilevskiy 15.00 40.00
GE8 Filip Gustavsson 10.00 25.00
GE9 Karel Vejmelka 6.00 15.00
GE10 Igor Shesterkin 20.00 50.00
GE11 Logan Thompson 12.00 30.00
GE12 Tristan Jarry 10.00 25.00
GE13 Samuel Ersson 10.00 25.00
GE14 Juuse Saros 12.00 30.00
GE15 Jordan Binnington 15.00 40.00
GE16 Stuart Skinner 12.00 30.00
GE17 Kaapo Kahkonen 10.00 25.00
GE18 Thatcher Demko 12.00 30.00
GE19 Pheonix Copley 6.00 15.00
GE20 Ilya Samsonov 10.00 25.00
GE21 Sergei Bobrovsky 15.00 40.00
GE22 Jacob Markstrom 10.00 25.00
GE23 Vitek Vanecek 10.00 25.00
GE24 Adin Hill 10.00 25.00
GE25 Linus Ullmark 10.00 25.00
GE26 Darcy Kuemper 10.00 25.00
GE27 Ville Husso 6.00 15.00
GE28 Pyotr Kochetkov 10.00 25.00
GE29 Jonathan Quick 20.00 50.00
GE30 Marc-Andre Fleury 20.00 50.00

2023-24 Metal Universe Goose Eggs Golden

*GOLDEN/25: .6X TO 1.5X BASIC
GE26 Darcy Kuemper 30.00 80.00

2023-24 Metal Universe Jambalaya

1OF20 Connor McDavid 100.00 250.00
2OF20 Connor Bedard 800.00 2000.00
3OF20 Jordan Kyrou 20.00 50.00
4OF20 Mitch Marner 30.00 80.00
5OF20 Sidney Crosby 80.00 200.00
6OF20 Alex Ovechkin 80.00 200.00
7OF20 Auston Matthews 80.00 200.00
8OF20 Erik Karlsson ERR Caufield Back 50.00 125.00
9OF20 Cole Caufield ERR Karlsson Back 50.00 125.00
10OF20 Kirill Kaprizov 60.00 150.00
11OF20 Matty Beniers 25.00 60.00
12OF20 Cale Makar 50.00 125.00
13OF20 Leon Draisaitl 60.00 150.00
14OF20 Nathan MacKinnon 80.00 200.00
15OF20 Tim Stutzle 25.00 60.00
16OF20 Nikita Kucherov 40.00 100.00
17OF20 Jack Hughes 50.00 125.00
18OF20 Rasmus Dahlin 25.00 60.00
19OF20 Ilya Sorokin 30.00 80.00
20OF20 Logan Cooley 60.00 150.00

2023-24 Metal Universe Martensite

MT1 Cole Caufield 8.00 20.00
MT2 Leon Draisaitl 12.00 30.00
MT3 Auston Matthews 15.00 40.00
MT4 Igor Shesterkin 8.00 20.00
MT5 Nathan MacKinnon 15.00 40.00
MT6 Alex Tuch 4.00 10.00
MT7 Roman Josi 4.00 10.00
MT8 Connor McDavid 30.00 80.00
MT9 Patrik Laine 5.00 12.00
MT10 Nick Suzuki 8.00 20.00
MT11 Jason Robertson 6.00 15.00
MT12 Juuse Saros 5.00 12.00
MT13 Ilya Sorokin 6.00 15.00
MT14 Martin Necas 6.00 15.00
MT15 Jake Oettinger 6.00 15.00
MT16 Kris Letang 5.00 12.00
MT17 Alex Ovechkin 30.00 80.00
MT18 Jordan Kyrou 4.00 10.00
MT19 Alex DeBrincat 5.00 12.00
MT20 Timo Meier 4.00 10.00
MT21 Mikko Rantanen 10.00 25.00
MT22 Joel Farabee 4.00 10.00
MT23 Artemi Panarin 8.00 20.00
MT24 Jack Hughes 10.00 25.00
MT25 Gabe Vilardi 4.00 10.00
MT26 Jakob Chychrun 4.00 10.00
MT27 Seth Jones 4.00 10.00
MT28 Quinn Hughes 10.00 25.00
MT29 Cale Makar 10.00 25.00
MT30 William Nylander 8.00 20.00
MT31 Matthew Tkachuk 8.00 20.00
MT32 Tage Thompson 5.00 12.00
MT33 Andrei Svechnikov 5.00 12.00
MT34 David Pastrnak 10.00 25.00
MT35 Nikolaj Ehlers 4.00 10.00
MT36 Bo Horvat 5.00 12.00
MT37 Anze Kopitar 6.00 15.00
MT38 Aleksander Barkov 6.00 15.00
MT39 Johnny Gaudreau 6.00 15.00
MT40 Jonathan Huberdeau 5.00 12.00
MT41 Colton Parayko 3.00 8.00
MT42 Clayton Keller 5.00 12.00
MT43 Mats Zuccarello 4.00 10.00
MT44 Brad Marchand 8.00 20.00
MT45 Elias Pettersson 6.00 15.00
MT46 Matty Beniers 5.00 12.00
MT47 Dylan Larkin 5.00 12.00
MT48 Tomas Hertl 4.00 10.00
MT49 Brayden Point 5.00 12.00
MT50 Trevor Zegras 4.00 10.00

2023-24 Metal Universe Meltdown

M1 Cale Makar 2.50 6.00
M2 William Nylander 2.00 5.00
M3 Alex Ovechkin 4.00 10.00
M4 Jake Oettinger 1.50 4.00
M5 Connor Bedard 8.00 20.00
M6 Carter Verhaeghe 1.00 2.50
M7 Ryan Nugent-Hopkins 1.25 3.00
M8 Matthew Knies 4.00 10.00
M9 Jamie Drysdale .75 2.00
M10 Tomas Hertl 1.00 2.50
M11 Auston Matthews 4.00 10.00
M12 Logan Cooley 3.00 8.00
M13 Yegor Sharangovich 1.00 2.50
M14 Nico Hischier 1.50 4.00
M15 Jared Spurgeon 1.00 2.50
M16 Victor Hedman 1.25 3.00
M17 Jason Zucker 1.00 2.50
M18 Roman Josi 1.00 2.50
M19 Sidney Crosby 4.00 10.00
M20 Wyatt Johnston 2.00 5.00
M21 J.T. Miller 1.25 3.00
M22 Leo Carlsson 3.00 8.00
M23 Jared McCann .75 2.00
M24 Adam Fantilli 3.00 8.00
M25 Connor McDavid 8.00 12.00

2023-24 Metal Universe Meltdown Gold

*GOLD/99: 1.2X TO 3X BASIC
M5 Connor Bedard 80.00 200.00

2023-24 Metal Universe Meltdown Spectrum

*SPECTRUM/199: .6X TO 1.5X BASIC
M5 Connor Bedard 40.00 100.00

2023-24 Metal Universe Meltdown Autographs

M1 Cale Makar SP 20.00 50.00
M4 Jake Oettinger 12.00 30.00
M5 Connor Bedard SP 500.00 1200.00
M7 Ryan Nugent-Hopkins 10.00 25.00
M8 Matthew Knies 30.00 80.00
M9 Jamie Drysdale SP 6.00 15.00
M10 Tomas Hertl 8.00 20.00
M11 Auston Matthews SP 50.00 125.00
M12 Logan Cooley 25.00 60.00
M13 Yegor Sharangovich 8.00 20.00
M14 Nico Hischier 12.00 30.00
M15 Jared Spurgeon 8.00 20.00
M17 Jason Zucker 8.00 20.00
M18 Roman Josi 8.00 20.00
M20 Wyatt Johnston 25.00 60.00
M22 Leo Carlsson SP 25.00 60.00
M23 Jared McCann 6.00 15.00

2023-24 Metal Universe Metal-X

MX1 Sidney Crosby 20.00 50.00
MX2 Auston Matthews 20.00 50.00
MX3 David Pastrnak 12.00 30.00
MX4 Nathan MacKinnon 20.00 50.00
MX5 Josh Morrissey 6.00 15.00
MX6 Alex Ovechkin 20.00 50.00
MX7 Jordan Kyrou 5.00 12.00
MX8 Brock Boeser 6.00 15.00
MX9 Connor McDavid 25.00 60.00
MX10 Sebastian Aho 8.00 20.00
MX11 Juraj Slafkovsky 10.00 25.00
MX12 Trevor Zegras 5.00 12.00
MX13 Cale Makar 12.00 30.00
MX14 Brady Tkachuk 8.00 20.00
MX15 Matthew Tkachuk 10.00 25.00
MX16 Jake Guentzel 8.00 20.00
MX17 Mika Zibanejad 6.00 15.00
MX18 Pierre-Luc Dubois 4.00 10.00
MX19 Mathew Barzal 6.00 15.00
MX20 Steven Stamkos 10.00 25.00
MX21 Ryan O'Reilly 5.00 12.00
MX22 Nick Suzuki 10.00 25.00
MX23 Leon Draisaitl 15.00 40.00
MX24 Mark Scheifele 8.00 20.00
MX25 Mark Stone 6.00 15.00
MX26 Logan Couture 6.00 15.00
MX27 Brad Marchand 10.00 25.00
MX28 Jack Hughes 12.00 30.00
MX29 Jake Oettinger 8.00 20.00
MX30 Matty Beniers 6.00 15.00
MX31 Adam Fox 6.00 15.00
MX32 Jacob Markstrom 5.00 12.00
MX33 Tyler Bertuzzi 4.00 10.00
MX34 Mattias Ekholm 4.00 10.00
MX35 Tage Thompson 6.00 15.00
MX36 Logan Cooley 15.00 40.00
MX37 Simon Nemec 10.00 25.00
MX38 Connor Zary 10.00 25.00
MX39 Luke Hughes 15.00 40.00
MX40 Tyson Foerster 10.00 25.00
MX41 Leo Carlsson 15.00 40.00
MX42 Matthew Knies 20.00 50.00
MX43 Devon Levi 12.00 30.00
MX44 Adam Fantilli 15.00 40.00
MX45 Connor Bedard 125.00 300.00

2023-24 Metal Universe Net-Rageous

1OF35NR Patrick Roy 80.00 200.00
2OF35NR Ilya Sorokin 25.00 60.00
3OF35NR Joey Daccord 15.00 40.00
4OF35NR Dominik Hasek 25.00 60.00
5OF35NR Jake Oettinger 25.00 60.00
6OF35NR Igor Shesterkin 60.00 150.00
7OF35NR Martin Brodeur 40.00 100.00
8OF35NR Andrei Vasilevskiy 25.00 60.00
9OF35NR Connor Hellebuyck 30.00 80.00
10OF35NR Linus Ullmark 15.00 40.00
11OF35NR Joonas Korpisalo 15.00 40.00
12OF35NR Tristan Jarry 15.00 40.00
13OF35NR Frederik Andersen 20.00 50.00
14OF35NR Ville Husso 10.00 25.00
15OF35NR Alexandar Georgiev 15.00 40.00
16OF35NR Jordan Binnington 30.00 80.00
17OF35NR Thatcher Demko 20.00 50.00
18OF35NR Karel Vejmelka 10.00 25.00
19OF35NR Philipp Grubauer 15.00 40.00
20OF35NR Juuse Saros 20.00 50.00
21OF35NR Pheonix Copley 10.00 25.00
22OF35NR Vitek Vanecek 15.00 40.00
23OF35NR Sergei Bobrovsky 25.00 60.00
24OF35NR Kaapo Kahkonen 15.00 40.00
25OF35NR Darcy Kuemper 15.00 40.00
26OF35NR Cal Petersen 10.00 25.00
27OF35NR Elvis Merzlikins 15.00 40.00
28OF35NR John Gibson 15.00 40.00
29OF35NR Adin Hill 15.00 40.00
30OF35NR Ilya Samsonov 15.00 40.00
31OF35NR Jacob Markstrom 15.00 40.00
32OF35NR Stuart Skinner 20.00 50.00
33OF35NR Marc-Andre Fleury 30.00 80.00
34OF35NR Devon Levi 40.00 100.00
35OF35NR Yaroslav Askarov 40.00 100.00

2023-24 Metal Universe NOYZ BOYZ

1OF20NB Auston Matthews 100.00 250.00
2OF20NB David Pastrnak 60.00 150.00
3OF20NB Connor McDavid 150.00 400.00
4OF20NB Sidney Crosby 100.00 250.00
5OF20NB Alex Ovechkin 125.00 300.00
6OF20NB Jack Hughes 60.00 150.00
7OF20NB Elias Pettersson 40.00 100.00
8OF20NB Nathan MacKinnon 100.00 250.00
9OF20NB Kirill Kaprizov 80.00 200.00
10OF20NB Brady Tkachuk 40.00 100.00
11OF20NB Trevor Zegras 25.00 60.00
12OF20NB Cale Makar 60.00 150.00
13OF20NB Cole Caufield 50.00 125.00
14OF20NB Jason Robertson 40.00 100.00
15OF20NB Mitch Marner 40.00 100.00
16OF20NB Igor Shesterkin 50.00 125.00
17OF20NB Matthew Tkachuk 50.00 125.00
18OF20NB Leon Draisaitl 80.00 200.00
19OF20NB Connor Bedard 600.00 1500.00
20OF20NB Adam Fantilli 80.00 200.00

2023-24 Metal Universe Palladium

P1 David Pastrnak 8.00 20.00
P2 Quinn Hughes 8.00 20.00
P3 Simon Nemec 6.00 15.00
P4 Logan Cooley 10.00 25.00
P5 Adam Fantilli 10.00 25.00
P6 Connor McDavid 15.00 40.00
P7 Cale Makar 8.00 20.00
P8 Alex Ovechkin 12.00 30.00
P9 Robert Thomas 3.00 8.00
P10 Connor Hellebuyck 6.00 15.00
P11 Sebastian Aho 5.00 12.00
P12 Jason Robertson 5.00 12.00
P13 Elias Pettersson 5.00 12.00
P14 Auston Matthews 12.00 30.00
P15 Tim Stutzle 4.00 10.00
P16 Quinton Byfield 4.00 10.00
P17 Alex Tuch 3.00 8.00
P18 Troy Terry 2.50 6.00
P19 Kirill Kaprizov 10.00 25.00
P20 Matty Beniers 4.00 10.00
P21 Leon Draisaitl 10.00 25.00
P22 Luke Hughes 10.00 25.00
P23 Artemi Panarin 6.00 15.00
P24 Jack Hughes 8.00 20.00
P25 Anze Kopitar 5.00 12.00
P26 Mitch Marner 5.00 12.00
P27 Jack Eichel 5.00 12.00
P28 Connor Bedard 150.00 400.00
P29 Steven Stamkos 6.00 15.00
P30 Clayton Keller 4.00 10.00

2023-24 Metal Universe Palladium Spectrum

*SPECTRUM/25: 1.2X TO 3X BASIC
P22 Luke Hughes 60.00 150.00

2023-24 Metal Universe Premium Player

*GOLD/99: 1X TO 2.5X BASIC
10F40PP Connor McDavid 8.00 20.00
20F40PP Leo Carlsson 5.00 12.00
30F40PP Alex Tuch 1.50 4.00
40F40PP Dylan Larkin 2.00 5.00
50F40PP Logan Cooley 5.00 12.00
60F40PP Kirill Kaprizov 5.00 12.00
70F40PP Mark Stone 2.00 5.00
80F40PP Alexis Lafreniere 2.50 6.00
90F40PP Leon Draisaitl 5.00 12.00
100F40PP Bowen Byram 2.00 5.00
110F40PP Jack Hughes 4.00 10.00
120F40PP Matthew Knies 6.00 15.00
130F40PP Kent Johnson 1.50 4.00
140F40PP Ryan Reaves 1.25 3.00
150F40PP Tristan Jarry 1.50 4.00
160F40PP Simon Edvinsson 3.00 8.00
170F40PP Frank Vatrano 1.25 3.00
180F40PP Jakob Pelletier 2.00 5.00
190F40PP Cole Sillinger 1.25 3.00
200F40PP Pavel Zacha 1.25 3.00
210F40PP Jake Guentzel 2.50 6.00
220F40PP Anze Kopitar 2.50 6.00
230F40PP Simon Nemec 3.00 8.00
240F40PP Brandon Hagel 1.25 3.00
250F40PP Pavel Buchnevich 1.25 3.00
260F40PP JJ Peterka 1.50 4.00
270F40PP Marc-Andre Fleury 3.00 8.00
280F40PP William Karlsson 2.00 5.00
290F40PP Ridly Greig 2.50 6.00
300F40PP Jonathan Huberdeau 2.00 5.00
310F40PP Zach Hyman 2.50 6.00
320F40PP Mikael Backlund 1.25 3.00
330F40PP Tyson Foerster 3.00 8.00
340F40PP Brandon Saad 1.25 3.00
350F40PP K'Andre Miller 1.25 3.00
360F40PP Mikhail Sergachev 1.25 3.00
370F40PP Danil Gushchin 1.50 4.00
380F40PP Jesper Bratt 1.50 4.00
390F40PP Andrei Kuzmenko 1.50 4.00
400F40PP Connor Bedard 30.00 80.00

2023-24 Metal Universe Quick Strike

*SPECTRUM/25: 1X TO 2.5X BASIC
QS1 Matthew Tkachuk 6.00 15.00
QS2 Luke Hughes 10.00 25.00
QS3 Artemi Panarin 6.00 15.00
QS4 Kirill Kaprizov 10.00 25.00
QS5 Auston Matthews 12.00 30.00
QS6 Dylan Cozens 3.00 8.00
QS7 Cole Caufield 6.00 15.00
QS8 Trevor Zegras 3.00 8.00
QS9 Tage Thompson 4.00 10.00
QS10 Jack Hughes 8.00 20.00
QS11 Leon Draisaitl 10.00 25.00
QS12 Bo Horvat 4.00 10.00
QS13 Roope Hintz 4.00 10.00
QS14 Sebastian Aho 5.00 12.00
QS15 Ivan Barbashev 2.50 6.00
QS16 Matty Beniers 4.00 10.00
QS17 Logan Cooley 10.00 25.00
QS18 Nazem Kadri 4.00 10.00
QS19 Elias Pettersson 5.00 12.00
QS20 Adam Fantilli 10.00 25.00
QS21 Chris Kreider 4.00 10.00
QS22 Tim Stutzle 4.00 10.00
QS23 David Pastrnak 8.00 20.00
QS24 Kyle Connor 5.00 12.00
QS25 Brayden Point 4.00 10.00
QS26 Zach Werenski 5.00 12.00
QS27 Leo Carlsson 10.00 25.00
QS28 Mikko Rantanen 8.00 20.00
QS29 Nathan MacKinnon 12.00 30.00
QS30 Adrian Kempe 3.00 8.00
QS31 Connor Bedard 80.00 200.00
QS32 Brady Tkachuk 5.00 12.00
QS33 Jason Robertson 5.00 12.00
QS34 Filip Forsberg 5.00 12.00
QS35 Carter Verhaeghe 3.00 8.00
QS36 Alex DeBrincat 4.00 10.00
QS37 Connor McDavid 15.00 40.00
QS38 Tomas Hertl 3.00 8.00
QS39 Nick Schmaltz 2.50 6.00
QS40 Sidney Crosby 12.00 30.00

2023-24 Metal Universe SkyBox Premium Prospects

*SAPPHIRE: .8X TO 2X BASIC
PP1 Connor Bedard 6.00 15.00
PP2 Logan Cooley 3.00 8.00
PP3 Adam Fantilli 3.00 8.00
PP4 Connor Zary 2.00 5.00
PP5 Marco Kasper 2.50 6.00
PP6 Pavel Mintyukov 1.50 4.00
PP7 Kevin Korchinski 1.50 4.00
PP8 Matt Savoie 2.00 5.00
PP9 Alex Laferriere 1.50 4.00
PP10 Yaroslav Askarov 2.50 6.00
PP11 Jiri Patera 1.50 4.00
PP12 Matthew Knies 4.00 10.00
PP13 Akito Hirose .75 2.00
PP14 Vincent Iorio 1.00 2.50
PP15 Samuel Bolduc 1.00 2.50
PP16 Matthew Coronato 1.50 4.00
PP17 Tyson Foerster 2.00 5.00
PP18 Aidan McDonough .75 2.00
PP19 Justin Sourdif 1.00 2.50
PP20 Fraser Minten 2.00 5.00
PP21 Dustin Wolf 3.00 8.00
PP22 Stanislav Svozil .75 2.00
PP23 Jonathan Gruden 1.00 2.50
PP24 Danil Gushchin 1.00 2.50
PP25 Leo Carlsson 3.00 8.00
PP26 Matthew Kessel .75 2.00
PP27 John Beecher 2.00 5.00
PP28 Brock Faber 2.50 6.00
PP29 Leevi Merilainen 1.00 2.50
PP30 Jackson LaCombe 1.00 2.50
PP31 Adam Ginning 1.00 2.50
PP32 William Dufour .75 2.00
PP33 Matt Murray 1.00 2.50
PP34 Simon Edvinsson 2.00 5.00
PP35 Wyatt Kaiser 1.00 2.50
PP36 Mackie Samoskevich 1.50 4.00
PP37 Jakob Pelletier 1.25 3.00
PP38 Lukas Rousek .75 2.00
PP39 Tye Kartye 1.50 4.00
PP40 Devon Levi 2.50 6.00
PP41 Simon Nemec 2.00 5.00
PP42 Matthew Poitras 2.00 5.00
PP43 Luke Evangelista 1.50 4.00
PP44 Sean Farrell 1.00 2.50
PP45 Ridly Greig 1.50 4.00
PP46 Owen Beck 1.50 4.00
PP47 Will Cuylle 1.50 4.00
PP48 Raphael Lavoie 1.00 2.50
PP49 Zach Benson 1.50 4.00
PP50 Luke Hughes 3.00 8.00

2023-24 Metal Universe SkyBox Premium Prospects Star Rubies

*RUBIES/50: 1.5X TO 4X BASIC
PP1 Connor Bedard 125.00 300.00

2023-24 Metal Universe Soul of the Game

10F35 Connor McDavid 12.00 30.00
20F35 Nick Suzuki 5.00 12.00
30F35 Sidney Crosby 10.00 25.00
40F35 Brent Burns 2.50 6.00
50F35 Jack Hughes 6.00 15.00
60F35 Brock Boeser 3.00 8.00
70F35 Aaron Ekblad 3.00 8.00
80F35 Auston Matthews 10.00 25.00
90F35 Tim Stutzle 3.00 8.00
100F35 Matty Beniers 3.00 8.00
110F35 Artemi Panarin 5.00 12.00
120F35 Jack Eichel 4.00 10.00
130F35 Alex Ovechkin 10.00 25.00
140F35 Kyle Connor 4.00 10.00
150F35 Erik Karlsson 3.00 8.00
160F35 Johnny Gaudreau 4.00 10.00
170F35 Drew Doughty 2.50 6.00
180F35 Mikko Rantanen 6.00 15.00
190F35 Juuse Saros 3.00 8.00
200F35 Anthony Duclair 2.00 5.00
210F35 Seth Jones 2.50 6.00
220F35 Jeremy Swayman 4.00 10.00
230F35 Moritz Seider 3.00 8.00
240F35 Jason Robertson 4.00 10.00
250F35 Rasmus Dahlin 3.00 8.00
260F35 Victor Hedman 3.00 8.00
270F35 Trevor Zegras 2.50 6.00
280F35 Jonathan Huberdeau 3.00 8.00
290F35 Clayton Keller 3.00 8.00
300F35 Jordan Kyrou 2.50 6.00
310F35 Kirill Kaprizov 8.00 20.00
320F35 Ilya Sorokin 4.00 10.00
330F35 Eric Lindros 4.00 10.00
340F35 Mario Lemieux 10.00 25.00
350F35 Wayne Gretzky 15.00 40.00

2023-24 Metal Universe Soul of the Game Gold

*GOLD/99: 1X TO 2.5X BASIC
10F35 Connor McDavid 60.00 150.00

2023-24 Metal Universe Soul of the Game Autographs

20F35 Nick Suzuki 15.00 40.00
40F35 Brent Burns 8.00 20.00
60F35 Brock Boeser 10.00 25.00
90F35 Tim Stutzle 10.00 25.00
100F35 Matty Beniers 10.00 25.00
120F35 Jack Eichel 12.00 30.00
180F35 Mikko Rantanen 20.00 50.00
190F35 Juuse Saros 10.00 25.00
220F35 Jeremy Swayman 12.00 30.00
280F35 Jonathan Huberdeau 10.00 25.00
330F35 Eric Lindros 12.00 30.00

2023-24 Metal Universe T Tauri Star

TTP1 Connor Bodard 6.00 15.00
TTP2 Jakob Pelletier 1.25 3.00
TTP3 Matthew Knies 4.00 10.00
TTP4 Brock Faber 2.50 6.00
TTP5 Owen Beck 1.50 4.00
TTP6 Simon Edvinsson 2.00 5.00
TTP7 Matthew Coronato 1.50 4.00
TTP8 Marco Kasper 2.50 6.00
TTP9 Leo Carlsson 3.00 8.00
TTP10 Logan Cooley 3.00 8.00
TTP11 William Dufour .75 2.00
TTP12 Ridly Greig 1.50 4.00
TTP13 Luke Hughes 3.00 8.00
TTP14 Tye Kartye 1.50 4.00
TTP15 Yaroslav Askarov 2.50 6.00
TTP16 Tyson Foerster 2.00 5.00
TTP17 Vincent Iorio 1.00 2.50
TTP18 Stanislav Svozil .75 2.00
TTP19 Luke Evangelista 1.50 4.00
TTP20 Adam Fantilli 3.00 8.00

2023-24 Metal Universe T Tauri Star Gold

*GOLD/99: 1X TO 2.5X BASIC
TTP1 Connor Bedard 40.00 100.00

2023-24 Metal Universe T Tauri Star Spectrum

*SPECTRUM/199: .5X TO 1.2X BASIC
TTP1 Connor Bedard 25.00 60.00

2023-24 Metal Universe T Tauri Star Autographs

TTP1 Connor Bedard SP 300.00 800.00
TTP3 Matthew Knies 25.00 60.00
TTP5 Owen Beck 10.00 25.00
TTP6 Simon Edvinsson 12.00 30.00
TTP7 Matthew Coronato 10.00 25.00
TTP8 Marco Kasper 15.00 40.00
TTP9 Leo Carlsson SP 20.00 50.00
TTP10 Logan Cooley SP 20.00 50.00
TTP12 Ridly Greig SP 10.00 25.00
TTP13 Luke Hughes SP 20.00 50.00
TTP14 Tye Kartye 10.00 25.00
TTP15 Yaroslav Askarov 15.00 40.00
TTP16 Tyson Foerster 12.00 30.00
TTP17 Vincent Iorio 6.00 15.00
TTP18 Stanislav Svozil 5.00 12.00

2023-24 Metal Universe The Business

10F25TB Sidney Crosby 25.00 60.00
20F25TB Rasmus Dahlin 8.00 20.00
30F25TB Logan Cooley 20.00 50.00
40F25TB Auston Matthews 25.00 60.00
50F25TB Nico Hischier 10.00 25.00
60F25TB Drew Doughty 6.00 15.00
70F25TB Miro Heiskanen 8.00 20.00
80F25TB Mark Stone 8.00 20.00
90F25TB Connor Bedard 125.00 300.00
100F25TB John Tavares 10.00 25.00
110F25TB Adam Fox 8.00 20.00
120F25TB Ilya Sorokin 10.00 25.00
130F25TB Robert Thomas 6.00 15.00
140F25TB Aleksander Barkov 10.00 25.00
150F25TB Vladimir Tarasenko 8.00 20.00
160F25TB Steven Stamkos 12.00 30.00
170F25TB J.T. Miller 8.00 20.00
180F25TB Marc-Andre Fleury 12.00 30.00
190F25TB Connor McDavid 30.00 80.00
200F25TB Travis Konecny 6.00 15.00
210F25TB Charlie McAvoy 8.00 20.00
220F25TB Seth Jones 6.00 15.00
230F25TB Evander Kane 6.00 15.00
240F25TB Adam Fantilli 20.00 50.00
250F25TB Alex Ovechkin 25.00 60.00

2023-24 Metal Universe Vivacity

10F40VC Connor McDavid 20.00 50.00
20F40VC Leo Carlsson 12.00 30.00
30F40VC Anze Kopitar 6.00 15.00
40F40VC Evgeni Malkin 8.00 20.00
50F40VC Trevor Zegras 4.00 10.00
60F40VC Andrei Svechnikov 5.00 12.00
70F40VC Jack Hughes 10.00 25.00
80F40VC David Pastrnak 10.00 25.00
90F40VC Auston Matthews 15.00 40.00
100F40VC Alex Ovechkin 15.00 40.00
110F40VC Jonathan Marchessault 5.00 12.00
120F40VC Sidney Crosby 15.00 40.00
130F40VC Steven Stamkos 8.00 20.00
140F40VC John Tavares 6.00 15.00
150F40VC Michael Bunting 4.00 10.00
160F40VC Brady Tkachuk 6.00 15.00
170F40VC Brad Marchand 8.00 20.00
180F40VC Wyatt Johnston 8.00 20.00
190F40VC Jared McCann 3.00 8.00
200F40VC Adam Fantilli 12.00 30.00
210F40VC Brock Nelson 4.00 10.00
220F40VC Owen Power 4.00 10.00
230F40VC Matt Boldy 6.00 15.00
240F40VC Moritz Seider 5.00 12.00
250F40VC Luke Hughes 12.00 30.00
260F40VC Brayden Point 5.00 12.00
270F40VC Lucas Raymond 6.00 15.00
280F40VC Nazem Kadri 5.00 12.00
290F40VC Clayton Keller 5.00 12.00
300F40VC Cole Caufield 8.00 20.00
310F40VC Logan Couture 5.00 12.00
320F40VC Vladimir Tarasenko 5.00 12.00
330F40VC Roman Josi 4.00 10.00
340F40VC Kirill Kaprizov 12.00 30.00
350F40VC Logan Cooley 12.00 30.00
360F40VC Juraj Slafkovsky 8.00 20.00
370F40VC Kyle Connor 6.00 15.00
380F40VC Quinn Hughes 10.00 25.00
390F40VC Mika Zibanejad 5.00 12.00
400F40VC Connor Bedard 100.00 250.00

2023-24 Metal Universe Z-Force

10F50 Leon Draisaitl 2.50 6.00
20F50 Sebastian Aho 1.25 3.00
30F50 Cole Caufield 1.50 4.00
40F50 David Pastrnak 2.00 5.00
50F50 Jake DeBrusk .75 2.00
60F50 Mitch Marner 1.25 3.00
70F50 Pierre-Luc Dubois .60 1.50
80F50 Brady Tkachuk 1.25 3.00
90F50 Owen Power .75 2.00
100F50 Johnny Gaudreau 1.25 3.00
110F50 Mikhail Sergachev .60 1.50
120F50 Connor McDavid 4.00 10.00
130F50 Ilya Sorokin 1.25 3.00
140F50 Alex Ovechkin 3.00 8.00
150F50 Steven Stamkos 1.50 4.00
160F50 Jack Eichel 1.25 3.00
170F50 Jack Hughes 2.00 5.00
180F50 Clayton Keller 1.00 2.50
190F50 Tim Stutzle 1.00 2.50
200F50 Mason McTavish .75 2.00
210F50 Elias Lindholm .75 2.00
220F50 Elias Pettersson 1.25 3.00
230F50 Auston Matthews 3.00 8.00
240F50 Filip Forsberg 1.25 3.00
250F50 Tage Thompson 1.00 2.50
260F50 Sidney Crosby 3.00 8.00
270F50 Quinn Hughes 2.00 5.00
280F50 Dylan Larkin 1.00 2.50
290F50 Jordan Kyrou .75 2.00
300F50 Matthew Tkachuk 1.50 4.00
310F50 Marc-Andre Fleury 1.50 4.00
320F50 Igor Shesterkin 1.50 4.00
330F50 Kevin Fiala .60 1.50
340F50 Nick Suzuki 1.50 4.00
350F50 Patrik Laine 1.00 2.50
360F50 Jason Robertson 1.25 3.00
370F50 Matty Beniers 1.00 2.50
380F50 Miro Heiskanen 1.00 2.50
390F50 Kirill Kaprizov 2.50 6.00
400F50 Seth Jarvis 1.00 2.50
410F50 Luke Hughes 2.50 6.00
420F50 Devon Levi 2.00 5.00
430F50 Logan Cooley 2.50 6.00
440F50 Matthew Knies 3.00 8.00
450F50 Yaroslav Askarov 2.00 5.00
460F50 Leo Carlsson 2.50 6.00
470F50 Simon Nemec 1.50 4.00
480F50 Ridly Greig 1.25 3.00
490F50 Adam Fantilli 2.50 6.00
500F50 Connor Bedard 15.00 40.00

2023-24 Metal Universe Z-Force Rave

*RAVE/399: .3X TO 1.5X BASIC
500F50 Connor Bedard 80.00 200.00

2023-24 Metal Universe Z-Force Super Rave

*SUPER RAVE/50: 3X TO 8X BASIC
120F50 Connor McDavid 80.00 200.00
140F50 Alex Ovechkin 60.00 150.00
230F50 Auston Matthews 40.00 100.00
260F50 Sidney Crosby 80.00 200.00
500F50 Connor Bedard 250.00 600.00

2024-25 Metal Universe

1 Matt Coronato .40 1.00
2 Trevor Moore .30 .75
3 Travis Konecny .50 1.25
4 Quinn Hughes 1.25 3.00
5 Kirill Marchenko .60 1.50
6 Roman Josi .50 1.25
7 Jordan Kyrou .50 1.25
8 Adam Fantilli .75 2.00
9 Luke Evangelista .40 1.00
10 Oliver Bjorkstrand .40 1.00
11 Alex Iafallo .30 .75
12 Seth Jarvis .60 1.50
13 Anze Kopitar .75 2.00
14 Joel Farabee .50 1.25
15 Jake DeBrusk .50 1.25
16 Ryan Strome .50 1.25
17 Alex DeBrincat .60 1.50
18 Noah Dobson .60 1.50
19 Auston Matthews 2.00 5.00
20 Jaccob Slavin .40 1.00
21 Brock Faber .60 1.50
22 Michael Bunting .50 1.25
23 Jack Eichel .75 2.00
24 Martin Necas .75 2.00
25 Matt Boldy .75 2.00
26 Kris Letang .60 1.50
27 William Karlsson .60 1.50
28 Connor Bedard 1.50 4.00
29 Mats Zuccarello .50 1.25
30 Evgeni Malkin 1.00 2.50
31 Mark Stone .60 1.50
32 Rasmus Dahlin .60 1.50
33 Aleksander Barkov .75 2.00
34 Josh Norris .50 1.25
35 Mikhail Sergachev .40 1.00
36 Tyler Bertuzzi .40 1.00
37 Nick Suzuki 1.00 2.50
38 Tyler Toffoli .50 1.25
39 John Carlson .50 1.25
40 Teuvo Teravainen .50 1.25
41 Juraj Slafkovsky 1.00 2.50
42 William Eklund .60 1.50
43 Pierre-Luc Dubois .40 1.00
44 Nathan MacKinnon 2.00 5.00
45 Kaiden Guhle .50 1.25
46 Fabian Zetterlund .30 .75
47 Dylan Strome .60 1.50
48 Jason Robertson .75 2.00
49 Nico Hischier .75 2.00
50 Jake Guentzel .75 2.00
51 Wyatt Johnston 1.00 2.50
52 Dawson Mercer .60 1.50
53 Jake Neighbours .50 1.25
54 JJ Peterka .50 1.25
55 Sam Reinhart 1.00 2.50
56 Tim Stutzle .60 1.50
57 Matias Maccelli .40 1.00
58 Yegor Sharangovich .50 1.25
59 Matthew Tkachuk 1.00 2.50
60 Drake Batherson .50 1.25
61 Kiefer Sherwood .30 .75
62 Mason McTavish .50 1.25
63 Mason Marchment .40 1.00
64 Luke Hughes .75 2.00
65 Nikita Kucherov 1.00 2.50
66 Pavel Zacha .40 1.00
67 Patrick Kane 1.00 2.50
68 Bo Horvat .60 1.50
69 Matthew Knies 1.00 2.50
70 Andrei Kuzmenko .50 1.25
71 Kevin Fiala .40 1.00
72 Morgan Frost .40 1.00
73 Brock Boeser .60 1.50
74 Brad Marchand 1.00 2.50
75 Connor McDavid 2.50 6.00
76 Artemi Panarin 1.00 2.50
77 William Nylander 1.00 2.50
78 Tage Thompson .60 1.50
79 Zach Hyman .75 2.00
80 K'Andre Miller .40 1.00
81 Logan Cooley .75 2.00
82 Kent Johnson .50 1.25
83 Jonathan Marchessault .60 1.50
84 Robert Thomas .50 1.25
85 Leo Carlsson .75 2.00
86 Dylan Larkin .60 1.50
87 Anders Lee .40 1.00
88 Brayden Point .60 1.50
89 Devon Toews .40 1.00
90 Steven Stamkos 1.00 2.50
91 Jared McCann .40 1.00
92 Mark Scheifele .75 2.00
93 Nikita Zadorov .30 .75
94 Leon Draisaitl 1.50 4.00
95 Alexis Lafreniere .75 2.00
96 John Tavares .75 2.00
97 Mikko Rantanen 1.25 3.00
98 Cole Caufield 1.00 2.50
99 Eeli Tolvanen .50 1.25
100 Kyle Connor .75 2.00
101 Lane Hutson RC 5.00 12.00
102 Mavrik Bourque RC 2.00 5.00
103 Nikita Chibrikov RC 1.00 2.50
104 Olen Zellweger RC 2.00 5.00
105 Seamus Casey RC 1.25 3.00
106 Kyle MacLean RC 1.00 2.50
107 Logan Morrison RC 1.00 2.50
108 Matt Rempe RC 2.00 5.00
109 Samuel Honzek RC 1.00 2.50
110 Liam Ohgren RC 2.00 5.00
111 Frank Nazar RC 3.00 8.00
112 Marshall Rifai RC 1.00 2.50
113 Akil Thomas RC 1.00 2.50
114 Phil Kemp RC 1.00 2.50
115 Logan Stankoven RC 2.50 6.00
116 Victor Mancini RC 1.00 2.50
117 Pierrick Dube RC 1.00 2.50
118 Luca Del Bel Belluz RC 1.00 2.50
119 Mason Morelli RC 1.00 2.50
120 Gavin Brindley RC 1.00 2.50
121 Rutger McGroarty RC 2.00 5.00
122 Brendan Brisson RC 1.25 3.00
123 Joshua Roy RC 1.50 4.00
124 Brian Halonen RC 1.00 2.50
125 Sam Colangelo RC 1.00 2.50
126 Shakir Mukhamadullin RC 1.25 3.00
127 Cutter Gauthier RC 2.50 6.00
128 Oskar Back RC 1.00 2.50
129 Vasily Ponomarev RC 1.00 2.50
130 Nikolai Kovalenko RC .75 2.00
131 Arshdeep Bains RC 1.25 3.00
132 Maxim Tsyplakov RC 1.50 4.00
133 Scott Morrow RC 1.25 3.00
134 Emil Lilleberg RC 1.00 2.50
135 Marat Khusnutdinov RC 1.00 2.50
136 Macklin Celebrini RC 5.00 12.00
137 Bradly Nadeau RC 1.50 4.00
138 Gage Goncalves RC 1.25 3.00
139 Matvei Michkov RC 4.00 10.00
140 Justin Brazeau RC 1.00 2.50
141 Zach Dean RC 1.00 2.50
142 Brennan Othmann RC 1.50 4.00
143 Will Smith RC 3.00 8.00
144 Ethan Del Mastro RC 1.00 2.50
145 Josh Doan RC 1.50 4.00
146 Zack Ostapchuk RC 1.00 2.50
147 Yan Kuznetsov RC 1.00 2.50
148 Conor Geekie RC 2.00 5.00
149 Zachary Bolduc RC 2.00 5.00
150 Ivan Fedotov RC 2.00 5.00

2024-25 Metal Universe Precious Metal Gems Red

*PMG RED/100: 10X TO 25X BASIC
*PMG RED RC/100: 5X TO 12X BASIC
101 Lane Hutson 250.00 600.00
143 Will Smith 100.00 250.00

2024-25 Metal Universe Purple Spectrum FX

*PURPLE/199: 1.2X TO 3X BASIC
*PURPLE RC/199: 1X TO 2.5X BASIC

2024-25 Metal Universe '13 Retro

PMG RED/90: 1.2X TO 3X BASIC
*PMG BLUE/50: 2X TO 5X BASIC
RT1 Logan Stankoven 15.00 40.00
RT2 Cutter Gauthier 15.00 40.00
RT3 Charlie McAvoy 8.00 20.00
RT4 Sebastian Aho 10.00 25.00
RT5 Mikko Rantanen 15.00 40.00
RT6 Adam Fantilli 10.00 25.00
RT7 Wyatt Johnston 12.00 30.00
RT8 Lucas Raymond 10.00 25.00
RT9 Zach Hyman 10.00 25.00
RT10 Sergei Bobrovsky 10.00 25.00
RT11 Anze Kopitar 10.00 25.00
RT12 Nick Suzuki 12.00 30.00
RT13 Filip Forsberg 10.00 25.00
RT14 Alexis Lafreniere 10.00 25.00
RT15 Brady Tkachuk 10.00 25.00
RT16 Evgeni Malkin 12.00 30.00
RT17 Victor Hedman 8.00 20.00
RT18 William Nylander 12.00 30.00
RT19 Quinn Hughes 15.00 40.00
RT20 Josh Morrissey 8.00 20.00

2024-25 Metal Universe Alphabetical

*SPECTRUM/199: .6X TO 1.5X BASIC
*GOLD/50: 1.5X TO 4X BASIC
A1 Sebastian Aho 1.50 4.00
A2 Aleksander Barkov 1.50 4.00
A3 Sidney Crosby 4.00 10.00
A4 Leon Draisaitl 3.00 8.00
A5 Jack Eichel 1.50 4.00
A6 Brock Faber 1.25 3.00
A7 Jake Guentzel 1.50 4.00
A8 Quinn Hughes 2.50 6.00
A9 Alex Iafallo .60 1.50
A10 Roman Josi 1.00 2.50
A11 Nikita Kucherov 2.00 5.00
A12 Dylan Larkin 1.25 3.00
A13 Connor McDavid 5.00 12.00
A14 Martin Necas 1.50 4.00
A15 Alex Ovechkin 4.00 10.00
A16 Artemi Panarin 2.00 5.00
A17 Jonathan Quick 1.25 3.00
A18 Sam Reinhart 2.00 5.00
A19 Tim Stutzle 1.25 3.00
A20 Matthew Tkachuk 2.00 5.00
A21 Linus Ullmark 1.00 2.50
A22 Andrei Vasilevskiy 1.50 4.00
A23 MacKenzie Weegar .75 2.00
A24 Arber Xhekaj 1.00 2.50
A25 Cam York .60 1.50
A26 Mats Zuccarello 1.00 2.50

2024-25 Metal Universe Alphabetical Autographs

A2 Aleksander Barkov 15.00 40.00
A4 Leon Draisaitl 30.00 80.00
A5 Jack Eichel 15.00 40.00
A7 Jake Guentzel 15.00 40.00
A8 Quinn Hughes 25.00 60.00
A9 Alex Iafallo 6.00 15.00
A10 Roman Josi 10.00 25.00
A11 Nikita Kucherov 20.00 50.00
A14 Martin Necas 15.00 40.00
A15 Alex Ovechkin 125.00 300.00
A20 Matthew Tkachuk 20.00 50.00
A22 Andrei Vasilevskiy 15.00 40.00
A23 MacKenzie Weegar 8.00 20.00
A24 Arber Xhekaj 10.00 25.00

2024-25 Metal Universe Autographs

1 Matt Coronato 5.00 12.00
4 Quinn Hughes 15.00 40.00
5 Kirill Marchenko 8.00 20.00
6 Roman Josi 6.00 15.00
8 Adam Fantilli 10.00 25.00
9 Luke Evangelista 5.00 12.00
10 Oliver Bjorkstrand 5.00 12.00
11 Alex Iafallo 4.00 10.00
12 Seth Jarvis 8.00 20.00
16 Ryan Strome 6.00 15.00
17 Alex DeBrincat 8.00 20.00
19 Auston Matthews 25.00 60.00
20 Jaccob Slavin 5.00 12.00
22 Michael Bunting 6.00 15.00
23 Jack Eichel 10.00 25.00
24 Martin Necas 10.00 25.00
25 Matt Boldy 10.00 25.00
26 Kris Letang 8.00 20.00
31 Mark Stone 8.00 20.00
33 Aleksander Barkov 10.00 25.00
37 Nick Suzuki 12.00 30.00
38 Tyler Toffoli 6.00 15.00
39 John Carlson 6.00 15.00
41 Juraj Slafkovsky 12.00 30.00
42 William Eklund 8.00 20.00
46 Fabian Zetterlund 4.00 10.00
50 Jake Guentzel 10.00 25.00
51 Wyatt Johnston 12.00 30.00
52 Dawson Mercer 8.00 20.00
53 Jake Neighbours 6.00 15.00
54 JJ Peterka 6.00 15.00
55 Sam Reinhart 12.00 30.00
57 Matias Maccelli 5.00 12.00
59 Matthew Tkachuk 12.00 30.00
61 Kiefer Sherwood 4.00 10.00
62 Mason McTavish 6.00 15.00
63 Mason Marchment 5.00 12.00
64 Luke Hughes 10.00 25.00
65 Nikita Kucherov 12.00 30.00
66 Pavel Zacha 5.00 12.00
69 Matthew Knies 12.00 30.00
73 Brock Boeser 8.00 20.00
75 Connor McDavid 60.00 150.00
78 Tage Thompson 8.00 20.00
80 K'Andre Miller 5.00 12.00
81 Logan Cooley 10.00 25.00
82 Kent Johnson 6.00 15.00
83 Jonathan Marchessault 8.00 20.00
84 Robert Thomas 6.00 15.00
87 Anders Lee 5.00 12.00
89 Devon Toews 5.00 12.00
91 Jared McCann 5.00 12.00
93 Nikita Zadorov 4.00 10.00
94 Leon Draisaitl 20.00 50.00
95 Alexis Lafreniere 10.00 25.00
96 John Tavares 10.00 25.00
97 Mikko Rantanen 15.00 40.00
99 Eeli Tolvanen 6.00 15.00
101 Lane Hutson 150.00 400.00
102 Mavrik Bourque 12.00 30.00
103 Nikita Chibrikov 6.00 15.00
104 Olen Zellweger 12.00 30.00
105 Seamus Casey 8.00 20.00
106 Kyle MacLean 6.00 15.00
107 Logan Morrison 6.00 15.00
108 Matt Rempe 12.00 30.00
109 Samuel Honzek 6.00 15.00
110 Liam Ohgren 12.00 30.00
111 Frank Nazar 20.00 50.00
112 Marshall Rifai 6.00 15.00
113 Akil Thomas 6.00 15.00
114 Phil Kemp 6.00 15.00
115 Logan Stankoven 15.00 40.00
116 Victor Mancini 6.00 15.00
117 Pierrick Dube 6.00 15.00
119 Mason Morelli 6.00 15.00
121 Rutger McGroarty 12.00 30.00
122 Brendan Brisson 8.00 20.00
124 Brian Halonen 6.00 15.00
125 Sam Colangelo 6.00 15.00
126 Shakir Mukhamadullin 8.00 20.00
129 Vasily Ponomarev 6.00 15.00
130 Nikolai Kovalenko 5.00 12.00
131 Arshdeep Bains 8.00 20.00
132 Maxim Tsyplakov 10.00 25.00
133 Scott Morrow 8.00 20.00
134 Emil Lilleberg 6.00 15.00
136 Macklin Celebrini 150.00 400.00
137 Bradly Nadeau 10.00 25.00
138 Gage Goncalves 8.00 20.00
139 Matvei Michkov 100.00 250.00
140 Justin Brazeau 6.00 15.00
141 Zach Dean 6.00 15.00
142 Brennan Othmann 10.00 25.00
143 Will Smith 20.00 50.00
144 Ethan Del Mastro 6.00 15.00
145 Josh Doan 10.00 25.00
147 Yan Kuznetsov 6.00 15.00
148 Conor Geekie 12.00 30.00
149 Zachary Bolduc 12.00 30.00

2024-25 Metal Universe Blast Furnace

BF1 Connor Bedard 4.00 10.00
BF2 J.T. Compher .75 2.00
BF3 Macklin Celebrini 6.00 15.00
BF4 Mason McTavish 1.25 3.00
BF5 Dylan Cozens 1.25 3.00
BF6 Wyatt Johnston 2.50 6.00
BF7 Nick Suzuki 2.50 6.00
BF8 Jack Hughes 3.00 8.00
BF9 Zach Hyman 2.00 5.00
BF10 Tomas Hertl 1.25 3.00
BF11 Seth Jarvis 1.50 4.00
BF12 Kevin Fiala 1.00 2.50
BF13 Matvei Michkov 5.00 12.00
BF14 Matthew Knies 2.50 6.00
BF15 Jared McCann 1.00 2.50
BF16 Drake Batherson 1.25 3.00
BF17 Rutger McGroarty 2.50 6.00
BF18 Brock Faber 1.50 4.00
BF19 Alexis Lafreniere 2.00 5.00
BF20 Anton Lundell 1.25 3.00
BF21 Samuel Honzek 1.25 3.00
BF22 Tyler Toffoli 1.25 3.00
BF23 Jett Luchanko 2.50 6.00
BF24 Ryan O'Reilly 1.25 3.00
BF25 Juraj Slafkovsky 2.50 6.00

2024-25 Metal Universe Blast Furnace Gold

*GOLD/50: 1.5X TO 4X BASIC
BF3 Macklin Celebrini 60.00 150.00

2024-25 Metal Universe Blast Furnace Speckle

*SPECKLE/199: .6X TO 1.5X BASIC
BF3 Macklin Celebrini 25.00 60.00

2024-25 Metal Universe Blast Furnace Autographs

BF1 Connor Bedard 80.00 200.00
BF2 J.T. Compher 6.00 15.00
BF4 Mason McTavish 10.00 25.00
BF5 Dylan Cozens 10.00 25.00
BF6 Wyatt Johnston 20.00 50.00
BF7 Nick Suzuki 20.00 50.00
BF8 Jack Hughes 25.00 60.00
BF10 Tomas Hertl 10.00 25.00
BF11 Seth Jarvis 12.00 30.00
BF14 Matthew Knies 20.00 50.00
BF15 Jared McCann 8.00 20.00
BF17 Rutger McGroarty 20.00 50.00
BF19 Alexis Lafreniere 15.00 40.00
BF20 Anton Lundell 10.00 25.00
BF21 Samuel Honzek 10.00 25.00
BF22 Tyler Toffoli 10.00 25.00
BF23 Jett Luchanko 20.00 50.00
BF24 Ryan O'Reilly 10.00 25.00
BF25 Juraj Slafkovsky 20.00 50.00

2024-25 Metal Universe Counterpoise

*SPECKLE/199: .8X TO 2X BASIC
*GOLD/50: 1.2X TO 3X BASIC
1 Juuse Saros 2.50 6.00
2 Ukko-Pekka Luukkonen 1.50 4.00
3 Pyotr Kochetkov 2.00 5.00
4 Marc-Andre Fleury 4.00 10.00
5 Jordan Binnington 3.00 8.00
6 Darcy Kuemper 2.00 5.00
7 Sergei Bobrovsky 3.00 8.00
8 Stuart Skinner 2.50 6.00
9 Connor Hellebuyck 4.00 10.00
10 Igor Shesterkin 4.00 10.00
11 Alex Lyon 1.50 4.00
12 Charlie Lindgren 1.50 4.00
13 Jake Oettinger 3.00 8.00
14 Adin Hill 2.00 5.00
15 Elvis Merzlikins 2.00 5.00
16 Thatcher Demko 2.50 6.00
17 Lukas Dostal 2.00 5.00
18 Jeremy Swayman 3.00 8.00
19 Ilya Sorokin 3.00 8.00
20 Jacob Markstrom 2.00 5.00
21 Joseph Woll 2.50 6.00
22 Joey Daccord 2.00 5.00
23 Samuel Montembeault 2.00 5.00
24 Tristan Jarry 2.00 5.00
25 Linus Ullmark 2.00 5.00
26 Dustin Wolf 3.00 8.00
27 Andrei Vasilevskiy 3.00 8.00
28 Petr Mrazek 1.50 4.00
29 Samuel Ersson 2.00 5.00
30 Alexandar Georgiev 2.00 5.00

2024-25 Metal Universe Counterpoise Autographs

1 Juuse Saros 12.00 30.00
3 Pyotr Kochetkov 10.00 25.00
4 Marc-Andre Fleury 30.00 80.00
7 Sergei Bobrovsky 15.00 40.00
8 Stuart Skinner 12.00 30.00
9 Connor Hellebuyck 20.00 50.00
10 Igor Shesterkin 20.00 50.00
11 Alex Lyon 8.00 20.00
12 Charlie Lindgren 8.00 20.00
13 Jake Oettinger 15.00 40.00
14 Adin Hill 10.00 25.00
16 Thatcher Demko 12.00 30.00
18 Jeremy Swayman 15.00 40.00
19 Ilya Sorokin 15.00 40.00
21 Joseph Woll 12.00 30.00
22 Joey Daccord 10.00 25.00
24 Tristan Jarry 10.00 25.00
26 Dustin Wolf 15.00 40.00
27 Andrei Vasilevskiy 15.00 40.00
28 Petr Mrazek 8.00 20.00
29 Samuel Ersson 10.00 25.00

2024-25 Metal Universe Dark Matter

DM1 Connor McDavid 30.00 80.00
DM2 Nathan MacKinnon 25.00 60.00
DM3 Auston Matthews 25.00 60.00
DM4 Macklin Celebrini 100.00 250.00
DM5 Kirill Kaprizov 20.00 50.00
DM6 Brayden Point 8.00 20.00
DM7 Nikita Kucherov 12.00 30.00
DM8 Evgeni Malkin 12.00 30.00
DM9 Matvei Michkov 100.00 250.00
DM10 Cole Caufield 12.00 30.00
DM11 Nazem Kadri 8.00 20.00
DM12 Mark Stone 8.00 20.00
DM13 Filip Forsberg 10.00 25.00
DM14 Rasmus Dahlin 8.00 20.00
DM15 Leon Draisaitl 20.00 50.00
DM16 Brad Marchand 12.00 30.00
DM17 Sam Reinhart 12.00 30.00
DM18 Will Smith 25.00 60.00
DM19 Connor Bedard 40.00 100.00
DM20 Steven Stamkos 12.00 30.00
DM21 Lucas Raymond 10.00 25.00
DM22 Mitch Marner 10.00 25.00
DM23 Mark Scheifele 10.00 25.00
DM24 Chris Kreider 8.00 20.00
DM25 David Pastrnak 15.00 40.00
DM26 Artemi Panarin 12.00 30.00
DM27 Frank Nazar 25.00 60.00
DM28 Roope Hintz 8.00 20.00
DM29 Evan Bouchard 8.00 20.00
DM30 Brad Lambert 8.00 20.00
DM31 Olen Zellweger 12.00 30.00
DM32 Alex Tuch 6.00 15.00
DM33 Cale Makar 15.00 40.00
DM34 Carter Verhaeghe 6.00 15.00
DM35 Vincent Trocheck 6.00 15.00
DM36 Adrian Kempe 6.00 15.00
DM37 Cutter Gauthier 25.00 60.00
DM38 Troy Terry 5.00 12.00
DM39 Lane Hutson 100.00 250.00
DM40 Joel Eriksson Ek 5.00 12.00
DM41 Yegor Sharangovich 6.00 15.00
DM42 Brennan Othmann 10.00 25.00
DM43 Liam Ohgren 12.00 30.00
DM44 Alex DeBrincat 8.00 20.00
DM45 Logan Stankoven 15.00 40.00

2024-25 Metal Universe Dawning

1 Jared McCann 1.00 2.50
2 Macklin Celebrini 6.00 15.00
3 K'Andre Miller 1.00 2.50
4 Anton Lundell 1.25 3.00

5 Pavel Zacha 1.00 2.50
6 Bryan Rust 1.25 3.00
7 Jonathan Marchessault 1.50 4.00
8 Matvei Michkov 5.00 12.00
9 Martin Necas 2.00 5.00
10 Alex DeBrincat 1.50 4.00
11 Alex Tuch 1.25 3.00
12 Wyatt Johnston 2.50 6.00
13 Seamus Casey 1.50 4.00
14 Noah Dobson 1.50 4.00
15 Trevor Moore .75 2.00
16 Cale Makar 3.00 8.00
17 Nick Suzuki 2.50 6.00
18 Zach Hyman 2.00 5.00
19 Brock Boeser 1.50 4.00
20 Mark Stone 1.50 4.00
21 Will Smith 4.00 10.00
22 Robert Thomas 1.25 3.00
23 Conor Geekie 2.50 6.00
24 Nico Hischier 2.00 5.00
25 Matt Boldy 2.00 5.00

2024-25 Metal Universe Dawning Gold

*GOLD/50: 1.5X TO 4X BASIC
2 Macklin Celebrini 30.00 80.00
8 Matvei Michkov 25.00 60.00
21 Will Smith 20.00 50.00

2024-25 Metal Universe Dawning Speckle

*SPECKLE/199: .6X TO 1.5X BASIC
2 Macklin Celebrini 20.00 50.00
8 Matvei Michkov 15.00 40.00

2024-25 Metal Universe Dawning Autographs

1 Jared McCann 8.00 20.00
2 Macklin Celebrini 150.00 400.00
3 K'Andre Miller 8.00 20.00
4 Anton Lundell 10.00 25.00
5 Pavel Zacha 8.00 20.00
7 Jonathan Marchessault 12.00 30.00
8 Matvei Michkov 125.00 300.00
9 Martin Necas 15.00 40.00
10 Alex DeBrincat 12.00 30.00
11 Alex Tuch 10.00 25.00
12 Wyatt Johnston 20.00 50.00
13 Seamus Casey 12.00 30.00
15 Trevor Moore 6.00 15.00
16 Cale Makar 25.00 60.00
17 Nick Suzuki 20.00 50.00
19 Brock Boeser 12.00 30.00
21 Will Smith 40.00 100.00
22 Robert Thomas 10.00 25.00
23 Conor Geekie 20.00 50.00
25 Matt Boldy 15.00 40.00

2024-25 Metal Universe Gen Z

*SPECTRUM/199: .6X TO 1.5X BASIC
*GOLD/50: 1.5X TO 4X BASIC
GZ1 Sebastian Aho 1.25 3.00
GZ2 Tage Thompson 1.00 2.50
GZ3 Jack Hughes 2.00 5.00
GZ4 Alex DeBrincat 1.00 2.50
GZ5 Mathew Barzal 1.00 2.50
GZ6 Matthew Tkachuk 1.50 4.00
GZ7 Alexis Lafreniere 1.25 3.00
GZ8 Juraj Slafkovsky 1.50 4.00
GZ9 Brady Tkachuk 1.25 3.00
GZ10 Auston Matthews 3.00 8.00
GZ11 Frank Nazar 2.50 6.00
GZ12 Mason McTavish .75 2.00
GZ13 Wyatt Johnston 1.50 4.00
GZ14 Tim Stutzle 1.00 2.50
GZ15 Matt Boldy 1.25 3.00
GZ16 Quinton Byfield 1.00 2.50
GZ17 Quinn Hughes 2.00 5.00
GZ18 Cutter Gauthier 2.00 5.00
GZ19 Logan Stankoven 2.00 5.00
GZ20 Connor Bedard 2.50 6.00

2024-25 Metal Universe Gen Z Autographs

GZ2 Tage Thompson 10.00 25.00
GZ3 Jack Hughes 20.00 50.00
GZ4 Alex DeBrincat 10.00 25.00
GZ6 Matthew Tkachuk 15.00 40.00
GZ7 Alexis Lafreniere 12.00 30.00
GZ8 Juraj Slafkovsky 15.00 40.00
GZ9 Brady Tkachuk 12.00 30.00
GZ11 Frank Nazar 25.00 60.00
GZ12 Mason McTavish 8.00 20.00
GZ15 Matt Boldy 12.00 30.00
GZ16 Quinton Byfield 10.00 25.00
GZ17 Quinn Hughes 20.00 50.00
GZ19 Logan Stankoven 20.00 50.00
GZ20 Connor Bedard 60.00 150.00

2024-25 Metal Universe Gold Bullion

GB1 Connor Hellebuyck 10.00 25.00
GB2 Connor Bedard 15.00 40.00
GB3 Kirill Kaprizov 15.00 40.00
GB4 Jordan Kyrou 5.00 12.00
GB5 Macklin Celebrini 100.00 250.00
GB6 Sebastian Aho 8.00 20.00
GB7 Igor Shesterkin 10.00 25.00
GB8 Clayton Keller 6.00 15.00
GB9 Jack Eichel 8.00 20.00
GB10 Travis Konecny 5.00 12.00
GB11 William Nylander 10.00 25.00
GB12 Jack Hughes 12.00 30.00
GB13 Alex Ovechkin 20.00 50.00
GB14 Matvei Michkov 80.00 200.00
GB15 Elias Pettersson 8.00 20.00
GB16 David Pastrnak 12.00 30.00
GB17 Brady Tkachuk 8.00 20.00
GB18 Mikko Rantanen 12.00 30.00
GB19 Jason Robertson 8.00 20.00
GB20 Brayden Point 6.00 15.00
GB21 Conor Geekie 10.00 25.00
GB22 Anze Kopitar 8.00 20.00
GB23 Rasmus Dahlin 6.00 15.00
GB24 Steven Stamkos 10.00 25.00
GB25 Mathew Barzal 6.00 15.00
GB26 Seamus Casey 6.00 15.00
GB27 Sidney Crosby 20.00 50.00
GB28 Connor McDavid 25.00 60.00
GB29 Kirill Marchenko 6.00 15.00
GB30 Auston Matthews 20.00 50.00
GB31 Dylan Larkin 6.00 15.00
GB32 Brad Marchand 10.00 25.00
GB33 Will Smith 15.00 40.00
GB34 Aleksander Barkov 8.00 20.00
GB35 Cole Caufield 10.00 25.00

2024-25 Metal Universe Liquid Gold

1 Nathan MacKinnon 200.00 500.00
2 Connor Bedard 150.00 400.00
3 David Pastrnak 125.00 300.00
4 Nick Suzuki 100.00 250.00
5 Quinn Hughes 125.00 300.00
7 Jack Hughes 125.00 300.00
8 Jack Eichel 80.00 200.00
9 Sebastian Aho 125.00 300.00
10 Mathew Barzal 60.00 150.00
11 Quinton Byfield 60.00 150.00
12 Nikita Kucherov 100.00 250.00
13 Auston Matthews 200.00 500.00
14 William Nylander 100.00 250.00
15 Connor McDavid 500.00 1200.00
16 Matthew Tkachuk 100.00 250.00
17 Sidney Crosby 250.00 600.00
18 Leon Draisaitl 150.00 400.00
19 Steven Stamkos 100.00 250.00
20 Artemi Panarin 100.00 250.00
21 Dylan Larkin 60.00 150.00
22 Brady Tkachuk 80.00 200.00
23 Wyatt Johnston 100.00 250.00
24 Kirill Kaprizov 150.00 400.00
25 Cale Makar 125.00 300.00

2024-25 Metal Universe Metalheads

MH1 Anaheim Ducks 20.00 50.00
MH2 Boston Bruins 20.00 50.00
MH3 Buffalo Sabres 20.00 50.00
MH4 Calgary Flames 20.00 50.00
MH5 Carolina Hurricanes 20.00 50.00
MH6 Chicago Blackhawks 20.00 50.00
MH7 Colorado Avalanche 20.00 50.00
MH8 Columbus Blue Jackets 20.00 50.00
MH9 Dallas Stars 20.00 50.00
MH10 Detroit Red Wings 20.00 50.00
MH11 Edmonton Oilers 20.00 50.00
MH12 Florida Panthers 30.00 80.00
MH13 Los Angeles Kings 20.00 50.00
MH14 Minnesota Wild 20.00 50.00
MH15 Montreal Canadiens 20.00 50.00
MH16 Nashville Predators 20.00 50.00
MH17 New Jersey Devils 20.00 50.00
MH18 New York Islanders 20.00 50.00
MH19 New York Rangers 20.00 50.00
MH20 Ottawa Senators 20.00 50.00
MH21 Philadelphia Flyers 20.00 50.00
MH22 Pittsburgh Penguins 20.00 50.00
MH23 San Jose Sharks 20.00 50.00
MH24 Seattle Kraken 50.00 125.00
MH25 St. Louis Blues 20.00 50.00
MH26 Tampa Bay Lightning 20.00 50.00
MH27 Toronto Maple Leafs 20.00 50.00
MH28 Utah Hockey Club 20.00 50.00
MH29 Vancouver Canucks 20.00 50.00
MH30 Vegas Golden Knights 20.00 50.00
MH31 Washington Capitals 20.00 50.00
MH32 Winnipeg Jets 20.00 50.00

2024-25 Metal Universe Microfibers

1 David Pastrnak 3.00 8.00
2 Evgeni Malkin 2.50 6.00
3 Sam Reinhart 2.50 6.00
4 Alex Ovechkin 5.00 12.00
5 Zach Hyman 2.00 5.00
6 Brock Boeser 1.50 4.00
7 Connor Bedard 4.00 10.00
8 Jake Guentzel 2.00 5.00
9 Filip Forsberg 2.00 5.00
10 Nathan MacKinnon 5.00 12.00
11 Nikita Kucherov 2.50 6.00
12 Mikko Rantanen 3.00 8.00
13 Brayden Point 1.50 4.00
14 Cale Makar 3.00 8.00
15 Auston Matthews 5.00 12.00
16 Artemi Panarin 2.50 6.00
17 Jason Robertson 2.00 5.00
18 Mitch Marner 2.00 5.00
19 Patrick Kane 2.50 6.00
20 William Nylander 2.50 6.00
21 Lucas Raymond 2.00 5.00
22 John Tavares 2.00 5.00
23 Kirill Kaprizov 4.00 10.00
24 Matthew Tkachuk 2.50 6.00
25 Connor Hellebuyck 2.50 6.00
26 Sidney Crosby 5.00 12.00
27 Nick Suzuki 2.50 6.00
28 Roman Josi 1.25 3.00
29 Sebastian Aho 2.00 5.00
30 Jordan Kyrou 1.25 3.00
31 Jack Hughes 3.00 8.00
32 Mathew Barzal 1.50 4.00
33 Aleksander Barkov 2.00 5.00
34 J.T. Miller 1.50 4.00
35 Steven Stamkos 2.50 6.00
36 Leon Draisaitl 4.00 10.00
37 Quinn Hughes 3.00 8.00
38 Jesper Bratt 1.25 3.00
39 Connor McDavid 6.00 15.00
40 Elias Pettersson 2.00 5.00

2024-25 Metal Universe On the Button

1 Auston Matthews 6.00 15.00
2 Sam Reinhart 3.00 8.00
3 Zach Hyman 2.50 6.00
4 Nathan MacKinnon 6.00 15.00
5 Artemi Panarin 3.00 8.00
6 Filip Forsberg 2.50 6.00
7 David Pastrnak 4.00 10.00
8 Kirill Kaprizov 5.00 12.00
9 Brayden Point 2.00 5.00
10 Nikita Kucherov 3.00 8.00
11 Mikko Rantanen 4.00 10.00
12 Sidney Crosby 6.00 15.00
13 Jonathan Marchessault 2.00 5.00
14 Leon Draisaitl 5.00 12.00
15 William Nylander 3.00 8.00
16 Steven Stamkos 3.00 8.00
17 Brock Boeser 2.00 5.00
18 Chris Kreider 2.00 5.00
19 J.T. Miller 2.00 5.00
20 Brady Tkachuk 2.50 6.00
21 Frank Vatrano 1.25 3.00
22 Sebastian Aho 2.50 6.00
23 Elias Pettersson 2.50 6.00
24 Carter Verhaeghe 1.50 4.00
25 Kyle Connor 2.50 6.00
26 Nick Suzuki 3.00 8.00
27 Clayton Keller 2.00 5.00
28 Dylan Larkin 2.00 5.00
29 Alex Ovechkin 6.00 15.00
30 Tyler Toffoli 1.50 4.00

2024-25 Metal Universe Points Per Game

*SPECKLE/199: .6X TO 1.5X BASIC
*GOLD/50: 1.2X TO 3X BASIC
PPG1 Nikita Kucherov 2.00 5.00
PPG2 Nathan MacKinnon 4.00 10.00
PPG3 Connor McDavid 5.00 12.00
PPG4 Artemi Panarin 2.00 5.00
PPG5 Auston Matthews 4.00 10.00
PPG6 Leon Draisaitl 3.00 8.00
PPG7 Mikko Rantanen 2.50 6.00
PPG8 Kirill Kaprizov 3.00 8.00
PPG9 Sidney Crosby 4.00 10.00
PPG10 Sam Reinhart 2.00 5.00
PPG11 Quinn Hughes 2.50 6.00
PPG12 Cale Makar 2.50 6.00
PPG13 Sebastian Aho 1.50 4.00
PPG14 Elias Pettersson 1.50 4.00
PPG15 Matthew Tkachuk 2.00 5.00
PPG16 Robert Thomas 1.00 2.50
PPG17 Mitch Marner 1.50 4.00
PPG18 Roman Josi 1.00 2.50
PPG19 Evan Bouchard 1.25 3.00
PPG20 David Pastrnak 2.50 6.00

2024-25 Metal Universe Points Per Game Autographs

PPG1 Nikita Kucherov 20.00 50.00
PPG7 Mikko Rantanen 25.00 60.00
PPG8 Kirill Kaprizov 30.00 80.00
PPG10 Sam Reinhart 20.00 50.00
PPG11 Quinn Hughes 25.00 60.00
PPG12 Cale Makar 25.00 60.00
PPG14 Elias Pettersson 15.00 40.00
PPG15 Matthew Tkachuk 20.00 50.00
PPG16 Robert Thomas 10.00 25.00
PPG18 Roman Josi 10.00 25.00

2024-25 Metal Universe Search Engines

*SPECTRUM/199: .6X TO 1.5X BASIC
*GOLD/50: 1.2X TO 3X BASIC
ST1 Wyatt Johnston 1.50 4.00
ST2 Logan Stankoven 2.00 5.00
ST3 Leo Carlsson 1.25 3.00
ST4 Juraj Slafkovsky 1.50 4.00
ST5 Seth Jarvis 1.00 2.50
ST6 Adam Fantilli 1.25 3.00
ST7 JJ Peterka .75 2.00
ST8 Matthew Knies 1.50 4.00
ST9 Connor Bedard 2.50 6.00
ST10 Dylan Holloway .75 2.00
ST11 Brock Faber 1.00 2.50
ST12 Quinton Byfield 1.00 2.50
ST13 Luke Evangelista .60 1.50
ST14 William Eklund 1.00 2.50
ST15 Jake Neighbours .75 2.00
ST16 Logan Cooley 1.25 3.00
ST17 Cole Perfetti .75 2.00
ST18 Cutter Gauthier 2.00 5.00
ST19 Mavrik Bourque 1.50 4.00
ST20 Frank Nazar 2.50 6.00
ST21 Liam Ohgren 1.50 4.00
ST22 Lane Hutson 4.00 10.00
ST23 Brennan Othmann 1.25 3.00
ST24 Josh Doan 1.25 3.00

2024-25 Metal Universe Search Engines Autographs

ST1 Wyatt Johnston 10.00 25.00
ST2 Logan Stankoven 12.00 30.00
ST4 Juraj Slafkovsky 15.00 40.00
ST5 Seth Jarvis 6.00 15.00
ST6 Adam Fantilli 8.00 20.00
ST7 JJ Peterka 5.00 12.00
ST8 Matthew Knies 10.00 25.00
ST10 Dylan Holloway 5.00 12.00
ST12 Quinton Byfield 6.00 15.00
ST13 Luke Evangelista 4.00 10.00
ST14 William Eklund 6.00 15.00
ST15 Jake Neighbours 5.00 12.00
ST16 Logan Cooley 8.00 20.00
ST17 Cole Perfetti 5.00 12.00
ST19 Mavrik Bourque 10.00 25.00
ST20 Frank Nazar 15.00 40.00
ST21 Liam Ohgren 10.00 25.00
ST23 Brennan Othmann 8.00 20.00
ST24 Josh Doan 8.00 20.00

2024-25 Metal Universe Silver Shots

*SPECTRUM/199: .6X TO 1.5X BASIC
*GOLD/50: 1.2X TO 3X BASIC
SS1 Frank Vatrano .60 1.50
SS2 Pavel Zacha .60 1.50
SS3 JJ Peterka .75 2.00
SS4 Andrei Kuzmenko .75 2.00
SS5 Seth Jarvis 1.00 2.50
SS6 Connor Bedard 2.50 6.00
SS7 Nathan MacKinnon 3.00 8.00
SS8 Kirill Marchenko 1.00 2.50
SS9 Wyatt Johnston 1.50 4.00
SS10 Dylan Larkin 1.00 2.50
SS11 Zach Hyman 1.25 3.00
SS12 Sam Reinhart 1.50 4.00
SS13 Trevor Moore .50 1.25
SS14 Matt Boldy 1.25 3.00
SS15 Nick Suzuki 1.50 4.00
SS16 Jonathan Marchessault 1.00 2.50
SS17 Jack Hughes 2.00 5.00
SS18 Brock Nelson .75 2.00
SS19 Artemi Panarin 1.50 4.00
SS20 Brady Tkachuk 1.25 3.00
SS21 Travis Konecny .75 2.00
SS22 Tyler Toffoli .75 2.00
SS23 Jared McCann .60 1.50
SS24 Robert Thomas .75 2.00
SS25 Jake Guentzel 1.25 3.00
SS26 John Tavares 1.25 3.00
SS27 Brock Boeser 1.00 2.50
SS28 William Karlsson 1.00 2.50
SS29 Alex Ovechkin 3.00 8.00
SS30 Kyle Connor 1.25 3.00

2024-25 Metal Universe Silver Shots Autographs

SS1 Frank Vatrano 5.00 12.00
SS2 Pavel Zacha 5.00 12.00
SS3 JJ Peterka 6.00 15.00
SS5 Seth Jarvis 8.00 20.00
SS8 Kirill Marchenko 8.00 20.00
SS9 Wyatt Johnston 12.00 30.00
SS14 Matt Boldy 10.00 25.00
SS15 Nick Suzuki 12.00 30.00
SS16 Jonathan Marchessault 8.00 20.00
SS17 Jack Hughes 15.00 40.00
SS18 Brock Nelson 6.00 15.00
SS20 Brady Tkachuk 10.00 25.00
SS23 Jared McCann 5.00 12.00
SS24 Robert Thomas 6.00 15.00
SS25 Jake Guentzel 10.00 25.00
SS26 John Tavares 10.00 25.00
SS27 Brock Boeser 8.00 20.00

2024-25 Metal Universe Skybox Premium Prospects

*RUBIES/50: 1.5X TO 4X BASIC
PP1 Joshua Roy 1.50 4.00
PP2 Macklin Celebrini 5.00 12.00
PP3 Brennan Othmann 1.50 4.00
PP4 Zack Ostapchuk 1.00 2.50
PP5 Marat Khusnutdinov 1.00 2.50
PP6 Matvei Michkov 4.00 10.00
PP7 Frank Nazar 3.00 8.00
PP8 Marshall Rifai 1.00 2.50
PP9 Liam Ohgren 2.00 5.00
PP10 Will Smith 3.00 8.00
PP11 Akil Thomas 1.00 2.50
PP12 Phil Kemp 1.00 2.50
PP13 Nikita Chibrikov 1.00 2.50
PP14 Olen Zellweger 2.00 5.00
PP15 Logan Morrison 1.00 2.50
PP16 Conor Geekie 2.00 5.00
PP17 Logan Stankoven 2.50 6.00
PP18 Pierrick Dube 1.00 2.50
PP19 Mavrik Bourque 2.00 5.00
PP20 Mason Morelli 1.00 2.50
PP21 Maxim Tsyplakov 1.50 4.00
PP22 Gavin Brindley 1.00 2.50
PP23 Brendan Brisson 1.25 3.00
PP24 Brian Halonen 1.00 2.50
PP25 Kyle MacLean 1.00 2.50
PP26 Seamus Casey 1.25 3.00
PP27 Sam Colangelo 1.00 2.50
PP28 Collin Graf 1.00 2.50
PP29 Cutter Gauthier 2.50 6.00
PP30 Shakir Mukhamadullin 1.25 3.00
PP31 Nikolai Kovalenko .75 2.00
PP32 Rutger McGroarty 2.00 5.00
PP33 Arshdeep Bains 1.25 3.00
PP34 Scott Morrow 1.25 3.00
PP35 Emil Lilleberg 1.00 2.50
PP36 Lane Hutson 5.00 12.00
PP37 Victor Mancini 1.00 2.50
PP38 Bradly Nadeau 1.50 4.00
PP39 Gage Goncalves 1.25 3.00
PP40 Justin Brazeau 1.00 2.50
PP41 Zachary Bolduc 2.00 5.00
PP42 Matt Rempe 2.00 5.00
PP43 Ethan Del Mastro 1.00 2.50
PP44 Oskar Back 1.00 2.50
PP45 Josh Doan 1.50 4.00
PP46 Ivan Fedotov 2.00 5.00
PP47 Samuel Honzek 1.00 2.50
PP48 Yan Kuznetsov 1.00 2.50
PP49 Zach Dean 1.00 2.50
PP50 Vasily Ponomarev 1.00 2.50

2024-25 Metal Universe Skybox Premium Prospects Autographs

*EMERALD/25: .6X TO 1.5X BASIC
PP1 Joshua Roy 10.00 25.00
PP2 Macklin Celebrini 125.00 300.00
PP3 Brennan Othmann 10.00 25.00
PP6 Matvei Michkov 125.00 300.00
PP7 Frank Nazar 20.00 50.00
PP8 Marshall Rifai 6.00 15.00
PP9 Liam Ohgren 12.00 30.00
PP10 Will Smith 40.00 100.00
PP11 Akil Thomas 6.00 15.00
PP12 Phil Kemp 6.00 15.00
PP13 Nikita Chibrikov 6.00 15.00
PP14 Olen Zellweger 12.00 30.00
PP15 Logan Morrison 6.00 15.00
PP16 Conor Geekie 12.00 30.00
PP17 Logan Stankoven 15.00 40.00
PP18 Pierrick Dube 6.00 15.00
PP19 Mavrik Bourque 12.00 30.00
PP20 Mason Morelli 6.00 15.00
PP21 Maxim Tsyplakov 10.00 25.00
PP23 Brendan Brisson 8.00 20.00
PP24 Brian Halonen 6.00 15.00
PP25 Kyle MacLean 6.00 15.00
PP26 Seamus Casey 8.00 20.00
PP27 Sam Colangelo 6.00 15.00
PP28 Collin Graf 6.00 15.00
PP30 Shakir Mukhamadullin 8.00 20.00
PP31 Nikolai Kovalenko 5.00 12.00
PP32 Rutger McGroarty 12.00 30.00
PP33 Arshdeep Bains 8.00 20.00
PP34 Scott Morrow 8.00 20.00
PP35 Emil Lilleberg 6.00 15.00
PP36 Lane Hutson 125.00 300.00
PP37 Victor Mancini 6.00 15.00
PP38 Bradly Nadeau 10.00 25.00
PP39 Gage Goncalves 8.00 20.00
PP40 Justin Brazeau 6.00 15.00
PP41 Zachary Bolduc 12.00 30.00
PP42 Matt Rempe 12.00 30.00
PP43 Ethan Del Mastro 6.00 15.00
PP45 Josh Doan 10.00 25.00
PP47 Samuel Honzek 6.00 15.00
PP48 Yan Kuznetsov 6.00 15.00
PP49 Zach Dean 6.00 15.00
PP50 Vasily Ponomarev 6.00 15.00

2024-25 Metal Universe Weaving

1 Nikita Kucherov 5.00 12.00
2 Connor McDavid 12.00 30.00
3 Nathan MacKinnon 10.00 25.00
4 Quinn Hughes 6.00 15.00
5 Artemi Panarin 5.00 12.00
6 Cale Makar 6.00 15.00
7 J.T. Miller 3.00 8.00
8 Leon Draisaitl 8.00 20.00
9 David Pastrnak 6.00 15.00
10 Mikko Rantanen 6.00 15.00
11 Evan Bouchard 3.00 8.00
12 Matthew Tkachuk 5.00 12.00
13 Roman Josi 2.50 6.00
14 Robert Thomas 2.50 6.00
15 Noah Dobson 3.00 8.00
17 Josh Morrissey 3.00 8.00
18 William Nylander 5.00 12.00
19 Aleksander Barkov 4.00 10.00
20 Mathew Barzal 3.00 8.00
21 Jesper Bratt 2.50 6.00
22 Adam Fox 3.00 8.00
23 Elias Pettersson 4.00 10.00
24 Sebastian Aho 4.00 10.00
25 Sidney Crosby 10.00 25.00
26 Vincent Trocheck 2.50 6.00
27 Tim Stutzle 3.00 8.00
28 Jason Robertson 4.00 10.00
29 Mats Zuccarello 2.50 6.00
30 Mike Matheson 1.50 4.00

2024-25 Metal Universe Z-Force

*RAVE/399: .6X TO 1.5X BASIC
1 Kirill Kaprizov 2.50 6.00
2 Frank Nazar 2.50 6.00
3 Connor Bedard 2.50 6.00
4 Jake Guentzel 1.25 3.00
5 Mikko Rantanen 2.00 5.00
6 Brayden Point 1.00 2.50
7 Sam Reinhart 1.50 4.00
8 Alex Ovechkin 3.00 8.00
9 Artemi Panarin 1.50 4.00
10 Brad Lambert 1.00 2.50
11 Aleksander Barkov 1.25 3.00
12 J.T. Miller 1.00 2.50
13 Zach Hyman 1.25 3.00
14 Brock Boeser 1.00 2.50
15 Leon Draisaitl 2.50 6.00
16 Quinn Hughes 2.00 5.00
17 Filip Forsberg 1.25 3.00
18 Brennan Othmann 1.25 3.00
19 Connor McDavid 4.00 10.00
20 Elias Pettersson 1.25 3.00
21 Lucas Raymond 1.25 3.00
22 John Tavares 1.25 3.00
23 Patrick Kane 1.50 4.00
24 William Nylander 1.50 4.00
25 David Pastrnak 2.00 5.00
26 Evgeni Malkin 1.50 4.00
27 Sebastian Aho 1.25 3.00
28 Robert Thomas .75 2.00
29 Steven Stamkos 1.50 4.00
30 Bradly Nadeau 1.25 3.00
31 Nick Suzuki 1.50 4.00
32 Logan Stankoven 2.00 5.00
33 Sidney Crosby 3.00 8.00
34 Mathew Barzal 1.00 2.50
35 Olen Zellweger 1.50 4.00
36 Matthew Tkachuk 1.50 4.00
37 Cutter Gauthier 2.00 5.00
38 Jesper Bratt .75 2.00
39 Liam Ohgren 1.50 4.00
40 Roman Josi .75 2.00
41 Gavin Brindley .75 2.00
42 Nathan MacKinnon 3.00 8.00
43 Nikita Kucherov 1.50 4.00
44 Igor Shesterkin 1.50 4.00
45 Cale Makar 2.00 5.00
46 Auston Matthews 3.00 8.00
47 Jack Hughes 2.00 5.00
48 Lane Hutson 4.00 10.00
49 Jason Robertson 1.25 3.00
50 Mitch Marner 1.25 3.00

2024-25 Metal Universe Z-Force Super Rave

*SUPER RAVE/50: 2.5X TO 6X BASIC
3 Connor Bedard 40.00 100.00
8 Alex Ovechkin 30.00 80.00
19 Connor McDavid 40.00 100.00
33 Sidney Crosby 30.00 80.00

1996 Metallic Ice Series

NNO Mike Modano 4.00 10.00

1972-73 Minnesota Fighting Saints Postcards WHA

COMPLETE SET (25) 35.00 70.00
1 Mike Antonovich 2.00 4.00
2 John Arbour 1.50 3.00
3 Terry Ball 1.50 3.00
4 Keith Christiansen 1.50 3.00
5 Wayne Connelly 2.50 5.00
6 Mike Curran 1.50 3.00
7 Craig Falkman 1.50 3.00
8 Ted Hampson 2.00 4.00
9 Jimmy Johnson 1.50 3.00
10 Bill Klatt 1.50 3.00
11 George Konik 1.50 3.00
12 Leonard Lilyholm 1.50 3.00
13 Bob MacMillan 1.50 3.00
14 Jack McCartan 2.50 5.00
15 Mike McMahon 1.50 3.00
16 George Morrison 1.50 3.00
17 Dick Paradise 1.50 3.00
18 Mel Pearson 1.50 3.00
19 Terry Ryan 1.50 3.00
20 Blaine Rydman 1.50 3.00
21 Frank Sanders 1.50 3.00
22 Glen Sonmor CO 1.50 3.00
23 Fred Speck 1.50 3.00
24 Bill Young 1.50 3.00
25 Carl Wetzel 1.50 3.00

1974-75 Minnesota Fighting Saints WHA

1 Mike Antonovich 2.00 4.00
2 John Arbour 1.50 3.00
5 Ron Busniuk 1.50 3.00
6 Wayne Connelly 2.00 4.00
7 Mike Curran 1.50 3.00
8 Gord Gallant 2.00 4.00
9 Gary Gambucci 1.50 3.00
10 John Garrett 5.00 10.00
11 Ted Hampson 2.00 4.00
12 Murray Heatley 1.50 3.00
13 Fran Huck 1.50 3.00
14 Jim Johnson 1.50 3.00
16 Mike McMahon 1.50 3.00
20 Rich Smith 1.50 3.00
23 Mike Walton 2.50 5.00

1982-83 Neilson's Gretzky

COMPLETE SET (50) 60.00 150.00
1 Discard Broken Stick 4.00 10.00
2 Handling the Puck 2.00 5.00
3 Offsides 2.00 5.00
4 Penalty Shot 2.00 5.00
5 Icing the Puck 2.00 5.00
6 Taping your Stick 2.00 5.00
7 Skates 2.00 5.00
8 The Helmet 2.00 5.00
9 Selecting Skates 2.00 5.00
10 Choosing a Stick
(with Gordie Howe) 15.00 30.00
11 General Equipment Care 2.00 5.00
12 The Hook Check
(with Marcel Dionne) 3.00 8.00
13 The Hip Check 2.00 5.00
14 Forward Skating
(With Mike Gartner) 4.00 10.00
15 Stopping 2.00 5.00
16 Sharp Turning 2.00 5.00
17 Fast Starts 2.00 5.00
18 Backward Skating 2.00 5.00
19 The Grip 2.00 5.00
20 The Wrist Shot 2.00 5.00
21 The Back Hand Shot 2.00 5.00
22 The Slap Shot 2.00 5.00
23 The Flip Shot 2.00 5.00
24 Pass Receiving 2.00 5.00
25 Faking 2.00 5.00
26 Puck Handling 2.00 5.00
27 Deflecting Shots 2.00 5.00
28 One On One 2.00 5.00
29 Keep Your Head Up 2.00 5.00
30 Passing to the Slot 2.00 5.00
31 Winning Face-Offs
(with Guy Lafleur
and Mike Bossy) 5.00 12.00
32 Forechecking 2.00 5.00
33 Body Checking 2.00 5.00
34 Breaking Out 2.00 5.00
35 The Drop Pass 2.00 5.00
36 Backchecking
(with Phil Esposito) 4.00 10.00
37 Using the Boards 2.00 5.00
38 The Power Play 3.00 8.00
39 Passing the Puck 2.00 5.00
40 Clear the Slot 2.00 5.00
41 Leg Lifts 2.00 5.00
42 Balance Exercise 2.00 5.00
43 Leg Stretches 2.00 5.00
44 Hip and Groin Stretch 2.00 5.00
45 Toe Touches
(with Mark Messier) 4.00 10.00
46 Goalie Warm Up Drill 2.00 5.00
47 Leg Exercises 2.00 5.00
48 Arm Exercises 2.00 5.00
49 Wrist Exercises 2.00 5.00
50 Flip Pass 3.00 8.00

2002 Nextel NHL All-Star Game

COMPLETE SET (4) 4.00 10.00
1 Rob Blake
Patrick Roy
Chris Pronger 1.60 4.00
2 Brendan Shanahan
Vincent Damphousse
Owen Nolan .80 2.00
3 Jaromir Jagr
Sergei Fedorov
Teemu Selanne 1.20 3.00
4 Nicklas Lidstrom
Dominik Hasek
Sandis Ozolinsh .80 2.00

1974-75 NHL Action Stamps

COMPLETE SET (324) 100.00 200.00
1 Eric Vail .25 .50
2 Jerry Byers .18 .35
3 Rey Comeau .18 .35
4 Curt Bennett .18 .35
5 Bob Murray .18 .35
6 Don Bouchard .50 1.00
7 Pat Quinn .50 1.00
8 Larry Romanchych .18 .35
9 Randy Manery .18 .35
10 Phil Myre .50 1.00
11 Buster Harvey .18 .35
12 Keith McCreary .18 .35
13 Jean Lemieux .18 .35
14 Arnie Brown .18 .35
15 Bob Leiter .18 .35
16 Jacques Richard .25 .50
17 Noel Price .18 .35
18 Tom Lysiak .38 .75
19 Bobby Orr 10.00 20.00
20 Al Sims .25 .50
21 Don Marcotte .18 .35
22 Terry O'Reilly .50 1.00
23 Carol Vadnais .18 .35
24 Gilles Gilbert .75 1.50
25 Bobby Schmautz .25 .50
26 Phil Esposito 2.50 5.00
27 Walt McKechnie .25 .50
28 Ken Hodge .38 .75
29 Dave Forbes .18 .35
30 Wayne Cashman .38 .75
31 Johnny Bucyk .75 1.50
32 Ross Brooks .25 .50
33 Dallas Smith .18 .35
34 Darryl Edestrand .18 .35
35 Gregg Sheppard .18 .35
36 Andre Savard .25 .50
37 Jim Schoenfeld .38 .75
38 Brian Spencer .38 .75
39 Rick Dudley .25 .50
40 Craig Ramsay .18 .35
41 Gary Bromley .38 .75
42 Lee Fogolin .18 .35
43 Jerry Korab .18 .35
44 Larry Mickey .18 .35
45 Roger Crozier .50 1.00
46 Larry Carriere .18 .35
47 Norm Gratton .18 .35
48 Jim Lorentz .18 .35
49 Rene Robert .38 .75
50 Gilbert Perreault
(74/75 season on back) 2.00 4.00
51 Mike Robitaille .18 .35
52 Don Luce .18 .35
53 Richard Martin .38 .75
54 Gerry Meehan .25 .50
55 Bruce Affleck .18 .35
56 Wayne King .18 .35
57 Joseph Johnston .18 .35
58 Ron Huston .18 .35
59 Dave Hrechkosy .18 .35
60 Stan Gilbertson .18 .35
61 Mike Christie .18 .35
62 Larry Wright .18 .35
63 Stan Weir .18 .35
64 Larry Patey .18 .35
65 Al MacAdam .25 .50
66 Ted McAneeley .18 .35
67 Jim Neilson .18 .35
68 Rick Hampton .18 .35
69 Len Frig .18 .35
70 Gilles Meloche .38 .75
71 Robert Stewart .18 .35
72 Craig Patrick .38 .75
73 Dennis Hull .38 .75
74 Dale Tallon .25 .50
75 Bill White .25 .50
76 Jim Pappin .18 .35
77 Cliff Koroll .18 .35
78 Tony Esposito 2.50 5.00
79 Doug Jarrett .18 .35
80 John Marks .18 .35
81 Stan Mikita 2.00 4.00
82 Darcy Rota .18 .35
83 J.P. Bordeleau .18 .35
84 Ivan Boldirev .18 .35
85 Germaine Gagnon UER .18 .35
86 Dick Redmond .18 .35
87 Pit Martin .18 .35
88 Keith Magnuson .25 .50
89 Phil Russell .18 .35
90 Chico Maki .25 .50
91 Jean Hamel .18 .35
92 Nick Libett .25 .50
93 Hank Nowak .18 .35
94 Guy Charron .25 .50
95 Bryan Watson .18 .35
96 Nelson Pyatt .18 .35
97 Billy Lochead .18 .35
98 Danny Grant .25 .50
99 Bill Hogaboam .18 .35
100 Jim Rutherford .50 1.00
101 Doug Grant .18 .35
102 Pierre Jarry .18 .35
103 Doug Roberts .18 .35
104 Red Berenson .38 .75
105 Marcel Dionne 1.75 3.50
106 Mickey Redmond .75 1.50
107 Jack Lynch .18 .35
108 Thommie Bergman .18 .35
109 Mike Corrigan .18 .35
110 Frank St.Marseille .18 .35
111 Gene Carr .18 .35
112 Neil Komadoski .18 .35
113 Gary Edwards .38 .75
114 Sheldon Kannegiesser .18 .35
115 Bob Murdoch .18 .35
116 Rogatien Vachon 1.25 3.00
117 Dave Hutchinson .18 .35
118 Tom Williams .18 .35
119 Butch Goring .38 .75
120 Bob Berry .25 .50
121 Dan Maloney .25 .50
122 Mike Murphy .18 .35
123 Juha Widing .25 .50
124 Don Kozak .18 .35
125 Bob Nevin .18 .35
126 Terry Harper .25 .50
127 Bill Goldsworthy .38 .75
128 Dennis O'Brien .18 .35
129 Dennis Hextall .25 .50
130 Murray Oliver .18 .35
131 Lou Nanne .25 .50
132 Fred Stanfield .18 .35
133 Jean-Paul Parise .25 .50
134 Tom Reid .18 .35
135 Fred Barrett .18 .35
136 Gary Bergman .18 .35
137 Barry Gibbs .18 .35
138 Cesare Maniago .50 1.00
139 Jude Drouin .18 .35
140 Blake Dunlop .18 .35
141 Henry Boucha .25 .50
142 Fern Rivard .18 .35
143 Chris Ahrens .18 .35
144 Don Martineau .18 .35
145 Jacques Lemaire .75 1.50
146 Peter Mahovlich .38 .75
147 Yvon Lambert .18 .35
148 Yvan Cournoyer 1.25 2.50
149 Michel Larocque .38 .75
150 Guy Lapointe .50 1.00
151 Steve Shutt 1.50 3.00
152 Guy Lafleur 3.50 7.00
153 Larry Robinson 1.00 2.00
154 Jacques Laperriere .38 .75
155 Chuck Lefley .18 .35
156 Henri Richard 1.25 2.50
157 Claude Larose .18 .35
158 Ken Dryden 6.00 12.00
159 Pierre Bouchard .18 .35

160 Murray Wilson .18 .35
161 Jim Roberts .25 .50
162 Serge Savard .50 1.00
163 Clark Gillies 1.25 2.50
164 Garry Howatt .18 .35
165 Ernie Hicke .18 .35
166 Craig Cameron .18 .35
167 Ralph Stewart .18 .35
168 Lorne Henning .18 .35
169 Glenn Resch .50 1.00
170 Bill MacMillan .18 .35
171 Doug Rombough .18 .35
172 Jean Potvin .18 .35
173 Gerry Hart .18 .35
174 Bert Marshall .18 .35
175 Billy Harris .18 .35
176 Bob Nystrom .38 .75
177 Dave Lewis .18 .35
178 Billy Smith 1.00 2.00
179 Denis Potvin 4.00 8.00
180 Ed Westfall .25 .50
181 Jerry Butler .18 .35
182 Bobby Rousseau .25 .50
183 Ron Harris .18 .35
184 Bill Fairbairn .18 .35
185 Derek Sanderson 1.50 3.00
186 Jean Ratelle 1.00 2.00
187 Greg Polis .18 .35
188 Rod Gilbert 1.00 2.00
189 Ed Giacomin 1.00 2.00
190 Rod Seiling .18 .35
191 Dale Rolfe .18 .35
192 Walt Tkaczuk .25 .50
193 Pete Stemkowski .25 .50
194 Gilles Villemure .38 .75
195 Ted Irvine .18 .35
196 Brad Park 1.00 2.00
197 Gilles Marotte .25 .50
198 Steve Vickers .25 .50
199 Ross Lonsberry .18 .35
200 Bob Kelly .25 .50
201 Reggie Leach .38 .75
202 Bernie Parent 1.75 3.50
203 Terry Crisp .38 .75
204 Bill Clement .50 1.00
205 Bill Barber .50 1.00
206 Dave Schultz .50 1.00
207 Ed Van Impe .18 .35
208 Jimmy Watson .25 .50
209 Tom Bladon .18 .35
210 Rick MacLeish .38 .75
211 Andre Dupont .25 .50
212 Orest Kindrachuk .25 .50
213 Gary Dornhoefer .38 .75
214 Joe Watson .25 .50
215 Don Saleski .18 .35
216 Bobby Clarke 3.00 6.00
217 Jean Pronovost .38 .75
218 Ab DeMarco .18 .35
219 Wayne Bianchin .18 .35
220 Dave Burrows .18 .35
221 Ron Lalonde .18 .35
222 Syl Apps .38 .75
223 Bob Kelly .18 .35
224 Chuck Arnason .18 .35
225 Steve Durbano .18 .35
226 Ron Schock .18 .35
227 Bob Paradise .18 .35
228 Ron Stackhouse .18 .35
229 Lowell MacDonald .25 .50
230 Bob Johnson .18 .35
231 Rick Kehoe .38 .75
232 Nelson Debenedet .18 .35
233 Vic Hadfield .25 .50
234 Denis Herron .50 1.00
235 Phil Roberto .18 .35
236 Floyd Thomson .18 .35
237 Don Awrey .10 .05
238 Rick Wilson .18 .35
239 John Davidson 1.50 3.00
240 Pierre Plante .18 .35
241 Barclay Plager .38 .75
242 Larry Giroux .18 .35
243 Bob Gassoff .38 .75
244 Dave Gardner .18 .35
245 Brian Ogilvie .18 .35
246 Ed Johnston .50 1.00
247 Bob Plager .25 .50
248 Wayne Merrick .18 .35
249 Larry Sacharuk .18 .35
250 Bill Collins .18 .35
251 Garnet Bailey .18 .35
252 Garry Unger .38 .75
253 Gary Sabourin .18 .35
254 Willie Brossart .18 .35
255 Tim Ecclestone .18 .35
256 Dave Keon .75 1.50
257 Darryl Sittler 1.50 3.00
258 Inge Hammarstrom .18 .35
259 Ian Turnbull .25 .50
260 Jim McKenny .18 .35
261 Norm Ullman .75 1.50
262 Doug Favell .50 1.00
263 Bob Neely .18 .35
264 Lanny McDonald 1.50 3.00
265 Dunc Wilson .38 .75
266 Errol Thompson .18 .35
267 Brian Glennie .18 .35
268 Bill Flett .18 .35
269 Borje Salming .75 1.50
270 Ron Ellis .25 .50
271 Dave Dunn .18 .35
272 Chris Oddleifson .18 .35
273 Barry Wilkins .18 .35
274 Gary Smith .38 .75
275 Dennis Ververgaert .18 .35
276 Jocelyn Guevremont .18 .35
277 Andre Boudrias .25 .50
278 John Gould .18 .35
279 Jim Wiley .18 .35
280 Bob Dailey .18 .35
281 Tracy Pratt .18 .35
282 Ken Lockett .18 .35
283 Paulin Bordeleau .18 .35
284 Gerry O'Flaherty .18 .35
285 Bryan McSheffrey .18 .35
286 Gregg Boddy .18 .35
287 Don Lever .25 .50
288 Dennis Kearns .18 .35
289 Robin Burns .18 .35
290 Gary Coalter .18 .35
291 John Wright .18 .35
292 Peter McDuffe .38 .75
293 Simon Nolet .18 .35
294 Ted Snell .18 .35
295 Gary Croteau .18 .35
296 Lynn Powis .18 .35
297 Dave Hudson .18 .35
298 Richard Lemieux .18 .35
299 Bryan Lefley .18 .35
300 Doug Horbul .18 .35
301 Brent Hughes .18 .35
302 Ed Gilbert .18 .35
303 Michel Plasse .38 .75
304 Dennis Patterson .18 .35
305 Randy Rota .18 .35
306 Chris Evans .18 .35
307 Bill Mikkelson .18 .35
308 Ron Low .50 1.00
309 Doug Mohns .25 .50
310 Joe Lundrigan .18 .35
311 Steve Atkinson .18 .35
312 Ron Anderson .18 .35
313 Mike Marson .38 .75
314 Lew Morrison .18 .35
315 Jack Egers .18 .35
316 Gordy Brooks .18 .35
317 Pete Laframboise .18 .35
318 Mike Bloom .18 .35
319 Bob Collyard .18 .35
320 Dave Kryskow .18 .35
321 Greg Joly .18 .35
322 Jim Hrycuik .18 .35
323 Bob Gryp .18 .35
324 Larry Fullan .18 .35
NNO Album 10.00 20.00

1974-75 NHL Action Stamps Update

COMPLETE SET (43) 25.00 50.00
1 Barry Gibbs .50 1.00
2 Henry Nowak .50 1.00
3 Jocelyn Guevremont .50 1.00
4 Bryan McSheffrey .50 1.00
5 Fred Stanfield .50 1.00
6 Dave Gardner .50 1.00
7 Morris Mott NEW .50 1.00
8 Gary Simmons NEW 2.00 4.00
9 Gary Bergman .75 1.50
10 Dave Kryskow .50 1.00
11 Walt McKechnie .50 1.00
12 Phil Roberto .50 1.00
13 Ted Snell .50 1.00
14 Guy Charron .75 1.50
15 Jean-Guy Lagace NEW .50 1.00
16 Denis Herron 2.00 4.00
17 Craig Cameron .50 1.00
18 John Flesch NEW .50 1.00
19 Norm Gratton .50 1.00
20 Ernie Hicke .50 1.00
21 Doug Rombough .50 1.00
22 Don Awrey .50 1.00
23 Wayne Thomas NEW 2.00 4.00
24 Jude Drouin .50 1.00
25 Jean Paul Parise .50 1.00
26 Rick Middleton NEW 2.50 5.00
27 Lew Morrison .50 1.00
28 Michel Plasse 2.00 4.00
29 Barry Wilkins .50 1.00
30 Red Berenson .75 1.50
31 Chris Evans .50 1.00
32 Claude Larose .50 1.00
33 Chuck Lefley .50 1.00
34 Craig Patrick .75 1.50
35 Dave Dunn .50 1.00
36 George Ferguson NEW .50 1.00
37 Rod Seiling .50 1.00
38 Ab Demarco .50 1.00
39 Gerry Meehan .50 1.00
40 Mike Robitaille .50 1.00
41 Willie Brossart .50 1.00
42 Ron Lalonde .50 1.00
43 Jack Lynch .50 1.00

1995-96 NHL Aces Playing Cards

COMPLETE SET (55) 6.00 15.00
1C Paul Coffey .25 .60
1D Wayne Gretzky 1.25 3.00
1H Eric Lindros .60 1.50
1S Patrick Roy 1.00 2.50
2C Scott Stevens .01 .05
2D Al MacInnis .01 .05
2H Craig Janney .01 .05
2S Kirk Muller .01 .05
3C Bill Ranford .05 .15
3D Mike Modano .25 .60
3H Doug Gilmour .25 .60
3S Steve Yzerman .60 1.50
4C Brian Bradley .01 .05
4D Alexandre Daigle .01 .05
4H Claude Lemieux .05 .15
4S Felix Potvin .15 .40
5C Ed Belfour .25 .60
5D Jeremy Roenick .25 .60
5H Trevor Linden .02 .10
5S Pat Lafontaine .05 .15
6C Brian Leetch .25 .60
6D Jason Arnott .02 .10
6H Geoff Sanderson .01 .05
6S Jim Carey .15 .40
7C Ron Francis .05 .15
7D Peter Bondra .25 .60
7H Paul Kariya .75 2.00
7S John Vanbiesbrouck .20 .50
8C Teemu Selanne .40 1.00
8D Ray Bourque .25 .60
8H Pierre Turgeon .05 .15
8S Alexei Yashin .15 .40
9C Martin Brodeur .50 1.25
9D Pavel Bure .50 1.25
9H Peter Forsberg .50 1.25
9S Chris Chelios .25 .60
10C Joe Nieuwendyk .07 .20
10D Mats Sundin .25 .60
10H Adam Oates .05 .15
10S Cam Neely .07 .20
11C Mark Messier .25 .60
11D Brett Hull .25 .60
11H Sergei Fedorov .40 1.00
11S Keith Tkachuk .25 .60
12C Mikael Renberg .05 .15
12D Jaromir Jagr .60 1.50
12H Mario Lemieux 1.00 2.50
12S John Leclair .30 .75
13C Joe Sakic .40 1.00
13D Dominik Hasek .40 1.00
13H Alexei Zhamnov .02 .10
13S Theo Fleury .25 .60
NNO Eastern Conference Logo .01 .05
NNO Checklist of Players in Deck .01 .05
NNO Western Conference Logo .01 .05

1996-97 NHL Aces Playing Cards

COMPLETE SET (55) 4.80 12.00
1 Daniel Alfredsson .10 .30
2 Jason Arnott .10 .30
3 Ray Bourque .30 .75
4 Rod Brind'Amour .10 .30
5 Martin Brodeur .30 .75
6 Pavel Bure .30 .75
7 Jim Carey .08 .25
8 Chris Chelios .10 .30
9 Vincent Damphousse .05 .15
10 Eric Daze .08 .25
11 Sergei Fedorov .30 .75
12 Ray Ferraro .02 .10
13 Theo Fleury .10 .30
14 Peter Forsberg .30 .75
15 Ron Francis .10 .30
16 Grant Fuhr .07 .20
17 Mike Gartner .05 .15
18 Doug Gilmour .10 .30
19 Travis Green .02 .10
20 Wayne Gretzky .75 2.00
21 Roman Hamrlik .05 .15
22 Brett Hull .15 .40
23 Jaromir Jagr .40 1.00
24 Ed Jovanovski .07 .20
25 Joe Juneau .07 .20
26 Paul Kariya .40 1.00
27 Pat LaFontaine .08 .25
28 Brian Leetch .10 .30
29 Mario Lemieux .60 1.50
30 Trevor Linden .10 .30
31 Eric Lindros .30 .75
32 Mark Messier .15 .40
33 Mike Modano .15 .40
34 Alexander Mogilny .08 .25
35 Owen Nolan .10 .30
36 Adam Oates .10 .30
37 Chris Osgood .10 .30
38 Daren Puppa .05 .15
39 Gary Roberts .05 .15
40 Jeremy Roenick .10 .30
41 Patrick Roy .60 1.50
42 Joe Sakic .30 .75
43 Teemu Selanne .30 .75
44 Brendan Shanahan .30 .75
45 Mats Sundin .10 .30
46 Jocelyn Thibault .08 .25
47 Keith Tkachuk .10 .30
48 Pierre Turgeon .08 .25
49 John Vanbiesbrouck .10 .30
50 Doug Weight .10 .30
51 Alexei Yashin .08 .25
52 Steve Yzerman .60 1.50
NNO Checklist .02 .10
NNO Western Conference .02 .10
NNO Eastern Conference .02 .10

1997-98 NHL Aces Playing Cards

COMPLETE SET (55) 0.00 20.00
1 Dominik Hasek .40 1.00
2 Mike Vernon .08 .25
3 Doug Gilmour .20 .50
4 Dimitri Kristich .02 .10
5 Mark Recchi .08 .25
6 Daniel Alfredsson .08 .25
7 Eric Lindros .08 .25
8 Keith Tkachuk .08 .25
9 Pavel Bure .30 .75
10 Brendan Shanahan .30 .75
11 Sandis Ozolinsh .02 .10
12 Mark Messier .30 .75
13 Patrick Roy .75 2.00
14 Paul Kariya .30 .75
15 Ray Bourque .40 1.00
16 Ryan Smyth .08 .25
17 Jarome Iginla .40 1.00
18 Chris Gratton .02 .10
19 Jeremy Roenick .40 1.00
20 Mike Modano .40 1.00
21 Doug Weight .08 .25
22 Jim Campbell .02 .10
23 Sheldon Kennedy .02 .10
24 Jason Arnott .02 .10
25 Peter Forsberg .40 1.00
26 Brian Leetch .40 1.00
27 Mike Peca .02 .10
28 Jere Lehtinen .08 .25
29 Trevor Linden .40 1.00
30 John Leclair .08 .25
31 Owen Nolan .08 .25
32 Pierre Turgeon .02 .10
33 Tony Amonte .02 .10
34 Alexei Yashin .02 .10
35 Mats Sundin .40 1.00
36 Jaromir Jagr .60 1.50
37 Wayne Gretzky 1.25 3.00
38 Martin Brodeur .60 1.50
39 Tony Granato .02 .10
40 Bryan Berard .02 .10
41 Geoff Sanderson .02 .10
42 Chris Chelios .20 .50
43 Felix Potvin .30 .75
44 Adam Oates .08 .25
45 Roman Hamrlik .02 .10
46 Theoren Fleury .08 .25
47 Vincent Damphousse .02 .10
48 Zigmund Palffy .08 .25
49 Saku Koivu .40 1.00
50 Teemu Selanne .40 1.00
51 John Vanbiesbrouck .20 .50
52 Vladimir Konstantinov .40 1.00
NNO Checklist .01 .01
NNO Eastern Conference .01 .01
NNO Western Conference .01 .01

1998-99 NHL Aces Playing Cards

COMPLETE SET (55) 6.00 15.00
1 Olaf Kolzig .20 .50
2 Marcel Cousineau .08 .25
3 Corey Schwab .08 .25
4 Dwayne Roloson .08 .25
5 Mark Fitzpatrick .08 .25
6 Guy Herbert .08 .25
7 Jamie McLennan .08 .25
8 Rick Tabaracci .08 .25
9 Jose Theodore .40 1.00
10 Grant Fuhr .40 1.00
11 Ed Belfour .40 1.00
12 Felix Potvin .40 1.00
13 Damian Rhodes .08 .25
14 Patrick Roy 1.00 2.50
15 Ken Wregget .08 .25
16 Bill Ranford .08 .25
17 Jamie Storr .08 .25
18 Chris Terreri .08 .25
19 Kelly Hrudey .08 .25
20 Ron Tugnutt .08 .25
21 Mike Vernon .08 .25
22 Mikhail Shtalenkov .08 .25
23 Darren Puppa .08 .25
24 Bryon Dafoe .08 .25
25 Arthurs Irbe .20 .50
26 Chris Osgood .20 .50
27 Dominik Hasek .60 1.50
28 Robbie Tallas .08 .25
29 Kirk McLean .08 .25
30 Peter Skudra .08 .25
31 Eric Fichaud .08 .25
32 Bob Essensa .08 .25
33 Sean Burke .08 .25
34 Jocelyn Thibault .08 .25
35 Ron Hextall .40 1.00
36 Nikolai Khabibulin .40 1.00
37 Mike Richter .40 1.00
38 Tommy Salo .08 .25
39 John Vanbiesbrouck .40 1.00
40 Curtis Joseph .40 1.00
41 Glenn Healy .08 .25
42 Mike Dunham .08 .25
43 Roman Turek .08 .25
44 Steve Shields .08 .25
45 Garth Snow .08 .25
46 Kevin Hodson .08 .25
47 Craig Billington .08 .25
48 Trevor Kidd .08 .25
49 Jeff Hackett .08 .25
50 Stephane Fiset .08 .25
51 Tom Barrasso .20 .50
52 Martin Brodeur .75 2.00
NNO Eastern Conference .01 .01
NNO Western Conference .01 .01
NNO Checklist .01 .01

1995-96 NHL Cool Trade

COMPLETE SET (20) 3.00 10.00
1 Cam Neely .20 .50
2 Wayne Gretzky 1.50 4.00
3 Jeremy Roenick .20 .50
4 Mario Lemieux 1.00 2.50
5 Mark Messier .30 .75
6 Ray Bourque .20 .50
7 Sergei Fedorov .40 1.00
8 Paul Kariya .40 1.00
9 Eric Lindros .40 1.00
10 Pavel Bure .30 .75
11 Chris Chelios .20 .50
12 Peter Forsberg .50 1.25
13 Saku Koivu .20 .50
14 Ed Belfour .20 .50
15 Brett Hull .30 .75
16 Patrick Roy 1.00 2.50
17 Doug Gilmour .20 .50
18 Martin Brodeur .40 1.00
19 Alexander Mogilny .20 .50
20 Jaromir Jagr .30 .75
RP1 Cam Neely .75 2.00
RP2 Wayne Gretzky 6.00 15.00
RP3 Jeremy Roenick 4.00 10.00
RP4 Mario Lemieux 3.00 8.00
RP5 Mark Messier 2.00 5.00
RP6 Ray Bourque 1.00 2.50
RP7 Sergei Fedorov 1.50 4.00
RP8 Paul Kariya 10.00 25.00
RP9 Eric Lindros 1.00 2.50
RP10 Pavel Bure 3.00 8.00
RP11 Chris Chelios .75 2.00
RP12 Peter Forsberg 1.25 3.00
RP13 Saku Koivu 4.00 10.00
RP14 Ed Belfour 1.00 2.50
RP15 Brett Hull 3.00 6.00
RP16 Patrick Roy 5.00 10.00
RP17 Doug Gilmour .75 2.00
RP18 Martin Brodeur 8.00 20.00
RP19 Alexander Mogilny 1.00 2.50
RP20 Jaromir Jagr 2.50 6.00

1996-97 NHL Pro Stamps

COMPLETE SET (130) 7.20 18.00
1 Stephane Fiset .05 .15
2 Peter Forsberg .20 .50
3 Claude Lemieux DP .05 .15
4 Mike Ricci .02 .10
5 Joe Sakic .15 .40
6 Ed Belfour .08 .25
7 Chris Chelios .08 .25
8 Joe Murphy .02 .10
9 Bernie Nicholls .02 .10
10 Jeremy Roenick DP .08 .25
11 Geoff Courtnall .02 .10
12 Brett Hull .15 .40
13 Al MacInnis .05 .15
14 Chris Pronger .05 .15
15 Esa Tikkanen .05 .15
16 Ray Bourque .08 .25
17 Blaine Lacher .05 .15
18 Cam Neely .07 .20
19 Adam Oates DP .07 .20
20 Kevin Stevens .02 .10
21 Valeri Bure .02 .10
22 Vincent Damphousse .05 .15
23 Mark Recchi .05 .15
24 Patrick Roy .30 .75
25 Pierre Turgeon .07 .20
26 Pavel Bure .15 .40
27 Trevor Linden .05 .15
28 Kirk McLean .05 .15
29 Alexander Mogilny .08 .25
30 Cliff Ronning .02 .10
31 Jason Allison .02 .10
32 Jim Carey .10 .30
33 Dale Hunter .02 .10
34 Joe Juneau DP .07 .20
35 Brendan Witt .02 .10
36 Martin Brodeur DP .15 .40
37 John MacLean .05 .15
38 Scott Niedermayer .05 .15
39 Stephane Richer .02 .10
40 Scott Stevens .05 .15
41 Patrik Carnback .02 .10
42 Guy Hebert .07 .20
43 Paul Kariya .25 .60
44 Oleg Tverdovsky .05 .15
45 Garry Valk .02 .10
46 Theo Fleury .07 .20
47 Trevor Kidd .05 .15
48 Joe Nieuwendyk .05 .15
49 Gary Roberts .02 .10
50 German Titov .02 .10
51 Rod Brind'Amour .05 .15
52 Ron Hextall .05 .15
53 John LeClair .10 .30
54 Eric Lindros .20 .50
55 Mikael Renberg .07 .20
56 Brett Lindros .02 .10
57 Wendel Clark .05 .15
58 Patrick Flatley .02 .10
59 Kirk Muller .02 .10
60 Mathieu Schneider .02 .10
61 Tim Cheveldae .05 .15
62 Dallas Drake .02 .10
63 Teemu Selanne .15 .40
64 Keith Tkachuk .10 .30
65 Alexei Zhamnov .05 .15
66 Rob Blake .05 .15
67 Wayne Gretzky DP .40 1.00
68 Jari Kurri .05 .15
69 Jamie Storr .05 .15
70 Rick Tocchet .05 .15
71 Brian Bradley .02 .10
72 Chris Gratton .05 .15
73 Roman Hamrlik .05 .15
74 Paul Ysebaert .02 .10
75 Rob Zamuner .02 .10
76 Dave Andreychuk .05 .15
77 Doug Gilmour .08 .25
78 Kenny Jonsson .05 .15
79 Felix Potvin .10 .30
80 Mats Sundin .07 .20
81 Jason Arnott .07 .20
82 Jason Bonsignore .02 .10
83 Todd Marchant .02 .10
84 Bill Ranford .07 .20
85 Doug Weight .07 .20
86 Jody Hull .02 .10
87 Bob Kudelski .02 .10
88 Scott Mellanby .05 .15
89 Rob Niedermayer .05 .15
90 John Vanbiesbrouck .08 .25
91 Ron Francis .07 .20
92 Jaromir Jagr .20 .50
93 Mario Lemieux DP .30 .75
94 Bryan Smolinski .02 .10
95 Sergei Zubov .02 .10
96 Adam Graves .05 .15
97 Brian Leetch .07 .20
98 Mark Messier DP .15 .40
99 Mike Richter .08 .25
100 Luc Robitaille .07 .20
101 Paul Coffey .07 .20
102 Sergei Fedorov DP .15 .40
103 Nicklas Lidstrom .05 .15
104 Ray Sheppard .02 .10
105 Steve Yzerman .20 .50
106 Donald Audette .02 .10
107 Dominik Hasek DP .15 .40
108 Yuri Khmylev .02 .10
109 Pat LaFontaine .05 .15
110 Alexei Zhitnik .02 .10
111 Radek Bonk .02 .10
112 Randy Cunneyworth .02 .10
113 Alexandre Daigle .05 .15
114 Steve Larouche .02 .10
115 Martin Straka .02 .10
116 Ulf Dahlen .02 .10
117 Pat Falloon .02 .10
118 Jeff Friesen .05 .15
119 Arturs Irbe DP .05 .15
120 Craig Janney .02 .10
121 Shane Churla .02 .10
122 Todd Harvey .02 .10
123 Derian Hatcher .02 .10
124 Mike Modano .07 .20
125 Andy Moog .07 .20
126 Sean Burke .05 .15
127 Andrew Cassels .02 .10
128 Geoff Sanderson .05 .15
129 Brendan Shanahan .15 .40
130 Darren Turcotte .02 .10

1994 NHLPA Phone Cards

COMPLETE SET (9) 16.00 40.00
1 Doug Gilmour 1.50 4.00
2 Brett Hull 2.00 5.00
3 Paul Kariya 3.00 8.00
4 Eric Lindros 2.50 6.00
5 Luc Robitaille 1.50 4.00
6 Jeremy Roenick 1.50 4.00
7 Patrick Roy 4.00 10.00
8 John Vanbiesbrouck 1.50 4.00
9 Team Ontario 1.25 3.00

2003 NHL Sticker Collection

COMPLETE SET (300) 25.00 50.00
1 Atlanta Thrashers Home Logo .10 .25
2 Atlanta Thrashers Away Logo .10 .25
3 Dany Heatley .20 .50
4 Ilya Kovalchuk .20 .50
5 Patrik Stefan .10 .25
6 Frantisek Kaberle .10 .25
7 Yannick Tremblay .10 .25
8 Tony Hrkac .10 .25
9 Shawn Mceachern .10 .25
10 Byron Dafoe .10 .25
11 Boston Bruins Home Logo .10 .25
12 Boston Bruins Away Logo .10 .25
13 Martin Lapointe .10 .25
14 Glen Murray .20 .50
15 Brian Rolston .10 .25
16 Sergei Samsonov .20 .50
17 Joe Thornton .40 1.00
18 Jozef Stumpel .10 .25
19 Nick Boynton .10 .25
20 Steve Shields .10 .25
21 Buffalo Sabres Home Logo .10 .25
22 Buffalo Sabres Away Logo .10 .25
23 Stu Barnes .10 .25
24 Curtis Brown .10 .25
25 Miroslav Satan .20 .50
26 Jochen Hecht .10 .25
27 Tim Connolly .10 .25
28 Jay McKee .10 .25
29 Chris Gratton .10 .25
30 Martin Biron .20 .50
31 Carolina Hurricanes Home Logo .10 .25
32 Carolina Hurricanes Away Logo .10 .25
33 Rod Brind'Amour .20 .50
34 Erik Cole .10 .25
35 Ron Francis .20 .50
36 Sami Kapanen .10 .25
37 Jeff O'Neill .10 .25
38 Bret Hedican .10 .25
39 Sean Hill .10 .25
40 Kevin Weekes .10 .25
41 Florida Panthers Home Logo .10 .25
42 Florida Panthers Away Logo .10 .25
43 Valeri Bure .10 .25
44 Olli Jokinen .10 .25
45 Marcus Nilsson .10 .25
46 Stephen Weiss .10 .25
47 Kristian Huselius .10 .25
48 Sandis Ozolinsh .10 .25
49 Jay Bouwmeester .20 .50
50 Roberto Luongo .60 1.50
51 Montreal Canadians Home Logo .10 .25
52 Montreal Canadians Away Logo .10 .25
53 Randy McKay .10 .25
54 Richard Zednik .10 .25
55 Doug Gilmour .40 1.00
56 Saku Koivu .40 1.00
57 Yanic Perreault .10 .25
58 Craig Rivet .10 .25
59 Patrice Brisebois .10 .25
60 Jose Theodore .30 .75
61 New Jersey Devils Home Logo .10 .25
62 New Jersey Devils Away Logo .10 .25
63 Patrik Elias .10 .25
64 Jeff Friesen .10 .25
65 Joe Nieuwendyk .20 .50
66 Sergei Brylin .10 .25
67 Jamie Langenbrunner .10 .25
68 Scott Stevens .10 .25
69 Scott Niedermayer .20 .50
70 Martin Brodeur .40 1.00
71 New York Islanders Home Logo .10 .25
72 New York Islanders Away Logo .10 .25
73 Shawn Bates .10 .25
74 Brad Isbister .10 .25
75 Mark Parrish .10 .25
76 Michael Peca .10 .25
77 Alexei Yashin .10 .25
78 Kenny Jonsson .10 .25
79 Roman Hamrlik .10 .25
80 Chris Osgood .20 .50
81 New York Rangers Home Logo .10 .25
82 New York Rangers Away Logo .10 .25
83 Pavel Bure .40 1.00
84 Bobby Holik .10 .25
85 Eric Lindros .40 1.00
86 Mark Messier .40 1.00
87 Petr Nedved .10 .25
88 Brian Leetch .20 .50
89 Darius Kasparitis .10 .25
90 Mike Richter .20 .50
91 Ottawa Senators Home Logo .10 .25
92 Ottawa Senators .10 .25
93 Daniel Alfredsson .20 .50
94 Jason Spezza .20 .50
95 Marian Hossa .30 .75
96 Magnus Arvedson .10 .25
97 Martin Havlat .20 .50
98 Wade Redden .10 .25
99 Chris Phillips .10 .25
100 Patrick Lalime .10 .25
101 Philadelphia Flyers Home Logo .10 .25
102 Philadelphia Flyers Away Logo .10 .25
103 Simon Gagne .20 .50
104 John LeClair .10 .25
105 Keith Primeau .10 .25
106 Mark Recchi .20 .50
107 Jeremy Roenick .40 1.00
108 Eric Desjardins .10 .25
109 Kim Johnsson .10 .25
110 Roman Cechmanek .10 .25
111 Pittsburgh Penguins Home Logo .10 .25
112 Pittsburgh Penguins Away Logo .10 .25
113 Jan Hrdina .10 .25
114 Alexei Kovalev .10 .25
115 Mario Lemieux .75 2.00
116 Alexei Morozov .10 .25
117 Wayne Primeau .10 .25
118 Michal Rozsival .10 .25
119 Dick Tarnstrom .10 .25
120 Johan Hedberg .10 .25
121 Tampa Bay Lightning Home Logo .10 .25
122 Tampa Bay Lightning Away Logo .10 .25
123 Dave Andreychuk .10 .25
124 Vincent Lecavalier .40 1.00
125 Vaclav Prospal .10 .25
126 Brad Richards .20 .50
127 Martin St. Louis .20 .50
128 Pavel Kubina .10 .25
129 Dan Boyle .10 .25
130 Nikolai Khabibulin .40 1.00
131 Toronto Maple Leafs Home Logo .10 .25
132 Toronto Maple Leafs Away Logo .10 .25
133 Mats Sundin .40 1.00
134 Tie Domi .10 .25
135 Darcy Tucker .10 .25
136 Alexander Mogilny .10 .25
137 Gary Roberts .10 .25
138 Tomas Kaberle .10 .25
139 Bryan McCabe .10 .25
140 Ed Belfour .40 1.00
141 Washington Capitals Home Logo .10 .25
142 Washington Capitals Away Logo .10 .25
143 Peter Bondra .10 .25
144 Jaromir Jagr .30 .75
145 Robert Lang .10 .25
146 Jeff Halpern .10 .25
147 Sergei Gonchar .10 .25
148 Dainius Zubrus .10 .25
149 Steve Konowalchuk .10 .25
150 Olaf Kolzig .20 .50
151 Anaheim Mighty Ducks Home Logo .10 .25
152 Anaheim Mighty Ducks Away Logo .10 .25
153 Paul Kariya .40 1.00
154 Matt Cullen .10 .25
155 Steve Rucchin .10 .25
156 Mike Leclerc .10 .25
157 Petr Sykora .10 .25
158 Stanislav Chistov .10 .25
159 Keith Carney .10 .25
160 Jean-Sebastien Giguere .20 .50
161 Calgary Flames Home Logo .10 .25
162 Calgary Flames Away Logo .10 .25
163 Craig Conroy .10 .25
164 Jarome Iginla .40 1.00
165 Chris Drury .20 .50
166 Martin Gelinas .10 .25
167 Stephane Yelle .10 .25
168 Denis Gauthier .10 .25
169 Bob Boughner .10 .25
170 Roman Turek .10 .25
171 Chicago Blackhawks Home Logo .10 .25
172 Chicago Blackhawks Away Logo .10 .25
173 Eric Daze .10 .25
174 Steve Sullivan .10 .25
175 Alexei Zhamnov .10 .25
176 Kyle Calder .10 .25
177 Phil Housley .10 .25
178 Tyler Arnason .10 .25
179 Lyle Odelein .10 .25
180 Jocelyn Thibault .20 .50
181 Colorado Avalanche Home Logo .10 .25
182 Colorado Avalanche Away Logo .10 .25
183 Peter Forsberg .40 1.00
184 Milan Hejduk .20 .50
185 Joe Sakic .40 1.00
186 Alex Tanguay .20 .50
187 Rob Blake .10 .25
188 Adam Foote .10 .25
189 Derek Morris .10 .25
190 Patrick Roy .75 2.00
191 Columbus Blue Jackets Home Logo .10 .25
192 Columbus Blue Jackets Away Logo .10 .25
193 Rick Nash .40 1.00
194 Geoff Sanderson .10 .25
195 Andrew Cassels .10 .25
196 Ray Whitney .10 .25
197 Luke Richardson .10 .25
198 Scott Lachance .10 .25
199 Mike Sillinger .10 .25
200 Marc Denis .10 .25
201 Dallas Stars Home Logo .10 .25
202 Dallas Stars Away Logo .10 .25
203 Ulf Dahlen .10 .25
204 Bill Guerin .10 .25
205 Mike Modano .30 .75
206 Pierre Turgeon .10 .25
207 Scott Young .10 .25
208 Sergei Zubov .10 .25

Card	Low	High
209 Darryl Sydor	.10	.25
210 Marty Turco	.20	.50
211 Detriot Red Wings Home Logo	.10	.25
212 Detriot Red Wings Away Logo	.10	.25
213 Sergei Fedorov	.20	.50
214 Brett Hull	.30	.75
215 Brendan Shanahan	.20	.50
216 Steve Yzerman	.75	2.00
217 Chris Chelios	.20	.50
218 Nicklas Lidstrom	.20	.50
219 Kris Draper	.10	.25
220 Curtis Joseph	.20	.50
221 Edmonton Oilers Home Logo	.10	.25
222 Edmonton Oilers Away Logo	.10	.25
223 Anson Carter	.10	.25
224 Mike Comrie	.10	.25
225 Ryan Smyth	.20	.50
226 Mike York	.10	.25
227 Eric Brewer	.10	.25
228 Jason Smith	.10	.25
229 Janne Niinimaa	.10	.25
230 Tommy Salo	.10	.25
231 Los Angeles Kings Home Logo	.10	.25
232 Los Angeles Kings Away Logo	.10	.25
233 Jason Allison	.10	.25
234 Adam Deadmarsh	.10	.25
235 Bryan Smolinski	.10	.25
236 Mathieu Schneider	.10	.25
237 Jaroslav Modry	.10	.25
238 Zigmund Palffy	.20	.50
239 Lubomir Visnovsky	.10	.25
240 Felix Potvin	.20	.50
241 Minnesota Wild Home Logo	.10	.25
242 Minnesota Wild Away Logo	.10	.25
243 Andrew Brunette	.10	.25
244 Marian Gaborik	.40	1.00
245 Cliff Ronning	.10	.25
246 Sergei Zholtok	.10	.25
247 Jim Dowd	.10	.25
248 Antti Laaksonen	.10	.25
249 Willie Mitchell	.10	.25
250 Manny Fernandez	.20	.50
251 Nashville Predators Home Logo	.10	.25
252 Nashville Predators Away Logo	.10	.25
253 Andreas Johansson	.10	.25
254 Greg Johnson	.10	.25
255 Denis Arkhipov	.10	.25
256 David Legwand	.10	.25
257 Vladimir Orszagh	.10	.25
258 Andy Delmore	.10	.25
259 Kimmo Timonen	.10	.25
260 Tomas Vokoun	.20	.50
261 Phoenix Coyotes Home Logo	.10	.25
262 Phoenix Coyotes Away Logo	.10	.25
263 Tony Amonte	.10	.25
264 Daniel Briere	.10	.25
265 Shane Doan	.10	.25
266 Daymond Langkow	.10	.25
267 Ladislav Nagy	.10	.25
268 Teppo Numminen	.10	.25
269 Danny Markov	.10	.25
270 Sean Burke	.20	.50
271 St. Louis Blues Home Logo	.10	.25
272 St. Louis Blues Away Logo	.10	.25
273 Pavol Demitra	.10	.25
274 Cory Stillman	.10	.25
275 Keith Tkachuk	.20	.50
276 Doug Weight	.10	.25
277 Al MacInnis	.20	.50
278 Chris Pronger	.20	.50
279 Eric Boguniecki	.10	.25
280 Brent Johnson	.10	.25
281 San Jose Sharks Home Logo	.10	.25
282 San Jose Sharks Away Logo	.10	.25
283 Vincent Damphousse	.10	.25
284 Adam Graves	.10	.25
285 Patrick Marleau	.20	.50
286 Owen Nolan	.10	.25
287 Teemu Selanne	.30	.75
288 Marco Sturm	.10	.25
289 Mike Ricci	.10	.25
290 Evgeni Nabokov	.20	.50
291 Vancouver Canucks Home Logo	.10	.25
292 Vancouver Canucks Away Logo	.10	.25
293 Todd Bertuzzi	.20	.50
294 Trevor Linden	.40	1.00
295 Brendan Morrison	.10	.25
296 Markus Naslund	.20	.50
297 Henrik Sedin	.10	.25
298 Ed Jovanovski	.10	.25
299 Mattias Ohlund	.10	.25
300 Dan Cloutier	.10	.25

1996 No Fear

Card	Low	High
COMPLETE SET (8)	5.00	12.00
2 Theoren Fleury HK	.40	1.00
3 Grant Fuhr HK	1.20	3.00

1972-73 Nordiques Postcards

Card	Low	High
COMPLETE SET (22)	20.00	40.00
1 Michel Archambeault	1.00	2.00
2 Serge Aubry	1.00	2.00
3 Yves Bergeron	1.00	2.00
4 Jacques Blain	1.00	2.00
5 Alain Caron	1.00	2.00
6 Ken Desjardine	1.00	2.00
7 Maurice Filion	1.00	2.00
8 Andre Gaudette	1.00	2.00
9 Jean-Guy Gendron	1.00	2.00
10 Rejean Giroux	1.00	2.00
11 Frank Golembrosky	1.00	2.00
12 Robert Guindon	1.00	2.00
13 Pierre Guite	1.00	2.00
14 Francois Lacombe	1.00	2.00
15 Paul Larose	1.00	2.00
16 Jacques Lemelin	1.00	2.00
17 Michel Parizeau	1.00	2.00
18 Jean Payette	1.00	2.00
19 Michel Rouleau	1.00	2.00
20 Pierre Roy	1.00	2.00
21 J.C. Tremblay	1.50	3.00
NNO Header Card	.50	1.00

1973-74 Nordiques Team Issue

Card	Low	High
COMPLETE SET (21)	25.00	50.00
1 Mike Archambault	1.25	2.50
2 Serge Aubry	1.25	2.50
3 Yves Bergeron	1.25	2.50
4 Jacques Blain	1.25	2.50
5 Richard Brodeur	4.00	8.00
6 Alain Caron	1.25	2.50
7 Ken Desjardine	1.25	2.50
8 Maurice Filion	1.25	2.50
9 Andre Gaudette	1.25	2.50
10 Jean-Guy Gendron	1.50	3.00
11 Rejean Giroux	1.25	2.50
12 Frank Golembrosky	1.25	2.50
13 Bob Guindon	1.25	2.50
14 Pierre Guite	1.25	2.50
15 Frank Lacombe	1.25	2.50
16 Paul Larose	1.25	2.50
17 Michel Parizeau	1.25	2.50
18 Jean Payette	1.25	2.50
19 Michel Rouleau	1.25	2.50
20 Pierre Roy	1.25	2.50
21 J.C. Tremblay	2.50	5.00

1976 Nordiques Marie Antoinette

Card	Low	High
COMPLETE SET (14)	30.00	60.00
1 Paul Baxter	2.00	4.00
2 Serge Bernier	2.00	4.00
3 Paulin Bordeleau	2.00	4.00
4 Andre Boudrias	2.50	5.00
5 Curt Brackenbury	2.00	4.00
6 Richard Brodeur	4.00	8.00
7 Real Cloutier	3.00	6.00
8 Charles Constantin	2.00	4.00
9 Bob Fitchner	2.00	4.00
10 Richard Grenier	2.00	4.00
11 Marc Tardif	3.00	6.00
12 Jean-Claude Tremblay	3.00	6.00
13 Steve Sutherland	2.00	4.00
14 Wally Weir	2.00	4.00

1976-77 Nordiques Postcards

Card	Low	High
COMPLETE SET (20)	15.00	30.00
1 Serge Aubry	.75	1.50
2 Paul Baxter	1.00	2.00
3 Jean Bernier	.75	1.50
4 Serge Bernier	1.50	3.00
5 Christian Bordeleau	.75	1.50
6 Paulin Bordeleau	1.00	2.00
7 Andre Boudrias	1.00	2.00
8 Curt Brackenbury	.75	1.50
9 Richard Brodeur	2.00	4.00
10 Real Cloutier	1.50	3.00
11 Charles Constantin	.75	1.50
12 Jim Dorey	1.00	2.00
13 Robert Fitchner	.75	1.50
14 Richard Grenier	.75	1.50
15 Francois Lacombe	.75	1.50
16 Pierre Roy	.75	1.50
17 Steve Sutherland	.75	1.50
18 Marc Tardif	1.50	3.00
19 J.C. Tremblay	1.50	3.00
20 Wally Weir	.75	1.50

1980-81 Nordiques Postcards

Card	Low	High
COMPLETE SET (29)	20.00	40.00
1 Michel Bergeron	.40	1.00
2 Serge Bernier	.75	2.00
3 Daniel Bouchard	.40	1.00
4 Ron Chipperfield	.40	1.00
5 Kim Clackson	.60	1.50
6 Real Cloutier	.75	2.00
7 Alain Cote	.60	1.50
8 Michel Dion	.60	1.50
9 Andre Dupont	.60	1.50
10 Robbie Ftorek	.75	2.00
11 Michel Goulet	2.50	5.00
12 Ron Grahame	.40	1.00
13 Jamie Hislop	.40	1.00
14 Dale Hoganson	.40	1.00
15 Dale Hunter	2.50	5.00
16 Pierre Lacroix	.40	1.00
17 Garry Lariviere	.40	1.00
18 Richard Leduc	.40	1.00
19 Lee Norwood	.60	1.50
20 John Paddock	.60	1.50
21 Dave Pichette	.40	1.00
22 Michel Plasse	.75	2.00
23 Jacques Richard	.60	1.50
24 Normand Rochefort	.40	1.00
25 Anton Stastny	.75	2.00
26 Peter Stastny	4.00	8.00
27 Marc Tardif	.75	2.00
28 Wally Weir	.40	1.00
29 John Wensink	.60	1.50

1981-82 Nordiques Postcards

Card	Low	High
COMPLETE SET (21)	10.00	25.00
1 Pierre Aubry	.40	1.00
2 Michel Bergeron CO	.60	1.50
3 Daniel Bouchard	.75	2.00
4 Real Cloutier	.75	2.00
5 Alain Cote	.40	1.00
6 Andre Dupont	.40	1.00
7 Miroslav Frycer UER (Last and first names are reversed)	.40	1.00
8 Michel Goulet	1.50	4.00
9 Dale Hunter	1.25	3.00
10 Pierre Lacroix	.40	1.00
11 Mario Marois	.40	1.00
12 Dave Pichette	.40	1.00
13 Michel Plasse	.60	1.50
14 Jacques Richard	.60	1.50
15 Normand Rochefort	.40	1.00
16 Anton Stastny	.60	1.50
17 Peter Stastny	2.00	5.00
18 Marian Stastny	1.00	2.50
19 Marc Tardif	.60	1.50
20 Charles Thiffault CO	.30	.75
21 Wally Weir	.40	1.00

1982-83 Nordiques Postcards

Card	Low	High
COMPLETE SET (25)	10.00	25.00
1 Pierre Aubry	.30	.75
2 Michel Bergeron CO	.60	1.50
3 Daniel Bouchard	.20	.50
4 Real Cloutier	.75	2.00
5 Alain Cote	.30	.75
6 Andre Dupont	.40	1.00
7 John Garrett	.60	1.50
8 Michel Goulet	1.25	3.00
9 Jean Hamel	.30	.75
10 Dale Hunter	1.00	2.50
11 Rick Lapointe	.40	1.00
12 Clint Malarchuk	.75	2.00
13 Mario Marois	.30	.75
14 Randy Moller	.30	.75
15 Wilf Paiement	.40	1.00
16 Dave Pichette	.30	.75
17 Jacques Richard	.60	1.50
18 Normand Rochefort	.30	.75
19 Louis Sleigher	.30	.75
20 Anton Stastny	.60	1.50
21 Marian Stastny	.60	1.50
22 Peter Stastny	1.25	3.00
23 Marc Tardif	.60	1.50
24 Charles Thiffault ACO	.20	.50
25 Wally Weir	.30	.75

1983-84 Nordiques Postcards

Card	Low	High
COMPLETE SET (32)	10.00	25.00
1 Pierre Aubry	.30	.75
2 Michel Bergeron CO	.40	1.00
3 Dan Bouchard	.50	1.25
4 Real Cloutier	.60	1.50
5 Alain Cote	.30	.75
6 Andre Dore	.30	.75
7 Andre Dupont	.40	1.00
8 John Garrett	.50	1.25
9 Paul Gillis	.30	.75
10 Mario Gosselin	.50	1.25
11 Michel Goulet	1.00	2.50
12 Jean Hamel	.30	.75
13 Dale Hunter	.60	1.50
14 Rick Lapointe	.30	.75
15 Clint Malarchuk	.60	1.50
16 Jimmy Mann	.40	1.00
17 Mario Marois	.40	1.00
18 Randy Moller	.40	1.00
19 Wilf Paiement	.40	1.00
20 Dave Pichette	.30	.75
21 Pat Price	.30	.75
22 Jacques Richard	.40	1.00
23 Normand Rochefort	.30	.75
24 Jean-Francois Sauve	.30	.75
25 Andre Savard	.30	.75
26 Louis Sleigher	.30	.75
27 Anton Stastny	.40	1.00
28 Marian Stastny	.40	1.00
29 Peter Stastny	1.00	2.50
30 Marc Tardif	.50	1.25
31 Wally Weir	.30	.75
32 Blake Wesley	.30	.75

1984-85 Nordiques Postcards

Card	Low	High
COMPLETE SET (27)	8.00	20.00
1 Brent Ashton	.30	.75
2 Bruce Bell	.30	.75
3 Michel Bergeron CO	.40	1.00
4 Daniel Bouchard	.40	1.00
5 Alain Cote	.30	.75
6 Gord Donnelly	.30	.75
7 Luc Dufour	.30	.75
8 Jean-Marc Gaulin	.30	.75
9 Paul Gillis	.30	.75
10 Mario Gosselin	.40	1.00
11 Michel Goulet	1.00	2.50
12 Dale Hunter	.60	1.50
13 Guy Lapointe ACO	.40	1.00
14 Jimmy Mann	.30	.75
15 Mario Marois	.30	.75
16 Brad Maxwell	.30	.75
17 Randy Moller	.30	.75
18 Simon Nolet ACO	.30	.75
19 Wilf Paiement	.40	1.00
20 Pat Price	.30	.75
21 Normand Rochefort	.40	1.00
22 Jean-Francois Sauve	.30	.75
23 Andre Savard	.30	.75
24 Richard Sevigny	.40	1.00
25 Anton Stastny	.40	1.00
26 Marian Stastny	.40	1.00
27 Peter Stastny	1.00	2.50

1985-86 Nordiques General Foods

Card	Low	High
COMPLETE SET (27)	12.00	30.00
1 John Anderson	.40	1.00
2 Brent Ashton	.40	1.00
3 Michel Bergeron CO	.40	1.00
4 Alain Cote	.40	1.00
5 Gilbert Delorme	.40	1.00
6 Mike Eagles	.40	1.00
7 Steven Finn	.40	1.00
8 Jean-Marc Gaulin	.40	1.00
9 Paul Gillis	.40	1.00
10 Mario Gosselin	.60	1.50
11 Michel Goulet	1.00	2.50
12 Ron Harris CO	.20	.50
13 Dale Hunter	1.00	2.50
14 Mark Kumpel	.40	1.00
15 Clint Malarchuk	.60	1.50
16 Jimmy Mann	.40	1.00
17 Mario Marois	.40	1.00
18 Randy Moller	.40	1.00
19 Simon Nolet CO	.20	.50
20 Pat Price	.40	1.00
21 Normand Rochefort	.40	1.00
22 Jean-Francois Sauve	.40	1.00
23 Richard Sevigny	.60	1.50
24 David Shaw	.40	1.00
25 Anton Stastny	.60	1.50
26 Peter Stastny	1.50	4.00
27 Trevor Stienburg	.40	1.00

1985-86 Nordiques McDonald's

Card	Low	High
COMPLETE SET (22)	10.00	25.00
1 Brent Ashton	.40	1.00
2 Jeff Brown	1.00	2.50
3 Alain Cote	.40	1.00
4 Gilbert Delorme	.40	1.00
5 Gord Donnelly	.40	1.00
6 Mike Eagles	.40	1.00
7 Paul Gillis	.40	1.00
8 Mario Gosselin	.60	1.50
9 Michel Goulet	1.00	2.50
10 Dale Hunter	1.00	2.50
11 Mark Kumpel	.40	1.00
12 Jason Lafreniere	.40	1.00
13 Clint Malarchuk	.60	1.50
14 Randy Moller	.40	1.00
15 Robert Picard	.40	1.00
16 Pat Price	.40	1.00
17 Normand Rochefort	.40	1.00
18 Richard Sevigny	.60	1.50
19 David Shaw	.40	1.00
20 Risto Siltanen	.40	1.00
21 Anton Stastny	.60	1.50
22 Peter Stastny	1.50	4.00

1985-86 Nordiques Placemats

Card	Low	High
COMPLETE SET (6)	8.00	20.00
1 Brent Ashton, Randy Moller	1.25	3.00
2 Mario Gosselin, Clint Malarchuk	1.50	4.00
3 Dale Hunter, Michel Goulet	2.00	5.00
4 Pat Price, Robert Picard	1.25	3.00
5 Peter Stastny, Anton Stastny	2.00	5.00
6 Player Portraits: Dale Hunter, Michel Goulet, Peter Stastny, Anton Stastny, Brent Ashton, Randy Moller, Pat Price, Robert Picard, Mario Gosselin, Clint Malarchuk, Alain Cote, John Anderson	2.00	5.00

1985-86 Nordiques Provigo

Card	Low	High
COMPLETE SET (25)	8.00	20.00
1 John Anderson 14	.40	1.00
2 Brent Ashton 9	.30	.75
3 Wayne Babych 18	.40	1.00
4 Michel Bergeron CO	.30	.75
5 Alain Cote 19	.30	.75
6 Gilbert Delorme 6	.30	.75
7 Mike Eagles 11	.30	.75
8 Steven Finn 25	.30	.75
9 Paul Gillis 23	.30	.75
10 Mario Gosselin 33	.40	1.00
11 Michel Goulet 16	.75	2.00
12 Dale Hunter 32	.75	2.00
13 Mark Kumpel 17	.30	.75
14 Clint Malarchuk 30	.40	1.00
15 Jimmy Mann 10	.40	1.00
16 Mario Marois 22	.40	1.00
17 Randy Moller 21	.30	.75
18 Wilf Paiement 27	.40	1.00
19 Pat Price 7	.30	.75
20 Normand Rochefort 5	.30	.75
21 J.F. Sauve 15	.30	.75
22 Richard Sevigny 1	.40	1.00
23 David Shaw 4	.30	.75
24 Anton Stastny 20	.40	1.00
25 Peter Stastny 26	1.25	3.00
NNO Poster	2.00	5.00

1985-86 Nordiques Team Issue

Card	Low	High
COMPLETE SET (27)	10.00	25.00
1 Brent Ashton	.40	1.00
2 Michel Bergeron CO	.40	1.00
3 Jeff Brown	1.00	2.50
4 Alain Cote	.40	1.00
5 Gilbert Delorme	.40	1.00
6 Gord Donnelly	.40	1.00
7 Mike Eagles	.40	1.00
8 Paul Gillis	.40	1.00
9 Mario Gosselin	.60	1.50
10 Michel Goulet	1.00	2.50
11 Dale Hunter	1.00	2.50
12 Mark Kumpel	.40	1.00
13 Jason Lafreniere	.40	1.00
14 Clint Malarchuk	.60	1.50
15 Randy Moller	.40	1.00
16 Simon Nolet CO	.20	.50
17 Robert Picard	.40	1.00
18 Pat Price	.40	1.00
19 Ken Quinney	.40	1.00
20 Normand Rochefort	.40	1.00
21 Richard Sevigny	.60	1.50
22 David Shaw	.40	1.00
23 Risto Siltanen	.40	1.00
24 Anton Stastny	.60	1.50
25 Peter Stastny	1.50	4.00
26 Charles Thiffault CO	.20	.50
27 Richard Zemlak	.40	1.00

1986-87 Nordiques General Foods

Card	Low	High
COMPLETE SET (28)	10.00	25.00
1 Brent Ashton	.30	.75
2 Michel Bergeron CO	.60	1.50
3 Jeff Brown	.60	1.50
4 Alain Cote	.30	.75
5 Gilbert Delorme	.30	.75
6 Gord Donnelly	.30	.75
7 Mike Eagles	.30	.75
8 Paul Gillis	.30	.75
9 Mario Gosselin	.60	1.50
10 Michel Goulet	.75	2.00
11 Mike Hough	.30	.75
12 Dale Hunter	.60	1.50
13 Mark Kumpel	.30	.75
14 Jason Lafreniere	.30	.75
15 Clint Malarchuk	.50	1.25
16 Randy Moller	.30	.75
17 Simon Nolet CO	.20	.50
18 Robert Picard	.30	.75
19 Pat Price	.30	.75
20 Ken Quinney	.30	.75
21 Normand Rochefort	.30	.75
22 Richard Sevigny	.50	1.25
23 David Shaw	.30	.75
24 Risto Siltanen	.30	.75
25 Anton Stastny	.40	1.00
26 Peter Stastny	1.25	3.00
27 Charles Thiffault CO	.20	.50
28 Richard Zemlak	.40	1.00

1986-87 Nordiques McDonald's

Card	Low	High
COMPLETE SET (25)	12.00	30.00
1 John Anderson	.60	1.50
2 Brent Ashton	.40	1.00
3 Jeff Brown	.75	2.00
4 Alain Cote	.40	1.00
5 Gilbert Delorme	.40	1.00
6 Mike Eagles	.40	1.00
7 Steven Finn	.40	1.00
8 Paul Gillis	.40	1.00
9 Mario Gosselin	.60	1.50
10 Michel Goulet	1.00	2.50
11 Mike Hough	.40	1.00
12 Dale Hunter	.75	2.00
13 Mark Kumpel	.40	1.00
14 Alain Lemieux	.40	1.00
15 Clint Malarchuk	.60	1.50
16 Jimmy Mann	.60	1.50
17 Randy Moller	.40	1.00
18 Wilf Paiement	.60	1.50
19 Pat Price	.40	1.00
20 Normand Rochefort	.40	1.00
21 Jean-Francois Sauve	.40	1.00
22 Richard Sevigny	.60	1.50
23 David Shaw	.40	1.00
24 Anton Stastny	.60	1.50
25 Peter Stastny	1.50	4.00

1986-87 Nordiques Team Issue

Card	Low	High
COMPLETE SET (29)	8.00	20.00
1 Jeff Brown	.75	2.00
2 Alain Cote	.30	.75
3 Bill Derlago	.30	.75
4 Gord Donnelly	.30	.75
5 Mike Eagles	.30	.75
6 Steven Finn	.30	.75
7 Paul Gillis	.30	.75
8 Mario Gosselin	.40	1.00
9 Michel Goulet	.75	2.00
10 Mike Hough	.30	.75
11 Dale Hunter	.60	1.50
12 Jason Lafreniere	.30	.75
13 Clint Malarchuk	.50	1.25
14 Basil McRae	.40	1.00
15 Randy Moller	.30	.75
16 John Ogrodnick	.40	1.00
17 Robert Picard	.30	.75
18 Pat Price	.30	.75
19 Normand Rochefort	.30	.75
20 Richard Sevigny	.50	1.25
21 David Shaw	.30	.75
22 Doug Shedden	.30	.75
23 Risto Siltanen	.30	.75
24 Anton Stastny	.40	1.00
25 Peter Stastny	1.25	3.00

1986-87 Nordiques Yum-Yum

Card	Low	High
COMPLETE SET (10)	10.00	25.00
1 Alain Cote	.75	2.00
2 Gilbert Delorme	.75	2.00
3 Paul Gillis	.75	2.00
4 Michel Goulet	2.00	5.00
5 Dale Hunter	1.50	4.00
6 Clint Malarchuk	1.25	3.00
7 Robert Picard	.75	2.00
8 Normand Rochefort	.75	2.00
9 Anton Stastny	1.00	2.50
10 Peter Stastny	2.50	6.00

1987-88 Nordiques General Foods

Card	Low	High
COMPLETE SET (32)	8.00	20.00
1 Tommy Albelin 28	.20	.50
2 Jeff Brown 22	.50	1.25
3 Mario Brunetta 30	.30	.75
4 Terry Carkner 4	.30	.75
5 Alain Cote 19	.20	.50
6 Gord Donnelly 34	.20	.50
7 Gaetan Duchesne 14	.30	.75
8 Mike Eagles 11	.20	.50
9 Steven Finn 29	.20	.50
10 Paul Gillis 23	.20	.50
11 Mario Gosselin 33	.40	1.00
12 Michel Goulet 16	.75	2.00
13 Stephane Guerard 46	.20	.50
14 Alan Haworth 15	.20	.50
15 Mike Hough 18	.20	.50
16 Jeff Jackson 25	.20	.50
17 Stu Kulak 17	.20	.50
18 Jason Lafreniere 10	.20	.50
19 Lane Lambert 7	.20	.50
20 David Latta 27	.20	.50
21 Max Middendorf 12	.20	.50
22 Randy Moller 21	.20	.50
23 Robert Picard 24	.20	.50
24 Daniel Poudrier 2	.20	.50
25 Ken Quinney 54	.20	.50
26 Normand Rochefort 5	.20	.50
27 Richard Sevigny 1	.30	.75
28 Anton Stastny 20	.30	.75
29 Peter Stastny 26	1.25	3.00
30 Ron Tugnutt 50	1.50	4.00
31 Alain Chainey, Andre Savard, Guy Lapointe	.08	.25
32 Badaboum (Mascot)	.08	.25

1987-88 Nordiques Team Issue

Card	Low	High
COMPLETE SET (32)	15.00	30.00
1 Richard Sevigny	.75	2.00
2 Daniel Poudrier	.40	1.00
3 Terry Carkner	.40	1.00
4 Normand Rochefort	.40	1.00
5 Lane Lambert	.40	1.00
6 Jason Lafreniere	.40	1.00
7 Mike Eagles	.40	1.00
8 Max Middendorf	.40	1.00
9 Gaetan Duchesne	.40	1.00
10 Alan Haworth	.40	1.00
11 Michel Goulet	.75	2.00
12 Stu Kulak	.40	1.00
13 Mike Hough	.40	1.00
14 Alain Cote	.40	1.00
15 Anton Stastny	.75	2.00
16 Randy Moller	.40	1.00
17 Jeff Brown	.40	1.00
18 Paul Gillis	.40	1.00
19 Robert Picard	.40	1.00
20 Jeff Jackson	.40	1.00
21 Peter Stastny	1.50	4.00
22 David Latta	.40	1.00
23 Tommy Albelin	.40	1.00
24 Steven Finn	.40	1.00
25 Mario Brunetta	.40	1.00
26 Mario Gosselin	.75	2.00
27 Gord Donnelly	.40	1.00
28 Stephane Guerard	.40	1.00
29 Ron Tugnutt	.75	2.00
30 Ken Quinney	.40	1.00
31 Badaboum on sled	.08	.25
32 Alain Chainey, Andre Savard, Guy Lapointe	.20	.50

1987-88 Nordiques Yum-Yum

Card	Low	High
COMPLETE SET (10)	8.00	20.00
1 Alain Cote 19	.60	1.50
2 Paul Gillis 23	.60	1.50
3A Mario Gosselin 33 ERR (Reverse has number 83)	1.25	3.00
3B Mario Gosselin 33 COR	1.25	3.00
4 Michel Goulet 16	1.50	4.00
5 Alan Haworth 15 UER (Reverse has 38 for sweater number)	.60	1.50
6 Jason Lefreniere 10 UER (Reverse has 30 for sweater number)	.60	1.50
7 Robert Picard 24	.60	1.50
8 Normand Rochefort 5	.60	1.50
9 Anton Stastny 20	.75	2.00
10 Peter Stastny 26	2.00	5.00

1988-89 Nordiques General Foods

Card	Low	High
COMPLETE SET (31)	14.00	35.00
1 Tommy Albelin	.20	.50
2 Badaboum MASCOT	.20	.50
3 Joel Baillargeon	.20	.50
4 Jeff Brown	.30	.75
5 Mario Brunetta	.30	.75
6 Coaches: Serge Aubry, Ron Lapointe, Guy Lapointe, Alain Chainey	.20	.50
7 Alain Cote	.20	.50
8 Gord Donnelly	.30	.75
9 Daniel Dore	.20	.50
10 Gaetan Duchesne	.30	.75
11 Steven Finn	.20	.50
12 Marc Fortier	.20	.50
13 Paul Gillis	.20	.50
14 Mario Gosselin	.30	.75
15 Michel Goulet	.60	1.50
16 Jari Gronstrand	.20	.50
17 Stephane Guerard	.20	.50
18 Mike Hough	.20	.50
19 Jeff Jackson	.20	.50
20 Iiro Jarvi	.20	.50
21 Darin Kimble	.40	1.00
22 Lane Lambert	.20	.50
23 David Latta	.20	.50
24 Curtis Leschyshyn	.40	1.00
25 Bob Mason	.30	.75
26 Mario Marois	.20	.50
27 Ken McRae	.20	.50
28 Randy Moller	.20	.50
29 Robert Picard	.20	.50
30 Walt Poddubny	.30	.75
31 Joe Sakic	60.00	150.00
32 Greg Smyth	.20	.50
33 Anton Stastny	.40	1.00
34 Peter Stastny	1.00	2.50
35 Trevor Steinberg	.20	.50
36 Ron Tugnutt	.75	2.00
37 Mark Vermette	.20	.50
38 Team Picture	.40	1.00

1988-89 Nordiques Team Issue

Card	Low	High
COMPLETE SET (33)	15.00	30.00
1 Tommy Albelin	.20	.50
2 Serge Aubry CO, Ron Lapointe CO, Guy Lapointe CO, Alain Chainey CO	.30	.75
3 Badaboum (Mascot)	.08	.25
4 Joel Baillargeon	.20	.50
5 Jeff Brown	.60	1.50
6 Mario Brunetta	.30	.75
7 Alain Cote	.20	.50
8 Gord Donnelly	.30	.75
9 Daniel Dore	.20	.50
10 Gaetan Duchesne	.30	.75
11 Steven Finn	.20	.50
12 Marc Fortier	.20	.50
13 Paul Gillis	.20	.50
14 Mario Gosselin	.30	.75
15 Michel Goulet	.75	2.00
16 Jari Gronstrand	.20	.50
17 Stephane Guerard	.20	.50
18 Jeff Jackson	.20	.50
19 Iiro Jarvi	.20	.50
20 Lane Lambert	.20	.50
21 David Latta	.20	.50
22 Curtis Leschyshyn	.40	1.00
23 Bob Mason	.30	.75
24 Randy Moller	.20	.50
25 Robert Picard	.20	.50
26 Walt Poddubny	.30	.75
27 Joe Sakic	60.00	150.00
28 Greg Smyth	.20	.50
29 Anton Stastny	.30	.75
30 Peter Stastny	1.00	2.50
31 Trevor Steinburg	.20	.50
32 Mark Vermette	.20	.50
33 Team Photo	.75	2.00
34 Bobby Dollas	.20	.50
35 Mike Hough	.20	.50
36 Darin Kimble	.20	.50
37 Ken McRae	.20	.50
38 Martin Madded	.20	.50
39 Ron Tugnutt	.40	1.00
40 Mario Marois	.20	.50
41 Jean Perron	.20	.50

1989-90 Nordiques Team Issue

Card	Low	High
COMPLETE SET (39)	10.00	25.00
1 Serge Aubry	.20	.50
2 Michel Bergeron CO	.20	.50
3 Jeff Brown	.30	.75
4 Alain Chainey	.20	.50
5 Joe Cirella	.20	.50
6 Lucien DeBlois	.20	.50
7 Daniel Dore	.20	.50
8 Steven Finn	.20	.50
9 Stephane Fiset	.60	1.50
10 Bryan Fogarty	.20	.50
11 Marc Fortier	.20	.50
12 Paul Gillis	.20	.50
13 Michel Goulet	.40	1.00
14 Jari Gronstrand	.20	.50
15 Stephane Guerard	.20	.50
16 Mike Hough	.20	.50
17 Tony Hrkac	.20	.50
18 Jeff Jackson	.20	.50
19 Iiro Jarvi	.20	.50
20 Kevin Kaminski	.20	.50
21 Darin Kimble	.20	.50
22 Guy Lafleur	1.00	2.50
23 Guy Lapointe	.20	.50
24 David Latta	.20	.50
25 Brian Lawton	.20	.50
26 Curtis Leschyshyn	.30	.75
27 Claude Loiselle	.20	.50
28 Mario Marois	.20	.50
29 Tony McKegney	.20	.50
30 Ken McRae	.20	.50
31 Greg Millen	.30	.75
32 Randy Moller	.20	.50
33 Sergei Mylnikov	.30	.75
34 Michel Petit	.20	.50
35 Robert Picard	.20	.50
36 Joe Sakic	6.00	15.00
37 Peter Stastny	.60	1.50
38 Ron Tugnutt	.60	1.50
39 Team Picture	.20	.50

1989-90 Nordiques General Foods

Card	Low	High
COMPLETE SET (30)	10.00	25.00
1 Michel Bergeron CO	.20	.50
2 Jeff Brown	.30	.75
3 Joe Cirella	.20	.50
4 Lucien DeBlois	.20	.50
5 Daniel Dore	.20	.50
6 Steven Finn	.20	.50
7 Stephane Fiset	.60	1.50
8 Marc Fortier	.20	.50
9 Paul Gillis	.20	.50
10 Michel Goulet	.40	1.00
11 Jari Gronstrand	.20	.50
12 Stephane Guerard	.20	.50
13 Mike Hough	.20	.50
14 Jeff Jackson	.20	.50
15 Iiro Jarvi	.20	.50
16 Kevin Kaminski	.20	.50
17 Darin Kimble	.20	.50
18 Guy Lafleur	1.00	2.50
19 David Latta	.20	.50
20 Curtis Leschyshyn	.30	.75
21 Claude Loiselle	.20	.50
22 Mario Marois	.20	.50
23 Ken McRae	.20	.50
24 Sergei Mylnikov	.30	.75
25 Michel Petit	.20	.50
26 Robert Picard	.20	.50
27 Joe Sakic	6.00	15.00
28 Peter Stastny	.60	1.50
29 Ron Tugnutt	.60	1.50
30 Team Photo	.60	1.50

1989-90 Nordiques Police

Card	Low	High
COMPLETE SET (27)	8.00	20.00
1 Jeff Brown	.30	.75
2 Joe Cirella	.20	.50
3 Lucien DeBlois	.20	.50
4 Daniel Dore	.20	.50
5 Steven Finn	.20	.50
6 Stephane Fiset	.60	1.50
7 Marc Fortier	.20	.50
8 Paul Gillis	.20	.50
9 Michel Goulet	.40	1.00
10 Stephane Guerard	.20	.50
11 Mike Hough	.20	.50
12 Jeff Jackson	.20	.50
13 Iiro Jarvi	.20	.50
14 Darin Kimble	.20	.50
15 Guy Lafleur	1.00	2.50
16 David Latta	.20	.50
17 Curtis Leschyshyn	.30	.75
18 Claude Loiselle	.20	.50
19 Mario Marois	.20	.50
20 Ken McRae	.20	.50
21 Sergei Mylnikov	.30	.75
22 Michel Petit	.20	.50
23 Robert Picard	.20	.50
24 Jean-Marc Routhier	.20	.50
25 Joe Sakic	6.00	15.00
26 Peter Stastny	.60	1.50
27 Ron Tugnutt	.60	1.50

1990-91 Nordiques Petro-Canada

Card	Low	High
COMPLETE SET (28)	15.00	30.00
1 Aaron Broten	.20	.50
2 Dave Chambers CO	.20	.50
3 Joe Cirella	.30	.75
4 Lucien DeBlois	.20	.50
5 Steven Finn	.20	.50
6 Bryan Fogarty	.20	.50
7 Marc Fortier	.20	.50

8 Robbie Ftorek ACO .20 .50
9 Paul Gillis .20 .50
10 Scott Gordon .30 .75
11 Mike Hough .20 .50
12 Tony Hrkac .30 .75
13 Darin Kimble .30 .75
14 Guy Lafleur .75 2.00
15 Curtis Leschyshyn .20 .50
16 Claude Loiselle .20 .50
17 Jacques Martin ACO .20 .50
18 Tony McKegney .20 .50
19 Owen Nolan 1.00 2.50
20 Michel Petit .20 .50
21 Joe Sakic 2.00 5.00
22 Everett Sanipass .20 .50
23 Mats Sundin 1.25 3.00
24 John Tanner .30 .75
25 Ron Tugnutt .40 1.00
26 Daniel Vincelette .20 .50
27 Craig Wolanin .20 .50
28 Team Photo .30 .75
29 Shawn Anderson .20 .50
30 Jacques Cloutier .30 .75
31 Alexei Gusarov .20 .50
32 Jeff Jackson .20 .50
33 Claude Lapointe .20 .50
34 Stephane Morin .20 .50
35 Scott Pearson .20 .50
36 Ken Quinney .20 .50
37 Serge Roberge .20 .50
38 Tony Twist .40 1.00
39 Randy Velischek .20 .50
40 Wayne Van Dorp .40 1.00
41 Mark Vermette .20 .50
42 Badaboum MASCOT .08 .25

1990-91 Nordiques Team Issue

COMPLETE SET (25) 6.00 15.00
1 Joe Cirella .20 .50
2 Lucien DeBlois .20 .50
3 Daniel Dore .20 .50
4 Steven Finn .20 .50
5 Stephane Fiset .60 1.50
6 Bryan Fogarty .20 .50
7 Marc Fortier .20 .50
8 Paul Gillis .20 .50
9 Michel Goulet .50 1.25
10 Stephane Guerard .20 .50
11 Mike Hough .20 .50
12 Tony Hrkac .25 .60
13 Jeff Jackson .20 .50
14 Iiro Jarvi .20 .50
15 Kevin Kaminski .20 .50
16 Darin Kimble .25 .60
17 David Latta .20 .50
18 Curtis Leschyshyn .20 .50
19 Claude Loiselle .20 .50
20 Mario Marois .20 .50
21 Tony McKegney .20 .50
22 Ken McRae .20 .50
23 Michel Petit .20 .50
24 Peter Stastny .60 1.50
25 Ron Tugnutt .40 1.00

1991 Nordiques Panini Team Stickers

COMPLETE SET (32) 2.00 5.00
1 Joe Cirella .01 .05
2 Daniel Dore .01 .05
3 Steven Finn .01 .05
4 Bryan Fogarty .01 .05
5 Marc Fortier .01 .05
6 Paul Gillis .01 .05
7 Scott Gordon .02 .10
8 Stephane Guerard .01 .05
9 Mike Hough .01 .05
10 Tony Hrkac .01 .05
11 Darin Kimble .01 .05
12 Guy Lafleur .20 .50
13 Curtis Leschyshyn .02 .10
14 Claude Loiselle .01 .05
15 Tony McKegney .01 .05
16 Ken McRae .01 .05
17 Owen Nolan .20 .50
18 Joe Sakic .50 1.25
19 Everett Sanipass .01 .05
20 Mats Sundin .30 .75
21 John Tanner .02 .10
22 Ron Tugnutt .05 .15
23 Randy Velischek .01 .05
24 Craig Wolanin .01 .05
A Team Logo
Left Side .01 .05
B Team Logo
Right Side .01 .05
C Guy Lafleur
Upper Left Corner .08 .25
D Guy Lafleur
Lower Left Corner .08 .25
E Benoit Hogue
Upper Right Corner .02 .10
F Benoit Hogue
Lower Right Corner .02 .10
G Guy Lafleur .20 .50
H Mats Sundin .30 .75

1991-92 Nordiques Petro-Canada

COMPLETE SET (35) 8.00 20.00
1 Badaboum (Mascot) .08 .25
2 Don Barber .20 .50
3 Jacques Cloutier .30 .75
4 Steven Finn .20 .50
5 Stephane Fiset .50 1.25
6 Bryan Fogarty .20 .50
7 Adam Foote .40 1.00
8 Marc Fortier .20 .50
9 Alexei Gusarov .20 .50
10 Mike Hough .20 .50
11 Don Jackson ACO .08 .25
12 Valeri Kamensky .60 1.50
13 John Kordic .30 .75
14 Claude Lapointe .20 .50
15 Curtis Leschyshyn .25 .60
16 Jacques Martin ACO .20 .50
17 Mike McNeill .20 .50
18 Ken McRae .20 .50
19 Kip Miller .20 .50
20 Stephane Morin .20 .50
21 Owen Nolan .60 1.50
22 Pierre Page GM/CO .20 .50
23 Greg Paslawski .20 .50
24 Herb Raglan .20 .50
25 Joe Sakic 1.50 4.00
26 Doug Smail .20 .50
27 Greg Smyth .20 .50
28 Mats Sundin .75 2.00
29 Mikhail Tatarinov .20 .50
30 Ron Tugnutt .30 .75
31 Tony Twist .50 1.25
32 Wayne Van Dorp .20 .50
33 Randy Velischek .20 .50
34 Mark Vermette .20 .50
35 Craig Wolanin .20 .50

1992-93 Nordiques Petro-Canada

COMPLETE SET (39) 8.00 20.00
1 Badaboum (Mascot) .08 .25
2 Daniel Bouchard CO .20 .50
3 Gino Cavallini .20 .50
4 Jacques Cloutier .30 .75
5 Steve Duchesne .20 .50
6 Steven Finn .20 .50
7 Stephane Fiset .40 1.00
8 Adam Foote .40 1.00
9 Alexei Gusarov .20 .50
10 Ron Hextall .40 1.00
11 Mike Hough .20 .50
12 Kerry Huffman .20 .50
13 Tim Hunter .20 .50
14 Don Jackson ACO .08 .25
15 Valeri Kamensky .20 .50
16 David Karpa .20 .50
17 Andrei Kovalenko .20 .50
18 Claude Lapointe .20 .50
19 Curtis Leschyshyn .20 .50
20 Bill Lindsay .20 .50
21 Jacques Martin ACO .08 .25
22 Owen Nolan .40 1.00
23 Pierre Page GM/CO .08 .25
24 Scott Pearson .20 .50
25 Herb Raglan .20 .50
26 Mike Ricci .30 .75
27 Martin Rucinsky .20 .50
28 Joe Sakic 1.50 4.00
29 Andre Savard ACO .08 .25
30 Chris Simon .40 1.00
31 Mats Sundin .75 2.00
32 John Tanner .25 .60
33 Mikhail Tatarinov .20 .50
34 Tony Twist .30 .75
35 Wayne Van Dorp .30 .75
36 Mark Vermette .20 .50
37 Craig Wolanin .20 .50
38 Scott Young .30 .75
39 Team Photo .08 .25

1994-95 Nordiques Burger King

COMPLETE SET (28) 8.00 20.00
1 Badaboum .20 .50
2 Bob Bassen .20 .50
3 Wendel Clark .40 1.00
4 Adam Deadmarsh .40 1.00
5 Steven Finn .20 .50
6 Stephane Fiset .40 1.00
7 Adam Foote .30 .75
8 Peter Forsberg 2.00 5.00
9 Alexei Gusarov .20 .50
10 Valeri Kamensky .20 .50
11 Jon Klemm .20 .50
12 Andrei Kovalenko .20 .50
13 Uwe Krupp .20 .50
14 Claude Lapointe .20 .50
15 Janne Laukkanen .20 .50
16 Sylvain Lefebvre .20 .50
17 Curtis Leschyshyn .20 .50
18 Paul MacDermid .20 .50
19 Owen Nolan .60 1.50
20 Mike Ricci .30 .75
21 Martin Rucinsky .30 .75
22 Joe Sakic 1.25 3.00
23 Reggie Savage .20 .50
24 Chris Simon .20 .50
25 Jocelyn Thibault .60 1.50
26 Craig Wolanin .20 .50
27 Scott Young .30 .75
28 Team Card .20 .50

2001 Nortel All-Star Game Sheets

COMPLETE SET (12) 24.00 60.00
1 Jaromir Jagr 3.00 7.50
2 Peter Forsberg 3.00 7.50
3 Pavel Bure 1.00 2.50
4 Nicklas Lidstrom 1.00 2.50
5 Dominik Hasek 2.00 5.00
6 Sandis Ozolinsh .40 1.00
7 Paul Kariya 4.00 10.00
8 Joe Sakic 3.00 7.50
9 Theo Fleury 1.00 2.50
10 Ray Bourque 3.00 7.50
11 Patrick Roy 6.00 15.00
12 Chris Pronger 1.00 2.50

1970-71 North Stars Postcards

COMPLETE SET (10) 17.50 35.00
1 Barry Gibbs 1.00 2.00
2 Bill Goldsworthy 2.50 5.00
3 Danny Grant 2.00 4.00
4 Ted Harris 1.00 2.00
5 Cesare Maniago 3.00 6.00
6 Jean Paul Parise 1.50 3.00
7 Tom Reid 1.00 2.00
8 Bobby Rousseau 1.00 2.00
9 Tom Williams 1.00 2.00
10 Lorne Worsley 5.00 10.00

1972-73 North Stars Glossy Photos

COMPLETE SET (20) 10.00 20.00
1 Fred Barrett .50 1.00
2 Charlie Burns .50 1.00
3 Jude Drouin .50 1.00
4 Barry Gibbs .50 1.00
5 Bill Goldsworthy 1.25 2.50
6 Danny Grant .75 1.50
7 Ted Harris .50 1.00
8 Fred(Buster) Harvey .50 1.00
9 Dennis Hextall .75 1.50
10 Cesare Maniago 1.00 2.00
11 Doug Mohns .75 1.50
12 Lou Nanne .75 1.50
13 Bob Nevin .50 1.00
14 Dennis O'Brien .50 1.00
15 Murray Oliver .50 1.00
16 J.P. Parise .50 1.00
17 Dean Prentice .75 1.50
18 Tom Reid .50 1.00
19 Gump Worsley 2.50 5.00
20 W.Blair/J.Gordon .50 1.00

1973-74 North Stars Action Posters

COMPLETE SET (10) 10.00 20.00
1 Henry Boucha 1.00 2.00
2 Jude Drouin 1.00 2.00
3 Barry Gibbs 1.00 2.00
4 Bill Goldsworthy 1.50 3.00
5 Dennis Hextall 1.00 2.00
6 Cesare Maniago 1.50 3.00
7 Lou Nanne 1.50 3.00
8 Dennis O'Brien 1.00 2.00
9 J.P. Parise 1.50 3.00
10 Tom Reid 1.00 2.00

1973-74 North Stars Postcards

COMPLETE SET (20) 10.00 20.00
1 Fred Barrett .38 .75
2 Gary Bergman .38 .75
3 Jude Drouin .38 .75
4 Tony Featherstone .38 .75
5 Barry Gibbs .38 .75
6 Bill Goldsworthy .63 1.25
7 Danny Grant .38 .75
8 Buster Harvey .38 .75
9 Dennis Hextall .50 1.00
10 Parker MacDonald .38 .75
11 Cesare Maniago .50 1.00
12 Lou Nanne .50 1.00
13 Rod Norrish .38 .75
14 Dennis O'Brien .38 .75
15 Murray Oliver .38 .75
16 Jean-Paul Parise .38 .75
17 Dean Prentice .50 1.00
18 Tom Reid .38 .75
19 Fred Stanfield .63 1.25
20 Lorne Worsley 1.50 3.00

1978-79 North Stars Cloverleaf Dairy

COMPLETE SET (11) 60.00 120.00
1 Gilles Meloche
Gary Sargent 7.50 15.00
2 Fred Barrett and
Per-Olov Brasar 6.00 12.00
3 Jean-Paul Parise and
Greg Smith 6.00 12.00
4 Al MacAdam and
Kent-Erik Andersson 6.00 12.00
5 Gary Edwards and
Bobby Smith 12.50 25.00
6 Mike Polich and
Brad Maxwell 6.00 12.00
7 Steve Payne and
Glen Sharpley 6.00 12.00
8 Tim Young and
Kris Manery 6.00 12.00
9 Ron Zanussi and
Tom Younghans 6.00 12.00
10 Final Entry Panel 6.00 12.00
NNO Sweepstakes Promotion 2.50 5.00

1979-80 North Stars Postcards

COMPLETE SET (21) 10.00 20.00
1 Kent-Erik Andersson .38 .75
2 Fred Barrett .38 .75
3 Gary Edwards .75 1.50
4 Mike Fidler .38 .75
5 Craig Hartsburg 1.00 2.00
6 Al MacAdam .50 1.00
7 Kris Manery .38 .75
8 Brad Maxwell .38 .75
9 Tom McCarthy .50 1.00
10 Gilles Meloche 1.00 2.00
11 Steve Payne .50 1.00
12 Mike Polich .38 .75
13 Gary Sargent .50 1.00
14 Glen Sharpley .38 .75
15 Paul Shmyr .38 .75
16 Bobby Smith 1.50 3.00
17 Greg Smith .38 .75
18 Glen Sonmor CO .38 .75
19 Tim Young .50 1.00
20 Tom Younghans .38 .75
21 Ron Zanussi .38 .75

1980-81 North Stars Postcards

COMPLETE SET (24) 8.00 20.00
1 Kent-Erik Andersson .30 .75
2 Fred Barrett .30 .75
3 Don Beaupre 1.00 2.50
4 Jack Carlson 1.00 2.50
5 Steve Christoff .40 1.00
6 Mike Eaves .30 .75
7 Gary Edwards .60 1.50
8 Curt Giles .40 1.00
9 Craig Hartsburg .75 2.00
10 Al MacAdam .40 1.00
11 Brad Maxwell .30 .75
12 Tom McCarthy .30 .75
13 Gilles Meloche .60 1.50
14 Murray Oliver ACO
J.P. Parise ACO
Glen Sonmor CO .30 .75
15 Steve Payne .30 .75
16 Mike Polich .30 .75
17 Gary Sargent .40 1.00
18 Glen Sharpley .30 .75
19 Paul Shmyr .30 .75
20 Bobby Smith 1.00 2.50
21 Greg Smith .30 .75
22 Tim Young .30 .75
23 Tom Younghans .30 .75
24 Ron Zanussi .30 .75

1981-82 North Stars Postcards

COMPLETE SET (24) 10.00 25.00
1 Kent-Erik Andersson .30 .75
2 Fred Barrett .30 .75
3 Don Beaupre 1.00 2.50
4 Neal Broten 1.50 4.00
5 Jack Carlson .75 2.00
6 Steve Christoff .30 .75
7 Dino Ciccarelli 2.50 6.00
8 Mike Eaves .30 .75
9 Curt Giles .40 1.00
10 Anders Hakansson .30 .75
11 Craig Hartsburg .60 1.50
12 Al Macadam .30 .75
13 Brad Maxwell .30 .75
14 Kevin Maxwell .30 .75
15 Tom McCarthy .30 .75
16 Gilles Meloche .60 1.50
17 Bill Nyrop .30 .75
18 Steve Payne .30 .75
19 Brad Palmer .30 .75
20 Gordie Roberts .30 .75
21 Gary Sargent .30 .75
22 Bobby Smith .75 2.00
23 Glen Sonmor CO
J.P. Parise ACO
Murray Oliver ACO .30 .75
24 Tim Young .30 .75

1982-83 North Stars Postcards

COMPLETE SET (24) 10.00 25.00
1 Fred Barrett .30 .75
2 Don Beaupre .60 1.50
3 Brian Bellows 1.25 3.00
4 Neal Broten 1.00 2.50
5 Dino Ciccarelli 1.50 4.00
6 Dino Ciccarelli
Neal Broten 1.00 2.50
7 Jordy Douglas .30 .75
8 Mike Eaves .30 .75
9 George Ferguson .30 .75
10 Ron Friest .30 .75
11 Curt Giles .40 1.00
12 Craig Hartsburg .60 1.50
13 Al MacAdam .30 .75
14 Dan Mandich .30 .75
15 Brad Maxwell .30 .75
16 Tom McCarthy .30 .75
17 Gilles Meloche .60 1.50
18 Steve Payne .30 .75
19 Willi Plett .40 1.00
20 Gordie Roberts .30 .75
21 Gary Sargent .30 .75
22 Bobby Smith .75 2.00
23 Ken Solheim .30 .75
24 Tim Young .30 .75
25 Team Photo .60 1.50

1983-84 North Stars Postcards

COMPLETE SET (27) 8.00 20.00
1 Keith Acton .30 .75
2 Brent Ashton .30 .75
3 Don Beaupre .60 1.50
4 Brian Bellows .75 2.00
5 Neal Broten .75 2.00
6 Dino Ciccarelli 1.00 2.50
7 Jordy Douglas .30 .75
8 George Ferguson .30 .75
9 Curt Giles .40 1.00
10 Craig Hartsburg .40 1.00
11 Brian Lawton .30 .75
12 Craig Levie .30 .75
13 Lars Lindgren .30 .75
14 Al MacAdam .30 .75
15 Bill Mahoney CO .20 .50
16 Dan Mandich .30 .75
17 Dennis Maruk .50 1.25
18 Brad Maxwell .30 .75
19 Tom McCarthy .30 .75
20 Gilles Meloche .40 1.00
21 Mark Napier .30 .75
22 Steve Payne .30 .75
23 Willi Plett .40 1.00
24 Dave Richter .30 .75
25 Gordie Roberts .30 .75
26 Randy Velischek .30 .75
27 Team Photo .60 1.50

1984-85 North Stars 7-Eleven

COMPLETE SET (12) 3.00 8.00
1 Neal Broten .50 1.25
2 Willi Plett .30 .75
3 Craig Hartsburg .50 1.25
4 Brian Bellows .75 2.00
5 Gordie Roberts .20 .50
6 Keith Acton .30 .75
7 Paul Holmgren .30 .75
8 Gilles Meloche .30 .75
9 Dennis Maruk .50 1.25
10 Tom McCarthy .20 .50
11 Steve Payne .30 .75
12 Dino Ciccarelli .75 2.00

1984-85 North Stars Postcards

COMPLETE SET (29) 6.00 15.00
1 Keith Acton .30 .75
2 Don Beaupre .60 1.50
3 Brian Bellows .75 2.00
4 Scott Bjugstad .20 .50
5 Neal Broten .60 1.50
6 Dino Ciccarelli .75 2.00
7 Curt Giles .30 .75
8 Curt Giles w/captain's C .20 .50
9 Craig Hartsburg .60 1.50
10 Tom Hirsch .20 .50
11 Paul Holmgren .40 1.00
12 Brian Lawton .20 .50
13 Dan Mandich .20 .50
14 Dennis Maruk .60 1.50
15 Brad Maxwell .20 .50
16 Tom McCarthy .20 .50
17 Tony McKegney .20 .50
18 Roland Melanson .30 .75
19 Gilles Meloche .30 .75
20 Mark Napier .30 .75
21 Steve Payne .30 .75
22 Willi Plett .30 .75
23 Dave Richter .20 .50
24 Gordie Roberts .20 .50
25 Bob Rouse .20 .50
26 Gord Sherven .20 .50
27 Harold Snepsts .40 1.00
28 Ken Solheim .20 .50
29 Randy Velischek .20 .50

1985-86 North Stars 7-Eleven

COMPLETE SET (12) 3.00 8.00
1 Dino Ciccarelli .75 2.00
2 Scott Bjugstad .20 .50
3 Curt Giles .30 .75
4 Don Beaupre .40 1.00
5 Tony McKegney .20 .50
6 Neal Broten .60 1.50
7 Willi Plett .30 .75
8 Craig Hartsburg .40 1.00
9 Brian Bellows .40 1.00
10 Keith Acton .30 .75
11 Dave Langevin .20 .50
12 Dirk Graham .60 1.50

1985-86 North Stars Postcards

COMPLETE SET (27) 6.00 15.00
1 Keith Acton .30 .75
2 Don Beaupre .40 1.00
3 Brian Bellows .40 1.00
4 Bo Berglund .20 .50
5 Scott Bjugstad .20 .50
6 Neal Broten .60 1.50
7 Jon Casey .60 1.50
8 Dino Ciccarelli .75 2.00
9 Tim Coulis .20 .50
10 Curt Giles .30 .75
11 Dirk Graham .60 1.50
12 Mats Hallin .20 .50
13 Craig Hartsburg .40 1.00
14 Tom Hirsch .20 .50
15 Dave Langevin .20 .50
16 Brian Lawton .20 .50
17 Craig Levie .20 .50
18 Dan Mandich .20 .50
19 Dennis Maruk .40 1.00
20 Tom McCarthy .20 .50
21 Tony McKegney .20 .50
22 Roland Melanson .30 .75
23 Steve Payne .20 .50
24 Willi Plett .30 .75
25 Gordie Roberts .20 .50
26 Bob Rouse .30 .75
27 Gord Sherven .20 .50

1986-87 North Stars 7-Eleven

COMPLETE SET (12) 3.00 8.00
1 Neal Broten .40 1.00
2 Brian MacLellan .20 .50
3 Willi Plett .30 .75
4 Scott Bjugstad .20 .50
5 Don Beaupre .40 1.00
6 Dino Ciccarelli .75 2.00
7 Craig Hartsburg .40 1.00
8 Dennis Maruk .60 1.50
9 Bob Rouse .20 .50
10 Gordie Roberts .20 .50
11 Bob Brooke .20 .50
12 Brian Bellows .60 1.50

1987-88 North Stars Postcards

COMPLETE SET (31) 8.00 20.00
1 Keith Acton .25 .60
2 Dave Archibald .20 .50
3 Warren Babe .20 .50
4 Don Beaupre .40 1.00
5 Brian Bellows .40 1.00
6 Mike Berger .20 .50
7 Scott Bjugstad .20 .50
8 Bob Brooke .20 .50
9 Herb Brooks CO .30 .75
10 Neal Broten .40 1.00
11 Dino Ciccarelli .60 1.50
12 Larry DePalma .20 .50
13 Dave Gagner 1.00 2.50
14 Curt Giles .30 .75
15 Dirk Graham .40 1.00
16 Craig Hartsburg .40 1.00
17 Tom Hirsch .20 .50
18 Brian Lawton .20 .50
19 Brian MacLellan .20 .50
20 Dennis Maruk .30 .75
21 Basil McRae .30 .75
22 Frantisek Musil .20 .50
23 Steve Payne .25 .60
24 Pat Price .20 .50
25 Chris Pryor .20 .50
26 Gordie Roberts .20 .50
27 Bob Rouse .25 .60
28 Terry Ruskowski .25 .60
29 Kari Takko .30 .75
30 Ron Wilson .20 .50
31 Richard Zemlak .20 .50

1988-89 North Stars ADA

COMPLETE SET (23) 5.00 12.00
1 Brian Bellows .40 1.00
2 Bob Brooke .20 .50
3 Neal Broten .40 1.00
4 Jon Casey .60 1.50
5 Shawn Chambers .20 .50
6 Dino Ciccarelli .75 2.00
7 Larry DePalma .20 .50
8 Curt Fraser .20 .50
9 Link Gaetz .30 .75
10 Dave Gagner .75 2.00
11 Stewart Gavin .20 .50
12 Curt Giles .20 .50
13 Marc Habscheid .20 .50
14 Mark Hardy .20 .50
15 Craig Hartsburg .40 1.00
16 Brian MacLellan .20 .50
17 Moe Mantha .20 .50
18 Basil McRae .30 .75
19 Frantisek Musil .20 .50
20 Dusan Pasek .20 .50
21 Bob Rouse .20 .50
22 Terry Ruskowski .20 .50
23 Kari Takko .30 .75

1989-90 North Stars ADA

COMPLETE SET (23) 8.00 20.00
NNO Brian Bellows .20 .50
NNO Perry Berezan .08 .25
NNO Bob Brooke .08 .25
NNO Neal Broten .40 1.00
NNO Jon Casey .30 .75
NNO Shawn Chambers .08 .25
NNO Shane Churla .40 1.00
NNO Clark Donatelli .08 .25
NNO Gaetan Duchesne .08 .25
NNO Curt Fraser .08 .25
NNO Dave Gagner .20 .50
NNO Mike Gartner .30 .75
NNO Stewart Gavin .08 .25
NNO Curt Giles .20 .50
NNO Ken Leiter .08 .25
NNO Basil McRae .30 .75
NNO Mike Modano 4.00 10.00
NNO Larry Murphy .30 .75
NNO Frantisek Musil .08 .25
NNO Pierre Page .08 .25
NNO Ville Siren .08 .25
NNO Kari Takko .30 .75
NNO Mark Tinordi .08 .25

1990 Oakville Horton

1 Tim Horton 1.50 4.00

1979-80 Oilers Postcards

COMPLETE SET (24) 50.00 100.00
1 Brett Callighen .50 1.00
2 Colin Campbell 1.00 2.00
3 Ron Chipperfield .50 1.00
4 Cam Connor .50 1.00
5 Peter Driscoll .50 1.00
6 Dave Dryden 1.00 2.00
7 Bill Flett .50 1.00
8 Lee Fogolin .50 1.00
9 Wayne Gretzky 30.00 60.00
10 Al Hamilton .50 1.00
11 Doug Hicks .50 1.00
12 Dave Hunter .50 1.00
13 Kevin Lowe 2.00 4.00
14 Dave Lumley .50 1.00
15 Blair MacDonald .50 1.00
16 Kari Makkonen .50 1.00
17 Mark Messier 12.50 25.00
18A Ed Mio ERR 1.00 2.00
18B Ed Mio COR 1.00 2.00
19 Pat Price .50 1.00
20 Dave Semenko 1.00 2.00
21 Bobby Schmautz .50 1.00
22 Risto Siltanen .75 1.50
23 Stan Weir .50 1.00

1980-81 Oilers Zellers

1 Wayne Gretzky 500.00 1000.00
2 Dave Lumley 5.00 10.00
3 Blair MacDonald 5.00 10.00

1981-82 Oilers Red Rooster

COMPLETE SET (30) 25.00 60.00
1 Grant Fuhr 1.50 4.00
2 Lee Fogolin .20 .50
4 Kevin Lowe .60 1.50
5 Doug Hicks .20 .50
6 Garry Lariviere .20 .50
7 Paul Coffey 3.00 8.00
8 Risto Siltanen .20 .50
9 Glenn Anderson 1.25 3.00
10 Matti Hagman .20 .50
11 Mark Messier 3.00 8.00
12 Dave Hunter .20 .50
15 Curt Brackenbury .20 .50
16 Pat Hughes .20 .50
17 Jari Kurri 2.00 5.00
18 Brett Callighen .20 .50
20 Dave Lumley .20 .50
21 Stan Weir .20 .50
26 Mike Forbes .20 .50
27 Dave Semenko .40 1.00
30 Ron Low .40 1.00
35 Andy Moog 1.50 4.00
77 Garry Unger .30 .75
99A Wayne Gretzky 30.00 80.00
99B Wayne Gretzky 5.00 12.00
99C Wayne Gretzky 5.00 12.00
99D Wayne Gretzky 5.00 12.00
99E Wayne Gretzky 5.00 12.00
NNO Team Autographs .40 1.00
xx Glen Sather CO .30 .75
xx Billy Harris CO .20 .50
xx Ted Green CO .20 .50

1981-82 Oilers West Edmonton Mall

COMPLETE SET (9) 50.00 125.00
1 Lee Fogolin 1.50 4.00
2 Grant Fuhr 6.00 15.00
3 Wayne Gretzky 40.00 100.00
4 Billy Harris ACO 1.50 4.00
5 Charlie Huddy 2.00 5.00
6 Gary Lariviere 1.50 4.00
7 Dave Lumley 1.50 4.00
8 Risto Siltanen 1.50 4.00
9 Stan Weir 1.50 4.00

1982-83 Oilers Red Rooster

COMPLETE SET (30) 15.00 40.00
2 Lee Fogolin .20 .50
4 Kevin Lowe .40 1.00
6 Garry Lariviere .20 .50
7 Paul Coffey 1.50 4.00
9 Glenn Anderson .50 1.25
10 Jaroslav Pouzar .20 .50
11 Mark Messier 2.00 5.00
12 Dave Hunter .20 .50
13 Ken Linseman .20 .50
14 Laurie Boschman .20 .50
16 Pat Hughes .20 .50
17 Jari Kurri 1.25 3.00
20 Dave Lumley .20 .50
21 Randy Gregg .20 .50
22 Charlie Huddy .30 .75
23 Marc Habscheid .20 .50
24 Tom Roulston .20 .50
27 Dave Semenko .30 .75
29 Don Jackson .20 .50
30 Ron Low .30 .75
31 Grant Fuhr 1.00 2.50
35 Andy Moog 1.00 2.50
77 Garry Unger .30 .75
99A Wayne Gretzky 4.00 10.00
99B Wayne Gretzky 4.00 10.00
99C Wayne Gretzky 4.00 10.00
99D Wayne Gretzky 4.00 10.00
NNO Glen Sather CO .30 .75
NNO John Muckler ACO .20 .50
NNO Ted Green ACO .20 .50

1983-84 Oilers Dollars

COMPLETE SET (7) 30.00 75.00
H14 Wayne Gretzky 4.00 10.00
H15 Andy Moog 2.00 5.00
H16 Dave Hunter 1.25 3.00
H17 Ken Linseman SP 12.00 30.00
H18 Lee Fogolin SP 12.00 30.00
H19 Dave Semenko 2.00 5.00
H20 Mark Messier 3.00 8.00

1983-84 Oilers McDonald's

COMPLETE SET (25) 10.00 25.00
1 Ken Linseman 13 .20 .50
2 Dave Semenko 27 .20 .50
3 Andy Moog 35 .75 2.00
4 Raimo Summanen 25 .15 .40
5 Jari Kurri 17 .75 2.00
6 Rick Chartraw 6 .15 .40
7 Don Jackson 29 .15 .40
8 Dave Hunter 12 .15 .40
9 Charlie Huddy 22 .20 .50
10 Emery Award .15 .40
11 Pat Conacher 15 .15 .40
12 Lee Fogolin 2 .15 .40
13 Kevin Lowe 4 .30 .75
14 Randy Gregg 21 .20 .50
15 Pat Hughes 16 .15 .40
16 Kevin McClelland 24 .15 .40
17 Willy Lindstrom 19 .15 .40
18 Mark Messier 11 1.50 4.00
19 Grant Fuhr 31 .75 2.00
20 Coaches
Ted Green
Glen Sather
John Muckler .30 .75
21 Wayne Gretzky 99 4.00 10.00
22 Dave Lumley 20 .15 .40
23 Jaroslav Pouzar 10 .15 .40
24 Glenn Anderson 9 .40 1.00
25 Paul Coffey 7 1.00 2.50
xx Playoff Album 1.25 3.00

1984-85 Oilers Red Rooster

COMPLETE SET (30) 12.00 30.00
2 Lee Fogolin .15 .40
4 Kevin Lowe .20 .50
7 Paul Coffey 1.00 2.50
8 Dave Lumley .15 .40
9 Glenn Anderson .40 1.00
10 Jaroslav Pouzar .15 .40
11 Mark Messier 1.50 4.00
12 Dave Hunter .15 .40
16 Pat Hughes .15 .40
17 Jari Kurri .75 2.00
18 Mark Napier .15 .40
19 Willy Lindstrom .15 .40
20 Billy Carroll .15 .40
21 Randy Gregg .15 .40
22 Charlie Huddy .15 .40
23 Marc Habscheid .15 .40
24 Kevin McClelland .15 .40
26 Mike Krushelnyski .15 .40
27 Dave Semenko .20 .50
28 Larry Melnyk .15 .40
29 Don Jackson .15 .40
31 Grant Fuhr .75 2.00
35 Andy Moog .75 2.00
99A Wayne Gretzky
You try to be aware 3.00 8.00
99B Wayne Gretzky 3.00 8.00
99C Wayne Gretzky 3.00 8.00
00D Wayne Gretzky 3.00 8.00
NNO Ted Green ACO .15 .40
NNO John Muckler ACO .15 .40
NNO Glen Sather CO P1
(Facsimile autograph .20 .50
NNO Glen Sather CO P2
(No facsimile autograph 2.00 5.00

1984-85 Oilers Team Issue

COMPLETE SET (23) 12.00 30.00
1 Glenn Anderson .50 1.25
2 Billy Carroll .20 .50
3 Paul Coffey 1.25 3.00
4 Lee Fogolin .20 .50
5 Grant Fuhr .75 2.00
6 Randy Gregg .20 .50
7 Wayne Gretzky 4.00 10.00
8 Charlie Huddy .20 .50
9 Pat Hughes .20 .50
10 Dave Hunter .20 .50
11 Don Jackson .20 .50
12 Mike Krushelnyski .30 .75
13 Jari Kurri .75 2.00
14 Willy Lindstrom .20 .50
15 Kevin Lowe .40 1.00
16 Dave Lumley .20 .50
17 Kevin McClelland .20 .50
18 Larry Melnyk .20 .50
19 Mark Messier 2.00 5.00
20 Andy Moog .75 2.00
21 Mark Napier .20 .50
22 Jaroslav Pouzar .20 .50
23 Dave Semenko .30 .75

1985-86 Oilers Red Rooster

COMPLETE SET (30) 15.00 40.00
2 Lee Fogolin .15 .40
4 Kevin Lowe .20 .50
5 Steve Smith .60 1.50
7 Paul Coffey 1.00 2.50
8 Gord Sherven .15 .40
9 Glenn Anderson .30 .75
10 Esa Tikkanen 1.25 3.00
11 Mark Messier 1.50 4.00
12 Dave Hunter .15 .40
14 Craig MacTavish .30 .75
17 Jari Kurri .75 2.00
18 Mark Napier .20 .50

19 Mike Rogers .15 .40
20 Dave Lumley .15 .40
21 Randy Gregg .15 .40
22 Charlie Huddy .15 .40
24 Kevin McClelland .15 .40
25 Raimo Summanen .15 .40
26 Mike Krushelnyski .15 .40
27 Dave Semenko .20 .50
29 Don Jackson .15 .40
31 Grant Fuhr .75 2.00
33 Marty McSorley 1.00 2.50
35 Andy Moog .75 2.00
99A Wayne Gretzky 3.00 8.00
99B Wayne Gretzky 3.00 8.00
99C Wayne Gretzky 3.00 8.00
NNO Bob McCammon ACO .15 .40
NNO John Muckler ACO .15 .40
NNO Glen Sather CO .20 .50

1986-87 Oilers Red Rooster

COMPLETE SET (30) 10.00 25.00
2 Lee Fogolin .15 .40
4 Kevin Lowe .20 .50
5 Steve Smith .30 .75
6 Jeff Beukeboom .20 .50
7 Paul Coffey .75 2.00
8 Stu Kulak .15 .40
9 Glenn Anderson .30 .75
10 Esa Tikkanen .75 2.00
11 Mark Messier 1.25 3.00
12 Dave Hunter .15 .40
14 Craig MacTavish .40 1.00
15 Steve Graves .15 .40
17 Jari Kurri .60 1.50
18 Danny Gare .20 .50
21 Randy Gregg .15 .40
22 Charlie Huddy .20 .50
24 Kevin McClelland .15 .40
25 Raimo Summanen .15 .40
26 Mike Krushelnyski .15 .40
28 Craig Muni .15 .40
31 Grant Fuhr .60 1.50
33 Marty McSorley .75 2.00
35A Andy Moog .60 1.50
35B Andy Moog .60 1.50
65 Mark Napier .20 .50
99A Wayne Gretzky 3.00 8.00
99B Wayne Gretzky 3.00 8.00
NNO Ted Green ACO 3.00 8.00
NNO John Muckler ACO .08 .25
NNO Glen Sather CO .20 .50

1986-87 Oilers Team Issue

COMPLETE SET (24) 15.00 40.00
2 Lee Fogolin .20 .50
4 Kevin Lowe .30 .75
5 Steve Smith .30 .75
6 Jeff Beukeboom .30 .75
7 Paul Coffey 1.25 3.00
8 Stu Kulak .20 .50
9 Glenn Anderson .40 1.00
10 Esa Tikkanen 1.25 3.00
11 Mark Messier 2.00 5.00
12 Dave Hunter .20 .50
14 Craig MacTavish .40 1.00
17 Jari Kurri 1.00 2.50
20 Jaroslav Pouzar .20 .50
21 Randy Gregg .20 .50
22 Charlie Huddy .20 .50
24 Kevin McClelland .20 .50
25 Raimo Summanen .20 .50
26 Mike Krushelnyski .20 .50
28 Craig Muni .20 .50
31 Grant Fuhr 1.00 2.50
33 Marty McSorley 1.25 3.00
35 Andy Moog 1.00 2.50
65 Mark Napier .30 .75
99 Wayne Gretzky 6.00 15.00

1987-88 Oilers Team Issue

COMPLETE SET (22) 12.00 30.00
4 Kevin Lowe .30 .75
5 Steve Smith .40 1.00
6 Jeff Beukeboom .40 1.00
9 Glenn Anderson .40 1.00
10 Esa Tikkanen .60 1.50
11 Mark Messier 1.50 4.00
12 Dave Hannan .20 .50
14 Craig MacTavish .30 .75
17 Jari Kurri .75 2.00
18 Craig Simpson .40 1.00
19 Normand Lacombe .20 .50
22 Charlie Huddy .20 .50
23 Keith Acton .30 .75
24 Kevin McClelland .20 .50
26 Mike Krushelnyski .20 .50
28 Craig Muni .20 .50
29 Daryl Reaugh .30 .75
30 Warren Skorodenski .30 .75
31 Grant Fuhr .75 2.00
33 Marty McSorley .60 1.50
36 Selmar Odelein .20 .50
99 Wayne Gretzky 6.00 15.00

1988-89 Oilers Tenth Anniversary

COMPLETE SET (164) 50.00 125.00
1 Garry Unger .40 1.00
2 Chris Joseph .20 .50
3 Raimo Summanen .20 .50
4 Mike Zanier .30 .75
5 Kevin Lowe .60 1.50
6 Dave Semenko .40 1.00
7 Peter Driscoll .20 .50
8 Ken Solheim .20 .50
9 Glenn Anderson 1.00 2.50
10 Curt Brackenbury .20 .50
11 Ron Shudra .20 .50
12 Gord Sherven .20 .50
13 Randy Gregg .30 .75
14 Larry Melnyk .20 .50
15 Tom Roulston .20 .50
16 Billy Carroll .20 .50
17 Jeff Beukeboom .30 .75
18 Jaroslav Pouzar .20 .50
19 Jeff Brubaker .20 .50
20 Danny Gare .30 .75
21 Craig MacTavish .30 .75
22 Reijo Routsalainen .30 .75
23 Willy Lindstrom .20 .50
24 Pat Hughes .20 .50
25 Jim Wiemer .20 .50
26 Selmar Odelein .20 .50
27 Kent Nilsson .40 1.00
28 Mark Napier .30 .75
29 Esa Tikkanen 1.00 2.50
30 John Miner .20 .50
31 Tom McMurchy .20 .50
32 Steve Graves .20 .50
33 Craig Muni .20 .50
34 Moe Mantha .20 .50
35 Dave Lumley .30 .75
36 Ron Low .30 .75
37 Marty McSorley 1.00 2.50
38 Steve Dykstra .20 .50
39 Risto Jalo .20 .50
40 Dave Hunter .20 .50
41 Jari Kurri 2.00 5.00
42 Lee Fogolin .20 .50
43 Moe Lemay .20 .50
44 Stu Kulak .20 .50
45 Charlie Huddy .30 .75
46 Wayne Gretzky 15.00 40.00
47 Ken Linseman .30 .75
48 Risto Siltanen .30 .75
49 Glen Sather .40 1.00
50 Brett Callighen .20 .50
51 Eddie Mio .30 .75
52 Ken Hammond .20 .50
53 Jimmy Carson .30 .75
54 Paul Coffey 2.00 5.00
55 Wayne Gretzky 1050th 10.00 25.00
56 Reed Larson .20 .50
57 Ted Green .30 .75
58 Matti Hagman .20 .50
59 Marc Habscheid .20 .50
60 Bill Ranford 2.00 5.00
61 Mark Lamb .20 .50
62 Daryl Reaugh .40 1.00
63 Al Hamilton .20 .50
64 Paul Coffey's 47th 1.25 3.00
65 Grant Fuhr 2.00 5.00
66 Stan Weir .20 .50
67 Ken Berry .20 .50
68 John Muckler CO .30 .75
69 Doug Smith .20 .50
70 Lance Nethery .20 .50
71 Bill Flett .20 .50
72 Mike Forbes .20 .50
73 Martin Gelinas .40 1.00
74 Ron Chipperfield .20 .50
75 Reg Kerr .20 .50
76 Don Jackson .20 .50
77 Keith Acton .30 .75
78 Gary Edwards .30 .75
79 Mike Krushelnyski .30 .75
80 Trainers
Lyle Kulchisky
Peter Millar
Barrie Stafford .20 .50
81 Normand Lacombe .20 .50
82 Pat Price .20 .50
83 Dave Hannan .20 .50
84 Garry Lariviere .20 .50
85 Greg Adams .20 .50
86 Poul Popiel .20 .50
87 Tom Gorence .20 .50
88 Geoff Courtnall .75 2.00
89 Mark Messier 3.00 8.00
90 Dave Dryden .30 .75
91 Andy Moog 2.00 5.00
92 Jim Ennis .20 .50
93 Craig Simpson .40 1.00
94 Laurie Boschman .20 .50
95 Doug Hicks .20 .50
96 Rick Chartraw .20 .50
97 1984 Stanley Cup Champs .40 1.00
98 Ron Carter .20 .50
99 Blair MacDonald .20 .50
100 Dean Clark .20 .50
101 Glen Cochrane .20 .50
102 Lindsay Middlebrook .20 .50
103 Ron Areshenkoff .20 .50
104 Billy Harris CO .20 .50
105 Conn Smythe Trophy .30 .75
106 John Blum .20 .50
107 Wayne Bianchin .20 .50
108 Tom Bladon .20 .50
109 Kevin McClelland .20 .50
110 Roy Sommer .20 .50
111 Mike Toal .20 .50
112 Don Ashby .20 .50
113 Don Nachbaur .20 .50
114 1985 Stanley Cup Champs .40 1.00
115 Jim Corsi .20 .50
116 John Hughes .20 .50
117 Coach of the Year Glen Sather .40 1.00
118 Bob Dupuis .20 .50
119 Jim Harrison .20 .50
120 Don Murdoch .20 .50
121 Steve Smith .40 1.00
122 Pete Lopresti .20 .50
123 Colin Campbell .40 1.00
124 Bryan Watson .20 .50
125 John Bednarski .20 .50
126 1987 Stanley Cup Champs (Marty McSorley) .40 1.00
127 Scott Metcalfe .20 .50
128 Mike Rogers .20 .50
129 Dan Newman .20 .50
130 Fuhr's 75th .75 2.00
131 Warren Skorodenski .30 .75
132 Todd Strueby .20 .50
133 Kelly Buchberger .40 1.00
134 Cam Connor .20 .50
135 Dean Hopkins .20 .50
136 Mike Moller .20 .50
137 1988 Stanley Cup Champs (Wayne Gretzky) 3.00 8.00
138 Bryon Baltimore .20 .50
139 Pat Conacher .20 .50
140 Ray Cote .20 .50
141 Walt Poddubny .20 .50
142 Jim Playfair .20 .50
143 Nick Fotiu .20 .50
144 Kari Makkonen .20 .50
145 Dave Brown .30 .75
146 Terry Martin .20 .50
147 Francois Leroux .20 .50
148 Kari Jalonen .20 .50
149 Tomas Jonsson .30 .75
150 Dave Donnelly .20 .50
151 Mike Ware .20 .50
152 Don Cutts .20 .50
153 Miroslav Frycer .20 .50
154 Bruce MacGregor GM .20 .50
155 Kim Issel .20 .50
156 Marco Baron .30 .75
157 Doug Halward .20 .50
158 Barry Fraser DIR .20 .50
159 Alan May .20 .50
160 Bobby Schmautz .20 .50
161 Craig Redmond .20 .50
162 Oilers Host '89 All-Star Game .30 .75
163 Alex Tidey .20 .50
164 Wayne Van Dorp .20 .50

1988-89 Oilers Team Issue

COMPLETE SET (27) 8.00 20.00
1 Glenn Anderson .40 1.00
2 Jeff Beukeboom .40 1.00
3 Dave Brown .30 .75
4 Kelly Buchberger .40 1.00
5 Jimmy Carson .30 .75
6 Miroslav Frycer .20 .50
7 Grant Fuhr .75 2.00
8 Randy Gregg .30 .75
9 Doug Halward .20 .50
10 Charlie Huddy .30 .75
11 Dave Hunter .20 .50
12 Tomas Jonsson .30 .75
13 Chris Joseph .20 .50
14 Jari Kurri .60 1.50
15 Normand Lacombe .20 .50
16 Mark Lamb .20 .50
17 John LeBlanc .20 .50
18 Kevin Lowe .30 .75
19 Craig MacTavish .30 .75
20 Kevin McClelland .20 .50
21 Mark Messier 1.50 4.00
22 Craig Muni .20 .50
23 Bill Ranford 1.25 3.00
24 Craig Redmond .20 .50
25 Craig Simpson .30 .75
26 Steve Smith .40 1.00
27 Esa Tikkanen .60 1.50

1989-90 Oilers Team Issue

COMPLETE SET (24) 10.00 25.00
1 Glenn Anderson .30 .75
2 Jeff Beukeboom .25 .60
3 Dave Brown .25 .60
4 Kelly Buchberger .25 .60
5 Peter Eriksson .15 .40
6 Grant Fuhr .60 1.50
7 Martin Gelinas .75 2.00
8 Adam Graves 1.50 4.00
9 Randy Gregg .25 .60
10 Charlie Huddy .25 .60
11 Petr Klima .30 .75
12 Jari Kurri .60 1.50
13 Normand Lacombe .15 .40
14 Mark Lamb .15 .40
15 Kevin Lowe .25 .60
16 Craig Mactavish .25 .60
17 Mark Messier 1.25 3.00
18 Craig Muni .15 .40
19 Joe Murphy .75 2.00
20 Bill Ranford .75 2.00
21 Craig Simpson .25 .60
22 Geoff Smith .25 .60
23 Steve Smith .30 .75
24 Esa Tikkanen .30 .75

1990-91 Oilers IGA

COMPLETE SET (30) 14.00 35.00
1 Glenn Anderson .60 1.50
2 Jeff Beukeboom .30 .75
3 Dave Brown .40 1.00
4 Kelly Buchberger .40 1.00
5 Martin Gelinas .40 1.00
6 Adam Graves 1.50 4.00
7 Ted Green CO SP 1.25 3.00
8 Charlie Huddy .30 .75
9 Chris Joseph .30 .75
10 Petr Klima .20 .50
11 Mark Lamb .20 .50
12 Ken Linseman .30 .75
13 Ron Low CO SP 1.25 3.00
14 Kevin Lowe .50 1.25
15 Craig MacTavish .30 .75
16 Mark Messier 2.50 6.00
17 Joey Moss .20 .50
18 John Muckler CO SP 1.25 3.00
19 Craig Muni .20 .50
20 Joe Murphy .30 .75
21 Bill Ranford 1.25 3.00
22 Anatoli Semenov .20 .50
23 Craig Simpson .20 .50
24 Geoff Smith .20 .50
25 Steve Smith .40 1.00
26 Kari Takko .30 .75
27 Esa Tikkanen .60 1.50
28 Training Staff SP .60 1.50
29 Edmonton Oilers Year-by-Year Record .20 .50
30 Checklist Card SP 1.25 3.00

1991 Oilers Panini Team Stickers

COMPLETE SET (32) 1.50 4.00
1 Glenn Anderson .07 .20
2 Jeff Beukeboom .01 .05
3 Dave Brown .01 .05
4 Kelly Buchberger .02 .10
5 Martin Gelinas .02 .10
6 Adam Graves .15 .40
7 Charlie Huddy .01 .05
8 Chris Joseph .01 .05
9 Petr Klima .02 .10
10 Mark Lamb .01 .05
11 Ken Linesman .01 .05
12 Kevin Lowe .05 .15
13 Craig MacTavish .02 .10
14 Mark Messier .20 .50
15 Craig Muni .01 .05
16 Joe Murphy .02 .10
17 Bill Ranford .15 .40
18 Eldon Reddick .02 .10
19 Anatoli Semenov .01 .05
20 Craig Simpson .02 .10
21 Geoff Smith .01 .05
22 Steve Smith .02 .10
23 Esa Tikkanen .07 .20
24 Oilers In Action .05 .15
A Team Logo Left Side .01 .05
B Team Logo Right Side .01 .05
C Oilers in Action Upper Left Corner .01 .05
D Oilers in Action Lower Left Corner .01 .05
E Bill Ranford Upper Right Corner .08 .25
F Bill Ranford Lower Right Corner .08 .25
G Mark Messier .20 .50
H Action in the Crease .05 .15

1991-92 Oilers IGA

COMPLETE SET (30) 8.00 20.00
1 Josef Beranek .20 .50
2 Kelly Buchberger .30 .75
3 Vincent Damphousse .60 1.50
4 Louie DeBrusk .20 .50
5 Martin Gelinas .30 .75
6 Peter Ing .25 .60
7 Petr Klima .20 .50
8 Mark Lamb .20 .50
9 Kevin Lowe .30 .75
10 Norm Maciver .20 .50
11 Craig MacTavish .30 .75
12 Troy Mallette .20 .50
13 Dave Manson .40 1.00
14 Scott Mellanby .40 1.00
15 Craig Muni .20 .50
16 Joe Murphy .30 .75
17 Bill Ranford .75 2.00
18 Steven Rice .20 .50
19 Luke Richardson .20 .50
20 Anatoli Semenov .20 .50
21 David Shaw .20 .50
22 Craig Simpson .30 .75
23 Geoff Smith .20 .50
24 Scott Thornton .20 .50
25 Esa Tikkanen .40 1.00
26 Training Staff SP .60 1.50
27 Ted Green CO SP 1.00 2.50
28 Ron Low CO SP 1.00 2.50
29 Kevin Primeau CO SP 1.00 2.50
30 Checklist Card SP 1.00 2.50

1991-92 Oilers Team Issue

COMPLETE SET (28) 6.00 15.00
1 Josef Beranek .20 .50
2 Jeff Beukeboom .20 .50
3 Kelly Buchberger .30 .75
4 Vincent Damphousse .60 1.50
5 Louie DeBrusk .20 .50
6 Martin Gelinas .20 .50
7 Peter Ing .25 .60
8 Chris Joseph .20 .50
9 Petr Klima .20 .50
10 Mark Lamb .20 .50
11 Kevin Lowe .30 .75
12 Norm Maciver .20 .50
13 Craig MacTavish .20 .50
14 Troy Mallette .20 .50
15 Dave Manson .40 1.00
16 Scott Mellanby .40 1.00
17 Craig Muni .20 .50
18 Joe Murphy .30 .75
19 Bill Ranford .75 2.00
20 Pokey Reddick .30 .75
21 Steve Rice .20 .50
22 Luke Richardson .20 .50
23 Martin Rucinsky .60 1.50
24 Anatoli Semenov .20 .50
25 Craig Simpson .20 .50
26 Geoff Smith .20 .50
27 Scott Thornton .20 .50
28 Esa Tikkanen .40 1.00

1992-93 Oilers IGA

COMPLETE SET (30) 6.00 15.00
1 Checklist .08 .25
2 Joseph Beranek .20 .50
3 Kelly Buchberger .30 .75
4 Shayne Corson .40 1.00
5 Louie DeBrusk .20 .50
6 Martin Gelinas .30 .75
7 Brent Gilchrist .20 .50
8 Brian Glynn .20 .50
9 Greg Hawgood .20 .50
10 Petr Klima .20 .50
11 Chris Joseph .20 .50
12 Craig MacTavish .20 .50
13 Dan Currie .20 .50
14 Dave Manson .20 .50
15 Scott Mellanby .20 .50
16 Craig Muni .20 .50
17 Bernie Nicholls .30 .75
18 Bill Ranford .40 1.00
19 Luke Richardson .20 .50
20 Craig Simpson .25 .60
21 Geoff Smith .20 .50
22 Vladimir Vujtek .20 .50
23 Esa Tikkanen .40 1.00
24 Ron Tugnutt .60 1.50
25 Shaun Van Allen .20 .50
26 Glen Sather GM .20 .50
27 Ted Green CO .20 .50
28 Ron Low CO .20 .50
29 Kevin Primeau CO .08 .25
30 Oilers Yearly Record .08 .25

1992-93 Oilers Team Issue

COMPLETE SET (22) 4.80 12.00
1 Kelly Buchberger .25 .60
2 Zdeno Ciger .20 .50
3 Shayne Corson .30 .75
4 Louie DeBrusk .20 .50
5 Todd Elik .20 .50
6 Brian Glynn .20 .50
7 Mike Hudson .20 .50
8 Chris Joseph .20 .50
9 Igor Kravchuk .20 .50
10 Francois Leroux .20 .50
11 Craig MacTavish .20 .50
12 Dave Manson .20 .50
13 Shjon Podein .20 .50
14 Bill Ranford .40 1.00
15 Steve Rice .20 .50
16 Luke Richardson .20 .50
17 Craig Simpson .25 .60
18 Geoff Smith .20 .50
19 Kevin Todd .20 .50
20 Vladimir Vujtek .20 .50
21 Doug Weight .75 2.00
22 Brad Werenka .20 .50

1996-97 Oilers Postcards

COMPLETE SET (27) 6.00 15.00
2 Boris Mironov .20 .50
4 Kevin Lowe .20 .50
5 Greg de Vries .20 .50
6 Jeff Norton .15 .40
7 Jason Arnott .40 1.00
8 Sean Brown .15 .40
10 Steve Kelly .20 .50
14 Mats Lindgren .20 .50
16 Kelly Buchberger .20 .50
17 Rem Murray .20 .50
18 Miroslav Satan .60 1.50
19 Boyd Devereaux .40 1.00
21 Mariusz Czerkawski .20 .50
22 Luke Richardson .20 .50
23 Dan McGillis .20 .50
24 Bryan Marchment .20 .50
25 Mike Grier .60 1.50
26 Todd Marchant .20 .50
29 Louie DeBrusk .15 .40
30 Bob Essensa .30 .75
31 Curtis Joseph .75 2.00
34 Donald Dufresne .15 .40
37 Dean McAmmond .15 .40
39 Doug Weight .40 1.00
51 Andrei Kovalenko .20 .50
85 Petr Klima .15 .40
94 Ryan Smyth .75 2.00

2000-01 Oilers Postcards

COMPLETE SET (25) 5.00 12.00
1 Eric Brewer .20 .50
2 Tom Poti .20 .50
3 Frank Musil .20 .50
4 Josh Green .20 .50
5 Domenic Pittis .20 .50
6 Rem Murray .20 .50
7 Ethan Moreau .20 .50
8 Jason Smith .20 .50
9 Anson Carter .75 2.00
10 Sean Brown .20 .50
11 Mike Grier .30 .75
12 Todd Marchant .20 .50
13 Georges Laraque .75 2.00
14 Dominic Roussel .20 .50
15 Scott Ferguson .20 .50
16 Dan LaCouture .20 .50
17 Sergei Zholtok .20 .50
18 Tommy Salo .40 1.00
19 Shawn Horcoff .20 .50
20 Doug Weight .40 1.00
21 Janne Niinimaa .20 .50
22 Paul Comrie .20 .50
23 Igor Ulanov .20 .50
24 Mike Comrie .20 .50
25 Ryan Smyth 1.00 2.50

2001-02 Oilers Postcards

COMPLETE SET (23) 5.00 12.00
1 Shawn Horcoff .20 .50
2 Josh Green .20 .50
3 Domenic Pittis .20 .50
4 Marty Reasoner .30 .75
5 Rem Murray .20 .50
6 Ethan Moreau .20 .50
7 Jochen Hecht .20 .50
8 Jason Smith .20 .50
9 Anson Carter .60 1.50
10 Sean Brown .20 .50
11 Steve Staios .20 .50
12 Mike Grier .30 .75
13 Todd Marchant .20 .50
14 Georges Laraque .60 1.50
15 Jussi Markkanen .20 .50
16 Scott Ferguson .20 .50
17 Tommy Salo .40 1.00
18 Janne Niinimaa .20 .50
19 Mike Comrie .20 .50
20 Ryan Smyth 1.00 2.50
21 Eric Brewer .20 .50
22 Tom Poti .20 .50
23 Daniel Cleary .20 .50

2002-03 Oilers Postcards

COMPLETE SET (22) 8.00 20.00
1 Eric Brewer .20 .50
2 Daniel Cleary .20 .50
3 Ales Pisa .20 .50
4 Shawn Horcoff .20 .50
5 Mike York .20 .50
6 Ethan Moreau .20 .50
7 Marty Reasoner .20 .50
8 Jason Smith .20 .50
9 Anson Carter .40 1.00
10 Steve Staios .20 .50
11 Todd Marchant .20 .50
12 Georges Laraque .60 1.50
14 Jussi Markkanen .40 1.00
15 Scott Ferguson .20 .50
16 Jiri Dopita .20 .50
17 Tommy Salo .40 1.00
18 Brian Swanson .20 .50
19 Janne Niinimaa .20 .50
20 Ales Hemsky 1.25 3.00
21 Mike Comrie .75 2.00
22 Ryan Smyth .75 2.00
113 Jason Chimera .20 .50

2003-04 Oilers Postcards

COMPLETE SET (22) 8.00 20.00
1 Marc-Andre Bergeron .30 .75
2 Eric Brewer .30 .75
3 Jason Chimera .20 .50
4 Ty Conklin .40 1.00
5 Cory Cross .30 .75
6 Radek Dvorak .30 .75
7 Scott Ferguson .20 .50
8 Ales Hemsky .60 1.50
9 Shawn Horcoff .20 .50
10 Brad Isbister .30 .75
11 Georges Laraque .40 1.00
12 Ethan Moreau .40 1.00
13 Fernando Pisani .40 1.00
14 Marty Reasoner .30 .75
15 Tommy Salo .40 1.00
16 Alexei Semenov .30 .75
17 Jason Smith .20 .50
18 Ryan Smyth .75 2.00
19 Steve Staios .30 .75
20 Jarret Stoll .40 1.00
21 Raffi Torres .40 1.00
22 Mike York .40 1.00

1932-33 O'Keefe Maple Leafs

COMPLETE SET (20) 6000.00 12000.00
1 Lorne Chabot 250.00 600.00
2 Red Horner 250.00 600.00
3 Alex Levinsky 200.00 500.00
4 Hap Day 200.00 500.00
5 Andy Blair 200.00 500.00
6 Ace Bailey 500.00 1200.00
7 King Clancy 500.00 1200.00
8 Harold Cotton 250.00 600.00
9 Charlie Conacher 400.00 1000.00
10 Joe Primeau 400.00 1000.00
11 Harvey Jackson 400.00 1000.00
12 Frank Finnigan 200.00 500.00
14 Bob Gracie 200.00 500.00
16 Harold Darragh 200.00 500.00
17 Benny Grant 200.00 500.00
18 Fred Robertson 200.00 500.00
19 Conn Smythe 400.00 1000.00
20 Dick Irvin 300.00 800.00
NNO Ken Doraty 250.00 600.00
NNO Bill Thoms 250.00 600.00

1933-34 O-Pee-Chee V304A Red

COMPLETE SET (48) 9000.00 15000.00
WRAPPER (1-CENT) 175.00 350.00
1 Danny Cox RC 125.00 300.00
2 Joe Lamb RC 80.00 200.00
3 Eddie Shore RC 2500.00 6000.00
4 Ken Doraty RC 80.00 200.00
5 Fred Hitchman 80.00 200.00
6 Nels Stewart RC 400.00 1000.00
7 Walter Galbraith RC 80.00 200.00
8 Dit Clapper RC 400.00 1000.00
9 Harry Oliver RC 200.00 500.00
10 Red Horner RC 125.00 300.00
11 Alex Levinsky RC 80.00 200.00
12 Joe Primeau RC 300.00 800.00
13 Ace Bailey RC 300.00 600.00
14 George Patterson RC 40.00 100.00
15 George Hainsworth RC 250.00 500.00
16 Ott Heller RC 60.00 150.00
17 Art Somers RC 60.00 150.00
18 Lorne Chabot RC 150.00 400.00
19 Johnny Gagnon RC 80.00 200.00
20 Pit Lepine RC 125.00 300.00
21 Wildor Larochelle RC 125.00 300.00
22 Georges Mantha RC 250.00 600.00
23 Howie Morenz 1200.00 3000.00
24 Syd Howe RC 300.00 800.00
25 Frank Finnigan 60.00 150.00
26 Bill Touhey RC 60.00 150.00
27 Cooney Weiland RC 150.00 400.00
28 Leo Bourgeault RC 100.00 250.00
29 Normie Himes RC 60.00 150.00
30 Johnny Sheppard RC 60.00 150.00
31 King Clancy 500.00 1200.00
32 Hap Day 125.00 300.00
33 Harvey Jackson RC 200.00 500.00
34 Charlie Conacher RC 300.00 800.00
35 Harold Cotton RC 80.00 200.00
36 Butch Keeling RC 60.00 150.00
37 Murray Murdoch RC 80.00 200.00
38 Bill Cook UER RC 150.00 400.00
39 Ivan Johnson RC 150.00 400.00
40 Happy Emms RC 60.00 150.00
41 Bert McInenly RC 60.00 150.00
42 John Sorrell RC 100.00 250.00
43 Bill Phillips RC 150.00 400.00
44 Charley McVeigh RC 125.00 300.00
45 Roy Worters RC 250.00 600.00
46 Albert Leduc RC 80.00 200.00
47 Nick Wasnie RC 60.00 150.00
48 Armand Mondou RC 80.00 200.00

1933-34 O-Pee-Chee V304B

COMPLETE SET (24) 2500.00 6000.00
WRAPPER (1-CENT) 175.00 350.00
49 Babe Siebert RC 300.00 800.00
50 Aurel Joliat 300.00 800.00
51 Larry Aurie RC 100.00 250.00
52 Ebbie Goodfellow RC 150.00 400.00
53 John Roach 80.00 200.00
54 Bill Beveridge RC 300.00 800.00
55 Earl Robinson RC 300.00 800.00
56 Jimmy Ward RC 60.00 150.00
57 Archie Wilcox RC 60.00 150.00
58 Lorne Duguid RC 60.00 150.00
59 Dave Kerr RC 80.00 200.00
60 Baldy Northcott RC 200.00 500.00
61 Marvin Wentworth RC 150.00 400.00
62 Dave Trottier RC 60.00 150.00
63 Wally Kilrea RC 100.00 250.00
64 Glen Brydson RC 60.00 150.00
65 Vernon Ayres RC 60.00 150.00
66 Bob Gracie RC 60.00 150.00
67 Vic Ripley RC 100.00 250.00
68 Tiny Thompson RC 600.00 1500.00
69 Alex Smith RC 60.00 150.00
70 Andy Blair RC 60.00 150.00
71 Cecil Dillon RC 80.00 200.00
72 Bun Cook RC 250.00 600.00

1935-36 O-Pee-Chee V304C

COMPLETE SET (24) 1200.00 3000.00
WRAPPER (1-CENT) 175.00 350.00
73 Wilfred Cude RC 80.00 200.00
74 Jack McGill RC 60.00 150.00
75 Russ Blinco RC 80.00 200.00
76 Hooley Smith 125.00 300.00
77 Herb Cain RC 50.00 125.00
78 Gus Marker RC 150.00 400.00
79 Lynn Patrick RC 80.00 200.00
80 Johnny Gottselig 50.00 125.00
81 Marty Barry 60.00 150.00
82 Sylvio Mantha 150.00 400.00
83 Flash Hollett RC 80.00 200.00
84 Nick Metz RC 60.00 150.00
85 Bill Thoms 100.00 250.00
86 Hec Kilrea 60.00 150.00
87 Pep Kelly RC 60.00 150.00
88 Art Jackson RC 60.00 150.00
89 Allan Shields RC 60.00 150.00
90 Buzz Boll 80.00 200.00
91 Jean Pusie RC 150.00 400.00
92 Roger Jenkins RC 100.00 250.00
93 Arthur Coulter RC 125.00 300.00
94 Art Chapman 50.00 125.00
95 Paul Haynes 60.00 150.00
96 Leroy Goldsworthy RC 80.00 200.00

1936-37 O-Pee-Chee V304D

COMPLETE SET (36) 8000.00 20000.00
WRAPPER (1-CENT) 175.00 350.00
97 Turk Broda RC 4000.00 10000.00
98 Sweeney Schriner RC 500.00 1200.00
99 Jack Shill RC 80.00 200.00
100 Bob Davidson RC 150.00 400.00
101 Syl Apps RC 1200.00 3000.00
102 Lionel Conacher 250.00 600.00
103 Jimmy Fowler RC 125.00 300.00
104 Al Murray RC 100.00 250.00
105 Neil Colville RC 600.00 1500.00
106 Paul Runge RC 80.00 200.00
107 Mike Karakas RC 300.00 800.00
108 John Gallagher RC 100.00 250.00
109 Alex Shibicky RC 125.00 300.00
110 Herb Cain 125.00 300.00
111 Bill McKenzie 200.00 500.00
112 Harold Jackson 125.00 300.00
113 Art Wiebe RC 80.00 200.00
114 Joffre Desilets RC 100.00 250.00
115 Earl Robinson 125.00 300.00
116 Cy Wentworth 100.00 250.00
117 Ebbie Goodfellow 150.00 400.00
118 Eddie Shore 800.00 2000.00
119 Buzz Boll 100.00 250.00
120 Wilfred Cude 125.00 300.00
121 Howie Morenz 800.00 2000.00
122 Red Horner 250.00 600.00
123 Charlie Conacher 400.00 1000.00
124 Busher Jackson 300.00 800.00
125 King Clancy 400.00 1000.00
126 Dave Trottier 125.00 300.00
127 Russ Blinco 80.00 200.00
128 Lynn Patrick 200.00 500.00
129 Aurel Joliat 300.00 800.00
130 Baldy Northcott 100.00 250.00
131 Larry Aurie 125.00 300.00
132 Hooley Smith 150.00 400.00

1937-38 O-Pee-Chee V304E

COMPLETE SET (48) 3000.00 8000.00
WRAPPER (1-CENT) 150.00 300.00
133 Turk Broda 400.00 600.00
134 Red Horner 125.00 200.00
135 Jimmy Fowler 60.00 100.00
136 Bob Davidson 150.00 400.00
137 Reg. Hamilton RC 60.00 100.00
138 Charlie Conacher 400.00 1000.00
139 Busher Jackson 175.00 300.00
140 Buzz Boll 60.00 100.00
141 Syl Apps 250.00 400.00
142 Gordie Drillon RC 175.00 300.00
143 Bill Thoms 150.00 400.00
144 Nick Metz 60.00 100.00
145 Pep Kelly 60.00 100.00
146 Murray Armstrong RC 150.00 400.00
147 Murph Chamberlain RC 60.00 100.00
148 Des Smith RC 100.00 250.00
149 Wilfred Cude 90.00 150.00
150 Babe Siebert 150.00 400.00
151 Bill MacKenzie 80.00 200.00
152 Aurel Joliat 300.00 500.00
153 Georges Mantha 60.00 100.00
154 Johnny Gagnon 60.00 100.00
155 Paul Haynes 125.00 300.00
156 Joffre Desilets 125.00 300.00
157 George Allen Brown RC 150.00 400.00
158 Paul Drouin RC 60.00 100.00
159 Pit Lepine 250.00 600.00
160 Toe Blake RC 500.00 800.00
161 Bill Beveridge 90.00 150.00
162 Allan Shields 125.00 300.00
163 Cy Wentworth 125.00 200.00
164 Stew Evans RC 125.00 300.00
165 Earl Robinson 150.00 400.00
166 Baldy Northcott 90.00 150.00
167 Paul Runge 60.00 100.00
168 Dave Trottier 125.00 300.00
169 Russ Blinco 60.00 100.00
170 Jimmy Ward 60.00 100.00
171 Bob Gracie 60.00 100.00
172 Herb Cain 150.00 400.00
173 Gus Marker 60.00 100.00
174 Walter Buswell RC 150.00 400.00
175 Carl Voss RC 125.00 200.00
176 Rod Lorraine RC 60.00 100.00
177 Armand Mondou 60.00 100.00
178 Cliff Goupille RC 60.00 100.00
179 Jerry Shannon RC 60.00 100.00
180 Tom Cook RC 125.00 200.00

1939-40 O-Pee-Chee V301-1

COMPLETE SET (100) 4000.00 7000.00
1 Reg Hamilton 35.00 60.00
2 Turk Broda 175.00 300.00
3 Bingo Kampman RC 25.00 50.00

4 Gordie Drillon 50.00 80.00
5 Bob Davidson 25.00 50.00
6 Syl Apps 125.00 200.00
7 Pete Langelle RC 25.00 50.00
8 Don Metz RC 25.00 50.00
9 Pep Kelly 25.00 50.00
10 Red Horner 60.00 100.00
11 Wally Stanowsky RC 80.00 200.00
12 Murph Chamberlain 25.00 50.00
13 Bucko MacDonald 25.00 50.00
14 Sweeney Schriner 60.00 100.00
15 Billy Taylor RC 25.00 50.00
16 Gus Marker 25.00 50.00
17 Hooley Smith 60.00 100.00
18 Art Chapman 25.00 50.00
19 Murray Armstrong 25.00 50.00
20 Busher Jackson 90.00 150.00
21 Buzz Boll 30.00 80.00
22 Cliff(Red) Goupille 25.00 50.00
23 Rod Lorraine 25.00 50.00
24 Paul Drouin 25.00 50.00
25 Johnny Gagnon 25.00 50.00
26 Georges Mantha 25.00 50.00
27 Armand Mondou 25.00 50.00
28 Claude Bourque RC 25.00 50.00
29 Ray Getliffe RC 25.00 50.00
30 Cy Wentworth 50.00 80.00
31 Paul Haynes 25.00 50.00
32 Walter Buswell 25.00 50.00
33 Ott Heller 25.00 50.00
34 Arthur Coulter 35.00 60.00
35 Clint Smith RC 60.00 100.00
36 Lynn Patrick 60.00 100.00
37 Dave Kerr 50.00 80.00
38 Murray Patrick RC 25.00 50.00
39 Neil Colville 60.00 100.00
40 Jack Portland RC 25.00 50.00
41 Flash Hollett 25.00 50.00
42 Herb Cain 50.00 80.00
43 Mud Bruneteau 25.00 50.00
44 Joffre DeSilets 25.00 50.00
45 Mush March 25.00 50.00
46 Cully Dahlstrom RC 25.00 50.00
47 Mike Karakas 35.00 60.00
48 Bill Thoms 25.00 50.00
49 Art Wiebe 25.00 50.00
50 Johnny Gottselig 25.00 50.00
51 Nick Metz 25.00 50.00
52 Jack Church RC 25.00 50.00
53 Bob Heron RC 25.00 50.00
54 Hank Goldup RC 25.00 50.00
55 Jimmy Fowler 25.00 50.00
56 Charlie Sands 25.00 50.00
57 Marty Barry 35.00 60.00
58 Doug Young 25.00 50.00
59 Charlie Conacher 150.00 250.00
60 John Sorrell 25.00 50.00
61 Tommy Anderson RC 25.00 50.00
62 Lorne Carr 25.00 50.00
63 Earl Robertson RC 35.00 60.00
64 Wilfy Field RC 25.00 50.00
65 Jimmy Orlando RC 25.00 50.00
66 Ebbie Goodfellow 35.00 60.00
67 Jack Keating RC 25.00 50.00
68 Sid Abel RC 250.00 400.00
69 Gus Giesebrecht RC 25.00 50.00
70 Don Deacon RC 25.00 50.00
71 Hec Kilrea 25.00 50.00
72 Syd Howe 60.00 100.00
73 Eddie Wares RC 25.00 50.00
74 Carl Liscombe RC 25.00 50.00
75 Tiny Thompson 90.00 150.00
76 Earl Seibert RC 25.00 50.00
77 Des Smith RC 25.00 50.00
78 Les Cunningham RC 25.00 50.00
79 George Allen RC 25.00 50.00
80 Bill Carse RC 25.00 50.00
81 Bill McKenzie 25.00 50.00
82 Ab DeMarco RC 25.00 50.00
83 Phil Watson 30.00 50.00
84 Alf Pike RC 25.00 50.00
85 Babe Pratt RC 50.00 80.00
86 Bryan Hextall Sr. RC 50.00 80.00
87 Kilby MacDonald RC 25.00 50.00
88 Alex Shibicky 25.00 50.00
89 Dutch Hiller RC 25.00 50.00
90 Mac Colville 25.00 50.00
91 Roy Conacher RC 60.00 100.00
92 Cooney Weiland 60.00 100.00
93 Art Jackson 25.00 50.00
94 Woody Dumart RC 75.00 150.00
95 Dit Clapper 125.00 200.00
96 Mel Hill RC 25.00 50.00
97 Frank Brimsek RC 150.00 300.00
98 Bill Cowley RC 75.00 150.00
99 Bobby Bauer RC 50.00 100.00
100 Eddie Shore 400.00 600.00

1940-41 O-Pee-Chee V301-2

COMPLETE SET (50) 1500.00 4000.00
101 Toe Blake 60.00 150.00
102 Charlie Sands 20.00 50.00
103 Wally Stanowski 15.00 40.00
104 Jack Adams 60.00 150.00
105 Johnny Mowers RC 15.00 40.00
106 Johnny Quilty RC 60.00 150.00
107 Billy Taylor 30.00 80.00
108 Turk Broda 60.00 150.00
109 Bingo Kampman 40.00 100.00
110 Gordie Drillon 50.00 125.00
111 Don Metz 50.00 125.00
112 Paul Haynes 30.00 80.00
113 Gus Marker 15.00 40.00
114 Alex Singbush RC 20.00 50.00
115 Alex Motter RC 30.00 80.00
116 Ken Reardon RC 80.00 200.00
117 Pete Langelle 40.00 100.00
118 Syl Apps 80.00 200.00
119 Reg. Hamilton 15.00 40.00
120 Cliff(Red) Goupille 40.00 100.00
121 Joe Benoit RC 60.00 150.00
122 Sweeney Schriner 40.00 100.00
123 Joe Carveth RC 40.00 100.00
124 Jack Stewart RC 80.00 200.00
125 Elmer Lach RC 300.00 800.00
126 Jack Schewchuk RC 30.00 80.00
127 Norman Larson RC 30.00 80.00
128 Don Grosso RC 50.00 125.00
129 Lester Douglas RC 25.00 60.00
130 Turk Broda 100.00 250.00
131 Max Bentley RC 150.00 400.00
132 Milt Schmidt RC 150.00 400.00
133 Nick Metz 40.00 100.00
134 Jack Crawford RC 30.00 80.00
135 Bill Benson RC 20.00 50.00
136 Lynn Patrick 80.00 200.00
137 Cully Dahlstrom 30.00 80.00
138 Mud Bruneteau 60.00 150.00
139 Dave Kerr 40.00 100.00
140 Bob(Red) Heron 40.00 100.00
141 Nick Metz 40.00 100.00
142 Ott Heller 50.00 125.00
143 Phil Hergesheimer RC 15.00 40.00
144 Tony Demers RC 30.00 80.00
145 Archie Wilder RC 30.00 80.00
146 Syl Apps 80.00 200.00
147 Ray Getliffe 25.00 60.00
148 Lex Chisholm RC 15.00 40.00
149 Eddie Wiseman RC 30.00 80.00
150 Paul Goodman RC 25.00 60.00

1968-69 O-Pee-Chee

COMMON CARD 3.00 8.00
SEMISTARS 4.00 10.00
UNLISTED STARS 5.00 12.00
1 Doug Harvey 100.00 250.00
2 Bobby Orr 300.00 800.00
3 Don Awrey UER 6.00 15.00
4 Ted Green 6.00 15.00
5 Johnny Bucyk 30.00 80.00
6 Derek Sanderson 50.00 125.00
7 Phil Esposito 15.00 40.00
8 Ken Hodge 6.00 15.00
9 John McKenzie 6.00 15.00
10 Fred Stanfield 15.00 40.00
11 Tom Williams 6.00 15.00
12 Denis DeJordy 6.00 15.00
13 Doug Jarrett 6.00 15.00
14 Gilles Marotte 25.00 60.00
15 Pat Stapleton 6.00 15.00
16 Bobby Hull 30.00 80.00
17 Chico Maki 6.00 15.00
18 Pit Martin 6.00 15.00
19 Doug Mohns 40.00 100.00
20 John Ferguson 15.00 40.00
21 Jim Pappin 6.00 15.00
22 Ken Wharram 6.00 15.00
23 Roger Crozier 10.00 25.00
24 Bob Baun 8.00 20.00
25 Gary Bergman 12.00 30.00
26 Kent Douglas 12.00 30.00
27 Ron Harris RC 6.00 15.00
28 Alex Delvecchio 15.00 40.00
29 Gordie Howe 125.00 300.00
30 Bruce MacGregor 6.00 15.00
31 Frank Mahovlich 25.00 60.00
32 Dean Prentice 6.00 15.00
33 Pete Stemkowski 10.00 25.00
34 Terry Sawchuk 30.00 80.00
35 Larry Cahan 6.00 15.00
36 Real Lemieux RC 6.00 15.00
37 Bill White RC 6.00 15.00
38 Gord Labossiere RC 6.00 15.00
39 Ted Irvine RC 6.00 15.00
40 Eddie Joyal 10.00 25.00
41 Dale Rolfe RC 6.00 15.00
42 Lowell MacDonald RC 6.00 15.00
43 Skip Krake UER 6.00 15.00
44 Terry Gray 10.00 25.00
45 Cesare Maniago 6.00 15.00
46 Mike McMahon 6.00 15.00
47 Wayne Hillman 6.00 15.00
48 Larry Hillman 6.00 15.00
49 Bob Woytowich 12.00 30.00
50 Wayne Connelly 6.00 15.00
51 Claude Larose 12.00 30.00
52 Danny Grant UER
John Vanderburg pictured 10.00 25.00
53 Andre Boudrias RC 20.00 50.00
54 Roy Cullen RC 6.00 15.00
55 Parker MacDonald 6.00 15.00
56 Gump Worsley 15.00 40.00
57 Terry Harper 6.00 15.00
58 Jacques Laperriere 10.00 25.00
59 J.C. Tremblay 6.00 15.00
60 Ralph Backstrom 8.00 20.00
61 Checklist 1 125.00 300.00
62 Yvan Cournoyer 60.00 150.00
63 Jacques Lemaire 10.00 25.00
64 Mickey Redmond RC 80.00 200.00
65 Bobby Rousseau 10.00 25.00
66 Gilles Tremblay 6.00 15.00
67 Ed Giacomin 8.00 20.00
68 Arnie Brown 12.00 30.00
69 Harry Howell 10.00 25.00
70 Al Hamilton RC 6.00 15.00
71 Rod Seiling 15.00 40.00
72 Rod Gilbert 6.00 15.00
73 Phil Goyette 10.00 25.00
74 Larry Jeffrey 6.00 15.00
75 Don Marshall 6.00 15.00
76 Bob Nevin 6.00 15.00
77 Jean Ratelle 12.00 30.00
78 Charlie Hodge 6.00 15.00
79 Bert Marshall 10.00 25.00
80 Billy Harris 6.00 15.00
81 Carol Vadnais 6.00 15.00
82 Howie Young 6.00 15.00
83 John Brenneman RC 6.00 15.00
84 Gerry Ehman 6.00 15.00
85 Ted Hampson 6.00 15.00
86 Bill Hicke 6.00 15.00
87 Gary Jarrett 6.00 15.00
88 Doug Roberts 12.00 30.00
89 Bernie Parent RC 300.00 800.00
90 Joe Watson 6.00 15.00
91 Ed Van Impe 10.00 25.00
92 Larry Zeidel 6.00 15.00
93 John Miszuk RC 6.00 15.00
94 Gary Dornhoefer 6.00 15.00
95 Leon Rochefort RC 6.00 15.00
96 Brit Selby 6.00 15.00
97 Forbes Kennedy 8.00 20.00
98 Ed Hoekstra RC 6.00 15.00
99 Garry Peters 8.00 20.00
100 Les Binkley RC 10.00 25.00
101 Leo Boivin 8.00 20.00
102 Earl Ingarfield 8.00 20.00
103 Lou Angotti 6.00 15.00
104 Andy Bathgate 6.00 15.00
105 Wally Boyer 6.00 15.00
106 Ken Schinkel 15.00 40.00
107 Ab McDonald 10.00 25.00
108 Charlie Burns 6.00 15.00
109 Val Fonteyne 6.00 15.00
110 Noel Price 6.00 15.00
111 Glenn Hall 8.00 20.00
112 Bob Plager RC 10.00 25.00
113 Jim Roberts 6.00 15.00
114 Red Berenson 6.00 15.00
115 Larry Keenan 6.00 15.00
116 Camille Henry 6.00 15.00
117 Gary Sabourin RC 6.00 15.00
118 Ron Schock 20.00 50.00
119 Gary Veneruzzo RC 6.00 15.00
120 Gerry Melnyk 10.00 25.00
121 Checklist 2 150.00 400.00
122 Johnny Bower 10.00 25.00
123 Tim Horton 60.00 150.00
124 Pierre Pilote 6.00 15.00
125 Marcel Pronovost 20.00 50.00
126 Ron Ellis 6.00 15.00
127 Paul Henderson 6.00 15.00
128 Al Arbour 6.00 15.00
129 Bob Pulford 6.00 15.00
130 Floyd Smith 6.00 15.00
131 Norm Ullman 25.00 60.00
132 Mike Walton 12.00 30.00
133 Ed Johnston DP 10.00 25.00
134 Glen Sather 8.00 20.00
135 Ed Westfall DP 6.00 15.00
136 Dallas Smith DP 6.00 15.00
137 Eddie Shack DP 10.00 25.00
138 Gary Doak DP 6.00 15.00
139 Ron Murphy DP 6.00 15.00
140 Gerry Cheevers DP 15.00 40.00
141 Bob Falkenberg RC 6.00 15.00
142 Garry Unger DP RC 12.00 30.00
143 Peter Mahovlich DP 12.00 30.00
144 Roy Edwards 8.00 20.00
145 Gary Bauman DP RC 6.00 15.00
146 Bob McCord DP 6.00 15.00
147 Elmer Vasko DP 6.00 15.00
148 Bill Goldsworthy RC 20.00 50.00
149 Jean-Paul Parise RC 25.00 60.00
150 Dave Dryden 6.00 15.00
151 Howie Young DP 6.00 15.00
152 Matt Ravlich DP 6.00 15.00
153 Dennis Hull DP 6.00 15.00
154 Eric Nesterenko DP 6.00 15.00
155 Stan Mikita DP 12.00 30.00
156 Bob Wall DP 6.00 15.00
157 Dave Amadio RC 6.00 15.00
158 Howie Hughes DP RC 12.00 30.00
159 Bill Flett RC 6.00 15.00
160 Doug Robinson 6.00 15.00
161 Dick Duff DP 8.00 20.00
162 Ted Harris DP 6.00 15.00
163 Claude Provost DP 6.00 15.00
164 Rogatien Vachon DP 40.00 100.00
165 Henri Richard DP 20.00 50.00
166 Jean Beliveau DP 50.00 125.00
167 Reg Fleming DP 6.00 15.00
168 Ron Stewart DP 6.00 15.00
169 Dave Balon 6.00 15.00
170 Orland Kurtenbach DP 10.00 25.00
171 Vic Hadfield DP 6.00 15.00
172 Jim Neilson DP 6.00 15.00
173 Bryan Watson DP 20.00 50.00
174 George Swarbrick DP RC 6.00 15.00
175 Joe Szura RC 6.00 15.00
176 Gary Smith RC 40.00 100.00
177 Barclay Plager UER DP RC 6.00 15.00
178 Tim Ecclestone DP RC 5.00 12.00
179 Jean-Guy Talbot DP 6.00 15.00
180 Ab McDonald DP 6.00 15.00
181 Jacques Plante DP 25.00 60.00
182 Bill McCreary RC 6.00 15.00
183 Allan Stanley DP 6.00 15.00
184 Andre Lacroix RC 6.00 15.00
185 Jean-Guy Gendron DP 6.00 15.00
186 Jim Johnson RC 6.00 15.00
187 Simon Nolet RC 6.00 15.00
188 Joe Daley DP RC 8.00 20.00
189 John Arbour DP RC 6.00 15.00
190 Billy Dea DP 6.00 15.00
191 Bob Dillabough DP 6.00 15.00
192 Bob Woytowich DP 6.00 15.00
193 Keith McCreary RC 6.00 15.00
194 Murray Oliver DP 6.00 15.00
195 Larry Mickey RC 6.00 15.00
196 Bill Sutherland DP RC 6.00 15.00
197 Bruce Gamble DP 10.00 25.00
198 Dave Keon DP 15.00 40.00
199 Gump Worsley AS1 40.00 100.00
200 Bobby Orr AS1 60.00 150.00
201 Tim Horton AS1 12.00 30.00
202 Stan Mikita AS1 12.00 30.00
203 Gordie Howe AS1 25.00 60.00
204 Bobby Hull AS1 20.00 50.00
205 Ed Giacomin AS2 8.00 20.00
206 J.C. Tremblay AS2 10.00 25.00
207 Jim Neilson AS2 6.00 15.00
208 Phil Esposito AS2 20.00 50.00
209 Rod Gilbert AS2 12.00 30.00
210 Johnny Bucyk AS2 6.00 15.00
211 Stan Mikita Triple 12.00 30.00
212 Worsley/Vachon Vezina 25.00 60.00
213 D.Sanderson Calder 20.00 50.00
214 B.Orr Norris 60.00 150.00
215 G.Hall Smythe 6.00 15.00
216 C.Provost Masterson 20.00 50.00

1968-69 O-Pee-Chee Puck Stickers

COMPLETE SET (22) 250.00 500.00
COMMON CARD (1-22) 5.00 10.00
1 Stan Mikita 10.00 25.00
2 Frank Mahovlich 10.00 25.00
3 Bobby Hull 25.00 50.00
4 Bobby Orr 125.00 250.00
5 Phil Esposito 15.00 30.00
6 Gump Worsley 10.00 20.00
7 Jean Beliveau 15.00 30.00
8 Elmer Vasko 7.50 15.00
9 Rod Gilbert 10.00 20.00
10 Roger Crozier 10.00 20.00
11 Lou Angotti 7.50 15.00
12 Charlie Hodge 7.50 15.00
13 Glenn Hall 10.00 25.00
14 Doug Harvey 10.00 25.00
15 Jacques Plante 25.00 50.00
16 Allan Stanley 7.50 15.00
17 Johnny Bower 15.00 30.00
18 Tim Horton 15.00 30.00
19 Dave Keon 15.00 40.00
20 Terry Sawchuk 25.00 50.00
21 Henri Richard 10.00 25.00
22 Gordie Howe Special 30.00 60.00

1969-70 O-Pee-Chee

COMMON CARD 3.00 8.00
SEMISTARS 4.00 10.00
UNLISTED STARS 5.00 12.00
1 Gump Worsley 80.00 200.00
2 Ted Harris 6.00 15.00
3 Jacques Laperriere 6.00 15.00
4 Serge Savard RC 80.00 200.00
5 J.C. Tremblay 25.00 60.00
6 Yvan Cournoyer 4.00 10.00
7 John Ferguson 4.00 10.00
8 Jacques Lemaire 6.00 15.00
9 Bobby Rousseau 6.00 15.00
10 Jean Beliveau 40.00 100.00
11 Dick Duff 6.00 15.00
12 Glenn Hall 5.00 12.00
13 Bob Plager 4.00 10.00
14 Ron Anderson RC 4.00 10.00
15 Jean-Guy Talbot 4.00 10.00
16 Andre Boudrias 15.00 40.00
17 Camille Henry 4.00 10.00
18 Ab McDonald 4.00 10.00
19 Gary Sabourin 4.00 10.00
20 Red Berenson 6.00 15.00
21 Phil Goyette 4.00 10.00
22 Gerry Cheevers 25.00 60.00
23 Ted Green 4.00 10.00
24 Bobby Orr 100.00 250.00
25 Dallas Smith 4.00 10.00
26 Johnny Bucyk 20.00 50.00
27 Ken Hodge 20.00 50.00
28 John McKenzie 4.00 10.00
29 Ed Westfall 4.00 10.00
30 Phil Esposito 12.00 30.00
31 Checklist 2 60.00 150.00
32 Fred Stanfield 4.00 10.00
33 Ed Giacomin 6.00 15.00
34 Arnie Brown 4.00 10.00
35 Jim Neilson 6.00 15.00
36 Rod Seiling 4.00 10.00
37 Rod Gilbert 5.00 12.00
38 Vic Hadfield 10.00 25.00
39 Don Marshall 4.00 10.00
40 Bob Nevin 4.00 10.00
41 Ron Stewart 15.00 40.00
42 Jean Ratelle 12.00 30.00
43 Walt Tkaczuk RC 25.00 60.00
44 Bruce Gamble 4.00 10.00
45 Jim Dorey RC 4.00 10.00
46 Ron Ellis 20.00 50.00
47 Paul Henderson 4.00 10.00
48 Brit Selby 10.00 25.00
49 Floyd Smith 4.00 10.00
50 Mike Walton 4.00 10.00
51 Dave Keon 60.00 150.00
52 Murray Oliver 20.00 50.00
53 Bob Pulford 4.00 10.00
54 Norm Ullman 4.00 10.00
55 Roger Crozier 20.00 50.00
56 Roy Edwards 12.00 30.00
57 Bob Baun 8.00 20.00
58 Gary Bergman 4.00 10.00
59 Carl Brewer 4.00 10.00
60 Wayne Connelly 4.00 10.00
61 Gordie Howe 40.00 100.00
62 Frank Mahovlich 12.00 30.00
63 Bruce MacGregor 6.00 15.00
64 Ron Harris 4.00 10.00
65 Pete Stemkowski 4.00 10.00
66 Denis DeJordy 12.00 30.00
67 Doug Jarrett 10.00 25.00
68 Gilles Marotte 4.00 10.00
69 Pat Stapleton 4.00 10.00
70 Bobby Hull 30.00 80.00
71 Dennis Hull 4.00 10.00
72 Doug Mohns 30.00 80.00
73 Howie Menard RC 4.00 10.00
74 Ken Wharram 4.00 10.00
75 Pit Martin 4.00 10.00
76 Stan Mikita 20.00 50.00
77 Charlie Hodge 10.00 25.00
78 Gary Smith 4.00 10.00
79 Harry Howell 8.00 20.00
80 Bert Marshall 10.00 25.00
81 Doug Roberts 4.00 10.00
82 Carol Vadnais 4.00 10.00
83 Gerry Ehman 20.00 50.00
84 Brian Perry RC 4.00 10.00
85 Gary Jarrett 4.00 10.00
86 Ted Hampson 12.00 30.00
87 Earl Ingarfield 4.00 10.00
88 Doug Favell RC 6.00 15.00
89 Bernie Parent 40.00 100.00
90 Larry Hillman 12.00 30.00
91 Wayne Hillman 8.00 20.00
92 Ed Van Impe 4.00 10.00
93 Joe Watson 4.00 10.00
94 Gary Dornhoefer 12.00 30.00
95 Reg Fleming 4.00 10.00
96 Ralph McSweyn RC 4.00 10.00
97 Jim Johnson 8.00 20.00
98 Andre Lacroix 8.00 20.00
99 Gerry Desjardins RC 5.00 12.00
100 Dale Rolfe 4.00 10.00
101 Bill White 4.00 10.00
102 Bill Flett 4.00 10.00
103 Ted Irvine 12.00 30.00
104 Ross Lonsberry 4.00 10.00
105 Leon Rochefort 25.00 60.00
106 Bryan Campbell RC 15.00 40.00
107 Dennis Hextall RC 4.00 10.00
108 Eddie Joyal 4.00 10.00
109 Gord Labossiere 4.00 10.00
110 Les Binkley 25.00 60.00
111 Tracy Pratt RC 10.00 25.00
112 Bryan Watson 4.00 10.00
113 Bob Blackburn RC 4.00 10.00
114 Keith McCreary 4.00 10.00
115 Dean Prentice 4.00 10.00
116 Glen Sather 4.00 10.00
117 Ken Schinkel 4.00 10.00
118 Wally Boyer 15.00 40.00
119 Val Fonteyne 4.00 10.00
120 Ron Schock 4.00 10.00
121 Cesare Maniago 4.00 10.00
122 Leo Boivin 4.00 10.00
123 Bob McCord 4.00 10.00
124 John Miszuk 4.00 10.00
125 Danny Grant 12.00 30.00
126 Bill Collins RC 4.00 10.00
127 Jean-Paul Parise 4.00 10.00
128 Tom Williams 4.00 10.00
129 Charlie Burns 4.00 10.00
130 Ray Cullen 10.00 25.00
131 Danny O'Shea RC 25.00 20.00
132 Checklist 1 300.00 800.00
133 Jim Pappin 4.00 10.00
134 Lou Angotti 6.00 15.00
135 Terry Cafery RC 4.00 10.00
136 Eric Nesterenko 4.00 10.00
137 Chico Maki 4.00 10.00
138 Tony Esposito RC 80.00 200.00
139 Eddie Shack 5.00 12.00
140 Bob Wall 4.00 10.00
141 Skip Krake 4.00 10.00
142 Howie Hughes 4.00 10.00
143 Jimmy Peters RC 4.00 10.00
144 Brent Hughes RC 4.00 10.00
145 Bill Hicke 4.00 10.00
146 Norm Ferguson RC 6.00 15.00
147 Dick Mattiussi RC 4.00 10.00
148 Mike Laughton RC 4.00 10.00
149 Gene Ubriaco RC 4.00 10.00
150 Bob Dillabough 4.00 10.00
151 Bob Woytowich 4.00 10.00
152 Joe Daley 4.00 10.00
153 Duane Rupp 4.00 10.00
154 Bryan Hextall RC 8.00 20.00
155 Jean Pronovost RC 10.00 25.00
156 Jim Morrison 4.00 10.00
157 Alex Delvecchio 5.00 12.00
158 Paul Popiel 4.00 10.00
159 Garry Unger 10.00 25.00
160 Garry Monahan 6.00 15.00
161 Matt Ravlich 8.00 20.00
162 Nick Libett RC 4.00 10.00
163 Henri Richard 20.00 50.00
164 Terry Harper 20.00 50.00
165 Rogatien Vachon 6.00 15.00
166 Ralph Backstrom 4.00 10.00
167 Claude Provost 10.00 25.00
168 Gilles Tremblay 6.00 15.00
169 Jean-Guy Gendron 5.00 12.00
170 Earl Heiskala RC 4.00 10.00
171 Garry Peters 4.00 10.00
172 Bill Sutherland 4.00 10.00
173 Dick Cherry RC 6.00 15.00
174 Jim Roberts 4.00 10.00
175 Noel Picard RC 15.00 40.00
176 Barclay Plager 6.00 15.00
177 Frank St. Marseille RC 4.00 10.00
178 Al Arbour 15.00 40.00
179 Tim Ecclestone 4.00 10.00
180 Jacques Plante 15.00 40.00
181 Bill McCreary 4.00 10.00
182 Tim Horton 30.00 80.00
183 Rick Ley RC 4.00 10.00
184 Wayne Carleton 4.00 10.00
185 Marv Edwards RC 4.00 10.00
186 Pat Quinn RC 6.00 15.00
187 Johnny Bower 15.00 40.00
188 Orland Kurtenbach 5.00 12.00
189 Terry Sawchuk UER 25.00 60.00
190 Real Lemieux 4.00 10.00
191 Dave Balon 4.00 10.00
192 Al Hamilton 15.00 40.00
193A G.Howe Mr. HK ERR 25.00 60.00
193B G.Howe Mr. HK COR 40.00 100.00
194 Claude Larose 4.00 10.00
195 Bill Goldsworthy 8.00 20.00
196 Bob Barlow RC 4.00 10.00
197 Ken Broderick RC 8.00 20.00
198 Lou Nanne RC 8.00 20.00
199 Tom Polonic RC 4.00 10.00
200 Ed Johnston 4.00 10.00
201 Derek Sanderson 20.00 50.00
202 Gary Doak 8.00 20.00
203 Don Awrey 6.00 15.00
204 Ron Murphy 4.00 10.00
205A P.Esposito Double ERR 10.00 25.00
205B P.Esposito Double COR 20.00 50.00
206 Alex Delvecchio Byng 4.00 10.00
207 J.Plante/G.Hall Vezina 12.00 30.00
208 Danny Grant Calder 4.00 10.00
209 Bobby Orr Norris 30.00 80.00
210 Serge Savard Smythe 4.00 10.00
211 Glenn Hall AS 6.00 15.00
212 Bobby Orr AS 80.00 200.00
213 Tim Horton AS 25.00 60.00
214 Phil Esposito AS 20.00 50.00
215 Gordie Howe AS 20.00 50.00
216 Bobby Hull AS 12.00 30.00
217 Ed Giacomin AS 5.00 12.00
218 Ted Green AS 4.00 10.00
219 Ted Harris AS 4.00 10.00
220 Jean Beliveau AS 12.00 30.00
221 Yvan Cournoyer AS 12.00 30.00
222 Frank Mahovlich AS 6.00 15.00
223 Art Ross Trophy 25.00 60.00
224 Hart Trophy 4.00 10.00
225 Lady Byng Trophy 25.00 60.00
226 Vezina Trophy 4.00 10.00
227 Calder Trophy 5.00 12.00
228 James Norris Trophy 40.00 100.00
229 Conn Smythe Trophy 5.00 12.00
230 Prince of Wales 4.00 10.00
231 The Stanley Cup 40.00 100.00

1969-70 O-Pee-Chee Four-in-One

COMPLETE SET (18) 600.00 1000.00
COMMON CARD (1-18) 30.00 60.00
1 Baun/Schink/Hort/Parent 30.00 60.00
2 Bink/Hodge/Flem/Laper 30.00 60.00
3 Courn/Neil/Sabo/Misz 30.00 60.00
4 Gamb/Vadn/Mahov/Hillman 30.00 60.00
5 Giac/Beliv/Joyal/Boivin 30.00 60.00
6 Goye/Jarret/Green/Hicke 30.00 60.00
7 Hamp/Brewer/DeJordy/Roche 30.00 60.00
8 Hodge/Quinn/Sand/Rupp 30.00 60.00
9 Ingfld/Robrts/Wors/Hull 50.00 100.00
10 Lacro/Wall/Savard/Croz 30.00 60.00
11 Mani/Orr/Keon/Gendron 150.00 300.00
12 McCr/Larose/Gilb/Cheev 30.00 60.00
13 Mikita/Arbo/Seili/Schock 30.00 60.00
14 Mohn/Woyt/Howe/Desj 75.00 150.00
15 Nev/Plante/Walt/Cullen 30.00 60.00
16 Pulf/Rich/Beren/Shack 40.00 80.00
17 Stapl/Grant/Marsh/Ratel 30.00 60.00
18 VanImp/Rolf/Delv/Espo 30.00 60.00

1969-70 O-Pee-Chee Stamps

COMPLETE SET (26) 125.00 250.00
COMMON CARD (1-26) 4.00 8.00
1 Jean Beliveau 7.50 15.00
2 Red Berenson 4.00 8.00
3 Les Binkley 5.00 10.00
4 Yvan Cournoyer 6.00 12.00
5 Ray Cullen 4.00 8.00
6 Gerry Desjardins 5.00 10.00
7 Phil Esposito 7.50 15.00
8 Ed Giacomin 6.00 12.00
9 Rod Gilbert 6.00 12.00
10 Danny Grant 4.00 8.00
11 Glenn Hall 7.50 15.00
12 Ted Hampson 4.00 8.00
13 Ken Hodge 4.00 8.00
14 Gordie Howe 20.00 40.00
15 Bobby Hull 15.00 30.00
16 Eddie Joyal 4.00 8.00
17 Dave Keon 7.50 15.00
18 Andre Lacroix 4.00 8.00
19 Frank Mahovlich 6.00 12.00
20 Keith McCreary 4.00 8.00
21 Stan Mikita 7.50 15.00
22 Bobby Orr 25.00 60.00
23 Bernie Parent 7.50 15.00
24 Jean Ratelle 5.00 10.00
25 Norm Ullman 5.00 10.00
26 Carol Vadnais 4.00 8.00

1970-71 O-Pee-Chee

1 Gerry Cheevers 20.00 50.00
2 Johnny Bucyk 30.00 80.00
3 Bobby Orr 200.00 500.00
4 Don Awrey 8.00 20.00
5 Fred Stanfield 5.00 12.00
6 John McKenzie 4.00 10.00
7 Wayne Cashman RC 25.00 60.00
8 Ken Hodge 8.00 20.00
9 Wayne Carleton 4.00 10.00
10 Garnet Bailey RC 5.00 12.00
11 Phil Esposito 15.00 40.00
12 Lou Angotti 4.00 10.00
13 Jim Pappin 4.00 10.00
14 Dennis Hull 6.00 15.00
15 Bobby Hull 25.00 60.00
16 Doug Mohns 3.00 8.00
17 Pat Stapleton 4.00 10.00
18 Pit Martin 4.00 10.00
19 Eric Nesterenko 4.00 10.00
20 Stan Mikita 12.00 30.00
21 Roy Edwards 15.00 40.00
22 Frank Mahovlich 10.00 25.00
23 Ron Harris 3.00 8.00
24 Checklist 1 125.00 300.00
25 Pete Stemkowski 3.00 8.00
26 Garry Unger 3.00 8.00
27 Bruce MacGregor 3.00 8.00
28 Larry Jeffrey 3.00 8.00
29 Gordie Howe 60.00 150.00
30 Billy Dea 3.00 8.00
31 Denis DeJordy 10.00 25.00
32 Matt Ravlich 5.00 12.00
33 Dave Amadio 3.00 8.00
34 Gilles Marotte 4.00 10.00
35 Eddie Shack 10.00 25.00
36 Bob Pulford 10.00 25.00
37 Ross Lonsberry 4.00 10.00
38 Gord Labossiere 3.00 8.00
39 Eddie Joyal 3.00 8.00
40 Gump Worsley 25.00 60.00
41 Bob McCord 3.00 8.00
42 Leo Boivin 4.00 10.00
43 Tom Reid RC 3.00 8.00
44 Charlie Burns 3.00 8.00
45 Bob Barlow 3.00 8.00
46 Bill Goldsworthy 4.00 10.00
47 Danny Grant 8.00 20.00
48 Norm Beaudin RC 3.00 8.00
49 Rogatien Vachon 10.00 25.00
50 Yvan Cournoyer 10.00 25.00
51 Serge Savard 12.00 30.00
52 Jacques Laperriere 6.00 15.00
53 Terry Harper 3.00 8.00
54 Ralph Backstrom 4.00 10.00
55 Jean Beliveau 10.00 25.00
56 Claude Larose 3.00 8.00
57 Jacques Lemaire 10.00 25.00
58 Peter Mahovlich 8.00 20.00
59 Tim Horton 15.00 40.00
60 Bob Nevin 3.00 8.00
61 Dave Balon 3.00 8.00
62 Vic Hadfield 4.00 10.00
63 Rod Gilbert 10.00 25.00
64 Ron Stewart 3.00 8.00
65 Ted Irvine 3.00 8.00
66 Arnie Brown 3.00 8.00
67 Brad Park RC 30.00 80.00
68 Ed Giacomin 15.00 40.00
69 Gary Smith 4.00 10.00
70 Carol Vadnais 4.00 10.00
71 Doug Roberts 3.00 8.00
72 Harry Howell 4.00 10.00
73 Joe Szura 3.00 8.00
74 Mike Laughton 3.00 8.00
75 Gary Jarrett 3.00 8.00
76 Bill Hicke 3.00 8.00
77 Paul Andrea RC 3.00 8.00
78 Bernie Parent 30.00 80.00
79 Joe Watson 3.00 8.00
80 Ed Van Impe 3.00 8.00
81 Larry Hillman 3.00 8.00
82 George Swarbrick 3.00 8.00
83 Bill Sutherland 3.00 8.00
84 Andre Lacroix 4.00 10.00
85 Gary Dornhoefer 10.00 25.00
86 Jean-Guy Gendron 3.00 8.00
87 Al Smith RC 4.00 10.00
88 Bob Woytowich 3.00 8.00
89 Duane Rupp 3.00 8.00
90 Jim Morrison 3.00 8.00
91 Ron Schock 3.00 8.00
92 Ken Schinkel 3.00 8.00
93 Keith McCreary 3.00 8.00
94 Bryan Hextall 4.00 10.00
95 Wayne Hicks RC 3.00 8.00
96 Gary Sabourin 3.00 8.00
97 Ernie Wakely RC 4.00 10.00
98 Bob Wall 3.00 8.00
99 Barclay Plager 5.00 12.00
100 Jean-Guy Talbot 3.00 8.00
101 Gary Veneruzzo 3.00 8.00
102 Tim Ecclestone 3.00 8.00
103 Red Berenson 6.00 15.00
104 Larry Keenan 3.00 8.00
105 Bruce Gamble 12.00 30.00
106 Jim Dorey 3.00 8.00
107 Mike Pelyk RC 3.00 8.00
108 Rick Ley 4.00 10.00
109 Mike Walton 3.00 8.00
110 Norm Ullman 10.00 25.00
111A Brit Selby no trade 3.00 8.00
111B Brit Selby trade 12.00 30.00
112 Garry Monahan 3.00 8.00
113 George Armstrong 10.00 25.00
114 Gary Doak 6.00 15.00
115 Darryl Sly RC 3.00 8.00
116 Wayne Maki 3.00 8.00
117 Orland Kurtenbach 3.00 8.00
118 Murray Hall 3.00 8.00
119 Marc Reaume 3.00 8.00
120 Pat Quinn 10.00 25.00
121 Andre Boudrias 6.00 15.00
122 Paul Popiel 3.00 8.00
123 Paul Terbenche 3.00 8.00
124 Howie Menard 3.00 8.00
125 Gerry Meehan RC 8.00 20.00
126 Skip Krake 3.00 8.00
127 Phil Goyette 3.00 8.00
128 Reg Fleming 3.00 8.00
129 Don Marshall 10.00 25.00
130 Bill Inglis RC 3.00 8.00
131 Gilbert Perreault RC 125.00 300.00
132 Checklist 2 200.00 500.00
133 Ed Johnston 4.00 10.00
134 Ted Green 8.00 20.00
135 Rick Smith RC 3.00 8.00
136 Derek Sanderson 30.00 80.00
137 Dallas Smith 8.00 20.00
138 Don Marcotte RC 8.00 20.00
139 Ed Westfall 4.00 10.00
140 Floyd Smith 3.00 8.00
141 Randy Wyrozub RC 3.00 8.00
142 Cliff Schmautz RC 3.00 8.00
143 Mike McMahon 3.00 8.00
144 Jim Watson 3.00 8.00
145 Roger Crozier 12.00 30.00
146 Tracy Pratt 3.00 8.00
147 Cliff Koroll RC 4.00 10.00
148 Gerry Pinder RC 4.00 10.00
149 Chico Maki 3.00 8.00
150 Doug Jarrett 3.00 8.00
151 Keith Magnuson RC 12.00 30.00
152 Gerry Desjardins 4.00 10.00
153 Tony Esposito 15.00 40.00
154 Gary Bergman 3.00 8.00
155 Tom Webster RC 4.00 10.00
156 Dale Rolfe 3.00 8.00
157 Alex Delvecchio 8.00 20.00
158 Nick Libett 3.00 8.00
159 Wayne Connelly 3.00 8.00
160 Mike Byers RC 3.00 8.00
161 Bill Flett 3.00 8.00
162 Larry Mickey 3.00 8.00
163 Noel Price 3.00 8.00
164 Larry Cahan 3.00 8.00
165 Jack Norris RC 4.00 10.00
166 Ted Harris 3.00 8.00
167 Murray Oliver 3.00 8.00
168 Jean-Paul Parise 4.00 10.00
169 Tom Williams 3.00 8.00
170 Bobby Rousseau 3.00 8.00
171 Jude Drouin RC 4.00 10.00
172 Walt McKechnie RC 4.00 10.00
173 Cesare Maniago 4.00 10.00
174 Rejean Houle RC 8.00 20.00
175A Mickey Redmond trade 4.00 10.00
175B Mickey Redmond no trade 12.00 30.00
176 Henri Richard 15.00 40.00
177 Guy Lapointe RC 30.00 80.00
178 J.C. Tremblay 6.00 15.00
179 Marc Tardif RC 10.00 25.00
180 Walt Tkaczuk 8.00 20.00
181 Jean Ratelle 6.00 15.00
182 Pete Stemkowski 3.00 8.00
183 Gilles Villemure 4.00 10.00
184 Rod Seiling 3.00 8.00
185 Jim Neilson 3.00 8.00
186 Dennis Hextall 4.00 10.00
187 Gerry Ehman 3.00 8.00
188 Bert Marshall 3.00 8.00
189 Gary Croteau RC 3.00 8.00
190 Ted Hampson 3.00 8.00
191 Earl Ingarfield 3.00 8.00
192 Dick Mattiussi 3.00 8.00
193 Earl Heiskala 3.00 8.00
194 Simon Nolet 3.00 8.00
195 Bobby Clarke RC 125.00 300.00
196 Garry Peters 3.00 8.00
197 Lew Morrison RC 3.00 8.00
198 Wayne Hillman 3.00 8.00
199 Doug Favell 10.00 25.00
200 Les Binkley 4.00 10.00

201 Dean Prentice	3.00	8.00
202 Jean Pronovost	4.00	10.00
203 Wally Boyer	3.00	8.00
204 Bryan Watson	3.00	8.00
205 Glen Sather	4.00	10.00
206 Lowell MacDonald	3.00	8.00
207 Andy Bathgate	6.00	15.00
208 Val Fonteyne	3.00	8.00
209 Jim Lorentz RC	3.00	8.00
210 Glenn Hall	10.00	25.00
211 Bob Plager	8.00	20.00
212 Noel Picard	3.00	8.00
213 Jim Roberts	4.00	10.00
214 Frank St.Marseille	3.00	8.00
215 Ab McDonald	3.00	8.00
216 Brian Glennie RC	3.00	8.00
217 Paul Henderson	4.00	10.00
218 Darryl Sittler RC	150.00	400.00
219 Dave Keon	8.00	20.00
220 Jim Harrison RC	3.00	8.00
221 Ron Ellis	4.00	10.00
222 Jacques Plante	20.00	50.00
223 Bob Baun	15.00	40.00
224 George Gardner RC	3.00	8.00
225 Dale Tallon RC	4.00	10.00
226 Rosaire Paiement RC	3.00	8.00
227 Mike Corrigan RC	3.00	8.00
228 Ray Cullen	3.00	8.00
229 Charlie Hodge	4.00	10.00
230 Len Lunde	3.00	8.00
231 Terry Sawchuk Mem	25.00	60.00
232 Bruins Team Champs	12.00	30.00
233 Espo/Cashman/Hodge	30.00	80.00
234 Tony Esposito AS1	15.00	40.00
235 Bobby Hull AS1	15.00	40.00
236 Bobby Orr AS1	30.00	80.00
237 Phil Esposito AS1	12.00	30.00
238 Gordie Howe AS1	25.00	60.00
239 Brad Park AS1	12.00	30.00
240 Stan Mikita AS2	10.00	25.00
241 John McKenzie AS2	4.00	10.00
242 Frank Mahovlich AS2	3.00	8.00
243 Carl Brewer AS2	3.00	8.00
244 Ed Giacomin AS2	8.00	20.00
245 Jacques Laperriere AS2	4.00	10.00
246 Bobby Orr Hart	40.00	100.00
247 Tony Esposito Calder	15.00	40.00
248A B.Orr Norris Howe	50.00	125.00
248B B.Orr Norris no Howe	50.00	125.00
249 Bobby Orr Ross	50.00	125.00
250 Tony Esposito Vezina	15.00	40.00
251 Phil Goyette Lady Byng	3.00	8.00
252 Bobby Orr Smythe	50.00	125.00
253 Pit Martin Bill Masterton Trophy	3.00	8.00
254 Stanley Cup Trophy	25.00	60.00
255 Wales Trophy	4.00	10.00
256 Conn Smythe Trophy	12.00	30.00
257 James Norris Trophy	80.00	200.00
258 Calder Trophy	4.00	10.00
259 Vezina Trophy	10.00	25.00
260 Lady Byng Trophy	4.00	10.00
261 Hart Trophy	12.00	30.00
262 Art Ross Trophy	15.00	40.00
263 Clarence Campbell Bowl	25.00	60.00
264 John Ferguson	10.00	25.00

1970-71 O-Pee-Chee Deckle

COMPLETE SET (48)	200.00	400.00
1 Pat Quinn	2.00	5.00
2 Eddie Shack	3.00	6.00
3 Eddie Joyal	2.00	5.00
4 Bobby Orr	40.00	80.00
5 Derek Sanderson	6.00	12.00
6 Phil Esposito	7.50	15.00
7 Fred Stanfield	2.00	5.00
8 Bob Woytowich	2.00	5.00
9 Ron Schock	2.00	5.00
10 Les Binkley	3.00	6.00
11 Roger Crozier	3.00	6.00
12 Reg Fleming	2.00	5.00
13 Charlie Burns	2.00	5.00
14 Bobby Rousseau	2.00	5.00
15 Leo Boivin	2.00	5.00
16 Garry Unger	2.00	5.00
17 Frank Mahovlich	5.00	10.00
18 Gordie Howe	25.00	50.00
19 Jacques Lemaire	3.00	8.00
20 Jacques Laperriere	2.00	5.00
21 Jean Beliveau	10.00	20.00
22 Rogatien Vachon	4.00	10.00
23 Yvan Cournoyer	3.00	8.00
24 Henri Richard	6.00	12.00
25 Red Berenson	2.00	5.00
26 Frank St.Marseille	2.00	5.00
27 Glenn Hall	5.00	10.00
28 Gary Sabourin	2.00	5.00
29 Doug Mohns	2.00	5.00
30 Bobby Hull	20.00	40.00
31 Ray Cullen	2.00	5.00
32 Tony Esposito	10.00	20.00
33 Gary Dornhoefer	2.00	5.00
34 Ed Van Impe	2.00	5.00
35 Doug Favell	3.00	6.00
36 Carol Vadnais	2.00	5.00
37 Harry Howell	2.00	5.00
38 Bill Hicke	2.00	5.00
39 Rod Gilbert	3.00	6.00
40 Jean Ratelle	3.00	6.00
41 Walt Tkaczuk	3.00	6.00
42 Ed Giacomin	4.00	8.00
43 Brad Park	6.00	15.00
44 Bruce Gamble	3.00	6.00
45 Orland Kurtenbach	2.00	5.00
46 Ron Ellis	2.00	6.00
47 Dave Keon	5.00	10.00
48 Norm Ullman	3.00	6.00

1971-72 O-Pee-Chee

1 Paul Popiel	6.00	15.00
2 Pierre Bouchard RC	50.00	125.00
3 Don Awrey	3.00	8.00
4 Paul Curtis RC	3.00	8.00
5 Guy Trottier RC	4.00	10.00
6 Paul Shmyr RC	4.00	10.00
7 Fred Stanfield	4.00	10.00
8 Mike Robitaille RC	3.00	8.00
9 Vic Hadfield	12.00	30.00
10 Jim Harrison	3.00	8.00
11 Bill White	3.00	8.00
12 Andre Boudrias	3.00	8.00
13 Gary Sabourin	3.00	8.00
14 Arnie Brown	6.00	15.00
15 Yvan Cournoyer	40.00	100.00
16 Bryan Hextall	8.00	20.00
17 Gary Croteau	3.00	8.00
18 Gilles Villemure	4.00	10.00
19 Serge Bernier RC	10.00	25.00
20 Phil Esposito	20.00	50.00
21 Tom Reid	3.00	8.00
22 Doug Barrie RC	3.00	8.00
23 Eddie Joyal	3.00	8.00
24 Dunc Wilson RC	6.00	15.00
25 Pat Stapleton	4.00	10.00
26 Garry Unger	20.00	50.00
27 Al Smith	8.00	20.00
28 Bob Woytowich	3.00	8.00
29 Marc Tardif	4.00	10.00
30 Norm Ullman	6.00	15.00
31 Tom Williams	3.00	8.00
32 Ted Harris	3.00	8.00
33 Andre Lacroix	8.00	20.00
34 Mike Byers	3.00	8.00
35 Johnny Bucyk	15.00	40.00
36 Roger Crozier	10.00	25.00
37 Alex Delvecchio	12.00	30.00
38 Frank St.Marseille	3.00	8.00
39 Pit Martin	4.00	10.00
40 Brad Park	12.00	30.00
41 Greg Polis RC	3.00	8.00
42 Orland Kurtenbach	3.00	8.00
43 Jim McKenny RC	3.00	8.00
44 Bob Nevin	3.00	8.00
45 Ken Dryden RC	250.00	600.00
46 Carol Vadnais	6.00	15.00
47 Bill Flett	3.00	8.00
48 Jim Johnson	3.00	8.00
49 Al Hamilton	3.00	8.00
50 Bobby Hull	30.00	80.00
51 Chris Bordeleau RC	3.00	8.00
52 Tim Ecclestone	3.00	8.00
53 Rod Seiling	3.00	8.00
54 Gerry Cheevers	25.00	60.00
55 Bill Goldsworthy	4.00	10.00
56 Ron Schock	3.00	8.00
57 Jim Dorey	3.00	8.00
58 Wayne Maki	3.00	8.00
59 Terry Harper	3.00	8.00
60 Gilbert Perreault	20.00	50.00
61 Ernie Hicke RC	3.00	8.00
62 Wayne Hillman	3.00	8.00
63 Denis DeJordy	4.00	10.00
64 Ken Schinkel	3.00	8.00
65 Derek Sanderson	12.00	30.00
66 Barclay Plager	8.00	20.00
67 Paul Henderson	15.00	40.00
68 Jude Drouin	3.00	8.00
69 Keith Magnuson	20.00	50.00
70 Ron Harris	3.00	8.00
71 Jacques Lemaire	8.00	20.00
72 Doug Favell	4.00	10.00
73 Bert Marshall	3.00	8.00
74 Ted Irvine	3.00	8.00
75 Walt Tkaczuk	4.00	10.00
76 Bob Berry RC	6.00	15.00
77 Syl Apps RC	6.00	15.00
78 Tom Webster	6.00	15.00
79 Danny Grant	8.00	20.00
80 Dave Keon	20.00	50.00
81 Ernie Wakely	15.00	40.00
82 John McKenzie	4.00	10.00
83 Ron Stackhouse RC	3.00	8.00
84 Peter Mahovlich	20.00	50.00
85 Dennis Hull	4.00	10.00
86 Juha Widing RC	3.00	8.00
87 Gary Doak	3.00	8.00
88 Phil Goyette	3.00	8.00
89 Lew Morrison	3.00	8.00
90 Ab DeMarco RC	3.00	8.00
91 Red Berenson	8.00	20.00
92 Mike Pelyk	3.00	8.00
93 Gary Jarrett	3.00	8.00
94 Bob Pulford	8.00	20.00
95 Dan Johnson RC	3.00	8.00
96 Eddie Shack	6.00	15.00
97 Jean Ratelle	6.00	15.00
98 Jim Pappin	3.00	8.00
99 Roy Edwards	10.00	25.00
100 Bobby Orr	100.00	250.00
101 Ted Hampson	3.00	8.00
102 Mickey Redmond	25.00	60.00
103 Bob Plager	6.00	15.00
104 Barry Ashbee RC	4.00	10.00
105 Frank Mahovlich	20.00	50.00
106 Dick Redmond RC	3.00	8.00
107 Tracy Pratt	3.00	8.00
108 Ralph Backstrom	4.00	10.00
109 Murray Hall	3.00	8.00
110 Tony Esposito	30.00	80.00
111 Checklist Card	400.00	1000.00
112 Jim Neilson	3.00	8.00
113 Ron Ellis	4.00	10.00
114 Bobby Clarke	40.00	100.00
115 Ken Hodge	4.00	10.00
116 Jim Roberts	10.00	25.00
117 Cesare Maniago	6.00	15.00
118 Jean Pronovost	4.00	10.00
119 Gary Bergman	3.00	8.00
120 Henri Richard	25.00	60.00
121 Ross Lonsberry	3.00	8.00
122 Pat Quinn	6.00	15.00
123 Rod Gilbert	6.00	15.00
124 Walt McKechnie	10.00	25.00
125 Stan Mikita	20.00	50.00
126 Ed Van Impe	3.00	8.00
127 Terry Crisp RC	8.00	20.00
128 Fred Barrett RC	3.00	8.00
129 Wayne Cashman	10.00	25.00
130 J.C. Tremblay	4.00	10.00
131 Bernie Parent	15.00	40.00
132 Bryan Watson	20.00	50.00
133 Marcel Dionne RC	125.00	300.00
134 Ab McDonald	4.00	10.00
135 Leon Rochefort	4.00	10.00
136 Serge Lajeunesse RC	4.00	10.00
137 Joe Daley	5.00	12.00
138 Brian Conacher	12.00	30.00
139 Bill Collins	8.00	20.00
140 Nick Libett	4.00	10.00
141 Bill Sutherland	5.00	12.00
142 Bill Hicke	4.00	10.00
143 Serge Savard	15.00	40.00
144 Jacques Laperriere	8.00	20.00
145 Guy Lapointe	12.00	30.00
146 Claude Larose UER	15.00	40.00
147 Rejean Houle	6.00	15.00
148 Guy Lafleur UER RC	250.00	600.00
149 Dale Hoganson RC	8.00	20.00
150 Al McDonough RC	4.00	10.00
151 Gilles Marotte	8.00	20.00
152 Butch Goring RC	30.00	80.00
153 Harry Howell	5.00	12.00
154 Real Lemieux	6.00	15.00
155 Gary Edwards RC	6.00	15.00
156 Rogatien Vachon	10.00	25.00
157 Mike Corrigan	4.00	10.00
158 Floyd Smith	4.00	10.00
159 Dave Dryden	12.00	30.00
160 Gerry Meehan	8.00	20.00
161 Richard Martin RC	20.00	50.00
162 Steve Atkinson RC	6.00	15.00
163 Ron Anderson	5.00	12.00
164 Dick Duff	5.00	12.00
165 Jim Watson	4.00	10.00
166 Don Luce RC	4.00	10.00
167 Larry Mickey	6.00	15.00
168 Larry Hillman	5.00	12.00
169 Ed Westfall	10.00	25.00
170 Dallas Smith	4.00	10.00
171 Mike Walton	4.00	10.00
172 Ed Johnston	5.00	12.00
173 Ted Green	10.00	25.00
174 Rick Smith	6.00	15.00
175 Reggie Leach RC	30.00	80.00
176 Don Marcotte	8.00	20.00
177 Bobby Sheehan RC	5.00	12.00
178 Wayne Carleton	4.00	10.00
179 Norm Ferguson	4.00	10.00
180 Don O'Donoghue RC	10.00	25.00
181 Gary Kurt RC	5.00	12.00
182 Joey Johnston RC	4.00	10.00
183 Stan Gilbertson RC	4.00	10.00
184 Craig Patrick RC	8.00	20.00
185 Gerry Pinder	8.00	20.00
186 Tim Horton	40.00	100.00
187 Darryl Edestrand RC	10.00	25.00
188 Keith McCreary	8.00	20.00
189 Val Fonteyne	4.00	10.00
190 S.Kannegiesser RC	4.00	10.00
191 Nick Harbaruk RC	4.00	10.00
192 Les Binkley	10.00	25.00
193 Darryl Sittler	30.00	80.00
194 Rick Ley	4.00	10.00
195 Jacques Plante	15.00	40.00
196 Bob Baun	30.00	80.00
197 Brian Glennie	6.00	15.00
198 Brian Spencer RC	6.00	15.00
199 Don Marshall	5.00	12.00
200 Denis Dupere RC	4.00	10.00
201 Bruce Gamble	12.00	30.00
202 Gary Dornhoefer	4.00	10.00
203 Bob Kelly RC	8.00	20.00
204 Jean-Guy Gendron	4.00	10.00
205 Brent Hughes	5.00	12.00
206 Simon Nolet	4.00	10.00
207 Rick MacLeish RC	20.00	50.00
208 Doug Jarrett	4.00	10.00
209 Cliff Koroll	8.00	20.00
210 Chico Maki	8.00	20.00
211 Danny O'Shea	4.00	10.00
212 Lou Angotti	5.00	12.00
213 Eric Nesterenko	5.00	12.00
214 Bryan Campbell	4.00	10.00
215 Bill Fairbairn RC	4.00	10.00
216 Bruce MacGregor	8.00	20.00
217 Pete Stemkowski	4.00	10.00
218 Bobby Rousseau	4.00	10.00
219 Dale Rolfe	4.00	10.00
220 Ed Giacomin	8.00	20.00
221 Glen Sather	5.00	12.00
222 Carl Brewer	5.00	12.00
223 George Morrison RC	8.00	20.00
224 Noel Picard	8.00	20.00
225 Peter McDuffe RC	25.00	60.00
226 Brit Selby	4.00	10.00
227 Jim Lorentz	5.00	12.00
228 Phil Roberto RC	4.00	10.00
229 Dave Balon	4.00	10.00
230 Barry Wilkins RC	4.00	10.00
231 Dennis Kearns RC	12.00	30.00
232 Jocelyn Guevremont RC	5.00	12.00
233 Rosaire Paiement	8.00	20.00
234 Dale Tallon	4.00	10.00
235 George Gardner	8.00	20.00
236 Ron Stewart	4.00	10.00
237 Wayne Connelly	4.00	10.00
238 Charlie Burns	10.00	25.00
239 Murray Oliver	4.00	10.00
240 Lou Nanne	8.00	20.00
241 Gump Worsley	8.00	20.00
242 Doug Mohns	10.00	25.00
243 Jean-Paul Parise	4.00	10.00
244 Dennis Hextall	8.00	20.00
245 Bobby Orr Double	40.00	100.00
246 Gilbert Perreault Calder	15.00	40.00
247 Phil Esposito Ross	8.00	20.00
248 Giacmn/Ville Vezina	12.00	30.00
249 Johnny Bucyk Byng	8.00	20.00
250 Ed Giacomin AS1	12.00	30.00
251 Bobby Orr AS1	30.00	80.00
252 J.C. Tremblay AS1	12.00	30.00
253 Phil Esposito AS1 UER	10.00	25.00
254 Ken Hodge AS1	5.00	12.00
255 Johnny Bucyk AS1	6.00	15.00
256 Jacques Plante AS2 UER	12.00	30.00
257 Brad Park AS2	5.00	12.00
258 Pat Stapleton AS2	5.00	12.00
259 Dave Keon AS2	12.00	30.00
260 Yvan Cournoyer AS2	5.00	12.00
261 Bobby Hull AS2	15.00	40.00
262 Gordie Howe Retires	40.00	100.00
263 Jean Beliveau Retires	30.00	80.00
264 Checklist Card	150.00	400.00

1971-72 O-Pee-Chee/Topps Booklets

COMPLETE SET (24)	50.00	125.00
1 Bobby Hull	6.00	15.00
2 Phil Esposito	3.00	6.00
3 Dale Tallon	1.25	3.00
4 Jacques Plante	4.00	8.00
5 Roger Crozier	1.25	3.00
6 Henri Richard	1.25	3.00
7 Ed Giacomin	2.50	5.00
8 Gilbert Perreault	3.00	6.00
9 Greg Polis	1.25	3.00
10 Bobby Clarke	5.00	10.00
11 Danny Grant	1.25	3.00
12 Alex Delvecchio	1.25	3.00
13 Tony Esposito	3.00	6.00
14 Garry Unger	1.25	3.00
15 Frank St.Marseille	1.25	3.00
16 Dave Keon	2.50	5.00
17 Ken Dryden	8.00	20.00
18 Rod Gilbert	1.25	3.00
19 Juha Widing	1.25	3.00
20 Orland Kurtenbach	1.25	3.00
21 Jude Drouin	1.25	3.00
22 Gary Smith	1.25	3.00
23 Gordie Howe	8.00	20.00
24 Bobby Orr	10.00	25.00

1971-72 O-Pee-Chee Posters

COMPLETE SET (24)	600.00	1000.00
1 Bobby Orr	125.00	250.00
2 Bob Pulford	10.00	20.00
3 Dave Keon	15.00	30.00
4 Yvan Cournoyer	15.00	30.00
5 Dale Tallon	10.00	20.00
6 Richard Martin	7.50	15.00
7 Rod Gilbert	15.00	30.00
8 Tony Esposito	20.00	40.00
9 Bobby Hull	25.00	50.00
10 Red Berenson	7.50	15.00
11 Norm Ullman	8.00	20.00
12 Orland Kurtenbach	7.50	15.00
13 Guy Lafleur	50.00	100.00
14 Gilbert Perreault	20.00	40.00
15 Jacques Plante	25.00	50.00
16 Bruce Gamble	10.00	25.00
17 Walt McKechnie	7.50	15.00
18 Tim Horton	25.00	50.00
19 Jean Ratelle	15.00	30.00
20 Garry Unger	7.50	15.00
21 Phil Esposito	25.00	50.00
22 Ken Dryden	75.00	150.00
23 Gump Worsley	15.00	30.00
24 Montreal Canadiens	20.00	40.00

1972-73 O-Pee-Chee

COMPLETE SET (340)	900.00	1500.00
1 Johnny Bucyk DP	15.00	40.00
2 Rene Robert RC	8.00	12.00
3 Gary Croteau	4.00	10.00
4 Pat Stapleton	4.00	10.00
5 Ron Harris	4.00	10.00
6 Checklist 1	25.00	60.00
7 Playoff Game 1	6.00	15.00
8 Marcel Dionne	10.00	25.00
9 Bob Berry	4.00	10.00
10 Lou Nanne	4.00	10.00
11 Marc Tardif	4.00	10.00
12 Jean Ratelle	4.00	10.00
13 Craig Cameron RC	4.00	10.00
14 Bobby Clarke	15.00	40.00
15 Jim Rutherford RC	10.00	25.00
16 Andre Dupont RC	4.00	10.00
17 Mike Pelyk	4.00	10.00
18 Dunc Wilson	4.00	10.00
19 Checklist 2	25.00	60.00
20 Playoff Game 2	4.00	10.00
21 Dallas Smith	4.00	10.00
22 Gerry Meehan	4.00	10.00
23 Rick Smith UER	4.00	10.00
24 Pit Martin	4.00	10.00
25 Keith McCreary	4.00	10.00
26 Alex Delvecchio	4.00	10.00
27 Gilles Marotte	4.00	10.00
28 Gump Worsley	4.00	10.00
29 Yvan Cournoyer	4.00	10.00
30 Playoff Game 3	4.00	10.00
31 Vic Hadfield	4.00	10.00
32 Tom Miller RC	4.00	10.00
33 Ed Van Impe	4.00	10.00
34 Greg Polis	4.00	10.00
35 Barclay Plager	4.00	10.00
36 Ron Ellis	4.00	10.00
37 Jocelyn Guevremont	4.00	10.00
38 Playoff Game 4	4.00	10.00
39 Carol Vadnais	4.00	10.00
40 Steve Atkinson	4.00	10.00
41 Ivan Boldirev RC	4.00	10.00
42 Jim Pappin	4.00	10.00
43 Phil Myre RC	20.00	50.00
44 Yvan Cournoyer IA	4.00	10.00
45 Nick Libett	4.00	10.00
46 Juha Widing	4.00	10.00
47 Jude Drouin	4.00	10.00
48A Jean Ratelle IA Def	4.00	10.00
48B Jean Ratelle IA Cent	4.00	10.00
49 Ken Hodge	4.00	10.00
50 Roger Crozier	4.00	10.00
51 Reggie Leach	4.00	10.00
52 Dennis Hull	4.00	10.00
53 Larry Hale RC	4.00	10.00
54 Playoff Game 5	4.00	10.00
55 Tim Ecclestone	4.00	10.00
56 Butch Goring	4.00	10.00
57 Danny Grant	4.00	10.00
58 Bobby Orr IA	40.00	100.00
59 Guy Lafleur	60.00	150.00
60 Jim Neilson	4.00	10.00
61 Brian Spencer	4.00	10.00
62 Joe Watson	4.00	10.00
63 Playoff Game 6	4.00	10.00
64 Jean Pronovost	4.00	10.00
65 Frank St.Marseille	4.00	10.00
66 Bob Baun	4.00	10.00
67 Paul Popiel	4.00	10.00
68 Wayne Cashman	4.00	10.00
69 Tracy Pratt	4.00	10.00
70 Stan Gilbertson	4.00	10.00
71 Keith Magnuson	4.00	10.00
72 Ernie Hicke	4.00	10.00
73 Gary Doak	4.00	10.00
74 Mike Corrigan	4.00	10.00
75 Doug Mohns	4.00	10.00
76 Phil Esposito IA	8.00	20.00
77 Jacques Lemaire	4.00	10.00
78 Pete Stemkowski	4.00	10.00
79 Bill Mikkelson RC	4.00	10.00
80 Rick Foley RC	4.00	10.00
81 Ron Schock	4.00	10.00
82 Phil Roberto	4.00	10.00
83 Jim McKenny	4.00	10.00
84 Wayne Maki	4.00	10.00
85A Brad Park IA Cent	8.00	20.00
85B Brad Park IA Def	5.00	12.00
86 Guy Lapointe	4.00	10.00
87 Bill Fairbairn	4.00	10.00
88 Terry Crisp	4.00	10.00
89 Doug Favell	4.00	10.00
90 Bryan Watson	4.00	10.00
91 Gary Sabourin	4.00	10.00
92 Jacques Plante	15.00	40.00
93 Andre Boudrias	4.00	10.00
94 Mike Walton	4.00	10.00
95 Don Luce	4.00	10.00
96 Joey Johnston	4.00	10.00
97 Doug Jarrett	4.00	10.00
98 Bill MacMillan RC	4.00	10.00
99 Mickey Redmond	4.00	10.00
100 Rogatien Vachon UER	4.00	10.00
101 Barry Gibbs RC	4.00	10.00
102 Frank Mahovlich DP	4.00	10.00
103 Bruce MacGregor	4.00	10.00
104 Ed Westfall	4.00	10.00
105 Rick MacLeish	5.00	12.00
106 Nick Harbaruk	4.00	10.00
107 Jack Egers RC	4.00	10.00
108 Dave Keon	4.00	10.00
109 Barry Wilkins	4.00	10.00
110 Walt Tkaczuk	4.00	10.00
111 Phil Esposito	10.00	25.00
112 Gilles Meloche RC	20.00	50.00
113 Gary Edwards	4.00	10.00
114 Brad Park	10.00	25.00
115 Syl Apps DP	4.00	10.00
116 Jim Lorentz	4.00	10.00
117 Gary Smith	4.00	10.00
118 Ted Harris	4.00	10.00
119 Gerry Desjardins DP	4.00	10.00
120 Garry Unger	4.00	10.00
121 Dale Tallon	4.00	10.00
122 Bill Plager RC	4.00	10.00
123 Red Berenson DP	4.00	10.00
124 Peter Mahovlich DP	4.00	10.00
125 Simon Nolet	4.00	10.00
126 Paul Henderson	4.00	10.00
127 Hart Trophy Winners	4.00	10.00
128 Frank Mahovlich IA	4.00	10.00
129 Bobby Orr	30.00	80.00
130 Bert Marshall	4.00	10.00
131 Ralph Backstrom	4.00	10.00
132 Gilles Villemure	4.00	10.00
133 Dave Burrows RC	4.00	10.00
134 Calder Trophy Winners	4.00	10.00
135 Dallas Smith IA	4.00	10.00
136 Gilbert Perreault DP	10.00	25.00
137 Tony Esposito DP	12.00	30.00
138 Cesare Maniago DP	4.00	10.00
139 Gerry Hart RC	4.00	10.00
140 Jacques Caron RC	4.00	10.00
141 Orland Kurtenbach	4.00	10.00
142 Norris Trophy Winners	4.00	10.00
143 Lew Morrison	4.00	10.00
144 Arnie Brown	4.00	10.00
145 Ken Dryden DP	20.00	50.00
146 Gary Dornhoefer	4.00	10.00
147 Norm Ullman	5.00	12.00
148 Art Ross Trophy	4.00	10.00
149 Orland Kurtenbach IA	4.00	10.00
150 Fred Stanfield	4.00	10.00
151 Dick Redmond DP	4.00	10.00
152 Serge Bernier	4.00	10.00
153 Rod Gilbert	5.00	12.00
154 Duane Rupp	4.00	10.00
155 Vezina Trophy Winners	4.00	10.00
156 Stan Mikita IA	5.00	12.00
157 Richard Martin DP	8.00	20.00
158 Bill White DP	4.00	10.00
159 Bill Goldsworthy DP	4.00	10.00
160 Jack Lynch RC	4.00	10.00
161 Bob Plager DP	4.00	10.00
162 Dave Balon UER	4.00	10.00
163 Noel Price	4.00	10.00
164 Gary Bergman DP	4.00	10.00
165 Pierre Bouchard	4.00	10.00
166 Ross Lonsberry	4.00	10.00
167 Denis Dupere	4.00	10.00
168 Byng Trophy Winners DP	4.00	10.00
169 Ken Hodge	4.00	10.00
170 Don Awrey DP	4.00	10.00
171 Marshall Johnston DP RC	4.00	10.00
172 Terry Harper	4.00	10.00
173 Ed Giacomin	4.00	10.00
174 Bryan Hextall DP	4.00	10.00
175 Conn Smythe Trophy Winners	4.00	10.00
176 Larry Hillman	4.00	10.00
177 Stan Mikita DP	8.00	20.00
178 Charlie Burns	4.00	10.00
179 Brian Marchinko	4.00	10.00
180 Noel Picard DP	4.00	10.00
181 Bobby Schmautz RC	4.00	10.00
182 Richard Martin IA UER	4.00	10.00
183 Pat Quinn	4.00	10.00
184 Denis DeJordy UER	4.00	10.00
185 Serge Savard	10.00	25.00
186 Eddie Shack	4.00	10.00
187 Bill Flett	4.00	10.00
188 Darryl Sittler	12.00	30.00
189 Gump Worsley IA	4.00	10.00
190 Checklist 2	20.00	50.00
191 Garnet Bailey DP	4.00	10.00
192 Walt McKechnie	4.00	10.00
193 Harry Howell	4.00	10.00
194 Rod Seiling	4.00	10.00
195 Darryl Edestrand	4.00	10.00
196 Tony Esposito IA	8.00	20.00
197 Tim Horton	8.00	20.00
198 Chico Maki DP	4.00	10.00
199 Jean-Paul Parise	4.00	10.00
200 Germaine Gagnon UER RC	4.00	10.00
201 Danny O'Shea	4.00	10.00
202 Richard Lemieux RC	4.00	10.00
203 Dan Bouchard RC	10.00	25.00
204 Leon Rochefort	4.00	10.00
205 Jacques Laperriere	4.00	10.00
206 Barry Ashbee	4.00	10.00
207 Garry Monahan	4.00	10.00
209 Dave Keon IA	5.00	12.00
210 Rejean Houle	4.00	10.00
211 Dave Hudson RC	4.00	10.00
212 Ted Irvine	4.00	10.00
213 Don Saleski RC	5.00	12.00
214 Lowell MacDonald	4.00	10.00
215 Mike Murphy RC	4.00	10.00
216 Brian Glennie	4.00	10.00
217 Bobby Lalonde RC	4.00	10.00
218 Bob Leiter	4.00	10.00
219 Don Marcotte	4.00	10.00
220 Jim Schoenfeld RC	10.00	25.00
221 Craig Patrick	4.00	10.00
222 Cliff Koroll	4.00	10.00
223 Guy Charron RC	4.00	10.00
224 Jim Peters	4.00	10.00
225 Dennis Hextall	4.00	10.00
226 Tony Esposito AS1	10.00	25.00
227 Orr/Park AS1	25.00	60.00
228 Bobby Hull AS1	20.00	50.00
229 Rod Gilbert AS1	4.00	10.00
230 Phil Esposito AS1	10.00	25.00
231 Claude Larose UER	4.00	10.00
232 Jim Mair RC	4.00	10.00
233 Bobby Rousseau	4.00	10.00
234 Brent Hughes	4.00	10.00
235 Al McDonough	4.00	10.00
236 Chris Evans RC	4.00	10.00
237 Pierre Jarry RC	4.00	10.00
238 Don Tannahill RC	4.00	10.00
239 Rey Comeau RC	4.00	10.00
240 Gregg Sheppard UER RC	4.00	10.00
241 Dave Dryden	4.00	10.00
242 Ted McAneeley RC	4.00	10.00
243 Lou Angotti	4.00	10.00
244 Len Fontaine RC	4.00	10.00
245 Bill Lesuk RC	4.00	10.00
246 Fred Harvey RC	4.00	10.00
247 Ken Dryden AS2	12.00	30.00
248 Bill White AS2	4.00	10.00
249 Pat Stapleton AS2	4.00	10.00
250 Ratel/Cour/Hadfld LL	5.00	12.00
251 Henri Richard	12.00	30.00
252 Bryan Lefley RC	4.00	10.00
253 Stanley Cup Trophy	80.00	200.00
254 Steve Vickers RC	8.00	20.00
255 Wayne Hillman	4.00	10.00
256 Ken Schinkel UER	4.00	10.00
257 Kevin O'Shea RC	4.00	10.00
258 Ron Low RC	10.00	25.00
259 Don Lever RC	30.00	80.00
260 Randy Manery RC	4.00	10.00
261 Ed Johnston	30.00	80.00
262 Craig Ramsay RC	8.00	20.00
263 Pete Laframboise RC	4.00	10.00
264 Dan Maloney RC	6.00	15.00
265 Bill Collins	4.00	10.00
266 Paul Curtis	4.00	10.00
267 Bob Nevin	4.00	10.00
268 Watson/Magnuson LL	4.00	10.00
269 Jim Roberts	4.00	10.00
270 Brian Lavender RC	4.00	10.00
271 Dale Rolfe	4.00	10.00
272 Espo/Hadf/B.Hull LL	12.00	30.00
273 Michel Belhumeur RC	10.00	25.00
274 Eddie Shack	4.00	10.00
275 Wayne Stephenson RC UER	20.00	50.00
276 Bruins SC Winner	25.00	60.00
277 Rick Kehoe RC	8.00	20.00
278 Gerry O'Flaherty RC	4.00	10.00
279 Jacques Richard RC	6.00	15.00
280 Espo/Orr/Ratelle LL	15.00	40.00
281 Nick Beverley RC	5.00	12.00
282 Larry Carriere RC	4.00	10.00
283 Orr/Espo/Ratelle LL	15.00	40.00
284 Rick Smith IA	4.00	10.00
285 Jerry Korab RC	6.00	15.00
286 Espo/Villem/Worsley LL	10.00	25.00
287 Ron Stackhouse	4.00	10.00
288 Barry Long RC	4.00	10.00
289 Dean Prentice	30.00	80.00
290 Norm Beaudin	6.00	15.00
291 Mike Amodeo RC	8.00	20.00
292 Jim Harrison	12.00	30.00
293 J.C. Tremblay	8.00	20.00
294 Murray Hall	8.00	20.00
295 Bart Crashley	8.00	20.00
296 Wayne Connelly	10.00	25.00
297 Bobby Sheehan	10.00	25.00
298 Ron Anderson	8.00	20.00
299 Chris Bordeleau	8.00	20.00
300 Les Binkley	8.00	20.00
301 Ron Walters	10.00	25.00
302 Jean-Guy Gendron	8.00	20.00
303 Gord Labossiere	10.00	25.00
304 Gerry Odrowski	8.00	20.00
305 Mike McMahon	8.00	20.00
306 Gary Kurt	20.00	50.00
307 Larry Cahan	8.00	20.00
308 Wally Boyer	8.00	20.00
309 Bob Charlebois RC	8.00	20.00
310 Bob Falkenberg	8.00	20.00
311 Jean Payette RC	8.00	20.00
312 Ted Taylor	8.00	20.00
313 Joe Szura	8.00	20.00
314 George Morrison	10.00	25.00
315 Wayne Rivers	8.00	20.00
316 Reg Fleming	8.00	20.00
317 Larry Hornung RC	8.00	20.00
318 Ron Climie RC	8.00	20.00
319 Val Fonteyne	8.00	20.00
320 Michel Archambault RC	8.00	20.00
321 Ab McDonald	8.00	20.00
322 Bob Leduc RC	10.00	25.00
323 Bob Wall	8.00	20.00
324 Alain Caron RC	8.00	20.00
325 Bob Woytowich	8.00	20.00
326 Guy Trottier	8.00	20.00
327 Bill Hicke	8.00	20.00
328 Guy Dufour RC	8.00	20.00
329 Wayne Rutledge RC	20.00	50.00
330 Gary Veneruzzo	8.00	20.00
331 Fred Speck RC	8.00	20.00
332 Ron Ward RC	8.00	20.00
333 Rosaire Paiement	10.00	25.00
334A Checklist 3 ERR	50.00	125.00
334B Checklist 3 COR	40.00	100.00
335 Michel Parizeau RC	10.00	25.00
336 Bobby Hull	30.00	80.00
337 Wayne Carleton	8.00	20.00
338 John McKenzie	8.00	20.00
339 Jim Dorey	8.00	20.00
340 Gerry Cheevers	20.00	50.00
341 Gerry Pinder	12.00	30.00

1972-73 O-Pee-Chee Player Crests

COMPLETE SET (22)	100.00	200.00
1 Pat Quinn	3.00	10.00
2 Phil Esposito	8.00	20.00
3 Bobby Orr	30.00	80.00
4 Richard Martin	2.50	6.00
5 Stan Mikita	4.00	10.00
6 Bill White	2.50	6.00
7 Red Berenson	2.50	6.00
8 Gary Bergman	2.50	6.00
9 Gary Edwards	2.50	6.00
10 Bill Goldsworthy	2.50	6.00
11 Jacques Laperriere	2.50	6.00
12 Ken Dryden	20.00	40.00
13 Ed Westfall	2.50	6.00
14 Walt Tkaczuk	2.50	6.00
15 Brad Park	5.00	12.00
16 Doug Favell	5.00	12.00
17 Eddie Shack	5.00	10.00
18 Jacques Caron	2.50	6.00
19 Paul Henderson	4.00	10.00
20 Jim Harrison	2.50	6.00
21 Dale Tallon	2.50	6.00
22 Orland Kurtenbach	2.50	6.00

1972-73 O-Pee-Chee Team Canada

COMPLETE SET (28)	150.00	300.00
1 Don Awrey	3.00	8.00
2 Red Berenson	3.00	8.00
3 Gary Bergman	3.00	8.00
4 Wayne Cashman	4.00	10.00
5 Bobby Clarke	12.50	25.00
6 Yvan Cournoyer	7.50	15.00
7 Ken Dryden	25.00	50.00
8 Ron Ellis	5.00	12.00
9 Phil Esposito	12.50	25.00
10 Tony Esposito	15.00	30.00
11 Rod Gilbert	5.00	12.00
12 Bill Goldsworthy	3.00	8.00
13 Vic Hadfield	3.00	8.00
14 Paul Henderson	15.00	30.00
15 Dennis Hull	3.00	8.00
16 Guy Lapointe	3.00	8.00
17 Frank Mahovlich	7.50	15.00
18 Pete Mahovlich	3.00	8.00
19 Stan Mikita	10.00	20.00
20 Jean-Paul Parise	3.00	8.00
21 Brad Park	5.00	12.00
22 Gilbert Perreault	3.00	8.00
23 Jean Ratelle	5.00	12.00
24 Mickey Redmond	5.00	12.00
25 Serge Savard	4.00	10.00
26 Rod Seiling	3.00	8.00
27 Pat Stapleton	3.00	8.00
28 Bill White	3.00	8.00

1972-73 O-Pee-Chee Team Logos

COMPLETE SET (30)	550.00	1000.00
1 NHL Logo	10.00	25.00
2 Atlanta Flames SP	100.00	200.00
3 Boston Bruins	5.00	12.00
4 Buffalo Sabres	5.00	12.00
5 California Seals	10.00	25.00
6 Chicago Blackhawks	5.00	12.00
7 Detroit Red Wings	5.00	12.00
8 Los Angeles Kings	5.00	12.00
9 Minnesota North Stars	6.00	15.00
10 Montreal Canadiens	5.00	12.00
11 New York Islanders SP	60.00	120.00
12 New York Rangers	6.00	15.00
13 Philadelphia Flyers	5.00	12.00
14 Pittsburgh Penguins	6.00	15.00
15 St. Louis Blues	5.00	12.00
16 Toronto Maple Leafs	5.00	12.00
17 Vancouver Canucks	8.00	20.00
18 WHA Logo SP	30.00	60.00
19 Chicago Cougars SP	30.00	60.00
20 Cleveland Crusaders SP	40.00	80.00
21 Edmonton Oilers SP	40.00	80.00
22 Houston Aeros SP	40.00	80.00
23 Los Angeles Sharks SP	30.00	60.00
24 Minnesota Fighting Saints SP	50.00	100.00
25 New England Whalers SP	40.00	80.00
26 New York Raiders SP	30.00	60.00
27 Ottawa Nationals SP	40.00	80.00
28 Phila. Blazers SP	40.00	80.00
29 Quebec Nordiques SP	30.00	60.00
30 Winnipeg Jets SP	50.00	100.00

1973-74 O-Pee-Chee

COMPLETE SET (264)	300.00	500.00
1 Alex Delvecchio	5.00	12.00
2 Gilles Meloche	4.00	10.00
3 Phil Roberto	4.00	10.00
4 Orland Kurtenbach	4.00	10.00
5 Gilles Marotte	4.00	10.00
6 Stan Mikita	15.00	40.00

7 Paul Henderson	4.00	10.00
8 Gregg Sheppard	4.00	10.00
9 Rod Seiling	4.00	10.00
10 Red Berenson	4.00	10.00
11 Jean Pronovost	4.00	10.00
12 Dick Redmond	4.00	10.00
13 Keith McCreary	4.00	10.00
14 Bryan Watson	4.00	10.00
15 Garry Unger	4.00	10.00
16 Neil Komadoski RC	4.00	10.00
17 Marcel Dionne	8.00	20.00
18 Ernie Hicke	4.00	10.00
19 Andre Boudrias	4.00	10.00
20 Bill Flett	4.00	10.00
21 Marshall Johnston	4.00	10.00
22 Gerry Meehan	4.00	10.00
23 Ed Johnston	4.00	10.00
24 Serge Savard	12.00	30.00
25 Walt Tkaczuk	4.00	10.00
26 Ken Hodge	4.00	10.00
27 Norm Ullman	5.00	12.00
28 Cliff Koroll	4.00	10.00
29 Rey Comeau	4.00	10.00
30 Bobby Orr	25.00	60.00
31 Wayne Stephenson	4.00	10.00
32 Dan Maloney	4.00	10.00
33 Henry Boucha RC	4.00	10.00
34 Gerry Hart	4.00	10.00
35 Bobby Schmautz	4.00	10.00
36 Ross Lonsberry	4.00	10.00
37 Ted McAneeley	4.00	10.00
38 Don Luce	4.00	10.00
39 Jim McKenny	4.00	10.00
40 Jacques Laperriere	4.00	10.00
41 Bill Fairbairn	4.00	10.00
42 Craig Cameron	4.00	10.00
43 Bryan Hextall	4.00	10.00
44 Chuck Lefley RC	4.00	10.00
45 Dan Bouchard	4.00	10.00
46 Jean-Paul Parise	4.00	10.00
47 Barclay Plager	4.00	10.00
48 Mike Corrigan	4.00	10.00
49 Nick Libett	4.00	10.00
50 Bobby Clarke	6.00	15.00
51 Bert Marshall	4.00	10.00
52 Craig Patrick	4.00	10.00
53 Richard Lemieux	4.00	10.00
54 Tracy Pratt	4.00	10.00
55 Ron Ellis	4.00	10.00
56 Jacques Lemaire	6.00	15.00
57 Steve Vickers	4.00	10.00
58 Carol Vadnais	4.00	10.00
59 Jim Rutherford	4.00	10.00
60 Rick Kehoe	4.00	10.00
61 Pat Quinn	4.00	10.00
62 Bill Goldsworthy	4.00	10.00
63 Dave Dryden	4.00	10.00
64 Rogatien Vachon	15.00	40.00
65 Gary Bergman	4.00	10.00
66 Bernie Parent	12.00	30.00
67 Ed Westfall	4.00	10.00
68 Ivan Boldirev	4.00	10.00
69 Don Tannahill	4.00	10.00
70 Gilbert Perreault	20.00	50.00
71 Mike Pelyk	4.00	10.00
72 Guy Lafleur	8.00	20.00
73 Pit Martin	4.00	10.00
74 Gilles Gilbert RC	5.00	12.00
75 Jim Lorentz	4.00	10.00
76 Syl Apps	4.00	10.00
77 Phil Myre	4.00	10.00
78 Bill White	4.00	10.00
79 Jack Egers	4.00	10.00
80 Terry Harper	4.00	10.00
81 Bill Barber RC	20.00	50.00
82 Roy Edwards	4.00	10.00
83 Brian Spencer	4.00	10.00
84 Reggie Leach	4.00	10.00
85 Wayne Cashman	4.00	10.00
86 Jim Schoenfeld	5.00	12.00
87 Henri Richard	20.00	50.00
88 Dennis O'Brien RC	4.00	10.00
89 Al McDonough	4.00	10.00
90 Tony Esposito	12.00	30.00
91 Joe Watson	4.00	10.00
92 Flames Team	4.00	10.00
93 Bruins Team	4.00	10.00
94 Sabres Team	4.00	10.00
95 Golden Seals Team	4.00	10.00
96 Blackhawks Team	8.00	20.00
97 Red Wings Team	4.00	10.00
98 Kings Team	4.00	10.00
99 North Stars Team	10.00	25.00
100 Canadiens Team	4.00	10.00
101 Islanders Team	4.00	10.00
102 Rangers Team	4.00	10.00
103 Flyers Team	4.00	10.00
104 Penguins Team	4.00	10.00
105 Blues Team	4.00	10.00
106 Maple Leafs Team	8.00	20.00
107 Canucks Team	6.00	15.00
108 Vic Hadfield	4.00	10.00
109 Tom Reid	4.00	10.00
110 Hilliard Graves RC	4.00	10.00
111 Don Lever	4.00	10.00
112 Jim Pappin	4.00	10.00
113 Andre Dupont	4.00	10.00
114 Guy Lapointe	4.00	10.00
115 Dennis Hextall	4.00	10.00
116 Checklist 1	20.00	50.00
117 Bob Leiter	4.00	10.00
118 Ab DeMarco	4.00	10.00
119 Gilles Villemure	4.00	10.00
120 Phil Esposito	8.00	20.00
121 Mike Robitaille	4.00	10.00
122 Real Lemieux	4.00	10.00
123 Jim Neilson	4.00	10.00
124 Steve Durbano RC	4.00	10.00
125 Jude Drouin	4.00	10.00
126 Gary Smith	4.00	10.00
127 Cesare Maniago	4.00	10.00
128 Lowell MacDonald	4.00	10.00
129 Checklist 2	40.00	100.00
130 Billy Harris RC	4.00	10.00
131 Randy Manery	4.00	10.00
132 Darryl Sittler	15.00	40.00
133 P.Espo/MacLeish LL	4.00	10.00
134 P.Espo/B.Clarke LL	8.00	20.00
135 P.Espo/B.Clarke LL	15.00	40.00
136 K.Dryden/T.Espo LL	8.00	20.00
137 Schultz/Schnfeld LL	4.00	10.00
138 P.Espo/MacLeish LL	4.00	10.00
139 Rene Robert	4.00	10.00
140 Dave Burrows	4.00	10.00
141 Jean Ratelle	5.00	12.00
142 Billy Smith RC	30.00	80.00
143 Jocelyn Guevremont	4.00	10.00
144 Tim Ecclestone	4.00	10.00
145 Frank Mahovlich	8.00	20.00
146 Rick MacLeish	5.00	12.00
147 Johnny Bucyk	8.00	20.00
148 Bob Plager	4.00	10.00
149 Curt Bennett RC	4.00	10.00
150 Dave Keon	10.00	25.00
151 Keith Magnuson	4.00	10.00
152 Walt McKechnie	4.00	10.00
153 Roger Crozier	4.00	10.00
154 Ted Harris	4.00	10.00
155 Butch Goring	4.00	10.00
156 Rod Gilbert	6.00	15.00
157 Yvan Cournoyer	12.00	30.00
158 Doug Favell	4.00	10.00
159 Juha Widing	4.00	10.00
160 Ed Giacomin	8.00	20.00
161 Germaine Gagnon UER	4.00	10.00
162 Dennis Kearns	4.00	10.00
163 Bill Collins	4.00	10.00
164 Peter Mahovlich	4.00	10.00
165 Brad Park	20.00	50.00
166 Dave Schultz RC	10.00	25.00
167 Dallas Smith	4.00	10.00
168 Gary Sabourin	4.00	10.00
169 Jacques Richard	4.00	10.00
170 Brian Glennie	4.00	10.00
171 Dennis Hull	4.00	10.00
172 Joey Johnston	4.00	10.00
173 Richard Martin	6.00	15.00
174 Barry Gibbs	4.00	10.00
175 Bob Berry	4.00	10.00
176 Greg Polis	4.00	10.00
177 Dale Rolfe	4.00	10.00
178 Gerry Desjardins	4.00	10.00
179 Bobby Lalonde	4.00	10.00
180 Mickey Redmond	4.00	10.00
181 Jim Roberts	4.00	10.00
182 Gary Dornhoefer	4.00	10.00
183 Derek Sanderson	6.00	15.00
184 Brent Hughes	4.00	10.00
185 Larry Romanchych RC	4.00	10.00
186 Pierre Jarry	4.00	10.00
187 Doug Jarrett	4.00	10.00
188 Bob Stewart RC	4.00	10.00
189 Tim Horton	15.00	40.00
190 Fred Harvey	4.00	10.00
191 Series A/Cand/Sabr	4.00	10.00
192 Series B/Flyrs/Stars	4.00	10.00
193 Series C/Hwks/Blues	4.00	10.00
194 Series D/Rngr/Bruins	4.00	10.00
195 Series E/Cndn/Flyr	4.00	10.00
196 Series F/Blckh/Rngr	4.00	10.00
197 Series G/Cndn/Hawk	4.00	10.00
198 Canadiens Champs	5.00	12.00
199 Gary Edwards	4.00	10.00
200 Ron Schock	4.00	10.00
201 Bruce MacGregor	4.00	10.00
202 Bob Nystrom RC	30.00	80.00
203 Jerry Korab	4.00	10.00
204 Thommie Bergman RC	4.00	10.00
205 Bill Lesuk	4.00	10.00
206 Ed Van Impe	4.00	10.00
207 Doug Roberts	4.00	10.00
208 Chris Evans	4.00	10.00
209 Lynn Powis RC	4.00	10.00
210 Denis Dupere	4.00	10.00
211 Dale Tallon	4.00	10.00
212 Stan Gilbertson	4.00	10.00
213 Craig Ramsay	4.00	10.00
214 Danny Grant	4.00	10.00
215 Doug Volmar RC	4.00	10.00
216 Darryl Edestrand	4.00	10.00
217 Pete Stemkowski	4.00	10.00
218 Lorne Henning RC	4.00	10.00
219 Bryan McSheffrey RC	4.00	10.00
220 Guy Charron	4.00	10.00
221 Wayne Thomas RC	8.00	20.00
222 Simon Nolet	4.00	10.00
223 Fred O'Donnell RC	4.00	10.00
224 Lou Angotti	4.00	10.00
225 Arnie Brown	4.00	10.00
226 Garry Monahan	4.00	10.00
227 Chico Maki	4.00	10.00
228 Gary Croteau	4.00	10.00
229 Paul Terbenche	4.00	10.00
230 Gump Worsley	8.00	20.00
231 Jim Peters	4.00	10.00
232 Jack Lynch	4.00	10.00
233 Bobby Rousseau	4.00	10.00
234 Dave Hudson	4.00	10.00
235 Gregg Boddy RC	4.00	10.00
236 Ron Stackhouse	4.00	10.00
237 Larry Robinson RC	100.00	250.00
238 Bobby Taylor RC	12.00	30.00
239 Nick Beverley	4.00	10.00
240 Don Awrey	4.00	10.00
241 Doug Mohns	4.00	10.00
242 Eddie Shack	5.00	12.00
243 Phil Russell RC	5.00	12.00
244 Pete Laframboise	4.00	10.00
245 Steve Atkinson	4.00	10.00
246 Lou Nanne	4.00	10.00
247 Yvon Labre RC	4.00	10.00
248 Ted Irvine	4.00	10.00
249 Tom Miller	4.00	10.00
250 Gerry O'Flaherty	4.00	10.00
251 Larry Johnston RC	4.00	10.00
252 Michel Plasse RC	8.00	20.00
253 Bob Kelly	4.00	10.00
254 Terry O'Reilly RC	25.00	60.00
255 Pierre Plante RC	4.00	10.00
256 Noel Price	4.00	10.00
257 Dunc Wilson	4.00	10.00
258 J.P. Bordeleau RC	4.00	10.00
259 Terry Murray RC	4.00	10.00
260 Larry Carriere	4.00	10.00
261 Pierre Bouchard	4.00	10.00
262 Frank St.Marseille	4.00	10.00
263 Checklist 3	15.00	40.00
264 Fred Barrett	4.00	10.00

1973-74 O-Pee-Chee Rings

COMPLETE SET (17)	75.00	175.00
1 Vancouver Canucks	3.00	8.00
2 Montreal Canadiens	5.00	12.00
3 Toronto Maple Leafs	3.00	8.00
4 NHL Logo	3.00	8.00
5 Minnesota North Stars	3.00	8.00
6 New York Rangers	3.00	8.00
7 California Seals	8.00	20.00
8 Pittsburgh Penguins	5.00	12.00
9 Philadelphia Flyers	3.00	8.00
10 Chicago Blackhawks	3.00	8.00
11 Boston Bruins	3.00	8.00
12 Los Angeles Kings	3.00	8.00
13 Detroit Red Wings	3.00	8.00
14 St. Louis Blues	3.00	8.00
15 Buffalo Sabres	3.00	8.00
16 Atlanta Flames	8.00	20.00
17 New York Islanders	3.00	8.00

1973-74 O-Pee-Chee Team Logos

COMPLETE SET (17)	25.00	60.00
1 NHL Logo	2.00	5.00
2 Atlanta Flames	6.00	15.00
3 Boston Bruins	3.00	6.00
4 Buffalo Sabres	2.00	5.00
5 California Seals	5.00	10.00
6 Chicago Blackhawks	2.00	5.00
7 Detroit Red Wings	3.00	6.00
8 Los Angeles Kings	2.00	5.00
9 Minnesota North Stars	3.00	6.00
10 Montreal Canadiens	3.00	6.00
11 New York Islanders	5.00	10.00
12 New York Rangers	2.00	5.00
13 Philadelphia Flyers	2.00	5.00
14 Pittsburgh Penguins	3.00	6.00
15 St. Louis Blues	2.00	5.00
16 Toronto Maple Leafs	3.00	6.00
17 Vancouver Canucks	2.00	5.00

1973-74 O-Pee-Chee WHA Posters

COMPLETE SET (20)	50.00	100.00
1 Al Smith	2.50	5.00
2 J.C. Tremblay	2.50	5.00
3 Guy Dufour	1.50	3.00
4 Pat Stapleton	2.50	5.00
5 Rosaire Paiement	1.50	3.00
6 Gerry Cheevers	5.00	10.00
7 Gerry Pinder	2.00	4.00
8 Wayne Carleton	1.50	3.00
9 Bob Leduc	1.50	3.00
10 Andre Lacroix	2.50	5.00
11 Jim Harrison	1.50	3.00
12 Ron Climie	1.50	3.00
13 Gordie Howe	12.50	25.00
14 The Howe Family	12.50	25.00
15 Mike Walton	2.00	4.00
16 Bobby Hull	10.00	20.00
17 Chris Bordeleau	1.50	3.00
18 Claude St.Sauveur	1.50	3.00
19 Bryan Campbell	1.50	3.00
20 Marc Tardif	2.50	5.00

1974-75 O-Pee-Chee

COMPLETE SET (396)	300.00	500.00
1 P.Espo/Gldswrthy LL	30.00	80.00
2 B.Orr/D.Hextall LL	15.00	40.00
3 P.Espo/B.Clarke LL	5.00	12.00
4 Favell/B.Parent LL	4.00	10.00
5 Watson/D.Schulz LL	4.00	10.00
6 Redmond/MacLsh LL	4.00	10.00
7 Gary Bromley RC	4.00	10.00
8 Bill Barber	5.00	12.00
9 Emile Francis CO	4.00	10.00
10 Gilles Gilbert	4.00	10.00
11 John Davidson RC	20.00	50.00
12 Ron Ellis	4.00	10.00
13 Syl Apps	4.00	10.00
14 Richard/Lysiak TL	4.00	10.00
15 Dan Bouchard	4.00	10.00
16 Ivan Boldirev	4.00	10.00
17 Gary Coalter RC	4.00	10.00
18 Bob Berry	4.00	10.00
19 Red Berenson	4.00	10.00
20 Stan Mikita	5.00	12.00
21 Fred Shero CO RC	20.00	50.00
22 Gary Smith	4.00	10.00
23 Bill Mikkelson	4.00	10.00
24 Jacques Lemaire UER	4.00	10.00
25 Gilbert Perreault	20.00	50.00
26 Cesare Maniago	4.00	10.00
27 Bobby Schmautz	4.00	10.00
28 Espo/Orr/Bucyk TL	10.00	25.00
29 Steve Vickers	4.00	10.00
30 Lowell MacDonald UER	4.00	10.00
31 Fred Stanfield	4.00	10.00
32 Ed Westfall	4.00	10.00
33 Curt Bennett	4.00	10.00
34 Bep Guidolin CO	4.00	10.00
35 Cliff Koroll	4.00	10.00
36 Gary Croteau	4.00	10.00
37 Mike Corrigan	4.00	10.00
38 Henry Boucha	4.00	10.00
39 Ron Low	4.00	10.00
40 Darryl Sittler	15.00	40.00
41 Tracy Pratt	4.00	10.00
42 Martin/Robert TL	4.00	10.00
43 Larry Carriere	4.00	10.00
44 Gary Dornhoefer	4.00	10.00
45 Denis Herron RC	5.00	12.00
46 Doug Favell	4.00	10.00
47 Dave Gardner RC	4.00	10.00
48 Morris Mott RC	4.00	10.00
49 Marc Boileau CO	4.00	10.00
50 Brad Park	8.00	20.00
51 Bob Leiter	4.00	10.00
52 Tom Reid	4.00	10.00
53 Serge Savard	4.00	10.00
54 Checklist 1-132 UER	80.00	200.00
55 Terry Harper	4.00	10.00
56 Seals Leaders	4.00	10.00
57 Guy Charron	4.00	10.00
58 Pit Martin	4.00	10.00
59 Chris Evans	4.00	10.00
60 Bernie Parent	5.00	12.00
61 Jim Lorentz	4.00	10.00
62 Dave Kryskow RC	4.00	10.00
63 Lou Angotti CO	4.00	10.00
64 Bill Flett	4.00	10.00
65 Vic Hadfield	4.00	10.00
66 Wayne Merrick RC	4.00	10.00
67 Andre Dupont	4.00	10.00
68 Tom Lysiak RC	4.00	10.00
69 Pappin/Mikita/Bord TL	4.00	10.00
70 Guy Lapointe	4.00	10.00
71 Gerry O'Flaherty	4.00	10.00
72 Marcel Dionne	15.00	40.00
73 Butch Deadmarsh RC	10.00	25.00
74 Butch Goring	4.00	10.00
75 Keith Magnuson	4.00	10.00
76 Red Kelly CO	4.00	10.00
77 Pete Stemkowski	4.00	10.00
78 Jim Roberts	4.00	10.00
79 Don Luce	4.00	10.00
80 Don Awrey	4.00	10.00
81 Rick Kehoe	4.00	10.00
82 Billy Smith	20.00	50.00
83 Jean-Paul Parise	4.00	10.00
84 Rdmnd/Dnne/Hoga TL	4.00	10.00
85 Ed Van Impe	4.00	10.00
86 Randy Manery	4.00	10.00
87 Barclay Plager	4.00	10.00
88 Inge Hammarstrom RC	4.00	10.00
89 Ab DeMarco	4.00	10.00
90 Bill White	4.00	10.00
91 Al Arbour CO	4.00	10.00
92 Bob Stewart	4.00	10.00
93 Jack Egers	4.00	10.00
94 Don Lever	4.00	10.00
95 Reggie Leach	4.00	10.00
96 Dennis O'Brien	4.00	10.00
97 Peter Mahovlich	4.00	10.00
98 Grng/St.Mrsle/Kzk TL	4.00	10.00
99 Gerry Meehan	4.00	10.00
100 Bobby Orr	50.00	125.00
101 Jean Potvin RC	4.00	10.00
102 Rod Seiling	4.00	10.00
103 Keith McCreary	4.00	10.00
104 Phil Maloney CO RC	4.00	10.00
105 Denis Dupere	4.00	10.00
106 Steve Durbano	4.00	10.00
107 Bob Plager UER	4.00	10.00
108 Chris Oddleifson RC	4.00	10.00
109 Jim Neilson	4.00	10.00
110 Jean Pronovost	4.00	10.00
111 Don Kozak RC	4.00	10.00
112 Gldswrthy/Hxtall TL	4.00	10.00
113 Jim Pappin	4.00	10.00
114 Richard Lemieux	4.00	10.00
115 Dennis Hextall	4.00	10.00
116 Bill Hogaboam RC	4.00	10.00
117 Vrgrt/Schmt/Boud TL	4.00	10.00
118 Jimmy Anderson CO	4.00	10.00
119 Walt Tkaczuk	4.00	10.00
120 Mickey Redmond	4.00	10.00
121 Jim Schoenfeld	4.00	10.00
122 Jocelyn Guevremont	4.00	10.00
123 Bob Nystrom	4.00	10.00
124 Cour/F.Mahov/Lrse TL	4.00	10.00
125 Lew Morrison	4.00	10.00
126 Terry Murray	4.00	10.00
127 Richard Martin AS	4.00	10.00
128 Ken Hodge AS	4.00	10.00
129 Phil Esposito AS	4.00	10.00
130 Bobby Orr AS	15.00	40.00
131 Brad Park AS	4.00	10.00
132 Gilles Gilbert AS	4.00	10.00
133 Lowell MacDonald AS	4.00	10.00
134 Bill Goldsworthy AS	4.00	10.00
135 Bobby Clarke AS	6.00	15.00
136 Bill White AS	4.00	10.00
137 Dave Burrows AS	4.00	10.00
138 Bernie Parent AS	4.00	10.00
139 Jacques Richard	4.00	10.00
140 Yvan Cournoyer	4.00	10.00
141 R.Gilbert/B.Park TL	4.00	10.00
142 Rene Robert	4.00	10.00
143 J. Bob Kelly RC	4.00	10.00
144 Ross Lonsberry	4.00	10.00
145 Jean Ratelle	4.00	10.00
146 Dallas Smith	4.00	10.00
147 Bernie Geoffrion CO	4.00	10.00
148 Ted McAneeley	4.00	10.00
149 Pierre Plante	4.00	10.00
150 Dennis Hull	4.00	10.00
151 Dave Keon	4.00	10.00
152 Dave Dunn RC	4.00	10.00
153 Michel Belhumeur	4.00	10.00
154 Clarke/D.Schultz TL	4.00	10.00
155 Ken Dryden	30.00	80.00
156 John Wright RC	4.00	10.00
157 Larry Romanchych	4.00	10.00
158 Ralph Stewart RC	4.00	10.00
159 Mike Robitaille	4.00	10.00
160 Ed Giacomin	4.00	10.00
161 Don Cherry CO RC	50.00	125.00
162 Checklist 133-264	15.00	40.00
163 Rick MacLeish	4.00	10.00
164 Greg Polis	4.00	10.00
165 Carol Vadnais	4.00	10.00
166 Pete Laframboise	4.00	10.00
167 Ron Schock	4.00	10.00
168 Lanny McDonald RC	40.00	100.00
169 Scouts Emblem	4.00	10.00
170 Tony Esposito	30.00	80.00
171 Pierre Jarry	4.00	10.00
172 Dan Maloney	4.00	10.00
173 Peter McDuffe	4.00	10.00
174 Danny Grant	4.00	10.00
175 John Stewart RC	4.00	10.00
176 Floyd Smith CO	4.00	10.00
177 Bert Marshall	4.00	10.00
178 Chuck Lefley UER	4.00	10.00
179 Gilles Villemure	4.00	10.00
180 Borje Salming RC	60.00	150.00
181 Doug Mohns	4.00	10.00
182 Barry Wilkins	4.00	10.00
183 MacDonald/Apps TL	4.00	10.00
184 Gregg Sheppard	4.00	10.00
185 Joey Johnston	4.00	10.00
186 Dick Redmond	4.00	10.00
187 Simon Nolet	4.00	10.00
188 Ron Stackhouse	4.00	10.00
189 Marshall Johnston	4.00	10.00
190 Richard Martin	4.00	10.00
191 Andre Boudrias	4.00	10.00
192 Steve Atkinson	4.00	10.00
193 Nick Libett	4.00	10.00
194 Bob Murdoch Kings RC	4.00	10.00
195 Denis Potvin RC	40.00	100.00
196 Dave Schultz	4.00	10.00
197 Unger/Plante TL	4.00	10.00
198 Jim McKenny	4.00	10.00
199 Gerry Hart	4.00	10.00
200 Phil Esposito	40.00	100.00
201 Rod Gilbert	4.00	10.00
202 Jacques Laperriere	4.00	10.00
203 Barry Gibbs	4.00	10.00
204 Billy Reay CO	4.00	10.00
205 Gilles Meloche	4.00	10.00
206 Wayne Cashman	4.00	10.00
207 Dennis Ververgaert RC	4.00	10.00
208 Phil Roberto	4.00	10.00
209 Quarter Finals	4.00	10.00
210 Quarter Finals	4.00	10.00
211 Quarter Finals	4.00	10.00
212 Quarter Finals	4.00	10.00
213 Semi-Finals	4.00	10.00
214 Semi-Finals	4.00	10.00
215 Stanley Cup Finals	4.00	10.00
216 Flyers Champions	4.00	10.00
217 Joe Watson	4.00	10.00
218 Wayne Stephenson	4.00	10.00
219 Sittlr/Ullmn/Hend TL	4.00	10.00
220 Bill Goldsworthy	4.00	10.00
221 Don Marcotte	4.00	10.00
222 Alex Delvecchio CO	4.00	10.00
223 Stan Gilbertson	4.00	10.00
224 Mike Murphy	4.00	10.00
225 Jim Rutherford	4.00	10.00
226 Phil Russell	4.00	10.00
227 Lynn Powis	4.00	10.00
228 Billy Harris	4.00	10.00
229 Bob Pulford CO	4.00	10.00
230 Ken Hodge	4.00	10.00
231 Bill Fairbairn	4.00	10.00
232 Guy Lafleur	20.00	50.00
233 Harr/Stw/Ptvn TL UER	4.00	10.00
234 Fred Barrett	4.00	10.00
235 Rogatien Vachon	15.00	40.00
236 Norm Ullman	4.00	10.00
237 Garry Unger	4.00	10.00
238 Jack Gordon CO RC	4.00	10.00
239 Johnny Bucyk	4.00	10.00
240 Bob Dailey RC	4.00	10.00
241 Dave Burrows	4.00	10.00
242 Len Frig RC	4.00	10.00
243 Henri Richard Mstrsn	4.00	10.00
244 Phil Esposito Hart	4.00	10.00
245 Johnny Bucyk Byng	4.00	10.00
246 Phil Esposito Ross	5.00	12.00
247 Wales Trophy	4.00	10.00
248 Bobby Orr Norris	12.00	30.00
249 Bernie Parent Vezina	4.00	10.00
250 Philadelphia Flyers SC	15.00	40.00
251 Bernie Parent Smythe	4.00	10.00
252 Denis Potvin Calder	5.00	12.00
253 Campbell Trophy	4.00	10.00
254 Pierre Bouchard	4.00	10.00
255 Jude Drouin	4.00	10.00
256 Capitals Emblem	4.00	10.00
257 Michel Plasse	4.00	10.00
258 Juha Widing	4.00	10.00
259 Bryan Watson	4.00	10.00
260 Bobby Clarke UER	5.00	12.00
261 Scotty Bowman CO RC	25.00	60.00
262 Craig Patrick	4.00	10.00
263 Craig Cameron	4.00	10.00
264 Ted Irvine	4.00	10.00
265 Ed Johnston	4.00	10.00
266 Dave Forbes RC	4.00	10.00
267 Red Wings Team CL	4.00	10.00
268 Rick Dudley RC	4.00	10.00
269 Darcy Rota RC	4.00	10.00
270 Phil Myre	4.00	10.00
271 Larry Brown RC	4.00	10.00
272 Bob Neely RC	4.00	10.00
273 Jerry Byers RC	4.00	10.00
274 Penguins Team CL	4.00	10.00
275 Glenn Goldup RC	4.00	10.00
276 Ron Harris	4.00	10.00
277 Joe Lundrigan RC	4.00	10.00
278 Mike Christie RC	4.00	10.00
279 Doug Rombough RC	4.00	10.00
280 Larry Robinson	15.00	40.00
281 Blues Team CL	4.00	10.00
282 John Marks RC	4.00	10.00
283 Don Saleski	4.00	10.00
284 Rick Wilson RC	4.00	10.00
285 Andre Savard RC	4.00	10.00
286 Pat Quinn	4.00	10.00
287 Kings Team CL	4.00	10.00
288 Norm Gratton	4.00	10.00
289 Ian Turnbull RC	4.00	10.00
290 Derek Sanderson	4.00	10.00
291 Murray Oliver	4.00	10.00
292 Wilf Paiement RC	4.00	10.00
293 Nelson Debenedet RC	4.00	10.00
294 Greg Joly RC	4.00	10.00
295 Terry O'Reilly	4.00	10.00
296 Rey Comeau	4.00	10.00
297 Michel Larocque RC	30.00	80.00
298 Floyd Thomson RC	4.00	10.00
299 Jean-Guy Lagace RC	4.00	10.00
300 Flyers Team CL	4.00	10.00
301 Al MacAdam RC	4.00	10.00
302 George Ferguson RC	4.00	10.00
303 Jimmy Watson RC	4.00	10.00
304 Rick Middleton RC	15.00	40.00
305 Craig Ramsay UER	4.00	10.00
306 Hilliard Graves	4.00	10.00
307 Islanders Team CL	4.00	10.00
308 Blake Dunlop RC	4.00	10.00
309 J.P. Bordeleau	4.00	10.00
310 Brian Glennie	4.00	10.00
311 Checklist 265-396 UER	30.00	80.00
312 Doug Roberts	4.00	10.00
313 Darryl Edestrand	4.00	10.00
314 Ron Anderson	4.00	10.00
315 Blackhawks Team CL	4.00	10.00
316 Steve Shutt RC	40.00	100.00
317 Doug Horbul RC	4.00	10.00
318 Billy Lochead RC	4.00	10.00
319 Fred Harvey	4.00	10.00
320 Gene Carr RC	4.00	10.00
321 Henri Richard	4.00	10.00
322 Canucks Team CL	4.00	10.00
323 Tim Ecclestone	4.00	10.00
324 Dave Lewis RC	4.00	10.00
325 Lou Nanne	4.00	10.00
326 Bobby Rousseau	4.00	10.00
327 Dunc Wilson	4.00	10.00
328 Brian Spencer	4.00	10.00
329 Rick Hampton RC	4.00	10.00
330 Canadiens Team CL UER	4.00	10.00
331 Jack Lynch	4.00	10.00
332 Garnet Bailey	4.00	10.00
333 Al Sims RC	4.00	10.00
334 Orest Kindrachuk RC	4.00	10.00
335 Dave Hudson	4.00	10.00
336 Bob Murray RC	4.00	10.00
337 Sabres Team CL	4.00	10.00
338 Sheldon Kannegiesser	4.00	10.00
339 Bill MacMillan	4.00	10.00
340 Paulin Bordeleau RC	4.00	10.00
341 Dale Rolfe	4.00	10.00
342 Yvon Lambert RC	4.00	10.00
343 Bob Paradise RC	4.00	10.00
344 Germaine Gagnon UER	4.00	10.00
345 Yvon Labre	4.00	10.00
346 Chris Ahrens RC	4.00	10.00
347 Doug Grant RC	4.00	10.00
348 Blaine Stoughton RC	4.00	10.00
349 Gregg Boddy	4.00	10.00
350 Bruins Team CL	4.00	10.00
351 Doug Jarrett	4.00	10.00
352 Terry Crisp	4.00	10.00
353 Glenn Resch UER RC	20.00	50.00
354 Jerry Korab	4.00	10.00
355 Stan Weir RC	4.00	10.00
356 Noel Price	4.00	10.00
357 Bill Clement RC	8.00	20.00
358 Neil Komadoski	4.00	10.00
359 Murray Wilson RC	4.00	10.00
360 Dale Tallon UER	4.00	10.00
361 Gary Doak	4.00	10.00
362 Randy Rota RC	4.00	10.00
363 North Stars Team CL	4.00	10.00
364 Bill Collins	4.00	10.00
365 Thommie Bergman UER	4.00	10.00
366 Dennis Kearns	4.00	10.00
367 Lorne Henning	4.00	10.00
368 Gary Sabourin	4.00	10.00
369 Mike Bloom RC	4.00	10.00
370 Rangers Team CL	4.00	10.00
371 Gary Simmons RC	5.00	12.00
372 Dwight Bialowas RC	4.00	10.00
373 Gilles Marotte	4.00	10.00
374 Frank St.Marseille	4.00	10.00
375 Garry Howatt RC	4.00	10.00
376 Ross Brooks RC	4.00	10.00
377 Flames Team CL	4.00	10.00
378 Bob Nevin	4.00	10.00
379 Lyle Moffat RC	4.00	10.00
380 Bob Kelly	4.00	10.00
381 John Gould RC	4.00	10.00
382 Dave Fortier RC	4.00	10.00
383 Jean Hamel RC	4.00	10.00
384 Bert Wilson RC	4.00	10.00
385 Chuck Arnason RC	4.00	10.00
386 Bruce Cowick RC	4.00	10.00
387 Ernie Hicke	4.00	10.00
388 Bob Gainey RC	40.00	100.00
389 Vic Venasky RC	4.00	10.00
390 Maple Leafs Team CL	4.00	10.00
391 Eric Vail RC	4.00	10.00
392 Bobby Lalonde	4.00	10.00
393 Jerry Butler RC	4.00	10.00
394 Tom Williams	4.00	10.00
395 Chico Maki	4.00	10.00
396 Tom Bladon RC	5.00	12.00

1974-75 O-Pee-Chee WHA

COMPLETE SET (66)	75.00	200.00
1 Gord/Mark/Marty Howe	25.00	60.00
2 Bruce MacGregor	3.00	8.00
3 Wayne Dillon RC	3.00	8.00
4 Ulf Nilsson RC	5.00	12.00
5 Serge Bernier	3.00	8.00
6 Bryan Campbell	3.00	8.00
7 Rosaire Paiement	3.00	8.00
8 Tom Webster	3.00	8.00
9 Gerry Pinder	3.00	8.00
10 Mike Walton	3.00	8.00
11 Norm Beaudin	3.00	8.00
12 Bob Whitlock RC	3.00	8.00
13 Wayne Rivers	3.00	8.00
14 Gerry Odrowski	3.00	8.00
15 Ron Climie	3.00	8.00
16 Tom Simpson RC	3.00	8.00
17 Anders Hedberg RC	12.00	30.00
18 J.C. Tremblay	3.00	8.00
19 Mike Pelyk	3.00	8.00
20 Dave Dryden	3.00	8.00
21 Ron Ward	3.00	8.00
22 Larry Lund RC	3.00	8.00
23 Ron Buchanan RC	3.00	8.00
24 Pat Hickey RC	3.00	8.00
25 Danny Lawson RC	3.00	8.00
26 Bob Guindon RC	3.00	8.00
27 Gene Peacosh RC	3.00	8.00
28 Fran Huck	3.00	8.00
29 Al Hamilton	3.00	8.00
30 Gerry Cheevers	6.00	15.00
31 Heikki Riihiranta RC	3.00	8.00
32 Don Burgess RC	3.00	8.00
33 John French RC	3.00	8.00
34 Jim Wiste RC	3.00	8.00
35 Pat Stapleton	5.00	12.00
36 J.P. LeBlanc RC	3.00	8.00
37 Mike Antonovich RC	3.00	8.00
38 Joe Daley	3.00	8.00
39 Ross Perkins RC	3.00	8.00
40 Frank Mahovlich	5.00	12.00
41 Rejean Houle	3.00	8.00
42 Ron Chipperfield RC	4.00	10.00
43 Marc Tardif	3.00	8.00
44 Murray Keogan RC	3.00	8.00
45 Wayne Carleton	3.00	8.00
46 Andre Gaudette RC	3.00	8.00
47 Ralph Backstrom	3.00	8.00
48 Don McLeod RC	3.00	8.00
49 Vaclav Nedomansky RC	40.00	100.00
50 Bobby Hull	20.00	50.00
51 Rusty Patenaude RC	3.00	8.00
52 Michel Parizeau	3.00	8.00
53 Checklist	8.00	20.00
54 Wayne Connelly	3.00	8.00
55 Gary Veneruzzo	3.00	8.00
56 Dennis Sobchuk RC	3.00	8.00
57 Paul Henderson	3.00	8.00
58 Andy Brown RC	12.00	30.00
59 Paul Popiel	3.00	8.00
60 Andre Lacroix	3.00	8.00
61 Gary Jarrett	3.00	8.00
62 Claude St.Sauveur RC	3.00	8.00
63 Real Cloutier RC	4.00	10.00
64 Jacques Plante	10.00	25.00
65 Gilles Gratton RC	5.00	12.00
66 Lars-Erik Sjoberg RC	5.00	12.00

1975-76 O-Pee-Chee

COMPLETE SET (396)	200.00	400.00
1 Stanley Cup Finals	5.00	12.00
2 Semi-Finals	3.00	8.00
3 Semi-Finals	3.00	8.00
4 Quarter Finals	3.00	8.00
5 Quarter Finals	3.00	8.00
6 Quarter Finals	3.00	8.00
7 Quarter Finals	3.00	8.00
8 Curt Bennett	3.00	8.00
9 Johnny Bucyk	3.00	8.00
10 Gilbert Perreault	5.00	12.00
11 Darryl Edestrand	3.00	8.00
12 Ivan Boldirev	3.00	8.00
13 Nick Libett	3.00	8.00
14 Jim McElmury RC	3.00	8.00
15 Frank St.Marseille	3.00	8.00
16 Blake Dunlop	3.00	8.00
17 Yvon Lambert	3.00	8.00
18 Gerry Hart	3.00	8.00
19 Steve Vickers	3.00	8.00
20 Rick MacLeish	3.00	8.00
21A Bob Paradise NoTR	3.00	8.00
21B Bob Paradise TR	3.00	8.00
22 Red Berenson	3.00	8.00
23 Lanny McDonald	5.00	12.00
24 Mike Robitaille	3.00	8.00
25 Ron Low	3.00	8.00
26A Bryan Hextall NoTR	3.00	8.00
26B Bryan Hextall TR	3.00	8.00
27A Carol Vadnais NoTR	3.00	8.00
27B Carol Vadnais TR	3.00	8.00
28 Jim Lorentz	3.00	8.00
29 Gary Simmons	3.00	8.00
30 Stan Mikita	6.00	15.00
31 Bryan Watson	3.00	8.00
32 Guy Charron	3.00	8.00
33 Bob Murdoch	3.00	8.00
34 Norm Gratton	3.00	8.00
35 Ken Dryden	25.00	60.00
36 Jean Potvin	3.00	8.00
37 Rick Middleton	3.00	8.00
38 Ed Van Impe	3.00	8.00
39 Rick Kehoe	3.00	8.00
40 Garry Unger	3.00	8.00
41 Ian Turnbull	3.00	8.00
42 Dennis Ververgaert	3.00	8.00
43 Mike Marson RC	3.00	8.00
44 Randy Manery	3.00	8.00
45 Gilles Gilbert	3.00	8.00
46 Rene Robert	3.00	8.00
47 Bob Stewart	3.00	8.00
48 Pit Martin	3.00	8.00
49 Danny Grant	3.00	8.00
50 Peter Mahovlich	3.00	8.00
51 Dennis Patterson RC	3.00	8.00
52 Mike Murphy	3.00	8.00
53 Dennis O'Brien	3.00	8.00
54 Garry Howatt	3.00	8.00
55 Ed Giacomin	3.00	8.00
56 Andre Dupont	3.00	8.00
57 Chuck Arnason	3.00	8.00
58 Bob Gassoff RC	3.00	8.00
59 Ron Ellis	3.00	8.00
60 Andre Boudrias	3.00	8.00
61 Yvon Labre	3.00	8.00
62 Hilliard Graves	3.00	8.00
63 Wayne Cashman	3.00	8.00
64 Danny Gare RC	3.00	8.00
65 Rick Hampton	3.00	8.00
66 Darcy Rota	3.00	8.00
67 Bill Hogaboam	3.00	8.00
68 Denis Herron	3.00	8.00
69 Sheldon Kannegiesser	3.00	8.00
70 Yvan Cournoyer	3.00	8.00
71 Ernie Hicke	3.00	8.00
72 Bert Marshall	3.00	8.00
73 Derek Sanderson	3.00	8.00
74 Tom Bladon	3.00	8.00
75 Ron Schock	3.00	8.00
76 Larry Sacharuk RC	3.00	8.00
77 George Ferguson	3.00	8.00
78 Ab DeMarco	3.00	8.00
79 Tom Williams	3.00	8.00
80 Phil Roberto	3.00	8.00
81 Bruins Team	3.00	8.00
82 Seals Team	3.00	8.00
83 Sabres Team	3.00	8.00
84 Blackhawks Team	3.00	8.00

Card	Low	High
85 Flames Team	3.00	8.00
86 Kings Team	3.00	8.00
87 Red Wings Team	3.00	8.00
88 Scouts Team	3.00	8.00
89 North Stars Team	3.00	8.00
90 Canadiens Team	3.00	8.00
91 Maple Leafs Team	3.00	8.00
92 Islanders Team	3.00	8.00
93 Penguins Team	3.00	8.00
94 Rangers Team	3.00	8.00
95 Flyers Team	3.00	8.00
96 Blues Team	3.00	8.00
97 Canucks Team	3.00	8.00
98 Capitals Team	3.00	8.00
99 Checklist 1-110	6.00	15.00
100 Bobby Orr	12.00	30.00
101 Germain Gagnon UER	3.00	8.00
102 Phil Russell	3.00	8.00
103 Billy Lochead	3.00	8.00
104 Robin Burns RC	3.00	8.00
105 Gary Edwards	3.00	8.00
106 Dwight Bialowas	3.00	8.00
107 Doug Risebrough UER RC	3.00	8.00
108 Dave Lewis	3.00	8.00
109 Bill Fairbairn	3.00	8.00
110 Ross Lonsberry	3.00	8.00
111 Ron Stackhouse	3.00	8.00
112 Claude Larose	3.00	8.00
113 Don Luce	3.00	8.00
114 Errol Thompson RC	3.00	8.00
115 Gary Smith	3.00	8.00
116 Jack Lynch	3.00	8.00
117 Jacques Richard	3.00	8.00
118 Dallas Smith	3.00	8.00
119 Dave Gardner	3.00	8.00
120 Mickey Redmond	3.00	8.00
121 John Marks	3.00	8.00
122 Dave Hudson	3.00	8.00
123 Bob Nevin	3.00	8.00
124 Fred Barrett	3.00	8.00
125 Gerry Desjardins	3.00	8.00
126 Guy Lafleur UER	6.00	15.00
127 Jean-Paul Parise	3.00	8.00
128 Walt Tkaczuk	3.00	8.00
129 Gary Dornhoefer	3.00	8.00
130 Syl Apps	3.00	8.00
131 Bob Plager	3.00	8.00
132 Stan Weir	3.00	8.00
133 Tracy Pratt	3.00	8.00
134 Jack Egers	3.00	8.00
135 Eric Vail	3.00	8.00
136 Al Sims	3.00	8.00
137 Larry Patey RC	3.00	8.00
138 Jim Schoenfeld	3.00	8.00
139 Cliff Koroll	3.00	8.00
140 Marcel Dionne	5.00	12.00
141 Jean-Guy Lagace	3.00	8.00
142 Juha Widing	3.00	8.00
143 Lou Nanne	3.00	8.00
144 Serge Savard	3.00	8.00
145 Glenn Resch	3.00	8.00
146 Ron Greschner RC	3.00	8.00
147 Dave Schultz	3.00	8.00
148 Barry Wilkins	3.00	8.00
149 Floyd Thomson	3.00	8.00
150 Darryl Sittler	5.00	12.00
151 Paulin Bordeleau	3.00	8.00
152 Ron Lalonde RC	3.00	8.00
153 Larry Romanchych	3.00	8.00
154 Larry Carriere	3.00	8.00
155 Andre Savard	3.00	8.00
156 Dave Hrechkosy RC	3.00	8.00
157 Bill White	3.00	8.00
158 Dave Kryskow	3.00	8.00
159 Denis Dupere	3.00	8.00
160 Rogatien Vachon	3.00	8.00
161 Doug Rombough	3.00	8.00
162 Murray Wilson	3.00	8.00
163 Bob Bourne RC	3.00	8.00
164 Gilles Marotte	3.00	8.00
165 Vic Hadfield	3.00	8.00
166 Reggie Leach	3.00	8.00
167 Jerry Butler	3.00	8.00
168 Inge Hammarstrom	3.00	8.00
169 Chris Oddleifson	3.00	8.00
170 Greg Joly	3.00	8.00
171 Checklist 111-220	5.00	12.00
172 Pat Quinn	3.00	8.00
173 Dave Forbes	3.00	8.00
174 Len Frig	3.00	8.00
175 Richard Martin	3.00	8.00
176 Keith Magnuson	3.00	8.00
177 Dan Maloney	3.00	8.00
178 Craig Patrick	3.00	8.00
179 Tom Williams	3.00	8.00
180 Bill Goldsworthy	3.00	8.00
181 Steve Shutt	3.00	8.00
182 Ralph Stewart	3.00	8.00
183 John Davidson	3.00	8.00
184 Bob Kelly	3.00	8.00
185 Ed Johnston	3.00	8.00
186 Dave Burrows	3.00	8.00
187 Dave Dunn	3.00	8.00
188 Dennis Kearns	3.00	8.00
189 Bill Clement	3.00	8.00
190 Gilles Meloche	3.00	8.00
191 Bob Leiter	3.00	8.00
192 Jerry Korab	3.00	8.00
193 Joey Johnston	3.00	8.00
194 Walt McKechnie	3.00	8.00
195 Wilf Paiement	3.00	8.00
196 Bob Berry	3.00	8.00
197 Dean Talafous RC	3.00	8.00
198 Guy Lapointe	3.00	8.00
199 Clark Gillies RC	20.00	50.00
200A Phil Esposito NoTR	5.00	12.00
200B Phil Esposito TR	3.00	8.00
201 Greg Polis	3.00	8.00
202 Jimmy Watson	3.00	8.00
203 Gord McRae RC	3.00	8.00
204 Lowell MacDonald	3.00	8.00
205 Barclay Plager	3.00	8.00
206 Don Lever	3.00	8.00
207 Bill Mikkelson	3.00	8.00
208 Espo/Lafleur/Martin LL	3.00	8.00
209 Clarke/Orr/P.Mahv LL	5.00	12.00
210 Orr/Espo/Dionne LL	12.00	30.00
211 Schltz/Dupnt/Rssll LL	3.00	8.00
212 Espo/Martin/Grant LL	3.00	8.00
213 Parnt/Vach/Drydn LL	5.00	12.00
214 Barry Gibbs	3.00	8.00
215 Ken Hodge	3.00	8.00
216 Jocelyn Guevremont	3.00	8.00
217 Warren Williams RC	3.00	8.00
218 Dick Redmond	3.00	8.00
219 Jim Rutherford	3.00	8.00
220 Simon Nolet	3.00	8.00
221 Butch Goring	3.00	8.00
222 Glen Sather	3.00	8.00
223 Mario Tremblay UER RC	3.00	8.00
224 Jude Drouin	3.00	8.00
225 Rod Gilbert	3.00	8.00
226 Bill Barber	3.00	8.00
227 Gary Inness RC	3.00	8.00
228 Wayne Merrick	3.00	8.00
229 Rod Seiling	3.00	8.00
230 Tom Lysiak	3.00	8.00
231 Bob Dailey	3.00	8.00
232 Michel Belhumeur	3.00	8.00
233 Bill Hajt RC	3.00	8.00
234 Jim Pappin	3.00	8.00
235 Gregg Sheppard	3.00	8.00
236A Gary Bergman NoTR	3.00	8.00
236B Gary Bergman TR	3.00	8.00
237 Randy Rota	3.00	8.00
238 Neil Komadoski	3.00	8.00
239 Craig Cameron	3.00	8.00
240 Tony Esposito	5.00	12.00
241 Larry Robinson	5.00	12.00
242 Billy Harris	3.00	8.00
243A Jean Ratelle NoTR	3.00	8.00
243B Jean Ratelle TR	3.00	8.00
244 Ted Irvine UER	3.00	8.00
245 Bob Neely	3.00	8.00
246 Bobby Lalonde	3.00	8.00
247 Ron Jones RC	3.00	8.00
248 Rey Comeau	3.00	8.00
249 Michel Plasse	3.00	8.00
250 Bobby Clarke	5.00	12.00
251 Bobby Schmautz	3.00	8.00
252 Peter McNab RC	3.00	8.00
253 Al MacAdam	3.00	8.00
254 Dennis Hull	3.00	8.00
255 Terry Harper	3.00	8.00
256 Peter McDuffe	3.00	8.00
257 Jean Hamel	3.00	8.00
258 Jacques Lemaire	3.00	8.00
259 Bob Nystrom	3.00	8.00
260A Brad Park NoTR	3.00	8.00
260B Brad Park TR	3.00	8.00
261 Cesare Maniago	3.00	8.00
262 Don Saleski	3.00	8.00
263 J. Bob Kelly	3.00	8.00
264 Bob Hess RC	3.00	8.00
265 Blaine Stoughton	3.00	8.00
266 John Gould	3.00	8.00
267A Checklist 221-330	20.00	50.00
267B Checklist 331-396	20.00	50.00
268 Dan Bouchard	3.00	8.00
269 Don Marcotte	3.00	8.00
270 Jim Neilson	3.00	8.00
271 Craig Ramsay	3.00	8.00
272 Grant Mulvey RC	3.00	8.00
273 Larry Giroux RC	3.00	8.00
274 Real Lemieux	3.00	8.00
275 Denis Potvin	5.00	12.00
276 Don Kozak	3.00	8.00
277 Tom Reid	3.00	8.00
278 Bob Gainey	5.00	12.00
279 Nick Beverley	3.00	8.00
280 Jean Pronovost	3.00	8.00
281 Joe Watson	3.00	8.00
282 Chuck Lefley	3.00	8.00
283 Borje Salming	5.00	12.00
284 Garnet Bailey	3.00	8.00
285 Gregg Boddy	3.00	8.00
286 Bobby Clarke AS1	3.00	8.00
287 Denis Potvin AS1	3.00	8.00
288 Bobby Orr AS1	25.00	60.00
289 Richard Martin AS1	3.00	8.00
290 Guy Lafleur AS1	5.00	12.00
291 Bernie Parent AS1	3.00	8.00
292 Phil Esposito AS2	3.00	8.00
293 Guy Lapointe AS2	3.00	8.00
294 Borje Salming AS2	3.00	8.00
295 Steve Vickers AS2	3.00	8.00
296 Rene Robert AS2	3.00	8.00
297 Rogatien Vachon AS2	3.00	8.00
298 Buster Harvey RC	3.00	8.00
299 Gary Sabourin	3.00	8.00
300 Bernie Parent	3.00	8.00
301 Terry O'Reilly	3.00	8.00
302 Ed Westfall	3.00	8.00
303 Pete Stemkowski	3.00	8.00
304 Pierre Bouchard	3.00	8.00
305 Pierre Larouche RC	12.00	30.00
306 Lee Fogolin RC	3.00	8.00
307 Gerry O'Flaherty	3.00	8.00
308 Phil Myre	3.00	8.00
309 Pierre Plante	3.00	8.00
310 Dennis Hextall	3.00	8.00
311 Jim McKenny	3.00	8.00
312 Vic Venasky	3.00	8.00
313 Vail/Lysiak TL	3.00	8.00
314 P.Espo/Orr/Bucyk TL	8.00	20.00
315 R.Martin/R.Robert TL	3.00	8.00
316 Hrchsy/Pley/Weir TL	3.00	8.00
317 S.Mikita/J.Pappin TL	3.00	8.00
318 D.Grant/M.Dionne TL	3.00	8.00
319 Nolet/Pmnt/Charn TL	3.00	8.00
320 Nevin/Wdng/Brry TL	3.00	8.00
321 Gldswrthy/Hextall TL	3.00	8.00
322 Lafleur/P.Mahov TL	3.00	8.00
323 Nystrm/Potvin/Gill TL	3.00	8.00
324 Vick/Gilbert/Ratle TL	3.00	8.00
325 R.Leach/B.Clarke TL	3.00	8.00
326 Pronovost/Schock TL	3.00	8.00
327 G.Unger/Sacharuk TL	3.00	8.00
328 Darryl Sittler TL	3.00	8.00
329 Lever/Boudrias TL	3.00	8.00
330 Williams/Bailey TL	3.00	8.00
331 Noel Price	3.00	8.00
332 Fred Stanfield	3.00	8.00
333 Doug Jarrett	3.00	8.00
334 Gary Coalter	3.00	8.00
335 Murray Oliver	3.00	8.00
336 Dave Fortier	3.00	8.00
337 Terry Crisp UER	3.00	8.00
338 Bert Wilson	3.00	8.00
339 John Grisdale RC	3.00	8.00
340 Ken Broderick	3.00	8.00
341 Frank Spring RC	3.00	8.00
342 Mike Korney RC	3.00	8.00
343 Gene Carr	3.00	8.00
344 Don Awrey	3.00	8.00
345 Pat Hickey	3.00	8.00
346 Colin Campbell RC	3.00	8.00
347 Wayne Thomas	3.00	8.00
348 Bob Gryp RC	3.00	8.00
349 Bill Flett	3.00	8.00
350 Roger Crozier	3.00	8.00
351 Dale Tallon	3.00	8.00
352 Larry Johnston	3.00	8.00
353 John Flesch RC	3.00	8.00
354 Lorne Henning	3.00	8.00
355 Wayne Stephenson	3.00	8.00
356 Rick Wilson	3.00	8.00
357 Garry Monahan	3.00	8.00
358 Gary Doak	3.00	8.00
359A Pierre Jarry NoTR	3.00	8.00
359B Pierre Jarry TR	3.00	8.00
360 George Pesut RC	3.00	8.00
361 Mike Corrigan	3.00	8.00
362 Michel Larocque	3.00	8.00
363 Wayne Dillon	3.00	8.00
364 Pete Laframboise	3.00	8.00
365 Brian Glennie	3.00	8.00
366 Mike Christie	3.00	8.00
367 Jean Lemieux RC	3.00	8.00
368 Gary Bromley	3.00	8.00
369 J.P. Bordeleau	3.00	8.00
370 Ed Gilbert RC	3.00	8.00
371 Chris Ahrens	3.00	8.00
372 Billy Smith	5.00	12.00
373 Larry Goodenough RC	3.00	8.00
374 Leon Rochefort	3.00	8.00
375 Doug Gibson RC	3.00	8.00
376 Mike Bloom	3.00	8.00
377 Larry Brown	3.00	8.00
378 Jim Roberts	3.00	8.00
379 Gilles Villemure	3.00	8.00
380 Dennis Owchar RC	3.00	8.00
381 Doug Favell	3.00	8.00
382 Stan Gilbertson UER	3.00	8.00
383 Ed Kea RC	3.00	8.00
384 Brian Spencer	3.00	8.00
385 Mike Veisor RC	3.00	8.00
386 Bob Murray	3.00	8.00
387 Andre St.Laurent RC	3.00	8.00
388 Rick Chartraw RC	3.00	8.00
389 Orest Kindrachuk	3.00	8.00
390 Dave Hutchinson RC	3.00	8.00
391 Glenn Goldup	3.00	8.00
392 Jerry Holland RC	3.00	8.00
393 Peter Sturgeon RC	3.00	8.00
394 Alain Daigle RC	3.00	8.00
396 Harold Snepsts RC	12.00	30.00

1975-76 O-Pee-Chee WHA

Card	Low	High
COMPLETE SET (132)	250.00	400.00
1 Bobby Hull	12.00	30.00
2 Dale Hoganson	2.50	6.00
3 Serge Aubry	2.50	6.00
4 Ron Chipperfield	2.50	6.00
5 Paul Shmyr	2.50	6.00
6 Perry Miller RC	2.50	6.00
7 Mark Howe RC	25.00	60.00
8 Mike Rogers RC	2.50	6.00
9 Bryon Baltimore	2.50	6.00
10 Andre Lacroix	2.50	6.00
11 Nick Harbaruk	2.50	6.00
12 John Garrett RC	5.00	12.00
13 Lou Nistico RC	2.50	6.00
14 Rick Ley	2.50	6.00
15 Veli-Pekka Ketola RC	5.00	12.00
16 Real Cloutier	2.50	6.00
17 Pierre Guite RC	2.50	6.00
18 Duane Rupp	2.50	6.00
19 Robbie Ftorek RC	8.00	20.00
20 Gerry Cheevers	25.00	60.00
21 John Schella RC	2.50	6.00
22 Bruce MacGregor	2.50	6.00
23 Ralph Backstrom	2.50	6.00
24 Gene Peacosh	2.50	6.00
25 Pierre Roy	2.50	6.00
26 Mike Walton	2.50	6.00
27 Vaclav Nedomansky	2.50	6.00
28 Christer Abrahamsson RC	4.00	10.00
29 Thommie Bergman	2.50	6.00
30 Marc Tardif	2.50	6.00
31 Bryan Campbell	2.50	6.00
32 Don McLeod	8.00	20.00
33 Al McDonough	2.50	6.00
34 Jacques Plante	10.00	25.00
35 Andre Hinse RC	2.50	6.00
36 Eddie Joyal	2.50	6.00
37 Ken Baird RC	2.50	6.00
38 Wayne Rivers	2.50	6.00
39 Ron Buchanan	2.50	6.00
40 Anders Hedberg	2.50	6.00
41 Rick Smith	2.50	6.00
42 Paul Henderson	2.50	6.00
43 Wayne Carleton	2.50	6.00
44 Richard Brodeur RC	5.00	12.00
45 John Hughes RC	2.50	6.00
46 Larry Israelson RC	2.50	6.00
47 Jim Harrison	2.50	6.00
48 Cam Connor RC	2.50	6.00
49 Al Hamilton	2.50	6.00
50 Ron Grahame RC	2.50	6.00
51 Frank Rochon RC	2.50	6.00
52 Ron Climie	2.50	6.00
53 Murray Heatley RC	2.50	6.00
54 John Arbour	2.50	6.00
55 Jim Shaw RC	2.50	6.00
56 Larry Pleau RC	2.50	6.00
57 Ted Green	2.50	6.00
58 Rick Dudley	2.50	6.00
59 Butch Deadmarsh	2.50	6.00
60 Serge Bernier	2.50	6.00
61 Ron Grahame AS	2.50	6.00
62 J.C. Tremblay AS	2.50	6.00
63 Kevin Morrison AS	2.50	6.00
64 Andre Lacroix AS	2.50	6.00
65 Bobby Hull AS	8.00	20.00
66 Gordie Howe AS	8.00	20.00
67 Gerry Cheevers AS	4.00	10.00
68 Poul Popiel AS	2.50	6.00
69 Barry Long AS	2.50	6.00
70 Serge Bernier AS	2.50	6.00
71 Marc Tardif AS	2.50	6.00
72 Anders Hedberg AS	2.50	6.00
73 Ron Ward	2.50	6.00
74 Michel Cormier RC	2.50	6.00
75 Marty Howe RC	2.50	6.00
76 Rusty Patenaude	2.50	6.00
77 John McKenzie	2.50	6.00
78 Mark Napier RC	2.50	6.00
79 Henry Boucha	2.50	6.00
80 Kevin Morrison RC	2.50	6.00
81 Tom Simpson	2.50	6.00
82 Brad Selwood RC	2.50	6.00
83 Ulf Nilsson	2.50	6.00
84 Rejean Houle	2.50	6.00
85 Normand Lapointe RC UER	2.50	6.00
86 Danny Lawson	2.50	6.00
87 Gary Jarrett	2.50	6.00
88 Al McLeod RC	2.50	6.00
89 Gord Labossiere	2.50	6.00
90 Barry Long	2.50	6.00
91 Rick Morris RC	2.50	6.00
92 Norm Ferguson	2.50	6.00
93 Bob Whitlock	2.50	6.00
94 Jim Dorey	2.50	6.00
95 Tom Webster	2.50	6.00
96 Gordie Gallant	2.50	6.00
97 Dave Keon	2.50	6.00
98 Ron Plumb RC	2.50	6.00
99 Rick Jodzio RC	2.50	6.00
100 Gordie Howe	12.00	30.00
101 Joe Daley	2.50	6.00
102 Wayne Muloin RC	2.50	6.00
103 Gavin Kirk RC	2.50	6.00
104 Dave Dryden	2.50	6.00
105 Bob Liddington RC	2.50	6.00
106 Rosaire Paiement	2.50	6.00
107 John Sheridan	4.00	10.00
108 Nick Fotiu RC	5.00	12.00
109 Lars-Erik Sjoberg	2.50	6.00
110 Frank Mahovlich	2.50	6.00
111 Mike Antonovich	2.50	6.00
112 Paul Terbenche	2.50	6.00
113 Rich Leduc RC	2.50	6.00
114 Jack Norris	2.50	6.00
115 Dennis Sobchuk	2.50	6.00
116 Chris Bordeleau	2.50	6.00
117 Doug Barrie	2.50	6.00
118 Hugh Harris RC	2.50	6.00
119 Cam Newton RC	2.50	6.00
120 Poul Popiel	2.50	6.00
121 Fran Huck	2.50	6.00
122 Tony Featherstone	2.50	6.00
123 Bob Woytowich	2.50	6.00
124 Claude St.Sauveur	2.50	6.00
125 Heikki Riihiranta	6.00	15.00
126 Gary Kurt	2.50	6.00
127 Thommy Abrahamsson RC	2.50	6.00
128 Danny Gruen RC	2.50	6.00
129 Jacques Locas RC	2.50	6.00
130 J.C. Tremblay	2.50	6.00
131 Checklist Card	12.00	30.00
132 Ernie Wakely	4.00	10.00

1976-77 O-Pee-Chee

Card	Low	High
COMPLETE SET (396)	150.00	300.00
1 Leach/Lafleur/Larou LL	5.00	12.00
2 Clarke/Lafleur/Perr LL	5.00	12.00
3 Lafleur/Clarke/Perr LL	3.00	8.00
4 Durbno/Watsn/Schltz LL	3.00	8.00
5 Espo/Lafleur/Potvin LL	3.00	8.00
6 Dryden/Resch/Laroc LL	6.00	15.00
7 Gary Doak	3.00	8.00
8 Jacques Richard	3.00	8.00
9 Wayne Dillon	3.00	8.00
10 Bernie Parent	3.00	8.00
11 Ed Westfall	3.00	8.00
12 Dick Redmond	3.00	8.00
13 Bryan Hextall	3.00	8.00
14 Jean Pronovost	3.00	8.00
15 Peter Mahovlich	3.00	8.00
16 Danny Grant	3.00	8.00
17 Phil Myre	3.00	8.00
18 Wayne Merrick	3.00	8.00
19 Steve Durbano	3.00	8.00
20 Derek Sanderson	3.00	8.00
21 Mike Murphy	3.00	8.00
22 Borje Salming	3.00	8.00
23 Mike Walton	3.00	8.00
24 Randy Manery	3.00	8.00
25 Ken Hodge	3.00	8.00
26 Mel Bridgman RC	3.00	8.00
27 Jerry Korab	3.00	8.00
28 Gilles Gratton	3.00	8.00
29 Andre St.Laurent	3.00	8.00
30 Yvan Cournoyer	3.00	8.00
31 Phil Russell	3.00	8.00
32 Dennis Hextall	3.00	8.00
33 Lowell MacDonald	3.00	8.00
34 Dennis O'Brien	3.00	8.00
35 Gerry Meehan	3.00	8.00
36 Gilles Meloche	3.00	8.00
37 Wilf Paiement	3.00	8.00
38 Bob MacMillan RC	3.00	8.00
39 Ian Turnbull	3.00	8.00
40 Rogatien Vachon	3.00	8.00
41 Nick Beverley	3.00	8.00
42 Rene Robert	3.00	8.00
43 Andre Savard	3.00	8.00
44 Bob Gainey	3.00	8.00
45 Joe Watson	3.00	8.00
46 Billy Smith	8.00	20.00
47 Darcy Rota	3.00	8.00
48 Rick Lapointe RC	3.00	8.00
49 Pierre Jarry	3.00	8.00
50 Syl Apps	3.00	8.00
51 Eric Vail	3.00	8.00
52 Greg Joly	3.00	8.00
53 Don Lever	3.00	8.00
54 Bob Murdoch Seals	3.00	8.00
55 Denis Herron	3.00	8.00
56 Mike Bloom	3.00	8.00
57 Bill Fairbairn	3.00	8.00
58 Fred Stanfield	3.00	8.00
59 Steve Shutt	3.00	8.00
60 Brad Park	3.00	8.00
61 Gilles Villemure	3.00	8.00
62 Bert Marshall	3.00	8.00
63 Chuck Lefley	3.00	8.00
64 Simon Nolet	3.00	8.00
65 Reggie Leach RB	3.00	8.00
66 Darryl Sittler RB	3.00	8.00
67 Bryan Trottier RB	3.00	8.00
68 Garry Unger RB	3.00	8.00
69 Ron Low	3.00	8.00
70 Bobby Clarke	3.00	8.00
71 Michel Bergeron RC	3.00	8.00
72 Ron Stackhouse	3.00	8.00
73 Bill Hogaboam	3.00	8.00
74 Bob Murdoch Kings	3.00	8.00
75 Steve Vickers	3.00	8.00
76 Pit Martin	3.00	8.00
77 Gerry Hart	3.00	8.00
78 Craig Ramsay	3.00	8.00
79 Michel Larocque	3.00	8.00
80 Jean Ratelle	3.00	8.00
81 Don Saleski	3.00	8.00
82 Bill Clement	3.00	8.00
83 Dave Burrows	3.00	8.00
84 Wayne Thomas	3.00	8.00
85 John Gould	3.00	8.00
86 Dennis Maruk RC	3.00	8.00
87 Ernie Hicke	3.00	8.00
88 Jim Rutherford	3.00	8.00
89 Dale Tallon	3.00	8.00
90 Rod Gilbert	3.00	8.00
91 Marcel Dionne	8.00	20.00
92 Chuck Arnason	3.00	8.00
93 Jean Potvin	3.00	8.00
94 Don Luce	3.00	8.00
95 Johnny Bucyk	3.00	8.00
96 Larry Goodenough	3.00	8.00
97 Mario Tremblay	3.00	8.00
98 Nelson Pyatt RC	3.00	8.00
99 Brian Glennie	3.00	8.00
100 Tony Esposito	3.00	8.00
101 Dan Maloney	3.00	8.00
102 Dunc Wilson	3.00	8.00
103 Dean Talafous	3.00	8.00
104 Ed Staniowski RC	3.00	8.00
105 Dallas Smith	3.00	8.00
106 Jude Drouin	3.00	8.00
107 Pat Hickey	3.00	8.00
108 Jocelyn Guevremont	3.00	8.00
109 Doug Risebrough	3.00	8.00
110 Reggie Leach	3.00	8.00
111 Dan Bouchard	3.00	8.00
112 Chris Oddleifson	3.00	8.00
113 Rick Hampton	3.00	8.00
114 John Marks	3.00	8.00
115 Bryan Trottier RC	25.00	60.00
116 Checklist 1-132	12.00	30.00
117 Greg Polis	3.00	8.00
118 Peter McNab	3.00	8.00
119 Jim Roberts Mont	3.00	8.00
120 Gerry Cheevers	3.00	8.00
121 Rick MacLeish	3.00	8.00
122 Billy Lochead	3.00	8.00
123 Tom Reid	3.00	8.00
124 Rick Kehoe	3.00	8.00
125 Keith Magnuson	3.00	8.00
126 Clark Gillies	3.00	8.00
127 Rick Middleton	3.00	8.00
128 Bill Hajt	3.00	8.00
129 Jacques Lemaire	3.00	8.00
130 Terry O'Reilly	3.00	8.00
131 Andre Dupont	3.00	8.00
132 Flames Team	3.00	8.00
133 Bruins Team	3.00	8.00
134 Sabres Team	3.00	8.00
135 Seals Team	3.00	8.00
136 Blackhawks Team	3.00	8.00
137 Red Wings Team	3.00	8.00
138 Scouts Team	3.00	8.00
139 Kings Team	3.00	8.00
140 North Stars Team	3.00	8.00
141 Canadiens Team	3.00	8.00
142 Islanders Team	3.00	8.00
143 Rangers Team	3.00	8.00
144 Flyers Team	3.00	8.00
145 Penguins Team	3.00	8.00
146 Blues Team	3.00	8.00
147 Maple Leafs Team	3.00	8.00
148 Canucks Team	3.00	8.00
149 Capitals Team	3.00	8.00
150 Dave Schultz	3.00	8.00
151 Larry Robinson	6.00	15.00
152 Al Smith	3.00	8.00
153 Bob Nystrom	3.00	8.00
154 Ron Greschner	3.00	8.00
155 Gregg Sheppard	3.00	8.00
156 Alain Daigle	3.00	8.00
157 Ed Van Impe	3.00	8.00
158 Tim Young RC	3.00	8.00
159 Bryan Lefley	3.00	8.00
160 Ed Giacomin	3.00	8.00
161 Yvon Labre	3.00	8.00
162 Jim Lorentz	3.00	8.00
163 Guy Lafleur	5.00	12.00
164 Tom Bladon	3.00	8.00
165 Wayne Cashman	3.00	8.00
166 Pete Stemkowski	3.00	8.00
167 Grant Mulvey	3.00	8.00
168 Yves Belanger RC	3.00	8.00
169 Bill Goldsworthy	3.00	8.00
170 Denis Potvin	3.00	8.00
171 Nick Libett	3.00	8.00
172 Michel Plasse	3.00	8.00
173 Lou Nanne	3.00	8.00
174 Tom Lysiak	3.00	8.00
175 Dennis Ververgaert	3.00	8.00
176A Gary Simmons ERR		
(Team transferred to Colorado)	3.00	8.00
177 Pierre Bouchard	3.00	8.00
178 Bill Barber	3.00	8.00
179 Darryl Edestrand	3.00	8.00
180 Gilbert Perreault	3.00	8.00
181 Dave Maloney RC	3.00	8.00
182 Jean-Paul Parise	3.00	8.00
183 Jim Harrison	3.00	8.00
184 Pete Lopresti RC	3.00	8.00
185 Don Kozak	3.00	8.00
186 Guy Charron	3.00	8.00
187 Stan Gilbertson	3.00	8.00
188 Bill Nyrop RC	3.00	8.00
189 Bobby Schmautz	3.00	8.00
190 Wayne Stephenson	3.00	8.00
191 Brian Spencer	3.00	8.00
192 Gilles Marotte	3.00	8.00
193 Lorne Henning	3.00	8.00
194 Bob Neely	3.00	8.00
195 Dennis Hull	3.00	8.00
196 Walt McKechnie	3.00	8.00
197 Curt Ridley RC	3.00	8.00
198 Dwight Bialowas	3.00	8.00
199 Pierre Larouche	3.00	8.00
200 Ken Dryden	25.00	60.00
201 Ross Lonsberry	3.00	8.00
202 Curt Bennett	3.00	8.00
203 Hartland Monahan RC	3.00	8.00
204 John Davidson	3.00	8.00
205 Serge Savard	3.00	8.00
206 Garry Howatt	3.00	8.00
207 Darryl Sittler	3.00	8.00
208 J.P. Bordeleau	3.00	8.00
209 Henry Boucha	3.00	8.00
210 Richard Martin	3.00	8.00
211 Vic Venasky	3.00	8.00
212 Buster Harvey	3.00	8.00
213 Bobby Orr	25.00	60.00
214 Martin/Perreault/Robert	3.00	8.00
215 Barber/Clarke/Leach	3.00	8.00
216 Gillies/Trottier/Harris	3.00	8.00
217 Gainey/Jarvis/Roberts	3.00	8.00
218 Bicentennial Line	3.00	8.00
219 Bob Kelly	3.00	8.00
220 Walt Tkaczuk	3.00	8.00
221 Dave Lewis	3.00	8.00
222 Danny Gare	3.00	8.00
223 Guy Lapointe	3.00	8.00
224 Hank Nowak RC	3.00	8.00
225 Stan Mikita	3.00	8.00
226 Vic Hadfield	3.00	8.00
227 Bernie Wolfe RC	3.00	8.00
228 Bryan Watson	3.00	8.00
229 Ralph Stewart	3.00	8.00
230 Gerry Desjardins	3.00	8.00
231 John Bednarski RC	3.00	8.00
232 Yvon Lambert	3.00	8.00
233 Orest Kindrachuk	3.00	8.00
234 Don Marcotte	3.00	8.00
235 Bill White	3.00	8.00
236 Red Berenson	3.00	8.00
237 Al MacAdam	3.00	8.00
238 Rick Blight RC	3.00	8.00
239 Butch Goring	3.00	8.00
240 Cesare Maniago	3.00	8.00
241 Jim Schoenfeld	3.00	8.00
242 Cliff Koroll	3.00	8.00
243 Scott Garland RC	3.00	8.00
244 Rick Chartraw	3.00	8.00
245 Phil Esposito	3.00	8.00
246 Dave Forbes	3.00	8.00
247 Jimmy Watson	3.00	8.00
248 Ron Schock	3.00	8.00
249 Fred Barrett	3.00	8.00
250 Glenn Resch	3.00	8.00
251 Ivan Boldirev	3.00	8.00
252 Billy Harris	3.00	8.00
253 Lee Fogolin	3.00	8.00
254 Murray Wilson	3.00	8.00
255 Gilles Gilbert	3.00	8.00
256 Gary Dornhoefer	3.00	8.00
257 Carol Vadnais	3.00	8.00
258 Checklist 133-264	12.00	30.00
259 Errol Thompson	3.00	8.00
260 Garry Unger	3.00	8.00
261 J. Bob Kelly	3.00	8.00
262 Terry Harper	3.00	8.00
263 Blake Dunlop	3.00	8.00
264 Canadiens Champs	3.00	8.00
265 Richard Mulhern RC	3.00	8.00
266 Gary Sabourin	3.00	8.00
267 Bill McKenzie UER RC	3.00	8.00
268 Mike Corrigan	3.00	8.00
269 Rick Smith	3.00	8.00
270 Stan Weir	3.00	8.00
271 Ron Sedlbauer RC	3.00	8.00
272 Jean Lemieux	3.00	8.00
273 Hilliard Graves	3.00	8.00
274 Dave Gardner	3.00	8.00
275 Tracy Pratt	3.00	8.00
276 Frank St.Marseille	3.00	8.00
277 Bob Hess	3.00	8.00
278 Bobby Lalonde	3.00	8.00
279 Tony White RC	3.00	8.00
280 Rod Seiling	3.00	8.00
281 Larry Romanchych	3.00	8.00
282 Ralph Klassen RC	3.00	8.00
283 Gary Croteau	3.00	8.00
284 Neil Komadoski	3.00	8.00
285 Ed Johnston	3.00	8.00
286 George Ferguson	3.00	8.00
287 Gerry O'Flaherty	3.00	8.00
288 Jack Lynch	3.00	8.00
289 Pat Quinn	3.00	8.00
290 Gene Carr	3.00	8.00
291 Bob Stewart	3.00	8.00
292 Doug Favell	3.00	8.00
293 Rick Wilson	3.00	8.00
294 Jack Valiquette RC	3.00	8.00
295 Garry Monahan	3.00	8.00
296 Michel Belhumeur	3.00	8.00
297 Larry Carriere	3.00	8.00
298 Fred Ahern RC	3.00	8.00
299 Dave Hudson	3.00	8.00
300 Bob Berry	3.00	8.00
301 Bob Gassoff	3.00	8.00
302 Jim McKenny	3.00	8.00
303 Gord Smith RC	3.00	8.00
304 Garnet Bailey	3.00	8.00
305 Bruce Affleck RC	3.00	8.00
306 Doug Halward RC	3.00	8.00
307 Lew Morrison	3.00	8.00
308 Bob Sauve RC	3.00	8.00
309 Bob Murray RC	3.00	8.00
310 Claude Larose	3.00	8.00
311 Don Awrey	3.00	8.00
312 Bill MacMillan	3.00	8.00
313 Doug Jarvis RC	3.00	8.00
314 Dennis Owchar	3.00	8.00
315 Jerry Holland	3.00	8.00
316 Guy Chouinard RC	3.00	8.00
317 Gary Smith	3.00	8.00
318 Pat Price RC	3.00	8.00
319 Tom Williams	3.00	8.00
320 Larry Patey	3.00	8.00
321 Claire Alexander	3.00	8.00
322 Larry Bolonchuk RC	3.00	8.00
323 Bob Sirois RC	3.00	8.00
324 Joe Zanussi RC	3.00	8.00
325 Joey Johnston	3.00	8.00
326 J.P. LeBlanc	3.00	8.00
327 Craig Cameron	3.00	8.00
328 Dave Fortier	3.00	8.00
329 Ed Gilbert	3.00	8.00
330 John Van Boxmeer RC	3.00	8.00
331 Gary Inness	3.00	8.00
332 Bill Flett	3.00	8.00
333 Mike Christie	3.00	8.00
334 Denis Dupere	3.00	8.00
335 Sheldon Kannegiesser	3.00	8.00
336 Jerry Butler	3.00	8.00
337 Gord McRae	3.00	8.00
338 Dennis Kearns	3.00	8.00
339 Ron Lalonde	3.00	8.00
340 Jean Hamel	3.00	8.00
341 Barry Gibbs	3.00	8.00
342 Mike Pelyk	3.00	8.00
343 Rey Comeau	3.00	8.00
344 Jim Neilson	3.00	8.00
345 Phil Roberto	3.00	8.00
346 Dave Hutchinson	3.00	8.00
347 Ted Irvine	3.00	8.00
348 Lanny McDonald	3.00	8.00
349 Jim Moxey RC	3.00	8.00
350 Bob Dailey	3.00	8.00
351 Tim Ecclestone	3.00	8.00
352 Len Frig	3.00	8.00
353 Randy Rota	3.00	8.00
354 Juha Widing	3.00	8.00
355 Larry Brown	3.00	8.00
356 Floyd Thomson	3.00	8.00
357 Richard Nantais RC	3.00	8.00
358 Inge Hammarstrom	3.00	8.00
359 Mike Robitaille	3.00	8.00
360 Rejean Houle	3.00	8.00
361 Ed Kea	3.00	8.00
362 Bob Girard RC	3.00	8.00
363 Bob Murray Vancv	3.00	8.00
364 Dave Hrechkosy	3.00	8.00
365 Gary Edwards	3.00	8.00
366 Harold Snepsts	3.00	8.00
367 Pat Boutette RC	3.00	8.00
368 Bob Paradise	3.00	8.00
369 Bob Plager	3.00	8.00
370 Tim Jacobs RC	3.00	8.00
371 Pierre Plante	3.00	8.00
372 Colin Campbell	3.00	8.00
373 Tiger Williams RC	15.00	40.00
374 Ab DeMarco	3.00	8.00
375 Mike Lampman RC	3.00	8.00
376 Mark Heaslip RC	3.00	8.00
377 Checklist Card	5.00	12.00
378 Bert Wilson	3.00	8.00
379 Bntt/Lysk/Qnn/St.S TL	3.00	8.00
380 Gre/Perrlt/Mrtin TL	3.00	8.00
381 Bucyk/Ratle/O'Rei TL	3.00	8.00
382 Mrtn/Tin/Rsll/Kroll TL	3.00	8.00
383 Seals/McAd/Mrdch TL	3.00	8.00
384 Charron/Durbano TL	3.00	8.00
385 Brgrn/McKch/Wtsn TL	3.00	8.00
386 Dione/Htch/Corrig TL	3.00	8.00
387 Hoga/Yng/O'Brien TL	3.00	8.00
388 Lafir/P.Mahv/Rise TL	3.00	8.00
389 Gillies/Potvin/How TL	3.00	8.00
390 Gilbert/Vick/Espo TL	3.00	8.00
391 Leach/Clrke/Brbr TL	3.00	8.00
392 Lrch/Apps/Schck TL	3.00	8.00
393 Lefly/Ungr/Gssf TL	3.00	8.00
394 Thmpsn/Sittlr/Will TL	3.00	8.00
395 Vgrt/Odl/Krns/Snpst TL	3.00	8.00
396 Pyatt/Mhn/Lbr/Whte TL	3.00	8.00

1976-77 O-Pee-Chee WHA

Card	Low	High
COMPLETE SET (132)	100.00	200.00
1 Tardif/Clout/Nedom LL	5.00	12.00
2 Tardif/Trembl/Nils LL	4.00	10.00
3 Tardif/B.Hull/Nils LL	5.00	12.00
4 Penalties Leaders	2.50	6.00
5 Tardif/B.Hull/Nils LL	5.00	12.00
6 Goals Against Avg. Leaders	2.50	6.00
7 Barry Long	2.50	6.00
8 Danny Lawson	2.50	6.00
9 Ulf Nilsson	4.00	10.00
10 Kevin Morrison	2.50	6.00
11 Gerry Pinder	2.50	6.00
12 Richard Brodeur	4.00	10.00
13 Robbie Ftorek	5.00	12.00
14 Tom Webster	2.50	6.00
15 Marty Howe	4.00	10.00
16 Bryan Campbell	2.50	6.00
17 Rick Dudley	2.50	6.00
18 Jim Turkiewicz RC	2.50	6.00
19 Rusty Patenaude	2.50	6.00
20 Joe Daley	2.50	6.00
21 Gary Veneruzzo	2.50	6.00
22 Chris Evans	2.50	6.00
23 Mike Antonovich	2.50	6.00

24 Jim Dorey 2.50 6.00
25 John Gray RC 2.50 6.00
26 Larry Pleau 2.50 6.00
27 Poul Popiel 2.50 6.00
28 Renald Leclerc RC 2.50 6.00
29 Dennis Sobchuk 2.50 6.00
30 Lars-Erik Sjoberg 2.50 6.00
31 Wayne Wood RC 2.50 6.00
32 Ron Chipperfield 2.50 6.00
33 Tim Sheehy RC 2.50 6.00
34 Brent Hughes 2.50 6.00
35 Ron Ward 2.50 6.00
36 Ron Huston RC 2.50 6.00
37 Rosaire Paiement 2.50 6.00
38 Terry Ruskowski RC 4.00 10.00
39 Hugh Harris 2.50 6.00
40 J.C. Tremblay 2.50 6.00
41 Rich Leduc 2.50 6.00
42 Peter Sullivan RC 2.50 6.00
43 Jerry Rollins RC 2.50 6.00
44 Ken Broderick 2.50 6.00
45 Peter Driscoll RC 2.50 6.00
46 Joe Noris RC 2.50 6.00
47 Al McLeod 2.50 6.00
48 Bruce Landon RC 2.50 6.00
49 Chris Bordeleau 2.50 6.00
50 Gordie Howe 10.00 25.00
51 Thommie Bergman 2.50 6.00
52 Dave Keon 4.00 10.00
53 Butch Deadmarsh 2.50 6.00
54 Bryan Maxwell 2.50 6.00
55 John Garrett 2.50 6.00
56 Glen Sather 2.50 6.00
57 John Miszuk 2.50 6.00
58 Heikki Riihiranta 2.50 6.00
59 Richard Grenier RC 2.50 6.00
60 Gene Peacosh 2.50 6.00
61 Joe Daley AS 2.50 6.00
62 J.C. Tremblay AS 2.50 6.00
63 Lars-Erik Sjoberg AS 2.50 6.00
64 Vaclav Nedomansky AS 2.50 6.00
65 Bobby Hull AS 8.00 20.00
66 Anders Hedberg AS 2.50 6.00
67 Chris Abrahamsson AS 2.50 6.00
68 Kevin Morrison AS 2.50 6.00
69 Paul Shmyr AS 2.50 6.00
70 Andre Lacroix AS 2.50 6.00
71 Gene Peacosh AS 2.50 6.00
72 Gordie Howe AS 8.00 20.00
73 Bob Nevin 2.50 6.00
74 Richard Lemieux 2.50 6.00
75 Mike Ford RC 2.50 6.00
76 Real Cloutier 2.50 6.00
77 Al McDonough 2.50 6.00
78 Del Hall RC 2.50 6.00
79 Thommy Abrahamsson 2.50 6.00
80 Andre Lacroix 2.50 6.00
81 Frank Hughes RC 2.50 6.00
82 Reg Thomas RC 2.50 6.00
83 Dave Inkpen RC 2.50 6.00
84 Paul Henderson 4.00 10.00
85 Dave Dryden 2.50 6.00
86 Lynn Powis 2.50 6.00
87 Andre Boudrias 2.50 6.00
88 Veli-Pekka Ketola 2.50 6.00
89 Cam Connor 2.50 6.00
90 Claude St.Sauveur 2.50 6.00
91 Garry Swain RC 2.50 6.00
92 Ernie Wakely 2.50 6.00
93 Blair MacDonald RC 2.50 6.00
94 Ron Plumb 2.50 6.00
95 Mark Howe 8.00 20.00
96 Peter Marrin RC 4.00 10.00
97 Al Hamilton 2.50 6.00
98 Paulin Bordeleau 2.50 6.00
99 Gavin Kirk 2.50 6.00
100 Bobby Hull 8.00 20.00
101 Rick Ley 2.50 6.00
102 Gary Kurt 2.50 6.00
103 John McKenzie 2.50 6.00
104 Al Karlander RC 2.50 6.00
105 John French 2.50 6.00
106 John Hughes 2.50 6.00
107 Ron Grahame 2.50 6.00
108 Mark Napier 2.50 6.00
109 Serge Bernier 2.50 6.00
110 Christer Abrahamsson 2.50 6.00
111 Frank Mahovlich 6.00 15.00
112 Ted Green 2.50 6.00
113 Rick Jodzio 2.50 6.00
114 Michel Dion RC 5.00 12.00
115 Rich Preston RC 2.50 6.00
116 Pekka Rautakallio RC 5.00 12.00
117 Checklist Card 5.00 12.00
118 Marc Tardif 2.50 6.00
119 Doug Barrie 2.50 6.00
120 Vaclav Nedomansky 2.50 6.00
121 Bill Lesuk 2.50 6.00
122 Wayne Connelly 2.50 6.00
123 Pierre Guite 2.50 6.00
124 Ralph Backstrom 2.50 6.00
125 Anders Hedberg 4.00 10.00
126 Norm Ullman 4.00 10.00
127 Steve Sutherland RC 2.50 6.00
128 John Schella 2.50 6.00
129 Don McLeod 2.50 6.00
130 Canadian Finals 5.00 12.00
131 U.S. Finals 4.00 10.00
132 World Trophy Final 2.50 6.00

1977-78 O-Pee-Chee

COMPLETE SET (396) 75.00 150.00
1 Shutt/Lafleur/Dionne LL 2.50 6.00
2 Lafleur/Dionne/Sal/ LL 2.50 6.00
3 Lafleur/Dionne/Shutt LL 2.50 6.00
4 Wills/Polnch/Gassoff LL 2.50 6.00
5 McDonald/Espo/Will LL 2.50 6.00
6 Laroc/Dryden/Resch LL 2.50 6.00
7 Perr/Shutt/Lafleur LL 2.50 6.00
8 Dryden/Vach/Parent LL 2.50 6.00
9 Brian Spencer 2.50 6.00
10 Denis Potvin AS2 2.50 6.00
11 Nick Fotiu 2.50 6.00
12 Bob Murray 2.50 6.00
13 Pete Lopresti 2.50 6.00
14 J. Bob Kelly 2.50 6.00
15 Rick MacLeish 2.50 6.00
16 Terry Harper 2.50 6.00
17 Willi Plett RC 2.50 6.00
18 Peter McNab 2.50 6.00
19 Wayne Thomas 2.50 6.00
20 Pierre Bouchard 2.50 6.00
21 Dennis Maruk 2.50 6.00
22 Mike Murphy 2.50 6.00
23 Cesare Maniago 2.50 6.00
24 Paul Gardner RC 2.50 6.00
25 Rod Gilbert 2.50 6.00
26 Orest Kindrachuk 2.50 6.00
27 Bill Hajt 2.50 6.00
28 John Davidson 2.50 6.00
29 Jean-Paul Parise 2.50 6.00
30 Larry Robinson AS1 4.00 10.00
31 Yvon Labre 2.50 6.00
32 Walt McKechnie 2.50 6.00
33 Rick Kehoe 2.50 6.00
34 Randy Holt RC 2.50 6.00
35 Garry Unger 2.50 6.00
36 Lou Nanne 2.50 6.00
37 Dan Bouchard 2.50 6.00
38 Darryl Sittler 2.50 6.00
39 Bob Murdoch 2.50 6.00
40 Jean Ratelle 2.50 6.00
41 Dave Maloney 2.50 6.00
42 Danny Gare 2.50 6.00
43 Jimmy Watson 2.50 6.00
44 Tom Williams 2.50 6.00
45 Serge Savard 2.50 6.00
46 Derek Sanderson 2.50 6.00
47 John Marks 2.50 6.00
48 Al Cameron RC 2.50 6.00
49 Dean Talafous 2.50 6.00
50 Glenn Resch 2.50 6.00
51 Ron Schock 2.50 6.00
52 Gary Croteau 2.50 6.00
53 Gerry Meehan 2.50 6.00
54 Ed Staniowski 2.50 6.00
55 Phil Esposito UER 2.50 6.00
56 Dennis Ververgaert 2.50 6.00
57 Rick Wilson 2.50 6.00
58 Jim Lorentz 2.50 6.00
59 Bobby Schmautz 2.50 6.00
60 Guy Lapointe AS2 2.50 6.00
61 Ivan Boldirev 2.50 6.00
62 Bob Nystrom 2.50 6.00
63 Rick Hampton 2.50 6.00
64 Jack Valiquette 2.50 6.00
65 Bernie Parent 2.50 6.00
66 Dave Burrows 2.50 6.00
67 Butch Goring 2.50 6.00
68A Checklist 1-132 ERR 2.50 6.00
68B Checklist 1-132 COR 2.50 6.00
69 Murray Wilson 2.50 6.00
70 Ed Giacomin 2.50 6.00
71 Flames Team 2.50 6.00
72 Bruins Team 2.50 6.00
73 Sabres Team 2.50 6.00
74 Blackhawks Team 2.50 6.00
75 Barons Team 2.50 6.00
76 Rockies Team 2.50 6.00
77 Red Wings Team 2.50 6.00
78 Kings Team 2.50 6.00
79 North Stars Team 2.50 6.00
80 Canadiens Team 2.50 6.00
81 Islanders Team 2.50 6.00
82 Rangers Team 2.50 6.00
83 Flyers Team 2.50 6.00
84 Penguins Team 2.50 6.00
85 Blues Team 2.50 6.00
86 Maple Leafs Team 2.50 6.00
87 Canucks Team 2.50 6.00
88 Capitals Team 2.50 6.00
89 Keith Magnuson 2.50 6.00
90 Walt Tkaczuk 2.50 6.00
91 Bill Nyrop 2.50 6.00
92 Michel Plasse 2.50 6.00
93 Bob Bourne 2.50 6.00
94 Lee Fogolin 2.50 6.00
95 Gregg Sheppard 2.50 6.00
96 Hartland Monahan 2.50 6.00
97 Curt Bennett 2.50 6.00
98 Bob Dailey 2.50 6.00
99 Bill Goldsworthy 2.50 6.00
100 Ken Dryden AS1 12.00 30.00
101 Grant Mulvey 2.50 6.00
102 Pierre Larouche 2.50 6.00
103 Nick Libett 2.50 6.00
104 Rick Smith 2.50 6.00
105 Bryan Trottier 6.00 15.00
106 Pierre Jarry 2.50 6.00
107 Red Berenson 2.50 6.00
108 Jim Schoenfeld 2.50 6.00
109 Gilles Meloche 2.50 6.00
110 Lanny McDonald AS2 2.50 6.00
111 Don Lever 2.50 6.00
112 Greg Polis 2.50 6.00
113 Gary Sargent RC 2.50 6.00
114 Earl Anderson RC 2.50 6.00
115 Bobby Clarke 2.50 6.00
116 Dave Lewis 2.50 6.00
117 Darcy Rota 2.50 6.00
118 Andre Savard 2.50 6.00
119 Denis Herron 2.50 6.00
120 Steve Shutt AS1 2.50 6.00
121 Mel Bridgman 2.50 6.00
122 Buster Harvey 2.50 6.00
123 Roland Eriksson RC 2.50 6.00
124 Dale Tallon 2.50 6.00
125 Gilles Gilbert 2.50 6.00
126 Billy Harris 2.50 6.00
127 Tom Lysiak 2.50 6.00
128 Jerry Korab 2.50 6.00
129 Bob Gainey 2.50 6.00
130 Will Paiement 2.50 6.00
131 Tom Bladon 2.50 6.00
132 Ernie Hicke 2.50 6.00
133 J.P. LeBlanc 2.50 6.00
134 Mike Milbury RC 4.00 10.00
135 Pit Martin 2.50 6.00
136 Steve Vickers 2.50 6.00
137 Don Awrey 2.50 6.00
138 Bernie Wolfe 2.50 6.00
139 Doug Jarvis 2.50 6.00
140 Borje Salming AS1 2.50 6.00
141 Bob MacMillan 2.50 6.00
142 Wayne Stephenson 2.50 6.00
143 Dave Forbes 2.50 6.00
144 Jean Potvin 2.50 6.00
145 Guy Charron 2.50 6.00
146 Cliff Koroll 2.50 6.00
147 Danny Grant 2.50 6.00
148 Bill Hogaboam 2.50 6.00
149 Al MacAdam 2.50 6.00
150 Gerry Desjardins 2.50 6.00
151 Yvon Lambert 2.50 6.00
152 Rick Lapointe 2.50 6.00
153 Ed Westfall 2.50 6.00
154 Carol Vadnais 2.50 6.00
155 Johnny Bucyk 2.50 6.00
156 J.P. Bordeleau 2.50 6.00
157 Ron Stackhouse 2.50 6.00
158 Glen Sharpley RC 2.50 6.00
159 Michel Bergeron 2.50 6.00
160 Rogatien Vachon AS2 2.50 6.00
161 Fred Stanfield 2.50 6.00
162 Gerry Hart 2.50 6.00
163 Mario Tremblay 2.50 6.00
164 Andre Dupont 2.50 6.00
165 Don Marcotte 2.50 6.00
166 Wayne Dillon 2.50 6.00
167 Claude Larose 2.50 6.00
168 Eric Vail 2.50 6.00
169 Tom Edur RC 2.50 6.00
170 Tony Esposito 2.50 6.00
171 Andre St.Laurent 2.50 6.00
172 Dan Maloney 2.50 6.00
173 Dennis O'Brien 2.50 6.00
174 Blair Chapman RC 2.50 6.00
175 Dennis Kearns 2.50 6.00
176 Wayne Merrick 2.50 6.00
177 Michel Larocque 2.50 6.00
178 Bob Kelly 2.50 6.00
179 Dave Farrish RC 2.50 6.00
180 Richard Martin AS2 2.50 6.00
181 Gary Doak 2.50 6.00
182 Jude Drouin 2.50 6.00
183 Barry Dean RC 2.50 6.00
184 Gary Smith 2.50 6.00
185 Reggie Leach 2.50 6.00
186 Ian Turnbull 2.50 6.00
187 Vic Venasky 2.50 6.00
188 Wayne Bianchin RC 2.50 6.00
189 Doug Risebrough 2.50 6.00
190 Brad Park 2.50 6.00
191 Craig Ramsay 2.50 6.00
192 Ken Hodge 2.50 6.00
193 Phil Myre 2.50 6.00
194 Garry Howatt 2.50 6.00
195 Stan Mikita 2.50 6.00
196 Garnet Bailey 2.50 6.00
197 Dennis Hextall 2.50 6.00
198 Nick Beverley 2.50 6.00
199 Larry Patey 2.50 6.00
200 Guy Lafleur AS1 20.00 50.00
201 Don Edwards RC 2.50 6.00
202 Gary Dornhoefer 2.50 6.00
203 Bob Paradise 2.50 6.00
204 Alex Pirus RC 2.50 6.00
205 Peter Mahovlich 2.50 6.00
206 Bert Marshall 2.50 6.00
207 Gilles Gratton 2.50 6.00
208 Alain Daigle 2.50 6.00
209 Chris Oddleifson 2.50 6.00
210 Gilbert Perreault AS2 2.50 6.00
211 Mike Palmateer RC 15.00 40.00
212 Billy Lochead 2.50 6.00
213 Dick Redmond 2.50 6.00
214 Guy Lafleur RB 2.50 6.00
215 Ian Turnbull RB 2.50 6.00
216 Guy Lafleur RB 2.50 6.00
217 Steve Shutt RB 2.50 6.00
218 Guy Lafleur RB 2.50 6.00
219 Lorne Henning 2.50 6.00
220 Terry O'Reilly 2.50 6.00
221 Pat Hickey 2.50 6.00
222 Rene Robert 2.50 6.00
223 Tim Young 2.50 6.00
224 Dunc Wilson 2.50 6.00
225 Dennis Hull 2.50 6.00
226 Rod Seiling 2.50 6.00
227 Bill Barber 2.50 6.00
228 Dennis Polonich RC 2.50 6.00
229 Billy Smith 2.50 6.00
230 Yvan Cournoyer 2.50 6.00
231 Don Luce 2.50 6.00
232 Mike McEwen RC 2.50 6.00
233 Don Saleski 2.50 6.00
234 Wayne Cashman 2.50 6.00
235 Phil Russell 2.50 6.00
236 Mike Corrigan 2.50 6.00
237 Guy Chouinard 2.50 6.00
238 Steve Jensen RC 2.50 6.00
239 Jim Rutherford 2.50 6.00
240 Marcel Dionne AS1 2.50 6.00
241 Rejean Houle 2.50 6.00
242 Jocelyn Guevremont 2.50 6.00
243 Jim Harrison 2.50 6.00
244 Don Murdoch RC 2.50 6.00
245 Rick Green RC 2.50 6.00
246 Rick Middleton 2.50 6.00
247 Joe Watson 2.50 6.00
248 Syl Apps 2.50 6.00
249 Checklist 133-264 4.00 10.00
250 Clark Gillies 2.50 6.00
251 Bobby Orr 25.00 60.00
252 Nelson Pyatt 2.50 6.00
253 Gary McAdam RC 2.50 6.00
254 Jacques Lemaire 2.50 6.00
255 Bob Girard 2.50 6.00
256 Ron Greschner 2.50 6.00
257 Ross Lonsberry 2.50 6.00
258 Dave Gardner 2.50 6.00
259 Rick Blight 2.50 6.00
260 Gerry Cheevers 2.50 6.00
261 Jean Pronovost 2.50 6.00
262 Cup Semi-Finals 2.50 6.00
263 Cup Semi-Finals 2.50 6.00
264 Canadiens Champs 2.50 6.00
265 Rick Bowness RC 2.50 6.00
266 George Ferguson 2.50 6.00
267 Mike Kitchen RC 2.50 6.00
268 Bob Berry 2.50 6.00
269 Greg Smith RC 2.50 6.00
270 Stan Jonathan RC 2.50 6.00
271 Dwight Bialowas 2.50 6.00
272 Pete Stemkowski 2.50 6.00
273 Greg Joly 2.50 6.00
274 Ken Houston RC 2.50 6.00
275 Brian Glennie 2.50 6.00
276 Ed Johnston 2.50 6.00
277 John Grisdale 2.50 6.00
278 Craig Patrick 2.50 6.00
279 Ken Breitenbach RC 2.50 6.00
280 Fred Ahern 2.50 6.00
281 Jim Roberts 2.50 6.00
282 Harvey Bennett RC 2.50 6.00
283 Ab DeMarco 2.50 6.00
284 Pat Boutette 2.50 6.00
285 Bob Plager 2.50 6.00
286 Hilliard Graves 2.50 6.00
287 Gordie Lane RC 2.50 6.00
288 Ron Andruff RC 2.50 6.00
289 Larry Brown 2.50 6.00
290 Mike Fidler RC 2.50 6.00
291 Fred Barrett 2.50 6.00
292 Bill Clement 2.50 6.00
293 Errol Thompson 2.50 6.00
294 Doug Grant 2.50 6.00
295 Harold Snepsts 2.50 6.00
296 Rick Bragnalo RC 2.50 6.00
297 Bryan Lefley 2.50 6.00
298 Gene Carr 2.50 6.00
299 Bob Stewart 2.50 6.00
300 Lew Morrison 2.50 6.00
301 Ed Kea 2.50 6.00
302 Scott Garland 2.50 6.00
303 Bill Fairbairn 2.50 6.00
304 Larry Carriere 2.50 6.00
305 Ron Low 2.50 6.00
306 Tom Reid 2.50 6.00
307 Paul Holmgren RC 2.50 6.00
308 Pat Price 2.50 6.00
309 Kirk Bowman RC 2.50 6.00
310 Bobby Simpson RC 2.50 6.00
311 Ron Ellis 2.50 6.00
312 Rick Bourbonnais RC UER 2.50 6.00
313 Bobby Lalonde 2.50 6.00
314 Tony White 2.50 6.00
315 John Van Boxmeer 2.50 6.00
316 Don Kozak 2.50 6.00
317 Jim Neilson 2.50 6.00
318 Terry Martin RC 2.50 6.00
319 Barry Gibbs 2.50 6.00
320 Inge Hammarstrom 2.50 6.00
321 Darryl Edestrand 2.50 6.00
322 Flames Logo 2.50 6.00
323 Bruins Logo 2.50 6.00
324 Sabres Logo 2.50 6.00
325 Blackhawks Logo 2.50 6.00
326 Barons Logo 2.50 6.00
327 Rockies Logo 2.50 6.00
328 Red Wings Logo 2.50 6.00
329 Kings Logo 2.50 6.00
330 North Stars Logo 2.50 6.00
331 Canadiens Logo 2.50 6.00
332 Islanders Logo 2.50 6.00
333 Rangers Logo 2.50 6.00
334 Flyers Logo 2.50 6.00
335 Penguins Logo 2.50 6.00
336 Blues Logo 2.50 6.00
337 Maple Leafs Logo 2.50 6.00
338 Canucks Logo 2.50 6.00
339 Capitals Logo 2.50 6.00
340 Chuck Lefley 2.50 6.00
341 Garry Monahan 2.50 6.00
342 Bryan Watson 2.50 6.00
343 Dave Hudson 2.50 6.00
344 Neil Komadoski 2.50 6.00
345 Gary Edwards 2.50 6.00
346 Rey Comeau 2.50 6.00
347 Bob Neely 2.50 6.00
348 Jean Hamel 2.50 6.00
349 Jerry Butler 2.50 6.00
350 Mike Walton 2.50 6.00
351 Bob Sirois 2.50 6.00
352 Jim McElmury 2.50 6.00
353 Dave Schultz 2.50 6.00
354 Doug Palazzari RC 2.50 6.00
355 David Shand RC 2.50 6.00
356 Stan Weir 2.50 6.00
357 Mike Christie 2.50 6.00
358 Floyd Thomson 2.50 6.00
359 Larry Goodenough 2.50 6.00
360 Bill Riley RC 2.50 6.00
361 Doug Hicks RC 2.50 6.00
362 Dan Newman RC 2.50 6.00
363 Rick Chartraw 2.50 6.00
364 Tim Ecclestone 2.50 6.00
365 Don Ashby RC 2.50 6.00
366 Jacques Richard 2.50 6.00
367 Yves Belanger 2.50 6.00
368 Ron Sedlbauer 2.50 6.00
369 Jack Lynch UER 2.50 6.00
370 Doug Favell 2.50 6.00
371 Bob Murdoch 2.50 6.00
372 Ralph Klassen 2.50 6.00
373 Richard Mulhern 2.50 6.00
374 Jim McKenny 2.50 6.00
375 Mike Bloom 2.50 6.00
376 Bruce Affleck 2.50 6.00
377 Gerry O'Flaherty 2.50 6.00
378 Ron Lalonde 2.50 6.00
379 Chuck Arnason 2.50 6.00
380 Dave Hutchinson 2.50 6.00
381A Checklist ERR 4.00 10.00
381B Checklist COR 4.00 10.00
382 John Gould 2.50 6.00
383 Tiger Williams 2.50 6.00
384 Len Frig 2.50 6.00
385 Pierre Plante 2.50 6.00
386 Ralph Stewart 2.50 6.00
387 Gord Smith 2.50 6.00
388 Dennis Dupere 2.50 6.00
389 Randy Manery 2.50 6.00
390 Lowell MacDonald 2.50 6.00
391 Dennis Owchar 2.50 6.00
392 Jim Roberts RC 2.50 6.00
393 Mike Veisor 2.50 6.00
394 Bob Hess 2.50 6.00
395 Curt Ridley 2.50 6.00
396 Mike Lampman 2.50 6.00

1977-78 O-Pee-Chee WHA

COMPLETE SET (66) 35.00 70.00
1 Gordie Howe 20.00 50.00
2 Jean Bernier RC 4.00 10.00
3 Anders Hedberg 5.00 12.00
4 Ken Broderick 4.00 10.00
5 Joe Noris 4.00 10.00
6 Blaine Stoughton 4.00 10.00
7 Claude St.Sauveur 4.00 10.00
8 Real Cloutier 2.50 6.00
9 Joe Daley 2.50 6.00
10 Ron Chipperfield 2.50 6.00
11 Wayne Rutledge 2.50 6.00
12 Mark Napier 2.50 6.00
13 Rich Leduc 2.50 6.00
14 Don McLeod 2.50 6.00
15 Ulf Nilsson 2.50 6.00
16 Blair MacDonald 2.50 6.00
17 Mike Rogers 2.50 6.00
18 Gary Inness 2.50 6.00
19 Larry Lund 2.50 6.00
20 Marc Tardif 2.50 6.00
21 Lars-Erik Sjoberg 2.50 6.00
22 Bryan Campbell 2.50 6.00
23 John Garrett 2.50 6.00
24 Ron Plumb 2.50 6.00
25 Mark Howe 8.00 20.00
26 Garry Lariviere RC 2.50 6.00
27 Peter Sullivan 2.50 6.00
28 Dave Dryden 2.50 6.00
29 Reg Thomas 2.50 6.00
30 Andre Lacroix 2.50 6.00
31 Paul Henderson 2.50 6.00
32 Paulin Bordeleau 2.50 6.00
33 Juha Widing 2.50 6.00
34 Mike Antonovich 2.50 6.00
35 Robbie Ftorek 4.00 10.00
36 Rosaire Paiement 2.50 6.00
37 Terry Ruskowski 2.50 6.00
38 Richard Brodeur 2.50 6.00
39 Willy Lindstrom RC 2.50 6.00
40 Al Hamilton 4.00 10.00
41 John McKenzie 2.50 6.00
42 Wayne Wood 2.50 6.00
43 Claude Larose 2.50 6.00
44 J.C. Tremblay 2.50 6.00
45 Gary Bromley 4.00 10.00
46 Ken Baird 2.50 6.00
47 Bobby Sheehan 4.00 10.00
48 Don Larway RC 2.50 6.00
49 Al Smith 2.50 6.00
50 Bobby Hull 20.00 50.00
51 Peter Marrin 2.50 6.00
52 Norm Ferguson 2.50 6.00
53 Dennis Sobchuk 2.50 6.00
54 Norm Dube RC 2.50 6.00
55 Tom Webster 2.50 6.00
56 Jim Park RC 2.50 6.00
57 Dan Labraaten RC 2.50 6.00
58 Checklist Card 6.00 15.00
59 Paul Shmyr 2.50 6.00
60 Serge Bernier 2.50 6.00
61 Frank Mahovlich 4.00 10.00
62 Michel Dion 4.00 10.00
63 Poul Popiel 4.00 10.00
64 Lyle Moffat 4.00 10.00
65 Marty Howe 4.00 10.00
66 Don Burgess 5.00 12.00

1978-79 O-Pee-Chee

COMPLETE SET (396) 100.00 200.00
1 Mike Bossy HL 6.00 15.00
2 Phil Esposito HL 2.50 6.00
3 Guy Lafleur HL 2.50 6.00
4 Darryl Sittler HL 2.50 6.00
5 Garry Unger HL 2.50 6.00
6 Gary Edwards 2.50 6.00
7 Rick Blight 2.50 6.00
8 Larry Patey 2.50 6.00
9 Craig Ramsay 2.50 6.00
10 Bryan Trottier 4.00 10.00
11 Don Murdoch 2.50 6.00
12 Phil Russell 2.50 6.00
13 Doug Jarvis 2.50 6.00
14 Gene Carr 2.50 6.00
15 Bernie Parent 2.50 6.00
16 Perry Miller 2.50 6.00
17 Kent-Erik Andersson RC 2.50 6.00
18 Gregg Sheppard 2.50 6.00
19 Dennis Owchar 2.50 6.00
20 Rogatien Vachon 2.50 6.00
21 Dan Maloney 2.50 6.00
22 Guy Charron 2.50 6.00
23 Dick Redmond 2.50 6.00
24 Checklist 1-132 4.00 10.00
25 Anders Hedberg 2.50 6.00
26 Mel Bridgman 2.50 6.00
27 Lee Fogolin 2.50 6.00
28 Gilles Meloche 2.50 6.00
29 Garry Howatt 2.50 6.00
30 Darryl Sittler 2.50 6.00
31 Curt Bennett 2.50 6.00
32 Andre St.Laurent 2.50 6.00
33 Blair Chapman 2.50 6.00
34 Keith Magnuson 2.50 6.00
35 Pierre Larouche 2.50 6.00
36 Michel Plasse 2.50 6.00
37 Gary Sargent 2.50 6.00
38 Mike Walton 2.50 6.00
39 Robert Picard RC 2.50 6.00
40 Terry O'Reilly 2.50 6.00
41 Dave Farrish 2.50 6.00
42 Gary McAdam 2.50 6.00
43 Joe Watson 2.50 6.00
44 Yves Belanger 2.50 6.00
45 Steve Jensen 2.50 6.00
46 Bob Stewart 2.50 6.00
47 Darcy Rota 2.50 6.00
48 Dennis Hextall 2.50 6.00
49 Bert Marshall 2.50 6.00
50 Ken Dryden 10.00 25.00
51 Peter Mahovlich 2.50 6.00
52 Dennis Ververgaert 2.50 6.00
53 Inge Hammarstrom 2.50 6.00
54 Doug Favell 2.50 6.00
55 Steve Vickers 2.50 6.00
56 Syl Apps 2.50 6.00
57 Errol Thompson 2.50 6.00
58 Don Luce 2.50 6.00
59 Mike Milbury 2.50 6.00
60 Yvan Cournoyer 2.50 6.00
61 Kirk Bowman 2.50 6.00
62 Billy Smith 2.50 6.00
63 Lafleur/Bossy/Shutt LL 6.00 15.00
64 Trott/Lafleur/Sitt LL 2.50 6.00
65 Lafleur/Trott/Sitt LL 2.50 6.00
66 Schltz/Will/Polnich LL 2.50 6.00
67 Bossy/Espo/Shutt LL 4.00 10.00
68 Dryden/Parent/Gilb LL 4.00 10.00
69 Lafleur/Barber/Sitt LL 2.50 6.00
70 Parent/Dryden/Espo LL 4.00 10.00
71 Bob Kelly 2.50 6.00
72 Ron Stackhouse 2.50 6.00
73 Wayne Dillon 2.50 6.00
74 Jim Rutherford 2.50 6.00
75 Stan Mikita 2.50 6.00
76 Bob Gainey 2.50 6.00
77 Gerry Hart 2.50 6.00
78 Lanny McDonald 2.50 6.00
79 Brad Park 2.50 6.00
80 Richard Martin 2.50 6.00
81 Bernie Wolfe 2.50 6.00
82 Bob MacMillan 2.50 6.00
83 Brad Maxwell RC 2.50 6.00
84 Mike Fidler 2.50 6.00
85 Carol Vadnais 2.50 6.00
86 Don Lever 2.50 6.00
87 Phil Myre 2.50 6.00
88 Paul Gardner 2.50 6.00
89 Bob Murray 2.50 6.00
90 Guy Lafleur 4.00 10.00
91 Bob Murdoch 2.50 6.00
92 Ron Ellis 2.50 6.00
93 Jude Drouin 2.50 6.00
94 Jocelyn Guevremont 2.50 6.00
95 Gilles Gilbert 2.50 6.00
96 Bob Sirois 2.50 6.00
97 Tom Lysiak 2.50 6.00
98 Andre Dupont 2.50 6.00
99 Per-Olov Brasar RC 2.50 6.00
100 Phil Esposito 2.50 6.00
101 J.P. Bordeleau 2.50 6.00
102 Pierre Mondou RC 2.50 6.00
103 Wayne Bianchin 2.50 6.00
104 Dennis O'Brien 2.50 6.00
105 Glenn Resch 2.50 6.00
106 Dennis Polonich 2.50 6.00
107 Kris Manery RC 2.50 6.00
108 Bill Hajt 2.50 6.00
109 Jere Gillis RC 2.50 6.00
110 Garry Unger 2.50 6.00
111 Nick Beverley 2.50 6.00
112 Pat Hickey 2.50 6.00
113 Rick Middleton 2.50 6.00
114 Orest Kindrachuk 2.50 6.00
115 Mike Bossy RC 50.00 125.00
116 Pierre Bouchard 2.50 6.00
117 Alain Daigle 2.50 6.00
118 Terry Martin 2.50 6.00
119 Tom Edur 2.50 6.00
120 Marcel Dionne 2.50 6.00
121 Barry Beck RC 2.50 6.00
122 Billy Lochead 2.50 6.00
123 Paul Harrison RC 2.50 6.00
124 Wayne Cashman 2.50 6.00
125 Rick MacLeish 2.50 6.00
126 Bob Bourne 2.50 6.00
127 Ian Turnbull 2.50 6.00
128 Gerry Meehan 2.50 6.00
129 Eric Vail 2.50 6.00
130 Gilbert Perreault 2.50 6.00
131 Bob Dailey 2.50 6.00
132 Dale McCourt RC 2.50 6.00
133 John Wensink RC 2.50 6.00
134 Bill Nyrop 2.50 6.00
135 Ivan Boldirev 2.50 6.00
136 Lucien DeBlois RC 2.50 6.00
137 Brian Spencer 2.50 6.00
138 Tim Young 2.50 6.00
139 Ron Sedlbauer 2.50 6.00
140 Gerry Cheevers 2.50 6.00
141 Dennis Maruk 2.50 6.00
142 Barry Dean 2.50 6.00
143 Bernie Federko RC 15.00 40.00
144 Stefan Persson RC 2.50 6.00
145 Wilf Paiement 2.50 6.00
146 Dale Tallon 2.50 6.00
147 Yvon Lambert 2.50 6.00
148 Greg Joly 2.50 6.00
149 Dean Talafous 2.50 6.00
150 Don Edwards 2.50 6.00
151 Butch Goring 2.50 6.00
152 Tom Bladon 2.50 6.00
153 Bob Nystrom 2.50 6.00
154 Ron Greschner 2.50 6.00
155 Jean Ratelle 2.50 6.00
156 Russ Anderson RC 2.50 6.00
157 John Marks 2.50 6.00
158 Michel Larocque 2.50 6.00
159 Paul Woods RC 2.50 6.00
160 Mike Palmateer 2.50 6.00
161 Jim Lorentz 2.50 6.00
162 Dave Lewis 2.50 6.00
163 Harvey Bennett 2.50 6.00
164 Rick Smith 2.50 6.00
165 Reggie Leach 2.50 6.00
166 Wayne Thomas 2.50 6.00
167 Dave Forbes 2.50 6.00
168 Doug Wilson RC 12.00 30.00
169 Dan Bouchard 2.50 6.00
170 Steve Shutt 2.50 6.00
171 Mike Kaszycki RC 2.50 6.00
172 Denis Herron 2.50 6.00
173 Rick Bowness 2.50 6.00
174 Rick Hampton 2.50 6.00
175 Glen Sharpley 2.50 6.00
176 Bill Barber 2.50 6.00
177 Ron Duguay RC 4.00 10.00
178 Jim Schoenfeld 2.50 6.00
179 Pierre Plante 2.50 6.00
180 Jacques Lemaire 2.50 6.00
181 Stan Jonathan 2.50 6.00
182 Billy Harris 2.50 6.00
183 Chris Oddleifson 2.50 6.00
184 Jean Pronovost 2.50 6.00
185 Fred Barrett 2.50 6.00
186 Ross Lonsberry 2.50 6.00
187 Mike McEwen 2.50 6.00
188 Rene Robert 2.50 6.00
189 J. Bob Kelly 2.50 6.00
190 Serge Savard 2.50 6.00
191 Dennis Kearns 2.50 6.00
192 Flames Team 2.50 6.00
193 Bruins Team 2.50 6.00
194 Sabres Team 2.50 6.00
195 Blackhawks Team 2.50 6.00
196 Rockies Team 2.50 6.00
197 Red Wings Team 2.50 6.00
198 Kings Team 2.50 6.00
199 North Stars Team 2.50 6.00
200 Canadiens Team 2.50 6.00
201 Islanders Team 2.50 6.00
202 Rangers Team 2.50 6.00
203 Flyers Team 2.50 6.00
204 Penguins Team 2.50 6.00
205 Blues Team 2.50 6.00
206 Maple Leafs Team 2.50 6.00
207 Canucks Team 2.50 6.00
208 Capitals Team 2.50 6.00
209 Danny Gare 2.50 6.00
210 Larry Robinson 2.50 6.00
211 John Davidson 2.50 6.00
212 Peter McNab 2.50 6.00
213 Rick Kehoe 2.50 6.00
214 Terry Harper 2.50 6.00
215 Bobby Clarke 2.50 6.00
216 Bryan Maxwell UER 2.50 6.00
217 Ted Bulley RC 2.50 6.00
218 Red Berenson 2.50 6.00
219 Ron Grahame 2.50 6.00
220 Clark Gillies 2.50 6.00
221 Dave Maloney 2.50 6.00
222 Derek Smith RC 2.50 6.00
223 Wayne Stephenson 2.50 6.00
224 John Van Boxmeer 2.50 6.00
225 Dave Schultz 2.50 6.00
226 Reed Larson RC 2.50 6.00
227 Rejean Houle 2.50 6.00
228 Doug Hicks 2.50 6.00
229 Mike Murphy 2.50 6.00
230 Pete Lopresti 2.50 6.00
231 Jerry Korab 2.50 6.00
232 Ed Westfall 2.50 6.00
233 Greg Malone RC 2.50 6.00
234 Paul Holmgren 2.50 6.00
235 Walt Tkaczuk 2.50 6.00
236 Don Marcotte 2.50 6.00
237 Ron Low 2.50 6.00
238 Rick Chartraw 2.50 6.00
239 Cliff Koroll 2.50 6.00
240 Borje Salming 2.50 6.00
241 Roland Eriksson 2.50 6.00
242 Ric Seiling RC 2.50 6.00
243 Jim Bedard RC 2.50 6.00
244 Peter Lee RC 2.50 6.00
245 Denis Potvin 2.50 6.00
246 Greg Polis 2.50 6.00
247 Jimmy Watson 2.50 6.00
248 Bobby Schmautz 2.50 6.00
249 Doug Risebrough 2.50 6.00
250 Tony Esposito 2.50 6.00
251 Nick Libett 2.50 6.00
252 Ron Zanussi RC 2.50 6.00
253 Andre Savard 2.50 6.00
254 Dave Burrows 2.50 6.00
255 Ulf Nilsson 2.50 6.00
256 Richard Mulhern 2.50 6.00
257 Don Saleski 2.50 6.00
258 Wayne Merrick 2.50 6.00
259 Checklist 133-264 4.00 10.00
260 Guy Lapointe 2.50 6.00
261 Grant Mulvey 2.50 6.00
262 Stanley Cup Semifinals 2.50 6.00
263 Stanley Cup Semifinals 2.50 6.00
264 Stanley Cup Finals 2.50 6.00
265 Bob Sauve 2.50 6.00
266 Randy Manery 2.50 6.00
267 Bill Fairbairn 2.50 6.00
268 Garry Monahan 2.50 6.00
269 Colin Campbell 2.50 6.00
270 Dan Newman 2.50 6.00
271 Dwight Foster RC 2.50 6.00
272 Larry Carriere 2.50 6.00
273 Michel Bergeron 2.50 6.00
274 Scott Garland 2.50 6.00
275 Bill McKenzie 2.50 6.00
276 Garnet Bailey 2.50 6.00
277 Ed Kea 2.50 6.00
278 Dave Gardner 2.50 6.00
279 Bruce Affleck 2.50 6.00
280 Bruce Boudreau RC 2.50 6.00
281 Jean Hamel 2.50 6.00
282 Kurt Walker RC 2.50 6.00
283 Denis Dupere 2.50 6.00
284 Gordie Lane 2.50 6.00
285 Bobby Lalonde 2.50 6.00
286 Pit Martin 2.50 6.00
287 Jean Potvin 2.50 6.00
288 Jimmy Jones RC 2.50 6.00
289 Dave Hutchinson 2.50 6.00
290 Pete Stemkowski 2.50 6.00
291 Mike Christie 2.50 6.00
292 Bill Riley 2.50 6.00
293 Rey Comeau 2.50 6.00
294 Jack McIlhargey RC 2.50 6.00
295 Tom Younghans RC 2.50 6.00
296 Mario Faubert RC 2.50 6.00
297 Checklist 265-396 4.00 10.00
298 Rob Palmer RC 2.50 6.00
299 Dave Hudson 2.50 6.00
300 Bobby Orr 20.00 50.00
301 Lorne Stamler RC 2.50 6.00
302 Curt Ridley 2.50 6.00

303 Greg Smith 2.50 6.00
304 Jerry Butler 2.50 6.00
305 Gary Doak 2.50 6.00
306 Danny Grant 2.50 6.00
307 Mark Suzor RC 2.50 6.00
308 Rick Bragnalo 2.50 6.00
309 John Gould 2.50 6.00
310 Sheldon Kannegiesser 2.50 6.00
311 Bobby Sheehan 2.50 6.00
312 Randy Carlyle RC 4.00 10.00
313 Lorne Henning 2.50 6.00
314 Tom Williams 2.50 6.00
315 Ron Andruff 2.50 6.00
316 Bryan Watson 2.50 6.00
317 Willi Plett 2.50 6.00
318 John Grisdale 2.50 6.00
319 Brian Sutter RC 5.00 12.00
320 Trevor Johansen RC 2.50 6.00
321 Vic Venasky 2.50 6.00
322 Rick Lapointe 2.50 6.00
323 Ron Delorme RC 2.50 6.00
324 Yvon Labre 2.50 6.00
325 Bryan Trottier AS UER 4.00 10.00
326 Guy Lafleur AS 2.50 6.00
327 Clark Gillies AS 2.50 6.00
328 Borje Salming AS 2.50 6.00
329 Larry Robinson AS 2.50 6.00
330 Ken Dryden AS 4.00 10.00
331 Darryl Sittler AS 2.50 6.00
332 Terry O'Reilly AS 2.50 6.00
333 Steve Shutt AS 2.50 6.00
334 Denis Potvin AS 2.50 6.00
335 Serge Savard AS 2.50 6.00
336 Don Edwards AS 2.50 6.00
337 Glenn Goldup 2.50 6.00
338 Mike Kitchen 2.50 6.00
339 Bob Girard 2.50 6.00
340 Guy Chouinard 2.50 6.00
341 Randy Holt 2.50 6.00
342 Jim Roberts 2.50 6.00
343 Dave Logan RC 2.50 6.00
344 Walt McKechnie 2.50 6.00
345 Brian Glennie 2.50 6.00
346 Ralph Klassen 2.50 6.00
347 Gord Smith 2.50 6.00
348 Ken Houston 2.50 6.00
349 Bob Manno RC 2.50 6.00
350 Jean-Paul Parise 2.50 6.00
351 Don Ashby 2.50 6.00
352 Fred Stanfield 2.50 6.00
353 Dave Taylor RC 8.00 20.00
354 Nelson Pyatt 2.50 6.00
355 Blair Stewart RC 2.50 6.00
356 David Shand 2.50 6.00
357 Hilliard Graves 2.50 6.00
358 Bob Hess 2.50 6.00
359 Tiger Williams 2.50 6.00
360 Larry Wright RC 2.50 6.00
361 Larry Brown 2.50 6.00
362 Gary Croteau 2.50 6.00
363 Rick Green 2.50 6.00
364 Bill Clement 2.50 6.00
365 Gerry O'Flaherty 2.50 6.00
366 John Baby RC 2.50 6.00
367 Nick Fotiu 2.50 6.00
368 Pat Price 2.50 6.00
369 Bert Wilson 2.50 6.00
370 Bryan Lefley 2.50 6.00
371 Ron Lalonde 2.50 6.00
372 Bobby Simpson 2.50 6.00
373 Doug Grant 2.50 6.00
374 Pat Boutette 2.50 6.00
375 Bob Paradise 2.50 6.00
376 Mario Tremblay 2.50 6.00
377 Darryl Edestrand 2.50 6.00
378 Andy Spruce RC 2.50 6.00
379 Jack Brownschidle RC 2.50 6.00
380 Harold Snepsts 2.50 6.00
381 Al MacAdam 2.50 6.00
382 Neil Komadoski 2.50 6.00
383 Don Awrey 2.50 6.00
384 Ron Schock 2.50 6.00
385 Gary Simmons 2.50 6.00
386 Fred Ahern 2.50 6.00
387 Larry Bolonchuk 2.50 6.00
388 Brad Gassoff RC 2.50 6.00
389 Chuck Arnason 2.50 6.00
390 Barry Gibbs 2.50 6.00
391 Jack Valiquette 2.50 6.00
392 Doug Halward 2.50 6.00
393 Hartland Monahan 2.50 6.00
394 Rod Seiling 2.50 6.00
395 George Ferguson 2.50 6.00
396 Al Cameron 2.50 6.00

1979-80 O-Pee-Chee

COMPLETE SET (396) 1200.00 3000.00
1 Bossy/Dionne/Lafleur LL 40.00 100.00
2 Trott/Lafleur/Dionne LL 3.00 8.00
3 Trott/Dionne/Lafleur LL 4.00 10.00
4 Williams/Holt/Schultz LL 2.00 5.00
5 Bossy/Dionne/Gardner LL 5.00 12.00
6 Dryden/Resch/Parent LL 15.00 40.00
7 Lafleur/Bossy/Trott/ LL 3.00 8.00
8 Dryden/Espo/Parent LL 8.00 20.00
9 Greg Malone 2.00 5.00
10 Rick Middleton 2.00 5.00
11 Greg Smith 2.00 5.00
12 Rene Robert 2.00 5.00
13 Doug Risebrough 2.00 5.00
14 Bob Kelly 2.00 5.00
15 Walt Tkaczuk 2.00 5.00
16 John Marks 2.00 5.00
17 Willie Huber RC 2.00 5.00
18 Wayne Gretzky UER RC 1500.00 4000.00
19 Ron Sedlbauer 2.00 5.00
20 Glenn Resch AS2 2.00 5.00
21 Blair Chapman 2.00 5.00
22 Ron Zanussi 2.00 5.00
23 Brad Park 3.00 8.00
24 Yvon Lambert 2.00 5.00
25 Andre Savard 2.00 5.00
26 Jimmy Watson 2.00 5.00
27 Hal Philipoff RC 2.00 5.00
28 Dan Bouchard 2.00 5.00
29 Bob Sirois 2.00 5.00
30 Ulf Nilsson 2.00 5.00
31 Mike Murphy 2.00 5.00
32 Stefan Persson 2.00 5.00
33 Garry Unger 2.00 5.00
34 Rejean Houle 2.00 5.00
35 Barry Beck 2.00 5.00
36 Tim Young 2.00 5.00
37 Rick Dudley 2.00 5.00
38 Wayne Stephenson 2.00 5.00
39 Peter McNab 2.00 5.00
40 Borje Salming AS2 2.00 5.00
41 Tom Lysiak 2.00 5.00
42 Don Maloney RC 2.00 5.00
43 Mike Rogers 2.00 5.00
44 Dave Lewis 2.00 5.00
45 Peter Lee 2.00 5.00
46 Marty Howe 2.00 5.00
47 Serge Bernier 2.00 5.00
48 Paul Woods 2.00 5.00
49 Bob Sauve 2.00 5.00
50 Larry Robinson AS1 3.00 8.00
51 Tom Gorence RC 2.00 5.00
52 Gary Sargent 2.00 5.00
53 Thomas Gradin RC 2.00 5.00
54 Dean Talafous 2.00 5.00
55 Bob Murray 2.00 5.00
56 Bob Bourne 2.00 5.00
57 Larry Patey 2.00 5.00
58 Ross Lonsberry 2.00 5.00
59 Rick Smith UER 2.00 5.00
60 Guy Chouinard 2.00 5.00
61 Danny Gare 2.00 5.00
62 Jim Bedard 2.00 5.00
63 Dale McCourt UER 2.00 5.00
64 Steve Payne RC 2.00 5.00
65 Pat Hughes RC 2.00 5.00
66 Mike McEwen 2.00 5.00
67 Reg Kerr RC 2.00 5.00
68 Walt McKechnie 2.00 5.00
69 Michel Plasse 2.00 5.00
70 Denis Potvin AS1 2.00 5.00
71 Dave Dryden 2.00 5.00
72 Gary McAdam 2.00 5.00
73 Andre St.Laurent 2.00 5.00
74 Jerry Korab 2.00 5.00
75 Rick MacLeish 2.00 5.00
76 Dennis Kearns 2.00 5.00
77 Jean Pronovost 2.00 5.00
78 Ron Greschner 2.00 5.00
79 Wayne Cashman 2.00 5.00
80 Tony Esposito 3.00 8.00
81 Jets Logo CL 20.00 50.00
82 Oilers Logo CL 40.00 100.00
83 Stanley Cup Finals 12.00 30.00
84 Brian Sutter 2.00 5.00
85 Gerry Cheevers 2.00 5.00
86 Pat Hickey 2.00 5.00
87 Mike Kaszycki 2.00 5.00
88 Grant Mulvey 2.00 5.00
89 Derek Smith 2.00 5.00
90 Steve Shutt 2.00 5.00
91 Robert Picard 2.00 5.00
92 Dan Labraaten 2.00 5.00
93 Glen Sharpley 2.00 5.00
94 Denis Herron 2.00 5.00
95 Reggie Leach 2.00 5.00
96 John Van Boxmeer 2.00 5.00
97 Tiger Williams 2.00 5.00
98 Butch Goring 2.00 5.00
99 Don Marcotte 2.00 5.00
100 Bryan Trottier AS1 3.00 8.00
101 Serge Savard AS2 2.00 5.00
102 Cliff Koroll 2.00 5.00
103 Gary Smith 2.00 5.00
104 Al MacAdam 2.00 5.00
105 Don Edwards 2.00 5.00
106 Errol Thompson 2.00 5.00
107 Andre Lacroix 2.00 5.00
108 Marc Tardif 2.00 5.00
109 Rick Kehoe 2.00 5.00
110 John Davidson 2.00 5.00
111 Behn Wilson RC 2.00 5.00
112 Doug Jarvis 2.00 5.00
113 Tom Rowe RC 2.00 5.00
114 Mike Milbury 2.00 5.00
115 Billy Harris 2.00 5.00
116 Greg Fox RC 2.00 5.00
117 Curt Fraser RC 2.00 5.00
118 Jean-Paul Parise 2.00 5.00
119 Ric Seiling 2.00 5.00
120 Darryl Sittler 2.00 5.00
121 Rick Lapointe 2.00 5.00
122 Jim Rutherford 2.00 5.00
123 Mario Tremblay 2.00 5.00
124 Randy Carlyle 2.00 5.00
125 Bobby Clarke 3.00 8.00
126 Wayne Thomas 2.00 5.00
127 Ivan Boldirev 2.00 5.00
128 Ted Bulley 2.00 5.00
129 Dick Redmond 2.00 5.00
130 Clark Gillies AS1 2.00 5.00
131 Checklist 1-132 25.00 60.00
132 Vaclav Nedomansky 2.00 5.00
133 Richard Mulhern 2.00 5.00
134 Dave Schultz 2.00 5.00
135 Guy Lapointe 2.00 5.00
136 Gilles Meloche 2.00 5.00
137 Randy Pierce RC 2.00 5.00
138 Cam Connor 2.00 5.00
139 George Ferguson 2.00 5.00
140 Bill Barber 2.00 5.00
141 Terry Ruskowski UER 2.00 5.00
142 Wayne Babych RC 2.00 5.00
143 Phil Russell 2.00 5.00
144 Bobby Schmautz 2.00 5.00
145 Carol Vadnais 2.00 5.00
146 John Tonelli RC 8.00 20.00
147 Peter Marsh RC 2.00 5.00
148 Thommie Bergman 2.00 5.00
149 Richard Martin 2.00 5.00
150 Ken Dryden AS1 10.00 25.00
151 Kris Manery 2.00 5.00
152 Guy Charron 2.00 5.00
153 Lanny McDonald 2.00 5.00
154 Ron Stackhouse 2.00 5.00
155 Stan Mikita 3.00 8.00
156 Paul Holmgren 2.00 5.00
157 Perry Miller 2.00 5.00
158 Gary Croteau 2.00 5.00
159 Dave Maloney 2.00 5.00
160 Marcel Dionne AS2 3.00 8.00
161 Mike Bossy RB 3.00 8.00
162 Don Maloney RB 2.00 5.00
163 Whalers Logo CL 6.00 15.00
164 Brad Park RB 2.00 5.00
165 Bryan Trottier RB 2.00 5.00
166 Al Hill RC 2.00 5.00
167 Gary Bromley UER 2.00 5.00
168 Don Murdoch 2.00 5.00
169 Wayne Merrick 2.00 5.00
170 Bob Gainey 2.00 5.00
171 Jim Schoenfeld 2.00 5.00
172 Gregg Sheppard 2.00 5.00
173 Dan Bolduc RC 2.00 5.00
174 Blake Dunlop 2.00 5.00
175 Gordie Howe 15.00 40.00
176 Richard Brodeur 2.00 5.00
177 Tom Younghans 2.00 5.00
178 Andre Dupont 2.00 5.00
179 Ed Johnstone RC 2.00 5.00
180 Gilbert Perreault 2.00 5.00
181 Bob Lorimer RC 2.00 5.00
182 John Wensink 2.00 5.00
183 Lee Fogolin 2.00 5.00
184 Greg Carroll RC 2.00 5.00
185 Bobby Hull 10.00 25.00
186 Harold Snepsts 2.00 5.00
187 Peter Mahovlich 2.00 5.00
188 Eric Vail 2.00 5.00
189 Phil Myre 2.00 5.00
190 Wilf Paiement 2.00 5.00
191 Charlie Simmer RC 5.00 12.00
192 Per-Olov Brasar 2.00 5.00
193 Lorne Henning 2.00 5.00
194 Don Luce 2.00 5.00
195 Steve Vickers 2.00 5.00
196 Bob Miller RC 2.00 5.00
197 Mike Palmateer 2.00 5.00
198 Nick Libett 2.00 5.00
199 Pat Ribble RC 2.00 5.00
200 Guy Lafleur AS1 6.00 15.00
201 Mel Bridgman 2.00 5.00
202 Morris Lukowich RC 2.00 5.00
203 Don Lever 2.00 5.00
204 Tom Bladon 2.00 5.00
205 Garry Howatt 2.00 5.00
206 Bobby Smith RC 8.00 20.00
207 Craig Ramsay 2.00 5.00
208 Ron Duguay 2.00 5.00
209 Gilles Gilbert 2.00 5.00
210 Bob MacMillan 2.00 5.00
211 Pierre Mondou 2.00 5.00
212 J.P. Bordeleau 2.00 5.00
213 Reed Larson 2.00 5.00
214 Dennis Ververgaert 2.00 5.00
215 Bernie Federko 8.00 20.00
216 Mark Howe 4.00 10.00
217 Bob Nystrom 2.00 5.00
218 Orest Kindrachuk 2.00 5.00
219 Mike Fidler 2.00 5.00
220 Phil Esposito 2.00 5.00
221 Bill Hajt 2.00 5.00
222 Mark Napier 2.00 5.00
223 Dennis Maruk 2.00 5.00
224 Dennis Polonich 2.00 5.00
225 Jean Ratelle 2.00 5.00
226 Bob Dailey 2.00 5.00
227 Alain Daigle 2.00 5.00
228 Ian Turnbull 2.00 5.00
229 Jack Valiquette 2.00 5.00
230 Mike Bossy AS2 12.00 30.00
231 Brad Maxwell 2.00 5.00
232 Dave Taylor 3.00 8.00
233 Pierre Larouche 2.00 5.00
234 Rod Schutt RC 2.00 5.00
235 Rogatien Vachon 2.00 5.00
236 Ryan Walter RC 2.00 5.00
237 Checklist 133-264 UER 20.00 50.00
238 Terry O'Reilly 2.00 5.00
239 Real Cloutier 2.00 5.00
240 Anders Hedberg 2.00 5.00
241 Ken Linseman RC 3.00 8.00
242 Billy Smith 2.00 5.00
243 Rick Chartraw 2.00 5.00
244 Flames Team 3.00 8.00
245 Bruins Team 3.00 8.00
246 Sabres Team 3.00 8.00
247 Blackhawks Team 3.00 8.00
248 Rockies Team 3.00 8.00
249 Red Wings Team 3.00 8.00
250 Kings Team 3.00 8.00
251 North Stars Team 3.00 8.00
252 Canadiens Team 8.00 20.00
253 Islanders Team 3.00 8.00
254 Rangers Team 3.00 8.00
255 Flyers Team 3.00 8.00
256 Penguins Team 3.00 8.00
257 Blues Team 3.00 8.00
258 Maple Leafs Team 3.00 8.00
259 Canucks Team 4.00 10.00
260 Capitals Team 3.00 8.00
261 Nordiques Team 5.00 12.00
262 Jean Hamel 2.00 5.00
263 Stan Jonathan 2.00 5.00
264 Russ Anderson 2.00 5.00
265 Gordie Roberts RC 2.00 5.00
266 Bill Flett 2.00 5.00
267 Robbie Ftorek 2.00 5.00
268 Mike Amodeo 2.00 5.00
269 Vic Venasky 2.00 5.00
270 Bob Manno 2.00 5.00
271 Dan Maloney 2.00 5.00
272 Al Sims 2.00 5.00
273 Greg Polis 2.00 5.00
274 Doug Favell 2.00 5.00
275 Pierre Plante 2.00 5.00
276 Bob Murdoch 2.00 5.00
277 Lyle Moffat 2.00 5.00
278 Jack Brownschidle 2.00 5.00
279 Dave Keon 2.00 5.00
280 Darryl Edestrand 2.00 5.00
281 Greg Millen RC 4.00 10.00
282 John Gould 2.00 5.00
283 Rich Leduc 2.00 5.00
284 Ron Delorme 2.00 5.00
285 Gord Smith 2.00 5.00
286 Nick Fotiu 2.00 5.00
287 Kevin McCarthy RC 2.00 5.00
288 Jimmy Jones 2.00 5.00
289 Pierre Bouchard 2.00 5.00
290 Wayne Bianchin 2.00 5.00
291 Garry Lariviere 2.00 5.00
292 Steve Jensen 2.00 5.00
293 John Garrett 2.00 5.00
294 Hilliard Graves 2.00 5.00
295 Bill Clement 2.00 5.00
296 Michel Larocque 2.00 5.00
297 Bob Stewart 2.00 5.00
298 Doug Patey RC 2.00 5.00
299 Dave Farrish 2.00 5.00
300 Al Smith 2.00 5.00
301 Billy Lochead 2.00 5.00
302 Dave Hutchinson 2.00 5.00
303 Bill Riley 2.00 5.00
304 Barry Gibbs 2.00 5.00
305 Chris Oddleifson 2.00 5.00
306 J. Bob Kelly UER 2.00 5.00
307 Al Hangsleben RC 2.00 5.00
308 Curt Brackenbury RC 2.00 5.00
309 Rick Green 2.00 5.00
310 Ken Houston 2.00 5.00
311 Greg Joly 2.00 5.00
312 Bill Lesuk 2.00 5.00
313 Bill Stewart RC 2.00 5.00
314 Rick Ley 2.00 5.00
315 Brett Callighen RC 2.00 5.00
316 Michel Dion 2.00 5.00
317 Randy Manery 2.00 5.00
318 Barry Dean 2.00 5.00
319 Pat Boutette 2.00 5.00
320 Mark Heaslip 2.00 5.00
321 Dave Inkpen 2.00 5.00
322 Jere Gillis 2.00 5.00
323 Larry Brown 2.00 5.00
324 Alain Cote RC 2.00 5.00
325 Gordie Lane 2.00 5.00
326 Bobby Lalonde 2.00 5.00
327 Ed Staniowski 2.00 5.00
328 Ron Plumb 2.00 5.00
329 Jude Drouin 2.00 5.00
330 Rick Hampton 2.00 5.00
331 Stan Weir 2.00 5.00
332 Blair Stewart 2.00 5.00
333 Mike Polich RC 2.00 5.00
334 Jean Potvin 2.00 5.00
335 Jordy Douglas RC 2.00 5.00
336 Joel Quenneville RC 2.00 5.00
337 Glen Hanlon RC 3.00 8.00
338 Dave Hoyda RC 2.00 5.00
339 Colin Campbell 2.00 5.00
340 John Smrke 2.00 5.00
341 Brian Glennie 2.00 5.00
342 Don Kozak 2.00 5.00
343 Yvon Labre 2.00 5.00
344 Curt Bennett 2.00 5.00
345 Mike Christie 2.00 5.00
346 Checklist 265-396 12.00 30.00
347 Pat Price 2.00 5.00
348 Ron Low 2.00 5.00
349 Mike Antonovich 2.00 5.00
350 Roland Eriksson 2.00 5.00
351 Bob Murdoch 2.00 5.00
352 Rob Palmer 2.00 5.00
353 Brad Gassoff 2.00 5.00
354 Bruce Boudreau 3.00 8.00
355 Al Hamilton 2.00 5.00
356 Blaine Stoughton 2.00 5.00
357 John Baby 2.00 5.00
358 Gary Inness 2.00 5.00
359 Wayne Dillon 2.00 5.00
360 Darcy Rota 2.00 5.00
361 Brian Engblom RC 2.00 5.00
362 Bill Hogaboam 2.00 5.00
363 Dave Debol RC 2.00 5.00
364 Pete Lopresti 2.00 5.00
365 Gerry Hart 2.00 5.00
366 Syl Apps 2.00 5.00
367 Jack McIlhargey 2.00 5.00
368 Willy Lindstrom 2.00 5.00
369 Don Laurence RC 2.00 5.00
370 Chuck Luksa RC 2.00 5.00
371 Dave Semenko RC 12.00 30.00
372 Paul Baxter RC 2.00 5.00
373 Ron Ellis 2.00 5.00
374 Leif Svensson RC 2.00 5.00
375 Dennis O'Brien 2.00 5.00
376 Glenn Goldup 2.00 5.00
377 Terry Richardson 2.00 5.00
378 Peter Sullivan 2.00 5.00
379 Doug Hicks 2.00 5.00
380 Jamie Hislop RC 2.00 5.00
381 Jocelyn Guevremont 2.00 5.00
382 Willi Plett 2.00 5.00
383 Larry Goodenough 2.00 5.00
384 Jim Warner RC 2.00 5.00
385 Rey Comeau 2.00 5.00
386 Barry Melrose RC 12.00 30.00
387 Dave Hunter RC 2.00 5.00
388 Wally Weir RC 2.00 5.00
389 Mario Lessard RC 2.00 5.00
390 Ed Kea 2.00 5.00
391 Bob Stephenson RC 2.00 5.00
392 Dennis Hextall 2.00 5.00
393 Jerry Butler 2.00 5.00
394 David Shand 2.00 5.00
395 Rick Blight 2.00 5.00
396 Lars-Erik Sjoberg 3.00 8.00

1980-81 O-Pee-Chee

COMPLETE SET (396) 250.00 600.00
1 Philadelphia Flyers RB .60 1.50
2 Ray Bourque RB 5.00 12.00
3 Wayne Gretzky RB 40.00 100.00
4 Charlie Simmer RB .60 1.50
5 Billy Smith RB .40 1.00
6 Jean Ratelle .40 1.00
7 Dave Maloney .30 .75
8 Phil Myre .40 1.00
9 Ken Morrow OLY RC 1.25 3.00
10 Guy Lafleur 1.25 3.00
11 Bill Derlago RC .30 .75
12 Doug Wilson .60 1.50
13 Craig Ramsay .25 .60
14 Pat Boutette .25 .60
15 Eric Vail .25 .60
16 Mike Foligno TL .75 2.00
17 Bobby Smith .75 2.00
18 Rick Kehoe .30 .75
19 Joel Quenneville .25 .60
20 Marcel Dionne .75 2.00
21 Kevin McCarthy .25 .60
22 Jim Craig OLY RC 4.00 10.00
23 Steve Vickers .25 .60
24 Ken Linseman .40 1.00
25 Mike Bossy 12.00 30.00
26 Serge Savard .50 1.25
27 Grant Mulvey TL .30 .75
28 Pat Hickey .25 .60
29 Peter Sullivan .25 .60
30 Blaine Stoughton .30 .75
31 Mike Liut RC 15.00 40.00
32 Blair MacDonald .25 .60
33 Rick Green .25 .60
34 Al MacAdam .30 .75
35 Robbie Ftorek .25 .60
36 Dick Redmond .25 .60
37 Ron Duguay .30 .75
38 Danny Gare TL .30 .75
39 Brian Propp RC 8.00 20.00
40 Bryan Trottier 1.00 2.50
41 Rich Preston .25 .60
42 Pierre Mondou .25 .60
43 Reed Larson .25 .60
44 George Ferguson .25 .60
45 Guy Chouinard .40 1.00
46 Billy Harris .25 .60
47 Gilles Meloche .40 1.00
48 Blair Chapman .25 .60
49 Mike Gartner TL 2.50 6.00
50 Darryl Sittler .50 1.25
51 Richard Martin .40 1.00
52 Ivan Boldirev .25 .60
53 Craig Norwich RC .25 .60
54 Dennis Polonich .25 .60
55 Bobby Clarke .60 1.50
56 Terry O'Reilly .40 1.00
57 Carol Vadnais .25 .60
58 Bob Gainey .50 1.25
59 Blaine Stoughton TL .30 .75
60 Billy Smith .40 1.00
61 Mike O'Connell RC .60 1.50
62 Lanny McDonald .50 1.25
63 Lee Fogolin .25 .60
64 Rocky Saganiuk RC .25 .60
65 Rolf Edberg RC .25 .60
66 Paul Shmyr .25 .60
67 Michel Goulet RC 20.00 50.00
68 Dan Bouchard .40 1.00
69 Mark Johnson OLY RC .50 1.25
70 Reggie Leach .30 .75
71 Bernie Federko TL .75 2.00
72 Peter Mahovlich .40 1.00
73 Anders Hedberg .40 1.00
74 Brad Park .30 .75
75 Clark Gillies .40 1.00
76 Doug Jarvis .25 .60
77 John Garrett .40 1.00
78 Dave Hutchinson .25 .60
79 John Anderson RC .50 1.25
80 Gilbert Perreault .40 1.00
81 Marcel Dionne AS1 .75 2.00
82 Guy Lafleur AS1 1.25 3.00
83 Charlie Simmer AS1 .60 1.50
84 Larry Robinson AS1 .40 1.00
85 Borje Salming AS1 .40 1.00
86 Tony Esposito AS1 .60 1.50
87 Wayne Gretzky AS2 30.00 80.00
88 Danny Gare AS2 .30 .75
89 Steve Shutt AS2 .30 .75
90 Barry Beck AS2 .30 .75
91 Mark Howe AS2 .60 1.50
92 Don Edwards AS2 .30 .75
93 Tom McCarthy RC .25 .60
94 P.McNab/R.Middleton TL .40 1.00
95 Mike Palmateer .40 1.00
96 Jim Schoenfeld .40 1.00
97 Jordy Douglas .25 .60
98 Keith Brown RC .30 .75
99 Dennis Ververgaert .25 .60
100 Phil Esposito .60 1.50
101 Jack Brownschidle .25 .60
102 Bob Nystrom .25 .60
103 Steve Christoff OLY RC .40 1.00
104 Rob Palmer .25 .60
105 Tiger Williams .30 .75
106 Kent Nilsson TL .30 .75
107 Morris Lukowich .40 1.00
108 Jack Valiquette .25 .60
109 Richie Dunn RC .25 .60
110 Rogatien Vachon .50 1.25
111 Mark Napier .25 .60
112 Gordie Roberts .25 .60
113 Stan Jonathan .25 .60
114 Brett Callighen .25 .60
115 Rick MacLeish .40 1.00
116 Ulf Nilsson .40 1.00
117 Rick Kehoe TL .30 .75
118 Dan Maloney .25 .60
119 Terry Ruskowski .25 .60
120 Denis Potvin .40 1.00
121 Wayne Stephenson .40 1.00
122 Rich Leduc .25 .60
123 Checklist 1-132 3.00 8.00
124 Don Lever .25 .60
125 Jim Rutherford .40 1.00
126 Ray Allison RC .25 .60
127 Mike Ramsey OLY RC 1.25 3.00
128 Stan Smyl TL .60 1.50
129 Al Secord RC 3.00 8.00
130 Denis Herron .40 1.00
131 Bob Dailey .25 .60
132 Dean Talafous .25 .60
133 Ian Turnbull .25 .60
134 Ron Sedlbauer .25 .60
135 Tom Bladon .25 .60
136 Bernie Federko 1.50 4.00
137 Dave Taylor 1.50 4.00
138 Bob Lorimer .25 .60
139 A.MacAdam/S.Payne TL .30 .75
140 Ray Bourque RC 80.00 200.00
141 Glen Hanlon .40 1.00
142 Willy Lindstrom .25 .60
143 Mike Rogers .25 .60
144 Tony McKegney RC .30 .75
145 Behn Wilson .25 .60
146 Lucien DeBlois .25 .60
147 Dave Burrows .25 .60
148 Paul Woods .25 .60
149 Phil Esposito TL .60 1.50
150 Tony Esposito .60 1.50
151 Pierre Larouche .40 1.00
152 Brad Maxwell .25 .60
153 Stan Weir .25 .60
154 Ryan Walter .25 .60
155 Dale Hoganson .25 .60
156 Anders Kallur RC .25 .60
157 Paul Reinhart RC .75 2.00
158 Greg Millen .40 1.00
159 Ric Seiling .25 .60
160 Mark Howe .60 1.50
161 Goals Leaders .60 1.50
162 Gretzky/Dionne/Lafleur LL 25.00 60.00
163 Dionne/Gretzky/Lafleur LL 25.00 60.00
164 Penalty Minutes LL .40 1.00
165 Sim/Dnne/Gre/Shtt/Stlr LL .75 2.00
166 Goals Against Avg. LL .40 1.00
167 Game-Winning Goals LL .30 .75
168 Espo/Chvrs/Sve/Vach LL .60 1.50
169 Perry Turnbull RC .25 .60
170 Barry Beck .30 .75
171 Charlie Simmer TL .60 1.50
172 Paul Holmgren .30 .75
173 Willie Huber .25 .60
174 Tim Young .25 .60
175 Gilles Gilbert .40 1.00
176 Dave Christian OLY RC 1.25 3.00
177 Lars Lindgren RC .25 .60
178 Real Cloutier .30 .75
179 Laurie Boschman RC .30 .75
180 Steve Shutt .30 .75
181 Bob Murray .25 .60
182 Wayne Gretzky TL 25.00 60.00
183 John Van Boxmeer .25 .60
184 Nick Fotiu .40 1.00
185 Mike McEwen .25 .60
186 Greg Malone .25 .60
187 Mike Foligno RC 2.00 5.00
188 Dave Langevin RC .25 .60
189 Mel Bridgman .25 .60
190 John Davidson .40 1.00
191 Mike Milbury .25 .60
192 Ron Zanussi .25 .60
193 Darryl Sittler TL .50 1.25
194 John Marks .25 .60
195 Mike Gartner RC 15.00 40.00
196 Dave Lewis .25 .60
197 Kent Nilsson RC 2.50 6.00
198 Rick Ley .25 .60
199 Derek Smith .25 .60
200 Bill Barber .40 1.00
201 Guy Lapointe .40 1.00
202 Vaclav Nedomansky .25 .60
203 Don Murdoch .25 .60
204 Mike Bossy TL 1.25 3.00
205 Pierre Hamel RC .40 1.00
206 Mike Eaves RC .25 .60
207 Doug Halward .25 .60
208 Stan Smyl RC .60 1.50
209 Mike Zuke RC .25 .60
210 Borje Salming .40 1.00
211 Walt Tkaczuk .40 1.00
212 Grant Mulvey .30 .75
213 Rob Ramage RC 3.00 8.00
214 Tom Rowe .25 .60
215 Don Edwards .30 .75
216 G.Lafleur/P.Larouche TL 1.00 3.00
217 Dan Labraaten .25 .60
218 Glen Sharpley .25 .60
219 Stefan Persson .25 .60
220 Peter McNab .30 .75
221 Doug Hicks .25 .60
222 Bengt Gustafsson RC .25 .60
223 Michel Dion .40 1.00
224 Jimmy Watson .25 .60
225 Wilf Paiement .25 .60
226 Phil Russell .25 .60
227 Morris Lukowich TL .40 1.00
228 Ron Stackhouse .25 .60
229 Ted Bulley .25 .60
230 Larry Robinson .40 1.00
231 Don Maloney .25 .60
232 Rob McClanahan OLY RC .30 .75
233 Al Sims .25 .60
234 Errol Thompson .25 .60
235 Glenn Resch .40 1.00
236 Bob Miller .25 .60
237 Gary Sargent .25 .60
238 Real Cloutier TL .30 .75
239 Rene Robert .50 1.25
240 Charlie Simmer .60 1.50
241 Thomas Gradin .25 .60
242 Rick Vaive RC 15.00 40.00
243 Ron Wilson RC .25 .60
244 Brian Sutter .75 2.00
245 Dale McCourt .25 .60
246 Yvon Lambert .25 .60
247 Tom Lysiak .25 .60
248 Ron Greschner .25 .60
249 Reggie Leach TL .30 .75
250 Wayne Gretzky 125.00 300.00
251 Rick Middleton .40 1.00
252 Al Smith .40 1.00
253 Fred Barrett .25 .60
254 Butch Goring .40 1.00
255 Robert Picard .25 .60
256 Marc Tardif .25 .60
257 Checklist 133-264 3.00 6.00
258 Barry Long .25 .60
259 Rene Robert TL .50 1.25
260 Danny Gare .30 .75
261 Rejean Houle .25 .60
262 Islanders/Sabres .30 .75
263 Flyers/North Stars .30 .75
264 Stanley Cup Finals .50 1.25
265 Bobby Lalonde .25 .60
266 Bob Sauve .40 1.00
267 Bob MacMillan .25 .60
268 Greg Fox .25 .60
269 Hardy Astrom RC .50 1.25
270 Greg Joly .25 .60
271 Dave Lumley RC .25 .60
272 Dave Keon .40 1.00
273 Garry Unger .40 1.00
274 Steve Payne .25 .60
275 Doug Risebrough .25 .60
276 Bob Bourne .25 .60
277 Ed Johnstone .25 .60
278 Peter Lee .25 .60
279 Pete Peeters RC 2.50 6.00
280 Ron Chipperfield .25 .60
281 Wayne Babych .40 1.00
282 David Shand .25 .60
283 Jere Gillis .25 .60
284 Dennis Maruk .40 1.00
285 Jude Drouin .25 .60
286 Mike Murphy .25 .60
287 Curt Fraser .25 .60
288 Gary McAdam .25 .60
289 Mark Messier UER RC 125.00 300.00
290 Vic Venasky .25 .60
291 Per-Olov Brasar .25 .60
292 Orest Kindrachuk .25 .60
293 Dave Hunter .25 .60
294 Steve Jensen .25 .60
295 Chris Oddleifson .25 .60
296 Larry Playfair RC .25 .60
297 Mario Tremblay .25 .60
298 Gilles Lupien RC .25 .60
299 Pat Price .25 .60
300 Jerry Korab .25 .60
301 Darcy Rota .25 .60
302 Don Luce .25 .60
303 Ken Houston .25 .60
304 Brian Engblom .25 .60
305 John Tonelli .75 2.00
306 Doug Sulliman RC .25 .60
307 Rod Schutt .25 .60
308 Norm Barnes RC .25 .60
309 Serge Bernier .25 .60
310 Larry Patey .40 1.00
311 Dave Farrish .25 .60
312 Harold Snepsts .40 1.00
313 Bob Sirois .25 .60
314 Peter Marsh .25 .60
315 Risto Siltanen RC .25 .60
316 Andre St.Laurent .25 .60
317 Craig Hartsburg RC 2.50 6.00
318 Wayne Cashman .40 1.00
319 Lindy Ruff RC 2.50 6.00
320 Willi Plett .40 1.00
321 Ron Delorme .25 .60
322 Gaston Gingras RC .25 .60
323 Gordie Lane .25 .60
324 Doug Soetaert RC .40 1.00
325 Gregg Sheppard .25 .60
326 Mike Busniuk RC .25 .60
327 Jamie Hislop .25 .60
328 Ed Staniowski .25 .60
329 Ron Ellis .40 1.00
330 Gary Bromley UER .40 1.00
331 Mark Lofthouse RC .25 .60
332 Dave Hoyda .25 .60
333 Ron Low .25 .60
334 Barry Gibbs .25 .60
335 Gary Edwards 1.25 3.00
336 Don Marcotte .25 .60
337 Bill Hajt .25 .60
338 Brad Marsh RC 2.00 5.00
339 J.P. Bordeleau .25 .60
340 Randy Pierce .25 .60
341 Eddie Mio RC .50 1.25
342 Randy Manery .25 .60
343 Tom Younghans .25 .60
344 Rod Langway RC 12.00 30.00
345 Wayne Merrick .25 .60
346 Steve Baker RC .40 1.00
347 Pat Hughes .25 .60
348 Al Hill .25 .60
349 Gerry Hart .25 .60
350 Richard Mulhern .25 .60
351 Jerry Butler .25 .60
352 Guy Charron .25 .60
353 Jimmy Mann RC .40 1.00
354 Brad McCrimmon RC 2.00 5.00
355 Rick Dudley .25 .60
356 Pekka Rautakallio .25 .60
357 Tim Trimper RC .25 .60
358 Mike Christie .25 .60
359 John Ogrodnick RC 2.00 5.00
360 Dave Semenko 1.50 4.00
361 Mike Veisor .40 1.00
362 Syl Apps .25 .60
363 Mike Polich .25 .60
364 Rick Chartraw .25 .60
365 Steve Tambellini RC .40 1.00
366 Ed Hospodar RC .25 .60
367 Randy Carlyle .40 1.00
368 Tom Gorence .25 .60
369 Pierre Plante .25 .60
370 Blake Dunlop .25 .60
371 Mike Kaszycki .25 .60
372 Rick Blight .25 .60
373 Pierre Bouchard .25 .60
374 Gary Doak .25 .60
375 Andre Savard .25 .60
376 Bill Clement .40 1.00
377 Reg Kerr .25 .60
378 Walt McKechnie .25 .60
379 George Lyle RC .25 .60
380 Colin Campbell .25 .60
381 Dave Debol .25 .60
382 Glenn Goldup .25 .60
383 Kent-Erik Andersson .25 .60
384 Tony Currie RC .25 .60
385 Richard Sevigny RC 6.00 15.00

386 Garry Howatt .25 .60
387 Cam Connor .25 .60
388 Ross Lonsberry .25 .60
389 Frank Bathe RC .25 .60
390 John Wensink .25 .60
391 Paul Harrison .40 1.00
392 Dennis Kearns .25 .60
393 Pat Ribble .25 .60
394 Markus Mattsson RC .40 1.00
395 Chuck Lefley .25 .60
396 Checklist 265-396 4.00 10.00

1980-81 O-Pee-Chee Super

COMPLETE SET (24) 20.00 40.00
1 Brad Park 1.00 2.50
2 Gilbert Perreault .60 1.50
3 Kent Nilsson .40 1.00
4 Tony Esposito .75 2.00
5 Lanny McDonald .60 1.50
6 Pete Mahovlich .30 .75
7 Wayne Gretzky 6.00 15.00
8 Marcel Dionne 1.00 2.50
9 Bob Gainey 1.25 3.00
10 Guy Lafleur 2.50 6.00
11 Larry Robinson .75 2.00
12 Mike Bossy 3.00 6.00
13 Denis Potvin .60 1.50
14 Phil Esposito 1.25 3.00
15 Anders Hedberg .30 .75
16 Bobby Clarke 1.25 3.00
17 Marc Tardif .20 .50
18 Bernie Federko .60 1.50
19 Borje Salming .40 1.00
20 Darryl Sittler .75 2.00
21 Ian Turnbull .20 .50
22 Glen Hanlon .25 .60
23 Mike Palmateer .60 1.50
24 Morris Lukowich .20 .50

1981-82 O-Pee-Chee

COMPLETE SET (396) 125.00 250.00
1 Ray Bourque 20.00 50.00
2 Rick Middleton .25 .60
3 Dwight Foster .25 .60
4 Steve Kasper RC .75 2.00
5 Peter McNab .25 .60
6 Mike O'Connell .30 .75
7 Terry O'Reilly .30 .75
8 Brad Park .30 .75
9 Dick Redmond .25 .60
10 Rogatien Vachon .40 1.00
11 Wayne Cashman .30 .75
12 Mike Gillis RC .30 .75
13 Stan Jonathan .25 .60
14 Don Marcotte .25 .60
15 Brad McCrimmon .30 .75
16 Mike Milbury .25 .60
17 Ray Bourque SA 3.00 8.00
18 Rick Middleton SA .25 .60
19 Rick Middleton TL .25 .60
20 Danny Gare .25 .60
21 Don Edwards .25 .60
22 Tony McKegney .25 .60
23 Bob Sauve .30 .75
24 Andre Savard .25 .60
25 Derek Smith .25 .60
26 John Van Boxmeer .25 .60
27 Danny Gare SA .25 .60
28 Danny Gare TL .25 .60
29 Richie Dunn .25 .60
30 Gilbert Perreault .40 1.00
31 Craig Ramsay .25 .60
32 Ric Seiling .25 .60
33 Guy Chouinard .30 .75
34 Kent Nilsson .25 .60
35 Willi Plett .25 .60
36 Paul Reinhart .25 .60
37 Pat Riggin RC .50 1.25
38 Eric Vail .25 .60
39 Bill Clement .30 .75
40 Jamie Hislop .25 .60
41 Randy Holt .25 .60
42 Dan Labraaten .25 .60
43 Kevin Lavallee RC .25 .60
44 Rejean Lemelin RC 2.50 6.00
45 Don Lever .25 .60
46 Bob MacMillan .25 .60
47 Brad Marsh .30 .75
48 Bob Murdoch .25 .60
49 Jim Peplinski RC 1.25 3.00
50 Pekka Rautakallio .25 .60
51 Phil Russell .25 .60
52 Kent Nilsson SA .25 .60
53 Kent Nilsson TL .25 .60
54 Tony Esposito .30 .75
55 Keith Brown .25 .60
56 Ted Bulley .25 .60
57 Tim Higgins RC .25 .60
58 Reg Kerr .25 .60
59 Tom Lysiak .25 .60
60 Grant Mulvey .25 .60
61 Bob Murray .25 .60
62 Terry Ruskowski .25 .60
63 Denis Savard RC 15.00 40.00
64 Glen Sharpley .25 .60
65 Darryl Sutter RC 1.00 2.50
66 Doug Wilson .30 .75
67 Tony Esposito SA .30 .75
68 Murray Bannerman RC .50 1.25
69 Greg Fox .25 .60
70 John Marks .25 .60
71 Peter Marsh .25 .60
72 Al Secord .30 .75
73 Tom Lysia TL .25 .60
74 Lucien DeBlois .25 .60
75 Paul Gagne RC .25 .60
76 Merlin Malinowski RC .25 .60
77 Lanny McDonald .25 .60
78 Joel Quenneville .25 .60
79 Rob Ramage .30 .75
80 Glenn Resch .30 .75
81 Steve Tambellini .25 .60
82 Ron Delorme .25 .60
83 Mike Kitchen .25 .60
84 Yvon Vautour RC .25 .60
85 Lanny McDonald TL .25 .60
86 Dale McCourt .25 .60
87 Mike Foligno .30 .75
88 Gilles Gilbert .30 .75
89 Willie Huber .25 .60
90 Mark Kirton RC .25 .60
91 Jim Korn RC .25 .60
92 Reed Larson .25 .60
93 Gary McAdam .25 .60
94 Vaclav Nedomansky .25 .60
95 John Ogrodnick .25 .60
96 Dale McCourt SA .25 .60
97 Jean Hamel .25 .60
98 Glen Hicks RC .25 .60
99 Larry Lozinski RC .30 .75
100 George Lyle .25 .60
101 Perry Miller .25 .60
102 Brad Maxwell .25 .60
103 Brad Smith RC .30 .75
104 Paul Woods .25 .60
105 Dale McCourt TL .25 .60
106 Wayne Gretzky 50.00 125.00
107 Jari Kurri RC 30.00 80.00
108 Glenn Anderson RC 20.00 50.00
109 Curt Brackenbury .25 .60
110 Brett Callighen .25 .60
111 Paul Coffey RC 25.00 60.00
112 Lee Fogolin .25 .60
113 Matti Hagman RC .25 .60
114 Doug Hicks .25 .60
115 Dave Hunter .25 .60
116 Garry Lariviere .25 .60
117 Kevin Lowe RC 12.00 30.00
118 Mark Messier 20.00 50.00
119 Eddie Mio .30 .75
120 Andy Moog RC 20.00 50.00
121 Dave Semenko .30 .75
122 Risto Siltanen .25 .60
123 Garry Unger .30 .75
124 Stan Weir .25 .60
125 Wayne Gretzky SA 25.00 60.00
126 Wayne Gretzky TL 20.00 50.00
127 Mike Rogers .25 .60
128 Mark Howe .40 1.00
129 Dave Keon .40 1.00
130 Warren Miller RC .25 .60
131 Al Sims .25 .60
132 Blaine Stoughton .30 .75
133 Rick MacLeish .30 .75
134 Greg Millen .30 .75
135 Mike Rogers SA .25 .60
136 Mike Fidler .25 .60
137 John Garrett .25 .60
138 Don Nachbaur RC .25 .60
139 Tom Rowe .25 .60
140 Mike Rogers TL .25 .60
141 Marcel Dionne .50 1.25
142 Charlie Simmer .25 .60
143 Dave Taylor .60 1.50
144 Billy Harris .25 .60
145 Jerry Korab .25 .60
146 Mario Lessard .30 .75
147 Don Luce .25 .60
148 Larry Murphy RC 15.00 40.00
149 Mike Murphy .25 .60
150 Marcel Dionne SA .50 1.25
151 Charlie Simmer SA .25 .60
152 Dave Taylor SA .30 .75
153 Jim Fox RC .30 .75
154 Steve Jensen .25 .60
155 Greg Terrion RC .25 .60
156 Marcel Dionne TL .50 1.25
157 Bobby Smith .25 .60
158 Kent-Erik Andersson .25 .60
159 Don Beaupre RC 2.00 5.00
160 Steve Christoff .25 .60
161 Dino Ciccarelli RC 6.00 15.00
162 Craig Hartsburg .25 .60
163 Al MacAdam .25 .60
164 Tom McCarthy .25 .60
165 Gilles Meloche .30 .75
166 Steve Payne .25 .60
167 Gordie Roberts .25 .60
168 Greg Smith .25 .60
169 Tim Young .25 .60
170 Bobby Smith SA .25 .60
171 Mike Eaves .25 .60
172 Mike Polich .25 .60
173 Tom Younghans .25 .60
174 Bobby Smith TL .25 .60
175 Brian Engblom .25 .60
176 Bob Gainey .30 .75
177 Guy Lafleur 1.00 2.50
178 Mark Napier .25 .60
179 Larry Robinson .40 1.00
180 Steve Shutt .25 .60
181 Keith Acton RC .50 1.25
182 Gaston Gingras .25 .60
183 Rejean Houle .25 .60
184 Doug Jarvis .25 .60
185 Yvon Lambert .25 .60
186 Rod Langway .60 1.50
187 Pierre Larouche .30 .75
188 Pierre Mondou .25 .60
189 Robert Picard .25 .60
190 Doug Risebrough .25 .60
191 Richard Sevigny .25 .60
192 Mario Tremblay .25 .60
193 Doug Wickenheiser RC .60 1.50
194 Bob Gainey SA .30 .75
195 Guy Lafleur SA 1.25 3.00
196 Larry Robinson SA .40 1.00
197 Steve Shutt TL .25 .60
198 Mike Bossy 1.50 4.00
199 Denis Potvin .40 1.00
200 Bryan Trottier .60 1.50
201 Bob Bourne .25 .60
202 Clark Gillies .40 1.00
203 Butch Goring .30 .75
204 Anders Kallur .25 .60
205 Ken Morrow .30 .75
206 Stefan Persson .25 .60
207 Billy Smith .40 1.00
208 Mike Bossy SA .60 1.50
209 Denis Potvin SA .40 1.00
210 Bryan Trottier SA .40 1.00
211 Duane Sutter RC .60 1.50
212 Gordie Lane .25 .60
213 Dave Langevin .25 .60
214 Bob Lorimer .25 .60
215 Mike McEwen .25 .60
216 Wayne Merrick .25 .60
217 Bob Nystrom .25 .60
218 John Tonelli .40 1.00
219 Mike Bossy TL 1.25 3.00
220 Barry Beck .40 1.00
221 Mike Allison RC .25 .60
222 John Davidson .40 1.00
223 Ron Duguay .30 .75
224 Ron Greschner .25 .60
225 Anders Hedberg .25 .60
226 Ed Johnstone .25 .60
227 Dave Maloney .25 .60
228 Don Maloney .25 .60
229 Ulf Nilsson .40 1.00
230 Barry Beck SA .40 1.00
231 Steve Baker .40 1.00
232 Jere Gillis .25 .60
233 Ed Hospodar .25 .60
234 Tom Laidlaw RC .40 1.00
235 Dean Talafous .25 .60
236 Carol Vadnais .25 .60
237 Anders Hedberg TL .25 .60
238 Bill Barber .25 .60
239 Behn Wilson .25 .60
240 Bobby Clarke .60 1.50
241 Bob Dailey .25 .60
242 Paul Holmgren .30 .75
243 Reggie Leach .40 1.00
244 Ken Linseman .40 1.00
245 Pete Peeters .60 1.50
246 Brian Propp .75 2.00
247 Bill Barber SA .25 .60
248 Mel Bridgman .25 .60
249 Mike Busniuk .25 .60
250 Tom Gorence .25 .60
251 Tim Kerr RC 2.50 6.00
252 Rick St.Croix RC .40 1.00
253 Bill Barber TL .25 .60
254 Rick Kehoe .25 .60
255 Pat Boutette .25 .60
256 Randy Carlyle .40 1.00
257 Paul Gardner .25 .60
258 Peter Lee .25 .60
259 Rod Schutt .25 .60
260 Rick Kehoe SA .25 .60
261 Mario Faubert .25 .60
262 George Ferguson .25 .60
263 Ross Lonsberry .25 .60
264 Greg Malone .25 .60
265 Pat Price .25 .60
266 Ron Stackhouse .25 .60
267 Rick Kehoe TL .25 .60
268 Jacques Richard .25 .60
269 Peter Stastny RC 15.00 40.00
270 Dan Bouchard .40 1.00
271 Kim Clackson RC .40 1.00
272 Alain Cote .25 .60
273 Andre Dupont .25 .60
274 Robbie Ftorek .25 .60
275 Michel Goulet 1.25 3.00
276 Dale Hoganson .25 .60
277 Dale Hunter RC 4.00 10.00
278 Pierre Lacroix .25 .60
279 Mario Marois RC .25 .60
280 Dave Pichette RC .25 .60
281 Michel Plasse .40 1.00
282 Anton Stastny RC .50 1.25
283 Marc Tardif .25 .60
284 Wally Weir .25 .60
285 Jacques Richard SA .25 .60
286 Peter Stastny SA 2.00 5.00
287 Peter Stastny TL 1.25 3.00
288 Bernie Federko .60 1.50
289 Mike Liut .60 1.50
290 Wayne Babych .25 .60
291 Blair Chapman .25 .60
292 Tony Currie .25 .60
293 Blake Dunlop .25 .60
294 Ed Kea .25 .60
295 Rick Lapointe .25 .60
296 Jorgen Pettersson RC .25 .60
297 Brian Sutter .40 1.00
298 Perry Turnbull .25 .60
299 Mike Zuke .25 .60
300 Bernie Federko SA .30 .75
301 Mike Liut SA .40 1.00
302 Jack Brownschidle .25 .60
303 Larry Patey .25 .60
304 Bernie Federko TL .30 .75
305 Bill Derlago .25 .60
306 Wilf Paiement .25 .60
307 Borje Salming .40 1.00
308 Darryl Sittler .50 1.25
309 Ian Turnbull .25 .60
310 Rick Vaive .40 1.00
311 Wilf Paiement SA .25 .60
312 Darryl Sittler SA .50 1.25
313 John Anderson .25 .60
314 Laurie Boschman .40 1.00
315 Jiri Crha RC .50 1.25
316 Vitezslav Duris RC .25 .60
317 Dave Farrish .25 .60
318 Pat Hickey .25 .60
319 Michel Larocque .40 1.00
320 Dan Maloney .25 .60
321 Terry Martin .25 .60
322 Rene Robert .40 1.00
323 Rocky Saganiuk .25 .60
324 Ron Sedlbauer .25 .60
325 Ron Zanussi .25 .60
326 Wilf Paiement TL .25 .60
327 Thomas Gradin .25 .60
328 Stan Smyl .40 1.00
329 Ivan Boldirev .25 .60
330 Per-Olov Brasar UER
(Brent Ashton pictured) .25 .60
331 Richard Brodeur .40 1.00
332 Jerry Butler .25 .60
333 Colin Campbell .25 .60
334 Curt Fraser .25 .60
335 Doug Halward .25 .60
336 Glen Hanlon .40 1.00
337 Dennis Kearns .25 .60
338 Rick Lanz RC UER .25 .60
339 Pat Ribble .25 .60
340 Blair MacDonald .25 .60
341 Kevin McCarthy .25 .60
342 Gerry Minor RC .25 .60
343 Darcy Rota .25 .60
344 Harold Snepsts .25 .60
345 Tiger Williams .25 .60
346 Thomas Gradin TL .25 .60
347 Mike Gartner 5.00 12.00
348 Rick Green .25 .60
349 Bob Kelly .25 .60
350 Dennis Maruk .25 .60
351 Mike Palmateer .25 .60
352 Ryan Walter .25 .60
353 Bengt Gustafsson .25 .60
354 Al Hangsleben .25 .60
355 Jean Pronovost .40 1.00
356 Dennis Ververgaert .25 .60
357 Dennis Maruk TL .25 .60
358 Dave Babych RC .60 1.50
359 Dave Christian .25 .60
360 Dave Christian SA .25 .60
361 Rick Bowness .40 1.00
362 Rick Dudley .25 .60
363 Norm Dupont RC .25 .60
364 Dan Geoffrion RC .25 .60
365 Pierre Hamel .30 .75
366 Dave Hoyda UER
(Photo actually
Doug Lecuyer) .25 .60
367 Doug Lecuyer RC .25 .60
368 Willy Lindstrom .25 .60
369 Barry Long .25 .60
370 Morris Lukowich .25 .60
371 Kris Manery .25 .60
372 Jimmy Mann .30 .75
373 Moe Mantha RC .30 .75
374 Markus Mattsson .30 .75
375 Don Spring RC .25 .60
376 Tim Trimper .25 .60
377 Ron Wilson .25 .60
378 Dave Christian TL .25 .60
379 Checklist 1-132 3.00 8.00
380 Checklist 133-264 3.00 8.00
381 Checklist 265-396 3.00 8.00
382 Mike Bossy LL 1.25 3.00
383 Wayne Gretzky LL 25.00 60.00
384 Wayne Gretzky LL 25.00 60.00
385 Tiger Williams LL .25 .60
386 Mike Bossy LL 1.25 3.00
387 Richard Sevigny LL .25 .60
388 Mike Bossy LL 1.25 3.00
389 Don Edward
Glenn Resch LL .30 .75
390 Mike Bossy RB 1.25 3.00
391 Dionne/Sims/Taylor RB 1.00 2.50
392 Wayne Gretzky RB 15.00 40.00
393 Larry Murphy RB 1.25 3.00
394 Mike Palmateer RB .25 .60
395 Peter Stastny RB 1.25 3.00
396 Bob Manno .30 .75

1982-83 O-Pee-Chee

COMPLETE SET (396) 60.00 120.00
1 Wayne Gretzky HL 12.00 30.00
2 Mike Bossy HL .40 1.00
3 Dale Hawerchuk HL 2.00 5.00
4 Mikko Leinonen HL .20 .50
5 Bryan Trottier HL .40 1.00
6 Rick Middleton .30 .75
7 Ray Bourque 5.00 12.00
8 Wayne Cashman .30 .75
9 Bruce Crowder RC .20 .50
10 Keith Crowder RC .20 .50
11 Tom Fergus RC .30 .75
12 Steve Kasper .20 .50
13 Normand Lovoillo RC .60 1.50
14 Don Marcotte .20 .50
15 Rick Middleton .30 .75
16 Peter McNab .20 .50
17 Mike O'Connell .20 .50
18 Terry O'Reilly .30 .75
19 Brad Park .30 .75
20 Barry Pederson RC .60 1.50
21 Brad Palmer RC .20 .50
22 Pete Peeters .40 1.00
23 Rogatien Vachon .40 1.00
24 Ray Bourque IA 2.00 5.00
25 Gilbert Perreault TL .40 1.00
26 Mike Foligno .30 .75
27 Yvon Lambert .20 .50
28 Dale McCourt .20 .50
29 Tony McKegney .20 .50
30 Gilbert Perreault .40 1.00
31 Lindy Ruff .20 .50
32 Mike Ramsey .20 .50
33 J.F. Sauve RC .20 .50
34 Bob Sauve .30 .75
35 Ric Seiling .20 .50
36 John Van Boxmeer .20 .50
37 John Van Boxmeer IA .20 .50
38 Lanny McDonald .30 .75
39 Mel Bridgman .20 .50
40 Mel Bridgman IA .20 .50
41 Guy Chouinard .20 .50
42 Steve Christoff .20 .50
43 Denis Cyr RC .20 .50
44 Bill Clement .30 .75
45 Richie Dunn .20 .50
46 Don Edwards .20 .50
47 Jamie Hislop .20 .50
48 Steve Konroyd RC .30 .75
49 Kevin Lavallee .20 .50
50 Rejean Lemelin .20 .50
51 Lanny McDonald .30 .75
52 Lanny McDonald IA .30 .75
53 Bob Murdoch .20 .50
54 Kent Nilsson .30 .75
55 Jim Peplinski .20 .50
56 Paul Reinhart .20 .50
57 Doug Risebrough .20 .50
58 Phil Russell .20 .50
59 Howard Walker RC .20 .50
60 Al Secord .30 .75
61 Murray Bannerman .30 .75
62 Keith Brown .20 .50
63 Doug Crossman RC .40 1.00
64 Tony Esposito .40 1.00
65 Greg Fox .20 .50
66 Tim Higgins .20 .50
67 Reg Kerr .20 .50
68 Tom Lysiak .20 .50
69 Grant Mulvey .20 .50
70 Bob Murray .20 .50
71 Rich Preston .20 .50
72 Terry Ruskowski .20 .50
73 Denis Savard 1.50 4.00
74 Al Secord .30 .75
75 Glen Sharpley .20 .50
76 Darryl Sutter .30 .75
77 Doug Wilson .30 .75
78 Doug Wilson IA .30 .75
79 John Ogrodnick .20 .50
80 John Barrett RC .20 .50
81 Mike Blaisdell RC .20 .50
82 Colin Campbell .20 .50
83 Danny Gare .30 .75
84 Gilles Gilbert .30 .75
85 Willie Huber .20 .50
86 Greg Joly .20 .50
87 Mark Kirton .20 .50
88 Reed Larson .20 .50
89 Reed Larson IA .20 .50
90 Reggie Leach .30 .75
91 Walt McKechnie .20 .50
92 John Ogrodnick .20 .50
93 Mark Osborne RC .30 .75
94 Jim Schoenfeld .30 .75
95 Derek Smith .20 .50
96 Greg Smith .20 .50
97 Eric Vail .20 .50
98 Paul Woods .20 .50
99 Wayne Gretzky TL 10.00 25.00
100 Glenn Anderson 1.00 2.50
101 Paul Coffey 3.00 8.00
102 Paul Coffey IA 2.50 6.00
103 Brett Callighen .20 .50
104 Lee Fogolin .20 .50
105 Grant Fuhr RC 25.00 60.00
106 Wayne Gretzky 30.00 80.00
107 Wayne Gretzky IA 15.00 40.00
108 Matti Hagman .20 .50
109 Pat Hughes .20 .50
110 Dave Hunter .20 .50
111 Jari Kurri 8.00 20.00
112 Ron Low .20 .50
113 Kevin Lowe UER .60 1.50
114 Dave Lumley .20 .50
115 Ken Linseman .30 .75
116 Garry Lariviere .20 .50
117 Mark Messier 8.00 20.00
118 Tom Roulston RC .20 .50
119 Dave Semenko .30 .75
120 Garry Unger .30 .75
121 Checklist 1-132 1.00 2.50
122 Blaine Stoughton .30 .75
123 Ron Francis RC 15.00 40.00
124 Chris Kotsopoulos RC .20 .50
125 Pierre Larouche .30 .75
126 Greg Millen .30 .75
127 Warren Miller .20 .50
128 Merlin Malinowski .20 .50
129 Risto Siltanen .20 .50
130 Blaine Stoughton .30 .75
131 Blaine Stoughton IA .30 .75
132 Doug Sulliman .20 .50
133 Blake Wesley RC .20 .50
134 Steve Tambellini .20 .50
135 Brent Ashton RC .30 .75
136 Aaron Broten RC .20 .50
137 Joe Cirella RC .30 .75
138 Dwight Foster .20 .50
139 Paul Gagne .20 .50
140 Garry Howatt .20 .50
141 Don Lever .20 .50
142 Bob Lorimer .20 .50
143 Bob MacMillan .20 .50
144 Rick Meagher RC .30 .75
145 Glenn Resch .30 .75
146 Glenn Resch IA .30 .75
147 Steve Tambellini .20 .50
148 Carol Vadnais .20 .50
149 Marcel Dionne TL .40 1.00
150 Dan Bonar RC .20 .50
151 Steve Bozek RC .30 .75
152 Marcel Dionne .40 1.00
153 Marcel Dionne IA .40 1.00
154 Jim Fox .20 .50
155 Mark Hardy RC .30 .75
156 Mario Lessard .20 .50
157 Dave Lewis .20 .50
158 Larry Murphy 1.25 3.00
159 Charlie Simmer .20 .50
160 Doug Smith RC .20 .50
161 Dave Taylor .30 .75
162 Dino Ciccarelli TL .40 1.00
163 Don Beaupre .40 1.00
164 Neal Broten RC 12.00 30.00
165 Dino Ciccarelli 1.25 3.00
166 Curt Giles RC .60 1.50
167 Craig Hartsburg .20 .50
168 Brad Maxwell .20 .50
169 Tom McCarthy .20 .50
170 Gilles Meloche .30 .75
171 Al MacAdam .20 .50
172 Steve Payne .20 .50
173 Willi Plett .20 .50
174 Gordie Roberts .20 .50
175 Bobby Smith .30 .75
176 Bobby Smith IA .30 .75
177 Tim Young .20 .50
178 Mark Napier .20 .50
179 Keith Acton .20 .50
180 Keith Acton IA .20 .50
181 Bob Gainey .40 1.00
182 Gaston Gingras .20 .50
183 Rick Green .20 .50
184 Rejean Houle .20 .50
185 Mark Hunter RC .30 .75
186 Guy Lafleur .40 1.00
187 Guy Lafleur IA .40 1.00
188 Pierre Mondou .20 .50
189 Mark Napier .20 .50
190 Robert Picard .20 .50
191 Larry Robinson .40 1.00
192 Steve Shutt .20 .50
193 Mario Tremblay .20 .50
194 Ryan Walter .20 .50
195 Rick Wamsley RC .60 1.50
196 Doug Wickenheiser .20 .50
197 Mike Bossy TL .40 1.00
198 Bob Bourne .20 .50
199 Mike Bossy .40 1.00
200 Butch Goring .30 .75
201 Clark Gillies .40 1.00
202 Tomas Jonsson RC .20 .50
203 Anders Kallur .20 .50
204 Dave Langevin .20 .50
205 Wayne Merrick .20 .50
206 Ken Morrow .30 .75
207 Mike McEwen .20 .50
208 Bob Nystrom .20 .50
209 Stefan Persson .20 .50
210 Denis Potvin .40 1.00
211 Billy Smith .40 1.00
212 Duane Sutter .20 .50
213 John Tonelli .40 1.00
214 Bryan Trottier .40 1.00
215 Bryan Trottier IA .40 1.00
216 Brent Sutter RC .60 1.50
217 Ron Duguay .30 .75
218 Kent-Erik Andersson .20 .50
219 Barry Beck .20 .50
220 Barry Beck IA .20 .50
221 Ron Duguay .30 .75
222 Nick Fotiu .30 .75
223 Robbie Ftorek .20 .50
224 Ron Greschner .20 .50
225 Anders Hedberg .30 .75
226 Ed Johnstone .20 .50
227 Tom Laidlaw .20 .50
228 Dave Maloney .20 .50
229 Don Maloney .20 .50
230 Eddie Mio .30 .75
231 Mark Pavelich RC .40 1.00
232 Mike Rogers .30 .75
233 Reijo Ruotsalainen RC .40 1.00
234 Steve Weeks RC .40 1.00
235 Wayne Gretzky LL 12.00 30.00
236 Paul Gardner LL .20 .50
237 W.Gretzky/M.Goulet LL 10.00 25.00
238 Paul Baxter LL .20 .50
239 Denis Herron LL .30 .75
240 Wayne Gretzky LL 10.00 25.00
241 Denis Herron LL .30 .75
242 Wayne Gretzky LL 12.00 30.00
243 Wayne Gretzky LL 12.00 30.00
244 Bill Barber TL .30 .75
245 Fred Arthur RC .20 .50
246 Bill Barber .30 .75
247 Bill Barber IA .30 .75
248 Bobby Clarke .60 1.50
249 Ron Flockhart RC .30 .75
250 Tom Gorence .20 .50
251 Paul Holmgren .30 .75
252 Mark Howe .40 1.00
253 Tim Kerr .60 1.50
254 Brad Marsh .20 .50
255 Brad McCrimmon .30 .75
256 Brian Propp .60 1.50
257 Darryl Sittler .40 1.00
258 Rick St.Croix .20 .50
259 Jimmy Watson .20 .50
260 Behn Wilson .20 .50
261 Checklist 133-264 1.00 2.50
262 Mike Bullard .40 1.00
263 Pat Boutette .20 .50
264 Mike Bullard RC .40 1.00
265 Randy Carlyle .20 .50
266 Randy Carlyle IA .20 .50
267 Michel Dion .30 .75
268 George Ferguson .20 .50
269 Paul Gardner .20 .50
270 Denis Herron .30 .75
271 Rick Kehoe .30 .75
272 Greg Malone .20 .50
273 Rick MacLeish .30 .75
274 Pat Price .20 .50
275 Ron Stackhouse .20 .50
276 Peter Stastny TL .30 .75
277 Pierre Aubry RC .20 .50
278 Dan Bouchard .30 .75
279 Real Cloutier .20 .50
280 Real Cloutier IA .20 .50
281 Alain Cote .20 .50
282 Andre Dupont .20 .50
283 John Garrett .20 .50
284 Michel Goulet .75 2.00
285 Dale Hunter .75 2.00
286 Pierre Lacroix .20 .50
287 Mario Marois .20 .50
288 Wilf Paiement .20 .50
289 Dave Pichette .20 .50
290 Jacques Richard .20 .50
291 Normand Rochefort RC .20 .50
292 Peter Stastny .30 .75
293 Peter Stastny IA .30 .75
294 Anton Stastny .30 .75
295 Marian Stastny RC .30 .75
296 Marc Tardif .20 .50
297 Wally Weir .20 .50
298 Brian Sutter .30 .75
299 Wayne Babych .20 .50
300 Jack Brownschidle .20 .50
301 Blake Dunlop .20 .50
302 Bernie Federko .30 .75
303 Bernie Federko IA .30 .75
304 Pat Hickey .20 .50
305 Guy Lapointe .30 .75
306 Mike Liut .40 1.00
307 Joe Mullen RC 12.00 30.00
308 Larry Patey .20 .50
309 Jorgen Pettersson .20 .50
310 Rob Ramage .20 .50
311 Brian Sutter .30 .75
312 Perry Turnbull .20 .50
313 Mike Zuke .20 .50
314 Rick Vaive .20 .50
315 John Anderson .20 .50
316 Normand Aubin RC .20 .50
317 Jim Benning RC .20 .50
318 Fred Boimistruck RC .20 .50
319 Bill Derlago .20 .50
320 Bill Derlago IA .20 .50
321 Miroslav Frycer RC .20 .50
322 Billy Harris .20 .50
323 Jim Korn .20 .50
324 Michel Larocque .30 .75
325 Bob Manno .20 .50
326 Dan Maloney .20 .50
327 Bob McGill RC .30 .75
328 Barry Melrose .30 .75
329 Terry Martin .20 .50
330 Rene Robert .30 .75
331 Rocky Saganiuk .20 .50
332 Borje Salming .40 1.00
333 Greg Terrion .20 .50
334 Vincent Tremblay RC .20 .50
335 Rick Vaive .20 .50
336 Rick Vaive IA .20 .50
337 Thomas Gradin .20 .50
338 Ivan Boldirev .20 .50
339 Richard Brodeur .30 .75
340 Richard Brodeur IA .30 .75
341 Tony Currie .20 .50
342 Marc Crawford RC .75 2.00
343 Curt Fraser .20 .50
344 Thomas Gradin .20 .50
345 Thomas Gradin IA .20 .50
346 Ivan Hlinka UER RC .30 .75
347 Ron Delorme .20 .50
348 Rick Lanz .25 .60
349 Lars Lindgren .20 .50
350 Blair MacDonald .20 .50
351 Kevin McCarthy .20 .50
352 Gerry Minor .20 .50
353 Lars Molin RC .20 .50
354 Gary Lupul RC .20 .50
355 Darcy Rota .20 .50
356 Stan Smyl .20 .50
357 Harold Snepsts .20 .50
358 Tiger Williams .20 .50
359 Dennis Maruk .30 .75
360 Ted Bulley .20 .50
361 Bobby Carpenter RC .60 1.50
362 Brian Engblom .20 .50
363 Mike Gartner 2.00 5.00
364 Bengt Gustafsson .20 .50
365 Doug Hicks .20 .50
366 Ken Houston .20 .50
367 Doug Jarvis .20 .50
368 Rod Langway .40 1.00
369 Dennis Maruk .30 .75
370 Dennis Maruk IA .30 .75
371 Dave Parro RC .30 .75
372 Pat Riggin .30 .75
373 Chris Valentine RC .20 .50
374 Dale Hawerchuk TL 1.00 3.00
375 Dave Babych .20 .50
376 Dave Babych IA .20 .50
377 Dave Christian .20 .50
378 Norm Dupont .20 .50
379 Lucien DeBlois .20 .50
380 Dale Hawerchuk RC 15.00 40.00
381 Dale Hawerchuk IA 1.00 3.00
382 Craig Levie RC .20 .50
383 Morris Lukowich .20 .50
384 Willy Lindstrom .20 .50
385 Bengt Lundholm RC .20 .50
386 Paul MacLean UER RC .40 1.00
387 Bryan Maxwell .20 .50
388 Doug Smail RC .30 .75
389 Doug Soetaert .30 .75
390 Serge Savard .40 1.00
391 Thomas Steen RC 1.25 3.00
392 Don Spring .20 .50
393 Ed Staniowski .20 .50
394 Tim Trimper .20 .50
395 Tim Watters RC .30 .75
396 Checklist 265-396 1.00 2.50

1983-84 O-Pee-Chee

COMPLETE SET (396) 40.00 100.00
1 Mike Bossy TL .40 1.00
2 Denis Potvin HL .20 .50
3 Mike Bossy .40 1.00
4 Bob Bourne .10 .30
5 Billy Carroll RC .10 .30
6 Clark Gillies .20 .50
7 Butch Goring .20 .50
8 Mats Hallin RC .10 .30
9 Tomas Jonsson .10 .30
10 Gordie Lane .10 .30
11 Dave Langevin .10 .30
12 Rollie Melanson RC .40 1.00
13 Ken Morrow .10 .30
14 Bob Nystrom .10 .30
15 Stefan Persson .10 .30
16 Denis Potvin .30 .75
17 Billy Smith .20 .50
18 Brent Sutter .30 .75
19 Duane Sutter .10 .30
20 John Tonelli .20 .50
21 Bryan Trottier .30 .75
22 Wayne Gretzky TL 12.00 30.00
23 M.Messier/W.Gretzky HL 20.00 50.00
24 Glenn Anderson .60 1.50
25 Paul Coffey 4.00 10.00
26 Lee Fogolin .10 .30
27 Grant Fuhr 3.00 8.00
28 Randy Gregg RC .30 .75
29 Wayne Gretzky 25.00 60.00
30 Charlie Huddy RC .40 1.00
31 Pat Hughes .10 .30
32 Dave Hunter .10 .30
33 Don Jackson RC .10 .30
34 Jari Kurri 3.00 8.00
35 Willy Lindstrom .10 .30
36 Ken Linseman .20 .50
37 Kevin Lowe .30 .75
38 Dave Lumley .10 .30
39 Mark Messier 2.50 6.00
40 Andy Moog 3.00 6.00
41 Jaroslav Pouzar RC .10 .30
42 Tom Roulston .10 .30

Card	Low	High
43 Rick Middleton SL	.20	.50
44 Pete Peeters HL	.20	.50
45 Ray Bourque UER	5.00	10.00
46 Bruce Crowder	.10	.30
47 Keith Crowder	.10	.30
48 Luc Dufour RC	.20	.50
49 Tom Fergus	.10	.30
50 Steve Kasper	.10	.30
51 Gord Kluzak RC	.30	.75
52 Mike Krushelnyski RC	.20	.50
53 Peter McNab	.10	.30
54 Rick Middleton	.20	.50
55 Mike Milbury	.20	.50
56 Mike O'Connell	.10	.30
57 Barry Pederson	.10	.30
58 Pete Peeters	.20	.50
59 Jim Schoenfeld	.20	.50
60 Tony McKegney SL	.10	.30
61 Bob Sauve HL	.20	.50
62 Real Cloutier	.10	.30
63 Mike Foligno	.20	.50
64 Bill Hajt	.10	.30
65 Phil Housley RC	10.00	25.00
66 Dale McCourt	.10	.30
67 Gilbert Perreault	.30	.75
68 Brent Peterson RC	.10	.30
69 Craig Ramsay	.10	.30
70 Mike Ramsey	.10	.30
71 Bob Sauve	.20	.50
72 Ric Seiling	.10	.30
73 John Van Boxmeer	.10	.30
74 Lanny McDonald SL	.20	.50
75 Lanny McDonald HL	.20	.50
76 Ed Beers RC	.10	.30
77 Steve Bozek	.10	.30
78 Guy Chouinard	.10	.30
79 Mike Eaves	.10	.30
80 Don Edwards	.10	.30
81 Kari Eloranta RC	.10	.30
82 Dave Hindmarch RC	.10	.30
83 Jamie Hislop	.10	.30
84 Jim Jackson RC	.10	.30
85 Steve Konroyd	.10	.30
86 Rejean Lemelin	.30	.75
87 Lanny McDonald	.20	.50
88 Greg Meredith RC	.10	.30
89 Kent Nilsson	.20	.50
90 Jim Peplinski	.10	.30
91 Paul Reinhart	.10	.30
92 Doug Risebrough	.10	.30
93 Steve Tambellini	.10	.30
94 Mickey Volcan RC	.10	.30
95 Al Secord SL	.20	.50
96 Denis Savard HL	.20	.50
97 Murray Bannerman	.20	.50
98 Keith Brown	.10	.30
99 Tony Esposito	.30	.75
100 Dave Feamster RC	.10	.30
101 Greg Fox	.10	.30
102 Curt Fraser	.10	.30
103 Bill Gardner RC	.10	.30
104 Tim Higgins	.10	.30
105 Steve Larmer UER RC	3.00	8.00
106 Steve Ludzik UER RC	.75	2.00
107 Tom Lysiak	.10	.30
108 Bob Murray	.10	.30
109 Rick Paterson RC	.10	.30
110 Rich Preston	.10	.30
111 Denis Savard	1.00	2.50
112 Al Secord	.20	.50
113 Darryl Sutter	.10	.30
114 Doug Wilson	.30	.75
115 John Ogrodnick SL	.10	.30
116 Corrado Micalef HL	.10	.30
117 John Barrett	.10	.30
118 Ivan Boldirev	.10	.30
119 Colin Campbell	.10	.30
120 Murray Craven RC	.30	.75
121 Ron Duguay	.10	.30
122 Dwight Foster	.10	.30
123 Danny Gare	.20	.50
124 Ed Johnstone	.10	.30
125 Reed Larson	.10	.30
126 Corrado Micalef RC	.10	.30
127 Eddie Mio	.20	.50
128 John Ogrodnick	.10	.30
129 Brad Park	.20	.50
130 Greg Smith	.10	.30
131 Ken Solheim RC	.10	.30
132 Bob Manno	.10	.30
133 Paul Woods	.10	.30
134 Checklist 1-132	1.00	2.50
135 Blaine Stoughton SL	.20	.50
136 Blaine Stoughton HL	.20	.50
137 Richie Dunn	.10	.30
138 Ron Francis	3.00	6.00
139 Marty Howe	.20	.50
140 Mark Johnson	.10	.30
141 Paul Lawless RC	.10	.30
142 Merlin Malinowski	.10	.30
143 Greg Millen	.20	.50
144 Ray Neufeld RC	.10	.30
145 Joel Quenneville	.10	.30
146 Risto Siltanen	.10	.30
147 Blaine Stoughton	.20	.50
148 Doug Sulliman	.10	.30
149 Bob Sullivan RC	.10	.30
150 Marcel Dionne TL	.20	.50
151 Marcel Dionne HL	.20	.50
152 Marcel Dionne	.30	.75
153 Daryl Evans RC	.10	.30
154 Jim Fox	.10	.30
155 Mark Hardy	.10	.30
156 Gary Laskoski RC	.10	.30
157 Kevin Lavallee	.10	.30
158 Dave Lewis	.10	.30
159 Larry Murphy	.60	1.50
160 Bernie Nicholls RC	6.00	15.00
161 Terry Ruskowski	.10	.30
162 Charlie Simmer	.20	.50
163 Dave Taylor	.30	.75
164 Dino Ciccarelli TL	.20	.50
165 Brian Bellows HL	.30	.75
166 Don Beaupre	.30	.75
167 Brian Bellows RC	2.00	5.00
168 Neal Broten	.30	.75
169 Steve Christoff	.10	.30
170 Dino Ciccarelli	1.00	2.50
171 George Ferguson	.10	.30
172 Craig Hartsburg	.10	.30
173 Al MacAdam	.10	.30
174 Dennis Maruk	.20	.50
175 Brad Maxwell	.10	.30
176 Tom McCarthy	.10	.30
177 Gilles Meloche	.20	.50
178 Steve Payne	.10	.30
179 Willi Plett	.10	.30
180 Gordie Roberts	.10	.30
181 Bobby Smith	.20	.50
182 Mark Napier SL	.10	.30
183 Guy Lafleur HL	.30	.75
184 Keith Acton	.10	.30
185 Guy Carbonneau RC	12.00	30.00
186 Gilbert Delorme RC	.10	.30
187 Bob Gainey	.30	.75
188 Rick Green	.10	.30
189 Guy Lafleur	.30	.75
190 Craig Ludwig RC	.40	1.00
191 Pierre Mondou	.10	.30
192 Mark Napier	.10	.30
193 Mats Naslund UER RC	3.00	8.00
194 Chris Nilan RC	.60	1.50
195 Larry Robinson	.20	.50
196 Bill Root RC	.10	.30
197 Richard Sevigny	.20	.50
198 Steve Shutt	.10	.30
199 Mario Tremblay	.10	.30
200 Ryan Walter	.10	.30
201 Rick Wamsley	.20	.50
202 Doug Wickenheiser	.10	.30
203 Wayne Gretzky Hart	10.00	25.00
204 Wayne Gretzky Ross	8.00	20.00
205 Mike Bossy Byng	.30	.75
206 Steve Larmer Calder	1.25	3.00
207 Rod Langway Norris	.10	.30
208 Lanny McDonald Masterton	.10	.30
209 Pete Peeters Vezina	.10	.30
210 Mike Bossy RB	.30	.75
211 Marcel Dionne RB	.20	.50
212 Wayne Gretzky RB	10.00	25.00
213 Pat Hughes RB	.10	.30
214 Rick Middleton RB	.20	.50
215 Wayne Gretzky LL	10.00	25.00
216 Wayne Gretzky LL	10.00	25.00
217 Wayne Gretzky LL	10.00	25.00
218 Brian Propp LL	.10	.30
219 Paul Gardner Al Secord LL	.10	.30
220 Randy Holt LL	.10	.30
221 Pete Peeters LL	.20	.50
222 Pete Peeters LL	.20	.50
223 Steve Tambellini TL	.10	.30
224 Don Lever HL	.10	.30
225 Brent Ashton	.10	.30
226 Mel Bridgman	.10	.30
227 Aaron Broten	.10	.30
228 Murray Brumwell RC	.10	.30
229 Garry Howatt	.10	.30
230 Jeff Larmer RC	.10	.30
231 Don Lever	.10	.30
232 Bob Lorimer	.10	.30
233 Ron Low	.10	.30
234 Bob MacMillan	.10	.30
235 Hector Marini RC	.10	.30
236 Glenn Resch	.20	.50
237 Phil Russell	.10	.30
238 Mark Pavelich SL	.20	.50
239 Mark Pavelich HL	.20	.50
240 Bill Baker RC	.30	.75
241 Barry Beck	.10	.30
242 Mike Blaisdell	.10	.30
243 Nick Fotiu	.20	.50
244 Robbie Ftorek	.10	.30
245 Anders Hedberg	.20	.50
246 Willie Huber	.10	.30
247 Tom Laidlaw	.10	.30
248 Mikko Leinonen RC	.10	.30
249 Dave Maloney	.10	.30
250 Don Maloney	.10	.30
251 Rob McClanahan	.10	.30
252 Mark Osborne	.10	.30
253 Mark Pavelich	.20	.50
254 Mike Rogers	.10	.30
255 Reijo Ruotsalainen	.10	.30
256 Checklist 133-264	1.00	2.50
257 Darryl SittlerSL	.20	.50
258 Darryl Sittler HL	.20	.50
259 Ray Allison	.10	.30
260 Bill Barber	.20	.50
261 Lindsay Carson RC	.10	.30
262 Bobby Clarke	.30	.75
263 Doug Crossman	.10	.30
264 Ron Flockhart	.10	.30
265 Bob Froese RC	.30	.75
266 Paul Holmgren	.20	.50
267 Mark Howe	.30	.75
268 Pelle Lindbergh RC	20.00	50.00
269 Brad Marsh	.10	.30
270 Brad McCrimmon	.20	.50
271 Brian Propp	.30	.75
272 Darryl Sittler	.30	.75
273 Mark Taylor RC	.10	.30
274 Rick Kehoe SL	.20	.50
275 Paul Gardner HL	.10	.30
276 Pat Boutette	.10	.30
277 Mike Bullard	.10	.30
278 Randy Carlyle	.10	.30
279 Michel Dion	.10	.30
280 Paul Gardner	.10	.30
281 Dave Hannan RC	.20	.50
282 Rick Kehoe	.20	.50
283 Randy Boyd RC	.10	.30
284 Greg Malone	.10	.30
285 Doug Shedden RC	.20	.50
286 Andre St.Laurent	.10	.30
287 Michel Goulet TL	.30	.75
288 Michel Goulet HL	.30	.75
289 Pierre Aubry	.10	.30
290 Dan Bouchard	.20	.50
291 Alain Cote	.10	.30
292 Michel Goulet	.30	.75
293 Dale Hunter	.30	.75
294 Rick Lapointe	.10	.30
295 Mario Marois	.10	.30
296 Tony McKegney	.10	.30
297 Randy Moller RC	.10	.30
298 Wilf Paiement	.10	.30
299 Dave Pichette	.10	.30
300 Normand Rochefort	.10	.30
301 Louis Sleigher RC	.10	.30
302 Anton Stastny	.20	.50
303 Marian Stastny	.20	.50
304 Peter Stastny	.60	1.50
305 Marc Tardif	.10	.30
306 Wally Weir	.10	.30
307 Blake Wesley	.10	.30
308 Brian Sutter SL	.20	.50
309 Mike Liut HL	.20	.50
310 Wayne Babych	.10	.30
311 Jack Brownschidle	.10	.30
312 Mike Crombeen RC	.10	.30
313 Andre Dore RC	.10	.30
314 Blake Dunlop	.10	.30
315 Bernie Federko	.30	.75
316 Mike Liut	.30	.75
317 Joe Mullen	1.00	2.50
318 Jorgen Pettersson	.10	.30
319 Rob Ramage	.10	.30
320 Brian Sutter	.20	.50
321 Perry Turnbull	.10	.30
322 Mike Zuke	.10	.30
323 Rick Vaive SL	.10	.30
324 Rick Vaive HL	.10	.30
325 John Anderson	.10	.30
326 Jim Benning	.10	.30
327 Bill Derlago	.10	.30
328 Dan Daoust RC	.10	.30
329 Dave Farrish	.10	.30
330 Miroslav Frycer	.10	.30
331 Stewart Gavin RC	.10	.30
332 Gaston Gingras	.10	.30
333 Billy Harris	.10	.30
334 Peter Inhacak RC	.10	.30
335 Jim Korn	.10	.30
336 Terry Martin	.10	.30
337 Frank Nigro RC	.10	.30
338 Mike Palmateer	.20	.50
339 Walt Poddubny RC	.20	.50
340 Rick St.Croix	.10	.30
341 Borje Salming	.20	.50
342 Greg Terrion	.10	.30
343 Rick Vaive	.10	.30
344 Darcy Rota SL	.10	.30
345 Darcy Rota HL	.10	.30
346 Richard Brodeur	.20	.50
347 Jiri Bubla RC	.10	.30
348 Ron Delorme	.10	.30
349 John Garrett	.10	.30
350 Thomas Gradin	.10	.30
351 Doug Halward	.10	.30
352 Mark Kirton	.10	.30
353 Rick Lanz	.10	.30
354 Lars Lindgren	.10	.30
355 Gary Lupul	.10	.30
356 Kevin McCarthy	.10	.30
357 Jim Nill RC	.10	.30
358 Darcy Rota	.10	.30
359 Stan Smyl	.10	.30
360 Harold Snepsts	.10	.30
361 Patrik Sundstrom RC	.20	.50
362 Tony Tanti RC	.30	.75
363 Tiger Williams	.20	.50
364 Mike Gartner TL	.30	.75
365 Rod Langway HL	.20	.50
366 Bobby Carpenter	.10	.30
367 Dave Christian	.10	.30
368 Brian Engblom	.10	.30
369 Mike Gartner	1.50	4.00
370 Bengt Gustafsson	.10	.30
371 Ken Houston	.10	.30
372 Doug Jarvis	.10	.30
373 Al Jensen RC	.30	.75
374 Rod Langway	.20	.50
375 Craig Laughlin RC	.20	.50
376 Scott Stevens RC	8.00	20.00
377 Dale Hawerchuk TL	.30	.75
378 Lucien DeBlois HL	.10	.30
379 Scott Arniel RC	.10	.30
380 Dave Babych	.10	.30
381 Laurie Boschman	.10	.30
382 Wade Campbell RC	.10	.30
383 Lucien DeBlois	.10	.30
384 Murray Eaves RC	.10	.30
385 Dale Hawerchuk	1.50	4.00
386 Morris Lukowich	.10	.30
387 Bengt Lundholm	.10	.30
388 Paul MacLean	.10	.30
389 Brian Mullen RC	.20	.50
390 Doug Smail	.10	.30
391 Doug Soetaert	.20	.50
392 Don Spring	.10	.30
393 Thomas Steen	.30	.75
394 Tim Watters	.10	.30
395 Tim Young	.10	.30
396 Checklist 265-396	1.00	2.50

1984-85 O-Pee-Chee

Card	Low	High
COMPLETE SET (396)	150.00	400.00
1 Ray Bourque	3.00	8.00
2 Keith Crowder	.20	.50
3 Luc Dufour	.30	.75
4 Tom Fergus	.20	.50
5 Doug Keans RC	.30	.75
6 Gord Kluzak	.20	.50
7 Ken Linseman	.30	.75
8 Nevin Markwart RC	.20	.50
9 Rick Middleton	.30	.75
10 Mike Milbury	.20	.50
11 Jim Nill	.20	.50
12 Mike O'Connell	.20	.50
13 Terry O'Reilly	.30	.75
14 Barry Pederson	.20	.50
15 Pete Peeters	.30	.75
16 Dave Silk RC	.20	.50
17 Dave Andreychuk RC	10.00	25.00
18 Tom Barrasso RC	12.00	30.00
19 Real Cloutier	.20	.50
20 Mike Foligno	.30	.75
21 Bill Hajt	.20	.50
22 Gilles Hamel RC	.20	.50
23 Phil Housley	.30	.75
24 Gilbert Perreault	.40	1.00
25 Brent Peterson	.20	.50
26 Larry Playfair	.20	.50
27 Craig Ramsay	.20	.50
28 Mike Ramsey	.20	.50
29 Lindy Ruff	.20	.50
30 Bob Sauve	.30	.75
31 Ric Seiling	.20	.50
32 Murray Bannerman	.30	.75
33 Keith Brown	.20	.50
34 Curt Fraser	.20	.50
35 Bill Gardner	.20	.50
36 Jeff Larmer	.20	.50
37 Steve Larmer	1.00	2.50
38 Steve Ludzik	.20	.50
39 Tom Lysiak	.20	.50
40 Bob MacMillan	.20	.50
41 Bob Murray	.20	.50
42 Troy Murray RC	.40	1.00
43 Jack O'Callahan RC	.30	.75
44 Rick Paterson	.20	.50
45 Denis Savard	.40	1.00
46 Al Secord	.30	.75
47 Darryl Sutter	.20	.50
48 Doug Wilson	.30	.75
49 John Barrett	.30	.75
50 Ivan Boldirev	.20	.50
51 Colin Campbell	.20	.50
52 Ron Duguay	.30	.75
53 Dwight Foster	.20	.50
54 Danny Gare	.20	.50
55 Ed Johnstone	.20	.50
56 Kelly Kisio RC	.30	.75
57 Lane Lambert	.20	.50
58 Reed Larson	.20	.50
59 Bob Manno	.20	.50
60 Randy Ladouceur RC	.20	.50
61 Eddie Mio	.30	.75
62 John Ogrodnick	.20	.50
63 Brad Park	.30	.75
64 Greg Smith	.20	.50
65 Greg Stefan RC	.30	.75
66 Paul Woods	.30	.75
67 Steve Yzerman RC	40.00	100.00
68 Bob Crawford RC	.20	.50
69 Richie Dunn	.20	.50
70 Ron Francis	1.50	4.00
71 Marty Howe	.20	.50
72 Mark Johnson	.20	.50
73 Chris Kotsopoulos	.20	.50
74 Greg Malone	.20	.50
75 Greg Millen	.30	.75
76 Ray Neufeld	.20	.50
77 Joel Quenneville	.20	.50
78 Risto Siltanen	.20	.50
79 Sylvain Turgeon RC	.30	.75
80 Mike Zuke	.20	.50
81 Steve Christoff	.20	.50
82 Marcel Dionne	.40	1.00
83 Brian Engblom	.20	.50
84 Jim Fox	.20	.50
85 Anders Hakansson RC	.20	.50
86 Mark Hardy	.20	.50
87 Brian MacLellan RC	.20	.50
88 Bernie Nicholls	.75	2.00
89 Terry Ruskowski	.20	.50
90 Charlie Simmer	.20	.50
91 Doug Smith	.20	.50
92 Dave Taylor	.30	.75
93 Keith Acton	.20	.50
94 Don Beaupre	.30	.75
95 Brian Bellows	.30	.75
96 Neal Broten	.40	1.00
97 Dino Ciccarelli	.40	1.00
98 Craig Hartsburg	.20	.50
99 Tom Hirsch RC	.20	.50
100 Paul Holmgren	.30	.75
101 Dennis Maruk	.30	.75
102 Brad Maxwell	.20	.50
103 Tom McCarthy	.20	.50
104 Gilles Meloche	.30	.75
105 Mark Napier	.20	.50
106 Steve Payne	.20	.50
107 Gordie Roberts	.20	.50
108 Harold Snepsts	.20	.50
109 Mel Bridgman	.20	.50
110 Joe Cirella	.20	.50
111 Tim Higgins	.20	.50
112 Don Lever	.20	.50
113 Dave Lewis	.20	.50
114 Bob Lorimer	.20	.50
115 Ron Low	.20	.50
116 Jan Ludvig RC	.20	.50
117 Gary McAdam	.20	.50
118 Rich Preston	.20	.50
119 Glenn Resch	.30	.75
120 Phil Russell	.20	.50
121 Pat Verbeek RC	5.00	12.00
122 Mike Bossy	.40	1.00
123 Bob Bourne	.20	.50
124 Pat Flatley RC	.40	1.00
125 Greg Gilbert RC	.30	.75
126 Clark Gillies	.40	1.00
127 Butch Goring	.30	.75
128 Tomas Jonsson	.20	.50
129 Pat LaFontaine RC	20.00	50.00
130 Rollie Melanson	.30	.75
131 Ken Morrow	.20	.50
132 Bob Nystrom	.20	.50
133 Stefan Persson	.20	.50
134 Denis Potvin	.40	1.00
135 Billy Smith	.40	1.00
136 Brent Sutter	.20	.50
137 Duane Sutter	.20	.50
138 John Tonelli	.30	.75
139 Bryan Trottier	.40	1.00
140 Barry Beck	.20	.50
141 Ron Greschner	.20	.50
142 Glen Hanlon	.30	.75
143 Anders Hedberg	.30	.75
144 Tom Laidlaw	.20	.50
145 Pierre Larouche	.30	.75
146 Dave Maloney	.20	.50
147 Don Maloney	.20	.50
148 Mark Osborne	.20	.50
149 Larry Patey	.20	.50
150 James Patrick RC	.40	1.00
151 Mark Pavelich	.20	.50
152 Mike Rogers	.20	.50
153 Reijo Ruotsalainen	.20	.50
154 Blaine Stoughton	.30	.75
155 Peter Sundstrom RC	.30	.75
156 Bill Barber	.30	.75
157 Doug Crossman	.20	.50
158 Thomas Eriksson RC	.20	.50
159 Bob Froese	.30	.75
160 Paul Guay RC	.20	.50
161 Mark Howe	.40	1.00
162 Tim Kerr	.20	.50
163 Brad Marsh	.20	.50
164 Brad McCrimmon	.30	.75
165 Dave Poulin RC	.60	1.50
166 Brian Propp	.30	.75
167 Ilkka Sinisalo RC	.30	.75
168 Darryl Sittler	.40	1.00
169 Rich Sutter RC	.30	.75
170 Ron Sutter RC	.40	1.00
171 Pat Boutette	.20	.50
172 Mike Bullard	.20	.50
173 Michel Dion	.30	.75
174 Ron Flockhart	.20	.50
175 Greg Fox	.20	.50
176 Denis Herron	.30	.75
177 Rick Kehoe	.30	.75
178 Kevin McCarthy	.20	.50
179 Tom Roulston	.20	.50
180 Mark Taylor	.20	.50
181 Wayne Babych	.20	.50
182 Tim Bothwell RC	.20	.50
183 Kevin Lavallee	.20	.50
184 Bernie Federko	.30	.75
185 Doug Gilmour RC	15.00	40.00
186 Terry Johnson RC	.20	.50
187 Mike Liut	.20	.50
188 Joe Mullen	.60	1.50
189 Jorgen Pettersson	.20	.50
190 Rob Ramage	.20	.50
191 Dwight Schofield RC	.20	.50
192 Brian Sutter	.30	.75
193 Doug Wickenheiser	.20	.50
194 Bobby Carpenter	.30	.75
195 Dave Christian	.20	.50
196 Bob Gould RC	.20	.50
197 Mike Gartner	1.00	3.00
198 Bengt Gustafsson	.20	.50
199 Alan Haworth RC	.20	.50
200 Doug Jarvis	.20	.50
201 Al Jensen	.30	.75
202 Rod Langway	.30	.75
203 Craig Laughlin	.20	.50
204 Larry Murphy	.30	.75
205 Pat Riggin	.30	.75
206 Scott Stevens	1.00	3.00
207 Michel Goulet AS	.30	.75
208 Wayne Gretzky AS	20.00	50.00
209 Mike Bossy AS	.40	1.00
210 Rod Langway AS	.30	.75
211 Ray Bourque AS	1.00	3.00
212 Tom Barrasso AS	1.50	4.00
213 Mark Messier AS	2.00	5.00
214 Bryan Trottier AS	.40	1.00
215 Jari Kurri AS	.75	2.00
216 Denis Potvin AS	.40	1.00
217 Paul Coffey AS	.60	1.50
218 Pat Riggin AS	.30	.75
219 Ed Beers	.20	.50
220 Steve Bozek	.20	.50
221 Mike Eaves	.20	.50
222 Don Edwards	.30	.75
223 Kari Eloranta	.20	.50
224 Dave Hindmarch	.20	.50
225 Jim Jackson	.20	.50
226 Steve Konroyd	.20	.50
227 Richard Kromm RC	.20	.50
228 Rejean Lemelin	.20	.50
229 Hakan Loob RC	1.00	3.00
230 Jamie Macoun RC	.30	.75
231 Lanny McDonald	.30	.75
232 Kent Nilsson	.30	.75
233 Jim Peplinski	.20	.50
234 Dan Quinn RC	.40	1.00
235 Paul Reinhart	.20	.50
236 Doug Risebrough	.20	.50
237 Steve Tambellini	.20	.50
238 Glenn Anderson	.30	.75
239 Paul Coffey	2.50	6.00
240 Lee Fogolin	.20	.50
241 Grant Fuhr	2.50	6.00
242 Randy Gregg	.20	.50
243 Wayne Gretzky	15.00	40.00
244 Charlie Huddy	.30	.75
245 Pat Hughes	.20	.50
246 Dave Hunter	.20	.50
247 Don Jackson	.20	.50
248 Mike Krushelnyski	.20	.50
249 Jari Kurri	2.00	5.00
250 Willy Lindstrom	.20	.50
251 Kevin Lowe	.40	1.00
252 Dave Lumley	.20	.50
253 Kevin McClelland RC	.20	.50
254 Mark Messier	2.50	6.00
255 Andy Moog	1.50	4.00
256 Jaroslav Pouzar	.20	.50
257 Guy Carbonneau	.40	1.00
258 John Chabot RC	.20	.50
259 Chris Chelios RC	20.00	50.00
260 Lucien DeBlois	.20	.50
261 Bob Gainey	.40	1.00
262 Rick Green	.20	.50
263 Jean Hamel	.20	.50
264 Guy Lafleur	.40	1.00
265 Craig Ludwig	.20	.50
266 Pierre Mondou	.20	.50
267 Mats Naslund	.40	1.00
268 Chris Nilan	.20	.50
269 Steve Penney RC	.30	.75
270 Larry Robinson	.40	1.00
271 Bill Root	.20	.50
272 Steve Shutt	.20	.50
273 Bobby Smith	.30	.75
274 Mario Tremblay	.20	.50
275 Ryan Walter	.20	.50
276 Bo Berglund RC	.20	.50
277 Dan Bouchard	.30	.75
278 Alain Cote	.20	.50
279 Andre Dore	.20	.50
280 Michel Goulet	.30	.75
281 Dale Hunter	.30	.75
282 Mario Marois	.20	.50
283 Tony McKegney	.20	.50
284 Randy Moller	.20	.50
285 Wilf Paiement	.20	.50
286 Pat Price	.20	.50
287 Normand Rochefort	.20	.50
288 Andre Savard	.20	.50
289 Richard Sevigny	.20	.50
290 Louis Sleigher	.20	.50
291 Anton Stastny	.30	.75
292 Marian Stastny	.30	.75
293 Peter Stastny	.30	.75
294 Blake Wesley	.20	.50
295 John Anderson	.20	.50
296 Jim Benning	.20	.50
297 Allan Bester UER RC	.30	.75
298 Rich Costello RC	.20	.50
299 Dan Daoust	.20	.50
300 Bill Derlago	.20	.50
301 Dave Farrish	.20	.50
302 Stewart Gavin	.20	.50
303 Gaston Gingras	.20	.50
304 Jim Korn	.20	.50
305 Gary Leeman RC	.40	1.00
306 Terry Martin	.20	.50
307 Gary Nylund RC	.20	.50
308 Mike Palmateer	.30	.75
309 Walt Poddubny	.20	.50
310 Rick St.Croix	.20	.50
311 Borje Salming	.40	1.00
312 Greg Terrion	.20	.50
313 Rick Vaive	.20	.50
314 Richard Brodeur	.30	.75
315 Jiri Bubla	.20	.50
316 Ron Delorme	.20	.50
317 John Garrett	.30	.75
318 Jere Gillis	.20	.50
319 Thomas Gradin	.20	.50
320 Doug Halward	.20	.50
321 Rick Lanz	.20	.50
322 Moe Lemay RC	.20	.50
323 Gary Lupul	.20	.50
324 Al MacAdam	.20	.50
325 Rob McClanahan	.20	.50
326 Peter McNab	.20	.50
327 Cam Neely RC	20.00	50.00
328 Darcy Rota	.20	.50
329 Andy Schliebener RC	.20	.50
330 Stan Smyl	.20	.50
331 Patrik Sundstrom	.20	.50
332 Tony Tanti	.20	.50
333 Scott Arniel	.20	.50
334 Dave Babych	.20	.50
335 Laurie Boschman	.20	.50
336 Wade Campbell	.20	.50
337 Randy Carlyle	.20	.50
338 Jordy Douglas	.20	.50
339 Dale Hawerchuk	1.00	3.00
340 Morris Lukowich	.20	.50
341 Bengt Lundholm	.20	.50
342 Paul MacLean	.20	.50
343 Andrew McBain RC	.20	.50
344 Brian Mullen	.20	.50
345 Robert Picard	.20	.50
346 Doug Smail	.20	.50
347 Doug Soetaert	.30	.75
348 Thomas Steen	.20	.50
349 Perry Turnbull	.20	.50
350 Tim Watters	.20	.50
351 Tim Young	.20	.50
352 Rick Middleton SL	.30	.75
353 Dave Andreychuk TL	1.00	3.00
354 Ed Beers SL	.20	.50
355 Denis Savard TL	.40	1.00
356 John Ogrodnick SL	.20	.50
357 Wayne Gretzky TL	20.00	50.00
358 Charlie Simmer SL	.20	.50
359 Brian Bellows TL	.30	.75
360 Guy Lafleur TL	.40	1.00
361 Mel Bridgman SL	.20	.50
362 Mike Bossy TL	.40	1.00
363 Pierre Larouche SL	.30	.75
364 Tim Kerr SL	.20	.50
365 Mike Bullard SL	.20	.50
366 Michel Goulet TL	.30	.75
367 Federko/Mullen UER SL	.60	1.50
368 Rick Vaive	.20	.50
369 Tony Tanti	.20	.50
370 Mike Gartner TL	1.00	3.00
371 Paul MacLean SL	.20	.50
372 Sylvain Turgeon SL	.30	.75
373 Wayne Gretzky Ross	2.00	5.00
374 Wayne Gretzky Hart	2.00	5.00
375 Tom Barrasso Calder	1.50	4.00
376 Mike Bossy Byng	.40	1.00
377 Rod Langway Norris	.30	.75
378 Brad Park TW	.30	.75
379 Tom Barrasso Vezina	1.50	4.00
380 Wayne Gretzky LL	10.00	25.00
381 Wayne Gretzky LL	10.00	25.00
382 Wayne Gretzky LL	10.00	25.00
383 Wayne Gretzky LL	10.00	25.00
384 Michel Goulet LL	.30	.75
385 Steve Yzerman LL	8.00	20.00
386 Pat Riggin LL	.30	.75
387 Rollie Melanson LL	.30	.75
388 Wayne Gretzky RB	8.00	20.00
389 Denis Potvin RB	.40	1.00
390 Brad Park RB	.30	.75
391 Michel Goulet RB	.30	.75
392 Pat LaFontaine RB	1.00	3.00
393 Dale Hawerchuk RB	1.00	3.00
394 Checklist 1-132	1.00	2.50
395 Checklist 133-264 UER (185 Gilmore)	1.00	2.50
396 Checklist 265-396	1.00	2.50

1984-85 O-Pee-Chee Stanley Cup Sweepstakes Entry

Card	Low	High
1 Centreman	.75	2.00
2 Left Wing	.75	2.00
3 Right Defense	.75	2.00
4 Right Wing	.75	2.00
5 Instant Winner	50.00	100.00

1985-86 O-Pee-Chee

Card	Low	High
COMPLETE SET (264)	250.00	600.00
1 Lanny McDonald	.75	2.00
2 Mike O'Connell	.30	.75
3 Curt Fraser	.30	.75
4 Steve Penney	.30	.75
5 Brian Engblom	.30	.75
6 Ron Sutter	.30	.75
7 Joe Mullen	.30	.75
8 Rod Langway	.30	.75
9 Mario Lemieux RC	150.00	400.00
10 Dave Babych	.30	.75
11 Bob Nystrom	.30	.75
12 Andy Moog	2.50	6.00
13 Dino Ciccarelli	.30	.75
14 Dwight Foster	.30	.75
15 James Patrick	.30	.75
16 Thomas Gradin	.30	.75
17 Mike Foligno	.30	.75
18 Mario Gosselin RC	.30	.75
19 Mike Zuke	.30	.75
20 John Anderson	.30	.75
21 Dave Pichette	.30	.75
22 Nick Fotiu	.30	.75
23 Tom Lysiak	.25	.60
24 Peter Zezel RC	1.00	2.50
25 Denis Potvin	.30	.75
26 Bob Carpenter	.25	.60
27 Murray Bannerman	.25	.60
28 Gordie Roberts	.25	.60
29 Steve Yzerman	15.00	40.00
30 Phil Russell	.25	.60
31 Peter Stastny	.25	.60
32 Craig Ramsay	.25	.60
33 Terry Ruskowski	.25	.60
34 Kevin Dineen RC	2.50	6.00
35 Mark Howe	.30	.75
36 Glenn Resch	.25	.60
37 Danny Gare	.25	.60
38 Doug Bodger RC	.25	.60
39 Mike Rogers	.30	.75
40 Ray Bourque	3.00	8.00
41 John Tonelli	.25	.60
42 Mel Bridgman	.30	.75
43 Sylvain Turgeon	.25	.60
44 Mark Johnson	.30	.75
45 Doug Wilson	.25	.60
46 Mike Gartner	1.50	4.00
47 Brent Peterson	.30	.75
48 Paul Reinhart	.25	.60
49 Mike Krushelnyski	.30	.75
50 Brian Bellows	.25	.60
51 Chris Chelios	3.00	8.00
52 Barry Pederson	.30	.75
53 Murray Craven	.25	.60
54 Pierre Larouche	.25	.60
55 Reed Larson	.25	.60
56 Pat Verbeek	.25	.60
57 Randy Carlyle	.25	.60
58 Ray Neufeld	.25	.60
59 Keith Brown	.30	.75
60 Bryan Trottier	.30	.75
61 Jim Fox	.30	.75
62 Scott Stevens	1.50	4.00
63 Phil Housley	.25	.60
64 Rick Middleton	.25	.60
65 Steve Payne	.20	.50
66 Dave Lewis	.25	.60
67 Mike Bullard	.25	.60
68 Stan Smyl	.25	.60
69 Mark Pavelich	.25	.60
70 John Ogrodnick	.25	.60
71 Bill Derlago	.25	.60
72 Brad Marsh	.25	.60
73 Denis Savard	.30	.75
74 Mark Fusco RC	.25	.60
75 Pete Peeters	.25	.60
76 Doug Gilmour	4.00	10.00
77 Mike Ramsey	.25	.60
78 Anton Stastny	.25	.60
79 Steve Kasper	.20	.50
80 Bryan Erickson RC	.25	.60
81 Clark Gillies	.30	.75
82 Keith Acton	.25	.60
83 Pat Flatley	.25	.60
84 Kirk Muller RC	1.50	4.00
85 Paul Coffey	2.00	5.00
86 Ed Olczyk RC	.30	.75
87 Charlie Simmer	.20	.50
88 Mike Liut	.20	.50
89 Dave Maloney	.30	.75
90 Marcel Dionne	.40	1.00
91 Tim Kerr	.20	.50
92 Ivan Boldirev	.30	.75
93 Ken Morrow	.20	.50
94 Don Maloney	.30	.75
95 Rejean Lemelin	.20	.50
96 Curt Giles	.30	.75
97 Bob Bourne	.20	.50
98 Joe Cirella	.30	.75
99 Dave Christian	.20	.50
100 Darryl Sutter	.30	.75
101 Kelly Kisio	.30	.75
102 Mats Naslund	.30	.75
103 Joel Quenneville	.30	.75
104 Bernie Federko	.25	.60
105 Tom Barrasso	.30	.75
106 Rick Vaive	.30	.75
107 Brent Sutter	.30	.75
108 Wayne Babych	.25	.60
109 Dale Hawerchuk	1.50	4.00
110 Pelle Lindbergh Mem.	20.00	50.00
111 Dennis Maruk	.20	.50
112 Reijo Ruotsalainen	.20	.50
113 Tom Fergus	.20	.50

114 Bob Murray .20 .50
115 Patrik Sundstrom .25 .60
116 Ron Duguay .25 .60
117 Alan Haworth .20 .50
118 Greg Malone .20 .50
119 Bill Hajt .20 .50
120 Wayne Gretzky 40.00 100.00
121 Craig Redmond RC .20 .50
122 Kelly Hrudey RC 8.00 20.00
123 Tomas Sandstrom RC 2.50 6.00
124 Neal Broten .25 .60
125 Moe Mantha .25 .60
126 Greg Gilbert .25 .60
127 Bruce Driver RC .30 .75
128 Dave Poulin .25 .60
129 Morris Lukowich .25 .60
130 Mike Bossy .30 .75
131 Larry Playfair .25 .60
132 Steve Larmer .25 .60
133 Doug Keans .25 .60
134 Bob Manno .30 .75
135 Brian Sutter .30 .75
136 Pat Riggin .30 .75
137 Pat LaFontaine 2.50 6.00
138 Barry Beck .30 .75
139 Rich Preston .30 .75
140 Ron Francis 2.00 5.00
141 Brian Propp .30 .75
142 Don Beaupre .30 .75
143 Dave Andreychuk .30 .75
144 Ed Beers .25 .60
145 Paul MacLean .25 .60
146 Troy Murray .30 .75
147 Larry Robinson .30 .75
148 Bernie Nicholls .30 .75
149 Glen Hanlon .30 .75
150 Michel Goulet .30 .75
151 Doug Jarvis .30 .75
152 Warren Young RC .25 .60
153 Tony Tanti .25 .60
154 Tomas Jonsson .25 .60
155 Jari Kurri 2.00 5.00
156 Tony McKegney .25 .60
157 Greg Stefan .25 .60
158 Brad McCrimmon .25 .60
159 Keith Crowder .20 .50
160 Gilbert Perreault .30 .75
161 Tim Bothwell .25 .60
162 Bob Crawford .25 .60
163 Paul Gagne .25 .60
164 Dan Daoust .25 .60
165 Checklist 1-132 3.00 8.00
166 Tim Bernhardt RC .25 .60
167 Gord Kluzak .20 .50
168 Glenn Anderson .25 .60
169 Bob Gainey .25 .60
170 Brent Ashton .25 .60
171 Ron Flockhart .25 .60
172 Gary Nylund .25 .60
173 Moe Lemay .25 .60
174 Bob Sauve .25 .60
175 Doug Smail .25 .60
176 Dan Quinn .25 .60
177 Mark Messier 2.50 6.00
178 Jay Wells RC .20 .50
179 Dale Hunter .20 .50
180 Richard Brodeur .20 .50
181 Bobby Smith .20 .50
182 Ron Greschner .20 .50
183 Don Edwards .20 .50
184 Hakan Loob .20 .50
185 Dave Ellett RC .30 .75
186 Denis Herron .30 .75
187 Charlie Huddy .30 .75
188 Ilkka Sinisalo .30 .75
189 Doug Halward .25 .60
190 Craig Laughlin .25 .60
191 Carey Wilson RC .25 .00
192 Craig Ludwig .25 .60
193 Bob MacMillan .25 .60
194 Mario Marois .25 .60
195 Brian Mullen .25 .60
196 Rob Ramage .25 .60
197 Rick Lanz .20 .50
198 Miroslav Frycer .25 .60
199 Randy Gregg .20 .50
200 Corrado Micalef .25 .60
201 Jamie Macoun .25 .60
202 Bob Brooke RC .25 .60
203 Billy Carroll .25 .60
204 Brian MacLellan .25 .60
205 Alain Cole .25 .60
206 Thomas Steen .25 .60
207 Grant Fuhr 2.50 6.00
208 Rich Sutter .25 .60
209 Al MacAdam .25 .60
210 Al Iafrate RC 6.00 15.00
211 Pierre Mondou .30 .75
212 Randy Hillier RC .30 .75
213 Mike Eaves .20 .50
214 Dave Taylor .20 .50
215 Robert Picard .20 .50
216 Randy Ladouceur .20 .50
217 Willy Lindstrom .20 .50
218 Torrie Robertson RC .25 .60
219 Tom Kurvers RC .25 .60
220 John Garrett .25 .60
221 Greg Millen .20 .50
222 Richard Kromm .20 .50
223 Bob Janecyk RC .20 .50
224 Brad Maxwell .20 .50
225 Mike McPhee RC .20 .50
226 Brian Hayward RC .25 .60
227 Duane Sutter .25 .60
228 Cam Neely 4.00 10.00
229 Doug Wickenheiser .25 .60
230 Rollie Melanson .25 .60
231 Bruce Bell RC .25 .60
232 Harold Snepsts .25 .60
233 Guy Carbonneau .25 .60
234 Doug Sulliman .25 .60
235 Lee Fogolin .30 .75
236 Larry Murphy .30 .75
237 Al MacInnis RC 20.00 50.00
238 Don Lever .30 .75
239 Kevin Lowe .30 .75
240 Randy Moller .30 .75
241 Doug Lidster RC .30 .75
242 Craig Hartsburg .25 .60
243 Doug Risebrough .25 .60
244 John Chabot .25 .60
245 Mario Tremblay .25 .60
246 Dan Bouchard .25 .60
247 Doug Shedden .25 .60
248 Borje Salming .30 .75
249 Aaron Broten .30 .75
250 Jim Benning .20 .50
251 Laurie Boschman .20 .50
252 George McPhee RC .25 .60
253 Mark Napier .30 .75
254 Perry Turnbull .30 .75
255 Warren Skorodenski RC .25 .60
256 Checklist 133-264 6.00 15.00
257 Wayne Gretzky LL 15.00 40.00
258 Wayne Gretzky LL 15.00 40.00
259 Wayne Gretzky LL 15.00 8.00
260 Tim Kerr LL .20 .50
261 Jari Kurri LL .50 1.25
262 Mario Lemieux LL 20.00 50.00
263 Tom Barrasso LL .30 .75
264 Warren Skorodenski LL .25 .60

1985-86 O-Pee-Chee Box Bottoms

COMPLETE SET (16) 40.00 100.00
A Brian Bellows .30 .75
B Ray Bourque 2.00 5.00
C Bob Carpenter .20 .50
D Chris Chelios 2.00 5.00
E Marcel Dionne .75 2.00
F Ron Francis 1.25 3.00
G Wayne Gretzky 12.00 30.00
H Tim Kerr .20 .50
I Mario Lemieux 40.00 100.00
J John Ogrodnick .20 .50
K Gilbert Perreault .40 1.00
L Glenn Resch .40 1.00
M Reijo Ruotsalainen .20 .50
N Brian Sutter .30 .75
O John Tonelli .20 .50
P Doug Wilson .30 .75

1986-87 O-Pee-Chee

COMPLETE SET (264) 150.00 400.00
1 Ray Bourque 2.50 5.00
2 Pat LaFontaine 1.25 3.00
3 Wayne Gretzky 25.00 60.00
4 Lindy Ruff .08 .25
5 Brad McCrimmon .08 .25
6 Tiger Williams .20 .50
7 Denis Savard .50 1.25
8 Lanny McDonald .20 .50
9 John Vanbiesbrouck RC 10.00 25.00
10 Greg Adams RC .60 1.50
11 Steve Yzerman 10.00 25.00
12 Craig Hartsburg .08 .25
13 John Anderson .08 .25
14 Bob Bourne .08 .25
15 Kjell Dahlin RC .08 .25
16 Dave Andreychuk .50 1.25
17 Rob Ramage .08 .25
18 Ron Greschner .08 .25
19 Bruce Driver .20 .50
20 Peter Stastny .20 .50
21 Dave Christian .08 .25
22 Doug Keans .08 .25
23 Scott Bjugstad RC .08 .25
24 Doug Bodger .08 .25
25 Troy Murray .08 .25
26 Al Iafrate .40 1.00
27 Kelly Hrudey .40 1.00
28 Doug Jarvis .08 .25
29 Rich Sutter .08 .25
30 Marcel Dionne .20 .50
31 Curt Fraser .08 .25
32 Doug Lidster .08 .25
33 Brian MacLellan .08 .25
34 Barry Pederson .08 .25
35 Craig Laughlin .08 .25
36 Ilkka Sinisalo .08 .25
37 John MacLean RC 1.50 4.00
38 Brian Mullen .08 .25
39 Duane Sutter .08 .25
40 Brian Engblom .08 .25
41 Chris Cichocki RC .08 .25
42 Gordie Roberts .08 .25
43 Ron Francis 1.00 2.50
44 Joe Mullen .40 1.00
45 Moe Mantha .08 .25
46 Pat Verbeek .08 .25
47 Clint Malarchuk RC .60 1.50
48 Bob Brooke .08 .25
49 Darryl Sutter .08 .25
50 Stan Smyl .08 .25
51 Greg Stefan .20 .50
52 Bill Hajt .08 .25
53 Patrick Roy RC 125.00 300.00
54 Gord Kluzak .08 .25
55 Bob Froese .08 .25
56 Grant Fuhr 1.00 2.50
57 Mark Hunter .08 .25
58 Dana Murzyn RC .40 1.00
59 Mike Gartner .40 1.00
60 Dennis Maruk .08 .25
61 Rich Preston .08 .25
62 Larry Robinson .08 .25
63 Dave Taylor .08 .25
64 Bob Murray .08 .25
65 Ken Morrow .08 .25
66 Mike Ridley RC .40 1.00
67 John Tucker RC .20 .50
68 Miroslav Frycer .08 .25
69 Danny Gare .20 .50
70 Randy Burridge RC .40 1.00
71 Dave Poulin .08 .25
72 Brian Sutter .20 .50
73 Dave Babych .08 .25
74 Dale Hawerchuk .50 1.25
75 Brian Bellows .40 1.00
76 Dave Pasin RC .08 .25
77 Pete Peeters .20 .50
78 Tomas Jonsson .08 .25
79 Gilbert Perreault .20 .50
80 Glenn Anderson .50 1.25
81 Don Maloney .08 .25
82 Ed Olczyk .08 .25
83 Mike Bullard .08 .25
84 Tom Fergus .08 .25
85 Dave Lewis .08 .25
86 Brian Propp .20 .50
87 John Ogrodnick .08 .25
88 Kevin Dineen .40 1.00
89 Don Beaupre .20 .50
90 Mike Bossy .60 1.50
91 Tom Barrasso .40 1.00
92 Michel Goulet .20 .50
93 Doug Gilmour 2.50 5.00
94 Kirk Muller .40 1.00
95 Larry Melnyk RC .08 .25
96 Bob Gainey .40 1.00
97 Steve Kasper .08 .25
98 Petr Klima RC .40 1.00
99 Neal Broten .20 .50
100 Al Secord .08 .25
101 Bryan Erickson .08 .25
102 Rejean Lemelin .20 .50
103 Sylvain Turgeon .20 .50
104 Bob Nystrom .08 .25
105 Bernie Federko .20 .50
106 Doug Wilson .20 .50
107 Alan Haworth .08 .25
108 Jari Kurri 1.00 2.50
109 Ron Sutter .08 .25
110 Reed Larson .08 .25
111 Terry Ruskowski .08 .25
112 Mark Johnson .08 .25
113 James Patrick .08 .25
114 Paul MacLean .08 .25
115 Mike Ramsey .08 .25
116 Kelly Kisio .08 .25
117 Brent Sutter .08 .25
118 Joel Quenneville .08 .25
119 Curt Giles .08 .25
120 Tony Tanti .08 .25
121 Doug Sulliman .08 .25
122 Mario Lemieux 30.00 80.00
123 Mark Howe .20 .50
124 Bob Sauve .20 .50
125 Anton Stastny .20 .50
126 Scott Stevens .40 1.00
127 Mike Foligno .08 .25
128 Reijo Ruotsalainen .08 .25
129 Denis Potvin .20 .50
130 Keith Crowder .08 .25
131 Bob Janecyk .20 .50
132 John Tonelli .08 .25
133 Mike Liut .08 .25
134 Tim Kerr .20 .50
135 Al Jensen .08 .25
136 Mel Bridgman .08 .25
137 Paul Coffey 1.50 4.00
138 Dino Ciccarelli .40 1.00
139 Steve Larmer .40 1.00
140 Mike O'Connell .08 .25
141 Clark Gillies .20 .50
142 Phil Russell .08 .25
143 Dirk Graham RC .60 1.50
144 Randy Carlyle .08 .25
145 Charlie Simmer .08 .25
146 Ron Flockhart .08 .25
147 Tom Laidlaw .08 .25
148 Dave Tippett RC .08 .25
149 Wendel Clark RC 30.00 80.00
150 Bob Carpenter .08 .25
151 Bill Watson RC .08 .25
152 Roberto Romano RC .08 .25
153 Doug Shedden .08 .25
154 Phil Housley .40 1.00
155 Bryan Trottier .40 1.00
156 Patrik Sundstrom .08 .25
157 Rick Middleton .20 .50
158 Glenn Resch .20 .50
159 Bernie Nicholls .20 .50
160 Ray Ferraro RC 2.50 6.00
161 Mats Naslund .20 .50
162 Pat Flatley .08 .25
163 Joe Cirella .08 .25
164 Rod Langway .20 .50
165 Checklist 1-132 1.25 3.00
166 Carey Wilson .08 .25
167 Murray Craven .08 .25
168 Paul Gillis RC .08 .25
169 Borje Salming .08 .25
170 Perry Turnbull .08 .25
171 Chris Chelios 2.00 5.00
172 Keith Acton .08 .25
173 Al MacInnis 3.00 6.00
174 Russ Courtnall RC 1.50 4.00
175 Brad Marsh .20 .50
176 Guy Carbonneau .20 .50
177 Ray Neufeld .08 .25
178 Craig MacTavish RC .75 2.00
179 Rick Lanz .08 .25
180 Murray Bannerman .08 .25
181 Brent Ashton .08 .25
182 Jim Peplinski .08 .25
183 Mark Napier .08 .25
184 Laurie Boschman .08 .25
185 Larry Murphy .40 1.00
186 Mark Messier .75 2.00
187 Risto Siltanen .08 .25
188 Bobby Smith .20 .50
189 Gary Suter RC 1.25 3.00
190 Peter Zezel .08 .25
191 Rick Vaive .08 .25
192 Dale Hunter .20 .50
193 Mike Krushelnyski .08 .25
194 Scott Arniel .08 .25
195 Larry Playfair .08 .25
196 Doug Risebrough .08 .25
197 Kevin Lowe .20 .50
198 Checklist 133-264 1.25 3.00
199 Chris Nilan .08 .25
200 Paul Cyr RC .08 .25
201 Ric Seiling .08 .25
202 Doug Smith .08 .25
203 Jamie Macoun .08 .25
204 Dan Quinn .08 .25
205 Paul Reinhart .08 .25
206 Keith Brown .08 .25
207 Jack O'Callahan .08 .25
208 Steve Richmond RC .08 .25
209 Warren Young .08 .25
210 Lee Fogolin .08 .25
211 Charlie Huddy .08 .25
212 Andy Moog 1.00 2.50
213 Wayne Babych .08 .25
214 Torrie Robertson .08 .25
215 Jim Fox .08 .25
216 Phil Sykes RC .08 .25
217 Jay Wells .08 .25
218 Dave Langevin .08 .25
219 Steve Payne .08 .25
220 Craig Ludwig .08 .25
221 Mike McPhee .08 .25
222 Steve Penney .08 .25
223 Mario Tremblay .08 .25
224 Ryan Walter .08 .25
225 Alain Chevrier RC .08 .25
226 Uli Hiemer RC .08 .25
227 Tim Higgins .08 .25
228 Billy Smith .20 .50
229 Richard Kromm .08 .25
230 Tomas Sandstrom .40 1.00
231 Jim Johnson RC .08 .25
232 Willy Lindstrom .08 .25
233 Alain Cote .08 .25
234 Gilbert Delorme .08 .25
235 Mario Gosselin .20 .50
236 David Shaw RC .40 1.00
237 Dave Barr RC .40 1.00
238 Ed Beers .08 .25
239 Charlie Bourgeois RC .08 .25
240 Rick Wamsley .08 .25
241 Dan Daoust .08 .25
242 Brad Maxwell .08 .25
243 Gary Nylund .08 .25
244 Greg Terrion .08 .25
245 Steve Thomas RC 2.00 5.00
246 Richard Brodeur .20 .50
247 Joel Otto UER RC .40 1.00
248 Doug Halward .08 .25
249 Moe Lemay UER
Photo is Joel Otto .08 .25
250 Cam Neely 2.00 5.00
251 Brent Peterson .08 .25
252 Petri Skriko RC .40 1.00
253 Greg C.Adams RC .20 .50
254 Bill Derlago .08 .25
255 Brian Hayward .20 .50
256 Doug Smail .08 .25
257 Thomas Steen .08 .25
258 Jari Kurri LL .40 1.00
259 Wayne Gretzky LL 15.00 40.00
260 Wayne Gretzky LL 15.00 40.00
261 Tim Kerr LL .08 .25
262 Kjell Dahlin LL .08 .25
263 Bob Froese LL .20 .50
264 Bob Froese LL .20 .50

1986-87 O-Pee-Chee Box Bottoms

COMPLETE SET (16) 16.00 40.00
A Greg Adams .20 .50
B Mike Bossy .60 1.50
C Dave Christian .08 .25
D Mike Foligno .20 .50
E Michel Goulet .30 .75
F Wayne Gretzky 8.00 20.00
G Tim Kerr .08 .25
H Jari Kurri 1.00 2.50
I Mario Lemieux 8.00 20.00
J Lanny McDonald .30 .75
K Bernie Nicholls .30 .75
L Mike Ridley .30 .75
M Larry Robinson .30 .75
N Denis Savard .30 .75
O Brian Sutter .08 .25
P Bryan Trottier .40 1.00

1987-88 O-Pee-Chee

COMPLETE SET (264) 60.00 120.00
COMP.FACT.SET (264) 75.00 150.00
1 Denis Potvin .30 .75
2 Rick Tocchet RC 4.00 10.00
3 Dave Andreychuk .30 .75
4 Stan Smyl .25 .60
5 Dave Babych .25 .60
6 Pat Verbeek .25 .60
7 Esa Tikkanen RC 3.00 8.00
8 Mike Ridley .25 .60
9 Randy Carlyle UER
(Misspelled Calryle .25 .60
on card front)
10 Greg Paslawski RC .25 .60
11 Neal Broten .25 .60
12 Wendel Clark 2.50 6.00
13 Bill Ranford RC 4.00 10.00
14 Doug Wilson .25 .60
15 Mario Lemieux 12.00 30.00
16 Mats Naslund .20 .50
17 Mel Bridgman .25 .60
18 James Patrick .25 .60
19 Rollie Melanson .25 .60
20 Lanny McDonald .25 .60
21 Peter Stastny .25 .60
22 Murray Craven .25 .60
23 Ulf Samuelsson RC 2.50 6.00
24 Michael Thelven RC .25 .60
25 Scott Stevens .30 .75
26 Petr Klima .25 .60
27 Brent Sutter .25 .60
28 Tomas Sandstrom .25 .60
29 Tim Bothwell .25 .60
30 Bob Carpenter .25 .60
31 Brian MacLellan .25 .60
32 John Chabot .25 .60
33 Phil Housley .25 .60
34 Patrik Sundstrom .25 .60
35 Dave Ellett .25 .60
36 John Vanbiesbrouck 3.00 8.00
37 Dave Lewis .25 .60
38 Tom McCarthy .25 .60
39 Dave Poulin .25 .60
40 Mike Foligno .25 .60
41 Gordie Roberts .25 .60
42 Luc Robitaille RC 20.00 50.00
43 Duane Sutter .25 .60
44 Pete Peeters .25 .60
45 John Anderson .25 .60
46 Aaron Broten .25 .60
47 Keith Brown .25 .60
48 Bobby Smith .25 .60
49 Don Maloney .25 .60
50 Mark Hunter .25 .60
51 Moe Mantha .25 .60
52 Charlie Simmer .20 .50
53 Wayne Gretzky 15.00 40.00
54 Mark Howe .30 .75
55 Bob Gould .25 .60
56 Steve Yzerman 10.00 25.00
57 Larry Playfair .25 .60
58 Alain Chevrier .25 .60
59 Steve Larmer .25 .60
60 Bryan Trottier .30 .75
61 Stewart Gavin .30 .75
62 Russ Courtnall .30 .75
63 Mike Ramsey .30 .75
64 Bob Brooke .30 .75
65 Rick Wamsley .30 .75
66 Ken Morrow .20 .50
67 Gerard Gallant UER RC .30 .75
68 Kevin Hatcher RC .75 2.00
69 Cam Neely 1.00 2.50
70 Sylvain Turgeon .20 .50
71 Peter Zezel .30 .75
72 Al MacInnis 2.00 5.00
73 Terry Ruskowski .30 .75
74 Troy Murray .30 .75
75 Jim Fox .30 .75
76 Kelly Kisio .30 .75
77 Michel Goulet .30 .75
78 Tom Barrasso .30 .75
79 Bruce Driver .30 .75
80 Craig Simpson RC .50 1.25
81 Dino Ciccarelli .30 .75
82 Gary Nylund .30 .75
83 Bernie Federko .25 .60
84 John Tonelli .30 .75
85 Brad McCrimmon .30 .75
86 Dave Tippett .30 .75
87 Ray Bourque 2.00 5.00
88 Dave Christian .20 .50
89 Glen Hanlon .30 .75
90 Brian Curran RC .30 .75
91 Paul MacLean .30 .75
92 Jimmy Carson RC .30 .75
93 Willie Huber .30 .75
94 Brian Bellows .25 .60
95 Doug Jarvis .30 .75
96 Clark Gillies .30 .75
97 Tony Tanti .30 .75
98 Pelle Eklund RC .30 .75
99 Paul Coffey 1.50 4.00
100 Brent Ashton .30 .75
101 Mark Johnson .30 .75
102 Greg Johnston RC .30 .75
103 Ron Flockhart .30 .75
104 Ed Olczyk .30 .75
105 Mike Bossy 1.00 2.50
106 Chris Chelios 1.50 4.00
107 Gilles Meloche .30 .75
108 Rod Langway .30 .75
109 Ray Ferraro .30 .75
110 Ron Duguay .25 .60
111 Al Secord .25 .60
112 Mark Messier .60 1.50
113 Ron Sutter .30 .75
114 Darren Veitch RC .30 .75
115 Rick Middleton .30 .75
116 Doug Sulliman .30 .75
117 Dennis Maruk .30 .75
118 Dave Taylor .30 .75
119 Kelly Hrudey .30 .75
120 Tom Fergus .20 .50
121 Christian Ruuttu RC .20 .50
122 Brian Benning RC .20 .50
123 Adam Oates RC 10.00 25.00
124 Kevin Dineen .30 .75
125 Doug Bodger .30 .75
126 Joe Mullen .30 .75
127 Denis Savard .30 .75
128 Brad Marsh .30 .75
129 Marcel Dionne .40 1.00
130 Bryan Erickson .30 .75
131 Reed Larson .30 .75
132 Don Beaupre .30 .75
133 Larry Murphy .25 .60
134 John Ogrodnick .30 .75
135 Greg Adams .30 .75
136 Pat Flatley .30 .75
137 Scott Arniel .20 .50
138 Dana Murzyn .20 .50
139 Greg C. Adams .20 .50
140 Bob Sauve .20 .50
141 Mike O'Connell .20 .50
142 Walt Poddubny .20 .50
143 Paul Reinhart .20 .50
144 Tim Kerr .20 .50
145 Brian Lawton RC .20 .50
146 Gino Cavallini RC .20 .50
147 Doug Keans .20 .50
148 Jari Kurri .25 .60
149 Dale Hawerchuk .40 1.00
150 Randy Cunneyworth RC .25 .60
151 Jay Wells .20 .50
152 Mike Liut .20 .50
153 Steve Konroyd .20 .50
154 John Tucker .20 .50
155 Rick Vaive .20 .50
156 Bob Murray .20 .50
157 Kirk Muller .20 .50
158 Brian Propp .20 .50
159 Ron Greschner .20 .50
160 Rob Ramage .20 .50
161 Craig Laughlin .20 .50
162 Steve Kasper .20 .50
163 Patrick Roy 12.00 30.00
164 Shawn Burr RC .25 .60
165 Craig Hartsburg .25 .60
166 Dean Evason RC .25 .60
167 Bob Bourne .20 .50
168 Mike Gartner .40 1.00
169 Ron Hextall RC 20.00 50.00
170 Joe Cirella .25 .60
171 Dan Quinn .25 .60
172 Tony McKegney .25 .60
173 Pat LaFontaine .30 .75
174 Allen Pedersen RC .25 .60
175 Doug Gilmour .40 1.00
176 Gary Suter .25 .60
177 Barry Pederson .25 .60
178 Grant Fuhr .50 1.25
179 Wayne Presley RC .25 .60
180 Wilf Paiement .25 .60
181 Doug Smail .30 .75
182 Doug Crossman .30 .75
183 Bernie Nicholls UER
(Misspelled Nichols
on both sides) .30 .75
184 Dirk Graham UER
(Misspelled Dick) .30 .75
185 Anton Stastny .30 .75
186 Greg Stefan .30 .75
187 Ron Francis .40 1.00
188 Steve Thomas .30 .75
189 Kelly Miller RC .30 .75
190 Tomas Jonsson .30 .75
191 John MacLean .30 .75
192 Larry Robinson .30 .75
193 Doug Wickenheiser .25 .60
194 Keith Crowder .20 .50
195 Bob Froese .20 .50
196 Jim Johnson .25 .60
197 Checklist 1-132 .60 1.50
198 Checklist 133-264 .60 1.50
199 Glenn Anderson .25 .60
200 Kevin Lowe .25 .60
201 Kevin McClelland .20 .50
202 Mike Krushelnyski .20 .50
203 Craig MacTavish .20 .50
204 Andy Moog .75 2.00
205 Marty McSorley RC 3.00 8.00
206 Craig Muni RC .20 .50
207 Charlie Huddy .20 .50
208 Hakan Loob .20 .50
209 Jim Peplinski .20 .50
210 Mike Bullard .20 .50
211 Carey Wilson .20 .50
212 Joel Otto .20 .50
213 Neil Sheehy RC .20 .50
214 Jamie Macoun .20 .50
215 Mike Vernon RC 20.00 50.00
216 Steve Bozek .20 .50
217 Daniel Berthiaume RC .20 .50
218 Gilles Hamel .20 .50
219 Tim Watters .20 .50
220 Mario Marois .25 .60
221 Thomas Steen .25 .60
222 Laurie Boschman .25 .60
223 Steve Rooney RC .25 .60
224 Ron Wilson .25 .60
225 Fredrik Olausson RC .25 .60
226 Jim Kyte RC .25 .60
227 Claude Lemieux RC 8.00 20.00
228 Bob Gainey .25 .60
229 Gaston Gingras .25 .60
230 Brian Hayward .25 .60
231 Ryan Walter .25 .60
232 Guy Carbonneau .25 .60
233 Stephane Richer RC 3.00 8.00
234 Rick Green .25 .60
235 Brian Skrudland RC .75 2.00
236 Allan Bester .25 .60
237 Borje Salming .30 .75
238 Al Iafrate .25 .60
239 Rick Lanz .25 .60
240 Gary Leeman .25 .60
241 Greg Terrion .25 .60
242 Ken Wregget RC 1.25 3.00
243 Vincent Damphousse RC 8.00 20.00
244 Chris Kotsopoulos .25 .60
245 Dale Hunter .25 .60
246 Clint Malarchuk .25 .60
247 Paul Gillis .25 .60
248 Robert Picard .25 .00
249 Doug Shedden .25 .60
250 Mario Gosselin .25 .60
251 Randy Moller .25 .60
252 David Shaw .25 .60
253 Mike Eagles RC .25 .60
254 Alain Cote .25 .60
255 Petri Skriko .25 .60
256 Doug Lidster .20 .50
257 Richard Brodeur UER
(Photo actually
Frank Caprice) .20 .50
258 Rich Sutter .20 .50
259 Steve Tambellini .20 .50
260 Jim Benning .20 .50
261 Dave Richter RC .20 .50
262 Michel Petit RC .20 .50
263 Brent Peterson .25 .60
264 Jim Sandlak RC .25 .60

1987-88 O-Pee-Chee Box Bottoms

COMPLETE SET (16) 14.00 35.00
A Wayne Gretzky 6.00 15.00
B Tim Kerr .15 .40
C Steve Yzerman 3.00 8.00
D Luc Robitaille 3.00 8.00
E Doug Gilmour .75 2.00
F Ray Bourque .75 2.00
G Joe Mullen .30 .75
H Larry Murphy .30 .75
I Dale Hawerchuk .40 1.00
J Ron Francis .75 2.00
K Walt Poddubny .08 .25
L Mats Naslund .20 .50
M Michel Goulet .30 .75
N Denis Savard .30 .75
O Bryan Trottier .40 1.00
P Russ Courtnall .30 .75

1987-88 O-Pee-Chee Minis

COMPLETE SET (42) 8.00 20.00
1 Glenn Anderson .08 .25
2 Brian Benning .02 .10
3 Daniel Berthiaume .05 .15
4 Ray Bourque .40 1.00
5 Shawn Burr .02 .10
6 Jimmy Carson .05 .15
7 Dino Ciccarelli .08 .25
8 Paul Coffey .40 1.00
9 Pelle Eklund .02 .10
10 Ron Francis .40 1.00
11 Doug Gilmour .40 1.00
12 Michel Goulet .08 .25
13 Wayne Gretzky 2.50 6.00
14 Glen Hanlon .05 .15
15 Brian Hayward .05 .15
16 Ron Hextall .75 2.00
17 Phil Housley .08 .25
18 Mark Howe .05 .15
19 Doug Jarvis .02 .10
20 Tim Kerr .05 .15
21 Jari Kurri .20 .50
22 Pat LaFontaine .20 .50
23 Mario Lemieux 3.00 8.00
24 Mike Liut .07 .20
25 Kevin Lowe .05 .15
26 Al MacInnis .15 .40
27 Brad McCrimmon .02 .10
28 Mark Messier .60 1.50
29 Joe Mullen .08 .25
30 Craig Muni .02 .10
31 Larry Murphy .08 .25
32 Dave Poulin .05 .15
33 Brian Propp .05 .15
34 Paul Reinhart .05 .15
35 Luc Robitaille 1.50 4.00
36 Patrick Roy 4.00 10.00
37 Christian Ruuttu .02 .10
38 Tomas Sandstrom .08 .25
39 Denis Savard .08 .25
40 Petri Skriko .02 .10
41 Bryan Trottier .20 .50
42 Checklist 1-42 .02 .10

1988-89 O-Pee-Chee

COMPLETE SET (264) 80.00 200.00
COMP.FACT.SET (264) 125.00 300.00
1 Mario Lemieux 8.00 20.00
2 Bob Joyce RC .30 .75
3 Joel Quenneville .25 .60
4 Tony McKegney .25 .60
5 Stephane Richer .25 .60
6 Mark Howe .30 .75
7 Brent Sutter .25 .60
8 Gilles Meloche .25 .60
9 Jimmy Carson .25 .60
10 John MacLean .25 .60
11 Gary Leeman .25 .60
12 Gerard Gallant .25 .60
13 Marcel Dionne .40 1.00
14 Dave Christian .20 .50
15 Gary Nylund .25 .60
16 Joe Nieuwendyk RC 6.00 15.00
17 Billy Smith .30 .75
18 Christian Ruuttu .25 .60
19 Randy Cunneyworth .25 .60
20 Brian Lawton .25 .60
21 Scott Mellanby RC 1.00 2.50
22 Peter Stastny .25 .60
23 Gord Kluzak .20 .50
24 Sylvain Turgeon .25 .60
25 Clint Malarchuk .25 .60
26 Denis Savard .30 .75
27 Craig Simpson .25 .60
28 Petr Klima .25 .60
29 Pat Verbeek .25 .60
30 Moe Mantha .25 .60
31 Chris Nilan .20 .50
32 Barry Pederson .25 .60
33 Randy Burridge .25 .60
34 Ron Hextall 1.00 2.50
35 Gaston Gingras .25 .00
36 Kevin Dineen .25 .60
37 Tom Laidlaw .25 .60
38 Paul MacLean .25 .60
39 John Chabot .25 .60
40 Lindy Ruff .25 .60
41 Dan Quinn .25 .60
42 Don Beaupre .25 .60
43 Gary Suter .25 .60
44 Mikko Makela RC .25 .60
45 Mark Johnson .25 .60
46 Dave Taylor .25 .60
47 Ulf Dahlen RC .25 .60
48 Jeff Sharples RC .25 .60
49 Chris Chelios .75 2.00
50 Mike Gartner .40 1.00
51 Darren Pang RC 1.00 2.50
52 Ron Francis .40 1.00
53 Ken Morrow .20 .50
54 Michel Goulet .25 .60
55 Ray Sheppard RC 1.00 2.50
56 Doug Gilmour .40 1.00
57 David Shaw .25 .60
58 Cam Neely .75 2.00
59 Grant Fuhr .50 1.25
60 Scott Stevens .30 .75
61 Bob Brooke .30 .75
62 Dave Hunter .30 .75
63 Alan Kerr RC .30 .75
64 Brad Marsh .30 .75
65 Dale Hawerchuk .40 1.00
66 Brett Hull RC 12.00 30.00
67 Patrik Sundstrom .30 .75
68 Greg Stefan .30 .75
69 James Patrick .30 .75
70 Dale Hunter .30 .75
71 Al Iafrate .30 .75
72 Bob Carpenter .25 .60
73 Ray Bourque 1.00 2.50
74 John Tucker .30 .75
75 Carey Wilson .30 .75
76 Joe Mullen .30 .75
77 Rick Vaive .30 .75
78 Shawn Burr .30 .75
79 Murray Craven .30 .75
80 Clark Gillies .30 .75
81 Bernie Federko .25 .60
82 Tony Tanti .30 .75
83 Greg Gilbert .30 .75

84 Kirk Muller .30 .75
85 Dave Tippett .30 .75
86 Kevin Hatcher .30 .75
87 Rick Middleton .30 .75
88 Bobby Smith .30 .75
89 Doug Wilson .25 .60
90 Scott Arniel .20 .50
91 Brian Mullen .30 .75
92 Mike O'Connell .20 .50
93 Mark Messier .60 1.50
94 Sean Burke RC 2.00 5.00
95 Brian Bellows .25 .60
96 Doug Bodger .20 .50
97 Bryan Trottier .30 .75
98 Anton Stastny .20 .50
99A Checklist 1-99
(found in vending cases) .30 .75
99B Checklist 1-132
(found in wax cases) .30 .75
100 Dave Poulin .20 .50
101 Bob Bourne .20 .50
102 John Vanbiesbrouck .30 .75
103 Allen Pedersen .20 .50
104 Mike Ridley .20 .50
105 Andrew McBain .20 .50
106 Troy Murray .20 .50
107 Tom Barrasso .20 .50
108 Tomas Jonsson .20 .50
109 Rob Brown RC .20 .50
110 Hakan Loob .20 .50
111 Ilkka Sinisalo .20 .50
112 Dave Archibald RC .20 .50
113 Doug Halward .20 .50
114 Ray Ferraro .20 .50
115 Doug Brown RC .20 .50
116 Patrick Roy 12.00 30.00
117 Greg Millen .20 .50
118 Ken Linseman .20 .50
119 Phil Housley .25 .60
120 Wayne Gretzky UER 10.00 25.00
121 Tomas Sandstrom .20 .50
122 Brendan Shanahan RC 12.00 30.00
123 Pat LaFontaine .30 .75
124 Luc Robitaille 2.50 6.00
125 Ed Olczyk .20 .50
126 Ron Sutter .20 .50
127 Mike Liut .20 .50
128 Brent Ashton .20 .50
129 Tony Hrkac RC .20 .50
130 Kelly Miller .20 .50
131 Alan Haworth .20 .50
132 Dave McLlwain RC .20 .50
133 Mike Ramsey .20 .50
134 Bob Sweeney RC .25 .60
135 Dirk Graham .25 .60
136 Ulf Samuelsson .25 .60
137 Petri Skriko .25 .60
138 Aaron Broten .25 .60
139 Jim Fox .25 .60
140 Randy Wood RC .25 .60
141 Larry Murphy .25 .60
142 Daniel Berthiaume .25 .60
143 Kelly Kisio .25 .60
144 Neal Broten .25 .60
145 Reed Larson .25 .60
146 Peter Zezel .25 .60
147 Jari Kurri .25 .60
148 Jim Johnson .25 .60
149 Gino Cavallini .25 .60
150 Glen Hanlon .25 .60
151 Bengt Gustafsson .25 .60
152 Mike Bullard .25 .60
153 John Ogrodnick .25 .60
154 Steve Larmer .25 .60
155 Kelly Hrudey .25 .60
156 Mats Naslund .20 .50
157 Bruce Driver .25 .60
158 Randy Hillier .25 .60
159 Craig Hartsburg .25 .60
160 Rollie Melanson .25 .60
161 Adam Oates 2.00 5.00
162 Greg Adams .20 .50
163 Dave Andreychuk .30 .75
164 Dave Babych .25 .60
165 Brian Noonan RC .25 .60
166 Glen Wesley RC .25 .60
167 Dave Ellett .25 .60
168 Brian Propp .25 .60
169 Bernie Nicholls .25 .60
170 Walt Poddubny .25 .60
171 Steve Konroyd .25 .60
172 Doug Sulliman .25 .60
173 Mario Gosselin .25 .60
174 Brian Benning .25 .60
175 Dino Ciccarelli .25 .60
176 Steve Kasper .20 .50
177 Rick Tocchet .75 2.00
178 Brad McCrimmon .25 .60
179 Paul Coffey .60 1.50
180 Pete Peeters .25 .60
181 Bob Probert RC 10.00 25.00
182 Steve Duchesne RC .75 2.00
183 Russ Courtnall .25 .60
184 Mike Foligno .25 .60
185 Wayne Presley .25 .60
186 Rejean Lemelin .20 .50
187 Mark Hunter .25 .60
188 Joe Cirella .25 .60
189 Glenn Anderson .25 .60
190 John Anderson .20 .50
191 Pat Flatley .20 .50
192 Rod Langway .20 .50
193 Brian MacLellan .25 .60
194 Pierre Turgeon RC 10.00 25.00
195 Brian Hayward .25 .60
196 Steve Yzerman 8.00 20.00
197 Doug Crossman .25 .60
198A Checklist 100-198
(Found in vending cases) .30 .75
198B Checklist 133-264 UER
(Found in wax cases) .30 .75
199 Greg C. Adams .25 .60
200 Laurie Boschman .25 .60
201 Jeff Brown RC .25 .60
202 Garth Butcher RC .25 .60
203 Guy Carbonneau .25 .60
204 Randy Carlyle .25 .60
205 Alain Cote .25 .60
206 Keith Crowder .20 .50
207 Vincent Damphousse .75 2.00
208 Gaetan Duchesne RC .25 .60
209 Iain Duncan RC .25 .60
210 Tommy Albelin RC .25 .60
211 Pelle Eklund .25 .60
212 Jan Erixon RC .25 .60
213 Paul Fenton RC .25 .60
214 Tom Fergus .20 .50
215 Dave Gagner RC .50 1.25
216 Bob Gainey .25 .60
217 Stewart Gavin .25 .60
218 Charlie Huddy .25 .60
219 Jeff Jackson RC .25 .60
220 Uwe Krupp RC .50 1.25
221 Mike Krushelnyski .25 .60
222 Tom Kurvers .25 .60
223 Jason Lafreniere RC .25 .60
224 Lane Lambert .25 .60
225 Rick Lanz .20 .50
226 Brad Lauer RC .25 .60
227 Claude Lemieux 1.25 3.00
228 Doug Lidster .25 .60
229 Kevin Lowe UER .25 .60
230 Craig Ludwig .25 .60
231 Al MacInnis .60 1.50
232 Craig MacTavish .25 .60
233 Mario Marois
misspelled Marios .25 .60
234 Lanny McDonald .25 .60
235 Rick Meagher .25 .60
236 Craig Muni .25 .60
237 Mike McPhee .20 .50
238 Ric Nattress RC .20 .50
239 Ray Neufeld .20 .50
240 Lee Norwood RC .20 .50
241 Mark Osborne UER
(Misspelled Osbourne .20 .50
242 Joel Otto .20 .50
243 Jim Peplinski .20 .50
244 Rob Ramage .20 .50
245 Luke Richardson RC .20 .50
246 Larry Robinson .30 .75
247 Borje Salming .30 .75
248 David Saunders RC .20 .50
249 Al Secord .20 .50
250 Charlie Simmer .20 .50
251 Doug Smail .20 .50
252 Steve Smith UER RC .20 .50
253 Stan Smyl .20 .50
254 Thomas Steen .20 .50
255 Rich Sutter .20 .50
256 Petr Svoboda RC .20 .50
257 Peter Taglianetti RC .20 .50
258 Steve Tambellini .20 .50
259 Steve Thomas .20 .50
260 Esa Tikkanen .60 1.50
261 Mike Vernon .60 1.50
262 Ryan Walter .20 .50
263 Doug Wickenheiser .20 .50
264 Ken Wregget .25 .60

1988-89 O-Pee-Chee Box Bottoms

COMPLETE SET (16) 6.00 15.00
A Ron Francis .40 1.00
B Wayne Gretzky 3.00 8.00
C Pat LaFontaine .40 1.00
D Bobby Smith .15 .40
E Bernie Federko .15 .40
F Kirk Muller .30 .75
G Ed Olczyk .08 .25
H Denis Savard .30 .75
I Ray Bourque .75 2.00
J Murray Craven
Brian Propp .08 .25
K Dale Hawerchuk .30 .75
L Steve Yzerman 2.00 5.00
M Dave Andreychuk .20 .50
N Mike Gartner .30 .75
O Hakan Loob .15 .40
P Luc Robitaille .60 1.50

1988-89 O-Pee-Chee Minis

COMPLETE SET (46) 8.00 20.00
1 Tom Barrasso .08 .25
2 Bob Bourne .01 .05
3 Ray Bourque .30 .75
4 Guy Carbonneau .05 .15
5 Jimmy Carson .02 .10
6 Paul Coffey .30 .75
7 Ulf Dahlen .05 .15
8 Marcel Dionne .15 .40
9 Grant Fuhr .20 .50
10 Michel Goulet .08 .25
11 Wayne Gretzky 2.50 6.00
12 Dale Hawerchuk .15 .40
13 Brian Hayward .05 .15
14 Ron Hextall .20 .50
15 Tony Hrkac .01 .05
16 Brett Hull 2.00 5.00
17 Steve Larmer .08 .25
18 Rejean Lemelin .05 .15
19 Mario Lemieux 2.00 5.00
20 Mike Liut .05 .15
21 Hakan Loob .08 .25
22 Al MacInnis .08 .25
23 Paul MacLean .02 .10
24 Brad McCrimmon .01 .05
25 Mark Messier .60 1.50
26 Mats Naslund .08 .25
27 Cam Neely .30 .75
28 Bernie Nicholls .08 .25
29 Joe Nieuwendyk .75 2.00
30 Pete Peeters .05 .15
31 Stephane Richer .15 .40
32 Luc Robitaille .30 .75
33 Patrick Roy 2.00 5.00
34 Denis Savard .15 .40
35 Ray Sheppard .20 .50
36 Craig Simpson .02 .10
37 Peter Stastny .15 .40
38 Greg Stefan .02 .10
39 Scott Stevens .08 .25
40 Gary Suter .05 .15
41 Petr Svoboda .02 .10
42 John Vanbiesbrouck 1.25 3.00
43 Pat Verbeek .15 .40
44 Mike Vernon .20 .50
45 Carey Wilson .01 .05
46 Checklist Card .01 .05

1989-90 O-Pee-Chee

COMPLETE SET (330) 60.00 150.00
COMP.FACT.SET (330) 100.00 250.00
*WHITE BACKS: 6X TO 15X BASIC CARDS
1 Mario Lemieux 1.25 3.00
2 Ulf Dahlen .30 .75
3 Terry Carkner RC .30 .75
4 Tony McKegney .30 .75
5 Denis Savard .30 .75
6 Derek King RC .30 .75
7 Lanny McDonald .30 .75
8 John Tonelli .30 .75
9 Tom Kurvers .30 .75
10 Dave Archibald .30 .75
11 Peter Sidorkiewicz RC .30 .75
12 Esa Tikkanen .30 .75
13 Dave Barr .30 .75
14 Brent Sutter .30 .75
15 Cam Neely .30 .75
16 Calle Johansson RC .25 .60
17 Patrick Roy 1.00 2.50
18 Dale DeGray RC .25 .60
19 Phil Bourque RC .25 .60
20 Kevin Dineen .25 .60
21 Mike Bullard .25 .60
22 Gary Leeman .25 .60
23 Greg Stefan .25 .60
24 Brian Mullen .25 .60
25 Pierre Turgeon .60 1.50
26 Bob Rouse RC .25 .60
27 Peter Zezel .25 .60
28 Jeff Brown .25 .60
29 Andy Brickley RC .25 .60
30 Mike Gartner .40 1.00
31 Darren Pang .25 .60
32 Pat Verbeek .25 .60
33 Petri Skriko .25 .60
34 Tom Laidlaw .25 .60
35 Randy Wood .25 .60
36 Tom Barrasso .25 .60
37 John Tucker .25 .60
38 Andrew McBain .25 .60
39 David Shaw .25 .60
40 Rejean Lemelin .20 .50
41 Dino Ciccarelli .25 .60
42 Jeff Sharples .25 .60
43 Jari Kurri .25 .60
44 Murray Craven .25 .60
45 Cliff Ronning RC 1.00 2.50
46 Dave Babych .25 .60
47 Bernie Nicholls .25 .60
48 Jon Casey RC .25 .60
49 Al MacInnis .40 1.00
50 Bob Errey RC .25 .60
51 Glen Wesley .25 .60
52 Dirk Graham .25 .60
53 Guy Carbonneau .25 .60
54 Tomas Sandstrom .25 .60
55 Rod Langway .25 .60
56 Patrik Sundstrom .25 .60
57 Michel Goulet .25 .60
58 Dave Taylor .25 .60
59 Phil Housley .25 .60
60 Pat LaFontaine .30 .75
61 Kirk McLean RC .40 1.00
62 Ken Linseman .25 .60
63 Randy Cunneyworth .25 .60
64 Tony Hrkac .25 .60
65 Mark Messier .60 1.50
66 Carey Wilson .25 .60
67 Stephen Leach RC .25 .60
68 Christian Ruuttu .25 .60
69 Dave Ellett .25 .60
70 Ray Ferraro .25 .60
71 Colin Patterson RC .25 .60
72 Tim Kerr .20 .50
73 Bob Joyce .25 .60
74 Doug Gilmour .40 1.00
75 Lee Norwood .25 .60
76 Dale Hunter .25 .60
77 Jim Johnson .25 .60
78 Mike Foligno .30 .75
79 Al Iafrate .30 .75
80 Rick Tocchet .30 .75
81 Greg Hawgood RC .30 .75
82 Steve Thomas .30 .75
83 Steve Yzerman .75 2.00
84 Mike McPhee .30 .75
85 David Volek RC .30 .75
86 Brian Benning .30 .75
87 Neal Broten .30 .75
88 Luc Robitaille .30 .75
89 Trevor Linden RC 8.00 20.00
90 James Patrick .30 .75
91 Brian Lawton .30 .75
92 Sean Burke .30 .75
93 Scott Stevens .30 .75
94 Pat Elynuik RC .30 .75
95 Paul Coffey .30 .75
96 Jan Erixon .30 .75
97 Mike Liut .20 .50
98 Wayne Presley .30 .75
99 Craig Simpson .30 .75
100 Kjell Samuelsson RC .30 .75
101 Shawn Burr .30 .75
102 John MacLean .30 .75
103 Tom Fergus .20 .50
104 Mike Krushelnyski .30 .75
105 Gary Nylund .30 .75
106 Dave Andreychuk .30 .75
107 Bernie Federko .25 .60
108 Gary Suter .25 .60
109 Dave Gagner .30 .75
110 Ray Bourque .50 1.25
111 Geoff Courtnall RC .60 1.50
112 Doug Wilson .25 .60
113 Joe Sakic RC 4.00 10.00
114 John Vanbiesbrouck .30 .75
115 Dave Poulin .30 .75
116 Rick Meagher .20 .50
117 Kirk Muller .20 .50
118 Mats Naslund .20 .50
119 Ray Sheppard .20 .50
120 Jeff Norton RC .25 .60
121 Randy Burridge .20 .50
122 Dale Hawerchuk .40 1.00
123 Steve Duchesne .20 .50
124 John Anderson .20 .50
125 Rick Vaive .20 .50
126 Randy Hillier .20 .50
127 Jimmy Carson .20 .50
128 Larry Murphy .25 .60
129 Paul MacLean .20 .50
130 Joe Cirella .20 .50
131 Kelly Miller .20 .50
132 Alain Chevrier .20 .50
133 Ed Olczyk .20 .50
134 Dave Tippett .20 .50
135 Bob Sweeney .20 .50
136 Brian Leetch RC 8.00 20.00
137 Greg Millen .20 .50
138 Joe Nieuwendyk .25 .60
139 Brian Propp .20 .50
140 Mike Ramsey .20 .50
141 Mike Allison .20 .50
142 Shawn Chambers RC .20 .50
143 Peter Stastny .25 .60
144 Glen Hanlon .20 .50
145 John Cullen RC .25 .60
146 Kevin Hatcher .25 .60
147 Brendan Shanahan .30 .75
148 Paul Reinhart .25 .60
149 Bryan Trottier .30 .75
150 Dave Manson RC .25 .60
151 Marc Habscheid RC .25 .60
152 Dan Quinn .25 .60
153 Stephane Richer .25 .60
154 Doug Bodger .25 .60
155 Ron Hextall .30 .75
156 Wayne Gretzky 8.00 20.00
157 Steve Tuttle RC .30 .75
158 Charlie Huddy .30 .75
159 Dave Christian .20 .50
160 Andy Moog .30 .75
161 Tony Granato RC .30 .75
162 Sylvain Cote RC .30 .75
163 Mike Vernon .40 1.00
164 Steve Chiasson RC .25 .60
165 Mike Ridley .25 .60
166 Kelly Hrudey .25 .60
167 Bob Carpenter .25 .60
168 Zarley Zalapski RC .25 .60
169 Derek Laxdal RC .30 .75
170 Clint Malarchuk .30 .75
171 Kelly Kisio .30 .75
172 Gerard Gallant .30 .75
173 Ron Sutter .30 .75
174 Chris Chelios .30 .75
175 Ron Francis .40 1.00
176 Gino Cavallini .25 .60
177 Brian Bellows .25 .60
178 Greg C. Adams .25 .60
179 Steve Larmer .25 .60
180 Aaron Broten .25 .60
181 Brent Ashton .25 .60
182 Gerald Diduck RC .25 .60
183 Paul MacDermid RC .25 .60
184 Walt Poddubny .25 .60
185 Adam Oates .30 .75
186 Brett Hull .40 1.00
187 Scott Arniel .20 .50
188 Bobby Smith .25 .60
189 Guy Lafleur .40 1.00
190 Craig Janney RC .40 1.00
191 Mark Howe .30 .75
192 Grant Fuhr .50 1.25
193 Rob Brown .20 .50
194 Steve Kasper .20 .50
195 Pete Peeters .20 .50
196 Joe Mullen .20 .50
197 Checklist 1-110 .20 .50
198 Checklist 111-220 .20 .50
199 Keith Crowder .20 .50
200 Daren Puppa RC .40 1.00
201 Benoit Hogue RC .20 .50
202 Gary Roberts RC .40 1.00
203 Brad McCrimmon .20 .50
204 Rick Wamsley .20 .50
205 Joel Otto .20 .50
206 Jim Peplinski .20 .50
207 Jamie Macoun .20 .50
208 Brian MacLellan .20 .50
209 Scott Young RC .50 1.25
210 Ulf Samuelsson .20 .50
211 Joel Quenneville UER
Misspelled Quennville .20 .50
212 Tim Watters .20 .50
213 Curt Giles .20 .50
214 Stewart Gavin .20 .50
215 Bob Brooke .25 .60
216 Basil McRae RC .25 .60
217 Frantisek Musil RC .25 .60
218 Adam Creighton RC .25 .60
219 Troy Murray .25 .60
220 Steve Konroyd .25 .60
221 Duane Sutter .25 .60
222 Trent Yawney RC .25 .60
223 Mike O'Connell .30 .75
224 Jim Nill .30 .75
225 John Chabot .30 .75
226 Glenn Anderson .25 .60
227 Kevin Lowe .30 .75
228 Steve Smith .25 .60
229 Randy Gregg .25 .60
230 Craig MacTavish .25 .60
231 Craig Muni .25 .60
232 Theo Fleury RC 5.00 12.00
233 Bill Ranford .25 .60
234 Claude Lemieux .25 .60
235 Larry Robinson .30 .75
236 Craig Ludwig .25 .60
237 Brian Hayward .25 .60
238 Petr Svoboda .25 .60
239 Russ Courtnall .25 .60
240 Ryan Walter .25 .60
241 Tommy Albelin .25 .60
242 Doug Brown .25 .60
243 Ken Daneyko RC .25 .60
244 Mark Johnson .25 .60
245 Randy Velischek RC .25 .60
246 Brad Dalgarno RC .25 .60
247 Mikko Makela .25 .60
248 Shayne Corson RC .50 1.25
249 Marc Bergevin RC .25 .60
250 Pat Flatley .20 .50
251 Michel Petit .20 .50
252 Mark Hardy .20 .50
253 Scott Mellanby .20 .50
254 Keith Acton .20 .50
255 Ken Wregget .20 .50
256 Gord Dineen RC .20 .50
257 Dave Hannan .20 .50
258 Mario Gosselin .20 .50
259 Randy Moller .20 .50
260 Mario Marois .20 .50
261 Robert Picard .20 .50
262 Marc Fortier RC .20 .50
263 Ron Tugnutt RC .75 2.00
264 Iiro Jarvi RC .20 .50
265 Paul Gillis .25 .60
266 Mike Hough RC .25 .60
267 Jim Sandlak .25 .60
268 Greg Paslawski .25 .60
269 Paul Cavallini RC .25 .60
270 Gaston Gingras .25 .60
271 Allan Bester .25 .60
272 Vincent Damphousse .25 .60
273 Daniel Marois RC .25 .60
274 Mark Osborne UER
Misspelled Osbourne .30 .75
275 Craig Laughlin .25 .60
276 Brad Marsh .25 .60
277 Dan Daoust .25 .60
278 Borje Salming .30 .75
279 Chris Kotsopoulos .25 .60
280 Tony Tanti .25 .60
281 Barry Pederson .25 .60
282 Rich Sutter .25 .60
283 Stan Smyl .25 .60
284 Doug Lidster .25 .60
285 Steve Weeks .20 .50
286 Harold Snepsts .20 .50
287 Brian Bradley RC .25 .60
288 Larry Melnyk .25 .60
289 Bob Gould .25 .60
290 Thomas Steen .25 .60
291 Randy Carlyle .25 .60
292 Hannu Jarvenpaa RC .20 .50
293 Iain Duncan .20 .50
294 Doug Smail .20 .50
295 Jim Kyte .25 .60
296 Daniel Berthiaume .25 .60
297 Peter Taglianetti .25 .60
298 Bruins/Janney .25 .60
299 Buffalo Sabres .25 .60
300 Calgary Flames .25 .60
301 Chicago Blackhawks .25 .60
302 Detroit Red Wings .25 .60
303 Edmonton Oilers .25 .60
304 Hartford Whalers .25 .60
305 Los Angeles Kings .25 .60
306 Minnesota North Stars .25 .60
307 Montreal Canadiens .25 .60
308 New Jersey Devils .25 .60
309 New York Islanders .25 .60
310 New York Rangers .25 .60
311 Flyers/Hextall .25 .60
312 Penguins/Lemieux .30 .75
313 Nordiques/Sakic .30 .75
314 St. Louis Blues .25 .60
315 Toronto Maple Leafs .25 .60
316 Vancouver Canucks
Action Scene/(Jim Sandlak,
Ray Bourque defending) .25 .60
317 Washington Capitals .25 .60
318 Winnipeg Jets .25 .60
319 Mario Lemieux Ross 1.25 3.00
320 Wayne Gretzky Hart 2.00 5.00
321 Brian Leetch Calder 1.00 2.50
322 Patrick Roy Vezina 1.00 2.50
323 Norris Trophy .25 .60
324 Lady Byng Trophy .25 .60
325 Wayne Gretzky HL 2.00 5.00
326 Brian Leetch HL UER 1.00 2.50
327 Mario Lemieux HL 1.25 3.00
328 1988-89 Highlight .25 .60
329 Coupe Stanley Cup .25 .60
330 Checklist 221-330 .25 .60

1989-90 O-Pee-Chee Box Bottoms

COMPLETE SET (16) 4.00 10.00
A Mario Lemieux 1.50 4.00
B Mike Ridley .08 .25
C Tomas Sandstrom .08 .25
D Petri Skriko .08 .25
E Wayne Gretzky 1.50 4.00
F Brett Hull .75 2.00
G Tim Kerr .08 .25
H Mats Naslund .08 .25
I Jari Kurri .20 .50
J Steve Larmer .20 .50
K Cam Neely .30 .75
L Steve Yzerman .75 2.00
M Kevin Dineen .08 .25
N Dave Gagner .15 .40
O Joe Mullen .15 .40
P Pierre Turgeon .30 .75

1989-90 O-Pee-Chee Sticker Back Cards

COMPLETE SET (76) 3.00 8.00
1 Greg Hawgood .02 .10
2 Craig Janney .08 .25
3 Bob Joyce .02 .10
4 Benoit Hogue .07 .20
5 Jiri Hrdina .02 .10
6 Peter Sidorkiewicz .07 .20
7 Scott Young .08 .25
8 Sean Burke .10 .30
9 Dave Volek .02 .10
10 Tony Granato .07 .20
11 Brian Leetch .40 1.00
12 Gord Murphy .02 .10
13 John Cullen .07 .20
14 Zarley Zalapski .07 .20
15 Iiro Jarvi .02 .10
16 Joe Sakic .60 1.50
17 Vincent Riendeau .07 .20
18 Dan Marois .02 .10
19 Trevor Linden .30 .75
20 Pat Elynuik .02 .10
21 Bob Essensa .07 .20
22 Checklist .02 .10
23 Joe Mullen .07 .20
24 Mario Lemieux .60 1.50
25 Gerard Gallant .02 .10
26 Chris Chelios .20 .50
27 Al MacInnis .08 .25
28 Patrick Roy .60 1.50
29 Geoff Courtnall .08 .25
30 Wayne Gretzky .75 2.00
31 Rob Brown .02 .10
32 Steve Duchesne .08 .25
33 Ray Bourque .20 .50
34 Mike Vernon .08 .25
Q35 Trivia Question 35 .01 .05
Q36 Trivia Question 36 .01 .05
Q37 Trivia Question 37 .01 .05
Q38 Trivia Question 38 .01 .05
Q39 Trivia Question 39 .01 .05
Q40 Trivia Question 40 .01 .05
Q41 Trivia Question 41 .01 .05
Q42 Trivia Question 42 .01 .05
Q43 Trivia Question 43 .01 .05
Q44 Trivia Question 44 .01 .05
Q45 Trivia Question 45 .01 .05
Q46 Trivia Question 46 .01 .05
Q47 Trivia Question 47 .01 .05
Q48 Trivia Question 48 .01 .05
Q49 Trivia Question 49 .01 .05
Q50 Trivia Question 50 .01 .05
Q51 Trivia Question 51 .01 .05
Q52 Trivia Question 52 .01 .05
Q53 Trivia Question 53 .01 .05
Q54 Trivia Question 54 .01 .05
Q55 Trivia Question 55 .01 .05
A56 Trivia Answer 56 .01 .05
A57 Trivia Answer 57 .01 .05
A58 Trivia Answer 58 .01 .05
A59 Trivia Answer 59 .01 .05
A60 Trivia Answer 60 .01 .05
A61 Trivia Answer 61 .01 .05
A62 Trivia Answer 62 .01 .05
A63 Trivia Answer 63 .01 .05
A64 Trivia Answer 64 .01 .05
A65 Trivia Answer 65 .01 .05
A66 Trivia Answer 66 .01 .05
A67 Trivia Answer 67 .01 .05
A68 Trivia Answer 68 .01 .05
A69 Trivia Answer 69 .01 .05
A70 Trivia Answer 70 .01 .05
A71 Trivia Answer 71 .01 .05
A72 Trivia Answer 72 .01 .05
A73 Trivia Answer 73 .01 .05
A74 Trivia Answer 74 .01 .05
A75 Trivia Answer 75 .01 .05
A76 Trivia Answer 76 .01 .05

1990-91 O-Pee-Chee

1 Wayne Gretzky Indy 1.25 3.00
2 Wayne Gretzky Oilers 1.25 3.00
3 Wayne Gretzky LA 1.25 3.00
4 Brett Hull HL .40 1.00
5 Jari Kurri HL .25 .60
6 Bryan Trottier HL .20 .50
7 Jeremy Roenick RC .60 1.50
8 Brian Propp .20 .50
9 Jim Hrivnak RC .20 .50
10 Mick Vukota RC .20 .50
11 Tom Kurvers .20 .50
12 Ulf Dahlen .20 .50
13 Bernie Nicholls .15 .40
14 Peter Sidorkiewicz .20 .50
15 Peter Zezel .20 .50
16 Mike Hartman RC .20 .50
17 Kings Team .15 .40
18 Jim Sandlak .20 .50
19 Rob Brown .40 1.00
20 Paul Ranheim RC .20 .50
21 Rick Zombo RC .20 .50
22 Paul Gillis .15 .40
23 Brian Hayward .20 .50
24 Brent Ashton .20 .50
25 Mark Lamb .20 .50
26 Rick Tocchet .20 .50
27 Slava Fetisov RC .40 1.00
28 Denis Savard .20 .50
29 Chris Chelios .20 .50
30 Janne Ojanen RC .20 .50
31 Don Maloney .20 .50
32 Allan Bester .20 .50
33 Geoff Smith RC .20 .50
34 Daniel Shank RC .20 .50
35 Mikael Andersson RC .20 .50
36 Gino Cavallini .20 .50
37 Rob Murphy RC .20 .50
38 Flames Team .25 .60
39 Laurie Boschman .15 .40
40 Craig Wolanin RC .15 .40
41 Phil Bourque .15 .40
42 Alexander Mogilny RC .60 1.50
43 Ray Bourque .30 .75
44 Mike Liut .12 .30
45 Ron Sutter .15 .40
46 Bob Kudelski RC .15 .40
47 Larry Murphy .15 .40
48 Darren Turcotte RC .15 .40
49 Paul Ysebaert RC .15 .40
50 Alan Kerr .15 .40
51 Randy Carlyle .15 .40
52 Iiro Jarvi .15 .40
53 Don Barber RC .15 .40
54 Carey Wilson .15 .40
55 Joey Kocur RC .40 1.00
56 Steve Larmer .15 .40
57 Paul Cavallini .15 .40
58 Shayne Corson .15 .40
59 Canucks Team .15 .40
60 Sergei Makarov RC .40 1.00
61 Kjell Samuelsson .15 .40
62 Tony Granato .12 .30
63 Tom Fergus .12 .30
64 Martin Gelinas RC .40 1.00
65 Tom Barrasso .15 .40
66 Pierre Turgeon .15 .40
67 Randy Cunneyworth .15 .40
68 Michal Pivonka RC .15 .40
69 Cam Neely .20 .50
70 Brian Bellows .15 .40
71 Pat Elynuik .15 .40
72 Doug Crossman .15 .40
73 Sylvain Turgeon .15 .40
74 Shawn Burr .15 .40
75 John Vanbiesbrouck .20 .50
76 Steve Bozek .15 .40
77 Brett Hull .40 1.00
78 Zarley Zalapski .15 .40
79 Wendel Clark .30 .75
80 Flyers Team .20 .50
81 Kelly Miller .12 .30
82 Mark Pederson RC .20 .50
83 Adam Creighton .12 .30
84 Scott Young .12 .30
85 Petr Klima .12 .30
86 Steve Duchesne .12 .30
87 Joe Nieuwendyk .15 .40
88 Andy Brickley .12 .30
89 Phil Housley .15 .40
90 Neal Broten .12 .30
91 Al Iafrate .12 .30
92 Steve Thomas .12 .30
93 Guy Carbonneau .12 .30
94 Steve Chiasson .12 .30
95 Mike Tomlak RC .20 .50
96 Roger Johansson RC .20 .50
97 Randy Wood .12 .30
98 Jim Johnson .12 .30
99 Bob Sweeney .12 .30
100 Dino Ciccarelli .20 .50
101 Rangers Team .20 .50
102 Mike Ramsey .12 .30
103 Kelly Hrudey .12 .30
104 Dave Ellett .12 .30
105 Bob Brooke .12 .30
106 Greg Adams .12 .30
107 Joe Cirella .12 .30
108 Jari Kurri .25 .60
109 Pete Peeters .12 .30
110 Paul MacLean .15 .40
111 Doug Wilson .15 .40
112 Pat Verbeek .15 .40
113 Bob Beers RC .15 .40
114 Mike O'Connell .15 .40
115 Brian Bradley .15 .40
116 Paul Coffey .20 .50
117 Doug Brown .15 .40
118 Aaron Broten .15 .40
119 Bob Essensa RC .30 .75
120 Wayne Gretzky 1.25 3.00
121 Vincent Damphousse .15 .40
122 Nordiques Team .15 .40
123 Mike Foligno .15 .40
124 Russ Courtnall .20 .50
125 Rick Meagher .15 .40
126 Craig Fisher RC .20 .50
127 Al MacInnis .25 .60
128 Derek King .20 .50
129 Dale Hunter .20 .50
130 Mark Messier UER .40 1.00
131 James Patrick UER
should be orange border .20 .50
132 Checklist 1-132 .20 .50
133 Red Wings Team .60 1.50
134 Barry Pederson .15 .40
135 Gary Leeman .15 .40
136 Doug Gilmour .25 .60
137 Mike McPhee .15 .40
138 Bob Murray .15 .40
139 Bob Carpenter .15 .40
140 Sean Burke .15 .40
141 Dale Hawerchuk .25 .60
142 Guy Lafleur .25 .60
143 Lindy Ruff .15 .40
144 Whalers Team .20 .50
145 Glenn Anderson .15 .40
146 Dave Chyzowski RC .15 .40
147 Kevin Hatcher .15 .40
148 Rick Vaive .15 .40
149 Adam Oates .20 .50
150 Garth Butcher .15 .40
151 Basil McRae .12 .30
152 Ilkka Sinisalo .15 .40
153 Steve Kasper .12 .30
154 Greg Paslawski .15 .40
155 Brad Marsh .15 .40
156 Esa Tikkanen .15 .40
157 Tony Tanti .15 .40
158 Mario Marois UER .15 .40
159 Sylvain Lefebvre RC .15 .40
160 Troy Murray .15 .40
161 Gary Roberts .20 .50
162 Randy Ladouceur .20 .50
163 John Chabot .20 .50
164 Calle Johansson .20 .50
165 Bruins Team .30 .75
166 Jeff Norton .20 .50
167 Mike Krushelnyski .20 .50
168 Dave Gagner .20 .50
169 Dave Andreychuk .20 .50
170 Dave Capuano RC .20 .50
171 Curtis Joseph RC .60 1.50
172 Bruce Driver .20 .50
173 Scott Mellanby .20 .50
174 John Ogrodnick .20 .50
175 Mario Lemieux .75 2.00
176 Marc Fortier .15 .40
177 Vincent Riendeau RC .20 .50
178 Mark Johnson .15 .40
179 Dirk Graham .15 .40
180 Jets Team .20 .50
181 Robb Stauber RC .20 .50

182 Christian Ruuttu .15 .40
183 Dave Tippett .15 .40
184 Pat LaFontaine .20 .50
185 Mark Howe .20 .50
186 Stephane Richer .20 .50
187 Jan Erixon .20 .50
188 Neil Sheehy .20 .50
189 Craig MacTavish .15 .40
190 Randy Burridge .15 .40
191 Bernie Federko .15 .40
192 Shawn Chambers .15 .40
193 Mark Messier AS1 .40 1.00
194 Luc Robitaille AS1 .20 .50
195 Brett Hull AS1 .40 1.00
196 Ray Bourque AS1 .30 .75
197 Al MacInnis AS1 .25 .60
198 Patrick Roy AS1 .50 1.25
199 Wayne Gretzky AS2 1.25 3.00
200 Brian Bellows AS2 .15 .40
201 Cam Neely AS2 .20 .50
202 Paul Coffey AS2 .20 .50
203 Doug Wilson AS2 .15 .40
204 Daren Puppa AS2 .15 .40
205 Gary Suter .12 .30
206 Ed Olczyk .20 .50
207 Doug Lidster .20 .50
208 John Cullen .20 .50
209 Luc Robitaille .20 .50
210 Tim Kerr .12 .30
211 Scott Stevens .20 .50
212 Craig Janney .20 .50
213 Kevin Dineen .20 .50
214 Jimmy Waite RC .20 .50
215 Benoit Hogue .20 .50
216 Curtis Leschyshyn RC .15 .40
217 Brad Lauer .15 .40
218 Joe Mullen .15 .40
219 Patrick Roy .50 1.25
220 Blues Team .20 .50
221 Brian Leetch .25 .60
222 Steve Yzerman .60 1.50
223 Stephane Beauregard RC .15 .40
224 John MacLean .15 .40
225 Trevor Linden .20 .50
226 Bill Ranford .15 .40
227 Mark Osborne .15 .40
228 Curt Giles .15 .40
229 Mikko Makela .15 .40
230 Bob Errey .15 .40
231 Jimmy Carson .15 .40
232 Kay Whitmore RC .15 .40
233 Gary Nylund .15 .40
234 Jiri Hrdina RC .15 .40
235 Stephen Leach .15 .40
236 Greg Hawgood .15 .40
237 Jocelyn Lemieux RC .15 .40
238 Daren Puppa .15 .40
239 Kelly Kisio .15 .40
240 Craig Simpson .15 .40
241 Maple Leafs Team .15 .40
242 Fredrik Olausson .15 .40
243 Ron Hextall .20 .50
244 Sergio Momesso RC .15 .40
245 Kirk Muller .15 .40
246 Petr Svoboda .15 .40
247 Daniel Berthiaume .15 .40
248 Andrew McBain .15 .40
249 Jeff Jackson UER .15 .40
250 Randy Gilhen RC .12 .30
251 Oilers
Adam Graves .40 1.00
252 Rick Bennett RC .12 .30
253 Don Beaupre .12 .30
254 Pelle Eklund .12 .30
255 Greg Gilbert .12 .30
256 Gordie Roberts .12 .30
257 Kirk McLean .12 .30
258 Brent Sutter .15 .40
259 Brendan Shanahan .20 .50
260 Todd Krygier RC .15 .40
261 Larry Robinson UER .20 .50
262 Sabres Team .15 .40
263 Dave Christian .12 .30
264 Checklist 133-264 .20 .50
265 Jamie Macoun .15 .40
266 Glen Hanlon .15 .40
267 Daniel Marois .15 .40
268 Doug Smail .15 .40
269 Jon Casey .20 .50
270 Brian Skrudland .15 .40
271 Michel Petit .15 .40
272 Dan Quinn .15 .40
273 Geoff Courtnall .15 .40
274 Mike Bullard .15 .40
275 Randy Gregg .15 .40
276 Keith Brown .15 .40
277 Troy Mallette RC .15 .40
278 Steve Tuttle .15 .40
279 Brad Shaw RC .15 .40
280 Mark Recchi RC .60 1.50
281 John Tonelli .15 .40
282 Doug Bodger .15 .40
283 Thomas Steen .15 .40
284 Devils Team .40 1.00
285 Lee Norwood .15 .40
286 Brian MacLellan .15 .40
287 Bobby Smith .15 .40
288 Rob Cimetta RC .15 .40
289 Rob Zettler RC .15 .40
290 David Reid RC .20 .50
291 Bryan Trottier .20 .50
292 Brian Mullen .20 .50
293 Paul Reinhart .20 .50
294 Andy Moog .20 .50
295 Jeff Brown .20 .50
296 Ryan Walter .20 .50
297 Trent Yawney .20 .50
298 John Druce RC .20 .50
299 Dave McLlwain .20 .50
300 David Volek .20 .50
301 Tomas Sandstrom .20 .50
302 Gord Murphy RC .20 .50
303 Lou Franceschetti RC .20 .50
304 Dana Murzyn .20 .50
305 North Stars Team .20 .50
306 Patrik Sundstrom .15 .40
307 Kevin Lowe .20 .50
308 Dave Barr .20 .50
309 Wendell Young RC .20 .50
310 Darrin Shannon RC .20 .50
311 Ron Francis .25 .60
312 Stephane Fiset RC .40 1.00
313 Paul Fenton .20 .50
314 Dave Taylor .20 .50
315 Islanders Team .20 .50
316 Petri Skriko .20 .50
317 Rob Ramage .20 .50
318 Murray Craven .20 .50
319 Gaetan Duchesne .20 .50
320 Brad McCrimmon .20 .50
321 Grant Fuhr .30 .75
322 Gerard Gallant .12 .30
323 Tommy Albelin .12 .30
324 Scott Arniel .12 .30
325 Mike Keane RC .12 .30
326 Penguins Team .20 .50
327 Mike Ridley .12 .30
328 Dave Babych .12 .30
329 Michel Goulet .12 .30
330 Mike Richter RC .60 1.50
331 Garry Galley RC .12 .30
332 Rod Brind'Amour RC .40 1.00
333 Tony McKegney .12 .30
334 Peter Stastny .15 .40
335 Greg Millen .15 .40
336 Ray Ferraro .15 .40
337 Miloslav Horava RC .15 .40
338 Paul MacDermid .15 .40
339 Craig Coxe RC .15 .40
340 Dave Snuggerud RC .15 .40
341 Mike Lalor RC .15 .40
342 Marc Habscheid .15 .40
343 Rejean Lemelin .12 .30
344 Charlie Huddy .15 .40
345 Ken Linseman .15 .40
346 Canadiens Team .20 .50
347 Troy Loney RC .20 .50
348 Mike Modano RC .60 1.50
349 Jeff Reese RC .20 .50
350 Pat Flatley .20 .50
351 Mike Vernon .15 .40
352 Todd Elik RC .20 .50
353 Rod Langway .20 .50
354 Moe Mantha .20 .50
355 Keith Acton .20 .50
356 Scott Pearson RC .20 .50
357 Perry Berezan RC .20 .50
358 Alexei Kasatonov RC .20 .50
359 Igor Larionov RC .40 1.00
360 Kevin Stevens RC .40 1.00
361 Yves Racine RC .20 .50
362 Dave Poulin .20 .50
363 Blackhawks Team .20 .50
364 Yvon Corriveau RC .15 .40
365 Brian Benning .15 .40
366 Hubie McDonough RC .15 .40
367 Ron Tugnutt .15 .40
368 Steve Smith .15 .40
369 Joel Otto .15 .40
370 Dave Lowry RC .15 .40
371 Clint Malarchuk .15 .40
372 Mathieu Schneider RC .15 .40
373 Mike Gartner .25 .60
374 John Tucker .15 .40
375 Chris Terreri RC .40 1.00
376 Dean Evason .15 .40
377 Jamie Leach RC .15 .40
378 Jacques Cloutier RC .15 .40
379 Glen Wesley .15 .40
380 Vladimir Krutov RC .40 1.00
381 Terry Carkner .15 .40
382 John McIntyre RC .15 .40
383 Ville Siren RC .15 .40
384 Joe Sakic .60 1.50
385 Teppo Numminen RC .40 1.00
386 Theo Fleury .25 .60
387 Glen Featherstone RC .15 .40
388 Stephan Lebeau RC .15 .40
389 Kevin McClelland .15 .40
390 Uwe Krupp .20 .50
391 Mark Janssens RC .20 .50
392 Marty McSorley .15 .40
393 Vladimir Ruzicka RC .20 .50
394 Capitals Team .20 .50
395 Mark Fitzpatrick RC .15 .40
396 Checklist 265-396 .20 .50
397 Dave Manson .20 .50
398 Bob Gould .20 .50
399 Bill Houlder RC .20 .50
400 Glenn Healy RC .40 1.00
401 John Kordic RC .40 1.00
402 Stewart Gavin .20 .50
403 David Shaw .20 .50
404 Ed Kastelic RC .20 .50
405 Rich Sutter .20 .50
406 Grant Ledyard RC .20 .50
407 Steve Weeks .20 .50
408 Randy Hillier .20 .50
409 Rick Wamsley .20 .50
410 Doug Houda RC .20 .50
411 Ken McRae RC .20 .50
412 Craig Ludwig .20 .50
413 Doug Evans RC .20 .50
414 Ken Baumgartner RC .20 .50
415 Ken Wregget .20 .50
416 Eric Weinrich RC .20 .50
417 Mike Allison .15 .40
418 Joel Quenneville .15 .40
419 Larry Melnyk .15 .40
420 Colin Patterson .15 .40
421 Gerald Diduck .15 .40
422 Brent Gilchrist RC .15 .40
423 Craig Muni .15 .40
424 Mike Hudson RC .15 .40
425 Eric Desjardins RC .40 1.00
426 Walt Poddubny .15 .40
427 Mike Hough .15 .40
428 Luke Richardson .15 .40
429 Joe Murphy RC .15 .40
430 Tim Cheveldae RC .15 .40
431 Adam Burt RC .15 .40
432 Kelly Chase RC .40 1.00
433 Robert Nordmark RC .15 .40
434 Tim Hunter RC .15 .40
435 Peter Taglianetti .15 .40
436 Alain Chevrier .15 .40
437 Darin Kimble RC .40 1.00
438 David Maley RC .20 .50
439 Jim Wiemer RC .20 .50
440 Nick Kypreos RC .20 .50
441 Lucien DeBlois .15 .40
442 Mario Gosselin .15 .40
443 Neil Wilkinson RC .15 .40
444 Mark Kumpel RC .12 .30
445 Sergei Mylnikov RC .12 .30
446 Ray Sheppard .12 .30
447 Ron Greschner .12 .30
448 Craig Berube RC .12 .30
449 Dave Hannan .12 .30
450 Jim Korn .12 .30
451 Claude Lemieux .12 .30
452 Eldon Reddick RC .40 1.00
453 Randy Velischek .12 .30
454 Chris Nilan .12 .30
455 Jim Benning .12 .30
456 Wayne Presley .12 .30
457 Jon Morris RC .12 .30
458 Clark Donatelli RC .12 .30
459 Ric Nattress .12 .30
460 Rob Murray RC .12 .30
461 Tim Watters .12 .30
462 Checklist 397-528 .20 .50
463 Derrick Smith RC .15 .40
464 Lyndon Byers RC .15 .40
465 Jeff Chychrun RC .15 .40
466 Duane Sutter .15 .40
467 Conn Smythe Trophy .15 .40
468 Anatoli Semenov RC .15 .40
469 Konstantin Kurashov RC .15 .40
470 Gord Dineen .15 .40
471 Jeff Beukeboom RC .15 .40
472 Andrei Lomakin RC .15 .40
473 Doug Sulliman .15 .40
474 Alexander Kerch RC .15 .40
475 Norris Trophy .30 .75
476 Keith Crowder .12 .30
477 Oleg Znarok RC .15 .40
478 Dimitri Zinovyev RC .15 .40
479 Igor Esmantovich RC .15 .40
480 Adam Graves RC .40 1.00
481 Petr Prajsler RC .15 .40
482 Sergei Yashin RC .15 .40
483 Jeff Bloemberg RC .15 .40
484 Yuri Strakhov RC .15 .40
485 Sergei B. Makarov RC .15 .40
486 Jennings Trophy .20 .50
487 Sergei Zaltsev RC .15 .40
488 Selke Trophy .15 .40
489 Yuri Kusnetsov RC .15 .40
490 Tom Chorske RC .15 .40
491 Igor Akulinin RC .15 .40
492 Mikhail Panin RC .15 .40
493 Sergei Nemchinov RC .15 .40
494 Vladimir Yurzinov RC .15 .40
495 Gord Kluzak .12 .30
496 Sergei Skosyrev RC .15 .40
497 Jeff Parker RC .15 .40
498 Tom Tilley RC .15 .40
499 Alexander Smirnov RC .15 .40
500 Alexander Lysenko RC .15 .40
501 Arturs Irbe UER RC .75 2.00
502 Alexei Frolikov RC .15 .40
503 Sergei Makarov Calder .40 1.00
504 Nikolai Varjanov RC .15 .40
505 Allen Pedersen .12 .30
506 Vladimir Shashov RC .15 .40
507 Tim Bergland RC .15 .40
508 Gennady Lebedev RC .20 .50
509 Rod Buskas RC .20 .50
510 Grant Jennings RC .20 .50
511 Ulf Samuelsson .20 .50
512 Patrick Roy Vezina .50 1.25
513 Brett Hull Byng .40 1.00
514 Dimitri Mironov RC .20 .50
515 Randy Moller .20 .50
516 Kerry Huffman RC .20 .50
517 Gilbert Delorme .20 .50
518 Greg C. Adams .20 .50
519 Hart Trophy .40 1.00
520 Sheldon Kennedy RC .20 .50
521 Harijs Vitolins RC .20 .50
522 Wayne Gretzky Ross 1.25 3.00
523 Dmitri Frolov RC .20 .50
524 Tom Laidlaw .20 .50
525 Oleg Bratash RC .20 .50
526 Kris King RC .20 .50
527 Wayne Van Dorp RC .20 .50
528 Chris Dahlquist RC .20 .50

1990-91 O-Pee-Chee Box Bottoms

COMPLETE SET (16) 5.00 12.00
A Alexander Mogilny .30 .75
B Jon Casey .15 .40
C Paul Coffey .30 .75
D Wayne Gretzky 1.50 4.00
E Patrick Roy 1.00 2.50
F Mike Modano .40 1.00
G Mario Lemieux 1.00 2.50
H Al MacInnis .20 .50
I Ray Bourque .30 .75
J Steve Yzerman 1.00 2.50
K Darren Turcotte .08 .25
L Mike Vernon .20 .50
M Pierre Turgeon .20 .50
N Doug Wilson .08 .25
O Don Beaupre .15 .40
P Sergei Makarov .20 .50

1990-91 O-Pee-Chee Red Army

COMPLETE SET (22) 5.00 12.00
1R Ilya Byalsin .15 .40
2R Vladimir Malakhov .15 .40
3R Andrei Khomutov .15 .40
4R Valeri Kamensky .20 .50
5R Dimitri Motkov .15 .40
6R Evgeny Shastin .15 .40
7R Arturs Irbe UER .60 1.50
8R Igor Chibirev .15 .40
9R Maxim Mikhailovsky .20 .50
10R Viacheslav Bykov .15 .40
11R Central Red Army Team .15 .40
12R Central Red Army Team .15 .40
13R Valeri Shirjaev .15 .40
14R Igor Maslennikov .15 .40
15R Igor Malykhin .15 .40
16R Dimitri Khristich .15 .40
17R Viktor Tikhonov CO .30 .75
18R Eugeny Davydov .15 .40
19R Sergei Fedorov 1.25 3.00
20R Pavel Kostichkin .15 .40
21R Vladimir Konstantinov .60 1.50
22R Checklist Card .15 .40

1991-92 O-Pee-Chee

*O-PEE-CHEE: .5X TO 1.25X TOPPS

1991-92 O-Pee-Chee Inserts

1S Link Gaetz .12 .30
2S Bengt Gustafsson .12 .30
3S Dan Keczmer .12 .30
4S Dean Kolstad .12 .30
5S Peter Lappin .12 .30
6S Jeff Madill .12 .30
7S Mike McHugh .12 .30
8S Jarmo Myllys UER .12 .30
9S Doug Zmolek .12 .30
10S Sharks Checklist .08 .25
11R Vadim Brezgunov .12 .30
12R Vyacheslav Butsayev .12 .30
13R Ilya Byakin .12 .30
14R Igor Chibirev .12 .30
15R Victor Gordiouk .12 .30
16R Yuri Khmylev .12 .30
17R Pavel Kostichkin .12 .30
18R Andrei Kovalenko .12 .30
19R Igor Kravchuk .15 .40
20R Igor Malykhin .12 .30
21R Igor Maslennikov .12 .30
22R Maxim Mikhailovsky .12 .30
23R Dimitri Mironov .12 .30
24R Sergei Nemchinov .12 .30
25R Alexander Prokopjev .12 .30
26R Igor Stelnov .12 .30
27R Sergei Vostrikov .12 .30
28R Sergei Zubov .12 .30
29R Central Red Army Team .05 .15
30R Central Red Army Team .12 .30
31R Alexander Andreivsky .12 .30
32R Igor Dorofeyev .12 .30
33R Alexander Galchenyuk .12 .30
34R Roman Ilyin .12 .30
35R Alexander Karpovtsev .12 .30
36R Ravil Khaidarov .12 .30
37R Igor Korolytov .12 .30
38R Andrei Kovalyov .12 .30
39R Yuri Leonov .12 .30
40R Andrei Lomakin UER
name misspelled .12 .30
41R Evgeny Popikhin .12 .30
42R Alexander Semak .15 .40
43R Mikhail Shtalenkov .12 .30
44R Sergei Sorokin .12 .30
45R Andrei Trefilov .12 .30
46R Ravil Yakubov .12 .30
47R Alexander Yudin .12 .30
48R Alexei Zhamnov .12 .30
49R Andrei Basalgin .12 .30
50R Lev Berdichevsky .12 .30
51R Konstantin Kapkaikin .12 .30
52R Konstantin Kurashov .12 .30
53R Andrei Kvartalnov UER .12 .30
54R Albert Malgin .12 .30
55R Nikolai Maslov .12 .30
56R Anatoli Naida .12 .30
57R Roman Oksiuta .12 .30
58R Sergei Selyanin .12 .30
59R Valeri Shiryev .12 .30
60R Alexander Smirnov .12 .30
61R Leonid Trukhno .12 .30
62R Igor Ulanov UER .15 .40
63R Andrei Yakovenko .12 .30
64R Oleg Yashin .12 .30
65R Valeri Zelepukin .15 .40
66R Russian Checklist .05 .15

1992-93 O-Pee-Chee

1 Kevin Todd .12 .30
2 Robert Kron .12 .30
3 David Volek .12 .30
4 Teppo Numminen .12 .30
5 Paul Coffey .20 .50
6 Luc Robitaille .20 .50
7 Steven Finn .12 .30
8 Gord Hynes .12 .30
9 Dave Ellett .12 .30
10 Alexander Godynyuk .12 .30
11 Darryl Sydor .12 .30
12 Randy Carlyle .15 .40
13 Chris Chelios .20 .50
14 Kent Manderville .12 .30
15 Wayne Gretzky 1.25 3.00
16 Jon Casey .12 .30
17 Mark Tinordi .12 .30
18 Dale Hunter .15 .40
19 Martin Gelinas UER .12 .30
20 Todd Elik .12 .30
21 Bob Sweeney .12 .30
22 Chris Dahlquist .15 .40
23 Joe Mullen .15 .40
24 Shawn Burr .12 .30
25 Pavel Bure .20 .50
26 Randy Gilhen .12 .30
27 Brian Bradley .12 .30
28 Don Beaupre .15 .40
29 Kevin Stevens .15 .40
30 Michal Pivonka .12 .30
31 Grant Fuhr .30 .75
32 Steve Larmer .12 .30
33 Gary Leeman .12 .30
34 Tony Tanti .12 .30
35 Denis Savard .20 .50
36 Paul Ranheim .12 .30
37 Andrei Lomakin .12 .30
38 Perry Anderson .12 .30
39 Stu Barnes .12 .30
40 Don Sweeney .12 .30
41 Jamie Baker .12 .30
42 Ray Ferraro .12 .30
43 Bobby Clarke 70 .30 .75
44 Kelly Hrudey .15 .40
45 Brian Skrudland .15 .40
46 Paul Ysebaert .12 .30
47 Pierre Turgeon .15 .40
48 Keith Brown .15 .40
49 Rod Brind'Amour .12 .30
50 Wayne McBean .12 .30
51 Doug Lidster .15 .40
52 Bernie Nicholls .15 .40
53 Daren Puppa .15 .40
54 Joe Sakic .40 1.00
55 Joe Sakic 89 .40 1.00
56 Dave Manson .12 .30
57 Denis Potvin 74 .20 .50
58 Daniel Marois .12 .30
59 Martin Brodeur .50 1.25
60 Brent Sutter .12 .30
61 Steve Yzerman .50 1.25
62 Neal Broten .15 .40
63 Darcy Wakaluk .15 .40
64 Troy Murray .12 .30
65 Tony Granato .12 .30
66 Frank Musil .15 .40
67 Claude Lemieux .12 .30
68 Brian Benning .12 .30
69 Stephane Matteau .12 .30
70 Tomas Forslund .12 .30
71 Dmitri Mironov .12 .30
72 Gary Roberts .12 .30
73 Felix Potvin .40 1.00
74 Glen Murray UER .15 .40
75 Stephane Fiset .12 .30
76 Stephane Richer .15 .40
77 Jeff Reese .12 .30
78 Marc Bureau .15 .40
79 Derek King .12 .30
80 Dave Gagner .15 .40
81 Ed Belfour .20 .50
82 Joel Otto .12 .30
83 Anatoli Semenov .12 .30
84 Ron Hextall .20 .50
85 Adam Creighton .12 .30
86 Kris King .12 .30
87 Brett Hull .40 1.00
88 Zdeno Ciger .12 .30
89 Petr Nedved .15 .40
90 Sergei Makarov .12 .30
91 Tomas Sandstrom .15 .40
92 Steve Heinze .12 .30
93 Robert Reichel .12 .30
94 Cliff Ronning .12 .30
95 Eric Weinrich .12 .30
96 Wendel Clark .30 .75
97 Rick Zombo .12 .30
98 Ric Nattress .15 .40
99 Theo Fleury .30 .75
100 Joe Murphy .12 .30
101 Gord Murphy .15 .40
102 Jaromir Jagr .40 1.00
103 Mike Craig .12 .30
104 John Cullen .12 .30
105 John Druce .12 .30
106 Peter Bondra .20 .50
107 Bryan Trottier 76 .20 .50
108 Steve Smith .12 .30
109 Petr Svoboda .15 .40
110 Mats Sundin .20 .50
111 Patrick Roy 86 .50 1.25
112 Steve Leach .12 .30
113 Jacques Cloutier .15 .40
114 Doug Weight .40 1.00
115 Frank Pietrangelo .15 .40
116 Guy Hebert RC .30 .75
117 Donald Audette .15 .40
118 Craig MacTavish .12 .30
119 Grant Fuhr 82 .30 .75
120 Trevor Linden .20 .50
121 Fredrik Olausson .12 .30
122 Geoff Sanderson .15 .40
123 Derian Hatcher .12 .30
124 Brett Hull 88 .40 1.00
125 Kelly Buchberger .12 .30
126 Ray Bourque .30 .75
127 Murray Craven .12 .30
128 Tim Cheveldae .12 .30
129 Ulf Dahlen .12 .30
130 Bryan Trottier .20 .50
131 Bob Carpenter .15 .40
132 Benoit Hogue .12 .30
133 Claude Vilgrain .15 .40
134 Glenn Anderson .15 .40
135 Marty McInnis .12 .30
136 Rob Pearson .12 .30
137 Bill Ranford .15 .40
138 Mario Lemieux .75 2.00
139 Bob Bassen .12 .30
140 Scott Mellanby .12 .30
141 Dave Andreychuk .20 .50
142 Kelly Miller .12 .30
143 Gaetan Duchesne .12 .30
144 Mike Sullivan .12 .30
145 Kevin Hatcher .12 .30
146 Doug Bodger .12 .30
147 Craig Berube .12 .30
148 Rick Tocchet .15 .40
149 Luciano Borsato .12 .30
150 Glen Wesley .12 .30
151 Mike Donnelly .12 .30
152 Jimmy Carson .12 .30
153 Jocelyn Lemieux .12 .30
154 Ray Sheppard .12 .30
155 Tony Amonte .15 .40
156 Adrien Plavsic .12 .30
157 Mark Pederson .12 .30
158 Adam Graves .12 .30
159 Igor Larionov .12 .30
160 Steve Chiasson .12 .30
161 Igor Kravchuk .12 .30
162 Slava Fetisov .12 .30
163 Gerard Gallant .12 .30
164 Patrick Roy .50 1.25
165 Ken Sutton .12 .30
166 Mathieu Schneider .12 .30
167 Larry Robinson 73 .20 .50
168 Jim Sandlak .12 .30
169 Joey Kocur .12 .30
170 Rob Brown .12 .30
171 Luke Richardson .15 .40
172 Adam Oates 87 .20 .50
173 Uwe Krupp .12 .30
174 Cam Neely .20 .50
175 Peter Sidorkiewicz .12 .30
176 Geoff Courtnall .12 .30
177 Doug Gilmour .25 .60
178 Josef Beranek .12 .30
179 Michel Picard .15 .40
180 Terry Carkner .15 .40
181 Nelson Emerson .12 .30
182 Perry Berezan .12 .30
183 Checklist C .01 .05
184 Andy Moog .20 .50
185 Michel Petit .12 .30
186 Mark Greig .15 .40
187 Paul Coffey 81 .20 .50
188 Ron Francis .25 .60
189 Joe Juneau .12 .30
190 Jeff Odgers .12 .30
191 Darryl Sittler 75 .25 .60
192 Vincent Damphousse .15 .40
193 Greg Paslawski .12 .30
194 Tony Esposito 69 .20 .50
195 Sergei Fedorov .30 .75
196 Doug Smail .12 .30
197 Pat Verbeek .12 .30
198 Dominic Roussel .15 .40
199 Mike McPhee .12 .30
200 Kevin Dineen .12 .30
201 Pat Elynuik .12 .30
202 Tom Kurvers .12 .30
203 Chris Joseph .12 .30
204 Mark Fitzpatrick .15 .40
205 Jari Kurri .20 .50
206 Guy Carbonneau .15 .40
207 Jan Erixon .15 .40
208 Mark Messier .40 1.00
209 Larry Murphy .15 .40
210 Dirk Graham .12 .30
211 Ron Tugnutt .15 .40
212 Dale Hawerchuk .25 .60
213 Dave Babych .15 .40
214 Mikael Andersson .12 .30
215 James Patrick .12 .30
216 Peter Stastny .15 .40
217 Bernie Parent 68 .25 .60
218 Jeff Hackett .15 .40
219 Dave Lowry .15 .40
220 Wayne Gretzky 79 1.25 3.00
221 Brent Gilchrist .12 .30
222 Andrew Cassels .12 .30
223 Calle Johansson .12 .30
224 Joe Reekie .12 .30
225 Craig Simpson .12 .30
226 Bob Essensa .15 .40
227 Pat Falloon .12 .30
228 Vladimir Ruzicka .12 .30
229 Igor Ulanov .12 .30
230 Kjell Samuelsson .15 .40
231 Shayne Corson .15 .40
232 Kelly Kisio .15 .40
233 Gordie Roberts .15 .40
234 Brian Noonan .12 .30
235 Slava Kozlov .15 .40
236 Checklist B .01 .05
237 Jeff Beukeboom .12 .30
238 Steve Konroyd .15 .40
239 Patrice Brisebois .12 .30
240 Mario Lemieux Smythe .75 2.00
241 Dana Murzyn .12 .30
242 Pelle Eklund .15 .40
243 Rob Blake .15 .40
244 Brendan Shanahan .20 .50
245 Mike Gartner HL .25 .60
246 David Bruce .12 .30
247 Mike Vernon .15 .40
248 Zarley Zalapski .12 .30
249 Dino Ciccarelli .15 .40
250 David Williams RC .12 .30
251 Scott Stevens 83 .20 .50
252 Bob Probert .20 .50
253 Mikhail Tatarinov .12 .30
254 Bobby Holik .15 .40
255 Tony Amonte 91 .15 .40
256 Brad May .12 .30
257 Philippe Bozon .12 .30
258 Mark Messier 80 .40 1.00
259 Mike Richter .20 .50
260 Brian Mullen .12 .30
261 Marty McSorley .15 .40
262 Glenn Healy .15 .40
263 Russ Romaniuk .12 .30
264 Dan Quinn .15 .40
265 Jyrki Lumme .12 .30
266 Valeri Kamensky .12 .30
267 Vladimir Konstantinov .20 .50
268 Peter Ahola .12 .30
269 Guy Larose .12 .30
270 Ulf Samuelsson .12 .30
271 Dale Craigwell .12 .30
272 Adam Oates .20 .50
273 Pat MacLeod .12 .30
274 Mike Keane .12 .30
275 John Vanbiesbrouck .20 .50
276 Brian Lawton .15 .40
277 Sylvain Cote .15 .40
278 Gary Suter .12 .30
279 Alexander Mogilny .15 .40
280 Garth Butcher .15 .40
281 Doug Wilson .15 .40
282 Chris Terreri .15 .40
283 Phil Esposito 77 UER .20 .50
284 Russ Courtnall .12 .30
285 Pat LaFontaine .20 .50
286 Dimitri Khristich .12 .30
287 John LeBlanc RC .15 .40
288 Randy Velischek .12 .30
289 Dave Christian .12 .30
290 Kevin Haller .12 .30
291 Kevin Miller .12 .30
292 Mario Lemieux 85 .75 2.00
293 Stephan Lebeau .12 .30
294 Marcel Dionne 71 .25 .60
295 Barry Pederson .12 .30
296 Steve Duchesne .12 .30
297 Yves Racine .12 .30
298 Phil Housley .15 .40
299 Randy Ladouceur .12 .30
300 Mike Gartner .25 .60
301 Dominik Hasek .30 .75
302 Kevin Lowe .15 .40
303 Sylvain Lefebvre .12 .30
304 J.J. Daigneault .12 .30
305 Mike Ridley .12 .30
306 Curtis Leschyshyn .15 .40
307 Gilbert Dionne .12 .30
308 Bill Guerin RC .40 1.00
309 Gerald Diduck .15 .40
310 Rick Wamsley .12 .30
311 Pat Jablonski UER .15 .40
312 Jay More .12 .30
313 Mike Modano .50 1.25
314 Checklist A .01 .05
315 Slyvain Turgeon .12 .30
316 Sergei Nemchinov .12 .30
317 Garry Galley .12 .30
318 Paul Coffey HL .20 .50
319 Esa Tikkanen .12 .30
320 Claude LaPointe .12 .30
321 Steve Yzerman 84 .50 1.25
322 Mark Lamb .12 .30
323 Bob Errey .15 .40
324 Pavel Bure 92 .20 .50
325 Craig Janney .15 .40
326 Bob Kudelski .15 .40
327 Kirk Muller .12 .30
328 Jim Paek .15 .40
329 Mike Ricci .12 .30
330 Al MacInnis .25 .60
331 Mike Hudson .12 .30
332 Darrin Shannon .12 .30
333 Doug Brown .15 .40
334 Corey Millen .12 .30
335 Mike Krushelnyski .12 .30
336 Scott Stevens .20 .50
337 Peter Zezel .12 .30
338 Geoff Smith .12 .30
339 Curtis Joseph .25 .60
340 Tom Barrasso .15 .40
341 Al Iafrate .15 .40
342 Kirk McLean .12 .30
343 Gerry Cheevers 72 .20 .50
344 Norm Maciver .12 .30
345 Jeremy Roenick .30 .75
346 Keith Tkachuk UER .20 .50
347 Rod Langway .15 .40
348 Ray Bourque HL .30 .75
349 Kirk McLean .12 .30
350 Brian Propp .12 .30
351 John Ogrodnick .12 .30
352 Benoit Brunet .12 .30
353 Alexei Kasatonov .12 .30
354 Joe Nieuwendyk .15 .40
355 Joe Sacco .12 .30
356 Tom Fergus .12 .30
357 Dan Lambert .12 .30
358 Michel Goulet .15 .40
359 Shawn McEachern .12 .30
360 Eric Desjardins .15 .40
361 Paul Stanton .12 .30
362 Ron Sutter .12 .30
363 Derrick Smith .12 .30
364 Paul Broten .12 .30
365 Greg Adams .12 .30
366 Rob Zettler .12 .30
367 Dave Poulin .12 .30
368 Keith Acton .15 .40
369 Nicklas Lidstrom .15 .40
370 Randy Burridge .12 .30
371 Jamie Macoun .15 .40
372 Craig Billington .15 .40
373 Mark Recchi .25 .60
374 Kris Draper .12 .30
375 Ed Olczyk .12 .30
376 Tom Draper .12 .30
377 Sergio Momesso .12 .30
378 Brian Leetch .15 .40
379 Paul Cavallini .12 .30
380 Paul Fenton .15 .40
381 Dean Evason .12 .30
382 Owen Nolan .20 .50
383 Jeremy Roenick 90 .30 .75
384 Brian Bellows .15 .40
385 Thomas Steen .12 .30
386 John LeClair .20 .50
387 Darren Turcotte .12 .30
388 James Black .12 .30
389 Alexei Gusarov .12 .30
390 Scott Lachance .12 .30
391 Mike Bossy 78 .20 .50
392 Mike Hough .15 .40
393 Grant Ledyard .12 .30
394 Tom Fitzgerald .12 .30
395 Steve Thomas .15 .40
396 Bobby Smith .15 .40

1992-93 O-Pee-Chee 25th Anniversary

1 Bernie Parent .20 .50
2 Tony Esposito .15 .40
3 Bobby Clarke .25 .60
4 Marcel Dionne .20 .50
5 Gerry Cheevers .15 .40
6 Larry Robinson .15 .40
7 Denis Potvin .15 .40
8 Darryl Sittler .20 .50
9 Bryan Trottier .15 .40
10 Phil Esposito .15 .40
11 Mike Bossy .15 .40
12 Wayne Gretzky 1.00 2.50
13 Mark Messier .30 .75
14 Paul Coffey .15 .40
15 Grant Fuhr .25 .60

16 Scott Stevens .15 .40
17 Steve Yzerman .40 1.00
18 Mario Lemieux .60 1.50
19 Patrick Roy .40 1.00
20 Adam Oates .15 .40
21 Brett Hull .30 .75
22 Joe Sakic .30 .75
23 Jeremy Roenick .25 .60
24 Tony Amonte .12 .30
25 Pavel Bure .15 .40
NNO Checklist .07 .20

1992-93 O-Pee-Chee Trophy Winners

COMPLETE SET (4) 2.00 5.00
1 Pavel Bure .60 1.50
2 Brian Leetch .20 .50
3 Mark Messier .25 .60
4 Patrick Roy 1.00 2.50

1993 O-Pee-Chee Canadiens Hockey Fest

COMPLETE SET (66) 28.00 70.00
1 Montreal Forum 1924 .40 1.00
2 Emile Bouchard .08 .25
3 Henri Richard .75 2.00
4 Serge Savard .20 .50
5 Toe Blake CO HL .75 2.00
6 Maurice Richard HL 2.00 5.00
7 Stephan Lebeau .08 .25
8 Kevin Haller .08 .25
9 Guy Carbonneau .20 .50
10 Jacques Demers CO .15 .40
11 Serge Savard .20 .50
12 Montreal Forum 1968 .40 1.00
13 Howie Morenz 2.00 5.00
14 Jean Beliveau 1.25 3.00
15 Jacques Laperriere .20 .50
16 Bob Gainey .30 .75
17 Guy Lafleur HL .75 2.00
18 Jacques Raymond .08 .25
19 Sean Hill .08 .25
20 Eric Desjardins .15 .40
21 Aurel Joliat .75 2.00
22 Doug Harvey .75 2.00
23 Yvan Cournoyer .30 .75
24 Frank Mahovlich HL .40 1.00
25 J.J. Daigneault .08 .25
26 Kirk Muller .15 .40
27 Jean Beliveau 1.50 4.00
28 Georges Vezina 2.00 5.00
29 Maurice Richard 3.00 8.00
30 Patrick Roy 5.00 12.00
31 Benoit Brunet .08 .25
32 Jacques Plante HL 1.25 3.00
33 Ralph Backstrom .08 .25
34 Elmer Lach .40 1.00
35 Stanley Cup Champions .20 .50
36 Jacques Laperriere .20 .50
37 Montreal Individual Records--Playoffs .08 .25
38 Vincent Damphousse .30 .75
39 Frank Mahovlich .75 2.00
40 Jacques Plante 2.00 5.00
41 Stanley Cup Champions Montreal .20 .50
42 Kenny Reardon .30 .75
43 Claude Provost .08 .25
44 Jean Beliveau HL 1.00 2.50
45 Edward Ronan .08 .25
46 Canadiens NHL Individual Records .08 .25
47 Bill Durnan .75 2.00
48 Stanley Cup .20 .50
49 Patrice Brisebois .08 .25
50 Denis Savard .30 .75
51 Ken Dryden 2.00 5.00
52 Lou Fontinato .15 .40
53 Jean-Guy Talbot .20 .50
54 BoomBoom Geoffrion .75 2.00
55 Joe Malone .40 1.00
56 Oleg Petrov .08 .25
57 Guy Lafleur 1.00 2.50
58 Bert Olmstead .20 .50
59 The Dream Team Jacques 2.00 5.00
60 Brian Bellows .15 .40
61 Henri Richard HL .40 1.00
62 Jacques Lemaire .30 .75
63 Dickie Moore .60 1.50
64 Lorne Worsley .60 1.50
65 Toe Blake .75 2.00
66 Checklist Card .02 .10

1993 O-Pee-Chee Canadiens Panel

1 Canadiens Panel 6.00 15.00

1999-00 O-Pee-Chee

COMPLETE SET (286) 20.00 50.00
*O-PEE-CHEE: .5X TO 1.2X TOPPS

1999-00 O-Pee-Chee All-Topps

COMPLETE SET (15) 20.00 40.00
*O-PEE-CHEE: .4X TO 1X TOPPS
AT1 Dominik Hasek 1.50 4.00
AT2 Martin Brodeur 2.00 5.00
AT3 Ray Bourque 1.25 3.00
AT4 Al MacInnis .60 1.50
AT5 Nicklas Lidstrom .75 2.00
AT6 Brian Leetch .75 2.00
AT7 John LeClair 1.00 2.50
AT8 Paul Kariya 2.00 5.00
AT9 Keith Tkachuk .75 2.00
AT10 Eric Lindros 1.25 3.00
AT11 Peter Forsberg 2.00 5.00
AT12 Steve Yzerman 4.00 10.00
AT13 Jaromir Jagr 1.25 3.00
AT14 Teemu Selanne 1.50 4.00
AT15 Pavel Bure 1.00 2.50

1999-00 O-Pee-Chee Autographs

TA1 John LeClair 20.00 50.00
TA2 Dominik Hasek 30.00 80.00
TA3 Curtis Joseph 15.00 40.00
TA4 Alexei Yashin 12.00 30.00
TA5 Mats Sundin 15.00 40.00
TA6 Chris Drury 12.00 30.00
TA7 Milan Hejduk 15.00 40.00
TA8 Marian Hossa 15.00 40.00
TA9 Vincent Lecavalier 12.00 30.00
TA10 Joe Thornton 20.00 50.00

1999-00 O-Pee-Chee Ice Masters

COMPLETE SET (20) 40.00 80.00
*O-PEE-CHEE: .4X TO 1X TOPPS
IM1 Joe Sakic 5.00 12.00
IM2 Dominik Hasek 5.00 12.00
IM3 Eric Lindros 3.00 8.00
IM4 Jaromir Jagr 3.00 8.00
IM5 John LeClair 2.00 5.00
IM6 Mats Sundin 2.00 5.00
IM7 Ray Bourque 3.00 8.00
IM8 Mike Modano 3.00 8.00
IM9 Peter Forsberg 4.00 10.00
IM10 Brian Leetch 2.00 5.00
IM11 Martin Brodeur 6.00 15.00
IM12 Al MacInnis 1.50 4.00
IM13 Paul Kariya 4.00 10.00
IM14 Alexei Yashin 1.50 4.00
IM15 Steve Yzerman 10.00 25.00
IM16 Ed Belfour 4.00 10.00
IM17 Keith Tkachuk 2.00 5.00
IM18 Patrick Roy 10.00 25.00
IM19 Nicklas Lidstrom 4.00 10.00
IM20 Teemu Selanne 3.00 8.00

1999-00 O-Pee-Chee Now Starring

COMPLETE SET (15) 10.00 20.00
*O-PEE-CHEE: .4X TO 1X TOPPS

1999-00 O-Pee-Chee A-Men

COMPLETE SET (6) 5.00 12.00
*O-PEE-CHEE: .4X TO 1X TOPPS

1999-00 O-Pee-Chee Fantastic Finishers

COMPLETE SET (6) 3.00 8.00
*O-PEE-CHEE: .4X TO 1X TOPPS

1999-00 O-Pee-Chee Ice Futures

COMPLETE SET (6) 1.25 3.00
*O-PEE-CHEE: .4X TO 1X TOPPS

1999-00 O-Pee-Chee Positive Performers

COMPLETE SET (6) 2.50 6.00
*O-PEE-CHEE: .4X TO 1X TOPPS

1999-00 O-Pee-Chee Postmasters

COMPLETE SET (6) 5.00 12.00
*O-PEE-CHEE: .4X TO 1X TOPPS

1999-00 O-Pee-Chee Top of the World

COMPLETE SET (20) 30.00 80.00
*O-PEE-CHEE: .4X TO 1X TOPPS

2000-01 O-Pee-Chee

*FOIL/100: 8X TO 20X BASIC INSERTS
1 Jaromir Jagr .60 1.50
2 Patrick Roy .50 1.25
3 Paul Kariya .20 .50
4 Mats Sundin .20 .50
5 Ron Francis .25 .60
6 Pavel Bure .20 .50
7 John LeClair .20 .50
8 Olaf Kolzig .20 .50
9 Chris Pronger .20 .50
10 Jeremy Roenick .30 .75
11 Owen Nolan .20 .50
12 Theo Fleury .25 .60
13 Zigmund Palffy .20 .50
14 Patrik Stefan .15 .40
15 Jarome Iginla .25 .60
16 Joe Thornton .30 .75
17 Tony Amonte .15 .40
18 Mike Modano .30 .75
19 Alexander Mogilny .15 .40
20 Mark Messier .40 1.00
21 Dominik Hasek .30 .75
22 Steve Yzerman .50 1.25
23 Marian Hossa .20 .50
24 David Legwand .20 .50
25 Jose Theodore .20 .50
26 Vincent Lecavalier .20 .50
27 Mike Ricci .12 .30
28 Scott Stevens .20 .50
29 Kevin Weekes .12 .30
30 Sean Burke .12 .30
31 Alexei Kovalev .15 .40
32 Trevor Linden .20 .50
33 Joe Juneau .12 .30
34 Niklas Sundstrom .12 .30
35 Dan Cloutier .15 .40
36 Drake Berehowsky .12 .30
37 Jonas Hoglund .12 .30
38 Sami Kapanen .12 .30
39 Matthew Barnaby .12 .30
40 Anson Carter .15 .40
41 Miroslav Satan .12 .30
42 Mark Recchi .25 .60
43 Pavol Demitra .25 .60
44 Peter Bondra .20 .50
45 Mike Richter .20 .50
46 Guy Hebert .15 .40
47 Robert Svehla .12 .30
48 Martin Skoula .15 .40
49 Ed Belfour .20 .50
50 Alexei Zhamnov .15 .40
51 Fred Brathwaite .15 .40
52 Andrew Brunette .12 .30
53 Byron Dafoe .15 .40
54 Claude Lemieux .15 .40
55 Sergei Berezin .12 .30
56 Felix Potvin .30 .75
57 Rod Brind'Amour .20 .50
58 Doug Gilmour .25 .60
59 Brett Hull .40 1.00
60 Nicklas Lidstrom .20 .50
61 Mike York .12 .30
62 Al MacInnis .25 .60
63 Brian Boucher .15 .40
64 Teemu Selanne .40 1.00
65 Mike Vernon .15 .40
66 Bill Guerin .20 .50
67 Ray Bourque .30 .75
68 Bryan McCabe .12 .30
69 Ray Ferraro .12 .30
70 Stephane Fiset .12 .30
71 Sergei Gonchar .12 .30
72 Mattias Ohlund .12 .30
73 Todd Marchant .12 .30
74 Derek Morris .12 .30
75 Brian Rolston .15 .40
76 Damian Rhodes .12 .30
77 Chris Drury .15 .40
78 Curtis Joseph .25 .60
79 Teppo Numminen .12 .30
80 Petr Nedved .15 .40
81 Doug Weight .20 .50
82 Arturs Irbe .15 .40
83 Chris Osgood .20 .50
84 Chris Gratton .12 .30
85 Jocelyn Thibault .15 .40
86 Oleg Tverdovsky .12 .30
87 Derian Hatcher .15 .40
88 Ray Whitney .15 .40
89 Saku Koivu .20 .50
90 Cliff Ronning .12 .30
91 Claude Lapointe .12 .30
92 Fredrik Modin .12 .30
93 Chris Simon .12 .30
94 Todd Harvey .15 .40
95 Martin Rucinsky .12 .30
96 Valeri Bure .15 .40
97 Brad Isbister .12 .30
98 Daymond Langkow .12 .30
99 Todd Bertuzzi .15 .40
100 Roman Turek .15 .40
101 Kenny Jonsson .12 .30
102 Mike Dunham .12 .30
103 Rob Blake .20 .50
104 Darius Kasparaitis .15 .40
105 Daniel Alfredsson .20 .50
106 Bobby Holik .12 .30
107 Tommy Salo .15 .40
108 Sergei Samsonov .15 .40
109 Joe Sakic .40 1.00
110 Bryan Smolinski .15 .40
111 Luc Robitaille .20 .50
112 Ryan Smyth .15 .40
113 Eric Daze .15 .40
114 Mariusz Czerkawski .12 .30
115 Brendan Shanahan .20 .50
116 Brian Rafalski .12 .30
117 Mark Parrish .12 .30
118 Jamie Langenbrunner .15 .40
119 Peter Forsberg .40 1.00
120 Phil Housley .15 .40
121 Jeff O'Neill .15 .40
122 Stu Barnes .15 .40
123 Glen Murray .15 .40
124 Jeff Hackett .12 .30
125 Sergei Fedorov .30 .75
126 Kyle McLaren .12 .30
127 Michael Nylander .12 .30
128 Sergei Zubov .15 .40
129 Steve Rucchin .12 .30
130 Nelson Emerson .12 .30
131 Martin Brodeur .50 1.25
132 Mike Grier .12 .30
133 Paul Coffey .20 .50
134 Radek Bonk .15 .40
135 Marc Savard .12 .30
136 Milan Hejduk .15 .40
137 Curtis Brown .12 .30
138 Viktor Kozlov .15 .40
139 Jason Woolley .12 .30
140 Adam Foote .15 .40
141 Radek Dvorak .15 .40
142 Jason Arnott .15 .40
143 German Titov .12 .30
144 Scott Thornton .15 .40
145 Brendan Morrison .20 .50
146 Keith Tkachuk .20 .50
147 Patrik Elias .20 .50
148 Donald Audette .15 .40
149 Jochen Hecht .12 .30
150 Dave Scatchard .12 .30
151 Tom Barrasso .15 .40
152 Adam Deadmarsh .12 .30
153 Brian Leetch .15 .40
154 Sergei Krivokrasov .12 .30
155 Randy Robitaille .12 .30
156 Petr Sykora .15 .40
157 Dave Andreychuk .20 .50
158 Mathieu Biron .12 .30
159 Sergei Zholtok .12 .30
160 Shawn McEachern .12 .30
161 Steve Shields .12 .30
162 Petr Svoboda .12 .30
163 Nikolai Antropov .15 .40
164 Michal Handzus .12 .30
165 Martin Straka .15 .40
166 Shane Doan .15 .40
167 Eric Desjardins .15 .40
168 Peter Schaefer .12 .30
169 Adam Oates .20 .50
170 Scott Niedermayer .20 .50
171 Dallas Drake .12 .30
172 Josh Green .12 .30
173 Mike Sillinger .12 .30
174 Adam Graves .15 .40
175 Lubos Bartecko .12 .30
176 Steve Konowalchuk .12 .30
177 Jozef Stumpel .12 .30
178 Vincent Damphousse .15 .40
179 Tomas Kaberle .12 .30
180 Maxim Afinogenov .12 .30
181 Marty McInnis .15 .40
182 Chris Chelios .20 .50
183 Joe Nieuwendyk .15 .40
184 Petr Buzek .12 .30
185 Calle Johansson .12 .30
186 Jeff Friesen .12 .30
187 Paul Mara .12 .30
188 Markus Naslund .20 .50
189 Scott Young .12 .30
190 Trevor Letowski .12 .30
191 Steve Thomas .12 .30
192 Martin Biron .15 .40
193 Jason Allison .15 .40
194 Bob Probert .20 .50
195 Jere Lehtinen .15 .40
196 Tom Poti .12 .30
197 Eric Lindros .30 .75
198 Rob Niedermayer .15 .40
199 Gary Roberts .12 .30
200 Richard Zednik .12 .30
201 Dainius Zubrus .12 .30
202 Tom Fitzgerald .12 .30
203 Scott Gomez .15 .40
204 Travis Green .12 .30
205 Pierre Turgeon .15 .40
206 Ed Jovanovski .15 .40
207 Trevor Kidd .12 .30
208 Jan Hrdina .12 .30
209 Valeri Zelepukin .12 .30
210 Vaclav Prospal .12 .30
211 Matt Cullen .12 .30
212 Karlis Skrastins .12 .30
213 Robyn Regehr .12 .30
214 Darren McCarty .12 .30
215 John Madden .15 .40
216 Scott Mellanby .12 .30
217 Tim Connolly .12 .30
218 Pat Verbeek .15 .40
219 Richard Matvichuk .12 .30
220 Rick Tocchet .15 .40
221 Jan Hlavac .12 .30
222 Jeff Halpern .12 .30
223 Patrick Marleau .20 .50
224 Robert Lang .12 .30
225 Wade Redden .12 .30
226 Stephane Richer .12 .30
227 Kim Johnsson .12 .30
228 Greg Adams .12 .30
229 Alex Tanguay .15 .40
230 Andre Savage .12 .30
231 Slava Kozlov .15 .40
232 Steve Sullivan .12 .30
233 Alexander Selivanov .12 .30
234 Tommy Westlund .12 .30
235 Darcy Tucker .12 .30
236 Simon Gagne .20 .50
237 Brad Stuart .15 .40
238 Jean-Sebastien Aubin .15 .40
239 Mike Johnson .12 .30
240 Shayne Corson .15 .40
241 Michael Peca .15 .40
242 Keith Primeau .15 .40
243 Martin Lapointe .15 .40
244 Tie Domi .15 .40
245 Janne Niinimaa .12 .30
246 Brenden Morrow .15 .40
247 Sandis Ozolinsh .12 .30
248 Ron Tugnutt .15 .40
249 Andrei Nazarov .12 .30
250 Bates Battaglia .12 .30
251 Yannick Tremblay .12 .30
252 Grant Fuhr .30 .75
253 Cory Stillman .12 .30
254 Jason Wiemer .12 .30
255 Martin Gelinas .12 .30
256 Mike Keane .15 .40
257 Ethan Moreau .12 .30
258 Jason Smith .12 .30
259 Kelly Buchberger .15 .40
260 Benoit Brunet .12 .30
261 Brian Savage .12 .30
262 Sheldon Souray .12 .30
263 Greg Johnson .12 .30
264 Magnus Arvedson .12 .30
265 Patrick Lalime .15 .40
266 Wayne Primeau .12 .30
267 Igor Korolev .12 .30
268 Yanic Perreault .12 .30
269 Adrian Aucoin .12 .30
270 Andrew Cassels .12 .30
271 Roberto Luongo .30 .75
272 Harold Druken .12 .30
273 Marc Denis .15 .40
274 Oleg Saprykin .12 .30
275 Glen Metropolit .12 .30
276 Mark Eaton .12 .30
277 Dmitri Yakushin .12 .30
278 Scott Hannan .12 .30
279 Dave Tanabe .12 .30
280 Jiri Fischer .12 .30
281 Dmitri Nabokov .12 .30
282 Ivan Novoseltsev .12 .30
283 Manny Fernandez .12 .30
284 Maxim Balmochnyk .12 .30
285 Brian Campbell .12 .30
286 Sergei Varlamov .12 .30
287 Ville Nieminen RC .12 .30
288 Colin White RC .12 .30
289 Mike Fisher .12 .30
290 Matt Elich RC .15 .40
291 Zenith Komarniski .12 .30
292 Eric Nickulas RC .12 .30
293 Steven McCarthy .12 .30
294 Jason Krog .12 .30
295 Robert Esche .12 .30
296 Adam Mair .12 .30
297 Ladislav Nagy .12 .30
298 S.Vyshedkevich RC .12 .30
299 Steve Begin .12 .30
300 Brad Ference .12 .30
301 Andy Delmore .12 .30
302 Brent Sopel RC .20 .50
303 Evgeni Nabokov .15 .40
304 David Gosselin RC .15 .40
305 Tavis Hansen .12 .30
306 Ray Giroux .12 .30
307 Serge Aubin RC .15 .40
308 Shane Willis .12 .30
309 Vitali Vishnevski .12 .30
310 Richard Jackman .12 .30
311 Petr Schastlivy .12 .30
312 Ryan Bonni .12 .30
313 Alexei Tezikov .12 .30
314 Zac Bierk .12 .30
315 Mike Ribeiro .12 .30
316 Darryl Laplante .12 .30
317 Kyle Calder .12 .30
318 Dimitri Kalinin .12 .30
319 Jean-Sebastien Giguere .20 .50
320 Willie Mitchell RC .20 .50
321 Stephen Valiquette RC .15 .40
322 Brian Willsie .12 .30
323 Jarkko Ruutu .12 .30
324 Jon Sim .12 .30
325 Jonathan Girard .12 .30
326 Martin Brodeur HL .50 1.25
327 Ray Bourque HL .30 .75
328 The Bure Brothers HL .20 .50
329 Steve Yzerman HL .50 1.25
330 Brett Hull HL .40 1.00

2000-01 O-Pee-Chee 1000 Point Club

PC1 Mark Messier 1.00 2.50
PC2 Steve Yzerman 1.25 3.00
PC3 Ron Francis .60 1.50
PC4 Paul Coffey .50 1.25
PC5 Ray Bourque .75 2.00
PC6 Doug Gilmour .60 1.50
PC7 Adam Oates .50 1.25
PC8 Larry Murphy .40 1.00
PC9 Dave Andreychuk .50 1.25
PC10 Luc Robitaille .50 1.25
PC11 Phil Housley .40 1.00
PC12 Brett Hull 1.00 2.50
PC13 Al MacInnis .60 1.50
PC14 Pierre Turgeon .40 1.00
PC15 Joe Sakic 1.00 2.50
PC16 Pat Verbeek .40 1.00

2000-01 O-Pee-Chee Combos

TC1 P.Bure/V.Bure .75 2.00
TC2 T.Selanne/P.Kariya 1.50 4.00
TC3 J.LeClair/T.Amonte .75 2.00
TC4 C.Joseph/D.Hasek 1.25 3.00
TC5 M.Modano/P.Forsberg 1.50 4.00
TC6 R.Bourque/C.Pronger 1.25 3.00
TC7 V.Lecavalier/J.Thornton 1.25 3.00
TC8 P.Roy/M.Brodeur 2.00 5.00
TC9 S.Yzerman/B.Hull 2.00 5.00
TC10 J.Jagr/M.Lemieux 3.00 8.00

2000-01 O-Pee-Chee Hobby Masters

HM1 Martin Brodeur 1.25 3.00
HM2 Pavel Bure .50 1.25
HM3 Peter Forsberg 1.00 2.50
HM4 Dominik Hasek .75 2.00
HM5 Jaromir Jagr 1.50 4.00
HM6 Curtis Joseph .60 1.50
HM7 Paul Kariya .50 1.25
HM8 Mike Modano .75 2.00
HM9 Patrick Roy 1.25 3.00
HM10 Steve Yzerman 1.25 3.00

2000-01 O-Pee-Chee NHL Draft

D1 Vincent Lecavalier .75 2.00
D2 Eric Lindros 1.25 3.00
D3 Mike Modano 1.25 3.00
D4 Owen Nolan .75 2.00
D5 Patrik Stefan .60 1.50
D6 Mats Sundin .75 2.00
D7 Joe Thornton 1.25 3.00
D8 Pavel Bure .75 2.00
D9 Anson Carter .60 1.50
D10 Pavol Demitra 1.00 2.50
D11 Doug Gilmour 1.00 2.50
D12 Dominik Hasek 1.25 3.00
D13 Brett Hull 1.50 4.00
D14 Luc Robitaille .75 2.00

2000-01 O-Pee-Chee Own the Game

OTG1 Jaromir Jagr 1.50 4.00
OTG2 Pavel Bure .50 1.25
OTG3 Mark Recchi .60 1.50
OTG4 Paul Kariya .50 1.25
OTG5 Teemu Selanne 1.00 2.50
OTG6 Owen Nolan .50 1.25
OTG7 Tony Amonte .40 1.00
OTG8 Mike Modano .75 2.00
OTG9 Joe Sakic 1.00 2.50
OTG10 Steve Yzerman 1.25 3.00
OTG11 Martin Brodeur 1.25 3.00
OTG12 Roman Turek .40 1.00
OTG13 Olaf Kolzig .50 1.25
OTG14 Curtis Joseph .60 1.50
OTG15 Arturs Irbe .40 1.00
OTG16 Patrick Roy 1.25 3.00
OTG17 Ed Belfour .50 1.25
OTG18 Chris Osgood .50 1.25
OTG19 Guy Hebert .40 1.00
OTG20 Steve Shields .30 .75
OTG21 Scott Gomez .40 1.00
OTG22 Alex Tanguay .40 1.00
OTG23 Mike York .30 .75
OTG24 Simon Gagne .50 1.25
OTG25 Jan Hlavac .30 .75
OTG26 Trevor Letowski .30 .75
OTG27 Brad Stuart .40 1.00
OTG28 Maxim Afinogenov .30 .75
OTG29 Tim Connolly .30 .75
OTG30 Jochen Hecht .30 .75

2001-02 O-Pee-Chee

*UPDATES: .5X TO 1.2X BASIC CARDS
1 Mario Lemieux .75 2.00
2 Steve Yzerman .50 1.25
3 Martin Brodeur .50 1.25
4 Brian Leetch .15 .40
5 Tony Amonte .15 .40
6 Bill Guerin .20 .50
7 Olaf Kolzig .20 .50
8 Pavel Bure .20 .50
9 Patrick Marleau .20 .50
10 Mariusz Czerkawski .12 .30
11 Teemu Selanne .40 1.00
12 Alex Tanguay .15 .40
13 Keith Primeau .15 .40
14 Alexei Yashin Senator .15 .40
14U Alexei Yashin Islander .15 .40
15 Markus Naslund .20 .50
16 Chris Pronger .20 .50
17 Sergei Zubov .15 .40
18 Marian Gaborik .20 .50
19 Mats Sundin .20 .50
20 Kevin Weekes .15 .40
21 J-P Dumont .12 .30
22 Nicklas Lidstrom .20 .50
23 Ron Francis .25 .60
24 Doug Weight Oilers .20 .50
24U Doug Weight Blues .20 .50
25 Zigmund Palffy .20 .50
26 Jason Allison .15 .40
27 Joe Sakic .40 1.00
28 Paul Kariya .20 .50
29 Marian Hossa .20 .50
30 Owen Nolan .20 .50
31 Jason Arnott .15 .40
32 Jaromir Jagr Pens .60 1.50
32U Jaromir Jagr Caps .60 1.50
33 Justin Williams .15 .40
34 Peter Bondra .20 .50
35 Chris Drury .15 .40
36 Radek Bonk .12 .30
37 Theo Fleury .25 .60
38 Keith Tkachuk .20 .50
39 Rick DiPietro .15 .40
40 Ed Jovanovski .15 .40
41 Scott Stevens .20 .50
42 John LeClair .20 .50
43 Jochen Hecht .12 .30
44 Vincent Lecavalier .20 .50
45 Henrik Sedin .25 .60
46 David Aebischer .15 .40
47 Patrick Roy .50 1.25
48 Valeri Bure .12 .30
49 Dominik Hasek Sabres .30 .75
49U Dominik Hasek Red Wings .30 .75
50 Ray Ferraro .12 .30
51 Milan Hejduk .15 .40
52 Mike Modano .30 .75
53 Sergei Fedorov .30 .75
54 Luc Robitaille .20 .50
55 Mark Messier .40 1.00
56 Sean Burke .12 .30
57 Jeff Friesen .12 .30
58 Alexander Mogilny Devils .15 .40
58U Alexander Mogilny Leafs .15 .40
59 Roman Cechmanek .15 .40
60 Martin Straka .12 .30
61 Pavol Demitra .25 .60
62 Curtis Joseph .25 .60
63 Daniel Sedin .25 .60
64 Brad Richards .20 .50
65 Simon Gagne .20 .50
66 Saku Koivu .20 .50
67 Jamie McLennan .12 .30
68 Roberto Luongo .30 .75
69 Brendan Shanahan .20 .50
70 Espen Knutsen .12 .30
71 Rob Blake .20 .50
72 Steve Sullivan .12 .30
73 Arturs Irbe .15 .40
74 Maxim Afinogenov .12 .30
75 Patrik Stefan .15 .40
76 Scott Gomez .15 .40
77 Brad Isbister .12 .30
78 Robert Lang .12 .30
79 Pierre Turgeon Blues .15 .40
79U Pierre Turgeon Stars .15 .40
80 Gary Roberts .12 .30
81 Adam Oates .20 .50
82 Evgeni Nabokov .15 .40
83 Petr Nedved .15 .40
84 Mike Dunham .15 .40
85 Chris Osgood Red Wing .20 .50
85U Chris Osgood Islander .20 .50
86 Brett Hull Stars .40 1.00
86U Brett Hull Red Wings .40 1.00
87 Peter Forsberg .40 1.00
88 Joe Thornton .30 .75
89 Ray Bourque .30 .75
90 Ed Belfour .20 .50
91 Patrik Elias .20 .50
92 Michael York .12 .30
93 Martin Havlat .15 .40
94 Jeremy Roenick Coyotes .30 .75
94U Jeremy Roenick Flyers .30 .75
95 Alexei Kovalev .15 .40
96 Al MacInnis .25 .60
97 Marco Sturm .12 .30
98 Jose Theodore .20 .50
99 Joe Nieuwendyk .15 .40
100 Darren McCarty .12 .30
101 Mark Recchi .25 .60
102 Daniel Alfredsson .20 .50
103 Miroslav Satan .15 .40
104 Sergei Samsonov .15 .40
105 Roman Turek Blues .15 .40
105U Roman Turek Flames .15 .40
106 Jarome Iginla .25 .60
107 Jeff O'Neill .15 .40
108 Tommy Salo .15 .40
109 Petr Sykora .12 .30
110 Adam Deadmarsh .12 .30
111 Oleg Tverdovsky .12 .30
112 Damian Rhodes .15 .40
113 Bob Probert .20 .50
114 Jere Lehtinen .15 .40
115 Cale Hulse .12 .30
116 Andy Sutton .12 .30
117 Wade Redden .12 .30
118 Brad Stuart .12 .30
119 Tomas Kaberle .12 .30
120 Sergei Gonchar .12 .30
121 Jean-Sebastien Aubin .15 .40
122 Adam Graves .15 .40
123 Teppo Numminen .12 .30
124 Martin Rucinsky .12 .30
125 Scott Young .12 .30
126 Pat Verbeek .15 .40
127 Michael Nylander .12 .30
128 Marc Savard .12 .30
129 Brian Rolston .15 .40
130 Sandis Ozolinsh .12 .30
131 Mike Grier .12 .30
132 Eric Belanger .12 .30
133 Patrick Lalime .15 .40
134 Steve Thomas .12 .30
135 Viktor Kozlov .12 .30
136 Manny Legace .15 .40
137 Oleg Saprykin .12 .30
138 Sami Kapanen .12 .30
139 Janne Niinimaa .12 .30
140 Scott Hartnell .12 .30
141 Tim Connolly .12 .30
142 Travis Green .12 .30
143 Matthew Barnaby .12 .30
144 Brendan Morrison .15 .40
145 Darcy Tucker .12 .30
146 Gary Suter .12 .30
147 Mattias Ohlund .12 .30
148 Patric Kjellberg .12 .30
149 Lubomir Visnovsky .12 .30
150 Claude Lapointe .12 .30
151 Martin Skoula .15 .40
152 Mike Vernon .15 .40
153 Stu Barnes .15 .40
154 Brenden Morrow .15 .40
155 Jim Dowd .12 .30
156 Shane Doan .15 .40
157 Peter Schaefer .12 .30
158 Jeff Halpern .12 .30
159 Sergei Berezin .12 .30
160 Mike Ricci .12 .30
161 Radek Dvorak .15 .40
162 Brian Savage .12 .30
163 Bryan Smolinski .12 .30
164 Derian Hatcher .12 .30
165 Shane Willis .12 .30
166 Ron Tugnutt .15 .40
167 Peter Worrell .12 .30
168 Richard Zednik .15 .40
169 Todd Marchant .12 .30
170 Andrew Brunette .12 .30
171 Derek Morris .12 .30
172 Kyle Calder .12 .30
173 Felix Potvin .30 .75
174 Bobby Holik .12 .30
175 Manny Fernandez .12 .30
176 Rick Tocchet .12 .30
177 Jonas Hoglund .12 .30
178 Todd Bertuzzi .20 .50
179 Garth Snow .15 .40
180 Cliff Ronning .12 .30
181 Martin Lapointe .12 .30
182 Jason Smith .12 .30
183 Byron Dafoe .15 .40
184 Rob Niedermayer .15 .40
185 Steve Rucchin .12 .30
186 Alexei Zhamnov .15 .40
187 Mike Richter .20 .50
188 Michal Handzus .12 .30
189 Pavel Kubina .12 .30
190 Donald Brashear .12 .30
191 Trevor Letowski .12 .30
192 Randy McKay .12 .30
193 Trevor Linden .20 .50
194 Mike Sillinger .12 .30
195 David Vyborny .12 .30
196 Dave Tanabe .12 .30
197 Scott Niedermayer .20 .50
198 Anson Carter .15 .40
199 Mike Leclerc .12 .30
200 Dave Scatchard .12 .30
201 Jan Hrdina .12 .30
202 Brian Holzinger .12 .30
203 Steve Konowalchuk .12 .30
204 Tie Domi .15 .40
205 Brent Johnson .15 .40
206 Shawn McEachern .12 .30
207 Jozef Stumpel .12 .30
208 Jamie Langenbrunner .12 .30
209 Jocelyn Thibault .15 .40
210 Donald Audette .12 .30
211 Serge Aubin .12 .30
212 Andrew Cassels .12 .30
213 Tyson Nash .12 .30
214 Colin White .12 .30
215 Tom Poti .12 .30
216 Rod Brind'Amour .20 .50
217 Fred Brathwaite .15 .40
218 Marc Denis .15 .40
219 Roman Simicek .12 .30
220 Jan Hlavac .12 .30
221 Darius Kasparaitis .12 .30
222 Vincent Damphousse .15 .40
223 Bob Boughner .12 .30
224 Yanic Perreault .12 .30
225 Chris Simon .12 .30
226 Chris Gratton .12 .30
227 Josef Vasicek .12 .30
228 Slava Kozlov .15 .40
229 Kelly Buchberger .15 .40
230 Jeff Hackett .15 .40
231 Taylor Pyatt .12 .30
232 Niklas Sundstrom .15 .40
233 Dan Cloutier .15 .40
234 Eric Daze .15 .40
235 Ryan Smyth .15 .40
236 Marty McInnis .15 .40
237 John Madden .15 .40
238 Claude Lemieux .15 .40
239 Steve Heinze .12 .30
240 Nikolai Antropov .12 .30
241 Cory Stillman .12 .30
242 Geoff Sanderson .12 .30
243 Trevor Kidd .12 .30
244 David Legwand .15 .40
245 Eric Desjardins .15 .40
246 Fredrik Modin .12 .30
247 Brett Clark .12 .30
248 Bryan Muir .12 .30
249 Ron Sutter .15 .40
250 Ken Klee .12 .30
251 Steve Halko .12 .30
252 Steve McKenna .12 .30
253 Marc Bergevin .12 .30
254 Scott Lachance .12 .30
255 Jamie Rivers .12 .30
256 Dixon Ward .12 .30
257 Gord Murphy .12 .30
258 Bret Hedican .12 .30
259 Bob Corkum .12 .30
260 Brent Sopel .12 .30
261 Todd Simpson .12 .30
262 Reid Simpson .12 .30
263 Chris McAlpine .12 .30

264 Deron Quint .12 .30
265 Josh Holden .12 .30
266 Mike Mottau .12 .30
267 Jakub Cutta .12 .30
268 Maxime Ouellet .20 .50
269 Peter Smrek RC .12 .30
270 Daniel Corso .12 .30
271 Rostislav Klesla .12 .30
272 Mika Noronen .12 .30
273 Kris Beech .12 .30
274 Sheldon Keefe .12 .30
275 Miikka Kiprusoff .20 .50
276 Mathieu Garon .15 .40
277 Jason Chimera RC .12 .30
278 Mark Bell .12 .30
279 Chris Nielsen .12 .30
280 Eric Chouinard .12 .30
281 Pierre Dagenais .12 .30
282 Branislav Mezei .12 .30
283 Milan Kraft .12 .30
284 Tomas Kloucek .12 .30
285 Petr Schastlivy .12 .30
286 Lee Goren .12 .30
287 Daniel Tkaczuk .12 .30
288 Andreas Lilja .12 .30
289 Tomas Divisek RC .15 .40
290 Alexei Ponikarovsky .12 .30
291 Mikael Samuelsson RC .15 .40
292 Petr Svoboda .15 .40
293 Mike Comrie .15 .40
294 Johan Hedberg .15 .40
295 Tyler Moss .12 .30
296 Martin Spanhel RC .12 .30
297 Mike Brown .15 .40
298 Derek Gustafson .12 .30
299 Matt Pettinger .12 .30
300 Mike Commodore .12 .30
301 Antti-Jussi Niemi .12 .30
302 Brad Tapper .12 .30
303 Rick Berry .12 .30
304 Andrew Raycroft .15 .40
305 Bryan Allen .12 .30
306 Ivan Novoseltsev .12 .30
307 Jason Williams .12 .30
308 Gregg Naumenko .12 .30
309 Jiri Bicek .12 .30
310 Mathieu Darche RC .20 .50
311 Brian Campbell .12 .30
312 Jeff Farkas .12 .30
313 Rico Fata .12 .30
314 Kristian Kudroc .12 .30
315 Roman Cechmanek AS .15 .40
316 Nicklas Lidstrom AS .20 .50
317 Ray Bourque AS .30 .75
318 Joe Sakic AS .40 1.00
319 Patrick Elias AS .20 .50
320 Jaromir Jagr AS .60 1.50
321 J.Madden/R.McKay .15 .40
322 Mark Recchi .25 .60
323 Vincent Damphousse .15 .40
324 Patrick Roy .50 1.25
325 Jaromir Jagr .60 1.50
326 Mario Lemieux .75 2.00
327 Mario Lemieux .75 2.00
328 Mario Lemieux .75 2.00
329 Mario Lemieux .75 2.00
330 Mario Lemieux .75 2.00
331 Ilya Kovalchuk RC 4.00 10.00
332 Dan Blackburn RC 1.00 2.50
333 Vaclav Nedorost RC .75 2.00
334 Krys Kolanos RC .75 2.00
335 Kristian Huselius RC 1.25 3.00
336 Martin Erat RC 1.00 2.50
337 Timo Parssinen RC 1.00 2.50
338 Scott Nichol RC .75 2.00
339 Nick Schultz RC .75 2.00
340 Jukka Hentunen RC .75 2.00
341 Pascal Dupuis RC 1.25 3.00
342 Radek Martinek RC .75 2.00
343 Scott Clemmensen RC .75 2.00
344 Jeff Jillson RC .75 2.00
345 Brian Sutherby RC .75 2.00
346 Nikita Alexeev RC .75 2.00
347 Niklas Hagman RC 1.00 2.50
348 Erik Cole RC 1.50 4.00
349 Pavel Datsyuk RC 15.00 40.00
350 Ilja Bryzgalov RC 2.00 5.00
351 Chris Neil RC 1.00 2.50
352 Mark Rycroft RC 1.00 2.50
353 Kamil Piros RC .75 2.00
354 Niko Kapanen RC 1.25 3.00
355 Jiri Dopita RC .75 2.00
356 Andreas Salomonsson RC .75 2.00
357 Ivan Ciernik RC .75 2.00
358 Jaroslav Bednar RC .75 2.00
359 Ty Conklin RC 1.25 3.00
360 Raffi Torres RC 1.25 3.00

2001-02 O-Pee-Chee Heritage Parallel

*OPC HERITAGE: 1X TO 2.5X OPC
55 Mark Messier 1.00 2.50

2001-02 O-Pee-Chee Heritage Parallel Limited

*LIMITED/50: 15X TO 40X BASIC OPC
55 Mark Messier 15.00 40.00

2001-02 O-Pee-Chee Premier Parallel

*OPC PREMIER: 1.5X TO 4X BASIC OPC
55 Mark Messier 1.50 4.00

2001-02 O-Pee-Chee Jumbos

1 Mario Lemieux 2.00 5.00
2 Steve Yzerman 2.00 5.00
3 Martin Brodeur .75 2.00
4 Paul Kariya 1.00 2.50
5 Patrick Roy 2.00 5.00
6 Curtis Joseph .75 2.00
7 Martin Havlat .75 2.00
8 Mike Comrie .40 1.00

2002-03 O-Pee-Chee

*1-330 VETERANS: .4X TO 1X TOPPS
*331-340 ROOKIES: .5X TO 1.2X TOPPS RC
19 Ron Francis .25 .60
242 Mark Messier .40 1.00
315 Ron Francis .25 .60

2002-03 O-Pee-Chee Jumbos

COMPLETE SET (25) 30.00 60.00
1 Joe Thornton 2.00 5.00
2 Jarome Iginla 1.25 3.00
3 Roman Turek .75 2.00
4 Ron Francis .75 2.00
5 Patrick Roy 4.00 10.00
6 Joe Sakic 3.00 8.00
7 Steve Yzerman 4.00 10.00
8 Brendan Shanahan 2.00 5.00
9 Mike Comrie 1.25 3.00
10 Ryan Smyth .75 2.00
11 Paul Kariya 2.00 5.00
12 Jose Theodore 1.25 3.00
13 Saku Koivu 1.25 3.00
14 Martin Brodeur 2.00 5.00
15 Mike Peca .40 1.00
16 Daniel Alfredsson .40 1.00
17 Martin Havlat 1.25 3.00
18 Sean Burke .75 2.00
19 Mario Lemieux 4.00 10.00
20 Owen Nolan .75 2.00
21 Chris Pronger .75 2.00
22 Mats Sundin 1.25 3.00
23 Curtis Joseph 1.25 3.00
24 Markus Naslund .75 2.00
25 Todd Bertuzzi .75 2.00

2002-03 O-Pee-Chee Premier Blue

*1-330 VETS/500: 4X TO 10X OPC
*331-340 ROOKIE/500: 2X TO 5X OPC

2002-03 O-Pee-Chee Premier Red

*1-330 VETS/100: 6X TO 15X OPC
*331-340 ROOKIE/100: 4X TO 10X OPC
242 Mark Messier 6.00 15.00

2002-03 O-Pee-Chee Factory Set

COMPLETE FACTORY SET 30.00 60.00
*VETS: .6X TO 1.5X BASIC OPC
*ROOKIES: .8X TO 2X BASIC OPC
242 Mark Messier .60 1.50

2002-03 O-Pee-Chee Hometown Heroes

COMPLETE SET (20) 6.00 15.00
*FACT.SET: .4X TO 1X BASIC INSERTS
HHC1 Jarome Iginla .40 1.00
HHC2 Ed Jovanovski .40 1.00
HHC3 Ryan Smyth .40 1.00
HHC4 Mike York .40 1.00
HHC5 Mats Sundin .50 1.25
HHC6 Todd Bertuzzi .40 1.00
HHC7 Markus Naslund .40 1.00
HHC8 Saku Koivu .40 1.00
HHC9 Jose Theodore .50 1.25
HHC10 Daniel Alfredsson .40 1.00
HHC11 Patrick Lalime .40 1.00
HHC12 Roman Turek .40 1.00
HHC13 Mike Comrie .40 1.00
HHC14 Tommy Salo .40 1.00
HHC15 Anson Carter .40 1.00
HHC16 Doug Gilmour .40 1.00
HHC17 Yanic Perreault .40 1.00
HHC18 Radek Bonk .40 1.00
HHC19 Darcy Tucker .40 1.00
HHC20 Curtis Joseph .60 1.50

2003-04 O-Pee-Chee

*O-PEE-CHEE: .5X TO 1.2X TOPPS
250 Ron Francis .25 .60
331 Patrice Bergeron RC 12.00 30.00

2003-04 O-Pee-Chee Blue

*VETS/500: 3X TO 8X BASIC TOPPS
*309-317 ROOKIES/500: 1.5X TO 4X TOPPS RC
*331-340 ROOKIES/500: .8X TO 2X TOPPS RC

2003-04 O-Pee-Chee Gold

*VETS/50: 10X TO 25X BASIC CARDS
*309-317 ROOKIES/50: 6X TO 12X BASIC RC
*331-340 ROOKIES/50: 2.5X TO 6X BASIC RC

2003-04 O-Pee-Chee Red

*VETS/100: 6X TO 15X BASIC CARDS
*309-317 ROOKIES/100: 3X TO 8X BASIC RC
*331-340 ROOKIES/100: 1.5X TO 4X BASIC RC

2006-07 O-Pee-Chee

1 Chris Pronger .20 .50
2 Samuel Pahlsson .12 .30
3 Andy McDonald .15 .40
4 Todd Fedoruk .12 .30
5 Teemu Selanne .40 1.00
6 Chris Kunitz .20 .50
7 Scott Niedermayer .20 .50
8 Corey Perry .30 .75
9 Sean O'Donnell .12 .30
10 Ryan Getzlaf .20 .50
11 Francois Beauchemin .12 .30
12 Dustin Penner .15 .40
13 Rob Niedermayer .15 .40
14 Todd Marchant .12 .30
15 Ilya Bryzgalov .20 .50
16 Stanislav Chistov .12 .30
17 Jean-Sebastien Giguere .20 .50
18 Andy Sutton .12 .30
19 Steve Rucchin .12 .30
20 Greg de Vries .12 .30
21 Vitaly Vishnevski .12 .30
22 Ilya Kovalchuk .20 .50
23 Scott Mellanby .12 .30
24 Jim Slater .12 .30
25 Kari Lehtonen .15 .40
26 Johan Hedberg .15 .40
27 Niclas Havelid .12 .30
28 Marian Hossa .20 .50
29 Bobby Holik .12 .30
30 Garnet Exelby .12 .30
31 Steve McCarthy .12 .30
32 Niko Kapanen .12 .30
33 Slava Kozlov .12 .30
34 P.J. Axelsson .12 .30
35 Hannu Toivonen .15 .40
36 Patrice Bergeron .25 .60
37 Tim Thomas .20 .50
38 Marc Savard .12 .30
39 Nathan Dempsey .12 .30
40 Glen Murray .15 .40
41 Brad Stuart .12 .30
42 Shean Donovan .12 .30
43 Marco Sturm .12 .30
44 Mark Mowers .12 .30
45 Paul Mara .12 .30
46 Andrew Alberts .12 .30
47 Brad Boyes .12 .30
48 Wayne Primeau .12 .30
49 Milan Jurcina .12 .30
50 Jason York .12 .30
51 Zdeno Chara .20 .50
52 Jiri Novotny .12 .30
53 Derek Roy .12 .30
54 Teppo Numminen .12 .30
55 Jason Pominville .12 .30
56 Henrik Tallinder .12 .30
57 Adam Mair .12 .30
58 Daniel Briere .20 .50
59 Chris Drury .15 .40
60 Ryan Miller .20 .50
61 Ales Kotalik .12 .30
62 Thomas Vanek .15 .40
63 Brian Campbell .15 .40
64 Paul Gaustad .12 .30
65 Jaroslav Spacek .12 .30
66 Jochen Hecht .12 .30
67 Maxim Afinogenov .12 .30
68 Martin Biron .15 .40
69 Robyn Regehr .12 .30
70 Dion Phaneuf .15 .40
71 Miikka Kiprusoff .20 .50
72 Jamie Lundmark .12 .30
73 Roman Hamrlik .12 .30
74 Kristian Huselius .12 .30
75 Darren McCarty .12 .30
76 Stephane Yelle .12 .30
77 Marcus Nilson .12 .30
78 Daymond Langkow .12 .30
79 Jamie McLennan .15 .40
80 Tony Amonte .15 .40
81 Chuck Kobasew .12 .30
82 Jarome Iginla .25 .60
83 Alex Tanguay .12 .30
84 Andrew Ference .12 .30
85 Matthew Lombardi .12 .30
86 Jeff Friesen .12 .30
87 Glen Wesley .12 .30
88 Cory Stillman .12 .30
89 John Grahame .12 .30
90 Erik Cole .12 .30
91 Chad Larose .12 .30
92 Andrew Ladd .12 .30
93 Craig Adams .12 .30
94 Eric Staal .25 .60
95 Rod Brind'Amour .20 .50
96 Mike Commodore .12 .30
97 Ray Whitney .15 .40
98 Justin Williams .15 .40
99 Kevyn Adams .12 .30
100 Cam Ward .20 .50
101 Eric Belanger .12 .30
102 Scott Walker .12 .30
103 Bret Hedican .12 .30
104 Tim Gleason .12 .30
105 Adrian Aucoin .12 .30
106 Nikolai Khabibulin .20 .50
107 Michal Handzus .15 .40
108 Tuomo Ruutu .20 .50
109 Martin Lapointe .12 .30
110 Jim Vandermeer .12 .30
111 Martin Havlat .12 .30
112 Bryan Smolinski .12 .30
113 Michael Holmqvist .12 .30
114 Rene Bourque .12 .30
115 Brandon Bochenski .12 .30
116 Patrick Sharp .20 .50
117 Brent Seabrook .12 .30
118 Duncan Keith .15 .40
119 Jeffrey Hamilton .12 .30
120 Radim Vrbata .12 .30
121 Joe Sakic .40 1.00
122 Petr Budaj .12 .30
123 Tyler Arnason .12 .30
124 Mark Rycroft .12 .30
125 John-Michael Liles .12 .30
126 Milan Hejduk .15 .40
127 Andrew Brunette .12 .30
128 Ian Laperriere .12 .30
129 Antti Laaksonen .12 .30
130 Marek Svatos .12 .30
131 Wojtek Wolski .12 .30
132 Patrice Brisebois .12 .30
133 Pierre Turgeon .15 .40
134 Brett McLean .12 .30
135 Karlis Skrastins .12 .30
136 Brad Richardson .12 .30
137 Brett Clark .12 .30
138 Jose Theodore .20 .50
139 Rick Nash .20 .50
140 Nikolai Zherdev .12 .30
141 Rostislav Klesla .12 .30
142 David Vyborny .12 .30
143 Anders Eriksson .12 .30
144 Adam Foote .12 .30
145 Jody Shelley .12 .30
146 Duvie Westcott .12 .30
147 Gilbert Brule .15 .40
148 Jason Chimera .12 .30
149 Pascal Leclaire .15 .40
150 Manny Malhotra .12 .30
151 Ron Hainsey .12 .30
152 Anson Carter .15 .40
153 Fredrik Modin .12 .30
154 Dan Fritsche .12 .30
155 Sergei Fedorov .30 .75
156 Marty Turco .20 .50
157 Jussi Jokinen .12 .30
158 Steve Ott .12 .30
159 Jaroslav Modry .12 .30
160 Patrik Stefan .12 .30
161 Matthew Barnaby .12 .30
162 Jeff Halpern .12 .30
163 Eric Lindros .30 .75
164 Sergei Zubov .15 .40
165 Darryl Sydor .12 .30
166 Brenden Morrow .15 .40
167 Antti Miettinen .12 .30
168 Jere Lehtinen .12 .30
169 Philippe Boucher .12 .30
170 Mike Ribeiro .12 .30
171 Stu Barnes .12 .30
172 Mike Modano .30 .75
173 Dominik Hasek .30 .75
174 Tomas Holmstrom .15 .40
175 Johan Franzen .15 .40
176 Robert Lang .12 .30
177 Mathieu Schneider .12 .30
178 Nicklas Lidstrom .20 .50
179 Chris Osgood .20 .50
180 Jason Williams .12 .30
181 Mikael Samuelsson .12 .30
182 Chris Chelios .20 .50
183 Pavel Datsyuk .30 .75
184 Dan Cleary .15 .40
185 Kirk Maltby .12 .30
186 Kris Draper .12 .30
187 Andreas Lilja .12 .30
188 Brett Lebda .12 .30
189 Jiri Hudler .20 .50
190 Henrik Zetterberg .25 .60
191 Ales Hemsky .15 .40
192 Fernando Pisani .12 .30
193 Joffrey Lupul .12 .30
194 Dwayne Roloson .15 .40
195 Matt Greene .12 .30
196 Jason Smith .12 .30
197 Ethan Moreau .12 .30
198 Jarret Stoll .15 .40
199 Jussi Markkanen .12 .30
200 Brad Winchester .12 .30
201 Marc-Andre Bergeron .12 .30
202 Raffi Torres .12 .30
203 Petr Sykora .15 .40
204 Shawn Horcoff .12 .30
205 Steve Staios .12 .30
206 Ryan Smyth .15 .40
207 Jay Bouwmeester .12 .30
208 Ed Belfour .20 .50
209 Ruslan Salei .12 .30
210 Stephen Weiss .12 .30
211 Rostislav Olesz .12 .30
212 Mike Van Ryn .12 .30
213 Jozef Stumpel .12 .30
214 Nathan Horton .20 .50
215 Alexander Auld .12 .30
216 Juraj Kolnik .12 .30
217 Martin Gelinas .12 .30
218 Joe Nieuwendyk .15 .40
219 Gary Roberts .12 .30
220 Todd Bertuzzi .20 .50
221 Chris Gratton .12 .30
222 Bryan Allen .12 .30
223 Olli Jokinen .20 .50
224 Alexander Frolov .15 .40
225 Mathieu Garon .15 .40
226 Dustin Brown .20 .50
227 Lubomir Visnovsky .12 .30
228 Sean Avery .12 .30
229 Brent Sopel .12 .30
230 Craig Conroy .12 .30
231 Aaron Miller .12 .30
232 Scott Thornton .12 .30
233 Mattias Norstrom .12 .30
234 Dan Cloutier .15 .40
235 Mike Cammalleri .12 .30
236 Oleg Tverdovsky .12 .30
237 Derek Armstrong .12 .30
238 Tom Kostopoulos .12 .30
239 Rob Blake .20 .50
240 Marian Gaborik .20 .50
241 Derek Boogaard .12 .30
242 Brian Rolston .15 .40
243 Keith Carney .12 .30
244 Mark Parrish .12 .30
245 Wes Walz .12 .30
246 Todd White .12 .30
247 Pierre-Marc Bouchard .20 .50
248 Nick Schultz .12 .30
249 Kurtis Foster .12 .30
250 Pascal Dupuis .12 .30
251 Mikko Koivu .15 .40
252 Manny Fernandez .12 .30
253 Wyatt Smith .12 .30
254 Brent Burns .20 .50
255 Kim Johnsson .12 .30
256 Pavol Demitra .25 .60
257 Michael Ryder .12 .30
258 David Aebischer .15 .40
259 Andrei Markov .20 .50
260 Alexander Perezhogin .12 .30
261 Sheldon Souray .12 .30
262 Cristobal Huet .15 .40
263 Chris Higgins .12 .30
264 Steve Begin .12 .30
265 Radek Bonk .12 .30
266 Janne Niinimaa .12 .30
267 Mike Komisarek .12 .30
268 Tomas Plekanec .12 .30
269 Sergei Samsonov .15 .40
270 Alexei Kovalev .12 .30
271 Craig Rivet .12 .30
272 Mathieu Dandenault .12 .30
273 Mike Johnson .12 .30
274 Saku Koivu .20 .50
275 Tomas Vokoun .15 .40
276 Scott Hartnell .12 .30
277 Marek Zidlicky .12 .30
278 Josef Vasicek .12 .30
279 Jordin Tootoo .20 .50
280 Ryan Suter .12 .30
281 Martin Erat .15 .40
282 David Legwand .12 .30
283 Kimmo Timonen .12 .30
284 Chris Mason .12 .30
285 Steve Sullivan .12 .30
286 Jason Arnott .15 .40
287 Dan Hamhuis .15 .40
288 J.P. Dumont .12 .30
289 Darcy Hordichuk .12 .30
290 Paul Kariya .20 .50
291 Martin Brodeur .50 1.25
292 Brian Gionta .12 .30
293 Paul Martin .12 .30
294 John Madden .12 .30
295 Brian Rafalski .15 .40
296 Colin White .12 .30
297 Zach Parise .20 .50
298 Jay Pandolfo .12 .30
299 Jamie Langenbrunner .12 .30
300 Scott Gomez .15 .40
301 Sergei Brylin .12 .30
302 Scott Clemmensen .12 .30
303 Jim Fahey .12 .30
304 Erik Rasmussen .12 .30
305 Brad Lukowich .12 .30
306 Patrik Elias .20 .50
307 Rick DiPietro .15 .40
308 Jason Blake .12 .30
309 Tom Poti .12 .30
310 Trent Hunter .12 .30
311 Brendan Witt .12 .30
312 Chris Simon .12 .30
313 Arron Asham .12 .30
314 Alexei Yashin .15 .40
315 Mike Sillinger .12 .30
316 Alexei Zhitnik .12 .30
317 Jeff Tambellini .12 .30
318 Mike Dunham .15 .40
319 Mike York .12 .30
320 Shawn Bates .12 .30
321 Viktor Kozlov .12 .30
322 Miroslav Satan .12 .30
323 Henrik Lundqvist .50 1.25
324 Fedor Tyutin .12 .30
325 Michal Rozsival .12 .30
326 Michael Nylander .12 .30
327 Sandis Ozolinsh .12 .30
328 Matt Cullen .12 .30
329 Brendan Shanahan .20 .50
330 Darius Kasparaitis .15 .40
331 Kevin Weekes .15 .40
332 Petr Prucha .15 .40
333 Martin Straka .12 .30
334 Aaron Ward .12 .30
335 Marek Malik .12 .30
336 Blair Betts .12 .30
337 Jason Ward .12 .30
338 Jaromir Jagr .60 1.50
339 Dany Heatley .15 .40
340 Wade Redden .12 .30
341 Peter Schaefer .12 .30
342 Mike Fisher .12 .30
343 Ray Emery .15 .40
344 Tom Preissing .12 .30
345 Patrick Eaves .12 .30
346 Daniel Alfredsson .20 .50
347 Chris Phillips .12 .30
348 Andrej Meszaros .12 .30
349 Martin Gerber .15 .40
350 Joe Corvo .12 .30
351 Antoine Vermette .15 .40
352 Chris Neil .12 .30
353 Anton Volchenkov .12 .30
354 Chris Kelly .15 .40
355 Jason Spezza .20 .50
356 Simon Gagne .20 .50
357 Antero Niittymaki .15 .40
358 Joni Pitkanen .12 .30
359 Jeff Carter .15 .40
360 Randy Jones .12 .30
361 R.J. Umberger .12 .30
362 Mike Knuble .12 .30
363 Derian Hatcher .12 .30
364 Sami Kapanen .12 .30
365 Frederick Meyer .12 .30
366 Mike Richards .15 .40
367 Robert Esche .15 .40
368 Randy Robitaille .12 .30
369 Stefan Ruzicka .12 .30
370 Geoff Sanderson .12 .30
371 Kyle Calder .12 .30
372 Peter Forsberg .40 1.00
373 Curtis Joseph .25 .60
374 Ladislav Nagy .12 .30
375 Nick Boynton .12 .30
376 Dave Scatchard .12 .30
377 Derek Morris .12 .30
378 Mike Comrie .15 .40
379 Ed Jovanovski .12 .30
380 Georges Laraque .12 .30
381 Oleg Saprykin .12 .30
382 Keith Ballard .12 .30
383 Steven Reinprecht .12 .30
384 Jeremy Roenick .30 .75
385 Zbynek Michalek .12 .30
386 Owen Nolan .20 .50
387 Fredrik Sjostrom .12 .30
388 David Leneveu .15 .40
389 Shane Doan .15 .40
390 Marc-Andre Fleury .40 1.00
391 Sergei Gonchar .12 .30
392 Dominic Moore .12 .30
393 Ryan Whitney .15 .40
394 Nils Ekman .12 .30
395 Brooks Orpik .12 .30
396 Mark Eaton .12 .30
397 Jocelyn Thibault .15 .40
398 Andre Roy .12 .30
399 Colby Armstrong .12 .30
400 Ryan Malone .12 .30
401 Jarkko Ruutu .12 .30
402 Mark Recchi .25 .60
403 John LeClair .20 .50
404 Josef Melichar .12 .30
405 Sidney Crosby .75 2.00
406 Jonathan Cheechoo .15 .40
407 Steve Bernier .12 .30
408 Evgeni Nabokov .15 .40
409 Marcel Goc .12 .30
410 Christian Ehrhoff .12 .30
411 Mark Bell .12 .30
412 Mike Grier .12 .30
413 Patrick Marleau .20 .50
414 Scott Hannan .12 .30
415 Mark Smith .12 .30
416 Milan Michalek .12 .30
417 Ville Nieminen .12 .30
418 Kyle McLaren .12 .30
419 Vesa Toskala .15 .40
420 Josh Gorges .12 .30
421 Joe Thornton .30 .75
422 Keith Tkachuk .20 .50
423 Barret Jackman .12 .30
424 Lee Stempniak .12 .30
425 Jay McClement .12 .30
426 Dallas Drake .12 .30
427 Curtis Sanford .15 .40
428 Petr Cajanek .12 .30
429 Eric Brewer .12 .30
430 Bill Guerin .20 .50
431 Jamal Mayers .12 .30
432 Manny Legace .15 .40
433 Christian Backman .12 .30
434 Martin Rucinsky .15 .40
435 Dennis Wideman .12 .30
436 Jay McKee .12 .30
437 Doug Weight .20 .50
438 Brad Richards .20 .50
439 Ruslan Fedotenko .12 .30
440 Johan Holmqvist .20 .50
441 Filip Kuba .12 .30
442 Dimitry Afanasenkov .12 .30
443 Ryan Craig .12 .30
444 Dan Boyle .12 .30
445 Paul Ranger .12 .30
446 Marc Denis .15 .40
447 Vaclav Prospal .12 .30
448 Tim Taylor .12 .30
449 Martin St. Louis .20 .50
450 Cory Sarich .12 .30
451 Nikita Alexeev .12 .30
452 Nolan Pratt .12 .30
453 Vincent Lecavalier .20 .50
454 Mats Sundin .20 .50
455 Darcy Tucker .15 .40
456 Kyle Wellwood .15 .40
457 Nik Antropov .15 .40
458 Tomas Kaberle .12 .30
459 Hal Gill .12 .30
460 Jean-Sebastien Aubin .15 .40
461 Matt Stajan .12 .30
462 Alexander Steen .12 .30
463 Bryan McCabe .12 .30
464 Jeff O'Neill .12 .30
465 Wade Belak .12 .30
466 Michael Peca .15 .40
467 Carlo Colaiacovo .12 .30
468 Chad Kilger .12 .30
469 Alexei Ponikarovsky .12 .30
470 Andrew Raycroft .15 .40
471 Roberto Luongo .30 .75
472 Ryan Kesler .20 .50
473 Jan Bulis .12 .30
474 Matt Cooke .12 .30
475 Sami Salo .12 .30
476 Brendan Morrison .12 .30
477 Henrik Sedin .25 .60
478 Daniel Sedin .25 .60
479 Mattias Ohlund .12 .30
480 Willie Mitchell .12 .30
481 Dany Sabourin .12 .30
482 Lukas Krajicek .12 .30
483 Marc Chouinard .12 .30
484 Trevor Linden .20 .50
485 Taylor Pyatt .12 .30
486 Markus Naslund .20 .50
487 Olaf Kolzig .20 .50
488 Donald Brashear .12 .30
489 Chris Clark .12 .30
490 Dainius Zubrus .12 .30
491 Matt Pettinger .15 .40
492 Jamie Heward .12 .30
493 Bryan Muir .12 .30
494 Steve Eminger .12 .30
495 Brian Pothier .12 .30
496 Brian Sutherby .12 .30
497 Richard Zednik .12 .30
498 Brent Johnson .15 .40
499 Matt Bradley .12 .30
500 Alexander Ovechkin .75 2.00
501 Dustin Byfuglien RC 2.00 5.00
502 Yan Stastny RC .75 2.00
503 Mark Stuart RC .75 2.00
504 Eric Fehr RC 1.25 3.00
505 Bill Thomas RC .75 2.00
506 Joel Perrault RC .75 2.00
507 Frank Doyle RC 1.00 2.50
508 Carsen Germyn RC .75 2.00
509 Ryan Potulny RC .75 2.00
510 David Printz RC .75 2.00
511 Rob Collins RC .75 2.00
512 Steve Regier RC .75 2.00
513 Matt Koalska RC .75 2.00
514 Ryan Caldwell RC .75 2.00
515 Masi Marjamaki RC .75 2.00
516 Cole Jarrett RC .75 2.00
517 Konstantin Pushkarev RC 1.00 2.50
518 Ben Ondrus RC .75 2.00
519 Brendan Bell RC .75 2.00
520 Ian White RC 1.00 2.50
521 Jeremy Williams RC .75 2.00
522 Marc-Antoine Pouliot RC .75 2.00
523 Noah Welch RC .75 2.00
524 Michel Ouellet RC .75 2.00
525 Shea Weber RC 2.00 5.00
526 Jarkko Immonen RC 1.00 2.50
527 David Liffiton RC .75 2.00
528 Tomas Kopecky RC 1.00 2.50
529 Billy Thompson RC .75 2.00
530 Filip Novak RC .75 2.00
531 Matt Carle RC .75 2.00
532 Dan Jancevski RC .75 2.00
533 Erik Reitz RC .75 2.00
534 Miroslav Kopriva RC .75 2.00
535 Jonas Johansson RC .75 2.00
536 Shane O'Brien RC .75 2.00
537 Ryan Shannon RC .75 2.00
538 Patrick O'Sullivan RC 1.25 3.00
539 Anze Kopitar RC 4.00 10.00
540 John Oduya RC 1.25 3.00
541 Travis Zajac RC 1.50 4.00
542 Fredrik Norrena RC .75 2.00
543 Phil Kessel RC 2.50 6.00
544 Guillaume Latendresse RC 1.25 3.00
545 Nigel Dawes RC .75 2.00
546 Jordan Staal RC 3.00 8.00
547 Kristopher Letang RC 3.00 8.00
548 Paul Stastny RC 2.00 5.00
549 Niklas Backstrom RC 1.50 4.00
550 D.J. King RC .75 2.00
551 Marc-Edouard Vlasic RC 1.25 3.00
552 Patrick Thoresen RC .75 2.00
553 Ladislav Smid RC .75 2.00
554 Loui Eriksson RC 1.50 4.00
555 Patrick Fischer RC .75 2.00
556 Mikko Lehtonen RC 1.00 2.50
557 Roman Polak RC 1.00 2.50
558 Luc Bourdon RC 1.25 3.00
559 Keith Yandle RC 2.00 5.00
560 Enver Lisin RC .75 2.00
561 Adam Burish RC 1.25 3.00
562 Alexei Kaigorodov RC .75 2.00
563 Alex Brooks RC .75 2.00
564 Evgeni Malkin RC 5.00 12.00
565 Nate Thompson RC .75 2.00
566 Janis Sprukts RC .75 2.00
567 Alexander Radulov RC 1.50 4.00
568 Alexei Mikhnov RC .75 2.00
569 Dave Bolland RC 1.25 3.00
570 Michael Blunden RC .75 2.00
571 Lars Jonsson RC .75 2.00
572 Triston Grant RC .75 2.00
573 Matt Lashoff RC .75 2.00
574 Dustin Boyd RC .75 2.00
575 Brandon Prust RC .75 2.00
576 Alexander Edler RC 1.25 3.00
577 Jan Hejda RC .75 2.00
578 Drew Stafford RC 1.25 3.00
579 Kelly Guard RC 1.00 2.50
580 Patrick Coulombe RC .75 2.00
581 Nathan McIver RC .75 2.00
582 Mike Brown RC .75 2.00
583 Jean-Francois Racine RC 1.00 2.50
584 Adam Dennis RC .75 2.00
585 Drew Larman RC .75 2.00
586 Mike Card RC .75 2.00
587 Michael Funk RC .75 2.00
588 Stefan Liv RC .75 2.00
589 David Booth RC 1.00 2.50
590 Blair Jones RC .75 2.00
591 Jussi Timonen RC 1.00 2.50
592 David McKee RC .75 2.00
593 Michael Ryan RC .75 2.00
594 Peter Harrold RC .75 2.00
595 Joe Pavelski RC 4.00 10.00
596 Karl Goehring RC 1.00 2.50
597 Benoit Pouliot RC 1.00 2.50
598 Jesse Schultz RC .75 2.00
599 Jeff Drouin-Deslauriers RC .75 2.00
600 Martin Houle RC 1.00 2.50
601 Joe Thornton .30 .75
602 Jonathan Cheechoo .15 .40
603 Wade Redden .12 .30
604 Michal Rozsival .12 .30
605 Ilya Kovalchuk .20 .50
606 Marian Hossa .20 .50
607 Sean Avery .12 .30
608 Martin Brodeur .50 1.25
609 Miikka Kiprusoff .20 .50
610 Cristobal Huet .15 .40
611 Eric Staal .25 .60
612 Fernando Pisani .12 .30
613 Dwayne Roloson .15 .40
614 Ilya Bryzgalov .20 .50
615 Alexander Ovechkin .75 2.00
616 P.Eaves/A.Kaigorodov .75 2.00
617 K.Ballard/K.Yandle .75 2.00
618 D.Phaneuf/L.Bourdon .75 2.00
619 J.Jokinen/L.Eriksson .75 2.00
620 M.Svatos/P.Stastny .75 2.00
621 S.Crosby/E.Malkin 2.00 5.00
622 C.Higgins/G.Latendresse .75 2.00
623 B.Boyes/P.Kessel .75 2.00
624 A.Ovechkin/E.Malkin 1.25 3.00
625 P.Prucha/N.Dawes .75 2.00
626 A.Meszaros/L.Smid .75 2.00
627 J.Carter/P.O'Sullivan .75 2.00
628 Z.Parise/T.Zajac .75 2.00
629 R.Whitney/N.Welch .75 2.00
630 R.Suter/C.Weber .75 2.00
631 J.Gorges/M.Carle .75 2.00
632 R.Getzlaf/R.Shannon 1.00 2.50
633 M.Richards/R.Potulny .75 2.00
634 P.LeClaire/F.Norrena .75 2.00
635 B.Winchester/M.Pouliot .75 2.00
636 M.Koivu/A.Kopitar 1.00 2.50
637 A.Alberts/M.Stuart .75 2.00
638 T.Vanek/D.Stafford 1.00 2.50
639 J.Franzen/T.Kopecky .75 2.00
640 C.Colaiacovo/I.White .75 2.00
641 F.Beauchemin/S.O'Brien .75 2.00
642 S.Bernier/E.Fehr .75 2.00
643 C.Perry/J.Staal 1.25 3.00
644 A.Steen/P.Thoresen .75 2.00
645 B.Seabrook/K.Letang .75 2.00
646 Teemu Selanne .40 1.00
647 Joe Sakic .40 1.00
648 Mike Modano .30 .75
649 Eric Lindros .30 .75
650 Dominik Hasek .30 .75
651 Nicklas Lidstrom .20 .50
652 Chris Chelios .20 .50
653 Joe Nieuwendyk .15 .40
654 Ed Belfour .20 .50
655 Rob Blake .20 .50
656 Saku Koivu .20 .50
657 Paul Kariya .20 .50
658 Martin Brodeur .50 1.25
659 Jaromir Jagr .60 1.50
660 Brendan Shanahan .20 .50
661 Daniel Alfredsson .20 .50
662 Peter Forsberg .40 1.00
663 Jeremy Roenick .30 .75
664 Curtis Joseph .25 .60
665 Sidney Crosby .75 2.00
666 Mark Recchi .25 .60
667 Doug Weight .20 .50
668 Keith Tkachuk .20 .50
669 Mats Sundin .20 .50
670 Markus Naslund .20 .50
671 Teemu Selanne .40 1.00
672 Ilya Kovalchuk .20 .50
673 Patrice Bergeron .25 .60
674 Ryan Miller .20 .50
675 Miikka Kiprusoff .20 .50

676 Eric Staal .25 .60
677 Nikolai Khabibulin .20 .50
678 Rick Nash .20 .50
679 Joe Sakic .40 1.00
680 Mike Modano .30 .75
681 Nicklas Lidstrom .20 .50
682 Ryan Smyth .15 .40
683 Olli Jokinen .20 .50
684 Rob Blake .20 .50
685 Marian Gaborik .20 .50
686 Saku Koivu .20 .50
687 Martin Brodeur .50 1.25
688 Paul Kariya .20 .50
689 Miroslav Satan .15 .40
690 Jaromir Jagr .60 1.50
691 Daniel Alfredsson .20 .50
692 Peter Forsberg .40 1.00
693 Shane Doan .15 .40
694 Sidney Crosby .75 2.00
695 Patrick Marleau .20 .50
696 Keith Tkachuk .20 .50
697 Vincent Lecavalier .20 .50
698 Mats Sundin .20 .50
699 Markus Naslund .20 .50
700 Alexander Ovechkin .75 2.00

2006-07 O-Pee-Chee Rainbow

*RAINBOW: 10X to 25X BASE HI
5 Teemu Selanne 12.00 30.00
121 Joe Sakic 25.00 60.00
173 Dominik Hasek 15.00 40.00
291 Martin Brodeur 25.00 60.00
405 Sidney Crosby 25.00 60.00
500 Alexander Ovechkin 30.00 80.00
539 Anze Kopitar 40.00 100.00
544 Guillaume Latendresse 10.00 25.00
546 Jordan Staal 12.00 30.00
548 Paul Stastny 15.00 40.00
564 Evgeni Malkin 40.00 100.00
567 Alexander Radulov 12.00 30.00
608 Martin Brodeur 25.00 60.00
615 Alexander Ovechkin 40.00 100.00
621 S.Crosby/E.Malkin 50.00 100.00
624 A.Ovechkin/E.Malkin 15.00 40.00
643 C.Perry/J.Staal 10.00 25.00
647 Joe Sakic 15.00 40.00
650 Dominik Hasek 10.00 25.00
658 Martin Brodeur 12.00 30.00
665 Sidney Crosby 25.00 60.00
679 Joe Sakic 15.00 40.00
687 Martin Brodeur 12.00 30.00
694 Sidney Crosby 25.00 60.00
700 Alexander Ovechkin 20.00 50.00

2006-07 O-Pee-Chee Autographs

AAH Ales Hemsky 6.00 15.00
AAM Andy McDonald 10.00 25.00
AAN Antero Niittymaki SP 40.00 80.00
AAR Andrew Raycroft SP 20.00 50.00
ABB Brad Boyes SP 30.00 60.00
ABG Brian Gionta 6.00 15.00
ABM Brendan Morrison 6.00 15.00
ABO Bobby Orr SP 400.00 700.00
ACC Chris Campoli 6.00 15.00
ACH Cristobal Huet 12.00 30.00
ACK Chris Kunitz 8.00 20.00
ACS Cory Stillman 8.00 20.00
ACW Cam Ward SP 40.00 100.00
ADB Daniel Briere 15.00 30.00
ADH Dany Heatley SP 30.00 60.00
ADR Dwayne Roloson 12.00 30.00
AEM Evgeni Malkin 125.00 200.00
AGB Gilbert Brule SP 20.00 50.00
AHA Dominik Hasek SP 40.00 80.00
AHT Hannu Toivonen 12.00 30.00
AIK Ilya Kovalchuk SP 30.00 80.00
AJA Jason Arnott 6.00 15.00
AJC Jeff Carter 10.00 25.00
AJI Jarome Iginla SP 40.00 80.00
AJL John-Michael Liles 6.00 15.00
AJS Jordan Staal 12.00 30.00
AKB Keith Ballard 6.00 15.00
AKC Kyle Calder 10.00 25.00
AKO Mikko Koivu 6.00 15.00
AMC Mike Cammalleri 10.00 25.00
AMG Marian Gaborik SP 50.00 100.00
AMP Marc-Antoine Pouliot 8.00 20.00
AMR Mike Richards 10.00 25.00
AMS Marek Svatos 6.00 15.00
ANA Rick Nash 20.00 50.00
ANH Nathan Horton 10.00 25.00
ANL Nicklas Lidstrom SP 40.00 100.00
APB Pierre-Marc Bouchard 6.00 15.00
APK Phil Kessel SP 60.00 125.00
APP Petr Prucha 8.00 20.00
APS Paul Stastny 30.00 60.00
ARB Rob Blake 10.00 25.00
ARL Roberto Luongo SP 75.00 150.00
ARM Ryan Malone 8.00 20.00
ARN Robert Nilsson 6.00 15.00
ARS Ryan Smyth 8.00 20.00
ASB Steve Bernier 10.00 25.00
ASW Stephen Weiss 6.00 15.00
AWR Wade Redden 6.00 15.00
AWW Wojtek Wolski 12.00 30.00

2006-07 O-Pee-Chee Swatches

SAA Arron Asham 5.00 12.00
SAE David Aebischer 6.00 15.00
SAF Alexander Frolov 5.00 12.00
SAH Ales Hemsky 6.00 15.00
SAM Andrej Meszaros 5.00 12.00
SAO Alexander Ovechkin 15.00 40.00
SAS Alexander Steen 5.00 12.00
SAT Alex Tanguay 5.00 12.00
SAY Alexei Yashin 6.00 15.00
SBB Brandon Bochenski 5.00 12.00
SBM Brendan Morrison 5.00 12.00
SBS Brad Stuart 5.00 12.00
SCC Chris Chelios 8.00 20.00
SCD Chris Drury 6.00 15.00
SCH Jonathan Cheechoo 6.00 15.00
SCK Chuck Kobasew 5.00 12.00
SCP Chris Pronger 8.00 20.00
SDA Daniel Alfredsson 8.00 20.00
SDE Pavol Demitra 10.00 25.00
SDH Dominik Hasek 12.00 30.00
SDK Duncan Keith 6.00 15.00
SDT Darcy Tucker 6.00 15.00
SDW Doug Weight 8.00 20.00
SEN Evgeni Nabokov 6.00 15.00
SES Eric Staal 10.00 25.00
SFP Fernando Pisani 5.00 12.00
SGA Mathieu Garon 6.00 15.00
SGL Guy Lafleur SP 50.00 125.00
SGM Glen Murray 6.00 15.00
SGR Gary Roberts 5.00 12.00
SHA Martin Havlat 5.00 12.00
SHE Milan Hejduk 6.00 15.00
SHO Shawn Horcoff 5.00 12.00
SHS Henrik Sedin 10.00 25.00
SHT Hannu Toivonen 6.00 15.00
SJA Jason Arnott 6.00 15.00
SJB Jay Bouwmeester 5.00 12.00
SJC Jeff Carter 6.00 15.00
SJG Jean-Sebastien Giguere 8.00 20.00
SJI Jarome Iginla 10.00 25.00
SJJ Jaromir Jagr 25.00 60.00
SJL Jere Lehtinen 5.00 12.00
SJP Joni Pitkanen 5.00 12.00
SJR Jeremy Roenick 12.00 30.00
SJS Jason Spezza 8.00 20.00
SKL Kari Lehtonen 6.00 15.00
SLE Jordan Leopold 5.00 12.00
SLX Mario Lemieux SP 25.00 60.00
SMA Maxim Afinogenov 5.00 12.00
SMB Martin Brodeur 20.00 50.00
SMC Mike Cammalleri 5.00 12.00
SMD Marc Denis 6.00 15.00
SMF Manny Fernandez 5.00 12.00
SMG Marian Gaborik 8.00 20.00
SMH Marian Hossa 8.00 20.00
SMI Miroslav Satan 6.00 15.00
SML Manny Legace 6.00 15.00
SMM Mike Modano 12.00 30.00
SMN Markus Naslund 8.00 20.00
SMR Mark Recchi 10.00 25.00
SMS Martin St. Louis SP 25.00 60.00
SMT Marty Turco 8.00 20.00
SNL Nicklas Lidstrom 8.00 20.00
SOJ Olli Jokinen 8.00 20.00
SOT Steve Ott 5.00 12.00
SPB Patrice Bergeron 10.00 25.00
SPD Pavel Datsyuk 12.00 30.00
SPF Peter Forsberg 15.00 40.00
SPK Paul Kariya 8.00 20.00
SPL Pascal LeClaire 6.00 15.00
SPM Patrick Marleau 8.00 20.00
SPR Patrick Roy 20.00 50.00
SPS Peter Stastny 6.00 15.00
SRB Rod Brind`Amour 8.00 20.00
SRD Rick DiPietro 6.00 15.00
SRE Robert Esche 6.00 15.00
SRF Ruslan Fedotenko 5.00 12.00
SRI Mike Ribeiro 5.00 12.00
SRK Rostislav Klesla 5.00 12.00
SRL Robert Lang 5.00 12.00
SRM Ryan Miller 8.00 20.00
SRN Rick Nash 8.00 20.00
SRS Ryan Smyth 6.00 15.00
SRY Michael Ryder 5.00 12.00
SSA Joe Sakic 10.00 25.00
SSB Steve Bernier 5.00 12.00
SSC Sidney Crosby SP 90.00 150.00
SSD Shane Doan 6.00 15.00
SSF Sergei Fedorov 12.00 30.00
SSG Scott Gomez 6.00 15.00
SSH Brendan Shanahan 8.00 20.00
SSO Sandis Ozolinsh 5.00 12.00
SSS Sergei Samsonov 6.00 15.00
SST Martin Straka 5.00 12.00
SSU Mats Sundin 8.00 20.00
STR Tuomo Ruutu 8.00 20.00
STS Teemu Selanne 15.00 40.00
STV Tomas Vokoun 6.00 15.00
SVL Vincent Lecavalier 8.00 20.00
SZC Zdeno Chara 8.00 20.00

2007-08 O-Pee-Chee

1 Jean-Sebastien Giguere .20 .50
2 Andy McDonald .15 .40
3 Teemu Selanne .40 1.00
4 Travis Moen .12 .30
5 George Parros .12 .30
6 Samuel Pahlsson .12 .30
7 Rob Niedermayer .15 .40
8 Scott Niedermayer .20 .50
9 Francois Beauchemin .12 .30
10 Dustin Penner .15 .40
11 Ryan Getzlaf .20 .50
12 Corey Perry .30 .75
13 Chris Kunitz .20 .50
14 Chris Pronger .20 .50
15 Ilya Bryzgalov .20 .50
16 Mathieu Schneider .12 .30
17 Todd Bertuzzi .20 .50
18 Marian Hossa .20 .50
19 Bobby Holik .12 .30
20 Eric Belanger .12 .30
21 Ken Klee .12 .30
22 Alexei Zhitnik .12 .30
23 Johan Hedberg .15 .40
24 Steve Rucchin .12 .30
25 Ilya Kovalchuk .20 .50
26 Niclas Havelid .12 .30
27 Jim Slater .12 .30
28 Kari Lehtonen .15 .40
29 Garnet Exelby .12 .30
30 Slava Kozlov .12 .30
31 Chris Thorburn .12 .30
32 Pascal Dupuis .12 .30
33 Andy Sutton .12 .30
34 Patrice Bergeron .25 .60
35 Phil Kessel .20 .50
36 Manny Fernandez .12 .30
37 Aaron Ward .12 .30
38 Zdeno Chara .20 .50
39 Glen Murray .15 .40
40 Marco Sturm .12 .30
41 Chuck Kobasew .12 .30
42 P.J. Axelsson .12 .30
43 Dennis Wideman .12 .30
44 Tim Thomas .20 .50
45 Andrew Ference .12 .30
46 Mark Mowers .12 .30
47 Marc Savard .12 .30
48 Brandon Bochenski .12 .30
49 Andrew Alberts .12 .30
50 Shean Donovan .12 .30
51 Ryan Miller .20 .50
52 Thomas Vanek .15 .40
53 Derek Roy .12 .30
54 Jochen Hecht .12 .30
55 Dmitri Kalinin .12 .30
56 Jason Pominville .12 .30
57 Daniel Paille .12 .30
58 Drew Stafford .12 .30
59 Brian Campbell .15 .40
60 Nathan Paetsch .12 .30
61 Jocelyn Thibault .15 .40
62 Andrew Peters .12 .30
63 Teppo Numminen .12 .30
64 Tim Connolly .12 .30
65 Ales Kotalik .12 .30
66 Maxim Afinogenov .12 .30
67 Jarome Iginla .25 .60
68 Matthew Lombardi .12 .30
69 Rhett Warrener .12 .30
70 Robyn Regehr .12 .30
71 Daymond Langkow .12 .30
72 David Hale .12 .30
73 Miikka Kiprusoff .20 .50
74 Stephane Yelle .12 .30
75 Adrian Aucoin .12 .30
76 Mark Giordano .20 .50
77 Alex Tanguay .15 .40
78 Kristian Huselius .12 .30
79 Owen Nolan .20 .50
80 Dion Phaneuf .15 .40
81 Craig Conroy .12 .30
82 Cory Sarich .12 .30
83 Cam Ward .20 .50
84 Ray Whitney .15 .40
85 Erik Cole .12 .30
86 Mike Commodore .12 .30
87 Eric Staal .25 .60
88 Chad Larose .12 .30
89 Justin Williams .15 .40
90 Tim Gleason .12 .30
91 Andrew Ladd .12 .30
92 David Tanabe .12 .30
93 John Grahame .12 .30
94 Cory Stillman .12 .30
95 Craig Adams .12 .30
96 Rod Brind`Amour .20 .50
97 Scott Walker .12 .30
98 Jeffrey Hamilton .12 .30
99 Glen Wesley .12 .30
100 Martin Havlat .20 .50
101 Rene Bourque .12 .30
102 Andrei Zyuzin .12 .30
103 Duncan Keith .15 .40
104 Jim Vandermeer .12 .30
105 Patrick Sharp .20 .50
106 Martin Lapointe .12 .30
107 Tuomo Ruutu .20 .50
108 Patrick Lalime .15 .40
109 Jason Williams .12 .30
110 Radim Vrbata .12 .30
111 Brent Seabrook .12 .30
112 Robert Lang .12 .30
113 Cam Barker .12 .30
114 Sergei Samsonov .15 .40
115 Nikolai Khabibulin .20 .50
116 Nikita Alexeev .12 .30
117 Joe Sakic .40 1.00
118 Peter Budaj .15 .40
119 Andrew Brunette .12 .30
120 John-Michael Liles .12 .30
121 Ian Laperriere .12 .30
122 Scott Hannan .12 .30
123 Marek Svatos .12 .30
124 Brett Clark .12 .30
125 Jose Theodore .20 .50
126 Jordan Leopold .12 .30
127 Tyler Arnason .12 .30
128 Wojtek Wolski .15 .40
129 Kurt Sauer .12 .30
130 Paul Stastny .15 .40
131 Brad Richardson .12 .30
132 Ryan Smyth .15 .40
133 Milan Hejduk .15 .40
134 Rick Nash .20 .50
135 Nikolai Zherdev .12 .30
136 Jody Shelley .12 .30
137 Adam Foote .12 .30
138 Ole-Kristian Tollefsen .12 .30
139 Jason Chimera .12 .30
140 Fredrik Norrena .12 .30
141 Sergei Fedorov .30 .75
142 Rostislav Klesla .12 .30
143 Dan Fritsche .12 .30
144 Fredrik Modin .12 .30
145 Manny Malhotra .12 .30
146 Jiri Novotny .12 .30
147 David Vyborny .12 .30
148 Alexander Svitov .12 .30
149 Gilbert Brule .15 .40
150 Pascal Leclaire .15 .40
151 Mike Modano .30 .75
152 Sergei Zubov .15 .40
153 Mike Smith .20 .50
154 Jussi Jokinen .12 .30
155 Philippe Boucher .12 .30
156 Trevor Daley .12 .30
157 Antti Miettinen .12 .30
158 Steve Ott .12 .30
159 Brenden Morrow .15 .40
160 Loui Eriksson .12 .30
161 Todd Fedoruk .12 .30
162 Mike Ribeiro .12 .30
163 Jere Lehtinen .12 .30
164 Stu Barnes .12 .30
165 Jeff Halpern .12 .30
166 Mattias Norstrom .12 .30
167 Marty Turco .20 .50
168 Nicklas Lidstrom .20 .50
169 Dan Cleary .15 .40
170 Kris Draper .12 .30
171 Chris Osgood .20 .50
172 Andreas Lilja .12 .30
173 Henrik Zetterberg .25 .60
174 Brett Lebda .12 .30
175 Chris Chelios .20 .50
176 Tomas Holmstrom .15 .40
177 Pavel Datsyuk .30 .75
178 Jiri Hudler .15 .40
179 Kyle Quincey .12 .30
180 Valtteri Filppula .12 .30
181 Brian Rafalski .15 .40
182 Johan Franzen .15 .40
183 Mikael Samuelsson .12 .30
184 Dominik Hasek .30 .75
185 Ales Hemsky .15 .40
186 Mathieu Garon .15 .40
187 Jarret Stoll .15 .40
188 Ladislav Smid .12 .30
189 Marc-Antoine Pouliot .12 .30
190 Matt Greene .12 .30
191 Joni Pitkanen .12 .30
192 Marty Reasoner .12 .30
193 Shawn Horcoff .12 .30
194 Steve Staios .12 .30
195 Ethan Moreau .12 .30
196 Patrick Thoresen .12 .30
197 Dwayne Roloson .15 .40
198 Fernando Pisani .12 .30
199 Geoff Sanderson .12 .30
200 Jean-Francois Jacques .12 .30
201 Raffi Torres .12 .30
202 Olli Jokinen .15 .40
203 Mike Van Ryn .12 .30
204 Stephen Weiss .12 .30
205 Bryan Allen .12 .30
206 Richard Zednik .12 .30
207 Steve Montador .12 .30
208 Alexander Auld .12 .30
209 Nathan Horton .20 .50
210 Ruslan Salei .12 .30
211 Rostislav Olesz .12 .30
212 David Booth .12 .30
213 Gregory Campbell .12 .30
214 Noah Welch .12 .30
215 Brett McLean .12 .30
216 Tomas Vokoun .15 .40
217 Jay Bouwmeester .12 .30
218 Radek Dvorak .12 .30
219 Rob Blake .20 .50
220 Patrick O'Sullivan .15 .40
221 Derek Armstrong .12 .30
222 Dan Cloutier .15 .40
223 Scott Thornton .12 .30
224 Michal Handzus .15 .40
225 Anze Kopitar .30 .75
226 Dustin Brown .20 .50
227 Raitis Ivanans .12 .30
228 Kyle Calder .12 .30
229 Brad Stuart .12 .30
230 Mike Cammalleri .15 .40
231 Ladislav Nagy .12 .30
232 Jason LaBarbera .15 .40
233 Lubomir Visnovsky .12 .30
234 Alexander Frolov .12 .30
235 Marian Gaborik .20 .50
236 Kim Johnsson .12 .30
237 Niklas Backstrom .20 .50
238 Branko Radivojevic .12 .30
239 Dominic Moore .12 .30
240 Pavol Demitra .25 .60
241 Nick Schultz .12 .30
242 Brian Rolston .15 .40
243 Josh Harding .20 .50
244 Derek Boogaard .12 .30
245 Kurtis Foster .12 .30
246 Stephane Veilleux .12 .30
247 Keith Carney .12 .30
248 Mikko Koivu .15 .40
249 Mark Parrish .12 .30
250 Brent Burns .20 .50
251 Pierre-Marc Bouchard .20 .50
252 Saku Koivu .20 .50
253 Chris Higgins .12 .30
254 Mike Komisarek .12 .30
255 Maxim Lapierre .12 .30
256 Guillaume Latendresse .15 .40
257 Bryan Smolinski .12 .30
258 Sheldon Souray .12 .30
259 Andrei Kostitsyn .15 .40
260 Cristobal Huet .15 .40
261 Michael Ryder .12 .30
262 Andrei Markov .20 .50
263 Josh Gorges .12 .30
264 Alexander Perezhogin .12 .30
265 Tomas Plekanec .12 .30
266 Roman Hamrlik .12 .30
267 Mark Streit .12 .30
268 Alexei Kovalev .15 .40
269 Jerred Smithson .12 .30
270 Jason Arnott .15 .40
271 Dan Hamhuis .15 .40
272 Jordin Tootoo .20 .50
273 Darcy Hordichuk .12 .30
274 Vernon Fiddler .12 .30
275 Steve Sullivan .12 .30
276 Shea Weber .15 .40
277 Alexander Radulov .20 .50
278 Marek Zidlicky .12 .30
279 David Legwand .15 .40
280 Radek Bonk .12 .30
281 Ryan Suter .15 .40
282 Chris Mason .15 .40
283 Greg de Vries .12 .30
284 J.P. Dumont .12 .30
285 Martin Erat .12 .30
286 Brian Gionta .12 .30
287 Travis Zajac .12 .30
288 Johnny Oduya .15 .40
289 Jamie Langenbrunner .12 .30
290 Colin White .12 .30
291 Sergei Brylin .12 .30
292 Dainius Zubrus .12 .30
293 Jay Pandolfo .12 .30
294 Cam Janssen .12 .30
295 Martin Brodeur .50 1.25
296 Zach Parise .20 .50
297 Paul Martin .12 .30
298 John Madden .12 .30
299 Mike Rupp .12 .30
300 Kevin Weekes .15 .40
301 Patrik Elias .20 .50
302 Rick DiPietro .15 .40
303 Mike Sillinger .12 .30
304 Marc-Andre Bergeron .12 .30
305 Mike Comrie .15 .40
306 Jon Sim .12 .30
307 Chris Campoli .12 .30
308 Ruslan Fedotenko .12 .30
309 Bill Guerin .20 .50
310 Trent Hunter .12 .30
311 Radek Martinek .12 .30
312 Frederick Meyer .12 .30
313 Richard Park .12 .30
314 Jeff Tambellini .12 .30
315 Wade Dubielewicz .15 .40
316 Brendan Witt .12 .30
317 Andy Hilbert .12 .30
318 Miroslav Satan .15 .40
319 Jaromir Jagr .60 1.50
320 Sean Avery .12 .30
321 Michal Rozsival .12 .30
322 Petr Prucha .12 .30
323 Matt Cullen .12 .30
324 Marcel Hossa .12 .30
325 Paul Mara .12 .30
326 Scott Gomez .15 .40
327 Blair Betts .12 .30
328 Colton Orr .12 .30
329 Marek Malik .12 .30
330 Chris Drury .15 .40
331 Martin Straka .12 .30
332 Nigel Dawes .12 .30
333 Ryan Hollweg .12 .30
334 Fedor Tyutin .12 .30
335 Henrik Lundqvist .50 1.25
336 Dany Heatley .15 .40
337 Wade Redden .12 .30
338 Joe Corvo .12 .30
339 Jason Spezza .20 .50
340 Patrick Eaves .12 .30
341 Chris Kelly .15 .40
342 Mike Fisher .12 .30
343 Ray Emery .15 .40
344 Andrej Meszaros .12 .30
345 Peter Schaefer .12 .30
346 Anton Volchenkov .12 .30
347 Chris Neil .12 .30
348 Chris Phillips .12 .30
349 Christoph Schubert .12 .30
350 Antoine Vermette .12 .30
351 Martin Gerber .15 .40
352 Daniel Alfredsson .20 .50
353 Jason Smith .12 .30
354 Simon Gagne .20 .50
355 Antero Niittymaki .15 .40
356 Joffrey Lupul .12 .30
357 Jeff Carter .15 .40
358 Ben Eager .12 .30
359 Scott Hartnell .12 .30
360 Martin Biron .15 .40
361 Mike Richards .15 .40
362 Kimmo Timonen .12 .30
363 R.J. Umberger .12 .30
364 Daniel Briere .20 .50
365 Scottie Upshall .12 .30
366 Mike Knuble .12 .30
367 Shane Doan .15 .40
368 Niko Kapanen .12 .30
369 Mathias Tjarnqvist .12 .30
370 Zbynek Michalek .12 .30
371 Fredrik Sjostrom .12 .30
372 Bill Thomas .12 .30
373 Josh Gratton .12 .30
374 Mikael Tellqvist .15 .40
375 Derek Morris .12 .30
376 Kevyn Adams .12 .30
377 Michael Zigomanis .12 .30
378 Ed Jovanovski .15 .40
379 David Leneveu .15 .40
380 Steven Reinprecht .12 .30
381 Nick Boynton .12 .30
382 Keith Ballard .12 .30
383 Marc-Andre Fleury .40 1.00
384 Jordan Staal .15 .40
385 Gary Roberts .12 .30
386 Georges Laraque .15 .40
387 Ryan Whitney .15 .40
388 Petr Sykora .15 .40
389 Jarkko Ruutu .12 .30
390 Evgeni Malkin .40 1.00
391 Brooks Orpik .12 .30
392 Maxime Talbot .12 .30
393 Mark Recchi .25 .60
394 Ryan Malone .12 .30
395 Colby Armstrong .12 .30
396 Sergei Gonchar .12 .30
397 Erik Christensen .12 .30
398 Darryl Sydor .12 .30
399 Sidney Crosby .75 2.00
400 Evgeni Nabokov .15 .40
401 Milan Michalek .12 .30
402 Marc-Edouard Vlasic .12 .30
403 Patrick Marleau .20 .50
404 Christian Ehrhoff .12 .30
405 Pat Rissmiller .12 .30
406 Craig Rivet .12 .30
407 Jonathan Cheechoo .15 .40
408 Joe Pavelski .25 .60
409 Curtis Brown .12 .30
410 Mike Grier .12 .30
411 Kyle McLaren .12 .30
412 Steve Bernier .12 .30
413 Matt Carle .12 .30
414 Marcel Goc .15 .40
415 Ryane Clowe .12 .30
416 Joe Thornton .30 .75
417 Manny Legace .15 .40
418 Brad Boyes .12 .30
419 Eric Brewer .12 .30
420 Jay McClement .12 .30
421 Martin Rucinsky .12 .30
422 Jay McKee .12 .30
423 Petr Cajanek .12 .30
424 Doug Weight .20 .50
425 Christian Backman .12 .30
426 Jamal Mayers .12 .30
427 Jeff Woywitka .12 .30
428 Lee Stempniak .12 .30
429 David Backes .12 .30
430 Barret Jackman .12 .30
431 Paul Kariya .20 .50
432 Keith Tkachuk .20 .50
433 Bryce Salvador .12 .30
434 Vincent Lecavalier .20 .50
435 Paul Ranger .12 .30
436 Vaclav Prospal .12 .30
437 Shane O'Brien .12 .30
438 Michel Ouellet .12 .30
439 Marc Denis .15 .40
440 Jason Ward .12 .30
441 Martin St. Louis .20 .50
442 Blair Jones .12 .30
443 Filip Kuba .12 .30
444 Ryan Craig .12 .30
445 Tim Taylor .12 .30
446 Dan Boyle .12 .30
447 Nick Tarnasky .12 .30
448 Johan Holmqvist .15 .40
449 Brad Richards .20 .50
450 Andre Roy .12 .30
451 Mats Sundin .20 .50
452 Kyle Wellwood .15 .40
453 Bryan McCabe .12 .30
454 Jason Blake .12 .30
455 Ian White .12 .30
456 Alexei Ponikarovsky .12 .30
457 Hal Gill .12 .30
458 Pavel Kubina .12 .30
459 Andrew Raycroft .15 .40
460 Alexander Steen .12 .30
461 Nik Antropov .15 .40
462 Mark Bell .12 .30
463 Carlo Colaiacovo .12 .30
464 Matt Stajan .12 .30
465 Tomas Kaberle .12 .30
466 Vesa Toskala .15 .40
467 Darcy Tucker .15 .40
468 Roberto Luongo .30 .75
469 Sami Salo .12 .30
470 Ryan Kesler .20 .50
471 Trevor Linden .20 .50
472 Kevin Bieksa .15 .40
473 Matt Cooke .12 .30
474 Aaron Miller .12 .30
475 Henrik Sedin .25 .60
476 Mattias Ohlund .12 .30
477 Brendan Morrison .12 .30
478 Willie Mitchell .12 .30
479 Curtis Sanford .15 .40
480 Markus Naslund .20 .50
481 Taylor Pyatt .12 .30
482 Alexandre Burrows .12 .30
483 Lukas Krajicek .12 .30
484 Daniel Sedin .25 .60
485 Alexander Ovechkin .75 2.00
486 Chris Clark .12 .30
487 Milan Jurcina .12 .30
488 Boyd Gordon .12 .30
489 Michael Nylander .12 .30
490 Donald Brashear .12 .30
491 Shaone Morrisonn .12 .30
492 Steve Eminger .12 .30
493 Olaf Kolzig .20 .50
494 Matt Pettinger .12 .30
495 Viktor Kozlov .12 .30
496 Brooks Laich .12 .30
497 Mike Green .15 .40
498 Jakub Klepis .12 .30
499 Brent Johnson .15 .40
500 Alexander Semin .20 .50
501 Bobby Ryan RC 1.50 4.00
502 Drew Miller RC .75 2.00
503 Aaron Rome RC .75 2.00
504 Ryan Carter RC .60 1.50
505 Jonas Hiller RC 1.25 3.00
506 Kent Huskins RC .60 1.50
507 Bjorn Melin RC .60 1.50
508 Bryan Little RC 1.00 2.50
509 Brett Sterling RC .60 1.50
510 Tobias Enstrom RC 1.00 2.50
511 David Krejci RC 2.00 5.00
512 Jonathan Sigalet RC .60 1.50
513 Milan Lucic RC 2.50 6.00
514 Curtis McElhinney RC 1.00 2.50
515 David Moss RC 1.00 2.50
516 Tomi Maki RC .60 1.50
517 Jonathan Toews RC 4.00 10.00
518 Patrick Kane RC 8.00 20.00
519 Colin Fraser RC .60 1.50
520 Bryan Bickell RC 1.25 3.00
521 Magnus Johansson RC .60 1.50
522 Pierre Parenteau RC .75 2.00
523 Jonas Nordqvist RC .60 1.50
524 David Koci RC .60 1.50
525 Tyler Weiman RC .75 2.00
526 Jaroslav Hlinka RC .75 2.00
527 Jeff Finger RC .60 1.50
528 Kris Russell RC 1.00 2.50
529 Danny Bois RC .60 1.50
530 Tomas Popperle RC .60 1.50
531 Marc Methot RC .60 1.50
532 Jared Boll RC .75 2.00
533 Curtis Glencross RC 1.00 2.50
534 Matt Niskanen RC 1.00 2.50
535 Tobias Stephan RC .75 2.00
536 Joel Lundqvist RC .60 1.50
537 Krys Barch RC .75 2.00
538 Chris Conner RC .60 1.50
539 Matt Ellis RC .75 2.00
540 Sam Gagner RC 1.25 3.00
541 Andrew Cogliano RC .75 2.00
542 Rob Schremp RC .75 2.00
543 Tom Gilbert RC .75 2.00
544 Bryan Young RC .60 1.50
545 Zack Stortini RC .60 1.50
546 Sebastien Bisaillon RC .60 1.50
547 Martin Lojek RC .60 1.50
548 Cory Murphy RC .60 1.50
549 Jack Johnson RC .75 2.00
550 Jonathan Bernier RC 1.25 3.00
551 Lauri Tukonen RC .60 1.50
552 Brady Murray RC .60 1.50
553 John Zeiler RC .60 1.50
554 Gabe Gauthier RC .60 1.50
555 Shay Stephenson RC .60 1.50
556 Joe Piskula RC .60 1.50
557 Petr Kalus RC .60 1.50
558 James Sheppard RC .60 1.50
559 Joel Ward RC 1.00 2.50
560 Carey Price RC 10.00 25.00
561 Kyle Chipchura RC 1.00 2.50
562 Jaroslav Halak RC 2.00 5.00
563 Duncan Milroy RC .60 1.50
564 Ville Koistinen RC .60 1.50
565 Rich Peverley RC .60 1.50
566 Nicklas Bergfors RC .60 1.50
567 Andy Greene RC .75 2.00
568 Mark Fraser RC .60 1.50
569 David Clarkson RC .60 1.50
570 Rod Pelley RC .60 1.50
571 Frans Nielsen RC 1.00 2.50
572 Marc Staal RC 1.00 2.50
573 Brandon Dubinsky RC 1.25 3.00
574 Ryan Callahan RC 1.25 3.00
575 Daniel Girardi RC .75 2.00
576 Nick Foligno RC 1.25 3.00
577 Brian Elliott RC 1.25 3.00
578 Ryan Parent RC .60 1.50
579 Scott Munroe RC .60 1.50
580 Denis Tolpeko RC .60 1.50
581 Riley Cote RC .75 2.00
582 Nathan Guenin RC .75 2.00
583 Peter Mueller RC .75 2.00
584 Martin Hanzal RC .75 2.00
585 Craig Weller RC .60 1.50
586 Daniel Winnik RC .75 2.00
587 Daniel Carcillo RC .75 2.00
588 Mark Mancari RC .60 1.50
589 Torrey Mitchell RC .75 2.00
590 Thomas Plihal RC .60 1.50
591 Erik Johnson RC 1.00 2.50
592 Darcy Campbell RC .60 1.50
593 Steve Wagner RC .60 1.50
594 Matt Smaby RC .60 1.50
595 Mike Lundin RC .60 1.50
596 Mason Raymond RC 1.00 2.50
597 Jannik Hansen RC .75 2.00
598 Nicklas Backstrom RC 2.00 5.00
599 Jeff Schultz RC .75 2.00
600 Jamie Hunt RC .60 1.50

2007-08 O-Pee-Chee Micromotion

*MICRO: 2.5X TO 6X

2007-08 O-Pee-Chee Micromotion Black

*MICRO BLACK: 6X TO 15X
*MICRO BLACK ROOKIES: 1.2X TO 3X

2007-08 O-Pee-Chee Silver

*SILVER: 1X TO 2.5X

2007-08 O-Pee-Chee 3x5 Toys R' Us

TRU1 Saku Koivu 4.00 10.00
TRU2 Michael Ryder 2.50 6.00
TRU3 Guillaume Latendresse 3.00 8.00
TRU4 Cristobal Huet 3.00 8.00
TRU5 Alexei Kovalev 3.00 8.00
TRU6 Chris Higgins 2.50 6.00
TRU7 Miikka Kiprusoff 4.00 10.00
TRU8 Jarome Iginla 5.00 12.00
TRU9 Dion Phaneuf 3.00 8.00
TRU10 Alex Tanguay 3.00 8.00
TRU11 Daymond Langkow 2.50 6.00
TRU12 Kristian Huselius 2.50 6.00
TRU13 Ray Emery 3.00 8.00
TRU14 Dany Heatley 3.00 8.00
TRU15 Daniel Alfredsson 4.00 10.00
TRU16 Jason Spezza 4.00 10.00
TRU17 Wade Redden 2.50 6.00
TRU18 Mike Fisher 2.50 6.00
TRU19 Roberto Luongo 6.00 15.00
TRU20 Markus Naslund 4.00 10.00
TRU21 Daniel Sedin 5.00 12.00
TRU22 Henrik Sedin 5.00 12.00
TRU23 Brendan Morrison 2.50 6.00
TRU24 Ryan Kesler 4.00 10.00
TRU25 Mats Sundin 4.00 10.00
TRU26 Jason Blake 2.50 6.00
TRU27 Darcy Tucker 3.00 8.00
TRU28 Alexander Steen 2.50 6.00
TRU29 Tomas Kaberle 2.50 6.00
TRU30 Vesa Toskala 3.00 8.00
TRU31 Ales Hemsky 3.00 8.00
TRU32 Dwayne Roloson 3.00 8.00
TRU33 Joni Pitkanen 2.50 6.00
TRU34 Geoff Sanderson 2.50 6.00
TRU35 Jarret Stoll 3.00 8.00
TRU36 Shawn Horcoff 2.50 6.00
TRU37 Sidney Crosby 15.00 40.00
TRU38 Martin Brodeur 10.00 25.00
TRU39 Nicklas Lidstrom 4.00 10.00
TRU40 Evgeni Malkin 8.00 20.00
TRU41 Scott Niedermayer 4.00 10.00
TRU42 Sidney Crosby 15.00 40.00

2007-08 O-Pee-Chee Bobby Orr Panoramic Cards

COMPLETE SET (6) 30.00 60.00
COMMON ORR 6.00 15.00

2007-08 O-Pee-Chee In Action

COMPLETE SET (20) 12.00 30.00
IA1 Sidney Crosby 2.00 5.00
IA2 Alexander Ovechkin 2.00 5.00
IA3 Evgeni Malkin 1.00 2.50
IA4 Dany Heatley .40 1.00
IA5 Rick Nash .50 1.25
IA6 Ilya Kovalchuk .50 1.25
IA7 Vincent Lecavalier .50 1.25
IA8 Jaromir Jagr 1.50 4.00
IA9 Thomas Vanek .40 1.00
IA10 Jarome Iginla .60 1.50
IA11 Henrik Zetterberg .60 1.50
IA12 Michael Ryder .30 .75
IA13 Mats Sundin .50 1.25
IA14 Joe Sakic 1.00 2.50
IA15 Martin Brodeur 1.25 3.00
IA16 Roberto Luongo .75 2.00
IA17 Ray Emery .40 1.00
IA18 Ryan Miller .50 1.25
IA19 Joe Thornton .75 2.00
IA20 Ryan Getzlaf .50 1.25

2007-08 O-Pee-Chee Materials Quad

QMANGE Alf/Nied/Gig/Emery 8.00 20.00
QMASHE Alf/Spez/Heat/Emery 8.00 20.00
QMASOW Antro/Staj/Ond/White 6.00 15.00
QMBEGP Brod/Eli/Gion/Parise 20.00 50.00
QMBFCK Blake/Frol/Cam/Kopit 12.00 30.00
QMBJBH Belf/Jos/Brod/Hasek 20.00 50.00
QMCBMA Con/Afino/Miller/Vanek 8.00 20.00
QMCBTK Char/Berg/Thorn/Kess 10.00 25.00
QMCHOD Chel/Hasek/Osg/Drap 12.00 30.00
QMDGHB Dem/Gab/Hall/Bouch 10.00 25.00
QMDLAF Leg/Arn/Fors/Dumont 15.00 40.00
QMDNLW Doan/Nash/Lom/Ward 8.00 20.00
QMGBRC Gag/Briere/Rich/Cart 8.00 20.00
QMGFCM Gonc/Fleu/Cros/Malk 15.00 40.00
QMITKP Iginla/Tang/Kipr/Phan 10.00 25.00
QMJBWH Jok/Bouw/Weiss/Hort 8.00 20.00
QMJDSB Jovo/Doan/Sjo/Bell 6.00 15.00
QMJHEH Jagr/Hejd/Elias/Havlat 25.00 60.00
QMJHSH Jagr/Hoss/St. Lo/Heat 25.00 60.00
QMJROM Jack/Ray/Ov/Malkin 25.00 60.00
QMJSLP Jagr/Strak/Lund/Pruc 25.00 60.00
QMKHHK Koivu/Huet/Higg/Kov 8.00 20.00
QMKMOJ Kolz/Morr/Ov/Jurcina 15.00 40.00
QMKOMR Kov/Ov/Malk/Radu 12.00 30.00
QMLHDZ Lids/Holm/Dats/Zett 10.00 25.00
QMLLMK Luo/Lind/Morr/Kesler 12.00 30.00
QMLNFB LeClr/Nash/Fed/Brule 12.00 30.00
QMLNMG Lids/Nied/McC/Gonc 8.00 20.00
QMLREK Luon/Ray/Emery/Kipr 12.00 30.00
QMLRSC Lecav/Rich/St. L/Craig 8.00 20.00
QMMLRT Mo/Leht/Rib/Turco 12.00 30.00
QMMTNC Marl/Thor/Nab/Chee 12.00 30.00
QMNSDS Nasl/Sedin/Ohl/Sedin 10.00 25.00
QMRNGW Rich/Nied/Gig/Ward 8.00 20.00
QMSBTI Sakic/Brod/Thorn/Ig 20.00 50.00
QMSCCL Still/Commo/Cole/Ladd 5.00 12.00
QMSDRD Sakic/Dem/Rich/Dats 15.00 40.00
QMSGDH Guer/Sat/DiPie/Hunt 8.00 20.00
QMSHRH Stoll/Horc/Rolo/Hem 6.00 15.00
QMSHRK Sam/Havl/Ruut/Khabi 8.00 20.00
QMSHSB Sakic/Hejd/Svat/Bud 15.00 40.00
QMSJSS Sakic/Shan/Jagr/Sun 25.00 60.00
QMSKAI Sundin/Koivu/Alf/Ig 10.00 25.00
QMSLHO Sel/Lecav/Heat/Ov 15.00 40.00
QMSLKJ Sel/Leht/Koivu/Jokin 15.00 40.00
QMSLTC Sak/Lecav/Thorn/Cros 15.00 40.00
QMSMKB Sav/Murr/Kob/Boch 6.00 15.00
QMSMSR Sel/Mo/Sund/Recchi 15.00 40.00
QMSNGG Sel/Nied/Gig/Getzlaf 15.00 40.00
QMSNLF Sund/Nas/Lids/Fors 15.00 40.00
QMSOVM Sedin/Ov/Van/Malk 12.00 30.00
QMSSKW Sharp/Seab/Keith/Will 8.00 20.00
QMSTMS Sun/Tuck/McC/Steen 8.00 20.00
QMTFSC Thorn/Fors/St. L/Cros 20.00 50.00
QMTLLW Theo/Leo/Lile/Wolski 8.00 20.00
QMTPPP Torr/Pisan/Pit/Pouliot 5.00 12.00
QMVSZP Vyb/Shel/Zher/Picard 6.00 15.00
QMWBSW Will/Brind/Staal/Ward 10.00 25.00
QMWJLB Weight/Jack/Leg/Boy 8.00 20.00
QMZMOJ Zubov/Morr/Ott/Jok 6.00 15.00

2007-08 O-Pee-Chee Record Breakers

COMPLETE SET (10) 8.00 20.00
RB1 Mike Modano .75 2.00
RB2 Martin Brodeur 1.25 3.00
RB3 Paul Stastny .40 1.00
RB4 Vincent Lecavalier .50 1.25
RB5 Sidney Crosby 2.00 5.00
RB6 Sheldon Souray .30 .75
RB7 Evgeni Malkin 1.00 2.50
RB8 Jaromir Jagr 1.50 4.00
RB9 Alexander Ovechkin 2.00 5.00
RB10 Roberto Luongo .75 2.00

2007-08 O-Pee-Chee Season Highlights

COMPLETE SET (19) 10.00 25.00
SH1 Scott Niedermayer .50 1.25
SH2 Daniel Alfredsson .50 1.25
SH3 Ryan Miller .50 1.25
SH4 Evgeni Malkin 1.00 2.50
SH5 Joe Sakic 1.00 2.50
SH6 Daniel Briere .50 1.25
SH7 Sidney Crosby 2.00 5.00
SH8 Brendan Shanahan .50 1.25
SH9 Jaromir Jagr 1.50 4.00
SH10 Mats Sundin .50 1.25
SH11 Teemu Selanne 1.00 2.50
SH12 Dean McAmmond .30 .75
SH13 Jean-Sebastien Giguere .50 1.25
SH14 Wade Dubielewicz .40 1.00
SH15 Sidney Crosby 2.00 5.00
SH16 Roberto Luongo .75 2.00
SH17 Dominik Hasek .75 2.00
SH18 Joe Thornton .75 2.00
SH19 Nicklas Lidstrom .50 1.25
SH20 Jordan Staal .40 1.00

2007-08 O-Pee-Chee Signatures

SAB Adam Burish 8.00 20.00
SAD Adam Dennis 8.00 20.00
SAE Alexander Edler 6.00 15.00
SAF Alexander Frolov 6.00 15.00
SAO Alexander Ovechkin SP 40.00 100.00
SAT Alex Tanguay SP 8.00 20.00
SBA Christian Backman 6.00 15.00
SBJ Blair Jones 6.00 15.00
SBM Brenden Morrow 8.00 20.00
SBO Ben Ondrus 6.00 15.00
SBP Benoit Pouliot 6.00 15.00
SBR Alex Brooks 6.00 15.00
SBW Ben Walter 6.00 15.00
SCK Chuck Kobasew 6.00 15.00
SCP Chris Phillips 6.00 15.00
SCT Chris Thorburn 6.00 15.00
SCW Cam Ward 10.00 25.00
SDB Dave Bolland 8.00 20.00
SDH Dany Heatley SP 8.00 20.00
SDL Drew Larman 6.00 15.00
SDS Drew Stafford 6.00 15.00
SDW Doug Weight 10.00 25.00
SEC Erik Christensen 6.00 15.00
SEL Patrik Elias 10.00 25.00
SEM Evgeni Malkin 20.00 50.00
SES Eric Staal SP 12.00 30.00
SFN Filip Novak 6.00 15.00
SFP Fernando Pisani 6.00 15.00
SGA Simon Gagne SP 10.00 25.00
SGH Gordie Howe SP 30.00 80.00
SHL Henrik Lundqvist SP 25.00 60.00
SIW Ian White 6.00 15.00
SJC Jeff Carter 8.00 20.00
SJG Jean-Sebastien Giguere SP 10.00 25.00
SJI Jarome Iginla SP 12.00 30.00
SJM Jay McClement 6.00 15.00
SJP Joe Pavelski 12.00 30.00
SJS Jordan Staal 8.00 20.00
SJT Joe Thornton SP 15.00 40.00
SMC Mike Cammalleri 8.00 20.00
SMG Marian Gaborik SP 10.00 25.00
SMH Marian Hossa SP 10.00 25.00
SMJ Milan Jurcina 6.00 15.00
SML Mario Lemieux SP 40.00 100.00
SMM Mark Messier SP 20.00 50.00
SMO Michel Ouellet 6.00 15.00
SMP Marc-Antoine Pouliot 6.00 15.00
SMR Michael Ryder 6.00 15.00
SMV Marc-Edouard Vlasic 6.00 15.00
SNG Niklas Grossman 6.00 15.00
SNZ Nikolai Zherdev 6.00 15.00
SOR Bobby Orr SP 40.00 100.00
SPE Corey Perry 15.00 40.00
SPM Paul Mara 6.00 15.00
SPR Brandon Prust 6.00 15.00
SPS Paul Stastny 8.00 20.00
SRA Paul Ranger 6.00 15.00
SRC Ryan Clowe SP 6.00 15.00
SRG Ryan Getzlaf 10.00 25.00
SRI Mike Richards 8.00 20.00
SRM Ryan Malone 6.00 15.00
SRN Rick Nash SP 10.00 25.00
SRY Ryan Miller 10.00 25.00
SSB Steve Bernier 6.00 15.00
SSC Sidney Crosby SP 40.00 100.00
SSG Scott Gomez 8.00 20.00
SSO Shane O'Brien 6.00 15.00
SST Martin St. Louis SP 10.00 25.00
SSW Shea Weber 8.00 20.00
STV Tomas Vokoun 8.00 20.00
SVL Vincent Lecavalier SP 10.00 25.00
SWW Wojtek Wolski 8.00 20.00

2007-08 O-Pee-Chee Stat Leaders

COMPLETE SET (20) 12.00 30.00
SL1 Selanne/Lecavalier/Heatley 1.00 2.50
SL2 Thornton/Savard/Crosby 2.00 5.00
SL3 Lecavalier/Thornton/Crosby 2.00 5.00
SL4 Lidstrom/Alfredsson/Vanek .50 1.25
SL5 Selanne/Kovalchuk/Souray 1.00 2.50
SL6 Lecavalier/Draper/Staal .50 1.25
SL7 Selanne/Zetterberg/Heatley 1.00 2.50
SL8 Neil/Gratton/Eager .30 .75
SL9 Brodeur/Hasek/Backstrom 1.25 3.00
SL10 Brodeur/Luongo/Kiprusoff 1.25 3.00
SL11 Brodeur/Mason/Backstrom 1.25 3.00
SL12 Brodeur/Hasek/Kiprusoff 1.25 3.00
SL13 Alfredsson/McDonald/Datsyuk .75 2.00
SL14 Lidstrom/Spezza/Heatley .50 1.25
SL15 Alfredsson/Spezza/Heatley .50 1.25
SL16 Pronger/Numminen/Pahlsson .50 1.25
SL17 Drury/Alfredsson/Getzlaf .50 1.25
SL18 Hasek/Giguere/Emery .75 2.00
SL19 Hasek/Luongo/Turco .75 2.00
SL20 Niedermayer/Gonchar/Souray .50 1.25

2007-08 O-Pee-Chee Team Checklists

COMPLETE SET (30) 20.00 50.00
CL1 Anaheim Ducks 1.00 2.50
CL2 Atlanta Thrashers 1.00 2.50
CL3 Boston Bruins 1.00 2.50
CL4 Buffalo Sabres 1.00 2.50
CL5 Calgary Flames 1.00 2.50
CL6 Carolina Hurricanes 1.00 2.50
CL7 Chicago Blackhawks 1.00 2.50
CL8 Colorado Avalanche 1.00 2.50
CL9 Columbus Blue Jackets 1.00 2.50
CL10 Dallas Stars 1.00 2.50
CL11 Detroit Red Wings 1.00 2.50
CL12 Edmonton Oilers 1.00 2.50
CL13 Florida Panthers 1.00 2.50
CL14 Los Angeles Kings 1.00 2.50
CL15 Minnesota Wild 1.00 2.50
CL16 Montreal Canadiens 1.00 2.50
CL17 Nashville Predators 1.00 2.50
CL18 New Jersey Devils 1.00 2.50
CL19 New York Islanders 1.00 2.50
CL20 New York Rangers 1.00 2.50
CL21 Ottawa Senators 1.00 2.50
CL22 Philadelphia Flyers 1.00 2.50
CL23 Phoenix Coyotes 1.00 2.50
CL24 Pittsburgh Penguins 1.00 2.50
CL25 San Jose Sharks 1.00 2.50
CL26 St. Louis Blues 1.00 2.50
CL27 Tampa Bay Lightning 1.00 2.50
CL28 Toronto Maple Leafs 1.00 2.50
CL29 Vancouver Canucks 1.00 2.50
CL30 Washington Capitals 1.00 2.50

2008-09 O-Pee-Chee

1 Markus Naslund .20 .50
2 Dan Hinote .12 .30
3 Pascal Dupuis .12 .30
4 Frantisek Kaberle .12 .30
5 Derek Morris .12 .30
6 Scottie Upshall .12 .30
7 Richard Park .12 .30
8 Josh Gorges .12 .30
9 Rob Blake .20 .50
10 Cory Murphy .12 .30
11 Sheldon Souray .12 .30
12 Mike Modano .30 .75
13 Wojtek Wolski .15 .40
14 Hal Gill .12 .30
15 Dustin Boyd .12 .30
16 Jason Pominville .12 .30
17 Slava Kozlov .12 .30
18 Sidney Crosby .75 2.00
19 Kamil Kreps .12 .30
20 Bryan McCabe .12 .30
21 Kari Ramo .15 .40
22 Joe Pavelski .25 .60
23 Mikael Tellqvist .15 .40
24 Braydon Coburn .12 .30
25 Nigel Dawes .12 .30
26 Jay Pandolfo .12 .30
27 Niklas Backstrom .20 .50
28 Shaone Morrisonn .12 .30
29 Bryan Allen .12 .30
30 Jiri Hudler .15 .40
31 Marc-Andre Bergeron .12 .30
32 Pascal Leclaire .15 .40
33 Tim Gleason .12 .30
34 Patrice Bergeron .25 .60
35 Eric Perrin .12 .30
36 Francois Beauchemin .12 .30
37 Fredrik Norrena .12 .30
38 Mats Sundin .20 .50
39 Jay McClement .12 .30
40 Jarkko Ruutu .12 .30
41 Ladislav Smid .12 .30
42 Daniel Carcillo .12 .30
43 Ryan Parent .12 .30
44 Antoine Vermette .12 .30
45 Brendan Shanahan .20 .50
46 Josef Vasicek .12 .30
47 Roman Hamrlik .12 .30
48 Michal Handzus .15 .40
49 Ales Hemsky .15 .40
50 Brooks Orpik .12 .30
51 Scott Parker .12 .30
52 Chad Larose .12 .30
53 Ryan Miller .20 .50
54 Tobias Enstrom .12 .30
55 George Parros .12 .30
56 Viktor Kozlov .12 .30
57 Kyle Wellwood .15 .40
58 Evgeni Nabokov .15 .40
59 Corey Perry .30 .75
60 Boyd Gordon .12 .30
61 Dan Cleary .15 .40
62 Mike Fisher .12 .30
63 John Madden .12 .30
64 Tomas Plekanec .12 .30
65 Nathan Horton .15 .40
66 Dwayne Roloson .15 .40
67 Niklas Kronwall .15 .40
68 Radim Vrbata .12 .30
69 Manny Malhotra .12 .30
70 Martin Havlat .20 .50
71 Curtis Joseph .25 .60
72 Saku Koivu .20 .50
73 Bryan Little .15 .40
74 Marc-Edouard Vlasic .12 .30
75 Jonas Hiller .15 .40
76 Brendan Morrison .12 .30
77 Nikolai Antropov .15 .40
78 Ryan Johnson .12 .30
79 Craig Rivet .12 .30
80 Marian Hossa .20 .50
81 Simon Gagne .20 .50
82 Cory Stillman .12 .30
83 Chris Campoli .12 .30
84 Zach Parise .20 .50
85 David Legwand .15 .40
86 Andrei Kostitsyn .15 .40
87 Maxim Afinogenov .12 .30
88 Kyle Calder .12 .30
89 Henrik Zetterberg .25 .60
90 Rostislav Klesla .12 .30
91 Travis Zajac .12 .30
92 Brent Seabrook .12 .30
93 Toni Lydman .12 .30
94 Todd White .12 .30
95 Tomas Fleischmann .12 .30
96 Devin Setoguchi .15 .40
97 Henrik Sedin .25 .60
98 Boyd Devereaux .12 .30
99 Michel Ouellet .12 .30
100 Matt Carle .12 .30
101 Zbynek Michalek .12 .30
102 Scott Gomez .15 .40
103 Dainius Zubrus .12 .30
104 Nikolai Khabibulin .20 .50
105 James Sheppard .12 .30
106 Richard Zednik .20 .50
107 Chris Osgood .20 .50
108 Alexander Semin .20 .50
109 Paul Stastny .15 .40
110 Justin Williams .15 .40
111 Eric Nystrom .12 .30
112 Tuukka Rask .25 .60
113 Mathieu Schneider .12 .30
114 Mikael Samuelsson .12 .30
115 Vincent Lecavalier .20 .50
116 Eric Brewer .12 .30
117 Pat Rissmiller .12 .30
118 Niko Kapanen .12 .30
119 Jaromir Jagr .60 1.50
120 Paul Martin .12 .30
121 Guillaume Latendresse .12 .30
122 Pierre-Marc Bouchard .20 .50
123 Olli Jokinen .15 .40
124 Brian Rafalski .15 .40
125 Rob Niedermayer .15 .40
126 Jiri Novotny .12 .30
127 Matt Cullen .12 .30
128 Tim Thomas .20 .50
129 Dennis Wideman .12 .30
130 Garnet Exelby .12 .30
131 Nicklas Lidstrom .20 .50
132 Sami Salo .12 .30
133 Alexei Ponikarovsky .12 .30
134 Paul Ranger .12 .30
135 Andy McDonald .15 .40
136 Chris Kunitz .20 .50
137 Mike Richards .20 .50
138 Andrej Meszaros .12 .30
139 Michal Rozsival .12 .30
140 Brendan Witt .12 .30
141 Marek Zidlicky .12 .30
142 Mark Parrish .12 .30
143 Craig Anderson .20 .50
144 Mathieu Garon .15 .40
145 Brett Lebda .12 .30
146 Loui Eriksson .12 .30
147 Marek Svatos .12 .30
148 Scott Walker .12 .30
149 Anders Eriksson .12 .30
150 Aaron Ward .12 .30
151 Nicklas Backstrom .20 .50
152 Anton Stralman .12 .30
153 Dmitri Kalinin .12 .30
154 Mike Grier .12 .30
155 Keith Yandle .12 .30
156 Ray Emery .15 .40
157 Chris Drury .15 .40
158 Blake Comeau .12 .30
159 Kevin Weekes .15 .40
160 Marian Gaborik .20 .50
161 Rostislav Olesz .12 .30
162 Tomas Kopecky .12 .30
163 Jason Chimera .12 .30
164 Tuomo Ruutu .20 .50
165 Henrik Tallinder .12 .30
166 Matt Stajan .12 .30
167 Marc Savard .12 .30
168 Alexei Zhitnik .12 .30
169 Scott Niedermayer .20 .50
170 Mike Green .15 .40
171 Pavel Kubina .12 .30
172 David Perron .15 .40
173 Jaroslav Halak .20 .50
174 Torrey Mitchell .12 .30
175 Shane Doan .15 .40
176 Johnny Oduya .12 .30
177 Carey Price .40 1.00
178 David Backes .12 .30
179 Martin Skoula .12 .30
180 David Booth .12 .30
181 Kris Draper .12 .30
182 Paul Gaustad .12 .30
183 Donald Brashear .12 .30
184 Roberto Luongo .30 .75
185 Brooks Laich .12 .30
186 Craig MacDonald .12 .30
187 Patrick Marleau .20 .50
188 Steven Reinprecht .12 .30
189 Chris Kelly .15 .40
190 Ryan Hollweg .12 .30
191 Andy Hilbert .12 .30
192 Andy Greene .12 .30
193 Jason Arnott .15 .40
194 Nick Schultz .15 .40
195 Jozef Stumpel .12 .30
196 Matt Niskanen .15 .40
197 John-Michael Liles .12 .30
198 Dave Bolland .15 .40
199 Patrick Eaves .12 .30
200 Cory Sarich .12 .30
201 Marco Sturm .12 .30
202 Martin St. Louis .20 .50
203 Jeff Schultz .12 .30
204 Alexander Steen .15 .40
205 Shane O'Brien .12 .30
206 Thomas Greiss .15 .40
207 Nick Boynton .12 .30
208 Daniel Girardi .12 .30
209 Alex Kovalev .15 .40
210 Henrik Lundqvist .50 1.25
211 Shea Weber .15 .40
212 Mikko Koivu .15 .40
213 Karlis Skrastins .12 .30
214 Jere Lehtinen .12 .30
215 Fredrik Modin .12 .30
216 Peter Budaj .15 .40
217 Andrew Ladd .15 .40
218 Joe Corvo .12 .30
219 Zdeno Chara .20 .50
220 Sean O'Donnell .12 .30
221 Ian White .12 .30
222 Andre Roy .12 .30
223 Steve Wagner .12 .30
224 Ty Conklin .15 .40
225 Daniel Winnik .12 .30
226 Jason Spezza .20 .50
227 Martin Brodeur .50 1.25
228 Ryan Callahan .12 .30
229 Ryan O'Byrne .12 .30
230 Brian Rolston .15 .40
231 Ladislav Nagy .12 .30
232 Tomas Holmstrom .15 .40
233 Kris Russell .12 .30
234 Jason LaBarbera .15 .40
235 Ben Guite .12 .30
236 Rene Bourque .12 .30
237 David Moss .12 .30
238 Jaroslav Spacek .12 .30
239 Jean-Sebastien Giguere .20 .50
240 Jason Blake .12 .30
241 Dan Boyle .12 .30
242 Joe Thornton .30 .75
243 Ilya Bryzgalov .15 .40
244 Martin Gerber .15 .40
245 Andy Sutton .12 .30
246 Patrik Elias .20 .50
247 Mike Komisarek .12 .30
248 Eric Belanger .12 .30
249 Andrew Raycroft .15 .40
250 David Vyborny .12 .30
251 Pavel Datsyuk .30 .75
252 Ron Hainsey .12 .30
253 Patrick Sharp .20 .50
254 Mike Sillinger .12 .30
255 Adrian Aucoin .12 .30
256 Thomas Vanek .15 .40
257 Derek Armstrong .12 .30
258 Teemu Selanne .40 1.00
259 Ryan Kesler .20 .50
260 Darcy Tucker .15 .40
261 Alexander Frolov .12 .30
262 Erik Johnson .12 .30
263 Willie Mitchell .12 .30
264 Ryan Whitney .20 .50
265 Jeff Carter .15 .40
266 Bruno Gervais .12 .30
267 Brent Sopel .12 .30
268 Martin Erat .12 .30
269 Raitis Ivanans .12 .30
270 Drew Stafford .12 .30
271 Robert Nilsson .12 .30
272 Lee Stempniak .12 .30
273 Dan Fritsche .12 .30
274 Ryan Smyth .15 .40
275 Owen Nolan .20 .50
276 David Krejci .20 .50
277 Jim Slater .12 .30
278 Alexander Ovechkin .75 2.00
279 Drew MacIntyre .20 .50
280 Stephane Robidas .12 .30
281 Manny Legace .20 .50
282 Jordan Staal .15 .40
283 Scott Hartnell .12 .30
284 Brandon Dubinsky .12 .30
285 Bill Guerin .20 .50
286 R.J. Umberger .12 .30
287 Ryan Suter .15 .40
288 Lubomir Visnovsky .12 .30
289 Joni Pitkanen .12 .30
290 Dominik Hasek .30 .75
291 Niklas Hagman .12 .30
292 Jordan Leopold .12 .30
293 Miroslav Satan .20 .50
294 Erik Cole .12 .30
295 Kristian Huselius .12 .30
296 Kari Lehtonen .25 .60
297 Mason Raymond .12 .30
298 Marc Denis .15 .40
299 Dan Ellis .12 .30
300 Randy Jones .12 .30
301 Cam Ward .20 .50
302 Tom Gilbert .12 .30
303 Daniel Alfredsson .20 .50
304 Radek Martinek .12 .30
305 Vernon Fiddler .12 .30
306 Tyler Kennedy .15 .40
307 Patrick O'Sullivan .15 .40
308 Chris Thorburn .12 .30
309 Dany Heatley .15 .40
310 Denis Grebeshkov .12 .30
311 Steve Ott .12 .30
312 Ian Laperriere .12 .30
313 Adam Burish .15 .40
314 Stephane Yelle .12 .30
315 Ilya Kovalchuk .20 .50
316 Brian Willsie .15 .40
317 Olaf Kolzig .20 .50
318 Daniel Sedin .25 .60
319 Filip Kuba .12 .30
320 Chris Neil .12 .30
321 Hannu Toivonen .15 .40
322 Milan Michalek .12 .30
323 Mark Eaton .12 .30
324 Dean McAmmond .12 .30
325 Marc Staal .15 .40
326 Mike Rupp .12 .30
327 Kim Johnsson .12 .30
328 Stephen Weiss .12 .30
329 Chris Chelios .20 .50
330 Mike Ribeiro .12 .30
331 Tyler Arnason .12 .30
332 Duncan Keith .15 .40
333 Rod Brind'Amour .20 .50
334 Peter Schaefer .12 .30
335 Colby Armstrong .12 .30
336 Ryan Carter .12 .30
337 Lukas Krajicek .12 .30
338 Mike Smith .15 .40
339 Maxime Talbot .20 .50
340 Steve Downie .12 .30
341 Christoph Schubert .12 .30
342 Jeff Halpern .12 .30
343 Jeff Tambellini .12 .30
344 Jordin Tootoo .12 .30
345 Anze Kopitar .30 .75
346 Evgeni Malkin .40 1.00
347 Zach Stortini .12 .30
348 Dustin Penner .15 .40
349 Trevor Daley .12 .30
350 Milan Hejduk .15 .40
351 Corey Crawford .25 .60
352 Robyn Regehr .12 .30
353 Daniel Paille .12 .30
354 Milan Lucic .30 .75
355 Chris Pronger .20 .50
356 Taylor Pyatt .12 .30
357 Jussi Jokinen .15 .40
358 Petr Sykora .15 .40
359 Jack Johnson .15 .40
360 Daymond Langkow .12 .30
361 Antero Niittymaki .15 .40
362 Trent Hunter .12 .30
363 Aaron Voros .12 .30
364 Craig Conroy .12 .30
365 Brett McLean .12 .30
366 Jarret Stoll .15 .40
367 Marty Turco .20 .50
368 Gilbert Brule .12 .30
369 Joe Sakic .40 1.00
370 Mike Knuble .12 .30
371 Jarome Iginla .25 .60
372 Stephane Veilleux .12 .30
373 Mark Stuart .12 .30
374 Mattias Ohlund .12 .30
375 Mike Lundin .12 .30
376 Sergei Gonchar .12 .30
377 Ed Jovanovski .15 .40
378 Kimmo Timonen .12 .30
379 Rick DiPietro .15 .40
380 J.P. Dumont .12 .30
381 Mattias Norstrom .12 .30
382 Andrei Markov .20 .50
383 Josh Harding .15 .40
384 Steve Staios .12 .30
385 Francis Bouillon .15 .40
386 Brenden Morrow .15 .40
387 Scott Hannan .12 .30
388 Dustin Byfuglien .20 .50
389 Bret Hedican .12 .30
390 Matthew Lombardi .12 .30
391 Derek Roy .12 .30
392 Phil Kessel .20 .50
393 Milan Jurcina .12 .30
394 Nick Foligno .20 .50
395 Jiri Tlusty .12 .30
396 Jonathan Cheechoo .15 .40
397 Peter Mueller .15 .40
398 Daniel Briere .12 .30
399 Anton Volchenkov .12 .30
400 Brian Pothier .12 .30
401 Sergei Brylin .12 .30
402 Sergei Kostitsyn .12 .30
403 Tomas Vokoun .15 .40
404 Valtteri Filppula .12 .30
405 Bobby Ryan .15 .40
406 Antti Miettinen .12 .30
407 Nikolai Zherdev .12 .30
408 Jack Skille .15 .40
409 Jochen Hecht .15 .40
410 Chuck Kobasew .12 .30
411 Brad Richards .20 .50
412 Todd Bertuzzi .20 .50
413 Trevor Linden .20 .50
414 Nick Tarnasky .12 .30
415 Brian Campbell .12 .30
416 Marc-Andre Fleury .40 1.00
417 Martin Biron .15 .40
418 Dan Hamhuis .15 .40
419 Petr Prucha .12 .30
420 David Clarkson .15 .40
421 Scott Nichol .12 .30
422 Christian Backman .12 .30
423 Brent Burns .20 .50
424 Pavol Demitra .25 .60
425 Sam Gagner .12 .30
426 Fernando Pisani .12 .30
427 Philippe Boucher .12 .30
428 Peter Forsberg .40 1.00
429 Cam Barker .12 .30
430 Miikka Kiprusoff .20 .50
431 Clarke MacArthur .12 .30
432 Glen Murray .15 .40
433 Ruslan Fedotenko .12 .30
434 Ales Kotalik .12 .30
435 Vesa Toskala .25 .60
436 Keith Tkachuk .20 .50
437 Ryan Malone .12 .30
438 Joffrey Lupul .12 .30
439 Chris Phillips .12 .30
440 Frederick Meyer .15 .40
441 P.J. Axelsson .12 .30
442 Colin White .12 .30
443 Chris Mason .15 .40
444 Mark Streit .12 .30
445 Andrew Cogliano .12 .30
446 Michael Ryder .12 .30
447 Rick Nash .20 .50
448 Patrick Kane .40 1.00
449 Steve Bernier .12 .30
450 Alexandre Burrows .15 .40
451 Ondrej Pavelec .25 .60
452 Alexander Edler .12 .30
453 Tomas Kaberle .12 .30
454 Jay McKee .12 .30
455 Christian Ehrhoff .12 .30
456 Kristopher Letang .25 .60
457 Vaclav Prospal .12 .30
458 Fedor Tyutin .12 .30
459 Jamie Langenbrunner .15 .40
460 Barret Jackman .12 .30
461 Chris Higgins .15 .40
462 Kyle Brodziak .12 .30
463 Mike Cammalleri .15 .40
464 Johan Franzen .15 .40
465 Jared Boll .20 .50
466 Andrew Brunette .12 .30
467 Robert Lang .12 .30
468 Glen Wesley .12 .30
469 Tim Connolly .12 .30
470 Niclas Havelid .12 .30
471 Cristobal Huet .15 .40
472 Kevin Bieksa .15 .40
473 Jason Ward .12 .30
474 Brad Boyes .12 .30
475 Brian Gionta .15 .40
476 Kyle McLaren .12 .30
477 Keith Ballard .12 .30
478 Wade Redden .12 .30
479 Martin Straka .12 .30
480 Radek Bonk .12 .30
481 Ray Whitney .15 .40
482 Kurtis Foster .12 .30
483 Dustin Brown .20 .50
484 Mike Van Ryn .12 .30
485 Sergei Zubov .15 .40
486 T.J. Hensick .15 .40
487 Eric Staal .25 .60
488 Alexander Radulov .15 .40
489 Alex Tanguay .12 .30
490 Manny Fernandez .12 .30
491 Jamal Mayers .12 .30
492 Colton Orr .12 .30
493 Jay Bouwmeester .12 .30
494 Jonathan Toews .30 .75
495 Ryan Getzlaf .20 .50
496 Checklist .12 .30
497 Checklist .12 .30
498 Checklist .12 .30
499 Checklist .12 .30
500 Checklist .12 .30
501 Sami Lepisto RC 1.00 2.50
502 Mike Brown RC 1.25 3.00
503 Zach Fitzgerald RC 1.25 3.00
504 Robbie Earl RC .75 2.00
505 Darryl Boyce RC 1.00 2.50
506 Alex Foster RC 1.00 2.50
507 Mike Iggulden RC 1.00 2.50
508 Tom Cavanagh RC 1.00 2.50
509 Alex Goligoski RC 1.50 4.00
510 Jon Filewich RC 1.00 2.50
511 Ryan Stone RC .75 2.00
512 Chris Minard RC 1.25 3.00
513 Kyle Turris RC 2.00 5.00
514 Claude Giroux RC 2.50 6.00
515 Kyle Greentree RC 1.25 3.00
516 Brian Lee RC 1.00 2.50
517 Ilya Zubov RC 1.00 2.50
518 Jesse Winchester RC .75 2.00
519 Kyle Okposo RC 1.50 4.00
520 Mike Mole RC 1.00 2.50
521 Jack Hillen RC 1.00 2.50
522 Jordan LaVallee RC 1.25 3.00
523 Matt D'Agostini RC 1.00 2.50
524 Corey Locke RC 1.00 2.50
525 Brian Boyle RC 1.00 2.50
526 Teddy Purcell RC 1.00 2.50
527 Danny Taylor RC 1.00 2.50
528 Erik Ersberg RC 1.00 2.50
529 Shawn Matthias RC 1.25 3.00
530 David Brine RC .75 2.00
531 Tyler Plante RC 1.00 2.50
532 Theo Peckham RC 1.00 2.50
533 Tom Sestito RC 1.25 3.00
534 Justin Abdelkader RC 2.00 5.00
535 Jonathan Ericsson RC 1.25 3.00
536 Darren Helm RC 1.25 3.00
537 Mattias Ritola RC 1.00 2.50
538 Garrett Stafford RC 1.25 3.00
539 Mark Fistric RC 1.00 2.50
540 B.J. Crombeen RC .75 2.00
541 Derick Brassard RC 1.25 3.00
542 Steve Mason RC 2.00 5.00
543 Adam Pineault RC 1.00 2.50
544 Dan LaCosta RC 1.25 3.00
545 Andrew Murray RC 1.00 2.50
546 Clay Wilson RC .75 2.00
547 Cody McLeod RC 1.00 2.50
548 Jordan Hendry RC 1.00 2.50
549 Niklas Hjalmarsson RC 1.25 3.00
550 Brandon Nolan RC 1.00 2.50
551 Tim Conboy RC 1.00 2.50
552 Joey Mormina RC 1.00 2.50
553 Joe Jensen RC 1.25 3.00
554 Tim Ramholt RC 1.00 2.50
555 Marc-Andre Gragnani RC 1.00 2.50
556 Pascal Pelletier RC .75 2.00
557 Boris Valabik RC 1.25 3.00
558 Colin Stuart RC 1.00 2.50
559 Kevin Doell RC .75 2.00
560 Andrew Ebbett RC .75 2.00
561 Checklist .15 .40
562 Dale Hawerchuk 1.00 2.50
563 Bobby Hull 1.50 4.00
564 Richard Brodeur .60 1.50
565 Borje Salming .75 2.00
566 Johnny Bower .75 2.00
567 Eddie Shack .75 2.00
568 Doug Wilson .60 1.50
569 Peter Stastny .60 1.50
570 Mario Lemieux 3.00 8.00
571 Joe Mullen .60 1.50
572 Ron Hextall .75 2.00
573 Rick MacLeish .60 1.50
574 Bernie Parent 1.00 2.50
575 Mark Messier 1.50 4.00
576 Brian Leetch .60 1.50
577 Mike Bossy .75 2.00
578 Pat LaFontaine .75 2.00
579 Guy Lafleur 1.00 2.50
580 Jean Beliveau .75 2.00
581 Frank Mahovlich .75 2.00
582 Dino Ciccarelli .75 2.00
583 Rogie Vachon 1.00 2.50
584 Wayne Gretzky 5.00 12.00
585 Glenn Anderson .60 1.50
586 Grant Fuhr 1.25 3.00
587 Luc Robitaille .75 2.00
588 Scotty Bowman .75 2.00
589 Alex Delvecchio .75 2.00
590 Patrick Roy 2.00 5.00
591 Jari Kurri .75 2.00
592 Denis Savard .75 2.00
593 Tony Esposito .75 2.00
594 Stan Mikita 1.00 2.50
595 Lanny McDonald .75 2.00
596 Gilbert Perreault .75 2.00
597 Ray Bourque 1.25 3.00
598 Cam Neely .75 2.00
599 Phil Esposito 1.25 3.00
600 Bobby Orr 3.00 8.00
601 Steve Montador .12 .30
602 Brendan Morrison .12 .30
603 Mathieu Schneider .12 .30
604 Ron Hainsey .12 .30
605 Michael Ryder .12 .30
606 Patrick Lalime .12 .30
607 Craig Rivet .12 .30
608 Teppo Numminen .12 .30
609 Todd Bertuzzi .20 .50
610 Mike Cammalleri .15 .40
611 Curtis Glencross .12 .30
612 Rene Bourque .12 .30
613 Jarome Iginla .25 .60
614 Joni Pitkanen .12 .30
615 Brian Campbell .12 .30
616 Cristobal Huet .15 .40
617 Adam Foote .12 .30
618 Darcy Tucker .15 .40
619 Andrew Raycroft .15 .40
620 Joe Sakic .40 1.00
621 Kristian Huselius .12 .30
622 R.J. Umberger .12 .30
623 Mike Commodore .12 .30
624 Sean Avery .12 .30
625 Mark Parrish .12 .30
626 Marian Hossa .20 .50
627 Ty Conklin .15 .40
628 Lubomir Visnovsky .12 .30
629 Erik Cole .12 .30
630 Jeff Drouin-Deslauriers .12 .30
631 Keith Ballard .12 .30
632 Cory Stillman .12 .30
633 Bryan McCabe .12 .30
634 Jarret Stoll .15 .40
635 Andrew Brunette .12 .30
636 Owen Nolan .20 .50
637 Marek Zidlicky .12 .30
638 Marc-Andre Bergeron .12 .30
639 Craig Weller .12 .30
640 Antti Miettinen .12 .30
641 Alex Tanguay .12 .30
642 Marc Denis .15 .40
643 Georges Laraque .15 .40
644 Robert Lang .12 .30
645 Joel Ward .12 .30
646 Brian Rolston .15 .40
647 Doug Weight .20 .50
648 Mark Streit .12 .30
649 Nikolai Zherdev .12 .30
650 Wade Redden .12 .30
651 Markus Naslund .20 .50
652 Filip Kuba .12 .30
653 Alex Auld .12 .30
654 Alexandre Picard .12 .30
655 Ryan Shannon .12 .30
656 Jason Smith .12 .30
657 Brendan Bell .12 .30
658 Samuel Pahlsson .12 .30

659 Matt Carle .12 .30
660 Arron Asham .12 .30
661 Ossi Vaananen .12 .30
662 Olli Jokinen .15 .40
663 Joakim Lindstrom .12 .30
664 Todd Fedoruk .12 .30
665 Ken Klee .12 .30
666 Eric Godard .12 .30
667 Miroslav Satan .20 .50
668 Ruslan Fedotenko .12 .30
669 Matt Cooke .12 .30
670 Sidney Crosby .75 2.00
671 Evgeni Malkin .40 1.00
672 Rob Blake .20 .50
673 Dan Boyle .12 .30
674 Jody Shelley .12 .30
675 Chris Mason .15 .40
676 Andy McDonald .15 .40
677 David Koci .12 .30
678 Andy Wozniewski .12 .30
679 Matt Foy .12 .30
680 Brad Winchester .12 .30
681 Mark Recchi .25 .60
682 Radim Vrbata .12 .30
683 Ryan Malone .12 .30
684 Vaclav Prospal .12 .30
685 Andrej Meszaros .12 .30
686 Gary Roberts .12 .30
687 Olaf Kolzig .20 .50
688 Steve Eminger .12 .30
689 Vincent Lecavalier .20 .50
690 Curtis Joseph .25 .60
691 Jeff Finger .12 .30
692 Ryan Hollweg .12 .30
693 Niklas Hagman .12 .30
694 Pavol Demitra .25 .60
695 Steve Bernier .12 .30
696 Shane O'Brien .12 .30
697 Darcy Hordichuk .12 .30
698 Rob Davison .12 .30
699 Jose Theodore .20 .50
700 Checklist .15 .40
701 Checklist .15 .40
702 Bret Hedican .12 .30
703 Cory Schneider RC 3.00 8.00
704 Jason Williams .12 .30
705 Karl Alzner RC .75 2.00
706 Johan Hedberg .15 .40
707 Erik Christensen .12 .30
708 Stephane Yelle .12 .30
709 Andrew Ference .12 .30
710 Andrej Sekera .12 .30
711 Andrew Peters .12 .30
712 Wayne Primeau .12 .30
713 Brandon Prust .12 .30
714 Sergei Samsonov .15 .40
715 Michael Leighton .15 .40
716 Nathan Gerbe RC 1.25 3.00
717 Kris Versteeg .12 .30
718 Aaron Johnson .12 .30
719 Ben Eager .12 .30
720 David Jones .12 .30
721 Brett Clark .12 .30
722 Raffi Torres .12 .30
723 Michael Peca .15 .40
724 Kenndal McArdle RC 1.00 2.50
725 Kirk Maltby .12 .30
726 Ethan Moreau .12 .30
727 Marc-Antoine Pouliot .12 .30
728 Wade Belak .12 .30
729 Kyle Quincey .12 .30
730 Matt Greene .12 .30
731 Derek Boogaard .12 .30
732 Cal Clutterbuck .12 .30
733 Maxim Lapierre .12 .30
734 Pekka Rinne .20 .50
735 Scott Clemmensen .12 .30
736 Mike Comrie .15 .40
737 Joey MacDonald .20 .50
738 Michal Repik RC 1.25 3.00
739 Jesse Winchester .12 .30
740 Riley Cote .12 .30
741 Dany Sabourin .12 .30
742 Brad Lukowich .12 .30
743 Brian Boucher .15 .40
744 Doug Murray .12 .30
745 Adam Hall .12 .30
746 Mikhail Grabovski .12 .30
747 Mike Van Ryn .12 .30
748 Chris Stewart RC 1.25 3.00
749 Zach Bogosian RC 1.50 4.00
750 Nathan Oystrick RC 1.25 3.00
751 Blake Wheeler RC 3.00 8.00
752 Adam Pardy RC 1.00 2.50
753 Zach Boychuk RC 1.25 3.00
754 Brandon Sutter RC 1.25 3.00
755 Dwight Helminen RC 1.25 3.00
756 Patrick Dwyer RC 1.25 3.00
757 Nikita Filatov RC 1.25 3.00
758 Jakub Voracek RC 2.50 6.00
759 Derek Dorsett RC 1.50 4.00
760 James Neal RC 2.50 6.00
761 Fabian Brunnstrom RC 1.00 2.50
762 Steve MacIntyre RC 1.25 3.00
763 Michael Frolik RC 1.25 3.00
764 Wayne Simmonds RC 2.00 5.00
765 Oscar Moller RC 1.00 2.50
766 Drew Doughty RC 3.00 8.00
767 Colton Gillies RC 1.00 2.50
768 Patric Hornqvist RC 1.25 3.00
769 Ryan Jones RC 1.25 3.00
770 Pierre-Luc Letourneau-Leblond RC .75 2.00
771 Patrick Davis RC 1.00 2.50
772 Anssi Salmela RC 1.25 3.00
773 Matthew Halischuk RC .75 2.00
774 Petr Vrana RC .75 2.00
775 Josh Bailey RC 1.50 4.00
776 Brett Skinner RC 1.00 2.50
777 Mitch Fritz RC 1.00 2.50
778 Jared Ross RC 1.25 3.00
779 Andreas Nodl RC .75 2.00
780 Luca Sbisa RC .75 2.00
781 Darroll Powe RC 1.25 3.00
782 Ben Maxwell RC 1.25 3.00
783 Kevin Porter RC 1.00 2.50
784 Viktor Tikhonov RC 1.00 2.50
785 Mikkel Boedker RC 1.50 4.00
786 Janne Pesonen RC 1.00 2.50
787 Brad Staubitz RC 1.00 2.50
788 Jamie McGinn RC 1.25 3.00
789 Ben Bishop RC 2.00 5.00
790 T.J. Oshie RC 2.50 6.00
791 Patrik Berglund RC 1.00 2.50
792 Chris Porter RC 1.25 3.00
793 Alex Pietrangelo RC 2.00 5.00
794 Vladimir Mihalik RC .75 2.00
795 Steven Stamkos RC 5.00 12.00
796 John Mitchell RC 1.00 2.50
797 Jonas Frogren RC .75 2.00
798 Luke Schenn RC 1.50 4.00
799 Nikolai Kulemin RC 1.25 3.00
800 Simeon Varlamov RC 2.50 6.00

2008-09 O-Pee-Chee 1979-80 Retro

COMPLETE SET (800) 300.00 600.00
COMP.SER.1 SET (600) 200.00 400.00
COMP.UPDATE SET (200) 100.00 200.00
*1-500/601-747 RETRO: 2X TO 5X
*510-560/748-800 ROOKIE: .6X TO 1.5X
*561-600 RETRO SP: .8X TO 2X
151 Nicklas Backstrom 1.25 3.00

2008-09 O-Pee-Chee 1979-80 Retro Blank Backs

*1-500/601-747 BLANK: 25X TO 60X BASE
*501-560/748-800 ROOKIE: 4X TO 10X
*561-600 BLANK SP: 5X TO 12X BASE
151 Nicklas Backstrom 15.00 40.00

2008-09 O-Pee-Chee 1979-80 Retro Rainbow

*RAINBOW VETS: 8X TO 20X BASE
*RAINBOW ROOKIES: 2X TO 5X BASE
*RAINBOW RETIRED: 2.5X TO 6X BASE
151 Nicklas Backstrom 5.00 12.00

2008-09 O-Pee-Chee Gold

*1-500/601-747 GOLD: 2.5X TO 6X BASE
*501-560/748-800 ROOKIE: .6X TO 1.5X
*561-600 GOLD SP: 1X TO 2.5X BASE
151 Nicklas Backstrom 1.50 4.00
795 Steven Stamkos 20.00 50.00

2008-09 O-Pee-Chee Metal

*METAL: 1.5X TO 4X BASE
*METAL ROOKIE: .5X TO 1.2X BASE RC
*METAL 561-600: .8X TO 2X BASE
151 Nicklas Backstrom 1.00 2.50

2008-09 O-Pee-Chee Metal X

*METAL X: 3X TO 8 X BASE
*METAL X ROOKIE: 1X TO 2.5X BASE RC
*METAL X 561-600: 1.2X TO 3X BASE
151 Nicklas Backstrom 2.00 5.00

2008-09 O-Pee-Chee All-Rookie Team

COMPLETE SET (6) 8.00 20.00
ARTCP Carey Price 1.50 4.00
ARTJT Jonathan Toews 1.25 3.00
ARTNB Nicklas Backstrom .75 2.00
ARTPK Patrick Kane 1.50 4.00
ARTTE Tobias Enstrom .50 1.25
ARTTG Tom Gilbert .50 1.25

2008-09 O-Pee-Chee Autographed Buybacks

BBAG Andy Greene 10.00 25.00
BBBE Brian Elliott 12.00 30.00
BBBR Bobby Ryan 12.00 30.00
BBCG Clark Gillies 15.00 40.00
BBCM Cory Murphy 8.00 20.00
BBDC Daniel Carcillo 10.00 25.00
BBDG Daniel Girardi 12.00 30.00
BBDH Dale Hawerchuk 15.00 40.00
BBDS Denis Savard 89-90 OPC 12.00 30.00
BBDW Doug Wilson 8.00 20.00
BBDY Ron Duguay 10.00 25.00
BBGF Grant Fuhr 25.00 60.00
BBGP Gilbert Perreault 15.00 40.00
BBHA Jaroslav Halak 12.00 30.00
BBJJ Jack Johnson 20.00 40.00
BBJS James Sheppard 10.00 25.00
BBLI Bryan Little 12.00 30.00
BBLT Lauri Tukonen 12.00 30.00
BBMB Mike Bossy 25.00 60.00
BBMC Curtis McElhinney 10.00 25.00
BBMD Lanny McDonald 89-90 OPC 15.00 40.00
BBMF Mark Fraser 8.00 20.00
BBMK Mark Mancari 8.00 20.00
BBMR Mason Raymond 20.00 50.00
BBMS Marc Staal 15.00 40.00
BBNB Neal Broten 89-90 OPC 25.00 50.00
BBPE Phil Esposito 20.00 50.00
BBPP Pete Peeters 12.00 30.00
BBPS Peter Stastny 15.00 40.00
BBPV Rich Peverley 10.00 25.00
BBRC Ryan Carter 8.00 20.00
BBRL Rod Langway 80-81 OPC 15.00 40.00
BBRO Luc Robitaille 89-90 OPC 12.00 30.00
BBRP Rod Pelley 8.00 20.00
BBRS Rob Schremp 15.00 40.00
BBRY Ryan Callahan 12.00 30.00
BBSG Sam Gagner 25.00 60.00
BBSM Matt Smaby 8.00 20.00
BBST Brett Sterling 8.00 20.00
BBSW Steve Wagner 10.00 25.00
BBTE Tobias Enstrom 20.00 50.00
BBTO Terry O'Reilly 25.00 60.00
BBTW Tyler Weiman 12.00 30.00
BBVK Ville Koistinen 8.00 20.00

2008-09 O-Pee-Chee Box Bottoms

IGIN/LUON/KOVAL/GABK 2.50 6.00
LECAV/NASH/STAAL/LUNDQ 1.50 4.00
BROD/THORN/ZETTER/TOEWS 1.50 4.00
OVECH/ALFRED/PRICE/SUND 2.50 6.00
STAM/SUTT/FILA/OKPOSO 2.50 6.00
VORCK/BOEDK/GILLIES/SCHEN 1.50 4.00
BRUNN/BRASS/OSHI/BOGO 2.00 5.00
TURRIS/WHEEL/BOYC/DOUGH 2.00 5.00
NNO Steven Stamkos U .60 1.50
NNO Brandon Sutter U .15 .40
NNO Nikita Filatov U .15 .40
NNO Kyle Okposo U .20 .50
NNO Jakub Voracek U .30 .75
NNO Mikkel Boedker U .20 .50
NNO Colton Gillies U .12 .30
NNO Luke Schenn U .20 .50
NNO Fabian Brunnstrom U .12 .30
NNO Derick Brassard U .15 .40
NNO T.J. Oshie U .30 .75
NNO Zach Bogosian U .20 .50
NNO Kyle Turris U .25 .60
NNO Blake Wheeler U .40 1.00
NNO Zach Boychuk U .15 .40
NNO Drew Doughty U .40 1.00
NNO Daniel Alfredsson .15 .40
NNO Martin Brodeur .40 1.00
NNO Marian Gaborik .15 .40
NNO Jarome Iginla .20 .50
NNO Ilya Kovalchuk .15 .40
NNO Vincent LeCavalier .15 .40
NNO Henrik Lundqvist .40 1.00
NNO Roberto Luongo .25 .60
NNO Rick Nash .15 .40
NNO Alexander Ovechkin .60 1.50
NNO Carey Price .30 .75
NNO Eric Staal .20 .50
NNO Mats Sundin .15 .40
NNO Joe Thornton .25 .60
NNO Jonathan Toews .25 .60
NNO Henrik Zetterberg .20 .50

2008-09 O-Pee-Chee First Team All-Stars

COMPLETE SET (6) 8.00 20.00
1STAO Alexander Ovechkin 5.00 12.00
1STDP Dion Phaneuf 1.00 2.50
1STEM Evgeni Malkin 2.50 6.00
1STEN Evgeni Nabokov 1.00 2.50
1STJI Jarome Iginla 1.50 4.00
1STNL Nicklas Lidstrom 1.25 3.00

2008-09 O-Pee-Chee Materials Triple

3MADR Radulov/Arnott/Dumont 6.00 15.00
3MASH Heatley/Alfreds/Spezz 6.00 15.00
3MASZ Alfredssn/Zetter/Sedin 8.00 20.00
3MBBJ Brown/Blake/Johnson 6.00 15.00
3MBBK Kopitar/Brown/Blake 10.00 25.00
3MBBP Price/Bouilln/Brisebs 12.00 30.00
3MBCP Phan/Cammalleri/Bertuz 6.00 15.00
3MBDL Brodr/Lundq/DiPiet 15.00 40.00
3MBEP Brodeur/Parise/Elias 15.00 40.00
3MBHH Higgins/Bouillon/Hamrlik 5.00 12.00
3MBLG Brodeur/Luong/Gigur 15.00 40.00
3MBLR Briere/Richards/Lupul 6.00 15.00
3MBOT Turris/Okposo/Brassard 10.00 25.00
3MBPM Salming/Forsbrg/Sundn 12.00 30.00
3MBRE Brind'Amour/Ruutu/Eavs 6.00 15.00
3MBSP Boyes/Perron/Stempniak 5.00 12.00
3MBSW Staal/Ward/Brind'Amour 8.00 20.00
3MCBP Connolly/Paille/Bernier 4.00 10.00
3MCFH Hunter/Comrie/Fedotenko 5.00 12.00
3MCHO Hasek/Osgood/Chelios 10.00 25.00
3MCOK Crosby/Ovechkin/Kane 25.00 60.00
3MCPC Parise/Cole/Carle 6.00 15.00
3MCRL Lidstrm/Chelio/Rafalsk 6.00 15.00
3MCSK Kopitar/Stoll/Calder 10.00 25.00
3MDGK Gaborik/Koivu/Demitra 8.00 20.00
3MDMJ Doan/Mueller/Jokinen 5.00 12.00
3MDSG DiPietro/Satan/Guerin 6.00 15.00
3MFCM Crosby/Malkin/Fleury 25.00 60.00
3MFCT Thoms/Ferndz/Chara 6.00 15.00
3MFIN Selanne/Koivu/Koivu 12.00 30.00
3MFTW Forsberg/Wolski/Tucker 12.00 30.00
3MGAC Gionta/Clarkson/Asham 5.00 12.00
3MGCM Crosby/Malkin/Gnchr 25.00 60.00
3MGKM Getzlaf/Mueller/Kopitar 10.00 25.00
3MGLN Gagne/Lupul/Niittymaki 6.00 15.00
3MGNL Lundqv/Naslund/Gomez 15.00 40.00
3MGRC Gagne/Richards/Carter 6.00 15.00
3MGRP Gomez/Redden/Prucha 5.00 12.00
3MGSD Drury/Gomez/Straka 5.00 12.00
3MGWL Gonchar/Whitney/Letang 8.00 20.00
3MHGS Gaborik/Hossa/Svatos 6.00 15.00
3MHHG Gagner/Hemsky/Horcoff 5.00 12.00
3MHLH Lidstrm/Hossa/Holmstrm 6.00 15.00
3MHMS Hossa/Staal/Malone 6.00 15.00
3MHSD Holmstrom/Draper/Stuart 5.00 12.00
3MHSG Gaborik/Hossa/Satan 6.00 15.00
3MHSV Heatley/Vanek/Steen 5.00 12.00
3MHTK Kane/Toews/Havlat 12.00 30.00
3MHTS Stastny/Hejduk/Tucker 5.00 12.00
3MIGS Iginla/Gagne/Staal 8.00 20.00
3MISH Iginla/St. Louis/Heatley 8.00 20.00
3MITP Iginla/Tanguay/Phaneuf 8.00 20.00
3MJBH Brodeur/Hasek/Joseph 15.00 40.00
3MJDM Mueller/Doan/Jokinen 5.00 12.00
3MJEM Jagr/Elias/Michalek 20.00 50.00
3MJLJ Legace/Johnson/Jackmn 6.00 15.00
3MJNJ Johnson/Johnson/Niskanen 5.00 12.00
3MJTS Toskala/Joseph/Stajan 8.00 20.00
3MKGH Kolzig/Huet/Green 6.00 15.00
3MKKP Koivu/Price/Kovalev 12.00 30.00
3MKLE Koval/Leht/Enstrom 8.00 20.00
3MKMC Malone/Kolzig/Carle 6.00 15.00
3MKOR Koval/Ovech/Radulov 25.00 60.00
3MKPK Koivu/Komisarek/Plekanec 6.00 15.00
3MKSF Fedorov/Semin/Kozlov 10.00 25.00
3MKTB Kariya/Tkachuk/Boyes 6.00 15.00
3MKWP Kariya/Perron/Woznw 6.00 15.00
3MKZO Ovech/Koval/Zherdev 25.00 60.00
3MLCT Lecav/Cheechoo/Toews 10.00 25.00
3MLDZ Zetter/Lidstrm/Dtsyuk 10.00 25.00
3MLEZ Legwand/Erat/Zidlicky 5.00 12.00
3MLMK Kesler/Linden/Morrison 6.00 15.00
3MLMO Morrow/Lehtinen/Ott 5.00 12.00
3MLNP Lidstrom/Phan/Nieder 6.00 15.00
3MLNZ Nash/Zherdev/Leclaire 6.00 15.00
3MLOB Luongo/Ohlund/Bernier 10.00 25.00
3MLOE Luongo/Ohlund/Edler 10.00 25.00
3MLRV Luongo/Toskala/Roloson 10.00 25.00
3MLSJ Lecav/St.Louis/Jokin 6.00 15.00
3MLSW Lang/Sharp/Williams 6.00 15.00
3MLTT Lecav/Thornton/Toews 12.00 30.00
3MMCM Cheechoo/Marleau/Michalek 6.00 15.00
3MMCW McCabe/White/Colaiacovo 4.00 10.00
3MMFG Mason/Fistric/Goligoski 10.00 25.00
3MMHK Kovalev/Higgins/Markov 6.00 15.00
3MMKL Murray/Kobasew/Lucic 10.00 25.00
3MMKP Modano/Kariya/Parise 10.00 25.00
3MMRR Modano/Ribeiro/Richards 10.00 25.00
3MMRT Modano/Roenick/Tkachuk 10.00 25.00
3MMSS Spezza/Stajan/Matthias 6.00 15.00
3MMVS Miller/Vanek/Stafford 6.00 15.00
3MNJL Iginla/Lombardi/Nolan 8.00 20.00
3MNLR Lehtonen/Niittymaki/Rask 8.00 20.00
3MNSS Naslund/Sedin/Sedin 8.00 20.00
3MPRB Rolston/Bouchard/Parrish 6.00 15.00
3MPRM Redden/Phillips/Meszaros 4.00 10.00
3MRCL Craig/Lundin/Recchi 8.00 20.00
3MRDS Spezza/Doan/Richards 6.00 15.00
3MRGH Heatley/Gerber/Redden 5.00 12.00
3MRHA Recchi/Holik/Armstrong 8.00 20.00
3MRHL Ryder/Latendresse/Higgins 4.00 10.00
3MRK1 Stamks/Dghty/Bogsian 20.00 50.00
3MRK2 Brassard/Turris/Okposo 10.00 25.00
3MRTL Ryder/Thomas/Lucic 10.00 25.00
3MSAS Steen/Antropov/Stajan 5.00 12.00
3MSBK Bergeron/Savard/Kessel 8.00 20.00
3MSBR Brind'Am/Samsonov/Ruutu 6.00 15.00
3MSBS Staal/Briere/Sakic 6.00 15.00
3MSBT Sundin/Tucker/Blake 6.00 15.00
3MSCW Cole/Williams/Samsonov 5.00 12.00
3MSDL Doan/Smyth/Lupul 5.00 12.00
3MSFB Forsb/Sund/Backstrm 12.00 30.00
3MSFS Sakic/Forsberg/Smyth 12.00 30.00
3MSGN Selanne/Getzlaf/Nieder 12.00 30.00
3MSJL Jagr/Shanahan/Lundq 20.00 50.00
3MSKA Sundin/Koivu/Alfredsson 6.00 15.00
3MSKK Khabibulin/Sharp/Keith 6.00 15.00
3MSKT Kariya/Shanahan/Selanne 12.00 30.00
3MSLB Sakic/Budaj/Liles 12.00 30.00
3MSLJ Selanne/Lehtinen/Jokinen 12.00 30.00
3MSNG Giguere/Selanne/Nieder 12.00 30.00
3MSOB Ovech/Bckstrm/Semin 12.00 30.00
3MSSS Staal/Staal/Staal 8.00 20.00
3MSWS Stastny/Svatos/Wolski 5.00 12.00
3MTLU Leclaire/Umberger/Torres 5.00 12.00
3MTRM Thorntn/Roenik/Mrl 10.00 25.00
3MTTL Toivonen/Lehtonen/Toskala 8.00 20.00
3MVKB Vyborny/Brule/Klesla 4.00 10.00
3MVWH Vokoun/Weiss/Horton 5.00 12.00
3MWPG Getzlaf/Perry/Weight 10.00 25.00
3MWPG Weight/Parise/Gomez 6.00 15.00
3MZBW Weiss/Bouwmeester/Zednik 6.00 15.00
3MZEG Giroux/Zubov/Earl 12.00 30.00
3MZKA Khabibulin/Zherdev/Antropov 6.00 15.00
3MZRT Turco/Ribeiro/Zubov 6.00 15.00
3MZTN Turco/Zubov/Niskanen 6.00 15.00

2008-09 O-Pee-Chee Oversized Cards

COMPLETE SET (42) 15.00 40.00
TRU1 Alexander Ovechkin 2.00 5.00
TRU2 Markus Naslund .50 1.25
TRU3 Roberto Luongo .75 2.00
TRU4 Mats Sundin .50 1.25
TRU5 Vincent Lecavalier .50 1.25
TRU6 Martin St. Louis .50 1.25
TRU7 Joe Thornton .75 2.00
TRU8 Sidney Crosby 2.00 5.00
TRU9 Evgeni Malkin 1.00 2.50
TRU10 Marc-Andre Fleury 1.00 2.50
TRU11 Shane Doan .40 1.00
TRU12 Mike Richards .40 1.00
TRU13 Brendan Shanahan .50 1.25
TRU14 Jaromir Jagr 1.50 4.00
TRU15 Henrik Lundqvist 1.25 3.00
TRU16 Martin Brodeur 1.25 3.00
TRU17 Alexander Radulov .50 1.25
TRU18 Saku Koivu .50 1.25
TRU19 Carey Price 1.00 2.50
TRU20 Marian Gaborik .50 1.25
TRU21 Anze Kopitar .75 2.00
TRU22 Sam Gagner .30 .75
TRU23 Andrew Cogliano .30 .75
TRU24 Henrik Zetterberg .60 1.50
TRU25 Nicklas Lidstrom .50 1.25
TRU26 Pavel Datsyuk .75 2.00
TRU27 Dominik Hasek .75 2.00
TRU28 Mike Modano .75 2.00
TRU29 Marty Turco .50 1.25
TRU30 Brad Richards .50 1.25
TRU31 Rick Nash .50 1.25
TRU32 Paul Stastny .40 1.00
TRU33 Joe Sakic 1.00 2.50
TRU34 Patrick Kane 1.00 2.50
TRU35 Jonathan Toews .75 2.00
TRU36 Eric Staal .60 1.50
TRU37 Jarome Iginla .60 1.50
TRU38 Miikka Kiprusoff .50 1.25
TRU39 Ryan Miller .50 1.25
TRU40 Patrice Bergeron .60 1.50
TRU41 Ilya Kovalchuk .50 1.25
TRU42 Ryan Getzlaf .50 1.25

2008-09 O-Pee-Chee Season Highlights

COMPLETE SET (19) 20.00 50.00
SH1 Alexander Ovechkin 4.00 10.00
SH2 Alexander Ovechkin 4.00 10.00
SH3 Andrew Cogliano .60 1.50
SH4 Chris Chelios 1.00 2.50
SH5 Evgeni Nabokov .75 2.00
SH6 Jarome Iginla 1.25 3.00
SH7 Jarome Iginla 1.25 3.00
SH8 Jeremy Roenick 1.50 4.00
SH9 Joe Sakic 2.00 5.00
SH10 Marian Gaborik 1.00 2.50
SH11 Martin Brodeur 2.50 6.00
SH12 Mats Sundin 1.00 2.50
SH13 Mike Modano 1.50 4.00
SH14 Paul Kariya 1.00 2.50
SH15 Robert Nilsson .60 1.50
SH16 Sidney Crosby 4.00 10.00
SH17 Carey Price 2.00 5.00
SH18 Johan Franzen .75 2.00
SH19 Jonathan Toews 1.50 4.00

2008-09 O-Pee-Chee Second Team All-Stars

COMPLETE SET (6) 5.00 12.00
2NDAK Alex Kovalev 1.25 3.00
2NDBC Brian Campbell 1.25 3.00
2NDHZ Henrik Zetterberg 2.00 5.00
2NDJT Joe Thornton 2.50 6.00
2NDMB Martin Brodeur 4.00 10.00
2NDZC Zdeno Chara 1.50 4.00

2008-09 O-Pee-Chee Signatures

SAK Anze Kopitar 15.00 40.00
SAO Alexander Ovechkin 40.00 100.00
SBC Blake Comeau 6.00 15.00
SBD Brandon Dubinsky 6.00 15.00
SBE Jonathan Bernier 8.00 20.00
SBL Michael Blunden 6.00 15.00
SBO Bobby Orr 100.00 200.00
SBR Bobby Ryan 8.00 20.00
SBY Dustin Byfuglien 10.00 25.00
SCA Casey Borer 10.00 25.00
SCB Cam Barker 6.00 15.00
SCD Chris Drury 8.00 20.00
SCH Chris Higgins 6.00 15.00
SCK Chris Kunitz 10.00 25.00
SCM Cory Murphy 6.00 15.00
SDA Daniel Carcillo 6.00 15.00
SDB Dan Boyle 6.00 15.00
SDC Dan Cleary 8.00 20.00
SDG Daniel Girardi 6.00 15.00
SDJ David Jones 6.00 15.00
SDP Daniel Paille 6.00 15.00
SDS Daniel Sedin 12.00 30.00
SDU Dustin Penner 8.00 20.00
SEJ Erik Johnson 6.00 15.00
SEN Eric Nystrom 6.00 15.00
SFN Frans Nielsen 6.00 15.00
SGL Guillaume Latendresse 6.00 15.00
SGM Greg Moore 6.00 15.00
SHA Josh Harding 10.00 25.00
SHE T.J. Hensick 8.00 20.00
SHI Jonas Hiller 8.00 20.00
SHL Jaroslav Hlinka 6.00 15.00
SHS Henrik Sedin 12.00 30.00
SHZ Henrik Zetterberg 12.00 30.00
SJB Jared Boll 6.00 15.00
SJC Jeff Carter 8.00 20.00
SJH Jaroslav Halak 10.00 25.00
SJJ Jack Johnson 6.00 15.00
SJO Johnny Boychuk 8.00 20.00
SJP Jason Pominville 6.00 15.00
SJS Jack Skille 8.00 20.00
SJT Jiri Tlusty 6.00 15.00
SKA Petr Kalus 8.00 20.00
SKC Kyle Chipchura 8.00 20.00
SKE Phil Kessel 10.00 25.00
SKY Keith Yandle 6.00 15.00
SLK Lukas Kaspar 6.00 15.00
SMA Mark Fraser 8.00 20.00
SMAN Mark Mancari 8.00 20.00
SMB Martin Brodeur 25.00 60.00
SME Matt Ellis 6.00 15.00
SMI Milan Michalek 6.00 15.00
SML Matt Lashoff 6.00 15.00
SMM Marc Methot 6.00 15.00
SMN Matt Niskanen 8.00 20.00
SMR Mike Ribeiro 6.00 15.00
SMS Matt Smaby 8.00 20.00
SMT Marty Turco 10.00 25.00
SNA Evgeni Nabokov 8.00 20.00
SNB Nicklas Backstrom 10.00 25.00
SNG Niklas Grossman 6.00 15.00
SNH Nathan Horton 8.00 20.00
SNI Nicklas Bergfors 15.00 40.00
SNK Niklas Kronwall 8.00 20.00
SOP Ondrej Pavelec 12.00 30.00
SPA Ryan Parent 6.00 15.00
SPB Peter Budaj 8.00 20.00
SPE David Perron 8.00 20.00
SPI Pierre-Marc Bouchard 10.00 25.00
SPK Patrick Kane 20.00 50.00
SPM Peter Mueller 8.00 20.00
SPS Paul Stastny 8.00 20.00
SRC Ryan Callahan 6.00 15.00
SRG Ryan Getzlaf 10.00 25.00
SRI Mike Richards 8.00 20.00
SRO Rostislav Olesz 6.00 15.00
SRP Rod Pelley 6.00 15.00
SRS Ryan Smyth 8.00 20.00
SRY Ryan Carter 6.00 15.00
SSC Sidney Crosby 80.00 150.00
SSD Steve Downie 10.00 25.00
SSE Devin Setoguchi 8.00 20.00
SSG Sam Gagner 6.00 15.00
SSH James Sheppard 6.00 15.00
SSJ Jordan Staal 8.00 20.00
SSK Sergei Kostitsyn 6.00 15.00
SSM Matt Stajan 6.00 15.00
SST Drew Stafford 6.00 15.00
STA Maxime Talbot 6.00 15.00
STE Tobias Enstrom 6.00 15.00
STG Tom Gilbert 6.00 15.00
STH Joe Thornton 15.00 40.00
STK Tomas Kaberle 6.00 15.00
STO Jonathan Toews 15.00 40.00
STP Tomas Plihal 8.00 20.00
STR Tuukka Rask 12.00 30.00
STS Tobias Stephan 8.00 20.00
STV Tomas Vokoun 8.00 20.00
STW Tyler Weiman 6.00 15.00
STY Tyler Kennedy 8.00 20.00
OPSAB Adam Burish 8.00 20.00
OPSAE Andrew Ebbett 6.00 15.00
OPSBB Brian Boyle 8.00 20.00
OPSBE Brendan Bell 6.00 15.00
OPSBG Brian Gionta 6.00 15.00
OPSBJ Jonathan Bernier 8.00 20.00
OPSBL Brian Lee 8.00 20.00
OPSBM Brenden Morrow 8.00 20.00
OPSBO Brad Boyes 6.00 15.00
OPSBW Blake Wheeler 25.00 60.00
OPSCG Colton Gillies 8.00 20.00
OPSCP Chris Phillips 6.00 15.00
OPSCR Sidney Crosby 80.00 150.00
OPSDC David Clarkson 8.00 20.00
OPSDG Daniel Girardi 6.00 15.00
OPSDL Dan LaCosta 10.00 25.00
OPSDP Daniel Paille 6.00 15.00
OPSDU Dustin Boyd 6.00 15.00
OPSEF Eric Fehr 6.00 15.00
OPSEL Patrik Elias 10.00 25.00
OPSFB Fabian Brunnstrom 8.00 20.00
OPSFR Michael Frolik 10.00 25.00
OPSHA Michal Handzus 8.00 20.00
OPSHE Josh Hennessy 6.00 15.00
OPSJA Jarret Stoll 8.00 20.00
OPSJD Jeff Drouin-Deslauriers 6.00 15.00
OPSJH Jannik Hansen 10.00 25.00
OPSJI Jarome Iginla 12.00 30.00
OPSJJ Jack Johnson 6.00 15.00
OPSJL John-Michael Liles 6.00 15.00
OPSJM Jamie McGinn 10.00 25.00
OPSJO Joel Perrault 6.00 15.00
OPSJP Jason Pominville 6.00 15.00
OPSJS James Sheppard 6.00 15.00
OPSJT Jiri Tlusty 6.00 15.00
OPSKD Kris Draper 6.00 15.00
OPSKN Kevin Nastiuk 6.00 15.00
OPSKQ Kyle Quincey 6.00 15.00
OPSKT Kyle Turris 15.00 40.00
OPSKV Kris Versteeg 6.00 15.00
OPSLA Drew Larman 6.00 15.00
OPSLI Bryan Little 8.00 20.00
OPSLS Luke Schenn 12.00 30.00
OPSMA Mark Fraser 8.00 20.00
OPSMB Mikkel Boedker 12.00 30.00
OPSMC Bryan McCabe 6.00 15.00
OPSME Matt Ellis 6.00 15.00
OPSMF Mark Fistric 8.00 20.00
OPSMG Martin Gerber 8.00 20.00
OPSMH Martin Havlat 10.00 25.00
OPSMI Mike Iggulden 8.00 20.00
OPSMK Mike Knuble 6.00 15.00
OPSMM Mark Mancari 8.00 20.00
OPSMP Marc-Antoine Pouliot 6.00 15.00
OPSMR Mattias Ritola 8.00 20.00
OPSMS Marco Sturm 6.00 15.00
OPSNB Nicklas Backstrom 10.00 25.00
OPSND Nigel Dawes 6.00 15.00
OPSNF Nikita Filatov 10.00 25.00
OPSNK Nikolai Kulemin 10.00 25.00
OPSNW Noah Welch 6.00 15.00
OPSOP Ondrej Pavelec 12.00 30.00
OPSPA Dimitri Patzold 6.00 15.00
OPSPD Dustin Penner 8.00 20.00
OPSPO Ryan Potulny 6.00 15.00
OPSRA Mason Raymond 6.00 15.00
OPSRC Ryane Clowe 6.00 15.00
OPSRP Rich Peverley 8.00 20.00
OPSSA Miroslav Satan 10.00 25.00
OPSSC Marek Schwarz 10.00 25.00
OPSSM Stefan Meyer 6.00 15.00
OPSSS Steven Stamkos 40.00 100.00
OPSSW Steve Wagner 6.00 15.00
OPSTG Tom Gilbert 6.00 15.00
OPSTO T.J. Oshie 20.00 50.00
OPSTS Tom Sestito 10.00 25.00
OPSTW Tyler Weiman 6.00 15.00
OPSVF Valtteri Filppula 6.00 15.00
OPSVT Viktor Tikhonov 8.00 20.00
OPSZB Zach Bogosian 12.00 30.00

2008-09 O-Pee-Chee Stat Leaders

COMPLETE SET (14) 12.00 30.00
SL1 Ovechkin/Malkin/Iginla 3.00 8.00
SL2 Ovechkin/Kovalchuk/Iginla 3.00 8.00
SL3 Thornton/Datsyuk/Savard 1.25 3.00
SL4 Datsyuk/Lidstrom/Heatley 1.25 3.00
SL5 Carcillo/Boll/Burish .60 1.50
SL6 Lidstrom/Gonchar/Streit .75 2.00
SL7 Nabokov/Brodeur/Kiprusoff 2.00 5.00
SL8 Osgood/Giguere/Hasek 1.25 3.00
SL9 Lundqvist/Leclaire/Nabokov 2.00 5.00
SL10 Ellis/Conklin/Giguere .75 2.00
SL11 Kane/Backstrom/Toews 1.50 4.00
SL12 Crosby/Zetterberg/Hossa 3.00 8.00
SL13 Franzen/Zetterberg/Hossa 1.00 2.50
SL14 Osgood/Fleury/Turco 1.50 4.00

2008-09 O-Pee-Chee Team Checklists

COMPLETE SET (30) 20.00 50.00
CL1 Anaheim Ducks 1.25 3.00
CL2 Atlanta Thrashers 1.25 3.00
CL3 Boston Bruins 1.25 3.00
CL4 Buffalo Sabres 1.25 3.00
CL5 Calgary Flames 1.25 3.00
CL6 Carolina Hurricanes 1.25 3.00
CL7 Chicago Blackhawks 1.25 3.00
CL8 Colorado Avalanche 1.25 3.00
CL9 Columbus Blue Jackets 1.25 3.00
CL10 Dallas Stars 1.25 3.00
CL11 Detroit Red Wings 1.25 3.00
CL12 Edmonton Oilers 1.25 3.00
CL13 Florida Panthers 1.25 3.00
CL14 Los Angeles Kings 1.25 3.00
CL15 Minnesota Wild 1.25 3.00
CL16 Montreal Canadiens 1.25 3.00
CL17 Nashville Predators 1.25 3.00
CL18 New Jersey Devils 1.25 3.00
CL19 New York Islanders 1.25 3.00
CL20 New York Rangers 1.25 3.00
CL21 Ottawa Senators 1.25 3.00
CL22 Philadelphia Flyers 1.25 3.00
CL23 Phoenix Coyotes 1.25 3.00
CL24 Pittsburgh Penguins 1.25 3.00
CL25 San Jose Sharks 1.25 3.00
CL26 St. Louis Blues 1.25 3.00
CL27 Tampa Bay Lightning 1.25 3.00
CL28 Toronto Maple Leafs 1.25 3.00
CL29 Vancouver Canucks 1.25 3.00
CL30 Washington Capitals 1.25 3.00

2008-09 O-Pee-Chee Trophy Cards

COMPLETE SET (19) 15.00 40.00
AWDAL Art Ross 1.00 2.50
AWDAO Hart Memorial 1.00 2.50
AWDDA Lady Byng 1.00 2.50
AWDDE Roger Crozier 1.00 2.50
AWDDR Clarence Campbell 1.00 2.50
AWDDW Stanley Cup 1.00 2.50
AWDHO William Jennings 1.00 2.50
AWDHZ Conn Smythe 1.00 2.50
AWDJB Bill Masterton 1.00 2.50
AWDMB Vezina 1.00 2.50
AWDNL James Norris 1.00 2.50
AWDOA Maurice Richard 1.00 2.50
AWDOV Lester B Pearson 1.00 2.50
AWDPD Frank J Selke 1.00 2.50
AWDPK Calder 1.00 2.50
AWDPP Prince of Whales 1.00 2.50
AWDPV Plus Minus Award 1.00 2.50
AWDRE Presidents' Trophy 1.00 2.50
AWDVL King Clancy Memorial Trophy 1.00 2.50

2008-09 O-Pee-Chee Wayne Gretzky Panoramic Cards

COMMON GRETAZKY 8.00 20.00

2008-09 O-Pee-Chee Wayne Gretzky Retro Cards

COMPLETE SET (4) 150.00 300.00
COMMON GRETZKY 40.00 80.00

2008-09 O-Pee-Chee Winter Classic Highlights

WC1 Buffalo Sabres 4.00 10.00
WC2 Brian Campbell 4.00 10.00
WC3 Brian Campbell 4.00 10.00
WC4 Erik Christensen 3.00 8.00
WC5 Ty Conklin 4.00 10.00
WC6 Ty Conklin 4.00 10.00
WC7 Ty Conklin 4.00 10.00
WC8 Daniel Paille 3.00 8.00
WC9 Sidney Crosby 8.00 20.00
WC10 Sidney Crosby 8.00 20.00
WC11 Pittsburgh Penguins 4.00 10.00
WC12 Paul Gaustad 3.00 8.00
WC13 Sergei Gonchar 3.00 8.00
WC14 Sergei Gonchar 3.00 8.00
WC15 Tyler Kennedy 4.00 10.00
WC16 Ales Kotalik 3.00 8.00
WC17 Buffalo Sabres 4.00 10.00
WC18 Georges Laraque 4.00 10.00
WC19 Evgeni Malkin 10.00 25.00
WC20 Ryan Malone 3.00 8.00
WC21 Ryan Miller 5.00 12.00
WC22 Derek Roy 3.00 8.00
WC23 Michael Ryan 3.00 8.00
WC24 Colby Armstrong 3.00 8.00
WC25 Jaroslav Spacek 3.00 8.00
WC26 Jordan Staal 4.00 10.00
WC27 Ralph Wilson Stadium 3.00 8.00
WC28 Thomas Vanek 4.00 10.00
WC29 Jason Pominville 3.00 8.00
WC30 Maxim Afinogenov 3.00 8.00
WC31 Jordan Staal SP 10.00 25.00
WC32 Ryan Miller SP 12.00 30.00
WC33 Evgeni Malkin SP 20.00 50.00
WC34 Thomas Vanek SP 10.00 25.00
WC35 Thomas Vanek SP 10.00 25.00
WC36 Evgeni Malkin SP 25.00 60.00
WC37 Sidney Crosby SP 15.00 40.00
WC38 Sidney Crosby SP 15.00 40.00
WC39 Sidney Crosby SP 15.00 40.00
WC40 Sidney Crosby SP 15.00 40.00

2009-10 O-Pee-Chee

1 Roberto Luongo .30 .75
2 Zdeno Chara .20 .50
3 Patrick Lalime .15 .40
4 Sergei Samsonov .15 .40
5 Troy Brouwer .12 .30
6 Mike Commodore .12 .30
7 Marian Hossa .20 .50
8 Alexander Ovechkin .75 2.00
9 Alexander Frolov .15 .40
10 Colton Gillies .20 .50
11 Jamie Langenbrunner .12 .30
12 Paul Mara .12 .30
13 Scottie Upshall .12 .30
14 Jordan Staal .15 .40
15 Anton Stralman .12 .30
16 Andrej Meszaros .12 .30
17 Henrik Sedin .25 .60
18 Karl Alzner .12 .30
19 Jonathan Toews .30 .75
20 Jim Slater .12 .30
21 Andrew Ference .12 .30
22 David Moss .15 .40
23 Bruno Gervais .12 .30
24 David Jones .12 .30
25 James Neal .12 .30
26 Ty Conklin .15 .40
27 Gregory Campbell .12 .30
28 Jonathan Quick .25 .60
29 Roman Hamrlik .12 .30
30 Martin Brodeur .50 1.25
31 Carey Price .40 1.00
32 Alex Auld .15 .40
33 Martin Hanzal .15 .40
34 Eric Godard .12 .30
35 Chris Mason .15 .40
36 Tomas Kaberle .12 .30
37 Erik Cole .12 .30
38 Joel Ward .12 .30
39 Colby Armstrong .12 .30
40 Stephane Yelle .12 .30
41 Craig Conroy .12 .30
42 Mike Comrie .15 .40
43 Cody McLeod .12 .30
44 Loui Eriksson .12 .30
45 Jiri Tlusty .12 .30
46 Cory Stillman .12 .30
47 Erik Ersberg .15 .40
48 Sergei Kostitsyn .12 .30
49 Brendan Shanahan .20 .50
50 Scott Gomez .15 .40
51 Chris Phillips .12 .30
52 Steven Reinprecht .12 .30
53 Ryan Whitney .12 .30
54 T.J. Oshie .20 .50
55 Alexei Ponikarovsky .12 .30
56 Willie Mitchell .12 .30
57 David Legwand .15 .40
58 Brendan Mikkelson .12 .30
59 Milan Lucic .15 .40
60 Adam Mair .12 .30
61 Joni Pitkanen .15 .40
62 Ryan Smyth .15 .40
63 Michael Peca .15 .40
64 Jiri Hudler .15 .40
65 Sam Gagner .12 .30
66 Patrick O'Sullivan .15 .40
67 Josh Harding .20 .50
68 Dainius Zubrus .12 .30
69 Daniel Alfredsson .20 .50
70 Daniel Briere .20 .50
71 Alex Goligoski .15 .40
72 Brian Boucher .15 .40
73 Paul Ranger .12 .30

74 Mats Sundin .20 .50
75 Rick Rypien .20 .50
76 Zbynek Michalek .12 .30
77 Corey Perry .30 .75
78 Zach Bogosian .15 .40
79 Ales Kotalik .12 .30
80 Cory Sarich .12 .30
81 Andrew Ladd .12 .30
82 Andrew Raycroft .15 .40
83 Fabian Brunnstrom .15 .40
84 Ales Hemsky .15 .40
85 Keith Ballard .12 .30
86 Marek Zidlicky .12 .30
87 Sidney Crosby .75 2.00
88 Patrick Kane .40 1.00
89 Daniel Girardi .12 .30
90 Jeff Carter .15 .40
91 Viktor Tikhonov .15 .40
92 Dan Boyle .12 .30
93 Barret Jackman .12 .30
94 Nikolai Kulemin .12 .30
95 Alexander Semin .20 .50
96 Wade Belak .12 .30
97 Jonas Hiller .15 .40
98 Chuck Kobasew .12 .30
99 Craig Rivet .12 .30
100 Adam Pardy .12 .30
101 Milan Hejduk .15 .40
102 Kris Russell .12 .30
103 Brian Rafalski .12 .30
104 Dwayne Roloson .15 .40
105 Kyle Quincey .12 .30
106 Niklas Backstrom .20 .50
107 Johnny Oduya .15 .40
108 Jason Spezza .20 .50
109 Luca Sbisa .20 .50
110 Kristopher Letang .25 .60
111 Evgeni Nabokov .15 .40
112 Evgeni Artyukhin .12 .30
113 Kevin Bieksa .15 .40
114 Donald Brashear .12 .30
115 Jonas Frogren .15 .40
116 Rob Niedermayer .12 .30
117 Patrice Bergeron .25 .60
118 Jochen Hecht .12 .30
119 Chad LaRose .12 .30
120 Paul Stastny .15 .40
121 Jared Boll .12 .30
122 Nicklas Lidstrom .12 .30
123 Jeff Drouin-Deslauriers .12 .30
124 Michal Handzus .15 .40
125 Andrei Markov .20 .50
126 David Clarkson .12 .30
127 Filip Kuba .12 .30
128 Martin Biron .15 .40
129 Pascal Dupuis .12 .30
130 Brad Boyes .12 .30
131 Ty Wishart .12 .30
132 Pavol Demitra .25 .60
133 Matt Bradley .12 .30
134 Steve Montador .12 .30
135 Matt Hunwick .12 .30
136 Jarome Iginla .25 .60
137 Justin Williams .15 .40
138 Wojtek Wolski .12 .30
139 Rostislav Klesla .20 .50
140 Johan Franzen .15 .40
141 Robert Nilsson .12 .30
142 Drew Doughty .25 .60
143 Robert Lang .12 .30
144 John Madden .12 .30
145 Antoine Vermette .12 .30
146 Antero Niittymaki .20 .50
147 Marc-Andre Fleury .40 1.00
148 Keith Tkachuk .20 .50
149 Mike Smith .20 .50
150 Alexandre Burrows .12 .30
151 Boyd Gordon .12 .30
152 Teemu Selanne .40 1.00
153 Phil Kessel .20 .50
154 Teppo Numminen .12 .30
155 Eric Staal .25 .60
156 Ben Eager .15 .40
157 Jakub Voracek .15 .40
158 Marty Turco .20 .50
159 Tom Gilbert .12 .30
160 Craig Anderson .20 .50
161 James Sheppard .12 .30
162 Zach Parise .20 .50
163 Trevor Smith .12 .30
164 Colton Orr .12 .30
165 Joffrey Lupul .12 .30
166 Chris Drury .15 .40
167 Christian Ehrhoff .12 .30
168 Ryan Malone .12 .30
169 Justin Pogge .20 .50
170 Tomas Fleischmann .12 .30
171 Kyle Brodziak .12 .30
172 Ilya Kovalchuk .20 .50
173 Tim Thomas .20 .50
174 Mike Cammalleri .15 .40
175 Brandon Sutter .12 .30
176 John-Michael Liles .12 .30
177 Nikita Filatov .15 .40
178 Mikael Samuelsson .12 .30
179 Steve Staios .12 .30
180 Oscar Moller .12 .30
181 Alex Kovalev .15 .40
182 Paul Martin .12 .30
183 Mike Fisher .12 .30
184 Arron Asham .12 .30
185 Mathieu Garon .20 .50
186 David Perron .15 .40
187 Ryan Bayda .12 .30
188 Steve Bernier .12 .30
189 Jean-Pierre Dumont .12 .30
190 Todd White .12 .30
191 Manny Fernandez .12 .30
192 Daymond Langkow .12 .30
193 Zach Boychuk .15 .40
194 Marek Svatos .15 .40
195 Steve Mason .15 .40
196 Tomas Holmstrom .15 .40
197 Marc-Antoine Pouliot .15 .40
198 Wayne Simmonds .25 .60
199 Andrei Kostitsyn .15 .40
200 Brian Rolston .15 .40
201 Chris Kelly .15 .40
202 Riley Cote .12 .30
203 Tyler Kennedy .15 .40
204 Patrik Berglund .12 .30
205 Vladimir Mihalik .20 .50
206 Alexander Edler .12 .30
207 Martin Erat .12 .30
208 Slava Kozlov .12 .30
209 P.J. Axelsson .12 .30
210 Todd Bertuzzi .20 .50
211 Dennis Seidenberg .12 .30
212 Jordan Leopold .12 .30
213 Pascal Leclaire .20 .50
214 Niklas Kronwall .15 .40
215 Stephen Weiss .12 .30
216 Trevor Lewis .12 .30
217 Saku Koivu .20 .50
218 Colin White .12 .30
219 Alexandre Picard .12 .30
220 Shane Doan .15 .40
221 Matt Cooke .12 .30
222 David Backes .12 .30
223 Nik Antropov .15 .40
224 Jannik Hansen .12 .30
225 Shea Weber .15 .40
226 Brad Winchester .12 .30
227 Boris Valabik .20 .50
228 Derek Roy .15 .40
229 Mark Giordano .20 .50
230 Patrick Sharp .20 .50
231 Adam Foote .12 .30
232 Steve Ott .12 .30
233 Brad Stuart .12 .30
234 Radek Dvorak .12 .30
235 Antti Miettinen .12 .30
236 Patrice Brisebois .12 .30
237 Bill Guerin .20 .50
238 Michal Rozsival .12 .30
239 Brian Lee .20 .50
240 Mikkel Boedker .12 .30
241 Patrick Marleau .20 .50
242 Carlo Colaiacovo .12 .30
243 Lee Stempniak .12 .30
244 Shane O'Brien .12 .30
245 Vernon Fiddler .12 .30
246 Tobias Enstrom .12 .30
247 Thomas Vanek .15 .40
248 Matthew Lombardi .12 .30
249 Kris Versteeg .12 .30
250 Darcy Tucker .15 .40
251 Trevor Daley .12 .30
252 Chris Osgood .20 .50
253 Michael Frolik .15 .40
254 Mikko Koivu .20 .50
255 Maxim Lapierre .12 .30
256 Doug Weight .20 .50
257 Brandon Dubinsky .12 .30
258 Brian Elliott .15 .40
259 Keith Yandle .12 .30
260 Joe Thornton .30 .75
261 Manny Legace .15 .40
262 Niklas Hagman .12 .30
263 Cory Schneider .20 .50
264 Dan Hamhuis .15 .40
265 Sami Salo .20 .50
266 Dennis Wideman .12 .30
267 Maxim Afinogenov .12 .30
268 Rod Brind'Amour .20 .50
269 Nikolai Khabibulin .20 .50
270 Fredrik Modin .12 .30
271 Tobias Stephan .12 .30
272 Denis Grebeshkov .12 .30
273 Dustin Brown .20 .50
274 Benoit Pouliot .12 .30
275 Patrik Elias .20 .50
276 Rick DiPietro .15 .40
277 Henrik Lundqvist .50 1.25
278 Kimmo Timonen .12 .30
279 Petr Sykora .15 .40
280 Jonathan Cheechoo .15 .40
281 Steve Eminger .12 .30
282 John Mitchell .12 .30
283 Sergei Fedorov .30 .75
284 Fernando Pisani .12 .30
285 Travis Moen .12 .30
286 Michael Ryder .12 .30
287 Ryan Miller .20 .50
288 Tuomo Ruutu .12 .30
289 Cristobal Huet .20 .50
290 Jason Arnott .15 .40
291 Pavel Datsyuk .30 .75
292 Dustin Penner .12 .30
293 Anze Kopitar .30 .75
294 Marian Gaborik .12 .30
295 Travis Zajac .12 .30
296 Joey MacDonald .15 .40
297 Stephen Valiquette .12 .30
298 Braydon Coburn .12 .30
299 Miroslav Satan .12 .30
300 Mike Grier .12 .30
301 Steven Stamkos .40 1.00
302 Daniel Sedin .25 .60
303 Milan Jurcina .12 .30
304 Cal Clutterbuck .12 .30
305 Ryan Getzlaf .20 .50
306 Kari Lehtonen .15 .40
307 Jason Pominville .12 .30
308 Dustin Boyd .12 .30
309 Brian Campbell .15 .40
310 Brett Clark .12 .30
311 Stephane Robidas .12 .30
312 Brett Lebda .12 .30
313 Bryan McCabe .15 .40
314 Pierre-Marc Bouchard .20 .50
315 Max Pacioretty .20 .50
316 Trent Hunter .12 .30
317 Ryan Callahan .12 .30
318 Ilya Zubov .12 .30
319 Kyle Turris .20 .50
320 Devin Setoguchi .15 .40
321 Jay McClement .12 .30
322 Mikhail Grabovski .12 .30
323 George Parros .12 .30
324 Jordin Tootoo .20 .50
325 Scott Niedermayer .20 .50
326 Mathieu Schneider .12 .30
327 Clarke MacArthur .12 .30
328 Curtis Glencross .12 .30
329 Duncan Keith .15 .40
330 Rick Nash .20 .50
331 Jere Lehtinen .15 .40
332 Shawn Horcoff .12 .30
333 Anthony Stewart .12 .30
334 Eric Belanger .12 .30
335 Jaroslav Halak .20 .50
336 Kyle Okposo .12 .30
337 Nigel Dawes .12 .30
338 Mike Richards .15 .40
339 Daniel Carcillo .12 .30
340 Joe Pavelski .25 .60
341 Martin St. Louis .20 .50
342 Ian White .15 .40
343 Mike Green .15 .40
344 Dan Ellis .12 .30
345 Francois Beauchemin .12 .30
346 Blake Wheeler .20 .50
347 Daniel Paille .15 .40
348 Joe Corvo .12 .30
349 Jack Skille .12 .30
350 Manny Malhotra .12 .30
351 Henrik Zetterberg .25 .60
352 Ethan Moreau .12 .30
353 Jarret Stoll .15 .40
354 Derek Boogaard .12 .30
355 Brian Gionta .12 .30
356 Dany Heatley .15 .40
357 Matt Carle .15 .40
358 Ruslan Fedotenko .12 .30
359 Jeremy Roenick .30 .75
360 Jussi Jokinen .12 .30
361 Ryan Kesler .20 .50
362 Jose Theodore .20 .50
363 Derek Morris .12 .30
364 Bobby Ryan .15 .40
365 Eric Perrin .12 .30
366 Jaroslav Spacek .12 .30
367 Miikka Kiprusoff .20 .50
368 Cam Barker .12 .30
369 Kristian Huselius .12 .30
370 Matt Niskanen .15 .40
371 Sheldon Souray .12 .30
372 Shawn Matthias .20 .50
373 Owen Nolan .20 .50
374 Chris Higgins .12 .30
375 Andy Hilbert .12 .30
376 Aaron Voros .12 .30
377 Simon Gagne .20 .50
378 Mike Weaver .12 .30
379 Milan Michalek .12 .30
380 Vincent Lecavalier .20 .50
381 Jeff Finger .12 .30
382 Viktor Kozlov .12 .30
383 Pekka Rinne .20 .50
384 Chris Kunitz .20 .50
385 David Krejci .20 .50
386 Paul Gaustad .15 .40
387 Ray Whitney .15 .40
388 Brent Seabrook .12 .30
389 Derick Brassard .12 .30
390 Darryl Sydor .12 .30
391 Andrew Cogliano .12 .30
392 Tomas Vokoun .15 .40
393 Brent Burns .20 .50
394 Matt D'Agostini .15 .40
395 Josh Bailey .15 .40
396 Lauri Korpikoski .12 .30
397 Mike Knuble .12 .30
398 Evgeni Malkin .40 1.00
399 Marc-Edouard Vlasic .12 .30
400 Vaclav Prospal .12 .30
401 Vesa Toskala .20 .50
402 Michael Nylander .12 .30
403 Anton Babchuk .15 .40
404 Rich Peverley .15 .40
405 Marco Sturm .12 .30
406 Adrian Aucoin .12 .30
407 Martin Havlat .15 .40
408 Chris Stewart .15 .40
409 Mike Modano .30 .75
410 Chris Chelios .20 .50
411 Jay Bouwmeester .12 .30
412 Jack Johnson .12 .30
413 Guillaume Latendresse .15 .40
414 Mark Streit .12 .30
415 Jamal Mayers .12 .30
416 Chris Neil .12 .30
417 Ed Jovanovski .15 .40
418 Philippe Boucher .12 .30
419 Paul Kariya .20 .50
420 Dominic Moore .20 .50
421 Mattias Ohlund .12 .30
422 Radek Bonk .12 .30
423 Jean-Sebastien Giguere .20 .50
424 Johan Hedberg .15 .40
425 Drew Stafford .12 .30
426 Robyn Regehr .12 .30
427 Dave Bolland .15 .40
428 Peter Budaj .15 .40
429 Brenden Morrow .15 .40
430 Kirk Maltby .12 .30
431 Michal Repik .12 .30
432 Andrew Brunette .12 .30
433 Mike Komisarek .15 .40
434 Richard Park .12 .30
435 Wade Redden .12 .30
436 Jesse Winchester .15 .40
437 Enver Lisin .12 .30
438 Ryane Clowe .12 .30
439 Mason Raymond .12 .30
440 Pavel Kubina .12 .30
441 Nicklas Backstrom .20 .50
442 Patric Hornqvist .12 .30
443 Ron Hainsey .12 .30
444 Mark Stuart .12 .30
445 Dion Phaneuf .15 .40
446 Brooks Orpik .12 .30
447 Tyler Arnason .12 .30
448 Brad Richards .20 .50
449 Valtteri Filppula .12 .30
450 Nathan Horton .20 .50
451 Raitis Ivanans .12 .30
452 Tomas Plekanec .12 .30
453 Bobby Holik .12 .30
454 Nikolai Zherdev .12 .30
455 Jarkko Ruutu .12 .30
456 Peter Mueller .15 .40
457 Maxime Talbot .12 .30
458 Andy McDonald .15 .40
459 Marc Staal .12 .30
460 Kyle Wellwood .15 .40
461 Ryan Suter .15 .40
462 Chris Pronger .20 .50
463 Marc Savard .12 .30
464 Tim Connolly .12 .30
465 Curtis McElhinney .12 .30
466 Dustin Byfuglien .20 .50
467 R.J. Umberger .15 .40
468 Sergei Zubov .12 .30
469 Lubomir Visnovsky .12 .30
470 Kenndal McArdle .15 .40
471 Marc-Andre Bergeron .12 .30
472 Alexander Steen .12 .30
473 Chris Campoli .12 .30
474 Marc Staal .12 .30
475 Scott Hartnell .12 .30
476 Ilya Bryzgalov .15 .40
477 Rob Blake .20 .50
478 Mark Recchi .25 .60
479 Luke Schenn .20 .50
480 Brooks Laich .12 .30
481 Steve Sullivan .12 .30
482 Bryan Little .20 .50
483 Jason Blake .12 .30
484 Rene Bourque .12 .30
485 Cam Ward .20 .50
486 T.J. Hensick .12 .30
487 Mike Ribeiro .12 .30
488 Dan Cleary .20 .50
489 David Booth .12 .30
490 Brian Boyle .12 .30
491 Alex Tanguay .12 .30
492 Scott Clemmensen .15 .40
493 Brendan Witt .12 .30
494 Nick Foligno .15 .40
495 Olli Jokinen .15 .40
496 Checklist .12 .30
497 Checklist .12 .30
498 Checklist .12 .30
499 Checklist .12 .30
500 Checklist .12 .30
501 Yannick Weber RC 1.25 3.00
502 Ville Leino RC 1.00 2.50
503 Troy Bodie RC 1.00 2.50
504 Tom Wandell RC 1.25 3.00
505 Tim Wallace RC .75 2.00
506 Tim Stapleton RC 1.25 3.00
507 T.J. Galiardi RC 1.25 3.00
508 Spencer Machacek RC 1.25 3.00
509 Sean Collins RC 1.00 2.50
510 Scott Lehman RC .75 2.00
511 Christian Hanson RC 1.25 3.00
512 Riley Armstrong RC 1.00 2.50
513 Riku Helenius RC 1.25 3.00
514 Phil Oreskovic RC 1.25 3.00
515 Peter Regin RC 1.00 2.50
516 Mike Santorelli RC 1.25 3.00
517 Mike McKenna RC 1.00 2.50
518 Mikael Backlund RC 2.00 5.00
519 Michal Neuvirth RC 2.00 5.00
520 Michael Vernace RC 1.00 2.50
521 Matt Hendricks RC 1.00 2.50
522 Matt Beleskey RC 1.00 2.50
523 Luca Caputi RC 1.25 3.00
524 Kurtis McLean RC 1.00 2.50
525 Kris Chucko RC .75 2.00
526 Kevin Westgarth RC 1.00 2.50
527 Kevin Quick RC .75 2.00
528 John Scott RC 1.25 3.00
529 Joel Rechlicz RC .75 2.00
530 Jhonas Enroth RC 1.50 4.00
531 Jesse Joensuu RC 1.00 2.50
532 Jay Beagle RC 1.50 4.00
533 Jaime Sifers RC 1.00 2.50
534 Taylor Chorney RC 1.25 3.00
535 Grant Lewis RC .75 2.00
536 Derek Peltier RC .75 2.00
537 Davis Drewiske RC 1.25 3.00
538 David Van Der Gulik RC 1.00 2.50
539 David Schlemko RC 1.00 2.50
540 John Negrin RC 1.25 3.00
541 Cal O'Reilly RC 1.00 2.50
542 Byron Bitz RC 1.00 2.50
543 Ivan Vishnevskiy RC .75 2.00
544 Brian Salcido RC .75 2.00
545 Brandon Segal RC 1.00 2.50
546 Ben Lovejoy RC 1.25 3.00
547 Artem Anisimov RC .75 2.00
548 Antti Niemi RC 2.00 5.00
549 Andrew MacDonald RC .75 2.00
550 Alexander Sulzer RC .75 2.00
551 Wayne Gretzky L 5.00 12.00
552 Denis Potvin L .75 2.00
553 Steve Shutt L .75 2.00
554 Dale Hawerchuk L 1.00 2.50
555 Don Cherry L .75 2.00
556 Stan Mikita L 1.00 2.50
557 Al MacInnis L 1.00 2.50
558 Denis Savard L .75 2.00
559 Bernie Federko L .60 1.50
560 Darryl Sutter L .60 1.50
561 Alex Delvecchio L .75 2.00
562 Rod Langway L .60 1.50
563 Johnny Bucyk L .75 2.00
564 Mark Messier L 1.50 4.00
565 Ted Lindsay L .60 1.50
566 Bobby Hull L 1.50 4.00
567 Scotty Bowman L .75 2.00
568 Clark Gillies L .75 2.00
569 Red Kelly L .75 2.00
570 Gilbert Perreault L .75 2.00
571 Terry O'Reilly L .60 1.50
572 Jean Beliveau L .75 2.00
573 Ron Ellis L .50 1.25
574 Harry Howell L .60 1.50
575 Guy Carbonneau L 1.25 3.00
576 Butch Bouchard L .60 1.50
577 Frank Mahovlich L .75 2.00
578 Lanny McDonald L .75 2.00
579 Peter Stastny L .60 1.50
580 Dick Duff L .60 1.50
581 Grant Fuhr L 1.25 3.00
582 Cam Neely L .75 2.00
583 Rogie Vachon L 1.00 2.50
584 Phil Esposito L 1.25 3.00
585 Theoren Fleury L 1.25 3.00
586 Bobby Orr L 3.00 8.00
587 Johnny Bower L .75 2.00
588 Luc Robitaille L .75 2.00
589 Jari Kurri L .75 2.00
590 Doug Wilson L .60 1.50
591 Borje Salming L .75 2.00
592 Marty McSorley L .60 1.50
593 Bob Bourne L .50 1.25
594 Doug Gilmour L 1.00 2.50
595 Mike Bossy L .75 2.00
596 Bobby Clarke L 1.25 3.00
597 Mario Lemieux L 3.00 8.00
598 Patrick Roy L 2.00 5.00
599 Tony Esposito L .75 2.00
600 Gordie Howe L 2.50 6.00
601 Justin Williams .15 .40
602 Jason Williams .12 .30
603 Rob Scuderi .12 .30
604 Aaron Ward .12 .30
605 Rickard Wallin .12 .30
606 Niclas Wallin .12 .30
607 Stephane Veilleux .12 .30
608 Ole-Kristian Tollefsen .12 .30
609 Alex Tanguay .12 .30
610 Petr Sykora .15 .40
611 Darryl Sydor .12 .30
612 Jaroslav Spacek .12 .30
613 Ryan Smyth .15 .40
614 Dennis Seidenberg .12 .30
615 Jeff Schultz .12 .30
616 Rob Schremp .12 .30
617 Luca Sbisa .20 .50
618 Mikael Samuelsson .12 .30
619 Dwayne Roloson .15 .40
620 Andrew Raycroft .15 .40
621 Kyle Quincey .12 .30
622 Vaclav Prospal .12 .30
623 Chris Pronger .20 .50
624 Wayne Primeau .12 .30
625 Roman Polak .12 .30
626 Patrick O'Sullivan .15 .40
627 Colton Orr .12 .30
628 Mattias Ohlund .12 .30
629 Antero Niittymaki .20 .50
630 Rob Niedermayer .12 .30
631 Scott Nichol .12 .30
632 Cory Murphy .12 .30
633 Matt Moulson .15 .40
634 Brendan Morrison .15 .40
635 Steve Montador .12 .30
636 Travis Moen .12 .30
637 Drew Miller .12 .30
638 Milan Michalek .12 .30
639 Steve McCarthy .12 .30
640 Paul Mara .12 .30
641 Manny Malhotra .12 .30
642 John Madden .12 .30
643 Joey MacDonald .15 .40
644 Joffrey Lupul .12 .30
645 Pascal Leclaire .20 .50
646 Ian Laperriere .12 .30
647 Robert Lang .12 .30
648 Quintin Laing .15 .40
649 Jason LaBarbera .15 .40
650 Pavel Kubina .12 .30
651 Alex Kovalev .15 .40
652 Ales Kotalik .12 .30
653 Lauri Korpikoski .12 .30
654 Mike Komisarek .15 .40
655 Saku Koivu .20 .50
656 Chuck Kobasew .12 .30
657 Mike Knuble .12 .30
658 Nikolai Khabibulin .20 .50
659 Phil Kessel .20 .50
660 Boyd Kane .12 .30
661 Ryan Johnson .12 .30
662 Brent Johnson .12 .30
663 Cam Janssen .12 .30
664 Marian Hossa .20 .50
665 Darcy Hordichuk .12 .30
666 Chris Higgins .12 .30
667 Dany Heatley .15 .40
668 Martin Havlat .15 .40
669 Jeff Halpern .12 .30
670 Scott Gomez .15 .40
671 Brian Gionta .12 .30
672 Hal Gill .12 .30
673 Mathieu Garon .20 .50
674 Marian Gaborik .20 .50
675 Maxim Afinogenov .12 .30
676 Todd Fedoruk .12 .30
677 Garnet Exelby .12 .30
678 Ray Emery .15 .40
679 Christian Ehrhoff .12 .30
680 Andrew Ebbett .12 .30
681 Steve Downie .12 .30
682 Nigel Dawes .12 .30
683 Ty Conklin .12 .30
684 Mike Comrie .15 .40
685 Scott Clemmensen .15 .40
686 Jonathan Cheechoo .15 .40
687 Mike Cammalleri .15 .40
688 Jay Bouwmeester .12 .30
689 Chris Bourque .20 .50
690 Paul Bissonnette .12 .30
691 Martin Biron .15 .40
692 Todd Bertuzzi .20 .50
693 Marc-Andre Bergeron .12 .30
694 Francois Beauchemin .12 .30
695 Alex Auld .12 .30
696 Keith Aucoin .25 .60
697 Evgeni Artyukhin .12 .30
698 Nik Antropov .15 .40
699 Craig Anderson .20 .50
700 Checklist .12 .30
701 Checklist .12 .30
702 Toni Lydman .12 .30
703 Brian McGrattan .12 .30
704 Matt Ellis .12 .30
705 Fredrik Sjostrom .12 .30
706 Tomas Kopecky .15 .40
707 Brent Sopel .12 .30
708 Bryan Bickell .12 .30
709 Niklas Hjalmarsson .12 .30
710 Henrik Tallinder .12 .30
711 Nathan Paetsch .12 .30
712 Mike Grier .12 .30
713 Jordan Hendry .15 .40
714 Aaron Johnson .12 .30
715 Johnny Boychuk .15 .40
716 Derek Morris .12 .30
717 Daniel Paille .15 .40
718 Steve Begin .12 .30
719 Ondrej Pavelec .25 .60
720 Christoph Schubert .12 .30
721 Eric Boulton .12 .30
722 Chris Thorburn .12 .30
723 Ryan Carter .12 .30
724 Erik Christensen .12 .30
725 Sheldon Brookbank .12 .30
726 Petteri Nokelainen .12 .30
727 Nick Boynton .12 .30
728 Ruslan Salei .12 .30
729 Scott Hannan .12 .30
730 David Koci .12 .30
731 Stephane Yelle .12 .30
732 Tom Kostopoulos .12 .30
733 Georges Laraque .15 .40
734 Ryan Shannon .15 .40
735 Anton Volchenkov .12 .30
736 Steve MacIntyre .12 .30
737 Gilbert Brule .25 .60
738 Jean-Francois Jacques .12 .30
739 Derek Meech .12 .30
740 Jimmy Howard .25 .60
741 Kyle Chipchura .15 .40
742 Matt Carkner .12 .30
743 Ryan Stone .12 .30
744 Anton Stralman .12 .30
745 Derek Dorsett .15 .40
746 Patrick Eaves .12 .30
747 Brad May .12 .30
748 Mathieu Roy .12 .30
749 Tanner Glass .12 .30
750 Shean Donovan .12 .30
751 Craig Adams .12 .30
752 Martin Skoula .12 .30
753 Steven Zalewski RC .40 1.00
754 Matthew Corrente RC .40 1.00
755 Bryan Rodney RC .40 1.00
756 Ryan Vesce RC .40 1.00
757 David Sloane RC .50 1.25
758 Lars Eller RC .50 1.25
759 Tyson Strachan RC .30 .75
760 Wes O'Neill RC .50 1.25
761 Matt Climie RC .40 1.00
762 Daniel Larsson RC .40 1.00
763 James Wright RC .50 1.25
764 Teemu Laakso RC .30 .75
765 Devan Dubnyk RC .75 2.00
766 Jason Demers RC .75 2.00
767 Benn Ferriero RC .50 1.25
768 Frazer McLaren RC .40 1.00
769 Johan Backlund RC .50 1.25
770 Mika Pyorala RC .40 1.00
771 Tyler Myers RC .75 2.00
772 Ryan O'Reilly RC 1.00 2.50
773 Jamie Benn RC 1.50 4.00
774 Dmitry Kulikov RC .50 1.25
775 Alec Martinez RC .60 1.50
776 Matt Gilroy RC .50 1.25
777 Michael Del Zotto RC .50 1.25
778 Jay Rosehill RC .50 1.25
779 Sergei Shirokov RC .30 .75
780 Tyler Ennis RC .60 1.50
781 Chris Butler RC .50 1.25
782 James Reimer RC 1.25 3.00
783 Perttu Lindgren RC .40 1.00
784 Bobby Sanguinetti RC .30 .75
785 Braden Holtby RC 1.25 3.00
786 Ryan Wilson RC .50 1.25
787 Aaron Gagnon RC .30 .75
788 Viktor Stalberg RC .50 1.25
789 Erik Karlsson RC 1.50 4.00
790 Brad Marchand RC 10.00 25.00
791 Colin Wilson RC .50 1.25
792 Michael Grabner RC .50 1.25
793 Tyler Bozak RC .75 2.00
794 Logan Couture RC 1.00 2.50
795 Evander Kane RC 1.00 2.50
796 Jonas Gustavsson RC .60 1.50
797 Victor Hedman RC 3.00 8.00
798 James van Riemsdyk RC 1.00 2.50
799 Matt Duchene RC 1.00 2.50
800 John Tavares RC 3.00 8.00

2009-10 O-Pee-Chee Rainbow

*SINGLES: 2.5X TO 6X BASIC CARDS
*ROOKIES: .6X TO 1.5X BASIC
*LEGENDS: 1X TO 2.5X BASIC
*UPD (601-752): 3X TO 8X BASIC CARDS
*UPD ROOKIES (753-800): 2X TO 5X

162 Zach Parise 1.50 4.00
441 Nicklas Backstrom 1.50 4.00
501 Yannick Weber 2.00 5.00
523 Luca Caputi 2.00 5.00
800 John Tavares 10.00 25.00

2009-10 O-Pee-Chee Retro

*SINGLES: 2X TO 5X BASIC CARDS
*ROOKIES: .5 X TO 1.2X BASIC CARDS
*LEGENDS: .8X TO 2X BASIC CARDS

441 Nicklas Backstrom 1.25 3.00

2009-10 O-Pee-Chee Retro Blank Backs

*BLANK: 25X TO 60X BASIC CARDS
*BLANK RCs: 4X TO 10X BASIC CARDS
*BLANK SPs: 5X TO 12X BASIC CARDS

COMMON CLs 4.00 10.00
441 Nicklas Backstrom 15.00 40.00

2009-10 O-Pee-Chee Retro Rainbow

*SINGLES: 6X TO 15X BASIC CARDS
*ROOKIES: 1.2X TO 3X BASIC
*LEGENDS: 2.5X TO 6X BASIC

441 Nicklas Backstrom 4.00 10.00

2009-10 O-Pee-Chee All Rookie Team

COMPLETE SET (6) 6.00 15.00
ART1 Steve Mason .60 1.50
ART2 Drew Doughty 1.00 2.50
ART3 Luke Schenn .75 2.00
ART4 Patrik Berglund .50 1.25
ART5 Bobby Ryan .60 1.50
ART6 Kris Versteeg .50 1.25

2009-10 O-Pee-Chee All Star Team

COMPLETE SET (12) 10.00 25.00
AST1 Tim Thomas .75 2.00
AST2 Mike Green .60 1.50
AST3 Zdeno Chara .75 2.00
AST4 Evgeni Malkin 1.50 4.00
AST5 Jarome Iginla 1.00 2.50
AST6 Alexander Ovechkin 3.00 8.00
AST7 Steve Mason .60 1.50
AST8 Nicklas Lidstrom .50 1.25
AST9 Dan Boyle .50 1.25
AST10 Pavel Datsyuk 1.25 3.00
AST11 Marian Hossa .75 2.00
AST12 Zach Parise .75 2.00

2009-10 O-Pee-Chee Box Bottoms

COMPLETE SET (16) 6.00 15.00
IGINLA/LECV/KOVAL/NASH 1.25 3.00
BRIND'A/MALKIN/ZETTER/STAMKOS 1.25 3.00
OVECH/LNGO/TOEWS/SCHENN 1.50 4.00
CRSBY/THRNTN/PRICE/LDSTRM 1.50 4.00
NNO Jarome Iginla .30 .75
NNO Vincent Lecavalier .25 .60
NNO Ilya Kovalchuk .25 .60
NNO Rick Nash .25 .60
NNO Rod Brind'Amour .25 .60
NNO Evgeni Malkin .50 1.25
NNO Henrik Zetterberg .30 .75
NNO Steven Stamkos .50 1.25
NNO Alexander Ovechkin 1.00 2.50
NNO Roberto Luongo .40 1.00
NNO Jonathan Toews .40 1.00
NNO Luke Schenn .25 .60
NNO Sidney Crosby 1.00 2.50
NNO Joe Thornton .40 1.00
NNO Carey Price .50 1.25
NNO Nicklas Lidstrom .15 .40

2009-10 O-Pee-Chee Buyback Autographs

BBCG Claude Giroux '08-09 30.00 60.00
BBHW Dale Hawerchuk '08-09 LL 10.00 25.00

2009-10 O-Pee-Chee Canadian Heroes

COMPLETE SET (42) 15.00 40.00
CBBC Braydon Coburn .50 1.25
CBBK Becky Kellar .50 1.25
CBCH Chris Mason .60 1.50
CBCL Charline Labonte .50 1.25
CBCM Carla MacLeod .50 1.25
CBCO Caroline Ouellette .50 1.25
CBCP Chris Phillips .50 1.25
CBCS Colleen Sostorics .60 1.50
CBCW Catherine Ward .50 1.25
CBDD Drew Doughty 1.00 2.50
CBDH Dan Hamhuis .60 1.50
CBDR Dwayne Roloson .60 1.50
CBGA Gillian Apps .50 1.25
CBGF Gillian Ferrari .50 1.25
CBGK Gina Kingsbury .50 1.25
CBHA Josh Harding .75 2.00
CBHE Dany Heatley .60 1.50
CBHI Haley Irwin .50 1.25
CBHW Hayley Wickenheiser .50 1.25
CBIW Ian White .60 1.50
CBJB Jennifer Botterill .75 2.00
CBJH Jayna Hefford .50 1.25
CBJS Jason Spezza .75 2.00
CBKS Kim St. Pierre .50 1.25
CBLS Luke Schenn .75 2.00
CBMA Meghan Agosta .50 1.25
CBML Matthew Lombardi .50 1.25
CBMM Meaghan Mikkelson .50 1.25
CBMP Marie-Philip Poulin 2.50 6.00
CBMS Martin St. Louis .75 2.00
CBMV Marc-Edouard Vlasic .50 1.25
CBRJ Rebecca Johnston .50 1.25
CBRO Derek Roy .50 1.25
CBSD Shane Doan .60 1.50
CBSH Shawn Horcoff .50 1.25
CBSS Shannon Szabados .50 1.25
CBST Steven Stamkos 1.50 4.00
CBSU Scottie Upshall .50 1.25
CBSV Sarah Vaillancourt .50 1.25
CBSW Shea Weber .60 1.50
CBTB Tessa Bonhomme .50 1.25
CBTZ Travis Zajac .50 1.25

2009-10 O-Pee-Chee Canadian Heroes Autographs

CBACP Carey Price 150.00 300.00
CBADD Drew Doughty 30.00 80.00
CBADH Dany Heatley 30.00 80.00
CBADP Dion Phaneuf 25.00 60.00
CBAGH Gordie Howe 125.00 250.00
CBAHA Josh Harding 25.00 60.00
CBAJI Jarome Iginla 125.00 250.00
CBAJT Jonathan Toews 75.00 150.00
CBALS Luke Schenn 50.00 100.00
CBAML Mario Lemieux 125.00 250.00
CBAMM Mark Messier 100.00 200.00
CBAMR Mike Richards 60.00 150.00
CBAPR Patrick Roy 250.00 400.00
CBARB Ray Bourque 125.00 250.00
CBARN Rick Nash 125.00 250.00
CBASC Sidney Crosby 125.00 250.00
CBAST Steven Stamkos 100.00 200.00
CBAWG Wayne Gretzky 400.00 600.00

2009-10 O-Pee-Chee Canadian Heroes Foil

CBH1 Wayne Gretzky 12.00 30.00
CBH2 Gordie Howe 10.00 25.00
CBH3 Bobby Orr 12.00 30.00
CBH4 Steven Stamkos 6.00 15.00
CBH5 Mark Messier 6.00 15.00
CBH6 Sidney Crosby 12.00 30.00
CBH7 Phil Esposito 5.00 12.00
CBH8 Tony Esposito 3.00 8.00
CBH9 Gilbert Perreault 3.00 8.00
CBH10 Lanny McDonald 3.00 8.00
CBH11 Ray Bourque 5.00 12.00
CBH12 Theoren Fleury 5.00 12.00
CBH13 Luc Robitaille 3.00 8.00
CBH14 Manon Rheaume 8.00 20.00
CBH15 Mike Bossy 3.00 8.00
CBH16 Bobby Clarke 5.00 12.00
CBH17 Patrick Roy 8.00 20.00
CBH18 Mario Lemieux 12.00 30.00
CBH19 Joe Thornton 5.00 12.00
CBH20 Jarome Iginla 4.00 10.00
CBH21 Vincent Lecavalier 3.00 8.00
CBH22 Ryan Getzlaf 3.00 8.00
CBH23 Patrick Marleau 3.00 8.00
CBH24 Martin St. Louis 3.00 8.00
CBH25 Mike Richards 2.50 6.00
CBH26 Shane Doan 2.50 6.00
CBH27 Jonathan Toews 5.00 12.00
CBH28 Steve Mason 2.50 6.00
CBH29 Martin Brodeur 8.00 20.00
CBH30 Marc-Andre Fleury 6.00 15.00
CBH31 Roberto Luongo 5.00 12.00
CBH32 Mike Green 2.50 6.00
CBH33 Brian Campbell 2.50 6.00
CBH34 Scott Niedermayer 3.00 8.00
CBH35 Dion Phaneuf 2.50 6.00
CBH36 Joe Sakic 6.00 15.00
CBH37 Marty Turco 3.00 8.00
CBH38 Carey Price 8.00 20.00
CBH39 Jason Spezza 3.00 8.00
CBH40 Rick Nash 3.00 8.00

2009-10 O-Pee-Chee In Action

COMPLETE SET (12) 12.00 30.00
ACT1 Sidney Crosby 3.00 8.00
ACT2 Evgeni Malkin 1.50 4.00
ACT3 Alexander Ovechkin 3.00 8.00
ACT4 Jarome Iginla 1.00 2.50
ACT5 Bobby Ryan .60 1.50
ACT6 Jonathan Toews 1.25 3.00
ACT7 Ilya Kovalchuk .75 2.00
ACT8 Henrik Zetterberg 1.00 2.50
ACT9 Ales Hemsky .60 1.50
ACT10 Zach Parise .75 2.00
ACT11 Dany Heatley .60 1.50
ACT12 Mikko Koivu .75 2.00

2009-10 O-Pee-Chee Materials

JBEES Wheel/Savard/Berg/Kessl 8.00 20.00
JBLUE Perrn/Tkac/Berglnd/Kariya 6.00 15.00
JBOLT St.L/Stamk/Prospl/Lecav 12.00 30.00
JBOST Ferndz/Ryder/Lucic/Rask 4.00 10.00
JCANE Ward/Staal/Cole/Brind 8.00 20.00
JCAPS Ovech/Grn/Back/Flsch 25.00 60.00
JCATS Booth/Hortn/Wiss/Vokn 6.00 15.00
JCNDS Kovalv/Kost/Mrkv/Kmsk 6.00 15.00
JCNKS Edler/Sedin/Bksa/Luong 10.00 25.00
JCOLO Sakic/Svts/Ststny/Wlski 12.00 30.00
JCYTE Lmbrdi/Bdkr/Muelr/Doan 5.00 12.00
JDEVL Clrksn/Brodr/Elias/Parise 15.00 40.00
JDRFT Dougty/Schn/Bdkr/Stmk 12.00 30.00
JDUCK Prnger/Perry/Gigre/Gtzlf 10.00 25.00
JEURO Sundn/Kolzig/Fdrv/Slne 12.00 30.00
JFLAM Phanf/Iginla/Kprsff/Jokin 8.00 20.00
JFLYR Ntymki/Crtr/Rchr/Ggne 6.00 15.00
JGCML Mario/Messi/Crsby/Gretz 60.00 125.00
JHABS Tang/Prce/Koivu/Plknc 12.00 30.00
JHAWK Sbrk/Toews/Kne/Sharp 12.00 30.00
JJACK Vorck/Umbrgr/Nsh/Klsla 6.00 15.00
JKING Frolv/Kpitr/Dghty/Brwn 10.00 25.00
JKMLP Tucker/Ignla/Niedr/Doan 8.00 20.00
JLEAF Blake/Schn/Stjn/Tskla 6.00 15.00
JLGND Howe/Messier/Roy/Gretz 60.00 125.00
JOILR Coglio/Poul/Ggnr/Horcff 8.00 20.00
JPENS Malkn/Staal/Flry/Crosby 25.00 60.00
JRBLF Fleury/Brdr/Roy/Luongo 15.00 40.00
JRNGR Dubin/Lund/Staal/Nslnd 15.00 40.00
JSABR Roy/Pomin/Miller/Vanek 6.00 15.00
JSBBS Shanahn/Skic/Brdr/Blke 15.00 40.00
JSENS Campli/Phillips/Htly/Spez 6.00 15.00
JSHRK Setog/Nabk/Trntn/Marlu 10.00 25.00
JSTAR Turco/Niskn/Mdno/Zubv 10.00 25.00
JTHRS Little/Koval/Leht/Enstrom 6.00 15.00
JVANC Sndin/Ohlnd/Luong/Bern 10.00 25.00
JWILD Gabrik/Koiv/Noln/Bouch 6.00 15.00
JWING Zetter/Hossa/Lids/Datsyk 10.00 25.00
JWNGS Raflski/Cheli/Osgd/Draper 6.00 15.00
JPREDS Legwnd/Rine/Web/Sullivn 6.00 15.00

2009-10 O-Pee-Chee Record Breakers

COMPLETE SET (10) 10.00 25.00
RB1 Zdeno Chara .75 2.00
RB2 Alexander Ovechkin 3.00 8.00
RB3 Steve Mason .60 1.50
RB4 Patrik Elias .75 2.00
RB5 Jarome Iginla 1.00 2.50
RB6 Miikka Kiprusoff .75 2.00
RB7 Mike Green .60 1.50
RB8 Martin Brodeur 2.00 5.00
RB9 Brendan Shanahan .75 2.00
RB10 Mike Richards .60 1.50

2009-10 O-Pee-Chee Signatures

SAP Adam Pineault 8.00 20.00
SBB Ben Bishop 8.00 20.00
SBL Brian Lee 10.00 25.00
SBM Brendan Mikkelson 6.00 15.00
SBO Bobby Orr 80.00 200.00
SBR Brian Boyle 6.00 15.00
SBS Brandon Sutter 6.00 15.00
SBU Peter Budaj 8.00 20.00
SBW Blake Wheeler 10.00 25.00
SCB Cam Barker 6.00 15.00
SCG Colton Gillies 10.00 25.00
SCK Chris Kunitz 10.00 25.00
SCL David Clarkson 8.00 20.00
SCO Cory Schneider 10.00 25.00
SCP Carey Price 20.00 50.00
SCS Chris Stewart 8.00 20.00
SDC Daniel Carcillo 6.00 15.00
SDD Drew Doughty 12.00 30.00
SDJ David Jones 6.00 15.00
SDP Dion Phaneuf 8.00 20.00
SDR Dwayne Roloson 8.00 20.00
SDS Daniel Sedin 12.00 30.00
SEN Evgeni Nabokov 8.00 20.00
SFB Fabian Brunnstrom 8.00 20.00
SGA Marian Gaborik 10.00 25.00
SGH Gordie Howe 60.00 150.00
SGI Claude Giroux 10.00 25.00
SGL Guillaume Latendresse 8.00 20.00
SHL Henrik Lundqvist 30.00 80.00
SHS Henrik Sedin 12.00 30.00
SHU Matt Hunwick 6.00 15.00
SJB Josh Bailey 8.00 20.00
SJD Jean-Pierre Dumont 6.00 15.00
SJH Jonas Hiller 8.00 20.00
SJI Jarome Iginla 12.00 30.00
SJM Jamie McGinn 8.00 20.00
SJN James Neal 6.00 15.00
SJP Justin Pogge 10.00 25.00
SJS Jack Skille 6.00 15.00
SJT Joe Thornton 15.00 40.00
SJV Jakub Voracek 8.00 20.00
SKA Karl Alzner 6.00 15.00
SKE Tyler Kennedy 8.00 20.00
SKM Kenndal McArdle 8.00 20.00
SKO Kyle Okposo 6.00 15.00
SKV Kris Versteeg 6.00 15.00
SLS Luke Schenn 10.00 25.00
SMA Steve Mason 8.00 20.00
SMB Mikkel Boedker 6.00 15.00
SMD Matt D'Agostini 8.00 20.00
SMG Mike Green 8.00 20.00
SMH Matthew Halischuk 8.00 20.00
SMI Michael Peca 8.00 20.00
SMK Mike Knuble 6.00 15.00
SMM Milan Michalek 6.00 15.00
SMN Markus Naslund 10.00 25.00
SMO Brendan Morrison 8.00 20.00
SMP Max Pacioretty 10.00 25.00
SMR Michal Repik 8.00 20.00
SMS Marc Staal 6.00 15.00
SMX Ben Maxwell 8.00 20.00
SNB Nicklas Backstrom 10.00 25.00
SNF Nikita Filatov 8.00 20.00
SNG Nathan Gerbe 8.00 20.00
SNI Matt Niskanen 8.00 20.00
SNK Nikolai Kulemin 6.00 15.00
SPB Patrik Berglund 6.00 15.00
SPD Pavel Datsyuk 15.00 40.00
SPE Patrik Elias 10.00 25.00
SPH Chris Phillips 6.00 15.00
SPI Alex Pietrangelo 8.00 20.00
SPO Jason Pominville 6.00 15.00
SRI Mike Ribeiro 6.00 15.00
SRS Ryan Smyth 8.00 20.00
SRY Bobby Ryan 8.00 20.00
SSC Sidney Crosby 60.00 150.00
SSD Steve Downie 6.00 15.00
SSG Simon Gagne 10.00 25.00
SSM Matt Smaby 8.00 20.00
SSS Steven Stamkos 20.00 50.00
SST Marco Sturm 6.00 15.00
SSV Simeon Varlamov 10.00 25.00
SSW Stephen Weiss 6.00 15.00
STE Tobias Enstrom 10.00 25.00
STG Tom Gilbert 6.00 15.00
STH Tomas Holmstrom 8.00 20.00
STK Tim Kennedy 8.00 20.00
STL Trevor Lewis 6.00 15.00
STO T.J. Oshie 10.00 25.00
STV Tomas Vokoun 8.00 20.00
STW Ty Wishart 8.00 20.00
SVT Viktor Tikhonov 8.00 20.00
SWG Wayne Gretzky 250.00 450.00
SZA Zach Boychuk 8.00 20.00
SZB Zach Bogosian 8.00 20.00

2009-10 O-Pee-Chee Stat Leaders

COMPLETE SET (17) 15.00 40.00
SL1 Evgeni Malkin 1.50 4.00
SL2 Alexander Ovechkin 3.00 8.00
SL3 Evgeni Malkin 1.50 4.00
SL4 Mike Richards .60 1.50
SL5 David Krejci .75 2.00
SL6 Daniel Carcillo .50 1.25
SL7 Thomas Vanek .60 1.50
SL8 Alexander Ovechkin 3.00 8.00
SL9 Jeff Carter .60 1.50
SL10 Alexander Ovechkin 3.00 8.00
SL11 Cal Clutterbuck .50 1.25
SL12 Evgeni Malkin 1.50 4.00
SL13 Steve Mason .60 1.50
SL14 Miikka Kiprusoff .75 2.00
SL15 Tim Thomas .75 2.00
SL16 Tim Thomas .75 2.00
SL17 Henrik Lundqvist 2.00 5.00

2009-10 O-Pee-Chee Top Draws Triple Jerseys

TJATL E.Kane/Antropov/Koval 15.00 40.00
TJBOS Ryder/Lucic/Rask 15.00 40.00
TJCGY Pelech/Backlund/Chucko 12.00 30.00
TJGR8 Lemieux/Yzermn/Gretzky 50.00 120.00
TJHOF Shutt/Stastny/McDonald 12.00 30.00
TJBEES Neely/Oates/Bourque 20.00 50.00
TJBUFF Vanek/Pominville/Roy 15.00 40.00
TJCALG MacInnis/Fleury/McDon 12.00 30.00
TJCAPS Green/Ovechkin/Back 20.00 50.00
TJCOUV Bernier/Grabnr/Shirokv 15.00 40.00
TJDALL Benn/Modano/Turco 12.00 30.00
TJNEXT van Riems/Tavr/Duchn 20.00 50.00
TJPHIL van Riems/Bartulis/Girx 15.00 40.00
TJRANG Gilroy/Anisimov/Del Zot 20.00 50.00
TJSANJ Ferriero/Coutre/Demrs 12.00 30.00
TJCANES Staal/Brind/Ward 15.00 40.00
TJFLAME Iginla/Kiprusoff/Phanf 12.00 30.00
TJFLYER Richards/Carter/Emery 15.00 40.00
TJHTOWN Holmstrm/Osgd/Franzn 15.00 40.00
TJKINGS Martinez/Frolov/Smyth 15.00 40.00
TJROOKD Hedman/Myers/Karlssn 15.00 40.00
TJROOKF Duchen/van Rms/Kane 12.00 30.00
TJROOKG Niemi/Gustav/Enroth 15.00 40.00
TJTHRSH Kane/Machck/Koval 15.00 40.00
TJPHILLY van Rms/Cartr/Rchrds 15.00 40.00

2009-10 O-Pee-Chee Trophy Winners

COMPLETE SET (13) 6.00 15.00
TW1 Alexander Ovechkin 3.00 8.00
TW2 Alexander Ovechkin 3.00 8.00
TW3 Alexander Ovechkin 3.00 8.00
TW4 Steve Sullivan .50 1.25
TW5 Tim Thomas .75 2.00
TW6 Pavel Datsyuk 1.25 3.00
TW7 Pavel Datsyuk 1.25 3.00
TW8 Zdeno Chara .75 2.00
TW9 Steve Mason .60 1.50
TW10 Evgeni Malkin 1.50 4.00
TW11 Ethan Moreau .50 1.25
TW12 Evgeni Malkin 1.50 4.00
TW13 Pittsburgh Penguins 2.00 5.00

2010-11 O-Pee-Chee

1 Corey Perry .30 .75
2 T.J. Oshie .20 .50
3 Sami Salo .12 .30
4 Mikhail Grabovski .12 .30
5 Carey Price .40 1.00
6 Saku Koivu .20 .50
7 Dainius Zubrus .12 .30
8 Sidney Crosby .75 2.00
9 Brandon Sutter .12 .30
10 Cal Clutterbuck .12 .30
11 Tyler Ennis .12 .30
12 Marco Sturm .12 .30
13 Steve Sullivan .12 .30
14 Lubomir Visnovsky .12 .30
15 Scott Parse .12 .30
16 Ben Eager .12 .30
17 Fernando Pisani .12 .30
18 Jonas Hiller .15 .40
19 Brian Rolston .15 .40
20 Ryan Suter .15 .40
21 Niklas Hjalmarsson .12 .30
22 Johnny Oduya .15 .40
23 Chris Higgins .12 .30
24 Matt Niskanen .15 .40
25 Niklas Backstrom .20 .50
26 Luca Caputi .15 .40
27 John Madden .12 .30
28 Mike Commodore .12 .30
29 Luca Sbisa .15 .40
30 Eric Belanger .12 .30
31 Joffrey Lupul .12 .30
32 Brian Elliott .15 .40
33 Fedor Tyutin .12 .30
34 Rostislav Klesla .12 .30
35 Zenon Konopka .15 .40
36 Milan Lucic .20 .50
37 Craig Rivet .12 .30
38 Francois Beauchemin .12 .30
39 Bobby Sanguinetti .12 .30
40 Zach Bogosian .15 .40
41 Logan Couture .25 .60
42 Pekka Rinne .20 .50
43 Mike Grier .12 .30
44 Mike Smith .20 .50
45 Craig Anderson .20 .50
46 Tomas Plekanec .12 .30
47 Pavel Datsyuk .30 .75
48 Brent Sopel .12 .30
49 Chad LaRose .12 .30
50 Alexander Frolov .12 .30
51 Thomas Vanek .15 .40
52 Scott Hannan .12 .30
53 Jay McKee .12 .30
54 Mason Raymond .12 .30
55 Michael Leighton .15 .40
56 Michael Del Zotto .15 .40
57 Colin White .12 .30
58 Doug Murray .12 .30
59 Ville Leino .15 .40
60 Henrik Lundqvist .50 1.25
61 Sam Gagner .12 .30
62 Ondrej Pavelec .20 .50
63 Kyle Cumiskey .12 .30
64 Steve Bernier .12 .30
65 Andy Greene .12 .30
66 Patrick Marleau .20 .50
67 Christian Ehrhoff .12 .30
68 Marty Turco .20 .50
69 Ryan Whitney .12 .30
70 Tomas Holmstrom .12 .30
71 Drew Doughty .25 .60
72 Tom Kostopoulos .12 .30
73 Patric Hornqvist .12 .30
74 Ron Hainsey .12 .30
75 Paul Stastny .15 .40
76 Miikka Kiprusoff .20 .50
77 Erik Christensen .12 .30
78 Phil Kessel .20 .50
79 T.J. Galiardi .15 .40
80 Niklas Hagman .12 .30
81 Michal Handzus .15 .40
82 Jason Arnott .15 .40
83 Ryan Malone .12 .30
84 Joe Corvo .12 .30
85 Anton Stralman .12 .30
86 John-Michael Liles .12 .30
87 Nikolai Kulemin .12 .30
88 Mike Green .15 .40
89 Jeff Deslauriers .12 .30
90 Martin Brodeur .50 1.25
91 David Legwand .15 .40
92 Henrik Zetterberg .25 .60
93 Ivan Vishnevskiy .12 .30
94 Robyn Regehr .12 .30
95 Brian Gionta .12 .30
96 Artem Anisimov .12 .30
97 Drew Stafford .12 .30
98 Matt Carle .15 .40
99 Ales Hemsky .15 .40
100 Cam Barker .12 .30
101 Tom Poti .12 .30
102 J.P. Dumont .12 .30
103 Steve Montador .12 .30
104 Kimmo Timonen .12 .30
105 Jonas Gustavsson .25 .60
106 Tom Wandell .12 .30
107 Bruno Gervais .12 .30
108 Blake Wheeler .20 .50
109 Tyler Bozak .12 .30
110 Scottie Upshall .12 .30
111 Jonathan Bernier .15 .40
112 Alex Tanguay .12 .30
113 Scott Nichol .12 .30
114 Joni Pitkanen .15 .40
115 Matthew Lombardi .12 .30
116 Jonathan Ericsson .12 .30
117 David Steckel .12 .30
118 Tuomo Ruutu .15 .40
119 Josh Gorges .12 .30
120 Bobby Ryan .15 .40
121 Jonathan Toews .30 .75
122 Jaroslav Spacek .12 .30
123 Jack Johnson .12 .30
124 Andrej Meszaros .12 .30
125 Jay McClement .12 .30
126 Anze Kopitar .30 .75
127 David Krejci .20 .50
128 Roman Hamrlik .12 .30
129 Brooks Orpik .12 .30
130 Patrick O'Sullivan .12 .30
131 Dustin Byfuglien .20 .50
132 Patrik Berglund .12 .30
133 Rob Schremp .12 .30
134 Bryan Allen .12 .30
135 Mike Ribeiro .12 .30
136 Valtteri Filppula .12 .30
137 Eric Nystrom .12 .30
138 Scott Hartnell .12 .30
139 Ian White .15 .40
140 Jarret Stoll .15 .40
141 Zbynek Michalek .12 .30
142 Michael Frolik .12 .30
143 Radim Vrbata .12 .30
144 Samuel Pahlsson .12 .30
145 Ryan Smyth .15 .40
146 Ryan Jones .12 .30
147 Radek Dvorak .12 .30
148 Matt Gilroy .12 .30
149 Dan Boyle .12 .30
150 Milan Michalek .12 .30
151 Dany Heatley .15 .40
152 Josh Bailey .15 .40
153 Johan Hedberg .15 .40
154 Curtis McElhinney .12 .30
155 Alex Kovalev .15 .40
156 Adam Foote .12 .30
157 Dave Bolland .15 .40
158 Toby Petersen .12 .30
159 Jamie Langenbrunner .12 .30
160 Dominic Moore .12 .30
161 Tuukka Rask .25 .60
162 Matt Stajan .12 .30
163 David Backes .12 .30
164 Maxime Talbot .12 .30
165 Claude Giroux .20 .50
166 Gilbert Brule .20 .50
167 Ray Whitney .15 .40
168 Tom Pyatt .12 .30
169 Marek Zidlicky .12 .30
170 Daniel Sedin .25 .60
171 Shawn Horcoff .12 .30
172 Dennis Seidenberg .12 .30
173 Simon Gagne .20 .50
174 Anton Volchenkov .12 .30
175 Guillaume Latendresse .15 .40
176 B.J. Crombeen .12 .30
177 Jason Spezza .20 .50
178 Alexander Semin .20 .50
179 Peter Mueller .15 .40
180 Colby Armstrong .12 .30
181 Troy Brouwer .12 .30
182 Zdeno Chara .20 .50
183 Alexandre Burrows .12 .30
184 Frans Nielsen .12 .30
185 Andrew Ebbett .12 .30
186 Tobias Enstrom .12 .30
187 Tyler Kennedy .12 .30
188 Fabian Brunnstrom .12 .30
189 Vernon Fiddler .12 .30
190 Ryan Kesler .20 .50
191 Teemu Selanne .40 1.00
192 Dmitry Kulikov .15 .40
193 Mark Stuart .12 .30
194 Corey Crawford .25 .60
195 Carl Gunnarsson .12 .30
196 Alexander Edler .12 .30
197 Adam Burish .12 .30
198 Ian Laperriere .12 .30
199 Semyon Varlamov .20 .50
200 Colin Wilson .15 .40
201 Erik Johnson .12 .30
202 Pierre-Marc Bouchard .20 .50
203 Brooks Laich .12 .30
204 Wojtek Wolski .12 .30
205 Shane O'Brien .12 .30
206 Dan Ellis .15 .40
207 Martin Erat .12 .30
208 Antti Miettinen .12 .30
209 Ilya Bryzgalov .15 .40
210 Cory Schneider .20 .50
211 Tomas Fleischmann .12 .30
212 Cody McLeod .12 .30
213 Daniel Paille .12 .30
214 Kris Draper .12 .30
215 Chris Phillips .12 .30
216 Kyle Brodziak .12 .30
217 Patrick Dwyer .12 .30
218 Tom Gilbert .12 .30
219 Jarome Iginla .25 .60
220 John Carlson .20 .50
221 Sean O'Donnell .12 .30
222 Daniel Winnik .12 .30
223 Maxim Lapierre .12 .30
224 Roberto Luongo .30 .75
225 Niclas Bergfors .15 .40
226 Vaclav Prospal .12 .30
227 Matt Cooke .12 .30
228 Jay Bouwmeester .12 .30
229 Niclas Wallin .12 .30
230 Steven Reinprecht .12 .30
231 David Jones .12 .30
232 Jaroslav Halak .20 .50
233 Mikael Backlund .15 .40
234 Bryan McCabe .12 .30
235 Andy McDonald .15 .40
236 Jordan Staal .15 .40
237 Brad Richards .20 .50
238 Milan Hejduk .15 .40
239 Scott Clemmensen .15 .40
240 Marian Gaborik .20 .50
241 Nathan Horton .15 .40
242 Zach Boychuk .15 .40
243 Mattias Ohlund .12 .30
244 Derek Morris .12 .30
245 Erik Karlsson .25 .60
246 Daymond Langkow .12 .30
247 Lee Stempniak .12 .30
248 Cody Franson .12 .30
249 Jordan Leopold .12 .30
250 Nicklas Lidstrom .20 .50
251 R.J. Umberger .12 .30
252 Tomas Kopecky .15 .40
253 Kris Russell .12 .30
254 Keith Ballard .12 .30
255 Wayne Simmonds .25 .60
256 Tyler Myers .12 .30
257 Patrick Sharp .20 .50
258 Alex Auld .15 .40
259 Arron Asham .12 .30
260 Justin Williams .15 .40
261 Chris Butler .12 .30
262 Brian Campbell .12 .30
263 Derek Dorsett .12 .30
264 Ilya Kovalchuk .20 .50
265 Andrei Markov .20 .50
266 Brent Seabrook .12 .30
267 Marc Savard .12 .30
268 Rene Bourque .12 .30
269 Tim Gleason .12 .30
270 Shea Weber .15 .40
271 Dan Hamhuis .15 .40
272 Kristopher Letang .25 .60
273 Vincent Lecavalier .20 .50
274 Marian Hossa .20 .50
275 Brad Richardson .12 .30
276 Jarkko Ruutu .12 .30
277 Chris Osgood .20 .50
278 Benoit Pouliot .12 .30
279 Alexander Steen .12 .30
280 Shane Doan .15 .40
281 Nicklas Backstrom .20 .50
282 Mike Komisarek .12 .30
283 Kristian Huselius .12 .30
284 Sheldon Souray .12 .30
285 Craig Conroy .12 .30
286 Alexander Ovechkin .75 2.00
287 Brandon Dubinsky .12 .30
288 Greg Zanon .12 .30
289 Jiri Hudler .15 .40
290 James Neal .12 .30
291 Joe Thornton .30 .75
292 Todd White .12 .30
293 Alex Pietrangelo .15 .40
294 Matt Walker .12 .30
295 Matt Hunwick .12 .30
296 David Booth .12 .30
297 Jason Blake .12 .30
298 Pascal Dupuis .12 .30
299 Curtis Glencross .12 .30
300 Matt Carkner .15 .40
301 Mike Knuble .12 .30
302 Blake Comeau .12 .30
303 Daniel Carcillo .12 .30
304 Adrian Aucoin .12 .30
305 Luke Schenn .20 .50
306 Daniel Girardi .12 .30
307 Paul Ranger .12 .30
308 George Parros .15 .40
309 Sean Avery .15 .40
310 Matt Bradley .12 .30
311 Trevor Daley .12 .30
312 Sergei Kostitsyn .12 .30
313 Jeff Carter .15 .40
314 Craig Adams .12 .30
315 Chris Drury .15 .40
316 Duncan Keith .15 .40
317 Martin St. Louis .20 .50
318 Sergei Gonchar .12 .30
319 Bryce Salvador .12 .30
320 Dustin Penner .12 .30
321 Chris Kunitz .20 .50
322 Mikael Samuelsson .12 .30
323 Kyle Quincey .12 .30
324 Matt Cullen .12 .30
325 Ryan Shannon .12 .30
326 David Moss .12 .30
327 Marc-Edouard Vlasic .12 .30
328 Evander Kane .20 .50
329 Brian Rafalski .12 .30
330 Stephane Robidas .12 .30
331 Cory Stillman .12 .30
332 Zach Parise .20 .50
333 Andrew Ladd .12 .30
334 Jean-Sebastien Giguere .20 .50
335 Joe Pavelski .25 .60
336 Braydon Coburn .12 .30
337 Dion Phaneuf .15 .40
338 Milan Jurcina .12 .30
339 Clarke MacArthur .12 .30
340 Ethan Moreau .12 .30
341 Chris Stewart .15 .40
342 James Wisniewski .12 .30
343 Alexei Ponikarovsky .12 .30
344 Martin Biron .15 .40
345 Dan Sexton .15 .40
346 David Perron .15 .40
347 Devin Setoguchi .15 .40
348 Mike Richards .15 .40
349 Colin Fraser .12 .30
350 Brenden Morrow .15 .40
351 Mike Modano .30 .75
352 Daniel Alfredsson .20 .50
353 Mark Recchi .25 .60
354 Karlis Skrastins .12 .30
355 Andrew Brunette .12 .30
356 Francis Bouillon .12 .30
357 Barret Jackman .12 .30
358 Manny Malhotra .15 .40
359 Keith Yandle .12 .30
360 Marc-Andre Fleury .40 1.00
361 Jared Boll .12 .30
362 Ryane Clowe .12 .30
363 Antti Niemi .15 .40
364 Colton Orr .12 .30
365 Jason Pominville .12 .30
366 Todd Bertuzzi .15 .40
367 Nick Boynton .12 .30
368 Tomas Vokoun .15 .40
369 Mikko Koivu .20 .50
370 Erik Cole .12 .30
371 Johan Franzen .15 .40
372 Steven Stamkos .40 1.00
373 Kari Lehtonen .15 .40
374 James van Riemsdyk .15 .40
375 Kurtis Foster .12 .30
376 Paul Gaustad .12 .30
377 Kent Huskins .12 .30
378 Teddy Purcell .12 .30
379 Brad Boyes .12 .30
380 Chris Mason .15 .40
381 Derick Brassard .12 .30
382 Karl Alzner .12 .30
383 Michal Rozsival .12 .30
384 Petr Prucha .12 .30
385 Patrick Kane .40 1.00
386 David Clarkson .12 .30
387 Jim Howard .25 .60
388 Travis Moen .12 .30
389 Jakub Voracek .15 .40
390 John Mitchell .12 .30
391 Evgeni Malkin .40 1.00
392 Michael Ryder .12 .30
393 Nick Foligno .15 .40
394 Ryan Miller .20 .50
395 Brett Clark .12 .30
396 Mark Streit .12 .30
397 Dustin Brown .20 .50
398 Eric Staal .25 .60
399 Toni Lydman .12 .30
400 Roman Polak .12 .30
401 Daniel Briere .20 .50
402 Todd Marchant .12 .30
403 Jason Chimera .12 .30
404 Pascal Leclaire .15 .40
405 Steve Ott .12 .30
406 Ryan O'Reilly .20 .50
407 John Scott .12 .30
408 Mark Giordano .20 .50
409 Mike Lundin .12 .30
410 Tim Connolly .12 .30
411 Olli Jokinen .15 .40
412 Ryan Getzlaf .20 .50
413 Derek Roy .12 .30
414 Kevin Bieksa .20 .50
415 Dwayne Roloson .15 .40
416 Pavel Kubina .12 .30
417 Scott Gomez .15 .40
418 Eric Fehr .12 .30
419 Jonathan Quick .25 .60
420 Raffi Torres .12 .30
421 Andrei Kostitsyn .15 .40
422 Sergei Samsonov .15 .40
423 Ryan Callahan .12 .30
424 Steve Downie .12 .30
425 Brent Burns .20 .50
426 Jochen Hecht .12 .30
427 Rob Scuderi .12 .30
428 Matt Duchene .20 .50
429 Chris Kelly .15 .40
430 Matt Moulson .15 .40
431 Doug Weight .20 .50
432 Rostislav Olesz .12 .30
433 Nick Schultz .12 .30
434 Chris Neil .12 .30
435 Steve Mason .15 .40
436 Filip Kuba .12 .30
437 Trent Hunter .12 .30
438 Jussi Jokinen .12 .30
439 Tim Thomas .20 .50
440 Kris Versteeg .12 .30
441 Patrik Elias .20 .50
442 Zach Stortini .12 .30
443 Kevin Klein .12 .30
444 Kyle Okposo .12 .30
445 Fredrik Sjostrom .12 .30
446 Cam Ward .20 .50
447 Dustin Boyd .12 .30
448 Jason Demers .12 .30
449 Joel Ward .12 .30
450 Ed Jovanovski .12 .30
451 Matt Beleskey .15 .40
452 Nikita Filatov .12 .30
453 Ryan Parent .12 .30
454 Matt Greene .12 .30
455 Alex Goligoski .15 .40
456 Loui Eriksson .12 .30
457 John Tavares .30 .75
458 Jeff Schultz .12 .30
459 Antoine Vermette .12 .30
460 Andrew Cogliano .12 .30
461 Nikolai Khabibulin .15 .40
462 Paul Martin .12 .30
463 Nik Antropov .15 .40
464 Niklas Kronwall .15 .40
465 Jamie Benn .25 .60
466 Hal Gill .12 .30
467 Victor Hedman .25 .60
468 Henrik Tallinder .12 .30
469 Martin Hanzal .12 .30
470 Anton Babchuk .12 .30
471 Dan Cleary .20 .50
472 Travis Zajac .12 .30
473 Antero Niittymaki .15 .40
474 Mike Cammalleri .20 .50
475 Taylor Pyatt .12 .30
476 Martin Havlat .15 .40
477 Sean Bergenheim .12 .30
478 Marc Staal .12 .30
479 Willie Mitchell .12 .30
480 Chris Pronger .20 .50
481 Mike Fisher .12 .30
482 Dennis Wideman .12 .30
483 Henrik Sedin .25 .60
484 Eric Brewer .12 .30
485 Rick Nash .20 .50
486 Rich Peverley .20 .50
487 Rob Niedermayer .12 .30
488 Carlo Colaiacovo .12 .30
489 Peter Regin .15 .40
490 Stephen Weiss .15 .40
491 Brad Stuart .12 .30
492 Mark Eaton .12 .30
493 Patrice Bergeron .25 .60
494 Bryan Little .20 .50
495 Jason Strudwick .12 .30
496 Checklist .12 .30
497 Checklist .12 .30
498 Checklist .12 .30
499 Checklist .12 .30
500 Checklist .12 .30
501 Dana Tyrell RC 1.00 2.50
502 Jordan Caron RC 1.25 3.00
503 Nino Niederreiter RC 1.50 4.00
504 P.K. Subban RC 3.00 8.00
505 Justin Falk RC .75 2.00
506 Brandon Pirri RC 1.00 2.50
507 Robin Lehner RC 2.00 5.00
508 Taylor Hall RC 2.50 6.00
509 Oliver Ekman-Larsson RC 1.50 4.00
510 Nazem Kadri RC 3.00 8.00
511 Marcus Johansson RC 1.50 4.00
512 Cam Fowler RC 2.50 6.00
513 Sergei Bobrovsky RC 4.00 10.00
514 Kyle Clifford RC 1.25 3.00
515 Jared Cowen RC 1.00 2.50
516 Brandon Yip RC 1.00 2.50
517 Matt Taormina RC 1.00 2.50
518 Jamie McBain RC 1.00 2.50
519 Jordan Eberle RC 2.50 6.00
520 Alexander Burmistrov RC 1.00 2.50
521 Dustin Tokarski RC 1.00 2.50
522 Philip Larsen RC 1.00 2.50
523 Nick Spaling RC 1.00 2.50
524 Jake Muzzin RC 2.50 6.00
525 Ryan Reaves RC 1.25 3.00
526 Maxim Noreau RC .75 2.00
527 Zach Hamill RC 1.00 2.50
528 Henrik Karlsson RC 1.00 2.50
529 Jacob Josefson RC 1.00 2.50
530 Luke Adam RC 1.00 2.50
531 Eric Tangradi RC 1.00 2.50
532 Alexander Urbom RC 1.00 2.50
533 Alexander Vasyunov RC 1.00 2.50
534 Matt Martin RC 1.50 4.00
535 Tommy Wingels RC 1.00 2.50
536 Tyler Seguin RC 3.00 8.00
537 Alex Plante RC 1.00 2.50
538 Derek Stepan RC 1.25 3.00
539 Zac Dalpe RC 1.25 3.00
540 T.J. Brodie RC 1.00 2.50
541 Nick Leddy RC 1.25 3.00
542 Mark Olver RC 1.00 2.50
543 Anders Lindback RC 1.00 2.50
544 Nick Johnson RC .75 2.00
545 Cody Almond RC 1.00 2.50
546 Nick Palmieri RC 1.00 2.50
547 Brayden Schenn RC 2.50 6.00
548 Jeff Skinner RC 2.50 6.00
549 Evan Brophey RC 1.00 2.50
550 Magnus Paajarvi RC 1.25 3.00
551 Dominik Hasek L 1.25 3.00
552 Mark Messier L 1.50 4.00
553 Luc Robitaille L .75 2.00
554 Gilbert Perreault L .75 2.00
555 Doug Gilmour L 1.00 2.50
556 Denis Savard L .75 2.00
557 Markus Naslund L .75 2.00
558 Guy Lafleur L 1.00 2.50
559 Jari Kurri L .75 2.00
560 Bobby Hull L 1.50 4.00
561 Phil Esposito L 1.25 3.00
562 Mike Bossy L .75 2.00
563 Stan Mikita L 1.00 2.50
564 Ray Bourque L 1.25 3.00
565 Johnny Bucyk L .75 2.00
566 Marcel Dionne L 1.00 2.50
567 Larry Robinson L .75 2.00
568 Red Kelly L .75 2.00
569 Tony Esposito L .75 2.00
570 Grant Fuhr L 1.25 3.00
571 Peter Stastny L .60 1.50
572 Brian Leetch L .60 1.50
573 Borje Salming L .75 2.00
574 Frank Mahovlich L .75 2.00
575 Andy Bathgate L .75 2.00
576 Al MacInnis L 1.00 2.50
577 Ted Lindsay L .75 2.00
578 Darryl Sittler L 1.00 2.50
579 Alex Delvecchio L .75 2.00
580 Brent Sutter L .50 1.25
581 Adam Oates L .75 2.00
582 Dale Hawerchuk L 1.00 2.50
583 Joe Mullen L .60 1.50
584 Bob Bourne L .50 1.25
585 Ron Hextall L .75 2.00
586 Guy Carbonneau L .75 2.00
587 Doug Wilson L .60 1.50
588 Butch Bouchard L .60 1.50
589 Dave Schultz L .75 2.00
590 Clark Gillies L .75 2.00
591 Cam Neely L .75 2.00
592 Rogie Vachon L 1.00 2.50
593 Johnny Bower L .75 2.00
594 Patrick Roy L 2.00 5.00
595 Steve Yzerman L 2.00 5.00
596 Mario Lemieux L 3.00 8.00
597 Bobby Orr L 3.00 8.00
598 Gordie Howe L 2.50 6.00
599 Wayne Gretzky L 5.00 12.00
600 Rookies Checklist .15 .40
601 Cory Emmerton RC 1.25 3.00
602 Eric Wellwood RC 1.25 3.00
603 Evgeny Grachev RC 1.00 2.50
604 Ian Cole RC 1.00 2.50
605 Jacob Markstrom RC 2.50 6.00
606 Jan Mursak RC 2.00 5.00
607 Keith Aulie RC 1.00 2.50
608 Kevin Shattenkirk RC 2.00 5.00

609 Linus Omark RC 1.25 3.00
610 Marcel Mueller RC 1.25 3.00
611 Mats Zuccarello RC 2.00 5.00
612 Matt Calvert RC 1.50 4.00
613 Matt Hackett RC 1.25 3.00
614 Mattias Tedenby RC 1.00 2.50
615 Patrice Cormier RC 1.25 3.00
616 Ryan McDonagh RC 2.50 6.00
617 Stefan Della Rovere RC 1.00 2.50
618 Thomas McCollum RC 1.25 3.00
619 Tomas Tatar RC 2.50 6.00
620 Travis Hamonic RC 1.25 3.00

2010-11 O-Pee-Chee Retro

COMPLETE SET (620) 200.00 300.00
COMP.UPD.SET (20) 20.00 50.00
*RETRO 1-500: 2X TO 5X BASE
*RETRO ROOKIES 501-550: .5X TO 1.2X
*RETRO LEGENDS 551-600: .8X TO 2X
*RETRO UPD.ROOKIES 601-620: .5X TO 1.2X
194 Corey Crawford 1.50 4.00
281 Nicklas Backstrom 1.25 3.00

2010-11 O-Pee-Chee Retro Black Rainbow

*BLACK RAINBOW 1-500: 6X TO 15X BASE
*BLACK RAIN.501-550: 1.2X TO 3X BASE RC
*BLACK RAIN.551-600: 2.5X TO 6X BASE
*BLACK RAIN.601-620: 1.2X TO 3X BASE RC
194 Corey Crawford 5.00 12.00
281 Nicklas Backstrom 4.00 10.00
504 P.K. Subban 30.00 80.00
508 Taylor Hall 30.00 80.00
519 Jordan Eberle 40.00 80.00
536 Tyler Seguin 40.00 80.00

2010-11 O-Pee-Chee Retro Rainbow

*RAINBOW 1-500: 2.5X TO 6X BASE
*RAINBOW 501-550: .6X TO 1.5X BASE RC
*RAINBOW 551-600: 1X TO 2.5X BASE
*RAINBOW 601-620: .6X TO 1.5X BASE RC
194 Corey Crawford 2.00 5.00
281 Nicklas Backstrom 1.50 4.00

2010-11 O-Pee-Chee All Rookie Team

COMPLETE SET (6) 6.00 15.00
AR1 Jim Howard 1.00 2.50
AR2 Tyler Myers .50 1.25
AR3 Michael Del Zotto .60 1.50
AR4 John Tavares 1.25 3.00
AR5 Matt Duchene .75 2.00
AR6 Niclas Bergfors .60 1.50

2010-11 O-Pee-Chee Box Bottoms

COMPLETE SET (16) 5.00 12.00
PANEL: TWS/MLK/TVRS/MARL 1.25 3.00
PANEL: CRSBY/STMK/DCH/KAD 1.50 4.00
PANEL: OVCH/KNE/BRDR/DGH 1.50 4.00
PANEL: LNGO/IGN/DATS/GRN 1.25 3.00
NNO Jonathan Toews .40 1.00
NNO Evgeni Malkin .50 1.25
NNO John Tavares .40 1.00
NNO Patrick Marleau .25 .60
NNO Sidney Crosby 1.00 2.50
NNO Steven Stamkos .50 1.25
NNO Matt Duchene .25 .60
NNO Nazem Kadri .60 1.50
NNO Alexander Ovechkin 1.00 2.50
NNO Patrick Kane .50 1.25
NNO Martin Brodeur .60 1.50
NNO Drew Doughty .30 .75
NNO Roberto Luongo .40 1.00
NNO Jarome Iginla .30 .75
NNO Pavel Datsyuk .40 1.00
NNO Mike Green .20 .50

2010-11 O-Pee-Chee In Action

COMP.SET w/o SPs (30) 75.00 150.00
IA1 Pavel Datsyuk 5.00 12.00
IA2 Alexandre Burrows 2.00 5.00
IA3 Alexander Semin 3.00 8.00
IA4 Tomas Plekanec 2.00 5.00
IA5 Jarome Iginla 4.00 10.00
IA6 Chris Pronger 3.00 8.00
IA7 Marc-Andre Fleury 6.00 15.00
IA8 Ilya Bryzgalov 2.50 6.00
IA9 Carey Price 6.00 15.00
IA10 Henrik Lundqvist 8.00 20.00
IA11 Jim Howard 4.00 10.00
IA12 Matt Duchene 3.00 8.00
IA13 Anze Kopitar 5.00 12.00
IA14 Drew Doughty 4.00 10.00
IA15 Nicklas Backstrom 3.00 8.00
IA16 Mike Green 2.50 6.00
IA17 Martin St. Louis 3.00 8.00
IA18 Brad Richards 3.00 8.00
IA19 Patrick Marleau 3.00 8.00
IA20 Ryan Getzlaf 3.00 8.00
IA21 Phil Kessel 3.00 8.00
IA22 Joe Thornton 5.00 12.00
IA23 Mike Richards 2.50 6.00
IA24 Dustin Penner 2.00 5.00
IA25 Paul Stastny 2.50 6.00
IA26 Daniel Alfredsson 3.00 8.00
IA27 Daniel Sedin 4.00 10.00
IA28 Mikko Koivu 3.00 8.00
IA29 Eric Staal 4.00 10.00
IA30 Jeff Carter 2.50 6.00
IA31 Rick Nash SP 6.00 15.00
IA32 Ryan Miller SP 6.00 15.00
IA33 Jonathan Toews SP 10.00 25.00
IA34 Henrik Sedin SP 8.00 20.00
IA35 Steven Stamkos SP 12.00 30.00
IA36 Patrick Kane SP 12.00 30.00
IA37 Marian Gaborik SP 6.00 15.00
IA38 Martin Brodeur SP 15.00 40.00
IA39 Alexander Ovechkin SP 25.00 60.00
IA40 Sidney Crosby SP 25.00 60.00

2010-11 O-Pee-Chee Season Highlights

COMPLETE SET (15) 12.00 30.00
SH1 Nicklas Lidstrom .75 2.00
SH2 Alexander Ovechkin 3.00 8.00
SH3 Keith Tkachuk .75 2.00
SH4 Mike Cammalleri .75 2.00
SH5 Paul Kariya .75 2.00
SH6 Martin Brodeur 2.00 5.00
SH7 Scott Niedermayer .75 2.00
SH8 Teemu Selanne 1.50 4.00
SH9 Martin Brodeur 2.00 5.00
SH10 Sidney Crosby 3.00 8.00
SH11 Henrik Sedin 1.00 2.50
SH12 Alexander Ovechkin 3.00 8.00
SH13 Mike Richards .60 1.50
SH14 Steven Stamkos 1.50 4.00
SH15 Patrick Kane 1.50 4.00

2010-11 O-Pee-Chee Signatures

OSAC Andrew Cogliano 5.00 12.00
OSAM Al MacInnis SP 50.00 100.00
OSAO Alexander Ovechkin SP 40.00 100.00
OSBA Barry Melrose 6.00 15.00
OSBH Bobby Hull SP 15.00 40.00
OSBL Brian Leetch SP 25.00 60.00
OSBM Brad Marchand 12.00 30.00
OSBO Bobby Orr SP 125.00 200.00
OSBR Bobby Ryan 6.00 15.00
OSBS Bobby Sanguinetti 5.00 12.00
OSCH Christian Hanson 5.00 12.00
OSCS Cory Schneider 8.00 20.00
OSCW Colin Wilson 6.00 15.00
OSDC Daniel Carcillo 5.00 12.00
OSDL Dan LaCosta 5.00 12.00
OSDO Don Cherry SP 25.00 60.00
OSDP Daniel Paille SP 15.00 40.00
OSDS Devin Setoguchi 6.00 15.00
OSEK Erik Karlsson 10.00 25.00
OSET Eric Tangradi 4.00 10.00
OSEV Evander Kane 8.00 20.00
OSGI Jean-Sebastien Giguere SP 25.00 60.00
OSJB Johnny Bucyk 8.00 20.00
OSJE Jhonas Enroth 8.00 20.00
OSJI Jarome Iginla 12.00 30.00
OSJV James van Riemsdyk 6.00 15.00
OSKC Kris Chucko 5.00 12.00
OSMA Andrei Markov 8.00 20.00
OSMD Matt Duchene 8.00 20.00
OSMF Mark Fraser 5.00 12.00
OSMG Matt Gilroy 5.00 12.00
OSMH Matt Hendricks 5.00 12.00
OSMN Michal Neuvirth 6.00 15.00
OSMR Mike Ribeiro 5.00 12.00
OSMS Michael Sauer 5.00 12.00
OSNB Nicklas Backstrom 8.00 20.00
OSNH Nathan Horton 6.00 15.00
OSNK Nazem Kadri 25.00 60.00
OSPE Phil Esposito SP 15.00 40.00
OSPK Patrick Kane 25.00 60.00
OSPS P.K. Subban 12.00 30.00
OSRH Riku Helenius 5.00 12.00
OSRO Ryan O'Reilly 8.00 20.00
OSSC Sidney Crosby SP 100.00 200.00
OSSG Simon Gagne 10.00 25.00
OSSH Sergei Shirokov 6.00 15.00
OSSL Marc Staal 5.00 12.00
OSSS Steven Stamkos SP 20.00 50.00
OSST Peter Stastny 12.00 30.00
OSSV Marek Svatos 5.00 12.00
OSSW Chris Stewart 6.00 15.00
OSSY Steve Yzerman SP 60.00 120.00
OSTM Tyler Myers 5.00 12.00
OSVH Victor Hedman 10.00 25.00
OSYW Yannick Weber 5.00 12.00

2010-11 O-Pee-Chee Souvenirs

SV1ST Kne/Stam/Crsby/Tvres 25.00 60.00
SVATL Kane/Antr/Enstm/Byfg 6.00 15.00
SVCAR Jokin/Staal/Wrd/Cole 10.00 25.00
SVCBJ Mason/Nash/Brsrd/Vrck 6.00 15.00
SVCGY Bou/Stajan/Iginla/Kiprsff 8.00 20.00
SVCHI Hosa/Tws/Seabrk/Kne 15.00 40.00
SVDRW Lids/Holms/Osgd/Zetter 8.00 20.00
SVEDM Cogli/Horcf/Khbib/Ggnr 5.00 12.00
SVFLA Booth/Vokn/Stillmn/Weiss 8.00 20.00
SVGR8 Yzer/Gretzky/Mess/Lem 30.00 80.00
SVLAK Anze/Johnsn/Brwn/Dghty 10.00 25.00
SVMTL Hamr/Price/Plekan/Kost 12.00 30.00
SVNYR Lundq/Staal/Drury/Gabrik 6.00 15.00
SVRUS Ovch/Semin/Kvlck/Kvalv 25.00 60.00
SVSJS Setog/Thrn/Heat/Pavlsk 10.00 25.00
SVSTL Jckmn/Kriya/Jhnsn/Back 8.00 20.00
SVSWE Lids/Zettr/Bckstrm/Lndq 15.00 40.00
SVTML McDon/Salm/Sittler/Mahv 10.00 25.00
SVUSA Parise/Backs/Keslr/Kane 12.00 30.00
SVVAN Tambl/Sedin/Luong/Sdin 10.00 25.00
SV2002 Bowman/Holms/Yzer/Lids 15.00 40.00
SVBEES Hortn/Thmas/Rask/Chra 15.00 40.00
SVBUFF Miller/Roy/Stafford/Vanek 8.00 20.00
SVCAPS Backs/Semin/Ovch/Green 15.00 40.00
SVHABS Price/Kost/Hamr/Gionta 10.00 25.00
SVLEAF Kessl/Kaberl/Gigre/Kulem 12.00 30.00
SVPENS Fleury/Malkn/Crsby/Staal 20.00 50.00
SVPITT Mullen/Lemx/Crsby/Malkn 20.00 50.00
SVPRED Webr/Dumnt/Rin/Lgwnd 8.00 20.00
SVSCUP Carter/Rchrds/Kane/Tws 10.00 25.00
SVSENS Kovlv/Folig/Leclre/Spez 8.00 20.00
SVWILD Backs/Koivu/Bouch/Havlt 10.00 25.00

2010-11 O-Pee-Chee Stat Kings

COMPLETE SET (20) 12.00 30.00
SK1 Sidney Crosby 3.00 8.00
SK2 Steven Stamkos 1.50 4.00
SK3 Henrik Sedin 1.00 2.50
SK4 Henrik Sedin 1.00 2.50
SK5 Zenon Konopka .60 1.50
SK6 Steven Stamkos 1.50 4.00
SK7 Alexander Ovechkin 3.00 8.00
SK8 Dany Heatley .60 1.50
SK9 Mike Green .60 1.50
SK10 Mike Green .60 1.50
SK11 Matt Duchene .75 2.00
SK12 Jeff Schultz .50 1.25
SK13 Cal Clutterbuck .50 1.25
SK14 Daniel Briere .75 2.00
SK15 Mike Cammalleri .75 2.00
SK16 Martin Brodeur 2.00 5.00
SK17 Tuukka Rask 1.00 2.50
SK18 Tuukka Rask 1.00 2.50
SK19 Martin Brodeur 2.00 5.00
SK20 Craig Anderson .75 2.00

2010-11 O-Pee-Chee Team Leaders

COMPLETE SET (30) 15.00 40.00
TL1 Hiller/Ryan/Getzlaf .75 2.00
TL2 Hedberg/Kovalchuk/Enstrom .75 2.00
TL3 Rask/Chara/Sturm 1.00 2.50
TL4 Connolly/Miller/Vanek .75 2.00
TL5 Iginla/Iginla/Kiprusoff 1.00 2.50
TL6 Staal/Ward/Jokinen 1.00 2.50
TL7 Niemi/Kane/Kane 1.50 4.00
TL8 Anderson/Stastny/Stewart .60 1.50
TL9 Huselius/Mason/Nash .75 2.00
TL10 Turco/Eriksson/Richards .75 2.00
TL11 Datsyuk/Howard/Zetterberg 1.25 3.00
TL12 Penner/Penner/Deslauriers .50 1.25
TL13 Horton/Vokoun/Weiss .60 1.50
TL14 Kopitar/Kopitar/Quick 1.25 3.00
TL15 Latendresse/Backstrom/Koivu .75 2.00
TL16 Gomez/Gionta/Halak .75 2.00
TL17 Sullivan/Rinne/Hornqvist .75 2.00
TL18 Parise/Parise/Brodeur 2.00 5.00
TL19 Roloson/Moulson/Streit .60 1.50
TL20 Gaborik/Gaborik/Lundqvist 2.00 5.00
TL21 Elliott/Fisher/Alfredsson .75 2.00
TL22 Carter/Pronger/Leighton .75 2.00
TL23 Vrbata/Doan/Bryzgalov .60 1.50
TL24 Fleury/Crosby/Crosby 3.00 8.00
TL25 Marleau/Thornton/Nabokov 1.25 3.00
TL26 Mason/Steen/McDonald .60 1.50
TL27 Stamkos/Niittymaki/St. Louis 1.50 4.00
TL28 Kessel/Kaberle/Gustavsson 1.00 2.50
TL29 Sedin/Luongo/Burrows 1.25 3.00
TL30 Backstrom/Ovechkin/Theodore 3.00 8.00

2010-11 O-Pee-Chee Trophy Winners

COMPLETE SET (13) 10.00 25.00
TW1 Henrik Sedin 1.00 2.50
TW2 Alexander Ovechkin 3.00 8.00
TW3 S.Stamkos/S.Crosby 3.00 8.00
TW4 Duncan Keith .60 1.50
TW5 Ryan Miller .75 2.00
TW6 Tyler Myers .50 1.25
TW7 Pavel Datsyuk 1.25 3.00
TW8 Martin St. Louis .75 2.00
TW9 Jose Theodore .75 2.00
TW10 Martin Brodeur 2.00 5.00
TW11 Shane Doan .60 1.50
TW12 Jonathan Toews 1.25 3.00
TW13 Henrik Sedin 1.00 2.50

2010-11 O-Pee-Chee Winter Classic

COMPLETE SET (16) 10.00 25.00
WC1 Daniel Briere .75 2.00
WC2 Scott Hartnell .50 1.25
WC3 Jeff Carter .60 1.50
WC4 Mike Richards .60 1.50
WC5 Chris Pronger .75 2.00
WC6 Daniel Carcillo .50 1.25
WC7 Michael Leighton .60 1.50
WC8 B.Clarke/B.Orr 3.00 8.00
WC9 Mark Recchi 1.00 2.50
WC10 Marco Sturm .50 1.25
WC11 Zdeno Chara .75 2.00
WC12 Patrice Bergeron 1.00 2.50
WC13 Marc Savard .50 1.25
WC14 David Krejci .75 2.00
WC15 Shawn Thornton .50 1.25
WC16 Tim Thomas .75 2.00

2011-12 O-Pee-Chee

1 Scott Hartnell .12 .30
2 Paul Mara .12 .30
3 Marian Hossa .20 .50
4 Duncan Keith .15 .40
5 Henrik Zetterberg .25 .60
6 Maxime Talbot .12 .30
7 Brian Campbell .12 .30
8 Todd Bertuzzi .15 .40
9 J.P. Dumont .12 .30
10 Claude Giroux .20 .50
11 Chris Phillips .12 .30
12 Dan Cleary .12 .30
13 Jordan Staal .15 .40
14 Ryan Kesler .20 .50
15 George Parros .15 .40
16 Joe Thornton .30 .75
17 Johan Franzen .15 .40
18 Patrick Kane .40 1.00
19 Mike Richards .15 .40
20 Patrick Sharp .20 .50
21 Jeff Carter .15 .40
22 Dan Boyle .12 .30
23 Daniel Sedin .25 .60
24 Henrik Sedin .25 .60
25 Eric Staal .25 .60
26 Pascal Dupuis .12 .30
27 Olli Jokinen .15 .40
28 Guillaume Latendresse .12 .30
29 Jonathan Toews .30 .75
30 Kris Versteeg .12 .30
31 Roberto Luongo .30 .75
32 Patrick Marleau .20 .50
33 Martin St. Louis .20 .50
34 Saku Koivu .20 .50
35 Cam Ward .20 .50
36 Tomas Holmstrom .12 .30
37 Antti Niemi .15 .40
38 Matt Cullen .12 .30
39 Raffi Torres .12 .30
40 Tim Thomas .20 .50
41 Jarome Iginla .25 .60
42 Joe Pavelski .20 .50
43 Fernando Pisani .12 .30
44 Chris Drury .15 .40
45 Brian Gionta .12 .30
46 Ryan Smyth .15 .40
47 Alexander Ovechkin .75 2.00
48 Daniel Briere .20 .50
49 Marc-Andre Fleury .40 1.00
50 Sidney Crosby .75 2.00
51 Jonas Hiller .15 .40
52 Adam McQuaid .12 .30
53 Steve Ott .12 .30
54 Andrei Loktionov .15 .40
55 Erik Cole .12 .30
56 Alec Martinez .12 .30
57 Lauri Korpikoski .12 .30
58 Keith Yandle .12 .30
59 Jay Bouwmeester .12 .30
60 Jay McClement .12 .30
61 Toni Lydman .12 .30
62 Brian Elliott .15 .40
63 Shawn Horcoff .12 .30
64 Devan Dubnyk .15 .40
65 Nate Thompson .12 .30
66 Douglas Murray .12 .30
67 Matt Hendricks .12 .30
68 Nick Schultz .12 .30
69 Jamie McBain .12 .30
70 Jannik Hansen .15 .40
71 Matt Calvert .12 .30
72 Victor Hedman .25 .60
73 Shea Weber .15 .40
74 David Perron .15 .40
75 David Clarkson .12 .30
76 Travis Zajac .12 .30
77 Michael Grabner .15 .40
78 Kevin Bieksa .15 .40
79 Viktor Stalberg .12 .30
80 Jim Howard .25 .60
81 Ryan McDonagh .12 .30
82 Valtteri Filppula .12 .30
83 Chris Pronger .20 .50
84 Ian White .12 .30
85 Tomas Kaberle .12 .30
86 Jason Pominville .12 .30
87 Filip Kuba .12 .30
88 Clarke MacArthur .12 .30
89 Niclas Bergfors .15 .40
90 Ron Hainsey .12 .30
91 Bobby Butler .15 .40
92 Jeff Halpern .12 .30
93 James Reimer .20 .50
94 Jamie Benn .20 .50
95 Dustin Brown .20 .50
96 Jonathan Quick .25 .60
97 Mikkel Boedker .12 .30
98 Michal Rozsival .12 .30
99 T.J. Galiardi .15 .40
100 John-Michael Liles .12 .30
101 Jordan Eberle .20 .50
102 Ryan Whitney .12 .30
103 Torrey Mitchell .12 .30
104 David Booth .12 .30
105 Mathieu Garon .12 .30
106 Alexander Edler .12 .30
107 John Carlson .20 .50
108 Mike Santorelli .12 .30
109 Nick Spaling .12 .30
110 B.J. Crombeen .12 .30
111 Nikita Nikitin .12 .30
112 Adam Mair .12 .30
113 Dennis Wideman .12 .30
114 Trent Hunter .12 .30
115 Radek Martinek .12 .30
116 Niklas Kronwall .15 .40
117 Ryan Callahan .15 .40
118 Jack Skille .15 .40
119 James van Riemsdyk .15 .40
120 Daniel Paille .12 .30
121 Drew Stafford .12 .30
122 Mike Weber .12 .30
123 Mikhail Grabovski .12 .30
124 Brett Lebda .12 .30
125 Jim Slater .12 .30
126 P.K. Subban .25 .60
127 Ryan Shannon .12 .30
128 Adam Burish .12 .30
129 Tuomo Ruutu .15 .40
130 Kyle Clifford .12 .30
131 Tom Pyatt .12 .30
132 Michal Handzus .12 .30
133 Sean Bergenheim .12 .30
134 Ryan Getzlaf .20 .50
135 Eric Belanger .12 .30
136 Vincent Lecavalier .20 .50
137 Mark Giordano .20 .50
138 Ryan O'Reilly .12 .30
139 Scott Clemmensen .15 .40
140 Joni Pitkanen .15 .40
141 Brandon McMillan .12 .30
142 Devin Setoguchi .12 .30
143 Rene Bourque .12 .30
144 Martin Havlat .15 .40
145 Alexander Semin .20 .50
146 Jared Boll .12 .30
147 Fedor Tyutin .12 .30
148 Cody Franson .12 .30
149 Marty Reasoner .12 .30
150 Ian Cole .12 .30
151 Dmitry Kulikov .12 .30
152 Martin Brodeur .50 1.25
153 Travis Hamonic .15 .40
154 Niklas Hjalmarsson .12 .30
155 Brandon Prust .12 .30
156 Pavel Datsyuk .30 .75
157 Evgeni Malkin .40 1.00
158 David Krejci .20 .50
159 Derek Roy .12 .30
160 Sergei Gonchar .12 .30
161 Braden Holtby .25 .60
162 Nazem Kadri .25 .60
163 Andrew Ladd .12 .30
164 Dustin Byfuglien .20 .50
165 Ondrej Pavelec .20 .50
166 Michal Neuvirth .15 .40
167 Travis Moen .12 .30
168 Tyler Kennedy .12 .30
169 Kari Lehtonen .15 .40
170 Steve Downie .12 .30
171 Anze Kopitar .30 .75
172 Shane Doan .15 .40
173 Lubomir Visnovsky .12 .30
174 Jeff Skinner .25 .60
175 Cory Sarich .12 .30
176 Cam Fowler .20 .50
177 Matt Duchene .20 .50
178 David Jones .12 .30
179 Corey Perry .30 .75
180 Ryan Malone .12 .30
181 Ales Hemsky .15 .40
182 James Neal .12 .30
183 Dustin Penner .15 .40
184 Andrew Brunette .12 .30
185 Luca Sbisa .15 .40
186 Mikko Koivu .15 .40
187 Sami Salo .12 .30
188 Troy Brouwer .12 .30
189 R.J. Umberger .12 .30
190 Martin Erat .12 .30
191 Colin Wilson .15 .40
192 Patrik Berglund .12 .30
193 Patric Hornqvist .12 .30
194 Ty Conklin .15 .40
195 Zach Parise .20 .50
196 Colin White .12 .30
197 Josh Bailey .15 .40
198 Taylor Pyatt .12 .30
199 Artem Anisimov .12 .30
200 Brian Rafalski .12 .30
201 Wojtek Wolski .12 .30
202 Michael Sauer .12 .30
203 Jiri Hudler .15 .40
204 Kimmo Timonen .12 .30
205 Chris Kunitz .20 .50
206 Brent Johnson .15 .40
207 Zdeno Chara .20 .50
208 Tim Connolly .12 .30
209 Jhonas Enroth .20 .50
210 Tyler Bozak .12 .30
211 Jason Arnott .15 .40
212 Nik Antropov .15 .40
213 Zach Bogosian .15 .40
214 Jaroslav Spacek .12 .30
215 Chris Neil .12 .30
216 Antti Miettinen .12 .30
217 Loui Eriksson .12 .30
218 Wayne Simmonds .25 .60
219 Martin Hanzal .12 .30
220 Matt Stajan .12 .30
221 Milan Hejduk .15 .40
222 Jiri Tlusty .12 .30
223 Andrew Cogliano .12 .30
224 Kyle Quincey .12 .30
225 Joe Corvo .12 .30
226 Gilbert Brule .12 .30
227 Bobby Ryan .15 .40
228 Trevor Daley .12 .30
229 Jarret Stoll .15 .40
230 Ray Whitney .12 .30
231 Robyn Regehr .12 .30
232 Kevin Porter .12 .30
233 Brandon Sutter .12 .30
234 Brandon Yip .12 .30
235 Steven Stamkos .40 1.00
236 Sam Gagner .12 .30
237 Francois Beauchemin .12 .30
238 Cory Stillman .12 .30
239 Paul Stastny .15 .40
240 Dominic Moore .12 .30
241 Alexandre Burrows .12 .30
242 Alex Tanguay .15 .40
243 Marc-Andre Bergeron .12 .30
244 Cody Hodgson .25 .60
245 Kurtis Foster .12 .30
246 Jussi Jokinen .12 .30
247 Michael Frolik .12 .30
248 Derick Brassard .12 .30
249 Evgeny Dadonov .12 .30
250 Rick Nash .20 .50
251 Luke Schenn .20 .50
252 Alexander Burmistrov .15 .40
253 Jason Chimera .12 .30
254 Anthony Stewart .12 .30
255 Marcus Johansson .15 .40
256 Brooks Laich .12 .30
257 Mathieu Perreault .12 .30
258 Roman Hamrlik .12 .30
259 Daniel Alfredsson .20 .50
260 Tomas Plekanec .12 .30
261 Jose Theodore .20 .50
262 Manny Malhotra .15 .40
263 Dave Bolland .15 .40
264 Jakub Voracek .15 .40
265 Shawn Matthias .12 .30
266 Kris Russell .12 .30
267 Francis Bouillon .12 .30
268 Alex Pietrangelo .15 .40
269 Mattias Tedenby .20 .50
270 Zenon Konopka .15 .40
271 Al Montoya .12 .30
272 Brad Stuart .12 .30
273 Mike Knuble .12 .30
274 Braydon Coburn .12 .30
275 Karl Alzner .12 .30
276 Jochen Hecht .12 .30
277 Dwayne Roloson .15 .40
278 Bryan Little .12 .30
279 Carey Price .40 1.00
280 Benoit Pouliot .30 .75
281 Teemu Selanne .40 1.00
282 Evander Kane .20 .50
283 Niklas Hagman .12 .30
284 Tim Gleason .12 .30
285 Nick Leddy .25 .60
286 Erik Johnson .12 .30
287 Derek Dorsett .12 .30
288 Mike Ribeiro .12 .30
289 Nicklas Lidstrom .25 .60
290 Drew Doughty .25 .60
291 Dennis Seidenberg .12 .30
292 Derek Stepan .12 .30
293 Dion Phaneuf .15 .40
294 Eric Nystrom .12 .30
295 Erik Karlsson .25 .60
296 Blake Comeau .12 .30
297 Blake Wheeler .20 .50
298 Brad Boyes .12 .30
299 Brandon Dubinsky .12 .30
300 Miikka Kiprusoff .20 .50
301 Daniel Winnik .12 .30
302 Adrian Aucoin .12 .30
303 Alex Goligoski .15 .40
304 Alexander Steen .12 .30
305 Mason Raymond .12 .30
306 Mats Zuccarello .20 .50
307 Matt Carkner .15 .40
308 Mike Fisher .12 .30
309 Nicklas Backstrom .20 .50
310 Brenden Morrow .15 .40
311 Niklas Backstrom .20 .50
312 Nikolai Kulemin .12 .30
313 Radim Vrbata .12 .30
314 Oliver Ekman-Larsson .20 .50
315 Andrej Meszaros .12 .30
316 Anders Lindback .15 .40
317 Andreas Nodl .12 .30
318 Antero Niittymaki .15 .40
319 Brent Burns .20 .50
320 Brent Seabrook .12 .30
321 Brian Boyle .12 .30
322 Brian Lee .15 .40
323 Brooks Orpik .12 .30
324 Michal Repik .12 .30
325 Stephane Robidas .12 .30
326 Jonathan Bernier .15 .40
327 Tomas Fleischmann .12 .30
328 Teddy Purcell .12 .30
329 Ladislav Smid .12 .30
330 Cal Clutterbuck .12 .30
331 Logan Couture .25 .60
332 Mikael Backlund .15 .40
333 Christian Ehrhoff .12 .30
334 Antoine Vermette .12 .30
335 Cal O'Reilly .12 .30
336 Carlo Colaiacovo .12 .30
337 Rod Pelley .12 .30
338 Kyle Okposo .12 .30
339 Patrick Eaves .12 .30
340 Henrik Lundqvist .50 1.25
341 Matt Carle .15 .40
342 Eric Tangradi .12 .30
343 Nathan Horton .20 .50
344 Jamal Mayers .12 .30
345 Mike Komisarek .15 .40
346 Milan Michalek .12 .30
347 Jamie Langenbrunner .12 .30
348 Justin Williams .15 .40
349 Lee Stempniak .12 .30
350 Chad LaRose .12 .30
351 Dana Tyrell .12 .30
352 Taylor Hall .20 .50
353 John Madden .12 .30
354 Ryane Clowe .12 .30
355 Marek Zidlicky .12 .30
356 Keith Ballard .12 .30
357 Steve Mason .15 .40
358 Ryan Suter .15 .40
359 Jason Garrison .12 .30
360 Johan Hedberg .15 .40
361 P.A. Parenteau .12 .30
362 Marian Gaborik .20 .50
363 Darroll Powe .12 .30
364 Tyler Seguin .25 .60
365 Chris Butler .12 .30
366 Carl Gunnarsson .12 .30
367 Jason Spezza .20 .50
368 Josh Gorges .12 .30
369 Pekka Rinne .20 .50
370 Patrice Bergeron .25 .60
371 Willie Mitchell .12 .30
372 Tyler Myers .12 .30
373 Tyler Ennis .12 .30
374 Ty Wishart .12 .30
375 Tuukka Rask .25 .60
376 Matt Moulson .12 .30
377 Tom Wandell .12 .30
378 Tom Gilbert .12 .30
379 Tobias Enstrom .12 .30
380 Thomas Vanek .15 .40
381 Theo Peckham .12 .30
382 T.J. Oshie .20 .50
383 Chris Kelly .15 .40
384 Stephen Weiss .15 .40
385 David Backes .12 .30
386 Mark Stuart .12 .30
387 Sergei Bobrovsky .30 .75
388 Andy McDonald .12 .30
389 David Steckel .12 .30
390 Anton Stralman .12 .30
391 Anton Volchenkov .12 .30
392 Arron Asham .12 .30
393 Barret Jackman .12 .30
394 Brad Marchand .40 1.00
395 Brett Clark .12 .30
396 Brian Rolston .15 .40
397 Cam Barker .12 .30
398 Chris Mason .15 .40
399 Chris Stewart .15 .40
400 Cody McCormick .12 .30
401 Colby Armstrong .12 .30
402 Colton Orr .12 .30
403 Corey Crawford .25 .60
404 Cory Schneider .20 .50
405 Simon Gagne .20 .50
406 Dan Hamhuis .15 .40
407 Ryan Miller .20 .50
408 Robin Lehner .15 .40
409 Rich Peverley .20 .50
410 Sergei Kostitsyn .12 .30
411 Linus Omark .20 .50
412 Jason Demers .12 .30
413 Mikael Samuelsson .12 .30
414 Kristian Huselius .12 .30
415 Justin Abdelkader .12 .30
416 Peter Regin .12 .30
417 Mark Dekanich .12 .30
418 Kevin Shattenkirk .15 .40
419 Ilya Kovalchuk .20 .50
420 Jacob Markstrom .20 .50
421 Andrew MacDonald .12 .30
422 Erik Christensen .12 .30
423 Daniel Carcillo .12 .30
424 Matt Cooke .12 .30
425 Paul Gaustad .12 .30
426 Jonas Gustavsson .20 .50
427 Scott Gomez .15 .40
428 Andrei Kostitsyn .15 .40
429 Michael Ryder .12 .30
430 Andrew Raycroft .15 .40
431 Andy Greene .12 .30
432 Brad Richards .20 .50
433 Jack Johnson .12 .30
434 Curtis Glencross .12 .30
435 Dany Heatley .15 .40
436 Steve Sullivan .12 .30
437 Dainius Zubrus .12 .30
438 John Tavares .30 .75
439 Jonathan Ericsson .12 .30
440 Michael Del Zotto .12 .30
441 Brian Boucher .15 .40
442 Matt Niskanen .15 .40
443 Phil Kessel .20 .50
444 Patrice Cormier .12 .30
445 Michael Cammalleri .15 .40
446 Max Pacioretty .20 .50
447 Keith Aulie .15 .40
448 Mark Letestu .15 .40
449 Ville Leino .15 .40
450 Johnny Boychuk .15 .40
451 Mark Fistric .12 .30
452 Rob Scuderi .12 .30
453 Kyle Turris .12 .30
454 Magnus Paajarvi .15 .40
455 Pierre-Marc Bouchard .20 .50
456 Marc-Edouard Vlasic .12 .30
457 Greg Zanon .12 .30
458 Samuel Pahlsson .12 .30
459 Ray Emery .15 .40
460 David Legwand .15 .40
461 Matt D'Agostini .12 .30
462 Patrik Elias .20 .50
463 Jeff Schultz .12 .30
464 Mike Weaver .12 .30
465 Henrik Tallinder .12 .30
466 Jesse Joensuu .12 .30
467 Pavel Kubina .12 .30
468 Bryan Bickell .12 .30
469 Jason Blake .12 .30
470 Marc Staal .12 .30
471 Darren Helm .12 .30
472 Mike Comrie .12 .30
473 Milan Lucic .20 .50
474 Mike Green .15 .40
475 Johnny Oduya .15 .40
476 James Wisniewski .12 .30
477 Semyon Varlamov .20 .50
478 Alex Kovalev .15 .40
479 Lars Eller .12 .30
480 Matt Greene .12 .30
481 Sergei Samsonov .15 .40
482 Anton Babchuk .12 .30
483 Rick DiPietro .15 .40
484 Kristopher Letang .25 .60
485 Joffrey Lupul .12 .30
486 Nick Foligno .15 .40
487 Derek Morris .12 .30
488 Liam Reddox .12 .30
489 Jordin Tootoo .15 .40
490 Jaroslav Halak .20 .50
491 David Moss .12 .30
492 Matt Martin .12 .30
493 Frans Nielsen .12 .30
494 Sean Avery .15 .40
495 Daniel Girardi .12 .30
496 Checklist .12 .30
497 Checklist .12 .30
498 Checklist .12 .30
499 Checklist .12 .30
500 Checklist .12 .30
501 Dale Hawerchuk L 1.00 2.50
502 Mike Gartner L 1.00 2.50
503 Richard Brodeur L .75 2.00
504 Tony Tanti L .75 2.00
505 Al Iafrate L .60 1.50
506 Brett Hull L 1.50 4.00
507 Mario Lemieux L 3.00 8.00
508 Bobby Clarke L 1.25 3.00
509 Eric Lindros L 1.25 3.00
510 Reggie Leach L .60 1.50
511 Bill Barber L .75 2.00
512 Rick MacLeish L .60 1.50
513 Dave Schultz L .75 2.00
514 Tim Kerr L .50 1.25
515 Mark Messier L 1.50 4.00
516 Andy Bathgate L .75 2.00
517 Mike Bossy L .75 2.00
518 Denis Potvin L .75 2.00
519 Patrick Roy L 2.00 5.00
520 Jean Beliveau L .75 2.00
521 Guy Lafleur L 1.00 2.50
522 Larry Robinson L .75 2.00
523 Claude Lemieux L .60 1.50
524 Russ Courtnall L .50 1.25
525 Neal Broten L .60 1.50
526 Marcel Dionne L 1.00 2.50
527 Rogie Vachon L 1.00 2.50
528 Bernie Nicholls L .60 1.50
529 Dave Taylor L .60 1.50
530 Ron Francis L 1.00 2.50
531 Wayne Gretzky L 5.00 12.00
532 Jari Kurri L .75 2.00
533 Bill Ranford L .75 2.00
534 Paul Coffey L .75 2.00
535 Ted Lindsay L .75 2.00
536 Red Kelly L .75 2.00
537 Igor Larionov L .75 2.00
538 Alex Delvecchio L .75 2.00
539 Joe Sakic L 1.50 4.00
540 Bobby Hull L 1.50 4.00
541 Stan Mikita L 1.00 2.50
542 Doug Wilson L .60 1.50
543 Steve Larmer L .60 1.50
544 Bobby Orr L 3.00 8.00
545 Ray Bourque L 1.50 4.00
546 Phil Esposito L 1.25 3.00
547 Johnny Bucyk L .75 2.00
548 Cam Neely L .75 2.00
549 Milt Schmidt L .60 1.50
550 Brad Park L .60 1.50

551 Todd Ford RC 1.25 3.00
552 Cody Hodgson RC 1.50 4.00
553 Yann Suave RC 1.00 2.50
554 Joe Colborne RC 1.00 2.50
555 Ben Scrivens RC 1.00 2.50
556 Matt Frattin RC 1.00 2.50
557 Alex Stalock .75 2.00
558 Brian Strait RC 1.25 3.00
559 Joe Vitale RC 1.00 2.50
560 Ben Holmstrom RC 1.00 2.50
561 Erik Gustafsson RC 1.25 3.00
562 Zac Rinaldo RC 1.00 2.50
563 Patrick Wiercioch RC 1.00 2.50
564 Erik Condra RC 1.00 2.50
565 Roman Wick RC 1.25 3.00
566 Colin Greening RC 1.00 2.50
567 Andre Benoit RC 1.25 3.00
568 Stephane Da Costa RC 1.00 2.50
569 Cam Talbot RC 2.50 6.00
570 Matt Campanale RC 1.00 2.50
571 Shane Sims RC 1.00 2.50
572 Mikko Koskinen RC 1.25 3.00
573 Jamie Doornbosch RC 1.00 2.50
574 Mark Katic RC 1.00 2.50
575 Justin DiBenedetto RC .75 2.00
576 Adam Henrique RC 2.50 6.00
577 Jonathon Blum RC 1.00 2.50
578 Blake Geoffrion RC 1.00 2.50
579 Aaron Palushaj RC 1.00 2.50
580 Brendon Nash RC 1.00 2.50
581 Drew Bagnall RC 1.00 2.50
582 Carson McMillan RC 1.25 3.00
583 Hugh Jessiman RC 1.00 2.50
584 Scott Timmins RC 1.00 2.50
585 Teemu Hartikainen RC 1.00 2.50
586 Chris Vande Velde RC 1.50 4.00
587 Tomas Vincour RC 1.00 2.50
588 Colton Sceviour RC 1.00 2.50
589 John Moore RC 1.00 2.50
590 Tomas Kubalik RC 1.00 2.50
591 Cameron Gaunce RC .75 2.00
592 Marcus Kruger RC 1.50 4.00
593 Greg Nemisz RC 1.00 2.50
594 Lance Bouma RC 1.00 2.50
595 Paul Postma RC 1.00 2.50
596 Andrei Zubarev RC 1.25 3.00
597 Carl Klingberg RC 1.00 2.50
598 Timo Pielmeier 1.25 3.00
599 Jean-Philippe Levasseur 1.00 2.50
600 Checklist .50 1.25
601 Semyon Varlamov .40 1.00
602 Jeff Carter .30 .75
603 Mike Richards .30 .75
604 Jaromir Jagr 1.25 3.00
605 Ilya Bryzgalov .40 1.00
606 Tomas Vokoun .30 .75
607 Ondrej Pavelec .40 1.00
608 Dustin Byfuglien .40 1.00
609 Alexander Burmistrov .30 .75
610 Evander Kane .40 1.00
611 Gabriel Landeskog RC 3.00 8.00
612 Ryan Johansen RC 3.00 8.00
613 Zack Kassian RC 1.25 3.00
614 Ryan Nugent-Hopkins RC 4.00 10.00
615 Erik Gudbranson RC 1.25 3.00
616 Craig Smith RC 1.25 3.00
617 Adam Larsson RC 1.25 3.00
618 David Rundblad RC 1.00 2.50
619 Mika Zibanejad RC 3.00 8.00
620 Sean Couturier RC 2.00 5.00
621 Matt Read RC 1.25 3.00
622 Brett Connolly RC 1.00 2.50
623 Louis Leblanc RC 1.00 2.50
624 Cody Eakin RC 1.50 4.00
625 Mark Scheifele RC 4.00 10.00

2011-12 O-Pee-Chee Black Rainbow

*1-500 VETS: 6X TO 15X BASIC CARDS
*501-600 LEGENDS : 2.5X TO 6X BASE
*551-599 ROOKIES: 1.5X TO 4X BASE RC
244 Cody Hodgson 15.00 40.00
309 Nicklas Backstrom 4.00 10.00
403 Corey Crawford 5.00 12.00
552 Cody Hodgson 15.00 40.00

2011-12 O-Pee-Chee Rainbow

*1-500 VETS: 2.5X TO 6X BASIC CARDS
*501-600 LEGENDS: 1X TO 2.5X BASE
*551-599 ROOKIES: .6X TO 1.5X BASE
244 Cody Hodgson 6.00 15.00
309 Nicklas Backstrom 1.50 4.00
403 Corey Crawford 2.00 5.00
552 Cody Hodgson 6.00 15.00

2011-12 O-Pee-Chee Retro

*1-500 VETS: 2X TO 5X BASIC CARDS
*501-550 LEGENDS: .8X TO 2X BASE
*551-600 ROOKIES: .5X TO 1.2X BASE
*601-610 VETS: 2X TO 5X BASIC CARDS
*611-625 ROOKIES: .6X TO 1.5X BASE
309 Nicklas Backstrom 1.25 3.00
403 Corey Crawford 1.50 4.00

2011-12 O-Pee-Chee Box Bottoms

COMPLETE SET (16) 6.00 15.00
1 Patrice Bergeron .30 .75
2 Martin Brodeur .60 1.50
3 Sidney Crosby 1.00 2.50
4 Claude Giroux .25 .60
5 Taylor Hall .25 .60
6 Jarome Iginla .30 .75
7 Patrick Kane .50 1.25
8 Ryan Kesler .25 .60
9 Henrik Lundqvist .60 1.50
10 Roberto Luongo .40 1.00
11 Alexander Ovechkin 1.00 2.50
12 Carey Price .50 1.25
13 Martin St. Louis .25 .60
14 Steven Stamkos .50 1.25
15 Jonathan Toews .40 1.00
16 Henrik Zetterberg .30 .75
P1 Stamkos/Iginla/Zett/Lundq 1.50 4.00
P2 Ovech/Keslr/Brod/Girox 1.50 4.00
P3 Toews/Luong/Berg/Hall 1.50 4.00
P4 Sid/Kane/St.Louis/Price 1.50 4.00

2011-12 O-Pee-Chee In Action

A1 Corey Perry 5.00 12.00
A2 Nathan Horton 3.00 8.00
A3 Derek Roy 2.00 5.00
A4 Jeff Skinner 4.00 10.00
A5 Patrick Sharp 3.00 8.00
A6 Matt Duchene 3.00 8.00
A7 Rick Nash 3.00 8.00
A8 Brad Richards 3.00 8.00
A9 Pavel Datsyuk 5.00 12.00
A10 Henrik Zetterberg 4.00 10.00
A11 Jordan Eberle 3.00 8.00
A12 Taylor Hall 3.00 8.00
A13 Drew Doughty 4.00 10.00
A14 Mikko Koivu 2.50 6.00
A15 P.K. Subban 4.00 10.00
A16 Ilya Kovalchuk 3.00 8.00
A17 John Tavares 5.00 12.00
A18 Marian Gaborik 3.00 8.00
A19 Jason Spezza 3.00 8.00
A20 Erik Karlsson 4.00 10.00
A21 Mike Richards 2.50 6.00
A22 Jeff Carter 2.50 6.00
A23 Evgeni Malkin 6.00 15.00
A24 Logan Couture 4.00 10.00
A25 Antti Niemi 2.50 6.00
A26 Phil Kessel 3.00 8.00
A27 Daniel Sedin 4.00 10.00
A28 Alexandre Burrows 2.00 5.00
A29 Alexander Semin 3.00 8.00
A30 Nicklas Backstrom 3.00 8.00
A31 Alexander Ovechkin SP 25.00 60.00
A32 Roberto Luongo SP 12.00 30.00
A33 Ryan Kesler SP 6.00 15.00
A34 Steven Stamkos SP 12.00 30.00
A35 Sidney Crosby SP 25.00 60.00
A36 Henrik Lundqvist SP 10.00 25.00
A37 Martin Brodeur SP 15.00 40.00
A38 Carey Price SP 12.00 30.00
A39 Patrick Kane SP 12.00 30.00
A40 Jonathan Toews SP 15.00 40.00

2011-12 O-Pee-Chee League Leaders

COMPLETE SET (10) 8.00 20.00
LL1 Perry/Stamkos/Iginla 1.50 4.00
LL2 Sedin/St. Louis/Sedin 1.00 2.50
LL3 Sedin/St. Louis/Perry 1.25 3.00
LL4 Konopka/Neil/Peckham .60 1.50
LL5 Sedin/Stamkos/Selanne 1.50 4.00
LL6 Clutterbuck/Ruutu/Brown .75 2.00
LL7 Luongo/Price/Ward 1.50 4.00
LL8 Thomas/Luongo/Rinne 1.25 3.00
LL9 Thomas/Rinne/Luongo 1.25 3.00
LL10 Lundqvist/Thomas/Price 2.00 5.00

2011-12 O-Pee-Chee Marquee Legends

COMPLETE SET (10) 15.00 40.00
L1 Paul Coffey 1.50 4.00
L2 Eric Lindros 2.50 6.00
L3 Bobby Orr 6.00 15.00
L4 Bobby Hull 3.00 8.00
L5 Wayne Gretzky 10.00 25.00
L6 Mario Lemieux 6.00 15.00
L7 Patrick Roy 4.00 10.00
L8 Ron Francis 2.00 5.00
L9 Mike Bossy 1.50 4.00
L10 Bobby Clarke 2.50 6.00

2011-12 O-Pee-Chee Playoff Beard

*BEARD: 2.5X TO 6X BASE
1 Scott Hartnell 1.00 2.50
2 Paul Mara 1.00 2.50
3 Marian Hossa 1.50 4.00
4 Duncan Keith 1.25 3.00
5 Henrik Zetterberg 2.00 5.00
6 Maxime Talbot 1.00 2.50
7 Brian Campbell 1.00 2.50
8 Todd Bertuzzi 1.25 3.00
9 J.P. Dumont 1.00 2.50
10 Claude Giroux 1.50 4.00
11 Chris Phillips 1.00 2.50
12 Dan Cleary 1.50 4.00
13 Jordan Staal 1.25 3.00
14 Ryan Kesler 1.25 3.00
15 George Parros 1.25 3.00
16 Joe Thornton 2.50 6.00
17 Johan Franzen 1.25 3.00
18 Patrick Kane 3.00 8.00
19 Mike Richards 1.25 3.00
20 Patrick Sharp 1.50 4.00
21 Jeff Carter 1.25 3.00
22 Dan Boyle 1.00 2.50
23 Daniel Sedin 2.00 5.00
24 Henrik Sedin 2.00 5.00
25 Eric Staal 2.00 5.00
26 Pascal Dupuis 1.00 2.50
27 Olli Jokinen 1.25 3.00
28 Guillaume Latendresse 1.25 3.00
29 Jonathan Toews 2.50 6.00
30 Kris Versteeg 1.00 2.50
31 Roberto Luongo 2.50 6.00
32 Patrick Marleau 1.50 4.00
33 Martin St. Louis 1.50 4.00
34 Saku Koivu 1.50 4.00
35 Cam Ward 1.50 4.00
36 Tomas Holmstrom 1.00 2.50
37 Antti Niemi 1.25 3.00
38 Matt Cullen 1.00 2.50
39 Raffi Torres 1.00 2.50
40 Tim Thomas 1.50 4.00
41 Jarome Iginla 2.00 5.00
42 Joe Pavelski 2.00 5.00
43 Fernando Pisani 1.00 2.50
44 Chris Drury 1.25 3.00
45 Brian Gionta 1.00 2.50
46 Ryan Smyth 1.50 4.00
47 Alexander Ovechkin 6.00 15.00
48 Daniel Briere 1.50 4.00
49 Marc-Andre Fleury 3.00 8.00
50 Sidney Crosby 6.00 15.00

2011-12 O-Pee-Chee Signatures

OSAH Ales Hemsky B 10.00 25.00
OSAK Arturs Kulda E 5.00 12.00
OSAL Andrew Ladd D 5.00 12.00
OSAO Alexander Ovechkin B 60.00 120.00
OSAS Alex Stalock D 5.00 12.00
OSBM Brett MacLean E 5.00 12.00
OSDB David Backes C 5.00 12.00
OSDS Drayson Bowman D 5.00 12.00
OSJA Jamie Arniel E 6.00 15.00
OSJM Justin Mercier E 5.00 12.00
OSJO Jim O'Brien D 8.00 20.00
OSJV Jakub Voracek D 6.00 15.00
OSKD Kaspars Daugavins D 5.00 12.00
OSKS Kevin Shattenkirk D 5.00 12.00
OSKV Kris Versteeg C 5.00 12.00
OSMA Jacob Markstrom E 8.00 20.00
OSMT Mattias Tedenby E 5.00 12.00
OSMZ Mats Zuccarello E 15.00 40.00
OSPB Patrik Berglund E 5.00 12.00
OSPM Peter Mueller C 6.00 15.00
OSRB Richard Bachman E 6.00 15.00
OSRM Ryan McDonagh E 8.00 20.00
OSTM Thomas McCollum E 6.00 15.00
OSTT Tomas Tatar E 10.00 25.00
OPCAL Andrew Ladd Upd. B 8.00 20.00
OPCAO A.Ovechkin Upd. A 100.00 175.00
OPCBM Brett MacLean Upd. B 8.00 20.00
OPCBO Bobby Orr Upd. A 250.00 400.00
OPCDB D.Bowman Upd. B 8.00 20.00
OPCGL G.Latendresse Upd. A 40.00 80.00
OPCJM J.Markstrom Upd. B 10.00 25.00
OPCMU Peter Mueller Upd. B 10.00 25.00
OPCNH Nathan Horton Upd. A 15.00 40.00
OPCRY Nugent-Hopkins Upd. A 150.00 250.00
OPCSC Sidney Crosby Upd. A 150.00 250.00
OPCSW Stephen Weiss Upd. A 12.00 30.00
OPCTM T.McCollum Upd. A 15.00 40.00

2011-12 O-Pee-Chee Souvenirs

#1#2 Gret/Lem/Crsby/Ovch A 300.00 400.00
BLUES Halk/Brgl/Bcks/Perr E 6.00 15.00
BOLTS Stmks/Lecv/St.L/Hdm E 10.00 25.00
BOS Chra/Berg/Rask/Thms E 12.00 30.00
BUF Vanek/Myrs/Grbe/Enn E 5.00 12.00
CAPS Ovch/Bckstr/Smin/Grn C 25.00 60.00
CBJ Brass/Nash/Vrck/Filat E 8.00 20.00
CGY Igni/Kipr/Bwmtr/Brque E 8.00 20.00
CHI Tws/Kne/Hossa/Sbrk E 12.00 30.00
DAL Benn/Rich/Erik/Gligki E 6.00 15.00
DET Zettr/Frnzn/Lidstr/Dtsy D 10.00 25.00
FLYER Brre/Crtr/Hrtnll/Crcillo E 12.00 30.00
GR8 Lem/Mess/Sakc/Yzrm A 125.00 250.00
LAK Qck/Dghty/Kptr/Smyth E 10.00 25.00
LBBR Sbn/Prce/Plkn/Cmmlri D 12.00 30.00
NASH Rne/Wber/Ster/Hrnq E 8.00 20.00
NJD Zajc/Elias/Prse/Clrksn E 10.00 25.00
NUCKS Lngo/Brrws/Kslr/Edlr E 10.00 25.00
NYI Bley/Mlson/Okps/DiPtr E 8.00 20.00
NYR Lndq/Staal/Gbrik/Stpn E 15.00 40.00
OTT Spez/Flino/Alfrd/Gnchr E 6.00 15.00
PENS Mlkn/Staal/Crsby/Flry D 25.00 60.00
POE1 Tvres/Hdgsn/Ebrl/Kne E 15.00 40.00
POE2 Sbn/Myrs/Ptrnglo/Aie E 8.00 20.00
POE3 Crmr/Benn/Dlla/Bychk E 6.00 15.00
SABRE Roy/Mill/Stff/Pmnvlle E 6.00 15.00
SJS Thrnt/Htley/Mrl/Stchi E 10.00 25.00
VAN Keslr/Sedins/Hodgson E 15.00 40.00
WILD Thdre/Bchr/Kvu/Bcks E 6.00 15.00
WPG Byfgln/Pvlc/Kne/Enstr E 10.00 25.00

2011-12 O-Pee-Chee Team Canada Signatures

TCAC Andrew Cogliano A 40.00 80.00
TCAH Adam Henrique Upd. B 30.00 60.00
TCAP Alex Pietrangelo A 40.00 80.00
TCBC Brett Connolly Upd. B 30.00 60.00
TCBO Bobby Orr A 300.00 500.00
TCBS Brandon Sutter C 6.00 15.00
TCBY Brayden Schenn A 25.00 60.00
TCCA Jordan Caron C 12.00 30.00
TCCE Cody Eakin Upd. B 25.00 50.00
TCCH Cody Hodgson B 12.00 30.00
TCCM Clarke MacArthur Upd. B 25.00 50.00
TCDD Drew Doughty A 40.00 80.00
TCDR Sean Couturier Upd. A 20.00 50.00
TCEG Derek Roy Upd. B 15.00 40.00
TCEK Evander Kane A 15.00 40.00
TCGL Guillaume Latendresse B 15.00 40.00
TCGN Erik Gudbranson Upd. A 25.00 50.00
TCJC Jared Cowen B 10.00 25.00
TCJE Jordan Eberle A 60.00 120.00
TCJT John Tavares A 50.00 120.00
TCKA Jeff Skinner Upd. A 40.00 80.00
TCKA Karl Alzner B 6.00 15.00
TCLC Logan Couture A 30.00 60.00
TCMD Matt Duchene A 40.00 80.00
TCMS Marco Scandella C 6.00 15.00
TCMT Maxime Talbot A 15.00 40.00
TCPC Patrice Cormier C 12.00 30.00
TCPM Patrick Marleau A 50.00 100.00
TCPS P.K. Subban A 75.00 150.00
TCRJ Keith Aulie Upd. B 10.00 25.00
TCRJ Ryan Johansen Upd. A 30.00 80.00
TCRY R.Nugent-Hopkins Upd. A 100.00 200.00
TCSC Sidney Crosby A 125.00 250.00
TCSD Stefan Della Rovere B 20.00 50.00
TCSG Simon Gagne A 50.00 120.00
TCSS Steven Stamkos A 75.00 150.00
TCTE Tyler Ennis C 6.00 15.00
TCTH Travis Hamonic B 8.00 20.00
TCWG Wayne Gretzky A 250.00 600.00

2011-12 O-Pee-Chee Team Leaders

COMPLETE SET (30) 20.00 50.00
TL1 Perry/Getzlaf/Selanne/Hiller 1.50 4.00
TL2 Ladd/Enstrom/Ladd/Pavelec .75 2.00
TL3 Lucic/Krejci/Chara/Thomas .75 2.00
TL4 Vanek/Vanek/Stafford/Miller .75 2.00
TL5 Iginla/Tanguay/Iginla/Kiprsff 1.00 2.50
TL6 Staal/Staal/Staal/Ward 1.00 2.50
TL7 Sharp/Kane/Sharp/Crawford 1.50 4.00
TL8 Jones/Dchne/Hejdk/Budaj .75 2.00
TL9 Nash/Nash/Umbrgr/Mason .75 2.00
TL10 Morrw/Ribro/Erkssn/Lehton .60 1.50
TL11 Franzn/Zettr/Hlmstrm/Hwrd 1.00 2.50
TL12 Hall/Hmsky/Hall/Dubnyk .60 1.50
TL13 Booth/Weiss/Booth/Vokoun .60 1.50
TL14 Brown/Kopitar/Smyth/Quick 1.25 3.00
TL15 Havlt/Koivu/Brns/Bckstrm .75 2.00
TL16 Gionta/Plek/Subban/Price 1.50 4.00
TL17 Kostitsyn/Suter/Erat/Rinne .75 2.00
TL18 Kovalchuk/Elias/Brodeur 2.00 5.00
TL19 Grabnr/Tavrs/Mlson/Mntya 1.25 3.00
TL20 Dubinsky/Callahan/Lundqv 2.00 5.00
TL21 Spezza/Alfredsson/Elliott .75 2.00
TL22 Carter/Giroux/Bobrovsky 1.25 3.00
TL23 Yandle/Doan/Bryzgalov .75 2.00
TL24 Letang/Crosby/Fleury 3.00 8.00
TL25 Mrleau/Thrntn/Htly/Niemi 1.25 3.00
TL26 Backs/Pietr/Brglnd/Halak .75 2.00
TL27 St. Louis/Stamkos/Roloson 1.50 4.00
TL28 MacArthur/Kessel/Reimer .75 2.00
TL29 Kesler/Sedins/Luongo 1.25 3.00
TL30 Ovechkin/Knuble/Neuvirth 3.00 8.00

2011-12 O-Pee-Chee Trophy Winners

COMPLETE SET (10) 6.00 15.00
TW1 Corey Perry 1.25 3.00
TW2 Daniel Sedin 1.00 2.50
TW3 Daniel Sedin 1.00 2.50
TW4 Corey Perry 1.25 3.00
TW5 Nicklas Lidstrom .50 1.25
TW6 Tim Thomas .75 2.00
TW7 Tim Thomase .75 2.00
TW8 Jeff Skinner 1.00 2.50
TW9 Ryan Kesler .75 2.00
TW10 Martin St. Louis .75 2.00

2012-13 O-Pee-Chee

1 Marian Gaborik .20 .50
2 Matt Moulson .12 .30
3 Ryan Nugent-Hopkins .25 .60
4 Justin Williams .15 .40
5 Luca Sbisa .15 .40
6 Duncan Keith .15 .40
7 Martin Brodeur .50 1.25
8 Johnny Boychuk .15 .40
9 Kris Versteeg .12 .30
10 Marco Scandella .12 .30
11 Bryan Bickell .12 .30
12 Anton Stralman .12 .30
13 Mikael Backlund .15 .40
14 Alex Goligoski .12 .30
15 Todd Bertuzzi .15 .40
16 Carl Hagelin .12 .30
17 Oliver Ekman-Larsson .20 .50
18 Miikka Kiprusoff .20 .50
19 Blake Geoffrion .20 .50
20 Thomas Vanek .15 .40
21 Jaroslav Halak .20 .50
22 Mark Stuart .12 .30
23 Jared Cowen .20 .50
24 Michael Grabner .15 .40
25 Alexandre Burrows .15 .40
26 Dan Ellis .15 .40
27 Tim Gleason .12 .30
28 Vaclav Prospal .12 .30
29 Tom Pyatt .12 .30
30 Ryan Whitney .12 .30
31 Rostislav Klesla .12 .30
32 Eric Staal .25 .60
33 Kari Lehtonen .15 .40
34 Marcel Goc .15 .40
35 Devin Setoguchi .15 .40
36 Torrey Mitchell .12 .30
37 Dmitry Orlov .20 .50
38 Zdeno Chara .20 .50
39 Nathan Gerbe .12 .30
40 Max Pacioretty .20 .50
41 Carl Gunnarsson .12 .30
42 Kyle Brodziak .12 .30
43 Daniel Winnik .12 .30
44 Teddy Purcell .12 .30
45 Erik Condra .12 .30
46 Patric Hornqvist .12 .30
47 Dave Bolland .15 .40
48 Ed Jovanovski .12 .30
49 Andrew Ladd .12 .30
50 Brett Connolly .12 .30
51 Jean-Sebastien Giguere .20 .50
52 Brayden Schenn .20 .50
53 Raphael Diaz .12 .30
54 Marc-Andre Gragnani .12 .30
55 Kristopher Letang .25 .60
56 Steve Mason .15 .40
57 Jhonas Enroth .20 .50
58 Loui Eriksson .12 .30
59 Alex Tanguay .15 .40
60 Willie Mitchell .15 .40
61 Arron Asham .12 .30
62 Karl Alzner .12 .30
63 Jamie McBain .12 .30
64 Patrick Marleau .20 .50
65 Jonas Gustavsson .20 .50
66 Milan Michalek .12 .30
67 Patrik Berglund .12 .30
68 Marc Methot .12 .30
69 Mason Raymond .12 .30
70 Stephane Robidas .12 .30
71 P.K. Subban .25 .60
72 Henrik Sedin .25 .60
73 Sean Couturier .15 .40
74 David Clarkson .12 .30
75 Chad LaRose .12 .30
76 Ryan O'Reilly .12 .30
77 Saku Koivu .20 .50
78 Dion Phaneuf .15 .40
79 Nathan Horton .20 .50
80 Jonathan Ericsson .12 .30
81 Shawn Horcoff .12 .30
82 Mark Fayne .12 .30
83 Scott Hartnell .12 .30
84 Dennis Wideman .12 .30
85 Matt D'Agostini .12 .30
86 Ryane Clowe .12 .30
87 Mike Smith .20 .50
88 Jason Garrison .12 .30
89 Al Montoya .12 .30
90 Alexander Radulov .20 .50
91 Tobias Enstrom .12 .30
92 Chris Kunitz .20 .50
93 Shane O'Brien .12 .30
94 Teemu Selanne .40 1.00
95 Sergei Bobrovsky .30 .75
96 Ryan Callahan .12 .30
97 Rob Scuderi .15 .40
98 Johan Franzen .15 .40
99 David Legwand .15 .40
100 Steve Ott .12 .30
101 Nikolai Khabibulin .20 .50
102 Matt Read .15 .40
103 Pascal Dupuis .12 .30
104 Mike Richards .15 .40
105 Derek Roy .12 .30
106 Johnny Oduya .15 .40
107 Tomas Kaberle .12 .30
108 Andrew MacDonald .12 .30
109 Ryan Jones .15 .40
110 David Backes .12 .30
111 Chris Phillips .12 .30
112 Tomas Fleischmann .12 .30
113 George Parros .15 .40
114 Alexander Steen .12 .30
115 Shea Weber .15 .40
116 Niklas Backstrom .15 .40
117 Jaromir Jagr .60 1.50
118 Erik Cole .12 .30
119 David Krejci .20 .50
120 Brad Richards .20 .50
121 Milan Hejduk .15 .40
122 Andrei Kostitsyn .15 .40
123 Jonathan Toews .30 .75
124 Corey Perry .30 .75
125 Josh Bailey .15 .40
126 Antoine Vermette .12 .30
127 Matt Greene .12 .30
128 Kyle Okposo .12 .30
129 Douglas Murray .12 .30
130 Shawn Thornton .12 .30
131 Brent Seabrook .12 .30
132 Trevor Daley .12 .30
133 James Reimer .20 .50
134 Craig Smith .12 .30
135 Dan Boyle .12 .30
136 Benoit Pouliot .12 .30
137 Zach Bogosian .15 .40
138 Jannik Hansen .15 .40
139 R.J. Umberger .12 .30
140 Taylor Hall .20 .50
141 Jeff Skinner .25 .60
142 Ryan Malone .12 .30
143 David Perron .15 .40
144 Kyle Clifford .12 .30
145 Jordin Tootoo .15 .40
146 Brent Burns .20 .50
147 Brandon Dubinsky .12 .30
148 Robyn Regehr .12 .30
149 Boyd Gordon .12 .30
150 Kyle Turris .12 .30
151 Drew Miller .12 .30
152 Tyler Bozak .12 .30
153 Lauri Korpikoski .12 .30
154 John Carlson .20 .50
155 Josh Harding .20 .50
156 Christian Ehrhoff .12 .30
157 Scott Clemmensen .15 .40
158 Dustin Byfuglien .20 .50
159 Shane Doan .15 .40
160 Derek Mackenzie .12 .30
161 Nick Leddy .12 .30
162 Jiri Tlusty .12 .30
163 Olli Jokinen .15 .40
164 B.J. Crombeen .12 .30
165 Ian White .15 .40
166 Marc-Andre Fleury .40 1.00
167 David Jones .12 .30
168 Alexander Ovechkin .75 2.00
169 Jake Gardiner .12 .30
170 Tanner Glass .12 .30
171 Braydon Coburn .12 .30
172 Kevin Bieksa .15 .40
173 Andy Greene .12 .30
174 Darren Helm .12 .30
175 Brandon Prust .12 .30
176 Brooks Laich .12 .30
177 Guillaume Latendresse .15 .40
178 Jan Hejda .12 .30
179 Brandon Sutter .12 .30
180 Jay Bouwmeester .12 .30
181 Mike Commodore .12 .30
182 Johan Hedberg .15 .40
183 Marc Staal .12 .30
184 Pavel Datsyuk .30 .75
185 Travis Moen .12 .30
186 Tim Thomas .20 .50
187 Curtis Sanford .15 .40
188 Anze Kopitar .30 .75
189 Eric Brewer .12 .30
190 Ryan Kesler .20 .50
191 Cam Fowler .20 .50
192 Brenden Morrow .15 .40
193 Craig Anderson .20 .50
194 Mike Green .15 .40
195 Stephen Weiss .15 .40
196 Matt Stajan .12 .30
197 Matt Niskanen .15 .40
198 Fedor Tyutin .12 .30
199 Nicklas Lidstrom .20 .50
200 Ilya Kovalchuk .20 .50
201 Matt Martin .12 .30
202 Raffi Torres .12 .30
203 Mikhail Grabovski .12 .30
204 Jason Chimera .12 .30
205 Corey Crawford .25 .60
206 Logan Couture .25 .60
207 Valtteri Filppula .12 .30
208 Ryan Suter .15 .40
209 Blake Comeau .12 .30
210 Nikolai Kulemin .12 .30
211 Ville Leino .15 .40
212 Brian Rolston .15 .40
213 Ruslan Fedotenko .12 .30
214 Ray Whitney .15 .40
215 Kyle Wellwood .15 .40
216 Manny Malhotra .15 .40
217 Joel Ward .12 .30
218 Jamie Langenbrunner .12 .30
219 Francois Beauchemin .12 .30
220 Chris Kelly .15 .40
221 Cam Ward .20 .50
222 Jonathan Quick .25 .60
223 P.A. Parenteau .12 .30
224 Kimmo Timonen .12 .30
225 Michal Handzus .12 .30
226 Bobby Butler .15 .40
227 Ryan Getzlaf .20 .50
228 Stefan Elliott .15 .40
229 Evgeni Malkin .40 1.00
230 Patrick Kane .40 1.00
231 Derick Brassard .12 .30
232 Jamie Benn .20 .50
233 Lars Eller .12 .30
234 Michael Cammalleri .15 .40
235 Toni Lydman .12 .30
236 T.J. Oshie .20 .50
237 Paul Martin .12 .30
238 Matt Ellis .12 .30
239 Steven Stamkos .40 1.00
240 Jakub Voracek .15 .40
241 Jack Johnson .12 .30
242 Gabriel Landeskog .25 .60
243 Mark Giordano .20 .50
244 Jim Slater .12 .30
245 Drew Stafford .12 .30
246 Cody Franson .12 .30
247 Mathieu Darche .12 .30
248 Tom Gilbert .12 .30
249 Marc-Andre Bergeron .12 .30
250 Mike Fisher .15 .40
251 Jeff Carter .15 .40
252 Brent Johnson .15 .40
253 Milan Jurcina .15 .40
254 Ryan Smyth .15 .40
255 Brian Gionta .12 .30
256 Adam Larsson .20 .50
257 Andrej Meszaros .12 .30
258 Chris Higgins .12 .30
259 Steve Sullivan .12 .30
260 Colin Greening .12 .30
261 Brian Lee .15 .40
262 Daymond Langkow .12 .30
263 Devan Dubnyk .15 .40
264 Erik Gudbranson .15 .40
265 Roberto Luongo .30 .75
266 Hal Gill .12 .30
267 Tuukka Rask .25 .60
268 Nicklas Backstrom .20 .50
269 Adam Henrique .15 .40
270 Nick Johnson .15 .40
271 Corey Potter .15 .40
272 Vernon Fiddler .12 .30
273 Nik Antropov .15 .40
274 Filip Kuba .12 .30
275 Joey MacDonald .15 .40
276 Jamie McGinn .12 .30
277 Thomas Greiss .15 .40
278 Viatcheslav Voynov .20 .50
279 Artem Anisimov .12 .30
280 Braden Holtby .25 .60
281 Brad Marchand .40 1.00
282 Jay Harrison .12 .30
283 Victor Hedman .25 .60
284 Jiri Hudler .15 .40
285 Daniel Carcillo .12 .30
286 Radek Dvorak .12 .30
287 Matt Cullen .12 .30
288 Henrik Lundqvist .50 1.25
289 Jason Arnott .15 .40
290 Mattias Tedenby .12 .30
291 Daniel Alfredsson .20 .50
292 Jose Theodore .20 .50
293 Niklas Hjalmarsson .12 .30
294 Matthew Halischuk .12 .30
295 Mike Santorelli .12 .30
296 Anthony Stewart .12 .30
297 Simon Gagne .20 .50
298 Nick Foligno .15 .40
299 Matt Cooke .12 .30
300 Lubomir Visnovsky .12 .30
301 Bryan Little .20 .50
302 Chris Butler .12 .30
303 Ryan Miller .20 .50
304 Brett Clark .12 .30
305 Erik Christensen .15 .40
306 Mike Komisarek .15 .40
307 Joe Corvo .12 .30
308 Evgeni Nabokov .12 .30
309 Derek Dorsett .12 .30
310 Rene Bourque .12 .30
311 Antti Niemi .15 .40
312 Evander Kane .20 .50
313 Brian Boyle .12 .30
314 Henrik Zetterberg .25 .60
315 Dustin Penner .12 .30
316 Cory Schneider .20 .50
317 Wayne Simmonds .25 .60
318 Eric Belanger .12 .30
319 Sean Bergenheim .12 .30
320 Peter Mueller .12 .30
321 Petr Sykora .12 .30
322 Mike Ribeiro .15 .40
323 Mikko Koivu .12 .30
324 Matt Hendricks .12 .30
325 Mark Letestu .15 .40
326 Kyle Quincey .12 .30
327 Jason Spezza .20 .50
328 Paul Stastny .12 .30
329 Ryan McDonagh .12 .30
330 T.J. Galiardi .12 .30
331 Sheldon Souray .12 .30
332 Tyler Seguin .25 .60
333 Steve Staios .12 .30
334 Peter Budaj .12 .30
335 Alexander Semin .20 .50
336 Clarke MacArthur .12 .30
337 Chris Stewart .15 .40
338 Maxime Talbot .12 .30
339 Andrei Loktionov .15 .40
340 Patrice Bergeron .25 .60
341 Niklas Hagman .12 .30
342 Roman Horak .12 .30
343 Pierre-Marc Bouchard .20 .50
344 Ryan Johansen .15 .40
345 Marcus Johansson .12 .30
346 Pekka Rinne .20 .50
347 Niklas Kronwall .15 .40
348 Dwayne Roloson .15 .40
349 Andrew Cogliano .12 .30
350 Alex Pietrangelo .12 .30
351 Keith Yandle .12 .30
352 Marian Hossa .20 .50
353 Tomas Kopecky .15 .40
354 Derek Stepan .12 .30
355 Erik Johnson .12 .30
356 Dan Hamhuis .15 .40
357 Zenon Konopka .15 .40
358 Jussi Jokinen .12 .30
359 Zbynek Michalek .12 .30
360 Tomas Holmstrom .12 .30
361 Drew Doughty .25 .60
362 Luke Adam .15 .40
363 Sam Gagner .12 .30
364 Martin St. Louis .20 .50
365 Luke Schenn .20 .50
366 Tom Wandell .12 .30
367 Henrik Tallinder .12 .30
368 Sidney Crosby .75 2.00
369 Marc-Edouard Vlasic .12 .30
370 Bobby Ryan .15 .40
371 Zack Smith .12 .30
372 Brad Boyes .12 .30
373 Daniel Briere .20 .50
374 Josh Gorges .15 .40
375 Nick Spaling .12 .30
376 Theo Peckham .12 .30
377 Chris Mason .15 .40
378 Martin Hanzal .12 .30
379 Darroll Powe .12 .30
380 Curtis Glencross .12 .30
381 Rich Peverley .20 .50
382 Alexander Burmistrov .15 .40
383 Barret Jackman .12 .30
384 Brian Campbell .12 .30
385 Michael Del Zotto .12 .30
386 David Booth .12 .30
387 Marek Zidlicky .12 .30
388 Tyler Kennedy .12 .30
389 Steve Downie .12 .30
390 Nikita Nikitin .12 .30
391 Ray Emery .15 .40
392 Jordan Leopold .12 .30
393 Derek Morris .12 .30
394 Zach Parise .20 .50
395 Mark Streit .12 .30
396 Phil Kessel .20 .50
397 Michael Ryder .12 .30
398 Daniel Girardi .12 .30
399 Sami Salo .12 .30
400 Joni Pitkanen .15 .40
401 Tyler Myers .12 .30
402 Cody McLeod .12 .30
403 Tuomo Ruutu .15 .40
404 Matt Carle .15 .40
405 Brooks Orpik .12 .30
406 Radim Vrbata .12 .30
407 Daniel Sedin .25 .60
408 Eric Nystrom .12 .30
409 Nino Niederreiter .12 .30
410 Patrik Elias .20 .50
411 James Wisniewski .12 .30
412 T.J. Brodie .12 .30
413 Erik Karlsson .25 .60
414 Claude Giroux .20 .50
415 Dan Cleary .20 .50
416 Shawn Matthias .12 .30
417 Dainius Zubrus .12 .30
418 Zack Kassian .12 .30
419 Jonas Hiller .15 .40
420 Ron Hainsey .12 .30
421 Dominic Moore .12 .30
422 Steve Montador .12 .30
423 Milan Lucic .20 .50
424 Mathieu Garon .15 .40
425 Colin Wilson .15 .40
426 Matt Beleskey .12 .30
427 Chris Neil .12 .30
428 Joffrey Lupul .12 .30
429 Anton Volchenkov .12 .30
430 Dustin Brown .20 .50
431 Alexander Edler .12 .30
432 Cody Hodgson .12 .30
433 Dennis Seidenberg .12 .30
434 Martin Biron .15 .40
435 Martin Havlat .15 .40
436 John Moore .12 .30
437 James van Riemsdyk .15 .40
438 Jarome Iginla .25 .60
439 Martin Erat .12 .30
440 Tomas Plekanec .12 .30
441 Frans Nielsen .12 .30
442 Troy Brouwer .12 .30
443 James Neal .12 .30
444 Jared Spurgeon .20 .50
445 Matt Duchene .20 .50
446 Dmitry Kulikov .12 .30
447 Ilya Bryzgalov .20 .50
448 John Tavares .30 .75
449 Ondrej Pavelec .20 .50
450 Jarret Stoll .15 .40
451 Kevin Shattenkirk .12 .30
452 Chris Campoli .12 .30
453 Adrian Aucoin .12 .30
454 Patrick Sharp .20 .50
455 Brad Stuart .12 .30
456 John-Michael Liles .12 .30
457 Tim Jackman .12 .30
458 Jaroslav Spacek .12 .30
459 Carey Price .40 1.00
460 Tomas Vokoun .15 .40
461 Kevin Klein .12 .30
462 Marcus Kruger .12 .30
463 Sergei Gonchar .12 .30
464 Travis Hamonic .15 .40
465 Tim Connolly .12 .30
466 Joe Thornton .30 .75
467 Jordan Staal .15 .40
468 Kris Russell .12 .30
469 Michal Neuvirth .15 .40
470 Dany Heatley .20 .50
471 Blake Wheeler .20 .50
472 Viktor Stalberg .12 .30
473 Ladislav Smid .12 .30
474 Justin Faulk .15 .40
475 David Desharnais .12 .30
476 Grant Clitsome .12 .30
477 Jordan Eberle .20 .50
478 Semyon Varlamov .20 .50
479 Vincent Lecavalier .20 .50
480 Mikkel Boedker .12 .30
481 Jim Howard .25 .60

482 Cal Clutterbuck .12 .30
483 Lee Stempniak .12 .30
484 Ales Hemsky .15 .40
485 Sergei Kostitsyn .12 .30
486 Brian Elliott .15 .40
487 Joe Pavelski .25 .60
488 Brad Richardson .12 .30
489 Tim Brent .12 .30
490 Nick Schultz .12 .30
491 Richard Bachman .15 .40
492 Rick Nash .20 .50
493 Nate Thompson .12 .30
494 Jason Pominville .12 .30
495 Mikael Samuelsson .12 .30
496 Checklist .12 .30
497 Checklist .12 .30
498 Checklist .12 .30
499 Checklist .12 .30
500 Checklist .12 .30
501 Bobby Orr L 3.00 8.00
502 Cam Neely L .75 2.00
503 Johnny Bucyk L .75 2.00
504 Milt Schmidt L .60 1.50
505 Phil Esposito L 1.25 3.00
506 Ray Bourque L 1.25 3.00
507 Bobby Hull L 1.50 4.00
508 Denis Savard L .75 2.00
509 Doug Wilson L .60 1.50
510 Stan Mikita L 1.00 2.50
511 Alex Delvecchio L .75 2.00
512 Red Kelly L .75 2.00
513 Ted Lindsay L .75 2.00
514 Bill Ranford L .75 2.00
515 Mark Messier L 1.50 4.00
516 Paul Coffey L .75 2.00
517 Ron Francis L 1.00 2.50
518 Jari Kurri L .75 2.00
519 Marcel Dionne L 1.00 2.50
520 Rogie Vachon L 1.00 2.50
521 Dino Ciccarelli L .75 2.00
522 Mike Modano L 1.25 3.00
523 Neal Broten L .60 1.50
524 Guy Lafleur L 1.00 2.50
525 Jean Beliveau L .75 2.00
526 Larry Robinson L .75 2.00
527 Claude Lemieux L .60 1.50
528 Scott Niedermayer L .75 2.00
529 Brent Sutter L .50 1.25
530 Bryan Trottier L .75 2.00
531 Denis Potvin L .75 2.00
532 Duane Sutter L .50 1.25
533 Mike Bossy L .75 2.00
534 Andy Bathgate L .75 2.00
535 Brad Park L .60 1.50
536 Bill Barber L .60 1.50
537 Bobby Clarke L 1.25 3.00
538 Dave Schultz L .75 2.00
539 Eric Lindros L 1.25 3.00
540 Tim Kerr L .50 1.25
541 Peter Stastny L .60 1.50
542 Brendan Shanahan L .75 2.00
543 Brett Hull L 1.50 4.00
544 Tony Twist L .50 1.25
545 Curtis Joseph L 1.00 2.50
546 Wendel Clark L 1.25 3.00
547 Markus Naslund L .75 2.00
548 Richard Brodeur L .75 2.00
549 Mike Gartner L 1.00 2.50
550 Dale Hawerchuk L 1.00 2.50
551 Checklist .75 2.00
552 Carter Camper RC .75 2.00
553 Maxime Sauve RC .75 2.00
554 Lane MacDermid RC 1.00 2.50
555 Torey Krug RC 2.50 6.00
556 Michael Hutchinson RC 1.25 3.00
557 Travis Turnbull RC .75 2.00
558 Sven Baertschi RC 1.25 3.00
559 Akim Aliu RC 1.00 2.50
560 Jeremy Welsh RC 1.00 2.50
561 Brandon Bollig RC .75 2.00
562 Tyson Barrie RC 2.50 6.00
563 Mike Connolly RC 1.00 2.50
564 Dalton Prout RC .75 2.00
565 Cody Goloubef RC .75 2.00
566 Shawn Hunwick RC .75 2.00
567 Ryan Garbutt RC .75 2.00
568 Reilly Smith RC 2.50 6.00
569 Brenden Dillon RC 1.00 2.50
570 Scott Glennie RC 1.00 2.50
571 Riley Sheahan RC 1.25 3.00
572 Philippe Cornet RC 1.00 2.50
573 Colby Robak RC .75 2.00
574 Jordan Nolan RC .75 2.00
575 Kristopher Foucault RC .75 2.00
576 Jason Zucker RC 2.00 5.00
577 Tyler Cuma RC .75 2.00
578 Chay Genoway RC .75 2.00
579 Gabriel Dumont RC 1.00 2.50
580 Robert Mayer RC 1.25 3.00
581 Chet Pickard RC 1.00 2.50
582 Aaron Ness RC .75 2.00
583 Casey Cizikas RC 1.00 2.50
584 Matt Donovan RC 1.00 2.50
585 Chris Kreider RC 3.00 8.00
586 Brandon Manning RC 1.00 2.50
587 Michael Stone RC 1.00 2.50
588 Matt Watkins RC .75 2.00
589 Tyson Sexsmith RC .75 2.00
590 Jake Allen RC 2.50 6.00
591 Jaden Schwartz RC 2.50 6.00
592 J.T. Brown RC 1.00 2.50
593 Carter Ashton RC .75 2.00
594 Ryan Hamilton RC .75 2.00
595 Jussi Rynnas RC .75 2.00
596 Joe Sakic MR 1.50 4.00
597 Mario Lemieux MR 3.00 8.00
598 Patrick Roy MR 2.00 5.00
599 Pelle Lindbergh MR .60 1.50
600 Wayne Gretzky MR 5.00 12.00

2012-13 O-Pee-Chee Black Rainbow

*1-500 VETS: 6X TO 15X BASIC CARDS
*501-600 LEGENDS: 2.5X TO 6X BASIC CARDS
*552-595 ROOKIES: 1.5X TO 4X BASIC CARDS
205 Corey Crawford 5.00 12.00
268 Nicklas Backstrom 4.00 10.00
558 Sven Baertschi 5.00 12.00
585 Chris Kreider 15.00 40.00

2012-13 O-Pee-Chee Rainbow

*1-500 VETS: 2.5X TO 6X BASIC CARDS
*501-600 LEGENDS: 1X TO 2.5X BASIC CARDS
*552-595 ROOKIES: .6X TO 1.5X BASIC CARDS
205 Corey Crawford 2.00 5.00
268 Nicklas Backstrom 1.50 4.00

2012-13 O-Pee-Chee Red

*1-500 VETS: 6X TO 15X BASIC CARDS
*501-600 LEGENDS: 2.5X TO 6X BASIC CARDS
*552-595 ROOKIES: 2.5X TO 6X BASIC CARDS
205 Corey Crawford 5.00 12.00
268 Nicklas Backstrom 4.00 10.00

2012-13 O-Pee-Chee Retro

*1-500 VETS: 2X TO 5X BASIC CARDS
*501-600 LEGENDS: .8X TO 2X BASIC CARDS
*552-595 ROOKIES: .5X TO 1.2X BASIC CARDS
205 Corey Crawford 1.50 4.00
268 Nicklas Backstrom 1.25 3.00
346 Pekka Rinne 1.25 3.00

2012-13 O-Pee-Chee All Stars

AS1 Alexander Ovechkin 20.00 50.00
AS2 Bobby Hull 10.00 25.00
AS3 Bobby Orr 20.00 50.00
AS4 Brad Marchand 10.00 25.00
AS5 Brett Hull 10.00 25.00
AS6 Bryan Trottier 5.00 12.00
AS7 Carey Price 12.00 30.00
AS8 Claude Giroux 5.00 12.00
AS9 Curtis Joseph 6.00 15.00
AS10 Daniel Sedin 6.00 15.00
AS11 Dominik Hasek 8.00 20.00
AS12 Ed Belfour 5.00 12.00
AS13 Eric Lindros 8.00 20.00
AS14 Evgeni Malkin 10.00 25.00
AS15 Henrik Lundqvist 12.00 30.00
AS16 Henrik Sedin 6.00 15.00
AS17 Henrik Zetterberg 6.00 15.00
AS18 Ilya Kovalchuk 5.00 12.00
AS19 Jarome Iginla 6.00 15.00
AS20 Jean Beliveau 5.00 12.00
AS21 Jeff Skinner 6.00 15.00
AS22 Joe Sakic 10.00 25.00
AS23 John Tavares 8.00 20.00
AS24 Jonathan Toews 10.00 25.00
AS25 Jordan Eberle 5.00 12.00
AS26 Mario Lemieux 20.00 50.00
AS27 Mark Messier 10.00 25.00
AS28 Martin Brodeur 12.00 30.00
AS29 Matt Duchene 5.00 12.00
AS30 Mike Gartner 6.00 15.00
AS31 Nicklas Backstrom 5.00 12.00
AS32 Nicklas Lidstrom 5.00 12.00
AS33 Ondrej Pavelec 5.00 12.00
AS34 P.K. Subban 6.00 15.00
AS35 Patrice Bergeron 6.00 15.00
AS36 Patrick Kane 10.00 25.00
AS37 Paul Coffey 5.00 12.00
AS38 Rick Nash 5.00 12.00
AS39 Roberto Luongo 8.00 20.00
AS40 Ron Francis 6.00 15.00
AS41 Ryan Miller 5.00 12.00
AS42 Ryan Nugent-Hopkins 6.00 15.00
AS43 Sidney Crosby 25.00 50.00
AS44 Steven Stamkos 10.00 25.00
AS45 Taylor Hall 5.00 12.00
AS46 Tim Thomas 5.00 12.00
AS47 Tyler Seguin 6.00 15.00
AS48 Wayne Gretzky 40.00 80.00
AS49 Zach Parise 5.00 12.00
AS50 Zdeno Chara 5.00 12.00

2012-13 O-Pee-Chee Black and White

1 Alex Ovechkin 100.00 250.00
2 Alexandre Burrows 15.00 40.00
3 Antti Niemi 20.00 50.00
4 Bobby Orr 90.00 150.00
5 Brett Hull 50.00 125.00
6 Carey Price 50.00 125.00
7 Claude Giroux 25.00 60.00
8 Curtis Joseph 30.00 80.00
9 Daniel Alfredsson 25.00 60.00
10 Drew Doughty 30.00 80.00
11 Eric Lindros 40.00 100.00
12 Erik Karlsson 30.00 80.00
13 Henrik Lundqvist 60.00 150.00
14 Ilya Kovalchuk 25.00 60.00
15 Jaromir Jagr 80.00 200.00
16 Jason Spezza 25.00 60.00
17 Joe Sakic 50.00 125.00
18 John Tavares 40.00 100.00
19 Jonathan Toews 30.00 80.00
20 Jordan Eberle 25.00 60.00
21 Mario Lemieux 60.00 120.00
22 Martin Brodeur 60.00 150.00
23 Milan Lucic 25.00 60.00
24 Nicklas Lidstrom 25.00 60.00
25 Ondrej Pavelec 25.00 60.00
26 P.K. Subban 30.00 80.00
27 Patrick Roy 100.00 175.00
28 Patrick Sharp 25.00 60.00
29 Pavel Datsyuk 40.00 100.00
30 Pelle Lindbergh 20.00 50.00
31 Roberto Luongo 40.00 100.00
32 Ryan Nugent-Hopkins 100.00 200.00
33 Sidney Crosby 125.00 200.00
35 Wayne Gretzky 100.00 200.00
36 Wendel Clark 40.00 100.00

2012-13 O-Pee-Chee Blaster Box Bottoms

1 Sidney Crosby A 1.00 2.50
2 Jonathan Toews A .40 1.00
3 Ryan Nugent-Hopkins B .30 .75
4 Alex Ovechkin B 1.00 2.50
5 Martin Brodeur C .60 1.50
6 Steven Stamkos C .50 1.25
P1 S.Crosby/J.Toews 1.00 2.50
P2 A.Ovechkin/Nugent-Hopkins .75 2.00
P3 M.Brodeur/S.Stamkos .75 2.00

2012-13 O-Pee-Chee Buyback Autographs

8 A.Ovechkin 09-10 OPCR/22 40.00 80.00
87 S.Crosby 09-10 OPCR/20 75.00 135.00

2012-13 O-Pee-Chee League Leaders

LL Bergeron/Seguin/Chara 8.00 20.00
LLGL Stamkos/Malkin/Gaborik 12.00 30.00
LLSO Quick/Elliott/Smith 8.00 20.00
LLSV Elliott/Schndr/Lndqvst 15.00 40.00
LLAST Sedin/Giroux/Karlsson 8.00 20.00
LLPIM Dorsett/Rinaldo/Konopka 5.00 12.00
LLPNT Malkin/Stamkos/Giroux 12.00 30.00
LLPPG Neal/Hartnell/Perry 8.00 20.00
LLWIN Rinne/Fleury/Lundqvist 10.00 25.00

2012-13 O-Pee-Chee Marquee Legends Gold

G1 Bobby Orr 25.00 60.00
G2 Bobby Hull 12.00 30.00
G3 Patrick Roy 15.00 40.00
G4 Joe Sakic 12.00 30.00
G5 Mark Messier 12.00 30.00
G6 Wayne Gretzky 15.00 40.00
G7 Jean Beliveau 6.00 15.00
G8 Eric Lindros 10.00 25.00
G9 Mario Lemieux 25.00 60.00
G10 Brett Hull 12.00 30.00

2012-13 O-Pee-Chee Pop Ups

COMMON CARD (PU1-PU50) 1.25 3.00
UNLISTED STARS 1.50 4.00
PU1 Corey Perry 2.50 6.00
PU2 Bobby Orr 6.00 15.00
PU3 Tyler Seguin 2.00 5.00
PU4 Tim Thomas 1.50 4.00
PU5 Ryan Miller 1.50 4.00
PU6 Jarome Iginla 2.00 5.00
PU7 Jeff Skinner 2.00 5.00
PU8 Jonathan Toews 2.50 6.00
PU9 Marian Hossa 1.50 4.00
PU10 Patrick Kane 3.00 8.00
PU11 Matt Duchene 1.50 4.00
PU12 Rick Nash 1.50 4.00
PU13 Jamie Benn 1.50 4.00
PU14 Henrik Zetterberg 2.00 5.00
PU15 Jim Howard 2.00 5.00
PU16 Nicklas Lidstrom 1.50 4.00
PU17 Pavel Datsyuk 2.50 6.00
PU18 Ryan Nugent-Hopkins 2.00 5.00
PU19 Paul Coffey 1.50 4.00
PU20 Taylor Hall 1.50 4.00
PU21 Wayne Gretzky 10.00 25.00
PU22 Brendan Shanahan 1.50 4.00
PU23 Ron Francis 2.00 5.00
PU24 Anze Kopitar 2.50 6.00
PU25 Drew Doughty 2.00 5.00
PU26 Jean Beliveau 1.50 4.00
PU27 Carey Price 3.00 8.00
PU28 Patrick Roy 4.00 10.00
PU29 P.K. Subban 2.00 5.00
PU30 Ilya Kovalchuk 1.50 4.00
PU31 Martin Brodeur 4.00 10.00
PU32 Zach Parise 1.50 4.00
PU33 John Tavares 2.50 6.00
PU34 Henrik Lundqvist 4.00 10.00
PU35 Mark Messier 3.00 8.00
PU36 Daniel Alfredsson 1.50 4.00
PU37 Claude Giroux 1.50 4.00
PU38 Eric Lindros 2.50 6.00
PU39 Pelle Lindbergh 3.00 8.00
PU40 Evgeni Malkin 3.00 8.00
PU41 Mario Lemieux 6.00 15.00
PU42 Sidney Crosby 6.00 15.00
PU43 Jaroslav Halak 1.50 4.00
PU44 Steven Stamkos 3.00 8.00
PU45 Phil Kessel 1.50 4.00
PU46 Daniel Sedin 2.00 5.00
PU47 Henrik Sedin 2.00 5.00
PU48 Roberto Luongo 2.50 6.00
PU49 Alexander Ovechkin 3.00 8.00
PU50 Ondrej Pavelec 1.50 4.00

2012-13 O-Pee-Chee Retro Hobby Box Bottoms

1 Sidney Crosby A 1.00 2.50
2 Pavel Datsyuk A .40 1.00
3 John Tavares A .40 1.00
4 Tim Thomas A .25 .60
5 Phil Kessel B .25 .60
6 Gabriel Landeskog B .30 .75
7 Henrik Lundqvist B .60 1.50
8 Alex Ovechkin B 1.00 2.50
9 Claude Giroux C .25 .60
10 Ryan Nugent-Hopkins C .30 .75
11 Carey Price C .50 1.25
12 Steven Stamkos C .50 1.25
13 Martin Brodeur D .60 1.50
14 Evgeni Malkin D .50 1.25
15 Eric Staal D .30 .75
16 Jonathan Toews D .40 1.00
P1 Crsby/Dtsyk/Tvres/Thmas 1.50 4.00
P2 Ovch/Kssl/Lndqst/Lndskg 1.25 3.00
P3 Stmkos/RNH/Girx/Price 1.50 4.00
P4 Tws/Brdr/Mlkin/E.Staal 1.25 3.00

2012-13 O-Pee-Chee Signatures

OPCAO Alexander Ovechkin A 50.00 100.00
OPCCS Cory Schneider B 15.00 40.00
OPCDH Dale Hawerchuk A 20.00 50.00
OPCEK Evander Kane B 10.00 25.00
OPCEN Evgeni Nabokov C 8.00 20.00
OPCGL Gabriel Landeskog A 20.00 50.00
OPCJE Jonathan Ericsson D 5.00 12.00
OPCJH Jonas Hiller C 6.00 15.00
OPCJP Joe Pavelski B 12.00 30.00
OPCKA Karl Alzner D 5.00 12.00
OPCKC Kyle Clifford D 5.00 12.00
OPCMA Matt Hackett B 8.00 20.00
OPCMB Matt Beleskey D 5.00 12.00
OPCMF Michael Frolik D 5.00 12.00
OPCMH Marian Hossa A 40.00 100.00
OPCML Maxim Lapierre D 6.00 15.00
OPCMN Markus Naslund A 20.00 50.00
OPCMS Matt Stajan C 5.00 12.00
OPCNF Nick Foligno D 6.00 15.00
OPCNG Nicklas Grossman D 5.00 12.00
OPCPM Peter Mueller C 6.00 15.00
OPCPR Pekka Rinne A 25.00 50.00
OPCRO Ryan O'Reilly D 8.00 20.00
OPCSG Sam Gagner D 6.00 15.00
OPCSS Steven Stamkos B 30.00 60.00
OPCSW Stephen Weiss D 6.00 15.00

2012-13 O-Pee-Chee Sport Royalty Autographs

WG Wayne Gretzky B 300.00 800.00

2012-13 O-Pee-Chee Stickers

COMPLETE SET (100) 40.00 80.00
S1 Teemu Selanne 1.25 3.00
S2 Ryan Getzlaf .60 1.50
S3 Bobby Ryan .50 1.25
S4 Jonas Hiller .50 1.25
S5 Corey Perry 1.00 2.50
S6 Tyler Seguin .75 2.00
S7 Zdeno Chara .60 1.50
S8 Tim Thomas .60 1.50
S9 David Krejci .60 1.50
S10 Nathan Horton .60 1.50
S11 Brad Marchand 1.25 3.00
S12 Bobby Orr 2.50 6.00
S13 Tyler Myers .40 1.00
S14 Thomas Vanek .50 1.25
S15 Ryan Miller .60 1.50
S16 Michael Cammalleri .50 1.25
S17 Jarome Iginla .75 2.00
S18 Miikka Kiprusoff .60 1.50
S19 Eric Staal .75 2.00
S20 Cam Ward .60 1.50
S21 Jeff Skinner .75 2.00
S22 Duncan Keith .50 1.25
S23 Corey Crawford .75 2.00
S24 Jonathan Toews 1.00 2.50
S25 Patrick Kane 1.25 3.00
S26 Marian Hossa .60 1.50
S27 Gabriel Landeskog .75 2.00
S28 Jean-Sebastien Giguere .60 1.50
S29 Matt Duchene .60 1.50
S30 Paul Stastny .50 1.25
S31 Joe Sakic 1.25 3.00
S32 Rick Nash .60 1.50
S33 Jamie Benn .60 1.50
S34 Brenden Morrow .50 1.25
S35 Jim Howard .75 2.00
S36 Henrik Zetterberg .75 2.00
S37 Pavel Datsyuk 1.00 2.50
S38 Nicklas Lidstrom .60 1.50
S39 Johan Franzen .50 1.25
S40 Ryan Nugent-Hopkins .75 2.00
S41 Sam Gagner .40 1.00
S42 Paul Coffey .60 1.50
S43 Jordan Eberle .60 1.50
S44 Taylor Hall .60 1.50
S45 Ryan Smyth .50 1.25
S46 Wayne Gretzky 4.00 10.00
S47 Stephen Weiss .50 1.25
S48 Tomas Fleischmann .40 1.00
S49 Drew Doughty .75 2.00
S50 Anze Kopitar 1.00 2.50
S51 Mike Richards .50 1.25
S52 Dany Heatley .50 1.25
S53 Mikko Koivu .50 1.25
S54 Niklas Backstrom .50 1.25
S55 Patrick Roy 1.50 4.00
S56 Carey Price 1.25 3.00
S57 P.K. Subban .75 2.00
S58 Jean Beliveau .60 1.50
S59 Pekka Rinne .60 1.50
S60 Shea Weber .50 1.25
S61 Martin Brodeur 1.50 4.00
S62 Zach Parise .60 1.50
S63 Ilya Kovalchuk .60 1.50
S64 P.A. Parenteau .40 1.00
S65 Evgeni Nabokov .50 1.25
S66 John Tavares 1.00 2.50
S67 Mark Messier 1.25 3.00
S68 Henrik Lundqvist 1.50 4.00
S69 Marian Gaborik .60 1.50
S70 Jason Spezza .60 1.50
S71 Daniel Alfredsson .60 1.50
S72 Jaromir Jagr 2.00 5.00
S73 Claude Giroux .60 1.50
S74 Eric Lindros 1.00 2.50
S75 Pelle Lindbergh .50 1.25
S76 Mario Lemieux 2.50 6.00
S77 Sidney Crosby 2.50 6.00
S78 Evgeni Malkin 1.25 3.00
S79 Marc-Andre Fleury 1.25 3.00
S80 Joe Thornton 1.00 2.50
S81 Patrick Marleau .60 1.50
S82 Logan Couture .75 2.00
S83 Jaroslav Halak .60 1.50
S84 Steven Stamkos 1.25 3.00
S85 James Reimer .60 1.50
S86 Dion Phaneuf .50 1.25
S87 Phil Kessel .60 1.50
S88 Ryan Kesler .60 1.50
S89 Roberto Luongo 1.00 2.50
S90 Daniel Sedin .75 2.00
S91 Henrik Sedin .75 2.00
S92 Alexandre Burrows .40 1.00
S93 Alexander Semin .60 1.50
S94 Alexander Ovechkin 2.50 6.00
S95 Nicklas Backstrom .60 1.50
S96 Mike Green .50 1.25
S97 Andrew Ladd .40 1.00
S98 Alexander Burmistrov .50 1.25
S99 Ondrej Pavelec .60 1.50
S100 Evander Kane .60 1.50

2012-13 O-Pee-Chee Team Canada Signatures

TCAH Adam Henrique C 10.00 25.00
TCBC Brett Connolly C 8.00 20.00
TCBO Bobby Orr A 350.00 500.00
TCCD Calvin de Haan C 8.00 20.00
TCCE Cody Eakin C 8.00 20.00
TCCJ Curtis Joseph A 50.00 100.00
TCCO Sean Couturier B 15.00 40.00
TCDO Shane Doan C 10.00 25.00
TCDP Dion Phaneuf B 10.00 25.00
TCEB Ed Belfour A 40.00 80.00
TCGF Grant Fuhr A 40.00 80.00
TCJC Jared Cowen B 30.00 60.00
TCJH Josh Harding C 12.00 30.00
TCKT Kyle Turris B 12.00 30.00
TCLC Logan Couture B 30.00 60.00
TCLL Louis Leblanc B 50.00 100.00
TCMF Marcus Foligno C 12.00 30.00
TCMS Martin St. Louis B 20.00 40.00
TCNA Rick Nash B 40.00 80.00
TCRE Ryan Ellis C 8.00 20.00
TCRS Ryan Smyth B 15.00 40.00
TCSC Sidney Crosby A 250.00 400.00
TCSD Simon Despres C 10.00 25.00
TCSG Simon Gagne B 20.00 40.00
TCSS Steven Stamkos B 30.00 80.00
TCSW Stephen Weiss C 10.00 25.00
TCWG Wayne Gretzky A 400.00 1000.00
TCZK Zack Kassian C 10.00 25.00

2012-13 O-Pee-Chee Team Logo Patches

TL1 NHL primary 10.00 25.00
TL2 Eastern Conf primary 8.00 20.00
TL3 Western Conf primary 8.00 20.00
TL4 Anaheim Ducks primary 10.00 25.00
TL5 Boston Bruins primary 15.00 40.00
TL6 Buffalo Sabres primary 10.00 25.00
TL7 Calgary Flames primary 15.00 40.00
TL8 Hurricanes primary 10.00 25.00
TL9 Blackhawks primary 12.00 30.00
TL10 Avalanche primary 12.00 30.00
TL11 Blue Jackets primary 10.00 25.00
TL12 Dallas Stars primary 10.00 25.00
TL13 Red Wings primary 15.00 40.00
TL14 Edmonton Oilers primary 12.00 30.00
TL15 Florida Panthers primary 8.00 20.00
TL16 L.A. Kings primary 15.00 30.00
TL17 Minnesota Wild primary 10.00 25.00
TL18 Canadiens primary 15.00 40.00
TL19 Nash. Predators primary 8.00 20.00
TL20 NJ Devils primary 12.00 30.00
TL21 NY Islanders primary 12.50 30.00
TL22 NY Rangers primary 10.00 25.00
TL23 Ottawa Senators primary 10.00 25.00
TL24 Flyers primary 10.00 25.00
TL25 Phoenix Coyotes primary 8.00 20.00
TL26 Penguins primary 15.00 40.00
TL27 SJ Sharks primary 10.00 25.00
TL28 St. Louis Blues primary 10.00 25.00
TL29 T.B. Lightning primary 15.00 40.00
TL30 Maple Leafs primary 12.00 30.00
TL31 Canucks primary 8.00 20.00
TL32 Capitals primary 10.00 25.00
TL33 Winnipeg Jets primary 20.00 40.00
TL34 NHL primary 10.00 25.00
TL35 Eastern Conference alt 8.00 20.00
TL36 Western Conference alt 8.00 20.00
TL37 Playoffs primary 10.00 25.00
TL38 Stanley Cup Final alt 10.00 25.00
TL39 All-Star Game primary 10.00 25.00
TL40 All-Star Game alt 10.00 25.00
TL41 Winter Classic alt 15.00 30.00
TL42 Heritage Classic alt 15.00 50.00
TL43 Boston Bruins alt 15.00 30.00
TL44 Boston Bruins script 15.00 30.00
TL45 Chicago Blackhawks alt 20.00 40.00
TL46 Minnesota Wild script 15.00 30.00
TL47 Canadiens script 20.00 40.00
TL48 Que Nordiques alt 30.00 60.00
TL49 Maple Leafs second 25.00 60.00
TL50 Winnipeg Jets script 20.00 40.00
TL51 Atl Thrashers 10ANN 20.00 40.00
TL52 Buffalo Sabres 10ANN 25.00 50.00
TL53 Calgary Flames 10ANN 20.00 40.00
TL54 Avalanche 10ANN 20.00 40.00
TL55 Edmonton Oilers 10ANN 30.00 60.00
TL56 Hart Whalers 10ANN 25.00 50.00
TL57 Nash Predators 10ANN 20.00 40.00
TL58 NJ Devils 10ANN 30.00 80.00
TL59 Ottawa Senators 10ANN 20.00 40.00
TL60 Que Nordiques 10ANN 25.00 50.00
TL61 SJ Sharks 10ANN 20.00 40.00
TL62 Winnipeg Jets 10ANN 30.00 60.00
TL63 Atlanta Flames primary 30.00 60.00
TL64 Cal. Golden Seals primary 30.00 80.00
TL65 Colorado Rockies primary 40.00 80.00
TL66 K.C. Scouts primary 50.00 120.00
TL67 LA Kings primary 30.00 60.00
TL68 North Stars primary 40.00 80.00
TL69 N.Y. Islanders primary 40.00 80.00
TL70 Penguins primary 40.00 80.00
TL71 St. Louis Blues primary 60.00 120.00
TL72 Canucks primary 50.00 100.00
TL73 Capitals primary 30.00 80.00
TL74 Boston Bruins primary 100.00 200.00
TL75 Blackhawks primary 50.00 100.00
TL76 Detroit Cougars primary 60.00 125.00
TL77 Red Wings primary 50.00 100.00
TL78 Hamilton Tigers primary 25.00 50.00
TL79 Canadiens primary 50.00 100.00
TL80 Maroons primary 50.00 100.00
TL81 N.Y. Americans primary 100.00 175.00
TL82 N.Y. Rangers primary 30.00 80.00
TL83 Ottawa Senators primary 50.00 100.00
TL84 St. Louis Eagles primary 40.00 80.00
TL85 Toronto Arenas primary 40.00 80.00
TL86 Maple Leafs primary 60.00 120.00
TL87 Avalanche Joe Sakic 40.00 80.00
TL88 Oilers Gretzky HOF 100.00 200.00
TL89 Oilers Messier 11 40.00 80.00
TL90 L.A. Kings Gretzky 802 150.00 300.00
TL91 N.J. Devils Brodeur 552 75.00 125.00
TL92 N.Y. Rangers Gretzky 75.00 150.00
TL93 N.Y. Rangers Shanahan 40.00 80.00
TL94 St. Louis Blues Hull 75.00 150.00
TL95 Caps 9-11 Memorial 175.00 300.00
TL96 Winn.Jets Memories 75.00 150.00

2013-14 O-Pee-Chee

1 Phil Kessel .20 .50
2 Benoit Pouliot .12 .30
3 Semyon Varlamov .20 .50
4 Andrew Ference .12 .30
5 Jonathan Bernier .15 .40
6 Daniel Girardi .12 .30
7 Douglas Murray .12 .30
8 Ray Whitney .15 .40
9 Daniel Briere .20 .50
10 Johan Franzen .15 .40
11 Pavel Bure .20 .50
12 Nick Spaling .12 .30
13 Dwight King .12 .30
14 Devin Setoguchi .15 .40
15 Andrej Sekera .12 .30
16 Patrick Dwyer .12 .30
17 John-Michael Liles .12 .30
18 Michael Grabner .15 .40
19 Guillaume Latendresse .15 .40
20 Derick Brassard .12 .30
21 Matt Read .12 .30
22 Duncan Keith .15 .40
23 Colin Wilson .15 .40
24 Jordan Eberle .20 .50
25 Drayson Bowman .12 .30
26 Jordin Tootoo .15 .40
27 Justin Williams .15 .40
28 Kyle Wellwood .15 .40
29 Larry Robinson .20 .50
30 Tyler Kennedy .12 .30
31 Kevin Klein .12 .30
32 Loui Eriksson .12 .30
33 Alexander Semin .20 .50
34 Cody Franson .12 .30
35 Erik Condra .12 .30
36 Nik Antropov .15 .40
37 Peter Holland .12 .30
38 Drew Miller .12 .30
39 Henrik Sedin .25 .60
40 Curtis Glencross .12 .30
41 Mike Richards .15 .40
42 Ryane Clowe .12 .30
43 Carl Gunnarsson .12 .30
44 Evgeni Nabokov .20 .50
45 James Wisniewski .12 .30
46 Brian Gionta .12 .30
47 Scott Hartnell .12 .30
48 Shawn Matthias .12 .30
49 Jonathan Toews .30 .75
50 Luc Robitaille .20 .50
51 Joey MacDonald .12 .30
52 Alex Pietrangelo .15 .40
53 Brayden Schenn .20 .50
54 Paul Gaustad .12 .30
55 Radim Vrbata .12 .30
56 Mark Fistric .12 .30
57 Cory Emmerton .12 .30
58 Matt Carle .15 .40
59 John Carlson .20 .50
60 Zenon Konopka .15 .40
61 Jiri Tlusty .12 .30
62 Alex Tanguay .12 .30
63 Viktor Stalberg .12 .30
64 Daniel Alfredsson .20 .50
65 Colin McDonald .15 .40
66 Dennis Seidenberg .12 .30
67 Steven Stamkos .40 1.00
68 R.J. Umberger .12 .30
69 Rob Scuderi .12 .30
70 Nikolai Khabibulin .20 .50
71 Jaroslav Halak .20 .50
72 Steve Ott .12 .30
73 Joni Pitkanen .15 .40
74 Henrik Zetterberg .25 .60
75 Jason Chimera .12 .30
76 Victor Hedman .25 .60
77 Sergei Bobrovsky .30 .75
78 Oliver Ekman-Larsson .20 .50
79 Mark Messier .40 1.00
80 Martin Erat .12 .30
81 Wayne Simmonds .25 .60
82 Jordan Leopold .12 .30
83 Craig Smith .12 .30
84 Matt Cooke .12 .30
85 Jay McClement .12 .30
86 Fedor Tyutin .12 .30
87 Rick Nash .20 .50
88 Kyle Turris .12 .30
89 Andrew MacDonald .12 .30
90 Bobby Orr .75 2.00
91 Vernon Fiddler .12 .30
92 Joffrey Lupul .12 .30
93 Patrik Berglund .12 .30
94 Braden Holtby .25 .60
95 Patrick Kane .40 1.00
96 Steve Sullivan .12 .30
97 Martin Hanzal .12 .30
98 Cam Atkinson .20 .50
99 James Sheppard .12 .30
100 T.J. Oshie .20 .50
101 Brooks Orpik .12 .30
102 Derek Roy .12 .30
103 Mike Weber .12 .30
104 Blake Comeau .12 .30
105 Colton Orr .12 .30
106 Jussi Jokinen .12 .30
107 Patrice Bergeron .25 .60
108 Justin Abdelkader .15 .40
109 Robin Lehner .15 .40
110 Teemu Selanne .40 1.00
111 Peter Mueller .12 .30
112 Cal Clutterbuck .12 .30
113 Troy Brouwer .12 .30
114 Mike Bossy .20 .50
115 Paul Martin .12 .30
116 Joe Pavelski .25 .60
117 Tom Pyatt .12 .30
118 Jan Hejda .12 .30
119 Brandon Sutter .12 .30
120 Marcus Foligno .15 .40
121 Pierre-Marc Bouchard .20 .50
122 Chris Neil .12 .30
123 Filip Kuba .12 .30
124 David Perron .15 .40
125 Jonathan Ericsson .12 .30
126 Doug Gilmour .25 .60
127 P.K. Subban .25 .60
128 Sheldon Souray .12 .30
129 Marc Staal .12 .30
130 Stephen Gionta .12 .30
131 Tom Gilbert .12 .30
132 Jacob Markstrom .20 .50
133 Jim Howard .25 .60
134 Jay Harrison .12 .30
135 Chris Kelly .12 .30
136 Mark Letestu .15 .40
137 Nick Schultz .12 .30
138 Taylor Pyatt .12 .30
139 Mikhail Grabovski .12 .30
140 Tomas Kopecky .15 .40
141 Mikkel Boedker .12 .30
142 Cody Eakin .12 .30
143 Dustin Byfuglien .20 .50
144 Richard Clune .12 .30
145 Kevin Bieksa .15 .40
146 Anton Volchenkov .12 .30
147 Francois Beauchemin .12 .30
148 Gregory Campbell .12 .30
149 Carey Price .40 1.00
150 Casey Cizikas .12 .30
151 Reilly Smith .20 .50
152 Marc-Andre Fleury .40 1.00
153 Brian Campbell .12 .30
154 Brandon Saad .15 .40
155 Clayton Stoner .12 .30
156 Jakub Kindl .12 .30
157 Zack Smith .12 .30
158 Alexander Edler .12 .30
159 Andrew Ladd .12 .30
160 Raffi Torres .12 .30
161 John Tavares .30 .75
162 Dmitry Kulikov .12 .30
163 Ryan Ellis .15 .40
164 Teddy Purcell .12 .30
165 Tyson Barrie .12 .30
166 Mathieu Perreault .12 .30
167 Dale Hawerchuk .25 .60
168 Marian Hossa .20 .50
169 Luca Sbisa .15 .40
170 Shawn Horcoff .12 .30
171 James Neal .12 .30
172 Mike Fisher .12 .30
173 Henrik Lundqvist .50 1.25
174 Brett Hull .40 1.00
175 Stephen Weiss .15 .40
176 Saku Koivu .20 .50
177 Sam Gagner .12 .30
178 Mike Ribeiro .12 .30
179 Tuukka Rask .25 .60
180 Marc Methot .12 .30
181 David Backes .12 .30
182 Jiri Hudler .15 .40
183 Steve Yzerman .50 1.25
184 Shea Weber .15 .40
185 Philip Larsen .12 .30
186 Brad Marchand .40 1.00
187 Jamie McBain .12 .30
188 Ryan Nugent-Hopkins .25 .60
189 Chris Phillips .12 .30
190 Mike Green .15 .40
191 Frans Nielsen .12 .30
192 Ruslan Fedotenko .12 .30
193 Kyle Brodziak .12 .30
194 Ryan Carter .12 .30
195 Niklas Hjalmarsson .12 .30
196 Marcel Goc .15 .40
197 Ryan McDonagh .12 .30
198 Joe Corvo .12 .30
199 Dion Phaneuf .15 .40
200 Tomas Vokoun .15 .40
201 Craig Anderson .20 .50
202 Dan Hamhuis .15 .40
203 Logan Couture .25 .60
204 Kari Lehtonen .15 .40
205 Vincent Lecavalier .20 .50
206 Devan Dubnyk .15 .40
207 Roman Josi .20 .50
208 Barret Jackman .12 .30
209 Evgeni Malkin .40 1.00
210 Dany Heatley .15 .40
211 Jochen Hecht .12 .30
212 Marcus Johansson .15 .40
213 Matt Calvert .12 .30
214 Boyd Gordon .12 .30
215 Alexandre Burrows .12 .30
216 Erik Johnson .12 .30
217 Erik Karlsson .25 .60
218 Eric Brewer .12 .30
219 Tomas Fleischmann .12 .30
220 Brandon Prust .12 .30
221 Daniel Winnik .12 .30
222 Brent Burns .20 .50
223 Andrew Shaw .12 .30
224 Torrey Mitchell .12 .30
225 Gustav Nyquist .12 .30
226 Patrick Wiercioch .12 .30
227 Trevor Daley .12 .30
228 Nazem Kadri .25 .60
229 Keith Yandle .12 .30
230 Mark Stuart .12 .30
231 Michael Del Zotto .12 .30
232 Nick Foligno .15 .40
233 David Desharnais .12 .30
234 Bryan Bickell .12 .30
235 Jakub Voracek .15 .40
236 Brian McGrattan .12 .30
237 Rob Klinkhammer .12 .30
238 Joel Ward .12 .30
239 Marian Gaborik .20 .50
240 Ryan Miller .20 .50
241 Josh Gorges .15 .40
242 Travis Hamonic .12 .30
243 Carl Hagelin .12 .30
244 Tobias Enstrom .12 .30
245 Scott Gomez .15 .40
246 Corey Crawford .25 .60
247 Francis Bouillon .12 .30
248 Miikka Kiprusoff .20 .50
249 Nate Thompson .12 .30
250 Lauri Korpikoski .12 .30
251 Alexander Ovechkin .75 2.00
252 Jake Muzzin .20 .50
253 Ryan Kesler .20 .50
254 Pascal Dupuis .12 .30
255 Ray Bourque .30 .75
256 Kimmo Timonen .12 .30
257 Andy McDonald .15 .40
258 Corey Perry .30 .75
259 Matt Hendricks .12 .30
260 Marcus Kruger .12 .30
261 Milan Hejduk .15 .40
262 Tyler Ennis .12 .30
263 John Moore .12 .30
264 Kris Versteeg .12 .30
265 Chad LaRose .12 .30
266 David Legwand .15 .40
267 Daniel Sedin .25 .60

268 Martin St. Louis .20 .50
269 Patrick Eaves .12 .30
270 James van Riemsdyk .15 .40
271 Jay Bouwmeester .12 .30
272 Nicklas Backstrom .20 .50
273 Andre Benoit .12 .30
274 Nikita Nikitin .12 .30
275 Brad Boyes .12 .30
276 Andrei Markov .12 .30
277 Matt Beleskey .12 .30
278 Brian Elliott .15 .40
279 Chris Butler .12 .30
280 Ilya Kovalchuk .20 .50
281 Lubomir Visnovsky .12 .30
282 Ray Emery .15 .40
283 Mikko Koivu .15 .40
284 Dominik Hasek .30 .75
285 Alex Goligoski .12 .30
286 Marc-Edouard Vlasic .12 .30
287 Vaclav Prospal .12 .30
288 Antoine Vermette .12 .30
289 David Jones .12 .30
290 Brian Boyle .12 .30
291 Kris Letang .25 .60
292 Justin Peters .12 .30
293 Simon Gagne .20 .50
294 Rich Peverley .12 .30
295 Gabriel Landeskog .25 .60
296 Adam Larsson .20 .50
297 Kyle Okposo .12 .30
298 Martin Havlat .15 .40
299 Maxime Talbot .12 .30
300 B.J. Crombeen .12 .30
301 Karl Alzner .12 .30
302 Eric Staal .25 .60
303 Ryan Whitney .12 .30
304 Kyle Clifford .12 .30
305 Sean Couturier .15 .40
306 Matthew Lombardi .12 .30
307 Michael Ryder .12 .30
308 Brenden Morrow .15 .40
309 Dan Cleary .20 .50
310 Theoren Fleury .25 .60
311 Cory Schneider .20 .50
312 Johan Hedberg .15 .40
313 Matt Martin .12 .30
314 Cody Hodgson .12 .30
315 Tyler Seguin .25 .60
316 Brent Seabrook .12 .30
317 Ryan O'Reilly .20 .50
318 Patrick Roy .50 1.25
319 Ryan Garbutt .12 .30
320 Jack Johnson .12 .30
321 Lee Stempniak .12 .30
322 Patrick Sharp .20 .50
323 Milan Lucic .20 .50
324 Anders Lindback .12 .30
325 Eric Tangradi .12 .30
326 Jamie Benn .20 .50
327 Tyler Bozak .12 .30
328 Martin Brodeur .50 1.25
329 Roberto Luongo .30 .75
330 Pekka Rinne .20 .50
331 Clarke MacArthur .12 .30
332 Michal Neuvirth .15 .40
333 Colin Greening .12 .30
334 Robyn Regehr .12 .30
335 Bryce Salvador .12 .30
336 Jared Spurgeon .20 .50
337 Grant Clitsome .12 .30
338 Nikolai Kulemin .12 .30
339 Jonas Hiller .15 .40
340 Derek Stepan .12 .30
341 David Krejci .20 .50
342 Jack Skille .15 .40
343 Andy Greene .12 .30
344 Dan Ellis .15 .40
345 Nick Bonino .12 .30
346 Eric Lindros .30 .75
347 Ladislav Smid .12 .30
348 Chris Higgins .12 .30
349 Matt Frattin .15 .40
350 Steve Begin .12 .30
351 John Mitchell .12 .30
352 Anton Khudobin .20 .50
353 Tim Jackman .12 .30
354 Patrik Elias .20 .50
355 Drew Doughty .25 .60
356 Ryan Smyth .15 .40
357 Aaron Palushaj .15 .40
358 Thomas Vanek .15 .40
359 Derek Morris .12 .30
360 Marek Zidlicky .12 .30
361 Niklas Kronwall .15 .40
362 Matt Moulson .12 .30
363 Matt Cullen .12 .30
364 Matt Stajan .12 .30
365 Zac Rinaldo .15 .40
366 Antti Niemi .15 .40
367 Shane Doan .15 .40
368 Eric Nystrom .12 .30
369 Josh Bailey .15 .40
370 Vladimir Sobotka .12 .30
371 Brandon Dubinsky .12 .30
372 Bobby Clarke .30 .75
373 Cam Fowler .12 .30
374 Matt Duchene .20 .50
375 Brandon Yip .12 .30
376 Ryan Callahan .12 .30
377 Justin Faulk .15 .40
378 Jason LaBarbera .15 .40
379 Cody McLeod .12 .30
380 Kyle Palmieri .15 .40
381 Sami Salo .12 .30
382 Valtteri Filppula .12 .30
383 Zdeno Chara .20 .50
384 Ilya Bryzgalov .20 .50
385 Jeff Skinner .25 .60
386 Ben Scrivens .15 .40
387 Joe Thornton .30 .75
388 Jarret Stoll .15 .40
389 Anton Stralman .12 .30
390 Jannik Hansen .15 .40
391 Jeff Petry .20 .50
392 P.A. Parenteau .12 .30
393 Ales Hemsky .12 .30
394 Ian White .15 .40
395 Michal Handzus .12 .30
396 Ryan Getzlaf .20 .50
397 Wayne Gretzky 1.25 3.00
398 Tyler Myers .12 .30
399 Brad Stuart .12 .30
400 George Parros .15 .40
401 Mason Raymond .12 .30
402 Adrian Aucoin .12 .30
403 Daniel Paille .12 .30
404 Travis Zajac .12 .30
405 Taylor Hall .20 .50
406 Jamie McGinn .12 .30
407 Evander Kane .20 .50
408 Alexei Emelin .12 .30
409 Magnus Paajarvi .15 .40
410 Erik Cole .12 .30
411 Christian Ehrhoff .12 .30
412 Jeff Carter .15 .40
413 Ryan Johansen .15 .40
414 Eric Fehr .12 .30
415 David Moss .12 .30
416 David Clarkson .12 .30
417 Ville Leino .15 .40
418 Nick Leddy .12 .30
419 Andrew Cogliano .12 .30
420 Gabriel Bourque .12 .30
421 Jonathan Quick .25 .60
422 Nathan Horton .20 .50
423 Paul Coffey .20 .50
424 Nathan Gerbe .12 .30
425 Ryan Suter .15 .40
426 Ryan Malone .12 .30
427 Rene Bourque .12 .30
428 Alexander Burmistrov .15 .40
429 Sergei Kostitsyn .12 .30
430 Nicklas Lidstrom .20 .50
431 Mike Smith .20 .50
432 Bryan Trottier .20 .50
433 Paul Stastny .15 .40
434 Jaden Schwartz .25 .60
435 Artem Anisimov .12 .30
436 Michael Cammalleri .15 .40
437 Bobby Ryan .15 .40
438 Rostislav Klesla .12 .30
439 Jason Garrison .12 .30
440 Max Pacioretty .20 .50
441 Olli Jokinen .15 .40
442 Zach Parise .20 .50
443 Chris Kunitz .20 .50
444 Anze Kopitar .30 .75
445 Kevin Shattenkirk .12 .30
446 Jakob Silfverberg .12 .30
447 Andrei Loktionov .12 .30
448 Tommy Wingels .12 .30
449 Lars Eller .12 .30
450 Ondrej Pavelec .20 .50
451 Drew Stafford .12 .30
452 Pavel Datsyuk .30 .75
453 Dustin Brown .20 .50
454 Alexander Steen .12 .30
455 Ben Bishop .15 .40
456 Erik Gudbranson .12 .30
457 Maxim Lapierre .12 .30
458 Adam Henrique .15 .40
459 Jordan Staal .15 .40
460 Milan Michalek .12 .30
461 Dave Bolland .12 .30
462 Adam Burish .12 .30
463 Mark Streit .12 .30
464 Jaromir Jagr .60 1.50
465 James Reimer .20 .50
466 Jason Pominville .12 .30
467 Trevor Lewis .12 .30
468 Stephane Robidas .12 .30
469 Dennis Wideman .12 .30
470 Bryan Little .20 .50
471 Kyle Chipchura .12 .30
472 Roman Polak .12 .30
473 Tomas Plekanec .12 .30
474 Mark Giordano .20 .50
475 Sidney Crosby .75 2.00
476 Blake Wheeler .20 .50
477 Luke Schenn .20 .50
478 Niklas Backstrom .20 .50
479 Brad Richards .20 .50
480 Sergei Gonchar .12 .30
481 Cam Ward .20 .50
482 Jarome Iginla .25 .60
483 Keaton Ellerby .12 .30
484 Dan Boyle .12 .30
485 Raphael Diaz .12 .30
486 Patric Hornqvist .12 .30
487 T.J. Brodie .12 .30
488 Claude Giroux .20 .50
489 Scott Clemmensen .15 .40
490 Joe Sakic .40 1.00
491 Slava Voynov .15 .40
492 Justin Falk .12 .30
493 Chris Stewart .15 .40
494 Ron Hainsey .12 .30
495 Patrick Marleau .20 .50
496 Checklist .12 .30
497 Checklist .12 .30
498 Checklist .12 .30
499 Checklist .12 .30
500 Checklist .12 .30
501 Nail Yakupov RC 4.00 10.00
502 Ryan Murphy RC 1.25 3.00
503 Jon Rheault RC .75 2.00
504 Sean Collins RC 1.00 2.50
505 Roman Cervenka RC 1.00 2.50
506 Quinton Howden RC 1.00 2.50
507 Matt Anderson RC .75 2.00
508 Matt Tennyson RC .75 2.00
509 Christian Thomas RC 1.00 2.50
510 Chris Brown RC .75 2.00
511 Mark Barberio RC .75 2.00
512 Zach Redmond RC 1.00 2.50
513 Steve Pinizzotto RC 1.25 3.00
514 Calvin Pickard RC 1.50 4.00
515 Jean-Gabriel Pageau RC 1.25 3.00
516 Darcy Kuemper RC 2.50 6.00
517 Viktor Fasth RC 1.25 3.00
518 Brett Bellemore RC 1.00 2.50
519 Dan DeKeyser RC 1.50 4.00
520 Brendan Gallagher RC 3.00 8.00
521 Oliver Lauridsen RC 1.00 2.50
522 Leo Komarov RC 1.25 3.00
523 Michal Jordan RC .75 2.00
524 Nick Petrecki RC .75 2.00
525 Filip Forsberg RC 4.00 10.00
526 Michael Sgarbossa RC .75 2.00
527 Mikhail Grigorenko RC .75 2.00
528 Emerson Etem RC 1.25 3.00
529 Alex Chiasson RC 1.25 3.00
530 Ben Street RC 1.00 2.50
531 Dougie Hamilton RC 2.00 5.00
532 Mark Arcobello RC 1.00 2.50
533 Victor Bartley RC 1.00 2.50
534 Beau Bennett RC 1.50 4.00
535 Steve Oleksy RC 1.25 3.00
536 Radko Gudas RC 1.25 3.00
537 Vladimir Tarasenko RC 3.00 8.00
538 Eric Gryba RC 1.00 2.50
539 Jarred Tinordi RC 1.25 3.00
540 Eric Selleck RC 1.00 2.50
541 Patrick Bordeleau RC 1.25 3.00
542 Sami Vatanen RC 1.25 3.00
543 Brian Lashoff RC 1.00 2.50
544 Drew Shore RC 1.00 2.50
545 Cameron Schilling RC .75 2.00
546 David Dziurzynski RC 1.25 3.00
547 Mike Kostka RC 1.00 2.50
548 Anthony Peluso RC .75 2.00
549 Thomas Hickey RC 1.00 2.50
550 Daniel Bang RC 1.00 2.50
551 Greg Pateryn RC 1.25 3.00
552 Tye McGinn RC 1.25 3.00
553 Stefan Matteau RC 1.00 2.50
554 Charlie Coyle RC 2.00 5.00
555 Jonathan Huberdeau RC 3.00 8.00
556 Petr Mrazek RC 2.50 6.00
557 Max Reinhart RC 1.25 3.00
558 Rickard Rakell RC 1.25 3.00
559 Anders Lee RC 2.00 5.00
560 Tyler Toffoli RC 2.50 6.00
561 Tyler Johnson RC 2.50 6.00
562 Philipp Grubauer RC 3.00 8.00
563 Brian Flynn RC 1.00 2.50
564 Mark Pysyk RC .75 2.00
565 Ryan Spooner RC 1.25 3.00
566 Cory Conacher RC .75 2.00
567 Andrej Sustr RC .75 2.00
568 Justin Schultz RC 1.25 3.00
569 Jamie Oleksiak RC 1.00 2.50
570 Jamie Tardif RC .75 2.00
571 Michael Caruso RC .75 2.00
572 Derek Grant RC 1.00 2.50
573 Nicklas Jensen RC 1.00 2.50
574 Dmitrij Jaskin RC 1.25 3.00
575 Alex Galchenyuk RC 3.00 8.00
576 Jonas Brodin RC 1.50 4.00
577 Richard Panik RC 1.25 3.00
578 J.T. Miller RC 3.00 8.00
579 Nathan Beaulieu RC .75 2.00
580 Ondrej Palat RC 2.00 5.00
581 Scott Laughton RC 1.25 3.00
582 Austin Watson RC 1.00 2.50
583 Jordan Schroeder RC 1.25 3.00
584 Chris Terry RC .75 2.00
585 Jonathan Audy-Marchessault RC 3.00 8.00
586 Christopher Nilstorp RC 1.00 2.50
587 Harri Pesonen RC 1.00 2.50
588 Matthew Irwin RC 1.00 2.50
589 Johan Larsson RC 1.50 4.00
590 Damien Brunner RC 1.00 2.50
591 Mikael Granlund RC 2.00 5.00
592 Chad Ruhwedel RC .75 2.00
593 Alex Killorn RC 2.00 5.00
594 Nicolas Blanchard RC 1.00 2.50
595 Nick Bjugstad RC 1.50 4.00
596 Ben Hanowski RC 1.00 2.50
597 Antoine Roussel RC 1.00 2.50
598 Sami Aittokallio RC 1.25 3.00
599 Jack Campbell RC 3.00 8.00
600 Checklist .75 2.00
601 Checklist .75 2.00
602 Jaromir Jagr 4.00 10.00
603 Daniel Briere 1.25 3.00
604 Bobby Ryan 1.00 2.50
605 David Perron 1.00 2.50
606 Loui Eriksson .75 2.00
607 Daniel Alfredsson 1.25 3.00
608 Tyler Seguin 1.50 4.00
609 David Clarkson .75 2.00
610 Jonathan Bernier 1.00 2.50
611 Cory Schneider 1.25 3.00
612 Vincent Lecavalier 1.25 3.00
613 Sean Monahan RC 1.50 4.00
614 Antti Raanta RC 2.00 5.00
615 Aleksander Barkov RC 3.00 8.00
616 Martin Jones RC 1.50 4.00
617 Mathew Dumba RC .60 1.50
618 Freddie Hamilton RC 1.00 2.50
619 Lucas Lessio RC .60 1.50
620 Nathan MacKinnon RC 4.00 10.00
621 Carl Soderberg RC 1.00 2.50
622 Jacob Trouba RC 1.50 4.00
623 Ryan Strome RC 1.50 4.00
624 Tomas Jurco RC 1.25 3.00
625 Tomas Hertl RC 3.00 8.00
626 Ryan Murray RC 1.50 4.00
627 Reto Berra RC 1.00 2.50
628 Michael Bournival RC 1.00 2.50
629 Rasmus Ristolainen RC 1.50 4.00
630 Olli Maatta RC 1.50 4.00
631 Marek Mazanec RC 1.00 2.50
632 Jon Merrill RC 1.00 2.50
633 Matt Nieto RC .75 2.00
634 Valeri Nichushkin RC 2.00 5.00
635 Nikita Zadorov RC .60 1.50
636 Seth Jones RC 2.00 5.00
637 Elias Lindholm RC 2.50 6.00
638 Jesper Fast RC 1.00 2.50
639 Morgan Rielly RC 2.50 6.00
640 Justin Fontaine RC 1.00 2.50
641 Boone Jenner RC 2.00 5.00
642 Zemgus Girgensons RC 1.50 4.00

2013-14 O-Pee-Chee Black Rainbow

*1-500 VETS: 8X TO 20X BASIC CARDS
*501-600 ROOK: 1.5X TO 4X BASIC RC
246 Corey Crawford 6.00 15.00
501 Nail Yakupov 15.00 40.00
575 Alex Galchenyuk 40.00 80.00

2013-14 O-Pee-Chee Rainbow

*1-500 VETS: 2.5X TO 6X BASIC CARDS
*501-600 ROOKIES: .5X TO 1.2X BASIC RC
246 Corey Crawford 2.00 5.00

2013-14 O-Pee-Chee Red

*1-500 VETS: 6X TO 15X BASIC CARDS
*501-600 ROOKIES: 1.2X TO 3X BASIC RC
*601-612 VETS: 1.5X TO 4X BASIC CARDS
*613-642 ROOK: 2X TO 5X BASIC RC
246 Corey Crawford 5.00 12.00

2013-14 O-Pee-Chee Retro

*1-500 VETS: 2X TO 5X BASIC CARDS
*501-600 ROOK: .5X TO 1.2X BASIC RC
*601-612 VETS: .6X TO 1.5X BASIC CARDS
*613-642 ROOK: .6X TO 1.5X BASIC RC
246 Corey Crawford 1.50 4.00

2013-14 O-Pee-Chee Blaster Box Bottoms

AG Alex Galchenyuk .60 1.50
AO Alexander Ovechkin 1.25 3.00
NY Nail Yakupov .50 1.25
SC Sidney Crosby 1.25 3.00
SS Steven Stamkos .60 1.50
VT Vladimir Tarasenko .60 1.50

2013-14 O-Pee-Chee Buyback Autographs

8 Ovechkin '09-10 OPC/23 75.00 125.00
87 Crosby '09-10 OPC/20 100.00 200.00

2013-14 O-Pee-Chee Glossy

1 Teemu Selanne 50.00 125.00
2 Corey Perry 40.00 100.00
3 Bobby Orr 75.00 135.00
4 Milan Lucic 25.00 60.00
5 Zdeno Chara 25.00 60.00
6 Tyler Seguin 30.00 80.00
7 Brad Marchand 50.00 125.00
8 Theo Fleury 30.00 80.00
9 Miikka Kiprusoff 25.00 60.00
10 Jarome Iginla 30.00 80.00
11 Jonathan Toews 50.00 100.00
12 Patrick Sharp 25.00 60.00
13 Patrick Kane 50.00 125.00
14 Matt Duchene 25.00 60.00
15 Brett Hull 40.00 80.00
16 Nicklas Lidstrom 25.00 60.00
17 Pavel Datsyuk 40.00 100.00
18 Jimmy Howard 30.00 80.00
19 Nail Yakupov 75.00 135.00
20 Jordan Eberle 25.00 60.00
21 Ryan Nugent-Hopkins 50.00 100.00
22 Wayne Gretzky 125.00 225.00
23 Taylor Hall 25.00 60.00
24 Pavel Bure 40.00 100.00
25 Jonathan Huberdeau 50.00 100.00
26 Drew Doughty 30.00 80.00
27 Mike Richards 20.00 50.00
28 Jonathan Quick 30.00 80.00
29 Mikko Koivu 20.00 50.00
30 Alex Galchenyuk 90.00 150.00
31 Carey Price 50.00 100.00
32 Patrick Roy 75.00 135.00
33 Pekka Rinne 25.00 60.00
34 Ilya Kovalchuk 25.00 60.00
35 Martin Brodeur 40.00 100.00
36 John Tavares 40.00 100.00
37 Henrik Lundqvist 60.00 150.00
38 Chris Kreider 30.00 80.00
39 Jason Spezza 25.00 60.00
40 Erik Karlsson 30.00 80.00
41 Pelle Lindbergh 20.00 50.00
42 Brayden Schenn 25.00 60.00
43 Eric Lindros 40.00 80.00
44 Mario Lemieux 50.00 100.00
45 Evgeni Malkin 40.00 80.00
46 Sidney Crosby 75.00 150.00
47 Joe Sakic 40.00 80.00
48 Mats Sundin 25.00 60.00
50 Steven Stamkos 40.00 80.00
51 Nazem Kadri 30.00 80.00
52 Wendel Clark 40.00 100.00
53 Alexandre Burrows 15.00 40.00
54 Roberto Luongo 40.00 100.00
55 Daniel Sedin 30.00 80.00
56 Henrik Sedin 30.00 80.00
57 Alex Ovechkin 50.00 100.00
58 Braden Holtby 30.00 80.00
59 Ondrej Pavelec 25.00 60.00
60 Evander Kane 25.00 60.00

2013-14 O-Pee-Chee League Leaders

LL Dpuis/Kntz/Toews 5.00 12.00
LLA St.Louis/Crsby/Bckstrm 12.00 30.00
LLSO Hwrd/Rask/Rinne 5.00 12.00
LLGAA Andrsn/Brner/Crwfrd 4.00 10.00
LLGLS Ovchkn/Stmks/Tvres 12.00 30.00
LLPIM Orr/Neil/Brown 3.00 8.00
LLPPG Ovchkn/Stmks/Vnek 12.00 30.00
LLPTS St. Louis/Stmks/Crsby 12.00 30.00
LLRPTS Ykpv/Hbrdeau/Cncher 4.00 10.00
LLWINS Lndqvst/Nmi/Bckstrm 8.00 20.00

2013-14 O-Pee-Chee Marquee Legends

ML1 Wayne Gretzky 12.00 30.00
ML2 Bobby Orr 10.00 25.00
ML3 Steve Yzerman 10.00 25.00
ML4 Patrick Roy 10.00 25.00
ML5 Mark Messier 8.00 20.00
ML6 Joe Sakic 8.00 20.00
ML7 Eric Lindros 6.00 15.00
ML8 Theoren Fleury 5.00 12.00
ML9 Dominik Hasek 6.00 15.00
ML10 Pavel Bure 4.00 10.00

2013-14 O-Pee-Chee Retro Hobby Box Bottoms

1 Sidney Crosby A 1.00 2.50
2 Ryan Getzlaf A .25 .60
3 Jonathan Huberdeau A .40 1.00
4 Henrik Lundqvist A .60 1.50
5 Martin Brodeur B .60 1.50
6 Alex Galchenyuk B .40 1.00
7 Steven Stamkos B .50 1.25
8 Henrik Zetterberg B .30 .75
9 Patrick Kane C .50 1.25
10 Alexander Ovechkin C 1.00 2.50
11 Carey Price C .50 1.25
12 Vladimir Tarasenko C .40 1.00
13 Tuukka Rask D .30 .75
14 John Tavares D .40 1.00
15 Jonathan Toews D .40 1.00
16 Nail Yakupov D .30 .75
P1 Crosby/Getlaf/Huber/Lund 1.25 3.00
P2 Brodr/Galch/Stamk/Zettr 1.25 3.00
P3 Kane/Ovch/Price/Taras 1.25 3.00
P4 Rask/Tavr/Toews/Yakpv 1.25 3.00

2013-14 O-Pee-Chee Rings

R1 Anaheim Ducks 1.50 4.00
R2 Boston Bruins 2.00 5.00
R3 Buffalo Sabres 1.50 4.00
R4 Calgary Flames 1.50 4.00
R5 Carolina Hurricanes 1.50 4.00
R6 Chicago Blackhawks 1.50 4.00
R7 Colorado Avalanche 1.50 4.00
R8 Columbus Blue Jackets 1.50 4.00
R9 Dallas Stars 1.50 4.00
R10 Detroit Red Wings 1.50 4.00
R11 Edmonton Oilers 2.00 5.00
R12 Florida Panthers 1.50 4.00
R13 Los Angeles Kings 1.50 4.00
R14 Minnesota Wild 1.50 4.00
R15 Montreal Canadiens 2.00 5.00
R16 Nashville Predators 1.50 4.00
R17 New Jersey Devils 1.50 4.00
R18 New York Islanders 1.50 4.00
R19 New York Rangers 1.50 4.00
R20 Ottawa Senators 1.50 4.00
R21 Philadelphia Flyers 1.50 4.00
R22 Phoenix Coyotes 1.50 4.00
R23 Pittsburgh Penguins 2.00 5.00
R24 San Jose Sharks 1.50 4.00
R25 St. Louis Blues 1.50 4.00
R26 Tampa Bay Lightning 1.50 4.00
R27 Toronto Maple Leafs 2.00 5.00
R28 Vancouver Canucks 1.50 4.00
R29 Washington Capitals 1.50 4.00
R30 Winnipeg Jets 1.50 4.00
R31 Wayne Gretzky 12.00 30.00
R32 Bobby Orr 8.00 20.00
R33 Mario Lemieux 8.00 20.00
R34 Patrick Roy 5.00 12.00
R35 Dave Schultz 2.00 5.00
R36 Terry O'Reilly 1.50 4.00
R37 Tie Domi 1.50 4.00
R38 Bob Probert 2.00 5.00
R39 Marty McSorley 1.50 4.00
R40 Daniel Carcillo 1.25 3.00
R41 Zenon Konopka 1.50 4.00
R42 George Parros 1.50 4.00
R43 Sidney Crosby 8.00 20.00
R44 Alexander Ovechkin 8.00 20.00
R45 Jonathan Toews 3.00 8.00
R46 Steven Stamkos 4.00 10.00
R47 Martin Brodeur 5.00 12.00
R48 Henrik Lundqvist 5.00 12.00
R49 Carey Price 4.00 10.00
R50 Jonathan Quick 2.50 6.00

2013-14 O-Pee-Chee Signatures

USAG Alex Galchenyuk B 2 40.00 80.00
USJH Jonathan Huberdeau B 2 75.00 125.00
USTH Tomas Hertl B 2 15.00 40.00
USVN Valeri Nichushkin B 2 20.00 40.00
OPCAB Adam Burish C 3.00 8.00
OPCAG Alex Goligoski B 8.00 20.00
OPCBL Brian Lee C 3.00 8.00
OPCBM Brayden McNabb C 3.00 8.00
OPCBO Bobby Orr A 175.00 300.00
OPCBS Brendan Smith B 5.00 12.00
OPCCK Chris Kunitz B 8.00 20.00
OPCCO Cal O'Reilly C 3.00 8.00
OPCDC Daniel Carcillo C 3.00 8.00
OPCEN Evgeni Nabokov B 8.00 20.00
OPCET Eric Tangradi C 4.00 10.00
OPCHS Harri Saferi C 3.00 8.00
OPCJB Josh Bailey C 4.00 10.00
OPCJE Jonathan Ericsson B 5.00 12.00
OPCJF Justin Falk C 3.00 8.00
OPCLB Lance Bouma C 3.00 8.00
OPCLI Leland Irving B 6.00 15.00
OPCMI Brendan Mikkelson C 3.00 8.00
OPCML Mario Lemieux A 100.00 175.00
OPCMS Mark Streit B 6.00 15.00
OPCNG Nicklas Grossman C 3.00 8.00
OPCPR Patrick Roy A 100.00 175.00
OPCRW Roman Wick C 3.00 8.00
OPCSU Mats Sundin A 50.00 100.00
OPCTL Trevor Lewis C 3.00 8.00
OPCVF Valtteri Filppula C 3.00 8.00
OPCVS Viktor Stalberg B 5.00 12.00
OPCWG Wayne Gretzky A 300.00 800.00
OPCYS Yann Sauve C 3.00 8.00

2013-14 O-Pee-Chee Sport Royalty Autographs

BO Bobby Orr 150.00 300.00

2013-14 O-Pee-Chee Stamps

STAO Alexander Ovechkin 15.00 40.00
STAP Alex Pietrangelo 3.00 8.00
STBO Bobby Orr 10.00 25.00
STCG Claude Giroux 4.00 10.00
STCP Corey Perry 6.00 15.00
STCS Cory Schneider 4.00 10.00
STDD Drew Doughty 5.00 12.00
STDS Daniel Sedin 5.00 12.00
STEK Erik Karlsson 5.00 12.00
STEL Eric Lindros 6.00 15.00
STEM Evgeni Malkin 8.00 20.00
STHL Henrik Lundqvist 10.00 25.00
STHS Henrik Sedin 5.00 12.00
STHZ Henrik Zetterberg 5.00 12.00
STIK Ilya Kovalchuk 4.00 10.00
STJB Jamie Benn 4.00 10.00
STJH Jim Howard 5.00 12.00
STJI Jarome Iginla 5.00 12.00
STJJ Jack Johnson 2.50 6.00
STJO Joe Sakic 8.00 20.00
STJQ Jonathan Quick 5.00 12.00
STJS Jeff Skinner 5.00 12.00
STJT Jonathan Toews 6.00 15.00
STKA Evander Kane 4.00 10.00
STKE Phil Kessel 4.00 10.00
STMB Martin Brodeur 10.00 25.00
STMD Matt Duchene 4.00 10.00
STML Mario Lemieux 15.00 40.00
STMM Mark Messier 8.00 20.00
STMS Mats Sundin 4.00 10.00
STOP Ondrej Pavelec 4.00 10.00
STPB Pavel Bure 4.00 10.00
STPC Paul Coffey 4.00 10.00
STPD Pavel Datsyuk 6.00 15.00
STPK Patrick Kane 8.00 20.00
STPR Carey Price 8.00 20.00
STPS P.K. Subban 5.00 12.00
STRF Ron Francis 5.00 12.00
STRM Ryan Miller 4.00 10.00
STRN Ryan Nugent-Hopkins 5.00 12.00
STRO Patrick Roy 10.00 25.00
STSC Sidney Crosby 15.00 40.00
STSS Steven Stamkos 8.00 20.00
STTA John Tavares 6.00 15.00
STTD Tie Domi 3.00 8.00
STTH Taylor Hall 4.00 10.00
STTS Tyler Seguin 5.00 12.00
STWG Wayne Gretzky 20.00 50.00
STZC Zdeno Chara 4.00 10.00
STZP Zach Parise 4.00 10.00

2013-14 O-Pee-Chee Stickers

SAB Alexandre Burrows .50 1.25
SAN Antti Niemi .60 1.50
SAO Alexander Ovechkin 3.00 8.00
SBC Bobby Clarke 1.25 3.00
SBE Jean Beliveau .75 2.00
SBH Braden Holtby 1.00 2.50
SBM Brad Marchand 1.50 4.00
SBO Bobby Orr 3.00 8.00
SBR Bobby Ryan .60 1.50
SBU Alexander Burmistrov .60 1.50
SCA Carey Price 1.50 4.00
SCC Corey Crawford 1.00 2.50
SCG Claude Giroux .75 2.00
SCK Chris Kreider 1.00 2.50
SCP Corey Perry 1.25 3.00
SCW Cam Ward .75 2.00
SDA Daniel Alfredsson .75 2.00
SDD Drew Doughty 1.00 2.50
SDH Dany Heatley .60 1.50
SDK David Krejci .75 2.00
SDP Dion Phaneuf .60 1.50
SDS Daniel Sedin 1.00 2.50
SEK Evander Kane .75 2.00
SEL Eric Lindros 1.25 3.00
SEM Evgeni Malkin 1.50 4.00
SES Eric Staal 1.00 2.50
SGL Gabriel Landeskog 1.00 2.50
SGR Mike Green .60 1.50
SHA Jaroslav Halak .75 2.00
SHL Henrik Lundqvist 2.00 5.00
SHO Jim Howard 1.00 2.50
SHS Henrik Sedin 1.00 2.50
SHZ Henrik Zetterberg 1.00 2.50
SIK Ilya Kovalchuk .75 2.00
SJA Jaromir Jagr 2.50 6.00
SJB Jamie Benn .75 2.00
SJE Jordan Eberle .75 2.00
SJF Johan Franzen .60 1.50
SJH Jonas Hiller .60 1.50
SJI Jarome Iginla 1.00 2.50
SJJ Jack Johnson .50 1.25
SJN James Neal .50 1.25
SJO Joe Thornton 1.25 3.00
SJQ Jonathan Quick 1.00 2.50
SJS Jeff Skinner 1.00 2.50
SJT Jonathan Toews 1.25 3.00
SKE Duncan Keith .60 1.50
SKO Mikko Koivu .60 1.50
SKV Kris Versteeg .50 1.25
SLC Logan Couture 1.00 2.50
SMB Martin Brodeur 2.00 5.00
SMC Michael Cammalleri .60 1.50
SMD Matt Duchene .75 2.00
SMF Marc-Andre Fleury 1.50 4.00
SMG Marian Gaborik .75 2.00
SMH Marian Hossa .75 2.00
SMI Mike Bossy .75 2.00
SMK Miikka Kiprusoff .75 2.00
SML Mario Lemieux 3.00 8.00
SMM Mark Messier 1.50 4.00
SMO Brenden Morrow .60 1.50
SMR Mike Richards .60 1.50
SMS Mark Scheifele 1.25 3.00
SNB Niklas Backstrom .60 1.50
SNH Nathan Horton .75 2.00
SNL Nicklas Lidstrom .75 2.00
SOP Ondrej Pavelec .75 2.00
SPB Pavel Bure .75 2.00
SPC Paul Coffey .75 2.00
SPD Pavel Datsyuk 1.25 3.00
SPH Phil Kessel .75 2.00
SPK Patrick Kane 1.50 4.00
SPM Patrick Marleau .75 2.00
SPR Patrick Roy 2.00 5.00
SPS Paul Stastny .60 1.50
SRG Ryan Getzlaf .75 2.00
SRI Pekka Rinne .75 2.00
SRK Ryan Kesler .75 2.00
SRM Ryan Miller .75 2.00
SRN Ryan Nugent-Hopkins 1.00 2.50
SRS Ryan Smyth .60 1.50
SSA Joe Sakic 1.50 4.00
SSC Sidney Crosby 3.00 8.00
SSE Tyler Seguin 1.00 2.50
SSG Sam Gagner .50 1.25
SSP Jason Spezza .75 2.00
SSS Steven Stamkos 1.50 4.00
SSU P.K. Subban 1.00 2.50
SSW Stephen Weiss .60 1.50
STA John Tavares 1.25 3.00
STD Tie Domi .60 1.50
STH Taylor Hall .75 2.00
STM Tyler Myers .50 1.25
STR Tuukka Rask 1.00 2.50
STS Teemu Selanne 1.50 4.00
STV Thomas Vanek .60 1.50
SWE Shea Weber .60 1.50
SWG Wayne Gretzky 5.00 12.00
SZC Zdeno Chara .75 2.00
SZP Zach Parise .75 2.00

2013-14 O-Pee-Chee Team Canada Signatures

TCAH Adam Henrique B 30.00 60.00
TCAP Alex Pietrangelo B 20.00 50.00
TCAT Alex Tanguay C 12.00 30.00
TCCA Carter Ashton D 4.00 10.00
TCCD Calvin de Haan E 4.00 10.00
TCCE Cody Eakin E 4.00 10.00
TCCS Chris Stewart D 5.00 12.00
TCDH Dale Hawerchuk B 30.00 60.00
TCDO Dylan Olsen B 15.00 40.00
TCDP Dion Phaneuf B 15.00 40.00
TCJB Jamie Benn B 25.00 50.00
TCJH Josh Harding E 6.00 15.00
TCJT John Tavares C 30.00 60.00
TCKA Keith Aulie E 4.00 10.00
TCLL Louis Leblanc D 4.00 10.00
TCMF Marcus Foligno C 15.00 40.00
TCMH Matthew Halischuk E 4.00 10.00
TCMR Mike Ribeiro E 4.00 10.00
TCMS Martin St. Louis C 20.00 50.00
TCRE Ryan Ellis E 5.00 12.00
TCRN Ryan Nugent-Hopkins A 100.00 175.00
TCSC Sean Couturier B 25.00 50.00
TCSM Shawn Matthias E 5.00 12.00
TCSS Steven Stamkos B 30.00 80.00
TCTM Tyler Myers D 4.00 10.00
TCWC Wendel Clark C 40.00 80.00
TCWG Wayne Gretzky A 300.00 800.00
TCZK Zack Kassian D 8.00 20.00

2013-14 O-Pee-Chee Team Logo Patches

TL101 NHL alternate 10.00 25.00
TL102 All-Star Game 80-81 primary 12.00 30.00
TL103 All-Star Game 90-91 primary 12.00 30.00
TL104 NHL Draft 06 primary 12.00 30.00
TL105 NHL Draft 12 primary 10.00 25.00
TL106 Winter Classic primary 10.00 25.00
TL107 Atl. Thrashers primary 10.00 25.00
TL108 Boston Bruins primary 15.00 40.00
TL109 Boston Bruins alt 12.00 30.00
TL110 Buffalo Sabres primary 10.00 25.00
TL111 Calgary Flames primary 10.00 25.00
TL112 Calgary Flames alt 10.00 25.00
TL113 Blue Jackets primary 10.00 25.00
TL114 Blue Jackets alt 10.00 25.00
TL115 Red Wings Hockeytown 40.00 40.00
TL116 Edmonton Oilers primary 12.00 30.00
TL117 Edmonton Oilers alt 15.00 40.00
TL118 Harford Whalers primary 12.00 30.00
TL119 Harford Whalers script 12.00 30.00
TL120 L.A. Kings primary 12.00 30.00
TL121 L.A. Kings primary 15.00 40.00
TL122 North Stars alt 15.00 40.00
TL123 Montreal Canadiens alt 20.00 50.00
TL124 Nash Predators primary 10.00 25.00
TL125 Nash Predators alt 10.00 25.00
TL126 NJ Devils primary 10.00 25.00
TL127 N.Y. Islanders alt 10.00 25.00
TL128 N.Y. Islanders primary 10.00 25.00
TL129 N.Y. Rangers alt 12.00 30.00
TL130 Ottaway Senators alt 10.00 25.00
TL131 Ottaway Senators primary 10.00 25.00
TL132 Flyers script 10.00 25.00
TL133 Flyers alt 15.00 40.00
TL134 Phoenix Coyotes alt 10.00 25.00
TL135 Phoenix Coyotes alt 10.00 25.00
TL136 Penguins primary 10.00 25.00
TL137 Penguins script 10.00 25.00
TL138 Que Nordiques alt 15.00 40.00
TL139 Que Nordiques alt 12.00 30.00
TL140 S.J. Sharks primary 10.00 25.00
TL141 St. Louis Blues primary 12.00 30.00
TL142 St. Louis Blues alt 12.00 30.00
TL143 T.B. Lighting primary 10.00 25.00
TL144 Maple Leafs primary 12.00 30.00
TL145 Maple Leafs secondary 12.00 30.00
TL146 Canucks primary 12.00 30.00
TL147 Canucks alt 15.00 40.00
TL148 Capitals primary 15.00 40.00
TL149 Winnipeg Jets alt 12.00 30.00
TL150 Winnipeg Jets primary 12.00 30.00
TL151 Buffalo Sabres 25ANN 30.00 60.00
TL152 Calgary Flames 25ANN 20.00 40.00
TL153 Edmonton Oilers 25ANN 25.00 50.00
TL154 L.A. Kings 30ANN 15.00 40.00
TL155 N.J. Devils 25ANN 20.00 40.00
TL156 N.Y. Islanders 25ANN 20.00 40.00
TL157 Flyers 40ANN 60.00 100.00
TL158 Penguins 25ANN 25.00 50.00
TL159 St. Louis Blues 25ANN 30.00 60.00
TL160 Canucks 25ANN 20.00 40.00
TL161 Canucks 40ANN 20.00 40.00
TL162 Capitals 25ANN 25.00 50.00
TL163 Golden Seals alt 40.00 100.00
TL164 Golden Seals primary 40.00 80.00
TL165 Cleveland Barons primary 30.00 60.00
TL166 CO Rockies alt 15.00 40.00
TL167 CO Rockies script 30.00 60.00
TL168 L.A. Kings alt 40.00 80.00
TL169 Penguins primary 25.00 50.00
TL170 Canucks alt 25.00 50.00
TL171 Boston Bruins primary 50.00 100.00
TL172 Blackhawks primary 30.00 60.00
TL173 N.Y. Rangers primary 35.00 60.00
TL174 Maple Leafs primary 35.00 60.00
TL175 Maple Leafs secondary 25.00 50.00
TL176 Maple Leafs primary 30.00 60.00
TL177 Boston Bruins primary 40.00 80.00
TL178 Boston Bruins primary 75.00 125.00
TL179 Blackhawks primary 75.00 125.00
TL180 Red Wings primary 100.00 200.00
TL182 Canadiens primary 60.00 120.00
TL183 Canadiens alt 60.00 120.00
TL184 Canadiens primary 60.00 120.00
TL185 N.Y. Americans primary 60.00 100.00
TL186 N.Y. Americans primary 60.00 100.00
TL187 Maple Leafs secondary 75.00 150.00
TL188 Toronto St. Pats primary 60.00 100.00
TL189 Brooklyn Americans primary 125.00250.00
TL190 Detroit Cougars alt 150.00 250.00
TL191 Detroit Falcons primary 50.00 125.00
TL192 Wanderers primary 150.00 250.00
TL193 Quakers primary 150.00 250.00

TL194 Pirates primary 150.00 250.00
TL195 Pirates alt 150.00 300.00
TL196 Toronto St. Pats primary 150.00 250.00

2014-15 O-Pee-Chee

1 Martin Brodeur .50 1.25
2 Teemu Selanne .40 1.00
3 Jean-Sebastien Giguere .20 .50
4 Daniel Alfredsson .20 .50
5 Jaromir Jagr .60 1.50
6 Jarret Stoll .15 .40
7 Andrew Ference .12 .30
8 Chris Kreider .25 .60
9 P.K. Subban .25 .60
10 Brent Seabrook .12 .30
11 Milan Lucic .20 .50
12 Ryan Garbutt .12 .30
13 Bobby Ryan .15 .40
14 Dany Heatley .15 .40
15 Mark Letestu .15 .40
16 Oliver Ekman-Larsson .20 .50
17 Tyler Ennis .12 .30
18 Sean Monahan .12 .30
19 Cam Ward .20 .50
20 Sean Bergenheim .12 .30
21 Kyle Palmieri .15 .40
22 Craig Smith .12 .30
23 Tom Sestito .12 .30
24 Jarome Iginla .25 .60
25 Olli Jokinen .15 .40
26 Teddy Purcell .12 .30
27 Mason Raymond .12 .30
28 Mikkel Boedker .12 .30
29 Jamie McGinn .12 .30
30 Ryan McDonagh .12 .30
31 Rich Peverley .20 .50
32 Marian Hossa .20 .50
33 Calvin de Haan .12 .30
34 Viktor Fasth .15 .40
35 Max Pacioretty .20 .50
36 Marcel Goc .12 .30
37 Jonas Brodin .12 .30
38 Pavel Datsyuk .30 .75
39 Luke Schenn .20 .50
40 Tyler Toffoli .20 .50
41 Carl Hagelin .12 .30
42 Joe Thornton .30 .75
43 Andy Greene .12 .30
44 Brock Nelson .20 .50
45 Alexander Ovechkin .75 2.00
46 Elias Lindholm .20 .50
47 Sven Baertschi .12 .30
48 Jimmy Hayes .12 .30
49 Alex Pietrangelo .15 .40
50 Marc-Andre Fleury .40 1.00
51 Brian Flynn .12 .30
52 Nathan Horton .20 .50
53 Nino Niederreiter .12 .30
54 Alex Killorn .12 .30
55 Zdeno Chara .20 .50
56 Ben Smith .15 .40
57 Frederik Andersen .25 .60
58 Jordan Eberle .20 .50
59 Shawn Matthias .12 .30
60 Radim Vrbata .12 .30
61 Ryan O'Reilly .20 .50
62 Dustin Brown .20 .50
63 Alex Chiasson .15 .40
64 Roman Josi .20 .50
65 Jonas Gustavsson .15 .40
66 Jiri Hudler .15 .40
67 Wayne Simmonds .25 .60
68 Chris Stewart .15 .40
69 Brandon Pirri .12 .30
70 Lubomir Visnovsky .12 .30
71 Vladimir Tarasenko .25 .60
72 Andrei Markov .15 .40
73 Jordan Staal .15 .40
74 Tommy Wingels .12 .30
75 Darcy Kuemper .20 .50
76 Jake Gardiner .12 .30
77 Michael Ryder .12 .30
78 Brandon Dubinsky .12 .30
79 Mats Zuccarello-Aasen .20 .50
80 Jared Cowen .12 .30
81 Mike Green .15 .40
82 Tobias Enstrom .12 .30
83 Ondrej Palat .15 .40
84 Corey Perry .30 .75
85 Alexandre Burrows .12 .30
86 Alexei Emelin .12 .30
87 David Krejci .20 .50
88 Viktor Stalberg .12 .30
89 Antoine Vermette .12 .30
90 Ladislav Smid .12 .30
91 Ben Scrivens .15 .40
92 P.A. Parenteau .12 .30
93 Dwight King .12 .30
94 Zemgus Girgensons .15 .40
95 Jamie Benn .20 .50
96 David Legwand .15 .40
97 Matt Niskanen .12 .30
98 Matt Read .15 .40
99 Joffrey Lupul .12 .30
100 Justin Faulk .15 .40
101 Nick Bjugstad .12 .30
102 Evgeni Nabokov .15 .40
103 Bryan Bickell .12 .30
104 Artem Anisimov .12 .30
105 Matt Irwin .12 .30
106 Alex Galchenyuk .12 .30
107 Derick Brassard .12 .30
108 Cam Fowler .20 .50
109 Patrik Elias .20 .50
110 Ryan Smyth .15 .40
111 Mikko Koivu .15 .40
112 Zack Smith .12 .30
113 Andrew Ladd .12 .30
114 Jaroslav Halak .15 .40
115 Nate Thompson .12 .30
116 Michael Del Zotto .12 .30
117 Shane Doan .15 .40
118 Jaden Schwartz .25 .60
119 Sergei Gonchar .12 .30
120 Maxime Talbot .12 .30
121 Mike Santorelli .12 .30
122 Eric Staal .25 .60
123 Chad Johnson .15 .40
124 Dennis Wideman .12 .30
125 Cory Conacher .12 .30
126 Brayden Schenn .20 .50
127 Niklas Kronwall .15 .40
128 Sidney Crosby .75 2.00
129 Trevor Lewis .12 .30
130 James Reimer .20 .50
131 James Wisniewski .12 .30
132 Tomas Fleischmann .12 .30
133 Daniel Briere .15 .40
134 Andrew Shaw .15 .40
135 Ryan Ellis .12 .30
136 Frans Nielsen .12 .30
137 Ben Lovejoy .12 .30
138 Tomas Hertl .20 .50
139 Erik Karlsson .25 .60
140 Brian Boyle .12 .30
141 Michael Frolik .12 .30
142 Nick Holden .12 .30
143 Brooks Laich .12 .30
144 Andrej Sekera .12 .30
145 Brian Elliott .15 .40
146 Erik Cole .12 .30
147 Gabriel Bourque .15 .40
148 Danny DeKeyser .12 .30
149 Jussi Jokinen .12 .30
150 Scott Hartnell .12 .30
151 Tuukka Rask .25 .60
152 Jannik Hansen .15 .40
153 Tyler Bozak .12 .30
154 Al Montoya .12 .30
155 Josh Gorges .12 .30
156 Marian Gaborik .20 .50
157 Drew Stafford .12 .30
158 Jack Johnson .12 .30
159 Zach Parise .20 .50
160 Pat Maroon .12 .30
161 Derek Stepan .12 .30
162 Ryan Malone .12 .30
163 Kyle Okposo .12 .30
164 Nathan MacKinnon .75 2.00
165 Roberto Luongo .30 .75
166 Kyle Turris .20 .50
167 Patrik Berglund .12 .30
168 Adam Henrique .15 .40
169 Ryan Jones .12 .30
170 Patrick Kane .40 1.00
171 Martin Havlat .15 .40
172 Alex Goligoski .15 .40
173 Joe Colborne .12 .30
174 Eric Fehr .12 .30
175 Andrej Meszaros .12 .30
176 Pascal Dupuis .12 .30
177 Willie Mitchell .12 .30
178 Eddie Lack .15 .40
179 Vincent Lecavalier .20 .50
180 Mark Stuart .12 .30
181 Rene Bourque .12 .30
182 Riley Nash .12 .30
183 Ryan Suter .15 .40
184 Nick Spaling .12 .30
185 Ryan Murray .12 .30
186 Ryan Callahan .12 .30
187 Milan Michalek .12 .30
188 Matt Beleskey .12 .30
189 Tanner Pearson .12 .30
190 Lee Stempniak .12 .30
191 Alexander Steen .12 .30
192 Mike Ribeiro .12 .30
193 Tyson Barrie .12 .30
194 Torey Krug .15 .40
195 Cory Schneider .20 .50
196 Nick Leddy .12 .30
197 Tyler Kennedy .12 .30
198 Jonathan Huberdeau .25 .60
199 Jonathan Ericsson .12 .30
200 Matt Stajan .12 .30
201 Cody Hodgson .12 .30
202 Nicklas Backstrom .20 .50
203 Martin Jones .15 .40
204 Brian Gionta .12 .30
205 Drayson Bowman .12 .30
206 Alexander Edler .12 .30
207 Ryan Nugent-Hopkins .25 .60
208 Chris Neil .12 .30
209 Henrik Lundqvist .50 1.25
210 Brenden Dillon .12 .30
211 Mikael Granlund .15 .40
212 Cam Atkinson .20 .50
213 Carter Hutton .15 .40
214 Sami Vatanen .12 .30
215 Sean Couturier .12 .30
216 Thomas Greiss .15 .40
217 James Neal .12 .30
218 Steve Ott .12 .30
219 J.T. Brown .12 .30
220 Erik Johnson .12 .30
221 Tuomo Ruutu .12 .30
222 Daniel Paille .12 .30
223 Justin Braun .12 .30
224 Michael Cammalleri .15 .40
225 James van Riemsdyk .15 .40
226 Slava Voynov .20 .50
227 Aleksander Barkov .30 .75
228 Marcus Foligno .12 .30
229 Zach Bogosian .15 .40
230 Casey Cizikas .12 .30
231 Peter Budaj .15 .40
232 Martin St. Louis .20 .50
233 Jiri Tlusty .12 .30
234 Niklas Hjalmarsson .12 .30
235 Jeff Petry .20 .50
236 Dustin Penner .12 .30
237 Eric Nystrom .12 .30
238 Kari Lehtonen .15 .40
239 Brenden Morrow .15 .40
240 Matthieu Perreault .12 .30
241 Boone Jenner .20 .50
242 Steve Mason .15 .40
243 Gustav Nyquist .12 .30
244 Marco Scandella .12 .30
245 Martin Erat .12 .30
246 Paul Martin .12 .30
247 Ryane Clowe .12 .30
248 Curtis Glencross .12 .30
249 Loui Eriksson .12 .30
250 Ales Hemsky .12 .30
251 Cody McLeod .12 .30
252 Anze Kopitar .30 .75
253 Chris Higgins .12 .30
254 Erik Gudbranson .12 .30
255 Jhonas Enroth .12 .30
256 Jonathan Toews .30 .75
257 Evander Kane .20 .50
258 David Desharnais .12 .30
259 Patrick Dwyer .12 .30
260 John Moore .12 .30
261 Valeri Nichushkin .20 .50
262 Jakob Silfverberg .12 .30
263 Boyd Gordon .12 .30
264 Fedor Tyutin .12 .30
265 Valtteri Filppula .12 .30
266 Antti Niemi .15 .40
267 Anders Lee .20 .50
268 John Carlson .12 .30
269 Paul Bissonnette .12 .30
270 Johan Franzen .15 .40
271 Matt Bartkowski .12 .30
272 Phil Kessel .20 .50
273 John Mitchell .12 .30
274 Travis Zajac .12 .30
275 Matt Moulson .12 .30
276 Colin Wilson .12 .30
277 Mark Giordano .20 .50
278 Mark Streit .12 .30
279 Mike Richards .15 .40
280 Tom Gilbert .12 .30
281 Robin Lehner .15 .40
282 Kevin Shattenkirk .12 .30
283 Devin Setoguchi .15 .40
284 Andre Benoit .12 .30
285 Daniel Sedin .25 .60
286 Ryan Murphy .12 .30
287 Kris Versteeg .12 .30
288 Brooks Orpik .12 .30
289 Ville Leino .15 .40
290 Nick Foligno .15 .40
291 Anton Stralman .12 .30
292 Ray Whitney .15 .40
293 Victor Hedman .25 .60
294 Mark Arcobello .12 .30
295 Tomas Plekanec .12 .30
296 Hampus Lindholm .12 .30
297 Jim Howard .25 .60
298 Patrick Marleau .20 .50
299 Matt Martin .12 .30
300 Adam McQuaid .12 .30
301 Mikael Backlund .15 .40
302 Josh Harding .15 .40
303 Lauri Korpikoski .12 .30
304 David Clarkson .12 .30
305 Troy Brouwer .12 .30
306 Kimmo Timonen .12 .30
307 Jason Spezza .20 .50
308 Dainius Zubrus .12 .30
309 Christopher Tanev .12 .30
310 Matt Cullen .12 .30
311 Dylan Olsen .12 .30
312 Michal Neuvirth .15 .40
313 Brandon Saad .15 .40
314 Vladimir Sobotka .12 .30
315 Jake Muzzin .20 .50
316 Bryan Little .12 .30
317 Steven Stamkos .40 1.00
318 Brad Richards .20 .50
319 Tim Thomas .20 .50
320 Craig Adams .12 .30
321 Anton Belov .20 .50
322 Thomas Vanek .15 .40
323 Carl Soderberg .12 .30
324 Marc-Edouard Vlasic .12 .30
325 Matt Calvert .12 .30
326 Brendan Smith .12 .30
327 Braden Holtby .25 .60
328 Charlie Coyle .20 .50
329 Colin Greening .12 .30
330 Jeff Skinner .25 .60
331 Saku Koivu .20 .50
332 Carl Gunnarsson .12 .30
333 Paul Stastny .15 .40
334 Michael Raffl .12 .30
335 Antti Raanta .20 .50
336 Thomas Hickey .12 .30
337 Henrik Sedin .25 .60
338 Justin Schultz .15 .40
339 Brad Boyes .12 .30
340 T.J. Oshie .20 .50
341 Martin Hanzal .12 .30
342 Seth Jones .20 .50
343 Kris Russell .12 .30
344 Benoit Pouliot .12 .30
345 Blake Wheeler .20 .50
346 Radko Gudas .12 .30
347 Alex Stalock .15 .40
348 Mark Pysyk .12 .30
349 Kris Letang .25 .60
350 Reilly Smith .20 .50
351 Justin Williams .15 .40
352 Eric Gelinas .15 .40
353 Carey Price .40 1.00
354 Ryan Johansen .15 .40
355 Karl Alzner .12 .30
356 Jordie Benn .15 .40
357 Matt Duchene .20 .50
358 Clarke MacArthur .12 .30
359 Derek Roy .12 .30
360 Kyle Quincey .12 .30
361 Morgan Rielly .20 .50
362 Anton Khudobin .20 .50
363 Rob Klinkhammer .12 .30
364 David Perron .15 .40
365 Erik Haula .12 .30
366 Ryan Kesler .20 .50
367 Johnny Oduya .15 .40
368 Cal Clutterbuck .20 .50
369 T.J. Brodie .15 .40
370 Braydon Coburn .12 .30
371 Ondrej Pavelec .20 .50
372 Chris Kunitz .20 .50
373 Nick Bonino .12 .30
374 Patric Hornqvist .12 .30
375 Rick Nash .20 .50
376 Dan Boyle .12 .30
377 Robyn Regehr .12 .30
378 Richard Panik .12 .30
379 Brendan Gallagher .20 .50
380 Mika Zibanejad .25 .60
381 Marek Zidlicky .12 .30
382 Derek Morris .12 .30
383 Drew Miller .12 .30
384 Joel Ward .12 .30
385 Antoine Roussel .12 .30
386 Sergei Bobrovsky .30 .75
387 Dougie Hamilton .15 .40
388 Nikolai Kulemin .12 .30
389 Patrick Sharp .12 .30
390 Joe Pavelski .25 .60
391 Jared Spurgeon .20 .50
392 Henrik Tallinder .12 .30
393 David Backes .15 .40
394 Ben Bishop .15 .40
395 Jason Garrison .12 .30
396 Alexander Semin .20 .50
397 Dmitry Kulikov .12 .30
398 Claude Giroux .20 .50
399 Dustin Byfuglien .20 .50
400 Nail Yakupov .12 .30
401 Marc Staal .12 .30
402 Karri Ramo .15 .40
403 Damien Brunner .12 .30
404 Jan Hejda .12 .30
405 Dave Bolland .12 .30
406 Cody Ceci .12 .30
407 Michael Grabner .15 .40
408 Corey Crawford .25 .60
409 Logan Couture .25 .60
410 David Moss .12 .30
411 Mikhail Grabovski .12 .30
412 Cody Eakin .12 .30
413 Patrice Bergeron .25 .60
414 Tomas Tatar .12 .30
415 Lars Eller .12 .30
416 Evgeni Malkin .40 1.00
417 Ryan Miller .20 .50
418 Matt Cooke .12 .30
419 Andrew Cogliano .12 .30
420 Mike Fisher .12 .30
421 Nikita Kucherov .40 1.00
422 Steve Downie .12 .30
423 Drew Doughty .25 .60
424 Jamie McBain .12 .30
425 David Jones .12 .30
426 Semyon Varlamov .20 .50
427 Chris Phillips .12 .30
428 Zack Kassian .12 .30
429 Dion Phaneuf .15 .40
430 Marcus Kruger .12 .30
431 Brian Campbell .12 .30
432 Mark Scheifele .30 .75
433 Jason Demers .12 .30
434 Tom Wilson .20 .50
435 Brandon Sutter .12 .30
436 Taylor Hall .20 .50
437 Cam Talbot .20 .50
438 Shea Weber .15 .40
439 Ryan Strome .20 .50
440 Steve Bernier .12 .30
441 Henrik Zetterberg .25 .60
442 Jason Pominville .12 .30
443 R.J. Umberger .12 .30
444 Matt Carle .12 .30
445 Jonas Hiller .15 .40
446 Nazem Kadri .25 .60
447 Brandon Prust .12 .30
448 Ron Hainsey .12 .30
449 Johnny Boychuk .15 .40
450 Jeff Carter .15 .40
451 Jakub Voracek .15 .40
452 Brandon Bollig .15 .40
453 Olli Maatta .12 .30
454 Craig Anderson .20 .50
455 Jesse Winchester .12 .30
456 Barret Jackman .12 .30
457 Brent Burns .20 .50
458 Trevor Daley .12 .30
459 Dan Hamhuis .12 .30
460 Tyler Johnson .12 .30
461 Christian Ehrhoff .12 .30
462 Jason Chimera .12 .30
463 Jacob Trouba .15 .40
464 Bryce Salvador .12 .30
465 Gabriel Landeskog .25 .60
466 Pekka Rinne .20 .50
467 Sam Gagner .12 .30
468 Keith Yandle .12 .30
469 Rob Scuderi .12 .30
470 Justin Fontaine .15 .40
471 T.J. Galiardi .12 .30
472 David Savard .12 .30
473 Daniel Girardi .12 .30
474 Andrew MacDonald .12 .30
475 Josh Bailey .15 .40
476 Ryan Getzlaf .20 .50
477 Justin Abdelkader .15 .40
478 Jonathan Bernier .15 .40
479 Nathan Gerbe .12 .30
480 Jay Bouwmeester .12 .30
481 Duncan Keith .15 .40
482 Kevin Bieksa .12 .30
483 Scottie Upshall .12 .30
484 Mike Smith .20 .50
485 Grant Clitsome .12 .30
486 Brad Marchand .40 1.00
487 Sami Salo .12 .30
488 Marc Methot .12 .30
489 Tyler Seguin .25 .60
490 Andrew Desjardins .12 .30
491 John Tavares .30 .75
492 Cody Franson .12 .30
493 Marcus Johansson .15 .40
494 Jonathan Quick .25 .60
495 Tyler Myers .12 .30
496 Checklist 1 .12 .30
497 Checklist 2 .12 .30
498 Checklist 3 .12 .30
499 Checklist 4 .12 .30
500 Checklist 5 .12 .30
501 Andrey Makarov RC 1.25 3.00
502 Adam Pageri RC 1.00 2.50
503 Ty Rattie RC 1.25 3.00
504 Jake McCabe RC 1.25 3.00
505 Vincent Trocheck RC 2.50 6.00
506 Pal Carey RC .75 2.00
507 Teuvo Teravainen RC 2.00 5.00
508 Oscar Klefbom RC 2.50 6.00
509 Laurent Brossoit RC 1.25 3.00
510 Connor Knapp RC .75 2.00
511 Calle Jarnkrok RC 1.25 3.00
512 Brandon Gormley RC 1.25 3.00
513 Andrew Campbell RC 1.00 2.50
514 Markus Granlund RC 2.00 5.00
515 Joonas Nattinen RC 1.25 3.00
516 Landon Ferraro RC .75 2.00
517 Phil Varone RC 1.00 2.50
518 Nicolas Deschamps RC 1.25 3.00
519 Cedric Paquette RC 1.25 3.00
520 Bill Arnold RC 1.00 2.50
521 Alexander Khokhlachev RC 1.25 3.00
522 Patrik Nemeth RC 1.25 3.00
523 Kristers Gudlevskis RC 1.25 3.00
524 Jonathan Racine RC 1.25 3.00
525 Corban Knight RC 1.25 3.00
526 Simon Moser RC .75 2.00
527 Matt Carey RC 1.00 2.50
528 Petter Granberg RC 1.00 2.50
529 Andrew Hammond RC 2.00 5.00
530 Nathan Lieuwen RC 1.25 3.00
531 Joey Hishon RC 1.50 4.00
532 Joni Ortio RC 1.50 4.00
533 Evgeny Kuznetsov RC 3.00 8.00
534 Mitch Callahan RC .75 2.00
535 Kellan Lain RC .75 2.00
536 Greg McKegg RC 1.00 2.50
537 Christian Folin RC 1.00 2.50
538 Matt Lindblad RC 1.00 2.50
539 Colton Sissons RC 1.25 3.00
540 Peter LeBlanc RC .75 2.00
541 Johan Sundstrom RC 1.25 3.00
542 Scott Mayfield RC 1.00 2.50
543 Tyler Wotherspoon RC 1.25 3.00
544 Johnny Gaudreau RC 8.00 20.00
545 Teemu Pulkkinen RC 1.50 4.00
546 Vladislav Namestnikov RC 2.00 5.00
547 Ryan Sproul RC 1.25 3.00
548 Mike Halmo RC .75 2.00
549 Joe Whitney RC .75 2.00
550 Mark Visentin RC 1.25 3.00
551 Rogie Vachon 1.25 3.00
552 Brian Bellows .75 2.00
553 Scotty Bowman 1.00 2.50
554 John LeClair 1.00 2.50
555 Steve Yzerman 2.50 6.00
556 Olaf Kolzig 1.00 2.50
557 Mike Bossy 1.00 2.50
558 Phil Esposito 1.50 4.00
559 Mike Modano 1.50 4.00
560 Guy Carbonneau 1.00 2.50
561 Adam Oates 1.00 2.50
562 Brian Leetch .75 2.00
563 Trevor Linden 1.00 2.50
564 Guy Lafleur 1.25 3.00
565 Bill Guerin 1.00 2.50
566 Jeremy Roenick 1.50 4.00
567 Bobby Hull 2.00 5.00
568 Bill Ranford 1.00 2.50
569 Tony Esposito 1.00 2.50
570 Stan Mikita 1.25 3.00
571 Bobby Orr 2.50 6.00
572 Rob Brown .75 2.00
573 Doug Harvey 1.00 2.50
574 Al MacInnis 1.25 3.00
575 Felix Potvin 1.50 4.00
576 Doug Gilmour 1.25 3.00
577 Mike Richter 1.00 2.50
578 Arturs Irbe .75 2.00
579 Jean Beliveau 1.00 2.50
580 Nicklas Lidstrom 1.00 2.50
581 Grant Fuhr 1.50 4.00
582 Pierre Turgeon .75 2.00
583 Dominik Hasek 1.50 4.00
584 Joe Sakic 2.00 5.00
585 Ray Bourque 1.50 4.00
586 Mike Gartner 1.25 3.00
587 Wayne Gretzky 6.00 15.00
588 Vincent Damphousse .75 2.00
589 Ron Francis 1.25 3.00
590 Patrick Roy 2.50 6.00
591 Jari Kurri 1.00 2.50
592 Larry Robinson 1.00 2.50
593 Dwayne Roloson .60 1.50
594 Doug Wilson .75 2.00
595 Richard Brodeur 1.00 2.50
596 Darryl Sittler 1.25 3.00
597 Terry O'Reilly .75 2.00
598 Eric Lindros 1.50 4.00
599 Peter Forsberg 2.00 5.00
600 Checklist .40 1.00
601 Sidney Crosby AW 20.00 50.00
602 Sidney Crosby AW 20.00 50.00
603 Tuukka Rask AW 6.00 15.00
604 Duncan Keith AW 4.00 10.00
605 Alex Ovechkin AW 20.00 50.00
606 Nathan MacKinnon AW 20.00 50.00
607 Patrice Bergeron AW 6.00 15.00
608 Justin Williams AW 4.00 10.00
609 Sidney Crosby AW 20.00 50.00
610 Wayne Gretzky AT 60.00 150.00
611 Nicklas Lidstrom AT 10.00 25.00
612 Jean Beliveau AT 10.00 25.00
613 Mario Lemieux AT 40.00 100.00
614 Dominik Hasek AT 15.00 40.00
615 Mike Bossy AT 10.00 25.00
616 Bobby Orr AT 40.00 100.00
617 Patrick Roy AT 25.00 60.00
618 Wayne Gretzky GO 50.00 125.00

2014-15 O-Pee-Chee Rainbow

*1-500 VETS: 2.5X TO 6X BASIC CARDS
*501-550 ROOKIES: .5X TO 1.2X BASIC RC
*551-600 LEGEND.6 TO 1.5X BASIC LGD
202 Nicklas Backstrom 1.50 4.00
544 Johnny Gaudreau 10.00 25.00

2014-15 O-Pee-Chee Red

*1-500 VETS: 5X TO 12X BASIC CARDS
*501-550 ROOKIES: 1X TO 2.5X BASIC CARDS
*551-600 LEGEND: 2X TO 5X BASIC LEG
202 Nicklas Backstrom 3.00 8.00
408 Corey Crawford 4.00 10.00
544 Johnny Gaudreau 15.00 40.00
571 Bobby Orr 30.00 60.00
587 Wayne Gretzky 30.00 60.00

2014-15 O-Pee-Chee Retro

*1-500 VETS: 2X TO 5X BASIC CARDS
*501-550 ROOK: .5X TO 1.2X BASIC RC
*551-600 LEGEND: .6X TO 1.5X BASIC LGD
202 Nicklas Backstrom 1.25 3.00
408 Corey Crawford 1.50 4.00

2014-15 O-Pee-Chee Black Rainbow

*1-500 VETS/100: 6X TO 15X BASIC CARDS
*501-550 ROOK/100: 1.2X TO 3X BASIC RC
*551-600 LGD/100: 2X TO 5X BASIC LGD
202 Nicklas Backstrom 4.00 10.00
544 Johnny Gaudreau 20.00 50.00
587 Wayne Gretzky 20.00 50.00
590 Patrick Roy 12.00 30.00

2014-15 O-Pee-Chee 3-D

1 Jaromir Jagr 100.00 250.00
2 Pavel Datsyuk 50.00 125.00
3 Carey Price 60.00 150.00
4 Evgeni Malkin 60.00 150.00
5 Steve Yzerman 80.00 200.00
6 Alex Ovechkin 125.00 300.00
7 Jonathan Toews 50.00 120.00
8 Jordan Eberle 30.00 80.00
9 Arturs Irbe 25.00 60.00
10 P.K. Subban 40.00 100.00
11 Rick Nash 30.00 80.00
12 Bobby Orr 125.00 300.00
13 Anze Kopitar 50.00 125.00
14 Henrik Zetterberg 40.00 100.00
15 Ryan Nugent-Hopkins 40.00 100.00
16 Bobby Hull 60.00 150.00
17 Brett Hull 60.00 150.00
18 Martin Brodeur 80.00 200.00
19 Curtis Joseph 40.00 100.00
20 Wayne Gretzky 200.00 500.00
21 Mario Lemieux 125.00 300.00
22 Ryan Miller 30.00 80.00
23 Sidney Crosby 125.00 300.00
24 Nathan MacKinnon 125.00 300.00
25 Pavel Bure 40.00 100.00
26 Felix Potvin 50.00 125.00
27 Phil Kessel 30.00 80.00
28 Teemu Selanne 60.00 150.00
29 Shea Weber 25.00 60.00
30 Erik Karlsson 40.00 100.00
31 Steven Stamkos 60.00 150.00
32 Taylor Hall 30.00 80.00
33 Jonathan Quick 30.00 80.00
34 Henrik Lundqvist 80.00 200.00
35 Mats Sundin 30.00 80.00
36 John Tavares 50.00 125.00
37 Ryan Getzlaf 30.00 80.00
38 Ray Bourque 50.00 125.00
39 Patrick Roy 80.00 200.00
40 Joe Sakic 60.00 150.00
41 Patrick Kane 60.00 150.00
42 Zdeno Chara 30.00 80.00

2014-15 O-Pee-Chee Blaster Box Bottoms

AO Alexander Ovechkin B 2.00 5.00
CP Carey Price A 1.00 2.50
EM Evgeni Malkin A 1.00 2.50
HL Henrik Lundqvist B 1.25 3.00
JQ Jonathan Quick C .60 1.50
JT Jonathan Toews C .75 2.00

2014-15 O-Pee-Chee Mini Tall Boys

1 Erik Karlsson 5.00 12.00
2 Nazem Kadri 5.00 12.00
3 Martin Brodeur 10.00 25.00
4 Vladislav Namestnikov 4.00 10.00
5 Ryan Getzlaf 4.00 10.00
6 Carey Price 8.00 20.00
7 Alexander Ovechkin 15.00 40.00
8 P.K. Subban 5.00 12.00
9 Zdeno Chara 4.00 10.00
10 Jonathan Bernier 3.00 8.00
11 Phil Kessel 4.00 10.00
12 John Tavares 6.00 15.00
13 Pavel Datsyuk 6.00 15.00
14 Sidney Crosby 15.00 40.00
15 Steven Stamkos 8.00 20.00
16 Claude Giroux 4.00 10.00
17 Tuukka Rask 5.00 12.00
18 Ryan Miller 4.00 10.00
19 Patrick Kane 8.00 20.00
20 Nathan MacKinnon 8.00 20.00
21 Teemu Selanne 8.00 20.00
22 Taylor Hall 4.00 10.00
23 Valeri Nichushkin 2.00 5.00
24 Henrik Lundqvist 10.00 25.00
25 Jonathan Toews 6.00 15.00
26 Evgeny Kuznetsov 8.00 20.00
27 Evgeni Malkin 8.00 20.00
28 Jonathan Quick 5.00 12.00
29 Jaromir Jagr 12.00 30.00
30 Brandon Gormley 4.00 10.00
31 Brett Hull 12.50 25.00
32 Pavel Bure 6.00 15.00
33 Joe Sakic 8.00 20.00
34 Mario Lemieux 8.00 20.00
35 Mark Messier 10.00 25.00
36 Dominik Hasek 6.00 15.00
37 Arturs Irbe 4.00 10.00
38 Nicklas Lidstrom 4.00 10.00
39 Wayne Gretzky 30.00 60.00
40 Bobby Orr 25.00 50.00
41 Steve Yzerman 10.00 25.00
42 Patrick Roy 20.00 40.00

2014-15 O-Pee-Chee Retro Hobby Box Bottoms

AG Alex Galchenyuk B .15 .40
AO Alexander Ovechkin C 1.00 2.50
CG Claude Giroux B .25 .60
CP Carey Price A .50 1.25
EM Evgeni Malkin A .50 1.25
HL Henrik Lundqvist C .60 1.50
HZ Henrik Zetterberg D .30 .75
JQ Jonathan Quick D .30 .75
JT Jonathan Toews B .40 1.00
NM Nathan MacKinnon C 1.00 2.50
NY Nail Yakupov D .15 .40
PK Phil Kessel A .25 .60
RG Ryan Getzlaf C .25 .60
SS Steven Stamkos D .50 1.25
VT Vladimir Tarasenko A .30 .75
MAF Marc-Andre Fleury B .50 1.25

2014-15 O-Pee-Chee Signatures

SAL Alex Pietrangelo A 12.00 30.00
SAP Aaron Palushaj E 10.00 25.00
SCK Chris Kreider B 10.00 25.00
SDG Daniel Girardi E 5.00 12.00
SHE Milan Hejduk A 12.00 30.00
SHO Peter Holland E 5.00 12.00
SJA Justin Abdelkader C 6.00 15.00
SJB Jordie Benn E 5.00 12.00
SJF Justin Faulk C 6.00 15.00
SJG John Gibson E 8.00 20.00
SJO Johnny Oduya D 6.00 15.00
SJS Jack Skille E 6.00 15.00
SJT Jiri Tlusty B 5.00 12.00
SKS Kevin Shattenkirk D 5.00 12.00
SLS Luke Schenn A 8.00 20.00
SMH Martin Hanzal D 5.00 12.00
SMK Mike Kostka E 8.00 20.00
SML Maxim Lapierre E 5.00 12.00
SMP Magnus Paajarvi A 8.00 20.00
SNG Nathan Gerbe D 5.00 12.00
SPH Patric Hornqvist C 5.00 12.00
SRD Raphael Diaz E 5.00 12.00
SRE Ray Emery E 6.00 15.00
SSB Sergei Bobrovsky A 25.00 60.00
SSH Shawn Horcoff E 5.00 12.00
SSS Sheldon Souray E 5.00 12.00
STR Tuukka Rask B 10.00 25.00
STV Tomas Vokoun B 6.00 15.00

2014-15 O-Pee-Chee Sport Royalty Autographs

SRAIS Sidney Crosby 125.00 200.00

2014-15 O-Pee-Chee Stickers

ST1 Seth Jones .75 2.00
ST2 Pavel Bure .75 2.00
ST3 Henrik Zetterberg 1.00 2.50
ST4 Martin Brodeur 2.00 5.00
ST5 Patrick Kane 1.50 4.00
ST6 Corey Crawford 1.00 2.50
ST7 Martin St. Louis .75 2.00
ST8 Steven Stamkos 1.50 4.00
ST9 P.K. Subban 1.00 2.50
ST10 Jordan Eberle .75 2.00
ST11 Alex Galchenyuk .50 1.25
ST12 Duncan Keith .60 1.50
ST13 Joe Sakic 1.50 4.00
ST14 Bobby Hull 1.50 4.00
ST15 Marian Hossa .75 2.00
ST16 Luc Robitaille .75 2.00
ST17 Nail Yakupov .50 1.25
ST18 Erik Karlsson 1.00 2.50
ST19 Mario Lemieux 3.00 8.00
ST20 Marian Gaborik .75 2.00
ST21 Shea Weber .60 1.50
ST22 Sergei Bobrovsky 1.25 3.00
ST23 Peter Forsberg 1.50 4.00
ST24 Teuvo Teravainen 1.25 3.00
ST25 Darryl Sittler 1.00 2.50
ST26 Danny DeKeyser .50 1.25
ST27 Mark Messier 1.50 4.00
ST28 David Backes .50 1.25
ST29 Jonathan Bernier .60 1.50
ST30 Nathan MacKinnon 3.00 8.00
ST31 Brett Hull 1.50 4.00
ST32 Pekka Rinne .75 2.00
ST33 Curtis Joseph 1.00 2.50
ST34 Jacob Trouba .60 1.50
ST35 Tuukka Rask 1.00 2.50
ST36 Ron Francis 1.00 2.50
ST37 Mike Modano 1.25 3.00
ST38 Dominik Hasek 1.25 3.00
ST39 Jonas Hiller .60 1.50
ST40 Patrick Sharp .75 2.00
ST41 Bobby Clarke 1.25 3.00
ST42 Dustin Byfuglien .75 2.00
ST43 Jonathan Quick 1.00 2.50
ST44 Tyler Seguin 1.00 2.50
ST45 Tomas Hertl .75 2.00
ST46 Ray Bourque 1.25 3.00
ST47 John Tavares 1.25 3.00
ST48 Evgeny Kuznetsov 2.00 5.00
ST49 Zach Parise .75 2.00
ST50 Nazem Kadri 1.00 2.50
ST51 Ryan Miller .75 2.00
ST52 Ryan Nugent-Hopkins .75 2.00
ST53 Vladimir Tarasenko 1.25 3.00
ST54 Joe Pavelski .75 2.00
ST55 Mats Sundin .75 2.00
ST56 Roberto Luongo 1.25 3.00
ST57 James van Riemsdyk .60 1.50
ST58 Nicklas Lidstrom .75 2.00
ST59 Ryan Getzlaf .75 2.00
ST60 Joe Thornton 1.25 3.00
ST61 Steve Yzerman 2.00 5.00
ST62 Shane Doan .60 1.50
ST63 Jason Spezza .75 2.00
ST64 Ryan Suter .60 1.50
ST65 Patrick Roy 2.00 5.00
ST66 Mike Bossy .75 2.00
ST67 Matt Duchene .75 2.00
ST68 Antti Niemi .60 1.50
ST69 Carey Price 1.50 4.00
ST70 Phil Kessel .75 2.00
ST71 Marcel Dionne 1.00 2.50
ST72 Brandon Gormley .75 2.00
ST73 Teemu Selanne 1.50 4.00
ST74 Mike Gartner 1.00 2.50
ST75 Calle Jarnkrok .75 2.00
ST76 Claude Giroux .75 2.00
ST77 Henrik Lundqvist 2.00 5.00
ST78 Sidney Crosby 3.00 8.00
ST79 Cam Neely .75 2.00
ST80 Alexander Ovechkin 3.00 8.00
ST81 Taylor Hall .75 2.00
ST82 Jamie Benn .75 2.00
ST83 Patrice Bergeron 1.00 2.50
ST84 Evgeni Malkin 1.50 4.00
ST85 Evander Kane .75 2.00
ST86 Grant Fuhr .75 2.00

ST87 Brendan Gallagher .75 2.00
ST88 Ryan Kesler .75 2.00
ST89 Jonathan Toews 1.25 3.00
ST90 Vladislav Namestnikov 1.25 3.00
ST91 Arturs Irbe .60 1.50
ST92 Oscar Klefbom 1.50 4.00
ST93 Brian Leetch .60 1.50
ST94 Jaromir Jagr 2.50 6.00
ST95 Corey Perry 1.25 3.00
ST96 John LeClair .75 2.00
ST97 Sean Monahan .50 1.25
ST98 Pavel Datsyuk 1.25 3.00
ST99 Wayne Gretzky 5.00 12.00
ST100 Drew Doughty 1.00 2.50

2014-15 O-Pee-Chee Team Canada Signatures

TCSAB Alexandre Burrows D 6.00 15.00
TCSAH Adam Henrique A 8.00 20.00
TCSAL Andrew Ladd D 6.00 15.00
TCSBH Braden Holtby E 12.00 30.00
TCSBO Bobby Orr B 100.00 200.00
TCSBS Brayden Schenn E 10.00 25.00
TCSCK Chris Kunitz D 10.00 25.00
TCSDP Dion Phaneuf A 8.00 20.00
TCSGL Guy Lafleur A 12.00 30.00
TCSJB Jonathan Bernier D 8.00 20.00
TCSJG Jean-Sebastien Giguere A 10.00 25.00
TCSJT John Tavares B 15.00 40.00
TCSLA Guillaume Latendresse C 6.00 15.00
TCSLC Logan Couture A 12.00 30.00
TCSLR Larry Robinson B 10.00 25.00
TCSMH Matthew Halischuk E 6.00 15.00
TCSMR Mike Ribeiro C 6.00 15.00
TCSMS Martin St. Louis A 10.00 25.00
TCSMU Ryan Murray C 6.00 15.00
TCSRM Ryan Murphy D 6.00 15.00
TCSRT Raffi Torres E 6.00 15.00
TCSRV Rogie Vachon B 12.00 30.00
TCSSG Simon Gagne A 8.00 20.00
TCSSM Steve Mason A 8.00 20.00
TCSSS Steve Shutt B 8.00 20.00
TCSTP Teddy Purcell D 6.00 15.00
TCSWG Wayne Gretzky B 250.00 600.00

2014-15 O-Pee-Chee Team Logo Patches

201 NHL 2005-06 Alt 15.00 40.00
202 Eastern Conf primary 10.00 40.00
203 Western Conf. primary 10.00 40.00
204 Winter Classic primary 10.00 40.00
205 Ducks alt 10.00 40.00
206 Ducks alt 10.00 40.00
207 Thrashers Inaugural 10.00 40.00
208 Bruins alt 15.00 40.00
209 Sabres alt 10.00 40.00
210 Sabres script 10.00 40.00
211 Flames alt 10.00 40.00
212 Flames script 10.00 40.00
213 Hurricanes script 10.00 40.00
214 Blackhawks alt 10.00 40.00
215 Avalanche secondary 10.00 40.00
216 Avalanche script 10.00 40.00
217 Blue Jackets alt 10.00 40.00
218 Stars primary 10.00 40.00
219 Stars secondary 10.00 40.00
220 Red Wings primary 10.00 40.00
221 Oilers alt 10.00 40.00
222 Oilers alt 10.00 40.00
223 Panthers alt 10.00 40.00
224 Panthers secondary 10.00 40.00
225 Panthers secondary 10.00 40.00
226 Whalers alt 10.00 40.00
227 Kings primary 10.00 40.00
228 Wild Inaugural 10.00 40.00
229 Wild primary 10.00 40.00
230 Predators Inaugural 10.00 40.00
231 Predators alt 10.00 40.00
232 Predators alt 10.00 40.00
233 Predators secondary 10.00 40.00
234 Devils script 15.00 40.00
235 Islanders primary 10.00 40.00
236 Rangers alt 15.00 40.00
237 Senators alt 10.00 40.00
238 Senators alt 10.00 40.00
239 Coyotes Inaugural 10.00 40.00
240 Sharks green 10.00 40.00
241 Sharks white 10.00 40.00
242 Blues primary 10.00 40.00
243 Blues primary 10.00 40.00
244 Lightning primary 10.00 40.00
245 Maple Leafs alt 10.00 40.00
246 Canucks primary 10.00 40.00
247 Capitals primary 15.00 40.00
248 Capitals alt 10.00 40.00
249 Jets primary 10.00 40.00
250 Jets alt 15.00 40.00
251 Bruins 80th Anniv. 25.00 50.00
252 Bruins 90th Anniv. 30.00 60.00
253 Blackhawks 75th Anniv. 20.00 40.00
254 Red Wings 50th Anniv. 25.00 50.00
255 Red Wings 75th Anniv. 25.00 50.00
256 Canadiens 75th Anniv. 30.00 60.00
257 Canadiens 100th Anniv. 30.00 60.00
258 Rangers 85th Anniv. 25.00 50.00
259 Maple Leafs 50th Anniv. 25.00 50.00
260 Maple Leafs 75th Anniv. 25.00 50.00
261 NHL 75th Anniv. 20.00 40.00
262 Stanley Cup 100th Anniv. 25.00 50.00
263 NHL alt 20.00 50.00
264 Campbell Conf. primary 20.00 50.00
265 Wales Conf. primary 20.00 50.00
266 Bruins primary 30.00 60.00
267 Sabres primary 20.00 50.00
268 Golden Seals primary 50.00 100.00
269 Blackhawks alt 60.00 120.00
270 Blackhawks alt 60.00 100.00
271 Kings primary 30.00 60.00
272 Seals secondary 30.00 60.00
273 North Stars primary 50.00 100.00
274 Canadiens script 30.00 60.00
275 Rangers primary 50.00 100.00
276 Penguins primary 60.00 120.00
277 Maple Leafs alt 60.00 120.00
278 Maple Leafs primary 30.00 60.00
279 Bruins primary 60.00 150.00
280 Bruins primary 75.00 150.00
281 Cougars alt 100.00 200.00
282 Red Wings V for Victory 25.00 60.00
283 Canadiens primary 90.00 150.00
284 Canadiens primary 100.00 200.00
285 Maroons alt 75.00 150.00
286 Americans primary 40.00 100.00
287 Senators World Champs 40.00 100.00
288 Eagles alt 150.00 250.00
289 St. Pats primary 60.00 150.00
290 Bruins Boston Gardens 80.00 200.00
291 Hurricanes Francis 10 40.00 100.00
292 Red Wings Believe 150.00 650.00
293 Oilers Glenn Anderson 9 100.00 200.00
294 Whalers Thanks 250.00 350.00
295 Kings Gretzky 99 150.00 250.00
296 Kings Luc Robitaille 20 150.00 250.00
297 Maple Leafs Gardens 150.00 250.00
298 Thrashers Cartoon 100.00 200.00
299 Sabres Cartoon 100.00 200.00
300 Red Wings Cartoon 100.00 200.00

2014-15 O-Pee-Chee V Series A

S1 Jaromir Jagr 6.00 15.00
S2 Phil Kessel 2.00 5.00
S3 Jonathan Quick 2.50 6.00
S4 Martin Brodeur 5.00 12.00
S5 Nathan MacKinnon 8.00 20.00
S6 Mike Gartner 2.50 6.00
S7 Brian Bellows 1.50 4.00
S8 Patrick Kane 4.00 10.00
S9 Dominik Hasek 3.00 8.00
S10 Pavel Bure 2.00 5.00
S11 Pekka Rinne 2.00 5.00
S12 Evgeny Kuznetsov 5.00 12.00
S13 Alexander Ovechkin 8.00 20.00
S14 Steven Stamkos 4.00 10.00
S15 Ryan Miller 2.00 5.00
S16 Zdeno Chara 2.00 5.00
S17 Ed Belfour 2.00 5.00
S18 Jonathan Toews 3.00 8.00
S19 Sergei Bobrovsky 3.00 8.00
S20 Mats Sundin 2.00 5.00
S21 Alexander Steen 1.25 3.00
S22 Tyler Seguin 2.50 6.00
S23 Patrice Bergeron 2.50 6.00
S24 Henrik Lundqvist 5.00 12.00
S25 Wayne Gretzky 12.00 30.00
S26 Sidney Crosby 8.00 20.00
S27 Carey Price 4.00 10.00
S28 Pavel Datsyuk 3.00 8.00
S29 Steve Yzerman 5.00 12.00
S30 Bobby Hull 4.00 10.00
S31 John LeClair 2.00 5.00
S32 Mike Bossy 2.00 5.00
S33 Mario Lemieux 8.00 20.00
S34 Rick Nash 2.00 5.00
S35 Evgeni Malkin 4.00 10.00
S36 Mark Messier 4.00 10.00
S37 Ryan Getzlaf 2.00 5.00
S38 Teuvo Teravainen 3.00 8.00
S39 Brad Marchand 4.00 10.00
S40 John Tavares 3.00 8.00
S41 Claude Giroux 2.00 5.00
S42 Ryan Nugent-Hopkins 2.50 6.00
S43 P.K. Subban 2.50 6.00
S44 Drew Doughty 2.50 6.00
S45 Grant Fuhr 3.00 8.00

2015-16 O-Pee-Chee

1 Scott Darling .15 .40
2 Francois Beauchemin .12 .30
3 Jaroslav Halak AS .20 .50
4 Niklas Hjalmarsson .12 .30
5 David Perron .15 .40
6 David Booth .12 .30
7 Darren Helm .12 .30
8 Michael Stone .12 .30
9 Jeff Petry .20 .50
10 Erik Haula .12 .30
11 Ben Smith .12 .30
12 Jaromir Jagr .60 1.50
13 Michael Del Zotto .12 .30
14 Eric Nystrom .12 .30
15 Maxime Talbot .12 .30
16 Curtis McElhinney .12 .30
17 Kyle Clifford .12 .30
18 Andy Greene .12 .30
19 Kari Lehtonen .15 .40
20 T.J. Brodie .12 .30
21 Jake Allen .20 .50
22 Andrew Ference .12 .30
23 John Mitchell .12 .30
24 Mikhail Grabovski .12 .30
25 Jonathan Drouin AS .15 .40
26 Tyler Ennis .12 .30
27 Chris Kreider .25 .60
28 Ryan Kesler .20 .50
29 Mathieu Perreault .12 .30
30 Chris Kunitz .20 .50
31 Aleksander Barkov .30 .75
32 P.K. Subban .25 .60
33 Mike Santorelli .12 .30
34 Andrew Shaw .12 .30
35 Braden Holtby .25 .60
36 Jonathan Ericsson .12 .30
37 Scott Hartnell .12 .30
38 Eric Staal .25 .60
39 Steve Mason .15 .40
40 Jay Bouwmeester .12 .30
41 Nick Bonino .12 .30
42 Andrej Nestrasil .12 .30
43 Morgan Rielly .20 .50
44 Michael Cammalleri .15 .40
45 Bryan Little .15 .40
46 Patrik Berglund .12 .30
47 Matt Carle .12 .30
48 Dennis Wideman .12 .30
49 Curtis Glencross .12 .30
50 Evgeni Malkin .40 1.00
51 Checklist .12 .30
52 Bobby Ryan AS .15 .40
53 Rick Nash AS .20 .50
54 Loui Eriksson .12 .30
55 Alec Martinez .12 .30
56 Nathan Beaulieu .12 .30
57 Jason Zucker .20 .50
58 Brayden Schenn .20 .50
59 Ales Hemsky .12 .30
60 Peter Holland .12 .30
61 Antti Niemi .15 .40
62 Alexander Wennberg .12 .30
63 Niklas Kronwall .15 .40
64 Cody McLeod .12 .30
65 Mika Zibanejad .25 .60
66 Ben Scrivens .15 .40
67 Nate Thompson .12 .30
68 Nicklas Backstrom .20 .50
69 Ryan McDonagh .12 .30
70 Shea Weber AS .15 .40
71 Johnny Oduya .15 .40
72 Mikael Backlund .15 .40
73 Trevor Lewis .12 .30
74 Chris Higgins .12 .30
75 Oliver Ekman-Larsson AS .20 .50
76 Patrice Bergeron AS .25 .60
77 Cam Ward .20 .50
78 James Reimer .20 .50
79 Nail Yakupov .12 .30
80 Tomas Jurco .12 .30
81 Kevin Shattenkirk AS .12 .30
82 Sean Bergenheim .12 .30
83 James Wisniewski .12 .30
84 Jhonas Enroth .20 .50
85 Joel Ward .12 .30
86 Joe Thornton .30 .75
87 Josh Bailey .15 .40
88 Jimmy Hayes .12 .30
89 Evander Kane .20 .50
90 Scott Gomez .15 .40
91 Brayden McNabb .12 .30
92 Craig Smith .12 .30
93 Steve Downie .12 .30
94 Tobias Enstrom .12 .30
95 Sergei Bobrovsky .30 .75
96 Karl Alzner .12 .30
97 Brad Richardson .12 .30
98 Sean Monahan .12 .30
99 Victor Rask .12 .30
100 Steven Stamkos AS .40 1.00
101 Jason Pominville .12 .30
102 Jarome Iginla .25 .60
103 Sergei Gonchar .12 .30
104 Kevin Hayes .15 .40
105 Patrick Sharp .20 .50
106 Andrew MacDonald .12 .30
107 Michael Hutchinson .12 .30
108 Frans Nielsen .12 .30
109 Jakob Silfverberg .12 .30
110 Jaden Schwartz .25 .60
111 Tuukka Rask .25 .60
112 Teddy Purcell .12 .30
113 Andrew Hammond .25 .60
114 Paul Martin .12 .30
115 Jared Spurgeon .20 .50
116 Tom Wilson .20 .50
117 Mason Raymond .12 .30
118 Tomas Hertl .20 .50
119 John Klingberg .20 .50
120 Leo Komarov .12 .30
121 Rasmus Ristolainen .12 .30
122 Mikkel Boedker .12 .30
123 Brian Boyle .12 .30
124 Radim Vrbata AS .12 .30
125 Aaron Ekblad AS .25 .60
126 Justin Abdelkader .15 .40
127 Michael Ryder .12 .30
128 Michael Frolik .12 .30
129 Anders Lee .20 .50
130 Roman Josi .20 .50
131 Matt Duchene .20 .50
132 Marian Hossa .20 .50
133 Andre Burakovsky .12 .30
134 David Pastrnak .50 1.25
135 Dominic Moore .12 .30
136 Nathan Gerbe .12 .30
137 Matt Hendricks .12 .30
138 Ben Bishop .15 .40
139 Joe Pavelski .25 .60
140 Steve Bernier .12 .30
141 Roman Polak .12 .30
142 Max Pacioretty .20 .50
143 Brian Elliott AS .15 .40
144 Matt Moulson .12 .30
145 Claude Giroux AS .20 .50
146 Devan Dubnyk .15 .40
147 Blake Comeau .12 .30
148 Erik Cole .12 .30
149 Colin Wilson .12 .30
150 Jonathan Quick .25 .60
151 Checklist .12 .30
152 Kevan Miller .12 .30
153 Kyle Palmieri .15 .40
154 Mark Giordano AS .20 .50
155 Leon Draisaitl .60 1.50
156 Johan Franzen .15 .40
157 Kevin Connauton .12 .30
158 Jussi Jokinen .12 .30
159 Mark Streit .12 .30
160 Anders Lindback .12 .30
161 Mark Stuart .12 .30
162 Duncan Keith AS .15 .40
163 Valtteri Filppula .12 .30
164 Lars Eller .12 .30
165 Colton Sceviour .12 .30
166 Marco Scandella .12 .30
167 Carl Hagelin .12 .30
168 Jannik Hansen .12 .30
169 Robin Lehner .15 .40
170 Bryce Salvador .12 .30
171 Logan Couture .25 .60
172 Nick Spaling .12 .30
173 Dave Bolland .12 .30
174 Adam Lowry .15 .40
175 Pavel Datsyuk .30 .75
176 Gabriel Landeskog .25 .60
177 Brock Nelson .20 .50
178 Derek Roy .12 .30
179 Sam Reinhart .40 1.00
180 Cody Ceci .12 .30
181 Marcus Johansson .15 .40
182 Vladislav Namestnikov .12 .30
183 Marian Gaborik .20 .50
184 Daniel Sedin .25 .60
185 Tomas Fleischmann .12 .30
186 Shane Doan .15 .40
187 Elias Lindholm .20 .50
188 Drew Stafford .12 .30
189 Kris Versteeg .12 .30
190 Taylor Beck .12 .30
191 Nikolai Kulemin .12 .30
192 Markus Granlund .15 .40
193 Jack Johnson .12 .30
194 Evgeny Kuznetsov .25 .60
195 Tomas Tatar .12 .30
196 Cody Eakin .12 .30
197 Alex Pietrangelo .15 .40
198 Ryan Carter .12 .30
199 Dennis Seidenberg .12 .30
200 Carey Price AS .40 1.00
201 Curtis Lazar .12 .30
202 Marc-Andre Fleury AS .40 1.00
203 Pat Maroon .12 .30
204 Patrick Kane AS .40 1.00
205 Ryan Miller .20 .50
206 Zach Redmond .12 .30
207 Gustav Nyquist .12 .30
208 Derek Stepan .12 .30
209 Anton Stralman .12 .30
210 Jason Spezza .20 .50
211 Andrej Sekera .12 .30
212 Justin Braun .12 .30
213 Brandon Pirri .12 .30
214 Josh Gorges .12 .30
215 Andrew Cogliano .12 .30
216 Lance Bouma .12 .30
217 Nino Niederreiter .12 .30
218 Kyle Okposo .12 .30
219 Lee Stempniak .12 .30
220 Carter Hutton .15 .40
221 Boone Jenner .20 .50
222 Mark Arcobello .12 .30
223 Nathan MacKinnon .75 2.00
224 Brooks Orpik .12 .30
225 Vladimir Tarasenko AS .25 .60
226 Phil Kessel AS .20 .50
227 Zdeno Chara .20 .50
228 Patric Hornqvist .12 .30
229 Tomas Plekanec .12 .30
230 Drew Doughty AS .25 .60
231 Teuvo Teravainen .20 .50
232 Vernon Fiddler .12 .30
233 Adam Henrique .15 .40
234 Connor Murphy .12 .30
235 Derick Brassard .12 .30
236 Mike Hoffman AS .12 .30
237 Frederik Andersen .25 .60
238 Dmitry Kulikov .12 .30
239 Jim Howard .25 .60
240 David Jones .12 .30
241 Matt Cullen .12 .30
242 Jordan Eberle .20 .50
243 Mike Weber .12 .30
244 Nick Foligno AS .15 .40
245 Jordan Staal .15 .40
246 Nikita Kucherov .40 1.00
247 Shawn Matthias .12 .30
248 Martin Havlat .15 .40
249 Seth Griffith .12 .30
250 John Tavares AS .30 .75
251 Checklist .12 .30
252 Andrew Ladd .12 .30
253 Joe Colborne .12 .30
254 David Backes .12 .30
255 Bo Horvat .25 .60
256 Michael Raffl .12 .30
257 Ryan O'Reilly .20 .50
258 Eric Fehr .12 .30
259 Keith Yandle .12 .30
260 Dion Phaneuf .15 .40
261 Danny DeKeyser .12 .30
262 Dustin Brown .20 .50
263 Michal Neuvirth .15 .40
264 Lauri Korpikoski .12 .30
265 Marcus Kruger .12 .30
266 Jason Demers .12 .30
267 Alex Chiasson .15 .40
268 Richard Panik .12 .30
269 Marko Dano .12 .30
270 Jason Garrison .12 .30
271 Brad Richards .20 .50
272 Niklas Svedberg .15 .40
273 Vincent Lecavalier .20 .50
274 Troy Brouwer .12 .30
275 Zach Parise .20 .50
276 Seth Jones .20 .50
277 Riley Sheahan .12 .30
278 John Gibson .20 .50
279 Damon Severson .12 .30
280 Calvin Pickard .20 .50
281 Anze Kopitar AS .30 .75
282 Jiri Hudler .15 .40
283 Riley Nash .12 .30
284 Christopher Tanev .12 .30
285 Daniel Girardi .12 .30
286 Nick Leddy .12 .30
287 Brian Flynn .12 .30
288 Tobias Rieder .12 .30
289 Viktor Fasth .15 .40
290 Steve Ott .12 .30
291 Ray Emery .15 .40
292 Chris Stewart .12 .30
293 Matt Calvert .12 .30
294 Daniel Winnik .12 .30
295 Marcus Foligno .15 .40
296 Torey Krug .15 .40
297 Vincent Trocheck .20 .50
298 Mark Stone .25 .60
299 Jay McClement .12 .30
300 Jonathan Toews AS .30 .75
301 Brendan Gallagher .20 .50
302 Brooks Laich .12 .30
303 Tanner Pearson .12 .30
304 Milan Lucic .15 .40
305 Joakim Lindstrom .12 .30
306 Taylor Hall .20 .50
307 Alex Killorn .12 .30
308 Alex Stalock .12 .30
309 Artem Anisimov .12 .30
310 Daniel Briere .15 .40
311 Erik Condra .12 .30
312 Andrei Markov .12 .30
313 Alexander Steen .12 .30
314 Derrick Pouliot .12 .30
315 Derek Dorsett .12 .30
316 Jiri Tlusty .12 .30
317 Hampus Lindholm .12 .30
318 Mike Ribeiro .12 .30
319 Jake Muzzin .20 .50
320 Erik Gudbranson .12 .30
321 Ondrej Palat .15 .40
322 Tommy Wingels .12 .30
323 Tyson Barrie .12 .30
324 Kyle Turris .15 .40
325 Johnny Gaudreau AS .30 .75
326 Anton Khudobin .20 .50
327 Darcy Kuemper .20 .50
328 Brian Gionta .12 .30
329 Cam Talbot .20 .50
330 Brad Marchand .40 1.00
331 Alex Goligoski .12 .30
332 Jake Gardiner .12 .30
333 Cory Schneider .20 .50
334 Tyler Toffoli .20 .50
335 Ondrej Pavelec .20 .50
336 Barret Jackman .12 .30
337 Matt Beleskey .12 .30
338 Luke Schenn .20 .50
339 Marek Zidlicky .12 .30
340 Mike Smith .20 .50
341 Justin Fontaine .12 .30
342 Kimmo Timonen .12 .30
343 Tyler Kennedy .12 .30
344 Victor Hedman .25 .60
345 Barclay Goodrow .12 .30
346 Tyler Bozak .12 .30
347 Trevor Daley .12 .30
348 Devante Smith-Pelly .15 .40
349 Willie Mitchell .12 .30
350 Henrik Lundqvist .50 1.25
351 Checklist .12 .30
352 Jared Cowen .12 .30
353 Ryan Ellis .12 .30
354 Thomas Vanek .15 .40
355 Dustin Byfuglien AS .20 .50
356 Alexander Edler .12 .30
357 Mike Green .15 .40
358 Matt Stajan .12 .30
359 Matt Martin .12 .30
360 Oscar Klefbom .30 .75
361 Travis Zajac .12 .30
362 David Desharnais .12 .30
363 Cody Hodgson .12 .30
364 Marc-Edouard Vlasic .12 .30
365 Sam Gagner .12 .30
366 David Savard .12 .30
367 Beau Bennett .12 .30
368 Martin Jones .15 .40
369 Semyon Varlamov .20 .50
370 Brian Campbell .12 .30
371 Jonathan Bernier .15 .40
372 Corey Perry .30 .75
373 Calle Jarnkrok .15 .40
374 Brendan Smith .12 .30
375 Carl Soderberg .12 .30
376 Cedric Paquette .12 .30
377 Alexandre Burrows .12 .30
378 Wayne Simmonds .25 .60
379 Charlie Coyle .20 .50
380 Matt Nieto .12 .30
381 Dmitrij Jaskin .12 .30
382 Alexei Emelin .12 .30
383 Ryan Nugent-Hopkins AS .25 .60
384 Nicolas Deslauriers .12 .30
385 Shawn Horcoff .12 .30
386 Martin Erat .12 .30
387 David Krejci .20 .50
388 Chris Neil .12 .30
389 Jeff Skinner .25 .60
390 Christian Ehrhoff .12 .30
391 Eddie Lack .15 .40
392 Antoine Vermette .12 .30
393 Cody Franson .12 .30
394 Boyd Gordon .12 .30
395 Ryan Strome .20 .50
396 Matt Read .12 .30
397 Dan Boyle .12 .30
398 Melker Karlsson .12 .30
399 Jori Lehtera .12 .30
400 Alexander Ovechkin AS .75 2.00
401 Patrik Elias AS .20 .50
402 P.A. Parenteau .12 .30
403 Mikael Granlund .15 .40
404 Dougie Hamilton .15 .40
405 Nazem Kadri .25 .60
406 Ryan Callahan .12 .30
407 Dwight King .12 .30
408 Cam Atkinson .20 .50
409 Mark Scheifele .30 .75
410 R.J. Umberger .12 .30
411 Corey Crawford AS .25 .60
412 Zemgus Girgensons AS .15 .40
413 Brenden Dillon .12 .30
414 Henrik Sedin .25 .60
415 Marc Staal .12 .30
416 Nick Holden .12 .30
417 Jamie Benn .20 .50
418 Ron Hainsey .12 .30
419 Justin Schultz .15 .40
420 Jonas Hiller .15 .40
421 Mike Fisher .12 .30
422 David Legwand .15 .40
423 Sean Couturier .15 .40
424 Brad Boyes .12 .30
425 Henrik Zetterberg .25 .60
426 Brandon Sutter .12 .30
427 Matt Niskanen .15 .40
428 Simon Despres .12 .30
429 Martin Hanzal .12 .30
430 Brandon Prust .12 .30
431 Johnny Boychuk .15 .40
432 Brandon Saad .15 .40
433 James Neal .12 .30
434 Kris Russell .12 .30
435 Ryan Suter AS .15 .40
436 Erik Karlsson .25 .60
437 Joffrey Lupul .12 .30
438 Brett Connolly .12 .30
439 Benoit Pouliot .12 .30
440 Jeff Carter .15 .40
441 Paul Stastny .15 .40
442 Justin Faulk AS .15 .40
443 Adam Larsson .20 .50
444 Blake Wheeler .20 .50
445 Dan Hamhuis .12 .30
446 Fedor Tyutin .12 .30
447 Nick Bjugstad .12 .30
448 Nikita Zadorov .12 .30
449 Kyle Chipchura .12 .30
450 Ryan Getzlaf AS .20 .50
451 Checklist .12 .30
452 Andrei Vasilevskiy .30 .75
453 Kevin Klein .12 .30
454 Kris Letang .25 .60
455 Craig Anderson .20 .50
456 Jakub Voracek AS .15 .40
457 Bryan Bickell .12 .30
458 Erik Johnson .12 .30
459 Reilly Smith .20 .50
460 Filip Forsberg AS .30 .75
461 John Carlson .20 .50
462 Antoine Roussel .12 .30
463 James van Riemsdyk .15 .40
464 Justin Williams .15 .40
465 Brent Burns AS .20 .50
466 Jiri Sekac AS .12 .30
467 Travis Hamonic .12 .30
468 Calvin de Haan .12 .30
469 Eric Gelinas .12 .30
470 Linden Vey .12 .30
471 Roberto Luongo AS .30 .75
472 Alex Galchenyuk .12 .30
473 Jonathan Huberdeau .25 .60
474 Ryan Johansen AS .15 .40
475 Martin St. Louis .20 .50
476 Tyler Myers .12 .30
477 Karri Ramo .15 .40
478 Zach Bogosian .15 .40
479 Jay Beagle .12 .30
480 Alexander Semin .20 .50
481 Alex Tanguay .12 .30
482 Cam Fowler .20 .50
483 John Moore .12 .30
484 Petr Mrazek .20 .50
485 Jacob Trouba .15 .40
486 Chris Vande Velde .12 .30
487 Nikita Nikitin .12 .30
488 Dale Weise .12 .30
489 Clarke MacArthur .12 .30
490 Jon Merrill .12 .30
491 Patrick Marleau .20 .50
492 Mikko Koivu .15 .40
493 Tyler Johnson .12 .30
494 Tyler Seguin AS .25 .60
495 Pekka Rinne .20 .50
496 T.J. Oshie .20 .50
497 Thomas Hickey .12 .30
498 Brent Seabrook AS .12 .30
499 Mats Zuccarello .20 .50
500 Sidney Crosby .75 2.00
501 Louis Domingue RC 1.25 3.00
502 Malcolm Subban RC 2.00 5.00
503 Alex Biega RC .75 2.00
504 Mike Lee RC .75 2.00
505 David Wolf RC 1.00 2.50
506 Ryan Hartman RC 1.50 4.00
507 Josh Anderson RC 2.50 6.00
508 Nick Shore RC .75 2.00
509 Jacob de la Rose RC 1.25 3.00
510 Anthony Bitetto RC .75 2.00
511 Mackenzie Skapski RC 1.25 3.00
512 Shane Prince RC .75 2.00
513 Anthony Stolarz RC 3.00 8.00
514 Petr Straka RC .75 2.00
515 Daniil Tarasov RC 1.00 2.50
516 Luke Witkowski RC .75 2.00
517 Antoine Bibeau RC 1.25 3.00
518 Ronalds Kenins RC .75 2.00
519 Jean-Francois Berube RC 1.00 2.50
520 Brian Ferlin RC .75 2.00
521 Jordan Oesterle RC .75 2.00
522 Kael Mouillierat RC .75 2.00
523 Matt Puempel RC 1.00 2.50
524 Brendan Ranford RC 1.00 2.50
525 Henrik Samuelsson RC .75 2.00
526 Emile Poirier RC 1.00 2.50
527 Oscar Dansk RC 1.50 4.00
528 Oscar Lindberg RC 1.25 3.00
529 Mark Alt RC .75 2.00
530 Chris Driedger RC 1.00 2.50
531 Sam Brittain RC 1.25 3.00
532 Rasmus Rissanen RC .75 2.00
533 Andrew MacWilliam RC .75 2.00
534 Kevin Fiala RC 1.50 4.00
535 Danny Biega RC .75 2.00
536 Andrew Miller RC 1.00 2.50
537 Viktor Arvidsson RC 1.25 3.00
538 Nick Cousins RC 1.25 3.00
539 Casey Bailey RC 1.25 3.00
540 Sam Bennett RC 4.00 10.00
541 Stefan Noesen RC .75 2.00
542 Kyle Baun RC 1.25 3.00
543 Slater Koekkoek RC .75 2.00
544 Andrew Copp RC 1.25 3.00
545 Brett Kulak RC 1.00 2.50
546 Duncan Siemens RC 1.25 3.00
547 Stanislav Galiev RC 1.25 3.00
548 David Musil RC 1.00 2.50
549 Bryan Lerg RC .75 2.00
550 Michael Paliotta RC .75 2.00
551 Brett Hull 2.00 5.00
552 Patrick Roy 2.50 6.00
553 Mike Modano 1.50 4.00
554 Bobby Hull 2.00 5.00
555 Andy Moog 1.00 2.50
556 John Vanbiesbrouck 1.00 2.50
557 Bobby Orr 4.00 10.00
558 Marty McSorley .75 2.00
559 Mario Lemieux 4.00 10.00
560 Teemu Selanne 2.00 5.00
561 Martin Brodeur 2.50 6.00
562 Mike Bossy 1.00 2.50
563 Steve Yzerman 2.50 6.00
564 Trevor Linden 1.00 2.50
565 Jean Beliveau 1.00 2.50
566 Mark Messier 2.00 5.00
567 Mike Gartner 1.25 3.00
568 Nicklas Lidstrom 1.00 2.50
569 Pierre Turgeon .75 2.00
570 Mats Sundin 1.00 2.50
571 Curtis Joseph 1.25 3.00
572 Brad Park .75 2.00
573 Adam Oates 1.00 2.50
574 Terry Sawchuk 1.00 2.50
575 Pelle Lindbergh .75 2.00
576 Olaf Kolzig 1.00 2.50
577 Darryl Sittler 1.25 3.00
578 Vincent Damphousse .75 2.00
579 Grant Fuhr 1.50 4.00
580 Arturs Irbe .75 2.00
581 Felix Potvin 1.50 4.00
582 Rob Brown .60 1.50
583 Wayne Gretzky 6.00 15.00
584 Chris Chelios 1.00 2.50
585 Tom Barrasso 1.00 2.50
586 Ray Bourque 1.50 4.00
587 Cam Neely 1.00 2.50
588 Pete Peeters .75 2.00
589 Marcel Dionne 1.25 3.00
590 Mike Liut .60 1.50
591 Steve Larmer .75 2.00
592 Dave Schultz 1.00 2.50
593 Denis Savard 1.00 2.50
594 Phil Esposito 1.50 4.00
595 Doug Harvey 1.00 2.50
596 Doug Weight 1.00 2.50
597 Brian Bellows .75 2.00
598 Wendel Clark 1.50 4.00
599 Denis Potvin 1.00 2.50
600 Checklist .12 .30
601 Carey Price AW 10.00 25.00
602 Jamie Benn AW 5.00 12.00
603 Carey Price AW 10.00 25.00
604 Erik Karlsson AW 8.00 20.00
605 Alexander Ovechkin AW 20.00 50.00
606 Aaron Ekblad AW 6.00 15.00
607 Patrice Bergeron AW 6.00 15.00
608 Duncan Keith AW 10.00 25.00
609 Carey Price AW 20.00 50.00
610 Wayne Gretzky AT 30.00 80.00
611 Bobby Orr AT 20.00 50.00
612 Brad Park AT 4.00 10.00
613 Mark Messier AT 10.00 25.00
614 Mario Lemieux AT 20.00 50.00
615 Cam Neely AT 5.00 12.00
616 Curtis Joseph AT 6.00 15.00
617 Vincent Damphousse AT 4.00 10.00
618 Stanley Cup 12.00 30.00

2015-16 O-Pee-Chee Rainbow

*1-500 VETS: 2.5X TO 6X BASIC CARDS
*501-550 ROOKIES: .5X TO 1.2X BASIC RC
*551-600 LEGENDS: .6X TO 1.5X BASIC SP
25 Jonathan Drouin AS 1.25 3.00
68 Nicklas Backstrom 1.50 4.00
194 Evgeny Kuznetsov 2.00 5.00
411 Corey Crawford AS 2.00 5.00
506 Ryan Hartman 2.00 5.00

2015-16 O-Pee-Chee Rainbow Black

*1-500 VETS/100: 6X TO 15X BASIC CARDS
*501-550 ROOKIE/100: 1.2X TO 3X BASIC RC
*551-600 LEGEND/100: 1.5X TO 4X BASIC SP
25 Jonathan Drouin AS 3.00 8.00
68 Nicklas Backstrom 4.00 10.00
194 Evgeny Kuznetsov 5.00 12.00
411 Corey Crawford AS 5.00 12.00
506 Ryan Hartman 5.00 12.00
583 Wayne Gretzky 15.00 40.00

2015-16 O-Pee-Chee Red

*1-500 VETS: 5X TO 12X BASIC CARDS
*501-550 ROOKIES: 1X TO 2.5X BASIC RC
*551-600 LEGENDS: 1.5X TO 4X BASIC RC
25 Jonathan Drouin AS 2.50 6.00
68 Nicklas Backstrom 3.00 8.00
194 Evgeny Kuznetsov 4.00 10.00
411 Corey Crawford AS 4.00 10.00
506 Ryan Hartman 4.00 10.00
540 Sam Bennett 12.00 30.00
552 Patrick Roy 12.00 30.00
557 Bobby Orr 12.00 30.00
583 Wayne Gretzky 15.00 40.00

2015-16 O-Pee-Chee Retro

*1-500 VETS: 1.5X TO 4X BASIC CARDS
*501-550 ROOKIES: .4X TO 1X BASIC RC
*551-600 LEGENDS: .5X TO 1.2X BASIC SP

2015-16 O-Pee-Chee All-Star Glossy

AS1 N.Foligno/J.Toews .75 2.00
AS2 Nick Foligno .75 2.00
AS3 Patrick Kane 2.00 5.00
AS4 Drew Doughty 1.25 3.00
AS5 Ryan Johansen .75 2.00
AS6 Duncan Keith .75 2.00
AS7 Anze Kopitar 1.50 4.00
AS8 Steven Stamkos 2.00 5.00
AS9 Phil Kessel 1.00 2.50
AS10 Carey Price 2.00 5.00
AS11 Claude Giroux 1.00 2.50
AS12 Dustin Byfuglien 1.00 2.50
AS13 Marc-Andre Fleury 2.00 5.00
AS14 Brian Elliott .75 2.00
AS15 Brent Burns 1.00 2.50
AS16 Jonathan Drouin .75 2.00
AS17 Jiri Sekac .60 1.50
AS18 Kevin Shattenkirk .60 1.50
AS19 Bobby Ryan .75 2.00
AS20 Radim Vrbata .60 1.50
AS21 Oliver Ekman-Larsson 1.00 2.50
AS22 Zemgus Girgensons .75 2.00
AS23 Alexander Ovechkin 4.00 10.00
AS24 Ryan Nugent-Hopkins 1.25 3.00
AS25 Jonathan Toews 1.50 4.00
AS26 Ryan Getzlaf 1.00 2.50
AS27 Rick Nash 1.00 2.50
AS28 Tyler Seguin 1.25 3.00
AS29 Shea Weber .75 2.00
AS30 Jakub Voracek .75 2.00
AS31 Corey Crawford 1.25 3.00
AS32 John Tavares 1.50 4.00
AS33 Roberto Luongo 1.50 4.00
AS34 Brent Seabrook .60 1.50
AS35 Vladimir Tarasenko 1.25 3.00
AS36 Patrice Bergeron 1.25 3.00

AS37 Jaroslav Halak 1.00 2.50
AS38 Johnny Gaudreau 1.50 4.00
AS39 Mike Hoffman .60 1.50
AS40 Aaron Ekblad 1.25 3.00
AS41 Patrik Elias 1.00 2.50
AS42 Ryan Suter .75 2.00
AS43 Mark Giordano 1.00 2.50
AS44 Justin Faulk .75 2.00
AS45 Filip Forsberg 1.50 4.00
AS46 Jonathan Drouin FS 1.00 2.50
AS47 Ryan Johansen Brk 1.00 2.50
AS48 Patrick Kane Acc 2.50 6.00
AS49 Shea Weber HS 1.00 2.50
AS50 Ryan Johansen MVP 1.00 2.50

2015-16 O-Pee-Chee Buyback Autographs

199 N.Lidstrom 12-13 Rtr/20 75.00 125.00

2015-16 O-Pee-Chee Draft Pick Puzzle

COMMON PUZZLE 2.00 5.00
OPCCM Connor McDavid/97 500.00 800.00

2015-16 O-Pee-Chee Mini Glossy

1 Ryan Getzlaf 3.00 8.00
2 Oliver Ekman-Larsson 3.00 8.00
3 Patrice Bergeron 4.00 10.00
4 Zemgus Girgensons 2.50 6.00
5 Johnny Gaudreau 5.00 12.00
6 Jiri Hudler 2.50 6.00
7 Patrick Kane 6.00 15.00
8 Jonathan Toews 5.00 12.00
9 Jarome Iginla 5.00 12.00
10 Tyler Seguin 4.00 10.00
11 Henrik Zetterberg 4.00 10.00
12 Jordan Eberle 3.00 8.00
13 Taylor Hall 3.00 8.00
14 Aaron Ekblad 4.00 10.00
15 Tyler Toffoli 3.00 8.00
16 Max Pacioretty 4.00 10.00
17 P.K. Subban 5.00 12.00
18 Filip Forsberg 5.00 12.00
19 Pekka Rinne 3.00 8.00
20 John Tavares 5.00 12.00
21 Kyle Okposo 2.00 5.00
22 Keith Yandle 2.00 5.00
23 Rick Nash 3.00 8.00
24 Pavel Datsyuk 4.00 10.00
25 Erik Karlsson 4.00 10.00
26 Jakub Voracek 2.50 6.00
27 Claude Giroux 4.00 10.00
28 Sidney Crosby 12.00 30.00
29 Evgeni Malkin 6.00 15.00
30 Vladimir Tarasenko 4.00 10.00
31 Tyler Johnson 2.00 5.00
32 Steven Stamkos 6.00 15.00
33 James van Riemsdyk 2.50 6.00
34 Nazem Kadri 4.00 10.00
35 Ryan Miller 3.00 8.00
36 Alexander Ovechkin 12.00 30.00
37 Wayne Gretzky 15.00 40.00
38 Bobby Orr 6.00 15.00
39 Martin Brodeur 8.00 20.00
40 Mario Lemieux 10.00 25.00
41 Steve Yzerman 6.00 15.00
42 Patrick Roy 10.00 25.00

2015-16 O-Pee-Chee Box Bottoms

32 P.K. Subban HOB .30 .75
50 Evgeni Malkin HOB .50 1.25
53 Rick Nash AS HOB .25 .60
70 Shea Weber AS HOB .20 .50
76 Patrice Bergeron AS HOB .30 .75
100 Steven Stamkos AS HOB .50 1.25
145 Claude Giroux AS HOB .25 .60
150 Jonathan Quick BL/HOB .30 .75
200 Carey Price AS BL HOB .50 1.25
204 Patrick Kane AS HOB .50 1.25
226 Phil Kessel AS HOB .25 .60
239 Jim Howard HOB .20 .50
250 John Tavares AS BL .60 1.50
383 Ryan Nugent-Hopkins AS HOB .30 .75
400 Alexander Ovechkin AS HOB 1.00 2.50
436 Erik Karlsson HOB .30 .75
450 Ryan Getzlaf AS HOB .25 .60
463 James van Riemsdyk BL .30 .75
494 Tyler Seguin AS HOB .30 .75
495 Pekka Rinne BL .40 1.00
500 Sidney Crosby BL 1.50 4.00

2015-16 O-Pee-Chee Glossy Rookies

R1 Connor McDavid 50.00 120.00
R2 Robby Fabbri 2.50 6.00
R3 Dylan Larkin 6.00 15.00
R4 Artemi Panarin 8.00 20.00
R5 Jake Virtanen 2.50 6.00
R6 Sam Bennett 6.00 15.00
R7 Zachary Fucale 1.50 4.00
R8 Max Domi 4.00 10.00
R9 Nikolaj Ehlers 4.00 10.00
R10 Jack Eichel 8.00 20.00

2015-16 O-Pee-Chee Glossy Rookies Black

COMPLETE SET (10)
*BLACK: 1X TO 2.5X BASIC INSERTS
R1 Connor McDavid 150.00 400.00

2015-16 O-Pee-Chee Glossy Rookies Red

COMPLETE SET (10)
*RED: .6X TO 1.5X BASIC INSERTS
R1 Connor McDavid 100.00 250.00

2015-16 O-Pee-Chee Signatures

SAV Andrei Vasilevskiy E 12.00 30.00
SBR Brett Ritchie E 3.00 8.00
SCC Charlie Coyle E 5.00 12.00
SCF Cody Franson D 3.00 8.00
SCG Cody Goloubef E 3.00 8.00
SCH Carl Hagelin B 6.00 15.00
SDS Derek Stepan B 6.00 15.00
SJE Jordie Benn E 3.00 8.00
SJH Jonathan Huberdeau B 10.00 25.00
SJM John Moore E 3.00 8.00
SJS Justin Schultz D 4.00 10.00
SKQ Kyle Quincey E 3.00 8.00
SKT Kyle Turris E 4.00 10.00
SLE Lars Eller E 3.00 8.00
SLK Lauri Korpikoski E 3.00 8.00
SMB Matt Beleskey E 3.00 8.00
SMG Mikael Granlund C 6.00 15.00
SMN Matt Nieto E 3.00 8.00
SMR Mikhail Grigorenko D 3.00 8.00
SPB Derrick Pouliot D 3.00 8.00
SRK Ryan Kesler B 10.00 25.00
SRM Ryan McDonagh C 8.00 20.00
SSL Scott Laughton C 8.00 20.00
STH Tomas Hertl B 10.00 25.00
SZR Zach Redmond E 3.00 8.00

2015-16 O-Pee-Chee Sport Royalty Autographs

GAO Alexander Ovechkin 100.00 200.00

2015-16 O-Pee-Chee Team Canada Signatures

TCSAC Andrew Cogliano E 4.00 10.00
TCSBD Brenden Dillon E 4.00 10.00
TCSBJ Boone Jenner E 6.00 15.00
TCSBS Ben Scrivens B 8.00 20.00
TCSCS Sean Couturier D 6.00 15.00
TCSDH Dougie Hamilton D 6.00 15.00
TCSDN Darnell Nurse D 6.00 15.00
TCSDP Derrick Pouliot D 5.00 12.00
TCSJB Jonathan Bernier B 8.00 20.00
TCSJC Jared Cowen D 5.00 12.00
TCSJH Jonathan Huberdeau C 12.00 30.00
TCSJN James Neal C 8.00 20.00
TCSJU Justin Schultz B 8.00 20.00
TCSJZ Jason Spezza B 20.00 40.00
TCSKT Kyle Turris D 6.00 15.00
TCSLL Louis Leblanc D 5.00 12.00
TCSLS Luke Schenn C 10.00 25.00
TCSMD Matt Duchene C 10.00 25.00
TCSMJ Martin Jones E 6.00 15.00
TCSMR Morgan Rielly D 15.00 30.00
TCSRJ Ryan Johansen C 8.00 20.00
TCSRS Ryan Spooner E 5.00 12.00
TCSSH Scott Hartnell C 6.00 15.00
TCSSW Shea Weber C 8.00 20.00
TCSTH Thomas Hickey E 4.00 10.00

2015-16 O-Pee-Chee Patches

P1 Corey Perry 8.00 20.00
P2 Ryan Getzlaf 5.00 12.00
P3 Oliver Ekman-Larsson 5.00 12.00
P4 Patrice Bergeron 6.00 15.00
P5 Zemgus Girgensons 4.00 10.00
P6 Jonas Hiller 4.00 10.00
P7 Eric Staal 6.00 15.00
P8 Patrick Kane 10.00 25.00
P9 Marian Hossa 5.00 12.00
P10 Nathan MacKinnon 20.00 50.00
P11 Sergei Bobrovsky 8.00 20.00
P12 Jamie Benn 5.00 12.00
P13 Jim Howard 6.00 15.00
P14 Pavel Datsyuk 8.00 20.00
P15 Jordan Eberle 5.00 12.00
P16 Jaromir Jagr 15.00 40.00
P17 Anze Kopitar 8.00 20.00
P18 Jonathan Quick 6.00 15.00
P19 Zach Parise 5.00 12.00
P20 Max Pacioretty 5.00 12.00
P21 P.K. Subban 6.00 15.00
P22 Filip Forsberg 8.00 20.00
P23 Adam Henrique 4.00 10.00
P24 John Tavares 8.00 20.00
P25 Rick Nash 5.00 12.00
P26 Henrik Lundqvist 12.00 30.00
P27 Bobby Ryan 4.00 10.00
P28 Claude Giroux 5.00 12.00
P29 Marc-Andre Fleury 10.00 25.00
P30 Sidney Crosby 20.00 50.00
P31 Joe Pavelski 6.00 15.00
P32 Vladimir Tarasenko 8.00 20.00
P33 Tyler Johnson 3.00 8.00
P34 Steven Stamkos 10.00 25.00
P35 Phil Kessel 6.00 15.00
P36 James van Riemsdyk 4.00 10.00
P37 Daniel Sedin 6.00 15.00
P38 Nicklas Backstrom 5.00 12.00
P39 Alexander Ovechkin 20.00 50.00
P40 Bryan Little 4.00 10.00
P41 Wayne Gretzky 25.00 50.00
P42 Mark Messier 10.00 25.00
P43 Mario Lemieux 25.00 60.00
P44 Patrick Roy 30.00 60.00
P45 Brett Hull 12.00 30.00
P46 Malcolm Subban 10.00 25.00
P47 Jacob de la Rose 6.00 15.00
P48 Kevin Fiala 8.00 20.00
P49 Matt Puempel 5.00 12.00
P50 Ryan Hartman 8.00 20.00
P51 Ryan Getzlaf 8.00 20.00
P52 Evgeni Malkin 15.00 40.00
P53 Alexander Ovechkin 30.00 80.00
P54 Steven Stamkos 15.00 40.00
P55 Jonathan Toews 12.00 30.00
P56 Carey Price 15.00 40.00
P57 Tuukka Rask 10.00 25.00
P58 Johnny Gaudreau 12.00 30.00
P59 Henrik Zetterberg 10.00 25.00
P60 Aaron Ekblad 10.00 25.00
P61 Jonathan Quick 10.00 25.00
P62 Pekka Rinne 8.00 20.00
P63 Jaromir Jagr 25.00 60.00
P64 John Tavares 12.00 30.00
P65 Martin St. Louis 8.00 20.00
P66 Erik Karlsson 10.00 25.00
P67 Jakub Voracek 6.00 15.00
P68 Sidney Crosby 30.00 80.00
P69 Logan Couture 10.00 25.00
P70 Vladimir Tarasenko 10.00 25.00
P71 Jonathan Bernier 6.00 15.00
P72 Ryan Miller 8.00 20.00
P73 Blake Wheeler 8.00 20.00
P74 Shea Weber 6.00 15.00
P75 Tyler Seguin 10.00 25.00
P76 Wayne Gretzky 75.00 135.00
P77 Bobby Orr 50.00 100.00
P78 Steve Yzerman 50.00 100.00
P79 Pavel Bure 30.00 60.00
P80 Grant Fuhr 25.00 50.00
P81 Mark Messier 25.00 60.00
P82 Mario Lemieux 50.00 100.00
P83 Patrick Roy 50.00 100.00
P84 Teemu Selanne 25.00 50.00
P85 Felix Potvin 40.00 80.00
P86 Sidney Crosby 60.00 120.00
P87 Alexander Ovechkin 50.00 100.00
P88 Steven Stamkos 50.00 100.00
P89 Jonathan Toews 50.00 100.00
P90 Carey Price 50.00 120.00

2015-16 O-Pee-Chee V Series B

S1 Jonathan Quick 2.00 5.00
S2 Pekka Rinne 1.50 4.00
S3 Mark Messier 3.00 8.00
S4 Curtis Joseph 2.00 5.00
S5 Steven Stamkos 3.00 8.00
S6 Carey Price 3.00 8.00
S7 Aaron Ekblad 2.00 5.00
S8 Zdeno Chara 1.50 4.00
S9 Sidney Crosby 6.00 15.00
S10 Pierre Turgeon 1.25 3.00
S11 Tyler Seguin 2.00 5.00
S12 Jakub Voracek 1.25 3.00
S13 Ryan Getzlaf 1.50 4.00
S14 Tyler Johnson 1.00 2.50
S15 Vladimir Tarasenko 2.00 5.00
S16 John Tavares 2.50 6.00
S17 Rick Nash 1.50 4.00
S18 Wayne Gretzky 10.00 25.00
S19 Evgeni Malkin 3.00 8.00
S20 Claude Giroux 1.50 4.00
S21 Patrick Kane 3.00 8.00
S22 Joe Pavelski 2.00 5.00
S23 Ryan Miller 1.50 4.00
S24 Brett Hull 3.00 8.00
S25 Jiri Hudler 1.25 3.00
S26 Johnny Gaudreau 2.50 6.00
S27 Jonathan Bernier 1.25 3.00
S28 Jonathan Drouin 1.25 3.00
S29 John Carlson 1.50 4.00
S30 Filip Forsberg 2.50 6.00
S31 Michael Hutchinson 1.00 2.50
S32 Corey Crawford 2.00 5.00
S33 James van Riemsdyk 1.25 3.00
S34 Jamie Benn 1.50 4.00
S35 Corey Perry 2.50 6.00
S36 Nikita Kucherov 3.00 8.00
S37 Jaromir Jagr 5.00 12.00
S38 Malcolm Subban 2.50 6.00
S39 Ryan Hartman 2.00 5.00
S40 Jacob de la Rose 1.50 4.00

2015-16 O-Pee-Chee Woodies

WW23 Evgeni Malkin 40.00 80.00

2016-17 O-Pee-Chee

1 Jonathan Quick .25 .60
2 Colton Sceviour .15 .40
3 Ben Hutton .20 .50
4 Sergei Kalinin .12 .30
5 Ryan Callahan .12 .30
6 Andrew Shaw .12 .30
7 Cody Ceci .12 .30
8 Deryk Engelland .12 .30
9 Matt Moulson .12 .30
10 Nicolas Petan .12 .30
11 J.T. Miller .25 .60
12 Henrik Sedin .25 .60
13 Wayne Simmonds .25 .60
14 Johnny Boychuk .15 .40
15 Andreas Athanasiou .20 .50
16 Sami Vatanen .15 .40
17 Kris Russell .12 .30
18 Jordan Staal .15 .40
19 Brett Connolly .15 .40
20 Beau Bennett .12 .30
21 Brent Burns .20 .50
22 Trevor Lewis .12 .30
23 Brandon Sutter .12 .30
24 Louis Domingue .15 .40
25 Leon Draisaitl .60 1.50
26 Josh Bailey .15 .40
27 Jonathan Huberdeau .25 .60
28 Mark Scheifele .30 .75
29 Roman Josi .20 .50
30 Kris Versteeg .12 .30
31 Max Domi .20 .50
32 Ryan O'Reilly .20 .50
33 Craig Anderson .20 .50
34 Kevin Hayes .15 .40
35 Damon Severson .12 .30
36 Rickard Rakell .12 .30
37 Boone Jenner .20 .50
38 Joni Ortio .15 .40
39 Ian Cole .12 .30
40 Dan Hamhuis .12 .30
41 John Tavares .30 .75
42 Henrik Zetterberg .25 .60
43 Calle Jarnkrok .15 .40
44 Jason Pominville .15 .40
45 Garret Sparks .12 .30
46 Johnny Oduya .12 .30
47 Jake Allen .20 .50
48 Nikita Zadorov .12 .30
49 Brian Campbell .12 .30
50 Valtteri Filppula .12 .30
51 Trevor Daley .12 .30
52 Brendan Smith .12 .30
53 Andrei Markov .15 .40
54 Dustin Brown .20 .50
55 Jamie Benn .25 .60
56 Ryan Suter .15 .40
57 Nicklas Backstrom .20 .50
58 Willie Mitchell .12 .30
59 Michal Rozsival .15 .40
60 Chris Kreider .25 .60
61 Frederik Andersen .25 .60
62 Nick Leddy .12 .30
63 Brendan Gallagher .20 .50
64 Carter Hutton .15 .40
65 Zemgus Girgensons .12 .30
66 Cam Talbot .20 .50
67 Brian Dumoulin .15 .40
68 Joe Thornton .30 .75
69 Colin Miller .12 .30
70 Andrei Vasilevskiy .30 .75
71 Milan Michalek .12 .30
72 Tom Wilson .20 .50
73 Mike Brown .12 .30
74 John Klingberg .20 .50
75 Derick Brassard .12 .30
76 Ryan Ellis .15 .40
77 Erik Johnson .12 .30
78 Jaromir Jagr .60 1.50
79 Zach Bogosian .15 .40
80 Joel Ward .12 .30
81 Alex Tanguay .12 .30
82 Jake Muzzin .20 .50
83 Olli Maatta .12 .30
84 Brad Marchand .40 1.00
85 Danny DeKeyser .12 .30
86 Patrik Berglund .12 .30
87 Andre Burakovsky .12 .30
88 Joonas Korpisalo .20 .50
89 James Neal .20 .50
90 Mattias Janmark .12 .30
91 Marc-Andre Fleury .40 1.00
92 Martin Marincin .15 .40
93 Marc Staal .12 .30
94 Andrew Cogliano .12 .30
95 J.T. Brown .12 .30
96 Luke Glendening .12 .30
97 David Krejci .20 .50
98 Justin Braun .12 .30
99 Erik Gudbranson .12 .30
100 Anze Kopitar .30 .75
101 Rick Nash .15 .40
102 Joakim Nordstrom .12 .30
103 Matt Read .12 .30
104 Brad Richardson .12 .30
105 Michael Grabner .15 .40
106 Carey Price .40 1.00
107 Evgeny Medvedev .12 .30
108 Matt Niskanen .12 .30
109 Jordan Eberle .20 .50
110 Checklist 1-110 .12 .30
111 Mikael Granlund .15 .40
112 Niklas Hjalmarsson .12 .30
113 Marek Zidlicky .12 .30
114 Tyler Johnson .12 .30
115 Devante Smith-Pelly .15 .40
116 Matt Stajan .12 .30
117 Tyler Myers .12 .30
118 Ryan McDonagh .12 .30
119 Francois Beauchemin .15 .40
120 Adam McQuaid .12 .30
121 Jean-Gabriel Pageau .12 .30
122 Jhonas Enroth .20 .50
123 Jamie McGinn .12 .30
124 Dion Phaneuf .15 .40
125 Josh Gorges .12 .30
126 Teddy Purcell .12 .30
127 Brian Boyle .12 .30
128 Justin Fontaine .15 .40
129 Benoit Pouliot .15 .40
130 Jori Lehtera .12 .30
131 Michael Stone .12 .30
132 Ryan Kesler .20 .50
133 Elias Lindholm .20 .50
134 Jeff Carter .15 .40
135 Keith Kinkaid .12 .30
136 Braydon Coburn .12 .30
137 Barret Jackman .12 .30
138 Tobias Enstrom .12 .30
139 Troy Brouwer .12 .30
140 Derek Mackenzie .12 .30
141 Jason Spezza .20 .50
142 Rick Nash .20 .50
143 Paul Martin .15 .40
144 Cam Fowler .20 .50
145 Dalton Prout .12 .30
146 Marian Hossa .20 .50
147 Nathan Gerbe .12 .30
148 Mark Pysyk .12 .30
149 Dwight King .15 .40
150 John Mitchell .12 .30
151 Jaroslav Halak .20 .50
152 Karl Alzner .12 .30
153 Roman Polak .12 .30
154 John-Michael Liles .15 .40
155 Jay McClement .12 .30
156 Trevor van Riemsdyk .15 .40
157 Sam Reinhart .40 1.00
158 Patrik Elias .20 .50
159 Jay Bouwmeester .12 .30
160 Stefan Matteau .12 .30
161 Mathieu Perreault .12 .30
162 Connor Murphy .12 .30
163 Dennis Wideman .12 .30
164 Oscar Lindberg .12 .30
165 Evgeni Malkin .40 1.00
166 Connor McDavid 1.00 2.50
167 Shawn Matthias .12 .30
168 Kevan Miller .12 .30
169 Jarret Stoll .15 .40
170 Dale Weise .12 .30
171 Matt Bartkowski .12 .30
172 Mark Stuart .12 .30
173 Joonas Donskoi .12 .30
174 Pavel Datsyuk .30 .75
175 Braden Holtby .25 .60
176 Patric Hornqvist .12 .30
177 Brian Elliott .15 .40
178 Mikael Backlund .15 .40
179 Valeri Nichushkin .20 .50
180 Blake Wheeler .20 .50
181 Jannik Hansen .12 .30
182 Rasmus Ristolainen .20 .50
183 Ryan Spooner .15 .40
184 P.K. Subban .25 .60
185 Matt Duchene .20 .50
186 Brenden Dillon .12 .30
187 Kevin Bieksa .15 .40
188 Calvin de Haan .12 .30
189 Nick Bonino .12 .30
190 Oliver Ekman-Larsson .20 .50
191 Adam Lowry .12 .30
192 Mark Letestu .12 .30
193 Sven Baertschi .12 .30
194 Victor Rask .12 .30
195 William Karlsson .25 .60
196 Chris Neil .12 .30
197 Antti Raanta .20 .50
198 Nino Niederreiter .12 .30
199 Frans Nielsen .12 .30
200 Taylor Hall .20 .50
201 Nick Spaling .12 .30
202 Riley Sheahan .12 .30
203 Jacob Markstrom .20 .50
204 Loui Eriksson .12 .30
205 Nathan MacKinnon .75 2.00
206 Lars Eller .12 .30
207 Adam Henrique .15 .40
208 Dmitry Kulikov .15 .40
209 Nick Foligno .15 .40
210 Steve Mason .15 .40
211 Jonathan Toews .30 .75
212 Drew Stafford .12 .30
213 Henrik Lundqvist .50 1.25
214 Viktor Arvidsson .12 .30
215 Antoine Vermette .20 .50
216 Vincent Lecavalier .20 .50
217 Jaccob Slavin .15 .40
218 Jason Garrison .15 .40
219 Adam Larsson .20 .50
220 Checklist 111-220 .12 .30
221 Joffrey Lupul .12 .30
222 Kris Letang .25 .60
223 Patrice Bergeron .25 .60
224 Andrej Sekera .12 .30
225 Jonas Hiller .12 .30
226 Daniel Winnik .15 .40
227 Alexandre Burrows .12 .30
228 Cody Franson .12 .30
229 Roberto Luongo .30 .75
230 Shea Weber .15 .40
231 Niklas Kronwall .15 .40
232 Eric Staal .25 .60
233 Alexander Wennberg .12 .30
234 Joe Colborne .12 .30
235 Kyle Okposo .15 .40
236 Vladimir Tarasenko .25 .60
237 Ryan Nugent-Hopkins .25 .60
238 Alec Martinez .15 .40
239 Chris Kunitz .20 .50
240 Ron Hainsey .15 .40
241 Jordan Martinook .12 .30
242 Al Montoya .15 .40
243 Mathew Dumba .15 .40
244 Brent Seabrook .12 .30
245 Zdeno Chara .20 .50
246 Jarome Iginla .25 .60
247 Ben Bishop .15 .40
248 Antti Niemi .15 .40
249 John Gibson .20 .50
250 Joseph Blandisi .15 .40
251 Eddie Lack .15 .40
252 Jake McCabe .15 .40
253 Pekka Rinne .20 .50
254 Sergei Bobrovsky .30 .75
255 Thomas Vanek .15 .40
256 Torey Krug .15 .40
257 Calvin Pickard .20 .50
258 Alexander Steen .12 .30
259 Vincent Trocheck .20 .50
260 Evander Kane .20 .50
261 Mark Streit .15 .40
262 Karri Ramo .12 .30
263 Jonathan Ericsson .12 .30
264 Mark Stone .25 .60
265 Christopher Tanev .12 .30
266 Filip Forsberg .30 .75
267 Casey Cizikas .12 .30
268 Martin Hanzal .15 .40
269 Brooks Laich .12 .30
270 Michael Frolik .15 .40
271 Ales Hemsky .15 .40
272 Robin Lehner .15 .40
273 Philipp Grubauer .20 .50
274 Jiri Hudler .15 .40
275 Andrew Ladd .12 .30
276 Shea Theodore .25 .60
277 Chris Thorburn .12 .30
278 Derek Stepan .12 .30
279 Paul Gaustad .12 .30
280 Jake Virtanen .25 .60
281 Tyler Seguin .25 .60
282 Patrick Marleau .20 .50
283 Sidney Crosby .75 2.00
284 Brett Pesce .12 .30
285 Erik Karlsson .25 .60
286 Luke Schenn .20 .50
287 Michael Cammalleri .15 .40
288 Phil Kessel .20 .50
289 Corey Crawford .25 .60
290 Jyrki Jokipakka .12 .30
291 Dylan Larkin .25 .60
292 Carl Soderberg .12 .30
293 James van Riemsdyk .12 .30
294 Carl Gunnarsson .12 .30
295 Justin Faulk .12 .30
296 Milan Lucic .15 .40
297 Ondrej Pavelec .20 .50
298 Mike Richards .15 .40
299 Mike Smith .20 .50
300 Marco Scandella .12 .30
301 Mike Hoffman .12 .30
302 Jordie Benn .12 .30
303 Seth Jones .20 .50
304 Joe Pavelski .25 .60
305 Nick Bjugstad .12 .30
306 Mattias Ekholm .15 .40
307 Noah Hanifin .20 .50
308 Brayden McNabb .12 .30
309 Michal Neuvirth .15 .40
310 T.J. Oshie .25 .60
311 Teuvo Teravainen .20 .50
312 Mika Zibanejad .20 .50
313 Josh Manson .15 .40
314 Charlie Coyle .12 .30
315 Nick Holden .12 .30
316 Chris Tierney .12 .30
317 Pat Maroon .12 .30
318 Colin Wilson .12 .30
319 Jim Howard .25 .60
320 Thomas Hickey .12 .30
321 Scottie Upshall .12 .30
322 Tyler Toffoli .12 .30
323 Sean Couturier .15 .40
324 Mike Condon .20 .50
325 Curtis Lazar .12 .30
326 Teemu Pulkkinen .12 .30
327 Tomas Fleischmann .15 .40
328 Erik Haula .15 .40
329 Dmitry Orlov .20 .50
330 Checklist 221-330 .12 .30
331 Brandon Dubinsky .12 .30
332 Marian Gaborik .20 .50
333 Travis Zajac .12 .30
334 Kevin Connauton .15 .40
335 Mikhail Grabovski .12 .30
336 Peter Holland .12 .30
337 Matt Beleskey .15 .40
338 Reilly Smith .20 .50
339 Shawn Horcoff .12 .30
340 Blake Comeau .12 .30
341 Victor Hedman .25 .60
342 Sam Gagner .12 .30
343 Sam Bennett .30 .75
344 Michael Hutchinson .12 .30
345 Nail Yakupov .12 .30
346 Tyler Bozak .12 .30
347 Carl Hagelin .12 .30
348 Cody Eakin .12 .30
349 Dan Boyle .12 .30
350 David Backes .12 .30
351 Cory Schneider .20 .50
352 Miikka Salomaki .12 .30
353 Jared Spurgeon .20 .50
354 Alexei Emelin .12 .30
355 Patrick Kane .40 1.00
356 Aleksander Barkov .30 .75
357 Scott Laughton .12 .30
358 Matt Hunwick .15 .40
359 Justin Abdelkader .15 .40
360 Lee Stempniak .12 .30
361 Cam Atkinson .20 .50
362 Tobias Rieder .12 .30
363 Vernon Fiddler .12 .30
364 Micheal Ferland .12 .30
365 Tanner Pearson .15 .40
366 Brandon Saad .15 .40
367 Nikita Kucherov .40 1.00
368 Gabriel Landeskog .25 .60
369 Andy Greene .12 .30
370 Andrew Hammond .15 .40
371 Jimmy Hayes .12 .30
372 Matt Nieto .12 .30
373 Dmitrij Jaskin .12 .30
374 Tyler Ennis .12 .30
375 Brad Richards .20 .50
376 Matt Calvert .12 .30
377 Justin Williams .15 .40
378 Jeff Skinner .25 .60
379 Anders Lee .20 .50
380 Derek Dorsett .12 .30
381 Aaron Ekblad .25 .60
382 Tyson Barrie .12 .30
383 David Jones .12 .30
384 Daniel Girardi .12 .30
385 Jake Gardiner .12 .30
386 Jaden Schwartz .25 .60
387 Jeff Petry .12 .30
388 Alexander Burmistrov .12 .30
389 Marcus Johansson .20 .50
390 Riley Nash .12 .30
391 Matt Hendricks .12 .30
392 Marc Methot .15 .40
393 Bo Horvat .25 .60
394 Ryan Strome .20 .50
395 Kevin Klein .12 .30
396 Nathan Beaulieu .12 .30
397 David Schlemko .12 .30
398 Robby Fabbri .12 .30
399 Brandon Pirri .12 .30
400 David Savard .12 .30
401 Torrey Mitchell .12 .30
402 Rob Scuderi .12 .30
403 Radim Vrbata .12 .30
404 Mats Zuccarello .20 .50
405 Tommy Wingels .12 .30
406 Ondrej Palat .15 .40
407 Kevin Shattenkirk .12 .30
408 Shayne Gostisbehere .20 .50
409 Griffin Reinhart .12 .30
410 T.J. Brodie .15 .40
411 Jay Beagle .12 .30
412 Mikkel Boedker .12 .30
413 Jakub Voracek .15 .40
414 Ty Rattie .12 .30
415 Brad Boyes .12 .30
416 Devan Dubnyk .15 .40
417 Jakob Silfverberg .12 .30
418 Ryan Miller .20 .50
419 Erik Gustafsson .12 .30
420 Nikolai Kulemin .12 .30
421 Johnny Gaudreau .30 .75
422 Jesper Fast .12 .30
423 Claude Giroux .20 .50
424 Nate Schmidt .12 .30
425 Petr Mrazek .20 .50
426 Logan Couture .25 .60
427 Alex Pietrangelo .15 .40
428 Jason Demers .12 .30
429 Zach Parise .20 .50
430 Jonathan Drouin .15 .40
431 Alexander Ovechkin .75 2.00
432 Michael Raffl .12 .30
433 Andrew Desjardins .15 .40
434 Andrej Sustr .12 .30
435 Dominic Moore .12 .30
436 Tuukka Rask .25 .60
437 Alex Galchenyuk .20 .50
438 Leo Komarov .12 .30
439 Radko Gudas .25 .60
440 Checklist 331-440 .12 .30
441 Mike Ribeiro .12 .30
442 Jonas Brodin .12 .30
443 Dustin Byfuglien .20 .50
444 Vladislav Namestnikov .12 .30
445 John Moore .12 .30
446 Martin Jones .25 .60
447 John Carlson .20 .50
448 Artem Anisimov .12 .30
449 Ryan Murray .12 .30
450 Gustav Nyquist .12 .30
451 Cody McLeod .12 .30
452 Sean Monahan .12 .30
453 Alexander Edler .12 .30
454 Patrick Sharp .15 .40
455 Ryan Johansen .15 .40
456 Cal Clutterbuck .12 .30
457 Keith Yandle .12 .30
458 Marcus Kruger .12 .30
459 Tomas Plekanec .12 .30
460 Brian Gionta .12 .30
461 Lauri Korpikoski .12 .30
462 Radek Faksa .12 .30
463 Jussi Jokinen .20 .50
464 Mike Fisher .12 .30
465 Andrew Copp .12 .30
466 Brooks Orpik .12 .30
467 Zack Smith .12 .30
468 Reto Berra .12 .30
469 P.A. Parenteau .12 .30
470 Shane Doan .15 .40
471 Dougie Hamilton .15 .40
472 Kyle Palmieri .15 .40
473 Matt Cullen .20 .50
474 Scott Darling .15 .40
475 Brayden Schenn .20 .50
476 Mikhail Grigorenko .12 .30
477 Ryan Reaves .12 .30
478 Darren Helm .12 .30
479 James Reimer .20 .50
480 Sven Andrighetto .15 .40
481 Anton Stralman .15 .40
482 Craig Smith .12 .30
483 David Pastrnak .50 1.25
484 David Perron .15 .40
485 Scott Hartnell .12 .30
486 Brandon Davidson .12 .30
487 Darcy Kuemper .20 .50
488 Travis Hamonic .12 .30
489 Marcus Foligno .15 .40
490 Bryan Rust .20 .50
491 Daniel Sedin .25 .60
492 Nazem Kadri .25 .60
493 Reid Boucher .12 .30
494 Jason Chimera .12 .30
495 Mark Giordano .20 .50
496 Darnell Nurse .15 .40
497 Marc-Edouard Vlasic .15 .40
498 Jack Johnson .12 .30
499 Anthony Duclair .15 .40
500 Alex Killorn .12 .30
501 Kyle Turris .15 .40
502 Andrej Nestrasil .15 .40
503 Drew Doughty .25 .60
504 Ben Lovejoy .12 .30
505 Nick Schultz .12 .30
506 Sergei Plotnikov .12 .30
507 Ryan Getzlaf .20 .50
508 Oscar Klefbom .30 .75
509 Carl Soderberg .12 .30
510 Mike Green .15 .40
511 Jack Eichel .30 .75
512 Paul Stastny .15 .40
513 Patrick Wiercioch .15 .40
514 Yannick Weber .12 .30
515 Antoine Roussel .12 .30
516 Connor Hellebuyck .40 1.00
517 Viktor Stalberg .15 .40
518 Matt Carle .12 .30
519 Jakub Kindl .12 .30
520 Semyon Varlamov .20 .50
521 Matt Murray .30 .75
522 Hampus Lindholm .12 .30
523 Duncan Keith .15 .40
524 Brock Nelson .20 .50
525 David Desharnais .12 .30
526 Jonathan Bernier .15 .40
527 Nikolaj Ehlers .20 .50
528 Jared McCann .15 .40
529 Jason Zucker .20 .50
530 Jacob Trouba .15 .40
531 Michael Del Zotto .12 .30
532 Corey Perry .30 .75
533 Tomas Tatar .12 .30
534 Nick Shore .12 .30
535 Bryan Little .15 .40
536 Morgan Rielly .20 .50
537 Max Pacioretty .20 .50
538 Justin Schultz .12 .30
539 Colton Parayko .15 .40
540 Artemi Panarin .40 1.00
541 Kari Lehtonen .12 .30
542 Cam Ward .20 .50
543 Alex Petrovic .12 .30
544 Evgeny Kuznetsov .25 .60
545 Bobby Ryan .15 .40
546 Mikko Koivu .15 .40
547 Dennis Seidenberg .12 .30
548 Tomas Hertl .20 .50
549 Thomas Greiss .15 .40
550 Checklist 441-550 .12 .30
551 Mike Reilly RC 1.00 2.50
552 Mark McNeill RC 1.25 3.00
553 J.C. Lipon RC 1.25 3.00
554 Daniel Altshuller RC 1.00 2.50
555 Chris Bigras RC 1.00 2.50
556 Oliver Bjorkstrand RC 1.50 4.00
557 Esa Lindell RC 1.50 4.00
558 Brendan Leipsic RC 1.00 2.50
559 Hudson Fasching RC 1.25 3.00
560 Oliver Kylington RC 1.00 2.50
561 Zach Hyman RC 4.00 10.00
562 Justin Bailey RC 1.25 3.00
563 Connor Brown RC 2.00 5.00
564 Oskar Sundqvist RC 1.25 3.00
565 Alan Quine RC 1.25 3.00
566 Kevin Gravel RC 1.50 4.00
567 Alex Friesen RC 1.50 4.00
568 Sonny Milano RC 1.50 4.00
569 Marek Hrivik RC 1.50 4.00
570 Kasperi Kapanen RC 2.00 5.00
571 Michael Matheson RC 1.25 3.00
572 Pontus Aberg RC 1.50 4.00
573 Nick Paul RC 1.25 3.00
574 Ryan Pulock RC 1.25 3.00
575 Garnet Hathaway RC 1.50 4.00
576 William Nylander RC 5.00 12.00
577 Jared Coreau RC 1.50 4.00
578 Darren Dietz RC 1.50 4.00
579 Nikita Soshnikov RC .75 2.00
580 Aaron Dell RC 1.25 3.00
581 Kyle Rau RC 1.50 4.00
582 Steven Santini RC 1.00 2.50
583 Noel Acciari RC 1.50 4.00

584 Josh Morrissey RC 3.00 8.00
585 Charlie Lindgren RC 2.00 5.00
586 Tobias Lindberg RC 2.00 5.00
587 Anthony Mantha RC 2.50 6.00
588 Trevor Carrick RC 1.25 3.00
589 Scott Kosmachuk RC 1.25 3.00
590 Nikita Tryamkin RC 1.00 2.50
591 Dominik Simon RC 1.00 2.50
592 Steve Michalek RC 1.50 4.00
593 Rinat Valiev RC 1.50 4.00
594 Jason Dickinson RC 1.00 2.50
595 Frederik Gauthier RC 1.00 2.50
596 Miles Wood RC 1.00 2.50
597 Nic Dowd RC 1.00 2.50
598 Sergey Tolchinsky RC 1.00 2.50
599 Evan Rodrigues RC 2.00 5.00
600 Pavel Zacha RC 2.00 5.00
601 Connor McDavid SH 5.00 12.00
602 Corey Perry SH 1.50 4.00
603 Alexander Ovechkin SH 4.00 10.00
604 Steven Stamkos SH 2.00 5.00
605 Patrick Kane SH 2.00 5.00
606 Henrik Zetterberg SH 1.25 3.00
607 Patrick Marleau SH 1.00 2.50
608 Drew Doughty SH 1.25 3.00
609 Jarome Iginla SH 1.25 3.00
610 Joe Thornton SH 1.50 4.00
611 Jonathan Quick SH 1.25 3.00
612 Braden Holtby SH 1.25 3.00
613 Jaromir Jagr SH 3.00 8.00
614 Jonathan Toews SH 1.50 4.00
615 Daniel Sedin SH 1.25 3.00
616 Anaheim Ducks CL .25 .60
617 Arizona Coyotoes CL .25 .60
618 Boston Bruins CL .25 .60
619 Buffalo Sabres CL .25 .60
620 Calgary Flames CL .25 .60
621 Carolina Hurricanes CL .25 .60
622 Chicago Blackhawks CL .25 .60
623 Colorado Avalanche CL .25 .60
624 Columbus Blue Jackets CL .25 .60
625 Dallas Stars CL .25 .60
626 Detroit Red Wings CL .25 .60
627 Edmonton Oilers CL .25 .60
628 Florida Panthers CL .25 .60
629 Los Angeles Kings CL .25 .60
630 Minnesota Wild CL .25 .60
631 Montreal Canadiens CL .25 .60
632 Nashville Predators CL .25 .60
633 New Jersey Devils CL .25 .60
634 New York Islanders CL .25 .60
635 New York Rangers CL .25 .60
636 Ottawa Senators CL .25 .60
637 Philadelphia Flyers CL .25 .60
638 Pittsburgh Penguins CL .25 .60
639 San Jose Sharks CL .25 .60
640 St. Louis Blues CL .25 .60
641 Tampa Bay Lightning CL .25 .60
642 Toronto Maple Leafs CL .25 .60
643 Vancouver Canucks CL .25 .60
644 Washington Capitals CL .25 .60
645 Winnipeg Jets CL .25 .60
646 Artemi Panarin LL 2.00 5.00
647 Derek Dorsett LL .60 1.50
648 Tyler Toffoli LL 1.00 2.50
649 Jean-Gabriel Pageau LL .60 1.50
650 Alexander Ovechkin LL 4.00 10.00
651 Jonathan Toews LL 1.50 4.00
652 Joe Pavelski LL 1.25 3.00
653 Brian Elliott LL .75 2.00
654 Ben Bishop LL .75 2.00
655 Corey Crawford LL 1.25 3.00
656 Braden Holtby LL 1.25 3.00
657 Erik Karlsson LL 1.25 3.00
658 Alexander Ovechkin LL 4.00 10.00
659 Patrick Kane LL 2.00 5.00
660 Checklist 551-660 .60 1.50
661A Patrick Kane - Hart Trophy 15.00 40.00
661B Taylor Hall .50 1.25
662A Braden Holtby - Vezina Trophy 10.00 25.00
662B David Backes .30 .75
663A Drew Doughty - Norris Trophy 10.00 25.00
663B Kyle Okposo .30 .75
664A Patrick Kane - Art Ross Trophy 15.00 40.00
664B Mikkel Boedker .30 .75
665A Alex Ovechkin - Rocket Richard Trophy 30.00 80.00
665B Milan Lucic .40 1.00
666A Anze Kopitar - Frank J. Selke Trophy 12.00 30.00
666B Shea Weber .40 1.00
667A Patrick Kane - Ted Lindsay Award 15.00 40.00
667B P.K. Subban .60 1.50
668A Sidney Crosby - Conn Smythe Trophy 30.00 80.00
668B Frederik Andersen .60 1.50
669A Artemi Panarin - Calder Trophy 15.00 40.00
669B Thomas Vanek .40 1.00
670A Bobby Hull 15.00 40.00
670B David Perron .75 2.00
671A Dominik Hasek 12.00 30.00
671B Tyler Motte RC 1.00 2.50
672A Nicklas Lidstrom 8.00 20.00
672B Mitch Marner RC 3.00 8.00
673A Patrick Roy 20.00 50.00
673B Zach Sanford RC 1.00 2.50
674A Mike Modano 12.00 30.00
674B A.J. Greer RC 1.00 2.50
675A Steve Yzerman 20.00 50.00
675B Jake Guentzel RC 3.00 8.00
676A Chris Chelios 8.00 20.00
676B Kyle Connor RC 3.00 8.00
677A Milt Schmidt 8.00 20.00
677B Artturi Lehkonen RC 1.25 3.00
678A Sidney Crosby 30.00 80.00
678B Zach Werenski RC 3.00 8.00
679 Patrik Laine RC 2.50 6.00
680 Nikita Zaitsev RC 1.00 2.50
681 Matthew Tkachuk RC 4.00 10.00
682 Brayden Point RC 2.50 6.00
683 Thomas Chabot RC 2.00 5.00
684 Jimmy Vesey RC 1.50 4.00
685 Danton Heinen RC .75 2.00
686 Ivan Provorov RC 1.50 4.00
687 Sebastian Aho RC 3.00 8.00
688 Dylan Strome RC 2.50 6.00
689 Mathew Barzal RC 3.00 8.00
690 Julius Honka RC 1.00 2.50
691 Jakob Chychrun RC 2.00 5.00
692 Travis Konecny RC 2.00 5.00
693 Kevin Labanc RC 1.00 2.50
694 Auston Matthews RC 10.00 25.00
695 Tom Kuhnhackl RC .75 2.00
696 Christian Dvorak RC 1.25 3.00
697 Joel Eriksson Ek RC 1.50 4.00
698 Jacob Larsson RC 1.50 4.00
699 Anthony DeAngelo RC .75 2.00
700 Pavel Buchnevich RC 1.50 4.00
701 Nick Schmaltz RC 1.25 3.00
702 Troy Stecher RC 1.00 2.50
703 Brandon Carlo RC 1.50 4.00
704 Jesse Puljujarvi RC 2.00 5.00
705 Anthony Beauvillier RC 1.00 2.50
706 Drake Caggiula RC 1.00 2.50
707 Mikhail Sergachev RC 1.50 4.00
708 Nick Baptiste RC 1.00 2.50
709 Denis Malgin RC .75 2.00
710 Nick Lappin RC 1.00 2.50

2016-17 O-Pee-Chee Rainbow Black

*1-550 VETS: 6X TO 15X BASIC CARDS
*551-710 ROOKIES: 1.2X TO 3X BASIC CARDS
601-660 SH/LL 1.5X TO 4X BASIC SP
57 Nicklas Backstrom 3.00 8.00
289 Corey Crawford 4.00 10.00
430 Jonathan Drouin 2.50 6.00
544 Evgeny Kuznetsov 4.00 10.00
655 Corey Crawford LL 4.00 10.00
672 Mitch Marner 50.00 125.00
679 Patrik Laine 50.00 120.00
694 Auston Matthews 100.00 225.00

2016-17 O-Pee-Chee Retro

*1-550 VETS: 2.5X TO 1.2X BASIC CARDS
*551-600 ROOKIES: .6X TO 1.5X BASIC CARDS
601-660 SH/LL .6X TO 1.50X BASIC SP
694 Auston Matthews 15.00 40.00

2016-17 O-Pee-Chee Patches

P1 John Gibson 5.00 12.00
P2 Max Domi 5.00 12.00
P3 David Krejci 5.00 12.00
P4 Jack Eichel 8.00 20.00
P5 Sam Bennett 8.00 20.00
P6 Noah Hanifin 5.00 12.00
P7 Jonathan Toews 8.00 20.00
P8 Duncan Keith 4.00 10.00
P9 Artemi Panarin 10.00 25.00
P10 Gabriel Landeskog 6.00 15.00
P11 Brandon Saad 4.00 10.00
P12 Tyler Seguin 6.00 15.00
P13 John Klingberg 5.00 12.00
P14 Dylan Larkin 6.00 15.00
P15 Connor McDavid 25.00 60.00
P16 Taylor Hall 5.00 12.00
P17 Aleksander Barkov 8.00 20.00
P18 Drew Doughty 6.00 15.00
P19 Jeff Carter 4.00 10.00
P20 Ryan Suter 4.00 10.00
P21 Carey Price 10.00 25.00
P22 Brendan Gallagher 5.00 12.00
P23 Pekka Rinne 5.00 12.00
P24 Shea Weber 4.00 10.00
P25 Cory Schneider 5.00 12.00
P26 Jaroslav Halak 5.00 12.00
P27 Mats Zuccarello 5.00 12.00
P28 Derek Stepan 3.00 8.00
P29 Erik Karlsson 6.00 15.00
P30 Wayne Simmonds 6.00 15.00
P31 Kris Letang 6.00 15.00
P32 Evgeni Malkin 10.00 25.00
P33 Logan Couture 6.00 15.00
P34 Alex Pietrangelo 4.00 10.00
P35 Victor Hedman 6.00 15.00
P36 Morgan Rielly 5.00 12.00
P37 Henrik Sedin 6.00 15.00
P38 Evgeny Kuznetsov 6.00 15.00
P39 Braden Holtby 6.00 15.00
P40 Dustin Byfuglien 5.00 12.00
P41 Wayne Gretzky LEG 40.00 100.00
P42 Jari Kurri LEG 6.00 15.00
P43 Joe Sakic LEG 12.00 30.00
P44 Dominik Hasek LEG 10.00 25.00
P45 Steve Yzerman LEG 15.00 40.00
P46 Mike Reilly 5.00 12.00
P47 William Nylander 25.00 60.00
P48 Michael Matheson 6.00 15.00
P49 Chris Bigras 5.00 12.00
P50 Nick Paul 8.00 20.00
P51 Shea Weber '16 AS 6.00 15.00
P52 Braden Holtby '16 AS 10.00 25.00
P53 Patrick Kane '16 AS 15.00 40.00
P54 Taylor Hall '16 AS 8.00 20.00
P55 Jaromir Jagr '16 AS 25.00 60.00
P56 Drew Doughty '16 AS 10.00 25.00
P57 Johnny Gaudreau '16 AS 12.00 30.00
P58 Justin Faulk '16 AS 6.00 15.00
P59 Dylan Larkin '16 AS 10.00 25.00
P60 Tyler Seguin '16 AS 10.00 25.00
P61 Carey Price '15 AS 12.00 30.00
P62 Anze Kopitar '15 AS 10.00 25.00
P63 Jonathan Toews '15 AS 10.00 25.00
P64 Steven Stamkos '15 AS 12.00 30.00
P65 John Tavares '15 AS 10.00 25.00
P66 Claude Giroux '12 AS 6.00 15.00
P67 Phil Kessel '12 AS 6.00 15.00
P68 Jason Spezza '12 AS 6.00 15.00
P69 Henrik Lundqvist '12 AS 15.00 40.00
P70 James Neal '12 AS 4.00 10.00
P71 Brent Burns '11 AS 6.00 15.00
P72 Rick Nash '11 AS 6.00 15.00
P73 Patrick Sharp '11 AS 5.00 12.00
P74 Mike Green '11 AS 5.00 12.00
P75 Duncan Keith '11 AS 5.00 12.00
P76 Joe Thornton '09 AS 10.00 25.00
P77 Evgeni Malkin '09 AS 12.00 30.00
P78 Zach Parise '09 AS 6.00 15.00
P79 Ryan Getzlaf '09 AS 6.00 15.00
P80 Jeff Carter '09 AS 5.00 12.00
P81 Pavel Datsyuk '08 AS 10.00 25.00
P82 Jarome Iginla '08 AS 8.00 20.00
P83 Eric Staal '08 AS 8.00 20.00
P84 Marian Hossa '08 AS 6.00 15.00
P85 Corey Perry '08 AS 10.00 25.00
P86 Wayne Gretzky '88 AS 250.00 600.00
P87 Larry Robinson '88 AS 40.00 100.00
P88 Patrick Roy '88 AS 100.00 250.00
P89 Steve Yzerman '88 AS 100.00 250.00
P90 Mario Lemieux '88 AS 150.00 400.00

2016-17 O-Pee-Chee Playing Cards

2C Daniel Sedin 1.50 4.00
2D Shayne Gostisbehere 1.25 3.00
2H Morgan Rielly 1.25 3.00
2S Brad Marchand 2.50 6.00
3C Henrik Sedin 1.50 4.00
3D Dylan Larkin 1.50 4.00
3H Mats Zuccarello 1.25 3.00
3S Adam Henrique 1.00 2.50
4C Mark Scheifele 2.00 5.00
4D Aleksander Barkov 2.00 5.00
4H Ryan Suter 1.00 2.50
4S Brian Elliott 1.00 2.50
5C Brandon Saad 1.00 2.50
5D Ben Bishop 1.00 2.50
5H Henrik Zetterberg 1.50 4.00
5S Brent Burns 1.25 3.00
6C Dustin Byfuglien 1.25 3.00
6D Sean Monahan .75 2.00
6H Shea Weber 1.00 2.50
6S Zach Parise 1.25 3.00
7C Pekka Rinne 1.25 3.00
7D Anze Kopitar 2.00 5.00
7H Cory Schneider 1.25 3.00
7S Claude Giroux 1.25 3.00
8C Matt Duchene 1.25 3.00
8D Patrice Bergeron 1.50 4.00
8H Johnny Gaudreau 2.00 5.00
8S Oliver Ekman-Larsson 1.25 3.00
9C Artemi Panarin 2.50 6.00
9D Taylor Hall 1.25 3.00
9H Nathan MacKinnon 5.00 12.00
9S Tyler Seguin 1.50 4.00
AC Connor McDavid 8.00 20.00
AD Sidney Crosby 6.00 15.00
AH Henrik Lundqvist 4.00 10.00
AS Erik Karlsson 2.00 5.00
JC Jamie Benn 1.25 3.00
JD Ryan Getzlaf 1.25 3.00
JH Joe Thornton 2.00 5.00
JS Vladimir Tarasenko 1.50 4.00
KC Jack Eichel 2.00 5.00
KD Alexander Ovechkin 5.00 12.00
KH Steven Stamkos 2.50 6.00
KS Jonathan Toews 2.00 5.00
QC Drew Doughty 1.50 4.00
QD Jaromir Jagr 4.00 10.00
QH Patrick Kane 2.50 6.00
QS John Tavares 2.00 5.00
10C Corey Perry 2.00 5.00
10D Braden Holtby 1.50 4.00
10H Evgeni Malkin 2.50 6.00
10S Carey Price 2.50 6.00

2016-17 O-Pee-Chee Puck Stickers

1 Teemu Selanne 3.00 8.00
2 Oliver Ekman-Larsson 1.50 4.00
3 Patrice Bergeron 2.00 5.00
4 Jack Eichel 2.50 6.00
5 Sam Bennett 2.50 6.00
6 Rod Brind'Amour 1.50 4.00
7 Patrick Kane 3.00 8.00
8 Matt Duchene 1.50 4.00
9 Brandon Saad 1.25 3.00
10 Jamie Benn 1.50 4.00
11 Henrik Zetterberg 2.00 5.00
12 Connor McDavid 8.00 20.00
13 Aaron Ekblad 2.00 5.00
14 Drew Doughty 2.00 5.00
15 Ryan Suter 1.25 3.00
16 P.K. Subban 2.00 5.00
17 Filip Forsberg 2.50 6.00
18 Adam Henrique 1.25 3.00
19 Jaroslav Halak 1.50 4.00
20 Mark Messier 3.00 8.00
21 Bobby Ryan 1.25 3.00
22 Jakub Voracek 1.25 3.00
23 Mario Lemieux 6.00 15.00
24 Brent Burns 1.50 4.00
25 Jake Allen 1.50 4.00
26 Victor Hedman 2.00 5.00
27 Morgan Rielly 1.50 4.00
28 Bo Horvat 2.00 5.00
29 Evgeny Kuznetsov 2.00 5.00
30 Blake Wheeler 1.50 4.00

2016-17 O-Pee-Chee Glossy Rookies

R1 Auston Matthews 8.00 20.00
R2 Mitch Marner 3.00 8.00
R3 Zach Werenski 3.00 8.00
R4 William Nylander 4.00 10.00
R5 Matthew Tkachuk 4.00 10.00
R6 Jesse Puljujarvi 2.00 5.00
R7 Jimmy Vesey 1.50 4.00
R8 Travis Konecny 2.00 5.00
R9 Pavel Zacha 1.50 4.00
R10 Patrik Laine 2.50 6.00

2016-17 O-Pee-Chee Signatures

SAA Andy Andreoff E 4.00 10.00
SAB Aleksander Barkov D 8.00 20.00
SAH Andrew Hammond D 4.00 10.00
SAS Andrew Shaw C 5.00 12.00
SBB Brent Burns B 10.00 25.00
SBC Barclay Goodrow E 3.00 8.00
SCG Claude Giroux B 10.00 25.00
SDD David Desharnais D 3.00 8.00
SDK David Krejci D 5.00 12.00
SFC Frank Corrado E 4.00 10.00
SJC Joe Colborne B 6.00 15.00
SJF Justin Fontaine E 4.00 10.00
SJH Jiri Hudler D 4.00 10.00
SJP Jean-Gabriel Pageau E 3.00 8.00
SJV James van Riemsdyk B 8.00 20.00
SKT Kyle Turris E 4.00 10.00
SMB Matt Beleskey D 4.00 10.00
SMD Matt Duchene B 10.00 25.00
SMM Matt Moulson D 3.00 8.00
SMR Morgan Rielly D 5.00 12.00
SMS Mark Scheifele E 8.00 20.00
SND Nicolas Deslauriers E 3.00 8.00
SNF Nick Foligno D 4.00 10.00
SOK Oscar Klefbom D 8.00 20.00
STJ Tyler Johnson D 3.00 8.00
STP Teemu Pulkkinen C 5.00 12.00
STT Tyler Toffoli C 8.00 20.00
USAB Anthony Beauvillier E 5.00 12.00
USBP Brayden Point E 12.00 30.00
USDH Danton Heinen E 4.00 10.00
USHF Hudson Fasching E 5.00 12.00
USJP Jesse Puljujarvi B 20.00 50.00
USKC Kyle Connor C 25.00 60.00
USMA Anthony Mantha C 15.00 40.00
USMM Mitch Marner C 50.00 125.00
USMT Matthew Tkachuk C 30.00 80.00
USMW Miles Wood E 4.00 10.00
USNS Nick Schmaltz D 6.00 15.00
USPB Pavel Buchnevich D 8.00 20.00
USPL Patrik Laine B 125.00 250.00
USPZ Pavel Zacha C 12.00 30.00
USSM Sonny Milano E 6.00 15.00
USTM Tyler Motte E 5.00 12.00
USWN William Nylander C 30.00 80.00
USZW Zach Werenski D 15.00 40.00

2016-17 O-Pee-Chee Team Canada Signatures

TCSAD Anthony Duclair E 5.00 12.00
TCSAE Aaron Ekblad B 20.00 50.00
TCSAH Adam Henrique C 8.00 20.00
TCSAP Alex Pietrangelo C 8.00 20.00
TCSBG Brendan Gallagher B 15.00 40.00
TCSCW Cam Ward C 10.00 25.00
TCSDN Darnell Nurse B 12.00 30.00
TCSES Eric Staal C 12.00 30.00
TCSJH Jonathan Huberdeau D 8.00 20.00
TCSJS Jordan Staal C 8.00 20.00
TCSJV Jake Virtanen C 12.00 30.00
TCSKT Kyle Turris D 5.00 12.00
TCSMR Morgan Rielly E 6.00 15.00
TCSMS Mark Scheifele D 10.00 25.00
TCSRF Robby Fabbri E 4.00 10.00
TCSRN Rick Nash B 15.00 40.00
TCSSB Sam Bennett C 15.00 40.00
TCSSK Jeff Skinner C 12.00 30.00
TCSSM Sean Monahan C 6.00 15.00
TCSTH Taylor Hall B 15.00 40.00
TCSTT Tyler Toffoli E 6.00 15.00

2016-17 O-Pee-Chee V Series C

S1 Cory Schneider 1.50 4.00
S2 Justin Faulk 1.25 3.00
S3 Claude Giroux 1.50 4.00
S4 Ryan Johansen 1.25 3.00
S5 Mike Modano 2.50 6.00
S6 Brandon Saad 1.25 3.00
S7 Sidney Crosby 6.00 15.00
S8 Victor Hedman 2.00 5.00
S9 Corey Perry 2.50 6.00
S10 Tyler Seguin 2.00 5.00
S11 Connor McDavid 8.00 20.00
S12 Patrick Kane 3.00 8.00
S13 Nathan MacKinnon 6.00 15.00
S14 John Tavares 2.50 6.00
S15 Alex Pietrangelo 1.25 3.00
S16 Oliver Ekman-Larsson 1.50 4.00
S17 Pavel Bure 1.50 4.00
S18 Carey Price 3.00 8.00
S19 Wayne Gretzky 10.00 25.00
S20 Bobby Orr 6.00 15.00
S21 Artemi Panarin 3.00 8.00
S22 Patrice Bergeron 2.00 5.00
S23 Taylor Hall 1.50 4.00
S24 Morgan Rielly 1.50 4.00
S25 P.K. Subban 2.00 5.00
S26 Joe Pavelski 2.00 5.00
S27 Dylan Larkin 2.00 5.00
S28 Dustin Byfuglien 1.50 4.00
S29 Jack Eichel 2.50 6.00
S30 Henrik Lundqvist 4.00 10.00
S31 Ryan Suter 1.25 3.00
S32 Aleksander Barkov 2.50 6.00
S33 Sean Monahan 1.00 2.50
S34 Vladimir Tarasenko 2.00 5.00
S35 Alexander Ovechkin 6.00 15.00
S36 Ryan Getzlaf 1.50 4.00
S37 Erik Karlsson 2.00 5.00
S38 Daniel Sedin 2.00 5.00
S39 Drew Doughty 2.00 5.00
S40 Mario Lemieux 6.00 15.00

2017-18 O-Pee-Chee

1 Auston Matthews .75 2.00
2 Tyler Seguin .25 .60
3 Kevin Shattenkirk .12 .30
4 Marian Hossa .20 .50
5 Evgeni Malkin .40 1.00
6 Cam Talbot .20 .50
7 Jeff Carter .15 .40
8 Max Pacioretty .20 .50
9 Tom Pyatt .12 .30
10 Nicklas Backstrom .20 .50
11 Slater Koekkoek .12 .30
12 Alan Quine .12 .30
13 Marc-Andre Fleury .40 1.00
14 Sven Andrighetto .12 .30
15 Patrik Laine .25 .60
16 Jakub Voracek .15 .40
17 Mike Fisher .12 .30
18 Eric Staal .25 .60
19 Patrik Berglund .12 .30
20 Lawson Crouse .12 .30
21 William Carrier .12 .30
22 Matthew Tkachuk .40 1.00
23 Elias Lindholm .20 .50
24 Marian Gaborik .20 .50
25 Brent Burns .20 .50
26 David Perron .15 .40
27 Connor Carrick .15 .40
28 Jack Skille .12 .30
29 Micheal Ferland .12 .30
30 Henrik Zetterberg .25 .60
31 Jakob Silfverberg .12 .30
32 Sam Gagner .12 .30
33 Adam Larsson .20 .50
34 Ben Bishop .15 .40
35 Adam Henrique .15 .40
36 Craig Anderson .20 .50
37 Nikita Kucherov .40 1.00
38 Cody Eakin .12 .30
39 Martin Jones .15 .40
40 Leo Komarov .12 .30
41 Josh Bailey .15 .40
42 Mikko Rantanen .50 1.25
43 Andrew Copp .12 .30
44 David Pastrnak .50 1.25
45 Paul Stastny .15 .40
46 Ryan Getzlaf .20 .50
47 Joonas Donskoi .12 .30
48 Patric Hornqvist .12 .30
49 Anthony Beauvillier .12 .30
50 Carey Price .40 1.00
51 Colton Sissons .12 .30
52 Devante Smith-Pelly .15 .40
53 Matt Dumba .12 .30
54 Reilly Smith .20 .50
55 Dustin Brown .20 .50
56 Mike Green .15 .40
57 Devin Shore .12 .30
58 Noah Hanifin .20 .50
59 Trevor van Riemsdyk .15 .40
60 Brandon Carlo .15 .40
61 Christian Dvorak .15 .40
62 John Gibson .20 .50
63 Pekka Rinne .20 .50
64 Mats Zuccarello .20 .50
65 Vladimir Tarasenko .25 .60
66 Vincent Trocheck .20 .50
67 Teuvo Teravainen .20 .50
68 Sam Reinhart .40 1.00
69 Loui Eriksson .12 .30
70 J.T. Brown .15 .40
71 Nick Cousins .12 .30
72 Matt Cullen .15 .40
73 Jannik Hansen .15 .40
74 Bo Horvat .25 .60
75 Erik Karlsson .25 .60
76 Ryan Strome .20 .50
77 Calle Jarnkrok .15 .40
78 Jason Zucker .20 .50
79 Darren Helm .12 .30
80 Ryan Nugent-Hopkins .25 .60
81 Dougie Hamilton .15 .40
82 Evander Kane .20 .50
83 Ryan Spooner .15 .40
84 Antoine Vermette .15 .40
85 Cam Atkinson .20 .50
86 Anthony DeAngelo .12 .30
87 Jay Beagle .12 .30
88 Ivan Provorov .15 .40
89 Ryan McDonagh .12 .30
90 Andrei Markov .12 .30
91 Curtis McKenzie .12 .30
92 Mathieu Perreault .12 .30
93 Justin Williams .15 .40
94 Radim Vrbata .12 .30
95 Artemi Panarin .40 1.00
96 Oscar Lindberg .15 .40
97 Connor McDavid 1.00 2.50
98 Michael Cammalleri .15 .40
99 Colton Sceviour .12 .30
100 Checklist .12 .30
101 Alexander Ovechkin .75 2.00
102 Henrik Sedin .25 .60
103 Blake Wheeler .20 .50
104 Austin Watson .15 .40
105 Matt Murray .30 .75
106 Mike Hoffman .12 .30
107 Jimmy Vesey .15 .40
108 Calvin de Haan .12 .30
109 Pavel Zacha .15 .40
110 Ryan Johansen .15 .40
111 Phillip Danault .20 .50
112 Jason Pominville .12 .30
113 David Krejci .20 .50
114 Aleksander Barkov .30 .75
115 Jordan Eberle .20 .50
116 Gustav Nyquist .12 .30
117 Antoine Roussel .12 .30
118 Brandon Dubinsky .12 .30
119 Mikhail Grigorenko .12 .30
120 Richard Panik .12 .30
121 Sebastian Aho .30 .75
122 Sean Monahan .12 .30
123 Drew Stafford .12 .30
124 Anze Kopitar .30 .75
125 Oliver Ekman-Larsson .20 .50
126 Nikolaj Ehlers .20 .50
127 Joel Eriksson Ek .15 .40
128 Oliver Bjorkstrand .15 .40
129 William Nylander .40 1.00
130 Jonathan Drouin .15 .40
131 Roberto Luongo .30 .75
132 Jake Virtanen .20 .50
133 Danny DeKeyser .12 .30
134 Jakub Vrana .20 .50
135 Mikko Koivu .15 .40
136 Nikita Soshnikov .12 .30
137 Joe Pavelski .25 .60
138 Phil Kessel .20 .50
139 Claude Giroux .20 .50
140 Henrik Lundqvist .50 1.25
141 Jason Chimera .12 .30
142 Craig Smith .12 .30
143 Brendan Gallagher .20 .50
144 Mikael Granlund .15 .40
145 Mark Pysyk .12 .30
146 Drake Caggiula .15 .40
147 Riley Sheahan .12 .30
148 Esa Lindell .15 .40
149 Rene Bourque .12 .30
150 Marcus Kruger .12 .30
151 Brock McGinn .12 .30
152 Troy Brouwer .12 .30
153 Brian Gionta .12 .30
154 Zdeno Chara .20 .50
155 Jordan Martinook .12 .30
156 Alexander Wennberg .12 .30
157 Matt Nieto .12 .30
158 Brayden Point .25 .60
159 Kevin Labanc .12 .30
160 Chad Johnson .12 .30
161 Jaden Schwartz .25 .60
162 Jacob Trouba .15 .40
163 Michael Chaput .15 .40
164 Paul Martin .12 .30
165 Patrick Eaves .15 .40
166 Ian Cole .12 .30
167 Travis Konecny .20 .50
168 Chris Wideman .12 .30
169 Michael Grabner .12 .30
170 John Tavares .30 .75
171 Kyle Palmieri .15 .40
172 John Carlson .20 .50
173 Alexander Radulov .20 .50
174 Erik Haula .12 .30
175 Derek Forbort .12 .30
176 Jason Demers .12 .30
177 Andrej Sekera .12 .30
178 Andreas Athanasiou .20 .50
179 John Klingberg .20 .50
180 William Karlsson .25 .60
181 Tuukka Rask .25 .60
182 Gabriel Landeskog .25 .60
183 Duncan Keith .15 .40
184 Lee Stempniak .12 .30
185 Michael Frolik .12 .30
186 Kyle Okposo .12 .30
187 Louis Domingue .12 .30
188 Zach Hyman .30 .75
189 Hampus Lindholm .12 .30
190 Stefan Noesen .12 .30
191 Tomas Hertl .20 .50
192 Matthew Benning .12 .30
193 Colton Parayko .15 .40
194 Nicolas Petan .12 .30
195 Lars Eller .12 .30
196 James Neal .12 .30
197 Kris Letang .25 .60
198 Mark Stone .25 .60
199 J.T. Miller .25 .60
200 Checklist .12 .30
201 Jonathan Toews .30 .75
202 Victor Rask .12 .30
203 Johnny Gaudreau .30 .75
204 Jake McCabe .12 .30
205 Brad Marchand .40 1.00
206 Tobias Rieder .12 .30
207 Alexander Steen .12 .30
208 Tyler Toffoli .20 .50
209 Brett Pesce .12 .30
210 Niklas Hjalmarsson .12 .30
211 Andreas Martinsen .12 .30
212 Shane Doan .15 .40
213 Nikita Zaitsev .15 .40
214 Steve Mason .15 .40
215 Cedric Paquette .12 .30
216 Joel Edmundson .12 .30
217 Darnell Nurse .15 .40
218 David Schlemko .12 .30
219 Ondrej Kase .12 .30
220 Adam Lowry .15 .40
221 Daniel Winnik .12 .30
222 Jacob Markstrom .20 .50
223 Morgan Rielly .20 .50
224 Nick Bonino .12 .30
225 Brayden Schenn .20 .50
226 Brady Skjei .15 .40
227 Anders Lee .20 .50
228 Travis Zajac .12 .30
229 Viktor Arvidsson .12 .30
230 Andrew Shaw .12 .30
231 Tanner Pearson .15 .40
232 Jonathan Marchessault .25 .60
233 Leon Draisaitl .60 1.50
234 Brett Ritchie .12 .30
235 Seth Jones .20 .50
236 Tyson Barrie .12 .30
237 Vincent Hinostroza .12 .30
238 Justin Faulk .15 .40
239 Matt Moulson .12 .30
240 David Backes .12 .30
241 Jonathan Bernier .15 .40
242 Shea Weber .15 .40
243 Nazem Kadri .25 .60
244 Vladislav Namestnikov .12 .30
245 Josh Anderson .15 .40
246 Mark Scheifele .30 .75
247 Sven Baertschi .12 .30
248 Melker Karlsson .12 .30
249 Jay Bouwmeester .12 .30
250 Matt Niskanen .15 .40
251 Blake Comeau .12 .30
252 Troy Stecher .12 .30
253 Conor Sheary .20 .50
254 Dion Phaneuf .15 .40
255 Derek Stepan .12 .30
256 Cory Schneider .20 .50
257 Mattias Ekholm .15 .40
258 Zach Parise .20 .50
259 Corey Crawford .25 .60
260 Corey Perry .30 .75
261 Nick Shore .12 .30
262 Michael Matheson .15 .40
263 Benoit Pouliot .12 .30
264 Dylan Larkin .25 .60
265 Jason Spezza .20 .50
266 Brandon Saad .15 .40
267 Brent Seabrook .12 .30
268 Sam Bennett .30 .75
269 Jack Eichel .30 .75
270 Derick Brassard .12 .30
271 Brendan Perlini .15 .40
272 Andrew Ladd .12 .30
273 Victor Hedman .25 .60
274 Jonathan Quick .25 .60
275 Connor Hellebuyck .40 1.00
276 Braden Holtby .25 .60
277 Daniel Sedin .25 .60
278 Mikkel Boedker .12 .30
279 Anthony Mantha .15 .40
280 Scott Wilson .12 .30
281 Sean Couturier .15 .40
282 Mike Condon .15 .40
283 Austin Czarnik .20 .50
284 Pavel Buchnevich .15 .40
285 Thomas Greiss .15 .40
286 Logan Couture .25 .60
287 Andrew Cogliano .12 .30
288 John Moore .12 .30
289 Ryan Ellis .15 .40
290 Artturi Lehkonen .15 .40
291 Jonas Brodin .12 .30
292 Jake Muzzin .20 .50
293 Jussi Jokinen .15 .40
294 Mark Letestu .15 .40
295 Xavier Ouellet .15 .40
296 Stephen Johns .15 .40
297 David Savard .12 .30
298 Joe Colborne .15 .40
299 Chris Stewart .15 .40
300 Checklist .12 .30
301 Sidney Crosby .75 2.00
302 Radko Gudas .15 .40
303 Zack Smith .12 .30
304 Nick Holden .15 .40
305 P.K. Subban .25 .60
306 Nathan Beaulieu .12 .30
307 Trevor Lewis .12 .30
308 Oscar Klefbom .15 .40
309 Jaromir Jagr .60 1.50
310 Tomas Tatar .12 .30
311 Patrick Sharp .15 .40
312 Nick Foligno .15 .40
313 Matt Duchene .20 .50
314 Artem Anisimov .12 .30
315 Kris Versteeg .12 .30
316 Rasmus Ristolainen .12 .30
317 Patrice Bergeron .25 .60
318 Max Domi .20 .50
319 Rickard Rakell .15 .40
320 Ryan Miller .20 .50
321 Cody Ceci .12 .30
322 Cody Franson .12 .30
323 Johnny Boychuk .15 .40
324 Keith Kinkaid .12 .30
325 Matt Calvert .12 .30
326 Martin Hanzal .15 .40
327 Cam Ward .20 .50
328 Peter Budaj .12 .30
329 Mitch Marner .30 .75
330 Chris Kreider .25 .60
331 Robby Fabbri .12 .30
332 Brandon Sutter .12 .30
333 Matt Beleskey .12 .30
334 Josh Morrissey .25 .60
335 Andre Burakovsky .12 .30
336 Johan Larsson .15 .40
337 Joe Thornton .30 .75
338 Jake Guentzel .30 .75
339 Jean-Gabriel Pageau .12 .30
340 Brandon Pirri .12 .30
341 Carter Hutton .15 .40
342 Nick Leddy .12 .30
343 Taylor Hall .20 .50
344 Filip Forsberg .30 .75
345 Alex Galchenyuk .12 .30
346 Nino Niederreiter .12 .30
347 Drew Doughty .25 .60
348 Anton Slepyshev .12 .30
349 Alex Killorn .12 .30
350 Justin Abdelkader .15 .40
351 Radek Faksa .15 .40
352 Calvin Pickard .20 .50
353 Tanner Kero .12 .30
354 Jaccob Slavin .15 .40
355 Ryan Reaves .12 .30
356 Riley Nash .12 .30
357 Jakob Chychrun .20 .50
358 Josh Manson .12 .30
359 Mark Giordano .20 .50
360 Valtteri Filppula .12 .30
361 Evgeny Kuznetsov .25 .60
362 Tyler Bozak .12 .30
363 Milan Lucic .20 .50
364 Scott Hartnell .12 .30
365 Alex Pietrangelo .15 .40
366 Dustin Byfuglien .20 .50
367 Alexander Edler .12 .30
368 Carl Hagelin .12 .30
369 Wayne Simmonds .25 .60
370 Rick Nash .20 .50
371 Casey Cizikas .12 .30
372 Juuse Saros .25 .60
373 Alexei Emelin .12 .30
374 Marcus Johansson .15 .40
375 Ryan Suter .15 .40
376 Kyle Clifford .12 .30
377 Thomas Vanek .15 .40
378 Petr Mrazek .20 .50
379 Ondrej Palat .15 .40
380 Jack Johnson .12 .30
381 Francois Beauchemin .12 .30
382 Ryan Hartman .12 .30
383 Jordan Staal .15 .40
384 Marcus Foligno .15 .40
385 Dominic Moore .12 .30
386 Nick Ritchie .12 .30
387 Michael Del Zotto .12 .30
388 Jamie McGinn .12 .30
389 Steven Stamkos .40 1.00
390 Kari Lehtonen .15 .40
391 Steven Santini .12 .30
392 Chris Tierney .12 .30
393 Brett Connolly .12 .30
394 Jeff Petry .20 .50
395 Frederik Andersen .25 .60
396 Chris Kunitz .20 .50
397 Beau Bennett .12 .30
398 Jonathan Huberdeau .25 .60
399 Alex Chiasson .15 .40
400 Checklist .12 .30
401 Patrick Kane .40 1.00
402 Ryan Kesler .20 .50
403 Torey Krug .15 .40
404 Zemgus Girgensons .15 .40
405 Jamie Benn .20 .50
406 Zack Kassian .12 .30
407 Alec Martinez .12 .30
408 Jared Spurgeon .20 .50
409 Tomas Plekanec .12 .30
410 Roman Josi .20 .50
411 Miles Wood .12 .30
412 Mika Zibanejad .25 .60
413 Bryan Rust .20 .50
414 Ben Hutton .12 .30
415 Tom Wilson .20 .50
416 Timo Meier .20 .50
417 Zach Sanford .12 .30
418 Robin Lehner .15 .40

419 Anthony Duclair .15 .40
420 P.A. Parenteau .12 .30
421 Dale Weise .12 .30
422 Andrei Vasilevskiy .30 .75
423 Alexandre Burrows .12 .30
424 Kevin Bieksa .15 .40
425 Colin Miller .12 .30
426 Brian Elliott .15 .40
427 Carl Soderberg .12 .30
428 Luke Glendening .12 .30
429 Keith Yandle .12 .30
430 Jarome Iginla .25 .60
431 Daniel Carr .12 .30
432 Damon Severson .12 .30
433 Nikolay Kulemin .12 .30
434 Ryan Dzingel .12 .30
435 Justin Schultz .20 .50
436 Patrick Maroon .20 .50
437 Dmitry Orlov .20 .50
438 Joel Armia .12 .30
439 Connor Brown .15 .40
440 Tyler Johnson .12 .30
441 Jori Lehtera .12 .30
442 Curtis Lazar .12 .30
443 Dennis Seidenberg .12 .30
444 Jim Howard .25 .60
445 Joseph Cramarossa .12 .30
446 Sami Vatanen .12 .30
447 Tim Schaller .12 .30
448 Mikael Backlund .15 .40
449 Derek Ryan .15 .40
450 Dennis Rasmussen .15 .40
451 Boone Jenner .20 .50
452 Antti Niemi .15 .40
453 Patrick Maroon .15 .40
454 Aaron Ekblad .25 .60
455 Charlie Coyle .20 .50
456 Paul Byron .15 .40
457 Colin Wilson .15 .40
458 Jake Gardiner .12 .30
459 Kevin Hayes .15 .40
460 Shayne Gostisbehere .20 .50
461 Trevor Daley .15 .40
462 Marc-Edouard Vlasic .12 .30
463 Cam Fowler .20 .50
464 Bryan Little .15 .40
465 Devan Dubnyk .15 .40
466 Markus Granlund .15 .40
467 Bobby Ryan .15 .40
468 Nail Yakupov .12 .30
469 James van Riemsdyk .15 .40
470 Kevin Fiala .15 .40
471 Brock Nelson .20 .50
472 Jesper Fast .12 .30
473 T.J. Oshie .20 .50
474 Matt Read .15 .40
475 Sergei Bobrovsky .30 .75
476 Joel Ward .15 .40
477 Nic Dowd .12 .30
478 Alex Goligoski .15 .40
479 Kyle Connor .30 .75
480 Patrick Wiercioch .15 .40
481 Jake Allen .20 .50
482 Joseph Blandisi .15 .40
483 Torrey Mitchell .15 .40
484 Anton Stralman .15 .40
485 Joakim Nordstrom .12 .30
486 Niklas Kronwall .15 .40
487 Kyle Turris .20 .50
488 Mike Smith .20 .50
489 Frank Vatrano .20 .50
490 Ryan O'Reilly .20 .50
491 T.J. Brodie .15 .40
492 Jeff Skinner .25 .60
493 Nick Schmaltz .15 .40
494 James Reimer .20 .50
495 Zach Werenski .30 .75
496 Brian Boyle .12 .30
497 Frans Nielsen .12 .30
498 Jesse Puljujarvi .20 .50
499 Nathan MacKinnon .75 2.00
500 Checklist .12 .30
501 Alexander Nylander RC 1.50 4.00
502 Valentin Zykov RC 1.00 2.50
503 Robert Hagg RC 1.00 2.50
504 Brock Boeser RC 2.50 6.00
505 Colin White RC 1.25 3.00
506 Marcus Sorensen RC .75 2.00
507 Ivan Barbashev RC 1.25 3.00
508 Carter Rowney RC .75 2.00
509 J.T. Compher RC 1.00 2.50
510 Evgeny Svechnikov RC 2.00 5.00
511 Jack Roslovic RC 1.25 3.00
512 Jake Dotchin RC .75 2.00
513 Josh Ho-Sang RC 1.25 3.00
514 Alexandre Carrier RC .75 2.00
515 Gabriel Carlsson RC .75 2.00
516 Christian Fischer RC 1.25 3.00
517 Kalle Kossila RC .75 2.00
518 Jakob Forsbacka-Karlsson RC 1.00 2.50
519 Ian McCoshen RC 1.00 2.50
520 Alex Tuch RC 2.50 6.00
521 Samuel Morin RC .60 1.50
522 Eric Comrie RC .75 2.00
523 Peter Cehlarik RC 1.00 2.50
524 Robbie Russo RC 1.00 2.50
525 Adrian Kempe RC 2.00 5.00
526 Remi Elie RC .75 2.00
527 Griffen Molino RC .75 2.00
528 Jordan Schmaltz RC 1.25 3.00
529 Rasmus Andersson RC 1.00 2.50
530 Nicolas Kerdiles RC 1.00 2.50
531 Chris DiDomenico RC .75 2.00
532 Paul LaDue RC .75 2.00
533 Tyson Jost RC 2.00 5.00
534 T.J. Tynan RC .75 2.00
535 Nikita Scherbak RC 1.25 3.00
536 Charlie McAvoy RC 2.50 6.00
537 Lucas Wallmark RC 1.00 2.50
538 Denis Gurianov RC 2.50 6.00
539 Jonny Brodzinski RC 1.00 2.50
540 Clayton Keller RC 2.50 6.00
541 Mike Vecchione RC .75 2.00
542 Jon Gillies RC 1.00 2.50
543 Blake Coleman RC 1.00 2.50
544 John Hayden RC .75 2.00
545 Riley Barber RC 1.00 2.50
546 C.J. Smith RC .75 2.00
547 Connor Jones RC .75 2.00
548 Alex Nedeljkovic RC 1.50 4.00
549 Dan Renouf RC .75 2.00
550 Vladislav Kamenev RC 1.00 2.50
551 Sidney Crosby SH 4.00 10.00
552 Marian Hossa SH 1.00 2.50
553 Jaromir Jagr SH 3.00 8.00
554 Auston Matthews SH 4.00 10.00
555 Connor McDavid SH 5.00 12.00
556 Joe Thornton SH 1.50 4.00
557 Patrick Marleau SH 1.00 2.50
558 Mitch Marner SH 1.50 4.00
559 Henrik Lundqvist SH 2.50 6.00
560 Alexander Ovechkin SH 4.00 10.00
561 Anaheim Ducks CL .25 .60
562 Arizona Coyotes CL .25 .60
563 Boston Bruins CL .25 .60
564 Buffalo Sabres CL .25 .60
565 Calgary Flames CL .25 .60
566 Carolina Hurricanes CL .25 .60
567 Chicago Blackhawks CL .25 .60
568 Colorado Avalanche CL .25 .60
569 Columbus Blue Jackets CL .25 .60
570 Dallas Stars CL .25 .60
571 Detroit Red Wings CL .25 .60
572 Edmonton Oilers CL .25 .60
573 Florida Panthers CL .25 .60
574 Los Angeles Kings CL .25 .60
575 Minnesota Wild CL .25 .60
576 Montreal Canadiens CL .25 .60
577 Nashville Predators CL .25 .60
578 New Jersey Devils CL .25 .60
579 New York Islanders CL .25 .60
580 New York Rangers CL .25 .60
581 Ottawa Senators CL .25 .60
582 Philadelphia Flyers CL .25 .60
583 Pittsburgh Penguins CL .25 .60
584 San Jose Sharks CL .25 .60
585 St. Louis Blues CL .25 .60
586 Tampa Bay Lightning CL .25 .60
587 Toronto Maple Leafs CL .25 .60
588 Vancouver Canucks CL .25 .60
589 Washington Capitals CL .25 .60
590 Winnipeg Jets CL .25 .60
591 Connor McDavid LL 5.00 12.00
592 Braden Holtby LL 1.25 3.00
593 Sidney Crosby LL 4.00 10.00
594 Mark Borowiecki LL .60 1.50
595 Brent Burns LL 1.00 2.50
596 Ryan Suter LL .75 2.00
597 Sergei Bobrovsky LL 1.50 4.00
598 Auston Matthews LL 4.00 10.00
599 Connor McDavid LL 5.00 12.00
600 Checklist LL .25 .60
601 Marc-Andre Fleury .50 1.25
602 Brayden Schenn .25 .60
603 Jaromir Jagr .75 2.00
604 Chris Kunitz .25 .60
605 Jonathan Drouin .20 .50
606 Alexander Radulov .25 .60
607 Patrick Marleau .25 .60
608 Kevin Shattenkirk .15 .40
609 Brandon Saad .20 .50
610 Artemi Panarin .50 1.25
611 Kailer Yamamoto RC 3.00 8.00
612 Alex Iafallo RC 1.25 3.00
613 Travis Sanheim RC 1.25 3.00
614 Oscar Fantenberg RC 1.25 3.00
615 Andreas Borgman RC 1.25 3.00
616 Jake DeBrusk RC 3.00 8.00
617 Kurtis MacDermid RC 1.25 3.00
618 Tage Thompson RC 3.00 8.00
619 Andrei Mironov RC 1.25 3.00
620 Haydn Fleury RC 1.25 3.00
621 Tucker Poolman RC 1.25 3.00
622 Victor Mete RC 1.25 3.00
623 Dylan Ferguson RC 1.25 3.00
624 Luke Kunin RC 1.25 3.00
625 Logan Brown RC 1.25 3.00
626 Madison Bowey RC .75 2.00
627 Jesper Bratt RC 2.50 6.00
628 Giovanni Fiore RC 1.25 3.00
629 Samuel Girard RC 1.25 3.00
630 Nathan Walker RC 1.25 3.00
631 Janne Kuokkanen RC 1.25 3.00
632 Pierre-Luc Dubois RC 2.00 5.00
633 Martin Necas RC 4.00 10.00
634 Anders Bjork RC 1.50 4.00
635 Vince Dunn RC 1.50 4.00
636 Will Butcher RC 1.50 4.00
637 Calle Rosen RC 1.25 3.00
638 Christian Jaros RC 1.00 2.50
639 Filip Chytil RC 1.25 3.00
640 Nolan Patrick RC 2.50 6.00
641 Jan Rutta RC 1.25 3.00
642 Owen Tippett RC 2.50 6.00
643 Christian Djoos RC 1.25 3.00
644 Brendan Lemieux RC 1.25 3.00
645 Alex DeBrincat RC 3.00 8.00
646 Viktor Antipin RC 1.25 3.00
647 Alex Formenton RC 1.25 3.00
648 Alex Kerfoot RC 2.50 6.00
649 Nico Hischier RC 4.00 10.00
650 Alex Tuch RC 3.00 8.00

2017-18 O-Pee-Chee Rainbow Black

*VETS/100: 2.5X TO 6X BASIC CARDS
*SP/RC/100: 1X TO 2.5X BASIC CARDS
1 Auston Matthews 20.00 50.00
504 Brock Boeser 50.00 125.00
554 Auston Matthews SH 20.00 50.00
598 Auston Matthews LL 25.00 60.00

2017-18 O-Pee-Chee Red

504 Brock Boeser 15.00 40.00

2017-18 O-Pee-Chee Hobby Box Bottoms

AO Alex Ovechkin G4 2.00 5.00
BB Brent Burns G2 .50 1.25
CG Claude Giroux G3 .50 1.25
CM Connor McDavid G2 2.50 6.00
CP Carey Price G3 1.00 2.50
EK Erik Karlsson G1 .60 1.50
EM Evgeni Malkin G3 1.00 2.50
HS Henrik Sedin G1 .60 1.50
JB Jamie Benn G4 .50 1.25
JQ Jonathan Quick G2 .60 1.50
JT Jonathan Toews G3 .75 2.00
MM Mitch Marner G4 .75 2.00
PK Patrick Kane G1 1.00 2.50
PL Patrick Laine G1 .60 1.50
SS Steven Stamkos G2 1.00 2.50
SW Shea Weber G4 .40 1.00

2017-18 O-Pee-Chee Glossy Rookies

R1 Josh Ho-Sang 1.00 2.50
R2 Brock Boeser 2.00 5.00
R3 Pierre-Luc Dubois 1.25 3.00
R4 Charlie McAvoy 2.00 5.00
R5 Alex DeBrincat 2.00 5.00
R6 Will Butcher 1.00 2.50
R7 Nolan Patrick 1.50 4.00
R8 Tyson Jost 1.50 4.00
R9 Nico Hischier 2.50 6.00
R10 Clayton Keller 2.00 5.00

2017-18 O-Pee-Chee Mini

M1 Nicklas Backstrom .75 2.00
M2 Mitch Marner 1.25 3.00
M3 Brayden Schenn .75 2.00
M4 Phil Kessel .75 2.00
M5 Alex Galchenyuk .50 1.25
M6 Jack Eichel 1.25 3.00
M7 Sean Monahan .50 1.25
M8 Aleksander Barkov 1.25 3.00
M9 Tyler Seguin 1.00 2.50
M10 Cam Talbot .75 2.00
M11 Anthony Mantha .60 1.50
M12 Ryan Getzlaf .75 2.00
M13 David Pastrnak 2.00 5.00
M14 Jeff Carter .60 1.50
M15 Artemi Panarin 1.50 4.00
M16 Eric Staal 1.00 2.50
M17 Kyle Turris .75 2.00
M18 Filip Forsberg 1.25 3.00
M19 Shea Weber .60 1.50
M20 Joe Pavelski 1.00 2.50
M21 Daniel Sedin 1.00 2.50
M22 Nikita Kucherov 1.50 4.00
M23 Loui Eriksson .50 1.25
M24 Mark Scheifele 1.25 3.00
M25 Oliver Ekman-Larsson .75 2.00
M26 Kyle Palmieri .60 1.50
M27 Jeff Skinner 1.00 2.50
M28 Mikko Rantanen 2.00 5.00
M29 Jake Allen .75 2.00
M30 Andrew Ladd .50 1.25
M31 Tuukka Rask 1.00 2.50
M32 Derek Stepan .50 1.25
M33 William Nylander 1.50 4.00
M34 Logan Couture 1.00 2.50
M35 Anze Kopitar .75 2.00
M36 Ryan O'Reilly .75 2.00
M37 Cam Atkinson .75 2.00
M38 Devan Dubnyk .60 1.50
M39 Patrik Laine 1.00 2.50
M40 Matt Murray 1.25 3.00
M41 Tomas Tatar .50 1.25
M42 Leon Draisaitl 2.50 6.00
M43 Corey Perry 1.25 3.00
M44 Jonathan Drouin .60 1.50
M45 Evgeny Kuznetsov 1.00 2.50
M46 Tyson Jost 1.50 4.00
M47 Nikita Scherbak 1.00 2.50
M48 Evgeny Svechnikov 1.50 4.00
M49 Brock Boeser 2.00 5.00
M50 Ivan Barbashev 1.00 2.50
M51 Clayton Keller SP 4.00 10.00
M52 Alexander Nylander SP 2.50 6.00
M53 Auston Matthews SP 6.00 15.00
M54 Jonathan Toews SP 2.50 6.00
M55 Brent Burns SP 1.50 4.00
M56 Sergei Bobrovsky SP 2.50 6.00
M57 Taylor Hall SP 1.50 4.00
M58 Jamie Benn SP 1.50 4.00
M59 Evgeni Malkin SP 3.00 8.00
M60 Henrik Zetterberg SP 2.00 5.00
M61 Nathan MacKinnon SP 6.00 15.00
M62 Max Pacioretty SP 1.50 4.00
M63 Erik Karlsson SP 2.00 5.00
M64 Vladimir Tarasenko SP 2.00 5.00
M65 Alexander Ovechkin SP 6.00 15.00
M66 Carey Price RARE 5.00 12.00
M67 Patrick Kane RARE 5.00 12.00
M68 Henrik Sedin RARE 3.00 8.00
M69 Brad Marchand RARE 5.00 12.00
M70 Sidney Crosby RARE 10.00 25.00
M71 Johnny Gaudreau RARE 4.00 10.00
M72 Henrik Lundqvist RARE 6.00 15.00
M73 Jaromir Jagr RARE 8.00 20.00
M74 John Tavares RARE 4.00 10.00
M75 P.K. Subban RARE 3.00 8.00
M76 Steven Stamkos RARE 5.00 12.00
M77 Connor McDavid RARE 12.00 30.00

2017-18 O-Pee-Chee Mini Back Variation

M1 Nicklas Backstrom 3.00 8.00
M2 Mitch Marner 5.00 12.00
M3 Brayden Schenn 3.00 8.00
M4 Phil Kessel 3.00 8.00
M5 Alex Galchenyuk 2.00 5.00
M6 Jack Eichel 5.00 12.00
M7 Sean Monahan 2.00 5.00
M8 Aleksander Barkov 5.00 12.00
M9 Tyler Seguin 4.00 10.00
M10 Cam Talbot 3.00 8.00
M11 Anthony Mantha 2.50 6.00
M12 Ryan Getzlaf 3.00 8.00
M13 David Pastrnak 8.00 20.00
M14 Jeff Carter 2.50 6.00
M15 Artemi Panarin 6.00 15.00
M16 Eric Staal 4.00 10.00
M17 Kyle Turris 3.00 8.00
M18 Filip Forsberg 5.00 12.00
M19 Shea Weber 2.50 6.00
M20 Joe Pavelski 4.00 10.00
M21 Daniel Sedin 4.00 10.00
M22 Nikita Kucherov 6.00 15.00
M23 Loui Eriksson 2.00 5.00
M24 Mark Scheifele 5.00 12.00
M25 Oliver Ekman-Larsson 3.00 8.00
M26 Kyle Palmieri 2.50 6.00
M27 Jeff Skinner 4.00 10.00
M28 Mikko Rantanen 8.00 20.00
M29 Jake Allen 3.00 8.00
M30 Andrew Ladd 2.00 5.00
M31 Tuukka Rask 4.00 10.00
M32 Derek Stepan 2.00 5.00
M33 William Nylander 6.00 15.00
M34 Logan Couture 4.00 10.00
M35 Anze Kopitar 5.00 12.00
M36 Ryan O'Reilly 3.00 8.00
M37 Cam Atkinson 3.00 8.00
M38 Devan Dubnyk 2.50 6.00
M39 Patrik Laine 4.00 10.00
M40 Matt Murray 5.00 12.00
M41 Tomas Tatar 2.00 5.00
M42 Leon Draisaitl 10.00 25.00
M43 Corey Perry 5.00 12.00
M44 Jonathan Drouin 2.50 6.00
M45 Evgeny Kuznetsov 4.00 10.00
M46 Tyson Jost 6.00 15.00
M47 Nikita Scherbak 4.00 10.00
M48 Evgeny Svechnikov 6.00 15.00
M49 Brock Boeser 8.00 20.00
M50 Ivan Barbashev 4.00 10.00
M51 Clayton Keller 8.00 20.00
M52 Alexander Nylander 5.00 12.00
M53 Auston Matthews 12.00 30.00
M54 Jonathan Toews 5.00 12.00
M55 Brent Burns 3.00 8.00
M56 Sergei Bobrovsky 5.00 12.00
M57 Taylor Hall 3.00 8.00
M58 Jamie Benn 3.00 8.00
M59 Evgeni Malkin 6.00 15.00
M60 Henrik Zetterberg 4.00 10.00
M61 Nathan MacKinnon 12.00 30.00
M62 Max Pacioretty 3.00 8.00
M63 Erik Karlsson 4.00 10.00
M64 Vladimir Tarasenko 4.00 10.00
M65 Alexander Ovechkin 12.00 30.00
M66 Carey Price 6.00 15.00
M67 Patrick Kane 6.00 15.00
M68 Henrik Sedin 4.00 10.00
M69 Brad Marchand 6.00 15.00
M70 Sidney Crosby 12.00 30.00
M71 Johnny Gaudreau 5.00 12.00
M72 Henrik Lundqvist 8.00 20.00
M73 Jaromir Jagr 10.00 25.00
M74 John Tavares 5.00 12.00
M75 P.K. Subban 4.00 10.00
M76 Steven Stamkos 6.00 15.00
M77 Connor McDavid 25.00 60.00

2017-18 O-Pee-Chee Patches

P1 Corey Perry 12.00 30.00
P2 Mike Smith 8.00 20.00
P3 Patrice Bergeron 10.00 25.00
P4 Ryan O'Reilly 8.00 20.00
P5 Sean Monahan 5.00 12.00
P6 Sebastian Aho 12.00 30.00
P7 Artemi Panarin 15.00 40.00
P8 Matt Duchene 8.00 20.00
P9 Nick Foligno 6.00 15.00
P10 Tyler Seguin 10.00 25.00
P11 Dylan Larkin 10.00 25.00
P12 Connor McDavid 40.00 100.00
P13 Aaron Ekblad 10.00 25.00
P14 Jeff Carter 6.00 15.00
P15 Devan Dubnyk 6.00 15.00
P16 Shea Weber 6.00 15.00
P17 Filip Forsberg 10.00 25.00
P18 Kyle Palmieri 6.00 15.00
P19 Andrew Ladd 5.00 12.00
P20 Derek Stepan 5.00 12.00
P21 Mike Hoffman 5.00 12.00
P22 Jakub Voracek 6.00 15.00
P23 Sidney Crosby 30.00 80.00
P24 Joe Pavelski 10.00 25.00
P25 Jaden Schwartz 10.00 25.00
P26 Nikita Kucherov 15.00 40.00
P27 Mitch Marner 12.00 30.00
P28 Daniel Sedin 10.00 25.00
P29 Alexander Ovechkin 30.00 80.00
P30 Patrik Laine 10.00 25.00
P31 Ivan Barbashev 15.00 40.00
P32 Vladislav Kamenev 12.00 30.00
P33 Nikita Scherbak 15.00 40.00
P34 Alex Tuch 30.00 80.00
P35 Nicolas Kerdiles 12.00 30.00
P36 Riley Barber 12.00 30.00
P37 Clayton Keller 30.00 80.00
P38 Christian Fischer 15.00 40.00
P39 Adrian Kempe 25.00 60.00
P40 Peter Cehlarik 12.00 30.00
P41 Sidney Crosby 100 40.00 100.00
P42 Carey Price 100 20.00 50.00
P43 Jonathan Toews 100 20.00 50.00
P44 Jaromir Jagr 100 30.00 80.00
P45 Connor McDavid 100 150.00 250.00
P46 Vladimir Tarasenko 100 12.00 30.00
P47 Claude Giroux 100 10.00 25.00
P48 Roberto Luongo 100 15.00 40.00
P49 John Tavares 100 10.00 25.00
P50 P.K. Subban 100 12.00 30.00
P51 Steven Stamkos 100 20.00 50.00
P52 Henrik Zetterberg 100 10.00 25.00
P53 Henrik Sedin 100 12.00 30.00
P54 Brent Burns 100 10.00 25.00
P55 Auston Matthews 100 80.00 150.00
P56 Henrik Lundqvist 100 25.00 60.00
P57 Ryan Kesler 100 10.00 25.00
P58 Anze Kopitar 100 15.00 40.00
P59 Brad Marchand 100 20.00 50.00
P60 Patrick Kane 100 20.00 50.00
P61 Erik Karlsson 100 12.00 30.00
P62 Nathan MacKinnon 100 40.00 100.00
P63 Johnny Gaudreau 100 15.00 40.00
P64 Oliver Ekman-Larsson 100 10.00 25.00
P65 Max Pacioretty 100 10.00 25.00
P66 Taylor Hall 100 10.00 25.00
P67 Jamie Benn 100 10.00 25.00
P68 Evgeni Malkin 100 20.00 50.00
P69 Tuukka Rask 100 10.00 25.00
P70 Alexander Ovechkin 100 40.00 100.00
P71 Wayne Gretzky 100 150.00 400.00
P72 Mark Messier 100 50.00 125.00
P73 Steve Yzerman 100 60.00 150.00
P74 Mike Bossy 100 25.00 60.00
P75 Daryl Sittler 100 20.00 50.00
P76 Mario Lemieux 100 100.00 250.00
P77 Bobby Orr 100 100.00 250.00
P78 Milt Schmidt 100 25.00 60.00
P79 Patrick Roy 100 60.00 150.00
P80 Stan Mikita 100 30.00 80.00
P81 Johnny Bower 100 25.00 60.00
P82 Eddie Shore 100 25.00 60.00
P83 Stormy 50.00 125.00
P84 Hunter 50.00 125.00
P85 Howler 50.00 125.00
P86 Sabretooth 50.00 125.00
P87 Victor E. Green 40.00 100.00
P88 Sparky The Dragon 50.00 125.00

2017-18 O-Pee-Chee Playing Cards

2C Vincent Trocheck 1.25 3.00
2D Loui Eriksson .75 2.00
2H Jakub Voracek 1.00 2.50
2S Mike Hoffman .75 2.00
3C Jaden Schwartz 1.50 4.00
3D Cam Atkinson 1.25 3.00
3H Gustav Nyquist .75 2.00
3S Ryan O'Reilly 1.25 3.00
4C Jeff Skinner 1.50 4.00
4D Logan Couture 1.50 4.00
4H Max Domi 1.25 3.00
4S Derek Stepan .75 2.00
5C Henrik Sedin 1.50 4.00
5D Sergei Bobrovsky 2.00 5.00
5H Shea Weber 1.00 2.50
5S Victor Hedman 1.50 4.00
6C Mark Scheifele 2.00 5.00
6D Ryan Johansen 1.00 2.50
6H Ryan Kesler 1.25 3.00
6S Nicklas Backstrom 1.25 3.00
7C Alex Galchenyuk .75 2.00
7D Jeff Carter 1.00 2.50
7H Devan Dubnyk 1.00 2.50
7S Brad Marchand 2.50 6.00
8C William Nylander 2.50 6.00
8D Wayne Simmonds 1.50 4.00
8H Johnny Gaudreau 2.00 5.00
8S Taylor Hall 1.25 3.00
9C Joe Pavelski 1.50 4.00
9D David Pastrnak 3.00 8.00
9H Nathan MacKinnon 5.00 12.00
9S Tyler Seguin 1.50 4.00
AC Connor McDavid 20.00 50.00
AD Sidney Crosby 15.00 40.00
AH Alexander Ovechkin 8.00 20.00
AS Auston Matthews 15.00 40.00
JC Nikita Kucherov 2.50 6.00
JD Corey Crawford 1.50 4.00
JH Leon Draisaitl 4.00 10.00
JS Vladimir Tarasenko 1.50 4.00
KC Patrik Laine 1.50 4.00
KD Jaromir Jagr 4.00 10.00
KH Patrick Kane 2.50 6.00
KS Henrik Lundqvist 3.00 8.00
QC Mitch Marner 2.00 5.00
QD Henrik Zetterberg 1.50 4.00
QH Jonathan Quick 1.50 4.00
QS John Tavares 2.00 5.00
10C P.K. Subban 1.50 4.00
10D Ryan Getzlaf 1.25 3.00
10H Phil Kessel 1.25 3.00
10S Max Pacioretty 1.25 3.00

2017-18 O-Pee-Chee Playing Cards Foil

*SINGLES: 6X TO 1.5X BASIC INSERTS
AC Connor McDavid 25.00 60.00
AD Sidney Crosby 25.00 60.00
AH Alexander Ovechkin 12.00 30.00
AS Auston Matthews 25.00 60.00

2017-18 O-Pee-Chee Retro Award Winners

AWAM Auston Matthews Calder 30.00 80.00
AWBB Brent Burns Norris 25.00 60.00
AWCM Connor McDavid Hart 40.00 100.00
AWCO Connor McDavid Art Ross 40.00 100.00
AWMC Connor McDavid Ted Lindsay 40.00 100.00
AWSB Sergei Bobrovsky Vezina 15.00 40.00
AWSC Sidney Crosby Richard 30.00 80.00

2017-18 O-Pee-Chee Retro Cup Captain

CCSC Sidney Crosby 40.00 100.00

2017-18 O-Pee-Chee Retro Top 10 Point Seasons

T1 Wayne Gretzky '85-86 25.00 60.00
T2 Wayne Gretzky '81-82 25.00 60.00
T3 Wayne Gretzky '84-85 25.00 60.00
T4 Wayne Gretzky '83-84 25.00 60.00
T5 Mario Lemieux '88-89 15.00 40.00
T6 Wayne Gretzky '82-83 25.00 60.00
T7 Wayne Gretzky '86-87 25.00 60.00
T8 Mario Lemieux '87-88 15.00 40.00
T9 Wayne Gretzky '88-89 25.00 60.00
T10 Wayne Gretzky '80-81 25.00 60.00

2017-18 O-Pee-Chee Team Logo Patches

301 NHL Centennial Classic '16-17 30.00 80.00
302 Pittsburgh Penguins '16-17 50th Season 150.00 250.00
303 New York Rangers '16-17 90th Anniversary 80.00 150.00
304 St. Louis Blues '16-17 50th Anniversary 60.00 150.00
305 Toronto Maple Leafs '16-17 100th Anniversary 60.00 150.00
306 Vegas Golden Knights Logo 80.00 150.00
307 LA Kings '16-17 50th Anniversary 80.00 150.00
308 Philadelphia Flyers '16-17 50th Season 80.00 150.00
309 Detroit Red Wings Joe Louis Arena Farewell 60.00 150.00
310 Florida Panthers '16-17 Primary 60.00 150.00

2018-19 O-Pee-Chee

1 Connor McDavid 1.25 3.00
2 Drew Doughty .30 .75
3 Mikko Rantanen .60 1.50
4 Nikita Kucherov .50 1.25
5 Sidney Crosby 1.00 2.50
6 Dylan Larkin .30 .75
7 Marc-Andre Fleury .50 1.25
8 Aleksander Barkov .40 1.00
9 Patrik Laine .30 .75
10 Oliver Ekman-Larsson .25 .60
11 David Pastrnak .60 1.50
12 Johnny Gaudreau .40 1.00
13 Wayne Simmonds .25 .60
14 Mitch Marner .40 1.00
15 Carey Price .50 1.25
16 Ryan O'Reilly .25 .60
17 Evgeny Kuznetsov .30 .75
18 Jeff Skinner .30 .75
19 Tyler Seguin .30 .75
20 Patrick Kane .50 1.25
21 Devan Dubnyk .20 .50
22 Oliver Bjorkstrand .20 .50
23 P.K. Subban .30 .75
24 Nico Hischier .40 1.00
25 Joe Pavelski .30 .75
26 Ryan Getzlaf .25 .60
27 Mathew Barzal .30 .75
28 Mark Stone .30 .75
29 Mats Zuccarello .25 .60
30 Vladimir Tarasenko .30 .75
31 Brock Boeser .30 .75
32 Anton Stralman .20 .50
33 Brayden McNabb .15 .40
34 Nazem Kadri .30 .75
35 Tuukka Rask .30 .75
36 Aaron Ekblad .30 .75
37 Brendan Leipsic .15 .40
38 Daniel Sedin .30 .75
39 Sam Reinhart .50 1.25
40 Logan Couture .30 .75
41 Brayden Schenn .25 .60
42 Shayne Gostisbehere .25 .60
43 Josh Bailey .20 .50
44 Justin Williams .20 .50
45 Matt Murray .25 .60
46 Semyon Varlamov .25 .60
47 John Klingberg .25 .60
48 Brayden Point .30 .75
49 Adrian Kempe .25 .60
50 Erik Karlsson .30 .75
51 Austin Watson .15 .40
52 John Hayden .15 .40
53 Jonathan Marchessault .30 .75
54 Jeff Petry .25 .60
55 Clayton Keller .30 .75
56 Dougie Hamilton .20 .50
57 John Carlson .25 .60
58 Nikolaj Ehlers .25 .60
59 Eric Staal .25 .60
60 Kyle Palmieri .20 .50
61 Viktor Arvidsson .15 .40
62 Pavel Buchnevich .20 .50
63 Sonny Milano .20 .50
64 Sean Kuraly .15 .40
65 Mike Hoffman .15 .40
66 Ondrej Kase .15 .40
67 Anders Lee .20 .50
68 Brent Burns .25 .60
69 Jacob Markstrom .25 .60
70 Brad Marchand .50 1.25
71 Jake Allen .25 .60
72 Tyler Bozak .15 .40
73 Pontus Aberg .15 .40
74 Max Domi .25 .60
75 Teuvo Teravainen .25 .60
76 Chris Kreider .30 .75
77 Travis Konecny .25 .60
78 Cory Schneider .25 .60
79 Nicklas Backstrom .25 .60
80 Jonathan Huberdeau .30 .75
81 Ryan Callahan .15 .40
82 Jim Howard .30 .75
83 Tyler Motte .15 .40
84 Derick Brassard .15 .40
85 Jordan Eberle .25 .60
86 Phillip Danault .25 .60
87 Jason Zucker .25 .60
88 Evander Kane .25 .60
89 Erik Gustafsson .15 .40
90 Jesse Puljujarvi .25 .60
91 Roman Josi .25 .60
92 Matthew Tkachuk .50 1.25
93 Jaden Schwartz .30 .75
94 William Karlsson .30 .75
95 Matt Duchene .25 .60
96 Victor Hedman .30 .75
97 Tyson Barrie .15 .40
98 Jesper Bratt .25 .60
99 Connor Hellebuyck .50 1.25
101 Vincent Trocheck .25 .60
102 Patrice Bergeron .30 .75
103 Jonathan Quick .30 .75
104 Devin Shore .15 .40
105 Auston Matthews 1.00 2.50
106 Josh Manson .15 .40
107 Luke Glendening .15 .40
108 Artturi Lehkonen .20 .50
109 David Perron .20 .50
110 Evgeni Malkin .50 1.25
111 Derek Stepan .15 .40
112 Kyle Okposo .15 .40
113 Anthony Duclair .20 .50
114 Sean Monahan .15 .40
115 Mikael Granlund .20 .50
116 Sebastian Aho .40 1.00
117 Filip Forsberg .40 1.00
118 Alex Kerfoot .20 .50
119 Martin Jones .20 .50
120 Braden Holtby .30 .75
121 Claude Giroux .25 .60
122 Mika Zibanejad .30 .75
123 Nick Leddy .15 .40
124 Ryan Dzingel .20 .50
125 Alexander Wennberg .15 .40
126 Alex Pietrangelo .20 .50
127 Ryan Strome .25 .60
128 Tristan Jarry .25 .60
129 Ryan Spooner .20 .50
130 Tyler Johnson .15 .40
131 Blake Wheeler .25 .60
132 Reilly Smith .25 .60
133 Tyler Toffoli .25 .60
134 Jake Virtanen .20 .50
135 Taylor Hall .25 .60
136 Kevin Hayes .20 .50
137 Ryan Suter .20 .50
138 Keith Yandle .15 .40
139 Rasmus Ristolainen .15 .40
140 William Nylander .50 1.25
141 Ryan Johansen .20 .50
142 Zack Kassian .15 .40
143 Mikael Backlund .15 .40
144 Christian Dvorak .15 .40
145 Shea Weber .25 .60
146 Cam Fowler .25 .60
147 Anton Forsberg .15 .40
148 Mattias Janmark .15 .40
149 Torey Krug .20 .50
150 Mark Scheifele .40 1.00
151 T.J. Oshie .25 .60
152 Tyson Jost .20 .50
153 Jordan Staal .20 .50
154 Tyler Bertuzzi .20 .50
155 Roberto Luongo .40 1.00
156 Tomas Hertl .25 .60
157 Jakub Voracek .20 .50
158 Josh Anderson .20 .50
159 Scott Hartnell .15 .40
160 Steven Stamkos .50 1.25
161 Brandon Montour .30 .75
162 Juuse Saros .30 .75
163 Phil Kessel .25 .60
164 Erik Haula .15 .40
165 Kevin Labanc .15 .40
166 Nate Thompson .20 .50
167 Alexander Steen .15 .40
168 Brock Nelson .25 .60
169 James van Riemsdyk .20 .50
170 Henrik Lundqvist .60 1.50
171 Bobby Ryan .20 .50
172 Danton Heinen .20 .50
173 Kevin Fiala .20 .50
174 Will Butcher .20 .50
175 Petr Mrazek .25 .60
176 Mark Giordano .25 .60
177 Brandon Sutter .15 .40
178 Matthew Benning .15 .40
179 Matt Dumba .15 .40
180 Corey Crawford .25 .60
181 Trevor Daley .20 .50
182 Ryan Pulock .20 .50
183 Jordie Benn .15 .40
184 Jason Pominville .15 .40
185 Evgenii Dadonov .15 .40
186 Elias Lindholm .25 .60
187 Lars Eller .15 .40
188 Adam Henrique .20 .50
189 Alex Goligoski .15 .40
190 Joe Thornton .40 1.00
191 Ivan Provorov .20 .50
192 Boone Jenner .20 .50
193 Riley Nash .15 .40
194 Kyle Connor .40 1.00
195 Patrick Marleau .25 .60
196 Samuel Girard .15 .40
197 Kris Letang .30 .75
198 Trevor Lewis .15 .40
199 James Neal .15 .40
200 Checklist .15 .40
201 Alexander Ovechkin 1.00 2.50
202 Julhar Khaira .15 .40
203 T.J. Brodie .15 .40
204 Yanni Gourde .20 .50
205 Nathan MacKinnon 1.00 2.50
206 Nick Bjugstad .15 .40
207 Alexander Radulov .25 .60
208 Nicolas Deslauriers .15 .40
209 Patrick Sharp .20 .50
210 Henrik Zetterberg .30 .75
211 Andrew Cogliano .15 .40
212 Bryan Little .15 .40
213 Marco Scandella .15 .40
214 Tom Wilson .25 .60
215 Nolan Patrick .25 .60
216 Morgan Rielly .25 .60
217 Malcolm Subban .20 .50
218 Christian Fischer .15 .40
219 Ryan Nugent-Hopkins .30 .75
220 Jake Guentzel .40 1.00
221 Mikko Koivu .25 .60
222 Jake DeBrusk .25 .60
223 Sergei Bobrovsky .40 1.00
224 Alec Martinez .20 .50
225 Craig Smith .15 .40
226 Miles Wood .15 .40
227 Chris Tierney .15 .40
228 Victor Rask .15 .40
229 Colton Parayko .20 .50
230 Gabriel Landeskog .30 .75
231 Anthony Beauvillier .15 .40
232 Jean-Gabriel Pageau .15 .40
233 Connor Murphy .15 .40
234 Patric Hornqvist .15 .40
235 Martin Frk .15 .40
236 Cam Talbot .25 .60
237 Derrick Pouliot .15 .40
238 Calle Jarnkrok .15 .40
239 Sam Bennett .40 1.00
240 Antti Niemi .15 .40
241 Thomas Vanek .20 .50
242 Hampus Lindholm .15 .40
243 Tanner Pearson .20 .50
244 Dustin Byfuglien .25 .60
245 Jared Spurgeon .25 .60
246 Dmitry Orlov .25 .60
247 Valtteri Filppula .15 .40
248 Brendan Perlini .15 .40
249 Alex Killorn .15 .40
250 Jamie Benn .25 .60
251 David Desharnais .15 .40
252 Michael Matheson .20 .50
253 Jake Gardiner .15 .40
254 Danny DeKeyser .15 .40

255 Pierre-Edouard Bellemare .15 .40
256 Benoit Pouliot .15 .40
257 Brent Seabrook .15 .40
258 Bryan Rust .25 .60
259 Derek Forbort .15 .40
260 Kyle Turris .20 .50
261 Michael Cammalleri .15 .40
262 Sami Vatanen .15 .40
263 Mikkel Boedker .15 .40
264 Nick Ritchie .15 .40
265 David Krejci .25 .60
266 Vladimir Sobotka .20 .50
267 Charlie Coyle .25 .60
268 Andrew Ladd .15 .40
269 Jesper Fast .15 .40
270 Brandon Dubinsky .15 .40
271 Tom Pyatt .20 .50
272 Michael Del Zotto .20 .50
273 Michael Frolik .20 .50
274 Kyle Brodziak .20 .50
275 Max Pacioretty .25 .60
276 Scott Laughton .15 .40
277 Timo Meier .25 .60
278 Zach Hyman .40 1.00
279 Jason Demers .20 .50
280 Pekka Rinne .25 .60
281 Carl Soderberg .15 .40
282 Mikhail Sergachev .20 .50
283 Colin Miller .15 .40
284 Esa Lindell .20 .50
285 Ryan Miller .25 .60
286 Vincent Hinostroza .20 .50
287 Mathieu Perreault .15 .40
288 Matt Niskanen .20 .50
289 Brian Gibbons .20 .50
290 Jeff Carter .20 .50
291 Nate Schmidt .20 .50
292 Riley Sheahan .15 .40
293 Evan Rodrigues .20 .50
294 Oscar Klefbom .20 .50
295 Justin Faulk .20 .50
296 Jared McCann .20 .50
297 Nino Niederreiter .15 .40
298 Nail Yakupov .15 .40
299 Charlie McAvoy .30 .75
300 Checklist .15 .40
301 Anthony Mantha .20 .50
302 Connor Brown .20 .50
303 Andrew Shaw .15 .40
304 Christian Folin .20 .50
305 Jonathan Toews .40 1.00
306 Mark Jankowski .15 .40
307 Antoine Vermette .15 .40
308 Jason Spezza .25 .60
309 Ondrej Palat .20 .50
310 Adam Larsson .25 .60
311 Tyler Myers .15 .40
312 Jakub Vrana .25 .60
313 Joel Eriksson Ek .20 .50
314 Carl Hagelin .15 .40
315 Artemi Panarin .50 1.25
316 Michael Raffl .20 .50
317 Curtis McElhinney .15 .40
318 Marcus Foligno .20 .50
319 Alex Tuch .25 .60
320 Derek Ryan .20 .50
321 Zemgus Girgensons .20 .50
322 Mattias Ekholm .20 .50
323 Jamie McGinn .20 .50
324 Radek Faksa .20 .50
325 Ben Bishop .20 .50
326 Nick Cousins .15 .40
327 David Backes .15 .40
328 Justin Braun .20 .50
329 Stefan Noesen .15 .40
330 Cam Atkinson .25 .60
331 Vince Dunn .20 .50
332 Rickard Rakell .20 .50
333 Olli Maatta .15 .40
334 Joel Armia .15 .40
335 Thomas Hickey .20 .50
336 Andy Andreoff .20 .50
337 Kevin Shattenkirk .15 .40
338 Joonas Donskoi .15 .40
339 Gustav Nyquist .15 .40
340 Vladislav Namestnikov .15 .40
341 Charles Hudon .20 .50
342 Kris Russell .15 .40
343 J.T. Miller .30 .75
344 Mike Smith .20 .50
345 Cody Ceci .15 .40
346 Thomas Chabot .25 .60
347 Chris Kunitz .20 .50
348 Oskar Sundqvist .15 .40
349 Erik Johnson .15 .40
350 Loui Eriksson .15 .40
351 Artem Anisimov .15 .40
352 Cody Eakin .15 .40
353 Niklas Hjalmarsson .15 .40
354 Denis Malgin .15 .40
355 Ryan Kesler .25 .60
356 Brian Elliott .20 .50
357 Colton Sissons .15 .40
358 Dan Hamhuis .20 .50
359 Brett Connolly .15 .40
360 John Tavares .40 1.00
361 Conor Sheary .25 .60
362 Zdeno Chara .25 .60
363 Brian Boyle .20 .50
364 Kyle Clifford .15 .40
365 Jimmy Vesey .20 .50
366 Josh Morrissey .30 .75
367 Tomas Plekanec .15 .40
368 Tyler Pitlick .15 .40
369 Marian Gaborik .25 .60
370 Alex Galchenyuk .15 .40
371 Sam Gagner .15 .40
372 Deryk Engelland .20 .50
373 Antoine Roussel .15 .40
374 Ron Hainsey .20 .50
375 Noah Hanifin .25 .60
376 Seth Jones .25 .60
377 Colton Sceviour .20 .50
378 Marc-Edouard Vlasic .15 .40
379 Frederik Andersen .30 .75
380 Marcus Johansson .20 .50
381 Tage Thompson .30 .75
382 Kevin Connauton .20 .50
383 Ryan Ellis .20 .50
384 Robin Lehner .20 .50
385 Mike Green .20 .50
386 Brandon Saad .20 .50
387 Troy Brouwer .15 .40
388 Tim Schaller .20 .50
389 Andrei Vasilevskiy .40 1.00
390 Jack Eichel .40 1.00
391 Cam Ward .25 .60
392 Justin Schultz .20 .50
393 Dion Phaneuf .20 .50
394 Jacob Trouba .20 .50
395 Shea Theodore .30 .75
396 Jakob Silfverberg .15 .40
397 Jay Beagle .15 .40
398 Matt Nieto .20 .50
399 Nick Bonino .15 .40
400 Checklist .15 .40
401 Darnell Nurse .20 .50
402 Anders Bjork .20 .50
403 James Reimer .25 .60
404 Nikita Zaitsev .20 .50
405 Jonathan Drouin .20 .50
406 Justin Abdelkader .20 .50
407 Duncan Keith .20 .50
408 Anze Kopitar .40 1.00
409 Remi Elie .20 .50
410 Pierre-Luc Dubois .20 .50
411 Brian Dumoulin .15 .40
412 Jakob Chychrun .25 .60
413 Matt Cullen .20 .50
414 Tomas Tatar .15 .40
415 Louis Domingue .20 .50
416 Alex Iafallo .15 .40
417 Jordan Weal .15 .40
418 Andrew Copp .15 .40
419 Ryan Hartman .15 .40
420 Josh Ho-Sang .20 .50
421 Keith Kinkaid .15 .40
422 J.T. Compher .15 .40
423 Brady Skjei .20 .50
424 Philipp Grubauer .25 .60
425 Milan Lucic .20 .50
426 Craig Anderson .20 .50
427 Ivan Barbashev .20 .50
428 Michael Stone .20 .50
429 Chandler Stephenson .20 .50
430 Scott Darling .20 .50
431 Blake Coleman .20 .50
432 Andreas Athanasiou .20 .50
433 Nick Foligno .20 .50
434 Derek Grant .15 .40
435 Alexander Edler .15 .40
436 Dominik Simon .15 .40
437 Chris Wagner .15 .40
438 Jonas Brodin .15 .40
439 Robert Hagg .15 .40
440 Rick Nash .25 .60
441 Brett Ritchie .15 .40
442 Richard Panik .15 .40
443 Jaroslav Halak .25 .60
444 Brandon Carlo .20 .50
445 Mark Pysyk .20 .50
446 Marc Staal .15 .40
447 Christian Djoos .20 .50
448 Dustin Brown .25 .60
449 Chad Johnson .20 .50
450 Alex DeBrincat .30 .75
451 Kasperi Kapanen .20 .50
452 Sven Baertschi .20 .50
453 Jamie Oleksiak .20 .50
454 Nikita Zadorov .15 .40
455 Haydn Fleury .15 .40
456 Ryan McDonagh .15 .40
457 Paul Byron .15 .40
458 John Gibson .25 .60
459 Ryan Carpenter .15 .40
460 Nick Shore .15 .40
461 Frans Nielsen .15 .40
462 Carter Hutton .20 .50
463 Nikita Soshnikov .20 .50
464 Colin Wilson .20 .50
465 Paul Stastny .20 .50
466 Patrick Maroon .20 .50
467 Aaron Dell .15 .40
468 Drake Caggiula .20 .50
469 Bo Horvat .30 .75
470 Henrik Sedin .30 .75
471 Kari Lehtonen .20 .50
472 Joel Edmundson .15 .40
473 Jori Lehtera .15 .40
474 Jussi Jokinen .20 .50
475 Anton Khudobin .25 .60
476 Ian Cole .15 .40
477 Fredrik Claesson .20 .50
478 Tommy Wingels .20 .50
479 Darren Helm .15 .40
480 Jack Roslovic .15 .40
481 Jimmy Hayes .15 .40
482 Adam Pelech .15 .40
483 Tom Kuhnhackl .15 .40
484 Eric Fehr .15 .40
485 Zach Werenski .40 1.00
486 Leon Draisaitl .75 2.00
487 Connor Brickley .15 .40
488 Oscar Lindberg .20 .50
489 Brock McGinn .15 .40
490 Corey Perry .40 1.00
491 Alex Stalock .15 .40
492 Alex Chiasson .20 .50
493 Nick Schmaltz .20 .50
494 Jake Muzzin .25 .60
495 Micheal Ferland .15 .40
496 Sven Andrighetto .20 .50
497 Antti Raanta .25 .60
498 Zach Parise .25 .60
499 Brendan Gallagher .25 .60
500 Checklist .15 .40
501 Casey Mittelstadt RC 2.00 5.00
502 Joe Hicketts RC 1.00 2.50
503 Nicolas Roy RC .60 1.50
504 Dylan Sikura RC 1.25 3.00
505 Henrik Borgstrom RC 1.50 4.00
506 Oskar Lindblom RC 1.50 4.00
507 Carl Dahlstrom RC .75 2.00
508 Daniel Brickley RC 1.00 2.50
509 Ryan Lomberg RC 1.00 2.50
510 Adam Gaudette RC 1.50 4.00
511 Travis Dermott RC 1.50 4.00
512 Sami Niku RC .75 2.00
513 Samuel Montembeault RC 2.00 5.00
514 Neal Pionk RC 1.00 2.50
515 Jordan Greenway RC 1.00 2.50
516 Michael Dal Colle RC 1.00 2.50
517 Victor Ejdsell RC .75 2.00
518 Philip Holm RC .75 2.00
519 Shane Gersich RC .75 2.00
520 Lias Andersson RC 1.50 4.00
521 Warren Foegele RC 1.00 2.50
522 Dylan Gambrell RC 1.00 2.50
523 Justin Holl RC 1.00 2.50
524 Christian Wolanin RC .75 2.00
525 Anthony Cirelli RC 1.50 4.00
526 John Gilmour RC .60 1.50
527 Zach Whitecloud RC .75 2.00
528 Eric Robinson RC .75 2.00
529 Landon Bow RC .75 2.00
530 Eeli Tolvanen RC 2.00 5.00
531 Morgan Klimchuk RC 1.00 2.50
532 Mitch Reinke RC .75 2.00
533 Mackenzie Blackwood RC 2.00 5.00
534 Ashton Sautner RC .75 2.00
535 Andreas Johnsson RC 1.25 3.00
536 Noah Juulsen RC 1.00 2.50
537 Tomas Hyka RC 1.00 2.50
538 Maxim Mamin RC 1.00 2.50
539 Louie Belpedio RC .75 2.00
540 Ethan Bear RC 1.50 4.00
541 Dillon Heatherington RC 1.00 2.50
542 Marcus Pettersson RC 1.00 2.50
543 Scott Foster RC 25.00 60.00
544 Tyrell Goulbourne RC .75 2.00
545 Troy Terry RC 1.50 4.00
546 Dominic Turgeon RC 1.00 2.50
547 Matthew Highmore RC 1.00 2.50
548 Spencer Foo RC .75 2.00
549 Zach Aston-Reese RC 1.50 4.00
550 Ryan Donato RC 1.50 4.00
551 Alexander Ovechkin SH 4.00 10.00
552 Evgeni Malkin SH 2.00 5.00
553 Roberto Luongo SH 1.50 4.00
554 Connor McDavid SH 5.00 12.00
555 Connor Hellebuyck SH 2.00 5.00
556 Mathew Barzal SH 1.25 3.00
557 D.Sedin/H.Sedin SH 1.25 3.00
558 Carey Price SH 2.00 5.00
559 Sidney Crosby SH 4.00 10.00
560 Taylor Hall SH 1.00 2.50
561 Tampa Bay Lightning CL .15 .40
562 Boston Bruins CL .15 .40
563 Toronto Maple Leafs CL .15 .40
564 Florida Panthers CL .15 .40
565 Detroit Red Wings CL .15 .40
566 Montreal Canadiens CL .15 .40
567 Ottawa Senators CL .15 .40
568 Buffalo Sabres CL .15 .40
569 Washington Capitals CL .15 .40
570 Pittsburgh Penguins CL .15 .40
571 Columbus Blue Jackets CL .15 .40
572 Philadelphia Flyers CL .15 .40
573 New Jersey Devils CL .15 .40
574 Carolina Hurricanes CL .15 .40
575 New York Rangers CL .15 .40
576 New York Islanders CL .15 .40
577 Nashville Predators CL .15 .40
578 Winnipeg Jets CL .15 .40
579 Minnesota Wild CL .15 .40
580 Colorado Avalanche CL .15 .40
581 St. Louis Blues CL .15 .40
582 Dallas Stars CL .15 .40
583 Chicago Blackhawks CL .15 .40
584 Vegas Golden Knights CL .15 .40
585 San Jose Sharks CL .15 .40
586 Los Angeles Kings CL .15 .40
587 Anaheim Ducks CL .15 .40
588 Calgary Flames CL .15 .40
589 Edmonton Oilers CL .15 .40
590 Vancouver Canucks CL .15 .40
591 Arizona Coyotes CL .15 .40
592 Alexander Ovechkin LL 4.00 10.00
593 William Karlsson LL 1.25 3.00
594 Connor Hellebuyck LL 2.00 5.00
595 Connor McDavid LL 5.00 12.00
596 Carter Hutton LL .75 2.00
597 Patrik Laine LL 1.25 3.00
598 Frederik Andersen LL 1.25 3.00
599 Claude Giroux LL 1.00 2.50
600 Mathew Barzal LL 1.25 3.00
601 John Tavares .40 1.00
602 Mike Hoffman .15 .40
603 Tyler Bozak .15 .40
604 Noah Hanifin .25 .60
605 Mikkel Boedker .15 .40
606 Ryan O'Reilly .25 .60
607 Alex Galchenyuk .15 .40
608 Dougie Hamilton .20 .50
609 Max Domi .25 .60
610 Erik Karlsson .30 .75
611 Elias Pettersson RC 4.00 10.00
612 Par Lindholm RC 1.25 3.00
613 Christoffer Ehn RC 1.00 2.50
614 Andrei Svechnikov RC 3.00 8.00
615 Ilya Lyubushkin RC 1.00 2.50
616 Sheldon Dries RC 1.00 2.50
617 Brett Howden RC 1.50 4.00
618 Austin Wagner RC 1.00 2.50
619 Dominik Kahun RC 1.25 3.00
620 Mathieu Joseph RC 1.50 4.00
621 Jordan Kyrou RC 2.50 6.00
622 Maxime Comtois RC 1.25 3.00
623 Jesperi Kotkaniemi RC 2.50 6.00
624 Jacob MacDonald RC 1.00 2.50
625 Evan Bouchard RC 3.00 8.00
626 Juho Lammikko RC 1.00 2.50
627 Sam Steel RC 1.25 3.00
628 Miro Heiskanen RC 3.00 8.00
629 Kiefer Sherwood RC 1.00 2.50
630 Roope Hintz RC 3.00 8.00
631 Luke Johnson RC 1.00 2.50
632 Brady Tkachuk RC 4.00 10.00
633 Dennis Cholowski RC 1.25 3.00
634 Henri Jokiharju RC 1.00 2.50
635 Kristian Vesalainen RC 1.50 4.00
636 Jaret Anderson-Dolan RC 1.00 2.50
637 Libor Sulak RC 1.00 2.50
638 Robert Thomas RC 2.50 6.00
639 Dillon Dube RC 1.50 4.00
640 Michael Rasmussen RC 1.50 4.00
641 Maxime Lajoie RC 2.00 5.00
642 Rourke Chartier RC 1.00 2.50
643 Filip Hronek RC 1.25 3.00
644 Antti Suomela RC 1.00 2.50
645 Mikhail Vorobyev RC 1.00 2.50
646 Juuso Riikola RC 1.00 2.50
647 Igor Ozhiganov RC 1.00 2.50
648 Juuso Valimaki RC 1.25 3.00
649 Isac Lundestrom RC 1.00 2.50
650 Rasmus Dahlin RC 3.00 8.00

2018-19 O-Pee-Chee Glossy Rookies

R1 Rasmus Dahlin 3.00 8.00
R2 Ryan Donato 2.00 5.00
R3 Brady Tkachuk 4.00 10.00
R4 Eeli Tolvanen 2.50 6.00
R5 Casey Mittelstadt 2.50 6.00
R6 Miro Heiskanen 3.00 8.00
R7 Jesperi Kotkaniemi 2.50 6.00
R8 Andrei Svechnikov 3.00 8.00
R9 Michael Rasmussen 1.50 4.00
R10 Elias Pettersson 4.00 10.00

2018-19 O-Pee-Chee HOF Logo Patches

HOF1 Yvan Cournoyer 20.00 50.00
HOF2 Paul Coffey 20.00 50.00
HOF3 Mark Messier 40.00 100.00
HOF4 Mats Sundin 20.00 50.00
HOF5 Dave Andreychuk 20.00 50.00
HOF6 Ted Lindsay 20.00 50.00
HOF7 Howie Morenz 20.00 50.00
HOF8 Tim Horton 30.00 80.00
HOF9 Patrick Roy SP 50.00 125.00
HOF10 Mario Lemieux SP 80.00 200.00

2018-19 O-Pee-Chee Marquee Legends

ML1 Wayne Gretzky 20.00 50.00
ML2 Borje Salming 8.00 20.00
ML3 Teemu Selanne 15.00 40.00
ML4 Peter Forsberg 8.00 20.00
ML5 Patrick Roy 15.00 40.00
ML6 Denis Savard 10.00 25.00
ML7 Bernie Parent 12.00 30.00
ML8 Bobby Orr 20.00 50.00
ML9 Ted Lindsay 8.00 20.00
ML10 Maurice Richard 20.00 50.00

2018-19 O-Pee-Chee Mini

M1 Dylan Larkin 1.00 2.50
M2 Alex DeBrincat 1.00 2.50
M3 Brad Marchand 1.50 4.00
M4 Jonathan Quick 1.00 2.50
M5 Gabriel Landeskog 1.00 2.50
M6 Artemi Panarin 1.50 4.00
M7 Jonathan Drouin .60 1.50
M8 Derek Stepan .50 1.25
M9 Viktor Arvidsson .50 1.25
M10 Ryan Nugent-Hopkins 1.00 2.50
M11 Matt Murray .75 2.00
M12 Jack Eichel 1.25 3.00
M13 Ben Bishop .60 1.50
M14 Aleksander Barkov 1.25 3.00
M15 Mikko Rantanen 2.00 5.00
M16 Sebastian Aho 1.25 3.00
M17 Steven Stamkos 1.50 4.00
M18 Johnny Gaudreau 1.25 3.00
M19 Mathew Barzal 1.00 2.50
M20 Jason Zucker .75 2.00
M21 Mitch Marner 1.25 3.00
M22 Nikolaj Ehlers .75 2.00
M23 Matt Duchene .75 2.00
M24 Brayden Schenn .75 2.00
M25 Rickard Rakell .60 1.50
M26 Claude Giroux .75 2.00
M27 Mats Zuccarello .75 2.00
M28 Nico Hischier 1.25 3.00
M29 Daniel Sedin 1.00 2.50
M30 William Karlsson 1.00 2.50
M31 T.J. Oshie .75 2.00
M32 Corey Crawford .60 1.50
M33 Aaron Ekblad 1.00 2.50
M34 Clayton Keller 1.00 2.50
M35 Eric Staal .75 2.00
M36 Wayne Simmonds .75 2.00
M37 James Neal .50 1.25
M38 Matthew Tkachuk 1.50 4.00
M39 Pekka Rinne .75 2.00
M40 Patrice Bergeron 1.00 2.50
M41 John Gibson .75 2.00
M42 Jake Guentzel 1.25 3.00
M43 Nazem Kadri 1.00 2.50
M44 Teuvo Teravainen .75 2.00
M45 Braden Holtby 1.00 2.50
M46 Logan Couture 1.00 2.50
M47 Joe Thornton 1.25 3.00
M48 Jaden Schwartz 1.00 2.50
M49 Erik Karlsson 1.00 2.50
M50 Andrei Vasilevskiy 1.25 3.00
M51 Sidney Crosby SP 6.00 15.00
M52 Patrick Kane SP 3.00 8.00
M53 Henrik Sedin SP 2.00 5.00
M54 John Tavares SP 2.50 6.00
M55 Brent Burns SP 1.50 4.00
M56 P.K. Subban SP 2.00 5.00
M57 Henrik Lundqvist SP 4.00 10.00
M58 Carey Price SP 3.00 8.00
M59 Brendan Gallagher SP 1.50 4.00
M60 Tyler Seguin SP 2.00 5.00
M61 Oliver Ekman-Larsson SP 1.50 4.00
M62 Leon Draisaitl SP 5.00 12.00
M63 Henrik Zetterberg SP 2.00 5.00
M64 Taylor Hall SP 1.50 4.00
M65 Patrik Laine SP 2.00 5.00
M66 Alexander Ovechkin RARE 10.00 25.00
M67 Jonathan Toews RARE 4.00 10.00
M68 Brock Boeser RARE 3.00 8.00
M69 Auston Matthews RARE 10.00 25.00
M70 Connor McDavid RARE 12.00 30.00
M71 Nikita Kucherov RARE 5.00 12.00
M72 Marc-Andre Fleury RARE 5.00 12.00
M73 Evgeni Malkin RARE 5.00 12.00
M74 Vladimir Tarasenko RARE 3.00 8.00
M75 Jamie Benn RARE 2.50 6.00
M76 Nathan MacKinnon RARE 10.00 25.00
M77 Anze Kopitar RARE 4.00 10.00

2018-19 O-Pee-Chee Mini Back Variation

M1 Dylan Larkin 4.00 10.00
M2 Alex DeBrincat 4.00 10.00
M3 Brad Marchand 6.00 15.00
M4 Jonathan Quick 4.00 10.00
M5 Gabriel Landeskog 4.00 10.00
M6 Artemi Panarin 6.00 15.00
M7 Jonathan Drouin 2.50 6.00
M8 Derek Stepan 2.00 5.00
M9 Viktor Arvidsson 2.00 5.00
M10 Ryan Nugent-Hopkins 4.00 10.00
M11 Matt Murray 3.00 8.00
M12 Jack Eichel 5.00 12.00
M13 Ben Bishop 2.50 6.00
M14 Aleksander Barkov 5.00 12.00
M15 Mikko Rantanen 8.00 20.00
M16 Sebastian Aho 5.00 12.00
M17 Steven Stamkos 6.00 15.00
M18 Johnny Gaudreau 5.00 12.00
M19 Mathew Barzal 4.00 10.00
M20 Jason Zucker 3.00 8.00
M21 Mitch Marner 5.00 12.00
M22 Nikolaj Ehlers 3.00 8.00
M23 Matt Duchene 3.00 8.00
M24 Brayden Schenn 3.00 8.00
M25 Rickard Rakell 2.50 6.00
M26 Claude Giroux 3.00 8.00
M27 Mats Zuccarello 3.00 8.00
M28 Nico Hischier 5.00 12.00
M29 Daniel Sedin 4.00 10.00
M30 William Karlsson 4.00 10.00
M31 T.J. Oshie 3.00 8.00
M32 Corey Crawford 2.50 6.00
M33 Aaron Ekblad 4.00 10.00
M34 Clayton Keller 4.00 10.00
M35 Eric Staal 3.00 8.00
M36 Wayne Simmonds 3.00 8.00
M37 James Neal 2.00 5.00
M38 Matthew Tkachuk 6.00 15.00
M39 Pekka Rinne 3.00 8.00
M40 Patrice Bergeron 4.00 10.00
M41 John Gibson 3.00 8.00
M42 Jake Guentzel 5.00 12.00
M43 Nazem Kadri 4.00 10.00
M44 Teuvo Teravainen 3.00 8.00
M45 Braden Holtby 4.00 10.00
M46 Logan Couture 4.00 10.00
M47 Joe Thornton 5.00 12.00
M48 Jaden Schwartz 4.00 10.00
M49 Erik Karlsson 4.00 10.00
M50 Andrei Vasilevskiy 5.00 12.00
M51 Sidney Crosby 12.00 30.00
M52 Patrick Kane 6.00 15.00
M53 Henrik Sedin 4.00 10.00
M54 John Tavares 5.00 12.00
M55 Brent Burns 3.00 8.00
M56 P.K. Subban 4.00 10.00
M57 Henrik Lundqvist 8.00 20.00
M58 Carey Price 6.00 15.00
M59 Brendan Gallagher 3.00 8.00
M60 Tyler Seguin 4.00 10.00
M61 Oliver Ekman-Larsson 3.00 8.00
M62 Leon Draisaitl 10.00 25.00
M63 Henrik Zetterberg 4.00 10.00
M64 Taylor Hall 3.00 8.00
M65 Patrik Laine 4.00 10.00
M66 Alexander Ovechkin 12.00 30.00
M67 Jonathan Toews 5.00 12.00
M68 Brock Boeser 4.00 10.00
M69 Auston Matthews 12.00 30.00
M70 Connor McDavid 15.00 40.00
M71 Nikita Kucherov 6.00 15.00
M72 Marc-Andre Fleury 6.00 15.00
M73 Evgeni Malkin 6.00 15.00
M74 Vladimir Tarasenko 4.00 10.00
M75 Jamie Benn 3.00 8.00
M76 Nathan MacKinnon 12.00 30.00
M77 Anze Kopitar 5.00 12.00

2018-19 O-Pee-Chee Patches

P1 Henrik Sedin 10.00 25.00
P2 Curtis Joseph 10.00 25.00
P3 Joe Nieuwendyk 6.00 15.00
P4 Adam Graves 8.00 20.00
P5 Ray Bourque 12.00 30.00
P6 Craig Anderson 6.00 15.00
P7 Max Pacioretty 8.00 20.00
P8 Phil Kessel 8.00 20.00
P9 Pat LaFontaine 8.00 20.00
P10 Dave Taylor 6.00 15.00
P11 Vancouver Canucks 5.00 12.00
P12 Washington Capitals 6.00 15.00
P13 Colorado Avalanche 5.00 12.00
P14 Pittsburgh Penguins 10.00 25.00
P15 Edmonton Oilers 15.00 40.00
P16 Patrice Bergeron 10.00 25.00
P17 Ryan Kesler 8.00 20.00
P18 Pavel Datsyuk 12.00 30.00
P19 Doug Gilmour 10.00 25.00
P20 Guy Carbonneau 8.00 20.00
P21 Jonathan Quick 10.00 25.00
P22 Corey Crawford 6.00 15.00
P23 Roberto Luongo 12.00 30.00
P24 Ed Belfour 8.00 20.00
P25 Andy Moog 8.00 20.00
P26 Alexander Ovechkin 30.00 80.00
P27 Steven Stamkos 15.00 40.00
P28 Rick Nash 8.00 20.00
P29 Jarome Iginla 10.00 25.00
P30 Pavel Bure 8.00 20.00
P31 Patrick Kane 15.00 40.00
P32 Daniel Sedin 10.00 25.00
P33 Joe Sakic 15.00 40.00
P34 Marcel Dionne 10.00 25.00
P35 Phil Esposito 12.00 30.00
P36 Connor McDavid 40.00 100.00
P37 Joe Thornton 12.00 30.00
P38 Jaromir Jagr 25.00 60.00
P39 Stan Mikita 8.00 20.00
P40 Dickie Moore 8.00 20.00
P41 Johnny Gaudreau 12.00 30.00
P42 Pierre Turgeon 6.00 15.00
P43 Jari Kurri 8.00 20.00
P44 Johnny Bucyk 8.00 20.00
P45 Alex Delvecchio 8.00 20.00
P46 Duncan Keith 6.00 15.00
P47 Henrik Zetterberg 10.00 25.00
P48 Mike Vernon 6.00 15.00
P49 Brian Leetch 6.00 15.00
P50 Bernie Parent 10.00 25.00
P51 Erik Karlsson 10.00 25.00
P52 Nicklas Lidstrom 8.00 20.00
P53 Denis Potvin 6.00 15.00
P54 Harry Howell 6.00 15.00
P55 Bobby Orr 30.00 80.00
P56 Auston Matthews 30.00 80.00
P57 Teemu Selanne 15.00 40.00
P58 Mike Bossy 8.00 20.00
P59 Peter Stastny 6.00 15.00
P60 Tony Esposito 8.00 20.00
P61 Tuukka Rask 10.00 25.00
P62 Dominik Hasek 12.00 30.00
P63 Glenn Hall 8.00 20.00
P64 Martin Brodeur 20.00 50.00
P65 Jacques Plante 8.00 20.00
P66 Carey Price 15.00 40.00
P67 Evgeni Malkin 15.00 40.00
P68 Wayne Gretzky 50.00 125.00
P69 Bobby Clarke 12.00 30.00
P70 Bobby Hull 15.00 40.00
P71 Sidney Crosby 30.00 80.00
P72 Anze Kopitar 12.00 30.00
P73 Jonathan Toews 12.00 30.00
P74 Rob Blake 8.00 20.00
P75 Brett Hull 15.00 40.00
P76 Steve Yzerman 20.00 50.00
P77 Wayne Gretzky 50.00 125.00
P78 Bryan Trottier 8.00 20.00
P79 Frank Mahovlich 8.00 20.00
P80 Jean Beliveau 8.00 20.00

2018-19 O-Pee-Chee Retro Award Winners

AWCM Connor McDavid 12.00 30.00
AWMB Mathew Barzal 8.00 20.00
AWPR Pekka Rinne 8.00 20.00
AWTH Taylor Hall 8.00 20.00
AWVH Victor Hedman 8.00 20.00

2018-19 O-Pee-Chee Retro Cup Captain

CCAO Alex Ovechkin 25.00 60.00

2018-19 O-Pee-Chee Team Logo Patches

311 Edmonton Oilers 100.00 200.00
312 Los Angeles Kings 40.00 100.00
313 Vegas Golden Knights 40.00 100.00
314 Carolina Hurricanes 40.00 100.00
315 Tampa Bay Lightning 30.00 80.00
316 Dallas Stars 30.00 80.00
317 San Jose Sharks 50.00 120.00
318 Washington Capitals 40.00 100.00
319 Arizona Coyotes 25.00 60.00
320 New York Rangers 60.00 150.00

2019-20 O-Pee-Chee

*BLUE: .6X TO 1.5X BASIC CARDS
*BLUE.RC: .6X TO 1.5X BASIC CARDS
*GOLD: 1.5X TO 4X BASIC CARDS
*GOLD.RC: 1X TO 2.5X BASIC CARDS
*RETRO: 1.5X TO 4X BASIC CARDS
*RETRO.RC: .8X TO 2X BASIC CARDS
*RETRO.BLK/100: 2.5X TO 6X BASIC CARDS
*RETRO.BLK.RC/100: 5X TO 12X BASIC CARDS
1 Nikita Zaitsev .15 .40
2 Nico Hischier .40 1.00
3 Ryan Hartman .15 .40
4 Ryan Callahan .15 .40
5 Bobby Ryan .20 .50
6 Zdeno Chara .25 .60
7 Victor Rask .15 .40
8 James van Riemsdyk .20 .50
9 Ryan Suter .20 .50
10 Adam Henrique .20 .50
11 Max Pacioretty .25 .60
12 Oscar Klefbom .25 .60
13 T.J. Oshie .25 .60
14 Antti Raanta .25 .60
15 Kris Letang .30 .75
16 Ryan Dzingel .20 .50
17 Derick Brassard .15 .40
18 Josh Bailey .20 .50
19 Bryan Rust .25 .60
20 Reilly Smith .25 .60
21 Chris Kreider .30 .75
22 Paul Byron .15 .40
23 Semyon Varlamov .25 .60
24 Vincent Trocheck .25 .60
25 Jake Muzzin .25 .60
26 Jaroslav Halak .25 .60
27 Jesper Bratt .25 .60
28 David Krejci .25 .60
29 Jakob Silfverberg .15 .40
30 Erik Haula .15 .40
31 Ondrej Palat .20 .50
32 Connor Brown .20 .50
33 Blake Coleman .20 .50
34 Linus Ullmark .25 .60
35 Blake Wheeler .25 .60
36 Alex DeBrincat .30 .75
37 Vladimir Tarasenko .30 .75
38 Hampus Lindholm .15 .40
39 Marco Scandella .15 .40
40 Jesperi Kotkaniemi .25 .60
41 Tyler Toffoli .25 .60
42 Alex Goligoski .20 .50
43 Jordan Binnington .40 1.00
44 Valeri Nichushkin .25 .60
45 Brayden McNabb .20 .50
46 Dennis Cholowski .20 .50
47 Henri Jokiharju .15 .40
48 Brett Pesce .15 .40
49 Filip Forsberg .40 1.00
50 Nikolay Goldobin .20 .50
51 Drake Batherson .25 .60
52 Jaden Schwartz .30 .75
53 Travis Konecny .25 .60
54 Justin Williams .20 .50
55 Cody Eakin .15 .40
56 Michael Grabner .20 .50
57 Nate Schmidt .20 .50
58 Henrik Lundqvist .60 1.50
59 Johnny Boychuk .20 .50
60 Justin Schultz .25 .60
61 Ian Cole .15 .40
62 Brandon Dubinsky .15 .40
63 J.T. Compher .15 .40
64 Carter Hart .25 .60
65 Micheal Ferland .15 .40
66 Matt Niskanen .20 .50
67 Neal Pionk .15 .40
68 Henrik Borgstrom .20 .50
69 Ryan Johansen .20 .50
70 Cal Clutterbuck .15 .40
71 Oliver Ekman-Larsson .25 .60
72 Brandon Saad .20 .50
73 Calle Jarnkrok .15 .40
74 Jakub Vrana .25 .60
75 Mikko Koskinen .15 .40
76 Loui Eriksson .15 .40
77 Vladislav Namestnikov .15 .40
78 Rasmus Dahlin .30 .75
79 Connor Hellebuyck .50 1.25
80 Brenden Dillon .15 .40
81 Pierre-Luc Dubois .20 .50
82 Nicklas Backstrom .25 .60
83 Joonas Korpisalo .25 .60
84 Jordan Eberle .25 .60
85 Erik Gudbranson .15 .40
86 Andrew Shaw .15 .40
87 Oliver Bjorkstrand .20 .50
88 Sven Baertschi .15 .40
89 Andrei Vasilevskiy .40 1.00
90 Jaccob Slavin .20 .50
91 Rasmus Ristolainen .15 .40
92 Matt Martin .15 .40
93 Garret Sparks .15 .40
94 Brent Burns .25 .60
95 Anthony Mantha .20 .50
96 Travis Sanheim .15 .40
97 Cody Ceci .15 .40
98 Niklas Hjalmarsson .15 .40
99 Mackenzie Blackwood .25 .60
100 Checklist .15 .40
101 Marc-Andre Fleury .50 1.25
102 Juuse Saros .30 .75
103 Frank Vatrano .20 .50
104 Brian Dumoulin .15 .40
105 Tom Wilson .25 .60
106 Robin Lehner .20 .50
107 P.K. Subban .30 .75
108 Ryan Reaves .15 .40
109 Mathew Barzal .30 .75
110 Victor Hedman .30 .75
111 Andrew Cogliano .15 .40
112 Jake Guentzel .40 1.00
113 Lars Eller .15 .40
114 Radek Faksa .20 .50
115 Nikolaj Ehlers .25 .60
116 Frans Nielsen .15 .40
117 Anders Lee .20 .50
118 Marc Staal .15 .40
119 Adam Larsson .20 .50
120 Philipp Grubauer .25 .60
121 Joe Pavelski .30 .75
122 Devin Shore .15 .40
123 Brock Boeser .30 .75
124 Brandon Tanev .20 .50
125 Derek Stepan .15 .40
126 Tuukka Rask .30 .75
127 Aaron Ekblad .30 .75
128 Dustin Brown .25 .60
129 Anthony Duclair .20 .50
130 Ryan Nugent-Hopkins .30 .75
131 Matt Calvert .15 .40
132 Shea Weber .25 .60
133 Tanner Pearson .25 .60
134 Oskar Sundqvist .15 .40
135 Bo Horvat .30 .75
136 Michal Kempny .15 .40
137 Jonathan Ericsson .15 .40
138 T.J. Brodie .20 .50
139 Duncan Keith .20 .50
140 Ryan Strome .25 .60
141 Ryan Donato .20 .50
142 Wayne Simmonds .25 .60
143 Jake DeBrusk .25 .60
144 Matt Duchene .25 .60
145 John Moore .15 .40
146 Corey Perry .40 1.00
147 John Carlson .25 .60
148 Zach Werenski .40 1.00
149 Viktor Arvidsson .15 .40
150 Travis Dermott .20 .50
151 Lawson Crouse .15 .40
152 Chris Tierney .20 .50
153 Jim Howard .30 .75
154 Joe Thornton .40 1.00
155 Sidney Crosby 1.00 2.50
156 Tomas Hertl .25 .60
157 Drew Doughty .30 .75
158 Ryan Miller .25 .60
159 Anton Stralman .15 .40
160 Kyle Connor .40 1.00
161 Brett Connolly .15 .40
162 Sean Monahan .15 .40
163 Patrick Marleau .25 .60
164 Erik Gustafsson .15 .40
165 Alex Killorn .15 .40
166 Victor Mete .15 .40
167 Zach Aston-Reese .25 .60
168 Mike Hoffman .15 .40
169 Joel Eriksson Ek .20 .50
170 Dylan Larkin .30 .75
171 Warren Foegele .20 .50
172 Jake Virtanen .25 .60
173 Ryan Murray .20 .50
174 Brandon Carlo .20 .50
175 Jonathan Toews .40 1.00
176 Craig Anderson .20 .50
177 Paul Stastny .20 .50
178 Phillip Danault .25 .60
179 Filip Chytil .20 .50
180 Jonathan Marchessault .30 .75
181 Olli Maatta .15 .40
182 Erik Karlsson .30 .75
183 Alexander Ovechkin 1.00 2.50

184 Johnny Gaudreau .40 1.00
185 Josh Manson .15 .40
186 Seth Jones .25 .60
187 Ryan Pulock .20 .50
188 Kyle Palmieri .20 .50
189 Joonas Donskoi .15 .40
190 Dylan Strome .30 .75
191 Elias Lindholm .25 .60
192 Evgeni Malkin .50 1.25
193 Cory Schneider .25 .60
194 Bryan Little .20 .50
195 Nolan Patrick .25 .60
196 Pierre-Edouard Bellemare .15 .40
197 Lias Andersson .20 .50
198 Brock Nelson .25 .60
199 Pavel Buchnevich .20 .50
200 Checklist .15 .40
201 David Backes .15 .40
202 Shea Theodore .30 .75
203 Carl Hagelin .15 .40
204 Andy Greene .15 .40
205 Kevin Fiala .20 .50
206 Matt Nieto .15 .40
207 Sebastian Aho .40 1.00
208 Nikita Kucherov .50 1.25
209 Justin Faulk .20 .50
210 Brent Seabrook .15 .40
211 Jared Spurgeon .25 .60
212 Brian Boyle .20 .50
213 Marcus Pettersson .15 .40
214 Jonathan Drouin .20 .50
215 James Reimer .25 .60
216 David Savard .15 .40
217 Alex Galchenyuk .15 .40
218 Mats Zuccarello .25 .60
219 Steven Stamkos .50 1.25
220 Jake Allen .25 .60
221 Carter Hutton .20 .50
222 Jujhar Khaira .15 .40
223 Braydon Coburn .15 .40
224 Andreas Athanasiou .20 .50
225 Troy Stecher .15 .40
226 Thomas Greiss .20 .50
227 Jason Zucker .25 .60
228 Brendan Gallagher .25 .60
229 J.T. Miller .30 .75
230 Jeff Skinner .25 .60
231 Elias Pettersson .40 1.00
232 Jared McCann .20 .50
233 Casey Cizikas .15 .40
234 Artemi Panarin .50 1.25
235 Joel Edmundson .15 .40
236 Colton Parayko .20 .50
237 Yanni Gourde .20 .50
238 Daniel Sprong .15 .40
239 Michael Rasmussen .15 .40
240 Jay Beagle .15 .40
241 Colin Wilson .20 .50
242 Colin White .15 .40
243 Travis Boyd .15 .40
244 Kyle Clifford .15 .40
245 Charlie McAvoy .30 .75
246 Morgan Rielly .25 .60
247 Cam Ward .25 .60
248 Miro Heiskanen .30 .75
249 Patrice Bergeron .30 .75
250 Kyle Okposo .15 .40
251 Carey Price .50 1.25
252 Jordan Staal .20 .50
253 Jordan Greenway .15 .40
254 Alexander Wennberg .15 .40
255 Dion Phaneuf .20 .50
256 Frederik Andersen .30 .75
257 Miles Wood .15 .40
258 Kevan Miller .15 .40
259 Mattias Janmark .15 .40
260 Marc-Edouard Vlasic .15 .40
261 Brady Tkachuk .40 1.00
262 Travis Hamonic .15 .40
263 Antti Niemi .20 .50
264 Jay Bouwmeester .15 .40
265 Connor Murphy .20 .50
266 Alex Iafallo .15 .40
267 Devan Dubnyk .20 .50
268 Tobias Rieder .15 .40
269 Sam Bennett .40 1.00
270 Nick Leddy .15 .40
271 Mark Pysyk .15 .40
272 Pekka Rinne .25 .60
273 Ivan Provorov .20 .50
274 Teuvo Teravainen .25 .60
275 Robert Thomas .25 .60
276 Zach Parise .25 .60
277 Patrik Nemeth .20 .50
278 Madison Bowey .15 .40
279 Brad Marchand .50 1.25
280 Brayden Schenn .25 .60
281 Ben Bishop .20 .50
282 Patric Hornqvist .15 .40
283 Anthony Beauvillier .15 .40
284 Joakim Nordstrom .15 .40
285 Vince Dunn .20 .50
286 Mitch Marner .40 1.00
287 Sean Couturier .20 .50
288 Ryan Getzlaf .25 .60
289 Andre Burakovsky .15 .40
290 Thomas Chabot .25 .60
291 Jonathan Huberdeau .30 .75
292 Christian Dvorak .20 .50
293 Dmitry Kulikov .20 .50
294 Rickard Rakell .20 .50
295 Mathieu Perreault .15 .40
296 Evgenii Dadonov .15 .40
297 Patrick Maroon .25 .60
298 Charlie Coyle .25 .60
299 Alexandar Georgiev .25 .60
300 Checklist .15 .40
301 Dustin Byfuglien .25 .60
302 Jason Pominville .15 .40
303 Jeff Carter .20 .50
304 Noah Juulsen .15 .40
305 Jamie Benn .25 .60
306 Vladimir Sobotka .15 .40
307 David Rittich .20 .50
308 David Pastrnak .60 1.50
309 Carl Soderberg .15 .40
310 Marcus Kruger .15 .40
311 Kris Russell .15 .40
312 Jimmy Vesey .20 .50
313 Vincent Hinostroza .15 .40
314 Connor McDavid 1.25 3.00
315 Corey Crawford .25 .60
316 Kasperi Kapanen .20 .50
317 Marcus Johansson .20 .50
318 Jacob Trouba .20 .50
319 Michael Stone .15 .40
320 Dmitry Orlov .25 .60
321 Josh Morrissey .30 .75
322 Ryan Ellis .20 .50
323 Jonathan Quick .30 .75
324 Nick Bonino .15 .40
325 Richard Panik .15 .40
326 Marcus Foligno .20 .50
327 Jake Gardiner .15 .40
328 Alexander Steen .15 .40
329 Zemgus Girgensons .20 .50
330 Erik Johnson .15 .40
331 Timo Meier .25 .60
332 Brady Skjei .20 .50
333 Chris Kunitz .15 .40
334 Evgeny Kuznetsov .30 .75
335 Cam Fowler .25 .60
336 Justin Braun .15 .40
337 Trevor van Riemsdyk .20 .50
338 Mike Smith .15 .40
339 Cam Atkinson .25 .60
340 Jean-Gabriel Pageau .15 .40
341 Torey Krug .20 .50
342 William Nylander .50 1.25
343 Kevin Labanc .15 .40
344 Jack Campbell .25 .60
345 Mikkel Boedker .15 .40
346 Sami Vatanen .15 .40
347 Colton Sceviour .15 .40
348 Alex Pietrangelo .20 .50
349 Alec Martinez .15 .40
350 Mike Green .20 .50
351 Casey DeSmith .20 .50
352 Mathieu Joseph .15 .40
353 Claude Giroux .25 .60
354 Trevor Daley .15 .40
355 Antoine Roussel .15 .40
356 Mikael Backlund .20 .50
357 Shayne Gostisbehere .25 .60
358 Eeli Tolvanen .25 .60
359 Dmitrij Jaskin .15 .40
360 Mark Giordano .25 .60
361 Ben Harpur .15 .40
362 Christopher Tanev .15 .40
363 Damon Severson .20 .50
364 Esa Lindell .20 .50
365 Brian Elliott .20 .50
366 Blake Comeau .15 .40
367 Artem Anisimov .15 .40
368 Gabriel Landeskog .30 .75
369 Nick Bjugstad .15 .40
370 Trevor Lewis .15 .40
371 Kevin Shattenkirk .15 .40
372 Kyle Turris .20 .50
373 Martin Jones .20 .50
374 Deryk Engelland .15 .40
375 Markus Nutivaara .15 .40
376 Max Domi .25 .60
377 Roberto Luongo .40 1.00
378 Milan Lucic .20 .50
379 Sam Reinhart .50 1.25
380 Ryan McDonagh .15 .40
381 Calvin de Haan .15 .40
382 Anthony Cirelli .20 .50
383 Michael Del Zotto .20 .50
384 Ilya Kovalchuk .25 .60
385 Phil Kessel .25 .60
386 Mikhail Sergachev .20 .50
387 Jacob Markstrom .20 .50
388 Ben Lovejoy .15 .40
389 Jason Demers .15 .40
390 Ondrej Kase .15 .40
391 Tomas Tatar .15 .40
392 Brandon Montour .30 .75
393 Pavel Zacha .20 .50
394 Jordie Benn .15 .40
395 Brett Howden .15 .40
396 Roman Josi .25 .60
397 Alexander Radulov .25 .60
398 Jesse Puljujarvi .25 .60
399 Zack Smith .15 .40
400 Checklist .15 .40
401 Zach Hyman .40 1.00
402 Andrew MacDonald .15 .40
403 Darcy Kuemper .25 .60
404 Anze Kopitar .40 1.00
405 Zach Bogosian .20 .50
406 Nick Seeler .15 .40
407 Patrik Laine .30 .75
408 Gustav Nyquist .15 .40
409 Travis Zajac .15 .40
410 Jason Spezza .25 .60
411 Mikko Rantanen .60 1.50
412 Jack Eichel .40 1.00
413 Justin Abdelkader .20 .50
414 Conor Sheary .25 .60
415 Mika Zibanejad .30 .75
416 Leo Komarov .15 .40
417 Mark Stone .30 .75
418 John Gibson .25 .60
419 Danny DeKeyser .15 .40
420 Eric Staal .25 .60
421 Nick Ritchie .15 .40
422 Boone Jenner .25 .60
423 Mattias Ekholm .20 .50
424 Kyle Brodziak .15 .40
425 Derek Forbort .15 .40
426 Mikko Koivu .25 .60
427 Craig Smith .15 .40
428 Jakub Voracek .20 .50
429 John Tavares .40 1.00
430 Nathan MacKinnon 1.00 2.50
431 Roope Hintz .30 .75
432 William Karlsson .30 .75
433 Maxime Lajoie .20 .50
434 Dominik Kahun .15 .40
435 Matt Murray .25 .60
436 Dougie Hamilton .20 .50
437 Aleksander Barkov .40 1.00
438 Patrick Kane .50 1.25
439 Colin Miller .15 .40
440 Darnell Nurse .20 .50
441 Logan Couture .30 .75
442 Radko Gudas .20 .50
443 Michael Frolik .20 .50
444 Mark Scheifele .40 1.00
445 Nazem Kadri .30 .75
446 Michael Matheson .15 .40
447 Adam Lowry .20 .50
448 Brayden Point .30 .75
449 Thomas Vanek .20 .50
450 Tyson Jost .20 .50
451 Brandon Sutter .15 .40
452 Matt Dumba .15 .40
453 Nino Niederreiter .15 .40
454 Brad Richardson .15 .40
455 Sergei Bobrovsky .40 1.00
456 Noah Hanifin .25 .60
457 Petr Mrazek .25 .60
458 Alexander Edler .15 .40
459 Clayton Keller .30 .75
460 Tyson Barrie .15 .40
461 Alex Tuch .25 .60
462 Tyler Myers .15 .40
463 Auston Matthews 1.00 2.50
464 Matthew Tkachuk .50 1.25
465 Melker Karlsson .15 .40
466 Niklas Kronwall .15 .40
467 Thomas Hickey .15 .40
468 Tyler Bozak .15 .40
469 Mikael Granlund .20 .50
470 James Neal .15 .40
471 Oskar Lindblom .20 .50
472 Leon Draisaitl .75 2.00
473 Casey Mittelstadt .25 .60
474 Dylan DeMelo .15 .40
475 Ryan Kesler .25 .60
476 Andrei Svechnikov .30 .75
477 Braden Holtby .30 .75
478 Evander Kane .25 .60
479 Keith Yandle .15 .40
480 Tyler Seguin .30 .75
481 Will Butcher .20 .50
482 Jonas Brodin .15 .40
483 Andrej Sekera .15 .40
484 David Perron .20 .50
485 Robert Hagg .15 .40
486 Nick Schmaltz .20 .50
487 John Klingberg .25 .60
488 Mark Borowiecki .15 .40
489 Ryan O'Reilly .25 .60
490 Denis Malgin .15 .40
491 Andrew Ladd .15 .40
492 Jeff Petry .25 .60
493 Andreas Johnsson .25 .60
494 Tyler Johnson .15 .40
495 Curtis McElhinney .15 .40
496 Jack Roslovic .15 .40
497 Kevin Hayes .20 .50
498 Taylor Hall .25 .60
499 Alex Chiasson .20 .50
500 Checklist .15 .40
501 Filip Zadina RC 1.25 3.00
502 Brandon Gignac RC .60 1.50
503 Kevin Stenlund RC .60 1.50
504 Ryan Poehling RC 1.25 3.00
505 Brogan Rafferty RC .75 2.00
506 Matt Roy RC .75 2.00
507 Mackenzie MacEachern RC .75 2.00
508 Alexandre Texier RC .75 2.00
509 Guillaume Brisebois RC .75 2.00
510 Nico Sturm RC .60 1.50
511 Max Veronneau RC .60 1.50
512 Trent Frederic RC .75 2.00
513 Philippe Myers RC .60 1.50
514 Blake Lizotte RC .75 2.00
515 Joey Daccord RC 1.50 4.00
516 Ryan Lindgren RC .60 1.50
517 Jake Chelios RC .60 1.50
518 Josh Brown RC .60 1.50
519 Quinn Hughes RC 4.00 10.00
520 Victor Olofsson RC 1.50 4.00
521 Kole Sherwood RC .75 2.00
522 Karson Kuhlman RC .75 2.00
523 Josh Teves RC .60 1.50
524 Zack MacEwen RC .60 1.50
525 Rudolfs Balcers RC .75 2.00
526 William Borgen RC .60 1.50
527 Max Jones RC .75 2.00
528 Cale Makar RC 4.00 10.00
529 Dennis Gilbert RC .60 1.50
530 Joel L'Esperance RC .75 2.00
531 Vitaly Abramov RC .75 2.00
532 Mark Friedman RC .60 1.50
533 Adam Johnson RC .60 1.50
534 Jacob Middleton RC .60 1.50
535 Carl Grundstrom RC .75 2.00
536 Josh Currie RC .60 1.50
537 Nathan Bastian RC .75 2.00
538 Rem Pitlick RC .75 2.00
539 Brady Keeper RC .75 2.00
540 Jimmy Schuldt RC .60 1.50
541 Kevin Boyle RC .75 2.00
542 Ryan Kuffner RC .75 2.00
543 Teddy Blueger RC .75 2.00
544 Erik Brannstrom RC .75 2.00
545 Dante Fabbro RC .75 2.00
546 Taro Hirose RC .75 2.00
547 Zach Senyshyn RC .75 2.00
548 Riley Stillman RC .75 2.00
549 Libor Hajek RC .60 1.50
550 Colton White RC 1.00 2.50
551 Anaheim Ducks TC .15 .40
552 Arizona Coyotes TC .15 .40
553 Boston Bruins TC .15 .40
554 Buffalo Sabres TC .15 .40
555 Calgary Flames TC .15 .40
556 Carolina Hurricanes TC .15 .40
557 Chicago Blackhawks TC .15 .40
558 Colorado Avalanche TC .15 .40
559 Columbus Blue Jackets TC .15 .40
560 Dallas Stars TC .15 .40
561 Detroit Red Wings TC .15 .40
562 Edmonton Oilers TC .15 .40
563 Florida Panthers TC .15 .40
564 Los Angeles Kings TC .15 .40
565 Minnesota Wild TC .15 .40
566 Montreal Canadiens TC .15 .40
567 Nashville Predators TC .15 .40
568 New Jersey Devils TC .15 .40
569 New York Islanders TC .15 .40
570 New York Rangers TC .15 .40
571 Ottawa Senators TC .15 .40
572 Philadelphia Flyers TC .15 .40
573 Pittsburgh Penguins TC .15 .40
574 San Jose Sharks TC .15 .40
575 St. Louis Blues TC .15 .40
576 Tampa Bay Lightning TC .15 .40
577 Toronto Maple Leafs TC .15 .40
578 Vancouver Canucks TC .15 .40
579 Vegas Golden Knights TC .15 .40
580 Washington Capitals TC .15 .40
581 Winnipeg Jets TC .15 .40
582 Alexander Ovechkin LL 2.50 6.00
583 Nikita Kucherov LL 1.25 3.00
584 Nikita Kucherov LL 1.25 3.00
585 Brayden Point LL .75 2.00
586 Phil Kessel LL .60 1.50
587 Ben Bishop LL .50 1.25
588 Sergei Bobrovsky LL 1.00 2.50
589 Andrei Vasilevskiy LL 1.00 2.50
590 Elias Pettersson LL 1.00 2.50
591 John Tavares SH 1.00 2.50
592 Jesperi Kotkaniemi SH .60 1.50
593 Marc-Andre Fleury SH 1.25 3.00
594 Elias Pettersson SH 1.00 2.50
595 Joe Thornton SH 1.00 2.50
596 Ryan Miller SH .60 1.50
597 Patrick Kane SH 1.25 3.00
598 Sidney Crosby SH 2.50 6.00
599 Alexander Ovechkin SH 2.50 6.00
600 Carey Price SH 1.25 3.00
601 P.K. Subban .30 .75
602 Semyon Varlamov .25 .60
603 Jacob Trouba .20 .50
604 Joe Pavelski .30 .75
605 Mats Zuccarello .25 .60
606 Corey Perry .40 1.00
607 Sergei Bobrovsky .40 1.00
608 Matt Duchene .25 .60
609 Nazem Kadri .30 .75
610 Artemi Panarin .50 1.25
611 Jack Hughes RC 4.00 10.00
612 Kirby Dach RC 1.50 4.00
613 Joel Farabee RC 1.25 3.00
614 Klim Kostin RC .75 2.00
615 Oliver Wahlstrom RC 1.25 3.00
616 Adam Boqvist RC .75 2.00
617 Morgan Frost RC 1.25 3.00
618 Ilya Mikheyev RC 1.25 3.00
619 Nicolas Hague RC .75 2.00
620 Danil Yurtaykin RC .60 1.50
621 Tobias Bjornfot RC .75 2.00
622 Adam Fox RC 2.00 5.00
623 Martin Fehervary RC .60 1.50
624 Connor Clifton RC .75 2.00
625 Ville Heinola RC 1.00 2.50
626 Elvis Merzlikins RC 1.50 4.00
627 Barrett Hayton RC 1.50 4.00
628 Dmytro Timashov RC .75 2.00
629 David Gustafsson RC .60 1.50
630 Dominik Kubalik RC 1.50 4.00
631 Emil Bemstrom RC .75 2.00
632 Carter Verhaeghe RC 1.25 3.00
633 Carsen Twarynski RC .60 1.50
634 Noah Dobson RC 2.00 5.00
635 Nikita Gusev RC 1.25 3.00
636 Cale Fleury RC 1.00 2.50
637 Jakob Lilja RC .60 1.50
638 Mario Ferraro RC .60 1.50
639 Nick Caamano RC .60 1.50
640 Gaetan Haas RC .60 1.50
641 Scott Sabourin RC .60 1.50
642 Cody Glass RC 1.25 3.00
643 Rasmus Sandin RC 1.25 3.00
644 Conor Timmins RC .75 2.00
645 Joakim Nygard RC .60 1.50
646 Connor Bunnaman RC .60 1.50
647 Nick Suzuki RC 3.00 8.00
648 Lean Bergmann RC .60 1.50
649 Jesper Boqvist RC .60 1.50
650 Kaapo Kakko RC 1.25 3.00

2019-20 O-Pee-Chee Box Bottoms

1 Connor McDavid
Jack Eichel
Carter Hart 1.50 4.00
2 John Tavares
Nathan MacKinnon
Carey Price 1.25 3.00
3 Patrick Kane
Johnny Gaudreau
Filip Zadina .60 1.50
4 Steven Stamkos
Elias Pettersson
Marc-Andre Fleury .60 1.50

2019-20 O-Pee-Chee '19 Stanley Cup Final Moments

1 Sean Kuraly 6.00 15.00
2 Carl Gunnarsson 6.00 15.00
3 Torey Krug 8.00 20.00
4 Ryan O'Reilly 10.00 25.00
5 Zdeno Chara 10.00 25.00
6 Jordan Binnington 15.00 40.00
7 Brad Marchand 20.00 50.00
8 Tuukka Rask 12.00 30.00
9 Alex Pietrangelo 8.00 20.00
10 Jordan Binnington 15.00 40.00
11 Ryan O'Reilly 10.00 25.00
12 St. Louis Blues 6.00 15.00

2019-20 O-Pee-Chee Caramel Minis

*CARAMEL: .5X TO 1.25X BASIC INSERTS
*CARAMEL.SP: .5X TO 1.25X BASIC INSERTS
*CARAMEL.SSP: .5X TO 1.25X BASIC INSERTS
C1 Elias Pettersson 1.25 3.00
C2 Pekka Rinne .75 2.00
C3 Henrik Lundqvist 2.00 5.00
C4 Steven Stamkos 1.50 4.00
C5 Claude Giroux .75 2.00
C6 Mark Giordano .75 2.00
C7 Robin Lehner .60 1.50
C8 Jack Eichel 1.25 3.00
C9 P.K. Subban 1.00 2.50
C10 Marc-Andre Fleury 1.50 4.00
C11 Mikko Rantanen 2.00 5.00
C12 Joe Thornton 1.25 3.00
C13 Brayden Point 1.00 2.50
C14 Braden Holtby 1.00 2.50
C15 John Gibson .75 2.00
C16 Jonathan Toews 1.25 3.00
C17 Ryan O'Reilly .75 2.00
C18 Jonathan Huberdeau 1.00 2.50
C19 Sebastian Aho 1.25 3.00
C20 Evgeni Malkin 1.50 4.00
C21 Sean Monahan .50 1.25
C22 Mitch Marner 1.25 3.00
C23 Max Domi .75 2.00
C24 Brad Marchand 1.50 4.00
C25 Brent Burns .75 2.00
C26 Drew Doughty 1.00 2.50
C27 Erik Karlsson 1.00 2.50
C28 Blake Wheeler .75 2.00
C29 John Tavares 2.50 6.00
C30 Carey Price 3.00 8.00
C31 Mark Scheifele 2.50 6.00
C32 Leon Draisaitl 5.00 12.00
C33 Nathan MacKinnon 6.00 15.00
C34 Johnny Gaudreau 2.50 6.00
C35 Sidney Crosby 6.00 15.00
C36 Connor McDavid 12.00 30.00
C37 Auston Matthews 10.00 25.00
C38 Patrick Kane 5.00 12.00
C39 Nikita Kucherov 5.00 12.00
C40 Alexander Ovechkin 10.00 25.00

2019-20 O-Pee-Chee Glossy Rookies

*COPPER: .5X TO 1.25X BASIC
*GOLD: .6X TO 1.5X BASIC
R1 Cale Makar 5.00 12.00
R2 Erik Brannstrom 1.00 2.50
R3 Dante Fabbro 1.00 2.50
R4 Max Jones 1.00 2.50
R5 Filip Zadina 1.50 4.00
R6 Carl Grundstrom 1.00 2.50
R7 Alexandre Texier 1.00 2.50
R8 Ryan Poehling 1.50 4.00
R9 Trent Frederic 1.00 2.50
R10 Quinn Hughes 5.00 12.00
R11 Kaapo Kakko 1.50 4.00
R12 Kirby Dach 2.00 5.00
R13 Nick Suzuki 4.00 10.00
R14 Rasmus Sandin 1.50 4.00
R15 Cody Glass 1.50 4.00
R16 Victor Olofsson 2.00 5.00
R17 Barrett Hayton 2.00 5.00
R18 Nikita Gusev 1.50 4.00
R19 Ville Heinola 1.25 3.00
R20 Jack Hughes 5.00 12.00

2019-20 O-Pee-Chee Hall of Fame Patches

HOF1 Michel Goulet 12.00 30.00
HOF2 Johnny Bower 12.00 30.00
HOF3 Bobby Clarke 20.00 50.00
HOF4 Brian Leetch 10.00 25.00
HOF5 Luc Robitaille 12.00 30.00
HOF6 Martin St. Louis 12.00 30.00
HOF7 Bryan Trottier 12.00 30.00
HOF8 Charlie Conacher 12.00 30.00
HOF9 Martin Brodeur SP 50.00 125.00
HOF10 Bobby Orr SP 80.00 200.00

2019-20 O-Pee-Chee In Action

L1 Connor McDavid 40.00 100.00
L2 Nikita Kucherov 15.00 40.00
L3 Patrick Kane 15.00 40.00
L4 Sidney Crosby 30.00 80.00
L5 Auston Matthews 30.00 80.00

2019-20 O-Pee-Chee OPC Platinum Preview

P1 Connor McDavid 5.00 12.00
P2 Erik Karlsson 1.25 3.00
P3 Nathan MacKinnon 4.00 10.00
P4 Steven Stamkos 2.00 5.00
P5 Auston Matthews 4.00 10.00
P6 Jonathan Toews 1.50 4.00
P7 Carey Price 2.00 5.00
P8 Tyler Seguin 1.25 3.00
P9 Brad Marchand 2.00 5.00
P10 Alex Ovechkin 4.00 10.00
P11 Brock Boeser 1.25 3.00
P12 Anze Kopitar 1.50 4.00
P13 Jack Eichel 1.50 4.00
P14 Max Pacioretty 1.00 2.50
P15 Sidney Crosby 4.00 10.00

2019-20 O-Pee-Chee Patches

P1 Patrice Bergeron 10.00 25.00
P2 Henrik Zetterberg 10.00 25.00
P3 Lanny McDonald 8.00 20.00
P4 Bryan Trottier 8.00 20.00
P5 Brendan Shanahan 8.00 20.00
P6 Brian Boyle 6.00 15.00
P7 Mario Lemieux 30.00 80.00
P8 Bobby Clarke 12.00 30.00
P9 Jean Ratelle 6.00 15.00
P10 Brad Park 6.00 15.00
P11 Filip Forsberg 12.00 30.00
P12 Henrik Lundqvist 20.00 50.00
P13 Patrice Bergeron 10.00 25.00
P14 Nicklas Lidstrom 8.00 20.00
P15 Chris Pronger 8.00 20.00
P16 Anze Kopitar 10.00 25.00
P17 Jonathan Toews 12.00 30.00
P18 Rod Brind'Amour 8.00 20.00
P19 Jere Lehtinen 6.00 15.00
P20 Guy Carbonneau 8.00 20.00
P21 Martin Brodeur 20.00 50.00
P22 Braden Holtby 10.00 25.00
P23 Patrick Roy 20.00 50.00
P24 Carey Price 15.00 40.00
P25 John Gibson 8.00 20.00
P26 Alexander Ovechkin 30.00 80.00
P27 Ilya Kovalchuk 8.00 20.00
P28 Corey Perry 12.00 30.00
P29 Sidney Crosby 30.00 80.00
P30 Teemu Selanne 15.00 40.00
P31 Connor McDavid 40.00 100.00
P32 Jaromir Jagr 25.00 60.00
P33 Mario Lemieux 30.00 80.00
P34 Carey Price 15.00 40.00
P35 Sidney Crosby 30.00 80.00
P36 Connor McDavid 40.00 100.00
P37 Patrick Kane 15.00 40.00
P38 Wayne Gretzky 50.00 125.00
P39 Guy Lafleur 10.00 25.00
P40 Jamie Benn 8.00 20.00
P41 Wayne Gretzky 50.00 125.00
P42 Brett Hull 15.00 40.00
P43 Marcel Dionne 10.00 25.00
P44 Joe Sakic 15.00 40.00
P45 Bobby Hull 20.00 50.00
P46 Alexander Ovechkin 30.00 80.00
P47 Sidney Crosby 30.00 80.00
P48 Reggie Leach 8.00 20.00
P49 Bobby Orr 30.00 80.00
P50 Butch Goring 6.00 15.00
P51 Victor Hedman 10.00 25.00
P52 Brent Burns 8.00 20.00
P53 Scott Niedermayer 8.00 20.00
P54 Chris Pronger 8.00 20.00
P55 Larry Robinson 8.00 20.00
P56 Mathew Barzal 10.00 25.00
P57 Patrick Kane 15.00 40.00
P58 Martin Brodeur 20.00 50.00
P59 Luc Robitaille 8.00 20.00
P60 Brian Leetch 6.00 15.00
P61 Pekka Rinne 8.00 20.00
P62 Henrik Lundqvist 20.00 50.00
P63 Patrick Roy 20.00 50.00
P64 Terry Sawchuk 8.00 20.00
P65 Sergei Bobrovsky 12.00 30.00
P66 Connor McDavid 40.00 100.00
P67 Taylor Hall 8.00 20.00
P68 Bobby Orr 30.00 80.00
P69 Andy Bathgate 6.00 15.00
P70 Jacques Plante 8.00 20.00
P71 Alexander Ovechkin 30.00 80.00
P72 Ted Lindsay 8.00 20.00
P73 Patrice Bergeron 10.00 25.00
P74 Mark Messier 15.00 40.00
P75 Martin Brodeur 20.00 50.00
P76 Scott Niedermayer 8.00 20.00
P77 Doug Gilmour 10.00 25.00
P78 Patrick Roy 20.00 50.00
P79 Patrick Kane 15.00 40.00
P80 Terry Sawchuk 8.00 20.00

2019-20 O-Pee-Chee Playing Cards

2C Rasmus Dahlin 2.00 5.00
2D Miro Heiskanen 2.00 5.00
2H Nico Hischier 2.50 6.00
2S Brady Tkachuk 2.50 6.00
3C Mathew Barzal 2.00 5.00
3D Dylan Larkin 2.00 5.00
3H Clayton Keller 2.00 5.00
3S Max Domi 1.50 4.00
4C Sebastian Aho 2.50 6.00
4D Zach Parise 1.50 4.00
4H Pekka Rinne 1.50 4.00
4S Jonathan Huberdeau 2.00 5.00
5C John Gibson 1.50 4.00
5D Aleksander Barkov 2.50 6.00
5H Seth Jones 1.50 4.00
5S Ryan O'Reilly 1.50 4.00
6C Brock Boeser 2.00 5.00
6D Elias Pettersson 2.50 6.00
6H Leon Draisaitl 5.00 12.00
6S Jonathan Quick 2.00 5.00
7C P.K. Subban 2.00 5.00
7D David Pastrnak 4.00 10.00
7H Sean Monahan 1.00 2.50
7S Mitch Marner 2.50 6.00
8C Blake Wheeler 1.50 4.00
8D Drew Doughty 2.00 5.00
8H Brent Burns 1.50 4.00
8S Tyler Seguin 2.00 5.00
9C Braden Holtby 2.00 5.00
9D Taylor Hall 1.50 4.00
9H Mikko Rantanen 4.00 10.00
9S Brayden Point 2.00 5.00
AC Alexander Ovechkin 6.00 15.00
AD Connor McDavid 8.00 20.00
AH Auston Matthews 6.00 15.00
AS Sidney Crosby 6.00 15.00
JC Brad Marchand 3.00 8.00
JD Jack Eichel 2.50 6.00
JH Carey Price 3.00 8.00
JS Johnny Gaudreau 2.50 6.00
KC John Tavares 2.50 6.00
KD Henrik Lundqvist 4.00 10.00
KH Patrick Kane 3.00 8.00
KS Nathan MacKinnon 6.00 15.00
QC Evgeni Malkin 3.00 8.00
QD Nikita Kucherov 3.00 8.00
QH Patrice Bergeron 2.00 5.00
QS Jonathan Toews 2.50 6.00
10C Steven Stamkos 3.00 8.00
10D Mark Scheifele 2.50 6.00
10H Claude Giroux 1.50 4.00
10S Marc-Andre Fleury 3.00 8.00

2019-20 O-Pee-Chee Team Logo Patch Update

321 Colorado Avalanche 40.00 100.00
322 St. Louis Blues 40.00 100.00
323 Columbus Blue Jackets 40.00 100.00
324 Arizona Coyotes 40.00 100.00
325 Florida Panthers 40.00 100.00
326 Nashville Predators 40.00 100.00
327 Ottawa Senators 40.00 100.00
328 New York Islanders 40.00 100.00
329 Chicago Blackhawks 40.00 100.00
330 Anaheim Ducks 40.00 100.00

2020-21 O-Pee-Chee

1 Leon Draisaitl .75 2.00
2 Denis Gurianov .30 .75
3 Andre Burakovsky .15 .40
4 Bo Horvat .30 .75
5 Juuse Saros .30 .75
6 Derek Grant .15 .40
7 Oscar Klefbom .25 .60
8 Josh Archibald .15 .40
9 Phillip Danault .25 .60
10 Max Jones .15 .40
11 Jake Allen .25 .60
12 Travis Zajac .15 .40
13 Carey Price .50 1.25
14 Michael Matheson .15 .40
15 Micheal Ferland .15 .40
16 Craig Anderson .20 .50
17 Adam Erne .15 .40
18 Duncan Keith .20 .50
19 Ian Cole .15 .40
20 Brendan Gallagher .25 .60
21 Vladislav Gavrikov .15 .40
22 Aleksander Barkov .40 1.00
23 Cody Ceci .15 .40
24 Corey Perry .40 1.00
25 Wayne Simmonds .25 .60
26 Andrei Vasilevskiy .40 1.00
27 Steven Stamkos .50 1.25
28 Filip Chytil .20 .50
29 Joonas Donskoi .15 .40
30 Marc-Edouard Vlasic .15 .40
31 Elias Pettersson .40 1.00
32 Josh Bailey .20 .50
33 Connor McDavid 1.25 3.00
34 Zack Kassian .15 .40
35 Philippe Myers .15 .40
36 Ryan Reaves .15 .40
37 Sergei Bobrovsky .40 1.00
38 Miles Wood .15 .40
39 Brayden Schenn .25 .60
40 Brady Tkachuk .40 1.00
41 Ryan Poehling .25 .60
42 Mike Reilly .15 .40
43 Patrice Bergeron .30 .75
44 Eric Staal .25 .60
45 Kyle Clifford .15 .40
46 Loui Eriksson .15 .40
47 P.K. Subban .30 .75
48 Nico Hischier .40 1.00
49 Kyle Okposo .15 .40
50 Jon Merrill .15 .40
51 Kevin Hayes .20 .50
52 Ben Bishop .20 .50
53 Jeff Skinner .25 .60
54 Ilya Kovalchuk .25 .60
55 Alex Tuch .25 .60
56 Aaron Ekblad .30 .75
57 William Nylander .50 1.25
58 Gabriel Landeskog .30 .75
59 Blake Wheeler .25 .60
60 Justin Schultz .25 .60
61 Anton Khudobin .25 .60
62 Henrik Lundqvist .60 1.50
63 Mike Hoffman .15 .40
64 Joel Eriksson Ek .20 .50
65 Josh Manson .15 .40
66 Jamie Benn .25 .60
67 Vladislav Namestnikov .15 .40
68 Ondrej Palat .25 .60
69 Sebastian Aho .40 1.00
70 Jack Hughes .60 1.50
71 Brock Boeser .30 .75
72 Madison Bowey .15 .40
73 Casey Cizikas .15 .40
74 Sam Reinhart .50 1.25
75 Kevin Fiala .20 .50
76 Travis Sanheim .15 .40
77 Joe Pavelski .30 .75
78 Conor Sheary .25 .60
79 Tom Wilson .25 .60
80 David Rittich .20 .50
81 Tomas Hertl .25 .60
82 Garnet Hathaway .20 .50
83 Mike Smith .15 .40
84 Jordan Eberle .25 .60
85 Mikael Granlund .20 .50
86 Seth Jones .25 .60
87 Jake Muzzin .25 .60
88 Sean Couturier .20 .50
89 Nate Schmidt .20 .50
90 Jakub Vrana .25 .60
91 Chandler Stephenson .20 .50
92 Ryan Murray .20 .50
93 Dominik Kahun .15 .40
94 Adam Lowry .20 .50
95 Givani Smith .15 .40
96 Cam Fowler .25 .60
97 Claude Giroux .25 .60
98 Ondrej Kase .15 .40
99 Carter Hutton .20 .50
100 Checklist .15 .40
101 Matthew Tkachuk .50 1.25
102 Josh Morrissey .30 .75
103 Colton Parayko .20 .50
104 Nick Schmaltz .20 .50
105 Anthony Mantha .20 .50
106 Matt Roy .15 .40
107 Blake Lizotte .15 .40
108 David Pastrnak .60 1.50
109 Matt Murray .25 .60
110 Marc-Andre Fleury .50 1.25
111 Thatcher Demko .30 .75
112 Rasmus Sandin .20 .50
113 Jamie Oleksiak .20 .50
114 Mitch Marner .40 1.00
115 Jesper Fast .15 .40
116 Scott Mayfield .15 .40
117 Andrei Svechnikov .30 .75
118 J.T. Miller .30 .75
119 Evander Kane .25 .60
120 Anze Kopitar .40 1.00
121 Marcus Sorensen .20 .50
122 Nikolaj Ehlers .25 .60
123 Ryan Strome .25 .60
124 Rickard Rakell .20 .50
125 Pavel Francouz .40 1.00
126 Dylan DeMelo .15 .40
127 Auston Matthews 1.00 2.50
128 Ryan Graves .20 .50
129 Alex Galchenyuk .15 .40
130 Evgeny Kuznetsov .30 .75
131 Ivan Provorov .20 .50
132 Marcus Johansson .20 .50
133 Nikita Gusev .20 .50
134 Mats Zuccarello .25 .60
135 Alexander Texier .20 .50
136 T.J. Oshie .25 .60

137 Nicklas Backstrom .25 .60
138 Kyle Connor .40 1.00
139 Jordan Staal .20 .50
140 Shea Theodore .30 .75
141 Zach Sanford .15 .40
142 Frank Vatrano .20 .50
143 Chris Driedger .15 .40
144 Devan Dubnyk .20 .50
145 Andy Greene .15 .40
146 Andreas Johnsson .25 .60
147 Jacob Trouba .20 .50
148 Alex Iafallo .15 .40
149 Ryan Nugent-Hopkins .30 .75
150 Tanner Pearson .25 .60
151 Justin Williams .20 .50
152 Calle Jarnkrok .15 .40
153 Matt Dumba .15 .40
154 Mikhail Sergachev .20 .50
155 Ben Hutton .15 .40
156 Jesper Boqvist .15 .40
157 Max Domi .25 .60
158 Sam Bennett .40 1.00
159 Alex DeBrincat .30 .75
160 Darcy Kuemper .25 .60
161 Mark Stone .30 .75
162 Johnny Gaudreau .40 1.00
163 Tony DeAngelo .15 .40
164 Jonathan Quick .30 .75
165 Mikael Backlund .20 .50
166 Jakob Chychrun .25 .60
167 Evgeni Malkin .50 1.25
168 Carter Verhaeghe .25 .60
169 Corey Crawford .25 .60
170 John Klingberg .25 .60
171 Nathan MacKinnon 1.00 2.50
172 Jared Spurgeon .25 .60
173 Nick Foligno .20 .50
174 Semyon Varlamov .25 .60
175 Dominik Kubalik .25 .60
176 Ryan Donato .20 .50
177 Samuel Girard .15 .40
178 Cam Talbot .25 .60
179 Joel Farabee .25 .60
180 Kevin Labanc .15 .40
181 Michael Raffl .15 .40
182 Elias Lindholm .25 .60
183 Philipp Grubauer .25 .60
184 Marcus Foligno .20 .50
185 Matt Grzelcyk .20 .50
186 Connor Hellebuyck .50 1.25
187 Tyler Toffoli .25 .60
188 Nathan Beaulieu .15 .40
189 Tyson Jost .20 .50
190 Radko Gudas .20 .50
191 Jonathan Toews .40 1.00
192 Matt Nieto .15 .40
193 Andrew Mangiapane .25 .60
194 Igor Shesterkin .50 1.25
195 Vincent Trocheck .25 .60
196 Blake Coleman .20 .50
197 Torey Krug .20 .50
198 Jaroslav Halak .25 .60
199 Samuel Blais .15 .40
200 Checklist .15 .40
201 Jonas Brodin .15 .40
202 Colton Sceviour .15 .40
203 Emil Bemstrom .15 .40
204 Tyson Barrie .15 .40
205 Pavel Buchnevich .20 .50
206 Jake Guentzel .40 1.00
207 Pavel Zacha .20 .50
208 Brendan Lemieux .20 .50
209 Milan Lucic .20 .50
210 Christopher Tanev .15 .40
211 Antti Raanta .25 .60
212 Jesper Bratt .25 .60
213 Phil Kessel .25 .60
214 Shea Weber .25 .60
215 Aaron Dell .15 .40
216 Jake McCabe .15 .40
217 Nikolai Prokhorkin .15 .40
218 Adam Gaudette .20 .50
219 Justin Faulk .20 .50
220 Viktor Arvidsson .15 .40
221 Alexander Steen .15 .40
222 Gaetan Haas .15 .40
223 Alexander Radulov .25 .60
224 Ilya Mikheyev .20 .50
225 Carl Soderberg .15 .40
226 John Tavares .40 1.00
227 Pierre-Luc Dubois .20 .50
228 Michal Kempny .15 .40
229 Alex Goligoski .20 .50
230 Jake Gardiner .15 .40
231 Patrik Laine .30 .75
232 Dougie Hamilton .20 .50
233 James van Riemsdyk .20 .50
234 Travis Dermott .20 .50
235 Victor Olofsson .25 .60
236 Zach Werenski .40 1.00
237 Tyler Seguin .30 .75
238 Brandon Montour .30 .75
239 Trevor Daley .15 .40
240 Miro Heiskanen .30 .75
241 Drew Doughty .30 .75
242 Ryan McDonagh .15 .40
243 Mattias Janmark .15 .40
244 Mathieu Perreault .15 .40
245 Ryan Pulock .20 .50
246 James Reimer .25 .60
247 Carter Rowney .15 .40
248 David Savard .15 .40
249 Oskar Lindblom .20 .50
250 Nikita Kucherov .50 1.25
251 Brett Pesce .15 .40
252 Devin Shore .15 .40
253 Patrick Kane .50 1.25
254 Craig Smith .15 .40
255 Jake DeBrusk .25 .60
256 Nikita Zaitsev .15 .40
257 Lars Eller .15 .40
258 Christian Dvorak .20 .50
259 Laurent Brossoit .15 .40
260 Kirby Dach .25 .60
261 Nick Jensen .15 .40
262 Chris Kreider .30 .75
263 Jaden Schwartz .30 .75
264 Mark Giordano .25 .60
265 Tyler Bozak .15 .40
266 Filip Forsberg .40 1.00
267 Vladimir Tarasenko .30 .75
268 Tyler Bertuzzi .25 .60
269 Taylor Hall .25 .60
270 Nicolas Hague .15 .40
271 Devon Toews .20 .50
272 Reilly Smith .25 .60
273 Radim Simek .15 .40
274 T.J. Brodie .20 .50
275 Andrew Shaw .15 .40
276 Robin Lehner .20 .50
277 Kaapo Kakko .25 .60
278 Ryan Dzingel .20 .50
279 Kasperi Kapanen .20 .50
280 Kris Letang .30 .75
281 Evgenii Dadonov .15 .40
282 Patric Hornqvist .15 .40
283 Elvis Merzlikins .25 .60
284 Derek Stepan .15 .40
285 Jeff Carter .20 .50
286 Rocco Grimaldi .15 .40
287 Adam Boqvist .20 .50
288 Anders Lee .20 .50
289 Sidney Crosby 1.00 2.50
290 Alec Martinez .15 .40
291 Jonathan Huberdeau .30 .75
292 Jonathan Drouin .20 .50
293 Thomas Chabot .25 .60
294 Kyle Palmieri .20 .50
295 Cody Eakin .15 .40
296 Artturi Lehkonen .20 .50
297 Adam Larsson .15 .40
298 Noel Acciari .15 .40
299 Richard Panik .15 .40
300 Checklist .15 .40
301 Dominik Simon .15 .40
302 Erik Cernak .15 .40
303 Cody Glass .20 .50
304 John Gibson .25 .60
305 Travis Hamonic .15 .40
306 Thomas Greiss .20 .50
307 Braden Holtby .30 .75
308 Patrik Nemeth .20 .50
309 Jonathan Bernier .20 .50
310 Connor Brown .20 .50
311 Anthony Bitetto .15 .40
312 Mikko Rantanen .60 1.50
313 Filip Zadina .20 .50
314 Alex Chiasson .20 .50
315 Brock Nelson .25 .60
316 Artem Anisimov .15 .40
317 Andrew Copp .20 .50
318 Danny DeKeyser .15 .40
319 Jean-Gabriel Pageau .15 .40
320 Anthony Duclair .20 .50
321 Matt Niskanen .20 .50
322 Nazem Kadri .30 .75
323 Quinn Hughes .60 1.50
324 Danton Heinen .20 .50
325 Tyler Myers .15 .40
326 Jaccob Slavin .20 .50
327 Ryan Getzlaf .25 .60
328 Jeff Petry .20 .50
329 Pekka Rinne .25 .60
330 Mika Zibanejad .30 .75
331 Dillon Dube .15 .40
332 Ilya Samsonov .25 .60
333 Brad Marchand .50 1.25
334 Stephen Johns .15 .40
335 Robert Thomas .25 .60
336 Colin White .15 .40
337 Travis Konecny .25 .60
338 Jakob Silfverberg .15 .40
339 Yanni Gourde .20 .50
340 Charlie McAvoy .30 .75
341 Nick Leddy .15 .40
342 Niklas Hjalmarsson .15 .40
343 Chris Tierney .15 .40
344 Esa Lindell .20 .50
345 Tomas Tatar .20 .50
346 Dustin Brown .25 .60
347 Justin Abdelkader .20 .50
348 Noah Hanifin .25 .60
349 Oskar Sundqvist .15 .40
350 Filip Hronek .15 .40
351 Brandon Carlo .20 .50
352 Austin Wagner .15 .40
353 Frederik Andersen .30 .75
354 Alexander Nylander .20 .50
355 Brandon Sutter .15 .40
356 Mackenzie Blackwood .25 .60
357 Cam Atkinson .25 .60
358 Robby Fabbri .15 .40
359 Andreas Athanasiou .15 .40
360 Zach Hyman .40 1.00
361 Nino Niederreiter .20 .50
362 Alex Kerfoot .20 .50
363 Paul Stastny .20 .50
364 Jake Virtanen .25 .60
365 Ron Hainsey .15 .40
366 Erik Gustafsson .15 .40
367 Hampus Lindholm .15 .40
368 Drake Caggiula .20 .50
369 Tyler Johnson .20 .50
370 David Perron .20 .50
371 Jonathan Marchessault .30 .75
372 Linus Ullmark .20 .50
373 Derick Brassard .15 .40
374 Brent Burns .25 .60
375 Adam Henrique .20 .50
376 Zdeno Chara .25 .60
377 Martin Necas .40 1.00
378 Alexander Edler .15 .40
379 Alex Stalock .15 .40
380 Kailer Yamamoto .25 .60
381 Patrick Maroon .25 .60
382 Alex Ovechkin 1.00 2.50
383 Cal Clutterbuck .15 .40
384 Mark Scheifele .40 1.00
385 Erik Johnson .15 .40
386 John Marino .25 .60
387 Carl Hagelin .15 .40
388 Brandon Saad .20 .50
389 Anthony Beauvillier .15 .40
390 Mathew Barzal .30 .75
391 Karson Kuhlman .15 .40
392 Logan Couture .30 .75
393 Jack Roslovic .15 .40
394 Brendan Smith .15 .40
395 Kyle Turris .20 .50
396 Nick Suzuki .50 1.25
397 Carter Hart .25 .60
398 Patrick Marleau .25 .60
399 Rasmus Ristolainen .15 .40
400 Checklist .15 .40
401 Adam Pelech .15 .40
402 Petr Mrazek .25 .60
403 Markus Nutivaara .15 .40
404 Alex Pietrangelo .20 .50
405 Joe Thornton .40 1.00
406 Oliver Ekman-Larsson .20 .50
407 Jason Zucker .25 .60
408 Teuvo Teravainen .20 .50
409 Warren Foegele .20 .50
410 Bryan Rust .25 .60
411 Oliver Bjorkstrand .20 .50
412 Cale Makar .60 1.50
413 Dmitry Kulikov .20 .50
414 Dmitry Orlov .25 .60
415 Rasmus Dahlin .30 .75
416 David Krejci .25 .60
417 Artemi Panarin .50 1.25
418 Dylan Larkin .30 .75
419 Ivan Barbashev .20 .50
420 Kyle Capobianco .20 .50
421 Jimmy Vesey .20 .50
422 Ryan Johansen .20 .50
423 Roope Hintz .30 .75
424 Brett Connolly .15 .40
425 Jared McCann .20 .50
426 Max Pacioretty .25 .60
427 Dante Fabbro .15 .40
428 Sean Monahan .15 .40
429 Nick Holden .20 .50
430 Brian Dumoulin .20 .50
431 Connor Murphy .20 .50
432 Clayton Keller .30 .75
433 Tuukka Rask .30 .75
434 Jacob Markstrom .25 .60
435 Erik Gudbranson .15 .40
436 Jack Eichel .40 1.00
437 William Karlsson .30 .75
438 Matt Calvert .25 .60
439 Erik Karlsson .30 .75
440 Jordan Binnington .40 1.00
441 Anders Bjork .15 .40
442 Dylan Strome .30 .75
443 Jakub Voracek .25 .60
444 Tristan Jarry .25 .60
445 Joonas Korpisalo .25 .60
446 Roman Josi .25 .60
447 Damon Severson .15 .40
448 Jim Howard .30 .75
449 Paul Byron .15 .40
450 Ethan Bear .15 .40
451 Sami Vatanen .25 .60
452 Jan Rutta .15 .40
453 Mattias Ekholm .20 .50
454 Zach Parise .25 .60
455 Matt Duchene .25 .60
456 Timo Meier .25 .60
457 Nick Bonino .20 .50
458 Dylan Gambrell .15 .40
459 Mikko Koskinen .25 .60
460 Morgan Rielly .25 .60
461 Jason Demers .15 .40
462 John Carlson .25 .60
463 Nate Thompson .15 .40
464 Alexandar Georgiev .25 .60
465 Adrian Kempe .25 .60
466 Ryan O'Reilly .25 .60
467 Brayden Point .30 .75
468 Anders Nilsson .15 .40
469 James Neal .15 .40
470 Martin Jones .20 .50
471 Adam Fox .30 .75
472 Boone Jenner .25 .60
473 Ben Chiarot .15 .40
474 Jay Bouwmeester .15 .40
475 Victor Hedman .30 .75
476 Derek Forbort .15 .40
477 Charlie Coyle .25 .60
478 Anthony Cirelli .20 .50
479 Radek Faksa .15 .40
480 Mikko Koivu .20 .50
481 Shayne Gostisbehere .25 .60
482 Darnell Nurse .20 .50
483 Caleb Jones .15 .40
484 Conor Garland .20 .50
485 Gustav Nyquist .15 .40
486 Brayden McNabb .15 .40
487 Neal Pionk .15 .40
488 Will Butcher .15 .40
489 Zach Aston-Reese .25 .60
490 Alex Killorn .15 .40
491 Ryan Ellis .20 .50
492 Kevin Shattenkirk .15 .40
493 Ryan Suter .20 .50
494 Brady Skjei .20 .50
495 Keith Yandle .15 .40
496 Joel Edmundson .15 .40
497 Zemgus Girgensons .20 .50
498 Michael Frolik .20 .50
499 Anton Stralman .15 .40
500 Checklist .15 .40
501 Timothy Liljegren RC 1.00 2.50
502 Kieffer Bellows RC .75 2.00
503 Jonas Johansson RC .75 2.00
504 Liam Foudy RC 1.00 2.50
505 Tyler Benson RC 1.00 2.50
506 Jake Evans RC 1.00 2.50
507 Maxim Letunov RC .75 2.00
508 Anthony Angello RC .75 2.00
509 Matiss Kivlenieks RC 1.25 3.00
510 Keegan Kolesar RC .75 2.00
511 Jason Robertson RC 2.50 6.00
512 Alexander True RC .75 2.00
513 Gustav Lindstrom RC .75 2.00
514 Alexander Yelesin RC .75 2.00
515 Andrei Chibisov RC .60 1.50
516 Egor Korshkov RC .60 1.50
517 Martin Kaut RC 1.00 2.50
518 Gabe Vilardi RC 1.50 4.00
519 Josh Norris RC 1.50 4.00
520 Lucas Carlsson RC .75 2.00
521 Gage Quinney RC .60 1.50
522 Mikey Anderson RC 1.00 2.50
523 Jani Hakanpaa RC .60 1.50
524 Morgan Geekie RC 1.00 2.50
525 Nikolai Knyzhov RC .75 2.00
526 Nicolas Beaudin RC 1.00 2.50
527 Brandon Hagel RC 1.25 3.00
528 Michael DiPietro RC 1.25 3.00
529 Calvin Thurkauf RC .75 2.00
530 Jansen Harkins RC .75 2.00
531 Patrick Roy ML 1.00 2.50
532 Peter Forsberg ML .75 2.00
533 Nicklas Lidstrom ML .40 1.00
534 Dominik Hasek ML .60 1.50
535 Henrik Zetterberg ML .50 1.25
536 Mats Sundin ML .40 1.00
537 Ray Bourque ML .60 1.50
538 Cam Neely ML .40 1.00
539 Martin Brodeur ML 1.00 2.50
540 Bobby Hull ML 1.00 2.50
541 Grant Fuhr ML .60 1.50
542 Mark Messier ML .75 2.00
543 Steve Yzerman ML 1.00 2.50
544 Joe Sakic ML .75 2.00
545 Teemu Selanne ML .75 2.00
546 Gordie Howe ML 1.25 3.00
547 Jaromir Jagr ML 1.25 3.00
548 Bobby Orr ML 1.50 4.00
549 Mike Modano ML .60 1.50
550 Wayne Gretzky ML 2.50 6.00
551 Anaheim Ducks CL .15 .40
552 Arizona Coyotes CL .15 .40
553 Boston Bruins CL .15 .40
554 Buffalo Sabres CL .15 .40
555 Calgary Flames CL .15 .40
556 Carolina Hurricanes CL .15 .40
557 Chicago Blackhawks CL .15 .40
558 Colorado Avalanche CL .15 .40
559 Columbus Blue Jackets CL .15 .40
560 Dallas Stars CL .15 .40
561 Detroit Red Wings CL .15 .40
562 Edmonton Oilers CL .15 .40
563 Florida Panthers CL .15 .40
564 Los Angeles Kings CL .15 .40
565 Minnesota Wild CL .15 .40
566 Montreal Canadiens CL .15 .40
567 Nashville Predators CL .15 .40
568 New Jersey Devils CL .15 .40
569 New York Islanders CL .15 .40
570 New York Rangers CL .15 .40
571 Ottawa Senators CL .15 .40
572 Philadelphia Flyers CL .15 .40
573 Pittsburgh Penguins CL .15 .40
574 San Jose Sharks CL .15 .40
575 St. Louis Blues CL .15 .40
576 Tampa Bay Lightning CL .15 .40
577 Toronto Maple Leafs CL .15 .40
578 Vancouver Canucks CL .15 .40
579 Vegas Golden Knights CL .15 .40
580 Washington Capitals CL .15 .40
581 Winnipeg Jets CL .15 .40
582 Alex Ovechkin LL 2.50 6.00
583 Leon Draisaitl LL 2.00 5.00
584 Leon Draisaitl LL 2.00 5.00
585 David Pastrnak LL 1.50 4.00
586 John Carlson LL .60 1.50
587 Anton Khudobin LL .60 1.50
588 Connor Hellebuyck LL 1.25 3.00
589 Andrei Vasilevskiy LL 1.00 2.50
590 Quinn Hughes LL 1.50 4.00
591 Alex Ovechkin SH 2.50 6.00
592 Joe Thornton SH 1.00 2.50
593 Andrei Svechnikov SH .75 2.00
594 Ryan Getzlaf SH .60 1.50
595 Zdeno Chara SH .60 1.50
596 Marc-Andre Fleury SH 1.25 3.00
597 Henrik Lundqvist SH 1.00 2.50
598 Taylor Hall SH .60 1.50
599 Patrick Kane SH 1.25 3.00
600 Checklist .15 .40

2020-21 O-Pee-Chee Blue

*BLUE: .75X TO 2X BASIC

2020-21 O-Pee-Chee Retro

*RETRO: .6X TO 1.5X BASIC

2020-21 O-Pee-Chee Retro Black

*RETRO.BLK: 2X TO 5X BASIC
509 Matiss Kivlenieks 8.00 20.00

2020-21 O-Pee-Chee #1 Draft Pick Bounty Puzzle

OPC1 Redemption Card 1 10.00 25.00
OPC2 Redemption Card 2 10.00 25.00
OPC3 Redemption Card 3 10.00 25.00
OPC4 Redemption Card 4 10.00 25.00
OPC5 Redemption Card 5 10.00 25.00
OPC6 Redemption Card 6 10.00 25.00
OPC7 Redemption Card 7 10.00 25.00
OPC8 Redemption Card 8 10.00 25.00
OPC9 Redemption Card 9 10.00 25.00

2020-21 O-Pee-Chee '11 Stanley Cup Final Moments

SC1 Roberto Luongo 25.00 60.00
SC2 Alexander Edler 10.00 25.00
SC3 Alexandre Burrows 10.00 25.00
SC4 Milan Lucic 12.00 30.00
SC5 David Krejci 15.00 40.00
SC6 Brad Marchand 20.00 50.00
SC7 Zdeno Chara 15.00 40.00

2020-21 O-Pee-Chee Glossy Rookie Phenoms

GRR1 Redemption Card 100.00 250.00

2020-21 O-Pee-Chee Hall of Fame Patches

HOF1 Willie O'Ree 15.00 40.00
HOF2 Martin Brodeur 30.00 80.00
HOF3 Patrick Roy 50.00 125.00
HOF4 Bobby Orr 50.00 125.00
HOF5 Dominik Hasek 20.00 50.00
HOF6 Mario Lemieux 50.00 125.00
HOF7 Wayne Gretzky 80.00 200.00
HOF8 Chris Chelios 12.00 30.00

2020-21 O-Pee-Chee OPC Premier Tallboys

*YELLOW: .75X TO 2X BASIC
P1 Nikita Kucherov 1.50 4.00
P2 John Tavares 1.25 3.00
P3 Artemi Panarin 1.50 4.00
P4 Andrei Vasilevskiy 1.25 3.00
P5 Nicklas Backstrom .75 2.00
P6 David Pastrnak 2.00 5.00
P7 Mark Scheifele 1.25 3.00
P8 Roman Josi .75 2.00
P9 Aleksander Barkov 1.25 3.00
P10 Claude Giroux .75 2.00
P11 Jack Eichel 1.25 3.00
P12 Brent Burns .75 2.00
P13 Brayden Point 1.00 2.50
P14 Tyler Seguin 1.00 2.50
P15 Blake Wheeler .75 2.00
P16 Sebastian Aho 1.25 3.00
P17 Mitch Marner 1.25 3.00
P18 Anze Kopitar 1.25 3.00
P19 John Carlson .75 2.00
P20 Taylor Hall .75 2.00
P21 Brad Marchand 1.50 4.00
P22 Sean Monahan .50 1.25
P23 Ryan O'Reilly .75 2.00
P24 Steven Stamkos 1.50 4.00
P25 Patrice Bergeron 1.00 2.50
P26 Evgeni Malkin 1.50 4.00
P27 Johnny Gaudreau 1.25 3.00
P28 Seth Jones .75 2.00
P29 Quinn Hughes 2.00 5.00
P30 Mark Stone 1.00 2.50
P31 Ben Bishop .60 1.50
P32 Elias Pettersson 1.25 3.00
P33 Vladimir Tarasenko 1.00 2.50
P34 Cale Makar 2.00 5.00
P35 Henrik Lundqvist 2.00 5.00
P36 Victor Hedman 1.00 2.50
P37 Josh Norris SP 4.00 10.00
P38 Jason Robertson SP 6.00 15.00
P39 Timothy Liljegren SP 2.50 6.00
P40 Gabe Vilardi SP 4.00 10.00
P41 Martin Kaut SP 2.50 6.00
P42 Nicolas Beaudin SP 2.50 6.00
P43 Lucas Carlsson SP 2.00 5.00
P44 Liam Foudy SP 2.50 6.00
P45 Connor McDavid SP 8.00 20.00
P46 Alex Ovechkin SP 6.00 15.00
P47 Nathan MacKinnon SP 6.00 15.00
P48 Sidney Crosby SP 6.00 15.00
P49 Leon Draisaitl SP 5.00 12.00
P50 Auston Matthews SP 6.00 15.00

2020-21 O-Pee-Chee Patches

P1 Olaf Kolzig 8.00 20.00
P2 Nick Foligno 6.00 15.00
P3 Jarome Iginla 10.00 25.00
P4 Jason Zucker 8.00 20.00
P5 Saku Koivu 8.00 20.00
P6 Robin Lehner 6.00 15.00
P7 Teemu Selanne 15.00 40.00
P8 Jaromir Jagr 15.00 40.00
P9 Devan Dubnyk 6.00 15.00
P10 Saku Koivu 8.00 20.00
P11 Nikita Kucherov 15.00 40.00
P12 Alexandre Burrows 5.00 12.00
P13 Joe Thornton 12.00 30.00
P14 Mike Modano 12.00 30.00
P15 Alex Ovechkin 12.00 30.00
P16 Ryan O'Reilly 8.00 20.00
P17 Steve Yzerman 20.00 50.00
P18 Dirk Graham 6.00 15.00
P19 Anze Kopitar 12.00 30.00
P20 Patrice Bergeron 10.00 25.00
P21 Robin Lehner 6.00 15.00
P22 Jonathan Quick 10.00 25.00
P23 Martin Brodeur 20.00 50.00
P24 Dominik Hasek 12.00 30.00
P25 Jaroslav Halak 8.00 20.00
P26 Alex Ovechkin 12.00 30.00
P27 Steven Stamkos 15.00 40.00
P28 Jarome Iginla 10.00 25.00
P29 Jonathan Cheechoo 6.00 15.00
P30 Sidney Crosby 30.00 80.00
P31 Nikita Kucherov 15.00 40.00
P32 Evgeni Malkin 12.00 30.00
P33 Connor McDavid 20.00 50.00
P34 Sidney Crosby 30.00 80.00
P35 Wayne Gretzky 20.00 50.00
P36 Nikita Kucherov 15.00 40.00
P37 Mario Lemieux 12.00 30.00
P38 Peter Forsberg 15.00 40.00
P39 Bobby Hull 20.00 50.00
P40 Jarome Iginla 10.00 25.00
P41 Aleksander Barkov 12.00 30.00
P42 William Karlsson 10.00 25.00
P43 Mats Naslund 5.00 12.00
P44 Anze Kopitar 12.00 30.00
P45 Ryan O'Reilly 8.00 20.00
P46 Ryan O'Reilly 8.00 20.00
P47 Jonathan Quick 10.00 25.00
P48 Steve Yzerman 20.00 50.00
P49 Jonathan Toews 12.00 30.00
P50 Evgeni Malkin 12.00 30.00
P51 Mark Giordano 8.00 20.00
P52 Drew Doughty 10.00 25.00
P53 Duncan Keith 6.00 15.00
P54 Zdeno Chara 8.00 20.00
P55 Ray Bourque 12.00 30.00
P56 Elias Pettersson 12.00 30.00
P57 Nathan MacKinnon 15.00 40.00
P58 Mario Lemieux 12.00 30.00
P59 Bobby Orr 30.00 80.00
P60 Artemi Panarin 15.00 40.00
P61 Andrei Vasilevskiy 12.00 30.00
P62 Olaf Kolzig 8.00 20.00
P63 Braden Holtby 10.00 25.00
P64 Grant Fuhr 12.00 30.00
P65 Martin Brodeur 20.00 50.00
P66 Nikita Kucherov 15.00 40.00
P67 Sidney Crosby 30.00 80.00
P68 Alex Ovechkin 12.00 30.00
P69 Joe Sakic 40.00 100.00
P70 Guy Lafleur 10.00 25.00
P71 Ryan O'Reilly 8.00 20.00
P72 Pavel Datsyuk 12.00 30.00
P73 Sidney Crosby 30.00 80.00
P74 Mats Naslund 5.00 12.00
P75 Bobby Orr 30.00 80.00
P76 Jonathan Quick 10.00 25.00
P77 Mike Modano 12.00 30.00
P78 Eric Staal 8.00 20.00
P79 Joe Sakic 40.00 100.00
P80 Wayne Gretzky 20.00 50.00
P81 Gnash 60.00 150.00
P82 Gritty SP 120.00 300.00

2020-21 O-Pee-Chee Playing Cards

2CLUBS Alex Pietrangelo 1.25 3.00
3CLUBS Kirby Dach 1.50 4.00
4CLUBS Anze Kopitar 2.50 6.00
5CLUBS Eric Staal 1.50 4.00
6CLUBS Taylor Hall 1.50 4.00
7CLUBS Mark Scheifele 2.50 6.00
8CLUBS Jordan Binnington 2.50 6.00
9CLUBS Carey Price 3.00 8.00
ACLUBS Auston Matthews 6.00 15.00
JCLUBS Elias Pettersson 2.50 6.00
KCLUBS Nathan MacKinnon 6.00 15.00
QCLUBS Jonathan Toews 2.50 6.00
10CLUBS David Pastrnak 4.00 10.00
2HEARTS Kaapo Kakko 1.25 3.00
2SPADES Quinn Hughes 4.00 10.00
3HEARTS Pekka Rinne 1.50 4.00
3SPADES Pierre-Luc Dubois 1.25 3.00
4HEARTS Brady Tkachuk 2.50 6.00
4SPADES Mitch Marner 2.50 6.00
5HEARTS Joe Thornton 2.50 6.00
5SPADES Matthew Tkachuk 3.00 8.00
6HEARTS Tyler Seguin 2.00 5.00
6SPADES Brock Boeser 2.00 5.00
7HEARTS Ryan Getzlaf 1.50 4.00
7SPADES Dylan Larkin 2.00 5.00
8HEARTS Nico Hischier 2.50 6.00
8SPADES Erik Karlsson 2.00 5.00
9HEARTS Claude Giroux 1.50 4.00
9SPADES Jack Eichel 2.50 6.00
AHEARTS Sidney Crosby 6.00 15.00
ASPADES Connor McDavid 8.00 20.00
JHEARTS Steven Stamkos 3.00 8.00
JSPADES Nikita Kucherov 3.00 8.00
KHEARTS Patrick Kane 3.00 8.00
KSPADES Leon Draisaitl 5.00 12.00
QHEARTS John Tavares 2.50 6.00
QSPADES Marc-Andre Fleury 3.00 8.00
10DIAMONDS Brad Marchand 3.00 8.00
10HEARTS Artemi Panarin 3.00 8.00
10SPADES Johnny Gaudreau 2.50 6.00
2DIAMONDS Carter Hart 1.50 4.00
3DIAMONDS Cale Makar 4.00 10.00
4DIAMONDS Aleksander Barkov 2.50 6.00
5DIAMONDS Jonathan Huberdeau 2.00 5.00
6DIAMONDS Ryan O'Reilly 1.50 4.00
7DIAMONDS Dougie Hamilton 1.25 3.00
8DIAMONDS Mathew Barzal 2.00 5.00
9DIAMONDS John Carlson 1.50 4.00
ADIAMONDS Alex Ovechkin 6.00 15.00
JDIAMONDS Patrice Bergeron 2.00 5.00
KDIAMONDS Evgeni Malkin 3.00 8.00
QDIAMONDS Henrik Lundqvist 4.00 10.00

2020-21 O-Pee-Chee Retro Cup Captain

CC1 Zdeno Chara 40.00 100.00

2020-21 O-Pee-Chee Team Logo Patch Update

331 Buffalo Sabres 40.00 100.00
332 Vancouver Canucks 40.00 100.00
333 Calgary Flames 40.00 100.00
334 Edmonton Oilers 40.00 100.00
335 Carolina Hurricanes 40.00 100.00
336 Boston Bruins 50.00 125.00
337 Los Angeles Kings 40.00 100.00
338 Colorado Avalanche 40.00 100.00
339 Nashville Predators 40.00 100.00
340 Dallas Stars 40.00 100.00

2021-22 O-Pee-Chee

1 Connor McDavid 1.25 3.00
2 Artemi Panarin .50 1.25
3 Alex Ovechkin 1.00 2.50
4 Kirill Kaprizov .75 2.00
5 Tim Stutzle .30 .75
6 Steven Stamkos .50 1.25
7 Auston Matthews 1.00 2.50
8 Evgeni Malkin .50 1.25
9 Jack Eichel .40 1.00
10 Carey Price .50 1.25
11 Erik Karlsson .30 .75
12 Sebastian Aho .40 1.00
13 Mikko Rantanen .60 1.50
14 Tyler Seguin .30 .75
15 Dylan Larkin .30 .75
16 Jonathan Huberdeau .30 .75
17 John Gibson .25 .60
18 Brad Marchand .50 1.25
19 Nathan MacKinnon 1.00 2.50
20 Adam Fox .30 .75
21 Jake Guentzel .40 1.00
22 Claude Giroux .25 .60
23 Jean-Gabriel Pageau .15 .40
24 Thomas Chabot .25 .60
25 Sean Couturier .20 .50
26 Tomas Hertl .25 .60
27 Ryan Johansen .20 .50
28 Vladimir Tarasenko .30 .75
29 Victor Hedman .30 .75
30 Alexis Lafreniere .40 1.00
31 Kirby Dach .25 .60
32 Patrik Laine .30 .75
33 Andrei Vasilevskiy .40 1.00
34 Mats Zuccarello .25 .60
35 Brock Boeser .30 .75
36 Mark Stone .30 .75
37 Johnny Gaudreau .40 1.00
38 Max Pacioretty .25 .60
39 Connor Hellebuyck .50 1.25
40 Brock Nelson .25 .60
41 Chris Kreider .30 .75
42 Jason Zucker .25 .60
43 Joel Farabee .25 .60
44 Kevin Labanc .15 .40
45 Nicklas Backstrom .25 .60
46 Keith Yandle .15 .40
47 Adrian Kempe .25 .60
48 Kyle Connor .40 1.00
49 Kevin Lankinen .25 .60
50 Jordan Binnington .40 1.00
51 Adin Hill .25 .60
52 Nico Hischier .40 1.00
53 Charlie Coyle .25 .60
54 Jordan Eberle .25 .60
55 Colin White .20 .50
56 Max Domi .25 .60
57 Aaron Ekblad .30 .75
58 Yanni Gourde .20 .50
59 Braden Holtby .30 .75
60 Michael Bunting .25 .60
61 Jason Robertson .40 1.00
62 Tyson Barrie .15 .40
63 Brendan Gallagher .25 .60
64 Ryan Reaves .20 .50
65 Bowen Byram .30 .75
66 Ilya Mikheyev .20 .50
67 Dylan Cozens .25 .60
68 Nikolaj Ehlers .25 .60
69 Andreas Athanasiou .20 .50
70 Anders Lee .20 .50
71 Reilly Smith .25 .60
72 Lawson Crouse .15 .40
73 Vitek Vanecek .25 .60
74 Linus Ullmark .25 .60
75 Nils Hoglander .20 .50
76 Ryan Strome .25 .60
77 Phil Kessel .25 .60
78 Pierre Engvall .15 .40
79 Kyle Capobianco .15 .40
80 Cam Fowler .25 .60
81 Jordan Staal .20 .50
82 Nick Suzuki .50 1.25
83 Cody Glass .20 .50
84 Patric Hornqvist .15 .40
85 Pavel Buchnevich .20 .50
86 Tuukka Rask .30 .75
87 Dominik Kubalik .25 .60
88 Bobby Ryan .20 .50
89 Hampus Lindholm .15 .40
90 Ryan Getzlaf .25 .60
91 William Carrier .15 .40
92 Jaden Schwartz .20 .50
93 Kaapo Kahkonen .25 .60
94 Carter Verhaeghe .25 .60
95 Cal Clutterbuck .15 .40
96 Cale Makar .60 1.50
97 Nazem Kadri .30 .75
98 Jesper Bratt .25 .60
99 Kevin Rooney .20 .50
100 Checklist .15 .40
101 Adam Larsson .15 .40
102 Eric Robinson .15 .40
103 Gabe Vilardi .25 .60
104 Lars Eller .15 .40
105 Dillon Dube .15 .40
106 Kevin Fiala .20 .50
107 Tomas Nosek .15 .40
108 Carter Hart .25 .60
109 Calle Jarnkrok .15 .40
110 Bryan Rust .25 .60
111 Jakub Voracek .25 .60
112 Roope Hintz .30 .75
113 Victor Rask .15 .40
114 Shea Weber .25 .60
115 Mikko Koskinen .25 .60
116 Colin Miller .15 .40
117 Devon Toews .20 .50
118 Duncan Keith .25 .60
119 Jacob Trouba .20 .50
120 Alec Martinez .15 .40
121 Jeff Skinner .25 .60
122 Semyon Varlamov .25 .60
123 Miles Wood .15 .40
124 Chandler Stephenson .20 .50
125 Andrei Svechnikov .30 .75
126 Sean Monahan .20 .50
127 Tristan Jarry .25 .60
128 Blake Lizotte .15 .40
129 Alex Iafallo .15 .40
130 Carl Hagelin .15 .40
131 Anthony Beauvillier .15 .40
132 Zach Werenski .40 1.00
133 Martin Jones .20 .50
134 Dylan Strome .30 .75
135 Nicolas Deslauriers .15 .40
136 Blake Coleman .20 .50
137 Valeri Nichushkin .25 .60
138 Seth Jones .25 .60
139 Jakub Vrana .25 .60
140 Nick Leddy .15 .40
141 Paul Stastny .20 .50
142 Matt Roy .15 .40
143 Vincent Trocheck .25 .60
144 Anthony Duclair .20 .50
145 Erik Haula .15 .40
146 Tyson Jost .20 .50
147 Adam Pelech .15 .40
148 Jesse Puljujarvi .25 .60
149 David Gustafsson .15 .40
150 Viktor Arvidsson .15 .40
151 Mike Hoffman .15 .40
152 J.T. Compher .15 .40
153 Milan Lucic .20 .50
154 Timo Meier .25 .60
155 Brandon Tanev .20 .50
156 Jakob Chychrun .25 .60
157 Nico Sturm .15 .40
158 Tomas Tatar .15 .40
159 Pius Suter .20 .50
160 Dustin Brown .25 .60
161 Gabriel Landeskog .30 .75
162 Casey Cizikas .20 .50
163 Radek Faksa .20 .50
164 Luke Kunin .15 .40
165 Andrew Copp .20 .50
166 Colin Blackwell .20 .50
167 Tom Wilson .25 .60
168 Rasmus Dahlin .30 .75
169 Nick Ritchie .15 .40
170 Jacob Larsson .20 .50
171 Danny DeKeyser .15 .40
172 J.T. Miller .30 .75

173 Josh Morrissey .30 .75
174 Mikael Backlund .20 .50
175 Ryan Miller .20 .50
176 Paul Byron .20 .50
177 Morgan Rielly .25 .60
178 Rocco Grimaldi .15 .40
179 Noah Dobson .30 .75
180 Casey DeSmith .20 .50
181 Owen Tippett .15 .40
182 Jeff Carter .20 .50
183 Ian Mitchell .15 .40
184 Michael Del Zotto .20 .50
185 Mikael Granlund .20 .50
186 Andreas Johnsson .20 .50
187 Radko Gudas .15 .40
188 Jamie Benn .25 .60
189 Evgenii Dadonov .20 .50
190 Connor Ingram .15 .40
191 Carl Grundstrom .15 .40
192 Adam Erne .15 .40
193 Ryan Suter .20 .50
194 Jason Dickinson .20 .50
195 Ryan Pulock .20 .50
196 Kevin Shattenkirk .15 .40
197 Mathieu Perreault .15 .40
198 Matthew Tkachuk .50 1.25
199 Tyler Bozak .15 .40
200 Checklist .15 .40
201 Brayden Schenn .25 .60
202 Thomas Greiss .20 .50
203 Marc-Edouard Vlasic .15 .40
204 Jake DeBrusk .25 .60
205 Justin Schultz .20 .50
206 Kaapo Kakko .20 .50
207 Jason Spezza .25 .60
208 Christopher Tanev .15 .40
209 Maxime Comtois .20 .50
210 Jonathan Drouin .20 .50
211 Eeli Tolvanen .25 .60
212 Adam Henrique .20 .50
213 Philipp Grubauer .25 .60
214 Jaret Anderson-Dolan .15 .40
215 Vladislav Gavrikov .15 .40
216 Filip Hronek .15 .40
217 Victor Olofsson .25 .60
218 Andre Burakovsky .15 .40
219 Alex Galchenyuk .15 .40
220 Brett Pesce .15 .40
221 Teddy Blueger .15 .40
222 Rasmus Andersson .20 .50
223 Filip Chytil .15 .40
224 Dmitry Orlov .25 .60
225 Andrew Cogliano .15 .40
226 Ryan Ellis .15 .40
227 Erik Cernak .15 .40
228 Mike Smith .15 .40
229 Mario Ferraro .15 .40
230 Brenden Dillon .15 .40
231 Troy Stecher .15 .40
232 Vince Dunn .20 .50
233 Corey Perry .40 1.00
234 Alex Chiasson .20 .50
235 Ilya Samsonov .25 .60
236 Noel Acciari .15 .40
237 Drew Doughty .30 .75
238 Zdeno Chara .25 .60
239 Clayton Keller .30 .75
240 Ville Husso .15 .40
241 Boone Jenner .25 .60
242 Pavel Zacha .20 .50
243 Dante Fabbro .15 .40
244 Ryan Hartman .15 .40
245 Neal Pionk .15 .40
246 Josh Archibald .15 .40
247 Brandon Hagel .20 .50
248 Robby Fabbri .15 .40
249 Zach Hyman .40 1.00
250 Samuel Girard .15 .40
251 Trevor Moore .15 .40
252 Mikey Anderson .20 .50
253 Jeff Petry .25 .60
254 Derek Forbort .15 .40
255 Matt Dumba .20 .50
256 Justin Holl .15 .40
257 Josh Manson .15 .40
258 Jonathan Marchessault .30 .75
259 Alexander Radulov .25 .60
260 Elvis Merzlikins .25 .60
261 Oliver Wahlstrom .15 .40
262 Alexandar Georgiev .25 .60
263 Anton Stralman .15 .40
264 Chris Tierney .20 .50
265 Mattias Ekholm .20 .50
266 Anthony Mantha .20 .50
267 Charlie McAvoy .30 .75
268 Alex Killorn .15 .40
269 Alexandre Texier .15 .40
270 Elias Lindholm .25 .60
271 Patrick Marleau .20 .50
272 Cam Atkinson .25 .60
273 Erik Brannstrom .15 .40
274 Nino Niederreiter .15 .40
275 Sam Bennett .40 1.00
276 Conor Garland .20 .50
277 Zach Sanford .15 .40
278 Gustav Forsling .25 .60
279 Tyler Bertuzzi .20 .50
280 Connor Brown .20 .50
281 Joel Eriksson Ek .20 .50
282 Colton Sissons .15 .40
283 Janne Kuokkanen .15 .40
284 Jack Campbell .25 .60
285 Denis Gurianov .30 .75
286 Ondrej Palat .20 .50
287 Ryan Lindgren .15 .40
288 Jake Muzzin .25 .60
289 John Carlson .25 .60
290 Joe Thornton .40 1.00
291 Shea Theodore .30 .75
292 Cal Petersen .15 .40
293 Kailer Yamamoto .25 .60
294 Jake Evans .15 .40
295 Alex DeBrincat .30 .75
296 Brandon Sutter .15 .40
297 K'Andre Miller .20 .50
298 Jordan Greenway .15 .40
299 Artem Zub .15 .40
300 Checklist .15 .40
301 Sam Reinhart .50 1.25
302 Robert Thomas .25 .60
303 Tage Thompson .30 .75
304 Nikita Zaitsev .15 .40
305 Ryan Graves .15 .40
306 Josh Anderson .20 .50
307 Christian Fischer .15 .40
308 P.K. Subban .30 .75
309 Ryan Donato .20 .50
310 Jared Spurgeon .25 .60
311 Jonathan Bernier .25 .60
312 Darnell Nurse .20 .50
313 Zach Aston-Reese .15 .40
314 Jeremy Lauzon .15 .40
315 Frank Vatrano .20 .50
316 Matt Murray .25 .60
317 Anthony Cirelli .20 .50
318 John Leonard .15 .40
319 Nick Schmaltz .20 .50
320 Zach Whitecloud .15 .40
321 William Nylander .50 1.25
322 Jake Bean .15 .40
323 Oliver Bjorkstrand .20 .50
324 Daniel Sprong .15 .40
325 Sam Gagner .15 .40
326 Malcolm Subban .20 .50
327 Craig Smith .15 .40
328 Matt Martin .15 .40
329 Jordan Kyrou .25 .60
330 Nikita Zadorov .15 .40
331 Kyle Clifford .15 .40
332 Yegor Sharangovich .25 .60
333 Rickard Rakell .20 .50
334 Nikolai Knyzhov .15 .40
335 Noah Hanifin .25 .60
336 Drake Batherson .25 .60
337 Nate Schmidt .15 .40
338 Taylor Hall .25 .60
339 Brady Tkachuk .40 1.00
340 Miro Heiskanen .30 .75
341 Andrew Mangiapane .25 .60
342 Mason Marchment .20 .50
343 Jonathan Quick .30 .75
344 Ryan Nugent-Hopkins .30 .75
345 Jake Allen .25 .60
346 Josh Norris .25 .60
347 Chris Driedger .15 .40
348 Shayne Gostisbehere .25 .60
349 Philipp Kurashev .20 .50
350 T.J. Brodie .15 .40
351 Brayden Point .30 .75
352 Carson Soucy .15 .40
353 Josh Bailey .20 .50
354 Thatcher Demko .30 .75
355 Joe Pavelski .30 .75
356 Adam Lowry .20 .50
357 Samuel Blais .15 .40
358 Nick Cousins .15 .40
359 Ty Smith .25 .60
360 Alex Nedeljkovic .20 .50
361 Vladislav Namestnikov .15 .40
362 Cam Talbot .25 .60
363 Patrick Maroon .15 .40
364 Eetu Luostarinen .15 .40
365 Christian Dvorak .20 .50
366 Connor Murphy .15 .40
367 Alexander Wennberg .15 .40
368 Nolan Foote .15 .40
369 Nick Paul .15 .40
370 Cody Eakin .15 .40
371 Joel Edmundson .15 .40
372 David Perron .20 .50
373 Igor Shesterkin .50 1.25
374 Mackenzie Blackwood .25 .60
375 Niklas Hjalmarsson .15 .40
376 Matt Grzelcyk .20 .50
377 Garnet Hathaway .15 .40
378 Jonas Brodin .15 .40
379 Brandon Saad .20 .50
380 Nicolas Aube-Kubel .15 .40
381 Mark Giordano .25 .60
382 Travis Sanheim .15 .40
383 Calvin de Haan .15 .40
384 Adam Boqvist .15 .40
385 Michael McLeod .15 .40
386 Scott Mayfield .15 .40
387 Anton Khudobin .25 .60
388 Marco Scandella .15 .40
389 Jack Roslovic .15 .40
390 Dominik Kahun .15 .40
391 Alex Goligoski .20 .50
392 Phillip Danault .25 .60
393 Andrej Sekera .15 .40
394 James Reimer .15 .40
395 Teuvo Teravainen .20 .50
396 Jared McCann .20 .50
397 Nicolas Hague .15 .40
398 Brian Elliott .15 .40
399 Rudolfs Balcers .15 .40
400 Checklist .15 .40
401 Oliver Ekman-Larsson .20 .50
402 John Klingberg .25 .60
403 Ryan McDonagh .15 .40
404 Rasmus Ristolainen .15 .40
405 Cody Ceci .15 .40
406 Mason Appleton .15 .40
407 Filip Zadina .20 .50
408 Brent Burns .25 .60
409 Jakob Silfverberg .15 .40
410 Sean Walker .15 .40
411 Martin Necas .40 1.00
412 Jacob Markstrom .25 .60
413 Ethan Bear .15 .40
414 Conor Sheary .25 .60
415 Damon Severson .15 .40
416 Tyler Myers .15 .40
417 Sean Kuraly .15 .40
418 Sidney Crosby 1.00 2.50
419 Jaroslav Halak .25 .60
420 Ivan Provorov .20 .50
421 Quinn Hughes .60 1.50
422 Dougie Hamilton .20 .50
423 Esa Lindell .20 .50
424 Kasperi Kapanen .20 .50
425 Justin Faulk .20 .50
426 Mathieu Joseph .15 .40
427 Marcus Foligno .20 .50
428 Kevin Hayes .20 .50
429 MacKenzie Weegar .20 .50
430 Troy Terry .30 .75
431 Joonas Korpisalo .25 .60
432 Jesper Fast .15 .40
433 Evgeny Kuznetsov .30 .75
434 Alex Kerfoot .20 .50
435 Brian Dumoulin .15 .40
436 Joonas Donskoi .15 .40
437 Emil Bemstrom .15 .40
438 William Karlsson .30 .75
439 Nick Foligno .15 .40
440 Michael Matheson .15 .40
441 Frederik Andersen .30 .75
442 Scott Laughton .15 .40
443 David Krejci .25 .60
444 Tyler Johnson .15 .40
445 Robin Lehner .20 .50
446 Jakub Zboril .15 .40
447 Jake Oettinger .40 1.00
448 Tanner Pearson .25 .60
449 Darcy Kuemper .25 .60
450 Blake Comeau .15 .40
451 Pierre-Edouard Bellemare .15 .40
452 Colton Parayko .20 .50
453 Jacob Slavin .20 .50
454 Blake Wheeler .25 .60
455 Kyle Okposo .15 .40
456 Derek Grant .15 .40
457 Zach Parise .25 .60
458 T.J. Oshie .25 .60
459 Jamie Oleksiak .20 .50
460 Alex Tuch .20 .50
461 Marc-Andre Fleury .50 1.25
462 Filip Forsberg .40 1.00
463 John Marino .25 .60
464 James van Riemsdyk .20 .50
465 Casey Mittelstadt .25 .60
466 Philippe Myers .20 .50
467 Bo Horvat .30 .75
468 Mikhail Sergachev .20 .50
469 Warren Foegele .15 .40
470 Oskar Lindblom .20 .50
471 Pierre-Luc Dubois .20 .50
472 Connor Clifton .15 .40
473 Torey Krug .20 .50
474 Evander Kane .25 .60
475 Alexander Romanov .20 .50
476 Logan Couture .30 .75
477 Travis Konecny .25 .60
478 Kris Letang .30 .75
479 Jake Gardiner .15 .40
480 Anze Kopitar .40 1.00
481 Tyler Toffoli .25 .60
482 Roman Josi .25 .60
483 Matt Duchene .25 .60
484 Mark Scheifele .40 1.00
485 Alex Pietrangelo .20 .50
486 Mika Zibanejad .30 .75
487 Mathew Barzal .30 .75
488 Sergei Bobrovsky .40 1.00
489 Patrick Kane .50 1.25
490 John Tavares .40 1.00
491 Patrice Bergeron .30 .75
492 Jack Hughes .60 1.50
493 Ryan O'Reilly .25 .60
494 David Pastrnak .60 1.50
495 Aleksander Barkov .40 1.00
496 Elias Pettersson .40 1.00
497 Barclay Goodrow .15 .40
498 Mitch Marner .40 1.00
499 Leon Draisaitl .75 2.00
500 Checklist .15 .40
501 Joe Veleno RC 1.00 2.50
502 Tanner Jeannot RC .75 2.00
503 Lane Pederson RC .75 2.00
504 Kole Lind RC 1.00 2.50
505 Spencer Knight RC 1.50 4.00
506 Cole Caufield RC 3.00 8.00
507 Quinton Byfield RC 2.00 5.00
508 Ukko-Pekka Luukkonen RC 1.25 3.00
509 Jacob Bryson RC .75 2.00
510 Veini Vehvilainen RC .75 2.00
511 Jan Jenik RC 1.00 2.50
512 Joey Keane RC .60 1.50
513 Zac Jones RC 1.00 2.50
514 Wade Allison RC .75 2.00
515 Ross Colton RC 1.00 2.50
516 Dakota Joshua RC .75 2.00
517 Radim Zohorna RC .75 2.00
518 Ivan Chekhovich RC .60 1.50
519 Tarmo Reunanen RC .75 2.00
520 Morgan Barron RC .60 1.50
521 Arttu Ruotsalainen RC .75 2.00
522 Tyce Thompson RC .75 2.00
523 Wyatt Kalynuk RC .75 2.00
524 Mattias Samuelsson RC .75 2.00
525 Jeremy Swayman RC 2.50 6.00
526 Alex Barre-Boulet RC .75 2.00
527 Filip Gustavsson RC 1.50 4.00
528 Jacob Bernard-Docker RC .75 2.00
529 David Farrance RC .75 2.00
530 Shane Pinto RC 1.25 3.00
531 Calen Addison RC .75 2.00
532 Rasmus Kupari RC .75 2.00
533 Grigori Denisenko RC 1.00 2.50
534 Jamie Drysdale RC 1.25 3.00
535 Trevor Zegras RC 1.50 4.00
536 Alex Newhook RC 1.25 3.00
537 Cam York RC .75 2.00
538 Logan Thompson RC 2.00 5.00
539 Garrett Pilon RC 1.00 2.50
540 Joshua Dunne RC .75 2.00
541 Kirill Kaprizov 1.25 3.00
542 Pius Suter .30 .75
543 Nils Hoglander .30 .75
544 Ilya Sorokin .60 1.50
545 Jason Robertson .60 1.50
546 Josh Norris .40 1.00
547 Tim Stutzle .50 1.25
548 Alexis Lafreniere .60 1.50
549 Dylan Cozens .40 1.00
550 Yegor Sharangovich .40 1.00
551 Anaheim Ducks .15 .40
552 Arizona Coyotes .15 .40
553 Boston Bruins .15 .40
554 Buffalo Sabres .15 .40
555 Calgary Flames .15 .40
556 Carolina Hurricanes .15 .40
557 Chicago Blackhawks .15 .40
558 Colorado Avalanche .15 .40
559 Columbus Blue Jackets .15 .40
560 Dallas Stars .15 .40
561 Detroit Red Wings .15 .40
562 Edmonton Oilers .15 .40
563 Florida Panthers .15 .40
564 Los Angeles Kings .15 .40
565 Minnesota Wild .15 .40
566 Montreal Canadiens .15 .40
567 Nashville Predators .15 .40
568 New Jersey Devils .15 .40
569 New York Islanders .15 .40
570 New York Rangers .15 .40
571 Ottawa Senators .15 .40
572 Philadelphia Flyers .15 .40
573 Pittsburgh Penguins .15 .40
574 San Jose Sharks .15 .40
575 St. Louis Blues .15 .40
576 Tampa Bay Lightning .15 .40
577 Toronto Maple Leafs .15 .40
578 Vancouver Canucks .15 .40
579 Vegas Golden Knights .15 .40
580 Washington Capitals .15 .40
581 Winnipeg Jets .15 .40
582 Auston Matthews 2.50 6.00
583 Connor McDavid 3.00 8.00
584 Connor McDavid 3.00 8.00
585 Leon Draisaitl 2.00 5.00
586 Tyson Barrie .40 1.00
587 Alex Nedeljkovic .50 1.25
588 Philipp Grubauer .60 1.50
589 Andrei Vasilevskiy 1.00 2.50
590 Kirill Kaprizov 2.00 5.00
591 Patrick Marleau .50 1.25
592 Patrick Kane 1.25 3.00
593 Marc-Andre Fleury 1.25 3.00
594 Sidney Crosby 2.50 6.00
595 David Pastrnak 1.50 4.00
596 Joe Thornton 1.00 2.50
597 Anze Kopitar 1.00 2.50
598 Nicklas Backstrom .60 1.50
599 Connor McDavid 3.00 8.00
600 Kirill Kaprizov 2.00 5.00
601 Marc-Andre Fleury .50 1.25
602 Duncan Keith .20 .50
603 Alex Nedeljkovic .20 .50
604 Keith Yandle .15 .40
605 Seth Jones .25 .60
606 Joe Thornton .40 1.00
607 Phillip Danault .25 .60
608 Zach Parise .25 .60
609 Sam Reinhart .50 1.25
610 Ryan Suter .20 .50
611 William Eklund RC 2.00 5.00
612 Benoit-Olivier Groulx RC .75 2.00
613 Cole Perfetti RC 1.50 4.00
614 Jake Neighbours RC 1.50 4.00
615 Cole Sillinger RC 1.25 3.00
616 Nils Lundkvist RC .75 2.00
617 Taylor Raddysh RC 1.25 3.00
618 Dawson Mercer RC 2.00 5.00
619 Vasily Podkolzin RC 1.00 2.50
620 Anton Lundell RC 1.50 4.00
621 Moritz Seider RC 2.00 5.00
622 Vladimir Tkachev RC .75 2.00
623 Philip Tomasino RC 1.00 2.50
624 Hendrix Lapierre RC .75 2.00
625 Jonathan Dahlen RC .75 2.00
626 Mason McTavish RC 1.50 4.00
627 Lucas Raymond RC 2.50 6.00
628 Yegor Chinakhov RC 1.25 3.00
629 Jake Leschyshyn RC .75 2.00
630 Boris Katchouk RC .60 1.50
631 Ivan Prosvetov RC .75 2.00
632 Parker Kelly RC .75 2.00
633 Matthew Phillips RC .75 2.00
634 Marian Studenic RC .75 2.00
635 Jack Ahcan RC .75 2.00
636 Matt Kiersted RC .60 1.50
637 Jeffrey Viel RC .75 2.00
638 Maksim Sushko RC .75 2.00
639 Mike Hardman RC .75 2.00
640 Jonah Gadjovich RC .75 2.00
641 Tanner Laczynski RC .75 2.00
642 Daniel Walcott RC .75 2.00
643 Simon Benoit RC .75 2.00
644 Michael Houser RC .75 2.00
645 Sampo Ranta RC .75 2.00
646 Jesse Ylonen RC .75 2.00
647 Karel Vejmelka RC 1.00 2.50
648 Oskar Steen RC 1.00 2.50
649 Brinson Pasichnuk RC .75 2.00
650 Adam Ruzicka RC .75 2.00

2021-22 O-Pee-Chee Neon Green

*GREEN (1-500): 3X TO 8X BASIC CARDS
*GREEN (501-550,582-600): 2X TO 5X BASIC CARDS
530 Shane Pinto 60.00 125.00
535 Trevor Zegras 80.00 200.00

2021-22 O-Pee-Chee Hall of Fame Patches

HOF1 Guy Carbonneau 20.00 50.00
HOF2 Doug Gilmour 25.00 60.00
HOF3 Mark Recchi 20.00 50.00
HOF4 Brett Hull 30.00 80.00
HOF5 Al MacInnis 25.00 60.00
HOF6 Grant Fuhr 30.00 80.00
HOF7 Pat LaFontaine 20.00 50.00
HOF8 Steve Yzerman 50.00 125.00

2021-22 O-Pee-Chee OPC Premier Tallboys

P1 Connor McDavid 4.00 10.00
P2 Auston Matthews 3.00 8.00
P3 Jonathan Toews 1.25 3.00
P4 Nathan MacKinnon 3.00 8.00
P5 Carey Price 1.50 4.00
P6 Evgeni Malkin 1.50 4.00
P7 Patrice Bergeron 1.00 2.50
P8 John Tavares 1.25 3.00
P9 Jack Hughes 2.00 5.00
P10 Quinn Hughes 2.00 5.00
P11 Sebastian Aho 1.25 3.00
P12 Jonathan Huberdeau 1.00 2.50
P13 Miro Heiskanen 1.00 2.50
P14 Andrei Vasilevskiy 1.25 3.00
P15 John Carlson .75 2.00
P16 Roman Josi .75 2.00
P17 Brayden Point 1.00 2.50
P18 Kyle Connor 1.25 3.00
P19 Nikita Kucherov 1.50 4.00
P20 David Pastrnak 2.00 5.00
P21 Victor Hedman 1.00 2.50
P22 Mark Scheifele 1.25 3.00
P23 Ryan O'Reilly .75 2.00
P24 Brady Tkachuk 1.25 3.00
P25 Anze Kopitar 1.25 3.00
P26 Aleksander Barkov 1.25 3.00
P27 Cale Makar 2.00 5.00
P28 Steven Stamkos 1.50 4.00
P29 Jack Eichel 1.25 3.00
P30 Elias Pettersson 1.25 3.00
P31 MarcAndre Fleury 1.50 4.00
P32 Artemi Panarin 1.50 4.00
P33 Patrick Kane 1.50 4.00
P34 Alex Ovechkin 3.00 8.00
P35 Sidney Crosby 3.00 8.00
P36 Jamie Drysdale SP 4.00 10.00
P37 Cole Caufield SP 10.00 25.00
P38 Quinton Byfield SP 6.00 15.00
P39 Spencer Knight SP 5.00 12.00
P40 Trevor Zegras SP 5.00 12.00
P41 Yegor Sharangovich SP 2.50 6.00
P42 Ty Smith SP 2.50 6.00
P43 Gabe Vilardi SP 2.50 6.00
P44 Philipp Kurashev SP 2.00 5.00
P45 Josh Norris SP 2.50 6.00
P46 Jason Robertson SP 4.00 10.00
P47 Ilya Sorokin SP 4.00 10.00
P48 Nils Hoglander SP 2.00 5.00
P49 Pius Suter SP 2.00 5.00
P50 Arthur Kaliyev SP 2.50 6.00
P51 Alexander Romanov SP 2.00 5.00
P52 Dylan Cozens SP 2.50 6.00
P53 Alexis Lafreniere SP 4.00 10.00
P54 Tim Stutzle SP 3.00 8.00
P55 Kirill Kaprizov SP 6.00 15.00

2021-22 O-Pee-Chee Patches

P1 Matt Dumba 8.00 20.00
P2 Henrik Sedin 12.00 30.00
P3 Daniel Sedin 12.00 30.00
P4 Trevor Linden 10.00 25.00
P5 Kevin Lowe 10.00 25.00
P6 Bobby Ryan 8.00 20.00
P7 Max Pacioretty 10.00 25.00
P8 Phil Kessel 10.00 25.00
P9 Teemu Selanne 20.00 50.00
P10 Henri Richard 10.00 25.00
P11 David Pastrnak 25.00 60.00
P12 Evgeny Kuznetsov 12.00 30.00
P13 Patrick Kane 20.00 50.00
P14 Chris Chelios 10.00 25.00
P15 Mark Messier 20.00 50.00
P16 Sean Couturier 8.00 20.00
P17 Michael Peca 10.00 25.00
P18 Troy Murray 10.00 25.00
P19 Bobby Clarke 15.00 40.00
P20 Steve Kasper 6.00 15.00
P21 Tuukka Rask 12.00 30.00
P22 Thomas Greiss 8.00 20.00
P23 Frederik Andersen 12.00 30.00
P24 Martin Brodeur 25.00 60.00
P25 Dominik Hasek 15.00 40.00
P26 David Pastrnak 25.00 60.00
P27 Milan Hejduk 10.00 25.00
P28 Pavel Bure 10.00 25.00
P29 Leon Draisaitl 30.00 80.00
P30 Alex Ovechkin 40.00 100.00
P31 Leon Draisaitl 30.00 80.00
P32 Sidney Crosby 40.00 100.00
P33 Martin St. Louis 10.00 25.00
P34 Evgeni Malkin 20.00 50.00
P35 Jarome Iginla 12.00 30.00
P36 Nathan MacKinnon 40.00 100.00
P37 Martin St. Louis 10.00 25.00
P38 Joe Mullen 10.00 25.00
P39 Stan Mikita 10.00 25.00
P40 Butch Goring 10.00 25.00
P41 Victor Hedman 12.00 30.00
P42 Patrick Kane 20.00 50.00
P43 Nicklas Lidstrom 10.00 25.00
P44 Patrick Roy 25.00 60.00
P45 Wayne Gretzky 60.00 150.00
P46 Roman Josi 10.00 25.00
P47 P.K. Subban 12.00 30.00
P48 Duncan Keith 8.00 20.00
P49 Al MacInnis 12.00 30.00
P50 Chris Chelios 10.00 25.00
P51 Cale Makar 25.00 60.00
P52 Aaron Ekblad 12.00 30.00
P53 Gabriel Landeskog 12.00 30.00
P54 Evgeni Malkin 20.00 50.00
P55 Alex Ovechkin 40.00 100.00
P56 Connor Hellebuyck 20.00 50.00
P57 Carey Price 20.00 50.00
P58 Ed Belfour 10.00 25.00
P59 Bernie Parent 12.00 30.00
P60 Tony Esposito 10.00 25.00
P61 Leon Draisaitl 30.00 80.00
P62 Jaromir Jagr 30.00 80.00
P63 Eric Lindros 15.00 40.00
P64 Dominik Hasek 15.00 40.00
P65 Mark Messier 20.00 50.00
P66 Victor Hedman 12.00 30.00
P67 Nicklas Lidstrom 10.00 25.00
P68 Martin St. Louis 10.00 25.00
P69 Jaromir Jagr 30.00 80.00
P70 Mike Bossy 10.00 25.00
P71 Yvan Cournoyer 10.00 25.00
P72 Bobby Clarke 15.00 40.00
P73 Johnny Bucyk 10.00 25.00
P74 Johnny Bower 10.00 25.00
P75 Glenn Hall 10.00 25.00
P76 Seattle Kraken 60.00 150.00

2021-22 O-Pee-Chee Playing Cards

JOKER Gnash 8.00 20.00
JOKER Gritty 8.00 20.00
2CLUBS Kyle Connor 2.50 6.00
3CLUBS Nico Hischier 2.50 6.00
4CLUBS Nick Schmaltz 1.25 3.00
5CLUBS John Carlson 1.50 4.00
6CLUBS Mark Scheifele 2.50 6.00
7CLUBS Matthew Tkachuk 3.00 8.00
8CLUBS Sebastian Aho 2.50 6.00
9CLUBS Quinn Hughes 4.00 10.00
JCLUBS Jack Hughes 4.00 10.00
KCLUBS Carey Price 3.00 8.00
QCLUBS MarcAndre Fleury 3.00 8.00
10CLUBS Cale Makar 4.00 10.00
2HEARTS Kirill Kaprizov 5.00 12.00
2SPADES Brent Burns 1.50 4.00
3HEARTS John Gibson 1.50 4.00
3SPADES Brock Boeser 2.00 5.00
4HEARTS Mathew Barzal 2.00 5.00
4SPADES Tyler Seguin 2.00 5.00
5HEARTS Jordan Binnington 2.50 6.00
5SPADES Jonathan Huberdeau 2.00 5.00
6HEARTS Alex DeBrincat 2.00 5.00
6SPADES Max Pacioretty 1.50 4.00
7HEARTS Anze Kopitar 2.50 6.00
7SPADES Ryan O'Reilly 1.50 4.00
8HEARTS Aleksander Barkov 2.50 6.00
8SPADES Patrik Laine 2.00 5.00
9HEARTS Nikita Kucherov 3.00 8.00
9SPADES John Tavares 2.50 6.00
JHEARTS Artemi Panarin 3.00 8.00
JSPADES Patrice Bergeron 2.00 5.00
KHEARTS Leon Draisaitl 5.00 12.00
KSPADES Patrick Kane 3.00 8.00
QHEARTS Elias Pettersson 2.50 6.00
QSPADES Evgeni Malkin 3.00 8.00
10DIAMONDS Brad Marchand 3.00 8.00
10HEARTS Steven Stamkos 3.00 8.00
10SPADES David Pastrnak 4.00 10.00
2DIAMONDS Andrei Vasilevskiy 2.50 6.00
3DIAMONDS Dylan Larkin 2.00 5.00
4DIAMONDS Claude Giroux 1.50 4.00
5DIAMONDS Nick Suzuki 3.00 8.00
6DIAMONDS Vladimir Tarasenko 2.00 5.00
7DIAMONDS Mark Stone 2.00 5.00
8DIAMONDS Brady Tkachuk 2.50 6.00
9DIAMONDS Mitch Marner 2.50 6.00
ACECLUBS Alex Ovechkin 6.00 15.00
ACEDIAMONDS Sidney Crosby 6.00 15.00
ACEHEARTS Connor McDavid 15.00 40.00
ACESPADES Auston Matthews 6.00 15.00
JDIAMONDS Jack Eichel 2.50 6.00
KDIAMONDS Nathan MacKinnon 6.00 15.00
QDIAMONDS Jonathan Toews 2.50 6.00

2021-22 O-Pee-Chee Retro Black

*RETRO.BLK: 2X TO 5X BASIC
530 Shane Pinto 40.00 100.00
535 Trevor Zegras 60.00 150.00

2021-22 O-Pee-Chee Team Logo Patch Update

341 Willie O'Ree 50.00 125.00
342 Buffalo Sabres 50.00 125.00
343 Ottawa Senators 50.00 125.00
344 Calgary Flames 50.00 125.00
345 Winnipeg Jets 50.00 125.00
346 Columbus Blue Jackets 50.00 125.00
347 Minnesota Wild 50.00 125.00
348 Arizona Coyotes 50.00 125.00
349 Colorado Avalanche 50.00 125.00
350 San Jose Sharks 50.00 125.00

2022-23 O-Pee-Chee

1 Trevor Zegras .25 .60
2 Alex DeBrincat .30 .75
3 Kirill Kaprizov .75 2.00
4 Leon Draisaitl .75 2.00
5 Michael Bunting .25 .60
6 Nazem Kadri .30 .75
7 David Pastrnak .60 1.50
8 Alex Ovechkin 1.00 2.50
9 Tyler Toffoli .25 .60
10 Jake Guentzel .40 1.00
11 Steven Stamkos .50 1.25
12 Jordan Kyrou .25 .60
13 Anton Lundell .25 .60
14 Sebastian Aho .40 1.00
15 Brad Marchand .50 1.25
16 Igor Shesterkin .50 1.25
17 Nathan MacKinnon 1.00 2.50
18 Patrick Kane .50 1.25
19 Anze Kopitar .40 1.00
20 Elias Pettersson .40 1.00
21 Brent Burns .25 .60
22 Brendan Gallagher .25 .60
23 Jordan Eberle .25 .60
24 Jack Hughes .60 1.50
25 Joel Farabee .25 .60
26 Clayton Keller .30 .75
27 Ryan Johansen .20 .50
28 Moritz Seider .30 .75
29 Cale Makar .60 1.50
30 Jean-Gabriel Pageau .15 .40
31 Mark Scheifele .40 1.00
32 Alexander Wennberg .15 .40
33 Mats Zuccarello .25 .60
34 Auston Matthews 1.00 2.50
35 Andrei Svechnikov .30 .75
36 Patrik Laine .30 .75
37 Alexis Lafreniere .40 1.00
38 Nico Hischier .40 1.00
39 Andrei Vasilevskiy .40 1.00
40 Tanner Jeannot .15 .40
41 Jonathan Marchessault .30 .75
42 Logan Couture .30 .75
43 Taylor Hall .25 .60
44 Conor Garland .20 .50
45 Spencer Knight .25 .60
46 Travis Konecny .25 .60
47 Pierre-Luc Dubois .20 .50
48 Joe Pavelski .30 .75
49 Brock Nelson .25 .60
50 Peyton Krebs .20 .50
51 Ilya Sorokin .40 1.00
52 Mark Stone .30 .75
53 Philipp Grubauer .25 .60
54 Petr Mrazek .20 .50
55 Tyler Bertuzzi .20 .50
56 John Tavares .40 1.00
57 Ryan Hartman .15 .40
58 John Carlson .25 .60
59 Alex Tuch .25 .60
60 Mike Hoffman .15 .40
61 Jaccob Slavin .20 .50
62 Tim Stutzle .30 .75
63 Darnell Nurse .20 .50
64 Kyle Connor .40 1.00
65 Artemi Panarin .50 1.25
66 Ivan Provorov .20 .50
67 Jonathan Huberdeau .30 .75
68 Quinton Byfield .30 .75
69 Seth Jones .25 .60
70 Dougie Hamilton .20 .50
71 Matt Duchene .25 .60
72 Chandler Stephenson .20 .50
73 Jeff Skinner .25 .60
74 Tomas Hertl .25 .60
75 Miro Heiskanen .30 .75
76 Quinn Hughes .60 1.50
77 Jamie Drysdale .20 .50
78 Elias Lindholm .25 .60
79 Drew Doughty .30 .75
80 Dylan Larkin .30 .75
81 Troy Terry .20 .50
82 Torey Krug .20 .50
83 Shayne Gostisbehere .25 .60
84 Nikita Kucherov .50 1.25
85 Jakub Voracek .20 .50
86 Johnny Gaudreau .40 1.00
87 Sidney Crosby 1.00 2.50
88 Jason Robertson .40 1.00
89 Vladimir Tarasenko .30 .75
90 Zach Werenski .40 1.00
91 Josh Anderson .20 .50
92 Claude Giroux .25 .60
93 Vasily Podkolzin .15 .40
94 Kasperi Kapanen .20 .50
95 Alex Newhook .20 .50
96 Sam Reinhart .50 1.25
97 Connor McDavid 1.25 3.00
98 Tom Wilson .25 .60
99 Adrian Kempe .25 .60
100 Checklist .15 .40
101 Mitch Marner .40 1.00
102 Noah Dobson .30 .75
103 Brandon Hagel .20 .50
104 Oliver Wahlstrom .15 .40
105 Dylan Cozens .25 .60
106 Tomas Tatar .15 .40
107 Oliver Bjorkstrand .20 .50
108 Brock Boeser .30 .75
109 Jack Eichel .40 1.00
110 Drake Batherson .25 .60
111 Adam Fox .30 .75
112 Morgan Rielly .25 .60
113 Charlie McAvoy .30 .75
114 T.J. Oshie .25 .60
115 Zach Hyman .40 1.00
116 Seth Jarvis .30 .75
117 Gabriel Landeskog .30 .75
118 Filip Forsberg .40 1.00
119 Isac Lundestrom .15 .40
120 Nikolaj Ehlers .25 .60
121 Phillip Danault .25 .60
122 Nick Suzuki .50 1.25
123 Alex Killorn .15 .40
124 Noah Hanifin .25 .60
125 Jamie Benn .25 .60
126 William Karlsson .30 .75
127 Mathew Barzal .30 .75
128 John Gibson .25 .60
129 Evgeny Kuznetsov .30 .75
130 Dylan Strome .30 .75
131 Alexander Barabanov .15 .40
132 Tage Thompson .30 .75
133 Ryan O'Reilly .25 .60
134 Victor Hedman .30 .75
135 Tristan Jarry .25 .60
136 Boone Jenner .25 .60
137 Sonny Milano .20 .50
138 Blake Wheeler .25 .60
139 William Nylander .50 1.25
140 Matthew Tkachuk .50 1.25
141 Dawson Mercer .30 .75
142 Chris Kreider .30 .75
143 Ryan Nugent-Hopkins .30 .75
144 Cole Caufield .50 1.25
145 Phil Kessel .25 .60
146 Patrice Bergeron .30 .75
147 Elvis Merzlikins .25 .60
148 Josh Norris .25 .60
149 Jordan Staal .20 .50
150 Connor Hellebuyck .50 1.25
151 Alex Iafallo .15 .40
152 Roman Josi .25 .60
153 Jacob Markstrom .25 .60
154 Erik Karlsson .30 .75
155 Jonathan Toews .40 1.00
156 Robert Thomas .25 .60
157 Yegor Sharangovich .25 .60
158 Aleksander Barkov .40 1.00
159 Tanner Pearson .25 .60
160 Jeremy Swayman .40 1.00
161 Nicklas Backstrom .25 .60
162 Sean Couturier .20 .50
163 Samuel Girard .15 .40
164 Brayden Point .30 .75
165 Alex Nedeljkovic .20 .50
166 Mika Zibanejad .30 .75
167 Tyler Seguin .30 .75
168 Jared McCann .20 .50
169 Lucas Raymond .40 1.00
170 Joel Eriksson Ek .20 .50
171 Viktor Arvidsson .15 .40
172 Jason Zucker .25 .60
173 Rasmus Dahlin .30 .75
174 Thomas Chabot .25 .60
175 Aaron Ekblad .30 .75
176 David Perron .20 .50
177 Juuse Saros .30 .75
178 John Marino .25 .60
179 Mikko Rantanen .60 1.50
180 Nick Schmaltz .20 .50
181 Kevin Fiala .20 .50
182 Anders Lee .20 .50
183 Max Pacioretty .25 .60
184 Teuvo Teravainen .25 .60
185 J.T. Miller .30 .75

186 Tyson Barrie .15 .40
187 Connor Brown .20 .50
188 Yanni Gourde .20 .50
189 Roope Hintz .30 .75
190 Cam Atkinson .25 .60
191 Sergei Bobrovsky .40 1.00
192 Jared Spurgeon .25 .60
193 Timo Meier .25 .60
194 Filip Hronek .15 .40
195 Brady Tkachuk .40 1.00
196 Bo Horvat .30 .75
197 T.J. Brodie .15 .40
198 Carey Price .50 1.25
199 Anthony Cirelli .20 .50
200 Checklist .15 .40
201 Jesse Puljujarvi .25 .60
202 Jamie Oleksiak .20 .50
203 Barclay Goodrow .15 .40
204 Martin Necas .40 1.00
205 Carter Verhaeghe .25 .60
206 Robby Fabbri .15 .40
207 Justin Holl .15 .40
208 Radek Faksa .20 .50
209 Kirby Dach .25 .60
210 Andrew Copp .15 .40
211 Gustav Nyquist .15 .40
212 Shea Theodore .30 .75
213 Jesper Bratt .25 .60
214 Jordan Binnington .40 1.00
215 Colin White .20 .50
216 Bowen Byram .30 .75
217 Jonathan Dahlen .15 .40
218 Artturi Lehkonen .20 .50
219 Frederick Gaudreau .15 .40
220 Brian Dumoulin .15 .40
221 Sean Monahan .15 .40
222 Connor McMichael .25 .60
223 Jesperi Kotkaniemi .25 .60
224 Kyle Palmieri .20 .50
225 Jeff Petry .25 .60
226 Evan Bouchard .30 .75
227 Cam Fowler .25 .60
228 Philip Tomasino .15 .40
229 Nick Bonino .15 .40
230 Nils Hoglander .20 .50
231 Kevin Lankinen .25 .60
232 Taylor Raddysh .20 .50
233 Filip Chytil .20 .50
234 Rudolfs Balcers .15 .40
235 Anthony Duclair .20 .50
236 Neal Pionk .15 .40
237 Adam Erne .15 .40
238 Brandon Saad .20 .50
239 John Klingberg .25 .60
240 Artem Zub .15 .40
241 Alex Pietrangelo .20 .50
242 Jonathan Drouin .20 .50
243 Alex Turcotte .15 .40
244 Jake DeBrusk .25 .60
245 Damon Severson .15 .40
246 Jonas Brodin .15 .40
247 Denis Gurianov .30 .75
248 David Kampf .15 .40
249 Maxime Comtois .20 .50
250 Mikael Granlund .20 .50
251 Marcus Pettersson .15 .40
252 Sean Kuraly .15 .40
253 Mark Giordano .25 .60
254 Ryan Ellis .15 .40
255 Josh Bailey .20 .50
256 Anthony Mantha .20 .50
257 Andrew Mangiapane .25 .60
258 Calle Jarnkrok .15 .40
259 Gabe Vilardi .25 .60
260 Dominik Kubalik .25 .60
261 Oliver Ekman-Larsson .15 .40
262 Kyle Okposo .15 .40
263 Cole Perfetti .25 .60
264 Matt Nieto .20 .50
265 Shane Pinto .20 .50
266 Andreas Johnsson .20 .50
267 Conor Sheary .25 .60
268 Ryan Reaves .20 .50
269 Jack Campbell .25 .60
270 Carter Hart .25 .60
271 Christian Dvorak .20 .50
272 Devon Toews .20 .50
273 Brady Skjei .15 .40
274 Casey Mittelstadt .25 .60
275 Erik Cernak .15 .40
276 Pius Suter .20 .50
277 Hampus Lindholm .15 .40
278 Evgenii Dadonov .15 .40
279 Duncan Keith .20 .50
280 Nick Ritchie .15 .40
281 Kevin Shattenkirk .15 .40
282 Anthony Beauvillier .15 .40
283 Brandon Duhaime .15 .40
284 Trevor Moore .15 .40
285 Alex Kerfoot .20 .50
286 Sam Bennett .40 1.00
287 Teddy Blueger .15 .40
288 Rickard Rakell .20 .50
289 J.T. Compher .15 .40
290 Jacob Peterson .15 .40
291 Matt Grzelcyk .20 .50
292 Justin Faulk .20 .50
293 Blake Coleman .20 .50
294 Colton Sissons .15 .40
295 Victor Olofsson .25 .60
296 Alexandre Texier .15 .40
297 P.K. Subban .30 .75
298 Andrew Ladd .20 .50
299 Pavel Francouz .20 .50
300 Checklist .15 .40
301 Victor Soderstrom .15 .40
302 Mario Ferraro .15 .40
303 Nino Niederreiter .15 .40
304 Josh Morrissey .30 .75
305 Alex Formenton .20 .50
306 Adam Henrique .20 .50
307 Jake Evans .15 .40
308 Joonas Donskoi .15 .40
309 Scott Mayfield .15 .40
310 William Carrier .15 .40
311 Joe Veleno .20 .50
312 Calen Addison .15 .40
313 Tyler Myers .15 .40
314 Mike Matheson .15 .40
315 Vladislav Gavrikov .15 .40
316 Kailer Yamamoto .25 .60
317 Dmitry Orlov .25 .60
318 Pavel Zacha .20 .50
319 Bryan Rust .25 .60
320 Colton Parayko .20 .50
321 Jacob Trouba .20 .50
322 Ryan Suter .20 .50
323 Jasper Weatherby .15 .40
324 Marc-Andre Fleury .50 1.25
325 Jesper Fast .15 .40
326 Rasmus Asplund .15 .40
327 William Eklund .30 .75
328 Eeli Tolvanen .25 .60
329 Erik Johnson .15 .40
330 Christopher Tanev .15 .40
331 Pierre Engvall .15 .40
332 Keith Yandle .15 .40
333 Arthur Kaliyev .25 .60
334 Jake Allen .25 .60
335 Brandon Carlo .20 .50
336 Ryan Strome .25 .60
337 Brock McGinn .15 .40
338 Tony DeAngelo .15 .40
339 Ondrej Palat .20 .50
340 Pierre-Edouard Bellemare .15 .40
341 Joe Thornton .40 1.00
342 Garnet Hathaway .15 .40
343 Darcy Kuemper .25 .60
344 Adam Pelech .15 .40
345 Rasmus Andersson .20 .50
346 Vince Dunn .20 .50
347 Ryan Graves .15 .40
348 Filip Zadina .20 .50
349 Robin Lehner .20 .50
350 Ryan Lindgren .15 .40
351 Victor Mete .15 .40
352 Mattias Ekholm .20 .50
353 Henri Jokiharju .15 .40
354 Cole Sillinger .20 .50
355 Thatcher Demko .30 .75
356 Derek Grant .15 .40
357 Ivan Barbashev .20 .50
358 Cal Petersen .15 .40
359 Ryan McDonagh .15 .40
360 Jake McCabe .15 .40
361 Craig Smith .15 .40
362 Dylan DeMelo .15 .40
363 Warren Foegele .15 .40
364 Evan Rodrigues .20 .50
365 Travis Sanheim .15 .40
366 Ondrej Kase .15 .40
367 Ty Smith .25 .60
368 Dmitry Kulikov .15 .40
369 Evgeni Malkin .50 1.25
370 MacKenzie Weegar .20 .50
371 Lawson Crouse .15 .40
372 Matt Roy .15 .40
373 K'Andre Miller .20 .50
374 Luke Schenn .25 .60
375 Casey Cizikas .20 .50
376 Logan O'Connor .25 .60
377 Michael Amadio .15 .40
378 Dante Fabbro .15 .40
379 Parker Kelly .15 .40
380 Karel Vejmelka .15 .40
381 Brayden Schenn .25 .60
382 Oliver Kylington .15 .40
383 Vincent Trocheck .25 .60
384 Mikhail Sergachev .20 .50
385 Michael Rasmussen .15 .40
386 Jake Bean .15 .40
387 Jaden Schwartz .20 .50
388 Brandon Montour .30 .75
389 Ilya Samsonov .25 .60
390 Reilly Smith .25 .60
391 Jake Oettinger .40 1.00
392 Oskar Lindblom .20 .50
393 MacKenzie Entwistle .15 .40
394 Cody Ceci .15 .40
395 Jakob Silfverberg .15 .40
396 Zemgus Girgensons .15 .40
397 Erik Haula .15 .40
398 Matt Dumba .15 .40
399 Nate Schmidt .15 .40
400 Checklist .15 .40
401 Max Domi .25 .60
402 Nils Lundkvist .15 .40
403 Sam Carrick .15 .40
404 Nico Daws .20 .50
405 Kyle Burroughs .15 .40
406 Mattias Samuelsson .15 .40
407 Braden Holtby .30 .75
408 Pavel Buchnevich .20 .50
409 Corey Perry .40 1.00
410 Matt Murray .25 .60
411 Connor Murphy .20 .50
412 Jordan Oesterle .15 .40
413 Danton Heinen .15 .40
414 Jordan Greenway .15 .40
415 Yegor Chinakhov .20 .50
416 Derek Ryan .15 .40
417 Brenden Dillon .15 .40
418 David Savard .15 .40
419 Rasmus Kupari .15 .40
420 Mackenzie Blackwood .25 .60
421 Adin Hill .25 .60
422 Marcus Foligno .20 .50
423 Frederik Andersen .30 .75
424 Vitek Vanecek .25 .60
425 Anders Bjork .15 .40
426 Dan Vladar .20 .50
427 Filip Gustavsson .25 .60
428 Gustav Forsling .25 .60
429 Scott Perunovich .15 .40
430 Jack Roslovic .15 .40
431 Alexandre Carrier .15 .40
432 Zach Whitecloud .15 .40
433 Linus Ullmark .25 .60
434 Brandon Tanev .20 .50
435 Scott Laughton .15 .40
436 Wayne Simmonds .25 .60
437 Michael McCarron .25 .60
438 Jeff Carter .20 .50
439 Adam Larsson .25 .60
440 Matthew Highmore .20 .50
441 Sammy Blais .15 .40
442 Patric Hornqvist .15 .40
443 Trevor van Riemsdyk .20 .50
444 Ethan Bear .15 .40
445 James Reimer .15 .40
446 Ross Colton .20 .50
447 Derek Forbort .15 .40
448 Marco Scandella .15 .40
449 Sam Steel .20 .50
450 Logan Stanley .15 .40
451 Dillon Dube .15 .40
452 Jonas Siegenthaler .15 .40
453 Mike Smith .15 .40
454 Lassi Thomson .15 .40
455 Joel Edmundson .15 .40
456 Adam Boqvist .15 .40
457 Dylan Coghlan .15 .40
458 Caleb Jones .15 .40
459 Nick Leddy .15 .40
460 Luke Kunin .15 .40
461 James van Riemsdyk .20 .50
462 Noah Gregor .15 .40
463 Robin Salo .15 .40
464 Morgan Geekie .15 .40
465 Zdeno Chara .25 .60
466 Nic Dowd .15 .40
467 Alexander Romanov .20 .50
468 Kole Lind .15 .40
469 Andre Burakovsky .15 .40
470 Kris Letang .30 .75
471 Tobias Bjornfot .15 .40
472 Niko Mikkola .15 .40
473 Spencer Martin .15 .40
474 Cam Talbot .25 .60
475 Patrick Maroon .15 .40
476 Givani Smith .15 .40
477 Zac Jones .15 .40
478 Jakob Chychrun .25 .60
479 Yakov Trenin .15 .40
480 Eric Robinson .20 .50
481 Nicolas Roy .15 .40
482 Mike Reilly .15 .40
483 Antti Raanta .25 .60
484 Semyon Varlamov .25 .60
485 Zack Kassian .15 .40
486 Milan Lucic .20 .50
487 Kevin Hayes .20 .50
488 Josh Mahura .15 .40
489 Esa Lindell .20 .50
490 Ryan Poehling .25 .60
491 Jakub Vrana .20 .50
492 Adam Lowry .20 .50
493 Joel Kiviranta .15 .40
494 Mason Appleton .15 .40
495 Sean Durzi .15 .40
496 Philipp Kurashev .20 .50
497 Janis Moser .15 .40
498 Carson Soucy .15 .40
499 Aliaksei Protas .15 .40
500 Checklist .15 .40
501 Connor McDavid AS 2.00 5.00
502 Auston Matthews AS 1.50 4.00
503 Jordan Kyrou AS .40 1.00
504 Leon Draisaitl AS 1.25 3.00
505 Troy Terry AS .30 .75
506 Claude Giroux AS .40 1.00
507 Jake Guentzel AS .60 1.50
508 Jonathan Huberdeau AS .50 1.25
509 Dylan Larkin AS .50 1.25
510 Jack Hughes AS 1.00 2.50
511 Tristan Jarry AS .40 1.00
512 Nick Suzuki AS .75 2.00
513 Brady Tkachuk AS .60 1.50
514 Steven Stamkos AS .75 2.00
515 Victor Hedman AS .50 1.25
516 Patrice Bergeron AS .50 1.25
517 Kyle Connor AS .60 1.50
518 Kirill Kaprizov AS 1.25 3.00
519 Alex DeBrincat AS .50 1.25
520 Nazem Kadri AS .50 1.25
521 Clayton Keller AS .50 1.25
522 Andrei Vasilevskiy AS .60 1.50
523 Rasmus Dahlin AS .50 1.25
524 Johnny Gaudreau AS .60 1.50
525 Jordan Eberle AS .40 1.00
526 Sebastian Aho AS .60 1.50
527 Thatcher Demko AS .50 1.25
528 Mark Stone AS .50 1.25
529 Cam Talbot AS .40 1.00
530 Roman Josi AS .40 1.00
531 Joe Pavelski AS .50 1.25
532 Evgeny Kuznetsov AS .50 1.25
533 Adam Pelech AS .25 .60
534 Tom Wilson AS .40 1.00
535 Zach Werenski AS .60 1.50
536 Adrian Kempe AS .40 1.00
537 Timo Meier AS .40 1.00
538 Jonathan Marchessault AS .50 1.25
539 Chris Kreider AS .50 1.25
540 Cale Makar AS 1.00 2.50
541 Matt Boldy RC 2.50 6.00
542 Jack Quinn RC 1.25 3.00
543 Lukas Reichel RC 1.50 4.00
544 Marco Rossi RC 2.00 5.00
545 Jacob Perreault RC .75 2.00
546 Samuel Fagemo RC .60 1.50
547 Braden Schneider RC 1.25 3.00
548 Brayden Tracey RC .60 1.50
549 Dylan Samberg RC .75 2.00
550 Vladislav Kolyachonok RC .60 1.50
551 Trey Fix-Wolansky RC .75 2.00
552 Isaac Ratcliffe RC .75 2.00
553 Kaedan Korczak RC .60 1.50
554 Lukas Dostal RC 1.50 4.00
555 Matias Maccelli RC 1.25 3.00
556 Jordan Spence RC .75 2.00
557 Erik Kallgren RC .75 2.00
558 Alex Vlasic RC .60 1.50
559 Noah Cates RC .75 2.00
560 Marc McLaughlin RC .75 2.00
561 Ronnie Attard RC .75 2.00
562 Jordan Harris RC 1.00 2.50
563 Mads Sogaard RC 1.00 2.50
564 Nick Abruzzese RC .75 2.00
565 Filip Hallander RC .75 2.00
566 Owen Power RC 1.50 4.00
567 Kent Johnson RC 1.50 4.00
568 Matty Beniers RC 2.00 5.00
569 Bobby Brink RC .75 2.00
570 Thomas Bordeleau RC .75 2.00
571 Reilly Walsh RC .75 2.00
572 Dylan Holloway RC 1.50 4.00
573 Pyotr Kochetkov RC 1.50 4.00
574 Jack McBain RC .75 2.00
575 Jake Christiansen RC .75 2.00
576 Jake Sanderson RC 2.00 5.00
577 Jakub Lauko RC 1.00 2.50
578 Arber Xhekaj RC 1.50 4.00
579 Andrei Kuzmenko RC 1.50 4.00
580 Pavol Regenda RC .75 2.00
581 Filip Roos RC .60 1.50
582 Cole Koepke RC .75 2.00
583 Elmer Soderblom RC 1.50 4.00
584 Nils Aman RC .75 2.00
585 Hunter Drew RC .75 2.00
586 Kaiden Guhle RC 1.50 4.00
587 Michael Eyssimont RC .75 2.00
588 Fredrik Karlstrom RC .60 1.50
589 Valtteri Puustinen RC .60 1.50
590 Chase Pearson RC .60 1.50
591 Mark Kastelic RC .60 1.50
592 Zack Hayes RC .60 1.50
593 Nathan Smith RC .60 1.50
594 David Jiricek RC 1.50 4.00
595 Dylan Guenther RC 2.00 5.00
596 Nikita Okhotiuk RC .60 1.50
597 Wyatt Johnston RC 3.00 8.00
598 Brandt Clarke RC 1.50 4.00
599 Juraj Slafkovsky RC 4.00 10.00
600 Shane Wright RC 2.00 5.00

2022-23 O-Pee-Chee Blue

*BLUE: .75X TO 2X BASIC

2022-23 O-Pee-Chee Neon Pink

*PINK.VETS: 2.5X TO 6X BASIC
*PINK.AS: 3X TO 8X BASIC
*PINK.RC: 2.5X TO 6X BASIC
541 Matt Boldy 25.00 60.00
566 Owen Power 30.00 80.00
568 Matty Beniers 60.00 150.00
599 Juraj Slafkovsky 50.00 125.00
600 Shane Wright 30.00 80.00

2022-23 O-Pee-Chee Rainbow

*RAINBOW/350: 1.25X TO 3X BASIC
568 Matty Beniers 30.00 80.00
573 Pyotr Kochetkov 10.00 25.00
597 Wyatt Johnston 15.00 40.00
599 Juraj Slafkovsky 25.00 60.00

2022-23 O-Pee-Chee Rainbow Black

*RNBW.BLACK.AS: 3X TO 8X BASIC
*RNBW.BLACK.RC: 2.5X TO 6X BASIC
541 Matt Boldy 30.00 80.00
568 Matty Beniers 50.00 125.00
586 Kaiden Guhle 15.00 40.00
597 Wyatt Johnston 25.00 60.00
599 Juraj Slafkovsky 30.00 80.00
600 Shane Wright 25.00 60.00

2022-23 O-Pee-Chee Red

*RED: 1.5X TO 4X BASIC

2022-23 O-Pee-Chee Yellow

*YELLOW.VETS/AS: .75X TO 2X BASIC
*YELLOW.RC: 1X TO 2.5X BASIC
568 Matty Beniers 25.00 60.00

2022-23 O-Pee-Chee 3-D Marquee Rookies

3DAK Andrei Kuzmenko 50.00 125.00
3DBE Matty Beniers 125.00 300.00
3DDH Dylan Holloway 30.00 80.00
3DJQ Jack Quinn 25.00 60.00
3DJS Juraj Slafkovsky 100.00 250.00
3DKJ Kent Johnson 30.00 80.00
3DLR Lukas Reichel 30.00 80.00
3DMB Matt Boldy 50.00 125.00
3DMR Marco Rossi 40.00 100.00
3DOP Owen Power 30.00 80.00
3DSA Jake Sanderson 40.00 100.00
3DSW Shane Wright 40.00 100.00

2022-23 O-Pee-Chee Hall of Fame Logo Patches

HOF1 Jarome Iginla 10.00 25.00
HOF2 Peter Stastny 6.00 15.00
HOF3 Sergei Zubov 6.00 15.00
HOF4 Teemu Selanne 15.00 40.00
HOF5 Borje Salming 8.00 20.00
HOF6 Tony Esposito 8.00 20.00

2022-23 O-Pee-Chee O-Pee-Chee Platinum Previews

*RAINBOW: .5X TO 1.2X BASIC
*BLUE: .75 X TO 2X BASIC
*VIOLET: 1X TO 2.5X BASIC
*PINK: 1.2X TO 3X BASIC
*COSMIC: 2X TO 5X BASIC
*RED/60: 2.5X TO 6X BASIC
PAM Auston Matthews 3.00 8.00
PAO Alex Ovechkin 3.00 8.00
PCM Connor McDavid 4.00 10.00
PDG Dylan Guenther 2.00 5.00
PLD Leon Draisaitl 2.50 6.00
PMB Matt Boldy 2.50 6.00
PMR Marco Rossi 2.00 5.00
PSC Sidney Crosby 3.00 8.00

2022-23 O-Pee-Chee O-Pee-Chee Platinum Previews Seismic Gold

*GOLD/25: 8X TO 20X BASIC
PMB Matt Boldy 125.00 300.00

2022-23 O-Pee-Chee OPC Premier

P2 Alex DeBrincat 1.00 2.50
P3 Kirill Kaprizov 2.50 6.00
P4 Leon Draisaitl 2.50 6.00
P5 Ryan O'Reilly .75 2.00
P6 Alex Ovechkin 3.00 8.00
P7 Patrick Kane 1.50 4.00
P8 Nathan MacKinnon 3.00 8.00
P9 Sebastian Aho 1.25 3.00
P10 Jordan Eberle .75 2.00
P11 Cale Makar 2.00 5.00
P12 Brad Marchand 1.50 4.00
P13 Mitch Marner 1.25 3.00
P14 Andrei Svechnikov 1.00 2.50
P15 Jason Robertson 1.25 3.00
P16 Jack Hughes 2.00 5.00
P17 Artemi Panarin 1.50 4.00
P18 Andrei Vasilevskiy 1.25 3.00
P19 Aleksander Barkov 1.25 3.00
P20 Robert Thomas .75 2.00
P21 Quinn Hughes 2.00 5.00
P22 Jonathan Huberdeau 1.00 2.50
P23 Anze Kopitar 1.25 3.00
P24 Cole Caufield 1.50 4.00
P25 Brady Tkachuk 1.25 3.00
P26 Victor Hedman 1.00 2.50
P27 Tim Stutzle 1.00 2.50
P28 Max Pacioretty .75 2.00
P29 Matthew Tkachuk 1.50 4.00
P30 Nico Hischier 1.25 3.00
P31 Adam Fox 1.00 2.50
P32 Mark Scheifele 1.25 3.00
P33 Troy Terry .60 1.50
P34 Moritz Seider 1.00 2.50
P35 Michael Bunting .75 2.00
P36 Brayden Point 1.00 2.50
P37 Kyle Connor 1.25 3.00
P38 Chris Kreider 1.00 2.50
P39 William Karlsson 1.00 2.50
P40 Dylan Larkin 1.00 2.50
P41 Miro Heiskanen 1.00 2.50
P42 Nicklas Backstrom .75 2.00
P43 Anton Lundell .75 2.00
P44 Kris Letang 1.00 2.50
P45 Jack Eichel 1.25 3.00
P46 Nikita Kucherov 1.50 4.00
P47 John Tavares 1.25 3.00
P48 Nick Suzuki 1.50 4.00
P49 William Nylander 1.50 4.00
P50 Mikko Rantanen 2.00 5.00
P51 Jake Guentzel 1.25 3.00
P52 Nazem Kadri 1.00 2.50
P53 Brendan Gallagher .75 2.00
P54 Yanni Gourde .60 1.50
P55 Lucas Raymond 1.25 3.00
P56 Tom Wilson .75 2.00
P57 Jordan Kyrou .75 2.00
P58 Rasmus Dahlin 1.00 2.50
P59 Kevin Fiala .60 1.50
P60 Josh Norris .75 2.00
P61 Brent Burns .75 2.00
P62 Elias Lindholm .75 2.00
P63 Conor Garland .60 1.50
P64 Spencer Knight .75 2.00
P65 Elias Pettersson 1.25 3.00
P66 Connor McDavid 4.00 10.00
P67 David Pastrnak 2.00 5.00
P68 Sidney Crosby 3.00 8.00
P69 Mathew Barzal 1.00 2.50
P70 Logan Couture 1.00 2.50
P71 Taylor Hall .75 2.00
P72 Clayton Keller 1.00 2.50
P73 Tyler Seguin 1.00 2.50
P74 Ryan Nugent-Hopkins 1.00 2.50
P75 Jeremy Swayman 1.25 3.00
P76 Matt Boldy 2.50 6.00
P77 Jack Quinn 1.25 3.00
P78 Marco Rossi 2.00 5.00
P79 Samuel Fagemo .60 1.50
P80 Lukas Dostal 1.50 4.00
P81 Braden Schneider 1.25 3.00
P82 Brayden Tracey .60 1.50
P83 Jacob Perreault .75 2.00
P84 Matty Beniers 2.00 5.00
P85 Lukas Reichel 1.50 4.00
P86 Owen Power 1.50 4.00
P87 Dylan Holloway 1.50 4.00
P88 Nick Abruzzese .75 2.00
P89 Kent Johnson 1.50 4.00
P90 Thomas Bordeleau .75 2.00
P91 Noah Cates .75 2.00
P92 Shane Wright 2.00 5.00
P93 Juraj Slafkovsky 4.00 10.00
P94 Jake Sanderson 2.00 5.00
P95 Wyatt Johnston 3.00 8.00
P96 Dylan Guenther 2.00 5.00
P97 Kaiden Guhle 1.50 4.00
P98 Bobby Brink .75 2.00
P99 Brandt Clarke 1.50 4.00
P100 Andrei Kuzmenko 1.50 4.00

2022-23 O-Pee-Chee OPC Premier Rainbow

*RAINBOW: 3X TO 8X BASIC
P84 Matty Beniers 50.00 125.00
P93 Juraj Slafkovsky 40.00 100.00

2022-23 O-Pee-Chee Patches

P1 Doug Weight 8.00 20.00
P2 Vincent Lecavalier 8.00 20.00
P3 Trevor Linden 8.00 20.00
P4 Dave Taylor 6.00 15.00
P5 Kevin Lowe 8.00 20.00
P6 Steve Yzerman 12.00 30.00
P7 Cam Neely 8.00 20.00
P8 Butch Goring 8.00 20.00
P9 Rod Gilbert 8.00 20.00
P10 Serge Savard 8.00 20.00
P11 Nathan MacKinnon 10.00 25.00
P12 Wayne Gretzky 25.00 60.00
P13 Chris Chelios 8.00 20.00
P14 Paul Coffey 8.00 20.00
P15 Cam Neely 8.00 20.00
P16 Michael Peca 8.00 20.00
P17 Jaroslav Halak 8.00 20.00
P18 Grant Fuhr 12.00 30.00
P19 Billy Smith 8.00 20.00
P20 Bob Sauve 8.00 20.00
P21 Patrick Roy 15.00 40.00
P22 Connor McDavid 20.00 50.00
P23 Sidney Crosby 15.00 40.00
P24 Evgeni Malkin 12.00 30.00
P25 Alex Ovechkin 12.00 30.00
P26 Guy Lafleur 10.00 25.00
P27 Marcel Dionne 10.00 25.00
P28 Bryan Trottier 8.00 20.00
P29 Phil Esposito 12.00 30.00
P30 Jean Beliveau 8.00 20.00
P31 Ted Lindsay 8.00 20.00
P32 Jaccob Slavin 6.00 15.00
P33 Martin St. Louis 8.00 20.00
P34 Mike Bossy 8.00 20.00
P35 Jean Ratelle 6.00 15.00
P36 Rick Middleton 8.00 20.00
P37 Andrei Vasilevskiy 12.00 30.00
P38 Scott Niedermayer 8.00 20.00
P39 Joe Sakic 8.00 20.00
P40 Glenn Hall 8.00 20.00
P41 Ron Hextall 8.00 20.00
P42 Mario Lemieux 15.00 40.00
P43 Billy Smith 8.00 20.00
P44 Guy Lafleur 10.00 25.00
P45 Adam Fox 10.00 25.00
P46 Al MacInnis 10.00 25.00
P47 Chris Chelios 8.00 20.00
P48 Rod Langway 8.00 20.00
P49 Rob Blake 8.00 20.00
P50 Kirill Kaprizov 15.00 40.00
P51 Jonathan Huberdeau 10.00 25.00
P52 Jeff Skinner 8.00 20.00
P53 Joe Nieuwendyk 6.00 15.00
P54 Steve Larmer 6.00 15.00
P55 Marc-Andre Fleury 15.00 40.00
P56 Ed Belfour 8.00 20.00
P57 Ron Hextall 8.00 20.00
P58 John Vanbiesbrouck 8.00 20.00
P59 Billy Smith 8.00 20.00
P60 Denis Herron 6.00 15.00
P61 Bob Sauve 8.00 20.00
P62 Bernie Parent 10.00 25.00
P63 Ed Giacomin 8.00 20.00
P64 Glenn Hall 8.00 20.00
P65 Connor McDavid 20.00 50.00
P66 Corey Perry 12.00 30.00
P67 Joe Thornton 12.00 30.00
P68 Chris Pronger 8.00 20.00
P69 Brett Hull 8.00 20.00
P70 Andrei Vasilevskiy 12.00 30.00
P71 Evgeni Malkin 12.00 30.00
P72 Scott Niedermayer 8.00 20.00
P73 Brendan Shanahan 8.00 20.00
P74 Nicklas Lidstrom 8.00 20.00
P75 Patrick Kane 15.00 40.00
P76 Mark Recchi 8.00 20.00
P77 Jari Kurri 8.00 20.00
P78 Mike Bossy 8.00 20.00
P79 Guy Lafleur 10.00 25.00
P80 Aleksander Barkov 12.00 30.00

2022-23 O-Pee-Chee Playing Cards

JOKER Wild Wing 4.00 10.00
JOKER Bailey 4.00 10.00
2CLUBS Joel Farabee 1.50 4.00
3CLUBS Matty Beniers 4.00 10.00
4CLUBS Ryan O'Reilly 1.50 4.00
5CLUBS Jason Robertson 2.50 6.00
6CLUBS Brady Tkachuk 2.50 6.00
7CLUBS Jordan Eberle 1.50 4.00
8CLUBS Artemi Panarin 3.00 8.00
9CLUBS Tristan Jarry 1.50 4.00
JCLUBS Chris Kreider 2.00 5.00
KCLUBS Nathan MacKinnon 6.00 15.00
QCLUBS Brad Marchand 3.00 8.00
10CLUBS Matt Boldy 5.00 12.00
2HEARTS Tanner Jeannot 1.00 2.50
2SPADES Clayton Keller 2.00 5.00
3HEARTS Alex DeBrincat 2.00 5.00
3SPADES Dylan Larkin 2.00 5.00
4HEARTS Patrik Laine 2.00 5.00
4SPADES Roman Josi 1.50 4.00
5HEARTS Nick Suzuki 3.00 8.00
5SPADES Brent Burns 1.50 4.00
6HEARTS Elias Pettersson 2.50 6.00
6SPADES Mathew Barzal 2.00 5.00
7HEARTS Taylor Hall 1.50 4.00
7SPADES Mitch Marner 2.50 6.00
8HEARTS Jonathan Huberdeau 2.00 5.00
8SPADES Kyle Connor 2.50 6.00
9HEARTS Igor Shesterkin 3.00 8.00
9SPADES Owen Power 3.00 8.00
JHEARTS Jack Eichel 2.50 6.00
JSPADES Steven Stamkos 3.00 8.00
KHEARTS Patrick Kane 3.00 8.00
KSPADES Leon Draisaitl 5.00 12.00
QHEARTS Quinn Hughes 4.00 10.00
QSPADES Kirill Kaprizov 5.00 12.00
10DIAMONDS Lucas Raymond 2.50 6.00
10HEARTS Moritz Seider 2.00 5.00
10SPADES Trevor Zegras 1.50 4.00
2DIAMONDS Jack Quinn 2.50 6.00
3DIAMONDS Michael Bunting 1.50 4.00
4DIAMONDS Cole Caufield 3.00 8.00
5DIAMONDS Johnny Gaudreau 2.50 6.00
6DIAMONDS Jordan Kyrou 1.50 4.00
7DIAMONDS Anze Kopitar 2.50 6.00
8DIAMONDS Jack Hughes 4.00 10.00
9DIAMONDS Darcy Kuemper 1.50 4.00
ACECLUBS Sidney Crosby 6.00 15.00
ACEDIAMONDS Alex Ovechkin 6.00 15.00
ACEHEARTS Auston Matthews 6.00 15.00
ACESPADES Connor McDavid 8.00 20.00
JDIAMONDS Andrei Vasilevskiy 2.50 6.00
KDIAMONDS Cale Makar 4.00 10.00
QDIAMONDS Sebastian Aho 2.50 6.00

2022-23 O-Pee-Chee Retro

1 Trevor Zegras .40 1.00
2 Alex DeBrincat .50 1.25
3 Kirill Kaprizov 1.25 3.00
4 Leon Draisaitl 1.25 3.00
5 Michael Bunting .40 1.00
6 Nazem Kadri .50 1.25
7 David Pastrnak 1.00 2.50
8 Alex Ovechkin 1.50 4.00
9 Tyler Toffoli .40 1.00
10 Jake Guentzel .60 1.50
11 Steven Stamkos .75 2.00
12 Jordan Kyrou .40 1.00
13 Anton Lundell .40 1.00
14 Sebastian Aho .60 1.50
15 Brad Marchand .75 2.00
16 Igor Shesterkin .75 2.00
17 Nathan MacKinnon 1.50 4.00
18 Patrick Kane .75 2.00
19 Anze Kopitar .60 1.50
20 Elias Pettersson .60 1.50
21 Brent Burns .40 1.00
22 Brendan Gallagher .40 1.00
23 Jordan Eberle .40 1.00
24 Jack Hughes 1.00 2.50
25 Joel Farabee .40 1.00
26 Clayton Keller .50 1.25
27 Ryan Johansen .30 .75
28 Moritz Seider .50 1.25
29 Cale Makar 1.00 2.50
30 Jean-Gabriel Pageau .25 .60
31 Mark Scheifele .60 1.50
32 Alexander Wennberg .25 .60
33 Mats Zuccarello .40 1.00
34 Auston Matthews 1.50 4.00
35 Andrei Svechnikov .50 1.25
36 Patrik Laine .50 1.25
37 Alexis Lafreniere .60 1.50
38 Nico Hischier .60 1.50
39 Andrei Vasilevskiy .60 1.50
40 Tanner Jeannot .25 .60
41 Jonathan Marchessault .50 1.25
42 Logan Couture .50 1.25
43 Taylor Hall .40 1.00
44 Conor Garland .30 .75
45 Spencer Knight .40 1.00
46 Travis Konecny .40 1.00
47 Pierre-Luc Dubois .30 .75
48 Joe Pavelski .50 1.25
49 Brock Nelson .40 1.00
50 Peyton Krebs .30 .75
51 Ilya Sorokin .60 1.50
52 Mark Stone .50 1.25
53 Philipp Grubauer .40 1.00
54 Petr Mrazek .30 .75
55 Tyler Bertuzzi .30 .75
56 John Tavares .60 1.50
57 Ryan Hartman .25 .60
58 John Carlson .40 1.00
59 Alex Tuch .40 1.00
60 Mike Hoffman .25 .60
61 Jaccob Slavin .30 .75
62 Tim Stutzle .50 1.25
63 Darnell Nurse .30 .75
64 Kyle Connor .60 1.50
65 Artemi Panarin .75 2.00
66 Ivan Provorov .30 .75
67 Jonathan Huberdeau .50 1.25
68 Quinton Byfield .50 1.25
69 Seth Jones .40 1.00
70 Dougie Hamilton .30 .75
71 Matt Duchene .40 1.00
72 Chandler Stephenson .30 .75
73 Jeff Skinner .40 1.00
74 Tomas Hertl .40 1.00
75 Miro Heiskanen .50 1.25
76 Quinn Hughes 1.00 2.50
77 Jamie Drysdale .30 .75
78 Elias Lindholm .40 1.00
79 Drew Doughty .50 1.25
80 Dylan Larkin .50 1.25
81 Troy Terry .30 .75
82 Torey Krug .30 .75
83 Shayne Gostisbehere .40 1.00
84 Nikita Kucherov .75 2.00
85 Jakub Voracek .30 .75
86 Johnny Gaudreau .60 1.50
87 Sidney Crosby 1.50 4.00
88 Jason Robertson .60 1.50
89 Vladimir Tarasenko .50 1.25
90 Zach Werenski .60 1.50
91 Josh Anderson .30 .75
92 Claude Giroux .40 1.00
93 Vasily Podkolzin .25 .60
94 Kasperi Kapanen .30 .75
95 Alex Newhook .30 .75
96 Sam Reinhart .75 2.00
97 Connor McDavid 2.00 5.00
98 Tom Wilson .40 1.00
99 Adrian Kempe .40 1.00
100 Checklist .25 .60
101 Mitch Marner .60 1.50
102 Noah Dobson .50 1.25
103 Brandon Hagel .30 .75
104 Oliver Wahlstrom .25 .60
105 Dylan Cozens .40 1.00
106 Tomas Tatar .25 .60
107 Oliver Bjorkstrand .30 .75
108 Brock Boeser .50 1.25
109 Jack Eichel .60 1.50
110 Drake Batherson .40 1.00
111 Adam Fox .50 1.25
112 Morgan Rielly .40 1.00
113 Charlie McAvoy .50 1.25
114 T.J. Oshie .40 1.00
115 Zach Hyman .60 1.50
116 Seth Jarvis .50 1.25
117 Gabriel Landeskog .50 1.25
118 Filip Forsberg .60 1.50
119 Isac Lundestrom .25 .60
120 Nikolaj Ehlers .40 1.00
121 Phillip Danault .40 1.00
122 Nick Suzuki .75 2.00
123 Alex Killorn .25 .60
124 Noah Hanifin .40 1.00
125 Jamie Benn .40 1.00
126 William Karlsson .50 1.25
127 Mathew Barzal .50 1.25
128 John Gibson .40 1.00
129 Evgeny Kuznetsov .50 1.25
130 Dylan Strome .50 1.25
131 Alexander Barabanov .25 .60
132 Tage Thompson .50 1.25
133 Ryan O'Reilly .40 1.00
134 Victor Hedman .50 1.25
135 Tristan Jarry .40 1.00
136 Boone Jenner .40 1.00
137 Sonny Milano .30 .75
138 Blake Wheeler .40 1.00
139 William Nylander .75 2.00
140 Matthew Tkachuk .75 2.00
141 Dawson Mercer .50 1.25
142 Chris Kreider .50 1.25
143 Ryan Nugent-Hopkins .50 1.25
144 Cole Caufield .75 2.00
145 Phil Kessel .40 1.00
146 Patrice Bergeron .50 1.25
147 Elvis Merzlikins .40 1.00

148 Josh Norris .40 1.00
149 Jordan Staal .30 .75
150 Connor Hellebuyck .75 2.00
151 Alex Iafallo .25 .60
152 Roman Josi .40 1.00
153 Jacob Markstrom .40 1.00
154 Erik Karlsson .50 1.25
155 Jonathan Toews .60 1.50
156 Robert Thomas .40 1.00
157 Yegor Sharangovich .40 1.00
158 Aleksander Barkov .60 1.50
159 Tanner Pearson .40 1.00
160 Jeremy Swayman .60 1.50
161 Nicklas Backstrom .40 1.00
162 Sean Couturier .30 .75
163 Samuel Girard .25 .60
164 Brayden Point .50 1.25
165 Alex Nedeljkovic .30 .75
166 Mika Zibanejad .50 1.25
167 Tyler Seguin .50 1.25
168 Jared McCann .30 .75
169 Lucas Raymond .60 1.50
170 Joel Eriksson Ek .30 .75
171 Viktor Arvidsson .25 .60
172 Jason Zucker .40 1.00
173 Rasmus Dahlin .50 1.25
174 Thomas Chabot .40 1.00
175 Aaron Ekblad .50 1.25
176 David Perron .30 .75
177 Juuse Saros .50 1.25
178 John Marino .40 1.00
179 Mikko Rantanen 1.00 2.50
180 Nick Schmaltz .30 .75
181 Kevin Fiala .30 .75
182 Anders Lee .30 .75
183 Max Pacioretty .40 1.00
184 Teuvo Teravainen .40 1.00
185 J.T. Miller .50 1.25
186 Tyson Barrie .25 .60
187 Connor Brown .30 .75
188 Yanni Gourde .30 .75
189 Roope Hintz .50 1.25
190 Cam Atkinson .40 1.00
191 Sergei Bobrovsky .60 1.50
192 Jared Spurgeon .40 1.00
193 Timo Meier .40 1.00
194 Filip Hronek .25 .60
195 Brady Tkachuk .60 1.50
196 Bo Horvat .50 1.25
197 T.J. Brodie .25 .60
198 Carey Price .75 2.00
199 Anthony Cirelli .30 .75
200 Checklist .25 .60
201 Jesse Puljujarvi .40 1.00
202 Jamie Oleksiak .30 .75
203 Barclay Goodrow .25 .60
204 Martin Necas .60 1.50
205 Carter Verhaeghe .40 1.00
206 Robby Fabbri .25 .60
207 Justin Holl .25 .60
208 Radek Faksa .30 .75
209 Kirby Dach .40 1.00
210 Andrew Copp .30 .75
211 Gustav Nyquist .25 .60
212 Shea Theodore .50 1.25
213 Jesper Bratt .40 1.00
214 Jordan Binnington .60 1.50
215 Colin White .30 .75
216 Bowen Byram .50 1.25
217 Jonathan Dahlen .25 .60
218 Arturri Lehkonen .30 .75
219 Frederick Gaudreau .25 .60
220 Brian Dumoulin .25 .60
221 Sean Monahan .25 .60
222 Connor McMichael .40 1.00
223 Jesperi Kotkaniemi .40 1.00
224 Kyle Palmieri .30 .75
225 Jeff Petry .40 1.00
226 Evan Bouchard .50 1.25
227 Cam Fowler .40 1.00
228 Philip Tomasino .50 1.25
229 Nick Bonino .25 .60
230 Nils Hoglander .25 .60
231 Kevin Lankinen .40 1.00
232 Taylor Raddysh .30 .75
233 Filip Chytil .30 .75
234 Rudolfs Balcers .25 .60
235 Anthony Duclair .30 .75
236 Neal Pionk .25 .60
237 Adam Erne .25 .60
238 Brandon Saad .30 .75
239 John Klingberg .40 1.00
240 Artem Zub .25 .60
241 Alex Pietrangelo .30 .75
242 Jonathan Drouin .30 .75
243 Alex Turcotte .25 .60
244 Jake DeBrusk .40 1.00
245 Damon Severson .25 .60
246 Jonas Brodin .25 .60
247 Dmitry Gurianov .50 1.25
248 David Kampf .25 .60
249 Maxime Comtois .30 .75
250 Mikael Granlund .30 .75
251 Marcus Pettersson .25 .60
252 Sean Kuraly .25 .60
253 Mark Giordano .40 1.00
254 Ryan Ellis .25 .60
255 Josh Bailey .30 .75
256 Anthony Mantha .30 .75
257 Andrew Mangiapane .40 1.00
258 Calle Jarnkrok .25 .60
259 Gabe Vilardi .40 1.00
260 Dominik Kubalik .40 1.00
261 Oliver Ekman-Larsson .25 .60
262 Kyle Okposo .25 .60
263 Cole Perfetti .40 1.00
264 Matt Nieto .30 .75
265 Shane Pinto .30 .75
266 Andreas Johnsson .30 .75
267 Conor Sheary .40 1.00
268 Ryan Reaves .30 .75
269 Jack Campbell .40 1.00
270 Carter Hart .40 1.00
271 Christian Dvorak .30 .75
272 Devon Toews .30 .75
273 Brady Skjei .25 .60
274 Casey Mittelstadt .40 1.00
275 Erik Cernak .25 .60
276 Pius Suter .30 .75
277 Hampus Lindholm .30 .75
278 Evgenii Dadonov .25 .60
279 Duncan Keith .30 .75
280 Nick Ritchie .25 .60
281 Kevin Shattenkirk .25 .60
282 Anthony Beauvillier .25 .60
283 Brandon Duhaime .25 .60
284 Trevor Moore .25 .60
285 Alex Kerfoot .30 .75
286 Sam Bennett .60 1.50
287 Teddy Blueger .25 .60
288 Rickard Rakell .30 .75
289 J.T. Compher .25 .60
290 Jacob Peterson .25 .60
291 Matt Grzelcyk .30 .75
292 Justin Faulk .30 .75
293 Blake Coleman .30 .75
294 Colton Sissons .25 .60
295 Victor Olofsson .40 1.00
296 Alexandre Texier .25 .60
297 P.K. Subban .50 1.25
298 Andrew Ladd .30 .75
299 Pavel Francouz .30 .75
300 Checklist .25 .60
301 Victor Soderstrom .25 .60
302 Mario Ferraro .25 .60
303 Nino Niederreiter .25 .60
304 Josh Morrissey .50 1.25
305 Alex Formenton .40 1.00
306 Adam Henrique .30 .75
307 Jake Evans .25 .60
308 Joonas Donskoi .25 .60
309 Scott Mayfield .25 .60
310 William Carrier .25 .60
311 Joe Veleno .30 .75
312 Calen Addison .50 1.25
313 Tyler Myers .25 .60
314 Mike Matheson .25 .60
315 Vladislav Gavrikov .25 .60
316 Kailer Yamamoto .40 1.00
317 Dmitry Orlov .40 1.00
318 Pavel Zacha .30 .75
319 Bryan Rust .40 1.00
320 Colton Parayko .30 .75
321 Jacob Trouba .30 .75
322 Ryan Suter .30 .75
323 Jasper Weatherby .25 .60
324 Marc-Andre Fleury .75 2.00
325 Jesper Fast .25 .60
326 Rasmus Asplund .25 .60
327 William Eklund .50 1.25
328 Eeli Tolvanen .40 1.00
329 Erik Johnson .25 .60
330 Christopher Tanev .25 .60
331 Pierre Engvall .25 .60
332 Keith Yandle .25 .60
333 Arthur Kaliyev .40 1.00
334 Jake Allen .40 1.00
335 Brandon Carlo .30 .75
336 Ryan Strome .40 1.00
337 Brock McGinn .25 .60
338 Tony DeAngelo .25 .60
339 Ondrej Palat .30 .75
340 Pierre-Edouard Bellemare .25 .60
341 Joe Thornton .60 1.50
342 Garnet Hathaway .30 .75
343 Darcy Kuemper .40 1.00
344 Adam Pelech .25 .60
345 Rasmus Andersson .30 .75
346 Vince Dunn .30 .75
347 Ryan Graves .25 .60
348 Filip Zadina .30 .75
349 Robin Lehner .30 .75
350 Ryan Lindgren .25 .60
351 Victor Mete .30 .75
352 Mattias Ekholm .30 .75
353 Henri Jokiharju .30 .75
354 Cole Sillinger .30 .75
355 Thatcher Demko .50 1.25
356 Derek Grant .25 .60
357 Ivan Barbashev .30 .75
358 Cal Petersen .25 .60
359 Ryan McDonagh .25 .60
360 Jake McCabe .25 .60
361 Craig Smith .25 .60
362 Dylan DeMelo .25 .60
363 Warren Foegele .25 .60
364 Evan Rodrigues .30 .75
365 Travis Sanheim .30 .75
366 Ondrej Kase .25 .60
367 Ty Smith .40 1.00
368 Dmitry Kulikov .25 .60
369 Evgeni Malkin .75 2.00
370 MacKenzie Weegar .30 .75
371 Lawson Crouse .30 .75
372 Matt Roy .25 .60
373 K'Andre Miller .30 .75
374 Luke Schenn .40 1.00
375 Casey Cizikas .30 .75
376 Logan O'Connor .40 1.00
377 Michael Amadio .25 .60
378 Dante Fabbro .25 .60
379 Parker Kelly .25 .60
380 Karel Vejmelka .25 .60
381 Brayden Schenn .40 1.00
382 Oliver Kylington .25 .60
383 Vincent Trocheck .40 1.00
384 Mikhail Sergachev .30 .75
385 Michael Rasmussen .25 .60
386 Jake Bean .30 .75
387 Jaden Schwartz .30 .75
388 Brandon Montour .50 1.25
389 Ilya Samsonov .40 1.00
390 Reilly Smith .40 1.00
391 Jake Oettinger .60 1.50
392 Oskar Lindblom .30 .75
393 MacKenzie Entwistle .25 .60
394 Cody Ceci .25 .60
395 Jakob Silfverberg .25 .60
396 Zemgus Girgensons .40 1.00
397 Erik Haula .25 .60
398 Matt Dumba .25 .60
399 Nate Schmidt .25 .60
400 Checklist .25 .60
401 Max Domi .40 1.00
402 Nils Lundkvist .25 .60
403 Sam Carrick .25 .60
404 Nico Daws .30 .75
405 Kyle Burroughs .25 .60
406 Mattias Samuelsson .25 .60
407 Braden Holtby .50 1.25
408 Pavel Buchnevich .30 .75
409 Corey Perry .60 1.50
410 Matt Murray .40 1.00
411 Connor Murphy .30 .75
412 Jordan Oesterle .25 .60
413 Danton Heinen .25 .60
414 Jordan Greenway .25 .60
415 Yegor Chinakhov .30 .75
416 Derek Ryan .25 .60
417 Brenden Dillon .25 .60
418 David Savard .25 .60
419 Rasmus Kupari .25 .60
420 Mackenzie Blackwood .40 1.00
421 Adin Hill .40 1.00
422 Marcus Foligno .30 .75
423 Frederik Andersen .50 1.25
424 Vitek Vanecek .40 1.00
425 Anders Bjork .25 .60
426 Dan Vladar .30 .75
427 Filip Gustavsson .40 1.00
428 Gustav Forsling .40 1.00
429 Scott Perunovich .25 .60
430 Jack Roslovic .25 .60
431 Alexandre Carrier .25 .60
432 Zach Whitecloud .25 .60
433 Linus Ullmark .40 1.00
434 Brandon Tanev .25 .60
435 Scott Laughton .25 .60
436 Wayne Simmonds .40 1.00
437 Michael McCarron .40 1.00
438 Jeff Carter .30 .75
439 Adam Larsson .40 1.00
440 Matthew Highmore .30 .75
441 Sammy Blais .30 .75
442 Patric Hornqvist .25 .60
443 Trevor van Riemsdyk .30 .75
444 Ethan Bear .25 .60
445 James Reimer .25 .60
446 Ross Colton .30 .75
447 Derek Forbort .25 .60
448 Marco Scandella .30 .75
449 Sam Steel .30 .75
450 Logan Stanley .25 .60
451 Dillon Dube .25 .60
452 Jonas Siegenthaler .25 .60
453 Mike Smith .25 .60
454 Lassi Thomson .25 .60
455 Joel Edmundson .25 .60
456 Adam Boqvist .25 .60
457 Dylan Coghlan .25 .60
458 Caleb Jones .25 .60
459 Nick Leddy .25 .60
460 Luke Kunin .25 .60
461 James van Riemsdyk .30 .75
462 Noah Gregor .25 .60
463 Robin Salo .25 .60
464 Morgan Geekie .25 .60
465 Zdeno Chara .40 1.00
466 Nic Dowd .25 .60
467 Alexander Romanov .30 .75
468 Kole Lind .25 .60
469 Andre Burakovsky .25 .60
470 Kris Letang .50 1.25
471 Tobias Bjornfot .25 .60
472 Niko Mikkola .25 .60
473 Spencer Martin .25 .60
474 Cam Talbot .40 1.00
475 Patrick Maroon .25 .60
476 Givani Smith .25 .60
477 Zac Jones .25 .60
478 Jakob Chychrun .40 1.00
479 Yakov Trenin .30 .75
480 Eric Robinson .25 .60
481 Nicolas Roy .25 .60
482 Mike Reilly .25 .60
483 Antti Raanta .40 1.00
484 Semyon Varlamov .40 1.00
485 Zack Kassian .25 .60
486 Milan Lucic .30 .75
487 Kevin Hayes .30 .75
488 Josh Mahura .25 .60
489 Esa Lindell .30 .75
490 Ryan Poehling .40 1.00
491 Jakub Vrana .30 .75
492 Adam Lowry .30 .75
493 Joel Kiviranta .25 .60
494 Mason Appleton .25 .60
495 Sean Durzi .25 .60
496 Philipp Kurashev .25 .60
497 Janis Moser .25 .60
498 Carson Soucy .25 .60
499 Aliaksei Protas .25 .60
500 Checklist .25 .60
501 Connor McDavid AS 3.00 8.00
502 Auston Matthews AS 2.50 6.00
503 Jordan Kyrou AS .60 1.50
504 Leon Draisaitl AS 2.00 5.00
505 Troy Terry AS .50 1.25
506 Claude Giroux AS .60 1.50
507 Jake Guentzel AS 1.00 2.50
508 Jonathan Huberdeau AS .75 2.00
509 Dylan Larkin AS .75 2.00
510 Jack Hughes AS 1.50 4.00
511 Tristan Jarry AS .60 1.50
512 Nick Suzuki AS 1.25 3.00
513 Brady Tkachuk AS 1.00 2.50
514 Steven Stamkos AS 1.25 3.00
515 Victor Hedman AS .75 2.00
516 Patrice Bergeron AS .75 2.00
517 Kyle Connor AS 1.00 2.50
518 Kirill Kaprizov AS 2.00 5.00
519 Alex DeBrincat AS .75 2.00
520 Nazem Kadri AS .75 2.00
521 Clayton Keller AS .75 2.00
522 Andrei Vasilevskiy AS 1.00 2.50
523 Rasmus Dahlin AS .75 2.00
524 Johnny Gaudreau AS 1.00 2.50
525 Jordan Eberle AS .60 1.50
526 Sebastian Aho AS 1.00 2.50
527 Thatcher Demko AS .75 2.00
528 Mark Stone AS .75 2.00
529 Cam Talbot AS .60 1.50
530 Roman Josi AS .60 1.50
531 Joe Pavelski AS .75 2.00
532 Evgeny Kuznetsov AS .75 2.00
533 Adam Pelech AS .40 1.00
534 Tom Wilson AS .60 1.50
535 Zach Werenski AS 1.00 2.50
536 Adrian Kempe AS .60 1.50
537 Timo Meier AS .60 1.50
538 Jonathan Marchessault AS .75 2.00
539 Chris Kreider AS .75 2.00
540 Cale Makar AS 1.50 4.00
541 Matt Boldy 8.00 20.00
542 Jack Quinn 4.00 10.00
543 Lukas Reichel 5.00 12.00
544 Marco Rossi 6.00 15.00
545 Jacob Perreault 2.50 6.00
546 Samuel Fagemo 2.00 5.00
547 Braden Schneider 4.00 10.00
548 Brayden Tracey 2.00 5.00
549 Dylan Samberg 2.50 6.00
550 Vladislav Kolyachonok 2.00 5.00
551 Trey Fix-Wolansky 2.50 6.00
552 Isaac Ratcliffe 2.50 6.00
553 Kaedan Korczak 2.00 5.00
554 Lukas Dostal 5.00 12.00
555 Matias Maccelli 4.00 10.00
556 Jordan Spence 2.50 6.00
557 Erik Kallgren 2.50 6.00
558 Alex Vlasic 2.00 5.00
559 Noah Cates 2.50 6.00
560 Marc McLaughlin 2.50 6.00
561 Ronnie Attard 2.50 6.00
562 Jordan Harris 3.00 8.00
563 Mads Sogaard 3.00 8.00
564 Nick Abruzzese 2.50 6.00
565 Filip Hallander 2.50 6.00
566 Owen Power 5.00 12.00
567 Kent Johnson 5.00 12.00
568 Matty Beniers 6.00 15.00
569 Bobby Brink 2.50 6.00
570 Thomas Bordeleau 2.50 6.00
571 Reilly Walsh 2.50 6.00
572 Dylan Holloway 5.00 12.00
573 Pyotr Kochetkov 5.00 12.00
574 Jack McBain 2.50 6.00
575 Jake Christiansen 2.50 6.00
576 Jake Sanderson 6.00 15.00
577 Jakub Lauko 3.00 8.00
578 Arber Xhekaj 5.00 12.00
579 Andrei Kuzmenko 5.00 12.00
580 Pavol Regenda 2.50 6.00
581 Filip Roos 2.00 5.00
582 Cole Koepke 2.50 6.00
583 Elmer Soderblom 5.00 12.00
584 Nils Aman 2.50 6.00
585 Hunter Drew 2.50 6.00
586 Kaiden Guhle 5.00 12.00
587 Michael Eyssimont 2.50 6.00
588 Fredrik Karlstrom 2.00 5.00
589 Valtteri Puustinen 2.00 5.00
590 Chase Pearson 2.00 5.00
591 Mark Kastelic 2.00 5.00
592 Zack Hayes 2.00 5.00
593 Nathan Smith 2.00 5.00
594 David Jiricek 5.00 12.00
595 Dylan Guenther 6.00 15.00
596 Nikita Okhotiuk 2.00 5.00
597 Wyatt Johnston 10.00 25.00
598 Brandt Clarke 5.00 12.00
599 Juraj Slafkovsky 12.00 30.00
600 Shane Wright 6.00 15.00

2022-23 O-Pee-Chee Retro Black

*RETRO/AS: 1.2 X TO 3X BASIC
*RETRO RC: .75X TO 2X BASIC
501 Connor McDavid AS 20.00 50.00
512 Nick Suzuki AS 10.00 25.00
541 Matt Boldy 30.00 80.00
568 Matty Beniers 40.00 100.00
599 Juraj Slafkovsky 50.00 125.00
600 Shane Wright 25.00 60.00

2022-23 O-Pee-Chee Team Logo Patches

351 Florida Panthers 80.00 200.00
352 Arizona Coyotes 80.00 200.00
353 Heritage Classic 80.00 200.00
354 Stanley Cup 80.00 200.00
355 Stadium Series 80.00 200.00
356 Minnesota Wild 80.00 200.00
357 St. Louis Blues 80.00 200.00
358 Vegas Golden Knights 80.00 200.00
359 Buffalo Sabres 80.00 200.00
360 Washington Capitals 80.00 200.00
361 Los Angeles Kings 80.00 200.00
362 Winnipeg Jets 80.00 200.00
363 Vancouver Canucks 80.00 200.00
364 Anaheim Ducks 80.00 200.00

2022-23 O-Pee-Chee Top Rookie Bounty Puzzle

OPC1 Redemption Card 6.00 15.00
OPC2 Redemption Card 6.00 15.00
OPC3 Redemption Card 6.00 15.00
OPC4 Redemption Card 6.00 15.00
OPC5 Redemption Card 6.00 15.00
OPC6 Redemption Card 6.00 15.00
OPC7 Redemption Card 6.00 15.00
OPC8 Redemption Card 6.00 15.00
OPC9 Redemption Card 6.00 15.00

2023-24 O-Pee-Chee

1 Connor McDavid 1.25 3.00
2 Cale Makar .60 1.50
3 Sebastian Aho .40 1.00
4 Matthew Tkachuk .50 1.25
5 Johnny Gaudreau .40 1.00
6 Jack Hughes .60 1.50
7 Mitch Marner .40 1.00
8 Alex Ovechkin 1.00 2.50
9 Nathan MacKinnon 1.00 2.50
10 Steven Stamkos .50 1.25
11 Leon Draisaitl .75 2.00
12 Mason McTavish .25 .60
13 Joe Pavelski .30 .75
14 Cole Caufield .50 1.25
15 Jonathan Toews .40 1.00
16 Marc-Andre Fleury .50 1.25
17 Brad Marchand .50 1.25
18 Nick Suzuki .50 1.25
19 Clayton Keller .30 .75
20 Aleksander Barkov .40 1.00
21 Vitek Vanecek .25 .60
22 Robert Thomas .25 .60
23 Spencer Knight .25 .60
24 Alexis Lafreniere .40 1.00
25 Elias Lindholm .25 .60
26 Owen Tippett .25 .60
27 Andrei Kuzmenko .25 .60
28 Ryan Nugent-Hopkins .30 .75
29 Kris Letang .30 .75
30 Matias Maccelli .20 .50
31 J.T. Compher .15 .40
32 Max Domi .25 .60
33 Noah Cates .15 .40
34 Dylan Strome .30 .75
35 Filip Forsberg .40 1.00
36 Mats Zuccarello .25 .60
37 Nicklas Backstrom .25 .60
38 Bo Horvat .30 .75
39 Reilly Smith .25 .60
40 Matty Beniers .30 .75
41 Jack Roslovic .15 .40
42 Juraj Slafkovsky .50 1.25
43 John Gibson .25 .60
44 Dylan Larkin .30 .75
45 Kevin Hayes .20 .50
46 Jack Quinn .20 .50
47 Andre Burakovsky .15 .40
48 Quinn Hughes .60 1.50
49 Alex Newhook .20 .50
50 Jack Campbell .25 .60
51 Ville Husso .15 .40
52 J.T. Miller .30 .75
53 Ilya Sorokin .40 1.00
54 Jake Guentzel .40 1.00
55 Dawson Mercer .30 .75
56 Karel Vejmelka .15 .40
57 Martin Necas .40 1.00
58 Jeremy Swayman .40 1.00
59 Alex Pietrangelo .30 .75
60 Max Pacioretty .25 .60
61 Alex Tuch .25 .60
62 Seth Jones .25 .60
63 Pyotr Kochetkov .25 .60
64 Mikael Backlund .20 .50
65 Brandon Hagel .20 .50
66 Jake Sanderson .30 .75
67 Chris Kreider .30 .75
68 Kaiden Guhle .25 .60
69 Ryan O'Reilly .25 .60
70 William Eklund .30 .75
71 Patrice Bergeron .30 .75
72 Cam Fowler .25 .60
73 Nikolaj Ehlers .25 .60
74 Dougie Hamilton .25 .60
75 Jacob Markstrom .25 .60
76 Josh Morrissey .30 .75
77 Shane Wright .30 .75
78 Jeff Skinner .25 .60
79 Tomas Hertl .25 .60
80 Victor Hedman .30 .75
81 Kyle Connor .40 1.00
82 Kevin Fiala .20 .50
83 Jordan Binnington .40 1.00
84 Moritz Seider .30 .75
85 Owen Power .25 .60
86 Jake Oettinger .40 1.00
87 Matt Duchene .25 .60
88 Miro Heiskanen .30 .75
89 Andrei Vasilevskiy .40 1.00
90 Kirby Dach .25 .60
91 Dylan Guenther .25 .60
92 Kirill Marchenko .30 .75
93 Cole Perfetti .25 .60
94 Mark Scheifele .40 1.00
95 Colton Parayko .20 .50
96 Matt Boldy .40 1.00
97 Michael Bunting .25 .60
98 Lucas Raymond .40 1.00
99 Scott Laughton .15 .40
100 Checklist .15 .40
101 Auston Matthews 1.00 2.50
102 Trevor Zegras .25 .60
103 David Pastrnak .60 1.50
104 Jason Robertson .40 1.00
105 Sidney Crosby 1.00 2.50
106 Kirill Kaprizov .75 2.00
107 Adam Fox .40 1.00
108 Elias Pettersson .40 1.00
109 Jack Eichel .40 1.00
110 Evgeni Malkin .50 1.25
111 Anze Kopitar .40 1.00
112 Artemi Panarin .50 1.25
113 Mikko Rantanen .60 1.50
114 Andrei Svechnikov .40 1.00
115 Marco Rossi .20 .50
116 Jonatan Berggren .20 .50
117 Roope Hintz .30 .75
118 Tyler Seguin .30 .75
119 Blake Coleman .20 .50
120 Yegor Sharangovich .20 .50
121 Jonathan Huberdeau .30 .75
122 Jesper Bratt .25 .60
123 Aaron Ekblad .25 .60
124 Adrian Kempe .25 .60
125 Seth Jarvis .30 .75
126 Taylor Raddysh .30 .75
127 Devon Toews .20 .50
128 Lukas Reichel .25 .60
129 Juuse Saros .30 .75
130 Charlie McAvoy .30 .75
131 Mikhail Sergachev .20 .50
132 K'Andre Miller .25 .60
133 Boone Jenner .25 .60
134 Erik Karlsson .30 .75
135 Claude Giroux .30 .75
136 Logan Couture .30 .75
137 Rickard Rakell .20 .50
138 Gabe Vilardi .20 .50
139 Jared Spurgeon .20 .50
140 Jonathan Marchessault .30 .75
141 Brent Burns .25 .60
142 Taylor Hall .30 .75
143 Sergei Bobrovsky .40 1.00
144 William Nylander .50 1.25
145 Logan Thompson .30 .75
146 Brady Tkachuk .40 1.00
147 Patrik Laine .30 .75
148 Igor Shesterkin .50 1.25
149 Rasmus Dahlin .30 .75
150 Dan Vladar .20 .50
151 Mikael Granlund .20 .50
152 Tage Thompson .30 .75
153 Patrick Kane .50 1.25
154 Travis Konecny .25 .60
155 Chandler Stephenson .20 .50
156 Pavel Buchnevich .20 .50
157 Dylan Holloway .25 .60
158 Brock Boeser .30 .75
159 Yanni Gourde .20 .50
160 Roman Josi .25 .60
161 Thatcher Demko .30 .75
162 Nico Hischier .40 1.00
163 Tim Stutzle .30 .75
164 Philipp Grubauer .25 .60
165 Anders Lee .20 .50
166 Vladimir Tarasenko .30 .75
167 Calen Addison .15 .40
168 Zach Hyman .40 1.00
169 Tristan Jarry .25 .60
170 Darnell Nurse .20 .50
171 Brock Nelson .25 .60
172 Jared McCann .20 .50
173 Jonathan Quick .30 .75
174 Darcy Kuemper .20 .50
175 Jordan Kyrou .25 .60
176 Mathew Barzal .30 .75
177 Carter Verhaeghe .25 .60
178 Josh Bailey .20 .50
179 Lawson Crouse .15 .40
180 Alex DeBrincat .30 .75
181 Carter Hart .25 .60
182 Evgeny Kuznetsov .30 .75
183 Quinton Byfield .30 .75
184 Kent Johnson .25 .60
185 Juuso Parssinen .15 .40
186 Linus Ullmark .25 .60
187 Drew Doughty .25 .60
188 Josh Anderson .20 .50
189 Tyler Toffoli .20 .50
190 David Perron .20 .50
191 Torey Krug .20 .50
192 Nikita Kucherov .50 1.25
193 Troy Terry .20 .50
194 Christian Dvorak .15 .40
195 Dominik Kubalik .15 .40
196 Connor Hellebuyck .50 1.25
197 John Tavares .40 1.00
198 Jordan Eberle .25 .60
199 Nick Schmaltz .20 .50
200 Checklist .15 .40
201 Derek Ryan .15 .40
202 Isac Lundestrom .15 .40
203 Adam Henrique .20 .50
204 Jason Dickinson .15 .40
205 James van Riemsdyk .20 .50
206 Joe Veleno .20 .50
207 Drake Batherson .25 .60
208 Brenden Dillon .15 .40
209 Calle Rosen .15 .40
210 Mark Kastelic .20 .50
211 Damon Severson .15 .40
212 Tyler Myers .15 .40
213 Peyton Krebs .20 .50
214 Ryan Reaves .20 .50
215 Adam Larsson .15 .40
216 Nikita Zadorov .25 .60
217 Ryan Lindgren .15 .40
218 Brendan Gallagher .25 .60
219 Alexandar Georgiev .25 .60
220 Jordan Martinook .15 .40
221 Jason Zucker .20 .50
222 Jesper Boqvist .15 .40
223 William Carrier .15 .40
224 Nate Schmidt .15 .40
225 Michael Matheson .15 .40
226 Ryan Lomberg .15 .40
227 Jeff Carter .20 .50
228 Jean-Gabriel Pageau .15 .40
229 Zack Kassian .15 .40
230 Philip Tomasino .15 .40
231 Nicolas Hague .15 .40
232 Nils Lundkvist .15 .40
233 Braden Schneider .20 .50
234 Brady Skjei .15 .40
235 Noah Hanifin .15 .40
236 Kevin Shattenkirk .15 .40
237 Cole Sillinger .20 .50
238 Nick Perbix .15 .40
239 Shane Pinto .20 .50
240 Jordan Harris .15 .40
241 Justin Faulk .15 .40
242 Timothy Liljegren .15 .40
243 Alex Killorn .20 .50
244 Sam Steel .15 .40
245 David Jiricek .25 .60
246 Tyler Johnson .15 .40
247 Anthony Duclair .20 .50
248 Morgan Frost .20 .50
249 Anthony Mantha .20 .50
250 Adam Lowry .20 .50
251 Brayden Schenn .25 .60
252 Brandon Tanev .20 .50
253 Mattias Ekholm .20 .50
254 Jordan Staal .20 .50
255 Nino Niederreiter .15 .40
256 Danton Heinen .15 .40
257 Barrett Hayton .25 .60
258 Rasmus Sandin .20 .50
259 Marco Scandella .15 .40
260 Pierre-Olivier Joseph .15 .40
261 Brian Dumoulin .15 .40
262 Matt Roy .15 .40
263 Miles Wood .15 .40
264 Wyatt Johnston .50 1.25
265 Austin Watson .15 .40
266 Corey Perry .40 1.00
267 Jalen Chatfield .15 .40
268 Jonas Brodin .15 .40
269 Anthony Cirelli .20 .50
270 Paul Stastny .20 .50
271 Trevor van Riemsdyk .20 .50
272 Ryan Pulock .20 .50
273 Brandon Saad .20 .50
274 Brandon Montour .30 .75
275 Jamie Benn .25 .60
276 Blake Wheeler .25 .60
277 Trent Frederic .15 .40
278 Mario Ferraro .15 .40
279 Bryan Rust .25 .60
280 Alexander Wennberg .15 .40
281 Jan Rutta .15 .40
282 Evgeny Svechnikov .15 .40
283 Noah Gregor .15 .40
284 Ethan Bear .15 .40
285 Radek Faksa .15 .40
286 Samuel Girard .15 .40
287 Alex Kerfoot .15 .40
288 Joel Armia .15 .40
289 Sean Durzi .15 .40
290 Sheldon Dries .15 .40
291 Vince Dunn .15 .40
292 Daniel Sprong .15 .40
293 Scott Mayfield .15 .40
294 Adam Boqvist .15 .40
295 Nicolas Roy .15 .40
296 Colton Sissons .15 .40
297 Bowen Byram .30 .75
298 Barclay Goodrow .15 .40
299 Ryan Hartman .15 .40
300 Checklist .15 .40
301 Marcus Foligno .20 .50
302 Andrew Ladd .20 .50
303 Anton Lundell .25 .60
304 Ty Dellandrea .15 .40
305 Nick Foligno .15 .40
306 Sean Couturier .20 .50
307 Mason Marchment .20 .50
308 Connor Dewar .15 .40
309 Matt Dumba .15 .40
310 Eetu Luostarinen .15 .40
311 Tomas Tatar .15 .40
312 Nico Sturm .15 .40
313 Jeremy Lauzon .15 .40
314 Adam Pelech .15 .40
315 MacKenzie Weegar .15 .40
316 Jaccob Slavin .15 .40
317 Stuart Skinner .30 .75
318 Hampus Lindholm .15 .40
319 Ryan McDonagh .15 .40
320 Kevin Labanc .15 .40
321 Ryan Johansen .15 .40
322 Liam O'Brien .15 .40
323 Ryan Suter .15 .40
324 Noah Dobson .20 .50
325 William Karlsson .30 .75
326 Erik Cernak .15 .40
327 Jamie Drysdale .20 .50
328 Tyler Bertuzzi .15 .40
329 Cody Glass .15 .40
330 Andrew Copp .15 .40
331 Josh Norris .25 .60
332 Erik Haula .15 .40
333 David Savard .15 .40
334 Frank Vatrano .20 .50
335 Justin Schultz .15 .40
336 Mike Hoffman .15 .40
337 Travis Boyd .15 .40
338 Erik Gudbranson .15 .40
339 Sammy Blais .15 .40
340 Cody Ceci .15 .40
341 Oliver Bjorkstrand .20 .50
342 Brock McGinn .15 .40
343 Nick Paul .15 .40
344 Ryan Strome .15 .40
345 Noel Acciari .15 .40
346 Artem Zub .15 .40
347 Nazem Kadri .30 .75
348 Andreas Athanasiou .15 .40
349 Pavel Zacha .15 .40
350 Pierre-Luc Dubois .15 .40
351 Rasmus Ristolainen .15 .40
352 Brett Kulak .15 .40
353 Ondrej Palat .20 .50
354 Sean Kuraly .15 .40
355 Brett Pesce .15 .40
356 Marc-Edouard Vlasic .15 .40
357 Joel Farabee .25 .60
358 Conor Sheary .25 .60
359 Emil Bemstrom .15 .40
360 Jani Hakanpaa .15 .40
361 Nick Cousins .15 .40
362 Olli Maatta .15 .40
363 Kyle Okposo .15 .40
364 Erik Johnson .15 .40
365 Jesper Fast .15 .40
366 Casey Mittelstadt .25 .60
367 Mikey Anderson .20 .50
368 Ryan Graves .15 .40
369 Marcus Pettersson .15 .40
370 Adam Erne .15 .40
371 Boris Katchouk .15 .40
372 Elvis Merzlikins .25 .60
373 Jake DeBrusk .15 .40
374 Phil Kessel .15 .40
375 John Marino .15 .40
376 Ilya Mikheyev .20 .50
377 Jaden Schwartz .15 .40
378 Paul Cotter .25 .60
379 Vincent Trocheck .25 .60
380 Travis Sanheim .15 .40
381 Cole Smith .15 .40
382 David Kampf .15 .40
383 Neal Pionk .15 .40
384 Dakota Joshua .15 .40
385 Nick Leddy .15 .40
386 Sonny Milano .20 .50
387 Nils Aman .15 .40
388 Jake Walman .15 .40
389 Dylan Cozens .25 .60
390 J.J. Moser .15 .40
391 Kaapo Kakko .20 .50
392 Ukko-Pekka Luukkonen .20 .50
393 Jordan Greenway .15 .40
394 Colin Blackwell .15 .40
395 Jakub Vrana .20 .50
396 Michael Amadio .15 .40

398 Matt Benning .15 .40
399 Jamie Oleksiak .20 .50
400 Checklist .15 .40
401 Alexander Romanov .20 .50
402 Jesperi Kotkaniemi .25 .60
403 Dillon Dube .15 .40
404 Gustav Forsling .25 .60
405 Jake Allen .25 .60
406 T.J. Oshie .25 .60
407 Warren Foegele .15 .40
408 Sam Bennett .40 1.00
409 Andrew Peeke .15 .40
410 Charlie Coyle .25 .60
411 John Carlson .25 .60
412 Brandon Carlo .20 .50
413 Oliver Ekman-Larsson .15 .40
414 Artturi Lehkonen .20 .50
415 Arthur Kaliyev .25 .60
416 Phillip Danault .25 .60
417 Connor Murphy .20 .50
418 Klim Kostin .15 .40
419 Logan O'Connor .25 .60
420 Andrew Mangiapane .25 .60
421 Alexander Barabanov .15 .40
422 Derek Grant .15 .40
423 Rasmus Andersson .20 .50
424 David Krejci .25 .60
425 Evan Bouchard .30 .75
426 Steven Lorentz .15 .40
427 Casey Cizikas .20 .50
428 Eric Robinson .15 .40
429 Jakob Chychrun .25 .60
430 Kailer Yamamoto .25 .60
431 Jacob Trouba .20 .50
432 Valeri Nichushkin .25 .60
433 Liam Foudy .20 .50
434 Esa Lindell .20 .50
435 Ben Chiarot .15 .40
436 Jimmy Vesey .20 .50
437 Mason Appleton .15 .40
438 Josh Manson .15 .40
439 Jonathan Drouin .20 .50
440 Victor Olofsson .25 .60
441 Brayden Point .30 .75
442 Mark Giordano .25 .60
443 Philipp Kurashev .20 .50
444 Thomas Chabot .25 .60
445 Nick Jensen .15 .40
446 Trevor Moore .15 .40
447 Jordan Oesterle .15 .40
448 Patrick Maroon .15 .40
449 Pius Suter .20 .50
450 Nikita Zaitsev .15 .40
451 Filip Hronek .15 .40
452 Frederick Gaudreau .15 .40
453 Ivan Provorov .20 .50
454 Filip Chytil .20 .50
455 Mika Zibanejad .30 .75
456 Travis Hamonic .20 .50
457 Mattias Samuelsson .15 .40
458 Viktor Arvidsson .15 .40
459 Henri Jokiharju .15 .40
460 Colin Miller .15 .40
461 Jonas Siegenthaler .15 .40
462 Mark Stone .30 .75
463 Mathieu Joseph .15 .40
464 Ross Colton .20 .50
465 Juuso Valimaki .15 .40
466 Kyle Palmieri .20 .50
467 Conor Garland .20 .50
468 Maxime Comtois .20 .50
469 Tom Wilson .25 .60
470 Dylan DeMelo .15 .40
471 Alex Iafallo .15 .40
472 Petr Mrazek .20 .50
473 Anthony Beauvillier .15 .40
474 Alexey Toropchenko .15 .40
475 Stefan Noesen .15 .40
476 Simon Benoit .15 .40
477 Tomas Nosek .15 .40
478 Morgan Rielly .25 .60
479 Kaapo Kahkonen .25 .60
480 Jeff Petry .25 .60
481 Denis Malgin .15 .40
482 Blake Lizotte .15 .40
483 JJ Peterka .25 .60
484 Sam Reinhart .50 1.25
485 Ryan McLeod .15 .40
486 Evander Kane .25 .60
487 T.J. Brodie .15 .40
488 Trevor Lewis .15 .40
489 Zach Aston-Reese .15 .40
490 Joel Eriksson Ek .20 .50
491 Robby Fabbri .15 .40
492 Yakov Trenin .15 .40
493 Nic Dowd .15 .40
494 Shea Theodore .30 .75
495 Thomas Novak .15 .40
496 Calle Jarnkrok .15 .40
497 Wade Allison .15 .40
498 Christian Fischer .15 .40
499 Jujhar Khaira .15 .40
500 Checklist .15 .40
501 Connor McDavid AS 2.00 5.00
502 Sidney Crosby AS 1.50 4.00
503 Alex Ovechkin AS 1.50 4.00
504 Nikita Kucherov AS .75 2.00
505 David Pastrnak AS 1.00 2.50
506 Jack Hughes AS 1.00 2.50
507 Artemi Panarin AS .75 2.00
508 Andrei Svechnikov AS .50 1.25
509 Nick Suzuki AS .75 2.00
510 Brady Tkachuk AS .60 1.50
511 Matthew Tkachuk AS .75 2.00
512 Rasmus Dahlin AS .50 1.25
513 Linus Ullmark AS .40 1.00
514 Andrei Vasilevskiy AS .60 1.50
515 Dylan Larkin AS .50 1.25
516 Johnny Gaudreau AS .60 1.50
517 Mitch Marner AS .60 1.50
518 Brock Nelson AS .40 1.00
519 Igor Shesterkin AS .75 2.00
520 Ilya Sorokin AS .60 1.50
521 Adam Fox AS .50 1.25
522 Josh Morrissey AS .50 1.25
523 Kirill Kaprizov AS 1.25 3.00
524 Juuse Saros AS .50 1.25
525 Cale Makar AS 1.00 2.50
526 Aleksander Barkov AS .60 1.50
527 Mikko Rantanen AS 1.00 2.50
528 Jason Robertson AS .60 1.50
529 Connor Hellebuyck AS .75 2.00
530 Clayton Keller AS .50 1.25
531 Nathan MacKinnon AS 1.50 4.00
532 Chandler Stephenson AS .30 .75
533 Logan Thompson AS .50 1.25
534 Kevin Fiala AS .30 .75
535 Bo Horvat AS .50 1.25
536 Nazem Kadri AS .50 1.25
537 Troy Terry AS .30 .75
538 Leon Draisaitl AS 1.25 3.00
539 Elias Pettersson AS .60 1.50
540 Erik Karlsson AS .50 1.25
541 Yaroslav Askarov RC 2.00 5.00
542 Jakob Pelletier RC 1.00 2.50
543 Ridly Greig RC 1.25 3.00
544 Vincent Desharnais RC 1.00 2.50
545 David Gust RC .75 2.00
546 Arnaud Durandeau RC .75 2.00
547 Cole Guttman RC .75 2.00
548 Owen Beck RC 1.25 3.00
549 Milos Kelemen RC .75 2.00
550 Luke Philp RC .75 2.00
551 Jaxson Stauber RC .75 2.00
552 Joona Koppanen RC .60 1.50
553 Jonathan Gruden RC .75 2.00
554 William Dufour RC .60 1.50
555 Samuel Bolduc RC .75 2.00
556 Wyatt Kaiser RC .75 2.00
557 Billy Sweezey RC .75 2.00
558 Will Cuylle RC 1.25 3.00
559 Arturs Silovs RC 1.50 4.00
560 Sean Farrell RC .75 2.00
561 Bobby McMann RC 1.25 3.00
562 Luke Evangelista RC 1.25 3.00
563 Simon Edvinsson RC 1.50 4.00
564 Egor Afanasyev RC .75 2.00
565 Hunter McKown RC .75 2.00
566 Jiri Patera RC 1.25 3.00
567 Tyson Foerster RC 1.50 4.00
568 Nikita Nesterenko RC .75 2.00
569 Aidan McDonough RC .60 1.50
570 Vincent Iorio RC .75 2.00
571 Michael Kesselring RC .75 2.00
572 Luke Hughes RC 2.50 6.00
573 Matthew Knies RC 3.00 8.00
574 Dustin Wolf RC 2.50 6.00
575 Matthew Coronato RC 1.25 3.00
576 Devon Levi RC 2.00 5.00
577 Joel Teasdale RC .75 2.00
578 Tye Kartye RC 1.25 3.00
579 Drew Helleson RC .75 2.00
580 Brock Faber RC 2.00 5.00
581 Marco Kasper RC 2.00 5.00
582 Connor Bedard RC 60.00 150.00
583 Adam Fantilli RC 2.50 6.00
584 Logan Cooley RC 2.50 6.00
585 John Beecher RC 1.50 4.00
586 Jackson LaCombe RC .75 2.00
587 Kevin Korchinski RC 1.25 3.00
588 Matthew Poitras RC 1.50 4.00
589 Fraser Minten RC 1.50 4.00
590 Waltteri Merela RC .75 2.00
591 Zach Benson RC 1.25 3.00
592 Mackie Samoskevich RC 1.25 3.00
593 Pavel Mintyukov RC 1.25 3.00
594 Emil Andrae RC .75 2.00
595 Uvis Balinskis RC .75 2.00
596 Adam Ginning RC .75 2.00
597 Matt Murray RC .75 2.00
598 Stanislav Svozil RC .60 1.50
599 Leo Carlsson RC 2.50 6.00
600 Checklist .50 1.25

2023-24 O-Pee-Chee Blue

*BLUE: .6X TO 1.5X BASIC
582 Connor Bedard 80.00 200.00

2023-24 O-Pee-Chee Purple

*PURPLE/49: 5X TO 12X BASIC
*PURP AS/RC: 4X TO 10X BASIC
561 Bobby McMann 25.00 60.00
572 Luke Hughes 30.00 80.00
573 Matthew Knies 30.00 80.00
578 Tye Kartye 40.00 100.00
580 Brock Faber 30.00 80.00
582 Connor Bedard 500.00 1200.00
583 Adam Fantilli 50.00 125.00
584 Logan Cooley 30.00 80.00
588 Matthew Poitras 30.00 80.00
589 Fraser Minten 12.00 30.00
591 Zach Benson 20.00 50.00
599 Leo Carlsson 30.00 80.00

2023-24 O-Pee-Chee Rainbow

*RAINBOW/350: 1.2X TO 3X BASIC
582 Connor Bedard 150.00 400.00

2023-24 O-Pee-Chee Rainbow Black

*RNBW BLK/100: 3X TO 8X BASIC
561 Bobby McMann 20.00 50.00
572 Luke Hughes 25.00 60.00
573 Matthew Knies 20.00 50.00
578 Tye Kartye 20.00 50.00
580 Brock Faber 25.00 60.00
582 Connor Bedard 400.00 1000.00
583 Adam Fantilli 40.00 100.00
584 Logan Cooley 20.00 50.00
588 Matthew Poitras 20.00 50.00
589 Fraser Minten 12.00 30.00
591 Zach Benson 15.00 40.00
599 Leo Carlsson 30.00 80.00

2023-24 O-Pee-Chee Red

*RED: 1.5X TO 4X BASIC
582 Connor Bedard 100.00 250.00

2023-24 O-Pee-Chee Yellow

*YELLOW.VETS/AS: .75X TO 2X BASIC
*YELLOW.RC: 1X TO 2.5X BASIC
582 Connor Bedard 100.00 250.00

2023-24 O-Pee-Chee '23-24 OPC Platinum Previews

*RAINBOW: .5X TO 1.2X BASIC
*BLUE:.75 X TO 2X BASIC
*VIOLET: 1X TO 2.5X BASIC
*PINK: 1.2X TO 3X BASIC
PAM Auston Matthews 3.00 8.00
PAO Alex Ovechkin 3.00 8.00
PCB Connor Bedard 40.00 100.00
PCM Connor McDavid 4.00 10.00
PKK Kirill Kaprizov 2.50 6.00
PLC Logan Cooley 2.50 6.00
PLH Luke Hughes 2.50 6.00
PMA Cale Makar 2.00 5.00
PYA Yaroslav Askarov 2.00 5.00

2023-24 O-Pee-Chee '23-24 OPC Platinum Previews Cosmic

*COSMIC: 2X TO 5X BASIC
PCB Connor Bedard 125.00 300.00

2023-24 O-Pee-Chee '23-24 OPC Platinum Previews Red Prism

*RED/50: 2.5X TO 6X BASIC
PCB Connor Bedard 150.00 400.00
PLC Logan Cooley 25.00 60.00
PLH Luke Hughes 20.00 50.00
PYA Yaroslav Askarov 15.00 40.00

2023-24 O-Pee-Chee '23-24 OPC Platinum Previews Seismic Gold

*GOLD/25: 6X TO 15X BASIC
PCB Connor Bedard 600.00 1500.00
PYA Yaroslav Askarov 30.00 80.00

2023-24 O-Pee-Chee 3-D Marquee Rookies

3DCB Connor Bedard 400.00 1000.00
3DDL Devon Levi 50.00 125.00
3DJP Jakob Pelletier 25.00 60.00
3DKN Matthew Knies 30.00 80.00
3DLC Logan Cooley 60.00 150.00
3DLH Luke Hughes 60.00 150.00
3DMC Matthew Coronato 30.00 80.00
3DMK Marco Kasper 50.00 125.00
3DOB Owen Beck 30.00 80.00
3DTF Tyson Foerster 40.00 100.00
3DVI Dustin Wolf 60.00 150.00
3DYA Yaroslav Askarov 30.00 80.00

2023-24 O-Pee-Chee Hall of Fame Logo Patches

HOF1 Eric Lindros 15.00 40.00
HOF2 Joe Sakic 20.00 50.00
HOF3 Ron Francis 12.00 30.00
HOF4 Jari Kurri 10.00 25.00
HOF5 Marcel Dionne 12.00 30.00
HOF6 Lanny McDonald 10.00 25.00

2023-24 O-Pee-Chee OPC Premier

P1 Jordan Kyrou 1.00 2.50
P2 Linus Ullmark 1.00 2.50
P3 Kyle Connor 1.50 4.00
P4 Juraj Slafkovsky 2.00 5.00
P5 Marc-Andre Fleury 2.00 5.00
P6 Joe Pavelski 1.25 3.00
P7 Jonathan Huberdeau 1.25 3.00
P8 Sebastian Aho 1.50 4.00
P9 Igor Shesterkin 2.00 5.00
P10 Nathan MacKinnon 4.00 10.00
P11 Cale Makar 2.50 6.00
P12 Jack Eichel 1.50 4.00
P13 Trevor Zegras 1.00 2.50
P14 Cole Caufield 2.00 5.00
P15 Moritz Seider 1.25 3.00
P16 Matty Beniers 1.25 3.00
P17 Carter Hart 1.00 2.50
P18 Tage Thompson 1.25 3.00
P19 Clayton Keller 1.25 3.00
P20 Roman Josi 1.00 2.50
P21 Alexis Lafreniere 1.50 4.00
P22 Erik Karlsson 1.25 3.00
P23 Johnny Gaudreau 1.50 4.00
P24 Patrick Kane 2.00 5.00
P25 Aleksander Barkov 1.50 4.00
P26 Nick Suzuki 2.00 5.00
P27 Mitch Marner 1.50 4.00
P28 Andrei Vasilevskiy 1.50 4.00
P29 Brad Marchand 2.00 5.00
P30 Andrei Svechnikov 1.25 3.00
P31 Alex Ovechkin 4.00 10.00
P32 Ilya Sorokin 1.50 4.00
P33 Quinn Hughes 2.50 6.00
P34 Tim Stutzle 1.25 3.00
P35 Michael Bunting 1.00 2.50
P36 Jonathan Toews 1.50 4.00
P37 Matthew Tkachuk 2.00 5.00
P38 Brady Tkachuk 1.50 4.00
P39 Rasmus Dahlin 1.25 3.00
P40 Elias Pettersson 1.50 4.00
P41 Artemi Panarin 2.00 5.00
P42 Evgeni Malkin 2.00 5.00
P43 Kirill Kaprizov 3.00 8.00
P44 Auston Matthews 4.00 10.00
P45 Connor McDavid 5.00 12.00
P46 Sidney Crosby 4.00 10.00
P47 John Tavares 1.50 4.00
P48 Nikita Kucherov 2.00 5.00
P49 Leon Draisaitl 3.00 8.00
P50 Jason Robertson 1.50 4.00
P51 David Pastrnak 2.50 6.00
P52 Jack Hughes 2.50 6.00
P53 Anze Kopitar 1.50 4.00
P54 Mason McTavish 1.00 2.50
P55 Nico Hischier 1.50 4.00
P56 Lucas Raymond 1.50 4.00
P57 Nick Schmaltz .75 2.00
P58 Mikko Rantanen 2.50 6.00
P59 Owen Power 1.00 2.50
P60 Dylan Larkin 1.25 3.00
P61 Josh Morrissey 1.25 3.00
P62 Jared McCann .75 2.00
P63 Tyler Toffoli 1.00 2.50
P64 Mathew Barzal 1.25 3.00
P65 Filip Forsberg 1.50 4.00
P66 Dylan Strome 1.25 3.00
P67 Logan Couture 1.25 3.00
P68 Seth Jones 1.00 2.50
P69 Chandler Stephenson .75 2.00
P70 Robert Thomas 1.00 2.50
P71 Patrik Laine 1.25 3.00
P72 Kevin Fiala .75 2.00
P73 Bo Horvat 1.25 3.00
P74 Logan Thompson 1.25 3.00
P75 Travis Konecny 1.00 2.50
P76 Egor Afanasyev 1.00 2.50
P77 Ridly Greig 1.50 4.00
P78 Luke Evangelista 1.50 4.00
P79 Jakob Pelletier 1.25 3.00
P80 Tye Kartye 1.50 4.00
P81 Owen Beck 1.50 4.00
P82 Simon Edvinsson 2.00 5.00
P83 Tyson Foerster 2.00 5.00
P84 Devon Levi 2.50 6.00
P85 Dustin Wolf 3.00 8.00
P86 Matthew Coronato 1.50 4.00
P87 Luke Hughes 3.00 8.00
P88 Matthew Knies 4.00 10.00
P89 Marco Kasper 2.50 6.00
P90 Sean Farrell 1.00 2.50
P91 Connor Bedard 80.00 200.00
P92 Kevin Korchinski 1.50 4.00
P93 Adam Fantilli 3.00 8.00
P94 Logan Cooley 3.00 8.00
P95 Mackie Samoskevich 1.50 4.00
P96 Pavel Mintyukov 1.50 4.00
P97 Zach Benson 1.50 4.00
P98 Alex Laferriere 1.50 4.00
P99 John Beecher 2.00 5.00
P100 Leo Carlsson 3.00 8.00

2023-24 O-Pee-Chee OPC Premier Diamond Rainbow

*RNBW/75: 2X TO 5X BASIC
*RNBW RC/75: 3X TO 8X BASIC
P80 Tye Kartye 20.00 50.00
P85 Dustin Wolf 25.00 60.00
P87 Luke Hughes 30.00 80.00
P91 Connor Bedard 500.00 1200.00
P93 Adam Fantilli 40.00 100.00
P94 Logan Cooley 20.00 50.00
P99 John Beecher 12.00 30.00
P100 Leo Carlsson 40.00 100.00

2023-24 O-Pee-Chee Patches

P1 Carey Price 10.00 25.00
P2 Cam Neely 5.00 12.00
P3 Adam Graves 4.00 10.00
P4 Larry Robinson 5.00 12.00
P5 Aleksander Barkov 8.00 20.00
P6 Luc Robitaille 5.00 12.00
P7 Mark Messier 10.00 25.00
P8 Marc-Andre Fleury 10.00 25.00
P9 Martin Brodeur 12.00 30.00
P10 Mike Vernon 4.00 10.00
P11 Connor McDavid 20.00 50.00
P12 Bobby Orr 15.00 40.00
P13 Gordie Howe 12.00 30.00
P14 Bernie Geoffrion 4.00 10.00
P15 Phil Esposito 8.00 20.00
P16 Kyle Connor 8.00 20.00
P17 Joe Mullen 5.00 12.00
P18 Mike Bossy 5.00 12.00
P19 Rick Kehoe 4.00 10.00
P20 Larry Robinson 5.00 12.00
P21 Patrick Roy 12.00 30.00
P22 Wayne Gretzky 25.00 60.00
P23 Mark Messier 10.00 25.00
P24 Mike Bossy 5.00 12.00
P25 Claude Lemieux 5.00 12.00
P26 Brian Leetch 4.00 10.00
P27 Cale Makar 12.00 30.00
P28 Ray Bourque 8.00 20.00
P29 Paul Coffey 5.00 12.00
P30 Moritz Seider 6.00 15.00
P31 Dale Hawerchuk 6.00 15.00
P32 Denis Potvin 5.00 12.00
P33 Peter Forsberg 10.00 25.00
P34 Igor Shesterkin 10.00 25.00
P35 Tony Esposito 5.00 12.00
P36 Rogie Vachon 5.00 12.00
P37 Johnny Bower 5.00 12.00
P38 Turk Broda 5.00 12.00
P39 Maurice Richard 10.00 25.00
P40 Auston Matthews 15.00 40.00
P41 Patrick Kane 10.00 25.00
P42 Mario Lemieux 15.00 40.00
P43 Phil Esposito 8.00 20.00
P44 Gordie Howe 12.00 30.00
P45 Auston Matthews 15.00 40.00
P46 Patrice Bergeron 6.00 15.00
P47 Chris Chelios 5.00 12.00
P48 Mats Sundin 5.00 12.00
P49 Jarome Iginla 6.00 15.00
P50 Sidney Crosby 15.00 40.00
P51 Shane Doan 4.00 10.00
P52 Jonathan Toews 8.00 20.00
P53 Shea Weber 5.00 12.00
P54 Nick Foligno 3.00 8.00
P55 Wayne Simmonds 5.00 12.00
P56 Mark Giordano 5.00 12.00
P57 Patrice Bergeron 6.00 15.00
P58 Anze Kopitar 8.00 20.00
P59 Cale Makar 12.00 30.00
P60 Maurice Richard 10.00 25.00
P61 Martin Brodeur 12.00 30.00
P62 Mark Messier 10.00 25.00
P63 Clark Gillies 5.00 12.00
P64 Denis Potvin 5.00 12.00
P65 Bobby Clarke 8.00 20.00
P66 Phil Esposito 8.00 20.00
P67 Johnny Bower 5.00 12.00
P68 Sid Abel 5.00 12.00
P69 Buoy 20.00 50.00

2023-24 O-Pee-Chee Playing Cards

10DIAMONDS Elias Pettersson 2.50 6.00
ACEDIAMONDS Auston Matthews 6.00 15.00
JOKER Buoy White Sweater 5.00 12.00
JOKER Buoy Green Sweater 5.00 12.00
2CLUBS Jordan Kyrou 1.50 4.00
3CLUBS Luke Hughes 5.00 12.00
4CLUBS Kyle Connor 2.50 6.00
5CLUBS Juraj Slafkovsky 3.00 8.00
6CLUBS Marc-Andre Fleury 3.00 8.00
7CLUBS Joe Pavelski 2.00 5.00
8CLUBS Jonathan Huberdeau 2.00 5.00
9CLUBS Sebastian Aho 2.50 6.00
JCLUBS Igor Shesterkin 3.00 8.00
KCLUBS Nathan MacKinnon 6.00 15.00
QCLUBS Cale Makar 4.00 10.00
10CLUBS Cole Caufield 3.00 8.00
2HEARTS Moritz Seider 2.00 5.00
2SPADES Matty Beniers 2.00 5.00
3HEARTS Carter Hart 1.50 4.00
3SPADES Tage Thompson 2.00 5.00
4HEARTS Clayton Keller 2.00 5.00
4SPADES Roman Josi 1.50 4.00
5HEARTS Alexis Lafreniere 2.50 6.00
5SPADES Logan Couture 2.00 5.00
6HEARTS Johnny Gaudreau 2.50 6.00
6SPADES Patrick Kane 3.00 8.00
7HEARTS Aleksander Barkov 2.50 6.00
7SPADES Nick Suzuki 3.00 8.00
8HEARTS Mitch Marner 2.50 6.00
8SPADES Andrei Vasilevskiy 2.50 6.00
9HEARTS Brad Marchand 3.00 8.00
9SPADES Andrei Svechnikov 2.00 5.00
JHEARTS John Tavares 2.50 6.00
JSPADES Nikita Kucherov 3.00 8.00
KHEARTS Leon Draisaitl 5.00 12.00
KSPADES Jason Robertson 2.50 6.00
QHEARTS David Pastrnak 4.00 10.00
QSPADES Jack Hughes 4.00 10.00
10HEARTS Jack Eichel 2.50 6.00
10SPADES Trevor Zegras 1.50 4.00
2DIAMONDS Ilya Sorokin 2.50 6.00
3DIAMONDS Quinn Hughes 4.00 10.00
4DIAMONDS Tim Stutzle 2.00 5.00
5DIAMONDS Michael Bunting 1.50 4.00
6DIAMONDS Jonathan Toews 2.50 6.00
7DIAMONDS Matthew Tkachuk 3.00 8.00
8DIAMONDS Brady Tkachuk 2.50 6.00
9DIAMONDS Rasmus Dahlin 2.00 5.00
ACECLUBS Alex Ovechkin 6.00 15.00
ACEHEARTS Connor McDavid 8.00 20.00
ACESPADES Sidney Crosby 6.00 15.00
JDIAMONDS Artemi Panarin 3.00 8.00
KDIAMONDS Kirill Kaprizov 5.00 12.00
QDIAMONDS Evgeni Malkin 3.00 8.00

2023-24 O-Pee-Chee Retro

1 Connor McDavid 2.00 5.00
2 Cale Makar 1.00 2.50
3 Sebastian Aho .60 1.50
4 Matthew Tkachuk .75 2.00
5 Johnny Gaudreau .60 1.50
6 Jack Hughes 1.00 2.50
7 Mitch Marner .60 1.50
8 Alex Ovechkin 1.50 4.00
9 Nathan MacKinnon 1.50 4.00
10 Steven Stamkos .75 2.00
11 Leon Draisaitl 1.25 3.00
12 Mason McTavish .40 1.00
13 Joe Pavelski .50 1.25
14 Cole Caufield .75 2.00
15 Jonathan Toews .60 1.50
16 Marc-Andre Fleury .75 2.00
17 Brad Marchand .75 2.00
18 Nick Suzuki .75 2.00
19 Clayton Keller .50 1.25
20 Aleksander Barkov .60 1.50
21 Vitek Vanecek .40 1.00
22 Robert Thomas .40 1.00
23 Spencer Knight .40 1.00
24 Alexis Lafreniere .60 1.50
25 Elias Lindholm .40 1.00
26 Owen Tippett .25 .60
27 Andrei Kuzmenko .40 1.00
28 Ryan Nugent-Hopkins .50 1.25
29 Kris Letang .50 1.25
30 Matias Maccelli .30 .75
31 J.T. Compher .25 .60
32 Max Domi .40 1.00
33 Noah Cates .25 .60
34 Dylan Strome .50 1.25
35 Filip Forsberg .60 1.50
36 Mats Zuccarello .40 1.00
37 Nicklas Backstrom .40 1.00
38 Bo Horvat .50 1.25
39 Reilly Smith .40 1.00
40 Matty Beniers .50 1.25
41 Jack Roslovic .25 .60
42 Juraj Slafkovsky .75 2.00
43 John Gibson .40 1.00
44 Dylan Larkin .50 1.25
45 Kevin Hayes .30 .75
46 Jack Quinn .30 .75
47 Andre Burakovsky .25 .60
48 Quinn Hughes 1.00 2.50
49 Alex Newhook .30 .75
50 Jack Campbell .40 1.00
51 Ville Husso .25 .60
52 J.T. Miller .50 1.25
53 Ilya Sorokin .60 1.50
54 Jake Guentzel .60 1.50
55 Dawson Mercer .50 1.25
56 Karel Vejmelka .25 .60
57 Martin Necas .60 1.50
58 Jeremy Swayman .60 1.50
59 Alex Pietrangelo .30 .75
60 Max Pacioretty .40 1.00
61 Alex Tuch .40 1.00
62 Seth Jones .40 1.00
63 Pyotr Kochetkov .40 1.00
64 Mikael Backlund .30 .75
65 Brandon Hagel .30 .75
66 Jake Sanderson .50 1.25
67 Chris Kreider .50 1.25
68 Kaiden Guhle .40 1.00
69 Ryan O'Reilly .40 1.00
70 William Eklund .50 1.25
71 Patrice Bergeron .50 1.25
72 Cam Fowler .40 1.00
73 Nikolaj Ehlers .40 1.00
74 Dougie Hamilton .30 .75
75 Jacob Markstrom .40 1.00
76 Josh Morrissey .50 1.25
77 Shane Wright .50 1.25
78 Jeff Skinner .40 1.00
79 Tomas Hertl .40 1.00
80 Victor Hedman .50 1.25
81 Kyle Connor .60 1.50
82 Kevin Fiala .30 .75
83 Jordan Binnington .60 1.50
84 Moritz Seider .50 1.25
85 Owen Power .40 1.00
86 Jake Oettinger .60 1.50
87 Matt Duchene .40 1.00
88 Miro Heiskanen .50 1.25
89 Andrei Vasilevskiy .60 1.50
90 Kirby Dach .40 1.00
91 Dylan Guenther .50 1.25
92 Kirill Marchenko .50 1.25
93 Cole Perfetti .40 1.00
94 Mark Scheifele .60 1.50
95 Colton Parayko .30 .75
96 Matt Boldy .60 1.50
97 Michael Bunting .40 1.00
98 Lucas Raymond .60 1.50
99 Scott Laughton .25 .60
100 Checklist .25 .60
101 Auston Matthews 1.50 4.00
102 Trevor Zegras .40 1.00
103 David Pastrnak 1.00 2.50
104 Jason Robertson .60 1.50
105 Sidney Crosby 1.50 4.00
106 Kirill Kaprizov 1.25 3.00
107 Adam Fox .50 1.25
108 Elias Pettersson .60 1.50
109 Jack Eichel .60 1.50
110 Evgeni Malkin .75 2.00
111 Anze Kopitar .60 1.50
112 Artemi Panarin .75 2.00
113 Mikko Rantanen 1.00 2.50
114 Andrei Svechnikov .50 1.25
115 Marco Rossi .50 1.25
116 Jonatan Berggren .30 .75
117 Roope Hintz .50 1.25
118 Tyler Seguin .50 1.25
119 Blake Coleman .30 .75
120 Yegor Sharangovich .40 1.00
121 Jonathan Huberdeau .50 1.25
122 Jesper Bratt .40 1.00
123 Aaron Ekblad .50 1.25
124 Adrian Kempe .40 1.00
125 Seth Jarvis .50 1.25
126 Taylor Raddysh .30 .75
127 Devon Toews .30 .75
128 Lukas Reichel .40 1.00
129 Juuse Saros .50 1.25
130 Charlie McAvoy .50 1.25
131 Mikhail Sergachev .30 .75
132 K'Andre Miller .30 .75
133 Boone Jenner .40 1.00
134 Erik Karlsson .50 1.25
135 Claude Giroux .40 1.00
136 Logan Couture .50 1.25
137 Rickard Rakell .30 .75
138 Gabe Vilardi .40 1.00
139 Jared Spurgeon .40 1.00
140 Jonathan Marchessault .50 1.25
141 Brent Burns .40 1.00
142 Taylor Hall .40 1.00
143 Sergei Bobrovsky .60 1.50
144 William Nylander .75 2.00
145 Logan Thompson .50 1.25
146 Brady Tkachuk .60 1.50
147 Patrik Laine .50 1.25
148 Igor Shesterkin .75 2.00
149 Rasmus Dahlin .50 1.25
150 Dan Vladar .30 .75
151 Mikael Granlund .30 .75
152 Tage Thompson .50 1.25
153 Patrick Kane .75 2.00
154 Travis Konecny .40 1.00
155 Chandler Stephenson .30 .75
156 Pavel Buchnevich .30 .75
157 Dylan Holloway .40 1.00
158 Brock Boeser .50 1.25
159 Yanni Gourde .30 .75
160 Roman Josi .40 1.00
161 Thatcher Demko .50 1.25
162 Nico Hischier .60 1.50
163 Tim Stutzle .50 1.25
164 Philipp Grubauer .40 1.00
165 Anders Lee .30 .75
166 Vladimir Tarasenko .50 1.25
167 Calen Addison .25 .60
168 Zach Hyman .60 1.50
169 Tristan Jarry .40 1.00
170 Darnell Nurse .30 .75
171 Brock Nelson .40 1.00
172 Jared McCann .30 .75
173 Jonathan Quick .50 1.25
174 Darcy Kuemper .40 1.00
175 Jordan Kyrou .40 1.00
176 Mathew Barzal .50 1.25
177 Carter Verhaeghe .40 1.00
178 Josh Bailey .30 .75
179 Lawson Crouse .25 .60
180 Alex DeBrincat .50 1.25
181 Carter Hart .40 1.00
182 Evgeny Kuznetsov .50 1.25
183 Quinton Byfield .50 1.25
184 Kent Johnson .40 1.00
185 Juuso Parssinen .25 .60
186 Linus Ullmark .40 1.00
187 Drew Doughty .40 1.00
188 Josh Anderson .30 .75
189 Tyler Toffoli .40 1.00
190 David Perron .30 .75
191 Torey Krug .30 .75
192 Nikita Kucherov .75 2.00
193 Troy Terry .30 .75
194 Christian Dvorak .30 .75
195 Dominik Kubalik .40 1.00
196 Connor Hellebuyck .75 2.00
197 John Tavares .60 1.50
198 Jordan Eberle .40 1.00
199 Nick Schmaltz .30 .75
200 Checklist .25 .60
201 Derek Ryan .25 .60
202 Isac Lundestrom .25 .60
203 Adam Henrique .30 .75
204 Jason Dickinson .25 .60
205 James van Riemsdyk .30 .75
206 Joe Veleno .30 .75
207 Drake Batherson .40 1.00
208 Brenden Dillon .25 .60
209 Calle Rosen .25 .60
210 Mark Kastelic .30 .75
211 Damon Severson .25 .60
212 Tyler Myers .25 .60
213 Peyton Krebs .30 .75
214 Ryan Reaves .30 .75
215 Adam Larsson .40 1.00
216 Nikita Zadorov .25 .60
217 Ryan Lindgren .25 .60
218 Brendan Gallagher .40 1.00
219 Alexandar Georgiev .40 1.00
220 Jordan Martinook .25 .60
221 Jason Zucker .40 1.00
222 Jesper Boqvist .25 .60
223 William Carrier .25 .60
224 Nate Schmidt .25 .60
225 Michael Matheson .25 .60
226 Ryan Lomberg .25 .60
227 Jeff Carter .30 .75
228 Jean-Gabriel Pageau .25 .60
229 Zack Kassian .25 .60
230 Philip Tomasino .25 .60
231 Nicolas Hague .25 .60
232 Nils Lundkvist .25 .60
233 Braden Schneider .30 .75
234 Brady Skjei .25 .60
235 Noah Hanifin .40 1.00
236 Kevin Shattenkirk .25 .60
237 Cole Sillinger .30 .75
238 Nick Perbix .25 .60
239 Shane Pinto .30 .75
240 Jordan Harris .25 .60
241 Justin Faulk .30 .75
242 Timothy Liljegren .25 .60
243 Alex Killorn .25 .60
244 Sam Steel .30 .75
245 David Jiricek .40 1.00
246 Tyler Johnson .25 .60
247 Anthony Duclair .30 .75
248 Morgan Frost .30 .75
249 Anthony Mantha .30 .75
250 Adam Lowry .30 .75
251 Brayden Schenn .40 1.00
252 Brandon Tanev .30 .75
253 Mattias Ekholm .30 .75
254 Jordan Staal .30 .75
255 Nino Niederreiter .25 .60
256 Danton Heinen .25 .60
257 Barrett Hayton .40 1.00
258 Rasmus Sandin .30 .75
259 Marco Scandella .25 .60
260 Pierre-Olivier Joseph .25 .60
261 Brian Dumoulin .25 .60
262 Matt Roy .25 .60
263 Miles Wood .25 .60
264 Wyatt Johnston .75 2.00
265 Austin Watson .25 .60
266 Corey Perry .60 1.50
267 Jalen Chatfield .25 .60
268 Jonas Brodin .25 .60
269 Anthony Cirelli .30 .75
270 Paul Stastny .30 .75
271 Trevor van Riemsdyk .30 .75
272 Ryan Pulock .30 .75
273 Brandon Saad .30 .75
274 Brandon Montour .50 1.25
275 Jamie Benn .40 1.00
276 Blake Wheeler .40 1.00
277 Trent Frederic .25 .60
278 Mario Ferraro .25 .60
279 Bryan Rust .40 1.00
280 Alexander Wennberg .25 .60
281 Jan Rutta .25 .60
282 Evgeny Svechnikov .25 .60
283 Noah Gregor .25 .60
284 Ethan Bear .25 .60
285 Radek Faksa .30 .75
286 Samuel Girard .25 .60
287 Alex Kerfoot .30 .75
288 Joel Armia .25 .60
289 Sean Durzi .25 .60
290 Sheldon Dries .25 .60
291 Vince Dunn .30 .75
292 Daniel Sprong .25 .60
293 Scott Mayfield .25 .60
294 Adam Boqvist .25 .60
295 Nicolas Roy .25 .60
296 Colton Sissons .25 .60
297 Bowen Byram .50 1.25
298 Barclay Goodrow .25 .60
299 Ryan Hartman .25 .60
300 Checklist .25 .60
301 Marcus Foligno .30 .75
302 Andrew Ladd .30 .75
303 Anton Lundell .40 1.00
304 Ty Dellandrea .25 .60
305 Nick Foligno .25 .60
306 Sean Couturier .30 .75
307 Mason Marchment .30 .75
308 Connor Dewar .25 .60
309 Matt Dumba .25 .60
310 Eetu Luostarinen .25 .60
311 Tomas Tatar .25 .60
312 Nico Sturm .25 .60
313 Jeremy Lauzon .25 .60
314 Adam Pelech .25 .60
315 MacKenzie Weegar .30 .75
316 Jaccob Slavin .30 .75
317 Stuart Skinner .50 1.25
318 Hampus Lindholm .25 .60
319 Ryan McDonagh .25 .60
320 Kevin Labanc .25 .60
321 Ryan Johansen .30 .75
322 Liam O'Brien .25 .60
323 Ryan Suter .30 .75
324 Noah Dobson .50 1.25
325 William Karlsson .50 1.25
326 Erik Cernak .25 .60
327 Jamie Drysdale .30 .75
328 Tyler Bertuzzi .30 .75
329 Cody Glass .30 .75
330 Andrew Copp .25 .60
331 Josh Norris .40 1.00
332 Erik Haula .25 .60
333 David Savard .25 .60
334 Frank Vatrano .30 .75
335 Justin Schultz .30 .75
336 Mike Hoffman .25 .60
337 Travis Boyd .25 .60
338 Erik Gudbranson .25 .60
339 Sammy Blais .25 .60
340 Cody Ceci .25 .60
341 Oliver Bjorkstrand .30 .75
342 Brock McGinn .25 .60

343 Nick Paul .25 .60
344 Ryan Strome .40 1.00
345 Noel Acciari .25 .60
346 Artem Zub .25 .60
347 Nazem Kadri .50 1.25
348 Andreas Athanasiou .30 .75
349 Pavel Zacha .30 .75
350 Pierre-Luc Dubois .30 .75
351 Rasmus Ristolainen .25 .60
352 Brett Kulak .25 .60
353 Ondrej Palat .30 .75
354 Sean Kuraly .25 .60
355 Brett Pesce .25 .60
356 Marc-Edouard Vlasic .25 .60
357 Joel Farabee .40 1.00
358 Conor Sheary .40 1.00
359 Emil Bemstrom .25 .60
360 Jani Hakanpaa .30 .75
361 Nick Cousins .25 .60
362 Olli Maatta .25 .60
363 Kyle Okposo .25 .60
364 Erik Johnson .25 .60
365 Jesper Fast .25 .60
366 Casey Mittelstadt .40 1.00
367 Mikey Anderson .30 .75
368 Ryan Graves .25 .60
369 Marcus Pettersson .25 .60
370 Adam Erne .25 .60
371 Boris Katchouk .25 .60
372 Elvis Merzlikins .40 1.00
373 Jake DeBrusk .40 1.00
374 Phil Kessel .40 1.00
375 John Marino .40 1.00
376 Ilya Mikheyev .30 .75
377 Jaden Schwartz .30 .75
378 Paul Cotter .25 .60
379 Vincent Trocheck .40 1.00
380 Travis Sanheim .25 .60
381 Cole Smith .25 .60
382 David Kampf .25 .60
383 Neal Pionk .25 .60
384 Dakota Joshua .25 .60
385 Nick Leddy .25 .60
386 Sonny Milano .30 .75
387 Nils Aman .25 .60
388 Jake Walman .25 .60
389 Dylan Cozens .40 1.00
390 J.J. Moser .25 .60
391 Kaapo Kakko .30 .75
392 Ukko-Pekka Luukkonen .30 .75
393 Jordan Greenway .25 .60
394 Colin Blackwell .25 .60
395 Jakub Vrana .30 .75
396 Michael Amadio .25 .60
397 Jakob Silfverberg .25 .60
398 Matt Benning .25 .60
399 Jamie Oleksiak .30 .75
400 Checklist .25 .60
401 Alexander Romanov .30 .75
402 Jesperi Kotkaniemi .40 1.00
403 Dillon Dube .25 .60
404 Gustav Forsling .40 1.00
405 Jake Allen .40 1.00
406 T.J. Oshie .40 1.00
407 Warren Foegele .25 .60
408 Sam Bennett .60 1.50
409 Andrew Peeke .25 .60
410 Charlie Coyle .40 1.00
411 John Carlson .40 1.00
412 Brandon Carlo .30 .75
413 Oliver Ekman-Larsson .25 .60
414 Artturi Lehkonen .30 .75
415 Arthur Kaliyev .40 1.00
416 Phillip Danault .40 1.00
417 Connor Murphy .30 .75
418 Klim Kostin .25 .60
419 Logan O'Connor .40 1.00
420 Andrew Mangiapane .40 1.00
421 Alexander Barabanov .25 .60
422 Derek Grant .25 .60
423 Rasmus Andersson .30 .75
424 David Krejci .40 1.00
425 Evan Bouchard .50 1.25
426 Steven Lorentz .25 .60
427 Casey Cizikas .30 .75
428 Eric Robinson .25 .60
429 Jakob Chychrun .40 1.00
430 Kailer Yamamoto .40 1.00
431 Jacob Trouba .30 .75
432 Valeri Nichushkin .40 1.00
433 Liam Foudy .30 .75
434 Esa Lindell .30 .75
435 Ben Chiarot .25 .60
436 Jimmy Vesey .30 .75
437 Mason Appleton .25 .60
438 Josh Manson .25 .60
439 Jonathan Drouin .30 .75
440 Victor Olofsson .40 1.00
441 Brayden Point .50 1.25
442 Mark Giordano .40 1.00
443 Philipp Kurashev .30 .75
444 Thomas Chabot .40 1.00
445 Nick Jensen .25 .60
446 Trevor Moore .25 .60
447 Jordan Oesterle .25 .60
448 Patrick Maroon .25 .60
449 Pius Suter .30 .75
450 Nikita Zaitsev .25 .60
451 Filip Hronek .25 .60
452 Frederick Gaudreau .25 .60
453 Ivan Provorov .30 .75
454 Filip Chytil .30 .75
455 Mika Zibanejad .50 1.25
456 Travis Hamonic .30 .75
457 Mattias Samuelsson .25 .60
458 Viktor Arvidsson .25 .60
459 Henri Jokiharju .25 .60
460 Colin Miller .25 .60
461 Jonas Siegenthaler .25 .60
462 Mark Stone .50 1.25
463 Mathieu Joseph .25 .60
464 Ross Colton .30 .75
465 Juuso Valimaki .25 .60
466 Kyle Palmieri .30 .75
467 Conor Garland .30 .75
468 Maxime Comtois .30 .75
469 Tom Wilson .40 1.00
470 Dylan DeMelo .25 .60
471 Alex Iafallo .25 .60
472 Petr Mrazek .30 .75
473 Anthony Beauvillier .25 .60
474 Alexey Toropchenko .25 .60
475 Stefan Noesen .25 .60
476 Simon Benoit .25 .60
477 Tomas Nosek .25 .60
478 Morgan Rielly .40 1.00
479 Kaapo Kahkonen .40 1.00
480 Jeff Petry .40 1.00
481 Denis Malgin .25 .60
482 Blake Lizotte .25 .60
483 JJ Peterka .40 1.00
484 Sam Reinhart .75 2.00
485 Ryan McLeod .25 .60
486 Evander Kane .40 1.00
487 T.J. Brodie .25 .60
488 Trevor Lewis .25 .60
489 Zach Aston-Reese .25 .60
490 Joel Eriksson Ek .30 .75
491 Robby Fabbri .25 .60
492 Yakov Trenin .25 .60
493 Nic Dowd .25 .60
494 Shea Theodore .50 1.25
495 Thomas Novak .25 .60
496 Calle Jarnkrok .25 .60
497 Wade Allison .25 .60
498 Christian Fischer .25 .60
499 Jujhar Khaira .25 .60
500 Checklist .25 .60
501 Connor McDavid AS 3.00 8.00
502 Sidney Crosby AS 2.50 6.00
503 Alex Ovechkin AS 2.50 6.00
504 Nikita Kucherov AS 1.25 3.00
505 David Pastrnak AS 1.50 4.00
506 Jack Hughes AS 1.50 4.00
507 Artemi Panarin AS 1.25 3.00
508 Andrei Svechnikov AS .75 2.00
509 Nick Suzuki AS 1.25 3.00
510 Brady Tkachuk AS 1.00 2.50
511 Matthew Tkachuk AS 1.25 3.00
512 Rasmus Dahlin AS .75 2.00
513 Linus Ullmark AS .60 1.50
514 Andrei Vasilevskiy AS 1.00 2.50
515 Dylan Larkin AS .75 2.00
516 Johnny Gaudreau AS 1.00 2.50
517 Mitch Marner AS 1.00 2.50
518 Brock Nelson AS .60 1.50
519 Igor Shesterkin AS 1.25 3.00
520 Ilya Sorokin AS 1.00 2.50
521 Adam Fox AS .75 2.00
522 Josh Morrissey AS .75 2.00
523 Kirill Kaprizov AS 2.00 5.00
524 Juuse Saros AS .75 2.00
525 Cale Makar AS 1.50 4.00
526 Aleksander Barkov AS 1.00 2.50
527 Mikko Rantanen AS 1.50 4.00
528 Jason Robertson AS 1.00 2.50
529 Connor Hellebuyck AS 1.25 3.00
530 Clayton Keller AS .75 2.00
531 Nathan MacKinnon AS 2.50 6.00
532 Chandler Stephenson AS .50 1.25
533 Logan Thompson AS .75 2.00
534 Kevin Fiala AS .50 1.25
535 Bo Horvat AS .75 2.00
536 Nazem Kadri AS .75 2.00
537 Troy Terry AS .50 1.25
538 Leon Draisaitl AS 2.00 5.00
539 Elias Pettersson AS 1.00 2.50
540 Erik Karlsson AS .75 2.00
541 Yaroslav Askarov 6.00 15.00
542 Jakob Pelletier 3.00 8.00
543 Ridly Greig 4.00 10.00
544 Vincent Desharnais 3.00 8.00
545 David Gust 2.50 6.00
546 Arnaud Durandeau 2.50 6.00
547 Cole Guttman 2.50 6.00
548 Owen Beck 4.00 10.00
549 Milos Kelemen 2.50 6.00
550 Luke Philp 2.50 6.00
551 Jaxson Stauber 2.50 6.00
552 Joona Koppanen 2.00 5.00
553 Jonathan Gruden 2.50 6.00
554 William Dufour 2.00 5.00
555 Samuel Bolduc 2.50 6.00
556 Wyatt Kaiser 2.50 6.00
557 Billy Sweezey 2.50 6.00
558 Will Cuylle 4.00 10.00
559 Arturs Silovs 5.00 12.00
560 Sean Farrell 2.50 6.00
561 Bobby McMann 4.00 10.00
562 Luke Evangelista 4.00 10.00
563 Simon Edvinsson 5.00 12.00
564 Egor Afanasyev 2.50 6.00
565 Hunter McKown 2.50 6.00
566 Jiri Patera 4.00 10.00
567 Tyson Foerster 5.00 12.00
568 Nikita Nesterenko 2.50 6.00
569 Aidan McDonough 2.00 5.00
570 Vincent Iorio 2.50 6.00
571 Michael Kesselring 2.50 6.00
572 Luke Hughes 8.00 20.00
573 Matthew Knies 10.00 25.00
574 Dustin Wolf 8.00 20.00
575 Matthew Coronato 4.00 10.00
576 Devon Levi 6.00 15.00
577 Joel Teasdale 2.50 6.00
578 Tye Kartye 4.00 10.00
579 Drew Helleson 2.50 6.00
580 Brock Faber 6.00 15.00
581 Marco Kasper 6.00 15.00
582 Connor Bedard 80.00 200.00
583 Adam Fantilli 8.00 20.00
584 Logan Cooley 8.00 20.00
585 John Beecher 5.00 12.00
586 Jackson LaCombe 2.50 6.00
587 Kevin Korchinski 4.00 10.00
588 Matthew Poitras 5.00 12.00
589 Fraser Minten 5.00 12.00
590 Waltteri Merela 2.50 6.00
591 Zach Benson 4.00 10.00
592 Mackie Samoskevich 4.00 10.00
593 Pavel Mintyukov 4.00 10.00
594 Emil Andrae 2.50 6.00
595 Uvis Balinskis 2.50 6.00
596 Adam Ginning 2.50 6.00
597 Matt Murray 2.50 6.00
598 Stanislav Svozil 2.00 5.00
599 Leo Carlsson 8.00 20.00
600 Checklist 1.50 4.00

2023-24 O-Pee-Chee Retro Black

*BLACK/100: 1.2X TO 3X BASIC
*BLACK AS: 2X TO 5X BASIC
*BLACK RC: 1X TO 2.5X BASIC
561 Bobby McMann 25.00 60.00
580 Brock Faber 30.00 80.00
582 Connor Bedard 400.00 1000.00
588 Matthew Poitras 20.00 50.00
599 Leo Carlsson 40.00 100.00

2023-24 O-Pee-Chee Team Logo Patches

365 Stadium Series 20.00 50.00
366 Global Series Finland 20.00 50.00
367 Global Series Sweden 20.00 50.00
368 Global Series Czech Republic 20.00 50.00
369 Global Series Germany 20.00 50.00
370 All Star Game 20.00 50.00
371 Winter Classic 20.00 50.00
372 Pittsburgh Penguins 20.00 50.00
373 Boston Bruins 20.00 50.00
374 Arizona Coyotes 20.00 50.00
375 Buffalo Sabres 20.00 50.00
376 Carolina Hurricanes 20.00 50.00
377 New Jersey Devils 20.00 50.00
378 Eastern Conference 20.00 50.00
379 Western Conference 20.00 50.00
380 Atlantic Division 20.00 50.00
381 Central Division 20.00 50.00
382 Metropolitan Division 20.00 50.00
383 Pacific Division 20.00 50.00
384 New York Islanders 20.00 50.00
385 Vancouver Canucks 20.00 50.00
386 Calgary Flames 20.00 50.00
387 Seattle Kraken 20.00 50.00
388 Tampa Bay Lightning 20.00 50.00
389 Kansas City Scouts 20.00 50.00

2023-24 O-Pee-Chee Top Rookie Bounty

OPC1 Redemption Card 15.00 40.00
OPC2 Redemption Card 15.00 40.00
OPC3 Redemption Card 15.00 40.00
OPC4 Redemption Card 15.00 40.00
OPC5 Redemption Card 15.00 40.00
OPC6 Redemption Card 15.00 40.00
OPC7 Redemption Card 15.00 40.00
OPC8 Redemption Card 15.00 40.00
OPC9 Redemption Card 15.00 40.00

2023-24 O-Pee-Chee Top Rookie Bounty Award

*BLACK/100: .6X TO 1.5X BASIC
BACB Connor Bedard 150.00 400.00

2023-24 O-Pee-Chee Wood Variants

WAM Auston Matthews 25.00 60.00
WAO Alex Ovechkin 25.00 60.00
WCB Connor Bedard 150.00 400.00
WCM Connor McDavid 50.00 125.00
WGH Gordie Howe 40.00 100.00
WJP Jakob Pelletier 12.00 30.00
WJR Jason Robertson 15.00 40.00
WJS Joe Sakic 20.00 50.00
WKK Kirill Kaprizov 30.00 80.00
WLD Leon Draisaitl 12.00 30.00
WLH Luke Hughes 25.00 60.00
WMA Cale Makar 25.00 60.00
WMB Martin Brodeur 25.00 60.00
WMC Matthew Coronato 15.00 40.00
WML Mario Lemieux 25.00 60.00
WMM Mitch Marner 15.00 40.00
WMN Matthew Knies 40.00 100.00
WNM Nathan MacKinnon 15.00 40.00
WSC Sidney Crosby 40.00 100.00
WWG Wayne Gretzky 40.00 100.00

2023-24 O-Pee-Chee Wood Variants Cherry

*CHERRY: .5X TO 1.2X BASIC
WAM Auston Matthews 40.00 100.00
WGH Gordie Howe 60.00 150.00
WLD Leon Draisaitl 20.00 50.00
WMB Martin Brodeur 40.00 100.00
WML Mario Lemieux 40.00 100.00
WNM Nathan MacKinnon 25.00 60.00
WWG Wayne Gretzky 60.00 150.00

2024-25 O-Pee-Chee

1 Nathan MacKinnon 1.00 2.50
2 Jordan Greenway .15 .40
3 Matt Boldy .40 1.00
4 Bryan Rust .25 .60
5 Adrian Kempe .25 .60
6 Brady Tkachuk .40 1.00
7 Auston Matthews 1.00 2.50
8 Joel Farabee .25 .60
9 Mason Appleton .15 .40
10 Artturi Lehkonen .20 .50
11 Jared McCann .20 .50
12 Oliver Kylington .15 .40
13 Troy Terry .20 .50
14 Reilly Smith .25 .60
15 Jacob Middleton .15 .40
16 Tyler Seguin .30 .75
17 Niko Mikkola .15 .40
18 Vincent Desharnais .15 .40
19 Sam Lafferty .15 .40
20 Brandt Clarke .25 .60
21 Kris Letang .30 .75
22 Evan Rodrigues .20 .50
23 Rasmus Dahlin .30 .75
24 Connor McDavid 1.25 3.00
25 Philip Tomasino .15 .40
26 Mikko Rantanen .60 1.50
27 Fraser Minten .25 .60
28 Drew O'Connor .15 .40
29 Trent Frederic .15 .40
30 Pyotr Kochetkov .25 .60
31 Warren Foegele .15 .40
32 Kevin Korchinski .20 .50
33 Brock Boeser .30 .75
34 Klim Kostin .15 .40
35 Filip Forsberg .40 1.00
36 Nick Bjugstad .15 .40
37 William Nylander .50 1.25
38 Joel Hofer .15 .40
39 Jonatan Berggren .20 .50
40 David Savard .15 .40
41 Jackson LaCombe .15 .40
42 Martin Pospisil .15 .40
43 Vladislav Gavrikov .15 .40
44 Roope Hintz .30 .75
45 Jakob Chychrun .25 .60
46 Fabian Zetterlund .15 .40
47 Adam Pelech .15 .40
48 Tyson Foerster .25 .60
49 Jiri Kulich .25 .60
50 Claude Giroux .25 .60
51 Tyler Bertuzzi .20 .50
52 Aaron Ekblad .30 .75
53 Kevin Bahl .15 .40
54 John Carlson .25 .60
55 Jacob Bernard-Docker .15 .40
56 Tyson Barrie .15 .40
57 Ryan Poehling .25 .60
58 Anders Lee .20 .50
59 Oskar Sundqvist .15 .40
60 Erik Gustafsson .15 .40
61 Joe Veleno .20 .50
62 John Beecher .25 .60
63 Scott Wedgewood .20 .50
64 Mikey Anderson .20 .50
65 Timo Meier .25 .60
66 Jordan Binnington .40 1.00
67 Mikael Granlund .20 .50
68 Eetu Luostarinen .15 .40
69 Cale Makar .60 1.50
70 Joonas Korpisalo .25 .60
71 Alexander Romanov .20 .50
72 Nick Robertson .25 .60
73 Igor Shesterkin .50 1.25
74 Jesper Bratt .25 .60
75 Michael Amadio .15 .40
76 Jason Dickinson .15 .40
77 Jan Rutta .15 .40
78 Mitch Marner .40 1.00
79 Kasperi Kapanen .20 .50
80 Jake Guentzel .40 1.00
81 Charlie Lindgren .20 .50
82 Brayden Schenn .25 .60
83 Andrew Mangiapane .25 .60
84 Jamie Drysdale .20 .50
85 Mason McTavish .25 .60
86 Tomas Tatar .15 .40
87 Mark Scheifele .40 1.00
88 Bo Horvat .30 .75
89 Dakota Joshua .15 .40
90 Jeff Skinner .25 .60
91 Philipp Grubauer .25 .60
92 Nick Paul .15 .40
93 Drew Doughty .25 .60
94 Cam Atkinson .25 .60
95 Tristan Luneau .15 .40
96 Sean Monahan .15 .40
97 Danton Heinen .15 .40
98 Alexander Holtz .25 .60
99 Kevin Stenlund .20 .50
100 Checklist .15 .40
101 Vincent Trocheck .25 .60
102 Jesperi Kotkaniemi .25 .60
103 Brock Faber .30 .75
104 Luke Hughes .40 1.00
105 Alex Ovechkin 1.00 2.50
106 Noah Dobson .30 .75
107 Jack Eichel .40 1.00
108 Joey Daccord .25 .60
109 Luke Philp .15 .40
110 Ryan Pulock .20 .50
111 Filip Hronek .15 .40
112 Nikita Kucherov .50 1.25
113 Connor Hellebuyck .50 1.25
114 Aliaksei Protas .15 .40
115 Simon Edvinsson .25 .60
116 Marcus Foligno .20 .50
117 Sean Durzi .15 .40
118 Nick Foligno .15 .40
119 Devon Toews .20 .50
120 Matias Maccelli .20 .50
121 Oliver Bjorkstrand .20 .50
122 Ivan Barbashev .20 .50
123 Calen Addison .15 .40
124 Travis Sanheim .15 .40
125 Boone Jenner .25 .60
126 Phillip Danault .25 .60
127 Lukas Dostal .25 .60
128 Erik Cernak .15 .40
129 Connor Dewar .15 .40
130 Paul Cotter .15 .40
131 Jakob Pelletier .15 .40
132 Dougie Hamilton .20 .50
133 T.J. Oshie .25 .60
134 David Perron .20 .50
135 Isac Lundestrom .15 .40
136 Dylan Guenther .30 .75
137 Ilya Samsonov .25 .60
138 Lawson Crouse .15 .40
139 Connor McMichael .25 .60
140 Alex Vlasic .15 .40
141 Charlie Coyle .25 .60
142 Andrew Copp .15 .40
143 Andrei Kuzmenko .25 .60
144 Conor Garland .20 .50
145 Tristan Jarry .25 .60
146 Frederick Gaudreau .15 .40
147 Trevor Moore .15 .40
148 Alex Killorn .15 .40
149 Sam Bennett .40 1.00
150 Rasmus Sandin .20 .50
151 Matthew Knies .50 1.25
152 Tye Kartye .20 .50
153 Jimmy Vesey .20 .50
154 Tage Thompson .30 .75
155 Neal Pionk .15 .40
156 Connor Bedard .75 2.00
157 Morgan Frost .20 .50
158 Ryan Hartman .15 .40
159 Brandon Tanev .20 .50
160 Ville Husso .15 .40
161 Aleksander Barkov .40 1.00
162 Corey Perry .40 1.00
163 Nicolas Roy .15 .40
164 Matthew Tkachuk .50 1.25
165 Logan Couture .30 .75
166 David Rittich .15 .40
167 Adam Fantilli .40 1.00
168 Tim Stutzle .30 .75
169 Ilya Sorokin .40 1.00
170 Leon Draisaitl .75 2.00
171 William Borgen .15 .40
172 Sergei Bobrovsky .40 1.00
173 Cole Perfetti .25 .60
174 Elias Pettersson .40 1.00
175 Trevor Zegras .25 .60
176 Jonathan Drouin .20 .50
177 Joel Eriksson Ek .20 .50
178 Marcus Pettersson .15 .40
179 Cam Talbot .25 .60
180 Jalen Chatfield .15 .40
181 Sean Couturier .20 .50
182 Michael Rasmussen .15 .40
183 Yegor Sharangovich .25 .60
184 Thatcher Demko .30 .75
185 Mike Hoffman .15 .40
186 Brent Burns .25 .60
187 Parker Kelly .15 .40
188 Shane Wright .30 .75
189 Darnell Nurse .20 .50
190 Dmitri Voronkov .15 .40
191 Luke Kunin .15 .40
192 Dustin Wolf .40 1.00
193 Liam O'Brien .15 .40
194 Casey Mittelstadt .25 .60
195 Filip Gustavsson .25 .60
196 Jordan Kyrou .25 .60
197 Jean-Gabriel Pageau .15 .40
198 Andrei Vasilevskiy .40 1.00
199 Tyler Johnson .15 .40
200 Checklist .15 .40
201 Blake Coleman .20 .50
202 Brandon Montour .30 .75
203 Mark Stone .30 .75
204 Petr Mrazek .20 .50
205 Erik Haula .15 .40
206 Brandon Saad .20 .50
207 Quinn Hughes .60 1.50
208 J.T. Compher .15 .40
209 Colton Sissons .15 .40
210 Anthony Mantha .20 .50
211 Dylan DeMelo .15 .40
212 Joseph Woll .30 .75
213 Ondrej Palat .20 .50
214 Mikhail Sergachev .20 .50
215 Jesper Fast .20 .50
216 Mason Marchment .20 .50
217 Kevin Hayes .20 .50
218 Alex Newhook .20 .50
219 Elias Lindholm .25 .60
220 Brock Nelson .25 .60
221 Tanner Jeannot .15 .40
222 Scott Laughton .15 .40
223 Vladimir Tarasenko .30 .75
224 Matt Savoie .25 .60
225 Samuel Girard .15 .40
226 Pavel Mintyukov .20 .50
227 Brendan Gallagher .25 .60
228 Tom Wilson .25 .60
229 Semyon Varlamov .25 .60
230 Jake McCabe .15 .40
231 Lukas Reichel .25 .60
232 Owen Tippett .15 .40
233 Adam Lowry .20 .50
234 Nick Perbix .15 .40
235 Mathieu Joseph .15 .40
236 Alex DeBrincat .30 .75
237 Ryan O'Reilly .25 .60
238 Torey Krug .20 .50
230 Ross Colton .20 .50
240 Zach Werenski .40 1.00
241 Miro Heiskanen .30 .75
242 Jake Evans .15 .40
243 Vince Dunn .20 .50
244 Frederik Andersen .30 .75
245 Gabe Vilardi .25 .60
246 Frank Vatrano .20 .50
247 Stefan Noesen .15 .40
248 Alex Tuch .25 .60
249 Jacob Trouba .20 .50
250 Jack McBain .15 .40
251 Justin Barron .20 .50
252 John Tavares .40 1.00
253 Brad Marchand .50 1.25
254 Philipp Kurashev .20 .50
255 Sebastian Aho .40 1.00
256 Marc-Andre Fleury .50 1.25
257 Teddy Blueger .15 .40
258 Rasmus Ristolainen .15 .40
259 Hudson Fasching .15 .40
260 Jake Oettinger .40 1.00
261 Nazem Kadri .30 .75
262 Pierre Engvall .15 .40
263 Jamie Benn .25 .60
264 Darcy Kuemper .25 .60
265 Jason Zucker .25 .60
266 Alex Pietrangelo .20 .50
267 Brady Skjei .15 .40
268 Cole Caufield .50 1.25
269 Anthony Cirelli .20 .50
270 Ilya Mikheyev .20 .50
271 Ryan Suter .20 .50
272 Pavel Zacha .20 .50
273 William Eklund .30 .75
274 Seth Jarvis .30 .75
275 Bobby Brink .15 .40
276 Kevin Fiala .20 .50
277 Marco Rossi .30 .75
278 Brayden Point .30 .75
279 Alexis Lafreniere .40 1.00
280 Jordan Martinook .15 .40
281 Jonathan Huberdeau .30 .75
282 Morgan Geekie .15 .40
283 Mika Zibanejad .30 .75
284 Dawson Mercer .30 .75
285 Anze Kopitar .40 1.00
286 Hendrix Lapierre .15 .40
287 Drake Batherson .25 .60
288 Jaccob Slavin .20 .50
289 Kirill Kaprizov .75 2.00
290 Chris Kreider .30 .75
291 Mackenzie Blackwood .25 .60
292 Matt Dumba .15 .40
293 Luke Schenn .25 .60
294 Mikael Backlund .20 .50
295 Ryan Nugent-Hopkins .30 .75
296 Viktor Arvidsson .15 .40
297 Josh Norris .25 .60
298 Nick Schmaltz .20 .50
299 Alexandar Georgiev .25 .60
300 Checklist .15 .40
301 Michael Eyssimont .15 .40
302 Kaapo Kakko .20 .50
303 Pavel Dorofeyev .15 .40
304 Roman Josi .25 .60
305 Matt Roy .15 .40
306 Jack Quinn .20 .50
307 Andrei Svechnikov .30 .75
308 Connor Ingram .15 .40
309 Victor Olofsson .25 .60
310 Nikita Zaitsev .15 .40
311 Dmitry Orlov .25 .60
312 Erik Gudbranson .15 .40
313 Pierre-Luc Dubois .20 .50
314 Gabriel Landeskog .30 .75
315 Lars Eller .15 .40
316 Daniel Sprong .15 .40
317 Sean Walker .15 .40
318 Max Domi .25 .60
319 Tyler Toffoli .25 .60
320 Radko Gudas .15 .40
321 Marcus Johansson .15 .40
322 Noel Acciari .15 .40
323 Jonathan Marchessault .30 .75
324 Laurent Brossoit .15 .40
325 Matt Duchene .25 .60
326 Jonas Brodin .15 .40
327 Jake Neighbours .25 .60
328 Casey Cizikas .20 .50
329 Oliver Ekman-Larsson .15 .40
330 Jack Roslovic .15 .40
331 Stuart Skinner .30 .75
332 Bobby McMann .20 .50
333 Eeli Tolvanen .25 .60
334 Mattias Samuelsson .15 .40
335 Ryan Donato .20 .50
336 Kyle Palmieri .20 .50
337 Alexey Toropchenko .15 .40
338 Steven Stamkos .50 1.25
339 Sam Reinhart .50 1.25
340 Ryan McLeod .15 .40
341 Calle Jarnkrok .15 .40
342 Filip Chytil .20 .50
343 Rasmus Andersson .20 .50
344 Alex Laferriere .15 .40
345 Shea Theodore .30 .75
346 Josh Anderson .20 .50
347 Dylan Cozens .25 .60
348 Pavel Buchnevich .20 .50
349 T.J. Brodie .15 .40
350 Alexander Wennberg .15 .40
351 Erik Brannstrom .15 .40
352 Juuse Saros .30 .75
353 Jacob Markstrom .25 .60
354 William Karlsson .30 .75
355 Kirby Dach .25 .60
356 Andre Burakovsky .15 .40
357 Elvis Merzlikins .25 .60
358 Zach Benson .20 .50
359 Zach Hyman .40 1.00
360 Nikolaj Ehlers .25 .60
361 Victor Hedman .30 .75
362 Jordan Harris .15 .40
363 Luke Glendening .15 .40
364 Adin Hill .25 .60
365 Evgenii Dadonov .15 .40
366 Jonas Siegenthaler .15 .40
367 Michael Bunting .25 .60
368 Matthew Poitras .25 .60
369 Anton Lundell .25 .60
370 Alex Kerfoot .20 .50
371 Kaiden Guhle .25 .60
372 Jake Sanderson .30 .75
373 Nicolas Deslauriers .15 .40
374 Adam Henrique .20 .50
375 Evgeni Malkin .50 1.25
376 Nico Sturm .15 .40
377 Colton Parayko .20 .50
378 Josh Morrissey .30 .75
379 Isak Rosen .15 .40
380 Shane Pinto .20 .50
381 Travis Konecny .25 .60
382 Quinton Byfield .30 .75
383 J.J. Moser .15 .40
384 Mats Zuccarello .25 .60
385 Samuel Montembeault .25 .60
386 Emil Bemstrom .15 .40
387 Tyler Myers .15 .40
388 Kevin Shattenkirk .15 .40
309 James van Riemsdyk .20 .50
390 Nico Hischier .40 1.00
391 Yanni Gourde .20 .50
392 Robby Fabbri .15 .40
393 Michael Carcone .15 .40
394 Cole Sillinger .20 .50
395 Logan O'Connor .25 .60
396 Kyle Connor .40 1.00
397 Noah Hanifin .25 .60
398 Alex Iafallo .15 .40
399 Mattias Ekholm .20 .50
400 Checklist .15 .40
401 Jordan Eberle .25 .60
402 Connor Zary .25 .60
403 Linus Ullmark .25 .60
404 Nic Dowd .15 .40
405 Bowen Byram .30 .75
406 Pius Suter .20 .50
407 Samuel Ersson .25 .60
408 John Gibson .25 .60
409 Gustav Nyquist .15 .40
410 Ryan McDonagh .15 .40
411 Patrick Maroon .15 .40
412 K'Andre Miller .20 .50
413 Anthony Duclair .20 .50
414 Nino Niederreiter .20 .50
415 JJ Peterka .25 .60
416 Thomas Chabot .25 .60
417 Jake DeBrusk .25 .60
418 Leo Carlsson .40 1.00
419 Patrik Laine .30 .75
420 Moritz Seider .30 .75
421 Robert Thomas .25 .60
422 John Marino .25 .60
423 Jason Robertson .40 1.00
424 Kiefer Sherwood .15 .40
425 Morgan Rielly .25 .60
426 Thomas Harley .25 .60
427 Kirill Marchenko .30 .75
428 Alex Lyon .20 .50
429 Rickard Rakell .20 .50
430 Logan Thompson .30 .75
431 Adam Fox .30 .75
432 Ryan Strome .25 .60
433 Evander Kane .25 .60
434 Mario Ferraro .15 .40
435 Mathew Barzal .30 .75
436 Chandler Stephenson .20 .50
437 Brett Leason .15 .40
438 Kent Johnson .25 .60
439 Logan Cooley .50 1.25
440 Shayne Gostisbehere .25 .60
441 Nick Suzuki .50 1.25
442 Jack Hughes .60 1.50
443 Teuvo Teravainen .25 .60
444 Sonny Milano .20 .50
445 Owen Power .25 .60
446 Dylan Larkin .30 .75
447 Michael Kesselring .15 .40
448 Jared Spurgeon .25 .60
449 Charlie McAvoy .30 .75
450 Jake Allen .25 .60
451 Jaden Schwartz .20 .50
452 J.T. Miller .30 .75
453 Dylan Strome .30 .75
454 Alex Nylander .20 .50
455 Devon Levi .30 .75
456 Tomas Hertl .25 .60
457 Vitek Vanecek .25 .60
458 Alex Nedeljkovic .20 .50
459 Luke Evangelista .20 .50
460 Lucas Raymond .40 1.00
461 Seth Jones .25 .60
462 Yegor Chinakhov .20 .50
463 Nils Hoglander .20 .50
464 Carter Verhaeghe .25 .60
465 Juraj Slafkovsky .50 1.25
466 Thomas Novak .15 .40
467 Marc-Edouard Vlasic .15 .40
468 Sidney Crosby 1.00 2.50
469 Evan Bouchard .30 .75
470 Simon Nemec .30 .75
471 Filip Zadina .20 .50
472 Michael Matheson .15 .40
473 Matty Beniers .30 .75
474 Jake Walman .15 .40
475 Miles Wood .15 .40
476 Jonathan Quick .30 .75
477 Brandon Hagel .20 .50
478 Taylor Hall .25 .60
479 MacKenzie Weegar .20 .50
480 Artemi Panarin .50 1.25
481 Christopher Tanev .15 .40
482 Ivan Miroshnichenko .20 .50
483 Clayton Keller .30 .75
484 Erik Karlsson .30 .75
485 Martin Necas .30 .75
486 Jack Johnson .15 .40
487 Vladislav Namestnikov .15 .40
488 Wyatt Johnston .50 1.25
489 Valeri Nichushkin .25 .60
490 Jeremy Swayman .40 1.00
491 Gustav Forsling .25 .60
492 Arber Xhekaj .25 .60
493 Patrick Kane .50 1.25
494 David Jiricek .25 .60
495 Will Cuylle .20 .50
496 David Pastrnak .60 1.50
107 Miro Heiskanen .30 .75
498 Ridly Greig .20 .50
499 Hampus Lindholm .15 .40
500 Checklist .15 .40
501 David Pastrnak AS 1.00 2.50
502 Frank Vatrano AS .30 .75
503 Filip Forsberg AS .60 1.50
504 Jeremy Swayman AS .60 1.50
505 Connor Hellebuyck AS .75 2.00
506 Quinn Hughes AS 1.00 2.50
507 Clayton Keller AS .50 1.25
508 Kirill Kaprizov AS 1.25 3.00
509 Leon Draisaitl AS 1.25 3.00
510 Brock Boeser AS .50 1.25
511 Igor Shesterkin AS .75 2.00
512 Cale Makar AS 1.00 2.50
513 Sergei Bobrovsky AS .60 1.50
514 Kyle Connor AS .60 1.50
515 Jake Oettinger AS .60 1.50
516 Sebastian Aho AS .60 1.50
517 Robert Thomas AS .40 1.00
518 Cam Talbot AS .40 1.00
519 William Nylander AS .75 2.00
520 Oliver Bjorkstrand AS .30 .75
521 Nick Suzuki AS .75 2.00
522 Nikita Kucherov AS .75 2.00
523 Mitch Marner AS .60 1.50
524 Alexandar Georgiev AS .40 1.00
525 Boone Jenner AS .40 1.00
526 Thatcher Demko AS .50 1.25
527 Alex DeBrincat AS .50 1.25
528 Sidney Crosby AS 1.50 4.00
529 Sam Reinhart AS .75 2.00
530 Brady Tkachuk AS .60 1.50
531 Mathew Barzal AS .50 1.25
532 Nathan MacKinnon AS 1.50 4.00
533 Rasmus Dahlin AS .50 1.25
534 Elias Pettersson AS .60 1.50
535 Auston Matthews AS 1.50 4.00
536 Travis Konecny AS .40 1.00
537 Connor McDavid AS 2.00 5.00
538 Jesper Bratt AS .40 1.00
539 Tom Wilson AS .40 1.00
540 Tomas Hertl AS .40 1.00
541 Jesper Wallstedt RC 2.00 5.00
542 Josh Doan RC 1.25 3.00
543 Kyle MacLean RC .75 2.00

544 Lukas Cormier RC .75 2.00
545 Macklin Celebrini RC 10.00 25.00
546 Cutter Gauthier RC 2.00 5.00
547 Matvei Michkov RC 8.00 20.00
548 Scott Morrow RC 1.00 2.50
549 Lane Hutson RC 6.00 15.00
550 Ruslan Iskhakov RC .75 2.00
551 Zack Ostapchuk RC .75 2.00
552 Will Smith RC 2.50 6.00
553 Zachary Bolduc RC 1.25 3.00
554 Akil Thomas RC .75 2.00
555 Joshua Roy RC 1.25 3.00
556 Shakir Mukhamadullin RC 1.00 2.50
557 Gage Goncalves RC 1.00 2.50
558 Marshall Rifai RC .75 2.00
559 Logan Mailloux RC 1.50 4.00
560 Adam Klapka RC .75 2.00
561 Jackson Blake RC 1.50 4.00
562 Mavrik Bourque RC 1.50 4.00
563 Rutger McGroarty RC 1.50 4.00
564 Frank Nazar RC 2.50 6.00
565 Seamus Casey RC 1.00 2.50
566 Bradly Nadeau RC 1.25 3.00
567 Emil Lilleberg RC .75 2.00
568 Collin Graf RC .75 2.00
569 Aku Raty RC .75 2.00
570 Brendan Brisson RC 1.00 2.50
571 Maxim Tsyplakov RC 1.25 3.00
572 Logan Stankoven RC 2.00 5.00
573 Arshdeep Bains RC 1.00 2.50
574 Matt Rempe RC 1.50 4.00
575 Maxwell Crozier RC .75 2.00
576 Liam Ohgren RC 1.50 4.00
577 Sam Colangelo RC .75 2.00
578 Zach Dean RC .75 2.00
579 Brennan Othmann RC 1.25 3.00
580 Brian Halonen RC .75 2.00
581 Conor Geekie RC 1.25 3.00
582 Justin Brazeau RC .75 2.00
583 Ivan Fedotov RC 1.25 3.00
584 Logan Morrison RC .75 2.00
585 Brad Lambert RC 1.00 2.50
586 Graeme Clarke RC .75 2.00
587 Olen Zellweger RC 1.50 4.00
588 Landon Slaggert RC .75 2.00
589 Jett Luchanko RC 1.50 4.00
590 Luca Del Bel Belluz RC .75 2.00
591 Mason Morelli RC .75 2.00
592 Declan Carlile RC .75 2.00
593 Nikita Chibrikov RC .75 2.00
594 Vasily Ponomarev RC .75 2.00
595 Phil Kemp RC .75 2.00
596 Marat Khusnutdinov RC .75 2.00
597 Pierrick Dube RC .75 2.00
598 Georgi Romanov RC 1.25 3.00
599 Gavin Brindley RC .75 2.00
600 Checklist .50 1.25

2024-25 O-Pee-Chee Blue

*BLUE: .6X TO 1.5X BASIC
545 Macklin Celebrini 25.00 60.00

2024-25 O-Pee-Chee Orange

*ORANGE/25: 8X TO 20X BASIC
*ORANGE RC/25: 5X TO 12X BASIC
*ORANGE AS/25: 5X TO 12X BASIC
545 Macklin Celebrini 200.00 500.00
546 Cutter Gauthier 40.00 100.00
547 Matvei Michkov 150.00 400.00
549 Lane Hutson 150.00 400.00
552 Will Smith 80.00 200.00

2024-25 O-Pee-Chee Rainbow

*RAINBOW/350: 1.2X TO 3X BASIC
547 Matvei Michkov 30.00 80.00

2024-25 O-Pee-Chee Rainbow Black

*RNBW BLK/100: 3X TO 8X BASIC

2024-25 O-Pee-Chee Rainbow Green

*RNBW GRN/33: 4X TO 10X BASIC
547 Matvei Michkov 100.00 250.00
549 Lane Hutson 80.00 200.00
552 Will Smith 40.00 100.00

2024-25 O-Pee-Chee Red

*RED: 1.5X TO 4X BASIC
547 Matvei Michkov 40.00 100.00
549 Lane Hutson 30.00 80.00

2024-25 O-Pee-Chee Variations Black and White Test Proof

*B&W: 2X TO 5X BASIC
*B&W RC: 2.5X TO 6X BASIC

2024-25 O-Pee-Chee Variations Draft

*DRAFT RC: 2X TO 5X BASIC

2024-25 O-Pee-Chee Variations End of Game Three Stars

*3 STARS: 5X TO 12X BASIC

2024-25 O-Pee-Chee Variations Goal Scoring Celebration

*GOAL CELEB: 6X TO 15X BASIC

2024-25 O-Pee-Chee Variations Helmet Off

*HELMET OFF: 6X TO 15X BASIC

2024-25 O-Pee-Chee Yellow

*YELLOW: .8X TO 2X BASIC
*YELLOW RC: 1X TO 2.5X BASIC

2024-25 O-Pee-Chee '24-25 OPC Platinum Previews

*RAINBOW: .5X TO 1.2X BASIC
*SUNSET: .8X TO 2X BASIC
PAM Auston Matthews 3.00 8.00
PAO Alex Ovechkin 3.00 8.00
PCG Cutter Gauthier 2.00 5.00
PCM Connor McDavid 4.00 10.00
PDP David Pastrnak 2.00 5.00
PJW Jesper Wallstedt 2.00 5.00
PLS Logan Stankoven 2.00 5.00
PMC Macklin Celebrini 10.00 25.00
PSC Sidney Crosby 3.00 8.00

2024-25 O-Pee-Chee '24-25 OPC Platinum Previews Cosmic

*COSMIC/65: 2X TO 5X BASIC
PCG Cutter Gauthier 15.00 40.00
PMC Macklin Celebrini 100.00 250.00

2024-25 O-Pee-Chee '24-25 OPC Platinum Previews Matte Pink

*PINK/75: 1.5X TO 4X BASIC
PCG Cutter Gauthier 12.00 30.00
PMC Macklin Celebrini 50.00 125.00

2024-25 O-Pee-Chee '24-25 OPC Platinum Previews Red Prism

*RED/50: 2.5X TO 6X BASIC
PCG Cutter Gauthier 20.00 50.00

2024-25 O-Pee-Chee '24-25 OPC Platinum Previews Seismic Gold

*GOLD/25: 6X TO 15X BASIC

2024-25 O-Pee-Chee '24-25 OPC Platinum Previews Violet Pixels

*VIOLET/99: 1.2X TO 3X BASIC
PCG Cutter Gauthier 10.00 25.00
PMC Macklin Celebrini 40.00 100.00

2024-25 O-Pee-Chee 3-D Marquee Rookies

3DBB Brendan Brisson 20.00 50.00
3DBO Brennan Othmann 25.00 60.00
3DCG Cutter Gauthier 40.00 100.00
3DFN Frank Nazar 50.00 125.00
3DJR Joshua Roy 25.00 60.00
3DJW Jesper Wallstedt 40.00 100.00
3DLS Logan Stankoven 40.00 100.00
3DMB Mavrik Bourque 30.00 80.00
3DMC Macklin Celebrini 125.00 300.00
3DMM Matvei Michkov 100.00 250.00
3DOZ Olen Zellweger 30.00 80.00
3DWS Will Smith 50.00 125.00

2024-25 O-Pee-Chee First Round Draft Patches

DP1 Connor Bedard 25.00 60.00
DP2 Adam Fantilli 12.00 30.00
DP3 Leo Carlsson 12.00 30.00
DP4 Zach Benson 6.00 15.00
DP5 Pavel Mintyukov 6.00 15.00
DP6 Matt Savoie 8.00 20.00
DP7 Juraj Slafkovsky 15.00 40.00
DP8 Logan Cooley 15.00 40.00
DP9 Shane Wright 10.00 25.00
DP10 Owen Power 8.00 20.00
DP11 Luke Hughes 12.00 30.00
DP12 Brennan Othmann 12.00 30.00
DP13 Quinton Byfield 10.00 25.00
DP14 Alexis Lafreniere 12.00 30.00
DP15 Brendan Brisson 10.00 25.00
DP16 Shakir Mukhamadullin 10.00 25.00
DP17 Steven Stamkos 15.00 40.00
DP18 Patrick Kane 15.00 40.00
DP19 Nicklas Backstrom 8.00 20.00
DP20 Trevor Zegras 8.00 20.00
DP21 Evgeni Malkin 15.00 40.00
DP22 Marc-Andre Fleury 15.00 40.00
DP23 Jack Hughes 20.00 50.00
DP24 Cole Caufield 15.00 40.00
DP25 Matt Boldy 12.00 30.00

2024-25 O-Pee-Chee Glo-Pee-Chee

GLO1 Nathan MacKinnon 40.00 100.00
GLO2 Cutter Gauthier 25.00 60.00
GLO3 Auston Matthews 40.00 100.00
GLO4 Connor McDavid 50.00 125.00
GLO5 David Pastrnak 25.00 60.00
GLO6 Mavrik Bourque 20.00 50.00
GLO7 Connor Bedard 30.00 80.00
GLO8 Kirill Kaprizov 30.00 80.00
GLO9 Alex Ovechkin 40.00 100.00
GLO10 Elias Pettersson 15.00 40.00
GLO11 Logan Stankoven 25.00 60.00
GLO12 Nick Suzuki 20.00 50.00
GLO13 Cale Makar 25.00 60.00
GLO14 Sidney Crosby 40.00 100.00
GLO15 Brendan Brisson 12.00 30.00
GLO16 Jack Hughes 25.00 60.00
GLO17 Leon Draisaitl 30.00 80.00
GLO18 Jason Robertson 15.00 40.00
GLO19 Zachary Bolduc 15.00 40.00
GLO20 Mitch Marner 15.00 40.00

2024-25 O-Pee-Chee OPC Premier

P1 Sidney Crosby 4.00 10.00
P2 Luke Hughes 1.50 4.00
P3 Andrei Vasilevskiy 1.50 4.00
P4 Nick Suzuki 2.00 5.00
P5 Artemi Panarin 2.00 5.00
P6 Jared McCann .75 2.00
P7 Nathan MacKinnon 4.00 10.00
P8 Jordan Kyrou 1.00 2.50
P9 Kirill Kaprizov 3.00 8.00
P10 Zach Hyman 1.50 4.00
P11 J.T. Miller 1.25 3.00
P12 Auston Matthews 4.00 10.00
P13 William Eklund 1.25 3.00
P14 Steven Stamkos 2.00 5.00
P15 Nico Hischier 1.50 4.00
P16 Matthew Tkachuk 2.00 5.00
P17 Matt Boldy 1.50 4.00
P18 Lucas Raymond 1.50 4.00
P19 Adrian Kempe 1.00 2.50
P20 Ilya Sorokin 1.50 4.00
P21 Connor Hellebuyck 2.00 5.00
P22 Aleksander Barkov 1.50 4.00
P23 Filip Forsberg 1.50 4.00
P24 Travis Konecny 1.00 2.50
P25 Quinn Hughes 2.50 6.00
P26 Roope Hintz 1.25 3.00
P27 Mikko Rantanen 2.50 6.00
P28 Jonathan Marchessault 1.25 3.00
P29 Andrei Svechnikov 1.25 3.00
P30 Brayden Point 1.25 3.00
P31 David Pastrnak 2.50 6.00
P32 Connor McDavid 5.00 12.00
P33 Wyatt Johnston 2.00 5.00
P34 Rasmus Dahlin 1.25 3.00
P35 Mark Scheifele 1.50 4.00
P36 Brock Boeser 1.25 3.00
P37 Sebastian Aho 1.50 4.00
P38 Igor Shesterkin 2.00 5.00
P39 Nikita Kucherov 2.00 5.00
P40 Tim Stutzle 1.25 3.00
P41 Dylan Larkin 1.25 3.00
P42 Cole Caufield 2.00 5.00
P43 Alex Ovechkin 4.00 10.00
P44 Leon Draisaitl 3.00 8.00
P45 Roman Josi 1.00 2.50
P46 Robert Thomas 1.00 2.50
P47 Jesper Bratt 1.00 2.50
P48 Moritz Seider 1.25 3.00
P49 Kyle Connor 1.50 4.00
P50 Jack Eichel 1.50 4.00
P51 Brady Tkachuk 1.50 4.00
P52 Jake Oettinger 1.50 4.00
P53 Nazem Kadri 1.25 3.00
P54 Alexis Lafreniere 1.50 4.00
P55 Sam Reinhart 2.00 5.00
P56 Evgeni Malkin 2.00 5.00
P57 Evan Bouchard 1.25 3.00
P58 Mason McTavish 1.00 2.50
P59 Jack Hughes 2.50 6.00
P60 Marc-Andre Fleury 2.00 5.00
P61 John Tavares 1.50 4.00
P62 Brad Marchand 2.00 5.00
P63 Jason Robertson 1.50 4.00
P64 Mitch Marner 1.50 4.00
P65 Anze Kopitar 1.50 4.00
P66 Connor Bedard 3.00 8.00
P67 Clayton Keller 1.25 3.00
P68 Elias Pettersson 1.50 4.00
P69 Adam Fantilli 1.50 4.00
P70 Brock Faber 1.25 3.00
P71 Cale Makar 2.50 6.00
P72 Mathew Barzal 1.25 3.00
P73 Brandon Hagel .75 2.00
P74 Tage Thompson 1.25 3.00
P75 William Nylander 2.00 5.00
P76 Zachary Bolduc 1.50 4.00
P77 Brendan Brisson 1.25 3.00
P78 Ivan Fedotov 1.50 4.00
P79 Matt Rempe 2.00 5.00
P80 Shakir Mukhamadullin 1.25 3.00
P81 Jesper Wallstedt 2.50 6.00
P82 Josh Doan 1.50 4.00
P83 Zack Ostapchuk 1.00 2.50
P84 Mavrik Bourque 2.00 5.00
P85 Frank Nazar 3.00 8.00
P86 Marat Khusnutdinov 1.00 2.50
P87 Brennan Othmann 1.50 4.00
P88 Cutter Gauthier 2.50 6.00
P89 Akil Thomas 1.00 2.50
P90 Joshua Roy 1.50 4.00
P91 Zach Dean 1.00 2.50
P92 Logan Stankoven 2.50 6.00
P93 Olen Zellweger 2.00 5.00
P94 Collin Graf 1.00 2.50
P95 Mason Morelli 1.00 2.50
P96 Macklin Celebrini 25.00 60.00
P97 Will Smith 3.00 8.00
P98 Matvei Michkov 20.00 50.00
P99 Seamus Casey 1.25 3.00
P100 Rutger McGroarty 2.00 5.00

2024-25 O-Pee-Chee OPC Premier Diamond Rainbow

*DIAMOND/75: 2X TO 5X BASIC
*DIAMOND RC/75: 3X TO 8X BASIC
P97 Will Smith 40.00 100.00

2024-25 O-Pee-Chee Playing Cards

2DIAMONDS Mavrik Bourque 3.00 8.00
3DIAMONDS Logan Cooley 3.00 8.00
4DIAMONDS Thatcher Demko 2.00 5.00
5DIAMONDS Sam Reinhart 3.00 8.00
6DIAMONDS Jared McCann 1.25 3.00
7DIAMONDS Robert Thomas 1.50 4.00
9DIAMONDS Jack Eichel 2.50 6.00
8DIAMONDS Brady Tkachuk 2.50 6.00
KDIAMONDS Kirill Kaprizov 5.00 12.00
ADIAMONDS Nikita Kucherov 3.00 8.00
10DIAMONDS Mikko Rantanen 4.00 10.00
JDIAMONDS Mathew Barzal 2.00 5.00
QDIAMONDS William Nylander 3.00 8.00
JOKER Iceburgh 5.00 12.00
JOKER Youppi 5.00 12.00
2CLUBS Cutter Gauthier 4.00 10.00
3CLUBS Brock Faber 2.00 5.00
4CLUBS Tim Stutzle 2.00 5.00
5CLUBS Tage Thompson 2.00 5.00
6CLUBS Dylan Larkin 2.00 5.00
7CLUBS Brad Marchand 3.00 8.00
8CLUBS Jack Hughes 4.00 10.00
9CLUBS Jason Robertson 2.50 6.00
ACLUBS Nathan MacKinnon 6.00 15.00
JCLUBS Brayden Point 2.00 5.00
KCLUBS David Pastrnak 4.00 10.00
QCLUBS Leon Draisaitl 5.00 12.00
10CLUBS Quinn Hughes 4.00 10.00
2HEARTS Logan Stankoven 4.00 10.00
2SPADES Adam Fantilli 2.50 6.00
3HEARTS William Eklund 2.00 5.00
3SPADES Luke Hughes 2.50 6.00
4HEARTS Nazem Kadri 2.00 5.00
4SPADES Leo Carlsson 2.50 6.00
5HEARTS Nick Suzuki 3.00 8.00
5SPADES Filip Forsberg 2.50 6.00
6HEARTS Steven Stamkos 3.00 8.00
6SPADES Adrian Kempe 1.50 4.00
7HEARTS Zach Hyman 2.50 6.00
7SPADES Travis Konecny 1.50 4.00
8HEARTS Matthew Tkachuk 3.00 8.00
8SPADES Cole Caufield 3.00 8.00
9HEARTS Sebastian Aho 2.50 6.00
9SPADES Aleksander Barkov 2.50 6.00
AHEARTS Auston Matthews 6.00 15.00
ASPADES Connor McDavid 8.00 20.00
JHEARTS Connor Bedard 5.00 12.00
JSPADES Elias Pettersson 2.50 6.00
KHEARTS Artemi Panarin 3.00 8.00
KSPADES Sidney Crosby 6.00 15.00
QHEARTS Cale Makar 4.00 10.00
QSPADES Alex Ovechkin 6.00 15.00
10HEARTS Connor Hellebuyck 3.00 8.00
10SPADES Mitch Marner 2.50 6.00

2024-25 O-Pee-Chee Retro

1 Nathan MacKinnon 1.50 4.00
2 Jordan Greenway .25 .60
3 Matt Boldy .60 1.50
4 Bryan Rust .40 1.00
5 Adrian Kempe .40 1.00
6 Brady Tkachuk .60 1.50
7 Auston Matthews 1.50 4.00
8 Joel Farabee .40 1.00
9 Mason Appleton .25 .60
10 Artturi Lehkonen .30 .75
11 Jared McCann .30 .75
12 Oliver Kylington .25 .60
13 Troy Terry .30 .75
14 Reilly Smith .40 1.00
15 Jacob Middleton .25 .60
16 Tyler Seguin .50 1.25
17 Niko Mikkola .25 .60
18 Vincent Desharnais .25 .60
19 Sam Lafferty .25 .60
20 Brandt Clarke .40 1.00
21 Kris Letang .50 1.25
22 Evan Rodrigues .30 .75
23 Rasmus Dahlin .50 1.25
24 Connor McDavid 2.00 5.00
25 Philip Tomasino .25 .60
26 Mikko Rantanen 1.00 2.50
27 Fraser Minten .40 1.00
28 Drew O'Connor .25 .60
29 Trent Frederic .25 .60
30 Pyotr Kochetkov .40 1.00
31 Warren Foegele .25 .60
32 Kevin Korchinski .30 .75
33 Brock Boeser .50 1.25
34 Klim Kostin .25 .60
35 Filip Forsberg .60 1.50
36 Nick Bjugstad .25 .60
37 William Nylander .75 2.00
38 Joel Hofer .25 .60
39 Jonatan Berggren .30 .75
40 David Savard .25 .60
41 Jackson LaCombe .25 .60
42 Martin Pospisil .25 .60
43 Vladislav Gavrikov .25 .60
44 Roope Hintz .50 1.25
45 Jakob Chychrun .40 1.00
46 Fabian Zetterlund .25 .60
47 Adam Pelech .25 .60
48 Tyson Foerster .40 1.00
49 Jiri Kulich .40 1.00
50 Claude Giroux .40 1.00
51 Tyler Bertuzzi .30 .75
52 Aaron Ekblad .50 1.25
53 Kevin Bahl .25 .60
54 John Carlson .40 1.00
55 Jacob Bernard-Docker .25 .60
56 Tyson Barrie .25 .60
57 Ryan Poehling .40 1.00
58 Anders Lee .30 .75
59 Oskar Sundqvist .25 .60
60 Erik Gustafsson .25 .60
61 Joe Veleno .30 .75
62 John Beecher .40 1.00
63 Scott Wedgewood .30 .75
64 Mikey Anderson .30 .75
65 Timo Meier .40 1.00
66 Jordan Binnington .60 1.50
67 Mikael Granlund .30 .75
68 Eetu Luostarinen .25 .60
69 Cale Makar 1.00 2.50
70 Joonas Korpisalo .40 1.00
71 Alexander Romanov .30 .75
72 Nick Robertson .40 1.00
73 Igor Shesterkin .75 2.00
74 Jesper Bratt .40 1.00
75 Michael Amadio .25 .60
76 Jason Dickinson .25 .60
77 Jan Rutta .25 .60
78 Mitch Marner .60 1.50
79 Kasperi Kapanen .30 .75
80 Jake Guentzel .60 1.50
81 Charlie Lindgren .30 .75
82 Brayden Schenn .40 1.00
83 Andrew Mangiapane .40 1.00
84 Jamie Drysdale .30 .75
85 Mason McTavish .40 1.00
86 Tomas Tatar .25 .60
87 Mark Scheifele .60 1.50
88 Bo Horvat .50 1.25
89 Dakota Joshua .25 .60
90 Jeff Skinner .40 1.00
91 Philipp Grubauer .40 1.00
92 Nick Paul .25 .60
93 Drew Doughty .40 1.00
94 Cam Atkinson .40 1.00
95 Tristan Luneau .25 .60
96 Sean Monahan .25 .60
97 Danton Heinen .25 .60
98 Alexander Holtz .40 1.00
99 Kevin Stenlund .30 .75
100 Checklist .25 .60
101 Vincent Trocheck .40 1.00
102 Jesperi Kotkaniemi .40 1.00
103 Brock Faber .50 1.25
104 Luke Hughes .60 1.50
105 Alex Ovechkin 1.50 4.00
106 Noah Dobson .50 1.25
107 Jack Eichel .60 1.50
108 Joey Daccord .40 1.00
109 Luke Philp .25 .60
110 Ryan Pulock .30 .75
111 Filip Hronek .25 .60
112 Nikita Kucherov .75 2.00
113 Connor Hellebuyck .75 2.00
114 Aliaksei Protas .25 .60
115 Simon Edvinsson .40 1.00
116 Marcus Foligno .30 .75
117 Sean Durzi .25 .60
118 Nick Foligno .25 .60
119 Devon Toews .30 .75
120 Matias Maccelli .30 .75
121 Oliver Bjorkstrand .30 .75
122 Ivan Barbashev .30 .75
123 Calen Addison .25 .60
124 Travis Sanheim .25 .60
125 Boone Jenner .40 1.00
126 Phillip Danault .40 1.00
127 Lukas Dostal .40 1.00
128 Erik Cernak .25 .60
129 Connor Dewar .25 .60
130 Paul Cotter .25 .60
131 Jakob Pelletier .25 .60
132 Dougie Hamilton .30 .75
133 T.J. Oshie .40 1.00
134 David Perron .30 .75
135 Isac Lundestrom .25 .60
136 Dylan Guenther .50 1.25
137 Ilya Samsonov .40 1.00
138 Lawson Crouse .25 .60
139 Connor McMichael .40 1.00
140 Alex Vlasic .25 .60
141 Charlie Coyle .40 1.00
142 Andrew Copp .25 .60
143 Andrei Kuzmenko .40 1.00
144 Conor Garland .30 .75
145 Tristan Jarry .40 1.00
146 Frederick Gaudreau .25 .60
147 Trevor Moore .25 .60
148 Alex Killorn .25 .60
149 Sam Bennett .60 1.50
150 Rasmus Sandin .30 .75
151 Matthew Knies .75 2.00
152 Tye Kartye .30 .75
153 Jimmy Vesey .30 .75
154 Tage Thompson .50 1.25
155 Neal Pionk .25 .60
156 Connor Bedard 1.25 3.00
157 Morgan Frost .30 .75
158 Ryan Hartman .25 .60
159 Brandon Tanev .30 .75
160 Ville Husso .25 .60
161 Aleksander Barkov .60 1.50
162 Corey Perry .60 1.50
163 Nicolas Roy .25 .60
164 Matthew Tkachuk .75 2.00
165 Logan Couture .50 1.25
166 David Rittich .25 .60
167 Adam Fantilli .60 1.50
168 Tim Stutzle .50 1.25
169 Ilya Sorokin .60 1.50
170 Leon Draisaitl 1.25 3.00
171 William Borgen .25 .60
172 Sergei Bobrovsky .60 1.50
173 Cole Perfetti .40 1.00
174 Elias Pettersson .60 1.50
175 Trevor Zegras .40 1.00
176 Jonathan Drouin .30 .75
177 Joel Eriksson Ek .30 .75
178 Marcus Pettersson .25 .60
179 Cam Talbot .40 1.00
180 Jalen Chatfield .25 .60
181 Sean Couturier .30 .75
182 Michael Rasmussen .25 .60
183 Yegor Sharangovich .40 1.00
184 Thatcher Demko .50 1.25
185 Mike Hoffman .25 .60
186 Brent Burns .40 1.00
187 Parker Kelly .25 .60
188 Shane Wright .50 1.25
189 Darnell Nurse .30 .75
190 Dmitri Voronkov .25 .60
191 Luke Kunin .25 .60
192 Dustin Wolf .60 1.50
193 Liam O'Brien .25 .60
194 Casey Mittelstadt .40 1.00
195 Filip Gustavsson .40 1.00
196 Jordan Kyrou .40 1.00
197 Jean-Gabriel Pageau .25 .60
198 Andrei Vasilevskiy .60 1.50
199 Tyler Johnson .25 .60
200 Checklist .25 .60
201 Blake Coleman .30 .75
202 Brandon Montour .50 1.25
203 Mark Stone .50 1.25
204 Petr Mrazek .30 .75
205 Erik Haula .25 .60
206 Brandon Saad .30 .75
207 Quinn Hughes 1.00 2.50
208 J.T. Compher .25 .60
209 Colton Sissons .25 .60
210 Anthony Mantha .30 .75
211 Dylan DeMelo .25 .60
212 Joseph Woll .50 1.25
213 Ondrej Palat .30 .75
214 Mikhail Sergachev .30 .75
215 Jesper Fast .30 .75
216 Mason Marchment .30 .75
217 Kevin Hayes .30 .75
218 Alex Newhook .30 .75
219 Elias Lindholm .40 1.00
220 Brock Nelson .40 1.00
221 Tanner Jeannot .25 .60
222 Scott Laughton .25 .60
223 Vladimir Tarasenko .50 1.25
224 Matt Savoie .40 1.00
225 Samuel Girard .25 .60
226 Pavel Mintyukov .30 .75
227 Brendan Gallagher .40 1.00
228 Tom Wilson .40 1.00
229 Semyon Varlamov .40 1.00
230 Jake McCabe .25 .60
231 Lukas Reichel .40 1.00
232 Owen Tippett .25 .60
233 Adam Lowry .30 .75
234 Nick Perbix .25 .60
235 Mathieu Joseph .25 .60
236 Alex DeBrincat .50 1.25
237 Ryan O'Reilly .40 1.00
238 Torey Krug .30 .75
239 Ross Colton .30 .75
240 Zach Werenski .60 1.50
241 Miro Heiskanen .50 1.25
242 Jake Evans .25 .60
243 Vince Dunn .30 .75
244 Frederik Andersen .50 1.25
245 Gabe Vilardi .40 1.00
246 Frank Vatrano .30 .75
247 Stefan Noesen .25 .60
248 Alex Tuch .40 1.00
249 Jacob Trouba .30 .75
250 Jack McBain .25 .60
251 Justin Barron .30 .75
252 John Tavares .60 1.50
253 Brad Marchand .75 2.00
254 Philipp Kurashev .30 .75
255 Sebastian Aho .60 1.50
256 Marc-Andre Fleury .75 2.00
257 Teddy Blueger .25 .60
258 Rasmus Ristolainen .25 .60
259 Hudson Fasching .25 .60
260 Jake Oettinger .60 1.50
261 Nazem Kadri .50 1.25
262 Pierre Engvall .25 .60
263 Jamie Benn .40 1.00
264 Darcy Kuemper .40 1.00
265 Jason Zucker .40 1.00
266 Alex Pietrangelo .30 .75
267 Brady Skjei .25 .60
268 Cole Caufield .75 2.00
269 Anthony Cirelli .30 .75
270 Ilya Mikheyev .30 .75
271 Ryan Suter .30 .75
272 Pavel Zacha .30 .75
273 William Eklund .50 1.25
274 Seth Jarvis .50 1.25
275 Bobby Brink .25 .60
276 Kevin Fiala .30 .75
277 Marco Rossi .50 1.25
278 Brayden Point .50 1.25
279 Alexis Lafreniere .60 1.50
280 Jordan Martinook .25 .60
281 Jonathan Huberdeau .50 1.25
282 Morgan Geekie .25 .60
283 Mika Zibanejad .50 1.25
284 Dawson Mercer .50 1.25
285 Anze Kopitar .60 1.50
286 Hendrix Lapierre .25 .60
287 Drake Batherson .40 1.00
288 Jaccob Slavin .30 .75
289 Kirill Kaprizov 1.25 3.00
290 Chris Kreider .50 1.25
291 Mackenzie Blackwood .40 1.00
292 Matt Dumba .25 .60
293 Luke Schenn .40 1.00
294 Mikael Backlund .30 .75
295 Ryan Nugent-Hopkins .50 1.25
296 Viktor Arvidsson .25 .60
297 Josh Norris .40 1.00
298 Nick Schmaltz .30 .75
299 Alexandar Georgiev .40 1.00
300 Checklist .25 .60
301 Michael Eyssimont .25 .60
302 Kaapo Kakko .30 .75
303 Pavel Dorofeyev .25 .60
304 Roman Josi .40 1.00
305 Matt Roy .25 .60
306 Jack Quinn .30 .75
307 Andrei Svechnikov .50 1.25
308 Connor Ingram .25 .60
309 Victor Olofsson .40 1.00
310 Nikita Zaitsev .25 .60
311 Dmitry Orlov .40 1.00
312 Erik Gudbranson .25 .60
313 Pierre-Luc Dubois .30 .75
314 Gabriel Landeskog .50 1.25
315 Lars Eller .25 .60
316 Daniel Sprong .25 .60
317 Sean Walker .25 .60
318 Max Domi .40 1.00
319 Tyler Toffoli .40 1.00
320 Radko Gudas .25 .60
321 Marcus Johansson .25 .60
322 Noel Acciari .25 .60
323 Jonathan Marchessault .50 1.25
324 Laurent Brossoit .25 .60
325 Matt Duchene .40 1.00
326 Jonas Brodin .25 .60
327 Jake Neighbours .40 1.00
328 Casey Cizikas .30 .75
329 Oliver Ekman-Larsson .25 .60
330 Jack Roslovic .25 .60
331 Stuart Skinner .50 1.25
332 Bobby McMann .30 .75
333 Eeli Tolvanen .40 1.00
334 Mattias Samuelsson .25 .60
335 Ryan Donato .30 .75
336 Kyle Palmieri .30 .75
337 Alexey Toropchenko .25 .60
338 Steven Stamkos .75 2.00
339 Sam Reinhart .75 2.00
340 Ryan McLeod .25 .60
341 Calle Jarnkrok .25 .60
342 Filip Chytil .30 .75
343 Rasmus Andersson .30 .75
344 Alex Laferriere .25 .60
345 Shea Theodore .50 1.25
346 Josh Anderson .30 .75
347 Dylan Cozens .40 1.00
348 Pavel Buchnevich .30 .75
349 T.J. Brodie .25 .60
350 Alexander Wennberg .25 .60
351 Erik Brannstrom .25 .60
352 Juuse Saros .50 1.25
353 Jacob Markstrom .40 1.00
354 William Karlsson .50 1.25
355 Kirby Dach .40 1.00
356 Andre Burakovsky .25 .60
357 Elvis Merzlikins .40 1.00
358 Zach Benson .30 .75
359 Zach Hyman .60 1.50
360 Nikolaj Ehlers .40 1.00
361 Victor Hedman .50 1.25
362 Jordan Harris .25 .60
363 Luke Glendening .25 .60
364 Adin Hill .40 1.00
365 Evgenii Dadonov .25 .60
366 Jonas Siegenthaler .25 .60
367 Michael Bunting .40 1.00
368 Matthew Poitras .40 1.00
369 Anton Lundell .40 1.00
370 Alex Kerfoot .30 .75
371 Kaiden Guhle .40 1.00
372 Jake Sanderson .50 1.25
373 Nicolas Deslauriers .25 .60
374 Adam Henrique .30 .75
375 Evgeni Malkin .75 2.00
376 Nico Sturm .25 .60
377 Colton Parayko .30 .75
378 Josh Morrissey .50 1.25
379 Isak Rosen .25 .60
380 Shane Pinto .30 .75
381 Travis Konecny .40 1.00
382 Quinton Byfield .50 1.25
383 J.J. Moser .25 .60
384 Mats Zuccarello .40 1.00
385 Samuel Montembeault .40 1.00
386 Emil Bemstrom .25 .60
387 Tyler Myers .25 .60
388 Kevin Shattenkirk .25 .60
389 James van Riemsdyk .30 .75
390 Nico Hischier .60 1.50
391 Yanni Gourde .30 .75
392 Robby Fabbri .25 .60
393 Michael Carcone .25 .60
394 Cole Sillinger .30 .75
395 Logan O'Connor .40 1.00
396 Kyle Connor .60 1.50
397 Noah Hanifin .40 1.00
398 Alex Iafallo .25 .60
399 Mattias Ekholm .30 .75
400 Checklist .25 .60
401 Jordan Eberle .40 1.00
402 Connor Zary .40 1.00
403 Linus Ullmark .40 1.00
404 Nic Dowd .25 .60
405 Bowen Byram .50 1.25
406 Pius Suter .30 .75
407 Samuel Ersson .40 1.00
408 John Gibson .40 1.00
409 Gustav Nyquist .25 .60
410 Ryan McDonagh .25 .60
411 Patrick Maroon .25 .60
412 K'Andre Miller .30 .75
413 Anthony Duclair .30 .75
414 Nino Niederreiter .30 .75
415 JJ Peterka .40 1.00
416 Thomas Chabot .40 1.00
417 Jake DeBrusk .40 1.00
418 Leo Carlsson .60 1.50
419 Patrik Laine .50 1.25
420 Moritz Seider .50 1.25
421 Robert Thomas .40 1.00
422 John Marino .40 1.00
423 Jason Robertson .60 1.50
424 Kiefer Sherwood .25 .60
425 Morgan Rielly .40 1.00
426 Thomas Harley .40 1.00
427 Kirill Marchenko .50 1.25
428 Alex Lyon .30 .75
429 Rickard Rakell .30 .75
430 Logan Thompson .50 1.25
431 Adam Fox .50 1.25
432 Ryan Strome .40 1.00
433 Evander Kane .40 1.00
434 Mario Ferraro .25 .60
435 Mathew Barzal .50 1.25
436 Chandler Stephenson .30 .75
437 Brett Leason .25 .60
438 Kent Johnson .40 1.00
439 Logan Cooley .60 1.50
440 Shayne Gostisbehere .40 1.00
441 Nick Suzuki .75 2.00
442 Jack Hughes 1.00 2.50
443 Teuvo Teravainen .40 1.00
444 Sonny Milano .30 .75
445 Owen Power .40 1.00
446 Dylan Larkin .50 1.25
447 Michael Kesselring .25 .60
448 Jared Spurgeon .40 1.00
449 Charlie McAvoy .50 1.25
450 Jake Allen .40 1.00
451 Jaden Schwartz .30 .75
452 J.T. Miller .50 1.25
453 Dylan Strome .50 1.25
454 Alex Nylander .30 .75
455 Devon Levi .50 1.25
456 Tomas Hertl .40 1.00
457 Vitek Vanecek .40 1.00
458 Alex Nedeljkovic .30 .75
459 Luke Evangelista .30 .75
460 Lucas Raymond .60 1.50
461 Seth Jones .40 1.00
462 Yegor Chinakhov .30 .75
463 Nils Hoglander .30 .75
464 Carter Verhaeghe .40 1.00
465 Juraj Slafkovsky .75 2.00
466 Thomas Novak .25 .60
467 Marc-Edouard Vlasic .25 .60
468 Sidney Crosby 1.50 4.00
469 Evan Bouchard .50 1.25
470 Simon Nemec .50 1.25
471 Filip Zadina .30 .75
472 Michael Matheson .25 .60
473 Matty Beniers .50 1.25
474 Jake Walman .25 .60
475 Miles Wood .25 .60
476 Jonathan Quick .50 1.25
477 Brandon Hagel .30 .75
478 Taylor Hall .40 1.00
479 MacKenzie Weegar .30 .75
480 Artemi Panarin .75 2.00
481 Christopher Tanev .25 .60
482 Ivan Miroshnichenko .30 .75
483 Clayton Keller .50 1.25
484 Erik Karlsson .50 1.25
485 Martin Necas .50 1.25
486 Jack Johnson .25 .60
487 Vladislav Namestnikov .25 .60
488 Wyatt Johnston .75 2.00
489 Valeri Nichushkin .40 1.00
490 Jeremy Swayman .60 1.50
491 Gustav Forsling .40 1.00
492 Arber Xhekaj .40 1.00
493 Patrick Kane .75 2.00
494 David Jiricek .40 1.00
495 Will Cuylle .30 .75
496 David Pastrnak 1.00 2.50
497 Miro Heiskanen .50 1.25
498 Ridly Greig .30 .75
499 Hampus Lindholm .25 .60
500 Checklist .25 .60
501 David Pastrnak AS 1.50 4.00
502 Frank Vatrano AS .50 1.25
503 Filip Forsberg AS 1.00 2.50
504 Jeremy Swayman AS 1.00 2.50
505 Connor Hellebuyck AS 1.25 3.00
506 Quinn Hughes AS 1.50 4.00
507 Clayton Keller AS .75 2.00

508 Kirill Kaprizov AS 2.00 5.00
509 Leon Draisaitl AS 2.00 5.00
510 Brock Boeser AS .75 2.00
511 Igor Shesterkin AS 1.25 3.00
512 Cale Makar AS 1.50 4.00
513 Sergei Bobrovsky AS 1.00 2.50
514 Kyle Connor AS 1.00 2.50
515 Jake Oettinger AS 1.00 2.50
516 Sebastian Aho AS 1.00 2.50
517 Robert Thomas AS .60 1.50
518 Cam Talbot AS .60 1.50
519 William Nylander AS 1.25 3.00
520 Oliver Bjorkstrand AS .50 1.25
521 Nick Suzuki AS 1.25 3.00
522 Nikita Kucherov AS 1.25 3.00
523 Mitch Marner AS 1.00 2.50
524 Alexandar Georgiev AS .60 1.50
525 Boone Jenner AS .60 1.50
526 Thatcher Demko AS .75 2.00
527 Alex DeBrincat AS .75 2.00
528 Sidney Crosby AS 2.50 6.00
529 Sam Reinhart AS 1.25 3.00
530 Brady Tkachuk AS 1.00 2.50
531 Mathew Barzal AS .75 2.00
532 Nathan MacKinnon AS 2.50 6.00
533 Rasmus Dahlin AS .75 2.00
534 Elias Pettersson AS 1.00 2.50
535 Auston Matthews AS 2.50 6.00
536 Travis Konecny AS .60 1.50
537 Connor McDavid AS 3.00 8.00
538 Jesper Bratt AS .60 1.50
539 Tom Wilson AS .60 1.50
540 Tomas Hertl AS .60 1.50
541 Jesper Wallstedt 6.00 15.00
542 Josh Doan 4.00 10.00
543 Kyle MacLean 2.50 6.00
544 Lukas Cormier 2.50 6.00
545 Macklin Celebrini 20.00 50.00
546 Cutter Gauthier 6.00 15.00
547 Matvei Michkov 15.00 40.00
548 Scott Morrow 3.00 8.00
549 Lane Hutson 12.00 30.00
550 Ruslan Iskhakov 2.50 6.00
551 Zack Ostapchuk 2.50 6.00
552 Will Smith 8.00 20.00
553 Zachary Bolduc 4.00 10.00
554 Akil Thomas 2.50 6.00
555 Joshua Roy 4.00 10.00
556 Shakir Mukhamadullin 3.00 8.00
557 Gage Goncalves 3.00 8.00
558 Marshall Rifai 2.50 6.00
559 Logan Mailloux 5.00 12.00
560 Adam Klapka 2.50 6.00
561 Jackson Blake 5.00 12.00
562 Mavrik Bourque 5.00 12.00
563 Rutger McGroarty 5.00 12.00
564 Frank Nazar 8.00 20.00
565 Seamus Casey 3.00 8.00
566 Bradly Nadeau 4.00 10.00
567 Emil Lilleberg 2.50 6.00
568 Collin Graf 2.50 6.00
569 Aku Raty 2.50 6.00
570 Brendan Brisson 3.00 8.00
571 Maxim Tsyplakov 4.00 10.00
572 Logan Stankoven 6.00 15.00
573 Arshdeep Bains 3.00 8.00
574 Matt Rempe 5.00 12.00
575 Maxwell Crozier 2.50 6.00
576 Liam Ohgren 5.00 12.00
577 Sam Colangelo 2.50 6.00
578 Zach Dean 2.50 6.00
579 Brennan Othmann 4.00 10.00
580 Brian Halonen 2.50 6.00
581 Conor Geekie 5.00 12.00
582 Justin Brazeau 2.50 6.00
583 Ivan Fedotov 4.00 10.00
584 Logan Morrison 2.50 6.00
585 Brad Lambert 3.00 8.00
586 Graeme Clarke 2.50 6.00
587 Olen Zellweger 5.00 12.00
588 Landon Slaggert 2.50 6.00
589 Jett Luchanko 5.00 12.00
590 Luca Del Bel Belluz 2.50 6.00
591 Mason Morelli 2.50 6.00
592 Declan Carlile 2.50 6.00
593 Nikita Chibrikov 2.50 6.00
594 Vasily Ponomarev 2.50 6.00
595 Phil Kemp 2.50 6.00
596 Marat Khusnutdinov 2.50 6.00
597 Pierrick Dube 2.50 6.00
598 Georgi Romanov 3.00 8.00
599 Gavin Brindley 2.50 6.00
600 Checklist 1.50 4.00

2024-25 O-Pee-Chee Retro Black

*BLACK/100: 1.5X TO 4X BASIC
*BLACK AS: 2X TO 5X BASIC
*BLACK RC: 1X TO 2.5X BASIC
545 Macklin Celebrini 125.00 300.00
547 Matvei Michkov 125.00 300.00
549 Lane Hutson 80.00 200.00

2024-25 O-Pee-Chee Retro Blank Back

*BLANK: 2.5X TO 6X BASIC
*BLANK AS: 2.5X TO 6X BASIC
*BLANK RC: 1.2X TO 3X BASIC
545 Macklin Celebrini 200.00 500.00
547 Matvei Michkov 150.00 400.00
549 Lane Hutson 125.00 300.00

2024-25 O-Pee-Chee Team Logo Patches

390 Boston Bruins Centennial 25.00 60.00
391 Anaheim Ducks 30th Anniversary 25.00 60.00
392 Nashville Predators 25th Anniversary 25.00 60.00
393 Stadium Series 25.00 60.00
394 New York Rangers 25.00 60.00
395 Winter Classic 25.00 60.00
396 Vegas Golden Knights 25.00 60.00
397 Seattle Kraken 25.00 60.00
398 Winter Classic '23-24 Alternate 25.00 60.00
399 San Jose Sharks 25.00 60.00
400 Minnesota Wild 25.00 60.00
401 Nashville Predators 25.00 60.00
402 Buffalo Sabres 25.00 60.00
403 All Star Game 25.00 60.00
404 NHL Centennial Logo 25.00 60.00
405 Anaheim Ducks 25.00 60.00
406 NHL Millenium Logo 25.00 60.00
407 All Star Game 25.00 60.00
408 All Star Game 25.00 60.00
409 All Star Game 25.00 60.00
410 Heritage Classic 25.00 60.00
411 Heritage Classic 20th Anniversary 25.00 60.00
412 Edmonton Oilers 25.00 60.00
413 Calgary Flames 25.00 60.00
414 Stadium Series '23-24 Alternate 25.00 60.00

2024-25 O-Pee-Chee Top Rookie Bounty Award

BAMC Macklin Celebrini 30.00 80.00

2024-25 O-Pee-Chee Top Rookie Bounty Award Black

BACE Macklin Celebrini 80.00 200.00

2024-25 O-Pee-Chee Top Rookie Bounty Award Autograph

BAAMC Macklin Celebrini 400.00 1000.00

2024-25 O-Pee-Chee Top Rookie Bounty Puzzle

OPC1 Redemption Card 10.00 25.00
OPC2 Redemption Card 10.00 25.00
OPC3 Redemption Card 10.00 25.00
OPC4 Redemption Card 10.00 25.00
OPC5 Redemption Card 10.00 25.00
OPC6 Redemption Card 10.00 25.00
OPC7 Redemption Card 10.00 25.00
OPC8 Redemption Card 10.00 25.00
OPC9 Redemption Card 10.00 25.00

2018-19 O-Pee-Chee Coast to Coast

1 Jonathan Toews .60 1.50
2 James Neal .25 .60
3 David Pastrnak 1.00 2.50
4 Ilya Kovalchuk .30 .75
5 Brendan Gallagher .40 1.00
6 Ryan Johansen .30 .75
7 Nico Hischier .60 1.50
8 Joe Thornton .60 1.50
9 Andrei Vasilevskiy .60 1.50
10 Mikael Granlund .30 .75
11 Andreas Athanasiou .30 .75
12 John Klingberg .40 1.00
13 Cam Atkinson .40 1.00
14 Gabriel Landeskog .50 1.25
15 Sebastian Aho .60 1.50
16 Mark Stone .50 1.25
17 Nicklas Backstrom .40 1.00
18 Nikolaj Ehlers .40 1.00
19 Ryan O'Reilly .40 1.00
20 William Karlsson .50 1.25
21 Ryan Getzlaf .40 1.00
22 Kyle Okposo .25 .60
23 Jordan Eberle .40 1.00
24 Jakub Voracek .30 .75
25 Jake Guentzel .60 1.50
26 Milan Lucic .30 .75
27 Jonathan Huberdeau .50 1.25
28 Patrick Marleau .40 1.00
29 Noah Hanifin .40 1.00
30 Tyler Toffoli .40 1.00
31 Bo Horvat .50 1.25
32 Mark Giordano .40 1.00
33 Filip Forsberg .60 1.50
34 Travis Konecny .40 1.00
35 Tyler Johnson .25 .60
36 Brandon Saad .30 .75
37 Brad Marchand .75 2.00
38 Marc-Edouard Vlasic .25 .60
39 Reilly Smith .40 1.00
40 Jeff Carter .30 .75
41 Logan Couture .50 1.25
42 Mikko Rantanen 1.00 2.50
43 Eric Staal .40 1.00
44 Dustin Byfuglien .40 1.00
45 Alex Pietrangelo .40 1.00
46 T.J. Oshie .40 1.00
47 Brayden Schenn .40 1.00
48 Frederik Andersen .50 1.25
49 Tomas Tatar .25 .60
50 Sergei Bobrovsky .60 1.50
51 Anthony Beauvillier .25 .60
52 Kyle Connor .60 1.50
53 Sean Monahan .25 .60
54 Kasperi Kapanen .30 .75
55 Jordan Staal .30 .75
56 Kris Letang .50 1.25
57 Morgan Rielly .40 1.00
58 Ryan Nugent-Hopkins .50 1.25
59 Pavel Buchnevich .30 .75
60 Alex Galchenyuk .25 .60
61 Alex DeBrincat .50 1.25
62 Mike Hoffman .25 .60
63 Kyle Palmieri .30 .75
64 Nolan Patrick .40 1.00
65 Max Domi .30 .75
66 Pierre-Luc Dubois .30 .75
67 Loui Eriksson .25 .60
68 Mikko Koivu .40 1.00
69 Thomas Chabot .40 1.00
70 Elias Lindholm .40 1.00
71 John Gibson .40 1.00
72 Charlie McAvoy .50 1.25
73 John Tavares .60 1.50
74 Sean Couturier .30 .75
75 Evander Kane .40 1.00
76 Drake Caggiula .30 .75
77 John Carlson .40 1.00
78 Alexander Radulov .40 1.00
79 Sam Reinhart .75 2.00
80 Jesse Puljujarvi .30 .75
81 Tyson Jost .30 .75
82 Duncan Keith .40 1.00
83 Connor Hellebuyck .75 2.00
84 Aaron Ekblad .50 1.25
85 Jaden Schwartz .50 1.25
86 Matt Murray .40 1.00
87 Craig Anderson .30 .75
88 Alex Kerfoot .30 .75
89 Jonathan Marchessault .50 1.25
90 Bobby Ryan .30 .75
91 Shea Weber .40 1.00
92 Dougie Hamilton .30 .75
93 Mika Zibanejad .50 1.25
94 Brandon Sutter .25 .60
95 Matthew Tkachuk .75 2.00
96 Cam Talbot .40 1.00
97 James van Riemsdyk .30 .75
98 William Nylander .75 2.00
99 Braden Holtby .50 1.25
100 Corey Crawford .30 .75
101 Connor McDavid 2.00 5.00
102 Steven Stamkos .75 2.00
103 Johnny Gaudreau .60 1.50
104 Artemi Panarin .75 2.00
105 Nathan MacKinnon 1.50 4.00
106 Tyler Seguin .50 1.25
107 Dylan Larkin .50 1.25
108 Anze Kopitar .60 1.50
109 P.K. Subban .50 1.25
110 Carey Price .75 2.00
111 Taylor Hall .40 1.00
112 Erik Karlsson .50 1.25
113 Victor Hedman .50 1.25
114 Brock Boeser .50 1.25
115 Marc-Andre Fleury .75 2.00
116 Patrik Laine .50 1.25
117 Mathew Barzal .50 1.25
118 Patrice Bergeron .50 1.25
119 Clayton Keller .50 1.25
120 Sidney Crosby 1.50 4.00
121 Brent Burns .40 1.00
122 Max Pacioretty .40 1.00
123 Jonathan Quick .50 1.25
124 Blake Wheeler .40 1.00
125 Auston Matthews 1.50 4.00
126 Vladimir Tarasenko .50 1.25
127 Evgeny Kuznetsov .50 1.25
128 Mark Scheifele .60 1.50
129 Tuukka Rask .50 1.25
130 Patrick Kane .75 2.00
131 Corey Perry .60 1.50
132 Jamie Benn .40 1.00
133 Nikita Kucherov .75 2.00
134 Anthony Mantha .30 .75
135 Roberto Luongo .60 1.50
136 Zach Parise .40 1.00
137 Teuvo Teravainen .40 1.00
138 Matt Duchene .40 1.00
139 Claude Giroux .40 1.00
140 Jack Eichel .60 1.50
141 Phil Kessel .40 1.00
142 Mitch Marner .60 1.50
143 Leon Draisaitl 1.25 3.00
144 Pekka Rinne .40 1.00
145 Drew Doughty .50 1.25
146 Aleksander Barkov .60 1.50
147 Evgeni Malkin .75 2.00
148 Jonathan Drouin .30 .75
149 Henrik Lundqvist 1.00 2.50
150 Alexander Ovechkin 1.50 4.00
151 Rasmus Dahlin RC 2.00 5.00
152 Travis Dermott RC 1.25 3.00
153 Robert Thomas RC 1.50 4.00
154 Henrik Borgstrom RC 1.25 3.00
155 Casey Mittelstadt RC 1.50 4.00
156 Anthony Cirelli RC 1.25 3.00
157 Brett Howden RC 1.00 2.50
158 Dillon Dube RC 1.00 2.50
159 Sam Steel RC .75 2.00
160 Elias Pettersson RC 2.50 6.00
161 Zach Aston-Reese RC 1.25 3.00
162 Dylan Sikura RC 1.00 2.50
163 Noah Juulsen RC .75 2.00
164 Michael Dal Colle RC .75 2.00
165 Andrei Svechnikov RC 2.00 5.00
166 Michael McLeod RC .60 1.50
167 Kristian Vesalainen RC 1.00 2.50
168 Isac Lundestrom RC .60 1.50
169 Maxime Lajoie RC 1.25 3.00
170 Ryan Donato RC 1.25 3.00
171 Henri Jokiharju RC .60 1.50
172 Andreas Johnsson RC 1.00 2.50
173 Jordan Greenway RC .75 2.00
174 Eeli Tolvanen RC 1.50 4.00
175 Brady Tkachuk RC 2.50 6.00
176 Maxime Comtois RC .75 2.00
177 Evan Bouchard RC 2.00 5.00
178 Dennis Cholowski RC .75 2.00
179 Lias Andersson RC 1.25 3.00
180 Miro Heiskanen RC 2.00 5.00
181 Warren Foegele RC .75 2.00
182 Adam Gaudette RC 1.25 3.00
183 Jordan Kyrou RC 1.50 4.00
184 Ilya Samsonov RC 1.50 4.00
185 Michael Rasmussen RC 1.00 2.50
186 Jakub Zboril RC .60 1.50
187 Drake Batherson RC 1.50 4.00
188 Juuso Valimaki RC .75 2.00
189 Jake Bean RC .75 2.00
190 Jesperi Kotkaniemi RC 1.50 4.00
191 Wayne Gretzky 20.00 50.00
192 Jean Beliveau 3.00 8.00
193 Steve Yzerman 8.00 20.00
194 Frank Mahovlich 3.00 8.00
195 Mario Lemieux 12.00 30.00
196 Joe Sakic 6.00 15.00
197 Darryl Sittler 4.00 10.00
198 Teemu Selanne 6.00 15.00
199 Mike Bossy 3.00 8.00
200 Bobby Orr 12.00 30.00
201 Maurice Richard 6.00 15.00
202 Pavel Bure 3.00 8.00
203 Jarome Iginla 4.00 10.00
204 Paul Coffey 3.00 8.00
205 Mark Messier 6.00 15.00
206 Chris Chelios 3.00 8.00
207 Marcel Dionne 4.00 10.00
208 Ray Bourque 5.00 12.00
209 Dale Hawerchuk 4.00 10.00
210 Patrick Roy 8.00 20.00

2018-19 O-Pee-Chee Coast to Coast Autographs

1 Jonathan Toews C 30.00 80.00
2 James Neal C 8.00 20.00
5 Brendan Gallagher A 80.00 200.00
6 Ryan Johansen D 10.00 25.00
8 Joe Thornton C 20.00 50.00
9 Andrei Vasilevskiy C 20.00 50.00
15 Sebastian Aho D 20.00 50.00
16 Mark Stone C 15.00 40.00
18 Nikolaj Ehlers D 12.00 30.00
20 William Karlsson C 15.00 40.00
24 Jakub Voracek C 10.00 25.00
25 Jake Guentzel A 20.00 50.00
27 Jonathan Huberdeau A 15.00 40.00
28 Patrick Marleau C 12.00 30.00
29 Noah Hanifin D 12.00 30.00
30 Tyler Toffoli C 12.00 30.00
31 Bo Horvat D 15.00 40.00
32 Mark Giordano D 12.00 30.00
34 Travis Konecny D 12.00 30.00
35 Tyler Johnson D 8.00 20.00
39 Reilly Smith C 12.00 30.00
41 Logan Couture D 15.00 40.00
42 Mikko Rantanen D 30.00 80.00
50 Sergei Bobrovsky C 20.00 50.00
52 Kyle Connor A 20.00 50.00
53 Sean Monahan C 8.00 20.00
58 Ryan Nugent-Hopkins C 15.00 40.00
59 Pavel Buchnevich C 10.00 25.00
63 Kyle Palmieri D 10.00 25.00
65 Max Domi D 12.00 30.00
66 Pierre-Luc Dubois C 12.00 30.00
73 John Tavares C 20.00 50.00
77 John Carlson C 12.00 30.00
78 Alexander Radulov C 12.00 30.00
80 Jesse Puljujarvi D 12.00 30.00
81 Tyson Jost D 10.00 25.00
82 Duncan Keith A 10.00 25.00
83 Connor Hellebuyck C 25.00 60.00
84 Aaron Ekblad C 15.00 40.00
87 Craig Anderson D 10.00 25.00
88 Alex Kerfoot D 10.00 25.00
89 Jonathan Marchessault C 15.00 40.00
90 Bobby Ryan D 10.00 25.00
95 Matthew Tkachuk C 25.00 60.00
101 Connor McDavid B 60.00 150.00
103 Johnny Gaudreau B 20.00 50.00
104 Artemi Panarin C 25.00 60.00
108 Anze Kopitar B 20.00 50.00
110 Carey Price B 60.00 150.00
111 Taylor Hall B 12.00 30.00
114 Brock Boeser B 15.00 40.00
115 Marc-Andre Fleury B 25.00 60.00
116 Patrik Laine C 15.00 40.00
117 Mathew Barzal A 15.00 40.00
119 Clayton Keller C 15.00 40.00
122 Max Pacioretty B 12.00 30.00
125 Auston Matthews B 50.00 125.00
126 Vladimir Tarasenko B 15.00 40.00
127 Evgeny Kuznetsov C 15.00 40.00
128 Mark Scheifele B 20.00 50.00
130 Patrick Kane B 25.00 60.00
132 Jamie Benn B 12.00 30.00
133 Nikita Kucherov C 25.00 60.00
142 Mitch Marner C 25.00 60.00
143 Leon Draisaitl C 40.00 100.00
146 Aleksander Barkov B 20.00 50.00
147 Evgeni Malkin B 25.00 60.00
148 Jonathan Drouin C 10.00 25.00
149 Henrik Lundqvist B 30.00 80.00
153 Robert Thomas D 25.00 60.00
154 Henrik Borgstrom E 20.00 50.00
155 Casey Mittelstadt D 25.00 60.00
156 Anthony Cirelli E 20.00 50.00
157 Brett Howden E 15.00 40.00
158 Dillon Dube E 12.00 30.00
159 Sam Steel D 12.00 30.00
160 Elias Pettersson D 150.00 250.00
161 Zach Aston-Reese E 20.00 50.00
162 Dylan Sikura D 10.00 25.00
163 Noah Juulsen E 10.00 25.00
164 Michael Dal Colle D 12.00 30.00
165 Andrei Svechnikov D 30.00 80.00
166 Michael McLeod E 12.00 30.00
167 Kristian Vesalainen E 15.00 40.00
168 Isac Lundestrom D 10.00 25.00
169 Maxime Lajoie D 20.00 50.00
171 Henri Jokiharju D 20.00 50.00
172 Andreas Johnsson D 15.00 40.00
174 Eeli Tolvanen D 25.00 60.00
175 Brady Tkachuk D 40.00 100.00
176 Maxime Comtois D 12.00 30.00
177 Evan Bouchard E 30.00 80.00
178 Dennis Cholowski E 12.00 30.00
179 Lias Andersson D 12.00 30.00
180 Miro Heiskanen D 30.00 80.00
181 Warren Foegele E 12.00 30.00
183 Jordan Kyrou E 25.00 60.00
184 Ilya Samsonov E 25.00 60.00
185 Michael Rasmussen D 15.00 40.00
186 Jakub Zboril E 12.00 30.00
187 Drake Batherson E 25.00 60.00
189 Jake Bean E 12.00 30.00
190 Jesperi Kotkaniemi D 25.00 60.00
191 Wayne Gretzky B 250.00 600.00
193 Steve Yzerman B 150.00 250.00
195 Mario Lemieux B 50.00 125.00
196 Joe Sakic B 50.00 120.00
197 Darryl Sittler C 15.00 40.00
198 Teemu Selanne B 30.00 80.00
199 Mike Bossy C 50.00 125.00
200 Bobby Orr C 50.00 125.00
203 Jarome Iginla C 15.00 40.00
204 Paul Coffey B 12.00 30.00
205 Mark Messier B 25.00 60.00
206 Chris Chelios C 12.00 30.00
207 Marcel Dionne C 15.00 40.00
208 Ray Bourque B 20.00 50.00
209 Dale Hawerchuk C 12.00 30.00
210 Patrick Roy B 30.00 80.00

2018-19 O-Pee-Chee Coast to Coast Autographs Extended

ABG Brendan Gaunce F 6.00 15.00
ABR Brett Ritchie F 6.00 15.00
ABS Brady Skjei E 8.00 20.00
ACW Colin White E 6.00 15.00
ADH Danton Heinen E 8.00 20.00
ADS Daniel Sprong F 6.00 15.00
AJA Josh Anderson F 8.00 20.00
AJD Jacob de la Rose F 6.00 15.00
AJM Jake McCabe F 8.00 20.00
AJW Jordan Weal F 6.00 15.00
ALC Lawson Crouse F 6.00 15.00
ALD Louis Domingue F 6.00 15.00
ANP Nicolas Petan F 6.00 15.00
AOK Oscar Klefbom F 8.00 20.00
ARF Radek Faksa F 8.00 20.00
ARH Ryan Hartman F 6.00 15.00
ASN Stefan Noesen F 6.00 15.00
ATS Travis Sanheim E 6.00 15.00

2018-19 O-Pee-Chee Coast to Coast Canadiana Vintage Map Relics

VRMB Manitoba 1895 and 1911 D 25.00 60.00
VRNB New Brunswick 1859 B 25.00 60.00
VRON Ontario 1866 A 25.00 60.00
VRQC Quebec 1890 and 1895 D 25.00 60.00
VRAB1 Alberta, Edmonton 1912 C 25.00 60.00
VRAB2 Alberta, Calgary 1912 C 25.00 60.00
VRBC1 British Columbia , Vancover 1863 C 25.00 60.00
VRBC2 British Columbia, Victoria 1898 C 25.00 60.00

2018-19 O-Pee-Chee Coast to Coast Franchise Heroes

G1 C.McDavid/W.Gretzky 10.00 25.00
G2 A.Matthews/D.Sittler 6.00 15.00
G3 V.Tarasenko/B.Hull 3.00 8.00
G4 C.Giroux/B.Clarke 2.50 6.00
G5 D.Larkin/S.Yzerman 4.00 10.00
G6 J.Benn/M.Modano 3.00 8.00
G7 C.Price/P.Roy 4.00 10.00
G8 N.MacKinnon/P.Forsberg 6.00 15.00
G9 A.Kopitar/M.Dionne 2.50 6.00
G10 A.Ovechkin/M.Gartner 6.00 15.00
G11 J.Toews/B.Hull 3.00 8.00
G12 J.Gaudreau/J.Iginla 2.50 6.00
G13 J.Eichel/D.Hasek 2.50 6.00
G14 S.Stamkos/D.Andreychuk 3.00 8.00
G15 B.Boeser/P.Bure 2.00 5.00
G16 M.Barzal/M.Bossy 2.00 5.00
G17 H.Lundqvist/M.Messier 4.00 10.00
G18 P.Bergeron/B.Orr 6.00 15.00
G19 R.Getzlaf/T.Selanne 3.00 8.00
G20 S.Crosby/M.Lemieux 6.00 15.00

2018-19 O-Pee-Chee Coast to Coast Iconic Captains

IC1 Wayne Gretzky 80.00 200.00
IC2 Mark Messier 25.00 60.00
IC3 Jean Beliveau 12.00 30.00
IC4 Mario Lemieux 50.00 125.00
IC5 Steve Yzerman 30.00 80.00
IC6 Connor McDavid 100.00 200.00
IC7 Sidney Crosby 50.00 125.00
IC8 Alex Ovechkin 50.00 120.00
IC9 Jonathan Toews 20.00 50.00
IC10 Anze Kopitar 20.00 50.00
IC11 Claude Giroux 12.00 30.00
IC12 Steven Stamkos 25.00 60.00
IC14 Jamie Benn 12.00 30.00
IC15 Gabriel Landeskog 15.00 40.00
IC16 Joe Pavelski 15.00 40.00
IC17 Jack Eichel 20.00 50.00

2018-19 O-Pee-Chee Coast to Coast Landmarks of the North

LN1 Vancouver, B.C. .75 2.00
LN2 Queen Charlotte Islands .75 2.00
LN3 Victoria .75 2.00
LN4 MacMillan Provincial Park .75 2.00
LN5 Capilano Suspension Bridge .75 2.00
LN6 The Discovery Islands .75 2.00
LN7 Yoho National Park .75 2.00
LN8 Legislature Building .75 2.00
LN9 Waterton Lakes National Park .75 2.00
LN10 Dinosaur Provincial Park .75 2.00
LN11 Yellowknife .75 2.00
LN12 Banff National Park .75 2.00
LN13 Canadian Badlands .75 2.00
LN14 Heritage Park Historical Village .75 2.00
LN15 Jasper National Park .75 2.00
LN16 Big Muddy Valley .75 2.00
LN17 Prince Albert National Park .75 2.00
LN18 Saskatoon .75 2.00
LN19 Winnipeg, Manitoba .75 2.00
LN20 Toronto, Ontario .75 2.00
LN21 Georgian Bay .75 2.00
LN22 Parliament Hill .75 2.00
LN23 Niagara Falls .75 2.00
LN24 Agawa Canyon .75 2.00
LN25 Ottawa (Ontario) .75 2.00
LN26 Quebec City .75 2.00
LN27 Les Iles de la Madeleine .75 2.00
LN28 Saint Joseph's Oratory .75 2.00
LN29 Mingan Archipelago National Park .75 2.00
LN30 Montreal, Quebec .75 2.00
LN31 Laurentian Mountains .75 2.00
LN32 Saguenay- Lac Saint-Jean .75 2.00
LN33 Eastern Townships .75 2.00
LN34 St. John's .75 2.00
LN35 Nahanni National Park Reserve .75 2.00
LN36 Halifax .75 2.00
LN37 Cape Breton .75 2.00
LN38 Bay of Fundy .75 2.00
LN39 Prince Edward Island National Park .75 2.00
LN40 Whitehorse .75 2.00

2018-19 O-Pee-Chee Coast to Coast Landmarks of the North Map Relics

NRBNP Banff National Park G 15.00 40.00
NRBOF Bay of Fundy D 15.00 40.00
NRCBI Cape Breton Island F 15.00 40.00
NRGBO Georgian Bay C 15.00 40.00
NRJNP Jasper National Park G 15.00 40.00
NRLIM Les Iles de la Madeleine D 15.00 40.00
NRLMQ Laurentian Mountains C 15.00 40.00
NRMAP Mingan Archipelago National Park B 20.00 50.00
NRMTL Montreal, Quebec G 15.00 40.00
NRNFO Niagara Falls A 25.00 60.00
NRPAP Prince Albert National Park A 25.00 60.00
NRQCI Queen Charlotte Islands B 15.00 40.00
NRSAS Saskatoon G 15.00 40.00
NRSTJ St. John's F 15.00 40.00
NRTOR Toronto, Ontario G 15.00 40.00
NRVAN Vancouver, B.C. G 15.00 40.00
NRVIC Victoria G 15.00 40.00
NRWLP Waterton Lakes National Park E 15.00 40.00
NRWPG Winnipeg, Manitoba F 15.00 40.00
NRWYT Whitehorse D 15.00 40.00
NRYNP Yoho National Park C 15.00 40.00

2018-19 O-Pee-Chee Coast to Coast Pride of the North

P1 Jonathan Toews 1.00 2.50
P2 James Neal .40 1.00
P3 Logan Couture .75 2.00
P4 Patrick Marleau .60 1.50
P5 Nathan MacKinnon 2.50 6.00
P6 Max Domi .60 1.50
P7 Brayden Schenn .60 1.50
P8 Jeff Skinner .75 2.00
P9 Matt Murray .60 1.50
P10 Tyler Seguin .60 1.50
P11 Jonathan Marchessault .75 2.00
P12 Brad Marchand 1.25 3.00
P13 Claude Giroux .60 1.50
P14 Jeff Carter .50 1.25
P15 Roberto Luongo 1.00 2.50
P16 Joe Thornton 1.00 2.50
P17 Mathew Barzal .75 2.00
P18 Ryan Johansen .50 1.25
P19 Mark Scheifele 1.00 2.50
P20 Taylor Hall .60 1.50
P21 Alex Pietrangelo .50 1.25
P22 Dylan Strome .75 2.00
P23 Anthony Mantha .50 1.25
P24 Matt Duchene .60 1.50
P25 Mitch Marner 1.00 2.50
P26 Ryan Nugent-Hopkins .75 2.00
P27 Ryan Getzlaf .60 1.50
P28 Duncan Keith .60 1.50
P29 Wayne Simmonds .60 1.50
P30 Steven Stamkos 1.25 3.00
P31 Eric Staal .60 1.50
P32 Mark Stone .75 2.00
P33 Shea Weber .60 1.50
P34 Jordan Eberle .60 1.50
P35 Brendan Gallagher .60 1.50
P36 Sean Monahan .40 1.00
P37 Patrice Bergeron .75 2.00
P38 Kris Letang .75 2.00
P39 Drew Doughty .75 2.00
P40 P.K. Subban .75 2.00
P41 Ryan O'Reilly .60 1.50
P42 Braden Holtby .75 2.00
P43 Aaron Ekblad .75 2.00
P44 Nolan Patrick .60 1.50
P45 Corey Crawford .50 1.25
P46 Sidney Crosby SP 6.00 15.00
P47 Connor McDavid SP 6.00 15.00
P48 Carey Price SP 6.00 15.00
P49 John Tavares SP 6.00 15.00
P50 Marc-Andre Fleury SP 10.00 25.00
P51 Mario Lemieux SP 6.00 15.00
P52 Bobby Orr SP 10.00 25.00
P53 Patrick Roy SP 6.00 15.00
P54 Steve Yzerman SP 6.00 15.00
P55 Wayne Gretzky SP 12.00 30.00

2018-19 O-Pee-Chee Coast to Coast Transparent All Stars

CCA1 Auston Matthews 12.00 30.00
CCA2 Steven Stamkos 8.00 20.00
CCA3 Jack Eichel 6.00 15.00
CCA4 Brad Marchand 8.00 20.00
CCA5 Nikita Kucherov 8.00 20.00
CCA6 Aleksander Barkov 6.00 15.00
CCA7 Carey Price 8.00 20.00
CCA8 Andrei Vasilevskiy 6.00 15.00
CCA9 Sidney Crosby 15.00 40.00
CCA10 Alexander Ovechkin 15.00 40.00
CCA11 Claude Giroux 4.00 10.00
CCA12 Kris Letang 5.00 12.00
CCA13 Braden Holtby 5.00 12.00
CCA14 Henrik Lundqvist 10.00 25.00
CCA15 Patrick Kane 8.00 20.00
CCA16 Nathan MacKinnon 15.00 40.00
CCA17 P.K. Subban 5.00 12.00
CCA18 Tyler Seguin 5.00 12.00
CCA19 Brayden Schenn 4.00 10.00
CCA20 Blake Wheeler 4.00 10.00
CCA21 Pekka Rinne 4.00 10.00
CCA22 Connor Hellebuyck 8.00 20.00
CCA23 Connor McDavid 20.00 50.00
CCA24 Anze Kopitar 6.00 15.00
CCA25 Brock Boeser 5.00 12.00
CCA26 Johnny Gaudreau 6.00 15.00
CCA27 Brent Burns 4.00 10.00
CCA28 Drew Doughty 5.00 12.00
CCA29 Rickard Rakell 3.00 8.00
CCA30 Marc-Andre Fleury 8.00 20.00

2018-19 O-Pee-Chee Coast to Coast Transparent Rookies

CCR1 Elias Pettersson 30.00 80.00
CCR2 Rasmus Dahlin 15.00 40.00
CCR3 Brady Tkachuk 20.00 50.00
CCR4 Jesperi Kotkaniemi 12.00 30.00
CCR5 Casey Mittelstadt 12.00 30.00
CCR6 Miro Heiskanen 15.00 40.00
CCR7 Ryan Donato 10.00 25.00
CCR8 Andrei Svechnikov 15.00 40.00
CCR9 Andreas Johnsson 8.00 20.00
CCR10 Maxime Lajoie 10.00 25.00
CCRWG Wayne Gretzky 250.00 350.00

2018-19 O-Pee-Chee Coast to Coast VS Black

VS25 Rasmus Dahlin 30.00 80.00
VS26 Brady Tkachuk 30.00 80.00
VS27 Elias Pettersson 30.00 80.00
VS28 Jesperi Kotkaniemi 20.00 50.00

1998-99 O-Pee-Chee Chrome

*VETS: 1X TO 2.5X BASIC CARDS
*RC: .8X TO 2X BASIC CARDS
1 Peter Forsberg .60 1.50
2 Petr Sykora .20 .50
3 Byron Dafoe .25 .60
4 Ron Francis .40 1.00
5 Alexei Yashin .25 .60
6 Dave Ellett .25 .60
7 Jamie Langenbrunner .30 .75
8 Doug Weight .30 .75
9 Jason Woolley .20 .50
10 Paul Coffey .30 .75
11 Uwe Krupp .20 .50
12 Tomas Sandstrom .20 .50
13 Scott Mellanby .20 .50
14 Vladimir Tsyplakov .20 .50
15 Martin Rucinsky .20 .50
16 Mikael Renberg .25 .60
17 Marco Sturm .20 .50
18 Eric Lindros .50 1.25
19 Sean Burke .20 .50
20 Martin Brodeur .75 2.00
21 Boyd Devereaux .20 .50
22 Kelly Buchberger .20 .50
23 Scott Stevens .30 .75
24 Jamie Storr .25 .60
25 Anders Eriksson .20 .50
26 Gary Suter .20 .50
27 Theo Fleury .40 1.00
28 Steve Leach .20 .50
29 Felix Potvin .50 1.25
30 Brett Hull .60 1.50
31 Mike Grier .20 .50
32 Cale Hulse .20 .50
33 Larry Murphy .25 .60
34 Rick Tocchet .25 .60
35 Eric Desjardins .25 .60
36 Igor Kravchuk .20 .50
37 Rob Niedermayer .20 .50
38 Bryan Smolinski .20 .50
39 Valeri Kamensky .25 .60
40 Ryan Smyth .25 .60
41 Bruce Driver .20 .50
42 Mike Johnson .20 .50
43 Rob Zamuner .20 .50
44 Steve Duchesne .20 .50
45 Martin Straka .20 .50
46 Bill Houlder .20 .50
47 Craig Conroy .20 .50
48 Guy Hebert .25 .60
49 Colin Forbes .20 .50
50 Mike Modano .50 1.25
51 Jamie Pushor .20 .50
52 Jarome Iginla .40 1.00
53 Paul Kariya .30 .75
54 Mattias Ohlund .20 .50
55 Sergei Berezin .20 .50
56 Peter Zezel .20 .50
57 Teppo Numminen .20 .50
58 Dale Hunter .20 .50
59 Sandy Moger .20 .50
60 John LeClair .30 .75
61 Wade Redden .20 .50
62 Patrik Elias .30 .75
63 Rob Blake .25 .60
64 Todd Marchant .20 .50
65 Claude Lemieux .25 .60
66 Trevor Kidd .25 .60
67 Sergei Fedorov .50 1.25
68 Joe Sakic .60 1.50
69 Derek Morris .20 .50
70 Alexei Morozov .20 .50
71 Mats Sundin .30 .75
72 Daymond Langkow .20 .50
73 Kevin Hatcher .20 .50
74 Damian Rhodes .20 .50
75 Brian Leetch .25 .60
76 Saku Koivu .30 .75
77 Rick Tabaracci .20 .50
78 Bernie Nicholls .20 .50
79 Alyn McCauley .20 .50
80 Patrice Brisebois .20 .50
81 Bret Hedican .20 .50
82 Sandy McCarthy .20 .50
83 Viktor Kozlov .20 .50
84 Derek King .20 .50
85 Alexander Selivanov .20 .50
86 Mike Vernon .25 .60
87 Jeff Beukeboom .20 .50
88 Tommy Salo .25 .60
89 Adam Graves .20 .50
90 Randy McKay .20 .50
91 Rich Pilon .20 .50
92 Richard Zednik .20 .50
93 Jeff Hackett .20 .50
94 Michael Peca .20 .50
95 Brent Gilchrist .20 .50
96 Stu Grimson .20 .50
97 Bob Probert .30 .75
98 Stu Barnes .20 .50
99 Ruslan Salei .20 .50
100 Al MacInnis .40 1.00
101 Ken Daneyko .20 .50
102 Paul Ranheim .20 .50
103 Marty McInnis .20 .50
104 Marian Hossa .30 .75
105 Darren McCarty .20 .50
106 Guy Carbonneau .20 .50
107 Dallas Drake .20 .50
108 Sergei Samsonov .25 .60
109 Teemu Selanne .60 1.50
110 Checklist .20 .50
111 Jaromir Jagr 1.00 2.50
112 Joe Thornton .50 1.25
113 Jon Klemm .20 .50
114 Grant Fuhr .50 1.25
115 Nikolai Khabibulin .30 .75
116 Rod Brind'Amour .30 .75
117 Trevor Linden .30 .75
118 Vincent Damphousse .25 .60
119 Dino Ciccarelli .25 .60
120 Pat Verbeek .20 .50
121 Sandis Ozolinsh .20 .50
122 Garth Snow .25 .60
123 Ed Belfour .30 .75
124 Keith Primeau .25 .60
125 Jason Allison .25 .60
126 Peter Bondra .30 .75
127 Ulf Samuelsson .25 .60
128 Jeff Friesen .20 .50
129 Jason Bonsignore .20 .50
130 Daniel Alfredsson .30 .75
131 Bobby Holik .20 .50
132 Jozef Stumpel .20 .50
133 Brian Bellows .20 .50
134 Chris Osgood .30 .75
135 Alexei Zhamnov .20 .50
136 Mattias Norstrom .20 .50

Card		
137 Drake Berehowsky	.20	.50
138 Mark Messier	.60	1.50
139 Geoff Courtnall	.25	.60
140 Marc Bureau	.20	.50
141 Don Sweeney	.20	.50
142 Wendel Clark	.50	1.25
143 Scott Niedermayer	.30	.75
144 Chris Therien	.20	.50
145 Kirk Muller	.20	.50
146 Wayne Primeau	.20	.50
147 Tony Granato	.20	.50
148 Derian Hatcher	.20	.50
149 Daniel Briere	.25	.60
150 Fredrik Olausson	.20	.50
151 Joe Juneau	.20	.50
152 Michal Grosek	.20	.50
153 Janne Laukkanen	.20	.50
154 Keith Tkachuk	.30	.75
155 Marty McSorley	.25	.60
156 Owen Nolan	.30	.75
157 Mark Tinordi	.20	.50
158 Steve Washburn	.20	.50
159 Luke Richardson	.20	.50
160 Kris King	.20	.50
161 Joe Nieuwendyk	.25	.60
162 Travis Green	.20	.50
163 Dominik Hasek	.50	1.25
164 Dimitri Khristich	.20	.50
165 Dave Manson	.20	.50
166 Chris Chelios	.30	.75
167 Claude LaPointe	.20	.50
168 Kris Draper	.20	.50
169 Brad Isbister	.20	.50
170 Patrick Marleau	.30	.75
171 Jeremy Roenick	.50	1.25
172 Darren Langdon	.20	.50
173 Kevin Dineen	.20	.50
174 Luc Robitaille	.30	.75
175 Steve Yzerman	.75	2.00
176 Sergei Zubov	.25	.60
177 Ed Jovanovski	.25	.60
178 Sami Kapanen	.20	.50
179 Adam Oates	.30	.75
180 Pavel Bure	.30	.75
181 Chris Pronger	.30	.75
182 Pat Falloon	.20	.50
183 Darcy Tucker	.20	.50
184 Zigmund Palffy	.30	.75
185 Curtis Brown	.20	.50
186 Curtis Joseph	.40	1.00
187 Valeri Zelepukin	.20	.50
188 Russ Courtnall	.20	.50
189 Adam Foote	.20	.50
190 Patrick Roy	.75	2.00
191 Cory Stillman	.20	.50
192 Alexei Zhitnik	.20	.50
193 Olaf Kolzig	.30	.75
194 Mark Fitzpatrick	.20	.50
195 Eric Daze	.25	.60
196 Zarley Zalapski	.20	.50
197 Niklas Sundstrom	.20	.50
198 Bryan Berard	.25	.60
199 Jason Arnott	.25	.60
200 Mike Richter	.30	.75
201 Ken Baumgartner	.20	.50
202 Jason Dawe	.20	.50
203 Nicklas Lidstrom	.40	1.00
204 Tony Amonte	.25	.60
205 Kjell Samuelsson	.20	.50
206 Ray Bourque	.50	1.25
207 Alexander Mogilny	.25	.60
208 Pierre Turgeon	.25	.60
209 Tom Barrasso	.25	.60
210 Richard Matvichuk	.20	.50
211 Sergei Krivokrasov	.20	.50
212 Ted Drury	.20	.50
213 Matthew Barnaby	.20	.50
214 Denis Pederson	.20	.50
215 John Vanbiesbrouck	.30	.75
216 Brendan Shanahan	.30	.75
217 Jocelyn Thibault	.25	.60
218 Nelson Emerson	.20	.50
219 Wayne Gretzky	2.00	5.00
220 Checklist	.20	.50
221 Ramzi Abid RC	.50	1.25
222 Mark Bell RC	.50	1.25
223 Michael Henrich RC	.50	1.25
224 Vincent Lecavalier	1.50	4.00
225 Rico Fata	.60	1.50
226 Bryan Allen	.50	1.25
227 Daniel Tkaczuk	.50	1.25
228 Brad Stuart RC	.50	1.25
229 Derrick Walser RC	.50	1.25
230 Jonathan Cheechoo RC	.75	2.00
231 Sergei Varlamov	.50	1.25
232 Scott Gomez RC	.75	2.00
233 Jeff Heerema RC	.50	1.25
234 David Legwand	.50	1.25
235 Manny Malhotra	.75	2.00
236 Michael Rupp RC	.60	1.50
237 Alex Tanguay	.60	1.50
238 Mathieu Biron RC	.60	1.50
239 Bujar Amidovski RC	.60	1.50
240 Brian Finley RC	.50	1.25
241 Philippe Sauve RC	.60	1.50
242 Jiri Fischer RC	.60	1.50

1998-99 O-Pee-Chee Chrome Blast From the Past

*REFRACTORS: 1X TO 2.5X BASIC INSERTS

Card		
1 Wayne Gretzky	30.00	80.00
2 Mark Messier	10.00	25.00
3 Ray Bourque	8.00	20.00
4 Patrick Roy	12.00	30.00
5 Grant Fuhr	8.00	20.00
6 Brett Hull	10.00	25.00
7 Gordie Howe	15.00	40.00
8 Stan Mikita	10.00	25.00
9 Bobby Hull	10.00	25.00
10 Phil Esposito	10.00	25.00

1998-99 O-Pee-Chee Chrome Board Members

*REFRACTORS: .8X TO 2X BASIC INSERTS

Card		
B1 Chris Pronger	2.00	5.00
B2 Chris Chelios	2.00	5.00
B3 Brian Leetch	1.50	4.00
B4 Ray Bourque	3.00	8.00
B5 Mattias Ohlund	1.25	3.00
B6 Nicklas Lidstrom	2.50	6.00
B7 Sergei Zubov	1.50	4.00
B8 Scott Niedermayer	2.00	5.00
B9 Larry Murphy	1.50	4.00
B10 Sandis Ozolinsh	1.25	3.00
B11 Rob Blake	2.00	5.00
B12 Scott Stevens	2.00	5.00
B13 Derian Hatcher	1.25	3.00
B14 Kevin Hatcher	1.25	3.00
B15 Wade Redden	1.25	3.00

1998-99 O-Pee-Chee Chrome Season's Best

*REFRACTORS: .8X TO 2X BASIC INSERTS

Card		
SB1 Dominik Hasek	2.50	6.00
SB2 Martin Brodeur	4.00	10.00
SB3 Ed Belfour	1.50	4.00
SB4 Curtis Joseph	2.00	5.00
SB5 Jeff Hackett	1.00	2.50
SB6 Tom Barrasso	1.25	3.00
SB7 Mike Johnson	1.00	2.50
SB8 Sergei Samsonov	1.25	3.00
SB9 Patrik Elias	1.50	4.00
SB10 Patrick Marleau	1.50	4.00
SB11 Mattias Ohlund	1.00	2.50
SB12 Marco Sturm	1.00	2.50
SB13 Teemu Selanne	3.00	8.00
SB14 Peter Bondra	1.50	4.00
SB15 Pavel Bure	1.50	4.00
SB16 John LeClair	1.50	4.00
SB17 Zigmund Palffy	1.50	4.00
SB18 Keith Tkachuk	1.50	4.00
SB19 Jaromir Jagr	5.00	12.00
SB20 Wayne Gretzky	10.00	25.00
SB21 Peter Forsberg	3.00	8.00
SB22 Ron Francis	2.00	5.00
SB23 Adam Oates	1.50	4.00
SB24 Jozef Stumpel	1.00	2.50
SB25 Chris Pronger	1.50	4.00
SB26 Larry Murphy	1.25	3.00
SB27 Jason Allison	1.25	3.00
SB28 John LeClair	1.50	4.00
SB29 Randy McKay	1.25	3.00
SB30 Dainius Zubrus	1.00	2.50

1999-00 O-Pee-Chee Chrome

Card		
COMPLETE SET (297)	200.00	400.00
*OPC CHROME: .6X TO 1.5X TOPPS CHROME		
23 Ron Francis	.60	1.50

1999-00 O-Pee-Chee Chrome All Topps

Card		
COMPLETE SET (15)	15.00	40.00
*O-PEE-CHEE: .4X TO 1X TOPPS CHROME		
*REFRACTORS: 1.2X TO 3X OPC INSERTS		

1999-00 O-Pee-Chee Chrome Ice Masters

Card		
COMPLETE SET (20)	25.00	50.00
*O-PEE-CHEE: .4X TO 1X TOPPS CHROME		
*REFRACTORS: 1.2X TO 3X OPC INSERTS		

1999-00 O-Pee-Chee Chrome A-Men

Card		
COMPLETE SET (6)	10.00	20.00
*O-PEE-CHEE: .4X TO 1X TOPPS CHROME		
*REFRACTORS: 1.2X TO 3X OPC INSERTS		

1999-00 O-Pee-Chee Chrome Fantastic Finishers

Card		
COMPLETE SET (6)	6.00	15.00
*O-PEE-CHEE: .4X TO 1X TOPPS CHROME		
*REFRACTORS: 1.2X TO 3X OPC INSERTS		

1999-00 O-Pee-Chee Chrome Ice Futures

Card		
COMPLETE SET (6)	5.00	12.00
*O-PEE-CHEE: .4X TO 1X TOPPS CHROME		
*REFRACTORS: 1.2X TO 3X OPC INSERTS		

1999-00 O-Pee-Chee Chrome Positive Performers

Card		
COMPLETE SET (6)	3.00	8.00
*O-PEE-CHEE: .4X TO 1X TOPPS CHROME		
*REFRACTORS: 1.2X TO 3X OPC INSERTS		

1999-00 O-Pee-Chee Chrome Postmasters

Card		
COMPLETE SET (6)	10.00	20.00
*O-PEE-CHEE: .4X TO 1X TOPPS CHROME		
*REFRACTORS: 1.2X TO 3X OPC INSERTS		

2014-15 O-Pee-Chee Platinum

Card		
1 Martin Brodeur	1.00	2.50
2 Alex Galchenyuk	.25	.60
3 Milan Lucic	.40	1.00
4 Mikko Koivu	.30	.75
5 Shane Doan	.30	.75
6 Eric Staal	.50	1.25
7 Brayden Schenn	.40	1.00
8A Sidney Crosby	1.50	4.00
8B Sidney Crosby SP	8.00	20.00
9 Bobby Ryan	.30	.75
10 Tomas Hertl	.40	1.00
11 Erik Karlsson	.50	1.25
12 Scott Hartnell	.25	.60
13 Tuukka Rask	.50	1.25
14 Tyler Bozak	.25	.60
15 Marian Gaborik	.40	1.00
16 Zach Parise	.40	1.00
17 Emerson Etem	.30	.75
18 Derek Stepan	.25	.60
19 Kyle Okposo	.25	.60
20A Nathan MacKinnon	1.50	4.00
20B Nathan MacKinnon SP	8.00	20.00
21 Roberto Luongo	.60	1.50
22 Kyle Turris	.40	1.00
23 Adam Henrique	.30	.75
24 Tyler Ennis	.25	.60
25A Patrick Kane	.75	2.00
25B Patrick Kane SP	8.00	20.00
26 Nino Niederreiter	.25	.60
27A Sean Monahan	.25	.60
27B Sean Monahan SP	2.00	5.00
28 Ryan Callahan	.25	.60
29 Cam Ward	.40	1.00
30 Alexander Steen	.25	.60
31 Cory Schneider	.40	1.00
32 Jonathan Huberdeau	.50	1.25
33 Matt Beleskey	.25	.60
34 Cody Hodgson	.25	.60
35 Nicklas Backstrom	.40	1.00
36A Ryan Nugent-Hopkins	.50	1.25
36B Ryan Nugent-Hopkins SP	8.00	20.00
37 Henrik Lundqvist	1.00	2.50
38 Sean Couturier	.30	.75
39 James Neal	.25	.60
40 Michael Cammalleri	.30	.75
41A James van Riemsdyk	.30	.75
41B James van Riemsdyk SP	2.50	6.00
42 Aleksander Barkov	.60	1.50
43A Martin St. Louis	.40	1.00
43B Martin St. Louis SP	3.00	8.00
44 Kari Lehtonen	.30	.75
45 Jarome Iginla	.50	1.25
46 Steve Mason	.30	.75
47 Gustav Nyquist	.25	.60
48A Anze Kopitar	.60	1.50
48B Anze Kopitar SP	6.00	15.00
49A Jonathan Toews	.60	1.50
49B Jonathan Toews	5.00	12.00
50 Evander Kane	.40	1.00
51 Valeri Nichushkin	.40	1.00
52 Valtteri Filppula	.25	.60
53 Antti Niemi	.30	.75
54A Phil Kessel	.40	1.00
54B Phil Kessel SP	3.00	8.00
55 Daniel Sedin	.50	1.25
56 Tomas Plekanec	.25	.60
57 Jim Howard	.50	1.25
58 Patrick Marleau	.40	1.00
59 P.A. Parenteau	.25	.60
60 Jason Spezza	.40	1.00
61 Bryan Little	.40	1.00
62 Steven Stamkos	.75	2.00
63 Brad Richards	.40	1.00
64 Marian Hossa	.40	1.00
65 Thomas Vanek	.30	.75
66 Marc-Edouard Vlasic	.25	.60
67 Braden Holtby	.50	1.25
68 Jeff Skinner	.50	1.25
69 Paul Stastny	.30	.75
70 Henrik Sedin	.50	1.25
71 T.J. Oshie	.40	1.00
72A Seth Jones	.40	1.00
72B Seth Jones SP	3.00	8.00
73 Blake Wheeler	.40	1.00
74 Kris Letang	.50	1.25
75 Max Pacioretty	.40	1.00
76A Carey Price	.75	2.00
76B Carey Price SP	12.00	30.00
77 Ryan Johansen	.30	.75
78A Matt Duchene	.40	1.00
78B Matt Duchene SP	3.00	8.00
79 David Perron	.30	.75
80 Ryan Kesler	.40	1.00
81 Ondrej Pavelec	.40	1.00
82 Chris Kunitz	.40	1.00
83 Patric Hornqvist	.25	.60
84 Rick Nash	.40	1.00
85 Brendan Gallagher	.40	1.00
86A Pavel Datsyuk	.60	1.50
86B Pavel Datsyuk SP	5.00	12.00
87 Joel Ward	.25	.60
88 Sergei Bobrovsky	.60	1.50
89 Patrick Sharp	.40	1.00
90 Luke Schenn	.40	1.00
91A Joe Pavelski	.50	1.25
91B Joe Pavelski SP	4.00	10.00
92 David Backes	.25	.60
93 Ben Bishop	.30	.75
94A Claude Giroux	.40	1.00
94B Claude Giroux SP	3.00	8.00
95 Dustin Byfuglien	.40	1.00
96 Tomas Tatar	.25	.60
97 Tyler Toffoli	.40	1.00
98 Nail Yakupov	.25	.60
99 Corey Crawford	.50	1.25
100A Logan Couture	.50	1.25
100B Logan Couture SP	4.00	10.00
101 Patrice Bergeron	.50	1.25
102A Evgeni Malkin	.75	2.00
102B Evgeni Malkin SP	6.00	15.00
103 Ryan Miller	.40	1.00
104 Joe Thornton	.60	1.50
105 Drew Doughty	.50	1.25
106 Semyon Varlamov	.40	1.00
107A Dion Phaneuf	.30	.75
107B Dion Phaneuf SP	2.50	6.00
108 Mark Scheifele	.60	1.50
109A Taylor Hall	.40	1.00
109B Taylor Hall SP	3.00	8.00
110A Shea Weber	.30	.75
110B Shea Weber SP	2.50	6.00
111 Ryan Strome	.40	1.00
112 Henrik Zetterberg	.50	1.25
113 Jason Pominville	.25	.60
114 Nazem Kadri	.50	1.25
115A Alexander Ovechkin	1.50	4.00
115B Alexander Ovechkin SP	8.00	20.00
116 Jeff Carter	.30	.75
117 Jakub Voracek	.30	.75
118 Craig Anderson	.40	1.00
119 Tyler Johnson	.25	.60
120 Gabriel Landeskog	.50	1.25
121A Pekka Rinne	.40	1.00
121B Pekka Rinne SP	3.00	8.00
122 Keith Yandle	.25	.60
123 Ryan Getzlaf	.40	1.00
124A Jonathan Bernier	.30	.75
124B Jonathan Bernier SP	2.50	6.00
125 Duncan Keith	.30	.75
126 Mike Smith	.40	1.00
127A Tyler Seguin	.50	1.25
127B Tyler Seguin SP	4.00	10.00
128 Alex Pietrangelo	.30	.75
129 John Tavares	.60	1.50
130 Jonathan Quick	.50	1.25
131 Tyler Myers	.25	.60
132 Jaromir Jagr	1.25	3.00
133 Marc-Andre Fleury	.75	2.00
134 Zdeno Chara	.40	1.00
135 Frederik Andersen	.50	1.25
136 Jordan Eberle	.40	1.00
137 Ryan O'Reilly	.40	1.00
138 Jiri Hudler	.30	.75
139 Wayne Simmonds	.50	1.25
140 Vladimir Tarasenko	.50	1.25
141 Brandon Dubinsky	.25	.60
142 Mats Zuccarello	.40	1.00
143 Mike Green	.30	.75
144 Ondrej Palat	.30	.75
145 Corey Perry	.60	1.50
146 Alexandre Burrows	.25	.60
147 David Krejci	.40	1.00
148 Antoine Vermette	.25	.60
149 P.K. Subban	.50	1.25
150 Jamie Benn	.40	1.00
151 Scott Darling RC	1.50	4.00
152 Mirco Mueller RC	.75	2.00
153A Ty Rattie RC	.75	2.00
153B Ty Rattie SP	3.00	8.00
154A Sven Andrighetto RC	1.00	2.50
154B Josh McCabe SP	3.00	8.00
155A Vincent Trocheck RC	1.50	4.00
155B Vincent Trocheck SP	6.00	15.00
156 Stuart Percy RC	.75	2.00
157A Teuvo Teravainen RC	1.25	3.00
157B Teuvo Teravainen SP	5.00	12.00
158A Aaron Ekblad RC	2.00	5.00
158B Aaron Ekblad SP	8.00	20.00
159A Leon Draisaitl RC	10.00	25.00
159B Leon Draisaitl SP	20.00	50.00
160 Josh Jooris RC	.75	2.00
161A Calle Jarnkrok RC	.75	2.00
161B Calle Jarnkrok SP	3.00	8.00
162A Brandon Gormley RC	.75	2.00
162B Brandon Gormley SP	3.00	8.00
163 Andre Burakovsky RC	1.25	3.00
164 Adam Lowry RC	1.25	3.00
165 Jori Lehtera RC	1.00	2.50
166 Andrei Vasilevskiy RC	15.00	40.00
167A Adam Clendening RC	.75	2.00
167B Oscar Klefbom SP	6.00	15.00
168 Shayne Gostisbehere RC	1.50	4.00
169A Anthony Duclair RC	1.25	3.00
169B Anthony Duclair SP	8.00	20.00
170 Ryan Sproul RC	.75	2.00
171A Alexander Khokhlachev RC	.75	2.00
171B Alexander Khokhlachev SP	3.00	8.00
172 Barclay Goodrow RC	.75	2.00
173A Bo Horvat RC	2.00	5.00
173B Bo Horvat SP	10.00	25.00
174 Derrick Pouliot RC	1.00	2.50
175A Corban Knight RC	.75	2.00
175B Corban Knight SP	3.00	8.00
176 Curtis McKenzie RC	.60	1.50
177 David Pastrnak RC	4.00	10.00
178 Kevin Hayes RC	2.00	5.00
179 Kerby Rychel RC	.60	1.50
180 Brett Ritchie RC	.75	2.00
181A Rocco Grimaldi RC	.75	2.00
181B Joey Hishon SP	4.00	10.00
182 Tobias Rieder RC	.75	2.00
183A Evgeny Kuznetsov RC	2.00	5.00
183B Evgeny Kuznetsov SP	10.00	25.00
184 Jiri Sekac RC	.60	1.50
185A Jonathan Drouin RC	1.50	4.00
185B Jonathan Drouin SP	12.00	30.00
186A Curtis Lazar RC	.75	2.00
186B Curtis Lazar SP	3.00	8.00
187 Marko Dano RC	.75	2.00
188A Alexander Wennberg RC	1.25	3.00
188B Alexander Wennberg SP	5.00	12.00
189 John Klingberg RC	1.50	4.00
190 Victor Rask RC	.75	2.00
191A Damon Severson RC	.75	2.00
191B Damon Severson SP	6.00	15.00
192A Griffin Reinhart RC	.75	2.00
192B Griffin Reinhart SP	3.00	8.00
193 Markus Granlund RC	1.25	3.00
194A Johnny Gaudreau RC	2.50	6.00
194B Johnny Gaudreau SP	10.00	25.00
195A Teemu Pulkkinen RC	1.00	2.50
195B Teemu Pulkkinen SP	4.00	10.00
196 Vladislav Namestnikov RC	1.25	3.00
197A Darnell Nurse RC	1.50	4.00
197B Darnell Nurse SP	6.00	15.00
198A Sam Reinhart RC	3.00	8.00
198B Sam Reinhart SP	12.00	30.00
199A Seth Griffith RC	1.00	2.50
199B Seth Griffith SP	4.00	10.00
200 William Karlsson RC	2.50	6.00

2014-15 O-Pee-Chee Platinum Black Ice

*VETS/65: 5X TO 12X BASIC CARDS
*ROOKIES/65:2.5X TO 6X BASIC CARDS

Card		
1 Martin Brodeur	15.00	40.00
8 Sidney Crosby	30.00	60.00
35 Nicklas Backstrom	5.00	12.00
115 Alexander Ovechkin	15.00	40.00
157 Teuvo Teravainen	30.00	60.00
159 Leon Draisaitl	80.00	200.00
168 Shayne Gostisbehere	20.00	40.00

2014-15 O-Pee-Chee Platinum Blue Cubes

*VETS/65: 4X TO 10X BASIC CARDS
*ROOKIES/65: 2X TO 5X BASIC CARDS

Card		
1 Martin Brodeur	8.00	20.00
8 Sidney Crosby	10.00	25.00
35 Nicklas Backstrom	4.00	10.00
159 Leon Draisaitl	50.00	125.00

2014-15 O-Pee-Chee Platinum Rainbow

*RAINBOW: .5X TO X 1.2BASIC CARDS

Card		
35 Nicklas Backstrom	.50	1.25
159 Leon Draisaitl	15.00	40.00

2014-15 O-Pee-Chee Platinum Red Prism

*VETS/135: 2X TO 5X BASIC CARDS
*ROOKIES/135: 1X TO 2.5X BASIC CARDS

Card		
1 Martin Brodeur	8.00	20.00
35 Nicklas Backstrom	2.00	5.00
159 Leon Draisaitl	80.00	200.00

2014-15 O-Pee-Chee Platinum Seismic Gold

*VETS/50: 4X TO 10X BASIC CARDS
*ROOKIES/50: 2X TO 5X BASIC CARDS

Card		
1 Martin Brodeur	10.00	25.00
8 Sidney Crosby	10.00	25.00
35 Nicklas Backstrom	4.00	10.00
76 Carey Price	8.00	20.00
132 Jaromir Jagr	10.00	25.00
159 Leon Draisaitl	60.00	150.00
177 David Pastrnak	20.00	50.00
194 Johnny Gaudreau	12.00	30.00

2014-15 O-Pee-Chee Platinum Legends

Card		
LS1 Wayne Gretzky	8.00	20.00
LS2 Steve Yzerman	6.00	15.00
LS3 Bobby Orr	8.00	20.00
LS4 Pierre Turgeon	1.50	4.00
LS5 Brett Hull	4.00	10.00
LS6 Doug Gilmour	2.50	6.00
LS7 Nicklas Lidstrom	2.00	5.00
LS8 Dominik Hasek	3.00	8.00
LS9 Guy Carbonneau	2.00	5.00
LS10 Stan Mikita	2.50	6.00
LS11 Marcel Dionne	2.50	6.00
LS12 Phil Esposito	3.00	8.00
LS13 Larry Robinson	2.00	5.00
LS14 Ray Bourque	3.00	8.00
LS15 Mike Gartner	2.50	6.00
LS16 Mario Lemieux	8.00	20.00
LS17 Mark Messier	4.00	10.00
LS18 Theoren Fleury	2.50	6.00
LS19 Patrick Roy	8.00	20.00
LS20 Jean Beliveau	2.00	5.00

2014-15 O-Pee-Chee Platinum Retro

*RAIN. VETS: 1.2X TO 3X BASIC INSERT
*RAIN. ROOKIES: .6X TO 1.5X BASIC INSERT
*RED VETS: 1.5X TO 4X BASIC INSERTS
*RED ROOK.: .75X TO 8X BASIC INSERTS
*BLACK VETS/100: 2X TO 5X BASIC INSERTS
*BLACK ROOK./100: 1X TO 2.5X BASIC INSERTS

Card		
1 Sidney Crosby	2.00	5.00
2 Ryan Getzlaf	.50	1.25
3 Claude Giroux	.50	1.25
4 T.J. Oshie	.50	1.25
5 Mikko Koivu	.40	1.00
6 David Backes	.30	.75
7 Sean Monahan	.30	.75
8 Anze Kopitar	.75	2.00
9 Ondrej Palat	.40	1.00
10 Martin St. Louis	.50	1.25
11 James van Riemsdyk	.40	1.00
12 Tyler Seguin	.60	1.50
13 Johan Franzen	.40	1.00
14 Shea Weber	.40	1.00
15 Jonathan Toews	.75	2.00
16 John Tavares	.75	2.00
17 Evgeni Malkin	1.00	2.50
18 Jonathan Bernier	.40	1.00
19 Joe Pavelski	.60	1.50
20 Ryan Nugent-Hopkins	.60	1.50
21 Seth Jones	.50	1.25
22 Matt Duchene	.50	1.25
23 Patrick Sharp	.50	1.25
24 Logan Couture	.60	1.50
25 Phil Kessel	.50	1.25
26 Pavel Datsyuk	.75	2.00
27 Nathan MacKinnon	2.00	5.00
28 Carey Price	1.00	2.50
29 Pekka Rinne	.50	1.25
30 Dion Phaneuf	.40	1.00
31 Tomas Hertl	.50	1.25
32 Nicklas Backstrom	.50	1.25
33 Tuukka Rask	.60	1.50
34 Tomas Plekanec	.30	.75
35 Patrick Kane	1.00	2.50
36 Paul Stastny	.40	1.00
37 Duncan Keith	.40	1.00
38 Taylor Hall	.50	1.25
39 Kari Lehtonen	.40	1.00
40 Adam Henrique	.40	1.00
41 Cody Hodgson	.30	.75
42 Henrik Zetterberg	.60	1.50
43 Ryan Miller	.50	1.25
44 Jason Spezza	.50	1.25
45 Chris Kunitz	.50	1.25
46 Gustav Nyquist	.30	.75
47 Sergei Bobrovsky	.75	2.00
48 Eric Staal	.60	1.50
49 Zdeno Chara	.50	1.25
50 Antti Niemi	.40	1.00
51 Evander Kane	.50	1.25
52 Bobby Ryan	.40	1.00
53 Zach Parise	.50	1.25
54 Keith Yandle	.30	.75
55 Corey Perry	.75	2.00
56 Patrice Bergeron	.60	1.50
57 Marian Gaborik	.50	1.25
58 Shane Doan	.40	1.00
59 Jonathan Quick	.60	1.50
60 Dustin Byfuglien	.50	1.25
61 Jarome Iginla	.60	1.50
62 Alexander Ovechkin	2.00	5.00
63 Drew Doughty	.60	1.50
64 Jordan Eberle	.50	1.25
65 Jamie Benn	.50	1.25
66 Alex Galchenyuk	.30	.75
67 Mats Zuccarello	.50	1.25
68 Henrik Lundqvist	1.25	3.00
69 P.K. Subban	.60	1.50
70 Steven Stamkos	1.00	2.50
71 Kevin Hayes	2.50	6.00
72 Darnell Nurse	2.00	5.00
73 Corban Knight	1.00	2.50
74 Bo Horvat	2.50	6.00
75 Sam Reinhart	4.00	10.00
76 Seth Griffith	1.25	3.00
77 Alexander Wennberg	1.50	4.00
78 Jiri Sekac	.75	2.00
79 Leon Draisaitl	15.00	40.00
80 Teuvo Teravainen	1.50	4.00
81 Griffin Reinhart	1.00	2.50
82 Brandon Gormley	1.00	2.50
83 Stuart Percy	1.00	2.50
84 William Karlsson	3.00	8.00
85 Aaron Ekblad	2.50	6.00
86 Evgeny Kuznetsov	2.50	6.00
87 Jori Lehtera	1.25	3.00
88 Oscar Klefbom	2.00	5.00
89 Curtis Lazar	1.00	2.50
90 Johnny Gaudreau	3.00	8.00
91 Vincent Trocheck	2.00	5.00
92 Mirco Mueller	1.00	2.50
93 Chris Tierney	1.00	2.50
94 Calle Jarnkrok	1.00	2.50
95 Andre Burakovsky	1.50	4.00
96 Alexander Khokhlachev	1.00	2.50
97 Teemu Pulkkinen	1.25	3.00
98 Joey Hishon	1.25	3.00
99 Ty Rattie	1.00	2.50
100 Anthony Duclair	1.50	4.00

2014-15 O-Pee-Chee Platinum Retro Rainbow Autographs

Card		
6 David Backes	4.00	10.00
8 Anze Kopitar	10.00	25.00
12 Tyler Seguin	15.00	40.00
14 Shea Weber	5.00	12.00
15 Jonathan Toews	60.00	120.00
16 John Tavares	15.00	40.00
23 Patrick Sharp	20.00	50.00
26 Pavel Datsyuk	15.00	40.00
28 Carey Price	75.00	150.00
31 Tomas Hertl	6.00	15.00
38 Taylor Hall	6.00	15.00
39 Kari Lehtonen	5.00	12.00
40 Adam Henrique	5.00	12.00
46 Gustav Nyquist	4.00	10.00
48 Eric Staal	8.00	20.00
52 Bobby Ryan	5.00	12.00
53 Zach Parise	8.00	20.00
55 Corey Perry	75.00	150.00
61 Jarome Iginla	12.00	30.00
62 Alexander Ovechkin	30.00	80.00
72 Darnell Nurse	15.00	30.00
74 Bo Horvat	20.00	50.00
75 Sam Reinhart	25.00	60.00
76 Seth Griffith	8.00	20.00
77 Alexander Wennberg	10.00	25.00
79 Leon Draisaitl	30.00	80.00
80 Teuvo Teravainen	10.00	25.00
82 Brandon Gormley	6.00	15.00
83 Stuart Percy	6.00	15.00
84 William Karlsson	20.00	50.00
85 Aaron Ekblad	15.00	40.00
86 Evgeny Kuznetsov	15.00	40.00
87 Jori Lehtera	8.00	20.00
89 Curtis Lazar	6.00	15.00
90 Johnny Gaudreau	100.00	250.00
91 Viccent Trocheck	12.00	30.00
92 Mirco Mueller	6.00	15.00
94 Calle Jarnkrok	6.00	15.00
96 Alexander Khokhlachev	6.00	15.00
98 Joey Hishon	8.00	20.00
99 Ty Rattie	6.00	15.00
100 Anthony Duclair	10.00	25.00

2014-15 O-Pee-Chee Platinum Rookie Autographs

Card		
RA1 Jonathan Drouin	20.00	50.00
RA2 Bo Horvat	15.00	40.00
RA3 Aaron Ekblad	8.00	20.00
RA4 Alexander Wennberg	5.00	12.00
RA5 Leon Draisaitl	80.00	200.00
RA6 Griffin Reinhart EXCH	3.00	8.00
RA7 Johnny Gaudreau	80.00	200.00
RA8 Teuvo Teravainen	5.00	12.00
RA9 Curtis Lazar	3.00	8.00
RA10 Evgeny Kuznetsov	15.00	40.00
RA11 Darnell Nurse	6.00	15.00
RA12 Stuart Percy	3.00	8.00
RA13 Ty Rattie	3.00	8.00
RA14 Brandon Gormley	3.00	8.00
RA15 Alexander Khokhlachev	3.00	8.00
RA16 Jiri Sekac EXCH	2.50	6.00
RA17 Seth Griffith	4.00	10.00
RA18 Anthony Duclair	5.00	12.00
RA19 Marko Dano	3.00	8.00
RA20 Adam Lowry	5.00	12.00
RA21 Andre Burakovsky EXCH	5.00	12.00
RA22 Victor Rask	3.00	8.00
RA23 Jori Lehtera	4.00	10.00
RA24 Mirco Mueller	3.00	8.00
RA25 Damon Severson	3.00	8.00
RA26 Calle Jarnkrok	3.00	8.00
RA27 Kevin Hayes	15.00	40.00
RA28 Corban Knight EXCH	3.00	8.00
RA29 Chris Tierney	3.00	8.00
RA30 William Karlsson	15.00	40.00

2014-15 O-Pee-Chee Platinum Rookie Autographs Black Ice

Card		
RA1 Jonathan Drouin	40.00	100.00
RA2 Bo Horvat	30.00	80.00
RA5 Leon Draisaitl	250.00	600.00
RA7 Johnny Gaudreau	125.00	300.00
RA16 Jiri Sekac EXCH	8.00	20.00
RA21 Andre Burakovsky EXCH	20.00	50.00
RA27 Kevin Hayes	25.00	60.00

2014-15 O-Pee-Chee Platinum Rookie Autographs Blue Rainbow

*BLUE/25: 1X TO 2.5X BASIC AU

Card		
RA1 Jonathan Drouin	100.00	200.00
RA2 Bo Horvat	60.00	150.00
RA3 Aaron Ekblad	100.00	200.00
RA5 Leon Draisaitl	150.00	400.00
RA7 Johnny Gaudreau	200.00	500.00
RA21 Andre Burakovsky EXCH	50.00	120.00
RA27 Kevin Hayes	40.00	100.00

2014-15 O-Pee-Chee Platinum Rookie Autographs Red Rainbow

*RED/50: 1X TO 2.5X BASIC AU

Card		
RA1 Jonathan Drouin	50.00	120.00
RA2 Bo Horvat	40.00	100.00
RA3 Aaron Ekblad	30.00	80.00
RA5 Leon Draisaitl	125.00	300.00
RA7 Johnny Gaudreau	150.00	400.00
RA21 Andre Burakovsky EXCH	25.00	60.00
RA27 Kevin Hayes	30.00	80.00

2014-15 O-Pee-Chee Platinum Superstars

Card		
PS1 John Tavares	3.00	8.00
PS2 Nathan MacKinnon	8.00	20.00
PS3 Claude Giroux	2.00	5.00
PS4 Zach Parise	2.00	5.00
PS5 Jonathan Toews	3.00	8.00
PS6 Patrick Kane	4.00	10.00
PS7 Phil Kessel	2.00	5.00
PS8 Shea Weber	1.50	4.00
PS9 Martin Brodeur	5.00	12.00
PS10 Martin St. Louis	2.00	5.00
PS11 Patrick Marleau	2.00	5.00
PS12 Carey Price	4.00	10.00
PS13 Tyler Seguin	2.50	6.00
PS14 Taylor Hall	2.00	5.00
PS15 Evgeni Malkin	4.00	10.00
PS16 Anze Kopitar	3.00	8.00
PS17 Corey Perry	3.00	8.00
PS18 Matt Duchene	2.00	5.00
PS19 Joe Pavelski	2.50	6.00
PS20 Jarome Iginla	2.50	6.00

2015-16 O-Pee-Chee Platinum

*PURPLE VETS: 8X TO 20X BASIC CARDS

Card		
1 Sidney Crosby	1.50	4.00
2 Oliver Ekman-Larsson	.40	1.00
3 Corey Crawford	.50	1.25
4 Ryan Nugent-Hopkins	.50	1.25
5 Rick Nash	.40	1.00
6 Loui Eriksson	.25	.60
7 Filip Forsberg	.60	1.50
8 Drew Doughty	.50	1.25
9 Patric Hornqvist	.25	.60
10 John Tavares	.60	1.50
11 Jason Spezza	.40	1.00
12 Mike Hoffman	.25	.60
13 Mike Smith	.40	1.00
14 Anders Lee	.40	1.00
15 Erik Karlsson	.50	1.25
16 Derek Stepan	.25	.60
17 Teuvo Teravainen	.40	1.00
18 Radim Vrbata	.25	.60
19 Joe Thornton	.60	1.50
20 Corey Perry	.60	1.50
21 Nazem Kadri	.50	1.25
22 Daniel Sedin	.50	1.25
23 James Neal	.25	.60
24 Brian Elliott	.30	.75
25 Evgeni Malkin	.75	2.00
26 Michael Cammalleri	.30	.75
27 Mark Scheifele	.60	1.50
28 Keith Yandle	.25	.60
29 Taylor Hall	.40	1.00
30 Claude Giroux	.40	1.00
31 Jonas Hiller	.30	.75
32 Frederik Andersen	.50	1.25
33 Henrik Sedin	.50	1.25
34 Max Pacioretty	.40	1.00
35 Zach Parise	.40	1.00
36 Mark Stone	.50	1.25
37 Jiri Hudler	.30	.75
38 Jaroslav Halak	.40	1.00
39 Cam Ward	.40	1.00
40 Henrik Zetterberg	.50	1.25
41 Shane Doan	.30	.75
42 Tyler Bozak	.25	.60
43 Semyon Varlamov	.40	1.00
44 Vladimir Tarasenko	.50	1.25
45 Jamie Benn	.40	1.00
46 Ryan Strome	.40	1.00
47 Nino Niederreiter	.25	.60
48 Andrew Hammond	.50	1.25
49 Kyle Okposo	.25	.60
50 Steven Stamkos	.75	2.00
51 Aaron Ekblad	.50	1.25
52 Jonathan Quick	.50	1.25
53 Ryan Kesler	.40	1.00
54 Kris Letang	.50	1.25
55 Tuukka Rask	.50	1.25
56 Brayden Schenn	.40	1.00
57 Blake Wheeler	.40	1.00
58 Nail Yakupov	.25	.60
59 James van Riemsdyk	.30	.75
60 Ryan Miller	.40	1.00
61 Bo Horvat	.50	1.25
62 Steve Mason	.30	.75
63 Ryan O'Reilly	.40	1.00
64 Sam Reinhart	.75	2.00
65 Johnny Gaudreau	.60	1.50
66 Victor Hedman	.50	1.25
67 Tyler Johnson	.25	.60
68 Jaromir Jagr	1.25	3.00
69 Matt Duchene	.40	1.00
70 Pavel Datsyuk	.60	1.50
71 Jaden Schwartz	.50	1.25
72 Pekka Rinne	.40	1.00
73 Eric Staal	.50	1.25
74 Patrice Bergeron	.50	1.25
75 Carey Price	.75	2.00
76 Joe Pavelski	.50	1.25
77 Jeff Carter	.30	.75
78 Kari Lehtonen	.30	.75
79 Milan Lucic	.30	.75
80 P.K. Subban	.50	1.25
81 Jonathan Bernier	.30	.75
82 Andrew Ladd	.25	.60
83 Patrik Elias	.40	1.00
84 Patrick Sharp	.40	1.00
85 Jarome Iginla	.50	1.25
86 Nicklas Backstrom	.40	1.00
87 Shea Weber	.30	.75
88 Sergei Bobrovsky	.60	1.50
89 David Backes	.25	.60
90 Tyler Seguin	.50	1.25
91 Brendan Gallagher	.40	1.00
92 Nick Foligno	.30	.75
93 Evgeny Kuznetsov	.50	1.25
94 Nikita Kucherov	.75	2.00
95 Nathan MacKinnon	1.50	4.00
96 Justin Abdelkader	.30	.75
97 Braden Holtby	.50	1.25
98 Adam Henrique	.30	.75
99 Ryan Johansen	.30	.75
100 Henrik Lundqvist	1.00	2.50
101 Thomas Vanek	.30	.75
102 Brad Marchand	.75	2.00
103 Jim Howard	.50	1.25
104 Matt Moulson	.25	.60
105 Anze Kopitar	.60	1.50
106 Martin Jones	.30	.75
107 Mark Giordano	.40	1.00
108 Kyle Turris	.30	.75
109 Gabriel Landeskog	.50	1.25
110 Roberto Luongo	.60	1.50
111 Mike Ribeiro	.25	.60

112 Zemgus Girgensons .30 .75
113 Cam Talbot .40 1.00
114 Marc-Andre Fleury .75 2.00
115 Chris Kreider .50 1.25
116 Derick Brassard .25 .60
117 Sean Monahan .25 .60
118 Logan Couture .50 1.25
119 Marcus Johansson .30 .75
120 Patrick Kane .75 2.00
121 Justin Faulk .30 .75
122 Ben Bishop .30 .75
123 Tomas Plekanec .25 .60
124 Duncan Keith .30 .75
125 Jonathan Toews .60 1.50
126 Bryan Little .30 .75
127 Jason Pominville .25 .60
128 Alex Galchenyuk .25 .60
129 Cory Schneider .40 1.00
130 Phil Kessel .40 1.00
131 Marian Gaborik .40 1.00
132 Alexandre Burrows .25 .60
133 Wayne Simmonds .50 1.25
134 Mike Green .30 .75
135 Bobby Ryan .30 .75
136 Matt Beleskey .25 .60
137 John Carlson .40 1.00
138 Jakub Voracek .30 .75
139 Jordan Eberle .40 1.00
140 Ryan Getzlaf .40 1.00
141 Alexander Steen .25 .60
142 Brandon Saad .30 .75
143 Gustav Nyquist .25 .60
144 Dion Phaneuf .30 .75
145 Marian Hossa .40 1.00
146 Dustin Byfuglien .40 1.00
147 Devan Dubnyk .30 .75
148 Tyler Ennis .25 .60
149 Ondrej Pavelec .40 1.00
150 Alexander Ovechkin 1.50 4.00
151 Mike Gartner 2.00 5.00
152 Doug Weight 1.50 4.00
153 Ron Francis 2.00 5.00
154 Felix Potvin 2.50 6.00
155 Mike Bossy 1.50 4.00
156 Grant Fuhr 2.50 6.00
157 Denis Potvin 1.50 4.00
158 John Vanbiesbrouck 1.50 4.00
159 Marcel Dionne 2.00 5.00
160 Cam Neely 1.50 4.00
161 Malcolm Subban C AU RC 10.00 25.00
162 Kevin Fiala E AU RC 8.00 20.00
163 Jacob de la Rose E AU RC 6.00 15.00
164 Henrik Samuelsson F AU RC 4.00 10.00
165 Dylan Larkin D AU RC 30.00 80.00
166 Sergei Plotnikov F AU RC 4.00 10.00
167 Nick Shore A AU RC 4.00 10.00
168 Matt Puempel E AU RC 5.00 12.00
169 Shane Prince E AU RC 4.00 10.00
170 Sam Bennett D AU RC 20.00 50.00
171 Nick Cousins E AU RC 6.00 15.00
172 Antoine Bibeau F AU RC 6.00 15.00
173 Nikolaj Ehlers D AU RC 12.00 30.00
174 Ryan Hartman F AU RC 8.00 20.00
175 Jordan Weal F AU RC 4.00 10.00
176 Jake Virtanen D AU RC 8.00 20.00
177 Ronalds Kenins F AU RC 4.00 10.00
178 Nicolas Petan D AU RC 6.00 15.00
179 Jared McCann E AU RC 8.00 20.00
180 Robby Fabbri C AU RC 8.00 20.00
181 Mikko Rantanen C AU RC 30.00 80.00
182 Nikolay Goldobin F AU RC 6.00 15.00
183 Daniel Sprong E AU RC 8.00 20.00
184 Emile Poirier F AU RC 5.00 12.00
185 Viktor Arvidsson F AU RC 6.00 15.00
186 Artemi Panarin B AU RC 25.00 60.00
187 Noah Hanifin A AU RC 12.00 30.00
188 Connor Hellebuyck A AU RC 25.00 60.00
189 Max Domi B AU RC 12.00 30.00
190 Connor McDavid C AU RC 800.00 2000.00

2015-16 O-Pee-Chee Platinum Black Ice

*VETS/99: 5X TO 12X BASIC CARDS
SP/50: 1.5X TO 4X BASIC CARDS
*ROOKIES/50: .75X TO 2X BASIC CARDS
165 Dylan Larkin AU 100.00 200.00
174 Ryan Hartman AU 15.00 40.00
190 Connor McDavid AU 3000.00 8000.00

2015-16 O-Pee-Chee Platinum Rainbow

*VETS: .5X TO 1.25X BASIC CARDS
*SP: .5X TO 1.25X BASIC CARDS
*ROOKIES: .5X TO 1.25X BASIC CARDS
*VETS STATED ODDS 1:5 H 1:10 B
*SP STATED ODDS 1:160 H 1:1,600 B
3 Corey Crawford .60 1.50
86 Nicklas Backstrom .50 1.25
93 Evgeny Kuznetsov .60 1.50
165 Dylan Larkin C AU 25.00 60.00
174 Ryan Hartman E AU 10.00 25.00
181 Mikko Rantanen C AU 50.00 125.00
190 Connor McDavid B AU 800.00 2000.00

2015-16 O-Pee-Chee Platinum Red Prism

*VETS/149: 2X TO 5X BASIC CARDS
SP/75: 1X TO 2.5X BASIC CARDS
*ROOKIES/75: .6X TO 1.6X BASIC CARDS
3 Corey Crawford 2.50 6.00
86 Nicklas Backstrom 2.00 5.00
93 Evgeny Kuznetsov 2.50 6.00
165 Dylan Larkin AU 60.00 150.00
174 Ryan Hartman AU 12.00 30.00
190 Connor McDavid AU 1500.00 4000.00

2015-16 O-Pee-Chee Platinum Traxx

*SINGLES: 1.5X TO 4X BASIC INSERTS
*SP: .6X TO 1.5X BASIC INSERTS
*RC: .6X TO 1.5X BASIC INSERTS
3 Corey Crawford 2.00 5.00
86 Nicklas Backstrom 1.50 4.00
93 Evgeny Kuznetsov 2.00 5.00
165 Dylan Larkin AU 30.00 80.00
174 Ryan Hartman AU 10.00 25.00
190 Connor McDavid AU 200.00 400.00

2015-16 O-Pee-Chee Platinum White Ice

*VETS: 2X TO 5X BASIC CARDS
*SP: 1X TO 2.5X BASIC CARDS
*ROOKIES: .6X TO 1.5X BASIC CARDS
3 Corey Crawford 2.50 6.00
86 Nicklas Backstrom 2.00 5.00
93 Evgeny Kuznetsov 2.50 6.00
165 Dylan Larkin AU 75.00 150.00
174 Ryan Hartman AU 12.00 30.00
190 Connor McDavid AU 550.00 650.00

2015-16 O-Pee-Chee Platinum Marquee Rookies

*RAINBOW: .5X TO 1.2X BASIC INSERTS
M1 Connor McDavid 50.00 125.00
M2 Emile Poirier 1.00 2.50
M3 Ryan Hartman 1.50 4.00
M4 Jacob de la Rose 1.25 3.00
M5 Malcolm Subban 2.00 5.00
M6 Kevin Fiala 1.50 4.00
M7 Garret Sparks 1.25 3.00
M8 Taylor Leier 1.25 3.00
M9 Shane Prince .75 2.00
M10 Sam Bennett 4.00 10.00
M11 Matt Puempel 1.00 2.50
M12 Brock McGinn 1.25 3.00
M13 Linus Ullmark 2.50 6.00
M14 Devin Shore 1.25 3.00
M15 Daniel Sprong 1.50 4.00
M16 Joonas Donskoi 1.25 3.00
M17 Mattias Janmark 1.25 3.00
M18 Nick Shore .75 2.00
M19 Nikolay Goldobin 1.25 3.00
M20 Jared McCann 1.50 4.00
M21 Hunter Shinkaruk 1.25 3.00
M22 Sergei Plotnikov .75 2.00
M23 Ben Hutton 1.25 3.00
M24 Colton Parayko 2.00 5.00
M25 Artemi Panarin 5.00 12.00
M26 Robby Fabbri 1.50 4.00
M27 Juuse Saros 3.00 8.00
M28 Stanislav Galiev 1.25 3.00
M29 Matt Murray 5.00 12.00
M30 Max Domi 2.50 6.00
M31 Chandler Stephenson 1.50 4.00
M32 Mike Condon 1.50 4.00
M33 Andreas Athanasiou 3.00 8.00
M34 Oscar Lindberg 1.25 3.00
M35 Brendan Gaunce 1.50 4.00
M36 Connor Hellebuyck 5.00 12.00
M37 Zachary Fucale 1.00 2.50
M38 Nikolaj Ehlers 2.50 6.00
M39 Mike McCarron 1.50 4.00
M40 Jake Virtanen 1.50 4.00
M41 Noah Hanifin 2.00 5.00
M42 Mikko Rantanen 6.00 15.00
M43 Nicolas Petan 1.25 3.00
M44 Gustav Olofsson 1.25 3.00
M45 Dylan Larkin 4.00 10.00
M46 Charles Hudon 1.25 3.00
M47 Adam Pelech 1.00 2.50
M48 Andrew Copp 1.25 3.00
M49 Nick Ritchie 1.25 3.00
M50 Jack Eichel 5.00 12.00

2015-16 O-Pee-Chee Platinum Marquee Rookies Black Ice

*BLACK ICE: 1X TO 2.5X BASIC INSERTS
M1 Connor McDavid 600.00 1500.00
M3 Ryan Hartman 5.00 12.00
M29 Matt Murray 40.00 80.00
M45 Dylan Larkin 25.00 60.00

2015-16 O-Pee-Chee Platinum Marquee Rookies Blue Cubes

*SINGLES: 1.25X TO 3X BASIC INSERTS
M1 Connor McDavid 1000.00 2500.00
M3 Ryan Hartman 6.00 15.00
M29 Matt Murray 40.00 80.00

2015-16 O-Pee-Chee Platinum Marquee Rookies Rainbow Purple

*PURPLE: 2.5X TO 6X BASIC INSERTS
M1 Connor McDavid 2000.00 5000.00

2015-16 O-Pee-Chee Platinum Marquee Rookies Red Prism

*RED PRISM: 1X TO 2.5X BASIC INSERTS
M1 Connor McDavid 500.00 1200.00

2015-16 O-Pee-Chee Platinum Marquee Rookies Seismic Gold

*SINGLES: 1.5X TO 4X BASIC INSERTS
M1 Connor McDavid 1500.00 4000.00
M3 Ryan Hartman 8.00 20.00
M25 Artemi Panarin 30.00 80.00
M29 Matt Murray 80.00 150.00
M45 Dylan Larkin 30.00 80.00
M50 Jack Eichel 30.00 80.00

2015-16 O-Pee-Chee Platinum Marquee Rookies Traxx

*TRAXX: .6X TO 1.5X BASIC INSERTS
M1 Connor McDavid 125.00 300.00

2015-16 O-Pee-Chee Platinum Marquee Rookies White Ice

*WHITE ICE: .75 X TO 2X BASIC INSERTS
M1 Connor McDavid 400.00 1000.00
M3 Ryan Hartman 4.00 10.00
M29 Matt Murray 25.00 60.00

2015-16 O-Pee-Chee Platinum Retro

*RAINBOW: .5X TO 1.25X BASIC INSERTS
*GOLD: 1.25X TO 3X BASIC INSERTS
R1 Wayne Gretzky 10.00 25.00
R2 Phil Esposito 2.50 6.00
R3 Martin Brodeur 4.00 10.00
R4 Bobby Orr 6.00 15.00
R5 Mike Bossy 1.50 4.00
R6 Doug Weight 1.50 4.00
R7 John Vanbiesbrouck 1.50 4.00
R8 Ray Bourque 2.50 6.00
R9 Glenn Anderson 1.25 3.00
R10 Steve Yzerman 4.00 10.00
R11 Marty Turco 1.50 4.00
R12 Mario Lemieux 6.00 15.00
R13 Bobby Hull 3.00 8.00
R14 Markus Naslund 1.50 4.00
R15 Marty McSorley 1.25 3.00
R16 Patrick Roy 4.00 10.00
R17 Cam Neely 1.50 4.00
R18 Denis Potvin 1.50 4.00
R19 Rob Blake 1.50 4.00
R20 Grant Fuhr 2.50 6.00
R21 John Tavares 2.50 6.00
R22 Sidney Crosby 6.00 15.00
R23 Alexander Ovechkin 6.00 15.00
R24 Jakub Voracek 1.25 3.00
R25 Jamie Benn 1.50 4.00
R26 Carey Price 3.00 8.00
R27 Steve Mason 1.25 3.00
R28 Taylor Hall 1.50 4.00
R29 Eric Staal 2.00 5.00
R30 Sean Monahan 1.00 2.50
R31 Anze Kopitar 2.50 6.00
R32 Joe Pavelski 2.00 5.00
R33 Jonathan Toews 2.50 6.00
R34 Zach Parise 1.50 4.00
R35 Jarome Iginla 2.00 5.00
R36 Bobby Ryan 1.25 3.00
R37 David Backes 1.00 2.50
R38 Ben Bishop 1.25 3.00
R39 Rick Nash 1.50 4.00
R40 Tyler Seguin 2.00 5.00
R41 Jiri Hudler 1.25 3.00
R42 Claude Giroux 1.50 4.00
R43 Steven Stamkos 3.00 8.00
R44 Evgeni Malkin 3.00 8.00
R45 Ryan Getzlaf 1.50 4.00
R46 Corey Perry 2.50 6.00
R47 Max Pacioretty 1.50 4.00
R48 Erik Karlsson 2.00 5.00
R49 Johnny Gaudreau 2.50 6.00
R50 Patrick Kane 3.00 8.00
R51 Filip Forsberg 2.50 6.00
R52 Devan Dubnyk 1.25 3.00
R53 Pekka Rinne 1.50 4.00
R54 Henrik Lundqvist 4.00 10.00
R55 Pavel Datsyuk 2.50 6.00
R56 Radim Vrbata 1.00 2.50
R57 Vladimir Tarasenko 3.00 8.00
R58 Phil Kessel 1.50 4.00
R59 Oliver Ekman-Larsson 1.50 4.00
R60 Patrice Bergeron 2.00 5.00
R61 Tyler Ennis 1.00 2.50
R62 Nick Foligno 1.25 3.00
R63 Jaromir Jagr 5.00 12.00
R64 Adam Henrique 1.25 3.00
R65 Andrew Ladd 1.00 2.50
R66 Henrik Zetterberg 2.00 5.00
R67 P.K. Subban 2.00 5.00
R68 Jonathan Bernier 1.25 3.00
R69 Andrew Hammond 2.00 5.00
R70 Jonathan Quick 2.00 5.00
R71 Malcolm Subban 2.50 6.00
R72 Emile Poirier 1.25 3.00
R73 Ryan Hartman 2.00 5.00
R74 Jacob de la Rose 1.50 4.00
R75 Sam Bennett 5.00 12.00
R76 Kevin Fiala 2.00 5.00
R77 Matt Puempel 1.25 3.00
R78 Noah Hanifin 2.50 6.00
R79 Artemi Panarin 6.00 15.00
R80 Nikolaj Ehlers 3.00 8.00
R81 Slater Koekkoek 1.00 2.50
R82 Oscar Lindberg 1.50 4.00
R83 Shane Prince 1.00 2.50
R84 Kyle Baun 1.50 4.00
R85 Max Domi 3.00 8.00
R86 Anthony Stolarz 4.00 10.00
R87 Josh Anderson 3.00 8.00
R88 Mikko Rantanen 8.00 20.00
R89 Connor Hellebuyck 6.00 15.00
R90 Dylan Larkin 5.00 12.00
R91 Daniel Sprong 2.00 5.00
R92 Antoine Bibeau 1.50 4.00
R93 Nikolay Goldobin 1.50 4.00
R94 Nick Cousins 1.50 4.00
R95 Robby Fabbri 2.00 5.00
R96 Ronalds Kenins 1.00 2.50
R97 Connor McDavid 60.00 150.00
R98 Nicolas Petan 1.50 4.00
R99 Jake Virtanen 2.00 5.00
R100 Jack Eichel 6.00 15.00

2015-16 O-Pee-Chee Platinum Retro Rainbow Gold

R73 Ryan Hartman 6.00 15.00
R97 Connor McDavid 400.00 1000.00

2015-16 O-Pee-Chee Platinum Retro Rainbow Orange

*ORANGE: 1.5X TO 4X BASIC INSERTS
R73 Ryan Hartman 10.00 25.00
R97 Connor McDavid 500.00 1200.00

2015-16 O-Pee-Chee Platinum Retro Rainbow Blue Autographs

R1 Wayne Gretzky A 300.00 800.00
R2 Phil Esposito A 10.00 25.00
R3 Martin Brodeur A 50.00 125.00
R4 Bobby Orr A 60.00 150.00
R5 Mike Bossy A 40.00 80.00
R6 Doug Weight C 6.00 15.00
R7 John Vanbiesbrouck C 6.00 15.00
R8 Ray Bourque 10.00 25.00
R9 Glenn Anderson 5.00 12.00
R10 Steve Yzerman A 30.00 80.00
R11 Marty Turco C 6.00 15.00
R12 Mario Lemieux C 50.00 125.00
R13 Bobby Hull 25.00 60.00
R14 Markus Naslund 6.00 15.00
R15 Marty McSorley C 5.00 12.00
R16 Patrick Roy A 50.00 120.00
R17 Cam Neely B 12.00 30.00
R18 Denis Potvin 6.00 15.00
R20 Grant Fuhr B 25.00 60.00
R21 John Tavares 10.00 25.00
R22 Sidney Crosby A 100.00 250.00
R23 Alexander Ovechkin A 60.00 150.00
R24 Jakub Voracek 5.00 12.00
R26 Carey Price B 50.00 100.00
R27 Steve Mason 5.00 12.00
R28 Taylor Hall B 50.00 100.00
R29 Eric Staal C 8.00 20.00
R30 Sean Monahan B 4.00 10.00
R31 Anze Kopitar 10.00 25.00
R32 Joe Pavelski C 8.00 20.00
R33 Jonathan Toews 10.00 25.00
R34 Zach Parise B 15.00 40.00
R35 Jarome Iginla B 8.00 20.00
R36 Bobby Ryan B 12.00 30.00
R37 David Backes A 15.00 40.00
R39 Rick Nash B 25.00 60.00
R41 Jiri Hudler D 5.00 12.00
R44 Evgeni Malkin A 12.00 30.00
R46 Corey Perry B 10.00 25.00
R47 Max Pacioretty C 15.00 40.00
R52 Devan Dubnyk D 5.00 12.00
R53 Pekka Rinne 6.00 15.00
R55 Pavel Datsyuk B 25.00 60.00
R62 Nick Foligno D 5.00 12.00
R63 Jaromir Jagr B 50.00 100.00
R64 Adam Henrique D 5.00 12.00
R65 Andrew Ladd D 4.00 10.00
R68 Jonathan Bernier C 5.00 12.00
R69 Andrew Hammond D 8.00 20.00
R71 Malcolm Subban 10.00 25.00
R72 Emile Poirier D 5.00 12.00
R73 Ryan Hartman D 8.00 20.00
R74 Jacob de la Rose C 6.00 15.00
R75 Sam Bennett C 20.00 50.00
R76 Kevin Fiala D 8.00 20.00
R77 Matt Puempel C 5.00 12.00
R78 Noah Hanifin C 10.00 25.00
R79 Artemi Panarin D 12.00 30.00
R80 Nikolaj Ehlers D 12.00 30.00
R81 Slater Koekkoek 4.00 10.00
R82 Oscar Lindberg C 6.00 15.00
R83 Shane Prince C 4.00 10.00
R84 Kyle Baun D 6.00 15.00
R86 Anthony Stolarz D 15.00 40.00
R88 Mikko Rantanen C 30.00 80.00
R89 Connor Hellebuyck B 25.00 60.00
R90 Dylan Larkin A 50.00 120.00
R91 Daniel Sprong C 8.00 20.00
R92 Antoine Bibeau D 6.00 15.00
R93 Nikolay Goldobin C 6.00 15.00
R94 Nick Cousins D 6.00 15.00
R95 Robby Fabbri 8.00 20.00
R96 Ronalds Kenins D 4.00 10.00
R97 Connor McDavid B 1200.00 3000.00
R98 Nicolas Petan D 6.00 15.00
R99 Jake Virtanen C 8.00 20.00

2015-16 O-Pee-Chee Platinum Superstars Die Cuts

SS1 Alexander Ovechkin 10.00 25.00
SS2 Sidney Crosby 10.00 25.00
SS3 Jakub Voracek 2.00 5.00
SS4 Max Pacioretty 2.50 6.00
SS5 Steven Stamkos 5.00 12.00
SS6 Bobby Ryan 2.00 5.00
SS7 Jamie Benn 2.50 6.00
SS8 Jonathan Toews 4.00 10.00
SS9 Vladimir Tarasenko 3.00 8.00
SS10 Taylor Hall 2.50 6.00
SS11 Joe Pavelski 3.00 8.00
SS12 Corey Perry 4.00 10.00
SS13 Johnny Gaudreau 4.00 10.00
SS14 Filip Forsberg 4.00 10.00
SS15 Mark Stone 3.00 8.00
SS16 Bobby Hull 5.00 12.00
SS17 Wayne Gretzky 15.00 40.00
SS18 Mike Bossy 2.50 6.00

2015-16 O-Pee-Chee Platinum Superstars Die Cuts Rainbow Autographs

SS1 Alexander Ovechkin B 50.00 120.00
SS2 Sidney Crosby A 150.00 250.00
SS3 Jakub Voracek 12.00 30.00
SS4 Max Pacioretty C 15.00 40.00
SS8 Jonathan Toews 25.00 60.00
SS10 Taylor Hall C 25.00 60.00
SS11 Joe Pavelski C 25.00 60.00
SS12 Corey Perry B 30.00 80.00
SS15 Mark Stone C 15.00 40.00
SS16 Bobby Hull 20.00 50.00
SS17 Wayne Gretzky A 400.00 1000.00
SS18 Mike Bossy B 20.00 50.00

2015-16 O-Pee-Chee Platinum Team Logo Die Cuts

T1 Ryan Getzlaf 2.50 6.00
T2 Shane Doan 2.00 5.00
T3 Patrice Bergeron 3.00 8.00
T4 Tyler Ennis 1.50 4.00
T5 Sean Monahan 1.50 4.00
T6 Eric Staal 2.00 5.00
T7 Jonathan Toews 4.00 10.00
T8 Jarome Iginla 3.00 8.00
T9 Nick Foligno 2.00 5.00
T10 Jamie Benn 2.50 6.00
T11 Pavel Datsyuk 2.50 6.00
T12 Taylor Hall 2.50 6.00
T13 Jaromir Jagr 8.00 20.00
T14 Anze Kopitar 2.50 6.00
T15 Devan Dubnyk 1.50 4.00
T16 Carey Price 5.00 12.00
T17 Pekka Rinne 2.50 6.00
T18 Cory Schneider 2.50 6.00
T19 John Tavares 4.00 10.00
T20 Rick Nash 2.50 6.00
T21 Erik Karlsson 3.00 8.00
T22 Jakub Voracek 2.00 5.00
T23 Sidney Crosby 10.00 25.00
T24 Joe Pavelski 3.00 8.00
T25 Vladimir Tarasenko 3.00 8.00
T26 Steven Stamkos 5.00 12.00
T27 James van Riemsdyk 2.00 5.00
T28 Ryan Miller 2.50 6.00
T29 Alexander Ovechkin 10.00 25.00
T30 Andrew Ladd 1.50 4.00
T31 Mike Modano 4.00 10.00
T32 Ron Francis 2.00 5.00
T33 Joe Sakic 5.00 12.00
T34 Teemu Selanne 5.00 12.00
T35 Mario Lemieux 10.00 25.00
T36 Wayne Gretzky 15.00 40.00

2015-16 O-Pee-Chee Platinum Trophied Talent Die Cuts

TT1 Wayne Gretzky 10.00 25.00
TT2 Bobby Orr 6.00 15.00
TT3 Teemu Selanne 3.00 8.00
TT4 Martin Brodeur 4.00 10.00
TT5 Patrick Roy 4.00 10.00
TT6 Carey Price 3.00 8.00
TT7 Jiri Hudler 1.25 3.00
TT8 Aaron Ekblad 2.00 5.00
TT9 Jamie Benn 1.50 4.00
TT10 Devan Dubnyk 1.25 3.00

2015-16 O-Pee-Chee Platinum Trophied Talent Die Cuts Rainbow Autographs

TT1 Wayne Gretzky A 400.00 1000.00
TT2 Bobby Orr A 80.00 150.00
TT3 Teemu Selanne B 30.00 80.00
TT5 Patrick Roy A 150.00 250.00
TT6 Carey Price B 80.00 150.00
TT7 Jiri Hudler C 20.00 50.00
TT8 Aaron Ekblad C 20.00 50.00
TT10 Devan Dubnyk 15.00 40.00

2016-17 O-Pee-Chee Platinum

1 Connor McDavid 2.00 5.00
2 Tyler Seguin .50 1.25
3 Nathan MacKinnon 1.50 4.00
4 Mika Zibanejad .50 1.25
5 Jonathan Toews .60 1.50
6 Brandon Saad .30 .75
7 Tuukka Rask .50 1.25
8 Anze Kopitar .60 1.50
9 Jonathan Huberdeau .50 1.25
10 Henrik Zetterberg .50 1.25
11 Filip Forsberg .60 1.50
12 Nino Niederreiter .25 .60
13 Jordan Staal .30 .75
14 Ryan Getzlaf .40 1.00
15 Oliver Ekman-Larsson .40 1.00
16 Adam Henrique .30 .75
17 Brock Nelson .40 1.00
18 Alex Galchenyuk .25 .60
19 Mark Stone .50 1.25
20 Johnny Gaudreau .60 1.50
21 Alexander Steen .25 .60
22 Brent Burns .40 1.00
23 Nikita Kucherov .75 2.00
24 Ryan O'Reilly .40 1.00
25 Sidney Crosby 1.50 4.00
26 Blake Wheeler .40 1.00
27 Leo Komarov .25 .60
28 Daniel Sedin .50 1.25
29 Shayne Gostisbehere .50 1.25
30 Braden Holtby .50 1.25
31 Jarome Iginla .50 1.25
32 David Backes .25 .60
33 Artemi Panarin .75 2.00
34 Justin Abdelkader .30 .75
35 Brendan Gallagher .40 1.00
36 Andre Burakovsky .25 .60
37 Taylor Hall .40 1.00
38 Ryan Nugent-Hopkins .50 1.25
39 Kris Letang .40 1.00
40 Jaromir Jagr 1.25 3.00
41 Drew Doughty .40 1.00
42 Logan Couture .50 1.25
43 Shane Doan .30 .75
44 Cam Atkinson .40 1.00
45 Jake Allen .40 1.00
46 Tyler Johnson .25 .60
47 Rickard Rakell .30 .75
48 James Neal .25 .60
49 Gabriel Landeskog .40 1.00
50 Patrick Kane .75 2.00
51 Anders Lee .40 1.00
52 Tomas Tatar .25 .60
53 Henrik Lundqvist 1.00 2.50
54 Jimmy Hayes .25 .60
55 Mikko Koivu .30 .75
56 Nazem Kadri .50 1.25
57 Jeff Skinner .50 1.25
58 Phil Kessel .50 1.25
59 Bo Horvat .50 1.25
60 P.K. Subban .50 1.25
61 Joe Thornton .60 1.50
62 Claude Giroux .60 1.50
63 Mark Scheifele .60 1.50
64 Jack Eichel .60 1.50
65 Jonathan Quick .50 1.25
66 Nicklas Backstrom .40 1.00
67 Aaron Ekblad .40 1.00
68 Vladimir Tarasenko .40 1.00
69 Kyle Okposo .25 .60
70 Max Pacioretty .40 1.00
71 Steven Stamkos .75 2.00
72 Pekka Rinne .50 1.25
73 Leon Draisaitl 1.25 3.00
74 John Gibson .40 1.00
75 Jamie Benn .40 1.00
76 Marcus Johansson .30 .75
77 Bobby Ryan .30 .75
78 Milan Lucic .30 .75
79 Erik Karlsson .40 1.00
80 Vincent Trocheck .40 1.00
81 Tomas Plekanec .25 .60
82 Rick Nash .25 .60
83 Sean Monahan .25 .60
84 Patric Hornqvist .25 .60
85 Patrick Marleau .40 1.00
86 Artem Anisimov .25 .60
87 Jake Virtanen .25 .60
88 Zach Parise .40 1.00
89 Kyle Palmieri .30 .75
90 Shea Weber .30 .75
91 Jeff Carter .25 .60
92 Patrice Bergeron .50 1.25
93 Morgan Rielly .40 1.00
94 Jakob Silfverberg .25 .60
95 Derek Stepan .25 .60
96 Dylan Larkin .50 1.25
97 Elias Lindholm .40 1.00
98 Ben Bishop .30 .75
99 Boone Jenner .40 1.00
100 Alexander Ovechkin 1.50 4.00
101 Robby Fabbri .25 .60
102 Andrew Ladd .25 .60
103 Sam Reinhart .75 2.00
104 Jordan Eberle .40 1.00
105 Wayne Simmonds .50 1.25
106 John Klingberg .40 1.00
107 Matt Duchene .40 1.00
108 Reilly Smith .40 1.00
109 Bryan Little .30 .75
110 Max Domi .40 1.00
111 Rasmus Ristolainen .25 .60
112 Tyler Toffoli .40 1.00
113 Gustav Nyquist .25 .60
114 Matt Murray .60 1.50
115 Ryan Kesler .40 1.00
116 Jean-Gabriel Pageau .25 .60
117 Joe Pavelski .50 1.25
118 Brian Elliott .30 .75
119 Duncan Keith .30 .75
120 Nikolaj Ehlers .40 1.00
121 Mats Zuccarello .40 1.00
122 David Pastrnak 1.00 2.50
123 Cory Schneider .40 1.00
124 Scott Hartnell .25 .60
125 Carey Price .75 2.00
126 Ondrej Palat .30 .75
127 Carl Soderberg .25 .60
128 Evgeny Kuznetsov .50 1.25
129 Jason Spezza .40 1.00
130 Sam Bennett .60 1.50
131 Devan Dubnyk .30 .75
132 Chris Kreider .50 1.25
133 Victor Rask .25 .60
134 Michael Raffl .25 .60
135 Corey Perry .60 1.50
136 Evgeni Malkin .75 2.00
137 Tyler Bozak .25 .60
138 Corey Crawford .50 1.25
139 Henrik Sedin .50 1.25
140 Anthony Duclair .30 .75
141 Tanner Pearson .30 .75
142 Mike Hoffman .25 .60
143 Ryan Johansen .30 .75
144 Jussi Jokinen .40 1.00
145 Petr Mrazek .40 1.00
146 Brad Marchand .75 2.00
147 Kevin Shattenkirk .25 .60
148 Patrick Sharp .30 .75
149 Martin Jones .30 .75
150 John Tavares .60 1.50
151 Auston Matthews RC 25.00 60.00
152 Matthew Tkachuk RC 4.00 10.00
153 Michael Matheson RC 1.00 2.50
154 Nick Schmaltz RC 1.25 3.00
155 William Nylander RC 4.00 10.00
156 Ivan Provorov RC 1.50 4.00
157 Chris Bigras RC .75 2.00
158 Danton Heinen RC .75 2.00
159 Oliver Bjorkstrand RC 1.25 3.00
160 Jesse Puljujarvi RC 2.00 5.00
161 Mikhail Sergachev RC 1.50 4.00
162 Frederik Gauthier RC .40 1.00
163 Brandon Carlo RC 1.50 4.00
164 Nikita Tryamkin RC .60 1.50
165 Hudson Fasching RC 1.00 2.50
166 Dylan Strome RC 2.50 6.00
167 Pavel Buchnevich RC 1.50 4.00
168 Tobias Lindberg RC 1.50 4.00
169 Jacob Larsson RC 1.50 4.00
170 Pavel Zacha RC 1.50 4.00
171 Anthony Beauvillier RC 1.00 2.50
172 Josh Morrissey RC 2.50 6.00
173 Sebastian Aho RC 3.00 8.00
174 Thomas Chabot RC 2.00 5.00
175 Connor Brown RC 1.50 4.00
176 Patrik Laine RC 2.50 6.00
177 Tom Kuhnhackl RC .75 2.00
178 Lawson Crouse RC .75 2.00
179 Trevor Carrick RC .40 1.00
180 Mitch Marner RC 3.00 8.00
181 Nick Sorensen RC .40 1.00
182 Sonny Milano RC 1.25 3.00
183 Gustav Forsling RC 2.00 5.00
184 Brayden Point RC 2.50 6.00
185 Anthony Mantha RC 2.00 5.00
186 Artturi Lehkonen RC 1.25 3.00
187 Kasperi Kapanen RC 1.50 4.00
188 Mathew Barzal RC 3.00 8.00
189 Nikita Soshnikov RC .60 1.50
190 Jimmy Vesey RC 1.00 2.50
191 Jakob Chychrun RC 2.00 5.00
192 Joel Eriksson Ek RC 1.50 4.00
193 Tyler Motte RC 1.00 2.50
194 Steven Santini RC .75 2.00
195 Brendan Leipsic RC .75 2.00
196 Zach Werenski RC 3.00 8.00
197 Kyle Connor RC 3.00 8.00
198 Zach Sanford RC 1.00 2.50
199 Travis Konecny RC 2.00 5.00
200 Christian Dvorak RC 1.25 3.00

2016-17 O-Pee-Chee Platinum Ice Blue Traxx

*TRAXX VET: 1.25X TO 3X BASIC CARDS
*TRAXX RC: .6X TO 1.5X BASIC CARDS
66 Nicklas Backstrom 1.25 3.00
128 Evgeny Kuznetsov 1.50 4.00
138 Corey Crawford 1.50 4.00
151 Auston Matthews 20.00 50.00

2016-17 O-Pee-Chee Platinum Rainbow Color Wheel

151 Auston Matthews 25.00 60.00

2016-17 O-Pee-Chee Platinum Rainbow Orange

*ORANGE/25: 5X TO 12X BASIC CARDS
*ORANGE RC/25: 3X TO 8X BASIC CARDS
1 Connor McDavid 40.00 100.00
66 Nicklas Backstrom 5.00 12.00
125 Carey Price 20.00 50.00
128 Evgeny Kuznetsov 6.00 15.00
138 Corey Crawford 6.00 15.00
151 Auston Matthews 100.00 200.00
176 Patrik Laine 50.00 120.00

2016-17 O-Pee-Chee Platinum Red Prism

*RED PRISM/199: 1.5X TO 4X BASIC CARDS
*RED PRISM RC/199: 1X TO 2.5X BASIC CARDS
1 Connor McDavid 15.00 40.00
66 Nicklas Backstrom 1.50 4.00
128 Evgeny Kuznetsov 2.00 5.00
138 Corey Crawford 2.00 5.00
151 Auston Matthews 30.00 80.00
155 William Nylander 15.00 40.00
176 Patrik Laine 25.00 60.00
180 Mitch Marner 20.00 50.00

2016-17 O-Pee-Chee Platinum Royal Blue Cubes

*BLUE CUBES/99: 2X TO 5X BASIC CARDS
*BLUE CUBES RC/99: 1.25X TO 3X BASIC CARDS
1 Connor McDavid 25.00 60.00
25 Sidney Crosby 6.00 15.00
66 Nicklas Backstrom 2.00 5.00
125 Carey Price 12.00 30.00
128 Evgeny Kuznetsov 2.50 6.00
138 Corey Crawford 2.50 6.00
151 Auston Matthews 40.00 100.00
155 William Nylander 20.00 50.00
176 Patrik Laine 30.00 80.00
180 Mitch Marner 25.00 60.00

2016-17 O-Pee-Chee Platinum Seismic Gold

*GOLD/50: 3X TO 10X BASIC CARDS
*GOLD RC/50: 2X TO 5X BASIC CARDS
1 Connor McDavid 30.00 80.00
50 Patrick Kane 8.00 20.00
66 Nicklas Backstrom 4.00 10.00
125 Carey Price 15.00 40.00
128 Evgeny Kuznetsov 5.00 12.00
138 Corey Crawford 5.00 12.00
151 Auston Matthews 90.00 150.00
155 William Nylander 25.00 60.00
173 Sebastian Aho 15.00 40.00
176 Patrik Laine 40.00 100.00
180 Mitch Marner 30.00 80.00

2016-17 O-Pee-Chee Platinum NHL Logo Crest Die Cuts

NHLLD1 Wayne Gretzky 6.00 15.00
NHLLD2 Bobby Orr 4.00 10.00
NHLLD3 Mario Lemieux 4.00 10.00
NHLLD4 Henrik Lundqvist 2.50 6.00
NHLLD5 Alexander Ovechkin 4.00 10.00
NHLLD6 Connor McDavid 5.00 12.00
NHLLD7 Jaromir Jagr 3.00 8.00
NHLLD8 Evgeni Malkin 2.00 5.00
NHLLD9 Patrick Kane 2.00 5.00
NHLLD10 Sidney Crosby 4.00 10.00
NHLLD11 Jamie Benn 1.00 2.50
NHLLD12 Henrik Zetterberg 1.25 3.00
NHLLD13 Jonathan Toews 1.50 4.00
NHLLD14 John Tavares 1.50 4.00
NHLLD15 Carey Price 2.00 5.00

2016-17 O-Pee-Chee Platinum Platinum Phenoms Die Cuts

OPPAK Anze Kopitar 3.00 8.00
OPPAL Andrew Ladd 1.25 3.00
OPPAM Auston Matthews 12.00 30.00
OPPBO Bobby Orr 8.00 20.00
OPPCH Carl Hagelin 1.25 3.00
OPPCM Connor McDavid 10.00 25.00
OPPCP Corey Perry 3.00 8.00
OPPDK David Krejci 2.00 5.00
OPPDS Dylan Strome 5.00 12.00
OPPHL Henrik Lundqvist 5.00 12.00
OPPHZ Henrik Zetterberg 2.50 6.00
OPPJP Joe Pavelski 2.50 6.00
OPPJT Jonathan Toews 3.00 8.00
OPPMM Mark Messier 4.00 10.00
OPPMU Matt Murray 3.00 8.00
OPPNM Nathan MacKinnon 8.00 20.00
OPPPL Patrik Laine 5.00 12.00
OPPPR Patrick Roy 5.00 12.00
OPPPZ Pavel Zacha 3.00 8.00
OPPSC Sidney Crosby 8.00 20.00
OPPSY Steve Yzerman 5.00 12.00
OPPTS Tyler Seguin 2.50 6.00
OPPWG Wayne Gretzky 12.00 30.00
OPPWN William Nylander 8.00 20.00
OPPZP Zach Parise 2.00 5.00

2016-17 O-Pee-Chee Platinum Puck Personas Die Cuts

PP1 Mario Lemieux 6.00 15.00
PP2 Martin Brodeur 4.00 10.00
PP3 Steve Yzerman 4.00 10.00
PP4 John Tavares 2.50 6.00
PP5 Roberto Luongo 2.50 6.00
PP6 Evgeni Malkin 3.00 8.00
PP7 Patrick Kane 3.00 8.00
PP8 Brent Burns 1.50 4.00
PP9 Alex Galchenyuk 1.00 2.50
PP10 Alexander Ovechkin 6.00 15.00
PP11 Mats Zuccarello 1.50 4.00
PP12 Matt Duchene 1.50 4.00
PP13 Max Pacioretty 1.50 4.00
PP14 Tyler Toffoli 1.50 4.00
PP15 Taylor Hall 1.50 4.00

2016-17 O-Pee-Chee Platinum Retro

R1 Henrik Zetterberg 2.00 5.00
R2 Andrew Ladd 1.00 2.50
R3 Alex Galchenyuk 1.00 2.50
R4 Ryan Spooner 1.25 3.00
R5 Sidney Crosby 6.00 15.00
R6 Ryan O'Reilly 1.50 4.00
R7 Nikita Kucherov 3.00 8.00
R8 David Krejci 1.50 4.00
R9 Wayne Simmonds 2.00 5.00
R10 Taylor Hall 1.50 4.00
R11 Jonathan Huberdeau 2.00 5.00
R12 Brent Burns 1.50 4.00
R13 Jake Muzzin 1.50 4.00
R14 Oliver Ekman-Larsson 1.50 4.00
R15 Jonathan Toews 2.50 6.00
R16 Jaroslav Halak 1.50 4.00
R17 Nathan MacKinnon 6.00 15.00
R18 Mark Scheifele 2.50 6.00
R19 Jamie Benn 1.50 4.00
R20 Henrik Lundqvist 4.00 10.00
R21 Aaron Ekblad 2.00 5.00
R22 Jake Allen 1.50 4.00
R23 Jaden Schwartz 2.00 5.00
R24 Victor Rask 1.00 2.50
R25 Connor McDavid 8.00 20.00
R26 Matt Murray 2.50 6.00
R27 Johnny Gaudreau 2.50 6.00

R28 Jason Pominville 1.00 2.50
R29 Roman Josi 1.50 4.00
R30 Alexander Ovechkin 6.00 15.00
R31 Roberto Luongo 2.50 6.00
R32 Tyler Toffoli 1.50 4.00
R33 Dylan Larkin 2.00 5.00
R34 Bo Horvat 2.00 5.00
R35 Sam Bennett 2.50 6.00
R36 Rasmus Ristolainen 1.00 2.50
R37 Noah Hanifin 1.50 4.00
R38 Mats Zuccarello 1.50 4.00
R39 Carl Hagelin 1.00 2.50
R40 Carey Price 3.00 8.00
R41 Morgan Rielly 1.50 4.00
R42 Kyle Palmieri 1.25 3.00
R43 Jason Spezza 1.50 4.00
R44 Brendan Gallagher 1.50 4.00
R45 Derek Stepan 1.00 2.50
R46 Jaromir Jagr 5.00 12.00
R47 John Tavares 2.50 6.00
R48 Leon Draisaitl 5.00 12.00
R49 Robby Fabbri 1.00 2.50
R50 Zach Parise 1.50 4.00
R51 Bobby Ryan 1.25 3.00
R52 Brandon Saad 1.25 3.00
R53 John Gibson 1.50 4.00
R54 Evgeny Kuznetsov 2.00 5.00
R55 Joe Pavelski 2.00 5.00
R56 Tyson Barrie 1.00 2.50
R57 Ryan Johansen 1.25 3.00
R58 Andrew Shaw 1.00 2.50
R59 Andreas Athanasiou 1.50 4.00
R60 Anze Kopitar 2.50 6.00
R61 Nino Niederreiter 1.00 2.50
R62 Boone Jenner 1.50 4.00
R63 Artemi Panarin 3.00 8.00
R64 Evgeni Malkin 3.00 8.00
R65 Pekka Rinne 1.50 4.00
R66 Auston Matthews 10.00 25.00
R67 Charlie Lindgren 2.50 6.00
R68 Dylan Strome 4.00 10.00
R69 Oliver Bjorkstrand 2.00 5.00
R70 Travis Konecny 3.00 8.00
R71 Michael Matheson 1.50 4.00
R72 Kyle Connor 5.00 12.00
R73 William Nylander 6.00 15.00
R74 Mikhail Sergachev 2.50 6.00
R75 Oliver Kylington 1.25 3.00
R76 Jesse Puljujarvi 3.00 8.00
R77 Sonny Milano 2.00 5.00
R78 Brayden Point 4.00 10.00
R79 Pavel Zacha 2.50 6.00
R80 Mathew Barzal 5.00 12.00
R81 Kasperi Kapanen 2.50 6.00
R82 Sebastian Aho 5.00 12.00
R83 Anthony Mantha 3.00 8.00
R84 Pavel Buchnevich 2.50 6.00
R85 Ryan Pulock 1.50 4.00
R86 Matthew Tkachuk 6.00 15.00
R87 Hudson Fasching 1.50 4.00
R88 Mitch Marner 5.00 12.00
R89 Josh Morrissey 4.00 10.00
R90 Zach Werenski 5.00 12.00
R91 Brendan Leipsic 1.25 3.00
R92 Ivan Provorov 2.50 6.00
R93 Justin Bailey 1.50 4.00
R94 Jimmy Vesey 2.50 6.00
R95 Connor Brown 2.50 6.00
R96 Jakob Chychrun 3.00 8.00
R97 Lawson Crouse 1.25 3.00
R98 Christian Dvorak 2.00 5.00
R99 Patrik Laine 4.00 10.00
R100 Joel Eriksson Ek 2.50 6.00

2016-17 O-Pee-Chee Platinum Retro Rainbow Black

R1 Henrik Zetterberg AU A 20.00 50.00
R3 Alex Galchenyuk AU A 25.00 60.00
R7 Nikita Kucherov AU C 15.00 40.00
R9 Wayne Simmonds AU B 25.00 60.00
R12 Brent Burns AU B 15.00 40.00
R16 Jaroslav Halak AU B 25.00 60.00
R18 Mark Scheifele AU C 15.00 40.00
R20 Henrik Lundqvist AU A 30.00 80.00
R26 Matt Murray AU C 20.00 50.00
R31 Roberto Luongo AU A 30.00 80.00
R34 Bo Horvat AU C 25.00 60.00
R45 Derek Stepan AU B 15.00 40.00
R46 Jaromir Jagr AU A 150.00 250.00
R47 John Tavares AU A 30.00 80.00
R48 Leon Draisaitl AU B 20.00 50.00
R50 Zach Parise AU A 40.00 100.00
R58 Andrew Shaw AU C 15.00 40.00
R67 Charlie Lindgren AU E 20.00 50.00
R68 Dylan Strome AU D 25.00 60.00
R70 Travis Konecny AU F 20.00 40.00
R74 Mikhail Sergachev AU D 20.00 50.00
R86 Matthew Tkachuk AU E 30.00 80.00
R94 Jimmy Vesey AU E 12.00 30.00
R100 Joel Eriksson Ek AU F 10.00 25.00

2016-17 O-Pee-Chee Platinum Retro Rainbow Gold

*GOLD/149: 1X TO 2.5X BASIC INSERTS
R54 Evgeny Kuznetsov 5.00 12.00
R66 Auston Matthews 50.00 120.00

2016-17 O-Pee-Chee Platinum Retro Rainbow Orange

*ORANGE/49: 2X TO 5X BASIC INSERTS
R25 Connor McDavid 30.00 80.00
R66 Auston Matthews 100.00 200.00

2016-17 O-Pee-Chee Platinum Rookie Autographs

RAB Anthony Beauvillier E 5.00 12.00
RAM Auston Matthews A 300.00 800.00
RAN Anthony Mantha A 20.00 50.00
RBA Mathew Barzal C 40.00 100.00
RBL Brendan Leipsic A 4.00 10.00
RBP Brayden Point A 30.00 80.00
RBR Connor Brown A 8.00 20.00
RCB Chris Bigras D 4.00 10.00
RCD Christian Dvorak E 6.00 15.00
RCL Charlie Lindgren C 12.00 30.00
RDS Dominik Simon E 4.00 10.00
REL Esa Lindell E 5.00 12.00
RHF Hudson Fasching C 5.00 12.00
RIP Ivan Provorov B 8.00 20.00
RJD Jason Dickinson A 4.00 10.00
RJM Josh Morrissey A 12.00 30.00
RJP Jesse Puljujarvi B 10.00 25.00
RJV Jimmy Vesey B 8.00 20.00
RKC Kyle Connor C 15.00 40.00
RLC Lawson Crouse E 4.00 10.00
RMA Michael Matheson A 8.00 20.00
RMM Mitch Marner A 100.00 250.00
RMR Mike Reilly E 4.00 10.00
RMS Mikhail Sergachev B 12.00 30.00
RMT Matthew Tkachuk B 20.00 50.00
RMW Miles Wood E 4.00 10.00
RNS Nikita Soshnikov C 3.00 8.00
ROB Oliver Bjorkstrand C 6.00 15.00
ROK Oliver Kylington E 4.00 10.00
ROS Oskar Sundqvist E 5.00 12.00
RPB Pavel Buchnevich A 8.00 20.00
RPL Patrik Laine B 80.00 150.00
RPZ Pavel Zacha A 8.00 20.00
RRP Ryan Pulock E 5.00 12.00
RSA Sebastian Aho D 25.00 60.00
RSC Nick Schmaltz C 12.00 30.00
RSM Sonny Milano E 6.00 15.00
RSS Steven Santini E 4.00 10.00
RST Dylan Strome A 12.00 30.00
RTC Trevor Carrick D 5.00 12.00
RTM Timo Meier E 10.00 25.00
RVR Jakub Vrana E 6.00 15.00
RWN William Nylander A 40.00 100.00
RZW Zach Werenski B 15.00 40.00

2016-17 O-Pee-Chee Platinum Rookie Autographs Rainbow

*RAINBOW: .5X TO 1.25X BASIC INSERTS
RAM Auston Matthews A 250.00 400.00
RJP Jesse Puljujarvi B 20.00 50.00
RMM Mitch Marner A 200.00 500.00
RMS Mikhail Sergachev B 25.00 60.00
RPL Patrik Laine B 80.00 150.00
RWN William Nylander A 60.00 150.00

2017-18 O-Pee-Chee Platinum

1 Sidney Crosby 1.50 4.00
2 Max Pacioretty .40 1.00
3 Brad Marchand .75 2.00
4 Nikita Kucherov .75 2.00
5 Henrik Lundqvist 1.00 2.50
6 Corey Perry .60 1.50
7 Tyler Seguin .50 1.25
8 Patrik Laine .50 1.25
9 Leon Draisaitl 1.25 3.00
10 Patrick Kane .75 2.00
11 Ryan O'Reilly .40 1.00
12 Evgeny Kuznetsov .50 1.25
13 Henrik Sedin .50 1.25
14 Jaden Schwartz .50 1.25
15 Sergei Bobrovsky .60 1.50
16 Adam Henrique .30 .75
17 Anthony Mantha .30 .75
18 Gabriel Landeskog .50 1.25
19 Aaron Ekblad .50 1.25
20 P.K. Subban .50 1.25
21 Sean Monahan .25 .60
22 Mikael Granlund .30 .75
23 Max Domi .40 1.00
24 Jeff Carter .30 .75
25 Auston Matthews 1.50 4.00
26 Matt Duchene .40 1.00
27 Wayne Simmonds .50 1.25
28 Sebastian Aho .60 1.50
29 Logan Couture .50 1.25
30 John Tavares .60 1.50
31 Marc-Andre Fleury .75 2.00
32 Ryan Kesler .40 1.00
33 Jake Guentzel .60 1.50
34 Jonathan Drouin .30 .75
35 Victor Hedman .50 1.25
36 David Krejci .40 1.00
37 Jamie Benn .40 1.00
38 Cam Talbot .40 1.00
39 Brandon Saad .30 .75
40 Taylor Hall .40 1.00
41 Chris Kreider .50 1.25
42 Jack Eichel .60 1.50
43 Jakub Voracek .30 .75
44 Nick Foligno .30 .75
45 Martin Jones .30 .75
46 Charlie Coyle .40 1.00
47 Nick Bonino .25 .60
48 Henrik Zetterberg .50 1.25
49 Johnny Gaudreau .60 1.50
50 Connor McDavid 2.00 5.00
51 Aleksander Barkov .60 1.50
52 Vladimir Tarasenko .50 1.25
53 James Neal .25 .60
54 Mark Scheifele .60 1.50
55 Anze Kopitar .60 1.50
56 Alex Galchenyuk .25 .60
57 Erik Karlsson .50 1.25
58 John Klingberg .40 1.00
59 Derek Stepan .25 .60
60 Mitch Marner .60 1.50
61 Loui Eriksson .25 .60
62 Scott Darling .30 .75
63 Nick Leddy .25 .60
64 Cam Fowler .40 1.00
65 Brent Burns .40 1.00
66 Evgeni Malkin .75 2.00
67 Nathan MacKinnon 1.50 4.00
68 Ryan Hartman .25 .60
69 T.J. Oshie .40 1.00
70 Steven Stamkos .75 2.00
71 Artemi Panarin .75 2.00
72 Dustin Byfuglien .40 1.00
73 Frans Nielsen .25 .60
74 Ryan Strome .40 1.00
75 Alexander Ovechkin 1.50 4.00
76 Matt Beleskey .25 .60
77 Alexander Radulov .40 1.00
78 Claude Giroux .40 1.00
79 Pekka Rinne .40 1.00
80 Nazem Kadri .50 1.25
81 Brayden Point .50 1.25
82 Mats Zuccarello .40 1.00
83 Oliver Ekman-Larsson .40 1.00
84 Brayden Schenn .40 1.00
85 Matthew Tkachuk .75 2.00
86 Cory Schneider .40 1.00
87 Christian Dvorak .30 .75
88 Duncan Keith .30 .75
89 Braden Holtby .50 1.25
90 Matt Murray .60 1.50
91 Reilly Smith .40 1.00
92 Jonathan Quick .50 1.25
93 Brandon Sutter .25 .60
94 Jonathan Huberdeau .50 1.25
95 Joe Thornton .60 1.50
96 Rickard Rakell .30 .75
97 Zach Parise .40 1.00
98 Brandon Dubinsky .25 .60
99 Tyson Barrie .25 .60
100 Carey Price .75 2.00
101 Sam Gagner .25 .60
102 Bobby Ryan .30 .75
103 Jason Pominville .25 .60
104 Jordan Eberle .40 1.00
105 Tuukka Rask .50 1.25
106 Nicklas Backstrom .40 1.00
107 Ryan Johansen .30 .75
108 William Nylander .75 2.00
109 Kevin Hayes .30 .75
110 Nick Bjugstad .25 .60
111 Andrei Vasilevskiy .60 1.50
112 Dylan Larkin .50 1.25
113 Nikolaj Ehlers .40 1.00
114 Jonathan Marchessault .50 1.25
115 Jeff Skinner .50 1.25
116 Sean Couturier .30 .75
117 Mikko Rantanen 1.00 2.50
118 David Pastrnak 1.00 2.50
119 Viktor Arvidsson .25 .60
120 Jaromir Jagr 1.25 3.00
121 Joe Pavelski .50 1.25
122 Alec Martinez .25 .60
123 Oscar Klefbom .30 .75
124 Ben Bishop .30 .75
125 Jonathan Toews .60 1.50
126 Andrew Ladd .25 .60
127 Kevin Shattenkirk .25 .60
128 William Karlsson .50 1.25
129 Cam Atkinson .40 1.00
130 Ryan Getzlaf .40 1.00
131 Kyle Palmieri .30 .75
132 Patrick Marleau .40 1.00
133 Mike Smith .40 1.00
134 Kyle Okposo .25 .60
135 Mike Hoffman .25 .60
136 Andreas Athanasiou .40 1.00
137 Andrew Shaw .25 .60
138 Justin Faulk .30 .75
139 Devan Dubnyk .30 .75
140 Phil Kessel .40 1.00
141 Mario Lemieux 1.50 4.00
142 Pavel Bure .40 1.00
143 Joe Sakic .75 2.00
144 Mark Recchi .50 1.25
145 Ed Belfour .50 1.25
146 Steve Yzerman 1.00 2.50
147 Teemu Selanne .75 2.00
148 Patrick Roy 1.00 2.50
149 Pat LaFontaine .40 1.00
150 Wayne Gretzky 2.50 6.00
151 Nico Hischier RC 3.00 8.00
152 Alex DeBrincat RC 2.50 6.00
153 Victor Mete RC 1.00 2.50
154 Adrian Kempe RC 2.00 5.00
155 Charlie McAvoy RC 2.50 6.00
156 Carter Rowney RC .75 2.00
157 Robert Hagg RC 1.00 2.50
158 Evgeny Svechnikov RC 2.00 5.00
159 Filip Chlapik RC .75 2.00
160 Clayton Keller RC 2.50 6.00
161 Jack Roslovic RC 1.25 3.00
162 Vince Dunn RC 1.25 3.00
163 Kailer Yamamoto RC 2.50 6.00
164 Samuel Girard RC 1.00 2.50
165 Brock Boeser RC 2.50 6.00
166 Rasmus Andersson RC 1.00 2.50
167 Logan Brown RC 1.00 2.50
168 Calle Rosen RC 1.00 2.50
169 Christian Jaros RC .75 2.00
170 Pierre-Luc Dubois RC 1.50 4.00
171 Samuel Blais RC 1.00 2.50
172 Anders Bjork RC 1.25 3.00
173 Travis Sanheim RC 1.00 2.50
174 Henrik Haapala RC 1.00 2.50
175 Will Butcher RC 1.25 3.00
176 Alex Kerfoot RC 2.00 5.00
177 Colin White RC 1.25 3.00
178 Luke Kunin RC 1.00 2.50
179 J.T. Compher RC 1.00 2.50
180 Alexander Nylander RC 1.50 4.00
181 Filip Chytil RC 1.00 2.50
182 Martin Necas RC 3.00 8.00
183 Andreas Borgman RC 1.00 2.50
184 Nikita Scherbak RC 1.25 3.00
185 Josh Ho-Sang RC 1.25 3.00
186 Ville Husso RC 1.25 3.00
187 Jake DeBrusk RC 2.50 6.00
188 Christian Djoos RC 1.00 2.50
189 John Hayden RC .75 2.00
190 Owen Tippett RC 2.00 5.00
191 Haydn Fleury RC 1.00 2.50
192 Tage Thompson RC 2.50 6.00
193 Alex Formenton RC 1.00 2.50
194 Alex Tuch RC 2.50 6.00
195 Tyson Jost RC 2.00 5.00
196 Eric Comrie RC .75 2.00
197 Jesper Bratt RC 2.00 5.00
198 Christian Fischer RC 1.25 3.00
199 Michael Amadio RC 1.00 2.50
200 Nolan Patrick RC 2.00 5.00

2017-18 O-Pee-Chee Platinum Orange Checkers

*ORANGE/25: 5X TO 12X BASIC CARDS
*ORANGE.RC/25: 2.5X TO 6X BASIC CARDS
165 Brock Boeser 60.00 150.00

2017-18 O-Pee-Chee Platinum Seismic Gold

*GOLD/50: 4X TO 10X BASIC CARDS
*GOLD.RC/50: 2X TO 5X BASIC CARDS
165 Brock Boeser 50.00 125.00

2017-18 O-Pee-Chee Platinum Destined For Glory

DG1 Connor McDavid 4.00 10.00
DG2 Matt Murray 1.25 3.00
DG3 Dylan Larkin 1.00 2.50
DG4 Jake Guentzel 1.25 3.00
DG5 Mitch Marner 1.25 3.00
DG6 Artemi Panarin 1.50 4.00
DG7 Jack Eichel 1.25 3.00
DG8 William Nylander 1.50 4.00
DG9 Anthony Mantha .60 1.50
DG10 Auston Matthews 6.00 15.00
DG11 Patrik Laine 1.00 2.50
DG12 Clayton Keller 2.00 5.00
DG13 Charlie McAvoy 2.00 5.00
DG14 Nico Hischier 2.50 6.00
DG15 Nolan Patrick 1.50 4.00

2017-18 O-Pee-Chee Platinum In Action

IA1 Alexander Ovechkin 4.00 10.00
IA2 Carey Price 1.50 4.00
IA3 Vladimir Tarasenko 1.00 2.50
IA4 Henrik Zetterberg 1.00 2.50
IA5 Auston Matthews 3.00 8.00
IA6 P.K. Subban 1.00 2.50
IA7 Jamie Benn .75 2.00
IA8 Johnny Gaudreau 1.25 3.00
IA9 Connor McDavid 4.00 10.00
IA10 Steven Stamkos 1.50 4.00
IA11 Brent Burns .75 2.00
IA12 Henrik Lundqvist 2.00 5.00
IA13 Sidney Crosby 3.00 8.00
IA14 Jonathan Drouin .60 1.50
IA15 Wayne Simmonds 1.00 2.50
IA16 Anze Kopitar 1.25 3.00
IA17 Patrick Kane 1.50 4.00
IA18 Mitch Marner 1.25 3.00
IA19 Matt Murray 1.25 3.00
IA20 John Tavares 1.25 3.00
IA21 Charlie McAvoy 2.00 5.00
IA22 Brock Boeser 2.00 5.00
IA23 Nico Hischier 2.50 6.00
IA24 Nolan Patrick 1.50 4.00
IA25 Pierre-Luc Dubois 1.25 3.00

2017-18 O-Pee-Chee Platinum Platinum Records

PR1 Wayne Gretzky 4.00 10.00
PR2 Wayne Gretzky 4.00 10.00
PR3 Wayne Gretzky 4.00 10.00
PR4 Wayne Gretzky 4.00 10.00
PR5 Wayne Gretzky 4.00 10.00
PR6 Teemu Selanne 1.25 3.00
PR7 Dave Andreychuk .60 1.50
PR8 Ian Turnbull .40 1.00
PR9 Darryl Sittler .75 2.00
PR10 Martin Brodeur 1.50 4.00
PR11 Auston Matthews 2.50 6.00
PR12 Jake Guentzel 1.00 2.50
PR13 Grant Fuhr 1.00 2.50
PR14 Mark Messier 1.25 3.00
PR15 Chris Chelios .60 1.50

2017-18 O-Pee-Chee Platinum Retro

R1 Auston Matthews 4.00 10.00
R2 Brad Marchand 2.00 5.00
R3 Johnny Gaudreau 1.50 4.00
R4 Oliver Ekman-Larsson 1.00 2.50
R5 Patrick Kane 2.00 5.00
R6 Vladimir Tarasenko 1.25 3.00
R7 Nathan MacKinnon 4.00 10.00
R8 Aleksander Barkov 1.50 4.00
R9 Brent Burns 1.00 2.50
R10 Jake Guentzel 1.50 4.00
R11 Max Pacioretty 1.00 2.50
R12 Henrik Lundqvist 2.50 6.00
R13 Jeff Skinner 1.25 3.00
R14 Steven Stamkos 2.00 5.00
R15 Tyler Seguin 1.25 3.00
R16 Cam Atkinson 1.00 2.50
R17 Daniel Sedin 1.25 3.00
R18 Jonathan Quick 1.25 3.00
R19 Nicklas Backstrom 1.00 2.50
R20 Connor McDavid 5.00 12.00
R21 Mikael Granlund .75 2.00
R22 P.K. Subban 1.25 3.00
R23 Anders Lee 1.00 2.50
R24 Corey Perry 1.50 4.00
R25 Shayne Gostisbehere 1.00 2.50
R26 Henrik Zetterberg 1.25 3.00
R27 Marc-Andre Fleury 2.00 5.00
R28 Adam Henrique .75 2.00
R29 Jack Eichel 1.50 4.00
R30 Erik Karlsson 1.25 3.00
R31 Nikolaj Ehlers 1.00 2.50
R32 Marcus Johansson .75 2.00
R33 Artemi Panarin 2.00 5.00
R34 Sidney Crosby 4.00 10.00
R35 Martin Jones .75 2.00
R36 Zdeno Chara 1.00 2.50
R37 Tyler Johnson .60 1.50
R38 Carey Price 2.00 5.00
R39 Jordan Eberle 1.00 2.50
R40 Mitch Marner 1.50 4.00
R41 Sean Monahan .60 1.50
R42 Ryan Kesler 1.00 2.50
R43 Mark Scheifele 1.50 4.00
R44 Jordan Staal .75 2.00
R45 Jakub Voracek .75 2.00
R46 Braden Holtby 1.25 3.00
R47 Drew Doughty 1.25 3.00
R48 Colton Parayko .75 2.00
R49 Conor Sheary 1.00 2.50
R50 Jonathan Toews 1.50 4.00
R51 Vincent Trocheck 1.00 2.50
R52 Loui Eriksson .60 1.50
R53 Tomas Tatar .60 1.50
R54 Devan Dubnyk .75 2.00
R55 Chris Kreider 1.25 3.00
R56 Jonathan Drouin .75 2.00
R57 James Neal .60 1.50
R58 John Tavares 1.50 4.00
R59 Viktor Arvidsson .60 1.50
R60 Kyle Okposo .60 1.50
R61 Ben Bishop .75 2.00
R62 Mikko Rantanen 2.50 6.00
R63 Kyle Turris 1.00 2.50
R64 Phil Kessel 1.00 2.50
R65 Frederik Andersen 1.25 3.00
R66 Nico Hischier 3.00 8.00
R67 Brock Boeser 2.50 6.00
R68 Alex DeBrincat 2.50 6.00
R69 Clayton Keller 2.50 6.00
R70 Nolan Patrick 2.00 5.00
R71 Tyson Jost 2.00 5.00
R72 Anders Bjork 1.25 3.00
R73 Colin White 1.25 3.00
R74 Filip Chytil 1.00 2.50
R75 Josh Ho-Sang 1.25 3.00
R76 Kailer Yamamoto 2.50 6.00
R77 Evgeny Svechnikov 2.00 5.00
R78 Logan Brown 1.00 2.50
R79 Ivan Barbashev 1.25 3.00
R80 Pierre-Luc Dubois 1.50 4.00
R81 Jack Roslovic 1.25 3.00
R82 Tage Thompson 2.50 6.00
R83 Alexander Nylander 1.50 4.00
R84 Jake DeBrusk 2.50 6.00
R85 Alex Tuch 2.50 6.00
R86 Jon Gillies 1.00 2.50
R87 J.T. Compher 1.00 2.50
R88 Riley Barber 1.00 2.50
R89 Remi Elie .75 2.00
R90 Christian Fischer 1.25 3.00
R91 Lucas Wallmark 1.00 2.50
R92 Jordan Schmaltz 1.25 3.00
R93 Mike Vecchione .75 2.00
R94 Gabriel Carlsson .75 2.00
R95 Nikita Scherbak 1.25 3.00
R96 Adrian Kempe 2.00 5.00
R97 Vladislav Kamenev 1.00 2.50
R98 Jakob Forsbacka-Karlsson 1.00 2.50
R99 Janne Kuokkanen 1.00 2.50
R100 Charlie McAvoy 2.50 6.00

2017-18 O-Pee-Chee Platinum Retro Rainbow Green

*GREEN/49: 2X TO 5X BASIC INSERTS
R67 Brock Boeser 40.00 100.00

2017-18 O-Pee-Chee Platinum Rookie Autographs

RAB Anders Bjork A 6.00 15.00
RAD Alex DeBrincat A 15.00 40.00
RAK Adrian Kempe A 10.00 25.00
RAN Alexander Nylander A 8.00 20.00
RAT Alex Tuch A 12.00 30.00
RBB Brock Boeser A 40.00 100.00
RBR Jesper Bratt B 15.00 40.00
RCF Christian Fischer B 6.00 15.00
RCK Clayton Keller A 20.00 50.00
RCM Charlie McAvoy A 25.00 60.00
RCW Colin White A 6.00 15.00
RDG Denis Gurianov C 12.00 30.00
RES Evgeny Svechnikov C 10.00 25.00
RFC Filip Chytil B 5.00 12.00
RHF Haydn Fleury C 5.00 12.00
RIB Ivan Barbashev C 6.00 15.00
RJB Jonny Brodzinski C 5.00 12.00
RJC J.T. Compher B 5.00 12.00
RJD Jake DeBrusk A 12.00 30.00
RJG Jon Gillies C 5.00 12.00
RJH Josh Ho-Sang A 6.00 15.00
RJK Jakob Forsbacka-Karlsson C 5.00 12.00
RJR Jack Roslovic C 6.00 15.00
RKE Alex Kerfoot B 10.00 25.00
RKU Janne Kuokkanen B 5.00 12.00
RKY Kailer Yamamoto A 12.00 30.00
RLB Logan Brown 5.00 12.00
RLK Luke Kunin B 5.00 12.00
RLW Lucas Wallmark 5.00 12.00
RMN Martin Necas B 15.00 40.00
RNS Nikita Scherbak C 6.00 15.00
ROT Owen Tippett A 10.00 25.00
RPD Pierre-Luc Dubois A 8.00 20.00
RSM Samuel Morin A 3.00 8.00
RTJ Tyson Jost A 10.00 25.00
RTS Travis Sanheim A 5.00 12.00
RTT Tage Thompson C 12.00 30.00
RVK Vladislav Kamenev B 5.00 12.00
RVM Victor Mete B 5.00 12.00
RVZ Valentin Zykov C 5.00 12.00
RWB Will Butcher B 6.00 15.00

2017-18 O-Pee-Chee Platinum Rookie Autographs Rainbow

*RAINBOW: .6X TO 1.5X BASIC INSERTS
RBB Brock Boeser A 60.00 150.00

2017-18 O-Pee-Chee Platinum Rookie Autographs Rainbow Seismic Gold

GOLD/25: 1.25X TO 3X BASIC INSERTS
RBB Brock Boeser 100.00 250.00

2017-18 O-Pee-Chee Platinum Rookie Autographs Red Prism

*RED/50: 1X TO 2.5X BASIC INSERTS

2018-19 O-Pee-Chee Platinum

1 Connor McDavid 2.00 5.00
2 Patrice Bergeron .50 1.25
3 Dylan Larkin .50 1.25
4 Jack Eichel .60 1.50
5 Erik Karlsson .50 1.25
6 Kyle Turris .30 .75
7 Andrei Vasilevskiy .60 1.50
8 Johnny Gaudreau .60 1.50
9 James van Riemsdyk .30 .75
10 Jonathan Toews .60 1.50
11 Aleksander Barkov .60 1.50
12 Ryan O'Reilly .40 1.00
13 Ryan Getzlaf .40 1.00
14 Gabriel Landeskog .50 1.25
15 Carey Price .75 2.00
16 Justin Williams .30 .75
17 Artemi Panarin .75 2.00
18 Max Pacioretty .40 1.00
19 Blake Wheeler .40 1.00
20 Sidney Crosby 1.50 4.00
21 Bobby Ryan .30 .75
22 Tyler Seguin .50 1.25
23 Mathew Barzal .50 1.25
24 Taylor Hall .40 1.00
25 Jonathan Quick .50 1.25
26 Zach Parise .40 1.00
27 Clayton Keller .50 1.25
28 Evgeny Kuznetsov .50 1.25
29 Brock Boeser .50 1.25
30 John Tavares .60 1.50
31 Mika Zibanejad .50 1.25
32 Milan Lucic .30 .75
33 Jake DeBrusk .40 1.00
34 Frans Nielsen .25 .60
35 Steven Stamkos .75 2.00
36 Jeff Skinner .50 1.25
37 Tomas Hertl .40 1.00
38 John Gibson .40 1.00
39 James Neal .25 .60
40 Patrick Kane .75 2.00
41 Christian Dvorak .30 .75
42 Sebastian Aho .60 1.50
43 Alex Kerfoot .30 .75
44 Pierre-Luc Dubois .30 .75
45 Jamie Benn .40 1.00
46 Keith Yandle .25 .60
47 Dustin Brown .40 1.00
48 Eric Staal .40 1.00
49 Tomas Tatar .25 .60
50 Alexander Ovechkin 1.50 4.00
51 Alex Pietrangelo .30 .75
52 Nolan Patrick .40 1.00
53 Patric Hornqvist .25 .60
54 Mark Stone .50 1.25
55 William Karlsson .50 1.25
56 Filip Forsberg .60 1.50
57 Morgan Rielly .40 1.00
58 Mark Scheifele .60 1.50
59 Anders Lee .30 .75
60 Nikita Kucherov .75 2.00
61 Bo Horvat .50 1.25
62 Leon Draisaitl 1.25 3.00
63 Brad Marchand .75 2.00
64 Rasmus Ristolainen .25 .60
65 Nico Hischier .60 1.50
66 Dougie Hamilton .30 .75
67 Pavel Buchnevich .30 .75
68 Joe Thornton .60 1.50
69 Marian Gaborik .40 1.00
70 John Carlson .40 1.00
71 Sergei Bobrovsky .60 1.50
72 Justin Abdelkader .30 .75
73 Brayden Schenn .40 1.00
74 Kyle Connor .60 1.50
75 Viktor Arvidsson .25 .60
76 Andreas Athanasiou .30 .75
77 Brock Nelson .40 1.00
78 Mike Hoffman .25 .60
79 Travis Konecny .40 1.00
80 Nathan MacKinnon 1.50 4.00
81 Loui Eriksson .25 .60
82 Alex DeBrincat .50 1.25
83 Jordan Eberle .40 1.00
84 Ryan Kesler .40 1.00
85 Mitch Marner .60 1.50
86 Jesper Bratt .40 1.00
87 Evander Kane .40 1.00
88 John Klingberg .40 1.00
89 Noah Hanifin .40 1.00
90 Alex Galchenyuk .25 .60
91 Mats Zuccarello .40 1.00
92 Ryan Nugent-Hopkins .50 1.25
93 Tyler Johnson .25 .60
94 Seth Jones .40 1.00
95 Connor Hellebuyck .75 2.00
96 Mikko Koivu .40 1.00
97 Mikkel Boedker .25 .60
98 Claude Giroux .40 1.00
99 Charlie McAvoy .50 1.25
100 Auston Matthews 1.50 4.00
101 Jason Spezza .40 1.00
102 Max Domi .40 1.00
103 Lars Eller .25 .60
104 Paul Stastny .30 .75
105 Matthew Tkachuk .75 2.00
106 Kyle Palmieri .30 .75
107 Dion Phaneuf .30 .75
108 Teuvo Teravainen .40 1.00
109 Brady Skjei .30 .75
110 Anze Kopitar .60 1.50
111 Kris Letang .50 1.25
112 Ryan McDonagh .25 .60
113 Derek Stepan .25 .60
114 Ilya Kovalchuk .30 .75
115 Evgeni Malkin .75 2.00
116 Sven Baertschi .30 .75
117 Alexander Wennberg .25 .60
118 Jonathan Drouin .30 .75
119 Mikael Backlund .30 .75
120 Marc-Andre Fleury .75 2.00
121 Mikko Rantanen 1.00 2.50
122 Kyle Okposo .25 .60
123 Anthony Mantha .30 .75
124 Ondrej Kase .25 .60
125 Brent Burns .40 1.00
126 Nick Schmaltz .30 .75
127 Frederik Andersen .50 1.25
128 Patrik Laine .50 1.25
129 David Krejci .40 1.00
130 Vladimir Tarasenko .50 1.25
131 Ryan Suter .30 .75
132 Corey Crawford .30 .75
133 Adam Larsson .40 1.00
134 Jake Guentzel .60 1.50
135 Pekka Rinne .40 1.00
136 Vincent Trocheck .40 1.00
137 Jonathan Marchessault .50 1.25
138 Brendan Gallagher .40 1.00
139 Josh Bailey .30 .75
140 Braden Holtby .50 1.25
141 Bobby Orr 1.50 4.00
142 Mark Messier .75 2.00
143 Brett Hull .75 2.00
144 Mario Lemieux 1.50 4.00
145 Darryl Sittler .50 1.25
146 Peter Forsberg .75 2.00
147 Marcel Dionne .50 1.25
148 Larry Robinson .40 1.00
149 Martin Brodeur 1.00 2.50
150 Wayne Gretzky 2.50 6.00
151 Elias Pettersson RC 3.00 8.00
152 Drake Batherson RC 2.00 5.00
153 Travis Dermott RC 1.50 4.00
154 Anthony Cirelli RC 1.50 4.00
155 Ryan Donato RC 1.50 4.00
156 Dillon Dube RC 1.25 3.00
157 Evan Bouchard RC 2.50 6.00
158 Lias Andersson RC 1.50 4.00
159 Isac Lundestrom RC .75 2.00
160 Rasmus Dahlin RC 2.50 6.00
161 Jordan Greenway RC 1.00 2.50
162 Henri Jokiharju RC .75 2.00
163 Jordan Kyrou RC 2.00 5.00
164 Henrik Borgstrom RC 1.50 4.00
165 Ilya Samsonov RC 2.00 5.00
166 Eeli Tolvanen RC 2.00 5.00
167 Noah Juulsen RC 1.00 2.50
168 Warren Foegele RC 1.00 2.50
169 Cal Petersen RC .75 2.00
170 Brady Tkachuk RC 3.00 8.00
171 Oskar Lindblom RC 1.50 4.00
172 Jakub Zboril RC 1.50 4.00
173 Maxime Comtois RC 1.00 2.50
174 Jeremy Lauzon RC 1.25 3.00
175 Miro Heiskanen RC 2.50 6.00
176 Dominik Kahun RC 1.00 2.50
177 Michael Rasmussen RC 1.25 3.00
178 Neal Pionk RC 1.00 2.50
179 Zach Aston-Reese RC 1.50 4.00
180 Jesperi Kotkaniemi RC 2.00 5.00
181 Antti Suomela RC .75 2.00
182 Sam Steel RC 1.00 2.50
183 Cooper Marody RC 1.00 2.50
184 Joey Anderson RC 1.00 2.50
185 Brett Howden RC 1.25 3.00
186 Alexandre Fortin RC .75 2.00
187 Maxime Lajoie RC 1.50 4.00
188 Kristian Vesalainen RC 1.25 3.00
189 Josh Mahura RC .75 2.00
190 Casey Mittelstadt RC 2.00 5.00
191 Juuso Valimaki RC 1.00 2.50
192 Michael Dal Colle RC 1.00 2.50
193 Adam Gaudette RC 1.50 4.00
194 Robert Thomas RC 2.00 5.00
195 Dennis Cholowski RC 1.00 2.50
196 Troy Terry RC 1.50 4.00
197 Andreas Johnsson RC 1.25 3.00
198 Dylan Sikura RC 1.25 3.00
199 Carter Hart RC 2.00 5.00
200 Andrei Svechnikov RC 2.50 6.00

2018-19 O-Pee-Chee Platinum Arctic Freeze

*ARTIC.VETS/79: 2X TO 5X BASIC CARDS
*ARTIC.RC/79: .75X TO 2X BASIC CARDS
85 Mitch Marner 15.00 40.00
100 Auston Matthews 12.00 30.00
160 Rasmus Dahlin 30.00 80.00
163 Jordan Kyrou 12.00 30.00
175 Miro Heiskanen 8.00 20.00
200 Andrei Svechnikov 8.00 20.00

2018-19 O-Pee-Chee Platinum Orange Checkers

*ORANGE.VET/25: 5X TO 12X BASIC CARDS
*ORANGE.RC/25: 2.5X TO 6X BASIC CARDS
150 Wayne Gretzky 40.00 100.00
151 Elias Pettersson 100.00 200.00
153 Travis Dermott 20.00 50.00
157 Evan Bouchard 30.00 80.00
165 Ilya Samsonov 25.00 60.00
180 Jesperi Kotkaniemi 30.00 80.00
182 Sam Steel 15.00 40.00
199 Carter Hart 100.00 200.00

2018-19 O-Pee-Chee Platinum Rainbow

*RAINBOW.VET: .6X TO 1.25X BASIC CARDS
*RAINBOW.RC: .6X TO 1.25X BASIC CARDS
151 Elias Pettersson 12.00 30.00

2018-19 O-Pee-Chee Platinum Red Prism

*RED.VET/199: 1.25X TO 3X BASIC CARDS
*RED.RC/199: 1X TO 2.5X BASIC CARDS
151 Elias Pettersson 15.00 40.00
163 Jordan Kyrou 15.00 40.00
199 Carter Hart 12.00 30.00

2018-19 O-Pee-Chee Platinum Seismic Gold

1 Connor McDavid 25.00 60.00
144 Mario Lemieux 15.00 40.00
151 Elias Pettersson 50.00 125.00
153 Travis Dermott 12.00 30.00
163 Jordan Kyrou 20.00 50.00
199 Carter Hart 60.00 150.00

2018-19 O-Pee-Chee Platinum In Action

IA1 Jonathan Toews 1.25 3.00
IA2 Erik Karlsson 1.00 2.50
IA3 Jonathan Quick 1.00 2.50
IA4 Evgeny Kuznetsov 1.00 2.50
IA5 Evgeni Malkin 1.50 4.00
IA6 Mitch Marner 1.25 3.00
IA7 Brad Marchand 1.50 4.00
IA8 Sean Couturier .60 1.50
IA9 Steven Stamkos 1.50 4.00
IA10 John Tavares 1.25 3.00
IA11 Dylan Larkin 1.00 2.50
IA12 Nico Hischier 1.25 3.00
IA13 Duncan Keith .60 1.50
IA14 Vincent Trocheck .75 2.00
IA15 Marc-Andre Fleury 1.50 4.00
IA16 Kevin Shattenkirk .50 1.25
IA17 Filip Forsberg 1.25 3.00
IA18 Andrei Vasilevskiy 1.25 3.00
IA19 Bobby Orr 3.00 8.00
IA20 Wayne Gretzky 5.00 12.00
IA21 Henrik Borgstrom 1.25 3.00
IA22 Jesperi Kotkaniemi 1.50 4.00
IA23 Brady Tkachuk 2.50 6.00
IA24 Andrei Svechnikov 2.00 5.00
IA25 Elias Pettersson 2.50 6.00

2018-19 O-Pee-Chee Platinum In Action Rainbow Autographs

IA1 Jonathan Toews A 60.00 150.00
IA5 Evgeni Malkin C 12.00 30.00
IA7 Brad Marchand D 20.00 50.00
IA10 John Tavares A 40.00 100.00
IA14 Vincent Trocheck D 6.00 15.00

IA15 Marc-Andre Fleury C 60.00 150.00
IA18 Andrei Vasilevskiy D 10.00 25.00
IA19 Bobby Orr D 25.00 60.00
IA20 Wayne Gretzky A 250.00 600.00
IA21 Henrik Borgstrom D 10.00 25.00
IA22 Jesperi Kotkaniemi D 30.00 80.00
IA23 Brady Tkachuk D 25.00 60.00
IA24 Andrei Svechnikov D 15.00 40.00
IA25 Elias Pettersson B 100.00 200.00

2018-19 O-Pee-Chee Platinum Net Magnets

NM1 Alexander Ovechkin 2.50 6.00
NM2 Nikita Kucherov 1.25 3.00
NM3 Patrick Kane 1.25 3.00
NM4 Anze Kopitar 1.00 2.50
NM5 Sidney Crosby 2.50 6.00
NM6 Tyler Seguin .75 2.00
NM7 Johnny Gaudreau 1.00 2.50
NM8 Patrik Laine .75 2.00
NM9 David Pastrnak 1.50 4.00
NM10 Connor McDavid 3.00 8.00
NM11 William Karlsson .75 2.00
NM12 Taylor Hall .60 1.50
NM13 Nathan MacKinnon 2.50 6.00
NM14 Vladimir Tarasenko .75 2.00
NM15 Auston Matthews 2.50 6.00

2018-19 O-Pee-Chee Platinum Net Magnets Rainbow Autographs

NM2 Nikita Kucherov C 20.00 50.00
NM11 William Karlsson C 20.00 50.00
NM14 Vladimir Tarasenko B 30.00 80.00

2018-19 O-Pee-Chee Platinum Retro

R1 Alexander Ovechkin 4.00 10.00
R2 Ilya Kovalchuk .75 2.00
R3 Connor Hellebuyck 2.00 5.00
R4 Jamie Benn 1.00 2.50
R5 Evgeni Malkin 2.00 5.00
R6 Jaccob Slavin .75 2.00
R7 Jonathan Marchessault 1.25 3.00
R8 Will Butcher .75 2.00
R9 Sean Monahan .60 1.50
R10 Carey Price 2.00 5.00
R11 William Nylander 2.00 5.00
R12 Zach Werenski 1.50 4.00
R13 Kevin Shattenkirk .60 1.50
R14 Jason Zucker 1.00 2.50
R15 Nikita Kucherov 2.00 5.00
R16 Jack Eichel 1.50 4.00
R17 Vincent Trocheck 1.00 2.50
R18 Tuukka Rask 1.25 3.00
R19 Darnell Nurse .75 2.00
R20 Erik Karlsson 1.25 3.00
R21 Nico Hischier 1.50 4.00
R22 Rickard Rakell .75 2.00
R23 Anthony Mantha .75 2.00
R24 Drew Doughty 1.25 3.00
R25 Patrick Kane 2.00 5.00
R26 Seth Jones 1.00 2.50
R27 Mikko Rantanen 2.50 6.00
R28 Matt Duchene 1.00 2.50
R29 Duncan Keith .75 2.00
R30 Alex Galchenyuk .60 1.50
R31 Reilly Smith 1.00 2.50
R32 Shea Weber 1.00 2.50
R33 Ryan Ellis .75 2.00
R34 Brandon Sutter .60 1.50
R35 Mathew Barzal 1.25 3.00
R36 Tobias Rieder .60 1.50
R37 Matthew Tkachuk 2.00 5.00
R38 Nikolaj Ehlers 1.00 2.50
R39 Dylan Larkin 1.25 3.00
R40 John Tavares 1.50 4.00
R41 Ryan O'Reilly 1.00 2.50
R42 Evgenii Dadonov .60 1.50
R43 Craig Anderson .75 2.00
R44 Ondrej Kase .60 1.50
R45 Logan Couture 1.25 3.00
R46 Danton Heinen .75 2.00
R47 Micheal Ferland .60 1.50
R48 T.J. Oshie 1.00 2.50
R49 Clayton Keller 1.25 3.00
R50 Auston Matthews 4.00 10.00
R51 Jeff Carter .75 2.00
R52 Victor Hedman 1.25 3.00
R53 Mike Green .75 2.00
R54 Vincent Hinostroza .75 2.00
R55 Evgeny Kuznetsov 1.25 3.00
R56 Erik Johnson .60 1.50
R57 Alexander Radulov 1.00 2.50
R58 P.K. Subban 1.25 3.00
R59 Max Pacioretty 1.00 2.50
R60 Connor McDavid 5.00 12.00
R61 Conor Sheary 1.00 2.50
R62 Nino Niederreiter .60 1.50
R63 James Neal .60 1.50
R64 Brock Boeser 1.25 3.00
R65 Sidney Crosby 4.00 10.00
R66 Rasmus Dahlin 2.50 6.00
R67 Maxime Comtois 1.00 2.50
R68 Adam Gaudette 1.50 4.00
R69 Brett Howden 1.25 3.00
R70 Jesperi Kotkaniemi 2.00 5.00
R71 Warren Foegele 1.00 2.50
R72 Victor Ejdsell .75 2.00
R73 Maxime Lajoie 1.50 4.00
R74 Robert Thomas 2.00 5.00
R75 Ryan Donato 1.50 4.00
R76 Travis Dermott 1.50 4.00
R77 Dennis Cholowski 1.00 2.50
R78 Henrik Borgstrom 1.50 4.00
R79 Anthony Cirelli 1.50 4.00
R80 Andrei Svechnikov 2.50 6.00
R81 Dylan Gambrell 1.00 2.50
R82 Eeli Tolvanen 2.00 5.00
R83 Evan Bouchard 2.50 6.00
R84 Noah Juulsen 1.00 2.50
R85 Miro Heiskanen 2.50 6.00
R86 Sam Steel 1.00 2.50
R87 Kristian Vesalainen 1.25 3.00
R88 Michael Rasmussen 1.25 3.00
R89 Michael Dal Colle 1.00 2.50
R90 Brady Tkachuk 3.00 8.00
R91 Jaret Anderson-Dolan .75 2.00
R92 Lias Andersson 1.50 4.00
R93 Juuso Valimaki 1.00 2.50
R94 Sami Niku .75 2.00
R95 Casey Mittelstadt 2.00 5.00
R96 Jordan Greenway 1.00 2.50
R97 Dylan Sikura 1.25 3.00
R98 Andreas Johnsson 1.25 3.00
R99 Daniel Brickley 1.00 2.50
R100 Elias Pettersson 3.00 8.00

2018-19 O-Pee-Chee Platinum Rookie Autographs

RAC Anthony Cirelli C 12.00 30.00
RAN Antti Suomela E 6.00 15.00
RAS Andrei Svechnikov A 20.00 50.00
RBH Brett Howden C 10.00 25.00
RBT Brady Tkachuk B 30.00 80.00
RCH Carter Hart B 100.00 200.00
RDB Daniel Brickley E 8.00 20.00
RDC Dennis Cholowski C 8.00 20.00
RDD Dillon Dube C 10.00 25.00
RDG Dylan Gambrell E 8.00 20.00
REB Evan Bouchard D 20.00 50.00
REP Elias Pettersson B 150.00 250.00
RET Eeli Tolvanen A 15.00 40.00
RHB Henrik Borgstrom D 12.00 30.00
RHJ Henri Jokiharju E 6.00 15.00
RJD Jaret Anderson-Dolan E 6.00 15.00
RJK Jesperi Kotkaniemi B 15.00 40.00
RKY Jordan Kyrou E 12.00 30.00
RMC Maxime Comtois E 8.00 20.00
RMH Miro Heiskanen A 50.00 125.00
RML Maxime Lajoie D 12.00 30.00
RMR Michael Rasmussen C 10.00 25.00
RNJ Noah Juulsen E 8.00 20.00
RNR Nicolas Roy E 5.00 12.00
RRT Robert Thomas C 15.00 40.00
RSF Spencer Foo E 6.00 15.00
RSS Sam Steel E 8.00 20.00
RTD Travis Dermott E 12.00 30.00
RTH Tomas Hyka E 8.00 20.00
RTT Troy Terry 15.00 40.00
RVE Victor Ejdsell E 6.00 15.00
RWF Warren Foegele E 8.00 20.00
RZA Zach Aston-Reese E 12.00 30.00

2018-19 O-Pee-Chee Platinum Rookie Autographs Red Prism

*RED/50: .75X TO 2X BASIC INSERTS
RAS Andrei Svechnikov 60.00 150.00
RCH Carter Hart 120.00 300.00
REP Elias Pettersson 250.00 350.00
RTT Troy Terry 40.00 100.00

2018-19 O-Pee-Chee Platinum Rookie Autographs Seismic Gold

*GOLD/50: 1X TO 2.5X BASIC INSERTS
RBT Brady Tkachuk 150.00 250.00
RCH Carter Hart 150.00 400.00
REP Elias Pettersson 300.00 500.00
RWF Warren Foegele 30.00 80.00

2018-19 O-Pee-Chee Platinum Rookie Autographs Violet Pixels

*VIOLET: .6X TO 1.5X BASIC INSERTS
RCH Carter Hart A 100.00 250.00
REP Elias Pettersson A 200.00 300.00
RWF Warren Foegele C 20.00 50.00

2018-19 O-Pee-Chee Platinum The Future is Now

FN1 Connor McDavid 4.00 10.00
FN2 Brock Boeser 1.00 2.50
FN3 Brayden Point 1.00 2.50
FN4 Alex Tuch .75 2.00
FN5 Auston Matthews 3.00 8.00
FN6 Jack Eichel 1.25 3.00
FN7 Sebastian Aho 1.25 3.00
FN8 Kyle Connor 1.25 3.00
FN9 Alex DeBrincat 1.00 2.50
FN10 Mathew Barzal 1.00 2.50
FN11 Casey Mittelstadt 1.50 4.00
FN12 Ryan Donato 1.25 3.00
FN13 Elias Pettersson 2.50 6.00
FN14 Jesperi Kotkaniemi 1.50 4.00
FN15 Rasmus Dahlin 2.00 5.00

2018-19 O-Pee-Chee Platinum The Future is Now Rainbow Autographs

FN1 Connor McDavid A 100.00 200.00
FN13 Elias Pettersson B 60.00 150.00
FN14 Jesperi Kotkaniemi C 30.00 80.00

2019-20 O-Pee-Chee Platinum

*RAINBOW.VET: .5X TO 1.25X BASIC CARDS
*RAINBOW.RC: .5X TO 1.25X BASIC RC
*SUNSET.VET: .6X TO 1.5X BASIC CARDS
*SUNSET.RC: .6X TO 1.5X BASIC RC
*PINK.VET: .6X TO 1.5X BASIC CARDS
*PINK.RC: .6X TO 1.5X BASIC RC
*VIOLET.VET/399: .75X TO 2X BASIC CARDS
*VIOLET.RC/399: .75X TO 2X BASIC RC
*RED.VET/199: 1.5X TO 4X BASIC CARDS
*RED.RC/199: .75X TO 2X BASIC RC
*ARCTIC.VET/99: 1.5X TO 4X BASIC CARDS
*ARCTIC.RC/99: 1X TO 2.5X BASIC RC
*GOLD.VET/50: 4X TO 10X BASIC CARDS
*GOLD.RC/50: 1.25X TO 4X BASIC RC
*ORANGE.VET: 8X TO 20X BASIC CARDS
*ORANGE.RC: 3X TO 8X BASIC RC
1 Sidney Crosby 1.50 4.00
2 Philipp Grubauer .40 1.00
3 Oliver Ekman-Larsson .40 1.00
4 Brock Boeser .50 1.25
5 Tomas Hertl .40 1.00
6 Ryan Johansen .30 .75
7 Zach Werenski .60 1.50
8 Artemi Panarin .75 2.00
9 Darnell Nurse .30 .75
10 Auston Matthews 1.50 4.00
11 Mark Scheifele .60 1.50
12 Jeff Carter .30 .75
13 Alex Tuch .40 1.00
14 Taylor Hall .40 1.00
15 William Karlsson .50 1.25
16 Kris Letang .50 1.25
17 Ryan Suter .30 .75
18 Travis Konecny .40 1.00
19 David Pastrnak 1.00 2.50
20 Jonathan Toews .60 1.50
21 Phil Kessel .40 1.00
22 Jonathan Marchessault .50 1.25
23 Mark Giordano .40 1.00
24 Jamie Benn .40 1.00
25 Alexander Ovechkin 1.50 4.00
26 Rickard Rakell .30 .75
27 Teuvo Teravainen .40 1.00
28 Anthony Mantha .30 .75
29 Filip Forsberg .60 1.50
30 Derek Stepan .25 .60
31 Miro Heiskanen .50 1.25
32 Mika Zibanejad .50 1.25
33 Brandon Saad .30 .75
34 Erik Karlsson .50 1.25
35 Alexander Edler .25 .60
36 Viktor Arvidsson .25 .60
37 Kyle Connor .60 1.50
38 Mikkel Boedker .25 .60
39 Steven Stamkos .75 2.00
40 Jonathan Quick .50 1.25
41 Connor Hellebuyck .75 2.00
42 Timo Meier .40 1.00
43 Oscar Klefbom .40 1.00
44 Anders Lee .30 .75
45 Henrik Lundqvist 1.00 2.50
46 Ryan Getzlaf .40 1.00
47 Sean Monahan .25 .60
48 Patrik Laine .50 1.25
49 Anze Kopitar .60 1.50
50 Patrick Kane .75 2.00
51 William Nylander .75 2.00
52 Ben Bishop .30 .75
53 Brent Burns .40 1.00
54 Brady Skjei .30 .75
55 J.T. Miller .50 1.25
56 Ryan Nugent-Hopkins .50 1.25
57 Eric Staal .40 1.00
58 Alex Pietrangelo .30 .75
59 Drew Doughty .50 1.25
60 John Gibson .40 1.00
61 Brock Nelson .40 1.00
62 Andreas Athanasiou .30 .75
63 Nicklas Backstrom .40 1.00
64 Jonathan Drouin .30 .75
65 John Tavares .60 1.50
66 Aleksander Barkov .60 1.50
67 Hampus Lindholm .25 .60
68 Brad Marchand .75 2.00
69 Dylan Larkin .50 1.25
70 Zach Parise .40 1.00
71 Nazem Kadri .50 1.25
72 Jesperi Kotkaniemi .40 1.00
73 Colton Parayko .30 .75
74 Jack Eichel .60 1.50
75 Nathan MacKinnon 1.50 4.00
76 Mark Stone .50 1.25
77 Rasmus Ristolainen .25 .60
78 Tyler Seguin .50 1.25
79 Mats Zuccarello .40 1.00
80 Artem Anisimov .25 .60
81 Pierre-Luc Dubois .30 .75
82 Andrei Vasilevskiy .60 1.50
83 Blake Wheeler .40 1.00
84 Ryan Ellis .30 .75
85 Devan Dubnyk .30 .75
86 Brendan Gallagher .40 1.00
87 Jonathan Huberdeau .50 1.25
88 Jake Guentzel .60 1.50
89 P.K. Subban .50 1.25
90 Jordan Eberle .40 1.00
91 Bo Horvat .50 1.25
92 Evgeni Malkin .75 2.00
93 Victor Hedman .50 1.25
94 Kyle Palmieri .30 .75
95 Robin Lehner .30 .75
96 Casey Mittelstadt .40 1.00
97 Gabriel Landeskog .50 1.25
98 Marc-Andre Fleury .75 2.00
99 Morgan Rielly .40 1.00
100 Nikita Kucherov .75 2.00
101 Tuukka Rask .50 1.25
102 Elias Lindholm .40 1.00
103 Leon Draisaitl 1.25 3.00
104 Jacob Trouba .30 .75
105 Jordan Binnington .60 1.50
106 Zdeno Chara .40 1.00
107 John Carlson .40 1.00
108 Sergei Bobrovsky .60 1.50
109 Andrei Svechnikov .50 1.25
110 Carter Hart .40 1.00
111 Patrice Bergeron .50 1.25
112 Alex DeBrincat .50 1.25
113 Rasmus Dahlin .50 1.25
114 Cam Fowler .40 1.00
115 Jaccob Slavin .30 .75
116 Claude Giroux .40 1.00
117 Evgeny Kuznetsov .50 1.25
118 Aaron Ekblad .50 1.25
119 Mitch Marner .60 1.50
120 Braden Holtby .50 1.25
121 Mikko Rantanen 1.00 2.50
122 Ryan O'Reilly .40 1.00
123 Jeff Skinner .40 1.00
124 Seth Jones .40 1.00
125 Carey Price .75 2.00
126 Brady Tkachuk .60 1.50
127 Clayton Keller .50 1.25
128 Nino Niederreiter .25 .60
129 Elias Pettersson .60 1.50
130 Logan Couture .50 1.25
131 Matthew Tkachuk .75 2.00
132 Max Domi .40 1.00
133 Gustav Nyquist .25 .60
134 Sebastian Aho .60 1.50
135 Johnny Gaudreau .60 1.50
136 Tyler Bertuzzi .30 .75
137 Evgenii Dadonov .25 .60
138 Sean Couturier .30 .75
139 Semyon Varlamov .40 1.00
140 Cam Atkinson .40 1.00
141 Vladimir Tarasenko .50 1.25
142 Thomas Chabot .40 1.00
143 Nico Hischier .60 1.50
144 Matt Duchene .40 1.00
145 Mathew Barzal .50 1.25
146 Matt Murray .40 1.00
147 Jakub Voracek .30 .75
148 Brayden Point .50 1.25
149 Joe Pavelski .50 1.25
150 Connor McDavid 2.00 5.00
151 Kirby Dach RC 2.00 5.00
152 Morgan Frost RC 1.50 4.00
153 Martin Fehervary RC .75 2.00
154 Mario Ferraro RC .75 2.00
155 Carter Verhaeghe RC 1.50 4.00
156 Teddy Blueger RC 1.00 2.50
157 David Gustafsson RC .75 2.00
158 Cale Fleury RC 1.25 3.00
159 Ville Heinola RC 1.25 3.00
160 Trevor Moore RC .75 2.00
161 Erik Brannstrom RC 1.00 2.50
162 Aleksi Saarela RC 1.00 2.50
163 Nico Sturm RC .75 2.00
164 Nick Suzuki RC 4.00 10.00
165 Noah Dobson RC 2.50 6.00
166 Emil Bemstrom RC 1.00 2.50
167 Max Jones RC 1.00 2.50
168 Joel L'Esperance RC 1.00 2.50
169 Conor Timmins RC 1.00 2.50
170 Adam Boqvist RC 1.00 2.50
171 Ilya Mikheyev RC 1.50 4.00
172 Sam Lafferty RC .75 2.00
173 Filip Zadina RC 1.50 4.00
174 Blake Lizotte RC 1.00 2.50
175 Cale Makar RC 5.00 12.00
176 Oliver Wahlstrom RC 1.50 4.00
177 Julien Gauthier RC 1.00 2.50
178 Adam Fox RC 2.50 6.00
179 Carl Grundstrom RC 1.00 2.50
180 Cody Glass RC 1.50 4.00
181 Barrett Hayton RC 2.00 5.00
182 Joel Farabee RC 1.50 4.00
183 Dante Fabbro RC 1.00 2.50
184 Nikita Gusev RC 1.50 4.00
185 Connor Clifton RC 1.00 2.50
186 Dominik Kubalik RC 2.00 5.00
187 Jesper Boqvist RC .75 2.00
188 Alexandre Texier RC 1.00 2.50
189 Vitaly Abramov RC 1.00 2.50
190 Quinn Hughes RC 5.00 12.00
191 Trent Frederic RC 1.00 2.50
192 Nicolas Hague RC 1.00 2.50
193 Nikolai Prokhorkin RC .75 2.00
194 Victor Olofsson RC 2.00 5.00
195 Philippe Myers RC .75 2.00
196 Tobias Bjornfot RC 1.00 2.50
197 Ryan Poehling RC 1.50 4.00
198 Taro Hirose RC 1.00 2.50
199 Kaapo Kakko RC 1.50 4.00
200 Jack Hughes RC 5.00 12.00

2019-20 O-Pee-Chee Platinum Best in the World

BW1 John Gibson .60 1.50
BW2 Artemi Panarin 1.25 3.00
BW3 John Tavares 1.00 2.50
BW4 Sergei Bobrovsky 1.00 2.50
BW5 Seth Jones .60 1.50
BW6 Connor McDavid 3.00 8.00
BW7 Steven Stamkos 1.25 3.00
BW8 Brad Marchand 1.25 3.00
BW9 Leon Draisaitl 2.00 5.00
BW10 Carey Price 1.25 3.00
BW11 Mark Stone .75 2.00
BW12 Henrik Lundqvist 1.50 4.00
BW13 Patrick Kane 1.25 3.00
BW14 Auston Matthews 2.50 6.00
BW15 Sidney Crosby 2.50 6.00

2019-20 O-Pee-Chee Platinum Best in the World Rainbow Autographs

BW3 John Tavares B 25.00 60.00
BW9 Leon Draisaitl B 30.00 80.00
BW11 Mark Stone C 20.00 50.00
BW12 Henrik Lundqvist B 40.00 100.00
BW14 Auston Matthews A 60.00 150.00

2019-20 O-Pee-Chee Platinum Calder Front Runners

CF1 Kaapo Kakko 1.25 3.00
CF2 Cale Makar 4.00 10.00
CF3 Victor Olofsson 1.50 4.00
CF4 Taro Hirose .60 1.50
CF5 Quinn Hughes 4.00 10.00
CF6 Adam Fox 2.00 5.00
CF7 Cody Glass 1.25 3.00
CF8 Alexandre Texier .75 2.00
CF9 Erik Brannstrom .75 2.00
CF10 Ryan Poehling 1.25 3.00
CF11 Dante Fabbro .75 2.00
CF12 Filip Zadina 1.25 3.00
CF13 Barrett Hayton 1.50 4.00
CF14 Nick Suzuki 3.00 8.00
CF15 Jack Hughes 4.00 10.00

2019-20 O-Pee-Chee Platinum Calder Front Runners Rainbow Autographs

CF2 Cale Makar A 40.00 100.00
CF3 Victor Olofsson C 15.00 40.00
CF4 Taro Hirose C 8.00 20.00
CF5 Quinn Hughes A 40.00 100.00
CF8 Alexandre Texier C 8.00 20.00
CF9 Erik Brannstrom B 8.00 20.00
CF10 Ryan Poehling B 12.00 30.00
CF12 Filip Zadina A 12.00 30.00
CF14 Nick Suzuki B 30.00 80.00
CF15 Jack Hughes A 40.00 100.00

2019-20 O-Pee-Chee Platinum Retro

R1 Connor McDavid 5.00 12.00
R2 Phil Kessel 1.00 2.50
R3 Aleksander Barkov 1.50 4.00
R4 Alex Tuch 1.00 2.50
R5 Ben Bishop .75 2.00
R6 Jack Eichel 1.50 4.00
R7 John Gibson 1.00 2.50
R8 Antti Raanta 1.00 2.50
R9 Brent Burns 1.00 2.50
R10 Leon Draisaitl 3.00 8.00
R11 Sebastian Aho 1.50 4.00
R12 Mathew Barzal 1.25 3.00
R13 John Tavares 1.50 4.00
R14 Blake Wheeler 1.00 2.50
R15 Andrei Vasilevskiy 1.50 4.00
R16 Mark Scheifele 1.50 4.00
R17 Claude Giroux 1.00 2.50
R18 Marc-Andre Fleury 2.00 5.00
R19 Erik Karlsson 1.25 3.00
R20 Steven Stamkos 2.00 5.00
R21 Jake Guentzel 1.50 4.00
R22 Teuvo Teravainen 1.00 2.50
R23 Sergei Bobrovsky 1.50 4.00
R24 Jakub Vrana 1.00 2.50
R25 Carey Price 2.00 5.00
R26 Matt Dumba .60 1.50
R27 Johnny Gaudreau 1.50 4.00
R28 Ryan O'Reilly 1.00 2.50
R29 Seth Jones 1.00 2.50
R30 Mikael Granlund .75 2.00
R31 Alex DeBrincat 1.25 3.00
R32 Brayden Point 1.25 3.00
R33 Timo Meier 1.00 2.50
R34 Auston Matthews 4.00 10.00
R35 Anders Lee .75 2.00
R36 Nico Hischier 1.50 4.00
R37 Nathan MacKinnon 4.00 10.00
R38 Jonathan Drouin .75 2.00
R39 Connor Hellebuyck 2.00 5.00
R40 Alexander Ovechkin 4.00 10.00
R41 Henrik Lundqvist 2.50 6.00
R42 Matthew Tkachuk 2.00 5.00
R43 Miro Heiskanen 1.25 3.00
R44 Patrick Kane 2.00 5.00
R45 Anze Kopitar 1.50 4.00
R46 Philipp Grubauer 1.00 2.50
R47 Ryan Dzingel .75 2.00
R48 Sidney Crosby 4.00 10.00
R49 Cam Atkinson 1.00 2.50
R50 Brad Marchand 2.00 5.00
R51 Kaapo Kakko 1.50 4.00
R52 Philippe Myers .75 2.00
R53 Rem Pitlick 1.00 2.50
R54 Ilya Mikheyev 1.50 4.00
R55 Erik Brannstrom 1.00 2.50
R56 Ryan Poehling 1.50 4.00
R57 Oliver Wahlstrom 1.50 4.00
R58 Riley Stillman 1.00 2.50
R59 Vitaly Abramov 1.00 2.50
R60 Mackenzie MacEachern 1.00 2.50
R61 Victor Olofsson 2.00 5.00
R62 Guillaume Brisebois 1.00 2.50
R63 Kole Sherwood 1.00 2.50
R64 Brady Keeper 1.00 2.50
R65 Barrett Hayton 2.00 5.00
R66 Noah Dobson 2.50 6.00
R67 Alexandre Texier 1.00 2.50
R68 Filip Zadina 1.50 4.00
R69 Karson Kuhlman 1.00 2.50
R70 Zack MacEwen .75 2.00
R71 Aleksi Saarela 1.00 2.50
R72 Max Jones 1.00 2.50
R73 Adam Fox 2.50 6.00
R74 Zach Senyshyn 1.00 2.50
R75 Taro Hirose 1.00 2.50
R76 Max Veronneau .75 2.00
R77 Carl Grundstrom 1.00 2.50
R78 Joel L'Esperance 1.00 2.50
R79 Jimmy Schuldt .75 2.00
R80 Trent Frederic 1.00 2.50
R81 Nathan Bastian 1.00 2.50
R82 Nico Sturm .75 2.00
R83 Quinn Hughes 5.00 12.00
R84 Cale Makar 5.00 12.00
R85 Libor Hajek .75 2.00
R86 Rudolfs Balcers 1.00 2.50
R87 Dante Fabbro 1.00 2.50
R88 Teddy Blueger 1.00 2.50
R89 Blake Lizotte 1.00 2.50
R90 Nick Suzuki 4.00 10.00
R91 Cody Glass 1.50 4.00
R92 Nikita Gusev 1.50 4.00
R93 Rasmus Sandin 1.50 4.00
R94 Nicolas Hague 1.00 2.50
R95 Jesper Boqvist .75 2.00
R96 Tobias Bjornfot 1.00 2.50
R97 Ville Heinola 1.25 3.00
R98 Dominik Kubalik 2.00 5.00
R99 Cale Fleury 1.25 3.00
R100 Jack Hughes 5.00 12.00

2019-20 O-Pee-Chee Platinum Retro Rainbow Autographs

R5 Ben Bishop C 8.00 20.00
R9 Brent Burns A 10.00 25.00
R10 Leon Draisaitl A 30.00 80.00
R13 John Tavares A 15.00 40.00
R16 Mark Scheifele B 15.00 40.00
R21 Jake Guentzel C 15.00 40.00
R22 Teuvo Teravainen C 10.00 25.00
R26 Matt Dumba C 6.00 15.00
R30 Mikael Granlund C 8.00 20.00
R36 Nico Hischier A 15.00 40.00
R39 Connor Hellebuyck C 20.00 50.00
R41 Henrik Lundqvist A 25.00 60.00
R43 Miro Heiskanen C 12.00 30.00
R46 Philipp Grubauer C 10.00 25.00
R47 Ryan Dzingel C 8.00 20.00
R49 Cam Atkinson C 10.00 25.00
R53 Rem Pitlick C 10.00 25.00
R54 Ilya Mikheyev B 15.00 40.00
R55 Erik Brannstrom B 10.00 25.00
R56 Ryan Poehling B 15.00 40.00
R57 Oliver Wahlstrom B 15.00 40.00
R59 Vitaly Abramov C 10.00 25.00
R61 Victor Olofsson C 20.00 50.00
R64 Brady Keeper C 10.00 25.00
R66 Noah Dobson C 25.00 60.00
R67 Alexandre Texier B 10.00 25.00
R69 Karson Kuhlman C 10.00 25.00
R72 Max Jones B 10.00 25.00
R75 Taro Hirose B 10.00 25.00
R76 Max Veronneau C 8.00 20.00
R77 Carl Grundstrom B 10.00 25.00
R79 Jimmy Schuldt C 8.00 20.00
R80 Trent Frederic C 10.00 25.00
R81 Nathan Bastian C 10.00 25.00
R82 Nico Sturm C 8.00 20.00
R85 Libor Hajek C 8.00 20.00
R88 Teddy Blueger C 10.00 25.00
R89 Blake Lizotte C 10.00 25.00
R93 Rasmus Sandin B 15.00 40.00
R96 Tobias Bjornfot B 10.00 25.00

2019-20 O-Pee-Chee Platinum Rookie Autographs

*RAINBOW: .5X TO 1.25X BASIC CARDS
*VIOLET: .6X TO 1.5X BASIC CARDS
*PINK: .75X TO 2X BASIC CARDS
*RED: 1X TO 2.5X BASIC CARDS
*GOLD: 1X TO 2.5X BASIC CARDS
RAT Alexandre Texier B 8.00 20.00
RAV Alexander Volkov C 6.00 15.00
RBE Emil Bemstrom B 8.00 20.00
RBG Brandon Gignac C 6.00 15.00
RBJ Tobias Bjornfot A 8.00 20.00
RBK Brady Keeper D 8.00 20.00
RBL Blake Lizotte D 8.00 20.00
RCC Connor Clifton D 8.00 20.00
RCM Cale Makar A 80.00 200.00
RDG David Gustafsson D 6.00 15.00
RDK Dominik Kubalik C 15.00 40.00
RDY Danil Yurtaykin D 6.00 15.00
REB Erik Brannstrom A 8.00 20.00
REM Elvis Merzlikins D 15.00 40.00
RFE Mario Ferraro B 6.00 15.00
RFZ Filip Zadina A 12.00 30.00
RGR Carl Grundstrom C 8.00 20.00
RJD Joey Daccord D 15.00 40.00
RJH Jack Hughes A 50.00 125.00
RJS Jimmy Schuldt C 6.00 15.00
RKD Kirby Dach A 15.00 40.00
RKF Kaden Fulcher D 8.00 20.00
RKK Karson Kuhlman D 8.00 20.00
RKO Klim Kostin D 8.00 20.00
RLB Lean Bergmann B 6.00 15.00
RLH Libor Hajek D 6.00 15.00
RMA Martin Fehervary D 6.00 15.00
RMF Morgan Frost A 12.00 30.00
RMJ Max Jones B 8.00 20.00
RMR Matt Roy B 8.00 20.00
RMV Max Veronneau D 6.00 15.00
RNB Nathan Bastian B 8.00 20.00
RND Noah Dobson B 20.00 50.00
RNS Nick Suzuki A 30.00 80.00
ROW Oliver Wahlstrom A 12.00 30.00
RPI Rem Pitlick D 8.00 20.00
RQH Quinn Hughes A 60.00 150.00
RRK Ryan Kuffner D 6.00 15.00
RRP Ryan Poehling A 12.00 30.00
RSA Rasmus Sandin A 12.00 30.00
RST Nico Sturm B 6.00 15.00
RTB Teddy Blueger B 8.00 20.00
RTH Taro Hirose A 8.00 20.00
RVA Vitaly Abramov B 8.00 20.00
RVO Victor Olofsson D 15.00 40.00
RZM Zack MacEwen D 6.00 15.00

2019-20 O-Pee-Chee Platinum Thrilling Finishes

TF1 Steven Stamkos 2.00 5.00
TF2 Connor McDavid 5.00 12.00
TF3 Mark Scheifele 1.50 4.00
TF4 Brayden Point 1.25 3.00
TF5 Cam Atkinson 1.00 2.50
TF6 Mark Stone 1.25 3.00
TF7 Alex DeBrincat 1.25 3.00
TF8 Sidney Crosby 4.00 10.00
TF9 Nathan MacKinnon 4.00 10.00
TF10 Viktor Arvidsson .60 1.50
TF11 Patrick Kane 2.00 5.00
TF12 Jake Guentzel 1.50 4.00
TF13 Aleksander Barkov 1.50 4.00
TF14 Alexander Ovechkin 4.00 10.00
TF15 Tomas Hertl 1.00 2.50
TF16 Joe Pavelski 1.25 3.00
TF17 Nikita Kucherov 2.00 5.00
TF18 Leon Draisaitl 3.00 8.00
TF19 Brad Marchand 2.00 5.00
TF20 Matthew Tkachuk 2.00 5.00
TF21 Jack Hughes 5.00 12.00
TF22 Cale Makar 5.00 12.00
TF23 Quinn Hughes 5.00 12.00
TF24 Filip Zadina 1.50 4.00
TF25 Kaapo Kakko 1.50 4.00

2019-20 O-Pee-Chee Platinum Thrilling Finishes Rainbow Autographs

TF3 Mark Scheifele A 15.00 40.00
TF5 Cam Atkinson B 10.00 25.00
TF6 Mark Stone B 12.00 30.00
TF12 Jake Guentzel B 15.00 40.00
TF22 Cale Makar B 50.00 125.00
TF24 Filip Zadina B 15.00 40.00

2020-21 O-Pee-Chee Platinum

1 Connor McDavid 2.00 5.00
2 Leon Draisaitl 1.25 3.00
3 Nikita Kucherov .75 2.00
4 Nathan MacKinnon 1.50 4.00
5 Auston Matthews 1.50 4.00
6 Vladimir Tarasenko .50 1.25
7 David Pastrnak 1.00 2.50
8 Jack Eichel .60 1.50
9 Carey Price .75 2.00
10 Quinn Hughes 1.00 2.50
11 Tyler Seguin .50 1.25
12 Claude Giroux .40 1.00
13 Patrice Bergeron .50 1.25
14 Blake Lizotte .25 .60
15 Dylan Larkin .50 1.25
16 Carter Hart .40 1.00
17 Erik Karlsson .50 1.25
18 Matthew Tkachuk .75 2.00
19 Anze Kopitar .60 1.50
20 Jonathan Huberdeau .50 1.25
21 Johnny Gaudreau .60 1.50
22 Victor Hedman .50 1.25
23 Shea Weber .40 1.00
24 Kris Letang .50 1.25
25 Ryan O'Reilly .40 1.00
26 Patrik Laine .50 1.25
27 David Perron .30 .75
28 Rasmus Dahlin .50 1.25
29 Filip Forsberg .60 1.50
30 Clayton Keller .50 1.25
31 Brent Burns .40 1.00
32 John Gibson .40 1.00
33 Derek Stepan .25 .60
34 Tuukka Rask .50 1.25
35 Victor Olofsson .40 1.00
36 Mark Giordano .40 1.00
37 Dougie Hamilton .30 .75
38 Kyle Connor .60 1.50
39 Jake Guentzel .60 1.50
40 Mark Stone .50 1.25
41 Bo Horvat .50 1.25
42 Morgan Rielly .40 1.00
43 Andrei Vasilevskiy .60 1.50
44 Miro Heiskanen .50 1.25
45 Colton Parayko .30 .75
46 Frederik Andersen .50 1.25
47 Tomas Hertl .40 1.00
48 Travis Konecny .40 1.00
49 Chris Kreider .50 1.25
50 Jordan Binnington .60 1.50
51 Jaccob Slavin .30 .75
52 Jakob Silfverberg .25 .60
53 Anders Lee .30 .75
54 P.K. Subban .50 1.25
55 Matt Duchene .40 1.00
56 Jesperi Kotkaniemi .40 1.00
57 Josh Bailey .30 .75
58 Adrian Kempe .40 1.00
59 Sergei Bobrovsky .60 1.50
60 Jonathan Marchessault .50 1.25
61 Valtteri Filppula .25 .60
62 Brayden Schenn .40 1.00
63 Gabriel Landeskog .50 1.25
64 Sean Couturier .30 .75
65 Dominik Kubalik .40 1.00
66 Zach Parise .40 1.00
67 Jesper Bratt .40 1.00
68 Jamie Benn .40 1.00
69 Pierre-Luc Dubois .30 .75
70 Darnell Nurse .30 .75
71 J.T. Miller .50 1.25
72 Bryan Rust .40 1.00
73 Anthony Mantha .30 .75
74 Thomas Chabot .40 1.00
75 Duncan Keith .30 .75
76 Phil Kessel .40 1.00
77 David Krejci .40 1.00
78 Seth Jones .40 1.00
79 Logan Couture .50 1.25
80 Blake Wheeler .40 1.00
81 Adam Henrique .30 .75
82 Jean-Gabriel Pageau .25 .60
83 T.J. Oshie .40 1.00
84 Zack Kassian .25 .60
85 Connor Brown .30 .75
86 Aaron Ekblad .50 1.25
87 Kyle Palmieri .30 .75
88 James van Riemsdyk .30 .75
89 Elias Lindholm .40 1.00
90 Joe Pavelski .50 1.25
91 Nazem Kadri .50 1.25
92 Jeff Skinner .40 1.00
93 Alex Iafallo .25 .60
94 Mats Zuccarello .40 1.00
95 William Karlsson .50 1.25
96 Taylor Hall .40 1.00
97 Nikolaj Ehlers .40 1.00
98 Tyler Toffoli .40 1.00
99 Torey Krug .30 .75
100 Alex Pietrangelo .30 .75
101 Tyler Bertuzzi .30 .75
102 Brayden Point .50 1.25
103 Zach Werenski .60 1.50
104 Brock Nelson .40 1.00
105 Sebastian Aho .60 1.50
106 Ryan Suter .30 .75
107 Adam Fox .50 1.25
108 Brady Tkachuk .60 1.50
109 Alexander Radulov .40 1.00
110 Brad Marchand .75 2.00
111 Elvis Merzlikins .40 1.00
112 Kevin Fiala .30 .75
113 Colin White .25 .60
114 Connor Hellebuyck .75 2.00
115 Nick Schmaltz .30 .75
116 Andrei Svechnikov .50 1.25
117 Sean Monahan .25 .60
118 Sam Reinhart .75 2.00
119 Ryan Getzlaf .40 1.00
120 Alex DeBrincat .50 1.25
121 Pekka Rinne .40 1.00
122 Nicklas Backstrom .40 1.00
123 Chris Tierney .30 .75
124 Marc-Andre Fleury .75 2.00
125 Mikko Rantanen 1.00 2.50
126 Brock Boeser .50 1.25
127 Drew Doughty .50 1.25
128 Brendan Gallagher .40 1.00
129 Max Pacioretty .40 1.00
130 Roman Josi .40 1.00
131 John Carlson .40 1.00
132 Aleksander Barkov .60 1.50
133 Mika Zibanejad .50 1.25
134 Jonathan Quick .50 1.25
135 Jakub Vrana .40 1.00
136 Ryan Nugent-Hopkins .50 1.25
137 Mark Scheifele .60 1.50
138 Mathew Barzal .50 1.25
139 John Tavares .60 1.50
140 Cale Makar 1.00 2.50
141 Evgeni Malkin .75 2.00
142 Jonathan Toews .60 1.50
143 Steven Stamkos .75 2.00
144 Mitch Marner .60 1.50
145 Patrick Kane .75 2.00
146 Nico Hischier .60 1.50
147 Artemi Panarin .75 2.00
148 Elias Pettersson .60 1.50
149 Sidney Crosby 1.50 4.00
150 Alex Ovechkin 1.50 4.00
151 Alexis Lafreniere RC 4.00 10.00
152 Bowen Byram RC 2.50 6.00
153 Nick Robertson RC 2.00 5.00
154 Connor McMichael RC 2.00 5.00
155 Victor Soderstrom RC 1.00 2.50
156 Vitali Kravtsov RC 2.50 6.00
157 Thomas Harley RC 2.00 5.00
158 Liam Foudy RC 1.25 3.00
159 Jason Robertson RC 3.00 8.00
160 Gabe Vilardi RC 2.00 5.00

161 Josh Norris RC 2.00 5.00
162 Timothy Liljegren RC 1.25 3.00
163 Peyton Krebs RC 2.00 5.00
164 Philipp Kurashev RC 1.50 4.00
165 Morgan Geekie RC 1.25 3.00
166 Shane Bowers RC 1.00 2.50
167 Ty Dellandrea RC 1.25 3.00
168 Ian Mitchell RC 1.00 2.50
169 Martin Kaut RC 1.25 3.00
170 Egor Zamula RC 1.00 2.50
171 Nicolas Beaudin RC 1.25 3.00
172 Michael DiPietro RC 1.50 4.00
178 Yegor Sharangovich RC 2.00 5.00
174 Alexander Alexeyev RC 1.00 2.50
175 Jake Oettinger RC 3.00 8.00
176 Dylan Coghlan RC 1.25 3.00
177 Pierre-Olivier Joseph RC 1.25 3.00
173 Ryan McLeod RC 1.00 2.50
179 Mikey Anderson RC 1.25 3.00
180 Connor Ingram RC 1.00 2.50
181 Kieffer Bellows RC 1.00 2.50
182 Gustav Lindstrom RC 1.00 2.50
183 Brandon Hagel RC 1.50 4.00
184 Steven Lorentz RC 1.00 2.50
185 Pavel Francouz RC 1.50 4.00
186 Calvin Thurkauf RC 1.00 2.50
187 Alex Belzile RC 1.00 2.50
188 Mikhail Berdin RC 1.25 3.00
189 Olli Juolevi RC 1.25 3.00
190 Philip Broberg RC 1.25 3.00
191 Cal Foote RC 1.50 4.00
192 Arthur Kaliyev RC 2.00 5.00
193 Ty Smith RC 2.00 5.00
194 Nils Hoglander RC 1.25 3.00
195 K'Andre Miller RC 2.50 6.00
196 Ilya Sorokin RC 3.00 8.00
197 Dylan Cozens RC 2.00 5.00
198 Alexander Romanov RC 1.50 4.00
199 Tim Stutzle RC 2.50 6.00
200 Kirill Kaprizov RC 5.00 12.00

2020-21 O-Pee-Chee Platinum Aquamarine

*AQUA/499: .75X TO 2X BASIC

2020-21 O-Pee-Chee Platinum Arctic Freeze

*ARCTIC/99: 1.5X TO 4X BASIC
*ARCTIC.RC/99: 1X TO 2.5X BASIC

2020-21 O-Pee-Chee Platinum Blue Surge

*BLUE: .75X TO 2X BASIC
1 Connor McDavid 12.00 30.00

2020-21 O-Pee-Chee Platinum Cosmic

*COSMIC/65: 4X TO 10X BASIC
*COSMIC.RC/65: 2X TO 5X BASIC
2 Leon Draisaitl 20.00 50.00
4 Nathan MacKinnon 25.00 60.00
5 Auston Matthews 25.00 60.00
149 Sidney Crosby 30.00 80.00
150 Alex Ovechkin 40.00 100.00
151 Alexis Lafreniere 100.00 250.00
153 Nick Robertson 20.00 50.00
154 Connor McMichael 20.00 50.00
194 Nils Hoglander 25.00 60.00
197 Dylan Cozens 25.00 60.00
200 Kirill Kaprizov 80.00 200.00

2020-21 O-Pee-Chee Platinum Matte Pink

*PINK: .6X TO 1.5X BASIC

2020-21 O-Pee-Chee Platinum Neon Yellow Surge

*NEON.YLW: .75X TO 2X BASIC
1 Connor McDavid 12.00 30.00

2020-21 O-Pee-Chee Platinum Orange Checkers

*ORANGE/25: 8X TO 20X BASIC
*ORANGE.RC/25: 4X TO 10X BASIC
1 Connor McDavid 300.00 800.00
149 Sidney Crosby 125.00 300.00
152 Bowen Byram 60.00 150.00
192 Arthur Kaliyev 50.00 125.00
194 Nils Hoglander 80.00 200.00
196 Ilya Sorokin 60.00 150.00

2020-21 O-Pee-Chee Platinum Rainbow

*RAINBOW: .5X TO 1.25X BASIC

2020-21 O-Pee-Chee Platinum Red Prism

*RED.PRISM/199: 1.5X TO 4X BASIC
*RED.PRISM.RC/199: .75X TO 2X BASIC

2020-21 O-Pee-Chee Platinum Red Surge

*RED.SURGE: .75X TO 2X BASIC
1 Connor McDavid 12.00 30.00

2020-21 O-Pee-Chee Platinum Seismic Gold

*SEIS.GOLD/50: 5X TO 12X BASIC
*SEIS.GOLD.RC/50: 2.5X TO 6X BASIC
1 Connor McDavid 300.00 800.00
2 Leon Draisaitl 25.00 60.00
4 Nathan MacKinnon 30.00 80.00
149 Sidney Crosby 125.00 300.00
150 Alex Ovechkin 125.00 300.00
151 Alexis Lafreniere 125.00 300.00
152 Bowen Byram 40.00 100.00
153 Nick Robertson 30.00 80.00
154 Connor McMichael 30.00 80.00
159 Jason Robertson 60.00 150.00
192 Arthur Kaliyev 30.00 80.00
194 Nils Hoglander 30.00 80.00
196 Ilya Sorokin 30.00 80.00
197 Dylan Cozens 30.00 80.00
200 Kirill Kaprizov 125.00 300.00

2020-21 O-Pee-Chee Platinum Sunset

*SUNSET: .6X TO 1.5X BASIC

2020-21 O-Pee-Chee Platinum Violet Pixels

*VIOLET/399: .75X TO 2X BASIC

2020-21 O-Pee-Chee Platinum Yellow Traxx

*YLW.TRAXX/249: 1X TO 2.5X BASIC

2020-21 O-Pee-Chee Platinum Best in the World

BW1 Connor McDavid 3.00 8.00
BW2 Marc-Andre Fleury 1.25 3.00
BW3 Sidney Crosby 2.50 6.00
BW4 Auston Matthews 2.50 6.00
BW5 Mark Scheifele 1.00 2.50
BW6 Patrick Kane 1.25 3.00
BW7 Sebastian Aho 1.00 2.50
BW8 Brent Burns .60 1.50
BW9 John Tavares 1.00 2.50
BW10 Carey Price 1.25 3.00
BW11 Artemi Panarin 1.25 3.00
BW12 Aleksander Barkov 1.00 2.50
BW13 Brad Marchand 1.25 3.00
BW14 Elias Pettersson 1.00 2.50
BW15 Andrei Vasilevskiy 1.00 2.50

2020-21 O-Pee-Chee Platinum Best in the World Rainbow Autographs

BW4 Auston Matthews B 200.00 500.00
BW5 Mark Scheifele C 25.00 60.00
BW8 Brent Burns C 15.00 40.00
BW9 John Tavares B 40.00 100.00
BW13 Brad Marchand C 30.00 80.00

2020-21 O-Pee-Chee Platinum Photo Driven

PD1 Connor McDavid 3.00 8.00
PD2 Sidney Crosby 2.50 6.00
PD3 Auston Matthews 2.50 6.00
PD4 Elias Pettersson 1.00 2.50
PD5 Carey Price 1.25 3.00
PD6 Brad Marchand 1.25 3.00
PD7 Artemi Panarin 1.25 3.00
PD8 Joe Pavelski .75 2.00
PD9 Andrei Svechnikov .75 2.00
PD10 Quinn Hughes 1.50 4.00
PD11 Brent Burns .60 1.50
PD12 Sebastian Aho 1.00 2.50
PD13 Ryan O'Reilly .60 1.50
PD14 Anze Kopitar 1.00 2.50
PD15 Nico Hischier 1.00 2.50
PD16 Brock Boeser .75 2.00
PD17 Carter Hart .60 1.50
PD18 Cale Makar 1.50 4.00
PD19 Tyler Seguin .75 2.00
PD20 Mark Stone .75 2.00
PD21 Peyton Krebs 1.25 3.00
PD22 Alexander Alexeyev .60 1.50
PD23 Ty Dellandrea .75 2.00
PD24 Nick Robertson 1.25 3.00
PD25 Bowen Byram 1.50 4.00

2020-21 O-Pee-Chee Platinum Photo Driven Rainbow Autographs

PD6 Brad Marchand B 40.00 100.00
PD8 Joe Pavelski C 25.00 60.00
PD9 Andrei Svechnikov B 25.00 60.00
PD11 Brent Burns C 20.00 50.00
PD14 Anze Kopitar B 30.00 80.00
PD15 Nico Hischier B 30.00 80.00
PD17 Carter Hart B 20.00 50.00
PD19 Tyler Seguin B 25.00 60.00
PD20 Mark Stone C 25.00 60.00
PD21 Peyton Krebs C 40.00 100.00
PD23 Ty Dellandrea C 10.00 25.00
PD24 Nick Robertson B 25.00 60.00
PD25 Bowen Byram B 50.00 125.00

2020-21 O-Pee-Chee Platinum Retro

*RAINBOW: .6X TO 1.5X BASIC
R1 Connor McDavid 5.00 12.00
R2 Auston Matthews 4.00 10.00
R3 Sidney Crosby 4.00 10.00
R4 Jonathan Toews 1.50 4.00
R5 Patrick Kane 2.00 5.00
R6 Carey Price 2.00 5.00
R7 John Tavares 1.50 4.00
R8 Connor Hellebuyck 2.00 5.00
R9 Elias Pettersson 1.50 4.00
R10 Brad Marchand 2.00 5.00
R11 Dylan Larkin 1.25 3.00
R12 Artemi Panarin 2.00 5.00
R13 Carter Hart 1.00 2.50
R14 Brent Burns 1.00 2.50
R15 Brock Boeser 1.25 3.00
R16 Matthew Tkachuk 2.00 5.00
R17 Sebastian Aho 1.50 4.00
R18 Andrei Svechnikov 1.25 3.00
R19 Tyler Seguin 1.25 3.00
R20 Joe Pavelski 1.25 3.00
R21 Miro Heiskanen 1.25 3.00
R22 Aleksander Barkov 1.50 4.00
R23 Anze Kopitar 1.50 4.00
R24 Nick Suzuki 2.00 5.00
R25 Zach Parise 1.00 2.50
R26 Brendan Gallagher 1.00 2.50
R27 Nico Hischier 1.50 4.00
R28 Brady Tkachuk 1.50 4.00
R29 Jake Guentzel 1.50 4.00
R30 Tomas Hertl 1.00 2.50
R31 Ryan O'Reilly 1.00 2.50
R32 Brayden Point 1.25 3.00
R33 Andrei Vasilevskiy 1.50 4.00
R34 Mark Stone 1.25 3.00
R35 Teuvo Teravainen 1.00 2.50
R36 Colton Parayko .75 2.00
R37 Mark Scheifele 1.50 4.00
R38 Dylan Strome 1.25 3.00
R39 Travis Konecny 1.00 2.50
R40 Quinn Hughes 2.50 6.00
R41 Cale Makar 2.50 6.00
R42 Jack Hughes 2.50 6.00
R43 Jakub Vrana 1.00 2.50
R44 Jean-Gabriel Pageau .60 1.50
R45 Phillip Danault 1.00 2.50
R46 Dustin Brown 1.00 2.50
R47 Sam Reinhart 2.00 5.00
R48 William Karlsson 1.25 3.00
R49 Roman Josi 1.00 2.50
R50 Ryan Nugent-Hopkins 1.25 3.00
R51 Mikhail Berdin 1.25 3.00
R52 Philipp Kurashev 1.50 4.00
R53 Timothy Liljegren 1.25 3.00
R54 Liam Foudy 1.25 3.00
R55 Gabe Vilardi 2.00 5.00
R56 Lucas Carlsson 1.00 2.50
R57 Kieffer Bellows 1.00 2.50
R58 Michael DiPietro 1.50 4.00
R59 Brandon Hagel 1.50 4.00
R60 Calvin Thurkauf 1.00 2.50
R61 Maxim Letunov 1.00 2.50
R62 Anthony Angello 1.00 2.50
R63 Alexander Yelesin 1.00 2.50
R64 Matiss Kivlenieks 1.50 4.00
R65 Gustav Lindstrom 1.00 2.50
R66 Egor Korshkov .75 2.00
R67 Keegan Kolesar 1.00 2.50
R68 Pierre-Olivier Joseph 1.25 3.00
R69 Nikolai Knyzhov 1.00 2.50
R70 Jani Hakanpaa .75 2.00
R71 Jonas Johansson 1.25 3.00
R72 Shane Bowers 1.00 2.50
R73 Peyton Krebs 2.00 5.00
R74 Alexander Alexeyev 1.00 2.50
R75 Jake Oettinger 3.00 8.00
R76 Reid Duke 1.25 3.00
R77 Vitali Kravtsov 2.50 6.00
R78 Steven Lorentz 1.00 2.50
R79 Dylan Coghlan 1.25 3.00
R80 Ty Dellandrea 1.25 3.00
R81 Victor Soderstrom 1.00 2.50
R82 Vitek Vanecek 2.00 5.00
R83 MacKenzie Entwistle 1.00 2.50
R84 Gage Quinney .75 2.00
R85 Jake Evans 1.25 3.00
R86 Bowen Byram 2.50 6.00
R87 Jansen Harkins 1.00 2.50
R88 Thomas Harley 2.00 5.00
R89 Olli Juolevi 1.25 3.00
R90 Tyler Benson 1.25 3.00
R91 Morgan Geekie 1.25 3.00
R92 Nicolas Beaudin 1.25 3.00
R93 Jason Robertson 3.00 8.00
R94 Martin Kaut 1.25 3.00
R95 Ryan McLeod 1.00 2.50
R96 Alex Belzile 1.00 2.50
R97 Connor Ingram 1.00 2.50
R98 Connor McMichael 2.00 5.00
R99 Josh Norris 2.00 5.00
R100 Nick Robertson 2.00 5.00

2020-21 O-Pee-Chee Platinum Retro Rainbow Blue

*RAIN.BLUE/149: 1.25X TO 3X BASIC
R1 Connor McDavid 25.00 60.00

2020-21 O-Pee-Chee Platinum Retro Rainbow Red Autographs

R7 John Tavares C 15.00 40.00
R10 Brad Marchand D 20.00 50.00
R13 Carter Hart C 10.00 25.00
R14 Brent Burns E 10.00 25.00
R16 Matthew Tkachuk E 20.00 50.00
R18 Andrei Svechnikov E 12.00 30.00
R19 Tyler Seguin C 12.00 30.00
R20 Joe Pavelski E 12.00 30.00
R23 Anze Kopitar C 15.00 40.00
R27 Nico Hischier E 15.00 40.00
R28 Brady Tkachuk E 15.00 40.00
R29 Jake Guentzel E 15.00 40.00
R34 Mark Stone D 12.00 30.00
R36 Colton Parayko E 8.00 20.00
R37 Mark Scheifele D 15.00 40.00
R46 Dustin Brown E 10.00 25.00
R47 Sam Reinhart E 20.00 50.00
R50 Ryan Nugent-Hopkins E 12.00 30.00
R54 Liam Foudy C 12.00 30.00
R59 Brandon Hagel C 15.00 40.00
R60 Calvin Thurkauf C 10.00 25.00
R61 Maxim Letunov C 10.00 25.00
R62 Anthony Angello C 10.00 25.00
R65 Gustav Lindstrom C 10.00 25.00
R67 Keegan Kolesar C 10.00 25.00
R69 Nikolai Knyzhov C 10.00 25.00
R72 Shane Bowers C 10.00 25.00
R73 Peyton Krebs A 20.00 50.00
R76 Reid Duke C 12.00 30.00
R78 Steven Lorentz C 10.00 25.00
R80 Ty Dellandrea C 12.00 30.00
R82 Vitek Vanecek C 20.00 50.00
R84 Gage Quinney C 8.00 20.00
R85 Jake Evans C 12.00 30.00
R86 Bowen Byram A 25.00 60.00
R89 Olli Juolevi C 12.00 30.00
R90 Tyler Benson C 12.00 30.00
R91 Morgan Geekie C 12.00 30.00
R92 Nicolas Beaudin C 12.00 30.00
R93 Jason Robertson B 60.00 150.00
R95 Ryan McLeod C 10.00 25.00
R96 Alex Belzile C 10.00 25.00
R99 Josh Norris A 20.00 50.00
R100 Nick Robertson B 20.00 50.00

2020-21 O-Pee-Chee Platinum Rookie Autographs

RAA Anthony Angello E 8.00 20.00
RAE Alex Belzile E 8.00 20.00
RAR Alexander Romanov B 12.00 30.00
RBB Bowen Byram B 20.00 50.00
RBH Brandon Hagel D 12.00 30.00
RCF Cal Foote D 12.00 30.00
RCI Connor Ingram D 8.00 20.00
RCM Connor McMichael B 15.00 40.00
RCT Calvin Thurkauf D 8.00 20.00
RDC Dylan Cozens B 15.00 40.00
RGL Gustav Lindstrom D 8.00 20.00
RGQ Gage Quinney E 6.00 15.00
RIM Ian Mitchell C 8.00 20.00
RIS Ilya Sorokin B 40.00 100.00
RJE Jake Evans B 10.00 25.00
RJH Jani Hakanpaa E 6.00 15.00
RJN Josh Norris B 15.00 40.00
RJR Jason Robertson B 40.00 100.00
RKE Keegan Kolesar E 8.00 20.00
RKI Matiss Kivlenieks E 12.00 30.00
RKK Kirill Kaprizov B 200.00 500.00
RKM K'Andre Miller B 20.00 50.00
RLC Lucas Carlsson E 8.00 20.00
RLF Liam Foudy C 10.00 25.00
RMA Mikey Anderson D 10.00 25.00
RMG Morgan Geekie D 10.00 25.00
RNB Nicolas Beaudin C 10.00 25.00
RNK Nikolai Knyzhov D 8.00 20.00
RNR Nick Robertson C 15.00 40.00
ROJ Olli Juolevi D 10.00 25.00
RPK Peyton Krebs C 15.00 40.00
RRD Reid Duke E 10.00 25.00
RSB Shane Bowers C 8.00 20.00
RSC Sasha Chmelevski D 8.00 20.00
RSL Steven Lorentz E 8.00 20.00
RST Tim Stutzle B 60.00 150.00
RTA Alexander True E 8.00 20.00
RTB Tyler Benson C 10.00 25.00
RTD Ty Dellandrea D 10.00 25.00
RTH Thomas Harley A 15.00 40.00
RTL Timothy Liljegren C 10.00 25.00
RTS Ty Smith B 15.00 40.00
RVV Vitek Vanecek C 15.00 40.00

2020-21 O-Pee-Chee Platinum Rookie Autographs Cosmic

*COSMIC/75: .6X TO 1.5X BASIC
RBB Bowen Byram 50.00 125.00
RDC Dylan Cozens 60.00 150.00
RIS Ilya Sorokin 80.00 200.00
RJR Jason Robertson 150.00 400.00
RKK Kirill Kaprizov 250.00 600.00
RST Tim Stutzle 125.00 300.00

2020-21 O-Pee-Chee Platinum Rookie Autographs Matte Pink

*PINK/99: .6X TO 1.5X BASIC
RAL Alexis Lafreniere 150.00 400.00
RBB Bowen Byram 50.00 125.00
RDC Dylan Cozens 50.00 125.00
RIS Ilya Sorokin 80.00 200.00
RJR Jason Robertson 100.00 250.00
RKK Kirill Kaprizov 250.00 600.00
RST Tim Stutzle 800.00 200.00

2020-21 O-Pee-Chee Platinum Rookie Autographs Rainbow

*RAINBOW: .5X TO 1.25X BASIC
RIS Ilya Sorokin B 80.00 200.00
RJR Jason Robertson D 200.00 500.00
RST Tim Stutzle A 100.00 250.00

2020-21 O-Pee-Chee Platinum Rookie Autographs Red Prism

*RED/50: .75X TO 2X BASIC
RDC Dylan Cozens 150.00 400.00
RIS Ilya Sorokin 100.00 250.00
RJR Jason Robertson 300.00 800.00
RKK Kirill Kaprizov 500.00 1200.00
RST Tim Stutzle 125.00 300.00

2020-21 O-Pee-Chee Platinum Rookie Autographs Seismic Gold

*SEIS.GOLD/25: 1X TO 2.5X BASIC
RAR Alexander Romanov 60.00 150.00
RCM Connor McMichael 150.00 400.00
RDC Dylan Cozens 200.00 500.00
RIS Ilya Sorokin 150.00 400.00
RJR Jason Robertson 600.00 1500.00
RMA Mikey Anderson 50.00 125.00
RST Tim Stutzle 150.00 400.00
RVV Vitek Vanecek 60.00 150.00

2020-21 O-Pee-Chee Platinum Rookie Autographs Violet Pixels

*VIOLET: .6X TO 1.5X BASIC
RIS Ilya Sorokin B 100.00 250.00
RJR Jason Robertson B 125.00 300.00
RKI Matiss Kivlenieks C 80.00 200.00
RST Tim Stutzle B 125.00 300.00

2020-21 O-Pee-Chee Platinum Sweet Selections

SS1 Ty Dellandrea .75 2.00
SS2 Bowen Byram 1.50 4.00
SS3 Peyton Krebs 1.25 3.00
SS4 Nick Robertson 1.25 3.00
SS5 Alexander Alexeyev .60 1.50
SS6 Josh Norris 1.25 3.00
SS7 Timothy Liljegren .75 2.00
SS8 Gabe Vilardi 1.25 3.00
SS9 Martin Kaut .75 2.00
SS10 Jason Robertson 2.00 5.00
SS11 Morgan Geekie .75 2.00
SS12 Nicolas Beaudin .75 2.00
SS13 Kieffer Bellows .60 1.50
SS14 Lucas Carlsson .60 1.50
SS15 Liam Foudy .75 2.00

2020-21 O-Pee-Chee Platinum Sweet Selections Rainbow Autographs

SS1 Ty Dellandrea 8.00 20.00
SS2 Bowen Byram 15.00 40.00
SS3 Peyton Krebs 12.00 30.00
SS4 Nick Robertson 12.00 30.00
SS10 Jason Robertson 40.00 100.00
SS11 Morgan Geekie 8.00 20.00
SS15 Liam Foudy 8.00 20.00

2021-22 O-Pee-Chee Platinum

1 Connor McDavid 2.00 5.00
2 Artemi Panarin .75 2.00
3 Alex Ovechkin 1.50 4.00
4 Kirill Kaprizov 1.25 3.00
5 Tim Stutzle .50 1.25
6 Steven Stamkos .75 2.00
7 Auston Matthews 1.50 4.00
8 Evgeni Malkin .75 2.00
9 Andrew Mangiapane .40 1.00
10 Carey Price .75 2.00
11 Erik Karlsson .50 1.25
12 Sebastian Aho .60 1.50
13 Mikko Rantanen 1.00 2.50
14 Tyler Seguin .50 1.25
15 Dylan Larkin .50 1.25
16 Jonathan Huberdeau .50 1.25
17 John Gibson .40 1.00
18 Brad Marchand .75 2.00
19 Nathan MacKinnon 1.50 4.00
20 Adam Fox .50 1.25
21 Jake Guentzel .60 1.50
22 Claude Giroux .40 1.00
23 Jean-Gabriel Pageau .25 .60
24 Thomas Chabot .40 1.00
25 Sean Couturier .30 .75
26 Tomas Hertl .40 1.00
27 Ryan Johansen .30 .75
28 James van Riemsdyk .30 .75
29 Victor Hedman .50 1.25
30 Alexis Lafreniere .60 1.50
31 Kirby Dach .40 1.00
32 Patrik Laine .50 1.25
33 Andrei Vasilevskiy .60 1.50
34 Mats Zuccarello .40 1.00
35 Brock Boeser .50 1.25
36 Mark Stone .50 1.25
37 Johnny Gaudreau .60 1.50
38 Max Pacioretty .40 1.00
39 Connor Hellebuyck .75 2.00
40 Brock Nelson .40 1.00
41 Chris Kreider .50 1.25
42 Jason Zucker .40 1.00
43 Joel Farabee .40 1.00
44 Darnell Nurse .30 .75
45 Nicklas Backstrom .40 1.00
46 Maxime Comtois .30 .75
47 Adrian Kempe .40 1.00
48 Kyle Connor .60 1.50
49 Kevin Lankinen .40 1.00
50 Jordan Binnington .60 1.50
51 P.K. Subban .50 1.25
52 Clayton Keller .50 1.25
53 Jeff Petry .40 1.00
54 Charlie McAvoy .50 1.25
55 Matt Dumba .30 .75
56 Max Domi .40 1.00
57 Aaron Ekblad .50 1.25
58 Jack Campbell .40 1.00
59 Alex Pietrangelo .30 .75
60 Alex Kerfoot .30 .75
61 Jason Robertson .60 1.50
62 Tyson Barrie .25 .60
63 Taylor Hall .40 1.00
64 Thatcher Demko .50 1.25
65 Casey Mittelstadt .40 1.00
66 Ivan Provorov .30 .75
67 Dylan Cozens .40 1.00
68 Cam Talbot .40 1.00
69 Brayden Point .50 1.25
70 Anders Lee .30 .75
71 Mikael Granlund .30 .75
72 Mika Zibanejad .50 1.25
73 Vitek Vanecek .40 1.00
74 Neal Pionk .25 .60
75 Ondrej Palat .30 .75
76 Ryan Strome .40 1.00
77 Phil Kessel .40 1.00
78 Mike Smith .25 .60
79 Martin Necas .60 1.50
80 Cam Fowler .40 1.00
81 Jordan Staal .30 .75
82 Nick Suzuki .75 2.00
83 Kris Letang .50 1.25
84 Drake Batherson .40 1.00
85 Alexander Romanov .30 .75
86 Robby Fabbri .25 .60
87 Sidney Crosby 1.50 4.00
88 Adam Henrique .30 .75
89 Jack Roslovic .25 .60
90 Ryan Getzlaf .40 1.00
91 Shea Theodore .50 1.25
92 Kaapo Kakko .30 .75
93 Josh Norris .40 1.00
94 Carter Verhaeghe .40 1.00
95 Cal Clutterbuck .25 .60
96 Cale Makar 1.00 2.50
97 Nazem Kadri .50 1.25
98 Jesper Bratt .40 1.00
99 Leon Draisaitl 1.25 3.00
100 Pavel Buchnevich .30 .75
101 Jonathan Toews .60 1.50
102 Nikita Kucherov .75 2.00
103 Gabe Vilardi .40 1.00
104 Dante Fabbro .25 .60
105 Dillon Dube .25 .60
106 Josh Anderson .30 .75
107 Kevin Fiala .30 .75
108 Carter Hart .40 1.00
109 Sergei Bobrovsky .60 1.50
110 Bryan Rust .40 1.00
111 William Nylander .75 2.00
112 Roope Hintz .50 1.25
113 Jacob Markstrom .40 1.00
114 Alex DeBrincat .50 1.25
115 Jared Spurgeon .40 1.00
116 Filip Hronek .25 .60
117 Devon Toews .30 .75
118 Victor Olofsson .40 1.00
119 Nick Schmaltz .30 .75
120 Alexandre Texier .25 .60
121 Quinn Hughes 1.00 2.50
122 Semyon Varlamov .40 1.00
123 Jordan Greenway .25 .60
124 Brent Burns .40 1.00
125 Andrei Svechnikov .50 1.25
126 Sean Monahan .25 .60
127 Tristan Jarry .40 1.00
128 Jonathan Quick .50 1.25
129 Alex Iafallo .25 .60
130 Mikhail Sergachev .30 .75
131 Anthony Beauvillier .25 .60
132 Zach Werenski .60 1.50
133 Rickard Rakell .30 .75
134 Connor Brown .30 .75
135 Brayden Schenn .40 1.00
136 Nino Niederreiter .25 .60
137 Drew Doughty .50 1.25
138 William Karlsson .50 1.25
139 Brady Tkachuk .60 1.50
140 Miro Heiskanen .50 1.25
141 Craig Smith .25 .60
142 Pavel Zacha .30 .75
143 Vincent Trocheck .40 1.00
144 Anthony Duclair .30 .75
145 Filip Zadina .30 .75
146 Tyson Jost .30 .75
147 Adam Pelech .25 .60
148 Jesse Puljujarvi .40 1.00
149 John Klingberg .40 1.00
150 Eeli Tolvanen .40 1.00
151 Jordan Kyrou .40 1.00
152 Colton Parayko .30 .75
153 Josh Bailey .30 .75
154 Timo Meier .40 1.00
155 Joe Pavelski .50 1.25
156 Jakob Chychrun .40 1.00
157 Oliver Bjorkstrand .30 .75
158 T.J. Oshie .40 1.00
159 Matt Grzelcyk .30 .75
160 Blake Wheeler .40 1.00
161 Gabriel Landeskog .50 1.25
162 Filip Forsberg .60 1.50
163 Marc-Edouard Vlasic .25 .60
164 Josh Norris .40 1.00
165 Andrew Copp .25 .60
166 Jack Hughes 1.00 2.50
167 Bo Horvat .50 1.25
168 Rasmus Dahlin .50 1.25
169 Morgan Rielly .40 1.00
170 Elias Lindholm .40 1.00
171 David Perron .30 .75
172 J.T. Miller .50 1.25
173 Logan Couture .50 1.25
174 Mackenzie Blackwood .40 1.00
175 Zach Hyman .60 1.50
176 Joe Thornton .60 1.50
177 Dougie Hamilton .30 .75
178 Alex Nedeljkovic .30 .75
179 Seth Jones .40 1.00
180 Marc-Andre Fleury .75 2.00
181 Tyler Toffoli .40 1.00
182 Roman Josi .40 1.00
183 Ryan Nugent-Hopkins .50 1.25
184 Mark Scheifele .60 1.50
185 Jonathan Marchessault .50 1.25
186 Nikolaj Ehlers .40 1.00
187 Mathew Barzal .50 1.25
188 Travis Konecny .40 1.00
189 John Carlson .40 1.00
190 John Tavares .60 1.50
191 Patrice Bergeron .50 1.25
192 Adam Erne .25 .60
193 Ryan O'Reilly .40 1.00
194 David Pastrnak 1.00 2.50
195 Aleksander Barkov .60 1.50
196 Elias Pettersson .60 1.50
197 Anze Kopitar .60 1.50
198 Matthew Tkachuk .75 2.00
199 Mitch Marner .60 1.50
200 Patrick Kane .75 2.00
201 Cole Caufield RC 4.00 10.00
202 Quinton Byfield RC 2.50 6.00
203 Trevor Zegras RC 2.00 5.00
204 Spencer Knight RC 2.00 5.00
205 Jeremy Swayman RC 3.00 8.00
206 Alex Newhook RC 1.50 4.00
207 Jamie Drysdale RC 1.50 4.00
208 Grigori Denisenko RC 1.25 3.00
209 Calen Addison RC 1.00 2.50
210 David Farrance RC 1.00 2.50
211 Zac Jones RC 1.25 3.00
212 Shane Pinto RC 1.50 4.00
213 Cam York RC 1.00 2.50
214 Ross Colton RC 1.25 3.00
215 Ukko-Pekka Luukkonen RC 1.50 4.00
216 Matthew Phillips RC 1.00 2.50
217 Joey Keane RC .75 2.00
218 Alex Barre-Boulet RC 1.00 2.50
219 Arttu Ruotsalainen RC 1.00 2.50
220 Tyce Thompson RC 1.00 2.50
221 Jacob Bryson RC 1.00 2.50
222 Mike Hardman RC 1.00 2.50
223 Wyatt Kalynuk RC 1.00 2.50
224 Sampo Ranta RC 1.00 2.50
225 Joe Veleno RC 1.25 3.00
226 Jesse Ylonen RC 1.00 2.50
227 Jacob Bernard-Docker RC 1.00 2.50
228 Kole Lind RC 1.25 3.00
229 Filip Gustavsson RC 2.00 5.00
230 Radim Zohorna RC 1.00 2.50
231 Morgan Barron RC .75 2.00
232 Rasmus Kupari RC 1.00 2.50
233 Wade Allison RC 1.00 2.50
234 Jan Jenik RC 1.25 3.00
235 Simon Benoit RC 1.00 2.50
236 Oskar Steen RC 1.25 3.00
237 Adam Ruzicka RC 1.00 2.50
238 Tanner Jeannot RC 1.00 2.50
239 Logan Thompson RC 2.50 6.00
240 Parker Kelly RC 1.00 2.50
241 Tarmo Reunanen RC 1.00 2.50
242 Dakota Joshua RC 1.00 2.50
243 Joshua Dunne RC 1.00 2.50
244 Tanner Laczynski RC 1.00 2.50
245 Brinson Pasichnuk RC 1.00 2.50
246 Jeffrey Viel RC 1.00 2.50
247 Jonah Gadjovich RC 1.00 2.50
248 William Lockwood RC 1.00 2.50
249 Brett Murray RC 1.00 2.50
250 Garrett Pilon RC 1.25 3.00
251 Marian Studenic RC 1.00 2.50
252 Jeremy Davies RC 1.00 2.50
253 Frederic Allard RC 1.00 2.50
254 Ivan Prosvetov RC 1.00 2.50
255 Matt Kiersted RC .75 2.00
256 Olle Alsing RC 1.00 2.50
257 Jackson Cates RC 1.00 2.50
258 Daniel Walcott RC 1.00 2.50
259 Jack Ahcan RC 1.00 2.50
260 Maksim Sushko RC 1.00 2.50
261 Keaton Middleton RC 1.00 2.50
262 Justin Richards RC 1.00 2.50
263 Kyle Burroughs RC 1.00 2.50
264 Mattias Samuelsson RC 1.00 2.50
265 Lane Pederson RC 1.00 2.50
266 Nils Lundkvist RC 1.00 2.50
267 Jake Leschyshyn RC 1.00 2.50
268 Jonathan Dahlen RC 1.00 2.50
269 Mason McTavish RC 2.00 5.00
270 Jasper Weatherby RC 1.00 2.50
271 Hendrix Lapierre RC 1.00 2.50
272 Taylor Raddysh RC 1.50 4.00
273 Benoit-Olivier Groulx RC 1.00 2.50
274 Pavel Dorofeyev RC 1.25 3.00
275 Boris Katchouk RC .75 2.00
276 Alex Turcotte RC 1.25 3.00
277 Jacob Peterson RC 1.00 2.50
278 Jake Neighbours RC 2.00 5.00
279 Maxwell Willman RC 1.00 2.50
280 Alexander Holtz RC 1.50 4.00
281 Karel Vejmelka RC 1.25 3.00
282 Dawson Mercer RC 2.50 6.00
283 Jonas Rondbjerg RC 1.00 2.50
284 Seth Jarvis RC 2.50 6.00
285 Cole Sillinger RC 1.50 4.00
286 Lucas Raymond RC 3.00 8.00
287 Moritz Seider RC 2.50 6.00
288 Scott Perunovich RC 1.00 2.50
289 Adam Beckman RC 1.00 2.50
290 Cole Perfetti RC 2.00 5.00
291 Riley Damiani RC 1.00 2.50
292 Philip Tomasino RC 1.25 3.00
293 Brandon Duhaime RC 1.00 2.50
294 Robin Salo RC 1.00 2.50
295 Lassi Thomson RC 1.00 2.50
296 Anton Lundell RC 2.00 5.00
297 Vasily Podkolzin RC 1.25 3.00
298 William Eklund RC 2.50 6.00
299 John-Jason Peterka RC 2.00 5.00
300 Thomas Novak RC 1.00 2.50

2021-22 O-Pee-Chee Platinum Arctic Freeze

*ARCTIC/99: 1.5X TO 4X BASIC
*ARCTIC RC/99: 1.2X TO 3X BASIC
1 Connor McDavid 30.00 80.00
201 Cole Caufield 80.00 200.00
202 Quinton Byfield 20.00 50.00
203 Trevor Zegras 60.00 150.00
204 Spencer Knight 15.00 40.00
205 Jeremy Swayman 25.00 60.00
286 Lucas Raymond 60.00 150.00
287 Moritz Seider 60.00 150.00

2021-22 O-Pee-Chee Platinum Blue Surge

*BLUE SURGE: .75X TO 2X BASIC
201 Cole Caufield 30.00 80.00

2021-22 O-Pee-Chee Platinum Cosmic

*COSMIC/65: 4X TO 10X BASIC
*COSMIC RC/65: 2X TO 5X BASIC
201 Cole Caufield 80.00 200.00
202 Quinton Byfield 25.00 60.00
203 Trevor Zegras 30.00 80.00
204 Spencer Knight 20.00 50.00
269 Mason McTavish 30.00 80.00
282 Dawson Mercer 20.00 50.00
284 Seth Jarvis 20.00 50.00
287 Moritz Seider 80.00 200.00
290 Cole Perfetti 20.00 50.00
298 William Eklund 25.00 60.00
299 John-Jason Peterka 20.00 50.00

2021-22 O-Pee-Chee Platinum Hot Magma

*HOT MAGMA/499: .75X TO 2X BASIC
1 Connor McDavid 12.00 30.00
201 Cole Caufield 40.00 100.00
203 Trevor Zegras 20.00 50.00
287 Moritz Seider 12.00 30.00

2021-22 O-Pee-Chee Platinum Matte Pink

*MATTE PINK: .6X TO 1.5X BASIC

2021-22 O-Pee-Chee Platinum Neon Yellow Surge

*NEON YLW SURGE: .75X TO 2X BASIC
201 Cole Caufield 30.00 80.00

2021-22 O-Pee-Chee Platinum Orange Checkers

*ORANGE/25: 8X TO 20X BASIC
*ORANGE RC/25: 4X TO 10X BASIC
1 Connor McDavid 300.00 800.00
203 Trevor Zegras 200.00 500.00
269 Mason McTavish 80.00 200.00
282 Dawson Mercer 100.00 250.00
284 Seth Jarvis 125.00 300.00
286 Lucas Raymond 250.00 600.00
287 Moritz Seider 250.00 600.00
290 Cole Perfetti 125.00 50.00
296 Anton Lundell 50.00 50.00
298 William Eklund 50.00 125.00
299 John-Jason Peterka 60.00 150.00

2021-22 O-Pee-Chee Platinum Rainbow

*RAINBOW: .5X TO 1.25X BASIC

2021-22 O-Pee-Chee Platinum Red Prism

*RED PRISM/199: 1.2X TO 3X BASIC
*RED PRISM RC/199: 1X TO 2.5X BASIC
1 Connor McDavid 25.00 60.00
201 Cole Caufield 50.00 125.00
203 Trevor Zegras 30.00 80.00
205 Jeremy Swayman 15.00 40.00
286 Lucas Raymond 30.00 80.00
287 Moritz Seider 30.00 80.00

2021-22 O-Pee-Chee Platinum Red Surge

*RED SURGE: .75X TO 2X BASIC
201 Cole Caufield 30.00 80.00

2021-22 O-Pee-Chee Platinum Seismic Gold

*SEISMIC GOLD/50: 5X TO 12X BASIC
*SEISMIC GOLD RC/50: 2.5X TO 6X BASIC
1 Connor McDavid 250.00 600.00
201 Cole Caufield 200.00 500.00
202 Quinton Byfield 60.00 150.00
203 Trevor Zegras 150.00 400.00
204 Spencer Knight 50.00 125.00
205 Jeremy Swayman 80.00 200.00
269 Mason McTavish 60.00 150.00
282 Dawson Mercer 80.00 200.00
284 Seth Jarvis 100.00 250.00
286 Lucas Raymond 200.00 500.00
287 Moritz Seider 200.00 500.00
290 Cole Perfetti 100.00 250.00
296 Anton Lundell 30.00 80.00
298 William Eklund 30.00 80.00
299 John-Jason Peterka 40.00 100.00

2021-22 O-Pee-Chee Platinum Sunset
*SUNSET: .6X TO 1.5X BASIC

2021-22 O-Pee-Chee Platinum Violet Pixels
*VIOLET/299: 1X TO 2.5X BASIC
1 Connor McDavid 20.00 50.00
201 Cole Caufield 50.00 125.00
203 Trevor Zegras 30.00 80.00
286 Lucas Raymond 15.00 40.00
287 Moritz Seider 30.00 80.00

2021-22 O-Pee-Chee Platinum Blue Rainbow Autographs
BAAL Anders Lee E 5.00 12.00
BAAT Alexandre Texier E 4.00 10.00
BABH Brandon Hagel E 5.00 12.00
BABJ Boone Jenner B 6.00 15.00
BABM Brad Marchand B 12.00 30.00
BABO Brock Boeser B 8.00 20.00
BABR Brayden Schenn C 6.00 15.00
BABS Bobby Smith A 6.00 15.00
BACA Cam Atkinson E 6.00 15.00
BACG Conor Garland D 5.00 12.00
BACM Casey Mittelstadt E 6.00 15.00
BACP Cal Petersen E 4.00 10.00
BADD Dick Duff B 6.00 15.00
BADS Dylan Strome D 8.00 20.00
BAGV Gabe Vilardi C 6.00 15.00
BAHO Nils Hoglander D 5.00 12.00
BAIL Isac Lundestrom C 4.00 10.00
BAJH Joel Hofer E 4.00 10.00
BAJK Joel Kiviranta E 4.00 10.00
BAJR Jack Roslovic E 4.00 10.00
BAJV Juuso Valimaki E 4.00 10.00
BAJZ Jakub Zboril E 4.00 10.00
BAKA Arthur Kaliyev E 6.00 15.00
BAKB Kieffer Bellows E 4.00 10.00
BAKK Keegan Kolesar E 4.00 10.00
BAKM K'Andre Miller E 5.00 12.00
BAKO Klim Kostin C 4.00 10.00
BAKP Kyle Palmieri E 5.00 12.00
BAKR Peyton Krebs E 5.00 12.00
BALF Liam Foudy E 5.00 12.00
BAMA Mason Appleton E 4.00 10.00
BAMC Connor McDavid A 200.00 500.00
BAMF Mario Ferraro D 4.00 10.00
BAMK Martin Kaut E 4.00 10.00
BAMM Matt Murray C 6.00 15.00
BAMN Martin Necas D 10.00 25.00
BAMS Mike Smith D 4.00 10.00
BANO Noah Hanifin E 4.00 10.00
BAPA Joe Pavelski E 8.00 20.00
BAPE Jeff Petry E 4.00 10.00
BAPF Peter Forsberg A 80.00 200.00
BAPJ Pierre-Olivier Joseph E 4.00 10.00
BAPN Patrik Nemeth E 4.00 10.00
BAPR Carey Price B 30.00 80.00
BAPS Pius Suter D 5.00 12.00
BARA Rasmus Asplund E 4.00 10.00
BARR Ryan Reaves E 5.00 12.00
BARS Ryan Suter D 5.00 12.00
BASL Steven Lorentz E 4.00 10.00
BATD Ty Dellandrea E 5.00 12.00
BATH Taylor Hall C 6.00 15.00
BATL Timothy Liljegren E 5.00 12.00
BATS Ty Smith E 6.00 15.00
BAVS Victor Soderstrom E 4.00 10.00
BAVV Vitek Vanecek E 6.00 15.00
BAYC Yvan Cournoyer B 6.00 15.00
BAYG Yanni Gourde C 5.00 12.00
BAYS Yegor Sharangovich E 6.00 15.00
BAZP Zach Parise C 6.00 15.00

2021-22 O-Pee-Chee Platinum Photo Driven
PD1 Patrice Bergeron .75 2.00
PD2 Alexis Lafreniere 1.00 2.50
PD3 Kris Letang .75 2.00
PD4 Brad Marchand 1.25 3.00
PD5 Jordan Binnington 1.00 2.50
PD6 Sebastian Aho 1.00 2.50
PD7 Nick Suzuki 1.25 3.00
PD8 Brock Boeser .75 2.00
PD9 Ryan O'Reilly .60 1.50
PD10 Alex DeBrincat .75 2.00
PD11 Spencer Knight 1.25 3.00
PD12 Trevor Zegras 1.25 3.00
PD13 Quinton Byfield 1.50 4.00
PD14 Alex Newhook 1.00 2.50
PD15 Jeremy Swayman 2.00 5.00

2021-22 O-Pee-Chee Platinum Photo Driven Rainbow Autographs
PD2 Alexis Lafreniere A 50.00 125.00
PD3 Kris Letang A 12.00 30.00
PD4 Brad Marchand A 25.00 60.00
PD7 Nick Suzuki B 50.00 125.00
PD8 Brock Boeser A 12.00 30.00
PD9 Ryan O'Reilly B 10.00 25.00
PD11 Spencer Knight A 40.00 100.00
PD13 Quinton Byfield A 50.00 125.00
PD14 Alex Newhook B 15.00 40.00
PD15 Jeremy Swayman B 60.00 150.00

2021-22 O-Pee-Chee Platinum Platinum Die Cuts
DC1 Connor McDavid 3.00 8.00
DC2 Patrick Kane 1.25 3.00
DC3 Auston Matthews 2.50 6.00
DC4 Sidney Crosby 2.50 6.00
DC5 Alex Ovechkin 2.50 6.00
DC6 David Pastrnak 1.50 4.00
DC7 Artemi Panarin 1.25 3.00
DC8 Alexis Lafreniere 1.00 2.50
DC9 Kirill Kaprizov 2.00 5.00
DC10 Quinn Hughes 1.50 4.00
DC12 Brad Marchand 1.25 3.00
DC13 Adam Fox .75 2.00
DC14 Anze Kopitar 1.00 2.50
DC15 Jonathan Huberdeau .75 2.00
DC16 Brock Boeser .75 2.00
DC17 Nick Suzuki 1.25 3.00
DC18 Miro Heiskanen .75 2.00
DC19 Andrei Svechnikov .75 2.00
DC20 Jason Robertson 1.00 2.50
DC21 Trevor Zegras 1.25 3.00
DC22 Cole Caufield 2.50 6.00
DC23 Quinton Byfield 1.50 4.00
DC24 Spencer Knight 1.25 3.00
DC25 Alex Newhook 1.00 2.50

2021-22 O-Pee-Chee Platinum Platinum Die Cuts Rainbow Autographs
DC8 Alexis Lafreniere D 15.00 40.00
DC12 Brad Marchand D 20.00 50.00
DC14 Anze Kopitar D 15.00 40.00
DC15 Jonathan Huberdeau D 12.00 30.00
DC16 Brock Boeser C 12.00 30.00
DC17 Nick Suzuki D 20.00 50.00
DC18 Miro Heiskanen D 12.00 30.00
DC19 Andrei Svechnikov D 12.00 30.00
DC23 Quinton Byfield C 25.00 60.00
DC24 Spencer Knight D 20.00 50.00
DC25 Alex Newhook D 15.00 40.00

2021-22 O-Pee-Chee Platinum Retro
*RAINBOW: .6X TO 1.5X BASIC
*BLUE/199: 1.2X TO 3X BASIC
*PINK: 2X TO 5X BASIC
R1 Connor McDavid 5.00 12.00
R2 Kris Letang 1.25 3.00
R3 Auston Matthews 4.00 10.00
R4 Patrick Kane 2.00 5.00
R5 Elias Pettersson 1.50 4.00
R6 Jeff Petry 1.00 2.50
R7 Bryan Rust 1.00 2.50
R8 Alex Ovechkin 4.00 10.00
R9 Sidney Crosby 4.00 10.00
R10 Oliver Bjorkstrand .75 2.00
R11 Josh Anderson .75 2.00
R12 Igor Shesterkin 2.00 5.00
R13 Artemi Panarin 2.00 5.00
R14 Quinn Hughes 2.50 6.00
R15 Jordan Kyrou 1.00 2.50
R16 Nick Suzuki 2.00 5.00
R17 Alex DeBrincat 1.25 3.00
R18 Nikita Kucherov 2.00 5.00
R19 Mark Scheifele 1.50 4.00
R20 Carter Hart 1.00 2.50
R21 Tim Stutzle 1.25 3.00
R22 Maxime Comtois .75 2.00
R23 Nathan MacKinnon 4.00 10.00
R24 Sebastian Aho 1.50 4.00
R25 Mikko Rantanen 2.50 6.00
R26 Tyler Bertuzzi .75 2.00
R27 Carter Verhaeghe 1.00 2.50
R28 Juuse Saros 1.25 3.00
R29 Oliver Wahlstrom .60 1.50
R30 Mathew Barzal 1.25 3.00
R31 Taylor Hall 1.00 2.50
R32 Drake Batherson 1.00 2.50
R33 Kevin Fiala .75 2.00
R34 Andrei Svechnikov 1.25 3.00
R35 Jack Hughes 2.50 6.00
R36 Joel Farabee 1.00 2.50
R37 Jason Robertson 1.50 4.00
R38 William Karlsson 1.25 3.00
R39 Patrik Laine 1.25 3.00
R40 Mike Smith .60 1.50
R41 Connor Hellebuyck 2.00 5.00
R42 Jake Guentzel 1.50 4.00
R43 Roope Hintz 1.25 3.00
R44 Ryan Nugent-Hopkins 1.25 3.00
R45 Filip Hronek .60 1.50
R46 Roman Josi 1.50 4.00
R47 Casey Mittelstadt 1.00 2.50
R48 John Carlson 1.00 2.50
R49 Kirill Kaprizov 3.00 8.00
R50 Jordan Binnington 1.00 2.50
R51 Mitch Marner 1.50 4.00
R52 Conor Garland .75 2.00
R53 Jonathan Toews 1.50 4.00
R54 Carey Price 2.00 5.00
R55 Evgeni Malkin 2.00 5.00
R56 John Tavares 1.50 4.00
R57 Patrice Bergeron 1.25 3.00
R58 David Pastrnak 2.50 6.00
R59 Cale Makar 2.50 6.00
R60 Leon Draisaitl 3.00 8.00
R61 Alexis Lafreniere 1.50 4.00
R62 Ty Smith 1.00 2.50
R63 Nick Robertson 1.00 2.50
R64 Jonathan Marchessault 1.25 3.00
R65 Jakob Chychrun 1.00 2.50
R66 Trevor Zegras 2.00 5.00
R67 Cole Caufield 4.00 10.00
R68 Quinton Byfield 2.50 6.00
R69 Spencer Knight 2.00 5.00
R70 Jeremy Swayman 3.00 8.00
R71 Alex Newhook 2.00 5.00
R72 Jamie Drysdale 1.50 4.00
R73 Calen Addison 1.00 2.50
R74 Grigori Denisenko 1.25 3.00
R75 Ross Colton 1.25 3.00
R76 Zac Jones 1.25 3.00
R77 David Farrance 1.00 2.50
R78 Filip Gustavsson 2.00 5.00
R79 Arttu Ruotsalainen 1.00 2.50
R80 Jacob Bernard-Docker 1.00 2.50
R81 Joe Veleno 1.25 3.00
R82 Ukko-Pekka Luukkonen 1.50 4.00
R83 Cam York 1.00 2.50
R84 Shane Pinto 1.50 4.00
R85 Ivan Prosvetov 1.00 2.50
R86 Rasmus Kupari 1.00 2.50
R87 Jesse Ylonen 1.00 2.50
R88 Morgan Barron .75 2.00
R89 Tyce Thompson 1.00 2.50
R90 Sampo Ranta 1.00 2.50
R91 Mike Hardman 1.00 2.50
R92 Wade Allison 1.00 2.50
R93 Wyatt Kalynuk 1.00 2.50
R94 Garrett Pilon 1.25 3.00
R95 Jack Ahcan 1.00 2.50
R96 Lucas Raymond 3.00 8.00
R97 Moritz Seider 2.50 6.00
R98 Anton Lundell 2.00 5.00
R99 Alexander Holtz 1.50 4.00
R100 Scott Perunovich 1.00 2.50

2021-22 O-Pee-Chee Platinum Retro Rainbow Red Autographs
R2 Kris Letang D 12.00 30.00
R6 Jeff Petry E 10.00 25.00
R16 Nick Suzuki D 20.00 50.00
R21 Tim Stutzle C 60.00 150.00
R26 Tyler Bertuzzi E 8.00 20.00
R31 Taylor Hall D 10.00 25.00
R33 Kevin Fiala D 8.00 20.00
R34 Andrei Svechnikov D 12.00 30.00
R38 William Karlsson C 12.00 30.00
R40 Mike Smith E 6.00 15.00
R41 Connor Hellebuyck D 20.00 50.00
R42 Jake Guentzel D 15.00 40.00
R43 Roope Hintz E 12.00 30.00
R45 Filip Hronek E 6.00 15.00
R46 Roman Josi C 10.00 25.00
R47 Casey Mittelstadt E 10.00 25.00
R54 Carey Price B 20.00 50.00
R56 John Tavares B 15.00 40.00
R59 Cale Makar C 25.00 60.00
R60 Leon Draisaitl B 30.00 80.00
R64 Jonathan Marchessault C 12.00 30.00
R68 Quinton Byfield B 80.00 200.00
R69 Spencer Knight B 20.00 50.00
R70 Jeremy Swayman D 40.00 100.00
R71 Alex Newhook B 15.00 40.00
R72 Jamie Drysdale C 15.00 40.00
R73 Calen Addison D 10.00 25.00
R74 Grigori Denisenko C 12.00 30.00
R75 Ross Colton D 12.00 30.00
R76 Zac Jones D 12.00 30.00
R78 Filip Gustavsson D 20.00 50.00
R80 Jacob Bernard-Docker D 10.00 25.00
R81 Joe Veleno D 12.00 30.00
R82 Ukko-Pekka Luukkonen D 15.00 40.00
R84 Shane Pinto D 15.00 40.00
R85 Ivan Prosvetov D 10.00 25.00
R86 Rasmus Kupari D 10.00 25.00
R87 Jesse Ylonen D 10.00 25.00
R88 Morgan Barron C 8.00 20.00
R89 Tyce Thompson D 10.00 25.00
R90 Sampo Ranta D 8.00 20.00
R93 Wyatt Kalynuk D 10.00 25.00
R94 Garrett Pilon D 12.00 30.00
R95 Jack Ahcan D 8.00 20.00
R98 Anton Lundell C 20.00 50.00
R99 Alexander Holtz B 15.00 40.00
R100 Scott Perunovich D 10.00 25.00

2021-22 O-Pee-Chee Platinum Rookie Autographs
*COSMIC: 1.2X TO 3X BASIC
RAB Alex Barre-Boulet E 8.00 20.00
RAD Adam Beckman E 8.00 20.00
RAH Alexander Holtz C 12.00 30.00
RAL Anton Lundell B 15.00 40.00
RAN Alex Newhook D 12.00 30.00
RAP Aliaksei Protas E 8.00 20.00
RAT Alex Turcotte B 10.00 25.00
RBE Jacob Bernard-Docker D 8.00 20.00
RBK Boris Katchouk D 6.00 15.00
RBL Brett Leason B 8.00 20.00
RCA Calen Addison C 8.00 20.00
RCC Cole Caufield A 80.00 200.00
RCP Cole Perfetti B 15.00 40.00
RCS Cole Sillinger C 12.00 30.00
RDM Dawson Mercer C 20.00 50.00
RES Egor Sokolov E 8.00 20.00
RFG Filip Gustavsson D 15.00 40.00
RGD Grigori Denisenko B 10.00 25.00
RGP Garrett Pilon E 10.00 25.00
RHL Hendrix Lapierre D 8.00 20.00
RIP Ivan Prosvetov B 8.00 20.00
RJA Jack Ahcan E 8.00 20.00
RJB Jacob Bryson E 8.00 20.00
RJD Jamie Drysdale B 12.00 30.00
RJJ Jan Jenik E 10.00 25.00
RJL Jake Leschyshyn B 8.00 20.00
RJN Jake Neighbours D 15.00 40.00
RJS Jeremy Swayman C 25.00 60.00
RJV Joe Veleno E 10.00 25.00
RJY Jesse Ylonen E 8.00 20.00
RKL Kole Lind E 10.00 25.00
RLP Lane Pederson C 8.00 20.00
RLT Logan Thompson E 20.00 50.00
RMB Morgan Barron C 6.00 15.00
RMM Mason McTavish A 15.00 40.00
RMS Mattias Samuelsson D 8.00 20.00
RNL Nils Lundkvist D 8.00 20.00
ROS Oskar Steen E 10.00 25.00
RPC Paul Cotter D 8.00 20.00
RPD Pavel Dorofeyev E 10.00 25.00
RPE Scott Perunovich E 8.00 20.00
RPJ John-Jason Peterka B 15.00 40.00
RPK Parker Kelly E 8.00 20.00
RPT Philip Tomasino D 10.00 25.00
RQB Quinton Byfield B 20.00 50.00
RRC Ross Colton D 8.00 20.00
RRK Rasmus Kupari C 8.00 20.00
RRM Ryan Merkley E 8.00 20.00
RRZ Radim Zohorna D 8.00 20.00
RSA Robin Salo B 8.00 20.00
RSE Moritz Seider B 20.00 50.00
RSJ Seth Jarvis C 20.00 50.00
RSK Spencer Knight C 15.00 40.00
RSP Shane Pinto D 12.00 30.00
RSR Sampo Ranta D 8.00 20.00
RTL Tanner Laczynski E 8.00 20.00
RTR Taylor Raddysh E 12.00 30.00
RTT Tyce Thompson E 8.00 20.00
RTZ Trevor Zegras B 60.00 150.00
RUL Ukko-Pekka Luukkonen E 12.00 30.00
RVP Vasily Podkolzin B 10.00 25.00
RWE William Eklund D 10.00 25.00
RWK Wyatt Kalynuk D 8.00 20.00
RZJ Zac Jones D 10.00 25.00

2021-22 O-Pee-Chee Platinum Rookie Autographs Blue Traxx
*BLUE: .6X TO 1.5X BASIC
RTZ Trevor Zegras A 150.00 400.00

2021-22 O-Pee-Chee Platinum Rookie Autographs Matte Pink
*PINK: 1X TO 2.5X BASIC
RCC Cole Caufield A 300.00 800.00
RSE Moritz Seider A 125.00 300.00
RTZ Trevor Zegras A 200.00 500.00

2021-22 O-Pee-Chee Platinum Rookie Autographs Rainbow
*RAINBOW: .5X TO 1.2X BASIC
RCC Cole Caufield A 200.00 500.00

2021-22 O-Pee-Chee Platinum Rookie Autographs Red Prism
*RED: .75X TO 2X BASIC
RJS Jeremy Swayman 60.00 150.00
RSE Moritz Seider 250.00 600.00
RSK Spencer Knight 80.00 200.00
RTZ Trevor Zegras 300.00 800.00

2021-22 O-Pee-Chee Platinum Rookie Autographs Seismic Gold
*SEISMIC GOLD: 1X TO 2.5X BASIC
RAH Alexander Holtz 125.00 300.00
RSK Spencer Knight 150.00 400.00
RWE William Eklund 100.00 250.00

2021-22 O-Pee-Chee Platinum Rookie Autographs Violet Pixels
*VIOLET: .75X TO 2X BASIC
RCC Cole Caufield A 250.00 600.00
RSE Moritz Seider A 100.00 250.00
RTZ Trevor Zegras A 150.00 400.00

2021-22 O-Pee-Chee Platinum Sweet Selections
SS1 Alex Newhook 1.00 2.50
SS2 Jeremy Swayman 2.00 5.00
SS3 Cole Caufield 2.50 6.00
SS4 Jamie Drysdale 1.00 2.50
SS5 Spencer Knight 1.25 3.00
SS6 Calen Addison .60 1.50
SS7 Quinton Byfield 1.50 4.00
SS8 Alex Barre-Boulet .60 1.50
SS9 Grigori Denisenko .75 2.00
SS10 Filip Gustavsson 1.25 3.00
SS11 Matthew Phillips .60 1.50
SS12 Arttu Ruotsalainen .60 1.50
SS13 Cam York .60 1.50
SS14 Joe Veleno .75 2.00
SS15 Ross Colton .75 2.00

2021-22 O-Pee-Chee Platinum Sweet Selections Rainbow Autographs
SS1 Alex Newhook 15.00 40.00
SS2 Jeremy Swayman 30.00 80.00
SS3 Cole Caufield 40.00 100.00
SS4 Jamie Drysdale 15.00 40.00
SS5 Spencer Knight 20.00 50.00
SS6 Calen Addison 10.00 25.00
SS7 Quinton Byfield 25.00 60.00
SS9 Grigori Denisenko 12.00 30.00
SS10 Filip Gustavsson 20.00 50.00
SS14 Joe Veleno 12.00 30.00
SS15 Ross Colton 12.00 30.00

2022-23 O-Pee-Chee Platinum
1 Trevor Zegras .40 1.00
2 Alex DeBrincat .50 1.25
3 Kirill Kaprizov 1.25 3.00
4 Leon Draisaitl 1.25 3.00
5 Michael Bunting .40 1.00
6 Nazem Kadri .50 1.25
7 David Pastrnak 1.00 2.50
8 Alex Ovechkin 1.50 4.00
9 Tyler Toffoli .40 1.00
10 Jake Guentzel .60 1.50
11 Steven Stamkos .75 2.00
12 Jordan Kyrou .40 1.00
13 Anton Lundell .40 1.00
14 Sebastian Aho .60 1.50
15 Brad Marchand .75 2.00
16 Igor Shesterkin .75 2.00
17 Nathan MacKinnon 1.50 4.00
18 Patrick Kane .75 2.00
19 Anze Kopitar .60 1.50
20 Elias Pettersson .60 1.50
21 Brent Burns .40 1.00
22 Brendan Gallagher .40 1.00
23 Jordan Eberle .40 1.00
24 Jack Hughes 1.00 2.50
25 Joel Farabee .40 1.00
26 Clayton Keller .50 1.25
27 Ryan Johansen .30 .75
28 Moritz Seider .50 1.25
29 Cale Makar 1.00 2.50
30 Jean-Gabriel Pageau .25 .60
31 Mark Scheifele .60 1.50
32 Alexander Wennberg .25 .60
33 Mats Zuccarello .40 1.00
34 Auston Matthews 1.50 4.00
35 Andrei Svechnikov .50 1.25
36 Patrik Laine .50 1.25
37 Alexis Lafreniere .60 1.50
38 Nico Hischier .60 1.50
39 Andrei Vasilevskiy .60 1.50
40 Tanner Jeannot .25 .60
41 Jonathan Marchessault .50 1.25
42 Logan Couture .50 1.25
43 Taylor Hall .40 1.00
44 Conor Garland .30 .75
45 Spencer Knight .40 1.00
46 Travis Konecny .40 1.00
47 Pierre-Luc Dubois .30 .75
48 Joe Pavelski .50 1.25
49 Brock Nelson .40 1.00
50 Peyton Krebs .30 .75
51 Ilya Sorokin .60 1.50
52 Mark Stone .50 1.25
53 Philipp Grubauer .40 1.00
54 Petr Mrazek .30 .75
55 Tyler Bertuzzi .30 .75
56 John Tavares .60 1.50
57 Ryan Hartman .25 .60
58 John Carlson .40 1.00
59 Alex Tuch .40 1.00
60 Mike Hoffman .25 .60
61 Jacob Slavin .30 .75
62 Tim Stutzle .50 1.25
63 Mike Smith .25 .60
64 Kyle Connor .60 1.50
65 Artemi Panarin .75 2.00
66 Ivan Provorov .30 .75
67 Jonathan Huberdeau .50 1.25
68 Quinton Byfield .50 1.25
69 Kirby Dach .40 1.00
70 Dougie Hamilton .30 .75
71 Matt Duchene .40 1.00
72 Chandler Stephenson .30 .75
73 Jeff Skinner .40 1.00
74 Tomas Hertl .40 1.00
75 Miro Heiskanen .50 1.25
76 Quinn Hughes 1.00 2.50
77 Jamie Drysdale .30 .75
78 Elias Lindholm .40 1.00
79 Drew Doughty .50 1.25
80 Dylan Larkin .50 1.25
81 Troy Terry .30 .75
82 Torey Krug .30 .75
83 Shayne Gostisbehere .40 1.00
84 Nikita Kucherov .75 2.00
85 Jakub Voracek .30 .75
86 Johnny Gaudreau .60 1.50
87 Sidney Crosby 1.50 4.00
88 Jason Robertson .60 1.50
89 Vladimir Tarasenko .50 1.25
90 Zach Werenski .60 1.50
91 Josh Anderson .30 .75
92 Claude Giroux .40 1.00
93 Vasily Podkolzin .25 .60
94 Kasperi Kapanen .30 .75
95 Alex Newhook .30 .75
96 Sam Reinhart .75 2.00
97 Connor McDavid 2.00 5.00
98 Tom Wilson .40 1.00
99 Adrian Kempe .40 1.00
100 Evgeni Malkin .75 2.00
101 Mitch Marner .60 1.50
102 Noah Dobson .50 1.25
103 Brandon Hagel .30 .75
104 Oliver Wahlstrom .25 .60
105 Dylan Cozens .40 1.00
106 Jesper Bratt .40 1.00
107 Oliver Bjorkstrand .30 .75
108 Brock Boeser .50 1.25
109 Jack Eichel .60 1.50
110 Drake Batherson .40 1.00
111 Adam Fox .50 1.25
112 Morgan Rielly .40 1.00
113 Charlie Coyle .40 1.00
114 Vitek Vanecek .40 1.00
115 Zach Hyman .60 1.50
116 Seth Jarvis .50 1.25
117 Gabriel Landeskog .50 1.25
118 Filip Forsberg .60 1.50
119 Isac Lundestrom .25 .60
120 Nikolaj Ehlers .40 1.00
121 Phillip Danault .40 1.00
122 Nick Suzuki .75 2.00
123 Mikhail Sergachev .30 .75
124 Blake Coleman .30 .75
125 Jamie Benn .40 1.00
126 William Karlsson .40 1.00
127 Mathew Barzal .50 1.25
128 John Gibson .40 1.00
129 Evgeny Kuznetsov .50 1.25
130 Philipp Kurashev .30 .75
131 Alexander Barabanov .25 .60
132 Tage Thompson .50 1.25
133 Ryan O'Reilly .40 1.00
134 Victor Hedman .60 1.50
135 Tristan Jarry .40 1.00
136 Boone Jenner .40 1.00
137 Sonny Milano .30 .75
138 Blake Wheeler .40 1.00
139 William Nylander .75 2.00
140 Matthew Tkachuk .75 2.00
141 Dawson Mercer .50 1.25
142 Chris Kreider .50 1.25
143 Ryan Nugent-Hopkins .75 2.00
144 Cole Caufield .75 2.00
145 Phil Kessel .40 1.00
146 Patrice Bergeron .50 1.25
147 Elvis Merzlikins .50 1.25
148 Josh Norris .40 1.00
149 Martin Necas .50 1.25
150 Connor Hellebuyck .75 2.00
151 Alex Iafallo .25 .60
152 Roman Josi .40 1.00
153 Jakob Markstrom .40 1.00
154 Erik Karlsson .50 1.25
155 Jonathan Toews .60 1.50
156 Robert Thomas .60 1.50
157 Yegor Sharangovich .40 1.00
158 Aleksander Barkov .60 1.50
159 Linus Ullmark .40 1.00
160 Jeremy Swayman .60 1.50
161 Nicklas Backstrom .40 1.00
162 Sean Couturier .30 .75
163 Samuel Girard .25 .60
164 Brayden Point .50 1.25
165 Alex Nedeljkovic .30 .75
166 Mika Zibanejad .50 1.25
167 Tyler Seguin .25 .60
168 Jared McCann .30 .75
169 Lucas Raymond .60 1.50
170 Joel Eriksson Ek .30 .75
171 Gabe Vilardi .40 1.00
172 Jason Zucker .40 1.00
173 Rasmus Dahlin .50 1.25
174 Thomas Chabot .40 1.00
175 Aaron Ekblad .50 1.25
176 Pavel Buchnevich .30 .75
177 Juuse Saros .50 1.25
178 John Marino .40 1.00
179 Mikko Rantanen 1.00 2.50
180 Nick Schmaltz .30 .75
181 Kevin Fiala .30 .75
182 Anders Lee .30 .75
183 Max Pacioretty .40 1.00
184 Teuvo Teravainen .40 1.00
185 J.T. Miller .50 1.25
186 Tyson Barrie .25 .60
187 Connor Brown .30 .75
188 Yanni Gourde .30 .75
189 Roope Hintz .50 1.25
190 Cam Atkinson .40 1.00
191 Sergei Bobrovsky .60 1.50
192 Jared Spurgeon .40 1.00
193 Timo Meier .40 1.00
194 Filip Hronek .25 .60
195 Brady Tkachuk .60 1.50
196 Bo Horvat .50 1.25
197 Nick Robertson .40 1.00
198 Max Domi .40 1.00
199 Anthony Cirelli .30 .75
200 Marc-Andre Fleury .75 2.00
201 Owen Power RC 2.00 5.00
202 Matt Boldy RC 3.00 8.00
203 Matty Beniers RC 2.50 6.00
204 Jack Quinn RC 1.50 4.00
205 Lukas Reichel RC 2.00 5.00
206 Kent Johnson RC 2.00 5.00
207 Dylan Holloway RC 2.00 5.00
208 Marco Rossi RC 2.50 6.00
209 Jacob Perreault RC 1.00 2.50
210 Lukas Dostal RC 2.00 5.00
211 Samuel Fagemo RC .75 2.00
212 Braden Schneider RC 1.50 4.00
213 Brayden Tracey RC .75 2.00
214 Hunter Drew RC 1.00 2.50
215 Nathan Smith RC .75 2.00
216 Jack McBain RC 1.00 2.50
217 Filip Hallander RC 1.00 2.50
218 Isaac Ratcliffe RC 1.00 2.50
219 Bobby Brink RC 1.00 2.50
220 Dylan Samberg RC 1.00 2.50
221 Vladislav Kolyachonok RC .75 2.00
222 Trey Fix-Wolansky RC 1.00 2.50
223 Reilly Walsh RC 1.00 2.50
224 Pyotr Kochetkov RC 2.00 5.00
225 Jordan Harris RC 1.25 3.00
226 Mark Kastelic RC .75 2.00
227 Thomas Bordeleau RC 1.00 2.50
228 Mads Sogaard RC 1.25 3.00
229 Nick Abruzzese RC 1.00 2.50
230 Zack Hayes RC .75 2.00
231 Michael Eyssimont RC 1.00 2.50
232 Marc McLaughlin RC 1.00 2.50
233 Matias Maccelli RC 1.50 4.00
234 Jordan Spence RC 1.00 2.50
235 Alex Vlasic RC .75 2.00
236 Erik Kallgren RC 1.00 2.50
237 Kaedan Korczak RC .75 2.00
238 Chase Pearson RC .75 2.00
239 Noah Cates RC 1.00 2.50
240 Ronnie Attard RC 1.00 2.50
241 Bokondji Imama RC .75 2.00
242 Viktor Lodin RC 1.00 2.50
243 Ben Meyers RC 1.00 2.50
244 Fredrik Karlstrom RC .75 2.00
245 Jeff Malott RC 1.00 2.50
246 Brandon Biro RC 1.50 4.00
247 Cole Reinhardt RC 1.00 2.50
248 Mitchell Chaffee RC .75 2.00
249 Carson Meyer RC .75 2.00
250 Hayden Hodgson RC .75 2.00
251 Linus Sandin RC .75 2.00
252 Valtteri Puustinen RC .75 2.00
253 Jakub Galvas RC 1.00 2.50
254 Jake Christiansen RC 1.00 2.50
255 Johnathan Kovacevic RC 1.00 2.50
256 Nikita Okhotiuk RC .75 2.00
257 Linus Hogberg RC .75 2.00
258 Brayden Pachal RC .75 2.00
259 Declan Chisholm RC 1.00 2.50
260 Jacob Moverare RC .75 2.00
261 Marcus Bjork RC 1.00 2.50
262 Matej Blumel RC 1.25 3.00
263 Juuso Parssinen RC 1.00 2.50
264 Nikita Alexandrov RC 1.00 2.50
265 Pontus Holmberg RC 1.00 2.50
266 Nick Blankenburg RC 1.00 2.50
267 Nick Perbix RC .75 2.00
268 Oskar Olausson RC 1.00 2.50
269 Lucas Johansen RC .75 2.00
270 Simon Holmstrom RC 1.00 2.50
271 Adam Raska RC 1.00 2.50
272 Nick DeSimone RC 1.00 2.50
273 Mac Hollowell RC 1.00 2.50
274 Nick Cicek RC 1.00 2.50
275 William Bitten RC 1.00 2.50
276 James Hamblin RC 1.00 2.50
277 Jean-Luc Foudy RC 1.00 2.50
278 Tyler Tucker RC 1.00 2.50
279 Dylan Wells RC 1.00 2.50
280 Aatu Raty RC 1.00 2.50
281 Filip Roos RC .75 2.00
282 Filip Kral RC 1.25 3.00
283 Pavol Regenda RC 1.00 2.50
284 Cole Koepke RC 1.00 2.50
285 Olle Lycksell RC 1.00 2.50
286 Nils Aman RC 1.00 2.50
287 Jonatan Berggren RC 1.50 4.00
288 Samuel Poulin RC 1.25 3.00
289 Jakub Lauko RC 1.25 3.00
290 Arber Xhekaj RC 2.00 5.00
291 Elmer Soderblom RC 2.00 5.00
292 Kaiden Guhle RC 2.00 5.00
293 David Jiricek RC 2.00 5.00
294 Wyatt Johnston RC 4.00 10.00
295 Andrei Kuzmenko RC 2.00 5.00
296 Brandt Clarke RC 2.00 5.00
297 Jake Sanderson RC 2.50 6.00
298 Dylan Guenther RC 2.50 6.00
299 Juraj Slafkovsky RC 5.00 12.00
300 Shane Wright RC 2.50 6.00

2022-23 O-Pee-Chee Platinum Aquamarine
*AQUAMRN/149: 1.2X TO 3X BASIC

2022-23 O-Pee-Chee Platinum Arctic Freeze
*ARCTIC/99: 1.5X TO 4X BASIC
*ARCTIC RC/99: 1.2X TO 3X BASIC

2022-23 O-Pee-Chee Platinum Cosmic
*COSMIC/65: 4X TO 10X BASIC
*COSMIC RC/65: 2.5X TO 6X BASIC
203 Matty Beniers 30.00 80.00
294 Wyatt Johnston 80.00 200.00
297 Jake Sanderson 20.00 50.00

2022-23 O-Pee-Chee Platinum Hot Magma
*HT MGMA/499: .75X TO 2X BASIC

2022-23 O-Pee-Chee Platinum Liquid Metal
*LQD MTL/349: 1X TO 2.5X BASIC

2022-23 O-Pee-Chee Platinum Matte Pink
*MATTE PINK: .6X TO 1.5X BASIC

2022-23 O-Pee-Chee Platinum Neon Yellow Surge
*NEON YLW: .75X TO 2X BASIC

2022-23 O-Pee-Chee Platinum Pond Hockey
*POND HKY: 6X TO 15X BASIC

2022-23 O-Pee-Chee Platinum Rainbow
*RAINBOW: .5X TO 1.2X BASIC

2022-23 O-Pee-Chee Platinum Red Prism
*RED/199: 1.2X TO 3X BASIC
*RED RC/199: 1X TO 2.5X BASIC

2022-23 O-Pee-Chee Platinum Sunset
*SUNSET: .6X TO 1.5X BASIC

2022-23 O-Pee-Chee Platinum Violet Pixels
*VIOLET/299: 1X TO 2.5X BASIC

2022-23 O-Pee-Chee Platinum Blue Rainbow Autographs
BAAE Aaron Ekblad SP 10.00 25.00
BAAF Alex Formenton 6.00 15.00
BAAL Anders Lee 6.00 15.00
BAAM Auston Matthews SP 125.00 300.00
BAAN Alex Nedeljkovic 6.00 15.00
BAAV Andrei Vasilevskiy SP 12.00 30.00
BABC Blake Coleman 6.00 15.00
BABG Brendan Gallagher 8.00 20.00
BABM Brad Marchand SP 15.00 40.00
BABS Brandon Saad 6.00 15.00
BACA Cayden Primeau 6.00 15.00
BACM Cale Makar SP 60.00 150.00
BADB Drake Batherson 8.00 20.00
BADC Dylan Cozens 8.00 20.00
BADK Darcy Kuemper 8.00 20.00
BADP David Perron 6.00 15.00
BAEB Evan Bouchard 10.00 25.00
BAEM Elvis Merzlikins 8.00 20.00
BAFO Marcus Foligno 6.00 15.00
BAHA Brandon Hagel 6.00 15.00
BAHE Tomas Hertl 8.00 20.00
BAHU Jonathan Huberdeau 10.00 25.00
BAIL Isac Lundestrom 5.00 12.00
BAIP Ivan Prosvetov 5.00 12.00
BAJB Josh Bailey 6.00 15.00
BAJG John Gibson 8.00 20.00
BAJH Jani Hakanpaa 6.00 15.00
BAJK Joel Kiviranta 5.00 12.00
BAJM John Marino 8.00 20.00
BAJN Josh Norris 8.00 20.00
BAJP Jeff Petry 8.00 20.00
BAJS Jaccob Slavin 6.00 15.00
BAJV James van Riemsdyk 6.00 15.00
BAKB Kasper Bjorkqvist 5.00 12.00
BAKD Kirby Dach 8.00 20.00
BAKF Kevin Fiala 6.00 15.00
BAKK Keegan Kolesar 5.00 12.00
BAKV Karel Vejmelka 5.00 12.00
BALI Kole Lind 5.00 12.00
BAMA Jacob Markstrom 8.00 20.00
BAMB Morgan Barron SP 5.00 12.00
BAMC Connor McDavid SP 200.00 500.00
BAMF Marc-Andre Fleury SP 15.00 40.00
BAMK Martin Kaut 5.00 12.00
BAMM Mason McTavish 8.00 20.00
BAMP Matthew Phillips 5.00 12.00
BANA Nicolas Aube-Kubel 5.00 12.00
BANE Alex Newhook 6.00 15.00
BANH Nils Hoglander 6.00 15.00
BANM Nick Merkley 5.00 12.00
BANO Noah Hanifin 8.00 20.00
BAPJ Pierre-Olivier Joseph 5.00 12.00
BAPR Carey Price SP 30.00 80.00
BAPS Pius Suter 6.00 15.00
BARD Riley Damiani 5.00 12.00
BARF Robby Fabbri 5.00 12.00
BARK Rasmus Kupari 5.00 12.00
BARL Robin Lehner 6.00 15.00
BARS Ryan Strome 8.00 20.00
BART Robert Thomas 8.00 20.00
BASJ Seth Jarvis 10.00 25.00
BASK Spencer Knight 8.00 20.00
BASM Sonny Milano 6.00 15.00
BASW Jeremy Swayman 30.00 80.00
BATH Thomas Harley 8.00 20.00
BATJ Tristan Jarry 8.00 20.00
BATL Timothy Liljegren 5.00 12.00
BATT Tage Thompson 10.00 25.00
BAVS Victor Soderstrom 5.00 12.00
BAZW Zach Werenski 12.00 30.00

2022-23 O-Pee-Chee Platinum Galvanized
G1 Connor McDavid 5.00 12.00
G2 Auston Matthews 4.00 10.00
G3 Leon Draisaitl 3.00 8.00
G4 Gabriel Landeskog 1.25 3.00
G5 Victor Hedman 1.25 3.00
G6 Taylor Hall 1.00 2.50
G7 Sebastian Aho 1.50 4.00
G8 Joe Pavelski 1.25 3.00
G9 Miro Heiskanen 1.25 3.00
G10 John Gibson 1.00 2.50
G11 Michael Bunting 1.00 2.50
G12 Kris Letang 1.25 3.00
G13 Lucas Raymond 1.50 4.00
G14 Seth Jarvis 1.25 3.00
G15 Jeremy Swayman 1.50 4.00
G16 Trevor Zegras 1.00 2.50
G17 Jordan Kyrou 1.00 2.50
G18 Clayton Keller 1.25 3.00
G19 Tage Thompson 1.25 3.00
G20 Cale Makar 2.50 6.00
G21 Alex Ovechkin 4.00 10.00
G22 Dylan Holloway 2.00 5.00

G23 Braden Schneider 1.50 4.00
G24 Lukas Dostal 2.00 5.00
G25 Kent Johnson 2.00 5.00

2022-23 O-Pee-Chee Platinum OPC Premier

OP1 Trevor Zegras 1.50 4.00
OP2 Kirill Kaprizov 5.00 12.00
OP3 Leon Draisaitl 5.00 12.00
OP4 Alex Ovechkin 6.00 15.00
OP5 Patrick Kane 3.00 8.00
OP6 Nathan MacKinnon 6.00 15.00
OP7 Cale Makar 4.00 10.00
OP8 Brad Marchand 3.00 8.00
OP9 Mitch Marner 2.50 6.00
OP10 Andrei Svechnikov 2.00 5.00
OP11 Jason Robertson 2.50 6.00
OP12 Jack Hughes 4.00 10.00
OP14 Andrei Vasilevskiy 2.50 6.00
OP15 Quinn Hughes 4.00 10.00
OP16 Anze Kopitar 2.50 6.00
OP17 Cole Caufield 3.00 8.00
OP18 Brady Tkachuk 2.50 6.00
OP19 Victor Hedman 2.00 5.00
OP20 Tim Stutzle 2.00 5.00
OP21 Moritz Seider 2.00 5.00
OP22 Jack Eichel 2.50 6.00
OP23 Nikita Kucherov 3.00 8.00
OP24 John Tavares 2.50 6.00
OP25 Nick Suzuki 3.00 8.00
OP26 Lucas Raymond 2.50 6.00
OP27 Jordan Kyrou 1.50 4.00
OP28 Rasmus Dahlin 2.00 5.00
OP29 Josh Norris 1.50 4.00
OP30 Elias Pettersson 2.50 6.00
OP31 Connor McDavid 8.00 20.00
OP32 David Pastrnak 4.00 10.00
OP33 Sidney Crosby 6.00 15.00
OP34 Clayton Keller 2.00 5.00
OP35 Jeremy Swayman 2.50 6.00
OP36 Matt Boldy 5.00 12.00
OP37 Marco Rossi 4.00 10.00
OP38 Matty Beniers 4.00 10.00
OP39 Owen Power 3.00 8.00
OP40 Dylan Holloway 3.00 8.00

2022-23 O-Pee-Chee Platinum Photo Driven

PD1 Alex Ovechkin 3.00 8.00
PD2 Connor McDavid 4.00 10.00
PD3 Carey Price 1.50 4.00
PD4 Igor Shesterkin 1.50 4.00
PD5 Sebastian Aho 1.25 3.00
PD6 Brad Marchand 1.50 4.00
PD7 Victor Hedman 1.00 2.50
PD8 Moritz Seider 1.00 2.50
PD9 Trevor Zegras .75 2.00
PD10 Marc-Andre Fleury 1.50 4.00
PD11 Gabriel Landeskog 1.00 2.50
PD12 Aaron Ekblad 1.00 2.50
PD13 Shane Wright 2.00 5.00
PD14 Matty Beniers 2.00 5.00
PD15 Owen Power 1.50 4.00

2022-23 O-Pee-Chee Platinum Retro

*RAINBOW: .6X TO 1.5X BASIC
*BLUE/199: 1.2X TO 3X BASIC
*PINK PULSAR: 2X TO 5X BASIC
R1 Trevor Zegras 1.00 2.50
R2 Kirill Kaprizov 3.00 8.00
R3 Leon Draisaitl 3.00 8.00
R4 Michael Bunting 1.00 2.50
R5 Alex Ovechkin 4.00 10.00
R6 Steven Stamkos 2.00 5.00
R7 Anton Lundell 1.00 2.50
R8 Vitek Vanecek 1.00 2.50
R9 Brad Marchand 2.00 5.00
R10 Igor Shesterkin 2.00 5.00
R11 Nathan MacKinnon 4.00 10.00
R12 Patrick Kane 2.00 5.00
R13 Anze Kopitar 1.50 4.00
R14 Elias Pettersson 1.50 4.00
R15 Brent Burns 1.00 2.50
R16 Jordan Eberle 1.00 2.50
R17 Jack Hughes 2.50 6.00
R18 Clayton Keller 1.25 3.00
R19 Moritz Seider 1.25 3.00
R20 Cale Makar 2.50 6.00
R21 Auston Matthews 4.00 10.00
R22 Andrei Svechnikov 1.25 3.00
R23 Alexis Lafreniere 1.50 4.00
R24 Andrei Vasilevskiy 1.50 4.00
R25 Tanner Jeannot .60 1.50
R26 Tage Thompson 1.25 3.00
R27 Taylor Hall 1.00 2.50
R28 Spencer Knight 1.00 2.50
R29 Joe Pavelski 1.25 3.00
R30 Peyton Krebs .75 2.00
R31 Ilya Sorokin 1.50 4.00
R32 Philipp Grubauer 1.00 2.50
R33 Tim Stutzle 1.25 3.00
R34 Kyle Connor 1.50 4.00
R35 Jonathan Huberdeau 1.25 3.00
R36 Miro Heiskanen 1.25 3.00
R37 Quinn Hughes 2.50 6.00
R38 Torey Krug .75 2.00
R39 Sidney Crosby 4.00 10.00
R40 Jason Robertson 1.50 4.00
R41 Zach Werenski 1.50 4.00
R42 Connor McDavid 5.00 12.00
R43 Tom Wilson 1.00 2.50
R44 Evgeni Malkin 2.00 5.00
R45 Brandon Hagel .75 2.00
R46 Dylan Cozens 1.00 2.50
R47 Jack Eichel 1.50 4.00
R48 Seth Jarvis 1.25 3.00
R49 Mathew Barzal 1.25 3.00
R50 John Gibson 1.00 2.50
R51 Ryan O'Reilly 1.00 2.50
R52 Victor Hedman 1.25 3.00
R53 Sonny Milano .75 2.00
R54 Matthew Tkachuk 2.00 5.00
R55 Dawson Mercer 1.25 3.00
R56 Cole Caufield 2.00 5.00
R57 Elvis Merzlikins 1.00 2.50
R58 Roman Josi 1.00 2.50
R60 Lucas Raymond 1.50 4.00
R61 Cam Atkinson 1.00 2.50
R62 Brady Tkachuk 1.50 4.00
R63 Nick Robertson 1.00 2.50
R64 Carey Price 2.00 5.00
R65 Marc-Andre Fleury 2.00 5.00
R66 Owen Power 2.00 5.00
R67 Matt Boldy 3.00 8.00
R68 Matty Beniers 2.50 6.00
R69 Jack Quinn 1.50 4.00
R70 Lukas Reichel 2.00 5.00
R71 Kent Johnson 2.00 5.00
R72 Dylan Holloway 2.00 5.00
R73 Marco Rossi 2.50 6.00
R74 Jacob Perreault 1.00 2.50
R75 Lukas Dostal 2.00 5.00
R76 Samuel Fagemo .75 2.00
R77 Braden Schneider 1.50 4.00
R78 Isaac Ratcliffe 1.00 2.50
R79 Bobby Brink 1.00 2.50
R80 Trey Fix-Wolansky 1.00 2.50
R81 Pyotr Kochetkov 2.00 5.00
R82 Thomas Bordeleau 1.00 2.50
R83 Mads Sogaard 1.25 3.00
R84 Marc McLaughlin 1.00 2.50
R85 Matias Maccelli 1.50 4.00
R86 Ronnie Attard 1.00 2.50
R87 Jonatan Berggren 1.50 4.00
R88 Samuel Poulin 1.25 3.00
R89 Jakub Lauko 1.25 3.00
R90 Arber Xhekaj 2.00 5.00
R91 Elmer Soderblom 2.00 5.00
R92 Kaiden Guhle 2.00 5.00
R93 David Jiricek 2.00 5.00
R94 Wyatt Johnston 4.00 10.00
R95 Andrei Kuzmenko 2.00 5.00
R96 Brandt Clarke 2.00 5.00
R97 Jake Sanderson 2.50 6.00
R98 Dylan Guenther 2.50 6.00
R99 Juraj Slafkovsky 5.00 12.00
R100 Shane Wright 2.50 6.00

2022-23 O-Pee-Chee Platinum Rookie Autographs

RAK Andrei Kuzmenko 15.00 40.00
RAR Aatu Raty 8.00 20.00
RAX Arber Xhekaj 15.00 40.00
RBB Bobby Brink 8.00 20.00
RBC Brandt Clarke 15.00 40.00
RBE Jonatan Berggren 12.00 30.00
RBM Matty Beniers SP 20.00 50.00
RBS Braden Schneider 12.00 30.00
RBT Brayden Tracey SP 6.00 15.00
RCP Chase Pearson 6.00 15.00
RDG Dylan Guenther 20.00 50.00
RDH Dylan Holloway 15.00 40.00
RDJ David Jiricek 15.00 40.00
RDS Dylan Samberg SP 8.00 20.00
REK Erik Kallgren 8.00 20.00
RES Elmer Soderblom 15.00 40.00
RFK Fredrik Karlstrom 6.00 15.00
RIR Isaac Ratcliffe 8.00 20.00
RJH Jordan Harris 10.00 25.00
RJM Jack McBain 8.00 20.00
RJQ Jack Quinn 12.00 30.00
RJS Jake Sanderson 20.00 50.00
RKG Kaiden Guhle 15.00 40.00
RKJ Kent Johnson 15.00 40.00
RKK Kaedan Korczak 6.00 15.00
RKM Kirill Marchenko 20.00 50.00
RLD Lukas Dostal 15.00 40.00
RMA Matias Maccelli 12.00 30.00
RMB Matt Boldy SP 25.00 60.00
RME Michael Eyssimont 8.00 20.00
RMK Mark Kastelic 6.00 15.00
RMR Marco Rossi 25.00 60.00
RMS Mads Sogaard 10.00 25.00
RNA Nick Abruzzese 8.00 20.00
RNC Noah Cates 8.00 20.00
RNP Nick Perbix 6.00 15.00
RNS Nathan Smith 6.00 15.00
ROO Oskar Olausson 8.00 20.00
ROP Owen Power SP 15.00 40.00
RPA Juuso Parssinen 8.00 20.00
RPK Pyotr Kochetkov 15.00 40.00
RPO Samuel Poulin 10.00 25.00
RRA Ronnie Attard 8.00 20.00
RSF Samuel Fagemo 6.00 15.00
RSL Juraj Slafkovsky SP 125.00 300.00
RSP Jordan Spence SP 8.00 20.00
RSW Shane Wright SP 20.00 50.00
RVP Valtteri Puustinen 6.00 15.00
RWJ Wyatt Johnston 50.00 125.00
RZH Zack Hayes 6.00 15.00

2022-23 O-Pee-Chee Platinum Rookie Autographs Blue Traxx

*BLUE: .5X TO 1.2X BASIC
RMB Matt Boldy SP 60.00 150.00
RSL Juraj Slafkovsky SP 200.00 500.00

2022-23 O-Pee-Chee Platinum Rookie Autographs Matte Pink

*PINK: .6X TO 1.5X BASIC
RBM Matty Beniers SP 80.00 200.00

2022-23 O-Pee-Chee Platinum Rookie Autographs Rainbow

*RAINBOW: .5X TO 1.2X BASIC
RMB Matt Boldy SP 60.00 150.00
RSL Juraj Slafkovsky SP 200.00 500.00

2022-23 O-Pee-Chee Platinum Rookie Autographs Violet Pixels

*VIOLET/99: .6X TO 1.5X BASIC
RBM Matty Beniers 80.00 200.00
RDH Dylan Holloway 30.00 80.00
RDJ David Jiricek 60.00 150.00
RJS Jake Sanderson 80.00 200.00
RLD Lukas Dostal 30.00 80.00
ROP Owen Power 60.00 150.00
RPK Pyotr Kochetkov 40.00 100.00
RWJ Wyatt Johnston 100.00 250.00

2022-23 O-Pee-Chee Platinum Sweet Selections

SS1 Owen Power 1.50 4.00
SS2 Matty Beniers 2.00 5.00
SS3 Jacob Perreault .75 2.00
SS4 Lukas Reichel 1.50 4.00
SS5 Kent Johnson 1.50 4.00
SS6 Juraj Slafkovsky 4.00 10.00
SS7 Brayden Tracey .60 1.50
SS8 Jack Quinn 1.25 3.00
SS9 Marco Rossi 2.00 5.00
SS10 Lukas Dostal 1.50 4.00
SS11 Braden Schneider 1.25 3.00
SS12 Matt Boldy 2.50 6.00
SS13 Mads Sogaard 1.00 2.50
SS14 Thomas Bordeleau .75 2.00
SS15 Shane Wright 2.00 5.00

2023-24 O-Pee-Chee Platinum

1 Auston Matthews 1.50 4.00
2 Cale Makar 1.00 2.50
3 John Tavares .60 1.50
4 Trevor Zegras .40 1.00
5 Leon Draisaitl 1.25 3.00
6 Jacob Markstrom .40 1.00
7 Dawson Mercer .50 1.25
8 Ryan O'Reilly .40 1.00
9 William Nylander .75 2.00
10 Jack Hughes 1.00 2.50
11 Bo Horvat .50 1.25
12 Shane Wright .50 1.25
13 Alexandar Georgiev .40 1.00
14 Jake Sanderson .50 1.25
15 Nathan MacKinnon 1.50 4.00
16 Michael Bunting .40 1.00
17 Tristan Jarry .40 1.00
18 Brendan Gallagher .40 1.00
19 Connor Hellebuyck .75 2.00
20 Elias Pettersson .60 1.50
21 Marc-Andre Fleury .75 2.00
22 Sean Monahan .25 .60
23 Brady Tkachuk .60 1.50
24 Morgan Frost .30 .75
25 Tyler Bertuzzi .30 .75
26 Drew Doughty .40 1.00
27 Victor Hedman .50 1.25
28 Ville Husso .25 .60
29 Quinn Hughes 1.00 2.50
30 Logan Couture .50 1.25
31 Sergei Bobrovsky .60 1.50
32 Thomas Novak .25 .60
33 Alex Tuch .40 1.00
34 Zach Werenski .60 1.50
35 Andrei Svechnikov .50 1.25
36 Charlie McAvoy .50 1.25
37 Jared Spurgeon .40 1.00
38 Jakob Chychrun .40 1.00
39 Matias Maccelli .30 .75
40 Mark Scheifele .60 1.50
41 Igor Shesterkin .75 2.00
42 Robert Thomas .40 1.00
43 Nick Schmaltz .30 .75
44 Jake DeBrusk .40 1.00
45 Adam Fox .50 1.25
46 Brent Burns .40 1.00
47 Linus Ullmark .40 1.00
48 Dylan Larkin .50 1.25
49 Thatcher Demko .50 1.25
50 Kyle Connor .60 1.50
51 Jared McCann .30 .75
52 Anton Lundell .40 1.00
53 Nick Suzuki .75 2.00
54 Tyler Toffoli .40 1.00
55 Alexis Lafreniere .60 1.50
56 Andreas Athanasiou .30 .75
57 Dylan Strome .50 1.25
58 Miro Heiskanen .50 1.25
59 Aleksander Barkov .60 1.50
60 Dylan Guenther .50 1.25
61 Noah Dobson .50 1.25
62 Evander Kane .40 1.00
63 Claude Giroux .40 1.00
64 Vitek Vanecek .40 1.00
65 Wyatt Johnston .75 2.00
66 T.J. Oshie .40 1.00
67 Mikko Rantanen 1.00 2.50
68 Valeri Nichushkin .40 1.00
69 Mikhail Sergachev .30 .75
70 Filip Forsberg .60 1.50
71 Stuart Skinner .50 1.25
72 Anders Lee .30 .75
73 Tage Thompson .50 1.25
74 Nino Niederreiter .25 .60
75 Timo Meier .40 1.00
76 Steven Stamkos .75 2.00
77 Joel Eriksson Ek .30 .75
78 Mario Ferraro .25 .60
79 Evan Bouchard .50 1.25
80 Jason Robertson .60 1.50
81 Jordan Eberle .40 1.00
82 Ilya Sorokin .60 1.50
83 Matt Boldy .60 1.50
84 Lucas Raymond .60 1.50
85 Nikolaj Ehlers .40 1.00
86 Evgeny Kuznetsov .50 1.25
87 Alexander Barabanov .25 .60
88 Juuse Saros .50 1.25
89 Jamie Drysdale .30 .75
90 Kirill Kaprizov 1.25 3.00
91 Brandon Montour .50 1.25
92 Sebastian Aho .60 1.50
93 Kris Letang .50 1.25
94 Dougie Hamilton .30 .75
95 Troy Terry .30 .75
96 Drake Batherson .40 1.00
97 William Eklund .50 1.25
98 Aaron Ekblad .50 1.25
99 Adrian Kempe .40 1.00
100 Connor McDavid 2.00 5.00
101 Mark Stone .50 1.25
102 Kent Johnson .40 1.00
103 Tom Wilson .40 1.00
104 Kaiden Guhle .40 1.00
105 Andrei Kuzmenko .40 1.00
106 Alex Pietrangelo .30 .75
107 K'Andre Miller .30 .75
108 Ryan Nugent-Hopkins .50 1.25
109 Pierre-Luc Dubois .30 .75
110 Mitch Marner .60 1.50
111 Jonathan Huberdeau .50 1.25
112 Chris Kreider .50 1.25
113 Jake Oettinger .60 1.50
114 Jonathan Marchessault .50 1.25
115 Pavel Buchnevich .30 .75
116 John Gibson .40 1.00
117 Juraj Slafkovsky .75 2.00
118 Martin Necas .60 1.50
119 Jordan Kyrou .40 1.00
120 Cole Perfetti .40 1.00
121 MacKenzie Weegar .30 .75
122 Carter Verhaeghe .40 1.00
123 Tomas Hertl .40 1.00
124 Brayden Point .50 1.25
125 Sidney Crosby 1.50 4.00
126 Nico Hischier .60 1.50
127 Owen Power .40 1.00
128 Kirill Marchenko .50 1.25
129 Colton Parayko .30 .75
130 Noah Cates .25 .60
131 Kevin Fiala .30 .75
132 Jack Eichel .60 1.50
133 Chandler Stephenson .30 .75
134 Artturi Lehkonen .30 .75
135 Cole Caufield .75 2.00
136 Joel Farabee .40 1.00
137 Clayton Keller .50 1.25
138 Artemi Panarin .75 2.00
139 Cam Fowler .40 1.00
140 Yegor Sharangovich .40 1.00
141 Johnny Gaudreau .60 1.50
142 Matthew Tkachuk .75 2.00
143 Owen Tippett .25 .60
144 Mathew Barzal .50 1.25
145 Ryan Hartman .25 .60
146 Anze Kopitar .60 1.50
147 Patrick Kane .75 2.00
148 Karel Vejmelka .25 .60
149 Brad Marchand .75 2.00
150 Alex Ovechkin 1.50 4.00
151 Josh Norris .40 1.00
152 Morgan Rielly .40 1.00
153 Mason McTavish .40 1.00
154 J.T. Miller .50 1.25
155 Mats Zuccarello .40 1.00
156 Roope Hintz .50 1.25
157 David Pastrnak 1.00 2.50
158 Jake Guentzel .60 1.50
159 William Karlsson .50 1.25
160 Rasmus Dahlin .50 1.25
161 Pavel Zacha .30 .75
162 Roman Josi .40 1.00
163 Josh Morrissey .50 1.25
164 Cole Sillinger .30 .75
165 Joe Pavelski .50 1.25
166 Logan Thompson .50 1.25
167 Brock Boeser .50 1.25
168 Philipp Grubauer .40 1.00
169 Travis Konecny .40 1.00
170 Erik Karlsson .50 1.25
171 Dylan Cozens .40 1.00
172 Samuel Ersson .40 1.00
173 Andrei Vasilevskiy .60 1.50
174 Lukas Reichel .40 1.00
175 Andre Burakovsky .25 .60
176 Nikita Kucherov .75 2.00
177 Nazem Kadri .50 1.25
178 Seth Jones .40 1.00
179 Elias Lindholm .40 1.00
180 Nicklas Backstrom .40 1.00
181 JJ Peterka .40 1.00
182 Quinton Byfield .50 1.25
183 Taylor Raddysh .30 .75
184 Jesper Bratt .40 1.00
185 Jordan Binnington .60 1.50
186 Tim Stutzle .50 1.25
187 Brayden Schenn .40 1.00
188 Evgeni Malkin .75 2.00
189 Mika Zibanejad .50 1.25
190 Alex DeBrincat .50 1.25
191 Seth Jarvis .50 1.25
192 Vladimir Tarasenko .50 1.25
193 Moritz Seider .50 1.25
194 Kirby Dach .40 1.00
195 Taylor Hall .40 1.00
196 Mattias Ekholm .30 .75
197 Patrik Laine .50 1.25
198 Anthony Duclair .30 .75
199 Ryan Reaves .30 .75
200 Matty Beniers .50 1.25
201 Connor Bedard RC 25.00 60.00
202 Logan Cooley RC 3.00 8.00
203 Adam Fantilli RC 3.00 8.00
204 Luke Hughes RC 3.00 8.00
205 Matthew Knies RC 4.00 10.00
206 Arnaud Durandeau RC 1.00 2.50
207 Egor Afanasyev RC 1.00 2.50
208 Jake Livingstone RC 1.00 2.50
209 Stanislav Svozil RC .75 2.00
210 Ridly Greig RC 1.50 4.00
211 Hunter McKown RC 1.00 2.50
212 David Gust RC 1.00 2.50
213 Will Cuylle RC 1.50 4.00
214 Luke Philp RC 1.00 2.50
215 Devon Levi RC 2.50 6.00
216 Elliot Desnoyers RC 1.00 2.50
217 Tye Kartye RC 1.50 4.00
218 Lukas Rousek RC .75 2.00
219 Tyler Kleven RC 1.00 2.50
220 Simon Edvinsson RC 2.00 5.00
221 Danil Gushchin RC 1.00 2.50
222 Tyler Angle RC 1.00 2.50
223 Pavel Mintyukov RC 1.50 4.00
224 Mason Lohrei RC 1.50 4.00
225 Owen Beck RC 1.50 4.00
226 Tristen Robins RC 1.00 2.50
227 Cole Guttman RC 1.00 2.50
228 Michael Kesselring RC 1.00 2.50
229 Samuel Knazko RC 1.00 2.50
230 Yaroslav Askarov RC 2.50 6.00
231 Jonathan Gruden RC 1.00 2.50
232 Matthew Kessel RC .75 2.00
233 Roby Jarventie RC 1.00 2.50
234 William Dufour RC .75 2.00
235 Luke Evangelista RC 1.50 4.00
236 Connor Zary RC 2.00 5.00
237 Jet Greaves RC 1.50 4.00
238 Tristan Luneau RC 1.00 2.50
239 Justin Sourdif RC 1.00 2.50
240 Dustin Wolf RC 3.00 8.00
241 Arturs Silovs RC 2.00 5.00
242 Hugh McGing RC 1.00 2.50
243 Simon Nemec RC 2.00 5.00
244 Adam Ginning RC 1.00 2.50
245 Olle Eriksson Ek RC 1.00 2.50
246 Wyatt Kaiser RC 1.00 2.50
247 Aidan McDonough RC .75 2.00
248 Nikita Nesterenko RC 1.00 2.50
249 Alex Laferriere RC 1.50 4.00
250 Marco Kasper RC 2.50 6.00
251 Ryan Johnson RC 1.25 3.00
252 Jaxson Stauber RC 1.00 2.50
253 Emil Andrae RC 1.00 2.50
254 Vincent Iorio RC 1.00 2.50
255 Bobby McMann RC 1.50 4.00
256 John Beecher RC 2.00 5.00
257 Walker Duehr RC .75 2.00
258 Hunter Shepard RC 1.00 2.50
259 Kevin Korchinski RC 1.50 4.00
260 Brock Faber RC 2.50 6.00
261 Jiri Kulich RC 2.00 5.00
262 Lucas Condotta RC 1.00 2.50
263 Vincent Desharnais RC 1.25 3.00
264 Maxence Guenette RC 1.00 2.50
265 Henry Thrun RC 1.00 2.50
266 Daemon Hunt RC 1.00 2.50
267 Sean Farrell RC 1.00 2.50
268 Jiri Patera RC 1.50 4.00
269 Mackie Samoskevich RC 1.50 4.00
270 John Ludvig RC 1.00 2.50
271 Martin Pospisil RC 1.25 3.00
272 Raphael Lavoie RC 1.00 2.50
273 Leevi Merilainen RC 1.00 2.50
274 Dmitri Voronkov RC 1.25 3.00
275 Tyson Foerster RC 2.00 5.00
276 Isak Rosen RC 1.00 2.50
277 Mikael Pyyhtia RC 1.00 2.50
278 Marc Del Gaizo RC 1.00 2.50
279 Uvis Balinskis RC 1.00 2.50
280 Matthew Coronato RC 1.50 4.00
281 Hardy Haman Aktell RC 1.00 2.50
282 Waltteri Merela RC 1.00 2.50
283 Milos Kelemen RC 1.00 2.50
284 Matt Murray RC 1.00 2.50
285 Cole McWard RC 1.00 2.50
286 Nick Swaney RC 1.00 2.50
287 Matt Tomkins RC 1.00 2.50
288 Jackson LaCombe RC 1.00 2.50
289 Ryker Evans RC 1.25 3.00
290 Matthew Poitras RC 2.00 5.00
291 Samuel Bolduc RC 1.00 2.50
292 Ty Emberson RC 1.00 2.50
293 Leo Carlsson RC 3.00 8.00
294 Ryan Shea RC 1.00 2.50
295 Jakob Pelletier RC 1.25 3.00
296 Fraser Minten RC 2.00 5.00
297 Matt Savoie RC 2.00 5.00
298 Akito Hirose RC .75 2.00
299 Joona Koppanen RC .75 2.00
300 Zach Benson RC 1.50 4.00

2023-24 O-Pee-Chee Platinum Arctic Freeze

*ARCTIC/99: 1.5X TO 4X BASIC
100 Connor McDavid 25.00 60.00
125 Sidney Crosby 15.00 40.00
150 Alex Ovechkin 12.00 30.00
201 Connor Bedard 300.00 800.00
202 Logan Cooley 40.00 100.00
203 Adam Fantilli 40.00 100.00
204 Luke Hughes 30.00 80.00
205 Matthew Knies 40.00 100.00
240 Dustin Wolf 20.00 50.00
260 Brock Faber 60.00 150.00
293 Leo Carlsson 30.00 80.00

2023-24 O-Pee-Chee Platinum Blue Fragments

*BLUE/125: 2X TO 5X BASIC
100 Connor McDavid 60.00 150.00
125 Sidney Crosby 15.00 40.00
150 Alex Ovechkin 20.00 50.00
201 Connor Bedard 400.00 1000.00
202 Logan Cooley 40.00 100.00
203 Adam Fantilli 40.00 100.00
204 Luke Hughes 30.00 80.00
205 Matthew Knies 40.00 100.00
240 Dustin Wolf 25.00 60.00
260 Brock Faber 60.00 150.00
293 Leo Carlsson 30.00 80.00

2023-24 O-Pee-Chee Platinum Cosmic

*COSMIC/65: 4X TO 10X BASIC
*COSMIC RC/65: 2.5X TO 6X BASIC
1 Auston Matthews 20.00 50.00
100 Connor McDavid 80.00 200.00
125 Sidney Crosby 25.00 60.00
150 Alex Ovechkin 25.00 60.00
201 Connor Bedard 600.00 1500.00
202 Logan Cooley 60.00 150.00
203 Adam Fantilli 60.00 150.00
204 Luke Hughes 60.00 150.00
205 Matthew Knies 60.00 150.00
240 Dustin Wolf 25.00 60.00
293 Leo Carlsson 80.00 200.00

2023-24 O-Pee-Chee Platinum Liquid Metal

*LQD METAL/399: 1X TO 2.5X BASIC
100 Connor McDavid 10.00 25.00
125 Sidney Crosby 8.00 20.00
201 Connor Bedard 200.00 500.00
202 Logan Cooley 12.00 30.00
203 Adam Fantilli 15.00 40.00
205 Matthew Knies 10.00 25.00
260 Brock Faber 12.00 30.00
293 Leo Carlsson 12.00 30.00

2023-24 O-Pee-Chee Platinum Matte Pink

*PINK: .6X TO 1.5X BASIC
201 Connor Bedard 80.00 200.00

2023-24 O-Pee-Chee Platinum Neon Yellow Surge

*YELLOW: .7X TO 2X BASIC
201 Connor Bedard 100.00 250.00

2023-24 O-Pee-Chee Platinum NHL Shield Variant

100 Connor McDavid 80.00 200.00
150 Alex Ovechkin 80.00 200.00
201 Connor Bedard 600.00 1500.00

2023-24 O-Pee-Chee Platinum Orange Checkers

*ORANGE/25: 8X TO 20X BASIC
*ORANGE RC/25: 4X TO 10X BASIC
1 Auston Matthews 50.00 125.00
2 Cale Makar 25.00 60.00
5 Leon Draisaitl 50.00 125.00
100 Connor McDavid 150.00 400.00
125 Sidney Crosby 50.00 125.00
150 Alex Ovechkin 80.00 200.00
202 Logan Cooley 150.00 400.00
203 Adam Fantilli 125.00 300.00
204 Luke Hughes 150.00 400.00
293 Leo Carlsson 150.00 400.00
300 Zach Benson 50.00 125.00

2023-24 O-Pee-Chee Platinum Rainbow

*RAINBOW: .5X TO 1.2X BASIC
201 Connor Bedard 60.00 150.00

2023-24 O-Pee-Chee Platinum Red Prism

*RED/199: 1.2X TO 3X BASIC
100 Connor McDavid 12.00 30.00
125 Sidney Crosby 10.00 25.00
201 Connor Bedard 300.00 800.00
202 Logan Cooley 25.00 60.00
203 Adam Fantilli 30.00 80.00
204 Luke Hughes 25.00 60.00
205 Matthew Knies 20.00 50.00
240 Dustin Wolf 15.00 40.00
260 Brock Faber 25.00 60.00
293 Leo Carlsson 25.00 60.00

2023-24 O-Pee-Chee Platinum Seismic Gold

*GOLD/50: 5X TO 12X BASIC
*GOLD RC/50: 2.5X TO 6X BASIC
1 Auston Matthews 30.00 80.00
2 Cale Makar 20.00 50.00
5 Leon Draisaitl 40.00 100.00
100 Connor McDavid 150.00 400.00
125 Sidney Crosby 50.00 125.00
150 Alex Ovechkin 80.00 200.00
202 Logan Cooley 125.00 300.00
203 Adam Fantilli 80.00 200.00
204 Luke Hughes 100.00 250.00
205 Matthew Knies 125.00 300.00
293 Leo Carlsson 125.00 300.00
300 Zach Benson 40.00 100.00

2023-24 O-Pee-Chee Platinum Sunset

*SUNSET: .6X TO 1.5X BASIC
201 Connor Bedard 60.00 150.00

2023-24 O-Pee-Chee Platinum Violet Pixels

*VIOLET/299: 1X TO 2.5X BASIC
100 Connor McDavid 10.00 25.00
125 Sidney Crosby 8.00 20.00
201 Connor Bedard 250.00 600.00
202 Logan Cooley 25.00 60.00
203 Adam Fantilli 20.00 50.00
204 Luke Hughes 15.00 40.00
205 Matthew Knies 20.00 50.00
240 Dustin Wolf 10.00 25.00
260 Brock Faber 20.00 50.00
293 Leo Carlsson 20.00 50.00

2023-24 O-Pee-Chee Platinum Blue Rainbow Autographs

BAAB Aleksander Barkov SP 12.00 30.00
BAAK Anze Kopitar SP 12.00 30.00
BAAL Anton Lundell 8.00 20.00
BAAN Alex Newhook 6.00 15.00
BAAR Alexander Romanov 6.00 15.00
BAAT Alex Tuch SP 8.00 20.00
BAAV Andrei Vasilevskiy SP 12.00 30.00
BAAX Arber Xhekaj 8.00 20.00
BABB Bowen Byram 10.00 25.00
BABC Brandt Clarke 8.00 20.00
BABM Brandon Montour 10.00 25.00
BACC Connor Clifton 5.00 12.00
BACH Connor Hellebuyck SP 15.00 40.00
BACN Cam Neely SP 8.00 20.00
BACP Colton Parayko 6.00 15.00
BADG Dylan Guenther 10.00 25.00
BADH Dany Heatley SP 6.00 15.00
BADJ Dakota Joshua 5.00 12.00
BADS Darryl Sittler SP 8.00 20.00
BADT Devon Toews 6.00 15.00
BAFG Filip Gustavsson 8.00 20.00
BAGV Gabe Vilardi 8.00 20.00
BAHO Simon Holmstrom 5.00 12.00
BAIS Ilya Samsonov 8.00 20.00
BAJA Jalen Chatfield 5.00 12.00
BAJB Jordan Binnington SP 12.00 30.00
BAJC John Carlson SP 8.00 20.00
BAJH Jonathan Huberdeau SP 10.00 25.00
BAJM Jacob Middleton 5.00 12.00
BAJN Jake Neighbours 8.00 20.00
BAJO Jake Oettinger SP 12.00 30.00
BAJP Jeff Petry 8.00 20.00
BAJW Joseph Woll 10.00 25.00
BAKA K'Andre Miller 6.00 15.00
BAKJ Kent Johnson SP 8.00 20.00
BAKL Kevin Labanc 5.00 12.00
BAKS Kiefer Sherwood 5.00 12.00
BAKV Karel Vejmelka 5.00 12.00
BALT Logan Thompson 10.00 25.00
BAMA Mikey Anderson 6.00 15.00
BAMB Morgan Barron 5.00 12.00
BAMC Cale Makar SP 20.00 50.00
BAMF Mario Ferraro 5.00 12.00
BAMI Michael Bunting 8.00 20.00
BAMO Josh Morrissey 10.00 25.00
BAMS Mark Stone SP 10.00 25.00
BANC Noah Cates SP 5.00 12.00
BAOB Oliver Bjorkstrand 6.00 15.00
BARC Ross Colton 6.00 15.00
BARO Ryan O'Reilly SP 8.00 20.00
BASB Scotty Bowman SP 8.00 20.00
BASO Ilya Sorokin SP 12.00 30.00
BASP Shane Pinto 6.00 15.00
BASW Shane Wright SP 10.00 25.00
BATA Tony Amonte SP 6.00 15.00
BATH Tomas Hertl SP 8.00 20.00
BATJ Tristan Jarry 8.00 20.00
BATM Timo Meier SP 8.00 20.00
BATN Thomas Novak 5.00 12.00
BATT Tyler Toffoli 8.00 20.00
BAWE William Eklund 10.00 25.00
BAYS Yegor Sharangovich 8.00 20.00

2023-24 O-Pee-Chee Platinum Photo Driven

*RED/85: .6X TO 1.5X BASIC
*GREEN/35: 1.5X TO 4X BASIC
PD1 Alex Ovechkin 3.00 8.00
PD2 Brent Burns .75 2.00
PD3 Jack Hughes 2.00 5.00
PD4 Mark Stone 1.00 2.50
PD5 Timo Meier .75 2.00
PD6 Auston Matthews 3.00 8.00
PD7 Leon Draisaitl 2.50 6.00
PD8 Cole Caufield 1.50 4.00
PD9 Sidney Crosby 3.00 8.00
PD10 Connor Hellebuyck 1.50 4.00
PD11 Matthew Tkachuk 1.50 4.00
PD12 Tage Thompson 1.00 2.50
PD13 Charlie McAvoy 1.00 2.50
PD14 Matty Beniers 1.00 2.50
PD15 Cale Makar 2.00 5.00

2023-24 O-Pee-Chee Platinum Photo Driven Autographs Rainbow

PD3 Jack Hughes 40.00 100.00

2023-24 O-Pee-Chee Platinum Retro

R1 Connor McDavid 5.00 12.00
R2 Andrei Vasilevskiy 1.50 4.00
R3 Trevor Zegras 1.00 2.50
R4 Roman Josi 1.00 2.50
R5 Patrik Laine 1.25 3.00
R6 Dylan Larkin 1.25 3.00
R7 Dylan Guenther 1.25 3.00
R8 Brock Nelson 1.00 2.50
R9 Mitch Marner 1.50 4.00
R10 Alex DeBrincat 1.25 3.00
R11 Seth Jones 1.00 2.50
R12 Logan Thompson 1.25 3.00
R13 Igor Shesterkin 2.00 5.00
R14 Cale Makar 2.50 6.00
R15 Teuvo Teravainen 1.00 2.50
R16 Sidney Crosby 4.00 10.00
R17 Anze Kopitar 1.50 4.00
R18 Quinn Hughes 2.50 6.00
R19 Leon Draisaitl 3.00 8.00
R20 Elias Pettersson 1.50 4.00
R21 Erik Karlsson 1.25 3.00
R22 Sebastian Aho 1.50 4.00
R23 Rasmus Dahlin 1.25 3.00
R24 Roope Hintz 1.25 3.00
R25 Mikko Rantanen 2.50 6.00
R26 Jared Spurgeon 1.00 2.50
R27 Casey Mittelstadt 1.00 2.50
R28 Nick Schmaltz .75 2.00
R29 Cole Perfetti 1.00 2.50
R30 Marc-Andre Fleury 2.00 5.00
R31 William Eklund 1.25 3.00
R32 Nico Hischier 1.50 4.00
R33 Kirill Kaprizov 3.00 8.00
R34 Jack Eichel 1.50 4.00
R35 Brad Marchand 2.00 5.00
R36 Jason Robertson 1.50 4.00
R37 Brayden Point 1.25 3.00
R38 Arber Xhekaj 1.00 2.50
R39 Tyler Bertuzzi .75 2.00
R40 JJ Peterka 1.00 2.50
R41 Pavel Buchnevich .75 2.00
R42 Vladimir Tarasenko 1.25 3.00
R43 Michael Bunting 1.00 2.50
R44 Nathan MacKinnon 4.00 10.00
R45 Jack Hughes 2.50 6.00
R46 Evgeny Kuznetsov 1.25 3.00
R47 Nikolaj Ehlers 1.00 2.50
R48 Carter Hart 1.00 2.50
R49 Matthew Tkachuk 2.00 5.00
R50 Taylor Raddysh .75 2.00
R51 Ryan O'Reilly 1.00 2.50
R52 Dawson Mercer 1.25 3.00
R53 Brendan Gallagher 1.00 2.50
R54 John Tavares 1.50 4.00
R55 Jordan Kyrou 1.00 2.50
R56 Cam Atkinson 1.00 2.50
R57 Troy Terry .75 2.00
R58 David Pastrnak 2.50 6.00
R59 Kevin Fiala .75 2.00
R60 Aaron Ekblad 1.25 3.00
R61 Shane Pinto .75 2.00
R62 Philipp Grubauer 1.00 2.50
R63 Kent Johnson 1.00 2.50
R64 Alex Ovechkin 4.00 10.00
R65 Jonathan Huberdeau 1.25 3.00
R66 Luke Hughes 3.00 8.00
R67 Owen Beck 1.50 4.00
R68 Luke Evangelista 1.50 4.00
R69 Will Cuylle 1.50 4.00
R70 Logan Cooley 3.00 8.00
R71 Tyson Foerster 2.00 5.00
R72 William Dufour .75 2.00
R73 Marco Kasper 2.50 6.00
R74 Ridly Greig 1.50 4.00
R75 Leo Carlsson 3.00 8.00
R76 Sean Farrell 1.00 2.50
R77 Dustin Wolf 3.00 8.00
R78 Arnaud Durandeau 1.00 2.50
R79 Leevi Merilainen 1.00 2.50
R80 Adam Fantilli 3.00 8.00
R81 Matthew Coronato 1.50 4.00
R82 Brock Faber 2.50 6.00
R83 Aidan McDonough .75 2.00
R84 Zach Benson 1.50 4.00
R85 Matthew Knies 4.00 10.00
R86 Jakob Pelletier 1.25 3.00
R87 Kevin Korchinski 1.50 4.00
R88 Lukas Rousek .75 2.00
R89 Elliot Desnoyers 1.00 2.50
R90 Simon Edvinsson 2.00 5.00
R91 Stanislav Svozil .75 2.00
R92 Tye Kartye 1.50 4.00

R93 Luke Philp 1.00 2.50
R94 Jonathan Gruden 1.00 2.50
R95 Yaroslav Askarov 2.50 6.00
R96 Jiri Patera 1.50 4.00
R97 Vincent Desharnais 1.25 3.00
R98 Samuel Bolduc 1.00 2.50
R99 Akito Hirose .75 2.00
R100 Connor Bedard 40.00 100.00

2023-24 O-Pee-Chee Platinum Retro Blue Pulsar

*BLUE/100: 2.5X TO 6X BASIC
R1 Connor McDavid 50.00 125.00
R66 Luke Hughes 30.00 80.00
R70 Logan Cooley 30.00 80.00
R80 Adam Fantilli 30.00 80.00
R82 Brock Faber 30.00 80.00
R85 Matthew Knies 25.00 60.00
R100 Connor Bedard 300.00 800.00

2023-24 O-Pee-Chee Platinum Retro Pink Pulsar

*PINK: 2X TO 5X BASIC
R1 Connor McDavid 40.00 100.00
R75 Leo Carlsson 30.00 80.00
R100 Connor Bedard 125.00 300.00

2023-24 O-Pee-Chee Platinum Retro Rainbow

*RAINBOW: .6X TO 1.5X BASIC
R100 Connor Bedard 80.00 200.00

2023-24 O-Pee-Chee Platinum Retro Autographs Red

R7 Dylan Guenther 10.00 25.00
R8 Brock Nelson 8.00 20.00
R25 Mikko Rantanen SP 20.00 50.00
R26 Jared Spurgeon 8.00 20.00
R27 Casey Mittelstadt 8.00 20.00
R30 Marc-Andre Fleury SP 50.00 125.00
R31 William Eklund 10.00 25.00
R32 Nico Hischier SP 25.00 60.00
R35 Brad Marchand SP 15.00 40.00
R50 Taylor Raddysh 6.00 15.00
R51 Ryan O'Reilly 8.00 20.00
R56 Cam Atkinson 8.00 20.00
R61 Shane Pinto 6.00 15.00
R63 Kent Johnson SP 8.00 20.00
R65 Jonathan Huberdeau 10.00 25.00
R70 Logan Cooley SP 60.00 150.00
R71 Tyson Foerster 15.00 40.00
R72 William Dufour 6.00 15.00
R74 Ridly Greig SP 12.00 30.00
R76 Sean Farrell SP 8.00 20.00
R77 Dustin Wolf SP 25.00 60.00
R78 Arnaud Durandeau 8.00 20.00
R80 Adam Fantilli SP 80.00 200.00
R81 Matthew Coronato SP 12.00 30.00
R83 Aidan McDonough 6.00 15.00
R85 Matthew Knies SP 40.00 100.00
R87 Kevin Korchinski SP 12.00 30.00
R89 Elliot Desnoyers 8.00 20.00
R92 Tye Kartye 12.00 30.00
R93 Luke Philp 8.00 20.00
R94 Jonathan Gruden 8.00 20.00
R96 Jiri Patera 12.00 30.00
R98 Samuel Bolduc 8.00 20.00
R99 Akito Hirose 6.00 15.00
R100 Connor Bedard SP 1200.00 3000.00

2023-24 O-Pee-Chee Platinum Rookie Autographs

RAD Arnaud Durandeau 8.00 20.00
RAF Adam Fantilli SP 60.00 150.00
RAG Adam Ginning 8.00 20.00
RAH Akito Hirose 6.00 15.00
RAM Aidan McDonough 6.00 15.00
RBF Brock Faber SP 60.00 150.00
RBM Bobby McMann 12.00 30.00
RCG Cole Guttman 8.00 20.00
RCM Cole McWard 8.00 20.00
RCO Logan Cooley SP 60.00 150.00
RCZ Connor Zary SP 15.00 40.00
RDL Devon Levi SP 20.00 50.00
RDU William Dufour 6.00 15.00
RDW Dustin Wolf SP 30.00 80.00
RED Elliot Desnoyers 8.00 20.00
RFM Fraser Minten 15.00 40.00
RGR Jet Greaves 12.00 30.00
RGU David Gust 8.00 20.00
RHT Henry Thrun 8.00 20.00
RHU Hugh McGing 8.00 20.00
RIM Ivan Miroshnichenko 12.00 30.00
RJG Jonathan Gruden 8.00 20.00
RJK Joona Koppanen 6.00 15.00
RJL Jackson LaCombe 8.00 20.00
RJS Jaxson Stauber 8.00 20.00
RKA Tye Kartye 12.00 30.00
RKE Milos Kelemen 8.00 20.00
RKK Kevin Korchinski SP 12.00 30.00
RKN Matthew Knies SP 50.00 125.00
RLC Leo Carlsson SP 60.00 150.00
RLE Luke Evangelista SP 12.00 30.00
RLH Luke Hughes SP 60.00 150.00
RLI Jake Livingstone 8.00 20.00
RLP Luke Philp 8.00 20.00
RMA Matthew Kessel 6.00 15.00
RMC Matthew Coronato 12.00 30.00
RMM Matt Murray 8.00 20.00
RMS Mackie Samoskevich 12.00 30.00
RNS Nick Swaney 8.00 20.00
ROE Olle Eriksson Ek 8.00 20.00
RPA Jiri Patera 12.00 30.00
RPM Pavel Mintyukov 12.00 30.00
RPO Matthew Poitras SP 15.00 40.00
RRG Ridly Greig 12.00 30.00
RRL Raphael Lavoie 8.00 20.00
RSA Matt Savoie SP 15.00 40.00
RSB Samuel Bolduc 8.00 20.00
RSF Sean Farrell SP 8.00 20.00
RSK Samuel Knazko 8.00 20.00
RTF Tyson Foerster 15.00 40.00
RTK Tyler Kleven 8.00 20.00
RTR Tristen Robins 8.00 20.00
RVI Vincent Iorio SP 8.00 20.00
RWD Walker Duehr 6.00 15.00

2023-24 O-Pee-Chee Platinum Rookie Autographs Cosmic

*COSMIC: .8X TO 2X BASIC
RAF Adam Fantilli/35 150.00 400.00
RBF Brock Faber/35 150.00 400.00
RCB Connor Bedard/35 2000.00 5000.00
RCO Logan Cooley/35 150.00 400.00
RCZ Connor Zary/35 60.00 150.00
RDL Devon Levi/35 100.00 250.00
RDW Dustin Wolf/35 100.00 250.00
RKN Matthew Knies/35 150.00 400.00
RLC Leo Carlsson/35 150.00 400.00
RLH Luke Hughes/35 150.00 400.00
RPM Pavel Mintyukov/35 60.00 150.00
RPO Matthew Poitras/35 80.00 200.00
RRG Ridly Greig/35 60.00 150.00
RSA Matt Savoie/35 60.00 150.00
RTF Tyson Foerster/35 50.00 125.00
RYA Yaroslav Askarov/35 100.00 250.00
RZB Zach Benson/35 60.00 150.00

2023-24 O-Pee-Chee Platinum Rookie Autographs Matte Pink

*PINK: .6X TO 1.5X BASIC
RAF Adam Fantilli SP 125.00 300.00
RBF Brock Faber SP 125.00 300.00
RCO Logan Cooley SP 125.00 300.00
RCZ Connor Zary SP 50.00 125.00
RDL Devon Levi SP 40.00 100.00
RDW Dustin Wolf SP 50.00 125.00
RKN Matthew Knies SP 125.00 300.00
RLC Leo Carlsson SP 125.00 300.00
RLH Luke Hughes SP 125.00 300.00

2023-24 O-Pee-Chee Platinum Rookie Autographs Rainbow

*RAINBOW: .5X TO 1.2X BASIC
RAF Adam Fantilli SP 100.00 250.00
RBF Brock Faber SP 100.00 250.00
RCO Logan Cooley SP 100.00 250.00
RDW Dustin Wolf SP 40.00 100.00
RKN Matthew Knies SP 100.00 250.00
RLC Leo Carlsson SP 100.00 250.00
RLH Luke Hughes SP 100.00 250.00

2023-24 O-Pee-Chee Platinum Rookie Autographs Red Prism

*RED: .8X TO 2X BASIC
RAF Adam Fantilli/30 200.00 500.00
RBF Brock Faber/30 150.00 400.00
RCB Connor Bedard/30 2000.00 5000.00
RCO Logan Cooley/30 150.00 400.00
RCZ Connor Zary/30 60.00 150.00
RDL Devon Levi/30 100.00 250.00
RDW Dustin Wolf/30 100.00 250.00
RKN Matthew Knies/30 150.00 400.00
RLC Leo Carlsson/30 150.00 400.00
RLH Luke Hughes/30 150.00 400.00
RPM Pavel Mintyukov/30 60.00 150.00
RPO Matthew Poitras/30 80.00 200.00
RRG Ridly Greig/30 60.00 150.00
RSA Matt Savoie/30 60.00 150.00
RTF Tyson Foerster/30 60.00 150.00
RYA Yaroslav Askarov/30 100.00 250.00
RZB Zach Benson/30 60.00 150.00

2023-24 O-Pee-Chee Platinum Rookie Autographs Seismic Gold

*GOLD/25: 1X TO 2.5X BASIC
RAF Adam Fantilli 250.00 600.00
RBF Brock Faber 200.00 500.00
RCB Connor Bedard 5000.00 12000.00
RCO Logan Cooley 200.00 500.00
RCZ Connor Zary 100.00 250.00
RDL Devon Levi 150.00 400.00
RDW Dustin Wolf 125.00 300.00
RFM Fraser Minten 100.00 250.00
RKN Matthew Knies 200.00 500.00
RLC Leo Carlsson 200.00 500.00
RLH Luke Hughes 200.00 500.00
RPM Pavel Mintyukov 80.00 200.00
RPO Matthew Poitras 150.00 400.00
RRG Ridly Greig 80.00 200.00
RSA Matt Savoie 80.00 200.00
RTF Tyson Foerster 80.00 200.00
RWC Will Cuylle 80.00 200.00
RYA Yaroslav Askarov 300.00 800.00
RZB Zach Benson 80.00 200.00

2023-24 O-Pee-Chee Platinum Rookie Autographs Sunset

*SUNSET: .5X TO 1.2X BASIC
RAF Adam Fantilli SP 100.00 250.00
RBF Brock Faber SP 100.00 250.00
RCO Logan Cooley SP 100.00 250.00
RDW Dustin Wolf SP 40.00 100.00
RKN Matthew Knies SP 100.00 250.00
RLC Leo Carlsson SP 100.00 250.00
RLH Luke Hughes SP 100.00 250.00

2023-24 O-Pee-Chee Platinum Rookie Autographs Violet Pixels

*VIOLET/99: .6X TO 1.5X BASIC
RBF Brock Faber 125.00 300.00
RCB Connor Bedard 1200.00 3000.00
RCO Logan Cooley 125.00 300.00
RCZ Connor Zary 50.00 125.00
RDL Devon Levi 60.00 150.00
RDW Dustin Wolf 80.00 200.00
RKN Matthew Knies 125.00 300.00
RLC Leo Carlsson 125.00 300.00
RLH Luke Hughes 125.00 300.00
RPM Pavel Mintyukov 40.00 100.00
RPO Matthew Poitras 40.00 100.00
RYA Yaroslav Askarov 80.00 200.00
RZB Zach Benson 40.00 100.00

2023-24 O-Pee-Chee Platinum Showmanship

S1 Connor McDavid 4.00 10.00
S2 Trevor Zegras .75 2.00
S3 Steven Stamkos 1.50 4.00
S4 Robert Thomas .75 2.00
S5 Brady Tkachuk 1.00 2.50
S6 Kyle Connor 1.25 3.00
S7 Clayton Keller 1.00 2.50
S8 Andrei Svechnikov 1.00 2.50
S9 Nick Suzuki 1.50 4.00
S10 Juuse Saros 1.00 2.50
S11 Nazem Kadri 1.00 2.50
S12 Linus Ullmark .75 2.00
S13 Miro Heiskanen 1.00 2.50
S14 J.T. Miller 1.00 2.50
S15 Tim Stutzle 1.00 2.50
S16 Marc-Andre Fleury 1.50 4.00
S17 Ilya Sorokin 1.25 3.00
S18 Jake Guentzel 1.25 3.00
S19 Adam Fox 1.00 2.50
S20 Patrik Laine 1.00 2.50
S21 Nathan MacKinnon 3.00 8.00
S22 Jake Oettinger 1.25 3.00
S23 Tomas Hertl .75 2.00
S24 Adrian Kempe .75 2.00
S25 Jacob Markstrom .75 2.00

2023-24 O-Pee-Chee Platinum Showmanship Autographs Rainbow

S5 Brady Tkachuk 15.00 40.00
S10 Juuse Saros 12.00 30.00
S15 Tim Stutzle 12.00 30.00
S16 Marc-Andre Fleury 40.00 100.00
S17 Ilya Sorokin 15.00 40.00
S22 Jake Oettinger 15.00 40.00
S23 Tomas Hertl 10.00 25.00

2023-24 O-Pee-Chee Platinum Sweet Selections

SS1 Luke Hughes 2.00 5.00
SS2 Jakob Pelletier .75 2.00
SS3 Tyson Foerster 1.25 3.00
SS4 Matthew Knies 2.50 6.00
SS5 Simon Edvinsson 1.25 3.00
SS6 Devon Levi 1.50 4.00
SS7 Luke Evangelista 1.00 2.50
SS8 Matthew Coronato 1.00 2.50
SS9 Connor Bedard 4.00 10.00
SS10 Brock Faber 1.50 4.00
SS11 Logan Cooley 2.00 5.00
SS12 Marco Kasper 1.50 4.00
SS13 Adam Fantilli 2.00 5.00
SS14 Ridly Greig 1.00 2.50
SS15 Yaroslav Askarov 1.50 4.00

2023-24 O-Pee-Chee Platinum Sweet Selections Green Pixel

*GREEN/35: 2.5X TO 6X BASIC
SS9 Connor Bedard 200.00 500.00

2023-24 O-Pee-Chee Platinum Sweet Selections Autographs Rainbow

SS3 Tyson Foerster 12.00 30.00
SS4 Matthew Knies SP 30.00 80.00
SS6 Devon Levi 25.00 60.00
SS8 Matthew Coronato 10.00 25.00
SS13 Adam Fantilli SP 50.00 125.00
SS14 Ridly Greig 10.00 25.00

2024-25 O-Pee-Chee Platinum

1 Connor McDavid 2.00 5.00
2 Connor Bedard 1.25 3.00
3 Brad Marchand .75 2.00
4 Tage Thompson .50 1.25
5 Patrick Kane .75 2.00
6 Matthew Tkachuk .75 2.00
7 Anze Kopitar .60 1.50
8 Sebastian Aho .60 1.50
9 Marco Rossi .50 1.25
10 Troy Terry .30 .75
11 Cole Caufield .75 2.00
12 Filip Forsberg .60 1.50
13 Jack Hughes 1.00 2.50
14 Artemi Panarin .75 2.00
15 Nick Schmaltz .30 .75
16 Brady Tkachuk .60 1.50
17 Elias Lindholm .40 1.00
18 Travis Konecny .40 1.00
19 William Eklund .50 1.25
20 Sidney Crosby 1.50 4.00
21 Colton Parayko .30 .75
22 Moritz Seider .50 1.25
23 Boone Jenner .40 1.00
24 Mathew Barzal .50 1.25
25 Alexandar Georgiev .40 1.00
26 Jack Eichel .60 1.50
27 Andrei Vasilevskiy .60 1.50
28 Jason Robertson .60 1.50
29 Victor Hedman .50 1.25
30 Marc-Andre Fleury .75 2.00
31 Mitch Marner .60 1.50
32 Michael Bunting .30 .75
33 Jake Neighbours .40 1.00
34 Brock Nelson .40 1.00
35 Elias Pettersson .60 1.50
36 Kyle Connor .50 1.25
37 Kevin Fiala .30 .75
38 Nazem Kadri .50 1.25
39 Nick Suzuki .75 2.00
40 Claude Giroux .40 1.00
41 JJ Peterka .40 1.00
42 Jake Walman .25 .60
43 Ryan Nugent-Hopkins .50 1.25
44 Erik Karlsson .50 1.25
45 Ryan O'Reilly .40 1.00
46 Lucas Raymond .60 1.50
47 Anders Lee .30 .75
48 Sam Bennett .30 .75
49 Owen Tippett .25 .60
50 Devon Toews .30 .75
51 David Perron .30 .75
52 Connor Zary .40 1.00
53 Jordan Binnington .50 1.25
54 Trevor Zegras .40 1.00
55 Fabian Zetterlund .25 .60
56 Ivan Barbashev .30 .75
57 Seth Jones .40 1.00
58 Trevor Moore .25 .60
59 Jonathan Huberdeau .50 1.25
60 Sam Reinhart .75 2.00
61 Frank Vatrano .30 .75
62 Linus Ullmark .40 1.00
63 Jesper Bratt .40 1.00
64 Wyatt Johnston .75 2.00
65 Dmitri Voronkov .25 .60
66 J.T. Miller .50 1.25
67 Jared McCann .30 .75
68 Vincent Trocheck .40 1.00
69 Jaccob Slavin .30 .75
70 Matthew Knies .75 2.00
71 Steven Stamkos .75 2.00
72 Igor Shesterkin .75 2.00
73 Tyler Toffoli .40 1.00
74 Yegor Sharangovich .40 1.00
75 Brandt Clarke .40 1.00
76 Sergei Bobrovsky .60 1.50
77 Alex Tuch .40 1.00
78 Bryan Rust .40 1.00
79 Lukas Dostal .40 1.00
80 John Tavares .60 1.50
81 Dylan Cozens .40 1.00
82 Brock Faber .50 1.25
83 Mark Stone .50 1.25
84 Adam Fantilli .60 1.50
85 Dawson Mercer .50 1.25
86 Tyson Foerster .40 1.00
87 Jamie Benn .40 1.00
88 Jake Guentzel .60 1.50
89 Nico Hischier .60 1.50
90 Nathan MacKinnon 1.50 4.00
91 Charlie Coyle .40 1.00
92 Brandon Hagel .30 .75
93 Robert Thomas .40 1.00
94 Martin Necas .60 1.50
95 Noah Hanifin .40 1.00
96 Samuel Montembeault .40 1.00
97 Dylan Strome .50 1.25
98 Tyler Bertuzzi .30 .75
99 Logan Cooley .60 1.50
100 Connor Hellebuyck .75 2.00
101 Jeremy Swayman .60 1.50
102 Aleksander Barkov .60 1.50
103 Quinton Byfield .50 1.25
104 Juraj Slafkovsky .75 2.00
105 Stuart Skinner .50 1.25
106 Kirill Kaprizov 1.25 3.00
107 Luke Hughes .60 1.50
108 Kent Johnson .30 .75
109 Ilya Sorokin .60 1.50
110 Alexis Lafreniere .60 1.50
111 Jake Sanderson .50 1.25
112 Andrei Kuzmenko .40 1.00
113 Dylan Larkin .50 1.25
114 Alex Ovechkin 1.50 4.00
115 Joel Farabee .40 1.00
116 Taylor Hall .40 1.00
117 Clayton Keller .50 1.25
118 Pavel Buchnevich .30 .75
119 Matt Boldy .60 1.50
120 Owen Power .50 1.25
121 Brayden Point .50 1.25
122 Mikael Granlund .30 .75
123 Chris Kreider .50 1.25
124 William Karlsson .50 1.25
125 Brock Boeser .50 1.25
126 Brent Burns .40 1.00
127 Tom Wilson .40 1.00
128 Juuse Saros .50 1.25
129 Noah Dobson .50 1.25
130 Nick Foligno .25 .60
131 Tyler Seguin .50 1.25
132 Charlie McAvoy .50 1.25
133 Gabe Vilardi .40 1.00
134 Carter Verhaeghe .40 1.00
135 Matias Maccelli .30 .75
136 Casey Mittelstadt .40 1.00
137 Drake Batherson .40 1.00
138 Leo Carlsson .60 1.50
139 Matty Beniers .50 1.25
140 MacKenzie Weegar .25 .60
141 Samuel Ersson .40 1.00
142 Mark Scheifele .60 1.50
143 Logan Thompson .50 1.25
144 Rasmus Dahlin .50 1.25
145 Alex DeBrincat .50 1.25
146 Evan Bouchard .50 1.25
147 Brendan Gallagher .40 1.00
148 Jordan Kyrou .40 1.00
149 Kirill Marchenko .40 1.00
150 Morgan Rielly .40 1.00
151 Kevin Korchinski .30 .75
152 Cole Perfetti .40 1.00
153 John Carlson .40 1.00
154 Roman Josi .40 1.00
155 Josh Morrissey .50 1.25
156 Mika Zibanejad .50 1.25
157 Dylan Guenther .50 1.25
158 Brady Skjei .25 .60
159 Oliver Bjorkstrand .30 .75
160 Matt Duchene .40 1.00
161 Darnell Nurse .30 .75
162 Devon Toews .30 .75
163 Mason McTavish .50 1.25
164 Jonathan Marchessault .50 1.25
165 Shane Wright .50 1.25
166 Thatcher Demko .50 1.25
167 Charlie Lindgren .30 .75
168 Cale Makar 1.00 2.50
169 Kris Letang .50 1.25
170 Filip Hronek .25 .60
171 Tomas Hertl .40 1.00
172 Cole Sillinger .30 .75
173 Mike Matheson .25 .60
174 Joel Eriksson Ek .30 .75
175 Quinn Hughes 1.00 2.50
176 Seth Jarvis .50 1.25
177 Adrian Kempe .50 1.25
178 Leon Draisaitl 1.25 3.00
179 Joey Daccord .40 1.00
180 Jaden Schwartz .30 .75
181 Mikhail Sergachev .30 .75
182 Zach Hyman .60 1.50
183 David Pastrnak 1.00 2.50
184 William Nylander .75 2.00
185 Logan Couture .50 1.25
186 Zach Benson .30 .75
187 Evgeni Malkin .75 2.00
188 Nikita Kucherov .75 2.00
189 Timo Meier .40 1.00
190 Pavel Mintyukov .30 .75
191 Jake Oettinger .60 1.50
192 Sean Couturier .30 .75
193 Auston Matthews 1.50 4.00
194 Drew Doughty .40 1.00
195 Tim Stutzle .50 1.25
196 Mikko Rantanen 1.00 2.50
197 J.T. Compher .25 .60
198 Bo Horvat .50 1.25
199 Andrei Svechnikov .50 1.25
200 Adam Fox .50 1.25
201 Cutter Gauthier RC 2.50 6.00
202 Logan Stankoven RC 2.50 6.00
203 Brennan Othmann RC 1.50 4.00
204 Jesper Wallstedt RC 2.50 6.00
205 Mavrik Bourque RC 2.00 5.00
206 Frank Nazar RC 3.00 8.00
207 Olen Zellweger RC 2.00 5.00
208 Joshua Roy RC 1.50 4.00
209 Shakir Mukhamadullin RC 1.25 3.00
210 Sam Colangelo RC 1.00 2.50
211 Aku Raty RC 1.00 2.50
212 Lian Bichsel RC 2.00 5.00
213 Denton Mateychuk RC 2.00 5.00
214 Matt Villalta RC 1.00 2.50
215 Owen Pickering RC 1.25 3.00
216 Fabian Lysell RC 2.50 6.00
217 Justin Brazeau RC 1.00 2.50
218 Adam Klapka RC 1.00 2.50
219 Yan Kuznetsov RC 1.00 2.50
220 Bradly Nadeau RC 1.50 4.00
221 Jackson Blake RC 2.00 5.00
222 Scott Morrow RC 1.25 3.00
223 Jakub Dobes RC 3.00 8.00
224 Ethan Del Mastro RC 1.00 2.50
225 Landon Slaggert RC 1.00 2.50
226 Jason Polin RC 1.00 2.50
227 Nikolai Kovalenko RC 1.00 2.50
228 Cameron Butler RC 1.00 2.50
229 Gavin Brindley RC 1.00 2.50
230 James Malatesta RC 1.00 2.50
231 Luca Del Bel Belluz RC 1.00 2.50
232 Phil Kemp RC 1.00 2.50
233 Akil Thomas RC 1.00 2.50
234 Lane Hutson RC 5.00 12.00
235 Liam Ohgren RC 2.00 5.00
236 Marat Khusnutdinov RC 1.00 2.50
237 Logan Mailloux RC 1.50 4.00
238 Fedor Svechkov RC 1.50 4.00
239 Graeme Clarke RC 1.00 2.50
240 Isaac Poulter RC 1.00 2.50
241 Kyle MacLean RC 1.00 2.50
242 Ruslan Iskhakov RC 1.00 2.50
243 Brandon Scanlin RC 1.00 2.50
244 Matt Rempe RC 2.00 5.00
245 Zack Ostapchuk RC 1.00 2.50
246 Ivan Fedotov RC 2.00 5.00
247 Jack St. Ivany RC 1.00 2.50
248 Collin Graf RC 1.00 2.50
249 Devin Cooley RC 1.00 2.50
250 Georgi Romanov RC 1.25 3.00
251 Logan Morrison RC 1.00 2.50
252 Zach Dean RC 1.00 2.50
253 Zachary Bolduc RC 2.00 5.00
254 Josh Doan RC 1.50 4.00
255 Declan Carlile RC 1.00 2.50
256 Emil Lilleberg RC 1.00 2.50
257 Gage Goncalves RC 1.25 3.00
258 Jack Thompson RC 1.00 2.50
259 Maxwell Crozier RC 1.00 2.50
260 Marshall Rifai RC 1.00 2.50
261 Arshdeep Bains RC 1.25 3.00
262 Brendan Brisson RC 1.25 3.00
263 Macklin Celebrini RC 5.00 12.00
264 Matvei Michkov RC 4.00 10.00
265 Lukas Cormier RC 1.00 2.50
266 Mason Morelli RC 1.00 2.50
267 Pierrick Dube RC 1.00 2.50
268 Brad Lambert RC 1.25 3.00
269 Nikita Chibrikov RC 1.25 3.00
270 Seamus Casey RC 1.25 3.00
271 Nolan Allan RC 1.00 2.50
272 Samuel Honzek RC 1.25 3.00
273 Ivan Ivan RC 1.00 2.50
274 Calum Ritchie RC 1.00 2.50
275 Victor Mancini RC 1.00 2.50
276 Rutger McGroarty RC 2.00 5.00
277 Maxim Tsyplakov RC 1.50 4.00
278 Will Smith RC 3.00 8.00
279 Andre Lee RC 1.00 2.50
280 Oliver Kapanen RC 1.00 2.50
281 Jonathan Lekkerimaki RC 2.50 6.00
282 Joel Blomqvist RC 1.25 3.00
283 Oskar Back RC 1.00 2.50
284 Jett Luchanko RC 2.00 5.00
285 Conor Geekie RC 2.00 5.00
286 Albert Johansson RC 1.00 2.50
287 Patrick Giles RC 1.00 2.50
288 Matt Stienburg RC 1.00 2.50
289 Daniil Misyul RC 1.00 2.50
290 Zachary L'Heureux RC 1.00 2.50
291 Maveric Lamoureux RC 1.50 4.00
292 Drew Commesso RC 1.25 3.00
293 Aleksei Kolosov RC 1.25 3.00
294 Ethan Cardwell RC .75 2.00
295 Noah Philp RC 1.00 2.50
296 Nikita Prishchepov RC 1.00 2.50
297 Isaiah George RC 1.25 3.00
298 Ales Stezka RC 1.00 2.50
299 Samuel Helenius RC 1.00 2.50
300 Sebastian Cossa RC 2.50 6.00

2024-25 O-Pee-Chee Platinum Arctic Freeze

*ARCTIC/99: 2X TO 5X BASIC
1 Connor McDavid 20.00 50.00
206 Frank Nazar 30.00 80.00
223 Jakub Dobes 25.00 60.00
234 Lane Hutson 60.00 150.00
263 Macklin Celebrini 100.00 250.00
264 Matvei Michkov 60.00 150.00
278 Will Smith 40.00 100.00
300 Sebastian Cossa 15.00 40.00

2024-25 O-Pee-Chee Platinum Blue Fragments

*BLUE/125: 1.5X TO 4X BASIC
1 Connor McDavid 20.00 50.00
206 Frank Nazar 20.00 50.00
223 Jakub Dobes 15.00 40.00
234 Lane Hutson 80.00 200.00
263 Macklin Celebrini 100.00 250.00
264 Matvei Michkov 60.00 150.00
278 Will Smith 30.00 80.00

2024-25 O-Pee-Chee Platinum Cosmic

*COSMIC/65: 4X TO 10X BASIC
*COSMIC RC/65: 2.5X TO 6X BASIC
1 Connor McDavid 25.00 60.00
206 Frank Nazar 80.00 200.00
223 Jakub Dobes 30.00 80.00
234 Lane Hutson 125.00 300.00
263 Macklin Celebrini 125.00 300.00
264 Matvei Michkov 80.00 200.00
300 Sebastian Cossa 20.00 50.00

2024-25 O-Pee-Chee Platinum Mixed Media Variant

*MX MEDIA: 10X TO 25X BASIC
*MX MEDIA RC: 6X TO 15X BASIC
263 Macklin Celebrini 125.00 300.00
264 Matvei Michkov 80.00 200.00

2024-25 O-Pee-Chee Platinum Neon Yellow Surge

*NEON YLW: .8X TO 2X BASIC
234 Lane Hutson 20.00 50.00
263 Macklin Celebrini 30.00 80.00
264 Matvei Michkov 25.00 60.00

2024-25 O-Pee-Chee Platinum Orange Checkers

*ORANGE/25: 8X TO 20X BASIC
*ORANGE RC/25: 4X TO 10X BASIC
1 Connor McDavid 200.00 500.00
2 Connor Bedard 100.00 250.00
20 Sidney Crosby 80.00 200.00
90 Nathan MacKinnon 50.00 125.00
114 Alex Ovechkin 60.00 150.00
178 Leon Draisaitl 40.00 100.00
193 Auston Matthews 50.00 125.00
201 Cutter Gauthier 100.00 250.00
202 Logan Stankoven 50.00 125.00
204 Jesper Wallstedt 30.00 80.00
206 Frank Nazar 150.00 400.00
216 Fabian Lysell 40.00 100.00
223 Jakub Dobes 50.00 125.00
263 Macklin Celebrini 800.00 2000.00
264 Matvei Michkov 250.00 600.00
281 Jonathan Lekkerimaki 50.00 125.00
300 Sebastian Cossa 50.00 125.00

2024-25 O-Pee-Chee Platinum Pink Magma

*PINK: .6X TO 1.5X BASIC
1 Connor McDavid 4.00 10.00
234 Lane Hutson 20.00 50.00
263 Macklin Celebrini 40.00 100.00
264 Matvei Michkov 20.00 50.00

2024-25 O-Pee-Chee Platinum Pond Hockey Variant

*POND HK: 6X TO 15X BASIC
263 Macklin Celebrini 125.00 300.00

2024-25 O-Pee-Chee Platinum Rainbow

*RAINBOW: .5X TO 1.2X BASIC
234 Lane Hutson 8.00 20.00
263 Macklin Celebrini 15.00 40.00

2024-25 O-Pee-Chee Platinum Red Prism

*RED/199: 1.2X TO 3X BASIC
1 Connor McDavid 12.00 30.00
206 Frank Nazar 12.00 30.00
234 Lane Hutson 60.00 150.00
263 Macklin Celebrini 80.00 200.00
264 Matvei Michkov 50.00 125.00
278 Will Smith 10.00 25.00

2024-25 O-Pee-Chee Platinum Seismic Gold

*GOLD/50: 5X TO 12X BASIC
*GOLD RC/50: 3X TO 8X BASIC
1 Connor McDavid 150.00 400.00
202 Logan Stankoven 30.00 80.00
206 Frank Nazar 125.00 300.00
216 Fabian Lysell 30.00 80.00
223 Jakub Dobes 40.00 100.00
234 Lane Hutson 200.00 500.00
263 Macklin Celebrini 600.00 1500.00
264 Matvei Michkov 200.00 500.00
281 Jonathan Lekkerimaki 50.00 125.00
300 Sebastian Cossa 40.00 100.00

2024-25 O-Pee-Chee Platinum Sunset

*SUNSET: .6X TO 1.5X BASIC
234 Lane Hutson 10.00 25.00
263 Macklin Celebrini 20.00 50.00
264 Matvei Michkov 15.00 40.00

2024-25 O-Pee-Chee Platinum Violet Pixels

*VIOLET/299: 1X TO 2.5X BASIC
1 Connor McDavid 8.00 20.00
234 Lane Hutson 40.00 100.00
263 Macklin Celebrini 60.00 150.00
264 Matvei Michkov 40.00 100.00

2024-25 O-Pee-Chee Platinum Blue Rainbow Autographs

BAAB Aleksander Barkov SP 12.00 30.00
BAAC Andrew Copp 5.00 12.00
BAAD Alex DeBrincat 10.00 25.00
BAAH Alexander Holtz 8.00 20.00
BAAK Andrei Kuzmenko 8.00 20.00
BAAL Anton Lundell 8.00 20.00
BAAM Auston Matthews SP 80.00 200.00
BAAP Aliaksei Protas 5.00 12.00
BAAT Alex Tuch 8.00 20.00
BABB Bobby Brink 5.00 12.00
BABC Blake Coleman 6.00 15.00
BABF Brock Faber 10.00 25.00
BABO Brock Boeser SP 10.00 25.00
BABS Brandon Saad 6.00 15.00
BABT Brady Tkachuk SP 12.00 30.00
BABU Michael Bunting 8.00 20.00
BACL Brandt Clarke 8.00 20.00
BACM Cale Makar SP 30.00 80.00
BACP Cole Perfetti 8.00 20.00
BACS Cole Sillinger 6.00 15.00
BADB Drake Batherson 8.00 20.00
BADG Dylan Guenther 10.00 25.00
BADJ David Jiricek 8.00 20.00
BAEP Elias Pettersson SP 12.00 30.00
BAFV Frank Vatrano 6.00 15.00
BAFZ Fabian Zetterlund 5.00 12.00
BAIS Ilya Sorokin 12.00 30.00
BAJA Tristan Jarry 8.00 20.00
BAJE Jordan Eberle 8.00 20.00
BAJG Jake Guentzel SP 12.00 30.00
BAJH Jack Hughes SP 20.00 50.00
BAJM Jonathan Marchessault 10.00 25.00
BAJN Jake Neighbours 8.00 20.00
BAJO Jake Oettinger SP 12.00 30.00
BAJP Jakob Pelletier 5.00 12.00
BAJQ Jack Quinn 6.00 15.00
BAJS Jake Sanderson SP 10.00 25.00
BAJT Jacob Trouba 5.00 12.00
BAJU Juuse Saros 10.00 25.00
BAJW Joseph Woll 10.00 25.00
BAKJ Kent Johnson 8.00 20.00
BAKK Kirill Kaprizov SP 50.00 125.00
BAKM Kirill Marchenko 10.00 25.00
BAKR Peyton Krebs 6.00 15.00
BALA Alexis Lafreniere SP 12.00 30.00
BALC Leo Carlsson 8.00 20.00
BALD Leon Draisaitl SP 60.00 150.00
BALI Charlie Lindgren 6.00 15.00
BAMB Matt Boldy SP 12.00 30.00
BAMC Jared McCann 6.00 15.00
BAMF Marc-Andre Fleury SP 15.00 40.00
BAMG Mikael Granlund 6.00 15.00
BAMH Miro Heiskanen SP 10.00 25.00
BAMI Matias Maccelli 6.00 15.00
BAMM Mason Marchment 6.00 15.00
BAMS Mark Stone SP 10.00 25.00
BAMT Mason McTavish SP 8.00 20.00
BAMW MacKenzie Weegar 5.00 12.00
BANC Noah Cates 5.00 12.00
BANE Nikolaj Ehlers 8.00 20.00
BANH Nils Hoglander 6.00 15.00
BANK Nikita Kucherov SP 15.00 40.00
BANS Nick Schmaltz 6.00 15.00
BAOP Owen Power SP 10.00 25.00
BAPA Artemi Panarin SP 15.00 40.00
BAPK Pyotr Kochetkov 8.00 20.00
BAPM Petr Mrazek SP 6.00 15.00
BARA Mikko Rantanen SP 20.00 50.00
BARG Ridly Greig 6.00 15.00
BARJ Roman Josi SP 8.00 20.00
BARR Ryan Reaves 6.00 15.00
BARS Ryan Strome 8.00 20.00
BASA Sebastian Aho SP 12.00 30.00
BASE Samuel Ersson 8.00 20.00
BASL Jacob Slavin 6.00 15.00
BASR Sam Reinhart SP 15.00 40.00
BAST Shea Theodore 10.00 25.00
BASU Nick Suzuki SP 25.00 60.00
BASW Shane Wright 10.00 25.00
BATJ Tanner Jeannot 5.00 12.00
BATK Matthew Tkachuk SP 15.00 40.00
BATM Timo Meier 8.00 20.00
BATR Taylor Raddysh 6.00 15.00
BATT Tage Thompson SP 10.00 25.00
BAWE William Eklund 10.00 25.00
BAWK William Karlsson 10.00 25.00

2024-25 O-Pee-Chee Platinum OPC Premier

OP1 Adam Fantilli 2.50 6.00
OP2 Alex Ovechkin 6.00 15.00
OP3 Artemi Panarin 3.00 8.00
OP4 Auston Matthews 6.00 15.00
OP5 Brad Marchand 3.00 8.00
OP6 Cale Makar 4.00 10.00
OP7 Cole Caufield 3.00 8.00
OP8 Connor Bedard 5.00 12.00
OP9 Connor McDavid 8.00 20.00
OP10 David Pastrnak 4.00 10.00
OP11 Elias Pettersson 2.50 6.00
OP12 Jack Eichel 2.50 6.00
OP13 Jason Robertson 2.50 6.00
OP14 Kirill Kaprizov 5.00 12.00
OP15 Leon Draisaitl 5.00 12.00
OP16 Marc-Andre Fleury 3.00 8.00
OP17 Nathan MacKinnon 6.00 15.00
OP18 Nikita Kucherov 3.00 8.00
OP19 Sidney Crosby 6.00 15.00
OP20 Sebastian Aho 2.50 6.00
OP21 Lane Hutson 25.00 60.00
OP22 Olen Zellweger 3.00 8.00
OP23 Logan Stankoven 4.00 10.00
OP24 Mavrik Bourque 3.00 8.00
OP25 Brendan Brisson 2.00 5.00
OP26 Cutter Gauthier 4.00 10.00
OP27 Frank Nazar 5.00 12.00
OP28 Liam Ohgren 3.00 8.00
OP29 Josh Doan 2.50 6.00
OP30 Brennan Othmann 2.50 6.00
OP31 Jesper Wallstedt 4.00 10.00
OP32 Zachary Bolduc 3.00 8.00
OP33 Macklin Celebrini 25.00 60.00
OP34 Matvei Michkov 10.00 25.00
OP35 Seamus Casey 2.00 5.00

2024-25 O-Pee-Chee Platinum Power Playmakers

*RAY/85: .8X TO 2X BASIC
*GREEN/35: 1.5X TO 4X BASIC
PM1 Roope Hintz .60 1.50
PM2 Jonathan Marchessault .60 1.50
PM3 John Tavares .75 2.00
PM4 Zach Hyman .75 2.00
PM5 Elias Pettersson .75 2.00
PM6 Mason McTavish .50 1.25
PM7 Artemi Panarin 1.00 2.50
PM8 Cole Perfetti .50 1.25
PM9 Aleksander Barkov .75 2.00
PM10 Matt Boldy .75 2.00
PM11 Kirill Kaprizov 1.50 4.00
PM12 Roman Josi .50 1.25
PM13 Jack Eichel .75 2.00
PM14 Leon Draisaitl 1.50 4.00
PM15 Mikko Rantanen 1.25 3.00

2024-25 O-Pee-Chee Platinum Power Playmakers Rainbow Autographs

PM2 Jonathan Marchessault 12.00 30.00
PM5 Elias Pettersson 15.00 40.00

PM6 Mason McTavish 10.00 25.00
PM7 Artemi Panarin 20.00 50.00
PM8 Cole Perfetti 10.00 25.00
PM11 Kirill Kaprizov 40.00 100.00
PM14 Leon Draisaitl SP 30.00 80.00

2024-25 O-Pee-Chee Platinum Retro

*PINK: 2X TO 5X BASIC
R1 Sidney Crosby 4.00 10.00
R2 Auston Matthews 4.00 10.00
R3 Alex Ovechkin 4.00 10.00
R4 Nathan MacKinnon 4.00 10.00
R5 Leon Draisaitl 3.00 8.00
R6 Kevin Fiala .75 2.00
R7 Pavel Zacha .75 2.00
R8 Jack Hughes 2.50 6.00
R9 Cale Makar 2.50 6.00
R10 Connor Bedard 3.00 8.00
R11 Kirill Kaprizov 3.00 8.00
R12 Nikita Kucherov 2.00 5.00
R13 Connor McDavid 5.00 12.00
R14 John Tavares 1.50 4.00
R15 Elias Pettersson 1.50 4.00
R16 Marc-Andre Fleury 2.00 5.00
R17 Alexis Lafreniere 1.50 4.00
R18 Shane Wright 1.25 3.00
R19 Morgan Frost .75 2.00
R20 Brad Marchand 2.00 5.00
R21 Quinn Hughes 2.50 6.00
R22 Frank Vatrano .75 2.00
R23 Chandler Stephenson .75 2.00
R24 Jason Dickinson .60 1.50
R25 Dylan Larkin 1.25 3.00
R26 Tim Stutzle 1.25 3.00
R27 Nick Suzuki 2.00 5.00
R28 Brady Tkachuk 1.50 4.00
R29 Matthew Tkachuk 2.00 5.00
R30 Joseph Woll 1.25 3.00
R31 Aleksander Barkov 1.50 4.00
R32 Sebastian Aho 1.50 4.00
R33 Artemi Panarin 2.00 5.00
R34 Sam Reinhart 2.00 5.00
R35 Zach Hyman 1.50 4.00
R36 Matt Boldy 1.50 4.00
R37 Luke Hughes 1.50 4.00
R38 Steven Stamkos 2.00 5.00
R39 Anze Kopitar 1.50 4.00
R40 Simon Edvinsson 1.00 2.50
R41 Noah Dobson 1.25 3.00
R42 Jake Oettinger 1.50 4.00
R43 Wyatt Johnston 2.00 5.00
R44 Colton Parayko .75 2.00
R45 Tage Thompson 1.25 3.00
R46 Mason McTavish 1.00 2.50
R47 Alex DeBrincat 1.25 3.00
R48 Roman Josi 1.00 2.50
R49 Evan Bouchard 1.25 3.00
R50 Ilya Sorokin 1.50 4.00
R51 Jordan Eberle 1.00 2.50
R52 Tristan Jarry 1.00 2.50
R53 Jordan Kyrou 1.00 2.50
R54 Bryan Rust 1.00 2.50
R55 Jake Sanderson 1.25 3.00
R56 David Pastrnak 2.50 6.00
R57 Andrei Kuzmenko 1.00 2.50
R58 Yegor Sharangovich 1.00 2.50
R59 William Eklund 1.25 3.00
R60 Alexander Holtz 1.00 2.50
R61 Kaiden Guhle 1.00 2.50
R62 Anton Lundell 1.00 2.50
R63 Kirill Marchenko 1.25 3.00
R64 Pyotr Kochetkov 1.00 2.50
R65 Matias Maccelli .75 2.00
R66 Olen Zellweger 2.00 5.00
R67 Logan Stankoven 2.50 6.00
R68 Brennan Othmann 1.50 4.00
R69 Jesper Wallstedt 2.50 6.00
R70 Mavrik Bourque 2.00 5.00
R71 Graeme Clarke 1.00 2.50
R72 Ivan Fedotov 2.00 5.00
R73 Josh Doan 1.50 4.00
R74 Zachary Bolduc 2.00 5.00
R75 Matt Rempe 2.00 5.00
R76 Akil Thomas 1.00 2.50
R77 Brendan Brisson 1.25 3.00
R78 Zach Dean 1.00 2.50
R79 Mason Morelli 1.00 2.50
R80 Logan Mailloux 1.50 4.00
R81 Liam Ohgren 2.00 5.00
R82 Shakir Mukhamadullin 1.25 3.00
R83 Arshdeep Bains 1.25 3.00
R84 Gage Goncalves 1.25 3.00
R85 Zack Ostapchuk 1.00 2.50
R86 Lukas Cormier 1.00 2.50
R87 Marat Khusnutdinov 1.00 2.50
R88 Cutter Gauthier 2.50 6.00
R89 Frank Nazar 3.00 8.00
R90 Lane Hutson 5.00 12.00
R91 Macklin Celebrini 5.00 12.00
R92 Matvei Michkov 4.00 10.00
R93 Will Smith 3.00 8.00
R94 Seamus Casey 1.25 3.00
R95 Rutger McGroarty 2.00 5.00
R96 Maxim Tsyplakov 1.50 4.00
R97 Conor Geekie 2.00 5.00
R98 Jett Luchanko 2.00 5.00
R99 Gavin Brindley 1.00 2.50
R100 Pierrick Dube 1.00 2.50

2024-25 O-Pee-Chee Platinum Retro Blue Luster

*BLUE/100: 2X TO 5X BASIC
R92 Matvei Michkov 50.00 125.00

2024-25 O-Pee-Chee Platinum Retro Rainbow

*RAINBOW: .6X TO 1.5X BASIC
R90 Lane Hutson 10.00 25.00
R91 Macklin Celebrini 12.00 30.00
R92 Matvei Michkov 10.00 25.00

2024-25 O-Pee-Chee Platinum Retro Autographs Red

R5 Leon Draisaitl SP 30.00 80.00
R7 Pavel Zacha 8.00 20.00
R9 Cale Makar SP 60.00 150.00
R11 Kirill Kaprizov SP 40.00 100.00
R12 Nikita Kucherov SP 20.00 50.00
R15 Elias Pettersson SP 15.00 40.00
R16 Marc-Andre Fleury SP 20.00 50.00
R18 Shane Wright 12.00 30.00
R19 Morgan Frost 8.00 20.00
R22 Frank Vatrano 8.00 20.00
R24 Jason Dickinson 6.00 15.00
R27 Nick Suzuki 20.00 50.00
R30 Joseph Woll 12.00 30.00
R33 Artemi Panarin SP 20.00 50.00
R34 Sam Reinhart 20.00 50.00
R37 Luke Hughes 15.00 40.00
R40 Simon Edvinsson 10.00 25.00
R42 Jake Oettinger 15.00 40.00
R44 Colton Parayko 8.00 20.00
R46 Mason McTavish 10.00 25.00
R50 Ilya Sorokin 15.00 40.00
R52 Tristan Jarry 10.00 25.00
R53 Jordan Kyrou 10.00 25.00
R55 Jake Sanderson 12.00 30.00
R58 Yegor Sharangovich 10.00 25.00
R59 William Eklund 12.00 30.00
R60 Alexander Holtz 10.00 25.00
R63 Kirill Marchenko 12.00 30.00
R64 Pyotr Kochetkov 10.00 25.00
R65 Matias Maccelli 8.00 20.00
R66 Olen Zellweger SP 20.00 50.00
R67 Logan Stankoven SP 40.00 100.00
R69 Jesper Wallstedt 40.00 100.00
R70 Mavrik Bourque 20.00 50.00
R71 Graeme Clarke 10.00 25.00
R72 Ivan Fedotov 20.00 50.00
R75 Matt Rempe 20.00 50.00
R76 Akil Thomas 10.00 25.00
R78 Zach Dean 10.00 25.00
R81 Liam Ohgren 20.00 50.00
R82 Shakir Mukhamadullin 12.00 30.00
R83 Arshdeep Bains 12.00 30.00
R85 Zack Ostapchuk 10.00 25.00
R86 Lukas Cormier 10.00 25.00
R87 Marat Khusnutdinov 10.00 25.00
R88 Cutter Gauthier SP 40.00 100.00
R89 Frank Nazar SP 80.00 200.00
R90 Lane Hutson 250.00 600.00
R91 Macklin Celebrini 300.00 800.00
R92 Matvei Michkov 150.00 400.00
R93 Will Smith 50.00 125.00
R100 Pierrick Dube 10.00 25.00

2024-25 O-Pee-Chee Platinum Rookie Autographs

RAB Arshdeep Bains SP 10.00 25.00
RAJ Albert Johansson 8.00 20.00
RAK Aleksei Kolosov 8.00 20.00
RAL Andre Lee 8.00 20.00
RAR Aku Raty 8.00 20.00
RAT Akil Thomas SP 8.00 20.00
RBH Brian Halonen 8.00 20.00
RCE Macklin Celebrini SP 300.00 800.00
RCG Collin Graf 8.00 20.00
RCO Devin Cooley 8.00 20.00
REC Ethan Cardwell 6.00 15.00
REL Emil Lilleberg 8.00 20.00
RFN Frank Nazar SP 30.00 80.00
RFS Fedor Svechkov 12.00 30.00
RGA Cutter Gauthier SP 20.00 50.00
RGC Graeme Clarke 8.00 20.00
RHE Samuel Helenius 8.00 20.00
RJB Joel Blomqvist 10.00 25.00
RJP Jason Polin 8.00 20.00
RJT Jack Thompson 8.00 20.00
RJW Jesper Wallstedt SP 20.00 50.00
RKL Adam Klapka 8.00 20.00
RLB Lian Bichsel SP 15.00 40.00
RLC Lukas Cormier 8.00 20.00
RLE Jonathan Lekkerimaki SP 20.00 50.00
RLH Lane Hutson SP 125.00 300.00
RLM Logan Morrison 8.00 20.00
RLO Liam Ohgren SP 15.00 40.00
RMB Mavrik Bourque SP 15.00 40.00
RMK Marat Khusnutdinov SP 8.00 20.00
RML Maveric Lamoureux 12.00 30.00
RMM Matvei Michkov SP 150.00 400.00
RMR Marshall Rifai 8.00 20.00
RMU Shakir Mukhamadullin 10.00 25.00
RNA Nolan Allan 8.00 20.00
RNC Nikita Chibrikov 8.00 20.00
ROZ Olen Zellweger SP 15.00 40.00
RPD Pierrick Dube 8.00 20.00
RPK Phil Kemp 8.00 20.00
RRE Matt Rempe 15.00 40.00
RSA Sam Colangelo 8.00 20.00
RSB Sebastian Cossa SP 30.00 80.00
RSH Samuel Honzek 8.00 20.00
RSM Scott Morrow 10.00 25.00
RSS Max Sasson 8.00 20.00
RST Logan Stankoven SP 20.00 50.00
RVM Victor Mancini 8.00 20.00
RVP Vasily Ponomarev 8.00 20.00
RWS Will Smith SP 80.00 200.00
RYK Yan Kuznetsov 8.00 20.00
RZD Zach Dean 8.00 20.00
RZL Zachary L'Heureux SP 10.00 25.00
RZO Zack Ostapchuk 8.00 20.00

2024-25 O-Pee-Chee Platinum Rookie Autographs Cosmic

*COSMIC/50: .8X TO 2X BASIC
RFN Frank Nazar 200.00 500.00
RJW Jesper Wallstedt 80.00 200.00
RLH Lane Hutson 400.00 1000.00
RSB Sebastian Cossa 80.00 200.00
RST Logan Stankoven 80.00 200.00
RWS Will Smith 250.00 600.00

2024-25 O-Pee-Chee Platinum Rookie Autographs Pink Magma

*PINK: .6X TO 1.5X BASIC
RLH Lane Hutson SP 250.00 600.00
RSB Sebastian Cossa 60.00 150.00

2024-25 O-Pee-Chee Platinum Rookie Autographs Rainbow

*RAINBOW: .5X TO 1.2X BASIC
RFN Frank Nazar 50.00 125.00
RLH Lane Hutson SP 200.00 500.00

2024-25 O-Pee-Chee Platinum Rookie Autographs Red Prism

*RED/30: 1X TO 2.5X BASIC
RFN Frank Nazar 250.00 600.00
RGA Cutter Gauthier 100.00 250.00
RJW Jesper Wallstedt 100.00 250.00
RLE Jonathan Lekkerimaki 80.00 200.00
RLH Lane Hutson 500.00 1200.00
RSB Sebastian Cossa 100.00 250.00
RST Logan Stankoven 100.00 250.00
RWS Will Smith 300.00 800.00

2024-25 O-Pee-Chee Platinum Rookie Autographs Seismic Gold

*GOLD/25: 1X TO 2.5X BASIC
RCE Macklin Celebrini 1500.00 4000.00
RFN Frank Nazar 250.00 600.00
RGA Cutter Gauthier 100.00 250.00
RJW Jesper Wallstedt 100.00 250.00
RLE Jonathan Lekkerimaki 80.00 200.00
RLH Lane Hutson 600.00 1500.00
RSB Sebastian Cossa 100.00 250.00
RST Logan Stankoven 100.00 250.00
RWS Will Smith 300.00 800.00

2024-25 O-Pee-Chee Platinum Rookie Autographs Sunset

*SUNSET: .5X TO 1.2X BASIC
RLH Lane Hutson SP 200.00 500.00

2024-25 O-Pee-Chee Platinum Rookie Autographs Violet Pixels

*VIOLET/65: .6X TO 1.5X BASIC
RFN Frank Nazar 150.00 400.00
RJW Jesper Wallstedt 60.00 150.00
RLH Lane Hutson 300.00 800.00
RSB Sebastian Cossa 80.00 200.00
RST Logan Stankoven 60.00 150.00
RWS Will Smith 150.00 400.00

2024-25 O-Pee-Chee Platinum Showmanship

S1 Jason Robertson 1.00 2.50
S2 Matthew Tkachuk 1.25 3.00
S3 Brady Tkachuk 1.00 2.50
S4 Nick Suzuki 1.25 3.00
S5 Trevor Moore .40 1.00
S6 Dylan Larkin .75 2.00
S7 Cole Sillinger .50 1.25
S8 Macklin Celebrini 3.00 8.00
S9 Quinn Hughes 1.50 4.00
S10 Logan Stankoven 1.50 4.00
S11 Tage Thompson .75 2.00
S12 Connor McDavid 3.00 8.00
S13 Kirill Kaprizov 2.00 5.00
S14 Cale Makar 1.50 4.00
S15 Leon Draisaitl 2.00 5.00
S16 Troy Terry .50 1.25
S17 Matvei Michkov 2.50 6.00
S18 David Pastrnak 1.50 4.00
S19 Nathan MacKinnon 2.50 6.00
S20 Alex Ovechkin 2.50 6.00
S21 Auston Matthews 2.50 6.00
S22 J.T. Compher .40 1.00
S23 Nikita Kucherov 1.25 3.00
S24 Lane Hutson 3.00 8.00
S25 Cutter Gauthier 1.50 4.00

2024-25 O-Pee-Chee Platinum Showmanship Rainbow Autographs

S4 Nick Suzuki 20.00 50.00
S8 Macklin Celebrini 250.00 600.00
S10 Logan Stankoven 25.00 60.00
S12 Connor McDavid 200.00 500.00
S13 Kirill Kaprizov SP 60.00 150.00
S14 Cale Makar 60.00 150.00
S15 Leon Draisaitl 40.00 100.00
S17 Matvei Michkov 125.00 300.00
S23 Nikita Kucherov 20.00 50.00
S24 Lane Hutson 150.00 400.00
S25 Cutter Gauthier 40.00 100.00

2024-25 O-Pee-Chee Platinum Sweet Selections

SS1 Cutter Gauthier 1.50 4.00
SS2 Lane Hutson 3.00 8.00
SS3 Brennan Othmann 1.00 2.50
SS4 Zachary Bolduc 1.25 3.00
SS5 Jesper Wallstedt 1.50 4.00
SS6 Liam Ohgren 1.25 3.00
SS7 Mavrik Bourque 1.25 3.00
SS8 Olen Zellweger 1.25 3.00
SS9 Josh Doan 1.00 2.50
SS10 Logan Stankoven 1.50 4.00
SS11 Macklin Celebrini 3.00 8.00
SS12 Matvei Michkov 2.50 6.00
SS13 Conor Geekie 1.25 3.00
SS14 Seamus Casey .75 2.00
SS15 Will Smith 2.00 5.00

2024-25 O-Pee-Chee Platinum Sweet Selections Green Ray

*GREEN/35: 3X TO 8X BASIC
SS12 Matvei Michkov 100.00 250.00

2024-25 O-Pee-Chee Platinum Sweet Selections Rainbow Autographs

SS1 Cutter Gauthier 15.00 40.00
SS2 Lane Hutson 200.00 500.00
SS5 Jesper Wallstedt 15.00 40.00
SS6 Liam Ohgren 12.00 30.00
SS7 Mavrik Bourque 12.00 30.00
SS8 Olen Zellweger 12.00 30.00
SS10 Logan Stankoven 15.00 40.00
SS11 Macklin Celebrini 150.00 400.00
SS12 Matvei Michkov 125.00 300.00
SS15 Will Smith 40.00 100.00

1990-91 OPC Premier

COMPLETE SET (132) 60.00 150.00
COMP.FACT.SET (132) 80.00 200.00
1 Scott Arniel .25 .60
2 Jergus Baca RC .30 .75
3 Brian Bellows .30 .75
4 Jean-Claude Bergeron RC .40 1.00
5 Daniel Berthiaume .30 .75
6 Rob Blake RC 2.50 6.00
7 Peter Bondra RC 1.50 4.00
8 Laurie Boschman .30 .75
9 Ray Bourque .60 1.50
10 Aaron Broten .30 .75
11 Greg Brown RC .40 1.00
12 Jimmy Carson .30 .75
13 Chris Chelios .40 1.00
14 Dino Ciccarelli .40 1.00
15 Zdeno Ciger RC .40 1.00
16 Paul Coffey .40 1.00
17 Danton Cole RC .40 1.00
18 Geoff Courtnall .30 .75
19 Mike Craig UER RC .40 1.00
20 John Cullen .40 1.00
21 Vincent Damphousse .30 .75
22 Gerald Diduck .30 .75
23 Kevin Dineen .40 1.00
24 Per Djoos RC .40 1.00
25 Tie Domi RC 1.50 4.00
26 Peter Douris RC .40 1.00
27 Rob DiMaio RC .40 1.00
28 Pat Elynuik .30 .75
29 Bob Essensa RC .60 1.50
30 Sergei Fedorov RC 4.00 10.00
31 Brent Fedyk RC .40 1.00
32 Ron Francis .50 1.25
33 Link Gaetz RC .40 1.00
34 Troy Gamble RC .40 1.00
35 Johan Garpenlov RC .40 1.00
36 Mike Gartner .50 1.25
37 Rick Green .40 1.00
38 Wayne Gretzky 2.50 6.00
39 Jeff Hackett RC .60 1.50
40 Dale Hawerchuk .50 1.25
41 Ron Hextall .40 1.00
42 Bruce Hoffort RC .40 1.00
43 Bobby Holik RC .40 1.00
44 Martin Hostak RC .40 1.00
45 Phil Housley .30 .75
46 Jody Hull RC .40 1.00
47 Brett Hull .75 2.00
48 Al Iafrate .25 .60
49 Peter Ing RC .40 1.00
50 Jaromir Jagr RC 12.00 30.00
51 Curtis Joseph RC 2.50 6.00
52 Robert Kron RC .40 1.00
53 Frantisek Kucera RC .40 1.00
54 Dale Kushner RC .40 1.00
55 Guy Lafleur .50 1.25
56 Pat LaFontaine .40 1.00
57 Mike Lalor RC .30 .75
58 Steve Larmer .30 .75
59 Jiri Latal RC .40 1.00
60 Jamie Leach RC .30 .75
61 Brian Leetch .50 1.25
62 Claude Lemieux .25 .60
63 Mario Lemieux 2.50 6.00
64 Craig Ludwig .40 1.00
65 Al MacInnis .50 1.25
66 Mikko Makela .30 .75
67 David Marcinyshyn RC .40 1.00
68 Stephane Matteau RC .40 1.00
69 Brad McCrimmon .40 1.00
70 Kirk McLean .25 .60
71 Mark Messier .75 2.00
72 Kelly Miller .25 .60
73 Kevin Miller RC .40 1.00
74 Mike Modano RC 3.00 8.00
75 Alexander Mogilny RC 1.25 3.00
76 Andy Moog .40 1.00
77 Joe Mullen .30 .75
78 Kirk Muller .30 .75
79 Pat Murray RC .40 1.00
80 Jarmo Myllys RC .40 1.00
81 Petr Nedved RC .40 1.00
82 Cam Neely .40 1.00
83 Bernie Nicholls .30 .75
84 Joe Nieuwendyk .30 .75
85 Chris Nilan .25 .60
86 Owen Nolan RC 1.25 3.00
87 Brian Noonan .40 1.00
88 Adam Oates .40 1.00
89 Greg Parks RC .40 1.00
90 Adrien Plavsic RC .40 1.00
91 Keith Primeau RC .60 1.50
92 Brian Propp .40 1.00
93 Dan Quinn .30 .75
94 Bill Ranford .30 .75
95 Robert Reichel RC .40 1.00
96 Mike Ricci RC .40 1.00
97 Steven Rice RC .40 1.00
98 Stephane Richer .40 1.00
99 Luc Robitaille .40 1.00
100 Jeremy Roenick RC 4.00 10.00
101 Patrick Roy 2.00 5.00
102 Joe Sakic 1.25 3.00
103 Denis Savard .40 1.00
104 Anatoli Semenov RC .30 .75
105 Brendan Shanahan .40 1.00
106 Ray Sheppard .25 .60
107 Mike Sillinger RC .40 1.00
108 Ilkka Sinisalo .30 .75
109 Bobby Smith .30 .75
110 Paul Stanton RC .40 1.00
111 Kevin Stevens RC .75 2.00
112 Scott Stevens .40 1.00
113 Alan Stewart RC .40 1.00
114 Mats Sundin RC 3.00 8.00
115 Brent Sutter .30 .75
116 Tim Sweeney RC .40 1.00
117 Peter Taglianetti .30 .75
118 John Tanner RC .40 1.00
119 Dave Tippett .30 .75
120 Rick Tocchet .40 1.00
121 Bryan Trottier .40 1.00
122 John Tucker .30 .75
123 Darren Turcotte RC .30 .75
124 Pierre Turgeon .30 .75
125 Randy Velischek .25 .60
126 Mike Vernon .30 .75
127 Wes Walz RC .40 1.00
128 Carey Wilson .30 .75
129 Doug Wilson .30 .75
130 Steve Yzerman 1.25 3.00
131 Peter Zezel .40 1.00
132 Checklist 1-132 .20 .50

1991-92 OPC Premier

COMPLETE SET (198) 6.00 15.00
COMP.FACT.SET (198) 8.00 20.00
1 Dale Hawerchuk .05 .15
2 Ray Sheppard .01 .05
3 Wayne Gretzky UER .60 1.50
4 John MacLean .05 .15
5 Pat Verbeek .01 .05
6 Doug Wilson .05 .15
7 Adam Oates .05 .15
8 Bob McGill .01 .05
9 Mike Vernon .05 .15
10 Glenn Anderson .05 .15
11 Tony Amonte RC .60 1.50
12 Stephen Leach .01 .05
13 Steve Duchesne .01 .05
14 Patrick Roy .50 1.25
15 Jarmo Myllys .01 .05
16 Yanic Dupre RC .01 .05
17 Chris Chelios .08 .25
18 Bill Ranford .05 .15
19 Ed Belfour .08 .25
20 Michel Picard RC .01 .05
21 Rob Zettler .01 .05
22 Kevin Todd RC .01 .05
23 Mike Ricci .08 .25
24 Jaromir Jagr .15 .40
25 Sergei Nemchinov .01 .05
26 Kevin Stevens .01 .05
27 Dan Quinn .01 .05
28 Adam Graves .05 .15
29 Pat Jablonski RC .05 .15
30 Scott Mellanby .01 .05
31 Tomas Forslund RC .01 .05
32 Doug Weight RC .50 1.25
33 Peter Ing .05 .15
34 Luc Robitaille .05 .15
35 Scott Niedermayer .01 .05
36 Dean Evason .01 .05
37 John Tonelli .01 .05
38 Ron Hextall .05 .15
39 Troy Mallette .01 .05
40 Tony Hrkac .01 .05
41 Ken Hodge Jr. .01 .05
42 Kip Miller .01 .05
43 Randy Burridge .01 .05
44 Rob Blake .05 .15
45 Sergei Makarov .01 .05
46 Luke Richardson .01 .05
47 Craig Berube .01 .05
48 Joe Nieuwendyk .05 .15
49 Brett Hull .10 .30
50 Phil Housley .05 .15
51 Mark Messier .08 .25
52 Jeremy Roenick .08 .25
53 Dave Christian .01 .05
54 Dave Barr .01 .05
55 Sergio Momesso .01 .05
56 Pat Falloon .01 .05
57 Brian Leetch .08 .25
58 Russ Courtnall .01 .05
59 Pierre Turgeon .05 .15
60 Steve Larmer .05 .15
61 Petr Klima .01 .05
62 Mikhail Tatarinov .01 .05
63 Rick Tocchet .05 .15
64 Pat LaFontaine .08 .25
65 Rob Pearson RC .01 .05
66 Glen Featherstone .01 .05
67 Pavel Bure .08 .25
68 Sergei Fedorov .15 .40
69 Kelly Kisio .01 .05
70 Joe Sakic .20 .50
71 Denis Savard .05 .15
72 Andrew Cassels .01 .05
73 Steve Yzerman .50 1.25
74 Todd Elik .01 .05
75 Troy Murray .01 .05
76 Rob Ramage .01 .05
77 Trevor Linden .05 .15
78 Mike Richter .08 .25
79 Paul Coffey .08 .25
80 Craig Ludwig .01 .05
81 Al MacInnis .05 .15
82 Tomas Sandstrom .01 .05
83 Tim Kerr .01 .05
84 Scott Stevens .05 .15
85 Steve Kasper .01 .05
86 Kirk Muller .01 .05
87 Pat MacLeod RC .01 .05
88 Kevin Hatcher .05 .15
89 Wayne Presley .01 .05
90 Darryl Sydor .05 .15
91 Tom Chorske .01 .05
92 Theo Fleury .01 .05
93 Craig Janney .05 .15
94 Rod Brind'Amour .08 .25
95 Ron Sutter .01 .05
96 Matt DelGuidice RC .01 .05
97 Rollie Melanson .05 .15
98 Tom Kurvers .01 .05
99 Bryan Marchment RC .05 .15
100 Grant Fuhr .08 .25
101 Geoff Courtnall .05 .15
102 Joel Otto .01 .05
103 Tom Barrasso .05 .15
104 Vincent Damphousse .01 .05
105 John LeClair RC .60 1.50
106 Gary Leeman .01 .05
107 Cam Neely .08 .25
108 Jeff Hackett .05 .15
109 Stu Barnes .01 .05
110 Neil Wilkinson .01 .05
111 Jari Kurri .08 .25
112 Jon Casey .05 .15
113 Stephane Richer .05 .15
114 Mario Lemieux .60 1.50
115 Brad Jones .01 .05
116 Wendel Clark .05 .15
117 Nicklas Lidstrom RC .60 1.50
118A Vladimir Konstantinov ERR RC 12.50 25.00
118B Vladimir Konstantinov COR RC .40 1.00
119 Ray Bourque .15 .40
120 Ron Francis .05 .15
121 Esa Tikkanen .01 .05
122 Randy Hillier .01 .05
123 Randy Gilhen .01 .05
124 Barry Pederson .01 .05
125 Charlie Huddy .01 .05
126 Gary Roberts .05 .15
127 John Cullen .01 .05
128 Dave Gagner .01 .05
129 Bob Kudelski .01 .05
130 Brendan Shanahan .08 .25
131 Dirk Graham .01 .05
132 Checklist 1-99 .01 .05
133 Andy Moog .08 .25
134 Gary Leeman ORIG6 .01 .05
135 Steve Larmer ORIG6 .05 .15
136 Steve Smith .01 .05
137 Dave Manson .01 .05
138 Nelson Emerson .01 .05
139 Doug Weight ORIG6 .08 .25
140 Uwe Krupp .01 .05
141 Peter Douris ORIG6 .01 .05
142 Steve Yzerman ORIG6 .30 .75
143 Derian Hatcher .05 .15
144 Vladimir Ruzicka ORIG6 .01 .05
145 Kirk Muller ORIG6 .01 .05
146 Darrin Shannon .01 .05
147 Mike Gartner ORIG6 .05 .15
148 Bob Carpenter ORIG6 .01 .05
149 Josef Beranek RC .01 .05
150 Chris Chelios ORIG6 .08 .25
151 Bob Rouse ORIG6 .01 .05
152 Guy Carbonneau ORIG6 .05 .15
153 Joe Mullen .05 .15
154 Ken Hodge Jr. ORIG6 .01 .05
155 Vladimir Konstantinov ORIG6 .08 .25
156 Brent Sutter .01 .05
157 Eric Desjardins ORIG6 .05 .15
158 Kirk McLean .05 .15
159 John Tonelli ORIG6 .01 .05
160 Rob Cimetta ORIG6 .01 .05
161 Shayne Corson .01 .05
162 Russ Romaniuk RC .01 .05
163 Nicklas Lidstrom ORIG6 .08 .25
164 Mike Gartner .05 .15
165 Curtis Joseph .08 .25
166 Brian Mullen .01 .05
167 Jimmy Carson .01 .05
168 Petr Svoboda ORIG6 .01 .05
169 Troy Crowder .01 .05
170 Patrick Roy ORIG6 .30 .75
171 Adam Creighton .01 .05
172 James Patrick ORIG6 .01 .05
173 Sergei Fedorov ORIG6 .15 .40
174 Jeremy Roenick ORIG6 .08 .25
175 Tim Cheveldae ORIG6 .05 .15
176 Dimitri Khristich .01 .05
177 Wendel Clark ORIG6 .08 .20
178 Andrei Lomakin .01 .05
179 Benoit Hogue .01 .05
180 Dave Ellett ORIG6 .01 .05
181 Mathieu Schneider ORIG6 .01 .05
182 Kay Whitmore .05 .15
183 Brian Leetch ORIG6 .08 .25
184 Sylvain Turgeon ORIG6 .01 .05
185 Brian Bradley ORIG6 .01 .05
186 John LeClair ORIG6 .20 .50
187 Paul Fenton .01 .05
188 Alain Cote ORIG6 .01 .05
189 Mike Krushelnyski ORIG6 .01 .05
190 Brian Bradley .01 .05
191 Grant Fuhr ORIG6 .08 .25
192 Ray Bourque ORIG6 .08 .25
193 Owen Nolan .08 .25
194 Russ Courtnall ORIG6 .01 .05
195 Steve Thomas .01 .05
196 Ed Olczyk .01 .05
197 Chris Terreri .05 .15
198 Checklist 100-198 .01 .05

1992-93 OPC Premier

1 Dave Christian .10 .25
2 Christian Ruuttu .10 .25
3 Vincent Damphousse .12 .30
4 Chris Lindberg .10 .25
5 Bill Lindsay RC .10 .25
6 Dmitri Kvartalnov RC .10 .25
7 Darcy Loewen .10 .25
8 Ed Courtenay .10 .25
9 Sergei Krivokrasov .10 .25
10 Shawn Antoski .10 .25
11 Andre Racicot .12 .30
12 Marty McInnis .10 .25
13 Alexei Zhamnov .12 .30
14 Keith Jones RC .15 .40
15 Steve Konowalchuk RC .12 .30
16 Darryl Sydor .10 .25
17 Janne Ojanen .10 .25
18 Doug Zmolek RC .10 .25
19 Michael Nylander RC .10 .25
20 Russ Courtnall .10 .25
21 Martin Straka RC .30 .75
22 Kevin Dahl RC .10 .25
23 Kent Manderville .10 .25
24 Steve Heinze .10 .25
25 Philippe Bozon .10 .25
26 Brent Fedyk .10 .25
27 Kris Draper .10 .25
28 Brad Schlegel .10 .25
29 Patric Kjellberg RC .15 .40
30 Ted Donato .10 .25
31 Vyatcheslav Butsayev RC .10 .25
32 Tyler Wright .10 .25
33 Tom Pederson RC .12 .30
34 Jim Hiller RC .10 .25
35 Chris Luongo RC .10 .25
36 Robert Petrovicky RC .10 .25
37 Jean-Francois Quintin RC .10 .25
38 Chris Dahlquist .12 .30
39 Daniel Laperriere RC .10 .25
40 Guy Hebert RC .25 .60
41 Ed Ronan RC .10 .25
42 Shawn Cronin .10 .25
43 Keith Tkachuk .15 .40
44 Dino Ciccarelli .12 .30
45 Doug Evans .10 .25
46 Roman Hamrlik RC .30 .75
47 Robert Lang RC .10 .25
48 Kerry Huffman .10 .25
49 Pat Conacher .10 .25
50 Dominik Hasek .25 .60
51 Dominic Roussel .12 .30
52 Glen Murray .12 .30
53 Igor Korolev RC .10 .25
54 Jiri Slegr .10 .25
55 Mikael Andersson .10 .25
56 Bob Babcock RC .10 .25
57 Ron Hextall .15 .40
58 Jeff Daniels .10 .25
59 Doug Crossman .12 .30
60 Viktor Gordijuk RC .10 .25
61 Adam Creighton .10 .25
62 Rob DiMaio .10 .25
63 Eric Weinrich .10 .25
64 Vitali Prokhorov RC .10 .25
65 Dimitri Yushkevich RC .10 .25
66 Evgeny Davydov .10 .25
67 Dixon Ward RC .12 .30
68 Teemu Selanne .30 .75
69 Rob Zamuner RC .12 .30
70 Joe Reekie .10 .25
71 Slava Kozlov .12 .30
72 Philippe Boucher .10 .25
73 Phil Bourque .10 .25
74 Yvon Corriveau .10 .25
75 Brian Bellows .12 .30
76 Wendell Young .12 .30
77 Bobby Holik .12 .30
78 Bob Carpenter .12 .30
79 Scott Lachance .10 .25
80 John Druce .10 .25
81 Keith Carney RC .30 .75
82 Neil Brady .10 .25
83 Richard Matvichuk RC .12 .30
84 Sergei Bautin RC .10 .25
85 Patrick Poulin .10 .25
86 Gordie Roberts .12 .30
87 Kay Whitmore .12 .30
88 Steph Beauregard .12 .30
89 Vladimir Malakhov .10 .25
90 Richard Smehlik RC .10 .25
91 Mike Ricci .10 .25
92 Sean Burke .12 .30
93 Andrei Kovalenko RC .25 .60
94 Shawn McEachern .10 .25
95 Pat Jablonski .12 .30
96 Oleg Petrov RC .10 .25
97 Glenn Mulvenna RC .10 .25
98 Jason Woolley RC .10 .25
99 Mark Greig .12 .30
100 Nikolai Borschevsky RC .10 .25
101 Joe Juneau .10 .25
102 Eric Lindros .25 .60
103 Darius Kasparaitis .10 .25
104 Sandis Ozolinsh .10 .25
105 Stan Drulia RC .10 .25
106 Mike Needham RC .10 .25
107 Norm Maciver .10 .25
108 Sylvain Lefebvre .10 .25
109 Tommy Sjodin RC .10 .25
110 Bob Sweeney .10 .25
111 Brian Mullen .10 .25
112 Peter Sidorkiewicz .10 .25
113 Scott Niedermayer .15 .40
114 Felix Potvin .30 .75
115 Robb Stauber .12 .30
116 Sylvain Turgeon .10 .25
117 Mark Janssens .10 .25
118 Darren Banks RC .10 .25
119 Pat Elynuik .10 .25
120 Bill Guerin RC .60 1.50
121 Reggie Savage .10 .25
122 Enrico Ciccone .10 .25
123 Chris Kontos RC .10 .25
124 Martin Rucinsky .10 .25
125 Alexei Zhitnik .10 .25
126 Alexei Kovalev .12 .30
127 Tim Kerr .10 .25
128 Guy Larose .10 .25
129 Brent Gilchrist .10 .25
130 Steve Duchesne .10 .25
131 Drake Berehowsky .10 .25
132 Checklist 1-132 .05 .15

1992-93 OPC Premier Star Performers

1 Ray Ferraro .12 .30
2 Dale Hunter .15 .40
3 Murray Craven .12 .30
4 Paul Coffey .20 .50
5 Jeremy Roenick .30 .75
6 Denis Savard .20 .50
7 Jon Casey .12 .30
8 Doug Gilmour .25 .60
9 Rod Brind'Amour .12 .30
10 Pavel Bure .20 .50
11 Joe Sakic .40 1.00
12 Pat Falloon .12 .30
13 Adam Oates .20 .50
14 Gary Roberts .12 .30
15 Mark Messier .40 1.00
16 Phil Housley .15 .40
17 Pat LaFontaine .20 .50
18 Stephane Richer .15 .40
19 Bill Ranford .15 .40
20 Sergei Fedorov .30 .75
21 Brett Hull .40 1.00
22 Mario Lemieux .75 2.00

1992-93 OPC Premier Top Rookies

COMPLETE SET (4) .60 1.50
1 Eric Lindros .20 .50
2 Roman Hamrlik .30 .75
3 Dominic Roussel .08 .25
4 Felix Potvin .60 1.50

1993-94 OPC Premier

1 Patrick Roy .40 1.00
2 Alexei Zhitnik .10 .25
3 Uwe Krupp .10 .25
4 Todd Gill .10 .25
5 Paul Stanton .10 .25
6 Petr Nedved .10 .25
7 Dale Hawerchuk .20 .50
8 Kevin Miller .10 .25
9 Nicklas Lidstrom .15 .40
10 Joe Sakic .30 .75
11 Thomas Steen .10 .25
12 Peter Bondra .15 .40
13 Brian Noonan .10 .25
14 Glen Featherstone .10 .25
15 Mike Vernon .12 .30
16 Janne Ojanen .10 .25
17 Neil Brady .10 .25
18 Dimitri Yushkevich .10 .25

19 Rob Zamuner .10 .25
20 Zarley Zalapski .10 .25
21 Mike Sullivan .10 .25
22 Jamie Baker .10 .25
23 Craig MacTavish .10 .25
24 Mark Tinordi .10 .25
25 Brian Leetch .12 .30
26 Brian Skrudland .10 .25
27 Keith Tkachuk .15 .40
28 Patrick Flatley .10 .25
29 Doug Bodger .10 .25
30 Felix Potvin .30 .75
31 Shawn Antoski .10 .25
32 Eric Desjardins .12 .30
33 Mike Donnelly .10 .25
34 Kjell Samuelsson .10 .25
35 Nelson Emerson .10 .25
36 Phil Housley .12 .30
37 Mario Lemieux LL .60 1.50
38 Shayne Corson .12 .30
39 Steve Smith .10 .25
40 Bob Kudelski .10 .25
41 Joe Cirella .10 .25
42 Sergei Nemchinov .10 .25
43 Kerry Huffman .10 .25
44 Bob Beers .10 .25
45 Al Iafrate .10 .25
46 Mike Modano .25 .60
47 Pat Verbeek .10 .25
48 Joel Otto .10 .25
49 Dino Ciccarelli .12 .30
50 Adam Oates .15 .40
51 Pat Elynuik .10 .25
52 Bobby Holik .10 .25
53 Johan Garpenlov .10 .25
54 Jeff Beukeboom .10 .25
55 Tommy Soderstrom .10 .25
56 Rob Blake .12 .30
57 Marty McInnis .10 .25
58 Dixon Ward .10 .25
59 Patrice Brisebois .10 .25
60 Ed Belfour .15 .40
61 Donald Audette .10 .25
62 Mike Ricci .10 .25
63 Fredrik Olausson .10 .25
64 Norm Maciver .10 .25
65 Andrew Cassels .10 .25
66 Tim Cheveldae .12 .30
67 David Reid .10 .25
68 Philippe Bozon .10 .25
69 Drake Berehowsky .10 .25
70 Tony Amonte .12 .30
71 Dave Manson .10 .25
72 Rick Tocchet .12 .30
73 Steve Kasper .10 .25
74 Assist Leader .15 .40
75 Ulf Dahlen .10 .25
76 Chris Lindberg .10 .25
77 Doug Wilson .12 .30
78 Mike Ridley .10 .25
79 Viacheslav Butsayev .10 .25
80 Scott Stevens .15 .40
81 Cliff Ronning .10 .25
82 Andrei Lomakin .10 .25
83 Shawn Burr .10 .25
84 Benoit Brunet .10 .25
85 Valeri Kamensky .12 .30
86 Randy Carlyle .10 .25
87 Chris Joseph .10 .25
88 Dirk Graham .10 .25
89 Ken Sutton .10 .25
90 Luc Robitaille AS .15 .40
91 Mario Lemieux AS .60 1.50
92 Teemu Selanne AS .30 .75
93 Ray Bourque AS .25 .60
94 Chris Chelios AS .15 .40
95 Ed Belfour AS .15 .40
96 Keith Jones .10 .25
97 Sylvain Turgeon .10 .25
98 Jim Johnson .10 .25
99 Michael Nylander .10 .25
100 Theo Fleury .10 .25
101 Shawn Chambers .10 .25
102 Alexander Semak .10 .25
103 Ron Sutter .10 .25
104 Glenn Anderson .12 .30
105 Jaromir Jagr .50 1.25
106 Adam Graves .10 .25
107 Nikolai Borschevsky .10 .25
108 Vladimir Konstantinov .12 .30
109 Robb Stauber .10 .25
110 Arturs Irbe .10 .25
111 Felix Potvin LL .30 .75
112 Darius Kasparaitis .10 .25
113 Kirk McLean .12 .30
114 Glen Wesley .10 .25
115 Rod Brind'Amour .12 .30
116 Mike Eagles .10 .25
117 Brian Bradley .10 .25
118 Dave Christian .10 .25
119 Randy Wood .10 .25
120 Craig Janney .10 .25
121 Eric Lindros SR .25 .60
122 Tommy Soderstrom SR .12 .30
123 Shawn McEachern SR .10 .25
124 Andrei Kovalenko SR .10 .25
125 Joe Juneau SR .10 .25
126 Felix Potvin SR .30 .75
127 Dixon Ward SR .10 .25
128 Alexei Zhamnov SR .12 .30
129 Vladimir Malakhov SR .10 .25
130 Teemu Selanne SR .30 .75
131 Neal Broten .10 .25
132 Ulf Samuelsson .10 .25
133 Mark Janssens .10 .25
134 Claude Lemieux .10 .25
135 Mike Richter .15 .40
136 Doug Weight .12 .30
137 Rob Pearson .10 .25
138 Sylvain Cote .10 .25
139 Mike Keane .10 .25
140 Benoit Hogue .10 .25
141 Michel Petit .10 .25
142 Mark Freer .10 .25
143 Doug Zmolek .10 .25
144 Tony Granato .10 .25
145 Paul Coffey .15 .40
146 Ted Donato .10 .25
147 Brent Sutter .10 .25
148 A.Mogilny
T.Selanne LL .30 .75
149 James Patrick .10 .25
150 Mikael Andersson .10 .25
151 Steve Duchesne .10 .25
152 Terry Carkner .10 .25
153 Russ Courtnall .10 .25
154 Brian Mullen .10 .25
155 Martin Straka .10 .25
156 Geoff Sanderson .12 .30
157 Mark Howe .15 .40
158 Stephane Richer .12 .30
159 Doug Crossman .10 .25
160 John Vanbiesbrouck .15 .40
161 Bob Essensa .12 .30
162 Wayne Presley .10 .25
163 Mathieu Schneider .10 .25
164 Jiri Slegr .10 .25
165 Stephane Fiset .12 .30
166 Wendell Young .10 .25
167 Kevin Dineen .10 .25
168 Sandis Ozolinsh .10 .25
169 Mike Krushelnyski .10 .25
170 Kevin Stevens AS .12 .30
171 Pat LaFontaine AS .15 .40
172 Alexander Mogilny AS .12 .30
173 Larry Murphy AS .12 .30
174 Al Iafrate AS .10 .25
175 Tom Barrasso AS .12 .30
176 Derek King .10 .25
177 Bob Probert .15 .40
178 Gary Suter .10 .25
179 David Shaw .10 .25
180 Luc Robitaille .15 .40
181 John LeClair .15 .40
182 Troy Murray .10 .25
183 Dave Gagner .12 .30
184 Darcy Loewen .10 .25
185 Mario Lemieux LL .60 1.50
186 Pat Jablonski .10 .25
187 Alexei Kovalev .12 .30
188 Todd Krygier .10 .25
189 Larry Murphy .12 .30
190 Pierre Turgeon .12 .30
191 Craig Ludwig .10 .25
192 Brad May .12 .30
193 John MacLean .12 .30
194 Ron Wilson .10 .25
195 Eric Weinrich .10 .25
196 Steve Chiasson .10 .25
197 Dmitri Kvartalnov .10 .25
198 Andrei Kovalenko .10 .25
199 Rob Gaudreau RC .15 .40
200 Evgeny Davydov .10 .25
201 Adrien Plavsic .10 .25
202 Brian Bellows .12 .30
203 Doug Evans .10 .25
204 Win Leader
Tom Barrasso .12 .30
205 Joe Nieuwendyk .12 .30
206 Jari Kurri .15 .40
207 Bob Rouse .10 .25
208 Yvon Corriveau .10 .25
209 John Blue .12 .30
210 Dimitri Khristich .10 .25
211 Brent Fedyk .10 .25
212 Jody Hull .10 .25
213 Chris Terreri .12 .30
214 Mike McPhee .10 .25
215 Chris Kontos .10 .25
216 Greg Gilbert .10 .25
217 Sergei Zubov .10 .25
218 Grant Fuhr .25 .60
219 Charlie Huddy .10 .25
220 Mario Lemieux .60 1.50
221 Sheldon Kennedy .10 .25
222 Curtis Joseph
St. Louis Blues
Save Pct. Leader .20 .50
223 Brad Dalgarno .10 .25
224 Bret Hedican .10 .25
225 Trevor Linden .15 .40
226 Darryl Sydor .10 .25
227 Jay More .10 .25
228 Dave Poulin .10 .25
229 Frank Musil .10 .25
230 Mark Recchi .20 .50
231 Craig Simpson .12 .30
232 Gino Cavallini .10 .25
233 Vincent Damphousse .12 .30
234 Luciano Borsato .10 .25
235 Dave Andreychuk .15 .40
236 Ken Daneyko .10 .25
237 Chris Chelios .15 .40
238 Andrew McBain .10 .25
239 Rick Tabaracci .10 .25
240 Steve Larmer .12 .30
241 Sean Burke .10 .25
242 Rob DiMaio .10 .25
243 Jim Paek .10 .25
244 Dave Lowry .10 .25
245 Alexander Mogilny .12 .30
246 Darren Turcotte .10 .25
247 Brendan Shanahan .15 .40
248 Peter Taglianetti .10 .25
249 Scott Mellanby .12 .30
250 Guy Carbonneau .10 .25
251 Claude LaPointe .10 .25
252 Pat Conacher .10 .25
253 Roger Johansson .10 .25
254 Cam Neely .15 .40
255 Garry Galley .10 .25
256 Keith Primeau .12 .30
257 Scott Lachance .10 .25
258 Bill Ranford .12 .30
259 Pat Falloon .10 .25
260 Pavel Bure .15 .40
261 Darrin Shannon .10 .25
262 Mike Foligno .10 .25
263 Checklist 1-132 .05 .15
264 Checklist 133-264 .05 .15
265 Peter Douris .10 .25
266 Warren Rychel .10 .25
267 Owen Nolan .15 .40
268 Mark Osborne .10 .25
269 Teppo Numminen .10 .25
270 Rob Niedermayer .12 .30
271 Mark Lamb .10 .25
272 Curtis Joseph .20 .50
273 Joe Murphy .10 .25
274 Bernie Nicholls .12 .30
275 Gord Roberts .10 .25
276 Al MacInnis .20 .50
277 Ken Wregget .10 .25
278 Calle Johansson .10 .25
279 Tom Kurvers .10 .25
280 Steve Yzerman .40 1.00
281 Roman Hamrlik .10 .25
282 Esa Tikkanen .12 .30
283 Darrin Madeley RC .15 .40
284 Robert Dirk .10 .25
285 Derek Plante RC .15 .40
286 Ron Tugnutt .12 .30
287 Frank Pietrangelo .12 .30
288 Paul DiPietro .10 .25
289 Alexander Godynyuk .10 .25
290 Kirk Maltby RC .15 .40
291 Olaf Kolzig .15 .40
292 Vitali Karamnov .10 .25
293 Alexei Gusarov .10 .25
294 Bryan Erickson .10 .25
295 Jocelyn Lemieux .10 .25
296 Bryan Trottier .15 .40
297 Dave Ellett .10 .25
298 Tim Watters .10 .25
299 Joe Juneau .10 .25
300 Steve Thomas .10 .25
301 Mark Greig .10 .25
302 Jeff Reese .10 .25
303 Steven King .10 .25
304 Don Beaupre .12 .30
305 Denis Savard .15 .40
306 Greg Smyth .10 .25
307 Jaroslav Modry RC .15 .40
308 Petr Svoboda .10 .25
309 Mike Craig .10 .25
310 Eric Lindros .25 .60
311 Dana Murzyn .10 .25
312 Sean Hill .10 .25
313 Andre Racicot .10 .25
314 John Vanbiesbrouck .15 .40
315 Doug Lidster .10 .25
316 Garth Butcher .10 .25
317 Alexei Yashin .10 .25
318 Sergei Fedorov .25 .60
319 Louie DeBrusk .10 .25
320 Dominik Hasek CZE .25 .60
321 Michal Pivonka .10 .25
322 Bobby Holik .10 .25
323 Roman Hamrlik CZE .10 .25
324 Petr Svoboda .10 .25
325 Jaromir Jagr CZE .50 1.25
326 Steven Finn .10 .25
327 Stephane Richer .12 .30
328 Claude Loiselle .10 .25
329 Joe Sacco .10 .25
330 Wayne Gretzky 1.00 2.50
331 Sylvain Lefebvre .10 .25
332 Sergei Bautin .10 .25
333 Craig Simpson .10 .25
334 Don Sweeney .10 .25
335 Dominic Roussel .12 .30
336 Scott Thomas RC .15 .40
337 Geoff Courtnall .10 .25
338 Tom Fitzgerald .10 .25
339 Kevin Haller .10 .25
340 Troy Loney .10 .25
341 Ronnie Stern .10 .25
342 Mark Astley RC .15 .40
343 Jeff Daniels .10 .25
344 Marc Bureau .10 .25
345 Micah Aivazoff RC .15 .40
346 Matthew Barnaby .12 .30
347 C.J. Young .10 .25
348 Dale Craigwell .10 .25
349 Ray Ferraro .10 .25
350 Ray Bourque .25 .60
351 Stu Barnes .10 .25
352 Alan Conroy RC .10 .25
353 Shawn McEachern .10 .25
354 Garry Valk .10 .25
355 Christian Ruuttu .10 .25
356 Darren Rumble .10 .25
357 Stu Grimson .10 .25
358 Alexander Karpovtsev .12 .30
359 Wendel Clark .25 .60
360 Michal Pivonka .10 .25
361 Peter Popovic RC .15 .40
362 Kevin Dahl .10 .25
363 Jeff Brown .10 .25
364 Daren Puppa .12 .30
365 Dallas Drake RC .15 .40
366 Dean McAmmond .10 .25
367 Martin Rucinsky .10 .25
368 Shane Churla .10 .25
369 Todd Ewen .10 .25
370 Kevin Stevens .12 .30
371 David Volek .10 .25
372 J.J. Daigneault .10 .25
373 Marc Bergevin .10 .25
374 Craig Billington .12 .30
375 Mike Gartner .20 .50
376 Jimmy Carson .10 .25
377 Bruce Driver .10 .25
378 Steve Heinze .10 .25
379 Patrick Carnback RC .15 .40
380 Wayne Gretzky CAN 1.00 2.50
381 Jeff Brown CAN .10 .25
382 Gary Roberts CAN .10 .25
383 Ray Bourque CAN .25 .60
384 Mike Gartner CAN .20 .50
385 Felix Potvin CAN .30 .75
386 Michel Goulet .10 .25
387 Dave Tippett .10 .25
388 Jim Waite .12 .30
389 Yuri Khmylev .10 .25
390 Doug Gilmour .20 .50
391 Brad McCrimmon .10 .25
392 Brent Severyn RC .15 .40
393 Jocelyn Thibault RC .15 .40
394 Boris Mironov .10 .25
395 Marty McSorley .12 .30
396 Shaun Van Allen .10 .25
397 Gary Leeman .10 .25
398 Ed Olczyk .10 .25
399 Darcy Wakaluk .10 .25
400 Murray Craven .10 .25
401 Martin Brodeur .40 1.00
402 Paul Laus RC .10 .25
403 Bill Houlder .10 .25
404 Robert Reichel .10 .25
405 Alexandre Daigle .10 .25
406 Brent Thompson .10 .25
407 Keith Acton .10 .25
408 Dave Karpa .10 .25
409 Igor Korolev .10 .25
410 Chris Gratton .12 .30
411 Vincent Riendeau .10 .25
412 Darren McCarty RC .25 .60
413 Bob Carpenter .12 .30
414 Joe Cirella .10 .25
415 Stephane Matteau .10 .25
416 Jozef Stumpel .10 .25
417 Rich Pilon .10 .25
418 Mattias Norstrom RC .15 .40
419 Dmitri Mironov .10 .25
420 Alexei Zhamnov .12 .30
421 Bill Guerin .15 .40
422 Greg Hawgood .10 .25
423 Randy Cunneyworth .10 .25
424 Ron Francis .20 .50
425 Brett Hull .30 .75
426 Tim Sweeney .10 .25
427 Mike Rathje .10 .25
428 Dave Babych .10 .25
429 Chris Tancill .10 .25
430 Mark Messier .30 .75
431 Bob Sweeney .10 .25
432 Terry Yake .10 .25
433 Joe Reekie .10 .25
434 Tomas Sandstrom .10 .25
435 Kevin Hatcher .10 .25
436 Bill Lindsay .10 .25
437 Jon Casey .12 .30
438 Dennis Vaske .10 .25
439 Allen Pedersen .10 .25
440 Pavel Bure RUS .15 .40
441 Sergei Fedorov RUS .25 .60
442 Arturs Irbe LAT .12 .30
443 Darius Kasparaitis .10 .25
444 Evgeny Davydov .10 .25
445 Vladimir Malakhov .10 .25
446 Tom Barrasso .12 .30
447 Jeff Norton .10 .25
448 David Emma .10 .25
449 Pelle Eklund .10 .25
450 Jeremy Roenick .25 .60
451 Jesse Belanger .10 .25
452 Vitali Prokhorov .10 .25
453 Arto Blomsten .10 .25
454 Peter Zezel .10 .25
455 Kelly Kisio .10 .25
456 Zdeno Ciger .10 .25
457 Greg Johnson .10 .25
458 Dave Archibald .10 .25
459 Vladimir Vujtek .10 .25
460 Mats Sundin .15 .40
461 Dan Keczmer .10 .25
462 Stephan Lebeau .10 .25
463 Dominik Hasek .25 .60
464 Kevin Lowe .10 .25
465 Gord Murphy .10 .25
466 Bryan Smolinski .10 .25
467 Josef Beranek .10 .25
468 Ron Hextall .15 .40
469 Randy Ladouceur .10 .25
470 Scott Niedermayer .15 .40
471 Kelly Hrudey .12 .30
472 Mike Needham .10 .25
473 John Tucker .10 .25
474 Kelly Miller .10 .25
475 Jyrki Lumme .10 .25
476 Andy Moog .15 .40
477 Glen Murray .12 .30
478 Mark Ferner RC .10 .25
479 John Cullen .10 .25
480 Gilbert Dionne .10 .25
481 Paul Ranheim .10 .25
482 Mike Hough .10 .25
483 Teemu Selanne .30 .75
484 Aaron Ward RC .15 .40
485 Chris Pronger .15 .40
486 Glenn Healy .12 .30
487 Curtis Leschyshyn .10 .25
488 Jim Montgomery RC .15 .40
489 Travis Green .10 .25
490 Pat LaFontaine .15 .40
491 Bobby Dollas RC .10 .25
492 Alexei Kasatonov .10 .25
493 Corey Millen .10 .25
494 Slava Kozlov .10 .25
495 Igor Kravchuk .10 .25
496 Dimitri Filimonov .10 .25
497 Jeff Odgers .10 .25
498 Joe Mullen .12 .30
499 Gary Shuchuk .10 .25
500 Jeremy Roenick USA .25 .60
501 Tom Barrasso USA .12 .30
502 Keith Tkachuk USA .15 .40
503 Phil Housley USA .12 .30
504 Tony Granato USA .10 .25
505 Brian Leetch USA .12 .30
506 Anatoli Semenov .10 .25
507 Steve Leach .10 .25
508 Brian Skrudland .10 .25
509 Kirk Muller .10 .25
510 Gary Roberts .10 .25
511 Gerard Gallant .10 .25
512 Joey Kocur .10 .25
513 Tie Domi .10 .25
514 Kay Whitmore .10 .25
515 Vladimir Malakhov .10 .25
516 Stewart Malgunas RC .10 .25
517 Jamie Macoun .10 .25
518 Alan May .10 .25
519 Guy Hebert .12 .30
520 Derian Hatcher .10 .25
521 Richard Smehlik .10 .25
522 Joby Messier RC .15 .40
523 Trent Klatt .10 .25
524 Tom Chorske .10 .25
525 Iain Fraser RC .15 .40
526 Dan Laperriere .10 .25
527 Checklist .05 .15
528 Checklist .05 .15

1993-94 OPC Premier Gold

*GOLD: 1X TO 2.5X BASIC CARDS

1993-94 OPC Premier Black Gold

1 Wayne Gretzky 8.00 20.00
2 Vincent Damphousse 1.25 3.00
3 Adam Oates 1.50 4.00
4 Phil Housley 1.00 2.50
5 Mike Vernon 1.25 3.00
6 Mats Sundin 1.50 4.00
7 Pavel Bure 3.00 8.00
8 Patrick Roy 4.00 10.00
9 Tom Barrasso 1.00 2.50
10 Alexander Mogilny 1.25 3.00
11 Doug Gilmour 1.50 4.00
12 Eric Lindros 6.00 15.00
13 Theo Fleury 1.50 4.00
14 Pat LaFontaine 1.25 3.00
15 Joe Sakic 2.00 5.00
16 Ed Belfour 1.50 4.00
17 Felix Potvin 3.00 8.00
18 Mario Lemieux 5.00 12.00
19 Jaromir Jagr 2.50 6.00
20 Teemu Selanne 2.50 6.00
21 Ray Bourque 1.50 4.00
22 Brett Hull 2.50 6.00
23 Steve Yzerman 2.50 6.00
24 Kirk Muller 1.00 2.50

1993-94 OPC Premier Team Canada

COMPLETE SET (19) 10.00 25.00
1 Brett Lindros .75 2.00
2 Manny Legace .75 2.00
3 Adrian Aucoin .60 1.50
4 Ken Lovsin .60 1.50
5 Craig Woodcroft .60 1.50
6 Derek Mayer .60 1.50
7 Fabian Joseph .60 1.50
8 Todd Brost .60 1.50
9 Chris Therien .75 2.00
10 Brad Turner .60 1.50
11 Trevor Sim .60 1.50
12 Todd Hlushko .60 1.50
13 Dwayne Norris .60 1.50
14 Chris Kontos .60 1.50
15 Petr Nedved .75 2.00
16 Brian Savage .75 2.00
17 Paul Kariya 1.50 4.00
18 Corey Hirsch .75 2.00
19 Todd Warriner .75 2.00

1994-95 OPC Premier

1 Mark Messier .20 .50
2 Darren Turcotte .05 .15
3 Mikhail Shtalenkov RC .05 .15
4 Rob Gaudreau .05 .15
5 Tony Amonte .07 .20
6 Stephane Quintal .05 .15
7 Iain Fraser .05 .15
8 Doug Weight .07 .20
9 German Titov .05 .15
10 Larry Murphy .07 .20
11 Danton Cole .05 .15
12 Pat Peake .05 .15
13 Chris Terreri .07 .20
14 Yuri Khmylev .05 .15
15 Paul Coffey .10 .25
16 Brian Savage .05 .15
17 Rod Brind'Amour .07 .20
18 Nathan Lafayette .05 .15
19 Gord Murphy .05 .15
20 Al Iafrate .05 .15
21 Kevin Miller .05 .15
22 Peter Zezel .05 .15
23 Sylvain Turgeon .05 .15
24 Mark Tinordi .05 .15
25 Jari Kurri .07 .20
26 Benoit Hogue .05 .15
27 Jeff Reese .05 .15
28 Brian Noonan .05 .15
29 Denis Tsygurov RC .10 .25
30 James Patrick .05 .15
31 Bob Corkum .05 .15
32 Valeri Kamensky .07 .20
33 Ray Whitney .05 .15
34 Joe Murphy .05 .15
35 Dominik Hasek AS .15 .40
36 Ray Bourque AS .15 .40
37 Brian Leetch AS .07 .20
38 Dave Andreychuk AS .05 .15
39 Pavel Bure AS .10 .25
40 Sergei Fedorov AS .15 .40
41 Bob Beers .05 .15
42 Byron Dafoe RC .30 .75
43 Lyle Odelein .07 .20
44 Markus Naslund .10 .25
45 Dean Chynoweth RC .05 .15
46 Trent Klatt .05 .15
47 Murray Craven .05 .15
48 Dave Mackey .05 .15
49 Norm Maciver .05 .15
50 Alexander Mogilny .07 .20
51 David Reid .05 .15
52 Nicklas Lidstrom .10 .25
53 Tom Fitzgerald .05 .15
54 Roman Hamrlik .05 .15
55 Wendel Clark .15 .40
56 Dominic Roussel .07 .20
57 Alexei Zhitnik .07 .20
58 Valeri Zelepukin .05 .15
59 Calle Johansson .05 .15
60 Craig Janney .07 .20
61 Randy Wood .05 .15
62 Curtis Leschyshyn .05 .15
63 Stephan Lebeau .05 .15
64 Dallas Drake .05 .15
65 Vincent Damphousse .07 .20
66 Scott Lachance .05 .15
67 Dirk Graham .05 .15
68 Kevin Smyth .05 .15
69 Denis Savard .10 .25
70 Mike Richter .10 .25
71 Ronnie Stern .05 .15
72 Kirk Maltby .05 .15
73 Kjell Samuelsson .05 .15
74 Neal Broten .07 .20
75 Trevor Linden .10 .25
76 Todd Elik .05 .15
77 Andrew McBain .05 .15
78 Alexei Kudashov .05 .15
79 Ken Daneyko .05 .15
80 D.Hasek
G.Fuhr GD .15 .40
81 Andy Moog
Dallas Stars
Darcy Wakaluk DUO
Dallas .10 .25
82 Vanbiesbrouck
Fitz. GD .10 .25
83 M.Brodeur
Terreri GD .25 .60
84 Tom Barrasso
Pittsburgh Penguins
Ken Wregget DUO .07 .20
85 Kirk McLean
Vancouver Canucks
Kay Whitmore DUO/ .07 .20
86 Darryl Sydor .05 .15
87 Chris Osgood .15 .40
88 Ted Donato .05 .15
89 Dave Lowry .05 .15
90 Mark Recchi .12 .30
91 Jim Montgomery .05 .15
92 Bill Houlder .05 .15
93 Richard Smehlik .05 .15
94 Benoit Brunet .05 .15
95 Teemu Selanne .20 .50
96 Paul Ranheim .05 .15
97 Andrei Kovalenko .05 .15
98 Grant Ledyard .05 .15
99 Brent Grieve RC .05 .15
100 Joe Juneau .05 .15
101 Martin Gelinas .05 .15
102 Jamie Macoun .05 .15
103 Craig MacTavish .05 .15
104 Micah Aivazoff .05 .15
105 Stephane Richer .07 .20
106 Eric Weinrich .05 .15
107 Pat Elynuik .05 .15
108 Tomas Sandstrom .05 .15
109 Darrin Madeley .05 .15
110 Al MacInnis .12 .30
111 Cam Stewart .05 .15
112 Dixon Ward .05 .15
113 Vlastimil Kroupa .05 .15
114 Rob DiMaio .05 .15
115 Pierre Turgeon .07 .20
116 Mike Hough .05 .15
117 John LeClair .10 .25
118 Dave Hannan .05 .15
119 Todd Ewen .05 .15
121 Dave Manson .05 .15
122 Jocelyn Lemieux .05 .15
123 Jocelyn Thibault .07 .20
124 Scott Pearson .05 .15
125 Patrick Roy AS .25 .60
126 Scott Stevens AS .10 .25
127 Al MacInnis AS .12 .30
128 Adam Graves AS .05 .15
129 Cam Neely AS .10 .25
130 Wayne Gretzky AS .60 1.50
131 Tom Chorske .05 .15
132 John Tucker .05 .15
133 Steve Smith .05 .15
134 Kay Whitmore .05 .15
135 Adam Oates .10 .25
136 Bill Berg .05 .15
137 Wes Walz .05 .15
138 Jeff Beukeboom .05 .15
139 Ron Francis .12 .30
140 Alexandre Daigle .05 .15
141 Josef Beranek .05 .15
142 Tom Pederson .05 .15
143 Jamie McLennan .07 .20
144 Scott Mellanby .07 .20
145 Slava Kozlov .07 .20
146 Marty McSorley .07 .20
147 Tim Sweeney .05 .15
148 Luciano Borsato .05 .15
149 Jason Dawe .05 .15
150 Wayne Gretzky LL .60 1.50
151 Pavel Bure LL .10 .25
152 Dominik Hasek LL .15 .40
153 Scott Stevens LL .10 .25
154 Wayne Gretzky LL .60 1.50
155 Mike Richter LL .10 .25
156 Dominik Hasek LL .15 .40
157 Ted Drury .05 .15
158 Peter Popovic .05 .15
159 Alexei Kasatonov .05 .15
160 Mats Sundin .10 .25
161 Brad Shaw .05 .15
162 Bret Hedican .05 .15
163 Mike McPhee .05 .15
164 Martin Straka .05 .15
165 Dmitri Mironov .05 .15
166 Andrei Trefilov .05 .15
167 Joe Reekie .05 .15
168 Gary Suter .05 .15
169 Greg Gilbert .05 .15
170 Igor Larinov .05 .15
171 Mike Sillinger .05 .15
172 Igor Kravchuk .05 .15
173 Glen Murray .07 .20
174 Shawn Chambers .05 .15
175 John MacLean .07 .20
176 Yves Racine .05 .15
177 Andrei Lomakin .05 .15
178 Patrick Flatley .05 .15
179 Igor Ulanov .05 .15
180 Pat LaFontaine .10 .25
181 Mathieu Schneider .05 .15
182 Peter Stastny .07 .20
183 Tony Granato .05 .15
184 Peter Douris .05 .15
185 Alexei Kovalev .07 .20
186 Geoff Courtnall .05 .15
187 Richard Matvichuk .05 .15
188 Troy Murray .05 .15
189 Todd Gill .05 .15
190 Martin Brodeur RS .25 .60
191 Mikael Renberg RS .07 .20
192 Alexei Yashin RS .07 .20
193 Jason Arnott RS .07 .20
194 Derek Plante RS .05 .15
195 Alexandre Daigle RS .05 .15
196 Bryan Smolinski RS .05 .15
197 Jesse Belanger RS .05 .15
198 Chris Pronger RS .10 .25
199 Chris Osgood RS .15 .40
200 Jeremy Roenick .15 .40
201 Johan Garpenlov .05 .15
202 Dave Karpa .05 .15
203 Darren McCarty .05 .15
204 Claude Lemieux .10 .25
205 Geoff Sanderson .07 .20
206 Tom Barrasso .07 .20
207 Kevin Dineen .05 .15
208 Sylvain Cote .05 .15
209 Brent Gretzky .05 .15
210 Shayne Corson .07 .20
211 Darius Kasparaitis .05 .15
212 Peter Andersson .05 .15
213 Robert Reichel .05 .15
214 Jozef Stumpel .05 .15
215 Brendan Shanahan .10 .25
216 Craig Muni .05 .15
217 Alexei Zhamnov .07 .20
218 Robert Lang .05 .15
219 Brian Bellows .07 .20
220 Steven King .05 .15
221 Sergei Zubov .07 .20
222 Kelly Miller .05 .15
223 Ilya Byakin .05 .15
224 Chris Tamer RC .05 .15
225 Doug Gilmour .12 .30
226 Shawn Antoski .05 .15
227 Andrew Cassels .05 .15
228 Craig Wolanin .05 .15
229 Jon Casey .07 .20
230 Mike Modano .15 .40
231 Bill Guerin .10 .25
232 Gaetan Duchesne .05 .15
233 Steve Dubinsky .05 .15
234 Jason Bowen .05 .15
235 Steve Yzerman .25 .60
236 Dave Poulin .05 .15
237 Michael Nylander .07 .20
238 Felix Potvin TF .15 .40
239 Sandis Ozolinsh FUT .05 .15
240 Scott Niedermayer FUT .10 .25
241 Eric Lindros TF .15 .40
242 Keith Tkachuk TF .10 .25
243 Teemu Selanne TF .20 .50
244 Marty McInnis .05 .15
245 Bob Kudelski .05 .15
246 Paul Cavallini .05 .15
247 Brian Bradley .05 .15
248 Robb Stauber .05 .15
249 Jay Wells .05 .15
250 Mario Lemieux .40 1.00
251 Tommy Albelin .05 .15
252 Paul DiPietro .05 .15
253 Mike Gartner .12 .30
254 Darrin Shannon .05 .15
255 Alexander Karpovtsev .05 .15
256 Dave Babych .05 .15
257 Greg Johnson .05 .15
258 Frank Musil .05 .15
259 Michal Pivonka .05 .15
260 Arturs Irbe .07 .20
261 Paul Broten .05 .15
262 Don Sweeney .05 .15
263 Doug Brown .05 .15
264 Bobby Dollas .05 .15
265 Brian Skrudland .05 .15
266 Dan Plante RC .05 .15
267 Chad Penney .05 .15
268 Steve Leach .05 .15
269 Damian Rhodes .07 .20
270 Glenn Anderson .07 .20
271 Randy McKay .05 .15
272 Jeff Brown .05 .15
273 Steve Konowalchuk .05 .15
276 Sergei Fedorov TOTG .15 .40
277 Adam Oates TOTG .10 .25
278 Mark Messier TOTG .20 .50
279 Doug Gilmour TOTG .12 .30
280 Wayne Gretzky TOTG .60 1.50
281 Rick Tocchet .07 .20
282 Guy Carbonneau .05 .15
283 Peter Bondra .10 .25
284 Valeri Karpov RC .05 .15
285 Ed Belfour .10 .25
286 Petr Nedved .07 .20
287 Mikael Andersson .05 .15
288 Boris Mironov .05 .15
289 Donald Audette .05 .15
290 Kevin Stevens .07 .20
291 Cliff Ronning .05 .15
292 Bruce Driver .05 .15
293 Mariusz Czerkawski RC .10 .25
294 Mikael Renberg .07 .20
295 Theo Fleury .10 .25
296 Robert Kron .05 .15
297 Wendel Clark .15 .40
298 Dave Gagner .07 .20
299 Ulf Dahlen .05 .15
300 Keith Tkachuk .10 .25
301 Mike Ridley .05 .15
302 Mike Vernon .07 .20
303 Troy Mallette .05 .15
304 Derek King .05 .15
305 Kirk Muller .05 .15
306 Rob Niedermayer .07 .20
307 Ian Laperriere RC .10 .25
308 Mike Donnelly .05 .15
309 Joe Sacco .05 .15
310 Patrick Roy TOTG .25 .60
311 Tom Barrasso .07 .20
312 Dominik Hasek TOTG .15 .40
313 Felix Potvin TOTG .15 .40
314 Mike Richter .10 .25
315 Bobby Holik .05 .15
316 Patrick Poulin .05 .15

317 Stephane Matteau .05 .15
318 Petr Klima .05 .15
319 Fredrik Olausson .05 .15
320 Dale Hawerchuk .12 .30
321 Jim Dowd .05 .15
322 Chris Therien .05 .15
323 Ravil Gusmanov RC .05 .15
324 Vincent Riendeau .05 .15
325 Pavel Bure .10 .25
326 Jimmy Carson .05 .15
327 Steve Chiasson .05 .15
328 Ken Wregget .07 .20
329 Kenny Jonsson .05 .15
330 Keith Primeau .07 .20
331 Bob Errey .05 .15
332 Derian Hatcher .05 .15
333 Stephane Fiset .07 .20
334 Brent Severyn .05 .15
335 Ray Ferraro .05 .15
336 Pavol Demitra .12 .30
337 Valeri Bure .05 .15
338 Guy Hebert .07 .20
339 Matt Johnson RC .05 .15
340 Curtis Joseph .12 .30
341 Rob Pearson .05 .15
342 Jeff Shantz .05 .15
343 Eric Charron RC .10 .25
344 Jason Smith .07 .20
345 M.Sundin
W.Clark TRA .15 .40
346 Rick Tocchet
Los Angeles Kings
Luc Robitaille
P .07 .20
347 Al MacInnis
St. Louis Blues
Phil Housley
Calgar .12 .30
348 Mike Vernon
Detroit Red Wings
Steve Chiasson
Ca .07 .20
349 Craig Simpson .05 .15
350 Adam Graves .05 .15
351 Kevin Haller .05 .15
352 Nelson Emerson .05 .15
353 Phil Housley .07 .20
354 Shawn McEachern .05 .15
355 Felix Potvin .15 .40
356 Sergio Momesso .10 .25
357 Glen Wesley .05 .15
358 David Shaw .05 .15
359 Terry Carkner .05 .15
360 John Vanbiesbrouck .10 .25
361 Dean Evason .05 .15
362 Michal Sykora .05 .15
363 Troy Loney .05 .15
364 Sylvain Lefebvre .05 .15
365 Alexei Yashin .10 .25
366 Gilbert Dionne .05 .15
367 Rick Tabaracci .07 .20
368 Paul Ysebaert .05 .15
369 Craig Johnson .05 .15
370 Scott Stevens .10 .25
371 Phillippe Boucher .05 .15
372 Garry Valk .05 .15
373 Jason Muzzatti .07 .20
374 Chris Joseph .05 .15
375 Wayne Gretzky .60 1.50
376 Teppo Numminen .05 .15
377 Oleg Petrov .05 .15
378 Patrik Juhlin RC .05 .15
379 Zarley Zalapski .05 .15
380 Martin Brodeur TOTF .25 .60
381 Chris Pronger TOTF .10 .25
382 Sergei Zubov TOTF .07 .20
383 Mikael Renberg TOTF .07 .20
384 Brett Lindros TOTF .05 .15
385 Peter Forsberg TOTF .20 .50
386 Brandon Convery .05 .15
387 Steve Heinze .05 .15
388 Glenn Healy .07 .20
389 Brian Benning .05 .15
390 Pat Verbeek .07 .20
391 Ulf Samuelsson .05 .15
392 Turner Stevenson .05 .15
393 Bob Rouse .05 .15
394 Steve Konroyd .05 .15
395 Russ Courtnall .05 .15
396 Sergei Makarov .05 .15
397 Kirk McLean .07 .20
398 Steven Finn .05 .15
399 Yan Kaminsky .05 .15
400 Eric Lindros .15 .40
401 Steve Duchesne .05 .15
402 John Slaney .05 .15
403 Bernie Nicholls
Chicago Black Hawks .07 .20
404 Kelly Buchberger .05 .15
405 Paul Kariya .10 .25
406 Michel Petit .05 .15
407 Cale Hulse RC .07 .20
408 Sheldon Kennedy .05 .15
409 Brad May .05 .15
410 Daren Puppa .07 .20
411 Janne Laukkanen .07 .20
412 Mats Sundin .10 .25
413 Trevor Kidd .07 .20
414 Greg Adams .05 .15
415 Pavel Bure TOTG .10 .25
416 Teemu Selanne TOTG .20 .50
417 Brett Hull TOTG .20 .50
418 Steve Larmer .07 .20
419 Cam Neely TOTG .10 .25
420 Ray Bourque .15 .40
421 Andrei Nikolishin .05 .15
422 Jim Paek .05 .15
423 John Cullen .05 .15
424 Darcy Wakaluk .07 .20
425 Peter Forsberg .20 .50
426 Yves Racine .05 .15
427 Jody Hull .05 .15
428 Ron Sutter .05 .15
429 Ray Sheppard .07 .20
430 Sandis Ozolinsh .05 .15
431 Brent Grieve .05 .15
432 Shaun Van Allen .05 .15
433 Craig Berube .05 .15
434 Vladislav Boulin RC .10 .25
435 Bill Ranford .07 .20
436 Denny Felsner .05 .15
437 Jamie Storr .07 .20
438 Brian Rolston .07 .20
439 Chris Gratton .05 .15
440 Dominik Hasek .15 .40
441 Garth Butcher .07 .20
442 Jyrki Lumme .05 .15
443 Sergei Nemchinov .05 .15
444 Tie Domi .07 .20
445 Gary Roberts .05 .15
446 Dave McLlwain .05 .15
447 John Gruden RC .05 .15
448 Vladimir Konstantinov .07 .20
449 Adam Deadmarsh .05 .15
450 Brian Leetch TOTG .07 .20
451 Scott Stevens .10 .25
452 Mark Tinordi .05 .15
453 Al Iafrate .05 .15
454 Ray Bourque TOTG .15 .40
455 Patrick Roy .25 .60
456 Viktor Gordiouk .07 .20
457 Owen Nolan .10 .25
458 Stu Barnes .05 .15
459 Zigmund Palffy .07 .20
460 Jaromir Jagr .30 .75
461 Andrei Nazarov .05 .15
462 Kelly Hrudey .07 .20
463 Jason Wiemer RC .05 .15
464 Oleg Tverdovsky .07 .20
465 Brett Hull .20 .50
466 Luke Richardson .05 .15
467 Jason Allison .07 .20
468 Dimitri Yushkevich .05 .15
469 Todd Simon RC .05 .15
470 Martin Brodeur .25 .60
471 Thomas Steen .05 .15
472 Vesa Viitakoski .07 .20
473 Todd Harvey .05 .15
474 Kent Manderville .05 .15
475 Chris Chelios .10 .25
476 Joby Messier .05 .15
477 Jassen Cullimore .05 .15
478 Jamie Pushor .07 .20
479 Bryan Smolinski .05 .15
480 Joe Sakic .20 .50
481 David Wilkie .07 .20
482 Craig Billington .07 .20
483 Pat Neaton .07 .20
484 Chris Pronger .10 .25
485 Brian Leetch POW .07 .20
486 Chris Chelios .10 .25
487 Jeff Brown .05 .15
488 Al MacInnis .12 .30
489 Paul Coffey .10 .25
490 Ray Bourque POW .15 .40
491 Phil Housley .07 .20
492 Larry Murphy .07 .20
493 Sergei Zubov POW .07 .20
494 Scott Stevens .10 .25
495 Steve Thomas .05 .15
496 Jim Waite .05 .15
497 Mike Keane .05 .15
498 Rob Blake .10 .25
499 John Lilley .05 .15
500 Brian Leetch .07 .20
501 Derek Plante .05 .15
502 Tim Cheveldae .07 .20
503 Vladimir Vujtek .05 .15
504 Esa Tikkanen .05 .15
505 Cam Neely .10 .25
506 Dale Hunter .05 .15
507 Marc Bergevin .05 .15
508 Joel Otto .05 .15
509 Brent Fedyk .05 .15
510 Dave Andreychuk .10 .25
511 Andy Moog .10 .25
512 Jaroslav Modry .05 .15
513 Sergei Krivokrasov .05 .15
514 Brett Lindros .05 .15
515 Cory Stillman RC .05 .15
516 Jon Rohloff RC .10 .25
517 Joe Mullen .07 .20
518 Evgeny Davydov .05 .15
519 Scott Young .05 .15
520 Sergei Fedorov .15 .40
521 Pat Falloon .05 .15
522 Bill Lindsay .05 .15
523 Ron Tugnutt .07 .20
524 Anatoli Semenov .05 .15
525 Geoff Courtnall .05 .15
526 Luc Robitaille .10 .25
527 Geoff Sanderson .07 .20
528 Esa Tikkanen .05 .15
529 Brendan Shanahan TOTG .10 .25
530 Jason Arnott .07 .20
531 Michal Grosek RC .05 .15
532 Steve Larmer .07 .20
533 Eric Fichaud RC .10 .25
534 Dimitri Khristich .05 .15
535 Garry Galley .05 .15
536 Aaron Gavey .05 .15
537 Joe Nieuwendyk .07 .20
538 Mike Craig .05 .15
539 Scott Niedermayer .10 .25
540 Luc Robitaille .10 .25
541 Dino Ciccarelli .07 .20
542 Sean Burke .07 .20
543 Jiri Slegr .05 .15
544 Jesse Belanger .05 .15
545 Sean Hill .05 .15
546 Vladimir Malakhov .05 .15
547 Jeff Friesen .05 .15
548 Mike Ricci .05 .15

1994-95 OPC Premier Finest Inserts

COMPLETE SET (23) 20.00 50.00
1 Patrik Carnback .60 1.50
2 Bryan Smolinski .60 1.50
3 Derek Plante .60 1.50
4 Alexander Karpovtsev .60 1.50
5 Trevor Kidd 1.25 3.00
6 Iain Fraser .60 1.50
7 Alexandre Daigle .60 1.50
8 Chris Osgood 2.00 5.00
9 Rob Niedermayer .60 1.50
10 Jason Arnott .60 1.50
11 Chris Pronger 2.00 5.00
12 Jesse Belanger .60 1.50
13 Oleg Petrov .60 1.50
14 Martin Brodeur 8.00 20.00
15 Alexei Yashin .60 1.50
16 Mikael Renberg 1.25 3.00
17 Boris Mironov .60 1.50
18 Damian Rhodes 1.25 3.00
19 Darren McCarty .60 1.50
20 Chris Gratton 1.25 3.00
21 Jamie McLennan .60 1.50
22 Nathan Lafayette .60 1.50
23 Jeff Shantz .60 1.50

1994-95 OPC Premier Special Effects

*OPC SE: .6X TO 1.5X TOPPS SPEC.EFFECT

2007-08 OPC Premier

1 Bernie Parent 3.00 8.00
2 Al MacInnis 3.00 8.00
3 Rob Blake 2.50 6.00
4 Bobby Orr 10.00 25.00
5 Denis Potvin 2.50 6.00
6 Nicklas Lidstrom 2.50 6.00
7 Phil Esposito 4.00 10.00
8 Cam Neely 2.50 6.00
9 Gordie Howe 8.00 20.00
10 Guy Lafleur 3.00 8.00
11 Mark Messier 5.00 12.00
12 Jarome Iginla 3.00 8.00
13 Mats Sundin 2.50 6.00
14 Brendan Shanahan 2.50 6.00
15 Dany Heatley 2.00 5.00
16 Bobby Clarke 4.00 10.00
17 Jari Kurri 2.50 6.00
18 Larry Robinson 2.50 6.00
19 Joe Sakic 5.00 12.00
20 Dino Ciccarelli 2.50 6.00
21 Borje Salming 2.50 6.00
22 Mike Bossy 2.50 6.00
23 Milan Hejduk 2.00 5.00
24 Bernie Federko 2.00 5.00
25 Stan Mikita 3.00 8.00
26 Peter Stastny 2.00 5.00
27 Frank Mahovlich 2.50 6.00
28 Alexander Semin 2.50 6.00
29 Marc-Andre Fleury 5.00 12.00
30 Martin Brodeur 6.00 15.00
31 Grant Fuhr 4.00 10.00
32 Billy Smith 2.50 6.00
33 Patrick Roy 6.00 15.00
34 Miikka Kiprusoff 2.50 6.00
35 Tony Esposito 2.50 6.00
36 Jean-Sebastien Giguere 2.50 6.00
37 Patrice Bergeron 3.00 8.00
38 Dominik Hasek 4.00 10.00
39 Henrik Zetterberg 3.00 8.00
40 Lee Stempniak 1.50 4.00
41 Keith Tkachuk 2.50 6.00
42 Alexander Ovechkin 10.00 25.00
43 Zach Parise 2.50 6.00
44 Andy Bathgate 2.00 5.00
45 Rick DiPietro 2.00 5.00
46 Alexander Radulov 2.50 6.00
47 Daniel Briere 2.50 6.00
48 Jason Spezza 2.50 6.00
49 Ray Emery 2.00 5.00
50 Marian Gaborik 2.50 6.00
51 Simon Gagne 2.50 6.00
52 Roberto Luongo 4.00 10.00
53 Saku Koivu 2.50 6.00
54 Paul Kariya 2.50 6.00
55 Lanny McDonald 2.50 6.00
56 Darryl Sittler 3.00 8.00
57 Scott Stevens 2.50 6.00
58 Joe Thornton 4.00 10.00
59 Mike Modano 4.00 10.00
60 Clark Gillies 2.50 6.00
61 Rick Nash 2.50 6.00
62 Dale Hawerchuk 3.00 8.00
63 Anze Kopitar 4.00 10.00
64 Gilbert Perreault 2.50 6.00
65 Daniel Alfredsson 2.50 6.00
66 Mario Lemieux 10.00 25.00
67 Brad Richards 2.50 6.00
68 Jaromir Jagr 8.00 20.00
69 Bobby Hull 5.00 12.00
70 Mark Recchi 3.00 8.00
71 Evgeni Malkin 5.00 12.00
72 Jordan Staal 2.00 5.00
73 Michael Ryder 1.50 4.00
74 Eric Staal 3.00 8.00
75 Olli Jokinen 2.00 5.00
76 Pavel Datsyuk 4.00 10.00
77 Ray Bourque 4.00 10.00
78 Vincent Lecavalier 2.50 6.00
79 Dwayne Roloson 2.00 5.00
80 Henrik Lundqvist 6.00 15.00
81 Phil Kessel 2.50 6.00
82 Tomas Vokoun 2.00 5.00
83 Steve Shutt 2.00 5.00
84 Thomas Vanek 2.00 5.00
85 Patrik Elias 2.50 6.00
86 Martin St. Louis 2.50 6.00
87 Sidney Crosby 10.00 25.00
88 Paul Stastny 2.00 5.00
89 Cam Ward 2.50 6.00
90 Marty Turco 2.50 6.00
91 Sergei Fedorov 4.00 10.00
92 Patrick Marleau 2.50 6.00
93 Jason Arnott 2.00 5.00
94 Jonathan Cheechoo 2.00 5.00
95 Ryan Getzlaf 2.50 6.00
96 Shane Doan 2.00 5.00
97 Ryan Miller 2.50 6.00
98 Markus Naslund 2.50 6.00
99 Wayne Gretzky 15.00 40.00
100 Alexander Frolov 1.50 4.00
101 Andrew Cogliano JSY AU RC 6.00 15.00
102 Andy Greene JSY AU RC 6.00 15.00
103 Anton Stralman JSY AU RC 5.00 12.00
104 Bobby Ryan JSY AU RC 12.00 30.00
105 Brandon Dubinsky JSY AU RC 10.00 25.00
106 Brian Elliott JSY AU RC 10.00 25.00
107 Bryan Little JSY AU RC 8.00 20.00
108 Carey Price JSY AU RC 50.00 125.00
109 Cory Murphy JSY AU RC 5.00 12.00
110 Curtis McElhinney JSY AU RC 8.00 20.00
111 Casey Borer JSY AU RC 5.00 12.00
112 David Krejci JSY AU RC 20.00 50.00
113 David Perron JSY AU RC 10.00 25.00
114 Drew Miller JSY AU RC 6.00 15.00
115 Erik Johnson JSY AU RC 8.00 20.00
116 Frans Nielsen JSY AU RC 8.00 20.00
117 Devin Setoguchi JSY AU RC 8.00 20.00
118 Jack Johnson JSY AU RC 6.00 15.00
119 James Sheppard JSY AU RC 5.00 12.00
120 Jannik Hansen JSY AU RC 6.00 15.00
121 Jared Boll JSY AU RC 6.00 15.00
122 Jaroslav Halak JSY AU RC 12.00 30.00
123 Jaroslav Hlinka JSY AU RC 6.00 15.00
124 Jiri Tlusty JSY AU RC 8.00 20.00
125 Jack Skille JSY AU RC 6.00 15.00
126 Jonathan Bernier JSY AU RC 12.00 30.00
127 Jonathan Sigalet JSY AU RC 5.00 12.00
128 Jonathan Toews JSY AU RC 75.00 135.00
129 Tuukka Rask JSY AU RC 25.00 50.00
130 Kyle Chipchura JSY AU RC 8.00 20.00
131 Lauri Tukonen JSY AU RC 5.00 12.00
132 Sergei Kostitsyn JSY AU RC 6.00 15.00
133 Marc Staal JSY AU RC 8.00 20.00
134 Martin Hanzal JSY AU RC 6.00 15.00
135 Mason Raymond JSY AU RC 8.00 20.00
136 T.J. Hensick JSY AU RC 6.00 15.00
137 Matt Niskanen JSY AU RC 8.00 20.00
138 Matt Smaby JSY AU RC 5.00 12.00
139 Milan Lucic JSY AU RC 12.00 30.00
140 Nick Foligno JSY AU RC 10.00 25.00
141 Nicklas Backstrom JSY AU RC 25.00 60.00
142 Nicklas Bergfors JSY AU RC 5.00 12.00
143 Ondrej Pavelec JSY AU RC 10.00 25.00
144 Patrick Kane JSY AU RC 80.00 200.00
145 Peter Mueller JSY AU RC 6.00 15.00
146 Petr Kalus JSY AU RC 5.00 12.00
147 Rob Schremp JSY AU RC 6.00 15.00
148 Rod Pelley JSY AU RC 5.00 12.00
149 Ryan Callahan JSY AU RC 10.00 25.00
150 Ryan Carter JSY AU RC 5.00 12.00
151 Steve Downie JSY AU RC 6.00 15.00
152 Sam Gagner JSY AU RC 10.00 25.00
153 Stefan Meyer JSY AU RC 6.00 15.00
154 Steve Wagner JSY AU RC 5.00 12.00
155 Tobias Enstrom JSY AU RC 8.00 20.00
156 Tobias Stephan JSY AU RC 6.00 15.00
157 David Jones JSY AU RC 5.00 12.00
158 Torrey Mitchell JSY AU RC 6.00 15.00
159 Tyler Weiman JSY AU RC 6.00 15.00
160 Ville Koistinen JSY AU RC 5.00 12.00

2007-08 OPC Premier Gold

*VETS/75: .4X TO 1X BASIC CARDS
*ROOK.JSY AU/50: .6X TO 1.5X BASIC RC
108 Carey Price JSY AU 100.00 175.00
128 Jonathan Toews JSY AU 125.00 200.00
144 Patrick Kane JSY AU 100.00 250.00

2007-08 OPC Premier Silver Spectrum

*SILVER SPECTRUM: .8X TO 2X
*SILVER SPECTRUM JSY AU: .6X TO 1.5X
108 Carey Price JSY AU 100.00 175.00
128 Jonathan Toews JSY AU 100.00 200.00

2007-08 OPC Premier Autographed Premier Stitchings

APSAB Andy Bathgate 12.00 30.00
APSAK Anze Kopitar 25.00 60.00
APSBC Bobby Clarke 25.00 60.00
APSBY Mike Bossy 25.00 60.00
APSCN Cam Neely 15.00 40.00
APSCW Cam Ward 15.00 40.00
APSDS Darryl Sittler 20.00 50.00
APSES Eric Staal 30.00 60.00
APSIK Ilya Kovalchuk 40.00 80.00
APSJB Johnny Bucyk 15.00 40.00
APSJC Jonathan Cheechoo 15.00 40.00
APSJG Jean-Sebastien Giguere 15.00 40.00
APSJI Jarome Iginla 20.00 50.00
APSLR Larry Robinson 12.00 30.00
APSMF Marc-Andre Fleury 30.00 80.00
APSMM Mike Modano 25.00 60.00
APSMN Markus Naslund 15.00 40.00
APSMR Michael Ryder 10.00 25.00
APSMS Martin St. Louis 15.00 40.00
APSMT Marty Turco 15.00 40.00
APSNL Nicklas Lidstrom 25.00 50.00
APSPS Peter Stastny 12.00 30.00
APSRN Rick Nash 20.00 50.00
APSSA Borje Salming 15.00 40.00
APSSD Shane Doan 12.00 30.00
APSSG Simon Gagne 15.00 40.00
APSSK Saku Koivu 25.00 50.00
APSSM Stan Mikita 20.00 50.00
APSST Paul Stastny 20.00 50.00
APSTV Thomas Vanek 15.00 40.00
APSVL Vincent Lecavalier 15.00 40.00
APSVO Tomas Vokoun 12.00 30.00

2007-08 OPC Premier Autographs Duos

PP2BC J.Bucyk/B.Clarke 10.00 25.00
PP2BF M.Brodeur/M.Fleury 25.00 60.00
PP2BK P.Bergeron/P.Kessel 12.00 30.00
PP2BT A.Bathgate/W.Tkaczuk 10.00 25.00
PP2CH B.Clarke/R.Hextall 15.00 40.00
PP2DF Lidstrom/Salming 10.00 25.00
PP2DH S.Doan/D.Heatley 8.00 20.00
PP2EJ E.Staal/J.Staal 12.00 30.00
PP2EM T.Esposito/S.Mikita 12.00 30.00
PP2FM B.Federko/J.Mullen 8.00 20.00
PP2FR G.Fuhr/B.Ranford 15.00 40.00
PP2FS M.Fleury/J.Staal 20.00 50.00
PP2GK M.Gaborik/P.Kalus 10.00 25.00
PP2GO B.Orr/G.Howe 40.00 100.00
PP2GS S.Gagne/M.St. Louis 10.00 25.00
PP2GT J.Giguere/M.Turco 10.00 25.00
PP2HK M.Hossa/I.Kovalchuk 10.00 25.00
PP2IC J.Iginla/J.Cheechoo 12.00 30.00
PP2IN J.Iginla/R.Nash 12.00 30.00
PP2IT J.Iginla/A.Tanguay 12.00 30.00
PP2KR Kovalchuk/Radulov 10.00 25.00
PP2LB Lecavalier/D.Boyle 10.00 25.00
PP2LK T.Lindsay/R.Kelly 10.00 25.00
PP2LR J.Lupul/M.Richards 8.00 20.00
PP2LS G.Lafleur/S.Shutt 12.00 30.00
PP2MB M.Modano/B.Morrow 15.00 40.00
PP2NB C.Neely/R.Bourque 15.00 40.00
PP2NK M.Naslund/R.Kesler 10.00 25.00
PP2OM A.Ovechkin/E.Malkin 40.00 100.00
PP2PG C.Perry/R.Getzlaf 15.00 40.00
PP2RG R.Nash/G.Brule 10.00 25.00
PP2RL Ryder/Latendresse 8.00 20.00
PP2SJ R.Schremp/J.Johnson 8.00 20.00
PP2SS M.Svatos/P.Stastny 8.00 20.00
PP2TB Tanguay/Bergeron 12.00 30.00
PP2VH T.Vokoun/D.Hasek 15.00 40.00
PP2VM Lecavalier/M.St. Louis 10.00 25.00

2007-08 OPC Premier Autographs Trios

PP3CKJ Cammallri/Kopitar/Johnson 25.00 60.00
PP3EHM Esposito/Hull/Mikita 75.00 150.00
PP3FKM Fuhr/Kurri/Messier 100.00 200.00
PP3GGP Giguere/Perry/Getzlaf 30.00 60.00
PP3GLC Gagne/Lupul/Carter 15.00 40.00
PP3HSH Hull/Steen/Hawer 50.00 100.00
PP3IGC Iginla/Gagne/Chech 25.00 60.00
PP3KRL Koivu/Ryder/Latendresse 20.00 50.00
PP3LHK Lindsay/Howe/Kelly 75.00 150.00
PP3LSB Lecavalier/St. Louis/Boyle 30.00 60.00
PP3LSR Lafleur/Shutt/Robinson 50.00 100.00
PP3MRM Modano/Ribeiro/Morrow 25.00 60.00
PP3NMK Naslund/Morrison/Kesler 15.00 40.00
PP3OGH Orr/Gretzky/Howe 600.00 1500.00
PP3RLO Lemieux/Roy/Orr 200.00 300.00
PP3SBK Savard/Bergeron/Kessel 50.00 100.00
PP3SHN St. Louis/Heatley/Nash 50.00 100.00
PP3WSW Williams/Staal/Ward 15.00 40.00

2007-08 OPC Premier Autographs Foursomes

PP4BHMH Belv/Hll/Mhv/Hwe 250.00 400.00
PP4DGHM Dne/Grt/Hwe/Msr 300.00 800.00
PP4DSFH Dne/Stst/Fdr/Hwr 75.00 150.00
PP4GSCN Ggn/St.L/Chc/Nsh 75.00 150.00
PP4HSGS Hsa/Stn/Gbk/Svt 100.00 200.00
PP4RBFE Roy/Brd/Fhr/Espo 200.00 350.00
PP4RUSS Ovch/Mlkn/Rdl/Kvl 125.00 200.00
PP4SPKS Svt/Prch/Kptr/Stny 125.00 200.00
PP4SSSS Staal/Stastny Bros. 125.00 200.00

2007-08 OPC Premier Original Six Signatures

O6AB Andy Bathgate 6.00 15.00
O6BD Bill Dineen 8.00 20.00
O6BH Bobby Hull 20.00 50.00
O6BO Bobby Orr 75.00 150.00
O6BS Borje Salming 8.00 20.00
O6DS Darryl Sittler 10.00 25.00
O6DW Doug Wilson 6.00 15.00
O6EG Ed Giacomin 8.00 20.00
O6EL Elmer Lach 6.00 15.00
O6FM Frank Mahovlich 8.00 20.00
O6GC Gerry Cheevers 8.00 20.00
O6GH Gordie Howe 30.00 80.00
O6GL Guy Lafleur 15.00 40.00
O6JB Jean Beliveau 50.00 100.00
O6LR Larry Robinson 6.00 15.00
O6MS Milt Schmidt 10.00 25.00
O6PH Paul Henderson 6.00 15.00
O6PP Pierre Pilote 10.00 25.00
O6RD Ron Duguay 6.00 15.00
O6RE Ron Ellis 6.00 15.00
O6RG Ron Greschner 5.00 12.00
O6RK Red Kelly 6.00 15.00
O6SS Steve Shutt 6.00 15.00
O6TE Tony Esposito 12.00 30.00
O6TL Ted Lindsay 10.00 25.00
O6TO Terry O'Reilly 6.00 15.00
O6WT Walt Tkaczuk 8.00 20.00

2007-08 OPC Premier Original Six Signatures Gold

*GOLD: .8X TO 2X BASE
O6BD Bill Dineen 12.00 30.00
O6BO Bobby Orr 100.00 200.00
O6GH Gordie Howe 60.00 120.00
O6RK Red Kelly 12.00 30.00
O6TL Ted Lindsay 12.00 30.00
O6TO Terry O'Reilly 8.00 20.00

2007-08 OPC Premier Original Six Signatures Silver

*SILVER: .6X TO 1.5X BASE
O6BH Bobby Hull 25.00 60.00
O6BO Bobby Orr 100.00 200.00
O6BS Borje Salming 12.00 30.00
O6DS Darryl Sittler 12.00 30.00
O6DW Doug Wilson 10.00 25.00
O6GH Gordie Howe 75.00 150.00

2007-08 OPC Premier Pairings Autographed Jerseys

PCAS C.Armstrong/J.Staal 15.00 40.00
PCBB J.Bucyk/R.Bourque 25.00 60.00
PCBP J.Bucyk/G.Perreault 12.00 30.00
PCBS M.Bossy/S.Shutt 12.00 30.00
PCCB Cammalleri/Brown 12.00 30.00
PCCK Cammalleri/Kopitar 12.00 30.00
PCCP C.Neely/P.Kessel 15.00 40.00
PCDF Lidstrom/Salming 25.00 50.00
PCDH M.Dionne/D.Hawerchuk 30.00 60.00
PCDN M.Dionne/B.Nicholls 15.00 40.00
PCEJ E.Malkin/J.Staal 25.00 60.00
PCFR G.Fuhr/B.Ranford 30.00 60.00
PCGD S.Gagne/S.Doan 10.00 25.00
PCHG M.Hossa/M.Gaborik 15.00 40.00
PCHK M.Hossa/I.Kovalchuk 20.00 50.00
PCIM J.Iginla/L.McDonald 30.00 60.00
PCIT J.Iginla/A.Tanguay 12.00 30.00
PCLB P.Leclaire/G.Brule 10.00 25.00
PCLG M.Lemieux/W.Gretzky 300.00 800.00
PCLM Leetch/Messier 60.00 120.00
PCLN P.Leclaire/R.Nash 12.00 30.00
PCLS Lecavalier/M.St. Louis 15.00 40.00
PCLT Lecavalier/Thornton 12.00 30.00
PCMB M.Turco/B.Morrow 15.00 40.00
PCMC M.Ryder/S.Shutt 12.00 30.00
PCMH MacInnis/Hawerchuk 12.00 30.00
PCMK B.Morrison/R.Kesler 15.00 40.00
PCMM M.Modano/J.Mullen 12.00 30.00
PCMO G.Lafleur/L.Robinson 25.00 60.00
PCMR M.Modano/M.Ribeiro 12.00 30.00
PCMS S.Mikita/D.Savard 15.00 40.00
PCNB R.Nash/G.Brule 12.00 30.00
PCNM M.Naslund/B.Morrison 15.00 40.00
PCNO C.Neely/A.Oates 25.00 50.00
PCNS Tanguay/Zetterberg 20.00 50.00
PCOM A.Ovechkin/E.Malkin 75.00 150.00
PCPD P.Stastny/D.Hawerchuk 30.00 60.00
PCPE P.Bergeron/E.Staal 15.00 40.00
PCPG C.Perry/R.Getzlaf 20.00 50.00
PCRB P.Roy/R.Bourque 60.00 120.00
PCRT M.Ribeiro/M.Turco 12.00 30.00
PCSH M.St. Louis/N.Horton 10.00 25.00
PCSM S.Gagne/A.Tanguay 12.00 30.00
PCSW M.Svatos/W.Wolski 12.00 30.00
PCWH T.Vokoun/N.Horton 12.00 30.00
PCWS J.Williams/E.Staal 12.00 30.00

2007-08 OPC Premier Pairings Autographed Jerseys Patch

PCAS C.Armstrong/J.Staal 15.00 40.00
PCBB J.Bucyk/R.Bourque 50.00 100.00
PCBP J.Bucyk/G.Perreault 15.00 40.00
PCBS M.Bossy/S.Shutt 20.00 50.00
PCCB Cammalleri/Brown 15.00 40.00
PCCP C.Neely/P.Kessel 30.00 60.00
PCDF Lidstrom/Salming 40.00 80.00
PCDH M.Dionne/D.Hawerchuk 25.00 50.00
PCEC E.Staal/C.Ward 40.00 80.00
PCEJ E.Malkin/J.Staal 25.00 60.00
PCGD S.Gagne/S.Doan 10.00 25.00
PCHG M.Hossa/M.Gaborik 40.00 80.00
PCHK M.Hossa/I.Kovalchuk 25.00 50.00
PCIM J.Iginla/L.McDonald 60.00 120.00
PCIT J.Iginla/A.Tanguay 25.00 60.00
PCKB R.Kesler/K.Bieksa 25.00 60.00
PCLB P.Leclaire/G.Brule 20.00 50.00
PCLM B.Leetch/M.Messier 60.00 120.00
PCLN P.Leclaire/R.Nash 20.00 50.00
PCLT Lecavalier/Thornton 25.00 60.00
PCMB M.Turco/B.Morrow 20.00 50.00
PCMH MacInnis/Hawerchuk 15.00 40.00
PCMK B.Morrison/R.Kesler 20.00 50.00
PCMM M.Modano/J.Mullen 12.00 30.00
PCMO G.Lafleur/L.Robinson 40.00 80.00
PCMR M.Modano/M.Ribeiro 15.00 40.00
PCMS S.Mikita/D.Savard 25.00 60.00
PCNB R.Nash/G.Brule 20.00 50.00
PCNM M.Naslund/B.Morrison 15.00 40.00
PCNO C.Neely/A.Oates 30.00 60.00
PCNS Tanguay/Zetterberg 40.00 80.00
PCOM A.Ovechkin/E.Malkin 100.00 200.00
PCPE P.Bergeron/E.Staal 15.00 40.00
PCRB P.Roy/R.Bourque 100.00 175.00
PCRT M.Ribeiro/M.Turco 15.00 40.00
PCSH M.St. Louis/N.Horton 15.00 40.00
PCSM S.Gagne/A.Tanguay 15.00 40.00
PCTR D.Tucker/A.Raycroft 20.00 50.00
PCWH T.Vokoun/N.Horton 20.00 50.00
PCWS J.Williams/E.Staal 12.00 30.00

2007-08 OPC Premier Penmanship

PPAK Anze Kopitar 12.00 30.00
PPBF Bernie Federko 6.00 15.00
PPCG Clark Gillies 8.00 20.00
PPDH Dany Heatley 6.00 15.00
PPDR Dwayne Roloson 6.00 15.00
PPEM Evgeni Malkin 15.00 40.00
PPHJ Milan Hejduk 8.00 20.00
PPHX Ron Hextall 8.00 20.00
PPIK Ilya Kovalchuk 10.00 25.00
PPJG Jean-Sebastien Giguere 8.00 20.00
PPJK Jari Kurri 8.00 20.00
PPJS Jordan Staal 10.00 25.00
PPMG Marian Gaborik 8.00 20.00
PPMN Markus Naslund 8.00 20.00
PPMT Marty Turco 8.00 20.00
PPNL Nicklas Lidstrom 12.00 30.00
PPPB Patrice Bergeron 8.00 20.00
PPPS Paul Stastny 6.00 15.00
PPRG Ryan Getzlaf 8.00 20.00
PPSC Sidney Crosby 75.00 150.00
PPSD Shane Doan 6.00 15.00
PPSG Simon Gagne 8.00 20.00
PPSK Saku Koivu 8.00 20.00
PPVL Vincent Lecavalier 8.00 20.00
PPVO Tomas Vokoun 6.00 15.00

2007-08 OPC Premier Penmanship Gold

*GOLD: .8X TO 2X BASE
PPEM Evgeni Malkin 40.00 80.00

2007-08 OPC Premier Penmanship Silver

*SILVER: .6X TO 1.5X BASE
PPEM Evgeni Malkin 30.00 80.00
PPSC Sidney Crosby 125.00 200.00

2007-08 OPC Premier Rare Remnants Triples

PTAJD Aebiscr/Jovanvski/Doan 15.00 40.00
PTAMV Afinogenov/Miller/Vanek 15.00 40.00
PTAVS Afinogenv/Vanek/Staffd 12.00 30.00
PTBES Brodeur/Elias/Stevens 20.00 50.00
PTBGP Brodeur/Gionta/Parise 15.00 40.00
PTBLB Blake/Lecav/Bourdon 15.00 40.00
PTBLK Brodeur/Luongo/Kiprusoff 20.00 50.00
PTBLM Beliveau/Lafleur/Mahov 15.00 40.00
PTBPS Bossy/Potvin/Smith 15.00 40.00
PTBRS Bourque/Robinsn/Stevns 15.00 40.00
PTBSW Brind'Amour/Staal/Ward 12.00 30.00
PTCFM Fleury/Crosby/Malkin 25.00 60.00
PTCGH Clarke/Gagne/Hextall 20.00 50.00
PTCMS Crosby/Malkin/Hextall 50.00 100.00
PTDFM Datsyuk/Fedorov/Malkin 15.00 40.00
PTDGK Demitra/Gaborik/Koivu 15.00 40.00
PTFBK Fernandz/Bergern/Kessel 12.00 30.00
PTFCK Frolov/Cammalleri/Kopitar 12.00 30.00
PTFCT Fernandz/Chara/Thomas 10.00 25.00
PTGBL Gagne/Briere/Lupul 15.00 40.00
PTGDP Gomez/Drury/Prucha 12.00 30.00
PTGRC Gagne/Richards/Carter 15.00 40.00
PTGSD Guerin/Satan/DiPietro 15.00 40.00
PTHDG Hossa/Demitra/Gaborik 12.00 30.00
PTHHK Huet/Higgins/Kovalev 12.00 30.00
PTHKL Hossa/Koval/Lehton 15.00 40.00
PTHLD Hasek/Lidstrom/Datsyuk 15.00 40.00
PTHRK Havlat/Ruutu/Khabibulin 12.00 30.00
PTHSW Hejduk/Svatos/Wolski 12.00 30.00
PTIKP Iginla/Kiprusoff/Phaneuf 10.00 25.00
PTJHE Jagr/Hasek/Elias 20.00 50.00
PTKOF Kolzig/Ovechkin/Fehr 15.00 40.00
PTKOR Koval/Ovech/Radulov 12.00 30.00
PTKRK Koivu/Ryder/Kovalev 12.00 30.00
PTKSK Koivu/Staal/Kopitar 15.00 40.00
PTKST Kariya/Tkachuk/Stemp 12.00 30.00
PTLEK Luongo/Emery/Kiprusoff 12.00 30.00
PTLHZ Lidstrm/Holmstrm/Zetter 15.00 40.00
PTLRS Lecavalier/Richards/St. Louis 12.00 30.00
PTMGM McDonald/Gilmour/Macln 12.00 30.00
PTMSR Modano/Sundin/Recchi 12.00 30.00
PTMTK Modano/Tkachuk/Kessel 15.00 40.00
PTNBO Neely/Bourque/Oates 15.00 40.00
PTNLM Naslund/Luongo/Morrison 10.00 25.00
PTNSS Naslund/Sedin/Sedin 10.00 25.00
PTNZF Nash/Zherdev/Fedorov 10.00 25.00
PTPGB Parrish/Gaborik/Bouchard 10.00 25.00
PTRLG Roy/Lemieux/Gretzky 75.00 150.00
PTROV Richards/Ott/Vaive 10.00 25.00
PTRRM Roberts/Recchi/Malone 15.00 40.00
PTSBS Spezza/Bergeron/Staal 10.00 25.00
PTSFA Sundin/Forsberg/Alfredsson 15.00 40.00
PTSHP Stoll/Hemsky/Pouliot 12.00 30.00
PTSJL Shanahan/Jagr/Lundqvist 10.00 25.00
PTSLJ Selanne/Lehtinen/Jokinen 15.00 40.00
PTSNG Selanne/Nieder/Giguere 15.00 40.00
PTSOH Stastny/Oates/Hawerchuk 10.00 25.00
PTSRT Sakic/Richards/Thornton 12.00 30.00
PTSSN Nolan/Sakic/Sundin 15.00 40.00
PTSTS Sakic/Theodore/Smyth 12.00 30.00
PTTSC Thornton/St.L/Crosby 20.00 50.00
PTVNB Vyborny/Nash/Brule 10.00 25.00

2007-08 OPC Premier Rare Remnants Quads

PQASHE Alf/Spez/Heat/Emry 25.00 60.00
PQBLMF Brodr/Luon/Miller/Flery 30.00 80.00
PQBSHS Brodr/Hask/Smith/Hxtl 30.00 80.00
PQCFMS Fleu/Crsby/Malkn/Stal 60.00 120.00
PQCWPS Cheli/Will/Prb/Stvns 25.00 60.00
PQGBBC Gag/Brier/Birn/Cartr 10.00 25.00
PQITKP Igin/Tang/Kipr/Phanf 20.00 50.00
PQJFIC Jagr/Fors/Igin/Crsby 60.00 120.00
PQLCGM Mrio/Crsby/Grtz/Mess 60.00 120.00
PQLNFB Lclre/Nsh/Fdrv/Brul 20.00 50.00
PQMTCC Mrlu/Thrn/Chec/Crle 25.00 60.00
PQRNWS BRch/Nder/Wrd/Stvns 25.00 60.00
PQSICM Sak/Igin/Crsby/Mess 40.00 100.00
PQSJDL Shan/Jgr/Druy/Lndq 50.00 100.00
PQSKBI Sakic/Krya/Brodr/Igin 20.00 50.00
PQSKRD Sakic/Krya/BRich/Dts 15.00 40.00
PQSOMA Selne/Alf/Ovch/Mlkn 60.00 120.00
PQSPNG Selne/Prng/Nder/Ggy 20.00 50.00
PQTNCO Thrn/Nsh/Crsby/Ovch 30.00 80.00

2007-08 OPC Premier Remnants Triples

*PATCH/15-35: 1X TO 2.5X JSY/50-100
PRAF Alexander Frolov/100 4.00 10.00
PRAK Alex Kovalev/100 5.00 12.00
PRAO Alexander Ovechkin/100 10.00 25.00
PRAS Alexander Steen/100 4.00 10.00
PRBL Rob Blake/100 6.00 15.00
PRBM Brendan Morrison/100 4.00 10.00
PRBO Mike Bossy/100 6.00 15.00
PRBR Rod Brind`Amour/100 6.00 15.00
PRBS Billy Smith/100 6.00 15.00
PRCH Jonathan Cheechoo/100 5.00 12.00
PRCW Cam Ward/100 6.00 15.00
PRDA Daniel Alfredsson/100 6.00 15.00
PRDE Pavol Demitra/100 8.00 20.00
PRDH Dale Hawerchuk/100 8.00 20.00
PRDL David Legwand/100 5.00 12.00
PRDR Dwayne Roloson/100 5.00 12.00
PRDS Darryl Sittler/100 8.00 20.00
PREB Ed Belfour/100 6.00 15.00
PREJ Ed Jovanovski/100 5.00 12.00
PREL Eric Lindros/100 8.00 20.00
PREM Evgeni Malkin/100 20.00 50.00
PRES Eric Staal/100 8.00 20.00
PRGA Simon Gagne/100 6.00 15.00
PRGP Gilbert Perreault/100 6.00 15.00
PRHA Dominik Hasek/100 10.00 25.00
PRHE Dany Heatley/75 8.00 20.00
PRHL Henrik Lundqvist/100 15.00 40.00
PRHM Milan Hejduk/100 5.00 12.00
PRHZ Henrik Zetterberg/100 8.00 20.00
PRIK Ilya Kovalchuk/100 6.00 15.00
PRJA Jason Arnott/100 5.00 12.00
PRJB Jay Bouwmeester/100 4.00 10.00
PRJC Jeff Carter/75 5.00 12.00
PRJG Jean-Sebastien Giguere/100 6.00 15.00
PRJI Jarome Iginla/100 8.00 20.00
PRJO Joe Sakic/100 8.00 20.00
PRJP Joni Pitkanen/100 4.00 10.00
PRJS Jason Spezza/100 6.00 15.00
PRJT Joe Thornton/100 10.00 25.00
PRJW Justin Williams/100 5.00 12.00
PRKL Kari Lehtonen/100 5.00 12.00
PRKO Mikko Koivu/100 5.00 12.00
PRLM Lanny McDonald/100 6.00 15.00
PRLR Larry Robinson/100 6.00 15.00
PRMA Martin Havlat/100 6.00 15.00
PRMB Martin Brodeur/100 15.00 40.00
PRMC Mike Cammalleri/100 5.00 12.00
PRMG Marian Gaborik/100 6.00 15.00
PRMH Marian Hossa/100 12.50 30.00
PRMI Mike Richards/100 5.00 12.00
PRMK Miikka Kiprusoff/100 6.00 15.00
PRML Mario Lemieux/100 25.00 60.00
PRMM Mike Modano/100 10.00 25.00
PRMN Markus Naslund/100 6.00 15.00
PRMR Mark Recchi/100 8.00 20.00
PRMS Marc Savard/100 4.00 10.00
PRMT Marty Turco/100 6.00 15.00
PRNH Nathan Horton/100 6.00 15.00
PRNL Nicklas Lidstrom/100 6.00 15.00
PROJ Olli Jokinen/100 5.00 12.00
PROK Olaf Kolzig/100 6.00 15.00
PRPB Patrice Bergeron/100 8.00 20.00
PRPD Pavel Datsyuk/100 8.00 20.00
PRPE Patrik Elias/100 6.00 15.00
PRPF Peter Forsberg/100 12.00 30.00
PRPI Pierre-Marc Bouchard/100 6.00 15.00
PRPK Paul Kariya/100 6.00 15.00
PRPM Patrick Marleau/100 6.00 15.00
PRPR Patrick Roy/100 15.00 40.00

Card	Low	High
PRPS Peter Stastny/100	5.00	12.00
PRRB Ray Bourque/100	10.00	25.00
PRRD Rick DiPietro/100	5.00	12.00
PRRI Mike Ribeiro/100	4.00	10.00
PRRL Roberto Luongo/100	10.00	25.00
PRRM Ryan Miller/100	6.00	15.00
PRRN Rick Nash/100	6.00	15.00
PRRS Ryan Smyth/100	5.00	12.00
PRRY Michael Ryder/100	4.00	10.00
PRSA Borje Salming/100	6.00	15.00
PRSC Sidney Crosby/100	30.00	80.00
PRSD Shane Doan/100	5.00	12.00
PRSE Sergei Samsonov/50	5.00	12.00
PRSF Sergei Fedorov/100	10.00	25.00
PRSG Scott Gomez/100	5.00	12.00
PRSH Brendan Shanahan/100	6.00	15.00
PRSK Saku Koivu/100	6.00	15.00
PRSM Miroslav Satan/100	5.00	12.00
PRSS Steve Shutt/100	5.00	12.00
PRST Martin St. Louis/100	6.00	15.00
PRSU Mats Sundin/100	6.00	15.00
PRSV Marek Svatos/100	4.00	10.00
PRTB Todd Bertuzzi/100	6.00	15.00
PRTH Tomas Holmstrom/100	5.00	12.00
PRTR Tuomo Ruutu/100	6.00	15.00
PRTS Teemu Selanne/100	12.00	30.00
PRTV Tomas Vokoun/100	5.00	12.00
PRVL Vincent Lecavalier/100	6.00	15.00

2007-08 OPC Premier Remnants Quads

*PATCH/20: .6X TO 1.5X QUAD/25

Card	Low	High
PRAF Alexander Frolov	12.00	30.00
PRAK Alex Kovalev	15.00	40.00
PRAO Alexander Ovechkin	25.00	60.00
PRAS Alexander Steen	12.00	30.00
PRBM Brendan Morrison	12.00	30.00
PRBO Mike Bossy	20.00	50.00
PRBR Rod Brind`Amour	20.00	50.00
PRBS Billy Smith	12.00	30.00
PRCH Jonathan Cheechoo	15.00	40.00
PRCW Cam Ward	20.00	50.00
PRDE Pavol Demitra	25.00	60.00
PRDH Dale Hawerchuk	25.00	60.00
PRDS Darryl Sittler	25.00	60.00
PREB Ed Belfour	20.00	50.00
PREJ Ed Jovanovski	15.00	40.00
PREL Eric Lindros	30.00	80.00
PREM Evgeni Malkin	20.00	50.00
PRES Eric Staal	25.00	60.00
PRGA Simon Gagne	20.00	50.00
PRHE Dany Heatley	20.00	50.00
PRHL Henrik Lundqvist	25.00	60.00
PRHM Milan Hejduk	15.00	40.00
PRHZ Henrik Zetterberg	20.00	50.00
PRIK Ilya Kovalchuk	12.00	30.00
PRJA Jason Arnott	15.00	40.00
PRJB Jay Bouwmeester	12.00	30.00
PRJC Jeff Carter	15.00	40.00
PRJG Jean-Sebastien Giguere	20.00	50.00
PRJI Jarome Iginla	20.00	50.00
PRJJ Jaromir Jagr	25.00	60.00
PRJO Joe Sakic	20.00	50.00
PRJP Joni Pitkanen	12.00	30.00
PRJS Jason Spezza	20.00	50.00
PRJT Joe Thornton	15.00	40.00
PRKL Kari Lehtonen	15.00	40.00
PRLM Lanny McDonald	12.00	30.00
PRLR Larry Robinson	20.00	50.00
PRMA Martin Havlat	12.00	30.00
PRMB Martin Brodeur	30.00	60.00
PRMC Mike Cammalleri	12.00	30.00
PRMG Marian Gaborik	20.00	50.00
PRMH Marian Hossa	20.00	50.00
PRMI Mike Richards	15.00	40.00
PRML Mario Lemieux	40.00	80.00
PRMM Mike Modano	12.00	30.00
PRMN Markus Naslund	20.00	50.00
PRMR Mark Recchi	25.00	60.00
PRMS Marc Savard	12.00	30.00
PRMT Marty Turco	20.00	50.00
PRNH Nathan Horton	12.00	30.00
PRNL Nicklas Lidstrom	20.00	50.00
PROJ Olli Jokinen	15.00	40.00
PROK Olaf Kolzig	12.00	30.00
PRPB Patrice Bergeron	25.00	60.00
PRPF Peter Forsberg	12.00	30.00
PRPI Pierre-Marc Bouchard	20.00	50.00
PRPK Paul Kariya	15.00	40.00
PRPM Patrick Marleau	20.00	50.00
PRPR Patrick Roy	30.00	80.00
PRPS Peter Stastny	15.00	40.00
PRRB Ray Bourque	30.00	80.00
PRRD Rick DiPietro	15.00	40.00
PRRI Mike Ribeiro	12.00	30.00
PRRM Ryan Miller	20.00	50.00
PRRN Rick Nash	20.00	50.00
PRRS Ryan Smyth	15.00	40.00
PRSA Borje Salming	20.00	50.00
PRSC Sidney Crosby	30.00	80.00
PRSD Shane Doan	15.00	40.00
PRSE Sergei Samsonov	15.00	40.00
PRSF Sergei Fedorov	30.00	80.00
PRSG Scott Gomez	15.00	40.00
PRSH Brendan Shanahan	12.00	30.00
PRSK Saku Koivu	20.00	50.00
PRSM Miroslav Satan/15	15.00	40.00
PRSS Steve Shutt	15.00	40.00
PRST Martin St. Louis	20.00	50.00
PRSU Mats Sundin	12.00	30.00
PRTH Tomas Holmstrom	12.00	30.00
PRTS Teemu Selanne	40.00	100.00
PRTV Tomas Vokoun	15.00	40.00
PRVL Vincent Lecavalier	15.00	40.00

2007-08 OPC Premier Stitchings

Card	Low	High
PSAB Andy Bathgate	5.00	12.00
PSAO Alexander Ovechkin	12.00	30.00
PSBC Bobby Clarke	10.00	25.00
PSBH Bobby Hull	12.00	30.00
PSBL Rob Blake	6.00	15.00
PSBO Bobby Orr	25.00	50.00
PSBP Bernie Parent	8.00	20.00
PSBR Brad Richards/25	12.50	30.00
PSBS Brendan Shanahan	6.00	15.00
PSCD Chris Drury	5.00	12.00
PSCN Cam Neely	6.00	15.00
PSCT Cyclone Taylor	6.00	15.00
PSDA Daniel Alfredsson	6.00	15.00
PSDH Dany Heatley	5.00	12.00
PSDS Darryl Sittler	6.00	15.00
PSEG Ed Giacomin	6.00	15.00
PSEJ Ed Jovanovski	5.00	12.00
PSEM Evgeni Malkin	12.00	30.00
PSES Eddie Shack	6.00	15.00
PSFN Frank Nighbor	6.00	15.00
PSGC Gerry Cheevers	6.00	15.00
PSGH Gordie Howe	12.00	30.00
PSGR Wayne Gretzky	20.00	50.00
PSIK Ilya Kovalchuk	6.00	15.00
PSJB Jean Beliveau	8.00	20.00
PSJI Jarome Iginla	8.00	20.00
PSJJ Jaromir Jagr	20.00	50.00
PSJL Jacques Lemaire	5.00	12.00
PSJS Jason Spezza	6.00	15.00
PSJT Joe Thornton	10.00	25.00
PSKL Kari Lehtonen	5.00	12.00
PSLR Larry Robinson	6.00	15.00
PSMA Martin Brodeur	10.00	25.00
PSMH Martin Havlat	6.00	15.00
PSMK Miikka Kiprusoff	6.00	15.00
PSML Mario Lemieux	12.00	30.00
PSMM Mark Messier	10.00	25.00
PSMS Mats Sundin	6.00	15.00
PSOK Olaf Kolzig	6.00	15.00
PSPD Pavel Datsyuk	10.00	25.00
PSPE Phil Esposito	10.00	25.00
PSPK Paul Kariya	6.00	15.00
PSPL Pat LaFontaine	6.00	15.00
PSPR Patrick Roy	20.00	40.00
PSRA Ray Bourque	10.00	25.00
PSRB Richard Brodeur	5.00	12.00
PSRK Red Kelly	6.00	15.00
PSRL Roberto Luongo	10.00	25.00
PSRO Patrick Roy	12.00	30.00
PSSA Joe Sakic	12.00	30.00
PSSF Sergei Fedorov	10.00	25.00
PSSM Billy Smith	6.00	15.00
PSST Jordan Staal	5.00	12.00
PSTE Tony Esposito	6.00	15.00
PSTS Teemu Selanne	12.00	30.00
PSVL Vincent Lecavalier	6.00	15.00
PSWA Wayne Gretzky	15.00	40.00
PSWG Wayne Gretzky/100	20.00	50.00

2007-08 OPC Premier Stitchings 25

*STITCHINGS/25: .6X TO 1.5X BASE JSY

2007-08 OPC Premier Stitchings 50

*STITCHINGS/50: .5X TO 1.2X BASE JSY

Card	Low	High
PSBR Brad Richards	8.00	20.00

2007-08 OPC Premier Stitchings Variation

*STITCHINGS/25: .6X TO 1.5X BASE JSY

Card	Low	High
PSAB Andy Bathgate	5.00	12.00
PSAO Alexander Ovechkin	12.00	30.00
PSBC Bobby Clarke	10.00	25.00
PSBH Bobby Hull	12.00	30.00
PSBL Rob Blake	6.00	15.00
PSBO Bobby Orr	25.00	60.00
PSBP Bernie Parent	8.00	20.00
PSBR Brad Richards	6.00	15.00
PSBS Brendan Shanahan	6.00	15.00
PSCD Chris Drury	5.00	12.00
PSCN Cam Neely	10.00	25.00
PSCT Cyclone Taylor	6.00	15.00
PSDA Daniel Alfredsson	6.00	15.00
PSDH Dany Heatley	5.00	12.00
PSDS Darryl Sittler	6.00	15.00
PSEG Ed Giacomin/50	6.00	15.00
PSEJ Ed Jovanovski	5.00	12.00
PSEM Evgeni Malkin	12.00	30.00
PSES Eddie Shack	6.00	15.00
PSFN Frank Nighbor	6.00	15.00
PSGC Gerry Cheevers	6.00	15.00
PSGR Wayne Gretzky	40.00	100.00
PSIK Ilya Kovalchuk	6.00	15.00
PSJB Jean Beliveau	8.00	20.00
PSJI Jarome Iginla	15.00	40.00
PSJJ Jaromir Jagr	20.00	50.00
PSJL Jacques Lemaire	5.00	12.00
PSJS Jason Spezza	6.00	15.00
PSJT Joe Thornton	10.00	25.00
PSKL Kari Lehtonen	5.00	12.00
PSLR Larry Robinson	6.00	15.00
PSMA Martin Brodeur	15.00	40.00
PSMH Martin Havlat	6.00	15.00
PSMK Miikka Kiprusoff	6.00	15.00
PSML Mario Lemieux	25.00	60.00
PSMM Mark Messier	12.00	30.00
PSMS Mats Sundin	6.00	15.00
PSOK Olaf Kolzig	6.00	15.00
PSPD Pavel Datsyuk	10.00	25.00
PSPE Phil Esposito	10.00	25.00
PSPK Paul Kariya	6.00	15.00
PSPR Patrick Roy	15.00	40.00
PSRA Ray Bourque	10.00	25.00
PSRB Richard Brodeur	5.00	12.00
PSRK Red Kelly	6.00	15.00
PSRL Roberto Luongo	10.00	25.00
PSRO Patrick Roy	15.00	40.00
PSSF Sergei Fedorov	10.00	25.00
PSSM Billy Smith	6.00	15.00
PSST Jordan Staal	5.00	12.00
PSTE Tony Esposito	6.00	15.00
PSTS Teemu Selanne	12.00	30.00
PSVL Vincent Lecavalier	6.00	15.00
PSWA Wayne Gretzky	40.00	100.00
PSWG Wayne Gretzky	25.00	60.00

2008-09 OPC Premier

Card	Low	High
COMP.SET w/o SPs (42)	175.00	300.00
1 Wayne Gretzky	12.00	30.00
2 Vincent Lecavalier	2.00	5.00
3 Tony Esposito	2.00	5.00
4 Sidney Crosby	8.00	20.00
5 Saku Koivu	2.00	5.00
6 Rick Nash	2.00	5.00
7 Ray Bourque	3.00	8.00
8 Phil Esposito	3.00	8.00
9 Peter Mueller	1.50	4.00
10 Pavel Datsyuk	3.00	8.00
11 Paul Stastny	1.50	4.00
12 Patrick Roy	5.00	12.00
13 Patrick Kane	4.00	10.00
14 Nicklas Lidstrom	2.00	5.00
15 Mike Bossy	2.00	5.00
16 Martin St. Louis	2.00	5.00
17 Martin Brodeur	5.00	12.00
18 Mark Messier	4.00	10.00
19 Mario Lemieux	8.00	20.00
20 Marian Gaborik	2.00	5.00
21 Jonathan Toews	3.00	8.00
22 Jonathan Cheechoo	1.50	4.00
23 Joe Thornton	3.00	8.00
24 Joe Sakic	4.00	10.00
25 Jarome Iginla	2.50	6.00
26 Jari Kurri	2.00	5.00
27 Ilya Kovalchuk	2.00	5.00
28 Henrik Zetterberg	2.50	6.00
29 Guy Lafleur	2.50	6.00
30 Grant Fuhr	3.00	8.00
31 Gordie Howe	6.00	15.00
32 Gilbert Perreault	2.00	5.00
33 Evgeni Malkin	4.00	10.00
34 Eric Staal	2.50	6.00
35 Dany Heatley	1.50	4.00
36 Dale Hawerchuk	2.50	6.00
37 Carey Price	4.00	10.00
38 Cam Neely	2.00	5.00
39 Bobby Orr	8.00	20.00
40 Bobby Hull	4.00	10.00
41 Bobby Clarke	3.00	8.00
42 Alexander Ovechkin	8.00	20.00
43 Zach Bogosian JSY AU RC	6.00	15.00
44 Blake Wheeler JSY AU RC	12.00	30.00
45 Zach Boychuk JSY AU RC	5.00	12.00
46 Brandon Sutter JSY AU RC	5.00	12.00
47 Nikita Filatov JSY AU RC	5.00	12.00
48 Jakub Voracek JSY AU RC	20.00	40.00
49 Derick Brassard JSY AU RC	5.00	12.00
50 Steve Mason JSY AU RC	12.00	30.00
51 Justin Pogge JSY AU RC	4.00	10.00
52 Fabian Brunnstrom JSY AU RC	4.00	10.00
53 James Neal JSY AU RC	15.00	30.00
54 Justin Abdelkader JSY AU RC	8.00	20.00
55 Darren Helm JSY AU RC	5.00	12.00
56 Mattias Ritola JSY AU RC	4.00	10.00
57 Michael Frolik JSY AU RC	5.00	12.00
58 Shawn Matthias JSY AU RC	5.00	12.00
59 Drew Doughty JSY AU RC	20.00	40.00
60 Oscar Moller JSY AU RC	4.00	10.00
61 Erik Ersberg JSY AU RC	4.00	10.00
62 Brian Boyle JSY AU RC	4.00	10.00
63 Colton Gillies JSY AU RC	4.00	10.00
64 Patric Hornqvist JSY AU RC	5.00	12.00
65 Ben Maxwell JSY AU RC	5.00	12.00
66 Josh Bailey JSY AU RC	6.00	15.00
67 Kyle Okposo JSY AU RC	6.00	15.00
68 Lauri Korpikoski JSY AU RC	3.00	8.00
69 Ilya Zubov JSY AU RC	4.00	10.00
70 Claude Giroux JSY AU RC	30.00	60.00
71 Luca Sbisa JSY AU RC	3.00	8.00
72 Viktor Tikhonov JSY AU RC	4.00	10.00
73 Mikkel Boedker JSY AU RC	6.00	15.00
74 Kyle Turris JSY AU RC	8.00	20.00
75 Alex Goligoski JSY AU RC	6.00	15.00
76 Jamie McGinn JSY AU RC	5.00	12.00
77 Alex Pietrangelo JSY AU RC	8.00	20.00
78 Patrik Berglund JSY AU RC	4.00	10.00
79 T.J. Oshie JSY AU RC	15.00	40.00
80 Ben Bishop JSY AU RC	12.50	25.00
81 Steven Stamkos JSY AU RC	80.00	200.00
82 Luke Schenn JSY AU RC	6.00	15.00
83 Nikolai Kulemin JSY AU RC	5.00	12.00
84 Cory Schneider JSY AU RC	12.00	30.00

2008-09 OPC Premier Gold Spectrum

*ROOKIE JSY AU/15: 1.2X TO 3X BASIC RC

2008-09 OPC Premier Silver

*SINGLES: .6X TO 1.5X BASIC CARDS

2008-09 OPC Premier Duos Autographs

Card	Low	High
PP2BF D.Brassard/N.Filatov	8.00	20.00
PP2BN F.Brunnstrom/J.Neal	12.00	30.00
PP2DH P.Datsyuk/M.Hossa EXCH	20.00	50.00
PP2DK A.Delvecchio/R.Kelly	12.00	30.00
PP2EN P.Esposito/C.Neely	30.00	80.00
PP2FA G.Fuhr/G.Anderson	12.00	30.00
PP2GG C.Gillies/C.Gillies	12.00	30.00
PP2GM W.Gretzky/M.Messier	200.00	500.00
PP2HE B.Hull/T.Esposito	50.00	100.00
PP2HO B.Orr/G.Howe	150.00	250.00
PP2KR J.Kurri/L.Robitaille	15.00	40.00
PP2KT J.Toews/P.Kane	125.00	200.00
PP2LN M.Naslund/H.Lundqvist	30.00	80.00
PP2LS V.Lecavalier/M.St. Louis	10.00	25.00
PP2MF E.Malkin/M.Fleury	30.00	80.00
PP2MK E.Malkin/I.Kovalchuk	20.00	50.00
PP2ML B.Leetch/M.Messier	50.00	100.00
PP2OB B.Orr/R.Bourque	100.00	200.00
PP2PV T.Vanek/G.Perreault	12.00	30.00
PP2RP C.Price/P.Roy	50.00	100.00
PP2SB Z.Boychuk/B.Sutter	12.00	30.00
PP2TC J.Cheechoo/J.Thornton	12.00	30.00
PP2TM K.Turris/P.Mueller	12.00	30.00
PP2ZL N.Lidstrom/H.Zetterberg	25.00	60.00

2008-09 OPC Premier Dynasty Duos Autographs

Card	Low	High
DDAF G.Fuhr/G.Anderson	20.00	50.00
DDBP M.Bossy/D.Potvin	12.00	30.00
DDDH T.Holmstrom/P.Datsyuk	20.00	50.00
DDGM M.Messier/W.Gretzky	200.00	500.00
DDLK T.Lindsay/R.Kelly	12.00	30.00
DDLS S.Shutt/G.Lafleur	15.00	40.00
DDMB F.Mahovlich/J.Bower	12.00	30.00
DDOE B.Orr/P.Esposito	100.00	200.00

2008-09 OPC Premier Dynasty Duos Autographs Gold Spectrum

*SINGLES: .6X TO 1.5X BASIC INSERTS

2008-09 OPC Premier Inductions Ink

Card	Low	High
PIAM Al MacInnis	10.00	25.00
PIBS Borje Salming	8.00	20.00
PIDS Denis Savard	8.00	20.00
PIJM Joe Mullen	6.00	15.00
PILM Lanny McDonald	8.00	20.00
PIMD Marcel Dionne	10.00	25.00
PIPS Peter Stastny	6.00	15.00
PIRB Ray Bourque	12.00	30.00
PISS Steve Shutt	8.00	20.00

2008-09 OPC Premier Inductions Ink Dual

Card	Low	High
2PIBP D.Potvin/M.Bossy	15.00	40.00
2PIDM M.Dionne/L.McDonald	20.00	50.00
2PIEL G.Lafleur/T.Esposito	20.00	50.00
2PIGL R.Langway/C.Gillies	15.00	40.00
2PIHB Beliveau/Howe EXCH	75.00	150.00
2PIKH J.Kurri/D.Hawerchuk	20.00	50.00
2PIMM Messier/MacInnis	30.00	80.00
2PIMS J.Mullen/D.Savard	15.00	40.00
2PIOH H.Howell/B.Orr	75.00	150.00

2008-09 OPC Premier Inductions Ink Gold Spectrum

*SINGLES: .5X TO 1.2X BASIC INSERTS

2008-09 OPC Premier Penmanship

Card	Low	High
PPAK Anze Kopitar	12.00	30.00
PPAO Alexander Ovechkin	40.00	80.00
PPCP Carey Price	25.00	50.00
PPDH Dany Heatley	8.00	20.00
PPEM Evgeni Malkin	25.00	60.00
PPHZ Henrik Zetterberg	12.00	30.00
PPJG Jean-Sebastien Giguere	8.00	20.00
PPJS Jordan Staal	6.00	15.00
PPMH Milan Hejduk	6.00	15.00
PPMR Mike Richards	6.00	15.00
PPMT Marty Turco	8.00	20.00
PPPK Patrick Kane	30.00	60.00
PPPS Paul Stastny	6.00	15.00
PPRG Ryan Getzlaf	8.00	20.00
PPRH Ron Hextall	10.00	25.00
PPSC Sidney Crosby	75.00	125.00
PPSG Simon Gagne	8.00	20.00
PPTH Joe Thornton	12.00	30.00
PPTV Thomas Vanek	6.00	15.00
PPVL Vincent Lecavalier	8.00	20.00

2008-09 OPC Premier Penmanship Gold Spectrum

*SINGLES: .6X TO 1.5X BASIC INSERTS

2008-09 OPC Premier Rare Remnants Triples

Card	Low	High
RR3BON Adam Oates		
Ray Bourque		
Cam Neely	20.00	50.00
RR3GML Mark Messier		
Wayne Gretzky		
Mario Lemieux	75.00	150.00
RR3LNG Ryan Getzlaf		
Rick Nash		
Vincent Lecavalier	12.00	30.00
RR3PMK Phil Kessel		
Peter Mueller		
Zach Parise	12.00	30.00
RR3RBH Martin Brodeur		
Dominik Hasek		
Patrick Roy	30.00	75.00
RR3RLB Patrick Roy		
Martin Brodeur		
Roberto Luongo	30.00	75.00
RR3SBV Fabian Brunnstrom		
Jakub Voracek		
Steven Stamkos	15.00	40.00
RR3SDB Zach Bogosian		
Drew Doughty		
Luke Schenn	20.00	50.00
RR3SRL Steve Shutt		
Rod Langway		
Larry Robinson	12.00	30.00
RR3SSB Patrice Bergeron		
Eric Staal		
Jason Spezza	15.00	40.00
RR3ZLH Henrik Zetterberg		
Nicklas Lidstrom		
Tomas Holmstrom	20.00	50.00

2008-09 OPC Premier Remnants Quads

Card	Low	High
PRAO Adam Oates	8.00	20.00
PRBS Borje Salming	8.00	20.00
PRCP Carey Price	15.00	40.00
PRDH Dale Hawerchuk	10.00	25.00
PRDS Darryl Sittler	10.00	25.00
PREM Evgeni Malkin	15.00	40.00
PRES Eric Staal	10.00	25.00
PRHA Dominik Hasek	12.00	30.00
PRHL Henrik Lundqvist	20.00	50.00
PRHZ Henrik Zetterberg	10.00	25.00
PRIK Ilya Kovalchuk	8.00	20.00
PRJC Jonathan Cheechoo	6.00	15.00
PRJI Jarome Iginla	10.00	25.00
PRKB Nicklas Backstrom	8.00	20.00
PRLM Lanny McDonald	8.00	20.00
PRLR Larry Robinson	8.00	20.00
PRMB Martin Brodeur	20.00	50.00
PRMG Marian Gaborik	8.00	20.00
PRMK Mikko Koivu	6.00	15.00
PRML Mario Lemieux	30.00	80.00
PRMM Mike Modano	12.00	30.00
PRMR Mike Richards	6.00	15.00
PRNL Nicklas Lidstrom	8.00	20.00
PROV Alexander Ovechkin	30.00	80.00
PRPB Patrice Bergeron	10.00	25.00
PRPM Peter Mueller	6.00	15.00
PRPR Patrick Roy	20.00	50.00
PRRB Ray Bourque	12.00	30.00
PRRL Roberto Luongo	12.00	30.00
PRRN Rick Nash	8.00	20.00
PRSC Sidney Crosby	30.00	80.00
PRSD Shane Doan	6.00	15.00
PRSG Simon Gagne	8.00	20.00
PRSK Saku Koivu	8.00	20.00
PRSS Steve Shutt	8.00	20.00
PRTR Tuomo Ruutu	8.00	20.00
PRVL Vincent Lecavalier	8.00	20.00
PRZP Marian Hossa	8.00	20.00

2008-09 OPC Premier Remnants Quads Gold

*GOLD: .5X TO 1.2X BASIC

Card	Low	High
PRKB Nicklas Backstrom	12.00	30.00

2008-09 OPC Premier Remnants Triples

*GOLD/35: .8X TO 2X BASIC TRIPLE

Card	Low	High
PRAO Adam Oates	5.00	12.00
PRBS Borje Salming	5.00	12.00
PRCP Carey Price	10.00	25.00
PRDH Dale Hawerchuk	6.00	15.00
PRDS Darryl Sittler	6.00	15.00
PREM Evgeni Malkin	10.00	25.00
PRES Eric Staal	6.00	15.00
PRHA Dominik Hasek	8.00	20.00
PRHL Henrik Lundqvist	12.00	30.00
PRHZ Henrik Zetterberg	6.00	15.00
PRIK Ilya Kovalchuk	5.00	12.00
PRJC Jonathan Cheechoo	4.00	10.00
PRJI Jarome Iginla	6.00	15.00
PRKB Nicklas Backstrom	5.00	12.00
PRLM Lanny McDonald	5.00	12.00
PRLR Larry Robinson	5.00	12.00
PRMB Martin Brodeur	12.00	30.00
PRMG Marian Gaborik	8.00	20.00
PRMK Mikko Koivu	4.00	10.00
PRML Mario Lemieux	20.00	50.00
PRMM Mike Modano	8.00	20.00
PRMR Mike Richards	4.00	10.00
PRNL Nicklas Lidstrom	5.00	12.00
PROV Alexander Ovechkin	20.00	50.00
PRPB Patrice Bergeron	6.00	15.00
PRPM Peter Mueller	4.00	10.00
PRPR Patrick Roy	12.00	30.00
PRRB Ray Bourque	8.00	20.00
PRRN Rick Nash	5.00	12.00
PRSC Sidney Crosby	20.00	50.00
PRSD Shane Doan	4.00	10.00
PRSG Simon Gagne	5.00	12.00
PRSK Saku Koivu	5.00	12.00
PRSS Steve Shutt	5.00	12.00
PRTR Tuomo Ruutu	5.00	12.00
PRVL Vincent Lecavalier	5.00	12.00
PRZP Marian Hossa	5.00	12.00

2008-09 OPC Premier Stitchings

*BLUE/25: .6X TO 1.5X STITCHINGS

Card	Low	High
PSBH Bobby Hull	6.00	15.00
PSBO Bobby Orr	12.00	30.00
PSCN Cam Neely	3.00	8.00
PSCP Carey Price	6.00	15.00
PSDH Dany Heatley	2.50	6.00
PSEM Evgeni Malkin	6.00	15.00
PSGH Gordie Howe	10.00	25.00
PSHL Henrik Lundqvist	8.00	20.00
PSHZ Henrik Zetterberg	4.00	10.00
PSIK Ilya Kovalchuk	3.00	8.00
PSJI Jarome Iginla	4.00	10.00
PSJS Joe Sakic	6.00	15.00
PSJT Joe Thornton	5.00	12.00
PSMB Martin Brodeur	8.00	20.00
PSME Mark Messier	6.00	15.00
PSMG Marian Gaborik	3.00	8.00
PSML Mario Lemieux	10.00	25.00
PSMM Mike Modano	4.00	10.00
PSOV Alexander Ovechkin	12.00	30.00
PSPD Pavel Datsyuk	5.00	12.00
PSPE Phil Esposito	5.00	12.00
PSPK Patrick Kane	6.00	15.00
PSPR Patrick Roy	8.00	20.00
PSRB Ray Bourque	5.00	12.00
PSRL Roberto Luongo	6.00	15.00
PSRN Rick Nash	3.00	8.00
PSSS Steven Stamkos	8.00	20.00
PSTO Jonathan Toews	5.00	12.00
PSVL Vincent Lecavalier	3.00	8.00
PSWG Wayne Gretzky	20.00	50.00

2008-09 OPC Premier Stitchings Autographs

Card	Low	High
APSBH Bobby Hull	30.00	60.00
APSBO Bobby Orr/15	125.00	200.00
APSCN Cam Neely	20.00	50.00
APSCP Carey Price	20.00	50.00
APSGH Gordie Howe/15	75.00	150.00
APSGP Gilbert Perreault	10.00	25.00
APSHZ Henrik Zetterberg	25.00	60.00
APSJI Jarome Iginla	10.00	25.00
APSJT Joe Thornton	12.00	30.00
APSMB Martin Brodeur	50.00	100.00
APSML Mario Lemieux/15	100.00	200.00
APSMM Mark Messier/15	50.00	100.00
APSPE Phil Esposito	20.00	50.00
APSPK Patrick Kane	15.00	40.00
APSPR Patrick Roy/15	75.00	150.00
APSTO Jonathan Toews	12.00	30.00
APSWG Wayne Gretzky/15	250.00	600.00

2008-09 OPC Premier Stitchings Variation

*VARIATION: .5X TO 1.2X STITCHINGS

2008-09 OPC Premier Trios

Card	Low	High
PP3BPF Price/Fleury/Brodeur	40.00	100.00
PP3BPG Gillies/Potvin/Bossy	50.00	100.00
PP3DVF Filatov/Voracek/Brassrd	30.00	60.00
PP3GOH Howe/Gretzky/Orr	300.00	800.00
PP3HTK Kane/Hull/Toews	100.00	175.00
PP3RFH Hextall/Roy/Fuhr	125.00	200.00

2009-10 OPC Premier

*GOLD/25: ..6X TO 1.5X BASIC CARDS
GOLD.RC/35: 1X TO 2.5X BASIC CARDS

Card	Low	High
1 Al MacInnis	1.50	4.00
2 Alexander Ovechkin	5.00	12.00
3 Anze Kopitar	2.00	5.00
4 Bobby Hull	2.50	6.00
5 Bobby Orr	5.00	12.00
6 Brian Leetch	1.00	2.50
7 Cam Neely	1.25	3.00
8 Carey Price	2.50	6.00
9 Dale Hawerchuk	1.50	4.00
10 Daniel Sedin	1.50	4.00
11 Dany Heatley	1.00	2.50
12 Dion Phaneuf	1.00	2.50
13 Eric Staal	1.50	4.00
14 Evgeni Malkin	2.50	6.00
15 Gordie Howe	4.00	10.00
16 Grant Fuhr	2.00	5.00
17 Guy Lafleur	1.50	4.00
18 Henrik Sedin	1.50	4.00
19 Henrik Zetterberg	1.50	4.00
20 Ilya Kovalchuk	1.25	3.00
21 Jari Kurri	1.25	3.00
22 Jarome Iginla	1.50	4.00
23 Jason Spezza	1.25	3.00
24 Jean Beliveau	1.25	3.00
25 Joe Thornton	2.00	5.00
26 Jonathan Toews	2.00	5.00
27 Luc Robitaille	1.25	3.00
28 Marc-Andre Fleury	2.50	6.00
29 Marian Gaborik	1.25	3.00
30 Mario Lemieux	5.00	12.00
31 Mark Messier	2.50	6.00
32 Martin Brodeur	3.00	8.00
33 Martin St. Louis	1.25	3.00
34 Marty Turco	1.25	3.00
35 Mike Richards	1.00	2.50
36 Nicklas Backstrom	1.25	3.00
37 Nicklas Lidstrom	.75	2.00
38 Patrick Kane	2.50	6.00
39 Patrick Roy	3.00	8.00
40 Paul Stastny	1.00	2.50
41 Pavel Datsyuk	2.00	5.00
42 Phil Esposito	2.00	5.00
43 Ray Bourque	2.00	5.00
44 Rick Nash	1.25	3.00
45 Roberto Luongo	2.00	5.00
46 Ron Hextall	1.25	3.00
47 Ryan Getzlaf	1.25	3.00
48 Ryan Miller	1.25	3.00
49 Saku Koivu	1.25	3.00
50 Sam Gagner	.75	2.00
51 Sidney Crosby	5.00	12.00
52 Steve Mason	1.00	2.50
53 Steve Yzerman	3.00	8.00
54 Steven Stamkos	2.50	6.00
55 Teemu Selanne	2.50	6.00
56 Thomas Vanek	1.00	2.50
57 Tony Esposito	1.25	3.00
58 Vincent Lecavalier	1.25	3.00
59 Walt Tkaczuk	1.00	2.50
60 Wayne Gretzky	8.00	20.00
61 John Tavares JSY AU RC	50.00	125.00
62 J.van Riemsdyk JSY AU RC	12.00	30.00
63 Evander Kane JSY AU RC	25.00	60.00
64 Victor Hedman JSY AU RC	15.00	40.00
65 Jonas Gustavsson JSY AU RC	8.00	20.00
66 Matt Duchene JSY AU RC	12.00	30.00
67 Colin Wilson JSY AU RC	6.00	15.00
68 T.J. Galiardi JSY AU RC	6.00	15.00
69 Yannick Weber JSY AU RC	6.00	15.00
70 Spencer Machacek JSY AU RC	6.00	15.00
71 Antti Niemi JSY AU RC	10.00	25.00
72 Viktor Stalberg JSY AU RC	6.00	15.00
73 Michael Del Zotto JSY AU RC	6.00	15.00
74 Dmitry Kulikov JSY AU RC	6.00	15.00
75 Jamie Benn JSY AU RC	20.00	50.00
76 Ryan O'Reilly JSY AU RC	12.00	30.00
77 Tyler Myers JSY AU RC	10.00	25.00
78 Erik Karlsson JSY AU RC	20.00	50.00
79 Matt Gilroy JSY AU RC	6.00	15.00
80 Sergei Shirokov JSY AU RC	4.00	10.00
81 Ville Leino JSY AU RC	5.00	12.00
82 Riku Helenius JSY AU RC	6.00	15.00
83 Mikael Backlund JSY AU RC	10.00	25.00
84 Michal Neuvirth JSY AU RC	10.00	25.00
85 Cody Franson JSY AU RC	6.00	15.00
86 Luca Caputi JSY AU RC	6.00	15.00
87 Kris Chucko JSY AU RC	4.00	10.00
88 Jhonas Enroth JSY AU RC	8.00	20.00
89 Ivan Vishnevskiy JSY AU RC	4.00	10.00
90 Jakub Kindl JSY AU RC	6.00	15.00
91 Artem Anisimov JSY AU RC	4.00	10.00
92 Taylor Chorney JSY AU RC	6.00	15.00
93 Benn Ferriero JSY AU RC	6.00	15.00
94 Cal O'Reilly JSY AU RC	5.00	12.00
95 Matthew Corrente JSY AU RC	5.00	12.00
96 Jason Demers JSY AU RC	10.00	25.00
97 Ryan Stoa JSY AU RC	5.00	12.00
98 Lars Eller JSY AU RC	6.00	15.00
99 Ryan O'Marra JSY AU RC	4.00	10.00
100 Logan Couture JSY AU RC	12.00	30.00
101 Brad Marchand JSY AU RC	80.00	200.00
102 Michael Grabner JSY AU RC	6.00	15.00

2009-10 OPC Premier Foursomes

Card	Low	High
AVKS Anism/Shirk/Kulk/Vshnv	5.00	12.00
CKWM Cout/Kan/Wlsn/Mrchd	20.00	50.00
CTDM Cornt/Tavrs/Zott/Myrs	20.00	50.00
DENG Gustv/Niem/Enrth/Dbnk	8.00	20.00
DKOM Ovch/Mlkn/Kovl/Datsk	20.00	50.00
DMKH Hdmn/Ztto/Karlssn/Myrs	15.00	40.00
EBHH Espo/Beliv/Hull/Howe	15.00	40.00
EMEB Enroth/Myers/Ennis/Butlr	8.00	20.00
FCMS Fleury/Sid/Malkn/Staal	20.00	50.00
GMCP Pric/Gmz/Cammllr/Mark	10.00	25.00
HGBS Gustv/Bzk/Stlbrg/Hnsn	8.00	20.00
ISHN Iginla/Htley/Nash/St.Lou	6.00	15.00
JIKP Iginl/Kprsff/Phanf/Jokn	6.00	15.00
KCOT Koval/Crsby/Ovch/Tvrs	20.00	50.00
LDZF Ldstrm/Dtsyk/Zttr/Frnzn	8.00	20.00
LSSK Sedn/Sedn/Ksler/Lngo	8.00	20.00
LTSS Spcz/Stl/Lcav/Thorntn	8.00	20.00
LYCO Mario/Yzer/Crsby/Ovch	20.00	50.00
LYGM Messi/Grtz/Mrio/Yzrmn	30.00	80.00
MPOV Rms/Mdno/Prse/Okps	10.00	25.00
MTNS Thorn/Mrleau/Set/Nbkv	8.00	20.00
NCTS Crsby/Nsh/Stamk/Tvrs	20.00	50.00
RBLF Roy/Brdr/Lngo/Fleury	12.00	30.00
RBTL Thms/Lcic/Berg/Rder	6.00	15.00
RCGV Riems/Rich/Cartr/Girx	10.00	25.00
SDSG Zott/Gilry/Sngti/Sauer	5.00	12.00
SGDO Ststny/Glrdi/Dchn/O'Re	10.00	25.00
SSGS Sedin/Sdin/Shrkv/Grb	6.00	15.00
TKDH Tavrs/Kne/Dchn/Hdmn	20.00	50.00
TWPM Masn/Prce/Wrd/Turco	10.00	25.00

2009-10 OPC Premier Rare Remnants Triples

*PATCH/25: .6X TO 1.5X BASIC JSY

Card	Low	High
PRTAN Antti Niemi	6.00	15.00
PRTAO Alexander Ovechkin	15.00	40.00
PRTBA Mikael Backlund	6.00	15.00
PRTBH Bobby Hull	8.00	20.00
PRTBL Brian Leetch	3.00	8.00
PRTBM Brad Marchand	15.00	40.00
PRTCN Cam Neely	4.00	10.00
PRTCP Carey Price	8.00	20.00
PRTCW Colin Wilson	4.00	10.00
PRTDB Derick Brassard	2.50	6.00
PRTDE Michael Del Zotto	4.00	10.00
PRTDH Dany Heatley	3.00	8.00
PRTDP Dion Phaneuf	3.00	8.00
PRTEK Evander Kane	8.00	20.00
PRTEM Evgeni Malkin	8.00	20.00
PRTES Eric Staal	5.00	12.00
PRTGH Gordie Howe	12.00	30.00
PRTGR Michael Grabner	4.00	10.00
PRTHL Henrik Lundqvist	10.00	25.00
PRTHZ Henrik Zetterberg	5.00	12.00
PRTIK Ilya Kovalchuk	4.00	10.00
PRTJB Jamie Benn	12.00	30.00
PRTJC Jeff Carter	3.00	8.00
PRTJG Jonas Gustavsson	5.00	12.00
PRTJI Jarome Iginla	5.00	12.00
PRTJS Jordan Staal	3.00	8.00
PRTJT Joe Thornton	6.00	15.00
PRTJV James van Riemsdyk	8.00	20.00
PRTKE Phil Kessel	4.00	10.00
PRTLC Logan Couture	8.00	20.00
PRTLE Lars Eller	4.00	10.00
PRTMB Martin Brodeur	10.00	25.00
PRTMD Matt Duchene	8.00	20.00
PRTMF Marc-Andre Fleury	8.00	20.00
PRTMG Marian Gaborik	4.00	10.00
PRTMK Miikka Kiprusoff	4.00	10.00
PRTML Mario Lemieux	15.00	40.00
PRTMM Mark Messier	8.00	20.00
PRTMO Mike Modano	6.00	15.00
PRTMR Mike Richards	3.00	8.00
PRTMS Martin St. Louis	4.00	10.00
PRTMT Marty Turco	4.00	10.00
PRTNB Nicklas Backstrom	4.00	10.00
PRTNL Nicklas Lidstrom	2.50	6.00
PRTPD Pavel Datsyuk	6.00	15.00
PRTPK Patrick Kane	8.00	20.00
PRTPM Patrick Marleau	4.00	10.00
PRTPR Patrick Roy	10.00	25.00
PRTPS Paul Stastny	3.00	8.00
PRTRB Ray Bourque	6.00	15.00
PRTRL Roberto Luongo	6.00	15.00
PRTRN Rick Nash	4.00	10.00
PRTRO Ryan O'Reilly	8.00	20.00
PRTSC Sidney Crosby	15.00	40.00
PRTSM Steve Mason	3.00	8.00
PRTSP Jason Spezza	4.00	10.00
PRTSS Steven Stamkos	8.00	20.00
PRTSY Steve Yzerman	10.00	25.00
PRTTA John Tavares	15.00	40.00
PRTTB Tyler Bozak	6.00	15.00
PRTTM Tyler Myers	6.00	15.00
PRTTO Jonathan Toews	6.00	15.00
PRTTT Tim Thomas	4.00	10.00
PRTTV Tomas Vokoun	3.00	8.00
PRTVH Victor Hedman	10.00	25.00
PRTVI Ville Leino	3.00	8.00
PRTVL Vincent Lecavalier	4.00	10.00
PRTWA Cam Ward	4.00	10.00
PRTWG Wayne Gretzky	25.00	60.00
PRTZP Zach Parise	4.00	10.00

2009-10 OPC Premier Remnants Quad Jerseys

Card	Low	High
PRQAO Alexander Ovechkin	25.00	60.00
PRQDP Dion Phaneuf	5.00	12.00
PRQEK Evander Kane	12.00	30.00
PRQEM Evgeni Malkin	12.00	30.00
PRQGH Gordie Howe	20.00	50.00
PRQHL Henrik Lundqvist	25.00	60.00
PRQHZ Henrik Zetterberg	8.00	20.00
PRQIK Ilya Kovalchuk	6.00	15.00
PRQJB Jamie Benn	10.00	25.00
PRQJC Jeff Carter	10.00	25.00
PRQJG Jonas Gustavsson	8.00	20.00
PRQJI Jarome Iginla	8.00	20.00
PRQJT John Tavares	25.00	60.00
PRQJV James van Riemsdyk	15.00	40.00
PRQMB Martin Brodeur	15.00	40.00
PRQMD Matt Duchene	15.00	40.00
PRQMF Marc-Andre Fleury	12.00	30.00
PRQMG Michael Grabner	6.00	15.00
PRQMK Miikka Kiprusoff	10.00	25.00
PRQML Mario Lemieux	20.00	50.00
PRQMM Mark Messier	12.00	30.00
PRQMR Mike Richards	25.00	60.00
PRQNB Nicklas Backstrom	6.00	15.00
PRQNL Nicklas Lidstrom	10.00	25.00
PRQPR Patrick Roy	15.00	40.00
PRQRL Roberto Luongo	10.00	25.00
PRQSC Sidney Crosby	25.00	60.00
PRQSS Steven Stamkos	12.00	30.00
PRQSY Steve Yzerman	15.00	40.00
PRQWG Wayne Gretzky	50.00	100.00

2009-10 OPC Premier Remnants Triple Autographs

Card	Low	High
AR3AO Alexander Ovechkin	40.00	100.00
AR3BH Bobby Hull	20.00	50.00
AR3BL Brian Leetch	12.00	30.00
AR3BW Blake Wheeler	10.00	25.00
AR3CN Cam Neely	10.00	25.00
AR3CP Carey Price	30.00	60.00
AR3CW Cam Ward	12.00	30.00
AR3DP Dion Phaneuf	8.00	20.00
AR3EM Evgeni Malkin	30.00	60.00
AR3ES Eric Staal	12.00	30.00
AR3GA Glenn Anderson	15.00	40.00
AR3GH Gordie Howe	60.00	120.00
AR3HL Henrik Lundqvist	25.00	60.00
AR3HZ Henrik Zetterberg	25.00	50.00
AR3JC Jeff Carter	8.00	20.00
AR3JI Jarome Iginla	12.00	30.00
AR3JK Jari Kurri	20.00	50.00
AR3JT Joe Thornton	15.00	40.00
AR3LR Luc Robitaille	20.00	50.00
AR3MB Martin Brodeur	50.00	100.00
AR3MF Marc-Andre Fleury	15.00	40.00
AR3MG Marian Gaborik	10.00	25.00
AR3ML Mario Lemieux	50.00	100.00
AR3MM Mark Messier	20.00	50.00
AR3NB Nicklas Backstrom	10.00	25.00
AR3NL Nicklas Lidstrom	15.00	40.00
AR3PD Pavel Datsyuk	15.00	40.00
AR3PR Patrick Roy	50.00	100.00
AR3RB Ray Bourque	25.00	60.00
AR3RM Ryan Miller	20.00	50.00
AR3RN Rick Nash	15.00	40.00
AR3SC Sidney Crosby	75.00	150.00

AR3SM Steve Mason 8.00 20.00
AR3SS Steven Stamkos 40.00 80.00
AR3SY Steve Yzerman 50.00 100.00
AR3TO Jonathan Toews 30.00 60.00
AR3VL Vincent Lecavalier 12.00 30.00
AR3WG Wayne Gretzky 150.00 400.00

2009-10 OPC Premier Signings

PSAA Artem Anisimov 4.00 10.00
PSAK Anze Kopitar 10.00 25.00
PSAN Antti Niemi 10.00 25.00
PSAT Alex Tanguay 4.00 10.00
PSBA David Backes 4.00 10.00
PSBH Bobby Hull 12.00 30.00
PSBL Brian Leetch 5.00 12.00
PSBO Bobby Orr 40.00 100.00
PSBR Martin Brodeur 15.00 40.00
PSBW Blake Wheeler 6.00 15.00
PSCP Carey Price 12.00 30.00
PSCR Sidney Crosby 60.00 150.00
PSCS Sidney Crosby 60.00 150.00
PSCW Cam Ward 6.00 15.00
PSDB Derick Brassard 4.00 10.00
PSDD Drew Doughty 8.00 20.00
PSDE Michael Del Zotto 6.00 15.00
PSDG Doug Gilmour 8.00 20.00
PSDH Dany Heatley 5.00 12.00
PSDP Dion Phaneuf 5.00 12.00
PSDS Daniel Sedin 8.00 20.00
PSEK Evander Kane 12.00 30.00
PSEM Evgeni Malkin 12.00 30.00
PSEP Phil Esposito 10.00 25.00
PSES Eric Staal 8.00 20.00
PSGA Glenn Anderson 5.00 12.00
PSGH Gordie Howe 20.00 50.00
PSGI Matt Gilroy 6.00 15.00
PSGO Scott Gomez 5.00 12.00
PSGP Gilbert Perreault 6.00 15.00
PSGR Mike Green 5.00 12.00
PSHL Henrik Lundqvist 15.00 40.00
PSHS Henrik Sedin 8.00 20.00
PSHZ Henrik Zetterberg 8.00 20.00
PSIK Ilya Kovalchuk 6.00 15.00
PSJA Jason Arnott 5.00 12.00
PSJB Jean Beliveau 6.00 15.00
PSJC Jeff Carter 5.00 12.00
PSJE Jhonas Enroth 8.00 20.00
PSJG Jonas Gustavsson 8.00 20.00
PSJI Jarome Iginla 8.00 20.00
PSJS Jordan Staal 5.00 12.00
PSJT Jonathan Toews 10.00 25.00
PSJV Jakub Voracek 5.00 12.00
PSKA Erik Karlsson 20.00 50.00
PSKE Phil Kessel 6.00 15.00
PSLE Vincent Lecavalier 6.00 15.00
PSLR Luc Robitaille 6.00 15.00
PSLS Luke Schenn 6.00 15.00
PSMB Mikael Backlund 10.00 25.00
PSMD Matt Duchene 12.00 30.00
PSME Mark Messier 12.00 30.00
PSMF Marc-Andre Fleury 12.00 30.00
PSMG Marian Gaborik 6.00 15.00
PSMH Milan Hejduk 5.00 12.00
PSML Mario Lemieux 25.00 60.00
PSMM Mike Modano 10.00 25.00
PSMN Markus Naslund 6.00 15.00
PSMR Mike Ribeiro 4.00 10.00
PSMS Martin St. Louis 6.00 15.00
PSMT Marty Turco 6.00 15.00
PSNB Nicklas Backstrom 6.00 15.00
PSNF Tony Esposito 6.00 15.00
PSNL Nicklas Lidstrom 4.00 10.00
PSOV Alexander Ovechkin 25.00 60.00
PSPB Patrice Bergeron 8.00 20.00
PSPD Pavel Datsyuk 10.00 25.00
PSPE Patrik Elias 6.00 15.00
PSPK Patrick Kane 12.00 30.00
PSPR Patrick Roy 30.00 80.00
PSPS Paul Stastny 5.00 12.00
PSRB Ray Bourque 10.00 25.00
PSRG Ryan Getzlaf 6.00 15.00
PSRI Mike Richards 5.00 12.00
PSRM Ryan Miller 6.00 15.00
PSRN Rick Nash 6.00 15.00
PSRO Ryan O'Reilly 12.00 30.00
PSRS Ryan Stoa 5.00 12.00
PSSC Sidney Crosby 60.00 150.00
PSSD Shane Doan 5.00 12.00
PSSG Sam Gagner 4.00 10.00
PSSH Sergei Shirokov 4.00 10.00
PSSI Simon Gagne 6.00 15.00
PSSK Saku Koivu 6.00 15.00
PSSM Steve Mason 5.00 12.00
PSSS Steven Stamkos 12.00 30.00
PSST Peter Stastny 5.00 12.00
PSSV Steve Shutt 6.00 15.00
PSSW Shea Weber 5.00 12.00
PSSY Steve Yzerman 15.00 40.00
PSTA John Tavares 25.00 60.00
PSTH Joe Thornton 10.00 25.00
PSTM Tyler Myers 10.00 25.00
PSTV Thomas Vanek 5.00 12.00
PSVA James van Riemsdyk 12.00 30.00
PSVH Victor Hedman 30.00 80.00
PSVL Ville Leino 5.00 12.00
PSVO Tomas Vokoun 5.00 12.00
PSWG Wayne Gretzky 200.00 500.00
PSZB Zach Bogosian 5.00 12.00

2009-10 OPC Premier Signings Duals

PS2BT J.Tavares/M.Bossy 50.00 100.00
PS2BV Vishnevskiy/Benn 10.00 25.00
PS2CV B.Clarke/J.Riemsdyk 20.00 50.00
PS2DW Dumont/Weber 10.00 25.00
PS2EO P.Esposito/B.Orr 75.00 150.00
PS2FF Foligno/Foligno 10.00 25.00
PS2FK G.Fuhr/J.Kurri 20.00 50.00
PS2FL V.Filppula/V.Leino 10.00 25.00
PS2GB N.Backstrom/M.Green 15.00 40.00
PS2GC Carter/Gagne 10.00 25.00
PS2GG Gillies/Gillies 10.00 25.00
PS2GL Gaborik/H.Lundqvist 30.00 80.00
PS2GM W.Gretzky/M.Messier 200.00 500.00
PS2GZ M.Gaborik/M.Zotto 15.00 40.00
PS2HD G.Howe/A.Delvecchio 60.00 100.00
PS2HG Gustavsson/C.Hanson 15.00 40.00
PS2HM B.Hull/S.Mikita 25.00 60.00
PS2HT B.Hull/J.Toews 40.00 80.00
PS2IB J.Iginla/M.Backlund 15.00 40.00
PS2JV J.Tavares/V.Hedman 50.00 100.00
PS2KS P.Kane/S.Stamkos 25.00 60.00
PS2KV P.Kane/J.Riemsdyk 25.00 60.00
PS2LB Leetch/Bathgate 10.00 25.00
PS2LE N.Lidstrom/J.Ericsson 8.00 20.00
PS2LG Gustavsson/Lundqvist 30.00 80.00
PS2LI V.Lecavalier/J.Iginla 20.00 50.00
PS2LK T.Lindsay/R.Kelly 20.00 40.00
PS2LS G.Lafleur/S.Shutt 15.00 40.00
PS2ME R.Miller/J.Enroth 15.00 40.00
PS2MH Hawerchuk/Mullen 15.00 40.00
PS2NW C.Neely/B.Wheeler 20.00 50.00
PS2OB B.Orr/R.Bourque 75.00 150.00
PS2OM A.Ovechkin/E.Malkin 100.00 200.00
PS2PP Stastny/Stastny 10.00 25.00
PS2RB P.Roy/M.Brodeur 30.00 80.00
PS2RC M.Richards/J.Carter 25.00 50.00
PS2RO Ovechkin/L.Robitaille 40.00 100.00
PS2SG S.Shirokov/M.Grabner 20.00 50.00
PS2SH V.Hedman/S.Stamkos 30.00 80.00
PS2SS M.St. Louis/S.Stamkos 30.00 60.00
PS2TD J.Tavares/M.Duchene 25.00 60.00
PS2VG T.Vanek/M.Grabner 15.00 40.00
PS2YL S.Yzerman/N.Lidstrom 60.00 120.00

2009-10 OPC Premier Stitchings

PSAC Andrew Cogliano 2.00 5.00
PSAO Alexander Ovechkin 8.00 20.00
PSBA Mikael Backlund 5.00 12.00
PSBF Benn Ferriero 10.00 25.00
PSBH Bobby Hull 6.00 15.00
PSBL Brian Leetch 2.50 6.00
PSBO Bobby Orr 12.00 30.00
PSBR Bobby Ryan 2.50 6.00
PSBW Blake Wheeler 3.00 8.00
PSCG Clark Gillies 3.00 8.00
PSCN Cam Neely 3.00 8.00
PSCP Carey Price 6.00 15.00
PSCW Cam Ward 3.00 8.00
PSDC Don Cherry 8.00 20.00
PSDH Dany Heatley 2.50 6.00
PSDP Denis Potvin 4.00 10.00
PSDP Dion Phaneuf 2.50 6.00
PSEM Evgeni Malkin 6.00 15.00
PSES Eric Staal 4.00 10.00
PSGH Gordie Howe 8.00 20.00
PSGP Gilbert Perreault 4.00 10.00
PSHL Henrik Lundqvist 8.00 20.00
PSHZ Henrik Zetterberg 4.00 10.00
PSIK Ilya Kovalchuk 3.00 8.00
PSJF Johan Franzen 2.50 6.00
PSJI Jarome Iginla 4.00 10.00
PSJK Jari Kurri 6.00 15.00
PSJN John Tavares 8.00 20.00
PSJS Jason Spezza 3.00 8.00
PSJT Joe Thornton 5.00 12.00
PSKA Paul Kariya 3.00 8.00
PSLR Luc Robitaille 4.00 10.00
PSLK Luke Schenn 3.00 8.00
PSMB Martin Brodeur 8.00 20.00
PSMD Matt Duchene 8.00 20.00
PSMF Marc-Andre Fleury 5.00 12.00
PSMG Marian Gaborik 3.00 8.00
PSMI Mike Bossy 2.50 6.00
PSMK Miikka Kiprusoff 3.00 8.00
PSML Mario Lemieux 8.00 20.00
PSMM Mark Messier 6.00 15.00
PSMN Markus Naslund 3.00 8.00
PSMO Mike Modano 5.00 12.00
PSMR Mike Richards 2.50 6.00
PSMS Martin St. Louis 3.00 8.00
PSNB Nicklas Backstrom 3.00 8.00
PSNL Nicklas Lidstrom 2.00 5.00
PSPD Pavel Datsyuk 6.00 15.00
PSPE Phil Esposito 5.00 12.00
PSPK Patrick Kane 6.00 15.00
PSPR Patrick Roy 8.00 20.00
PSRB Ray Bourque 5.00 12.00
PSRL Roberto Luongo 5.00 12.00
PSRM Ryan Miller 5.00 12.00
PSRN Rick Nash 3.00 8.00
PSSC Sidney Crosby 15.00 40.00
PSSG Sam Gagner 2.00 5.00
PSSM Steve Mason 2.50 6.00
PSSS Steven Stamkos 6.00 15.00
PSSY Steve Yzerman 8.00 20.00
PSTO Jonathan Toews 5.00 12.00
PSTS Teemu Selanne 6.00 15.00
PSTV Thomas Vanek 2.50 6.00
PSVL Vincent Lecavalier 3.00 8.00
PSWG Wayne Gretzky 15.00 40.00

2009-10 OPC Premier Stitchings Autographs

APSAC Andrew Cogliano 8.00 20.00
APSAO Alexander Ovechkin 60.00 120.00
APSBH Bobby Hull 20.00 50.00
APSBL Brian Leetch 12.00 30.00
APSBO Bobby Orr 100.00 150.00
APSBR Martin Brodeur 50.00 100.00
APSCG Clark Gillies 10.00 25.00
APSCN Cam Neely 15.00 40.00
APSCP Carey Price 20.00 50.00
APSCW Cam Ward 10.00 25.00
APSDC Don Cherry 60.00 120.00
APSDH Dany Heatley 15.00 40.00
APSDP Denis Potvin 8.00 20.00
APSEM Evgeni Malkin 50.00 100.00
APSES Eric Staal 15.00 40.00
APSGH Gordie Howe 60.00 120.00
APSGP Gilbert Perreault 12.00 30.00
APSGR Wayne Gretzky 250.00 600.00
APSHZ Henrik Zetterberg 30.00 60.00
APSJI Jarome Iginla 20.00 50.00
APSJK Jari Kurri 15.00 40.00
APSJN John Tavares 30.00 80.00
APSKA Patrick Kane 30.00 80.00
APSLK Luke Schenn 6.00 15.00
APSMA Mark Messier 30.00 60.00
APSMD Matt Duchene 40.00 80.00
APSMG Marian Gaborik 12.00 30.00
APSML Mario Lemieux 50.00 100.00
APSMM Mike Modano 15.00 40.00
APSMS Martin St. Louis 8.00 20.00
APSNB Nicklas Backstrom 6.00 15.00
APSNL Nicklas Lidstrom 15.00 40.00
APSPD Pavel Datsyuk 15.00 40.00
APSPE Phil Esposito 10.00 25.00
APSPH Dion Phaneuf 5.00 12.00
APSRB Ray Bourque/24 25.00 60.00
APSRM Ryan Miller 15.00 40.00
APSRN Rick Nash 15.00 40.00
APSRO Patrick Roy 40.00 80.00
APSRY Bobby Ryan 12.00 30.00
APSSC Sidney Crosby 100.00 200.00
APSSG Sam Gagner 8.00 20.00
APSSM Steve Mason 5.00 12.00
APSSS Steven Stamkos 25.00 50.00
APSSY Steve Yzerman 50.00 100.00
APSTH Joe Thornton 15.00 40.00
APSTV Thomas Vanek 12.00 30.00
APSTW Jonathan Toews 30.00 60.00
APSVL Vincent Lecavalier 12.00 30.00

2009-10 OPC Premier Trios Jerseys

*PATCH/15: 1X TO 2.5X TRIO JSY
3JAKA Afinogenv/Koval/Antropv 5.00 12.00
3JASK Alfredssn/Spez/Kovalv 8.00 20.00
3JBMR Robinsn/MacIns/Bourque 8.00 20.00
3JBSW Ward/Staal/Brind`Amour 8.00 20.00
3JCBP Pelech/Backlund/Chucko 8.00 20.00
3JCDF Couture/Demers/Ferriero 10.00 25.00
3JCTS Crosby/Stamkos/Tavares 40.00 80.00
3JCWM Marchnd/Wilsn/Couture 20.00 50.00
3JDGL Lundqvist/Gaborik/Drury 12.00 30.00
3JDMO Dubnyk/McDon/O'Mrra 8.00 20.00
3JDSG Zotto/Gilroy/Sauer 5.00 12.00
3JEME Enroth/Myers/Ennis 8.00 20.00
3JFCS Fleury/Crosby/Staal 12.00 30.00
3JFOW Wilson/O'Reilly/Franson 5.00 12.00
3JGBS Gustavs/Stalbrg/Bozak 8.00 20.00
3JGDO Duchne/O'Reilly/Galrdi 12.00 30.00
3JGKH Gustav/Hedmn/Karlssn 15.00 40.00
3JHTK Toews/Kane/Hossa 15.00 40.00
3JKAM Messier/Kurri/Anderson 12.00 30.00
3JKBS Kessel/Bozak/Stalberg 8.00 20.00
3JKLN Kiprusoff/Lehton/Niemi 8.00 20.00
3JKOM Ovech/Malkin/Koval 20.00 50.00
3JKSS Kurri/Selanne/Koivu 15.00 40.00
3JLAM Leetch/Andrsn/Messier 15.00 40.00
3JLCM Lemieux/Crosby/Malkin 20.00 50.00
3JLEG Lundq/Enroth/Gustav 12.00 30.00
3JLIN Lecavalier/Iginla/Nash 6.00 15.00
3JLMP Leetch/Modano/Parise 10.00 25.00
3JLPM Luongo/Price/Mason 12.50 30.00
3JLSH Hedmn/Salming/Lidstrm 12.00 30.00
3JLSS Lecav/St.Louis/Stamks 10.00 25.00
3JLVB Benn/Vishnev/Lindgren 15.00 40.00
3JLYM Lemieux/Yzermn/Messr 25.00 60.00
3JLYT Yzermn/Lemieux/Tavres 20.00 50.00
3JMGK McDnld/Gilmour/Kessel 12.00 30.00
3JMMG McDnld/Mullen/Gilmour 6.00 15.00
3JMTS Thrntn/Marleu/Setoguc 8.00 20.00
3JMVM Miller/Vanek/Myers 8.00 20.00
3JNBM Mason/Nash/Brassard 5.00 12.00
3JOCM Ovechkin/Crosby/Malkin 25.00 60.00
3JPKW Parise/Kane/Wilson 10.00 25.00
3JRBF Roy/Brodeur/Fleury 25.00 60.00
3JRBL Roy/Brodeur/Luongo 25.00 60.00
3JRCG Richards/Carter/Giroux 15.00 40.00
3JRCV Richrds/Carter/Riemsdyk 15.00 40.00
3JRDG Gretzky/Robitlle/Dionne 30.00 80.00
3JRNG Gretzky/Robitlle/Nicholls 30.00 80.00
3JSDG Zotto/Gilroy/Sanguinetti 5.00 12.00
3JSDO Stastny/Duchne/O'Reilly 10.00 25.00
3JSGH Satan/Gaborik/Hossa 12.00 30.00
3JSGR Getzlaf/Ryan/Selanne 10.00 25.00
3JSHN St. Louis/Heatley/Nash 5.00 12.00
3JSKK Spezza/Kovalev/Karlsson 15.00 40.00
3JSOG Semin/Ovechkin/Green 15.00 40.00
3JSSL Luongo/Sedin/Sedin 8.00 20.00
3JTDH Tavares/Hedmn/Duchne 15.00 40.00
3JTKD Tavares/Kane/Duchene 20.00 50.00
3JTVD Duchene/Tavares/Riems 20.00 50.00
3JVWG Riemsdyk/Wilson/Gilroy 10.00 25.00
3JYGM Yzerman/Gretzky/Messier 30.00 80.00
3JYLH Lidstrom/Howe/Yzerman 15.00 40.00
3JYZH Howe/Yzerman/Zetterberg 40.00 80.00

1981-82 O-Pee-Chee Stickers

COMPLETE SET (269) 20.00 50.00
1 The Stanley Cup FOIL .75 2.00
2 The Stanley Cup FOIL .75 2.00
3 The Stanley Cup FOIL .75 2.00
4 The Stanley Cup FOIL .75 2.00
5 The Stanley Cup FOIL .75 2.00
6 The Stanley Cup FOIL .75 2.00
7 Oilers vs. Islanders .20 .50
8 Oilers vs. Islanders .20 .50
9 Oilers vs. Islanders .20 .50
10 Oilers vs. Islanders .20 .50
11 Jari Kurri 1.50 4.00
12 Pat Riggin .10 .25
13 Flames vs. Flyers .08 .20
14 Flames vs. Flyers .08 .20
15 Flames vs. Flyers .08 .20
16 Flames vs. Flyers .08 .20
17 Stanley Cup Winner/1980-81 .08 .20
18 Stanley Cup Winner/1980-81 .08 .20
19 Conn Smythe Trophy FOIL .60 1.50
20 Butch Goring .08 .20
21 North Stars vs. Islanders .08 .20
22 Steve Payne .08 .20
23 North Stars vs. Islanders .08 .20
24 North Stars vs. Islanders .08 .20
25 North Stars vs. Islanders .08 .20
26 North Stars vs. Islanders .08 .20
27 Prince of Wales Trophy FOIL .60 1.50
28 Prince of Wales Trophy FOIL .60 1.50
29 Guy Lafleur .40 1.00
30 Bob Gainey .10 .25
31 Larry Robinson .20 .50
32 Steve Shutt .10 .25
33 Brian Engblom .08 .20
34 Doug Jarvis .08 .20
35 Yvon Lambert .08 .20
36 Mark Napier .08 .20
37 Rejean Houle .08 .20
38 Pierre Larouche .15 .40
39 Rod Langway .15 .40
40 Richard Sevigny .15 .40
41 Guy Lafleur .40 1.00
42 Larry Robinson .20 .50
43 Bob Gainey .15 .40
44 Steve Shutt .10 .25
45 Rick Middleton .10 .25
46 Peter McNab .08 .20
47 Rogatien Vachon .15 .40
48 Brad Park .15 .40
49 Ray Bourque 1.25 3.00
50 Terry O'Reilly .10 .25
51 Steve Kasper .08 .20
52 Dwight Foster .08 .20
53 Danny Gare .10 .25
54 Andre Savard .08 .20
55 Don Edwards .08 .20
56 Bob Sauve .10 .25
57 Tony McKegney .08 .20
58 John Van Boxmeer .08 .20
59 Derek Smith .08 .20
60 Gilbert Perreault .15 .40
61 Mike Rogers .08 .20
62 Mark Howe .15 .40
63 Blaine Stoughton .15 .40
64 Rick Ley .08 .20
65 Jordy Douglas .08 .20
66 Al Sims .08 .20
67 Norm Barnes .08 .20
68 John Garrett .10 .25
69 Peter Stastny .60 1.50
70 Anton Stastny .10 .25
71 Jacques Richard .08 .20
72 Robbie Ftorek .08 .20
73 Dan Bouchard .10 .25
74 Real Cloutier .08 .20
75 Michel Goulet .30 .75
76 Marc Tardif .08 .20
77 Capitals vs. Maple Leafs .08 .20
78 Capitals vs. Maple Leafs .08 .20
79 Capitals vs. Maple Leafs .08 .20
80 Capitals vs. Maple Leafs .08 .20
81 Whalers vs. Capitals .08 .20
82 Whalers vs. Capitals .08 .20
83 Canadiens vs. Capitals .08 .20
84 Dan Bouchard .10 .25
85 North Stars vs. Capitals .08 .20
86 North Stars vs. Capitals .08 .20
87 Bruins vs. Capitals .08 .20
88 Bobby Smith .10 .25
89 Don Beaupre .10 .25
90 Al MacAdam .08 .20
91 Craig Hartsburg .10 .25
92 Steve Payne .08 .20
93 Gilles Meloche .10 .25
94 Tim Young .08 .20
95 Tom McCarthy .08 .20
96 Wilf Paiement .08 .20
97 Darryl Sittler .15 .40
98 Borje Salming .15 .40
99 Bill Derlago .08 .20
100 Ian Turnbull .08 .20
101 Rick Vaive .10 .25
102 Dan Maloney .08 .20
103 Laurie Boschman .08 .20
104 Pat Hickey .08 .20
105 Michel Larocque .10 .25
106 Jiri Crha .08 .20
107 John Anderson .08 .20
108 Bill Derlago .08 .20
109 Darryl Sittler .10 .25
110 Wilf Paiement .08 .20
111 Borje Salming .10 .25
112 Denis Savard 1.00 2.50
113 Tony Esposito .30 .75
114 Tom Lysiak .10 .25
115 Keith Brown .08 .20
116 Glen Sharpley .08 .20
117 Terry Ruskowski .08 .20
118 Reg Kerr .08 .20
119 Bob Murray .08 .20
120 Dale McCourt .08 .20
121 John Ogrodnick .10 .25
122 Mike Foligno .10 .25
123 Gilles Gilbert .10 .25
124 Reed Larson .08 .20
125 Vaclav Nedomansky .08 .20
126 Willie Huber .08 .20
127 Jim Korn .08 .20
128 Bernie Federko .20 .50
129 Mike Liut .15 .40
130 Wayne Babych .08 .20
131 Blake Dunlop .08 .20
132 Mike Zuke .08 .20
133 Brian Sutter .10 .25
134 Rick Lapointe .08 .20
135 Jorgen Pettersson .08 .20
136 Dave Christian .10 .25
137 Dave Babych .08 .20
138 Morris Lukowich .08 .20
139 Norm Dupont .08 .20
140 Ron Wilson .08 .20
141 Dan Geoffrion .08 .20
142 Barry Long .08 .20
143 Pierre Hamel .08 .20
144 Charlie Simmer AS FOIL .60 1.50
145 Mark Howe AS FOIL .75 2.00
146 Don Beaupre AS FOIL .60 1.50
147 Marcel Dionne AS FOIL .75 2.00
148 Larry Robinson AS FOIL .75 2.00
149 Dave Taylor AS FOIL .60 1.50
150 Mike Bossy AS FOIL 1.00 2.50
151 Denis Potvin AS FOIL .75 2.00
152 Bryan Trottier AS FOIL .75 2.00
153 Mike Liut AS FOIL .60 1.50
154 Rob Ramage AS FOIL .60 1.50
155 Bill Barber AS FOIL .60 1.50
156 Campbell Bowl FOIL .60 1.50
157 Campbell Bowl FOIL .60 1.50
158 Mike Bossy .40 1.00
159 Denis Potvin .15 .40
160 Bryan Trottier .20 .50
161 Billy Smith .15 .40
162 Anders Kallur .08 .20
163 Bob Bourne .08 .20
164 Clark Gillies .08 .20
165 Ken Morrow .15 .40
166 Anders Hedberg .10 .25
167 Ron Greschner .10 .25
168 Barry Beck .08 .20
169 Ed Johnstone .08 .20
170 Don Maloney .10 .25
171 Ron Duguay .10 .25
172 Ulf Nilsson .08 .20
173 Dave Maloney .08 .20
174 Bill Barber .20 .50
175 Behn Wilson .08 .20
176 Ken Linseman .10 .25
177 Pete Peeters .20 .50
178 Bobby Clarke .40 1.00
179 Paul Holmgren .10 .25
180 Brian Propp .08 .20
181 Reggie Leach .10 .25
182 Rick Kehoe .08 .20
183 Randy Carlyle .08 .20
184 George Ferguson .08 .20
185 Peter Lee .08 .20
186 Rod Schutt .08 .20
187 Paul Gardner .08 .20
188 Ron Stackhouse .08 .20
189 Mario Faubert .08 .20
190 Mike Gartner .50 1.25
191 Dennis Maruk .08 .20
192 Ryan Walter .10 .25
193 Rick Green .08 .20
194 Mike Palmateer .15 .40
195 Bob Kelly .08 .20
196 Jean Pronovost .08 .20
197 Al Hangsleben .08 .20
198 Flames vs. Capitals .08 .20
199 Oilers vs. Islanders .40 1.00
200 Oilers vs. Islanders .40 1.00
201 Oilers vs. Islanders .40 1.00
202 Oilers vs. Islanders .40 1.00
203 Rangers vs. Islanders .08 .20
204 Rangers vs. Islanders .08 .20
205 Flyers vs. Capitals .08 .20
206 Flyers vs. Capitals .08 .20
207 Rangers vs. Capitals .08 .20
208 Canadiens vs. Capitals .08 .20
209 Wayne Gretzky 4.00 10.00
210 Mark Messier 2.00 5.00
211 Jari Kurri 1.50 4.00
212 Brett Callighen .08 .20
213 Matti Hagman .08 .20
214 Risto Siltanen .10 .25
215 Lee Fogolin .08 .20
216 Eddie Mio .08 .20
217 Glenn Anderson .60 1.50
218 Kent Nilsson .10 .25
219 Guy Chouinard .08 .20
220 Eric Vail .08 .20
221 Pat Riggin .10 .25
222 Willi Plett .08 .20
223 Pekka Rautakallio .08 .20
224 Paul Reinhart .10 .25
225 Brad Marsh .10 .25
226 Phil Russell .08 .20
227 Lanny McDonald .15 .40
228 Merlin Malinowski .08 .20
229 Rob Ramage .10 .25
230 Glenn Resch .15 .40
231 Ron Delorme .08 .20
232 Lucien DeBlois .08 .20
233 Paul Gagne .08 .20
234 Joel Quenneville .08 .20
235 Marcel Dionne .20 .50
236 Charlie Simmer .15 .40
237 Dave Taylor .15 .40
238 Mario Lessard .08 .20
239 Larry Murphy .50 1.25
240 Jerry Korab .08 .20
241 Mike Murphy .08 .20
242 Billy Harris .08 .20
243 Thomas Gradin .10 .25
244 Per-Olov Brasar .08 .20
245 Glen Hanlon .10 .25
246 Chris Oddleifson .08 .20
247 Tiger Williams .20 .50
248 Kevin McCarthy .08 .20
249 Dennis Kearns .08 .20
250 Harold Snepsts .15 .40
251 Art Ross Trophy FOIL .60 1.50
252 Wayne Gretzky 4.00 10.00
253 Mike Bossy .40 1.00
254 Norris Trophy FOIL .60 1.50
255 Randy Carlyle .08 .20
256 Richard Sevigny .15 .40
257 Vezina Trophy FOIL .60 1.50
258 Denis Herron .08 .20
259 Michel Larocque .10 .25
260 Lady Byng Trophy FOIL .60 1.50
261 Rick Kehoe .08 .20
262 Calder Trophy FOIL .60 1.50
263 Peter Stastny .60 1.50
264 Wayne Gretzky 4.00 10.00
265 Hart Trophy FOIL .60 1.50
266 Charlie Simmer .15 .40
267 Marcel Dionne .20 .50
268 Dave Taylor .15 .40
269 Bob Gainey .15 .40
xx Sticker Album 2.00 5.00

1982-83 O-Pee-Chee Stickers

COMPLETE SET (263) 18.00 45.00
*TOPPS: .4X TO 1X O-PEE-CHEE
1 Mike Bossy .20 .50
2 Conn Smythe Trophy FOIL .08 .25
3 1981-82 Stanley Cup Winners .01 .05
4 1981-82 Stanley Cup Winners .01 .05
5 Stanley Cup Finals .08 .25
6 Stanley Cup Finals .08 .25
7 Richard Brodeur .08 .25
8 Victory Victoire .01 .05
9 Stanley Cup Finals .08 .25
10 Stanley Cup Finals .08 .25
11 Canucks vs. Chicago .01 .05
12 Canucks vs. Chicago .01 .05
13 Canucks vs. Chicago .01 .05
14 Tom Lysiak .08 .25
15 Peter Stastny .30 .75
16 Islanders vs. Quebec .01 .05
17 Islanders vs. Quebec .01 .05
18 Islanders vs. Quebec .01 .05
19 Peter Stastny .30 .75
20 Marian Stastny .01 .05
21 Marc Tardif .08 .25
22 Wilf Paiement .01 .05
23 Real Cloutier .01 .05
24 Anton Stastny .08 .25
25 Michel Goulet .20 .50
26 Dale Hunter .08 .25
27 Dan Bouchard .08 .25
28 Guy Lafleur .20 .50
29 Guy Lafleur .20 .50
30 Mario Tremblay .08 .25
31 Larry Robinson .08 .25
32 Steve Shutt .08 .25
33 Steve Shutt .08 .25
34 Rod Langway .08 .25
35 Pierre Mondou .01 .05
36 Bob Gainey .08 .25
37 Rick Wamsley .08 .25
38 Mark Napier .08 .25
39 Mark Napier .08 .25
40 Doug Jarvis .08 .25
41 Denis Herron .08 .25
42 Keith Acton .01 .05
43 Keith Acton .01 .05
44 Prince of Wales Trophy FOIL .08 .25
45 Prince of Wales Trophy FOIL .08 .25
46 Denis Potvin .08 .25
47 Bryan Trottier .08 .25
48 Bryan Trottier .08 .25
49 John Tonelli .08 .25
50 Mike Bossy .20 .50
51 Mike Bossy .20 .50
52 Duane Sutter .08 .25
53 Bob Bourne .01 .05
54 Clark Gillies .08 .25
55 Clark Gillies .08 .25
56 Brent Sutter .08 .25
57 Anders Kallur .01 .05
58 Ken Morrow .08 .25
59 Bob Nystrom .08 .25
60 Billy Smith .08 .25
61 Billy Smith .08 .25
62 Rick Vaive .08 .25
63 Rick Vaive .08 .25
64 Jim Benning .01 .05
65 Miroslav Frycer .01 .05
66 Terry Martin .01 .05
67 Bill Derlago .01 .05
68 Bill Derlago .01 .05
69 Rocky Saganiuk .01 .05
70 Vincent Tremblay .01 .05
71 Bob Manno .01 .05
72 Dan Maloney .08 .25
73 John Anderson .01 .05
74 John Anderson .01 .05
75 Borje Salming .08 .25
76 Borje Salming .08 .25
77 Michel Larocque .08 .25
78 Rick Middleton .08 .25
79 Rick Middleton .08 .25
80 Keith Crowder .01 .05
81 Steve Kasper .08 .25
82 Brad Park .10 .30
83 Peter McNab .08 .25
84 Peter McNab .08 .25
85 Terry O'Reilly .08 .25
86 Ray Bourque .60 1.50
87 Ray Bourque .60 1.50
88 Tom Fergus .01 .05
89 Mike O'Connell .01 .05
90 Brad McCrimmon .08 .25
91 Don Marcotte .01 .05
92 Barry Pederson .08 .25
93 Barry Pederson .08 .25
94 Mark Messier 1.50 4.00
95 Grant Fuhr .75 2.00
96 Kevin Lowe .20 .50
97 Wayne Gretzky 2.50 6.00
98 Wayne Gretzky 2.50 6.00
99 Glenn Anderson .20 .50
100 Glenn Anderson .20 .50
101 Dave Lumley .01 .05
102 Dave Hunter .01 .05
103 Matti Hagman .01 .05
104 Paul Coffey .75 2.00
105 Paul Coffey .75 2.00
106 Lee Fogolin .01 .05
107 Ron Low .08 .25
108 Jari Kurri .40 1.00
109 Jari Kurri .40 1.00
110 Bill Barber .08 .25
111 Brian Propp .08 .25
112 Ken Linseman .08 .25
113 Ron Flockhart .08 .25
114 Darryl Sittler .08 .25
115 Bobby Clarke .20 .50
116 Paul Holmgren .08 .25
117 Pete Peeters .08 .25
118 Gilbert Perreault .08 .25
119 Dale McCourt .01 .05
120 Mike Foligno .08 .25
121 John Van Boxmeer .01 .05
122 Tony McKegney .08 .25
123 Ric Seiling .01 .05
124 Don Edwards .08 .25
125 Yvon Lambert .01 .05
126 Blaine Stoughton .08 .25
127 Pierre Larouche .08 .25
128 Doug Sulliman .01 .05
129 Ron Francis 1.25 3.00
130 Greg Millen .08 .25
131 Mark Howe .08 .25
132 Chris Kotsopoulos .01 .05
133 Garry Howatt .01 .05
134 Ron Duguay .08 .25
135 Barry Beck .08 .25
136 Mike Rogers .01 .05
137 Don Maloney .08 .25
138 Mark Pavelich .08 .25
139 Ed Johnstone .01 .05
140 Dave Maloney .01 .05
141 Steve Weeks .08 .25
142 Eddie Mio .08 .25
143 Rick Kehoe .08 .25
144 Randy Carlyle .08 .25
145 Paul Gardner .01 .05
146 Michel Dion .08 .25
147 Rick MacLeish .08 .25
148 Pat Boutette .08 .25
149 Mike Bullard .08 .25
150 George Ferguson .01 .05
151 Dennis Maruk .08 .25
152 Ryan Walter .08 .25
153 Mike Gartner .20 .50
154 Bob Carpenter .20 .50
155 Chris Valentine .01 .05
156 Rick Green .08 .25
157 Bengt Gustafsson .01 .05
158 Dave Parro .01 .05
159 Mark Messier AS FOIL 1.50 4.00
160 Paul Coffey AS FOIL 1.25 3.00
161 Grant Fuhr AS FOIL 1.25 3.00
162 Wayne Gretzky AS FOIL 4.00 10.00
163 Doug Wilson AS FOIL .20 .50
164 Dave Taylor AS FOIL .20 .50
165 Mike Bossy AS FOIL .40 1.00
166 Ray Bourque AS FOIL 1.00 2.50
167 Peter Stastny AS FOIL .40 1.00
168 Michel Dion AS FOIL .08 .25
169 Larry Robinson AS FOIL .20 .50
170 Bill Barber AS FOIL .20 .50
171 Denis Savard .20 .50
172 Doug Wilson .08 .25
173 Grant Mulvey .08 .25
174 Tom Lysiak .08 .25
175 Al Secord .08 .25
176 Reg Kerr .01 .05
177 Tim Higgins .01 .05
178 Terry Ruskowski .08 .25
179 John Ogrodnick .08 .25
180 Reed Larson .01 .05
181 Bob Sauve .08 .25
182 Mark Osborne .01 .05
183 Jim Schoenfeld .08 .25
184 Danny Gare .08 .25
185 Willie Huber .01 .05
186 Walt McKechnie .01 .05
187 Paul Woods .08 .25
188 Bobby Smith .08 .25
189 Dino Ciccarelli .30 .75
190 Neal Broten .20 .50
191 Steve Payne .08 .25
192 Craig Hartsburg .08 .25
193 Don Beaupre .08 .25
194 Steve Christoff .08 .25
195 Gilles Meloche .08 .25
196 Mike Liut .08 .25
197 Bernie Federko .08 .25
198 Brian Sutter .08 .25
199 Blake Dunlop .01 .05
200 Joe Mullen .40 1.00
201 Wayne Babych .01 .05
202 Jorgen Pettersson .01 .05
203 Perry Turnbull .01 .05
204 Dale Hawerchuk 1.00 2.50
205 Morris Lukowich .01 .05
206 Dave Christian .08 .25
207 Dave Babych .08 .25
208 Paul MacLean .08 .25
209 Willy Lindstrom .01 .05
210 Ed Staniowski .01 .05
211 Doug Soetaert .08 .25
212 Lucien DeBlois .01 .05
213 Mel Bridgman .08 .25
214 Lanny McDonald .08 .25
215 Guy Chouinard .08 .25
216 Jim Peplinski .08 .25
217 Kent Nilsson .08 .25
218 Pekka Rautakallio .08 .25
219 Paul Reinhart .08 .25
220 Kevin Lavallee .01 .05
221 Ken Houston .01 .05
222 Glenn Resch .08 .25
223 Rob Ramage .08 .25
224 Don Lever .01 .05
225 Bob MacMillan .01 .05
226 Steve Tambellini .01 .05
227 Brent Ashton .01 .05
228 Bob Lorimer .01 .05
229 Merlin Malinowski .01 .05
230 Marcel Dionne .08 .25
231 Dave Taylor .08 .25
232 Larry Murphy .20 .50
233 Steve Bozek .01 .05
234 Greg Terrion .01 .05
235 Jim Fox .01 .05
236 Mario Lessard .08 .25
237 Charlie Simmer .08 .25
238 Campbell Bowl FOIL .08 .25
239 Campbell Bowl FOIL .08 .25
240 Thomas Gradin .08 .25
241 Ivan Boldirev .01 .05
242 Stan Smyl .08 .25
243 Harold Snepsts .08 .25
244 Curt Fraser .01 .05
245 Lars Molin .01 .05
246 Kevin McCarthy .01 .05
247 Richard Brodeur .08 .25
248 Calder Trophy FOIL .08 .25
249 Dale Hawerchuk 1.00 2.50
250 Vezina Trophy FOIL .08 .25
251 Billy Smith .08 .25
252 Denis Herron Rick Wamsley .10 .25
253 Steve Kasper .08 .25

254 Doug Wilson .08 .25
255 Norris Trophy FOIL .08 .25
256 Wayne Gretzky 2.50 6.00
257 Wayne Gretzky 2.50 6.00
258 Wayne Gretzky 2.50 6.00
259 Wayne Gretzky 2.50 6.00
260 Hart Trophy FOIL .08 .25
261 Art Ross Trophy FOIL .08 .25
262 Rick Middleton .08 .25
263 Lady Byng Trophy FOIL .08 .25
NNO Sticker Album 2.00 5.00

1983-84 O-Pee-Chee Stickers

COMPLETE SET (330) 16.00 40.00
1 Marcel Dionne FOIL .20 .50
2 Guy Lafleur FOIL .40 1.00
3 Darryl Sittler FOIL .20 .50
4 Gilbert Perreault FOIL .20 .50
5 Bill Barber .08 .25
6 Steve Shutt .08 .25
7 Wayne Gretzky 2.50 6.00
8 Lanny McDonald .08 .25
9 Reggie Leach .08 .25
10 Mike Bossy .20 .50
11 Rick Kehoe .08 .25
12 Bobby Clarke .08 .25
13 Butch Goring .08 .25
14 Rick Middleton .08 .25
15 Conn Smythe
Trophy FOIL .05 .15
16 Billy Smith .08 .25
17 Lee Fogolin .01 .05
18 Stanley Cup Finals .08 .25
19 Stanley Cup Finals .08 .25
20 Stanley Cup Finals .08 .25
21 Stanley Cup Finals .08 .25
22 Stanley Cup FOIL .08 .25
23 Stanley Cup FOIL .08 .25
24 Stanley Cup FOIL .08 .25
25 Rick Vaive .08 .25
26 Rick Vaive .08 .25
27 Billy Harris .01 .05
28 Dan Daoust .01 .05
29 Dan Daoust .01 .05
30 John Anderson .01 .05
31 John Anderson .01 .05
32 Peter Ihnacak .01 .05
33 Borje Salming .08 .25
34 Borje Salming .08 .25
35 Bill Derlago .01 .05
36 Rick St.Croix .08 .25
37 Greg Terrion .01 .05
38 Miroslav Frycer .01 .05
39 Mike Palmateer .08 .25
40 Gaston Gingras .01 .05
41 Pete Peeters .08 .25
42 Pete Peeters .08 .25
43 Mike Krushelnyski .08 .25
44 Rick Middleton .08 .25
45 Rick Middleton .08 .25
46 Ray Bourque .40 1.00
47 Ray Bourque .40 1.00
48 Brad Park .08 .25
49 Barry Pederson .08 .25
50 Barry Pederson .08 .25
51 Peter McNab .08 .25
52 Mike O'Connell .01 .05
53 Steve Kasper .08 .25
54 Marty Howe .08 .25
55 Tom Fergus .01 .05
56 Keith Crowder .01 .05
57 Steve Shutt .08 .25
58 Guy Lafleur .20 .50
59 Guy Lafleur .20 .50
60 Larry Robinson .08 .25
61 Larry Robinson .08 .25
62 Ryan Walter .08 .25
63 Ryan Walter .08 .25
64 Mark Napier .01 .05
65 Mark Napier .08 .25
66 Bob Gainey .08 .25
67 Doug Wickenheiser .01 .05
68 Pierre Mondou .01 .05
69 Mario Tremblay .08 .25
70 Gilbert Delorme .01 .05
71 Mats Naslund .08 .25
72 Rick Wamsley .08 .25
73 Ken Morrow .08 .25
74 John Tonelli .08 .25
75 John Tonelli .08 .25
76 Bryan Trottier .08 .25
77 Bryan Trottier .08 .25
78 Mike Bossy .20 .50
79 Mike Bossy .20 .50
80 Bob Bourne .01 .05
81 Denis Potvin .08 .25
82 Denis Potvin .08 .25
83 Dave Langevin .01 .05
84 Clark Gillies .08 .25
85 Bob Nystrom .08 .25
86 Billy Smith .08 .25
87 Tomas Jonsson .01 .05
88 Rollie Melanson .08 .25
89 Wayne Gretzky 2.50 6.00
90 Wayne Gretzky 2.50 6.00
91 Willy Lindstrom .01 .05
92 Glenn Anderson .20 .50
93 Glenn Anderson .20 .50
94 Paul Coffey .40 1.00
95 Paul Coffey .40 1.00
96 Charlie Huddy .08 .25
97 Mark Messier .75 2.00
98 Mark Messier .75 2.00
99 Andy Moog .40 1.00
100 Lee Fogolin .01 .05
101 Kevin Lowe .08 .25
102 Ken Linseman .08 .25
103 Tom Roulston .01 .05
104 Jari Kurri .40 1.00
105 Darryl Sutter .08 .25
106 Denis Savard .08 .25
107 Denis Savard .08 .25
108 Steve Larmer .75 2.00
109 Bob Murray .01 .05
110 Tom Lysiak .08 .25
111 Al Secord .08 .25
112 Doug Wilson .08 .25
113 Murray Bannerman .08 .25
114 Gordie Roberts .01 .05
115 Tom McCarthy .01 .05
116 Bobby Smith .08 .25
117 Craig Hartsburg .08 .25
118 Dino Ciccarelli .20 .50
119 Dino Ciccarelli .20 .50
120 Neal Broten .08 .25
121 Steve Payne .01 .05
122 Don Beaupre .08 .25
123 Jorgen Pettersson .01 .05
124 Perry Turnbull .01 .05
125 Bernie Federko .08 .25
126 Mike Crombeen .01 .05
127 Brian Sutter .08 .25
128 Brian Sutter .08 .25
129 Mike Liut .08 .25
130 Rob Ramage .08 .25
131 Blake Dunlop .01 .05
132 Ivan Boldirev .01 .05
133 Dwight Foster .01 .05
134 Reed Larson .01 .05
135 Danny Gare .08 .25
136 Jim Schoenfeld .08 .25
137 John Ogrodnick .08 .25
138 John Ogrodnick .08 .25
139 Willie Huber .01 .05
140 Greg Smith .01 .05
141 Ed Beers .01 .05
142 Brian Bellows .20 .50
143 Jiri Bubla .01 .05
144 Daryl Evans .01 .05
145 Randy Gregg .01 .05
146 Jim Jackson .01 .05
147 Corrado Micalef .01 .05
148 Brian Mullen .08 .25
149 Frank Nigro .01 .05
150 Walt Poddubny .01 .05
151 Jaroslav Pouzar .01 .05
152 Patrik Sundstrom .08 .25
153 Denis Savard .20 .50
154 Dave Hunter .01 .05
155 Andy Moog .40 1.00
156 Al Secord .08 .25
157 Mark Messier .75 2.00
158 Glenn Anderson .20 .50
159 Jaroslav Pouzar .01 .05
160 Al Secord AS .01 .05
161 Wayne Gretzky AS 2.50 6.00
162 Lanny McDonald AS .08 .25
163 Dave Babych AS .01 .05
164 Murray Bannerman AS .08 .25
165 Doug Wilson AS .01 .05
166 Michel Goulet AS .08 .25
167 Peter Stastny AS .20 .50
168 Marian Stastny AS .08 .25
169 Denis Potvin AS .08 .25
170 Pete Peeters AS .08 .25
171 Mark Howe AS .08 .25
172 Luc Dufour .01 .05
173 Ray Bourque .40 1.00
174 Bob Bourne .01 .05
175 Denis Potvin .08 .25
176 Mike Bossy .20 .50
177 Butch Goring .08 .25
178 Brad Park .08 .25
179 Murray Brumwell .01 .05
180 Guy Carbonneau .40 1.00
181 Lindsay Carson .01 .05
182 Luc Dufour .01 .05
183 Bob Froese .08 .25
184 Mats Hallin .01 .05
185 Gord Kluzak .08 .25
186 Jeff Larmer .01 .05
187 Milan Novy .01 .05
188 Scott Stevens .75 2.00
189 Bob Sullivan .01 .05
190 Mark Taylor .01 .05
191 Darryl Sittler .08 .25
192 Ron Flockhart .01 .05
193 Brad McCrimmon .08 .25
194 Bill Barber .08 .25
195 Mark Howe .08 .25
196 Mark Howe .08 .25
197 Pelle Lindbergh 1.50 4.00
198 Bobby Clarke .08 .25
199 Brian Propp .08 .25
200 Ken Houston .01 .05
201 Rod Langway .08 .25
202 Al Jensen .08 .25
203 Brian Engblom .01 .05
204 Dennis Maruk .08 .25
205 Dennis Maruk .08 .25
206 Bob Carpenter .08 .25
207 Mike Gartner .20 .50
208 Doug Jarvis .08 .25
209 Eddie Mio .08 .25
210 Barry Beck .08 .25
211 Dave Maloney .08 .25
212 Don Maloney .08 .25
213 Mark Pavelich .08 .25
214 Mark Pavelich .01 .05
215 Anders Hedberg .08 .25
216 Reijo Ruotsalainen .01 .05
217 Mike Rogers .01 .05
218 Don Lever .01 .05
219 Steve Tambellini .01 .05
220 Bob MacMillan .01 .05
221 Hector Marini .01 .05
222 Glenn Resch .08 .25
223 Glenn Resch .08 .25
224 Carol Vadnais .01 .05
225 Joel Quenneville .01 .05
226 Aaron Broten .01 .05
227 Randy Carlyle .08 .25
228 Doug Shedden .01 .05
229 Greg Malone .01 .05
230 Paul Gardner .01 .05
231 Rick Kehoe .08 .25
232 Rick Kehoe .08 .25
233 Pat Boutette .01 .05
234 Michel Dion .08 .25
235 Mike Bullard .08 .25
236 Dale McCourt .01 .05
237 Mike Foligno .08 .25
238 Phil Housley .40 1.00
239 Tony McKegney .08 .25
240 Gilbert Perreault .08 .25
241 Gilbert Perreault .08 .25
242 Bob Sauve .08 .25
243 Mike Ramsey .08 .25
244 John Van Boxmeer .01 .05
245 Dan Bouchard .08 .25
246 Real Cloutier .01 .05
247 Marc Tardif .08 .25
248 Randy Moller .01 .05
249 Michel Goulet .08 .25
250 Michel Goulet .08 .25
251 Marian Stastny .08 .25
252 Anton Stastny .08 .25
253 Peter Stastny .20 .50
254 Mark Johnson .08 .25
255 Ron Francis .60 1.50
256 Doug Sulliman .01 .05
257 Risto Siltanen .01 .05
258 Blaine Stoughton .08 .25
259 Blaine Stoughton .08 .25
260 Ray Neufeld .01 .05
261 Pierre Lacroix .01 .05
262 Greg Millen .08 .25
263 Lanny McDonald .08 .25
264 Paul Reinhart .08 .25
265 Mel Bridgman .08 .25
266 Rejean Lemelin .08 .25
267 Kent Nilsson .08 .25
268 Kent Nilsson .08 .25
269 Doug Risebrough .08 .25
270 Kari Eloranta .01 .05
271 Phil Russell .01 .05
272 Darcy Rota .01 .05
273 Thomas Gradin .08 .25
274 Stan Smyl .08 .25
275 John Garrett .08 .25
276 Richard Brodeur .08 .25
277 Richard Brodeur .08 .25
278 Doug Halward .01 .05
279 Kevin McCarthy .01 .05
280 Rick Lanz .01 .05
281 Morris Lukowich .01 .05
282 Dale Hawerchuk .40 1.00
283 Paul MacLean .08 .25
284 Lucien DeBlois .01 .05
285 Dave Babych .08 .25
286 Dave Babych .01 .05
287 Doug Smail .01 .05
288 Doug Soetaert .01 .05
289 Thomas Steen .08 .25
290 Charlie Simmer .08 .25
291 Terry Ruskowski .08 .25
292 Bernie Nicholls .75 2.00
293 Jim Fox .01 .05
294 Marcel Dionne .08 .25
295 Marcel Dionne .08 .25
296 Gary Laskoski .01 .05
297 Jerry Korab .01 .05
298 Larry Murphy .20 .50
299 Hart Trophy FOIL .05 .15
300 Hart Trophy FOIL .05 .15
301 Wayne Gretzky 2.50 6.00
302 Bobby Clarke .08 .25
303 Lanny McDonald .08 .25
304 Lady Byng
Trophy FOIL .05 .15
305 Lady Byng
Trophy FOIL .05 .15
306 Mike Bossy .20 .50
307 Wayne Gretzky 2.50 6.00
308 Art Ross
Trophy FOIL .05 .15
309 Art Ross
Trophy FOIL .05 .15
310 Calder Trophy FOIL .05 .15
311 Calder Trophy FOIL .05 .15
312 Steve Larmer .60 1.50
313 Rod Langway .08 .25
314 Norris Trophy FOIL .05 .15
315 Norris Trophy FOIL .05 .15
316 Billy Smith .08 .25
317 Roland Melanson .08 .25
318 Pete Peeters .08 .25
319 Vezina Trophy FOIL .05 .15
320 Vezina Trophy FOIL .05 .15
321 Mike Bossy FOIL .20 .50
322 Mike Bossy FOIL .20 .50
323 Marcel Dionne FOIL .20 .50
324 Marcel Dionne FOIL .20 .50
325 Wayne Gretzky FOIL 3.00 8.00
326 Wayne Gretzky FOIL 3.00 8.00
327 Pat Hughes FOIL .05 .15
328 Pat Hughes FOIL .05 .15
329 Rick Middleton FOIL .05 .15
330 Rick Middleton FOIL .05 .15
xx Sticker Album 1.50 4.00

1984-85 O-Pee-Chee Stickers

COMPLETE SET (270) 16.00 40.00
1 Stanley Cup .20 .50
2 Stanley Cup .20 .50
3 Stanley Cup .20 .50
4 Stanley Cup .20 .50
5 Mark Messier .50 1.25
6 Maple Leafs Logo FOIL
23. Blackhawks Logo FOIL .30 .75
7 Borje Salming .05 .15
8 Borje Salming .05 .15
9 Dan Daoust .05 .15
10 Dan Daoust .05 .15
11 Rick Vaive .05 .15
12 Rick Vaive .05 .15
13 Dale McCourt .05 .15
14 Bill Derlago .05 .15
15 Gary Nylund .05 .15
16 Gary Nylund .05 .15
17 Jim Korn .05 .15
18 John Anderson .05 .15
19 Greg Terrion .05 .15
20 Allan Bester .08 .25
21 Jim Benning .05 .15
22 Mike Palmateer .08 .25
24 Denis Savard .20 .50
25 Denis Savard .20 .50
26 Bob Murray .05 .15
27 Doug Wilson .05 .15
28 Keith Brown .05 .15
29 Steve Larmer .20 .50
30 Darryl Sutter .05 .15
31 Tom Lysiak .05 .15
32 Murray Bannerman .08 .25
33 Red Wings Logo FOIL
43. North Stars Logo FOIL .20 .50
34 John Ogrodnick .05 .15
35 John Ogrodnick .05 .15
36 Reed Larson .05 .15
37 Steve Yzerman 5.00 12.00
38 Brad Park .08 .25
39 Ivan Boldirev .05 .15
40 Kelly Kisio .05 .15
41 Greg Stefan .08 .25
42 Ron Duguay .05 .15
44 Brian Bellows .08 .25
45 Brian Bellows .08 .25
46 Neal Broten .15 .40
47 Dino Ciccarelli .20 .50
48 Dennis Maruk .05 .15
49 Steve Payne .05 .15
50 Brad Maxwell .05 .15
51 Gilles Meloche .08 .25
52 Tom McCarthy .05 .15
53 Blues Logo FOIL
67. Devils Logo FOIL .15 .40
54 Bernie Federko .08 .25
55 Bernie Federko .08 .25
56 Brian Sutter .05 .15
57 Mike Liut .15 .40
58 Doug Wickenheiser .05 .15
59 Jorgen Pettersson .05 .15
60 Doug Gilmour 1.50 4.00
61 Joe Mullen .15 .40
62 Rob Ramage .05 .15
63 Wayne Gretzky FOIL
64. Michel Goulet FOIL 2.50 6.00
65 Pat Riggin FOIL
66. Denis Potvin FOIL .15 .40
68 Glenn Resch .08 .25
69 Glenn Resch .08 .25
70 Don Lever .05 .15
71 Mel Bridgman .05 .15
72 Bob MacMillan .05 .15
73 Pat Verbeek .20 .50
74 Joe Cirella .05 .15
75 Phil Russell .05 .15
76 Jan Ludvig .05 .15
77 Islanders Logo FOIL
94. Rangers Logo FOIL .15 .40
78 Denis Potvin .15 .40
79 Denis Potvin .15 .40
80 John Tonelli .05 .15
81 John Tonelli .05 .15
82 Mike Bossy .20 .50
83 Mike Bossy .20 .50
84 Butch Goring .05 .15
85 Bob Nystrom .05 .15
86 Bryan Trottier .15 .40
87 Bryan Trottier .15 .40
88 Brent Sutter .05 .15
89 Bob Bourne .05 .15
90 Greg Gilbert .05 .15
91 Billy Smith .15 .40
92 Rollie Melanson .08 .25
93 Ken Morrow .08 .25
95 Don Maloney .05 .15
96 Don Maloney .05 .15
97 Mark Pavelich .05 .15
98 Glen Hanlon .08 .25
99 Mike Rogers .05 .15
100 Barry Beck .05 .15
101 Reijo Ruotsalainen .05 .15
102 Anders Hedberg .05 .15
103 Pierre Larouche .08 .25
104 Flyers Logo FOIL
114. Penguins Logo FOIL .15 .40
105 Tim Kerr .05 .15
106 Tim Kerr .05 .15
107 Ron Sutter .08 .25
108 Darryl Sittler .08 .25
109 Mark Howe .15 .40
110 Dave Poulin .05 .15
111 Rich Sutter .08 .25
112 Brian Propp .05 .15
113 Bob Froese .08 .25
115 Ron Flockhart .05 .15
116 Ron Flockhart .05 .15
117 Rick Kehoe .05 .15
118 Mike Bullard .05 .15
119 Kevin McCarthy .05 .15
120 Doug Shedden .05 .15
121 Mark Taylor .05 .15
122 Denis Herron .05 .15
123 Tom Roulston .05 .15
124 Capitals Logo FOIL
146. Canadiens Logo FOIL .30 .75
125 Rod Langway .05 .15
126 Rod Langway .05 .15
127 Larry Murphy .08 .25
128 Al Jensen .05 .15
129 Doug Jarvis .05 .15
130 Bengt Gustafsson .05 .15
131 Mike Gartner .20 .50
132 Bob Carpenter .05 .15
133 Dave Christian .05 .15
134 Paul Coffey FOIL .50 1.25
135 Murray Bannerman FOIL .08 .25
136 Rob Ramage FOIL .08 .25
137 John Ogrodnick FOIL .08 .25
138 Wayne Gretzky FOIL 2.50 6.00
139 Rick Vaive FOIL .08 .25
140 Michel Goulet FOIL .20 .50
141 Peter Stastny FOIL .20 .50
142 Rick Middleton FOIL .08 .25
143 Ray Bourque FOIL .50 1.25
144 Pete Peeters FOIL .08 .25
145 Denis Potvin FOIL .20 .50
147 Larry Robinson .08 .25
148 Larry Robinson .08 .25
149 Guy Lafleur .20 .50
150 Guy Lafleur .20 .50
151 Bobby Smith .05 .15
152 Bobby Smith .05 .15
153 Bob Gainey .08 .25
154 Craig Ludwig .05 .15
155 Mats Naslund .08 .25
156 Mats Naslund .08 .25
157 Rick Wamsley .08 .25
158 Jean Hamel .05 .15
159 Ryan Walter .05 .15
160 Guy Carbonneau .15 .40
161 Mario Tremblay .05 .15
162 Pierre Mondou .05 .15
163 Nordiques Logo FOIL
180. Bruins Logo FOIL .15 .40
164 Peter Stastny .20 .50
165 Peter Stastny .20 .50
166 Mario Marois .05 .15
167 Mario Marois .05 .15
168 Michel Goulet .15 .40
169 Michel Goulet .15 .40
170 Andre Savard .05 .15
171 Tony McKegney .05 .15
172 Dan Bouchard .08 .25
173 Dan Bouchard .08 .25
174 Randy Moller .05 .15
175 Wilf Paiement .05 .15
176 Normand Rochefort .05 .15
177 Marian Stastny .05 .15
178 Anton Stastny .05 .15
179 Dale Hunter .08 .25
181 Rick Middleton .08 .25
182 Rick Middleton .08 .25
183 Ray Bourque .30 .75
184 Pete Peeters .08 .25
185 Mike O'Connell .05 .15
186 Gord Kluzak .05 .15
187 Barry Pederson .05 .15
188 Mike Krushelnyski .05 .15
189 Tom Fergus .05 .15
190 Whalers Logo FOIL
200. Sabres Logo FOIL .20 .50
191 Sylvain Turgeon .05 .15
192 Sylvain Turgeon .05 .15
193 Mark Johnson .05 .15
194 Greg Malone .05 .15
195 Mike Zuke .05 .15
196 Ron Francis .40 1.00
197 Bob Crawford .05 .15
198 Greg Millen .08 .25
199 Ray Neufeld .05 .15
201 Gilbert Perreault .15 .40
202 Gilbert Perreault .15 .40
203 Phil Housley .20 .50
204 Phil Housley .20 .50
205 Tom Barrasso .30 .75
206 Tom Barrasso .30 .75
207 Larry Playfair .05 .15
208 Bob Sauve .08 .25
209 Dave Andreychuk .40 1.00
210 Dave Andreychuk .40 1.00
211 Mike Ramsey .05 .15
212 Mike Foligno .05 .15
213 Lindy Ruff .05 .15
214 Bill Hajt .05 .15
215 Craig Ramsay .05 .15
216 Ric Seiling .05 .15
217 Hart Trophy FOIL
224. Selke Trophy FOIL .15 .40
218 Vezina Trophy FOIL
223. Masterton Trophy FOIL .15 .40
219 Jennings Trophy FOIL
221. Art Ross Trophy FOIL .15 .40
220 Calder Trophy FOIL
225. Lady Byng Trophy FOIL .15 .40
222 Norris Trophy FOIL
283. Jets Logo FOIL .15 .40
226 Wayne Gretzky
227. Tom Barrasso 1.50 4.00
228 Tom Barrasso
229. Wayne Gretzky 1.50 4.00
230 Rod Langway
231. Brad Park .08 .25
232 Al Jensen
233. Pat Riggin .08 .25
234 Doug Jarvis
235. Mike Bossy .15 .40
236 Flames Logo FOIL
246. Oilers Logo FOIL .15 .40
237 Lanny McDonald .08 .25
238 Lanny McDonald .08 .25
239 Steve Tambellini .05 .15
240 Rejean Lemelin .08 .25
241 Doug Risebrough .05 .15
242 Hakan Loob .08 .25
243 Ed Beers .05 .15
244 Mike Eaves .05 .15
245 Kent Nilsson .05 .15
247 Glenn Anderson .08 .25
248 Glenn Anderson .08 .25
249 Jari Kurri .20 .50
250 Jari Kurri .20 .50
251 Paul Coffey .30 .75
252 Paul Coffey .30 .75
253 Kevin Lowe .15 .40
254 Lee Fogolin .05 .15
255 Wayne Gretzky 1.50 4.00
256 Wayne Gretzky 1.50 4.00
257 Randy Gregg .05 .15
258 Charlie Huddy .05 .15
259 Grant Fuhr .20 .50
260 Willy Lindstrom .05 .15
261 Mark Messier .50 1.25
262 Andy Moog .20 .50
263 Kings Logo FOIL
273. Canucks Logo FOIL .15 .40
264 Marcel Dionne .08 .25
265 Marcel Dionne .08 .25
266 Charlie Simmer .05 .15
267 Dave Taylor .05 .15
268 Jim Fox .05 .15
269 Bernie Nicholls .20 .50
270 Terry Ruskowski .05 .15
271 Brian Engblom .05 .15
272 Mark Hardy .05 .15
274 Tony Tanti .05 .15
275 Tony Tanti .05 .15
276 Rick Lanz .05 .15
277 Richard Brodeur .08 .25
278 Doug Halward .05 .15
279 Patrik Sundstrom .08 .25
280 Darcy Rota .05 .15
281 Stan Smyl .05 .15
282 Thomas Gradin .05 .15
284 Dale Hawerchuk .20 .50
285 Dale Hawerchuk .20 .50
286 Scott Arniel .05 .15
287 Dave Babych .05 .15
288 Laurie Boschman .05 .15
289 Paul MacLean .05 .15
290 Lucien DeBlois .05 .15
291 Randy Carlyle .05 .15
292 Thomas Steen .05 .15
NNO Sticker Album 2.00 5.00

1985-86 O-Pee-Chee Stickers

COMPLETE SET (163) 16.00 40.00
1 Stanley Cup Finals .08 .25
2 Stanley Cup Finals .02 .10
3 Stanley Cup Finals .02 .10
4 Stanley Cup Finals .02 .10
5 Wayne Gretzky 2.00 5.00
6 Rick Vaive .02 .10
7 Bill Derlago .02 .10
8 Rick St. Croix
136. Doug Soetaert .02 .10
9 Tim Bernhardt
137. Mark Hunter .02 .10
10 John Anderson
138. Bob Gainey .02 .10
11 Dan Daoust
139. Petr Svoboda .02 .10
12 Borje Salming .02 .10
13 Al Iafrate
143. Dan Bouchard .20 .50
14 Gary Nylund
144. Mario Marois .02 .10
15 Bob McGill
145. Randy Moller .02 .10
16 Jim Benning
146. Mario Gosselin .08 .25
17 Stewart Gavin
148. Normand Rochefort .02 .10
18 Greg Terrion
149. Alain Cote .02 .10
19 Peter Ihnacak
150. Paul Gillis .02 .10
20 Russ Courtnall
151. Dale Hunter .20 .50
21 Miroslav Frycer .02 .10
22 Denis Savard .08 .25
23 Steve Yzerman
152. Wilf Paiement .75 2.00
24 Curt Fraser
153. Brent Ashton .02 .10
25 Doug Wilson .02 .10
26 Ed Olczyk
154. Brad Maxwell .08 .25
27 Murray Bannerman
155. J.F. Sauve .02 .10
28 Steve Larmer
158. Charlie Simmer .08 .25
29 Troy Murray
159. Rick Middleton .02 .10
30 Steve Yzerman 1.25 3.00
31 Greg Stefan
161. Mike O'Connell .02 .10
32 Ron Duguay
162. Terry O'Reilly .02 .10
33 Reed Larson
163. Keith Crowder .02 .10
34 Ivan Boldirev
164. Tom Fergus .02 .10
35 Danny Gare
166. Greg Malone .02 .10
36 Darryl Sittler
167. Bob Crawford .02 .10
37 John Ogrodnick .02 .10
38 Keith Acton .02 .10
39 Dino Ciccarelli
168. Kevin Dineen .08 .25
40 Neal Broten
160. Miko Liut .00 .25
41 Brian Bellows .08 .25
42 Steve Payne
170. Joel Quenneville .02 .10
43 Gordie Roberts
171. Ray Neufeld .02 .10
44 Harold Snepsts
175. Craig Ramsay .02 .10
45 Tony McKegney
176. Bill Hajt .02 .10
46 Brian Sutter .02 .10
47 Joe Mullen
177. Dave Maloney .08 .25
48 Doug Gilmour
178. Brent Peterson .40 1.00
49 Tim Bothwell
180. Mike Ramsey .02 .10
50 Mark Johnson
181. Bob Sauve .02 .10
51 Greg Millen
182. Ric Seiling .02 .10
52 Doug Wickenheiser
183. Paul Cyr .02 .10
53 Bernie Federko .02 .10
54 Wayne Gretzky FOIL
197. Vezina Trophy FOIL 1.50 4.00
55 Tom Barrasso FOIL
203. Hart Trophy FOIL .08 .25
56 Paul Coffey FOIL
204. Calder Trophy FOIL .20 .50
57 Mel Bridgman .02 .10
58 Phil Russell
184. John Tucker .02 .10
59 Dave Lewis
185. Gilles Hamel .02 .10
60 Paul Gagne
186. Malcolm Davis .02 .10
61 Glenn Resch
187. Dave Andreychuk .08 .25
62 Aaron Broten
189. Tom Barrasso .08 .25
63 Dave Pichette
190. Bob Sauve .02 .10
64 Kirk Muller .40 1.00
65 Bryan Trottier .08 .25
66 Mike Bossy .08 .25
67 Bob Bourne
191. Paul Coffey .08 .25
68 Clark Gillies
192. Craig Ramsay .02 .10
69 Bob Nystrom
193. Pelle Lindbergh .75 2.00
70 Denis Potvin
198. Wayne Gretzky 1.50 4.00
71 Brent Sutter .02 .10
72 Duane Sutter
199. Mario Lemieux 3.00 8.00
73 Pat Flatley
200. Anders Hedberg .02 .10
74 Pat LaFontaine
201. Jari Kurri .40 1.00
75 Greg Gilbert
202. Wayne Gretzky 1.50 4.00
76 Billy Smith
209. Paul Reinhart .08 .25
77 Gordie Lane
210. Rejean Lemelin .02 .10
78 Tomas Jonsson
211. Al MacInnis .75 2.00
79 Kelly Hrudey
212. Jamie Macoun .30 .75
80 John Tonelli .02 .10
81 Reijo Ruotsalainen .02 .10
82 Barry Beck
213. Carey Wilson .08 .25
83 James Patrick
214. Ed Beers .08 .25
84 Mark Pavelich .02 .10
85 Pierre Larouche .02 .10
86 Mike Rogers
219. Kevin Lowe .08 .25
87 Glen Hanlon
220. Andy Moog .08 .25
88 John Vanbiesbrouck
221. Grant Fuhr 1.25 3.00
89 Dave Poulin .02 .10
90 Brian Propp
223. Mike Krushelnyski .02 .10
91 Pelle Lindbergh
224. Billy Carroll .75 2.00
92 Brad McCrimmon
225. Randy Gregg .02 .10
93 Mark Howe
226. Willy Lindstrom .08 .25
94 Peter Zezel
227. Glenn Anderson .08 .25
95 Murray Craven
228. Mark Messier .20 .50
96 Tim Kerr .02 .10
97 Mario Lemieux 6.00 15.00
98 Moe Mantha
229. Pat Hughes .02 .10
99 Doug Bodger
230. Kevin McClelland .02 .10
100 Warren Young .02 .10
101 John Chabot
233. Brian Engblom .02 .10
102 Doug Shedden
234. Mark Hardy .02 .10
103 Wayne Babych
236. Jim Fox .02 .10
104 Mike Bullard
237. Terry Ruskowski .02 .10
105 Rod Langway .02 .10
106 Pat Riggin
238. Dave Taylor .02 .10
107 Scott Stevens
239. Bob Janecyk .08 .25
108 Alan Haworth
241. Patrik Sundstrom .02 .10
109 Doug Jarvis
242. Al MacAdam .02 .10
110 Dave Christian
243. Doug Halward .02 .10
111 Mike Gartner
244. Peter McNab .08 .25
112 Bob Carpenter .02 .10
113 Rod Langway FOIL .05 .15
114 Tom Barrasso FOIL .08 .25
115 Ray Bourque FOIL .40 1.00
116 John Tonelli FOIL .05 .15
117 Brent Sutter FOIL .05 .15
118 Mike Bossy FOIL .20 .50
119 John Ogrodnick FOIL .05 .15
120 Wayne Gretzky FOIL 2.00 5.00
121 Jari Kurri FOIL .30 .75
122 Doug Wilson FOIL .05 .15
123 Andy Moog FOIL .20 .50
124 Paul Coffey FOIL .40 1.00
125 Chris Chelios .40 1.00
126 Steve Penney .02 .10
127 Chris Nilan
245. Tony Tanti .02 .10
128 Ron Flockhart
246. Moe Lemay .02 .10
129 Tom Kurvers
249. Dave Babych .02 .10
130 Craig Ludwig
250. Paul MacLean .02 .10
131 Mats Naslund .02 .10
132 Bobby Smith
252. Robert Picard .02 .10
133 Pierre Mondou
253. Thomas Steen .02 .10
134 Mario Tremblay
254. Laurie Boschman .02 .10
135 Guy Carbonneau
255. Doug Smail .08 .25
140 Larry Robinson .08 .25
141 Michel Goulet .08 .25
142 Bruce Bell .02 .10
147 Anton Stastny .02 .10
156 Peter Stastny .08 .25
157 Ray Bourque .20 .50
160 Pete Peeters .02 .10
165 Sylvain Turgeon .02 .10
172 Ron Francis .20 .50
173 Phil Housley .08 .25
174 Mike Foligno .02 .10
179 Tom Barrasso .08 .25
188 Gilbert Perreault .08 .25
194 Jennings Trophy FOIL
205. Masterton Trophy FOIL .02 .10
195 Norris Trophy FOIL
206. Lady Byng Trophy FOIL .02 .10
196 Selke Trophy FOIL
207. Art Ross Trophy FOIL .02 .10
208 Kent Nilsson .02 .10

215 Lanny McDonald .08 .25
216 Charlie Huddy .02 .10
217 Paul Coffey .20 .50
222 Wayne Gretzky 2.00 5.00
231 Jari Kurri .20 .50
232 Bernie Nicholls .08 .25
235 Marcel Dionne .08 .25
240 Thomas Gradin .02 .10
247 Stan Smyl .02 .10
248 Dale Hawerchuk .20 .50
251 Randy Carlyle .02 .10
NNO Sticker Album 2.00 5.00

1986-87 O-Pee-Chee Stickers

COMPLETE SET (167) 15.00 40.00
1 Stanley Cup Action .20 .50
2 Stanley Cup Action .08 .25
3 Stanley Cup Action .08 .25
4 Stanley Cup Action .08 .25
5 Patrick Roy FOIL 6.00 15.00
6 Chris Chelios
151. Darryl Sutter .15 .40
7 Guy Carbonneau
152. Bob Sauve .02 .05
8 Larry Robinson .02 .10
9 Mario Tremblay FOIL
154. Troy Murray .02 .05
10 Tom Kurvers
155. Al Secord .02 .05
11 Mats Naslund .02 .10
12 Bob Gainey .30 .75
13 Bobby Smith .02 .10
14 Craig Ludwig
156. Ed Olczyk .08 .25
15 Mike McPhee
157. Steve Larmer .08 .25
16 Doug Soetaert
159. Danny Gare .02 .05
17 Petr Svoboda
160. Petr Svoboda .02 .05
18 Kjell Dahlin .02 .10
19 Patrick Roy 4.00 10.00
20 Alain Cote
161. Steve Yzerman 1.00 2.50
21 Mario Gosselin
162. Petr Klima .02 .05
22 Michel Goulet .08 .25
23 J.F. Sauve
163. Kelly Kisio .02 .05
24 Paul Gillis
164. Doug Shedden .02 .05
25 Brent Ashton .02 .10
26 Peter Stastny .08 .25
27 Anton Stastny .02 .10
28 Gilbert Delorme
167. Brian Bellows .02 .05
29 Risto Siltanen
168. Scott Bjugstad .02 .05
30 Robert Picard
170. Dennis Maruk .02 .05
31 David Shaw
171. Dirk Graham .08 .25
32 Dale Hunter .02 .10
33 Clint Malarchuk .15 .40
34 Ray Bourque .20 .50
35 Rick Middleton
172. Curt Giles .02 .05
36 Charlie Simmer
173. Craig Hartsburg .02 .05
37 Keith Crowder .02 .10
38 Barry Pederson
175. Brian Sutter .02 .05
39 Reed Larson
176. Ron Flockhart .02 .05
40 Steve Kasper
177. Doug Gilmour .20 .50
41 Pat Riggin
178. Charlie Bourgeois .02 .05
42 Mike Foligno .02 .10
43 Gilbert Perreault
179. Rick Wamsley .02 .05
44 Mike Ramsey
180. Rob Ramage .02 .05
45 Tom Barrasso
186. Bob Froese .15 .40
46 Brian Engblom
187. Darren Jensen .02 .05
47 Phil Housley
188. Paul Coffey .20 .50
48 John Tucker
189. Troy Murray .02 .05
49 Dave Andreychuk .08 .25
50 Dave Babych .02 .10
51 Ron Francis
190. John Vanbiesbrouck .40 1.00
52 Mike Liut
191. Wayne Gretzky 1.50 4.00
53 Sylvain Turgeon .02 .10
54 John Anderson
192. Gary Suter .02 .05
55 Joel Quenneville
193. Bob Froese .02 .05
56 Kevin Dineen
194. Mike Bossy .08 .25
57 Ray Ferraro
195. Wayne Gretzky 1.50 4.00
58 Action Sticker .02 .10
59 Action Sticker .02 .10
60 Action Sticker .02 .10
61 Action Sticker .02 .10
62 Action Sticker .02 .10
63 Action Sticker .02 .10
64 Action Sticker .02 .10
65 Action Sticker .02 .10
66 Andy Moog
197. Dave Lewis .15 .40
67 Grant Fuhr
198. Joe Cirella .15 .40
68 Paul Coffey .20 .50
69 Charlie Huddy
199. Rich Preston .02 .05
70 Kevin Lowe
200. Mark Johnson .08 .25
71 Lee Fogolin .02 .10
72 Wayne Gretzky 2.00 5.00
73 Jari Kurri .10 .30
74 Mike Krushelnyski
201. Kirk Muller .08 .25
75 Mark Napier
202. Pat Verbeek .08 .25
76 Craig MacTavish
204. Bob Nystrom .02 .05
77 Kevin McClelland
205. Clark Gillies .02 .05
78 Glenn Anderson .10 .30
79 Mark Messier .30 .75
80 Lanny McDonald .10 .30
81 John Tonelli
207. Pat Flatley .02 .05
82 Joe Mullen
208. Bob Bourne .08 .25
83 Reggie Lemelin .08 .25
84 Jim Peplinski
212. Kelly Hrudey .20 .50
85 Jamie Macoun
213. Billy Smith .08 .25
86 Al MacInnis
214. Tomas Jonsson .20 .50
87 Dan Quinn
215. Ken Morrow .02 .05
88 Marcel Dionne .08 .25
89 Jim Fox
217. Mike Bossy .15 .40
90 Dave Taylor
219. Bob Brooke .02 .05
91 Bob Janecyk
222. Ron Greschner .02 .05
92 Jay Wells
223. Tom Laidlaw .02 .05
93 Bryan Erickson
224. Larry Melnyk .02 .05
94 Tiger Williams
225. Reijo Ruotsalainen .02 .05
95 Bernie Nicholls .08 .25
96 Stan Smyl .02 .10
97 Doug Halward
227. Willy Lindstrom .02 .05
98 Richard Brodeur
228. Mike Bullard .02 .05
99 Tony Tanti .02 .10
100 Brent Peterson
229. Roberto Romano .02 .05
101 Patrik Sundstrom
230. John Chabot .02 .05
102 Doug Lidster
231. Moe Mantha .02 .05
103 Petri Skriko
232. Doug Bodger .02 .05
104 Dale Hawerchuk .08 .25
105 Bill Derlago
234. Glenn Resch .08 .25
106 Ray Neufeld
235. Brad Marsh .02 .05
107 Randy Carlyle
237. Doug Crossman .02 .05
108 Paul MacLean
238. Ilkka Sinisalo .02 .05
109 Brian Mullen
242. Rich Sutter .02 .05
110 Thomas Steen
243. Ron Sutter .02 .05
111 Laurie Boschman .02 .10
112 Paul Coffey FOIL
126. Kjell Dahlin FOIL .30 .75
113 Michel Goulet
127. Pelle Eklund FOIL .20 .50
114 John Vanbiesbrouck FOIL
128. Jim Johnson FOIL 1.25 3.00
115 Wayne Gretzky
129. Petr Klima FOIL 2.50 6.00
116 Mark Howe FOIL
130. Joel Otto FOIL .15 .40
117 Mike Bossy FOIL
131. Mike Ridley FOIL .30 .75
118 Jari Kurri FOIL
132. Patrick Roy FOIL 4.00 10.00
119 Ray Bourque FOIL
133. David Shaw FOIL .30 .75
120 Mario Lemieux FOIL
134. Gary Suter FOIL 2.50 6.00
121 Grant Fuhr FOIL
135. Steve Thomas FOIL .20 .50
122 Mats Naslund FOIL
182. Bob Froese FOIL .15 .40
123 Larry Robinson
183. Wayne Gretzky FOIL 2.00 5.00
124 Chris Cichocki FOIL
184. Mark Howe FOIL .15 .40
125 Wendel Clark FOIL
185. Jari Kurri FOIL 1.00 2.50
136 Borje Salming
244. Murray Craven .02 .05
137 Gary Nylund
245. Peter Zezel .02 .05
138 Rick Vaive .02 .10
139 Don Edwards
249. Rod Langway .02 .05
140 Steve Thomas
250. Bob Carpenter .08 .25
141 Wendel Clark .50 1.25
142 Miroslav Frycer .02 .10
143 Tom Fergus .02 .10
144 Marian Stastny
252. Al Jensen .02 .05
145 Brad Maxwell
253. Craig Laughlin .02 .05
146 Dan Daoust
254. Scott Stevens .08 .25
147 Greg Terrion
255. Alan Haworth .02 .05
148 Al Iafrate .15 .40
149 Russ Courtnall .08 .25
150 Denis Savard .08 .25
153 Doug Wilson .02 .10
158 John Ogrodnick .02 .10
165 Greg Stefan .02 .10
166 Neal Broten .08 .25
169 Dino Ciccarelli .08 .25
174 Bernie Federko .02 .10
181 Mark Hunter .02 .10
196 Greg Adams .02 .10
203 Mel Bridgman .02 .10
206 Pat LaFontaine .30 .75
209 Denis Potvin .08 .25
210 Duane Sutter .02 .10
211 Brent Sutter .02 .10
216 Bryan Trottier .08 .25
217 Mike Bossy .15 .40
218 John Vanbiesbrouck .75 2.00
221 Mike Ridley .08 .25
226 Terry Ruskowski .02 .10
233 Mario Lemieux 5.00 12.00
236 Bob Froese .02 .10
239 Brian Propp .02 .10
240 Tim Kerr .02 .10
241 Dave Poulin .40 1.00
246 Mark Howe .02 .10
247 Brad McCrimmon .02 .10
248 Dave Christian .02 .10
251 Mike Gartner .08 .25
NNO Sticker Album 1.50 4.00

1987-88 O-Pee-Chee Stickers

COMPLETE SET (168) 12.00 30.00
1 Ron Hextall MVP .08 .25
2 Stanley Cup Action .08 .25
3 Stanley Cup Action .08 .25
4 Stanley Cup Action .08 .25
5 Stanley Cup Action .08 .25
6 Mats Naslund .08 .25
7 Guy Carbonneau
146. Steve Dykstra .08 .25
8 Gaston Gingras
147. Dave Andreychuk .08 .25
9 Chris Chelios .20 .50
10 Bobby Smith .08 .25
11 Rick Green
149. Mike Ramsey .02 .10
12 Bob Gainey
150. Mike Foligno .08 .25
13 Patrick Roy 3.00 8.00
14 Kjell Dahlin
153. Greg Terrion .02 .10
15 Chris Nilan
154. Steve Thomas .08 .25
16 Larry Robinson .08 .25
17 Ryan Walter
157. Rick Lanz .02 .10
18 Petr Svoboda
158. Miroslav Frycer .02 .10
19 Claude Lemieux .60 1.50
20 Rob Ramage
160. Al Iafrate .08 .25
21 Mark Hunter
161. Gary Leeman .02 .10
22 Rick Wamsley
163. Todd Gill .02 .10
23 Greg Paslawski
164. Ken Wregget .10 .30
24 Bernie Federko .08 .25
25 Ron Flockhart
166. Craig Simpson .08 .25
26 Tim Bothwell
167. Terry Ruskowski .02 .10
27 Doug Gilmour .20 .50
28 Kelly Kisio
168. Gilles Meloche .02 .10
29 Don Maloney
169. John Chabot .02 .10
30 James Patrick
171. Moe Mantha .02 .10
31 Willie Huber
172. Jim Johnson .02 .10
32 Walt Poddubny .02 .10
33 John Vanbiesbrouck
178. Ray Bourque .20 .50
34 Marcel Dionne
179. Dave Poulin .08 .25
35 Tomas Sandstrom .08 .25
36 Joe Mullen .08 .25
37 Mike Bullard
180. Wayne Gretzky Hart Tr. 1.25 3.00
38 Neil Sheehy
181. Wayne Gretzky Ross Tr. 1.25 3.00
39 Paul Reinhart .02 .10
40 Al MacInnis .08 .25
41 Mike Vernon
182. Ron Hextall .20 .50
42 Joel Otto
183. Doug Jarvis .02 .10
43 Lanny McDonald .08 .25
44 Hakan Loob
184. Brian Hayward .08 .25
45 Carey Wilson
185. Patrick Roy 1.25 3.00
46 Jim Peplinski .02 .10
47 John Tonelli
186. Joe Mullen .08 .25
48 Jamie Macoun
187. Luc Robitaille .30 .75
49 Gary Suter .08 .25
50 Dennis Maruk
189. Richard Brodeur .02 .10
51 Don Beaupre
190. Dave Richter .08 .25
52 Neal Broten
193. Rich Sutter .08 .25
53 Brian Bellows
194. Jim Sandlak .08 .25
54 Craig Hartsburg .02 .10
55 Gordie Roberts
196. Michel Petit .02 .10
56 Steve Payne
197. Jim Benning .02 .10
57 Dino Ciccarelli .08 .25
58 Pat Verbeek
199. Brent Peterson .02 .10
59 Doug Sulliman
200. Garth Butcher .08 .25
60 Bruce Driver
202. Kevin Dineen .02 .10
61 Joe Cirella
203. Sylvain Turgeon .02 .10
62 Aaron Broten .02 .10
63 Alain Chevrier
204. John Anderson .02 .10
64 Mark Johnson
205. Ulf Samuelsson .08 .25
65 Kirk Muller .08 .25
66A Face-Off Action
(Jim Sandlak) .02 .10
66B Face-Off Action
(Steve Kasper) .02 .10
67 Action Sticker .02 .10
68 Action Sticker .02 .10
69 Murray Craven IA .02 .10
70 Bruins Action .02 .10
71 Islanders Action .02 .10
72 Action Sticker .02 .10
73 Action Sticker .02 .10
74 Al Secord
207. Doug Jarvis .02 .10
75 Bob Sauve
208. Dave Babych .02 .10
76 Ed Olczyk
210. Jimmy Carson .08 .25
77 Doug Wilson
211. Larry Playfair .02 .10
78 Denis Savard .08 .25
79 Troy Murray
212. Jay Wells .02 .10
80 Gary Nylund
213. Rollie Melanson .02 .10
81 Steve Larmer .08 .25
82 Jari Kurri .08 .25
83 Esa Tikkanen
215. Dave Taylor .20 .50
84 Kevin Lowe
216. Jim Fox .02 .10
85 Grant Fuhr .08 .25
86 Wayne Gretzky 1.50 4.00
87 Charlie Huddy
219. Jason Lafreniere .02 .10
88 Kent Nilsson
220. Mike Hough .02 .10
89 Paul Coffey .20 .50
90 Mike Krushelnyski
223. David Shaw .02 .10
91 Craig MacTavish
224. Bill Derlago .02 .10
92 Mark Messier .40 1.00
93 Andy Moog
226. Doug Shedden .08 .25
94 Randy Gregg
227. Basil McRae .02 .10
95 Glenn Anderson .08 .25
96 Peter Zezel
229. Randy Moller .08 .25
97 Brian Propp
230. Robert Picard .08 .25
98 Dave Poulin
232. Larry Murphy .08 .25
99 Brad McCrimmon
233. Scott Stevens .08 .25
100 Mark Howe .08 .25
101 Ron Hextall
234. Mike Ridley .20 .50
102 Ron Sutter
235. Dave Christian .02 .10
103 Tim Kerr .02 .10
104 Petr Klima
237. Bob Gould .08 .25
105 Adam Oates
238. Bob Mason .60 1.50
106 Gerard Gallant
240. Bryan Trottier .08 .25
107 Mike O'Connell
241. Brent Sutter .02 .10
108 Brent Ashton .02 .10
109 Glen Hanlon
242. Kelly Hrudey .08 .25
110 Harold Snepsts
243. Pat LaFontaine .20 .50
111 Steve Yzerman .40 1.00
112 Mark Howe
124. Brian Benning .08 .25
113 Michel Goulet
125. Shawn Burr .08 .25
114 Ron Hextall
126. Jimmy Carson .20 .50
115 Wayne Gretzky
127. Shayne Corson 1.25 3.00
116 Ray Bourque
128. Vincent Damphousse .20 .50
117 Jari Kurri
129. Ron Hextall .20 .50
118 Dino Ciccarelli
130. Jason Lafreniere .08 .25
119 Larry Murphy
131. Ken Leiter .08 .25
120 Mario Lemieux
132. Allen Pedersen 1.50 4.00
121 Mike Liut
133. Luc Robitaille .30 .75
122 Luc Robitaille
134. Christian Ruuttu .40 1.00
123 Al MacInnis
135. Jim Sandlak .08 .25
136 Keith Crowder
245. Pat Flatley .02 .10
137 Charlie Simmer
246. Ken Morrow .02 .10
138 Rick Middleton
248. Randy Carlyle .02 .10
139 Doug Keans
249. Daniel Berthiaume .08 .25
140 Ray Bourque .08 .25
141 Tom McCarthy
250. Mario Marois .02 .10
142 Reed Larson
251. Dave Ellett .02 .10
143 Cam Neely .20 .50
144 Christian Ruuttu
253. Gilles Hamel .02 .10
145 John Tucker
254. Doug Smail .02 .10
148 Tom Barrasso .08 .25
151 Phil Housley .08 .25
152 Wendel Clark .20 .50
155 Rick Vaive .02 .10
156 Russ Courtnall .08 .25
159 Tom Fergus .02 .10
162 Allan Bester .08 .25
165 Borje Salming .08 .25
170 Mario Lemieux 1.25 3.00
173 Dan Quinn .02 .10
174 Wayne Gretzky
176. Mark Howe 1.25 3.00
175 Brian Hayward
177. Luc Robitaille .30 .75
188 Barry Pederson .02 .10
191 Doug Lidster .02 .10
192 Petri Skriko .02 .10
195 Tony Tanti .02 .10
198 Stan Smyl .02 .10
201 Patrik Sundstrom .02 .10
206 Ron Francis .20 .50
209 Mike Liut .08 .25
214 Bernie Nicholls .08 .25
217 Luc Robitaille 1.25 3.00
218 John Ogrodnick .02 .10
221 Paul Gillis .02 .10
222 Peter Stastny .08 .25
225 Michel Goulet .08 .25
228 Anton Stastny .02 .10
231 Mario Gosselin .08 .25
236 Rod Langway .08 .25
239 Mike Gartner .08 .25
244 Mike Bossy .08 .25
247 Denis Potvin .08 .25
252 Paul MacLean .02 .10
255 Dale Hawerchuk .08 .25
NNO Sticker Album 1.50 4.00

1988-89 O-Pee-Chee Stickers

COMPLETE SET (182) 8.00 20.00
1 Wayne Gretzky MVP 1.50 4.00
2 Oilers/Bruins Action .02 .10
3 Oilers/Bruins Action .08 .25
4 Oilers/Bruins Action .08 .25
5 Oilers/Bruins Action .02 .10
6 Doug Wilson
135. Darren Pang .08 .25
7 Dirk Graham
136. Kirk McLean .08 .25
8 Darren Pang
137. Doug Smail .02 .10
9 Rick Vaive
138. Thomas Steen .02 .10
10 Troy Murray
139. Laurie Boschman .02 .10
11 Brian Noonan
140. Iain Duncan
Kirk McLean (back) .02 .10
12 Steve Larmer .08 .25
13 Denis Savard .08 .25
14 Mark Hunter
141. Ray Neufeld .02 .10
15 Brian Sutter
142. Mario Marois .02 .10
16 Brett Hull
145. Jim Kyte .75 2.00
17 Tony McKegney
146. Pokey Reddick .02 .10
18 Brian Benning
151. Roland Melanson
Darren Pang (back) .02 .10
19 Tony Hrkac
152. Steve Duchesne .08 .25
20 Doug Gilmour .20 .50
21 Bernie Federko .02 .10
22 Cam Neely .20 .50
23 Ray Bourque
Doug Brown (back) .20 .50
24 Rejean Lemelin
153. Bob Carpenter .02 .10
25 Gord Kluzak
154. Jim Fox .02 .10
26 Rick Middleton
155. Dave Taylor .08 .25
27 Steve Kasper
156. Bernie Nicholls .08 .25
28 Bob Sweeney
168. Mark Osborne .02 .10
29 Randy Burridge
169. Dan Daoust .02 .10
30 Bruins/Whalers Action .02 .10
31 Canadiens/Bruins
Action .02 .10
32 Canadiens/Bruins
Action .02 .10
33 Blues/Red Wings
Action .02 .10
34 Canadiens/Bruins
Action .02 .10
35 Canadiens/Bruins
Action .02 .10
36 Canadiens/Bruins
Action
Tony Hrkac (back) .02 .10
37 Canadiens/Bruins
Action .02 .10
38 Canadiens/Bruins
Action .02 .10
39 Larry Robinson
170. Tom Fergus .08 .25
40 Ryan Walter
171. Vincent Damphousse .08 .25
41 Guy Carbonneau
172. Wendel Clark .08 .25
42 Bob Gainey
173. Luke Richardson .08 .25
43 Claude Lemieux
176. Rick Lanz .20 .50
44 Petr Svoboda
177. Ken Wregget .08 .25
45 Patrick Roy 1.25 3.00
46 Bobby Smith .08 .25
47 Mike McPhee
182. Normand Rochefort .02 .10
48 Craig Ludwig
183. Lane Lambert .02 .10
49 Stephane Richer .08 .25
50 Mats Naslund .02 .10
51 Chris Chelios .20 .50
52 Brian Hayward .08 .25
53 Larry Melnyk
184. Tommy Albelin
David Archibald (back) .02 .10
54 Garth Butcher
185. Jason Lafreniere .02 .10
55 Kirk McLean
186. Alain Cote .08 .25
56 Doug Wickenheiser
187. Gaetan Duchesne .02 .10
57 Rich Sutter
190. Jeff Jackson .02 .10
58 Jim Benning
191. Mike Eagles .02 .10
59 Tony Tanti .02 .10
60 Stan Smyl .02 .10
61 David Saunders
196. Don Beaupre .08 .25
62 Steve Tambellini
197. Brian MacLellan .02 .10
63 Doug Lidster
Rob Brown (back) .02 .10
64 Petri Skriko .02 .10
65 Barry Pederson .02 .10
66 Greg Adams .02 .10
67 Mike Gartner .08 .25
68 Scott Stevens
Bob Sweeney (back) .08 .25
69 Rod Langway
198. Brian Lawton
Pierre Turgeon (back) .02 .10
70 Dave Christian
199. Craig Hartsburg .02 .10
71 Larry Murphy
200. Moe Mantha .02 .10
72 Clint Malarchuk
201. Neal Broten .08 .25
73 Dale Hunter
204. Mario Lemieux .60 1.50
74 Mike Ridley
205. Joe Nieuwendyk
Jeff Sharples (back) .08 .25
75 Kirk Muller .08 .25
76 Aaron Broten .02 .10
77 Bruce Driver
206. Brad McCrimmon .02 .10
78 John MacLean
207. Pete Peeters .08 .25
79 Joe Cirella
208. Norris Trophy Winner
Ray Bourque .08 .25
80 Doug Brown
209. Selke Trophy Winner
Guy Carbonneau .02 .10
81 Pat Verbeek
210. Hart Trophy Winner
Mario Lemieux
Brett Hull (back) 1.50 4.00
82 Sean Burke
211. Ross Trophy Winner
Mario Lemiuex .40 1.00
83 Joel Otto
212. Vezina Trophy Winner
Grant Fuhr .08 .25
84 Rob Ramage
213. Masterton Trophy Winner
Bob Bourne .02 .10
85 Lanny McDonald
215. Lady Byng Trophy Win
Mats Naslund
Glen Wesley (back) .08 .25
86 Mike Vernon
216. Calder Trophy Winner
Joe Nieuwendyk .20 .50
87 John Tonelli
217. Craig MacTavish .02 .10
88 Jim Peplinski
218. Chris Joseph .02 .10
89 Gary Suter .08 .25
90 Joe Nieuwendyk
Craig Janney (back) .40 1.00
91 Ric Nattress
219. Kevin Lowe .02 .10
92 Al MacInnis
220. Esa Tikkanen .20 .50
93 Mike Bullard .02 .10
94 Hakan Loob .02 .10
95 Joe Mullen .08 .25
96 Brad McCrimmon .02 .10
97 Brian Propp
221. Charlie Huddy .02 .10
98 Murray Craven
222. Geoff Courtnall .08 .25
99 Rick Tocchet
225. Steve Smith .20 .50
100 Doug Crossman
226. Mike Krushelnyski .02 .10
101 Brad Marsh
233. Paul Coffee .08 .25
102 Peter Zezel
234. Doug Bodger .02 .10
103 Ron Hextall .08 .25
104 Mark Howe .08 .25
105 Brent Sutter
235. Dave Hunter .02 .10
106 Alan Kerr
236. Dan Quinn .02 .10
107 Randy Wood
237. Rob Brown .02 .10
108 Mikko Makela
238. Gilles Meloche
Iain Duncan (back) .02 .10
109 Kelly Hrudey
241. John Vanbiesbrouck .20 .50
110 Steve Konroyd
242. Tomas Sandstrom .02 .10
111 Pat LaFontaine .20 .50
112 Bryan Trottier .08 .25
113 Gary Suter
243. David Shaw .02 .10
114 Luc Robitaille
244. Marcel Dionne .20 .50
115 Patrick Roy
245. Chris Nilan .60 1.50
116 Mario Lemieux
246. James Patrick .60 1.50
117 Ray Bourque
247. Bob Probert .20 .50
118 Hakan Loob
248. Mike O'Connell .02 .10
119 Mike Bullard
249. Jeff Sharples .02 .10
120 Brad McCrimmon
250. Brent Ashton .02 .10
121 Wayne Gretzky
251. Petr Klima .75 2.00
122 Grant Fuhr
252. Greg Stefan .08 .25
123 Craig Simpson
255. Phil Housley
Glenn Healy (back) .08 .25
124 Mark Howe
256. Christian Ruuttu .02 .10
125 Joe Nieuwendyk
257. Mike Foligno .08 .25
126 Ray Sheppard
258. Scott Arniel
Ulf Dahlen (back) .08 .25
127 Brett Hull
259. Tom Barrasso .75 2.00
128 Ulf Dahlen
260. Mike Ramsey .08 .25
129 Tony Hrkac
265. Ulf Samuelsson .02 .10
130 Bob Sweeney
266. Carey Wilson .02 .10
131 Rob Brown
267. Dave Babych .08 .25
132 Iain Duncan
268. Ray Ferraro .02 .10
133 Pierre Turgeon
269. Kevin Dineen .40 1.00
134 Calle Johansson
270. John Anderson
Joe Nieuwendyk (back) .02 .10
143 Dale Hawerchuk .08 .25
144 Paul MacLean .02 .10
147 Andrew McBain
Brian Noonan (back) .02 .10
148 Randy Carlyle .02 .10
149 Daniel Berthiaume .08 .25
150 Dave Ellett .02 .10
157 Luc Robitaille .30 .75
158 Jimmy Carson
Sean Burke (back) .20 .50
159 Canadiens/Bruins
Action .02 .10
160 Devils/Nordiques
Action .02 .10
161 Devils/Nordiques
Action
Ray Sheppard (back) .02 .10
162 Devils/North Stars
Action .02 .10
163 Oilers/Flames Action .02 .10
164 Oilers/Flames Action .02 .10
165 Oilers/Flames Action .02 .10
166 Oilers/Flames Action .02 .10
167 Canadiens/Bruins
Action .02 .10
174 Borje Salming .08 .25
175 Russ Courtnall .08 .25
178 Gary Leeman .02 .10
179 Al Secord .02 .10
180 Al Iafrate .08 .25
181 Ed Olczyk .02 .10
188 Michel Goulet .08 .25
189 Peter Stastny
Brian Leetch (back) .08 .25
192 Jeff Brown .20 .50
193 Mario Gosselin .08 .25
194 Anton Stastny .02 .10
195 Alan Haworth .02 .10
202 Dino Ciccarelli
Randy Wood (back) .08 .25
203 Brian Bellows .02 .10
223 Grant Fuhr .08 .25
224 Wayne Gretzky 1.50 4.00
227 Jari Kurri .08 .25
228 Craig Simpson .02 .10
229 Glenn Anderson .08 .25
230 Mark Messier .20 .50
231 Randy Cunneyworth .02 .10
232 Mario Lemieux 1.25 3.00
239 Kelly Kisio .02 .10
240 Walt Poddubny .02 .10
253 Steve Yzerman .40 1.00
254 Gerard Gallant
Calle Johansson (back) .08 .25
261 Dave Andreychuk .08 .25
262 Ray Sheppard .08 .25
263 Mike Liut .08 .25
264 Ron Francis .20 .50
NNO Sticker Album 1.25 3.00
214 Brian Hayward
Patrick Roy .60 1.50

1988-89 O-Pee-Chee Sticker Back Cards

COMPLETE SET (106) 3.00 8.00
1 David Archibald .02 .10
2 Doug Brown .02 .10
3 Rob Brown .02 .10
4 Sean Burke .07 .20
5 Ulf Dahlen .07 .20
6 Iain Duncan .02 .10
7 Glenn Healy .02 .10
8 Tony Hrkac .02 .10
9 Brett Hull 1.00 2.50
10 Craig Janney .07 .20
11 Calle Johansson .07 .20
12 Brian Leetch .40 1.00
13 Kirk McLean .10 .30
14 Joe Nieuwendyk .40 1.00
15 Brian Noonan .02 .10
16 Darren Pang .02 .10
17 Jeff Sharples .02 .10
18 Ray Sheppard .02 .10
19 Bob Sweeney .02 .10
20 Pierre Turgeon .20 .50
21 Glen Wesley .02 .10
22 Randy Wood .02 .10
A1 Answer 1 .01 .05
A2 Answer 2 .01 .05
A3 Answer 3 .01 .05
A4 Answer 4 .01 .05
A5 Answer 5 .01 .05
A6 Answer 6 .01 .05
A7 Answer 7 .01 .05
A8 Answer 8 .01 .05
A9 Answer 9 .01 .05
Q1 Question 1 .01 .05
Q2 Question 2 .01 .05
Q3 Question 3 .01 .05
Q4 Question 4 .01 .05
Q5 Question 5 .01 .05
Q6 Question 6 .01 .05
Q7 Question 7 .01 .05

Q8 Question 8 .01 .05
Q9 Question 9 .01 .05
A10 Answer 10 .01 .05
A11 Answer 11 .01 .05
A12 Answer 12 .01 .05
A13 Answer 13 .01 .05
A14 Answer 14 .01 .05
A15 Answer 15 .01 .05
A16 Answer 16 .01 .05
A17 Answer 17 .01 .05
A18 Answer 18 .01 .05
A19 Answer 19 .01 .05
A20 Answer 20 .01 .05
A21 Answer 21 .01 .05
A22 Answer 22 .01 .05
A23 Answer 23 .01 .05
A24 Answer 24 .01 .05
A25 Answer 25 .01 .05
A26 Answer 26 .01 .05
A27 Answer 27 .01 .05
A28 Answer 28 .01 .05
A29 Answer 29 .01 .05
A30 Answer 30 .01 .05
A31 Answer 31 .01 .05
A32 Answer 32 .01 .05
A33 Answer 33 .01 .05
A34 Answer 34 .01 .05
A35 Answer 35 .01 .05
A36 Answer 36 .01 .05
A37 Answer 37 .01 .05
A38 Answer 38 .01 .05
A39 Answer 39 .01 .05
A40 Answer 40 .01 .05
A41 Answer 41 .01 .05
A42 Answer 42 .01 .05
Q10 Question 10 .01 .05
Q11 Question 11 .01 .05
Q12 Question 12 .01 .05
Q13 Question 13 .01 .05
Q14 Question 14 .01 .05
Q15 Question 15 .01 .05
Q16 Question 16 .01 .05
Q17 Question 17 .01 .05
Q18 Question 18 .01 .05
Q19 Question 19 .01 .05
Q20 Question 20 .01 .05
Q21 Question 21 .01 .05
Q22 Question 22 .01 .05
Q23 Question 23 .01 .05
Q24 Question 24 .01 .05
Q25 Question 25 .01 .05
Q26 Question 26 .01 .05
Q27 Question 27 .01 .05
Q28 Question 28 .01 .05
Q29 Question 29 .01 .05
Q30 Question 30 .01 .05
Q31 Question 31 .01 .05
Q32 Question 32 .01 .05
Q33 Question 33 .01 .05
Q34 Question 34 .01 .05
Q35 Question 35 .01 .05
Q36 Question 36 .01 .05
Q37 Question 37 .01 .05
Q38 Question 38 .01 .05
Q39 Question 39 .01 .05
Q40 Question 40 .01 .05
Q41 Question 41 .01 .05
Q42 Question 42 .01 .05

1989-90 O-Pee-Chee Stickers

COMPLETE SET (182) 8.00 20.00
1 Flames/Canadiens action UL .02 .10
2 Flames/Canadiens action UR .08 .25
3 Flames/Canadiens action LL .02 .10
4 Flames/Canadiens action LR .02 .10
5 Al MacInnis Conn Smythe Trophy Win .08 .25
6 Flames/Canadiens action UL .02 .10
7 Flames/Canadiens action UR .02 .10
8 Flames/Canadiens action LL .02 .10
9 Flames/Canadiens action LR .02 .10
10 Darren Pang
150. Steve Duchesne
Tony Granato FS (back) .08 .25
11 Troy Murray
151. Dave Taylor .02 .10
12 Dirk Graham
152. Steve Kasper .02 .10
13 Dave Manson
153. Mike Krushelnyski .02 .10
14 Doug Wilson
156. Chris Chelios
Patrick Roy AS (back) .60 1.50
15 Steve Thomas
157. Gerard Gallant .02 .10
16 Denis Savard .08 .25
17 Steve Larmer .08 .25
18 Paul MacLean
158. Mario Lemieux .40 1.00
19 Paul Cavallini
159. Al MacInnis .02 .10
20 Cliff Ronning
160. Joe Mullen .08 .25
21 Gaston Gingras
161. Patrick Roy
Al MacInnis AS (back) .40 1.00
22 Brett Hull .40 1.00
23 Peter Zezel .02 .10
24 Brian Benning
162. Ray Bourque .08 .25
25 Tony Hrkac
163. Rob Brown .02 .10
26 Ken Linseman
164. Geoff Courtnall .02 .10
27 Glen Wesley
165. Steve Duchesne .02 .10
28 Randy Burridge
166. Wayne Gretzky .60 1.50
29 Craig Janney
167. Mike Vernon .08 .25
30 Andy Moog
170. David Reid .08 .25
31 Bob Joyce
171. Craig Laughlin .02 .10
32 Ray Bourque
Gerard Gallant AS (back) .20 .50
33 Cam Neely .20 .50
34 Sean Burke
174. Mark Osborne .02 .10
35 Pat Elynuik
175. Brad Marsh
Craig Janney FS (back) .20 .50
36 Tony Granato
176. Daniel Marois .02 .10
37 Benoit Hogue
177. Dan Daoust .08 .25
38 Craig Janney
180. Chris Kotsopoulos .08 .25
39 Brian Leetch
181. Derek Laxdal .20 .50
40 Trevor Linden
184. Jeff Jackson .20 .50
41 Joe Sakic
185. Mario Marois
Joe Sakic FS (back) 1.00 2.50
42 Peter Sidorkiewicz
188. Bob Mason .02 .10
43 Dave Volek
189. Marc Fortier .02 .10
44 Scott Young
190. Robert Picard .02 .10
45 Zarley Zalapski
191. Steven Finn .02 .10
46 Mats Naslund .02 .10
47 Bobby Smith
Wayne Gretzky AS (back) .75 2.00
48 Guy Carbonneau
194. Gaetan Duchesne .02 .10
49 Shayne Corson
195. Randy Moller .02 .10
50 Brian Hayward .02 .10
51 Stephane Richer .02 .10
52 Claude Lemieux
196. Mike Gartner .08 .25
53 Russ Courtnall
197. Jon Casey .08 .25
54 Petr Svoboda
198. Marc Habscheid
Chris Chelios AS (back) .20 .50
55 Larry Robinson
199. Larry Murphy
Mario Lemieux AS (back) .60 1.50
56 Chris Chelios .20 .50
57 Patrick Roy .60 1.50
58 Bob Gainey
200. Brian Bellows .02 .10
59 Mike McPhee
201. Dave Archibald .02 .10
60 Barry Pederson
Jiri Hrdina AS (back) .02 .10
61 Trevor Linden
Joe Mullen AS (back) .30 .75
62 Rich Sutter
204. Vezina Trophy .02 .10
63 Brian Bradley
205. Jennings Trophy
Bob Essensa FS (back) .08 .25
64 Kirk McLean
John Cullen FS (back) .08 .25
65 Paul Reinhart
Steve Duchesne AS (back) .08 .25
66 Robert Nordmark
206. Selke Trophy
Pat Elynuik FS (back) .02 .10
67 Steve Bozek
207. Masterton Trophy
Greg Hawgood FS (back) .02 .10
68 Stan Smyl
208. Mario Lemieux .40 1.00
69 Doug Lidster
209. Wayne Gretzky .01 1.50
70 Petri Skriko .02 .10
71 Tony Tanti .02 .10
72 Garth Butcher
210. Patrick Roy
Ray Bourque AS (back) .40 1.00
73 Larry Melnyk
212. Chris Chelios .08 .25
74 Kelly Miller
213. Guy Carbonneau .02 .10
75 Dino Ciccarelli
214. Joe Mullen .02 .10
76 Scott Stevens
215. Brian Leetch
Mike Vernon AS (back) .20 .50
77 Rod Langway
216. Tim Kerr
Benoit Hogue FS (back) .08 .25
78 Dave Christian
219. Esa Tikkanen .08 .25
79 Stephen Leach
220. Charlie Huddy .02 .10
80 Geoff Courtnall .08 .25
81 Mike Ridley .02 .10
82 Patrik Sundstrom
223. Steve Smith .02 .10
83 Kirk Muller
224. Kevin Lowe .02 .10
84 Tom Kurvers
225. Chris Joseph .02 .10
85 Walt Poddubny
226. Craig MacTavish .02 .10
86 Sean Burke .08 .25
87 John MacLean .02 .10
88 Aaron Broten (229)
Gordon Murphy FS .02 .10
89 Brendan Shanahan
230. Bill Ranford .40 1.00
90 Joe Mullen .08 .25
91 Brad McCrimmon
Brian Leetch FS (back) .40 1.00
92 Lanny McDonald
231. John Cullen .08 .25
93 Rick Wamsley
232. Zarley Zalapski .02 .10
94 Mike Vernon .08 .25
95 Al MacInnis .08 .25
96 Joel Otto
233. Bob Errey
Scott Young FS (back) .02 .10
97 Jiri Hrdina
234. Dan Quinn .02 .10
98 Gary Roberts
235. Tom Barrasso .08 .25
99 Jim Peplinski
236. Rob Brown .02 .10
100 Gary Suter .02 .10
101 Joe Nieuwendyk .08 .25
102 Colin Patterson
239. Carey Wilson
Dan Marois FS (back) .02 .10
103 Doug Gilmour
240. Brian Leetch .20 .50
104 Mike Bullard
241. Tony Granato .02 .10
105 Pelle Eklund
242. James Patrick .02 .10
106 Brian Propp
245. Guy Lafleur .08 .25
107 Ron Sutter
246. John Vanbiesbrouck
Geoff Courtnall AS (back) .20 .50
108 Rick Tocchet
247. Bernie Federko .08 .25
109 Mark Howe
248. Greg Stefan .02 .10
110 Tim Kerr .02 .10
111 Ron Hextall .08 .25
112 Mikko Makela
249. Mike O'Connell
Trevor Linden AS (back) .30 .75
113 Dave Volek
250. Dave Barr .08 .25
114 Gary Nylund
251. Lee Norwood .02 .10
115 Brent Sutter
252. Shawn Burr .02 .10
116 Derek King
255. Christian Ruuttu .08 .25
117 Gerald Diduck
256. Rick Vaive
Rob Brown AS (back) .02 .10
118 Bryan Trottier
Peter Sidorkiewicz FS (back) .08 .25
119 Pat LaFontaine .20 .50
120 Blues/Bruins action L .02 .10
121 Blues/Bruins action R .02 .10
122 Bruins/Rangers action L .02 .10
123 Bruins/Rangers action R .02 .10
124 Blackhawks action .02 .10
125 Bruins/Canadiens action
(Ray Bourque) .08 .25
126 Devils/Bruins action .02 .10
127 Flames/Devils action .02 .10
128 Canadiens/Flyers action .02 .10
129 Flyers/Oilers action .02 .10
130 Canucks/Bruins action L .02 .10
131 Canucks/Bruins action R .02 .10
132 North Stars/Bruins action L .02 .10
133 North Stars/Bruins action R .02 .10
134 Dale Hawerchuk .08 .25
135 Andrew McBain .02 .10
136 Iain Duncan
257. Doug Bodger .02 .10
137 Eldon Reddick
258. Dave Andreychuk .02 .10
138 Brent Ashton .02 .10
139 Dave Ellett .02 .10
140 Jim Kyte
259. Ray Sheppard .02 .10
141 Doug Smail
260. Mike Foligno .02 .10
142 Pat Elynuik
263. Ray Ferraro .02 .10
143 Randy Carlyle
264. Scott Young .02 .10
144 Thomas Steen .02 .10
145 Hannu Jarvenpaa .02 .10
146 Peter Taglianetti
265. Dave Babych
Vincent Riendeau FS (back) .02 .10
147 Laurie Boschman
266. Paul MacDermid .02 .10
148 Luc Robitaille
267. Mike Liut .20 .50
149 Kelly Hrudey
268. Dave Tippett .02 .10
154 Wayne Gretzky .75 2.00
155 Bernie Nicholls .02 .10
168 Gary Leeman .02 .10
169 Allan Bester .02 .10
172 Ed Olczyk .02 .10
173 Tom Fergus .02 .10
178 Al Iafrate .08 .25
179 Vincent Damphousse .08 .25
182 Peter Stastny .08 .25
183 Paul Gillis .02 .10
186 Michel Goulet .08 .25
187 Joe Sakic
Dave Volek FS (back) 1.50 4.00
192 Iiro Jarvi .02 .10
193 Jeff Brown .08 .25
202 Neal Broten .02 .10
203 Dave Gagner
Sean Burke FS (back) .20 .50
211 Patrick Roy
Brian Hayward
(Jennings Trophy Winners) .30 .75
217 Craig Simpson .02 .10
218 Glenn Anderson .02 .10
221 Jari Kurri .08 .25
222 Jimmy Carson .02 .10
227 Mark Messier .20 .50
228 Grant Fuhr .08 .25
237 Paul Coffey .20 .50
238 Mario Lemieux .60 1.50
243 Brian Mullen .02 .10
244 Tomas Sandstrom .02 .10
253 Gerard Gallant .02 .10
254 Steve Yzerman .30 .75
261 Phil Housley .08 .25
262 Pierre Turgeon .20 .50
269 Ron Francis .20 .50
270 Kevin Dineen .02 .10
NNO Sticker Album .75 2.00

2014-15 O-Pee-Chee Update

*RED VETS: 2.5X TO 6X BASIC INSERTS
*RED ROOK: 2.5X TO 6X BASIC INSERTS
*RETRO VETS: .6X TO 1.5X BASIC INSERTS
*RETRO ROOK: .5X TO 1.2X BASIC INSERTS
U1 Jason Spezza .75 2.00
U2 Jarome Iginla 1.00 2.50
U3 Ryan Kesler .75 2.00
U4 Ryan Miller .75 2.00
U5 James Neal .50 1.25
U6 Radim Vrbata .50 1.25
U7 Matt Niskanen .60 1.50
U8 Thomas Vanek .60 1.50
U9 Paul Stastny .60 1.50
U10 Brad Richards .75 2.00
U11 Matt Moulson .50 1.25
U12 Brooks Orpik .50 1.25
U13 Leon Draisaitl 5.00 12.00
U14 Derrick Pouliot 1.25 3.00
U15 Andrei Vasilevskiy 12.00 30.00
U16 Seth Griffith 1.25 3.00
U17 Adam Lowry 1.50 4.00
U18 Sam Reinhart 4.00 10.00
U19 Jiri Sekac .75 2.00
U20 Alexander Wennberg 1.50 4.00
U21 Curtis Lazar 1.00 2.50
U22 Shayne Gostisbehere 2.00 5.00
U23 Victor Rask 1.00 2.50
U24 Jori Lehtera 1.25 3.00
U25 Chris Tierney 1.00 2.50
U26 William Karlsson 3.00 8.00
U27 Jonathan Drouin 3.00 8.00
U28 Mirco Mueller 1.00 2.50
U29 Trevor van Riemsdyk 1.50 4.00
U30 Aaron Ekblad 2.50 6.00
U31 Darnell Nurse 2.00 5.00
U32 Curtis McKenzie .75 2.00
U33 Stuart Percy 1.00 2.50
U34 Bo Horvat 2.50 6.00
U35 Andre Burakovsky 1.50 4.00
U36 Rocco Grimaldi 1.00 2.50
U37 Kevin Hayes 2.50 6.00
U38 Tobias Rieder 1.00 2.50
U39 Damon Severson 1.00 2.50
U40 Marko Dano 1.00 2.50
U41 Anthony Duclair 1.50 4.00
U42 Griffin Reinhart 1.00 2.50

2014-15 O-Pee-Chee Update Signatures

USAB Andre Burakovsky C 6.00 15.00
USAD Anthony Duclair B 8.00 20.00
USAE Aaron Ekblad B 20.00 50.00
USAW Alexander Wennberg C 6.00 15.00
USBH Bo Horvat A 20.00 40.00
USCL Curtis Lazar C 12.00 30.00
USDN Darnell Nurse C 6.00 15.00
USDS Damon Severson C 6.00 15.00
USGR Griffin Reinhart C 4.00 10.00
USJD Jonathan Drouin B 30.00 60.00
USLD Leon Draisaitl B 40.00 100.00
USSR Sam Reinhart B 60.00 120.00

2015-16 O-Pee-Chee Update

U1 Ryan O'Reilly .75 2.00
U2 Dougie Hamilton .60 1.50
U3 Brandon Saad .60 1.50
U4 Patrick Sharp .75 2.00
U5 Mike Green .60 1.50
U6 Milan Lucic .60 1.50
U7 Phil Kessel .75 2.00
U8 Martin Jones .60 1.50
U9 Troy Brouwer .50 1.25
U10 T.J. Oshie .75 2.00
U11 Connor McDavid 40.00 100.00
U12 Nikolaj Ehlers 2.00 5.00
U13 Connor Brickley .75 2.00
U14 Anton Slepyshev .60 1.50
U15 Dylan DeMelo .75 2.00
U16 Jake Virtanen 1.25 3.00
U17 Matt O'Connor .75 2.00
U18 Colton Parayko 1.50 4.00
U19 Ben Hutton 1.00 2.50
U20 Dylan Larkin 3.00 8.00
U21 Colin Miller .75 2.00
U22 Joel Edmundson .75 2.00
U23 Sergei Plotnikov .60 1.50
U24 Robby Fabbri 1.25 3.00
U25 Brock McGinn 1.00 2.50
U26 Mike Condon 1.00 2.50
U27 Vincent Hinostroza .60 1.50
U28 Sergei Kalinin .60 1.50
U29 Nicolas Petan 1.00 2.50
U30 Mattias Janmark 1.00 2.50
U31 Chris Wideman 1.00 2.50
U32 Jared McCann 1.25 3.00
U33 Joonas Kemppainen .60 1.50
U34 Tyler Randell 1.00 2.50
U35 Max Domi 2.00 5.00
U36 Jordan Weal .60 1.50
U37 Andreas Athanasiou 2.50 6.00
U38 Chandler Stephenson 1.25 3.00
U39 Brendan Gaunce 1.25 3.00
U40 Daniel Sprong 1.25 3.00
U41 Joonas Donskoi 1.00 2.50
U42 Linus Ullmark 2.00 5.00
U43 Derek Forbort .75 2.00
U44 Radek Faksa 1.00 2.50
U45 Artemi Panarin 4.00 10.00
U46 Noah Hanifin 1.50 4.00
U47 Connor Hellebuyck 4.00 10.00
U48 Nikolay Goldobin 1.00 2.50
U49 Mikko Rantanen 5.00 12.00
U50 Jack Eichel 4.00 10.00

2015-16 O-Pee-Chee Update Rainbow Foil

*RAINBOW: .5X TO 1.2X BASIC INSERTS
U11 Connor McDavid 75.00 200.00

2015-16 O-Pee-Chee Update Rainbow Foil Black

*BLACK VETS/100: 1.5X TO 4X BASIC INSERTS
*BLACK ROOK/100: 1.2X TO 3X BASIC INSERTS
U11 Connor McDavid 250.00 600.00
U45 Artemi Panarin 40.00 80.00
U50 Jack Eichel 60.00 120.00

2015-16 O-Pee-Chee Update Red

*RED: 2.5X TO 6X BASIC INSERTS
U11 Connor McDavid 500.00 1200.00

2015-16 O-Pee-Chee Update Retro

*RETRO: .5X TO 1.2X BASIC INSERTS
U11 Connor McDavid 75.00 200.00

2015-16 O-Pee-Chee Update Signatures

COMPLETE SET (17)
USCS Carl Soderberg C 3.00 8.00
USDD Devan Dubnyk B 15.00 40.00
USDL David Legwand D 4.00 10.00
USEE Emerson Etem E 4.00 10.00
USGL Gabriel Landeskog C 6.00 15.00
USJQ Jonathan Quick B 30.00 80.00
USLA Dylan Larkin D 100.00 200.00
USMB Matt Beleskey C 6.00 15.00
USMD Matt Duchene C 10.00 25.00
USMF Matt Fraser E 4.00 10.00
USNG Nikolay Goldobin C 5.00 12.00
USOM Olli Maatta A 20.00 50.00
USRR Rickard Rakell A 8.00 20.00
USRS Ryan Spooner D 4.00 10.00
USSR Sam Reinhart D 10.00 25.00
USSU Ryan Suter B 10.00 25.00
USVT Vincent Trocheck E 5.00 12.00

1976 Old Timers

COMPLETE SET (18) 30.00 60.00
1 Gerry Abel 1.25 2.50
2 Sid Abel 4.00 8.00
3 Doug Barkley 1.25 2.50
4 Joe Carveth 1.25 2.50
5 Billy Dea 1.25 2.50
6 Alex Delvecchio 7.50 15.00
7 Bill Gadsby 1.25 2.50
8 Hal Jackson 1.25 2.50
9 Joe Klukay 1.25 2.50
10 Ted Lindsay 7.50 15.00
11 Jim Orlando 1.25 2.50
12 Marty Pavlich 1.25 2.50
13 Jim Peters 1.25 2.50
14 Marcel Pronovost 1.25 2.50
15 Marc Reaume 1.25 2.50
16 Leo Reise Jr. 1.25 2.50
17 Glen Skov 1.25 2.50
18 Jack Stewart 1.25 2.50

1999-00 Oscar Mayer Lunchables

COMPLETE SET (12) 6.00 15.00
1 Ray Bourque .60 1.50
2 Pavel Bure .75 2.00
3 Dominik Hasek .60 1.50
4 Jaromir Jagr 1.00 2.50
5 Curtis Joseph .40 1.00
6 Paul Kariya 1.25 3.00
7 Saku Koivu .30 .75
8 Eric Lindros 1.00 2.50
9 Al MacInnis .20 .50
10 Mark Messier .40 1.00
11 Mats Sundin .40 1.00
12 Alexei Yashin .25 .60

1997-98 Pacific

*COPPER: 2X TO 5X BASIC CARDS
1 Ray Bourque .25 .60
2 Brian Leetch .12 .30
3 Claude Lemieux .12 .30
4 Mike Modano .25 .60
5 Zigmund Palffy .15 .40
6 Nikolai Khabibulin .15 .40
7 Chris Chelios .15 .40
8 Teemu Selanne .30 .75
9 Paul Kariya .15 .40
10 John LeClair .15 .40
11 Mark Messier .30 .75
12 Jarome Iginla .20 .50
13 Petr Nedved .15 .40
14 Brendan Shanahan .15 .40
15 Dino Ciccarelli .15 .40
16 Brett Hull .30 .75
17 Wendel Clark .25 .60
18 Peter Bondra .15 .40
19 Steve Yzerman .40 1.00
20 Ed Belfour .15 .40
21 Peter Forsberg .30 .75
22 Mike Gartner .20 .50
23 Jim Carey .10 .25
24 Mike Vernon .12 .30
25 Vincent Damphousse .12 .30
26 Adam Graves .10 .25
27 Ron Hextall .15 .40
28 Keith Tkachuk .15 .40
29 Felix Potvin .25 .60
30 Martin Brodeur .40 1.00
31 Rod Brind'Amour .15 .40
32 Pierre Turgeon .12 .30
33 Patrick Roy .40 1.00
34 John Vanbiesbrouck .15 .40
35 Andy Moog .15 .40
36 Sergei Berezin .12 .30
37 Adam Oates .15 .40
38 Joe Sakic .30 .75
39 Dominik Hasek .25 .60
40 Patrick Lalime .12 .30
41 Bobby Dollas .10 .25
42 Kyle McLaren .10 .25
43 Wayne Primeau .12 .30
44 Stephane Richer .10 .25
45 Theo Fleury .20 .50
46 Kevin Miller .10 .25
47 Adam Deadmarsh .10 .25
48 Darryl Sydor .10 .25
49 Igor Larionov .10 .25
50 Radek Dvorak .12 .30
51 Andrei Kovalenko .10 .25
52 Keith Primeau .12 .30
53 Ray Ferraro .10 .25
54 David Wilkie .10 .25
55 Bobby Holik .10 .25
56 Tommy Salo .10 .25
57 Jeff Beukeboom .12 .30
58 Daniel Alfredsson .15 .40
59 Mikael Renberg .12 .30
60 Norm Maciver .10 .25
61 Darius Kasparaitis .12 .30
62 Geoff Courtnall .10 .25
63 Jeff Friesen .12 .30
64 Brian Bradley .10 .25
65 Tie Domi .12 .30
67 Martin Gelinas .10 .25
68 Jaromir Jagr .50 1.25
69 Steve Konowalchuk .12 .30
70 Brian Bellows .12 .30
71 Jozef Stumpel .10 .25
72 Darryl Shannon .10 .25
73 Todd Simpson .12 .30
74 Ulf Dahlen .10 .25
75 Sandis Ozolinsh .10 .25
76 Sergei Zubov .12 .30
77 Paul Coffey .15 .40
78 Nicklas Lidstrom .15 .40
79 Jason Arnott .12 .30
80 Ray Sheppard .12 .30
81 Sean Burke .10 .25
82 Vladimir Tsyplakov .12 .30
83 Darcy Tucker .15 .40
84 Dave Andreychuk .15 .40
85 Scott Lachance .12 .30
86 Niklas Sundstrom .12 .30
87 Ron Tugnutt .15 .40
88 Eric Lindros .25 .60
89 Alexander Mogilny .12 .30
90 Kris King .10 .25
91 Sergei Fedorov .25 .60
92 Ed Olczyk .10 .25
93 Doug Gilmour .20 .50
94 Ryan Smyth .12 .30
95 Scott Pellerin .10 .25
96 Pavel Bure .15 .40
97 Jeremy Roenick .25 .60
98 Todd Gill .12 .30
99 Wayne Gretzky 1.00 2.50
100 Roman Hamrlik .10 .25
101 Rob Zettler .10 .25
102 Sergei Nemchinov .10 .25
103 Sergei Gonchar .10 .25
104 Steve Rucchin .12 .30
105 Landon Wilson .10 .25
106 Anatoli Semenov .10 .25
107 Corey Millen .10 .25
108 Eric Daze .10 .25
109 Mike Ricci .10 .25
110 Jamie Langenbrunner .12 .30
111 Slava Fetisov .10 .25
112 Rem Murray .10 .25
113 Tom Fitzgerald .10 .25
114 Robert Kron .10 .25
115 Kevin Stevens .12 .30
116 Valeri Bure .10 .25
117 Bill Guerin .15 .40
118 Bryan McCabe .10 .25
119 Alexei Kovalev .12 .30
120 Alexei Yashin .12 .30
121 Eric Desjardins .10 .25
122 Teppo Numminen .10 .25
123 Ron Francis .20 .50
124 Chris Pronger .15 .40
125 Viktor Kozlov .12 .30
126 Corey Schwab .12 .30
127 Fredrik Modin .12 .30
128 Markus Naslund .15 .40
129 Dale Hunter .12 .30
130 Warren Rychel .12 .30
131 Anson Carter .10 .25
132 Miroslav Satan .10 .25
133 Trevor Kidd .10 .25
134 Sergei Krivokrasov .10 .25
135 Adam Foote .10 .25
136 Brent Gilchrist .15 .40
137 Chris Osgood .15 .40
138 Doug Weight .15 .40
139 Martin Straka .10 .25
140 Jeff O'Neill .12 .30
141 Byron Dafoe .12 .30
142 Brian Savage .10 .25
143 Lyle Odelein .10 .25
144 Niklas Andersson .10 .25
145 Luc Robitaille .15 .40
146 Damian Rhodes .12 .30
147 Garth Snow .12 .30
148 Craig Janney .10 .25
149 Fredrik Olausson .12 .30
150 Joe Murphy .12 .30
151 Owen Nolan .15 .40
152 Shawn Burr .10 .25
153 Dimitri Yushkevich .10 .25
154 Trevor Linden .15 .40
155 Joe Juneau .10 .25
156 Sean Pronger .10 .25
157 Jeff Odgers .10 .25
158 Brian Holzinger .12 .30
159 Dave Gagner .10 .25
160 Jeff Hackett .10 .25
161 Eric Lacroix .10 .25
162 Pat Verbeek .12 .30
163 Darren McCarty .12 .30
164 Mike Grier .12 .30
165 Per Gustafsson .12 .30
166 Andrew Cassels .10 .25
167 Vitali Yachmenev .12 .30
168 Jocelyn Thibault .12 .30
169 John MacLean .10 .25
170 Travis Green .12 .30
171 Ulf Samuelsson .15 .40
172 Bruce Gardiner RC .12 .30
173 Janne Niinimaa .12 .30
174 Jim Johnson .12 .30
175 Stu Barnes .10 .25
176 Harry York .12 .30
177 Al Iafrate .12 .30
178 Paul Ysebaert .12 .30
179 Mathieu Schneider .12 .30
180 Corey Hirsch .12 .30
181 Mark Tinordi .12 .30
182 Kevin Todd .10 .25
183 Tim Sweeney .10 .25
184 Donald Audette .12 .30
185 Jonas Hoglund .12 .30
186 Brent Sutter .10 .25
187 Scott Young .12 .30
188 Arturs Irbe .12 .30
189 Vladimir Konstantinov .10 .25
190 Mats Lindgren .10 .25
191 David Nemirovsky .10 .25
192 Sami Kapanen .12 .30
193 Rob Blake .15 .40
194 Sebastien Bordeleau .12 .30
195 Steve Thomas .12 .30
196 Bryan Smolinski .12 .30
197 Mike Richter .15 .40
198 Randy Cunneyworth .10 .25
199 Pat Falloon .10 .25
200 Cliff Ronning .10 .25
201 Ken Wregget .10 .25
202 Al MacInnis .20 .50
203 Tony Granato .10 .25
204 Rob Zamuner .10 .25
205 Mats Sundin .15 .40
206 Mike Ridley .10 .25
207 Sylvain Cote .10 .25
208 Joe Sacco .12 .30
209 Ted Donato .10 .25
210 Matthew Barnaby .10 .25
211 Cory Stillman .12 .30
212 Gary Suter .10 .25
213 Valeri Kamensky .12 .30
214 Derian Hatcher .12 .30
215 Jamie Pushor .10 .25
216 Mariusz Czerkawski .10 .25
217 Kirk Muller .10 .25
218 Kevin Dineen .12 .30
219 Dimitri Khristich .12 .30
220 Martin Rucinsky .12 .30
221 Denis Pederson .10 .25
222 Bryan Berard .10 .25
223 Alexander Karpovtsev .10 .25
224 Shawn McEachern .10 .25
225 Dale Hawerchuk .20 .50
226 Bob Corkum .12 .30
227 Kevin Hatcher .10 .25
228 Grant Fuhr .25 .60
229 Darren Turcotte .12 .30
230 Patrick Poulin .10 .25
231 Jamie Macoun .10 .25
232 Jyrki Lumme .12 .30
233 Bill Ranford .12 .30
234 Dmitri Mironov .12 .30
235 Mattias Timander .12 .30
236 Alexei Zhitnik .10 .25
237 Hnat Domenichelli .12 .30
238 Murray Craven .10 .25
239 Mike Keane .10 .25
240 Benoit Hogue .12 .30
241 Martin Lapointe .10 .25
242 Curtis Joseph .20 .50
243 Robert Svehla .12 .30
244 Glen Wesley .10 .25
245 Stephane Fiset .12 .30
246 Shayne Corson .12 .30
247 Scott Niedermayer .15 .40
248 Steve Webb RC .15 .40
249 Esa Tikkanen .10 .25
250 Alexandre Daigle .10 .25
251 Trent Klatt .12 .30
252 Oleg Tverdovsky .12 .30
253 Dave Roche .10 .25
254 Tony Twist .12 .30
255 Bernie Nicholls .12 .30
256 Rick Tabaracci .12 .30
257 Todd Warriner .12 .30
258 Kirk McLean .12 .30
259 Phil Housley .12 .30
260 Guy Hebert .12 .30
261 Steve Heinze .10 .25
262 Derek Plante .12 .30
263 German Titov .10 .25
264 Tony Amonte .12 .30
265 Uwe Krupp .10 .25
266 Joe Nieuwendyk .12 .30
267 Vyacheslav Kozlov .12 .30
268 Kelly Buchberger .12 .30
269 Rob Niedermayer .10 .25
270 Geoff Sanderson .12 .30
271 Jan Vopat .10 .25
272 Saku Koivu .15 .40
273 Scott Stevens .15 .40
274 Eric Fichaud .12 .30
275 Russ Courtnall .10 .25
276 Wade Redden .10 .25
277 Petr Svoboda .10 .25
278 Andreas Dackell .12 .30
279 Jason Woolley .12 .30
280 Stephane Matteau .10 .25
281 Stephen Guolla RC .10 .25
282 John Cullen .10 .25
283 Steve Sullivan .12 .30
284 Bret Hedican .10 .25
285 Michal Pivonka .10 .25
286 Darren Van Impe .12 .30
287 Rob DiMaio .10 .25
288 Garry Galley .10 .25
289 Kent Manderville .10 .25
290 Bob Probert .15 .40
291 Keith Jones .10 .25
292 Guy Carbonneau .15 .40
293 Tomas Sandstrom .10 .25
294 Daniel McGillis RC .12 .30
295 Brian Skrudland .10 .25
296 Stu Grimson .12 .30
297 Doug Zmolek .10 .25
298 Mark Recchi .20 .50
299 Valeri Zelepukin .12 .30
300 Derek Armstrong .10 .25
301 Eric Cairns RC .15 .40
302 Steve Duchesne .10 .25
303 Dainius Zubrus .12 .30
304 Deron Quint .10 .25
305 Joe Dziedzic .10 .25
306 Mike Peluso .10 .25
307 Andrei Nazarov .10 .25
308 Chris Gratton .10 .25
309 Mike Craig .10 .25
310 Lonny Bohonos .12 .30
311 Rick Tocchet .10 .25
312 Ted Drury .12 .30
313 Jean-Yves Roy .10 .25

314 Jason Dawe .12 .30
315 Jamie Allison .12 .30
316 Alexei Zhamnov .10 .25
317 Aaron Miller .10 .25
318 Todd Krygier .10 .25
319 Tomas Holmstrom .10 .25
320 Todd Marchant .12 .30
321 Scott Mellanby .12 .30
322 Marek Malik .10 .25
323 Dan Bylsma .12 .30
324 Stephane Quintal .12 .30
325 Ken Daneyko .12 .30
326 Robert Reichel .12 .30
327 Daniel Goneau .12 .30
328 Sergei Zholtok .12 .30
329 Kjell Samuelsson .10 .25
330 Shane Doan .12 .30
331 Radek Bonk .10 .25
332 Jim Campbell .10 .25
333 Marty McSorley .12 .30
334 Brantt Myhres .10 .25
335 Mike Johnson RC .12 .30
336 Mike Sillinger .10 .25
337 Kelly Hrudey .12 .30
338 Joel Bouchard .10 .25
339 Brian Noonan .10 .25
340 Dean Chynoweth .12 .30
341 Michael Peca .12 .30
342 Jeff Toms RC .10 .25
343 Denis Savard .15 .40
344 Stephane Yelle .10 .25
345 Grant Ledyard .10 .25
346 Ronnie Stern .10 .25
347 Petr Klima .10 .25
348 Johan Garpenlov .10 .25
349 Nelson Emerson .12 .30
350 Matt Johnson .10 .25
351 Ken Belanger RC .15 .40
CM1 Mark Messier .30 .75

1997-98 Pacific Emerald Green
*GREEN: 3X TO 8X BASIC CARDS

1997-98 Pacific Ice Blue
ICE BLUE/67: 20X TO 50X BASIC CARDS

1997-98 Pacific Red
*RED: 5X TO 12X BASIC CARDS

1997-98 Pacific Silver
*SILVER: 2.5X TO 6X BASIC CARDS

1997-98 Pacific Card-Supials
*MINIS: .4X TO .1X LARGE
1 Paul Kariya .60 1.50
2 Teemu Selanne 1.25 3.00
3 Jarome Iginla .75 2.00
4 Peter Forsberg 1.25 3.00
5 Mike Modano 1.00 2.50
6 Sergei Fedorov 1.00 2.50
7 Vladimir Konstantinov .40 1.00
8 Steve Yzerman 1.50 4.00
9 John Vanbiesbrouck .60 1.50
10 Martin Brodeur 1.50 4.00
11 Doug Gilmour .75 2.00
12 Wayne Gretzky 4.00 10.00
13 Mark Messier 1.25 3.00
14 John LeClair .60 1.50
15 Eric Lindros 1.00 2.50
16 Jeremy Roenick 1.00 2.50
17 Keith Tkachuk .60 1.50
18 Brett Hull 1.25 3.00
19 Felix Potvin 1.00 2.50
20 Pavel Bure .60 1.50

1997-98 Pacific Cramer's Choice
COMPLETE SET (10) 40.00 100.00
1 Paul Kariya 5.00 12.00
2 Dominik Hasek 8.00 20.00
3 Jarome Iginla 5.00 12.00
4 Peter Forsberg 10.00 25.00
5 Patrick Roy 20.00 50.00
6 Steve Yzerman 20.00 50.00
7 Wayne Gretzky 25.00 60.00
8 Mark Messier 5.00 12.00
9 Eric Lindros 6.00 15.00
10 Jaromir Jagr 8.00 20.00

1997-98 Pacific Gold Crown Die-Cuts
COMPLETE SET (20) 30.00 80.00
1 Paul Kariya 1.50 4.00
2 Teemu Selanne 1.25 3.00
3 Dominik Hasek 3.00 8.00
4 Michael Peca .75 2.00
5 Jarome Iginla 1.50 4.00
6 Chris Chelios .75 2.00
7 Peter Forsberg 2.00 5.00
8 Patrick Roy 8.00 20.00
9 Joe Sakic 3.00 8.00
10 Brendan Shanahan 1.50 4.00
11 Steve Yzerman 6.00 15.00
12 Ryan Smyth .75 2.00
13 John Vanbiesbrouck 1.25 3.00
14 Martin Brodeur 4.00 10.00
15 Wayne Gretzky 8.00 20.00
16 Mark Messier 1.50 4.00
17 Eric Lindros 1.25 3.00
18 Jaromir Jagr 2.00 5.00
19 Brett Hull 1.25 3.00
20 Pavel Bure 1.50 4.00

1997-98 Pacific In The Cage Laser Cuts
COMPLETE SET (20) 40.00 100.00
1 Guy Hebert 2.00 5.00
2 Dominik Hasek 5.00 12.00
3 Trevor Kidd 2.00 5.00
4 Jeff Hackett 2.00 5.00
5 Patrick Roy 8.00 20.00
6 Andy Moog 2.00 5.00
7 Chris Osgood 2.00 5.00
8 Mike Vernon 2.00 5.00
9 Curtis Joseph 4.00 10.00
10 John Vanbiesbrouck 4.00 10.00
11 Jocelyn Thibault 2.00 5.00
12 Martin Brodeur 6.00 15.00
13 Mike Richter 4.00 10.00
14 Ron Hextall 4.00 10.00
15 Garth Snow 2.00 5.00
16 Nikolai Khabibulin 4.00 10.00
17 Patrick Lalime 2.00 5.00
18 Grant Fuhr 4.00 10.00
19 Ed Belfour 4.00 10.00
20 Felix Potvin 4.00 10.00

1997-98 Pacific Slap Shots Die-Cuts
COMPLETE SET (36) 50.00 125.00
1A Paul Kariya 2.00 5.00
1B Jari Kurri 1.50 4.00
1C Teemu Selanne 1.50 4.00
2A Peter Forsberg 3.00 8.00
2B Joe Sakic 4.00 10.00
2C Claude Lemieux 1.00 2.50
3A Brendan Shanahan 2.00 5.00
3B Sergei Fedorov 2.00 5.00
3C Steve Yzerman 6.00 15.00
4A Mark Recchi 1.00 2.50
4B Vincent Damphousse 1.00 2.50
4C Stephane Richer 1.00 2.50
5A Wayne Gretzky 10.00 25.00
5B Mark Messier 2.00 5.00
5C Brian Leetch 1.50 4.00
6A Rod Brind'Amour 1.00 2.50
6B Eric Lindros 2.00 5.00
6C John LeClair 1.00 2.50
7A Keith Tkachuk 1.00 2.50
7B Jeremy Roenick 2.00 5.00
7C Mike Gartner 1.00 2.50
8A Petr Nedved 1.00 2.50
8B Ron Francis 1.00 2.50
8C Jaromir Jagr 3.00 8.00
9A Geoff Courtnall 1.00 2.50
9B Pierre Turgeon 1.00 2.50
9C Brett Hull 2.00 5.00
10A Wendel Clark 3.00 8.00
10B Mats Sundin 1.50 4.00
10C Sergei Berezin 1.00 2.50
11A Pavel Bure 2.50 6.00
11B Trevor Linden 1.50 4.00
11C Alexander Mogilny 1.00 2.50
12A Joe Juneau 1.00 2.50
12B Adam Oates 1.00 2.50
12C Peter Bondra 1.00 2.50

1997-98 Pacific Team Checklists
COMPLETE SET (26) 40.00 100.00
1 Teemu Selanne 2.00 5.00
2 Ray Bourque 2.00 5.00
3 Dominik Hasek 4.00 8.00
4 Jarome Iginla 2.50 6.00
5 Keith Primeau .75 2.00
6 Chris Chelios 1.25 3.00
7 Patrick Roy 6.00 15.00
8 Mike Modano 2.00 5.00
9 Steve Yzerman 5.00 12.00
10 Curtis Joseph 1.25 3.00
11 John Vanbiesbrouck 1.25 3.00
12 Rob Blake .75 2.00
13 Stephane Richer .75 2.00
14 Martin Brodeur 4.00 10.00
15 Zigmund Palffy 1.25 3.00
16 Wayne Gretzky 10.00 25.00
17 Alexandre Daigle .75 2.00
18 Eric Lindros 1.25 3.00
19 Jeremy Roenick 2.00 5.00
20 Jaromir Jagr 3.00 8.00
21 Brett Hull 2.00 5.00
22 Owen Nolan .75 2.00
23 Dino Ciccarelli .75 2.00
24 Felix Potvin 1.25 3.00
25 Pavel Bure 2.00 5.00
26 Peter Bondra .75 2.00

1998-99 Pacific
1 Damian Rhodes .20 .50
2 Mattias Ohlund .12 .30
3 Craig Ludwig .12 .30
4 Rob Blake .20 .50
5 Nicklas Lidstrom .25 .60
6 Calle Johansson .12 .30
7 Chris Chelios .20 .50
8 Teemu Selanne .40 1.00
9 Paul Kariya .20 .50
10 Pavel Bure .20 .50
11 Mark Messier .40 1.00
12 Peter Bondra .20 .50
13 Mats Sundin .20 .50
14 Brendan Shanahan .20 .50
15 Jamie Langenbrunner .12 .30
16 Brett Hull .40 1.00
17 Rod Brind'Amour .20 .50
18 Adam Deadmarsh .12 .30
19 Steve Yzerman .50 1.25
20 Ed Belfour .20 .50
21 Peter Forsberg .40 1.00
22 Dino Ciccarelli .20 .50
23 Brian Bellows .15 .40
24 Janne Niinimaa .12 .30
25 Joe Nieuwendyk .15 .40
26 Patrik Elias .20 .50
27 Michael Peca .12 .30
28 Tie Domi .15 .40
29 Felix Potvin .30 .75
30 Martin Brodeur .50 1.25
31 Grant Fuhr .30 .75
32 Trevor Linden .20 .50
33 Patrick Roy .50 1.25
34 John Vanbiesbrouck .20 .50
35 Tom Barrasso .15 .40
36 Matthew Barnaby .12 .30
37 Olaf Kolzig .20 .50
38 Pavol Demitra .25 .60
39 Dominik Hasek .30 .75
40 Chris Terreri .15 .40
41 Jason Allison .15 .40
42 Richard Smehlik .12 .30
43 Frank Banham .12 .30
44 Chris Pronger .20 .50
45 Matt Cullen .12 .30
46 Mike Rucinski RC .15 .40
47 Mike Crowley RC .15 .40
48 Scott Young .12 .30
49 Brian Savage .12 .30
50 Travis Green .12 .30
51 John LeClair .20 .50
52 Adam Foote .12 .30
53 Derek Morris .12 .30
54 Guy Hebert .15 .40
55 Chris Gratton .15 .40
56 Sergei Zubov .15 .40
57 Dave Karpa .12 .30
58 Sergei Varlamov .12 .30
59 Josef Marha .12 .30
60 Jason Marshall .12 .30
61 Jeff Nielsen RC .15 .40
62 Steve Rucchin .12 .30
63 Tomas Sandstrom .12 .30
64 Jason Bonsignore .12 .30
65 Mikhail Shtalenkov .12 .30
67 Tom Askey RC .15 .40
68 Jaromir Jagr .60 1.50
69 Per Axelsson .12 .30
70 Ken Baumgartner .12 .30
71 Jiri Slegr .12 .30
72 Mathieu Schneider .12 .30
73 Anson Carter .15 .40
74 Byron Dafoe .15 .40
75 Rob DiMaio .12 .30
76 Ted Donato .12 .30
77 Ray Bourque .30 .75
78 Dave Ellett .15 .40
79 Steve Heinze .12 .30
80 Geoff Sanderson .12 .30
81 Miroslav Satan .15 .40
82 Martin Straka .12 .30
83 Dimitri Khristich .12 .30
84 Grant Ledyard .12 .30
85 Cameron Mann .12 .30
86 Kyle McLaren .12 .30
87 Sergei Samsonov .15 .40
88 Eric Lindros .30 .75
89 Alexander Mogilny .15 .40
90 Joe Juneau .12 .30
91 Sergei Fedorov .30 .75
92 Rick Tocchet .15 .40
93 Doug Gilmour .25 .60
94 Ryan Smyth .15 .40
95 Alexei Morozov .12 .30
96 Phil Housley .15 .40
97 Jeremy Roenick .30 .75
98 Jay More .12 .30
99 Wayne Gretzky 1.25 3.00
100 Robbie Tallas .12 .30
101 Tim Taylor .12 .30
102 Joe Thornton .30 .75
103 Donald Audette .12 .30
104 Curtis Brown .12 .30
105 Michal Grosek .12 .30
106 Brian Holzinger .12 .30
107 Derek Plante .12 .30
108 Rob Ray .12 .30
109 Darryl Shannon .12 .30
110 Steve Shields .12 .30
111 Vaclav Varada .12 .30
112 Dixon Ward .15 .40
113 Jason Woolley .12 .30
114 Alexei Zhitnik .12 .30
115 Andrew Cassels .12 .30
116 Hnat Domenichelli .12 .30
117 Theo Fleury .25 .60
118 Denis Gauthier .12 .30
119 Cale Hulse .12 .30
120 Jarome Iginla .25 .60
121 Marty McInnis .12 .30
122 Tyler Moss .12 .30
123 Michael Nylander .15 .40
124 Dwayne Roloson .12 .30
125 Cory Stillman .12 .30
126 Rick Tabaracci .12 .30
127 German Titov .12 .30
128 Jason Wiemer .12 .30
129 Steve Chiasson .12 .30
130 Kevin Dineen .12 .30
131 Nelson Emerson .12 .30
132 Martin Gelinas .12 .30
133 Stu Grimson .12 .30
134 Sami Kapanen .12 .30
135 Trevor Kidd .12 .30
136 Robert Kron .12 .30
137 Jeff O'Neill .12 .30
138 Keith Primeau .15 .40
139 Paul Ranheim .12 .30
140 Gary Roberts .12 .30
141 Glen Wesley .12 .30
142 Tony Amonte .15 .40
143 Eric Daze .15 .40
144 Jeff Hackett .12 .30
145 Greg Johnson .12 .30
146 Chad Kilger .12 .30
147 Sergei Krivokrasov .12 .30
148 Christian LaFlamme .12 .30
149 Jean-Yves Leroux .15 .40
150 Dmitri Nabokov .12 .30
151 Jeff Shantz .12 .30
152 Gary Suter .12 .30
153 Eric Weinrich .12 .30
154 Todd White RC .15 .40
155 Alexei Zhamnov .12 .30
156 Wade Belak .12 .30
157 Craig Billington .12 .30
158 Rene Corbet .12 .30
159 Shean Donovan .12 .30
160 Valeri Kamensky .12 .30
161 Uwe Krupp .12 .30
162 Jari Kurri .12 .30
163 Eric Lacroix .12 .30
164 Claude Lemieux .15 .40
165 Eric Messier .12 .30
166 Jeff Odgers .12 .30
167 Sandis Ozolinsh .12 .30
168 Warren Rychel .12 .30
169 Joe Sakic .40 1.00
170 Stephane Yelle .12 .30
171 Greg Adams .12 .30
172 Jason Botterill .12 .30
173 Guy Carbonneau .12 .30
174 Shawn Chambers .12 .30
175 Manny Fernandez .12 .30
176 Derian Hatcher .12 .30
177 Benoit Hogue .12 .30
178 Mike Keane .12 .30
179 Jere Lehtinen .15 .40
180 Juha Lind .12 .30
181 Mike Modano .30 .75
182 Brian Skrudland .12 .30
183 Darryl Sydor .12 .30
184 Roman Turek .12 .30
185 Pat Verbeek .12 .30
186 Jamie Wright .12 .30
187 Doug Brown .12 .30
188 Kris Draper .12 .30
189 Anders Eriksson .12 .30
190 Slava Fetisov .12 .30
191 Brent Gilchrist .12 .30
192 Kevin Hodson .12 .30
193 Tomas Holmstrom .12 .30
194 Michael Knuble .12 .30
195 Joey Kocur .12 .30
196 Vyacheslav Kozlov .15 .40
197 Martin Lapointe .12 .30
198 Igor Larionov .20 .50
199 Kirk Maltby .12 .30
200 Norm Maracle RC .15 .40
201 Darren McCarty .12 .30
202 Dmitri Mironov .12 .30
203 Larry Murphy .15 .40
204 Chris Osgood .20 .50
205 Kelly Buchberger .12 .30
206 Bob Essensa .15 .40
207 Scott Fraser .12 .30
208 Mike Grier .12 .30
209 Bill Guerin .20 .50
210 Tony Hrkac .12 .30
211 Curtis Joseph .25 .60
212 Mats Lindgren .12 .30
213 Todd Marchant .12 .30
214 Dean McAmmond .12 .30
215 Craig Millar .12 .30
216 Boris Mironov .12 .30
217 Doug Weight .20 .50
218 Valeri Zelepukin .12 .30
219 Roman Hamrlik .12 .30
220 Radek Dvorak .12 .30
221 Dave Gagner .12 .30
222 Ed Jovanovski .15 .40
223 Viktor Kozlov .15 .40
224 Paul Laus .15 .40
225 Kirk McLean .15 .40
226 Scott Mellanby .12 .30
227 Kirk Muller .12 .30
228 Robert Svehla .12 .30
229 Steve Washburn .12 .30
230 Kevin Weekes .15 .40
231 Ray Whitney .12 .30
232 Peter Worrell RC .15 .40
233 Russ Courtnall .12 .30
234 Stephane Fiset .15 .40
235 Garry Galley .12 .30
236 Craig Johnson .12 .30
237 Ian Laperriere .12 .30
238 Donald MacLean .12 .30
239 Steve McKenna .12 .30
240 Sandy Moger .12 .30
241 Glen Murray .15 .40
242 Sean O'Donnell .12 .30
243 Yanic Perreault .12 .30
244 Luc Robitaille .20 .50
245 Jamie Storr .15 .40
246 Jozef Stumpel .12 .30
247 Vladimir Tsyplakov .12 .30
248 Benoit Brunet .12 .30
249 Shayne Corson .15 .40
250 Vincent Damphousse .15 .40
251 Eric Houde RC .15 .40
252 Saku Koivu .20 .50
253 Vladimir Malakhov .12 .30
254 Dave Manson .12 .30
255 Andy Moog .20 .50
256 Mark Recchi .25 .60
257 Martin Rucinsky .12 .30
258 Jocelyn Thibault .15 .40
259 Mick Vukota .12 .30
260 Dave Andreychuk .20 .50
261 Jason Arnott .15 .40
262 Mike Dunham .15 .40
263 Bobby Holik .12 .30
264 Randy McKay .15 .40
265 Brendan Morrison .12 .30
266 Scott Niedermayer .20 .50
267 Lyle Odelein .12 .30
268 Krzysztof Oliwa .12 .30
269 Denis Pederson .12 .30
270 Brian Rolston .15 .40
271 Sheldon Souray RC .25 .60
272 Scott Stevens .20 .50
273 Petr Sykora .12 .30
274 Steve Thomas .12 .30
275 Bryan Berard .15 .40
276 Zdeno Chara .20 .50
277 Vladimir Chebaturkin RC .15 .40
278 Tom Chorske .12 .30
279 Mariusz Czerkawski .12 .30
280 Jason Dawe .12 .30
281 Wade Flaherty .12 .30
282 Kenny Jonsson .12 .30
283 Sergei Nemchinov .12 .30
284 Zigmund Palffy .20 .50
285 Rich Pilon .12 .30
286 Robert Reichel .12 .30
287 Joe Sacco .12 .30
288 Tommy Salo .15 .40
289 Bryan Smolinski .12 .30
290 Jeff Beukeboom .12 .30
291 Dan Cloutier .15 .40
292 Bruce Driver .12 .30
293 Adam Graves .12 .30
294 Alexei Kovalev .15 .40
295 Pat LaFontaine .20 .50
296 Darren Langdon .12 .30
297 Brian Leetch .15 .40
298 Mike Richter .20 .50
299 Ulf Samuelsson .15 .40
300 Marc Savard .12 .30
301 Kevin Stevens .15 .40
302 Niklas Sundstrom .12 .30
303 Tim Sweeney .12 .30
304 Vladimir Vorobiev .12 .30
305 Daniel Alfredsson .20 .50
306 Magnus Arvedson .12 .30
307 Radek Bonk .12 .30
308 Andreas Dackell .12 .30
309 Bruce Gardiner .12 .30
310 Igor Kravchuk .12 .30
311 Denny Lambert .15 .40
312 Janne Laukkanen .12 .30
313 Shawn McEachern .12 .30
314 Chris Phillips .12 .30
315 Wade Redden .12 .30
316 Ron Tugnutt .12 .30
317 Shaun Van Allen .12 .30
318 Alexei Yashin .15 .40
319 Jason York .12 .30
320 Sergei Zholtok .12 .30
321 Sean Burke .12 .30
322 Paul Coffey .20 .50
323 Alexandre Daigle .12 .30
324 Eric Desjardins .15 .40
325 Colin Forbes .12 .30
326 Ron Hextall .20 .50
327 Trent Klatt .12 .30
328 Dan McGillis .12 .30
329 Joel Otto .12 .30
330 Shjon Podein .12 .30
331 Mike Sillinger .12 .30
332 Chris Therien .12 .30
333 Dainius Zubrus .12 .30
334 Bob Corkum .12 .30
335 Jim Cummins .12 .30
336 Jason Doig .12 .30
337 Dallas Drake .12 .30
338 Mike Gartner .25 .60
339 Brad Isbister .12 .30
340 Craig Janney .12 .30
341 Nikolai Khabibulin .20 .50
342 Teppo Numminen .12 .30
343 Cliff Ronning .12 .30
344 Keith Tkachuk .20 .50
345 Oleg Tverdovsky .20 .50
346 Jim Waite .12 .30
347 Juha Ylonen .12 .30
348 Stu Barnes .12 .30
349 Rob Brown .12 .30
350 Robert Dome .12 .30
351 Ron Francis .25 .60
352 Kevin Hatcher .12 .30
353 Alex Hicks .12 .30
354 Darius Kasparaitis .12 .30
355 Robert Lang .12 .30
356 Fredrik Olausson .12 .30
357 Ed Olczyk .12 .30
358 Peter Skudra .12 .30
359 Chris Tamer .12 .30
360 Ken Wregget .15 .40
361 Blair Atcheynum .12 .30
362 Jim Campbell .12 .30
363 Kelly Chase .12 .30
364 Craig Conroy .12 .30
365 Geoff Courtnall .15 .40
366 Steve Duchesne .15 .40
367 Todd Gill .12 .30
368 Al MacInnis .25 .60
369 Jamie McLennan .15 .40
370 Scott Pellerin .12 .30
371 Pascal Rheaume .12 .30
372 Jamie Rivers .12 .30
373 Darren Turcotte .15 .40
374 Pierre Turgeon .15 .40
375 Tony Twist .12 .30
376 Terry Yake .12 .30
377 Richard Brennan .12 .30
378 Murray Craven .12 .30
379 Jeff Friesen .12 .30
380 Tony Granato .12 .30
381 Bill Houlder .12 .30
382 Kelly Hrudey .12 .30
383 Alexander Korolyuk .12 .30
384 John MacLean .12 .30
385 Bryan Marchment .12 .30
386 Patrick Marleau .20 .50
387 Stephane Matteau .12 .30
388 Marty McSorley .15 .40
389 Bernie Nicholls .15 .40
390 Owen Nolan .20 .50
391 Mike Ricci .12 .30
392 Marco Sturm .12 .30
393 Mike Vernon .15 .40
394 Andrei Zyuzin .12 .30
395 Mikael Andersson .12 .30
396 Zac Bierk RC .25 .60
397 Enrico Ciccone .12 .30
398 Louie DeBrusk .12 .30
399 Karl Dykhuis .12 .30
400 Daymond Langkow .12 .30
401 Mike McBain .12 .30
402 Sandy McCarthy .12 .30
403 Daren Puppa .15 .40
404 Mikael Renberg .15 .40
405 Stephane Richer .12 .30
406 Alexander Selivanov .12 .30
407 Darcy Tucker .12 .30
408 Paul Ysebaert .12 .30
409 Rob Zamuner .12 .30
410 Sergei Berezin .15 .40
411 Wendel Clark .30 .75
412 Sylvain Cote .12 .30
413 Mike Johnson .12 .30
414 Derek King .12 .30
415 Kris King .12 .30
416 Igor Korolev .12 .30
417 Daniil Markov RC .15 .40
418 Alyn McCauley .12 .30
419 Fredrik Modin .12 .30
420 Martin Prochazka .12 .30
421 Jason Smith .12 .30
422 Steve Sullivan .12 .30
423 Yannick Tremblay .12 .30
424 Todd Bertuzzi .20 .50
425 Donald Brashear .12 .30
426 Bret Hedican .12 .30
427 Arturs Irbe .15 .40
428 Jyrki Lumme .12 .30
429 Brad May .12 .30
430 Bryan McCabe .12 .30
431 Markus Naslund .20 .50
432 Brian Noonan .12 .30
433 Dave Scatchard .12 .30
434 Garth Snow .15 .40
435 Scott Walker RC .15 .40
436 Peter Zezel .12 .30
437 Craig Berube .12 .30
438 Jeff Brown .12 .30
439 Andrew Brunette .15 .40
440 Jan Bulis .12 .30
441 Sergei Gonchar .12 .30
442 Dale Hunter .15 .40
443 Steve Konowalchuk .12 .30
444 Kelly Miller .12 .30
445 Adam Oates .20 .50
446 Bill Ranford .15 .40
447 Jaroslav Svejkovsky .12 .30
448 Esa Tikkanen .12 .30
449 Mark Tinordi .12 .30
450 Brendan Witt .12 .30
451 Richard Zednik .12 .30
S181 Mike Modano SAMPLE .30 .75

1998-99 Pacific Ice Blue
*VETERANS: 6X TO 15X BASIC CARDS
*ROOKIES: 1.2X TO 3X BASIC CARDS

1998-99 Pacific Red
*VETERANS: 3X TO 8X BASIC CARDS
*ROOKIES: 1.5X TO 4X BASIC CARDS

1998-99 Pacific Cramer's Choice
COMPLETE SET (10) 100.00 200.00
1 Sergei Samsonov 4.00 10.00
2 Dominik Hasek 8.00 20.00
3 Peter Forsberg 12.50 30.00
4 Patrick Roy 20.00 50.00
5 Mike Modano 6.00 15.00
6 Martin Brodeur 12.50 30.00
7 Wayne Gretzky 25.00 60.00
8 Eric Lindros 5.00 12.00
9 Jaromir Jagr 8.00 20.00
10 Pavel Bure 5.00 12.00

1998-99 Pacific Dynagon Ice Inserts
1 Paul Kariya .75 2.00
2 Teemu Selanne 1.50 4.00
3 Sergei Samsonov .60 1.50
4 Dominik Hasek 1.25 3.00
5 Peter Forsberg 1.50 4.00
6 Patrick Roy 2.00 5.00
7 Joe Sakic 1.50 4.00
8 Mike Modano 1.25 3.00
9 Sergei Fedorov 1.25 3.00
10 Steve Yzerman 2.00 5.00
11 Saku Koivu .75 2.00
12 Martin Brodeur 2.00 5.00
13 Wayne Gretzky 5.00 12.00
14 John LeClair .75 2.00
15 Eric Lindros 1.25 3.00
16 Jaromir Jagr 2.50 6.00
17 Pavel Bure .75 2.00
18 Mark Messier 1.50 4.00
19 Peter Bondra .75 2.00
20 Olaf Kolzig .75 2.00

1998-99 Pacific Titanium Ice
1 Paul Kariya 3.00 8.00
2 Teemu Selanne 6.00 15.00
3 Sergei Samsonov 2.50 6.00
4 Dominik Hasek 5.00 12.00
5 Peter Forsberg 6.00 15.00
6 Patrick Roy 8.00 20.00
7 Joe Sakic 6.00 15.00
8 Mike Modano 5.00 12.00
9 Sergei Fedorov 5.00 12.00
10 Steve Yzerman 8.00 20.00
11 Saku Koivu 3.00 8.00
12 Martin Brodeur 8.00 20.00
13 Wayne Gretzky 20.00 50.00
14 John LeClair 3.00 8.00
15 Eric Lindros 5.00 12.00
16 Jaromir Jagr 10.00 25.00
17 Pavel Bure 3.00 8.00
18 Mark Messier 6.00 15.00
19 Peter Bondra 3.00 8.00
20 Olaf Kolzig 3.00 8.00

1998-99 Pacific Gold Crown Die-Cuts
1 Paul Kariya 1.25 3.00
2 Teemu Selanne 2.50 6.00
3 Sergei Samsonov 1.00 2.50
4 Dominik Hasek 2.00 5.00
5 Michael Peca .75 2.00
6 Theo Fleury 1.50 4.00
7 Chris Chelios 1.25 3.00
8 Peter Forsberg 2.50 6.00
9 Patrick Roy 3.00 8.00
10 Joe Sakic 2.50 6.00
11 Ed Belfour 1.25 3.00
12 Mike Modano 2.00 5.00
13 Sergei Fedorov 2.00 5.00
14 Chris Osgood 1.25 3.00
15 Brendan Shanahan 1.25 3.00
16 Steve Yzerman 3.00 8.00
17 Saku Koivu 1.25 3.00
18 Martin Brodeur 3.00 8.00
19 Patrik Elias 1.25 3.00
20 Doug Gilmour 1.50 4.00
21 Trevor Linden 1.25 3.00
22 Zigmund Palffy 1.25 3.00
23 Wayne Gretzky 8.00 20.00
24 John LeClair 1.25 3.00
25 Eric Lindros 2.00 5.00
26 Dainius Zubrus .75 2.00
27 Keith Tkachuk 1.25 3.00
28 Tom Barrasso 1.00 2.50
29 Jaromir Jagr 4.00 10.00
30 Brett Hull 2.50 6.00
31 Felix Potvin 2.00 5.00
32 Mats Sundin 1.25 3.00
33 Pavel Bure 1.25 3.00
34 Mark Messier 2.50 6.00
35 Peter Bondra 1.25 3.00
36 Olaf Kolzig 1.25 3.00

1998-99 Pacific Martin Brodeur Show Promo
COMPLETE SET (1) 10.00
1 Martin Brodeur 4.00 10.00

1998-99 Pacific Team Checklists
1 Paul Kariya .30 .75
2 Sergei Samsonov .25 .60
3 Dominik Hasek .50 1.25
4 Theo Fleury .40 1.00
5 Keith Primeau .25 .60
6 Chris Chelios .30 .75
7 Patrick Roy .75 2.00
8 Mike Modano .50 1.25
9 Steve Yzerman .75 2.00
10 Ryan Smyth .25 .60
11 John Vanbiesbrouck .30 .75
12 Jozef Stumpel .20 .50
13 Saku Koivu .30 .75
14 Mike Dunham .25 .60
15 Martin Brodeur .75 2.00
16 Zigmund Palffy .30 .75
17 Wayne Gretzky 2.00 5.00
18 Alexei Yashin .25 .60
19 Eric Lindros .50 1.25
20 Keith Tkachuk .30 .75
21 Jaromir Jagr 1.00 2.50
22 Brett Hull .60 1.50
23 Patrick Marleau .30 .75
24 Rob Zamuner .20 .50
25 Mats Sundin .30 .75
26 Pavel Bure .30 .75
27 Olaf Kolzig .30 .75
28 Atlanta Thrashers .20 .50
29 Minnesota Wild .20 .50
30 Columbus Blue Jackets .20 .50

1998-99 Pacific Timelines
1 Teemu Selanne 3.00 8.00
2 Dominik Hasek 2.50 6.00
3 Peter Forsberg 3.00 8.00
4 Patrick Roy 4.00 10.00
5 Joe Sakic 3.00 8.00
6 Ed Belfour 1.50 4.00
7 Brendan Shanahan 1.50 4.00
8 Steve Yzerman 4.00 10.00
9 Mike Modano 2.50 6.00
10 Doug Gilmour 2.00 5.00
11 Wayne Gretzky 10.00 25.00
12 Pat LaFontaine 1.50 4.00
13 John LeClair 1.50 4.00
14 Eric Lindros 2.50 6.00
15 Keith Tkachuk 1.50 4.00
16 Jaromir Jagr 5.00 12.00
17 Brett Hull 3.00 8.00
18 Mats Sundin 1.50 4.00
19 Pavel Bure 1.50 4.00
20 Mark Messier 3.00 8.00

1998-99 Pacific Trophy Winners
1 Martin Brodeur 2.00 5.00
2 Dominik Hasek 1.25 3.00
3 Jaromir Jagr 2.50 6.00
4 Sergei Samsonov .60 1.50
5 Sergei Fedorov 1.25 3.00
6 Nicklas Lidstrom 1.00 2.50
7 Darren McCarty .50 1.25
8 Chris Osgood .75 2.00
9 Brendan Shanahan .75 2.00
10 Steve Yzerman 2.00 5.00

1999-00 Pacific
1 Matt Cullen .10 .25
2 Johan Davidsson .10 .25
3 Scott Ferguson RC .10 .25
4 Travis Green .10 .25
5 Stu Grimson .12 .30
6 Kevin Haller .10 .25
7 Guy Hebert .15 .40
8 Paul Kariya .15 .40
9 Marty McInnis .10 .25
10 Jim McKenzie .10 .25
11 Fredrik Olausson .10 .25
12 Dominic Roussel .10 .25
13 Steve Rucchin .10 .25
14 Ruslan Salei .10 .25
15 Tomas Sandstrom .10 .25
16 Teemu Selanne .30 .75
17 Jason Allison .12 .30
18 P.J. Axelsson .10 .25
19 Shawn Bates .10 .25
20 Ray Bourque .25 .60
21 Anson Carter .12 .30
22 Byron Dafoe .12 .30
23 Hal Gill .10 .25
24 Steve Heinze .10 .25
25 Dimitri Khristich .10 .25
26 Cameron Mann .10 .25
27 Kyle McLaren .10 .25
28 Sergei Samsonov .12 .30
29 Robbie Tallas .10 .25
30 Joe Thornton .25 .60
31 Landon Wilson .10 .25
32 J.Girard/A.Savage RC .10 .25
33 Stu Barnes .12 .30
34 Martin Biron .12 .30
35 Curtis Brown .10 .25
36 Michal Grosek .10 .25
37 Dominik Hasek .25 .60
38 Brian Holzinger .10 .25
39 Joe Juneau .10 .25
40 Jay McKee .10 .25
41 Michael Peca .12 .30
42 Erik Rasmussen .10 .25
43 Rob Ray .10 .25
44 Geoff Sanderson .12 .30
45 Miroslav Satan .12 .30
46 Darryl Shannon .10 .25
47 Vaclav Varada .10 .25
48 Dixon Ward .10 .25
49 Jason Woolley .10 .25
50 Alexei Zhitnik .10 .25
51 Fred Brathwaite .10 .25
52 Valeri Bure .10 .25
53 Andrew Cassels .10 .25
54 Rene Corbet .10 .25
55 Jean-Sebastien Giguere .15 .40
56 Phil Housley .12 .30
57 Jarome Iginla .20 .50
58 Derek Morris .10 .25
59 Andrei Nazarov .10 .25
60 Jeff Shantz .10 .25
61 Todd Simpson .10 .25
62 Cory Stillman .10 .25
63 Jason Wiemer .10 .25
64 Clarke Wilm .10 .25

65 Ken Wregget .10 .25
66 R.Fata RC/T.Garner .10 .25
67 Bates Battaglia .10 .25
68 Paul Coffey .15 .40
69 Kevin Dineen .10 .25
70 Ron Francis .20 .50
71 Martin Gelinas .10 .25
72 Arturs Irbe .12 .30
73 Sami Kapanen .10 .25
74 Trevor Kidd .10 .25
75 Andrei Kovalenko .10 .25
76 Robert Kron .10 .25
77 Kent Manderville .10 .25
78 Jeff O'Neill .10 .25
79 Keith Primeau .12 .30
80 Gary Roberts .10 .25
81 Ray Sheppard .10 .25
82 Glen Wesley .10 .25
83 Byron Ritchie RC
Craig MacDonald .15 .40
84 Tony Amonte .12 .30
85 Eric Daze .12 .30
86 J-P Dumont .12 .30
87 Anders Eriksson .10 .25
88 Mark Fitzpatrick .10 .25
89 Doug Gilmour .20 .50
90 J.Y. Leroux .10 .25
91 Dave Manson .10 .25
92 Josef Marha .10 .25
93 Dean McAmmond .10 .25
94 Boris Mironov .10 .25
95 Ed Olczyk .10 .25
96 Bob Probert .15 .40
97 Jocelyn Thibault .12 .30
98 Alexei Zhamnov .10 .25
99 Remi Royer
Ty Jones .10 .25
100 Craig Billington .10 .25
101 Adam Deadmarsh .10 .25
102 Chris Drury .12 .30
103 Theo Fleury .20 .50
104 Adam Foote .12 .30
105 Peter Forsberg .30 .75
106 Milan Hejduk .12 .30
107 Dale Hunter .12 .30
108 Valeri Kamensky .10 .25
109 Sylvain Lefebvre .10 .25
110 Claude Lemieux .12 .30
111 Aaron Miller .10 .25
112 Jeff Odgers .10 .25
113 Sandis Ozolinsh .10 .25
114 Patrick Roy .40 1.00
115 Joe Sakic .30 .75
116 Stephane Yelle .10 .25
117 Ed Belfour .15 .40
118 Derian Hatcher .12 .30
119 Benoit Hogue .10 .25
120 Brett Hull .30 .75
121 Mike Keane .12 .30
122 Jamie Langenbrunner .10 .25
123 Jere Lehtinen .12 .30
124 Brad Lukowich RC .12 .30
125 Grant Marshall .10 .25
126 Mike Modano .25 .60
127 Joe Nieuwendyk .12 .30
128 Derek Plante .10 .25
129 Darryl Sydor .12 .30
130 Roman Turek .12 .30
131 Pat Verbeek .12 .30
132 Sergei Zubov .12 .30
133 Jonathan Sim RC
Blake Sloan .15 .40
134 Doug Brown .10 .25
135 Chris Chelios .15 .40
136 Wendel Clark .25 .60
137 Kris Draper .12 .30
138 Sergei Fedorov .25 .60
139 Tomas Holmstrom .10 .25
140 Vyacheslav Kozlov .10 .25
141 Martin Lapointe .12 .30
142 Igor Larionov .15 .40
143 Nicklas Lidstrom .15 .40
144 Darren McCarty .10 .25
145 Larry Murphy .12 .30
146 Chris Osgood .15 .40
147 Bill Ranford .12 .30
148 Ulf Samuelsson .10 .25
149 Brendan Shanahan .15 .40
150 Aaron Ward .10 .25
151 Steve Yzerman .40 1.00
152 Josef Beranek .10 .25
153 Pat Falloon .12 .30
154 Mike Grier .10 .25
155 Bill Guerin .15 .40
156 Roman Hamrlik .10 .25
157 Chad Kilger .10 .25
158 Georges Laraque RC .30 .75
159 Todd Marchant .10 .25
160 Ethan Moreau .10 .25
161 Rem Murray .10 .25
162 Janne Niinimaa .10 .25
163 Tom Poti .10 .25
164 Tommy Salo .12 .30
165 Alexander Selivanov .10 .25
166 Ryan Smyth .12 .30
167 Doug Weight .15 .40
168 Steve Passmore RC .12 .30
169 Pavel Bure .15 .40
170 Sean Burke .10 .25
171 Dino Ciccarelli .15 .40
172 Radek Dvorak .10 .25
173 Viktor Kozlov .10 .25
174 Oleg Kvasha .10 .25
175 Paul Laus .10 .25
176 Bill Lindsay .10 .25
177 Kirk McLean .12 .30
178 Scott Mellanby .10 .25
179 Rob Niedermayer .10 .25
180 Mark Parrish .10 .25
181 Jaroslav Spacek .10 .25
182 Robert Svehla .10 .25
183 Ray Whitney .12 .30
184 Peter Worrell .10 .25
185 D.Boyle RC/M.Nilson .12 .30
186 Donald Audette .10 .25
187 Rob Blake .15 .40
188 Russ Courtnall .10 .25
189 Ray Ferraro .10 .25
190 Stephane Fiset .12 .30
191 Craig Johnson .10 .25
192 Olli Jokinen .12 .30
193 Glen Murray .12 .30
194 Mattias Norstrom .10 .25
195 Sean O'Donnell .10 .25
196 Luc Robitaille .15 .40
197 Pavel Rosa .10 .25
198 Jamie Storr .10 .25
199 Jozef Stumpel .10 .25
200 Vladimir Tsyplakov .10 .25
201 Benoit Brunet .10 .25
202 Shayne Corson .12 .30
203 Jeff Hackett .10 .25
204 Matt Higgins .10 .25
205 Saku Koivu .15 .40
206 Vladimir Malakhov .10 .25
207 Patrick Poulin .10 .25
208 Stephane Quintal .10 .25
209 Martin Rucinsky .10 .25
210 Brian Savage .10 .25
211 Turner Stevenson .10 .25
212 Jose Theodore .15 .40
213 Eric Weinrich .10 .25
214 Sergei Zholtok .10 .25
215 Dainius Zubrus .12 .30
216 Terry Ryan
Miloslav Guren .10 .25
217 Drake Berehowsky .10 .25
218 Sebastien Bordeleau .10 .25
219 Bob Boughner .10 .25
220 Andrew Brunette .10 .25
221 Patrick Cote .10 .25
222 Mike Dunham .10 .25
223 Tom Fitzgerald .10 .25
224 Jamie Heward .10 .25
225 Greg Johnson .10 .25
226 Patric Kjellberg .10 .25
227 Sergei Krivokrasov .10 .25
228 Denny Lambert .10 .25
229 David Legwand .10 .25
230 Mark Mowers RC .10 .25
231 Cliff Ronning .10 .25
232 Tomas Vokoun .15 .40
233 Scott Walker .10 .25
234 Jason Arnott .12 .30
235 Martin Brodeur .40 1.00
236 Ken Daneyko .10 .25
237 Patrik Elias .15 .40
238 Bobby Holik .10 .25
239 John Madden RC .15 .40
240 Randy McKay .10 .25
241 Brendan Morrison .12 .30
242 Scott Niedermayer .15 .40
243 Lyle Odelein .10 .25
244 Krzysztof Oliwa .10 .25
245 Jay Pandolfo .10 .25
246 Brian Rolston .12 .30
247 Vadim Sharifijanov .10 .25
248 Petr Sykora .12 .30
249 Chris Terreri .12 .30
250 Scott Stevens .15 .40
251 Eric Brewer .10 .25
252 Zdeno Chara .15 .40
253 Mariusz Czerkawski .10 .25
254 Wade Flaherty .10 .25
255 Kenny Jonsson .10 .25
256 Claude Lapointe .12 .30
257 Mark Lawrence .10 .25
258 Trevor Linden .15 .40
259 Mats Lindgren .10 .25
260 Warren Luhning .10 .25
261 Zigmund Palffy .15 .40
262 Rich Pilon .10 .25
263 Felix Potvin .25 .60
264 Barry Richter .10 .25
265 Bryan Smolinski .10 .25
266 Mike Watt .10 .25
267 Dan Cloutier .10 .25
268 Brent Fedyk .10 .25
269 Adam Graves .12 .30
270 Todd Harvey .10 .25
271 Mike Knuble .10 .25
272 Brian Leetch .12 .30
273 John MacLean .12 .30
274 Manny Malhotra .12 .30
275 Rumun Ndur .10 .25
276 Petr Nedved .10 .25
277 Peter Popovic .10 .25
278 Mike Richter .15 .40
279 Marc Savard .10 .25
280 Mathieu Schneider .10 .25
281 Kevin Stevens .12 .30
282 Niklas Sundstrom .10 .25
283 Daniel Alfredsson .15 .40
284 Magnus Arvedson .10 .25
285 Radek Bonk .10 .25
286 Andreas Dackell .10 .25
287 Bruce Gardiner .10 .25
288 Marian Hossa .15 .40
289 Andreas Johansson .10 .25
290 Igor Kravchuk .10 .25
291 Shawn McEachern .10 .25
292 Vaclav Prospal .10 .25
293 Wade Redden .10 .25
294 Damian Rhodes .10 .25
295 Sami Salo .12 .30
296 Ron Tugnutt .12 .30
297 Alexei Yashin .12 .30
298 Jason York .10 .25
299 Rod Brind'Amour .15 .40
300 Adam Burt .10 .25
301 Eric Desjardins .12 .30
302 Ron Hextall .15 .40
303 Jody Hull .10 .25
304 Keith Jones .10 .25
305 Daymond Langkow .12 .30
306 John LeClair .15 .40
307 Eric Lindros .25 .60
308 Sandy McCarthy .10 .25
309 Dan McGillis .10 .25
310 Mark Recchi .20 .50
311 Mikael Renberg .10 .25
312 Chris Therien .10 .25
313 John Vanbiesbrouck .15 .40
314 Valeri Zelepukin .10 .25
315 Greg Adams .10 .25
316 Keith Carney .10 .25
317 Bob Corkum .10 .25
318 Jim Cummins .10 .25
319 Shane Doan .12 .30
320 Dallas Drake .10 .25
321 Nikolai Khabibulin .12 .30
322 Jyrki Lumme .10 .25
323 Teppo Numminen .10 .25
324 Robert Reichel .10 .25
325 Jeremy Roenick .25 .60
326 Mikhail Shtalenkov .10 .25
327 Mike Stapleton .10 .25
328 Keith Tkachuk .15 .40
329 Rick Tocchet .12 .30
330 Oleg Tverdovsky .10 .25
331 Juha Ylonen .10 .25
332 R.Esche RC/S.Langkow .15 .40
333 Matthew Barnaby .10 .25
334 Tom Barrasso .15 .40
335 Rob Brown .10 .25
336 Kevin Hatcher .10 .25
337 Jan Hrdina .10 .25
338 Jaromir Jagr .50 1.25
339 Darius Kasparaitis .12 .30
340 Dan Kesa .10 .25
341 Alexei Kovalev .12 .30
342 Robert Lang .10 .25
343 Kip Miller .10 .25
344 Alexei Morozov .12 .30
345 Peter Skudra .12 .30
346 Jiri Slegr .10 .25
347 Martin Straka .10 .25
348 German Titov .10 .25
349 Brad Werenka .10 .25
350 J.S. Aubin RC
Brian Bonin .12 .30
351 Blair Atcheynum .10 .25
352 Lubos Bartecko .10 .25
353 Craig Conroy .10 .25
354 Geoff Courtnall .12 .30
355 Pavol Demitra .20 .50
356 Grant Fuhr .25 .60
357 Michal Handzus .12 .30
358 Al MacInnis .20 .50
359 Jamal Mayers .10 .25
360 Jamie McLennan .12 .30
361 Scott Pellerin .10 .25
362 Chris Pronger .15 .40
363 Pascal Rheaume .10 .25
364 Pierre Turgeon .12 .30
365 Tony Twist .12 .30
366 Scott Young .10 .25
367 J.Hecht RC/B.Johnson .25 .60
368 Tyson Nash RC
Marty Reasoner .10 .25
369 Vincent Damphousse .12 .30
370 Jeff Friesen .12 .30
371 Tony Granato .10 .25
372 Bill Houlder .10 .25
373 Alexander Korolyuk .10 .25
374 Bryan Marchment .12 .30
375 Patrick Marleau .15 .40
376 Stephane Matteau .10 .25
377 Joe Murphy .10 .25
378 Owen Nolan .15 .40
379 Mike Rathje .10 .25
380 Mike Ricci .10 .25
381 Steve Shields .12 .30
382 Ronnie Stern .10 .25
383 Marco Sturm .10 .25
384 Mike Vernon .12 .30
385 Scott Hannan RC
Shawn Heins .10 .25
386 Cory Cross .10 .25
387 Alexandre Daigle .10 .25
388 Colin Forbes .10 .25
389 Chris Gratton .10 .25
390 Kevin Hodson .10 .25
391 Pavel Kubina .10 .25
392 Vincent Lecavalier .15 .40
393 Michael Nylander .10 .25
394 Stephane Richer .12 .30
395 Corey Schwab .10 .25
396 Mike Sillinger .10 .25
397 Petr Svoboda .12 .30
398 Darcy Tucker .10 .25
399 Rob Zamuner .10 .25
400 Paul Mara RC
Mario Larocque .10 .25
401 Bryan Berard .10 .25
402 Sergei Berezin .10 .25
403 Lonny Bohonos .10 .25
404 Sylvain Cote .10 .25
405 Tie Domi .12 .30
406 Mike Johnson .12 .30
407 Curtis Joseph .20 .50
408 Tomas Kaberle .10 .25
409 Alexander Karpovtsev .10 .25
410 Derek King .10 .25
411 Igor Korolev .10 .25
412 Adam Mair RC .10 .25
413 Alyn McCauley .12 .30
414 Yanic Perreault .10 .25
415 Steve Sullivan .10 .25
416 Mats Sundin .15 .40
417 Steve Thomas .10 .25
418 Garry Valk .10 .25
419 Adrian Aucion .10 .25
420 Todd Bertuzzi .12 .30
421 Donald Brashear .10 .25
422 Dave Gagner .10 .25
423 Josh Holden .10 .25
424 Ed Jovanovski .12 .30
425 Bryan McCabe .12 .30
426 Mark Messier .30 .75
427 Alexander Mogilny .12 .30
428 Bill Muckalt .10 .25
429 Markus Naslund .15 .40
430 Mattias Ohlund .10 .25
431 Dave Scatchard .10 .25
432 Peter Schaefer .10 .25
433 Garth Snow .12 .30
434 Kevin Weekes .10 .25
435 Brian Bellows .12 .30
436 James Black .10 .25
437 Peter Bondra .15 .40
438 Jan Bulis .10 .25
439 Sergei Gonchar .10 .25
440 Benoit Gratton RC .10 .25
441 Calle Johansson .10 .25
442 Ken Klee .10 .25
443 Olaf Kolzig .15 .40
444 Steve Konowalchuk .10 .25
445 Andrei Nikolishin .10 .25
446 Adam Oates .15 .40
447 Jaroslav Svejkovsky .10 .25
448 Rick Tabaracci .10 .25
449 Richard Zednik .10 .25
450 Baumgartner/Tezikov RC .15 .40
451 Ladislav Kohn AG .10 .25
452 Petr Buzek AG .10 .25
453 Robyn Regehr AG .10 .25
454 David Tanabe AG .10 .25
455 Jiri Fischer AG .10 .25
456 Paul Comrie AG .25 .60
457 Brad Chartrand AG .10 .25
458 Scott Gomez AG .12 .30
459 Roberto Luongo AG .25 .60
460 Mike York AG .10 .25
462 Trevor Letowski AG .10 .25
463 Brad Stuart AG .12 .30
464 Ben Clymer AG .10 .25
465 Nikolai Antropov AG .40 1.00
466 Jeff Halpern AG .10 .25
235S Martin Brodeur Sample .75 2.00

1999-00 Pacific Copper

*COPPER/99: 8X TO 20X BASIC CARDS
426 Mark Messier 6.00 15.00

1999-00 Pacific Emerald Green

*GREEN/199: 6X TO 15X BASIC CARDS
426 Mark Messier 5.00 12.00

1999-00 Pacific Gold

*GOLD/199: 6X TO 15X BASIC CARDS
426 Mark Messier 5.00 12.00

1999-00 Pacific Ice Blue

*ICE BLUE/75: 10X TO 25X BASIC CARDS
426 Mark Messier 8.00 20.00

1999-00 Pacific Premiere Date

*PREM.DATE/46: 15X TO 40X BASIC CARDS
426 Mark Messier 12.00 30.00

1999-00 Pacific Red

*RED: 1X TO 2.5X BASIC CARDS

1999-00 Pacific Center Ice

COMPLETE SET (20) 12.00 30.00
1 Paul Kariya .75 2.00
2 Teemu Selanne .75 2.00
3 Dominik Hasek 1.50 4.00
4 Jarome Iginla 1.00 2.50
5 Theo Fleury .60 1.50
6 Peter Forsberg 2.00 5.00
7 Patrick Roy 4.00 10.00
8 Joe Sakic 1.50 4.00
9 Mike Modano 1.25 3.00
10 Brendan Shanahan .75 2.00
11 Steve Yzerman 4.00 10.00
12 Doug Weight .60 1.50
13 Trevor Linden .30 .75
14 Martin Brodeur 2.00 5.00
15 Alexei Yashin .30 .75
16 Eric Lindros .75 2.00
17 Jaromir Jagr 1.25 3.00
18 Curtis Joseph .75 2.00
19 Mats Sundin .75 2.00
20 Mark Messier .75 2.00

1999-00 Pacific Cramer's Choice

COMPLETE SET (10) 175.00 350.00
1 Paul Kariya 8.00 20.00
2 Dominik Hasek 15.00 40.00
3 Peter Forsberg 10.00 25.00
4 Patrick Roy 30.00 80.00
5 Joe Sakic 15.00 40.00
6 Mike Modano 12.50 30.00
7 Steve Yzerman 30.00 80.00
8 Eric Lindros 8.00 20.00
9 Jaromir Jagr 12.50 30.00
10 Curtis Joseph 8.00 20.00

1999-00 Pacific Gold Crown Die-Cuts

COMPLETE SET (36) 100.00 200.00
1 Paul Kariya 2.00 5.00
2 Teemu Selanne 2.00 5.00
3 Ray Bourque 3.00 8.00
4 Byron Dafoe 1.25 3.00
5 Dominik Hasek 4.00 10.00
6 Michael Peca 1.25 3.00
7 Chris Drury 1.25 3.00
8 Theo Fleury 1.25 3.00
9 Peter Forsberg 5.00 12.00
10 Milan Hejduk 1.25 3.00
11 Patrick Roy 10.00 25.00
12 Joe Sakic 4.00 10.00
13 Ed Belfour 2.00 5.00
14 Brett Hull 2.50 6.00
15 Mike Modano 2.50 6.00
16 Chris Chelios 1.25 3.00
17 Brendan Shanahan 2.00 5.00
18 Steve Yzerman 10.00 25.00
19 Pavel Bure 2.00 5.00
20 David Legwand 1.25 3.00
21 Martin Brodeur 6.00 15.00
22 Felix Potvin 2.00 5.00
23 Mike Richter 2.00 5.00
24 Alexei Yashin 1.25 3.00
25 John LeClair 1.25 3.00
26 Eric Lindros 2.00 5.00
27 Mark Recchi 1.25 3.00
28 John Vanbiesbrouck 1.25 3.00
29 Jeremy Roenick 2.50 6.00
30 Keith Tkachuk 1.25 3.00
31 Jaromir Jagr 3.00 8.00
32 Vincent Lecavalier 2.00 5.00
33 Sergei Berezin 1.25 3.00
34 Curtis Joseph 2.00 5.00
35 Mats Sundin 2.00 5.00
36 Mark Messier 2.00 5.00

1999-00 Pacific Home and Away

COMPLETE SET (20) 50.00 100.00
1 Paul Kariya 1.25 3.00
2 Teemu Selanne 1.25 3.00
3 Dominik Hasek 2.50 6.00
4 Peter Forsberg 3.00 8.00
5 Patrick Roy 6.00 15.00
6 Mike Modano 2.00 5.00
7 Steve Yzerman 6.00 15.00
8 John LeClair 1.25 3.00
9 Eric Lindros 1.25 3.00
10 Jaromir Jagr 2.00 5.00
11 Paul Kariya 1.25 3.00
12 Teemu Selanne 1.25 3.00
13 Dominik Hasek 2.50 6.00
14 Peter Forsberg 3.00 8.00
15 Patrick Roy 6.00 15.00
16 Mike Modano 2.00 5.00
17 Steve Yzerman 6.00 15.00
18 John LeClair 1.25 3.00
19 Eric Lindros 1.25 3.00
20 Jaromir Jagr 2.00 5.00

1999-00 Pacific In the Cage Net-Fusions

COMPLETE SET (20) 50.00 100.00
1 Guy Hebert 2.50 6.00
2 Byron Dafoe 2.00 5.00
3 Dominik Hasek 5.00 12.00
4 Arturs Irbe 2.00 5.00
5 Patrick Roy 12.50 30.00
6 Ed Belfour 3.00 8.00
7 Chris Osgood 3.00 8.00
8 Tommy Salo 2.50 6.00
9 Jeff Hackett 2.00 5.00
10 Martin Brodeur 6.00 15.00
11 Felix Potvin 3.00 8.00
12 Mike Richter 3.00 8.00
13 Ron Tugnutt 2.50 6.00
14 John Vanbiesbrouck 3.00 8.00
15 Nikolai Khabibulin 2.50 6.00
16 Tom Barrasso 2.00 5.00
17 Grant Fuhr 3.00 8.00
18 Mike Vernon 2.50 6.00
19 Curtis Joseph 3.00 8.00
20 Olaf Kolzig 2.50 6.00

1999-00 Pacific Past and Present

COMPLETE SET (20) 100.00 200.00
1 Paul Kariya 2.00 5.00
2 Teemu Selanne 2.00 5.00
3 Ray Bourque 3.00 8.00
4 Dominik Hasek 6.00 15.00
5 Theo Fleury 1.50 4.00
6 Peter Forsberg 8.00 20.00
7 Patrick Roy 12.00 30.00
8 Joe Sakic 6.00 15.00
9 Ed Belfour 2.00 5.00
10 Brett Hull 3.00 8.00
11 Mike Modano 3.00 8.00
12 Brendan Shanahan 2.00 5.00
13 Steve Yzerman 12.00 30.00
14 Pavel Bure 2.00 5.00
15 Martin Brodeur 8.00 20.00
16 John LeClair 1.50 4.00
17 Eric Lindros 2.00 5.00
18 John Vanbiesbrouck 1.50 4.00
19 Jaromir Jagr 4.00 10.00
20 Curtis Joseph 2.00 5.00

1999-00 Pacific Team Leaders

COMPLETE SET (28) 30.00 60.00
1 Paul Kariya 1.00 2.50
2 Atlanta Thrashers .40 1.00
3 Ray Bourque 1.50 4.00
4 Dominik Hasek 2.00 5.00
5 Jarome Iginla 1.25 3.00
6 Arturs Irbe .75 2.00
7 Doug Gilmour .75 2.00
8 Patrick Roy 5.00 12.00
9 Mike Modano 1.50 4.00
10 Steve Yzerman 5.00 12.00
11 Bill Guerin .75 2.00
12 Pavel Bure 1.00 2.50
13 Luc Robitaille .75 2.00
14 Saku Koivu 1.00 2.50
15 Mike Dunham .75 2.00
16 Martin Brodeur 2.50 6.00
17 Zigmund Palffy .75 2.00
18 Mike Richter 1.00 2.50
19 Alexei Yashin .40 1.00
20 Eric Lindros 1.00 2.50
21 Keith Tkachuk 1.00 2.50
22 Jaromir Jagr 1.50 4.00
23 Grant Fuhr .75 2.00
24 Mike Vernon .75 2.00
25 Vincent Lecavalier 1.00 2.50
26 Curtis Joseph 1.00 2.50
27 Mark Messier 1.00 2.50
28 Peter Bondra .75 2.00

2000-01 Pacific

1 Maxim Balmochnyk .12 .30
2 Matt Cullen .12 .30
3 Ted Donato .12 .30
4 Guy Hebert .15 .40
5 Paul Kariya .20 .50
6 Ladislav Kohn .12 .30
7 Marty McInnis .15 .40
8 Kip Miller .12 .30
9 Dominic Roussel .12 .30
10 Steve Rucchin .12 .30
11 Teemu Selanne .40 1.00
12 Oleg Tverdovsky .12 .30
13 Vitali Vishnevski .12 .30
14 Donald Audette .15 .40
15 Andrew Brunette .12 .30
16 Petr Buzek .12 .30
17 Hnat Domenichelli .12 .30
18 Ray Ferraro .12 .30
19 Steve Guolla .12 .30
20 Denny Lambert .12 .30
21 Damian Rhodes .12 .30
22 Mike Stapleton .12 .30
23 Patrik Stefan .15 .40
24 Per Svartvadet .12 .30
25 Dean Sylvester .12 .30
26 Yannick Tremblay .12 .30
27 B.Adams RC/Fankhouser .12 .30
28 Vasilijevs RC/Vyshedkevich RC .12 .30
29 Jason Allison .15 .40
30 Per Johan Axelsson .12 .30
31 Anson Carter .15 .40
32 Byron Dafoe .15 .40
33 Hal Gill .12 .30
34 John Grahame .12 .30
35 Steve Heinze .12 .30
36 Joe Hulbig .12 .30
37 Mike Knuble .12 .30
38 Kyle McLaren .12 .30
39 Eric Nickulas RC .12 .30
40 Brian Rolston .15 .40
41 Sergei Samsonov .15 .40
42 Andre Savage .12 .30
43 Joe Thornton .30 .75
44 Darren Van Impe .12 .30
45 N.Boynton/J.Aitken RC .12 .30
46 Maxim Afinogenov .12 .30
47 Stu Barnes .15 .40
48 Martin Biron .15 .40
49 Curtis Brown .12 .30
50 Doug Gilmour .25 .60
51 Chris Gratton .12 .30
52 Dominik Hasek .30 .75
53 Michael Peca .15 .40
54 Erik Rasmussen .12 .30
55 Rob Ray .12 .30
56 Geoff Sanderson .15 .40
57 Miroslav Satan .12 .30
58 Vladimir Tsyplakov .12 .30
59 Vaclav Varada .12 .30
60 Jason Woolley .12 .30
61 Fred Brathwaite .15 .40
62 Valeri Bure .15 .40
63 Bobby Dollas .12 .30
64 Jean-Sebastien Giguere .20 .50
65 Phil Housley .15 .40
66 Jarome Iginla .25 .60
67 Andreas Johansson .12 .30
68 Sergei Krivokrasov .12 .30
69 Bill Lindsay .12 .30
70 Derek Morris .12 .30
71 Andrei Nazarov .12 .30
72 Oleg Saprykin .12 .30
73 Marc Savard .12 .30
74 Jeff Shantz .12 .30
75 Cory Stillman .12 .30
76 Jason Wiemer .12 .30
77 C.Clark/S.Varlamov .12 .30
78 Bates Battaglia .12 .30
79 Rod Brind'Amour .20 .50
80 Paul Coffey .20 .50
81 Ron Francis .25 .60
82 Sean Hill .12 .30
83 Arturs Irbe .15 .40
84 Sami Kapanen .12 .30
85 Dave Karpa .12 .30
86 Andrei Kovalenko .12 .30
87 Robert Kron .12 .30
88 Jeff O'Neill .15 .40
89 Gary Roberts .12 .30
90 Dave Tanabe .12 .30
91 Tommy Westlund .12 .30
92 Tony Amonte .15 .40
93 Eric Daze .15 .40
94 Kevin Dean .12 .30
95 Michal Grosek .12 .30
96 Dean McAmmond .12 .30
97 Bryan McCabe .12 .30
98 Steven McCarthy .12 .30
99 Boris Mironov .12 .30
100 Michael Nylander .12 .30
101 Bob Probert .20 .50
102 Steve Sullivan .12 .30
103 Jocelyn Thibault .15 .40
104 Ryan Vandenbussche .12 .30
105 Alexei Zhamnov .15 .40
106 Dave Andreychuk .20 .50
107 Ray Bourque .30 .75
108 Adam Deadmarsh .12 .30
109 Marc Denis .15 .40
110 Greg DeVries .12 .30
111 Chris Drury .15 .40
112 Adam Foote .15 .40
113 Peter Forsberg .40 1.00
114 Alexei Gusarov .12 .30
115 Milan Hejduk .15 .40
116 Eric Messier .12 .30
117 Sandis Ozolinsh .12 .30
118 Shjon Podein .12 .30
119 Dave Reid .12 .30
120 Patrick Roy .50 1.25
121 Joe Sakic .40 1.00
122 Martin Skoula .15 .40
123 Alex Tanguay .15 .40
124 Stephane Yelle .12 .30
125 S.Aubin RC/V.Nieminen RC .15 .40
126 Ed Belfour .20 .50
127 Guy Carbonneau .15 .40
128 Sylvain Cote .12 .30
129 Manny Fernandez .12 .30
130 Derian Hatcher .15 .40
131 Brett Hull .40 1.00
132 Mike Keane .15 .40
133 Jamie Langenbrunner .15 .40
134 Jere Lehtinen .15 .40
135 Dave Manson .12 .30
136 Richard Matvichuk .12 .30
137 Mike Modano .30 .75
138 Brenden Morrow .15 .40
139 Joe Nieuwendyk .15 .40
140 Blake Sloan .12 .30
141 Darryl Sydor .15 .40
142 Scott Thornton .15 .40
143 Sergei Zubov ERR .15 .40
144 Doug Brown .12 .30
145 Chris Chelios .20 .50
146 Kris Draper .12 .30
147 Sergei Fedorov .30 .75
148 Tomas Holmstrom .15 .40
149 Vyacheslav Kozlov .15 .40
150 Darryl Laplante .12 .30
151 Martin Lapointe .15 .40
152 Igor Larionov .20 .50
153 Nicklas Lidstrom .20 .50
154 Kirk Maltby .12 .30
155 Darren McCarty .12 .30
156 Larry Murphy .15 .40
157 Chris Osgood .20 .50
158 Brendan Shanahan .20 .50
159 Pat Verbeek .15 .40
160 Jesse Wallin .12 .30
161 Ken Wregget .15 .40
162 Steve Yzerman .50 1.25
163 Boyd Devereaux .12 .30
164 Jim Dowd .12 .30
165 Mike Grier .12 .30
166 Bill Guerin .20 .50
167 Roman Hamrlik .12 .30
168 Georges Laraque .15 .40
169 Todd Marchant .12 .30
170 Ethan Moreau .12 .30
171 Tom Poti .12 .30
172 Tommy Salo .15 .40
173 Alexander Selivanov .12 .30
174 Ryan Smyth .15 .40
175 German Titov .12 .30
176 Doug Weight .20 .50
177 Pavel Bure .20 .50
178 Trevor Kidd .12 .30
179 Viktor Kozlov .15 .40
180 Oleg Kvasha .12 .30
181 Paul Laus .12 .30
182 Scott Mellanby .12 .30
183 Rob Niedermayer .15 .40
184 Ivan Novoseltsev .12 .30
185 Mark Parrish .12 .30
186 Mikhail Shtalenkov .12 .30
187 Robert Svehla .12 .30
188 Mike Vernon .15 .40
189 Ray Whitney .15 .40
190 Peter Worrell .12 .30
191 E.Boguniecki/B.Ference .12 .30
192 Aki Berg .12 .30
193 Rob Blake .20 .50
194 Kelly Buchberger .15 .40
195 Nelson Emerson .12 .30
196 Stephane Fiset .12 .30
197 Garry Galley .12 .30
198 Glen Murray .15 .40
199 Jan Nemecek .12 .30
200 Zigmund Palffy .20 .50
201 Luc Robitaille .20 .50
202 Bryan Smolinski .15 .40
203 Jamie Storr .15 .40
204 Jozef Stumpel .12 .30
205 Patrice Brisebois .12 .30
206 Benoit Brunet .12 .30
207 Shayne Corson .15 .40
208 Jeff Hackett .12 .30
209 Saku Koivu .20 .50
210 Trevor Linden .20 .50
211 Oleg Petrov .12 .30
212 Martin Rucinsky .12 .30
213 Brian Savage .12 .30
214 Sheldon Souray .12 .30
215 Jose Theodore .20 .50
216 Eric Weinrich .12 .30
217 Sergei Zholtok .12 .30
218 Dainius Zubrus .12 .30
219 Sebastien Bordeleau .12 .30
220 Mike Dunham .12 .30
221 Tom Fitzgerald .12 .30
222 Greg Johnson .12 .30
223 David Legwand .20 .50
224 Craig Millar .12 .30
225 Cliff Ronning .12 .30
226 Kimmo Timonen .12 .30
227 Tomas Vokoun .15 .40
228 Scott Walker .12 .30
229 A.Boikov RC/M.Moro RC .12 .30
230 D.Gosselin RC/C.Mason RC .25 .60
231 Jason Arnott .15 .40
232 Martin Brodeur .50 1.25
233 Patrik Elias .20 .50
234 Scott Gomez .15 .40
235 Bobby Holik .12 .30
236 Claude Lemieux .15 .40
237 John Madden .15 .40
238 Vladimir Malakhov .12 .30
239 Randy McKay .12 .30
240 Alexander Mogilny .15 .40
241 Scott Niedermayer .20 .50
242 Brian Rafalski .12 .30
243 Scott Stevens .20 .50
244 Petr Sykora .15 .40
245 Chris Terreri .12 .30
246 W.Mitchell RC/C.White RC .20 .50
247 Tim Connolly .12 .30
248 Mariusz Czerkawski .12 .30
249 Josh Green .12 .30
250 Brad Isbister .12 .30
251 Jason Krog .12 .30
252 Claude Lapointe .12 .30
253 Roberto Luongo .30 .75
254 Petr Mika RC .12 .30
255 Dave Scatchard .12 .30
256 Steve Valiquette RC .15 .40
257 Kevin Weekes .12 .30
258 Alexandre Daigle .15 .40
259 Radek Dvorak .15 .40
260 Theo Fleury .25 .60
261 Adam Graves .15 .40
262 Jan Hlavac .12 .30
263 Kim Johnsson .12 .30
264 Valeri Kamensky .12 .30
265 Brian Leetch .15 .40
266 John MacLean .15 .40
267 Kirk McLean .12 .30
268 Petr Nedved .15 .40
269 Mike Richter .20 .50
270 Mathieu Schneider .12 .30
271 Johan Witehall RC .12 .30
272 Mike York .12 .30
273 Daniel Alfredsson .20 .50
274 Magnus Arvedson .12 .30
275 Tom Barrasso .15 .40
276 Radek Bonk .15 .40
277 Mike Fisher .12 .30
278 Marian Hossa .20 .50
279 Jani Hurme RC .12 .30
280 Joe Juneau .12 .30
281 Patrick Lalime .15 .40
282 Grant Ledyard .12 .30
283 Shawn McEachern .12 .30

284 Chris Phillips .12 .30
285 Vaclav Prospal .12 .30
286 Wade Redden .12 .30
287 Sami Salo .12 .30
288 Alexei Yashin .15 .40
289 Jason York .12 .30
290 Rob Zamuner .12 .30
291 E.Goldmann RC/P.Schastlivy .12 .30
292 Craig Berube .12 .30
293 Brian Boucher .15 .40
294 Andy Delmore .12 .30
295 Eric Desjardins .15 .40
296 Simon Gagne .20 .50
297 Jody Hull .12 .30
298 Keith Jones .12 .30
299 Daymond Langkow .12 .30
300 John LeClair .20 .50
301 Eric Lindros .30 .75
302 Kent Manderville .12 .30
303 Dan McGillis .12 .30
304 Gino Odjick .12 .30
305 Keith Primeau .15 .40
306 Mark Recchi .25 .60
307 Chris Therien .12 .30
308 Rick Tocchet .15 .40
309 John Vanbiesbrouck .20 .50
310 Valeri Zelepukin .12 .30
311 Sean Burke .12 .30
312 Keith Carney .12 .30
313 Louie DeBrusk .12 .30
314 Shane Doan .15 .40
315 Dallas Drake .12 .30
316 Travis Green .12 .30
317 Nikolai Khabibulin .30 .75
318 Trevor Letowski .12 .30
319 Jyrki Lumme .12 .30
320 Mikael Renberg .12 .30
321 Jeremy Roenick .30 .75
322 Keith Tkachuk .20 .50
323 R.Esche/W.Smith .12 .30
324 Jean-Sebastien Aubin .15 .40
325 Matthew Barnaby .12 .30
326 Pat Falloon .15 .40
327 Jan Hrdina .12 .30
328 Jaromir Jagr .60 1.50
329 Darius Kasparaitis .15 .40
330 Alexei Kovalev .15 .40
331 Robert Lang .12 .30
332 Janne Laukkanen .12 .30
333 Stephen Leach .12 .30
334 Alexei Morozov .12 .30
335 Michal Rozsival .12 .30
336 Jiri Slegr .12 .30
337 Martin Straka .15 .40
338 Ron Tugnutt .15 .40
339 Lubos Bartecko .12 .30
340 Marc Bergevin .12 .30
341 Pavol Demitra .25 .60
342 Mike Eastwood .12 .30
343 Dave Ellett .12 .30
344 Michal Handzus .12 .30
345 Jochen Hecht .12 .30
346 Al MacInnis .25 .60
347 Jamie McLennan .12 .30
348 Tyson Nash .12 .30
349 Chris Pronger .20 .50
350 Marty Reasoner .12 .30
351 Stephane Richer .12 .30
352 Roman Turek .15 .40
353 Pierre Turgeon .15 .40
354 Scott Young .12 .30
355 D.Bekar RC/L.Nagy .12 .30
356 Vincent Damphousse .15 .40
357 Jeff Friesen .12 .30
358 Todd Harvey .15 .40
359 Alexander Korolyuk .12 .30
360 Patrick Marleau .20 .50
361 Stephane Matteau .12 .30
362 Evgeni Nabokov .15 .40
363 Owen Nolan .20 .50
364 Mike Ricci .12 .30
365 Steve Shields .12 .30
366 Brad Stuart .15 .40
367 Marco Sturm .12 .30
368 Gary Suter .12 .30
369 Dan Cloutier .15 .40
370 Stan Drulia .12 .30
371 Matt Elich RC .15 .40
372 Brian Holzinger .12 .30
373 Mike Johnson .12 .30
374 Ryan Johnson .12 .30
375 Dieter Kochan RC .12 .30
376 Pavel Kubina .12 .30
377 Vincent Lecavalier .20 .50
378 Fredrik Modin .12 .30
379 Wayne Primeau .12 .30
380 Cory Sarich .12 .30
381 Petr Svoboda .12 .30
382 K.Astashenko RC/K.Freadrich RC .12 .30
383 G.Dwyer/M.Posmyk .12 .30
384 Nikolai Antropov .15 .40
385 Sergei Berezin .12 .30
386 Wendel Clark .30 .75
387 Tie Domi .15 .40
388 Gerald Diduck .12 .30
389 Jeff Farkas .12 .30
390 Glenn Healy .12 .30
391 Jonas Hoglund .12 .30
392 Curtis Joseph .25 .60
393 Tomas Kaberle .12 .30
394 Alexander Karpovtsev .12 .30
395 Dimitri Khristich .12 .30
396 Igor Korolev .12 .30
397 Yanic Perreault .12 .30
398 DJ Smith .12 .30
399 Mats Sundin .20 .50
400 Steve Thomas .12 .30
401 Darcy Tucker .12 .30
402 Dimitri Yushkevich .12 .30
403 Adrian Aucoin .12 .30
404 Todd Bertuzzi .15 .40
405 Donald Brashear .12 .30
406 Andrew Cassels .12 .30
407 Harold Druken .12 .30
408 Ed Jovanovski .15 .40
409 Steve Kariya .12 .30
410 Trent Klatt .12 .30
411 Mark Messier .40 1.00
412 Markus Naslund .20 .50
413 Mattias Ohlund .12 .30
414 Felix Potvin .30 .75
415 Peter Schaefer .12 .30
416 Garth Snow .15 .40
417 A.Michaud/J.Ruutu .20 .50
418 Peter Bondra .20 .50
419 Martin Brochu RC .12 .30
420 Jan Bulis .12 .30
421 Sergei Gonchar .12 .30
422 Jeff Halpern .12 .30
423 Calle Johansson .12 .30
424 Ken Klee .12 .30
425 Olaf Kolzig .20 .50
426 Steve Konowalchuk .12 .30
427 Glen Metropolit .12 .30
428 Adam Oates .20 .50
429 Chris Simon .12 .30
430 Richard Zednik .12 .30
431 Jorgen Jonsson SF .12 .30
432 Teemu Selanne SF .40 1.00
433 Sami Kapanen SF .12 .30
434 Peter Forsberg SF .40 1.00
435 Jere Lehtinen SF .15 .40
436 Nicklas Lidstrom SF .20 .50
437 Janne Niinimaa SF .12 .30
438 Tommy Salo SF .15 .40
439 Saku Koivu SF .20 .50
440 Patric Kjellberg SF .12 .30
441 Olli Jokinen SF .15 .40
442 Kenny Jonsson SF .12 .30
443 Daniel Alfredsson SF .20 .50
444 Andreas Dackell SF .12 .30
445 Teppo Numminen SF .12 .30
446 Marcus Ragnarsson SF .12 .30
447 Niklas Sundstrom SF .12 .30
448 Mats Sundin SF .20 .50
449 Markus Naslund SF .20 .50
450 Ulf Dahlen SF .12 .30

2000-01 Pacific Copper

*COPPER/40: 10X TO 25X BASIC CARDS

2000-01 Pacific Gold

*GOLD/50: 6X TO 15X BASIC CARDS

2000-01 Pacific Ice Blue

*VETS: 10X TO 25X BASIC CARDS

2000-01 Pacific Premiere Date

*PREM.DATE/40: 10X TO 25X BASIC CARDS

2000-01 Pacific 2001: Ice Odyssey

1 Paul Kariya 1.50 4.00
2 Teemu Selanne 3.00 8.00
3 Martin Biron 1.25 3.00
4 Jarome Iginla 2.00 5.00
5 Chris Drury 1.25 3.00
6 Peter Forsberg 3.00 8.00
7 Milan Hejduk 1.25 3.00
8 Patrick Roy 4.00 10.00
9 Steve Yzerman 4.00 10.00
10 Pavel Bure 1.50 4.00
11 Jose Theodore 1.50 4.00
12 Martin Brodeur 4.00 10.00
13 Patrik Elias 1.50 4.00
14 Scott Gomez 1.25 3.00
15 Roberto Luongo 2.50 6.00
16 Marian Hossa 1.50 4.00
17 Brian Boucher 1.25 3.00
18 Jaromir Jagr 5.00 12.00
19 Vincent Lecavalier 1.50 4.00
20 Mats Sundin 1.50 4.00

2000-01 Pacific Autographs

57 Miroslav Satan/500 4.00 10.00
123 Alex Tanguay/250 5.00 12.00
126 Ed Belfour/250 6.00 15.00
137 Mike Modano/250 10.00 25.00
138 Brenden Morrow/500 5.00 12.00
169 Todd Marchant/250 4.00 10.00
172 Tommy Salo/500 5.00 12.00
215 Jose Theodore/250 6.00 15.00
223 David Legwand/250 6.00 15.00
233 Patrik Elias/500 6.00 15.00
234 Scott Gomez/500 5.00 12.00
251 Jason Krog/500 4.00 10.00
262 Jan Hlavac/500 4.00 10.00
272 Mike York/500 4.00 10.00
296 Simon Gagne/1000 6.00 15.00
300 John LeClair/250 10.00 25.00
352 Roman Turek/500 5.00 12.00
377 Vincent Lecavalier/1000 6.00 15.00
384 Nikolai Antropov/250 5.00 12.00

2000-01 Pacific Cramer's Choice

1 Paul Kariya 2.00 5.00
2 Teemu Selanne 4.00 10.00
3 Peter Forsberg 4.00 10.00
4 Patrick Roy 5.00 12.00
5 Steve Yzerman 5.00 12.00
6 Pavel Bure 2.00 5.00
7 Martin Brodeur 5.00 12.00
8 Scott Gomez 1.50 4.00
9 Jaromir Jagr 6.00 15.00
10 Mats Sundin 2.00 5.00

2000-01 Pacific Euro-Stars

1 Teemu Selanne 2.00 5.00
2 Dominik Hasek 1.50 4.00
3 Peter Forsberg 2.00 5.00
4 Sergei Fedorov 1.50 4.00
5 Pavel Bure 1.00 2.50
6 Jaromir Jagr 3.00 8.00
7 Pavol Demitra 1.25 3.00
8 Roman Turek .75 2.00
9 Mats Sundin 1.00 2.50
10 Olaf Kolzig 1.00 2.50

2000-01 Pacific Jerseys

1 Ray Bourque 4.00 10.00
2 Eric Messier 1.50 4.00
3 Patrick Roy 6.00 15.00
4 Joe Sakic 5.00 12.00
5 Mike Modano 4.00 10.00
6 Darryl Sydor 2.00 5.00
7 Brendan Shanahan 2.50 6.00
8 Steve Yzerman 6.00 15.00
9 Pavel Bure 2.50 6.00
10 Eric Desjardins 2.00 5.00
11 Daymond Langkow 1.50 4.00
12 Shane Doan 2.00 5.00
13 Jaromir Jagr 8.00 20.00
14 Mark Messier 5.00 12.00
15 Olaf Kolzig 2.50 6.00

2000-01 Pacific Gold Crown Die Cuts

1 Paul Kariya 2.00 5.00
2 Teemu Selanne 4.00 10.00
3 Joe Thornton 3.00 8.00
4 Dominik Hasek 3.00 8.00
5 Valeri Bure 1.50 4.00
6 Tony Amonte 1.50 4.00
7 Ray Bourque 3.00 8.00
8A Peter Forsberg 4.00 10.00
8B Milan Hejduk 1.50 4.00
9 Joe Sakic 4.00 10.00
10 Patrick Roy 5.00 12.00
11 Brett Hull 4.00 10.00
13 Mike Modano 3.00 8.00
14 Brendan Shanahan 2.00 5.00
15 Steve Yzerman 5.00 12.00
16 Pavel Bure 2.00 5.00
17 Luc Robitaille 2.00 5.00
18 Martin Brodeur 5.00 12.00
19 Scott Gomez 1.50 4.00
20 Roberto Luongo 3.00 8.00
21 Marian Hossa 2.00 5.00
22 Brian Boucher 1.50 4.00
23 John LeClair 2.00 5.00
24 Eric Lindros 3.00 8.00
25 Mark Recchi 2.50 6.00
26 Keith Tkachuk 2.00 5.00
27 Jeremy Roenick 3.00 8.00
28 Jaromir Jagr 6.00 15.00
29 Chris Pronger 2.00 5.00
30 Roman Turek 1.50 4.00
31 Owen Nolan 2.00 5.00
32 Vincent Lecavalier 2.00 5.00
33 Mats Sundin 2.00 5.00
34 Curtis Joseph 2.50 6.00
35 Mark Messier 4.00 10.00
36 Olaf Kolzig 2.00 5.00

2000-01 Pacific In the Cage Net-Fusions

1 Dominik Hasek 3.00 8.00
2 Fred Brathwaite 1.50 4.00
3 Patrick Roy 5.00 12.00
4 Mike Vernon 1.50 4.00
5 Stephane Fiset 1.25 3.00
6 Jeff Hackett 1.25 3.00
7 Martin Brodeur 5.00 12.00
8 Mike Richter 2.00 5.00
9 Brian Boucher 1.50 4.00
10 Curtis Joseph 2.50 6.00

2000-01 Pacific North American Stars

1 Paul Kariya 1.50 4.00
2 Joe Sakic 3.00 8.00
3 Patrick Roy 4.00 10.00
4 Mike Modano 2.50 6.00
5 Brendan Shanahan 1.50 4.00
6 Steve Yzerman 4.00 10.00
7 Martin Brodeur 4.00 10.00
8 Scott Gomez 1.25 3.00
9 John LeClair 1.50 4.00
10 Curtis Joseph 2.00 5.00

2000-01 Pacific Reflections

1 Paul Kariya 2.50 6.00
2 Teemu Selanne 5.00 12.00
3 Doug Gilmour 3.00 8.00
4 Ray Bourque 4.00 10.00
5 Peter Forsberg 5.00 12.00
6 Joe Sakic 5.00 12.00
7 Brett Hull 5.00 12.00
8 Mike Modano 4.00 10.00
9 Brendan Shanahan 2.50 6.00
10 Steve Yzerman 6.00 15.00
11 Pavel Bure 2.50 6.00
12 Zigmund Palffy 2.50 6.00
13 Scott Gomez 2.00 5.00
14 Marian Hossa 2.50 6.00
15 John LeClair 2.50 6.00
16 Eric Lindros 4.00 10.00
17 Jaromir Jagr 8.00 20.00
18 Vincent Lecavalier 2.50 6.00
19 Mats Sundin 2.50 6.00
20 Mark Messier 5.00 12.00

2001-02 Pacific

1 Matt Cullen .12 .30
2 Jim Cummins .12 .30
3 Jeff Friesen .12 .30
4 Jean-Sebastien Giguere .20 .50
5 Tony Hrkac .12 .30
6 Paul Kariya .20 .50
7 Mike Leclerc .12 .30
8 Marty McInnis .15 .40
9 Steve Rucchin .12 .30
10 Ruslan Salei .12 .30
11 Steve Shields .15 .40
12 Oleg Tverdovsky .12 .30
13 Bob Wren RC .12 .30
14 Andrew Brunette .12 .30
15 Hnat Domenichelli .12 .30
16 Ray Ferraro .12 .30
17 Stephen Guolla .12 .30
18 Milan Hnilicka .15 .40
19 Tomi Kallio .12 .30
20 Norm Maracle .12 .30
21 Rumun Ndur .12 .30
22 Jeff Odgers .12 .30
23 Damian Rhodes .15 .40
24 Jiri Slegr .12 .30
25 Patrik Stefan .15 .40
26 J.P. Vigier .12 .30
27 Jason Allison .15 .40
28 P.J. Axelsson .12 .30
29 Byron Dafoe .15 .40
30 John Grahame .15 .40
31 Bill Guerin .20 .50
32 Mike Knuble .12 .30
33 Andrei Kovalenko .12 .30
34 Eric Manlow .12 .30
35 Andrei Nazarov .12 .30
36 Brian Rolston .15 .40
37 Sergei Samsonov .15 .40
38 Peter Skudra .15 .40
39 Don Sweeney .12 .30
40 Joe Thornton .30 .75
41 Eric Weinrich .12 .30
42 Maxim Afinogenov .12 .30
43 Dave Andreychuk .20 .50
44 Donald Audette .12 .30
45 Stu Barnes .15 .40
46 Martin Biron .15 .40
47 J-P Dumont .12 .30
48 Doug Gilmour .25 .60
49 Chris Gratton .12 .30
50 Dominik Hasek .30 .75
51 Steve Heinze .12 .30
52 Erik Rasmussen .12 .30
53 Rob Ray .12 .30
54 Miroslav Satan .15 .40
55 Alexei Zhitnik .12 .30
56 Tommy Albelin .12 .30
57 Fred Brathwaite .15 .40
58 Valeri Bure .12 .30
59 Craig Conroy .12 .30
60 Phil Housley .15 .40
61 Jarome Iginla .25 .60
62 Dave Lowry .12 .30
63 Derek Morris .12 .30
64 Oleg Saprykin .12 .30
65 Marc Savard .12 .30
66 Daniel Tkaczuk .12 .30
67 Mike Vernon .15 .40
68 Jason Wiemer .12 .30
69 Bates Battaglia .12 .30
70 Rod Brind'Amour .20 .50
71 Ron Francis .25 .60
72 Martin Gelinas .12 .30
73 Kevin Hatcher .12 .30
74 Arturs Irbe .15 .40
75 Sami Kapanen .12 .30
76 Dave Karpa .12 .30
77 Tyler Moss .12 .30
78 Jeff O'Neill .15 .40
79 Sandis Ozolinsh .12 .30
80 Scott Pellerin .12 .30
81 Shane Willis .12 .30
82 Tony Amonte .15 .40
83 Mark Bell .12 .30
84 Eric Daze .15 .40
85 Steve Dubinsky .12 .30
86 Chris Herperger .12 .30
87 Michel Larocque .12 .30
88 Michael Nylander .12 .30
89 Steve Passmore .12 .30
90 Bob Probert .20 .50
91 Stephane Quintal .12 .30
92 Steve Sullivan .12 .30
93 Jocelyn Thibault .15 .40
94 Alexei Zhamnov .15 .40
95 David Aebischer .15 .40
96 Rick Berry .12 .30
97 Rob Blake .20 .50
98 Ray Bourque .30 .75
99 Chris Drury .15 .40
100 Adam Foote .15 .40
101 Peter Forsberg .40 1.00
102 Milan Hejduk .15 .40
103 Ville Nieminen .12 .30
104 Shjon Podein .12 .30
105 Steven Reinprecht .12 .30
106 Patrick Roy .50 1.25
107 Joe Sakic .40 1.00
108 Alex Tanguay .15 .40
109 Serge Aubin .12 .30
110 Mathieu Darche RC .20 .50
111 Matt Davidson RC .12 .30
112 Marc Denis .15 .40
113 Rostislav Klesla .12 .30
114 Espen Knutsen .12 .30
115 Chris Nielsen .12 .30
116 Geoff Sanderson .12 .30
117 Martin Spanhel RC .12 .30
118 Ron Tugnutt .15 .40
119 David Vyborny .12 .30
120 Ray Whitney .12 .30
121 Tyler Wright .12 .30
122 Ed Belfour .20 .50
123 Steve Gainey .12 .30
124 Derian Hatcher .12 .30
125 Sami Helenius .12 .30
126 Brett Hull .40 1.00
127 Jamie Langenbrunner .12 .30
128 Jere Lehtinen .15 .40
129 Brad Lukowich .12 .30
130 Grant Marshall .12 .30
131 Mike Modano .30 .75
132 Brenden Morrow .15 .40
133 Kirk Muller .15 .40
134 Joe Nieuwendyk .15 .40
135 Darryl Sydor .12 .30
136 Marty Turco .20 .50
137 Sergei Zubov .15 .40
138 Chris Chelios .20 .50
139 Sergei Fedorov .30 .75
140 Todd Gill .12 .30
141 Tomas Holmstrom .12 .30
142 Slava Kozlov .15 .40
143 Martin Lapointe .12 .30
144 Igor Larionov .20 .50
145 Manny Legace .15 .40
146 Nicklas Lidstrom .20 .50
147 Darren McCarty .12 .30
148 Chris Osgood .20 .50
149 Brendan Shanahan .20 .50
150 Pat Verbeek .15 .40
151 Aaron Ward .12 .30
152 Steve Yzerman .50 1.25
153 Anson Carter .15 .40
154 Jason Chimera RC .12 .30
155 Daniel Cleary .15 .40
156 Mike Comrie .15 .40
157 Mike Grier .12 .30
158 Shawn Horcoff .15 .40
159 Georges Laraque .15 .40
160 Todd Marchant .12 .30
161 Rem Murray .15 .40
162 Janne Niinimaa .12 .30
163 Dominic Roussel .12 .30
164 Tommy Salo .15 .40
165 Jason Smith .12 .30
166 Ryan Smyth .15 .40
167 Doug Weight .20 .50
168 Kevyn Adams .12 .30
169 Pavel Bure .20 .50
170 Anders Eriksson .12 .30
171 Trevor Kidd .12 .30
172 Viktor Kozlov .12 .30
173 Roberto Luongo .30 .75
174 Rob Niedermayer .15 .40
175 Marcus Nilsson .12 .30
176 Andrej Podkonicky RC .12 .30
177 Robert Svehla .12 .30
178 Peter Worrell .12 .30
179 Eric Belanger .12 .30
180 Adam Deadmarsh .12 .30
181 Stu Grimson .12 .30
182 Andreas Lilja .12 .30
183 Glen Murray .15 .40
184 Zigmund Palffy .20 .50
185 Felix Potvin .30 .75
186 Luc Robitaille .20 .50
187 Mathieu Schneider .12 .30
188 Bryan Smolinski .12 .30
189 Jamie Storr .15 .40
190 Jozef Stumpel .12 .30
191 Lubomir Visnovsky .12 .30
192 Jim Dowd .12 .30
193 Manny Fernandez .12 .30
194 Marian Gaborik .20 .50
195 Derek Gustafson .12 .30
196 Matt Johnson .12 .30
197 Filip Kuba .12 .30
198 Antti Laaksonen .12 .30
199 Jamie McLennan .12 .30
200 Lubomir Sekeras .12 .30
201 Wes Walz .12 .30
202 Francis Belanger RC .15 .40
203 Patrice Brisebois .12 .30
204 Jan Bulis .12 .30
205 Karl Dykhuis .12 .30
206 Mathieu Garon .15 .40
207 Jeff Hackett .15 .40
208 Chad Kilger .12 .30
209 Saku Koivu .20 .50
210 Oleg Petrov .12 .30
211 Martin Rucinsky .12 .30
212 Brian Savage .12 .30
213 Jose Theodore .20 .50
214 Richard Zednik .15 .40
215 Marian Cisar .12 .30
216 Mike Dunham .15 .40
217 Scott Hartnell .12 .30
218 Greg Johnson .12 .30
219 Patric Kjellberg .12 .30
220 David Legwand .15 .40
221 Cliff Ronning .12 .30
222 Tomas Vokoun .15 .40
223 Scott Walker .12 .30
224 Vitali Yachmenev .12 .30
225 Jason Arnott .15 .40
226 Jiri Bicek .12 .30
227 Martin Brodeur .50 1.25
228 Sergei Brylin .12 .30
229 Patrik Elias .20 .50
230 Scott Gomez .15 .40
231 Bobby Holik .12 .30
232 John Madden .15 .40
233 Randy McKay .12 .30
234 Jim McKenzie .12 .30
235 Alexander Mogilny .15 .40
236 Sergei Nemchinov .12 .30
237 Scott Niedermayer .20 .50
238 Scott Stevens .20 .50
239 Petr Sykora .12 .30
240 John Vanbiesbrouck .20 .50
241 Ed Ward .12 .30
242 Zdeno Chara .20 .50
243 Tim Connolly .12 .30
244 Mariusz Czerkawski .12 .30
245 Rick DiPietro .15 .40
246 Garry Galley .12 .30
247 Kevin Haller .12 .30
248 Roman Hamrlik .12 .30
249 Brad Isbister .12 .30
250 Kenny Jonsson .12 .30
251 Claude Lapointe .12 .30
252 Mark Parrish .12 .30
253 Dave Scatchard .12 .30
254 Chris Terreri .15 .40
255 Radek Dvorak .15 .40
256 Theo Fleury .25 .60
257 Adam Graves .15 .40
258 Guy Hebert .20 .50
259 Jan Hlavac .12 .30
260 Valeri Kamensky .12 .30
261 Brian Leetch .15 .40
262 Sylvain Lefebvre .12 .30
263 Sandy McCarthy .12 .30
264 Mark Messier .40 1.00
265 Petr Nedved .15 .40
266 Rich Pilon .12 .30
267 Mike Richter .20 .50
268 Mike York .12 .30
269 Daniel Alfredsson .20 .50
270 Magnus Arvedson .12 .30
271 Radek Bonk .12 .30
272 Martin Havlat .15 .40
273 Marian Hossa .20 .50
274 Jani Hurme .15 .40
275 Patrick Lalime .15 .40
276 Shawn McEachern .12 .30
277 Chris Phillips .12 .30
278 Wade Redden .12 .30
279 Andre Roy .12 .30
280 Mike Sillinger .12 .30
281 Alexei Yashin .15 .40
282 Rob Zamuner .12 .30
283 Brian Boucher .15 .40
284 Roman Cechmanek .15 .40
285 Eric Desjardins .15 .40
286 Ruslan Fedotenko .12 .30
287 Simon Gagne .20 .50
288 Daymond Langkow .15 .40
289 John LeClair .20 .50
290 Eric Lindros .30 .75
291 Dan McGillis .12 .30
292 Keith Primeau .15 .40
293 Paul Ranheim .12 .30
294 Mark Recchi .25 .60
295 Rick Tocchet .12 .30
296 Justin Williams .15 .40
297 Joel Bouchard .12 .30
298 Daniel Briere .15 .40
299 Sean Burke .12 .30
300 Keith Carney .12 .30
301 Shane Doan .15 .40
302 Robert Esche .12 .30
303 Michal Handzus .12 .30
304 Mike Johnson .12 .30
305 Joe Juneau .12 .30
306 Claude Lemieux .15 .40
307 Teppo Numminen .12 .30
308 Jeremy Roenick .30 .75
309 Landon Wilson .12 .30
310 Jean-Sebastien Aubin .15 .40
311 Jan Hrdina .12 .30
312 Jaromir Jagr .60 1.50
313 Darius Kasparaitis .12 .30
314 Alexei Kovalev .15 .40
315 Robert Lang .12 .30
316 Mario Lemieux .75 2.00
317 Garth Snow .15 .40
318 Kevin Stevens .15 .40
319 Martin Straka .12 .30
320 Sebastien Bordeleau .12 .30
321 Pavol Demitra .25 .60
322 Dallas Drake .12 .30
323 Jochen Hecht .12 .30
324 Brent Johnson .15 .40
325 Reed Low .12 .30
326 Al MacInnis .25 .60
327 Scott Mellanby .12 .30
328 Jaroslav Obsut RC .12 .30
329 Chris Pronger .20 .50
330 Darren Rumble .12 .30
331 Cory Stillman .12 .30
332 Keith Tkachuk .20 .50
333 Roman Turek .15 .40
334 Pierre Turgeon .15 .40
335 Scott Young .12 .30
336 Vincent Damphousse .15 .40
337 Miikka Kiprusoff .20 .50
338 Bryan Marchment .12 .30
339 Patrick Marleau .20 .50
340 Evgeni Nabokov .15 .40
341 Owen Nolan .20 .50
342 Jeff Norton .12 .30
343 Mike Ricci .12 .30
344 Teemu Selanne .40 1.00
345 Brad Stuart .12 .30
346 Marco Sturm .12 .30
347 Niklas Sundstrom .15 .40
348 Scott Thornton .15 .40
349 Matthew Barnaby .12 .30
350 Brian Holzinger .12 .30
351 Nikolai Khabibulin .20 .50
352 Alexander Kharitonov .12 .30
353 Pavel Kubina .12 .30
354 Kristian Kudroc .12 .30
355 Vincent Lecavalier .20 .50
356 Fredrik Modin .12 .30
357 Brad Richards .20 .50
358 Martin St. Louis .20 .50
359 Kevin Weekes .15 .40
360 Thomas Ziegler RC .15 .40
361 Sergei Berezin .12 .30
362 Shayne Corson .15 .40
363 Cory Cross .12 .30
364 Tie Domi .15 .40
365 Glenn Healy .12 .30
366 Jonas Hoglund .12 .30
367 Curtis Joseph .25 .60
368 Don MacLean .12 .30
369 Dave Manson .12 .30
370 Yanic Perreault .12 .30
371 Alexei Ponikarovsky .12 .30
372 Gary Roberts .12 .30
373 Mats Sundin .20 .50
374 Steve Thomas .12 .30
375 Darcy Tucker .12 .30
376 Murray Baron .12 .30
377 Todd Bertuzzi .20 .50
378 Donald Brashear .12 .30
379 Andrew Cassels .12 .30
380 Dan Cloutier .15 .40
381 Bob Essensa .15 .40
382 Ed Jovanovski .15 .40
383 Brendan Morrison .15 .40
384 Markus Naslund .20 .50
385 Mattias Ohlund .12 .30
386 Peter Schaefer .12 .30
387 Daniel Sedin .25 .60
388 Henrik Sedin .25 .60
389 Craig Billington .12 .30
390 Peter Bondra .20 .50
391 Ulf Dahlen .12 .30
392 Sergei Gonchar .12 .30
393 Jeff Halpern .12 .30
394 Dmitri Khristich .12 .30
395 Olaf Kolzig .20 .50
396 Steve Konowalchuk .12 .30
397 Trevor Linden .20 .50
398 Adam Oates .20 .50
399 Chris Simon .12 .30
400 Dainius Zubrus .12 .30
401 P.Kariya/J.Cummins .20 .50
402 R.Ferraro/J.Odgers .12 .30
403 J.Allison/K.Belanger .15 .40
404 J.Dumont/R.Ray .12 .30
405 J.Iginla/J.Wiemer .25 .60
406 R.Francis/D.Langdon .25 .60
407 S.Sullivan/B.Probert .20 .50
408 J.Sakic/S.Parker .40 1.00
409 M.Modano/G.Marshall .30 .75
410 S.Yzerman/D.McCarty .50 1.25
411 R.Smyth/G.Laraque .15 .40
412 P.Bure/P.Worrell .20 .50
413 Z.Palffy/S.Grimson .20 .50
414 P.Elias/C.White .20 .50
415 Czerkawski/Z.Chara .20 .50
416 T.Fleury/S.McCarthy .25 .60
417 M.Hossa/A.Roy .20 .50
418 J.Roenick/L.DeBrusk .30 .75
419 M.Lemieux/K.Oliwa .75 2.00
420 P.Turgeon/R.Low .15 .40
421 T.Selanne/Marchment .40 1.00
422 Lecavalier/M.Barnaby .20 .50
423 M.Sundin/T.Domi .20 .50
424 M.Naslund/D.Brashear .20 .50
425 P.Bondra/C.Simon .20 .50
426 J.Allison/J.Thornton .30 .75
427 J.Sakic/P.Roy .50 1.25
428 M.Modano/B.Hull .40 1.00
429 S.Fedorov/N.Lidstrom .30 .75
430 D.Weight/R.Smyth .20 .50
431 P.Bure/R.Luongo .30 .75
432 L.Robitaille/Z.Palffy .20 .50
433 P.Elias/A.Mogilny .20 .50
434 Czerkawski/R.DiPietro .15 .40
435 T.Fleury/B.Leetch .25 .60
436 A.Yashin/M.Hossa .20 .50
437 K.Primeau/Cechmanek .15 .40
438 J.Roenick/S.Burke .30 .75
439 J.Jagr/M.Lemieux .75 2.00
440 P.Turgeon/B.Johnson .15 .40
441 T.Selanne/E.Nabokov .40 1.00
442 M.Sundin/C.Joseph .25 .60
443 A.Oates/P.Bondra .20 .50
444 David Aebischer AU/500 10.00 25.00
445 Steven Reinprecht AU/500 8.00 20.00
446 Marty Turco AU/500 12.00 30.00
447 Marian Gaborik AU/500 15.00 40.00
448 Martin Havlat AU/500 10.00 25.00
449 Brent Johnson AU/500 10.00 25.00
450 Evgeni Nabokov AU/500 10.00 25.00
451 Brad Richards AU/500 12.00 30.00
452 Johan Hedberg SP 2.00 5.00
453 Timo Parssinen RC 1.50 4.00
454 Ilya Kovalchuk RC 6.00 15.00
455 Vaclav Nedorost RC 1.25 3.00
456 Kristian Huselius RC 2.00 5.00
457 Jaroslav Bednar RC 1.25 3.00
458 Dan Blackburn RC 1.50 4.00
459 Jiri Dopita RC 1.25 3.00
460 Krystofer Kolanos RC 1.25 3.00
461 Jeff Jillson RC 1.25 3.00
462 Nikita Alexeev RC 1.25 3.00

2001-02 Pacific Extreme LTD

*EXTREME/49: 8X TO 20X BASIC CARDS
264 Mark Messier 10.00 25.00

2001-02 Pacific Gold

*GOLD/100: 5X TO 12X BASIC CARDS

2001-02 Pacific Hobby LTD

*HOBBY LTD/99: 5X TO 12X BASIC CARDS
264 Mark Messier 4.00 10.00

2001-02 Pacific Premiere Date

*PREM.DATE/45: 8X TO 20X BASIC CARDS
264 Mark Messier 10.00 25.00

2001-02 Pacific Retail LTD

*LTD/149: 5X TO 12X BASIC CARDS
264 Mark Messier 6.00 15.00

2001-02 Pacific All-Stars

COMPLETE SET (20) 60.00 125.00
W1 Dominik Hasek 3.00 8.00
W2 Peter Forsberg 4.00 10.00
W3 Sergei Fedorov 3.00 8.00
W4 Pavel Bure 2.00 5.00
W5 Zigmund Palffy 1.25 3.00
W6 Marian Hossa 1.50 4.00
W7 Roman Cechmanek 3.00 8.00
W8 Alexei Kovalev 1.50 4.00
W9 Evgeni Nabokov 3.00 8.00
W10 Mats Sundin 1.50 4.00
NA1 Paul Kariya 1.50 4.00
NA2 Bill Guerin 1.25 3.00
NA3 Ray Bourque 6.00 15.00
NA4 Patrick Roy 8.00 20.00
NA5 Joe Sakic 3.00 8.00
NA6 Brett Hull 2.00 5.00
NA7 Doug Weight 1.25 3.00
NA8 Luc Robitaille 1.25 3.00
NA9 Martin Brodeur 4.00 10.00
NA10 Mario Lemieux 10.00 25.00

2001-02 Pacific Cramer's Choice

1 Paul Kariya 8.00 20.00
2 Ray Bourque 20.00 50.00
3 Patrick Roy 40.00 100.00
4 Joe Sakic 20.00 50.00
5 Steve Yzerman 30.00 80.00
6 Pavel Bure 10.00 25.00
7 Martin Brodeur 25.00 60.00
8 Jaromir Jagr 12.00 30.00
9 Mario Lemieux 40.00 100.00
10 Curtis Joseph 15.00 40.00

2001-02 Pacific Jerseys

1 Andre Savage/510 2.50 6.00
2 Eric Weinrich/510 2.50 6.00
3 Jay McKee/1135 2.50 6.00
4 Fred Brathwaite/1135 3.00 8.00
5 Marc Savard/760 2.50 6.00
6 Tony Amonte/1135 3.00 8.00
7 Alexei Zhamnov/1135 2.50 6.00
8 Chris Dingman/510 2.50 6.00
9 Joe Sakic/510 6.00 15.00
10 Derian Hatcher/1135 2.50 6.00
11 Jamie Langenbrunner/1135 2.50 6.00
12 Sergei Zubov/760 4.00 10.00
13 Mathieu Dandenault/1135 2.50 6.00
14 Chris Osgood/760 4.00 10.00
15 Doug Weight/260 3.00 8.00
16 Aaron Miller/510 2.50 6.00
17 Cliff Ronning/510 2.50 6.00
18 Bobby Holik/760 2.50 6.00
19 Mariusz Czerkawski/510 2.50 6.00
20 Chris Terreri/1135 2.50 6.00
21 Guy Hebert/760 3.00 8.00
22 Mike Richter/760 3.00 8.00
23 Mika Alatalo/510 2.50 6.00
24 Shane Doan/310 2.50 6.00
25 Jyrki Lumme/1135 2.50 6.00
26 Jan Hrdina/510 2.50 6.00
27 Jaromir Jagr/210 6.00 15.00
28 Mario Lemieux/110 20.00 50.00
29 Kip Miller/1135 2.50 6.00
30 Ian Moran/1135 2.50 6.00

31 Martin Straka/110 5.00 12.00
32 Cory Stillman/1135 2.50 6.00
33 Vincent Damphousse/1010 2.50 6.00
34 Teemu Selanne/1135 4.00 10.00
35 Mats Sundin/760 3.00 8.00
36 Dainius Zubrus/760 2.50 6.00

2001-02 Pacific Gold Crown Die-Cuts

COMPLETE SET (20) 60.00 125.00
1 Paul Kariya 1.50 4.00
2 Joe Thornton 2.50 6.00
3 Dominik Hasek 4.00 10.00
4 Ray Bourque 3.00 8.00
5 Peter Forsberg 5.00 12.00
6 Patrick Roy 8.00 20.00
7 Joe Sakic 4.00 10.00
8 Mike Modano 2.50 6.00
9 Sergei Fedorov 2.50 6.00
10 Steve Yzerman 8.00 20.00
11 Pavel Bure 1.50 4.00
12 Martin Brodeur 6.00 15.00
13 Rick DiPietro 1.50 4.00
14 Mark Messier 2.50 6.00
15 Marian Hossa 1.50 4.00
16 Jaromir Jagr 3.00 8.00
17 Mario Lemieux 12.00 30.00
18 Keith Tkachuk 1.50 4.00
19 Evgeni Nabokov 2.50 6.00
20 Curtis Joseph 1.50 4.00

2001-02 Pacific Heads Up Samples

NNO1 Martin Brodeur 1.25 3.00
NNO2 Mike Comrie 1.00 2.50
NNO3 Martin Havlat 1.00 2.50
NNO4 Mario Lemieux 1.25 3.00
NNO5 Evgeni Nabokov 1.00 2.50
NNO6 Patrick Roy 1.25 3.00
NNO7 Joe Sakic 1.00 2.50
NNO8 Teemu Selanne 1.00 2.50
NNO9 Brendan Shanahan 1.00 2.50

2001-02 Pacific Impact Zone

COMPLETE SET (20) 15.00 40.00
1 Paul Kariya 1.50 4.00
2 Byron Dafoe .75 2.00
3 Doug Gilmour .75 2.00
4 Dominik Hasek 3.00 8.00
5 Ron Francis .75 2.00
6 Ray Bourque 3.00 8.00
7 Patrick Roy 6.00 15.00
8 Ed Belfour 1.50 4.00
9 Derian Hatcher .40 1.00
10 Mike Modano 2.50 6.00
11 Chris Osgood .75 2.00
12 Martin Brodeur 4.00 10.00
13 Marian Hossa .75 2.00
14 Patrick Lalime .75 2.00
15 Roman Cechmanek .40 1.00
16 Chris Pronger .75 2.00
17 Tie Domi .40 1.00
18 Curtis Joseph 1.50 4.00
19 Mats Sundin 1.50 4.00
20 Andrew Cassels .40 1.00

2001-02 Pacific 97-98 Update

COMPLETE SET (7) 10.00 20.00
*GOLD/100: 8X TO 20X BASIC INSERT
66 Mario Lemieux 2.50 6.00
352 Mike LeClerc 1.25 3.00
353 Sergei Samsonov 1.50 4.00
354 Joe Thornton 2.50 6.00
355 Steve Shields 1.25 3.00
356 Patrik Elias 1.25 3.00
357 Marian Hossa 1.50 4.00

2001-02 Pacific Steel Curtain

COMPLETE SET (20) 30.00 60.00
1 Steve Shields 1.00 2.50
2 Byron Dafoe 1.00 2.50
3 Dominik Hasek 2.50 6.00
4 Jocelyn Thibault 1.00 2.50
5 Patrick Roy 6.00 15.00
6 Ed Belfour 1.25 3.00
7 Manny Legace 1.00 2.50
8 Tommy Salo 1.00 2.50
9 Roberto Luongo 1.50 4.00
10 Jose Theodore 1.50 4.00
11 Martin Brodeur 3.00 8.00
12 Rick DiPietro 1.00 2.50
13 Mike Richter 1.25 3.00
14 Patrick Lalime 1.00 2.50
15 Roman Cechmanek 1.00 2.50
16 Sean Burke 1.00 2.50
17 Roman Turek 1.00 2.50
18 Evgeni Nabokov 1.00 2.50
19 Curtis Joseph 1.25 3.00
20 Olaf Kolzig 1.00 2.50

2001-02 Pacific Top Draft Picks

COMPLETE SET (10) 10.00 25.00
1 Rick DiPietro .75 2.00
2 Patrik Stefan .40 1.00
3 Vincent Lecavalier 1.25 3.00
4 Joe Thornton 2.00 5.00
5 Eric Lindros 1.25 3.00
6 Owen Nolan .75 2.00
7 Mats Sundin 1.25 3.00
8 Mike Modano 2.00 5.00
9 Pierre Turgeon .75 2.00
10 Mario Lemieux 4.00 10.00

2001 Pacific Top Draft Picks Draft Day Promos

COMPLETE SET (10) 40.00 100.00
1 Rick DiPietro 6.00 15.00
2 Patrik Stefan 2.00 5.00
3 Vincent LeCavalier 4.80 12.00
4 Joe Thornton 6.00 15.00
5 Eric Lindros 4.80 12.00
6 Owen Nolan 4.00 10.00
7 Mats Sundin 4.80 12.00
8 Mike Modano 6.00 15.00
9 Pierre Turgeon 4.00 10.00
10 Mario Lemieux 12.00 30.00

2002-03 Pacific

COMPLETE SET (400) 50.00 100.00
1 Matt Cullen .12 .30
2 Jeff Friesen .12 .30
3 Jean-Sebastien Giguere .20 .50
4 Paul Kariya .20 .50
5 Mike Leclerc .12 .30
6 Andy McDonald .20 .50
7 Steve Rucchin .12 .30
8 Steve Shields .15 .40
9 German Titov .12 .30
10 Oleg Tverdovsky .12 .30
11 Jason York .12 .30
12 Lubos Bartecko .12 .30
13 Dany Heatley .15 .40
14 Milan Hnilicka .15 .40
15 Tony Hrkac .12 .30
16 Frantisek Kaberle .12 .30
17 Tomi Kallio .12 .30
18 Ilya Kovalchuk .25 .60
19 Jeff Odgers .12 .30
20 Damian Rhodes .12 .30
21 Patrik Stefan .15 .40
22 Daniel Tjarnqvist .12 .30
23 Nicholas Boynton .12 .30
24 Sean Brown .12 .30
25 Byron Dafoe .15 .40
26 Hal Gill .12 .30
27 John Grahame .12 .30
28 Bill Guerin .20 .50
29 Martin Lapointe .15 .40
30 Glen Murray .15 .40
31 Brian Rolston .15 .40
32 Sergei Samsonov .15 .40
33 P.J. Stock .12 .30
34 Jozef Stumpel .12 .30
35 Joe Thornton .30 .75
36 Maxim Afinogenov .12 .30
37 Stu Barnes .12 .30
38 Martin Biron .15 .40
39 Curtis Brown .12 .30
40 Tim Connolly .12 .30
41 J-P Dumont .12 .30
42 Chris Gratton .12 .30
43 Ales Kotalik .12 .30
44 Slava Kozlov .12 .30
45 Jay McKee .12 .30
46 Mika Noronen .15 .40
47 Rob Ray .12 .30
48 Miroslav Satan .20 .50
49 Alexei Zhitnik .15 .40
50 Bob Boughner .12 .30
51 Chris Clark .12 .30
52 Craig Conroy .12 .30
53 Denis Gauthier .12 .30
54 Jarome Iginla .25 .60
55 Toni Lydman .12 .30
56 Dean McAmmond .12 .30
57 Derek Morris .12 .30
58 Rob Niedermayer .15 .40
59 Marc Savard .12 .30
60 Roman Turek .20 .50
61 Mike Vernon .15 .40
62 Bates Battaglia .12 .30
63 Rod Brind'Amour .20 .50
64 Erik Cole .12 .30
65 Ron Francis .25 .60
66 Bret Hedican .12 .30
67 Arturs Irbe .15 .40
68 Sami Kapanen .12 .30
69 Jeff O'Neill .12 .30
70 Dave Tanabe .12 .30
71 Josef Vasicek .12 .30
72 Kevin Weekes .15 .40
73 Tony Amonte .15 .40
74 Mark Bell .12 .30
75 Kyle Calder .12 .30
76 Eric Daze .15 .40
77 Phil Housley .15 .40
78 Jon Klemm .12 .30
79 Boris Mironov .12 .30
80 Steve Passmore .12 .30
81 Bob Probert .20 .50
82 Steve Sullivan .12 .30
83 Jocelyn Thibault .15 .40
84 Steve Thomas .12 .30
85 Alexei Zhamnov .15 .40
86 David Aebischer .15 .40
87 Rob Blake .20 .50
88 Chris Drury .15 .40
89 Adam Foote .12 .30
90 Peter Forsberg .40 1.00
91 Milan Hejduk .15 .40
92 Darius Kasparaitis .12 .30
93 Scott Parker .12 .30
94 Steven Reinprecht .12 .30
95 Patrick Roy .50 1.25
96 Joe Sakic .40 1.00
97 Alex Tanguay .15 .40
98 Radim Vrbata .12 .30
99 Marc Denis .12 .30
100 Rostislav Klesla .15 .40
101 Espen Knutsen .12 .30
102 Grant Marshall .12 .30
103 Deron Quint .12 .30
104 Geoff Sanderson .12 .30
105 Jody Shelley .12 .30
106 Mike Sillinger .12 .30
107 Ron Tugnutt .15 .40
108 David Vyborny .12 .30
109 Ray Whitney .12 .30
110 Jason Arnott .15 .40
111 Ed Belfour .20 .50
112 Derian Hatcher .12 .30
113 Jere Lehtinen .20 .50
114 Mike Modano .30 .75
115 Brenden Morrow .12 .30
116 Kirk Muller .12 .30
117 Scott Pellerin .12 .30
118 Darryl Sydor .12 .30
119 Marty Turco .20 .50
120 Pierre Turgeon .15 .40
121 Pat Verbeek .12 .30
122 Sergei Zubov .15 .40
123 Chris Chelios .20 .50
124 Pavel Datsyuk .30 .75
125 Boyd Devereaux .12 .30
126 Kris Draper .12 .30
127 Sergei Fedorov .30 .75
128 Dominik Hasek .30 .75
129 Brett Hull .40 1.00
130 Igor Larionov .20 .50
131 Manny Legace .20 .50
132 Nicklas Lidstrom .20 .50
133 Luc Robitaille .20 .50
134 Brendan Shanahan .20 .50
135 Jiri Slegr .12 .30
136 Jason Williams .12 .30
137 Steve Yzerman .50 1.25
138 Eric Brewer .12 .30
139 Anson Carter .15 .40
140 Daniel Cleary .15 .40
141 Mike Comrie .20 .50
142 Mike Grier .12 .30
143 Jochen Hecht .12 .30
144 Georges Laraque .15 .40
145 Todd Marchant .12 .30
146 Jussi Markkanen .12 .30
147 Janne Niinimaa .12 .30
148 Tommy Salo .15 .40
149 Ryan Smyth .15 .40
150 Mike York .12 .30
151 Eric Beaudoin .12 .30
152 Valeri Bure .15 .40
153 Niklas Hagman .12 .30
154 Kristian Huselius .12 .30
155 Trevor Kidd .12 .30
156 Roberto Luongo .30 .75
157 Marcus Nilsson .12 .30
158 Sandis Ozolinsh .12 .30
159 Nick Smith .12 .30
160 Robert Svehla .12 .30
161 Stephen Weiss .20 .50
162 Jason Wiemer .12 .30
163 Peter Worrell .12 .30
164 Jason Allison .15 .40
165 Adam Deadmarsh .12 .30
166 Steve Heinze .12 .30
167 Craig Johnson .12 .30
168 Ian Laperriere .15 .40
169 Aaron Miller .12 .30
170 Jaroslav Modry .12 .30
171 Zigmund Palffy .20 .50
172 Felix Potvin .30 .75
173 Cliff Ronning .12 .30
174 Mathieu Schneider .12 .30
175 Bryan Smolinski .12 .30
176 Jamie Storr .12 .30
177 Andrew Brunette .12 .30
178 Hnat Domenichelli .12 .30
179 Jim Dowd .12 .30
180 Pascal Dupuis .12 .30
181 Manny Fernandez .12 .30
182 Marian Gaborik .20 .50
183 Darby Hendrickson .12 .30
184 Filip Kuba .12 .30
185 Antti Laaksonen .12 .30
186 Stacy Roest .12 .30
187 Dwayne Roloson .12 .30
188 Wes Walz .12 .30
189 Sergei Zholtok .12 .30
190 Donald Audette .12 .30
191 Sergei Berezin .12 .30
192 Patrice Brisebois .12 .30
193 Andreas Dackell .12 .30
194 Stephane Fiset .12 .30
195 Mathieu Garon .15 .40
196 Doug Gilmour .25 .60
197 Joe Juneau .12 .30
198 Saku Koivu .20 .50
199 Andrei Markov .20 .50
200 Yanic Perreault .12 .30
201 Oleg Petrov .12 .30
202 Mike Ribeiro .12 .30
203 Jose Theodore .20 .50
204 Richard Zednik .12 .30
205 Denis Arkhipov .12 .30
206 Andy Delmore .12 .30
207 Mike Dunham .15 .40
208 Martin Erat .12 .30
209 Stu Grimson .12 .30
210 Scott Hartnell .12 .30
211 Greg Johnson .12 .30
212 David Legwand .12 .30
213 Vladimir Orszagh .12 .30
214 Kimmo Timonen .12 .30
215 Tomas Vokoun .15 .40
216 Scott Walker .12 .30
217 Vitali Yachmenev .12 .30
218 Martin Brodeur .50 1.25
219 Sergei Brylin .12 .30
220 Patrik Elias .20 .50
221 Brian Gionta .12 .30
222 Scott Gomez .15 .40
223 Bobby Holik .12 .30
224 Jamie Langenbrunner .15 .40
225 John Madden .12 .30
226 Scott Niedermayer .20 .50
227 Joe Nieuwendyk .20 .50
228 Brian Rafalski .12 .30
229 Scott Stevens .20 .50
230 Petr Sykora .15 .40
231 John Vanbiesbrouck .20 .50
232 Adrian Aucoin .12 .30
233 Shawn Bates .12 .30
234 Mariusz Czerkawski .12 .30
235 Rick DiPietro .15 .40
236 Roman Hamrlik .12 .30
237 Brad Isbister .12 .30
238 Kenny Jonsson .12 .30
239 Kip Miller .12 .30
240 Chris Osgood .20 .50
241 Mark Parrish .12 .30
242 Michael Peca .15 .40
243 Garth Snow .15 .40
244 Raffi Torres .12 .30
245 Alexei Yashin .12 .30
246 Matthew Barnaby .12 .30
247 Bryan Berard .12 .30
248 Dan Blackburn .15 .40
249 Pavel Bure .20 .50
250 Radek Dvorak .12 .30
251 Theo Fleury .25 .60
252 Brian Leetch .15 .40
253 Eric Lindros .30 .75
254 Vladimir Malakhov .12 .30
255 Sandy McCarthy .12 .30
256 Mark Messier .40 1.00
257 Petr Nedved .12 .30
258 Mike Richter .20 .50
259 Martin Rucinsky .12 .30
260 Daniel Alfredsson .20 .50
261 Magnus Arvedson .12 .30
262 Chris Bala .12 .30
263 Radek Bonk .15 .40
264 Zdeno Chara .20 .50
265 Mike Fisher .12 .30
266 Martin Havlat .15 .40
267 Marian Hossa .20 .50
268 Jani Hurme .15 .40
269 Patrick Lalime .15 .40
270 Shawn McEachern .12 .30
271 Chris Phillips .12 .30
272 Wade Redden .12 .30
273 Sami Salo .12 .30
274 Todd White .12 .30
275 Brian Boucher .15 .40
276 Donald Brashear .12 .30
277 Roman Cechmanek .15 .40
278 Eric Desjardins .12 .30
279 Jiri Dopita .12 .30
280 Simon Gagne .20 .50
281 Kim Johnsson .12 .30
282 John LeClair .20 .50
283 Neil Little .12 .30
284 Adam Oates .20 .50
285 Keith Primeau .15 .40
286 Mark Recchi .25 .60
287 Jeremy Roenick .30 .75
288 Bill Tibbetts .12 .30
289 Eric Weinrich .12 .30
290 Justin Williams .15 .40
291 Daniel Briere .15 .40
292 Sean Burke .15 .40
293 Shane Doan .15 .40
294 Robert Esche .12 .30
295 Michal Handzus .15 .40
296 Mike Johnson .15 .40
297 Krystofer Kolanos .15 .40
298 Daymond Langkow .15 .40
299 Claude Lemieux .15 .40
300 Daniil Markov .12 .30
301 Ladislav Nagy .12 .30
302 Andrei Nazarov .15 .40
303 Teppo Numminen .12 .30
304 Brian Savage .12 .30
305 J-S Aubin .12 .30
306 Kris Beech .12 .30
307 Johan Hedberg .20 .50
308 Jan Hrdina .12 .30
309 Alexei Kovalev .15 .40
310 Milan Kraft .12 .30
311 Robert Lang .12 .30
312 Mario Lemieux .75 2.00
313 Alexei Morozov .12 .30
314 Toby Petersen .12 .30
315 Wayne Primeau .15 .40
316 Randy Robitaille .12 .30
317 Michal Rozsival .15 .40
318 Martin Straka .15 .40
319 Fred Brathwaite .15 .40
320 Pavol Demitra .25 .60
321 Dallas Drake .15 .40
322 Ray Ferraro .15 .40
323 Brent Johnson .15 .40
324 Reed Low .12 .30
325 Al MacInnis .25 .60
326 Scott Mellanby .12 .30
327 Chris Pronger .20 .50
328 Cory Stillman .12 .30
329 Keith Tkachuk .20 .50
330 Doug Weight .20 .50
331 Scott Young .12 .30
332 Vincent Damphousse .15 .40
333 Adam Graves .15 .40
334 Jeff Jillson .12 .30
335 Bryan Marchment .12 .30
336 Patrick Marleau .20 .50
337 Evgeni Nabokov .15 .40
338 Owen Nolan .20 .50
339 Mike Ricci .15 .40
340 Teemu Selanne .40 1.00
341 Brad Stuart .12 .30
342 Marco Sturm .12 .30
343 Gary Suter .12 .30
344 Scott Thornton .12 .30
345 Nikita Alexeev .12 .30
346 Dave Andreychuk .20 .50
347 Ben Clymer .12 .30
348 Nikolai Khabibulin .20 .50
349 Dieter Kochan .12 .30
350 Pavel Kubina .12 .30
351 Vincent Lecavalier .20 .50
352 Fredrik Modin .12 .30
353 Vaclav Prospal .12 .30
354 Brad Richards .20 .50
355 Martin St.Louis .20 .50
356 Shane Willis .12 .30
357 Tom Barrasso .15 .40
358 Shayne Corson .15 .40
359 Tie Domi .15 .40
360 Travis Green .12 .30
361 Curtis Joseph .15 .40
362 Tomas Kaberle .12 .30
363 Bryan McCabe .12 .30
364 Alyn McCauley .12 .30
365 Alexander Mogilny .15 .40
366 Robert Reichel .12 .30
367 Mikael Renberg .12 .30
368 Gary Roberts .12 .30
369 Corey Schwab .15 .40
370 Mats Sundin .20 .50
371 Darcy Tucker .12 .30
372 Dimitri Yushkevich .12 .30
373 Todd Bertuzzi .20 .50
374 Andrew Cassels .12 .30
375 Dan Cloutier .15 .40
376 Matt Cooke .12 .30
377 Jan Hlavac .12 .30
378 Ed Jovanovski .15 .40
379 Trevor Linden .15 .40
380 Brendan Morrison .15 .40
381 Markus Naslund .20 .50
382 Mattias Ohlund .12 .30
383 Daniel Sedin .25 .60
384 Henrik Sedin .25 .60
385 Peter Skudra .12 .30
386 Brent Sopel .12 .30
387 Craig Billington .12 .30
388 Peter Bondra .20 .50
389 Ulf Dahlen .12 .30
390 Sergei Gonchar .15 .40
391 Jeff Halpern .12 .30
392 Jaromir Jagr .60 1.50
393 Calle Johansson .12 .30
394 Dimitri Khristich .12 .30
395 Olaf Kolzig .20 .50
396 Steve Konowalchuk .12 .30
397 Andrei Nikolishin .12 .30
398 Stephen Peat .12 .30
399 Chris Simon .12 .30
400 Dainius Zubrus .12 .30
401 Stanislav Chistov RC 1.00 2.50
402 Alexei Smirnov RC 1.25 3.00
403 Chuck Kobasew RC 1.25 3.00
404 Rick Nash RC 6.00 15.00
405 Henrik Zetterberg RC 10.00 25.00
406 Ales Hemsky RC 4.00 10.00
407 Jay Bouwmeester RC 3.00 8.00
408 Alexander Frolov RC 2.50 6.00
409 P-M Bouchard RC 1.50 4.00
410 Alexander Svitov RC 1.00 2.50

2002-03 Pacific Blue

*BLUE/45: 8X TO 20X BASIC CARDS
256 Mark Messier 10.00 25.00

2002-03 Pacific Red

*RED: .6X TO 1.5X BASIC CARDS
256 Mark Messier .75 2.00

2002-03 Pacific Cramer's Choice

1 Dany Heatley 6.00 15.00
2 Ilya Kovalchuk 6.00 15.00
3 Joe Thornton 6.00 15.00
4 Peter Forsberg 10.00 25.00
5 Patrick Roy 25.00 60.00
6 Dominik Hasek 8.00 20.00
7 Steve Yzerman 25.00 60.00
8 Martin Brodeur 15.00 40.00
9 Mario Lemieux 30.00 75.00
10 Mats Sundin 4.00 10.00

2002-03 Pacific Impact Zone

COMPLETE SET (10) 8.00 15.00
1 Paul Kariya .40 1.00
2 Ilya Kovalchuk .50 1.25
3 Joe Thornton .60 1.50
4 Jarome Iginla .60 1.50
5 Joe Sakic .75 2.00
6 Brendan Shanahan .60 1.50
7 Saku Koivu .40 1.00
8 Eric Lindros .60 1.50
9 Mario Lemieux 2.50 6.00
10 Teemu Selanne .40 1.00

2002-03 Pacific Jerseys

*HOLOSILVER/40: 1X TO 2.5X BASIC JSY
1 Dany Heatley 5.00 12.00
2 Milan Hnilicka 3.00 8.00
3 Joe Thornton 6.00 15.00
4 Miroslav Satan 3.00 8.00
5 Roman Turek 3.00 8.00
6 Arturs Irbe 3.00 8.00
7 Tony Amonte 3.00 8.00
8 Steve Sullivan 3.00 8.00
9 Rob Blake 3.00 8.00
10 Chris Drury 3.00 8.00
11 Joe Sakic 8.00 20.00
12 Marc Denis 3.00 8.00
13 Ron Tugnutt 3.00 8.00
14 Jason Arnott 3.00 8.00
15 Mike Modano 6.00 15.00
16 Sergei Fedorov 6.00 12.00
17 Dominik Hasek 12.50 30.00
18 Jason Williams 3.00 8.00
19 Tommy Salo 3.00 8.00
20 Wade Flaherty 3.00 8.00
21 Jason Allison 3.00 8.00
22 Aaron Miller 3.00 8.00
23 Cliff Ronning 3.00 8.00
24 Manny Fernandez 3.00 8.00
25 Sergei Berezin 3.00 8.00
26 Yanic Perreault 3.00 8.00
27 Jose Theodore 5.00 12.00
28 Martin Erat 3.00 8.00
29 Jukka Hentunen 3.00 8.00
30 Jamie Langenbrunner SP 3.00 8.00
31 Joe Nieuwendyk SP 3.00 8.00
32 Michael Peca 3.00 8.00
33 Alexei Yashin 3.00 8.00
34 Pavel Bure 4.00 10.00
35 Theo Fleury 3.00 8.00
36 Mark Messier 4.00 10.00
37 Martin Havlat 2.50 6.00
38 Jiri Dopita 3.00 8.00
39 Simon Gagne 4.00 10.00
40 Adam Oates 3.00 8.00
41 Daymond Langkow 3.00 8.00
42 Mario Lemieux 10.00 25.00
43 Pavol Demitra 3.00 8.00
44 Ray Ferraro 3.00 8.00
45 Evgeni Nabokov 3.00 8.00
46 Fredrik Modin 3.00 8.00
47 Alexander Mogilny 3.00 8.00
48 Darcy Tucker 3.00 8.00
49 Dan Cloutier 3.00 8.00
50 Jaromir Jagr 6.00 15.00
NNO I.Kovalchuk AU/500 15.00 40.00

2002-03 Pacific Lamplighters

COMPLETE SET (14) 25.00 50.00
1 Dany Heatley 1.00 2.50
2 Ilya Kovalchuk 1.00 2.50
3 Joe Thornton 1.25 3.00
4 Jarome Iginla 1.00 2.50
5 Peter Forsberg 2.00 5.00
6 Joe Sakic 1.50 4.00
7 Steve Yzerman 3.00 8.00
8 Alexei Yashin .75 2.00
9 Pavel Bure 1.25 3.00
10 Eric Lindros .75 2.00
11 Mario Lemieux 4.00 10.00
12 Mats Sundin .75 2.00
13 Todd Bertuzzi .75 2.00
14 Jaromir Jagr 1.25 3.00

2002-03 Pacific Main Attractions

COMPLETE SET (20) 15.00 30.00
1 Paul Kariya .40 1.00
2 Ilya Kovalchuk 1.50 4.00
3 Joe Thornton .60 1.50
4 Jarome Iginla .60 1.50
5 Patrick Roy 2.00 5.00
6 Mike Modano .60 1.50
7 Steve Yzerman 2.00 5.00
8 Mike Comrie .30 .75
9 Jason Allison .30 .75
10 Jose Theodore .50 1.25
11 Martin Brodeur 1.50 4.00
12 Alexei Yashin .30 .75
13 Pavel Bure .60 1.50
14 Daniel Alfredsson .60 1.50
15 Jeremy Roenick .50 1.25
16 Mario Lemieux 2.50 6.00
17 Keith Tkachuk .40 1.00
18 Mats Sundin .40 1.00
19 Markus Naslund .40 1.00
20 Jaromir Jagr .60 1.50

2002-03 Pacific Maximum Impact

COMPLETE SET (16) 12.50 25.00
1 Roman Turek .30 .75
2 Patrick Roy 2.00 5.00
3 Dominik Hasek .75 2.00
4 Jose Theodore .60 1.50
5 Martin Brodeur 1.25 3.00
6 Sean Burke .30 .75
7 Evgeni Nabokov .30 .75
8 Curtis Joseph .40 1.00
9 Ilya Kovalchuk 1.50 4.00
10 Joe Thornton .60 1.50
11 Jarome Iginla .60 1.50
12 Joe Sakic .75 2.00
13 Steve Yzerman 2.00 5.00
14 Eric Lindros .40 1.00
15 Mario Lemieux 2.50 6.00
16 Mats Sundin .40 1.00

2002-03 Pacific Shining Moments

COMPLETE SET (10) 20.00 40.00
1 Dany Heatley 2.50 6.00
2 Ilya Kovalchuk 3.00 8.00
3 Erik Cole 1.50 4.00
4 Radim Vrbata 1.50 4.00
5 Pavel Datsyuk 2.50 6.00
6 Kristian Huselius 1.50 4.00
7 Stephen Weiss 1.50 4.00
8 Mike Ribeiro 1.50 4.00
9 Dan Blackburn 2.00 5.00
10 Krystofer Kolanos 1.50 4.00

2003-04 Pacific

1 Stanislav Chistov .12 .30
2 Martin Gerber .12 .30
3 Jean-Sebastien Giguere .20 .50
4 Niclas Havelid .12 .30
5 Paul Kariya .20 .50
6 Mike Leclerc .12 .30
7 Adam Oates .20 .50
8 Sandis Ozolinsh .12 .30
9 Steve Rucchin .12 .30
10 Petr Sykora .15 .40
11 Steve Thomas .12 .30
12 Byron Dafoe .15 .40
13 Joe DiPenta RC .15 .40
14 Dany Heatley .15 .40
15 Milan Hnilicka .12 .30
16 Ilya Kovalchuk .20 .50
17 Slava Kozlov .15 .40
18 Shawn McEachern .12 .30
19 Pasi Numminen .15 .40
20 Jeff Odgers .12 .30
21 Marc Savard .12 .30
22 Patrik Stefan .12 .30
23 P.J. Axelsson .12 .30
24 Bryan Berard .15 .40
25 Nick Boynton .12 .30
26 Jeff Hackett .15 .40
27 Mike Knuble .12 .30
28 Glen Murray .15 .40
29 Brian Rolston .15 .40
30 Sergei Samsonov .15 .40
31 Steve Shields .15 .40
32 P.J. Stock .12 .30
33 Jozef Stumpel .12 .30
34 Joe Thornton .30 .75
35 Milan Bartovic RC .15 .40
36 Martin Biron .15 .40
37 Daniel Briere .20 .50
38 Curtis Brown .12 .30
39 Tim Connolly .12 .30
40 J-P Dumont .12 .30
41 Ales Kotalik .12 .30
42 Ryan Miller .20 .50
43 Mika Noronen .15 .40
44 Taylor Pyatt .12 .30
45 Miroslav Satan .15 .40
46 Alexei Zhitnik .15 .40
47 Craig Conroy .12 .30
48 Chris Drury .15 .40
49 Martin Gelinas .12 .30
50 Jarome Iginla .25 .60
51 Chuck Kobasew .12 .30
52 Jordan Leopold .12 .30
53 Toni Lydman .12 .30
54 Dean McAmmond .12 .30
55 Jamie McLennan .12 .30
56 Roman Turek .15 .40
57 Stephane Yelle .12 .30
58 Ryan Bayda .12 .30
59 Rod Brind'Amour .20 .50
60 Erik Cole .12 .30
61 Ron Francis .25 .60
62 Jeff Heerema .12 .30
63 Sean Hill .12 .30
64 Arturs Irbe .15 .40
65 Jeff O'Neill .12 .30
66 Radim Vrbata .12 .30
67 Kevin Weekes .15 .40
68 Craig Andersson .20 .50
69 Tyler Arnason .12 .30
70 Mark Bell .12 .30
71 Kyle Calder .12 .30
72 Eric Daze .15 .40
73 Theoren Fleury .25 .60
74 Steve Passmore .12 .30
75 Chris Simon .12 .30
76 Steve Sullivan .12 .30
77 Jocelyn Thibault .15 .40
78 Alexei Zhamnov .15 .40
79 David Aebischer .15 .40
80 Bates Battaglia .12 .30
81 Rob Blake .20 .50
82 Adam Foote .12 .30
83 Peter Forsberg .40 1.00
84 Milan Hejduk .15 .40
85 Derek Morris .12 .30
86 Vaclav Nedorost .12 .30
87 Steven Reinprecht .12 .30
88 Patrick Roy .50 1.25
89 Joe Sakic .40 1.00
90 Alex Tanguay .15 .40
91 Andrew Cassels .12 .30
92 Marc Denis .15 .40
93 Rostislav Klesla .12 .30
94 Pascal Leclaire .12 .30
95 Kent McDonell RC .15 .40
96 Rick Nash .20 .50
97 Geoff Sanderson .12 .30
98 Mike Sillinger .12 .30
99 David Vyborny .12 .30
100 Ray Whitney .15 .40
101 Tyler Wright .12 .30
102 Jason Arnott .15 .40
103 Ulf Dahlen .12 .30
104 Bill Guerin .20 .50
105 Derian Hatcher .12 .30
106 Jere Lehtinen .15 .40
107 Mike Modano .30 .75
108 Brenden Morrow .15 .40
109 Steve Ott .12 .30
110 Ron Tugnutt .15 .40
111 Marty Turco .20 .50
112 Pierre Turgeon .15 .40
113 Scott Young .12 .30
114 Sergei Zubov .15 .40
115 Chris Chelios .20 .50
116 Pavel Datsyuk .30 .75
117 Sergei Fedorov .30 .75
118 Tomas Holmstrom .15 .40
119 Brett Hull .40 1.00
120 Curtis Joseph .25 .60
121 Igor Larionov .20 .50
122 Manny Legace .12 .30
123 Nicklas Lidstrom .20 .50
124 Luc Robitaille .20 .50
125 Mathieu Schneider .12 .30
126 Brendan Shanahan .20 .50
127 Steve Yzerman .50 1.25
128 Henrik Zetterberg .25 .60
129 Eric Brewer .12 .30
130 Jason Chimera .12 .30
131 Mike Comrie .15 .40
132 Ales Hemsky .20 .50
133 Brad Isbister .12 .30
134 Georges Laraque .15 .40
135 Todd Marchant .12 .30
136 Jussi Markkanen .12 .30
137 Tommy Salo .15 .40
138 Ryan Smyth .15 .40
139 Mike York .12 .30
140 Jaroslav Bednar .12 .30
141 Jay Bouwmeester .12 .30
142 Matt Cullen .12 .30
143 Jani Hurme .12 .30
144 Kristian Huselius .12 .30
145 Olli Jokinen .20 .50
146 Viktor Kozlov .12 .30
147 Roberto Luongo .30 .75
148 Marcus Nilsson .12 .30
149 Stephen Weiss .12 .30
150 Peter Worrell .12 .30
151 Jason Allison .15 .40
152 Jared Aulin .12 .30
153 Michael Cammalleri .20 .50
154 Adam Deadmarsh .12 .30
155 Alexander Frolov .15 .40
156 Cristobal Huet .15 .40
157 Jaroslav Modry .12 .30
158 Zigmund Palffy .20 .50
159 Felix Potvin .30 .75
160 Jamie Storr .15 .40
161 Pierre-Marc Bouchard .20 .50
162 Andrew Brunette .12 .30
163 Pascal Dupuis .12 .30
164 Manny Fernandez .12 .30
165 Marian Gaborik .20 .50
166 Filip Kuba .12 .30
167 Antti Laaksonen .12 .30
168 Richard Park .12 .30
169 Dwayne Roloson .15 .40
170 Cliff Ronning .12 .30
171 Wes Walz .12 .30
172 Sergei Zholtok .12 .30
173 Donald Audette .12 .30
174 Patrice Brisebois .12 .30
175 Jan Bulis .15 .40
176 Mathieu Garon .12 .30
177 Marcel Hossa .12 .30
178 Saku Koivu .20 .50
179 Andrei Markov .12 .30
180 Yanic Perreault .12 .30
181 Mike Ribeiro .12 .30
182 Niklas Sundstrom .12 .30
183 Jose Theodore .20 .50
184 Richard Zednik .12 .30
185 Denis Arkhipov .12 .30
186 Andy Delmore .12 .30
187 Adam Hall .12 .30
188 Scott Hartnell .12 .30
189 Andreas Johansson .12 .30
190 David Legwand .15 .40
191 Oleg Petrov .15 .40
192 Kimmo Timonen .12 .30
193 Scottie Upshall .15 .40
194 Tomas Vokoun .15 .40

195 Scott Walker .12 .30
196 Martin Brodeur .50 1.25
197 Patrik Elias .20 .50
198 Jeff Friesen .12 .30
199 Brian Gionta .12 .30
200 Scott Gomez .15 .40
201 Jamie Langenbrunner .15 .40
202 John Madden .12 .30
203 Scott Niedermayer .20 .50
204 Joe Nieuwendyk .15 .40
205 Brian Rafalski .15 .40
206 Scott Stevens .20 .50
207 Oleg Tverdovsky .12 .30
208 Arron Asham .12 .30
209 Shawn Bates .12 .30
210 Jason Blake .12 .30
211 Rick DiPietro .15 .40
212 Roman Hamrlik .12 .30
213 Mark Parrish .12 .30
214 Michael Peca .15 .40
215 Dave Scatchard .12 .30
216 Garth Snow .15 .40
217 Mattias Weinhandl .12 .30
218 Alexei Yashin .15 .40
219 Matthew Barnaby .12 .30
220 Dan Blackburn .15 .40
221 Pavel Bure .20 .50
222 Anson Carter .15 .40
223 Mike Dunham .15 .40
224 Bobby Holik .12 .30
225 Alex Kovalev .15 .40
226 Brian Leetch .15 .40
227 Eric Lindros .30 .75
228 Mark Messier .40 1.00
229 Petr Nedved .12 .30
230 Tom Poti .12 .30
231 Mike Richter .20 .50
232 Daniel Alfredsson .20 .50
233 Magnus Arvedson .12 .30
234 Radek Bonk .15 .40
235 Zdeno Chara .20 .50
236 Mike Fisher .12 .30
237 Martin Havlat .20 .50
238 Marian Hossa .20 .50
239 Patrick Lalime .15 .40
240 Martin Prusek .12 .30
241 Wade Redden .12 .30
242 Bryan Smolinski .12 .30
243 Jason Spezza .20 .50
244 Vaclav Varada .12 .30
245 Todd White .12 .30
246 Tony Amonte .15 .40
247 Donald Brashear .12 .30
248 Roman Cechmanek .15 .40
249 Eric Desjardins .15 .40
250 Robert Esche .12 .30
251 Simon Gagne .20 .50
252 Michal Handzus .15 .40
253 Kim Johnsson .12 .30
254 John LeClair .20 .50
255 Keith Primeau .15 .40
256 Mark Recchi .25 .60
257 Jeremy Roenick .30 .75
258 Zac Bierk .12 .30
259 Brian Boucher .15 .40
260 Sean Burke .12 .30
261 Shane Doan .15 .40
262 Chris Gratton .12 .30
263 Jan Hrdina .12 .30
264 Mike Johnson .12 .30
265 Daymond Langkow .12 .30
266 Ladislav Nagy .12 .30
267 Teppo Numminen .12 .30
268 Jeff Taffe .12 .30
269 Ramzi Abid .12 .30
270 Rico Fata .12 .30
271 Johan Hedberg .15 .40
272 Brian Holzinger .12 .30
273 Mathias Johansson .12 .30
274 Mario Lemieux .75 2.00
275 Alexei Morozov .12 .30
276 Martin Straka .12 .30
277 Tomas Surovy .12 .30
278 Dick Tarnstrom .12 .30
279 Eric Boguniecki .12 .30
280 Pavol Demitra .25 .60
281 Dallas Drake .12 .30
282 Barret Jackman .12 .30
283 Brent Johnson .15 .40
284 Al MacInnis .25 .60
285 Scott Mellanby .12 .30
286 Chris Osgood .20 .50
287 Chris Pronger .20 .50
288 Peter Sejna RC .15 .40
289 Cory Stillman .12 .30
290 Keith Tkachuk .20 .50
291 Doug Weight .20 .50
292 Jonathan Cheechoo .15 .40
293 Vincent Damphousse .15 .40
294 Niko Dimitrakos .12 .30
295 Miikka Kiprusoff .20 .50
296 Patrick Marleau .20 .50
297 Alyn McCauley .12 .30
298 Evgeni Nabokov .15 .40
299 Mike Ricci .12 .30
300 Teemu Selanne .40 1.00
301 Marco Sturm .12 .30
302 Vesa Toskala .12 .30
303 Dave Andreychuk .20 .50
304 Dan Boyle .12 .30
305 Ruslan Fedotenko .12 .30
306 John Grahame .12 .30
307 Nikolai Khabibulin .20 .50
308 Vincent Lecavalier .20 .50
309 Fredrik Modin .12 .30
310 Vaclav Prospal .12 .30
311 Brad Richards .20 .50
312 Martin St. Louis .20 .50
313 Alexander Svitov .12 .30
314 Nik Antropov .15 .40
315 Ed Belfour .20 .50
316 Tie Domi .15 .40
317 Doug Gilmour .25 .60
318 Tomas Kaberle .12 .30
319 Trevor Kidd .12 .30
320 Alexander Mogilny .15 .40
321 Owen Nolan .20 .50
322 Gary Roberts .12 .30
323 Matt Stajan RC .20 .50
324 Mats Sundin .20 .50
325 Robert Svehla .12 .30
326 Darcy Tucker .15 .40
327 Todd Bertuzzi .20 .50
328 Dan Cloutier .15 .40
329 Matt Cooke .12 .30
330 Ed Jovanovski .15 .40
331 Trent Klatt .12 .30
332 Trevor Linden .20 .50
333 Brendan Morrison .15 .40
334 Markus Naslund .20 .50
335 Daniel Sedin .25 .60
336 Henrik Sedin .25 .60
337 Peter Skudra .15 .40
338 Brent Sopel .12 .30
339 Sergei Berezin .12 .30
340 Peter Bondra .20 .50
341 Sebastien Charpentier .12 .30
342 Sergei Gonchar .12 .30
343 Mike Grier .12 .30
344 Jeff Halpern .12 .30
345 Jaromir Jagr .60 1.50
346 Olaf Kolzig .20 .50
347 Robert Lang .12 .30
348 Kip Miller .12 .30
349 Michael Nylander .12 .30
350 Dainius Zubrus .12 .30
351 Joffrey Lupul RC 1.50 4.00
352 Eric Staal RC 3.00 8.00
353 Tuomo Ruutu RC 1.00 2.50
354 Pavel Vorobiev RC .75 2.00
355 Nathan Horton RC 1.50 4.00
356 Dustin Brown RC 1.50 4.00
357 Jordin Tootoo RC 1.25 3.00
358 Marc-Andre Fleury RC 4.00 10.00
359 Milan Michalek RC 1.25 3.00
360 Boyd Gordon RC .75 2.00
361 Derek Roy RC 1.00 2.50
362 Matthew Lombardi RC .75 2.00
363 Nikolai Zherdev RC 1.25 3.00
364 Jiri Hudler RC 1.50 4.00
365 Niklas Kronwall RC 1.25 3.00
366 Fredrik Sjostrom RC 1.00 2.50
367 Ryan Malone RC 1.25 3.00
368 Ryan Kesler RC 2.50 6.00

2003-04 Pacific Blue

*BLUE/250: 1.2X TO 3X BASIC CARDS

2003-04 Pacific Red

*RED: .6X TO 1.5X BASIC CARDS
228 Mark Messier .75 2.00

2003-04 Pacific Cramer's Choice

1 Peter Forsberg 12.00 30.00
2 Patrick Roy 25.00 60.00
3 Rick Nash 12.00 30.00
4 Mike Modano 8.00 20.00
5 Steve Yzerman 20.00 50.00
6 Henrik Zetterberg 10.00 25.00
7 Martin Brodeur 20.00 50.00
8 Mario Lemieux 30.00 80.00
9 Markus Naslund 4.00 10.00
10 Jaromir Jagr 10.00 25.00

2003-04 Pacific In the Crease

COMPLETE SET (12) 10.00 20.00
1 Jean-Sebastien Giguere .60 1.50
2 Jocelyn Thibault .60 1.50
3 Patrick Roy 1.50 4.00
4 Marty Turco .60 1.50
5 Curtis Joseph .75 2.00
6 Jose Theodore 1.00 2.50
7 Martin Brodeur 1.25 3.00
8 Patrick Lalime .60 1.50
9 Roman Cechmanek .60 1.50
10 Sean Burke .60 1.50
11 Ed Belfour .75 2.00
12 Dan Cloutier .60 1.50

2003-04 Pacific Jerseys

*GOLD/50: 1X TO 2.5X BASIC JSY
1 Paul Kariya 2.50 6.00
2 Dany Heatley 3.00 8.00
3 Milan Hnilicka 2.00 5.00
4 Ilya Kovalchuk 3.00 8.00
5 Joe Thornton 5.00 12.00
6 J-P Dumont 2.00 5.00
7 Chris Drury 2.00 5.00
8 Peter Forsberg 6.00 15.00
9 Patrick Roy 10.00 25.00
10 Joe Sakic 5.00 12.00
11 Alex Tanguay 2.00 5.00
12 Geoff Sanderson 2.00 5.00
13 Mike Modano 3.00 8.00
14 Marty Turco 2.00 5.00
15 Brendan Shanahan 2.50 6.00
16 Steve Yzerman 8.00 20.00
17 Ryan Smyth 2.00 5.00
18 Ziggy Palffy 2.00 5.00
19 Filip Kuba 2.00 5.00
20 Saku Koivu 2.50 6.00
21 Jose Theodore 3.00 8.00
22 Scott Walker 2.00 5.00
23 Martin Brodeur 8.00 20.00
24 Alexei Yashin 2.00 5.00
25 Pavel Bure 2.50 6.00
26 Eric Lindros 2.50 6.00
27 Daniel Alfredsson 2.00 5.00
28 Jason Spezza 5.00 12.00
29 Roman Cechmanek 2.00 5.00
30 Jeremy Roenick 3.00 8.00
31 Mario Lemieux 10.00 25.00
32 Brent Johnson 2.00 5.00
33 Keith Tkachuk 2.50 6.00
34 Miikka Kiprusoff 2.00 5.00
35 Vincent Lecavalier 2.00 5.00
36 Fredrik Modin 2.00 5.00
37 Ed Belfour 3.00 8.00
38 Todd Bertuzzi 2.50 6.00
39 Dan Cloutier 2.00 5.00
40 Jaromir Jagr 3.00 8.00

2003-04 Pacific Main Attractions

1 Paul Kariya .60 1.50
2 Ilya Kovalchuk .75 2.00
3 Joe Thornton .75 2.00
4 Peter Forsberg 1.25 3.00
5 Mike Modano .75 2.00
6 Steve Yzerman 1.50 4.00
7 Marian Gaborik 1.00 2.50
8 Saku Koivu .60 1.50
9 Pavel Bure .60 1.50
10 Marian Hossa .60 1.50
11 John LeClair .60 1.50
12 Mario Lemieux 2.00 5.00
13 Teemu Selanne .60 1.50
14 Mats Sundin .60 1.50
15 Markus Naslund .60 1.50
16 Jaromir Jagr .75 2.00

2003-04 Pacific Marty Turco

COMPLETE SET (6) 8.00 15.00
COMMON CARD (1-6) 1.25 3.00

2003-04 Pacific Marty Turco Autographs

COMMON AUTO/99 (1-5) 15.00 40.00
COMMON AUTO/35 (6) 40.00 100.00

2003-04 Pacific Maximum Impact

COMPLETE SET (10) 10.00 20.00
1 Joe Thornton 1.25 3.00
2 Jarome Iginla 1.00 2.50
3 Rick Nash 1.00 2.50
4 Brendan Shanahan .75 2.00
5 Michael Peca .60 1.50
6 Eric Lindros .75 2.00
7 Mark Messier .75 2.00
8 Jeremy Roenick 1.00 2.50
9 Owen Nolan .60 1.50
10 Todd Bertuzzi .75 2.00

2003-04 Pacific Milestones

COMPLETE SET (8) 10.00 20.00
1 Patrick Roy 2.50 6.00
2 Joe Sakic 1.50 4.00
3 Mike Modano 1.25 3.00
4 Marty Turco .60 1.50
5 Brett Hull 1.00 2.50
6 Joe Nieuwendyk .60 1.50
7 Mats Sundin .75 2.00
8 Jaromir Jagr 1.25 3.00

2003-04 Pacific View from the Crease

COMPLETE SET (8) 15.00 30.00
1 Paul Kariya 1.25 3.00
2 Joe Thornton 2.00 5.00
3 Joe Sakic 2.50 6.00
4 Mike Modano 2.00 5.00
5 Sergei Fedorov 1.50 4.00
6 Brett Hull 1.50 4.00
7 Marian Gaborik 2.50 6.00
8 Todd Bertuzzi 1.25 3.00

2004-05 Pacific

COMPLETE SET (300) 15.00 40.00
1 Stanislav Chistov .12 .30
2 Sergei Fedorov .30 .75
3 Martin Gerber .15 .40
4 Jean-Sebastien Giguere .20 .50
5 Joffrey Lupul .12 .30
6 Vaclav Prospal .12 .30
7 Steve Rucchin .12 .30
8 Martin Skoula .12 .30
9 Petr Sykora .15 .40
10 Dany Heatley .15 .40
11 Ilya Kovalchuk .20 .50
12 Slava Kozlov .15 .40
13 Shawn McEachern .12 .30
14 Pasi Nurminen .15 .40
15 Ronald Petrovicky .12 .30
16 Randy Robitaille .12 .30
17 Marc Savard .12 .30
18 Patrik Stefan .12 .30
19 Patrice Bergeron .25 .60
20 Sergei Gonchar .15 .40
21 Mike Knuble .12 .30
22 Glen Murray .15 .40
23 Felix Potvin .30 .75
24 Andrew Raycroft .15 .40
25 Brian Rolston .15 .40
26 Sergei Samsonov .15 .40
27 Joe Thornton .30 .75
28 Maxim Afinogenov .12 .30
29 Martin Biron .15 .40
30 Daniel Briere .20 .50
31 Chris Drury .15 .40
32 J-P Dumont .12 .30
33 Jochen Hecht .12 .30
34 Mika Noronen .15 .40
35 Derek Roy .12 .30
36 Miroslav Satan .15 .40
37 Craig Conroy .12 .30
38 Shean Donovan .12 .30
39 Martin Gelinas .12 .30
40 Jarome Iginla .25 .60
41 Miikka Kiprusoff .20 .50
42 Jordan Leopold .12 .30
43 Matthew Lombardi .12 .30
44 Steven Reinprecht .12 .30
45 Chris Simon .12 .30
46 Rod Brind'Amour .20 .50
47 Erik Cole .12 .30
48 Sean Hill .12 .30
49 Jeff O'Neill .12 .30
50 Eric Staal .25 .60
51 Josef Vasicek .12 .30
52 Radim Vrbata .12 .30
53 Kevin Weekes .15 .40
54 Justin Williams .15 .40
55 Craig Andersson .20 .50
56 Tyler Arnason .12 .30
57 Mark Bell .12 .30
58 Bryan Berard .15 .40
59 Kyle Calder .12 .30
60 Eric Daze .15 .40
61 Brett McLean .12 .30
62 Tuomo Ruutu .15 .40
63 Jocelyn Thibault .15 .40
64 David Aebischer .15 .40
65 Rob Blake .20 .50
66 Peter Forsberg .40 1.00
67 Milan Hejduk .15 .40
68 Paul Kariya .20 .50
69 Joe Sakic .40 1.00
70 Tommy Salo .15 .40
71 Teemu Selanne .40 1.00
72 Alex Tanguay .15 .40
73 Andrew Cassels .12 .30
74 Marc Denis .15 .40
75 Anders Eriksson .12 .30
76 Trevor Letowski .12 .30
77 Manny Malhotra .12 .30
78 Todd Marchant .12 .30
79 Rick Nash .20 .50
80 David Vyborny .12 .30
81 Nikolai Zherdev .15 .40
82 Jason Arnott .15 .40
83 Valeri Bure .15 .40
84 Bill Guerin .20 .50
85 Jere Lehtinen .20 .50
86 Mike Modano .30 .75
87 Brenden Morrow .15 .40
88 Marty Turco .20 .50
89 Pierre Turgeon .15 .40
90 Sergei Zubov .15 .40
91 Pavel Datsyuk .30 .75
92 Kris Draper .12 .30
93 Brett Hull .40 1.00
94 Curtis Joseph .25 .60
95 Robert Lang .12 .30
96 Manny Legace .15 .40
97 Nicklas Lidstrom .20 .50
98 Brendan Shanahan .20 .50
99 Steve Yzerman .50 1.25
100 Ty Conklin .15 .40
101 Radek Dvorak .12 .30
102 Ales Hemsky .20 .50
103 Shawn Horcoff .15 .40
104 Ethan Moreau .12 .30
105 Petr Nedved .12 .30
106 Ryan Smyth .15 .40
107 Raffi Torres .12 .30
108 Mike York .12 .30
109 Jay Bouwmeester .12 .30
110 Niklas Hagman .15 .40
111 Nathan Horton .20 .50
112 Kristian Huselius .12 .30
113 Olli Jokinen .15 .40
114 Juraj Kolnik .12 .30
115 Roberto Luongo .30 .75
116 Mike Van Ryn .12 .30
117 Stephen Weiss .12 .30
118 Derek Armstrong .12 .30
119 Dustin Brown .20 .50
120 Roman Cechmanek .15 .40
121 Alexander Frolov .15 .40
122 Cristobal Huet .15 .40
123 Trent Klatt .12 .30
124 Ziggy Palffy .20 .50
125 Luc Robitaille .20 .50
126 Jozef Stumpel .12 .30
127 Andrew Brunette .12 .30
128 Brent Burns .20 .50
129 Alexandre Daigle .12 .30
130 Pascal Dupuis .12 .30
131 Manny Fernandez .12 .30
132 Marian Gaborik .20 .50
133 Filip Kuba .12 .30
134 Antti Laaksonen .12 .30
135 Dwayne Roloson .15 .40
136 Patrice Brisebois .12 .30
137 Saku Koivu .20 .50
138 Alex Kovalev .15 .40
139 Yanic Perreault .12 .30
140 Mike Ribeiro .12 .30
141 Michael Ryder .15 .40
142 Sheldon Souray .12 .30
143 Jose Theodore .20 .50
144 Richard Zednik .12 .30
145 Martin Erat .12 .30
146 Adam Hall .12 .30
147 Scott Hartnell .12 .30
148 David Legwand .15 .40
149 Steve Sullivan .12 .30
150 Jordin Tootoo .12 .30
151 Tomas Vokoun .15 .40
152 Scott Walker .12 .30
153 Marek Zidlicky .12 .30
154 Martin Brodeur .50 1.25
155 Patrik Elias .20 .50
156 Jeff Friesen .12 .30
157 Brian Gionta .12 .30
158 Scott Gomez .15 .40
159 Jamie Langenbrunner .15 .40
160 John Madden .12 .30
161 Scott Niedermayer .20 .50
162 Scott Stevens .20 .50
163 Adrian Aucoin .12 .30
164 Jason Blake .12 .30
165 Mariusz Czerkawski .12 .30
166 Rick DiPietro .15 .40
167 Trent Hunter .12 .30
168 Oleg Kvasha .12 .30
169 Mark Parrish .12 .30
170 Michael Peca .15 .40
171 Alexei Yashin .15 .40
172 Mike Dunham .15 .40
173 Jan Hlavac .12 .30
174 Bobby Holik .12 .30
175 Jaromir Jagr .60 1.50
176 Eric Lindros .30 .75
177 Mark Messier .40 1.00
178 Boris Mironov .12 .30
179 Tom Poti .12 .30
180 Fedor Tyutin .12 .30
181 Daniel Alfredsson .20 .50
182 Peter Bondra .20 .50
183 Zdeno Chara .20 .50
184 Martin Havlat .20 .50
185 Marian Hossa .20 .50
186 Patrick Lalime .15 .40
187 Wade Redden .12 .30
188 Bryan Smolinski .15 .40
189 Jason Spezza .20 .50
190 Tony Amonte .15 .40
191 Sean Burke .12 .30
192 Robert Esche .15 .40
193 Simon Gagne .20 .50
194 Michal Handzus .12 .30
195 John LeClair .20 .50
196 Joni Pitkanen .12 .30
197 Mark Recchi .25 .60
198 Jeremy Roenick .30 .75
199 Brian Boucher .15 .40
200 Mike Comrie .15 .40
201 Shane Doan .15 .40
202 Daymond Langkow .12 .30
203 Paul Mara .12 .30
204 Derek Morris .12 .30
205 Ladislav Nagy .12 .30
206 Fredrik Sjostrom .12 .30
207 Jeff Taffe .12 .30
208 Jean-Sebastien Aubin .12 .30
209 Rico Fata .12 .30
210 Marc-Andre Fleury .40 1.00
211 Ric Jackman .12 .30
212 Milan Kraft .12 .30
213 Mario Lemieux .75 2.00
214 Ryan Malone .12 .30
215 Aleksey Morozov .12 .30
216 Dick Tarnstrom .12 .30
217 Pavol Demitra .25 .60
218 Dallas Drake .12 .30
219 Barret Jackman .12 .30
220 Al MacInnis .25 .60
221 Chris Osgood .20 .50
222 Chris Pronger .20 .50
223 Mark Rycroft .12 .30
224 Keith Tkachuk .20 .50
225 Doug Weight .20 .50
226 Jonathan Cheechoo .15 .40
227 Vincent Damphousse .15 .40
228 Nils Ekman .12 .30
229 Alex Korolyuk .12 .30
230 Patrick Marleau .20 .50
231 Alyn McCauley .12 .30
232 Evgeni Nabokov .15 .40
233 Marco Sturm .12 .30
234 Vesa Toskala .12 .30
235 Dave Andreychuk .20 .50
236 John Grahame .15 .40
237 Nikolai Khabibulin .20 .50
238 Pavel Kubina .12 .30
239 Vincent Lecavalier .20 .50
240 Fredrik Modin .12 .30
241 Brad Richards .20 .50
242 Martin St. Louis .20 .50
243 Cory Stillman .12 .30
244 Ed Belfour .20 .50
245 Brian Leetch .15 .40
246 Bryan McCabe .12 .30
247 Alexander Mogilny .15 .40
248 Joe Nieuwendyk .15 .40
249 Owen Nolan .20 .50
250 Gary Roberts .12 .30
251 Mats Sundin .20 .50
252 Darcy Tucker .12 .30
253 Todd Bertuzzi .20 .50
254 Dan Cloutier .15 .40
255 Ed Jovanovski .15 .40
256 Trevor Linden .20 .50
257 Brendan Morrison .15 .40
258 Markus Naslund .20 .50
259 Mattias Ohlund .12 .30
260 Daniel Sedin .25 .60
261 Henrik Sedin .25 .60
262 Sebastien Charpentier .15 .40
263 Jeff Halpern .12 .30
264 Olaf Kolzig .20 .50
265 Kip Miller .12 .30
266 Maxime Ouellet .12 .30
267 Matt Pettinger .12 .30
268 Brian Willsie .12 .30
269 Brendan Witt .12 .30
270 Dainius Zubrus .12 .30
271 Chris Kunitz .25 .60
272 Kari Lehtonen .25 .60
273 Brett Lysak .12 .30
274 Matt Keith .12 .30
275 Adam Munro .12 .30
276 Mikhail Kuleshov .12 .30
277 John-Michael Liles .12 .30
278 Marek Svatos .12 .30
279 Dan Fritsche .12 .30
280 Greg Mauldin .12 .30
281 Mike Pandolfo .12 .30
282 Dan Ellis .15 .40
283 Mike Bishai .12 .30
284 Lukas Krajicek .12 .30
285 Denis Grebeshkov .12 .30
286 Tomas Plekanec .12 .30
287 Timofei Shishkanov .12 .30
288 Scottie Upshall .12 .30
289 Thomas Pihlman .12 .30
290 Aleksander Suglobov .12 .30
291 Jozef Balej .12 .30
292 Bryce Lampman .12 .30
293 Randy Jones .12 .30
294 Antero Niittymaki .12 .30
295 Mike Stutzel .12 .30
296 Niko Dimitrakos .12 .30
297 Marcel Goc RC .20 .50
298 Matt Stajan .12 .30
299 Alexander Semin .20 .50
300 Roman Tvrdon .12 .30

2004-05 Pacific Blue

*BLUE/250: 2X TO 5X BASIC CARDS

2004-05 Pacific Red

*RED: .8X TO 2X BASIC CARDS

2004-05 Pacific All-Stars

COMPLETE SET (12) 8.00 15.00
1 Ilya Kovalchuk .75 2.00
2 Joe Thornton .75 2.00
3 Joe Sakic 1.25 3.00
4 Rick Nash .75 2.00
5 Mike Modano 1.00 2.50
6 Marty Turco .50 1.25
7 Robert Lang .50 1.25
8 Nicklas Lidstrom .60 1.50
9 Jose Theodore .75 2.00
10 Martin Brodeur 1.50 4.00
11 Patrick Marleau .50 1.25
12 Martin St. Louis .50 1.25

2004-05 Pacific Cramer's Choice

1 Ilya Kovalchuk 12.00 30.00
2 Joe Thornton 12.00 30.00
3 Jarome Iginla 12.00 30.00
4 Joe Sakic 15.00 40.00
5 Rick Nash 12.00 30.00
6 Steve Yzerman 20.00 50.00
7 Martin Brodeur 15.00 40.00
8 Mario Lemieux 20.00 50.00
9 Martin St. Louis 8.00 20.00
10 Ed Belfour 8.00 20.00

2004-05 Pacific Global Connection

COMPLETE SET (8) 8.00 15.00
1 D.Heatley
I.Kovalchuk 1.25 3.00
2 S.Samsonov/J.Thornton 1.00 2.50
3 P.Forsberg/J.Sakic 1.50 4.00
4 P.Kariya/T.Selanne 1.00 2.50
5 P.Datsyuk/H.Zetterberg 1.25 3.00
6 B.Hull/N.Lidstrom 1.00 2.50
7 M.Havlat/M.Hossa 1.00 2.50
8 A.Mogilny/M.Sundin 1.00 2.50

2004-05 Pacific Gold Crown Die-Cuts

COMPLETE SET (8) 10.00 25.00
1 Ilya Kovalchuk 2.00 5.00
2 Andrew Raycroft 1.50 4.00
3 Eric Staal 2.50 6.00
4 Henrik Zetterberg 2.50 6.00
5 Michael Ryder 1.50 4.00
6 Jordin Tootoo 1.25 3.00
7 Jason Spezza 2.00 5.00
8 Jonathan Cheechoo 1.50 4.00

2004-05 Pacific In The Crease

COMPLETE SET (10) 8.00 15.00
1 Andrew Raycroft .75 2.00
2 Miikka Kiprusoff .75 2.00
3 David Aebischer .75 2.00
4 Marty Turco .75 2.00
5 Dominik Hasek 1.25 3.00
6 Roberto Luongo 1.25 3.00
7 Jose Theodore 1.25 3.00
8 Martin Brodeur 1.50 4.00
9 Nikolai Khabibulin 1.00 2.50
10 Ed Belfour 1.00 2.50

2004-05 Pacific Jerseys

*GOLD: 1X TO 2X
1 Sergei Fedorov 4.00 10.00
2 Patrice Bergeron 3.00 8.00
3 Sergei Samsonov 3.00 8.00
4 Joe Thornton 5.00 12.00
5 Ales Kotalik 2.00 5.00
6 Mark Bell 2.00 5.00
7 Jocelyn Thibault 2.00 5.00
8 Peter Forsberg 6.00 15.00
9 Paul Kariya 4.00 10.00
10 Joe Sakic 6.00 15.00
11 Mike Modano 5.00 12.00
12 Derian Hatcher 2.00 5.00
13 Jason Williams 2.00 5.00
14 Steve Yzerman 10.00 25.00
15 Ryan Smyth 2.00 5.00
16 Roberto Luongo 3.00 8.00
17 Vaclav Nedorost 2.00 5.00
18 Jason Allison 2.00 5.00
19 Alex Kovalev 2.00 5.00
20 Martin Brodeur 10.00 25.00
21 Alexei Yashin 2.00 5.00
22 Pavel Bure 3.00 8.00
23 Eric Lindros 4.00 10.00
24 Daniel Alfredsson 3.00 8.00
25 Martin Havlat 3.00 8.00
26 Jeff Hackett 2.00 5.00
27 Joni Pitkanen 2.00 5.00
28 Jeremy Roenick 3.00 8.00
29 Brent Johnson 2.00 5.00
30 Krystofer Kolanos 2.00 5.00
31 Kris Beech 2.00 5.00
32 Mike Eastwood 2.00 5.00
33 Rico Fata 2.00 5.00
34 Mario Lemieux 10.00 25.00
35 Chris Osgood 2.00 5.00
36 Peter Sejna 2.00 5.00
37 Vincent Lecavalier 3.00 8.00
38 Ed Belfour 3.00 8.00
39 Matt Stajan 1.50 4.00
40 Mats Sundin 3.00 8.00
41 Todd Bertuzzi 3.00 8.00
42 Dan Cloutier 2.00 5.00
43 Brendan Morrison 2.00 5.00
44 Olaf Kolzig 3.00 8.00
45 Kovy J/Iginla J/Nash AU 75.00 200.00

2004-05 Pacific Milestones

COMPLETE SET (6) 10.00 20.00
1 Steve Yzerman 3.00 8.00
2 Martin Brodeur 3.00 8.00
3 Jaromir Jagr 1.50 4.00
4 Mark Messier 1.00 2.50
5 Mario Lemieux 4.00 10.00
6 Ed Belfour 1.00 2.50

2004-05 Pacific Philadelphia

COMPLETE SET (16) 10.00 25.00
1 Sergei Fedorov 1.00 2.50
2 Joe Sakic 1.25 3.00
3 Chris Chelios .60 1.50
4 Dominik Hasek 1.00 2.50
5 Brett Hull 1.25 3.00
6 Steve Yzerman 1.50 4.00
7 Luc Robitaille .60 1.50
8 Jaromir Jagr 2.00 5.00
9 Eric Lindros 1.00 2.50
10 Mark Messier 1.25 3.00
11 John LeClair .60 1.50
12 Jeremy Roenick 1.00 2.50
13 Mario Lemieux 2.50 6.00
14 Keith Tkachuk .60 1.50
15 Ron Francis .75 2.00
16 Brian Leetch .50 1.25

2001-02 Pacific Adrenaline

1 Jeff Friesen .12 .30
2 Jean-Sebastien Giguere .20 .50
3 Paul Kariya .20 .50
4 Marty McInnis .15 .40
5 Steve Shields .15 .40
6 Oleg Tverdovsky .12 .30
7 Ray Ferraro .12 .30
8 Milan Hnilicka .15 .40
9 Tomi Kallio .12 .30
10 Damian Rhodes .15 .40
11 Patrik Stefan .15 .40
12 Byron Dafoe .15 .40
13 Bill Guerin .20 .50
14 Martin Lapointe .12 .30
15 Sergei Samsonov .15 .40
16 Jozef Stumpel .12 .30
17 Joe Thornton .30 .75
18 Stu Barnes .15 .40
19 Martin Biron .15 .40
20 Tim Connolly .12 .30
21 J-P Dumont .12 .30
22 Chris Gratton .12 .30
23 Slava Kozlov .15 .40
24 Miroslav Satan .15 .40
25 Jarome Iginla .25 .60
26 Derek Morris .12 .30
27 Rob Niedermayer .15 .40
28 Marc Savard .12 .30
29 Roman Turek .15 .40
30 Mike Vernon .15 .40
31 Rod Brind'Amour .20 .50
32 Ron Francis .25 .60
33 Martin Gelinas .12 .30
34 Arturs Irbe .15 .40
35 Sami Kapanen .12 .30
36 Jeff O'Neill .15 .40
37 Shane Willis .12 .30
38 Tony Amonte .15 .40
39 Eric Daze .15 .40
40 Michael Nylander .12 .30
41 Steve Sullivan .12 .30
42 Jocelyn Thibault .15 .40
43 Alexei Zhamnov .15 .40
44 David Aebischer .15 .40
45 Rob Blake .20 .50
46 Chris Drury .15 .40
47 Peter Forsberg .40 1.00
48 Milan Hejduk .15 .40
49 Patrick Roy .50 1.25
50 Joe Sakic .40 1.00
51 Alex Tanguay .15 .40
52 Marc Denis .15 .40
53 Rostislav Klesla .12 .30
54 Espen Knutsen .12 .30
55 Geoff Sanderson .12 .30
56 Ron Tugnutt .15 .40
57 Donald Audette .12 .30
58 Ed Belfour .20 .50
59 Mike Modano .30 .75
60 Joe Nieuwendyk .15 .40
61 Marty Turco .20 .50
62 Pierre Turgeon .15 .40
63 Chris Chelios .20 .50
64 Sergei Fedorov .30 .75
65 Dominik Hasek .30 .75
66 Brett Hull .40 1.00
67 Nicklas Lidstrom .20 .50
68 Luc Robitaille .20 .50
69 Brendan Shanahan .20 .50
70 Steve Yzerman .50 1.25
71 Eric Brewer .12 .30
72 Anson Carter .15 .40
73 Daniel Cleary .15 .40
74 Mike Comrie .15 .40
75 Mike Grier .12 .30
76 Jochen Hecht .12 .30
77 Tommy Salo .15 .40
78 Ryan Smyth .15 .40
79 Pavel Bure .20 .50
80 Valeri Bure .12 .30
81 Trevor Kidd .12 .30
82 Viktor Kozlov .12 .30
83 Roberto Luongo .30 .75
84 Marcus Nilsson .12 .30
85 Jason Allison .15 .40
86 Adam Deadmarsh .12 .30
87 Zigmund Palffy .20 .50
88 Felix Potvin .30 .75
89 Mathieu Schneider .12 .30
90 Bryan Smolinski .12 .30
91 Manny Fernandez .12 .30
92 Marian Gaborik .20 .50
93 Darby Hendrickson .12 .30
94 Lubomir Sekeras .12 .30
95 Wes Walz .12 .30
96 Joe Juneau .12 .30
97 Yanic Perreault .12 .30
98 Oleg Petrov .12 .30
99 Martin Rucinsky .12 .30
100 Brian Savage .12 .30
101 Jose Theodore .20 .50
102 Richard Zednik .15 .40
103 Mike Dunham .15 .40
104 Scott Hartnell .12 .30
105 Patric Kjellberg .12 .30
106 David Legwand .15 .40
107 Cliff Ronning .12 .30
108 Tomas Vokoun .15 .40
109 Scott Walker .12 .30
110 Jason Arnott .15 .40
111 Martin Brodeur .50 1.25
112 Sergei Brylin .12 .30
113 Patrik Elias .20 .50
114 Scott Gomez .15 .40
115 John Madden .15 .40
116 Randy McKay .12 .30
117 Scott Stevens .20 .50
118 Mariusz Czerkawski .12 .30
119 Rick DiPietro .15 .40
120 Brad Isbister .12 .30
121 Chris Osgood .20 .50
122 Michael Peca .15 .40
123 Alexei Yashin .15 .40
124 Radek Dvorak .15 .40
125 Theo Fleury .25 .60
126 Brian Leetch .15 .40
127 Eric Lindros .30 .75
128 Mark Messier .40 1.00
129 Petr Nedved .15 .40
130 Mike Richter .20 .50
131 Daniel Alfredsson .20 .50
132 Radek Bonk .12 .30
133 Martin Havlat .15 .40

134 Marian Hossa .20 .50
135 Patrick Lalime .15 .40
136 Shawn McEachern .12 .30
137 Wade Redden .12 .30
138 Roman Cechmanek .15 .40
139 Simon Gagne .20 .50
140 John LeClair .20 .50
141 Keith Primeau .15 .40
142 Mark Recchi .25 .60
143 Jeremy Roenick .30 .75
144 Justin Williams .15 .40
145 Sergei Berezin .12 .30
146 Sean Burke .12 .30
147 Shane Doan .15 .40
148 Michal Handzus .12 .30
149 Daymond Langkow .15 .40
150 Claude Lemieux .15 .40
151 Johan Hedberg .15 .40
152 Jan Hrdina .12 .30
153 Alexei Kovalev .15 .40
154 Robert Lang .12 .30
155 Mario Lemieux .75 2.00
156 Martin Straka .12 .30
157 Fred Brathwaite .15 .40
158 Pavol Demitra .25 .60
159 Brent Johnson .15 .40
160 Al MacInnis .25 .60
161 Chris Pronger .20 .50
162 Cory Stillman .12 .30
163 Keith Tkachuk .20 .50
164 Doug Weight .20 .50
165 Miikka Kiprusoff .20 .50
166 Patrick Marleau .20 .50
167 Evgeni Nabokov .15 .40
168 Owen Nolan .20 .50
169 Mike Ricci .12 .30
170 Teemu Selanne .40 1.00
171 Marco Sturm .12 .30
172 Brian Holzinger .12 .30
173 Nikolai Khabibulin .20 .50
174 Vincent Lecavalier .20 .50
175 Fredrik Modin .12 .30
176 Brad Richards .20 .50
177 Martin St. Louis .20 .50
178 Kevin Weekes .15 .40
179 Tie Domi .15 .40
180 Jonas Hoglund .12 .30
181 Curtis Joseph .25 .60
182 Tomas Kaberle .12 .30
183 Alexander Mogilny .15 .40
184 Gary Roberts .12 .30
185 Mats Sundin .20 .50
186 Darcy Tucker .12 .30
187 Todd Bertuzzi .20 .50
188 Andrew Cassels .12 .30
189 Dan Cloutier .15 .40
190 Brendan Morrison .15 .40
191 Markus Naslund .20 .50
192 Daniel Sedin .25 .60
193 Henrik Sedin .25 .60
194 Peter Bondra .20 .50
195 Sergei Gonchar .12 .30
196 Jeff Halpern .12 .30
197 Jaromir Jagr .60 1.50
198 Olaf Kolzig .20 .50
199 Steve Konowalchuk .12 .30
200 Adam Oates .20 .50
201 Ilja Bryzgalov RC 3.00 8.00
202 Timo Parssinen RC 1.50 4.00
203 I.Kovalchuk AU/500 RC 15.00 40.00
204 Kamil Piros RC 1.25 3.00
205 Erik Cole RC 2.50 6.00
206 Vaclav Nedorost RC 1.25 3.00
207 Pavel Datsyuk RC 12.00 30.00
208 Ty Conklin RC 2.00 5.00
209 Niklas Hagman RC 1.50 4.00
210 Kristian Huselius RC 2.00 5.00
211 Jaroslav Bednar RC 1.25 3.00
212 Nick Schultz RC 1.25 3.00
213 Martin Erat RC 1.50 4.00
214 Scott Clemmensen RC 1.25 3.00
215 Andreas Salomonsson RC 1.25 3.00
216 Radek Martinek RC 1.25 3.00
217 Dan Blackburn RC 1.50 4.00
218 Chris Neil RC 1.50 4.00
219 Pavel Brendl SP 1.25 3.00
220 Jiri Dopita RC 1.25 3.00
221 Krystofer Kolanos RC 1.25 3.00
222 Mark Rycroft RC 1.50 4.00
223 Jeff Jillson RC 1.25 3.00
224 Nikita Alexeev RC 1.25 3.00
225 Brian Sutherby RC 1.25 3.00

2001-02 Pacific Adrenaline Blue

*1-200 VETS/62: 6X TO 15X BASIC CARDS
*201-225 ROOKIES/62: .8X TO 2X
128 Mark Messier 8.00 20.00
203 Ilya Kovalchuk 12.00 30.00

2001-02 Pacific Adrenaline Premiere Date

*1-200 VETS/62: 6X TO 15X BASIC CARDS
*201-225 ROOKIES/62: .8X TO 2X
128 Mark Messier 8.00 20.00
203 Ilya Kovalchuk 12.00 30.00

2001-02 Pacific Adrenaline Red

*1-200 VETS/54: 8X TO 20X BASIC CARDS
*201-225 ROOKIE/54: 1X TO 2.5X
128 Mark Messier 10.00 25.00
203 Ilya Kovalchuk 15.00 40.00

2001-02 Pacific Adrenaline Retail

*RETAIL VETS: .4X TO 1X HOBBY
*RETAIL ROOKIES: .15X TO .4X HOBBY
128 Mark Messier .50 1.25
203 Ilya Kovalchuk RC 5.00 12.00

2001-02 Pacific Adrenaline Blade Runners

1 Paul Kariya 8.00 20.00
2 Patrick Roy 20.00 50.00
3 Joe Sakic 15.00 40.00
4 Dominik Hasek 12.00 30.00
5 Steve Yzerman 20.00 50.00
6 Pavel Bure 8.00 20.00
7 Martin Brodeur 20.00 50.00
8 Eric Lindros 12.00 30.00
9 Mario Lemieux 30.00 80.00
10 Jaromir Jagr 25.00 60.00

2001-02 Pacific Adrenaline Creased Lightning

COMPLETE SET (20) 15.00 40.00
1 Martin Biron .75 2.00
2 Arturs Irbe .75 2.00
3 Jocelyn Thibault .75 2.00
4 Patrick Roy 2.50 6.00
5 Ed Belfour 1.00 2.50
6 Dominik Hasek 1.50 4.00
7 Tommy Salo .75 2.00
8 Roberto Luongo 1.50 4.00
9 Felix Potvin 1.50 4.00
10 Jose Theodore 1.00 2.50
11 Martin Brodeur 2.50 6.00
12 Rick DiPietro .75 2.00
13 Mike Richter 1.00 2.50
14 Patrick Lalime .75 2.00
15 Roman Cechmanek .75 2.00
16 Sean Burke .75 2.00
17 Johan Hedberg .75 2.00
18 Brent Johnson .75 2.00
19 Evgeni Nabokov .75 2.00
20 Curtis Joseph 1.25 3.00

2001-02 Pacific Adrenaline Jerseys

1 Oleg Tverdovsky 2.00 5.00
2 Sergei Samsonov 4.00 10.00
3 J-P Dumont 2.00 5.00
4 Jay McKee 2.00 5.00
5 Jarome Iginla 6.00 15.00
6 Roman Turek 2.00 5.00
7 Tony Amonte 4.00 10.00
8 Alexei Zhamnov 2.00 5.00
9 Patrick Roy 12.50 30.00
10 Joe Sakic 8.00 20.00
11 Ed Belfour 4.00 10.00
12 Derian Hatcher 2.00 5.00
13 Joe Nieuwendyk 4.00 10.00
14 Pierre Turgeon 4.00 10.00
15 Brett Hull 6.00 15.00
16 Steve Yzerman 12.00 30.00
17 Jochen Hecht 2.00 5.00
18 Valeri Bure 2.00 5.00
19 Robert Svehla 2.00 5.00
20 Felix Potvin 5.00 12.00
21 Jamie McLennan 2.00 5.00
22 Saku Koivu 4.00 10.00
23 Patric Kjellberg 2.00 5.00
24 Kimmo Timonen 2.00 5.00
25 Martin Brodeur 8.00 20.00
26 Petr Sykora 2.00 5.00
27 Chris Osgood 4.00 10.00
28 Eric Lindros 5.00 12.00
29 Petr Nedved 2.00 5.00
30 Mike Richter 4.00 10.00
31 Zdeno Chara 2.50 6.00
32 John LeClair 2.00 5.00
33 Shane Doan 2.00 5.00
34 Daymond Langkow 2.00 5.00
35 Alexei Kovalev 2.00 5.00
36 Milan Kraft 2.00 5.00
37 Robert Lang 2.00 5.00
38 Mario Lemieux 12.00 30.00
39 Fred Brathwaite 2.00 5.00
40 Cory Stillman 2.00 5.00
41 Doug Weight 4.00 10.00
42 Scott Young 2.00 5.00
43 Teemu Selanne 4.00 10.00
44 Nikolai Khabibulin 4.00 10.00
45 Vincent Lecavalier 5.00 12.00
46 Shayne Corson 2.00 5.00
47 Mats Sundin 5.00 12.00
48 Dimitri Yushkevich 2.00 5.00
49 Andrew Cassels 2.00 5.00
50 Jaromir Jagr 8.00 20.00

2001-02 Pacific Adrenaline Playmakers

COMPLETE SET (10) 10.00 25.00
1 Joe Thornton 2.50 6.00
2 Milan Hejduk .75 2.00
3 Mike Modano 2.50 6.00
4 Brett Hull 1.50 4.00
5 Mike Comrie .75 2.00
6 Marian Gaborik 2.50 6.00
7 Martin Havlat 1.25 3.00
8 Teemu Selanne 1.50 4.00
9 Daniel Sedin 1.25 3.00
10 Henrik Sedin 1.25 3.00

2001-02 Pacific Adrenaline Power Play

COMPLETE SET (36) 8.00 20.00
1 Jean-Sebastien Giguere .20 .50
2 Steve Shields .20 .50
3 Milan Hnilicka .20 .50
4 Byron DaFoe .20 .50
5 Martin Biron .20 .50
6 Roman Turek .20 .50
7 Arturs Irbe .20 .50
8 Jocelyn Thibault .20 .50
9 Patrick Roy 1.50 4.00
10 Marc Denis .20 .50
11 Ron Tugnutt .20 .50
12 Ed Belfour .30 .75
13 Marty Turco .30 .75
14 Dominik Hasek .60 1.50
15 Tommy Salo .20 .50
16 Trevor Kidd .20 .50
17 Roberto Luongo .40 1.00
18 Felix Potvin .30 .75
19 Manny Fernandez .20 .50
20 Jose Theodore .40 1.00
21 Mike Dunham .20 .50
22 Martin Brodeur .75 2.00
23 Rick DiPietro .30 .75
24 Mike Richter .30 .75
25 Patrick Lalime .20 .50
26 Roman Cechmanek .20 .50
27 Sean Burke .20 .50
28 Johan Hedberg .20 .50
29 Fred Brathwaite .20 .50
30 Brent Johnson .20 .50
31 Miikka Kiprusoff .40 1.00
32 Evgeni Nabokov .20 .50
33 Nikolai Khabibulin .30 .75
34 Curtis Joseph .30 .75
35 Dan Cloutier .20 .50
36 Olaf Kolzig .40 1.00

2001-02 Pacific Adrenaline Rookie Report

COMPLETE SET (20) 15.00 40.00
1 Ilja Bryzgalov 1.25 3.00
2 Dany Heatley 3.00 8.00
3 Ilya Kovalchuk 8.00 20.00
4 Erik Cole 2.00 5.00
5 Mark Bell .40 1.00
6 Vaclav Nedorost .40 1.00
7 Rostislav Klesla .40 1.00
8 Pavel Datsyuk 5.00 12.00
9 Kristian Huselius .40 1.00
10 Jaroslav Bednar .40 1.00
11 Rick DiPietro 2.00 5.00
12 Dan Blackburn .40 1.00
13 Pavel Brendl .40 1.00
14 Krystofer Kolanos .40 1.00
15 Kris Beech .40 1.00
16 Johan Hedberg .40 1.00
17 Jeff Jillson .40 1.00
18 Miikka Kiprusoff 2.00 5.00
19 Nikita Alexeev .40 1.00
20 Brian Sutherby .40 1.00

2001-02 Pacific Adrenaline World Beaters

COMPLETE SET (20) 25.00 50.00
1 Paul Kariya .75 2.00
2 Chris Drury .60 1.50
3 Joe Sakic 1.25 3.00
4 Mike Modano 1.00 2.50
5 Brett Hull .75 2.00
6 Steve Yzerman 3.00 8.00
7 Pavel Bure .75 2.00
8 Zigmund Palffy .60 1.50
9 Marian Gaborik 1.50 4.00
10 Patrik Elias .60 1.50
11 Alexei Yashin .60 1.50
12 Eric Lindros 1.00 2.50
13 Martin Havlat .60 1.50
14 John LeClair .75 2.00
15 Alexei Kovalev .60 1.50
16 Mario Lemieux 4.00 10.00
17 Keith Tkachuk .75 2.00
18 Teemu Selanne .75 2.00
19 Mats Sundin .75 2.00
20 Jaromir Jagr 1.00 2.50

2003 Pacific All-Star Game-Used Goal Net Cards

COMPLETE SET (2) 20.00 40.00
1 North American All-Star Team 20.00 25.00
2 World All-Star Team 20.00 25.00

2001-02 Pacific Arena Exclusives

*ARENA/50: 8X TO 20X BASIC CARDS
*452 HEDBERG/50: .8X TO 2X BASIC CARDS
71 Ron Francis 6.00 15.00
264 Mark Messier 10.00 25.00
406 Ron Francis
Darren Langdon 6.00 15.00

2003 Pacific Atlantic City National Convention

COMPLETE SET (6) 12.50 30.00
1 Rick Nash
John LeClair 3.00 8.00
2 Henrik Zetterberg
Ilya Kovalchuk 4.00 10.00
3 Ryan Miller
Martin Brodeur 2.50 6.00
4 Jay Bouwmeester
Scott Stevens 2.00 5.00
5 Jason Spezza
Jeremy Roenick 3.00 8.00
6 Stanislav Chistov
Paul Kariya 2.00 5.00

2002 Pacific Calder Collection All-Star Fantasy

COMPLETE SET (10) 20.00 50.00
1 Dany Heatley 3.20 8.00
2 Ilya Kovalchuk 8.00 20.00
3 Erik Cole 2.40 6.00
4 Vaclav Nedorost 2.40 6.00
5 Kristian Huselius 2.40 6.00
6 Jaroslav Bednar 1.20 3.00
7 Martin Erat 1.20 3.00
8 Dan Blackburn 3.20 8.00
9 Krys Kolanos 2.40 6.00
10 Jeff Jillson 1.60 4.00

2003 Pacific Calder Collection NHL All-Star Block Party

COMPLETE SET 10.00 25.00
1 Stanislav Chistov .75 2.00
2 Chuck Kobasew .75 2.00
3 Jordan Leopold .75 2.00
4 Rick Nash 4.00 10.00
5 Henrik Zetterberg 4.00 10.00
6 Jay Bouwmeester 2.50 6.00
7 Alexander Frolov 2.00 5.00
8 P-M Bouchard 2.00 5.00
9 Jason Spezza 3.00 8.00
10 Alexander Svitov .75 2.00

2003 Pacific Calder Contenders NHL Entry Draft

COMPLETE SET 15.00 40.00
1 Stanislav Chistov .75 2.00
2 Ales Kotalik .75 2.00
3 Ryan Miller 2.00 5.00
4 Tyler Arnason .75 2.00
5 Pascal Leclaire 1.25 3.00
6 Rick Nash 4.00 10.00
7 Henrik Zetterberg 3.00 8.00
8 Ales Hemsky .75 2.00
9 Jay Bouwmeester 1.50 4.00
10 Jason Spezza 3.00 8.00

2002-03 Pacific Calder

COMP.SET w/o SP'S (100) 15.00 30.00
1 Dany Heatley .25 .60
2 Ilya Kovalchuk .40 1.00
3 Evgeni Nabokov .25 .60
4 Brad Richards .30 .75
5 Scott Gomez .25 .60
6 Brad Stuart .20 .50
7 Chris Drury .30 .75
8 Marian Hossa .30 .75
9 Sergei Samsonov .25 .60
10 Mattias Ohlund .20 .50
11 Bryan Berard .20 .50
12 Jarome Iginla .40 1.00
13 Daniel Alfredsson .30 .75
14 Eric Daze .20 .50
15 Peter Forsberg .60 1.50
16 Martin Brodeur .75 2.00
17 Jason Arnott .25 .60
18 Teemu Selanne .60 1.50
19 Pavel Bure .30 .75
20 Nicklas Lidstrom .30 .75
21 Ed Belfour .30 .75
22 Sergei Fedorov .50 1.25
23 Mike Modano .50 1.25
24 Brian Leetch .25 .60
25 Joe Nieuwendyk .25 .60
26 Luc Robitaille .30 .75
27 Mario Lemieux 1.25 3.00
28 Chris Chelios .30 .75
29 Steve Yzerman .75 2.00
30 Paul Kariya .30 .75
31 Joe Thornton .50 1.25
32 Theoren Fleury .40 1.00
33 Milan Hejduk .25 .60
34 Patrick Roy .75 2.00
35 Joe Sakic .60 1.50
36 Marty Turco .30 .75
37 Brett Hull .60 1.50
38 Curtis Joseph .40 1.00
39 Brendan Shanahan .30 .75
40 Mike Comrie .30 .75
41 Marian Gaborik .30 .75
42 Saku Koivu .30 .75
43 Jose Theodore .30 .75
44 Alexei Yashin .25 .60
45 Alex Kovalev .25 .60
46 Eric Lindros .50 1.25
47 Mark Messier .60 1.50
48 Tony Amonte .25 .60
49 Vincent Lecavalier .30 .75
50 Mats Sundin .30 .75
51 Markus Naslund .30 .75
52 Jaromir Jagr 1.00 2.50
53 Dan Snyder .20 .50
54 Lee Goren .20 .50
55 Ivan Huml .20 .50
56 Andrew Raycroft .25 .60
57 Ales Kotalik .20 .50
58 Mika Noronen .25 .60
59 Henrik Tallinder .20 .50
60 Pavel Brendl .20 .50
61 Jeff Heerema .20 .50
62 Jaroslav Svoboda .20 .50
63 Tyler Arnason .30 .75
64 Riku Hahl .20 .50
65 Vaclav Nedorost .20 .50
66 Niko Kapanen .25 .60
67 Jesse Wallin .20 .50
68 Jason Chimera .20 .50
69 Jani Rita .20 .50
70 Raffi Torres .20 .50
71 Jaroslav Bednar .20 .50
72 Stephen Weiss .30 .75
73 Joe Corvo .20 .50
74 Kyle Wanvig .20 .50
75 Mathieu Garon .25 .60
76 Marcel Hossa .20 .50
77 Jan Lasak .25 .60
78 Christian Berglund .20 .50
79 Jiri Bicek .20 .50
80 Michael Rupp .20 .50
81 Rick DiPietro .25 .60
82 Justin Mapletoft .20 .50
83 Mattias Weinhandl .20 .50
84 Jamie Lundmark .25 .60
85 Ales Pisa .20 .50
86 Toni Dahlman .20 .50
87 Eric Chouinard .20 .50
88 Ramzi Abid .20 .50
89 Sebastien Caron .25 .60
90 Dan Focht .20 .50
91 Barret Jackman .20 .50
92 Justin Papineau .20 .50
93 Jonathan Cheechoo .25 .60
94 Miikka Kiprusoff .30 .75
95 Vesa Toskala .20 .50
96 Karel Pilar .20 .50
97 Fedor Fedorov .20 .50
98 Sebastien Charpentier .20 .50
99 Joel Kwiatkowski .20 .50
100 Brian Sutherby .20 .50
101 Stanislav Chistov RC 1.00 2.50
102 Kurt Sauer RC 1.00 2.50
103 Alexei Smirnov RC 1.25 3.00
104 Shaone Morrisonn RC 1.00 2.50
105 Kris Vernarsky RC 1.00 2.50
106 Ryan Miller RC 5.00 12.00
107 Chuck Kobasew RC 1.25 3.00
108 Jordan Leopold RC 1.50 4.00
109 Ryan Bayda RC 1.00 2.50
110 Igor Radulov RC 1.00 2.50
111 Pascal Leclaire RC 1.25 3.00
112 Rick Nash RC 8.00 20.00
112AU Rick Nash AU/100 40.00 100.00
113 Jason Bacashihua RC 1.25 3.00
114 Steve Ott RC 1.00 2.50
115 Dmitri Bykov RC 1.00 2.50
116 Henrik Zetterberg RC 8.00 20.00
117 Ales Hemsky RC 4.00 10.00
118 Fernando Pisani RC 1.00 2.50
119 Jay Bouwmeester RC 3.00 8.00
120 Jared Aulin RC 1.00 2.50
121 Michael Cammalleri RC 3.00 8.00
122 Alexander Frolov RC 2.50 6.00
123 Cristobal Huet RC 2.00 5.00
124 P-M Bouchard RC 1.50 4.00
125 Stephane Veilleux RC 1.00 2.50
126 Ron Hainsey RC 1.00 2.50
127 Mike Komisarek RC 1.50 4.00
128 Vernon Fiddler RC 1.25 3.00
129 Adam Hall RC 1.00 2.50
130 Scottie Upshall RC 1.25 3.00
131 Eric Godard RC 1.00 2.50
132 Ray Emery RC 3.00 8.00
133 Jason Spezza RC 6.00 15.00
134 Anton Volchenkov RC 1.00 2.50
135 Dennis Seidenberg RC 1.50 4.00
136 Radovan Somik RC 1.00 2.50
137 Jim Vandermeer RC 1.00 2.50
138 Jeff Taffe RC 1.00 2.50
139 Brooks Orpik RC 1.00 2.50
140 Tomas Surovy RC 1.00 2.50
141 Curtis Sanford RC 1.50 4.00
142 Matt Walker RC 1.00 2.50
143 Niko Dimitrakos RC 1.00 2.50
144 Jim Fahey RC 1.00 2.50
145 Lynn Loyns RC 1.00 2.50
146 Alexander Svitov RC 1.00 2.50
147 Carlo Colaiacovo RC 1.50 4.00
148 Mikael Tellqvist RC 1.00 2.50
149 Steve Eminger RC 1.00 2.50
150 Alex Henry RC 1.25 3.00

2002-03 Pacific Calder Silver

*1-100 VETS/299: 1.5X TO 4X BASIC CARDS
*101-150 ROOKIES/299: .4X TO 1X BASIC RC
47 Mark Messier 2.50 6.00

2002-03 Pacific Calder Chasing Glory

COMPLETE SET (10) 8.00 20.00
1 Joe Thornton 1.25 3.00
2 Peter Forsberg 1.50 4.00
3 Patrick Roy 2.00 5.00
4 Mike Modano 1.25 3.00
5 Marty Turco .75 2.00
6 Martin Brodeur 2.00 5.00
7 Marian Hossa .75 2.00
8 Mario Lemieux 3.00 8.00
9 Ed Belfour .75 2.00
10 Markus Naslund .75 2.00

2002-03 Pacific Calder Hardware Heroes

COMPLETE SET (12) 8.00 20.00
1 Dany Heatley .60 1.50
2 Patrick Roy 2.00 5.00
3 Joe Sakic 1.00 2.50
4 Brett Hull .60 1.50
5 Nicklas Lidstrom .50 1.25
6 Steve Yzerman 2.00 5.00
7 Jose Theodore .60 1.50
8 Eric Lindros .50 1.25
9 Mark Messier .50 1.25
10 Mario Lemieux 2.50 6.00
11 Ed Belfour .50 1.25
12 Jaromir Jagr .75 2.00

2002-03 Pacific Calder Hart Stoppers

COMPLETE SET (8) 10.00 20.00
1 Joe Thornton 1.00 2.50
2 Peter Forsberg 1.50 4.00
3 Patrick Roy 2.00 5.00
4 Mike Modano 1.00 2.50
5 Marty Turco .60 1.50
6 Martin Brodeur 1.50 4.00
7 Marian Hossa .60 1.50
8 Markus Naslund .60 1.50

2002-03 Pacific Calder Jerseys

1 Dany Heatley 5.00 12.00
2 Patrik Stefan 3.00 8.00
3 Glen Murray 3.00 8.00
4 Joe Thornton 5.00 12.00
5 Miroslav Satan 3.00 8.00
6 Alexei Zhamnov 3.00 8.00
7 Peter Forsberg 8.00 20.00
8 Patrick Roy 8.00 20.00
9 Marty Turco 4.00 10.00
10 Luc Robitaille 3.00 8.00
11 Olli Jokinen 3.00 8.00
12 Yanic Perreault 3.00 8.00
13 Tomas Vokoun 3.00 8.00
14 Rick DiPietro 3.00 8.00
15 Daniel Alfredsson 3.00 8.00
16 Jason Spezza 6.00 15.00
17 Roman Cechmanek 3.00 8.00
18 Mario Lemieux 8.00 20.00
19 Valeri Bure 3.00 8.00
20 Doug Weight 3.00 8.00
21 Ed Belfour 4.00 10.00
22 Mats Sundin 4.00 10.00
23 Brendan Morrison 3.00 8.00
24 Markus Naslund 3.00 8.00
25 Jaromir Jagr 6.00 15.00

2002-03 Pacific Calder Reflections

COMPLETE SET (20) 12.00 30.00
1 Stanislav Chistov .50 1.25
2 Ivan Huml .50 1.25
3 Ales Kotalik .50 1.25
4 Ryan Miller 1.50 4.00
5 Jordan Leopold .75 2.00
6 Tyler Arnason .75 2.00
7 Pascal Leclaire .60 1.50
8 Rick Nash 1.50 4.00
9 Henrik Zetterberg 2.50 6.00
10 Ales Hemsky 1.00 2.50
11 Jay Bouwmeester .75 2.00
12 Stephen Weiss .75 2.00
13 Michael Cammalleri .75 2.00
14 Alexander Frolov .60 1.50
15 P-M Bouchard .75 2.00
16 Marcel Hossa .50 1.25
17 Rick DiPietro .60 1.50
18 Jason Spezza 1.50 4.00
19 Barret Jackman .50 1.25
20 Jonathan Cheechoo .60 1.50

2003-04 Pacific Calder

1 Sergei Fedorov .50 1.25
2 Jean-Sebastien Giguere .30 .75
3 Dany Heatley .25 .60
4 Ilya Kovalchuk .30 .75
5 Marc Savard .20 .50
6 Sergei Gonchar .20 .50
7 Glen Murray .25 .60
8 Andrew Raycroft .25 .60
9 Joe Thornton .50 1.25
10 Martin Biron .25 .60
11 Daniel Briere .30 .75
12 Mika Noronen .20 .50
13 Jarome Iginla .40 1.00
14 Miikka Kiprusoff .30 .75
15 Chuck Kobasew .20 .50
16 Erik Cole .20 .50
17 Josef Vasicek .20 .50
18 Justin Williams .25 .60
19 Tyler Arnason .20 .50
20 Mark Bell .20 .50
21 Kyle Calder .20 .50
22 Peter Forsberg .60 1.50
23 Milan Hejduk .25 .60
24 Paul Kariya .30 .75
25 Joe Sakic .60 1.50
26 Philippe Sauve .25 .60
27 Alex Tanguay .25 .60
28 Marc Denis .25 .60
29 Rick Nash .30 .75
30 Valeri Bure .20 .50
31 Bill Guerin .30 .75
32 Mike Modano .50 1.25
33 Marty Turco .30 .75
34 Pavel Datsyuk .50 1.25
35 Kris Draper .20 .50
36 Dominik Hasek .50 1.25
37 Brett Hull .60 1.50
38 Curtis Joseph .40 1.00
39 Robert Lang .20 .50
40 Brendan Shanahan .30 .75
41 Steve Yzerman .75 2.00
42 Ryan Smyth .25 .60
43 Raffi Torres .20 .50
44 Mike York .20 .50
45 Jay Bouwmeester .20 .50
46 Olli Jokinen .30 .75
47 Roberto Luongo .50 1.25
48 Roman Cechmanek .25 .60
49 Alexander Frolov .25 .60
50 Ziggy Palffy .30 .75
51 Alexandre Daigle .25 .60
52 Marian Gaborik .30 .75
53 Dwayne Roloson .25 .60
54 Saku Koivu .30 .75
55 Alex Kovalev .25 .60
56 Mike Ribeiro .20 .50
57 Michael Ryder .25 .60
58 Jose Theodore .30 .75
59 Scott Hartnell .20 .50
60 Scottie Upshall .25 .60
61 Tomas Vokoun .25 .60
62 Martin Brodeur .75 2.00
63 Patrik Elias .30 .75
64 Jeff Friesen .20 .50
65 Rick DiPietro .25 .60
66 Trent Hunter .20 .50
67 Jaromir Jagr 1.00 2.50
68 Eric Lindros .50 1.25
69 Mark Messier .60 1.50
70 Daniel Alfredsson .30 .75
71 Martin Havlat .30 .75
72 Marian Hossa .30 .75
73 Jason Spezza .30 .75
74 Mark Recchi .40 1.00
75 Jeremy Roenick .50 1.25
76 Brian Boucher .25 .60
77 Mike Comrie .25 .60
78 Shane Doan .25 .60
79 Ladislav Nagy .20 .50
80 Rico Fata .20 .50
81 Mario Lemieux 1.25 3.00
82 Pavol Demitra .40 1.00
83 Chris Osgood .30 .75
84 Keith Tkachuk .30 .75
85 Doug Weight .30 .75
86 Jonathan Cheechoo .25 .60
87 Patrick Marleau .30 .75
88 Evgeni Nabokov .25 .60
89 Nikolai Khabibulin .30 .75
90 Vincent Lecavalier .30 .75
91 Martin St. Louis .30 .75
92 Ed Belfour .30 .75
93 Owen Nolan .30 .75
94 Gary Roberts .20 .50
95 Mats Sundin .30 .75
96 Todd Bertuzzi .30 .75
97 Dan Cloutier .25 .60
98 Jason King .20 .50
99 Brendan Morrison .25 .60
100 Markus Naslund .30 .75
101 Chris Kunitz RC 2.00 5.00
102 Kari Lehtonen RC 4.00 10.00
103 Jason Pominville RC 2.50 6.00
104 Derek Roy RC 1.50 4.00
105 Brent Krahn RC 1.00 2.50
106 Eric Staal RC 5.00 12.00
107 Adam Munro RC 1.00 2.50
108 Tuomo Ruutu RC 1.50 4.00
109 Pavel Vorobiev RC 1.25 3.00
110 Cody McCormick RC 1.25 3.00
111 Dan Fritsche RC 1.00 2.50
112 Tim Jackman RC 1.25 3.00
113 Nikolai Zherdev RC 2.00 5.00
114 Dan Ellis RC 1.25 3.00
115 Jiri Hudler RC 2.50 6.00
116 Niklas Kronwall RC 2.00 5.00
117 Nathan Robinson RC 1.00 2.50
118 Doug Lynch RC 1.00 2.50
119 Scott Barney 1.00 2.50
120 Noah Clarke RC 1.00 2.50
121 Brent Burns RC 3.00 8.00
122 Dan Hamhuis RC 1.25 3.00
123 Timofei Shishkanov RC 1.00 2.50
124 Marek Zidlicky RC 1.00 2.50
125 Tuomas Pihlman RC 1.25 3.00
126 Jozef Balej RC 1.00 2.50
127 Dominic Moore RC 1.00 2.50
128 Chad Wiseman 1.00 2.50
129 Fredrik Sjostrom RC 1.50 4.00
130 Marc-Andre Fleury RC 8.00 20.00
131 Ryan Malone RC 2.00 5.00
132 Matt Murley RC 1.25 3.00
133 John Pohl RC 1.00 2.50
134 Milan Michalek RC 2.00 5.00
135 Kyle Wellwood RC 1.50 4.00
136 Wade Brookbank RC 1.25 3.00
137 Ryan Kesler RC 4.00 10.00
138 Peter Sarno RC 1.00 2.50
139 Alexander Semin RC 3.00 8.00
140 Rastislav Stana RC 1.50 4.00
141 Jean-Sebastien Giguere JSY 2.50 6.00
142 Ilya Kovalchuk JSY 8.00 20.00
143 Joe Thornton JSY/200 6.00 15.00
144 Jarome Iginla JSY 6.00 15.00
145 Peter Forsberg JSY 8.00 20.00
146 Milan Hejduk JSY 2.50 6.00
147 Rick Nash JSY/500 4.00 10.00
148 Marty Turco JSY 4.00 10.00
149 Roman Cechmanek JSY 2.50 6.00
150 Martin Brodeur JSY/200 12.00 30.00
151 Jaromir Jagr JSY 6.00 15.00
152 Daniel Alfredsson JSY/500 3.00 8.00
153 Marian Hossa JSY 3.00 8.00
154 Jeff Hackett JSY/500 2.50 6.00
155 Mario Lemieux JSY/66 25.00 60.00
156 Chris Osgood JSY/500 3.00 8.00
157 Vincent Lecavalier .30 .75
158 Ed Belfour JSY 3.00 8.00
159 Todd Bertuzzi JSY 3.00 8.00
160 Brendan Morrison JSY/500 2.50 6.00
161 Olaf Kolzig JSY 3.00 8.00
162 Joffrey Lupul JSY RC 5.00 12.00
163 Patrice Bergeron JSY RC 10.00 25.00
164 Matthew Lombardi JSY RC 2.50 6.00
165 Antti Miettinen JSY RC 3.00 8.00
166 Nathan Horton JSY RC 5.00 12.00
167 Dustin Brown JSY RC 5.00 12.00
168 Chris Higgins JSY RC 4.00 10.00
169 Jordin Tootoo JSY RC 4.00 10.00
170 Sean Bergenheim JSY RC 2.50 6.00
171 Antoine Vermette JSY RC 4.00 10.00
172 Joni Pitkanen JSY RC 3.00 8.00
173 Peter Sejna JSY RC 2.50 6.00
174 Matt Stajan JSY RC 3.00 8.00
175 Boyd Gordon JSY RC 2.50 6.00
176 Andrew Raycroft AU/250 10.00 25.00

2003-04 Pacific Calder Silver

*1-110 VETS/575: 1.5X TO 4X BASIC CARDS
*111-140 ROOKIE/575: .4X TO 1X BASIC RC

2003-04 Pacific Calder Reflections

COMPLETE SET 15.00 30.00
1 Joffrey Lupul 2.00 5.00
2 Patrice Bergeron 8.00 20.00
3 Andrew Raycroft 2.50 6.00
4 Eric Staal 2.50 6.00
5 Michael Ryder 2.00 5.00
6 Trent Hunter 2.00 5.00
7 Marc-Andre Fleury 4.00 10.00
8 Ryan Malone 2.00 5.00

2002-03 Pacific Complete

*RED/100: 6X TO 15X BASIC CARDS
1 Nicklas Lidstrom .20 .50
2 Mika Noronen .15 .40
3 Alexei Kovalev .15 .40
4 Jason Allison .15 .40
5 Erik Cole .12 .30
6 Sami Kapanen .12 .30
7 Marty Turco .20 .50
8 Brad Isbister .12 .30
9 Saku Koivu .20 .50
10 Jarome Iginla .25 .60
11 Jean-Sebastien Giguere .20 .50
12 Roman Turek .20 .50
13 Joe Sakic .40 1.00
14 Peter Bondra .20 .50
15 Dany Heatley .15 .40
16 Vincent Lecavalier .20 .50
17 Manny Fernandez .12 .30
18 Simon Gagne .20 .50
19 Rick DiPietro .15 .40
20 Mark Recchi .25 .60
21 Mike Richter .20 .50
22 Daymond Langkow .15 .40
23 Pavel Datsyuk .30 .75
24 Mark Messier .40 1.00
25 Ed Belfour .20 .50
26 Michael Peca .15 .40
27 Krystofer Kolanos .12 .30
28 Alexander Mogilny .15 .40
29 Martin Straka .15 .40
30 Shane Willis .12 .30
31 Alyn McCauley .12 .30
32 Ryan Smyth .15 .40
33 Tomi Kallio .12 .30
34 Doug Weight .20 .50
35 Nicholas Boynton .12 .30
36 Pascal Dupuis .12 .30
37 Jaroslav Svoboda .12 .30
38 Al MacInnis .25 .60
39 Peter Forsberg .40 1.00
40 Rostislav Klesla .12 .30
41 Kimmo Timonen .12 .30
42 Darren McCarty .15 .40
43 Brian Savage .12 .30
44 Ethan Moreau .12 .30
45 Peter Worrell .12 .30
46 Doug Gilmour .25 .60
47 David Aebischer .15 .40
48 Aaron Miller .12 .30
49 Nick Schultz .12 .30
50 Magnus Arvedson .12 .30
51 Cale Hulse .12 .30
52 Brian Gionta .12 .30
53 Trevor Linden .20 .50
54 Raffi Torres .12 .30
55 Jean-Sebastien Aubin .12 .30
56 Zdeno Chara .20 .50
57 Mattias Ohlund .12 .30
58 Travis Green .12 .30
59 Michael Nylander .12 .30
60 Andreas Dackell .12 .30
61 Craig Billington .12 .30
62 Chris Therien .12 .30
63 Eric Brewer .12 .30
64 Shayne Corson .15 .40
65 Patrice Brisebois .12 .30
66 Sean O'Donnell .12 .30
67 Sergei Varlamov .15 .40
68 Donald Brashear .12 .30
69 Vaclav Prospal .12 .30
70 Mike Ricci .12 .30

71 Fredrik Modin .12 .30
72 Stu Grimson .12 .30
73 Jeff Jillson .12 .30
74 Andre Roy .12 .30
75 Filip Kuba .12 .30
76 Martin Skoula .12 .30
77 Sandis Ozolinsh .12 .30
78 Robert Reichel .12 .30
79 Wes Walz .12 .30
80 Keith Carney .12 .30
81 Steve Kariya .12 .30
82 Dave Tanabe .12 .30
83 Robert Svehla .12 .30
84 Rob Ray .12 .30
85 Niklas Hagman .12 .30
86 Stu Barnes .12 .30
87 Scott Gomez .15 .40
88 Rob Niedermayer .15 .40
89 Dave Scatchard .12 .30
90 Petr Nedved .12 .30
91 Bob Probert .20 .50
92 Dallas Drake .15 .40
93 Mike Leclerc .12 .30
94 Janne Niinimaa .12 .30
95 Rob Zamuner .12 .30
96 Jim Dowd .12 .30
97 Richard Matvichuk .12 .30
98 Boyd Devereaux .12 .30
99 Jamie Storr .15 .40
100 Rem Murray .12 .30
101 Jaromir Jagr .60 1.50
102 Todd Bertuzzi .20 .50
103 Mike Modano .30 .75
104 Sergei Fedorov .30 .75
105 Ilya Kovalchuk .25 .60
106 Patrik Elias .20 .50
107 Marian Hossa .20 .50
108 Paul Kariya .20 .50
109 Manny Legace .20 .50
110 Milan Hejduk .15 .40
111 Adam Deadmarsh .12 .30
112 Owen Nolan .20 .50
113 Patrick Marleau .20 .50
114 Adam Oates .20 .50
115 Donald Audette .12 .30
116 Steven Reinprecht .12 .30
117 Jere Lehtinen .20 .50
118 Joe Nieuwendyk .15 .40
119 Roman Cechmanek .15 .40
120 Brian Rolston .15 .40
121 Chris Drury .20 .50
122 J-P Dumont .12 .30
123 Denis Arkhipov .12 .30
124 Sergei Zubov .15 .40
125 Scott Hartnell .12 .30
126 Espen Knutsen .12 .30
127 Slava Kozlov .12 .30
128 Roberto Luongo .30 .75
129 John LeClair .20 .50
130 Daniel Sedin .25 .60
131 Justin Williams .15 .40
132 Kyle Calder .12 .30
133 Bryan Smolinski .15 .40
134 Scott Mellanby .12 .30
135 Martin Lapointe .15 .40
136 Dwayne Roloson .12 .30
137 Niklas Sundstrom .12 .30
138 Ladislav Nagy .12 .30
139 Mathieu Schneider .12 .30
140 Scott Walker .12 .30
141 Marcus Nilsson .12 .30
142 Steve Thomas .12 .30
143 Kevin Weekes .15 .40
144 Vladimir Orszagh .12 .30
145 Brad Stuart .12 .30
146 Shawn Bates .12 .30
147 Oleg Tverdovsky .12 .30
148 Andy Delmore .12 .30
149 Stanislav Neckar .12 .30
150 Phil Housley .15 .40
151 Matt Cooke .12 .30
152 Scott Niedermayer .20 .50
153 Jeff Hackett .15 .40
154 Ruslan Fedotenko .12 .30
155 Daniel Cleary .15 .40
156 Martin Prusek .12 .30
157 Matt Cullen .12 .30
158 Jason Woolley .12 .30
159 Fred Brathwaite .15 .40
160 Adam Graves .15 .40
161 Kenny Jonsson .12 .30
162 Todd Marchant .12 .30
163 Jason Williams .12 .30
164 Joe Juneau .12 .30
165 Patrick Roy .50 1.25
166 Tie Domi .15 .40
167 Adrian Aucoin .12 .30
168 Dan Blackburn .15 .40
169 Vitali Yachmenev .12 .30
170 Derian Hatcher .15 .40
171 Mike Ribeiro .12 .30
172 Mike Van Ryn .12 .30
173 Brian Willsie .12 .30
174 Chris Phillips .12 .30
175 Jason York .12 .30
176 Kris Draper .12 .30
177 Sean Burke .12 .30
178 Kevin Dineen .12 .30
179 Toni Lydman .12 .30
180 Artem Chubarov .12 .30
181 Trevor Letowski .12 .30
182 P.J. Axelsson .12 .30
183 Lubos Bartecko .12 .30
184 Mike Knuble .12 .30
185 Ossi Vaananen .12 .30
186 David Vyborny .12 .30
187 Kevyn Adams .12 .30
188 Johan Hedberg .20 .50
189 Brent Gilchrist .15 .40
190 Eric Boguniecki .12 .30
191 Marcus Ragnarsson .12 .30
192 Eric Weinrich .12 .30
193 Yannick Tremblay .12 .30
194 Mike Keane .15 .40
195 Chad Kilger .12 .30
196 Glen Metropolit .12 .30
197 Stephane Quintal .12 .30
198 Tyler Arnason .20 .50
199 Jan Bulis .12 .30
200 Patric Kjellberg .12 .30
201 Eric Lindros .30 .75
202 Markus Naslund .20 .50
203 Ziggy Palffy .20 .50
204 Brian Rafalski .12 .30
205 Miroslav Satan .20 .50
206 Marian Gaborik .20 .50
207 Tony Amonte .15 .40
208 Tomas Kaberle .12 .30
209 Ray Whitney .15 .40
210 Ron Francis .25 .60
211 Steve Sullivan .12 .30
212 Bryan Berard .12 .30
213 Keith Primeau .15 .40
214 Vincent Damphousse .15 .40
215 Richard Zednik .12 .30
216 Ed Jovanovski .15 .40
217 Valeri Bure .15 .40
218 Jozef Stumpel .12 .30
219 Alexei Zhamnov .15 .40
220 Mariusz Czerkawski .12 .30
221 John Grahame .12 .30
222 Mark Parrish .12 .30
223 Mike York .12 .30
224 Chris Osgood .20 .50
225 Scott Young .12 .30
226 Derek Morris .12 .30
227 Brendan Morrison .15 .40
228 Mike Sillinger .12 .30
229 Todd White .12 .30
230 Tom Poti .12 .30
231 Sergei Zholtok .12 .30
232 Kip Miller .12 .30
233 Pasi Nurminen .12 .30
234 Michal Handzus .15 .40
235 Henrik Sedin .25 .60
236 Steve McCarthy .12 .30
237 Jeff Halpern .12 .30
238 Stephen Weiss .20 .50
239 Pavel Kubina .12 .30
240 Luc Robitaille .20 .50
241 Michal Rozsival .15 .40
242 Martin Gelinas .12 .30
243 Curtis Brown .12 .30
244 Steve Passmore .12 .30
245 Tony Hrkac .12 .30
246 Alexei Yashin .15 .40
247 Richard Park .12 .30
248 Viktor Kozlov .12 .30
249 Andrei Markov .20 .50
250 Dan Boyle .12 .30
251 Paul Mara .12 .30
252 Jeremy Roenick .30 .75
253 Randy McKay .12 .30
254 Tommy Salo .15 .40
255 Jaroslav Spacek .12 .30
256 Adam Foote .12 .30
257 Martin Erat .12 .30
258 Jamal Mayers .12 .30
259 Chris Neil .12 .30
260 Mark Bell .12 .30
261 Matt Bradley .12 .30
262 Boris Mironov .12 .30
263 Trevor Kidd .12 .30
264 Dave Andreychuk .20 .50
265 Jaroslav Modry .12 .30
266 Vaclav Varada .12 .30
267 Marty Murray .12 .30
268 Ben Clymer .12 .30
269 Mikael Renberg .12 .30
270 Sean Hill .12 .30
271 Eric Belanger .12 .30
272 Andy McDonald .20 .50
273 Miikka Kiprusoff .20 .50
274 Brad May .12 .30
275 Dan LaCouture .12 .30
276 Andy Sutton .12 .30
277 Kirk Maltby .12 .30
278 Kirk Muller .12 .30
279 Alex Tanguay .15 .40
280 Bryan Marchment .15 .40
281 Jason Smith .12 .30
282 Dan Bylsma .12 .30
283 Jyrki Lumme .12 .30
284 Chris Gratton .12 .30
285 Chris Clark .12 .30
286 David Legwand .15 .40
287 Alexander Khavanov .12 .30
288 Marc Chouinard .12 .30
289 Rob DiMaio .12 .30
290 Sean Avery .15 .40
291 Tommy Albelin .12 .30
292 Jean-Francois Fortin .12 .30
293 Matthew Barnaby .12 .30
294 Jan Hrdina .12 .30
295 Harold Druken .12 .30
296 Jody Hull .12 .30
297 Shjon Podein .12 .30
298 Jochen Hecht .12 .30
299 Glen Murray .15 .40
300 Sergei Brylin .12 .30
301 Pavel Bure .20 .50
302 Mike Comrie .20 .50
303 Mario Lemieux .75 2.00
304 Mats Sundin .20 .50
305 Jason Blake .12 .30
306 Robert Lang .12 .30
307 Bill Guerin .20 .50
308 Brad Richards .20 .50
309 Radek Bonk .15 .40
310 Craig Conroy .12 .30
311 Brett Hull .40 1.00
312 Dainius Zubrus .12 .30
313 Petr Sykora .15 .40
314 Craig Rivet .12 .30
315 Andrew Brunette .12 .30
316 Kristian Huselius .12 .30
317 Rod Brind'Amour .20 .50
318 Tim Connolly .12 .30
319 Anson Carter .15 .40
320 Cory Stillman .12 .30
321 Teppo Numminen .12 .30
322 Jason Arnott .15 .40
323 Oleg Petrov .12 .30
324 Shawn McEachern .12 .30
325 Scott Thornton .12 .30
326 Oleg Kvasha .12 .30
327 Byron Dafoe .15 .40
328 Glen Wesley .12 .30
329 Eric Messier .12 .30
330 Brad Lukowich .12 .30
331 Jon Klemm .12 .30
332 Tomas Vokoun .15 .40
333 Scott Hannan .12 .30
334 Mike Eastwood .12 .30
335 Peter Skudra .12 .30
336 Roman Hamrlik .12 .30
337 Josef Vasicek .12 .30
338 Bryan McCabe .12 .30
339 Igor Larionov .20 .50
340 Darryl Sydor .12 .30
341 Mike Fisher .12 .30
342 Greg Johnson .12 .30
343 Danny Markov .12 .30
344 Frantisek Kaberle .12 .30
345 Michal Grosek .12 .30
346 Ivan Novoseltsev .12 .30
347 Marty McInnis .12 .30
348 Eric Desjardins .12 .30
349 Jason Wiemer .12 .30
350 Fredrik Olausson .12 .30
351 Bill Muckalt .12 .30
352 Ville Nieminen .12 .30
353 Taylor Pyatt .12 .30
354 Mike Rathje .12 .30
355 Trent Klatt .12 .30
356 Bret Hedican .12 .30
357 Tyler Wright .12 .30
358 Greg deVries .12 .30
359 Lubomir Sekeras .12 .30
360 Jonas Hoglund .12 .30
361 Mike Grier .12 .30
362 Wade Redden .12 .30
363 Nik Antropov .15 .40
364 Philippe Boucher .12 .30
365 Clarke Wilm .12 .30
366 Erik Rasmussen .12 .30
367 Per Svartvadet .12 .30
368 Felix Potvin .30 .75
369 Igor Korolev .12 .30
370 Vladimir Malakhov .12 .30
371 Mathieu Dandenault .12 .30
372 Brent Johnson .15 .40
373 Shaun Van Allen .12 .30
374 Scott Pellerin .12 .30
375 Radim Vrbata .12 .30
376 Mike Johnson .15 .40
377 Mikael Samuelsson .12 .30
378 Radek Martinek .12 .30
379 Curtis Joseph .25 .60
380 Craig Johnson .12 .30
381 Kelly Buchberger .15 .40
382 Todd Harvey .12 .30
383 Jason Chimera .12 .30
384 Claude Lapointe .12 .30
385 Marc Denis .15 .40
386 Lyle Odelein .12 .30
387 Dimitri Kalinin .12 .30
388 Scott Nichol .12 .30
389 Tom Fitzgerald .12 .30
390 Darius Kasparaitis .12 .30
391 Bryan Allen .12 .30
392 Jamie McLennan .12 .30
393 Martin St. Louis .20 .50
394 Landon Wilson .12 .30
395 Kim Johnsson .12 .30
396 Pavel Trnka .12 .30
397 P.J. Stock .12 .30
398 Alexandre Daigle .12 .30
399 Andrew Cassels .12 .30
400 Wayne Primeau .15 .40
401 Theo Fleury .25 .60
402 Cliff Ronning .12 .30
403 Sergei Samsonov .15 .40
404 Jean-Francois Labbe .12 .30
405 Darcy Tucker .12 .30
406 Daniel Briere .15 .40
407 Marc Savard .12 .30
408 Blake Sloan .15 .40
409 Sergei Berezin .12 .30
410 Ron Tugnutt .15 .40
411 Jocelyn Thibault .15 .40
412 Jose Theodore .20 .50
413 Sheldon Keefe .12 .30
414 Yanic Perreault .12 .30
415 Jason Krog .12 .30
416 John Madden .12 .30
417 Jonathan Girard .12 .30
418 Niclas Havelid .12 .30
419 Daniel Alfredsson .20 .50
420 Dean McAmmond .12 .30
421 Brenden Morrow .15 .40
422 Dimitri Yushkevich .12 .30
423 Alexei Zhitnik .15 .40
424 Jani Hurme .15 .40
425 Antti Laaksonen .12 .30
426 Corey Schwab .15 .40
427 Geoff Sanderson .15 .40
428 Brian Leetch .15 .40
429 Brad Tapper .12 .30
430 Derek Armstrong .12 .30
431 Evgeni Nabokov .15 .40
432 Jan Hlavac .12 .30
433 Bob Boughner .12 .30
434 Andreas Johansson .12 .30
435 Jeff Odgers .12 .30
436 Teemu Selanne .40 1.00
437 Pavol Demitra .25 .60
438 Tomas Holmstrom .12 .30
439 Jeff Friesen .12 .30
440 Eric Boulton .12 .30
441 Oleg Saprykin .12 .30
442 Chris Chelios .20 .50
443 Stephane Yelle .12 .30
444 Martin Havlat .15 .40
445 Jeff O'Neill .12 .30
446 Dan Cloutier .15 .40
447 Nikolai Khabibulin .20 .50
448 Grant Marshall .12 .30
449 Pierre Turgeon .15 .40
450 Jamie Langenbrunner .15 .40
451 Steve Staios .12 .30
452 Alexei Morozov .12 .30
453 Shawn Horcoff .15 .40
454 Adam Mair .12 .30
455 Ruslan Salei .12 .30
456 Robert Esche .12 .30
457 Brent Sopel .12 .30
458 Aaron Ward .12 .30
459 Martin Biron .15 .40
460 Brian Boucher .15 .40
461 Richard Jackman .12 .30
462 Jarkko Ruutu .12 .30
463 Bates Battaglia .12 .30
464 Sergei Gonchar .15 .40
465 Martin Brodeur .50 1.25
466 Patrik Stefan .15 .40
467 Scott Stevens .20 .50
468 Gary Roberts .12 .30
469 Shane Doan .15 .40
470 Keith Tkachuk .20 .50
471 Brendan Witt .12 .30
472 Todd Fedoruk .12 .30
473 Patrick Lalime .15 .40
474 Mike Dunham .15 .40
475 Ulf Dahlen .12 .30
476 Olli Jokinen .20 .50
477 Garth Snow .15 .40
478 Sean Pronger .12 .30
479 Milan Kraft .12 .30
480 Aki Berg .12 .30
481 Steve Shields .15 .40
482 Sami Salo .12 .30
483 Brendan Shanahan .20 .50
484 Niclas Wallin .12 .30
485 Sandy McCarthy .12 .30
486 Olaf Kolzig .20 .50
487 Cory Sarich .12 .30
488 Zac Bierk .12 .30
489 Luke Richardson .12 .30
490 Colin White .12 .30
491 Reed Low .12 .30
492 Joe Thornton .30 .75
493 Rob Blake .20 .50
494 Bobby Holik .12 .30
495 Chris Simon .12 .30
496 Wade Belak .12 .30
497 Eric Daze .12 .30
498 Hal Gill .12 .30
499 Chris Pronger .20 .50
500 Steve Yzerman .50 1.25
501 Justin Papineau .12 .30
502 Alex Auld .12 .30
503 Niko Kapanen .15 .40
504 Michael Cammalleri .40 1.00
505 Sebastien Charpentier .12 .30
506 Stanislav Chistov .12 .30
507 Jiri Bicek .12 .30
508 Ryan Flinn .12 .30
509 Christian Berglund .12 .30
510 Vernon Fiddler .15 .40
511 Andrej Nedorost .12 .30
512 Lynn Loyns .12 .30
513 Niko Dimitrakos .12 .30
514 Ryan Bayda .12 .30
515 Curtis Sanford .20 .50
516 Pierre-Marc Bouchard .20 .50
517 Sebastien Caron .15 .40
518 Steve Ott .12 .30
519 Dan Snyder .12 .30
520 Mattias Weinhandl .12 .30
521 Henrik Zetterberg 1.25 3.00
522 Tomas Surovy .12 .30
523 Ales Hemsky .50 1.25
524 Jamie Lundmark .15 .40
525 Barret Jackman .12 .30
526 Toni Dahlman .12 .30
527 Jaroslav Bednar .12 .30
528 Ales Pisa .12 .30
529 Joel Kwiatkowski .12 .30
530 Jan Lasak .15 .40
531 Jim Fahey .12 .30
532 Pavel Brendl .12 .30
533 Stephane Veilleux .12 .30
534 Vaclav Nedorost .12 .30
535 Tomas Malec .12 .30
536 Jeff Heerema .12 .30
537 Dmitri Bykov .12 .30
538 Dennis Seidenberg .20 .50
539 Jonathan Cheechoo .15 .40
540 Fernando Pisani .12 .30
541 Riku Hahl .12 .30
542 Jani Rita .12 .30
543 Jim Vandermeer .12 .30
544 Jordan Leopold .20 .50
545 Joe Corvo .12 .30
546 Ales Kotalik .12 .30
547 Ryan Miller .75 2.00
548 Tomas Kurka .12 .30
549 Arturs Irbe .15 .40
550 Radovan Somik .12 .30
551 Mathieu Garon .15 .40
552 Jesse Wallin .12 .30
553 Steve Eminger .12 .30
554 Jason Bacashihua .15 .40
555 Ramzi Abid .12 .30
556 Marcel Hossa .12 .30
557 Rick Nash .75 2.00
558 Kris Vernarsky .12 .30
559 Brian Sutherby .12 .30
560 Adam Hall .12 .30
561 Eric Chouinard .12 .30
562 Henrik Tallinder .12 .30
563 Alexander Svitov .12 .30
564 Kurt Sauer .12 .30
565 Matt Walker .12 .30
566 Ray Emery .40 1.00
567 Eric Godard .12 .30
568 Jay Bouwmeester .40 1.00
569 Kip Brennan .12 .30
570 Mike Komisarek .20 .50
571 Alex Henry .15 .40
572 Scottie Upshall .15 .40
573 Chuck Kobasew .15 .40
574 Anton Volchenkov .12 .30
575 Carlo Colaiacovo .20 .50
576 Pascal Leclaire .15 .40
577 Jason Spezza .75 2.00
578 Jeff Taffe .12 .30
579 Alexander Frolov .30 .75
580 Shaone Morrisonn .12 .30
581 Ron Hainsey .12 .30
582 Alexei Smirnov .15 .40
583 Andrew Raycroft .15 .40
584 Brooks Orpik .12 .30
585 Dan Focht .12 .30
586 Fedor Fedorov .12 .30
587 Ivan Huml .12 .30
588 Jared Aulin .12 .30
589 Justin Mapletoft .12 .30
590 Karel Pilar .12 .30
591 Kyle Wanvig .12 .30
592 Lee Goren .12 .30
593 Cristobal Huet .25 .60
594 Mikael Tellqvist .12 .30
595 Igor Radulov .12 .30
596 Kirill Safronov .12 .30
597 Jerred Smithson .12 .30
598 Vesa Toskala .12 .30
599 Dick Tarnstrom .12 .30
600 Martin Gerber .20 .50

2003-04 Pacific Complete

*RED/100: 5X TO 12X BASIC CARDS
*RED STAR ROOKIES/100: 3X TO 8X

1 Donald Brashear .12 .30
2 Chris Gratton .12 .30
3 Alyn McCauley .12 .30
4 Mats Sundin .20 .50
5 Brenden Morrow .15 .40
6 Jaroslav Modry .12 .30
7 Brian Rafalski .15 .40
8 Mike Grier .12 .30
9 Marco Sturm .12 .30
10 Mike Comrie .15 .40
11 Derek Morris .12 .30
12 Scott Niedermayer .20 .50
13 Dainius Zubrus .12 .30
14 Jason Krog .12 .30
15 Brian Rolston .15 .40
16 Dany Heatley .15 .40
17 Dean McAmmond .12 .30
18 Glen Murray .15 .40
19 Adam Mair .12 .30
20 Tony Amonte .15 .40
21 David Vyborny .12 .30
22 Tyler Wright .12 .30
23 Doug Gilmour .25 .60
24 Andy Sutton .12 .30
25 Ivan Huml .12 .30
26 Olli Jokinen .20 .50
27 Kimmo Timonen .12 .30
28 Donald Audette .12 .30
29 Martin St. Louis .20 .50
30 Martin Skoula .12 .30
31 Wade Redden .12 .30
32 Kyle Calder .12 .30
33 Shawn Bates .12 .30
34 Brendan Shanahan .20 .50
35 Martin Havlat .20 .50
36 Radim Vrbata .12 .30
37 Eric Daze .15 .40
38 J-P Dumont .12 .30
39 Scott Mellanby .12 .30
40 Brad Richards .20 .50
41 Jason Allison .15 .40
42 Rostislav Klesla .12 .30
43 Tyler Arnason .12 .30
44 Henrik Sedin .25 .60
45 Markus Naslund .20 .50
46 Daniel Sedin .25 .60
47 Niklas Sundstrom .12 .30
48 Rod Brind'Amour .20 .50
49 Martin Straka .12 .30
50 Craig Conroy .12 .30
51 Tomas Kaberle .12 .30
52 Robyn Regehr .12 .30
53 Scott Hartnell .12 .30
54 Sergei Zholtok .12 .30
55 Pierre Turgeon .15 .40
56 Mike Ricci .12 .30
57 Brad Tapper .12 .30
58 Martin Gelinas .12 .30
59 Philippe Boucher .12 .30
60 Alex Tanguay .15 .40
61 Niclas Havelid .12 .30
62 Kristian Huselius .12 .30
63 Dave Lowry .12 .30
64 Tim Connolly .12 .30
65 Robert Lang .12 .30
66 Taylor Pyatt .12 .30
67 Bryan Smolinski .12 .30
68 Keith Primeau .15 .40
69 Anson Carter .15 .40
70 Dallas Drake .12 .30
71 Curtis Brown .12 .30
72 Nik Antropov .15 .40
73 Aaron Ward .12 .30
74 Tie Domi .15 .40
75 Mike Leclerc .12 .30
76 Tom Poti .12 .30
77 Kris Draper .12 .30
78 Joe Juneau .12 .30
79 Milan Kraft .12 .30
80 Marty Reasoner .12 .30
81 Shaun Van Allen .12 .30
82 Kenny Jonsson .12 .30
83 Alexander Khavanov .12 .30
84 Pavel Kubina .12 .30
85 Vladimir Malakhov .12 .30
86 Willie Mitchell .12 .30
87 Jason Smith .12 .30
88 Radoslav Suchy .12 .30
89 Mattias Timander .12 .30
90 Eric Weinrich .12 .30
91 Andrei Zyuzin .12 .30
92 Christian Berglund .12 .30
93 Jamie Lundmark .12 .30
94 Kirk Maltby .12 .30
95 Brian Savage .12 .30
96 Petr Schastlivy .12 .30
97 Ian Laperriere .12 .30
98 Alexei Morozov .12 .30
99 Justin Williams .15 .40
100 Jason Chimera .12 .30
101 Patrick Marleau .20 .50
102 Ryan Smyth .15 .40
103 Michal Handzus .15 .40
104 Brett Hull .40 1.00
105 Tom Fitzgerald .12 .30
106 Ben Clymer .12 .30
107 Rick Nash .20 .50
108 Scott Walker .12 .30
109 Rob Niedermayer .15 .40
110 Sergei Gonchar .12 .30
111 Chris Chelios .20 .50
112 Brian Leetch .15 .40
113 David Legwand .15 .40
114 Sean Hill .12 .30
115 Brad Isbister .12 .30
116 Pavel Datsyuk .30 .75
117 Alexei Yashin .15 .40
118 Jere Lehtinen .15 .40
119 Jason Spezza .20 .50
120 Daniel Briere .20 .50
121 Andreas Dackell .12 .30
122 Shane Doan .15 .40
123 Josef Vasicek .12 .30
124 Dan McGillis .12 .30
125 Geoff Sanderson .12 .30
126 Teemu Selanne .40 1.00
127 Andreas Johansson .12 .30
128 Al MacInnis .25 .60
129 Ruslan Fedotenko .12 .30
130 Scott Stevens .20 .50
131 Frantisek Kaberle .12 .30
132 Toni Lydman .12 .30
133 Kip Miller .12 .30
134 Dan Hinote .12 .30
135 Mike Modano .30 .75
136 Scott Thornton .15 .40
137 Eric Lindros .30 .75
138 Grant Marshall .12 .30
139 Vincent Damphousse .15 .40
140 Mario Lemieux .75 2.00
141 Patrice Brisebois .12 .30
142 Sergei Samsonov .15 .40
143 Sergei Zubov .15 .40
144 Alexei Zhamnov .15 .40
145 Oleg Kvasha .12 .30
146 Brendan Morrison .15 .40
147 Jason York .12 .30
148 Eric Boguniecki .12 .30
149 Henrik Zetterberg .25 .60
150 Nick Boynton .12 .30
151 Trevor Linden .20 .50
152 Joe Nieuwendyk .15 .40
153 Filip Kuba .12 .30
154 Matthew Barnaby .12 .30
155 Ales Hemsky .20 .50
156 Jan Bulis .12 .30
157 Yannick Tremblay .12 .30
158 Andre Roy .12 .30
159 Jaroslav Bednar .12 .30
160 Stephane Yelle .12 .30
161 Paul Mara .12 .30
162 Sandis Ozolinsh .12 .30
163 Trent Klatt .12 .30
164 Brian Gionta .12 .30
165 Jaroslav Spacek .12 .30
166 Rob Blake .20 .50
167 Ziggy Palffy .20 .50
168 Chris Clark .12 .30
169 John LeClair .20 .50
170 Landon Wilson .12 .30
171 Mark Bell .12 .30
172 Simon Gagne .20 .50
173 Michael Nylander .12 .30
174 Andy McDonald .15 .40
175 Todd Bertuzzi .20 .50
176 Dick Tarnstrom .12 .30
177 Radek Dvorak .15 .40
178 Antti Laaksonen .12 .30
179 Steve Rucchin .12 .30
180 Steve Sullivan .12 .30
181 Viktor Kozlov .12 .30
182 Miroslav Satan .15 .40
183 Lubomir Visnovsky .12 .30
184 Stephen Weiss .12 .30
185 John Madden .12 .30
186 Mike Knuble .12 .30
187 Michael Peca .15 .40
188 Adam Foote .12 .30
189 Steve McKenna .12 .30
190 Adam Deadmarsh .12 .30
191 Barret Jackman .12 .30
192 Marian Gaborik .20 .50
193 Zdeno Chara .20 .50
194 Chris Drury .15 .40
195 Sami Salo .12 .30
196 Daniel Tjarnqvist .12 .30
197 Vaclav Varada .12 .30
198 Shawn McEachern .12 .30
199 Kevyn Adams .12 .30
200 Roman Hamrlik .12 .30
201 Keith Carney .12 .30
202 Scott Gomez .15 .40
203 Marcus Nilsson .12 .30
204 Tomas Surovy .12 .30
205 Vladimir Orszagh .12 .30
206 Owen Nolan .20 .50
207 Matt Cooke .12 .30
208 Jeremy Roenick .30 .75
209 Andrew Cassels .12 .30
210 Jim Dowd .12 .30
211 Todd Marchant .12 .30
212 Joe Sakic .40 1.00
213 Krystofer Kolanos .12 .30
214 Chris Phillips .12 .30
215 Stanislav Chistov .12 .30
216 Steve Yzerman .50 1.25
217 Jamie Langenbrunner .15 .40
218 Daymond Langkow .12 .30
219 Jarome Iginla .25 .60
220 Darryl Sydor .12 .30
221 Mark Messier .40 1.00
222 Richard Matvichuk .12 .30
223 Jay Bouwmeester .12 .30
224 Sheldon Souray .12 .30
225 Niklas Hagman .12 .30
226 Bill Lindsay .12 .30
227 Ray Whitney .15 .40
228 Jordan Leopold .12 .30
229 Daniel Alfredsson .20 .50
230 Kyle McLaren .12 .30
231 Vincent Lecavalier .20 .50
232 Bobby Holik .12 .30
233 Adam Hall .12 .30
234 Mark Recchi .25 .60
235 Alexander Mogilny .15 .40
236 Alexei Zhitnik .15 .40
237 Jay McKee .12 .30
238 Jaromir Jagr .60 1.50
239 Ladislav Nagy .12 .30
240 Radek Bonk .15 .40
241 Mike Van Ryn .12 .30
242 Joe Thornton .30 .75
243 Peter Bondra .20 .50
244 Keith Tkachuk .20 .50
245 Luc Robitaille .20 .50
246 Alexandre Daigle .15 .40
247 Jason Blake .12 .30
248 Jonathan Cheechoo .15 .40
249 Alexander Frolov .15 .40
250 Danny Markov .12 .30
251 Oleg Saprykin .12 .30
252 Maxim Afinogenov .12 .30
253 Alexander Karpovtsev .12 .30
254 Peter Forsberg .40 1.00
255 Espen Knutsen .12 .30
256 Erik Cole .12 .30
257 Dan Boyle .12 .30
258 Marc Savard .12 .30
259 Adrian Aucoin .12 .30
260 Brian Holzinger .12 .30
261 Cory Stillman .12 .30
262 Mattias Ohlund .12 .30
263 Petr Sykora .15 .40
264 Jeff Halpern .12 .30
265 Patrik Stefan .12 .30
266 Jeff Jillson .12 .30
267 Mariusz Czerkawski .12 .30
268 Jeff O'Neill .12 .30
269 Brad Stuart .12 .30
270 Ron Francis .25 .60
271 Mike Johnson .12 .30
272 Richard Park .12 .30
273 Yanic Perreault .12 .30
274 Eric Belanger .12 .30
275 Stu Barnes .12 .30
276 Nathan Dempsey .12 .30
277 Bryan McCabe .12 .30
278 Andrew Brunette .12 .30
279 Ville Nieminen .12 .30
280 Greg Johnson .12 .30
281 Alex Kovalev .15 .40
282 Raffi Torres .12 .30
283 Drake Berehowsky .12 .30
284 Steve McCarthy .12 .30
285 Martin Erat .12 .30
286 Pavol Demitra .25 .60
287 Saku Koivu .20 .50
288 Milan Hejduk .15 .40
289 Sami Kapanen .12 .30
290 Nicklas Lidstrom .20 .50
291 Eric Brewer .12 .30
292 Martin Lapointe .15 .40
293 Andrei Markov .20 .50
294 Doug Weight .20 .50
295 Jason Arnott .15 .40
296 Mike York .12 .30
297 Jay Pandolfo .12 .30
298 Ed Jovanovski .15 .40
299 Bill Guerin .20 .50
300 Petr Cajanek .12 .30
301 Shawn Horcoff .12 .30
302 Ales Kotalik .12 .30
303 Chris Dingman .12 .30
304 Arron Asham .12 .30
305 Steve Staios .12 .30
306 Artem Chubarov .12 .30
307 Karlis Skrastins .12 .30
308 Nick Schultz .12 .30
309 Rico Fata .12 .30
310 Jan Hrdina .12 .30
311 Brendan Witt .12 .30
312 Lyle Odelein .12 .30
313 Pascal Dupuis .12 .30
314 Paul Kariya .20 .50
315 Petr Nedved .12 .30
316 Tim Taylor .12 .30
317 Ethan Moreau .12 .30
318 Shean Donovan .12 .30
319 Ruslan Salei .12 .30
320 Rem Murray .12 .30
321 Eric Nickulas .12 .30
322 Rob DiMaio .12 .30
323 Steven Reinprecht .12 .30
324 Cory Cross .12 .30
325 Kim Johnsson .12 .30
326 Chris Simon .12 .30
327 Gary Roberts .12 .30
328 Ken Klee .12 .30
329 Krzysztof Oliwa .12 .30
330 Marian Hossa .20 .50
331 Valeri Bure .12 .30
332 Bret Hedican .12 .30
333 Pavel Trnka .12 .30
334 Darcy Tucker .15 .40
335 Peter Schaefer .12 .30
336 Sergei Brylin .12 .30
337 Hal Gill .12 .30
338 Jason Woolley .12 .30
339 Mike Rathje .12 .30
340 Marty Murray .12 .30
341 Todd White .12 .30
342 Brent Sopel .12 .30
343 Glen Wesley .12 .30
344 Jozef Stumpel .12 .30
345 Scott Nichol .12 .30
346 Derrick Walser .12 .30
347 Marc Bergevin .12 .30
348 Richard Zednik .12 .30
349 Mike Ribeiro .12 .30
350 Mike Eastwood .12 .30
351 Trevor Letowski .12 .30
352 Fredrik Modin .12 .30
353 Mark Parrish .12 .30
354 Sandy McCarthy .12 .30
355 Tomas Holmstrom .15 .40
356 Dmitri Kalinin .12 .30

357 Janne Niinimaa .12 .30
358 Dave Andreychuk .12 .30
359 Boyd Devereaux .12 .30
360 Sergei Fedorov .30 .75
361 Josef Melichar .12 .30
362 Stephane Quintal .12 .30
363 Lasse Pirjeta .12 .30
364 Denis Arkhipov .12 .30
365 Matt Cullen .12 .30
366 Teppo Numminen .12 .30
367 Ilya Kovalchuk .20 .50
368 Reed Low .12 .30
369 Jochen Hecht .12 .30
370 Martin Rucinsky .12 .30
371 Mark Eaton .12 .30
372 Nils Ekman .12 .30
373 Slava Kozlov .15 .40
374 Scott Young .12 .30
375 Mathieu Schneider .12 .30
376 Scott Hannan .12 .30
377 Brad May .12 .30
378 Jeff Friesen .12 .30
379 P.J. Axelsson .12 .30
380 Brian Sutherby .12 .30
381 David Tanabe .12 .30
382 Pierre-Marc Bouchard .20 .50
383 Steve Konowalchuk .12 .30
384 Chris Pronger .20 .50
385 Craig Rivet .12 .30
386 Eric Desjardins .15 .40
387 Jody Shelley .12 .30
388 Vaclav Prospal .12 .30
389 Aaron Miller .12 .30
390 Deron Quint .12 .30
391 Joel Kwiatkowski .12 .30
392 Branko Radivojevic .12 .30
393 Niko Kapanen .12 .30
394 Wayne Primeau .12 .30
395 Patrik Elias .20 .50
396 Ronald Petrovicky .12 .30
397 Mike Cammalleri .20 .50
398 Bryan Berard .15 .40
399 Jason Doig .12 .30
400 Marcus Ragnarsson .12 .30
401 Aaron Downey .12 .30
402 Byron Dafoe .15 .40
403 Jean-Sebastien Giguere .20 .50
404 Dwayne Roloson .15 .40
405 Marc-Andre Fleury 2.00 5.00
406 Ray Emery .15 .40
407 Derek Armstrong .12 .30
408 Randy Robitaille .12 .30
409 Manny Fernandez .12 .30
410 Jeff Hackett .15 .40
411 Nikolai Khabibulin .20 .50
412 Tomas Vokoun .15 .40
413 Chris Neil .12 .30
414 Andrei Nikolishin .12 .30
415 Garth Snow .15 .40
416 Marty Turco .20 .50
417 Roberto Luongo .30 .75
418 Mikael Tellqvist .15 .40
419 Chris Osgood .20 .50
420 Jocelyn Thibault .15 .40
421 Olaf Kolzig .20 .50
422 Tommy Salo .15 .40
423 Corey Schwab .15 .40
424 Johan Hedberg .15 .40
425 Travis Green .12 .30
426 Pascal Leclaire .12 .30
427 Craig Andersson .20 .50
428 John Grahame .12 .30
429 Pasi Nurminen .15 .40
430 Trevor Kidd .12 .30
431 Scott Lachance .12 .30
432 Brent Johnson .12 .30
433 Jamie Storr .15 .40
434 Miikka Kiprusoff .20 .50
435 Cristobal Huet .15 .40
436 Jose Theodore .20 .50
437 Ty Conklin .15 .40
438 Curtis Joseph .25 .60
439 Jussi Markkanen .12 .30
440 Patrick Lalime .15 .40
441 Vesa Toskala .12 .30
442 Dan Cloutier .15 .40
443 Kevin Weekes .15 .40
444 Peter Worrell .15 .40
445 Zac Bierk .12 .30
446 Evgeni Nabokov .15 .40
447 Martin Biron .15 .40
448 Rick DiPietro .15 .40
449 Ed Belfour .20 .50
450 Martin Gerber .12 .30
451 Reinhard Divis .12 .30
452 Brian Finley .12 .30
453 Jason Bacashihua .12 .30
454 Mika Noronen .12 .30
455 Scott Clemmensen .12 .30
456 Brian Boucher .15 .40
457 Jason LaBarbera .12 .30
458 Mike Dunham .15 .40
459 Sean Burke .12 .30
460 Felix Potvin .30 .75
461 Martin Brodeur .50 1.25
462 Sebastien Caron .15 .40
463 Rob Zamuner .12 .30
464 Igor Larionov .20 .50
465 Andrew Raycroft .15 .40
466 Mathieu Garon .12 .30
467 Roman Turek .15 .40
468 Steve Passmore .12 .30
469 Chris Mason .12 .30
470 Jean-Sebastien Aubin .12 .30
471 Milan Hnilicka .12 .30
472 Steve Shields .15 .40
473 Arturs Irbe .15 .40
474 Ilja Bryzgalov .15 .40
475 Roman Cechmanek .15 .40
476 Steve Ott .12 .30
477 Mattias Weinhandl .12 .30
478 Brent Krahn .12 .30
479 Jamie McLennan .12 .30
480 Michael Leighton .12 .30
481 Ryan Miller .20 .50
482 Dominik Hasek .30 .75
483 Marc Denis .15 .40
484 Rastislav Stana .20 .50
485 Alex Auld .12 .30
486 Fred Brathwaite .15 .40
487 Martin Prusek .12 .30
488 Robert Esche .12 .30
489 Sebastien Charpentier .12 .30
490 David Aebischer .15 .40
491 Manny Legace .12 .30
492 Philippe Sauve .15 .40
493 Bob Boughner .12 .30
494 Maxime Ouellet .15 .40
495 Ron Tugnutt .15 .40
496 J.P. Vigier .12 .30
497 Steve Thomas .12 .30
498 Manny Malhotra .12 .30
499 Dany Sabourin .12 .30
500 Pavel Brendl .12 .30
501 Derek Roy .20 .50
502 Lawrence Nycholat .15 .40
503 Simon Gamache .12 .30
504 Dan Fritsche .12 .30
505 Chris Higgins .25 .60
506 Pierre Hedin .15 .40
507 Marc-Andre Fleury 2.00 5.00
508 Tony Salmelainen .12 .30
509 Ryan Kesler .50 1.25
510 John-Michael Liles .15 .40
511 Zbynek Michalek .12 .30
512 Trent Hunter .12 .30
513 Matthew Lombardi .15 .40
514 Matt Stajan .20 .50
515 Gregory Campbell .12 .30
516 Chad Wiseman .12 .30
517 Konstantin Koltsov .12 .30
518 Joffrey Lupul .75 2.00
519 Jeff MacMillan .15 .40
520 Wade Brookbank .15 .40
521 Timofei Shishkanov .12 .30
522 Eric Staal 1.50 4.00
523 Nathan Horton .75 2.00
524 Julien Vauclair .12 .30
525 Tom Preissing .15 .40
526 Kent McDonell .15 .40
527 Antoine Vermette .25 .60
528 Anton Babchuk .12 .30
529 Grant McNeill .12 .30
530 Chris Hajt .15 .40
531 Burke Henry .12 .30
532 Kyle Rossiter .15 .40
533 Joni Pitkanen .20 .50
534 Maxim Kondratiev .12 .30
535 Peter Sejna .15 .40
536 Sergei Zinovjev .12 .30
537 Nathan Robinson .12 .30
538 Tuomas Pihlman .15 .40
539 Lasse Kukkonen .12 .30
540 Tomas Plekanec .40 1.00
541 Alexander Semin 1.00 2.50
542 Fredrik Sjostrom .20 .50
543 Kari Lehtonen 1.25 3.00
544 Matt Murley .15 .40
545 Dustin Brown .30 .75
546 Tuomo Ruutu .20 .50
547 Dominic Moore .12 .30
548 Garnet Exelby .12 .30
549 Dan Hamhuis .15 .40
550 Ryan Malone .25 .60
551 Milan Michalek .60 1.50
552 Aaron Johnson .12 .30
553 Matthew Spiller .15 .40
554 Christian Ehrhoff .15 .40
555 Doug Lynch .12 .30
556 Andrew Peters .15 .40
557 Aleksander Suglobov .12 .30
558 Chuck Kobasew .12 .30
559 Sean Bergenheim .15 .40
560 Jason Pominville .75 2.00
561 Andrew Hutchinson .12 .30
562 Garrett Burnett .12 .30
563 Nikolai Zherdev .60 1.50
564 Tony Martensson .12 .30
565 Antti Miettinen .20 .50
566 Scott Barney .12 .30
567 Jordin Tootoo .60 1.50
568 Brad Leeb .12 .30
569 Peter Sarno .12 .30
570 Jed Ortmeyer .12 .30
571 Kyle Wellwood .20 .50
572 Brent Krahn .12 .30
573 Dmitri Afanasenkov .15 .40
574 Jarret Stoll .12 .30
575 Marek Zidlicky .12 .30
576 Karl Stewart .12 .30
577 Darryl Bootland .15 .40
578 Niklas Kronwall .25 .60
579 Paul Martin .12 .30
580 Adam Munro .15 .40
581 Pat Leahy .15 .40
582 Cody McCormick .15 .40
583 Jozef Balej .12 .30
584 Boyd Gordon .15 .40
585 Jason King .12 .30
586 Trevor Daley .20 .50
587 Robert Schnabel .15 .40
588 Chris Kunitz .25 .60
589 Mike Danton .12 .30
590 Mikhail Yakubov .12 .30
591 John Pohl .12 .30
592 Brent Burns .40 1.00
593 Patrice Bergeron 1.50 4.00
594 Jiri Hudler .75 2.00
595 David Hale .12 .30
596 Travis Moen .15 .40
597 Michael Ryder .15 .40
598 Tim Gleason .15 .40
599 Christian Backman .20 .50
600 Pavel Vorobiev .15 .40

1997-98 Pacific Dynagon

1 Brian Bellows .30 .75
2 Guy Hebert .30 .75
3 Paul Kariya .40 1.00
4 Steve Rucchin .30 .75
5 Teemu Selanne .75 2.00
6 Jason Allison .30 .75
7 Ray Bourque .60 1.50
8 Jim Carey .20 .50
9 Jozef Stumpel .20 .50
10 Dominik Hasek .60 1.50
11 Brian Holzinger .30 .75
12 Michael Peca .30 .75
13 Derek Plante .30 .75
14 Miroslav Satan .20 .50
15 Theo Fleury .40 1.00
16 Jonas Hoglund .30 .75
17 Jarome Iginla .40 1.00
18 Trevor Kidd .20 .50
19 German Titov .20 .50
20 Sean Burke .20 .50
21 Andrew Cassels .20 .50
22 Keith Primeau .30 .75
23 Geoff Sanderson .30 .75
24 Tony Amonte .30 .75
25 Chris Chelios .40 1.00
26 Eric Daze .20 .50
27 Jeff Hackett .20 .50
28 Ethan Moreau .20 .50
29 Peter Forsberg .75 2.00
30 Valeri Kamensky .30 .75
31 Claude Lemieux .30 .75
32 Sandis Ozolinsh .20 .50
33 Patrick Roy .75 2.00
34 Joe Sakic .75 2.00
35 Derian Hatcher .30 .75
36 Jamie Langenbrunner .30 .75
37 Mike Modano .60 1.50
38 Joe Nieuwendyk .30 .75
39 Darryl Sydor .20 .50
40 Sergei Zubov .30 .75
41 Sergei Fedorov .60 1.50
42 Vladimir Konstantinov .20 .50
43 Chris Osgood .40 1.00
44 Brendan Shanahan .40 1.00
45 Mike Vernon .30 .75
46 Steve Yzerman .75 2.00
47 Kelly Buchberger .30 .75
48 Mike Grier .30 .75
49 Curtis Joseph .40 1.00
50 Rem Murray .20 .50
51 Ryan Smyth .30 .75
52 Doug Weight .40 1.00
53 Ed Jovanovski .20 .50
54 Scott Mellanby .20 .50
55 Ray Sheppard .30 .75
56 Robert Svehla .30 .75
57 John Vanbiesbrouck .40 1.00
58 Rob Blake .40 1.00
59 Ray Ferraro .20 .50
60 Dimitri Khristich .30 .75
61 Vladimir Tsyplakov .30 .75
62 Vincent Damphousse .30 .75
63 Saku Koivu .40 1.00
64 Mark Recchi .40 1.00
65 Stephane Richer .20 .50
66 Jocelyn Thibault .30 .75
67 Dave Andreychuk .40 1.00
68 Martin Brodeur .75 2.00
69 Doug Gilmour .40 1.00
70 Bobby Holik .20 .50
71 John MacLean .20 .50
72 Bryan Berard .20 .50
73 Travis Green .30 .75
74 Zigmund Palffy .40 1.00
75 Tommy Salo .20 .50
76 Bryan Smolinski .30 .75
77 Adam Graves .20 .50
78 Wayne Gretzky 2.00 5.00
79 Alexei Kovalev .30 .75
80 Brian Leetch .30 .75
81 Mark Messier .75 2.00
82 Mike Richter .40 1.00
83 Daniel Alfredsson .40 1.00
84 Alexandre Daigle .20 .50
85 Wade Redden .20 .50
86 Damian Rhodes .30 .75
87 Alexei Yashin .30 .75
88 Rod Brind'Amour .40 1.00
89 Ron Hextall .40 1.00
90 John LeClair .40 1.00
91 Eric Lindros .60 1.50
92 Janne Niinimaa .30 .75
93 Garth Snow .30 .75
94 Dainius Zubrus .30 .75
95 Mike Gartner .40 1.00
96 Nikolai Khabibulin .40 1.00
97 Jeremy Roenick .60 1.50
98 Keith Tkachuk .40 1.00
99 Oleg Tverdovsky .30 .75
100 Ron Francis .40 1.00
101 Kevin Hatcher .20 .50
102 Jaromir Jagr 1.00 3.00
103 Patrick Lalime .30 .75
104 Petr Nedved .40 1.00
105 Jim Campbell .40 1.00
106 Grant Fuhr .60 1.50
107 Brett Hull .75 2.00
108 Pierre Turgeon .30 .75
109 Harry York .30 .75
110 Jeff Friesen .30 .75
111 Tony Granato .30 .75
112 Stephen Guolla RC .30 .75
113 Viktor Kozlov .30 .75
114 Owen Nolan .40 1.00
115 Dino Ciccarelli .40 1.00
116 John Cullen .20 .50
117 Chris Gratton .20 .50
118 Roman Hamrlik .30 .75
119 Daymond Langkow .20 .50
120 Sergei Berezin .30 .75
121 Wendel Clark .60 1.50
122 Felix Potvin .60 1.50
123 Steve Sullivan .30 .75
124 Mats Sundin .40 1.00
125 Pavel Bure .40 1.00
126 Martin Gelinas .20 .50
127 Trevor Linden .40 1.00
128 Kirk McLean .30 .75
129 Alexander Mogilny .40 1.00
130 Peter Bondra .40 1.00
131 Joe Juneau .20 .50
132 Steve Konowalchuk .30 .75
133 Adam Oates .40 1.00
134 Bill Ranford .30 .75
135 Paul Kariya
Teemu Selanne .75 2.00
136 Dominik Hasek
Mike Peca .60 1.50
137 T.Fleury/J.Iginla .40 1.00
138 P.Forsberg/P.Roy .75 2.00
139 B.Shanahan/S.Yzerman .75 2.00
140 W.Gretzky/M.Messier 2.00 5.00
141 J.LeClair/E.Lindros .60 1.50
142 J.Jagr/P.Lalime 1.00 3.00
143 J.Campbell/B.Hull .75 2.00
144 S.Berezin/M.Sundin .40 1.00
NNO1 Shawn Bates RC .30 .75
NNO2 Daniel Cleary .30 .75
NNO3 Marian Hossa RC .40 1.00
NNO4 Olli Jokinen RC .40 1.00
NNO5 Espen Knutsen RC .40 1.00
NNO6 Patrick Marleau .40 1.00
NNO7 Alyn McCauley .30 .75
NNO8 Mattias Ohlund .30 .75
NNO9 Chris Phillips .30 .75
NNO10 Erik Rasmussen .30 .75
NNO11 Sergei Samsonov .30 .75
NNO12 Joe Thornton .60 1.50

1997-98 Pacific Dynagon Copper

*VETS: 5X TO 12X BASIC CARDS
*ROOKIE STAR: 2X TO 5X BASIC CARDS

1997-98 Pacific Dynagon Dark Gray

*VETS: 5X TO 12X BASIC CARDS
*ROOKIE STAR: 2X TO 5X BASIC CARDS

1997-98 Pacific Dynagon Emerald Green

*VETS: 5X TO 12X BASIC CARDS
*ROOKIE STAR: 2X TO 5X BASIC CARDS

1997-98 Pacific Dynagon Ice Blue

*VETS: 8X TO 15X BASIC CARDS
*ROOKIE STAR: 2.5X TO 8X BASIC CARDS

1997-98 Pacific Dynagon Red

*VETS: 5X TO 12X BASIC CARDS
*ROOKIE STAR: 2X TO 5X BASIC CARDS

1997-98 Pacific Dynagon Silver

*VETS: 5X TO 12X BASIC CARDS
*ROOKIE STAR: 2X TO 5X BASIC CARDS

1997-98 Pacific Dynagon Best Kept Secrets

1 J.J. Daigneault .15 .40
2 Paul Kariya .20 .50
3 Dave Karpa .12 .30
4 Teemu Selanne .40 1.00
5 Ray Bourque .30 .75
6 Jim Carey .12 .30
7 Davis Payne .12 .30
8 Paxton Schafer .12 .30
9 Bob Boughner .12 .30
10 Dominik Hasek .30 .75
11 Brad May .12 .30
12 Cale Hulse .15 .40
13 Jarome Iginla .25 .60
14 James Patrick .12 .30
15 Zarley Zalapski .12 .30
16 Jeff Brown .15 .40
17 Keith Primeau .15 .40
18 Steven Rice .15 .40
19 James Black .12 .30
20 Chris Chelios .20 .50
21 Steve Dubinsky .12 .30
22 Steve Smith .12 .30
23 Craig Billington .12 .30
24 Peter Forsberg .40 1.00
25 Jon Klemm .12 .30
26 Patrick Roy .50 1.25
27 Joe Sakic .40 1.00
28 Neal Broten .12 .30
29 Richard Matvichuk .15 .40
30 Mike Modano .30 .75
31 Andy Moog .20 .50
32 Sergei Fedorov .30 .75
33 Kirk Maltby .12 .30
34 Brendan Shanahan .20 .50
35 Tim Taylor .15 .40
36 Steve Yzerman .50 1.25
37 Louie DeBrusk .12 .30
38 Joe Hulbig .12 .30
39 Ryan Smyth .15 .40
40 Mike Hough .12 .30
41 Jody Hull .12 .30
42 Paul Laus .12 .30
43 John Vanbiesbrouck .20 .50
44 Aki Berg .12 .30
45 Ray Ferraro .12 .30
46 Craig Johnson .12 .30
47 Ian Laperriere .12 .30
48 Vincent Damphousse .15 .40
49 Dave Manson .12 .30
50 Stephane Richer .12 .30
51 Craig Rivet .15 .40
52 Martin Brodeur .50 1.25
53 Jay Pandolfo .15 .40
54 Brian Rolston .15 .40
55 Doug Houda .15 .40
56 Brent Hughes .12 .30
57 Zigmund Palffy .20 .50
58 Adam Graves .12 .30
59 Wayne Gretzky 1.25 3.00
60 Chris Ferraro .12 .30
61 Glenn Healy .12 .30
62 Brian Leetch .15 .40
63 Mark Messier .40 1.00
64 Radim Bicanek .12 .30
65 Philip Crowe .12 .30
66 Christer Olsson .12 .30
67 Jason York .12 .30
68 Rod Brind'Amour .20 .50
69 John Druce .12 .30
70 Daniel Lacroix .12 .30
71 John LeClair .20 .50
72 Eric Lindros .30 .75
73 Murray Baron .12 .30
74 Mike Gartner .25 .60
75 Brad McCrimmon .12 .30
76 Keith Tkachuk .20 .50
77 Jaromir Jagr .60 1.50
78 Patrick Lalime .15 .40
79 Ian Moran .15 .40
80 Petr Nedved .20 .50
81 Brett Hull .40 1.00
82 Robert Petrovicky .15 .40
83 Pierre Turgeon .15 .40
84 Trent Yawney .12 .30
85 Tim Hunter .12 .30
86 Marcus Ragnarsson .12 .30
87 Dody Wood .12 .30
88 Dino Ciccarelli .20 .50
89 Alexander Selivanov .12 .30
90 Jason Wiemer .12 .30
91 Sergei Berezin .15 .40
92 Felix Potvin .30 .75
93 Mats Sundin .20 .50
94 Craig Wolanin .15 .40
95 Pavel Bure .20 .50
96 Troy Crowder .12 .30
97 Dana Murzyn .12 .30
98 Gino Odjick .12 .30
99 Craig Berube .12 .30
100 Peter Bondra .20 .50
101 Mike Eagles .15 .40
102 Andrei Nikolishin .12 .30
103 Paul Kariya .20 .50
104 Dominik Hasek .30 .75
105 Michael Peca .15 .40
106 M.Brodeur/M.Dunham .50 1.25
107 Bryan Berard .12 .30
108 Brian Leetch .15 .40
109 Tony Granato .12 .30
110 Trevor Linden .20 .50

1997-98 Pacific Dynagon Dynamic Duos

COMPLETE SET (30) 30.00 80.00
1A Paul Kariya 1.50 4.00
1B Teemu Selanne 1.50 4.00
2A Ray Bourque 2.00 5.00
2B Jim Carey .75 2.00
3A Dominik Hasek 3.00 8.00
3B Michael Peca .40 1.00
4A Theo Fleury .75 2.00
4B Jarome Iginla 2.00 5.00
5A Peter Forsberg 2.50 6.00
5B Claude Lemieux .40 1.00
6A Patrick Roy 8.00 20.00
6B Joe Sakic 3.00 8.00
7A Sergei Fedorov 1.50 4.00
7B Vladimir Konstantinov .75 2.00
8A Brendan Shanahan 1.50 4.00
8B Steve Yzerman 6.00 15.00
9A Bryan Berard .40 1.00
9B Zigmund Palffy .75 2.00
10A Wayne Gretzky 10.00 25.00
10B Mark Messier 1.50 4.00
11A Eric Lindros 1.50 4.00
11B Dainius Zubrus .40 1.00
12A Jeremy Roenick 2.00 5.00
12B Keith Tkachuk 1.25 3.00
13A Jaromir Jagr 2.50 6.00
13B Patrick Lalime .75 2.00
14A Jim Campbell .40 1.00
14B Brett Hull 1.50 4.00
15A Pavel Bure 1.50 4.00
15B Alexander Mogilny .75 2.00

1997-98 Pacific Dynagon Kings of the NHL

COMPLETE SET (10) 30.00 80.00
1 Paul Kariya 3.00 8.00
2 Peter Forsberg 6.00 15.00
3 Patrick Roy 12.00 30.00
4 Joe Sakic 6.00 15.00
5 John Vanbiesbrouck 2.50 6.00
6 Wayne Gretzky 20.00 50.00
7 Mark Messier 3.00 8.00
8 Eric Lindros 3.00 8.00
9 Jaromir Jagr 5.00 12.00
10 Pavel Bure 3.00 8.00

1997-98 Pacific Dynagon Stonewallers

COMPLETE SET (20) 25.00 60.00
1 Guy Hebert 1.25 3.00
2 Jim Carey 1.25 3.00
3 Dominik Hasek 4.00 10.00
4 Trevor Kidd 1.25 3.00
5 Jeff Hackett 1.25 3.00
6 Patrick Roy 10.00 25.00
7 Chris Osgood 1.25 3.00
8 Mike Vernon 1.50 4.00
9 Curtis Joseph 1.50 4.00
10 John Vanbiesbrouck 1.50 4.00
11 Jocelyn Thibault 1.25 3.00
12 Martin Brodeur 6.00 15.00
13 Tommy Salo 1.25 3.00
14 Mike Richter 1.50 4.00
15 Ron Hextall 1.50 4.00
16 Garth Snow 1.25 3.00
17 Nikolai Khabibulin 1.50 4.00
18 Patrick Lalime 1.25 3.00
19 Grant Fuhr 1.50 4.00
20 Felix Potvin 2.00 5.00

1997-98 Pacific Dynagon Tandems

COMPLETE SET (72) 60.00 150.00
1 W.Gretzky/E.Lindros 10.00 25.00
2 J.Sakic/P.Kariya 4.00 10.00
3 J.Iginla/M.Messier 4.00 10.00
4 P.Roy/D.Hasek 8.00 20.00
5 P.Forsberg/J.Jagr 4.00 10.00
6 B.Shanahan/K.Tkachuk 1.25 3.00
7 S.Yzerman/T.Selanne 4.00 10.00
8 S.Fedorov/B.Hull 4.00 10.00
9 D.Zubrus/P.Lalime .75 2.00
10 S.Berezin/M.Grier .75 2.00
11 Z.Palffy/C.Joseph 1.25 3.00
12 C.Osgood/M.Brodeur 4.00 10.00
13 J.Vanbiesbr./J.Thibault 1.25 3.00
14 S.Koivu/P.Bure 2.00 5.00
15 J.LeClair/P.Bondra 1.25 3.00
16 M.Sundin/J.Niinimaa 1.25 3.00
17 F.Potvin/J.Carey 3.00 8.00
18 Fuhr/Hull/Campbell 2.00 5.00
19 Gretzky/Messier/Leetch 8.00 20.00
20 Lindros/LeClair/B'Amour 2.00 5.00
21 Hasek/Peca/Satan 2.00 5.00
22 Jagr/Lalime/Nedved 2.00 5.00
23 Iginla/Fleury/Kidd 2.00 5.00
24 Kariya/Selanne/Hebert 2.00 5.00
25 Forsberg/Roy/Lemieux 8.00 20.00
26 Yzerman/Shanahan/Konst. 8.00 20.00
27 Sundin/Berezin/Clark 2.00 5.00
28 R.Bourque/D.Plante 2.00 5.00
29 B.Bellows/J.Allison .75 2.00
30 S.Rucchin/K.Primeau 1.00 2.50
31 J.Stumpel/E.Daze .75 2.00
32 B.Holzinger/J.Langenbrunner .75 2.00
33 M.Peca/T.Amonte .75 2.00
34 G.Titov/D.Sydor .75 2.00
35 T.Fleury/C.Chelios 1.25 3.00
36 J.Hoglund/D.Khristich .75 2.00
37 S.Burke/D.Andreychuk 1.00 2.50
38 G.Sanderson/D.Hatcher .75 2.00
39 A.Cassels/J.Hackett .75 2.00
40 E.Moreau/R.Ferraro .75 2.00
41 S.Ozolinsh/D.Gilmour 1.00 2.50
42 V.Kamensky/M.Modano 1.25 3.00
43 J.Nieuwendyk/V.Tsyplakov 1.00 2.50
44 S.Zubov/M.Vernon 1.00 2.50
45 R.Blake/B.Holik 1.00 2.50
46 V.Damphousse/D.Weight 1.00 2.50
47 M.Recchi/R.Smyth 1.00 2.50
48 S.Richer/J.MacLean .75 2.00
49 K.Buchberger/E.Jovanovski .75 2.00
50 R.Murray/O.Nolan .75 2.00
51 R.Svehla/B.Ranford .75 2.00
52 R.Sheppard/S.Sullivan .75 2.00
53 S.Mellanby/J.Cullen .75 2.00
54 G.Snow/A.Daigle .75 2.00
55 R.Hextall/A.Mogilny 1.25 3.00
56 K.McLean/A.Oates 1.00 2.50
57 J.Juneau/D.Ciccarelli 1.00 2.50
58 S.Konowalchuk/J.Campbell .75 2.00
59 T.Linden/P.Turgeon 1.25 3.00
60 M.Gelinas/J.Friesen .75 2.00
61 R.Hamrlik/H.York 1.00 2.50
62 K.Hatcher/C.Gratton .75 2.00
63 R.Francis/J.Roenick 1.50 4.00
64 N.Khabibulin/V.Kozlov 1.00 2.50
65 D.Langkow/M.Gartner .75 2.00
66 O.Tverdovsky/S.Guolla .75 2.00
67 T.Granato/T.Salo .75 2.00
68 B.Smolinski/W.Redden .75 2.00
69 A.Graves/D.Rhodes .75 2.00
70 M.Richter/A.Yashin 1.25 3.00
71 D.Alfredsson/B.Berard 1.00 2.50
72 T.Green/A.Kovalev .75 2.00

1998-99 Pacific Dynagon Ice

RED: 8X TO 2X BASIC CARDS
*BLUE/67: 8X TO 20X BASIC CARDS
1 Travis Green .10 .25
2 Guy Hebert .12 .30
3 Paul Kariya .15 .40
4 Steve Rucchin .12 .30
5 Tomas Sandstrom .10 .25
6 Teemu Selanne .30 .75
7 Jason Allison .12 .30
8 Ray Bourque .25 .60
9 Byron Dafoe .12 .30
10 Anson Carter .12 .30
11 Dimitri Khristich .10 .25
12 Antti Laaksonen RC .30 .75
13 Peter Nordstrom RC .12 .30
14 Sergei Samsonov .12 .30
15 Joe Thornton .25 .60
16 Matthew Barnaby .10 .25
17 Michal Grosek .10 .25
18 Dominik Hasek .25 .60
19 Brian Holzinger .10 .25
20 Michael Peca .10 .25
21 Miroslav Satan .12 .30
22 Vaclav Varada .10 .25
23 Andrew Cassels .10 .25
24 Rico Fata .12 .30
25 Theo Fleury .20 .50
26 Phil Housley .12 .30
27 Jarome Iginla .20 .50
28 Martin St. Louis RC .50 1.25
29 Ken Wregget .12 .30
30 Kevin Dineen .10 .25
31 Ron Francis .20 .50
32 Martin Gelinas .10 .25
33 Arturs Irbe .12 .30
34 Sami Kapanen .10 .25
35 Trevor Kidd .12 .30
36 Robert Kron .10 .25
37 Keith Primeau .12 .30
38 Tony Amonte .12 .30
39 Chris Chelios .15 .40
40 Eric Daze .12 .30
41 Doug Gilmour .20 .50
42 Jeff Hackett .10 .25
43 Ty Jones .10 .25
44 Bob Probert .15 .40
45 Adam Deadmarsh .12 .30
46 Chris Drury .12 .30
47 Peter Forsberg .30 .75
48 Milan Hejduk RC .25 .60
49 Valeri Kamensky .12 .30
50 Claude Lemieux .12 .30
51 Patrick Roy .40 1.00
52 Joe Sakic .30 .75
53 Ed Belfour .15 .40
54 Sergey Gusev RC .12 .30
55 Derian Hatcher .12 .30
56 Brett Hull .30 .75
57 Jamie Langenbrunner .12 .30
58 Jere Lehtinen .12 .30
59 Mike Modano .25 .60
60 Joe Nieuwendyk .12 .30
61 Sergei Zubov .12 .30
62 Sergei Fedorov .25 .60
63 Vyacheslav Kozlov .10 .25
64 Uwe Krupp .10 .25
65 Nicklas Lidstrom .20 .50
66 Darren McCarty .10 .25
67 Chris Osgood .15 .40
68 Brendan Shanahan .15 .40
69 Steve Yzerman .40 1.00
70 Bob Essensa .12 .30
71 Mike Grier .10 .25
72 Bill Guerin .15 .40
73 Roman Hamrlik .10 .25
74 Janne Niinimaa .10 .25
75 Tom Poti .10 .25
76 Ryan Smyth .12 .30
77 Doug Weight .15 .40
78 Sean Burke .10 .25
79 Dino Ciccarelli .15 .40
80 Dave Gagner .10 .25
81 Ed Jovanovski .12 .30
82 Viktor Kozlov .10 .25
83 Oleg Kvasha RC .15 .40
84 Paul Laus .12 .30
85 Mark Parrish RC .25 .60
86 Rob Blake .15 .40
87 Stephane Fiset .12 .30
88 Josh Green RC .15 .40
89 Yanic Perreault .10 .25
90 Luc Robitaille .15 .40
91 Jozef Stumpel .10 .25
92 Vladimir Tsyplakov .10 .25
93 Brad Brown .10 .25
94 Shayne Corson .12 .30
95 Vincent Damphousse .12 .30
96 Saku Koivu .15 .40
97 Mark Recchi .20 .50
98 Jocelyn Thibault .12 .30
99 Sergei Zholtok .10 .25
100 Andrew Brunette .12 .30
101 Mike Dunham .12 .30
102 Tom Fitzgerald .12 .30
103 Patrik Kjellberg .10 .25
104 Sergei Krivokrasov .10 .25
105 Darren Turcotte .12 .30
106 Dave Andreychuk .15 .40
107 Jason Arnott .12 .30
108 Martin Brodeur .40 1.00
109 Patrik Elias .15 .40
110 Bobby Holik .10 .25
111 Brendan Morrison .10 .25
112 Scott Stevens .15 .40
113 Bryan Berard .12 .30
114 Eric Brewer .15 .40
115 Trevor Linden .15 .40
116 Zigmund Palffy .15 .40
117 Robert Reichel .10 .25
118 Tommy Salo .12 .30
119 Bryan Smolinski .10 .25
120 Adam Graves .10 .25
121 Wayne Gretzky 1.00 2.50
122 Alexei Kovalev .12 .30
123 Brian Leetch .15 .40
124 Manny Malhotra .12 .30
125 Mike Richter .15 .40
126 Daniel Alfredsson .15 .40
127 Igor Kravchuk .10 .25
128 Shawn McEachern .10 .25
129 Vaclav Prospal .10 .25
130 Damian Rhodes .15 .40
131 Sami Salo RC .10 .25
132 Alexei Yashin .15 .40
133 Rod Brind'Amour .12 .30
134 Alexandre Daigle .10 .25
135 Chris Gratton .12 .30
136 Ron Hextall .15 .40
137 John LeClair .15 .40
138 Eric Lindros .25 .60
139 Mike Maneluk RC .10 .25
140 John Vanbiesbrouck .15 .40
141 Dainius Zubrus .10 .25
142 Brad Isbister .12 .30
143 Nikolai Khabibulin .15 .40
144 Jeremy Roenick .25 .60
145 Keith Tkachuk .15 .40
146 Rick Tocchet .12 .30
147 Oleg Tverdovsky .15 .40
148 Tom Barrasso .12 .30
149 Kevin Hatcher .10 .25
150 Jan Hrdina RC .20 .50
151 Jaromir Jagr .50 1.25
152 Alexei Morozov .10 .25
153 Jiri Slegr .10 .25
154 Martin Straka .10 .25
155 Jim Campbell .12 .30
156 Geoff Courtnall .12 .30
157 Grant Fuhr .25 .60
158 Michal Handzus RC .20 .50
159 Al MacInnis .20 .50
160 Jamie McLennan .12 .30
161 Chris Pronger .15 .40
162 Marty Reasoner .15 .40
163 Pierre Turgeon .12 .30
164 Jeff Friesen .12 .30
165 Tony Granato .10 .25
166 Scott Hannan RC .12 .30
167 Patrick Marleau .15 .40
168 Owen Nolan .15 .40
169 Marco Sturm .10 .25
170 Mike Vernon .12 .30
171 Wendel Clark .25 .60
172 John Cullen .10 .25
173 Vincent Lecavalier .30 .75
174 Stephane Richer .10 .25
175 Paul Ysebaert .10 .25
176 Rob Zamuner .10 .25
177 Sergei Berezin .12 .30
178 Tie Domi .12 .30
179 Mike Johnson .10 .25
180 Curtis Joseph .20 .50
181 Tomas Kaberle RC .20 .50
182 Igor Korolev .10 .25
183 Alyn McCauley .10 .25
184 Mats Sundin .15 .40
185 Todd Bertuzzi .15 .40
186 Donald Brashear .10 .25
187 Pavel Bure .15 .40
188 Matt Cooke RC .15 .40
189 Mark Messier .30 .75
190 Alexander Mogilny .12 .30
191 Mattias Ohlund .10 .25
192 Garth Snow .12 .30
193 Peter Bondra .15 .40
194 Matthew Herr RC .10 .25
195 Calle Johansson .10 .25
196 Joe Juneau .10 .25
197 Olaf Kolzig .15 .40
198 Adam Oates .15 .40
199 Jaroslav Svejkovsky .10 .25
200 Richard Zednik .10 .25

1998-99 Pacific Dynagon Ice Adrenaline Rush Bronze

*SILVER1/120: .5X TO 1.2X BRONZE/180
*RED/79: .8X TO 2X BRONZE/180
1 Paul Kariya 2.00 5.00
2 Teemu Selanne 4.00 10.00
3 Dominik Hasek 3.00 8.00
4 Peter Forsberg 4.00 10.00
5 Patrick Roy 5.00 12.00
6 Joe Sakic 4.00 10.00
7 Steve Yzerman 5.00 12.00
8 Wayne Gretzky 12.00 30.00
9 Eric Lindros 3.00 8.00
10 Jaromir Jagr 6.00 15.00

1998-99 Pacific Dynagon Ice Forward Thinking

1 Paul Kariya 1.00 2.50
2 Teemu Selanne 2.00 5.00
3 Michael Peca .60 1.50
4 Doug Gilmour 1.25 3.00
5 Peter Forsberg 2.00 5.00
6 Joe Sakic 2.00 5.00
7 Brett Hull 2.00 5.00
8 Mike Modano 1.50 4.00
9 Sergei Fedorov 1.50 4.00
10 Brendan Shanahan 1.00 2.50
11 Steve Yzerman 2.50 6.00
12 Saku Koivu 1.00 2.50
13 Wayne Gretzky 6.00 15.00
14 John LeClair 1.00 2.50
15 Eric Lindros 1.50 4.00
16 Jaromir Jagr 3.00 8.00
17 Vincent Lecavalier 2.00 5.00
18 Mats Sundin 1.00 2.50
19 Mark Messier 2.00 5.00
20 Peter Bondra 1.00 2.50

1998-99 Pacific Dynagon Ice Watchmen

1 Dominik Hasek 2.00 5.00
2 Patrick Roy 3.00 8.00
3 Ed Belfour 1.25 3.00
4 Chris Osgood 1.25 3.00
5 Martin Brodeur 3.00 8.00
6 Mike Richter 1.25 3.00
7 John Vanbiesbrouck 1.25 3.00
8 Grant Fuhr 2.00 5.00
9 Curtis Joseph 1.50 4.00
10 Olaf Kolzig 1.25 3.00

1998-99 Pacific Dynagon Ice Preeminent Players

1 Paul Kariya 2.00 5.00
2 Dominik Hasek 3.00 8.00
3 Peter Forsberg 4.00 10.00
4 Patrick Roy 5.00 12.00
5 Mike Modano 3.00 8.00
6 Steve Yzerman 5.00 12.00
7 Martin Brodeur 5.00 12.00
8 Wayne Gretzky 12.00 30.00
9 Eric Lindros 3.00 8.00
10 Jaromir Jagr 6.00 15.00

1998-99 Pacific Dynagon Ice Rookies

1 Chris Drury .75 2.00
2 Milan Hejduk 1.50 4.00
3 Mark Parrish 1.50 4.00
4 Brendan Morrison .60 1.50
5 Mike Maneluk .60 1.50
6 Jan Hrdina 1.25 3.00
7 Marty Reasoner 1.00 2.50
8 Vincent Lecavalier 2.00 5.00
9 Tomas Kaberle 1.25 3.00
10 Bill Muckalt .60 1.50

1998-99 Pacific Dynagon Ice Team Checklists

1 Paul Kariya .75 2.00
2 Ray Bourque 1.25 3.00
3 Dominik Hasek 1.25 3.00
4 Theo Fleury 1.00 2.50
5 Keith Primeau .60 1.50
6 Chris Chelios .75 2.00
7 Patrick Roy 2.00 5.00
8 Mike Modano 1.25 3.00
9 Steve Yzerman 2.00 5.00
10 Ryan Smyth .60 1.50
11 Dino Ciccarelli .75 2.00
12 Rob Blake .75 2.00
13 Saku Koivu .75 2.00
14 Mike Dunham .60 1.50
15 Martin Brodeur 2.00 5.00
16 Trevor Linden .75 2.00
17 Wayne Gretzky 5.00 12.00
18 Alexei Yashin .60 1.50
19 Eric Lindros 1.25 3.00
20 Keith Tkachuk .75 2.00
21 Jaromir Jagr 2.50 6.00
22 Grant Fuhr 1.25 3.00
23 Mike Vernon .60 1.50
24 Vincent Lecavalier 1.50 4.00
25 Mats Sundin .75 2.00
26 Mark Messier 1.50 4.00
27 Peter Bondra .75 2.00

1999-00 Pacific Dynagon Ice

COMPLETE SET (206) 15.00 40.00
COMP.SET w/o SP's (200) 35.00 70.00
1 Steve Kariya SP RC 1.50 4.00
2 Simon Gagne SP 2.50 6.00
3 Mike Fisher SP RC 2.50 6.00
4 Mike Ribeiro SP 1.50 4.00
5 Oleg Saprykin SP RC 4.00 10.00
6 Patrik Stefan SP RC 4.00 10.00
7 Ted Donato .08 .25
8 Niclas Havelid RC .30 .75
9 Guy Hebert .25 .60
10 Paul Kariya .30 .75
11 Steve Rucchin .08 .25
12 Teemu Selanne .30 .75
13 Oleg Tverdovsky .08 .25
14 Kelly Buchberger .08 .25
15 Nelson Emerson .08 .25
16 Ray Ferraro .08 .25
17 Norm Maracle .25 .60
18 Damian Rhodes .25 .60
19 Per Svartvadet RC .08 .25
20 Jason Allison .08 .25
21 Ray Bourque .50 1.25
22 Anson Carter .25 .60
23 Byron Dafoe .25 .60
24 John Grahame RC .60 1.50
25 Sergei Samsonov .25 .60
26 Joe Thornton .50 1.25
27 Stu Barnes .08 .25
28 Martin Biron .25 .60
29 Curtis Brown .08 .25
30 Michal Grosek .08 .25
31 Dominik Hasek .60 1.50
32 Michael Peca .25 .60
33 Miroslav Satan .25 .60
34 Valeri Bure .08 .25
35 Grant Fuhr .25 .60
36 Jarome Iginla .40 1.00
37 Derek Morris .08 .25
38 Marc Savard .08 .25
39 Cory Stillman .08 .25
40 Ron Francis .25 .60
41 Arturs Irbe .25 .60
42 Sami Kapanen .08 .25
43 Keith Primeau .08 .25
44 Dave Tanabe .08 .25
45 Tommy Westlund RC .25 .60
46 Tony Amonte .25 .60
47 Wendel Clark .08 .25
48 Eric Daze .25 .60
49 J-P Dumont .25 .60
50 Doug Gilmour .25 .60
51 Steve McCarthy .08 .25
52 Jocelyn Thibault .25 .60
53 Alexei Zhamnov .08 .25
54 Adam Deadmarsh .08 .25
55 Chris Drury .25 .60
56 Peter Forsberg .75 2.00
57 Milan Hejduk .30 .75
58 Dan Hinote RC .25 .60
59 Patrick Roy 1.50 4.00
60 Joe Sakic .60 1.50
61 Martin Skoula RC .75 2.00
62 Alex Tanguay .25 .60
63 Ed Belfour .30 .75
64 Derian Hatcher .08 .25
65 Brett Hull .40 1.00
66 Jamie Langenbrunner .08 .25
67 Jere Lehtinen .25 .60
68 Mike Modano .50 1.25
69 Joe Nieuwendyk .25 .60
70 Pavel Patera RC .08 .25
71 Yuri Butsayev RC .08 .25
72 Chris Chelios .30 .75
73 Sergei Fedorov .50 1.25
74 Vyacheslav Kozlov .08 .25
75 Nicklas Lidstrom .30 .75
76 Darren McCarty .08 .25
77 Chris Osgood .25 .60
78 Brendan Shanahan .30 .75
79 Steve Yzerman 1.50 4.00
80 Paul Comrie RC .25 .60
81 Mike Grier .08 .25
82 Tom Poti .08 .25
83 Bill Ranford .25 .60
84 Tommy Salo .25 .60
85 Ryan Smyth .08 .25
86 Doug Weight .25 .60
87 Pavel Bure .30 .75
88 Sean Burke .25 .60
89 Trevor Kidd .25 .60
90 Viktor Kozlov .08 .25
91 Ivan Novoseltsev RC .60 1.50
92 Mark Parrish .08 .25
93 Ray Whitney .08 .25
94 Jason Blake RC .25 .60
95 Rob Blake .25 .60
96 Stephane Fiset .25 .60
97 Zigmund Palffy .25 .60
98 Luc Robitaille .25 .60
99 Jozef Stumpel .25 .60
100 Shayne Corson .08 .25
101 Jeff Hackett .25 .60
102 Saku Koivu .30 .75
103 Trevor Linden .08 .25
104 Martin Rucinsky .08 .25
105 Brian Savage .08 .25
106 Mike Dunham .25 .60
107 Greg Johnson .08 .25
108 Sergei Krivokrasov .08 .25
109 David Legwand .25 .60
110 Ville Peltonen .08 .25
111 Cliff Ronning .08 .25
112 Scott Walker .08 .25
113 Jason Arnott .08 .25
114 Martin Brodeur .75 2.00
115 Patrik Elias .25 .60
116 Scott Gomez .08 .25
117 Bobby Holik .08 .25
118 Scott Niedermayer .08 .25
119 Brian Rafalski RC .60 1.50
120 Petr Sykora .08 .25
121 Mathieu Biron .25 .60
122 Tim Connolly .08 .25
123 Mariusz Czerkawski .08 .25
124 Olli Jokinen .25 .60
125 Jorgen Jonsson RC .08 .25
126 Kenny Jonsson .08 .25
127 Felix Potvin .30 .75
128 Theo Fleury .08 .25
129 Adam Graves .08 .25
130 Kim Johnsson RC .25 .60
131 Valeri Kamensky .25 .60
132 Brian Leetch .30 .75
133 Petr Nedved .25 .60
134 Mike Richter .30 .75
135 Mike York .08 .25
136 Daniel Alfredsson .25 .60
137 Magnus Arvedson .08 .25
138 Radek Bonk .08 .25
139 Marian Hossa .30 .75
140 Patrick Lalime .25 .60
141 Ron Tugnutt .25 .60
142 Alexei Yashin .08 .25
143 Rob Zamuner .08 .25
144 Brian Boucher .30 .75
145 Rod Brind'Amour .25 .60
146 Mark Eaton RC .30 .75
147 John LeClair .30 .75
148 Eric Lindros .30 .75
149 Mark Recchi .25 .60
150 John Vanbiesbrouck .25 .60
151 Travis Green .08 .25
152 Nikolai Khabibulin .25 .60
153 Jeremy Roenick .40 1.00
154 Mikhail Shtalenkov .25 .60
155 Keith Tkachuk .30 .75
156 Rick Tocchet .25 .60
157 Matthew Barnaby .08 .25
158 Tom Barrasso .25 .60
159 Jaromir Jagr .50 1.25
160 Alexei Kovalev .08 .25
161 Alexei Morozov .08 .25
162 Michal Rozsival RC .08 .25
163 Martin Straka .08 .25
164 German Titov .08 .25
165 Pavol Demitra .25 .60
166 Al MacInnis .25 .60
167 Chris Pronger .25 .60
168 Roman Turek .25 .60
169 Pierre Turgeon .25 .60
170 Scott Young .08 .25
171 Vincent Damphousse .08 .25
172 Jeff Friesen .08 .25
173 Patrick Marleau .30 .75
174 Owen Nolan .25 .60
175 Steve Shields .25 .60
176 Brad Stuart .25 .60
177 Niklas Sundstrom .08 .25
178 Mike Vernon .25 .60
179 Dan Cloutier .25 .60
180 Chris Gratton .08 .25
181 Vincent Lecavalier .30 .75
182 Fredrik Modin .08 .25
183 Darcy Tucker .08 .25
184 Nikolai Antropov RC .75 2.00
185 Sergei Berezin .08 .25
186 Tie Domi .25 .60
187 Jonas Hoglund .08 .25
188 Mike Johnson .08 .25
189 Curtis Joseph .30 .75
190 Mats Sundin .30 .75
191 Steve Thomas .08 .25
192 Andrew Cassels .08 .25
193 Artem Chubarov .08 .25
194 Mark Messier .30 .75
195 Alexander Mogilny .25 .60
196 Bill Muckalt .08 .25
197 Markus Naslund .30 .75
198 Kevin Weekes .25 .60
199 Peter Bondra .25 .60
200 Jan Bulis .08 .25
201 Jeff Halpern RC .75 2.00
202 Olaf Kolzig .25 .60
203 Adam Oates .25 .60
204 Chris Simon .08 .25
205 Alexander Volchkov RC .25 .60
206 Richard Zednik .08 .25
NNO Martin Brodeur SAMPLE 1.50 4.00

1999-00 Pacific Dynagon Ice Blue

*ICE BLUE 1-6: 2.5X TO 6X BASIC CARDS
*ICE BLUE 7-200: 15X TO 40X BASIC CARDS

1999-00 Pacific Dynagon Ice Copper

*COPPER 1-6: 1.5X TO 4X BASIC CARDS
*COPPER 7-200: 10X TO 25X BASIC CARDS

1999-00 Pacific Dynagon Ice Gold

*GOLD 1-6: .8X TO 2X BASIC SP
*GOLD 7-200: 4X TO 10X BASIC CARDS

1999-00 Pacific Dynagon Ice Premiere Date

*1-6 PREM.DATE: 2.5X TO 6X BASIC SP
*7-200 PREM.DATE: 15X TO 40X BASIC CARDS

1999-00 Pacific Dynagon Ice 2000 All-Star Preview

COMPLETE SET (20) 50.00 100.00
1 Paul Kariya 1.25 3.00
2 Teemu Selanne 1.25 3.00
3 Ray Bourque 2.00 5.00
4 Dominik Hasek 2.50 6.00
5 Patrick Roy 6.00 15.00
6 Joe Sakic 2.50 6.00
7 Nicklas Lidstrom 1.25 3.00
8 Steve Yzerman 6.00 15.00
9 Ed Belfour 1.25 3.00
10 Jere Lehtinen 1.00 2.50
11 Mike Modano 2.00 5.00
12 Pavel Bure 1.50 4.00
13 Martin Brodeur 3.00 8.00
14 John LeClair 1.50 4.00
15 Eric Lindros 2.00 5.00
16 Jaromir Jagr 2.00 5.00
17 Keith Tkachuk 1.25 3.00
18 Curtis Joseph 1.25 3.00
19 Mats Sundin 1.25 3.00
20 Peter Bondra 1.00 2.50

1999-00 Pacific Dynagon Ice Checkmates American

COMPLETE SET (30) 40.00 100.00
1 P.Kariya/S.Kariya .60 1.50
2 T.Selanne/B.Shanahan .60 1.50
3 P.Stefan/E.Lindros .60 1.50
4 T.Amonte/C.Pronger .60 1.50
5 C.Drury/P.Forsberg 3.00 8.00
6 J.Sakic/T.Fleury 2.50 6.00
7 S.Yzerman/C.Chelios 5.00 12.00
8 B.Hull/M.Peca 1.50 4.00
9 M.Modano/D.Hatcher 2.00 5.00
10 P.Bure/R.Bourque 1.50 4.00
11 Z.Palffy/K.Tkachuk 1.00 2.50
12 M.Hossa/J.LeClair 1.25 3.00
13 J.Jagr/M.Barnaby 2.00 5.00
14 P.Marleau/O.Nolan .60 1.50
15 M.Sundin/T.Domi 1.00 2.50
16 S.Kariya/P.Kariya .60 1.50
17 B.Shanahan/T.Selanne .60 1.50
18 E.Lindros/P.Stefan 1.25 3.00
19 C.Pronger/T.Amonte 1.00 2.50
20 P.Forsberg/C.Drury 3.00 8.00
21 T.Fleury/J.Sakic 2.50 6.00
22 C.Chelios/S.Yzerman 5.00 12.00
23 M.Peca/B.Hull 1.50 4.00
24 D.Hatcher/M.Modano 2.00 5.00
25 R.Bourque/P.Bure 1.50 4.00
26 K.Tkachuk/Z.Palffy 1.00 2.50
27 J.LeClair/M.Hossa 1.25 3.00
28 M.Barnaby/J.Jagr 2.00 5.00
29 O.Nolan/P.Marleau 1.25 3.00
30 T.Domi/M.Sundin 1.25 3.00

1999-00 Pacific Dynagon Ice Checkmates Canadian

COMPLETE SET (30) 40.00 80.00
1 Steve Kariya .60 1.50
2 Brendan Shanahan 2.00 5.00
3 Eric Lindros 2.00 5.00
4 Chris Pronger 1.00 2.50
5 Peter Forsberg 3.00 8.00
6 Theo Fleury .60 1.50
7 Chris Chelios 1.25 3.00
8 Michael Peca 1.00 2.50
9 Derian Hatcher .60 1.50
10 Ray Bourque 2.00 5.00
11 Keith Tkachuk 1.25 3.00
12 John LeClair 1.25 3.00
13 Matthew Barnaby .60 1.50
14 Owen Nolan 1.00 2.50
15 Tie Domi .60 1.50
16 Paul Kariya 1.25 3.00
17 Teemu Selanne 1.25 3.00
18 Patrik Stefan 1.00 2.50
19 Tony Amonte 1.00 2.50
20 Chris Drury 1.00 2.50
21 Joe Sakic 2.50 6.00
22 Steve Yzerman 5.00 12.00
23 Brett Hull 1.50 4.00
24 Mike Modano 2.00 5.00
25 Pavel Bure 1.50 4.00
26 Zigmund Palffy 1.00 2.50
27 Marian Hossa 1.25 3.00
28 Jaromir Jagr 2.00 5.00
29 Patrick Marleau 1.25 3.00
30 Mats Sundin 1.25 3.00

1999-00 Pacific Dynagon Ice Lamplighter Net-Fusions

COMPLETE SET (10) 40.00 80.00
1 Paul Kariya 2.50 6.00
2 Teemu Selanne 2.50 6.00
3 Patrik Stefan 2.00 5.00
4 Joe Sakic 5.00 12.00
5 Steve Yzerman 12.50 30.00
6 Pavel Bure 3.00 8.00
7 Theo Fleury 2.50 6.00
8 John LeClair 3.00 8.00
9 Eric Lindros 4.00 10.00
10 Jaromir Jagr 4.00 10.00

1999-00 Pacific Dynagon Ice Lords of the Rink

COMPLETE SET (10) 15.00 40.00
1 Paul Kariya 8.00 20.00
2 Teemu Selanne 10.00 25.00
3 Dominik Hasek 6.00 15.00
4 Peter Forsberg 8.00 20.00
5 Patrick Roy 15.00 40.00
6 Joe Sakic 8.00 20.00
7 Steve Yzerman 12.00 30.00
8 Martin Brodeur 10.00 25.00
9 Eric Lindros 6.00 15.00
10 Jaromir Jagr 6.00 15.00

1999-00 Pacific Dynagon Ice Masks

COMPLETE SET (10) 12.00 30.00
1 Patrick Roy 6.00 15.00
2 Martin Brodeur 5.00 12.00
3 Mike Richter 1.00 2.50
4 John Vanbiesbrouck 1.00 2.50
5 Curtis Joseph 1.00 2.50
6 Patrick Roy 6.00 15.00
7 Martin Brodeur 3.00 8.00
8 Mike Richter 1.00 2.50
9 John Vanbiesbrouck 1.00 2.50
10 Curtis Joseph 1.00 2.50

2002 Pacific Entry Draft

COMPLETE SET (10) 24.00 40.00
1 Ilya Kovalchuk 10.00 20.00
2 Erik Cole 3.20 5.00
3 Mark Bell 1.20 2.00
4 Marcel Hossa 2.00 3.00
5 Mike Ribeiro 1.20 2.00
6 Rick DiPietro 4.00 5.00
7 Raffi Torres 2.00 2.00
8 Dan Blackburn 4.00 5.00
9 Krys Kolanos 3.20 5.00
10 Jeff Jillson 2.00 3.00

2002-03 Pacific Exclusive

COMP.SET w/o SP's (175) 25.00 60.00
1 Jean-Sebastien Giguere .30 .75
2 Paul Kariya .30 .75
3 Adam Oates .30 .75
4 Petr Sykora .25 .60
5 Dany Heatley .25 .60
6 Milan Hnilicka .25 .60
7 Tomi Kallio .20 .50
8 Ilya Kovalchuk .40 1.00
9 Patrik Stefan .25 .60
10 Nick Boynton .20 .50
11 Glen Murray .25 .60
12 Brian Rolston .25 .60
13 Sergei Samsonov .25 .60
14 Steve Shields .25 .60
15 Joe Thornton .50 1.25
16 Martin Biron .25 .60
17 Tim Connolly .20 .50
18 J-P Dumont .20 .50
19 Mika Noronen .25 .60
20 Miroslav Satan .30 .75
21 Craig Conroy .20 .50
22 Chris Drury .30 .75
23 Jarome Iginla .40 1.00
24 Roman Turek .30 .75
25 Bates Battaglia .20 .50
26 Rod Brind'Amour .30 .75
27 Erik Cole .20 .50
28 Ron Francis .40 1.00
29 Arturs Irbe .25 .60
30 Sami Kapanen .20 .50
31 Jeff O'Neill .20 .50
32 Jaroslav Svoboda .20 .50
33 Josef Vasicek .20 .50
34 Mark Bell .20 .50
35 Eric Daze .20 .50
36 Theo Fleury .40 1.00
37 Jocelyn Thibault .25 .60
38 Alexei Zhamnov .25 .60
39 Rob Blake .30 .75
40 Peter Forsberg .60 1.50
41 Milan Hejduk .25 .60
42 Dean McAmmond .20 .50
43 Derek Morris .20 .50
44 Steven Reinprecht .20 .50
45 Patrick Roy .75 2.00
46 Joe Sakic .60 1.50
47 Alex Tanguay .25 .60
48 Radim Vrbata .20 .50
49 Andrew Cassels .20 .50
50 Marc Denis .25 .60
51 Rostislav Klesla .20 .50
52 Espen Knutsen .20 .50
53 Ray Whitney .25 .60
54 Jason Arnott .25 .60
55 Bill Guerin .30 .75
56 Jere Lehtinen .30 .75
57 Mike Modano .50 1.25
58 Marty Turco .30 .75
59 Pierre Turgeon .25 .60
60 Chris Chelios .30 .75
61 Pavel Datsyuk .50 1.25
62 Sergei Fedorov .50 1.25
63 Brett Hull .60 1.50
64 Curtis Joseph .40 1.00
65 Nicklas Lidstrom .30 .75
66 Luc Robitaille .30 .75
67 Brendan Shanahan .30 .75
68 Steve Yzerman .75 2.00
69 Anson Carter .25 .60
70 Mike Comrie .30 .75
71 Tommy Salo .25 .60
72 Jason Smith .20 .50
73 Ryan Smyth .25 .60
74 Mike York .20 .50
75 Valeri Bure .25 .60
76 Kristian Huselius .20 .50
77 Roberto Luongo .50 1.25
78 Stephen Weiss .30 .75
79 Jason Allison .25 .60
80 Adam Deadmarsh .20 .50
81 Zigmund Palffy .30 .75
82 Felix Potvin .50 1.25
83 Bryan Smolinski .25 .60
84 Andrew Brunette .20 .50
85 Pascal Dupuis .20 .50
86 Manny Fernandez .20 .50
87 Marian Gaborik .30 .75
88 Cliff Ronning .20 .50
89 Mariusz Czerkawski .20 .50
90 Marcel Hossa .20 .50
91 Saku Koivu .30 .75
92 Yanic Perreault .20 .50
93 Oleg Petrov .20 .50
94 Jose Theodore .30 .75
95 Richard Zednik .20 .50
96 Denis Arkhipov .20 .50
97 Mike Dunham .25 .60
98 Scott Hartnell .20 .50
99 Greg Johnson .20 .50
100 David Legwand .25 .60
101 Christian Berglund .20 .50
102 Martin Brodeur .75 2.00
103 Patrik Elias .30 .75
104 Jeff Friesen .20 .50
105 Joe Nieuwendyk .25 .60
106 Rick DiPietro .25 .60
107 Brad Isbister .20 .50
108 Chris Osgood .30 .75
109 Mark Parrish .20 .50
110 Michael Peca .25 .60
111 Alexei Yashin .25 .60
112 Dan Blackburn .25 .60
113 Pavel Bure .30 .75
114 Bobby Holik .20 .50
115 Brian Leetch .25 .60
116 Eric Lindros .50 1.25
117 Mark Messier .60 1.50
118 Mike Richter .30 .75
119 Daniel Alfredsson .30 .75
120 Radek Bonk .25 .60
121 Martin Havlat .25 .60
122 Marian Hossa .30 .75
123 Patrick Lalime .25 .60
124 Pavel Brendl .20 .50
125 Roman Cechmanek .25 .60
126 Simon Gagne .30 .75
127 John LeClair .30 .75
128 Mark Recchi .40 1.00
129 Jeremy Roenick .50 1.25
130 Tony Amonte .25 .60
131 Brian Boucher .25 .60
132 Daniel Briere .25 .60
133 Sean Burke .20 .50
134 Krystofer Kolanos .20 .50
135 Daymond Langkow .25 .60
136 Johan Hedberg .30 .75
137 Alexei Kovalev .25 .60
138 Mario Lemieux 1.25 3.00
139 Alexei Morozov .20 .50
140 Martin Straka .25 .60
141 Pavol Demitra .40 1.00
142 Barret Jackman .20 .50
143 Brent Johnson .25 .60
144 Al MacInnis .40 1.00
145 Chris Pronger .30 .75
146 Keith Tkachuk .30 .75
147 Doug Weight .30 .75
148 Vincent Damphousse .25 .60
149 Patrick Marleau .30 .75
150 Evgeni Nabokov .25 .60
151 Owen Nolan .30 .75
152 Teemu Selanne .60 1.50
153 Scott Thornton .20 .50
154 Dave Andreychuk .30 .75
155 Nikolai Khabibulin .30 .75
156 Vincent Lecavalier .30 .75
157 Brad Richards .30 .75
158 Shane Willis .20 .50
159 Ed Belfour .30 .75
160 Alyn McCauley .20 .50
161 Alexander Mogilny .25 .60
162 Gary Roberts .20 .50
163 Mats Sundin .30 .75
164 Darcy Tucker .20 .50
165 Todd Bertuzzi .30 .75
166 Dan Cloutier .25 .60
167 Ed Jovanovski .25 .60
168 Brendan Morrison .25 .60
169 Markus Naslund .30 .75
170 Peter Bondra .30 .75
171 Sergei Gonchar .25 .60
172 Jaromir Jagr 1.00 2.50
173 Olaf Kolzig .30 .75
174 Robert Lang .20 .50
175 Dainius Zubrus .20 .50
176 Martin Gerber RC 1.50 4.00
177 Dmitri Bykov RC 1.00 2.50
178 Ales Hemsky RC 4.00 10.00
179A Alex Henry RC 1.25 3.00
179B Jason Spezza RC 6.00 15.00
180 P-M Bouchard RC 1.50 4.00
181 Ron Hainsey RC 1.00 2.50
182 Adam Hall RC 1.00 2.50
183 Scottie Upshall RC 1.25 3.00
184 Mike Danton .20 .50
185 Jamie Lundmark .25 .60
186 Anton Volchenkov RC 1.00 2.50
187 Dennis Seidenberg RC 1.50 4.00
188 Patrick Sharp RC 3.00 8.00
189 Petr Cajanek .20 .50
190 Jonathan Cheechoo .25 .60
191 Fedor Fedorov .20 .50
192 Steve Eminger RC 1.00 2.50
193 Stanislav Chistov AU RC 2.50 6.00
194 Alexei Smirnov AU RC 3.00 8.00
195 Chuck Kobasew AU RC 3.00 8.00
196 Rick Nash AU RC 15.00 30.00
197 Henrik Zetterberg AU RC 15.00 40.00
198 Jay Bouwmeester AU RC 8.00 20.00
199 Alexander Frolov AU RC 6.00 15.00
200 Alexander Svitov AU RC 2.50 6.00

2002-03 Pacific Exclusive Blue

*BLUE/699: 1.5X TO 4X BASIC CARDS
*BLUE/699: .3X TO .8X BASIC RC

2002-03 Pacific Exclusive Gold

*VETS: 1X TO 2.5X BASIC CARDS
*ROOKIE SP's: .2X TO .5X BASIC RC
117 Mark Messier 1.50 4.00
193 Stanislav Chistov .50 1.25
194 Alexei Smirnov .60 1.50
195 Chuck Kobasew .60 1.50
196 Rick Nash 3.00 8.00
197 Henrik Zetterberg 5.00 12.00
198 Jay Bouwmeester 1.50 4.00
199 Alexander Frolov 1.25 3.00
200 Alexander Svitov .50 1.25

2002-03 Pacific Exclusive Retail

193 Stanislav Chistov RC .75 2.00
194 Alexei Smirnov RC 1.00 2.50
195 Chuck Kobasew RC 1.00 2.50
196 Rick Nash RC 5.00 12.00
197 Henrik Zetterberg RC 8.00 20.00
198 Jay Bouwmeester RC 2.50 6.00
199 Alexander Frolov RC 2.00 5.00
200 Alexander Svitov RC .75 2.00

2002-03 Pacific Exclusive Advantage

COMPLETE SET (15) 8.00 20.00
1 Jean-Sebastien Giguere .50 1.25
2 Roman Turek .50 1.25
3 Arturs Irbe .50 1.25
4 Patrick Roy 2.00 5.00
5 Marc Denis .50 1.25
6 Marty Turco .50 1.25
7 Curtis Joseph .60 1.50
8 Roberto Luongo 1.00 2.50
9 Felix Potvin .60 1.50
10 Jose Theodore .75 2.00
11 Martin Brodeur 1.50 4.00
12 Mike Richter .60 1.50
13 Brent Johnson .50 1.25
14 Evgeni Nabokov .50 1.25
15 Ed Belfour .60 1.50

2002-03 Pacific Exclusive Destined

COMPLETE SET (10) 6.00 15.00
1 Stanislav Chistov .60 1.50
2 Dany Heatley 1.25 3.00
3 Ilya Kovalchuk 1.50 4.00
4 Ivan Huml .60 1.50
5 Rick Nash 2.00 5.00
6 Pavel Datsyuk 1.50 3.50
7 Kristian Huselius .60 1.50
8 Stephen Weiss .75 2.00
9 Jamie Lundmark .60 1.50
10 Jonathan Cheechoo 1.25 3.00

2002-03 Pacific Exclusive Etched in Stone

COMPLETE SET (10) 12.00 30.00
1 Paul Kariya .75 2.00
2 Ron Francis .75 2.00
3 Patrick Roy 4.00 10.00
4 Joe Sakic 2.00 5.00
5 Brett Hull 1.25 3.00
6 Steve Yzerman 5.00 12.00
7 Martin Brodeur 3.00 8.00
8 Eric Lindros .75 2.00
9 Mario Lemieux 5.00 12.00
10 Jaromir Jagr 1.50 4.00

2002-03 Pacific Exclusive Great Expectations

COMPLETE SET (15) 12.50 25.00
1 Dany Heatley 1.25 3.00
2 Ilya Kovalchuk 1.25 3.00
3 Ivan Huml .75 2.00
4 Erik Cole .75 2.00
5 Radim Vrbata .75 2.00
6 Pavel Datsyuk 1.00 2.50
7 Mike Comrie .75 2.00
8 Kristian Huselius .75 2.00
9 Stephen Weiss .75 2.00
10 Marian Gaborik 1.50 4.00
11 Marcel Hossa .75 2.00
12 Rick DiPietro 1.00 2.50
13 Dan Blackburn .75 2.00
14 Krystofer Kolanos .75 2.00
15 Barret Jackman .75 2.00

2002-03 Pacific Exclusive Jerseys

COMMON CARD (1-25) 3.00 8.00
*GOLD/25: .8X TO 2X BASIC JERSEY
1 Tomi Kallio 3.00 8.00
2 Joe Thornton 8.00 20.00
3 Miroslav Satan 4.00 10.00
4 Theo Fleury 3.00 8.00
5 Milan Hejduk 5.00 12.00
6 Pierre Turgeon 4.00 10.00
7 Sergei Fedorov 8.00 20.00
8 Nicklas Lidstrom 5.00 12.00
9 Tommy Salo 4.00 10.00
10 Kristian Huselius 3.00 8.00
11 Roberto Luongo 8.00 20.00
12 Bryan Smolinski 3.00 8.00
13 Manny Fernandez 4.00 10.00
14 Mariusz Czerkawski 3.00 8.00
15 David Legwand 4.00 10.00
16 Bobby Holik 3.00 8.00
17 Eric Lindros 5.00 12.00
18 Marian Hossa 5.00 12.00
19 Michal Handzus 3.00 8.00
20 Alexei Kovalev 4.00 10.00
21 Keith Tkachuk 5.00 12.00
22 Patrick Marleau 4.00 10.00
23 Brad Richards 5.00 12.00
24 Mats Sundin 5.00 12.00
25 Olaf Kolzig 4.00 10.00

2002-03 Pacific Exclusive Maximum Overdrive

COMPLETE SET (20) 15.00 30.00
1 Paul Kariya .40 1.00
2 Dany Heatley .50 1.25
3 Ilya Kovalchuk .50 1.25
4 Joe Thornton .60 1.50
5 Jarome Iginla .60 1.50
6 Peter Forsberg 1.00 2.50
7 Joe Sakic .75 2.00
8 Mike Modano .60 1.50
9 Sergei Fedorov .75 2.00
10 Steve Yzerman 2.00 5.00
11 Saku Koivu .40 1.00
12 Patrik Elias .40 1.00
13 Alexei Yashin .40 1.00
14 Pavel Bure .40 1.00
15 Simon Gagne .40 1.00
16 Mario Lemieux 2.50 6.00
17 Teemu Selanne .40 1.00
18 Mats Sundin .40 1.00
19 Markus Naslund .40 1.00
20 Jaromir Jagr .60 1.50

2003-04 Pacific Exhibit

COMP.SET w/o SP's (150) 25.00 60.00
COMP.SET w/o JSYS (200) 25.00 60.00
1 Stanislav Chistov .15 .40
2 Mike Leclerc .15 .40
3 Adam Oates .25 .60
4 Sandis Ozolinsh .15 .40
5 Vaclav Prospal .15 .40
6 Steve Rucchin .15 .40
7 Steve Thomas .15 .40
8 Byron Dafoe .20 .50
9 Joe DiPenta RC .20 .50
10 Slava Kozlov .20 .50
11 Patrik Stefan .15 .40
12 Bryan Berard .20 .50
13 Mike Knuble .15 .40
14 Glen Murray .20 .50
15 Brian Rolston .20 .50
16 Milan Bartovic RC .20 .50
17 Daniel Briere .25 .60
18 Chris Drury .20 .50
19 J-P Dumont .15 .40
20 Ales Kotalik .15 .40
21 Ryan Miller .25 .60
22 Miroslav Satan .20 .50
23 Craig Conroy .15 .40
24 Martin Gelinas .15 .40
25 Roman Turek .20 .50
26 Rod Brind'Amour .25 .60
27 Erik Cole .15 .40
28 Arturs Irbe .20 .50
29 Jeff O'Neill .15 .40
30 Tyler Arnason .15 .40
31 Kyle Calder .15 .40
32 Eric Daze .20 .50
33 Theoren Fleury .30 .75
34 Alexei Zhamnov .20 .50
35 David Aebischer .20 .50
36 Rob Blake .25 .60
37 Milan Hejduk .20 .50
38 Derek Morris .15 .40
39 Teemu Selanne .50 1.25
40 Alex Tanguay .20 .50
41 Andrew Cassels .15 .40
42 Marc Denis .20 .50
43 Kent McDonell RC .20 .50
44 Geoff Sanderson .15 .40
45 Ray Whitney .20 .50
46 Jason Arnott .20 .50
47 Bill Guerin .25 .60
48 Jere Lehtinen .20 .50
49 Brenden Morrow .20 .50
50 Teppo Numminen .15 .40
51 Chris Chelios .25 .60
52 Pavel Datsyuk .40 1.00
53 Derian Hatcher .15 .40
54 Nicklas Lidstrom .25 .60
55 Brendan Shanahan .25 .60
56 Henrik Zetterberg .30 .75
57 Mike Comrie .20 .50
58 Ales Hemsky .25 .60
59 Georges Laraque .20 .50
60 Tommy Salo .20 .50
61 Mike York .15 .40
62 Jay Bouwmeester .15 .40
63 Kristian Huselius .15 .40

64 Olli Jokinen .25 .60
65 Stephen Weiss .15 .40
66 Jason Allison .20 .50
67 Roman Cechmanek .20 .50
68 Adam Deadmarsh .15 .40
69 Alexander Frolov .20 .50
70 Felix Potvin .40 1.00
71 Andrew Brunette .15 .40
72 Manny Fernandez .15 .40
73 Filip Kuba .15 .40
74 Dwayne Roloson .20 .50
75 Cliff Ronning .15 .40
76 Mathieu Garon .15 .40
77 Marcel Hossa .15 .40
78 Yanic Perreault .15 .40
79 Richard Zednik .15 .40
80 Scott Hartnell .15 .40
81 Andreas Johansson .15 .40
82 Tomas Vokoun .20 .50
83 Scott Walker .15 .40
84 Patrik Elias .25 .60
85 Jeff Friesen .15 .40
86 Scott Gomez .20 .50
87 Jamie Langenbrunner .20 .50
88 John Madden .15 .40
89 Joe Nieuwendyk .20 .50
90 Scott Stevens .25 .60
91 Jason Blake .15 .40
92 Rick DiPietro .20 .50
93 Roman Hamrlik .15 .40
94 Mark Parrish .15 .40
95 Dan Blackburn .20 .50
96 Anson Carter .20 .50
97 Mike Dunham .20 .50
98 Bobby Holik .15 .40
99 Alex Kovalev .20 .50
100 Tom Poti .15 .40
101 Daniel Alfredsson .25 .60
102 Zdeno Chara .25 .60
103 Mike Fisher .15 .40
104 Martin Havlat .25 .60
105 Bryan Smolinski .15 .40
106 Jason Spezza .25 .60
107 Todd White .15 .40
108 Tony Amonte .20 .50
109 Simon Gagne .25 .60
110 Jeff Hackett .20 .50
111 Keith Primeau .20 .50
112 Mark Recchi .30 .75
113 Shane Doan .20 .50
114 Chris Gratton .15 .40
115 Mike Johnson .15 .40
116 Daymond Langkow .15 .40
117 Johan Hedberg .20 .50
118 Aleksey Morozov .15 .40
119 Martin Straka .15 .40
120 Dick Tarnstrom .15 .40
121 Pavol Demitra .30 .75
122 Al MacInnis .30 .75
123 Chris Pronger .25 .60
124 Peter Sejna RC .20 .50
125 Keith Tkachuk .25 .60
126 Doug Weight .25 .60
127 Jonathan Cheechoo .20 .50
128 Vincent Damphousse .20 .50
129 Patrick Marleau .25 .60
130 Dave Andreychuk .25 .60
131 John Grahame .15 .40
132 Brad Richards .25 .60
133 Martin St. Louis .25 .60
134 Nik Antropov .20 .50
135 Tie Domi .20 .50
136 Doug Gilmour .30 .75
137 Alexander Mogilny .20 .50
138 Matt Stajan RC .25 .60
139 Darcy Tucker .20 .50
140 Dan Cloutier .20 .50
141 Ed Jovanovski .20 .50
142 Trevor Linden .25 .60
143 Brendan Morrison .20 .50
144 Daniel Sedin .30 .75
145 Henrik Sedin .30 .75
146 Sergei Berezin .15 .40
147 Peter Bondra .25 .60
148 Sebastien Charpentier .15 .40
149 Sergei Gonchar .15 .40
150 Michael Nylander .15 .40
151 Sergei Fedorov .75 2.00
152 Jean-Sebastien Giguere .50 1.25
153 Dany Heatley .40 1.00
154 Ilya Kovalchuk .50 1.25
155 Joe Thornton .75 2.00
156 Martin Biron .40 1.00
157 Jarome Iginla .60 1.50
158 Ron Francis .60 1.50
159 Jocelyn Thibault .40 1.00
160 Peter Forsberg 1.00 2.50
161 Paul Kariya .50 1.25
162 Patrick Roy 1.25 3.00
163 Joe Sakic 1.00 2.50
164 Rick Nash .50 1.25
165 Mike Modano .75 2.00
166 Marty Turco .50 1.25
167 Dominik Hasek .75 2.00
168 Brett Hull 1.00 2.50
169 Steve Yzerman 1.25 3.00
170 Ryan Smyth .40 1.00
171 Roberto Luongo .75 2.00
172 Ziggy Palffy .50 1.25
173 Marian Gaborik .50 1.25
174 Saku Koivu .50 1.25
175 Jose Theodore .50 1.25
176 David Legwand .40 1.00
177 Martin Brodeur 1.25 3.00
178 Michael Peca .40 1.00
179 Alexei Yashin .40 1.00
180 Pavel Bure .50 1.25
181 Eric Lindros .75 2.00
182 Mark Messier 1.00 2.50
183 Marian Hossa .50 1.25
184 Patrick Lalime .40 1.00
185 John LeClair .50 1.25
186 Jeremy Roenick .75 2.00
187 Sean Burke .30 .75
188 Mario Lemieux 2.00 5.00
189 Barret Jackman .30 .75
190 Chris Osgood .50 1.25
191 Evgeni Nabokov .40 1.00
192 Nikolai Khabibulin .50 1.25
193 Vincent Lecavalier .50 1.25
194 Ed Belfour .50 1.25
195 Owen Nolan .50 1.25
196 Mats Sundin .50 1.25
197 Todd Bertuzzi .50 1.25
198 Markus Naslund .50 1.25
199 Jaromir Jagr 1.50 4.00
200 Olaf Kolzig .50 1.25
201 Stanislav Chistov JSY 4.00 10.00
202 Martin Biron JSY 5.00 12.00
203 Eric Daze JSY 5.00 12.00
204 Milan Hejduk JSY 5.00 12.00
205 Bill Guerin JSY 6.00 15.00
206 Marty Turco JSY 6.00 15.00
207 Jason Allison JSY 5.00 12.00
208 Roman Cechmanek JSY 5.00 12.00
209 David Legwand JSY 5.00 12.00
210 Patrick Lalime JSY 5.00 12.00
211 Tony Amonte JSY 5.00 12.00
212 Jeff Hackett JSY 5.00 12.00
213 Sean Burke JSY 4.00 10.00
214 Chris Osgood JSY 6.00 15.00
215 Nikolai Khabibulin JSY 6.00 15.00
216 B.Hull JSY/B.Hull AU 12.00 30.00
217 Yzerman JSY/T.Espo AU 12.50 30.00
218 P.Roy JSY/Beliveau AU 30.00 60.00
219 Kovalchuk JSY/Lafleur AU 12.50 30.00
220 Heatley JSY/G.Hall AU 15.00 30.00
221 Lemieux JSY/J.Bower AU 15.00 40.00
222 Theodore JSY/Sittler AU 10.00 25.00
223 P.Kariya JSY/M.Dionne AU 10.00 25.00
224 Brodeur JSY/Mahovlich AU 20.00 50.00
225 J.Sakic JSY/B.Park AU 15.00 30.00
226 Joffrey Lupul RC 2.00 5.00
227 Patrice Bergeron RC 4.00 10.00
228 Matthew Lombardi RC 1.00 2.50
229 Eric Staal RC 4.00 10.00
230 Nikolai Zherdev RC 1.50 4.00
231 Nathan Horton RC 2.00 5.00
232 Brent Burns RC 2.50 6.00
233 Joni Pitkanen RC 1.25 3.00
234 Marc-Andre Fleury RC 6.00 15.00
235 Ryan Malone RC 1.50 4.00

2003-04 Pacific Exhibit Blue Backs

*1-150 BLUE/275: 2X TO 5X BASIC CARDS
*151-200 BLUE/425: 1X TO 2.5X BASIC CARDS

2003-04 Pacific Exhibit Yellow Backs

*YELLOW BACK: .6X TO 1.5X BASIC CARDS

2003-04 Pacific Exhibit History Makers

COMPLETE SET (8) 12.50 25.00
1 Paul Kariya .60 1.50
2 Peter Forsberg 1.50 4.00
3 Joe Sakic 1.25 3.00
4 Brett Hull .75 2.00
5 Steve Yzerman 2.50 6.00
6 Mario Lemieux 3.00 8.00
7 Todd Bertuzzi .60 1.50
8 Markus Naslund .60 1.50

2003-04 Pacific Exhibit Pursuing Prominence

COMPLETE SET (12) 8.00 15.00
1 Dany Heatley 1.00 2.50
2 Ilya Kovalchuk 1.00 2.50
3 Joe Thornton 1.00 2.50
4 Rick Nash 1.25 3.00
5 Henrik Zetterberg 1.25 3.00
6 Ales Hemsky .50 1.25
7 Jay Bouwmeester .50 1.25
8 Marian Gaborik 1.25 3.00
9 Marian Hossa .50 1.25
10 Jason Spezza 1.25 3.00
11 Barret Jackman .50 1.25
12 Vincent Lecavalier .50 1.25

2003-04 Pacific Exhibit Standing on Tradition

COMPLETE SET (10) 10.00 20.00
1 Jean-Sebastien Giguere .60 1.50
2 Jocelyn Thibault .60 1.50
3 Patrick Roy 2.50 6.00
4 Marty Turco .60 1.50
5 Dominik Hasek 1.50 4.00
6 Roberto Luongo 1.00 2.50
7 Jose Theodore .75 2.00
8 Martin Brodeur 2.00 5.00
9 Patrick Lalime .60 1.50
10 Ed Belfour .75 2.00

2001-02 Pacific Heads Up

1 Paul Kariya .25 .60
2 Steve Shields .20 .50
3 Ray Ferraro .15 .40
4 Milan Hnilicka .20 .50
5 Patrik Stefan .20 .50
6 Jason Allison .20 .50
7 Byron Dafoe .20 .50
8 Bill Guerin .25 .60
9 Sergei Samsonov .20 .50
10 Joe Thornton .40 1.00
11 J-P Dumont .15 .40
12 Jarome Iginla .30 .75
13 Marc Savard .15 .40
14 Roman Turek .20 .50
15 Ron Francis .30 .75
16 Arturs Irbe .20 .50
17 Jeff O'Neill .20 .50
18 Tony Amonte .20 .50
19 Steve Sullivan .15 .40
20 Jocelyn Thibault .20 .50
21 Rob Blake .25 .60
22 Chris Drury .20 .50
23 Peter Forsberg .50 1.25
24 Milan Hejduk .20 .50
25 Patrick Roy .60 1.50
26 Joe Sakic .50 1.25
27 Marc Denis .20 .50
28 Geoff Sanderson .15 .40
29 Ed Belfour .25 .60
30 Brett Hull .50 1.25
31 Mike Modano .40 1.00
32 Joe Nieuwendyk .20 .50
33 Pierre Turgeon .20 .50
34 Sergei Fedorov .40 1.00
35 Dominik Hasek .40 1.00
36 Chris Osgood .25 .60
37 Luc Robitaille .25 .60
38 Brendan Shanahan .25 .60
39 Steve Yzerman .60 1.50
40 Mike Comrie .20 .50
41 Tommy Salo .20 .50
42 Ryan Smyth .20 .50
43 Pavel Bure .25 .60
44 Roberto Luongo .40 1.00
45 Steve Heinze .15 .40
46 Zigmund Palffy .25 .60
47 Felix Potvin .40 1.00
48 Manny Fernandez .15 .40
49 Marian Gaborik .25 .60
50 Saku Koivu .25 .60
51 Brian Savage .15 .40
52 Jose Theodore .25 .60
53 Mike Dunham .20 .50
54 David Legwand .20 .50
55 Jason Arnott .20 .50
56 Martin Brodeur .60 1.50
57 Patrik Elias .25 .60
58 Scott Stevens .25 .60
59 Mariusz Czerkawski .15 .40
60 Rick DiPietro .20 .50
61 Mike Peca .20 .50
62 Alexei Yashin .20 .50
63 Theo Fleury .30 .75
64 Brian Leetch .20 .50
65 Mark Messier .50 1.25
66 Mike Richter .25 .60
67 Daniel Alfredsson .25 .60
68 Martin Havlat .20 .50
69 Marian Hossa .25 .60
70 Patrick Lalime .20 .50
71 Roman Cechmanek .20 .50
72 John LeClair .25 .60
73 Mark Recchi .30 .75
74 Jeremy Roenick .40 1.00
75 Sean Burke .15 .40
76 Johan Hedberg .20 .50
77 Alexei Kovalev .20 .50
78 Mario Lemieux 1.00 2.50
79 Fred Brathwaite .20 .50
80 Chris Pronger .25 .60
81 Keith Tkachuk .25 .60
82 Doug Weight .25 .60
83 Patrick Marleau .25 .60
84 Evgeni Nabokov .20 .50
85 Teemu Selanne .50 1.25
86 Nikolai Khabibulin .25 .60
87 Vincent Lecavalier .25 .60
88 Brad Richards .25 .60
89 Curtis Joseph .30 .75
90 Alexander Mogilny .20 .50
91 Gary Roberts .15 .40
92 Mats Sundin .25 .60
93 Dan Cloutier .20 .50
94 Markus Naslund .25 .60
95 Daniel Sedin .30 .75
96 Henrik Sedin .30 .75
97 Peter Bondra .25 .60
98 Jaromir Jagr .75 2.00
99 Olaf Kolzig .25 .60
100 Adam Oates .25 .60
101 Ilja Bryzgalov RC 3.00 8.00
102 Timo Parssinen RC 1.50 4.00
103 Ilya Kovalchuk RC 10.00 25.00
104 Erik Cole RC 2.50 6.00
105 Vaclav Nedorost RC 1.25 3.00
106 Pavel Datsyuk RC 20.00 50.00
107 Kristian Huselius RC 2.00 5.00
108 Jaroslav Bednar RC 1.25 3.00
109 Pascal Dupuis RC 2.00 5.00
110 Martin Erat RC 1.50 4.00
111 Scott Clemmensen RC 1.25 3.00
112 Dan Blackburn RC 1.50 4.00
113 Chris Neil RC 1.50 4.00
114 Pavel Brendl SP 1.25 3.00
115 Jiri Dopita RC 1.25 3.00
116 Krystofer Kolanos RC 1.25 3.00
117 Mark Rycroft RC 1.50 4.00
118 Jeff Jillson RC 1.25 3.00
119 Nikita Alexeev RC 1.25 3.00
120 Brian Sutherby RC 1.25 3.00

2001-02 Pacific Heads Up Blue

*BLUE/55: 8X TO 20X BASIC CARDS

2001-02 Pacific Heads Up Premiere Date

*PREM.DATE/105: 5X TO 12X BASIC CARDS
65 Mark Messier 8.00 20.00

2001-02 Pacific Heads Up Red

*RED/165: 4X TO 10X BASIC CARDS
65 Mark Messier 6.00 15.00

2001-02 Pacific Heads Up Silver

*SILVER/27: 12X TO 30X BASIC CARDS
65 Mark Messier 20.00 50.00

2001-02 Pacific Heads Up All-Star Net

1 Nabokov/Cechmanek 20.00 50.00
2 M.Brodeur/R.Blake 25.00 60.00
3 B.Guerin/D.Weight 20.00 50.00
4 P.Bure/Z.Palffy 12.00 30.00
5 P.Kariya/M.Sundin 10.00 25.00
6 C.Pronger/N.Lidstrom 12.00 30.00

2001-02 Pacific Heads Up Bobble Heads

1 Paul Kariya 12.50 30.00
2 Patrick Roy 15.00 40.00
3 Joe Sakic 12.50 30.00
4 Dominik Hasek 12.50 30.00
5 Steve Yzerman 15.00 40.00
7 Martin Brodeur 15.00 40.00
8 Mark Messier 12.50 30.00
9 Johan Hedberg 12.50 30.00
10 Mario Lemieux 20.00 50.00
11 Curtis Joseph 12.50 30.00
12 Jaromir Jagr 12.50 30.00

2001-02 Pacific Heads Up Breaking the Glass

COMPLETE SET (20) 30.00 60.00
1 Milan Hnilicka 1.25 3.00
2 Patrik Stefan 1.25 3.00
3 J-P Dumont 1.25 3.00
4 Shane Willis 1.25 3.00
5 David Aebischer 1.25 3.00
6 Chris Drury 1.25 3.00
7 Alex Tanguay 2.00 5.00
8 Marc Denis 1.25 3.00
9 Marty Turco 1.25 3.00
10 Mike Comrie 1.25 3.00
11 Roberto Luongo 1.50 4.00
12 Marian Gaborik 3.00 8.00
13 David Legwand 1.25 3.00
14 Rick DiPietro 1.25 3.00
15 Martin Havlat 1.25 3.00
16 Johan Hedberg 1.25 3.00
17 Evgeni Nabokov 1.25 3.00
18 Brad Richards 1.25 3.00
19 Daniel Sedin 2.00 5.00
20 Henrik Sedin 2.00 5.00

2001-02 Pacific Heads Up HD NHL

COMPLETE SET (20) 8.00 20.00
1 Paul Kariya .75 2.00
2 Peter Forsberg 2.00 5.00
3 Joe Sakic 1.50 4.00
4 Mike Modano 1.25 3.00
5 Steve Yzerman 4.00 10.00
6 Pavel Bure 1.00 2.50
7 Mario Lemieux 5.00 12.00
8 Teemu Selanne .75 2.00
9 Mats Sundin .75 2.00
10 Jaromir Jagr 1.25 3.00
11 Roman Turek .60 1.50
12 Ed Belfour .75 2.00
13 Chris Osgood .60 1.50
14 Tommy Salo .60 1.50
15 Felix Potvin .75 2.00
16 Jose Theodore 1.00 2.50
17 Martin Brodeur 2.00 5.00
18 Mike Richter .75 2.00
19 Roman Cechmanek .60 1.50
20 Curtis Joseph .75 2.00

2001-02 Pacific Heads Up Prime Picks

COMPLETE SET (10) 15.00 40.00
1 Mike Comrie 1.50 4.00
2 Roberto Luongo 4.00 10.00
3 Marian Gaborik 4.00 10.00
4 Rick DiPietro 1.50 4.00
5 Martin Havlat 1.50 4.00
6 Johan Hedberg 1.50 4.00
7 Evgeni Nabokov 1.50 4.00
8 Brad Richards 2.00 5.00
9 Daniel Sedin 2.50 6.00
10 Henrik Sedin 2.50 6.00

2001-02 Pacific Heads Up Quad Jerseys

1 Gig/Leclerc/Selanne/Hebert 6.00 15.00
2 Thorn/Sams/McLaren/Dafoe 8.00 20.00
3 Niedmyr/Holik/Axels/Sween 8.00 20.00
4 Hasek/Barnes/Czer/Jonsson 6.00 15.00
5 Iginla/V.Bure/Savard/Fata 6.00 15.00
6 Amonte/Daze/Thibault/Calder 6.00 15.00
7 Gig/Leclerc/Selanne/Hebert 6.00 15.00
8 Forsbrg/Sakic/Miller/Reid 10.00 25.00
9 Roy/Dingman/deVries/Klemm 8.00 20.00
10 Modano/Nieuw/Sydor/Hatch 6.00 15.00
11 Shan/Chelios/Dandnlt/Osgd 8.00 20.00
12 Brunet/Zholtok/Zubrus/Dahlen 6.00 15.00
13 Dunham/Legwnd/Fitz/Walker 6.00 15.00
14 Fleury/Leetch/Richtr/Nodvd 6.00 15.00
15 LeClair/Desjdns/Stevns/Millr 6.00 15.00
16 Roenick/Burke/Alatalo/Doan 6.00 15.00
17 Lemieux/Jagr/Hrdina/Kaspts 15.00 40.00
18 Straka/Kov/Aubin/Parent 6.00 15.00
19 Domi/Healy/Alfron/Cloutier 6.00 15.00
20 Roy/Jos./Hasek/Richter 20.00 50.00
21 Lemieux/Sakic/Moda./Bure 30.00 80.00
22 Weight/Cheli./Hatch./Ltch. 10.00 25.00
23 Zhitnik/Rasmsn/Ray/Smehlik 6.00 15.00
24 Lehtinen/Keane/Hogue/Sloan 6.00 15.00
25 York/Graves/Lefebvre/Malhtra 6.00 15.00
26 Burke/Nummin/Suchy/Lumme 6.00 15.00
27 Lecvalr/Primeau/Barnby/Kraft 6.00 15.00
28 Straka/Morzv/Berank/Bghnr 6.00 15.00
29 Kovalev/Rozsivl/Parent/Kasp 6.00 15.00

2001-02 Pacific Heads Up Rink Immortals

1 Paul Kariya 8.00 20.00
2 Patrick Roy 20.00 50.00
3 Joe Sakic 10.00 25.00
4 Brett Hull 8.00 20.00
5 Dominik Hasek 10.00 25.00
6 Steve Yzerman 15.00 40.00
7 Pavel Bure 6.00 15.00
8 Martin Brodeur 12.00 30.00
9 Mario Lemieux 25.00 60.00
10 Jaromir Jagr 10.00 25.00

2001-02 Pacific Heads Up Showstoppers

COMPLETE SET (20) 20.00 40.00
1 Steve Shields .60 1.50
2 Byron Dafoe .60 1.50
3 Roman Turek .60 1.50
4 Patrick Roy 4.00 10.00
5 Ed Belfour .75 2.00
6 Dominik Hasek 1.50 4.00
7 Chris Osgood .60 1.50
8 Tommy Salo .60 1.50
9 Roberto Luongo 1.00 2.50
10 Felix Potvin .75 2.00
11 Jose Theodore 1.00 2.50
12 Martin Brodeur 2.00 5.00
13 Rick DiPietro .60 1.50
14 Mike Richter .60 1.50
15 Patrick Lalime .60 1.50
16 Roman Cechmanek .60 1.50
17 Johan Hedberg .60 1.50
18 Evgeni Nabokov .60 1.50
19 Curtis Joseph .75 2.00
20 Olaf Kolzig .60 1.50

2001-02 Pacific Heads Up Stat Masters

COMPLETE SET (20) 25.00 50.00
1 Paul Kariya .60 1.50
2 Joe Thornton 1.00 2.50
3 Peter Forsberg 1.50 4.00
4 Joe Sakic 1.25 3.00
5 Brett Hull .75 2.00
6 Mike Modano 1.00 2.50
7 Steve Yzerman 3.00 8.00
8 Pavel Bure .75 2.00
9 Zigmund Palffy .50 1.25
10 Jason Arnott .50 1.25
11 Theo Fleury .50 1.25
12 Marian Hossa .60 1.50
13 Jeremy Roenick .75 2.00
14 Mario Lemieux 4.00 10.00
15 Keith Tkachuk .60 1.50
16 Teemu Selanne .60 1.50
17 Vincent Lecavalier .60 1.50
18 Brad Richards .50 1.25
19 Mats Sundin .60 1.50
20 Jaromir Jagr 1.00 2.50

2002-03 Pacific Heads Up

COMPLETE SET (145) 40.00 80.00
COMP.SET w/o SP's (125) 12.00 30.00
1 Jean-Sebastien Giguere .30 .75
2 Paul Kariya .30 .75
3 Adam Oates .30 .75
4 Dany Heatley .25 .60
5 Milan Hnilicka .25 .60
6 Ilya Kovalchuk .40 1.00
7 Byron Dafoe .25 .60
8 Glen Murray .25 .60
9 Brian Rolston .25 .60
10 Sergei Samsonov .25 .60
11 Joe Thornton .50 1.25
12 Martin Biron .25 .60
13 J-P Dumont .20 .50
14 Miroslav Satan .30 .75
15 Craig Conroy .20 .50
16 Jarome Iginla .40 1.00
17 Dean McAmmond .20 .50
18 Roman Turek .30 .75
19 Erik Cole .20 .50
20 Ron Francis .40 1.00
21 Arturs Irbe .25 .60
22 Sami Kapanen .20 .50
23 Jeff O'Neill .20 .50
24 Tony Amonte .25 .60
25 Eric Daze .20 .50
26 Jocelyn Thibault .25 .60
27 Alexei Zhamnov .25 .60
28 Rob Blake .30 .75
29 Chris Drury .30 .75
30 Peter Forsberg .60 1.50
31 Milan Hejduk .25 .60
32 Patrick Roy .75 2.00
33 Joe Sakic .60 1.50
34 Marc Denis .25 .60
35 Rostislav Klesla .20 .50
36 Ray Whitney .25 .60
37 Jason Arnott .25 .60
38 Bill Guerin .30 .75
39 Mike Modano .50 1.25
40 Marty Turco .30 .75
41 Sergei Fedorov .50 1.25
42 Dominik Hasek .50 1.25
43 Brett Hull .60 1.50
44 Curtis Joseph .40 1.00
45 Nicklas Lidstrom .30 .75
46 Luc Robitaille .30 .75
47 Brendan Shanahan .30 .75
48 Steve Yzerman .75 2.00
49 Mike Comrie .30 .75
50 Tommy Salo .25 .60
51 Ryan Smyth .25 .60
52 Kristian Huselius .20 .50
53 Roberto Luongo .50 1.25
54 Stephen Weiss .30 .75
55 Jason Allison .25 .60
56 Adam Deadmarsh .20 .50
57 Zigmund Palffy .30 .75
58 Felix Potvin .50 1.25
59 Andrew Brunette .20 .50
60 Manny Fernandez .20 .50
61 Marian Gaborik .30 .75
62 Donald Audette .20 .50
63 Doug Gilmour .40 1.00
64 Saku Koivu .30 .75
65 Yanic Perreault .20 .50
66 Jose Theodore .30 .75
67 Denis Arkhipov .20 .50
68 Scott Hartnell .20 .50
69 David Legwand .25 .60
70 Martin Brodeur .75 2.00
71 Patrik Elias .30 .75
72 Joe Nieuwendyk .25 .60
73 Chris Osgood .30 .75
74 Mark Parrish .20 .50
75 Michael Peca .25 .60
76 Alexei Yashin .25 .60
77 Daniel Blackburn .25 .60
78 Pavel Bure .30 .75
79 Theo Fleury .40 1.00
80 Bobby Holik .20 .50
81 Brian Leetch .25 .60
82 Eric Lindros .50 1.25
83 Mike Richter .30 .75
84 Daniel Alfredsson .30 .75
85 Radek Bonk .25 .60
86 Martin Havlat .25 .60
87 Marian Hossa .30 .75
88 Patrick Lalime .25 .60
89 Roman Cechmanek .25 .60
90 Simon Gagne .30 .75
91 John LeClair .30 .75
92 Mark Recchi .40 1.00
93 Jeremy Roenick .50 1.25
94 Daniel Briere .25 .60
95 Sean Burke .20 .50
96 Krystofer Kolanos .20 .50
97 Daymond Langkow .25 .60
98 Johan Hedberg .30 .75
99 Alexei Kovalev .25 .60
100 Mario Lemieux 1.25 3.00
101 Alexei Morozov .20 .50
102 Pavol Demitra .40 1.00
103 Brent Johnson .25 .60
104 Chris Pronger .30 .75
105 Keith Tkachuk .30 .75
106 Doug Weight .30 .75
107 Patrick Marleau .30 .75
108 Evgeni Nabokov .25 .60
109 Owen Nolan .30 .75
110 Teemu Selanne .60 1.50
111 Nikolai Khabibulin .30 .75
112 Vincent Lecavalier .30 .75
113 Brad Richards .30 .75
114 Ed Belfour .30 .75
115 Alyn McCauley .20 .50
116 Alexander Mogilny .25 .60
117 Gary Roberts .20 .50
118 Mats Sundin .30 .75
119 Todd Bertuzzi .30 .75
120 Dan Cloutier .25 .60
121 Brendan Morrison .25 .60
122 Markus Naslund .30 .75
123 Peter Bondra .30 .75
124 Jaromir Jagr 1.00 2.50
125 Olaf Kolzig .30 .75
126 Stanislav Chistov RC .60 1.50
127 Martin Gerber RC 1.00 2.50
128 Alexei Smirnov RC .75 2.00
129 Chuck Kobasew RC .75 2.00
130 Rick Nash RC 4.00 10.00
131 Dmitri Bykov RC .60 1.50
132 Henrik Zetterberg RC 6.00 15.00
133 Ales Hemsky RC 2.50 6.00
134 Jay Bouwmeester RC 2.00 5.00
135 Alexander Frolov RC 1.50 4.00
136 Sylvain Blouin RC .60 1.50
137 P-M Bouchard RC 1.00 2.50
138 Ron Hainsey RC .60 1.50
139 Scottie Upshall RC .75 2.00
140 Mike Danton SP .60 1.50
141 Ray Schultz RC .60 1.50
142 Anton Volchenkov RC .60 1.50
143 Dennis Seidenberg RC 1.00 2.50
144 Alexander Svitov RC .60 1.50
145 Steve Eminger RC .60 1.50

2002-03 Pacific Heads Up Blue

*BLUE/240: 2X TO 5X BASIC CARDS

2002-03 Pacific Heads Up Purple

*PURPLE/30: 12X TO 30X BASIC CARDS

2002-03 Pacific Heads Up Red

*RED/80: 6X TO 15X BASIC CARDS

2002-03 Pacific Heads Up Bobble Heads

1 Jason Allison 10.00 25.00
2 Pavel Bure 10.00 25.00
3 Mike Comrie 10.00 25.00
4 Peter Forsberg 15.00 50.00
5 Jarome Iginla 15.00 40.00
6 Saku Koivu 10.00 25.00
7 Ilya Kovalchuk 15.00 40.00
8 Eric Lindros 10.00 25.00
9 Evgeni Nabokov 10.00 25.00
10 Brendan Shanahan 10.00 25.00
11 Mats Sundin 10.00 25.00
12 Jose Theodore 15.00 40.00
13 Joe Thornton 15.00 40.00
14 Alexei Yashin 10.00 25.00

2002-03 Pacific Heads Up Etched in Time

1 Paul Kariya 6.00 15.00
2 Ilya Kovalchuk 12.50 30.00
3 Joe Thornton 8.00 20.00
4 Jarome Iginla 8.00 20.00
5 Ron Francis 6.00 15.00
6 Peter Forsberg 15.00 40.00
7 Patrick Roy 20.00 50.00
8 Joe Sakic 12.50 30.00
9 Dominik Hasek 12.00 30.00
10 Steve Yzerman 20.00 50.00
11 Martin Brodeur 15.00 40.00
12 Eric Lindros 6.00 15.00
13 Mario Lemieux 25.00 60.00
14 Mats Sundin 6.00 15.00
15 Jaromir Jagr 8.00 20.00

2002-03 Pacific Heads Up Head First

COMPLETE SET (16) 12.00 30.00
1 Dany Heatley 1.25 3.00
2 Ilya Kovalchuk 1.50 4.00
3 Sergei Samsonov .75 2.00
4 Joe Thornton 1.50 4.00
5 Stephen Weiss .75 2.00
6 Marian Gaborik 1.50 4.00
7 Scott Hartnell .75 2.00
8 Rick DiPietro 1.00 2.50
9 Raffi Torres .75 2.00
10 Dan Blackburn .75 2.00
11 Martin Havlat 1.00 2.50
12 Simon Gagne 1.25 3.00
13 Krystofer Kolanos .75 2.00
14 Vincent Lecavalier 1.25 3.00
15 Daniel Sedin 1.25 3.00
16 Henrik Sedin 1.25 3.00

2002-03 Pacific Heads Up Inside the Numbers

COMPLETE SET (24) 12.00 30.00
1 Adam Oates .60 1.50
2 Dany Heatley 1.00 2.50
3 Ilya Kovalchuk 1.00 2.50
4 Joe Thornton 1.25 3.00
5 Jarome Iginla 1.50 3.00
6 Ron Francis .60 1.50
7 Patrick Roy 3.00 8.00
8 Joe Sakic 1.50 4.00
9 Mike Modano 1.25 3.00
10 Dominik Hasek 1.50 4.00
11 Brendan Shanahan .75 2.00
12 Jose Theodore 1.00 2.50
13 Martin Brodeur 2.50 6.00
14 Alexei Yashin .60 1.50
15 Eric Lindros .75 2.00
16 Daniel Alfredsson .60 1.50
17 Mario Lemieux 4.00 10.00
18 Pavol Demitra .60 1.50
19 Evgeni Nabokov .60 1.50
20 Nikolai Khabibulin .75 2.00
21 Mats Sundin .75 2.00
22 Todd Bertuzzi .75 2.00
23 Markus Naslund .75 2.00
24 Jaromir Jagr 1.25 3.00

2002-03 Pacific Heads Up Postseason Picks

COMPLETE SET (10) 20.00 40.00
1 Erik Cole .75 2.00
2 Ron Francis .75 2.00
3 Peter Forsberg 2.00 5.00
4 Patrick Roy 4.00 10.00
5 Joe Sakic 1.50 4.00
6 Dominik Hasek 1.50 4.00
7 Brendan Shanahan 1.00 2.50
8 Steve Yzerman 4.00 10.00
9 Jose Theodore 1.00 2.50
10 Mats Sundin .75 2.00

2002-03 Pacific Heads Up Quad Jerseys

COMPLETE SET (36)
COMMON CARD (1-36) 5.00 12.00
1 Friesen/Tver/Allison/Deadmrsh 5.00 12.00
2 Kovlchk/Stefan/Hnilicka/Kallio 5.00 12.00
3 Sams/Thorntn/McLrn/Swney 5.00 12.00
4 Dumont/Biron/Mckee/Satan 5.00 12.00
5 Turek/Savrd/Comrie/Smyth 5.00 12.00
6 Franc/Irbe/Brdmour/O'Neill 12.50 30.00
7 Amonte/Daze/Bell/Sulli 5.00 12.00
8 Drury/Hejduk/Tngy/Nedrst 5.00 12.00
9 Blake/Sakic/Rbtlle/Fedorov 15.00 40.00
10 Denis/Tugntt/Klesla/Sandrsn 5.00 12.00
11 Belfour/Turco/Trgeon/Mdno 6.00 15.00
12 Hasek/Hull/Lidstrm/Williams 10.00 25.00
13 Allison/Palffy/Potvin/Smlnski 4.00 10.00
14 Gbrik/Kuba/McLnn/Ferndz 6.00 15.00
15 Theod/Prrlt/Berzn/Koivu 6.00 15.00
16 Erat/Legwnd/Walkr/Hntnen 5.00 12.00
17 Brodeur/Elias/Gomez/Stevens 12.50 30.00
18 Peca/Yash/Lndros/Fleury 5.00 12.00
19 Alfrdsson/Lalime/Havlat/Hossa 10.00 25.00
20 Oates/Roenk/Cech/Dopita 5.00 12.00
21 Klnos/Handzs/Lngkow/Doan 5.00 12.00
22 Hedbrg/Lang/Petrsn/Beech 5.00 12.00
23 Prngr/Tkck/Demtra/Vrlmov 5.00 12.00
24 Nabkv/Nolan/Kipsff/Marleau 8.00 20.00
25 Khabi/Richrd/Bure/Luongo 10.00 25.00
26 Cujo/Robrts/Moglny/Tuckr 10.00 25.00
27 Cltier/Brtzzi/D.Sedin/H.Sedin 8.00 20.00
28 Lemx/Prnger/Brodeur/Cujo 15.00 40.00
29 Guerin/Mdno/Hull/Leetch 12.50 30.00
30 Bure/Khabi./Fedrov/Yashin 12.50 30.00
31 Sundin/Alfr-son/Salo/Hdbrg 5.00 12.00
32 Jagr/Hasek/Hejduk/Elias 10.00 25.00
33 Selne/Lehtn./Lumme/Kallio 5.00 12.00
34 Bndra/Gbrik/Demitra/Plffy 8.00 20.00
35 Kovlchk/Heat./Klnos/Cole 10.00 25.00
36 Hslius/Dopita/Erat/Hntnen 5.00 12.00

2002-03 Pacific Heads Up Showstoppers

COMPLETE SET (20) 25.00 50.00
1 Jean-Sebastien Giguere .40 1.00
2 Byron Dafoe .40 1.00
3 Roman Turek .40 1.00
4 Arturs Irbe .40 1.00
5 Jocelyn Thibault .40 1.00
6 Patrick Roy 2.50 6.00
7 Marty Turco .40 1.00
8 Dominik Hasek 1.25 3.00
9 Curtis Joseph .60 1.50
10 Roberto Luongo .75 2.00
11 Felix Potvin .60 1.50
12 Jose Theodore .60 2.00
13 Martin Brodeur 1.50 4.00
14 Chris Osgood .60 1.50
15 Patrick Lalime .40 1.00
16 Sean Burke .40 1.00
17 Brent Johnson .40 1.00
18 Evgeni Nabokov .40 1.00
19 Nikolai Khabibulin .60 1.50
20 Dan Cloutier .40 1.00

2002-03 Pacific Heads Up Stat Masters

COMPLETE SET (15) 40.00 80.00
1 Paul Kariya 1.25 3.00
2 Dany Heatley 1.50 4.00
3 Ilya Kovalchuk 1.50 4.00
4 Joe Thornton 2.00 5.00
5 Jarome Iginla 1.50 4.00
6 Ron Francis 1.25 3.00
7 Joe Sakic 2.50 6.00
8 Brett Hull 1.50 4.00
9 Steve Yzerman 6.00 15.00
10 Pavel Bure 1.50 4.00
11 Eric Lindros 1.25 3.00
12 Mario Lemieux 8.00 20.00
13 Mats Sundin 1.25 3.00
14 Todd Bertuzzi 1.25 3.00
15 Jaromir Jagr 2.00 5.00

2003-04 Pacific Heads Up

COMPLETE SET (136) 30.00 80.00
COMP.SET w/o SP's (100) 15.00 30.00
1 Sergei Fedorov .60 1.50
2 Jean-Sebastien Giguere .40 1.00
3 Steve Rucchin .25 .60
4 Ilya Kovalchuk .40 1.00
5 Shawn McEachern .25 .60
6 Pasi Nurminen .30 .75
7 Mike Knuble .25 .60
8 Andrew Raycroft .30 .75
9 Brian Rolston .30 .75
10 Joe Thornton .60 1.50
11 Martin Biron .30 .75
12 Daniel Briere .40 1.00
13 J-P Dumont .25 .60
14 Jarome Iginla .50 1.25
15 Jamie McLennan .25 .60
16 Steven Reinprecht .25 .60
17 Ron Francis .50 1.25
18 Josef Vasicek .25 .60

19 Kevin Weekes .30 .75
20 Mark Bell .25 .60
21 Michael Leighton .25 .60
22 Jocelyn Thibault UER .30 .75
23 David Aebischer .30 .75
24 Peter Forsberg .75 2.00
25 Paul Kariya .40 1.00
26 Joe Sakic .75 2.00
27 Alex Tanguay .30 .75
28 Marc Denis .30 .75
29 Rick Nash .40 1.00
30 David Vyborny .25 .60
31 Bill Guerin .40 1.00
32 Mike Modano .60 1.50
33 Marty Turco .40 1.00
34 Pavel Datsyuk .60 1.50
35 Dominik Hasek .60 1.50
36 Brett Hull .75 2.00
37 Brendan Shanahan .40 1.00
38 Steve Yzerman 1.00 2.50
39 Henrik Zetterberg .50 1.25
40 Ty Conklin .30 .75
41 Ales Hemsky .40 1.00
42 Ryan Smyth .30 .75
43 Jay Bouwmeester .25 .60
44 Olli Jokinen .40 1.00
45 Roberto Luongo .60 1.50
46 Roman Cechmanek .30 .75
47 Cristobal Huet .30 .75
48 Ziggy Palffy .40 1.00
49 Pierre-Marc Bouchard .40 1.00
50 Marian Gaborik .40 1.00
51 Dwayne Roloson .30 .75
52 Saku Koivu .40 1.00
53 Mike Ribeiro .25 .60
54 Michael Ryder UER .30 .75
55 Jose Theodore .40 1.00
56 Scott Hartnell .25 .60
57 David Legwand .30 .75
58 Martin Brodeur 1.00 2.50
59 Patrik Elias .40 1.00
60 Jamie Langenbrunner .30 .75
61 Mariusz Czerkawski .25 .60
62 Rick DiPietro .30 .75
63 Trent Hunter .25 .60
64 Alexei Yashin .30 .75
65 Alex Kovalev .30 .75
66 Eric Lindros .60 1.50
67 Mark Messier .75 2.00
68 Daniel Alfredsson .40 1.00
69 Marian Hossa .40 1.00
70 Patrick Lalime .30 .75
71 Jason Spezza .40 1.00
72 Tony Amonte .30 .75
73 Robert Esche .25 .60
74 Jeremy Roenick .60 1.50
75 Justin Williams .30 .75
76 Sean Burke .25 .60
77 Ladislav Nagy .25 .60
78 Rico Fata .25 .60
79 Mario Lemieux 1.50 4.00
80 Barret Jackman .25 .60
81 Chris Osgood .40 1.00
82 Chris Pronger .40 1.00
83 Patrick Marleau .40 1.00
84 Alyn McCauley .25 .60
85 Marco Sturm .25 .60
86 Nikolai Khabibulin .40 1.00
87 Vincent Lecavalier .40 1.00
88 Martin St. Louis .40 1.00
89 Cory Stillman .25 .60
90 Ed Belfour .40 1.00
91 Alexander Mogilny .30 .75
92 Owen Nolan .40 1.00
93 Mats Sundin .40 1.00
94 Todd Bertuzzi .40 1.00
95 Dan Cloutier .30 .75
96 Jason King .25 .60
97 Brendan Morrison .30 .75
98 Markus Naslund .40 1.00
99 Jaromir Jagr 1.25 3.00
100 Robert Lang .25 .60
101 Joffrey Lupul RC 2.00 5.00
102 Patrice Bergeron RC 8.00 20.00
103 Pat Leahy RC 1.00 2.50
104 Brent Krahn RC .75 2.00
105 Matthew Lombardi RC 1.00 2.50
106 Eric Staal RC 4.00 10.00
107 Tuomo Ruutu RC 1.25 3.00
108 Mikhail Yakubov RC .75 2.00
109 Cody McCormick RC 1.00 2.50
110 Dan Fritsche RC .75 2.00
111 Nikolai Zherdev RC 1.50 4.00
112 Antti Miettinen RC 1.25 3.00
113 Darryl Bootland RC 1.00 2.50
114 Jiri Hudler RC 2.00 5.00
115 Nathan Robinson RC .75 2.00
116 Tony Salmelainen RC .75 2.00
117 Peter Sarno RC .75 2.00
118 Nathan Horton RC 2.00 5.00
119 Dustin Brown RC 2.00 5.00
120 Brent Burns RC 2.50 6.00
121 Christopher Higgins RC 1.50 4.00
122 Dan Hamhuis RC 1.00 2.50
123 Jordin Tootoo RC 1.50 4.00
124 Marek Zidlicky RC .75 2.00
125 Paul Martin RC 1.00 2.50
126 Dominic Moore RC .75 2.00
127 Antoine Vermette RC 1.50 4.00
128 Joni Pitkanen RC 1.25 3.00
129 Fredrik Sjostrom RC 1.25 3.00
130 Marc-Andre Fleury RC 5.00 12.00
131 John Pohl RC .75 2.00
132 Peter Sejna RC 1.00 2.50
133 Milan Michalek RC 1.50 4.00
134 Matt Stajan RC 1.25 3.00
135 Boyd Gordon RC 1.00 2.50
136 Alexander Semin RC 2.50 6.00

2003-04 Pacific Heads Up Hobby LTD

*1-100 VETS/299: 2X TO 5X BASIC CARDS
*101-136 ROOK/250: .6X TO 1.5X BASIC RC

2003-04 Pacific Heads Up Retail LTD

*STARS: .5X TO 1.2X
*ROOKIES: .25X TO .5X

2003-04 Pacific Heads Up Fast Forwards

*LTD: .75X TO 2X
1 Sergei Fedorov 1.00 2.50
2 Ilya Kovalchuk 1.00 2.50
3 Rick Nash 1.00 2.50
4 Mike Modano 1.25 3.00
5 Marian Gaborik 1.50 4.00
6 Marian Hossa .75 2.00
7 Jeremy Roenick 1.00 2.50
8 Alexander Mogilny .75 2.00
9 Markus Naslund .75 2.00

2003-04 Pacific Heads Up In Focus

*LTD: .75X TO 2X
1 Sergei Fedorov 1.00 2.50
2 Ilya Kovalchuk 1.00 2.50
3 Eric Staal 1.00 2.50
4 Joe Sakic 1.50 4.00
5 Alex Tanguay .75 2.00
6 Rick Nash 1.00 2.50
7 Henrik Zetterberg .75 2.00
8 Jay Bouwmeester .75 2.00
9 Jason Spezza .75 2.00
10 Todd Bertuzzi .75 2.00

2003-04 Pacific Heads Up Jerseys

1 Joffrey Lupul 3.00 8.00
2 Ilya Kovalchuk SP 8.00 20.00
3 Joe Thornton SP 10.00 25.00
4 Ales Kotalik 2.00 5.00
5 Ryan Miller 4.00 10.00
6 Matthew Lombardi 2.00 5.00
7 David Aebischer 3.00 8.00
8 Peter Forsberg SP 8.00 20.00
9 Antti Miettinen 2.00 5.00
10 Steve Yzerman SP 12.50 30.00
11 Ales Hemsky 2.00 5.00
12 Jay Bouwmeester 2.00 5.00
13 Nathan Horton 3.00 8.00
14 Dustin Brown 4.00 10.00
15 Ziggy Palffy 2.00 5.00
16 Chris Higgins 3.00 8.00
17 Jordin Tootoo 5.00 12.00
18 Martin Brodeur 10.00 25.00
19 Rick DiPietro 3.00 8.00
20 Jason Spezza 6.00 15.00
21 Antoine Vermette 2.00 5.00
22 Mario Lemieux SP 15.00 40.00
23 Barret Jackman 2.00 5.00
24 Owen Nolan 2.00 5.00
25 Boyd Gordon 2.00 5.00

2003-04 Pacific Heads Up Mini Sweaters

1 Marc-Andre Fleury 12.00 30.00
2 Ilya Kovalchuk 12.00 30.00
3 Joe Thornton 12.00 30.00
4 Peter Forsberg 12.00 30.00
5 Steve Yzerman 15.00 40.00
6 Martin Brodeur 15.00 40.00
7 Marian Gaborik 12.00 30.00
8 Ed Belfour 8.00 20.00
9 Todd Bertuzzi 8.00 20.00

2003-04 Pacific Heads Up Prime Prospects

COMPLETE SET (10) 10.00 20.00
*LTD: .6X TO 1.5X
1 Joffrey Lupul .75 2.00
2 Patrice Bergeron 1.50 4.00
3 Ryan Miller 1.25 3.00
4 Matthew Lombardi .40 1.00
5 Eric Staal 2.00 5.00
6 Philippe Sauve .40 1.00
7 Nikolai Zherdev 1.25 3.00
8 Jiri Hudler .75 2.00
9 Nathan Horton .75 2.00
10 Dustin Brown .50 1.25
11 Brent Burns .40 1.00
12 Christopher Higgins 1.25 3.00
13 Michael Ryder 1.25 3.00
14 Jordin Tootoo 1.25 3.00
15 Antoine Vermette .40 1.00
16 Joni Pitkanen .75 2.00
17 Marc-Andre Fleury 2.00 5.00
18 Milan Michalek .75 2.00
19 Matt Stajan .75 2.00
20 Jason King .40 1.00

2003-04 Pacific Heads Up Rink Immortals

*LTD: .75X TO 2X
1 Joe Thornton 1.00 2.50
2 Peter Forsberg 2.00 5.00
3 Joe Sakic 1.50 4.00
4 Dominik Hasek 1.50 4.00
5 Brett Hull 1.00 2.50
6 Steve Yzerman 2.50 6.00
7 Martin Brodeur 2.50 6.00
8 Mark Messier 1.00 2.50
9 Mario Lemieux 3.00 8.00
10 Ed Belfour 1.00 2.50

2003-04 Pacific Heads Up Stonewallers

*LTD: .75X TO 2X
1 Jean-Sebastien Giguere .60 1.50
2 Pasi Nurminen .60 1.50
3 David Aebischer .60 1.50
4 Marty Turco .60 1.50
5 Dominik Hasek 1.50 4.00
6 Jose Theodore 1.00 2.50
7 Martin Brodeur 2.50 6.00
8 Rick DiPietro .60 1.50
9 Patrick Lalime .60 1.50
10 Nikolai Khabibulin .75 2.00
11 Ed Belfour .75 2.00
12 Dan Cloutier .60 1.50

2001-02 Pacific High Voltage

COMPLETE SET (10) 20.00 50.00
1 Dany Heatley 2.50 6.00
2 Ilya Kovalchuk 10.00 25.00
3 Erik Cole 3.00 8.00
4 Vaclav Nedorost 2.50 6.00
5 Kristian Huselius 3.00 8.00
6 Martin Erat .75 2.00
7 Dan Blackburn 1.00 2.50
8 Krystofer Kolanos 2.50 6.00
9 Jeff Jillson 1.50 4.00
10 Nikita Alexeev 1.50 4.00

1997-98 Pacific Invincible

1 Brian Bellows .25 .60
2 Guy Hebert .25 .60
3 Paul Kariya .30 .75
4 Teemu Selanne .60 1.50
5 Darren Van Impe .25 .60
6 Jason Allison .25 .60
7 Ray Bourque .50 1.25
8 Jim Carey .20 .50
9 Ted Donato .20 .50
10 Jozef Stumpel .20 .50
11 Jason Dawe .25 .60
12 Dominik Hasek .50 1.25
13 Michael Peca .25 .60
14 Derek Plante .25 .60
15 Miroslav Satan .20 .50
16 Theo Fleury .40 1.00
17 Dave Gagner .20 .50
18 Jonas Hoglund .25 .60
19 Jarome Iginla .40 1.00
20 Trevor Kidd .20 .50
21 German Titov .20 .50
22 Sean Burke .20 .50
23 Andrew Cassels .20 .50
24 Derek King .25 .60
25 Keith Primeau .25 .60
26 Geoff Sanderson .25 .60
27 Tony Amonte .25 .60
28 Chris Chelios .30 .75
29 Eric Daze .20 .50
30 Jeff Hackett .20 .50
31 Ethan Moreau .20 .50
32 Alexei Zhamnov .20 .50
33 Adam Deadmarsh .20 .50
34 Peter Forsberg .60 1.50
35 Valeri Kamensky .25 .60
36 Claude Lemieux .25 .60
37 Sandis Ozolinsh .20 .50
38 Patrick Roy .75 2.00
39 Joe Sakic .60 1.50
40 Jamie Langenbrunner .25 .60
41 Mike Modano .50 1.25
42 Andy Moog .30 .75
43 Joe Nieuwendyk .25 .60
44 Pat Verbeek .25 .60
45 Sergei Zubov .25 .60
46 Sergei Fedorov .50 1.25
47 Vladimir Konstantinov .20 .50
48 Vyacheslav Kozlov .25 .60
49 Nicklas Lidstrom .30 .75
50 Chris Osgood .30 .75
51 Brendan Shanahan .30 .75
52 Mike Vernon .25 .60
53 Steve Yzerman .75 2.00
54 Jason Arnott .25 .60
55 Mike Grier .25 .60
56 Curtis Joseph .40 1.00
57 Rem Murray .20 .50
58 Ryan Smyth .25 .60
59 Doug Weight .30 .75
60 Ed Jovanovski .20 .50
61 Scott Mellanby .25 .60
62 Kirk Muller .20 .50
63 Ray Sheppard .25 .60
64 John Vanbiesbrouck .30 .75
65 Rob Blake .30 .75
66 Ray Ferraro .20 .50
67 Stephane Fiset .25 .60
68 Dimitri Khristich .25 .60
69 Vladimir Tsyplakov .25 .60
70 Vincent Damphousse .25 .60
71 Saku Koivu .30 .75
72 Mark Recchi .40 1.00
73 Stephane Richer .20 .50
74 Jocelyn Thibault .25 .60
75 Dave Andreychuk .30 .75
76 Martin Brodeur .75 2.00
77 Doug Gilmour .40 1.00
78 Bobby Holik .20 .50
79 Denis Pederson .20 .50
80 Bryan Berard .20 .50
81 Travis Green .25 .60
82 Zigmund Palffy .30 .75
83 Tommy Salo .20 .50
84 Bryan Smolinski .25 .60
85 Adam Graves .20 .50
86 Wayne Gretzky 2.00 5.00
87 Alexei Kovalev .25 .60
88 Brian Leetch .25 .60
89 Mark Messier .60 1.50
90 Mike Richter .30 .75
91 Luc Robitaille .30 .75
92 Daniel Alfredsson .30 .75
93 Alexandre Daigle .20 .50
94 Steve Duchesne .20 .50
95 Wade Redden .20 .50
96 Ron Tugnutt .30 .75
97 Alexei Yashin .25 .60
98 Rod Brind'Amour .30 .75
99 Paul Coffey .30 .75
100 Ron Hextall .30 .75
101 John LeClair .30 .75
102 Eric Lindros .50 1.25
103 Janne Niinimaa .25 .60
104 Mikael Renberg .25 .60
105 Dainius Zubrus .25 .60
106 Mike Gartner .40 1.00
107 Nikolai Khabibulin .30 .75
108 Jeremy Roenick .50 1.25
109 Keith Tkachuk .30 .75
110 Oleg Tverdovsky .25 .60
111 Ron Francis .40 1.00
112 Kevin Hatcher .20 .50
113 Jaromir Jagr 1.00 2.50
114 Patrick Lalime .25 .60
115 Petr Nedved .30 .75
116 Ed Olczyk .20 .50
117 Jim Campbell .20 .50
118 Geoff Courtnall .20 .50
119 Grant Fuhr .50 1.25
120 Brett Hull .60 1.50
121 Sergio Momesso .20 .50
122 Pierre Turgeon .25 .60
123 Ed Belfour .30 .75
124 Jeff Friesen .25 .60
125 Tony Granato .20 .50
126 Stephen Guolla RC .20 .50
127 Bernie Nicholls .25 .60
128 Owen Nolan .30 .75
129 Dino Ciccarelli .30 .75
130 John Cullen .20 .50
131 Chris Gratton .20 .50
132 Roman Hamrlik .20 .50
133 Daymond Langkow .20 .50
134 Paul Ysebaert .25 .60
135 Sergei Berezin .25 .60
136 Wendel Clark .50 1.25
137 Felix Potvin .50 1.25
138 Steve Sullivan .25 .60
139 Mats Sundin .30 .75
140 Pavel Bure .30 .75
141 Martin Gelinas .20 .50
142 Trevor Linden .30 .75
143 Kirk McLean .25 .60
144 Alexander Mogilny .25 .60
145 Peter Bondra .30 .75
146 Dale Hunter .25 .60
147 Joe Juneau .20 .50
148 Steve Konowalchuk .25 .60
149 Adam Oates .30 .75
150 Bill Ranford .25 .60
S41 Mike Modano Sample .50 1.25

1997-98 Pacific Invincible Copper

*COPPER: 3X TO 8X BASIC CARDS

1997-98 Pacific Invincible Emerald Green

*GREEN: 3X TO 8X BASIC CARDS

1997-98 Pacific Invincible Ice Blue

*ICE BLUE: 10X TO 25X BASIC CARDS

1997-98 Pacific Invincible Red

*RED: 4X TO 10X BASIC CARDS

1997-98 Pacific Invincible Silver

*SILVER: 4X TO 10X BASIC CARDS

1997-98 Pacific Invincible Attack Zone

COMPLETE SET (24) 50.00 100.00
1 Paul Kariya 2.50 6.00
2 Teemu Selanne 2.50 6.00
3 Michael Peca 1.00 2.50
4 Jarome Iginla 3.00 8.00
5 Peter Forsberg 6.00 15.00
6 Claude Lemieux 1.00 2.50
7 Joe Sakic 5.00 12.00
8 Mike Modano 4.00 10.00
9 Sergei Fedorov 4.00 10.00
10 Brendan Shanahan 2.50 6.00
11 Steve Yzerman 10.00 25.00
12 Bryan Berard 2.00 5.00
13 Zigmund Palffy 2.00 5.00
14 Wayne Gretzky 12.50 30.00
15 Brian Leetch 2.50 6.00
16 Mark Messier 2.50 6.00
17 John LeClair 2.50 6.00
18 Eric Lindros 3.00 8.00
19 Ron Francis 2.00 5.00
20 Jaromir Jagr 4.00 10.00
21 Brett Hull 3.00 8.00
22 Dino Ciccarelli 1.00 2.50
23 Pavel Bure 2.50 6.00
24 Alexander Mogilny 2.00 5.00

1997-98 Pacific Invincible Feature Performers

COMPLETE SET (36) 15.00 40.00
1 Paul Kariya 1.25 3.00
2 Teemu Selanne 1.25 3.00
3 Ray Bourque 2.00 5.00
4 Dominik Hasek 3.00 8.00
5 Jarome Iginla 2.00 5.00
6 Chris Chelios 1.25 3.00
7 Peter Forsberg 2.50 6.00
8 Claude Lemieux .40 1.00
9 Patrick Roy 6.00 15.00
10 Joe Sakic 3.00 8.00
11 Mike Modano 1.50 4.00
12 Sergei Fedorov 1.25 3.00
13 Vladimir Konstantinov 1.25 3.00
14 Brendan Shanahan 1.25 3.00
15 Mike Vernon .75 2.00
16 Steve Yzerman 4.00 10.00
17 John Vanbiesbrouck .75 2.00
18 Saku Koivu 1.25 3.00
19 Martin Brodeur 4.00 10.00
20 Zigmund Palffy .75 2.00
21 Wayne Gretzky 8.00 20.00
22 Mark Messier 1.25 3.00
23 Alexandre Daigle .40 1.00
24 John LeClair .75 2.00
25 Eric Lindros 1.25 3.00
26 Janne Niinimaa .40 1.00
27 Jeremy Roenick 2.00 5.00
28 Jaromir Jagr 2.50 6.00
29 Patrick Lalime .75 2.00
30 Jim Campbell .40 1.00
31 Brett Hull 1.25 3.00
32 Sergei Berezin .40 1.00
33 Felix Potvin 1.25 3.00
34 Mats Sundin 1.25 3.00
35 Alexander Mogilny .75 2.00
36 Peter Bondra .75 2.00

1997-98 Pacific Invincible NHL Regime

COMPLETE SET (220) 8.00 20.00
1 Ken Baumgartner .05 .15
2 Mark Janssens .05 .15
3 Jean-Francois Jomphe .05 .15
4 Paul Kariya .10 .30
5 Jason Marshall .05 .15
6 Richard Park .05 .15
7 Teemu Selanne .10 .30
8 Mikhail Shtalenkov .05 .15
9 Bob Beers .05 .15
10 Ray Bourque .20 .50
11 Jim Carey .05 .15
12 Brett Harkins .05 .15
13 Sheldon Kennedy .05 .15
14 Troy Mallette .05 .15
15 Sandy Moger .05 .15
16 Jon Rohloff .05 .15
17 Don Sweeney .05 .15
18 Randy Burridge .05 .15
19 Michal Grosek .05 .15
20 Dominik Hasek .25 .60
21 Rob Ray .05 .15
22 Steve Shields .08 .25
23 Richard Smehlik .05 .15
24 Dixon Ward .05 .15
25 Mike Wilson .05 .15
26 Tommy Albelin .05 .15
27 Aaron Gavey .05 .15
28 Todd Hlushko .05 .15
29 Jarome Iginla .15 .40
30 Yves Racine .05 .15
31 Dwayne Roloson .08 .25
32 Mike Sullivan .05 .15
33 Ed Ward .05 .15
34 Adam Burt .05 .15
35 Nelson Emerson .05 .15
36 Kevin Haller .05 .15
37 Derek King .05 .15
38 Curtis Leschyshyn .05 .15
39 Chris Murray .05 .15
40 Jason Muzzatti .05 .15
41 Keith Carney .05 .15
42 Chris Chelios .10 .30
43 Enrico Ciccone .05 .15
44 Jim Cummins .05 .15
45 Cam Russell .05 .15
46 Jeff Shantz .05 .15
47 Michal Sykora .05 .15
48 Chris Terreri .08 .25
49 Eric Weinrich .05 .15
50 Rene Corbet .05 .15
51 Peter Forsberg .30 .75
52 Alexei Gusarov .05 .15
53 Uwe Krupp .05 .15
54 Sylvain Lefebvre .05 .15
55 Eric Messier .08 .25
56 Patrick Roy .60 1.50
57 Joe Sakic .25 .60
58 Brent Severyn .05 .15
59 Greg Adams .05 .15
60 Todd Harvey .05 .15
61 Jere Lehtinen .05 .15
62 Craig Ludwig .05 .15
63 Mike Modano .20 .50
64 Andy Moog .08 .25
65 Dave Reid .05 .15
66 Roman Turek .05 .15
67 Doug Brown .05 .15
68 Kris Draper .05 .15
69 Sergei Fedorov .20 .50
70 Joey Kocur .05 .15
71 Kirk Maltby .05 .15
72 Bob Rouse .05 .15
73 Brendan Shanahan .10 .30
74 Aaron Ward .05 .15
75 Steve Yzerman .60 1.50
76 Greg DeVries .05 .15
77 Bob Essensa .08 .25
78 Kevin Lowe .05 .15
79 Bryan Marchment .05 .15
80 Dean McAmmond .05 .15
81 Boris Mironov .05 .15
82 Luke Richardson .05 .15
83 Ryan Smyth .08 .25
84 Terry Carkner .05 .15
85 Ed Jovanovski .05 .15
86 Bill Lindsay .05 .15
87 Dave Lowry .05 .15
88 Gord Murphy .05 .15
89 John Vanbiesbrouck .08 .25
90 Steve Washburn .05 .15
91 Chris Wells .05 .15
92 Philippe Boucher .05 .15
93 Steven Finn .05 .15
94 Mattias Norstrom .05 .15
95 Kai Nurminen .05 .15
96 Sean O'Donnell .05 .15
97 Yanic Perreault .05 .15
98 Jeff Shevalier .05 .15
99 Brad Smyth .05 .15
100 Brad Brown .05 .15
101 Jassen Cullimore .05 .15
102 Vincent Damphousse .05 .15
103 Vladimir Malakhov .05 .15
104 Peter Popovic .05 .15
105 Stephane Richer .08 .25
106 Turner Stevenson .05 .15
107 Jose Theodore .15 .40
108 Martin Brodeur .30 .75
109 Bob Carpenter .05 .15
110 Mike Dunham .08 .25
111 Patrik Elias .08 .25
112 Dave Ellett .05 .15
113 Doug Gilmour .08 .25
114 Randy McKay .05 .15
115 Todd Bertuzzi .10 .30
116 Kenny Jonsson .05 .15
117 Paul Kruse .05 .15
118 Claude Lapointe .05 .15
119 Zigmund Palffy .08 .25
120 Rich Pilon .05 .15
121 Dan Plante .05 .15
122 Dennis Vaske .05 .15
123 Shane Churla .05 .15
124 Bruce Driver .05 .15
125 Mike Eastwood .05 .15
126 Patrick Flatley .05 .15
127 Adam Graves .05 .15
128 Wayne Gretzky .75 2.00
129 Brian Leetch .10 .30
130 Doug Lidster .05 .15
131 Mark Messier .10 .30
132 Tom Chorske .05 .15
133 Sean Hill .05 .15
134 Denny Lambert .05 .15
135 Janne Laukkanen .05 .15
136 Frank Musil .05 .15
137 Lance Pitlick .05 .15
138 Shaun Van Allen .05 .15
139 Rod Brind'Amour .08 .25
140 Paul Coffey .10 .30
141 Karl Dykhuis .05 .15
142 Dan Kordic .05 .15
143 Daniel Lacroix .05 .15
144 John LeClair .10 .30
145 Eric Lindros .10 .30
146 Joel Otto .05 .15
147 Shjon Podein .05 .15
148 Chris Therien .05 .15
149 Shane Doan .05 .15
150 Dallas Drake .05 .15
151 Jeff Finley .05 .15
152 Mike Gartner .05 .15
153 Nikolai Khabibulin .08 .25
154 Darrin Shannon .05 .15
155 Mike Stapleton .05 .15
156 Keith Tkachuk .10 .30
157 Tom Barrasso .08 .25
158 Josef Beranek .05 .15
159 Alex Hicks .05 .15
160 Jaromir Jagr .20 .50
161 Patrick Lalime .08 .25
162 Francois Leroux .05 .15
163 Petr Nedved .08 .25
164 Roman Oksiuta .05 .15
165 Chris Tamer .05 .15
166 Marc Bergevin .05 .15
167 Jon Casey .08 .25
168 Craig Conroy .05 .15
169 Brett Hull .15 .40
170 Igor Kravchuk .05 .15
171 Stephen Leach .05 .15
172 Ricard Persson .05 .15
173 Pierre Turgeon .08 .25
174 Ed Belfour .10 .30
175 Doug Bodger .05 .15
176 Shean Donovan .05 .15
177 Bob Errey .05 .15
178 Todd Ewen .05 .15
179 Wade Flaherty .05 .15
180 Mike Rathje .05 .15
181 Ron Sutter .05 .15
182 Mikael Andersson .05 .15
183 Dino Ciccarelli .05 .15
184 Cory Cross .05 .15
185 Jamie Huscroft .05 .15
186 Rudy Poeschek .05 .15
187 Daren Puppa .08 .25
188 David Shaw .05 .15
189 Jay Wells .05 .15
190 Jamie Baker .05 .15
191 Sergei Berezin .08 .25
192 Brandon Convery .05 .15
193 Darby Hendrickson .05 .15
194 Matt Martin .05 .15
195 Felix Potvin .10 .30
196 Jason Smith .05 .15
197 Craig Wolanin .05 .15
198 Adrian Aucoin .05 .15
199 Dave Babych .05 .15
200 Donald Brashear .05 .15
201 Pavel Bure .10 .30
202 Chris Joseph .05 .15
203 Alexander Mogilny .08 .25
204 David Roberts .05 .15
205 Scott Walker .05 .15
206 Peter Bondra .08 .25
207 Andrew Brunette .08 .25
208 Calle Johansson .05 .15
209 Ken Klee .05 .15
210 Olaf Kolzig .08 .25
211 Kelly Miller .05 .15
212 Joe Reekie .05 .15
213 Chris Simon .05 .15
214 Brendan Witt .05 .15
215 Paul Kariya TL .10 .30
216 Peter Forsberg TL .10 .30
217 Patrick Roy TL .10 .30
218 Wayne Gretzky TL .10 .30
219 Eric Lindros TL .10 .30
220 Jaromir Jagr TL .10 .30

1997-98 Pacific Invincible Off The Glass

COMPLETE SET (20) 25.00 60.00
1 Paul Kariya 1.25 3.00
2 Teemu Selanne 1.25 3.00
3 Michael Peca .75 2.00
4 Jarome Iginla 2.00 5.00
5 Peter Forsberg 3.00 8.00
6 Joe Sakic 4.00 10.00
7 Sergei Fedorov 1.50 4.00
8 Brendan Shanahan 1.25 3.00
9 Steve Yzerman 6.00 15.00
10 Mike Grier .75 2.00
11 Saku Koivu 1.25 3.00
12 Wayne Gretzky 10.00 25.00
13 Mark Messier 1.50 4.00
14 Eric Lindros 1.25 3.00
15 Dainius Zubrus .75 2.00
16 Keith Tkachuk 1.25 3.00
17 Jaromir Jagr 3.00 8.00
18 Brett Hull 1.50 4.00
19 Sergei Berezin .75 2.00
20 Pavel Bure 1.50 4.00

2003-04 Pacific Invincible

COMPLETE SET (125)
COMP.SET w/o SP's (100) 12.00 30.00
1 Stanislav Chistov .25 .60
2 Sergei Fedorov .60 1.50
3 Jean-Sebastien Giguere .40 1.00
4 Dany Heatley .30 .75
5 Ilya Kovalchuk .40 1.00
6 Glen Murray .30 .75
7 Sergei Samsonov .30 .75
8 Joe Thornton .60 1.50
9 Martin Biron .30 .75
10 Ryan Miller .40 1.00
11 Miroslav Satan .30 .75
12 Craig Conroy .25 .60
13 Jarome Iginla .50 1.25
14 Roman Turek .30 .75
15 Ron Francis .50 1.25
16 Jeff O'Neill .25 .60
17 Eric Daze .30 .75
18 Jocelyn Thibault .30 .75
19 Alexei Zhamnov .30 .75
20 David Aebischer .30 .75
21 Peter Forsberg .75 2.00
22 Milan Hejduk .30 .75
23 Paul Kariya .40 1.00
24 Patrick Roy 1.00 2.50
25 Joe Sakic .75 2.00
26 Teemu Selanne .75 2.00
27 Marc Denis .30 .75
28 Rick Nash .40 1.00
29 Bill Guerin .40 1.00
30 Mike Modano .60 1.50
31 Marty Turco .40 1.00
32 Dominik Hasek .60 1.50
33 Brett Hull .75 2.00
34 Nicklas Lidstrom .40 1.00
35 Brendan Shanahan .40 1.00
36 Steve Yzerman 1.00 2.50
37 Henrik Zetterberg .50 1.25
38 Mike Comrie .30 .75
39 Ales Hemsky .40 1.00
40 Ryan Smyth .30 .75
41 Jay Bouwmeester .25 .60
42 Olli Jokinen .40 1.00
43 Roberto Luongo .60 1.50
44 Jason Allison .30 .75
45 Roman Cechmanek .30 .75
46 Zigmund Palffy .40 1.00
47 Manny Fernandez .25 .60
48 Marian Gaborik .40 1.00
49 Marcel Hossa .25 .60
50 Saku Koivu .40 1.00
51 Jose Theodore .40 1.00
52 David Legwand .30 .75
53 Scottie Upshall .30 .75
54 Tomas Vokoun .30 .75
55 Martin Brodeur 1.00 2.50
56 Patrik Elias .40 1.00
57 Jeff Friesen .25 .60
58 Jamie Langenbrunner .30 .75
59 Scott Stevens .40 1.00
60 Rick DiPietro .30 .75
61 Mark Parrish .25 .60
62 Michael Peca .30 .75
63 Alexei Yashin .30 .75
64 Pavel Bure .40 1.00
65 Alex Kovalev .30 .75
66 Eric Lindros .60 1.50
67 Mark Messier .75 2.00
68 Daniel Alfredsson .40 1.00
69 Marian Hossa .40 1.00
70 Patrick Lalime .30 .75
71 Jason Spezza .40 1.00
72 Tony Amonte .30 .75
73 Jeff Hackett .30 .75
74 John LeClair .40 1.00
75 Jeremy Roenick .60 1.50
76 Sean Burke .25 .60
77 Daymond Langkow .25 .60
78 Mario Lemieux 1.50 4.00
79 Pavol Demitra .50 1.25
80 Barret Jackman .25 .60
81 Chris Osgood .40 1.00
82 Doug Weight .40 1.00
83 Patrick Marleau .40 1.00
84 Evgeni Nabokov .30 .75
85 John Grahame .25 .60
86 Nikolai Khabibulin .40 1.00
87 Vincent Lecavalier .40 1.00
88 Martin St. Louis .40 1.00
89 Ed Belfour .40 1.00
90 Alexander Mogilny .30 .75
91 Owen Nolan .40 1.00
92 Mats Sundin .40 1.00
93 Todd Bertuzzi .40 1.00
94 Dan Cloutier .30 .75
95 Johan Hedberg .30 .75
96 Brendan Morrison .30 .75
97 Markus Naslund .40 1.00
98 Peter Bondra .40 1.00
99 Jaromir Jagr 1.25 3.00
100 Olaf Kolzig .40 1.00
101 Joffrey Lupul RC 3.00 8.00
102 Patrice Bergeron RC 6.00 15.00
103 Milan Bartovic RC 1.50 4.00
104 Matthew Lombardi RC 1.50 4.00
105 Eric Staal RC 6.00 15.00
106 Tuomo Ruutu RC 2.00 5.00
107 Pavel Vorobiev RC 1.50 4.00
108 Dan Fritsche RC 1.25 3.00
109 Kent McDonell RC 1.50 4.00
110 Antti Miettinen RC 2.00 5.00
111 Nathan Horton RC 3.00 8.00
112 Dustin Brown RC 3.00 8.00
113 Tim Gleason RC 1.50 4.00
114 Brent Burns RC 4.00 10.00
115 Christopher Higgins RC 2.50 6.00
116 Dan Hamhuis RC 1.50 4.00
117 Jordin Tootoo RC 2.50 6.00
118 Sean Bergenheim RC 1.50 4.00
119 Antoine Vermette RC 2.50 6.00
120 Joni Pitkanen RC 2.00 5.00
121 Marc-Andre Fleury RC 8.00 20.00
122 Peter Sejna RC 1.50 4.00
123 Milan Michalek RC 2.50 6.00
124 Matt Stajan RC 2.00 5.00
125 Boyd Gordon RC 1.50 4.00

2003-04 Pacific Invincible Blue

*1-100 VETS/350: 2X TO 5X BASIC CARDS
*101-125 ROOK/350: .5X TO 1.2X RC
67 Mark Messier 4.00 10.00

2003-04 Pacific Invincible Red

*1-100 VETS/850: 1.5X TO 4X BASIC CARDS
*101-125 ROOKIES/850: .3X TO .8X RC
67 Mark Messier 3.00 8.00

2003-04 Pacific Invincible Retail

*1-100 VETS: .4X TO 1X HOBBY
*101-125 ROOKIES: .25X TO .6X
67 Mark Messier .75 2.00

2003-04 Pacific Invincible Afterburners

1 Ilya Kovalchuk 1.25 3.00
2 Paul Kariya .75 2.00
3 Teemu Selanne .75 2.00
4 Mike Modano 1.25 3.00

5 Henrik Zetterberg 1.00 2.50
6 Marian Gaborik 1.25 3.00
7 Pavel Bure .75 2.00
8 Marian Hossa .75 2.00
9 Martin St. Louis .75 2.00
10 Markus Naslund .75 2.00

2003-04 Pacific Invincible Featured Performers

COMPLETE SET (30) 10.00 25.00
1 Jean-Sebastien Giguere .40 1.00
2 Dany Heatley .75 2.00
3 Joe Thornton 1.00 2.50
4 Miroslav Satan .40 1.00
5 Jarome Iginla .50 1.25
6 Ron Francis .40 1.00
7 Jocelyn Thibault .40 1.00
8 Peter Forsberg 1.50 4.00
9 Rick Nash .75 2.00
10 Mike Modano 1.00 2.50
11 Steve Yzerman 2.00 5.00
12 Ales Hemsky .40 1.00
13 Olli Jokinen .40 1.00
14 Ziggy Palffy .40 1.00
15 Marian Gaborik 1.25 3.00
16 Jose Theodore .50 1.25
17 David Legwand .40 1.00
18 Martin Brodeur 1.50 4.00
19 Michael Peca .40 1.00
20 Eric Lindros .40 1.00
21 Jason Spezza .75 2.00
22 Jeremy Roenick .50 1.25
23 Sean Burke .40 1.00
24 Mario Lemieux 2.50 6.00
25 Pavol Demitra .40 1.00
26 Patrick Marleau .40 1.00
27 Vincent Lecavalier .40 1.00
28 Mats Sundin .40 1.00
29 Todd Bertuzzi .40 1.00
30 Jaromir Jagr 1.00 2.50

2003-04 Pacific Invincible Freeze Frame

COMPLETE SET (24) 10.00 20.00
1 Jean-Sebastien Giguere .30 .75
2 Ryan Miller .60 1.50
3 Jocelyn Thibault .30 .75
4 Patrick Roy 2.00 5.00
5 Marc Denis .30 .75
6 Marty Turco .30 .75
7 Dominik Hasek 1.00 2.50
8 Roberto Luongo .60 1.50
9 Roman Cechmanek .30 .75
10 Jose Theodore .50 1.25
11 Tomas Vokoun .30 .75
12 Martin Brodeur 1.50 4.00
13 Rick DiPietro .30 .75
14 Garth Snow .30 .75
15 Mike Dunham .30 .75
16 Patrick Lalime .30 .75
17 Sean Burke .30 .75
18 Chris Osgood .30 .75
19 Evgeni Nabokov .30 .75
20 John Grahame .30 .75
21 Nikolai Khabibulin .30 .75
22 Ed Belfour .40 1.00
23 Dan Cloutier .30 .75
24 Olaf Kolzig .30 .75

2003-04 Pacific Invincible Jerseys

1 Byron Dafoe 2.50 6.00
2 Milan Hnilicka 2.50 6.00
3 Martin Biron 2.50 6.00
4 Jamie McLennan 2.50 6.00
5 Roman Turek 3.00 8.00
6 Patrick Roy SP 12.00 30.00
7 Fred Brathwaite SP 4.00 10.00
8 Marc Denis 3.00 8.00
9 Ron Tugnutt 3.00 8.00
10 Marty Turco 3.00 8.00
11 Dominik Hasek SP 10.00 25.00
12 Curtis Joseph 4.00 10.00
13 Roman Cechmanek 2.50 6.00
14 Felix Potvin 5.00 12.00
15 Manny Fernandez 3.00 8.00
16 Jose Theodore 4.00 10.00
17 Tomas Vokoun 3.00 8.00
18 Martin Brodeur 8.00 20.00
19 Rick DiPietro 4.00 10.00
20 Mike Richter 3.00 8.00
21 Patrick Lalime 2.50 6.00
22 Jeff Hackett 2.50 6.00
23 Sean Burke 3.00 8.00
24 Johan Hedberg 3.00 8.00
25 Brent Johnson 2.50 6.00
26 Chris Osgood 3.00 8.00
27 Miikka Kiprusoff 4.00 10.00
28 Evgeni Nabokov 4.00 10.00
29 Nikolai Khabibulin 3.00 8.00
30 Ed Belfour SP 6.00 15.00
31 Dan Cloutier 3.00 8.00
32 Olaf Kolzig 4.00 10.00

2003-04 Pacific Invincible New Sensations

1 Stanislav Chistov .60 1.50
2 Dany Heatley 1.25 3.00
3 Ilya Kovalchuk 1.25 3.00
4 Ales Kotalik .60 1.50
5 Ryan Miller .75 2.00
6 Chuck Kobasew .60 1.50
7 Jordan Leopold .60 1.50
8 Tyler Arnason .60 1.50
9 Rick Nash 1.00 2.50
10 Pavel Datsyuk .75 2.00
11 Henrik Zetterberg 1.00 2.50
12 Ales Hemsky .60 1.50
13 Jay Bouwmeester .60 1.50
14 Alexander Frolov .60 1.50
15 Marcel Hossa .60 1.50
16 Rick DiPietro .60 1.50
17 Mattias Weinhandl .60 1.50
18 Jason Spezza 1.00 2.50
19 Barret Jackman .60 1.50
20 Jonathan Cheechoo .75 2.00

2003-04 Pacific Invincible Top Line

1 Sergei Fedorov 1.50 3.00
2 Peter Forsberg 2.00 5.00
3 Paul Kariya 1.00 2.50
4 Joe Sakic 2.00 5.00
5 Brett Hull 1.25 3.00
6 Steve Yzerman 3.00 8.00
7 Marian Gaborik 2.00 5.00
8 Mario Lemieux 4.00 10.00
9 Markus Naslund 1.00 2.50
10 Jaromir Jagr 1.50 4.00

2002 Pacific Les Gardiens

COMPLETE SET (7) 30.00
*GOLD/99: .6X TO 1.5X BASIC CARDS
1 Jean-Sebastien Giguere 2.00 5.00
2 Jocelyn Thibault 2.00 3.00
3 Patrick Roy 4.80 10.00
4 Roberto Luongo 2.00 5.00
5 Jose Theodore 3.20 5.00
6 Martin Brodeur 4.00 8.00
7 Patrick Lalime 2.00 3.00

2003-04 Pacific Luxury Suite

1A Sergei Fedorov J/S-150 12.50 30.00
1B Sergei Fedorov J/P-100 15.00 40.00
2A Ilya Kovalchuk J/S-300 12.50 30.00
2B Ilya Kovalchuk J/P-100 15.00 40.00
3A Jarome Iginla J/S-150 15.00 40.00
3B Jarome Iginla J/P-100 20.00 50.00
4A Ron Francis P/S-65 30.00 80.00
5A Peter Forsberg J/S-150 15.00 40.00
5B Peter Forsberg J/P-100 20.00 50.00
6A Joe Sakic J/S-300 15.00 30.00
6B Joe Sakic J/P-100 20.00 50.00
7A Marc Denis P/S-175 12.50 30.00
8A Mike Modano J/S-150 15.00 40.00
8B Mike Modano J/P-100 15.00 40.00
9A Dominik Hasek P/S-30 50.00 100.00
9B Dominik Hasek S/B-20 50.00 100.00
10A Steve Yzerman J/S-150 30.00 80.00
10B Steve Yzerman J/P-100 30.00 80.00
11A Ziggy Palffy J/S-150 8.00 20.00
11B Ziggy Palffy J/P-100 12.50 30.00
12A Jose Theodore J/S-300 15.00 40.00
12B Jose Theodore J/P-100 20.00 50.00
13A Martin Brodeur J/S-300 15.00 40.00
13B Martin Brodeur J/P-100 25.00 60.00
14A Jason Spezza J/S-300 10.00 25.00
14B Jason Spezza J/P-50 25.00 60.00
15A Mike Comrie J/S-300 6.00 15.00
15B Mike Comrie J/P-50 10.00 25.00
16A Mario Lemieux J/S-100 30.00 80.00
17A Nikolai Khabibulin J/S-150 12.50 30.00
17B Nikolai Khabibulin J/P-50 25.00 60.00
18A Vincent Lecavalier J/S-100 15.00 40.00
18B Vincent Lecavalier J/P-50 25.00 60.00
19A Ed Belfour J/S-300 12.50 30.00
19B Ed Belfour J/P-50 15.00 40.00
20A Mats Sundin J/S-300 12.00 30.00
20B Mats Sundin J/P-50 15.00 40.00
21A Todd Bertuzzi J/S-300 12.50 30.00
21B Todd Bertuzzi J/P-50 20.00 50.00
22A Markus Naslund J/S-300 8.00 20.00
22B Markus Naslund J/P-50 15.00 40.00
23A Olaf Kolzig J/S-150 6.00 15.00
23B Olaf Kolzig J/P-50 15.00 40.00
24A S.Fedorov/J.Giguere J/J 8.00 20.00
24B S.Fedorov/J.Giguere P/P 12.50 30.00
25A Kovalchuk/Heatley J/J-475 10.00 25.00
25B Kovalchuk/Heatley P/P-50 30.00 80.00
26A J.Thornton/S.Samsonov J/J 8.00 20.00
26B J.Thornton/S.Samsonov P/P 15.00 40.00
26C J.Thornton/S.Samsonov J/S 12.50 30.00
27A R.Miller/A.Kotalik J/J 8.00 20.00
27B R.Miller/A.Kotalik P/P 15.00 40.00
28A P.Forsberg/J.Sakic J/J 10.00 25.00
28B P.Forsberg/J.Sakic P/P 40.00 100.00
29A P.Kariya/T.Selanne J/J 5.00 12.00
29B P.Kariya/T.Selanne P/P 25.00 60.00
30A P.Kariya/M.Hejduk J/J 10.00 25.00
30B P.Kariya/M.Hejduk P/P 25.00 60.00
31A T.Selanne/D.Aebischer J/J 8.00 20.00
31B T.Selanne/D.Aebischer P/P 15.00 40.00
32A M.Modano/M.Turco J/J 6.00 15.00
32B M.Modano/M.Turco P/P 15.00 40.00
33A B.Hull/B. Shanahan J/J 10.00 25.00
33B B.Hull/B. Shanahan P/P 20.00 50.00
34A C.Chelios/N.Lidstrom P/P 40.00 100.00
35A R.Smyth/A.Hemsky J/J 6.00 15.00
35B R.Smyth/A.Hemsky P/P 25.00 60.00
36A Bouwmeester/Luongo J/J 6.00 15.00
36B Bouwmeester/Luongo P/P 20.00 50.00
37A Palffy/Deadmarsh J/J-400 5.00 12.00
37B Palffy/Deadmarsh P/P 12.00 30.00
37C Palffy/Deadmarsh B/B 15.00 40.00
38A S.Koivu/J.Theodore J/J 10.00 25.00
38B S.Koivu/J.Theodore P/P 25.00 60.00
39A Vokoun/Walker J/J-350 5.00 12.00
39B Vokoun/Walker P/P 15.00 40.00
39C Vokoun/Walker J/S-100 8.00 20.00
40A M.Brodeur/P.Elias J/J 8.00 20.00
40B M.Brodeur/P.Elias P/P 30.00 80.00
41A A.Yashin/R.DiPietro J/J 8.00 20.00
41B A.Yashin/R.DiPietro P/P 20.00 50.00
42A Lindros/Leetch J/J 8.00 20.00
42B Lindros/Leetch P/P-75 20.00 50.00
43A M. Hossa/P.Lalime J/J 6.00 15.00
43B M. Hossa/P.Lalime P/P 20.00 50.00
44A J.Roenick/J.Hackett J/J 8.00 20.00
44B J.Roenick/J.Hackett P/P 15.00 40.00
45A Jackman/Pronger J/J-250 8.00 20.00
45B Jackman/Pronger P/P-50 20.00 50.00
46A D.Weight/C.Osgood J/J 8.00 20.00
46B D.Weight/C.Osgood P/P 20.00 50.00
47A N.Khabibulin/V.Lecavalier J/J 10.00 25.00
47B N.Khabibulin/V.Lecavalier P/P 15.00 40.00
48A Sundin/Mogilny J/J-500 6.00 15.00
48B Sundin/Mogilny P/P-25 25.00 60.00
49A B.Morrison/D.Cloutier J/J 6.00 15.00
49B B.Morrison/D.Cloutier P/P 12.50 30.00
50A J.Jagr/P.Bondra J/J-400 8.00 20.00
50B J.Jagr/P.Bondra P/P 25.00 60.00
51 Garrett Burnett RC 3.00 8.00
52 Tony Martensson RC 3.00 8.00
53 Sergei Zinovjev RC 3.00 8.00
54 Andrew Peters RC 3.00 8.00
55 Matthew Lombardi RC 3.00 8.00
56 Travis Moen RC 3.00 8.00
57 Pavel Vorobiev RC 3.00 8.00
58 Mikhail Yakubov RC 3.00 8.00
59 Cody McCormick RC 3.00 8.00
60 Dan Fritsche RC 3.00 8.00
61 Kent McDonell RC 3.00 8.00
62 Nikolai Zherdev RC 8.00 20.00
63 Darryl Bootland RC 3.00 8.00
64 Nathan Robinson RC 3.00 8.00
65 Tony Salmelainen RC 3.00 8.00
66 Peter Sarno RC 3.00 8.00
67 Gregory Campbell RC 3.00 8.00
68 Dan Hamhuis RC 3.00 8.00
69 Marek Zidlicky RC 3.00 8.00
70 David Hale RC 3.00 8.00
71 Paul Martin RC 3.00 8.00
72 Dominic Moore RC 3.00 8.00
73 Fredrik Sjostrom RC 3.00 8.00
74 Matt Murley RC 3.00 8.00
75 John Pohl RC 3.00 8.00
76 Tom Preissing RC 3.00 8.00
77 Maxim Kondratiev RC 3.00 8.00
78 Ryan Kesler RC 6.00 15.00
79 Alexander Semin RC 10.00 25.00
80 Rastislav Stana RC 4.00 10.00
81 Joffrey Lupul JSY AU RC 12.00 30.00
82 Patrice Bergeron JSY AU RC 80.00 200.00
83 Brent Krahn PCK AU RC 8.00 20.00
84 Eric Staal PCK AU RC 10.00 25.00
85 Tuomo Ruutu PCK AU RC 10.00 25.00
86 Antti Miettinen JSY AU RC 8.00 20.00
87 Jiri Hudler PCK AU RC 12.00 30.00
88 Nathan Horton JSY AU RC 15.00 40.00
89 Dustin Brown JSY AU RC 15.00 30.00
90 Brent Burns PCK AU RC 12.00 30.00
91 Chris Higgins JSY AU RC 12.50 30.00
92 Jordin Tootoo JSY AU RC 15.00 40.00
93 S.Bergenheim PCK AU RC 8.00 20.00
94 Antoine Vermette JSY AU RC 10.00 25.00
95 Joni Pitkanen JSY AU RC 8.00 20.00
96 M.Fleury PCK AU RC 40.00 80.00
97 Peter Sejna PCK AU RC 8.00 20.00
98 Milan Michalek PCK AU RC 15.00 40.00
99 Matt Stajan PCK AU RC 8.00 20.00
100 Boyd Gordon JSY AU RC 8.00 20.00

2003 Pacific Montreal International

COMPLETE SET (6) 15.00
1 Saku Koivu
Anthony Calvillo 2.00 5.00
2 Jose Theodore
Jermaine Copeland 2.00 5.00
3 Yanic Perreault
Ben Cahoon .75 2.00
4 Richard Zednik
Eric Lapointe .75 2.00
5 Jan Bulis
Bruno Heppell .75 2.00
6 Patrice Brisebois
Kevin Johnson .75 2.00

2003 Pacific Montreal Olympic Stadium Show

COMPLETE SET (8) 15.00 40.00
*GOLD/99: .8X TO 2X BASIC CARDS
1 Stanislav Chistov 1.25 3.00
2 Pascal Leclaire 1.25 3.00
3 Rick Nash 4.00 10.00
4 Henrik Zetterberg 4.00 10.00
5 Jay Bouwmeester 2.50 6.00
6 Alexander Frolov 1.25 3.00
7 Ron Hainsey 1.25 3.00
8 Jason Spezza 4.00 10.00

2004 Pacific Montreal International

COMPLETE SET (8) 6.00 15.00
*GOLD: 2X TO 4X BASIC CARDS
1 Patrice Bergeron 1.50 4.00
2 Eric Staal .75 2.00
3 Nathan Horton .75 2.00
4 Chris Higgins .40 1.00
5 Jordin Tootoo .75 2.00
6 Antoine Vermette .40 1.00
7 Joni Pitkanen .75 2.00
8 Marc-Andre Fleury 1.50 4.00

2004 Pacific NHL All-Star FANtasy

COMPLETE SET (10) 8.00 20.00
1 Joffrey Lupul .60 1.50
2 Patrice Bergeron 1.50 4.00
3 Eric Staal 1.00 2.50
4 Jiri Hudler .75 2.00
5 Brent Burns .60 1.50
6 Jordin Tootoo 1.00 2.50
7 Joni Pitkanen .75 2.00
8 Marc-Andre Fleury 1.50 4.00
9 Peter Sejna .40 1.00
10 Matt Stajan .75 2.00

2004 Pacific NHL All-Star Nets

*GOLD: 1X TO 2.5X BASIC CARDS
1 Eastern Team
Joe Thornton
Martin Brodeur
Marian 12.50 30.00
2 Western Team
Mike Modano
Marty Turco
Marian Gab 15.00 25.00

2004 Pacific NHL Draft All-Star Nets

COMPLETE SET (3) 60.00 125.00
1 I.Kovalchuk
R.Nash 20.00 50.00
2 M.St.Louis
J.Sakic 15.00 40.00
3 M.Turco
M.Brodeur 20.00 50.00

2004 Pacific NHL Draft Show Calder Reflections

COMPLETE SET (8)
1 Joffrey Lupul .75 2.00
2 Patrice Bergeron 1.50 4.00
3 Andrew Raycroft 1.25 3.00
4 Eric Staal .75 2.00
5 Michael Ryder .75 2.00
6 Trent Hunter .40 1.00
7 Marc-Andre Fleury 1.50 4.00
8 Ryan Malone .40 1.00

1997-98 Pacific Omega

COMPLETE SET (250) 12.00 30.00
1 Matt Cullen RC .12 .30
2 Guy Hebert .12 .30
3 Paul Kariya .15 .40
4 Dmitri Mironov .12 .30
5 Steve Rucchin .12 .30
6 Tomas Sandstrom .10 .25
7 Teemu Selanne .30 .75
8 Mikhail Shtalenkov .12 .30
9 Pavel Trnka .10 .25
10 Jason Allison .12 .30
11 Per Axelsson .15 .40
12 Ray Bourque .25 .60
13 Anson Carter .10 .25
14 Byron Dafoe .12 .30
15 Ted Donato .10 .25
16 Hal Gill RC .10 .25
17 Dimitri Khristich .12 .30
18 Sergei Samsonov .12 .30
19 Joe Thornton .25 .60
20 Jason Dawe .12 .30
21 Michal Grosek .10 .25
22 Dominik Hasek .25 .60
23 Brian Holzinger .12 .30
24 Michael Peca .12 .30
25 Derek Plante .12 .30
26 Miroslav Satan .10 .25
27 Steve Shields RC .15 .40
28 Andrew Cassels .10 .25
29 Theo Fleury .20 .50
30 Jarome Iginla .20 .50
31 Derek Morris RC .15 .40
32 Tyler Moss RC .12 .30
33 Michael Nylander .12 .30
34 Dwayne Roloson .12 .30
35 Cory Stillman .12 .30
36 Rick Tabaracci .12 .30
37 German Titov .10 .25
38 Bates Battaglia RC .12 .30
39 Nelson Emerson .12 .30
40 Martin Gelinas .10 .25
41 Sami Kapanen .12 .30
42 Trevor Kidd .10 .25
43 Kevin Dineen .12 .30
44 Keith Primeau .12 .30
45 Gary Roberts .12 .30
46 Tony Amonte .12 .30
47 Keith Carney .10 .25
48 Chris Chelios .15 .40
49 Eric Daze .10 .25
50 Brian Felsner .10 .25
51 Jeff Hackett .10 .25
52 Christian LaFlamme RC .15 .40
53 Alexei Zhamnov .10 .25
54 Craig Billington .10 .25
55 Adam Deadmarsh .10 .25
56 Peter Forsberg .30 .75
57 Valeri Kamensky .12 .30
58 Uwe Krupp .10 .25
59 Jari Kurri .15 .40
60 Claude Lemieux .12 .30
61 Eric Messier RC .15 .40
62 Jeff Odgers .10 .25
63 Sandis Ozolinsh .10 .25
64 Patrick Roy .40 1.00
65 Joe Sakic .30 .75
66 Greg Adams .12 .30
67 Ed Belfour .15 .40
68 Manny Fernandez .10 .25
69 Derian Hatcher .12 .30
70 Jamie Langenbrunner .12 .30
71 Jere Lehtinen .12 .30
72 Juha Lind RC .15 .40
73 Mike Modano .25 .60
74 Joe Nieuwendyk .12 .30
75 Darryl Sydor .10 .25
76 Pat Verbeek .12 .30
77 Sergei Zubov .12 .30
78 Slava Fetisov .10 .25
79 Brent Gilchrist .15 .40
80 Kevin Hodson .12 .30
81 Vyacheslav Kozlov .12 .30
82 Igor Larionov .10 .25
83 Nicklas Lidstrom .15 .40
84 Darren McCarty .12 .30
85 Larry Murphy .12 .30
86 Chris Osgood .15 .40
87 Brendan Shanahan .15 .40
88 Steve Yzerman .40 1.00
89 Kelly Buchberger .12 .30
90 Mike Grier .12 .30
91 Bill Guerin .15 .40
92 Roman Hamrlik .10 .25
93 Curtis Joseph .20 .50
94 Boris Mironov .10 .25
95 Ryan Smyth .12 .30
96 Doug Weight .15 .40
97 Dino Ciccarelli .15 .40
98 Dave Gagner .10 .25
99 Ed Jovanovski .10 .25
100 Scott Mellanby .12 .30
101 Robert Svehla .12 .30
102 John Vanbiesbrouck .15 .40
103 Steve Washburn .10 .25
104 Kevin Weekes RC .12 .30
105 Ray Whitney .12 .30
106 Rob Blake .15 .40
107 Stephane Fiset .12 .30
108 Garry Galley .10 .25
109 Steve McKenna RC .20 .50
110 Glen Murray .12 .30
111 Yanic Perreault .12 .30
112 Luc Robitaille .15 .40
113 Jamie Storr .12 .30
114 Jozef Stumpel .10 .25
115 Vladimir Tsyplakov .12 .30
116 Shayne Corson .12 .30
117 Vincent Damphousse .12 .30
118 Saku Koivu .15 .40
119 Vladimir Malakhov .10 .25
120 Andy Moog .15 .40
121 Mark Recchi .20 .50
122 Martin Rucinsky .12 .30
123 Brian Savage .10 .25
124 Jocelyn Thibault .12 .30
125 Jason Arnott .12 .30
126 Brad Bombardir RC .12 .30
127 Martin Brodeur .40 1.00
128 Patrik Elias RC .25 .60
129 Doug Gilmour .20 .50
130 Bobby Holik .10 .25
131 Randy McKay .12 .30
132 Scott Niedermayer .15 .40
133 Krzysztof Oliwa RC .15 .40
134 Scott Stevens .15 .40
135 Petr Sykora .10 .25
136 Bryan Berard .10 .25
137 Travis Green .12 .30
138 Bryan McCabe .10 .25
139 Sergei Nemchinov .10 .25
140 Zigmund Palffy .15 .40
141 Robert Reichel .12 .30
142 Tommy Salo .10 .25
143 Bryan Smolinski .12 .30
144 Adam Graves .10 .25
145 Wayne Gretzky 1.00 2.50
146 Pat LaFontaine .15 .40
147 Brian Leetch .12 .30
148 Mike Richter .15 .40
149 Kevin Stevens .12 .30
150 Niklas Sundstrom .12 .30
151 Tim Sweeney .10 .25
152 Daniel Alfredsson .15 .40
153 Magnus Arvedson .15 .40
154 Andreas Dackell .12 .30
155 Igor Kravchuk .10 .25
156 Shawn McEachern .10 .25
157 Damian Rhodes .12 .30
158 Ron Tugnutt .15 .40
159 Alexei Yashin .12 .30
160 Rod Brind'Amour .15 .40
161 Paul Coffey .15 .40
162 Eric Desjardins .10 .25
163 Colin Forbes .15 .40
164 Chris Gratton .10 .25
165 Ron Hextall .15 .40
166 Trent Klatt .12 .30
167 John LeClair .15 .40
168 Eric Lindros .25 .60
169 Joel Otto .10 .25
170 Garth Snow .12 .30
171 Dainius Zubrus .12 .30
172 Dallas Drake .12 .30
173 Mike Gartner .20 .50
174 Nikolai Khabibulin .15 .40
175 Teppo Numminen .10 .25
176 Jeremy Roenick .25 .60
177 Keith Tkachuk .15 .40
178 Rick Tocchet .10 .25
179 Oleg Tverdovsky .12 .30
180 Juha Ylonen .12 .30
181 Stu Barnes .10 .25
182 Tom Barrasso .12 .30
183 Rob Brown .12 .30
184 Ron Francis .20 .50
185 Kevin Hatcher .10 .25
186 Jaromir Jagr .50 1.25
187 Alexei Morozov .12 .30
188 Ed Olczyk .10 .25
189 Jim Campbell .10 .25
190 Geoff Courtnall .10 .25
191 Pavol Demitra .20 .50
192 Steve Duchesne .10 .25
193 Grant Fuhr .25 .60
194 Brett Hull .30 .75
195 Al MacInnis .20 .50
196 Chris Pronger .15 .40
197 Pascal Rheaume RC .12 .30
198 Jamie Rivers .12 .30
199 Pierre Turgeon .12 .30
200 Jeff Friesen .12 .30
201 Tony Granato .10 .25
202 John MacLean .10 .25
203 Patrick Marleau .15 .40
204 Marty McSorley .12 .30
205 Owen Nolan .15 .40
206 Marco Sturm RC .15 .40
207 Mike Vernon .12 .30
208 Andrei Zyuzin RC .10 .25
209 Karl Dykhuis .10 .25
210 Daymond Langkow .10 .25
211 Louie DeBrusk .10 .25
212 Daren Puppa .12 .30
213 Mikael Renberg .12 .30
214 Alexander Selivanov .10 .25
215 Paul Ysebaert .12 .30
216 Rob Zamuner .10 .25
217 Sergei Berezin .12 .30
218 Wendel Clark .25 .60
219 Marcel Cousineau .12 .30
220 Tie Domi .12 .30
221 Mike Johnson RC .12 .30
222 Igor Korolev .10 .25
223 Felix Potvin .25 .60
224 Mathieu Schneider .12 .30
225 Mats Sundin .15 .40
226 Yannick Tremblay RC .12 .30
227 Donald Brashear .12 .30
228 Pavel Bure .15 .40
229 Sean Burke .10 .25
230 Trevor Linden .15 .40
231 Mark Messier .30 .75
232 Alexander Mogilny .12 .30
233 Markus Naslund .15 .40
234 Mattias Ohlund .12 .30
235 Dave Scatchard RC .12 .30
236 Peter Bondra .15 .40
237 Andrew Brunette .12 .30
238 Phil Housley .12 .30
239 Dale Hunter .12 .30
240 Calle Johansson .12 .30
241 Joe Juneau .10 .25
242 Olaf Kolzig .15 .40
243 Adam Oates .15 .40
244 Richard Zednik .12 .30
245 Chris Chelios
Keith Tkachuk .15 .40
246 Mike Modano
Ed Belfour .25 .60
247 Teemu Selanne
Saku Koivu .30 .75
248 Eric Lindros
Shayne Corson .25 .60
249 Patrick Roy
Martin Brodeur .40 1.00
250 Wayne Gretzky
Mark Messier 1.00 2.50
NNO Mike Modano SAMPLE .25 .60

1997-98 Pacific Omega Copper

*COPPER: 2X TO 5X BASIC CARDS
*COPPER ROOKIE STAR: 1.2X TO 3X

1997-98 Pacific Omega Dark Gray

*DARK GRAY: 2X TO 5X BASIC CARDS
*DARK GRAY ROOKIE STAR: 1.2X TO 3X

1997-98 Pacific Omega Emerald Green

*GREEN: 2X TO 5X BASIC CARDS
*GREEN ROOKIE STAR: 1.2X TO 3X

1997-98 Pacific Omega Gold

*GOLD: 2X TO 5X BASIC CARDS
*GOLD ROOKIE STAR: 1.2X TO 3X BASIC CARDS

1997-98 Pacific Omega Ice Blue

*ICE BLUE VETS: 10X TO 25X BASIC CARDS
*ICE BLUE ROOKIE STAR: 6X TO 15X

1997-98 Pacific Omega Game Face

COMPLETE SET (20) 12.00 30.00
1 Paul Kariya .60 1.50
2 Teemu Selanne .60 1.50
3 Peter Forsberg 1.50 4.00
4 Joe Sakic 2.00 5.00
5 Mike Modano 1.25 3.00
6 Nicklas Lidstrom .60 1.50
7 Brendan Shanahan .60 1.50
8 Steve Yzerman 3.00 8.00
9 Ryan Smyth .50 1.25
10 Saku Koivu .60 1.50
11 Wayne Gretzky 4.00 10.00
12 John LeClair .60 1.50
13 Eric Lindros 1.25 3.00
14 Dainius Zubrus .60 1.50
15 Keith Tkachuk .60 1.50
16 Jaromir Jagr 1.25 3.00
17 Brett Hull .75 2.00
18 Pavel Bure .60 1.50
19 Mark Messier .60 1.50
20 Peter Bondra .50 1.25

1997-98 Pacific Omega No Scoring Zone

COMPLETE SET (10) 6.00 12.00
1 Dominik Hasek 1.00 2.50
2 Patrick Roy 2.50 6.00
3 Ed Belfour .50 1.25
4 Chris Osgood .40 1.00
5 John Vanbiesbrouck .40 1.00
6 Andy Moog .40 1.00
7 Martin Brodeur 1.25 3.00
8 Mike Richter .50 1.25
9 Ron Hextall .40 1.00
10 Felix Potvin .50 1.25

1997-98 Pacific Omega Silks

COMPLETE SET (12) 30.00 60.00
1 Paul Kariya 1.25 3.00
2 Teemu Selanne 2.50 6.00
3 Peter Forsberg 3.00 8.00
4 Patrick Roy 6.00 15.00
5 Joe Sakic 2.50 6.00
6 Steve Yzerman 6.00 15.00
7 Martin Brodeur 3.00 0.00
8 Wayne Gretzky 8.00 20.00
9 Eric Lindros 1.25 3.00
10 Jaromir Jagr 2.00 5.00
11 Pavel Bure 1.25 3.00
12 Mark Messier 1.25 3.00

1997-98 Pacific Omega Stick Handle Laser Cuts

COMPLETE SET (20) 60.00 120.00
1 Paul Kariya 5.00 12.00
2 Teemu Selanne 6.00 15.00
3 Theo Fleury 2.00 5.00
4 Chris Chelios 2.00 5.00
5 Peter Forsberg 6.00 15.00
6 Joe Sakic 4.00 10.00
7 Mike Modano 3.00 8.00
8 Brendan Shanahan 2.00 5.00
9 Steve Yzerman 12.50 30.00
10 Saku Koivu 2.00 5.00
11 Doug Gilmour 2.00 5.00
12 Zigmund Palffy 2.00 5.00
13 Wayne Gretzky 15.00 40.00
14 Pat LaFontaine 2.00 5.00
15 John LeClair 2.00 5.00
16 Eric Lindros 2.00 5.00
17 Jaromir Jagr 3.00 8.00
18 Mats Sundin 2.00 5.00
19 Pavel Bure 2.00 5.00
20 Mark Messier 2.00 5.00

1997-98 Pacific Omega Team Leaders

COMPLETE SET (20) 15.00 30.00
1 Paul Kariya .50 1.25
2 Ray Bourque .75 2.00
3 Theo Fleury .20 .50
4 Patrick Roy 2.50 6.00
5 Joe Sakic 1.00 2.50
6 Ed Belfour .50 1.25
7 Joe Nieuwendyk .40 1.00
8 Brendan Shanahan .50 1.25
9 Steve Yzerman 2.50 6.00
10 Ryan Smyth .40 1.00
11 Shayne Corson .20 .50
12 Mark Recchi .40 1.00
13 Martin Brodeur 1.25 3.00
14 Wayne Gretzky 3.00 8.00
15 Rod Brind'Amour .40 1.00
16 Eric Lindros .50 1.25
17 Chris Pronger .40 1.00
18 Felix Potvin .50 1.25
19 Pavel Bure .50 1.25
20 Mark Messier .50 1.25

1998-99 Pacific Omega

*RED: 1.5X TO 4X BASIC CARDS
*OPENING DAY: 10X TO 25X BASIC CARDS
1 Travis Green .12 .30
2 Stu Grimson .12 .30
3 Guy Hebert .15 .40
4 Paul Kariya .20 .50
5 Marty McInnis .12 .30
6 Fredrik Olausson .12 .30
7 Steve Rucchin .12 .30
8 Teemu Selanne .40 1.00
9 Johan Davidsson
Antti Aalto .12 .30
10 Jason Allison .15 .40
11 Ken Belanger .12 .30
12 Ray Bourque .30 .75
13 Anson Carter .15 .40
14 Byron Dafoe .15 .40
15 Steve Heinze .12 .30
16 Dimitri Khristich .12 .30
17 Sergei Samsonov .15 .40
18 Robbie Tallas .12 .30
19 Joe Thornton .30 .75
20 Matthew Barnaby .12 .30
21 Curtis Brown .12 .30
22 Michal Grosek .12 .30
23 Domink Hasek .30 .75
24 Brian Holzinger .12 .30
25 Micael Peca .12 .30
26 Rob Ray .12 .30
27 Geoff Sanderson .12 .30
28 Miroslav Satan .15 .40
29 Dixon Ward .15 .40
30 Valeri Bure .12 .30
31 Theo Fleury .25 .60
32 Jean-Sebastien Giguere .15 .40
33 Jarome Iginla .25 .60
34 Tyler Moss .12 .30
35 Cory Stillman .12 .30
36 Jason Wiemer .12 .30
37 Clarke Wilm RC .12 .30
38 M.St.Louis RC/R.Fata .60 1.50
39 Paul Coffey .20 .50
40 Ron Francis .25 .60
41 Martin Gelinas .12 .30
42 Arturs Irbe .15 .40
43 Sami Kapanen .12 .30
44 Trevor Kidd .12 .30
45 Keith Primeau .15 .40
46 Gary Roberts .12 .30
47 Ray Sheppard .12 .30
48 Tony Amonte .15 .40
49 Chris Chelios .20 .50
50 Eric Daze .15 .40
51 Nelson Emerson .12 .30
52 Doug Gilmour .25 .60
53 Mike Maneluk RC .12 .30
54 Bob Probert .20 .50
55 Jocelyn Thibault .15 .40
56 Alexei Zhamnov .12 .30
57 Todd White RC
Brad Brown .15 .40
58 Adam Deadmarsh .12 .30
59 Marc Denis .15 .40
60 Peter Forsberg .40 1.00
61 Claude Lemieux .15 .40
62 Jeff Odgers .12 .30
63 Sandis Ozolinsh .12 .30
64 Patrick Roy .50 1.25
65 Joe Sakic .40 1.00
66 Wade Belak RC
Scott Parker .12 .30
67 C.Drury/M.Hejduk RC .30 .75
68 Ed Belfour .20 .50
69 Derian Hatcher .12 .30
70 Brett Hull .40 1.00
71 Jamie Langenbrunner .12 .30
72 Jere Lehtinen .15 .40
73 Mike Modano .30 .75
74 Joe Nieuwendyk .15 .40
75 Darryl Sydor .12 .30
76 Roman Turek .12 .30
77 Sergei Zubov .15 .40
78 Sergei Gusev RC
Jamie Wright .12 .30
79 Sergei Fedorov .30 .75
80 Joey Kocur .12 .30
81 Martin LaPointe .12 .30
82 Igor Larionov .20 .50
83 Nicklas Lidstrom .25 .60
84 Darren McCarty .12 .30
85 Larry Murphy .15 .40
86 Chris Osgood .20 .50
87 Brendan Shanahan .20 .50
88 Steve Yzerman .50 1.25
89 N.Maracle RC/S.Roest RC .15 .40
90 Josef Beranek .12 .30
91 Sean Brown .12 .30
92 Bill Guerin .20 .50
93 Roman Hamrlik .12 .30
94 Janne Niinimaa .12 .30
95 Mikhail Shtalenkov .12 .30
96 Ryan Smyth .15 .40
97 Doug Weight .20 .50
98 Tom Poti
Craig Millar .12 .30
99 Pavel Bure .20 .50
100 Sean Burke .12 .30
101 Dino Ciccarelli .20 .50
102 Bret Hedican .12 .30
103 Viktor Kozlov .15 .40
104 Paul Laus .15 .40
105 Rob Niedermayer .12 .30
106 Mark Parrish RC .30 .75
107 Ray Whitney .12 .30
108 O.Kvasha RC/P.Worrell RC .20 .50
109 Rob Blake .20 .50
110 Stephane Fiset .15 .40
111 Glen Murray .15 .40
112 Luc Robitaille .20 .50
113 Jamie Storr .15 .40
114 Jozef Stumpel .12 .30
115 Vladimir Tsyplakov .12 .30
116 M.Visheau RC
J.Green RC .20 .50

117 Olli Jokinen RC
Pavel Rosa .15 .40
118 Benoit Brunet .12 .30
119 Shayne Corson .15 .40
120 Vincent Damphousse .15 .40
121 Jeff Hackett .12 .30
122 Matt Higgins RC .12 .30
123 Saku Koivu .20 .50
124 Mark Recchi .25 .60
125 Martin Rucinsky .12 .30
126 Brian Savage .12 .30
127 Andrew Brunette .15 .40
128 Mike Dunham .15 .40
129 Greg Johnson .12 .30
130 Sergei Krivokrasov .12 .30
131 Denny Lambert .15 .40
132 Cliff Ronning .12 .30
133 Tomas Vokoun .12 .30
134 Patrick Cote
Kimmo Timonen .12 .30
135 Jason Arnott .15 .40
136 Martin Brodeur .50 1.25
137 Patrik Elias .20 .50
138 Bobby Holik .12 .30
139 Brendan Morrison .12 .30
140 Krzysztof Oliwa .12 .30
141 Brian Rolston .15 .40
142 Vadim Sharifijanov .12 .30
143 Scott Stevens .20 .50
144 Petr Sykora .12 .30
145 Ted Donato .12 .30
146 Kenny Jonsson .12 .30
147 Trevor Linden .20 .50
148 Gino Odjick .12 .30
149 Zigmund Palffy .20 .50
150 Felix Potvin .30 .75
151 Robert Reichel .12 .30
152 Tommy Salo .15 .40
153 Mike Watt
Eric Brewer .20 .50
154 Dan Cloutier .15 .40
155 Adam Graves .12 .30
156 Wayne Gretzky 1.25 3.00
157 Todd Harvey .12 .30
158 Brian Leetch .15 .40
159 Manny Malhotra .20 .50
160 Petr Nedved .12 .30
161 Mike Richter .20 .50
162 Esa Tikkanen .12 .30
163 Daniel Alfredsson .20 .50
164 Marian Hossa .20 .50
165 Andreas Johansson .12 .30
166 Shawn McEachern .12 .30
167 Wade Redden .12 .30
168 Damian Rhodes .20 .50
169 Ron Tugnutt .12 .30
170 Alexei Yashin .15 .40
171 Patrick Traverse RC
Sami Salo .12 .30
172 Rod Brind'Amour .20 .50
173 Eric Desjardins .15 .40
174 Ron Hextall .20 .50
175 Keith Jones .12 .30
176 John LeClair .20 .50
177 Eric Lindros .30 .75
178 Mikael Renberg .15 .40
179 Dimitri Tertyshny RC .12 .30
180 John Vanbiesbrouck .20 .50
181 Dainius Zubrus .12 .30
182 Daniel Briere .15 .40
183 Dallas Drake .12 .30
184 Nikolai Khabibulin .20 .50
185 Jyrki Lumme .12 .30
186 Teppo Numminen .12 .30
187 Jeremy Roenick .30 .75
188 Keith Tkachuk .20 .50
189 Rick Tocchet .15 .40
190 Oleg Tverdovsky .20 .50
191 Jim Waite .12 .30
192 Jean-Sebastien Aubin RC .30 .75
193 Stu Barnes .12 .30
194 Tom Barrasso .15 .40
195 Jaromir Jagr .60 1.50
196 Alexei Kovalev .15 .40
197 Robert Lang .12 .30
198 Alexei Morozov .12 .30
199 Martin Straka .12 .30
200 J.Hrdina RC/M.Galanov RC .25 .60
201 Pavol Demitra .25 .60
202 Grant Fuhr .30 .75
203 Al MacInnis .25 .60
204 Jamie McLennan .15 .40
205 Chris Pronger .20 .50
206 Pierre Turgeon .15 .40
207 Tony Twist .12 .30
208 M.Reasoner RC/L.Bartecko .20 .50
209 Jeff Friesen .12 .30
210 Bryan Marchment .12 .30
211 Patrick Marleau .20 .50
212 Owen Nolan .20 .50
213 Mike Ricci .12 .30
214 Steve Shields .12 .30
215 Marco Sturm .12 .30
216 Mike Vernon .15 .40
217 Wendel Clark .30 .75
218 Chris Gratton .15 .40
219 Vincent Lecavalier .40 1.00
220 Sandy McCarthy .12 .30
221 Stephane Richer .12 .30
222 Darcy Tucker .12 .30
223 Rob Zamuner .12 .30
224 P.Kubina RC/Z.Bierk RC .25 .60
225 Bryan Berard .15 .40
226 Tie Domi .15 .40
227 Mike Johnson .12 .30
228 Curtis Joseph .25 .60
229 Igor Korolev .12 .30
230 Alyn McCauley .12 .30
231 Mats Sundin .20 .50
232 Steve Thomas .12 .30
233 T.Kaberle RC/D.Markov RC .25 .60
234 Adrian Aucoin .12 .30
235 Corey Hirsch .12 .30
236 Mark Messier .40 1.00
237 Alexander Mogilny .15 .40
238 Bill Muckalt RC .12 .30
239 Markus Naslund .20 .50
240 Mattias Ohlund .12 .30
241 Garth Snow .15 .40
242 Matt Cooke RC
Peter Schaefer .12 .30
243 Brian Bellows .15 .40
244 Craig Berube .12 .30
245 Peter Bondra .20 .50
246 Matt Herr RC .12 .30
247 Joe Juneau .12 .30
248 Olaf Kolzig .20 .50
249 Adam Oates .20 .50
250 Richard Zednik .12 .30
251 Last Game at MLG SP 2.00 5.00
252 First Game at ACC SP 2.00 5.00
S136 Martin Brodeur SAMPLE .50 1.25

1998-99 Pacific Omega Championship Spotlight

*GREEN/50: 1.5X TO 4X BASIC INSERTS
1 Paul Kariya 2.50 6.00
2 Dominik Hasek 4.00 10.00
3 Patrick Roy 6.00 15.00
4 Steve Yzerman 6.00 15.00
5 Pavel Bure 2.50 6.00
6 Martin Brodeur 6.00 15.00
7 Wayne Gretzky 15.00 40.00
8 Eric Lindros 4.00 10.00
9 Jaromir Jagr 8.00 20.00
10 Curtis Joseph 3.00 8.00

1998-99 Pacific Omega EO Portraits

1 Paul Kariya 1.00 2.50
2 Teemu Selanne 2.00 5.00
3 Dominik Hasek 1.50 4.00
4 Peter Forsberg 2.00 5.00
5 Patrick Roy 2.50 6.00
6 Joe Sakic 2.00 5.00
7 Brett Hull 2.00 5.00
8 Mike Modano 1.50 4.00
9 Sergei Fedorov 1.50 4.00
10 Brendan Shanahan 1.00 2.50
11 Steve Yzerman 2.50 6.00
12 Pavel Bure 1.00 2.50
13 Martin Brodeur 2.50 6.00
14 Wayne Gretzky 6.00 15.00
15 John LeClair 1.00 2.50
16 Eric Lindros 1.50 4.00
17 Keith Tkachuk 1.00 2.50
18 Jaromir Jagr 3.00 8.00
19 Mats Sundin 1.00 2.50
20 Mark Messier 2.00 5.00

1998-99 Pacific Omega Face to Face

1 P.Roy/M.Brodeur 4.00 10.00
2 W. Gretzky/P.Kariya 10.00 25.00
3 D.Hasek/J.Jagr 5.00 12.00
4 S.Fedorov/P.Bure 2.50 6.00
5 K.Tkachuk/B.Shanahan 1.50 4.00
6 S.Yzerman/J.Sakic 4.00 10.00
7 T.Selanne/S.Koivu 3.00 8.00
8 P.Forsberg/M.Sundin 3.00 8.00
9 M.Modano/J.LeClair 2.50 6.00
10 E.Lindros/M.Messier 3.00 8.00

1998-99 Pacific Omega Online

1 Paul Kariya .30 .75
2 Teemu Selanne .60 1.50
3 Ray Bourque .50 1.25
4 Dominik Hasek .50 1.25
5 Theo Fleury .40 1.00
6 Chris Chelios .30 .75
7 Doug Gilmour .40 1.00
8 Peter Forsberg .60 1.50
9 Patrick Roy .75 2.00
10 Joe Sakic .60 1.50
11 Ed Belfour .30 .75
12 Brett Hull .60 1.50
13 Mike Modano .50 1.25
14 Sergei Fedorov .50 1.25
15 Brendan Shanahan .30 .75
16 Steve Yzerman .75 2.00
17 Pavel Bure .30 .75
18 Saku Koivu .30 .75
19 Martin Brodeur .75 2.00
20 Brendan Morrison .20 .50
21 Zigmund Palffy .30 .75
22 Felix Potvin .50 1.25
23 Wayne Gretzky 2.00 5.00
24 Alexei Yashin .25 .60
25 John LeClair .30 .75
26 Eric Lindros .50 1.25
27 John Vanbiesbrouck .30 .75
28 Nikolai Khabibulin .30 .75
29 Keith Tkachuk .30 .75
30 Jaromir Jagr 1.00 2.50
31 Vincent Lecavalier .60 1.50
32 Curtis Joseph .40 1.00
33 Mats Sundin .30 .75
34 Mark Messier .60 1.50
35 Bill Muckalt .20 .50
36 Peter Bondra .30 .75

1998-99 Pacific Omega Planet Ice

*ICE/25-100: 1.25X TO 3X BASIC INSERTS
1 Ray Bourque 2.50 6.00
2 Chris Chelios 1.50 4.00
3 Vincent Lecavalier 3.00 8.00
4 Mark Parrish 2.50 6.00
5 Felix Potvin 2.50 6.00
6 Alexei Yashin 1.25 3.00
7 Ed Belfour 1.50 4.00
8 Peter Bondra 1.50 4.00
9 Brett Hull 3.00 8.00
10 Mark Messier 3.00 8.00
11 Mats Sundin 1.50 4.00
12 John Vanbiesbrouck 1.50 4.00
13 Sergei Fedorov 2.50 6.00
14 Curtis Joseph 2.00 5.00
15 John LeClair 1.50 4.00
16 Mike Modano 2.50 6.00
17 Brendan Shanahan 1.50 4.00
18 Keith Tkachuk 1.50 4.00
19 Martin Brodeur 4.00 10.00
20 Pavel Bure 1.50 4.00
21 Dominik Hasek 2.50 6.00
22 Joe Sakic 3.00 8.00
23 Teemu Selanne 3.00 8.00
24 Steve Yzerman 4.00 10.00
25 Peter Forsberg 3.00 8.00
26 Wayne Gretzky 10.00 25.00
27 Jaromir Jagr 5.00 12.00
28 Paul Kariya 1.50 4.00
29 Eric Lindros 2.50 6.00
30 Patrick Roy 4.00 10.00

1998-99 Pacific Omega Prism

COMPLETE SET (20) 20.00 40.00
1 Paul Kariya .60 1.50
2 Teemu Selanne .60 1.50
3 Dominik Hasek .60 1.50
4 Peter Forsberg 1.50 4.00
5 Patrick Roy 3.00 8.00
6 Joe Sakic 1.25 3.00
7 Mike Modano 1.00 2.50
8 Sergei Fedorov 1.00 2.50
9 Brendan Shanahan .60 1.50
10 Steve Yzerman 3.00 8.00
11 Pavel Bure .60 1.50
12 Martin Brodeur 1.50 4.00
13 Wayne Gretzky 4.00 10.00
14 Alexei Yashin .25 .60
15 John LeClair .60 1.50
16 Eric Lindros .60 1.50
17 Keith Tkachuk .60 1.50
18 Jaromir Jagr 1.00 2.50
19 Mats Sundin .60 1.50
20 Mark Messier .60 1.50

1999-00 Pacific Omega

COMPLETE SET (250) 30.00 60.00
1 Matt Cullen .12 .30
2 Guy Hebert .20 .50
3 Paul Kariya .20 .50
4 Marty McInnis .12 .30
5 Steve Rucchin .12 .30
6 Teemu Selanne .40 1.00
7 Pascal Trepanier .12 .30
8 L.Kohn
V.Vishnevski .15 .40
9 Andrew Brunette .12 .30
10 Nelson Emerson .12 .30
11 Ray Ferraro .12 .30
12 Damian Rhodes .12 .30
13 Patrik Stefan RC .20 .50
14 Dean Sylvester RC .12 .30
15 P.Buzek
S.Fankhouser RC .12 .30
16 Jason Allison .15 .40
17 Dave Andreychuk .20 .50
18 Ray Bourque .30 .75
19 Anson Carter .15 .40
20 Byron Dafoe .15 .40
21 Sergei Samsonov .15 .40
22 Joe Thornton .30 .75
23 J.GrahameRC
J.HendersonRC .15 .40
24 Maxim Afinogenov .12 .30
25 Martin Biron .15 .40
26 Curtis Brown .12 .30
27 Brian Campbell RC .20 .50
28 Dominik Hasek .30 .75
29 Dimitri Kalinin RC .12 .30
30 Michael Peca .15 .40
31 Miroslav Satan .15 .40
32 Rhett Warrener .12 .30
33 J.L.Grand-Pierre RC
D.Moravec RC .12 .30
34 Fred Brathwaite .12 .30
35 Valeri Bure .12 .30
36 Grant Fuhr .30 .75
37 Phil Housley .15 .40
38 Jarome Iginla .25 .60
39 Oleg Saprykin RC .20 .50
40 Marc Savard .12 .30
41 Cory Stillman .12 .30
42 T.Brigley RC
R.Regehr .12 .30
43 Ron Francis .25 .60
44 Sean Hill .12 .30
45 Arturs Irbe .15 .40
46 Sami Kapanen .12 .30
47 Curtis Leschyshyn .12 .30
48 Jeff O'Neill .12 .30
49 Gary Roberts .12 .30
50 D.Tanabe
T.Westlund RC .12 .30
51 Tony Amonte .15 .40
52 Eric Daze .15 .40
53 Doug Gilmour .25 .60
54 Michael Nylander .12 .30
55 Steve Sullivan .12 .30
56 Jocelyn Thibault .15 .40
57 Alexei Zhamnov .12 .30
58 J-P Dumont
M.Lamothe RC .15 .40
59 C.Herperger RC
S.McCarthy .12 .30
60 Adam Deadmarsh 2.00 5.00
61 Chris Drury .15 .40
62 Peter Forsberg .40 1.00
63 Milan Hejduk .15 .40
64 Sandis Ozolinsh .12 .30
65 Patrick Roy .50 1.25
66 Joe Sakic .40 1.00
67 Alex Tanguay .15 .40
68 M.Denis
M.Skoula RC .15 .40
69 S.Helenius RC
B.Willsie .15 .40
70 Ed Belfour .20 .50
71 Manny Fernandez .12 .30
72 Brett Hull .40 1.00
73 Jere Lehtinen .15 .40
74 Mike Modano .30 .75
75 Brenden Morrow .20 .50
76 Joe Nieuwendyk .15 .40
77 Sergei Zubov .15 .40
78 R.Christie RC
R.Lyashenko .12 .30
79 R.Jackman
A.Letang RC .20 .50
80 Chris Chelios .20 .50
81 Sergei Fedorov .30 .75
82 Igor Larionov .20 .50
83 Nicklas Lidstrom .20 .50
84 Chris Osgood .20 .50
85 Brendan Shanahan .20 .50
86 Pat Verbeek .15 .40
87 Ken Wregget .12 .30
88 Steve Yzerman .50 1.25
89 Paul Comrie RC .30 .75
90 Bill Guerin .20 .50
91 Tom Poti .12 .30
92 Bert Robertsson RC .12 .30
93 Tommy Salo .15 .40
94 Alexander Selivanov .12 .30
95 Ryan Smyth .15 .40
96 Doug Weight .20 .50
97 Pavel Bure .20 .50
98 Viktor Kozlov .12 .30
99 Mark Parrish .12 .30
100 Mikhail Shtalenkov .12 .30
101 Robert Svehla .12 .30
102 Mike Vernon .15 .40
103 Ray Whitney .15 .40
104 D.DuerdenRC/I.Nvsltsv RC .25 .60
105 J.Jakopin RC
F.Kuba RC .12 .30
106 Rob Blake .20 .50
107 Stephane Fiset .15 .40
108 Jaroslav Modry .12 .30
109 Glen Murray .15 .40
110 Zigmund Palffy .20 .50
111 Luc Robitaille .20 .50
112 Bryan Smolinski .12 .30
113 Jamie Storr .12 .30
114 Marko Tuomainen .12 .30
115 B.Chartrand RC
F.Kaberle .12 .30
116 Shayne Corson .15 .40
117 Craig Darby .12 .30
118 Jeff Hackett .12 .30
119 Saku Koivu .20 .50
120 Trevor Linden .20 .50
121 Martin Rucinsky .12 .30
122 Brian Savage .12 .30
123 Jose Theodore .20 .50
124 F.Bouillon RC
S.Robidas RC .20 .50
125 Mike Ribeiro
J.Ward .12 .30
126 Mike Dunham .12 .30
127 Patric Kjellberg .12 .30
128 Cliff Ronning .12 .30
129 Tomas Vokoun .20 .50
130 D.Legwand
R.Robitaille .12 .30
131 R.Lintner RC
K.Skrastins RC .12 .30
132 Jason Arnott .15 .40
133 Martin Brodeur .50 1.25
134 Patrik Elias .20 .50
135 Scott Gomez .15 .40
136 Bobby Holik .12 .30
137 Claude Lemieux .15 .40
138 Petr Sykora .15 .40
139 J.Madden RC
B.Rafalski RC .20 .50
140 Mariusz Czerkawski .12 .30
141 Brad Isbister .12 .30
142 Jorgen Jonsson RC .12 .30
143 Roberto Luongo .30 .75
144 Bill Muckalt .12 .30
145 Kevin Weekes .12 .30
146 T.Connolly
E.Korolev RC .12 .30
147 Alexandre Daigle .12 .30
148 Radek Dvorak .12 .30
149 Theo Fleury .25 .60
150 Adam Graves .15 .40
151 Brian Leetch .15 .40
152 Petr Nedved .12 .30
153 Mike Richter .20 .50
154 Michael York .12 .30
155 J.Hlavac
K.Johnsson RC .12 .30
156 Daniel Alfredsson .20 .50
157 Magnus Arvedson .12 .30
158 Radek Bonk .12 .30
159 Marian Hossa .20 .50
160 Patrick Lalime .15 .40
161 Shawn McEachern .12 .30
162 Petr Schastlivy RC .12 .30
163 Ron Tugnutt .15 .40
164 Shaun Van Allen .12 .30
165 Alexei Yashin .15 .40
166 M.Fisher RC
A.Roy RC .20 .50
167 Brian Boucher .20 .50
168 Eric Desjardins .15 .40
169 Simon Gagne .20 .50
170 Daymond Langkow .15 .40
171 John LeClair .20 .50
172 Eric Lindros .30 .75
173 Keith Primeau .15 .40
174 Mark Recchi .25 .60
175 Mikael Renberg .12 .30
176 John Vanbiesbrouck .20 .50
177 A.Delmore RC
M.Eaton RC .12 .30
178 Shane Doan .15 .40
179 Dallas Drake .12 .30
180 Robert Esche RC .20 .50
181 Travis Green .12 .30
182 Nikolai Khabibulin .15 .40
183 Teppo Numminen .12 .30
184 Jeremy Roenick .30 .75
185 Keith Tkachuk .20 .50
186 T.Letowski
R.Suchy RC .12 .30
187 Jan Hrdina .12 .30
188 Jaromir Jagr .60 1.50
189 Hans Jonsson RC .12 .30
190 Alexei Kovalev .15 .40
191 Martin Straka .12 .30
192 German Titov .12 .30
193 Tyler Wright .12 .30
194 J.S.Aubin
M.Rozsival RC .15 .40
195 Pavol Demitra .25 .60
196 Al MacInnis .25 .60
197 Jamie McLennan .15 .40
198 Tyson Nash RC .12 .30
199 Chris Pronger .20 .50
200 Todd Reirden RC .12 .30
201 Roman Turek .15 .40
202 Pierre Turgeon .15 .40
203 J.Hecht RC
L.Nagy RC .30 .75
204 Vincent Damphousse .15 .40
205 Jeff Friesen .15 .40
206 Todd Harvey .12 .30
207 Alexander Korolyuk .12 .30
208 Patrick Marleau .20 .50
209 Owen Nolan .20 .50
210 Steve Shields .15 .40
211 Gary Suter .12 .30
212 Evgeni Nabokov RC
Brad Stuart 2.50 6.00
213 Dan Cloutier .12 .30
214 Stan Drulia .12 .30
215 Chris Gratton .12 .30
216 Vincent Lecavalier .20 .50
217 Steve Martins RC .12 .30
218 Fredrik Modin .12 .30
219 Mike Sillinger .12 .30
220 B.Clymer RC
N.Ekman RC .12 .30
221 Nikolai Antropov RC .50 1.25
222 Sergei Berezin .12 .30
223 Tie Domi .15 .40
224 Jonas Hoglund .12 .30
225 Curtis Joseph .25 .60
226 Tomas Kaberle .12 .30
227 Dimitri Khristich .12 .30
228 Mats Sundin .20 .50
229 Steve Thomas .12 .30
230 A.Mair RC
D.Yakushin RC .12 .30
231 Todd Bertuzzi .15 .40
232 Andrew Cassels .12 .30
233 Steve Kariya RC .20 .50
234 Mark Messier .40 1.00
235 Alexander Mogilny .15 .40
236 Markus Naslund .20 .50
237 Felix Potvin .60 1.50
238 R.Bonni RC
Z.Komarniski .12 .30
239 H.Druken
P.Schaefer .12 .30
240 B.Leeb RC
A.Michaud RC .12 .30
241 Peter Bondra .20 .50
242 Jan Bulis .12 .30
243 Olaf Kolzig .20 .50
244 Steve Konowalchuk .12 .30
245 Adam Oates .20 .50
246 J.Halpern RC
G.Mtrplt RC .12 .30
247 A.Tezikov RC
A.Volchkov RC .20 .50
248 North American All-Stars .15 .40
249 World All-Stars .15 .40
250 P.Bure
V.Bure .20 .50
NNO Martin Brodeur SAMPLE .50 1.25

1999-00 Pacific Omega Copper

*VETS: 4X TO 10 BASE
*ROOKIES: 2X TO 5X BASE
234 Mark Messier 6.00 15.00

1999-00 Pacific Omega Gold

*VETS: 2X TO 5X BASE
*ROOKIES: 1X TO 2.5X BASE
234 Mark Messier 4.00 10.00

1999-00 Pacific Omega Ice Blue

*VETS: 5X TO 12X BASIC CARDS
*ROOKIES: 2.5X TO 6X BASIC CARDS
234 Mark Messier 6.00 15.00

1999-00 Pacific Omega Premiere Date

*VETS: 6X TO 15X BASE
*ROOKIES: 3X TO 8X BASE
234 Mark Messier 6.00 15.00

1999-00 Pacific Omega Cup Contenders

COMPLETE SET (20) 25.00 60.00
1 Paul Kariya 1.00 2.50
2 Dominik Hasek 1.50 4.00
3 Peter Forsberg 2.00 5.00
4 Patrick Roy 2.50 6.00
5 Joe Sakic 2.00 5.00
6 Brett Hull 2.00 5.00
7 Mike Modano 1.50 4.00
8 Sergei Fedorov 1.50 4.00
9 Brendan Shanahan 1.00 2.50
10 Steve Yzerman 2.50 6.00
11 Pavel Bure 1.00 2.50
12 Martin Brodeur 2.50 6.00
13 Theo Fleury 1.25 3.00
14 Mike Richter 1.00 2.50
15 John LeClair 1.00 2.50
16 Jeremy Roenick 1.50 4.00
17 Jaromir Jagr 3.00 8.00
18 Al MacInnis 1.25 3.00
19 Curtis Joseph 1.25 3.00
20 Mark Messier 2.00 5.00

1999-00 Pacific Omega EO Portraits

COMPLETE SET (20) 20.00 50.00
1 Paul Kariya 1.00 2.50
2 Teemu Selanne 2.00 5.00
3 Patrik Stefan 1.00 2.50
4 Dominik Hasek 1.50 4.00
5 Peter Forsberg 2.00 5.00
6 Patrick Roy 2.50 6.00
7 Mike Modano 1.50 4.00
8 Brendan Shanahan 1.00 2.50
9 Steve Yzerman 2.50 6.00
10 Pave Bure 1.00 2.50
11 Martin Brodeur 2.50 6.00
12 Scott Gomez .75 2.00
13 Eric Lindros 1.50 4.00
14 John Vanbiesbrouck 1.00 2.50
15 Keith Tkachuk 1.00 2.50
16 Jaromir Jagr 3.00 8.00
17 Vincent Lecavalier 1.00 2.50
18 Curtis Joseph 1.25 3.00
19 Mats Sundin 1.00 2.50
20 Mark Messier 2.00 5.00

1999-00 Pacific Omega Game-Used Jerseys

1 Teemu Selanne 10.00 25.00
2 Mike Modano 8.00 20.00
3 Steve Yzerman 10.00 25.00
4 Martin Brodeur 12.00 30.00
5 Mike Richter 5.00 12.00
6 John LeClair 5.00 12.00
7 Eric Lindros 8.00 20.00
8 John Vanbiesbrouck 5.00 12.00
9 Jaromir Jagr 15.00 40.00
10 Mats Sundin 5.00 12.00

1999-00 Pacific Omega NHL Generations

COMPLETE SET (10) 60.00 120.00
1 P.Kariya/S.Kariya 3.00 8.00
2 T.Selanne/M.Hejduk 6.00 15.00
3 P.Forsberg/C.Drury 6.00 15.00
4 P.Roy/R.Luongo 8.00 20.00
5 M.Modano/D.Legwand 5.00 12.00
6 S.Yzerman/S.Gomez 8.00 20.00
7 P.Bure/M.Hossa 3.00 8.00
8 J.LeClair/S.Gagne 3.00 8.00
9 E.Lindros/V.Lecavalier 5.00 12.00
10 J.Jagr/P.Stefan 10.00 25.00

1999-00 Pacific Omega North American All-Stars

COMPLETE SET (10) 8.00 20.00
1 Paul Kariya .75 2.00
2 Ray Bourque 1.25 3.00
3 Joe Sakic 1.50 4.00
4 Mike Modano 1.25 3.00
5 Brendan Shanahan .75 2.00
6 Steve Yzerman 2.00 5.00
7 Martin Brodeur 2.00 5.00
8 Scott Gomez .60 1.50
9 Curtis Joseph 1.00 2.50
10 Mark Messier 1.50 4.00

1999-00 Pacific Omega 5 Star Talents

COMPLETE SET (30) 20.00 40.00
1 Patrik Stefan .60 1.50
2 Alex Tanguay .50 1.25
3 David Legwand .40 1.00
4 Scott Gomez .50 1.25
5 Roberto Luongo 1.00 2.50
6 Steve Kariya .60 1.50
7 Brendan Shanahan .60 1.50
8 John LeClair .60 1.50
9 Eric Lindros 1.00 2.50
10 Keith Tkachuk .60 1.50
11 Owen Nolan .60 1.50
12 Mark Messier 1.25 3.00
13 Paul Kariya .60 1.50
14 Teemu Selanne 1.25 3.00
15 Pavel Bure .60 1.50
16 Theo Fleury .75 2.00
17 Marian Hossa .60 1.50
18 Jaromir Jagr 2.00 5.00
19 Peter Forsberg 1.25 3.00
20 Mike Modano 1.00 2.50
21 Steve Yzerman 1.50 4.00
22 Mark Recchi .75 2.00
23 Vincent Lecavalier .60 1.50
24 Mats Sundin .60 1.50
25 Dominik Hasek 1.00 2.50
26 Patrick Roy 1.50 4.00
27 Ed Belfour .60 1.50
28 Martin Brodeur 1.50 4.00
29 John Vanbiesbrouck .60 1.50
30 Curtis Joseph .75 2.00

1999-00 Pacific Omega 5 Star Talents Parallel

*1-6 PARALLEL/100: 2X TO 5X BASIC INSERT
*7-12 PARALLEL/75: 2.5X TO 6X BASIC INSERT
*13-18 PARALLEL/50: 3X TO 8X BASIC INSERT
*19-24 PARALLEL/25: 4X TO 10X BASIC INSERT
12 Mark Messier 8.00 20.00

1999-00 Pacific Omega World All-Stars

COMPLETE SET (10) 6.00 12.00
1 Teemu Selanne 1.50 4.00
2 Valeri Bure .50 1.25
3 Nicklas Lidstrom .75 2.00
4 Pavel Bure .75 2.00
5 Viktor Kozlov .50 1.25
6 Jaromir Jagr 2.50 6.00
7 Pavol Demitra 1.00 2.50
8 Roman Turek .60 1.50
9 Mats Sundin .75 2.00
10 Olaf Kolzig .75 2.00

1999-00 Pacific Prism

COMPLETE SET (150) 30.00 60.00
1 Guy Hebert .15 .40
2 Paul Kariya .20 .50
3 Mike Leclerc .10 .30
4 Steve Rucchin .10 .30
5 Teemu Selanne .20 .50
6 Andrew Brunette .15 .40
7 Petr Buzek .15 .40
8 Damian Rhodes .10 .30
9 Patrik Stefan RC .75 2.00
10 Jason Allison .10 .30
11 Dave Andreychuk .15 .40
12 Ray Bourque .30 .75
13 Byron Dafoe .15 .40
14 Sergei Samsonov .15 .40
15 Joe Thornton .30 .75
16 Maxim Afinogenov .10 .30
17 Martin Biron .15 .40
18 Curtis Brown .10 .30
19 Dominik Hasek .40 1.00
20 Michael Peca .10 .30
21 Miroslav Satan .15 .40
22 Valeri Bure .10 .30
23 Grant Fuhr .15 .40
24 Jarome Iginla .25 .60
25 Oleg Saprykin RC .60 1.50
26 Cory Stillman .10 .30
27 Bates Battaglia .10 .30
28 Ron Francis .10 .30
29 Arturs Irbe .15 .40
30 Sami Kapanen .10 .30
31 Keith Primeau .10 .30
32 Tony Amonte .15 .40
33 J-P Dumont .15 .40
34 Doug Gilmour .15 .40
35 Jocelyn Thibault .15 .40
36 Alexei Zhamnov .10 .30
37 Chris Drury .15 .40
38 Peter Forsberg .50 1.25
39 Milan Hejduk .20 .50
40 Patrick Roy 1.00 2.50
41 Joe Sakic .40 1.00
42 Alex Tanguay .15 .40
43 Ed Belfour .20 .50
44 Brett Hull .25 .60
45 Roman Lyashenko .10 .30
46 Mike Modano .30 .75
47 Joe Nieuwendyk .15 .40
48 Brendan Shanahan .20 .50
49 Chris Chelios .20 .50
50 Sergei Fedorov .30 .75
51 Jiri Fischer .10 .30
52 Nicklas Lidstrom .20 .50
53 Chris Osgood .15 .40
54 Steve Yzerman 1.00 2.50
55 Bill Guerin .10 .30
56 Tommy Salo .15 .40
57 Alexander Selivanov .10 .30
58 Ryan Smyth .10 .30
59 Doug Weight .15 .40
60 Pavel Bure .20 .50
61 Trevor Kidd .10 .30
62 Viktor Kozlov .15 .40
63 Mark Parrish .10 .30
64 Ray Whitney .15 .40
65 Rob Blake .15 .40
66 Stephane Fiset .15 .40
67 Frantisek Kaberle .10 .30
68 Zigmund Palffy .15 .40
69 Luc Robitaille .15 .40
70 Francis Bouillon RC .20 .50
71 Jeff Hackett .15 .40
72 Saku Koivu .20 .50
73 Trevor Linden .15 .40
74 Brian Savage .10 .30
75 Mike Dunham .15 .40
76 David Legwand .20 .50
77 Cliff Ronning .15 .40
78 Rob Valicevic RC .20 .50
79 Martin Brodeur .50 1.25
80 Patrik Elias .15 .40
81 Scott Gomez .10 .30
82 Bobby Holik .10 .30
83 Claude Lemieux .10 .30
84 Petr Sykora .10 .30
85 Tim Connolly .10 .30
86 Mariusz Czerkawski .10 .30
87 Brad Isbister .10 .30
88 Roberto Luongo .25 .60
89 Theo Fleury .10 .30
90 Jan Hlavac .10 .30
91 Brian Leetch .20 .50
92 Mike Richter .20 .50
93 Mike York .10 .30
94 Daniel Alfredsson .15 .40
95 Radek Bonk .10 .30
96 Marian Hossa .20 .50
97 Shawn McEachern .10 .30
98 Ron Tugnutt .15 .40
99 Alexei Yashin .10 .30
100 Brian Boucher .20 .50
101 Simon Gagne .20 .50
102 John LeClair .20 .50
103 Eric Lindros .20 .50
104 Mark Recchi .15 .40
105 John Vanbiesbrouck .15 .40
106 Mike Alatalo RC .20 .50
107 Travis Green .10 .30
108 Nikolai Khabibulin .15 .40
109 Jeremy Roenick .25 .60
110 Keith Tkachuk .20 .50
111 Rick Tocchet .15 .40
112 Jean-Sebastien Aubin .15 .40
113 Andrew Ference .10 .30
114 Jaromir Jagr .30 .75
115 Alexei Kovalev .10 .30
116 Martin Straka .10 .30
117 Pavol Demitra .15 .40
118 Jochen Hecht RC .75 2.00
119 Al MacInnis .15 .40
120 Chris Pronger .15 .40
121 Roman Turek .15 .40
122 Pierre Turgeon .15 .40
123 Vincent Damphousse .10 .30
124 Jeff Friesen .10 .30
125 Patrick Marleau .15 .40
126 Owen Nolan .15 .40
127 Steve Shields .15 .40
128 Brad Stuart .15 .40
129 Dan Cloutier .10 .30
130 Ben Clymer RC .20 .50
131 Chris Gratton .10 .30
132 Vincent Lecavalier .20 .50
133 Darcy Tucker .10 .30
134 Nikolai Antropov RC 1.25 3.00
135 Sergei Berezin .10 .30
136 Tie Domi .15 .40
137 Curtis Joseph .20 .50
138 Dimitri Khristich .10 .30
139 Mats Sundin .20 .50
140 Steve Kariya RC .60 1.50
141 Mark Messier .20 .50
142 Alfie Michaud RC .40 1.00
143 Alexander Mogilny .15 .40
144 Jarkko Ruutu RC .20 .50
145 Peter Schaefer .15 .40
146 Peter Bondra .15 .40
147 Jan Bulis .10 .30
148 Olaf Kolzig .15 .40
149 Glen Metropolit RC .60 1.50
150 Adam Oates .15 .40
NNO Martin Brodeur SAMPLE .75 2.00

1999-00 Pacific Prism Holographic Blue
*VETS: 6X TO 15X BASIC CARDS
*ROOKIES: 3X TO 8X BASIC CARDS

1999-00 Pacific Prism Holographic Gold
*VETS: 1.2X TO 3X BASIC CARDS
*ROOKIES: .8X TO 2X BASIC CARDS

1999-00 Pacific Prism Holographic Mirror
*VETS: 4X TO 10X BASIC CARDS
*ROOKIES: 2X TO 5X BASIC CARDS

1999-00 Pacific Prism Holographic Purple
*VETS: 5X TO 12X BASIC CARDS
*ROOKIES: 2.5X TO 6X BASIC CARDS

1999-00 Pacific Prism Premiere Date
*VETS: 8X TO 20X BASIC CARDS
*ROOKIES: 4X TO 10X BASIC CARDS

1999-00 Pacific Prism Clear Advantage
COMPLETE SET (20) 20.00 40.00
1 Paul Kariya .60 1.50
2 Teemu Selanne .60 1.50
3 Dominik Hasek 1.25 3.00
4 Peter Forsberg 1.50 4.00
5 Patrick Roy 3.00 8.00
6 Alex Tanguay .50 1.25
7 Brett Hull .75 2.00
8 Brendan Shanahan 1.00 2.50
9 Steve Yzerman 3.00 8.00
10 Pavel Bure .75 2.00
11 Zigmund Palffy .50 1.25
12 Martin Brodeur 1.50 4.00
13 Theo Fleury .50 1.25
14 Marian Hossa .60 1.50
15 John LeClair .75 2.00
16 Eric Lindros 1.00 2.50
17 Mark Recchi .50 1.25
18 Jaromir Jagr 1.00 2.50
19 Vincent Lecavalier .60 1.50
20 Mats Sundin .60 1.50

1999-00 Pacific Prism Ice Prospects
COMPLETE SET (10) 30.00 60.00
1 Patrik Stefan 3.00 8.00
2 Martin Biron 3.00 8.00
3 Alex Tanguay 3.00 8.00
4 David Legwand 3.00 8.00
5 Scott Gomez 3.00 8.00
6 Simon Gagne 3.00 8.00
7 Brad Stuart 3.00 8.00
8 Nikolai Antropov 3.00 8.00
9 Steve Kariya 3.00 8.00
10 Peter Schaefer 3.00 8.00

1999-00 Pacific Prism Dial-a-Stats
COMPLETE SET (10) 40.00 80.00
1 Paul Kariya 6.00 15.00
2 Teemu Selanne 6.00 15.00
3 Dominik Hasek 4.00 10.00
4 Peter Forsberg 5.00 12.00
5 Patrick Roy 10.00 25.00
6 Mike Modano 3.00 8.00
7 Steve Yzerman 10.00 25.00
8 Eric Lindros 3.00 8.00
9 Jaromir Jagr 3.00 8.00
10 Mark Messier 2.50 6.00

1999-00 Pacific Prism Sno-Globe Die-Cuts
COMPLETE SET (20) 20.00 40.00
1 Paul Kariya .60 1.50
2 Teemu Selanne .60 1.50
3 Ray Bourque 1.00 2.50
4 Dominik Hasek 1.25 3.00
5 Peter Forsberg 1.50 4.00
6 Patrick Roy 3.00 8.00
7 Joe Sakic 1.25 3.00
8 Ed Belfour .60 1.50
9 Mike Modano 1.00 2.50
10 Brendan Shanahan 1.00 2.50
11 Steve Yzerman 3.00 8.00
12 Pavel Bure .75 2.00
13 Martin Brodeur 1.50 4.00
14 Theo Fleury .60 1.50
15 John LeClair .75 2.00
16 Eric Lindros 1.00 2.50
17 John Vanbiesbrouck .60 1.50
18 Keith Tkachuk .60 1.50
19 Jaromir Jagr 1.00 2.50
20 Curtis Joseph .60 1.50

2003-04 Pacific Prism
COMP.SET w/o JSY's (100) 20.00 50.00
1 Stanislav Chistov .20 .50
2 Jean-Sebastien Giguere .30 .75
3 Adam Oates .30 .75
4 Petr Sykora .25 .60
5 Joe DiPenta RC 1.00 2.50
6 Slava Kozlov .25 .60
7 Marc Savard .20 .50
8 Patrik Stefan .20 .50
9 Jeff Hackett .25 .60
10 Mike Knuble .20 .50
11 Sergei Samsonov .25 .60
12 Steve Shields .25 .60
13 Milan Bartovic RC 1.00 2.50
14 Martin Biron .25 .60
15 Daniel Briere .30 .75
16 Ryan Miller .30 .75
17 Miroslav Satan .25 .60
18 Craig Conroy .20 .50
19 Roman Turek .25 .60
20 Ron Francis .40 1.00
21 Arturs Irbe .25 .60
22 Jeff O'Neill .20 .50
23 Tyler Arnason .20 .50
24 Theo Fleury .40 1.00
25 Jocelyn Thibault .25 .60
26 Alexei Zhamnov .25 .60
27 Rob Blake .30 .75
28 Alex Tanguay .25 .60
29 Marc Denis .25 .60
30 Kent McDonell RC 1.00 2.50
31 Rick Nash .30 .75
32 Geoff Sanderson .20 .50
33 Ray Whitney .25 .60
34 Jason Arnott .25 .60
35 Jere Lehtinen .25 .60
36 Pavel Datsyuk .50 1.25
37 Brett Hull .60 1.50
38 Curtis Joseph .40 1.00
39 Henrik Zetterberg .40 1.00
40 Ales Hemsky .30 .75
41 Tommy Salo .25 .60
42 Ryan Smyth .25 .60
43 Jay Bouwmeester .20 .50
44 Olli Jokinen .30 .75
45 Roberto Luongo .50 1.25
46 Stephen Weiss .20 .50
47 Michael Cammalleri .30 .75
48 Adam Deadmarsh .20 .50
49 Alexander Frolov .25 .60
50 Felix Potvin .50 1.25
51 Andrew Brunette .20 .50
52 Manny Fernandez .20 .50
53 Marian Gaborik .30 .75
54 Dwayne Roloson .25 .60
55 Cliff Ronning .20 .50
56 Marcel Hossa .20 .50
57 Yanic Perreault .20 .50
58 Scottie Upshall .25 .60
59 Tomas Vokoun .25 .60
60 Scott Walker .20 .50
61 Patrik Elias .30 .75
62 Jamie Langenbrunner .25 .60
63 John Madden .20 .50
64 Joe Nieuwendyk .25 .60
65 Scott Stevens .30 .75
66 Jason Blake .20 .50
67 Rick DiPietro .25 .60
68 Mark Parrish .20 .50
69 Mike Dunham .25 .60
70 Alex Kovalev .25 .60
71 Brian Leetch .25 .60
72 Mark Messier .60 1.50
73 Zdeno Chara .30 .75
74 Martin Havlat .30 .75
75 Todd White .20 .50
76 John LeClair .30 .75
77 Mark Recchi .40 1.00
78 Shane Doan .25 .60
79 Mike Johnson .20 .50
80 Johan Hedberg .25 .60
81 Martin Straka .20 .50
82 Pavol Demitra .40 1.00
83 Barret Jackman .20 .50
84 Al MacInnis .40 1.00
85 Peter Sejna RC 1.00 2.50
86 Keith Tkachuk .30 .75
87 Patrick Marleau .30 .75
88 Evgeni Nabokov .25 .60
89 Teemu Selanne .60 1.50
90 Dave Andreychuk .30 .75
91 Brad Richards .30 .75
92 Alexander Mogilny .25 .60
93 Owen Nolan .30 .75
94 Matt Stajan RC 1.25 3.00
95 Ed Jovanovski .25 .60
96 Daniel Sedin .40 1.00
97 Henrik Sedin .40 1.00
98 Peter Bondra .30 .75
99 Sergei Gonchar .20 .50
100 Olaf Kolzig .30 .75
101 Paul Kariya JSY/935 4.00 10.00
102 Dany Heatley JSY/924 3.00 8.00
103 Ilya Kovalchuk JSY/935 4.00 10.00
104 Glen Murray JSY/1185 3.00 8.00
105 Joe Thornton JSY/685 6.00 15.00
106 Chris Drury JSY/935 3.00 8.00
107 Jarome Iginla JSY/1183 5.00 12.00
108 Eric Daze JSY/1171 3.00 8.00
109 Milan Hejduk JSY/1183 3.00 8.00
110 Peter Forsberg JSY/685 8.00 20.00
111 Patrick Roy JSY/185 12.00 30.00
112 Joe Sakic JSY/935 8.00 20.00
113 Bill Guerin JSY/1136 4.00 10.00
114 Mike Modano JSY/935 6.00 15.00
115 Marty Turco JSY/685 4.00 10.00
116 Sergei Fedorov JSY/685 6.00 15.00
117 Brendan Shanahan JSY/935 4.00 10.00
118 Steve Yzerman JSY/185 15.00 40.00
119 Mike Comrie JSY/935 3.00 8.00
120 Jason Allison JSY/1176 3.00 8.00
121 Roman Cechmanek JSY/1185 3.00 8.00
122 Zigmund Palffy JSY/1060 4.00 10.00
123 Saku Koivu JSY/935 4.00 10.00
124 Jose Theodore JSY/1185 4.00 10.00
125 Richard Zednik JSY/1185 2.50 6.00
126 David Legwand JSY/1185 3.00 8.00
127 Martin Brodeur JSY/685 10.00 25.00
128 Michael Peca JSY/1185 3.00 8.00
129 Alexei Yashin JSY/1185 3.00 8.00
130 Pavel Bure JSY/935 4.00 10.00
131 Eric Lindros JSY/935 6.00 15.00
132 Daniel Alfredsson JSY/185 6.00 15.00
133 Marian Hossa JSY/185 6.00 15.00
134 Jason Spezza JSY/185 6.00 15.00
135 Tony Amonte JSY/1163 3.00 8.00
136 Jeremy Roenick JSY/1185 4.00 10.00
137 Sean Burke JSY/1185 2.50 6.00
138 Mario Lemieux JSY/305 12.00 30.00
139 Chris Osgood JSY/1185 4.00 10.00
140 Doug Weight JSY/1185 3.00 8.00
141 Nikolai Khabibulin JSY/1125 4.00 10.00
142 Vincent Lecavalier JSY/935 4.00 10.00
143 Martin St. Louis JSY/1185 4.00 10.00
144 Ed Belfour JSY/685 4.00 10.00
145 Mats Sundin JSY/685 4.00 10.00
146 Todd Bertuzzi JSY/935 4.00 10.00
147 Dan Cloutier JSY/1185 3.00 8.00
148 Brendan Morrison JSY/685 3.00 8.00
149 Markus Naslund JSY/185 6.00 15.00
150 Jaromir Jagr JSY/185 20.00 50.00
151 Joffrey Lupul RC 2.50 6.00
152 Patrice Bergeron RC 5.00 12.00
153 Matthew Lombardi RC 1.25 3.00
154 Eric Staal RC 5.00 12.00
155 Nikolai Zherdev RC 2.00 5.00
156 Jiri Hudler RC 2.50 6.00
157 Nathan Horton RC 2.50 6.00
158 Jordin Tootoo RC 2.00 5.00
159 Antoine Vermette RC 2.00 5.00
160 Marc-Andre Fleury RC 6.00 15.00

2003-04 Pacific Prism Blue
*1-100 VETS/325: 1.5X TO 4X BASIC CARDS
*ROOKIES/325: .5X TO 1.2X RC/975
*101-150 JSY/90: .8X TO 2X JSY/300-1185
*101-150 JSY/90: .5X TO 1.2X JSY/185
72 Mark Messier 2.50 6.00

2003-04 Pacific Prism Gold
*1-100 VETS/425: 1.2X TO 3X BASIC CARDS
*ROOKIES/425: .4X TO 1X RC/975
72 Mark Messier 2.00 5.00

2003-04 Pacific Prism Patches
*PATCH/50-75: 1X TO 2.5X BASE JERSEYS
118 Steve Yzerman SP 50.00 125.00

2003-04 Pacific Prism Red
*1-100 VETS/260: 2X TO 5X BASIC CARDS
*ROOKIES/260: .6X TO 1.5X RC/975
*101-150 JSY/75: .8X TO 2X JSY/300-1185
*101-150 JSY/75: .5X TO 1.2X JSY/185
72 Mark Messier 3.00 8.00

2003-04 Pacific Prism Retail Jerseys
*RETAIL/150: .6X TO 1.5X HOB JSY/300-1185
*RETAIL/150: .4X TO 1X HOB JSY/185

2003-04 Pacific Prism Crease Police
COMPLETE SET (8) 10.00 20.00
1 Jean-Sebastien Giguere 1.50 4.00
2 Patrick Roy 3.00 8.00
3 Marty Turco 1.50 4.00
4 Curtis Joseph 1.50 4.00
5 Jose Theodore 2.00 5.00
6 Martin Brodeur 2.50 6.00
7 Patrick Lalime 1.50 4.00
8 Ed Belfour 1.50 4.00

2003-04 Pacific Prism Paramount Prodigies
COMPLETE SET (20) 15.00 30.00
1 Stanislav Chistov .60 1.50
2 Jean-Sebastien Giguere .60 1.50
3 Dany Heatley 1.00 2.50
4 Ilya Kovalchuk 1.00 2.50
5 Tyler Arnason .60 1.50
6 Rick Nash 1.00 2.50
7 Pavel Datsyuk .75 2.00
8 Henrik Zetterberg 1.25 3.00
9 Mike Comrie .60 1.50
10 Ales Hemsky .60 1.50
11 Jay Bouwmeester .60 1.50
12 Stephen Weiss .60 1.50
13 Alexander Frolov .60 1.50
14 Marian Gaborik 1.00 2.50
15 David Legwand .60 1.50
16 Martin Havlat .60 1.50
17 Marian Hossa .75 2.00
18 Jason Spezza 1.00 2.50
19 Barret Jackman .60 1.50
20 Vincent Lecavalier .60 1.50

2003-04 Pacific Prism Rookie Revolution
COMPLETE SET (12) 8.00 15.00
1 Stanislav Chistov .40 1.00
2 Ales Kotalik .40 1.00
3 Ryan Miller 1.00 2.50
4 Tyler Arnason .40 1.00
5 Rick Nash 1.00 2.50
6 Henrik Zetterberg 1.00 2.50
7 Ales Hemsky .75 2.00
8 Jay Bouwmeester .60 1.50
9 Alexander Frolov .60 1.50
10 Pierre-Marc Bouchard .60 1.50
11 Jason Spezza 1.00 2.50
12 Jonathan Cheechoo .75 2.00

2003-04 Pacific Prism Stat Masters
COMPLETE SET (10) 8.00 15.00
1 Paul Kariya .40 1.00
2 Joe Thornton .50 1.25
3 Peter Forsberg 1.00 2.50
4 Milan Hejduk .40 1.00
5 Mike Modano .60 1.50
6 Steve Yzerman 1.50 4.00
7 Mario Lemieux 2.00 5.00
8 Todd Bertuzzi .40 1.00
9 Markus Naslund .60 1.50
10 Jaromir Jagr .60 1.50

2002-03 Pacific Quest For the Cup
COMP.SET w/o SP's (100) 20.00 40.00
1 Jean-Sebastien Giguere .30 .75
2 Paul Kariya .30 .75
3 Sandis Ozolinsh .20 .50
4 Dany Heatley .25 .60
5 Ilya Kovalchuk .40 1.00
6 Jeff Hackett .25 .60
7 Glen Murray .25 .60
8 Joe Thornton .50 1.25
9 Martin Biron .25 .60
10 Miroslav Satan .30 .75
11 Chris Drury .30 .75
12 Jarome Iginla .40 1.00
13 Roman Turek .20 .50
14 Ron Francis .40 1.00
15 Jeff O'Neill .20 .50
16 Eric Daze .20 .50
17 Theo Fleury .20 .50
18 Jocelyn Thibault .25 .60
19 Alexei Zhamnov .25 .60
20 Rob Blake .30 .75
21 Peter Forsberg .60 1.50
22 Milan Hejduk .60 1.50
23 Patrick Roy .75 2.00
24 Joe Sakic .60 1.50
25 Marc Denis .25 .60
26 Ray Whitney .25 .60
27 Bill Guerin .30 .75
28 Jere Lehtinen .30 .75
29 Mike Modano .50 1.25
30 Marty Turco .30 .75
30AU Marty Turco AU/500 5.00 12.00
31 Pierre Turgeon .25 .60
32 Sergei Fedorov .50 1.25
33 Brett Hull .60 1.50
34 Curtis Joseph .40 1.00
35 Nicklas Lidstrom .30 .75
36 Brendan Shanahan .30 .75
37 Steve Yzerman .75 2.00
38 Mike Comrie .30 .75
39 Tommy Salo .25 .60
40 Ryan Smyth .25 .60
41 Olli Jokinen .30 .75
42 Roberto Luongo .50 1.25
43 Jason Allison .25 .60
44 Zigmund Palffy .30 .75
45 Felix Potvin .50 1.25
46 Pascal Dupuis .20 .50
47 Manny Fernandez .20 .50
48 Marian Gaborik .30 .75
49 Cliff Ronning .20 .50
50 Saku Koivu .30 .75
51 Yanic Perreault .20 .50
52 Jose Theodore .30 .75
53 Richard Zednik .20 .50
54 David Legwand .25 .60
55 Tomas Vokoun .25 .60
56 Martin Brodeur .75 2.00
57 Patrik Elias .30 .75
58 Jeff Friesen .20 .50
59 Jamie Langenbrunner .25 .60
60 Rick DiPietro .25 .60
61 Michael Peca .25 .60
62 Alexei Yashin .25 .60
63 Pavel Bure .30 .75
64 Anson Carter .25 .60
65 Alexei Kovalev .25 .60
66 Eric Lindros .50 1.25
67 Mark Messier .60 1.50
68 Daniel Alfredsson .30 .75
69 Radek Bonk .25 .60
70 Martin Havlat .25 .60
71 Marian Hossa .30 .75
72 Patrick Lalime .25 .60
73 Tony Amonte .25 .60
74 Roman Cechmanek .25 .60
75 Simon Gagne .30 .75
76 Sami Kapanen .20 .50
77 Jeremy Roenick .50 1.25
78 Sean Burke .25 .60
79 Johan Hedberg .30 .75
80 Mario Lemieux 1.25 3.00
81 Pavol Demitra .40 1.00
82 Brent Johnson .25 .60
83 Cory Stillman .20 .50
84 Keith Tkachuk .30 .75
85 Doug Weight .30 .75
86 Evgeni Nabokov .25 .60
87 Teemu Selanne .60 1.50
88 Nikolai Khabibulin .30 .75
89 Vincent Lecavalier .30 .75
90 Martin St. Louis .30 .75
91 Ed Belfour .30 .75
92 Alexander Mogilny .25 .60
93 Mats Sundin .30 .75
94 Todd Bertuzzi .30 .75
95 Dan Cloutier .25 .60
96 Brendan Morrison .25 .60
97 Markus Naslund .30 .75
98 Jaromir Jagr 1.00 2.50
99 Olaf Kolzig .30 .75
100 Michael Nylander .20 .50
101 Stanislav Chistov RC .75 2.00
102 Martin Gerber RC 1.25 3.00
103 Kurt Sauer RC .75 2.00
104 Alexei Smirnov RC 1.00 2.50
105 Shaone Morrisonn RC .75 2.00
106 Tim Thomas RC 6.00 15.00
107 Ryan Miller RC 5.00 12.00
108 Chuck Kobasew RC 1.00 2.50
109 Jordan Leopold RC 1.25 3.00
110 Ryan Bayda RC .75 2.00
111 Tomas Malec RC .75 2.00
112 Pascal Leclaire RC 1.00 2.50
113 Rick Nash RC 6.00 15.00
114 Jason Bacashihua RC 1.00 2.50
115 Steve Ott RC .75 2.00
116 Dmitri Bykov RC .75 2.00
117 Henrik Zetterberg RC 8.00 20.00
118 Ales Hemsky RC 3.00 8.00
119 Fernando Pisani RC .75 2.00
120 Jay Bouwmeester RC 2.50 6.00
121 Kip Brennan SP .75 2.00
122 Michael Cammalleri RC 2.50 6.00
123 Alexander Frolov RC 2.00 5.00
124 P-M Bouchard RC 1.25 3.00
125 Stephane Veilleux RC .75 2.00
126 Ron Hainsey RC .75 2.00
127 Mike Komisarek RC 1.25 3.00
128 Vernon Fiddler RC 1.00 2.50
129 Adam Hall RC .75 2.00
130 Scottie Upshall RC 1.00 2.50
131 Eric Godard RC .75 2.00
132 Ray Emery RC 2.50 6.00
133 Jason Spezza RC 5.00 12.00
134 Anton Volchenkov RC .75 2.00
135 Dennis Seidenberg RC 1.25 3.00
136 Radovan Somik RC .75 2.00
137 Jim Vandermeer RC .75 2.00
138 Jeff Taffe RC .75 2.00
139 Brooks Orpik RC .75 2.00
140 Tomas Surovy RC .75 2.00
141 Dick Tarnstrom RC .75 2.00
142 Curtis Sanford RC 1.25 3.00
143 Matt Walker RC .75 2.00
144 Niko Dimitrakos RC .75 2.00
145 Jim Fahey RC .75 2.00
146 Lynn Loyns RC .75 2.00
147 Alexander Svitov RC .75 2.00
148 Carlo Colaiacovo RC 1.25 3.00
149 Mikael Tellqvist RC .75 2.00
150 Steve Eminger RC .75 2.00

2002-03 Pacific Quest For the Cup Gold
*1-100 VETS/325: 2X TO 5X BASIC CARDS
*101-150 ROOKIES/325: .5X TO 1.2X RC
67 Mark Messier 3.00 8.00

2002-03 Pacific Quest For the Cup Calder Contenders
COMPLETE SET (10) 8.00 20.00
1 Stanislav Chistov 1.00 2.50
2 Ales Kotalik 1.00 2.50
3 Ryan Miller 1.50 4.00
4 Tyler Arnason 1.00 2.50
5 Pascal Leclaire 1.00 2.50
6 Rick Nash 2.50 6.00
7 Henrik Zetterberg 2.50 6.00
8 Ales Hemsky 1.50 4.00
9 Jay Bouwmeester 1.50 4.00
10 Jason Spezza 2.50 6.00

2002-03 Pacific Quest For the Cup Chasing the Cup
COMPLETE SET (20) 10.00 20.00
1 Paul Kariya .50 1.25
2 Dany Heatley .60 1.50
3 Ilya Kovalchuk .60 1.50
4 Joe Thornton .75 2.00
5 Marty Turco .40 1.00
6 Curtis Joseph .50 1.25
7 Marian Gaborik 1.00 2.50
8 Jose Theodore .50 1.25
9 Alexei Yashin .40 1.00
10 Pavel Bure .50 1.25
11 Eric Lindros .50 1.25
12 Daniel Alfredsson .40 1.00
13 Marian Hossa .50 1.25
14 Jeremy Roenick .50 1.25
15 Teemu Selanne .50 1.25
16 Owen Nolan .40 1.00
17 Mats Sundin .50 1.25
18 Todd Bertuzzi .50 1.25
19 Brendan Morrison .40 1.00
20 Markus Naslund .40 1.00

2002-03 Pacific Quest For the Cup Jerseys
1 Dany Heatley 4.00 10.00
2 Glen Murray 3.00 8.00
3 Joe Thornton 5.00 12.00
4 Rob Blake 3.00 8.00
5 Peter Forsberg 8.00 20.00
6 Patrick Roy 10.00 25.00
7 Mike Modano 5.00 12.00
8 Marty Turco 3.00 8.00
9 Nicklas Lidstrom 4.00 10.00
10 Rick DiPietro 3.00 8.00
11 Mark Messier 4.00 10.00
12 Daniel Alfredsson 3.00 8.00
13 Marian Hossa 4.00 10.00
14 Jason Spezza 8.00 20.00
15 Roman Cechmanek 3.00 8.00
16 Jeremy Roenick 4.00 10.00
17 Mario Lemieux 12.50 30.00
18 Brent Johnson 3.00 8.00
19 Doug Weight 3.00 8.00
20 Martin St. Louis 3.00 8.00
21 Ed Belfour 4.00 10.00
22 Gary Roberts 3.00 8.00
23 Markus Naslund 4.00 10.00
24 Jaromir Jagr 4.00 10.00
25 Olaf Kolzig 3.00 8.00

2002-03 Pacific Quest For the Cup Raising the Cup
COMPLETE SET (12) 15.00 30.00
1 Peter Forsberg 1.50 4.00
2 Patrick Roy 2.50 6.00
3 Joe Sakic 1.00 2.50
4 Mike Modano .75 2.00
5 Sergei Fedorov .75 2.00
6 Brett Hull .75 2.00
7 Brendan Shanahan .60 1.50
8 Steve Yzerman 2.50 6.00
9 Martin Brodeur 2.50 6.00
10 Mark Messier .60 1.50
11 Mario Lemieux 3.00 8.00
12 Jaromir Jagr .75 2.00

2003-04 Pacific Quest for the Cup
COMP.SET w/o SP's 20.00 40.00
1 Sergei Fedorov .40 1.00
2 Jean-Sebastien Giguere .25 .60
3 Dany Heatley .40 1.00
4 Ilya Kovalchuk .40 1.00
5 Slava Kozlov .15 .40
6 Pasi Nurminen .25 .60
7 Mike Knuble .15 .40
8 Glen Murray .15 .40
9 Andrew Raycroft .25 .60
10 Joe Thornton .40 1.00
11 Daniel Briere .15 .40
12 Ales Kotalik .15 .40
13 Miroslav Satan .25 .60
14 Shean Donovan .15 .40
15 Jarome Iginla .40 1.00
16 Miikka Kiprusoff .25 .60
17 Erik Cole .15 .40
18 Ron Francis .25 .60
19 Tyler Arnason .25 .60
20 Mark Bell .15 .40
21 Kyle Calder .15 .40
22 David Aebischer .25 .60
23 Peter Forsberg .75 2.00
24 Milan Hejduk .30 .75
25 Paul Kariya .30 .75
26 Joe Sakic .60 1.50
27 Teemu Selanne .30 .75
28 Alex Tanguay .25 .60
29 Marc Denis .25 .60
30 Rick Nash .40 1.00
31 Bill Guerin .25 .60
32 Mike Modano .50 1.25
33 Marty Turco .25 .60
34 Pavel Datsyuk .30 .75
35 Kris Draper .15 .40
36 Dominik Hasek .60 1.50
37 Brett Hull .40 1.00
38 Curtis Joseph .30 .75
39 Robert Lang .25 .60
40 Brendan Shanahan .30 .75
41 Steve Yzerman 1.50 4.00
42 Ales Hemsky .25 .60
43 Ryan Smyth .15 .40
44 Raffi Torres .15 .40
45 Jay Bouwmeester .15 .40
46 Valeri Bure .15 .40
47 Olli Jokinen .25 .60
48 Roberto Luongo .40 1.00
49 Roman Cechmanek .25 .60
50 Alexander Frolov .15 .40
51 Ziggy Palffy .25 .60
52 Andrew Brunette .15 .40
53 Alexandre Daigle .15 .40
54 Marian Gaborik .60 1.50
55 Saku Koivu .30 .75
56 Mike Ribeiro .15 .40
57 Michael Ryder .15 .40
58 Sheldon Souray .15 .40
59 Jose Theodore .40 1.00
60 Martin Erat .15 .40
61 Scott Hartnell .15 .40
62 Tomas Vokoun .25 .60
63 Martin Brodeur .75 2.00
64 Patrik Elias .25 .60
65 Scott Stevens .25 .60
66 Rick DiPietro .25 .60
67 Trent Hunter .15 .40
68 Alexei Yashin .15 .40
69 Jaromir Jagr .50 1.25
70 Alex Kovalev .25 .60
71 Eric Lindros .30 .75
72 Daniel Alfredsson .25 .60
73 Peter Bondra .25 .60
74 Martin Havlat .25 .60
75 Marian Hossa .30 .75
76 Patrick Lalime .25 .60
77 Jason Spezza .30 .75
78 Tony Amonte .25 .60
79 Mark Recchi .25 .60
80 Jeremy Roenick .40 1.00
81 Shane Doan .15 .40
82 Ladislav Nagy .15 .40
83 Rico Fata .15 .40
84 Mario Lemieux 2.00 5.00
85 Pavol Demitra .25 .60
86 Keith Tkachuk .30 .75
87 Doug Weight .25 .60
88 Jonathan Cheechoo .20 .50
89 Patrick Marleau .25 .60
90 Evgeni Nabokov .25 .60
91 Nikolai Khabibulin .30 .75
92 Vincent Lecavalier .30 .75
93 Martin St. Louis .25 .60
94 Ed Belfour .30 .75
95 Owen Nolan .25 .60
96 Mats Sundin .30 .75
97 Todd Bertuzzi .30 .75
98 Jason King .15 .40
99 Brendan Morrison .25 .60
100 Markus Naslund .30 .75
101 Joffrey Lupul RC 2.00 5.00
102 Patrice Bergeron RC 8.00 20.00
103 Derek Roy RC 1.50 4.00
104 Brent Krahn RC 1.25 3.00
105 Matthew Lombardi RC 1.25 3.00
106 Eric Staal RC 5.00 12.00
107 Anton Babchuk RC 1.25 3.00
108 Tuomo Ruutu RC 2.00 5.00
109 Pavel Vorobiev RC 1.25 3.00
110 Mikhail Yakubov RC 1.25 3.00
111 Dan Fritsche RC 1.25 3.00
112 Nikolai Zherdev RC 2.50 6.00
113 Antti Miettinen RC 1.25 3.00
114 Darryl Bootland RC 1.25 3.00
115 Jiri Hudler RC 2.00 5.00
116 Nathan Robinson RC 1.25 3.00
117 Tony Salmelainen RC 1.25 3.00
118 Nathan Horton RC 3.00 8.00
119 Dustin Brown RC 1.50 4.00
120 Brent Burns RC 1.25 3.00
121 Christopher Higgins RC 3.00 8.00
122 Dan Hamhuis RC 1.25 3.00
123 Jordin Tootoo RC 3.00 8.00
124 Marek Zidlicky RC 1.25 3.00
125 David Hale RC 1.25 3.00
126 Paul Martin RC 1.25 3.00
127 Dominic Moore RC 1.25 3.00
128 Antoine Vermette RC 1.25 3.00
129 Joni Pitkanen RC 1.25 3.00
130 Fredrik Sjostrom RC 1.25 3.00
131 Marc-Andre Fleury RC 6.00 15.00
132 Ryan Malone RC 2.00 5.00
133 John Pohl RC 1.25 3.00
134 Peter Sejna RC 1.25 3.00
135 Milan Michalek RC 1.25 3.00
136 Matt Stajan RC 2.00 5.00
137 Ryan Kesler RC 2.50 6.00
138 Boyd Gordon RC 1.25 3.00
139 Alexander Semin RC 4.00 10.00
140 Rastislav Stana RC 1.25 3.00

2003-04 Pacific Quest for the Cup Blue
*STARS: 2X TO 5X BASE HI

2003-04 Pacific Quest for the Cup Calder Contenders
COMPLETE SET (20) 15.00 30.00
1 Patrice Bergeron 2.50 6.00
2 Andrew Raycroft 2.50 6.00
3 Matthew Lombardi 1.25 3.00
4 Eric Staal 2.00 5.00
5 Tuomo Ruutu 2.00 5.00
6 Philippe Sauve 1.25 3.00
7 Nikolai Zherdev 2.00 5.00
8 Jiri Hudler 1.25 3.00
9 Nathan Horton 1.50 4.00
10 Dustin Brown 1.50 4.00
11 Brent Burns 1.25 3.00
12 Michael Ryder 1.50 4.00
13 Jordin Tootoo 1.50 4.00
14 Trent Hunter 1.25 3.00
15 Antoine Vermette 1.25 3.00
16 Joni Pitkanen 1.25 3.00
17 Marc-Andre Fleury 3.00 8.00
18 Ryan Malone 1.25 3.00
19 Matt Stajan 1.50 4.00
20 Jason King 1.25 3.00

2003-04 Pacific Quest for the Cup Chasing the Cup
COMPLETE SET (9) 6.00 15.00
1 Dany Heatley 1.00 2.50
2 Ilya Kovalchuk 1.00 2.50
3 Joe Thornton 1.00 2.50
4 Paul Kariya .50 1.25
5 Rick Nash .60 1.50
6 Marty Turco .50 1.25
7 Jason Spezza .50 1.25
8 Mats Sundin .50 1.25
9 Todd Bertuzzi .50 1.25

2003-04 Pacific Quest for the Cup Connquest
COMPLETE SET (6) 8.00 15.00
1 Jean-Sebastien Giguere .75 2.00
2 Joe Sakic 1.50 4.00
3 Nicklas Lidstrom .75 2.00
4 Steve Yzerman 2.50 6.00
5 Scott Stevens .75 2.00
6 Mario Lemieux 3.00 8.00

2003-04 Pacific Quest for the Cup Jerseys
1 Ilya Kovalchuk SP 5.00 12.00
2 Joe Thornton 4.00 10.00
3 Jarome Iginla 3.00 8.00
4 Jocelyn Thibault 3.00 8.00
5 David Aebischer SP 4.00 10.00
6 Joe Sakic 5.00 12.00
7 Rick Nash 4.00 10.00
8 Marty Turco 2.50 6.00
9 Steve Yzerman SP 12.00 30.00
10 Ryan Smyth 2.50 6.00
11 Scott Walker 2.50 6.00
12 Patrik Elias 3.00 8.00
13 Jaromir Jagr 4.00 10.00
14 Martin Havlat 2.50 6.00
15 Jeff Hackett 2.50 6.00
16 Mario Lemieux SP 8.00 20.00
17 Nikolai Khabibulin 3.00 8.00
18 Ed Belfour SP 6.00 15.00
19 Dan Cloutier 2.50 6.00

2003-04 Pacific Quest for the Cup Raising the Cup
1 Sergei Fedorov .75 2.00
2 Rob Blake .60 1.50
3 Peter Forsberg 1.50 4.00
4 Milan Hejduk .60 1.50
5 Joe Sakic 1.25 3.00
6 Mike Modano 1.00 2.50
7 Dominik Hasek 1.25 3.00
8 Brett Hull .75 2.00
9 Nicklas Lidstrom .60 1.50
10 Brendan Shanahan .60 1.50
11 Steve Yzerman 2.00 5.00
12 Martin Brodeur 2.00 5.00
13 Scott Stevens .60 1.50
14 Mark Messier .60 1.50
15 Mario Lemieux 2.50 6.00

2003-04 Pacific Supreme
COMP.SET w/o SP's (100) 15.00 40.00
1 Sergei Fedorov .40 1.00
2 Jean-Sebastien Giguere .25 .60
3 Petr Sykora .20 .50
4 Dany Heatley .20 .50
5 Ilya Kovalchuk .25 .60
6 Glen Murray .20 .50
7 Sergei Samsonov .20 .50
8 Joe Thornton .40 1.00
9 Daniel Briere .25 .60
10 Chris Drury .20 .50
11 Ales Kotalik .15 .40
12 Ryan Miller .25 .60
13 Jarome Iginla .30 .75
14 Chuck Kobasew .15 .40
15 Ron Francis .30 .75
16 Jeff O'Neill .15 .40
17 Radim Vrbata .15 .40
18 Tyler Arnason .15 .40
19 Steve Sullivan .15 .40
20 Jocelyn Thibault .20 .50
21 Peter Forsberg .50 1.25
22 Milan Hejduk .20 .50
23 Paul Kariya .25 .60
24 Patrick Roy .60 1.50
25 Joe Sakic .50 1.25
26 Marc Denis .20 .50
27 Rick Nash .25 .60
28 Geoff Sanderson .20 .50
29 Jason Arnott .20 .50
30 Mike Modano .40 1.00
31 Marty Turco .25 .60
32 Dominik Hasek .40 1.00
33 Brett Hull .50 1.25
34 Ray Whitney .20 .50
35 Steve Yzerman .60 1.50
36 Henrik Zetterberg .30 .75
37 Mike Comrie .20 .50
38 Ales Hemsky .25 .60
39 Tommy Salo .20 .50
40 Ryan Smyth .20 .50
41 Jay Bouwmeester .15 .40
42 Olli Jokinen .20 .50
43 Roberto Luongo .40 1.00
44 Roman Cechmanek .20 .50
45 Alexander Frolov .20 .50
46 Ziggy Palffy .25 .60
47 Pierre-Marc Bouchard .25 .60
48 Marian Gaborik .25 .60
49 Dwayne Roloson .20 .50
50 Marcel Hossa .15 .40
51 Saku Koivu .25 .60
52 Jose Theodore .25 .60
53 Richard Zednik .15 .40
54 Andreas Johansson .15 .40
55 David Legwand .20 .50
56 Tomas Vokoun .20 .50
57 Martin Brodeur .60 1.50
58 Patrik Elias .25 .60
59 John Madden .15 .40
60 Jamie Langenbrunner .20 .50
61 Jason Blake .15 .40
62 Rick DiPietro .20 .50
63 Michael Peca .20 .50
64 Alexei Yashin .20 .50

65 Anson Carter .20 .50
66 Alex Kovalev .20 .50
67 Eric Lindros .40 1.00
68 Petr Nedved .15 .40
69 Daniel Alfredsson .25 .60
70 Marian Hossa .25 .60
71 Patrick Lalime .20 .50
72 Jason Spezza .25 .60
73 Tony Amonte .20 .50
74 John LeClair .25 .60
75 Jeremy Roenick .40 1.00
76 Sean Burke .15 .40
77 Mike Johnson .15 .40
78 Sebastien Caron .20 .50
79 Mario Lemieux 1.00 2.50
80 Pavol Demitra .30 .75
81 Barret Jackman .15 .40
82 Chris Pronger .25 .60
83 Keith Tkachuk .25 .60
84 Patrick Marleau .25 .60
85 Evgeni Nabokov .20 .50
86 Marco Sturm .15 .40
87 Nikolai Khabibulin .25 .60
88 Vincent Lecavalier .25 .60
89 Martin St. Louis .25 .60
90 Ed Belfour .25 .60
91 Alexander Mogilny .20 .50
92 Owen Nolan .25 .60
93 Mats Sundin .25 .60
94 Todd Bertuzzi .25 .60
95 Dan Cloutier .20 .50
96 Brendan Morrison .20 .50
97 Markus Naslund .25 .60
98 Peter Bondra .25 .60
99 Jaromir Jagr .75 2.00
100 Olaf Kolzig .25 .60
101 Garrett Burnett RC 1.25 3.00
102 Joffrey Lupul RC 3.00 8.00
102A Joffrey Lupul AU/375 8.00 20.00
103 Joe DiPenta RC 1.50 4.00
104 Patrice Bergeron RC 15.00 40.00
105 Milan Bartovic RC 1.50 4.00
106 Andrew Peters RC 1.50 4.00
107 Brent Krahn RC 1.25 3.00
108 Matthew Lombardi RC 1.50 4.00
109 Eric Staal RC 6.00 15.00
109A Eric Staal AU/375 15.00 40.00
110 Travis Moen RC 1.50 4.00
111 Tuomo Ruutu RC 2.00 5.00
111A Tuomo Ruutu AU/375 5.00 12.00
112 Pavel Vorobiev RC 1.50 4.00
113 Cody McCormick RC 1.50 4.00
114 Dan Fritsche RC 1.25 3.00
115 Kent McDonell RC 1.50 4.00
116 Antti Miettinen RC 2.00 5.00
117 Jiri Hudler RC 3.00 8.00
117A Jiri Hudler AU/375 8.00 20.00
118 Nathan Horton RC 3.00 8.00
118A Nathan Horton AU/375 8.00 20.00
119 Dustin Brown RC 3.00 8.00
119A Dustin Brown AU/375 12.50 30.00
120 Tim Gleason RC 1.50 4.00
121 Esa Pirnes RC 1.25 3.00
122 Brent Burns RC 4.00 10.00
123 Chris Higgins RC 2.50 6.00
123A Chris Higgins AU/375 6.00 15.00
124 Dan Hamhuis RC 1.50 4.00
125 Jordin Tootoo RC 2.50 6.00
125A Jordin Tootoo AU/375 6.00 15.00
126 Marek Zidlicky RC 1.25 3.00
127 David Hale RC 1.25 3.00
128 Paul Martin RC 1.50 4.00
129 Sean Bergenheim RC 1.50 4.00
130 Antoine Vermette RC 2.50 6.00
130A Antoine Vermette AU/375 6.00 15.00
131 Joni Pitkanen RC 2.00 5.00
131A Joni Pitkanen AU/375 5.00 12.00
132 Matthew Spiller RC 1.50 4.00
133 Marc-Andre Fleury RC 8.00 20.00
133A Marc-Andre Fleury AU/375 25.00 50.00
134 Matt Murley RC 1.50 4.00
135 Peter Sejna RC 1.50 4.00
135A Peter Sejna AU/375 4.00 10.00
136 Milan Michalek RC 2.50 6.00
136A Milan Michalek AU/375 6.00 15.00
137 Tom Preissing RC 1.50 4.00
138 Maxim Kondratiev RC 1.25 3.00
139 Matt Stajan RC 2.00 5.00
139A Matt Stajan AU 4.00 10.00
140 Boyd Gordon RC 1.50 4.00

2003-04 Pacific Supreme Blue

*1-100 VETS: 1.2X TO 3X BASIC CARDS
*101-140 ROOKIE/250: .8X TO 2X RC/775

2003-04 Pacific Supreme Red

*1-100 VETS: 1.5X TO 4X BASIC CARDS
*101-140 ROOKIE/425: .5X TO 1.2X RC/775

2003-04 Pacific Supreme Retail

*1-100 VETS: .4X TO 1X HOBBY GOLD
*101-140 ROOKIES: .25X TO .6X RC/775

2003-04 Pacific Supreme Generations

COMPLETE SET (24) 25.00 50.00
1 R.Francis/R.Vrbata 1.50 4.00
2 P.Roy/D.Aebischer 3.00 8.00
3 G.Sanderson/R.Nash 1.50 4.00
4 S.Yzerman/P.Datsyuk 4.00 10.00
5 B.Hull/H.Zetterberg 3.00 8.00
6 D.Alfredsson/J.Spezza 2.50 6.00
7 S.Burke/Z.Bierk 1.25 3.00
8 M.Lemieux/Marc-Andre Fleury 5.00 12.00
9 A.MacInnis/B.Jackman 1.50 4.00
10 V.Damphousse/J.Cheechoo 1.50 4.00
11 M.Sundin/N.Antropov 1.50 4.00
12 M.Naslund/D.Sedin 1.50 4.00

2003-04 Pacific Supreme Jerseys

1 Sergei Fedorov/500 4.00 10.00
2 Ilya Kovalchuk/500 4.00 10.00
3 Joe Thornton/400 5.00 12.00
4 Chris Drury/500 2.50 6.00
5 Miroslav Satan/500 2.50 6.00
6 Jarome Iginla/500 4.00 10.00
7 Eric Daze/500 2.50 6.00
8 Peter Forsberg/200 8.00 20.00
9 Paul Kariya/500 3.00 8.00
10 Patrick Roy/500 10.00 25.00
11 Brett Hull/500 4.00 10.00
12 Steve Yzerman/200 10.00 25.00
13 Mike Comrie/500 2.50 6.00
14 Ryan Smyth/500 2.50 6.00
15 Olli Jokinen/500 2.50 6.00
16 Jose Theodore/500 4.00 10.00
17 Pavel Bure/500 3.00 8.00
18 Eric Lindros/500 3.00 8.00
19 Tony Amonte/500 2.50 6.00
20 Jeremy Roenick/500 4.00 10.00
21 Mario Lemieux/500 10.00 25.00
22 Vincent Lecavalier/500 2.50 6.00
23 Mats Sundin/500 3.00 8.00
24 Markus Naslund/500 3.00 8.00
25 Jaromir Jagr/500 4.00 10.00

2003-04 Pacific Supreme Standing Guard

COMPLETE SET (12) 10.00 25.00
1 Jean-Sebastien Giguere 1.25 3.00
2 Jocelyn Thibault 1.25 3.00
3 Patrick Roy 3.00 8.00
4 Marc Denis 1.25 3.00
5 Marty Turco 1.25 3.00
6 Dominik Hasek 2.00 5.00
7 Roberto Luongo 2.00 5.00
8 Jose Theodore 2.00 5.00
9 Martin Brodeur 2.50 6.00
10 Patrick Lalime 1.25 3.00
11 Sean Burke 1.25 3.00
12 Ed Belfour 1.50 4.00

2003-04 Pacific Supreme Team

COMPLETE SET (10) 8.00 15.00
1 Joe Thornton .50 1.25
2 Peter Forsberg 1.00 2.50
3 Joe Sakic .60 1.50
4 Brett Hull .40 1.00
5 Steve Yzerman 2.00 5.00
6 Marian Gaborik .60 1.50
7 Mario Lemieux 2.50 6.00
8 Todd Bertuzzi .30 .75
9 Markus Naslund .30 .75
10 Jaromir Jagr .50 1.25

2002 Pacific Toronto Fall Expo

COMPLETE SET (10) 10.00 25.00
*GOLD: 1.5X TO 4X
1 Ed Belfour
Curtis Joseph 2.00 5.00
2 Jose Theodore
Patrick Roy 4.00 10.00
3 Roman Turek
Tommy Salo .60 1.50
4 Patrick Lalime
Dan Cloutier .60 1.50
5 Roberto Luongo
Nikolai Khabibulin 1.25 3.00
6 Martin Brodeur
Mike Richter 2.00 5.00
7 Jean-Sebastien Giguere
Felix Potvin 3.00 8.00
8 Marty Turco
Sean Burke 1.25 3.00
9 Martin Biron
Jocelyn Thibault .60 1.50
10 Brent Johnson
Evgeni Nabokov .60 1.50

2002 Pacific Toronto Spring Expo Rookie Collection

COMPLETE SET (10) 10.00 25.00
1 Dany Heatley 2.00 5.00
2 Ilya Kovalchuk 3.00 8.00
3 Mark Bell .75 2.00
4 Radim Vrbata .75 2.00
5 Rostislav Klesla 1.25 3.00
6 Pavel Datsyuk 3.00 8.00
7 Kristian Huselius .75 2.00
8 Raffi Torres .75 2.00
9 Dan Blackburn 1.25 3.00
10 Krystofer Kolanos .75 2.00

2003 Pacific Toronto Spring Expo

COMPLETE SET (8) 15.00 35.00
*GOLD/99: 1X TO 2.5X BASIC CARDS
1 Stanislav Chistov 1.00 2.50
2 Ryan Miller 1.50 4.00
3 Rick Nash 2.00 5.00
4 Henrik Zetterberg 3.00 8.00
5 Jay Bouwmeester 1.50 4.00
6 Mike Cammalleri 1.00 2.50
7 Jason Spezza 2.00 5.00
8 Carlo Colaiacovo 1.00 2.50

2003 Pacific Toronto Fall Expo

COMPLETE SET (6) 10.00 20.00
1 Todd Bertuzzi
Dave Dickenson 1.50 4.00
2 Jarome Iginla
Marcus Crandell 2.00 5.00
3 Ryan Smyth
Ricky Ray 1.25 3.00
4 Jose Theodore
Anthony Calvillo 2.00 5.00
5 Marian Hossa
Josh Ranek 1.25 3.00
6 Ed Belfour
Damon Allen 1.50 4.00

2004 Pacific National Convention

COMPLETE SET (6) 8.00 20.00
1 Ilya Kovalchuk 2.00 5.00
2 Joe Thornton 2.00 5.00
3 Rick Nash 2.00 5.00
4 Rick DiPietro .75 2.00
5 Marc-Andre Fleury 1.50 4.00
6 Vincent Lecavalier 1.25 3.00

2004 Pacific Toronto Spring Expo

*GOLD/99: .8X TO 2X BASIC CARDS
1 Patrice Bergeron 1.50 4.00
2 Eric Staal .75 2.00
3 Nathan Horton .75 2.00
4 Dustin Brown 1.00 2.50
5 Jordin Tootoo .75 2.00
6 Antoine Vermette .50 1.25
7 Marc-Andre Fleury 2.00 5.00
8 Matt Stajan .60 1.50

2004 Pacific WHA Autographs

1 Bobby Hull 15.00 30.00
2 Andre Lacroix 10.00 20.00

2010-11 Panini All Goalies

*UP CLOSE: 2X TO 5X BASE
1 Jonas Hiller .15 .40
2 Timo Pielmeier .20 .50
3 Dan Ellis .15 .40
4 Ray Emery .15 .40
5 Chris Mason .15 .40
6 Ondrej Pavelec .20 .50
7 Peter Mannino .15 .40
8 Tim Thomas .20 .50
9 Tuukka Rask .25 .60
10 Ryan Miller .20 .50
11 Patrick Lalime .15 .40
12 Jhonas Enroth .20 .50
13 Miikka Kiprusoff .20 .50
14 Henrik Karlsson .15 .40
15 Cam Ward .20 .50
16 Justin Peters .15 .40
17 Corey Crawford .25 .60
18 Marty Turco .20 .50
19 Brian Elliott .15 .40
20 Peter Budaj .15 .40
21 Steve Mason .15 .40
22 Mathieu Garon .15 .40
23 Kari Lehtonen .15 .40
24 Andrew Raycroft .15 .40
25 Richard Bachman .20 .50
26 Chris Osgood .20 .50
27 Jimmy Howard .25 .60
28 Joey MacDonald .15 .40
29 Jordan Pearce .25 .60
30 Thomas McCollum .20 .50
31 Nikolai Khabibulin .15 .40
32 Devan Dubnyk .15 .40
33 Martin Gerber .15 .40
34 Tomas Vokoun .15 .40
35 Jacob Markstrom .40 1.00
36 Scott Clemmensen .15 .40
37 Jonathan Bernier .15 .40
38 Jonathan Quick .25 .60
39 Matt Hackett .20 .50
40 Niklas Backstrom .20 .50
41 Jose Theodore .20 .50
42 Anton Khudobin .20 .50
43 Alex Auld .15 .40
44 Carey Price .40 1.00
45 Pekka Rinne .20 .50
46 Anders Lindback .15 .40
47 Mark Dekanich .15 .40
48 Jeff Frazee .25 .60
49 Johan Hedberg .15 .40
50 Martin Brodeur .50 1.25
51 Mike McKenna .15 .40
52 Rick DiPietro .15 .40
53 Nathan Lawson .15 .40
54 Kevin Poulin .20 .50
55 Al Montoya .15 .40
56 Henrik Lundqvist .50 1.25
57 Martin Biron .15 .40
58 Craig Anderson .20 .50
59 Pascal Leclaire .15 .40
60 Robin Lehner .30 .75
61 Mike Brodeur .15 .40
62 Curtis McElhinney .12 .30
63 Sergei Bobrovsky .60 1.50
64 Brian Boucher .15 .40
65 Michael Leighton .15 .40
66 Jason LaBarbera .15 .40
67 Ilya Bryzgalov .15 .40
68 Matt Climie .15 .40
69 Marc-Andre Fleury .40 1.00
70 Brent Johnson .15 .40
71 Antero Niittymaki .15 .40
72 Antti Niemi .15 .40
73 Alex Stalock .15 .40
74 J.P. Anderson .20 .50
75 Carter Hutton .40 1.00
76 Jaroslav Halak .20 .50
77 Ty Conklin .15 .40
78 Ben Bishop .15 .40
79 Dwayne Roloson .15 .40
80 Mike Smith .20 .50
81 Cedrick Desjardins .20 .50
82 James Reimer .20 .50
83 Jean-Sebastien Giguere .20 .50
84 Jonas Gustavsson .25 .60
85 Roberto Luongo .30 .75
86 Cory Schneider .20 .50
87 Semyon Varlamov .20 .50
88 Michal Neuvirth .15 .40
89 Braden Holtby .25 .60
90 Patrick Roy .50 1.25
91 Tony Esposito .20 .50
92 Ron Hextall .20 .50
93 Gerry Cheevers .20 .50
94 Jim Craig .15 .40
95 Ed Belfour .20 .50
96 Curtis Joseph .25 .60
97 Felix Potvin .30 .75
98 Grant Fuhr .30 .75
99 Richard Brodeur .20 .50
100 Tom Barrasso .20 .50

2010-11 Panini All Goalies Stopper Sweaters

1 Patrick Roy 10.00 25.00
2 Martin Brodeur 10.00 25.00
3 Roberto Luongo 6.00 15.00
4 Tim Thomas 4.00 10.00
5 Carey Price 8.00 20.00
6 Craig Anderson 4.00 10.00
7 Henrik Lundqvist 10.00 25.00
8 Pekka Rinne 4.00 10.00
9 Kari Lehtonen 3.00 8.00
10 Cam Ward 4.00 10.00
11 Devan Dubnyk 3.00 8.00
12 Mike Smith 4.00 10.00
13 Ondrej Pavelec 4.00 10.00
14 Cory Schneider 4.00 10.00
15 Andrew Raycroft 3.00 8.00
16 Peter Budaj 3.00 8.00
17 Brian Elliott 3.00 8.00
18 Miikka Kiprusoff 4.00 10.00

2012 Panini Black Friday Spokesman Jumbo Jerseys

GH Gordie Howe 8.00 20.00

2013 Panini Black Friday Rookie Materials

NM Nathan MacKinnon HK 10.00 25.00

2010 Panini Century Sports Stamp Autographs

18 Mike Bossy/40 15.00 40.00
20 Paul Coffey/50 10.00 25.00
22 Pierre Pilote/75 8.00 20.00
24 Gerry Cheevers/100 6.00 15.00
26 Bill Gadsby/75 6.00 15.00
37 Norm Ullman/85 10.00 20.00
38 Cammi Granato/50 20.00 50.00
41 Ray Bourque/52 20.00 50.00
42 Pat LaFontaine/39 40.00 80.00

2011-12 Panini Contenders

COMP.SET w/o SP's (100) 8.00 20.00
1 Roberto Luongo .60 1.50
2 Duncan Keith .30 .75
3 Dion Phaneuf .30 .75
4 Vincent Lecavalier .40 1.00
5 Nicklas Lidstrom .25 .60
6 Shea Weber .30 .75
7 Jeff Carter .30 .75
8 Teemu Selanne .75 2.00
9 Matt Duchene .40 1.00
10 Corey Perry .60 1.50
11 Daniel Alfredsson .40 1.00
12 Jarome Iginla .50 1.25
13 Pavel Datsyuk .60 1.50
14 Jordan Eberle .40 1.00
15 Dany Heatley .30 .75
16 Andrew Ladd .25 .60
17 Ryan Kesler .40 1.00
18 Marc Staal .25 .60
19 Joe Thornton .60 1.50
20 Chris Pronger .40 1.00
21 Loui Eriksson .25 .60
22 Dan Boyle .25 .60
23 Dustin Brown .40 1.00
24 Ryan Callahan .25 .60
25 Chris Stewart .30 .75
26 Martin St. Louis .40 1.00
27 Alex Pietrangelo .30 .75
28 Claude Giroux .40 1.00
29 Marc-Andre Fleury .75 2.00
30 Henrik Lundqvist 1.00 2.50
31 Carey Price .75 2.00
32 Kari Lehtonen .30 .75
33 Zdeno Chara .40 1.00
34 Miikka Kiprusoff .40 1.00
35 Nikolai Khabibulin .30 .75
36 Milan Lucic .40 1.00
37 Mike Smith .40 1.00
38 Jonas Hiller .30 .75
39 Al Montoya .25 .60
40 Henrik Zetterberg .50 1.25
41 Craig Anderson .40 1.00
42 David Backes .25 .60
43 Tim Thomas .40 1.00
44 Henrik Sedin .50 1.25
45 Jonathan Quick .50 1.25
46 David Krejci .40 1.00
47 Daniel Sedin .50 1.25
48 Danny Briere .40 1.00
49 Joe Pavelski .50 1.25
50 Corey Crawford .50 1.25
51 Jason Spezza .40 1.00
52 Mike Green .30 .75
53 Jeff Skinner .50 1.25
54 Anze Kopitar .60 1.50
55 Jason Pominville .25 .60
56 Semyon Varlamov .40 1.00
57 Tyler Myers .25 .60
58 Kris Letang .50 1.25
59 Eric Staal .50 1.25
60 Jose Theodore .40 1.00
61 Rick Nash .40 1.00
62 Patrik Elias .40 1.00
63 Brad Marchand .75 2.00
64 Mike Commodore .30 .75
65 Erik Karlsson .50 1.25
66 Martin Brodeur 1.00 2.50
67 Max Pacioretty .40 1.00
68 Jaromir Jagr 1.25 3.00
69 Taylor Hall .40 1.00
70 Ryan Miller .40 1.00
71 Evgeni Malkin .75 2.00
72 Luke Adam .30 .75
73 Michael Ryder .25 .60
74 T.J. Oshie .40 1.00
75 Brian Gionta .25 .60
76 P.K. Subban .50 1.25
77 Joffrey Lupul .25 .60
78 Marian Gaborik .40 1.00
79 James Reimer .40 1.00
80 Nik Antropov .30 .75
81 Phil Kessel .40 1.00
82 Mike Richards .30 .75
83 Ales Hemsky .30 .75
84 Mikhail Grabovski .25 .60
85 Jamie Benn .40 1.00
86 Ondrej Pavelec .40 1.00
87 Sidney Crosby 1.50 4.00
88 Patrick Kane .75 2.00
89 Ray Whitney .30 .75
90 Logan Couture .50 1.25
91 Steven Stamkos .75 2.00
92 John Tavares .60 1.50
93 Jimmy Howard .50 1.25
94 Ryan Smyth .30 .75
95 Cam Ward .40 1.00
96 Pierre-Marc Bouchard .40 1.00
97 Ryan Getzlaf .40 1.00
98 Alex Ovechkin 1.50 4.00
99 Jonathan Toews .60 1.50
100 Josh Harding .40 1.00
101 Corey Perry CC 2.50 6.00
102 Ryan Getzlaf CC 1.50 4.00
103 Nathan Horton CC 1.50 4.00
104 Patrice Bergeron CC 2.00 5.00
105 Tim Thomas CC 1.50 4.00
106 Ryan Miller CC 1.50 4.00
107 Jarome Iginla CC 2.00 5.00
108 Jonathan Toews CC 2.50 6.00
109 Matt Duchene CC 1.50 4.00
110 Pavel Datsyuk CC 2.50 6.00
111 Nicklas Lidstrom CC 1.00 2.50
112 Drew Doughty CC 2.00 5.00
113 Anze Kopitar CC 2.50 6.00
114 Dustin Brown CC 1.50 4.00
115 Carey Price CC 3.00 8.00
116 Scott Gomez CC 1.25 3.00
117 John Tavares CC 2.50 6.00
118 Brad Richards CC 1.50 4.00
119 Jaromir Jagr CC 5.00 12.00
120 Claude Giroux CC 1.50 4.00
121 James van Riemsdyk CC 1.25 3.00
122 Danny Briere CC 1.50 4.00
123 Ilya Bryzgalov CC 1.50 4.00
124 Chris Pronger CC 1.50 4.00
125 Shane Doan CC 1.25 3.00
126 Marc-Andre Fleury CC 3.00 8.00
127 Jordan Staal CC 1.25 3.00
128 Sidney Crosby CC 6.00 15.00
129 Kris Letang CC 2.00 5.00
130 James Neal CC 1.00 2.50
131 Evgeni Malkin CC 3.00 8.00
132 Patrick Marleau CC 1.50 4.00
133 Logan Couture CC 2.00 5.00
134 Dan Boyle CC 1.00 2.50
135 Joe Thornton CC 2.50 6.00
136 Martin St. Louis CC 1.50 4.00
137 Vincent Lecavalier CC 1.50 4.00
138 Steven Stamkos CC 3.00 8.00
139 Victor Hedman CC 2.00 5.00
140 Mikhail Grabovski CC 1.00 2.50
141 James Reimer CC 1.50 4.00
142 Phil Kessel CC 1.50 4.00
143 Ryan Kesler CC 1.50 4.00
144 Roberto Luongo CC 2.50 6.00
145 Henrik Sedin CC 2.00 5.00
146 Daniel Sedin CC 2.00 5.00
147 Alexander Semin CC 1.50 4.00
148 Alex Ovechkin CC 6.00 15.00
149 John Carlson CC 1.50 4.00
150 Tomas Vokoun CC 1.25 3.00
151 Steve Yzerman CC 4.00 10.00
152 Denis Savard CC 1.50 4.00
153 Patrick Roy CC 4.00 10.00
154 Mark Messier CC 3.00 8.00
155 Joe Sakic CC 3.00 8.00
156 Brendan Shanahan CC 1.50 4.00
157 Bryan Trottier CC 1.50 4.00
158 Luc Robitaille CC 1.50 4.00
159 Mario Lemieux CC 6.00 15.00
160 Curtis Joseph CC 2.00 5.00
161 Maxime Macenauer RC 1.50 4.00
162 Patrick Maroon RC 1.50 4.00
163 Corey Tropp RC 1.50 4.00
164 Lance Bouma RC 1.50 4.00
165 Cameron Gaunce RC 1.25 3.00
166 Colton Sceviour RC 1.50 4.00
167 Colten Teubert RC 1.50 4.00
168 Chris VandeVelde RC 2.50 6.00
169 Hugh Jessiman RC 1.50 4.00
170 Bracken Kearns RC 1.50 4.00
171 Scott Timmins RC 1.50 4.00
172 Carson McMillan RC 2.00 5.00
173 Drew Bagnall RC 1.50 4.00
174 Frederic St-Denis RC 1.50 4.00
175 Brendon Nash RC 1.50 4.00
176 Mattias Ekholm RC 3.00 8.00
177 Ryan Thang RC 1.25 3.00
178 Keith Kinkaid RC 1.50 4.00
179 Mikko Koskinen RC 2.00 5.00
180 Mark Katic RC 1.50 4.00
181 Shane Sims RC 1.50 4.00
182 Matt Campanale RC 1.50 4.00
183 Dmitry Orlov RC 4.00 10.00
184 Justin DiBenedetto RC 1.25 3.00
185 David Ullstrom RC 1.50 4.00
186 Kevin Marshall RC 1.50 4.00
187 Ben Holmstrom RC 1.50 4.00
188 Brian Strait RC 2.00 5.00
189 Harri Sateri RC 1.50 4.00
190 Todd Ford RC 2.00 5.00
191 Marc-Andre Bourdon RC 3.00 8.00
192 Anders Nilsson RC 1.50 4.00
193 Kris Fredheim RC 1.50 4.00
194 Paul Postma RC 1.50 4.00
195 Tomas Kundratek RC 2.00 5.00
196 Roman Josi RC 4.00 10.00
197 Stefan Elliott RC 1.50 4.00
198 Brayden McNabb RC 1.50 4.00
199 Bill Sweatt RC 1.50 4.00
200 T.J. Brennan RC 1.50 4.00
201 Smith-Pelly AU RC 4.00 10.00
202 Peter Holland AU RC 3.00 8.00
203 Greg Nemisz AU RC 3.00 8.00
204 Roman Horak AU RC 3.00 8.00
205 Justin Faulk AU RC 5.00 12.00
206 Brandon Saad AU RC 8.00 20.00
207 Marcus Kruger AU RC 5.00 12.00
208 G.Landeskog AU RC 12.00 30.00
209 Ryan Johansen AU RC 10.00 25.00
210 Cam Atkinson AU RC 8.00 20.00
211 John Moore AU RC 3.00 8.00
212 David Savard AU RC 3.00 8.00
213 Tomas Kubalik AU RC 3.00 8.00
214 Allen York AU RC 3.00 8.00
215 Tomas Vincour AU RC 3.00 8.00
216 Gustav Nyquist AU RC 12.00 30.00
217 Brendan Smith AU RC 6.00 15.00
218 R.Nugent-Hopkins AU RC 15.00 40.00
219 Carl Hagelin AU/763 RC 12.00 30.00
220 Ryan Ellis AU RC 3.00 8.00
221 Simon Despres AU RC 8.00 20.00
222 Gudbranson AU RC 4.00 10.00
223 Slava Voynov AU RC 3.00 8.00
224 Brett Bulmer AU RC 3.00 8.00
225 Aaron Palushaj AU RC 3.00 8.00
226 Alexei Emelin AU RC 3.00 8.00
227 Raphael Diaz AU RC 3.00 8.00
228 Craig Smith AU RC 4.00 10.00
229 Jonathon Blum AU RC 3.00 8.00
230 Blake Geoffrion AU RC 3.00 8.00
231 Adam Larsson AU RC 4.00 10.00
232 Adam Henrique AU RC 6.00 15.00
233 Tim Erixon AU RC 5.00 12.00
234 Cam Talbot AU RC 8.00 20.00
235 Mika Zibanejad AU RC 12.00 30.00
236 Stephane Da Costa AU RC 3.00 8.00
237 Patrick Wiercioch AU RC 3.00 8.00
238 Colin Greening AU RC 3.00 8.00
239 David Rundblad AU RC 3.00 8.00
240 Erik Condra AU RC 3.00 8.00
241 Sean Couturier AU RC 6.00 15.00
242 Matt Read AU RC 10.00 25.00
243 Zac Rinaldo AU RC 3.00 8.00
244 Erik Gustafsson AU RC 4.00 10.00
245 Calvin de Haan AU RC 3.00 8.00
246 Louis Leblanc AU RC 10.00 25.00
247 Joe Vitale AU RC 5.00 12.00
248 Robert Bortuzzo AU RC 5.00 12.00
249 Brett Connolly AU RC 5.00 12.00
250 Joe Colborne AU RC 5.00 12.00
251 Jake Gardiner AU RC 6.00 15.00
252 Matt Frattin AU RC 6.00 15.00
253 Ben Scrivens AU RC 6.00 15.00
254 Eddie Lack AU RC 6.00 15.00
255 Cody Hodgson AU RC 8.00 20.00
256 Yann Sauve AU RC 3.00 8.00
257 Cody Eakin AU RC 5.00 12.00
258 Carl Klingberg AU RC 3.00 8.00
259 Mark Scheifele AU RC 15.00 40.00
260 Zack Kassian AU RC 6.00 15.00
261 Andrew Shaw RC 5.00 12.00
262 Brad Malone RC 2.50 6.00
263 Cade Fairchild RC 1.25 3.00
264 Dylan Olsen RC 2.50 6.00
265 Gabriel Bourque RC 3.00 8.00
266 Iiro Tarkki RC 2.50 6.00
267 Jeremy Smith RC 3.00 8.00
268 Jimmy Hayes RC 3.00 8.00
269 Leland Irving RC 1.50 4.00
270 Marcus Foligno RC 3.00 8.00
271 Mike Hoffman RC 6.00 15.00
272 Mike Murphy RC 3.00 8.00
273 Riley Nash RC 1.50 4.00
274 Stu Bickel RC 1.50 4.00
275 Matt Fraser RC 2.00 5.00
276 Joakim Andersson RC 3.00 8.00
277 Brian Foster RC 2.50 6.00
278 Andre Petersson RC 2.00 5.00
279 Harry Zolnierczyk RC 1.50 4.00
280 Mark Borowiecki RC 2.00 5.00
281 Andy Miele RC 1.50 4.00
282 Anton Lander RC 1.50 4.00
283 Carl Sneep RC 2.50 6.00

2011-12 Panini Contenders Match Ups Booklet Autographs

3 Erixon/Calla/Larsn/Henrq 40.00 80.00
4 Segn/Rask/Kes/Clbrne SP 90.00 150.00
5 Grabv/Rmer/Subn/Price SP 40.00 100.00
6 Frattin/Gard/Grning/Cndra 10.00 25.00
7 Hall/Ebrle/Igin/Giord SP 40.00 100.00
8 Quick/Brwn/Hillr/Perry 40.00 80.00
10 Morrow/Leht/Seto/Bckstrm 12.00 30.00
11 Giroux/Read/Call/Stepan 50.00 100.00
12 Doan/Bisn/Kane/Klingbrg 20.00 50.00
13 Johan/Moore/Osh/Pietr 15.00 40.00
14 Smith/Howard/Varla/Land 50.00 120.00
15 Paajrvi/Landr/Karls/Bcklnd 15.00 40.00
16 Atknsn/Svrd/Scheif/Post 12.00 30.00
17 Kesler/Schn/Brown/Bernier 15.00 40.00
18 Jagr/Bryzg/Fleury/Malkin SP 125.00 250.00
19 Staal/Lund/Brdr/Parise SP 175.00 300.00
20 Ctre/Pavel/Selne/Perry SP 40.00 80.00
21 Andrsn/Grning/Eller/Diaz 12.00 30.00
22 Vanek/Miller/Bergrn/Thms 40.00 80.00
23 Sharp/Prngr/Giroux/Toews 75.00 150.00
24 Geof/Smith/Atkin/Jhnsn 12.00 30.00

2011-12 Panini Contenders NHL Ink

*GOLD/25: 1X TO 2.5X BASIC AU
*GOLD/25: .8X TO 2X BASIC AU SP
1 Teemu Selanne SP 12.00 30.00
2 Ray Bourque SP 10.00 25.00
3 Curtis Glencross 4.00 10.00
4 Greg Nemisz 5.00 12.00
5 Mark Giordano 6.00 15.00
6 Jarome Iginla SP 8.00 20.00
7 Roman Horak 5.00 12.00
8 Cam Ward 6.00 15.00
9 Justin Faulk 8.00 20.00
10 Viktor Stalberg 4.00 10.00
11 Marcus Kruger 8.00 20.00
13 John Moore 5.00 12.00
14 Kari Lehtonen SP 5.00 12.00
15 Tomas Vincour 5.00 12.00
16 Cory Emmerton SP 5.00 12.00
17 Jimmy Howard SP 8.00 20.00
18 Steve Yzerman SP 15.00 40.00
20 Teemu Hartikainen 5.00 12.00
21 Evgeny Dadonov 4.00 10.00
22 Anze Kopitar SP 10.00 25.00
23 Drew Doughty SP 8.00 20.00
24 Brett Bulmer 5.00 12.00
25 Nick Johnson 5.00 12.00
26 Cal Clutterbuck 4.00 10.00
27 Cody Almond 4.00 10.00
28 Devin Setoguchi 5.00 12.00
29 Max Pacioretty SP 6.00 15.00
30 Aaron Palushaj 5.00 12.00
31 Colin Wilson SP 5.00 12.00
32 Blake Geoffrion 5.00 12.00
33 Craig Smith 6.00 15.00
34 Adam Larsson 6.00 15.00
35 John Tavares SP 10.00 25.00
36 Derek Stepan SP 4.00 10.00
39 Robin Lehner 5.00 12.00
40 Colin Greening 5.00 12.00
41 David Rundblad 5.00 12.00
42 Erik Gustafsson 6.00 15.00
43 Zac Rinaldo 5.00 12.00
44 James van Riemsdyk SP 5.00 12.00
45 Chris Pronger SP 6.00 15.00
46 Claude Giroux SP 6.00 15.00
48 Jaromir Jagr SP 20.00 50.00
49 Matt Read 6.00 15.00
50 Sean Couturier 10.00 25.00
51 Andy Miele 5.00 12.00
52 Evgeni Malkin SP 12.00 30.00
53 James Neal 4.00 10.00
55 Mario Lemieux SP 25.00 60.00
56 Sidney Crosby SP 25.00 60.00
57 Patrick Marleau SP 6.00 15.00
58 Alex Pietrangelo 5.00 12.00
59 Matt Frattin 5.00 12.00
60 Dion Phaneuf SP 5.00 12.00
61 James Reimer SP 6.00 15.00
62 Carl Gunnarsson 4.00 10.00
63 Daniel Sedin SP 8.00 20.00
64 Henrik Sedin SP 8.00 20.00
65 Cody Eakin 8.00 20.00
66 Alex Ovechkin SP 25.00 60.00
67 Eric Fehr 4.00 10.00
68 Paul Postma 5.00 12.00
69 Mark Scheifele SP 20.00 50.00
70 Teemu Selanne SP 12.00 30.00

2011-12 Panini Contenders NHL Ink Duals

*GOLD/25: .6X TO 1.5X BASIC INSERTS
1 T.Hall/Nugent-Hopkins SP 30.00 80.00
2 J.Sakic/S.Yzerman SP EXCH 25.00 60.00
3 S.Couturier/M.Read 15.00 40.00
4 Z.Rinaldo/J.Shelley 8.00 20.00
5 B.Scrivens/M.Frattin 8.00 20.00
6 A.Henrique/A.Larsson 20.00 50.00
7 Nugent-Hop/Landeskog SP 30.00 80.00
8 B.Hull/B.Hull SP 20.00 50.00
9 B.Saad/B.Hull SP 20.00 50.00
10 R.McDonagh/T.Erixon 8.00 20.00
11 M.Scheifele/P.Postma 30.00 80.00
12 P.Roy/C.Price SP 25.00 60.00
13 T.Seguin/J.Caron SP 12.00 30.00
14 G.Landeskog/R.O'Reilly 25.00 60.00
15 J.Iginla/C.Glencross SP 12.00 30.00
16 D.Rundblad/Wiercioch 8.00 20.00
17 T.Myers/R.Miller SP 10.00 25.00
18 D.Doughty/J.Johnson SP 12.00 30.00
19 R.Johansen/J.Carter SP 25.00 60.00
20 C.Hodgson/Y.Sauve SP 12.00 30.00

2011-12 Panini Contenders NHL Ink Triples

1 Yzerman/Sakic/Trottier 75.00 150.00
2 Hull/Hawerchuk/Selanne 100.00 200.00
3 Sedin/Sedin/Luongo 30.00 60.00
4 Hall/Seguin/Gudbranson 30.00 80.00
5 Price/Subban/Cammalleri 25.00 50.00
6 Hall/Eberle/Schenn 50.00 100.00
7 Carlson/Gardiner/Stepan 40.00 100.00
8 Hedman/Seguin/Landskg 50.00 100.00
9 Tavares/Hall/Nugent-Hop 175.00 300.00
10 Modano/Belfour/Hull 60.00 125.00

2011-12 Panini Contenders Original Six Booklet Autographs

1 Chra/Tws/Phn/Lds/Gnt/Clhn 75.00 150.00
2 Yzrm/Svrd/Laf/Clrk/Brqe/Espo 100.00 175.00
3 Roy/Ptv/Chv/Dvdsn/Vch/Espo 200.00 350.00
4 Thm/Stl/Lids/Kne/Price/Kssl 50.00 100.00
6 Bwr/Fhr/Ptvn/Jsph/Blfr/Rmer 250.00 350.00

2011-12 Panini Contenders Patch Autographs

101 Corey Perry/100 15.00 30.00
102 Ryan Getzlaf/100 15.00 40.00
103 Nathan Horton/100 15.00 40.00
104 Patrice Bergeron/100 15.00 40.00
106 Ryan Miller/100 15.00 40.00
107 Jarome Iginla/100 25.00 60.00
108 Jonathan Toews/49 40.00 80.00
109 Matt Duchene/100 15.00 40.00
110 Pavel Datsyuk/100 20.00 50.00
111 Nicklas Lidstrom/100 30.00 60.00
112 Drew Doughty/100 20.00 50.00
113 Anze Kopitar/100 20.00 50.00
114 Dustin Brown/100 15.00 40.00
115 Carey Price/31 60.00 120.00
116 Scott Gomez/100 10.00 25.00
117 John Tavares/100 20.00 50.00
118 Brad Richards/100 15.00 40.00
119 Jaromir Jagr/50 40.00 100.00
120 Claude Giroux/100 25.00 50.00
121 James van Riemsdyk/100 12.00 30.00
122 Danny Briere/100 15.00 40.00
123 Ilya Bryzgalov/78 12.00 30.00
124 Chris Pronger/100 15.00 40.00
125 Shane Doan/100 12.00 30.00
126 Marc-Andre Fleury/100 12.00 30.00
127 Jordan Staal/100 12.00 30.00
128 Sidney Crosby/25 150.00 250.00
129 Kris Letang/100 25.00 50.00
130 James Neal/100 10.00 25.00
131 Evgeni Malkin/25 40.00 80.00
132 Patrick Marleau/100 15.00 40.00
133 Logan Couture/100 20.00 50.00
134 Dan Boyle/100 10.00 25.00
135 Joe Thornton/100 25.00 60.00
136 Martin St. Louis/100 15.00 40.00
137 Vincent Lecavalier/100 15.00 40.00
138 Steven Stamkos/100 30.00 60.00
139 Victor Hedman/100 20.00 50.00
140 Mikhail Grabovski/100 15.00 40.00
141 James Reimer/100 15.00 40.00
142 Phil Kessel/100 15.00 40.00
143 Ryan Kesler/100 15.00 40.00
144 Roberto Luongo/40 30.00 60.00
145 Henrik Sedin/100 10.00 25.00
146 Daniel Sedin/100 12.00 30.00
147 Alexander Semin/100 12.00 30.00
148 Alex Ovechkin/25 100.00 200.00
149 John Carlson/100 15.00 40.00
150 Tomas Vokoun/87 12.00 30.00
151 Steve Yzerman/50 40.00 100.00
152 Denis Savard/100 15.00 40.00
153 Patrick Roy/100 60.00 120.00
154 Mark Messier/25 30.00 60.00
155 Joe Sakic/100 25.00 60.00
156 Brendan Shanahan/25 50.00 100.00
157 Bryan Trottier/50 30.00 60.00
158 Luc Robitaille/90 15.00 40.00
159 Mario Lemieux/25 60.00 120.00
160 Curtis Joseph/100 25.00 50.00
201 Devante Smith-Pelly/100 10.00 25.00
202 Peter Holland/100 12.00 30.00
203 Greg Nemisz/100 8.00 20.00
204 Roman Horak /100 12.00 30.00

205 Justin Faulk/100 15.00 40.00
206 Brandon Saad/100 15.00 40.00
207 Marcus Kruger/100 12.00 30.00
208 Gabriel Landeskog/100 60.00 120.00
209 Ryan Johansen/76 25.00 60.00
210 Cam Atkinson/100 20.00 50.00
211 John Moore/100 8.00 20.00
212 David Savard/100 10.00 25.00
213 Tomas Kubalik/100 8.00 20.00
214 Allen York/100 10.00 25.00
215 Tomas Vincour/100 8.00 20.00
216 Gustav Nyquist/100 20.00 50.00
217 Brendan Smith/100 8.00 20.00
218 R.Nugent-Hopkins/100 75.00 150.00
219 Carl Hagelin/100 25.00 60.00
220 Ryan Ellis/100 8.00 20.00
221 Simon Despres/100 8.00 20.00
222 Erik Gudbranson/100 15.00 40.00
223 Slava Voynov/100 8.00 20.00
224 Brett Bulmer/100 8.00 20.00
225 Aaron Palushaj/100 8.00 20.00
226 Alexei Emelin/100 8.00 20.00
227 Raphael Diaz/100 8.00 20.00
228 Craig Smith/100 20.00 50.00
229 Jonathon Blum /100 8.00 20.00
230 Blake Geoffrion/100 8.00 20.00
231 Adam Larsson/100 30.00 60.00
232 Adam Henrique/100 30.00 80.00
233 Tim Erixon/100 8.00 20.00
234 Cam Talbot/100 20.00 50.00
235 Mika Zibanejad/100 15.00 40.00
236 Stephane Da Costa/100 8.00 20.00
237 Patrick Wiercioch/100 8.00 20.00
238 Colin Greening/100 8.00 20.00
239 David Rundblad/100 8.00 20.00
240 Erik Condra/100 8.00 20.00
241 Sean Couturier/100 15.00 40.00
242 Matt Read/100 12.00 30.00
243 Zac Rinaldo/100 8.00 20.00
244 Erik Gustafsson/100 10.00 25.00
245 Calvin de Haan/100 10.00 25.00
246 Louis Leblanc/100 15.00 40.00
247 Joe Vitale/100 15.00 40.00
248 Robert Bortuzzo/100 12.00 30.00
249 Brett Connolly/100 15.00 40.00
250 Joe Colborne/100 8.00 20.00
251 Jake Gardiner/100 15.00 40.00
252 Matt Frattin/100 8.00 20.00
253 Ben Scrivens/100 15.00 40.00
254 Eddie Lack/100 12.00 30.00
255 Cody Hodgson/100 12.00 30.00
256 Yann Sauve/25 25.00 50.00
257 Cody Eakin/100 15.00 40.00
258 Carl Klingberg/100 15.00 30.00
259 Mark Scheifele/100 40.00 100.00
260 Zack Kassian/100 10.00 25.00

2011-12 Panini Contenders Starting Line Ups Booklet Autographs

1 Pitt Penguins 125.00 200.00
3 Phil.Flyers 50.00 120.00
4 Buffalo Sabres 60.00 120.00
5 NJ Devils 200.00 350.00
6 SJ Sharks 90.00 150.00

2012-13 Panini Contenders Cup Contenders

1 Teemu Selanne 3.00 8.00
2 Vincent Lecavalier 1.50 4.00
3 Ryan Nugent-Hopkins 2.00 5.00
4 Matt Duchene 1.50 4.00
5 Loui Eriksson 1.00 2.50
6 Joe Thornton 2.50 6.00
7 Patrick Kane 3.00 8.00
8 Rick Nash 1.50 4.00
9 Henrik Sedin 2.00 5.00
10 Ryan Suter 1.25 3.00
11 Zdeno Chara 1.50 4.00
12 Jordan Staal 1.25 3.00
13 Nicklas Backstrom 1.50 4.00
14 Alex Pietrangelo 1.25 3.00
15 Ilya Kovalchuk 1.50 4.00
16 Jason Pominville 1.00 2.50
17 Milan Michalek 1.00 2.50
18 Mike Richards 1.25 3.00
19 Nazem Kadri 2.00 5.00
20 Andrei Markov 1.00 2.50
21 Henrik Zetterberg 2.00 5.00
22 Sidney Crosby 6.00 15.00
23 Evander Kane 1.50 4.00
24 Sean Couturier 1.25 3.00
25 Oliver Ekman-Larsson 1.50 4.00

2012-13 Panini Contenders Hart Contenders

1 Evgeni Malkin 3.00 8.00
2 Daniel Sedin 2.00 5.00
3 Corey Perry 2.50 6.00
4 Dustin Byfuglien 1.50 4.00
5 Alex Ovechkin 6.00 15.00
6 Claude Giroux 1.50 4.00
7 Patrick Marleau 1.50 4.00
8 Steven Stamkos 3.00 8.00
9 John Tavares 2.50 6.00
10 Jordan Eberle 1.50 4.00
11 Jonathan Toews 2.50 6.00
12 Phil Kessel 1.50 4.00
13 Anze Kopitar 2.50 6.00
14 Tyler Seguin 2.00 5.00
15 Jarome Iginla 2.00 5.00
16 Eric Staal 2.00 5.00
17 Marian Gaborik 1.50 4.00
18 Jaromir Jagr 5.00 12.00
19 Pavel Datsyuk 2.50 6.00
20 Zach Parise 1.50 4.00
21 Shea Weber 1.25 3.00
22 Gabriel Landeskog 2.00 5.00
23 David Backes 1.00 2.50
24 Shane Doan 1.25 3.00
25 Thomas Vanek 1.25 3.00

2012-13 Panini Contenders Legacies

1 Gordie Howe 6.00 15.00
2 Mark Messier 4.00 10.00
3 Bobby Clarke 3.00 8.00
4 Bobby Hull 4.00 10.00
5 Bernie Parent 2.50 6.00
6 Mario Lemieux 8.00 20.00
7 Stan Mikita 2.50 6.00
8 Eric Lindros 3.00 8.00
9 Larry Robinson 2.00 5.00
10 Cam Neely 2.00 5.00
11 Gilbert Perreault 2.00 5.00
12 Igor Larionov 2.00 5.00
13 Johnny Bower 2.00 5.00
14 Bernie Nicholls 1.50 4.00
15 Patrick Roy 5.00 12.00
16 Steve Yzerman 5.00 12.00
17 Joe Sakic 4.00 10.00
18 Brett Hull 4.00 10.00
19 Doug Gilmour 2.50 6.00
20 Joe Nieuwendyk 1.50 4.00
21 Phil Esposito 3.00 8.00
22 Yvan Cournoyer 2.00 5.00
23 Mike Richter 2.00 5.00
24 Pierre Turgeon 1.50 4.00
25 Curtis Joseph 2.50 6.00

2012-13 Panini Contenders Vezina Contenders

1 Pekka Rinne 1.50 4.00
2 Jonathan Quick 2.00 5.00
3 Cory Schneider 1.50 4.00
4 Miikka Kiprusoff 1.50 4.00
5 Semyon Varlamov 1.50 4.00
6 Marc-Andre Fleury 3.00 8.00
7 Jonas Hiller 1.25 3.00
8 Mike Smith 1.50 4.00
9 Jimmy Howard 2.00 5.00
10 Tuukka Rask 2.00 5.00
11 Brian Elliott 1.25 3.00
12 Carey Price 3.00 8.00
13 Craig Anderson 1.50 4.00
14 Martin Brodeur 4.00 10.00
15 Ondrej Pavelec 1.50 4.00
16 Ryan Miller 1.50 4.00
17 Devan Dubnyk 1.25 3.00
18 Henrik Lundqvist 4.00 10.00
19 Niklas Backstrom 1.25 3.00
20 Corey Crawford 2.00 5.00
21 Kari Lehtonen 1.25 3.00
22 Anders Lindback 1.00 2.50
23 Sergei Bobrovsky 2.50 6.00
24 Cam Ward 1.50 4.00
25 Ilya Bryzgalov 1.50 4.00

2013-14 Panini Contenders

COMP.SET w/o RC's (100) 10.00 25.00
1 Jonathan Toews .60 1.50
2 Marian Hossa .40 1.00
3 Patrick Kane .75 2.00
4 Corey Crawford .50 1.25
5 T.J. Oshie .40 1.00
6 Alex Pietrangelo .30 .75
7 Jaroslav Halak .40 1.00
8 Joe Thornton .60 1.50
9 Logan Couture .50 1.25
10 Patrick Marleau .40 1.00
11 Antti Niemi .30 .75
12 Teemu Selanne .75 2.00
13 Ryan Getzlaf .40 1.00
14 Jonas Hiller .30 .75
15 Corey Perry .60 1.50
16 Gabriel Landeskog .50 1.25
17 Matt Duchene .40 1.00
18 Semyon Varlamov .40 1.00
19 Shane Doan .30 .75
20 Keith Yandle .25 .60
21 Mike Smith .40 1.00
22 Zach Parise .40 1.00
23 Ryan Suter .30 .75
24 Josh Harding .40 1.00
25 Dustin Brown .40 1.00
26 Jeff Carter .30 .75
27 Drew Doughty .50 1.25
28 Jonathan Quick .50 1.25
29 Tuukka Rask .50 1.25
30 Zdeno Chara .40 1.00
31 Patrice Bergeron .50 1.25
32 Jarome Iginla .50 1.25
33 Sidney Crosby 1.50 4.00
34 Evgeni Malkin .75 2.00
35 Kris Letang .50 1.25
36 Marc-Andre Fleury .75 2.00
37 Martin St. Louis .40 1.00
38 Steven Stamkos .75 2.00
39 Ben Bishop .30 .75
40 Phil Kessel .40 1.00
41 Joffrey Lupul .25 .60
42 Jonathan Bernier .30 .75
43 James Reimer .40 1.00
44 Henrik Zetterberg .50 1.25
45 Pavel Datsyuk .60 1.50
46 Jimmy Howard .50 1.25
47 Daniel Alfredsson .40 1.00
48 Daniel Sedin .50 1.25
49 Henrik Sedin .50 1.25
50 Roberto Luongo .60 1.50
51 Alex Ovechkin 1.50 4.00
52 Nicklas Backstrom .40 1.00
53 Braden Holtby .50 1.25
54 Jamie Benn .40 1.00
55 Kari Lehtonen .30 .75
56 Tyler Seguin .50 1.25
57 Mike Fisher .25 .60
58 Shea Weber .30 .75
59 Pekka Rinne .40 1.00
60 Max Pacioretty .40 1.00
61 Lars Eller .25 .60
62 P.K. Subban .50 1.25
63 Carey Price .75 2.00
64 Patrik Elias .40 1.00
65 Martin Brodeur 1.00 2.50
66 Cory Schneider .40 1.00
67 Jaromir Jagr 1.25 3.00
68 Andrew Ladd .25 .60
69 Zach Bogosian .30 .75
70 Ondrej Pavelec .40 1.00
71 Rick Nash .40 1.00
72 Ryan Callahan .25 .60
73 Henrik Lundqvist 1.00 2.50
74 Claude Giroux .40 1.00
75 Sean Couturier .30 .75
76 Vincent Lecavalier .40 1.00
77 Jason Spezza .40 1.00
78 Bobby Ryan .30 .75
79 Craig Anderson .40 1.00
80 Eric Staal .50 1.25
81 Cam Ward .40 1.00
82 Jordan Staal .30 .75
83 Marian Gaborik .40 1.00
84 Jack Johnson .25 .60
85 Sergei Bobrovsky .60 1.50
86 John Tavares .60 1.50
87 Kyle Okposo .25 .60
88 Thomas Vanek .30 .75
89 Curtis Glencross .25 .60
90 T.J. Brodie .25 .60
91 Mike Cammalleri .30 .75
92 Tim Thomas .40 1.00
93 Brian Campbell .25 .60
94 Brad Boyes .25 .60
95 Jordan Eberle .40 1.00
96 Sam Gagner .25 .60
97 Taylor Hall .40 1.00
98 Drew Stafford .25 .60
99 Ryan Miller .40 1.00
100 Cody Hodgson .25 .60
101 Kevan Miller RC 2.50 6.00
102A Ben Hanowski RC 2.50 6.00
102B Ben Hanowski AU 3.00 8.00
103 Damien Brunner RC 2.50 6.00
104 Eric Selleck RC 2.50 6.00
105 Nicolas Blanchard RC 2.50 6.00
106 Sami Aittokallio RC 3.00 8.00
107 Zach Sill RC 3.00 8.00
108 Will Acton RC 2.50 6.00
109 Karl Stollery RC 2.50 6.00
110A Drew LeBlanc RC 2.00 5.00
110B Drew LeBlanc AU 2.50 6.00
111A Michael Latta RC 2.50 6.00
111B Michael Latta AU 3.00 8.00
112 Spencer Abbott RC 2.50 6.00
113 Luke Gazdic RC 2.50 6.00
114 Jean-Gabriel Pageau RC 3.00 8.00
115 Christopher Breen RC 2.50 6.00
116 Brett Bellemore RC 2.50 6.00
117A Ryan Stanton RC 3.00 8.00
117B Ryan Stanton AU 4.00 10.00
118 Patrick Holland RC 5.00 12.00
119A Jesper Fast RC 3.00 8.00
119B Jesper Fast AU 4.00 10.00
120 Eric Gelinas RC 3.00 8.00
121 Connor Carrick RC 2.50 6.00
122 Andrej Sustr RC 2.00 5.00
123A Michael Raffl RC 2.50 6.00
123B Michael Raffl AU 3.00 8.00
124A Matt Tennyson RC 2.00 5.00
124B Matt Tennyson AU 2.50 6.00
125 Carter Bancks RC 2.50 6.00
126A Dave Dziurzynski RC 2.50 6.00
126B Dave Dziurzynski AU SP2 3.00 8.00
127 Anton Belov RC 3.00 8.00
128A Greg Pateryn RC 3.00 8.00
128B Greg Pateryn AU 4.00 10.00
129 Brian Dumoulin RC 3.00 8.00
130 Justin Fontaine RC 3.00 8.00
131 Luke Glendening RC 3.00 8.00
132A Chris Terry RC 2.00 5.00
132B Chris Terry AU 2.50 6.00
133 Adam Almquist RC 2.00 5.00
134 Antti Raanta RC 6.00 15.00
135 Ben Chiarot RC 3.00 8.00
136 Brian Gibbons RC 3.00 8.00
137 Chad Billins RC 2.50 6.00
138 Connor Murphy RC 2.50 6.00
139 Darren Archibald RC 2.50 6.00
140A David Broll RC 3.00 8.00
140B David Broll AU SP2 4.00 10.00
141A Freddie Hamilton RC 3.00 8.00
141B Freddie Hamilton AU 4.00 10.00
142 Jamie Devane RC 2.50 6.00
143A Jayson Megna RC 3.00 8.00
143B Jayson Megna AU 4.00 10.00
144 Joakim Nordstrom RC 2.50 6.00
145 Jordan Szwarz RC 3.00 8.00
146 Linden Vey RC 2.00 5.00
147 Marek Mazanec RC 3.00 8.00
148 Michael Chaput RC 2.00 5.00
149 Nate Schmidt RC 2.50 6.00
150 Olli Maatta RC 5.00 12.00
151 Tyler Johnson AU RC 8.00 20.00
152 Michael Kostka AU RC 3.00 8.00
153 Oliver Lauridsen AU RC 3.00 8.00
154 Anders Lee AU RC 10.00 25.00
155 Taylor Beck AU RC 3.00 8.00
156 Jonathan Rheault AU RC 2.50 6.00
157 Alex Petrovic AU RC 3.00 8.00
158 Chris Brown AU RC 2.50 6.00
159 Joonas Rask AU RC 2.50 6.00
160 Ondrej Palat AU RC 6.00 15.00
161 J.Marchessault AU RC 10.00 25.00
162 Jason Missiaen AU RC 4.00 10.00
163 Victor Bartley AU RC 3.00 8.00
164 Calvin Pickard AU RC 5.00 12.00
165 Steve Oleksy AU RC 4.00 10.00
166 Kevin Henderson AU RC 3.00 8.00
167 Jeff Zatkoff AU RC 4.00 10.00
169 Joe Cannata AU RC 3.00 8.00
170 John Muse AU RC 4.00 10.00
171 Matthew Konan AU RC 4.00 10.00
172 Martin Jones AU RC 6.00 15.00
173 Mark Cundari AU RC 2.50 6.00
174 Harri Pesonen AU RC 3.00 8.00
175 Shawn Lalonde AU RC 4.00 10.00
176 Eric Hartzell AU RC 4.00 10.00
177 Cristopher Nilstorp AU RC 3.00 8.00
178 T.Pearson AU SP2 RC 4.00 10.00
179 Rickard Rakell AU SP2 RC 4.00 10.00
180 Nicklas Jensen AU SP2 RC 3.00 8.00
181 Sami Vatanen AU SP2 RC 4.00 10.00
182 Scott Laughton AU SP2 RC 5.00 12.00
183 Nick Bjugstad AU SP2 RC 5.00 12.00
184 Mark Pysyk AU RC 4.00 10.00
185 Jarred Tinordi AU SP2 RC 4.00 10.00
186 Quinton Howden AU SP2 RC 3.00 8.00
187 Jamie Oleksiak AU SP2 RC 3.00 8.00
188 Frank Corrado AU RC 2.50 6.00
189 Max Reinhart AU RC 4.00 10.00
190 Jared Staal AU RC 3.00 8.00
191 Dmitrij Jaskin AU RC 4.00 10.00
192 Stefan Matteau AU SP2 RC 3.00 8.00
193 Johan Gustafsson AU RC 5.00 12.00
194 Ben Street AU RC 3.00 8.00
195 Michael Caruso AU RC 2.50 6.00
196 Edward Pasquale AU RC 2.50 6.00
197 Carl Soderberg AU RC 4.00 10.00
198 Christian Thomas AU RC 3.00 8.00
199 Ryan Murphy AU RC 4.00 10.00
200 Nick Petrecki AU RC 2.50 6.00
201 Brian Lashoff AU RC 3.00 8.00
202 Anthony Peluso AU RC 2.50 6.00
203 Matt Irwin AU RC 3.00 8.00
204 J.Schroeder AU SP1 RC 4.00 10.00
205 Eric Gryba AU RC 3.00 8.00
206 Michael Sgarbossa AU RC 4.00 10.00
207 Dylan McIlrath AU SP2 RC 2.50 6.00
208 Philipp Grubauer AU RC 10.00 25.00
209 Richard Panik AU RC 4.00 10.00
210 Ryan Spooner AU RC 4.00 10.00
211 Igor Bobkov AU RC 3.00 8.00
212 Antoine Roussel AU RC 4.00 10.00
213 Cody Ceci AU SP2 RC 3.00 8.00
214 Petr Mrazek AU RC 8.00 20.00
215 D.DeKeyser AU SP2 RC 5.00 12.00
216 Drew Shore AU SP2 RC 3.00 8.00
217 Magnus Hellberg AU RC 4.00 10.00
218 John Gibson AU RC 10.00 25.00
219 Nikita Zadorov AU SP2 RC 2.50 6.00
220 J.T. Miller AU SP2 RC 10.00 25.00
221 Kevin Connauton AU RC 3.00 8.00
222 Xavier Ouellet AU SP2 RC 4.00 10.00
223 Tyler Pitlick AU RC 4.00 10.00
224 Darcy Kuemper AU RC EXCH 8.00 20.00
225 Josh Leivo AU RC 3.00 8.00
226A Alex Killorn AU SP2 RC 6.00 15.00
226B Alex Killorn AU/50* 10.00 25.00
227A Austin Watson AU SP2 RC 3.00 8.00
227B Austin Watson AU/50* 5.00 12.00
228A Boone Jenner AU SP2 RC 8.00 20.00
228B Boone Jenner AU/50* 12.00 30.00
229A Brock Nelson AU SP2 RC 8.00 20.00
229B Brock Nelson AU/50* 12.00 30.00
230A Charlie Coyle AU SP2 RC 6.00 15.00
230B Charlie Coyle AU/50* 10.00 25.00
231A E.Lindholm AU SP2 RC 10.00 25.00
231B Elias Lindholm AU/50* 15.00 40.00
232A Emerson Etem AU SP2 RC 4.00 10.00
232B Emerson Etem AU/50* 6.00 15.00
233A Filip Forsberg AU SP2 RC 12.00 30.00
233B Filip Forsberg AU/50* 20.00 50.00
234A Hampus Lindholm AU SP2 RC 6.00 15.00
234B Hampus Lindholm AU/50* 10.00 25.00
235A Jack Campbell AU SP1 RC 10.00 25.00
235B Jack Campbell AU/50* 15.00 40.00
236A Jonas Brodin AU SP1 RC 5.00 12.00
236B Jonas Brodin AU/50* 8.00 20.00
237A Viktor Fasth AU SP2 RC 4.00 10.00
237B Viktor Fasth AU/50* 6.00 15.00
238A Lucas Lessio AU RC 2.50 6.00
238B Lucas Lessio AU/50* 4.00 10.00
239A Mark Arcobello AU RC 4.00 10.00
239B Mark Arcobello AU/50* 6.00 15.00
240A Matt Dumba AU SP2 RC 2.50 6.00
240B Matt Dumba AU/50* 4.00 10.00
241A Johan Larsson AU SP2 RC 5.00 12.00
241B Johan Larsson AU/50* 8.00 20.00
242A Nathan Beaulieu AU SP2 RC 2.50 6.00
242B Nathan Beaulieu AU/50* 4.00 10.00
243A Reto Berra AU RC 4.00 10.00
243B Reto Berra AU/50* 6.00 15.00
245A Ryan Murray AU SP1 RC 6.00 15.00
245B Ryan Murray AU/50* 10.00 25.00
246A Jon Merrill AU SP2 RC 4.00 10.00
246B Jon Merrill AU/50* 6.00 15.00
247A Thomas Hickey AU SP1 RC 3.00 8.00
247B Thomas Hickey AU/50* 5.00 12.00
248A Tye McGinn AU SP2 RC 4.00 10.00
248B Tye McGinn AU/50* 6.00 16.00
249A Tyler Toffoli AU SP2 RC 8.00 20.00
249B Tyler Toffoli AU/50* 12.00 30.00
250A Z.Girgensons AU RC 6.00 15.00
250B Z.Girgensons AU/50* 10.00 25.00
251A F.Andersen AU SP2 RC 10.00 25.00
251B F.Andersen AU/50* 15.00 40.00
251C Frederik Andersen AU SP 30.00 80.00
252A Ryan Strome AU SP1 RC 6.00 15.00
252B Ryan Strome AU/50* 10.00 25.00
252C Ryan Strome AU SP 20.00 50.00
253A D.Hamilton AU SP2 RC 6.00 15.00
253B Dougie Hamilton AU/50* 10.00 25.00
253C Dougie Hamilton AU SP 20.00 50.00
254A M.Grigorenko AU SP1 RC 2.50 6.00
254B M.Grigorenko AU/50* 4.00 10.00
254C M.Grigorenko AU SP 8.00 20.00
255A S.Monahan AU SP2 RC 6.00 15.00
255B Sean Monahan AU/50* 10.00 25.00
255C Sean Monahan AU SP 20.00 50.00
256A N.MacKinnon AU SP1 RC 20.00 50.00
256B N.MacKinnon AU/50* 30.00 80.00
256C N.MacKinnon AU SP 60.00 150.00
257A Alex Chiasson AU SP2 RC 4.00 10.00
257B Alex Chiasson AU/50* 6.00 15.00
257C Alex Chiasson AU SP 12.00 30.00
258A V.Nichushkin AU SP2 C 8.00 20.00
258B Valeri Nichushkin AU/50* 12.00 30.00
258C V.Nichushkin AU SP 25.00 60.00
259A Tomas Jurco AU SP2 RC 5.00 12.00
259B Tomas Jurco AU/50* 8.00 20.00
259C Tomas Jurco AU SP 15.00 40.00
260A Justin Schultz AU SP2 RC 4.00 10.00
260B Justin Schultz AU/50* 6.00 15.00
260C Justin Schultz AU SP 12.00 30.00
261A Nail Yakupov AU SP1 RC 8.00 20.00
261B Nail Yakupov AU/50* 12.00 30.00
261C Nail Yakupov AU SP 25.00 60.00
262A A.Barkov AU SP1 RC 12.00 30.00
262B A.Barkov AU/50* 20.00 50.00
262C A.Barkov AU SP 40.00 100.00
263A J.Huberdeau AU SP1 RC 10.00 25.00
263B J.Huberdeau AU/50* 15.00 40.00
263C J.Huberdeau AU SP 30.00 80.00
264A M.Granlund AU SP1 RC 6.00 15.00
264B Mikael Granlund AU/50* 10.00 25.00
264C Mikael Granlund AU SP 20.00 50.00
265A A.glchenyuk AU SP1 RC 10.00 25.00
265B A.Galchenyuk AU/50* 15.00 40.00
265C Alex Galchenyuk AU SP 30.00 80.00
266A B.Gallagher AU SP2 RC 10.00 25.00
266B B.Gallagher AU/50* 15.00 40.00
266C B.Gallagher AU SP 30.00 80.00
267A Michael Bournival AU SP2 RC 4.00 10.00
267B Michael Bournival AU/50* 6.00 15.00
267C Michael Bournival AU SP 12.00 30.00
268A Seth Jones AU SP1 RC 8.00 20.00
268B Seth Jones AU/50* 12.00 30.00
268C Seth Jones AU SP 25.00 60.00
269A Cory Conacher AU SP2 RC 2.50 6.00
269B Cory Conacher AU/50* 4.00 10.00
269C Cory Conacher AU SP 8.00 20.00
270A Beau Bennett AU SP2 RC 5.00 12.00
270B Beau Bennett AU/50* 8.00 20.00
270C Beau Bennett AU SP 15.00 40.00
271A Tomas Hertl AU SP2 RC 8.00 20.00
271B Tomas Hertl AU/50* 12.00 30.00
271C Tomas Hertl AU SP 25.00 60.00
272A V.Tarasenko AU SP1 RC 10.00 25.00
272B V.Tarasenko AU/50* 15.00 40.00
272C Vladimir Tarasenko AU SP 30.00 80.00
273A Morgan Rielly AU SP2 RC 10.00 25.00
273B Morgan Rielly AU/50* 15.00 40.00
273C Morgan Rielly AU SP 30.00 80.00
274A Jacob Trouba AU SP2 RC 6.00 15.00
274B Jacob Trouba AU/50* 10.00 25.00
274C Jacob Trouba AU SP 20.00 50.00
275A Tom Wilson AU SP2 RC 8.00 20.00
275B Tom Wilson AU/50* 12.00 30.00
275C Tom Wilson AU SP 25.00 60.00
276 Brian Flynn AU RC 3.00 8.00
277 Calvin Heeter AU RC 3.00 8.00
278 Cameron Schilling AU RC 2.50 6.00
279 Chad Ruhwedel AU RC 2.50 6.00
280 Daniel Bang AU RC 3.00 8.00
281 Derek Grant AU RC 3.00 8.00
282 Jamie Tardif AU RC 2.50 6.00
283 Jason Akeson AU RC 3.00 8.00
284 Mark Barberio AU RC 2.50 6.00
285 Sean Collins AU SP2 RC 3.00 8.00
286 Taylor Fedun AU RC 5.00 12.00
287 Zach Redmond AU SP1 RC 3.00 8.00

2013-14 Panini Contenders Gold

*VETS/100: 2.5X TO 6X BASIC CARDS
*ROOKIES/100: .6X TO 1.5X BASIC CARDS/600
*ROOK AU/100: .6X TO 1.5X BASIC CARDS
4 Corey Crawford 3.00 8.00
52 Nicklas Backstrom 2.50 6.00

2013-14 Panini Contenders 3 vs 3 Autographs

33BM Boston Bruins Stars/100 15.00 40.00
33CD Calgary Flames Stars/25 25.00 60.00
33MW Minnesota Wild Stars/25 20.00 50.00
33TB Maple Leafs Stars/25 30.00 80.00
33ALA Anaheim Ducks Stars/100 25.00 60.00

2013-14 Panini Contenders Contending Classes Dual Signatures

CDAM M.Arcobello/S.Monahan 10.00 25.00
CDBD J.Brodin/M.Dumba 8.00 20.00
CDGB B.Gallagher/M.Bournival 15.00 40.00
CDGR A.Galchenyuk/M.Rielly 15.00 40.00
CDHL D.Hamilton/H.Lindholm 10.00 25.00
CDRN A.Roussel/V.Nichushkin 12.00 30.00
CDRT J.Trouba/Z.Redmond 10.00 25.00
CDSJ J.Schultz/S.Jones 12.00 30.00
CDTH T.Hertl/V.Tarasenko 15.00 40.00
CDYM N.Yakupov/N.MacKinnon 30.00 80.00

2013-14 Panini Contenders Cup Contenders

CC1 Evgeni Malkin 1.50 4.00
CC2 Teemu Selanne 1.50 4.00
CC3 Patrick Kane 1.50 4.00
CC4 Gabriel Landeskog 1.00 2.50
CC5 Tyler Seguin 1.00 2.50
CC6 Anze Kopitar 1.25 3.00
CC7 Mikhail Grabovski .50 1.25
CC8 Joe Thornton 1.25 3.00
CC9 T.J. Oshie .75 2.00
CC10 Daniel Sedin 1.00 2.50
CC11 Milan Lucic .75 2.00
CC12 Sidney Crosby 3.00 8.00
CC13 Martin St. Louis .75 2.00
CC14 James van Riemsdyk .60 1.50
CC15 Joffrey Lupul .50 1.25
CC16 Niklas Kronwall .60 1.50
CC17 Henrik Zetterberg 1.00 2.50
CC18 Max Pacioretty .75 2.00
CC19 Erik Karlsson 1.00 2.50
CC20 Patrick Sharp .75 2.00
CC21 Logan Couture 1.00 2.50
CC22 Oliver Ekman-Larsson .75 2.00
CC23 Zach Parise .75 2.00
CC24 Mike Richards .60 1.50
CC25 Steven Stamkos 1.50 4.00

2013-14 Panini Contenders Cup Contenders Patch Autographs

CCDS Daniel Sedin 12.00 30.00
CCEM Evgeni Malkin 20.00 50.00
CCGL Gabriel Landeskog 12.00 30.00
CCPK Patrick Kane EXCH 30.00 80.00
CCTS Tyler Seguin 12.00 30.00
CCAKO Anze Kopitar 15.00 40.00
CCJTH Joe Thornton 15.00 40.00
CCMGR Mikhail Grabovski 6.00 15.00

2013-14 Panini Contenders Eights Autographs

C8G Goalie Stars 50.00 125.00
C8C76 1970s Stars 25.00 60.00
C8CPT Canadiens Stars 80.00 200.00
C8FLA Florida Panthers Stars 15.00 40.00
C8NO9 Jersey 9 Stars 80.00 200.00
C8PIT Penguins Stars 80.00 200.00
C8STL St. Louis Blues Stars 25.00 60.00
C8TOR Maple Leafs Stars 30.00 80.00
C8USA USA Stars 40.00 100.00
C8WSH Capitals Stars 80.00 200.00

2013-14 Panini Contenders Fours Autographs

C4BOS Boston Bruins Stars 5.00 12.00
C4BRO Stall Brothers 8.00 20.00
C4BUF Buffalo Sabres Stars 4.00 10.00
C4CBJ Blue Jackets Stars 10.00 25.00
C4CHI Blackhawks Stars 6.00 15.00
C4COL Avalanche Stars 30.00 80.00
C4HFD Hartford Whalers Stars 8.00 20.00
C4MIN Minnesota Wild Stars 12.00 30.00
C4NYI NY Islanders Stars 6.00 15.00
C4NYR NY Rangers Stars 6.00 15.00
C4RK1 Plso/Rsk/Pckrd/Trba 10.00 25.00
C4RK2 Blieu/Ptrcki/Llnde/Mrrll 6.00 15.00
C4RK3 Rhlt/Pnk/Plt/Brkv 20.00 50.00
C4RK4 Ztkf/Bnntt/Knn/Lghtn 8.00 20.00
C4RK5 Strm/Kllm/Lndhm/Grgrn 15.00 40.00
C4RK6 Anaheim Ducks Stars 15.00 40.00
C4RK7 Florida Panthers Stars 15.00 40.00
C4SJS San Jose Sharks Stars 10.00 25.00
C4STL St. Louis Blues Stars 30.00 80.00
C4TBL TB Lightning Stars 12.00 30.00

2013-14 Panini Contenders Global Contenders Autographs

GCAN Antti Niemi/25 10.00 25.00
GCCH Carl Hagelin/25 8.00 20.00
GCCP Carey Price/25 25.00 60.00
GCDS Daniel Sedin/25 15.00 40.00
GCEM Evgeni Malkin/25 25.00 60.00
GCGL Gabriel Landeskog/25 15.00 40.00
GCHL Henrik Lundqvist/25 30.00 80.00
GCJQ Jonathan Quick/25 EXCH 15.00 40.00
GCJT John Tavares/25 20.00 50.00
GCMG Marian Gaborik/25 12.00 30.00
GCPB Patrice Bergeron
(inserted in 2013-14 Panini Prime) 15.00 40.00
GCPD Pavel Datsyuk/25 20.00 50.00
GCPK Patrick Kane/25 25.00 60.00
GCRM Ryan Miller/25 12.00 30.00
GCZP Zach Parise/25 12.00 30.00
GCJHA Jaroslav Halak/25 12.00 30.00
GCJHI Jonas Hiller/25 10.00 25.00
GCJTO Jonathan Toews/25 20.00 50.00
GCMDU Matt Duchene/25 12.00 30.00
GCOVI Alex Ovechkin/25 50.00 120.00
GCPKE Phil Kessel/25 12.00 30.00
GCSVO Slava Voynov/25 10.00 25.00
GCTMU Teemu Selanne/25 25.00 60.00

2013-14 Panini Contenders Hart Contenders

HC1 Patrice Bergeron 1.00 2.50
HC2 Cody Hodgson .50 1.25
HC3 Mike Cammalleri .60 1.50
HC4 Eric Staal 1.00 2.50
HC5 Jonathan Toews 1.25 3.00
HC6 Matt Duchene .75 2.00
HC7 Jamie Benn .75 2.00
HC8 Ryan Nugent-Hopkins 1.00 2.50
HC9 Anze Kopitar 1.25 3.00
HC10 Zach Parise .75 2.00
HC11 John Tavares 1.25 3.00
HC12 Claude Giroux .75 2.00
HC13 Sidney Crosby 3.00 8.00
HC14 Patrick Marleau .75 2.00
HC15 Martin St. Louis .75 2.00
HC16 Phil Kessel .75 2.00
HC17 Henrik Sedin 1.00 2.50
HC18 Alex Ovechkin 3.00 8.00
HC19 Brad Richards .75 2.00
HC20 Evander Kane .75 2.00
HC21 Corey Perry 1.25 3.00
HC22 Henrik Zetterberg 1.00 2.50
HC23 Carey Price 1.50 4.00
HC24 Alexander Steen .50 1.25
HC25 Keith Yandle .50 1.25

2013-14 Panini Contenders Hart Contenders Patch Autographs

HCBRI Brad Richards 12.00 30.00
HCCGX Claude Giroux EXCH 12.00 30.00
HCCHO Cody Hodgson 8.00 20.00
HCERS Eric Staal 15.00 40.00
HCEVK Evander Kane 12.00 30.00
HCJT John Tavares 20.00 50.00
HCJTO Jonathan Toews 20.00 50.00
HCMC Mike Cammalleri 10.00 25.00
HCMDU Matt Duchene 12.00 30.00
HCMSL Martin St. Louis 12.00 30.00
HCOVI Alex Ovechkin 50.00 120.00
HCPBE Patrice Bergeron 15.00 40.00
HCPKE Phil Kessel 12.00 30.00
HCPM Patrick Marleau 12.00 30.00
HCRNH Ryan Nugent-Hopkins 15.00 40.00
HCSC Sidney Crosby EXCH 50.00 125.00
HCZP Zach Parise 12.00 30.00

2013-14 Panini Contenders Legacies

CL1 Eric Lindros 1.25 3.00
CL2 Ron Francis 1.00 2.50
CL3 Stan Mikita 1.00 2.50
CL4 Gordie Howe 2.50 6.00
CL5 Pat LaFontaine .75 2.00
CL6 Marcel Dionne 1.00 2.50
CL7 Bobby Clarke 1.25 3.00
CL8 Mario Lemieux 3.00 8.00
CL9 Wendel Clark 1.25 3.00
CL10 Brett Hull 1.50 4.00
CL11 Ray Bourque 1.25 3.00
CL12 Joe Nieuwendyk .60 1.50
CL13 Bobby Hull 1.50 4.00
CL14 Joe Sakic 1.50 4.00
CL15 Mike Modano 1.25 3.00
CL16 Steve Yzerman 2.00 5.00
CL17 Jari Kurri .75 2.00
CL18 John Vanbiesbrouck .75 2.00
CL19 Jean Beliveau .75 2.00
CL20 Mike Bossy .75 2.00
CL21 Mark Messier 1.50 4.00
CL22 Dave Andreychuk .75 2.00
CL23 Johnny Bower .75 2.00
CL24 Trevor Linden .75 2.00
CL25 Olaf Kolzig .75 2.00

2013-14 Panini Contenders Match Ups Booklet Autographs

MAFHM Andr/Fsth/Hlbrg/Mzn/99 30.00 80.00
MBBHH Brkv/Bjg/Hbr/Hwdn/50 40.00 100.00
MBDRT Brdn/Dmb/Rdm/Trba/99 20.00 50.00
MBSSM Bcks/Shk/McDn/Stp/85 8.00 20.00
MCGEG Cmlri/Glncr/Ebrl/Ggn/99 12.00 30.00
MEFRA Etm/Fsth/Rkll/Andr/199 30.00 80.00
MFLVR Rstl/Frsb/Lndh/Vtnn/99 40.00 100.00
MGBBL Brdn/Lndh/Grn/Brkv/99 40.00 100.00
MGPGR Grg/Pysk/Grg/Rstln/99 20.00 50.00
MHBKJ Hbrd/Bjg/Klrn/Jhnsn/99 30.00 80.00
MHZLM Hrtzll/Ztk/Lghtn/McG/99 15.00 40.00
MJMFJ Jnnr/Mrry/Frsbrg/Jnes/99 40.00 100.00
MKSSS Slnne/Koivu/Sdn/Sdn/50 25.00 60.00
MMEBR Mllr/Enrth/Brnr/Rmr/175 12.00 30.00
MMMNH Mttu/Mrrll/Nlsn/Hcky/199 25.00 60.00
MPGTN Prse/Grnl/Tws/Nrds/50 20.00 50.00
MSMHL Stpn/McDn/Hgln/Lndq/25 30.00 80.00
MTJHN Trsnko/Jskn/Hrtl/Nto/99 30.00 80.00
MTNRM Tvrs/Nlsn/Rchrds/Mllr/50 30.00 80.00
MYAMR Arcb/Rnhrt/Ykv/Mnhn/50 25.00 60.00
MYSSH Sdrb/Hmltn/Schz/Ykv/50 25.00 60.00

2013-14 Panini Contenders NHL Ink

IMT Matt Tennyson
(inserted in 2013-14 Panini Prime) 3.00 8.00
ICC Cory Conacher 3.00 8.00
ICT Christian Thomas 4.00 10.00
IMBA Mikael Backlund 4.00 10.00
IMGB Michael Grabner 4.00 10.00
IMHT Michael Hutchinson 3.00 8.00
IMKO Matthew Konan 5.00 12.00
IMXM Maxime Macenauer 3.00 8.00
INMK Nathan MacKinnon 25.00 60.00
IRLY Morgan Rielly 12.00 30.00
IAB Aleksander Barkov 15.00 40.00
IAG Alex Galchenyuk 12.00 30.00
IAS Andrew Shaw 3.00 8.00
IASH Carter Ashton 3.00 8.00
IBCO Brett Connolly 3.00 8.00
IBJE Boone Jenner 10.00 25.00
IBLA Brian Lashoff 4.00 10.00
IBR Bobby Ryan 4.00 10.00
ICCI Casey Cizikas 3.00 8.00
ICCL Cal Clutterbuck 3.00 8.00
ICGE Chay Genoway 5.00 12.00
ICRU Chad Ruhwedel 3.00 8.00
ICSM Craig Smith 3.00 8.00
ICTE Chris Terry 3.00 8.00
ICWI Colin Wilson 4.00 10.00
IDBA Daniel Bang 4.00 10.00
IDBR Daniel Briere 5.00 12.00
IDDK Danny DeKeyser 6.00 15.00
IDP David Perron 4.00 10.00
IFA Frederik Andersen 12.00 30.00
IGB Gabriel Bourque 4.00 10.00
IGD Gabriel Dumont 3.00 8.00
IIB Igor Bobkov 4.00 10.00
IJAK Jason Akeson 4.00 10.00
IJCN Joe Cannata 4.00 10.00
IJCO Joe Colborne 3.00 8.00
IJFA Jesper Fast 5.00 12.00
IJH Jonathan Huberdeau 12.00 30.00
IJME Jon Merrill 5.00 12.00
IJMI Jason Missiaen 5.00 12.00
IJMU John Muse 5.00 12.00
IJSC Jaden Schwartz 6.00 15.00
IJSI Jakob Silfverberg 3.00 8.00
IJSZ Jordan Szwarz 5.00 12.00
IJTB J.T. Brown 3.00 8.00
IJTR Jacob Trouba 8.00 20.00
IKB Kevin Bieksa 4.00 10.00
IKH Kevin Henderson 4.00 10.00
IKK Keith Kinkaid 3.00 8.00
IMMO Matt Moulson 3.00 8.00
IMSC Mark Scheifele 8.00 20.00
INN Nino Niederreiter 3.00 8.00
INYQ Gustav Nyquist 3.00 8.00
IOL Oliver Lauridsen 4.00 10.00
IOP Ondrej Palat 8.00 20.00
IPCO Philippe Cornet 3.00 8.00
IREL Ryan Ellis 4.00 10.00
IRNA Riley Nash 3.00 8.00
IRSM Reilly Smith 5.00 12.00
ISB Sven Baertschi 4.00 10.00
ISJ Seth Jones 10.00 25.00
ISO Steve Oleksy 5.00 12.00
ISTA Ryan Stanton 5.00 12.00
ISVO Slava Voynov 4.00 10.00
ITBA Tyson Barrie 3.00 8.00
ITHE Tomas Hertl 10.00 25.00
ITK Torey Krug 4.00 10.00
ITT Tyler Toffoli 10.00 25.00
ITW Tom Wilson 10.00 25.00
IDDZ Dave Dziurzynski
(inserted in 2013-14 Panini Prime) 4.00 10.00

2013-14 Panini Contenders NHL Ink Duals

IDBM S.Baertschi/S.Monahan 10.00 25.00
IDBT D.Byfuglien/J.Trouba 10.00 25.00
IDCH L.Couture/T.Hertl 12.00 30.00
IDCS P.Coffey/J.Schultz 6.00 15.00
IDFF V.Fasth/J.Fast 6.00 15.00
IDGG B.Gionta/A.Galchenyuk 15.00 40.00
IDGR J.Gardiner/M.Rielly 15.00 40.00
IDGS B.Gallagher/M.St. Louis 15.00 40.00
IDHH D.Hamilton/F.Hamilton 10.00 25.00
IDJJ M.Jones/S.Jones 12.00 30.00
IDJM M.Jones/M.Mazanec 10.00 25.00
IDKH T.Krug/D.Hamilton 10.00 25.00
IDKT N.Kadri/K.Turris 8.00 20.00
IDLL E.Lindholm/H.Lindholm 15.00 40.00
IDRB J.Roenick/B.Bickell 10.00 25.00
IDSM J.Silfverberg/P.Maroon 4.00 10.00
IDTV T.Thomas/J.Vanbiesbrouck 6.00 15.00
IDWJ S.Weber/S.Jones 12.00 30.00

2013-14 Panini Contenders NHL Ink Triples

ITBSH Brodeur/Smith/Hextall 30.00 80.00
ITRSL Richards/St. Louis/Lecavalier 12.00 30.00
ITHNY Hll/Ngnt-Hp/Ykpv/25 25.00 60.00
ITPBS Pietrnglo/Bwmstr/Shtnkrk/25 10.00 25.00
ITSSS Staal/Staal/Staal/25 15.00 40.00

2013-14 Panini Contenders Norris Contenders

NC1 Torey Krug .60 1.50
NC2 Dougie Hamilton 1.25 3.00
NC3 Mark Giordano .75 2.00
NC4 Jonas Brodin 1.00 2.50
NC5 Ryan Murray 1.25 3.00
NC6 Justin Schultz .75 2.00
NC7 Slava Voynov .60 1.50
NC8 P.K. Subban 1.00 2.50
NC9 Roman Josi .75 2.00

NC10 Seth Jones 1.50 4.00
NC11 Marc Staal .50 1.25
NC12 Keith Yandle .50 1.25
NC13 Hampus Lindholm 1.25 3.00
NC14 Kris Letang 1.00 2.50
NC15 Dan Boyle .50 1.25
NC16 Alex Pietrangelo .60 1.50
NC17 Kevin Shattenkirk .50 1.25
NC18 Victor Hedman 1.00 2.50
NC19 Matthew Carle .60 1.50
NC20 Dustin Byfuglien .75 2.00

2013-14 Panini Contenders Norris Contenders Patch Autographs

NCAP Alex Pietrangelo 8.00 20.00
NCDH Dougie Hamilton 15.00 40.00
NCJB Jonas Brodin 12.00 30.00
NCKL Kris Letang 12.00 30.00
NCKS Kevin Shattenkirk 6.00 15.00
NCKY Keith Yandle 6.00 15.00
NCSJ Seth Jones 20.00 50.00
NCVH Victor Hedman 12.00 30.00
NCDBO Dan Boyle 6.00 15.00
NCHLI Hampus Lindholm 15.00 40.00
NCJUS Justin Schultz 10.00 25.00
NCMAS Marc Staal 6.00 15.00
NCMGI Mark Giordano 10.00 25.00
NCRJO Roman Josi 10.00 25.00
NCRMR Ryan Murray 15.00 40.00
NCSVO Slava Voynov 8.00 20.00

2013-14 Panini Contenders Patch Autographs

176 Eric Hartzell/100 8.00 20.00
177 Cristopher Nilstorp/100 6.00 15.00
178 Tanner Pearson/100 8.00 20.00
179 Rickard Rakell/100 8.00 20.00
180 Nicklas Jensen/100 6.00 15.00
181 Sami Vatanen/100 8.00 20.00
182 Scott Laughton/100 10.00 25.00
183 Nick Bjugstad/100 10.00 25.00
186 Quinton Howden/100 6.00 15.00
187 Jamie Oleksiak/100 6.00 15.00
188 Frank Corrado/100 5.00 12.00
189 Max Reinhart/100 8.00 20.00
190 Jared Staal/100 6.00 15.00
191 Dmitrij Jaskin/100 8.00 20.00
192 Stefan Matteau/100 6.00 15.00
193 Johan Gustafsson/100 10.00 25.00
194 Ben Street/100 6.00 15.00
195 Michael Caruso/100 5.00 12.00
196 Edward Pasquale/100 5.00 12.00
197 Carl Soderberg/100 8.00 20.00
198 Christian Thomas/100 6.00 15.00
200 Nick Petrecki/100 5.00 12.00
201 Brian Lashoff/100 6.00 15.00
202 Anthony Peluso/100 5.00 12.00
203 Matt Irwin/100 6.00 15.00
204 Jordan Schroeder/100 8.00 20.00
205 Eric Gryba/100 6.00 15.00
206 Michael Sgarbossa/100 8.00 20.00
207 Dylan McIlrath/100 5.00 12.00
208 Philipp Grubauer/100 20.00 50.00
209 Richard Panik/100 8.00 20.00
210 Ryan Spooner/100 8.00 20.00
211 Igor Bobkov/100 6.00 15.00
212 Antoine Roussel/100 8.00 20.00
213 Cody Ceci/100 6.00 15.00
214 Petr Mrazek/100 15.00 40.00
215 Danny DeKeyser/100 10.00 25.00
217 Magnus Hellberg/100 8.00 20.00
218 John Gibson/100 20.00 50.00
219 Nikita Zadorov/100 5.00 12.00
221 Kevin Connauton/100 6.00 15.00
222 Xavier Ouellet/49 8.00 20.00
224 Darcy Kuemper/100 15.00 40.00
226 Alex Killorn/100 12.00 30.00
227 Austin Watson/100 6.00 15.00
228 Boone Jenner/100 15.00 40.00
229 Brock Nelson/100 15.00 40.00
230 Charlie Coyle/100 12.00 30.00
231 Elias Lindholm/100 20.00 50.00
232 Emerson Etem/100 8.00 20.00
233 Filip Forsberg/100 25.00 60.00
234 Hampus Lindholm/100 12.00 30.00
235 Jack Campbell/100 20.00 50.00
236 Jonas Brodin/100 10.00 25.00
237 Viktor Fasth/100 8.00 20.00
239 Mark Arcobello/100 8.00 20.00
240 Matt Dumba/100 5.00 12.00
242 Nathan Beaulieu/100 5.00 12.00
243 Reto Berra/100 8.00 20.00
245 Ryan Murray/100 12.00 30.00
246 Jon Merrill/100 8.00 20.00
247 Thomas Hickey/100 6.00 15.00
248 Tye McGinn/100 8.00 20.00
249 Tyler Toffoli/100 15.00 40.00
250 Zemgus Girgensons/100 12.00 30.00
251 Frederik Andersen/100 20.00 50.00
252 Ryan Strome/100 12.00 30.00
253 Dougie Hamilton/100 12.00 30.00
254 Mikhail Grigorenko/100 5.00 12.00
255 Sean Monahan/100 12.00 30.00
256 Nathan MacKinnon/100 40.00 100.00
257 Alex Chiasson/100 8.00 20.00
258 Valeri Nichushkin/100 15.00 40.00
259 Tomas Jurco/100 10.00 25.00
260 Justin Schultz/100 8.00 20.00
261 Nail Yakupov/100 15.00 40.00
262 Aleksander Barkov/100 25.00 60.00
263 Jonathan Huberdeau/100 20.00 50.00
264 Mikael Granlund/100 12.00 30.00
265 Alex Galchenyuk/100 20.00 50.00
266 Brendan Gallagher/100 20.00 50.00
267 Michael Bournival/100 8.00 20.00
268 Seth Jones/100 15.00 40.00
269 Cory Conacher/100 5.00 12.00
270 Beau Bennett/100 10.00 25.00
271 Tomas Hertl/100 10.00 20.00
272 Vladimir Tarasenko/100 20.00 50.00
273 Morgan Rielly/100 20.00 50.00
274 Jacob Trouba/100 12.00 30.00
275 Tom Wilson/100 15.00 40.00

2013-14 Panini Contenders Rookie Ticket Recall Autographs

2 John Tavares/25 25.00 60.00
7 Patrick Kane/25 EXCH 25.00 60.00
8 Jeremy Roenick/25 25.00 60.00
10 Henrik Lundqvist/25 25.00 60.00

2013-14 Panini Contenders Selke Contenders

SC1 Ryan Getzlaf .75 2.00
SC2 Patrice Bergeron 1.00 2.50
SC3 Drew Stafford .50 1.25
SC4 Curtis Glencross .50 1.25
SC5 Jordan Staal .60 1.50
SC6 Jonathan Toews 1.25 3.00
SC7 Paul Stastny .60 1.50
SC8 Pavel Datsyuk 1.25 3.00
SC9 Dustin Brown .75 2.00
SC10 Scottie Upshall .50 1.25
SC11 Mike Fisher .50 1.25
SC12 Travis Zajac .50 1.25
SC13 Brad Richards .75 2.00
SC14 Shane Doan .60 1.50
SC15 Joe Pavelski 1.00 2.50
SC16 David Backes .50 1.25
SC17 Teddy Purcell .50 1.25
SC18 David Clarkson .50 1.25
SC19 Ryan Kesler .75 2.00
SC20 Andrew Ladd .50 1.25
SC21 Shawn Horcoff .50 1.25
SC22 Mikko Koivu .60 1.50
SC23 David Desharnais .50 1.25
SC24 Jakub Voracek .60 1.50
SC25 Clarke MacArthur .50 1.25

2013-14 Panini Contenders Selke Contenders Patch Autographs

SCAL Andrew Ladd/20 8.00 20.00
SCBRI Brad Richards/25 12.00 30.00
SCCG Curtis Glencross/25 8.00 20.00
SCDB David Backes/25 8.00 20.00
SCDUB Dustin Brown/25 12.00 30.00
SCJOS Jordan Staal/25 10.00 25.00
SCJP Joe Pavelski/25 15.00 40.00
SCJTO Jonathan Toews/25 20.00 50.00.
SCMF Mike Fisher/25 8.00 20.00
SCPB Patrice Bergeron/25 15.00 40.00
SCPD Pavel Datsyuk/25 20.00 50.00
SCRG Ryan Getzlaf/25 12.00 30.00
SCRK Ryan Kesler/25 12.00 30.00

2013-14 Panini Contenders Sixes Autographs

C6G Goalie Stars 40.00 100.00
C6V1 Sln/Sk/Brq/Ov/St.L/Wbr 60.00 150.00
C6BOS Boston Bruins Stars 20.00 50.00
C6DAL Dallas Stars 20.00 50.00
C6EDM Edmonton Oilers Stars 30.00 80.00
C6NSH Nashville Predators Stars 15.00 40.00
C6NYI New York Islanders Stars 30.00 80.00
C6NYR New York Rangers Stars 40.00 100.00
C6OLY Olympic Stars 30.00 80.00
C6OR6 Cnr/Str/Mta/Brq/Yz/Msr 40.00 100.00
C6PHI Philadelphia Flyers Stars 25.00 60.00
C6RK1 Crd/Jns/Sch/Arc/Ptl/Fs 15.00 40.00
C6RK2 Rookie Stars 1 50.00 125.00
C6RK3 Rookie Stars 2 40.00 100.00
C6RUS Russian Stars 60.00 150.00
C6STL St. Louis Blues Stars 20.00 50.00
C6SWE Ert/Sn/Lg/Sn/Sv/Lg 40.00 100.00
C6USG U.S. Goalie Stars 40.00 100.00
C6WIS Jsp/Chs/Hty/Str/Trs/Smt 20.00 50.00
C6WPG Winnipeg Jets Stars 25.00 60.00

2013-14 Panini Contenders Top of the Class Autographs

TCD DH/JS/JB/SJ/MR/JT 30.00 80.00
TCF1 NY/JH/AG/NM/SM/TH 60.00 150.00
TCF2 VT/EE/BB/AB/EL/BJ 40.00 100.00
TCF3 BG/AC/MG/MB/VN/ZG 30.00 80.00
TCFDG NY/DH/VF/NM/SJ/RB 60.00 150.00

2013-14 Panini Contenders Vezina Contenders

VC1 Jonas Hiller .60 1.50
VC2 Tuukka Rask 1.00 2.50
VC3 Ryan Miller .75 2.00
VC4 Semyon Varlamov .75 2.00
VC5 Cam Ward .75 2.00
VC6 Kari Lehtonen .60 1.50
VC7 Jimmy Howard 1.00 2.50
VC8 Jonathan Quick 1.00 2.50
VC9 Niklas Backstrom .60 1.50
VC10 Carey Price 1.50 4.00
VC11 Pekka Rinne .75 2.00
VC12 Martin Brodeur 2.00 5.00
VC13 Henrik Lundqvist 2.00 5.00
VC14 Craig Anderson .75 2.00
VC15 Mike Smith .75 2.00
VC16 Marc-Andre Fleury 1.50 4.00
VC17 Antti Niemi .60 1.50
VC18 Jaroslav Halak .75 2.00
VC19 Jonathan Bernier .60 1.50
VC20 Ondrej Pavelec .75 2.00
VC21 Sergei Bobrovsky 1.25 3.00
VC22 Corey Crawford 1.00 2.50
VC23 Ben Bishop .60 1.50
VC24 Roberto Luongo 1.25 3.00
VC25 Braden Holtby 1.00 2.50

2013-14 Panini Contenders Vezina Contenders Patch Autographs

VCAN Antti Niemi 12.00 30.00
VCCP Carey Price 25.00 50.00
VCHL Henrik Lundqvist 30.00 80.00
VCJQ Jonathan Quick EXCH 20.00 50.00
VCMB Martin Brodeur 50.00 100.00
VCMS Mike Smith 15.00 40.00
VCRM Ryan Miller 12.00 30.00
VCJBE Jonathan Bernier 12.00 30.00
VCJHA Jaroslav Halak 15.00 40.00
VCJHI Jonas Hiller 12.00 30.00
VCJHO Jimmy Howard 20.00 50.00
VCKLE Kari Lehtonen 12.00 30.00
VCMAF Marc-Andre Fleury 30.00 80.00

2013-14 Panini Contenders Winter Classic Contenders Autographs

WCNK Nazem Kadri 12.00 30.00
WCNL Nicklas Lidstrom 10.00 25.00
WCPD Pavel Datsyuk 15.00 40.00
WCSY Steve Yzerman 30.00 80.00
WCWC Wendel Clark 15.00 40.00
WCBSM Brendan Smith 6.00 15.00
WCCCH Chris Chelios 10.00 25.00
WCDDK Danny DeKeyser 12.00 30.00
WCDPH Dion Phaneuf 8.00 20.00
WCDSI Darryl Sittler 12.00 30.00
WCJBE Jonathan Bernier 8.00 20.00
WCJHO Jimmy Howard 12.00 30.00
WCJRE James Reimer EXCH 10.00 25.00
WCPKE Phil Kessel 10.00 25.00
WCRLY Morgan Rielly 25.00 60.00

2013-14 Panini Father's Day Autographs

TW Tom Wilson 3.00 8.00

2013-14 Panini Father's Day Private Signings

BJ Boone Jenner/25 8.00 20.00
BT Bryan Trottier/25 6.00 15.00
CC Chris Chelios/25 8.00 20.00
CN Cam Neely/25 10.00 25.00
CW Cam Ward/25 4.00 10.00
JH Jonathan Huberdeau/25 5.00 12.00
NM Nathan MacKinnon/25 100.00 200.00
NY Nail Yakupov/25 8.00 20.00
RB1 Ray Bourque/25 20.00 50.00
RM Ryan Murray/25 4.00 10.00
RS Ryan Strome/25 8.00 20.00
SM Sean Monohan/25 5.00 12.00
TH Tomas Hertl/25 40.00 80.00

2012 Panini National Convention ROY Materials

1 Gabriel Landeskog 5.00 12.00

2013 Panini National Convention Draft Day Materials

HK1 Nail Yakupov 8.00 20.00
HK2 Stefan Matteau 5.00 12.00
HK3 Tom Wilson 6.00 15.00
HK4 Scott Laughton 5.00 12.00

2013 Panini National Convention Rookie Materials

HK1 Dougie Hamilton 5.00 12.00
HK2 Ryan Murphy 4.00 10.00
HK3 Brandon Saad 5.00 12.00

2013 Panini National Convention Tools of the Trade Towels

JS Justin Schultz 5.00 12.00
NY Nail Yakupov 8.00 20.00

2013-14 Panini National Treasures

*SILVER/25: .5X TO 1.2X BASIC CARDS/199
1 Carey Price 4.00 10.00
2 Jamie Benn 2.00 5.00
3 Phil Kessel 2.00 5.00
4 Taylor Hall 2.00 5.00
5 Denis Potvin 2.00 5.00
6 Shea Weber 1.50 4.00
7 Paul Coffey 2.00 5.00
8 Teemu Selanne 4.00 10.00
9 Gordie Howe 6.00 15.00
10 Guy Lafleur 2.50 6.00
11 Mark Messier 4.00 10.00
12 Yvan Cournoyer 2.00 5.00
13 Pavel Datsyuk 3.00 8.00
14 Zach Parise 2.00 5.00
15 Ryan Getzlaf 2.00 5.00
16 Brett Hull 4.00 10.00
17 Roberto Luongo 3.00 8.00
18 John Tavares 3.00 8.00
19 Steve Yzerman 5.00 12.00
20 Luc Robitaille 2.00 5.00
21 Stan Mikita 2.50 6.00
22 Daniel Sedin 2.50 6.00
23 Evgeni Malkin 4.00 10.00
24 Joe Thornton 3.00 8.00
25 John Vanbiesbrouck 2.00 5.00
26 Jack Johnson 1.25 3.00
27 Cody Hodgson 1.25 3.00
28 Mike Smith 2.00 5.00
29 Alex Ovechkin 8.00 20.00
30 Martin Brodeur 5.00 12.00
31 Curtis Joseph 2.50 6.00
32 Jonathan Quick 2.50 6.00
33 Patrick Roy 5.00 12.00
34 Gilbert Perreault 2.00 5.00
35 Joe Nieuwendyk 1.50 4.00
36 Ron Francis 2.50 6.00
37 Ryan Callahan 1.25 3.00
38 Semyon Varlamov 2.00 5.00
39 Tyler Seguin 2.50 6.00
40 Anze Kopitar 3.00 8.00
41 Craig Anderson 2.00 5.00
42 David Backes 1.25 3.00
43 Corey Perry 3.00 8.00
44 Jonathan Toews 3.00 8.00
45 Pekka Rinne 2.00 5.00
46 Tuukka Rask 2.50 6.00
47 Henrik Lundqvist 5.00 12.00
48 Ed Belfour 2.00 5.00
49 Bobby Clarke 3.00 8.00
50 Marc-Andre Fleury 4.00 10.00
51 Patrick Marleau 2.00 5.00
52 Ryan Miller 2.00 5.00
53 Jeff Skinner 2.50 6.00
54 Henrik Sedin 2.50 6.00
55 Jonas Hiller 1.50 4.00
56 Cam Neely 2.00 5.00
57 Grant Fuhr 3.00 8.00
58 Eric Staal 2.50 6.00
59 Bobby Hull 4.00 10.00
60 Joe Sakic 4.00 10.00
61 Rick Nash 2.00 5.00
62 Henrik Zetterberg 2.50 6.00
63 Mike Modano 3.00 8.00
64 Ryan Nugent-Hopkins 2.50 6.00
65 Erik Karlsson 2.50 6.00
66 Mario Lemieux 8.00 20.00
67 Ryan Suter 1.50 4.00
68 Jaromir Jagr 6.00 15.00
69 Mike Fisher 1.25 3.00
70 Mike Bossy 2.00 5.00
71 Martin St. Louis 2.00 5.00
72 Sergei Bobrovsky 3.00 8.00
73 Jeremy Roenick 3.00 8.00
74 Shane Doan 1.50 4.00
75 Antti Niemi 1.50 4.00
76 P.K. Subban 2.50 6.00
77 Ray Bourque 3.00 8.00
78 Darryl Sittler 2.50 6.00
79 Nicklas Backstrom 2.00 5.00
80 Dustin Byfuglien 2.00 5.00
81 Lanny McDonald 2.00 5.00
82 Jarome Iginla 2.50 6.00
83 Andrew Ladd 1.25 3.00
84 Jordan Eberle 2.00 5.00
85 Claude Giroux 2.00 5.00
86 Matt Duchene 2.00 5.00
87 Sidney Crosby 6.00 15.00
88 Patrick Kane 4.00 10.00
89 Jason Spezza 2.00 5.00
90 Felix Potvin 3.00 8.00
91 Steven Stamkos 4.00 10.00
92 Pat LaFontaine 2.00 5.00
93 Doug Gilmour 2.50 6.00
94 Brendan Shanahan 2.00 5.00
95 Brian Leetch 1.50 4.00
96 Pavel Bure 2.00 5.00
97 Mike Cammalleri 1.50 4.00
98 Ron Hextall 2.00 5.00
99 Marcel Dionne 2.50 6.00
100 Wendel Clark 3.00 8.00
101 Brian Lashoff AU RC 4.00 10.00
102 Mark Arcobello AU RC 5.00 12.00
103 David Broll AU RC 5.00 12.00
104 Freddie Hamilton AU RC 5.00 12.00
105 Harri Pesonen AU RC 4.00 10.00
107 Jason Missiaen AU RC 5.00 12.00
108 Jeff Zatkoff AU RC 5.00 12.00
109 Jesper Fast AU RC 5.00 12.00
110 Joe Cannata AU RC 4.00 10.00
111 Johan Gustafsson AU RC 6.00 15.00
112 Johan Larsson AU RC 6.00 15.00
113 Joonas Rask AU RC 3.00 8.00
114 Jordan Szwarz AU RC 3.00 8.00
115 Michael Kostka AU RC 3.00 8.00
116 Michael Latta AU RC 4.00 10.00
117 Ondrej Palat AU RC 30.00 60.00
119 Radko Gudas AU RC 8.00 20.00
120 Rickard Rakell AU RC 5.00 12.00
121 Steve Oleksy AU RC 5.00 12.00
122 Taylor Beck AU RC 4.00 10.00
123 Taylor Fedun AU RC 6.00 15.00
124 Tye McGinn AU RC 5.00 12.00
125 Tyler Johnson AU RC 75.00 125.00
126 A.Barkov JSY AU RC 80.00 200.00
127 Alex Chiasson JSY AU RC 20.00 50.00
128 Alex Galchenyuk JSY AU RC 200.00 400.00
129 Alex Killorn JSY AU RC 30.00 80.00
130 Anthony Peluso JSY AU RC 12.00 30.00
131 Antoine Roussel JSY AU RC 20.00 50.00
132 Austin Watson JSY AU RC 15.00 40.00
133 Beau Bennett JSY AU RC 15.00 40.00
134 Boone Jenner JSY AU RC 30.00 80.00
135 B.Gallagher JSY AU RC 80.00 150.00
136 Brian Flynn JSY AU RC 12.00 30.00
137 Brock Nelson JSY AU RC 25.00 60.00
138 Calvin Pickard JSY AU RC 30.00 80.00
139 Cameron Schilling JSY AU RC 12.00 30.00
140 Carl Soderberg JSY AU RC 15.00 40.00
141 Charlie Coyle JSY AU RC 25.00 60.00
142 Chris Brown JSY AU RC 12.00 30.00
143 Christian Thomas JSY AU RC 12.00 30.00
144 Cody Ceci JSY AU RC 15.00 40.00
145 Cory Conacher JSY AU RC 12.00 30.00
146 Danny DeKeyser JSY AU RC 20.00 50.00
147 Darcy Kuemper JSY AU RC 25.00 60.00
148 Dmitrij Jaskin JSY AU RC 20.00 50.00
149 Dougie Hamilton JSY AU RC 40.00 100.00
150 Dylan McIlrath JSY AU RC 12.00 30.00
151 Edward Pasquale JSY AU RC 12.00 30.00
152 Elias Lindholm JSY AU RC 50.00 125.00
153 Emerson Etem JSY AU RC 12.00 30.00
154 Eric Hartzell JSY AU RC 12.00 30.00
155 Filip Forsberg JSY AU RC 90.00 150.00
156 Frank Corrado JSY AU RC 12.00 30.00
157 Frederik Andersen JSY AU RC 40.00 80.00
158 Hampus Lindholm JSY AU RC 25.00 60.00
159 J.T. Miller JSY AU RC 25.00 60.00
160 Jack Campbell JSY AU RC 50.00 120.00
161 Jacob Trouba JSY AU RC 30.00 80.00
162 Jamie Devane JSY AU RC 15.00 40.00
163 Jamie Oleksiak JSY AU RC 15.00 40.00
164 Jared Staal JSY AU RC 12.00 30.00
165 Jarred Tinordi JSY AU RC 20.00 50.00
166 Jayson Megna JSY AU RC 15.00 40.00
168 Joakim Nordstrom JSY AU RC 15.00 40.00
169 John Gibson JSY AU RC 75.00 150.00
170 Jon Merrill JSY AU RC 15.00 40.00
171 Jonas Brodin JSY AU RC 20.00 50.00
172 J.Huberdeau JSY AU RC 100.00 200.00
173 Jordan Schroeder JSY AU RC 20.00 50.00
174 Justin Schultz JSY AU RC 20.00 50.00
175 Kevin Connauton JSY AU RC 12.00 30.00
176 Lucas Lessio JSY AU RC 15.00 40.00
177 Magnus Hellberg JSY AU RC 20.00 50.00
178 Marek Mazanec JSY AU RC 20.00 50.00
179 Antti Raanta JSY AU RC 25.00 60.00
180 Mark Pysyk JSY AU RC 15.00 40.00
181 Martin Jones JSY AU RC EXCH 50.00 100.00
182 Matt Dumba JSY AU RC 12.00 30.00
183 Matt Nieto JSY AU RC 15.00 40.00
184 M.Bournival JSY AU RC 20.00 50.00
185 Michael Raffl JSY AU RC 15.00 40.00
186 Mikael Granlund JSY AU RC 60.00 120.00
187 M.Grigorenko JSY AU RC 12.00 30.00
188 Morgan Rielly JSY AU RC 50.00 100.00
189 Nail Yakupov JSY AU RC 200.00 400.00
190 Nathan Beaulieu JSY AU RC 12.00 30.00
191 N.MacKinnon JSY AU RC 800.00 2000.00
192 Nick Bjugstad JSY AU RC 30.00 80.00
193 Nick Petrecki JSY AU RC 15.00 40.00
194 Nicklas Jensen JSY AU RC 15.00 40.00
196 Nikita Zadorov JSY AU RC 12.00 30.00
197 Olli Maatta JSY AU RC 30.00 80.00
198 Petr Mrazek JSY AU RC 50.00 100.00
199 Philipp Grubauer JSY AU RC 12.00 30.00
200 Quinton Howden JSY AU RC 20.00 50.00
201 R.Ristolainen JSY AU RC 40.00 80.00
203 Reto Berra JSY AU RC 20.00 50.00
204 Richard Panik JSY AU RC 15.00 40.00
205 Ryan Murphy JSY AU RC 20.00 50.00
206 Ryan Murray JSY AU RC 20.00 50.00
207 Ryan Spooner JSY AU RC 20.00 50.00
208 Ryan Strome JSY AU RC 60.00 120.00
209 Sami Vatanen JSY AU RC 40.00 80.00
210 Scott Laughton JSY AU RC 20.00 50.00
211 Sean Monahan JSY AU RC 175.00 300.00
212 Seth Jones JSY AU RC 60.00 150.00
213 Stefan Matteau JSY AU RC 15.00 40.00
214 Tanner Pearson JSY AU RC 50.00 100.00
215 Thomas Hickey JSY AU RC 15.00 40.00
216 Tom Wilson JSY AU RC 40.00 100.00
217 Tomas Hertl JSY AU RC 100.00 200.00
218 Tomas Jurco JSY AU RC 25.00 60.00
219 Tyler Pitlick JSY AU RC 15.00 40.00
220 Tyler Toffoli JSY AU RC 100.00 175.00
221 Valeri Nichushkin JSY AU RC 30.00 80.00
222 Viktor Fasth JSY AU RC 20.00 50.00
224 Xavier Ouellet JSY AU RC 20.00 50.00
225 Z.Girgensons JSY AU RC 50.00 100.00

2013-14 Panini National Treasures Gold

*GOLD AU/25: .6X TO 1.5X BASIC AU/99
125 Tyler Johnson AU 125.00 200.00

2013-14 Panini National Treasures Rainbow

*RAINBOW AU/61-81: .4X TO 1X ROOK AU/99
*RAINBOW AU/30-58: .5X TO 1.2X ROOK AU/99
*RAINBOW AU/15-29: .6X TO 1.5X ROOK AU/99
*RAIN.JSY AU/60-83: .4X TO 1X RK JSY AU/99
*RAIN.JSY AU/30-59: .5X TO 1.2X RK JSY AU/99
*RAIN.JSY AU/15-29: .6X TO 1.5X RK JSY AU/99
126 A.Barkov JSY AU/16 200.00 400.00
128 A.Galchenyuk JSY AU/27 300.00 500.00
149 Dougie Hamilton JSY AU/27 40.00 100.00
169 John Gibson JSY AU/36 60.00 120.00
191 N.MacKinnon JSY AU/29 1000.00 2500.00
221 V.Nichushkin JSY AU/43 100.00 200.00

2013-14 Panini National Treasures Silver

*SILVER/25: .8X TO 2X BASIC CARDS/199
79 Nicklas Backstrom 4.00 10.00

2013-14 Panini National Treasures All Star Treasures Autographs

1 Gordie Howe/23 100.00 200.00
2 Ray Bourque/19 40.00 80.00
3 Paul Coffey/15 40.00 80.00

2013-14 Panini National Treasures Century Materials Jersey

*PRIME/50: .5X TO 1.2X BASIC JSY/99
*PATCH/25: .6X TO 1.5X BASIC JSY/99
1 Nathan MacKinnon/99 12.00 30.00
2 Pavel Bure/99 6.00 15.00
3 Sidney Crosby/99 12.00 30.00
4 Tomas Hertl/99 5.00 12.00
5 Paul Coffey/99 3.00 8.00
6 Alex Ovechkin/99 12.00 30.00
7 Antti Raanta/99 5.00 12.00
8 Marcel Dionne/99 4.00 10.00
9 Steven Stamkos/99 6.00 15.00
10 Tomas Jurco/99 3.00 8.00
11 Ron Francis/99 4.00 10.00
12 John Tavares/99 5.00 12.00
13 Mikael Granlund/99 4.00 10.00
14 Denis Potvin/99 3.00 8.00
15 Evgeni Malkin/99 6.00 15.00
16 Seth Jones/99 5.00 12.00
17 Steve Yzerman/99 8.00 20.00
18 Jeff Carter/99 2.50 6.00
19 Nail Yakupov/99 5.00 12.00
20 Mario Lemieux/99 10.00 25.00
21 Carey Price/99 6.00 15.00
22 Sean Monahan/99 6.00 15.00
23 Gordie Howe/25 15.00 40.00
24 Martin Brodeur/99 10.00 25.00
25 Morgan Rielly/99 6.00 15.00
26 Jeremy Roenick/99 5.00 12.00
27 Gabriel Landeskog/99 4.00 10.00
28 Valeri Nichushkin/99 5.00 12.00
29 Mike Modano/99 5.00 12.00
30 Patrick Kane/99 6.00 15.00
31 Alex Galchenyuk/99 6.00 15.00
32 Brett Hull/99 6.00 15.00
33 Jason Spezza/99 3.00 8.00
34 Damien Brunner/99 2.50 6.00
35 Joe Sakic/75 10.00 25.00
36 Claude Giroux/99 3.00 8.00
37 Jacob Trouba/99 4.00 10.00
38 Ron Francis/99 4.00 10.00
39 Daniel Sedin/99 4.00 10.00
40 Aleksander Barkov/99 8.00 20.00
41 Yvan Cournoyer/50 4.00 10.00
42 Marian Gaborik/99 3.00 8.00
43 Jonathan Huberdeau/99 6.00 15.00
44 Stan Mikita/99 4.00 10.00
45 Henrik Lundqvist/50 8.00 20.00
46 Elias Lindholm/99 6.00 15.00
47 Phil Esposito/99 5.00 12.00
48 Teemu Selanne/99 6.00 15.00
49 Olli Maatta/99 4.00 10.00
50 Mark Messier/99 6.00 15.00

2013-14 Panini National Treasures Cherry's Treasures Autographs

1 E.Lindros/D.Cherry/49 30.00 60.00
2 J.Tavares/D.Cherry/99 40.00 80.00
3 T.Seguin/D.Cherry/99 30.00 60.00
4 D.Gilmour/D.Cherry/99 30.00 60.00
5 D.Clarkson/D.Cherry/99 12.00 30.00
6 M.Messier/D.Cherry/49 40.00 80.00
7 S.Yzerman/D.Cherry/49 60.00 120.00
8 M.Duchene/D.Cherry/99 12.00 30.00
9 MacKinnon/D.Cherry/99 80.00 150.00
10 C.Neely/D.Cherry/49 30.00 60.00

2013-14 Panini National Treasures Colossal Jerseys

*PRIME/25: .6X TO 1.5X BASIC JSY/50
1 Nathan MacKinnon/50 10.00 25.00
2 Nail Yakupov/50 6.00 15.00
3 Tomas Hertl/50 6.00 15.00
4 Sean Monahan/50 6.00 15.00
5 Valeri Nichushkin/50 6.00 15.00
6 Alex Galchenyuk/50 8.00 20.00
7 Brendan Gallagher/50 6.00 15.00
8 Morgan Rielly/50 8.00 20.00
9 Tom Wilson/50 6.00 15.00
10 Ryan Strome/50 5.00 12.00
11 Tomas Jurco/50 4.00 10.00
12 John Gibson/50 6.00 15.00
13 Tanner Pearson/50 6.00 15.00
14 Boone Jenner/50 6.00 15.00
15 Jon Merrill/50 3.00 8.00
16 Martin Jones/50 4.00 10.00
17 Ryan Spooner/50 3.00 8.00
18 Brock Nelson/50 6.00 15.00
19 Jacob Trouba/50 5.00 12.00
20 Jonathan Huberdeau/25 6.00 15.00
21 Austin Watson/50 2.50 6.00
22 Mikhail Grigorenko/50 2.00 5.00
23 Mikael Granlund/50 5.00 12.00
24 Ryan Murray/50 5.00 12.00
25 Elias Lindholm/50 8.00 20.00
26 Gordie Howe/25 30.00 80.00
27 Jonathan Quick/50 6.00 15.00
28 Adam Henrique/50 3.00 8.00
29 Derek Stepan/50 2.50 6.00
30 Maxime Talbot/50 2.50 6.00
31 Vincent Lecavalier/50 4.00 10.00
32 Tyler Seguin/50 5.00 12.00
33 Jeremy Roenick/50 6.00 15.00
34 Ryan Kesler/50 4.00 10.00
35 Ron Hextall/50 5.00 12.00
36 Reilly Smith/50 4.00 10.00
37 Pierre Turgeon/50 3.00 8.00
38 Pekka Rinne/50 4.00 10.00
39 Paul Coffey/50 5.00 12.00
40 Patrick Marleau/50 4.00 10.00
41 Nazem Kadri/50 5.00 12.00
42 Mikael Backlund/50 3.00 8.00
43 Matt Duchene/50 4.00 10.00
44 Loui Eriksson/50 2.50 6.00
45 Jaromir Jagr/50 8.00 20.00
46 Sean Couturier/50 3.00 8.00
47 Taylor Hall/50 4.00 10.00
48 Steve Yzerman/25 10.00 25.00
49 Torey Krug/50 6.00 15.00
50 Chris Kreider/50 5.00 12.00

2013-14 Panini National Treasures Colossal Jerseys Autograph

1 Nathan MacKinnon/25 60.00 150.00
2 Nail Yakupov/25 20.00 50.00
3 Tomas Hertl/25 15.00 40.00
5 Valeri Nichushkin/25 12.00 30.00
6 Alex Galchenyuk/25 25.00 60.00
7 Brendan Gallagher/25 20.00 50.00
8 Morgan Rielly/25 15.00 40.00
9 Tom Wilson/25 15.00 40.00
10 Ryan Strome/25 12.00 30.00
11 Tomas Jurco/25 10.00 25.00
12 John Gibson/25 12.00 30.00
13 Tanner Pearson/25 8.00 20.00
14 Boone Jenner/25 15.00 40.00
15 Jon Merrill/25 8.00 20.00
16 Martin Jones/25 15.00 40.00
17 Ryan Spooner/25 8.00 20.00
18 Brock Nelson/25 15.00 40.00
19 Jacob Trouba/25 12.00 30.00
20 Jonathan Huberdeau/25 12.00 30.00
21 Austin Watson/25 6.00 15.00
22 Mikhail Grigorenko/25 10.00 25.00
23 Mikael Granlund/25 12.00 30.00
24 Ryan Murray/25 12.00 30.00
25 Elias Lindholm/25 10.00 25.00
27 Jonathan Quick/25 15.00 40.00
28 Adam Henrique/25 10.00 25.00
29 Derek Stepan/25 10.00 25.00
31 Vincent Lecavalier/25 10.00 25.00
32 Tyler Seguin/25 15.00 40.00
33 Jeremy Roenick/25 20.00 50.00
34 Ryan Kesler/25 12.00 30.00
35 Ron Hextall/25 20.00 50.00
36 Reilly Smith/25 12.00 30.00
37 Pierre Turgeon/25 10.00 25.00
38 Pekka Rinne/25 12.00 30.00
39 Paul Coffey/25 12.00 30.00
42 Mikael Backlund/25 EXCH 10.00 25.00
43 Matt Duchene/25 12.00 30.00
44 Loui Eriksson/25 8.00 20.00
45 Jaromir Jagr/25 40.00 80.00
46 Sean Couturier/25 10.00 25.00
47 Taylor Hall/25 20.00 50.00
49 Torey Krug/25 10.00 25.00
50 Chris Kreider/25 15.00 40.00

2013-14 Panini National Treasures Crazy 8's Jerseys

*PRIME/25: .6X TO 1.5X BASIC JSY/50
1 Atlantic Division 20.00 50.00
3 Central Division 20.00 50.00
4 Pacific Division 12.00 30.00
5 NHL Stars 12.00 30.00
7 Russian Stars 20.00 50.00
8 NHL Stars 15.00 40.00
9 NHL Stars 20.00 50.00
11 Colorado Stars 25.00 60.00
12 Edmonton Stars 20.00 50.00
13 Anaheim Stars 20.00 50.00
14 NHL Stars 12.00 30.00
15 NHL Stars 20.00 50.00
16 Sidney Crosby 40.00 100.00
MD Metropolitan Division 40.00 100.00
13D 2013 Draft Picks 30.00 80.00
SCF Blackhawks and Bruins 25.00 50.00

2013-14 Panini National Treasures Dual Autographs

*GOLD/15-25:.6X TO 1.5X AU/75-100
3 Silfverberg/R.Rakell/100 6.00 15.00
4 P.Elias/T.Ruutu/100 6.00 15.00
5 A.Peluso/E.Pasquale/100 4.00 10.00
6 C.Ward/E.Staal/100 8.00 20.00
7 R.Panik/V.Filppula/100 8.00 20.00
8 D.Phaneuf/J.Leivo/100 8.00 20.00
9 P.Datsyuk/P.Mrazek/100 12.00 30.00
10 A.Watson/Del Zotto/100 5.00 12.00
12 C.Pickard/C.Pickard/100 8.00 20.00
13 M.Mazanec/P.Mrazek/100 12.00 30.00
14 Markstrom/R.Luongo/100 10.00 25.00
15 B.Schenn/Z.Rinaldo/100 6.00 15.00
17 C.Neely/J.Iginla/100 8.00 20.00
18 J.Howard/P.Mrazek/100 10.00 25.00
20 J.Tavares/N.Yakupov/100 12.00 30.00
21 B.Ryan/J.Silfverberg/100 5.00 12.00
22 M.Foligno/N.Foligno/100 8.00 20.00
23 Galchenyuk/Yakupov/100 20.00 50.00
24 E.Lach/Y.Cournoyer/100 12.00 30.00
25 B.Richards/St. Louis/100 10.00 25.00
27 J.Reimer/J.Bower/100 10.00 25.00
28 J.Iginla/R.Spooner/100 8.00 20.00
29 B.Street/S.Baertschi/100 5.00 12.00
30 J.Johnson/N.Foligno/100 5.00 12.00
31 C.Emmerton/S.Weiss/100 5.00 12.00
32 B.Boyes/J.Rheault/100 4.00 10.00
33 C.Coyle/D.Kuemper/100 10.00 25.00
34 C.Coyle/Z.Parise/100 12.00 30.00
35 B.Gallagher/C.Thomas/75 12.00 30.00
36 Pesonen/S.Matteau/100 5.00 12.00
37 A.Lee/M.Grabner/100 10.00 25.00
38 J.Neal/Z.Rinaldo/100 5.00 12.00
40 M.Kostka/O.Palat/100 10.00 25.00
41 D.Gilmour/W.Clark/100 15.00 40.00
42 M.Naslund/T.Linden/100 12.00 30.00
43 C.Carrick/K.Alzner/100 5.00 12.00
44 M.Konan/T.McGinn/100 6.00 15.00
45 C.Simmer/M.Dionne/100 12.00 30.00

2013-14 Panini National Treasures Dual Memorabilia Autographs

*PRIME/25: .6X TO 1.5X BASIC JSY AU
1 Darcy Kuemper 15.00 40.00
2 Marc Staal 2.50 6.00
3 Cody Hodgson 2.50 6.00
4 Curtis Glencross 2.50 6.00
5 Austin Watson 3.00 8.00
6 Gordie Howe 60.00 120.00
7 Christian Thomas 3.00 8.00
8 Tye McGinn 4.00 10.00
9 Michael Kostka 3.00 8.00
10 Nick Petrecki 2.50 6.00
11 Anthony Peluso 2.50 6.00
12 Xavier Ouellet 4.00 10.00
13 Stefan Matteau 3.00 8.00
14 Anze Kopitar 10.00 25.00
15 Jay Bouwmeester 2.50 6.00
16 Eric Lindros 25.00 50.00
17 Brendan Shanahan 10.00 25.00
18 Dion Phaneuf 3.00 8.00
19 Jerry D'Amigo 4.00 10.00
20 Jason Missiaen 4.00 10.00
21 Mark Messier 20.00 50.00
22 Cam Neely 12.00 30.00
23 Cody Ceci 3.00 8.00
24 Petr Mrazek 8.00 20.00
25 Mark Giordano 4.00 10.00
26 Johan Franzen 3.00 8.00
27 Beau Bennett 5.00 12.00
28 Bryan Trottier 8.00 20.00
29 Mikael Granlund 10.00 25.00
30 Dan Boyle 5.00 12.00
31 Joakim Nordstrom 3.00 8.00
32 Brian Leetch 10.00 25.00
33 Pat LaFontaine 10.00 25.00
34 Magnus Hellberg 4.00 10.00
35 Connor Murphy 3.00 8.00
36 Tyler Ennis 2.50 6.00
37 Rogie Vachon 10.00 25.00
38 Jacob Markstrom 6.00 15.00
39 Stephen Weiss 3.00 8.00
40 Mikael Backlund 6.00 15.00
41 Logan Couture 5.00 12.00
42 Joe Nieuwendyk 8.00 20.00
43 Edward Pasquale 2.50 6.00
44 Max Pacioretty 8.00 20.00
45 David Krejci 10.00 25.00

2013-14 Panini National Treasures Dual Rookie Jumbo Patch Autographs

1 Yakupov/MacKinnon 125.00 250.00
2 Galchenyuk/Gallagher 75.00 150.00
3 A.Barkov/J.Huberdeau 30.00 80.00
5 M.Raffl/S.Laughton 15.00 40.00
6 Arcobello/S.Monahan 30.00 80.00
7 H.Lindholm/T.Hertl 30.00 80.00
8 J.Merrill/S.Matteau 15.00 40.00
10 M.Rielly/O.Maatta 40.00 80.00
11 J.Trouba/S.Jones 25.00 60.00
12 Roussel/Nichushkin 25.00 60.00

2013-14 Panini National Treasures Dual Stick Booklet Autographs

1 A.Ovechkin/E.Malkin/25 200.00 300.00
2 C.Joseph/F.Potvin/25 75.00 150.00
5 C.Neely/R.Bourque/20 100.00 200.00
6 T.Seguin/V.Nichushkin/25 40.00 80.00
12 E.Lindros/V.Lecavalier/25 60.00 120.00

2013-14 Panini National Treasures Frozen Treasures Jersey Autographs

1 Alex Ovechkin/25 60.00 120.00
3 John Tavares/35 25.00 60.00
4 Jonathan Toews/35 25.00 60.00
5 Pavel Datsyuk/35 25.00 60.00
6 Henrik Lundqvist/35 40.00 100.00
7 Carey Price/35 30.00 80.00
8 Claude Giroux/35 15.00 40.00
9 Cam Neely/35 15.00 40.00
10 Mario Lemieux/15 90.00 150.00
12 Jeremy Roenick/35 25.00 60.00
13 Mark Messier/15 50.00 100.00
14 Gabriel Landeskog/35 20.00 50.00
15 Brett Hull/35 30.00 60.00
16 Tyler Seguin/35 20.00 50.00
17 Ryan Getzlaf/35 15.00 40.00
18 Daniel Sedin/35 20.00 50.00
20 Martin Brodeur/35 40.00 100.00
21 Patrick Kane/35 40.00 80.00
22 Phil Kessel/35 15.00 40.00
23 Jonathan Quick/35 20.00 50.00

24 Ryan Miller/35 12.00 30.00
25 Joe Sakic/35 30.00 80.00

2013-14 Panini National Treasures Greatest Signatures

2 Don Cherry/25 60.00 120.00
3 Bobby Clarke/25 25.00 60.00
7 Cam Neely/25 15.00 40.00
9 Tony Esposito/25 40.00 100.00
10 Stan Mikita/25 40.00 80.00
11 Bernie Parent/25 20.00 50.00
12 Joe Sakic/25 30.00 80.00
13 Brett Hull/25 25.00 60.00
14 Bobby Hull/25 40.00 80.00
15 Curtis Joseph/25 20.00 50.00
17 Yvan Cournoyer/25 15.00 40.00
18 Charlie Simmer/25 10.00 25.00
19 Doug Gilmour/25 30.00 60.00
21 Wendel Clark/25 20.00 50.00
22 Milt Schmidt/25 20.00 50.00
23 Johnny Bower/25 15.00 40.00
24 Mike Bossy/25 15.00 40.00
25 Ray Bourque/25 25.00 60.00

2013-14 Panini National Treasures Icy Inscriptions

1 Matt Moulson 5.00 12.00
2 Dylan McIlrath 5.00 12.00
3 John Gibson 15.00 40.00
4 Matt Duchene 12.00 30.00
5 Andrew Ladd 5.00 12.00
6 Jesper Fast 5.00 12.00
7 Sergei Bobrovsky 8.00 20.00
9 Henrik Lundqvist 40.00 80.00
11 Eric Staal 10.00 25.00
12 Boone Jenner 15.00 40.00
13 Jason Spezza 8.00 20.00
14 Jon Merrill 8.00 20.00
15 Tyler Seguin 30.00 60.00

2013-14 Panini National Treasures Jumbo Jerseys Booklet

*PRIME/25: .6X TO 1.5X BASIC JSY/75-99
1 Tyler Seguin/99 10.00 25.00
2 Alex Ovechkin/99 25.00 60.00
3 Claude Giroux/99 6.00 15.00
4 Taylor Hall/99 6.00 15.00
5 Luc Robitaille/99 6.00 15.00
6 Dion Phaneuf/99 5.00 12.00
7 Sidney Crosby/99 25.00 60.00
8 Steve Yzerman/99 15.00 40.00
9 Jeremy Roenick/99 10.00 25.00
10 Mike Modano/99 10.00 25.00
11 Brad Richards/99 6.00 15.00
12 Evgeni Malkin/99 12.00 30.00
13 Jaromir Jagr/99 12.00 30.00
14 Joe Sakic/99 12.00 30.00
15 John Tavares/99 10.00 25.00
16 Jonathan Quick/99 8.00 20.00
17 Matt Duchene/99 6.00 15.00
18 Jonathan Toews/75 10.00 25.00
19 Patrice Bergeron/99 10.00 25.00
20 Ryan Getzlaf/99 6.00 15.00

2013-14 Panini National Treasures Jumbo Quad Patches Booklet

1 Brkv/Hbrd/Bgstd/Hwdn 50.00 100.00
2 Prry/Crtr/St. Louis/Shrp 25.00 60.00
3 Fwlr/Quick/Ststny/Prse 30.00 60.00
4 McKin/Mnhn/Hrtl/Nchsh 50.00 120.00
5 Glchny/Hbrd/Ykpv/Trsnk 40.00 80.00
6 Andrsn/Bbkv/Gbsn/Hillr 25.00 60.00
8 Hmltn/Trba/Schltz/Jnes 20.00 50.00
9 Lndq/Erksn/Jhnsn/Bckstr 25.00 60.00

2013-14 Panini National Treasures Jumbo Triple Patches Booklet

1 Hamilton/Bourque/Chara 30.00 60.00
2 Carter/Williams/Richards 25.00 50.00
3 Keith/Karlsson/Subban 30.00 60.00
4 Cogliano/Perry/Bonino 12.00 30.00
5 Yakpv/MacKin/RNH 50.00 120.00
6 Staal/Staal/Staal 12.00 30.00
7 Barkv/Lhtnen/Timon 30.00 80.00
8 MacInnis/Weber/Chara 12.00 30.00
9 Anismv/Dubnsky/Gabrk 25.00 50.00
10 Pysyk/Grigrnko/Grgnsns 25.00 60.00
11 Karlsn/Spzza/Michalek 15.00 40.00
12 Couture/Vlasic/Hertl 30.00 80.00

2013-14 Panini National Treasures Knights in the City Materials

1 J.Sakic/N.MacKinnon 6.00 15.00
2 D.Hamilton/R.Bourque 5.00 12.00
3 L.Robitaille/T.Toffoli 6.00 15.00
4 B.Gainey/B.Gallagher 10.00 25.00
5 Nieuwendyk/Monahan 5.00 12.00
6 M.Modano/V.Nichushkin 6.00 15.00
7 E.Lindholm/R.Francis 8.00 20.00
8 A.Raanta/E.Belfour 6.00 15.00
9 M.Bossy/R.Strome 5.00 12.00
10 Perreault/Girgensons 5.00 12.00
11 Galchenyuk/Cournoyer 8.00 20.00
12 M.Messier/N.Yakupov 6.00 15.00
13 A.Barkov/P.Bure 12.00 30.00
14 B.Clarke/S.Laughton 5.00 12.00
15 O.Maatta/P.Coffey 10.00 25.00
16 B.Hull/V.Tarasenko 12.00 30.00
17 S.Yzerman/T.Jurco 8.00 20.00
18 D.Gilmour/M.Rielly 8.00 20.00
19 M.Gartner/T.Wilson 6.00 15.00
20 M.Dionne/T.Pearson 4.00 10.00
21 B.Bennett/M.Lemieux 12.00 30.00
22 E.Lindros/M.Raffl 8.00 20.00
23 J.Devane/W.Clark 5.00 12.00
24 J.Thornton/T.Hertl 6.00 15.00
25 S.Jones/S.Weber 6.00 15.00

2013-14 Panini National Treasures Matchups Jerseys

*PRIME/25: .8X TO 2X BASIC JSY/99
1 Trouba/MacKinnon/99 8.00 20.00
2 Lemieux/M.Messier/99 10.00 25.00
3 C.Price/J.Quick/99 12.00 30.00
4 A.Raanta/M.Jones/99 5.00 12.00
5 G.Howe/J.Bucyk/25 20.00 50.00
6 Doughty/Karlsson/99 4.00 10.00
7 B.Gallagher/M.Rielly/99 6.00 15.00
8 B.Gainey/B.Clarke/99 6.00 15.00
9 Schneider/R.Luongo/99 6.00 15.00
10 Yakupov/Monahan/99 4.00 10.00
11 D.Potvin/P.Esposito/99 5.00 12.00
12 A.Kopitar/T.Selanne/99 8.00 20.00
13 M.Raffl/O.Maatta/99 6.00 15.00
14 F.Potvin/P.Roy/99 12.00 30.00
15 C.Giroux/E.Malkin/99 6.00 15.00
16 S.Jones/Nichushkin/99 5.00 12.00
17 B.Hull/J.Roenick/99 5.00 12.00
18 P.Kane/T.Oshie/99 6.00 15.00
19 T.Hertl/T.Toffoli/99 8.00 20.00
20 D.Sittler/G.Lafleur/99 6.00 15.00
21 Galchenyuk/Hamilton/99 10.00 25.00
22 B.Leetch/R.Bourque/99 5.00 12.00
23 Ovechkin/S.Stamkos/99 12.00 30.00
24 A.Barkov/S.Vatanen/99 8.00 20.00
25 E.Lindros/S.Yzerman/99 12.00 30.00

2013-14 Panini National Treasures Newfound Treasures Materials Autograph

NTAB Aleksander Barkov 10.00 25.00
NTAG Alex Galchenyuk 15.00 40.00
NTBJ Boone Jenner 12.00 30.00
NTCC Cody Ceci 5.00 12.00
NTEL Elias Lindholm 8.00 20.00
NTHL Hampus Lindholm 8.00 20.00
NTJC Jack Campbell 25.00 60.00
NTJG John Gibson 15.00 40.00
NTJH Jonathan Huberdeau 15.00 40.00
NTJM Jon Merrill 8.00 20.00
NTJT Jacob Trouba 10.00 25.00
NTMJ Martin Jones 12.00 30.00
NTMR Morgan Rielly 15.00 40.00
NTMRA Michael Raffl 10.00 25.00
NTNM Nathan MacKinnon 40.00 100.00
NTNY Nail Yakupov 15.00 40.00
NTOM Olli Maatta 10.00 25.00
NTRS Ryan Spooner 6.00 15.00
NTRST Ryan Strome 10.00 25.00
NTSM Sean Monahan 15.00 40.00
NTTH Tomas Hertl 12.00 30.00
NTTJ Tomas Jurco 15.00 40.00
NTVN Valeri Nichushkin 12.00 30.00
NTZG Zemgus Girgensons 10.00 25.00

2013-14 Panini National Treasures Newfound Treasures Materials Autograph Prime

NTNM Nathan MacKinnon 50.00 120.00

2013-14 Panini National Treasures NHL Gear Autographs

2 Tyler Seguin/50 25.00 50.00
3 Adam Henrique/99 6.00 15.00
4 Alex Ovechkin/25 60.00 120.00
6 Jonathan Toews/50 50.00 100.00
7 Adam Graves/49 10.00 25.00
9 Brenden Morrow/99 6.00 15.00
10 Brian Leetch/50 12.00 30.00
11 Cam Neely/50 15.00 40.00
12 Carey Price/50 25.00 60.00
14 Curtis Joseph/50 20.00 50.00
15 Dave Andreychuk/99 8.00 20.00
16 Derek Stepan/99 5.00 12.00
17 Devan Dubnyk/75 EXCH 15.00 30.00
18 Ed Belfour/50 20.00 50.00
19 Mike Modano/50 25.00 50.00
23 Vincent Lecavalier/50 10.00 25.00
24 Ray Bourque/50 30.00 80.00
25 Patrick Roy/25 60.00 120.00
26 Jeremy Roenick/25 25.00 60.00
27 Ryan Getzlaf/50 15.00 40.00
28 Bobby Ryan/50 8.00 20.00
20 Ryan Miller/50 10.00 25.00
30 Ryan Nugent-Hopkins/25 15.00 40.00
31 Jonathan Quick/25 25.00 60.00
32 Joe Thornton/25 20.00 50.00
33 John Tavares/25 25.00 60.00

2013-14 Panini National Treasures NHL Rookie Gear Autographs

1 Nail Yakupov 30.00 80.00
2 Nathan MacKinnon 40.00 100.00
3 Aleksander Barkov 15.00 40.00
4 Jonathan Huberdeau 15.00 40.00
5 Valeri Nichushkin 15.00 40.00
6 Sean Monahan 25.00 50.00
7 Tomas Hertl 20.00 50.00
8 John Gibson 15.00 40.00
9 Elias Lindholm 20.00 50.00
10 Tomas Jurco 12.00 30.00
11 Ryan Strome 10.00 25.00
12 Seth Jones 15.00 40.00
13 Jacob Trouba 12.00 30.00
14 Morgan Rielly 15.00 40.00
15 Michael Raffl 10.00 25.00
16 Tyler Toffoli 15.00 40.00
17 Hampus Lindholm 10.00 25.00
18 Ryan Murray 12.00 30.00
19 Alex Galchenyuk 30.00 60.00
20 Brendan Gallagher 15.00 40.00
21 Nicklas Jensen 6.00 15.00
22 Zemgus Girgensons 12.00 30.00
24 Martin Jones 12.00 30.00
26 Matt Dumba 5.00 12.00
27 Dougie Hamilton 15.00 40.00
28 Boone Jenner 15.00 40.00
29 Olli Maatta 20.00 50.00
30 Matt Nieto 8.00 20.00
31 Antoine Roussel 8.00 20.00
32 Mikael Granlund 12.00 30.00
33 Jon Merrill 8.00 20.00
34 Ryan Spooner 8.00 20.00

2013-14 Panini National Treasures Notable Nicknames

1 Ron Hextall/25 20.00 50.00
3 Ed Belfour/25 50.00 100.00
4 Johnny Bower/25 40.00 100.00
6 Pavel Datsyuk/25 30.00 80.00
7 Cam Ward/25 15.00 40.00
8 Tony Esposito/25 20.00 50.00
9 Doug Gilmour/25 20.00 50.00
12 Bobby Hull/25 60.00 120.00
13 Jarome Iginla/25 15.00 40.00
14 Curtis Joseph/25 40.00 100.00
16 Henrik Lundqvist/25 50.00 125.00
17 Stan Mikita/25 40.00 80.00
18 Ryan Nugent-Hopkins/25 25.00 60.00
20 Felix Potvin/25 60.00 120.00
21 James Reimer/25 50.00 100.00
22 Luc Robitaille/25 20.00 50.00
23 Jeremy Roenick/25 25.00 60.00
25 John Vanbiesbrouck/25 20.00 50.00

2013-14 Panini National Treasures Numbers Patch

1 Carey Price/31 15.00 40.00
3 Phil Kessel/81 8.00 20.00
15 Ryan Getzlaf/15 8.00 20.00
16 Brett Hull/16 15.00 40.00
18 John Tavares/91 12.00 30.00
19 Steve Yzerman/19 20.00 50.00
20 Luc Robitaille/20 8.00 20.00
21 Stan Mikita/21 10.00 25.00
22 Daniel Sedin/22 10.00 25.00
23 Evgeni Malkin/71 15.00 40.00
24 Joe Thornton/19 12.00 30.00
25 John Vanbiesbrouck/34 8.00 20.00
27 Cody Hodgson/19 5.00 12.00
28 Mike Smith/41 8.00 20.00
30 Martin Brodeur/30 20.00 50.00
31 Curtis Joseph/31 10.00 25.00
32 Jonathan Quick/32 10.00 25.00
33 Patrick Roy/33 20.00 50.00
35 Joe Nieuwendyk/25 6.00 15.00
37 Ryan Callahan/24 5.00 12.00
39 Tyler Seguin/91 10.00 25.00
41 Craig Anderson/41 8.00 20.00
42 David Backes/42 5.00 12.00
44 Jonathan Toews/19 12.00 30.00
45 Pekka Rinne/35 8.00 20.00
46 Tuukka Rask/40 10.00 25.00
47 Henrik Lundqvist/30 20.00 50.00
48 Ed Belfour/20 8.00 20.00
49 Bobby Clarke/16 12.00 30.00
50 Marc-Andre Fleury/29 15.00 40.00
52 Ryan Miller/39 8.00 20.00
53 Jeff Skinner/53 10.00 25.00
54 Henrik Sedin/33 10.00 25.00
57 Grant Fuhr/31 12.00 30.00
60 Joe Sakic/19 15.00 40.00
61 Rick Nash/61 8.00 20.00
62 Henrik Zetterberg/40 10.00 25.00
64 Ryan Nugent-Hopkins/93 10.00 25.00
65 Erik Karlsson/65 10.00 25.00
66 Mario Lemieux/66 30.00 80.00
67 Ryan Suter/20 6.00 15.00
68 Jaromir Jagr/68 25.00 60.00
70 Mike Bossy/22 8.00 20.00
71 Martin St. Louis/26 8.00 20.00
72 Sergei Bobrovsky/72 12.00 30.00
73 Jeremy Roenick/97 12.00 30.00
74 Shane Doan/19 6.00 15.00
75 Antti Niemi/31 6.00 15.00
76 P.K. Subban/76 10.00 25.00
77 Ray Bourque/77 12.00 30.00
78 Darryl Sittler/27 10.00 25.00
79 Nicklas Backstrom/19 8.00 20.00
80 Dustin Byfuglien/33 8.00 20.00
83 Andrew Ladd/16 5.00 12.00
85 Claude Giroux/28 8.00 20.00
87 Sidney Crosby/87 30.00 80.00
88 Patrick Kane/88 15.00 40.00
89 Jason Spezza/19 8.00 20.00
90 Felix Potvin/29 12.00 30.00
92 Pat LaFontaine/16 8.00 20.00
94 Brendan Shanahan/94 8.00 20.00
98 Ron Hextall/27 8.00 20.00
99 Marcel Dionne/16 10.00 25.00
100 Wendel Clark/17 12.00 30.00

2013-14 Panini National Treasures Past and Present Autographs

1 J.Tavares/M.Bossy/99 30.00 60.00
2 E.Staal/K.Primeau/99 15.00 40.00
3 C.Neely/R.Smith/99 12.00 30.00
4 F.Andersen/G.Hebert/99 30.00 80.00
6 C.Kreider/M.Messier/49 30.00 80.00
7 B.Federko/J.Schwartz/99 15.00 40.00
8 E.Lindros/M.Read/99 20.00 50.00
9 H.Lundqvist/M.Richter/99 30.00 80.00
10 C.Price/P.Roy/99 75.00 135.00
11 A.Killorn/D.Andreychuk/99 20.00 50.00
12 G.Howe/P.Datsyuk/49 60.00 120.00
13 C.Joseph/J.Bernier/99 20.00 50.00
14 J.Neal/R.Francis/99 15.00 40.00
15 R.Kesler/T.Linden/99 12.00 30.00

2013-14 Panini National Treasures Past Present and Future Autographs

1 Modano/Seguin/Nichushkin 20.00 50.00
2 Hamilton/Bourque/Krug 40.00 80.00
3 Messier/Yakupov/Hall 20.00 50.00
4 Sakic/Duchene/MacKinnon 60.00 120.00
5 Brown/Robitaille/Toffoli 20.00 50.00
6 Nieuwendyk/Backlund/Monahan 15.00 40.00
7 Tavares/Bossy/Strome 30.00 60.00
8 Giroux/Lindros/Laughton 20.00 50.00
9 Galchenyuk/Pacioretty/Cournoyer 30.00 80.00
10 Phaneuf/Gilmour/Rielly 25.00 60.00

2013-14 Panini National Treasures Phenoms Autographs

PEE1 Emerson Etem logo 3.00 8.00
PEE2 Emerson Etem draft 3.00 8.00
PJC1 Jack Campbell Stars 8.00 20.00
PJC2 Jack Campbell Texas SP 8.00 20.00
PMG Mikael Granlund 5.00 12.00
PMR Morgan Rielly SP 15.00 30.00
PNB1 Nathan Beaulieu logo 5.00 12.00
PNB2 Nathan Beaulieu draft 5.00 12.00
PQH1 Quinton Howden Panther 3.00 8.00
PQH2 Q.Howden Panther circle 3.00 8.00
PQH3 Quinton Howden draft 3.00 8.00
PQH4 Q.Howden NHLPA SP 3.00 8.00
PRM1 Ryan Murray logo 5.00 12.00
PRM2 R.Murray war cap SP 5.00 12.00
PRS1 Ryan Strome NYI 5.00 12.00
PRS2 Ryan Strome NHLPA 5.00 12.00
PTW Tom Wilson SP 6.00 15.00

2013-14 Panini National Treasures Quad Autographs

1 Glchn/Gllghr/Lflr/Crnyr/50 60.00 120.00
2 Schn/Rshill/Msn/McGn/50 12.00 30.00
3 Wrd/Sknnr/Jrdn/Gerbe/50 15.00 40.00
4 Prrn/Ebrle/RNH/Gagner/35 15.00 40.00
5 Oats/Chvrs/Lmlin/O'Rlly/35 20.00 50.00
6 Etm/Hbrt/Hllr/Ndrmyer/35 15.00 40.00
7 Sakc/Dchn/Sgrba/Hjdk/50 20.00 50.00
8 Wtsn/Pckrd/Mznc/Fshr/45 10.00 25.00
10 Brsrd/Mre/Diaz/McDngh/50 8.00 20.00
11 Crrck/Alznr/Grbv/Grbr/50 15.00 40.00
12 Hmhs/Mrkst/Cnta/Bksa/50 12.00 30.00
13 Hdgsn/Andrc/Flgn/Trgn/50 12.00 30.00
14 Wrd/Stl/Prmeau/Frncs/50 15.00 40.00
15 Galch/Hbrd/Grnl/Ykpv/20 40.00 100.00

2013-14 Panini National Treasures Retro Phenoms Autographs

RPCSM1 Craig Smith NP Logo SP 4.00 10.00
RPCSM2 Craig Smith tiger 3.00 8.00
RPJSI1 Jakob Silfverberg logo 3.00 8.00
RPJSI2 Jakob Silfverberg circle logo 3.00 8.00
RPJSI3 Jakob Silfverberg draft SP 4.00 10.00
RPJSK1 Jeff Skinner hurricanes 6.00 15.00
RPJSK2 Jeff Skinner Flag 6.00 15.00
RPTC1 Tyler Cuma wolf logo 4.00 10.00
RPTC2 Tyler Cuma circle logo SP 5.00 12.00
RPTC3 Tyler Cuma NHLPA SP 5.00 12.00

2013-14 Panini National Treasures Rookie Jumbo Jerseys Booklet Autographs

1 Nail Yakupov/99 15.00 40.00
2 Nathan MacKinnon/99 40.00 100.00
3 Tomas Hertl/99 15.00 40.00
4 Jonathan Huberdeau/75 12.00 30.00
5 Alex Galchenyuk/99 25.00 60.00
6 Brendan Gallagher/99 20.00 50.00
8 Sean Monahan/99 20.00 50.00
9 Seth Jones/99 15.00 40.00
10 Hampus Lindholm/99 8.00 20.00
11 Jacob Trouba/99 12.00 30.00
12 Morgan Rielly/99 15.00 40.00
13 Tomas Jurco/99 12.00 30.00
14 Jon Merrill/99 8.00 20.00
15 Ryan Strome/99 8.00 20.00
16 Elias Lindholm/99 12.00 30.00
17 Aleksander Barkov/99 12.00 30.00
18 Zemgus Girgensons/99 10.00 25.00
19 Tom Wilson/99 15.00 40.00
20 Ryan Spooner/99 8.00 20.00
21 Ryan Murray/99 12.00 30.00
22 Boone Jenner/99 10.00 25.00
23 Michael Bournival/99 8.00 20.00
24 Magnus Hellberg/99 8.00 20.00
25 Filip Forsberg/99 25.00 60.00
26 Mikael Granlund/99 12.00 30.00
27 Valeri Nichushkin/99 20.00 50.00
28 Darcy Kuemper/99 15.00 40.00
29 Ryan Murphy/99 8.00 20.00
30 Mark Arcobello/99 8.00 20.00
31 Dylan McIlrath/99 8.00 20.00
32 Martin Jones/99 10.00 25.00
33 John Gibson/99 15.00 40.00
34 Brock Nelson/99 12.00 30.00
35 Michael Raffl/99 6.00 15.00
36 Mikhail Grigorenko/99 12.00 30.00

2013-14 Panini National Treasures Rookie Jumbo Jerseys Booklet Autographs Patch

*PATCH/20-25: .6X TO 1.5X BASIC JSY AU/75-99
2 Nathan MacKinnon/25 60.00 150.00

2013-14 Panini National Treasures Rookie Jumbo Jerseys Booklet Autographs Prime

*PRIME/49: .5X TO 1.2X BASIC JSY AU/75-99
2 Nathan MacKinnon 40.00 100.00

2013-14 Panini National Treasures Rookie Riches Autographs

1 Nathan MacKinnon 30.00 80.00
2 Nail Yakupov 15.00 40.00
3 Sean Monahan 12.00 30.00
4 Tomas Hertl 15.00 40.00
5 Alex Galchenyuk 25.00 60.00
6 Jonathan Huberdeau 15.00 40.00
7 Valeri Nichushkin 12.00 30.00
8 Hampus Lindholm 10.00 25.00
9 Jacob Trouba 10.00 25.00
10 Filip Forsberg 20.00 50.00
11 Brendan Gallagher 15.00 40.00
12 Morgan Rielly 12.00 30.00
13 Aleksander Barkov 10.00 25.00
15 Martin Jones 12.00 30.00

2013-14 Panini National Treasures Rookie Timeline Jerseys

*PATCH/15-25: .8X TO 2X BASIC JSY/99
*PRIME/50: .5X TO 1.2X BASIC JSY/99
RTAB Aleksander Barkov 8.00 20.00
RTAR Antti Raanta 5.00 12.00
RTBG Brendan Gallagher 8.00 20.00
RTBJ Boone Jenner 5.00 12.00
RTCB Chris Brown 3.00 8.00
RTCC Charlie Coyle 4.00 10.00
RTDH Dougie Hamilton 4.00 10.00
RTDK Darcy Kuemper 4.00 10.00
RTDM Dylan McIlrath 2.50 6.00
RTDS Drew Shore 2.50 6.00
RTEL Elias Lindholm 6.00 15.00
RTEP Edward Pasquale 1.50 4.00
RTFA Frederik Andersen 6.00 15.00
RTJC Jack Campbell 6.00 15.00
RTJG John Gibson 6.00 15.00
RTJM Jon Merrill 3.00 8.00
RTJS Justin Schultz 2.50 6.00
RTJT Jacob Trouba 4.00 10.00
RTLL Lucas Lessio 2.50 6.00
RTMD Matt Dumba 1.50 4.00
RTMG1 Mikael Granlund 4.00 10.00
RTMG2 Mikhail Grigorenko 1.50 4.00
RTMH Magnus Hellberg 2.50 6.00
RTMJ Martin Jones 5.00 12.00
RTMP Mark Pysyk 2.50 6.00
RTMR1 Michael Raffl 2.00 5.00
RTMR2 Morgan Rielly 6.00 15.00
RTNB Nathan Beaulieu 1.50 4.00
RTNJ Nicklas Jensen 3.00 8.00
RTNM Nathan MacKinnon 12.00 30.00
RTNY Nail Yakupov 6.00 15.00
RTNZ Nikita Zadorov 1.50 4.00
RTOM Olli Maatta 6.00 15.00
RTPG Philipp Grubauer 6.00 15.00
RTPM Petr Mrazek 5.00 12.00
RTQH Quinton Howden 2.50 6.00
RTRB Reto Berra 4.00 10.00
RTRM1 Ryan Murphy 2.50 6.00
RTRM2 Ryan Murray 4.00 10.00
RTRS1 Ryan Spooner 5.00 12.00
RTRS2 Ryan Strome 5.00 12.00
RTSJ Seth Jones 5.00 12.00
RTSL Scott Laughton 3.00 8.00
RTSM1 Stefan Matteau 2.00 5.00
RTSM2 Sean Monahan 4.00 10.00
RTTH Tomas Hertl 8.00 20.00
RTTP Tanner Pearson 4.00 10.00
RTTT Tyler Toffoli 5.00 12.00
RTTW Tom Wilson 5.00 12.00
RTVN Valeri Nichushkin 5.00 12.00

2013-14 Panini National Treasures Scratching the Surface Autographs

2 Nathan MacKinnon 60.00 120.00

2013-14 Panini National Treasures Six Autographs

1 Russian Stars 50.00 100.00
2 Pittsburgh Stars 60.00 120.00
3 Dallas and Minnesota 20.00 50.00
4 Bruins and Canadiens 20.00 50.00
5 Flames and Oilers 30.00 60.00
6 Wings and Blackhawks 100.00 200.00
7 Penguins and Flyers 50.00 100.00
8 Panthers and Lightning 20.00 50.00
9 Toronto Maple Leafs 75.00 125.00

2013-14 Panini National Treasures Sweeter by the Dozen Jerseys

SDBOS Boston Stars 50.00 100.00
SDBUF Buffalo Stars 30.00 60.00
SDLA Kings/Ducks Stars 40.00 80.00
SDMTL Montreal Stars 75.00 150.00
SDNO1 NHL Stars 40.00 100.00
SDNOS NHL Stars 30.00 60.00
SDNY Devils/Rangers Stars 60.00 120.00
SDOR6 Original 6 Stars 30.00 60.00
SDRD1 1st Round Rookies 40.00 100.00
SDTOR Toronto Stars 90.00 150.00
SDWC Winter Classic 40.00 80.00

2013-14 Panini National Treasures Timeline Jerseys

*PRIME/35-50: .5X TO 1.2X BASIC JSY/99
*PRIME/25: .6X TO 1.5X BASIC JSY/99
*PRIME/15: 1.5X TO 4X BASIC JSY/99
*PATCH/20-25: .6X TO 1.5X BASIC JSY/99
TAF Adam Foote/99 6.00 15.00
TAM Al MacInnis/99 6.00 15.00
TAO Alex Ovechkin/99 10.00 25.00
TBB Brian Bellows/99 5.00 12.00
TBH Braden Holtby/99 6.00 15.00
TBL Brooks Laich/99 8.00 20.00
TBR Bobby Ryan/99 4.00 10.00
TBS Brendan Shanahan/99 8.00 20.00
TCC Chris Chelios/99 5.00 12.00
TCN Cam Neely/99 6.00 15.00
TCS1 Cory Schneider/99 5.00 12.00
TCS2 Charlie Simmer/99 3.00 8.00
TDC Dan Cloutier/99 4.00 10.00
TDG Doug Gilmour/00 8.00 20.00
TEK Erik Karlsson/99 8.00 20.00
TEL Eric Lindros/99 10.00 25.00
TEM Evgeni Malkin/99 10.00 25.00
TGH Gordie Howe/25 25.00 50.00
TGL1 Guy Lafleur/99 10.00 25.00
TGL2 Gabriel Landeskog/99 6.00 15.00
TGP Gilbert Perreault/99 10.00 25.00
TIL Igor Larionov/99 8.00 20.00
TJB Jamie Benn/99 5.00 12.00
TJS Jordan Staal/99 4.00 10.00
TJV John Vanbiesbrouck/99 8.00 20.00
TKL Ken Linseman/99 6.00 15.00
TLC Logan Couture/99 6.00 15.00
TLM Lanny McDonald/99 6.00 15.00
TMD Marcel Dionne/99 12.00 30.00
TML Milan Lucic/99 5.00 12.00
TNL Nicklas Lidstrom/99 8.00 20.00
TPC Paul Coffey/99 5.00 12.00
TPS1 Patrick Sharp/99 5.00 12.00
TPS2 P.K. Subban/99 8.00 20.00
TRB Rob Blake/99 5.00 12.00
TRF Ron Francis/99 6.00 15.00
TRL Reggie Leach/99 6.00 15.00
TRT Rick Tocchet/99 6.00 15.00
TSC Sidney Crosby/99 12.00 30.00
TSD Shane Doan/99 4.00 10.00
TSM Stan Mikita/99 8.00 20.00
TSS Steven Stamkos/99 6.00 15.00
TSW Shea Weber/99 4.00 10.00
TTB Tom Barrasso/99 12.00 30.00
TTO T.J. Oshie/99 6.00 15.00
TTR Tuukka Rask/99 8.00 20.00
TTS1 Tyler Seguin/99 10.00 25.00
TTS2 Teemu Selanne/99 12.00 30.00
TTT Tim Thomas/99 5.00 12.00
TVL Vincent Lecavalier/99 5.00 12.00

2013-14 Panini National Treasures Treasure Chest Jerseys Booklet

*PRIME/25: .5X TO 1.2X BASIC JSY/50
TCDRC Rookie Stars 80.00 150.00
TCPTS All Time Points Leaders 150.00 250.00
TCWIN 200 Win Goalies 150.00 250.00
TCPHI Philadelphia Stars 75.00 150.00
TCSTR Dallas/Minnesota Stars 75.00 150.00
TCCAN Team Canada 75.00 150.00
TCUSA Team USA 60.00 120.00
TCWJC Junior World Champs 50.00 120.00
TCRKS Rookie Stars 50.00 120.00

2013-14 Panini National Treasures Treasure Hunting Draft Plaques

1 Nathan MacKinnon/25 25.00 60.00
2 Aleksander Barkov/25 15.00 40.00
3 Seth Jones/25 10.00 25.00
4 Elias Lindholm/25 12.00 30.00
5 Sean Monahan/25 12.00 30.00
7 Valeri Nichushkin/25 10.00 25.00

2013-14 Panini National Treasures Treasured Trophies Autographs Art Ross

1 Gordie Howe 50.00 100.00
3 Marcel Dionne 20.00 50.00
4 Jaromir Jagr 50.00 100.00
5 Mario Lemieux 75.00 120.00
6 Martin St. Louis 15.00 40.00
7 Henrik Sedin 20.00 50.00
8 Daniel Sedin 20.00 50.00
9 Sidney Crosby 100.00 200.00

2013-14 Panini National Treasures Treasured Trophies Autographs Calder

1 Jonathan Huberdeau 15.00 40.00
2 Gabriel Landeskog 12.00 30.00
3 Jeff Skinner 20.00 50.00
5 Martin Brodeur 40.00 100.00
6 Ed Belfour 30.00 80.00
7 Brian Leetch 12.00 30.00
8 Joe Nieuwendyk 12.00 30.00
9 Luc Robitaille 15.00 40.00
10 Mario Lemieux 75.00 120.00

2013-14 Panini National Treasures Treasured Trophies Autographs Conn Smythe

2 Jonathan Quick EXCH 30.00 60.00
3 Al MacInnis 20.00 50.00
4 Jonathan Toews 50.00 100.00
5 Evgeni Malkin 30.00 80.00
6 Joe Nieuwendyk 12.00 30.00
7 Brad Richards 15.00 40.00
8 Ron Hextall 30.00 60.00
9 Jean-Sebastien Giguere 15.00 40.00
10 Brian Leetch 12.00 30.00

2013-14 Panini National Treasures Treasured Trophies Autographs Hart

1 Sidney Crosby 100.00 200.00
2 Alex Ovechkin EXCH 20.00 50.00
3 Mark Messier 40.00 80.00
4 Henrik Sedin 20.00 50.00
5 Joe Thornton 25.00 60.00
6 Martin St. Louis 15.00 40.00
7 Joe Sakic 25.00 60.00
8 Jaromir Jagr 50.00 100.00
9 Brett Hull 20.00 50.00
10 Mario Lemieux 75.00 120.00

2013-14 Panini National Treasures Treasured Trophies Autographs Lady Byng

1 Martin St. Louis 15.00 40.00
3 Brad Richards 15.00 40.00
4 Ron Francis 20.00 50.00
5 Joe Sakic 30.00 80.00
6 Pierre Turgeon 20.00 50.00
7 Brett Hull 20.00 50.00
8 Bobby Hull 25.00 60.00
9 Mike Bossy 15.00 40.00
10 Stan Mikita 25.00 60.00

2013-14 Panini National Treasures Treasured Trophies Autographs Norris

1 Nicklas Lidstrom 20.00 50.00
2 Chris Pronger 12.00 30.00
3 Al MacInnis 20.00 50.00
5 Brian Leetch 12.00 30.00
6 Chris Chelios 30.00 80.00
7 Paul Coffey 15.00 40.00
8 Ray Bourque 30.00 80.00
9 Denis Potvin 15.00 40.00
10 Larry Robinson 15.00 40.00

2013-14 Panini National Treasures Treasured Trophies Autographs Selke

1 Jonathan Toews 60.00 120.00
2 Patrice Bergeron EXCH 20.00 50.00
3 Ryan Kesler 20.00 50.00
5 Steve Yzerman 50.00 100.00
6 Ron Francis 20.00 50.00
7 Doug Gilmour 20.00 50.00
8 Bobby Clarke 30.00 80.00
9 Bob Gainey 15.00 40.00
10 Rod Brind'Amour 12.00 30.00

2013-14 Panini National Treasures Treasured Trophies Autographs Vezina

1 Henrik Lundqvist 40.00 100.00
2 Ron Hextall 30.00 60.00
3 Patrick Roy 75.00 150.00
4 Ryan Miller 12.00 30.00
5 Tim Thomas 20.00 50.00
6 Martin Brodeur EXCH 40.00 100.00
7 Ed Belfour 40.00 80.00
8 Grant Fuhr 20.00 50.00
9 John Vanbiesbrouck 50.00 100.00
10 Bernie Parent 20.00 50.00

2013-14 Panini National Treasures Trio Autographs

*GOLD/15-20: .5X TO 1.2X BASIC DUAL AU
1 Kmpr/Zucker/Granlnd/75 15.00 40.00
2 Kostka/Palat/Hedman/75 10.00 25.00
3 Ovchkn/Ykpov/Dtsyk/50 50.00 125.00
4 Yandle/Smith/Doan/60 12.00 30.00
5 Boyes/Shore/Luongo/75 10.00 25.00
6 Lrnov/Ykpov/Tretiak/75 30.00 80.00
7 Glncrss/Cndri/Brtschi/60 8.00 20.00
8 Wtsn/Frsbrg/Maznec/20 15.00 40.00
9 Hnrq/Andry/Matteau/25 12.00 30.00
10 Clarke/Howe/Kerr/50 15.00 40.00
11 Chlios/Rnick/Hebert/50 20.00 50.00
13 Jhnsn/Kessel/Vanek/25 15.00 40.00
14 Coyle/Kmper/Parise/75 25.00 60.00
15 Ptrnglo/Jskin/Reaves/50 12.00 30.00
16 Nchlls/Dghty/Robitlle/35 20.00 50.00
17 Emelin/Rbnsn/Savrd/50 15.00 40.00
18 Ryan/Andrsn/Gryba/50 12.00 30.00
19 Kuempr/Zatkff/Mrazk/75 15.00 40.00
20 Boyle/Irwin/Petrecki/25 12.00 30.00
21 Silfver/Eriksn/Lidstrm/75 12.00 30.00
22 Benn/Bwmstr/Toews/30 20.00 50.00
23 Glchnyk/Gllghr/Thomas/25 30.00 80.00
25 Prout/Johnson/Foligno/75 8.00 20.00

2013-14 Panini National Treasures Triple Memorabilia Autographs

1 Gordie Howe 40.00 100.00
2 Mark Messier 30.00 80.00
3 Joe Sakic 15.00 40.00
4 Alex Ovechkin 60.00 150.00
5 Pavel Datsyuk 25.00 60.00
6 Brendan Shanahan 15.00 40.00
7 Brad Richards 15.00 40.00
8 Cam Neely 12.00 30.00
9 Alex Galchenyuk 20.00 50.00
10 Teemu Selanne 30.00 80.00
11 Patrick Roy 40.00 100.00
12 Carey Price 30.00 80.00
13 Rick Nash 12.00 30.00
14 Bernie Parent 20.00 50.00
15 Bobby Clarke 25.00 60.00
16 Brendan Gallagher 12.00 30.00
17 Taylor Hall 15.00 40.00
18 Jeremy Roenick 25.00 60.00
19 Vladislav Tretiak 20.00 50.00
20 Ron Francis 20.00 50.00
21 Martin Brodeur 40.00 100.00
22 Yvan Cournoyer 12.00 30.00

2012 Panini NHL Draft

COMPLETE SET (8) 7.50 15.00
JJ Jaromir Jagr .60 1.50
ML Mario Lemieux 1.25 3.00
SS Steven Stamkos .75 2.00
TH Taylor Hall .75 2.00
MAF Marc-Andre Fleury .50 1.25
RNH Ryan Nugent-Hopkins 2.50 6.00
SC1 Mario Lemieux SP 2.00 5.00
SC2 Evgeni Malkin SP 1.25 3.00

2013-14 Panini Playbook

1 Ryan Getzlaf 2.00 5.00
2 Jakob Silfverberg 1.25 3.00
3 Corey Perry 3.00 8.00
4 Cam Fowler 2.00 5.00
5 Patrice Bergeron 2.50 6.00
6 Jarome Iginla 2.50 6.00
7 Zdeno Chara 2.00 5.00
8 Tuukka Rask 2.50 6.00
9 Cody Hodgson 1.25 3.00
10 Ryan Miller 2.00 5.00
11 Curtis Glencross 1.25 3.00
12 Mark Giordano 2.00 5.00
13 Eric Staal 2.50 6.00
14 Jordan Staal 1.50 4.00
15 Patrick Kane 4.00 10.00
16 Jonathan Toews 3.00 8.00
17 Marian Hossa 2.00 5.00
18 Corey Crawford 2.50 6.00
19 Matt Duchene 2.00 5.00
20 Gabriel Landeskog 2.50 6.00
21 Marian Gaborik 2.00 5.00
22 Sergei Bobrovsky 3.00 8.00
23 Tyler Seguin 2.50 6.00
24 Jamie Benn 2.00 5.00
25 Daniel Alfredsson 2.00 5.00
26 Henrik Zetterberg 2.50 6.00
27 Pavel Datsyuk 3.00 8.00
20 Jimmy Howard 2.50 6.00
29 Ryan Nugent-Hopkins 2.50 6.00
30 Taylor Hall 2.00 5.00
31 Jordan Eberle 2.00 5.00
32 Ilya Bryzgalov 2.00 5.00
33 Jacob Markstrom 2.00 5.00
34 Tim Thomas 2.00 5.00
35 Dustin Brown 2.00 5.00
36 Mike Richards 1.50 4.00
37 Drew Doughty 2.50 6.00
38 Jonathan Quick 2.50 6.00
39 Zach Parise 2.00 5.00
40 Ryan Suter 1.50 4.00
41 Max Pacioretty 2.00 5.00
42 Lars Eller 1.25 3.00
43 P.K. Subban 2.50 6.00
44 Carey Price 4.00 10.00
45 Shea Weber 1.50 4.00
46 Pekka Rinne 2.00 5.00
47 Jaromir Jagr 6.00 15.00
48 Martin Brodeur 5.00 12.00
49 John Tavares 3.00 8.00
50 Casey Cizikas 1.25 3.00
51 Derek Stepan 1.25 3.00
52 Rick Nash 2.00 5.00
53 Derick Brassard 1.25 3.00
54 Henrik Lundqvist 5.00 12.00
55 Bobby Ryan 1.50 4.00
56 Jason Spezza 2.00 5.00
57 Claude Giroux 2.00 5.00
58 Vincent Lecavalier 2.00 5.00
59 Shane Doan 1.50 4.00
60 Oliver Ekman-Larsson 2.00 5.00
61 Sidney Crosby 8.00 20.00
62 Evgeni Malkin 4.00 10.00
63 Kris Letang 2.50 6.00
64 Marc-Andre Fleury 4.00 10.00
65 Joe Thornton 3.00 8.00
66 Joe Pavelski 2.50 6.00
67 Logan Couture 2.50 6.00
68 Patrick Marleau 2.00 5.00
69 David Backes 1.25 3.00
70 Alex Pietrangelo 1.50 4.00
71 Steven Stamkos 4.00 10.00
72 Martin St. Louis 2.00 5.00
73 Nazem Kadri 2.50 6.00
74 Phil Kessel 2.00 5.00

75 David Clarkson 1.25 3.00
76 Jonathan Bernier 1.50 4.00
77 Daniel Sedin 2.50 6.00
78 Henrik Sedin 2.50 6.00
79 Ryan Kesler 2.00 5.00
80 Roberto Luongo 3.00 8.00
81 Alex Ovechkin 8.00 20.00
82 Nicklas Backstrom 2.00 5.00
83 Andrew Ladd 1.25 3.00
84 Dustin Byfuglien 2.00 5.00
85 Joe Sakic 4.00 10.00
86 Guy Lafleur 2.50 6.00
87 Mike Modano 3.00 8.00
88 Ed Belfour 2.00 5.00
89 Eric Lindros 3.00 8.00
90 Ron Hextall 2.00 5.00
91 Gordie Howe 6.00 15.00
92 Steve Yzerman 5.00 12.00
93 Pavel Bure 2.00 5.00
94 John Vanbiesbrouck 2.00 5.00
95 Mark Messier 4.00 10.00
96 Mike Richter 2.00 5.00
97 Doug Gilmour 2.50 6.00
98 Felix Potvin 3.00 8.00
99 Ray Bourque 3.00 8.00
100 Patrick Roy 5.00 12.00
101 Sami Vatanen JSY AU RC 8.00 20.00
102 Carl Soderberg JSY AU RC 8.00 20.00
103 M.Grigorenko JSY AU RC 5.00 12.00
104 Max Reinhart JSY AU RC EXCH 8.00 20.00
105 Jared Staal JSY AU RC 8.00 20.00
106 Emerson Etem JSY AU RC 8.00 20.00
107 Antoine Roussel JSY AU RC 8.00 20.00
108 Alex Chiasson JSY AU RC 8.00 20.00
109 Charlie Coyle JSY AU RC 12.00 30.00
110 Danny DeKeyser JSY AU RC 10.00 25.00
111 Petr Mrazek JSY AU RC 15.00 40.00
112 Nick Bjugstad JSY AU RC 10.00 25.00
113 Drew Shore JSY AU RC 6.00 15.00
114 Tanner Pearson JSY AU RC 8.00 20.00
115 Brock Nelson JSY AU RC 15.00 40.00
116 Jonas Brodin JSY AU RC 10.00 25.00
117 Mikael Granlund JSY AU RC 12.00 30.00
118 B.Gallagher JSY AU RC 20.00 50.00
119 Filip Forsberg JSY AU RC 20.00 50.00
120 Stefan Matteau JSY AU RC 6.00 15.00
121 Thomas Hickey JSY AU RC 6.00 15.00
122 J.T. Miller JSY AU RC EXCH 20.00 50.00
123 Viktor Fasth JSY AU RC 8.00 20.00
124 V.Tarasenko JSY AU RC 20.00 50.00
125 Dmitrij Jaskin JSY AU RC 8.00 20.00
126 Alex Killorn JSY AU RC 12.00 30.00
127 Cory Conacher JSY AU RC 5.00 12.00
129 Nicklas Jensen JSY AU RC 6.00 15.00
130 Tom Wilson JSY AU RC 15.00 40.00
131 Nail Yakupov JSY AU RC 15.00 40.00
132 Alex Galchenyuk JSY AU RC 40.00 80.00
133 Dougie Hamilton JSY AU RC 15.00 40.00
134 Justin Schultz JSY AU RC 8.00 20.00
135 Tyler Toffoli JSY AU RC 15.00 40.00
136 J.Huberdeau JSY AU RC 20.00 50.00
137 N.MacKinnon JSY AU RC 30.00 80.00
138 Seth Jones JSY AU RC 15.00 40.00
139 Morgan Rielly JSY AU RC 20.00 50.00
140 Aleksander Barkov JSY AU RC 15.00 40.00
141 Sean Monahan JSY AU RC 20.00 50.00
142 Valeri Nichushkin JSY AU RC 15.00 40.00
143 Ryan Murray JSY AU RC 8.00 20.00
144 Tomas Hertl JSY AU RC 15.00 40.00
145 Elias Lindholm JSY AU RC 20.00 50.00
146 Jacob Trouba JSY AU RC 15.00 40.00
147 Matt Dumba JSY AU RC 5.00 12.00
148 Scott Laughton JSY AU RC 10.00 25.00
149 Beau Bennett JSY AU RC 10.00 25.00
150 Boone Jenner JSY AU RC 15.00 40.00
151 Ryan Murphy JSY AU RC EXCH 8.00 20.00
152 Hampus Lindholm JSY AU RC 12.00 30.00
153 Joakim Nordstrom JSY AU RC 6.00 15.00
154 Olli Maatta JSY AU RC 12.00 30.00
155 Ryan Spooner JSY AU RC 8.00 20.00
156 Jack Campbell JSY AU RC 20.00 50.00
157 Nathan Beaulieu JSY AU RC 5.00 12.00
158 Jamie Oleksiak JSY AU RC 6.00 15.00
159 Z.Girgensons JSY AU RC EXCH 12.00 30.00
160 Jon Merrill JSY AU RC 8.00 20.00
161 John Gibson JSY AU RC 15.00 40.00
162 Matt Nieto JSY AU RC 6.00 15.00
163 Michael Bournival JSY AU RC 8.00 20.00
164 Anthony Peluso JSY AU RC 5.00 12.00
165 R.Strome JSY AU RC EXCH 20.00 40.00
166 Tomas Jurco JSY AU RC 10.00 25.00
167 Dylan McIlrath JSY AU RC 8.00 20.00
168 Lucas Lessio JSY AU RC 5.00 12.00

2013-14 Panini Playbook Gold

*GOLD/25: 1X TO 2.5X BASIC CARDS
18 Corey Crawford 6.00 15.00
82 Nicklas Backstrom 5.00 12.00

2013-14 Panini Playbook Rookie Jerseys Autographs Prime

*PRIME/25: .8X TO 2X BASIC JSY AU/199
135 Tyler Toffoli 40.00 100.00
137 Nathan MacKinnon 300.00 500.00
161 John Gibson 60.00 120.00

2013-14 Panini Playbook Armory

AAH Adam Henrique 15.00 40.00
ABH Brett Hull 40.00 100.00
AIL Igor Larionov 20.00 50.00
AJP Joe Pavelski 25.00 60.00
AMG Marian Gaborik 20.00 50.00
ABRI Brad Richards 20.00 50.00
ADST Derek Stepan 12.00 30.00
AJVR James van Riemsdyk 15.00 40.00
ALUC Luc Robitaille 20.00 50.00
AMHE Milan Hejduk 15.00 40.00
AMRI Mike Richards 15.00 40.00
AOVI Alex Ovechkin 80.00 200.00

2013-14 Panini Playbook AUTObiography

AUAL Andrew Ladd 4.00 10.00
AUAN Antti Niemi 5.00 12.00
AUBH Brett Hull 15.00 30.00
AUBR Bobby Ryan 5.00 12.00
AUBSD Brandon Saad 5.00 12.00
AUCN Cam Neely 12.50 25.00
AUDBR Daniel Briere 6.00 15.00
AUDCI Dino Ciccarelli 6.00 15.00
AUDP David Perron 5.00 12.00
AUDR Derek Roy 4.00 10.00
AUHL Henrik Lundqvist 20.00 40.00
AUJBE Jonathan Bernier 5.00 12.00
AUJCO Joe Colborne 4.00 10.00
AUJI Jarome Iginla 15.00 30.00
AUJM Jacob Markstrom 6.00 15.00
AUJNE James Neal 4.00 10.00
AUJP Joe Pavelski 8.00 20.00
AUJS Joe Sakic 12.00 30.00
AUJTO Jonathan Toews 20.00 50.00
AULE Loui Eriksson 12.00 30.00
AUMB Martin Brodeur 20.00 40.00
AUMS Mike Smith 8.00 20.00
AUMT Marty Turco 6.00 15.00
AUNL Nicklas Lidstrom 8.00 20.00
AUPB Pavel Bure 15.00 30.00
AURB Ray Bourque 20.00 40.00
AURK Ryan Kesler 6.00 15.00
AURNH Ryan Nugent-Hopkins 8.00 20.00
AUTE Tony Esposito 8.00 20.00
AUTL Trevor Linden 8.00 20.00
AUTS Tyler Seguin 12.50 25.00
AUTTH Tim Thomas 10.00 25.00
AUVL Vincent Lecavalier 8.00 20.00
AUYC Yvan Cournoyer 8.00 20.00

2013-14 Panini Playbook Breakout Jerseys

*PRIME/25: .6X TO 1.5X BASIC JSY/180-199
*PRIME/25: .5X TO 1.2X BASIC JSY/25
BAB Aleksander Barkov 6.00 15.00
BAG Alex Galchenyuk 8.00 20.00
BBB Beau Bennett 4.00 10.00
BBG Brendan Gallagher 8.00 20.00
BBJE Boone Jenner 6.00 15.00
BBNE Brock Nelson 6.00 15.00
BCB Chris Brown 2.00 5.00
BCON Cory Conacher 2.00 5.00
BDDK Danny DeKeyser/180 4.00 10.00
BDH Dougie Hamilton 6.00 15.00
BDMI Dylan McIlrath 2.00 5.00
BFA Frederik Andersen 8.00 20.00
BFC Frank Corrado 2.50 6.00
BFF Filip Forsberg/25 12.00 30.00
BJGI John Gibson 8.00 20.00
BJH Jonathan Huberdeau 6.00 15.00
BJME Jon Merrill 5.00 12.00
BJNO Joakim Nordstrom 2.50 6.00
BJTM J.T. Miller 8.00 20.00
BJTR Jacob Trouba 5.00 12.00
BJUS Justin Schultz 3.00 8.00
BMAR Mark Arcobello 3.00 8.00
BMGR Mikael Granlund 5.00 12.00
BMIK Mikhail Grigorenko 2.00 5.00
BNJ Nicklas Jensen 2.50 6.00
BNMK Nathan MacKinnon 10.00 25.00
BNY Nail Yakupov 5.00 12.00
BRBE Reto Berra 3.00 8.00
BRLY Morgan Rielly 6.00 15.00
BRMR Ryan Murray 5.00 12.00
BRS Ryan Strome 5.00 12.00
BSJ Seth Jones 6.00 15.00
BSL Scott Laughton 4.00 10.00
BSMO Sean Monahan 5.00 12.00
BTHE Tomas Hertl 8.00 20.00
BTJU Tomas Jurco 6.00 15.00
BTMG Tye McGinn 3.00 8.00
BTP Tanner Pearson 3.00 8.00
BTW Tom Wilson 6.00 15.00
BVN Valeri Nichushkin 6.00 15.00

2013-14 Panini Playbook Double Rookie Classbook Jerseys

*PRIME/50: .5X TO 1.2X BASIC DUAL
*PATCH/25: .8X TO 2X BASIC DUAL JSY
DRBD N.Beaulieu/J.Devane 8.00 20.00
DRBM B.Bennett/O.Maatta 15.00 40.00
DRCG C.Conacher/Z.Girgensons 12.00 30.00
DRDKR D.DeKeyser/M.Rielly 15.00 40.00
DREN E.Etem/M.Nieto 8.00 20.00
DRFD F.Forsberg/M.Dumba 15.00 40.00
DRGH A.Galchenyuk/T.Hertl 12.00 30.00
DRGM B.Gallagher/S.Monahan 15.00 40.00
DRGN M.Granlund/J.Nordstrom 8.00 20.00
DRGR M.Grigorenko/R.Ristolainen 12.00 30.00
DRHB J.Huberdeau/A.Barkov 12.00 30.00
DRHJ D.Hamilton/S.Jones 10.00 25.00
DRLJ S.Laughton/B.Jenner 15.00 40.00
DRMGS T.McGinn/R.Strome 12.00 30.00
DRMM J.Miller/J.Merrill 20.00 50.00
DRMU R.Murphy/R.Murray 8.00 20.00
DRPC A.Peluso/K.Connauton 6.00 15.00
DRPL T.Pearson/L.Lessio 8.00 20.00
DRSB R.Spooner/M.Bournival 8.00 20.00
DRST J.Schultz/J.Trouba 8.00 20.00
DRTM T.Toffoli/C.Murphy 10.00 25.00
DRTN V.Tarasenko/V.Nichushkin 12.00 30.00
DRTZ J.Tinordi/N.Zadorov 8.00 20.00
DRVL S.Vatanen/H.Lindholm 10.00 25.00
DRWL T.Wilson/E.Lindholm 20.00 50.00
DRYMK N.Yakupov/N.MacKinnon 15.00 40.00

2013-14 Panini Playbook Fabled Fabrics

FFBC Bobby Clarke 8.00 20.00
FFGH Gordie Howe 15.00 40.00
FFMD Marcel Dionne 6.00 15.00
FFPE Phil Esposito 8.00 20.00
FFRV Rogie Vachon 6.00 15.00
FFSM Stan Mikita 6.00 15.00
FFYC Yvan Cournoyer 5.00 12.00
FFBSA Borje Salming 5.00 12.00
FFBSY Mike Bossy 5.00 12.00
FFRMI Rick Middleton 3.00 8.00

2013-14 Panini Playbook First Drafts Signatures

FDZG Zemgus Girgensons 8.00 20.00
FDMG Mikhail Grigorenko
(inserted in 2013-14 Panini Prime) 3.00 8.00
FDJTM J.T. Miller 3.00 8.00
FDAB Aleksander Barkov 10.00 25.00
FDAG Alex Galchenyuk 12.00 30.00
FDAW Austin Watson 2.50 6.00
FDBB Beau Bennett 8.00 20.00
FDBNE Brock Nelson 6.00 15.00
FDCOY Charlie Coyle 5.00 12.00
FDDH Dougie Hamilton 10.00 25.00
FDEE Emerson Etem 3.00 8.00
FDELI Elias Lindholm 8.00 20.00
FDFF Filip Forsberg 12.00 30.00
FDHLI Hampus Lindholm 5.00 12.00
FDJB Jonas Brodin 4.00 10.00
FDJH Jonathan Huberdeau 6.00 15.00
FDJSC Jaden Schwartz 8.00 20.00
FDJT John Tavares 12.50 25.00
FDJTH Joe Thornton 10.00 25.00
FDJTR Jacob Trouba 10.00 25.00
FDMAF Marc-Andre Fleury 12.50 25.00
FDMDB Matt Dumba 2.00 5.00
FDMSC Mark Scheifele 10.00 25.00
FDNBE Nathan Beaulieu 5.00 12.00
FDNJ Nicklas Jensen 2.50 6.00
FDNMK Nathan MacKinnon 30.00 80.00
FDNY Nail Yakupov 10.00 25.00
FDOVI Alex Ovechkin 30.00 60.00
FDPK Patrick Kane 25.00 50.00
FDRLY Morgan Rielly 8.00 20.00
FDRMR Ryan Murray 5.00 12.00
FDRN Rick Nash 6.00 15.00
FDRNH Ryan Nugent-Hopkins 8.00 20.00
FDRSH Riley Sheahan 4.00 10.00
FDSB Sven Baertschi 5.00 12.00
FDSC Sidney Crosby 60.00 120.00
FDSJ Seth Jones 6.00 15.00
FDSL Scott Laughton 4.00 10.00
FDSMA Stefan Matteau 2.50 6.00
FDSMO Sean Monahan 5.00 12.00
FDTH Taylor Hall 6.00 15.00
FDTHE Tomas Hertl 6.00 15.00
FDTW Tom Wilson 6.00 15.00
FDVL Vincent Lecavalier 6.00 15.00
FDVN Valeri Nichushkin 6.00 15.00

2013-14 Panini Playbook First Round Edition Jerseys Autographs

*PRIME/25: .6X TO 1.5X BASIC JSY AU
FRAB Aleksander Barkov 12.00 30.00
FRAG Alex Galchenyuk 25.00 60.00
FRDH Dougie Hamilton 12.00 30.00
FRELI Elias Lindholm 6.00 15.00
FRFF Filip Forsberg 25.00 60.00
FRJH Jonathan Huberdeau 15.00 40.00
FRJTR Jacob Trouba 15.00 40.00
FRMDB Matt Dumba 10.00 25.00
FRMGR Mikael Granlund 12.00 30.00
FRMIK Mikhail Grigorenko 5.00 12.00
FRNMK Nathan MacKinnon 30.00 80.00
FRNY Nail Yakupov 15.00 40.00
FRRLY Morgan Rielly 12.00 30.00
FRRMP Ryan Murphy 8.00 20.00
FRRMR Ryan Murray 12.00 30.00
FRSJ Seth Jones 15.00 40.00
FRSMO Sean Monahan 10.00 25.00
FRTHE Tomas Hertl 15.00 40.00
FRTW Tom Wilson 10.00 25.00
FRVN Valeri Nichushkin 15.00 40.00
FRVT Vladimir Tarasenko 20.00 50.00

2013-14 Panini Playbook Limited Edition Jerseys

*PRIME/25: .6X TO 1.5X BASIC JSY/99
LEAH Adam Henrique 4.00 10.00
LEAP Alex Pietrangelo 4.00 10.00
LEAT Alex Tanguay 5.00 12.00
LEBN Bernie Nicholls 4.00 10.00
LEBR Bobby Ryan 4.00 10.00
LEBW Blake Wheeler 5.00 12.00
LECN Cam Neely 5.00 12.00
LEDS Daniel Sedin 6.00 15.00
LEEL Eric Lindros 8.00 20.00
LEGL Gabriel Landeskog 6.00 15.00
LEJJ Jaromir Jagr 6.00 15.00
LEJR Jeremy Roenick 8.00 20.00
LEJT John Tavares 8.00 20.00
LEMH Marian Hossa 5.00 12.00
LEML Mario Lemieux 8.00 20.00
LEMM Mark Messier 10.00 25.00
LEMO Mike Modano 8.00 20.00
LENL Nicklas Lidstrom 5.00 12.00
LEPB Pavel Bure 5.00 12.00
LEPC Paul Coffey 5.00 12.00
LERF Ron Francis 6.00 15.00
LERM Ryan Miller 5.00 12.00
LERN Rick Nash 5.00 12.00
LESC Sidney Crosby 10.00 25.00
LESK Saku Koivu 5.00 12.00
LESS Steven Stamkos 6.00 15.00
LESW Shea Weber 4.00 10.00
LESY Steve Yzerman 8.00 20.00
LETH Taylor Hall 5.00 12.00
LETS Tyler Seguin 6.00 15.00
LEABU Alexandre Burrows 3.00 8.00
LEAKO Anze Kopitar 8.00 20.00
LEAMI Al MacInnis 6.00 15.00
LEDKR David Krejci 5.00 12.00
LEDST Derek Stepan 3.00 8.00
LEJBE Jonathan Bernier 4.00 10.00
LEJHA Jaroslav Halak 5.00 12.00
LEJOS Jordan Staal 4.00 10.00
LEJTH Joe Thornton 8.00 20.00
LELEL Lars Eller 3.00 8.00
LEMGI Mark Giordano 5.00 12.00
LEMHZ Martin Hanzal 3.00 8.00
LEOVI Alex Ovechkin 20.00 50.00
LEPRI Pekka Rinne 5.00 12.00
LERBL Rob Blake 5.00 12.00
LERNH Ryan Nugent-Hopkins 6.00 15.00
LESJN Matt Stajan 3.00 8.00
LETTH Tim Thomas 5.00 12.00
LEVTR Vladislav Tretiak 10.00 25.00

2013-14 Panini Playbook Nicknames

NBH Brett Hull 20.00 40.00
NJTO Jonathan Toews 50.00 100.00
NJV John Vanbiesbrouck 30.00 80.00
NML Mario Lemieux 30.00 80.00
NOVI Alex Ovechkin 30.00 80.00
NPD Pavel Datsyuk 30.00 60.00
NSS Steven Stamkos 25.00 60.00
NSY Steve Yzerman 30.00 80.00
NTMU Teemu Selanne 40.00 80.00

013-14 Panini Playbook Signature Jerseys Booklet

*PRIME/25: .8X TO 2X BASIC JSY AU/100
SBDB David Backes/100 10.00 25.00
SBHL Henrik Lundqvist/100 30.00 60.00
SBJE Jordan Eberle/100 10.00 25.00
SBJHO Jimmy Howard/100 12.00 30.00
SBJT John Tavares/100 25.00 50.00
SBJTO Jonathan Toews/100 40.00 100.00
SBLC Logan Couture/100 8.00 20.00
SBMC Mike Cammalleri/100 8.00 20.00
SBMS Mike Smith/100 12.00 30.00
SBPK Patrick Kane/41 50.00 100.00
SBPS Patrick Sharp/100 30.00 60.00
SBRG Ryan Getzlaf/100 12.00 30.00
SBRK Ryan Kesler/100 12.00 30.00
SBSC Sidney Crosby/22 100.00 175.00
SBTS Tyler Seguin/100 30.00 60.00

2013-14 Panini Playbook Split Decisions Jerseys

*PRIME/25: .6X TO 1.5X BASIC JSY
SDBHY Braden Holtby 10.00 25.00
SDCP Carey Price 15.00 40.00
SDDDU Devan Dubnyk 6.00 15.00
SDHL Henrik Lundqvist 20.00 50.00
SDJHI Jonas Hiller 6.00 15.00
SDJQ Jonathan Quick 10.00 25.00
SDKLE Kari Lehtonen 6.00 15.00
SDLU Roberto Luongo 12.00 30.00
SDPR Patrick Roy 20.00 50.00
SDPRI Pekka Rinne 8.00 20.00
SDRHX Ron Hextall 8.00 20.00
SDSTM Steve Mason 6.00 15.00

2013-14 Panini Playbook Storied Signatures

STAD Alex Delvecchio 10.00 25.00
STBC Bobby Clarke 15.00 40.00
STBP Bernie Parent 15.00 30.00
STBT Bryan Trottier 10.00 25.00
STGH Gordie Howe 60.00 120.00
STLR Larry Robinson 8.00 20.00
STML Mario Lemieux 50.00 100.00
STMM Mark Messier 20.00 40.00
STPE Phil Esposito 15.00 30.00
STPR Patrick Roy 50.00 100.00
STSM Stan Mikita 12.00 30.00
STSY Steve Yzerman 40.00 80.00
STBSY Mike Bossy 15.00 30.00
STBWR Johnny Bower 10.00 25.00
STJET Bobby Hull 20.00 40.00

2013-14 Panini Playbook Then and Now Jerseys

*PRIME/25: .6X TO 1.5X BASIC JSY
TNCA Craig Anderson 12.00 30.00
TNCN Cam Neely 12.00 30.00
TNJFC Jeff Carter 10.00 25.00
TNJS Joe Sakic 25.00 60.00
TNJSG Jean-Sebastien Giguere 15.00 40.00
TNMRI Mike Richards 10.00 25.00
TNPB Pavel Bure 25.00 50.00
TNRB Ray Bourque 20.00 50.00
TNRN Rick Nash 12.00 30.00
TNSVA Semyon Varlamov 15.00 40.00
TNTMU Teemu Selanne 30.00 60.00
TNTS Tyler Seguin 15.00 40.00

2011-12 Panini Player of the Day

COMPLETE SET (5) 7.50 15.00
POD1 Alex Ovechkin 2.50 6.00
POD2 Tim Thomas .60 1.50
POD3 Steven Stamkos 1.25 3.00
POD4 Ryan Nugent-Hopkins 5.00 12.00
POD5 Gabriel Landeskog 1.50 4.00

2011-12 Panini Player of the Day Black Border

COMPLETE SET (9)
PODAH Adam Henrique 1.25 3.00
PODAP Aaron Palushaj .50 1.25
PODBG Blake Geoffrion .50 1.25
PODBS Brandon Saad 1.00 2.50
PODCK Carl Klingberg .50 1.25
PODGN Greg Nemisz .50 1.25
PODJM John Moore .50 1.25
PODMK Marcus Kruger .75 2.00
PODSC Sean Couturier 1.00 2.50
PODPKS P.K. Subban .75 2.00

2013-14 Panini Player of the Day

COMPLETE SET (17) 8.00 20.00
*THICK STOCK: .5X TO 1.2X BASIC CARDS
1 John Tavares .60 1.50
2 Steven Stamkos .75 2.00
3 Joe Thornton .60 1.50
4 Jamie Benn .40 1.00
5 Evgeni Malkin .75 2.00
6 Corey Crawford .50 1.25
7 Corey Perry .60 1.50
8 Henrik Zetterberg .50 1.25
RC1 Nail Yakupov .50 1.25
RC2 Nathan MacKinnon 1.25 3.00
RC3 Alex Galchenyuk .60 1.50
RC4 Sean Monahan .40 1.00
RC5 Jacob Trouba .40 1.00
RC6 Tomas Hertl .50 1.25
RC7 Aleksander Barkov .75 2.00
RC8 Morgan Rielly .60 1.50
RC9 Jean-Gabriel Pageau .25 .60

2013-14 Panini Player of the Day Autographs

BG Brian Gionta 3.00 8.00
BJ Boone Jenner 4.00 10.00
JT Jacob Trouba 8.00 20.00
NB Nick Bjugstad 3.00 8.00
PM Patrick Marleau 5.00 12.00
SM Sean Monahan 4.00 10.00
SS Steven Stamkos 15.00 40.00

2013-14 Panini Player of the Day Rookie Materials

1 Nicklas Jensen 2.00 5.00
3 Ryan Spooner 2.50 6.00
5 Petr Mrazek 5.00 12.00
9 Ryan Murray 4.00 10.00
AC Alex Chiasson 2.50 6.00
AW Austin Watson 2.00 5.00
JH Jonathan Huberdeau 6.00 15.00
JM J.T. Miller 6.00 15.00
JT Jarred Tinordi 2.50 6.00
NM Nathan MacKinnon 12.00 30.00

2010-11 Panini Preferred Player of the Day Autographs

PODJS Jeff Skinner 8.00 20.00
PODPK Phil Kessel 8.00 20.00

2011-12 Panini Preferred Player of the Day Autographs

PODDH Dany Heatley 15.00 40.00

2011-12 Panini Prime

1 Bobby Ryan 1.50 4.00
2 Corey Perry 3.00 8.00
3 Ryan Getzlaf 2.00 5.00
4 Cam Neely 2.00 5.00
5 Ray Bourque 3.00 8.00
6 Tim Thomas 2.00 5.00
7 Tyler Seguin 2.50 6.00
8 Gilbert Perreault 2.00 5.00
9 Ryan Miller 2.00 5.00
10 Tyler Myers 1.25 3.00
11 Jarome Iginla 2.50 6.00
12 Michael Cammalleri 1.50 4.00
13 Miikka Kiprusoff 2.00 5.00
14 Cam Ward 2.00 5.00
15 Eric Staal 2.50 6.00
16 Jeff Skinner 2.50 6.00
17 Bobby Hull 4.00 10.00
18 Ed Belfour 2.00 5.00
19 Jonathan Toews 3.00 8.00
20 Patrick Kane 4.00 10.00
21 Patrick Sharp 2.00 5.00
22 Joe Sakic 4.00 10.00
23 Matt Duchene 2.00 5.00
24 Patrick Roy 5.00 12.00
25 Jack Johnson 1.25 3.00
26 Rick Nash 2.00 5.00
27 Brenden Morrow 1.50 4.00
28 Brett Hull 4.00 10.00
29 Jamie Benn 2.00 5.00
30 Kari Lehtonen 1.50 4.00
31 Loui Eriksson 1.25 3.00
32 Gordie Howe 6.00 15.00
33 Henrik Zetterberg 2.50 6.00
34 Pavel Datsyuk 3.00 8.00
35 Steve Yzerman 5.00 12.00
36 Jordan Eberle 2.00 5.00
37 Mark Messier 4.00 10.00
38 Ryan Smyth 1.50 4.00
39 Taylor Hall 2.00 5.00
40 Ed Jovanovski 1.25 3.00
41 Kris Versteeg 1.25 3.00
42 Stephen Weiss 1.50 4.00
43 Anze Kopitar 3.00 8.00
44 Jeff Carter 1.50 4.00
45 Jonathan Quick 2.50 6.00
46 Mike Richards 1.50 4.00
47 Mikko Koivu 1.50 4.00
48 Niklas Backstrom 2.00 5.00
49 Carey Price 4.00 10.00
50 Erik Cole 1.25 3.00
51 Lars Eller 1.25 3.00
52 P.K. Subban 2.50 6.00
53 Pekka Rinne 2.00 5.00
54 Shea Weber 1.50 4.00
55 Ilya Kovalchuk 2.00 5.00
56 Martin Brodeur 5.00 12.00
57 Zach Parise 2.00 5.00
58 Bryan Trottier 2.00 5.00
59 John Tavares 3.00 8.00
60 Brad Richards 2.00 5.00
61 Henrik Lundqvist 5.00 12.00
62 Marian Gaborik 2.00 5.00
63 Daniel Alfredsson 2.00 5.00
64 Erik Karlsson 2.50 6.00
65 Jason Spezza 2.00 5.00
66 Bobby Clarke 3.00 8.00
67 Claude Giroux 2.00 5.00
68 Eric Lindros 3.00 8.00
69 Jaromir Jagr 6.00 15.00
70 Jeremy Roenick 3.00 8.00
71 Mike Smith 2.00 5.00
72 Shane Doan 1.50 4.00
73 Evgeni Malkin 4.00 10.00
74 Kris Letang 2.50 6.00
75 Marc-Andre Fleury 4.00 10.00
76 Mario Lemieux 8.00 20.00
77 Sidney Crosby 8.00 20.00
78 Antti Niemi 1.50 4.00
79 Joe Thornton 3.00 8.00
80 Logan Couture 2.50 6.00
81 Alex Pietrangelo 1.50 4.00
82 Jaroslav Halak 2.00 5.00
83 Martin St. Louis 2.00 5.00
84 Steven Stamkos 4.00 10.00
85 Vincent Lecavalier 2.00 5.00
86 Dion Phaneuf 1.50 4.00
87 Doug Gilmour 2.50 6.00
88 Joffrey Lupul 1.25 3.00
89 Phil Kessel 2.00 5.00
90 Daniel Sedin 2.50 6.00
91 Henrik Sedin 2.50 6.00
92 Roberto Luongo 3.00 8.00
93 Ryan Kesler 2.00 5.00
94 Alex Ovechkin 8.00 20.00
95 Mike Green 1.50 4.00
96 Tomas Vokoun 1.50 4.00
97 Alexander Burmistrov 1.50 4.00
98 Andrew Ladd 1.25 3.00
99 Dustin Byfuglien 2.00 5.00
100 Ondrej Pavelec 2.00 5.00
101 Smith-Pelly JSY AU RC 8.00 20.00
102 Peter Holland JSY AU RC 6.00 15.00
103 Cody Hodgson JSY AU RC 6.00 15.00
104 Roman Horak JSY AU RC 6.00 15.00
105 Greg Nemisz JSY AU RC 6.00 15.00
106 Justin Faulk JSY AU RC 10.00 25.00
107 Brandon Saad JSY AU RC 12.00 30.00
108 Marcus Kruger JSY AU RC 12.00 30.00
109 G.Landeskog JSY AU RC 15.00 40.00
110 C.Gaunce JSY AU RC 5.00 12.00
111 Ryan Johansen JSY AU RC 20.00 50.00
112 Tomas Kubalik JSY AU RC 6.00 15.00
113 John Moore JSY AU RC 6.00 15.00
114 Cam Atkinson JSY AU RC 15.00 40.00
115 Allen York JSY AU RC 8.00 20.00
116 David Savard JSY AU RC 6.00 15.00
117 Tomas Vincour JSY AU RC 6.00 15.00
118 Colton Sceviour JSY AU RC 6.00 15.00
119 Gustav Nyquist JSY AU RC 12.00 30.00
120 Brendan Smith JSY AU RC 6.00 15.00
121 Nug-Hopkins JSY AU RC 30.00 80.00
122 Hartikainen JSY AU RC 6.00 15.00
123 Anton Lander JSY AU RC 6.00 15.00
124 Erik Gudbranson
JSY AU RC EXCH 8.00 20.00
125 Slava Voynov JSY AU RC 6.00 15.00
126 Brett Bulmer JSY AU RC 6.00 15.00
127 Louis Leblanc JSY AU RC 6.00 15.00
128 Alexei Emelin JSY AU RC 6.00 15.00
129 Raphael Diaz JSY AU RC 6.00 15.00
130 B.Geoffrion JSY AU RC 6.00 15.00
131 Aaron Palushaj JSY AU RC 6.00 15.00
132 Craig Smith JSY AU RC 8.00 20.00
133 Ryan Ellis JSY AU RC 6.00 15.00
134 Jonathon Blum JSY AU RC 8.00 20.00
135 Adam Henrique JSY AU RC 15.00 40.00
136 Adam Larsson JSY AU RC 8.00 20.00
137 Calvin de Haan JSY AU RC 6.00 15.00
138 Carl Hagelin JSY AU RC 8.00 20.00
139 Tim Erixon JSY AU RC 6.00 15.00
140 Cam Talbot JSY AU RC 15.00 40.00
141 Mika Zibanejad JSY AU RC 10.00 25.00
142 Colin Greening JSY AU RC 6.00 15.00
143 Erik Condra JSY AU RC 6.00 15.00
144 S.Da Costa JSY AU RC 6.00 15.00
145 P.Wiercioch JSY AU RC 6.00 15.00
146 Sean Couturier JSY AU RC 12.00 30.00
147 Matt Read JSY AU RC 8.00 20.00
148 Erik Gustafsson JSY AU RC 8.00 20.00
149 Zac Rinaldo JSY AU RC 6.00 15.00
150 David Rundblad JSY AU RC 6.00 15.00
151 Simon Despres JSY AU RC 6.00 15.00
152 Joe Vitale JSY AU RC 6.00 15.00
153 R.Bortuzzo JSY AU RC 6.00 15.00
154 Harri Sateri JSY AU RC 6.00 15.00
155 Brett Connolly JSY AU RC 6.00 15.00
156 Jake Gardiner JSY AU RC 10.00 25.00
157 Joe Colborne JSY AU RC 6.00 15.00
158 Matt Frattin JSY AU RC 8.00 20.00
159 Ben Scrivens JSY AU RC 6.00 15.00
160 Zack Kassian JSY AU RC 10.00 25.00
161 Eddie Lack JSY AU RC 6.00 15.00
162 Yann Sauve JSY AU RC 6.00 15.00
163 Cody Eakin JSY AU RC 10.00 25.00
164 Dmitry Orlov JSY AU RC 15.00 40.00
165 Mark Scheifele JSY AU RC 25.00 60.00
166 Carl Klingberg JSY AU RC 6.00 15.00

2011-12 Panini Prime Rookies Hologold Patch Autographs

*HOLOGOLD/25: .6X TO 1.5X JSY AU/199
121 Ryan Nugent-Hopkins 125.00 250.00

2011-12 Panini Prime Rookies Holosilver Patch Autographs

*HOLOSILVER/50: .5X TO 1.2X JSY AU/199

2011-12 Panini Prime Silver

*1-100 VETS/25: 1X TO 2.5X BASIC CARDS

2011-12 Panini Prime Colors Patch Horizontal

5 Patrice Bergeron/24 15.00 40.00
6 Ray Bourque/16 20.00 50.00
7 Tim Thomas/18 12.00 30.00
8 Zdeno Chara/16 12.00 30.00
10 Tyler Seguin/19 15.00 40.00
11 Ryan Miller/25 12.00 30.00
12 Derek Roy/15 8.00 20.00
14 Cody Hodgson/15 15.00 40.00
17 Ron Francis/25 15.00 40.00
19 Stan Mikita/15 15.00 40.00
20 Gabriel Landeskog/25 30.00 80.00
21 Matt Duchene/19 12.00 30.00
22 Paul Stastny/22 10.00 25.00
26 Loui Eriksson/18 8.00 20.00
27 Brenden Morrow/20 10.00 25.00
28 Steve Yzerman/18 30.00 80.00
29 Henrik Zetterberg/17 15.00 40.00
30 Ryan Nugent-Hopkins/18 40.00 100.00
32 Ryan Smyth/22 10.00 25.00
35 Dustin Brown/17 12.00 30.00
37 Jonathan Bernier/19 10.00 25.00
40 Cal Clutterbuck/20 8.00 20.00
41 Carey Price/18 25.00 60.00
42 Colin Wilson/20 10.00 25.00
43 Pekka Rinne/25 12.00 30.00
47 Patrik Elias/20 12.00 30.00
48 Scott Niedermayer/20 12.00 30.00
50 Bryan Trottier/15 12.00 30.00
52 Kyle Okposo/24 8.00 20.00
54 Brandon Dubinsky/16 8.00 20.00
65 Danny Briere/16 12.00 30.00
68 Scott Hartnell/22 8.00 20.00
70 Jakub Voracek/18 10.00 25.00
72 Mike Smith/25 12.00 30.00
73 Shane Doan/16 10.00 25.00
74 Jaromir Jagr/16 40.00 100.00
76 Mario Lemieux/16 50.00 125.00
82 Logan Couture/28 15.00 40.00
83 Martin Havlat/16 10.00 25.00
85 Ryane Clowe/16 8.00 20.00
87 Brett Hull/19 25.00 60.00
88 David Backes/16 8.00 20.00
90 Steven Stamkos/18 25.00 60.00
94 Cory Schneider/19 12.00 30.00
95 Daniel Sedin/17 15.00 40.00
96 Henrik Sedin/17 15.00 40.00
98 Karl Alzner/18 8.00 20.00
99 Tomas Vokoun/23 10.00 25.00
100 Ondrej Pavelec/20 12.00 30.00

2011-12 Panini Prime Colors Patch Vertical

8 Zdeno Chara/20 15.00 40.00
9 Tuukka Rask/16 20.00 50.00
18 Patrick Kane/17 30.00 80.00
22 Paul Stastny/17 12.00 30.00
23 Milan Hejduk/18 12.00 30.00
24 Rick Nash/17 15.00 40.00
34 Anze Kopitar/20 25.00 60.00
36 Jeff Carter/18 12.00 30.00
38 Luc Robitaille/18 15.00 40.00
46 Martin Brodeur/16 40.00 100.00
49 Adam Larsson/23 15.00 40.00
60 Jason Spezza/18 15.00 40.00
61 Mika Zibanejad/21 40.00 100.00
63 Chris Pronger/18 15.00 40.00
71 Keith Yandle/20 10.00 25.00
77 Sidney Crosby/22 60.00 150.00
84 Patrick Marleau/16 15.00 40.00
85 Ryane Clowe/21 10.00 25.00
91 Vincent Lecavalier/17 15.00 40.00

2011-12 Panini Prime Combos Jerseys

*PATCH/25: .6X TO 1.5X DUAL JSY/225
*PRIME/50: .6X TO 1.5X DUAL JSY/225
1 B.Ryan/R.Getzlaf/225 3.00 8.00
2 D.Alfredsson/J.Spezza/225 3.00 8.00
3 L.Leblanc/R.Diaz/225 2.50 6.00
4 D.Keith/J.Toews/225 5.00 12.00
5 C.Perry/D.Smith-Pelly/225 5.00 12.00
6 B.Wheeler/M.Scheifele/225 10.00 25.00
7 P.Larsen/T.Vincour/225 2.50 6.00
8 H.Zetterberg/N.Lidstrom/225 4.00 10.00
9 J.Bernier/J.Quick/225 4.00 10.00
10 M.Read/S.Couturier/225 5.00 12.00
11 A.Miele/D.Rundblad/225 2.50 6.00
12 B.Scrivens/M.Frattin/225 2.50 6.00
13 D.Sedin/H.Sedin/225 4.00 10.00
14 M.Neuvirth/T.Vokoun/225 2.50 6.00
15 C.Atkinson/D.Savard/225 6.00 15.00
16 E.Kane/P.Kane/225 6.00 15.00
17 P.Esposito/T.Esposito/25 8.00 20.00
18 A.Ovechkin/A.Semin/225 12.00 30.00
19 C.de Haan/T.Hamonic/225 2.50 6.00
20 J.McBain/J.Faulk/225 4.00 10.00
21 J.Vitale/R.Bortuzzo/225 2.50 6.00
22 B.Schenn/L.Schenn/225 3.00 8.00
23 C.Perry/H.Sedin/225 5.00 12.00
24 B.Elliott/J.Halak/225 3.00 8.00
25 B.Saad/M.Kruger/225 5.00 12.00
26 J.Howard/P.Datsyuk/225 5.00 12.00
27 Y.Sauve/Z.Kassian/225 3.00 8.00
28 G.Nemisz/R.Horak/225 2.50 6.00
29 A.York/T.Kubalik/225 3.00 8.00
30 A.Palushaj/A.Emelin/225 2.50 6.00
31 C.Greening/S.Da Costa/225 2.50 6.00
32 S.Hartnell/Z.Rinaldo/225 2.50 6.00
33 C.Hodgson/Z.Kassian/225 4.00 10.00
34 D.Stafford/J.Pominville/225 2.00 5.00
35 T.Thomas/T.Rask/225 4.00 10.00
36 D.Doughty/S.Voynov/225 4.00 10.00
37 C.Smith/R.Suter/225 3.00 8.00
38 J.Staal/S.Despres/225 2.50 6.00
39 H.Sateri/J.Pavelski/225 4.00 10.00
40 B.Bulmer/D.Setoguchi/225 2.50 6.00
41 J.Moore/R.Johansen/225 8.00 20.00
42 C.Neil/P.Wiercioch/225 2.50 6.00
43 R.Malone/S.Stamkos/225 6.00 15.00
44 C.Joseph/G.Fuhr/225 5.00 12.00
45 B.Holtby/M.Green/225 4.00 10.00
46 C.Klingberg/O.Pavelec/225 3.00 8.00
47 E.Gudbranson/R.Ellis/225 3.00 8.00
48 RNH/S.Couturier/225 10.00 25.00
49 C.Teubert/E.Condra/225 2.50 6.00
50 B.Geoffrion/C.Price/225 6.00 15.00

2011-12 Panini Prime Namesakes Autographs

1 Aaron Palushaj/75 8.00 20.00
2 Adam Henrique/75 20.00 50.00
4 Alex Ovechkin/75 40.00 100.00
5 Anton Lander/75 8.00 20.00
6 Ben Scrivens/75 8.00 20.00
7 Blake Geoffrion/75 8.00 20.00
9 Bobby Ryan/25 8.00 20.00
10 Brandon Saad/25 15.00 40.00
11 Brendan Smith/75 8.00 20.00
12 Brenden Morrow/75 8.00 20.00
13 Brett Connolly/75 8.00 20.00
14 Brian Gionta/75 6.00 15.00
15 Cameron Gaunce/75 6.00 15.00
16 Cody Hodgson/75 12.00 30.00
17 Craig Anderson/75 10.00 25.00
18 Dany Heatley/75 8.00 20.00
19 David Rundblad/75 8.00 20.00
21 Devante Smith-Pelly/75 10.00 25.00
22 Dion Phaneuf/75 8.00 20.00
23 Dustin Brown/75 10.00 25.00
24 Erik Condra/75 8.00 20.00
26 Felix Potvin/75 15.00 40.00
27 Gabriel Landeskog/75 25.00 60.00
30 Harry Zolnierczyk/75 8.00 20.00
31 Jack Johnson/75 6.00 15.00
33 James Neal/25 6.00 15.00
34 James van Riemsdyk/75 8.00 20.00
35 Jarome Iginla/75 12.00 30.00
36 Jaroslav Halak/75 10.00 25.00
38 Jeremy Roenick/75 15.00 40.00
39 Joe Sakic/25 20.00 50.00
40 Jonas Hiller/75 8.00 20.00
41 Jonathan Bernier/75 8.00 20.00
42 Jonathan Quick/75 12.00 30.00
43 Jordan Staal/75 8.00 20.00
44 Jordin Tootoo/75 8.00 20.00
45 Nathan Gerbe/75 6.00 15.00
46 Loui Eriksson/75 6.00 15.00
47 Magnus Paajarvi/75 8.00 20.00
48 Marcus Kruger/75 12.00 30.00
49 Mark Scheifele/75 30.00 80.00
50 Martin Havlat/75 8.00 20.00
51 Matt Duchene/75 10.00 25.00
52 Matt Moulson/75 6.00 15.00
53 Michael Cammalleri/75 8.00 20.00
54 Michael Del Zotto/75 6.00 15.00
56 Nazem Kadri/7 12.00 30.00
57 Nikolai Khabibulin/75 8.00 20.00
58 Patrick Roy/25 40.00 100.00
59 Peter Holland/75 8.00 20.00
60 Ryan Ellis/75 8.00 20.00
61 Ryan Johansen/75 25.00 60.00
62 Ryan Nugent-Hopkins/75 30.00 80.00
63 Sean Couturier/75 15.00 40.00
65 Sidney Crosby/25 60.00 150.00
66 Simon Despres/75 8.00 20.00
67 Slava Voynov/75 8.00 20.00
69 Steve Yzerman/30 40.00 100.00
70 Tim Erixon/75 8.00 20.00
71 Tomas Kubalik/75 8.00 20.00

73 Zac Rinaldo/75 8.00 20.00
74 Zack Kassian/75 10.00 25.00
75 Robin Lehner/75 8.00 20.00
77 Ryan Kesler/75 10.00 25.00
78 Sam Gagner/75 6.00 15.00
79 Alex Pietrangelo/75 8.00 20.00
81 Brad Richards/50 10.00 25.00
82 Carl Hagelin/75 12.00 30.00
83 Carl Klingberg/75 8.00 20.00
84 Colin Greening/75 8.00 20.00
85 Craig Smith/50 10.00 25.00
86 Cody Eakin/50 12.00 30.00
88 Jake Gardiner/50 12.00 30.00
89 Jimmy Hayes/75 10.00 25.00
90 Lance Bouma/75 8.00 20.00
91 Leland Irving/75 8.00 20.00
92 Justin Faulk/85 12.00 30.00
93 Lars Eller/50 6.00 15.00
94 Matt Read/25 10.00 25.00
95 Pekka Rinne/50 10.00 25.00
96 Mark Messier/25 30.00 80.00
97 Louis Leblanc/75 8.00 20.00
98 Mario Lemieux/25 60.00 150.00
99 Gordie Howe/20 100.00 200.00
100 Jaromir Jagr/25 50.00 125.00

2011-12 Panini Prime Prime Time Rookies Jersey Autographs

*PRIME/15: .8X TO 2X BASIC AU/50
1 Ryan Nugent-Hopkins 20.00 50.00
2 Gabriel Landeskog 15.00 40.00
3 Sean Couturier 10.00 25.00
4 Mark Scheifele 20.00 50.00
5 Adam Henrique 12.00 30.00
6 Matt Read 12.00 30.00
7 Ryan Johansen 15.00 40.00
8 Craig Smith 6.00 15.00
9 Cody Eakin 8.00 20.00
10 Louis Leblanc 5.00 12.00
11 Gustav Nyquist 12.00 30.00
12 Jake Gardiner 12.00 30.00
13 Brett Connolly 8.00 20.00
14 Cody Hodgson 8.00 20.00
15 Zack Kassian 6.00 15.00
16 Carl Hagelin 8.00 20.00
17 Adam Larsson 10.00 25.00
18 Mika Zibanejad 15.00 40.00
20 Brandon Saad 10.00 25.00
21 Devante Smith-Pelly 6.00 15.00
22 Tomas Vincour 5.00 12.00
23 Colin Greening 8.00 20.00
24 Brett Bulmer 5.00 12.00
25 Peter Holland 5.00 12.00
26 Marcus Kruger 8.00 20.00
27 David Rundblad 5.00 12.00
28 Tim Erixon 5.00 12.00
29 Brendan Smith 5.00 12.00
30 Matt Frattin EXCH 10.00 25.00
31 John Moore 5.00 12.00
32 Roman Horak 5.00 12.00
33 Aaron Palushaj 5.00 12.00
34 Ryan Ellis 5.00 12.00
36 Slava Voynov 5.00 12.00
37 Harri Sateri 5.00 12.00
38 Simon Despres 5.00 12.00
39 Erik Gudbranson 6.00 15.00
40 Blake Geoffrion 5.00 12.00
41 Greg Nemisz 5.00 12.00
42 Anton Lander 5.00 12.00
43 Calvin de Haan 5.00 12.00
44 Justin Faulk 8.00 20.00
45 Cam Atkinson 12.00 30.00
46 Ben Scrivens 5.00 12.00
47 Erik Gustafsson 6.00 15.00
48 Eddie Lack 5.00 12.00
49 Carl Klingberg 5.00 12.00
50 Stephane Da Costa 5.00 12.00

2011-12 Panini Prime Prime Time Rookies Jerseys

*PRIME/25: .8X TO 2X BASIC JSY/99
1 Ryan Nugent-Hopkins 15.00 40.00
2 Gabriel Landeskog 12.00 30.00
3 Sean Couturier 6.00 15.00
4 Mark Scheifele 12.00 30.00
5 Adam Henrique 6.00 15.00
6 Matt Read 4.00 10.00
7 Ryan Johansen 10.00 25.00
8 Craig Smith 4.00 10.00
9 Cody Eakin 5.00 12.00
10 Louis Leblanc 6.00 15.00
11 Gustav Nyquist 6.00 15.00
12 Jake Gardiner 5.00 12.00
13 Brett Connolly 3.00 8.00
14 Cody Hodgson 6.00 15.00
15 Zack Kassian 4.00 10.00
16 Carl Hagelin 6.00 15.00
17 Adam Larsson 5.00 12.00
18 Mika Zibanejad 5.00 12.00
19 Joe Colborne 3.00 8.00
20 Brandon Saad 6.00 15.00
21 Devante Smith-Pelly 4.00 10.00
22 Tomas Vincour 3.00 8.00
23 Colin Greening 3.00 8.00
24 Brett Bulmer 3.00 8.00
25 Peter Holland 3.00 8.00
26 Marcus Kruger 5.00 12.00
27 David Rundblad 3.00 8.00
28 Tim Erixon 3.00 8.00
29 Brendan Smith 3.00 8.00
30 Matt Frattin 3.00 8.00
31 John Moore 3.00 8.00
32 Roman Horak 3.00 8.00
33 Aaron Palushaj 3.00 8.00
34 Ryan Ellis 3.00 8.00
35 Alexei Emelin 3.00 8.00
36 Slava Voynov 3.00 8.00
37 Harri Sateri 3.00 8.00
38 Simon Despres 3.00 8.00
39 Erik Gudbranson 4.00 10.00
40 Blake Geoffrion 3.00 8.00
41 Greg Nemisz 3.00 8.00
42 Anton Lander 3.00 8.00
43 Calvin de Haan 3.00 8.00
44 Justin Faulk 5.00 12.00
45 Cam Atkinson 8.00 20.00
46 Ben Scrivens 3.00 8.00
47 Erik Gustafsson 5.00 12.00
48 Eddie Lack 3.00 8.00
49 Carl Klingberg 3.00 8.00
50 Stephane Da Costa 3.00 8.00

2011-12 Panini Prime Quads Jerseys

*PRIME/15: .6X TO 1.5X BASIC QUAD/75
*PRIME/15: .5X TO 1.2X BASIC QUAD/25
1 Prong/Sakic/Mario/Yzermn 30.00 80.00
2 Prust/Boll/Martin/Thornton 5.00 12.00
3 Malkin/Neal/Gabrk/Stamks 12.00 30.00
4 Lndqvst/Quick/Smith/Rinn 20.00 50.00
5 Neil/Dorstt/Rinaldo/Konpk 6.00 15.00
6 Price/Hiller/Kiprsff/Smith 15.00 40.00
7 Richrds/Sakic/StLou/Dats 15.00 40.00
8 Ovech/Sedin/Malkin/Sedin 12.00 30.00
9 Joseph/Belfr/Brodr/Roy 20.00 50.00
10 Hull/Howe/Dion/Espo/25 40.00 100.00
11 Malkn/Zettr/Toews/Thoms 15.00 40.00
12 Jackman/Elliott/Halak/Oshie 8.00 20.00
13 Kunitz/Tangrdi/Vitle/Bortzzo 8.00 20.00
14 Zolnier/Read/Coutr/Rnldo 12.50 30.00
15 deHaan/Nielsn/DiPiet/Hamnc 6.00 15.00
16 Geoffrn/Price/LebInc/Diaz 15.00 40.00
17 Phanf/Gardnr/Reimr/Schn 10.00 25.00
18 Saad/Toews/Krugr/Kane 10.00 25.00
19 Smith/Nyqst/Hwrd/Ldstrm 10.00 25.00
20 Richd/Hgln/Zuccrl/DelZ 12.00 30.00

2011-12 Panini Prime Quads Jerseys Prime

1 Pronger/Sakic/Lemieux/Yzerman 40.00 100.00
2 Prust/Boll/Martin/Thornton 8.00 20.00
3 Malkin/Neal/Gaborik/Stamkos 25.00 60.00
4 Lundqvist/Quick/Smith/Rinne 30.00 80.00
5 Neil/Dorsett/Rinaldo/Konopka 12.00 30.00
6 Price/Hiller/Kiprusoff/Smith 30.00 80.00
7 Richards/Sakic/St. Louis/Datsyuk 30.00 80.00
8 Ovechkin/Sedin/Malkin/Sedin 60.00 150.00
9 Joseph/Belfour/Brodeur/Roy 30.00 80.00
10 Hull/Howe/Dionne/Esposito 50.00 120.00
11 Malkin/Zetterberg/Toews/Thomas 30.00 80.00
12 Jackman/Elliott/Halak/Oshie 15.00 40.00
13 Kunitz/Tangradi/Vitale/Bortuzzo 25.00 60.00
14 Zolnierczyk/Read
Couturier/Rinaldo 25.00 60.00
15 de Haan/Nielsen/DiPietro/Hamonic 12.0030.00
16 Geoffrion/Price/Leblanc/Diaz 30.00 80.00
17 Phaneuf/Gardiner/Reimer/Schenn 15.00 40.00
18 Saad/Toews/Kruger/Kane 20.00 50.00
19 Smith/Nyquist/Howard/Lidstrom 15.00 40.00
20 Richards/Hagelin
Zuccarello/Del Zotto 20.00 50.00

2011-12 Panini Prime Showcase Swatches

1 Ryan Nugent-Hopkins 30.00 80.00
2 Ryan Ellis 6.00 15.00
3 Adam Henrique 15.00 40.00
4 Greg Nemisz 6.00 15.00
5 Brendan Smith 6.00 15.00
6 Brett Connolly 6.00 15.00
7 Zack Kassian 8.00 20.00
8 Cody Eakin 10.00 25.00
9 Simon Despres 6.00 15.00
10 Joe Colborne 6.00 15.00
11 Gabriel Landeskog 15.00 40.00
12 David Rundblad 6.00 15.00
13 Mika Zibanejad 20.00 50.00
14 Carl Klingberg 6.00 15.00
15 Marcus Kruger 10.00 25.00
16 Tim Erixon 6.00 15.00
17 Justin Faulk 10.00 25.00
18 Jake Gardiner 10.00 25.00
19 Aaron Palushaj 6.00 15.00
20 John Moore 8.00 20.00
21 Erik Gudbranson 8.00 20.00
22 Bobby Ryan 8.00 20.00
23 Corey Perry 15.00 40.00
24 Milan Lucic 10.00 25.00
25 Zdeno Chara 10.00 25.00
26 Cody Hodgson 15.00 40.00
27 Ville Leino 8.00 20.00
28 Miikka Kiprusoff 10.00 25.00
29 Brandon Saad 12.00 30.00
30 Jonathan Toews 12.00 30.00
31 Erik Johnson 6.00 15.00
32 Joe Sakic 20.00 50.00
33 Rick Nash 12.00 30.00
34 Ryan Johansen 20.00 50.00
35 Henrik Zetterberg 12.00 30.00
36 Steve Yzerman 40.00 80.00
37 Anton Lander 6.00 15.00
38 Ryan Nugent-Hopkins 25.00 60.00
39 Taylor Hall 15.00 40.00
40 Erik Gudbranson 8.00 20.00
41 Kris Versteeg 6.00 15.00
42 Jeff Carter 8.00 20.00
43 Jonathan Quick 12.00 30.00
44 Brett Bulmer 8.00 20.00
45 Niklas Backstrom 10.00 25.00
46 Brian Gionta 6.00 15.00
47 Blake Geoffrion 8.00 20.00
48 Louis Leblanc 6.00 15.00
49 Craig Smith 10.00 25.00
50 Jonathon Blum 8.00 20.00
51 Ryan Suter 8.00 20.00
52 Adam Larsson 8.00 20.00
53 Martin Brodeur 25.00 60.00
54 Calvin de Haan 8.00 20.00
55 Henrik Lundqvist 25.00 60.00
56 Ryan Callahan 12.00 30.00
57 Colin Greening 8.00 20.00
58 Daniel Alfredsson 10.00 25.00
59 Erik Karlsson 12.00 30.00
60 Ilya Bryzgalov 12.00 30.00
61 Matt Read 8.00 20.00
62 Scott Hartnell 12.00 30.00
63 Sean Couturier 20.00 50.00
64 Mike Smith 10.00 25.00
65 Mikkel Boedker 6.00 15.00
66 James Neal 12.00 30.00
67 Joe Vitale 8.00 20.00
68 Sidney Crosby 40.00 100.00
69 Joe Pavelski 12.00 30.00
70 Patrick Marleau 10.00 25.00
71 David Backes 6.00 15.00
72 Martin St. Louis 10.00 25.00
73 Ben Scrivens 6.00 15.00
74 Joe Colborne 10.00 25.00
75 Luke Schenn 8.00 20.00
76 Matt Frattin 6.00 15.00
77 Ryan Kesler 12.00 30.00
78 Zack Kassian 8.00 20.00
79 Alex Ovechkin 15.00 40.00
80 Cody Eakin 10.00 25.00
81 Blake Wheeler 8.00 20.00
82 Mark Scheifele 15.00 40.00

2011-12 Panini Prime Showcase Jersey Prime Colors

*PATCH/15: .6X TO 1.5X PRIME COLOR/35
1 Ryan Nugent-Hopkins 25.00 60.00
2 Ryan Ellis 5.00 12.00
3 Adam Henrique 10.00 25.00
4 Greg Nemisz 5.00 12.00
5 Brendan Smith 5.00 12.00
6 Brett Connolly 5.00 12.00
7 Zack Kassian 6.00 15.00
8 Cody Eakin 8.00 20.00
9 Simon Despres 5.00 12.00
10 Joe Colborne 5.00 12.00
11 Gabriel Landeskog 15.00 40.00
12 David Rundblad 5.00 12.00
13 Mika Zibanejad 15.00 40.00
14 Carl Klingberg 5.00 12.00
15 Marcus Kruger 8.00 20.00
16 Tim Erixon 5.00 12.00
17 Justin Faulk 8.00 20.00
18 Jake Gardiner 8.00 20.00
19 Aaron Palushaj 5.00 12.00
20 John Moore 5.00 12.00

2011-12 Panini Prime Signatures

*GOLD/50: .5X TO 1.2X BASIC AU/99
*GOLD/50: .4X TO 1X BASIC AU/31
*HOLOSILVER/25: .6X TO 1.5X BASIC AU/99
*HOLOSILVER/25: .5X TO 1.2X BASIC AU/31
1 Alex Ovechkin/99 30.00 80.00
2 Gordie Howe/25 50.00 125.00
3 Mario Lemieux/99 40.00 100.00
4 Martin Brodeur/99 25.00 60.00
5 Aaron Palushaj/99 5.00 12.00
6 Sidney Crosby/25 60.00 150.00
8 Brandon Saad/99 10.00 25.00
9 Colten Teubert/99 5.00 12.00
11 Mike Modano/99 10.00 25.00
12 Brendan Smith/30 10.00 25.00
13 Brett Connolly/99 5.00 12.00
14 Cam Ward/99 6.00 15.00
15 Cameron Gaunce/99 4.00 10.00
16 Carl Hagelin/99 8.00 20.00
17 Chris Pronger/99 6.00 15.00
18 Dylan Olsen/31 8.00 20.00
19 Cody Hodgson/99 8.00 20.00
20 Colin Wilson/99 5.00 12.00
20 Colin Wilson
(inserted in 2013-14 Panini Prime) 5.00 12.00
21 David Rundblad/99 5.00 12.00
22 Craig Anderson/99 6.00 15.00
23 Dale Hawerchuk/99 8.00 20.00
24 Dion Phaneuf/99 5.00 12.00
25 Dustin Brown/99 6.00 15.00
26 Patrick Roy/99 25.00 60.00
27 Gilbert Perreault/99 6.00 15.00
28 Gustav Nyquist/99 12.00 30.00
29 Jack Johnson/99 4.00 10.00
30 Ben Scrivens/99 5.00 12.00
31 Roman Horak/99 5.00 12.00
32 Johnny Bucyk/99 6.00 15.00
34 Jonathon Blum/99 5.00 12.00
35 Matt Read/99 6.00 15.00
36 Devante Smith-Pelly/99 6.00 15.00
37 Marcus Kruger/99 8.00 20.00
38 Leland Irving/99 5.00 12.00
39 Louis Leblanc/99 5.00 12.00
40 Mark Scheifele/99 20.00 50.00
41 Sam Gagner/99 4.00 10.00
42 Martin Havlat/99 5.00 12.00
43 Niklas Backstrom/99 6.00 15.00
45 Pekka Rinne/50 6.00 15.00
46 Peter Holland/99 5.00 12.00
47 Raphael Diaz/99 5.00 12.00
48 Riley Nash/99 5.00 12.00
49 Roberto Luongo/99 10.00 25.00
50 Roman Josi/99 12.00 30.00
51 Ron Hextall/99 6.00 15.00
52 Ryan Ellis/99 5.00 12.00
53 Ryan Kesler/99 6.00 15.00
54 Ryan Smyth/99 5.00 12.00
55 Carl Klingberg/99 5.00 12.00
57 Sean Couturier/99 10.00 25.00
58 Semyon Varlamov/99 6.00 15.00
59 Bill Ranford/99 6.00 15.00
60 Simon Despres/99 5.00 12.00
61 Tim Erixon/99 5.00 12.00
62 Tomas Kubalik
(inserted in 2013-14 Panini Prime) 5.00 12.00
63 Jimmy Hayes/99 6.00 15.00
64 Anton Lander/99 5.00 12.00
65 Tyler Seguin/99 8.00 20.00
66 Paul Postma/99 5.00 12.00
67 Zach Parise/99 6.00 15.00
68 Zack Kassian/99 6.00 15.00
69 James van Riemsdyk/99 5.00 12.00
70 Peter Stastny/99 5.00 12.00

2011-12 Panini Prime Signatures Duals

*GOLD/15: .5X TO 1.2X BASIC DUAL/25
2 B.Hull/B.Hull 40.00 80.00
3 C.Price/P.Roy 60.00 120.00
5 E.Lindros/J.Tavares 30.00 60.00
9 C.Joseph/F.Potvin 30.00 80.00
10 C.Hagelin/T.Erixon 12.00 30.00
11 M.Modano/P.Datsyuk 30.00 60.00
12 J.Roenick/S.Mikita 25.00 60.00
13 R.Luongo/R.Kesler 25.00 60.00
15 D.Briere/C.Pronger 15.00 40.00
16 B.Nicholls/L.Robitaille 15.00 40.00
17 A.Graves/R.Gilbert 12.00 30.00
18 J.Bower/R.Vachon 30.00 80.00
20 K.Letang/S.Despres 60.00 120.00

2011-12 Panini Prime Trios Jerseys

*PATCH/15: .8X TO 2X TRIO/150
*PRIME/25: .6X TO 1.5X TRIO/150
*PRIME/15: .5X TO 1.2X TRIO/25
1 Kane/150/Miller/Parise 12.00 30.00
2 Brodr/150/Richrds/Nash 10.00 25.00
3 Alfrdssn/150/Lidstrm/Hrnqvst 6.00 15.00
4 Semin/150/Bryzglv/Datsyk 10.00 25.00
5 Kiprusoff/150/Koivu/Selanne 12.00 30.00
6 Elliott/150/Lundqvist/Quick 15.00 40.00
7 Elliott/150/Quick/Smith 8.00 20.00
8 Burrows/150/Bieksa/Kesler 6.00 15.00
9 Scrivns/150/Phanf/Gstvssn 6.00 15.00
10 Morrow/150/Sceviour/Vincour 5.00 12.00
11 Smith/150/Nyqust/Zettrbrg 10.00 25.00
12 StLouis/150/Stamks/Lecav 8.00 20.00
13 Pietrangelo/150/Crombeen/Oshie 6.00 15.00
14 Nemisz/150/Cammalleri/Horak 5.00 12.00
15 Bryzglv/150/Read/Coutur 10.00 25.00
16 Wheelr/150/Klingbrg/Scheif 20.00 50.00
17 Lander/150/Teubrt/Hartikn 5.00 12.00
18 Bulmer/150/Heatley/Palmieri 5.00 12.00
19 Miele/150/Rundblad/Yandle 5.00 12.00
20 Larssn/150/Greene/Brodr 8.00 20.00
21 Doughty/150/Quick/Voynv 8.00 20.00
22 de Haan/150/Nielsen/DiPietro 5.00 12.00
23 Hagelin/150/Gaborik/Erixon 8.00 20.00
24 Palshj/150/Geoffrn/LebInc 8.00 20.00
25 Holtby/150/Neuvirth/Vokn 8.00 20.00
26 Gaunce/150/Johnson/Stastny 5.00 12.00
27 Sateri/150/Marleau/Clowe 6.00 15.00
28 Greening/150/Condra/DaCsta 5.00 12.00
29 Emeln/150/Gorges/Diaz 5.00 12.00
30 Sidney Crosby/25 40.00 100.00

2012-13 Panini Prime

1 Craig Anderson 1.50 4.00
2 Dave Andreychuk 1.50 4.00
3 Artem Anisimov 1.00 2.50
4 David Backes 1.00 2.50
5 Mikael Backlund 1.25 3.00
6 Niklas Backstrom 1.25 3.00
7 Ed Belfour 1.50 4.00
8 Jamie Benn 1.50 4.00
9 Sergei Bobrovsky 2.50 6.00
10 Ray Bourque 2.50 6.00
11 Martin Brodeur 4.00 10.00
12 Pavel Bure 1.50 4.00
13 Alexander Burmistrov 1.25 3.00
14 Bobby Clarke 2.50 6.00
15 Scott Clemmensen 1.25 3.00
16 Logan Couture 2.00 5.00
17 Sidney Crosby 6.00 15.00
18 Pavel Datsyuk 2.50 6.00
19 Devan Dubnyk 1.25 3.00
20 Matt Duchene 1.50 4.00
21 Jordan Eberle 1.50 4.00
22 Loui Eriksson 1.00 2.50
23 Mike Fisher 1.00 2.50
24 Marc-Andre Fleury 3.00 8.00
25 Ryan Getzlaf 1.50 4.00
26 Doug Gilmour 2.00 5.00
27 Brian Gionta 1.00 2.50
28 Claude Giroux 1.50 4.00
29 Taylor Hall 1.50 4.00
30 Dale Hawerchuk 2.00 5.00
31 Adam Henrique 1.25 3.00
32 Cody Hodgson 1.00 2.50
33 Braden Holtby 2.00 5.00
34 Gordie Howe 5.00 12.00
35 Brett Hull 3.00 8.00
36 Jarome Iginla 2.00 5.00
37 Jaromir Jagr 5.00 12.00
38 Ryan Johansen 1.25 3.00
39 Ed Jovanovski 1.00 2.50
40 Patrick Kane 3.00 8.00
41 Erik Karlsson 2.00 5.00
42 Phil Kessel 1.50 4.00
43 Olaf Kolzig 1.50 4.00
44 Anze Kopitar 2.50 6.00
45 Andrew Ladd 1.00 2.50
46 Pat LaFontaine 1.50 4.00
47 Gabriel Landeskog 2.00 5.00
48 Adam Larsson 1.50 4.00
49 Brian Leetch 1.25 3.00
50 Mario Lemieux 6.00 15.00
51 Anders Lindback 1.00 2.50
52 Eric Lindros 2.50 6.00
53 Henrik Lundqvist 4.00 10.00
54 Al MacInnis 2.00 5.00
55 Evgeni Malkin 3.00 8.00
56 Mark Messier 3.00 8.00
57 Stan Mikita 2.00 5.00
58 Ryan Miller 1.50 4.00
59 Mike Modano 2.50 6.00
60 Matt Moulson 1.00 2.50
61 Kirk Muller 1.25 3.00
62 Rick Nash 1.50 4.00
63 Joe Nieuwendyk 1.25 3.00
64 Owen Nolan 1.50 4.00
65 Ryan Nugent-Hopkins 2.00 5.00
66 Alex Ovechkin 6.00 15.00
67 Max Pacioretty 1.50 4.00
68 Zach Parise 1.50 4.00
69 Ondrej Pavelec 1.50 4.00
70 Joe Pavelski 2.00 5.00
71 Alex Pietrangelo 1.25 3.00
72 Felix Potvin 2.50 6.00
73 Carey Price 3.00 8.00
74 Jonathan Quick 2.00 5.00
75 Tuukka Rask 2.00 5.00
76 Matt Read 1.25 3.00
77 James Reimer 1.50 4.00
78 Mike Richards 1.25 3.00
79 Pekka Rinne 1.50 4.00
80 Luc Robitaille 1.50 4.00
81 Patrick Roy 4.00 10.00
82 Bobby Ryan 1.25 3.00
83 Joe Sakic 3.00 8.00
84 Tyler Seguin 2.00 5.00
85 Teemu Selanne 3.00 8.00
86 Jeff Skinner 2.00 5.00
87 Billy Smith 1.50 4.00
88 Craig Smith 1.00 2.50
89 Mike Smith 1.50 4.00
90 Eric Staal 2.00 5.00
91 Steven Stamkos 3.00 8.00
92 Ryan Suter 1.25 3.00
93 John Tavares 2.50 6.00
94 Joe Thornton 2.50 6.00
95 Jonathan Toews 2.50 6.00
96 Keith Yandle 1.00 2.50
97 Cam Ward 1.50 4.00
98 Steve Yzerman 4.00 10.00
99 Henrik Zetterberg 2.00 5.00
100 Mika Zibanejad 2.00 5.00
101 Mat Clark JSY AU RC 2.50 6.00
102 Max Sauve JSY AU RC 2.00 5.00
103 Michael Hutchinson JSY AU RC 3.00 8.00
104 Torey Krug JSY AU RC 6.00 15.00
105 Carter Camper JSY AU RC 2.00 5.00
106 Lane MacDermid JSY AU RC 2.50 6.00
107 Travis Turnbull JSY AU RC 2.00 5.00
108 Akim Aliu JSY AU RC 2.50 6.00
109 Sven Baertschi JSY AU RC 3.00 8.00
110 Jeremy Welsh JSY AU RC 2.50 6.00
111 Brandon Bollig JSY AU RC 2.00 5.00
112 Mike Connolly JSY AU RC 2.50 6.00
113 Tyson Barrie JSY AU RC 6.00 15.00
114 Andrew Joudrey JSY AU RC 2.50 6.00
115 Cody Goloubef JSY AU RC 2.00 5.00
116 Dalton Prout JSY AU RC 2.00 5.00
117 Shawn Hunwick JSY AU RC 2.00 5.00
118 Brenden Dillon JSY AU RC 2.50 6.00
119 Reilly Smith JSY AU RC 6.00 15.00
120 Ryan Garbutt JSY AU RC 2.00 5.00
121 Scott Glennie JSY AU RC 2.50 6.00
122 Riley Sheahan JSY AU RC 3.00 8.00
123 Philippe Cornet JSY AU RC 2.50 6.00
124 Colby Robak JSY AU RC 2.00 5.00
125 Jordan Nolan JSY AU RC 2.00 5.00
126 Chay Genoway JSY AU RC 2.00 5.00
127 Jason Zucker JSY AU RC 5.00 12.00
128 Kris Foucault JSY AU RC 2.00 5.00
129 Tyler Cuma JSY AU RC 2.00 5.00
130 Gabriel Dumont JSY AU RC 2.50 6.00
131 Robert Mayer JSY AU RC 3.00 8.00
132 Chet Pickard JSY AU RC 2.50 6.00
133 Aaron Ness JSY AU RC 2.00 5.00
134 Casey Cizikas JSY AU RC 2.50 6.00
135 Matt Donovan JSY AU RC 2.50 6.00
136 Matt Watkins JSY AU RC 2.00 5.00
137 Chris Kreider JSY AU RC 20.00 50.00
138 Jakob Silfverberg JSY AU RC 4.00 10.00
139 Mark Stone JSY AU RC 8.00 20.00
140 Brandon Manning JSY AU RC 2.50 6.00
141 Michael Stone JSY AU RC 2.50 6.00
142 Tyson Sexsmith JSY AU RC 2.00 5.00
143 Jaden Schwartz JSY AU RC 6.00 15.00
144 Jake Allen JSY AU RC 6.00 15.00
145 J.T. Brown JSY AU RC 2.50 6.00
146 Carter Ashton JSY AU RC 2.00 5.00
147 Jussi Rynnas JSY AU RC 2.00 5.00
148 Ryan Hamilton JSY AU RC 2.00 5.00

2012-13 Panini Prime Colors Logo

1 Adam Foote/23 20.00 50.00
2 Alex Tanguay/26 25.00 60.00
3 Bobby Ryan/17 25.00 60.00
4 Brendan Shanahan/24 30.00 80.00
5 Cam Neely/22 30.00 80.00
6 Chris Chelios/19 30.00 80.00
7 Darryl Sydor/20 20.00 50.00
8 Dave Andreychuk/19 30.00 80.00
9 David Krejci/25 30.00 80.00
10 David Steckel/17 20.00 50.00
11 Dustin Byfuglien/24 30.00 80.00
12 Erik Johnson/17 20.00 50.00
13 Gabriel Landeskog/24 40.00 100.00
15 Jarome Iginla/26 40.00 100.00
16 Jay Bouwmeester/26 20.00 50.00
17 Jeremy Roenick/17 50.00 125.00
18 Jimmy Howard/17 40.00 100.00
19 Joe Sakic/27 60.00 150.00
20 Joe Thornton/21 50.00 125.00
21 Jonathan Quick/16 40.00 100.00
22 Kari Lehtonen/18 25.00 60.00
23 Loui Eriksson/18 20.00 50.00
24 Mario Lemieux/19 125.00 300.00
25 Matt Read/18 25.00 60.00
26 Matt Stajan/27 20.00 50.00
28 Miikka Kiprusoff/25 30.00 80.00
29 Mike Gartner/20 40.00 100.00
30 Milan Hejduk/26 25.00 60.00
31 Milan Lucic/20 30.00 80.00
32 Nathan Horton/22 30.00 80.00
33 Nick Fotiu/16 20.00 50.00
34 Nicklas Backstrom/18 30.00 80.00
35 Pat Falloon/25 20.00 50.00
36 Patrick Sharp/15 30.00 80.00
37 Paul Coffey/16 30.00 80.00
39 Pekka Rinne/18 30.00 80.00
40 Pierre Turgeon/29 25.00 60.00
42 Rod Brind'Amour/25 20.00 50.00
43 Ryan Kesler/29 30.00 80.00
44 Ryan O'Reilly/17 30.00 80.00
46 Shea Weber/18 25.00 60.00
47 Steve Downie/24 20.00 50.00
48 Teemu Selanne/17 60.00 150.00
49 Trevor Daley/21 20.00 50.00
50 Tuukka Rask/20 40.00 100.00
51 Tyler Seguin/21 40.00 100.00
52 Wayne Simmonds/18 40.00 100.00
53 Zac Rinaldo/18 25.00 60.00
54 Zach Parise/25 30.00 80.00
55 Zdeno Chara/20 30.00 80.00
56 Al Iafrate/16 25.00 60.00
57 Al MacInnis/18 40.00 100.00
58 Alex Ovechkin/20 125.00 300.00
59 Paul Coffey/15 30.00 80.00
60 Rob Blake/20 30.00 80.00
62 Alexandre Burrows/27 20.00 50.00
63 Brian Boyle/16 20.00 50.00
64 Brian Campbell/26 20.00 50.00
65 Brian Gionta/18 20.00 50.00
66 Cory Schneider/23 30.00 80.00
67 Daniel Alfredsson/20 30.00 80.00
68 David Legwand/16 25.00 60.00
69 Duncan Keith/17 25.00 60.00
70 Jason Spezza/21 30.00 80.00
71 Jonathan Toews/17 50.00 120.00
72 Joe Nieuwendyk/23 25.00 60.00
74 John Tavares/21 50.00 125.00
75 Mike Richards/18 25.00 60.00
76 Marian Hossa/23 30.00 80.00
77 Justin Williams/20 25.00 60.00
78 Marc-Edouard Vlasic/22 20.00 50.00
79 Ondrej Pavelec/24 30.00 80.00
80 Paul Bissonnette/22 20.00 50.00
81 Niklas Backstrom/22 25.00 60.00
82 Saku Koivu/20 30.00 80.00
83 Vincent Lecavalier/24 30.00 80.00
84 Tyler Ennis/18 20.00 50.00
85 Thomas Vanek/28 25.00 60.00
86 Stu Grimson/18 20.00 50.00
87 Scott Clemmensen/25 25.00 60.00
89 Grant Fuhr/21 50.00 125.00
90 Evgenii Dadonov/20 20.00 50.00
91 Milan Michalek/22 20.00 50.00
92 Marty McSorley/20 25.00 60.00
93 Chris Neil/23 20.00 50.00
94 Brett Hull/21 60.00 150.00
96 Frans Nielsen/22 20.00 50.00
97 Ray Bourque/17 50.00 125.00
98 Joe Pavelski/20 40.00 100.00
99 Jamie Benn/17 30.00 80.00
100 Curtis Glencross/25 20.00 50.00
101 Chris Kunitz/28 30.00 80.00
102 Derick Brassard/17 20.00 50.00
103 Marc-Andre Fleury/18 60.00 150.00
104 Henrik Lundqvist/15 80.00 200.00
105 Sidney Crosby/17 125.00 300.00
106 Ilya Kovalchuk/22 30.00 80.00
107 Andrei Markov/18 20.00 50.00
108 Keith Yandle/23 20.00 50.00
109 Corey Perry/18 50.00 120.00
110 David Backes/18 20.00 50.00
111 Scott Hartnell/18 20.00 50.00
112 Josh Gorges/15 25.00 60.00
113 Ray Emery/21 25.00 60.00
114 Taylor Hall/20 30.00 80.00
115 Sam Gagner/24 20.00 50.00
116 Jaroslav Halak/20 30.00 80.00
117 Karl Alzner/19 20.00 50.00
118 Kyle Okposo/22 20.00 50.00
119 Jason Pominville/20 20.00 50.00
120 Corey Crawford/23 40.00 100.00

2012-13 Panini Prime Dual Jerseys

1 A.Aliu/S.Baertschi/200 2.50 6.00
2 M.Brodeur/I.Kovalchuk/200 6.00 15.00
3 J.Rynnas/C.Ashton/200 1.50 4.00
4 R.Mayer/C.Price/200 5.00 12.00
5 R.Smith/R.Garbutt/200 5.00 12.00
6 T.Selanne/J.Jagr/100 8.00 20.00
7 J.Brown/S.Stamkos/200 5.00 12.00
8 D.Byfuglien/O.Pavelec/100 2.50 6.00
9 A.Ovechkin/B.Holtby/100 10.00 25.00
10 C.Kreider/D.Stepan/200 6.00 15.00
11 C.Fowler/J.Zucker/200 4.00 10.00
12 C.Goloubet/J.Benn/200 2.50 6.00
13 C.Hodgson/P.Subban/100 3.00 8.00
14 G.Howe/M.Messier/15 20.00 50.00
15 R.Hextall/M.Brodeur/200 6.00 15.00
16 J.Quick/W.Mitchell/200 3.00 8.00
17 M.Richards/D.King/100 2.00 5.00
18 R.Nash/M.Gaborik/100 2.50 6.00
19 C.Cizikas/J.Tavares/100 2.00 5.00
20 M.Fleury/C.Kunitz/100 5.00 12.00
21 M.Duchene/M.Connolly/100 2.50 6.00
22 T.Barrie/E.Johnson/200 5.00 12.00
23 T.Bozak/R.Hamilton/200 1.50 4.00
24 J.Zucker/T.Cuma/200 4.00 10.00
25 J.Allen/J.Schwartz/200 5.00 12.00
26 V.Lecavalier/D.Legwand/200 2.50 6.00
27 R.Sheahan/P.Datsyuk/200 4.00 10.00
28 B.Bollig/J.Toews/100 4.00 10.00
29 Sidney Crosby Dual/200 10.00 25.00
30 B.Gainey/P.Roy/100 6.00 15.00
31 P.Roy/J.Vanbiesbrouck/100 6.00 15.00
32 J.Mullen/J.Nieuwendyk/100 2.00 5.00
33 J.Silfverberg/M.Stone/200 6.00 15.00
34 M.Stone/K.Yandle/200 2.00 5.00
35 A.Joudrey/B.Marchand/200 5.00 12.00
36 M.Messier/S.Yzerman/50 6.00 15.00
37 R.Miller/B.Orpik/200 2.50 6.00
38 P.Datsyuk/B.Seabrook/200 4.00 10.00
39 D.Briere/D.Krejci/200 2.50 6.00
40 K.Alzner/C.Kunitz/200 2.50 6.00
41 K.Timonen/M.Staal/200 1.50 4.00
42 M.Watkins/M.Donovan/200 2.00 5.00
43 R.Brind'Amour/A.Hemsky/200 2.00 5.00
44 M.Hossa/M.Hejduk/100 2.50 6.00
45 S.Hunwick/D.Prout/200 1.50 4.00
46 M.Stone/M.Stone/200 6.00 15.00
47 E.Lindros/P.Falloon/200 4.00 10.00
48 M.Lemieux/P.Roy/100 10.00 25.00
49 P.Roy/M.Brodeur/100 6.00 15.00
50 B.Hull/M.Lemieux/100 10.00 25.00

2012-13 Panini Prime Gloves

1 Brandon Dubinsky 5.00 12.00
2 Brett Hull 15.00 40.00
3 Claude Giroux 8.00 20.00
4 Dany Heatley 6.00 15.00
5 Derek Stepan 5.00 12.00
6 Igor Larionov 8.00 20.00
7 Ilya Kovalchuk 8.00 20.00
8 James van Riemsdyk 6.00 15.00
9 Jeff Carter 6.00 15.00
10 Joffrey Lupul 5.00 12.00
11 Luc Robitaille 8.00 20.00
12 Matt Read 6.00 15.00
13 Matthew Carle 6.00 15.00
14 Mike Richards 6.00 15.00
15 Milan Hejduk 6.00 15.00
16 Patrick Kane 15.00 40.00
17 Sean Couturier 6.00 15.00
18 Marian Gaborik 8.00 20.00
19 Joe Thornton 12.00 30.00
20 Chris Chelios 8.00 20.00

2012-13 Panini Prime Namesakes Autographs

2 Andrew Joudrey/75 8.00 20.00
4 Cal Clutterbuck/75 6.00 15.00
5 Casey Cizikas/75 8.00 20.00
6 Chet Pickard/75 8.00 20.00
7 Chris Kreider/75 25.00 60.00
8 Daniel Carcillo/75 6.00 15.00
9 Gustav Nyquist/75 6.00 15.00
11 Jaden Schwartz/75 20.00 50.00
12 Jakob Silfverberg/75 12.00 30.00
13 James Reimer/75 10.00 25.00
14 James van Riemsdyk/75 8.00 20.00
15 Michael Stone/75 8.00 20.00
16 Raphael Diaz/75 6.00 15.00
18 Roman Josi/75 10.00 25.00
19 Ryan Garbutt/75 6.00 15.00
20 Ryan Hamilton/75 6.00 15.00
21 Scott Glennie/75 8.00 20.00
22 Sven Baertschi/75 10.00 25.00
23 Tyson Barrie/75 20.00 50.00
24 Brayden Schenn/75 10.00 25.00
25 Brett Hull/25 20.00 50.00
26 Cory Emmerton/75 6.00 15.00
27 Derek Roy/75 6.00 15.00
28 Jhonas Enroth/75 10.00 25.00
29 Jimmy Howard/75 12.00 30.00
30 Jordan Nolan/75 6.00 15.00
32 Nazem Kadri/75 12.00 30.00
33 Tony Esposito/75 10.00 25.00
34 Zach Parise/75 10.00 25.00
35 Vincent Lecavalier/75 10.00 25.00
37 Gabriel Dumont/75 8.00 20.00
38 Harri Sateri/75 8.00 20.00
40 J.T. Brown/75 8.00 20.00
41 John Tavares/25 15.00 40.00
42 Mark Stone/75 25.00 60.00
44 Mike Smith/75 10.00 25.00
45 Akim Aliu/75 8.00 20.00
46 Andrew Ladd/75 6.00 15.00
47 Travis Turnbull/75 6.00 15.00
48 Lane MacDermid/75 8.00 20.00

2012-13 Panini Prime Numbersakes Autographs

3 Joe Sakic/25 20.00 50.00
4 Chris Kreider/25 25.00 60.00
8 Sven Baertschi/25 10.00 25.00
9 Jakob Silfverberg/25 12.00 30.00
11 John Tavares/25 15.00 40.00
13 Leland Irving/25 8.00 20.00
14 Loui Eriksson/25 6.00 15.00
15 Cory Schneider/25 10.00 25.00
19 Alex Pietrangelo/25 8.00 20.00
21 Pavel Datsyuk/25 15.00 40.00
22 Martin St. Louis/25 10.00 25.00
23 Ben Scrivens/25 10.00 25.00
24 Eric Lindros/25 15.00 40.00
25 Steve Yzerman/25 25.00 60.00
27 Jaden Schwartz/25 20.00 50.00
28 Reilly Smith/25 20.00 50.00
29 John LeClair/25 10.00 25.00
30 Phil Kessel/25 10.00 25.00
31 Ryan Johansen/25 8.00 20.00
32 Brandon Saad/25 8.00 20.00
33 Sean Couturier/25 8.00 20.00
34 Alex Ovechkin/25 40.00 100.00
36 Jordan Eberle/25 10.00 25.00
37 Joe Pavelski/25 12.00 30.00
38 Jake Allen/25 20.00 50.00
40 Mika Zibanejad/25 12.00 30.00
41 Zach Parise/25 10.00 25.00
42 Ryan Garbutt/25 6.00 15.00
43 Ryan Miller/25 10.00 25.00
44 Michael Stone/25 8.00 20.00
45 Mike Smith/25 10.00 25.00
46 Ron Francis/25 12.00 30.00
47 Eric Staal/25 12.00 30.00
48 Tyson Barrie/25 20.00 50.00
49 Brad Boyes/25 6.00 15.00
50 Jordan Nolan/25 6.00 15.00

2012-13 Panini Prime Prime Time Rookies Jersey Autographs

1 Ryan Hamilton/50 3.00 8.00
2 Jussi Rynnas/50 3.00 8.00
3 Carter Ashton/50 3.00 8.00
4 J.T. Brown/50 4.00 10.00
5 Jake Allen
(inserted in 2013-14 Panini Prime) 10.00 25.00
6 Jaden Schwartz/50 10.00 25.00
7 Tyson Sexsmith/50 3.00 8.00
8 Michael Stone/50 4.00 10.00
9 Brandon Manning/50 4.00 10.00
10 Mark Stone/50 12.00 30.00
11 Jakob Silfverberg/50 6.00 15.00
12 Chris Kreider/50 12.00 30.00
13 Matt Watkins/50 3.00 8.00
14 Matt Donovan/50 4.00 10.00
15 Casey Cizikas/50 4.00 10.00
16 Aaron Ness/50 3.00 8.00
18 Robert Mayer/50 5.00 12.00
19 Gabriel Dumont/50 4.00 10.00
20 Tyler Cuma/50 3.00 8.00
21 Kris Foucault/50 3.00 8.00
22 Jason Zucker/50 8.00 20.00
23 Chay Genoway/50 3.00 8.00
24 Jordan Nolan/50 3.00 8.00
25 Colby Robak/50 3.00 8.00
26 Philippe Cornet/50 4.00 10.00
27 Riley Sheahan/50 5.00 12.00
28 Scott Glennie/50 4.00 10.00
29 Ryan Garbutt/50 3.00 8.00
30 Reilly Smith/50 10.00 25.00
31 Brenden Dillon/50 4.00 10.00
32 Shawn Hunwick/50 3.00 8.00
33 Dalton Prout/50 3.00 8.00
34 Cody Goloubef/50 3.00 8.00
35 Andrew Joudrey/50 4.00 10.00
36 Tyson Barrie/50 10.00 25.00
37 Mike Connolly/50 4.00 10.00
39 Jeremy Welsh/50 4.00 10.00
40 Sven Baertschi/50 5.00 12.00
41 Akim Aliu/50 4.00 10.00
42 Travis Turnbull/50 3.00 8.00
43 Lane MacDermid/50 4.00 10.00
44 Carter Camper/50 3.00 8.00
45 Torey Krug/50 10.00 25.00
46 Michael Hutchinson/50 5.00 12.00
47 Max Sauve/50 3.00 8.00
48 Mat Clark/50 4.00 10.00

2012-13 Panini Prime Prime Time Rookies Jerseys

1 Ryan Hamilton/99 1.50 4.00
2 Jussi Rynnas/99 1.50 4.00
3 Carter Ashton/99 1.50 4.00
4 J.T. Brown/99 2.00 5.00
5 Jake Allen/99 5.00 12.00
6 Jaden Schwartz/99 5.00 12.00
7 Tyson Sexsmith/99 1.50 4.00

8 Michael Stone/99 2.00 5.00
9 Brandon Manning/99 2.00 5.00
10 Mark Stone/99 6.00 15.00
11 Jakob Silfverberg/99 3.00 8.00
12 Chris Kreider/99 6.00 15.00
13 Matt Watkins/99 1.50 4.00
14 Matt Donovan/99 2.00 5.00
15 Casey Cizikas/99 2.00 5.00
16 Aaron Ness/99 1.50 4.00
17 Chet Pickard/25 3.00 8.00
18 Robert Mayer/99 2.50 6.00
19 Gabriel Dumont/99 2.00 5.00
20 Tyler Cuma/99 1.50 4.00
21 Kris Foucault/99 1.50 4.00
22 Jason Zucker/99 4.00 10.00
23 Chay Genoway/99 1.50 4.00
24 Jordan Nolan/99 1.50 4.00
25 Colby Robak/99 1.50 4.00
26 Philippe Cornet/99 2.00 5.00
27 Riley Sheahan/99 2.50 6.00
28 Scott Glennie/99 2.00 5.00
29 Ryan Garbutt/99 1.50 4.00
30 Reilly Smith/99 5.00 12.00
31 Brenden Dillon/99 2.00 5.00
32 Shawn Hunwick/99 1.50 4.00
33 Dalton Prout/99 1.50 4.00
34 Cody Goloubef/99 1.50 4.00
35 Andrew Joudrey/99 2.00 5.00
36 Tyson Barrie/99 5.00 12.00
37 Mike Connolly/99 2.00 5.00
38 Brandon Bollig/99 1.50 4.00
39 Jeremy Welsh/99 2.00 5.00
40 Sven Baertschi/99 2.50 6.00
41 Akim Aliu/99 2.00 5.00
42 Travis Turnbull/99 1.50 4.00
43 Lane MacDermid/99 2.00 5.00
44 Carter Camper/99 1.50 4.00
45 Torey Krug/99 5.00 12.00
46 Michael Hutchinson/99 2.50 6.00
47 Max Sauve/99 1.50 4.00
48 Mat Clark/99 2.00 5.00

2012-13 Panini Prime Quad Jerseys

1 Cmpr/Hmltn/Ryn/Htchn/50 5.00 12.00
2 Howe/Hull/Dnne/Grtnr/25 15.00 40.00
3 Mess/Brque/Coffy/Frncis/50 10.00 25.00
4 Prngr/Tws/Lngo/Mrlau/50 8.00 20.00
5 Rchrd/Brdr/Mrrw/Weber/50 12.00 30.00
6 Ltch/LeClr/LaFn/Mdano/50 8.00 20.00
7 Lemx/Fhr/ulet/Bourque/50 20.00 50.00
8 Clarke/Brbr/Prnt/Leach/50 8.00 20.00
9 Kerr/Hextall/Messr/Fuhr/50 10.00 25.00
10 Lemx/Francis/Jagr/Cofy/50 20.00 50.00
11 Yzer/Shan/Larnv/Lidstrm/50 12.00 30.00
12 Ovech/Mlkn/Staff/Dbnk/50 20.00 50.00
13 Ryan/Price/Kopitar/Staal/50 10.00 25.00
14 Belfr/Gilmr/Hwe/Nieuw/50 6.00 15.00
15 Hull/Leetch/Robit/Yzer/50 12.00 30.00
16 Jdrey/Golbf/Prt/Hnwck/50 4.00 10.00
17 Bchm/Hiller/Getzlf/Seln/50 10.00 25.00
18 Stl/Stl/Schnn/Schenn/50 5.00 12.00
19 Koivu/Koivu/Sdin/Sdin/50 6.00 15.00
20 Piet/Ovech/Brmstv/Tngy/50 20.00 50.00

2012-13 Panini Prime Quad Jerseys Prime

*PRIME/15: .6X TO 1.5X BASIC JSY/50
2 Howe/Hull/Dionne/Gartner/15 50.00 120.00

2012-13 Panini Prime Showcase Jersey Prime Colors

*PATCH/15: .8X TO 2X BASIC JSY/35
1 Carter Ashton 3.00 8.00
2 Jake Allen 10.00 25.00
3 Jussi Rynnas 3.00 8.00
4 Scott Glennie 4.00 10.00
5 Reilly Smith 10.00 25.00
6 Chris Kreider 8.00 20.00
7 Tyson Barrie 10.00 25.00
8 Jaden Schwartz 8.00 20.00

2012-13 Panini Prime Showcase Swatches

1 Chris Kreider/25 12.00 30.00
2 Jaden Schwartz/25 10.00 25.00
3 Pat Falloon/25 6.00 15.00
5 Alex Ovechkin/25 15.00 40.00
6 Al Iafrate/25 12.00 30.00
7 Al MacInnis/25 8.00 20.00
8 Alex Tanguay/25 8.00 20.00
9 Andrew Cogliano/25 6.00 15.00
10 Artem Anisimov/25 6.00 15.00
11 Akim Aliu/25 6.00 15.00
12 Anze Kopitar/25 15.00 40.00
13 Barret Jackman/25 8.00 20.00
14 Bernie Nicholls/25 8.00 20.00
15 Bobby Clarke/25 15.00 40.00
16 Bobby Ryan/25 8.00 20.00
17 Zach Parise/25 10.00 25.00
18 Wojtek Wolski/25 6.00 15.00
19 Wayne Simmonds/25 15.00 40.00
20 Wade Redden/25 6.00 15.00
21 Vincent Lecavalier/25 10.00 25.00
22 Valtteri Filppula/25 6.00 15.00
23 Tyson Barrie/25 10.00 25.00
24 Tyler Seguin/25 12.00 30.00
25 Tuukka Rask/25 12.00 30.00
26 Ilya Kovalchuk/25 10.00 25.00
27 Teemu Selanne/25 10.00 25.00
28 Taylor Hall/25 10.00 25.00
29 Stu Grimson/25 10.00 25.00
30 Steven Stamkos/25 20.00 50.00
31 Steve Yzerman/25 30.00 80.00
32 Sidney Crosby/25 40.00 80.00
33 Shea Weber/25 8.00 20.00
34 Shawn Horcoff/25 8.00 20.00
35 Saku Koivu/25 10.00 25.00
36 Ryan Miller/25 10.00 25.00
37 Ryan Kesler/25 10.00 25.00
38 Brandon Bollig/25 6.00 15.00
39 Brandon Prust/25 12.00 30.00
40 Brendan Shanahan/25 10.00 25.00
41 Brian Elliott/25 8.00 20.00
42 Jake Allen/25 10.00 25.00
43 James van Riemsdyk/25 8.00 20.00
44 Jamie Benn/25 10.00 25.00
45 Jonathan Quick/25 12.00 30.00
46 Jussi Rynnas/25 12.00 30.00
47 Luke Schenn/25 10.00 25.00
48 Martin Brodeur/25 25.00 60.00
49 Martin St. Louis/25 10.00 25.00
50 Nicklas Lidstrom/25 15.00 40.00
51 Ondrej Pavelec/25 10.00 25.00
52 Pavel Datsyuk/25 12.00 30.00
53 Ron Francis/25 12.00 30.00
54 Ryan Garbutt/25 6.00 15.00
55 Cal Clutterbuck/25 6.00 15.00
56 Cam Neely/25 10.00 25.00
57 Carey Price/25 20.00 50.00
58 Claude Giroux/25 12.00 30.00
59 Corey Perry/25 15.00 40.00
60 James Neal/25 6.00 15.00
61 Joe Thornton/25 12.00 30.00
62 Jonathan Toews/25 15.00 40.00
63 Sven Baertschi/25 5.00 12.00
64 Casey Cizikas/25 8.00 20.00
65 Brenden Morrow/25 8.00 20.00
66 Dany Heatley/25 8.00 20.00
67 Frans Nielsen/25 6.00 15.00
68 Jeremy Roenick/25 15.00 40.00
69 Joe Sakic/25 20.00 50.00
70 John LeClair/25 10.00 25.00
71 Kari Lehtonen/25 8.00 20.00
72 Matt Stajan/25 6.00 15.00
73 Milan Lucic/25 6.00 15.00
74 Henrik Lundqvist/25 25.00 60.00
75 Nikolai Kulemin/25 6.00 15.00
76 Patrick Marleau/25 10.00 25.00
77 Pekka Rinne/25 10.00 25.00
78 Roberto Luongo/25 15.00 40.00
79 Dustin Brown/25 10.00 25.00
80 Paul Bissonnette/25 12.00 30.00

2012-13 Panini Prime Signatures

*GOLD/25: .5X TO 1.2X BASIC AU/99
1 Adam Henrique/99 5.00 12.00
2 Akim Aliu/99 5.00 12.00
3 Alex Ovechkin/25 30.00 80.00
5 Andrew Joudrey/99 5.00 12.00
6 Andrew Ladd/99 4.00 10.00
7 Bobby Ryan/99 5.00 12.00
8 Brad Richards/50 6.00 15.00
10 Brayden Schenn/99 6.00 15.00
11 Brenden Dillon/99 5.00 12.00
12 Brett Hull/25 25.00 50.00
13 Cal Clutterbuck/99 4.00 10.00
14 Casey Cizikas/99 5.00 12.00
15 Chet Pickard/99 5.00 12.00
16 Chris Chelios/25 10.00 25.00
17 Chris Kreider/99 10.00 25.00
18 Cody Hodgson/99 2.50 6.00
19 Cory Schneider/99 5.00 12.00
20 Craig Smith/99 4.00 10.00
21 Eric Staal/50 8.00 20.00
25 Gustav Nyquist/99 8.00 20.00
26 J.T. Brown/99 4.00 10.00
27 Jaden Schwartz/99 6.00 15.00
28 Jakob Silfverberg/99 5.00 12.00
29 James Neal/99 8.00 20.00
30 Jamie Benn/50
(inserted in 2013-14 Panini Prime) 4.00 10.00
31 Jarome Iginla/50 20.00 40.00
32 Joe Pavelski/99 8.00 20.00
33 Joe Sakic/25 25.00 50.00
34 John LeClair/99 12.00 30.00
35 John Tavares/50 20.00 40.00
36 Jonathan Quick/50 12.00 30.00
37 Jordin Tootoo/99 6.00 15.00
38 Keith Primeau/99 6.00 15.00
39 Keith Yandle/99 6.00 15.00
40 Kyle Turris/99 4.00 10.00
41 Leland Irving/99 5.00 12.00
42 Loui Eriksson/99
(inserted in 2013-14 Panini Prime) 2.50 6.00
43 Marc-Andre Fleury/50 10.00 25.00
44 Mark Messier/25 25.00 60.00
45 Mark Stone/99 15.00 40.00
47 Martin St. Louis/50 6.00 15.00
48 Matt Duchene/50 8.00 20.00
49 Matt Read/99 5.00 12.00
50 Michael Stone/99 5.00 12.00
51 Mika Zibanejad/25 10.00 25.00
52 Michael Hutchinson/99 4.00 10.00
53 Mike Smith/99 6.00 15.00
54 Nazem Kadri/99 8.00 20.00
55 Reilly Smith/99 12.00 30.00
56 Riley Sheahan/99 4.00 10.00
57 Robert Mayer/99 4.00 10.00
58 Ryan Garbutt/99 5.00 12.00
59 Ryan Johansen/99 3.00 8.00
60 Ryan Nugent-Hopkins/99 10.00 25.00
62 Simon Despres/99 5.00 12.00
64 Sven Baertschi/99 4.00 10.00
65 Taylor Hall/50 20.00 40.00
66 Tomas Vokoun/50 12.00 30.00
67 Tony Esposito/50 15.00 40.00
68 Tyson Barrie/99 8.00 20.00
69 Zac Dalpe/99 4.00 10.00
70 Zack Kassian/99 4.00 10.00

2012-13 Panini Prime Signatures Duals

*GOLD/25: .6X TO 1.5X BASIC DUAL/50
1 C.Hagelin/C.Kreider/50 15.00 40.00
2 J.Schwartz/J.Allen/50 10.00 25.00
3 C.Ashton/J.Rynnas/50 8.00 20.00
5 L.Irving/S.Baertschi/50 6.00 15.00
6 C.Cizikas/J.Tavares/50 10.00 25.00
9 M.Read/S.Couturier/50 12.00 30.00
11 R.Smith/B.Dillon/50 25.00 60.00
12 T.Barrie/G.Landeskog/50 12.00 30.00
13 J.Rynnas/F.Potvin/50 20.00 50.00
14 R.Nugent-Hopkins/P.Cornet/50 12.00 30.00
16 J.Brown/B.Connolly/50 12.00 30.00
17 K.Foucault/J.Zucker/50 8.00 20.00
18 C.Pickard/P.Rinne/50 8.00 20.00
19 A.Kopitar/J.Nolan/50 20.00 50.00
20 J.Neal/M.Fleury/50 12.00 30.00

2012-13 Panini Prime Signatures Trios

1 Kreidr/Slfvrbrg/Btsch/25 25.00 60.00
3 Dilln/Smith/Glennie/25 10.00 25.00
6 Jsph/Ryns/Rmer/25 15.00 40.00
7 Cizikas/Wtkns/Ness/25 8.00 20.00
8 Quick/Brwn/Noln/25 25.00 60.00

2012-13 Panini Prime Skates

1 Adam Henrique 20.00 50.00
2 Igor Larionov 15.00 40.00
3 Joe Nieuwendyk 8.00 20.00
4 Mike Richards 8.00 20.00
5 Zach Parise 10.00 25.00
6 Alex Ovechkin 30.00 80.00
7 Ilya Kovalchuk 10.00 25.00
8 Brad Richards 15.00 40.00
9 Dan Girardi 6.00 15.00
10 Carl Hagelin 12.00 30.00
11 Joe Pavelski 12.00 30.00
12 Marian Gaborik 10.00 25.00

2012-13 Panini Prime Trios Jerseys

*PRIME/15-25: .8X TO 2X BASIC INSERTS/100
1 Sekera/Enroth/Ennis 6.00 15.00
2 Hodgson/Turnbull/Miller 5.00 12.00
3 Clarke/Lindros/Primeau 8.00 20.00
4 Schenn/Manning/Couturier 6.00 15.00
5 Richards/Staal/Lundqvist 6.00 15.00
6 Hagelin/Kreider/Girardi 6.00 15.00
7 Neely/Bourque/Middleton 10.00 25.00
8 Seguin/Rask/Chara 8.00 20.00
9 Hall/Hemsky/Horcoff 6.00 15.00
10 RNH/Cornet/Jones 6.00 15.00
11 Pacioretty/Gorges/Eller 6.00 15.00
12 Gionta/Markov/Dumont 8.00 20.00
13 Mayer/Price/Roy 10.00 25.00
14 Ness/Nielsen/LaFontaine 6.00 15.00
15 Keith/Emery/Crawford 10.00 25.00
16 Tavares/Donovan/Watkins 5.00 12.00
17 Cizikas/Nabokov/Visnovsky 5.00 12.00
18 Lindros/Ovechkin/RNH 10.00 25.00
19 Marleau/Ryan/Seguin 8.00 20.00
20 Toews/Duchene/LaFont 10.00 25.00
21 Miller/Kreider/Kessel 6.00 15.00
22 Eriksson/Landskg/Slfvrbrg 5.00 12.00
23 Hagelin/Alfredsson/Lidstrom 6.00 15.00
24 Allen/Smith/Goloubef 5.00 12.00
25 Barrie/Garbutt/Nolan 6.00 15.00
26 Datsyuk/Bryzglv/Ovechkin 6.00 15.00
27 Malkin/Kovalchuk/Kulemin 8.00 20.00
28 Allen/Schwartz/Jackman 6.00 15.00
29 Koivu/Perry/Clark 10.00 25.00
30 Iafrate/MacInnis/Chara 8.00 20.00

2013-14 Panini Prime

1 Ryan Getzlaf 1.25 3.00
2 Jakob Silfverberg .75 2.00
3 Corey Perry 2.00 5.00
4 Patrice Bergeron 1.50 4.00
5 Jarome Iginla 1.50 4.00
6 Torey Krug 1.00 2.50
7 Tuukka Rask 1.50 4.00
8 Cody Hodgson .75 2.00
9 Ryan Miller 1.25 3.00
10 Matt Moulson .75 2.00
11 Sven Baertschi 1.00 2.50
12 Mikael Backlund .75 2.00
13 Curtis Glencross .75 2.00
14 Eric Staal 1.50 4.00
15 Cam Ward 1.25 3.00
16 Nathan Gerbe .75 2.00
17 Jonathan Toews 2.50 6.00
18 Patrick Kane 2.50 6.00
19 Brandon Saad 1.00 2.50
20 Corey Crawford 1.50 4.00
21 Gabriel Landeskog 1.50 4.00
22 Matt Duchene 1.25 3.00
23 Patrick Roy 3.00 8.00
24 Joe Sakic 2.50 6.00
25 R.J. Umberger .75 2.00
26 Ryan Johansen 1.00 2.50
27 Sergei Bobrovsky 2.00 5.00
28 Tyler Seguin 1.50 4.00
29 Kari Lehtonen 1.00 2.50
30 Mike Modano 2.00 5.00
31 Pavel Datsyuk 2.00 5.00
32 Jimmy Howard 1.50 4.00
33 Gordie Howe 4.00 10.00
34 Steve Yzerman 2.50 6.00
35 Ryan Nugent-Hopkins 1.50 4.00
36 Taylor Hall 1.25 3.00
37 Jordan Eberle 1.25 3.00
38 Tim Thomas 1.25 3.00
39 Scottie Upshall .75 2.00
40 Brad Boyes .75 2.00
41 Jonathan Quick 2.50 6.00
42 Luc Robitaille 1.25 3.00
43 Anze Kopitar 2.00 5.00
44 Mikko Koivu 1.00 2.50
45 Zach Parise 1.25 3.00
46 Nino Niederreiter .75 2.00
47 Carey Price 2.50 6.00
48 Max Pacioretty 1.50 4.00
49 P.K. Subban 1.50 4.00
50 Pekka Rinne 1.25 3.00
51 Shea Weber 1.00 2.50
52 Colin Wilson 1.00 2.50
53 Jaromir Jagr 4.00 10.00
54 Martin Brodeur 3.00 8.00
55 Adam Henrique 1.00 2.50
56 John Tavares 2.00 5.00
57 Casey Cizikas .75 2.00
58 Thomas Vanek 1.25 3.00
59 Henrik Lundqvist 3.00 8.00
60 Brad Richards 1.25 3.00
61 Chris Kreider 1.50 4.00
62 Mark Messier 2.50 6.00
63 Bobby Ryan 1.00 2.50
64 Craig Anderson 1.25 3.00
65 Erik Karlsson 1.50 4.00
66 Vincent Lecavalier 1.25 3.00
67 Claude Giroux 1.25 3.00
68 Steve Mason 1.00 2.50
69 Eric Lindros 2.00 5.00
70 Mike Smith 1.00 2.50
71 Michael Stone 1.00 2.50
72 Keith Yandle .75 2.00
73 Sidney Crosby 5.00 12.00
74 Evgeni Malkin 2.50 6.00
75 Marc-Andre Fleury 2.50 6.00
76 Mario Lemieux 5.00 12.00
77 Derek Roy .75 2.00
78 Jaroslav Halak 1.25 3.00
79 Brett Hull 2.50 6.00
80 Patrick Marleau 1.25 3.00
81 Joe Thornton 2.00 5.00
82 Joe Pavelski 1.50 4.00
83 Antti Niemi 1.00 2.50
84 Martin St. Louis 1.25 3.00
85 Ben Bishop 1.00 2.50
86 Steven Stamkos 2.50 6.00
87 Dion Phaneuf 1.00 2.50
88 Phil Kessel 1.25 3.00
89 Nazem Kadri 1.50 4.00
90 James Reimer 1.25 3.00
91 Pavel Bure 1.25 3.00
92 Roberto Luongo 2.00 5.00
93 Ryan Kesler 1.25 3.00
94 Daniel Sedin 1.50 4.00
95 Alex Ovechkin 5.00 12.00
96 Braden Holtby 1.50 4.00
97 Nicklas Backstrom 1.25 3.00
98 Andrew Ladd .75 2.00
99 Dustin Byfuglien 1.25 3.00
100 Mark Scheifele 2.00 5.00
101 Viktor Fasth JSY AU RC 5.00 12.00
102 Jack Campbell JSY AU RC 12.00 30.00
103 Austin Watson JSY AU RC 4.00 10.00
104 Nathan Beaulieu JSY AU RC 3.00 8.00
106 Ryan Spooner JSY AU RC 5.00 12.00
107 Ryan Murphy JSY AU RC 5.00 12.00
108 Charlie Coyle JSY AU RC 8.00 20.00
109 Jordan Schroeder JSY AU RC 5.00 12.00
110 Igor Bobkov JSY AU RC 4.00 10.00
111 Beau Bennett JSY AU RC 6.00 15.00
112 Scott Laughton JSY AU RC 6.00 15.00
113 Emerson Etem JSY AU RC 5.00 12.00
114 Tyler Toffoli JSY AU RC 10.00 25.00
115 Quinton Howden JSY AU RC 4.00 10.00
116 Justin Schultz JSY AU RC 8.00 20.00
117 Alex Galchenyuk JSY AU RC 12.00 30.00
118 Jonathan Huberdeau JSY AU RC 12.00 30.00
119 Dougie Hamilton JSY AU RC 8.00 20.00
120 Nail Yakupov JSY AU RC 12.00 30.00
121 Tom Wilson JSY AU RC 10.00 25.00
122 Nicklas Jensen JSY AU RC 4.00 10.00
123 Leo Komarov JSY AU RC 5.00 12.00
124 Cory Conacher JSY AU RC 3.00 8.00
125 Alex Killorn JSY AU RC 8.00 20.00
126 Dmitrij Jaskin JSY AU RC 5.00 12.00
127 V.Tarasenko JSY AU RC EXCH 12.00 30.00
129 J.T. Miller JSY AU RC 12.00 30.00
130 Thomas Hickey JSY AU RC 4.00 10.00
131 Stefan Matteau JSY AU RC 4.00 10.00
132 Filip Forsberg JSY AU RC 15.00 40.00
133 Brendan Gallagher JSY AU RC 12.00 30.00
134 Mikael Granlund JSY AU RC 12.00 30.00
135 Jonas Brodin JSY AU RC 8.00 20.00
137 Tanner Pearson JSY AU RC 5.00 12.00
138 Drew Shore JSY AU RC 4.00 10.00
139 Nick Bjugstad JSY AU RC 6.00 15.00
140 Petr Mrazek JSY AU RC 10.00 25.00
141 Danny DeKeyser JSY AU RC 6.00 15.00
143 Alex Chiasson JSY AU RC 5.00 12.00
144 Antoine Roussel JSY AU RC 5.00 12.00
145 Tomas Jurco JSY AU RC 6.00 15.00
146 Jared Staal JSY AU RC 4.00 10.00
147 Max Reinhart JSY AU RC 5.00 12.00
148 Mikhail Grigorenko JSY AU RC 3.00 8.00
149 Carl Soderberg JSY AU RC 5.00 12.00
150 Sami Vatanen JSY AU RC 5.00 12.00
151 Jacob Trouba JSY AU RC 8.00 20.00
152 Morgan Rielly JSY AU RC 8.00 20.00
153 Tomas Hertl JSY AU RC 10.00 25.00
154 John Gibson JSY AU RC 12.00 30.00
155 Tye McGinn JSY AU RC 4.00 10.00
156 Michael Raffl JSY AU RC 4.00 10.00
157 Seth Jones JSY AU RC 10.00 25.00
158 Michael Bournival JSY AU RC 5.00 12.00
159 Jamie Oleksiak JSY AU RC 5.00 12.00
160 Matt Dumba JSY AU RC 3.00 8.00
162 Aleksander Barkov JSY AU RC 15.00 40.00
163 Martin Jones JSY AU RC 8.00 20.00
164 Xavier Ouellet JSY AU RC 3.00 8.00
165 Valeri Nichushkin JSY AU RC 10.00 25.00
166 Christian Thomas JSY AU RC 4.00 10.00
167 Boone Jenner JSY AU RC 10.00 25.00
168 Hampus Lindholm JSY AU RC 8.00 20.00
169 Elias Lindholm JSY AU RC 12.00 30.00
170 Ryan Murray JSY AU RC 8.00 20.00
171 Sean Monahan JSY AU RC 12.00 30.00
172 Zemgus Girgensons JSY AU RC 8.00 20.00
173 Joakim Nordstrom JSY AU RC 4.00 10.00
174 Frederik Andersen JSY AU RC 12.00 30.00
176 Anthony Peluso JSY AU RC 3.00 8.00
177 Olli Maatta JSY AU RC 8.00 20.00
178 Nathan MacKinnon JSY AU RC 25.00 60.00
179 Philipp Grubauer JSY AU RC 12.00 30.00
180 Edward Pasquale JSY AU RC 3.00 8.00
181 Frank Corrado JSY AU RC 3.00 8.00
182 Jamie Devane JSY AU RC 4.00 10.00
184 Nikita Zadorov JSY AU RC 3.00 8.00
186 Richard Panik JSY AU RC 5.00 12.00
187 Nick Petrecki JSY AU RC 3.00 8.00
188 Chris Brown JSY AU RC 3.00 8.00
189 Brock Nelson JSY AU RC 10.00 25.00
190 Rickard Rakell JSY AU RC 3.00 8.00
191 Dylan McIlrath JSY AU RC 3.00 8.00
192 Kevin Connauton JSY AU RC 4.00 10.00
193 Magnus Hellberg JSY AU RC 4.00 10.00
194 Mark Arcobello JSY AU RC 5.00 12.00
195 Reto Berra JSY AU RC 3.00 8.00
196 Ryan Strome JSY AU RC 8.00 20.00
197 Cody Ceci JSY AU RC 4.00 10.00
198 Mark Pysyk JSY AU RC 3.00 8.00
199 Jon Merrill JSY AU RC 5.00 12.00

2013-14 Panini Prime Hologold

*101-148 ROOKIES/50: .6X TO 1.5X BASIC RC
178 Nathan MacKinnon JSY AU 50.00 100.00
179 Philipp Grubauer JSY AU 25.00 60.00

2013-14 Panini Prime Holosilver

*VETS/50: .5X TO 1.2X BASIC CARDS
*ROOKIES/50: .5X TO 1.2X BASIC CARDS
20 Corey Crawford 3.00 8.00
97 Nicklas Backstrom 2.50 6.00
117 Alex Galchenyuk JSY AU 75.00 150.00
178 Nathan MacKinnon JSY AU 30.00 80.00
179 Philipp Grubauer JSY AU 20.00 50.00

2013-14 Panini Prime Colors Logo

PCAB Alexandre Burrows/35 15.00 40.00
PCAF Adam Foote/21 30.00 60.00
PCAH Adam Henrique/69 15.00 40.00
PCAM Al MacInnis/23 50.00 100.00
PCAN Antti Niemi/35 15.00 40.00
PCAO Alex Ovechkin/30 40.00 100.00
PCAP Alex Pietrangelo/15 15.00 40.00
PCAT Alex Tanguay/23 12.00 30.00
PCAZ1 Anze Kopitar/31 25.00 60.00
PCAZ2 Anze Kopitar/33 30.00 80.00
PCBBE Brian Bellows/34 15.00 40.00
PCBD Brenden Dillon/38 12.00 30.00
PCBHO Braden Holtby/32 25.00 60.00
PCBHU Brett Hull/34 40.00 80.00
PCBLA Brooks Laich/17 12.00 30.00
PCBLI Bryan Little/56 25.00 60.00
PCBT Bryan Trottier/26 20.00 50.00
PCBW Blake Wheeler/36 10.00 25.00
PCCA Craig Anderson/32 12.00 30.00
PCCG Claude Giroux/41 30.00 80.00
PCCH Chris Higgins/31 10.00 25.00
PCCN Cam Neely/40 75.00 150.00
PCCP Carey Price/19 75.00 120.00
PCCSC Cory Schneider/53 12.00 30.00
PCCSM Craig Smith/17 25.00 60.00
PCDA Daniel Alfredsson/15 20.00 50.00
PCDBRO Dustin Brown/54 30.00 80.00
PCDBRU Damien Brunner/22 15.00 40.00
PCDBY Dustin Byfuglien/42 20.00 50.00
PCDD Devan Dubnyk/41 10.00 25.00
PCDH Dan Hamhuis/40 30.00 60.00
PCDKE Duncan Keith/19 50.00 100.00
PCDKR David Krejci/53 12.00 30.00
PCDP Dion Phaneuf/41 15.00 40.00
PCDR Derek Roy/46 15.00 40.00
PCDSED Daniel Sedin/52 25.00 60.00
PCDSET Devin Setoguchi/32 12.00 30.00
PCEC Erik Cole/17 12.00 30.00
PCEF Eric Fehr/21 20.00 50.00
PCEK Erik Karlsson/34 20.00 50.00
PCEM Evgeni Malkin/37 30.00 80.00
PCGB Gabriel Bourque/15 15.00 40.00
PCGC Guy Carbonneau/19 20.00 50.00
PCGF Grant Fuhr/15 75.00 150.00
PCGH Gordie Howe/15 75.00 150.00
PCGP Gilbert Perreault/18 30.00 80.00
PCHZ Henrik Zetterberg/31 40.00 100.00
PCJBA Josh Bailey/23 30.00 60.00
PCJBO Jay Bouwmeester/31 12.00 30.00
PCJE Jordan Eberle/61 25.00 60.00
PCJI Jarome Iginla/52 25.00 60.00
PCJJ Jaromir Jagr/36 40.00 100.00
PDJM Jacob Markstrom/22 20.00 50.00
PCJQ Jonathan Quick/47 25.00 60.00
PCJR2 Jeremy Roenick/80 20.00 50.00
PCJSA Joe Sakic/51 20.00 50.00
PCJSG Jean-Sebastien Giguere/34 30.00 60.00
PCJSP Jason Spezza/57 12.00 30.00
PCJTA John Tavares/22 30.00 80.00
PCJTO Jonathan Toews/30 150.00 250.00
PCJV John Vanbiesbrouck/17 75.00 150.00
PCKLE Kris Letang/40 30.00 80.00
PCKLEH Kari Lehtonen/77 20.00 50.00
PCKO Kyle Okposo/28 25.00 60.00
PCKP Keith Primeau/61 12.00 30.00
PCKV Kris Versteeg/30 20.00 50.00
PCLR1 Luc Robitaille/17 25.00 60.00
PCLR2 Luc Robitaille/39 30.00 80.00
PCLS Luke Schenn/17 20.00 50.00
PCMAF Marc-Andre Fleury/38 25.00 60.00
PCMBA Mikael Backlund/71 12.00 30.00
PCMBO Mikkel Boedker/36 12.00 30.00
PCMBR Martin Brodeur/24 50.00 125.00
PCMDI Marcel Dionne/24 75.00 150.00
PCMDU Matt Duchene/23 40.00 80.00
PCMEV Marc-Edouard Vlasic/43 12.00 30.00
PCMGI Mark Giordano/70 10.00 25.00
PCMGR Mike Green/53 15.00 40.00
PCMHAN Martin Hanzal/39 15.00 40.00
PCMHAV Marty Havlat/15 15.00 40.00
PCML Milan Lucic/32 20.00 50.00
PCMN Michal Neuvirth/17 40.00 80.00
PCMP Max Pacioretty/36 25.00 60.00
PCMS Matt Stajan/25 12.00 30.00
PCMZ Mats Zuccarello/18 25.00 60.00
PCNB Nicklas Backstrom/36 25.00 60.00
PCPAP P.A. Parenteau/22 15.00 40.00
PCPB Patrice Bergeron/42 30.00 80.00
PCPB1 Pavel Bure/21 40.00 80.00
PCPC Paul Coffey/36 15.00 40.00
PCPK Patrick Kane/25 60.00 120.00
PCPKS P.K. Subban/35 40.00 80.00
PCPR Pekka Rinne/26 30.00 60.00
PCPSS Patrick Sharp/32 100.00 200.00
PCPST Paul Stastny/73 25.00 60.00
PCRB Rob Blake/36 20.00 50.00
PCRF Ron Francis/83 15.00 40.00
PCRH Ron Hextall/20 25.00 60.00
PCRMA Ryan Malone/39 10.00 25.00
PCRMI Ryan Miller/22 20.00 50.00
PCSB Sean Bergenheim/24 12.00 30.00
PCSCL Scott Clemmensen/45 15.00 40.00
PCSCO Sean Couturier/46 60.00 120.00
PCSCR Sidney Crosby/32 50.00 100.00
PCSD Shane Doan/46 15.00 40.00
PCSS Steven Stamkos/21 100.00 200.00
PCST Shawn Thornton/35 25.00 60.00
PCSW Shea Weber/51 25.00 60.00
PCSY Steve Yzerman/16 100.00 200.00
PCTB Tom Barrasso/23 40.00 80.00
PCTJO T.J. Oshie/30 20.00 50.00
PCTKE Tyler Kennedy/31 15.00 40.00
PCTKR Torey Krug/18 15.00 40.00
PCTR Tuukka Rask/27 25.00 60.00
PCTS Tyler Seguin/56 25.00 60.00
PCTSE Teemu Selanne/43 30.00 80.00
PCTV Thomas Vanek/71 20.00 50.00

2013-14 Panini Prime Colors Numbers

PCAF Adam Foote/18 12.00 30.00
PCAK1 Anze Kopitar/15 30.00 60.00
PCAK2 Anze Kopitar/24 40.00 80.00
PCAM Al MacInnis/20 25.00 60.00
PCAT Alex Tanguay/22 12.00 30.00
PCBBE Brian Bellows/32 30.00 60.00
PCBHU Brett Hull/26 50.00 100.00
PCBLA Brooks Laich/15 20.00 40.00
PCBLI Bryan Little/18 12.00 30.00
PCCA Craig Anderson/18 15.00 40.00
PCCG Claude Giroux/35 50.00 100.00
PCCSC Cory Schneider/30 15.00 40.00
PCDBR Dustin Brown/65 25.00 50.00
PCDK Duncan Keith/16 15.00 40.00
PCDK David Krejci/47 15.00 40.00
PCDR Derek Roy/22 12.00 30.00
PCDSED Daniel Sedin/49 15.00 40.00
PCDSET Devin Setoguchi/18 15.00 40.00
PCEF Eric Fehr/19 12.00 30.00
PCEK Erik Karlsson/29 20.00 50.00
PCGF Grant Fuhr/15 30.00 60.00
PCHZ Henrik Zetterberg/51 15.00 40.00
PCJB Jay Bouwmeester/23 12.00 30.00
PCJE Jordan Eberle/54 25.00 60.00
PCJE Josh Bailey/22 15.00 40.00
PCJF Johan Franzen/32 12.00 30.00
PCJI Jarome Iginla/49 20.00 50.00
PCJJ Jaromir Jagr/46 40.00 80.00
PCJQ Jonathan Quick/59 40.00 80.00
PCJR1 Jeremy Roenick/15 40.00 80.00
PCJR2 Jeremy Roenick/21 20.00 50.00
PCJSG Jean-Sebastien Giguere/24 20.00 50.00
PCJSP Jason Spezza/36 15.00 40.00
PCJTA John Tavares/19 30.00 80.00
PCKLEH Kari Lehtonen/82 10.00 25.00
PCKLET Kris Letang/32 25.00 60.00
PCKO Kyle Okposo/20 12.00 30.00
PCKP Keith Primeau/44 10.00 25.00
PCKV Kris Versteeg/24 15.00 40.00
PCLR1 Luc Robitaille/21 20.00 50.00
PCMAF Marc-Andre Fleury/17 40.00 100.00
PCMBA Mikael Backlund/37 12.00 30.00
PCMBO Mikkel Boedker/15 12.00 30.00
PCMBR Martin Brodeur/26 30.00 80.00
PCMD Matt Duchene/16 30.00 80.00
PCMD Marcel Dionne/22 50.00 100.00
PCMEV Marc-Edouard Vlasic/37 15.00 40.00
PCMGI Mark Giordano/24 20.00 50.00
PCMGR Mike Green/24 15.00 40.00
PCMHAV Marty Havlat/16 15.00 40.00
PCML Milan Lucic/26 15.00 40.00
PCMN Michal Neuvirth/15 15.00 40.00
PCMR Mike Richards/44 30.00 80.00
PCMZ Mats Zuccarello/24 20.00 50.00
PCNB Nicklas Backstrom/30 15.00 40.00
PCPAS Paul Stastny/69 12.00 30.00
PCPB Patrice Bergeron/38 40.00 80.00
PCPC Paul Coffey/37 15.00 40.00
PCPK Patrick Kane/57 40.00 80.00
PCPKS P.K. Subban/21 40.00 80.00
PCPR Pekka Rinne/26 15.00 40.00
PCPS Patrick Sharp/27 15.00 40.00
PCRF Ron Francis/64 15.00 40.00
PCRH Ron Hextall/18 25.00 50.00
PCRM Ryan Miller/25 15.00 40.00
PCSC Sean Couturier/26 25.00 60.00
PCSCL Scott Clemmensen/24 15.00 40.00
PCSCR Sidney Crosby/44 50.00 120.00
PCSK Saku Koivu/18 20.00 50.00
PCST Shawn Thornton/26 15.00 40.00
PCSW Shea Weber/22 12.00 30.00
PCTJO T.J. Oshie/20 25.00 50.00
PCTK Tyler Kennedy/32 10.00 25.00
PCTR Tuukka Rask/38 25.00 60.00
PCTSEG Tyler Seguin/58 15.00 40.00
PCTV Thomas Vanek/54 15.00 40.00

2013-14 Panini Prime Colors Patch

PCAF Adam Foote/38 30.00 60.00
PCAN Antti Niemi/20 15.00 40.00
PCAO Alex Ovechkin/17 75.00 150.00
PCAT Alex Tanguay/19 12.00 30.00
PCBD Brenden Dillon/18 12.00 30.00
PCBHU Brett Hull/18 40.00 80.00
PCBLA Brooks Laich/19 12.00 30.00
PCBW Blake Wheeler/15 20.00 50.00
PCCA Craig Anderson/35 15.00 40.00
PCCSC Cory Schneider/27 15.00 40.00
PCDA Daniel Alfredsson/18 20.00 50.00
PCDB Dustin Byfuglien/20 15.00 40.00
PCDBRO Dustin Brown/15 60.00 120.00
PCDH Dan Hamhuis/20 15.00 40.00
PCDK Duncan Keith/18 15.00 40.00
PCDKR David Krejci/25 30.00 60.00
PCDR Derek Roy/27 15.00 40.00
PCDSED Daniel Sedin/27 30.00 60.00
PCDSET Devin Setoguchi/17 30.00 60.00
PCEF Eric Fehr/22 12.00 30.00
PCEK Erik Karlsson/22 50.00 100.00
PCGC Guy Carbonneau/18 15.00 40.00
PCGL Gabriel Landeskog/22 30.00 80.00
PCJI Jarome Iginla/22 40.00 80.00
PCJP Justin Peters/20 15.00 40.00
PCJS Jason Spezza/37 25.00 50.00
PCJSG Jean-Sebastien Giguere/15 25.00 60.00
PCJTA John Tavares/17 60.00 120.00
PCJTO Jonathan Toews/15 60.00 120.00
PCKLE Kari Lehtonen/54 15.00 40.00
PCKO Kyle Okposo/16 25.00 50.00
PCKP Keith Primeau/16 15.00 40.00
PCLC Logan Couture/19 30.00 60.00
PCMB Mikael Backlund/29 25.00 60.00
PCMDU Matt Duchene/28 25.00 60.00
PCMEV Marc-Edouard Vlasic/22 20.00 50.00
PCMGI Mark Giordano/17 30.00 60.00
PCMGR Mike Green/31 30.00 60.00
PCMLE Mario Lemieux/27 75.00 150.00
PCNB Nicklas Backstrom/25 30.00 60.00
PCPBE Patrice Bergeron/28 150.00 300.00
PCPH Patric Hornqvist/20 12.00 30.00
PCPK Patrick Kane/18 60.00 120.00
PCPR Pekka Rinne/15 25.00 60.00
PCPSH Patrick Sharp/17 40.00 80.00
PCPST Paul Stastny/43 15.00 40.00
PCRB Ray Bourque/17 100.00 200.00
PCRF Ron Francis/37 20.00 50.00
PCRM Ryan Miller/18 40.00 80.00
PCRS Ryan Suter/27 30.00 60.00
PCRW Ray Whitney/19 15.00 40.00
PCSCL Scott Clemmensen/20 15.00 40.00
PCSG Sergei Gonchar/16 15.00 40.00
PCSS Steven Stamkos/16 60.00 120.00
PCSW Shea Weber/25 30.00 60.00
PCTR Tuukka Rask/28 25.00 60.00
PCTSEG Tyler Seguin/28 25.00 60.00
PCTV Thomas Vanek/36 30.00 80.00

2013-14 Panini Prime Coverage

CVAO Alex Ovechkin 30.00 80.00
CVBG Brian Gionta 8.00 20.00
CVBH Brett Hull 15.00 40.00
CVBRI Brad Richards 12.00 30.00
CVCC Chris Chelios 12.00 30.00
CVCG Claude Giroux 20.00 50.00
CVILA Igor Larionov 12.00 30.00
CVJB Jamie Benn 10.00 25.00
CVJLU Joffrey Lupul 8.00 20.00
CVJT Joe Thornton 20.00 50.00
CVJTM J.T. Miller 30.00 80.00
CVKL Kris Letang 40.00 100.00
CVLR Luc Robitaille 12.00 30.00
CVMR Mike Richards 12.00 30.00
CVMT Marty Turco 12.00 30.00
CVPD Pascal Dupuis 8.00 20.00
CVPE Patrik Elias 12.00 30.00
CVPK Patrick Kane 25.00 50.00

2013-14 Panini Prime Draft Hats

DHAB Aleksander Barkov/25 12.00 30.00
DHEL Elias Lindholm/25 10.00 25.00
DHNM Nathan MacKinnon/25 50.00 120.00
DHSJ Seth Jones/25 15.00 40.00
DHVN Valeri Nichushkin/20 15.00 40.00

2013-14 Panini Prime Dual Jerseys

*PATCH/25: 1.2X TO 3X JSY/150-200
*PRIME/50: .5X TO 1.2X JSY/150-200
*PRIME/25: .8X TO 2X JSY/100
DAB F.Andersen/I.Bobkov/200 10.00 25.00
DAP M.Arcobello/M.Pysyk/200 3.00 8.00
DBJ N.Backstrom/N.Jensen/200 4.00 10.00
DBL E.Belfour/R.Luongo/200 6.00 15.00
DBLE B.Bellows/M.Lemieux/200 15.00 40.00
DBM M.Messier/P.Bure/200 8.00 20.00
DCF M.A.Fleury/C.Crawford/200 8.00 20.00
DCG C.Ceci/E.Gryba/200 3.00 8.00
DCK Z.Chara/D.Keith/200 4.00 10.00
DGM D.Granlund/M.Dumba/200 4.00 10.00
DGS B.Gallagher/M.St.Louis/200 6.00 15.00
DHD S.Hartnell/S.Downie/200 2.50 6.00
DHH A.Henrique/T.Hall/200 4.00 10.00
DHHG G.Howe/M.Howe/100 20.00 50.00
DHM E.Hartzell/O.Maatta/200 6.00 15.00
DJH J.Jagr/T.Hertl/200 8.00 20.00
DJL B.Jenner/S.Laughton/200 8.00 20.00
DJO T.Jurco/X.Ouellet/200 4.00 10.00
DJR J.Jagr/J.Roenick/200 12.00 30.00
DKD P.Kessel/P.Datsyuk/150 5.00 12.00
DKG A.Kopitar/R.Getzlaf/200 5.00 12.00
DKM A.Killorn/N.MacKinnon/200 8.00 20.00
DLB H.Lundqvist/M.Brodeur/200 10.00 25.00
DLH H.Lindholm/T.Hertl/200 8.00 20.00
DLJ E.Lindholm/M.Jordan/200 4.00 12.00
DLM S.Laughton/T.McGinn/200 3.00 8.00
DLP E.Lindros/T.Pearson/200 6.00 15.00
DLT I.Larionov/V.Tretiak/200 8.00 20.00
DMJ M.Mazanec/S.Jones/200 5.00 12.00
DML J.Merrill/N.Lidstrom/200 4.00 10.00
DMM R.Murphy/R.Murray/200 4.00 10.00
DMR D.McIlrath/M.Rielly/200 4.00 10.00
DMY C.Murphy/K.Yandle/200 3.00 8.00
DNS B.Nelson/R.Strome/200 8.00 20.00
DON J.Oleksiak/V.Nichushkin/200 4.00 10.00
DOW A.Ovechkin/T.Wilson/200 15.00 40.00
DPT A.Peluso/J.Trouba/200 6.00 15.00
DRD M.Rielly/J.Devane/200 5.00 12.00
DRN A.Raanta/J.Nordstrom/200 8.00 20.00
DSC B.Shanahan/C.Chelios/200 8.00 20.00
DSH J.Sakic/Q.Howden/200 8.00 20.00
DSS D.Sedin/J.Spezza/200 5.00 12.00
DST V.Sobotka/V.Tarasenko/200 6.00 15.00
DSY S.Stamkos/N.Yakupov/200 6.00 15.00
DTC M.Turco/J.Campbell/200 6.00 15.00
DTN J.Tavares/R.Nash/200 6.00 15.00
DTT C.Thomas/J.Tinordi/200 4.00 10.00
DYB N.Yakupov/P.Bure/200 8.00 20.00
DYM S.Yzerman/S.Monahan/200 10.00 25.00

2013-14 Panini Prime Dual Rookie Class '13 Jerseys

13AG Alex Galchenyuk 10.00 25.00
13BB Beau Bennett 8.00 20.00
13BG Brendan Gallagher 6.00 15.00
13DH Dougie Hamilton 4.00 10.00
13EE Emerson Etem 4.00 10.00
13FA Frederik Andersen 6.00 15.00
13FF Filip Forsberg 8.00 20.00
13JH Jonathan Huberdeau 4.00 10.00
13JS Justin Schultz 2.50 6.00
13MG Mikhail Grigorenko 1.50 4.00
13NY Nail Yakupov 4.00 10.00
13RM Ryan Murphy 2.50 6.00
13SL Scott Laughton 3.00 8.00
13TW Tom Wilson 5.00 12.00
13VT Vladimir Tarasenko 5.00 12.00

2013-14 Panini Prime Dual Rookie Class '14 Jerseys

UNLISTED STARS/100 2.50 6.00
14AB Aleksander Barkov 8.00 20.00
14BJ Boone Jenner 5.00 12.00
14EL Elias Lindholm 5.00 12.00
14HL Hampus Lindholm 5.00 12.00
14JT Jacob Trouba 5.00 12.00
14MM Marek Mazanec 2.50 6.00
14MR Morgan Rielly 5.00 12.00
14NM Nathan MacKinnon 10.00 25.00
14OM Olli Maatta 4.00 10.00
14RM Ryan Murray 3.00 8.00
14SJ Seth Jones 6.00 15.00
14SM Sean Monahan 6.00 15.00
14TH Tomas Hertl 5.00 12.00
14VN Valeri Nichushkin 5.00 12.00
14ZG Zemgus Girgensons 4.00 10.00

2013-14 Panini Prime Dual Rookie Class '14 Jerseys Prime

*PRIME/25: .6X TO 1.5X BASIC INSERTS/100
14NM Nathan MacKinnon 20.00 50.00
14OM Olli Maatta 20.00 50.00

2013-14 Panini Prime Gloves

PGBD Brandon Dubinsky 2.50 6.00
PGBG Brian Gionta 2.50 6.00
PGBH Brett Hull 6.00 15.00
PGBR Brad Richards 4.00 10.00
PGCC Chris Chelios 6.00 15.00
PGCG Claude Giroux 10.00 25.00
PGCH Dany Heatley 3.00 8.00
PGIL Igor Larionov 4.00 10.00
PGJB Jamie Benn 3.00 8.00
PGJP Joe Pavelski 5.00 12.00
PGJR James van Riemsdyk 3.00 8.00
PGJT Joe Thornton 6.00 15.00
PGLR Luc Robitaille 4.00 10.00
PGMG Marian Gaborik 8.00 20.00
PGMR Mike Richards 3.00 8.00
PGPD Pascal Dupuis 5.00 12.00
PGPE Patrik Elias 4.00 10.00
PGPK Patrick Kane 8.00 20.00
PGSC Sean Couturier 3.00 8.00
PGTS Tyler Seguin 5.00 12.00

2013-14 Panini Prime Namesakes Autographs

NAAB Aleksander Barkov/75 30.00 80.00
NAAG Alex Galchenyuk/75 60.00 120.00
NAAK Alex Killorn/75 15.00 40.00
NAALAD Andrew Ladd/25 10.00 25.00
NAALAR Adam Larsson/75 10.00 25.00
NABB Beau Bennett/75 20.00 50.00
NABH Brett Hull/25 25.00 60.00
NABJ Boone Jenner/75 20.00 50.00
NABS Ben Scrivens/75 12.00 30.00
NADB Derick Brassard/75 15.00 40.00
NADD Danny DeKeyser/75 12.00 30.00
NADG Doug Gilmour/75 25.00 60.00
NADH Dougie Hamilton/75 15.00 40.00
NAEG Erik Gustafsson/75 6.00 15.00
NAELH Elias Lindholm/75 25.00 60.00
NAELR Eric Lindros/75 40.00 80.00
NAFA Frederik Andersen/75 25.00 60.00
NAGB Gabriel Bourque/75 10.00 25.00
NAGH Gordie Howe/20 80.00 200.00
NAHL Hampus Lindholm/75 15.00 40.00
NAJB Jonathan Bernier/75 15.00 40.00
NAJH Jonathan Huberdeau/75 15.00 40.00
NAJN Joe Nieuwendyk/75 12.00 30.00
NAJP Joe Pavelski/75 15.00 40.00
NAJR Jeremy Roenick/75 15.00 40.00
NAJS Justin Schultz/75 10.00 25.00
NAJT Jacob Trouba/75 15.00 40.00
NAMAF Marc-Andre Fleury/25 25.00 60.00
NAMG Michael Grabner/75 30.00 80.00
NAMM Mark Messier/25 25.00 60.00
NAMR Mike Richter/50 15.00 40.00
NANM Nathan MacKinnon/75 30.00 80.00
NANY Nail Yakupov/75 15.00 40.00
NARF Ron Francis/75 15.00 40.00
NARMA Robert Mayer/75 10.00 25.00
NARMU Ryan Murray/75 12.00 30.00
NASE Stefan Elliott/75 8.00 20.00
NASJ Seth Jones/75 15.00 40.00
NASM Sean Monahan/75 20.00 50.00
NATH Tomas Hertl/75 25.00 60.00
NATK Torey Krug/75 20.00 50.00
NAVL Vincent Lecavalier/75 10.00 25.00
NAVN Valeri Nichushkin/75
inserted in 2013-14
Panini National Treasures 15.00 40.00

2013-14 Panini Prime Numbersakes Autographs

NUAB Aleksander Barkov/25 20.00 50.00
NUAG Alex Galchenyuk/25 25.00 60.00
NUAK Alex Killorn/25 15.00 40.00
NUAR Antoine Roussel/25 20.00 50.00
NUBH Brett Hull/25 20.00 40.00
NUBS Brandon Saad/25 15.00 40.00
NUCJ Curtis Joseph/25 30.00 80.00
NUCN Cam Neely/25 12.00 30.00
NUDH Dougie Hamilton/25 20.00 50.00
NUEB Ed Belfour/25 30.00 60.00
NUEE Emerson Etem/25 15.00 40.00
NUEL Elias Lindholm/25 25.00 60.00
NUEM Evgeni Malkin/25 30.00 60.00
NUFP Felix Potvin/25 60.00 120.00
NUGL Gabriel Landeskog/25 15.00 40.00
NUHL Hampus Lindholm/25 15.00 40.00
NUJH Jonathan Huberdeau/25 25.00 60.00
NUJI Jarome Iginla/25 15.00 40.00
NUJJ Jaromir Jagr/25 60.00 120.00
NUJQ Jonathan Quick/25 30.00 80.00
NUJR Jeremy Roenick/25 20.00 50.00
NUJS Joe Sakic/25 30.00 80.00
NUJTO Jonathan Toews/25 30.00 60.00
NUJTR Jacob Trouba/25 30.00 80.00
NUMAF Marc-Andre Fleury/25 25.00 50.00
NUML Mario Lemieux/25 75.00 120.00
NUMME Mark Messier/25 30.00 80.00
NUMMO Mike Modano/25 20.00 50.00
NUMS Mike Smith/25 15.00 40.00
NUMSL Martin St. Louis/25 12.00 30.00
NUNM Nathan MacKinnon/25 60.00 150.00
NUNY Nail Yakupov/25 40.00 80.00
NUPK Phil Kessel/25 15.00 40.00
NUPR Patrick Roy/25 100.00 200.00
NURB Ray Bourque/25 40.00 80.00
NURG Ryan Getzlaf/25 12.00 30.00
NURH Ron Hextall/25 40.00 80.00
NURK Ryan Kesler/25 20.00 50.00
NURNH Ryan Nugent-Hopkins/25 30.00 80.00
NUSJ Seth Jones/25 20.00 50.00
NUTH Tomas Hertl/25 20.00 50.00
NUTL Trevor Linden/25 20.00 40.00
NUTS Tyler Seguin/25 30.00 80.00
NUVL Vincent Lecavalier/25 15.00 30.00

2013-14 Panini Prime Prime Time Rookies Jerseys

RKAB Aleksander Barkov/50 5.00 12.00
RKAC Alex Chiasson/50 3.00 8.00
RKAG Alex Galchenyuk/50 8.00 20.00
RKAK Alex Killorn/50 5.00 12.00
RKAP Anthony Peluso/50 2.00 5.00
RKAR Antoine Roussel/50 3.00 8.00
RKBB Beau Bennett/50 4.00 10.00
RKBG Brendan Gallagher/50 8.00 20.00
RKBJ Boone Jenner/50 6.00 15.00
RKBN Brock Nelson/50 6.00 15.00
RKDH Dougie Hamilton/50 5.00 12.00
RKEE Emerson Etem/50 3.00 8.00
RKEL Elias Lindholm/50 8.00 20.00
RKFA Frederik Andersen/50 8.00 20.00
RKFF Filip Forsberg/50 8.00 20.00
RKHL Hampus Lindholm/50 5.00 12.00
RKJC Jack Campbell/50 8.00 20.00
RKJH Jonathan Huberdeau/50 8.00 20.00
RKJME Jon Merrill/50 3.00 8.00
RKJMI J.T. Miller/50 8.00 20.00
RKJN Joakim Nordstrom/50 2.50 6.00
RKJS Justin Schultz/50 3.00 8.00
RKJS Jared Staal/50 2.50 6.00
RKJT Jacob Trouba/50 5.00 12.00
RKMD Matt Dumba/50 2.00 5.00
RKMGRA Mikael Granlund/50 5.00 12.00
RKMGRI Mikhail Grigorenko/50 2.00 5.00
RKMJ Martin Jones/50 5.00 12.00
RKMN Matt Nieto/50 2.50 6.00
KRMR Michael Raffl/50 2.50 6.00
RKMR Morgan Rielly/50 8.00 20.00
RKNJ Nicklas Jensen/50 2.50 6.00
RKNM Nathan MacKinnon/50 15.00 40.00
RKNY Nail Yakupov/50 6.00 15.00
RKPM Petr Mrazek/50 12.00 30.00
RKRMP Ryan Murphy/50 3.00 8.00
RKRMU Ryan Murray/50 5.00 12.00
RKRS Ryan Strome/50 5.00 12.00
RKSJ Seth Jones/50 6.00 15.00
RKSL Scott Laughton/50 6.00 15.00
RKSM Sean Monahan/50 5.00 12.00
RKTH Tomas Hertl/50 6.00 15.00
RKTJ Tomas Jurco/50 4.00 10.00
RKTP Tanner Pearson/50 3.00 8.00
RKTT Tyler Toffoli/50 6.00 15.00
RKTW Tom Wilson/50 8.00 20.00
RKVN Valeri Nichushkin/50 6.00 15.00
RKVT Vladimir Tarasenko/50 8.00 20.00
RKZG Zemgus Girgensons/50 8.00 20.00

2013-14 Panini Prime Quad Jerseys

QBLMS Brkv/Lndskg/Mrry/Sgn 8.00 20.00
QCBBB Cmpbl/Bgstd/Brgehm/Brkv 6.00 15.00
QEALV Etm/Andrsn/Lndhlm/Vtnn 8.00 20.00
QGGBB Glchnk/Gllgr/Brnvl/Bleu 10.00 25.00
QGGDD Glgski/Gnchr/Dln/Dly 8.00 20.00
QGONS Gtzl/ORlly/NgtHpkns/Strme 8.00 20.00
QHCST Hggns/Crdo/Schrdr/Tnv 5.00 12.00
QHTDG Hbrdu/Tws/Dchne/Glnyk 12.00 30.00
QJLCF Jgr/Lmeux/Cffy/Frncs 15.00 40.00
QJTSK Jhnsn/Tvrs/Stmks/Kne 10.00 25.00
QKHCH Klkv/Hwdn/Clmsn/Hbrdau 6.00 15.00
QLSOL Lmx/St.Ls/Ovchkn/Lndrs 20.00 50.00
QMNHY NgtHpkns/Ykpv/McKnn/Hll 15.00 40.00
QMSSS Mlkn/Sdn/Sdn/StLs 10.00 25.00
QOGPT Ovkn/Glnyk/Ptrnglo/Tngy 10.00 25.00
QPBSG Prry/Bchmn/Slnne/Gtzlf 8.00 20.00
QPTRP Plso/Trba/Rdmnd/Psqle 4.00 10.00
QRDVN Rbtlle/Dnne/Vchn/Nchlls 10.00 25.00
QSSSS Stl/Stl/Stl/Stl 10.00 25.00
QTMMJ Trba/Mrphy/Mller/Jnes 12.00 30.00

2013-14 Panini Prime Rookie Colors Logo

RPCAB Aleksander Barkov/46 50.00 100.00
RPCAR Antti Raanta/23 30.00 80.00
RPCBJ Boone Jenner/27 30.00 80.00
RPCCM Connor Murphy/44 8.00 20.00
RPCDH Dougie Hamilton/28 25.00 60.00
RPCEL Elias Lindholm/48 25.00 60.00
RPCJD Jamie Devane/19 12.00 30.00
RPCJH Jonathan Huberdeau/50 15.00 40.00
RPCJN Joakim Nordstrom/40 20.00 50.00
RPCJT Jacob Trouba/47 12.00 30.00
RPCMD Matt Dumba/48 12.00 30.00
RPCNJ Nicklas Jensen/28 12.00 30.00
RPCNM Nathan MacKinnon/25 60.00 150.00
RPCRMR Ryan Murray/50 20.00 50.00
RPCSJ Seth Jones/39 20.00 50.00
RPCSM Sean Monahan/40 15.00 40.00
RPCTH Tomas Hertl/37 20.00 50.00
RPCTP Tanner Pearson/20 15.00 40.00
RPCTW Tom Wilson/26 30.00 80.00

2013-14 Panini Prime Rookie Showcase Swatches

RSAG Alex Galchenyuk 15.00 40.00
RSAW Austin Watson 4.00 10.00
RSBB Beau Bennett 6.00 15.00
RSBG Brendan Gallagher 10.00 25.00
RSBJ Boone Jenner 8.00 20.00
RSCCN Cory Conacher 3.00 8.00
RSCCY Charlie Coyle 8.00 20.00
RSCT Christian Thomas 4.00 10.00
RSDH Dougie Hamilton 8.00 20.00
RSEE Emerson Etem 5.00 12.00
RSJC Jack Campbell 12.00 30.00
RSJH Jonathan Huberdeau 10.00 25.00
RSJM Jon Merrill 8.00 20.00
RSJSR Jordan Schroeder 5.00 12.00
RSJT Jarred Tinordi 5.00 12.00
RSMG Mikhail Grigorenko 6.00 15.00
RSMR Morgan Rielly 12.00 30.00
RSNB Nathan Beaulieu 3.00 8.00
RSNM Nathan MacKinnon 25.00 60.00
RSNY Nail Yakupov 10.00 25.00
RSPM Petr Mrazek 10.00 25.00
RSQH Quinton Howden 5.00 12.00
RSRMR Ryan Murray 8.00 20.00
RSSL Scott Laughton 6.00 15.00
RSSM Sean Monahan 8.00 20.00
TSTH Tomas Hertl 10.00 25.00
RSTJ Tomas Jurco 6.00 15.00
RSTP Tanner Pearson 5.00 12.00
RSTT Tyler Toffoli 10.00 25.00
RSTW Tom Wilson 10.00 25.00

2013-14 Panini Prime Showcase Jersey Patches

1 Nail Yakupov 25.00 50.00
2 Alex Galchenyuk 25.00 50.00
3 Justin Schultz 10.00 25.00
4 Scott Laughton 12.00 30.00
5 Emerson Etem 10.00 25.00
7 Austin Watson 8.00 20.00
8 Tomas Jurco 12.00 30.00
9 Jack Campbell 25.00 60.00
11 Nathan MacKinnon 40.00 80.00
12 Petr Mrazek 20.00 40.00
13 Mikhail Grigorenko 6.00 15.00
14 Tomas Hertl 15.00 40.00
15 Tom Wilson 20.00 50.00
16 Sean Monahan 15.00 40.00
17 Brendan Gallagher 30.00 60.00
18 Tanner Pearson 30.00 80.00
20 Cory Conacher 6.00 15.00
21 Matt Dumba 6.00 15.00
22 Ryan Spooner 10.00 25.00
23 Boone Jenner 20.00 50.00

2013-14 Panini Prime Showcase Swatches

1 Jordan Eberle/25 10.00 25.00
4 Jacob Markstrom/25 10.00 25.00
5 Mike Richards/25 8.00 20.00
6 Derek Stepan/25 6.00 15.00
7 Mark Giordano/25 10.00 25.00
11 Sidney Crosby/25 40.00 100.00
12 Jeff Carter/25 8.00 20.00
13 Nail Yakupov/25 10.00 25.00
14 Aleksander Barkov/25 8.00 20.00
15 Alex Galchenyuk/25 12.00 30.00
16 Valeri Nichushkin/25 10.00 25.00
17 Sean Monahan/25 8.00 20.00
18 Tomas Hertl/25 10.00 25.00
19 Brendan Gallagher/25 10.00 25.00
20 Nathan MacKinnon/25 25.00 60.00
21 Frederik Andersen/25 12.00 30.00
22 Seth Jones/25 10.00 25.00
24 Filip Forsberg/25 15.00 40.00
25 Tom Wilson/25 10.00 25.00
26 Steven Stamkos/25 12.00 30.00
27 John Tavares/25 15.00 40.00
28 Evgeni Malkin/25 20.00 50.00
30 Dan Cloutier/25 8.00 20.00
31 Jeremy Roenick/25 15.00 40.00
32 Mike Modano/25 15.00 40.00
33 Rob Blake/25 10.00 25.00
34 Tuukka Rask/25 12.00 30.00
35 Tyler Seguin/25 12.00 30.00
36 Jamie Benn/25 10.00 25.00
37 Brooks Laich/25 8.00 20.00
38 Kris Versteeg/25 6.00 15.00
39 Alex Pietrangelo/25 6.00 15.00
40 Steve Yzerman/25 25.00 60.00
41 Sean Couturier/25 8.00 20.00
42 Saku Koivu/25 10.00 25.00
43 Ron Hextall/25 10.00 25.00
44 Pavel Datsyuk/25 15.00 40.00
45 Tanner Pearson/25 6.00 15.00
46 Elias Lindholm/25 12.00 30.00
47 Marek Mazanec/25 5.00 12.00
48 Petr Mrazek/25 15.00 40.00
49 Mikhail Grigorenko/25 6.00 15.00
50 Alex Chiasson/25 5.00 12.00
51 Brian Bellows/25 8.00 20.00
52 Chris Chelios/25 12.00 30.00
53 Eric Lindros/25 25.00 50.00
55 Jean-Sebastien Giguere/25 10.00 25.00
56 Luc Robitaille/25 15.00 40.00
57 Nicklas Lidstrom/25 10.00 25.00
58 Patrick Roy/25 25.00 60.00
59 Brett Hull/25 12.00 30.00
60 Cam Fowler/25 10.00 25.00
61 Joe Thornton/25 15.00 40.00
62 Josh Gorges/25 8.00 20.00
64 Carey Price/25 20.00 50.00
65 Adam Foote/25 6.00 15.00

2013-14 Panini Prime Signatures Duals

SDCS C.Chelios/B.Shanahan 25.00 50.00
SDCT J.Campbell/M.Turco 10.00 25.00
SDGJ A.Galchenyuk/S.Jones 12.00 30.00
SDHJ T.Hertl/J.Jagr 30.00 80.00
SDHT D.Hamilton/J.Trouba 6.00 15.00
SDHY G.Howe/S.Yzerman 60.00 120.00
SDLJ S.Laughton/B.Jenner 8.00 20.00
SDLL E.Lindholm/H.Lindholm 10.00 25.00
SDLM G.Landeskog/N.MacKinnon 30.00 80.00
SDMM S.Matteau/S.Matteau 10.00 25.00
SDMY M.Messier/N.Yakupov 15.00 40.00
SDSG M.St.Louis/B.Gallagher 10.00 25.00
SDSS H.Sedin/D.Sedin 10.00 25.00
SDVF V.Fasth/F.Andersen 10.00 25.00
SDYM N.Yakupov/N.MacKinnon 60.00 120.00

2013-14 Panini Prime Signatures Duals Gold

SDHY G.Howe/Yzerman EXCH 75.00 150.00
SDMY M.Messier/N.Yakupov 40.00 80.00

2013-14 Panini Prime Signatures Gold

SNM Nathan MacKinnon/25 100.00 250.00

2013-14 Panini Prime Signatures Trios

1 Lemieux/Messier/Howe 175.00 300.00
2 Barkov/McKinn/Hertl 90.00 150.00
3 Yakupov/Glchnyk/Hbrdeau 40.00 100.00
6 Potvin/Reimer/Bernier 40.00 80.00
7 Lindros/LeClair/Hextall 50.00 100.00
8 Glchnyk/Gllaghr/Bournival 40.00 80.00
9 Yakupov/RNH/MacKinnon 75.00 150.00
10 Chiasson/Roussel/Nichushkin 20.00 40.00

2013-14 Panini Prime Skates

PSAC Alex Chiasson/50 4.00 10.00
PSAH Adam Henrique/25 6.00 15.00
PSAH Carl Hagelin/50 3.00 8.00
PSAO Alex Ovechkin/30 20.00 50.00
PSAR Antoine Roussel/50 5.00 12.00
PSBRI Brad Richards/25 8.00 20.00
PSDG Dan Girardi/50 3.00 8.00
PSDS Derek Stepan/50 3.00 8.00
PSIL Igor Larionov/50 5.00 12.00
PSJB Jamie Benn/50 5.00 12.00
PSJM J.T. Miller/40 12.00 30.00
PSJN Joe Nieuwendyk/50 4.00 10.00
PSJP Joe Pavelski/50 6.00 15.00
PSKL Kris Letang/50 12.00 30.00
PSMG Marian Gaborik/50 10.00 25.00
PSMR Mike Richards/50 4.00 10.00
PSPD Pascal Dupuis/50 8.00 20.00
PSRM Ryan McDonagh/50 5.00 12.00
PSZP Zach Parise/50 5.00 12.00

2013-14 Panini Prime Trios Jerseys

*PRIME/25: .6X TO 1.5X BASIC JSY/100

DGTJ Glchnyk/Trba/Jnes 8.00 20.00
EJWS Jagr/Whtny/Slnne 15.00 40.00
RLMD Lndskg/McKnn/Dchne 12.00 30.00
TBCL Brbr/Clrke/Lch 12.00 30.00
TBJS Brra/Jsi/Sbsa 5.00 12.00
TCGY Bcklnd/Mnhn/Nwndyk 6.00 15.00
TCMM Ctre/Mnhn/Mrzk 6.00 15.00
TCON Cmpbll/Olksk/Nchshkn 6.00 15.00
TEDM Schltz/Arcbllo/Ykpv 6.00 15.00
TEJL Ellr/Jnsn/Lrsn 4.00 10.00
TEMH Emry/Msn/Hxtll 6.00 15.00
TGBM Grnlnd/Brkv/Mtta 10.00 25.00
TGGR Grgrnko/Grgnsns/Rstlnn 8.00 20.00
TGJH Gbrk/Jrco/Hssa 6.00 15.00
THBC Hmltn/Brque/Chra 10.00 25.00
THNP Hrtl/Nto/Ptrcki 8.00 20.00
TKNK Kne/Nsh/Kdri 10.00 25.00
TLLF Lndhlm/Lndhlm/Frsbrg 15.00 40.00
TLMM Lndrs/Mrk/Mdno 8.00 20.00
TLPJ Lrssn/Ptrnglo/Jnes 4.00 10.00
TMMP Mrzk/Mznc/Pvlc 10.00 25.00
TNYR Mcllrth/Mllr/Fst 4.00 10.00
TOMN Ovchkn/Mlkn/Nchshkn 20.00 50.00
TPTS Prry/Tvrs/Stmks 5.00 12.00
TQMH Quck/Mllr/Hwrd 6.00 15.00
TRCC Rssl/Chssn/Cnntn 3.00 8.00
TRTP Rnhrt/Tlbt/Pcrtty 5.00 12.00
TSC Sidney Crosby 20.00 50.00
TSTL Roy/Ptrnglo/Trsnko 5.00 12.00
TVLM Vlchnkv/Lrssn/Mrrll 5.00 12.00

2011-12 Panini Private Signings

AA Artem Anisimov 8.00 20.00
AB Alexandre Burrows 10.00 25.00
AGO Alex Goligoski 8.00 20.00
AH Adam Henrique 30.00 60.00
AO1 Alex Ovechkin white helmet 50.00 100.00
AO2 Alex Ovechkin red helmet 75.00 150.00
AV Antoine Vermette 4.00 10.00
BAI Josh Bailey 6.00 15.00
BC Bobby Clarke 15.00 40.00
BE Brian Elliott 12.50 30.00
BEN Jamie Benn 6.00 15.00
BER Jonathan Bernier 10.00 25.00
BG Blake Geoffrion 8.00 20.00
BH1 Brett Hull Flames 20.00 40.00
BH2 Brett Hull Red Wings 25.00 50.00
BH3 Brett Hull Blues 30.00 60.00
BL1 Brian Leetch Bruins 10.00 25.00
BL2 Brian Leetch Rangers 12.00 30.00
BM Brenden Morrow 6.00 15.00
BOW Drayson Bowman 5.00 12.00
BP1 Brad Park 20.00 40.00
BP2 Brad Park 12.50 30.00
BP3 Bernie Parent 25.00 50.00
BR Brad Richards 6.00 15.00
BS Brendan Shanahan 30.00 80.00
BT1 Bryan Trottier 15.00 30.00
BY Dustin Byfuglien 8.00 20.00
CA Craig Anderson 6.00 15.00
CAR Daniel Carcillo 6.00 15.00
CG Claude Giroux 20.00 40.00
CHF Johnny Bucyk 10.00 25.00
CJ1 Curtis Joseph Oilers 30.00 60.00
CJ2 Curtis Joseph Blues 25.00 50.00
CJ3 Curtis Joseph Leafs 15.00 40.00
CM Chris Mason 6.00 15.00
CN2 Cam Neely 30.00 60.00
CNE Chris Neil 6.00 15.00
CO Colton Orr 25.00 50.00
CP1 Corey Perry 12.00 30.00
CP2 Carey Price 25.00 60.00
CPR Chris Pronger 20.00 50.00
CS Charlie Simmer 8.00 20.00
CSC Cory Schneider 8.00 20.00
DA Daniel Alfredsson 15.00 30.00
DB1 David Backes 6.00 15.00
DB2 Dan Bouchard 8.00 20.00
DBR Dustin Brown 6.00 15.00
DC2 Dino Ciccarelli 8.00 20.00
DD Drew Doughty 10.00 25.00
DE Dan Ellis 5.00 12.00
DG1 Doug Gilmour Leafs 25.00 50.00
DG2 Doug Gilmour Blues 20.00 50.00
DH Dany Heatley 30.00 60.00
DOR Derek Dorsett 5.00 12.00
DP Dustin Penner 4.00 10.00
DR Derek Roy 6.00 15.00
DRO Dwayne Roloson 5.00 12.00
DS Daniel Sedin 20.00 40.00
DS1 Denis Savard Hawks 12.00 30.00
DS2 Denis Savard Canadiens 15.00 40.00
DUC Matt Duchene 10.00 25.00
DYK2 Joe Nieuwendyk 10.00 25.00
EB2 Ed Belfour Stars 30.00 60.00
EB3 Ed Belfour Sharks 30.00 60.00
EG1 Ed Giacomin Red Wings 20.00 50.00
EG2 Ed Giacomin Rangers 15.00 40.00
EK Evander Kane 8.00 20.00
EM Evgeni Malkin 25.00 50.00
ENN Tyler Ennis 8.00 20.00
ES Eric Staal 8.00 20.00
FIS Mike Fisher 6.00 15.00
FN Frans Nielsen 4.00 10.00
FP1 Felix Potvin Leafs 20.00 40.00
FP2 Felix Potvin Canucks 30.00 60.00
GC Gerry Cheevers 15.00 40.00
GF2 Grant Fuhr 30.00 60.00
GH1 Glenn Hall Blackhawks 12.00 30.00
GH2 Glenn Hall Red Wings 12.00 30.00
GH3 Glenn Hall Blues 12.00 30.00
GJ1 Bobby Hull white jersey 15.00 40.00
GJ2 Bobby Hull red jersey 20.00 50.00
GL Guillaume Latendresse 5.00 12.00
GL1 Gabriel Landeskog 25.00 60.00
GL2 Gabriel Landeskog 30.00 60.00
GN Greg Nemisz 6.00 15.00
GP Gilbert Perreault 12.00 30.00
GRE Andy Greene 4.00 10.00
GRP1 Don Cherry Bruins 20.00 50.00
GRP2 Don Cherry Rockies 20.00 50.00
GUY1 Guy Lafleur Habs 15.00 40.00
GUY2 Guy Lafleur Nordiques 15.00 40.00
HAL Taylor Hall 60.00 120.00
HIL Jonas Hiller 6.00 15.00
HL Henrik Lundqvist 25.00 50.00
HR Henri Richard 50.00 100.00
HS Henrik Sedin 15.00 30.00
JAN Cam Janssen 4.00 10.00
JB Jean Beliveau 25.00 50.00
JE Jordan Eberle 50.00 100.00
JG Jake Gardiner 12.00 30.00
JH Jimmy Howard 12.00 30.00
JI1 Jarome Iginla red 15.00 40.00
JI2 Jarome Iginla white 12.00 30.00
JN James Neal 12.00 30.00
JP Joe Pavelski 8.00 20.00
JR Jeremy Roenick 50.00 100.00
JS1 Joe Sakic Nordiques 40.00 80.00
JS2 Joe Sakic Avs 40.00 80.00
JT Joe Thornton 12.00 30.00
JVR James van Riemsdyk 8.00 20.00
KH Ken Hodge 15.00 30.00
KL Kari Lehtonen 6.00 15.00
KM Kenndal McArdle 6.00 15.00
KP Keith Primeau 8.00 20.00
KR Kris Russell 4.00 10.00
LAF1 Pat LaFontaine Sabres 25.00 50.00
LAF2 Pat LaFontaine Islanders 15.00 40.00
LE Loui Eriksson 6.00 15.00
LEV Normand Leveille 12.00 30.00
LM Lanny McDonald 15.00 30.00
LR1 Luc Robitaille Red Wings 12.00 30.00
LR2 Luc Robitaille Kings 15.00 40.00
LR3 Luc Robitaille Penguins 12.00 30.00
LS Lee Stempniak 4.00 10.00
MB1 Martin Brodeur white 40.00 80.00
MB2 Martin Brodeur red 50.00 100.00
MC Matt Carkner 6.00 15.00
MD1 Marcel Dionne Red Wings 10.00 25.00
MD2 Marcel Dionne Kings 10.00 25.00
MF1 Marc-Andre Fleury 15.00 30.00
MF2 Michael Frolik 6.00 15.00
MG Marian Gaborik 15.00 40.00
MH Marian Hossa 12.00 30.00
MID Rick Middleton 8.00 20.00
MIK Stan Mikita 12.00 30.00
MK Mike Komisarek 6.00 15.00
ML Mario Lemieux 60.00 120.00
MLE Michael Leighton 8.00 20.00
MO Mike Modano 15.00 40.00
MP Max Pacioretty 8.00 20.00
MR Manon Rheaume 20.00 50.00
MS Mikael Samuelsson 6.00 15.00
MSL Martin St. Louis 20.00 40.00
MT Max Talbot 6.00 15.00
NG Nathan Gerbe 5.00 12.00
NL1 Nicklas Lidstrom 25.00 50.00
OP Ondrej Pavelec 15.00 30.00
PC Paul Coffey 30.00 60.00
PD Pavel Datsyuk 20.00 50.00
PE1 Phil Esposito Bruins 15.00 40.00
PE2 Phil Esposito Rangers 25.00 50.00
PH Patric Hornqvist 6.00 15.00
PK1 Patrick Kane red jersey 25.00 60.00
PK2 Patrick Kane black jersey 20.00 50.00
PKS P.K. Subban 50.00 100.00
PL Pascal Leclaire 6.00 15.00
PM Patrick Marleau 5.00 12.00
POT Denis Potvin 8.00 20.00
PR1 Patrick Roy Avs 50.00 100.00
PR2 Patrick Roy Habs 50.00 100.00
RAP Aaron Palushaj 5.00 12.00
RAY1 Ray Bourque COL 40.00 80.00
RAY2 Ray Bourque BOS 30.00 60.00
BRO Richard Brodeur 12.00 30.00
REG Peter Regin 5.00 12.00
REN Rene Bourque 8.00 20.00
RG Rod Gilbert 8.00 20.00
RIN Pekka Rinne 12.00 30.00
RK Ryan Kesler 15.00 40.00
RM1 Ryan Miller blue 10.00 25.00
RM2 Ryan Miller white 10.00 25.00
RN Rick Nash 15.00 40.00
RRN1 Ryan Nugent-Hopkins 75.00 150.00
RRN2 Ryan Nugent-Hopkins 100.00 200.00
RRN3 Ryan Nugent-Hopkins 50.00 100.00
RR Rick Rypien 15.00 40.00
RS Ryan Smyth 6.00 15.00
RV1 Rogie Vachon Bruins 10.00 25.00
RV2 Rogie Vachon Kings 10.00 25.00
SAN Derek Sanderson 10.00 25.00
SAV Marc Savard 6.00 15.00
SC1 Sidney Crosby white 100.00 200.00
SC2 Sidney Crosby black 100.00 200.00
SC3 Sidney Crosby blue 100.00 200.00
SCH Milt Schmidt 12.00 30.00
SD Shane Doan 6.00 15.00
SEG Tyler Seguin 30.00 80.00
SG Simon Gagne 8.00 20.00
SIT1 Darryl Sittler Flyers 12.00 30.00
SIT2 Darryl Sittler Leafs 12.00 30.00
SM Steve Mason 6.00 15.00
SO Steve Ott 20.00 40.00
SS Steven Stamkos 30.00 60.00
SV Semyon Varlamov 8.00 20.00
SW Shea Weber 6.00 15.00
SY1 Steve Yzerman Wings 75.00 150.00
SY2 Steve Yzerman GM 75.00 150.00
TAV John Tavares 20.00 40.00
TB Tom Barrasso 25.00 50.00
TE1 Tony Esposito Hawks 20.00 50.00
TE2 Tony Esposito Canadiens 30.00 75.00
TEO Jose Theodore 8.00 20.00
TG T.J. Galiardi 5.00 12.00
TL1 Trevor Linden Canucks 15.00 40.00
TL2 Trevor Linden Habs 15.00 40.00
TO Terry O'Reilly 12.00 30.00
TO2 Jonathan Toews 30.00 60.00
TS Teemu Selanne 25.00 50.00
TT Tim Thomas 40.00 80.00
VL Vincent Lecavalier 12.00 30.00
WS Wayne Simmonds 6.00 15.00
WW Wojtek Wolski 4.00 10.00
YC Yvan Cournoyer 30.00 60.00
ZB Zach Boychuk 4.00 10.00
ZP Zach Parise 12.00 30.00
ZS Zack Stortini 6.00 15.00
BAC Mikael Backlund 4.00 10.00
GET Ryan Getzlaf 10.00 25.00
LET Kristopher Letang 15.00 40.00
PLL Pierre-Luc Letourneau-Leblond 4.00 10.00
RBC Brett Connolly 10.00 25.00
RBS Brendan Smith 8.00 20.00
RCE Cody Eakin 6.00 15.00
RCK Carl Klingberg 6.00 15.00
RHL Jonathon Huberdeau 4.00 10.00
RJF Justin Faulk 6.00 15.00
RJJ Jack Johnson 5.00 12.00
RJM John Moore 5.00 12.00
RMK Marcus Kruger 8.00 20.00
RMZ Mika Zibanejad 8.00 20.00
RRE Ryan Ellis 5.00 12.00
RSD Simon Despres 6.00 15.00
RST Shawn Thornton 8.00 20.00
RZK Zack Kassian 10.00 25.00
THR Phil Kessel 10.00 25.00
JCR1 Jim Craig ATL 15.00 40.00
JCR2 Jim Craig BOS 15.00 40.00

2013-14 Panini Private Signings

PSAC Alex Chiasson D 5.00 12.00
PSAG Alex Galchenyuk D 20.00 50.00
PSAK Alex Killorn T 8.00 20.00
PSAR Antoine Roussel D 5.00 12.00
PSBB Beau Bennett TC 6.00 15.00
PSBG Brendan Gallagher D 20.00 40.00
PSBJ Nick Bjugstad D 6.00 15.00
PSBL Brian Lashoff T 4.00 10.00
PSCC Charlie Coyle TC 8.00 20.00
PSCC Cory Conacher D 3.00 8.00
PSCT Christian Thomas D 4.00 10.00
PSDD Danny DeKeyser D 6.00 15.00
PSDH Dougie Hamilton 8.00 20.00
PSDJ Dmitrij Jaskin T 5.00 12.00
PSDS Drew Shore TC 4.00 10.00
PSFF Filip Forsberg T 15.00 40.00
PSIF Jamie Tardif D 3.00 8.00
PSJB Jonas Brodin C 6.00 15.00
PSJC Jack Campbell D 12.00 30.00
PSJH Jonathan Huberdeau D 12.00 30.00
PSJM J.T. Miller T 12.00 30.00
PSJS Jared Staal T 4.00 10.00
PSJS Jordan Schroeder T 5.00 12.00
PSKO Mikhail Grigorenko D 3.00 8.00
PSMG Mikael Granlund T 8.00 20.00
PSMK Michael Kostka T 4.00 10.00
PSNB Nathan Beaulieu TC 3.00 8.00
PSNJ Nicklas Jensen D 4.00 10.00
PSNY Nail Yakupov T 20.00 40.00
PSOK Jamie Oleksiak D 4.00 10.00
PSPG Philipp Grubauer T 12.00 30.00
PSQH Quinton Howden T 4.00 10.00
PSRM Ryan Murphy TC 5.00 12.00
PSRP Richard Panik T 5.00 12.00
PSRR Rickard Rakell D 5.00 12.00
PSRS Ryan Spooner T 8.00 20.00
PSRZ Petr Mrazek D 10.00 25.00
PSSL Scott Laughton D 6.00 15.00
PSSM Stefan Matteau T 4.00 10.00
PSSO Carl Soderberg D 5.00 12.00
PSSV Sami Vatanen TC 5.00 12.00
PSTH Thomas Hickey T 4.00 10.00
PSTP Tanner Pearson D 5.00 12.00
PSTT Tyler Toffoli T 10.00 25.00
PSTW Tom Wilson D 6.00 15.00
PSVF Viktor Fasth D 5.00 12.00
PSZR Zach Redmond T 4.00 10.00

2012-13 Panini Prizm

1 Teemu Selanne 1.25 3.00
2 Bobby Ryan .50 1.25
3 Tyler Seguin .75 2.00
4 Tuukka Rask .75 2.00
5 Cody Hodgson .40 1.00
6 Jarome Iginla .75 2.00
7 Eric Staal .75 2.00
8 Jordan Staal .50 1.25
9 Patrick Kane 1.25 3.00
10 Jonathan Toews 1.00 2.50
11 Gabriel Landeskog .75 2.00
12 Matt Duchene .60 1.50
13 Ryan Johansen .50 1.25
14 Jaromir Jagr 2.00 5.00
15 Loui Eriksson .40 1.00
16 Pavel Datsyuk 1.00 2.50
17 Henrik Zetterberg .75 2.00
18 Jordan Eberle .60 1.50
19 Ryan Nugent-Hopkins .75 2.00
20 Stephen Weiss .50 1.25
21 Jonathan Quick .75 2.00
22 Anze Kopitar 1.00 2.50
23 Zach Parise .60 1.50
24 Mikko Koivu .50 1.25
25 Carey Price 1.25 3.00
26 Brian Gionta .40 1.00
27 Pekka Rinne .60 1.50
28 Adam Henrique .50 1.25
29 Martin Brodeur 1.50 4.00
30 John Tavares 1.00 2.50
31 Henrik Lundqvist 1.50 4.00
32 Rick Nash .60 1.50
33 Jason Spezza .60 1.50
34 Daniel Alfredsson .60 1.50
35 Claude Giroux .60 1.50
36 Sean Couturier .50 1.25
37 Mike Smith .60 1.50
38 Sidney Crosby 2.50 6.00
39 Marc-Andre Fleury 1.25 3.00
40 Joe Thornton 1.00 2.50
41 Joe Pavelski .75 2.00
42 Alex Pietrangelo .50 1.25
43 Brian Elliott .50 1.25
44 Steven Stamkos 1.25 3.00
45 Vincent Lecavalier .60 1.50
46 Phil Kessel .60 1.50
47 James Reimer .60 1.50
48 Cory Schneider .60 1.50
49 Daniel Sedin .75 2.00
50 Alex Ovechkin 2.50 6.00
51 Nicklas Backstrom .60 1.50
52 Andrew Ladd .40 1.00
53 Mat Clark RC 1.25 3.00
54 Carter Camper RC 1.00 2.50
55 Lane MacDermid RC 1.25 3.00
56 Max Sauve RC 1.00 2.50
57 Torey Krug RC 3.00 8.00
58 Michael Hutchinson RC 1.50 4.00
59 Travis Turnbull RC 1.00 2.50
60 Akim Aliu RC 1.25 3.00
61 Jeremy Welsh RC 1.25 3.00
62 Brandon Bollig RC 1.00 2.50
63 Tyson Barrie RC 3.00 8.00
64 Mike Connolly RC 1.25 3.00
65 Andrew Joudrey RC 1.25 3.00
66 Shawn Hunwick RC 1.00 2.50
67 Cody Goloubef RC 1.00 2.50
68 Dalton Prout RC 1.00 2.50
69 Ryan Garbutt RC 1.00 2.50
70 Reilly Smith RC 3.00 8.00
71 Scott Glennie RC 1.25 3.00
72 Brenden Dillon RC 1.25 3.00
73 Riley Sheahan RC 1.50 4.00
74 Philippe Cornet RC 1.25 3.00
75 Colby Robak RC 1.00 2.50
76 Jordan Nolan RC 1.00 2.50
77 Kris Foucault RC 1.00 2.50
78 Tyler Cuma RC 1.00 2.50
79 Chay Genoway RC 1.00 2.50
80 Jason Zucker RC 2.50 6.00
81 Robert Mayer RC 1.50 4.00
82 Gabriel Dumont RC 1.25 3.00
83 Chet Pickard RC 1.25 3.00
84 Aaron Ness RC 1.00 2.50
85 Casey Cizikas RC 1.25 3.00
86 Matt Donovan RC 1.25 3.00
87 Matt Watkins RC 1.00 2.50
88 Jakob Silfverberg RC 2.00 5.00
89 Mark Stone RC 4.00 10.00
90 Brandon Manning RC 1.25 3.00
91 Michael Stone RC 1.25 3.00
92 Tyson Sexsmith RC 1.00 2.50
93 Jake Allen RC 3.00 8.00
94 J.T. Brown RC 1.25 3.00
95 Carter Ashton RC 1.00 2.50
96 Ryan Hamilton RC 1.00 2.50
97 Jussi Rynnas RC 1.00 2.50
98 Sven Baertschi RC 1.50 4.00
99 Chris Kreider RC 4.00 10.00
100 Jaden Schwartz RC 3.00 8.00

2012-13 Panini Prizm Blue

*1-52 VETS/25: 2.5X TO 6X BASIC CARDS
*53-100 ROOKIES/25: 2X TO 5X BASIC RC

2012-13 Panini Prizm Pulsar Father's Day

*1-52 VETS: .8X TO 2X BASIC CARDS
*53-100 ROOKIES: .5X TO 1.2X BASIC RC

2012-13 Panini Prizm Rainbow

*1-52 VETS: .8X TO 2X BASIC CARDS
*53-100 ROOKIES: .5X TO 1.2X BASIC RC

2012-13 Panini Prizm Red

*1-52 VETS/50: 1.5X TO 4X BASIC CARDS
*53-100 ROOKIES/50: 1.2X TO 3X BASIC RC

2012-13 Panini Prizm Autographs

1 Adam Henrique SP B 10.00 25.00
2 Alex Ovechkin SP A 75.00 125.00
3 Paul Postma 4.00 10.00
4 Andrew Shaw 10.00 25.00
5 Brad Richards SP B 15.00 30.00
6 Marcus Kruger 8.00 20.00
7 Brian Elliott 5.00 12.00
8 Alexandre Burrows 15.00 30.00
9 Mikko Koskinen 4.00 10.00
10 Carl Hagelin 6.00 15.00
11 Chris Chelios SP B 15.00 30.00
12 Claude Giroux SP B 40.00 80.00
13 Mike Komisarek 5.00 12.00
14 Robert Bortuzzo 4.00 10.00
15 Colin Greening 5.00 12.00
16 Craig Smith 4.00 10.00
18 Gabriel Landeskog SP B 20.00 40.00
19 Anders Nilsson 4.00 10.00
20 Gustav Nyquist 8.00 20.00
21 Jack Johnson SP B 4.00 10.00
22 James Neal SP B 10.00 25.00
23 Carey Price SP A 20.00 40.00
24 John Tavares SP B 15.00 30.00
25 Tomas Kubalik 4.00 10.00
26 Jordan Eberle SP B 20.00 40.00
27 Louis Leblanc 8.00 20.00
28 Marcus Foligno 8.00 20.00
29 Matt Read 5.00 12.00
30 Eddie Lack 6.00 15.00
31 Nazem Kadri SP B 10.00 25.00
32 Luke Schenn SP B 8.00 20.00
33 Thomas McCollum 5.00 12.00
34 Pavel Datsyuk SP A 20.00 40.00
35 Rick Nash SP A 30.00 60.00
36 Jonathan Toews SP A 30.00 60.00
37 Matt Calvert 3.00 8.00
38 Ryan Kesler SP B 15.00 30.00
39 Ryan Nugent-Hopkins SP B 40.00 80.00
40 Sidney Crosby SP A 75.00 135.00
41 Simon Despres 4.00 10.00
42 Stephen Weiss 6.00 15.00
43 Lennart Petrell 4.00 10.00
44 Travis Zajac 4.00 10.00
46 Zack Kassian 8.00 20.00
47 Drew Doughty SP B 20.00 40.00
48 Dion Phaneuf SP B 5.00 12.00
50 Alex Pietrangelo 8.00 20.00
51 Zach Parise SP B 8.00 20.00
53 Mat Clark 4.00 10.00
54 Carter Camper 3.00 8.00
55 Lane MacDermid SP B 8.00 20.00
56 Max Sauve 3.00 8.00
57 Torey Krug 8.00 20.00
58 Michael Hutchinson 5.00 12.00
59 Travis Turnbull SP B 4.00 10.00
60 Akim Aliu 4.00 10.00
61 Jeremy Welsh SP B 5.00 12.00
62 Brandon Bollig 3.00 8.00
63 Tyson Barrie 10.00 25.00
64 Mike Connolly SP A 12.00 30.00
65 Andrew Joudrey 4.00 10.00
66 Shawn Hunwick SP B 4.00 10.00
67 Cody Goloubef 3.00 8.00
68 Dalton Prout 3.00 8.00
69 Ryan Garbutt SP B 4.00 10.00
70 Reilly Smith 10.00 25.00
71 Scott Glennie 4.00 10.00
72 Brenden Dillon 4.00 10.00
73 Riley Sheahan 5.00 12.00

74 Philippe Cornet 4.00 10.00
75 Colby Robak 3.00 8.00
76 Jordan Nolan 3.00 8.00
77 Kris Foucault 3.00 8.00
78 Tyler Cuma 3.00 8.00
79 Chay Genoway 3.00 8.00
80 Jason Zucker 8.00 20.00
81 Robert Mayer 5.00 12.00
82 Gabriel Dumont SP B 10.00 25.00
83 Chet Pickard SP B 5.00 12.00
84 Aaron Ness 3.00 8.00
85 Casey Cizikas 4.00 10.00
86 Matt Donovan 4.00 10.00
87 Matt Watkins 3.00 8.00
88 Jakob Silfverberg 6.00 15.00
89 Mark Stone 12.00 30.00
90 Brandon Manning 4.00 10.00
91 Michael Stone 4.00 10.00
92 Tyson Sexsmith 3.00 8.00
93 Jake Allen 10.00 25.00
94 J.T. Brown 4.00 10.00
95 Carter Ashton 3.00 8.00
96 Ryan Hamilton 6.00 15.00
97 Jussi Rynnas 8.00 20.00
98 Sven Baertschi 5.00 12.00
99 Chris Kreider 12.00 30.00
100 Jaden Schwartz 10.00 25.00

2013-14 Panini Prizm

*VET.PRIZM: 2.5X TO 6X BASIC CARDS
*RC.PRIZM: 1X TO 2.5X BASIC RC
*VET.BLUE: 2.5X TO 6X BASIC CARDS
*RC.BLUE: 1X TO 2.5X BASIC RC
*VET.BLUE.PULSAR: 2X TO 5X BASIC CARDS
*RC.BLUE.PULSAR: .8X TO 2X BASIC RC
*VETS.GREEN: 2.5X TO 6X BASIC CARDS
*RC.GREEN: 1X TO 2.5X BASIC RC
*VET.ORANGE/50: 6X TO 15X BASIC CARDS
*RC.ORANGE/50: 2X TO 5X BASIC RC
*RC.PURPLE: .8X TO 2X BASIC CARDS
*VET.RED: 2.5X TO 6X BASIC CARDS
*RC.RED: 1X TO 2.5X BASIC RC
*VET.RED.PULSAR: 2X TO 5X BASIC CARDS
*RC.RED.PULSAR: .8X TO 2X BASIC RC
1 Zdeno Chara .30 .75
2 Patrice Bergeron .40 1.00
3 Torey Krug .25 .60
4 Tuukka Rask .40 1.00
5 Brad Marchand .60 1.50
6 Milan Lucic .30 .75
7 David Krejci .30 .75
8 Thomas Vanek .25 .60
9 Ryan Miller .30 .75
10 Cody Hodgson .20 .50
11 Steve Ott .20 .50
12 Drew Stafford .20 .50
13 Tyler Myers .20 .50
14 Eric Staal .40 1.00
15 Jordan Staal .25 .60
16 Cam Ward .30 .75
17 Alexander Semin .30 .75
18 Jiri Tlusty .20 .50
19 Jeff Skinner .40 1.00
20 Tuomo Ruutu .25 .60
21 Jack Johnson .20 .50
22 Sergei Bobrovsky .50 1.25
23 Marian Gaborik .30 .75
24 R.J. Umberger .20 .50
25 Ryan Johansen .25 .60
26 Brandon Dubinsky .20 .50
27 Henrik Zetterberg .40 1.00
28 Pavel Datsyuk .50 1.25
29 Niklas Kronwall .25 .60
30 Jimmy Howard .40 1.00
31 Johan Franzen .25 .60
32 Daniel Cleary .30 .75
33 Jakub Kindl .20 .50
34 Erik Gudbranson .20 .50
35 Jacob Markstrom .30 .75
36 Brian Campbell .20 .50
37 Ed Jovanovski .20 .50
38 Kris Versteeg .20 .50
39 Max Pacioretty .30 .75
40 P.K. Subban .40 1.00
41 Carey Price .60 1.50
42 Brian Gionta .20 .50
43 Tomas Plekanec .20 .50
44 Andrei Markov .20 .50
45 David Desharnais .20 .50
46 Martin Brodeur .75 2.00
47 Patrik Elias .30 .75
48 Ilya Kovalchuk .30 .75
49 Adam Henrique .25 .60
50 Travis Zajac .20 .50
51 Dainius Zubrus .20 .50
52 Adam Larsson .30 .75
53 John Tavares .50 1.25
54 Matt Moulson .20 .50
55 Michael Grabner .25 .60
56 Evgeni Nabokov .30 .75
57 Josh Bailey .25 .60
58 Lubomir Visnovsky .20 .50
59 Kyle Okposo .20 .50
60 Henrik Lundqvist .75 2.00
61 Brad Richards .30 .75
62 Ryan Callahan .20 .50
63 Rick Nash .30 .75
64 Derick Brassard .20 .50
65 Carl Hagelin .20 .50
66 Marc Staal .20 .50
67 Derek Stepan .20 .50
68 Chris Phillips .20 .50
69 Erik Karlsson .40 1.00
70 Craig Anderson .30 .75
71 Mika Zibanejad .40 1.00
72 Jason Spezza .30 .75
73 Kyle Turris .20 .50
74 Milan Michalek .20 .50
75 Robin Lehner .25 .60
76 Claude Giroux .30 .75
77 Steve Mason .25 .60
78 Scott Hartnell .20 .50
79 Luke Schenn .30 .75
80 Jakub Voracek .25 .60
81 Sean Couturier .25 .60
82 Matt Read .20 .50
83 Brayden Schenn .30 .75
84 Sidney Crosby 1.25 3.00
85 Evgeni Malkin .60 1.50
86 Marc-Andre Fleury .60 1.50
87 Kris Letang .40 1.00
88 Tomas Vokoun .25 .60
89 James Neal .20 .50
90 Chris Kunitz .30 .75
91 Ben Bishop .25 .60
92 Martin St. Louis .30 .75
93 Steven Stamkos .60 1.50
94 Ryan Malone .20 .50
95 Victor Hedman .40 1.00
96 Joffrey Lupul .20 .50
97 Phil Kessel .30 .75
98 James van Riemsdyk .25 .60
99 Dion Phaneuf .25 .60
100 Nazem Kadri .40 1.00
101 James Reimer .30 .75
102 Jake Gardiner .20 .50
103 Alex Ovechkin 1.25 3.00
104 Nicklas Backstrom .30 .75
105 Braden Holtby .40 1.00
106 Brooks Laich .20 .50
107 Mike Green .25 .60
108 John Carlson .30 .75
109 Corey Perry .50 1.25
110 Cam Fowler .30 .75
111 Ryan Getzlaf .30 .75
112 Teemu Selanne .60 1.50
113 Francois Beauchemin .20 .50
114 Saku Koivu .30 .75
115 Jonas Hiller .25 .60
116 Mike Cammalleri .25 .60
117 Miikka Kiprusoff .30 .75
118 Curtis Glencross .20 .50
119 Dennis Wideman .20 .50
120 Jiri Hudler .25 .60
121 T.J. Brodie .20 .50
122 Jonathan Toews .50 1.25
123 Patrick Kane .60 1.50
124 Duncan Keith .25 .60
125 Marian Hossa .30 .75
126 Corey Crawford .40 1.00
127 Patrick Sharp .30 .75
128 Brent Seabrook .20 .50
129 Gabriel Landeskog .40 1.00
130 Milan Hejduk .25 .60
131 Semyon Varlamov .30 .75
132 Erik Johnson .20 .50
133 Matt Duchene .30 .75
134 Ryan O'Reilly .30 .75
135 Jamie Benn .30 .75
136 Erik Cole .20 .50
137 Kari Lehtonen .25 .60
138 Alex Goligoski .20 .50
139 Ray Whitney .25 .60
140 Taylor Hall .30 .75
141 Sam Gagner .20 .50
142 Jordan Eberle .30 .75
143 Devan Dubnyk .25 .60
144 Ryan Smyth .25 .60
145 Ryan Nugent-Hopkins .40 1.00
146 Nick Schultz .20 .50
147 Ladislav Smid .20 .50
148 Jonathan Quick .40 1.00
149 Dustin Brown .30 .75
150 Anze Kopitar .50 1.25
151 Drew Doughty .40 1.00
152 Mike Richards .25 .60
153 Jeff Carter .25 .60
154 Slava Voynov .25 .60
155 Mikko Koivu .25 .60
156 Zach Parise .30 .75
157 Jared Spurgeon .30 .75
158 Niklas Backstrom .25 .60
159 Ryan Suter .25 .60
160 Dany Heatley .25 .60
161 Josh Harding .30 .75
162 Jason Pominville .20 .50
163 Shea Weber .25 .60
164 Pekka Rinne .30 .75
165 David Legwand .25 .60
166 Mike Fisher .20 .50
167 Roman Josi .30 .75
168 Shane Doan .25 .60
169 Mike Smith .30 .75
170 Oliver Ekman-Larsson .30 .75
171 Mikkel Boedker .20 .50
172 Keith Yandle .20 .50
173 Logan Couture .40 1.00
174 Joe Thornton .50 1.25
175 Joe Pavelski .40 1.00
176 Dan Boyle .20 .50
177 Patrick Marleau .30 .75
178 Antti Niemi .25 .60
179 Alex Pietrangelo .25 .60
180 T.J. Oshie .30 .75
181 Kevin Shattenkirk .20 .50
182 David Backes .20 .50
183 Jay Bouwmeester .20 .50
184 Alexander Steen .20 .50
185 Chris Stewart .25 .60
186 Jake Allen .30 .75
187 Daniel Sedin .40 1.00
188 Ryan Kesler .30 .75
189 Alexandre Burrows .20 .50
190 Chris Higgins .20 .50
191 Henrik Sedin .40 1.00
192 Kevin Bieksa .25 .60
193 Roberto Luongo .50 1.25
194 Mason Raymond .20 .50
195 Andrew Ladd .20 .50
196 Ondrej Pavelec .30 .75
197 Evander Kane .30 .75
198 Mark Scheifele .50 1.25
199 Blake Wheeler .30 .75
200 Dustin Byfuglien .30 .75
201 Emerson Etem RC .75 2.00
202 Igor Bobkov RC .60 1.50
203 Rickard Rakell RC .75 2.00
204 Sami Vatanen RC .75 2.00
205 Viktor Fasth RC .75 2.00
206 Carl Soderberg RC .75 2.00
207 Dougie Hamilton RC 1.25 3.00
208 Ryan Spooner RC .75 2.00
209 Brian Flynn RC .60 1.50
210 Chad Ruhwedel RC .50 1.25
211 Johan Larsson RC 1.00 2.50
212 Mark Pysyk RC .75 2.00
213 Mikhail Grigorenko RC .50 1.25
214 Ben Hanowski RC .60 1.50
215 Mark Cundari RC .50 1.25
216 Maxwell Reinhart RC .75 2.00
217 Roman Cervenka RC .60 1.50
218 Chris Terry RC .50 1.25
219 Jared Staal RC .60 1.50
220 Michal Jordan RC .50 1.25
221 Ryan Murphy RC .75 2.00
222 Drew LeBlanc RC .50 1.25
223 Ryan Stanton RC .75 2.00
224 Calvin Pickard RC 1.00 2.50
225 Michael Sgarbossa RC .75 2.00
226 Patrick Bordeleau RC .75 2.00
227 Jonathan Audy-Marchessault RC 2.00 5.00
228 Sean Collins RC .60 1.50
229 Alex Chiasson RC .75 2.00
230 Antoine Roussel RC .75 2.00
231 Cristopher Nilstorp RC .60 1.50
232 Jack Campbell RC 2.00 5.00
233 Jamie Oleksiak RC .60 1.50
234 Brian Lashoff RC .60 1.50
235 Damien Brunner RC .60 1.50
236 Danny DeKeyser RC 1.00 2.50
237 Petr Mrazek RC 1.50 4.00
238 Justin Schultz RC .75 2.00
239 Mark Arcobello RC .75 2.00
240 Nail Yakupov RC 1.50 4.00
241 Alex Petrovic RC .60 1.50
242 Drew Shore RC .60 1.50
243 Jonathan Huberdeau RC 2.00 5.00
244 Nick Bjugstad RC 1.00 2.50
245 Quinton Howden RC .60 1.50
246 Tyler Toffoli RC 1.50 4.00
247 Charlie Coyle RC 1.25 3.00
248 Darcy Kuemper RC 1.50 4.00
249 Jonas Brodin RC 1.00 2.50
250 Mikael Granlund RC 1.25 3.00
251 Alex Galchenyuk RC 2.00 5.00
252 Brendan Gallagher RC 2.00 5.00
253 Jarred Tinordi RC .75 2.00
254 Nathan Beaulieu RC .50 1.25
255 Austin Watson RC .60 1.50
256 Filip Forsberg RC 2.50 6.00
257 Joonas Rask RC .50 1.25
258 Taylor Beck RC .60 1.50
259 Eric Gelinas RC .75 2.00
260 Harri Pesonen RC .60 1.50
261 Stefan Matteau RC .60 1.50
262 Anders Lee RC 1.25 3.00
263 Brock Nelson RC 1.50 4.00
264 Thomas Hickey RC .60 1.50
265 Christian Thomas RC .60 1.50
266 J.T. Miller RC 2.00 5.00
267 Cory Conacher RC .50 1.25
268 Dave Dziurzynski RC .60 1.50
269 Eric Gryba RC .60 1.50
270 Jean-Gabriel Pageau RC .75 2.00
271 Jason Akeson RC .60 1.50
272 Oliver Lauridsen RC .60 1.50
273 Scott Laughton RC 1.00 2.50
274 Tye McGinn RC .75 2.00
275 Chris Brown RC .50 1.25
276 Beau Bennett RC 1.00 2.50
277 Eric Hartzell RC .75 2.00
278 Matt Irwin RC .60 1.50
279 Matt Tennyson RC .50 1.25
280 Nick Petrecki RC .50 1.25
281 Dmitrij Jaskin RC .75 2.00
282 Vladimir Tarasenko RC 3.00 8.00
283 Alex Killorn RC 1.25 3.00
284 Ondrej Palat RC 1.25 3.00
285 Radko Gudas RC .75 2.00
286 Richard Panik RC .75 2.00
287 Tyler Johnson RC 1.50 4.00
288 Leo Komarov RC .75 2.00
289 Michael Kostka RC .60 1.50
290 Frank Corrado RC .50 1.25
291 Joe Cannata RC .60 1.50
292 Jordan Schroeder RC .75 2.00
293 Nicklas Jensen RC .60 1.50
294 Cameron Schilling RC .50 1.25
295 Philipp Grubauer RC 2.00 5.00
296 Steve Oleksy RC .75 2.00
297 Tom Wilson RC 1.50 4.00
298 Anthony Peluso RC .50 1.25
299 Eddie Pasquale RC .50 1.25
300 Zach Redmond RC .60 1.50
301 Loui Eriksson .20 .50
302 Jarome Iginla .40 1.00
303 Reilly Smith .30 .75
304 Matt Moulson .20 .50
305 Daniel Alfredsson .30 .75
306 Tim Thomas .30 .75
307 Daniel Briere .30 .75
308 Jaromir Jagr 1.00 2.50
309 Cory Schneider .30 .75
310 Thomas Vanek .25 .60
311 Bobby Ryan .25 .60
312 Vincent Lecavalier .30 .75
313 Jonathan Bernier .25 .60
314 David Clarkson .20 .50
315 Mason Raymond .20 .50
316 Tyler Seguin .40 1.00
317 Ilya Bryzgalov .30 .75
318 David Perron .25 .60
319 Mike Ribeiro .20 .50
320 Devin Setoguchi .25 .60
321 John Gibson RC 2.00 5.00
322 Hampus Lindholm RC 1.25 3.00
323 Kevan Miller RC .60 1.50
324 Jamie Tardif RC .50 1.25
325 Nikita Zadorov RC .50 1.25
326 Rasmus Ristolainen RC 1.25 3.00
327 Zemgus Girgensons RC 1.25 3.00
328 Ben Street RC .60 1.50
329 Reto Berra RC .75 2.00
330 Sean Monahan RC 1.25 3.00
331 Elias Lindholm RC 2.00 5.00
332 Nathan MacKinnon RC 8.00 20.00
333 John Muse RC .75 2.00
334 Antti Raanta RC 1.50 4.00
335 Joakim Nordstrom RC .60 1.50
336 Shawn Lalonde RC .75 2.00
337 Boone Jenner RC 1.50 4.00
338 Ryan Murray RC 1.25 3.00
339 Kevin Connauton RC .60 1.50
340 Valeri Nichushkin RC 1.50 4.00
341 Luke Glendening RC .75 2.00
342 Tomas Jurco RC 1.00 2.50
343 Xavier Ouellet RC .75 2.00
344 Anton Belov RC .75 2.00
345 Luke Gazdic RC .60 1.50
346 Martin Marincin RC .60 1.50
347 Taylor Fedun RC 1.00 2.50
348 Tyler Pitlick RC .75 2.00
349 Will Acton RC .60 1.50
350 Aleksander Barkov RC 2.50 6.00
351 Jonathan Rheault RC .50 1.25
352 Niklas Svedberg RC 1.50 4.00
353 Linden Vey RC .50 1.25
354 Martin Jones RC 1.25 3.00
355 Tanner Pearson RC .75 2.00
356 Erik Haula RC 1.00 2.50
357 Johan Gustafsson RC 1.00 2.50
358 Matt Dumba RC .50 1.25
359 Greg Pateryn RC .75 2.00
360 Michael Bournival RC .75 2.00
361 Patrick Holland RC 1.25 3.00
362 Daniel Bang RC .60 1.50
363 Kevin Henderson RC .60 1.50
364 Magnus Hellberg RC .75 2.00
365 Marek Mazanec RC .75 2.00
366 Seth Jones RC 1.50 4.00
367 Dylan McIlrath RC .50 1.25
368 Jon Merrill RC .75 2.00
369 Reid Boucher RC .75 2.00
370 Ryan Strome RC 1.25 3.00
371 Jason Missiaen RC .75 2.00
372 Jesper Fast RC .75 2.00
373 Cody Ceci RC .60 1.50
374 Derek Grant RC .60 1.50
375 Calvin Heeter RC .60 1.50
376 Michael Raffl RC .60 1.50
377 Connor Murphy RC .60 1.50
378 Jordan Szwarz RC .75 2.00
379 Lucas Lessio RC .50 1.25
380 Brian Dumoulin RC .75 2.00
381 Brian Gibbons RC .75 2.00
382 Jayson Megna RC .75 2.00
383 Jeff Zatkoff RC .75 2.00
384 Olli Maatta RC 2.50 6.00
385 Zach Sill RC .75 2.00
386 Freddie Hamilton RC .75 2.00
387 Matt Nieto RC .60 1.50
388 Tomas Hertl RC 2.50 6.00
389 Mark Barberio RC .50 1.25
390 Nikita Kucherov RC 40.00 100.00
391 David Broll RC .75 2.00
392 Jamie Devane RC .60 1.50
393 Jerry D'Amigo RC .75 2.00
394 Josh Leivo RC .60 1.50
395 Morgan Rielly RC 2.00 5.00
396 Connor Carrick RC .60 1.50
397 Michael Latta RC .60 1.50
398 Patrick Wey RC .60 1.50
399 Jacob Trouba RC 1.25 3.00
400 John Albert RC .60 1.50

2013-14 Panini Prizm Cracked Ice Toronto Fall Expo

*CRACKED ICE: .6X TO 1.5X BASIC RC

2013-14 Panini Prizm Cracked Ice Toronto Fall Expo VIP 30

*1-200 VETS/30: 8X TO 20X BASIC CARDS
*201-300 ROOK/30: 2.5X TO 6X BASIC RC
104 Nicklas Backstrom 8.00 20.00
126 Corey Crawford 10.00 25.00

2013-14 Panini Prizm Prizms

390 Nikita Kucherov 80.00 200.00

2013-14 Panini Prizm Autographs

*PRIZM/15-20: .6X TO 1.5X BASIC AU
A1S Eric Staal 8.00 20.00
AAY Allen York 4.00 10.00
AB4 Jean Beliveau 6.00 15.00
ABB1 Brandon Bollig 5.00 12.00
ABB2 Brett Bulmer 4.00 10.00
ABH Brett Hull 12.00 30.00
ABK Brad Park 5.00 12.00
ABM Basil McRae 4.00 10.00
ABR1 Bill Ranford 6.00 15.00
ABR2 Bobby Ryan 5.00 12.00
ABS Brendan Shanahan 6.00 15.00
ABT Bryan Trottier 6.00 15.00
ABU Brent Burns 6.00 15.00
ABV Alexander Burmistrov 5.00 12.00
ABZ Tyler Bozak 4.00 10.00
AC7 Chris Chelios 6.00 15.00
ACA Craig Anderson 6.00 15.00
ACD Cedrick Desjardins 5.00 12.00
ACG Chay Genoway 6.00 15.00
ACH Carl Hagelin 4.00 10.00
ACI David Krejci 6.00 15.00
ACK Chris Kreider 8.00 20.00
ACP Carey Price 12.00 30.00
ACS Cory Schneider 6.00 15.00
ACU Tyler Cuma 5.00 12.00
ACW Cam Ward 6.00 15.00
ADC Daniel Carcillo 4.00 10.00
ADG Doug Gilmour 8.00 20.00
ADP Dalton Prout 5.00 12.00
AEO Jose Theodore 6.00 15.00
AFV Jakob Silfverberg 4.00 10.00
AGC Gerry Cheevers 6.00 15.00
AGF Cody Goloubef 4.00 10.00
AGH Gordie Howe 20.00 50.00
AGI Mikhail Grabovski 4.00 10.00
AGL Gabriel Landeskog 8.00 20.00
AGS Gary Simmons 6.00 15.00
AGX Claude Giroux 6.00 15.00
AH9 Bobby Hull 12.00 30.00
AHJ Hugh Jessiman 5.00 12.00
AHS Harri Sateri 4.00 10.00
AHY Rich Peverley 6.00 15.00
AIU Akim Aliu 4.00 10.00
AJA Jake Allen 6.00 15.00
AJB Jamie Benn 6.00 15.00
AJD Justin DiBenedetto 4.00 10.00
AJE1 Jordan Eberle 6.00 15.00
AJE2 Borje Salming 6.00 15.00
AJF1 Joe Finley 4.00 10.00
AJF2 Johan Franzen 5.00 12.00
AJG1 Jean-Sebastien Giguere 6.00 15.00
AJG2 Jonas Gustavsson 5.00 12.00
AJJ Jaromir Jagr 20.00 50.00
AJN1 James Neal 4.00 10.00
AJN2 Jordan Nolan 5.00 12.00
AJQ Jonathan Quick 8.00 20.00
AJS Joe Sakic 12.00 30.00
AJT John Tavares 10.00 25.00
AKF Kris Foucault 4.00 10.00
AKP Keith Primeau 5.00 12.00
ALC Logan Couture 8.00 20.00
ALE Loui Eriksson 4.00 10.00
ALS Lee Stempniak 4.00 10.00
AM2 Al MacInnis 8.00 20.00
AMC Mat Clark 4.00 10.00
AMG Michael Grabner 5.00 12.00
AMH Matt Hunwick 4.00 10.00
AML Mario Lemieux 25.00 60.00
AMM2 Matt Moulson 4.00 10.00
AMM1 Mark Messier 12.00 30.00
AMS1 Mike Smith 6.00 15.00
AMS2 Michael Stone 5.00 12.00
AN8 Cam Neely 6.00 15.00
ANH Ryan Nugent-Hopkins 8.00 20.00
ANK Nazem Kadri 8.00 20.00
ANO Mark Giordano 6.00 15.00
AOB Jim O'Brien 4.00 10.00
AOP Ondrej Pavelec 6.00 15.00
AOV Alex Ovechkin 25.00 60.00
APB Pavel Bure 6.00 15.00
APC Patrice Cormier 4.00 10.00
APD Pavel Datsyuk 10.00 25.00
APE Corey Perry 10.00 25.00
APH Peter Holland 4.00 10.00
APK Patrick Kane 12.00 30.00
APP Corey Tropp 4.00 10.00
APR1 Chris Pronger 6.00 15.00
APR2 Patrick Roy 15.00 40.00
APS P.K. Subban 8.00 20.00
ARB1 Ray Bourque 10.00 25.00
ARB2 Rene Bourque 4.00 10.00
ARH Ryan Hamilton 4.00 10.00
ARJ Roman Josi 6.00 15.00
ARK1 Rick Kehoe 5.00 12.00
ARK2 Ryan Kesler 6.00 15.00
ARM Ryan Miller 6.00 15.00
ARN Rick Nash 6.00 15.00
ARS Riley Sheahan 4.00 10.00
ASB1 Sven Baertschi 5.00 12.00
ASB2 Sergei Bobrovsky 10.00 25.00
ASC1 Sean Couturier 5.00 12.00
ASC2 Sidney Crosby 25.00 60.00
ASE Stefan Elliott 5.00 12.00
ASG1 Sam Gagner 4.00 10.00
ASG2 Scott Glennie 4.00 10.00
ASI Darryl Sittler 8.00 20.00
AST Martin St. Louis 6.00 15.00
ASW Shea Weber 5.00 12.00
ASY Steve Yzerman 15.00 40.00
ASZ1 Greg Nemisz 4.00 10.00
ASZ2 Brad Staubitz 4.00 10.00
ATB1 Tyson Barrie 4.00 10.00
ATB2 T.J. Brennan 4.00 10.00
ATO T.J. Oshie 6.00 15.00
ATS Tyler Seguin 8.00 20.00
ATW Jonathan Toews 10.00 25.00
ATZ Jaden Schwartz 8.00 20.00
AUY Jussi Rynnas 4.00 10.00
AVL1 Martin Havlat 5.00 12.00
AVL2 Vincent Lecavalier 6.00 15.00
AVO Tomas Vokoun 5.00 12.00
AWL Drew Bagnall 4.00 10.00
AWN J.T. Brown 4.00 10.00
AYK Colby Robak 4.00 10.00
AZP Zach Parise 6.00 15.00

2013-14 Panini Prizm Cracked Ice Toronto Fall Expo Autographs

201 Emerson Etem 5.00 12.00
207 Dougie Hamilton 10.00 25.00
208 Ryan Spooner 6.00 15.00
232 Jack Campbell 15.00 40.00
237 Petr Mrazek 12.00 30.00
246 Tyler Toffoli 12.00 30.00
247 Charlie Coyle 10.00 25.00
253 Jarred Tinordi 6.00 15.00
254 Nathan Beaulieu 4.00 10.00
263 Brock Nelson 12.00 30.00
265 Christian Thomas 5.00 12.00
273 Scott Laughton 8.00 20.00
276 Beau Bennett 8.00 20.00
293 Nicklas Jensen 5.00 12.00

2013-14 Panini Prizm Endless Impressions

*PRIZM: .6X TO 1.5X BASIC INSERTS
*ORANGE/50: 1.2X TO 3X BASIC INSERTS
EI1 Gordie Howe 5.00 12.00
EI2 Bernie Parent 2.00 5.00
EI3 Johnny Bower 1.50 4.00
EI4 Bobby Hull 3.00 8.00
EI5 Mario Lemieux 6.00 15.00
EI6 Marcel Dionne 2.00 5.00
EI7 Stan Mikita 2.00 5.00
EI8 Johnny Bucyk 1.50 4.00
EI9 Patrick Roy 4.00 10.00
EI10 Mark Messier 3.00 8.00
EI11 Guy Lafleur 2.00 5.00
EI12 Billy Smith 1.50 4.00
EI13 Tony Esposito 1.50 4.00
EI14 Phil Esposito 2.50 6.00
EI15 Steve Yzerman 4.00 10.00

2013-14 Panini Prizm Immortalized

*PRIZM: .6X TO 1.5X BASIC INSERTS
*ORANGE/50: 1.2X TO 3X BASIC INSERTS
1 Sidney Crosby 6.00 15.00
2 Steve Yzerman 4.00 10.00
3 Jonathan Toews 2.50 6.00
4 Teemu Selanne 3.00 8.00
5 Joe Sakic 3.00 8.00
6 Patrick Roy 4.00 10.00
7 Mark Messier 3.00 8.00
8 Mike Richter 1.50 4.00
9 Brett Hull 3.00 8.00
10 Martin Brodeur 4.00 10.00
11 Patrice Bergeron 2.00 5.00
12 Bobby Clarke 2.50 6.00
13 Gordie Howe 5.00 12.00
14 Mike Bossy 1.50 4.00
15 Larry Robinson 1.50 4.00
16 Jonathan Quick 2.00 5.00
17 Martin St. Louis 1.50 4.00
18 Joe Nieuwendyk 1.25 3.00
19 Phil Esposito 2.50 6.00
20 Ray Bourque 2.50 6.00

2013-14 Panini Prizm Initial Impressions

*PRIZM: .8X TO 2X BASIC INSERTS
*ORANGE/50: 1.5X TO 4X BASIC INSERTS
II1 Nail Yakupov 2.00 5.00
II2 Jonathan Huberdeau 2.50 6.00
II3 Vladimir Tarasenko 2.50 6.00
II4 Alex Galchenyuk 2.50 6.00
II5 Dougie Hamilton 1.50 4.00
II6 Ryan Murphy 1.00 2.50
II7 Stefan Matteau .75 2.00
II8 Tyler Toffoli 2.00 5.00
II9 Cory Conacher .60 1.50
II10 Damien Brunner .75 2.00
II11 Viktor Fasth 1.00 2.50
II12 Justin Schultz 1.00 2.50
II13 Emerson Etem 1.00 2.50
II14 Scott Laughton 1.25 3.00
II15 Brendan Gallagher 2.50 6.00

2013-14 Panini Prizm Net Defenders

*PRIZM: .5X TO 1.2X BASIC INSERTS
*ORANGE/50: 1X TO 2.5X BASIC INSERTS
ND1 Henrik Lundqvist 5.00 12.00
ND2 Antti Niemi 1.50 4.00
ND3 Niklas Backstrom 1.50 4.00
ND4 Marc-Andre Fleury 4.00 10.00
ND5 Evgeni Nabokov 2.00 5.00
ND6 Braden Holtby 2.50 6.00
ND7 Sergei Bobrovsky 3.00 8.00
ND8 Jimmy Howard 2.50 6.00
ND9 Carey Price 4.00 10.00
ND10 Ondrej Pavelec 2.00 5.00
ND11 Corey Crawford 2.50 6.00
ND12 Tuukka Rask 2.50 6.00
ND13 James Reimer 2.00 5.00
ND14 Martin Brodeur 5.00 12.00
ND15 Jonathan Quick 2.50 6.00
ND16 Roberto Luongo 3.00 8.00
ND17 Ryan Miller 2.00 5.00
ND18 Jonas Hiller 1.50 4.00
ND19 Pekka Rinne 2.00 5.00
ND20 Mike Smith 2.00 5.00

2013-14 Panini Prizm Pivotal Players

*PRIZM: .6X TO 1.5X BASIC INSERTS
*ORANGE/50: 1.2X TO 3X BASIC INSERTS
PP1 Corey Perry 2.50 6.00
PP2 Patrice Bergeron 2.00 5.00
PP3 Cody Hodgson 1.00 2.50
PP4 Curtis Glencross 1.00 2.50
PP5 Alexander Semin 1.50 4.00
PP6 Patrick Kane 3.00 8.00
PP7 Gabriel Landeskog 2.00 5.00
PP8 Marian Gaborik 1.50 4.00
PP9 Jamie Benn 1.50 4.00
PP10 Henrik Zetterberg 2.00 5.00
PP11 Jordan Eberle 1.50 4.00
PP12 Jonathan Huberdeau 2.00 5.00
PP13 Jeff Carter 1.25 3.00
PP14 Zach Parise 1.50 4.00
PP15 P.K. Subban 2.00 5.00
PP16 Shea Weber 1.25 3.00
PP17 Martin Brodeur 4.00 10.00
PP18 John Tavares 2.50 6.00
PP19 Henrik Lundqvist 4.00 10.00
PP20 Erik Karlsson 2.00 5.00
PP21 Claude Giroux 1.50 4.00
PP22 Oliver Ekman-Larsson 1.50 4.00
PP23 Evgeni Malkin 3.00 8.00
PP24 Logan Couture 2.00 5.00
PP25 David Backes 1.00 2.50
PP26 Steven Stamkos 3.00 8.00
PP27 Nazem Kadri 2.00 5.00
PP28 Roberto Luongo 2.50 6.00
PP29 Alex Ovechkin 6.00 15.00
PP30 Andrew Ladd 1.00 2.50

2013-14 Panini Prizm Rookie Autographs

321 John Gibson 12.00 30.00
322 Hampus Lindholm 8.00 20.00
324 Jamie Tardif 3.00 8.00
325 Nikita Zadorov 3.00 8.00
327 Zemgus Girgensons 8.00 20.00
329 Reto Berra 5.00 12.00
330 Sean Monahan 8.00 20.00
331 Elias Lindholm 12.00 30.00
332 Nathan MacKinnon 40.00 100.00
333 John Muse 5.00 12.00
334 Antti Raanta 10.00 25.00
335 Joakim Nordstrom 4.00 10.00
336 Shawn Lalonde 5.00 12.00
337 Boone Jenner 10.00 25.00
338 Ryan Murray 8.00 20.00
339 Kevin Connauton 4.00 10.00
342 Tomas Jurco 6.00 15.00
347 Taylor Fedun 6.00 15.00
348 Tyler Pitlick 5.00 12.00
350 Aleksander Barkov 15.00 40.00
351 Jonathan Rheault 3.00 8.00
353 Linden Vey 3.00 8.00
354 Martin Jones 8.00 20.00
355 Tanner Pearson 5.00 12.00
358 Matt Dumba 3.00 8.00
359 Greg Pateryn 5.00 12.00
360 Michael Bournival 5.00 12.00
362 Daniel Bang 4.00 10.00
363 Kevin Henderson 4.00 10.00
366 Seth Jones 10.00 25.00
367 Dylan McIlrath 3.00 8.00
368 Jon Merrill 5.00 12.00
370 Ryan Strome 8.00 20.00
372 Jesper Fast 5.00 12.00
375 Calvin Heeter 4.00 10.00
376 Michael Raffl 4.00 10.00
378 Jordan Szwarz 5.00 12.00
379 Lucas Lessio 3.00 8.00
383 Jeff Zatkoff 5.00 12.00
386 Freddie Hamilton 5.00 12.00
387 Matt Nieto 4.00 10.00
388 Tomas Hertl 10.00 25.00
389 Mark Barberio 3.00 8.00
391 David Broll 5.00 12.00
392 Jamie Devane 4.00 10.00
394 Josh Leivo 4.00 10.00
395 Morgan Rielly 12.00 30.00
397 Michael Latta 4.00 10.00
399 Jacob Trouba 8.00 20.00
A2P Calvin Pickard 6.00 15.00
AAC Alex Chiasson 12.00 30.00
AAG Alex Galchenyuk 40.00 100.00
AAK Alex Killorn 8.00 20.00
AAM Jonathan Audy-Marchessault 12.00 30.00
AAR Antoine Roussel 5.00 12.00
AAW Austin Watson 4.00 10.00
ABB Beau Bennett 12.00 30.00
ABJ Nick Bjugstad 6.00 15.00
ABL Brian Lashoff 4.00 10.00
ACC Cory Conacher 3.00 8.00
ACN Cristopher Nilstorp 4.00 10.00
ACT Christian Thomas 4.00 10.00
ADH Dougie Hamilton 15.00 40.00
ADS Drew Shore 4.00 10.00
ADZ Dave Dziurzynski 4.00 10.00
AEE Emerson Etem 5.00 12.00
AEG Eric Gryba 4.00 10.00
AEP Eddie Pasquale 3.00 8.00
AEY Danny DeKeyser 10.00 25.00
AFA Frederik Andersen 12.00 30.00
AFF Filip Forsberg 10.00 25.00
AGA Brendan Gallagher 15.00 40.00
AGO Mikhail Grigorenko 12.00 30.00
AHI Thomas Hickey 4.00 10.00
AHP Harri Pesonen 4.00 10.00
AIJ Dmitrij Jaskin 5.00 12.00
AJC Jack Campbell 6.00 15.00
AJH Jonathan Huberdeau 15.00 40.00
AJL Johan Larsson 6.00 15.00
AJM J.T. Miller 12.00 30.00
AJO Jonas Brodin 6.00 15.00
AKK Michael Kostka 4.00 10.00
ALK Leo Komarov 5.00 12.00
AMA Mark Arcobello 5.00 12.00
AMC Michael Caruso 3.00 8.00
AMG Mikael Granlund 8.00 20.00
AMI Matt Irwin 4.00 10.00
AMJ Michal Jordan 3.00 8.00
ANB Nathan Beaulieu 3.00 8.00
ANJ Nicklas Jensen 4.00 10.00
ANP Nick Petrecki 3.00 8.00
ANY Nail Yakupov 30.00 80.00
ANZ Justin Schultz 5.00 12.00
AOE Jordan Schroeder 5.00 12.00
AOK Jamie Oleksiak 4.00 10.00
AOP Ondrej Palat 8.00 20.00
AOY Charlie Coyle 8.00 20.00
APG Philipp Grubauer 12.00 30.00
APM Petr Mrazek 10.00 25.00
APY Mark Pysyk 5.00 12.00
AQH Quinton Howden 4.00 10.00
ARG Radko Gudas 5.00 12.00
ARM Ryan Murphy 5.00 12.00
ARP Richard Panik 5.00 12.00
ARR Rickard Rakell 5.00 12.00
ASL Scott Laughton 6.00 15.00
ASO Carl Soderberg 5.00 12.00
ASP Ryan Spooner 8.00 20.00
ASV Sami Vatanen 5.00 12.00
ATB Taylor Beck 4.00 10.00
ATI Jarred Tinordi 5.00 12.00
ATM Tye McGinn 5.00 12.00
ATT Tyler Toffoli 10.00 25.00
AU2 Stefan Matteau 4.00 10.00
AUE Darcy Kuemper 6.00 15.00
AVB Victor Bartley 4.00 10.00
AVF Viktor Fasth 5.00 12.00
AVK Roman Cervenka 4.00 10.00
AVT Vladimir Tarasenko 30.00 60.00
AWN Chris Brown 3.00 8.00
AXW Maxwell Reinhart 5.00 12.00
AYP Anthony Peluso 3.00 8.00
AZR Zach Redmond 4.00 10.00

2013-14 Panini Prizm Rookie Autographs Prizms

*PRIZM/15-35: .8X TO 2X BASIC AU
ANY Nail Yakupov/15 125.00 200.00
AVT Vladimir Tarasenko/20 50.00 100.00

2013-14 Panini Prizm Cracked Ice Toronto Spring Expo

*301-320 VETS: 1.5X TO 4X BASIC CARDS
*321-400 ROOKIES: .8X TO 2X BASIC RC
332 Nathan MacKinnon 15.00 40.00
384 Olli Maatta 5.00 12.00
388 Tomas Hertl 5.00 12.00
390 Nikita Kucherov 100.00 250.00

2013-14 Panini Prizm Cracked Ice Toronto Spring Expo Autographs

321 John Gibson 25.00 50.00
322 Hampus Lindholm 8.00 20.00
324 Jamie Tardif 3.00 8.00
325 Nikita Zadorov 3.00 8.00
329 Reto Berra 5.00 12.00
330 Sean Monahan 8.00 20.00
332 Nathan MacKinnon 125.00 200.00
333 John Muse 5.00 12.00
336 Shawn Lalonde 5.00 12.00
337 Boone Jenner 10.00 25.00
338 Ryan Murray 8.00 20.00
339 Kevin Connauton 4.00 10.00
342 Tomas Jurco 6.00 15.00
347 Taylor Fedun 6.00 15.00
348 Tyler Pitlick 5.00 12.00
350 Aleksander Barkov 15.00 40.00
354 Martin Jones 8.00 20.00
355 Tanner Pearson 5.00 12.00
358 Matt Dumba 3.00 8.00
359 Greg Pateryn 5.00 12.00
360 Michael Bournival 5.00 12.00

362 Daniel Bang 4.00 10.00
365 Marek Mazanec 5.00 12.00
366 Seth Jones 10.00 25.00
367 Dylan McIlrath 3.00 8.00
368 Jon Merrill 5.00 12.00
370 Ryan Strome 8.00 20.00
372 Jesper Fast 5.00 12.00
375 Calvin Heeter 4.00 10.00
378 Jordan Szwarz 5.00 12.00
379 Lucas Lessio 3.00 8.00
383 Jeff Zatkoff 5.00 12.00
386 Freddie Hamilton 5.00 12.00
388 Tomas Hertl 10.00 25.00
389 Mark Barberio 3.00 8.00
391 David Broll 5.00 12.00
392 Jamie Devane 4.00 10.00
394 Josh Leivo 4.00 10.00

2011-12 Panini Rookie Anthology

COMP.SET w/o RC's (100) 10.00 25.00
1 Henrik Sedin .40 1.00
2 Phil Kessel .30 .75
3 Claude Giroux .30 .75
4 Joffrey Lupul .20 .50
5 Daniel Sedin .40 1.00
6 Steven Stamkos .60 1.50
7 Marian Hossa .30 .75
8 Evgeni Malkin .60 1.50
9 Jordan Eberle .30 .75
10 Jason Pominville .20 .50
11 Pavel Datsyuk .50 1.25
12 Jason Spezza .30 .75
13 Nicklas Backstrom .30 .75
14 Jonathan Toews .50 1.25
15 Jamie Benn .30 .75
16 Erik Karlsson .40 1.00
17 Patrick Sharp .30 .75
18 Thomas Vanek .25 .60
19 Teemu Selanne .60 1.50
20 Kris Versteeg .20 .50
21 Loui Eriksson .20 .50
22 Patrik Elias .30 .75
23 Scott Hartnell .20 .50
24 Tyler Seguin .40 1.00
25 Patrick Kane .60 1.50
26 James Neal .20 .50
27 Johan Franzen .25 .60
28 Ray Whitney .25 .60
29 John Tavares .50 1.25
30 Anze Kopitar .50 1.25
31 Corey Perry .50 1.25
32 Zach Parise .30 .75
33 Marian Gaborik .30 .75
34 Tomas Fleischmann .20 .50
35 Ilya Kovalchuk .30 .75
36 Patrice Bergeron .40 1.00
37 Matt Moulson .20 .50
38 Alex Ovechkin 1.25 3.00
39 Jaromir Jagr 1.00 2.50
40 Jarome Iginla .40 1.00
41 Daniel Alfredsson .30 .75
42 Mikko Koivu .25 .60
43 Joe Thornton .50 1.25
44 Brad Marchand .60 1.50
45 Ryan Smyth .25 .60
46 Henrik Zetterberg .40 1.00
47 Evander Kane .30 .75
48 Sidney Crosby 1.25 3.00
49 Brad Richards .30 .75
50 Martin St. Louis .30 .75
51 P.K. Subban .40 1.00
52 Erik Cole .20 .50
53 Milan Lucic .30 .75
54 Ryan Kesler .30 .75
55 Shea Weber .25 .60
56 Logan Couture .40 1.00
57 Rick Nash .30 .75
58 Taylor Hall .30 .75
59 David Backes .20 .50
60 Danny Briere .30 .75
61 Ryan O'Reilly .30 .75
62 Eric Staal .40 1.00
63 Milan Michalek .20 .50
64 Dion Phaneuf .25 .60
65 Blake Wheeler .30 .75
66 Ryan Getzlaf .30 .75
67 Shane Doan .25 .60
68 Alexander Steen .20 .50
69 Jeff Carter .25 .60
70 Jeff Skinner .40 1.00
71 Nicklas Lidstrom .20 .50
72 Pekka Rinne .30 .75
73 Craig Anderson .30 .75
74 Marc-Andre Fleury .60 1.50
75 Henrik Lundqvist .75 2.00
76 Jonathan Quick .40 1.00
77 Antti Niemi .25 .60
78 Miikka Kiprusoff .30 .75
79 Tim Thomas .30 .75
80 Roberto Luongo .50 1.25
81 Mike Smith .30 .75
82 Tomas Vokoun .25 .60
83 Ilya Bryzgalov .30 .75
84 Brian Elliott .25 .60
85 Carey Price .60 1.50
86 Kari Lehtonen .25 .60
87 Corey Crawford .40 1.00
88 Ondrej Pavelec .30 .75
89 Jose Theodore .30 .75
90 Semyon Varlamov .30 .75
91 Cam Ward .30 .75
92 Niklas Backstrom .30 .75
93 Martin Brodeur .75 2.00
94 Jonas Gustavsson .30 .75
95 Ryan Miller .30 .75
96 Jonas Hiller .25 .60
97 Tuukka Rask .40 1.00
98 Martin Biron .25 .60
99 Cory Schneider .30 .75
100 Jimmy Howard .40 1.00
101 Sean Couturier JSY AU RC 15.00 40.00
102 Adam Henrique JSY AU RC 15.00 40.00
103 Nugent-Hopkins JSY AU RC 60.00 120.00
104 C.Hodgson JSY AU RC 50.00 120.00
105 G. Landeskog JSY AU RC 30.00 80.00
106 Brett Connolly JSY AU RC 10.00 25.00
107 Craig Smith JSY AU RC 12.00 30.00
108 Carl Hagelin JSY AU RC 15.00 40.00
109 Adam Larsson JSY AU RC 15.00 40.00
110 Justin Faulk JSY AU RC 15.00 40.00
111 Brendan Smith JSY AU RC 10.00 25.00
112 Louis Leblanc JSY AU RC 10.00 25.00
113 Jake Gardiner JSY AU RC 12.00 30.00
114 Matt Read JSY AU RC 12.00 30.00
115 Mark Scheifele JSY AU RC 20.00 50.00
116 Zack Kassian JSY AU RC 6.00 15.00
117 Tim Erixon JSY AU RC 5.00 12.00
118 S.Despres JSY AU RC 5.00 12.00
119 Cody Eakin JSY AU RC 8.00 20.00
120 Ryan Ellis JSY AU RC 5.00 12.00
121 Greg Nemisz JSY AU RC 5.00 12.00
122 Colin Greening JSY AU RC 5.00 12.00
123 R.Johansen JSY AU RC 15.00 40.00
124 D.Smith-Pelly JSY AU RC 6.00 15.00
125 B.Saad JSY AU RC 12.00 30.00
126 Eddie Lack JSY AU RC 5.00 12.00
127 B.Geoffrion JSY AU RC 5.00 12.00
128 M.Kruger JSY AU RC 8.00 20.00
129 Harri Sateri JSY AU RC 5.00 12.00
130 S.Voynov JSY AU RC 5.00 12.00
131 Cam Atkinson JSY AU RC 12.00 30.00
132 Ben Scrivens JSY AU RC 8.00 20.00
133 Zac Rinaldo JSY AU RC 5.00 12.00
134 Matt Frattin JSY AU RC 5.00 12.00
135 David Savard JSY AU RC 5.00 12.00
136 E.Gudbranson JSY AU RC 8.00 20.00
137 C.de Haan JSY AU RC 5.00 12.00
138 A.Palushaj JSY AU RC 5.00 12.00
139 R.Bortuzzo JSY AU RC 5.00 12.00
140 Erik Condra JSY AU RC 5.00 12.00
141 G.Nyquist JSY AU RC 15.00 40.00
142 P.Wiercioch JSY AU RC 5.00 12.00
143 D.Rundblad JSY AU RC 5.00 12.00
144 J.Blum JSY AU RC 5.00 12.00
145 S.Da Costa JSY AU RC 5.00 12.00
146 T.Vincour JSY AU RC 5.00 12.00
147 Raphael Diaz JSY AU RC 5.00 12.00
148 Carl Klingberg JSY AU RC 5.00 12.00
149 E.Gustafsson JSY AU RC 6.00 15.00
150 M.Macenauer JSY AU RC 5.00 12.00
151 Allen York JSY AU RC 6.00 15.00
152 John Moore JSY AU RC 5.00 12.00
153 Tomas Kubalik JSY AU RC 5.00 12.00
154 Cam Talbot JSY AU RC 6.00 15.00
155 Brian Strait JSY AU RC 6.00 15.00
156 H.Zolnierczyk JSY AU RC 5.00 12.00
157 Joe Vitale JSY AU RC 5.00 12.00
158 Joe Colborne JSY AU RC 6.00 15.00
159 M.Zibanejad JSY AU RC 15.00 40.00
160 Andy Miele JSY AU RC 5.00 12.00
161 Peter Holland JSY AU RC 5.00 12.00
162 T.Hartikainen JSY AU RC 8.00 20.00
163 Brett Bulmer JSY AU RC 5.00 12.00
164 C.Sceviour JSY AU RC 5.00 12.00
165 C.Gaunce JSY AU RC 4.00 10.00

2011-12 Panini Rookie Anthology Draft Year Combo Jerseys

1 Selanne/Modano 10.00 25.00
2 Holmstrom/Nabokov 6.00 15.00
3 Datsyuk/Fisher 6.00 15.00
4 Zetterberg/Erat 5.00 12.00
5 D.Sedin/H.Sedin 6.00 15.00
6 Pominville/Spezza 6.00 15.00
7 McElhinney/Nash 4.00 10.00
8 Bergeron/Horton 5.00 12.00
9 A.Kostitsyn/Halak 4.00 10.00
10 M.Richards/Carter 6.00 15.00
11 Howard/Seabrook 5.00 12.00
12 Getzlaf/Perry 5.00 12.00
13 Ovechkin/Green 15.00 40.00
14 Quick/Ryan 5.00 12.00
15 Price/Neal 8.00 20.00
16 Ovechkin/Malkin 10.00 25.00
17 Stastny/Mercier 3.00 8.00
18 Setoguchi/Vlasic 3.00 8.00
19 Toews/J.Staal 6.00 15.00
20 Reimer/Varlamov 5.00 12.00
21 P.Kane/van Riemsdyk 8.00 20.00
22 Stamkos/Doughty 8.00 20.00
23 E.Kane/O'Reilly 6.00 15.00
24 Gagner/Simmonds 5.00 12.00
25 Cogliano/Bass 2.50 6.00
26 Price/M.Staal 12.00 30.00
27 Hossa/Marleau 6.00 15.00
28 Franzen/Olesz 3.00 8.00
29 Fisher/Neil 5.00 12.00
30 Carter/Horton 4.00 10.00
31 Halak/Howard 6.00 15.00
32 Olesz/N.Johnson 3.00 8.00
33 Neal/Cogliano 2.50 6.00
34 Enroth/Varlamov 4.00 10.00
35 Hall/Seguin 20.00 50.00
36 Nugent-Hopkins/Landeskog 12.00 30.00
37 Lecavalier/Legwand 4.00 10.00
38 W.Clark/Nieuwendyk 6.00 15.00
39 Simmonds/Palmieri 5.00 12.00
40 Toews/Frolik 6.00 15.00

2011-12 Panini Rookie Anthology Rookie Rivalry Dual Jerseys

1 Smith-Pelly/Voynov 3.00 8.00
2 Kassian/Palushaj 3.00 8.00
3 Geoffrion/B.Smith 5.00 12.00
4 Landeskog/Da Costa 6.00 15.00
5 Nemisz/Zibanejad 8.00 20.00
6 Erixon/de Haan 2.50 6.00
7 Kruger/Nyquist 6.00 15.00
8 Johansen/C.Smith 8.00 20.00
9 Eakin/Connolly 4.00 10.00
10 Gardiner/Palushaj 4.00 10.00
11 Hodgson/Saad 5.00 12.00
12 Gudbranson/Faulk 4.00 10.00
13 Holland/Voynov 2.50 6.00
14 Eakin/Gudbranson 4.00 10.00
15 Horak /Lack 3.00 8.00
16 Rinaldo/Vitale 5.00 12.00
17 Hagelin/Henrique 6.00 15.00
18 Atkinson/Blum 6.00 15.00
19 Larsson/Talbot 6.00 15.00
20 Rundblad/Zibanejad 6.00 15.00
21 Gaunce/Da Costa 2.50 6.00
22 Sceviour/Miele 2.50 6.00
23 Despres/Gustafsson 3.00 8.00
24 Couturier/Talbot 5.00 12.00
25 Leblanc/Scrivens 2.50 6.00
26 Sauve/Bulmer 4.00 10.00
27 Kubalik/Ellis 2.50 6.00
28 Frattin/Wiercioch 2.50 6.00
29 Read/Bortuzzo 5.00 12.00
30 Colborne/Emelin 2.50 6.00
31 Nugent-Hopkins/Hodgson 12.00 30.00
32 Moore/Blum 2.50 6.00
33 Vincour/Sateri 2.50 6.00
34 York/Ellis 3.00 8.00
35 Condra/Diaz 2.50 6.00
36 Jeffrey /Zolnierczyk 2.50 6.00
37 Kassian/Greening 3.00 8.00
38 Saad/Savard 5.00 12.00
39 York/Sateri 3.00 8.00
40 Scrivens/Lack 2.50 6.00
41 York/Talbot 6.00 15.00
42 Henrique/Gustafsson 5.00 12.00
43 Vitale/Read 5.00 12.00
44 Frattin/Rundblad 2.50 6.00
45 Eakin/Bortuzzo 4.00 10.00
46 Hodgson/Kruger 5.00 12.00
47 Hagelin/de Haan 6.00 15.00
48 Colborne/Condra 2.50 6.00
49 Despres/Rinaldo 5.00 12.00
50 Greening/Emelin 2.50 6.00
51 Smith-Pelly/Vincour 4.00 10.00
52 Nugent-Hopkins/Landeskog 12.00 30.00
53 Johansen/Nyquist 8.00 20.00
54 Leblanc/Zibanejad 8.00 20.00
55 C.Smith/Atkinson 6.00 15.00
56 Erixon/Despres 2.50 6.00
57 B.Smith/Read 5.00 12.00
58 Gardiner/Sauve 4.00 10.00
59 Geoffrion/Connolly 2.50 6.00
60 Couturier/Strait 5.00 12.00

2011-12 Panini Rookie Anthology Rookie Treasures Patches

*101-105 PATCH AU/15: .4X TO 1X AU RC/99
*106-115 PTCH AU/15: .5X TO 1.2X AU RC/199
*116-165 PTCH AU/15: 1X TO 2.5X AU RC/499

2012-13 Panini Rookie Anthology

COMP.SET w/o RC's (100) 10.00 25.00
1 Jaromir Jagr 1.00 2.50
2 Rick Nash .30 .75
3 Zach Parise .30 .75
4 Jordan Staal .25 .60
5 Colby Armstrong .20 .50
6 Peter Mueller .20 .50
7 Anders Lindback .20 .50
8 Sergei Bobrovsky .50 1.25
9 Alexander Semin .30 .75
10 Ryan Suter .25 .60
11 Ruslan Fedotenko .20 .50
12 Matthew Carle .25 .60
13 Olli Jokinen .25 .60
14 Jiri Hudler .25 .60
15 Sheldon Souray .20 .50
16 Jordin Tootoo .25 .60
17 George Parros .25 .60
18 Guillaume Latendresse .25 .60
19 Brad Boyes .20 .50
20 Jonas Gustavsson .30 .75
21 Teemu Selanne .60 1.50
22 Evander Kane .30 .75
23 Tyler Seguin .40 1.00
24 Alex Ovechkin 1.25 3.00
25 Ryan Miller .30 .75
26 Henrik Sedin .40 1.00
27 Jarome Iginla .40 1.00
28 Phil Kessel .30 .75
29 Eric Staal .40 1.00
30 Steven Stamkos .60 1.50
31 Jonathan Toews .50 1.25
32 Alex Pietrangelo .25 .60
33 Gabriel Landeskog .40 1.00
34 Joe Thornton .50 1.25
35 Jack Johnson .20 .50
36 Sidney Crosby 1.25 3.00
37 Loui Eriksson .20 .50
38 Mike Smith .30 .75
39 Pavel Datsyuk .50 1.25
40 Claude Giroux .30 .75
41 Ryan Nugent-Hopkins .40 1.00
42 Daniel Alfredsson .30 .75
43 Kris Versteeg .20 .50
44 Henrik Lundqvist .75 2.00
45 Jonathan Quick .40 1.00
46 John Tavares .50 1.25
47 Niklas Backstrom .25 .60
48 Martin Brodeur .75 2.00
49 Carey Price .60 1.50
50 Shea Weber .25 .60
51 Pekka Rinne .30 .75
52 Max Pacioretty .30 .75
53 Ilya Kovalchuk .30 .75
54 Matt Moulson .20 .50
55 Dustin Brown .30 .75
56 Marian Gaborik .30 .75
57 Scott Clemmensen .25 .60
58 Jason Spezza .30 .75
59 Jordan Eberle .30 .75
60 Ilya Bryzgalov .30 .75
61 Henrik Zetterberg .40 1.00
62 Shane Doan .25 .60
63 Kari Lehtonen .25 .60
64 Evgeni Malkin .60 1.50
65 Ryan Johansen .25 .60
66 Logan Couture .40 1.00
67 Matt Duchene .30 .75
68 Brian Elliott .25 .60
69 Patrick Kane .60 1.50
70 Vincent Lecavalier .30 .75
71 Cam Ward .30 .75
72 James Reimer .30 .75
73 Miikka Kiprusoff .30 .75
74 Ryan Kesler .30 .75
75 Cody Hodgson .20 .50
76 Braden Holtby .40 1.00
77 Tuukka Rask .40 1.00
78 Mark Scheifele .50 1.25
79 Corey Perry .50 1.25
80 Brayden Schenn .30 .75
81 Marc-Andre Fleury .60 1.50
82 Anze Kopitar .50 1.25
83 Adam Henrique .25 .60
84 Dion Phaneuf .25 .60
85 Cory Schneider .30 .75
86 P.K. Subban .40 1.00
87 Jimmy Howard .40 1.00
88 Taylor Hall .30 .75
89 Brad Richards .30 .75
90 David Backes .20 .50
91 Brandon Dubinsky .20 .50
92 Luke Schenn .30 .75
93 Eric Tangradi .20 .50
94 Steve Ott .20 .50
95 Derek Roy .20 .50
96 Artem Anisimov .20 .50
97 James van Riemsdyk .25 .60
98 Nick Foligno .25 .60
99 Brandon Sutter .20 .50
100 Mike Ribeiro .20 .50
101 M.Clark JSY AU/699 RC 4.00 10.00
102 C.Camper JSY AU/699 RC 3.00 8.00
103 MacDermid JSY AU/699 RC 4.00 10.00
104 M.Sauve JSY AU/499 RC 3.00 8.00
105 T.Krug JSY AU/699 RC 8.00 20.00
106 Hutchinson JSY AU/699 RC 5.00 12.00
107 T.Turnbull JSY AU/699 RC 3.00 8.00
108 A.Aliu JSY AU/499 RC 4.00 10.00
109 J.Welsh JSY AU/699 RC 4.00 10.00
110 B.Bollig JSY AU/499 RC 3.00 8.00
111 T.Barrie JSY AU/699 RC 10.00 25.00
112 M.Connolly JSY AU/699 RC 4.00 10.00
113 A.Joudrey JSY AU/499 RC 4.00 10.00
114 S.Hunwick JSY AU/699 RC 3.00 8.00
115 C.Goloubef JSY AU/699 RC 3.00 8.00
116 D.Prout JSY AU/699 RC 3.00 8.00
117 R.Garbutt JSY AU/699 RC 3.00 8.00
118 R.Smith JSY AU/499 RC 10.00 25.00
119 S.Glennie JSY AU/499 RC 4.00 10.00
120 B.Dillon JSY AU/699 RC 4.00 10.00
121 R.Sheahan JSY AU/499 RC 5.00 12.00
122 P.Cornet JSY AU/699 RC 4.00 10.00
123 C.Robak JSY AU/699 RC 3.00 8.00
124 J.Nolan JSY AU/499 RC 3.00 8.00
125 K.Foucault JSY AU/699 RC 3.00 8.00
126 T.Cuma JSY AU/699 RC 3.00 8.00
127 C.Genoway JSY AU/699 RC 3.00 8.00
128 J.Zucker JSY AU/699 RC 8.00 20.00
129 R.Mayer JSY AU/499 RC 5.00 12.00
130 G.Dumont JSY AU/699 RC 4.00 10.00
131 C.Pickard JSY AU/699 RC 4.00 10.00
132 A.Ness JSY AU/699 RC 3.00 8.00
133 C.Cizikas JSY AU/499 RC 4.00 10.00
134 M.Donovan JSY AU/499 RC 4.00 10.00
135 M.Watkins JSY AU/499 RC 3.00 8.00
136 Silfverberg JSY AU/499 RC 8.00 20.00
137 M.Stone JSY AU/499 RC 12.00 30.00
138 B.Manning JSY AU/699 RC 4.00 10.00
139 M.Stone JSY AU/699 RC 4.00 10.00
140 T.Sexsmith JSY AU/699 RC 3.00 8.00
141 J.Allen JSY AU/499 RC 10.00 25.00
142 J.Brown JSY AU/499 RC 4.00 10.00
143 C.Ashton JSY AU/499 RC 3.00 8.00
144 R.Hamilton JSY AU/499 RC 3.00 8.00
145 J.Rynnas JSY AU/499 RC 3.00 8.00
146 S.Baertschi JSY AU/199 RC 8.00 20.00
147 J.Schwartz JSY AU/199 RC 15.00 40.00
148 C.Kreider JSY AU/199 RC 20.00 50.00

2012-13 Panini Rookie Anthology Rookie Treasures Patches

*PATCH AU/99: .6X TO 1.5X JSY AU/499-699
*PATCH AU/50: .8X TO 2X JSY AU/499-699
*PATCH AU/25: .5X TO 1.2X JSY AU/199

2013-14 Panini Rookie Anthology

COMP.SET w/o RC's (100) 10.00 25.00
1 Ryan Getzlaf .30 .75
2 Jonas Hiller .25 .60
3 Corey Perry .50 1.25
4 Teemu Selanne .60 1.50
5 Patrice Bergeron .40 1.00
6 Zdeno Chara .30 .75
7 Jarome Iginla .40 1.00
8 Tuukka Rask .40 1.00
9 Tyler Ennis .20 .50
10 Drew Stafford .20 .50
11 Cody Hodgson .20 .50
12 Mike Cammalleri .25 .60
13 Mark Giordano .30 .75
14 Jiri Hudler .25 .60
15 Jeff Skinner .40 1.00
16 Eric Staal .40 1.00
17 Cam Ward .30 .75
18 Corey Crawford .40 1.00
19 Patrick Kane .60 1.50
20 Duncan Keith .25 .60
21 Jonathan Toews .50 1.25
22 Matt Duchene .30 .75
23 Gabriel Landeskog .40 1.00
24 Semyon Varlamov .30 .75
25 Sergei Bobrovsky .50 1.25
26 Marian Gaborik .30 .75
27 Ryan Johansen .25 .60
28 Jamie Benn .30 .75
29 Kari Lehtonen .25 .60
30 Tyler Seguin .40 1.00
31 Pavel Datsyuk .50 1.25
32 Jimmy Howard .40 1.00
33 Niklas Kronwall .25 .60
34 Henrik Zetterberg .40 1.00
35 Jordan Eberle .30 .75
36 Taylor Hall .30 .75
37 Ryan Nugent-Hopkins .40 1.00
38 Sam Gagner .20 .50
39 Brian Campbell .20 .50
40 Roberto Luongo .50 1.25
41 Scottie Upshall .20 .50
42 Drew Doughty .40 1.00
43 Anze Kopitar .50 1.25
44 Jonathan Quick .40 1.00
45 Mike Richards .25 .60
46 Josh Harding .30 .75
47 Zach Parise .30 .75
48 Ryan Suter .25 .60
49 Max Pacioretty .30 .75
50 Carey Price .60 1.50
51 P.K. Subban .40 1.00
52 Mike Fisher .20 .50
53 Pekka Rinne .30 .75
54 Shea Weber .25 .60
55 Martin Brodeur .75 2.00
56 Jaromir Jagr 1.00 2.50
57 Cory Schneider .30 .75
58 Evgeni Nabokov .30 .75
59 Kyle Okposo .20 .50
60 John Tavares .50 1.25
61 Henrik Lundqvist .75 2.00
62 Ryan McDonagh .20 .50
63 Rick Nash .30 .75
64 Brad Richards .30 .75
65 Erik Karlsson .40 1.00
66 Bobby Ryan .25 .60
67 Jason Spezza .30 .75
68 Sean Couturier .25 .60
69 Claude Giroux .30 .75
70 Vincent Lecavalier .30 .75
71 Shane Doan .25 .60
72 Mike Smith .30 .75
73 Keith Yandle .20 .50
74 Sidney Crosby 1.25 3.00
75 Marc-Andre Fleury .60 1.50
76 Kris Letang .40 1.00
77 Evgeni Malkin .60 1.50
78 Logan Couture .40 1.00
79 Patrick Marleau .30 .75
80 Antti Niemi .25 .60
81 Joe Thornton .50 1.25
82 David Backes .20 .50
83 Ryan Miller .30 .75
84 Alexander Steen .20 .50
85 Ben Bishop .25 .60
86 Martin St. Louis .30 .75
87 Steven Stamkos .60 1.50
88 Jonathan Bernier .25 .60
89 Phil Kessel .30 .75
90 Joffrey Lupul .20 .50
91 James Reimer .30 .75
92 Ryan Kesler .30 .75
93 Daniel Sedin .40 1.00
94 Henrik Sedin .40 1.00
95 Nicklas Backstrom .30 .75
96 Braden Holtby .40 1.00
97 Alex Ovechkin 1.25 3.00
98 Andrew Ladd .20 .50
99 Ondrej Pavelec .30 .75
100 Blake Wheeler .30 .75
101 Sami Vatanen JSY AU RC 4.00 10.00
102 F.Andersen JSY AU RC 10.00 25.00
103 H.Lindholm JSY AU RC 6.00 15.00
104 Emerson Etem JSY AU RC 4.00 10.00
105 Igor Bobkov JSY AU RC 3.00 8.00
106 Viktor Fasth JSY AU RC 4.00 10.00
107 Carl Soderberg JSY AU RC 8.00 20.00
108 Rickard Rakell JSY AU RC 4.00 10.00
109 D.Hamilton JSY AU RC 6.00 15.00
110 Ryan Spooner JSY AU RC 4.00 10.00
111 Mark Pysyk JSY AU RC 4.00 10.00
112 M.Grigorenko JSY AU RC 2.50 6.00
113 Nikita Zadorov JSY AU RC 2.50 6.00
115 Z.Girgensons JSY AU RC 6.00 15.00
116 Reto Berra JSY AU RC 4.00 10.00
117 Sean Monahan JSY AU RC 6.00 15.00
118 Max Reinhart JSY AU RC 4.00 10.00
119 Elias Lindholm JSY AU RC 10.00 25.00
120 Jared Staal JSY AU RC 3.00 8.00
121 Ryan Murphy JSY AU RC 4.00 10.00
122 Martin Jones JSY AU RC 6.00 15.00
123 J.Nordstrom JSY AU RC 3.00 8.00
124 Michael Kostka JSY AU RC 3.00 8.00
125 Calvin Pickard JSY AU RC 5.00 12.00
126 N.MacKinnon JSY AU RC 100.00 250.00
127 Boone Jenner JSY AU RC 8.00 20.00
128 Ryan Murray JSY AU RC 6.00 15.00
129 Alex Chiasson JSY AU RC 4.00 10.00
130 Antoine Roussel JSY AU RC 4.00 10.00
131 Jack Campbell JSY AU RC 10.00 25.00
132 Jamie Oleksiak JSY AU RC 3.00 8.00
133 Kevin Connauton JSY AU RC 3.00 8.00
134 V.Nichushkin JSY AU RC 8.00 20.00
135 Brian Lashoff JSY AU RC 3.00 8.00
136 C.Nilstorp JSY AU RC 3.00 8.00
137 D.DeKeyser JSY AU RC 5.00 12.00
138 Petr Mrazek JSY AU RC 8.00 20.00
139 Xavier Ouellet JSY AU RC 4.00 10.00
140 Justin Schultz JSY AU RC 4.00 10.00
141 Nail Yakupov JSY AU RC 8.00 20.00
142 Connor Murphy JSY AU RC 3.00 8.00
143 Mark Arcobello JSY AU RC 4.00 10.00
144 A.Barkov JSY AU RC 12.00 30.00
145 Drew Shore JSY AU RC 3.00 8.00
146 J.Huberdeau JSY AU RC 8.00 20.00
147 Nick Bjugstad JSY AU RC 5.00 12.00
148 Quinton Howden JSY AU RC 3.00 8.00
149 Tyler Toffoli JSY AU RC 8.00 20.00
150 John Gibson JSY AU RC 15.00 40.00
151 Tanner Pearson JSY AU RC 5.00 12.00
152 Charlie Coyle JSY AU RC 6.00 15.00
153 J.Gustafsson JSY AU RC 5.00 12.00
154 Jonas Brodin JSY AU RC EXCH 5.00 12.00
155 Mikael Granlund JSY AU RC 6.00 15.00
156 Matt Dumba JSY AU RC 2.50 6.00
157 B.Gallagher JSY AU RC 10.00 25.00
158 Michael Bournival JSY AU RC 4.00 10.00
159 Nathan Beaulieu JSY AU RC 2.50 6.00
160 Alex Galchenyuk JSY AU RC 10.00 25.00
162 Austin Watson JSY AU RC 3.00 8.00
163 Christian Thomas JSY AU RC 3.00 8.00
164 F.Forsberg JSY AU/125 RC 15.00 40.00
165 Marek Mazanec JSY AU RC 4.00 10.00
166 Seth Jones JSY AU RC 8.00 20.00
167 Jon Merrill JSY AU RC 4.00 10.00
168 Stefan Matteau JSY AU RC 3.00 8.00
169 Brock Nelson JSY AU RC 8.00 20.00
170 Thomas Hickey JSY AU RC 3.00 8.00
171 Jesper Fast JSY AU RC 4.00 10.00
172 J.T. Miller JSY AU RC 10.00 25.00
173 Cory Conacher JSY AU RC 2.50 6.00
174 Scott Laughton JSY AU RC 5.00 12.00
175 Lucas Lessio JSY AU RC 2.50 6.00
176 Olli Maatta JSY AU RC 6.00 15.00
177 Matt Nieto JSY AU RC 3.00 8.00
178 Eric Hartzell JSY AU RC 4.00 10.00
179 Tomas Hertl JSY AU RC 8.00 20.00
180 V.Tarasenko JSY AU RC 10.00 25.00
181 Alex Killorn JSY AU RC 6.00 15.00
182 Nick Petrecki JSY AU RC 2.50 6.00
184 Jamie Devane JSY AU RC 3.00 8.00
185 Darcy Kuemper JSY AU RC 8.00 20.00
186 Morgan Rielly JSY AU RC 10.00 25.00
188 Frank Corrado JSY AU RC 2.50 6.00
189 J.Schroeder JSY AU RC 4.00 10.00
190 Nicklas Jensen JSY AU RC 3.00 8.00
191 Philipp Grubauer JSY AU RC 10.00 25.00
192 Tom Wilson JSY AU RC 8.00 20.00
193 Jacob Trouba JSY AU RC 6.00 15.00
194 Zach Redmond JSY AU RC 3.00 8.00
195 E.Pasquale JSY AU RC 2.50 6.00
196 Tomas Jurco JSY AU RC 5.00 12.00
197 Ryan Strome JSY AU RC 8.00 20.00
198 Dylan McIlrath JSY AU RC 2.50 6.00
199 Cody Ceci JSY AU RC 3.00 8.00
200 M.Hellberg JSY AU RC 4.00 10.00

2013-14 Panini Rookie Anthology Gold

*GOLD/100: 4X TO 10X BASIC CARDS
18 Corey Crawford 4.00 10.00
95 Nicklas Backstrom 3.00 8.00

2013-14 Panini Rookie Anthology Rookie Patch Autographs

*PATCH/25: 1X TO 2.5X BASIC ROOKIE
126 Nathan MacKinnon/25 150.00 400.00

2013-14 Panini Rookie Anthology Rookie Prime Autographs

*PRIME/50: .6X TO 1.5X BASIC ROOKIES
*PRIME/15-25: .8X TO 2X BASIC ROOKIES
126 Nathan MacKinnon/50 125.00 300.00

2013-14 Panini Social Signatures

SSAK Anze Kopitar TC 10.00 25.00
SSAL Andrew Ladd TC 4.00 10.00
SSAM Andy Miele T 4.00 10.00
SSAO Alex Ovechkin PB 25.00 60.00
SSAS Andrew Shaw T 4.00 10.00
SSAS Anthony Stewart PB 4.00 10.00
SSBBO Brandon Bollig T 5.00 12.00
SSBC Brett Connolly PB 4.00 10.00
SSBE Brian Elliott PB 5.00 12.00
SSBG Brian Gionta PB 4.00 10.00
SSBH Brett Hull PB 12.00 30.00
SSBM Brenden Morrow PB 5.00 12.00
SSBR Brad Richards CR 6.00 15.00
SSCG Claude Giroux TC 6.00 15.00
SSCP Carey Price CR 12.00 30.00
SSCT Colten Teubert TC 4.00 10.00
SSDB David Backes PB 4.00 10.00
SSDP David Perron PB 5.00 12.00
SSDR Derek Roy PB 4.00 10.00
SSDS Derek Stepan PP 4.00 10.00
SSEC Erik Condra CR 4.00 10.00
SSEF Eric Fehr TC 4.00 10.00
SSEM Evgeni Malkin PB 12.00 30.00
SSGL Gabriel Landeskog PB 8.00 20.00
SSGP George Parros T 5.00 12.00
SSHL Henrik Lundqvist TC 15.00 40.00
SSJB Jamie Benn TC 6.00 15.00
SSJG Jake Gardiner TC 4.00 10.00
SSJHY Jimmy Hayes T 4.00 10.00
SSJL John-Michael Liles PB 4.00 10.00
SSJM Jacob Markstrom CR 6.00 15.00
SSJN James Neal PB 4.00 10.00
SSJQ Jonathan Quick TC 8.00 20.00
SSJR Jeremy Roenick PB 10.00 25.00
SSJS Jim Slater PB 4.00 10.00
SSJT John Tavares PB 10.00 25.00
SSJWA Joel Ward T 4.00 10.00
SSKS Kevin Shattenkirk T 4.00 10.00
SSKT Kyle Turris PB 4.00 10.00
SSLA Luke Adam TC 5.00 12.00
SSLC Logan Couture CR 8.00 20.00
SSMB Mikael Backlund PB 5.00 12.00
SSMF Mike Fisher CR 4.00 10.00
SSMG Marian Gaborik PB 6.00 15.00
SSMM Matt Moulson PB 4.00 10.00
SSMT Maxime Talbot CR 4.00 10.00
SSNBO Nick Bonino T 4.00 10.00
SSPK Phil Kessel PB 6.00 15.00
SSPP P.A. Parenteau CR 4.00 10.00
SSRGA Ryan Garbutt T 4.00 10.00
SSRIB Richard Bachman T 5.00 12.00
SSRJ Ryan Johansen TC 5.00 12.00
SSRK Ryan Kesler PB 6.00 15.00
SSRN Ryan Nugent-Hopkins PB 8.00 20.00
SSRT Rick Tocchet PB 5.00 12.00
SSRU R.J. Umberger TC 4.00 10.00
SSSO Steve Ott TC 4.00 10.00
SSSS Sheldon Souray TC 4.00 10.00
SSSU Scottie Upshall CR 4.00 10.00
SSTH Taylor Hall PB 6.00 15.00
SSTO T.J. Oshie CR 6.00 15.00
SSTS Tyler Seguin TC 8.00 20.00
SSVH Victor Hedman TC 8.00 20.00
SSVL Vincent Lecavalier CR 6.00 15.00
SSWW Wojtek Wolski PB 4.00 10.00
SSBS1 Brayden Schenn PB 6.00 15.00
SSBS2 Ben Scrivens CR 5.00 12.00
SSCA1 Craig Anderson PB 6.00 15.00
SSCA2 Colby Armstrong CR 4.00 10.00
SSJE1 Jordan Eberle PB 6.00 15.00
SSJE2 Jhonas Enroth PB 6.00 15.00
SSJJ1 Jaromir Jagr PB 20.00 50.00
SSJJ2 Jack Johnson CR 4.00 10.00
SSKA1 Keith Aulie PB 4.00 10.00
SSKA2 Karl Alzner CR 4.00 10.00
SSMC1 Matthew Carle PB 5.00 12.00
SSMC2 Mike Cammalleri PB 5.00 12.00
SSMR1 Mike Rupp CR 4.00 10.00
SSMR2 Matt Read TC 4.00 10.00

1979 Panini Stickers

COMPLETE SET (400) 30.00 80.00
1 Goal Disallowed .20 .40
2 Butt-Ending .10 .20
3 Slow Whistle .10 .20
4 Hooking .10 .20
5 Charging .10 .20
6 Misconduct Penalty .10 .20
7 Holding .10 .20
8 High-Sticking .10 .20
9 Tripping .10 .20
10 Cross-Checking .10 .20
11 Elbowing .10 .20
12 Icing (I) .10 .20
13 Icing (II) .10 .20
14 Boarding .10 .20
15 Kneeing .10 .20
16 Slashing .10 .20
17 Excessive Roughness .10 .20
18 Spearing .10 .20
19 Interference .10 .20
20 Poster .10 .20
21 Czech.-USSR 6-4 .25 .50
22 Czech.-USSR 6-4 .25 .50
23 USSR-Czech. 3-1 .25 .50
24 USSR-Czech. 3-1 .25 .50
25 USSR-Czech. 3-1 .25 .50
26 USSR-Czech. 3-1 .25 .50
27 Can-Sweden 3-2 .25 .50
28 Can-Sweden 3-2 .25 .50
29 USSR-Canada 5-1 .38 .75
30 USSR-Canada 5-1 .38 .75
31 Czech.-Canada 3-2 .25 .50
32 Czech.-Canada 3-2 .25 .50
33 USSR-Sweden 7-1 .25 .50
34 USSR-Sweden 7-1 .25 .50
35 USA-Finland 4-3 .25 .50
36 USA-Finland 4-3 .25 .50
37 Finland-DDR 7-2 .10 .20
38 DDR-BRD 0-0 .10 .20
39 DDR-BRD 0-0 .10 .20
40 Czechoslovakia .10 .20
41 Poland .10 .20
42 USSR .63 1.25
43 USA .63 1.25
44 Canada 2.50 5.00
45 Deutschland-BRD .10 .20
46 Finland .10 .20
47 Sweden .25 .50
48 Canada Team Picture (upper left) .50 1.00
49 Canada Team Picture (upper right) .50 1.00
50 Canada Team Picture (lower left) .50 1.00
51 Canada Team Picture (lower right) .50 1.00
52 Denis Herron 1.00 2.00
53 Dan Bouchard 1.00 2.00
54 Rick Hampton .25 .50
55 Robert Picard .25 .50
56 Brad Maxwell .25 .50
57 David Shand .25 .50
58 Dennis Kearns .25 .50
59 Tom Lysiak .50 1.00
60 Dennis Maruk 1.00 2.00
61 Marcel Dionne 3.00 6.00
62 Guy Charron .50 1.00
63 Glen Sharpley .25 .50
64 Jean Pronovost .50 1.00
65 Don Lever .25 .50
66 Bob MacMillan .38 .75
67 Wilf Paiement .50 1.00
68 Pat Hickey .38 .75
69 Mike Murphy .25 .50
70 Czechoslovakia Team Picture (upper left) .25 .50
71 Czechoslovakia Team Picture (upper right) .25 .50
72 Czechoslovakia Team Picture (lower left) .25 .50
73 Czechoslovakia Team Picture (lower right) .25 .50
74 Jiri Holecek .38 .75
75 Jiri Crha .50 1.00
76 Jiri Bubla .38 .75
77 Milan Kajki .10 .20
78 Miroslav Dvorak .25 .50
79 Milan Chalupa .25 .50
80 Frantisek Kaberle .20 .40
81 Jan Zajicek .10 .20
82 Jiri Novak .10 .20
83 Ivan Hlinka .30 .75
84 Peter Stastny 5.00 10.00
85 Milan Novy .25 .50
86 Vladimir Martinec .10 .20
87 Jaroslav Pouzar .25 .50
88 Pavel Richter .10 .20
89 Bohuslav Ebermann .10 .20
90 Marian Stastny .50 1.00
91 Frantisek Cernick .20 .40
92 FDR Team Picture (upper left) .10 .20
93 FDR Team Picture (upper right) .10 .20
94 FDR Team Picture (lower left) .10 .20
95 FDR Team Picture (lower right) .10 .20
96 Erich Weishaupt .10 .20
97 Bernhard Engelbrecht .10 .20
98 Ignaz Berndaner .10 .20
99 Robert Murray .10 .20
100 Udo Kiessling .25 .50
101 Klaus Auhuber .10 .20
102 Horst Kretschmer .10 .20
103 Erich Kuhnhackl .25 .50
104 Martin Wild .10 .20
105 Lorenz Funk, Sr .10 .20
106 M. Hinterstocker .10 .20
107 Alois Schloder .10 .20
108 Rainer Philipp .10 .20
109 H. Hinterstocker .10 .20
110 Franz Reindl .10 .20
111 Walter Koberle .25 .50
112 Johann Zach .10 .20
113 Marcus Kuhl .10 .20
114 Poland Team Picture (upper left) .10 .20

115 Poland Team Picture (upper right) .10 .20
116 Poland Team Picture (lower left) .10 .20
117 Poland Team Picture (lower right) .10 .20
118 Henryk Wojtynek .10 .20
119 T. Slowakiewicz .10 .20
120 Henryk Janiszewski .10 .20
121 Henryk Gruth .10 .20
122 Andr. Slowakiewicz .10 .20
123 Andrzej Eskrzycki .10 .20
124 Jerzy Potz .25 .50
125 Marek Marcinczak .10 .20
126 Jozef Batkiewicz .10 .20
127 Stefan Chowaniec .10 .20
128 Andrzej Malysiak .10 .20
129 Walenty Zietara .10 .20
130 Henryk Pytel .10 .20
131 Mieczyslaw Jaskierski .10 .20
132 Andrezei Zabawa .10 .20
133 Tadeusz Oboj .10 .20
134 Jan Piecko .10 .20
135 Leszek Tokarz .10 .20
136 USSR Team Picture (upper left) .38 .75
137 USSR Team Picture (upper right) .38 .75
138 USSR Team Picture (lower left) .38 .75
139 USSR Team Picture (lower right) .38 .75
140 Vladislav Tretiak 5.00 10.00
141 Slava Fetisov 4.00 8.00
142 Vladimir Lutchenko .50 1.00
143 Vasilij Pervukhin .38 .75
144 Valeri Vasiliev 1.00 2.00
145 Gennady Tsygankov .50 1.00
146 Juri Fedorov .20 .40
147 Vladimir Petrov 2.00 4.00
148 Vladimir Golikov .20 .40
149 Victor Zhluktov .25 .50
150 Boris Mikhailov 2.00 4.00
151 Valeri Kharlamov 3.00 6.00
152 Helmut Balderis .50 1.00
153 Sergej Kapustin .38 .75
154 Alexander Golikov .20 .40
155 Alexander Maltsev 2.00 4.00
156 Yuri Lebedev .38 .75
157 Sergei Makarov 2.50 5.00
158 Finland Team Picture (upper left) .10 .20
159 Finland Team Picture (upper right) .10 .20
160 Finland Team Picture (lower left) .10 .20
161 Finland Team Picture (lower right) .10 .20
162 Urpo Ylonen .25 .50
163 Antero Kivela .10 .20
164 Pekka Rautakallio .50 1.00
165 Timo Nummelin .10 .20
166 Risto Siltanen .50 1.00
167 Pekka Marjamaki .10 .20
168 Tapio Levo .20 .40
169 Lasse Litma .10 .20
170 Esa Peitonen .10 .20
171 Martti Jarkko .10 .20
172 Matti Hagman .25 .50
173 Seppo Repo .20 .40
174 Pertti Korvulahti .10 .20
175 Seppo Ahokainen .10 .20
176 Juhani Tamminen .20 .40
177 Jukka Porvari .10 .20
178 Mikko Leinonen .38 .75
179 Matti Rautiainen .10 .20
180 Sweden Team Picture (upper left) .25 .50
181 Sweden Team Picture (upper right) .25 .50
182 Sweden Team Picture (lower left) .25 .50
183 Sweden Team Picture (lower right) .25 .50
184 Goran Hogasta .20 .40
185 Hardy Astrom 1.00 2.00
186 Stig Ostling .20 .40
187 Ulf Weinstock .10 .20
188 Mats Waltin .10 .20
189 Stig Salming .25 .50
190 Lars Zetterstrom .10 .20
191 Lars Lindgren .25 .50
192 Leif Holmgren .10 .20
193 Roland Ericksson .10 .20
194 Rolf Edberg .10 .20
195 Per-Olov Brasar .25 .50
196 Mats Ahlberg .10 .20
197 Bengt Lundholm .25 .50
198 Lars Gunnar Lundberg .10 .20
199 Nils-Olov Olsson .10 .20
200 Kent-Erik Anderson .38 .75
201 Thomas Gradin .75 1.50
202 USA Team Picture (upper left) .38 .75
203 USA Team Picture (upper right) .38 .75
204 USA Team Picture (lower left) .38 .75
205 USA Team Picture (lower right) .38 .75
206 Peter Lopresti .38 .75
207 Jim Warden .25 .50
208 Dick Lamby .25 .50
209 Craig Norwich .25 .50
210 Glen Patrick .25 .50
211 Patrick Westrum .25 .50
212 Don Jackson .25 .50
213 Mark Johnson .50 1.00
214 Curt Bennett .25 .50
215 Dave Debol .25 .50
216 Bob Collyard .25 .50
217 Mike Fidler .25 .50
218 Tom Younghans .25 .50
219 Harvey Bennett .25 .50
220 Steve Jensen .38 .75
221 Jim Warner .25 .50
222 Mike Eaves .50 1.00
223 William Gilligan .25 .50
224 Poster .25 .50
225 Poland-Rom. 8-6 .10 .20
226 Poland-Rom. 8-6 .10 .20
227 Poland-Rom. 8-6 .10 .20
228 Poland-Rom. 8-6 .10 .20
229 Poland-Hun. 7-2 .10 .20
230 Poland-Hun. 7-2 .10 .20
231 Japan-Yug. 6-1 .10 .20
232 Japan-Yug. 6-1 .10 .20
233 Italy-Yug. 6-1 .10 .20
234 Italy-Yug. 6-1 .10 .20
235 Romania-Italy 5-5 .10 .20
236 Romania-Italy 5-5 .10 .20
237 Poland .10 .20
238 Poland .10 .20
239 Deutschland-DDR .10 .20
240 Hungary .10 .20
241 Netherland .10 .20
242 Romania .10 .20
243 Switzerland .10 .20
244 Japan .10 .20
245 Norway .10 .20
246 Austria .10 .20
247 DDR .10 .20
248 DDR .10 .20
249 Herzig Kraske .10 .20
250 Simon Peters .10 .20
251 Frenzel Lempio .10 .20
252 Fengler Slapke .10 .20
253 Patschinski Bielas 1 .10 .20
254 Peters Scholz .10 .20
255 Bogelsack Stasche .10 .20
256 Switzerland .10 .20
257 Switzerland .10 .20
258 Grubauer Anken .10 .20
259 Zenhausern Meyer .10 .20
260 Kolliker Locher .10 .20
261 Mattli Conte .10 .20
262 Holzer Dellsberger .10 .20
263 Horisberger Rossetti .10 .20
264 Berger Schmid .10 .20
265 Hungary .10 .20
266 Hungary .10 .20
267 Balagh Farkas .10 .20
268 Kovacs Hajzer .10 .20
269 Flora Kereszty .10 .20
270 Palla Meszoly .10 .20
271 Menyhart Havran .10 .20
272 Poth Muhr .10 .20
273 Buzas Pek .10 .20
274 Netherlands .10 .20
275 Netherlands .10 .20
276 Van Bilsen Krikke .10 .20
277 Van Soldt Peternousek .10 .20
278 Kolijn Van Den Broek .10 .20
279 Van Wieren Toren .10 .20
280 Van Onlangs Schaffer .10 .20
281 Janssen Van Der Griendt .10 .20
282 De Heer Koopmans .10 .20
283 Japan .10 .20
284 Japan .10 .20
285 Iwamoto Misaw .10 .20
286 Ito Tonozaki .10 .20
287 Hori Nakayama .10 .20
288 Tanaka Kyoya .10 .20
289 Kawamura Hoshino .10 .20
290 Misawa Sakurai .10 .20
291 Honma Hanzawa .10 .20
292 Norway .10 .20
293 Norway .10 .20
294 Walberg Goldstein .10 .20
295 Martinsen Molberg .10 .20
296 Nilsen Erevik .10 .20
297 Lien Roymark .10 .20
298 Eriksen Ovstedal .10 .20
299 Johansen Haraldsen .10 .20
300 Stethereng Throrkildsen .10 .20
301 Austria .10 .20
302 Austria .10 .20
303 Schilcherl Prohaska .10 .20
304 Hyytaienen Russ .10 .20
305 Staribacher Schneider .10 .20
306 Kotnauer Pok .10 .20
307 Sadjina Konig .10 .20
308 Mortl Pepeunig .10 .20
309 Schilchner Haiszan .10 .20
310 Romania .10 .20
311 Romania .10 .20
312 Hutan Netedu .10 .20
313 Antal Gall .10 .20
314 Lustinian Lonita .10 .20
315 Hutanu Halauca .10 .20
316 Tureanu Axinte .10 .20
317 Nagy Costea .10 .20
318 Nistor Olenici .10 .20
319 Poster .10 .20
320 Den.-Net 3-3 .10 .20
321 Den.-Net 3-3 .10 .20
322 Net.-Spain 19-0 .10 .20
323 Net.-Spain 19-0 .10 .20
324 Aus.-Den 7-4 .10 .20
325 Aus.-Den 7-4 .10 .20
326 Net.-Bul. 8-0 .10 .20
327 China-Den. 3-2 .10 .20
328 China-France 8-4 .10 .20
329 Bulgaria .10 .20
330 France .10 .20
331 Italy .10 .20
332 Yugoslavia .10 .20
333 Belgium .10 .20
334 China .10 .20
335 Denmark .10 .20
336 Spain .10 .20
337 Belgium .10 .20
338 Belgium .10 .20
339 Smeets Lauwers .10 .20
340 Adriaensen Zwikel .10 .20
341 Cuvelier Sarazin .10 .20
342 Vermeulen Voskertian .10 .20
343 Verschraegen Arnould .10 .20
344 Lejeune Langh .10 .20
345 Bulgaria .10 .20
346 Bulgaria .10 .20
347 Iliev Lazarov .10 .20
348 Iliev Krastinov .10 .20
349 Hristov Petrov .10 .20
350 Atanasov Nenov .10 .20
351 Todorov Stoilov .10 .20
352 Guerasimov Batchvarov .10 .20
353 China .10 .20
354 China .10 .20
355 Ting Wen Yung Ke .10 .20
356 Ke Shao Tang .10 .20
357 Ta Chun Ung Sheng .10 .20
358 Hsi Kiang Chang Shun .10 .20
359 Cheng Hsin Te Hsi .10 .20
360 Shu Ching Sheng Wen .10 .20
361 Denmark .10 .20
362 Denmark .10 .20
363 Hansen Holten Moller .10 .20
364 Andersen Pedersen .10 .20
365 Henriksen Hviid .10 .20
366 Nielsen Thomsen .10 .20
367 Nielsen Kahl .10 .20
368 Jensen Gjerding .10 .20
369 Spain .10 .20
370 Spain .10 .20
371 Estrada Lizarraga .10 .20
372 Gonzalez Munitiz .10 .20
373 Marin Aguado .10 .20
374 Raventos Encinas .10 .20
375 Capillas Sarazirar .10 .20
376 Labayen Plaza .10 .20
377 France .10 .20
378 France .10 .20
379 Maric Del Monaco .10 .20
380 Oprandi Combe .10 .20
381 Allard Le Blond .10 .20
382 Vassieux Rey .10 .20
383 Galiay Le Blond .10 .20
384 Vinard Smaniotto .10 .20
385 Italy .10 .20
386 Italy .10 .20
387 Tigliani Gasser .10 .20
388 Kostner Pasqualotto .10 .20
389 Lacedelli Polloni .10 .20
390 Insam De Toni .10 .20
391 Strohmaier Kasslatter .10 .20
392 De Marchi Pugliese .10 .20
393 Yugoslavia .10 .20
394 Yugoslavia .10 .20
395 Zbontar Scap .10 .20
396 Kumar Kosir .10 .20
397 Kavec Smolej .10 .20
398 Kafner Lepsa .10 .20
399 Poljansek Kosir .10 .20
400 Klemenc Jan .10 .20
xx Sticker Album 10.00 20.00

1987-88 Panini Stickers

1 Stanley Cup .05 .15
2 Bruins Action .05 .15
3 Bruins Emblem .05 .15
4 Doug Keans .05 .15
5 Bill Ranford .15 .40
6 Ray Bourque .30 .75
7 Reed Larson .10 .25
8 Mike Milbury .05 .15
9 Michael Thelven .07 .20
10 Cam Neely .30 .75
11 Charlie Simmer .05 .15
12 Rick Middleton .10 .25
13 Tom McCarthy .07 .20
14 Keith Crowder .05 .15
15 Steve Kasper .05 .15
16 Ken Linseman .05 .15
17 Dwight Foster .05 .15
18 Jay Miller .05 .15
19 Sabres Action .05 .15
20 Sabres Emblem .05 .15
21 Jacques Cloutier .05 .15
22 Tom Barrasso .10 .25
23 Daren Puppa .05 .15
24 Phil Housley .07 .20
25 Mike Ramsey .10 .25
26 Bill Hajt .05 .15
27 Dave Andreychuk .10 .25
28 Christian Ruuttu .10 .25
29 Mike Foligno .07 .20
30 John Tucker .05 .15
31 Adam Creighton .05 .15
32 Wilf Paiement .07 .20
33 Paul Cyr .05 .15
34 Clark Gillies .10 .25
35 Lindy Ruff .05 .15
36 Whalers Action .05 .15
37 Whalers Emblem .05 .15
38 Mike Liut .05 .15
39 Steve Weeks .05 .15
40 Dave Babych .07 .20
41 Ulf Samuelsson .30 .75
42 Dana Murzyn .10 .25
43 Ron Francis .12 .30
44 Kevin Dineen .10 .25
45 John Anderson .07 .20
46 Ray Ferraro .10 .25
47 Dean Evason .07 .20
48 Paul Lawless .05 .15
49 Stewart Gavin .10 .25
50 Sylvain Turgeon .10 .25
51 Dave Tippett .10 .25
52 Doug Jarvis .10 .25
53 Canadiens Action .05 .15
54 Canadiens Emblem .05 .15
55 Brian Hayward .07 .20
56 Patrick Roy .30 .75
57 Larry Robinson .10 .25
58 Chris Chelios .15 .40
59 Craig Ludwig .05 .15
60 Rick Green .07 .20
61 Mats Naslund .05 .15
62 Bobby Smith .07 .20
63 Claude Lemieux .30 .75
64 Guy Carbonneau .07 .20
65 Stephane Richer .15 .40
66 Mike McPhee .05 .15
67 Brian Skrudland .25 .60
68 Chris Nilan .05 .15
69 Bob Gainey .07 .20
70 Devils Action .05 .15
71 Devils Emblem .05 .15
72 Craig Billington .05 .15
73 Alain Chevrier .07 .20
74 Bruce Driver .10 .25
75 Joe Cirella .07 .20
76 Ken Daneyko .05 .15
77 Craig Wolanin .05 .15
78 Aaron Broten .07 .20
79 Kirk Muller .05 .15
80 John MacLean .10 .25
81 Pat Verbeek .07 .20
82 Doug Sulliman .10 .25
83 Mark Johnson .10 .25
84 Greg Adams .10 .25
85 Claude Loiselle .05 .15
86 Andy Brickley .07 .20
87 Islanders Action .05 .15
88 Islanders Emblem .05 .15
89 Billy Smith .05 .15
90 Kelly Hrudey .10 .25
91 Denis Potvin .10 .25
92 Tomas Jonsson .10 .25
93 Ken Leiter .05 .15
94 Ken Morrow .05 .15
95 Brian Curran .10 .25
96 Bryan Trottier .10 .25
97 Mike Bossy .10 .25
98 Pat LaFontaine .10 .25
99 Brent Sutter .07 .20
100 Mikko Makela .05 .15
101 Pat Flatley .10 .25
102 Duane Sutter .07 .20
103 Rich Kromm .05 .15
104 Rangers Action .05 .15
105 Rangers Emblem .05 .15
106 John Vanbiesbrouck .15 .40
107 James Patrick .07 .20
108 Ron Greschner .05 .15
109 Willie Huber .10 .25
110 Curt Giles .05 .15
111 Larry Melnyk .05 .15
112 Walt Poddubny .05 .15
113 Marcel Dionne .12 .30
114 Tomas Sandstrom .07 .20
115 Kelly Kisio .10 .25
116 Pierre Larouche .05 .15
117 Don Maloney .07 .20
118 Tony McKegney .07 .20
119 Ron Duguay .07 .20
120 Jan Erixon .05 .15
121 Flyers Action .05 .15
122 Flyers Emblem .05 .15
123 Ron Hextall .30 .75
124 Mark Howe .10 .25
125 Doug Crossman .10 .25
126 Brad McCrimmon .10 .25
127 Brad Marsh .10 .25
128 Tim Kerr .05 .15
129 Peter Zezel .10 .25
130 Dave Poulin .07 .20
131 Brian Propp .05 .15
132 Pelle Eklund .10 .25
133 Murray Craven .07 .20
134 Rick Tocchet .30 .75
135 Derrick Smith .05 .15
136 Ilkka Sinisalo .05 .15
137 Ron Sutter .10 .25
138 Penguins Action .05 .15
139 Penguins Emblem .05 .15
140 Gilles Meloche .10 .25
141 Doug Bodger .10 .25
142 Moe Mantha .07 .20
143 Jim Johnson .07 .20
144 Rod Buskas .05 .15
145 Randy Hillier .05 .15
146 Mario Lemieux .40 1.00
147 Dan Quinn .07 .20
148 Randy Cunneyworth .07 .20
149 Craig Simpson .15 .40
150 Terry Ruskowski .10 .25
151 John Chabot .07 .20
152 Bob Errey .05 .15
153 Dan Frawley .05 .15
154 Dave Hannan .05 .15
155 Nordiques Action .05 .15
156 Nordiques Emblem .05 .15
157 Mario Gosselin .07 .20
158 Clint Malarchuk .07 .20
159 Risto Siltanen .05 .15
160 Robert Picard .07 .20
161 Normand Rochefort .05 .15
162 Randy Moller .07 .20
163 Michel Goulet .10 .25
164 Peter Stastny .07 .20
165 John Ogrodnick .10 .25
166 Anton Stastny .10 .25
167 Paul Gillis .07 .20
168 Dale Hunter .07 .20
169 Alain Cote .07 .20
170 Mike Eagles .07 .20
171 Jason Lafreniere .05 .15
172 Capitals Action .05 .15
173 Capitals Emblem .05 .15
174 Pete Peeters .07 .20
175 Bob Mason .05 .15
176 Larry Murphy .07 .20
177 Scott Stevens .10 .25
178 Rod Langway .10 .25
179 Kevin Hatcher .25 .60
180 Mike Gartner .12 .30
181 Mike Ridley .07 .20
182 Craig Laughlin .05 .15
183 Gaetan Duchesne .05 .15
184 Dave Christian .05 .15
185 Greg Adams .10 .25
186 Kelly Miller .10 .25
187 Alan Haworth .05 .15
188 Lou Franceschetti .05 .15
189 Stanley Cup top half .05 .15
190 Stanley Cup bottom half .05 .15
191 Ron Hextall .30 .75
192 Wayne Gretzky .60 1.50
193 Brian Propp .05 .15
194 Mark Messier .20 .50
195 Flyers/Oilers Action .05 .15
196 Flyers/Oilers Action .05 .15
197 Gretzky Holding Cup .60 1.50
198 Gretzky Holding Cup .60 1.50
199 Gretzky Holding Cup .60 1.50
200 Gretzky Holding Cup .60 1.50
201 Flames Action .05 .15
202 Flames Emblem .05 .15
203 Mike Vernon .30 .75
204 Rejean Lemelin .05 .15
205 Al MacInnis .15 .40
206 Paul Reinhart .05 .15
207 Gary Suter .07 .20
208 Jamie Macoun .05 .15
209 Neil Sheehy .05 .15
210 Joe Mullen .10 .25
211 Carey Wilson .05 .15
212 Joel Otto .05 .15
213 Jim Peplinski .05 .15
214 Hakan Loob .05 .15
215 Lanny McDonald .07 .20
216 Tim Hunter .05 .15
217 Gary Roberts .05 .15
218 Blackhawks Action .05 .15
219 Blackhawks Emblem .05 .15
220 Bob Sauve .05 .15
221 Murray Bannerman .05 .15
222 Doug Wilson .07 .20
223 Bob Murray .05 .15
224 Gary Nylund .10 .25
225 Denis Savard .10 .25
226 Steve Larmer .07 .20
227 Troy Murray .10 .25
228 Wayne Presley .07 .20
229 Al Secord .10 .25
230 Ed Olczyk .10 .25
231 Curt Fraser .05 .15
232 Bill Watson .05 .15
233 Keith Brown .07 .20
234 Darryl Sutter .05 .15
235 Red Wings Action .05 .15
236 Red Wings Emblem .05 .15
237 Greg Stefan .10 .25
238 Glen Hanlon .10 .25
239 Darren Veitch .10 .25
240 Mike O'Connell .05 .15
241 Harold Snepsts .05 .15
242 Dave Lewis .07 .20
243 Steve Yzerman .30 .75
244 Brent Ashton .10 .25
245 Gerard Gallant .10 .25
246 Petr Klima .07 .20
247 Shawn Burr .07 .20
248 Adam Oates .30 .75
249 Mel Bridgman .07 .20
250 Tim Higgins .05 .15
251 Joey Kocur .05 .15
252 Oilers Action .05 .15
253 Oilers Emblem .05 .15
254 Grant Fuhr .15 .40
255 Andy Moog .25 .60
256 Paul Coffey .15 .40
257 Kevin Lowe .07 .20
258 Craig Muni .05 .15
259 Steve Smith .05 .15
260 Charlie Huddy .05 .15
261 Wayne Gretzky .60 1.50
262 Jari Kurri .05 .15
263 Mark Messier .20 .50
264 Esa Tikkanen .15 .40
265 Glenn Anderson .07 .20
266 Mike Krushelnyski .05 .15
267 Craig MacTavish .05 .15
268 Dave Hunter .05 .15
269 Kings Action .05 .15
270 Kings Emblem .05 .15
271 Roland Melanson .07 .20
272 Darren Eliot .05 .15
273 Grant Ledyard .05 .15
274 Jay Wells .05 .15
275 Mark Hardy .05 .15
276 Dean Kennedy .05 .15
277 Luc Robitaille .30 .75
278 Bernie Nicholls .10 .25
279 Jimmy Carson .10 .25
280 Dave Taylor .10 .25
281 Jim Fox .10 .25
282 Bryan Erickson .10 .25
283 Tiger Williams .05 .15
284 Sean McKenna .05 .15
285 Phil Sykes .05 .15
286 North Stars Action .05 .15
287 North Stars Emblem .05 .15
288 Kari Takko .05 .15
289 Don Beaupre .10 .25
290 Craig Hartsburg .07 .20
291 Ron Wilson .05 .15
292 Frantisek Musil .05 .15
293 Dino Ciccarelli .10 .25
294 Brian MacLellan .07 .20
295 Dirk Graham .10 .25
296 Brian Bellows .07 .20
297 Neal Broten .07 .20
298 Dennis Maruk .10 .25
299 Keith Acton .05 .15
300 Brian Lawton .05 .15
301 Bob Brooke .10 .25
302 Willi Plett .05 .15
303 Blues Action .05 .15
304 Blues Emblem .05 .15
305 Rick Wamsley .10 .25
306 Rob Ramage .05 .15
307 Ric Nattress .05 .15
308 Bruce Bell .05 .15
309 Charlie Bourgeois .05 .15
310 Jim Pavese .05 .15
311 Doug Gilmour .12 .30
312 Bernie Federko .07 .20
313 Mark Hunter .07 .20
314 Greg Paslawski .07 .20
315 Gino Cavallini .05 .15
316 Rick Meagher .05 .15
317 Ron Flockhart .10 .25
318 Doug Wickenheiser .07 .20
319 Jocelyn Lemieux .05 .15
320 Maple Leafs Action .05 .15
321 Maple Leafs Emblem .05 .15
322 Ken Wregget .15 .40
323 Allan Bester .07 .20
324 Todd Gill .05 .15
325 Al Iafrate .07 .20
326 Borje Salming .10 .25
327 Russ Courtnall .10 .25
328 Rick Vaive .05 .15
329 Steve Thomas .10 .25
330 Wendel Clark .15 .40
331 Gary Leeman .07 .20
332 Tom Fergus .05 .15
333 Vincent Damphousse .30 .75
334 Peter Ihnacak .05 .15
335 Brad Smith .05 .15
336 Miroslav Ihnacak .05 .15
337 Canucks Action .05 .15
338 Canucks Emblem .05 .15
339 Frank Caprice .05 .15
340 Richard Brodeur .05 .15
341 Doug Lidster .05 .15
342 Michel Petit .07 .20
343 Garth Butcher .05 .15
344 Dave Richter .07 .20
345 Tony Tanti .10 .25
346 Barry Pederson .07 .20
347 Petri Skriko .07 .20
348 Patrik Sundstrom .07 .20
349 Stan Smyl .07 .20
350 Rich Sutter .07 .20
351 Steve Tambellini .07 .20
352 Jim Sandlak .07 .20
353 Dave Lowry .05 .15
354 Jets Action .05 .15
355 Jets Emblem .05 .15
356 Daniel Berthiaume .05 .15
357 Pokey Reddick .05 .15
358 Dave Ellett .07 .20
359 Mario Marois .07 .20
360 Randy Carlyle .07 .20
361 Fredrick Olausson .07 .20
362 Jim Kyte .07 .20
363 Dale Hawerchuk .12 .30
364 Paul MacLean .10 .25
365 Thomas Steen .07 .20
366 Gilles Hamel .05 .15
367 Doug Smail .10 .25
368 Laurie Boschman .07 .20
369 Ray Neufeld .05 .15
370 Andrew McBain .05 .15
371 Wayne Gretzky .60 1.50
372 Hart Trophy .05 .15
373 Wayne Gretzky .60 1.50
374 Art Ross Trophy .05 .15
375 Jennings Trophy .05 .15
376A Brian Hayward .07 .20
376B Patrick Roy .30 .75
377 Vezina Trophy .05 .15
378 Ron Hextall .30 .75
379 Luc Robitaille .30 .75
380 Calder Trophy .05 .15
381 Ray Bourque .30 .75
382 Norris Trophy .05 .15
383 Lady Byng Trophy .05 .15
384 Joe Mullen .10 .25
385 Frank Selke Trophy .05 .15
386 Dave Poulin .07 .20
387 Doug Jarvis .10 .25
388 Masterton Trophy .05 .15
389 Wayne Gretzky .60 1.50
390 Emery Edge Award .05 .15
391 Flyers Team Photo (left half) .05 .15
392 Flyers Team Photo (right half) .05 .15
393 Prince of Wales Trophy .05 .15
394 Clarence S. Campbell Bowl .05 .15
395 Oilers Team Photo (left half .05 .15
396 Oilers Team Photo (right half .05 .15
NNO Sticker Album 2.00 5.00

1988-89 Panini Stickers

1 Road to the Cup Stanley Cup .05 .10
2 Flames Emblem .05 .10
3 Flames Uniform .05 .10
4 Mike Vernon .20 .50
5 Al MacInnis .20 .50
6 Brad McCrimmon .07 .20
7 Gary Suter .07 .20
8 Mike Bullard .07 .20
9 Hakan Loob .05 .15
10 Lanny McDonald .07 .20
11 Joe Mullen .10 .25
12 Joe Nieuwendyk .30 .75
13 Joel Otto .05 .15
14 Jim Peplinski .05 .15
15 Gary Roberts .05 .15
16 Flames Team LH .05 .10
17 Flames Team RH .05 .10
18 Blackhawks Emblem .05 .10
19 Blackhawks Uniform .05 .10
20 Bob Mason .05 .15
21 Darren Pang .30 .75
22 Bob Murray .05 .15
23 Gary Nylund .07 .20
24 Doug Wilson .07 .20
25 Dirk Graham .07 .20
26 Steve Larmer .07 .20
27 Troy Murray .05 .15
28 Brian Noonan .07 .20
29 Denis Savard .10 .25
30 Steve Thomas .05 .15
31 Rick Vaive .10 .25
32 Blackhawks Team LH .05 .10
33 Blackhawks Team RH .05 .10
34 Red Wings Emblem .05 .10
35 Red Wings Uniform .05 .10
36 Glen Hanlon .07 .20
37 Greg Stefan .10 .25
38 Jeff Sharples .07 .20
39 Darren Veitch .05 .15
40 Brent Ashton .05 .15
41 Shawn Burr .10 .25
42 John Chabot .07 .20
43 Gerard Gallant .07 .20
44 Petr Klima .07 .20
45 Adam Oates .20 .50
46 Bob Probert .30 .75
47 Steve Yzerman .30 .75
48 Red Wings Team LH .05 .10
49 Red Wings Team RH .05 .10
50 Oilers Emblem .05 .10
51 Oilers Uniform .05 .10
52 Grant Fuhr .15 .40
53 Charlie Huddy .07 .20
54 Kevin Lowe .07 .20
55 Steve Smith .05 .15
56 Jeff Beukeboom .05 .15
57 Glenn Anderson .07 .20
58 Wayne Gretzky .60 1.50
59 Jari Kurri .07 .20
60 Craig MacTavish .07 .20
61 Mark Messier .20 .50
62 Craig Simpson .07 .20
63 Esa Tikkanen .20 .50
64 Oilers Team LH .05 .10
65 Oilers Team RH .05 .10
66 Kings Emblem .05 .10

67 Kings Uniform .05 .10
68 Glenn Healy .05 .15
69 Roland Melanson .07 .20
70 Steve Duchesne .25 .60
71 Tom Laidlaw .07 .20
72 Jay Wells .05 .15
73 Mike Allison .05 .15
74 Bob Carpenter .07 .20
75 Jimmy Carson .07 .20
76 Jim Fox .07 .20
77 Bernie Nicholls .07 .20
78 Luc Robitaille .20 .50
79 Dave Taylor .07 .20
80 Kings Team LH .05 .10
81 Kings Team RH .05 .10
82 North Stars Emblem .05 .10
83 North Stars Uniform .05 .10
84 Don Beaupre .07 .20
85 Kari Takko .05 .15
86 Craig Hartsburg .07 .20
87 Frantisek Musil .05 .15
88 Dave Archibald .05 .15
89 Brian Bellows .07 .20
90 Scott Bjugstad .05 .15
91 Bob Brooke .10 .25
92 Neal Broten .07 .20
93 Dino Ciccarelli .07 .20
94 Brian Lawton .07 .20
95 Brian MacLellan .07 .20
96 North Stars Team LH .05 .10
97 North Stars Team RH .05 .10
98 Blues Emblem .05 .10
99 Blues Uniform .05 .10
100 Greg Millen .05 .15
101 Brian Benning .07 .20
102 Gordie Roberts .05 .15
103 Gino Cavallini .07 .20
104 Bernie Federko .07 .20
105 Doug Gilmour .12 .30
106 Tony Hrkac .05 .15
107 Brett Hull .30 .75
108 Mark Hunter .07 .20
109 Tony McKegney .07 .20
110 Rick Meagher .07 .20
111 Brian Sutter .05 .15
112 Blues Team LH .05 .10
113 Blues Team RH .05 .10
114 Maple Leafs Emblem .05 .10
115 Maple Leafs Uniform .05 .10
116 Allan Bester .05 .15
117 Ken Wregget .07 .20
118 Al Iafrate .10 .25
119 Luke Richardson .05 .15
120 Borje Salming .10 .25
121 Wendel Clark .15 .40
122 Russ Courtnall .07 .20
123 Vincent Damphousse .25 .60
124 Dan Daoust .05 .15
125 Gary Leeman .07 .20
126 Ed Olczyk .05 .15
127 Mark Osborne .05 .15
128 Maple Leafs Team LH .05 .10
129 Maple Leafs Team RH .05 .10
130 Canucks Emblem .05 .10
131 Canucks Uniform .05 .10
132 Kirk McLean .05 .15
133 Jim Benning .05 .15
134 Garth Butcher .07 .20
135 Doug Lidster .07 .20
136 Greg Adams .05 .15
137 David Bruce .05 .15
138 Barry Pederson .07 .20
139 Jim Sandlak .05 .15
140 Petri Skriko .07 .20
141 Stan Smyl .05 .15
142 Rich Sutter .05 .15
143 Tony Tanti .10 .25
144 Canucks Team LH .05 .10
145 Canucks Team RH .05 .10
146 Jets Emblem .05 .10
147 Jets Uniform .05 .10
148 Daniel Berthiaume .07 .20
149 Randy Carlyle .07 .20
150 Dave Ellett .07 .20
151 Mario Marois .07 .20
152 Peter Taglianetti .05 .15
153 Laurie Boschman .07 .20
154 Iain Duncan .07 .20
155 Dale Hawerchuk .12 .30
156 Paul MacLean .07 .20
157 Andrew McBain .05 .15
158 Doug Smail .05 .15
159 Thomas Steen .05 .15
160 Jets Team LH .05 .10
161 Jets Team RH .05 .10
162 Prince of Wales Trophy .05 .10
163 Caps/Flyers Action .05 .10
164 Bruins/Canadiens Action .05 .10
165 Caps/Devils Action .05 .10
166 Bruins/Devils Action LH .05 .10
167 Bruins/Devils Action RH .05 .10
168 Flames/Kings Action .05 .10
169 Clarence S. Campbell Bowl .05 .10
170 Oilers/Flames Action .05 .10
171 Blues/Red Wings Action .05 .10
172 Oilers/Red Wings Action .05 .10
173 Oilers/Red Wings Action .05 .10
174 Oilers Celebrate .05 .10
175 Oilers/Bruins Action .05 .10
176 Stanley Cup (top half) .05 .10
177 Stanley Cup (bottom half) .05 .10
178 Wayne Gretzky .60 1.50
178 Bruins Action .05 .10
179 Oilers/Bruins Action RH .05 .10
180 Oilers/Bruins Action LH .05 .10
181 Wayne Gretzky .60 1.50
182 Conn Smythe Trophy .05 .10
183 Oilers Celebrate UL .05 .10
184 Oilers Celebrate UR .05 .10
185 Oilers Celebrate LL .05 .10
186 Oilers Celebrate LR .05 .10
187 Flames Action .05 .10
188 Grant Fuhr .15 .40
189 Devils Action .05 .10
190 Marcel Dionne .12 .30
191 Cam Neely .25 .60
192 Capitals Action .05 .10
193 Wayne Gretzky .60 1.50
194 Jets/Bruins Action .05 .10
195 Bruins/Canadiens Action .05 .10
196 Blues Action .05 .10
197 Caps/Flyers Action .05 .10
198 Islanders Action .05 .10
199 Flames Action .05 .10
200 Penguins Action .05 .10
201 Bruins Emblem .05 .10
202 Bruins Uniform .05 .10
203 Rejean Lemelin .05 .15
204 Ray Bourque .30 .75
205 Gord Kluzak .05 .15
206 Michael Thelven .05 .15
207 Glen Wesley .07 .20
208 Randy Burridge .07 .20
209 Keith Crowder .05 .15
210 Steve Kasper .05 .15
211 Ken Linseman .05 .15
212 Jay Miller .05 .15
214 Bob Sweeney .07 .20
215 Bruins Team LH .05 .10
216 Bruins Team RH .05 .10
217 Sabres Emblem .05 .10
218 Sabres Uniform .05 .10
219 Tom Barrasso .05 .15
220 Phil Housley .07 .20
221 Calle Johansson .05 .15
222 Mike Ramsey .05 .15
223 Dave Andreychuk .10 .25
224 Scott Arniel .05 .15
225 Adam Creighton .05 .15
226 Mike Foligno .07 .20
227 Christian Ruuttu .07 .20
228 Ray Sheppard .30 .75
229 John Tucker .10 .25
230 Pierre Turgeon .40 1.00
231 Sabres Team LH .05 .10
232 Sabres Team RH .05 .10
233 Whalers Emblem .05 .10
234 Whalers Uniform .05 .10
235 Mike Liut .05 .15
236 Dave Babych .07 .20
237 Sylvain Cote .05 .15
238 Ulf Samuelsson .07 .20
239 John Anderson .05 .15
240 Kevin Dineen .07 .20
241 Ray Ferraro .05 .15
242 Ron Francis .12 .30
243 Paul MacDermid .05 .15
244 Dave Tippett .10 .25
245 Sylvain Turgeon .07 .20
246 Carey Wilson .10 .25
247 Whalers Team LH .05 .10
248 Whalers Team RH .05 .10
249 Canadiens Emblem .05 .10
250 Canadiens Uniform .05 .10
251 Brian Hayward .07 .20
252 Patrick Roy .30 .75
253 Chris Chelios .25 .60
254 Craig Ludwig .07 .20
255 Petr Svoboda .05 .15
256 Guy Carbonneau .07 .20
257 Claude Lemieux .20 .50
258 Mike McPhee .05 .15
259 Mats Naslund .05 .15
260 Stephane Richer .07 .20
261 Bobby Smith .10 .25
262 Ryan Walter .05 .15
263 Canadiens Team LH .05 .10
264 Canadiens Team RH .05 .10
265 Devils Emblem .05 .10
266 Devils Uniform .05 .10
267 Sean Burke .20 .50
268 Joe Cirella .07 .20
269 Bruce Driver .07 .20
270 Craig Wolanin .05 .15
271 Aaron Broten .07 .20
272 Doug Brown .05 .15
273 Claude Loiselle .05 .15
274 John MacLean .07 .20
275 Kirk Muller .10 .25
276 Brendan Shanahan .40 1.00
277 Patrik Sundstrom .10 .25
278 Pat Verbeek .07 .20
279 Devils Team LH .05 .10
280 Devils Team RH .05 .10
281 Islanders Emblem .05 .10
282 Islanders Uniform .05 .10
283 Kelly Hrudey .07 .20
284 Steve Konroyd .07 .20
285 Ken Morrow .05 .15
286 Pat Flatley .05 .15
287 Greg Gilbert .10 .25
288 Alan Kerr .10 .25
289 Derek King .05 .15
290 Pat LaFontaine .10 .25
291 Mikko Makela .07 .20
292 Brent Sutter .07 .20
293 Bryan Trottier .10 .25
294 Randy Wood .07 .20
295 Islanders Team .05 .10
296 Islanders Team .05 .10
297 Rangers Emblem .05 .10
298 Rangers Uniform .05 .10
299 Bob Froese .05 .15
300 John Vanbiesbrouck .10 .25
301 Brian Leetch .05 .15
302 Norm Maciver .05 .15
303 James Patrick .10 .25
304 Michel Petit .05 .15
305 Ulf Dahlen .07 .20
306 Jan Erixon .07 .20
307 Kelly Kisio .07 .20
308 Don Maloney .05 .15
309 Walt Poddubny .07 .20
310 Tomas Sandstrom .05 .15
311 Rangers Team LH .05 .10
312 Rangers Team RH .05 .10
313 Flyers Emblem .05 .10
314 Flyers Uniform .05 .10
315 Ron Hextall .20 .50
316 Mark Howe .10 .25
317 Kerry Huffman .05 .15
318 Kjell Samuelsson .05 .15
319 Dave Brown .05 .15
320 Murray Craven .10 .25
321 Tim Kerr .05 .15
322 Scott Mellanby .30 .75
323 Dave Poulin .05 .15
324 Brian Propp .07 .20
325 Ilkka Sinisalo .05 .15
326 Rick Tocchet .25 .60
327 Flyers Team LH .05 .10
328 Flyers Team RH .05 .10
329 Penguins Emblem .05 .10
330 Penguins Uniform .05 .10
331 Frank Pietrangelo .05 .15
332 Doug Bodger .05 .15
333 Paul Coffey .20 .50
334 Jim Johnson .07 .20
335 Ville Siren .05 .15
336 Rob Brown .05 .15
337 Randy Cunneyworth .07 .20
338 Dan Frawley .05 .15
339 Dave Hunter .10 .25
340 Mario Lemieux .40 1.00
341 Troy Loney .05 .15
342 Dan Quinn .07 .20
343 Penguins Team LH .05 .10
344 Penguins Team RH .05 .10
345 Nordiques Emblem .05 .10
346 Nordiques Uniform .05 .10
347 Mario Gosselin .07 .20
348 Tommy Albelin .07 .20
349 Jeff Brown .07 .20
350 Steven Finn .05 .15
351 Randy Moller .05 .15
352 Alain Cote .07 .20
353 Gaetan Duchesne .07 .20
354 Mike Eagles .05 .15
355 Michel Goulet .07 .20
356 Lane Lambert .07 .20
357 Anton Stastny .05 .15
358 Peter Stastny .07 .20
359 Nordiques Team LH .05 .10
360 Nordiques Team RH .05 .10
361 Capitals Emblem .05 .10
362 Capitals Uniform .05 .10
363 Clint Malarchuk .07 .20
364 Pete Peeters .07 .20
365 Kevin Hatcher .10 .25
366 Rod Langway .05 .15
367 Larry Murphy .07 .20
368 Scott Stevens .10 .25
369 Dave Christian .05 .15
370 Mike Gartner .12 .30
371 Bengt Gustafsson .07 .20
372 Dale Hunter .10 .25
373 Kelly Miller .05 .15
374 Mike Ridley .05 .15
375 Capitals Team LH .05 .10
376 Capitals Team RH .05 .10
377 Hockey Rink Schematic .05 .10
378 Hockey Rink Schematic .05 .10
379 Cross-checking .05 .10
380 Elbowing .05 .10
381 High-sticking .05 .10
382 Holding .05 .10
383 Hooking .05 .10
384 Interference .05 .10
385 Spearing .05 .10
386 Tripping .05 .10
387 Boarding .05 .10
388 Charging .05 .10
389 Delayed Calling of Penalty .05 .10
390 Kneeing .05 .10
391 Misconduct .05 .10
392 Roughing .05 .10
393 Slashing .05 .10
394 Unsportsmanlike Conduct .05 .10
395 Wash-out .05 .10
396 Icing .05 .10
397 Off-side .05 .10
398 Wash-out .05 .10
399 Bill Masterton Memorial Trophy Bob Bourne .05 .15
400 Hart Memorial Trophy Mario Lemieux .40 1.00
401 Art Ross Trophy Mario Lemieux .40 1.00
402 William M. Jennings Trophy Brian Hayward Patrick Roy .30 .75
403 Vezina Trophy Grant Fuhr .15 .40
404 Calder Memorial Trophy Joe Nieuwendyk .30 .75
405 James Norris Memorial Trophy Ray Bourque .30 .75
406 Lady Byng Trophy Mats Naslund .05 .15
407 Frank J. Selke Trophy Guy Carbonneau .07 .20
408 Emery Edge Award Brad McCrimmon .07 .20
NNO Sticker Album 2.00 5.00

1989-90 Panini Stickers

1 NHL Logo .05 .15
2 Playoff schedule .05 .15
3 Flames/Blackhawks action .05 .15
4 Flames/Canucks action .05 .15
5 Kings/Oilers action .05 .15
6 Vernon goal LH .12 .30
7 Vernon goal RH .12 .30
8 Bruins/Sabres action .05 .15
9 Canadiens/Bruins action .05 .15
10 Flyers score .05 .15
11 Canadiens/Flyers action LH .05 .15
12 Canadiens/Flyers action RH .05 .15
13 Canadiens/Flames action .05 .15
14 Canadiens celebration .05 .15
15 Canadiens/Flames action .05 .15
16 Canadiens/Flames action .05 .15
17 Flames celebration .05 .15
18 Flames/Canadiens action LH .05 .15
19 Flames/Canadiens action RH .05 .15
20 Al MacInnis Conn Smythe Trophy .12 .30
21 Stanley Cup Flames UL .05 .15
22 Stanley Cup Flames UR .05 .15
23 Stanley Cup Flames LL .05 .15
24 Stanley Cup Flames LR .05 .15
25 Stanley Cup .05 .15
26 Calgary Flames .05 .15
27 Joe Mullen .05 .15
28 Doug Gilmour .12 .30
29 Joe Nieuwendyk .07 .20
30 Gary Suter .07 .20
31 Flames team .05 .15
32 Al MacInnis .12 .30
33 Brad McCrimmon .05 .15
34 Mike Vernon .12 .30
35 Gary Roberts .12 .30
36 Colin Patterson .07 .20
37 Jim Peplinski .05 .15
38 Jamie Macoun .05 .15
39 Lanny McDonald .10 .25
40 Saddledome .05 .15
41 Chicago Blackhawks .05 .15
42 Darren Pang .07 .20
43 Steve Larmer .07 .20
44 Dirk Graham .07 .20
45 Doug Wilson .07 .20
46 Blackhawks/Oilers action (Ed Belfour shown) .05 .15
47 Dave Manson .07 .20
48 Troy Murray .07 .20
49 Denis Savard .10 .25
50 Steve Thomas .10 .25
51 Adam Creighton .07 .20
52 Wayne Presley .10 .25
53 Trent Yawney .07 .20
54 Alain Chevrier .05 .15
55 Chicago Stadium .05 .15
56 Detroit Red Wings .05 .15
57 Steve Yzerman .25 .60
58 Gerard Gallant .10 .25
59 Greg Stefan .07 .20
60 Dave Barr .10 .25
61 Red Wings Team .05 .15
62 Steve Chiasson .07 .20
63 Shawn Burr .10 .25
64 Rick Zombo .05 .15
65 Glen Hanlon .05 .15
66 Jeff Sharples .07 .20
67 Joey Kocur .05 .15
68 Lee Norwood .07 .20
69 Mike O'Connell .10 .25
70 Joe Louis Arena .05 .15
71 Edmonton Oilers .05 .15
72 Jimmy Carson .05 .15
73 Jari Kurri .07 .20
74 Mark Messier .20 .50
75 Craig Simpson .10 .25
76 Oilers/Flyers action .05 .15
77 Glenn Anderson .07 .20
78 Craig MacTavish .07 .20
79 Kevin Lowe .10 .25
80 Craig Muni .07 .20
81 Bill Ranford .07 .20
82 Charlie Huddy .10 .25
83 Steve Smith .07 .20
84 Normand Lacombe .05 .15
85 Northlands Coliseum .05 .15
86 L.A. Kings logo .05 .15
87 Wayne Gretzky .60 1.50
88 Bernie Nicholls .07 .20
89 Kelly Hrudey .07 .20
90 John Tonelli .10 .25
91 Oilers/Kings action .05 .15
92 Steve Kasper .05 .15
93 Steve Duchesne .05 .15
94 Mike Krushelnyski .10 .25
95 Luc Robitaille .10 .25
96 Ron Duguay .05 .15
97 Glenn Healy .05 .15
98 Dave Taylor .07 .20
99 Marty McSorley .07 .20
100 The Great Western Forum .05 .15
101 Minnesota North Stars .05 .15
102 Kari Takko .05 .15
103 Dave Gagner .10 .25
104 Mike Gartner .12 .30
105 Brian Bellows .07 .20
106 North Stars Team .05 .15
107 Neal Broten .10 .25
108 Larry Murphy .07 .20
109 Basil McRae .07 .20
110 Perry Berezan .05 .15
111 Shawn Chambers .05 .15
112 Curt Giles .05 .15
113 Stewart Gavin .05 .15
114 Jon Casey .07 .20
115 Metropolitan Sports Center .05 .15
116 St. Louis Blues .05 .15
117 Brett Hull .12 .30
118 Peter Zezel .07 .20
119 Tony Hrkac .07 .20
120 Vincent Riendeau .05 .15
121 Blues/Islanders action .05 .15
122 Cliff Ronning .30 .75
123 Gino Cavallini .07 .20
124 Brian Benning .10 .25
125 Rick Meagher .05 .15
126 Steve Tuttle .10 .25
127 Paul Cavallini .07 .20
128 Tom Tilley .05 .15
129 Greg Millen .05 .15
130 St. Louis Arena .05 .15
131 Toronto Maple Leafs .05 .15
132 Ed Olczyk .05 .15
133 Gary Leeman .07 .20
134 Vincent Damphousse .07 .20
135 Tom Fergus .05 .15
136 Maple Leafs action .05 .15
137 Daniel Marois .07 .20
138 Mark Osborne .10 .25
139 Allan Bester .07 .20
140 Al Iafrate .10 .25
141 Brad Marsh .07 .20
142 Luke Richardson .05 .15
143 Todd Gill .05 .15
144 Wendel Clark .15 .40
145 Maple Leafs Gardens .05 .15
146 Vancouver Canucks .05 .15
147 Petri Skriko .07 .20
148 Trevor Linden .30 .75
149 Tony Tanti .07 .20
150 Steve Weeks .05 .15
151 Canucks/Islanders action .05 .15
152 Brian Bradley .07 .20
153 Barry Pederson .07 .20
154 Greg Adams .07 .20
155 Kirk McLean .12 .30
156 Jim Sandlak .07 .20
157 Rich Sutter .07 .20
158 Garth Butcher .05 .15
159 Stan Smyl .07 .20
160 Pacific Coliseum .05 .15
161 Winnipeg Jets .05 .15
162 Dale Hawerchuk .12 .30
163 Thomas Steen .07 .20
164 Brent Ashton .07 .20
165 Pat Elynuik .10 .25
166 Jets/Islanders action .05 .15
167 Dave Ellett .07 .20
168 Randy Carlyle .07 .20
169 Laurie Boschman .05 .15
170 Iain Duncan .05 .15
171 Doug Smail .05 .15
172 Teppo Numminen .05 .15
173 Bob Essensa .05 .15
174 Peter Taglianetti .07 .20
175 Winnipeg Arena .05 .15
176 Steve Duchesne AS .05 .15
177 Luc Robitaille AS .10 .25
178 Mike Vernon AS .12 .30
179 Wayne Gretzky AS .60 1.50
180 Kevin Lowe AS .10 .25
181 Jari Kurri AS .07 .20
182 Cam Neely AS .10 .25
183 Paul Coffey AS .10 .25
184 Mario Lemieux AS .40 1.00
185 Sean Burke AS .10 .25
186 Rob Brown AS .05 .15
187 Ray Bourque AS .15 .40
188 Boston Bruins .05 .15
189 Greg Hawgood .10 .25
190 Ken Linseman .07 .20
191 Andy Moog .10 .25
192 Cam Neely .10 .25
193 Bruins/Flyers action .05 .15
194 Andy Brickley .07 .20
195 Rejean Lemelin .05 .15
196 Bob Carpenter .07 .20
197 Randy Burridge .05 .15
198 Craig Janney .12 .30
199 Bob Joyce .07 .20
200 Glen Wesley .07 .20
201 Ray Bourque .15 .40
202 Boston Garden .05 .15
203 Buffalo Sabres .05 .15
204 Pierre Turgeon .20 .50
205 Phil Housley .07 .20
206 Rick Vaive .05 .15
207 Christian Ruuttu .07 .20
208 Flyers/Sabres action .05 .15
209 Doug Bodger .07 .20
210 Mike Foligno .10 .25
211 Ray Sheppard .05 .15
212 John Tucker .07 .20
213 Scott Arniel .05 .15
214 Daren Puppa .12 .30
215 Dave Andreychuk .10 .25
216 Uwe Krupp .05 .15
217 Memorial Auditorium .05 .15
218 Hartford Whalers .05 .15
219 Kevin Dineen .07 .20
220 Peter Sidorkiewicz .10 .25
221 Ron Francis .12 .30
222 Ray Ferraro .07 .20
223 Islanders/Whalers action .05 .15
224 Scott Young .15 .40
225 Dave Babych .07 .20
226 Dave Tippett .05 .15
227 Paul MacDermid .07 .20
228 Ulf Samuelsson .05 .15
229 Sylvain Cote .10 .25
230 Jody Hull .05 .15
231 Don Maloney .05 .15
232 Hartford Civic Center .05 .15
233 Montreal Canadiens .05 .15
234 Mats Naslund .05 .15
235 Patrick Roy .30 .75
236 Bobby Smith .07 .20
237 Chris Chelios .10 .25
238 Flames/Canadiens action .05 .15
239 Stephane Richer .07 .20
240 Claude Lemieux .07 .20
241 Guy Carbonneau .07 .20
242 Shayne Corson .15 .40
243 Mike McPhee .10 .25
244 Petr Svoboda .07 .20
245 Larry Robinson .10 .25
246 Brian Hayward .07 .20
247 Montreal Forum .05 .15
248 New Jersey Devils .05 .15
249 John MacLean .10 .25
250 Patrik Sundstrom .07 .20
251 Kirk Muller .05 .15
252 Tom Kurvers .10 .25
253 Bruins/Devils action .05 .15
254 Aaron Broten .07 .20
255 Brendan Shanahan .10 .25
256 Sean Burke .10 .25
257 Tommy Albelin .07 .20
258 Ken Daneyko .07 .20
259 Randy Velischek .07 .20
260 Mark Johnson .07 .20
261 Jim Korn .05 .15
262 Brendan Byrne Arena .05 .15
263 New York Islanders .05 .15
264 Pat LaFontaine .10 .25
265 Mark Fitzpatrick .05 .15
266 Brent Sutter .10 .25
267 David Volek .10 .25
268 Islanders/Rangers action .05 .15
269 Bryan Trottier .10 .25
270 Mikko Makela .07 .20
271 Derek King .10 .25
272 Pat Flatley .05 .15
273 Jeff Norton .07 .20
274 Gerald Diduck .07 .20
275 Alan Kerr .05 .15
276 Jeff Hackett .05 .15
277 Nassau Veterans Memorial Coliseum .05 .15
278 New York Rangers .05 .15
279 Brian Leetch .30 .75
280 Carey Wilson .07 .20
281 Tomas Sandstrom .07 .20
282 John Vanbiesbrouck .10 .25
283 Oilers/Rangers action .05 .15
284 Bob Froese .05 .15
285 Tony Granato .10 .25
286 Brian Mullen .07 .20
287 Kelly Kisio .10 .25
288 Ulf Dahlen .10 .25
289 James Patrick .10 .25
290 John Ogrodnick .05 .15
291 Michel Petit .05 .15
292 Madison Square Garden .05 .15
293 Philadelphia Flyers .05 .15
294 Tim Kerr .05 .15
295 Rick Tocchet .10 .25
296 Pelle Eklund .05 .15
297 Terry Carkner .10 .25
298 Flyers/Canadiens action .05 .15
299 Ron Sutter .10 .25
300 Mark Howe .10 .25
301 Keith Acton .05 .15
302 Ron Hextall .10 .25
303 Gord Murphy .05 .15
304 Derrick Smith .05 .15
305 Dave Poulin .10 .25
306 Brian Propp .05 .15
307 The Spectrum .05 .15
308 Pittsburgh Penguins .05 .15
309 Mario Lemieux .40 1.00
310 Rob Brown .05 .15
311 Paul Coffey .10 .25
312 Tom Barrasso .07 .20
313 Penguins/Flyers action .05 .15
314 Dan Quinn .07 .20
315 Bob Errey .07 .20
316 John Cullen .07 .20
317 Phil Bourque .07 .20
318 Zarley Zalapski .07 .20
319 Troy Loney .05 .15
320 Jim Johnson .07 .20
321 Kevin Stevens .05 .15
322 Civic Arena .05 .15
323 Quebec Nordiques .05 .15
324 Peter Stastny .07 .20
325 Jeff Brown .07 .20
326 Michel Goulet .07 .20
327 Joe Sakic .30 .75
328 Flyers/Nordiques action .05 .15
329 Iiro Jarvi .05 .15
330 Paul Gillis .07 .20
331 Randy Moller .05 .15
332 Ron Tugnutt .25 .60
333 Robert Picard .05 .15
334 Curtis Leschyshyn .05 .15
335 Marc Fortier .05 .15
336 Mario Marois .05 .15
337 Le Colisee .05 .15
338 Washington Capitals .05 .15
339 Mike Ridley .07 .20
340 Geoff Courtnall .20 .50
341 Scott Stevens .10 .25
342 Dino Ciccarelli .07 .20
343 Capitals/Flames action .05 .15
344 Bob Mason .05 .15
345 Dave Christian .05 .15
346 Dale Hunter .07 .20
347 Kevin Hatcher .07 .20
348 Kelly Miller .05 .15
349 Stephen Leach .07 .20
350 Rod Langway .07 .20
351 Bob Rouse .07 .20
352 Capital Centre .05 .15
353 Calgary Flames .05 .15
354 Edmonton Oilers .05 .15
355 Winnipeg Jets .05 .15
356 Toronto Maple Leafs .05 .15
357 Buffalo Sabres .05 .15
358 Montreal Canadiens .05 .15
359 Quebec Nordiques .05 .15
360 New Jersey Devils .05 .15
361 Boston Bruins .05 .15
362 Hartford Whalers .05 .15
363 Vancouver Canucks .05 .15
364 Minnesota North Stars .05 .15
365 Los Angeles Kings .05 .15
366 St. Louis Blues .05 .15
367 Chicago Blackhawks .05 .15
368 Detroit Red Wings .05 .15
369 Pittsburgh Penguins .05 .15
370 Washington Capitals .05 .15
371 Philadelphia Flyers .05 .15
372 New York Rangers .05 .15
373 New York Islanders .05 .15
374 Wayne Gretzky .60 1.50
375 Mario Lemieux .40 1.00
376 Patrick Roy .30 .75
377 Tim Kerr .05 .15
378 Brian Leetch .30 .75
379 Chris Chelios .10 .25
380 Joe Mullen .05 .15
381 Guy Carbonneau .07 .20
382 Bryan Trottier .10 .25
383 Patrick Roy .30 .75
384 Joe Mullen .05 .15
NNO Sticker Album 1.00 2.50

1990-91 Panini Stickers

1 Prince of Wales .05 .15
2 Clarence Campbell .05 .15
3 Stanley Cup .05 .15
4 Dave Poulin .10 .25
5 Brian Propp .10 .25
6 Glen Wesley .07 .20
7 Bob Carpenter .07 .20
8 John Carter .07 .20
9 Cam Neely .10 .25
10 Greg Hawgood .07 .20
11 Andy Moog .10 .25
12 Boston Bruins logo .05 .15
13 Rejean Lemelin .05 .15
14 Craig Janney .10 .25
15 Bob Sweeney .05 .15
16 Andy Brickley .05 .15
17 Ray Bourque .15 .40
18 Dave Christian .05 .15
19 Dave Snuggerud .07 .20
20 Christian Ruuttu .07 .20
21 Phil Housley .07 .20
22 Uwe Krupp .10 .25
23 Rick Vaive .07 .20
24 Mike Ramsey .05 .15
25 Mike Foligno .07 .20
26 Clint Malarchuk .07 .20
27 Buffalo Sabres logo .05 .15
28 Pierre Turgeon .07 .20
29 Dave Andreychuk .10 .25
30 Scott Arniel .05 .15
31 Daren Puppa .07 .20
32 Mike Hartman .10 .25
33 Doug Bodger .07 .20
34 Scott Young .05 .15
35 Todd Krygier .07 .20
36 Pat Verbeek .07 .20
37 Dave Tippett .07 .20
38 Peter Sidorkiewicz .10 .25
39 Ron Francis .12 .30
40 Dave Babych .05 .15
41 Randy Ladouceur .10 .25
42 Hartford Whalers logo .05 .15
43 Kevin Dineen .10 .25
44 Dean Evason .07 .20
45 Ray Ferraro .07 .20
46 Mike Tomlak .10 .25
47 Mikael Andersson .10 .25
48 Brad Shaw .07 .20
49 Chris Chelios .10 .25
50 Petr Svoboda .07 .20
51 Patrick Roy .25 .60
52 Bobby Smith .07 .20
53 Stephane Richer .10 .25
54 Shayne Corson .07 .20
55 Brian Skrudland .07 .20
56 Russ Courtnall .10 .25
57 Montreal Canadiens logo .05 .15
58 Guy Carbonneau .05 .15
59 Sylvain Lefebvre .07 .20
60 Mathieu Schneider .07 .20
61 Brian Hayward .10 .25
62 Mats Naslund .05 .15
63 Mike McPhee .07 .20
64 Brendan Shanahan .10 .25
65 Patrik Sundstrom .07 .20
66 Mark Johnson .07 .20
67 Doug Brown .07 .20
68 Chris Terreri .20 .50
69 Bruce Driver .10 .25
70 Peter Stastny .07 .20
71 Sylvain Turgeon .07 .20
72 New Jersey Devils logo .05 .15
73 Kirk Muller .07 .20
74 John MacLean .07 .20
75 Slava Fetisov .20 .50
76 Tommy Albelin .05 .15
77 Sean Burke .07 .20
78 Janne Ojanen .10 .25
79 Randy Wood .05 .15
80 Gary Nylund .07 .20
81 Pat LaFontaine .10 .25
82 Pat Flatley .10 .25
83 Bryan Trottier .10 .25
84 Don Maloney .10 .25
85 Gerald Diduck .07 .20
86 Mark Fitzpatrick .07 .20
87 New York Islanders logo .05 .15
88 Glenn Healy .20 .50
89 Alan Kerr .07 .20
90 Brent Sutter .07 .20
91 Doug Crossman .07 .20
92 Hubie McDonough .07 .20
93 Jeff Norton .10 .25
94 Kelly Kisio .07 .20
95 Brian Leetch .12 .30
96 Brian Mullen .10 .25
97 James Patrick .10 .25
98 Mike Richter .30 .75
99 John Ogrodnick .10 .25
100 Troy Mallette .07 .20
101 Mark Janssens .10 .25
102 New York Rangers logo .05 .15
103 Mike Gartner .12 .30
104 Jan Erixon .10 .25
105 Carey Wilson .07 .20
106 Bernie Nicholls .07 .20
107 Darren Turcotte .07 .20
108 John Vanbiesbrouck .10 .25
109 Ron Sutter .07 .20
110 Kjell Samuelsson .07 .20
111 Ken Linseman .07 .20
112 Ken Wregget .10 .25
113 Pelle Eklund .05 .15
114 Terry Carkner .07 .20
115 Gord Murphy .10 .25
116 Murray Craven .10 .25
117 Philadelphia Flyers logo .05 .15
118 Ron Hextall .10 .25
119 Mike Bullard .07 .20

120 Tim Kerr .05 .15
121 Rick Tocchet .10 .25
122 Mark Howe .10 .25
123 Ilkka Sinisalo .07 .20
124 Tony Tanti .07 .20
125 John Cullen .10 .25
126 Zarley Zalapski .07 .20
127 Wendell Young .10 .25
128 Rob Brown .20 .50
129 Phil Bourque .07 .20
130 Mark Recchi .30 .75
131 Kevin Stevens .20 .50
132 Pittsburgh Penguins logo .05 .15
133 Bob Errey .07 .20
134 Tom Barrasso .07 .20
135 Paul Coffey .10 .25
136 Mario Lemieux .40 1.00
137 Randy Hillier .10 .25
138 Troy Loney .10 .25
139 Joe Sakic .30 .75
140 Lucien DeBlois .07 .20
141 Joe Cirella .05 .15
142 Ron Tugnutt .07 .20
143 Paul Gillis .07 .20
144 Bryan Fogarty .05 .15
145 Guy Lafleur .12 .30
146 Tony Hrkac .05 .15
147 Quebec Nordiques logo .05 .15
148 Michel Petit .07 .20
149 Tony McKegney .05 .15
150 Curtis Leschyshyn .07 .20
151 Claude Loiselle .05 .15
152 Mario Brunetta .05 .15
153 Marc Fortier .07 .20
154 Michal Pivonka .07 .20
155 Scott Stevens .10 .25
156 Kelly Miller .05 .15
157 John Tucker .07 .20
158 Don Beaupre .05 .15
159 Geoff Courtnall .07 .20
160 Alan May .05 .15
161 Dino Ciccarelli .10 .25
162 Washington Capitals logo .05 .15
163 Mike Ridley .05 .15
164 Bob Rouse .05 .15
165 Mike Liut .05 .15
166 Stephen Leach .07 .20
167 Kevin Hatcher .07 .20
168 Dale Hunter .10 .25
169 Prince of Wales .05 .15
170 Clarence Campbell .05 .15
171 Stanley Cup .05 .15
172 Doug Gilmour .12 .30
173 Brad McCrimmon .10 .25
174 Joe Nieuwendyk .07 .20
175 Mike Vernon .07 .20
176 Theo Fleury .12 .30
177 Gary Suter .05 .15
178 Jamie Macoun .07 .20
179 Gary Roberts .10 .25
180 Calgary Flames logo .05 .15
181 Paul Ranheim .10 .25
182 Jiri Hrdina .07 .20
183 Joe Mullen .07 .20
184 Sergei Makarov .20 .50
185 Al MacInnis .12 .30
186 Rick Wamsley .10 .25
187 Trent Yawney .10 .25
188 Greg Millen .07 .20
189 Doug Wilson .07 .20
190 Jocelyn Lemieux .07 .20
191 Dirk Graham .07 .20
192 Keith Brown .07 .20
193 Adam Creighton .05 .15
194 Steve Larmer .07 .20
195 Chicago Blackhawks logo .05 .15
196 Greg Gilbert .05 .15
197 Jacques Cloutier .07 .20
198 Denis Savard .10 .25
199 Dave Manson .10 .25
200 Troy Murray .07 .20
201 Jeremy Roenick .30 .75
202 Lee Norwood .07 .20
203 Glen Hanlon .07 .20
204 Marc Habscheid .07 .20
205 Gerard Gallant .05 .15
206 Rick Zombo .10 .25
207 Steve Chiasson .05 .15
208 Steve Yzerman .30 .75
209 Bernie Federko .07 .20
210 Detroit Red Wings logo .05 .15
211 Joey Kocur .20 .50
212 Tim Cheveldae .07 .20
213 Shawn Burr .07 .20
214 Jimmy Carson .07 .20
215 Mike O'Connell .07 .20
216 John Chabot .10 .25
217 Craig Muni .07 .20
218 Bill Ranford .07 .20
219 Mark Messier .20 .50
220 Craig MacTavish .07 .20
221 Charlie Huddy .07 .20
222 Jari Kurri .12 .30
223 Esa Tikkanen .07 .20
224 Kevin Lowe .10 .25
225 Edmonton Oilers logo .05 .15
226 Steve Smith .07 .20
227 Glenn Anderson .07 .20
228 Petr Klima .05 .15
229 Craig Simpson .07 .20
230 Grant Fuhr .15 .40
231 Randy Gregg .07 .20
232 Bob Kudelski .07 .20
233 Luc Robitaille .10 .25
234 Marty McSorley .07 .20
235 John Tonelli .07 .20
236 Dave Taylor .10 .25
237 Mikko Makela .07 .20
238 Steve Kasper .05 .15
239 Tony Granato .05 .15
240 Los Angeles Kings logo .05 .15
241 Steve Duchesne .05 .15
242 Wayne Gretzky .60 1.50
243 Tomas Sandstrom .10 .25
244 Larry Robinson .10 .25
245 Mike Krushelnyski .10 .25
246 Kelly Hrudey .05 .15
247 Aaron Broten .07 .20
248 Dave Gagner .10 .25
249 Basil McRae .05 .15
250 Curt Giles .07 .20
251 Larry Murphy .07 .20
252 Shawn Chambers .07 .20
253 Mike Modano .30 .75
254 Jon Casey .10 .25
255 North Stars logo .05 .15
256 Gaetan Duchesne .10 .25
257 Brian Bellows .07 .20
258 Frantisek Musil .05 .15
259 Don Barber .07 .20
260 Stewart Gavin .10 .25
261 Neal Broten .05 .15
262 Brett Hull .20 .50
263 Sergio Momesso .07 .20
264 Peter Zezel .10 .25
265 Gino Cavallini .10 .25
266 Rod Brind'Amour .20 .50
267 Mike Lalor .07 .20
268 Vincent Riendeau .10 .25
269 Gordie Roberts .05 .15
270 St. Louis Blues logo .05 .15
271 Paul MacLean .07 .20
272 Curtis Joseph .30 .75
273 Rick Meagher .07 .20
274 Jeff Brown .10 .25
275 Adam Oates .10 .25
276 Paul Cavallini .07 .20
277 Brad Marsh .07 .20
278 Mark Osborne .07 .20
279 Gary Leeman .07 .20
280 Rob Ramage .10 .25
281 Jeff Reese .10 .25
282 Tom Fergus .05 .15
283 Ed Olczyk .10 .25
284 Daniel Marois .07 .20
285 Maple Leafs logo .05 .15
286 Wendel Clark .15 .40
287 Tom Kurvers .10 .25
288 Gilles Thibaudeau .05 .15
289 Lou Franceschetti .10 .25
290 Al Iafrate .05 .15
291 Vincent Damphousse .07 .20
292 Stan Smyl .05 .15
293 Paul Reinhart .10 .25
294 Igor Larionov .20 .50
295 Doug Lidster .10 .25
296 Kirk McLean .05 .15
297 Andrew McBain .07 .20
298 Petri Skriko .10 .25
299 Trevor Linden .10 .25
300 Vancouver Canucks logo .05 .15
301 Steve Bozek .07 .20
302 Brian Bradley .07 .20
303 Greg Adams .05 .15
304 Vladimir Krutov .20 .50
305 Dan Quinn .07 .20
306 Jim Sandlak .10 .25
307 Teppo Numminen .20 .50
308 Doug Smail .07 .20
309 Greg Paslawski .07 .20
310 Dave Ellett .05 .15
311 Bob Essensa .15 .40
312 Pat Elynuik .07 .20
313 Paul Fenton .10 .25
314 Randy Carlyle .07 .20
315 Winnipeg Jets logo .05 .15
316 Thomas Steen .07 .20
317 Dale Hawerchuk .12 .30
318 Fredrik Olausson .07 .20
319 Dave McLlwain .10 .25
320 Laurie Boschman .07 .20
321 Brent Ashton .10 .25
322 Ray Bourque .15 .40
323 Patrick Roy .25 .60
324 Paul Coffey .10 .25
325 Brian Propp .10 .25
326 Mario Lemieux .40 1.00
327 Cam Neely .10 .25
328 Al MacInnis .12 .30
329 Mike Vernon .07 .20
330 Kevin Lowe .10 .25
331 Luc Robitaille .10 .25
332 Wayne Gretzky .60 1.50
333 Brett Hull .20 .50
334 Sergei Makarov .20 .50
335 Alexei Kasatonov .10 .25
336 Igor Larionov .20 .50
337 Vladimir Krutov .20 .50
338 Alexander Mogilny .30 .75
339 Slava Fetisov .20 .50
340 Mike Modano .30 .75
341 Mark Recchi .30 .75
342 Paul Ranheim .10 .25
343 Rod Brind'Amour .20 .50
344 Brad Shaw .07 .20
345 Mike Richter .30 .75
346 Hart Trophy .05 .15
347 Art Ross Trophy .05 .15
348 Calder Memorial Trophy .05 .15
349 Lady Byng Trophy .05 .15
350 Norris Trophy .05 .15
351 Vezina Trophy .05 .15
NNO Sticker Album 1.00 2.50

1991-92 Panini Stickers

1 NHL Logo .05 .15
2 NHLPA Logo .05 .15
3 NHL Logo 75th Anniversary (Left) .05 .15
4 NHL Logo 75th Anniversary (Right) .05 .15
5 Clarence Campbell Conference Logo .05 .15
6 Prince of Wales Conference Logo .05 .15
7 Stanley Cup Championship Logo .05 .15
8 Steve Larmer .07 .20
9 Ed Belfour .25 .60
10 Chris Chelios .10 .25
11 Michel Goulet .07 .20
12 Jeremy Roenick .15 .40
13 Adam Creighton .07 .20
14 Steve Thomas .07 .20
15 Dave Manson .07 .20
16 Dirk Graham .07 .20
17 Troy Murray .07 .20
18 Doug Wilson .07 .20
19 Wayne Presley .07 .20
20 Jocelyn Lemieux .07 .20
21 Keith Brown .07 .20
22 Curtis Joseph .12 .30
23 Jeff Brown .07 .20
24 Gino Cavallini .07 .20
25 Brett Hull .20 .50
26 Scott Stevens .10 .25
27 Dan Quinn .07 .20
28 Garth Butcher .07 .20
29 Bob Bassen .07 .20
30 Rod Brind'Amour .07 .20
31 Adam Oates .07 .20
32 Dave Lowry .07 .20
33 Rich Sutter .07 .20
34 Ron Wilson .07 .20
35 Paul Cavallini .07 .20
36 Trevor Linden .10 .25
37 Troy Gamble .05 .15
38 Geoff Courtnall .07 .20
39 Greg Adams .07 .20
40 Doug Lidster .07 .20
41 Dave Capuano .07 .20
42 Igor Larionov .07 .20
43 Tom Kurvers .07 .20
44 Sergio Momesso .07 .20
45 Kirk McLean .07 .20
46 Cliff Ronning .05 .15
47 Robert Kron .07 .20
48 Steve Bozek .07 .20
49 Petr Nedved .07 .20
50 Al MacInnis .12 .30
51 Theo Fleury .07 .20
52 Gary Roberts .07 .20
53 Joe Nieuwendyk .07 .20
54 Paul Ranheim .10 .25
55 Mike Vernon .07 .20
56 Carey Wilson .07 .20
57 Gary Suter .05 .15
58 Sergei Makarov .07 .20
59 Doug Gilmour .12 .30
60 Joel Otto .07 .20
61 Jamie Macoun .07 .20
62 Stephane Matteau .07 .20
63 Robert Reichel .20 .50
64 Ed Olczyk .07 .20
65 Phil Housley .07 .20
66 Pat Elynuik .07 .20
67 Fredrik Olausson .07 .20
68 Thomas Steen .07 .20
69 Paul MacDermid .07 .20
70 Brent Ashton .07 .20
71 Teppo Numminen .07 .20
72 Danton Cole .05 .15
73 Dave McLlwain .07 .20
74 Scott Arniel .05 .15
75 Bob Essensa .07 .20
76 Randy Carlyle .07 .20
77 Mark Osborne .07 .20
78 Wayne Gretzky .60 1.50
79 Tomas Sandstrom .07 .20
80 Steve Duchesne .05 .15
81 Kelly Hrudey .07 .20
82 Larry Robinson .10 .25
83 Tony Granato .05 .15
84 Marty McSorley .07 .20
85 Todd Elik .07 .20
86 Rob Blake .10 .25
87 Bob Kudelski .05 .15
88 Steve Kasper .05 .15
89 Dave Taylor .07 .20
90 John Tonelli .07 .20
91 Luc Robitaille .10 .25
92 Vincent Damphousse .07 .20
93 Brian Bradley .07 .20
94 Dave Ellett .07 .20
95 Daniel Marois .07 .20
96 Rob Ramage .07 .20
97 Mike Krushelnyski .07 .20
98 Michel Petit .07 .20
99 Peter Ing .07 .20
100 Lucien DeBlois .07 .20
101 Bob Rouse .07 .20
102 Wendel Clark .15 .40
103 Peter Zezel .05 .15
104 David Reid .05 .15
105 Aaron Broten .07 .20
106 Brian Hayward .07 .20
107 Neal Broten .07 .20
108 Brian Bellows .07 .20
109 Mark Tinordi .07 .20
110 Ulf Dahlen .07 .20
111 Doug Smail .07 .20
112 Dave Gagner .07 .20
113 Bobby Smith .07 .20
114 Brian Glynn .07 .20
115 Brian Propp .07 .20
116 Mike Modano .20 .50
117 Gaetan Duchesne .07 .20
118 Jon Casey .05 .15
119 Basil McRae .07 .20
120 Glenn Anderson .07 .20
121 Steve Smith .10 .25
122 Adam Graves .07 .20
123 Esa Tikkanen .07 .20
124 Mark Messier .07 .20
125 Bill Ranford .07 .20
126 Petr Klima .07 .20
127 Anatoli Semenov .07 .20
128 Martin Gelinas .07 .20
129 Charlie Huddy .07 .20
130 Craig Simpson .05 .15
131 Kevin Lowe .07 .20
132 Craig MacTavish .07 .20
133 Craig Muni .07 .20
134 Steve Yzerman .30 .75
135 Shawn Burr .07 .20
136 Tim Cheveldae .07 .20
137 Rick Zombo .07 .20
138 Marc Habscheid .07 .20
139 Jimmy Carson .07 .20
140 Brent Fedyk .07 .20
141 Yves Racine .07 .20
142 Gerard Gallant .05 .15
143 Steve Chiasson .07 .20
144 Johan Garpenlov .07 .20
145 Sergei Fedorov .15 .40
146 Bob Probert .10 .25
147 Rick Green .05 .15
148 Chicago Blackhawks Logo .05 .15
149 Detroit Red Wings Logo .05 .15
150 Minnesota North Stars Logo .05 .15
151 St. Louis Blues Logo .05 .15
152 Toronto Maple Leafs Logo .05 .15
153 Calgary Flames Logo .05 .15
154 Edmonton Oilers Logo .05 .15
155 Los Angeles Kings Logo .05 .15
156 San Jose Sharks Logo .05 .15
157 Vancouver Canucks Logo .05 .15
158 Winnipeg Jets Logo .05 .15
159 Boston Bruins Logo .05 .15
160 Buffalo Sabres Logo .05 .15
161 Hartford Whalers Logo .05 .15
162 Montreal Canadiens Logo .05 .15
163 Quebec Nordiques Logo .05 .15
164 New Jersey Devils Logo .05 .15
165 New York Islanders Logo .05 .15
166 New York Rangers Logo .05 .15
167 Philadelphia Flyers Logo .05 .15
168 Pittsburgh Penguins Logo .05 .15
169 Washington Capitals Logo .05 .15
170 Craig Janney .07 .20
171 Ray Bourque .15 .40
172 Rejean Lemelin .05 .15
173 Dave Christian .05 .15
174 Randy Burridge .07 .20
175 Garry Galley .07 .20
176 Cam Neely .10 .25
177 Bob Sweeney .05 .15
178 Ken Hodge Jr. .05 .15
179 Andy Moog .10 .25
180 Don Sweeney .05 .15
181 Bob Carpenter .07 .20
182 Glen Wesley .07 .20
183 Chris Nilan .05 .15
184 Patrick Roy .25 .60
185 Petr Svoboda .07 .20
186 Russ Courtnall .05 .15
187 Denis Savard .10 .25
188 Mike McPhee .07 .20
189 Eric Desjardins .10 .25
190 Mike Keane .05 .15
191 Stephan Lebeau .07 .20
192 J.J. Daigneault .05 .15
193 Stephane Richer .07 .20
194 Brian Skrudland .07 .20
195 Mathieu Schneider .07 .20
196 Shayne Corson .07 .20
197 Guy Carbonneau .07 .20
198 Kevin Hatcher .07 .20
199 Mike Ridley .07 .20
200 John Druce .07 .20
201 Don Beaupre .07 .20
202 Kelly Miller .07 .20
203 Dale Hunter .07 .20
204 Nick Kypreos .07 .20
205 Calle Johansson .07 .20
206 Michal Pivonka .07 .20
207 Dino Ciccarelli .07 .20
208 Al Iafrate .07 .20
209 Rod Langway .07 .20
210 Mikhail Tatarinov .07 .20
211 Stephen Leach .07 .20
212 Sean Burke .10 .25
213 John MacLean .07 .20
214 Lee Norwood .07 .20
215 Laurie Boschman .05 .15
216 Alexei Kasatonov .05 .15
217 Patrik Sundstrom .07 .20
218 Ken Daneyko .07 .20
219 Kirk Muller .05 .15
220 Peter Stastny .07 .20
221 Chris Terreri .07 .20
222 Brendan Shanahan .10 .25
223 Eric Weinrich .10 .25
224 Claude Lemieux .07 .20
225 Bruce Driver .07 .20
226 Tim Kerr .05 .15
227 Ron Hextall .10 .25
228 Pelle Eklund .07 .20
229 Rick Tocchet .07 .20
230 Gord Murphy .07 .20
231 Mike Ricci .05 .15
232 Derrick Smith .07 .20
233 Ron Sutter .07 .20
234 Murray Craven .07 .20
235 Terry Carkner .07 .20
236 Ken Wregget .07 .20
237 Keith Acton .07 .20
238 Scott Mellanby .07 .20
239 Kjell Samuelsson .07 .20
240 Jeff Hackett .07 .20
241 David Volek .07 .20
242 Craig Ludwig .07 .20
243 Pat LaFontaine .10 .25
244 Randy Wood .07 .20
245 Pat Flatley .07 .20
246 Brent Sutter .07 .20
247 Derek King .05 .15
248 Jeff Norton .07 .20
249 Glenn Healy .10 .25
250 Ray Ferraro .07 .20
251 Gary Nylund .07 .20
252 Joe Reekie .05 .15
253 Dave Chyzowski .05 .15
254 Mike Hough .07 .20
255 Mats Sundin .10 .25
256 Curtis Leschyshyn .07 .20
257 Joe Sakic .30 .75
258 Stephane Fiset .05 .15
259 Bryan Fogarty .07 .20
260 Alexei Gusarov .07 .20
261 Steven Finn .05 .15
262 Everett Sanipass .07 .20
263 Stephane Morin .07 .20
264 Craig Wolanin .07 .20
265 Randy Velischek .07 .20
266 Owen Nolan .10 .25
267 Ron Tugnutt .07 .20
268 Mario Lemieux .40 1.00
269 Kevin Stevens .07 .20
270 Larry Murphy .07 .20
271 Tom Barrasso .07 .20
272 Phil Bourque .07 .20
273 Scott Young .07 .20
274 Paul Stanton .07 .20
275 Jaromir Jagr .30 .75
276 Paul Coffey .10 .25
277 Ulf Samuelsson .07 .20
278 Joe Mullen .07 .20
279 Bob Errey .07 .20
280 Mark Recchi .12 .30
281 Ron Francis .12 .30
282 John Vanbiesbrouck .10 .25
283 Jan Erixon .07 .20
284 Brian Leetch .07 .20
285 Darren Turcotte .07 .20
286 Ray Sheppard .07 .20
287 James Patrick .07 .20
288 Bernie Nicholls .07 .20
289 Brian Mullen .07 .20
290 Mike Richter .10 .25
291 Kelly Kisio .07 .20
292 Mike Gartner .12 .30
293 John Ogrodnick .07 .20
294 David Shaw .07 .20
295 Troy Mallette .07 .20
296 Dale Hawerchuk .12 .30
297 Rick Vaive .05 .15
298 Daren Puppa .07 .20
299 Mike Ramsey .07 .20
300 Benoit Hogue .07 .20
301 Clint Malarchuk .07 .20
302 Mikko Makela .07 .20
303 Pierre Turgeon .07 .20
304 Alexander Mogilny .07 .20
305 Uwe Krupp .07 .20
306 Christian Ruuttu .07 .20
307 Doug Bodger .07 .20
308 Dave Snuggerud .05 .15
309 Dave Andreychuk .10 .25
310 Peter Sidorkiewicz .07 .20
311 Brad Shaw .05 .15
312 Dean Evason .07 .20
313 Pat Verbeek .07 .20
314 John Cullen .07 .20
315 Rob Brown .07 .20
316 Bobby Holik .10 .25
317 Todd Krygier .07 .20
318 Adam Burt .07 .20
319 Mike Tomlak .07 .20
320 Randy Cunneyworth .07 .20
321 Paul Cyr .07 .20
322 Zarley Zalapski .07 .20
323 Kevin Dineen .07 .20
324 Luc Robitaille .07 .20
325 Brett Hull .20 .50
326 All-Star Game Logo .05 .15
327 Wayne Gretzky .60 1.50
328 Mike Vernon .07 .20
329 Chris Chelios .10 .25
330 Al MacInnis .12 .30
331 Rick Tocchet .07 .20
332 Cam Neely .10 .25
333 Patrick Roy .25 .60
334 Joe Sakic .30 .75
335 Ray Bourque .15 .40
336 Paul Coffey .10 .25
337 Ed Belfour .25 .60
338 Mike Ricci .05 .15
339 Rob Blake .10 .25
340 Sergei Fedorov .15 .40
341 Ken Hodge Jr. .07 .20
342 Bobby Holik .10 .25
343 Robert Reichel .20 .50
344 Jaromir Jagr .30 .75
NNO Sticker Album .60 1.50

1992-93 Panini Stickers

1 Stanley Cup .05 .15
2 Blackhawks logo .05 .15
3 Ed Belfour .10 .25
4 Jeremy Roenick .15 .40
5 Steve Larmer .07 .20
6 Michel Goulet .07 .20
7 Dirk Graham .05 .15
8 Jocelyn Lemieux .05 .15
9 Brian Noonan .05 .15
10 Rob Brown .05 .15
11 Chris Chelios .10 .25
12 Steve Smith .05 .15
13 Keith Brown .05 .15
14 St. Louis Blues .05 .15
15 Curtis Joseph .12 .30
16 Brett Hull .20 .50
17 Brendan Shanahan .10 .25
18 Ron Wilson .07 .20
19 Rich Sutter .05 .15
20 Ron Sutter .05 .15
21 Dave Lowry .07 .20
22 Craig Janney .07 .20
23 Paul Cavallini .07 .20
24 Garth Butcher .07 .20
25 Jeff Brown .07 .20
26 Canucks Logo .05 .15
27 Kirk McLean .05 .15
28 Trevor Linden .10 .25
29 Geoff Courtnall .07 .20
30 Cliff Ronning .05 .15
31 Petr Nedved .07 .20
32 Igor Larionov .05 .15
33 Robert Kron .05 .15
34 Jim Sandlak .05 .15
35 Dave Babych .07 .20
36 Jyrki Lumme .05 .15
37 Doug Lidster .07 .20
38 Flames Logo .05 .15
39 Mike Vernon .05 .15
40 Joe Nieuwendyk .07 .20
41 Gary Leeman .05 .15
42 Robert Reichel .05 .15
43 Joel Otto .05 .15
44 Paul Ranheim .05 .15
45 Gary Roberts .05 .15
46 Theo Fleury .15 .40
47 Sergei Makarov .05 .15
48 Gary Suter .05 .15
49 Al MacInnis .12 .30
50 Jets Logo .05 .15
51 Bob Essensa .07 .20
52 Teppo Numminen .05 .15
53 Thomas Steen .05 .15
54 Pat Elynuik .05 .15
55 Ed Olczyk .05 .15
56 Danton Cole .07 .20
57 Troy Murray .05 .15
58 Darrin Shannon .05 .15
59 Russ Romaniuk .05 .15
60 Fredrik Olausson .05 .15
61 Phil Housley .07 .20
62 Kings Logo .05 .15
63 Kelly Hrudey .05 .15
64 Wayne Gretzky .60 1.50
65 Luc Robitaille .10 .25
66 Jari Kurri .10 .25
67 Tomas Sandstrom .05 .15
68 Tony Granato .05 .15
69 Bob Kudelski .07 .20
70 Corey Millen .05 .15
71 Rob Blake .07 .20
72 Paul Coffey .10 .25
73 Marty McSorley .07 .20
74 Maple Leafs Logo .05 .15
75 Grant Fuhr .15 .40
76 Glenn Anderson .07 .20
77 Doug Gilmour .12 .30
78 Mike Krushelnyski .05 .15
79 Wendel Clark .15 .40
80 Rob Pearson .05 .15
81 Peter Zezel .05 .15
82 Todd Gill .05 .15
83 Dave Ellett .05 .15
84 Mike Foligno .07 .20
85 Ken Baumgartner .05 .15
86 North Stars Logo .05 .15
87 Jon Casey .05 .15
88 Brian Bellows .07 .20
89 Neal Broten .07 .20
90 Dave Gagner .07 .20
91 Mike Modano .25 .60
92 Ulf Dahlen .05 .15
93 Brian Propp .05 .15
94 Jim Johnson .07 .20
95 Mike Craig .05 .15
96 Bobby Smith .07 .20
97 Mark Tinordi .05 .15
98 Oilers Logo .05 .15
99 Bill Ranford .07 .20
100 Joe Murphy .05 .15
101 Craig MacTavish .05 .15
102 Craig Simpson .05 .15
103 Esa Tikkanen .05 .15
104 Vincent Damphousse .07 .20
105 Petr Klima .05 .15
106 Martin Gelinas .05 .15
107 Kevin Lowe .07 .20
108 Dave Manson .05 .15
109 Bernie Nicholls .07 .20
110 Red Wings Logo .05 .15
111 Tim Cheveldae .05 .15
112 Steve Yzerman .25 .60
113 Sergei Fedorov .15 .40
114 Jimmy Carson .05 .15
115 Kevin Miller .05 .15
116 Gerard Gallant .05 .15
117 Keith Primeau .07 .20
118 Paul Ysebaert .05 .15
119 Yves Racine .05 .15
120 Steve Chiasson .05 .15
121 Ray Sheppard .05 .15
122 Sharks Logo .05 .15
123 Jeff Hackett .07 .20
124 Kelly Kisio .07 .20
125 Brian Mullen .05 .15
126 David Bruce .05 .15
127 Rob Zettler .05 .15
128 Neil Wilkinson .05 .15
129 Doug Wilson .07 .20
130 Jeff Odgers .05 .15
131 Dean Evason .05 .15
132 Brian Lawton .07 .20
133 Dale Craigwell .05 .15
134 Bruins Logo .05 .15
135 Andy Moog .10 .25
136 Adam Oates .10 .25
137 Dave Poulin .05 .15
138 Vladimir Ruzicka .05 .15
139 Jeff Lazaro .05 .15
140 Bob Carpenter .07 .20
141 Peter Douris .05 .15
142 Glen Murray .07 .20
143 Cam Neely .10 .25
144 Ray Bourque .15 .40
145 Glen Wesley .05 .15
146 Canadiens Logo .05 .15
147 Patrick Roy .25 .60
148 Kirk Muller .05 .15
149 Guy Carbonneau .07 .20
150 Shayne Corson .07 .20
151 Stephan Lebeau .05 .15
152 Denis Savard .10 .25
153 Brent Gilchrist .05 .15
154 Russ Courtnall .05 .15
155 Patrice Brisebois .05 .15
156 Eric Desjardins .07 .20
157 Matt Schneider .05 .15
158 Capitals Logo .05 .15
159 Don Beaupre .07 .20
160 Dino Ciccarelli .07 .20
161 Michal Pivonka .05 .15
162 Mike Ridley .05 .15
163 Randy Burridge .05 .15
164 Peter Bondra .10 .25
165 Dale Hunter .07 .20
166 Kelly Miller .05 .15
167 Kevin Hatcher .05 .15
168 Al Iafrate .07 .20
169 Rod Langway .07 .20
170 Devils Logo .05 .15
171 Chris Terreri .07 .20
172 Claude Lemieux .05 .15
173 Stephane Richer .07 .20
174 Peter Stastny .07 .20
175 Zdeno Ciger .05 .15
176 Alexander Semak .05 .15
177 Valeri Zelepukin .05 .15
178 Bruce Driver .07 .20
179 Scott Niedermayer .10 .25
180 Alexei Kasatonov .05 .15
181 Scott Stevens .10 .25
182 Flyers Logo .05 .15
183 Dominic Roussel .07 .20
184 Mike Ricci .05 .15
185 Mark Recchi .12 .30
186 Kevin Dineen .05 .15
187 Rod Brind'Amour .05 .15
188 Mark Pederson .05 .15
189 Pelle Eklund .07 .20
190 Terry Carkner .07 .20
191 Mark Howe .10 .25
192 Steve Duchesne .05 .15
193 Andrei Lomakin .05 .15
194 Islanders Logo .05 .15
195 Mark Fitzpatrick .07 .20
196 Pierre Turgeon .07 .20
197 Benoit Hogue .05 .15
198 Ray Ferraro .05 .15
199 Derek King .05 .15
200 David Volek .05 .15
201 Patrick Flatley .07 .20
202 Uwe Krupp .05 .15
203 Steve Thomas .07 .20
204 Adam Creighton .07 .20
205 Jeff Norton .07 .20
206 Nordiques Logo .05 .15
207 Stephane Fiset .05 .15
208 Mikhail Tatarinov .05 .15
209 Joe Sakic .20 .50
210 Owen Nolan .10 .25
211 Mike Hough .07 .20
212 Mats Sundin .10 .25
213 Claude Lapointe .05 .15
214 Stephane Morin .05 .15
215 Alexei Gusarov .05 .15
216 Steven Finn .05 .15
217 Curtis Leschyshyn .07 .20
218 Penguins Logo .05 .15
219 Tom Barrasso .07 .20
220 Mario Lemieux .40 1.00
221 Kevin Stevens .05 .15
222 Shawn McEachern .05 .15
223 Joe Mullen .07 .20
224 Ron Francis .12 .30
225 Phil Bourque .05 .15
226 Rick Tocchet .05 .15
227 Bryan Trottier .10 .25
228 Larry Murphy .07 .20
229 Ulf Samuelsson .05 .15
230 Rangers Logo .05 .15
231 Mike Richter .10 .25
232 John Vanbiesbrouck .10 .25
233 Mark Messier .20 .50
234 Sergei Nemchinov .05 .15
235 Darren Turcotte .05 .15
236 Doug Weight .20 .50
237 Mike Gartner .12 .30
238 Adam Graves .05 .15
239 Brian Leetch .07 .20
240 James Patrick .05 .15
241 Jan Erixon .05 .15
242 Sabres Logo .05 .15
243 Tom Draper .05 .15
244 Grant Ledyard .05 .15
245 Doug Bodger .05 .15
246 Pat LaFontaine .10 .25
247 Dale Hawerchuk .12 .30
248 Alexander Mogilny .07 .20
249 Dave Andreychuk .10 .25
250 Christian Ruuttu .05 .15
251 Randy Wood .05 .15
252 Brad May .05 .15
253 Mike Ramsey .05 .15
254 Whalers Logo .05 .15
255 Kay Whitmore .07 .20
256 Pat Verbeek .05 .15
257 John Cullen .05 .15
258 Mikael Andersson .05 .15
259 Yvon Corriveau .05 .15
260 Randy Cunneyworth .07 .20
261 Robert Holik .07 .20
262 Murray Craven .05 .15
263 Zarley Zalapski .05 .15
264 Adam Burt .05 .15
265 Brad Shaw .05 .15
266 Lightning Logo .05 .15
267 Lightning Jersey .05 .15
268 Senators Logo .05 .15
269 Senators Jersey .05 .15
270 Tony Amonte .07 .20
271 Pavel Bure .10 .25
272 Gilbert Dionne .05 .15
273 Pat Falloon .05 .15
274 Nicklas Lidstrom .07 .20
275 Kevin Todd .05 .15
276 Prince of Wales Conference Logo .05 .15
277 Patrick Roy AS .25 .60
278 Paul Coffey AS .10 .25
279 Ray Bourque AS .15 .40
280 Mario Lemieux AS .40 1.00
281 Kevin Stevens AS .07 .20
282 Jaromir Jagr AS .20 .50
283 Clarence Campbell Conference Logo .05 .15
284 Ed Belfour AS .10 .25
285 Al MacInnis AS .12 .30
286 Chris Chelios AS .10 .25
287 Wayne Gretzky AS .60 1.50

288 Luc Robitaille AS .10 .25
289 Brett Hull AS .20 .50
290 Pavel Bure .10 .25
291 Sergei Fedorov .15 .40
292 Dominik Hasek .15 .40
293 Robert Holik .07 .20
294 Jaromir Jagr .20 .50
295 Valeri Kamensky .05 .15
296 Alexander Semak .05 .15
297 Igor Kravchuk .05 .15
298 Nicklas Lidstrom .07 .20
299 Alexander Mogilny .07 .20
300 Petr Nedved .07 .20
301 Robert Reichel .05 .15
302 Mats Sundin .10 .25
303 Calder Trophy .05 .15
304 Hart Trophy .05 .15
305 Lady Byng Trophy .05 .15
306 Norris Trophy .05 .15
307 Selke Trophy .05 .15
308 Vezina Trophy .05 .15
A Igor Kravchuk .05 .15
B Nelson Emerson .05 .15
C Pavel Bure .10 .25
D Tomas Forslund .05 .15
E Luciano Borsato .05 .15
F Darryl Sydor .05 .15
G Felix Potvin .20 .50
H Derian Hatcher .05 .15
I Joseph Beranek .05 .15
J Nicklas Lidstrom .07 .20
K Pat Falloon .05 .15
L Joe Juneau .05 .15
M Gilbert Dionne .05 .15
N Dimitri Khristich .05 .15
O Kevin Todd .05 .15
P Eric Lindros .15 .40
Q Scott Lachance .05 .15
R Valeri Kamensky .05 .15
S Jaromir Jagr .20 .50
T Tony Amonte .07 .20
U Donald Audette .07 .20
V Geoff Sanderson .07 .20
NNO Sticker Album .60 1.50

1992-93 Panini Stickers French

COMPLETE SET (330)
1 Stanley Cup .07 .20
2 Blackhawks logo .02 .10
3 Ed Belfour .20 .50
4 Jeremy Roenick .20 .50
5 Steve Larmer .02 .10
6 Michel Goulet .07 .20
7 Dirk Graham .02 .10
8 Jocelyn Lemieux .02 .10
9 Brian Noonan .02 .10
10 Rob Brown .02 .10
11 Chris Chelios .20 .50
12 Steve Smith .02 .10
13 Keith Brown .02 .10
14 St. Louis Blues .02 .10
15 Curtis Joseph .20 .50
16 Brett Hull .30 .75
17 Brendan Shanahan .50 1.25
18 Ron Wilson .02 .10
19 Rich Sutter .02 .10
20 Ron Sutter .07 .20
21 Dave Lowry .02 .10
22 Craig Janney .02 .10
23 Paul Cavallini .02 .10
24 Garth Butcher .02 .10
25 Jeff Brown .02 .10
26 Canucks Logo .02 .10
27 Kirk McLean .07 .20
28 Trevor Linden .07 .20
29 Geoff Courtnall .02 .10
30 Cliff Ronning .02 .10
31 Petr Nedved .07 .20
32 Igor Larionov .07 .20
33 Robert Kron .02 .10
34 Jim Sandlak .02 .10
35 Dave Babych .02 .10
36 Jyrki Lumme .02 .10
37 Doug Lidster .02 .10
38 Flames Logo .02 .10
39 Mike Vernon .07 .20
40 Joe Nieuwendyk .07 .20
41 Gary Leeman .02 .10
42 Robert Reichel .02 .10
43 Joel Otto .02 .10
44 Paul Ranheim .02 .10
45 Gary Roberts .07 .20
46 Theo Fleury .20 .50
47 Sergei Makarov .02 .10
48 Gary Suter .07 .20
49 Al MacInnis .07 .20
50 Jets Logo .02 .10
51 Bob Essensa .07 .20
52 Teppo Numminen .02 .10
53 Thomas Steen .02 .10
54 Pat Elynuik .02 .10
55 Ed Olczyk .02 .10
56 Danton Cole .02 .10
57 Troy Murray .02 .10
58 Darrin Shannon .02 .10
59 Russ Romaniuk .02 .10
60 Fredrik Olausson .02 .10
61 Phil Housley .02 .10
62 Kings Logo .02 .10
63 Kelly Hrudey .07 .20
64 Wayne Gretzky .75 2.00
65 Luc Robitaille .07 .20
66 Jari Kurri .07 .20
67 Tomas Sandstrom .02 .10
68 Tony Granato .02 .10
69 Bob Kudelski .02 .10
70 Corey Millen .02 .10
71 Rob Blake .07 .20
72 Paul Coffey .20 .50
73 Marty McSorley .07 .20
74 Maple Leafs Logo .02 .10
75 Grant Fuhr .07 .20
76 Glenn Anderson .07 .20
77 Doug Gilmour .20 .50
78 Mike Krushelnyski .02 .10
79 Wendel Clark .07 .20
80 Rob Pearson .02 .10
81 Peter Zezel .02 .10
82 Todd Gill .02 .10
83 Dave Ellett .02 .10
84 Mike Foligno .02 .10
85 Ken Baumgartner .02 .10
86 North Stars Logo .02 .10
87 Jon Casey .07 .20
88 Brian Bellows .02 .10
89 Neal Broten .07 .20
90 Dave Gagner .02 .10
91 Mike Modano .30 .75
92 Ulf Dahlen .02 .10
93 Brian Propp .02 .10
94 Jim Johnson .02 .10
95 Mike Craig .02 .10
96 Bobby Smith .02 .10
97 Mark Tinordi .02 .10
98 Oilers Logo .02 .10
99 Bill Ranford .07 .20
100 Joe Murphy .07 .20
101 Craig MacTavish .02 .10
102 Craig Simpson .02 .10
103 Esa Tikkanen .07 .20
104 Vincent Damphousse .07 .20
105 Petr Klima .02 .10
106 Martin Gelinas .02 .10
107 Kevin Lowe .07 .20
108 Dave Manson .02 .10
109 Bernie Nicholls .07 .20
110 Red Wings Logo .02 .10
111 Tim Cheveldae .07 .20
112 Steve Yzerman .75 2.00
113 Sergei Fedorov .50 1.25
114 Jimmy Carson .02 .10
115 Kevin Miller .02 .10
116 Gerard Gallant .02 .10
117 Keith Primeau .07 .20
118 Paul Ysebaert .02 .10
119 Yves Racine .02 .10
120 Steve Chiasson .02 .10
121 Ray Sheppard .02 .10
122 Sharks Logo .02 .10
123 Jeff Hackett .07 .20
124 Kelly Kisio .02 .10
125 Brian Mullen .02 .10
126 David Bruce .02 .10
127 Rob Zettler .02 .10
128 Neil Wilkinson .02 .10
129 Doug Wilson .02 .10
130 Jeff Odgers .02 .10
131 Dean Evason .02 .10
132 Brian Lawton .02 .10
133 Dale Craigwell .02 .10
134 Bruins Logo .02 .10
135 Andy Moog .07 .20
136 Adam Oates .10 .30
137 Dave Poulin .02 .10
138 Vladimir Ruzicka .02 .10
139 Jeff Lazaro .02 .10
140 Bob Carpenter .02 .10
141 Peter Douris .02 .10
142 Glen Murray .02 .10
143 Cam Neely .20 .50
144 Ray Bourque .30 .75
145 Glen Wesley .02 .10
146 Canadiens Logo .02 .10
147 Patrick Roy .60 1.50
148 Kirk Muller .07 .20
149 Guy Carbonneau .07 .20
150 Shayne Corson .02 .10
151 Stephan Lebeau .02 .10
152 Denis Savard .07 .20
153 Brent Gilchrist .02 .10
154 Russ Courtnall .02 .10
155 Patrice Brisebois .02 .10
156 Eric Desjardins .07 .20
157 Matt Schneider .02 .10
158 Capitals Logo .02 .10
159 Don Beaupre .07 .20
160 Dino Ciccarelli .07 .20
161 Michal Pivonka .02 .10
162 Mike Ridley .02 .10
163 Randy Burridge .02 .10
164 Peter Bondra .20 .50
165 Dale Hunter .07 .20
166 Kelly Miller .02 .10
167 Kevin Hatcher .07 .20
168 Al Iafrate .07 .20
169 Rod Langway .02 .10
170 Devils Logo .02 .10
171 Chris Terreri .07 .20
172 Claude Lemieux .07 .20
173 Stephane Richer .07 .20
174 Peter Stastny .02 .10
175 Zdeno Ciger .02 .10
176 Alexander Semak .02 .10
177 Valeri Zelepukin .02 .10
178 Bruce Driver .02 .10
179 Scott Niedermayer .07 .20
180 Alexei Kasatonov .02 .10
181 Scott Stevens .07 .20
182 Flyers Logo .02 .10
183 Dominic Roussel .07 .20
184 Mike Ricci .02 .10
185 Mark Recchi .07 .20
186 Kevin Dineen .02 .10
187 Rod Brind'Amour .10 .30
188 Mark Pederson .02 .10
189 Pelle Eklund .02 .10
190 Terry Carkner .02 .10
191 Mark Howe .07 .20
192 Steve Duchesne .02 .10
193 Andrei Lomakin .02 .10
194 Islanders Logo .02 .10
195 Mark Fitzpatrick .07 .20
196 Pierre Turgeon .07 .20
197 Benoit Hogue .02 .10
198 Ray Ferraro .02 .10
199 Derek King .02 .10
200 David Volek .02 .10
201 Patrick Flatley .02 .10
202 Uwe Krupp .02 .10
203 Steve Thomas .02 .10
204 Adam Creighton .02 .10
205 Jeff Norton .02 .10
206 Nordiques Logo .02 .10
207 Stephane Fiset .07 .20
208 Mikhail Tatarinov .02 .10
209 Joe Sakic .50 1.25
210 Owen Nolan .07 .20
211 Mike Hough .02 .10
212 Mats Sundin .20 .50
213 Claude Lapointe .02 .10
214 Stephane Morin .02 .10
215 Alexei Gusarov .02 .10
216 Steven Finn .02 .10
217 Curtis Leschyshyn .02 .10
218 Penguins Logo .02 .10
219 Tom Barrasso .07 .20
220 Mario Lemieux .60 1.50
221 Kevin Stevens .02 .10
222 Shawn McEachern .02 .10
223 Joe Mullen .07 .20
224 Ron Francis .07 .20
225 Phil Bourque .02 .10
226 Rick Tocchet .07 .20
227 Bryan Trottier .07 .20
228 Larry Murphy .07 .20
229 Ulf Samuelsson .02 .10
230 Rangers Logo .02 .10
231 Mike Richter .20 .50
232 John Vanbiesbrouck .20 .50
233 Mark Messier .30 .75
234 Sergei Nemchinov .02 .10
235 Darren Turcotte .07 .20
236 Doug Weight .07 .20
237 Mike Gartner .07 .20
238 Adam Graves .07 .20
239 Brian Leetch .20 .50
240 James Patrick .02 .10
241 Jan Erixon .02 .10
242 Sabres Logo .02 .10
243 Tom Draper .02 .10
244 Grant Ledyard .02 .10
245 Doug Bodger .02 .10
246 Pat LaFontaine .20 .50
247 Dale Hawerchuk .07 .20
248 Alexander Mogilny .07 .20
249 Dave Andreychuk .07 .20
250 Christian Ruuttu .02 .10
251 Randy Wood .02 .10
252 Brad May .02 .10
253 Mike Ramsey .02 .10
254 Whalers Logo .02 .10
255 Kay Whitmore .07 .20
256 Pat Verbeek .07 .20
257 John Cullen .02 .10
258 Mikael Andersson .02 .10
259 Yvon Corriveau .02 .10
260 Randy Cunneyworth .02 .10
261 Robert Holik .07 .20
262 Murray Craven .02 .10
263 Zarley Zalapski .02 .10
264 Adam Burt .02 .10
265 Brad Shaw .02 .10
266 Lightning Logo .02 .10
267 Lightning Jersey .02 .10
268 Senators Logo .02 .10
269 Senators Jersey .02 .10
270 Tony Amonte .07 .20
271 Pavel Bure .60 1.50
272 Gilbert Dionne .07 .20
273 Pat Falloon .07 .20
274 Nicklas Lidstrom .20 .50
275 Kevin Todd .02 .10
276 Prince of Wales Conference Logo .02 .10
277 Patrick Roy AS .60 1.50
278 Paul Coffey AS .20 .50
279 Ray Bourque AS .30 .75
280 Mario Lemieux AS .60 1.50
281 Kevin Stevens AS .02 .10
282 Jaromir Jagr AS .75 2.00
283 Clarence Campbell Conference Logo .02 .10
284 Ed Belfour AS .20 .50
285 Al MacInnis AS .07 .20
286 Chris Chelios AS .20 .50
287 Wayne Gretzky AS .75 2.00
288 Luc Robitaille AS .07 .20
289 Brett Hull AS .20 .50
290 Pavel Bure .60 1.50
291 Sergei Fedorov .50 1.25
292 Dominik Hasek .50 1.25
293 Robert Holik .02 .10
294 Jaromir Jagr .75 2.00
295 Valeri Kamensky .02 .10
296 Alexander Semak .02 .10
297 Igor Kravchuk .02 .10
298 Nicklas Lidstrom .20 .50
299 Alexander Mogilny .07 .20
300 Petr Nedved .07 .20
301 Robert Reichel .02 .10
302 Mats Sundin .20 .50
303 Calder Trophy .02 .10
304 Hart Trophy .02 .10
305 Lady Byng Trophy .02 .10
306 Norris Trophy .02 .10
307 Selke Trophy .02 .10
308 Vezina Trophy .02 .10
A Igor Kravchuk .02 .10
B Nelson Emerson .20 .50
C Pavel Bure 1.00 2.50
D Tomas Forslund .20 .50
E Luciano Borsato .20 .50
F Darryl Sydor .30 .75
G Felix Potvin .60 1.50
H Derian Hatcher .20 .50
I Joseph Beranek .20 .50
J Nicklas Lidstrom .50 1.25
K Pat Falloon .30 .75
L Joe Juneau .30 .75
M Gilbert Dionne .40 1.00
N Dimitri Khristich .20 .50
O Kevin Todd .20 .50
P Eric Lindros .75 2.00
Q Scott Lachance .20 .50
R Valeri Kamensky .20 .50
S Jaromir Jagr .75 2.00
T Tony Amonte .30 .75
U Donald Audette .20 .50
V Geoff Sanderson .30 .75
NNO Sticker Album .60 1.50

1993-94 Panini Stickers

1 Bruins Logo .05 .15
2 Adam Oates .10 .25
3 Cam Neely .10 .25
4 Dave Poulin .05 .15
5 Steve Leach .05 .15
6 Glen Wesley .05 .15
7 Dmitri Kvartalnov .05 .15
8 Ted Donato .05 .15
9 Andy Moog .10 .25
10 Ray Bourque .15 .40
11 Don Sweeney .05 .15
12 Canadiens Logo .05 .15
13 Vincent Damphousse .07 .20
14 Kirk Muller .05 .15
15 Brian Bellows .07 .20
16 Stephan Lebeau .05 .15
17 Denis Savard .10 .25
18 Gilbert Dionne .05 .15
19 Guy Carbonneau .05 .15
20 Benoit Brunet .05 .15
21 Eric Desjardins .07 .20
22 Mathieu Schneider .05 .15
23 Capitals Logo .05 .15
24 Peter Bondra .10 .25
25 Mike Ridley .05 .15
26 Dale Hunter .05 .15
27 Michal Pivonka .05 .15
28 Dimitri Khristich .05 .15
29 Pat Elynuik .05 .15
30 Kelly Miller .05 .15
31 Calle Johansson .05 .15
32 Al Iafrate .05 .15
33 Don Beaupre .07 .20
34 Devils Logo .05 .15
35 Claude Lemieux .05 .15
36 Alexander Semak .05 .15
37 Stephane Richer .07 .20
38 Valeri Zelepukin .05 .15
39 Bernie Nicholls .07 .20
40 John MacLean .07 .20
41 Peter Stastny .07 .20
42 Scott Niedermayer .10 .25
43 Scott Stevens .10 .25
44 Bruce Driver .07 .20
45 Flyers Logo .05 .15
46 Mark Recchi .12 .30
47 Rod Brind'Amour .07 .20
48 Brent Fedyk .05 .15
49 Kevin Dineen .05 .15
50 Keith Acton .05 .15
51 Pelle Eklund .05 .15
52 Andrei Lomakin .05 .15
53 Garry Galley .05 .15
54 Terry Carkner .05 .15
55 Tommy Soderstrom .07 .20
56 Islanders Logo .05 .15
57 Steve Thomas .05 .15
58 Derek King .05 .15
59 Benoit Hogue .05 .15
60 Patrick Flatley .05 .15
61 Brian Mullen .05 .15
62 Marty McInnis .05 .15
63 Scott Lachance .05 .15
64 Jeff Norton .05 .15
65 Glenn Healy .07 .20
66 Mark Fitzpatrick .07 .20
67 Nordiques Logo .05 .15
68 Mats Sundin .10 .25
69 Mike Ricci .05 .15
70 Owen Nolan .10 .25
71 Andrei Kovalenko .05 .15
72 Valeri Kamensky .07 .20
73 Scott Young .05 .15
74 Martin Rucinsky .07 .20
75 Steven Finn .05 .15
76 Steve Duchesne .05 .15
77 Ron Hextall .10 .25
78 Penguins Logo .05 .15
79 Kevin Stevens .05 .15
80 Rick Tocchet .07 .20
81 Ron Francis .12 .30
82 Jaromir Jagr .30 .75
83 Joe Mullen .07 .20
84 Shawn McEachern .05 .15
85 Dave Tippett .05 .15
86 Larry Murphy .07 .20
87 Ulf Samuelsson .05 .15
88 Tom Barrasso .07 .20
89 Rangers Logo .05 .15
90 Tony Amonte .07 .20
91 Mike Gartner .12 .30
92 Adam Graves .05 .15
93 Sergei Nemchinov .05 .15
94 Darren Turcotte .05 .15
95 Esa Tikkanen .05 .15
96 Brian Leetch .07 .20
97 Kevin Lowe .05 .15
98 John Vanbiesbrouck .10 .25
99 Mike Richter .10 .25
100 Sabres Logo .05 .15
101 Pat LaFontaine .10 .25
102 Dale Hawerchuk .12 .30
103 Donald Audette .05 .15
104 Bob Sweeney .05 .15
105 Randy Wood .05 .15
106 Yuri Khmylev .05 .15
107 Wayne Presley .05 .15
108 Grant Fuhr .15 .40
109 Doug Bodger .05 .15
110 Richard Smehlik .05 .15
111 Senators Logo .05 .15
112 Norm Maciver .05 .15
113 Jamie Baker .05 .15
114 Bob Kudelski .05 .15
115 Jody Hull .05 .15
116 Mike Peluso .05 .15
117 Mark Lamb .05 .15
118 Mark Freer .05 .15
119 Neil Brady .05 .15
120 Brad Shaw .05 .15
121 Peter Sidorkiewicz .05 .15
122 Whalers Logo .05 .15
123 Andrew Cassels .05 .15
124 Pat Verbeek .05 .15
125 Terry Yake .05 .15
126 Patrick Poulin .05 .15
127 Mark Janssens .05 .15
128 Michael Nylander .05 .15
129 Zarley Zalapski .05 .15
130 Eric Weinrich .05 .15
131 Sean Burke .05 .15
132 Frank Pietrangelo .07 .20
133 Phil Housley BB .05 .15
134 Paul Coffey BB .10 .25
135 Larry Murphy BB .07 .20
136 Mario Lemieux BB .40 1.00
137 Pat LaFontaine BB .10 .25
138 Adam Oates BB .10 .25
139 Felix Potvin BB .20 .50
140 Ed Belfour BB .10 .25
141 Tom Barrasso BB .07 .20
142 Teemu Selanne BB .20 .50
143 Joe Juneau BB .05 .15
144 Eric Lindros BB .15 .40
145 Blackhawks Logo .05 .15
146 Steve Larmer .07 .20
147 Dirk Graham .05 .15
148 Michel Goulet .05 .15
149 Brian Noonan .05 .15
150 Stephane Matteau .05 .15
151 Brent Sutter .05 .15
152 Jocelyn Lemieux .05 .15
153 Chris Chelios .10 .25
154 Steve Smith .05 .15
155 Ed Belfour .10 .25
156 Blues Logo .05 .15
157 Craig Janney .07 .20
158 Brendan Shanahan .10 .25
159 Nelson Emerson .05 .15
160 Rich Sutter .05 .15
161 Ron Sutter .05 .15
162 Ron Wilson .05 .15
163 Bob Bassen .05 .15
164 Garth Butcher .05 .15
165 Jeff Brown .05 .15
166 Curtis Joseph .12 .30
167 Canucks Logo .05 .15
168 Cliff Ronning .05 .15
169 Murray Craven .05 .15
170 Geoff Courtnall .05 .15
171 Petr Nedved .05 .15
172 Trevor Linden .10 .25
173 Greg Adams .05 .15
174 Anatoli Semenov .05 .15
175 Jyrki Lumme .05 .15
176 Doug Lidster .05 .15
177 Kirk McLean .07 .20
178 Flames Logo .05 .15
179 Theo Fleury .10 .25
180 Robert Reichel .05 .15
181 Gary Roberts .07 .20
182 Joe Nieuwendyk .07 .20
183 Sergei Makarov .05 .15
184 Paul Ranheim .05 .15
185 Joel Otto .05 .15
186 Gary Suter .05 .15
187 Jeff Reese .05 .15
188 Mike Vernon .07 .20
189 Jets Logo .05 .15
190 Alexei Zhamnov .07 .20
191 Thomas Steen .05 .15
192 Darrin Shannon .05 .15
193 Keith Tkachuk .10 .25
194 Evgeny Davydov .05 .15
195 Luciano Borsato .05 .15
196 Phil Housley .07 .20
197 Teppo Numminen .05 .15
198 Fredrik Olausson .05 .15
199 Bob Essensa .07 .20
200 Kings Logo .05 .15
201 Luc Robitaille .10 .25
202 Jari Kurri .10 .25
203 Tony Granato .05 .15
204 Jimmy Carson .05 .15
205 Tomas Sandstrom .05 .15
206 Dave Taylor .05 .15
207 Corey Millen .05 .15
208 Marty McSorley .05 .15
209 Rob Blake .07 .20
210 Kelly Hrudey .07 .20
211 Lightning Logo .05 .15
212 John Tucker .05 .15
213 Chris Kontos .05 .15
214 Rob Zamuner .05 .15
215 Adam Creighton .05 .15
216 Mikael Andersson .05 .15
217 Bob Beers .05 .15
218 Rob DiMaio .05 .15
219 Shawn Chambers .05 .15
220 J.C. Bergeron .05 .15
221 Wendell Young .05 .15
222 Maple Leafs Logo .05 .15
223 Dave Andreychuk .10 .25
224 Nikolai Borschevsky .05 .15
225 Glenn Anderson .07 .20
226 John Cullen .05 .15
227 Wendel Clark .15 .40
228 Mike Foligno .05 .15
229 Mike Krushelnyski .05 .15
230 James Macoun .05 .15
231 Dave Ellett .05 .15
232 Felix Potvin .20 .50
233 Oilers Logo .05 .15
234 Petr Klima .05 .15
235 Doug Weight .07 .20
236 Shayne Corson .07 .20
237 Craig Simpson .05 .15
238 Todd Elik .05 .15
239 Zdeno Ciger .05 .15
240 Craig MacTavish .05 .15
241 Kelly Buchberger .05 .15
242 Dave Manson .05 .15
243 Scott Mellanby .07 .20
244 Red Wings Logo .05 .15
245 Dino Ciccarelli .07 .20
246 Sergei Fedorov .15 .40
247 Ray Sheppard .07 .20
248 Paul Ysebaert .10 .25
249 Bob Probert .10 .25
250 Keith Primeau .05 .15
251 Steve Chiasson .05 .15
252 Paul Coffey .10 .25
253 Nicklas Lidstrom .10 .25
254 Tim Cheveldae .07 .20
255 Sharks Logo .05 .15
256 Kelly Kisio .05 .15
257 Johan Garpenlov .05 .15
258 Robert Gaudreau .10 .25
259 Dean Evason .05 .15
260 Jeff Odgers .05 .15
261 Ed Courtenay .05 .15
262 Mike Sullivan .05 .15
263 Doug Zmolek .05 .15
264 Doug Wilson .07 .20
265 Brian Hayward .05 .15
266 Stars Logo .05 .15
267 Brian Propp .05 .15
268 Russ Courtnall .05 .15
269 Dave Gagner .07 .20
270 Ulf Dahlen .05 .15
271 Mike Craig .05 .15
272 Neal Broten .07 .20
273 Gaetan Duchesne .05 .15
274 Derian Hatcher .05 .15
275 Mark Tinordi .05 .15
276 Jon Casey .07 .20
A Joe Juneau .05 .15
B Patrick Roy .25 .60
C Kevin Hatcher .05 .15
D Chris Terreri .07 .20
E Eric Lindros .15 .40
F Pierre Turgeon .07 .20
G Joe Sakic .20 .50
H Mario Lemieux .40 1.00
I Mark Messier .20 .50
J Alexander Mogilny .07 .20
K Sylvain Turgeon .05 .15
L Geoff Sanderson .07 .20
M Jeremy Roenick .15 .40
N Brett Hull .20 .50
O Pavel Bure .10 .25
P Al MacInnis .12 .30
Q Teemu Selanne .20 .50
R Wayne Gretzky .60 1.50
S Brian Bradley .05 .15
T Doug Gilmour .12 .30
U Bill Ranford .07 .20
V Steve Yzerman .25 .60
W Pat Falloon .05 .15
X Mike Modano .15 .40

1994-95 Panini Stickers

1 Adam Oates .10 .25
2 Ted Donato .05 .15
3 Cam Neely .10 .25
4 Brent Hughes .05 .15
5 Bruins Logo .05 .15
6 Glen Wesley .05 .15
7 Al Iafrate .05 .15
8 Ray Bourque .15 .40
9 Jon Casey .07 .20
10 Guy Carbonneau .05 .15
11 Pierre Sevigny .05 .15
12 Kirk Muller .05 .15
13 Canadiens Logo .05 .15
14 Vincent Damphousse .07 .20
15 Gilbert Dionne .05 .15
16 Mathieu Schneider .05 .15
17 Eric Desjardins .07 .20
18 Patrick Roy .25 .60
19 Joe Juneau .05 .15
20 Dimitri Khristich .05 .15
21 Dale Hunter .05 .15
22 Capitals Logo .05 .15
23 Mike Ridley .05 .15
24 Peter Bondra .10 .25
25 Sylvain Cote .05 .15
26 Kevin Hatcher .05 .15
27 Don Beaupre .07 .20
28 Bernie Nicholls .07 .20
29 Alexander Semak .05 .15
30 John MacLean .07 .20
31 Devils Logo .05 .15
32 Stephane Richer .07 .20
33 Valeri Zelepukin .05 .15
34 Scott Stevens .10 .25
35 Martin Brodeur .25 .60
36 Chris Terreri .07 .20
37 Rod Brind'Amour .07 .20
38 Eric Lindros .15 .40
39 Mark Recchi .12 .30
40 Flyers Logo .05 .15
41 Kevin Dineen .05 .15
42 Brent Fedyk .05 .15
43 Garry Galley .05 .15
44 Ryan McGill .05 .15
45 Dominic Roussel .07 .20
46 Ray Ferraro .05 .15
47 Benoit Hogue .05 .15
48 Pierre Turgeon .07 .20
49 Islanders Logo .05 .15
50 Patrick Flatley .05 .15
51 Steve Thomas .05 .15
52 Darius Kasparaitis .05 .15
53 Vladimir Malakhov .05 .15
54 Ron Hextall .10 .25
55 Mats Sundin .10 .25
56 Joe Sakic .20 .50
57 Nordiques Logo .05 .15
58 Claude Lapointe .05 .15
59 Scott Young .05 .15
60 Valeri Kamensky .07 .20
61 Steven Finn .05 .15
62 Jocelyn Thibault .07 .20
63 Stephane Fiset .07 .20
64 Brian Skrudland .05 .15
65 Bob Kudelski .05 .15
66 Jody Hull .05 .15
67 Scott Mellanby .07 .20
68 Panthers Logo .05 .15
69 Dave Lowry .05 .15
70 Mike Hough .05 .15
71 Gord Murphy .05 .15
72 John Vanbiesbrouck .10 .25
73 Ron Francis .12 .30
74 Mario Lemieux .40 1.00
75 Penguins Logo .05 .15
76 Jaromir Jagr .30 .75
77 Rick Tocchet .07 .20
78 Kevin Stevens .05 .15
79 Ulf Samuelsson .05 .15
80 Larry Murphy .07 .20
81 Tom Barrasso .07 .20
82 Mark Messier .20 .50
83 Alexei Kovalev .07 .20
84 Rangers Logo .05 .15
85 Sergei Nemchinov .05 .15
86 Steve Larmer .07 .20
87 Adam Graves .05 .15
88 Brian Leetch .07 .20
89 Sergei Zubov .07 .20
90 Mike Richter .10 .25
91 Dale Hawerchuk .12 .30
92 Pat Lafontaine .10 .25
93 Donald Audette .05 .15
94 Alexander Mogilny .07 .20
95 Sabres Logo .05 .15
96 Yuri Khmylev .05 .15
97 Brad May .05 .15
98 Richard Smehlik .05 .15
99 Dominik Hasek .15 .40
100 Dave McLlwain .05 .15
101 Alexandre Daigle .05 .15
102 David Archibald .05 .15
103 Senators Logo .05 .15
104 Troy Murray .05 .15
105 Sylvain Turgeon .05 .15
106 Gord Dineen .05 .15
107 Darren Rumble .05 .15
108 Craig Billington .07 .20
109 Geoff Sanderson .07 .20
110 Andrew Cassels .05 .15
111 Whalers Logo .05 .15
112 Pat Verbeek .07 .20
113 Jim Sandlak .05 .15
114 Jocelyn Lemieux .05 .15
115 Brian Propp .05 .15
116 Frantisek Kucera .05 .15
117 Sean Burke .07 .20
118 Anatoli Semenov .05 .15
119 Stephan Lebeau .05 .15
120 Mighty Ducks Logo .05 .15
121 Terry Yake .05 .15
122 Joe Sacco .05 .15
123 Todd Ewen .05 .15
124 Troy Loney .05 .15
125 Sean Hill .05 .15
126 Guy Hebert .07 .20
127 Jeremy Roenick .15 .40
128 Tony Amonte .07 .20
129 Joe Murphy .05 .15
130 BlackHawks Logo .05 .15
131 Michel Goulet .05 .15
132 Paul Ysebaert .05 .15
133 Gary Suter .05 .15
134 Chris Chelios .10 .25
135 Ed Belfour .10 .25
136 Craig Janney .07 .20
137 Petr Nedved .07 .20
138 Blues Logo .05 .15
139 Kevin Miller .05 .15
140 Brett Hull .20 .50
141 Brendan Shanahan .10 .25
142 Phil Housley .07 .20
143 Steve Duchesne .05 .15
144 Curtis Joseph .12 .30
145 Cliff Ronning .05 .15
146 Pavel Bure .10 .25
147 Trevor Linden .10 .25
148 Canucks Logo .05 .15
149 Geoff Courtnall .05 .15
150 Gino Odjick .05 .15
151 Jyrki Lumme .05 .15
152 Jeff Brown .05 .15
153 Kirk McLean .07 .20
154 Robert Reichel .05 .15
155 Joel Otto .05 .15
156 Joe Nieuwendyk .07 .20
157 Flames Logo .05 .15
158 German Titov .05 .15
159 Theoren Fleury .10 .25
160 Gary Roberts .07 .20
161 Al MacInnis .12 .30
162 Mike Vernon .07 .20
163 Alexei Zhamnov .07 .20
164 Nelson Emerson .05 .15
165 Jets Logo .05 .15
166 Teemu Selanne .20 .50
167 Tie Domi .07 .20
168 Keith Tkachuk .10 .25
169 Teppo Numminen .05 .15
170 Stephane Quintal .05 .15
171 Tim Cheveldae .07 .20
172 Wayne Gretzky .60 1.50
173 Jari Kurri .07 .20
174 Luc Robitaille .10 .25
175 Kings Logo .05 .15
176 Tony Granato .05 .15
177 Rob Blake .10 .25
178 Marty McSorley .07 .20
179 Alexei Zhitnik .07 .20
180 Kelly Hrudey .07 .20
181 Denis Savard .10 .25
182 Brian Bradley .05 .15
183 Lightning Logo .05 .15
184 Danton Cole .05 .15
185 Petr Klima .05 .15
186 Mikael Andersson .05 .15
187 Shawn Chambers .05 .15
188 Roman Hamrlik .05 .15
189 Daren Puppa .07 .20
190 Doug Gilmour .12 .30
191 Mike Gartner .12 .30
192 Nikolai Borschevsky .05 .15
193 Maple Leafs Logo .05 .15
194 Dave Andreychuk .10 .25
195 Wendel Clark .15 .40
196 Sylvain Lefebvre .05 .15
197 Dave Ellett .05 .15
198 Felix Potvin .15 .40
199 Doug Weight .07 .20
200 Zdeno Ciger .05 .15
201 Kelly Buchberger .05 .15
202 Shayne Corson .07 .20
203 Oilers Logo .05 .15
204 Scott Pearson .05 .15
205 Igor Kravchuk .05 .15
206 Luke Richardson .05 .15

207 Bill Ranford .07 .20
208 Vyacheslav Kozlov .07 .20
209 Steve Yzerman .25 .60
210 Sergei Fedorov .15 .40
211 Ray Sheppard .07 .20
212 Red Wings Logo .05 .15
213 Bob Probert .10 .25
214 Keith Primeau .07 .20
215 Paul Coffey .10 .25
216 Nicklas Lidstrom .10 .25
217 Igor Larionov .05 .15
218 Todd Elik .05 .15
219 Pat Falloon .05 .15
220 Sharks Logo .05 .15
221 Ulf Dahlen .05 .15
222 Sergei Makarov .05 .15
223 Sandis Ozolinsh .05 .15
224 Jeff Norton .05 .15
225 Arturs Irbe .07 .20
226 Mike Modano .15 .40
227 Dave Gagner .07 .20
228 Mike Craig .05 .15
229 Stars Logo .05 .15
230 Russ Courtnall .05 .15
231 Derian Hatcher .05 .15
232 Mark Tinordi .05 .15
233 Craig Ludwig .05 .15
234 Darcy Wakaluk .07 .20
235 Pavel Bure
Brett Hull .20 .50
236 Sergei Fedorov
Dave Andreychuk .15 .40
237 Brendan Shanahan
Ray Sheppard .10 .25
238 Adam Graves
Cam Neely .10 .25
239 Mike Modano 50+ Goals .15 .40
A Bryan Smolinski .05 .15
B Oleg Petrov .05 .15
C Pat Peake .05 .15
D Jaroslav Modry .05 .15
E Mikael Renberg .07 .20
F Yan Kaminsky .05 .15
G Iain Fraser .05 .15
H Rob Niedermayer .07 .20
I Markus Naslund .10 .25
J Alexander Karpovtsev .05 .15
K Derek Plante .05 .15
L Alexei Yashin .10 .25
M Chris Pronger .10 .25
N Patrik Carnback .05 .15
O Jeff Shantz .05 .15
P Vitali Karamnov .05 .15
Q Nathan Lafayette .05 .15
R Trevor Kidd .07 .20
S Dave Tomlinson .05 .15
T Robert Lang .05 .15
U Chris Gratton .05 .15
V Alexei Kudashov .05 .15
W Jason Arnott .07 .20
X Chris Osgood .15 .40
Y Mike Rathje .05 .15
Z Jarkko Varvio .05 .15
AA Wayne Gretzky .60 1.50
BB Sergei Fedorov .15 .40
CC Adam Oates .10 .25
DD Mark Recchi .12 .30
EE Brendan Shanahan .10 .25
FF Doug Gilmour .12 .30
GG Pavel Bure .10 .25
HH Jeremy Roenick .15 .40
II Jaromir Jagr .30 .75
JJ Dave Andreychuk .10 .25

1995-96 Panini Stickers

1 Claude Lemieux .10 .25
2 Claude Lemieux .10 .25
3 Adam Oates .10 .25
4 Ted Donato .05 .15
5 Mariusz Czerkawski .05 .15
6 Sandy Moger .05 .15
7 Kevin Stevens .07 .20
8 Cam Neely .10 .25
9 Ray Bourque .15 .40
10 Bruins Logo .05 .15
11 Don Sweeney .05 .15
12 Al Iafrate .07 .20
13 Blaine Lacher .07 .20
14 Brian Holzinger .20 .50
15 Pat LaFontaine .10 .25
16 Derek Plante .05 .15
17 Yuri Khmylev .05 .15
18 Jason Dawe .05 .15
19 Donald Audette .07 .20
20 Alexei Zhitnik .05 .15
21 Sabres Logo .05 .15
22 Richard Smehlik .07 .20
23 Garry Galley .05 .15
24 Dominik Hasek .15 .40
25 Andrew Cassels .05 .15
26 Jimmy Carson .07 .20
27 Darren Turcotte .05 .15
28 Geoff Sanderson .05 .15
29 Andrei Nikolishin .05 .15
30 Kevin Smyth .05 .15
31 Brendan Shanahan .10 .25
32 Whalers Logo .05 .15
33 Steven Rice .05 .15
34 Frantisek Kucera .05 .15
35 Sean Burke .05 .15
36 Brian Savage .05 .15
37 Pierre Turgeon .07 .20
38 Vincent Damphousse .07 .20
39 Benoit Brunet .05 .15
40 Mike Keane .05 .15
41 Mark Recchi .12 .30
42 Vladimir Malakhov .05 .15
43 Canadiens Logo .05 .15
44 Patrice Brisebois .05 .15
45 Stephane Quintal .07 .20
46 Patrick Roy .25 .60
47 Alexandre Daigle .05 .15
48 Alexei Yashin .07 .20
49 Dan Quinn .07 .20
50 Radek Bonk .05 .15
51 Scott Levins .05 .15
52 Sylvain Turgeon .05 .15
53 Pavol Demitra .12 .30
54 Senators Logo .05 .15
55 Steve Larouche .05 .15
56 Sean Hill .05 .15
57 Don Beaupre .07 .20
58 Ron Francis .12 .30
59 Mario Lemieux .40 1.00
60 Bryan Smolinski .05 .15
61 Luc Robitaille .10 .25
62 Tomas Sandstrom .07 .20
63 Jaromir Jagr .30 .75
64 Joe Mullen .07 .20
65 Penguins Logo .05 .15
66 Ulf Samuelsson .05 .15
67 Dmitri Mironov .05 .15
68 Ken Wregget .07 .20
69 Stu Barnes .05 .15
70 Jesse Belanger .05 .15
71 Rob Niedermayer .07 .20
72 Brian Skrudland .05 .15
73 Dave Lowry .05 .15
74 Jody Hull .05 .15
75 Scott Mellanby .07 .20
76 Panthers Logo .05 .15
77 Gord Murphy .05 .15
78 Magnus Svensson .07 .20
79 John Vanbiesbrouck .10 .25
80 Neal Broten .07 .20
81 Bill Guerin .10 .25
82 Claude Lemieux .10 .25
83 John MacLean .07 .20
84 Randy McKay .05 .15
85 Stephane Richer .07 .20
86 Shawn Chambers .05 .15
87 Devils Logo .05 .15
88 Scott Niedermayer .10 .25
89 Scott Stevens .10 .25
90 Martin Brodeur .25 .60
91 Kirk Muller .07 .20
92 Derek King .07 .20
93 Patrick Flatley .05 .15
94 Brett Lindros .05 .15
95 Steve Thomas .07 .20
96 Darius Kasparaitis .05 .15
97 Scott Lachance .05 .15
98 Islanders Logo .05 .15
99 Mathieu Schneider .05 .15
100 Dennis Vaske .05 .15
101 Tommy Salo .15 .40
102 Mark Messier .20 .50
103 Ray Ferraro .05 .15
104 Petr Nedved .07 .20
105 Adam Graves .07 .20
106 Alexei Kovalev .07 .20
107 Steve Larmer .07 .20
108 Pat Verbeek .07 .20
109 Rangers Logo .05 .15
110 Brian Leetch .07 .20
111 Sergei Zubov .07 .20
112 Mike Richter .10 .25
113 Eric Lindros .15 .40
114 Rod Brind'Amour .10 .25
115 Joel Otto .05 .15
116 John LeClair .10 .25
117 Mikael Renberg .07 .20
118 Chris Therien .05 .15
119 Eric Desjardins .07 .20
120 Flyers Logo .05 .15
121 Dimitri Yushkevich .05 .15
122 Karl Dykhuis .05 .15
123 Ron Hextall .10 .25
124 Brian Bradley .07 .20
125 John Tucker .05 .15
126 Chris Gratton .05 .15
127 Alexander Semak .05 .15
128 Brian Bellows .07 .20
129 Paul Ysebaert .05 .15
130 Petr Klima .05 .15
131 Lightning Logo .05 .15
132 Alexander Selivanov .07 .20
133 Roman Hamrlik .05 .15
134 Daren Puppa .07 .20
135 Dale Hunter .07 .20
136 Michal Pivonka .05 .15
137 Steve Konowalchuk .07 .20
138 Joe Juneau .05 .15
139 Peter Bondra .10 .25
140 Keith Jones .07 .20
141 Sergei Gonchar .05 .15
142 Capitals Logo .05 .15
143 Calle Johansson .05 .15
144 Mark Tinordi .05 .15
145 Jim Carey .07 .20
146 Eric Lindros AW .15 .40
147 Paul Coffey AW .10 .25
148 Peter Forsberg AW .20 .50
149 Dominik Hasek AW .15 .40
150 Jaromir Jagr AW .30 .75
151 Peter Bondra LL .10 .25
152 Ron Francis LL .12 .30
153 Cam Neely LL .10 .25
154 Dominik Hasek LL .15 .40
155 Ian Laperriere LL .05 .15
156 Bernie Nicholls .07 .20
157 Jeremy Roenick .15 .40
158 Patrick Poulin .05 .15
159 Eric Daze .20 .50
160 Tony Amonte .07 .20
161 Sergei Krivokrasov .05 .15
162 Joe Murphy .05 .15
163 Blackhawks Logo .05 .15
164 Chris Chelios .10 .25
165 Gary Suter .05 .15
166 Ed Belfour .07 .20
167 Dave Gagner .05 .15
168 Mike Modano .15 .40
169 Todd Harvey .05 .15
170 Mike Donnelly .05 .15
171 Mike Kennedy .07 .20
172 Trent Klatt .05 .15
173 Derian Hatcher .07 .20
174 Stars Logo .05 .15
175 Kevin Hatcher .07 .20
176 Grant Ledyard .05 .15
177 Andy Moog .10 .25
178 Sergei Fedorov .15 .40
179 Steve Yzerman .25 .60
180 Vyacheslav Kozlov .07 .20
181 Keith Primeau .07 .20
182 Dino Ciccarelli .07 .20
183 Ray Sheppard .07 .20
184 Paul Coffey .10 .25
185 Red Wings Logo .05 .15
186 Nicklas Lidstrom .10 .25
187 Chris Osgood .10 .25
188 Mike Vernon .07 .20
189 Dale Hawerchuk .12 .30
190 Ian Laperriere .05 .15
191 David Roberts .05 .15
192 Esa Tikkanen .05 .15
193 Geoff Courtnall .05 .15
194 Brett Hull .20 .50
195 Steve Duchesne .05 .15
196 Blues Logo .05 .15
197 Al MacInnis .12 .30
198 Chris Pronger .10 .25
199 Jon Casey .07 .20
200 Doug Gilmour .12 .30
201 Mats Sundin .10 .25
202 Benoit Hogue .05 .15
203 Dave Andreychuk .10 .25
204 Mike Gartner .12 .30
205 Dave Ellett .05 .15
206 Todd Gill .05 .15
207 Maple Leafs Logo .05 .15
208 Kenny Jonsson .10 .25
209 Larry Murphy .07 .20
210 Felix Potvin .15 .40
211 Dallas Drake .05 .15
212 Alexei Zhamnov .10 .25
213 Mike Eastwood .05 .15
214 Keith Tkachuk .10 .25
215 Igor Korolev .05 .15
216 Nelson Emerson .05 .15
217 Teemu Selanne .20 .50
218 Jets Logo .05 .15
219 Dave Manson .05 .15
220 Teppo Numminen .05 .15
221 Nikolai Khabibulin .07 .20
222 Steve Rucchin .07 .20
223 Shaun Van Allen .05 .15
224 Patrik Carnback .05 .15
225 Peter Douris .05 .15
226 Todd Krygier .05 .15
227 Paul Kariya .10 .25
228 Bobby Dollas .05 .15
229 Ducks Logo .05 .15
230 Milos Holan .05 .15
231 Oleg Tverdovsky .10 .25
232 Guy Hebert .07 .20
233 Joe Nieuwendyk .07 .20
234 German Titov .07 .20
235 Paul Kruse .05 .15
236 Gary Roberts .05 .15
237 Theo Fleury .12 .30
238 Ronnie Stern .05 .15
239 Steve Chiasson .05 .15
240 Flames Logo .05 .15
241 Phil Housley .07 .20
242 Zarley Zalapski .05 .15
243 Trevor Kidd .07 .20
244 Peter Forsberg .20 .50
245 Mike Ricci .05 .15
246 Joe Sakic .20 .50
247 Wendel Clark .15 .40
248 Valeri Kamensky .07 .20
249 Owen Nolan .10 .25
250 Scott Young .05 .15
251 Avalanche Logo .05 .15
252 Uwe Krupp .07 .20
253 Curtis Leschyshyn .05 .15
254 Jocelyn Thibault .07 .20
255 Jason Arnott .07 .20
256 Jason Bonsignore .05 .15
257 Todd Marchant .05 .15
258 Scott Thornton .07 .20
259 Doug Weight .10 .25
260 Shayne Corson .07 .20
261 Kelly Buchberger .05 .15
262 Oilers Logo .05 .15
263 David Oliver .05 .15
264 Igor Kravchuk .05 .15
265 Curtis Joseph .12 .30
266 Wayne Gretzky .60 1.50
267 Tony Granato .05 .15
268 Dimitri Khristich .05 .15
269 John Druce .07 .20
270 Jari Kurri .10 .25
271 Rick Tocchet .07 .20
272 Rob Blake .07 .20
273 Kings Logo .05 .15
274 Marty McSorley .07 .20
275 Darryl Sydor .07 .20
276 Kelly Hrudey .07 .20
277 Craig Janney .05 .15
278 Jeff Friesen .05 .15
279 Viktor Kozlov .07 .20
280 Ray Whitney .07 .20
281 Ulf Dahlen .05 .15
282 Sergei Makarov .05 .15
283 Sandis Ozolinsh .05 .15
284 Sharks Logo .05 .15
285 Mike Rathje .07 .20
286 Michal Sykora .05 .15
287 Arturs Irbe .07 .20
288 Trevor Linden .10 .25
289 Mike Ridley .05 .15
290 Cliff Ronning .05 .15
291 Josef Beranek .05 .15
292 Roman Oksiuta .05 .15
293 Pavel Bure .10 .25
294 Alexander Mogilny .07 .20
295 Canucks Logo .05 .15
296 Russ Courtnall .05 .15
297 Jeff Brown .07 .20
298 Kirk McLean .07 .20
299 Peter Forsberg .20 .50
300 Paul Kariya .10 .25
301 Chris Therien .05 .15
302 Blaine Lacher .07 .20
303 Jim Carey .07 .20
304 Jeff Friesen .05 .15
305 Ian Laperriere .05 .15
306 Kenny Jonsson .10 .25

1996-97 Panini Stickers

1 Ray Bourque .15 .40
2 Bill Ranford .07 .20
3 Cam Neely .10 .25
4 Adam Oates .10 .25
5 Kyle McLaren .05 .15
6 Rick Tocchet .07 .20
7 Shawn McEachern .05 .15
8 Boston Logo .05 .15
9 Jozef Stumpel .05 .15
10 Ted Donato .05 .15
11 Dave Reid .05 .15
12 Donald Audette .05 .15
13 Garry Galley .05 .15
14 Dominik Hasek .15 .40
15 Pat LaFontaine .10 .25
16 Jason Dawe .05 .15
17 Alexei Zhitnik .05 .15
18 Brad May .05 .15
19 Buffalo Logo .05 .15
20 Matthew Barnaby .05 .15
21 Darryl Shannon .05 .15
22 Derek Plante .05 .15
23 Geoff Sanderson .07 .20
24 Sean Burke .05 .15
25 Nelson Emerson .05 .15
26 Brendan Shanahan .10 .25
27 Jeff Brown .05 .15
28 Andrew Cassels .05 .15
29 Hartford Logo .05 .15
30 Jeff O'Neill .05 .15
31 Robert Kron .05 .15
32 Andrei Nikolishin .05 .15
33 Brad McCrimmon .05 .15
34 Valeri Bure .05 .15
35 Vincent Damphousse .07 .20
36 Jocelyn Thibault .07 .20
37 Saku Koivu .10 .25
38 Mark Recchi .12 .30
39 Martin Rucinsky .05 .15
40 Pierre Turgeon .07 .20
41 Montreal Logo .05 .15
42 Andrei Kovalenko .05 .15
43 Peter Popovic .05 .15
44 Vladimir Malakhov .05 .15
45 Alexandre Daigle .05 .15
46 Daniel Alfredsson .10 .25
47 Damian Rhodes .07 .20
48 Alexei Yashin .07 .20
49 Radek Bonk .05 .10
50 Steve Duchesne .05 .15
51 Ottawa Logo .05 .15
52 Pavol Demitra .12 .30
53 Antti Tormanen .05 .15
54 Stanislav Neckar .05 .15
55 Randy Cunneyworth .05 .15
56 Petr Nedved .07 .20
57 Ron Francis .12 .30
58 Jaromir Jagr .30 .75
59 Mario Lemieux .40 1.00
60 Tom Barrasso .07 .20
61 Tomas Sandstrom .05 .15
62 Bryan Smolinski .05 .15
63 Pittsburgh Logo .05 .15
64 Sergei Zubov .07 .20
65 Dmitri Mironov .05 .15
66 Kevin Miller .05 .15
67 Scott Mellanby .07 .20
68 Ed Jovanovski .07 .20
69 Ray Sheppard .07 .20
70 John Vanbiesbrouck .10 .25
71 Radek Dvorak .07 .20
72 Rob Niedermayer .07 .20
73 Florida Logo .05 .15
74 Robert Svehla .05 .15
75 Johan Garpenlov .05 .15
76 Martin Straka .05 .15
77 Paul Laus .05 .15
78 Steve Thomas .05 .15
79 Martin Brodeur .25 .60
80 Scott Stevens .10 .25
81 Petr Sykora .05 .15
82 Dave Andreychuk .10 .25
83 Bill Guerin .10 .25
84 New Jersey Logo .05 .15
85 Phil Housley .07 .20
86 Scott Niedermayer .10 .25
87 Valeri Zelepukin .07 .20
88 John MacLean .07 .20
89 Todd Bertuzzi .10 .25
90 Eric Fichaud .07 .20
91 Zigmund Palffy .10 .25
92 Travis Green .07 .20
93 Kenny Jonsson .05 .15
94 Bryan McCabe .05 .15
95 Marty McInnis .05 .15
96 New York Islanders Logo .05 .15
97 Alexander Semak .05 .15
98 Niklas Andersson .05 .15
99 Scott Lachance .05 .15
100 Adam Graves .05 .15
101 Mark Messier .20 .50
102 Brian Leetch .07 .20
103 Mike Richter .10 .25
104 Alexei Kovalev .07 .20
105 Luc Robitaille .10 .25
106 New York Rangers Logo .05 .15
107 Ulf Samuelsson .05 .15
108 Niklas Sundstrom .05 .15
109 Jari Kurri .10 .25
110 Sergei Nemchinov .05 .15
111 Rod Brind'Amour .10 .25
112 John Leclair .10 .25
113 Ron Hextall .10 .25
114 Eric Lindros .15 .40
115 Eric Desjardins .07 .20
116 Dale Hawerchuk .12 .30
117 Philadelphia Logo .05 .15
118 Mikael Renberg .07 .20
119 Joel Otto .05 .15
120 Petr Svoboda .05 .15
121 Karl Dykhuis .05 .15
122 Brian Bradley .05 .15
123 Roman Hamrlik .05 .15
124 Chris Gratton .07 .20
125 Daren Puppa .07 .20
126 Petr Klima .05 .15
127 Alexander Selivanov .05 .15
128 Tampa Bay Logo .05 .15
129 Aaron Gavey .05 .15
130 Brian Bellows .07 .20
131 Rob Zamuner .05 .15
132 Mikael Andersson .05 .15
133 Peter Bondra .10 .25
134 Jim Carey .10 .25
135 Sergei Gonchar .05 .15
136 Brendan Witt .05 .15
137 Sylvain Cote .05 .15
138 Joe Juneau .05 .15
139 Michal Pivonka .05 .15
140 Washington Logo .05 .15
141 Andrew Brunette .12 .30
142 Calle Johansson .07 .20
143 Stefan Ustorf .05 .15
144 Mario Lemieux .40 1.00
145 Ron Francis .12 .30
146 Ron Hextall .10 .25
147 Vladimir Konstantinov .07 .20
148 Brian Leetch .07 .20
149 Gary Roberts .05 .15
150 Mario Lemieux .40 1.00
151 Chris Chelios .10 .25
152 Daniel Alfredsson .10 .25
153 Paul Kariya .10 .25
154 Jim Carey .10 .25
155 Joe Sakic .20 .50
156 Ed Belfour .10 .25
157 Chris Chelios .10 .25
158 Jeremy Roenick .15 .40
159 Eric Daze .07 .20
160 Tony Amonte .07 .20
161 Bernie Nicholls .07 .20
162 Chicago Logo .05 .15
163 Gary Suter .05 .15
164 Denis Savard .10 .25
165 Brent Sutter .05 .15
166 Keith Carney .05 .15
167 Derian Hatcher .05 .15
168 Mike Modano .15 .40
169 Joe Nieuwendyk .07 .20
170 Kevin Hatcher .05 .15
171 Benoit Hogue .05 .15
172 Grant Marshall .05 .15
173 Andy Moog .10 .25
174 Dallas Logo .05 .15
175 Jere Lehtinen .05 .15
176 Greg Adams .05 .15
177 Brent Gilchrist .05 .15
178 Sergei Fedorov .15 .40
179 Paul Coffey .10 .25
180 Chris Osgood .10 .25
181 Steve Yzerman .25 .60
182 Vladimir Konstantinov .07 .20
183 Slava Kozlov .05 .15
184 Detroit Logo .05 .15
185 Nicklas Lidstrom .12 .30
186 Keith Primeau .07 .20
187 Viacheslav Fetisov .05 .15
188 Igor Larionov .10 .25
189 Nikolai Khabibulin .07 .20
190 Chad Kilger .05 .15
191 Keith Tkachuk .10 .25
192 Oleg Tverdovsky .07 .20
193 Ed Olczyk .05 .15
194 Teppo Numminen .05 .15
195 Phoenix Logo .05 .15
196 Alexei Zhamnov .07 .20
197 Dave Manson .05 .15
198 Craig Janney .07 .20
199 Igor Korolev .05 .15
200 Wayne Gretzky .60 1.50
201 Chris Pronger .10 .25
202 Brett Hull .20 .50
203 Grant Fuhr .15 .40
204 Shayne Corson .07 .20
205 Geoff Courtnall .05 .15
206 St.Louis Logo .05 .15
207 Al MacInnis .12 .30
208 Christer Olsson .05 .15
209 Adam Creighton .05 .15
210 Tony Twist .05 .15
211 Felix Potvin .15 .40
212 Kirk Muller .05 .15
213 Wendel Clark .15 .40
214 Doug Gilmour .12 .30
215 Mike Gartner .12 .30
216 Larry Murphy .07 .20
217 Toronto Logo .05 .15
218 Mats Sundin .10 .25
219 Dave Gagner .10 .25
220 Mathieu Schneider .05 .15
221 Tie Domi .07 .20
222 Paul Kariya .10 .25
223 Guy Hebert .07 .20
224 Roman Oksiuta .05 .15
225 Teemu Selanne .20 .50
226 Steve Rucchin .05 .15
227 Bobby Dollas .05 .15
228 Anaheim Logo .05 .15
229 Darren Van Impe .05 .15
230 Fredrik Olausson .05 .15
231 Shaun Van Allen .05 .15
232 Joe Sacco .12 .30
233 Trevor Kidd .05 .15
234 Theoren Fleury .20 .50
235 German Titov .05 .15
236 James Patrick .05 .15
237 Michael Nylander .05 .15
238 Cory Stillman .05 .15
239 Calgary Logo .05 .15
240 Gary Roberts .05 .15
241 Jamie Huscroft .05 .15
242 Tommy Albelin .07 .20
243 Zarley Zalapski .05 .15
244 Peter Forsberg .20 .50
245 Joe Sakic .20 .50
246 Claude Lemieux .05 .15
247 Patrick Roy .25 .60
248 Valeri Kamensky .07 .20
249 Uwe Krupp .05 .15
250 Colorado Logo .05 .15
251 Sandis Ozolinsh .05 .15
252 Curtis Leschyshyn .05 .15
253 Scott Young .05 .15
254 Alexei Gusarov .05 .15
255 Curtis Joseph .12 .30
256 Bryan Marchment .05 .15
257 Doug Weight .10 .25
258 Jason Arnott .07 .20
259 Zdeno Ciger .05 .15
260 Miroslav Satan .05 .15
261 Mariusz Czerkawski .05 .15
262 Edmonton Logo .05 .15
263 Jiri Slegr .05 .15
264 Jeff Norton .07 .20
265 Boris Mironov .05 .15
266 Vitali Yachmenev .05 .15
267 Byron Dafoe .07 .20
268 Rob Blake .10 .25
269 Ray Ferraro .05 .15
270 Dimitri Khristich .05 .15
271 Kevin Todd .05 .15
272 Yanic Perreault .05 .15
273 Los Angeles Logo .05 .15
274 Tony Granato .05 .15
275 Jaroslav Modry .05 .15
276 Mattias Norstrom .05 .15
277 Owen Nolan .10 .25
278 Jeff Friesen .05 .15
279 Marcus Ragnarsson .05 .15
280 Chris Terreri .07 .20
281 Darren Turcotte .05 .15
282 Viktor Kozlov .05 .15
283 Ulf Dahlen .05 .15
284 San Jose Logo .05 .15
285 Michal Sykora .05 .15
286 Ray Whitney .05 .15
287 Shean Donovan .05 .15
288 Alexander Mogilny .07 .20
289 Pavel Bure .10 .25
290 Trevor Linden .10 .25
291 Kirk McLean .07 .20
292 Russ Courtnall .05 .15
293 Jyrki Lumme .05 .15
294 Vancouver Logo .05 .15
295 Cliff Ronning .05 .15
296 Markus Naslund .10 .25
297 Esa Tikkanen .05 .15
298 Josef Beranek .05 .15
299 Martin Biron .12 .30
300 Peter Ferraro .05 .15
301 Jason Bonsignore .05 .15
302 Jamie Storr .05 .15
303 Eric Fichaud .07 .20
304 Andrew Brunette .12 .30

1997-98 Panini Stickers

1 Rob DiMaio .05 .15
2 Jeff Odgers .05 .15
3 Jozef Stumpel .05 .15
4 Ted Donato .05 .15
5 Mattias Timander .07 .20
6 Bruins Logo Foil .05 .15
7 Don Sweeney .05 .15
8 Jim Carey .05 .15
9 Ray Bourque .15 .40
10 Dominik Hasek .15 .40
11 Alexei Zhitnik .05 .15
12 Derek Plante .07 .20
13 Michael Peca .07 .20
14 Darryl Shannon .05 .15
15 Sabres Logo Foil .05 .15
16 Donald Audette .07 .20
17 Michal Grosek .05 .15
18 Miroslav Satan .05 .15
19 Robert Kron .05 .15
20 Geoff Sanderson .07 .20
21 Andrew Cassels .05 .15
22 Marek Malik .05 .15
23 Derek King .07 .20
24 Hurricanes Logo Foil .05 .15
25 Sami Kapanen .07 .20
26 Alexander Godynyuk .05 .15
27 Keith Primeau .07 .20
28 Saku Koivu .10 .25
29 Vincent Damphousse .07 .20
30 Brian Savage .05 .15
31 Valeri Bure .05 .15
32 Mark Recchi .12 .30
33 Canadiens Logo Foil .05 .15
34 Vladimir Malakhov .05 .15
35 Peter Popovic .05 .15
36 Martin Rucinsky .07 .20
37 Radek Bonk .05 .15
38 Alexandre Daigle .05 .15
39 Sergei Zholtok .07 .20
40 Janne Laukkanen .07 .20
41 Daniel Alfredsson .10 .25
42 Senators Lolo Foil .05 .15
43 Alexei Yashin .07 .20
44 Frank Musil .05 .15
45 Steve Duchesne .05 .15
46 Darius Kasparaitis .07 .20
47 Jaromir Jagr .30 .75
48 Roman Oksiuta .05 .15
49 Kevin Hatcher .05 .15
50 Ron Francis .12 .30
51 Penguins Logo Foil .05 .15
52 Petr Nedved .10 .25
53 Andreas Johansson .05 .15
54 Fredrik Olausson .07 .20
55 Robert Svehla .07 .20
56 Radek Dvorak .07 .20
57 Martin Straka .05 .15
58 Kirk Muller .05 .15
59 Per Gustafsson .07 .20
60 Panthers Logo Foil .05 .15
61 Ray Sheppard .07 .20
62 Johan Garpenlov .05 .15
63 Scott Mellanby .07 .20
64 Martin Brodeur .25 .60
65 Bobby Holik .05 .15
66 Doug Gilmour .12 .30
67 Valeri Zelepukin .07 .20
68 Petr Sykora .05 .15
69 Devils Logo Foil .05 .15
70 John MacLean .05 .15
71 Dave Andreychuk .10 .25
72 Scott Niedermayer .10 .25
73 Zigmund Palffy .10 .25
74 Tommy Salo .05 .15
75 Niklas Andersson .05 .15
76 Kenny Jonsson .07 .20
77 Robert Reichel .07 .20
78 Islanders Logo Foil .05 .15
79 Travis Green .07 .20
80 Bryan Berard .05 .15
81 Bryan Smolinski .07 .20
82 Wayne Gretzky .60 1.50
83 Mark Messier .20 .50
84 Brian Leetch .07 .20
85 Alexei Kovalev .07 .20
86 Esa Tikkanen .05 .15
87 Rangers Logo Foil .05 .15
88 Ulf Samuelsson .10 .25
89 Niklas Sundstrom .07 .20
90 Alexander Karpovtsev .05 .15
91 Ron Hextall .10 .25
92 Eric Lindros .15 .40
93 Rod Brind'Amour .10 .25
94 Janne Niinimaa .07 .20
95 Dainius Zubrus .07 .20
96 Flyers Logo Foil .05 .15
97 Petr Svoboda .05 .15
98 John LeClair .10 .25
99 Mikael Renberg .07 .20
100 Dino Ciccarelli .10 .25
101 Roman Hamrlik .05 .15
102 Alexander Selivanov .05 .15
103 Chris Gratton .05 .15
104 Mikael Andersson .05 .15
105 Lightning Logo Foil .05 .15
106 Igor Ulanov .07 .20
107 John Cullen .05 .15
108 Rob Zamuner .05 .15
109 Peter Bondra .10 .25
110 Bill Ranford .07 .20
111 Michal Pivonka .05 .15
112 Sergei Gonchar .05 .15
113 Calle Johansson .07 .20
114 Capitals Logo Foil .05 .15
115 Dale Hunter .07 .20
116 Adam Oates .10 .25
117 Andrei Nikolishin .07 .20
118 Dominik Hasek Foil .15 .40
119 Bryan Berard Foil .05 .15
120 Brian Leetch Foil .07 .20
121 Paul Kariya Foil .10 .25
122 Michael Peca Foil .07 .20
123 Keith Tkachuk Foil .10 .25
124 Martin Brodeur Foil .25 .60
125 John LeClair Foil .10 .25
126 Miroslav Satan Foil .05 .15
127 Patrick Roy Foil .25 .60
128 Alexei Zhamnov .05 .15
129 Chris Chelios .10 .25
130 Ulf Dahlen .05 .15
131 Tony Amonte .07 .20
132 Michal Sykora .05 .15
133 Blackhawks Logo Foil .05 .15
134 Eric Weinrich .05 .15
135 Sergei Krivokrasov .05 .15
136 Eric Daze .05 .15
137 Pat Verbeek .07 .20
138 Sergei Zubov .07 .20
139 Mike Modano .15 .40
140 Darryl Sydor .05 .15
141 Dave Reid .05 .15
142 Stars Logo Foil .05 .15
143 Benoit Hogue .07 .20
144 Joe Nieuwendyk .07 .20
145 Jere Lehtinen .07 .20
146 Nicklas Lidstrom .10 .25
147 Vladimir Konstantinov .05 .15
148 Sergei Fedorov .15 .40
149 Steve Yzerman .25 .60
150 Tomas Sandstrom .05 .15
151 Red Wings Logo Foil .05 .15
152 Igor Larionov .05 .15
153 Vyacheslav Kozlov .07 .20
154 Brendan Shanahan .10 .25
155 Nikolai Khabibulin .10 .25
156 Teppo Numminen .05 .15
157 Jeremy Roenick .15 .40
158 Mike Gartner .12 .30
159 Igor Korolev .05 .15
160 Coyotes Logo Foil .05 .15
161 Craig Janney .05 .15
162 Keith Tkachuk .10 .25
163 Oleg Tverdovsky .07 .20
164 Pierre Turgeon .07 .20
165 Igor Kravchuk .05 .15
166 Robert Petrovicky .07 .20
167 Geoff Courtnall .05 .15
168 Brett Hull .20 .50
169 Blues Logo Foil .05 .15
170 Chris Pronger .10 .25
171 Joe Murphy .07 .20
172 Grant Fuhr .15 .40
173 Dimitri Yushkevich .05 .15
174 Wendel Clark .15 .40
175 Steve Sullivan .07 .20
176 Tie Domi .07 .20
177 Todd Warriner .07 .20
178 Maple Leafs Logo Foil .05 .15
179 Mats Sundin .10 .25
180 Sergei Berezin .07 .20
181 Fredrik Modin .07 .20
182 Dmitri Mironov .07 .20
183 Paul Kariya .10 .25
184 Steve Rucchin .07 .20
185 Darren Van Impe .07 .20
186 Joe Sacco .07 .20
187 Mighty Ducks Logo Foil .05 .15
188 Teemu Selanne .20 .50
189 Jari Kurri .10 .25
190 Brian Bellows .07 .20
191 Dave Gagner .05 .15
192 German Titov .05 .15
193 Marty McInnis .05 .15
194 Jarome Iginla .12 .30
195 Tommy Albelin .07 .20
196 Flames Logo Foil .05 .15
197 Joel Bouchard .05 .15
198 Jonas Hoglund .07 .20
199 Theoren Fleury .12 .30
200 Uwe Krupp .05 .15
201 Peter Forsberg .20 .50
202 Adam Foote .05 .15

203 Valeri Kamensky	.07	.20
204 Joe Sakic	.20	.50
205 Avalanche Logo Foil	.05	.15
206 Sandis Ozolinsh	.05	.15
207 Alexei Gusarov	.07	.20
208 Patrick Roy	.25	.60
209 Andrei Kovalenko	.05	.15
210 Jason Arnott	.07	.20
211 Mariusz Czerkawski	.05	.15
212 Ryan Smyth	.07	.20
213 Mats Lindgren	.05	.15
214 Oilers Logo Foil	.05	.15
215 Doug Weight	.10	.25
216 Boris Mironov	.05	.15
217 Petr Klima	.05	.15
218 Vladimir Tsyplakov	.07	.20
219 Mattias Norstrom	.07	.20
220 Rob Blake	.10	.25
221 Kai Nurminen	.05	.15
222 Vitali Yachmenev	.07	.20
223 Kings Logo Foil	.05	.15
224 Ray Ferraro	.05	.15
225 Kevin Stevens	.07	.20
226 Dimitri Khristich	.07	.20
227 Tony Granato	.05	.15
228 Bernie Nicholls	.07	.20
229 Doug Bodger	.05	.15
230 Owen Nolan	.10	.25
231 Viktor Kozlov	.07	.20
232 Sharks Logo Foil	.05	.15
233 Jeff Friesen	.07	.20
234 Marcus Ragnarsson	.05	.15
235 Andrei Nazarov	.05	.15
236 Pavel Bure	.10	.25
237 Alexander Mogilny	.07	.20
238 Martin Gelinas	.05	.15
239 Markus Naslund	.10	.25
240 David Roberts	.05	.15
241 Canucks Logo Foil	.05	.15
242 Trevor Linden	.10	.25
243 Mike Ridley	.05	.15
244 Jyrki Lumme	.07	.20
245 Janne Niinimaa	.07	.20
246 Patrick Lalime	.07	.20
247 Bryan Berard	.05	.15
248 Jim Campbell	.05	.15
249 Dainius Zubrus	.07	.20
250 Sergei Berezin	.07	.20
251 Mats Lindgren	.05	.15
252 Jarome Iginla	.12	.30

1998-99 Panini Photocards

1 Daniel Alfredsson	.20	.50
2 Jason Allison	.15	.40
3 Tony Amonte	.15	.40
4 Jason Arnott	.15	.40
5 Tom Barrasso	.15	.40
6 Stu Barnes	.12	.30
7 Ed Belfour	.20	.50
8 Bryan Berard	.15	.40
9 Rob Blake	.20	.50
10 Peter Bondra	.20	.50
11 Ray Bourque	.30	.75
12 Rod Brind'Amour	.20	.50
13 Martin Brodeur	.50	1.25
14 Andrew Brunette	.15	.40
15 Pavel Bure	.20	.50
16 Chris Chelios	.20	.50
17 Vincent Damphousse	.15	.40
18 Eric Daze	.15	.40
19 Detroit Red Wings	.20	.50
20 Mike Dunham	.15	.40
21 Sergei Fedorov	.30	.75
22 Stephane Fiset	.15	.40
23 Theo Fleury	.25	.60
24 Peter Forsberg	.40	1.00
25 Ron Francis	.25	.60
26 Jeff Friesen	.12	.30
27 Grant Fuhr	.30	.75
28 Doug Gilmour	.25	.60
29 Adam Graves	.12	.30
30 Wayne Gretzky	1.25	3.00
31 Michal Grosek	.12	.30
32 Dominik Hasek	.30	.75
33 Kevin Hatcher	.12	.30
34 Brett Hull	.40	1.00
35 Jaromir Jagr	.60	1.50
36 Mike Johnson	.12	.30
37 Curtis Joseph	.25	.60
38 Joe Juneau	.12	.30
39 Paul Kariya	.20	.50
40 Nikolai Khabibulin	.20	.50
41 Saku Koivu	.20	.50
42 Olaf Kolzig	.20	.50
43 Oleg Kvasha	.20	.50
44 Vincent Lecavalier	.40	1.00
45 John LeClair	.20	.50
46 Brian Leetch	.15	.40
47 Claude Lemieux	.20	.50
48 Trevor Linden	.20	.50
49 Eric Lindros	.30	.75
50 Al MacInnis	.25	.60
51 Mark Messier	.40	1.00
52 Mike Modano	.30	.75
53 Alexander Mogilny	.15	.40
54 Brendan Morrison	.12	.30
55 Scott Niedermayer	.20	.50
56 Joe Nieuwendyk	.15	.40
57 Adam Oates	.20	.50
58 Chris Osgood	.20	.50
59 Zigmund Palffy	.20	.50
60 Mark Parrish	.30	.75
61 Michael Peca	.12	.30
62 Yanic Perreault	.12	.30
63 Felix Potvin	.30	.75
64 Keith Primeau	.15	.40
65 Chris Pronger	.20	.50
66 Daren Puppa	.15	.40
67 Mark Recchi	.25	.60
68 Mike Richter	.20	.50
69 Luc Robitaille	.20	.50
70 Jeremy Roenick	.30	.75
71 Patrick Roy	.50	1.25
72 Joe Sakic	.40	1.00
73 Tommy Salo	.15	.40
74 Sergei Samsonov	.15	.40
75 Geoff Sanderson	.12	.30
76 Teemu Selanne	.40	1.00
77 Brendan Shanahan	.20	.50
78 Ryan Smyth	.15	.40
79 Garth Snow	.15	.40
80 Cory Stillman	.12	.30
81 Mats Sundin	.20	.50
82 Jocelyn Thibault	.15	.40
83 Joe Thornton	.30	.75
84 Keith Tkachuk	.20	.50
85 Pierre Turgeon	.15	.40
86 Oleg Tverdovsky	.20	.50
87 John Vanbiesbrouck	.20	.50
88 Mike Vernon	.15	.40
89 Doug Weight	.20	.50
90 Alexei Yashin	.15	.40
91 Steve Yzerman	.50	1.25
92 Steve Yzerman w/CUP	.50	1.25
93 Rob Blake AW	.20	.50
94 Martin Brodeur AW	.50	1.25
95 Ron Francis AW	.25	.60
96 Dominik Hasek AW	.30	.75
97 Jaromir Jagr AW	.60	1.50
98 Sergei Samsonov AW	.15	.40
99 Peter Bondra AS	.20	.50
100 Ray Bourque AS	.30	.75
101 Peter Forsberg AS	.40	1.00
102 Wayne Gretzky AS	1.25	3.00
103 Saku Koivu AS	.20	.50
104 Eric Lindros AS	.30	.75
105 Mark Messier AS	.40	1.00
106 Patrick Roy	.50	1.25
107 Teemu Selanne AS	.40	1.00
108 Mats Sundin AS	.20	.50

1998-99 Panini Stickers

1 Teemu Selanne	.20	.50
2 Peter Bondra	.10	.25
3 Wayne Gretzky	.60	1.50
4 Jaromir Jagr	.30	.75
5 Chris Pronger	.10	.25
6 Ed Belfour	.10	.25
7 Bruins logo	.05	.15
8 Dimitri Khristich	.05	.15
9 P.J. Axelsson	.05	.15
10 Byron Dafoe	.07	.20
11 Ted Donato	.05	.15
12 Ray Bourque	.15	.40
13 Sergei Samsonov	.07	.20
14 Jason Allison	.07	.20
15 Sabres logo	.05	.15
16 Miroslav Satan	.07	.20
17 Donald Audette	.05	.15
18 Michal Grosek	.05	.15
19 Dominik Hasek	.15	.40
20 Richard Smehlik	.05	.15
21 Mike Peca	.05	.15
22 Alexei Zhitnik	.05	.15
23 Hurricanes logo	.05	.15
24 Trevor Kidd	.05	.15
25 Nelson Emerson	.05	.15
26 Curtis Leschyshyn	.05	.15
27 Robert Kron	.05	.15
28 Gary Roberts	.05	.15
29 Sami Kapanen	.05	.15
30 Keith Primeau	.07	.20
31 Canadiens logo	.05	.15
32 Saku Koivu	.10	.25
33 Vladimir Malakhov	.05	.15
34 Mark Recchi	.12	.30
35 Jocelyn Thibault	.07	.20
36 Peter Popovic	.05	.15
37 Martin Rucinsky	.05	.15
38 Jonas Hoglund	.05	.15
39 Senators logo	.05	.15
40 Damian Rhodes	.10	.25
41 Radek Bonk	.05	.15
42 Daniel Alfredsson	.10	.25
43 Alexei Yashin	.07	.20
44 Magnus Arvedson	.05	.15
45 Janne Laukkanen	.05	.15
46 Igor Kravchuk	.05	.15
47 Penguins logo	.05	.15
48 Jaromir Jagr	.30	.75
49 Ron Francis	.12	.30
50 Darius Kasparaitis	.05	.15
51 Tom Barrasso	.07	.20
52 Martin Straka	.05	.15
53 Alexei Morozov	.05	.15
54 Fredrik Olausson	.05	.15
55 Panthers logo	.05	.15
56 Radek Dvorak	.05	.15
57 Robert Svehla	.05	.15
58 Ray Whitney	.05	.15
59 Dave Gagner	.05	.15
60 John Vanbiesbrouck	.10	.25
61 Ed Jovanovski	.07	.20
62 Viktor Kozlov	.07	.20
63 Devils logo	.05	.15
64 Petr Sykora	.05	.15
65 Scott Niedermayer	.10	.25
66 Dave Andreychuk	.10	.25
67 Martin Brodeur	.25	.60
68 Bobby Holik	.05	.15
69 Doug Gilmour	.12	.30
70 Patrik Elias	.10	.25
71 Islanders logo	.05	.15
72 Tommy Salo	.07	.20
73 Zigmund Palffy	.10	.25
74 Bryan Smolinski	.05	.15
75 Robert Reichel	.05	.15
76 Sergei Nemchinov	.05	.15
77 Kenny Jonsson	.05	.15
78 Bryan Berard	.07	.20
79 Rangers logo	.05	.15
80 Wayne Gretzky	.60	1.50
81 Adam Graves	.05	.15
82 Mike Richter	.10	.25
83 Brian Leetch	.07	.20
84 Alexei Kovalev	.07	.20
85 Ulf Samuelsson	.07	.20
86 Niklas Sundstrom	.05	.15
87 Flyers logo	.05	.15
88 John LeClair	.10	.25
89 Petr Svoboda	.05	.15
90 Rod Brind'Amour	.10	.25
91 Sean Burke	.05	.15
92 Dainius Zubrus	.05	.15
93 Alexandre Daigle	.05	.15
94 Eric Lindros	.15	.40
95 Lightning logo	.05	.15
96 Mark Fitzpatrick	.05	.15
97 Alexander Selivanov	.05	.15
98 Mikael Renberg	.07	.20
99 Rob Zamuner	.05	.15
100 Karl Dykhuis	.05	.15
101 Paul Ysebaert	.05	.15
102 Mikael Andersson	.05	.15
103 Capitals logo	.05	.15
104 Peter Bondra	.10	.25
105 Sergei Gonchar	.05	.15
106 Adam Oates	.10	.25
107 Calle Johansson	.05	.15
108 Olaf Kolzig	.10	.25
109 Esa Tikkanen	.05	.15
110 Andrei Nikolishin	.05	.15
111 Blackhawks logo	.05	.15
112 Alexei Zhamnov	.05	.15
113 Eric Daze	.07	.20
114 Chris Chelios	.10	.25
115 Jeff Hackett	.05	.15
116 Gary Suter	.05	.15
117 Eric Weinrich	.05	.15
118 Tony Amonte	.07	.20
119 Stars logo	.05	.15
120 Jere Lehtinen	.07	.20
121 Joe Nieuwendyk	.07	.20
122 Ed Belfour	.10	.25
123 Mike Modano	.15	.40
124 Sergei Zubov	.07	.20
125 Darryl Sydor	.05	.15
126 Pat Verbeek	.05	.15
127 Red Wings logo	.05	.15
128 Chris Osgood	.10	.25
129 Sergei Fedorov	.15	.40
130 Stanley Cup	.05	.15
131 Igor Larionov	.10	.25
132 Slava Kozlov	.05	.15
133 Brendan Shanahan	.10	.25
134 Nicklas Lidstrom	.12	.30
135 Steve Yzerman	.25	.60
136 Predators logo	.05	.15
137 Jan Vopat	.05	.15
138 Sergei Krivokrasov	.05	.15
139 Darren Turcotte	.07	.20
140 Tom Fitzgerald	.07	.20
141 Joel Bouchard	.05	.15
142 Scott Walker	.07	.20
143 Coyotes logo	.05	.15
144 Keith Tkachuk	.10	.25
145 Craig Janney	.05	.15
146 Oleg Tverdovsky	.10	.25
147 Nikolai Khabibulin	.10	.25
148 Teppo Numminen	.05	.15
149 Cliff Ronning	.05	.15
150 Jeremy Roenick	.15	.40
151 Blues logo	.05	.15
152 Brett Hull	.20	.50
153 Chris Pronger	.10	.25
154 Pierre Turgeon	.07	.20
155 Grant Fuhr	.15	.40
156 Geoff Courtnall	.07	.20
157 Pavol Demitra	.12	.30
158 Steve Duchesne	.07	.20
159 Maple Leafs logo	.05	.15
160 Fredrik Modin	.05	.15
161 Dimitri Yushkevich	.05	.15
162 Tie Domi	.07	.20
163 Igor Korolev	.05	.15
164 Mats Sundin	.10	.25
165 Felix Potvin	.15	.40
166 Sergei Berezin	.07	.20
167 Mighty Ducks logo	.05	.15
168 Guy Hebert	.07	.20
169 Teemu Selanne	.20	.50
170 Paul Kariya	.10	.25
171 Steve Rucchin	.05	.15
172 Tomas Sandstrom	.05	.15
173 Josef Marha	.05	.15
174 Ruslan Salei	.05	.15
175 Flames logo	.05	.15
176 Theo Fleury	.12	.30
177 Michael Nylander	.07	.20
178 German Titov	.05	.15
179 Rick Tabaracci	.05	.15
180 Cory Stillman	.05	.15
181 Jarome Iginla	.12	.30
182 Tommy Albelin	.05	.15
183 Avalanche logo	.05	.15
184 Patrick Roy	.25	.60
185 Peter Forsberg	.20	.50
186 Alexei Gusarov	.05	.15
187 Uwe Krupp	.05	.15
188 Valeri Kamensky	.05	.15
189 Joe Sakic	.20	.50
190 Sandis Ozolinsh	.05	.15
191 Oilers logo	.05	.15
192 Boris Mironov	.05	.15
193 Mats Lindgren	.05	.15
194 Andrei Kovalenko	.05	.15
195 Curtis Joseph	.12	.30
196 Roman Hamrlik	.05	.15
197 Doug Weight	.10	.25
198 Janne Niinimaa	.05	.15
199 Kings logo	.05	.15
200 Stephane Fiset	.07	.20
201 Jozef Stumpel	.05	.15
202 Aki Berg	.05	.15
203 Glen Murray	.07	.20
204 Vladimir Tsyplakov	.05	.15
205 Rob Blake	.10	.25
206 Mattias Norstrom	.05	.15
207 Sharks logo	.05	.15
208 Marcus Ragnarsson	.05	.15
209 Jeff Friesen	.05	.15
210 Owen Nolan	.10	.25
211 Mike Vernon	.07	.20
212 John MacLean	.05	.15
213 Andrei Zyuzin	.05	.15
214 Marco Sturm	.05	.15
215 Canucks logo	.05	.15
216 Pavel Bure	.10	.25
217 Alexander Mogilny	.07	.20
218 Arturs Irbe	.07	.20
219 Mark Messier	.20	.50
220 Markus Naslund	.10	.25
221 Mattias Ohlund	.05	.15
222 Jyrki Lumme	.05	.15
223 Dominik Hasek	.15	.40
224 Rob Blake	.10	.25
225 Sergei Samsonov	.07	.20
226 Jere Lehtinen	.07	.20
227 Ron Francis	.12	.30
228 Jamie McLennan	.07	.20

1999-00 Panini Stickers

1 NHL logo	.05	.15
2 NHLPA logo	.05	.15
3 Jaromir Jagr	.30	.75
4 Chris Drury	.07	.20
5 Al MacInnis	.12	.30
6 Dominik Hasek	.15	.40
7 Jere Lehtinen	.07	.20
8 Joe Nieuwendyk	.07	.20
9 Atlanta logo	.05	.15
10 Kelly Buchberger	.05	.15
11 Johan Garpenlov	.05	.15
12 Ray Ferraro	.05	.15
13 Nelson Emerson	.05	.15
14 Kevin Dean	.05	.15
15 Patrik Stefan	.10	.25
16 Per Svartvadet	.05	.15
17 Damian Rhodes	.05	.15
18 Andrew Brunette	.05	.15
19 Yannick Tremblay	.05	.15
20 Boston logo	.05	.15
21 Ray Bourque	.15	.40
22 Anson Carter	.07	.20
23 Byron Dafoe	.07	.20
24 Dave Andreychuk	.10	.25
25 Sergei Samsonov	.07	.20
26 Joe Thornton	.15	.40
27 Jason Allison	.07	.20
28 P.J. Axelsson	.05	.15
29 Kyle McLaren	.05	.15
30 Rob DiMaio	.05	.15
31 Buffalo logo	.05	.15
32 Dominik Hasek	.15	.40
33 Geoff Sanderson	.07	.20
34 Richard Smehlik	.05	.15
35 Alexei Zhitnik	.05	.15
36 Jason Woolley	.05	.15
37 Michael Peca	.07	.20
38 Miroslav Satan	.07	.20
39 Michal Grosek	.05	.15
40 Stu Barnes	.07	.20
41 Vaclav Varada	.05	.15
42 Carolina logo	.05	.15
43 Sami Kapanen	.05	.15
44 Ron Francis	.12	.30
45 Robert Kron	.05	.15
46 Andrei Kovalenko	.05	.15
47 Martin Gelinas	.05	.15
48 Glen Wesley	.05	.15
49 Kent Manderville	.05	.15
50 Gary Roberts	.05	.15
51 Tommy Westlund	.05	.15
52 Bates Battaglia	.05	.15
53 Florida logo	.05	.15
54 Sean Burke	.05	.15
55 Robert Svehla	.05	.15
56 Pavel Bure	.10	.25
57 Jaroslav Spacek	.05	.15
58 Radek Dvorak	.05	.15
59 Rob Niedermayer	.05	.15
60 Viktor Kozlov	.05	.15
61 Mark Parrish	.05	.15
62 Scott Mellanby	.05	.15
63 Oleg Kvasha	.05	.15
64 Montreal logo	.05	.15
65 Saku Koivu	.10	.25
66 Trevor Linden	.10	.25
67 Brian Savage	.05	.15
68 Martin Rucinsky	.05	.15
69 Scott Lachance	.05	.15
70 Scott Thornton	.05	.15
71 Mike Ribeiro	.05	.15
72 Jeff Hackett	.05	.15
73 Dainius Zubrus	.07	.20
74 Eric Weinrich	.05	.15
75 New Jersey logo	.05	.15
76 Scott Stevens	.10	.25
77 Sergei Nemchinov	.05	.15
78 Petr Sykora	.07	.20
79 Martin Brodeur	.25	.60
80 Claude Lemieux	.07	.20
81 Bobby Holik	.05	.15
82 Brian Rafalski	.10	.25
83 Scott Gomez	.07	.20
84 Jason Arnott	.07	.20
85 Ken Daneyko	.05	.15
86 NY Islanders logo	.05	.15
87 Jorgen Jonsson	.05	.15
88 Olli Jokinen	.07	.20
89 Zdeno Chara	.10	.25
90 Mats Lindgren	.05	.15
91 Felix Potvin	.15	.40
92 Kenny Jonsson	.05	.15
93 Tim Connolly	.05	.15
94 Mariusz Czerkawski	.05	.15
95 Gino Odjick	.05	.15
96 Brad Isbister	.05	.15
97 NY Rangers logo	.05	.15
98 Brian Leetch	.07	.20
99 Theo Fleury	.12	.30
100 Adam Graves	.07	.20
101 Mike Richter	.10	.25
102 Kim Johnsson	.05	.15
103 Kevin Stevens	.07	.20
104 Mathieu Schneider	.05	.15
105 Stephane Quintal	.05	.15
106 John MacLean	.07	.20
107 Kevin Hatcher	.05	.15
108 Ottawa logo	.05	.15
109 Janne Laukkanen	.05	.15
110 Andreas Dackell	.05	.15
111 Rob Zamuner	.05	.15
112 Daniel Alfredsson	.10	.25
113 Shawn McEachern	.05	.15
114 Marian Hossa	.10	.25
115 Magnus Arvedson	.05	.15
116 Radek Bonk	.05	.15
117 Ron Tugnutt	.07	.20
118 Igor Kravchuk	.05	.15
119 Philadelphia logo	.05	.15
120 Ulf Samuelsson	.05	.15
121 Eric Lindros	.15	.40
122 Mikael Renberg	.05	.15
123 Valeri Zelepukin	.05	.15
124 Rod Brind'Amour	.10	.25
125 John LeClair	.10	.25
126 Mark Recchi	.12	.30
127 Eric Desjardins	.07	.20
128 John Vanbiesbrouck	.10	.25
129 Simon Gagne	.10	.25
130 Pittsburgh logo	.05	.15
131 Jaromir Jagr	.30	.75
132 Jiri Slegr	.05	.15
133 Robert Lang	.05	.15
134 Alexei Kovalev	.07	.20
135 Darius Kasparaitis	.07	.20
136 Alexei Morozov	.07	.20
137 Tom Barrasso	.10	.25
138 Martin Straka	.05	.15
139 German Titov	.05	.15
140 Matthew Barnaby	.05	.15
141 Tampa Bay logo	.05	.15
142 Michael Nylander	.05	.15
143 Chris Gratton	.05	.15
144 Petr Svoboda	.07	.20
145 Stephane Richer	.07	.20
146 Pavel Kubina	.05	.15
147 Fredrik Modin	.05	.15
148 Vincent Lecavalier	.10	.25
149 Andrei Zyuzin	.05	.15
150 Dan Cloutier	.05	.15
151 Darcy Tucker	.05	.15
152 Toronto logo	.05	.15
153 Mats Sundin	.10	.25
154 Steve Thomas	.05	.15
155 Alexander Karpovtsev	.05	.15
156 Jonas Hoglund	.05	.15
157 Curtis Joseph	.12	.30
158 Yanic Perreault	.05	.15
159 Dimitri Khristich	.05	.15
160 Bryan Berard	.05	.15
161 Sergei Berezin	.05	.15
162 Tie Domi	.07	.20
163 Washington logo	.05	.15
164 Ulf Dahlen	.05	.15
165 Dmitri Mironov	.05	.15
166 Adam Oates	.10	.25
167 Peter Bondra	.10	.25
168 Joe Sacco	.05	.15
169 Sergei Gonchar	.05	.15
170 Calle Johansson	.05	.15
171 Chris Simon	.05	.15
172 Richard Zednik	.05	.15
173 Andrei Nikolishin	.05	.15
174 Anaheim logo	.05	.15
175 Paul Kariya	.10	.25
176 Teemu Selanne	.20	.50
177 Matt Cullen	.05	.15
178 Ted Donato	.05	.15
179 Niclas Havelid	.10	.25
180 Marty McInnis	.05	.15
181 Guy Hebert	.10	.25
182 Steve Rucchin	.05	.15
183 Oleg Tverdovsky	.05	.15
184 Pavel Trnka	.05	.15
185 Calgary logo	.05	.15
186 Grant Fuhr	.15	.40
187 Tommy Albelin	.05	.15
188 Steve Smith	.05	.15
189 Valeri Bure	.05	.15
190 Jarome Iginla	.12	.30
191 Cory Stillman	.05	.15
192 Derek Morris	.05	.15
193 Phil Housley	.07	.20
194 Marc Savard	.05	.15
195 Andrei Nazarov	.05	.15
196 Chicago logo	.05	.15
197 Bryan McCabe	.07	.20
198 Eric Daze	.07	.20
199 Anders Eriksson	.05	.15
200 Alexei Zhamnov	.05	.15
201 Doug Gilmour	.12	.30
202 Dean McAmmond	.05	.15
203 Tony Amonte	.07	.20
204 J-P Dumont	.07	.20
205 Wendel Clark	.15	.40
206 Bryan Muir	.05	.15
207 Colorado logo	.05	.15
208 Aelxei Gusarov	.05	.15
209 Peter Forsberg	.20	.50
210 Joe Sakic	.20	.50
211 Patrick Roy	.25	.60
212 Milan Hejduk	.07	.20
213 Sandis Ozolinsh	.05	.15
214 Adam Deadmarsh	.05	.15
215 Chris Drury	.07	.20
216 Alex Tanguay	.07	.20
217 Adam Foote	.07	.20
218 Dallas logo	.05	.15
219 Pavel Patera	.05	.15
220 Guy Carbonneau	.05	.15
221 Sergei Zubov	.07	.20
222 Joe Nieuwendyk	.07	.20
223 Darryl Sydor	.07	.20
224 Derian Hatcher	.07	.20
225 Brett Hull	.20	.50
226 Mike Modano	.15	.40
227 Ed Belfour	.10	.25
228 Jamie Langenbrunner	.05	.15
229 Detroit logo	.05	.15
230 Igor Larionov	.10	.25
231 Steve Yzerman	.25	.60
232 Sergei Fedorov	.15	.40
233 Nicklas Lidstrom	.10	.25
234 Brendan Shanahan	.10	.25
235 Larry Murphy	.07	.20
236 Slava Kozlov	.05	.15
237 Steve Duchesne	.05	.15
238 Chris Chelios	.10	.25
239 Chris Osgood	.10	.25
240 Edmonton logo	.05	.15
241 Tommy Salo	.07	.20
242 Tom Poti	.05	.15
243 Doug Weight	.10	.25
244 Ryan Smyth	.07	.20
245 Janne Niinimaa	.05	.15
246 Roman Hamrlik	.05	.15
247 Bill Guerin	.10	.25
248 Todd Marchant	.05	.15
249 Mike Grier	.05	.15
250 Bill Ranford	.07	.20
251 Los Angeles logo	.05	.15
252 Rob Blake	.10	.25
253 Mattias Norstrom	.05	.15
254 Frantisek Kaberle	.05	.15
255 Bryan Smolinski	.05	.15
256 Stephane Fiset	.07	.20
257 Zigmund Palffy	.10	.25
258 Luc Robitaille	.10	.25
259 Jozef Stumpel	.05	.15
260 Garry Galley	.05	.15
261 Glen Murray	.07	.20
262 Nashville logo	.05	.15
263 Ville Peltonen	.05	.15
264 Patric Kjellberg	.05	.15
265 Kimmo Timonen	.05	.15
266 Scott Walker	.05	.15
267 Dan Keczmer	.05	.15
268 David Legwand	.05	.15
269 Cliff Ronning	.05	.15
270 Sergei Krivokrasov	.05	.15
271 Tom Fitzgerald	.05	.15
272 Vitali Yachmenev	.05	.15
273 Phoenix logo	.05	.15
274 Mika Alatalo	.07	.20
275 Juha Ylonen	.05	.15
276 Keith Tkachuk	.10	.25
277 Travis Green	.05	.15
278 Stanislav Neckar	.05	.15
279 Jyrki Lumme	.05	.15
280 Teppo Numminen	.05	.15
281 Jeremy Roenick	.15	.40
282 Rick Tocchet	.07	.20
283 Shane Doan	.07	.20
284 St. Louis logo	.05	.15
285 Roman Turek	.07	.20
286 Chris Pronger	.10	.25
287 Al MacInnis	.12	.30
288 Scott Young	.05	.15
289 Marc Bergevin	.05	.15
290 Jochen Hecht	.15	.40
291 Craig Conroy	.05	.15
292 Pierre Turgeon	.07	.20
293 Pavol Demitra	.12	.30
294 Michal Handzus	.07	.20
295 San Jose logo	.05	.15
296 Jeff Friesen	.07	.20
297 Niklas Sundstrom	.05	.15
298 Mike Ricci	.05	.15
299 Gary Suter	.05	.15
300 Owen Nolan	.10	.25
301 Patrick Marleau	.10	.25
302 Marco Sturm	.05	.15
303 Vincent Damphousse	.07	.20
304 Brad Stuart	.07	.20
305 Mike Vernon	.07	.20
306 Vancouver logo	.05	.15
307 Mark Messier	.20	.50
308 Mattias Ohlund	.05	.15
309 Alexander Mogilny	.07	.20
310 Markus Naslund	.10	.25
311 Andrew Cassels	.05	.15
312 Adrian Aucoin	.05	.15
313 Steve Kariya	.10	.25
314 Peter Schaefer	.05	.15
315 Ed Jovanovski	.07	.20
316 Garth Snow	.07	.20
317 Jaromir Jagr	.30	.75
318 Teemu Selanne	.20	.50
319 Tony Amonte	.07	.20
320 Peter Forsberg	.20	.50
321 Paul Kariya	.10	.25
322 Alexei Yashin	.07	.20
323 Eric Lindros	.15	.40
324 Theo Fleury	.12	.30
325 John LeClair	.10	.25
326 Jason Allison	.07	.20
327 Joe Sakic	.20	.50
328 Pavol Demitra	.12	.30
329 Alexander Karpovtsev	.05	.15
330 Dimitri Khristich	.05	.15
331 Mark Messier	.20	.50
332 Brett Hull	.20	.50
333 Scott Pellerin	.05	.15
334 Brian Rolston	.07	.20
335 Miroslav Satan	.07	.20
336 Patrick Roy	.25	.60
337 John Vanbiesbrouck	.10	.25
338 Felix Potvin	.15	.40
339 Mike Dunham	.05	.15
340 Dominic Roussel	.05	.15
341 Al MacInnis	.12	.30
342 Ray Bourque	.15	.40
343 Adrian Aucoin	.05	.15
344 Sergei Gonchar	.05	.15
345 Phil Housley	.07	.20
346 Nicklas Lidstrom	.10	.25
347 Martin Brodeur	.25	.60
348 Ron Tugnutt	.07	.20
349 Dominik Hasek	.15	.40
350 Guy Hebert	.10	.25
351 Byron Dafoe	.07	.20
352 Curtis Joseph	.12	.30
353 Peter Schaefer	.05	.15
354 Scott Gomez	.07	.20
355 Alex Tanguay	.07	.20
356 Steve Kariya	.10	.25
357 Frantisek Kaberle	.05	.15
358 Brian Rafalski	.10	.25
359 Columbus logo	.05	.15
360 Minnesota logo	.05	.10

2000-01 Panini Stickers

1 NHL logo	.05	.15
2 NHLPA logo	.05	.15
3 Atlanta logo	.05	.15
4 Johan Garpenlov	.05	.15
5 Patrik Stefan	.07	.20
6 Andrew Brunette	.05	.15
7 Andreas Karlsson	.05	.15
8 Ray Ferraro	.05	.15
9 Petr Buzek	.05	.15
10 Boston logo	.05	.15
11 Sergei Samsonov	.07	.20
12 P.J. Axelsson	.05	.15
13 Anson Carter	.07	.20
14 Eric Nickulas	.05	.15
15 Mikko Eloranta	.05	.15
16 Joe Thornton	.15	.40
17 Buffalo logo	.05	.15
18 Dominik Hasek	.15	.40
19 Curtis Brown	.05	.15
20 Michael Peca	.07	.20
21 Vaclav Varada	.05	.15
22 Alexei Zhitnik	.07	.20
23 Miroslav Satan	.05	.15
24 Carolina logo	.05	.15
25 Sami Kapanen	.05	.15
26 Paul Coffey	.10	.25
27 Marek Malik	.05	.15
28 Andrei Kovalenko	.05	.15
29 Arturs Irbe	.07	.20
30 Ron Francis	.12	.30
31 Florida logo	.05	.15
32 Scott Mellanby	.05	.15
33 Viktor Kozlov	.07	.20
34 Jaroslav Spacek	.05	.15
35 Ray Whitney	.07	.20
36 Robert Svehla	.05	.15
37 Pavel Bure	.10	.25
38 Montreal logo	.05	.15
39 Saku Koivu	.10	.25
40 Trevor Linden	.10	.25
41 Karl Dykhuis	.05	.15
42 Sergei Zholtok	.05	.15
43 Martin Rucinsky	.05	.15
44 Dainius Zubrus	.05	.15
45 New Jersey logo	.05	.15
46 Alexander Mogilny	.07	.20
47 Petr Sykora	.07	.20
48 Martin Brodeur	.25	.60
49 Bobby Holik	.05	.15
50 Scott Gomez	.07	.20
51 Patrik Elias	.10	.25
52 NY Islanders logo	.05	.15
53 Brad Isbister	.05	.15
54 Mariusz Czerkawski	.05	.15
55 Mats Lindgren	.05	.15
56 Tim Connolly	.05	.15
57 Kenny Jonsson	.05	.15
58 Olli Jokinen	.07	.20
59 NY Rangers logo	.05	.15
60 Brian Leetch	.07	.20
61 Petr Nedved	.07	.20
62 Radek Dvorak	.07	.20
63 Valeri Kamensky	.05	.15
64 Theo Fleury	.12	.30
65 Jan Hlavac	.05	.15
66 Ottawa logo	.05	.15
67 Magnus Arvedson	.05	.15
68 Igor Kravchuk	.05	.15
69 Vaclav Prospal	.05	.15
70 Daniel Alfredsson	.10	.25
71 Shawn McEachern	.05	.15
72 Radek Bonk	.07	.20
73 Philadelphia logo	.05	.15
74 John LeClair	.10	.25
75 Eric Lindros	.15	.40
76 Mark Recchi	.12	.30
77 Daymond Langkow	.05	.15
78 Ulf Samuelsson	.05	.15
79 Valeri Zelepukin	.05	.15
80 Pittsburgh logo	.05	.15
81 Jaromir Jagr	.30	.75
82 Martin Straka	.07	.20
83 Alexei Morozov	.05	.15
84 Alexei Kovalev	.07	.20
85 Robert Lang	.05	.15
86 Darius Kasparaitis	.07	.20
87 Tampa Bay logo	.05	.15
88 Vincent Lecavalier	.10	.25
89 Fredrik Modin	.05	.15
90 Jaroslav Svejkovsky	.05	.15
91 Mike Johnson	.05	.15
92 Pavel Kubina	.05	.15
93 Petr Svoboda	.05	.15
94 Toronto logo	.05	.15
95 Mats Sundin	.10	.25
96 Darcy Tucker	.05	.15
97 Steve Thomas	.05	.15
98 Jonas Hoglund	.05	.15
99 Igor Korolev	.05	.15
100 Yanic Perreault	.05	.15
101 Washington logo	.05	.15
102 Peter Bondra	.10	.25
103 Sergei Gonchar	.05	.15
104 Joe Sacco	.05	.15
105 Ulf Dahlen	.05	.15
106 Adam Oates	.10	.25
107 Calle Johansson	.05	.15
108 Anaheim logo	.05	.15
109 Paul Kariya	.10	.25
110 Guy Hebert	.07	.20
111 Teemu Selanne	.20	.50
112 Ruslan Salei	.05	.15
113 Vitali Vishnevsky	.05	.15
114 Oleg Tverdovsky	.05	.15
115 Calgary logo	.05	.15
116 Valeri Bure	.07	.20
117 Jarome Iginla	.12	.30
118 Marc Savard	.05	.15
119 Andrei Nazarov	.05	.15
120 Phil Housley	.07	.20
121 Derek Morris	.05	.15
122 Chicago logo	.05	.15
123 Michael Nylander	.05	.15
124 Boris Mironov	.05	.15
125 Alexei Zhamnov	.07	.20
126 Tony Amonte	.07	.20
127 Michal Grosek	.05	.15
128 Steve Sullivan	.05	.15
129 Colorado logo	.05	.15
130 Peter Forsberg	.20	.50
131 Patrick Roy	.25	.60
132 Joe Sakic	.20	.50
133 Stephane Yelle	.05	.15
134 Sandis Ozolinsh	.05	.15
135 Milan Hejduk	.07	.20
136 Columbus logo	.05	.15
137 Geoff Sanderson	.07	.20
138 Ron Tugnutt	.07	.20
139 Radim Bicanek	.05	.15

140 Mattias Timander .05 .15
141 Krzsystof Oliwa .05 .15
142 Espen Knutsen .05 .15
143 Dallas logo .05 .15
144 Mike Modano .15 .40
145 Joe Nieuwendyk .07 .20
146 Sergei Zubov .07 .20
147 Richard Matvichuk .05 .15
148 Brett Hull .20 .50
149 Jamie Langenbrunner .07 .20
150 Detroit logo .05 .15
151 Sergei Fedorov .15 .40
152 Brendan Shanahan .10 .25
153 Nicklas Lidstrom .10 .25
154 Slava Kozlov .07 .20
155 Igor Larionov .10 .25
156 Steve Yzerman .25 .60
157 Edmonton logo .05 .15
158 Doug Weight .10 .25
159 German Titov .05 .15
160 Janne Niinimaa .05 .15
161 Roman Hamrlik .05 .15
162 Ryan Smyth .07 .20
163 Alexander Selivanov .05 .15
164 Los Angeles logo .05 .15
165 Rob Blake .10 .25
166 Luc Robitaille .10 .25
167 Ziggy Palffy .10 .25
168 Jozef Stumpel .05 .15
169 Glen Murray .07 .20
170 Mattias Norstrom .05 .15
171 Minnesota logo .05 .15
172 Curtis Leschyshyn .05 .15
173 Sergei Krivokrasov .05 .15
174 Antti Laaksonen .05 .15
175 Pavel Patera .05 .15
176 Sean O'Donnell .05 .15
177 Manny Fernandez .05 .15
178 Nashville logo .05 .15
179 Vitali Yachmenev .05 .15
180 Patric Kjellberg .05 .15
181 Ville Peltonen .05 .15
182 Cliff Ronning .05 .15
183 Greg Johnson .05 .15
184 Kimmo Timonen .05 .15
185 Phoenix logo .05 .15
186 Jeremy Roenick .15 .40
187 Jyrki Lumme .05 .15
188 Travis Green .05 .15
189 Teppo Numminen .05 .15
190 Keith Tkachuk .10 .25
191 Radoslav Suchy .05 .15
192 St, Louis logo .05 .15
193 Chris Pronger .10 .25
194 Pierre Turgeon .07 .20
195 Pavol Demitra .12 .30
196 Roman Turek .07 .20
197 Michal Handzus .05 .15
198 Stephane Richer .05 .15
199 San Jose logo .05 .15
200 Vincent Damphousse .07 .20
201 Niklas Sundstrom .05 .15
202 Stephane Matteau .05 .15
203 Marcus Ragnarsson .05 .15
204 Owen Nolan .10 .25
205 Alexander Korolyuk .05 .15
206 Vancouver logo .05 .15
207 Andrew Cassels .05 .15
208 Artem Chubarov .05 .15
208 Mark Messier .20 .50
210 Mattias Ohlund .05 .15
211 Todd Bertuzzi .07 .20
212 Markus Naslund .10 .25

2003-04 Panini Stickers

1 Slava Kozlov .07 .20
2 Marc Savard .05 .15
3 Pasi Nurminen .07 .20
4 Shawn McEachern .05 .15
5 Andy Sutton .05 .15
6 Dany Heatley .07 .20
7 Atlanta Thrashers Logo .05 .15
8 Ilya Kovalchuk .10 .25
9 Altanta Action part a .05 .15
10 Altanta Action part b .05 .15
11 Yannick Tremblay .05 .15
12 Randy Robitaille .05 .15
13 Patrik Stefan .05 .15
14 Sergei Samsonov .07 .20
15 Joe Thornton .15 .40
16 Nick Boynton .05 .15
17 Felix Potvin .15 .40
18 Glen Murray .07 .20
19 Mike Knuble .05 .15
20 Boston Bruins Logo .05 .15
21 Brian Rolston .07 .20
22 Patrice Bergeron .30 .75
23 Martin Lapointe .05 .15
24 Bruins Action Part a .05 .15
25 Bruins Action Part b .05 .15
26 Hal Gill .05 .15
27 Maxim Afinogenov .05 .15
28 Sabres Action Part a .05 .15
29 Sabres Action Part b .05 .15
30 Jean-Pierre Dumont .05 .15
31 Ales Kotalik .05 .15
32 Daniel Briere .10 .25
33 Buffalo Sabres Logo .05 .15
34 Tim Connolly .05 .15
35 Martin Biron .07 .20
36 Curtis Brown .05 .15
37 Chris Drury .07 .20
38 Miroslav Satan .07 .20
39 Alexei Zhitnik .07 .20
40 Rod Brind'Amour .10 .25
41 Kevin Weekes .07 .20
42 Radim Vrbata .05 .15
43 Eric Staal .30 .75
44 Kevyn Adams .05 .15
45 Bret Hedican .05 .15
46 Carolina Hurricanes Logo .05 .15
47 Eric Cole .05 .15
48 Hurricanes Action Part a .05 .15
49 Hurricanes Action Part b .05 .15
50 Josef Vasicek .05 .15
51 Ron Francis .12 .30
52 Jeff O'Neill .05 .15
53 Mathieu Biron .07 .20
54 Kristian Huselius .05 .15
55 Marcus Nilson .05 .15
56 Viktor Kozlov .05 .15
57 Jay Bouwmeester .05 .15
58 Nathan Horton .15 .40
59 Florida Panthers Logo .05 .15
60 Panthers Action Part a .05 .15
61 Panthers Action Part b .05 .15
62 Darcy Hordichuk .05 .15
63 Olli Jokinen .10 .25
64 Roberto Luongo .15 .40
65 Niklas Hagman .05 .15
66 Richard Zednik .05 .15
67 Saku Koivu .10 .25
68 Michael Ryder .07 .20
69 Patrice Brisebois .05 .15
70 Marcel Hossa .05 .15
71 Craig Rivet .05 .15
72 Montreal Canadiens Logo .05 .15
73 Canadiens Action Part a .05 .15
74 Canadiens Action Part b .05 .15
75 Chad Kilger .05 .15
76 Joe Juneau .05 .15
77 Jose Theodore .10 .25
78 Andrei Markov .10 .25
79 Patrik Elias .10 .25
80 Devils Action Part a .05 .15
81 Devils Action Part b .05 .15
82 Scott Gomez .07 .20
83 Scott Stevens .10 .25
84 Scott Niedermayer .10 .25
85 NewJersey Devils Logo .05 .15
86 Jamie Langenbrunner .07 .20
87 Brian Rafalski .07 .20
88 Martin Brodeur .25 .60
89 Brian Gionta .05 .15
90 John Madden .05 .15
91 Jeff Friesen .05 .15
92 Mariusz Czerkawski .05 .15
93 Rick DiPietro .07 .20
94 Alexei Yashin .07 .20
95 Adrian Aucoin .05 .15
96 Michael Peca .05 .15
97 Janne Niinimaa .05 .15
98 NewYork Islanders Logo .05 .15
99 Dave Scatchard .05 .15
100 Islanders Action Part a .05 .15
101 Islanders Action Part b .05 .15
102 Shawn Bates .05 .15
103 Jason Blake .05 .15
104 Roman Hamrlik .05 .15
105 Brian Leetch .07 .20
106 Alex Kovalev .05 .15
107 Tom Poti .05 .15
108 Matthew Barnaby .05 .15
109 Bobby Holik .05 .15
110 Mike Dunham .07 .20
111 NewYork Rangers Logo .05 .15
112 Mark Messier .20 .50
113 Rangers Action Part a .05 .15
114 Rangers Action Part b .05 .15
115 Petr Nedved .05 .15
116 Anson Carter .07 .20
117 Eric Lindros .15 .40
118 Daniel Alfredsson .10 .25
119 Senators Action Part a .05 .15
120 Senators Action Part b .05 .15
121 Marian Hossa .10 .25
122 Todd White .05 .15
123 Zdeno Chara .10 .25
124 Ottawa Senators Logo .05 .15
125 Radek Bonk .07 .20
126 Wade Redden .05 .15
127 Martin Havlat .10 .25
128 Chris Neil .05 .15
129 Patrick Lalime .07 .20
130 Jasson Spezza .05 .15
131 John Leclair .10 .25
132 Flyers Action Part a .05 .15
133 Flyers Action Part b .05 .15
134 Tony Amonte .07 .20
135 Jeff Hackett .07 .20
136 Mark Recchi .12 .30
137 Philadelphia Flyers Logo .05 .15
138 Simon Gagne .10 .25
139 Justin Williams .07 .20
140 Jeremy Roenick .15 .40
141 Keith Primeau .07 .20
142 Eric Desjardins .07 .20
143 Joni Pitkanen .10 .25
144 Mario Lemieux .40 1.00
145 Ryan Malone .12 .30
146 Marc-Andre Fleury .40 1.00
147 Konstantin Koltsov .05 .15
148 Rico Fata .05 .15
149 Ramzi Abid .05 .15
150 Pittsburgh Penguins Logo .05 .15
151 Penguins Action Part a .05 .15
152 Penguins Action Part b .05 .15
153 Aleksey Morozov .05 .15
154 Dick Tarnstrom .05 .15
155 Steve McKenna .05 .15
156 Brooks Orpik .05 .15
157 Fredrik Modin .05 .15
158 Vincent Lecavalier .10 .25
159 Dave Andreychuk .10 .25
160 Alexander Svitov .05 .15
161 Pavel Kubina .05 .15
162 Nikolai Khabibulin .10 .25
163 Tampa Bay Lightning Logo .05 .15
164 Martin St-louis .05 .15
165 Lightning Action Part a .05 .15
166 Lightning Action Part b .05 .15
167 Dan Boyle .05 .15
168 Brad Richards .10 .25
169 Cory Stillman .05 .15
170 Joe Nieuwendyk .07 .20
171 Tomas Kaberle .05 .15
172 Darcy Tucker .07 .20
173 Mats Sundin .10 .25
174 Bryan McCabe .05 .15
175 Ken Klee .05 .15
176 Toronto Maple Leafs Logo .05 .15
177 Gary Robers .05 .15
178 Maple Leafs Action Part a .05 .15
179 Maple Leafs Action Part b .05 .15
180 Alexander Mogilny .07 .20
181 Owen Nolan .10 .25
182 Ed Belfour .10 .25
183 Peter Bondra .10 .25
184 Jaromir Jagr .30 .75
185 Steve Eminger .05 .15
186 Capitals Action Part a .05 .15
187 Capitals Action Part b .05 .15
188 Olaf Kolzig .10 .25
189 Washington Capitals Logo .05 .15
190 Dainius Zubrus .05 .15
191 Sergei Gonchar .05 .15
192 Alexander Semin .20 .50
193 Brendan Witt .05 .15
194 Jeff Halpern .05 .15
195 Robert Lang .05 .15
196 Petr Sykora .07 .20
197 Jean-Sebastien Giguere .05 .15
198 Stanislav Chistov .05 .15
199 Mike Leclerc .05 .15
200 Vaclav Prospal .05 .15
201 Keith Carney .05 .15
202 Mighty Ducks of Anaheim Logo .05 .15
203 Sergei Fedorov .15 .40
204 Mighty Ducks Action Part a .05 .15
205 Mighty Ducks Action Part b .05 .15
206 Steve Rucchin .05 .15
207 Rob Niedermayer .07 .20
208 Sandis Ozolinsh .05 .15
209 Dean McAmmond .05 .15
210 Craig Conroy .05 .15
211 Chuck Kobasew .05 .15
212 Jarome Iginla .12 .30
213 Stephane Yelle .05 .15
214 Roman Turek .07 .20
215 Calgary Flames Logo .05 .15
216 Flames Action Part a .05 .15
217 Flames Action Part b .05 .15
218 Robyn Regehr .05 .15
219 Jordan Leopold .05 .15
220 Steven Reinprecht .05 .15
221 Denis Gauthier .05 .15
222 Alexei Zhamnov .07 .20
223 Mark Bell .05 .15
224 Bryan Berard .07 .20
225 Steve Sullivan .05 .15
226 Jocelyn Thibault .07 .20
227 Eric Daze .07 .20
228 Chicago BlackHawks Logo .05 .15
229 Blackhawks Action Part a .05 .15
230 Blackhawks Action Part b .05 .15
231 Ville Nieminen .05 .15
232 Tyler Arnason .05 .15
233 Kyle Calder .05 .15
234 Nathan Dempsey .05 .15
235 David Aebischer .07 .20
236 Rob Blake .10 .25
237 Adam Foote .05 .15
238 Teemu Selanne .20 .50
239 Peter Forsberg .20 .50
240 Alex Tanguay .07 .20
241 Colorado Avalanche Logo .05 .15
242 Joe Sakic .20 .50
243 Paul Kariya .10 .25
244 Milan Hejduk .07 .20
245 Derek Morris .05 .15
246 Avalanche Action Part a .05 .15
247 Avalanche Action Part b .05 .15
248 Darryl Sydor .05 .15
249 Blue Jackets Action Part a .05 .15
250 Blue Jackets Action Part b .05 .15
251 Espen Knutsen .05 .15
252 Rostislav Klesla .05 .15
253 Marc Denis .07 .20
254 Columbus Blue Jackets Logo .05 .15
255 Geoff Sanderson .05 .15
256 Jaroslav Spacek .05 .15
257 Rick Nash .10 .25
258 David Vyborny .05 .15
259 Jody Shelley .05 .15
260 Todd Marchant .05 .15
261 Sergei Zubov .07 .20
262 Stars Action Part a .05 .15
263 Stars Action Part b .05 .15
264 Jason Arnott .07 .20
265 Jere Lehtinen .07 .20
266 Teppo Numminen .05 .15
267 Dallas Stars Logo .05 .15
268 Stu Barnes .05 .15
269 Brenden Morrow .07 .20
270 Mike Modano .15 .40
271 Marty Turco .10 .25
272 Bill Guerin .10 .25
273 Niko Kapanen .05 .15
274 Steve Yzerman .25 .60
275 Ray Whitney .07 .20
276 Chris Chelios .10 .25
277 Brett Hull .20 .50
278 Pavel Datsyuk .15 .40
279 Brendan Shanahan .10 .25
280 Detroit Red Wings Logo .05 .15
281 Darren McCarty .05 .15
282 Dominik Hasek .15 .40
283 Kris Draper .05 .15
284 Red Wings Action Part a .05 .15
285 Red Wings Action Part b .05 .15
286 Nicklas Lidstrom .10 .25
287 George Laraque .05 .15
288 Eric Brewer .05 .15
289 Jason Smith .05 .15
290 Raffi Torres .05 .15
291 Oilers Action Part a .05 .15
292 Oilers Action Part b .05 .15
293 Edmonton Oilers Logo .05 .15
294 Mike York .05 .15
295 Fernando Pisani .05 .15
296 Ales Hemsky .10 .25
297 Ryan Smyth .07 .20
298 Shawn Horcoff .05 .15
299 Tommy Salo .07 .20
300 Roman Cechmanek .07 .20
301 Kings Action Part a .05 .15
302 Kings Action Part b .05 .15
303 Lubomir Visnovsky .05 .15
304 Adam Deadmarsh .05 .15
305 Aaron Miller .05 .15
306 Los Angeles Kings Logo .05 .15
307 Jason Allison .07 .20
308 Jaroslav Modry .05 .15
309 Mattias Norstrom .05 .15
310 Alexander Frolov .07 .20
311 Zigmund Palffy .10 .25
312 Ian Laperriere .05 .15
313 Sergei Zholtok .05 .15
314 Pierre-Marc Bouchard .10 .25
315 Dwayne Roloson .07 .20
316 Filip Kuba .05 .15
317 Andrew Brunette .05 .15
318 Marian Gaborik .10 .25
319 Minnesota Wild Logo .05 .15
320 Matt Johnson .05 .15
321 Wild Action Part a .05 .15
322 Wild Action Part b .05 .15
323 Willie Mitchell .05 .15
324 Darby Hendrickson .05 .15
325 Pascal Dupuis .05 .15
326 Adam Hall .05 .15
327 Predators Action Part a .05 .15
328 Predators Action Part b .05 .15
329 Kimmo Timonen .05 .15
330 Dan Hamhuis .07 .20
331 Marek Zidlicky .05 .15
332 Nashville Predators Logo .05 .15
333 Scott Walker .05 .15
334 David Legwand .07 .20
335 Scott Hartnell .05 .15
336 Tomas Vokoun .07 .20
337 Greg Johnson .05 .15
338 Jordin Tootoo .12 .30
339 Ossi Vaananen .05 .15
340 Ladislav Nagy .05 .15
341 Shane Doan .07 .20
342 Jan Hrdina .05 .15
343 Coyotes Action Part a .05 .15
344 Coyotes Action Part b .05 .15
345 Phoenix Coyotes Logo .05 .15
346 Sean Burke .05 .15
347 Mike Johnson .05 .15
348 Paul Mara .05 .15
349 Krys Kolanos .05 .15
350 Chris Gratton .05 .15
351 Daymond Langkow .05 .15
352 Chris Osgood .10 .25
353 Blues Action Part a .05 .15
354 Blues Action Part b .05 .15
355 Keith Tkachuk .10 .25
356 Doug Weight .10 .25
357 Chris Pronger .10 .25
358 St.Louis Blues Logo .05 .15
359 Al MacInnis .12 .30
360 Pavol Demitra .12 .30
361 Peter Sejna .07 .20
362 Dallas Drake .05 .15
363 Barret Jackman .05 .15
364 Petr Cajanek .05 .15
365 Vincent Damphousse .07 .20
366 Scott Thornton .07 .20
367 Evgeni Nabokov .07 .20
368 Mike Ricci .05 .15
369 Alyn McCauley .05 .15
370 Marco Sturm .05 .15
371 SanJose Sharks Logo .05 .15
372 Sharks Action Part a .05 .15
373 Sharks Action Part b .05 .15
374 Patrick Marleau .10 .25
375 Milan Michalek .12 .30
376 Jonathan Cheechoo .07 .20
377 Brad Stuart .05 .15
378 Todd Bertuzzi .10 .25
379 Canucks Action Part a .05 .15
380 Canucks Action Part b .05 .15
381 Brendan Morrison .07 .20
382 Markus Naslund .10 .25
383 Ed Jovanovski .07 .20
384 Vancouver Canucks Logo .05 .15
385 Mattias Ohlund .05 .15
386 Dan Cloutier .07 .20
387 Daniel Sedin .12 .30
388 Trevor Linden .10 .25
389 Matt Cooke .05 .15
390 Jason King .05 .15

2005-06 Panini Stickers

1 Sidney Crosby 3.00 8.00
2 Alexander Ovechkin 30.00 80.00
3 Mike Richards .20 .50
4 Dion Phaneuf .15 .40
5 Corey Perry .30 .75
6 Henrik Lundqvist .50 1.25
7 Ilya Kovalchuk .10 .25
8 Marian Hossa .10 .25
9 Bobby Holik .05 .15
10 Kari Lehtonen .07 .20
11 Marc Savard .05 .15
12 Jaroslav Modry .05 .15
13 Thrashers Team Logo .07 .20
14 Thrashers Action Shot A .07 .20
15 Thrashers Action Shot B .07 .20
16 Peter Bondra .10 .25
17 Slava Kozlov .05 .15
18 Patrik Stefan .05 .15
19 Joe Thornton .15 .40
20 Brian Leetch .07 .20
21 Sergei Samsonov .07 .20
22 Patrice Bergeron .12 .30
23 Glen Murray .07 .20
24 Bruins Team Logo .07 .20
25 Bruins Action Shot A .07 .20
26 Bruins Action Shot B .07 .20
27 Andrew Raycroft .07 .20
28 Jiri Slegr .05 .15
29 Shawn McEachern .05 .15
30 P.J. Axelsson .05 .15
31 Sabres Action Shot A .07 .20
32 Sabres Action Shot B .07 .20
33 Chris Drury .07 .20
34 Daniel Briere .10 .25
35 Ryan Miller .10 .25
36 Maxim Afinogenov .05 .15
37 J.P. Dumont .05 .15
38 Sabres Team Logo .07 .20
39 Jochen Hecht .05 .15
40 Thomas Vanek .20 .50
41 Andrew Peters .05 .15
42 Teppo Numminen .05 .15
43 Rod Brind'Amour .10 .25
44 Eric Staal .12 .30
45 Erik Cole .05 .15
46 Justin Williams .07 .20
47 Oleg Tverdovsky .05 .15
48 Hurricanes Action Shot A .07 .20
49 Hurricanes Action Shot B .07 .20
50 Hurricanes Team Logo .07 .20
51 Cory Stillman .07 .20
52 Ray Whitney .07 .20
53 Glen Wesley .05 .15
54 Martin Gerber .07 .20
55 Roberto Luongo .15 .40
56 Olli Jokinen .10 .25
57 Gary Roberts .05 .15
58 Joe Nieuwendyk .07 .20
59 Jay Bouwmeester .05 .15
60 Panthers Action Shot A .07 .20
61 Panthers Action Shot B .07 .20
62 Panthers Team Logo .07 .20
63 Nathan Horton .10 .25
64 Stephen Weiss .05 .15
65 Kristian Huselius .05 .15
66 Jozef Stumpel .05 .15
67 Canadiens Action Shot A .07 .20
68 Canadiens Action Shot B .07 .20
69 Jose Theodore .10 .25
70 Saku Koivu .10 .25
71 Alex Kovalev .07 .20
72 Michael Ryder .07 .20
73 Canadiens Team Logo .07 .20
74 Mike Ribeiro .05 .15
75 Sheldon Souray .05 .15
76 Richard Zednik .05 .15
77 Mathieu Dandenault .05 .15
78 Radek Bonk .05 .15
79 Martin Brodeur .25 .60
80 Scott Gomez .07 .20
81 Alexander Mogilny .07 .20
82 Vladimir Malakhov .05 .15
83 Brian Rafalski .07 .20
84 Jamie Langenbrunner .05 .15
85 Devils Team Logo .07 .20
86 Devils Action Shot A .07 .20
87 Devils Action Shot B .07 .20
88 Brian Gionta .05 .15
89 John Madden .05 .15
90 Zach Parise .25 .60
91 Alexei Yashin .07 .20
92 Rick DiPietro .07 .20
93 Miroslav Satan .07 .20
94 Jason Blake .05 .15
95 Mark Parrish .05 .15
96 Islanders Action Shot A .07 .20
97 Islanders Action Shot B .07 .20
98 Islanders Team Logo .07 .20
99 Trent Hunter .05 .15
100 Mike York .05 .15
101 Alexei Zhitnik .05 .15
102 Garth Snow .07 .20
103 Jaromir Jagr .30 .75
104 Michael Nylander .05 .15
105 Martin Straka .05 .15
106 Darius Kasparaitis .05 .15
107 Rangers Action Shot A .07 .20
108 Rangers Action Shot B .07 .20
109 Kevin Weekes .07 .20
110 Tom Poti .05 .15
111 Rangers Team Logo .07 .20
112 Martin Rucinsky .05 .15
113 Steve Rucchin .05 .15
114 Marek Malik .05 .15
115 Dany Heatley .07 .20
116 Jason Spezza .10 .25
117 Dominik Hasek .15 .40
118 Daniel Alfredsson .10 .25
119 Senators Action Shot A .07 .20
120 Senators Action Shot B .07 .20
121 Zdeno Chara .10 .25
122 Martin Havlat .10 .25
123 Senators Team Logo .07 .20
124 Mike Fisher .05 .15
125 Wade Redden .05 .15
126 Chris Phillips .05 .15
127 Flyers Action Shot A .07 .20
128 Flyers Action Shot B .07 .20
129 Peter Forsberg .20 .50
130 Keith Primeau .07 .20
131 Simon Gagne .10 .25
132 Robert Esche .07 .20
133 Joni Pitkanen .05 .15
134 Flyers Team Logo .07 .20
135 Derian Hatcher .05 .15
136 Mike Knuble .05 .15
137 Eric Desjardins .07 .20
138 Jeff Carter .15 .40
139 Sidney Crosby .07 .20
140 Mario Lemieux .40 1.00
141 Mark Recchi .12 .30
142 Zigmund Palffy .10 .25
143 Sergei Gonchar .05 .15
144 Penguins Action Shot A .07 .20
145 Penguins Action Shot B .07 .20
146 Penguins Team Logo .07 .20
147 Marc-Andre Fleury .20 .50
148 John LeClair .10 .25
149 Ryan Malone .05 .15
150 Dick Tarnstrom .05 .15
151 Vincent Lecavalier .10 .25
152 Brad Richards .10 .25
153 Martin St. Louis .10 .25
154 Lightning Action Shot A .07 .20
155 Lightning Action Shot B .07 .20
156 John Grahame .05 .15
157 Fredrik Modin .05 .15
158 Lightning Team Logo .07 .20
159 Ruslan Fedotenko .05 .15
160 Dan Boyle .05 .15
161 Pavel Kubina .05 .15
162 Dave Andreychuk .10 .25
163 Mats Sundin .10 .25
164 Ed Belfour .10 .25
165 Eric Lindros .15 .40
166 Darcy Tucker .07 .20
167 Jeff O'Neill .05 .15
168 Bryan McCabe .05 .15
169 Maple Leafs Team Logo .07 .20
170 Maple Leafs Action Shot A .07 .20
171 Maple Leafs Action Shot B .07 .20
172 Tie Domi .07 .20
173 Tomas Kaberle .05 .15
174 Matt Stajan .05 .15
175 Alexander Ovechkin 25.00 60.00
176 Olaf Kolzig .10 .25
177 Brian Sutherby .05 .15
178 Jeff Halpern .05 .15
179 Danius Zubrus .05 .15
180 Capitals Action Shot A .07 .20
181 Capitals Action Shot B .07 .20
182 Capitals Team Logo .07 .20
183 Brendan Witt .05 .15
184 Andrew Cassels .05 .15
185 Jeff Friesen .05 .15
186 Steve Eminger .05 .15
187 Jean Sebastien Giguere .10 .25
188 Ruslan Salei .05 .15
189 Scott Niedermayer .10 .25
190 Rob Niedermayer .07 .20
191 Sandis Ozolinsh .05 .15
192 Teemu Selanne .20 .50
193 Mighty Ducks Team Logo .07 .20
194 Mighty Ducks Action Shot A .07 .20
195 Mighty Ducks Action Shot B .07 .20
196 Joffrey Lupul .05 .15
197 Petr Sykora .07 .20
198 Ryan Getzlaf .25 .60
199 Jarome Iginla .12 .30
200 Miikka Kiprusoff .10 .25
201 Shean Donovan .05 .15
202 Roman Hamrlik .05 .15
203 Daymond Langkow .05 .15
204 Steven Reinprecht .05 .15
205 Flames Team Logo .07 .20
206 Flames Action Shot A .07 .20
207 Flames Action Shot B .07 .20
208 Chuck Kobasew .05 .15
209 Jordan Leopold .05 .15
210 Tony Amonte .07 .20
211 Tuomo Ruutu .10 .25
212 Nikolai Khabibulin .10 .25
213 Jassen Cullimore .05 .15
214 Adrian Aucoin .05 .15
215 Tyler Arnason .05 .15
216 Blackhawks Team Logo .07 .20
217 Matthew Barnaby .05 .15
218 Blackhawks Action Shot A .07 .20
219 Blackhawks Action Shot B .07 .20
220 Mark Bell .05 .15
221 Kyle Calder .05 .15
222 Martin Lapointe .05 .15
223 Joe Sakic .20 .50
224 Milan Hejduk .07 .20
225 Rob Blake .10 .25
226 Alex Tanguay .10 .25
227 David Aebischer .07 .20
228 John-Michael Liles .05 .15
229 Avalanche Team Logo .07 .20
230 Avalanche Action Shot A .07 .20
231 Avalanche Action Shot B .07 .20
232 Pierre Turgeon .07 .20
233 Andrew Brunette .05 .15
234 Steve Konowalchuk .05 .15
235 Rick Nash .10 .25
236 Adam Foote .05 .15
237 Marc Denis .07 .20
238 Nikolai Zherdev .05 .15
239 Dan Fritsche .05 .15
240 Manny Malhotra .07 .20
241 Blue Jackets Team Logo .07 .20
242 Blue Jackets Action Shot A .07 .20
243 Blue Jackets Action Shot B .07 .20
244 Bryan Berard .05 .15
245 David Vyborny .05 .15
246 Sergei Federov .15 .40
247 Mike Modano .15 .40
248 Bill Guerin .10 .25
249 Sergei Zubov .07 .20
250 Jere Lehtinen .07 .20
251 Jason Arnott .07 .20
252 Stars Team Logo .07 .20
253 Brenden Morrow .07 .20
254 Stars Action Shot A .07 .20
255 Stars Action Shot B .07 .20
256 Stu Barnes .05 .15
257 Antti Miettinen .05 .15
258 Marty Turco .10 .25
259 Steve Yzerman .25 .60
260 Brendan Shanahan .10 .25
261 Nicklas Lidstrom .10 .25
262 Kris Draper .12 .30
263 Robert Lang .05 .15
264 Pavel Datsyuk .15 .40
265 Red Wings Team Logo .07 .20
266 Red Wings Action Shot A .07 .20
267 Red Wings Action Shot B .07 .20
268 Chris Osgood .10 .25
269 Chris Chelios .10 .25
270 Henrik Zetterberg .12 .30
271 Ryan Smyth .07 .20
272 Chris Pronger .10 .25
273 Michael Peca .07 .20
274 Ty Conklin .07 .20
275 Georges Laraque .07 .20
276 Oilers Action Shot A .07 .20
277 Oilers Action Shot B .07 .20
278 Oilers Team Logo .07 .20
279 Ales Hemsky .07 .20
280 Jason Smith .07 .20
281 Steve Staios .05 .15
282 Radek Dvorak .05 .15
283 Luc Robitaille .10 .25
284 Jeremy Roenick .15 .40
285 Alexander Frolov .05 .15
286 Pavol Demitra .12 .30
287 Mattias Norstrom .05 .15
288 Kings Team Logo .07 .20
289 Kings Action Shot A .07 .20
290 Kings Action Shot B .07 .20
291 Lubomir Visnovsky .05 .15
292 Eric Belanger .05 .15
293 Mathieu Garon .07 .20
294 Mike Cammalleri .10 .25
295 Marian Gaborik .10 .25
296 Dwayne Roloson .07 .20
297 Marc Chouinard .05 .15
298 Brian Rolston .07 .20
299 Pierre-Marc Bouchard .10 .25
300 Willie Mitchell .05 .15
301 Wild Team Logo .07 .20
302 Wild Action Shot A .07 .20
303 Wild Action Shot B .07 .20
304 Manny Fernandez .05 .15
305 Alexandre Daigle .05 .15
306 Wes Walz .05 .15
307 Paul Kariya .10 .25
308 Steve Sullivan .05 .15
309 Tomas Vokoun .07 .20
310 Kimmo Timonen .05 .15
311 Marek Zidlicky .05 .15
312 Dan Hamuis .07 .20
313 David Legwand .07 .20
314 Predators Team Logo .07 .20
315 Scott Walker .05 .15
316 Predators Action Shot A .07 .20
317 Predators Action Shot B .07 .20
318 Greg Johnson .05 .15
319 Shane Doan .07 .20
320 Geoff Sanderson .05 .15
321 Mike Comrie .07 .20
322 Curtis Joseph .12 .30
323 Mike Ricci .05 .15
324 Paul Mara .05 .15
325 Coyotes Team Logo .07 .20
326 Coyotes Action Shot A .07 .20
327 Coyotes Action Shot B .07 .20
328 Oleg Saprykin .05 .15
329 Petr Nedved .05 .15
330 Derek Morris .05 .15
331 Blues Action Shot A .07 .20
332 Blues Action Shot B .07 .20
333 Doug Weight .10 .25
334 Keith Tkachuk .10 .25
335 Barret Jackman .05 .15
336 Eric Brewer .05 .15
337 Patrick Lalime .07 .20
338 Blues Team Logo .07 .20
339 Dallas Drake .05 .15
340 Scott Young .05 .15
341 Petr Cajanek .05 .15
342 Bryce Salvador .05 .15
343 Evgeni Nabokov .07 .20
344 Patrick Marleau .10 .25
345 Marco Sturm .05 .15
346 Brad Stuart .05 .15
347 Jonathan Cheechoo .07 .20
348 Scott Hannan .05 .15
349 Sharks Team Logo .07 .20
350 Sharks Action Shot A .07 .20
351 Sharks Action Shot B .07 .20
352 Alyn McCauley .05 .15
353 Niko Dimotrakos .05 .15
354 Wayne Primeau .05 .15
355 Markus Naslund .10 .25
356 Brendan Morrison .05 .15
357 Ed Jovanovski .07 .20
358 Todd Bertuzzi .10 .25
359 Dan Cloutier .07 .20
360 Canucks Action Shot A .07 .20
361 Canucks Action Shot B .07 .20
362 Canucks Team Logo .07 .20
363 Trevor Linden .10 .25
364 Daniel Sedin .12 .30
365 Henrik Sedin .12 .30
366 Mattias Ohlund .05 .15
367 Action Shot 1A .07 .20
368 Action Shot 1B .07 .20
369 Action Shot 2A .07 .20
370 Action Shot 2B .07 .20
371 Action Shot 3A .07 .20
372 Action Shot 3B .07 .20
373 Action Shot 4A .07 .20
374 Action Shot 4B .07 .20
375 Action Shot 5A .07 .20
376 Action Shot 5B .07 .20
377 Action Shot 6A .07 .20
378 Action Shot 6B .07 .20
379 Action Shot 7A .07 .20
380 Action Shot 7B .07 .20
381 Action Shot 8A .07 .20
382 Action Shot 8B .07 .20
383 Action Shot 9A .07 .20
384 Action Shot 9B .07 .20
385 Action Shot 10A .07 .20
386 Action Shot 10B .07 .20
387 Action Shot 11A .07 .20
388 Action Shot 11B .07 .20
389 Action Shot 12A .07 .20
390 Action Shot 12B .07 .20

2006-07 Panini Stickers

1 Atlanta Thrashers Puzzle Piece .05 .15
2 Atlanta Thrashers Puzzle Piece .05 .15
3 Atlanta Thrashers Team Logo .05 .15
4 Bobby Holik .05 .15
5 Marian Hossa .10 .25
6 Ilya Kovalchuk .10 .25
7 Vyacheslav Kozlov .05 .15
8 Scott Mellanby .05 .15
9 Kari Lehtonen .07 .20
10 Niclas Havelid .05 .15
11 Steve Rucchin .05 .15
12 Andy Sutton .05 .15
13 Boston Bruins Puzzle Piece .05 .15
14 Boston Bruins Puzzle Piece .05 .15
15 Boston Bruins Team Logo .05 .15
16 P.J. Axelsson .05 .15
17 Patrice Bergeron .12 .30
18 Brad Boyes .05 .15
19 Glen Murray .07 .20
20 Marc Savard .05 .15
21 Marco Sturm .05 .15
22 Zdeno Chara .10 .25
23 Brad Stuart .05 .15
24 Paul Mara .05 .15
25 Buffalo Sabres Puzzle Piece .05 .15
26 Buffalo Sabres Puzzle Piece .05 .15
27 Buffalo Sabres Team Logo .05 .15
28 Ryan Miller .10 .25
29 Chris Drury .07 .20
30 Maxim Afinogenov .05 .15
31 Ales Kotalik .05 .15
32 Daniel Briere .10 .25
33 Thomas Vanek .07 .20

34 Derek Roy .05 .15
35 Brian Campbell .07 .20
36 Tim Connolly .05 .15
37 Carolina Hurricanes Puzzle Piece .05 .15
38 Carolina Hurricanes Puzzle Piece .05 .15
39 Carolina Hurricanes Team Logo .05 .15
40 Cam Ward .10 .25
41 Rod Brind'Amour .10 .25
42 Erik Cole .05 .15
43 Eric Staal .12 .30
44 Cory Stillman .05 .15
45 Ray Whitney .07 .20
46 Justin Williams .07 .20
47 Frantisek Kaberle .05 .15
48 Bret Hedican .05 .15
49 Florida Panthers Puzzle Piece .05 .15
50 Florida Panthers Puzzle Piece .05 .15
51 Florida Panthers Team Logo .05 .15
52 Todd Bertuzzi .10 .25
53 Nathan Horton .10 .25
54 Olli Jokinen .10 .25
55 Joe Nieuwendyk .07 .20
56 Rostislav Olesz .05 .15
57 Gary Roberts .05 .15
58 Josef Stumpel .05 .15
59 Jay Bouwmeester .05 .15
60 Ed Belfour .10 .25
61 Montreal Canadiens Puzzle Piece .05 .15
62 Montreal Canadiens Puzzle Piece .05 .15
63 Montreal Canadiens Team Logo .05 .15
64 Saku Koivu .10 .25
65 Alexei Kovalev .07 .20
66 Chris Higgins .05 .15
67 Mike Ribeiro .05 .15
68 Michael Ryder .05 .15
69 Sergei Samsonov .07 .20
70 Andrei Markov .10 .25
71 Sheldon Souray .05 .15
72 Cristobal Huet .07 .20
73 New Jersey Devils Puzzle Piece .05 .15
74 New Jersey Devils Puzzle Piece .05 .15
75 New Jersey Devils Team Logo .05 .15
76 Martin Brodeur .25 .60
77 Brian Gionta .05 .15
78 Patrik Elias .10 .25
79 Scott Gomez .07 .20
80 Brian Rafalski .07 .20
81 Colin White .05 .15
82 Jamie Langenbrunner .05 .15
83 John Madden .05 .15
84 Zach Parise .10 .25
85 New York Islanders Puzzle Piece .05 .15
86 New York Islanders Puzzle Piece .05 .15
87 New York Islanders Team Logo .05 .15
88 Rick DiPietro .07 .20
89 Miroslav Satan .07 .20
90 Alexei Yashin .07 .20
91 Mike York .05 .15
92 Jason Blake .05 .15
93 Brendan Witt .05 .15
94 Alexei Zhitnik .05 .15
95 Mike Sillinger .05 .15
96 Trent Hunter .05 .15
97 New York Rangers Puzzle Piece .05 .15
98 New York Rangers Puzzle Piece .05 .15
99 New York Rangers Team Logo .05 .15
100 Jaromir Jagr .30 .75
101 Brendan Shanahan .10 .25
102 Henrik Lundqvist .25 .60
103 Marek Malik .05 .15
104 Michal Rozsival .05 .15
105 Petr Prucha .07 .20
106 Martin Straka .05 .15
107 Michael Nylander .05 .15
108 Darius Kasparaitis .05 .15
109 Ottawa Senators Puzzle Piece .05 .15
110 Ottawa Senators Puzzle Piece .05 .15
111 Ottawa Senators Team Logo .05 .15
112 Daniel Alfredsson .10 .25
113 Jason Spezza .10 .25
114 Dany Heatley .07 .20
115 Mike Fisher .05 .15
116 Patrick Eaves .05 .15
117 Chris Phillips .05 .15
118 Wade Redden .05 .15
119 Martin Gerber .07 .20
120 Ray Emery .07 .20
121 Philadelphia Flyers Puzzle Piece .05 .15
122 Philadelphia Flyers Puzzle Piece .05 .15
123 Philadelphia Flyers Team Logo .05 .15
124 Peter Forsberg .20 .50
125 Kyle Calder .05 .15
126 Simon Gagne .10 .25
127 Petr Nedved .05 .15
128 Derian Hatcher .05 .15
129 Joni Pitkanen .05 .15
130 Robert Esche .07 .20
131 Mike Knuble .05 .15
132 Jeff Carter .07 .20
133 Pittsburgh Penguins Puzzle Piece .05 .15
134 Pittsburgh Penguins Puzzle Piece .05 .15
135 Pittsburgh Penguins Team Logo .05 .15
136 Sidney Crosby 1.00 2.50
137 Mark Recchi .12 .30
138 Marc-Andre Fleury .20 .50
139 Sergei Gonchar .05 .15
140 Ronald Petrovicky .05 .15
141 John LeClair .10 .25
142 Ryan Malone .05 .15
143 Ryan Whitney .07 .20
144 Nils Ekman .05 .15
145 Tampa Bay Lightning Puzzle Piece .05 .15
146 Tampa Bay Lightning Puzzle Piece .05 .15
147 Tampa Bay Lightning Team Logo .05 .15
148 Marc Denis .07 .20
149 Vincent Lecavalier .10 .25
150 Brad Richards .10 .25
151 Vaclav Prospal .05 .15
152 Dan Boyle .05 .15
153 Martin St. Louis .10 .25
154 Filip Kuba .05 .15
155 Ruslan Fedotenko .05 .15
156 Cory Sarich .05 .15
157 Toronto Maple Leafs Puzzle Piece .05 .15
158 Toronto Maple Leafs Puzzle Piece .05 .15
159 Toronto Maple Leafs Team Logo .05 .15
160 Andrew Raycroft .07 .20
161 Mats Sundin .10 .25
162 Pavel Kubina .05 .15
163 Michael Peca .07 .20
164 Darcy Tucker .07 .20
165 Tomas Kaberle .05 .15
166 Bryan McCabe .05 .15
167 Jeff O'Neill .05 .15
168 Alexander Steen .05 .15
169 Washington Capitals Puzzle Piece .05 .15
170 Washington Capitals Puzzle Piece .05 .15
171 Washington Capitals Team Logo .05 .15
172 Alexander Ovechkin .40 1.00
173 Richard Zednik .05 .15
174 Dainius Zubrus .05 .15
175 Olaf Kolzig .10 .25
176 Chris Clark .05 .15
177 Matt Pettinger .07 .20
178 Ben Clymer .05 .15
179 Brian Sutherby .05 .15
180 Brian Pothier .05 .15
181 Anaheim Ducks Puzzle Piece .05 .15
182 Anaheim Ducks Puzzle Piece .05 .15
183 Anaheim Ducks Team Logo .05 .15
184 Chris Pronger .10 .25
185 Scott Niedermayer .10 .25
186 Jean-Sebastien Giguere .10 .25
187 Teemu Selanne .20 .50
188 Andy McDonald .07 .20
189 Rob Niedermayer .07 .20
190 Ilya Bryzgalov .10 .25
191 Ryan Getzlaf .10 .25
192 Chris Kunitz .10 .25
193 Calgary Flames Puzzle Piece .05 .15
194 Calgary Flames Puzzle Piece .05 .15
195 Calgary Flames Team Logo .05 .15
196 Jarome Iginla .12 .30
197 Miikka Kiprusoff .10 .25
198 Alex Tanguay .05 .15
199 Dion Phaneuf .07 .20
200 Tony Amonte .07 .20
201 Robyn Regehr .05 .15
202 Rhett Warrener .05 .15
203 Daymond Langkow .05 .15
204 Kristian Huselius .05 .15
205 Chicago Blackhawks Puzzle Piece .05 .15
206 Chicago Blackhawks Puzzle Piece .05 .15
207 Chicago Blackhawks Team Logo .05 .15
208 Nikolai Khabibulin .10 .25
209 Martin Havlat .05 .15
210 Tuomo Ruutu .10 .25
211 Michal Handzus .07 .20
212 Radim Vrbata .05 .15
213 Bryan Smolinski .05 .15
214 Patrick Sharp .10 .25
215 Adrian Aucoin .05 .15
216 Martin Lapointe .05 .15
217 Colorado Avalanche Puzzle Piece .05 .15
218 Colorado Avalanche Puzzle Piece .05 .15
219 Colorado Avalanche Team Logo .05 .15
220 Jose Theodore .10 .25
221 Joe Sakic .20 .50
222 Milan Hejduk .07 .20
223 Marek Svatos .05 .15
224 Pierre Turgeon .07 .20
225 Andrew Brunette .05 .15
226 Steve Konowalchuk .05 .15
227 John-Michael Liles .05 .15
228 Ian Laperriere .05 .15
229 Columbus Blue Jackets Puzzle Piece .05 .15
230 Columbus Blue Jackets Puzzle Piece .05 .15
231 Columbus Blue Jackets Team Logo .05 .15
232 Rick Nash .10 .25
233 Sergei Fedorov .15 .40
234 Fredrik Modin .05 .15
235 David Vyborny .05 .15
236 Adam Foote .05 .15
237 Rostislav Klesla .05 .15
238 Pascal Leclaire .07 .20
239 Nikolai Zherdev .05 .15
240 Jason Chimera .05 .15
241 Dallas Stars Puzzle Piece .05 .15
242 Dallas Stars Puzzle Piece .05 .15
243 Dallas Stars Team Logo .05 .15
244 Marty Turco .10 .25
245 Mike Modano .15 .40
246 Eric Lindros .15 .40
247 Sergei Zubov .07 .20
248 Jere Lehtinen .05 .15
249 Brenden Morrow .07 .20
250 Jaroslav Modry .05 .15
251 Stu Barnes .05 .15
252 Phillipe Boucher .05 .15
253 Detroit Red Wings Puzzle Piece .05 .15
254 Detroit Red Wings Puzzle Piece .05 .15
255 Detroit Red Wings Team Logo .05 .15
256 Dominik Hasek .15 .40
257 Pavel Datsyuk .15 .40
258 Chris Chelios .10 .25
259 Nicklas Lidstrom .10 .25
260 Henrik Zetterberg .12 .30
261 Robert Lang .05 .15
262 Mathieu Schneider .05 .15
263 Kris Draper .05 .15
264 Tomas Holmstrom .07 .20
265 Edmonton Oilers Puzzle Piece .05 .15
266 Edmonton Oilers Puzzle Piece .05 .15
267 Edmonton Oilers Team Logo .05 .15
268 Dwayne Roloson .07 .20
269 Ryan Smyth .07 .20
270 Jason Smith .05 .15
271 Joffrey Lupul .05 .15
272 Ales Hemsky .07 .20
273 Fernando Pisani .05 .15
274 Raffi Torres .05 .15
275 Shawn Horcoff .05 .15
276 Jarret Stoll .07 .20
277 Los Angeles Kings Puzzle Piece .05 .15
278 Los Angeles Kings Puzzle Piece .05 .15
279 Los Angeles Kings Team Logo .05 .15
280 Alexander Frolov .05 .15
281 Rob Blake .10 .25
282 Dan Cloutier .07 .20
283 Mattias Norstrom .05 .15
284 Lubomir Visnovsky .05 .15
285 Craig Conroy .05 .15
286 Sean Avery .05 .15
287 Mike Cammalleri .05 .15
288 Dustin Brown .10 .25
289 Minnesota Wild Puzzle Piece .05 .15
290 Minnesota Wild Puzzle Piece .05 .15
291 Minnesota Wild Team Logo .05 .15
292 Manny Fernandez .05 .15
293 Marian Gaborik .10 .25
294 Mark Parrish .05 .15
295 Pavol Demitra .12 .30
296 Brian Rolston .07 .20
297 Wes Walz .05 .15
298 Pierre-Marc Bouchard .10 .25
299 Todd White .05 .15
300 Martin Skoula .05 .15
301 Nashville Predators Puzzle Piece .05 .15
302 Nashville Predators Puzzle Piece .05 .15
303 Nashville Predators Team Logo .05 .15
304 Paul Kariya .10 .25
305 Jason Arnott .07 .20
306 Steve Sullivan .05 .15
307 Tomas Vokoun .07 .20
308 Marek Zidlicky .05 .15
309 David Legwand .07 .20
310 Martin Erat .05 .15
311 Kimmo Timonen .05 .15
312 Scott Hartnell .05 .15
313 Phoenix Coyotes Puzzle Piece .05 .15
314 Phoenix Coyotes Puzzle Piece .05 .15
315 Phoenix Coyotes Team Logo .05 .15
316 Ed Jovanovski .07 .20
317 Jeremy Roenick .15 .40
318 Curtis Joseph .12 .30
319 Shane Doan .07 .20
320 Mike Comrie .07 .20
321 Ladislav Nagy .05 .15
322 Nick Boynton .05 .15
323 Derek Morris .05 .15
324 Steve Reinprecht .05 .15
325 San Jose Sharks Puzzle Piece .05 .15
326 San Jose Sharks Puzzle Piece .05 .15
327 San Jose Sharks Team Logo .05 .15
328 Vesa Toskala .07 .20
329 Evgeni Nabokov .07 .20
330 Joe Thornton .15 .40
331 Jonathan Cheechoo .07 .20
332 Mark Bell .05 .15
333 Patrick Marleau .10 .25
334 Steve Bernier .05 .15
335 Scott Hannan .05 .15
336 Milan Michalek .05 .15
337 St. Louis Blues Puzzle Piece .05 .15
338 St. Louis Blues Puzzle Piece .05 .15
339 St. Louis Blues Team Logo .05 .15
340 Doug Weight .10 .25
341 Bill Guerin .10 .25
342 Martin Rucinsky .05 .15
343 Jay McKee .05 .15
344 Barret Jackman .05 .15
345 Eric Brewer .05 .15
346 Keith Tkachuk .10 .25
347 Manny Legace .07 .20
348 Petr Cajanek .05 .15
349 Vancouver Canucks Puzzle Piece .05 .15
350 Vancouver Canucks Puzzle Piece .05 .15
351 Vancouver Canucks Team Logo .05 .15
352 Roberto Luongo .15 .40
353 Jan Bulis .05 .15
354 Markus Naslund .10 .25
355 Brendan Morrison .05 .15
356 Daniel Sedin .12 .30
357 Henrik Sedin .12 .30
358 Mattias Ohlund .05 .15
359 Sami Salo .05 .15
360 Matt Cooke .05 .15

2008-09 Panini Stickers

1 Atlanta Thrashers Logo .05 .15
2 Kari Lehtonen .12 .30
3 Vyacheslav Kozlov .05 .15
4 Colby Armstrong .05 .15
5 Garnet Exelby .05 .15
6 Niclas Havelid .05 .15
7 Ilya Kovalchuk .10 .25
8 Todd White .05 .15
9 Tobias Enstrom .05 .15
10 Boston Bruins Logo .05 .15
11 Tim Thomas .10 .25
12 Zdeno Chara .10 .25
13 Patrice Bergeron .12 .30
14 Phil Kessel .10 .25
15 Dennis Wideman .05 .15
16 Marc Savard .05 .15
17 Marco Sturm .05 .15
18 Milan Lucic .15 .40
19 Buffalo Sabres Logo .05 .15
20 Ryan Miller .10 .25
21 Jason Pominville .05 .15
22 Derek Roy .05 .15
23 Tim Connolly .05 .15
24 Jaroslav Spacek .05 .15
25 Thomas Vanek .07 .20
26 Henrik Tallinder .05 .15
27 Drew Stafford .05 .15
28 Carolina Hurricanes Logo .05 .15
29 Cam Ward .10 .25
30 Frantisek Kaberle .05 .15
31 Joni Pitkanen .05 .15
32 Rod Brind'Amour .10 .25
33 Justin Williams .07 .20
34 Eric Staal .12 .30
35 Ray Whitney .07 .20
36 Patrick Eaves .05 .15
37 Florida Panthers Logo .05 .15
38 Tomas Vokoun .07 .20
39 Stephen Weiss .05 .15
40 Rostislav Olesz .05 .15
41 David Booth .05 .15
42 Jay Bouwmeester .05 .15
43 Nathan Horton .07 .20
44 Bryan Allen .05 .15
45 Shawn Matthias .10 .25
46 Montreal Canadiens Logo .05 .15
47 Carey Price .20 .50
48 Saku Koivu .10 .25
49 Andrei Markov .10 .25
50 Tomas Plekanec .05 .15
51 Christopher Higgins .05 .15
52 Alex Kovalev .07 .20
53 Mike Komisarek .05 .15
54 Andrei Kostitsyn .07 .20
55 New Jersey Devils Logo .05 .15
56 Martin Brodeur .25 .60
57 Paul Martin .05 .15
58 John Madden .05 .15
59 Patrik Elias .10 .25
60 Brian Gionta .05 .15
61 Zach Parise .10 .25
62 John Oduya .07 .20
63 Travis Zajac .05 .15
64 New York Islanders Logo .05 .15
65 Rick DiPietro .07 .20
66 Bill Guerin .10 .25
67 Chris Campoli .05 .15
68 Brendan Witt .05 .15
69 Mike Sillinger .05 .15
70 Mike Comrie .07 .20
71 Trent Hunter .05 .15
72 Kyle Okposo .12 .30
73 New York Rangers Logo .05 .15
74 Henrik Lundqvist .25 .60
75 Chris Drury .07 .20
76 Markus Naslund .10 .25
77 Marc Staal .05 .15
78 Michal Rozsival .05 .15
79 Scott Gomez .07 .20
80 Colton Orr .05 .15
81 Brandon Dubinsky .05 .15
82 Ottawa Senators Logo .05 .15
83 Martin Gerber .07 .20
84 Dany Heatley .07 .20
85 Jason Spezza .10 .25
86 Mike Fisher .05 .15
87 Chris Phillips .05 .15
88 Daniel Alfredsson .10 .25
89 Filip Kuba .05 .15
90 Nick Foligno .10 .25
91 Philadelphia Flyers Logo .05 .15
92 Martin Biron .07 .20
93 Mike Richards .07 .20
94 Simon Gagne .10 .25
95 Jeff Carter .07 .20
96 Kimmo Timonen .05 .15
97 Danny Briere .10 .25
98 Braydon Coburn .05 .15
99 Claude Giroux .20 .50
100 Pittsburgh Penguins Logo .05 .15
101 Marc-Andre Fleury .20 .50
102 Evgeni Malkin .20 .50
103 Petr Sykora .07 .20
104 Sergei Gonchar .05 .15
105 Jordan Staal .07 .20
106 Sidney Crosby .40 1.00
107 Ryan Whitney .10 .25
108 Kris Letang .12 .30
109 Tampa Bay Lightning Logo .05 .15
110 Mike Smith .10 .25
111 Vaclav Prospal .05 .15
112 Martin St-Louis .10 .25
113 Ryan Malone .05 .15
114 Paul Ranger .05 .15
115 Vincent Lecavalier .10 .25
116 Andrej Meszaros .05 .15
117 Steven Stamkos .40 1.00
118 Toronto Maple Leafs Logo .05 .15
119 Vesa Toskala .12 .30
120 Jason Blake .05 .15
121 Alex Steen .05 .15
122 Matt Stajan .05 .15
123 Tomas Kaberle .05 .15
124 Nik Antropov .07 .20
125 Pavel Kubina .05 .15
126 Jiri Tlusty .05 .15
127 Washington Capitals Logo .05 .15
128 Jose Theodore .10 .25
129 Mike Green .07 .20
130 Alexander Semin .10 .25
131 Sergei Fedorov .15 .40
132 Tom Poti .05 .15
133 Alex Ovechkin .40 1.00
134 Brooks Laich .05 .15
135 Nicklas Backstrom .10 .25
136 Anaheim Ducks Logo .05 .15
137 Jean-Sebastien Giguere .10 .25
138 Chris Pronger .10 .25
139 Corey Perry .15 .40
140 Chris Kunitz .10 .25
141 Scott Niedermayer .10 .25
142 Ryan Getzlaf .10 .25
143 George Parros .05 .15
144 Bobby Ryan .07 .20
145 Calgary Flames Logo .05 .15
146 Miikka Kiprusoff .10 .25
147 Dion Phaneuf .07 .20
148 Robyn Regehr .05 .15
149 Daymond Langkow .05 .15
150 Mike Cammalleri .07 .20
151 Jarome Iginla .12 .30
152 Matthew Lombardi .05 .15
153 Dustin Boyd .05 .15
154 Chicago Blackhawks Logo .05 .15
155 Cristobal Huet .07 .20
156 Brian Campbell .07 .20
157 Martin Havlat .10 .25
158 Duncan Keith .07 .20
159 Patrick Sharp .10 .25
160 Jonathan Toews .15 .40
161 Dustin Byfuglien .10 .25
162 Patrick Kane .20 .50
163 Colorado Avalanche Logo .05 .15
164 Peter Budaj .07 .20
165 Paul Stastny .07 .20
166 Ryan Smyth .07 .20
167 Milan Hejduk .07 .20
168 John-Michael Liles .05 .15
169 Joe Sakic .20 .50
170 Adam Foote .05 .15
171 T.J. Hensick .07 .20
172 Columbus Blue Jackets Logo .05 .15
173 Pascal Leclaire .07 .20
174 Fredrik Modin .05 .15
175 Rostislav Klesla .05 .15
176 Kris Russell .05 .15
177 Michael Peca .07 .20
178 Rick Nash .10 .25
179 Manny Malhotra .05 .15
180 Derick Brassard .10 .25
181 Dallas Stars Logo .05 .15
182 Marty Turco .10 .25
183 Brenden Morrow .07 .20
184 Mike Modano .15 .40
185 Sean Avery .05 .15
186 Philippe Boucher .05 .15
187 Mike Ribeiro .05 .15
188 Sergei Zubov .07 .20
189 Matt Niskanen .07 .20
190 Detroit Red Wings Logo .05 .15
191 Chris Osgood .10 .25
192 Nicklas Lidstrom .10 .25
193 Marian Hossa .10 .25
194 Pavel Datsyuk .15 .40
195 Brian Rafalski .07 .20
196 Henrik Zetterberg .12 .30
197 Johan Franzen .07 .20
198 Valtteri Filppula .05 .15
199 Edmonton Oilers Logo .05 .15
200 Mathieu Garon .07 .20
201 Sheldon Souray .05 .15
202 Shawn Horcoff .05 .15
203 Andrew Cogliano .05 .15
204 Dustin Penner .07 .20
205 Ales Hemsky .07 .20
206 Lubomir Visnovsky .05 .15
207 Sam Gagner .05 .15
208 Los Angeles Kings Logo .05 .15
209 Jason Labarbera .07 .20
210 Dustin Brown .10 .25
211 Tom Preissing .05 .15
212 Jack Johnson .05 .15
213 Alexander Frolov .05 .15
214 Anze Kopitar .15 .40
215 Patrick O'Sullivan .07 .20
216 Jonathan Bernier .07 .20
217 Minnesota Wild Logo .05 .15
218 Niklas Backstrom .10 .25
219 Brent Burns .10 .25
220 Pierre-Marc Bouchard .10 .25
221 Mikko Koivu .07 .20
222 Nick Schultz .05 .15
223 Marian Gaborik .10 .25
224 Derek Boogaard .05 .15
225 James Sheppard .05 .15
226 Nashville Predators Logo .05 .15
227 Dan Ellis .05 .15
228 J.P. Dumont .05 .15
229 Martin Erat .05 .15
230 David Legwand .07 .20
231 Shea Weber .07 .20
232 Jason Arnott .07 .20
233 Ryan Suter .07 .20
234 Ville Koistinen .07 .20
235 Phoenix Coyotes Logo .05 .15
236 Ilya Bryzgalov .07 .20
237 Olli Jokinen .07 .20
238 Peter Mueller .07 .20
239 Daniel Carcillo .05 .15
240 Ed Jovanovski .07 .20
241 Shane Doan .07 .20
242 Derek Morris .05 .15
243 Kyle Turris .15 .40
244 San Jose Sharks Logo .05 .15
245 Evgeni Nabokov .07 .20
246 Jonathan Cheechoo .07 .20
247 Patrick Marleau .10 .25
248 Milan Michalek .05 .15
249 Marc-Edouard Vlasic .05 .15
250 Joe Thornton .15 .40
251 Christian Ehrhoff .05 .15
252 Devin Setoguchi .07 .20
253 St. Louis Blues Logo .05 .15
254 Manny Legace .10 .25
255 Keith Tkachuk .10 .25
256 Andy McDonald .07 .20
257 Brad Boyes .05 .15
258 Eric Brewer .05 .15
259 Paul Kariya .10 .25
260 Erik Johnson .05 .15
261 David Perron .07 .20
262 Vancouver Canucks Logo .05 .15
263 Roberto Luongo .15 .40
264 Mattias Ohlund .05 .15
265 Kevin Bieksa .07 .20
266 Daniel Sedin .12 .30
267 Henrik Sedin .12 .30
268 Ryan Kesler .10 .25
269 Pavol Demitra .12 .30
270 Alexander Edler .05 .15

2009-10 Panini Stickers

1 NHLPA Logo .05 .15
2 NHL Logo .05 .15
3 EASTERN CONFERENCE Logo .05 .15
4 WESTERN CONFERENCE Logo .05 .15
5 Central Division CHAMPION .05 .15
6 Northwest Division Champion .05 .15
7 Pacific Division Champion .05 .15
8 Atlantic Division Champion .05 .15
9 Northeast Division Champion .05 .15
10 Southeast Division Champion .05 .15
11 Atlanta Thrashers Logo .05 .15
12 Kari Lehtonen .07 .20
13 Slava Kozlov .05 .15
14 Tobias Enstrom .10 .25
15 Colby Armstrong .05 .15
16 Chris Thorburn .05 .15
17 Zach Bogosian .07 .20
18 Ilya Kovalchuk SS .10 .25
19 Todd White .05 .15
20 Bryan Little .10 .25
21 Boston Bruins Logo .05 .15
22 Tim Thomas .10 .25
23 Zdeno Chara .10 .25
24 Milan Lucic .07 .20
25 Patrice Bergeron .12 .30
26 Michael Ryder .05 .15
27 Dennis Wideman .05 .15
28 Marc Savard SS .05 .15
29 David Krejci .10 .25
30 Blake Wheeler .10 .25
31 Buffalo Sabres Logo .05 .15
32 Ryan Miller .10 .25
33 Derek Roy .05 .15
34 Jason Pominville .05 .15
35 Thomas Vanek SS .07 .20
36 Tim ConnOlly .05 .15
37 Craig Rivet .05 .15
38 Drew Stafford .05 .15
39 Henrik Tallinder .05 .15
40 Patrick Kaleta .05 .15
41 Carolina Hurricanes Logo .05 .15
42 Cam Ward .10 .25
43 Rod Brindâ€™Amour .10 .25
44 Joni Pitkanen .07 .20
45 Joe Corvo .05 .15
46 Chad LaRose .05 .15
47 Erik Cole .05 .15
48 Eric Staal SS .12 .30
49 Ray Whitney .07 .20
50 Tuomo Ruutu .05 .15
51 Florida Panthers Logo .05 .15
52 Tomas Vokoun .07 .20
53 Stephen Weiss .05 .15
54 Nathan Horton SS .10 .25
55 Rostislav Olesz .05 .15
56 David Booth .05 .15
57 Keith Ballard .05 .15
58 Bryan McCabe .07 .20
59 Cory Stillman .05 .15
60 Michael Frolik .07 .20
61 Montreal Canadiens Logo .05 .15
62 Carey PRICE .20 .50
63 Scott Gomez SS .07 .20
64 Andrei MARKOV .10 .25
65 Andrei KOSTITSYN .07 .20
66 Tomas PLEKANEC .05 .15
67 Maxim Lapierre .05 .15
68 Guillaume Latendresse .07 .20
69 Roman Hamrlik .05 .15
70 Mike Cammalleri .07 .20
71 New Jersey Devils Logo .05 .15
72 Martin Brodeur .25 .60
73 Zach Parise SS .10 .25
74 Brian Rolston .07 .20
75 Patrik Elias .10 .25
76 Jamie Langenbrunner .05 .15
77 Travis Zajac .05 .15
78 Paul Martin .05 .15
79 Johnny Oduya .07 .20
80 David Clarkson .07 .20
81 New York Islanders Logo .05 .15
82 Rick DiPietro .07 .20
83 Kyle Okposo .05 .15
84 Brendan Witt .05 .15
85 Josh Bailey .07 .20
86 Trent Hunter .05 .15
87 Jeff Tambellini .05 .15
88 Mark Streit .05 .15
89 Sean Bergenheim .05 .15
90 Doug Weight .10 .25
91 New York Rangers Logo .05 .15
92 Henrik Lundqvist SS .25 .60
93 Brandon Dubinsky .05 .15
94 Marian Gaborik .10 .25
95 Chris Drury .07 .20
96 Marc Staal .05 .15
97 Sean Avery .07 .20
98 Ryan Callahan .05 .15
99 Wade Redden .05 .15
100 Michal Rozsival .05 .15
101 Ottawa Senators Logo .05 .15
102 Pascal LeClaire .10 .25
103 Alex Kovalev .07 .20
104 Daniel Alfredsson SS .10 .25
105 Chris Kelly .07 .20
106 Jason Spezza .10 .25
107 Mike Fisher .05 .15
108 Chris Phillips .05 .15
109 Filip Kuba .05 .15
110 Nick Foligno .07 .20
111 Philadelphia Flyers Logo .05 .15
112 Ray Emery .07 .20
113 Daniel Briere .10 .25
114 Simon Gagne .10 .25
115 Mike Richards .07 .20
116 Jeff Carter .07 .20
117 Claude Giroux .10 .25
118 Kimmo Timonen .07 .20
119 Braydon Coburn .05 .15
120 Scott Hartnell .05 .15
121 Pittsburgh Penguins Logo .05 .15
122 Marc-Andre Fleury .20 .50
123 Evgeni Malkin .20 .50
124 Tyler Kennedy .07 .20
125 Sidney Crosby SS .40 1.00
126 Jordan Staal .07 .20
127 Kris Letang .12 .30
128 Sergei Gonchar .05 .15
129 Maxime Talbot .05 .15
130 Brooks Orpik .05 .15
131 Tampa Bay Lightning Logo .05 .15
132 Mike Smith .10 .25
133 Martin St. Louis .10 .25
134 Vincent Lecavalier SS .10 .25
135 Steven Stamkos .20 .50
136 Alex Tanguay .05 .15
137 Ryan Malone .05 .15
138 Paul Ranger .05 .15
139 Andrej Meszaros .05 .15
140 Jeff HALPERN .05 .15
141 Toronto Maple Leafs Logo .05 .15
142 Vesa Toskala .10 .25
143 Jason Blake .05 .15
144 Luke Schenn SS .10 .25
145 Niklas Hagman .05 .15
146 Nikolai Kulemin .05 .15
147 Tomas Kaberle .05 .15
148 Mike Komisarek .07 .20
149 Matt STAJAN .05 .15
150 John Mitchell .05 .15
151 Washington Capitals Logo .05 .15
152 Semyon Varlamov .10 .25
153 Mike Green .07 .20
154 Nicklas Backstrom .10 .25
155 Alexander Semin .10 .25
156 Chris Clark .05 .15
157 David Steckel .05 .15
158 Alex Ovechkin SS .40 1.00
159 John Erskine .05 .15
160 Brooks Laich .05 .15
161 Anaheim Ducks Logo .05 .15
162 Jonas Hiller .07 .20
163 Ryan Whitney .05 .15
164 Corey Perry .15 .40
165 Ryan Getzlaf SS .10 .25
166 Scott Niedermayer .10 .25
167 Bobby Ryan .07 .20
168 George Parros .05 .15
169 Teemu Selanne .20 .50
170 Andrew Ebbett .05 .15
171 Calgary Flames Logo .05 .15
172 Miikka Kiprusoff .10 .25
173 Dion Phaneuf .07 .20
174 Jarome Iginla SS .12 .30
175 Robyn Regehr .07 .20
176 Daymond Langkow .05 .15
177 Rene Bourque .05 .15
178 Olli Jokinen .07 .20
179 Dustin Boyd .05 .15
180 Craig Conroy .05 .15
181 Chicago Blackhawks Logo .05 .15
182 Cristobal Huet .10 .25
183 Jonathan Toews SS .15 .40
184 Patrick Kane .20 .50
185 Brian Campbell .07 .20
186 Marian Hossa .10 .25
187 Duncan Keith .07 .20
188 Patrick Sharp .10 .25
189 Dustin Byfuglien .10 .25
190 Brent Seabrook .05 .15
191 Colorado Avalanche Logo .05 .15
192 Peter Budaj .07 .20
193 Chris Stewart .07 .20
194 Scott Hannan .05 .15
195 John-Michael Liles .05 .15
196 Paul Stastny SS .07 .20
197 Milan Hejduk .07 .20
198 Wojtek Wolski .05 .15
199 Adam Foote .05 .15
200 Marek Svatos .05 .15
201 Columbus Blue Jackets Logo .05 .15
202 Steve Mason .07 .20
203 Kristian Huselius .05 .15
204 Derick Brassard .05 .15
205 Rick Nash SS .10 .25
206 Rostislav Klesla .10 .25
207 Mike Commodore .05 .15
208 Nikita Filatov .07 .20
209 Jakub Voracek .07 .20
210 R.J. Umberger .07 .20
211 Dallas Stars Logo .05 .15
212 Marty Turco .10 .25
213 Mike Modano .15 .40
214 James Neal .05 .15
215 Brenden Morrow SS .07 .20
216 Mike Ribeiro .05 .15
217 Loui Eriksson .05 .15
218 Fabian Brunnstrom .07 .20
219 Matt Niskanen .07 .20
220 Brad Richards .10 .25
221 Detroit Red Wings Logo .05 .15
222 Chris Osgood .10 .25
223 Nicklas Lidstrom .05 .15
224 Pavel Datsyuk SS .15 .40
225 Henrik Zetterberg .12 .30
226 Dan Cleary .10 .25
227 Brian Rafalski .05 .15
228 Valterri Filppula .05 .15
229 Johan Franzen .07 .20
230 Tomas Holmstrom .07 .20
231 Edmonton Oilers Logo .05 .15
232 Nikolai Khabibulin .10 .25
233 Ales Hemsky SS .07 .20
234 Sam Gagner .05 .15
235 Sheldon Souray .05 .15
236 Shawn Horcoff .05 .15
237 Andrew Cogliano .05 .15
238 Patrick O'Sullivan .07 .20
239 Tom Gilbert .05 .15
240 Ethan Moreau .05 .15
241 Los Angeles Kings Logo .05 .15
242 Erik Ersberg .07 .20
243 Dustin Brown .10 .25
244 Justin Williams .07 .20
245 Jack Johnson .05 .15
246 Drew Doughty .12 .30
247 Alexander Frolov .07 .20
248 Ryan Smyth .07 .20
249 Anze Kopitar SS .15 .40
250 Wayne Simmonds .12 .30
251 Minnesota Wild Logo .05 .15
252 Niklas Backstrom .10 .25
253 Martin Havlat .07 .20
254 Brent Burns .10 .25
255 Pierre-Marc Bouchard .10 .25
256 Andrew Brunette .05 .15
257 Derek Boogaard .05 .15
258 Mikko Koivu SS .10 .25
259 Nick Schultz .05 .15
260 Cal Clutterbuck .05 .15
261 Nashville Predators Logo .05 .15
262 Pekka Rinne .10 .25
263 Jason Arnott .07 .20
264 J.P. Dumont .05 .15
265 Jordin Tootoo .10 .25
266 David Legwand .07 .20
267 Ryan Suter .07 .20
268 Shea Weber SS .07 .20
269 Dan Hamhuis .07 .20
270 Martin Erat .05 .15
271 Phoenix Coyotes Logo .05 .15
272 Ilya Bryzgalov .07 .20
273 Peter Mueller .07 .20
274 Kyle Turris .10 .25
275 Ed Jovanovski .05 .15
276 Martin Hanzal .07 .20
277 Mikkel Boedker .05 .15
278 Zbynek Michalek .05 .15
279 Shane Doan SS .07 .20
280 Viktor Tikhonov .07 .20
281 San Jose Sharks Logo .05 .15
282 Evgeni Nabokov .07 .20
283 Joe Pavelski .12 .30
284 Patrick Marleau .10 .25
285 Milan Michalek .05 .15
286 Joe Thornton SS .15 .40
287 Devin Setoguchi .07 .20

288 Ryane Clowe .05 .15
289 Rob Blake .10 .25
290 Dan Boyle .05 .15
291 St Louis Blues Logo .05 .15
292 Chris Mason .07 .20
293 Paul Kariya .10 .25
294 T.J. Oshie .10 .25
295 Brad Boyes SS .05 .15
296 Andy McDonald .07 .20
297 Keith Tkachuk .10 .25
298 Erik Johnson .05 .15
299 Barret Jackman .05 .15
300 David Backes .05 .15
301 Vancouver Canucks Logo .05 .15
302 Roberto Luongo SS .15 .40
303 Ryan Kesler .10 .25
304 Alexander Edler .05 .15
305 Mason Raymond .05 .15
306 Kevin Bieksa .07 .20
307 Daniel Sedin .12 .30
308 Henrik Sedin .12 .30
309 Alexandre Burrows .05 .15
310 Pavol Demitra .12 .30
311 James van Riemsdyk .20 .50
312 John Tavares .40 1.00
313 Ville Leino .07 .20
314 Michael Del Zotto .10 .25
315 Benn Ferriero .10 .25
316 Victor Hedman .25 .60
317 Matt Duchene .20 .50
318 Erik Karlsson .30 .75
319 Ryan O'Reilly .20 .50
320 Evander Kane .20 .50
321 Viktor Stalberg .10 .25
322 Jamie Benn .30 .75
323 Tyler Myers .15 .40
324 Sergei Shirokov .05 .15
325 Matt Gilroy .10 .25
326 Dmitry Kulikov .10 .25
327 James Wright .10 .25
328 Artem Anisimov .05 .15
329 Matt Halischuk .07 .20
330 Peter Regin .07 .20
331 Byron Bitz .07 .20
332 Mikael Backlund .15 .40
333 Kris Chucko .05 .15
334 Taylor Chorney .10 .25
335 Alec Martinez .12 .30
336 Yannick Weber .10 .25
337 Luca Caputi .10 .25
338 Teemu Laakso .05 .15
339 Jonas Gustavsson .12 .30
340 Jason Demers .15 .40
341 Season Opener .05 .15
342 Season Opener .05 .15
343 Winter Classic .05 .15
344 Winter Classic .05 .15
345 Winter Classic .05 .15
346 Winter Classic .05 .15
347 Alexander Ovechkin AW .40 1.00
348 Alexander Ovechkin AW .40 1.00
349 Martin Brodeur AW .25 .60
350 Martin Brodeur AW .25 .60
351 Martin Brodeur AW .25 .60
352 Martin Brodeur AW .25 .60
353 Pittsburgh Penguins East.Champs.05 .15
354 Detroit Red Wings West Champs.05 .15
355 Stanley Cup .05 .15
356 Stanley Cup .05 .15
357 Stanley Cup .05 .15
358 Stanley Cup .05 .15
359 Alexander Ovechkin AW .40 1.00
360 Zdeno Chara AW .10 .25
361 Tim Thomas AW .10 .25
362 Evgeni Malkin AW .20 .50
363 Steve Mason AW .07 .20
364 Pavel Datsyuk AW .15 .40

2010-11 Panini Stickers

1 NHL Logo Foil .07 .20
2 NHLPA Logo Foil .07 .20
3 Stanley Cup Foil .07 .20
4 Western Conference Logo Foil .07 .20
5 Western Conference Logo Foil .07 .20
6 Eastern Conference Logo Foil .07 .20
7 Atlanta Thrashers Foil .07 .20
8 Nik Antropov Foil .07 .20
9 Evander Kane .10 .25
10 Zach Bogosian .07 .20
11 Tobias Ensrom .05 .15
12 Ondrej Pavelec .10 .25
13 Rich Peverley .10 .25
14 Ron Hainsey .05 .15
15 Johnny Oduya .07 .20
16 Niclas Bergfors .07 .20
17 Boston Bruins Foil .07 .20
18 Marc Savard Foil .05 .15
19 Zdeno Chara .10 .25
20 Patrice Bergeron .12 .30
21 David Krejci .10 .25
22 Tuukka Rask .12 .30
23 Milan Lucic .10 .25
24 Dennis Seidenberg .05 .15
25 Marco Sturm .05 .15
26 Shawn Thornton .05 .15
27 Buffalo Sabres Foil .07 .20
28 Ryan Miller Foil .10 .25
29 Thomas Vanek .07 .20
30 Derek Roy .05 .15
31 Jason Pominville .05 .15
32 Tyler Myers .05 .15
33 Craig Rivet .05 .15
34 Tyler Ennis .05 .15
35 Patrick Kaleta .05 .15
36 Tim Connolly .05 .15
37 Carolina Hurricanes Foil .07 .20
38 Eric Staal Foil .12 .30
39 Cam Ward .10 .25
40 Tim Gleason .05 .15
41 Joni Pitkanen .07 .20
42 Tuomu Ruutu .07 .20
43 Chad LaRose .05 .15
44 Brandon Sutter .05 .15
45 Jussi Jokinen .05 .15
46 Sergei Samsonov .07 .20
47 Florida Panthers Foil .07 .20
48 Stephen Weiss Foil .07 .20
49 Rostislav Olesz .05 .15
50 David Booth .05 .15
51 Tomas Vokoun .07 .20
52 Bryan McCabe .05 .15
53 Shawn Matthias .05 .15
54 Cory Stillman .05 .15
55 Michael Frolik .05 .15
56 Dmitry Kulikov .07 .20
57 Montreal Canadiens Foil .07 .20
58 Michael Cammalleri Foil .10 .25
59 Scott Gomez .07 .20
60 Brian Gionta .05 .15
61 Tomas Plekanec .05 .15
62 Josh Gorges .05 .15
63 Andrei Markov .10 .25
64 Hal Gill .05 .15
65 Carey Price .20 .50
66 Travis Moen .05 .15
67 New Jersey Devils Foil .07 .20
68 Zach Parise Foil .10 .25
69 Martin Brodeur .25 .60
70 Travis Zajac .05 .15
71 Jamie Langenbrunner .05 .15
72 David Clarkson .05 .15
73 Andy Greene .05 .15
74 Colin White .05 .15
75 Patrik Elias .10 .25
76 Dainius Zubrus .05 .15
77 New York Islanders Foil .07 .20
78 John Tavares Foil .15 .40
79 Kyle Okposo .05 .15
80 Mark Streit .05 .15
81 Matt Moulson .07 .20
82 Dwayne Roloson .07 .20
83 Rick DiPietro .07 .20
84 Trent Hunter .05 .15
85 Josh Bailey .07 .20
86 Blake Comeau .05 .15
87 New York Rangers Foil .07 .20
88 Marian Gaborik Foil .10 .25
89 Henrik Lundqvist .25 .60
90 Marc Staal .05 .15
91 Daniel Girardi .05 .15
92 Brandon Dubinsky .05 .15
93 Ryan Callahan .05 .15
94 Sean Avery .07 .20
95 Michael Del Zotto .07 .20
96 Chris Drury .07 .20
97 Ottawa Senators Foil .07 .20
98 Daniel Alfredsson Foil .10 .25
99 Jason Spezza .10 .25
100 Mike Fisher .05 .15
101 Milan Michalek .05 .15
102 Chris Phillips .05 .15
103 Erik Karlsson .12 .30
104 Brian Elliot .07 .20
105 Alex Kovalev .07 .20
106 Jarkko Ruutu .05 .15
107 Philadelphia Flyers Foil .07 .20
108 Mike Richards Foil .07 .20
109 Jeff Carter .07 .20
110 Daniel Briere .10 .25
111 Claude Giroux .10 .25
112 Chris Pronger .10 .25
113 Kimmo Timonen .05 .15
114 Brian Boucher .07 .20
115 James van Riemsdyk .07 .20
116 Ville Leino .07 .20
117 Pittsburgh Penguins Foil .07 .20
118 Sidney Crosby Foil .40 1.00
119 Evgeni Malkin .20 .50
120 Marc-Andre Fleury .20 .50
121 Jordan Staal .07 .20
122 Kris Letang .12 .30
123 Matt Cooke .05 .15
124 Maxime Talbot .05 .15
125 Brooks Orpik .05 .15
126 Chris Kunitz .10 .25
127 Tampa Bay Lightning Foil .07 .20
128 Steven Stamkos Foil .20 .50
129 Vincent Lecavalier .10 .25
130 Martin St. Louis .10 .25
131 Victor Hedman .12 .30
132 Steve Downie .05 .15
133 Nate Thompson .05 .15
134 Mike Smith .10 .25
135 Ryan Malone .05 .15
136 Mattias Ohlund .05 .15
137 Toronto Maple Leafs Foil .07 .20
138 Phil Kessel Foil .10 .25
139 Dion Phaneuf .07 .20
140 Jonas Gustavsson .12 .30
141 Jean-Sebastien Giguere .10 .25
142 Luke Schenn .10 .25
143 Tyler Bozak .05 .15
144 Mike Komisarek .05 .15
145 Colton Orr .05 .15
146 Mikhail Grabovski .05 .15
147 Washington Capitals Foil .07 .20
148 Alex Ovechkin Foil .40 1.00
149 Alex Semin .10 .25
150 Nicklas Backstrom .10 .25
151 Mike Green .07 .20
152 Brooks Laich .05 .15
153 Jeff Schultz .05 .15
154 Semyon Varlamov .10 .25
155 Mike Knuble .05 .15
156 John Carlson .10 .25
157 Anaheim Ducks Foil .07 .20
158 Ryan Getzlaf Foil .10 .25
159 Corey Perry .15 .40
160 Jonas Hiller .07 .20
161 Bobby Ryan .07 .20
162 Lubomir Visnovsky .05 .15
163 George Parros .07 .20
164 Jason Blake .05 .15
165 Joffrey Lupul .05 .15
166 Teemu Selanne .20 .50
167 Calgary Flames Foil .07 .20
168 Jarome Iginla Foil .12 .30
169 Miikka Kiprusoff .10 .25
170 Jay Bouwmeester .05 .15
171 Matt Stajan .05 .15
172 Rene Bourque .05 .15
173 Robyn Regehr .05 .15
174 Mark Giordano .10 .25
175 Daymond Langkow .05 .15
176 Mikael Backlund .07 .20
177 Chicago Blackhawks Foil .07 .20
178 Jonathan Toews Foil .15 .40
179 Patrick Kane .20 .50
180 Tomas Kopecky .07 .20
181 Marian Hossa .10 .25
182 Duncan Keith .07 .20
183 Brent Seabrook .05 .15
184 Dave Bolland .07 .20
185 Bryan Bickell .05 .15
186 Patrick Sharp .10 .25
187 Colorado Avalanche Foil .07 .20
188 Paul Stastny Foil .07 .20
189 Matt Duchene .10 .25
190 Craig Anderson .10 .25
191 Ryan O'Reilly .10 .25
192 Milan Hejduk .07 .20
193 Chris Stewart .07 .20
194 Scott Hannan .05 .15
195 John-Michael Liles .05 .15
196 T.J. Galiardi .07 .20
197 Columbus Blue Jackets Foil .07 .20
198 Rick Nash Foil .10 .25
199 Kristian Huselius .05 .15
200 Steve Mason .07 .20
201 Jakub Voracek .07 .20
202 Antoine Vermette .05 .15
203 Kris Russell .05 .15
204 Mike Commodore .05 .15
205 R.J. Umberger .05 .15
206 Derick Brassard .05 .15
207 Dallas Stars Foil .07 .20
208 Brad Richards Foil .10 .25
209 Brenden Morrow .07 .20
210 Mike Ribeiro .05 .15
211 Loui Eriksson .05 .15
212 James Neal .05 .15
213 Jamie Benn .12 .30
214 Stephane Robidas .05 .15
215 Steve Ott .05 .15
216 Kari Lehtonen .07 .20
217 Detroit Red Wings Foil .07 .20
218 Pavel Datsyuk Foil .15 .40
219 Henrik Zetterberg .12 .30
220 Nicklas Lidstrom .10 .25
221 Brian Rafalski .05 .15
222 Jimmy Howard .12 .30
223 Johan Franzen .07 .20
224 Valtteri Filppula .05 .15
225 Tomas Holmstrom .05 .15
226 Niklas Kronwall .07 .20
227 Edmonton Oilers Foil .07 .20
228 Ales Hemsky Foil .07 .20
229 Dustin Penner .05 .15
230 Sam Gagner .05 .15
231 Ryan Whitney .05 .15
232 Andrew Cogliano .05 .15
233 Tom Gilbert .05 .15
234 Shawn Horcoff .05 .15
235 Jeff Deslauriers .05 .15
236 Zach Stortini .05 .15
237 Los Angeles Kings Foil .07 .20
238 Drew Doughty Foil .12 .30
239 Anze Kopitar .15 .40
240 Ryan Smyth .07 .20
241 Dustin Brown .10 .25
242 Jonathan Quick .12 .30
243 Jack Johnson .05 .15
244 Wayne Simmonds .12 .30
245 Jarret Stoll .07 .20
246 Matt Greene .05 .15
247 Minnesota Wild Foil .07 .20
248 Mikko Koivu Foil .10 .25
249 Niklas Backstrom .10 .25
250 Martin Havlat .07 .20
251 Brent Burns .10 .25
252 Marek Zidlicky .05 .15
253 Cal Clutterbuck .05 .15
254 Guillaume Latendresse .07 .20
255 Andrew Brunette .05 .15
256 Pierre-Marc Bouchard .10 .25
257 Nashville Predators Foil .07 .20
258 Shea Weber Foil .07 .20
259 Pekka Rinne .10 .25
260 Ryan Suter .07 .20
261 Martin Erat .05 .15
262 Patric Hornqvist .05 .15
263 David Legwand .07 .20
264 Colin Wilson .07 .20
265 Steve Sullivan .05 .15
266 Jordin Tootoo .07 .20
267 Phoenix Coyotes Foil .07 .20
268 Shane Doan Foil .07 .20
269 Radim Vrbata .05 .15
270 Vernon Fiddler .05 .15
271 Ilya Bryzgalov .07 .20
272 Ed Jovanovski .05 .15
273 Keith Yandle .05 .15
274 Wojtek Wolski .05 .15
275 Martin Hanzal .05 .15
276 Daniel Winnik .05 .15
277 San Jose Sharks Foil .07 .20
278 Joe Thornton Foil .15 .40
279 Dany Heatley .07 .20
280 Dan Boyle .05 .15
281 Joe Pavelski .12 .30
282 Devin Setoguchi .07 .20
283 Ryane Clowe .05 .15
284 Logan Couture .12 .30
285 Douglas Murray .05 .15
286 Thomas Greiss .07 .20
287 St Louis Blues Foil .07 .20
288 Erik Johnson Foil .05 .15
289 T.J. Oshie .10 .25
290 Brad Boyes .05 .15
291 David Backes .05 .15
292 Andy McDonald .07 .20
293 Barret Jackman .05 .15
294 Ty Conklin .07 .20
295 Alex Pietrangelo .07 .20
296 Jay McClement .05 .15
297 Vancouver Canucks Foil .07 .20
298 Henrik Sedin Foil .12 .30
299 Daniel Sedin .12 .30
300 Roberto Luongo .15 .40
301 Ryan Kesler .10 .25
302 Alex Burrows .05 .15
303 Kevin Bieksa .10 .25
304 Alexander Edler .05 .15
305 Mikael Samuelsson .05 .15
306 Mason Raymond .05 .15
307 Season Premiere 1 .07 .20
308 Season Premiere 1 .07 .20
309 Season premiere 2 .07 .20
310 Season premiere 2 .07 .20
311 Martin Brodeur .25 .60
312 Martin Brodeur .25 .60
313 Winter Classic .07 .20
314 Winter Classic .07 .20
315 Capitals' President Cup Winners.07 .20
316 Capitals' President Cup Winners.07 .20
317 Western Conf.Champs .07 .20
318 Western Conf.Champs .07 .20
319 Eastern Conf.Champs .07 .20
320 Eastern Conf.Champs .07 .20
321 Stanley Cup Champs .07 .20
322 Stanley Cup Champs .07 .20
323 Henrik Sedin ROSS .12 .30
324 Ryan Miller VEZINA .10 .25
325 Duncan Keith NORRIS .07 .20
326 Tyler Myers CALDER .05 .15
327 Pavel Datsyuk SELKE .15 .40
328 Martin St. Louis BING .10 .25
329 Sidney Crosby MESSIER .40 1.00
330 Jose Theodore MASTERSON .10 .25
331 Dave Tippett ADAMS .05 .15
332 Jonathan Toews CONN .15 .40
333 Shane Doan CLANCY .07 .20
334 Alexander Ovechkin LINDSAY .40 1.00
335 Nick Palmieri .07 .20
336 Zach Hamill .07 .20
337 Jamie McBain .07 .20
338 Justin Mercier .07 .20
339 Brayden Irwin .07 .20
340 Nick Bonino .10 .25
341 Philip Larsen .07 .20
342 Bobby Butler .07 .20
343 Maxim Noreau .05 .15
344 Nick Johnson .05 .15
345 Brock Trotter .15 .40
346 Matt Martin .12 .30
347 Jerome Samson .07 .20
348 Arturs Kulda .07 .20
349 Ryan Wilson .07 .20
350 Casey Wellman .07 .20
351 Evgeny dadonov .10 .25
352 P.K. Subban .25 .60
353 Nick Spaling .07 .20
354 Kyle Wilson .10 .25
355 James Wyman .07 .20
356 Dylan Reese .07 .20
357 Carter Hutton .20 .50
358 Jared Cowen .07 .20
359 Cody Almond .07 .20
360 Eric Tangradi .07 .20
361 Andrew Bodnarchuk .07 .20
362 Dustin Tokarski .07 .20
363 Nazem Kadri .25 .60
364 Anton Klementyev .07 .20

2011-12 Panini Stickers

1 NHL Logo .05 .15
2 NHLPA Logo .05 .15
3 Stanley Cup .05 .15
4 Stanley Cup Champions Bruins .05 .15
5 Western Conference Logo .05 .15
6 Chicago Blackhawks .05 .15
7 Columbus Blue Jackets .05 .15
8 Detroit Red Wings .05 .15
9 Nashville Predators .05 .15
10 St. Louis Blues .05 .15
11 Calgary Flames .05 .15
12 Colorado Avalanche .05 .15
13 Edmonton Oilers .05 .15
14 Minnesota Wild .05 .15
15 Vancouver Canucks .05 .15
16 Anaheim Ducks .05 .15
17 Dallas Stars .05 .15
18 Los Angeles Kings .05 .15
19 Phoenix Coyotes .05 .15
20 San Jose Sharks .05 .15
21 Eastern Conference Logo .05 .15
22 New Jersey Devils .05 .15
23 New York Islanders .05 .15
24 New York Rangers .05 .15
25 Philadelphia Flyers .05 .15
26 Pittsburgh Penguins .05 .15
27 Boston Bruins .05 .15
28 Buffalo Sabres .05 .15
29 Montreal Canadiens .05 .15
30 Ottawa Senators .05 .15
31 Toronto Maple Leafs .05 .15
32 Carolina Hurricanes .05 .15
33 Florida Panthers .05 .15
34 Tampa Bay Lightning .05 .15
35 Washington Capitals .05 .15
36 Winnipeg Jets .05 .15
37 Boston Bruins .05 .15
38 Tim Thomas .10 .25
39 Brad Marchand .20 .50
40 David Krejci .10 .25
41 Dennis Seidenberg .05 .15
42 Milan Lucic .10 .25
43 Nathan Horton .10 .25
44 Patrice Bergeron .12 .30
45 Tyler Seguin .12 .30
46 Zdeno Chara .10 .25
47 Buffalo Sabres .05 .15
48 Ryan Miller .10 .25
49 Brad Boyes .05 .15
50 Derek Roy .05 .15
51 Drew Stafford .05 .15
52 Jason Pominville .05 .15
53 Jochen Hecht .05 .15
54 Nathan Gerbe .05 .15
55 Thomas Vanek .07 .20
56 Tyler Myers .05 .15
57 Carolina Hurricanes .05 .15
58 Eric Staal .12 .30
59 Brandon Sutter .05 .15
60 Cam Ward .10 .25
61 Jamie McBain .05 .15
62 Jeff Skinner .12 .30
63 Tim Gleason .05 .15
64 Tuomo Ruutu .07 .20
65 Jussi Jokinen .05 .15
66 Chad Larose .05 .15
67 Florida Panthers .05 .15
68 Stephen Weiss .07 .20
69 David Booth .05 .15
70 Dmitry Kulikov .05 .15
71 Evgeny Dadonov .05 .15
72 Jacob Markstrom .10 .25
73 Jason Garrison .05 .15
74 Mike Santorelli .05 .15
75 Mike Weaver .05 .15
76 Jack Skille .07 .20
77 Montreal Canadiens .05 .15
78 Carey Price .20 .50
79 Andrei Kostitsyn .07 .20
80 Brian Gionta .05 .15
81 David Deshardnais .05 .15
82 Lars Eller .05 .15
83 Michael Cammalleri .07 .20
84 P.K. Subban .12 .30
85 Scott Gomez .07 .20
86 Tomas Plekanec .05 .15
87 New Jersey Devils .05 .15
88 Martin Brodeur .25 .60
89 Andy Greene .05 .15
90 Dainius Zubrus .05 .15
91 David Clarkson .05 .15
92 David Steckel .05 .15
93 Ilya Kovalchuk .10 .25
94 Mattias Tedenby .05 .15
95 Patrik Elias .10 .25
96 Travis Zajac .05 .15
97 New York Islanders .05 .15
98 John Tavares .15 .40
99 Frans Nielsen .05 .15
100 Kyle Okposo .05 .15
101 Mark Streit .05 .15
102 Matt Moulson .05 .15
103 Michael Grabner .07 .20
104 P.A. Parenteau .05 .15
105 Rick DiPietro .07 .20
106 Travis Hamonic .07 .20
107 New York Rangers .05 .15
108 Henrik Lundqvist .25 .60
109 Artem Anisimov .05 .15
110 Brandon Dubinsky .05 .15
111 Dan Girardi .05 .15
112 Derek Stepan .05 .15
113 Marc Staal .05 .15
114 Marian Gaborik .10 .25
115 Ryan Callahan .05 .15
116 Sean Avery .07 .20
117 Ottawa Senators .05 .15
118 Daniel Alfredsson .10 .25
119 Chris Neil .05 .15
120 Chris Phillips .05 .15
121 Craig Anderson .10 .25
122 Erik Karlsson .12 .30
123 Jason Spezza .10 .25
124 Milan Michalek .05 .15
125 Nick Foligno .07 .20
126 Sergei Gonchar .05 .15
127 Philadelphia Flyers .05 .15
128 Claude Giroux .10 .25
129 Blair Betts .05 .15
130 Chris Pronger .10 .25
131 Danny Briere .10 .25
132 James van Riemsdyk .07 .20
133 Kimmo Timonen .05 .15
134 Scott Hartnell .05 .15
135 Sergei Bobrovsky .15 .40
136 Jaromir Jagr .30 .75
137 Pittsburgh Penguins .05 .15
138 Sidney Crosby .40 1.00
139 Brooks Orpik .05 .15
140 Chris Kunitz .10 .25
141 Evgeni Malkin .20 .50
142 James Neal .05 .15
143 Jordan Staal .07 .20
144 Kris Letang .12 .30
145 Marc-Andre Fleury .20 .50
146 Mark Letestu .07 .20
147 Tampa Bay Lightning .05 .15
148 Steven Stamkos .20 .50
149 Martin St. Louis .10 .25
150 Mattias Ohlund .05 .15
151 Ryan Malone .05 .15
152 Dwayne Roloson .07 .20
153 Steve Downie .05 .15
154 Teddy Purcell .05 .15
155 Victor Hedman .12 .30
156 Vincent Lecavalier .10 .25
157 Toronto Maple Leafs .05 .15
158 James Reimer .10 .25
159 Colby Armstrong .05 .15
160 Dion Phaneuf .07 .20
161 Joffrey Lupul .05 .15
162 Luke Schenn .10 .25
163 Mikhail Grabovski .05 .15
164 Nikolai Kulemin .05 .15
165 Phil Kessel .10 .25
166 Tyler Bozak .05 .15
167 Washington Capitals .05 .15
168 Alex Ovechkin .40 1.00
169 Alexander Semin .10 .25
170 Brooks Laich .05 .15
171 Tomas Vokoun .07 .20
172 John Carlson .10 .25
173 Michal Neuvirth .07 .20
174 Mike Green .07 .20
175 Mike Knuble .05 .15
176 Nicklas Backstrom .10 .25
177 Winnipeg Jets .05 .15
178 Dustin Byfuglien .10 .25
179 Andrew Ladd .05 .15
180 Blake Wheeler .10 .25
181 Bryan Little .10 .25
182 Evander Kane .10 .25
183 Nik Antropov .07 .20
184 Ondrej Pavelec .10 .25
185 Tobias Enstrom .05 .15
186 Zach Bogosian .07 .20
187 Anaheim Ducks .05 .15
188 Corey Perry .15 .40
189 Bobby Ryan .07 .20
190 Cam Fowler .10 .25
191 Jonas Hiller .07 .20
192 Lubomir Visnovsky .05 .15
193 Luca Sbisa .07 .20
194 Saku Koivu .10 .25
195 George Parros .07 .20
196 Ryan Getzlaf .10 .25
197 Calgary Flames .05 .15
198 Jarome Iginla .12 .30
199 Alex Tanguay .05 .15
200 David Moss .05 .15
201 Daymond Langkow .05 .15
202 Jay Bouwmeester .05 .15
203 Mark Giordano .10 .25
204 Miikka Kiprusoff .10 .25
205 Olli Jokinen .07 .20
206 Rene Bourque .05 .15
207 Chicago Blackhawks .05 .15
208 Jonathan Toews .15 .40
209 Brent Seabrook .05 .15
210 Corey Crawford .12 .30
211 Dave Bolland .07 .20
212 Duncan Keith .07 .20
213 Marian Hossa .10 .25
214 Niklas Hjalmarsson .05 .15
215 Patrick Kane .20 .50
216 Patrick Sharp .10 .25
217 Colorado Avalanche .05 .15
218 Matt Duchene .10 .25
219 Daniel Winnik .05 .15
220 David Jones .05 .15
221 Erik Johnson .05 .15
222 Milan Hejduk .07 .20
223 Paul Stastny .07 .20
224 Ryan O'Reilly .10 .25
225 Brandon Yip .05 .15
226 Semyon Varlamov .10 .25
227 Columbus Blue Jackets .05 .15
228 Rick Nash .10 .25
229 Antoine Vermette .05 .15
230 Derick Brassard .05 .15
231 Matt Calvert .05 .15
232 Kris Russell .05 .15
233 Kristian Huselius .05 .15
234 Marc Methot .05 .15
235 R.J. Umberger .05 .15
236 Steve Mason .07 .20
237 Dallas Stars .05 .15
238 Loui Ericksson .05 .15
239 Alex Goligoski .07 .20
240 Brenden Morrow .07 .20
241 Jamie Benn .10 .25
242 Kari Lehtonen .07 .20
243 Mike Ribeiro .05 .15
244 Stephane Robidas .05 .15
245 Steve Ott .05 .15
246 Tom Wandell .05 .15
247 Detroit Red Wings .05 .15
248 Pavel Datsyuk .15 .40
249 Danny Cleary .10 .25
250 Henrik Zetterberg .12 .30
251 Jimmy Howard .12 .30
252 Johan Franzen .07 .20
253 Nicklas Lidstrom .05 .15
254 Niklas Kronwall .07 .20
255 Tomas Holmstrom .05 .15
256 Valtteri Filppula .05 .15
257 Edmonton Oilers .05 .15
258 Jordan Eberle .10 .25
259 Ales Hemsky .07 .20
260 Nikolai Khabibulin .07 .20
261 Ryan Jones .07 .20
262 Ryan Whitney .05 .15
263 Sam Gagner .05 .15
264 Shawn Horcoff .05 .15
265 Taylor Hall .10 .25
266 Tom Gilbert .05 .15
267 Los Angeles Kings .05 .15
268 Drew Doughty .12 .30
269 Anze Kopitar .15 .40
270 Dustin Brown .10 .25
271 Jack Johnson .05 .15
272 Jarret Stoll .07 .20
273 Jonathan Quick .12 .30
274 Justin Williams .07 .20
275 Kyle Clifford .05 .15
276 Mike Richards .07 .20
277 Minnesota Wild .05 .15
278 Mikko Koivu .07 .20
279 Nick Schultz .05 .15
280 Cal Clutterbuck .05 .15
281 Kyle Brodziak .05 .15
282 Marek Zidicky .05 .15
283 Matt Cullen .05 .15
284 Niklas Backstrom .10 .25
285 Pierre-Marc Bouchard .10 .25
286 Dany Heatley .07 .20
287 Nashville Predators .05 .15
288 Pekka Rinne .10 .25
289 Colin Wilson .07 .20
290 David Legwand .07 .20
291 Martin Erat .05 .15
292 Mike Fisher .05 .15
293 Patric Hornqvist .05 .15
294 Ryan Suter .07 .20
295 Sergei Kostitsyn .05 .15
296 Shea Weber .07 .20
297 Phoenix Coyotes .05 .15
298 Shane Doan .07 .20
299 Derek Morris .05 .15
300 Keith Yandle .05 .15
301 Lauri Korpikoski .05 .15
302 Lee Stempniak .05 .15
303 Martin Hanzal .05 .15
304 Mikkel Boedker .05 .15
305 Ray Whitney .07 .20
306 Taylor Pyatt .05 .15
307 San Jose Sharks .05 .15
308 Joe Thornton .15 .40
309 Antti Niemi .07 .20
310 Dan Boyle .05 .15
311 Joe Pavelski .12 .30
312 Logan Couture .12 .30
313 Marc-Edouard Vlasic .05 .15
314 Patrick Marleau .10 .25
315 Ryane Clowe .05 .15
316 Torrey Mitchell .05 .15
317 St. Louis Blues .05 .15
318 Jaroslav Halak .10 .25
319 Alex Pietrangelo .07 .20
320 Alexander Steen .05 .15
321 Andy McDonald .07 .20
322 T.J. Oshie .10 .25
323 Chris Stewart .07 .20
324 David Backes .05 .15
325 David Perron .07 .20
326 Patrik Berglund .05 .15
327 Vancouver Canucks .05 .15
328 Daniel Sedin .12 .30
329 Alexandre Burrows .05 .15
330 Kevin Bieksa .07 .20
331 Dan Hamhuis .07 .20
332 Henrik Sedin .12 .30
333 Mason Raymond .05 .15
334 Mikael Samuelsson .05 .15
335 Roberto Luongo .15 .40
336 Ryan Kesler .10 .25
337 Carey Price HC .20 .50
338 Jarome Iginla HC .12 .30
339 Sidney Crosby WC .40 1.00
340 Alex Ovechkin WC .40 1.00
341 Eric Staal H .12 .30
342 Mikko Koivu H .07 .20
343 Prague .05 .15
344 Prague 2 .05 .15
345 R.Nash/J.Thornton S .15 .40
346 Stockholm .05 .15
347 Boston Bruins .05 .15
348 Boston Bruins 2 .05 .15
349 Vancouver Canucks .05 .15
350 Vancouver Canucks 2 .05 .15
351 Zdeno Chara SC .10 .25
352 Boston Bruins 3 .05 .15
353 Boston Bruins 4 .05 .15
354 Boston Bruins 5 .05 .15
355 Patrick Kane AS FOIL .20 .50
356 Martin St. Louis AS FOIL .10 .25
357 Steven Stamkos AS FOIL .20 .50
358 Henrik Sedin AS FOIL .12 .30
359 Jonathan Toews AS FOIL .15 .40
360 Matt Duchene AS FOIL .10 .25
361 Nicklas Lidstrom AS FOIL .05 .15
362 Tim Thomas AS FOIL .10 .25
363 Eric Staal AS FOIL .12 .30
364 Jeff Skinner AS FOIL .12 .30
365 Daniel Sedin AS FOIL .12 .30
366 Alex Ovechkin AS FOIL .40 1.00
367 Claude Giroux AS FOIL .10 .25
368 Corey Perry AS FOIL .15 .40
369 Zdeno Chara AS FOIL .10 .25
370 Cam Ward AS FOIL .10 .25
371 Henrik Lundqvist AS FOIL .25 .60
372 Carey Price AS FOIL .20 .50
373 Alexander Burmistrov YS FOIL .07 .20
374 Tyler Ennis YS FOIL .05 .15
375 Linus Omark YS FOIL .10 .25
376 Magnus Paajarvi YS FOIL .07 .20
377 Mats Zuccarello YS FOIL .10 .25
378 Nazem Kadri YS FOIL .12 .30
379 Joe Colborne R FOIL .07 .20
380 Cody Hodgson R FOIL .12 .30
381 Aaron Palushaj R FOIL .07 .20
382 Marcus Kruger R FOIL .12 .30
383 Stephane Da Costa R FOIL .07 .20
384 Tomas Vincour R FOIL .07 .20

2012-13 Panini Stickers

1 NHL Logo .05 .15
2 NHLPA Logo .05 .15
3 Stanley Cup Champions Logo .05 .15
4 Eastern Conference .05 .15
5 Stanley Cup Logo .05 .15
6 Western Conference .05 .15
7 Rangers Division Champs .05 .15
8 Rangers Division Champs .05 .15
9 Devils Conference Champs .05 .15
10 Devils Conference Champs .05 .15
11 Bruins Division Champs .05 .15
12 Bruins Division Champs .05 .15
13 2011 Premier Sabres vs. Kings .05 .15
14 2011 Premier Sabres vs. Kings .05 .15
15 Panthers Division Champs .05 .15
16 Panthers Division Champs .05 .15
17 Cup Playoffs Panthers vs. Devils.05 .15
18 Cup Playoffs Panthers vs. Devils.05 .15
19 Blues Division Champs .05 .15
20 Blues Division Champs .05 .15
21 Cup Playoffs Coyotes vs. Predators.05 .15
22 Cup Playoffs Coyotes vs. Predators.05 .15
23 Canucks Division Champs .05 .15
24 Canucks Division Champs .05 .15
25 Heritage Classic Canadiens vs. Flames .05 .15
26 Heritage Classic Canadiens vs. Flames .05 .15
27 Kings Stanley Cup Champs .05 .15
28 Kings Stanley Cup Champs .05 .15
29 Sharks Division Champs .05 .15
30 Sharks Division Champs .05 .15
31 Zdeno Chara .10 .25
32 Brad Marchand .20 .50
33 David Krejci .10 .25
34 Milan Lucic .10 .25
35 Nathan Horton .10 .25
36 Patrice Bergeron .12 .30
37 Dennis Seidenberg .05 .15
38 Tuukka Rask .12 .30
39 Tyler Seguin .12 .30
40 Ryan Miller .10 .25
41 Steve Ott .05 .15
42 Drew Stafford .05 .15
43 Jhonas Enroth .10 .25
44 Nathan Gerbe .05 .15
45 Jason Pominville .05 .15
46 Thomas Vanek .07 .20
47 Tyler Ennis .05 .15
48 Tyler Myers .05 .15
49 Eric Staal .12 .30
50 Jordan Staal .07 .20
51 Cam Ward .10 .25
52 Chad LaRose .05 .15
53 Jamie McBain .05 .15
54 Jeff Skinner .12 .30
55 Jiri Tlusty .05 .15
56 Jussi Jokinen .05 .15
57 Alexander Semin .10 .25
58 Brian Campbell .05 .15
59 Jose Theodore .10 .25

60 Tomas Kopecky .07 .20
61 Stephen Weiss .07 .20
62 Sean Bergenheim .05 .15
63 Jacob Markstrom .10 .25
64 Kris Versteeg .05 .15
65 George Parros .07 .20
66 Tomas Fleischmann .05 .15
67 Carey Price .20 .50
68 David Desharnais .05 .15
69 Erik Cole .05 .15
70 Lars Eller .05 .15
71 Max Pacioretty .10 .25
72 P.K. Subban .12 .30
73 Rene Bourque .05 .15
74 Brian Gionta .05 .15
75 Tomas Plekanec .05 .15
76 Martin Brodeur .25 .60
77 Adam Henrique .07 .20
78 Adam Larsson .10 .25
79 Dainius Zubrus .05 .15
80 David Clarkson .05 .15
81 Ilya Kovalchuk .10 .25
82 Patrik Elias .10 .25
83 Travis Zajac .05 .15
84 Petr Sykora .07 .20
85 John Tavares .15 .40
86 Frans Nielsen .05 .15
87 Kyle Okposo .05 .15
88 Mark Streit .05 .15
89 Matt Moulson .05 .15
90 Michael Grabner .07 .20
91 Nino Neiderreiter .05 .15
92 Rick DiPietro .07 .20
93 Travis Hamonic .07 .20
94 Henrik Lundqvist .25 .60
95 Dan Girardi .05 .15
96 Brad Richards .10 .25
97 Rick Nash .10 .25
98 Carl Hagelin .05 .15
99 Derek Stepan .05 .15
100 Marian Gaborik .10 .25
101 Michael Del Zotto .05 .15
102 Ryan Callahan .05 .15
103 Daniel Alfredsson .10 .25
104 Chris Neil .05 .15
105 Colin Greening .05 .15
106 Craig Anderson .10 .25
107 Erik Karlsson .12 .30
108 Jason Spezza .10 .25
109 Milan Michalek .05 .15
110 Guilliaume Latendresse .07 .20
111 Mika Zibanejad .12 .30
112 Claude Giroux .10 .25
113 Chris Pronger .10 .25
114 Danny Briere .10 .25
115 Ilya Bryzgalov .10 .25
116 Luke Schenn .10 .25
117 Kimmo Timonen .05 .15
118 Matt Read .07 .20
119 Scott Hartnell .05 .15
120 Wayne Simmonds .12 .30
121 Sidney Crosby .40 1.00
122 Brooks Orpik .05 .15
123 Chris Kunitz .10 .25
124 James Neal .05 .15
125 Brandon Sutter .05 .15
126 Kris Letang .12 .30
127 Marc-Andre Fleury .20 .50
128 Pascal Dupuis .05 .15
129 Evgeni Malkin .20 .50
130 Steven Stamkos .20 .50
131 Mathieu Garon .07 .20
132 Anders Lindback .05 .15
133 Marc-Andre Bergeron .05 .15
134 Martin St. Louis .10 .25
135 Ryan Malone .05 .15
136 Teddy Purcell .05 .15
137 Victor Hedman .12 .30
138 Vincent Lecavalier .10 .25
139 Phil Kessel .10 .25
140 James van Riemsdyk .07 .20
141 Dion Phaneuf .07 .20
142 James Reimer .10 .25
143 Joffrey Lupul .05 .15
144 Ben Scrivens .10 .25
145 Mikhail Grabovski .05 .15
146 Jake Gardiner .05 .15
147 Tyler Bozak .05 .15
148 Alex Ovechkin .40 1.00
149 Karl Alzner .05 .15
150 Brooks Laich .05 .15
151 John Carlson .10 .25
152 Marcus Johansson .07 .20
153 Mike Ribeiro .10 .25
154 Mike Green .07 .20
155 Nicklas Backstrom .10 .25
156 Braden Holtby .12 .30
157 Evander Kane .10 .25
158 Alexander Burmistrov .07 .20
159 Andrew Ladd .05 .15
160 Blake Wheeler .10 .25
161 Bryan Little .10 .25
162 Dustin Byfuglien .10 .25
163 Olli Jokinen .07 .20
164 Ondrej Pavelec .10 .25
165 Tobias Enstrom .05 .15
166 Corey Perry .15 .40
167 Andrew Cogliano .05 .15
168 Bobby Ryan .07 .20
169 Cam Fowler .10 .25
170 Teemu Selanne .20 .50
171 Jonas Hiller .07 .20
172 Sheldon Souray .05 .15
173 Ryan Getzlaf .10 .25
174 Saku Koivu .10 .25
175 Jarome Iginla .12 .30
176 Alex Tanguay .07 .20
177 Curtis Glencross .05 .15
178 Jay Bouwmeester .05 .15
179 Dennis Wideman .05 .15
180 Mark Giordano .10 .25
181 Michael Cammalleri .07 .20
182 Miikka Kiprusoff .10 .25
183 Jiri Hudler .07 .20
184 Jonathan Toews FOIL .15 .40
185 Marcus Kruger .05 .15
186 Corey Crawford .12 .30
187 Viktor Stalberg .05 .15
188 Dave Bolland .07 .20
189 Duncan Keith .07 .20
190 Marian Hossa .10 .25
191 Patrick Kane .20 .50
192 Patrick Sharp .10 .25
193 Matt Duchene .10 .25
194 David Jones .05 .15
195 P.A. Parenteau .05 .15
196 Gabriel Landeskog .12 .30
197 Jean-Sebastien Giguere .10 .25
198 Milan Hejduk .07 .20
199 Paul Stastny .07 .20
200 Ryan O'Reilly .10 .25
201 Semyon Varlamov .10 .25
202 Vinny Prospal .05 .15
203 Derek Dorsett .05 .15
204 Derick Brassard .05 .15
205 Sergei Bobrovsky .15 .40
206 Nick Foligno .07 .20
207 R.J. Umberger .05 .15
208 Ryan Johansen .07 .20
209 Steve Mason .07 .20
210 Jack Johnson .05 .15
211 Jamie Benn .10 .25
212 Richard Bachman .07 .20
213 Brenden Morrow .07 .20
214 Kari Lehtonen .07 .20
215 Loui Eriksson .05 .15
216 Derek Roy .05 .15
217 Jaromir Jagr .30 .75
218 Ray Whitney .07 .20
219 Trevor Daley .05 .15
220 Pavel Datsyuk .15 .40
221 Danny Cleary .10 .25
222 Henrik Zetterberg .12 .30
223 Jimmy Howard .12 .30
224 Johan Franzen .07 .20
225 Jonas Gustavsson .10 .25
226 Niklas Kronwall .07 .20
227 Tomas Holmstrom .05 .15
228 Valtteri Filppula .05 .15
229 Jordan Eberle .10 .25
230 Ales Hemsky .07 .20
231 Nikolai Khabibulin .05 .15
232 Devan Dubnyk .07 .20
233 Ryan Nugent-Hopkins .12 .30
234 Ryan Smyth .07 .20
235 Sam Gagner .05 .15
236 Shawn Horcoff .05 .15
237 Taylor Hall .10 .25
238 Anze Kopitar .15 .40
239 Jeff Carter .07 .20
240 Jonathan Bernier .07 .20
241 Drew Doughty .12 .30
242 Dustin Brown .10 .25
243 Jarret Stoll .07 .20
244 Jonathan Quick .12 .30
245 Justin Williams .07 .20
246 Mike Richards .07 .20
247 Dany Heatley .07 .20
248 Ryan Suter .07 .20
249 Mikko Koivu .07 .20
250 Devin Setoguchi .07 .20
251 Josh Harding .10 .25
252 Kyle Brodziak .05 .15
253 Matt Cullen .05 .15
254 Niklas Backstrom .07 .20
255 Zach Parise .10 .25
256 Shea Weber .07 .20
257 David Legwand .07 .20
258 Craig Smith .05 .15
259 Martin Erat .05 .15
260 Mike Fisher .05 .15
261 Pekka Rinne .10 .25
262 Chris Mason .07 .20
263 Sergei Kostitsyn .05 .15
264 Patric Hornqvist .05 .15
265 Shane Doan .07 .20
266 Radim Vrbata .05 .15
267 Keith Yandle .05 .15
268 Lauri Korpikoski .05 .15
269 Martin Hanzal .05 .15
270 Mike Smith .10 .25
271 Mikkel Boedker .05 .15
272 Oliver Ekman-Larsson .10 .25
273 Paul Bissonnette .05 .15
274 Joe Thornton .15 .40
275 Antti Niemi .07 .20
276 Dan Boyle .05 .15
277 Joe Pavelski .12 .30
278 Logan Couture .12 .30
279 Martin Havlat .07 .20
280 Patrick Marleau .10 .25
281 Ryane Clowe .07 .20
282 Adam Burish .05 .15
283 David Backes .05 .15
284 Alex Pietrangelo .07 .20
285 Brian Elliott .07 .20
286 Chris Stewart .07 .20
287 David Perron .07 .20
288 Kevin Shattenkirk .05 .15
289 Patrik Berglund .05 .15
290 T.J. Oshie .10 .25
291 Jaroslav Halak .10 .25
292 Daniel Sedin .12 .30
293 Alexandre Burrows .05 .15
294 Cory Schneider .10 .25
295 Kevin Bieksa .07 .20
296 David Booth .05 .15
297 Henrik Sedin .12 .30
298 Alexander Edler .05 .15
299 Roberto Luongo .15 .40
300 Ryan Kesler .10 .25
301 Andrew Shaw YS .05 .15
302 Luke Adam YS .07 .20
303 Slava Voynov YS .10 .25
304 Cody Hodgson YS .05 .15
305 Gustav Nyquist YS .05 .15
306 Sean Couturier YS .07 .20
307 Carter Ashton .05 .15
308 Sven Baertschi .10 .25
309 Jaden Schwartz .05 .15
310 Brandon Bollig .05 .15
311 Jakob Silfverberg .12 .30
312 Chris Kreider .25 .60
313 Dion Phaneuf AS .07 .20
314 Erik Karlsson AS .12 .30
315 Carey Price AS .20 .50
316 Claude Giroux AS .10 .25
317 Corey Perry AS .15 .40
318 Daniel Sedin AS .12 .30
319 Evgeni Malkin AS .20 .50
320 Henrik Lundqvist AS .25 .60
321 Henrik Sedin AS .12 .30
322 Jarome Iginla AS .12 .30
323 John Tavares AS .15 .40
324 Tyler Seguin AS .12 .30
325 Kris Letang AS .12 .30
326 Patrick Kane AS .20 .50
327 Pavel Datsyuk AS .15 .40
328 Steven Stamkos AS .20 .50
329 Tim Thomas AS .10 .25
330 Zdeno Chara AS .10 .25

2012-13 Panini Stickers Team Logo Foils

A1 New Jersey Devils .15 .40
A2 New York Islanders .15 .40
A3 New York Rangers .15 .40
A4 Philadelphia Flyers .15 .40
A5 Pittsburgh Penguins .15 .40
A6 Boston Bruins .15 .40
A7 Buffalo Sabres .15 .40
A8 Montreal Canadiens .15 .40
A9 Ottawa Senators .15 .40
A10 Toronto Maple Leafs .15 .40
A11 Carolina Hurricanes .15 .40
A12 Florida Panthers .15 .40
A13 Tampa Bay Lightning .15 .40
A14 Washington Capitals .15 .40
A15 Winnipeg Jets .15 .40
A16 Chicago Blackhawks .15 .40
A17 Columbus Blue Jackets .15 .40
A18 Detroit Red Wings .15 .40
A19 Nashville Predators .15 .40
A20 St. Louis Blues .15 .40
A21 Calgary Flames .15 .40
A22 Colorado Avalanche .15 .40
A23 Edmonton Oilers .15 .40
A24 Minnesota Wild .15 .40
A25 Vancouver Canucks .15 .40
A26 Anaheim Ducks .15 .40
A27 Dallas Stars .15 .40
A28 Los Angeles Kings .15 .40
A29 Phoenix Coyotes .15 .40
A30 San Jose Sharks .15 .40
A31 Boston Bruins .15 .40
A32 Buffalo Sabres .15 .40
A33 Carolina Hurricanes .15 .40
A34 Florida Panthers .15 .40
A35 Montreal Canadiens .15 .40
A36 New Jersey Devils .15 .40
A37 New York Islanders .15 .40
A38 New York Rangers .15 .40
A39 Ottawa Senators .15 .40
A40 Philadelphia Flyers .15 .40
A41 Pittsburgh Penguins .15 .40
A42 Tampa Bay Lightning .15 .40
A43 Toronto Maple Leafs .15 .40
A44 Washington Capitals .15 .40
A45 Winnipeg Jets .15 .40
A46 Anaheim Ducks .15 .40
A47 Calgary Flames .15 .40
A48 Chicago Blackhawks .15 .40
A49 Colorado Avalanche .15 .40
A50 Columbus Blue Jackets .15 .40
A51 Dallas Stars .15 .40
A52 Detroit Red Wings .15 .40
A53 Edmonton Oilers .15 .40
A54 Los Angeles Kings .15 .40
A55 Minnesota Wild .15 .40
A56 Nashville Predators .15 .40
A57 Phoenix Coyotes .15 .40
A58 San Jose Sharks .15 .40
A59 St. Louis Blues .15 .40
A60 Vancouver Canucks .15 .40

2013-14 Panini Stickers

1 NHL Logo .07 .20
2 NHLPA Logo .07 .20
3 Stanley Cup Championship Logo .07 .20
4 Eastern Conference Logo .07 .20
5 Stanley Cup Logo .07 .20
6 Western Conference Logo .07 .20
7 Eastern Conference Action Puzzle .07 .20
8 Eastern Conference Action Puzzle .07 .20
9 Eastern Conference Action Puzzle .07 .20
10 Eastern Conference Action Puzzle .07 .20
11 Eastern Conference Action Puzzle .07 .20
12 Eastern Conference Action Puzzle .07 .20
13 Boston Bruins Eastern Conference Champs .07 .20
14 Boston Bruins Eastern Conference Champs .07 .20
15 Western Conference Action Puzzle .07 .20
16 Western Conference Action Puzzle .07 .20
17 Western Conference Action Puzzle .07 .20
18 Western Conference Action Puzzle .07 .20
19 Western Conference Action Puzzle .07 .20
20 Western Conference Action Puzzle .07 .20
21 Chicago Blackhawks Team Western Conference Champs Puzzle .07 .20
22 Chicago Blackhawks Team Western Conference Champs Puzzle .07 .20
23 Stanley Cup Finals Action Puzzle .07 .20
24 Stanley Cup Finals Action Puzzle .07 .20
25 Stanley Cup Finals Action Puzzle .07 .20
26 Stanley Cup Finals Action Puzzle .07 .20
27 Chicago Blackhawks Team Stanley Cup Champs Puzzle .07 .20
28 Chicago Blackhawks Team Stanley Cup Champs Puzzle .07 .20
29 Tuukka Rask .12 .30
30 Torey Krug .07 .20
31 Zdeno Chara FOIL .10 .25
32 Dennis Seidenberg .05 .15
33 Brad Marchand .20 .50
34 Milan Lucic .10 .25
35 Jarome Iginla .12 .30
36 David Krejci .10 .25
37 Patrice Bergeron .12 .30
38 Ryan Miller FOIL .10 .25
39 Christian Ehrhoff .05 .15
40 Tyler Myers .05 .15
41 Thomas Vanek .07 .20
42 Nathan Gerbe .05 .15
43 Drew Stafford .05 .15
44 Steve Ott .05 .15
45 Tyler Ennis .05 .15
46 Cody Hodgson .05 .15
47 Cam Ward .10 .25
48 Justin Faulk .07 .20
49 Jeff Skinner .12 .30
50 Alexander Semin .10 .25
51 Chad LaRose .05 .15
52 Eric Staal .12 .30
53 Tuomo Ruutu .07 .20
54 Jiri Tlusty .05 .15
55 Jordan Staal .07 .20
56 Sergei Bobrovsky .15 .40
57 Jack Johnson .05 .15
58 Tim Erixon .05 .15
59 R.J. Umberger .05 .15
60 Marian Gaborik FOIL .10 .25
61 Cam Atkinson .10 .25
62 Brandon Dubinsky .05 .15
63 Mark Letestu .07 .20
64 Ryan Johansen .07 .20
65 Jimmy Howard .12 .30
66 Niklas Kronwall .07 .20
67 Kyle Quincey .05 .15
68 Henrik Zetterberg .12 .30
69 Justin Abdelkader .07 .20
70 Danny Cleary .10 .25
71 Johan Franzen .07 .20
72 Daniel Alfredsson .10 .25
73 Pavel Datsyuk FOIL .15 .40
74 Jacob Markstrom .10 .25
75 Erik Gudbranson .05 .15
76 Ed Jovanovski .05 .15
77 Dmitry Kulikov .05 .15
78 Brian Campbell FOIL .05 .15
79 Tomas Fleischmann .05 .15
80 Tomas Kopecky .05 .15
81 Kris Versteeg .05 .15
82 Peter Mueller .05 .15
83 Carey Price FOIL .20 .50
84 Andrei Markov .05 .15
85 P.K. Subban .12 .30
86 Max Pacioretty .10 .25
87 Rene Bourque .05 .15
88 Brian Gionta .05 .15
89 David Desharnais .05 .15
90 Lars Eller .05 .15
91 Tomas Plekanec .05 .15
92 Martin Brodeur FOIL .25 .60
93 Cory Schneider .10 .25
94 Adam Larsson .10 .25
95 Bryce Salvador .05 .15
96 Ryan Carter .05 .15
97 Patrik Elias .10 .25
98 Dainius Zubrus .05 .15
99 Adam Henrique .07 .20
100 Travis Zajac .05 .15
101 Evgeni Nabokov .10 .25
102 Travis Hamonic .05 .15
103 Lubomir Visnovsky .05 .15
104 Matt Moulson .05 .15
105 Kyle Okposo .05 .15
106 Michael Grabner .07 .20
107 John Tavares FOIL .15 .40
108 Frans Nielsen .05 .15
109 Josh Bailey .07 .20
110 Henrik Lundqvist FOIL .25 .60
111 Marc Staal .05 .15
112 Michael Del Zotto .05 .15
113 Carl Hagelin .07 .20
114 Rick Nash .10 .25
115 Ryan Callahan .05 .15
116 Brian Boyle .05 .15
117 Derick Brassard .05 .15
118 Derek Stepan .05 .15
119 Craig Anderson FOIL .10 .25
120 Erik Karlsson .12 .30
121 Chris Phillips .05 .15
122 Milan Michalek .05 .15
123 Colin Greening .05 .15
124 Chris Neil .05 .15
125 Kyle Turris .05 .15
126 Jason Spezza .10 .25
127 Mika Zibanejad .12 .30
128 Steve Mason .07 .20
129 Braydon Coburn .05 .15
130 Kimmo Timonen .05 .15
131 Scott Hartnell .05 .15
132 Claude Giroux FOIL .10 .25
133 Matt Read .05 .15
134 Wayne Simmonds .12 .30
135 Vincent Lecavalier .10 .25
136 Sean Couturier .07 .20
137 Tomas Vokoun .07 .20
138 Marc-Andre Fleury .20 .50
139 Brooks Orpik .05 .15
140 Kris Letang .12 .30
141 Chris Kunitz .10 .25
142 James Neal .05 .15
143 Pascal Dupuis .05 .15
144 Sidney Crosby FOIL .40 1.00
145 Evgeni Malkin .20 .50
146 Ben Bishop .07 .20
147 Anders Lindback .05 .15
148 Victor Hedman .12 .30
149 Ryan Malone .05 .15
150 Teddy Purcell .05 .15
151 B.J. Crombeen .05 .15
152 Martin St. Louis .10 .25
153 Steven Stamkos FOIL .20 .50
154 Valtteri Filppula .05 .15
155 James Reimer .10 .25
156 Jonathan Bernier .07 .20
157 Dion Phaneuf .07 .20
158 Jake Gardiner .05 .15
159 James van Riemsdyk .07 .20
160 Joffrey Lupul .05 .15
161 Phil Kessel FOIL .10 .25
162 Tyler Bozak .05 .15
163 Nazem Kadri .12 .30
164 Michal Neuvirth .07 .20
165 Braden Holtby .12 .30
166 John Carlson .10 .25
167 Mike Green .07 .20
168 Karl Alzner .05 .15
169 Alex Ovechkin FOIL .40 1.00
170 Martin Erat .05 .15
171 Nicklas Backstrom .10 .25
172 Brooks Laich .05 .15
173 Jonas Hiller .07 .20
174 Cam Fowler .10 .25
175 Francois Beauchemin .05 .15
176 Corey Perry FOIL .15 .40
177 Teemu Selanne .20 .50
178 Nick Bonino .05 .15
179 Saku Koivu .10 .25
180 Andrew Cogliano .05 .15
181 Ryan Getzlaf .10 .25
182 Mark Giordano .10 .25
183 Dennis Wideman .05 .15
184 Curtis Glencross .05 .15
185 Sven Baertschi .07 .20
186 Jiri Hudler .05 .15
187 Lee Stempniak .05 .15
188 Michael Cammalleri FOIL .07 .20
189 Mikael Backlund .07 .20
190 Jiri Hudler .07 .20
191 Corey Crawford .12 .30
192 Duncan Keith .07 .20
193 Brent Seabrook .05 .15
194 Patrick Sharp .10 .25
195 Brandon Saad .07 .20
196 Bryan Bickell .05 .15
197 Marian Hossa .10 .25
198 Patrick Kane .20 .50
199 Jonathan Toews FOIL .15 .40
200 Semyon Varlamov .10 .25
201 Erik Johnson .05 .15
202 Gabriel Landeskog FOIL .12 .30
203 Alex Tanguay .05 .15
204 P.A. Parenteau .05 .15
205 Milan Hejduk .07 .20
206 Paul Stastny .07 .20
207 Ryan O'Reilly .10 .25
208 Matt Duchene .10 .25
209 Richard Bachman .07 .20
210 Kari Lehtonen .07 .20
211 Alex Goligoski .05 .15
212 Brenden Dillon .05 .15
213 Erik Cole .05 .15
214 Jamie Benn FOIL .10 .25
215 Tyler Seguin .12 .30
216 Ryan Garbutt .05 .15
217 Cody Eakin .05 .15
218 Devan Dubnyk .07 .20
219 Nick Schultz .05 .15
220 Ladislav Smid .05 .15
221 Taylor Hall FOIL .10 .25
222 Ryan Smyth .07 .20
223 Jordan Eberle .10 .25
224 Ales Hemsky .07 .20
225 Sam Gagner .05 .15
226 Ryan Nugent-Hopkins .12 .30
227 Jonathan Quick FOIL .12 .30
228 Slava Voynov .07 .20
229 Drew Doughty .12 .30
230 Justin Williams .07 .20
231 Dustin Brown .10 .25
232 Jarret Stoll .07 .20
233 Anze Kopitar .15 .40
234 Jeff Carter .07 .20
235 Mike Richards .07 .20
236 Josh Harding .10 .25
237 Nicklas Backstrom .07 .20
238 Ryan Suter .05 .15
239 Jared Spurgeon .05 .15
240 Dany Heatley .07 .20
241 Zach Parise FOIL .10 .25
242 Jason Pominville .05 .15
243 Torrey Mitchell .05 .15
244 Mikko Koivu .07 .20
245 Pekka Rinne FOIL .10 .25
246 Chris Mason .07 .20
247 Roman Josi .10 .25
248 Shea Weber .07 .20
249 Sergei Kostitsyn .05 .15
250 Gabriel Bourque .07 .20
251 David Legwand .07 .20
252 Craig Smith .05 .15
253 Mike Fisher .05 .15
254 Mike Smith .10 .25
255 Oliver Ekman-Larsson .10 .25
256 Keith Yandle .05 .15
257 Lauri Korpikoski .05 .15
258 Mikkel Boedker .05 .15
259 Shane Doan FOIL .07 .20
260 Radim Vrbata .05 .15
261 Martin Hanzal .05 .15
262 Antoine Vermette .05 .15
263 Antti Niemi .07 .20
264 Dan Boyle .05 .15
265 Brent Burns .10 .25
266 Marc-Edouard Vlasic .05 .15
267 Patrick Marleau .10 .25
268 Logan Couture FOIL .12 .30
269 Tommy Wingels .05 .15
270 Joe Thornton .15 .40
271 Joe Pavelski .12 .30
272 Brian Elliott .07 .20
273 Jaroslav Halak .10 .25
274 Jay Bouwmeester .05 .15
275 Alex Pietrangelo FOIL .07 .20
276 David Perron .07 .20
277 Alexander Steen .05 .15
278 T.J. Oshie .10 .25
279 Chris Stewart .07 .20
280 David Backes .05 .15
281 Roberto Luongo .15 .40
282 Alexander Edler .05 .15
283 Kevin Bieksa .07 .20
284 Jason Garrison .05 .15
285 Chris Higgins .05 .15
286 Daniel Sedin FOIL .12 .30
287 Alexandre Burrows .05 .15
288 Ryan Kesler .10 .25
289 Henrik Sedin .12 .30
290 Ondrej Pavelec .10 .25
291 Dustin Byfuglien .10 .25
292 Zach Bogosian .07 .20
293 Tobias Enstrom .05 .15
294 Evander Kane .10 .25
295 Andrew Ladd .05 .15
296 Blake Wheeler .10 .25
297 Nik Antropov .07 .20
298 Bryan Little .10 .25
299 Beau Bennett .12 .30
300 Jonas Brodin .12 .30
301 Damien Brunner .07 .20
302 Alex Chiasson .10 .25
303 Cory Conacher .05 .15
304 Emerson Etem .10 .25
305 Filip Forsberg .30 .75
306 Alex Galchenyuk .25 .60
307 Brendan Gallagher .25 .60
308 Mikael Granlund .15 .40
309 Mikhail Grigorenko .05 .15
310 Dougie Hamilton .15 .40
311 Thomas Hickey .07 .20
312 Jonathan Huberdeau .25 .60
313 Alex Killorn .15 .40
314 Danny DeKeyser .12 .30
315 Scott Laughton .12 .30
316 Ryan Murphy .10 .25
317 Jean-Gabriel Pageau .10 .25
318 Justin Schultz .12 .30
319 Vladimir Tarasenko .25 .60
320 Tyler Toffoli .20 .50
321 Tom Wilson .20 .50
322 Nail Yakupov .20 .50
323 Alex Ovechkin TW .40 1.00
324 Sergei Bobrovsky TW .15 .40
325 P.K. Subban TW .12 .30
326 Jonathan Huberdeau TW .25 .60
327 Martin St. Louis TW .05 .15
328 Alex Ovechkin TW .40 1.00

2013-14 Panini Stickers Team Logo Foils

A1 Boston Bruins/A2. Buffalo Sabres .15 .40
A3 Detroit Red Wings A4. Florida Panthers .15 .40
A5 Montreal Canadiens A6. Ottawa Senators .15 .40
A7 Tampa Bay Lightning A8. Toronto Maple Leafs .15 .40
A9 Carolina Hurricanes A10. Columbus Blue Jackets .15 .40
A11 New Jersey Devils A12. NY Islanders .15 .40
A13 NY Rangers/A14. Philadelphia Flyers .15 .40
A15 Pittsburgh Penguins/A16. Washington Capitals .15 .40
A17 Anaheim Ducks/A18. Calgary Flames .15 .40
A19 Edmonton Oilers/A20. L.A Kings .15 .40
A21 Phoenix Coyotes/A22. San Jose Sharks .15 .40
A23 Vancouver Canucks/A24. Chicago Blackhawks .15 .40
A25 Colorado Avalanche/A26. Dallas Stars .15 .40
A27 Minnesota Wild/A28. Nashville Predators .15 .40
A29 St. Louis Blues/A30. Winnipeg Jets .15 .40
A31 Boston Bruins/A32. Buffalo Sabres .15 .40
A33 Carolina Hurricanes/A34. Columbus Blue Jackets .15 .40
A35 Detroit Red Wings/A36. Florida Panthers .15 .40
A37 Montreal Canadiens/A38. New Jersey Devils .15 .40
A39 NY Islanders/A40. NY Rangers .15 .40
A41 Ottawa Senators/A42. Philadelphia Flyers .15 .40
A43 Pittsburgh Penguins/A44. Tampa Bay Lightning .15 .40
A45 Toronto Maple Leafs/A46. Washington Capitals .15 .40
A47 Anaheim Ducks/A48. Calgary Flames .15 .40
A49 Chicago Blackhawks/A50. Colorado Avalanche .15 .40
A51 Dallas Stars/A52. Edmonton Oilers .15 .40
A53 L.A Kings/A54. Minnesota Wild .15 .40
A55 Nashville Predators/A56. Phoenix Coyotes .15 .40
A57 San Jose Sharks/A58. St. Louis Blues .15 .40
A59 Vancouver Canucks/A60. Winnipeg Jets .15 .40

2014-15 Panini Stickers

1 NHL Logo FOIL .07 .20
2 Panini Logo FOIL .07 .20
3 NHLPA Logo FOIL .07 .20
4 Boston Bruins Home Jersey .07 .20
5 Boston Bruins Away Jersey .07 .20
6 Patrice Bergeron FOIL .12 .30
7 Boston Bruins Team Logo .07 .20
8 Tuukka Rask FOIL .12 .30
9 Tuukka Rask .12 .30
10 Zdeno Chara .10 .25
11 Dougie Hamilton .07 .20
12 Torey Krug .07 .20
13 Patrice Bergeron .12 .30
14 David Krejci .10 .25
15 Milan Lucic .10 .25
16 Brad Marchand .20 .50
17 Reilly Smith .10 .25
18 Buffalo Sabres Home Jersey .07 .20
19 Buffalo Sabres Away Jersey .07 .20
20 Matt Moulson FOIL .05 .15
21 Buffalo Sabres Team Logo .07 .20
22 Tyler Ennis FOIL .05 .15
23 Jhonas Enroth .10 .25
24 Michal Neuvirth .07 .20
25 Tyler Myers .05 .15
26 Tyler Ennis .05 .15
27 Brian Gionta .05 .15
28 Zemgus Girgensons .07 .20
29 Cody Hodgson .05 .15
30 Matt Moulson .05 .15
31 Drew Stafford .05 .15
32 Carolina Hurricanes Home Jersey .07 .20
33 Carolina Hurricans Away Jersey .07 .20
34 Eric Staal FOIL .12 .30
35 Carolina Hurricanes Team Logo .07 .20
36 Jeff Skinner FOIL .12 .30
37 Cam Ward .10 .25
38 Justin Faulk .07 .20
39 Nathan Gerbe .05 .15
40 Elias Lindholm .10 .25
41 Alexander Semin .10 .25
42 Jeff Skinner .12 .30
43 Eric Staal .12 .30
44 Jordan Staal .07 .20
45 Jiri Tlusty .05 .15
46 Columbus Blue Jackets Home Jersey .07 .20
47 Columbus Blue Jackets Away Jersey .07 .20
48 Sergei Bobrovsky FOIL .15 .40
49 Columbus Blue Jackets Team Logo .07 .20
50 Ryan Johansen FOIL .07 .20
51 Sergei Bobrovsky .15 .40
52 Jack Johnson .05 .15
53 Ryan Murray .05 .15
54 James Wisniewski .05 .15
55 Brandon Dubinsky .05 .15
56 Nick Foligno .07 .20
57 Scott Hartnell .05 .15
58 Boone Jenner .10 .25
59 Ryan Johansen .07 .20
60 Detroit Red Wings Home Jersey .07 .20
61 Detroit Red Wings Away Jersey .07 .20
62 Pavel Datsyuk FOIL .15 .40
63 Detroit Red Wings Team Logo .07 .20
64 Henrik Zetterberg FOIL .12 .30
65 Jimmy Howard .07 .20
66 Jonas Gustavsson .07 .20
67 Danny DeKeyser .07 .20
68 Niklas Kronwall .07 .20
69 Pavel Datsyuk .15 .40
70 Johan Franzen .07 .20
71 Gustav Nyquist .05 .15
72 Tomas Tatar .05 .15
73 Henrik Zetterberg .12 .30
74 Florida Panthers Home Team .07 .20
75 Florida Panthers Away Team .07 .20
76 Brian Campbell FOIL .05 .15
77 Florida Panthers Logo .07 .20
78 Roberto Luongo FOIL .15 .40
79 Roberto Luongo .15 .40
80 Brian Campbell .05 .15
81 Erik Gudbranson .05 .15
82 Aleksander Barkov .15 .40
83 Nick Bjugstad .05 .15
84 Tomas Fleischmann .05 .15
85 Jonathan Huberdeau .12 .30
86 Jussi Jokinen .05 .15
87 Scottie Upshall .05 .15
88 Montreal Canadiens Home Jersey .07 .20
89 Montreal Canadiens Away Jersey .07 .20
90 P.K. Subban FOIL .12 .30
91 Montreal Canadiens Team Logo .07 .20
92 Carey Price FOIL .20 .50
93 Carey Price .20 .50
94 Andrei Markov .05 .15
95 P.K Subban .07 .20
96 David Desharnais .05 .15
97 Lars Eller .05 .15
98 Alex Galchenyuk .05 .15
99 Brendan Gallagher .10 .25
100 Max Pacioretty .10 .25
101 Tomas Plekanec .05 .15
102 New Jersey Devils Home Jersey .07 .20
103 New Jersey Devils Away Jersey .07 .20
104 Jaromir Jagr FOIL .30 .75
105 New Jersey Devils Team Logo .07 .20
106 Cory Schneider FOIL .10 .25
107 Cory Schneider .10 .25
108 Marek Zidlicky .05 .15
109 Andy Greene .05 .15
110 Damien Brunner .05 .15
111 Mike Cammalleri .07 .20
112 Patrik Elias .10 .25
113 Adam Henrique .07 .20
114 Jaromir Jagr .30 .75
115 Travis Zajac .05 .15
116 New York Islanders Home Jersey .07 .20
117 New York Islanders Away Jersey .07 .20
118 Kyle Okposo FOIL .05 .15
119 New York Islanders Logo .07 .20
120 John Tavares FOIL .15 .40
121 Jaroslav Halak .10 .25
122 Travis Hamonic .05 .15
123 Thomas Hickey .05 .15
124 Josh Bailey .07 .20
125 Michael Grabner .07 .20
126 Frans Nielsen .05 .15
127 Kyle Okposo .05 .15
128 Ryan Strome .10 .25
129 John Tavares .15 .40
130 New York Rangers Home Jersey .07 .20
131 New York Rangers Away Jersey .07 .20
132 Mats Zuccarello-Aasen FOIL .10 .25
133 New York Rangers Team Logo .07 .20
134 Henrik Lundqvist FOIL .25 .60
135 Henrik Lundqvist .25 .60
136 Ryan McDonagh .05 .15
137 Marc Staal .05 .15
138 Derick Brassard .05 .15
139 Carl Hagelin .05 .15
140 Rick Nash .10 .25
141 Martin St. Louis .10 .25
142 Derek Stepan .05 .15

143 Mats Zuccarello-Aasen .10 .25
144 Ottawa Senators Home Jersey .07 .20
145 Ottawa Senators Away Jersey .07 .20
146 Bobby Ryan FOIL .07 .20
147 Ottawa Senators Team Logo .07 .20
148 Erik Karlsson FOIL .12 .30
149 Craig Anderson .10 .25
150 Cody Ceci .05 .15
151 Erik Karlsson .12 .30
152 Alex Chiasson .07 .20
153 Clarke MacArthur .05 .15
154 Milan Michalek .05 .15
155 Bobby Ryan .07 .20
156 Kyle Turris .10 .25
157 Mika Zibanejad .12 .30
158 Philadelphia Flyers Home Team.07 .20
159 Philadelphia Flyers Away Team.07 .20
160 Wayne Simmonds FOIL .12 .30
161 Philadelphia Flyers Logo .07 .20
162 Claude Giroux FOIL .10 .25
163 Steve Mason .07 .20
164 Luke Schenn .10 .25
165 Braydon Coburn .05 .15
166 Sean Couturier .07 .20
167 Claude Giroux .10 .25
168 Vincent Lecavalier .10 .25
169 Brayden Schenn .10 .25
170 Wayne Simmonds .12 .30
171 Jakub Voracek .07 .20
172 Pittsburgh Penguins Home Jersey.07 .20
173 Pittsburgh Penguins Away Jersey.07 .20
174 Marc-Andre Fleury FOIL .20 .50
175 Pittsburgh Penguins Logo .07 .20
176 Sidney Crosby FOIL .40 1.00
177 Marc-Andre Fleury .20 .50
178 Kris Letang .12 .30
179 Olli Maatta .05 .15
180 Beau Bennett .05 .15
181 Sidney Crosby .40 1.00
182 Pascal Dupuis .05 .15
183 Patric Hornqvist .05 .15
184 Chris Kunitz .10 .25
185 Evgeni Malkin .20 .50
186 Tampa Bay Lightning Home Jersey .07 .20
187 Tampa Bay Lightning Away Jersey.07 .20
188 Ben Bishop FOIL .07 .20
189 Tampa Bay Lightning Team Logo.07 .20
190 Steven Stamkos FOIL .20 .50
191 Ben Bishop .07 .20
192 Mathieu Carle .05 .15
193 Victor Hedman .12 .30
194 Brian Boyle .05 .15
195 Ryan Callahan .05 .15
196 Valtteri Filppula .05 .15
197 Tyler Johnson .05 .15
198 Ondrej Palat .07 .20
199 Steven Stamkos .20 .50
200 Toronto Maple Leafs Home Jersey.07 .20
201 Toronto Maple Leafs Away Jersey.07 .20
202 Phil Kessel FOIL .10 .25
203 Toronto Maple Leafs Logo .07 .20
204 James van Riemsdyk FOIL .07 .20
205 Jonathan Bernier .07 .20
206 James Reimer .10 .25
207 Jake Gardiner .05 .15
208 Dion Phaneuf .07 .20
209 David Clarkson .05 .15
210 Nazem Kadri .12 .30
211 Phil Kessel .10 .25
212 Joffrey Lupul .05 .15
213 James van Riemsdyk .07 .20
214 Washington Capitals Home Jersey.07 .20
215 Washington Capitals Away Jersey.07 .20
216 Nicklas Backstrom FOIL .10 .25
217 Washington Capitals Team Logo.07 .20
218 Alex Ovechkin FOIL .40 1.00
219 Braden Holtby .12 .30
220 Karl Alzner .05 .15
221 John Carlson .10 .25
222 Mike Green .07 .20
223 Nicklas Backstrom .10 .25
224 Troy Brouwer .05 .15
225 Brooks Laich .05 .15
226 Alex Ovechkin .40 1.00
227 Joel Ward .05 .15
228 Anaheim Ducks Home Jersey .07 .20
229 Anaheim Ducks Away Jersey .07 .20
230 Corey Perry FOIL .15 .40
231 Anaheim Ducks Team Logo .07 .20
232 Ryan Getzlaf FOIL .10 .25
233 Frederik Andersen .12 .30
234 Cam Fowler .10 .25
235 Hampus Lindholm .05 .15
236 Andrew Cogliano .05 .15
237 Ryan Getzlaf .10 .25
238 Ryan Kesler .10 .25
239 Kyle Palmieri .07 .20
240 Corey Perry .15 .40
241 Jakob Silfverberg .05 .15
242 Arizona Coyotes Home Jersey .07 .20
243 Arizona Coyotes Away Jersey .07 .20
244 Keith Yandle FOIL .05 .15
245 Arizona Coyotes Team Logo .07 .20
246 Mike Smith FOIL .10 .25
247 Mike Smith .10 .25
248 Oliver Ekman-Larsson .10 .25
249 Keith Yandle .05 .15
250 Mikkel Boedker .05 .15
251 Shane Doan .07 .20
252 Sam Gagner .05 .15
253 Martin Hanzal .05 .15
254 Lauri Korpikoski .05 .15
255 Antoine Vermette .05 .15
256 Calgary Flames Home Jersey .07 .20
257 Calgary Flames Away Jersey .07 .20
258 Jiri Hudler FOIL .07 .20
259 Calgary Flames Team Logo .07 .20
260 Mark Giordano FOIL .10 .25
261 Jonas Hiller .07 .20
262 T.J. Brodie .05 .15
263 Mark Giordano .10 .25
264 Dennis Wideman .05 .15
265 Mikael Backlund .07 .20
266 Curtis Glencross .05 .15
267 Jiri Hudler .07 .20
268 Sean Monahan .05 .15
269 Mason Raymond .05 .15
270 Chicago Blackhawks Home Jersey.07 .20
271 Chicago Blackhawks Away Jersey.07 .20
272 Jonathan Toews FOIL .15 .40
273 Chicago Blackhawks Logo .07 .20
274 Patrick Kane FOIL .20 .50
275 Corey Crawford .12 .30
276 Duncan Keith .07 .20
277 Brent Seabrook .05 .15
278 Marian Hossa .10 .25
279 Patrick Kane .20 .50
280 Brad Richards .10 .25
281 Patrick Sharp .10 .25
282 Andrew Shaw .05 .15
283 Jonathan Toews .15 .40
284 Colorado Avalanche Home Jersey.07 .20
285 Colorado Avalanche Away Jersey.07 .20
286 Nathan MacKinnon FOIL .40 1.00
287 Colorado Avalanche Team Logo .07 .20
288 Semyon Varlamov FOIL .10 .25
289 Semyon Varlamov .10 .25
290 Erik Johnson .05 .15
291 Tyson Barrie .05 .15
292 Matt Duchene .10 .25
293 Jarome Iginla .12 .30
294 Gabriel Landeskog .12 .30
295 Nathan MacKinnon .40 1.00
296 Jamie McGinn .05 .15
297 Ryan O'Reilly .10 .25
298 Dallas Stars Home Jersey .07 .20
299 Dallas Stars Away Jersey .07 .20
300 Jamie Benn FOIL .10 .25
301 Dallas Stars Team Logo .07 .20
302 Tyler Seguin FOIL .12 .30
303 Kari Lehtonen .07 .20
304 Brenden Dillon .05 .15
305 Alex Goligoski .05 .15
306 Jamie Benn .10 .25
307 Erik Cole .05 .15
308 Valeri Nichushkin .10 .25
309 Antoine Roussel .05 .15
310 Tyler Seguin .12 .30
311 Jason Spezza .10 .25
312 Edmonton Oilers Home Jersey .07 .20
313 Edmonton Oilers Away Jersey .07 .20
314 Jordan Eberle FOIL .10 .25
315 Edmonton Oilers Team Logo .07 .20
316 Taylor Hall FOIL .10 .25
317 Ben Scrivens .07 .20
318 Andrew Ference .05 .15
319 Justin Schultz .07 .20
320 Jordan Eberle .10 .25
321 Taylor Hall .10 .25
322 Ryan Nugent-Hopkins .12 .30
323 David Perron .07 .20
324 Teddy Purcell .05 .15
325 Nail Yakupov .05 .15
326 Los Angeles Kings Home Jersey.07 .20
327 Los Angeles Kings Away Jersey.07 .20
328 Drew Doughty FOIL .12 .30
329 Los Angeles Kings Logo .07 .20
330 Anze Kopitar FOIL .15 .40
331 Jonathan Quick .12 .30
332 Drew Doughty .12 .30
333 Slava Voynov .10 .25
334 Dustin Brown .10 .25
335 Jeff Carter .07 .20
336 Marian Gaborik .10 .25
337 Anze Kopitar .15 .40
338 Mike Richards .07 .20
339 Justin Williams .07 .20
340 Minnesota Wild Home Jersey .07 .20
341 Minnesota Wild Away Jersey .07 .20
342 Mikael Granlund FOIL .07 .20
343 Minnesota Wild Team Logo .07 .20
344 Zach Parise FOIL .10 .25
345 Nicklas Backstrom .10 .25
346 Josh Harding .07 .20
347 Ryan Suter .07 .20
348 Charlie Coyle .10 .25
349 Mikael Granlund .07 .20
350 Mikko Koivu .07 .20
351 Zach Parise .10 .25
352 Jason Pominville .05 .15
353 Thomas Vanek .07 .20
354 Nashville Predators Home Jersey.07 .20
355 Nashville Predators Away Jersey.07 .20
356 Pekka Rinne FOIL .10 .25
357 Nashville Predators Team Logo.07 .20
358 Shea Weber FOIL .07 .20
359 Pekka Rinne .10 .25
360 Seth Jones .10 .25
361 Roman Josi .10 .25
362 Shea Weber .07 .20
363 Mike Fisher .05 .15
364 James Neal .05 .15
365 Mike Ribeiro .05 .15
366 Craig Smith .05 .15
367 Colin Wilson .05 .15
368 San Jose Sharks Home Jersey .07 .20
369 San Jose Sharks Away Jersey .07 .20
370 Brent Burns FOIL .10 .25
371 San Jose Sharks Logo .07 .20
372 Joe Pavelski FOIL .12 .30
373 Antti Niemi .07 .20
374 Brent Burns .10 .25
375 Marc-Edouard Vlasic .05 .15
376 Logan Couture .12 .30
377 Tomas Hertl .10 .25
378 Patrick Marleau .10 .25
379 Joe Pavelski .12 .30
380 Joe Thornton .15 .40
381 Tommy Wingels .05 .15
382 St Louis Blues Home Jersey .07 .20
383 St Louis Blues Away Jersey .07 .20
384 David Backes FOIL .05 .15
385 St Louis Blues Team Logo .07 .20
386 T.J. Oshie FOIL .10 .25
387 Brian Elliott .07 .20
388 Jay Bouwmeester .05 .15
389 Alex Pietrangelo .07 .20
390 Kevin Shattenkirk .05 .15
391 David Backes .05 .15
392 T.J. Oshie .10 .25
393 Jaden Schwartz .12 .30
394 Alexander Steen .05 .15
395 Vladimir Tarasenko .12 .30
396 Vancouver Canucks Home Jersey .07 .20
397 Vancouver Canucks Away Jersey.07 .20
398 Daniel Sedin FOIL .12 .30
399 Vancouver Canucks Team Logo.07 .20
400 Henrik Sedin FOIL .12 .30
401 Ryan Miller .10 .25
402 Kevin Bieksa .07 .20
403 Alexander Edler .05 .15
404 Alexandre Burrows .05 .15
405 Jannik Hansen .07 .20
406 Chris Higgins .05 .15
407 Daniel Sedin .12 .30
408 Henrik Sedin .12 .30
409 Radim Vrbata .05 .15
410 Winnipeg Jets Home Jersey .07 .20
411 Winnipeg Jets Away Jersey .07 .20
412 Dustin Byfuglien FOIL .10 .25
413 Winnipeg Jets Team Logo .07 .20
414 Blake Wheeler FOIL .10 .25
415 Ondrej Pavelec .10 .25
416 Zach Bogosian .07 .20
417 Jacob Trouba .07 .20
418 Dustin Byfuglien .10 .25
419 Evander Kane .10 .25
420 Andrew Ladd .05 .15
421 Bryan Little .10 .25
422 Mark Scheifele .15 .40
423 Blake Wheeler .10 .25
424 Jake Allen RR .10 .25
425 John Gibson RR .10 .25
426 Johnny Gaudreau RR .30 .75
427 Brandon Gormley RR .10 .25
428 Evgeny Kuznetsov RR .25 .60
429 Calle Jarnkrok RR .10 .25
430 Tanner Pearson RR .05 .15
431 Nikita Zadorov RR .05 .15
432 Teuvo Teravainen RR .15 .40
433 2014 Winter Classic Logo .07 .20
434 Winter Classic Maple Leafs .07 .20
435 Winter Classic Lineup .07 .20
436 Winter Classic Jimmy Howard .07 .20
437 Winter Classic Jonathan Bernier.07 .20
438 Winter Classic Faceoff .07 .20
439 Winter Classic Goal .07 .20
440 Heritage Classic Logo .07 .20
441 Heritage Classic Ottawa Senators.07 .20
442 Heritage Classic Cannucks Lockers .07 .20
443 Heritage Classic Vancouver Cannucks .07 .20
444 Heritage Classic Save .07 .20
445 Heritage Classic 2 on 1 .07 .20
446 Heritage Classic Ottawa Wins .07 .20
447 Stadium Series Ducks vs. Kings.07 .20
448 Stadium Series Ducks Win .07 .20
449 Stadium Series Rangers vs. Devils.07 .20
450 Stadium Series Rangers Win .07 .20
451 Stadium Series Rangers vs. Islanders .07 .20
452 Stadium Series Rangers Win .07 .20
453 Stadium Series Penguins vs. Blackhawks .07 .20
454 Stadium Series Blackhawks Win.07 .20
455 Western Conference Final .07 .20
456 Western Conference First Round.07 .20
457 Western Conference Second Round .07 .20
458 Western Conference Second Round .07 .20
459 Western Conference First Round.07 .20
460 Western Conference First Round.07 .20
461 Western Conference First Round.07 .20
462 Eastern Conference Final .07 .20
463 Eastern Conference Second Round .07 .20
464 Eastern Conference Second Round .07 .20
465 Eastern Conference First Round.07 .20
466 Eastern Conference First Round.07 .20
467 Eastern Conference First Round.07 .20
468 Eastern Conference First Round.07 .20
469 Stanley Cup Finals Rangers 2; Kings 3 .07 .20
470 Stanley Cup Finals Rangers 4; Kings 5 .07 .20
471 Stanley Cup Finals Kings 3; Rangers 0 .07 .20
472 Stanley Cup Finals Kings 1; Rangers 0 .07 .20
473 Stanley Cup Finals Rangers 2; Kings 3 .07 .20
474 Stanley Cup MVP .07 .20
475 Stanley Cup Kings 1 .07 .20
476 Stanley Cup Kings 2 .07 .20
477 Art Ross Trophy .07 .20
478 Sidney Crosby Art Ross Winner .40 1.00
479 Rocket Richard Trophy .07 .20
480 Alex Ovechkin Rocket Richard Winner .40 1.00
481 Selke Trophy .07 .20
482 Patrice Bergeron Selke Trophy Winner .12 .30
483 Masterton Trophy .07 .20
484 Masterton Trophy Winner .07 .20
485 Hart Trophy .07 .20
486 Sidney Crosby Hart Trophy Winner .40 1.00
487 Vezina Trophy .07 .20
488 Tuukka Rask Vezina Winner .12 .30
489 Norris Trophy .07 .20
490 Duncan Keith Norris Trophy Winner .07 .20
491 Lady Byng Trophy .07 .20
492 Ryan O'Reilly Lady Byng Winner .10 .25
493 Calder Trophy .07 .20
494 Nathan MacKinnon Calder Winner .40 1.00
495 Stanley Cup Puzzle A .07 .20
496 Stanley Cup Puzzle B .07 .20
497 Stanley Cup Puzzle C .07 .20
498 Stanley Cup Puzzle D .07 .20
499 Stanley Cup Puzzle E .07 .20
500 Stanley Cup Puzzle F .07 .20

2015-16 Panini Stickers

1 Florida Panthers Washington Capitals Shootout SH.07 .20
2 Martin Brodeur SH .25 .60
3 Andrew Hammond SH .12 .30
4 Jaromir Jagr SH .30 .75
5 Jamie Benn SH .10 .25
6 Johnny Gaudreau Matt Stone SH .15 .40
7 Devan Dubnyk SH .07 .20
8 Carey Price SH .20 .50
9 Winnipeg Jets SH .07 .20
10 Bruins Jerseys .07 .20
11 Boston Bruins Logo .07 .20
12 Tuukka Rask FOIL .12 .30
13 Patrice Bergeron FOIL .12 .30
14 Zdeno Chara FOIL .10 .25
15 Tuukka Rask .12 .30
16 Zdeno Chara .10 .25
17 Torey Krug .07 .20
18 Patrice Bergeron .12 .30
19 Loui Eriksson .05 .15
20 David Krejci .10 .25
21 Brad Marchand .20 .50
22 David Pastrnak .25 .60
23 Dennis Seidenberg .05 .15
24 Sabres Jerseys .07 .20
25 Buffalo Sabres Logo .07 .20
26 Matt Moulson FOIL .05 .15
27 Tyler Ennis FOIL .05 .15
28 Zemgus Girgensons FOIL .07 .20
29 Robin Lehner .07 .20
30 Zach Bogosian .07 .20
31 Rasmus Ristolainen .05 .15
32 Tyler Ennis .05 .15
33 Marcus Foligno .07 .20
34 Brian Gionta .05 .15
35 Zemgus Girgensons .07 .20
36 Matt Moulson .05 .15
37 Ryan O'Reilly .10 .25
38 Hurricanes Jerseys .07 .20
39 Carolina Hurricanes Logo .07 .20
40 Eric Staal FOIL .12 .30
41 Justin Faulk FOIL .07 .20
42 Jeff Skinner FOIL .12 .30
43 Cam Ward .10 .25
44 Justin Faulk .07 .20
45 James Wisniewski .05 .15
46 Nathan Gerbe .05 .15
47 Elias Lindholm .10 .25
48 Victor Rask .05 .15
49 Jeff Skinner .12 .30
50 Eric Staal .12 .30
51 Jordan Staal .07 .20
52 Blue Jackets Jerseys .07 .20
53 Columbus Blue Jackets Logo .07 .20
54 Nick Foligno FOIL .07 .20
55 Jack Johnson FOIL .05 .15
56 Ryan Johansen FOIL .07 .20
57 Sergei Bobrovsky .15 .40
58 Jack Johnson .05 .15
59 David Savard .05 .15
60 Cam Atkinson .10 .25
61 Brandon Dubinsky .05 .15
62 Nick Foligno .07 .20
63 Scott Hartnell .05 .15
64 Boone Jenner .10 .25
65 Ryan Johansen .07 .20
66 Red Wings Jerseys .07 .20
67 Detroit Red Wings Logo .07 .20
68 Pavel Datsyuk FOIL .15 .40
69 Niklas Kronwall FOIL .07 .20
70 Henrik Zetterberg FOIL .12 .30
71 Jimmy Howard .12 .30
72 Petr Mrazek .10 .25
73 Danny DeKeyser .05 .15
74 Niklas Kronwall .07 .20
75 Justin Abdelkader .07 .20
76 Pavel Datsyuk .15 .40
77 Gustav Nyquist .05 .15
78 Tomas Tatar .05 .15
79 Henrik Zetterberg .12 .30
80 Panthers Jerseys .07 .20
81 Florida Panthers Logo .07 .20
82 Aaron Ekblad FOIL .12 .30
83 Jaromir Jagr FOIL .30 .75
84 Roberto Luongo FOIL .15 .40
85 Roberto Luongo .15 .40
86 Brian Campbell .05 .15
87 Aaron Ekblad .12 .30
88 Aleksander Barkov .15 .40
89 Nick Bjugstad .05 .15
90 Jonathan Huberdeau .12 .30
91 Jaromir Jagr .30 .75
92 Jussi Jokinen .05 .15
93 Brandon Pirri .05 .15
94 Canadiens Jerseys .07 .20
95 Montreal Canadiens Logo .07 .20
96 Carey Price FOIL .20 .50
97 Max Pacioretty FOIL .10 .25
98 P.K. Subban FOIL .12 .30
99 Carey Price .20 .50
100 Andrei Markov .05 .15
101 P.K. Subban .12 .30
102 David Desharnais .05 .15
103 Lars Eller .05 .15
104 Alex Galchenyuk .05 .15
105 Brendan Gallagher .10 .25
106 Max Pacioretty .10 .25
107 Tomas Plekanec .05 .15
108 Devils Jerseys .07 .20
109 New Jersey Devils Logo .07 .20
110 Cory Schneider FOIL .10 .25
111 Mike Cammalleri FOIL .07 .20
112 Adam Henrique FOIL .07 .20
113 Cory Schneider .10 .25
114 Eric Gelinas .05 .15
115 Andy Greene .05 .15
116 Adam Larsson .10 .25
117 Jon Merrill .05 .15
118 Mike Cammalleri .07 .20
119 Patrik Elias .10 .25
120 Adam Henrique .07 .20
121 Travis Zajac .05 .15
122 Islanders Jerseys .07 .20
123 New York Islanders Logo .07 .20
124 John Tavares FOIL .15 .40
125 Jaroslav Halak FOIL .10 .25
126 Kyle Okposo FOIL .05 .15
127 Jaroslav Halak .10 .25
128 Johnny Boychuk .07 .20
129 Travis Hamonic .05 .15
130 Nick Leddy .05 .15
131 Brock Nelson .10 .25
132 Frans Nielsen .05 .15
133 Kyle Okposo .05 .15
134 Ryan Strome .10 .25
135 John Tavares .15 .40
136 Rangers Jerseys .07 .20
137 New York Rangers Logo .07 .20
138 Henrik Lundqvist FOIL .25 .60
139 Derick Brassard FOIL .05 .15
140 Rick Nash FOIL .10 .25
141 Henrik Lundqvist .25 .60
142 Ryan McDonagh .05 .15
143 Keith Yandle .05 .15
144 Derick Brassard .05 .15
145 Chris Kreider .12 .30
146 J.T. Miller .12 .30
147 Rick Nash .10 .25
148 Derek Stepan .05 .15
149 Mats Zuccarello .10 .25
150 Senators Jerseys .07 .20
151 Ottawa Senators Logo .07 .20
152 Erik Karlsson FOIL .12 .30
153 Mike Hoffman FOIL .05 .15
154 Mark Stone FOIL .12 .30
155 Craig Anderson .10 .25
156 Andrew Hammond .12 .30
157 Cody Ceci .05 .15
158 Erik Karlsson .12 .30
159 Mike Hoffman .05 .15
160 Bobby Ryan .07 .20
161 Mark Stone .12 .30
162 Kyle Turris .07 .20
163 Mika Zibanejad .12 .30
164 Flyers Jerseys .07 .20
165 Philadelphia Flyers Logo .07 .20
166 Claude Giroux FOIL .10 .25
167 Steve Mason FOIL .07 .20
168 Jakub Voracek FOIL .07 .20
169 Steve Mason .07 .20
170 Luke Schenn .10 .25
171 Mark Streit .05 .15
172 Sean Couturier .07 .20
173 Claude Giroux .10 .25
174 Vincent Lecavalier .10 .25
175 Brayden Schenn .10 .25
176 Wayne Simmonds .12 .30
177 Jakub Voracek .07 .20
178 Penguins Jerseys .07 .20
179 Pittsburgh Penguins Logo .07 .20
180 Sidney Crosby FOIL .40 1.00
181 Marc-Andre Fleury FOIL .20 .50
182 Evgeni Malkin FOIL .20 .50
183 Marc-Andre Fleury .20 .50
184 Kris Letang .12 .30
185 Phil Kessel .10 .25
186 David Perron .07 .20
187 Sidney Crosby .40 1.00
188 Patric Hornqvist .05 .15
189 Chris Kunitz .10 .25
190 Evgeni Malkin .20 .50
191 Rob Scuderi .05 .15
192 Lightning Jerseys .07 .20
193 Tampa Bay Lightning Logo .07 .20
194 Steven Stamkos FOIL .20 .50
195 Ben Bishop FOIL .07 .20
196 Tyler Johnson FOIL .05 .15
197 Ben Bishop .07 .20
198 Victor Hedman .12 .30
199 Anton Stralman .05 .15
200 Ryan Callahan .05 .15
201 Valtteri Filppula .05 .15
202 Tyler Johnson .05 .15
203 Nikita Kucherov .20 .50
204 Ondrej Palat .07 .20
205 Steven Stamkos .20 .50
206 Maple Leafs Jerseys .07 .20
207 Toronto Maple Leafs Logo .07 .20
208 Tyler Bozak FOIL .05 .15
209 Morgan Rielly FOIL .10 .25
210 James van Riemsdyk FOIL .07 .20
211 Jonathan Bernier .07 .20
212 James Reimer .10 .25
213 Dion Phaneuf .07 .20
214 Morgan Rielly .10 .25
215 Tyler Bozak .05 .15
216 Nazem Kadri .12 .30
217 Jake Gardiner .05 .15
218 Joffrey Lupul .05 .15
219 James van Riemsdyk .07 .20
220 Capitals Jerseys .07 .20
221 Washington Capitals Logo .07 .20
222 Alex Ovechkin FOIL .40 1.00
223 Braden Holtby FOIL .12 .30
224 Nicklas Backstrom FOIL .10 .25
225 Braden Holtby .12 .30
226 Karl Alzner .05 .15
227 John Carlson .10 .25
228 Nicklas Backstrom .10 .25
229 T.J. Oshie .10 .25
230 Andre Burakovsky .05 .15
231 Marcus Johansson .07 .20
232 Evgeny Kuznetsov .12 .30
233 Alex Ovechkin .40 1.00
234 Ducks Jerseys .07 .20
235 Anaheim Ducks Logo .07 .20
236 Corey Perry FOIL .15 .40
237 Ryan Getzlaf FOIL .10 .25
238 Ryan Kesler FOIL .10 .25
239 Frederik Andersen .12 .30
240 Cam Fowler .10 .25
241 Hampus Lindholm .05 .15
242 Sami Vatanen .05 .15
243 Ryan Getzlaf .10 .25
244 Ryan Kesler .10 .25
245 Patrick Maroon .05 .15
246 Corey Perry .15 .40
247 Jakob Silfverberg .05 .15
248 Coyotes Jerseys .07 .20
249 Arizona Coyotes Logo .07 .20
250 Oliver Ekman-Larsson FOIL .10 .25
251 Shane Doan FOIL .07 .20
252 Martin Hanzal FOIL .05 .15
253 Mike Smith .10 .25
254 Oliver Ekman-Larsson .10 .25
255 Boyd Gordon .05 .15
256 Michael Stone .05 .15
257 Mikkel Boedker .05 .15
258 Shane Doan .07 .20
259 Martin Hanzal .05 .15
260 Antoine Vermette .05 .15
261 Tobias Rieder .05 .15
262 Flames Jerseys .07 .20
263 Calgary Flames Logo .07 .20
264 Johnny Gaudreau FOIL .15 .40
265 Jiri Hudler FOIL .07 .20
266 Sean Monahan FOIL .05 .15
267 Jonas Hiller .07 .20
268 T.J. Brodie .05 .15
269 Mark Giordano .10 .25
270 Dennis Wideman .05 .15
271 Mikael Backlund .07 .20
272 Lance Bouma .05 .15
273 Johnny Gaudreau .15 .40
274 Jiri Hudler .07 .20
275 Sean Monahan .05 .15
276 Blackhawks Jerseys .07 .20
277 Chicago Blackhawks Logo .07 .20
278 Jonathan Toews FOIL .15 .40
279 Marian Hossa FOIL .10 .25
280 Patrick Kane FOIL .20 .50
281 Corey Crawford .12 .30
282 Duncan Keith .07 .20
283 Brent Seabrook .05 .15
284 Marian Hossa .10 .25
285 Patrick Kane .20 .50
286 Niklas Hjalmarsson .05 .15
287 Teuvo Teravainen .10 .25
288 Andrew Shaw .05 .15
289 Jonathan Toews .15 .40
290 Avalanche Jerseys .07 .20
291 Colorado Avalanche Logo .07 .20
292 Gabriel Landeskog FOIL .12 .30
293 Semyon Varlamov FOIL .10 .25
294 Jarome Iginla FOIL .12 .30
295 Semyon Varlamov .10 .25
296 Tyson Barrie .05 .15
297 Erik Johnson .05 .15
298 Matt Duchene .10 .25
299 Jarome Iginla .12 .30
300 Gabriel Landeskog .12 .30
301 Nathan MacKinnon .40 1.00
302 Carl Soderberg .05 .15
303 Alex Tanguay .05 .15
304 Stars Jerseys .07 .20
305 Dallas Stars Logo .07 .20
306 Jamie Benn FOIL .10 .25
307 John Klingberg FOIL .10 .25
308 Tyler Seguin FOIL .12 .30
309 Antti Niemi .07 .20
310 Kari Lehtonen .07 .20
311 Alex Goligoski .05 .15
312 John Klingberg .10 .25
313 Jamie Benn .10 .25
314 Cody Eakin .05 .15
315 Patrick Sharp .10 .25
316 Tyler Seguin .12 .30
317 Jason Spezza .10 .25
318 Oilers Jerseys .07 .20
319 Edmonton Oilers Logo .07 .20
320 Jordan Eberle FOIL .10 .25
321 Ryan Nugent-Hopkins FOIL .12 .30
322 Taylor Hall FOIL .10 .25
323 Ben Scrivens .07 .20
324 Cam Talbot .10 .25
325 Justin Schultz .07 .20
326 Jordan Eberle .10 .25
327 Taylor Hall .10 .25
328 Ryan Nugent-Hopkins .12 .30
329 Benoit Pouliot .05 .15
330 Teddy Purcell .05 .15
331 Nail Yakupov .05 .15
332 Kings Jerseys .07 .20
333 Los Angeles Kings Logo .07 .20
334 Drew Doughty FOIL .12 .30
335 Jeff Carter FOIL .07 .20
336 Anze Kopitar FOIL .15 .40
337 Jonathan Quick .12 .30
338 Drew Doughty .12 .30
339 Jake Muzzin .10 .25
340 Dustin Brown .10 .25
341 Jeff Carter .07 .20
342 Marian Gaborik .10 .25
343 Anze Kopitar .15 .40
344 Milan Lucic .07 .20
345 Tyler Toffoli .10 .25
346 Wild Jerseys .07 .20
347 Minnesota Wild Logo .07 .20
348 Zach Parise FOIL .10 .25
349 Devan Dubnyk FOIL .07 .20
350 Ryan Suter FOIL .07 .20
351 Devan Dubnyk .07 .20
352 Jonas Brodin .05 .15
353 Matt Dumba .05 .15
354 Ryan Suter .07 .20
355 Mikael Granlund .07 .20
356 Mikko Koivu .07 .20
357 Zach Parise .10 .25
358 Jason Pominville .05 .15
359 Thomas Vanek .07 .20
360 Predators Jerseys .07 .20
361 Nashville Predators Logo .07 .20
362 Filip Forsberg FOIL .15 .40
363 Pekka Rinne FOIL .10 .25
364 Roman Josi FOIL .10 .25
365 Pekka Rinne .10 .25
366 Seth Jones .10 .25
367 Roman Josi .10 .25
368 Shea Weber .07 .20
369 Mike Fisher .05 .15
370 Filip Forsberg .15 .40
371 James Neal .05 .15
372 Craig Smith .05 .15
373 Colin Wilson .05 .15
374 Sharks Jerseys .07 .20
375 San Jose Sharks Logo .07 .20
376 Joe Pavelski FOIL .12 .30
377 Brent Burns FOIL .10 .25
378 Logan Couture FOIL .12 .30
379 Martin Jones .07 .20
380 Brent Burns .10 .25
381 Marc-Edouard Vlasic .05 .15
382 Logan Couture .12 .30
383 Tomas Hertl .10 .25
384 Patrick Marleau .10 .25
385 Joe Pavelski .12 .30
386 Joe Thornton .15 .40
387 Tommy Wingels .05 .15
388 Blues Jerseys .07 .20
389 St. Louis Blues Logo .07 .20
390 Vladimir Tarasenko FOIL .12 .30
391 Kevin Shattenkirk FOIL .05 .15
392 Alexander Steen FOIL .05 .15
393 Jake Allen .10 .25
394 Brian Elliott .07 .20
395 Alex Pietrangelo .07 .20
396 Kevin Shattenkirk .05 .15
397 David Backes .05 .15
398 Paul Stastny .07 .20
399 Jaden Schwartz .12 .30
400 Alexander Steen .05 .15
401 Vladimir Tarasenko .12 .30
402 Canucks Jerseys .07 .20
403 Vancouver Canucks Logo .07 .20
404 Daniel Sedin FOIL .12 .30
405 Henrik Sedin FOIL .12 .30
406 Radim Vrbata FOIL .05 .15
407 Ryan Miller .10 .25
408 Jannik Hansen .05 .15
409 Alexander Edler .05 .15
410 Christopher Tanev .05 .15
411 Chris Higgins .05 .15
412 Alexandre Burrows .05 .15
413 Daniel Sedin .12 .30
414 Henrik Sedin .12 .30
415 Radim Vrbata .05 .15
416 Jets Jerseys .07 .20
417 Winnipeg Jets Logo .07 .20
418 Andrew Ladd FOIL .05 .15
419 Mark Scheifele FOIL .15 .40
420 Blake Wheeler FOIL .10 .25
421 Michael Hutchinson .05 .15
422 Ondrej Pavelec .10 .25
423 Dustin Byfuglien .10 .25
424 Tyler Myers .05 .15
425 Jacob Trouba .07 .20
426 Andrew Ladd .05 .15
427 Bryan Little .07 .20
428 Mark Scheifele .15 .40
429 Blake Wheeler .10 .25
430 Winter Classic 1 .07 .20
431 Winter Classic 2 .07 .20
432 Winter Classic 3 .07 .20
433 2015 Winter Classic Logo .07 .20
434 Winter Classic 4 .07 .20
435 Stadium Series 1 .07 .20
436 Stadium Series Kings Win (Logan Couture)) .12 .30
437 Stadium Series 3 .07 .20
438 2015 Stadium Series Logo .07 .20
439 Stadium Series 4 .07 .20
440 Jonathan Drouin AS .07 .20
441 2015-16 All Star Game Logo .07 .20
442 Patrick Kane AS .20 .50
443 Ryan Johansen AS .07 .20
444 Shea Weber AS .07 .20
445 Jonathan Toews AS .15 .40
446 Ryan Johansen AS MVP .07 .20
447 Nick Foligno AS .07 .20
448 Corey Crawford AS .12 .30
449 Aaron Ekblad AS .12 .30
450 Mark Giordano AS .10 .25
451 Patrice Bergeron AS .12 .30
452 Rick Nash AS .10 .25
453 Tyler Seguin AS .12 .30
454 Vladimir Tarasenko AS .12 .30
455 John Tavares AS .15 .40
456 Jakub Voracek AS .07 .20
457 Carey Price AS .20 .50
458 Brent Burns AS .10 .25
459 Kevin Shattenkirk AS .05 .15
460 Zemgus Girgensons AS .07 .20
461 Claude Giroux AS .10 .25
462 Alex Ovechkin AS .40 1.00
463 Bobby Ryan AS .07 .20
464 Steven Stamkos AS .20 .50
465 Radim Vrbata AS .05 .15
466 Western Conference First Round.07 .20
467 Western Conference First Round.07 .20
468 Western Conference First Round.05 .15
469 Western Conference First Round.07 .20
470 Western Conference Second Round .07 .20
471 Western Conference Second Round .07 .20
472 Western Conference Finals .07 .20
473 Eastern Conference Finals .07 .20
474 Eastern Conference Second Round .07 .20
475 Eastern Conference Second Round .07 .20
476 Eastern Conference First Round.07 .20
477 Eastern Conference First Round.07 .20
478 Eastern Conference First Round.07 .20
479 Eastern Conference First Round.07 .20
480 Stanley Cup Finals Blackhawks 2; Lightning 1 .07 .20
481 Stanley Cup Finals Blackhawks 3; Lightning 4 .07 .20
482 Stanley Cup Finals Lightning 3; Blackhawks 2 .07 .20
483 Stanley Cup Finals Lightning 1; Blackhawks 2 .07 .20
484 Stanley Cup Finals Blackhawks 2; Lightning 1 .07 .20
485 Stanley Cup Finals Lightning 0; Blackhawks 2 .07 .20
486 Conn Smythe Trophy FOIL .07 .20
487 Duncan Keith Conn Smythe Winner .07 .20
488 Stanley Cup FOIL .07 .20
489 Blackhawks Champions 1 .07 .20
490 Blackhawks Champions 2 .07 .20
491 Blackhawks Champs Logo 1 (half team and Cup logo) .07 .20
492 Blackhawks Champs Logo 2

(half team and Cup logo) .07 .20
493 Carey Price
Hart Trophy Winner .30 .75
494 Jamie Benn
Art Ross Trophy Winner .15 .40
495 Alex Ovechkin
Rocket Richard Winner .60 1.50
496 Carey Price
Vezina Trophy Winner .30 .75
497 Erik Karlsson
Norris Trophy Winner .20 .50
498 Patrice Bergeron
Selke Trophy Winner .20 .50
499 Aaron Ekblad
Calder Trophy Winner .20 .50
500 Jiri Hudler
Lady Bing Trophy Winner .12 .30
501 Devan Dubnyk
Masterton Trophy Winner .12 .30
502 Sam Bennett RR .50 1.25
503 Kevin Fiala RR .20 .50
504 Darnell Nurse RR .12 .30
505 Matt Puempel RR .12 .30
506 Rated Rookie Logo .07 .20
507 Ty Rattie RR .10 .25
508 Griffin Reinhart RR .10 .25
509 Sam Reinhart RR .30 .75
510 Andrei Vasilevskiy RR .25 .60
511 Stanley Cup Puzzle A .07 .20
512 Stanley Cup Puzzle B .07 .20
513 Stanley Cup Puzzle C .07 .20
514 Stanley Cup Puzzle D .07 .20
515 Stanley Cup Puzzle E .07 .20
516 Stanley Cup Puzzle F .07 .20

2016-17 Panini Stickers

1 Patrick Kane
Hart Trophy Winner .20 .50
2 Patrick Kane
Art Ross Trophy Winner .20 .50
3 Alex Ovechkin
Rocket Richard Trophy Winner .40 1.00
4 Braden Holtby
Vezina Trophy Winner .12 .30
5 Drew Doughty
Norris Trophy Winner .12 .30
6 Anze Kopitar
Selke Trophy Winner .15 .40
7 Artemi Panarin
Calder Trophy Winner .20 .50
8 Anze Kopitar
Lady Byng Trophy Winner .15 .40
9 Jaromir Jagr
Masterton Trophy Winner .30 .75
10 Patrice Bergeron STAR .12 .30
11 David Krejci STAR .10 .25
12 Boston Bruins Logo .07 .20
13 Brad Marchand ILL .20 .50
14 Tuukka Rask STAR .12 .30
15 Tuukka Rask .12 .30
16 Zdeno Chara .10 .25
17 Torey Krug .07 .20
18 Matt Beleskey .07 .20
19 Patrice Bergeron .12 .30
20 David Backes .05 .15
21 David Krejci .10 .25
22 Brad Marchand .20 .50
23 David Pastrnak .25 .60
24 Jack Eichel STAR .15 .40
25 Sam Reinhart STAR .20 .50
26 Buffalo Sabres Logo .07 .20
27 Ryan O'Reilly ILL .10 .25
28 Rasmus Ristolainen STAR .05 .15
29 Robin Lehner .07 .20
30 Zach Bogosian .07 .20
31 Rasmus Ristolainen .05 .15
32 Jack Eichel .15 .40
33 Tyler Ennis .05 .15
34 Zemgus Girgensons .07 .20
35 Evander Kane .10 .25
36 Ryan O'Reilly .10 .25
37 Sam Reinhart .20 .50
38 Justin Faulk STAR .07 .20
39 Elias Lindholm STAR .10 .25
40 Carolina Hurricanes Logo .07 .20
41 Jeff Skinner ILL .12 .30
42 Jordan Staal STAR .07 .20
43 Cam Ward .10 .25
44 Justin Faulk .07 .20
45 Ron Hainsey .07 .20
46 Noah Hanifin .10 .25
47 Elias Lindholm .10 .25
48 Andrej Nestrasil .07 .20
49 Victor Rask .05 .15
50 Jeff Skinner .12 .30
51 Jordan Staal .07 .20
52 Cam Atkinson STAR .10 .25
53 Boone Jenner STAR .10 .25
54 Columbus Blue Jackets Logo .07 .20
55 Sergei Bobrovsky ILL .15 .40
56 Brandon Saad STAR .07 .20
57 Sergei Bobrovsky .15 .40
58 Jack Johnson .05 .15
59 Seth Jones .10 .25
60 David Savard .05 .15
61 Cam Atkinson .10 .25
62 Brandon Dubinsky .05 .15
63 Scott Hartnell .05 .15
64 Boone Jenner .10 .25
65 Brandon Saad .07 .20
66 Dylan Larkin STAR .12 .30
67 Niklas Kronwall STAR .07 .20
68 Detroit Red Wings Logo .07 .20
69 Henrik Zetterberg ILL .12 .30
70 Petr Mrazek STAR .10 .25
71 Jimmy Howard .12 .30
72 Petr Mrazek .10 .25
73 Mike Green .07 .20
74 Niklas Kronwall .07 .20
75 Justin Abdelkader .07 .20
76 Tomas Tatar .05 .15
77 Dylan Larkin .12 .30
78 Gustav Nyquist .05 .15
79 Henrik Zetterberg .12 .30
80 Aaron Ekblad STAR .12 .30
81 Jaromir Jagr STAR .30 .75
82 Florida Panthers Logo .07 .20
83 Roberto Luongo ILL .15 .40
84 Aleksander Barkov STAR .15 .40
85 Roberto Luongo .15 .40
86 Aaron Ekblad .12 .30
87 Aleksander Barkov .15 .40
88 Nick Bjugstad .05 .15
89 Jonathan Huberdeau .12 .30
90 Jaromir Jagr .30 .75
91 Jussi Jokinen .10 .25
92 Reilly Smith .10 .25
93 Vincent Trocheck .10 .25
94 Max Pacioretty STAR .10 .25
95 Alex Galchenyuk STAR .05 .15
96 Montreal Canadiens Logo .07 .20
97 Shea Weber ILL .07 .20
98 Carey Price STAR .20 .50
99 Carey Price .20 .50
100 Andrei Markov .05 .15
101 Shea Weber .07 .20
102 David Desharnais .05 .15
103 Andrew Shaw .05 .15
104 Alex Galchenyuk .05 .15
105 Brendan Gallagher .10 .25
106 Max Pacioretty .10 .25
107 Tomas Plekanec .05 .15
108 Travis Zajac STAR .05 .15
109 Cory Schneider STAR .10 .25
110 New Jersey Devils Logo .07 .20
111 Adam Henrique ILL .07 .20
112 Kyle Palmieri STAR .07 .20
113 Cory Schneider .10 .25
114 Andy Greene .05 .15
115 Taylor Hall .10 .25
116 John Moore .05 .15
117 Damon Severson .05 .15
118 Michael Cammalleri .07 .20
119 Adam Henrique .07 .20
120 Kyle Palmieri .07 .20
121 Travis Zajac .05 .15
122 Brock Nelson STAR .10 .25
123 Nick Leddy STAR .05 .15
124 New York Islanders Logo .07 .20
125 John Tavares ILL .15 .40
126 Anders Lee STAR .10 .25
127 Thomas Greiss .07 .20
128 Jaroslav Halak .10 .25
129 Johnny Boychuk .07 .20
130 Nick Leddy .05 .15
131 Anders Lee .10 .25
132 Brock Nelson .10 .25
133 Casey Cizikas .05 .15
134 Andrew Ladd .05 .15
135 John Tavares .15 .40
136 Mats Zuccarello STAR .10 .25
137 Ryan McDonagh STAR .05 .15
138 New York Rangers Logo .07 .20
139 Derek Stepan ILL .05 .15
140 Henrik Lundqvist STAR .25 .60
141 Henrik Lundqvist .25 .60
142 Ryan McDonagh .05 .15
143 Dan Girardi .05 .15
144 Mika Zibanejad .12 .30
145 Chris Kreider .12 .30
146 J.T. Miller .12 .30
147 Rick Nash .10 .25
148 Derek Stepan .05 .15
149 Mats Zuccarello .10 .25
150 Craig Anderson STAR .10 .25
151 Erik Karlsson STAR .12 .30
152 Ottawa Senators Logo .07 .20
153 Bobby Ryan ILL .07 .20
154 Mark Stone STAR .12 .30
155 Craig Anderson .10 .25
156 Cody Ceci .05 .15
157 Erik Karlsson .12 .30
158 Dion Phaneuf .07 .20
159 Mike Hoffman .05 .15
160 Bobby Ryan .07 .20
161 Mark Stone .12 .30
162 Kyle Turris .07 .20
163 Derick Brassard .05 .15
164 Jakub Voracek STAR .07 .20
165 Wayne Simmonds STAR .12 .30
166 Philadelphia Flyers Logo .07 .20
167 Claude Giroux ILL .10 .25
168 Shayne Gostisbehere STAR .10 .25
169 Steve Mason .07 .20
170 Michal Neuvirth .07 .20
171 Shayne Gostisbehere .10 .25
172 Mark Streit .07 .20
173 Sean Couturier .07 .20
174 Claude Giroux .10 .25
175 Brayden Schenn .10 .25
176 Wayne Simmonds .12 .30
177 Jakub Voracek .07 .20
178 Kris Letang STAR .12 .30
179 Phil Kessel STAR .10 .25
180 Pittsburgh Penguins Logo .07 .20
181 Sidney Crosby ILL .40 1.00
182 Evgeni Malkin STAR .20 .50
183 Marc-Andre Fleury .20 .50
184 Matt Murray .15 .40
185 Kris Letang .12 .30
186 Sidney Crosby .40 1.00
187 Carl Hagelin .05 .15
188 Patric Hornqvist .05 .15
189 Phil Kessel .10 .25
190 Chris Kunitz .10 .25
191 Evgeni Malkin .20 .50
192 Tyler Johnson STAR .05 .15
193 Ben Bishop STAR .07 .20
194 Tampa Bay Lightning Logo .07 .20
195 Victor Hedman ILL .12 .30
196 Steven Stamkos STAR .20 .50
197 Ben Bishop .07 .20
198 Andrei Vasilevskiy .15 .40
199 Victor Hedman .12 .30
200 Ryan Callahan .05 .15
201 Jonathan Drouin .07 .20
202 Tyler Johnson .05 .15
203 Nikita Kucherov .20 .50
204 Ondrej Palat .07 .20
205 Steven Stamkos .20 .50
206 James van Riemsdyk STAR .07 .20
207 Nazem Kadri STAR .12 .30
208 Toronto Maple Leafs Logo .07 .20
209 Morgan Rielly ILL .10 .25
210 Leo Komarov STAR .05 .15
211 Frederik Andersen .12 .30
212 Brooks Laich .05 .15
213 Jake Gardiner .05 .15
214 Morgan Rielly .10 .25
215 Tyler Bozak .05 .15
216 Nazem Kadri .12 .30
217 Leo Komarov .05 .15
218 William Nylander .40 1.00
219 James van Riemsdyk .07 .20
220 Braden Holtby STAR .12 .30
221 Evgeny Kuznetsov STAR .12 .30
222 Washington Capitals Logo .07 .20
223 Alex Ovechkin ILL .40 1.00
224 Nicklas Backstrom STAR .10 .25
225 Braden Holtby .12 .30
226 Karl Alzner .05 .15
227 John Carlson .10 .25
228 Matt Niskanen .07 .20
229 Nicklas Backstrom .10 .25
230 Evgeny Kuznetsov .12 .30
231 T.J. Oshie .10 .25
232 Alex Ovechkin .40 1.00
233 Justin Williams .07 .20
234 John Gibson .10 .25
235 Andrew Cogliano .05 .15
236 Cam Fowler .10 .25
237 Sami Vatanen .07 .20
238 Ryan Getzlaf .10 .25
239 Ryan Kesler .10 .25
240 Corey Perry .15 .40
241 Rickard Rakell .07 .20
242 Jakob Silfverberg .05 .15
243 Ryan Getzlaf STAR .10 .25
244 John Gibson STAR .10 .25
245 Ryan Kesler STAR .10 .25
246 Corey Perry ILL .15 .40
247 Anaheim Ducks Logo .07 .20
248 Louis Domingue .07 .20
249 Mike Smith .10 .25
250 Oliver Ekman-Larsson .10 .25
251 Michael Stone .05 .15
252 Shane Doan .07 .20
253 Max Domi .10 .25
254 Anthony Duclair .07 .20
255 Martin Hanzal .07 .20
256 Antoine Vermette .10 .25
257 Mike Smith STAR .10 .25
258 Oliver Ekman-Larsson STAR .10 .25
259 Shane Doan STAR .07 .20
260 Max Domi ILL .10 .25
261 Arizona Coyotes Logo .07 .20
262 Brian Elliott .07 .20
263 T.J. Brodie .07 .20
264 Mark Giordano .10 .25
265 Dougie Hamilton .07 .20
266 Mikael Backlund .07 .20
267 Sam Bennett .15 .40
268 Michael Frolik .07 .20
269 Johnny Gaudreau .15 .40
270 Sean Monahan .05 .15
271 Johnny Gaudreau STAR .15 .40
272 Mikael Backlund STAR .07 .20
273 Sean Monahan STAR .05 .15
274 Mark Giordano ILL .10 .25
275 Calgary Flames Logo .07 .20
276 Corey Crawford .12 .30
277 Duncan Keith .07 .20
278 Brent Seabrook .05 .15
279 Artem Anisimov .05 .15
280 Marian Hossa .10 .25
281 Patrick Kane .20 .50
282 Artemi Panarin .20 .50
283 Niklas Hjalmarsson .05 .15
284 Jonathan Toews .15 .40
285 Patrick Kane STAR .20 .50
286 Artemi Panarin STAR .20 .50
287 Duncan Keith STAR .07 .20
288 Jonathan Toews ILL .15 .40
289 Chicago Blackhawks Logo .07 .20
290 Semyon Varlamov .10 .25
291 Tyson Barrie .05 .15
292 Francois Beauchemin .07 .20
293 Erik Johnson .05 .15
294 Matt Duchene .10 .25
295 Jarome Iginla .12 .30
296 Gabriel Landeskog .12 .30
297 Nathan MacKinnon .40 1.00
298 Carl Soderberg .05 .15
299 Tyson Barrie STAR .05 .15
300 Nathan MacKinnon STAR .40 1.00
301 Gabriel Landeskog STAR .12 .30
302 Matt Duchene ILL .10 .25
303 Colorado Avalanche Logo .07 .20
304 Kari Lehtonen .07 .20
305 Antti Niemi .07 .20
306 Antoine Roussel .05 .15
307 John Klingberg .10 .25
308 Jamie Benn .10 .25
309 Cody Eakin .05 .15
310 Tyler Seguin .12 .30
311 Patrick Sharp .07 .20
312 Jason Spezza .10 .25
313 Jamie Benn STAR .10 .25
314 John Klingberg STAR .10 .25
315 Jason Spezza STAR .10 .25
316 Tyler Seguin ILL .12 .30
317 Dallas Stars Logo .07 .20
318 Cam Talbot .10 .25
319 Andrej Sekera .05 .15
320 Leon Draisaitl .30 .75
321 Jordan Eberle .10 .25
322 Adam Larsson .10 .25
323 Milan Lucic .07 .20
324 Connor McDavid .50 1.25
325 Ryan Nugent-Hopkins .12 .30
326 Benoit Pouliot .07 .20
327 Leon Draisaitl STAR .30 .75
328 Connor McDavid STAR .50 1.25
329 Jordan Eberle STAR .10 .25
330 Milan Lucic ILL .07 .20
331 Edmonton Oilers Logo .07 .20
332 Jonathan Quick .12 .30
333 Drew Doughty .12 .30
334 Jake Muzzin .10 .25
335 Dustin Brown .10 .25
336 Jeff Carter .07 .20
337 Anze Kopitar .15 .40
338 Marian Gaborik .10 .25
339 Tanner Pearson .07 .20
340 Tyler Toffoli .10 .25
341 Anze Kopitar STAR .15 .40
342 Tyler Toffoli STAR .10 .25
343 Drew Doughty STAR .12 .30
344 Jonathan Quick ILL .12 .30
345 Los Angeles Kings Logo .07 .20
346 Devan Dubnyk .07 .20
347 Ryan Suter .07 .20
348 Charlie Coyle .10 .25
349 Mikael Granlund .07 .20
350 Mikko Koivu .07 .20
351 Nino Niederreiter .05 .15
352 Zach Parise .10 .25
353 Jason Pominville .05 .15
354 Eric Staal .12 .30
355 Mikko Koivu STAR .07 .20
356 Ryan Suter STAR .07 .20
357 Devan Dubnyk STAR .07 .20
358 Zach Parise ILL .10 .25
359 Minnesota Wild Logo .07 .20
360 Pekka Rinne .10 .25
361 Roman Josi .10 .25
362 P.K. Subban .12 .30
363 Mike Fisher .05 .15
364 Filip Forsberg .15 .40
365 Ryan Johansen .07 .20
366 James Neal .05 .15
367 Mike Ribeiro .05 .15
368 Craig Smith .05 .15
369 Pekka Rinne STAR .10 .25
370 Filip Forsberg STAR .15 .40
371 James Neal STAR .05 .15
372 P.K. Subban ILL .12 .30
373 Nashville Predators Logo .07 .20
374 Martin Jones .07 .20
375 Brent Burns .10 .25
376 Marc-Edouard Vlasic .05 .15
377 Logan Couture .12 .30
378 Tomas Hertl .10 .25
379 Patrick Marleau .10 .25
380 Joe Pavelski .12 .30
381 Joe Thornton .15 .40
382 Joel Ward .07 .20
383 Joe Pavelski STAR .12 .30
384 Joe Thornton STAR .15 .40
385 Patrick Marleau STAR .10 .25
386 Brent Burns ILL .10 .25
387 San Jose Sharks Logo .07 .20
388 Jake Allen .10 .25
389 Jay Bouwmeester .05 .15
390 Alex Pietrangelo .07 .20
391 Kevin Shattenkirk .05 .15
392 Jaden Schwartz .12 .30
393 Robby Fabbri .05 .15
394 Paul Stastny .07 .20
395 Alexander Steen .05 .15
396 Vladimir Tarasenko .12 .30
397 Jake Allen STAR .10 .25
398 Alex Pietrangelo STAR .07 .20
399 Alexander Steen STAR .05 .15
400 Vladimir Tarasenko ILL .12 .30
401 St. Louis Blues Logo .07 .20
402 Ryan Miller .10 .25
403 Alexander Edler .05 .15
404 Loui Eriksson .05 .15
405 Christopher Tanev .05 .15
406 Alexandre Burrows .05 .15
407 Jannik Hansen .05 .15
408 Bo Horvat .12 .30
409 Daniel Sedin .12 .30
410 Henrik Sedin .12 .30
411 Ryan Miller STAR .10 .25
412 Henrik Sedin STAR .12 .30
413 Bo Horvat STAR .12 .30
414 Daniel Sedin ILL .12 .30
415 Vancouver Canucks Logo .07 .20
416 Ondrej Pavelec .10 .25
417 Dustin Byfuglien .10 .25
418 Tyler Myers .05 .15
419 Jacob Trouba .07 .20
420 Nikolaj Ehlers .10 .25
421 Bryan Little .07 .20
422 Mark Scheifele .15 .40
423 Drew Stafford .05 .15
424 Blake Wheeler .10 .25
425 Dustin Byfuglien STAR .10 .25
426 Jacob Trouba STAR .07 .20
427 Mark Scheifele STAR .15 .40
428 Blake Wheeler ILL .10 .25
429 Winnipeg Jets Logo .07 .20
430 Winter Classic 1 .07 .20
431 Winter Classic 2 .07 .20
432 Winter Classic Logo .07 .20
433 Winter Classic 3 .07 .20
434 Winter Classic 4 .07 .20
435 Stadium Series Minnesota 1 .07 .20
436 Stadium Series Minnesota 2 .07 .20
437 Stadium Series Minnesota Logo .07 .20
438 Stadium Series Minnesota 3 .07 .20
439 Stadium Series Minnesota 4 .07 .20
440 Stadium Series Colorado 1 .07 .20
441 Stadium Series Colorado 2 .07 .20
442 Stadium Series Colorado Logo .07 .20
443 Stadium Series Colorado 3 .07 .20
444 Stadium Series Colorado 4 .07 .20
445 Dylan Larkin
Fastest Skater .12 .30
446 All Star Game Logo .07 .20
447 P.K. Subban
Breakaway Challenge Winner .12 .30
448 John Tavares
Most Accurate Shooter .15 .40
449 John Scott
All-Star Game MVP .10 .25
450 Shea Weber
Hardest Shot .07 .20
451 Jamie Benn .10 .25
452 Dustin Byfuglien .10 .25
453 Patrick Kane .20 .50
454 Pekka Rinne .10 .25
455 Vladimir Tarasenko .12 .30
456 Brent Burns .10 .25
457 Johnny Gaudreau .15 .40
458 John Scott .10 .25
459 Corey Perry .15 .40
460 Jonathan Quick .12 .30
461 Patrice Bergeron .12 .30
462 Erik Karlsson .12 .30
463 Jaromir Jagr .30 .75
464 Roberto Luongo .15 .40
465 Steven Stamkos .20 .50
466 Claude Giroux .10 .25
467 Braden Holtby .12 .30
468 John Tavares .15 .40
469 Evgeni Malkin .20 .50
470 Ryan McDonagh .05 .15
471 Dallas Stars vs. Minnesota Wild .07 .20
472 St. Louis Blues vs.
Chicago Blackhawks .07 .20
473 Anaheim Ducks vs.
Nashville Predators .07 .20
474 Los Angeles Kings vs.
San Jose Sharks .07 .20
475 Dallas Stars vs. St. Louis Blues .07 .20
476 San Jose Sharks vs.
Nashville Predators .07 .20
477 St. Louis Blues vs.
San Jose Sharks .07 .20
478 Pittsburgh Penguins vs.
Tampa Bay Lightning .07 .20
479 Washington Capitals vs.
Pittsburgh Penguins .07 .20
480 Tampa Bay Lightning vs.
New York Islanders .07 .20
481 Washington Capitals vs.
Philadelphia Flyers .07 .20
482 Pittsburgh Penguins vs.
New York Rangers .07 .20
483 Florida Panthers vs.
New York Islanders .07 .20
484 Tampa Bay Lightning vs.
Detroit Red Wings .07 .20
485 Stanley Cup Finals Game 1 .07 .20
486 Stanley Cup Finals Game 2 .07 .20
487 Stanley Cup Finals Game 3 .07 .20
488 Stanley Cup Finals Game 4 .07 .20
489 Stanley Cup Finals Game 5 .07 .20
490 Stanley Cup Finals Game 6 .07 .20
491 Conn Smythe Trophy .07 .20
492 Sidney Crosby
Conn Smythe Trophy Winner .40 1.00
493 Stanley Cup .07 .20
494 Pittsburgh Penguins Team Photo
Left .07 .20
495 Pittsburgh Penguins Team Photo
Right .07 .20
496 Stanley Cup Champions Logo
Left .07 .20
497 Stanley Cup Champions Logo
Right .07 .20
498 Stanley Cup
Top Left .07 .20
499 Stanley Cup
Top Right .07 .20
500 Stanley Cup
Middle Left .07 .20
501 Stanley Cup
Middle Right .07 .20
502 Stanley Cup
Bottom Left .07 .20
503 Stanley Cup
Bottom Right .07 .20

2017-18 Panini Stickers

1 Connor McDavid
Hart Trophy Winner FOIL .50 1.25
2 Connor McDavid
Art Ross Trophy Winner FOIL .50 1.25
3 Sidney Crosby
Rocket Richard Trophy Winner FOIL .40 1.00
4 Sergei Bobrovsky
Vezina Trophy Winner FOIL .15 .40
5 Brent Burns
Norris Trophy Winner FOIL .10 .25
6 Patrice Bergeron
Selke Trophy Winner FOIL .12 .30
7 Auston Matthews
Calder Trophy Winner FOIL .40 1.00
8 Johnny Gaudreau
Lady Byng Trophy Winner FOIL .15 .40
9 Craig Anderson
Masterton Trophy Winner .07 .20
10 Boston Bruins Team Logo FOIL .07 .20
11 Zdeno Chara ILL .10 .25
12 David Pastrnak STAR .25 .60
13 Tuukka Rask STAR .12 .30
14 Brad Marchand STAR .20 .50
15 Tuukka Rask .12 .30
16 Brandon Carlo .07 .20
17 Zdeno Chara .10 .25
18 Torey Krug .07 .20
19 David Backes .05 .15
20 Patrice Bergeron .12 .30
21 David Krejci .10 .25
22 Brad Marchand .20 .50
23 David Pastrnak .25 .60
24 Buffalo Sabres Team Logo FOIL .07 .20
25 Evander Kane ILL .10 .25
26 Rasmus Ristolainen STAR .05 .15
27 Jack Eichel STAR .15 .40
28 Kyle Okposo STAR .05 .15
29 Robin Lehner .07 .20
30 Zach Bogosian .07 .20
31 Rasmus Ristolainen .05 .15
32 Jack Eichel .15 .40
33 Evander Kane .10 .25
34 Matt Moulson .05 .15
35 Kyle Okposo .05 .15
36 Ryan O'Reilly .10 .25
37 Sam Reinhart .20 .50
38 Carolina Hurricanes
Team Logo FOIL .07 .20
39 Justin Faulk ILL .07 .20
40 Jeff Skinner STAR .12 .30
41 Cam Ward STAR .10 .25
42 Sebastian Aho STAR .15 .40
43 Cam Ward .10 .25
44 Justin Faulk .07 .20
45 Noah Hanifin .10 .25
46 Justin Williams .07 .20
47 Sebastian Aho .15 .40
48 Elias Lindholm .10 .25
49 Victor Rask .05 .15
50 Jeff Skinner .12 .30
51 Jordan Staal .07 .20
52 Columbus Blue Jackets
Team Logo FOIL .07 .20
53 Seth Jones ILL .10 .25
54 Zach Werenski STAR .15 .40
55 Sergei Bobrovsky STAR .15 .40
56 Cam Atkinson STAR .10 .25
57 Sergei Bobrovsky .15 .40
58 Seth Jones .10 .25
59 Zach Werenski .15 .40
60 Cam Atkinson .10 .25
61 Brandon Dubinsky .05 .15
62 Nick Foligno .07 .20
63 Boone Jenner .10 .25
64 Artemi Panarin .20 .50
65 Alexander Wennberg .05 .15
66 Detroit Red Wings Team Logo FOIL .07 .20
67 Anthony Mantha ILL .07 .20
68 Henrik Zetterberg STAR .12 .30
69 Dylan Larkin STAR .12 .30
70 Mike Green STAR .07 .20
71 Jimmy Howard .12 .30
72 Petr Mrazek .10 .25
73 Mike Green .07 .20
74 Niklas Kronwall .07 .20
75 Andreas Athanasiou .10 .25
76 Dylan Larkin .12 .30
77 Anthony Mantha .07 .20
78 Frans Nielsen .05 .15
79 Henrik Zetterberg .12 .30
80 Florida Panthers Team Logo FOIL .07 .20
81 Vincent Trocheck ILL .10 .25
82 Keith Yandle STAR .05 .15
83 Aleksander Barkov STAR .15 .40
84 Jonathan Huberdeau STAR .12 .30
85 Roberto Luongo .15 .40
86 James Reimer .10 .25
87 Aaron Ekblad .12 .30
88 Keith Yandle .05 .15
89 Aleksander Barkov .15 .40
90 Jonathan Huberdeau .12 .30
91 Radim Vrbata .05 .15
92 Nick Bjugstad .05 .15
93 Vincent Trocheck .10 .25
94 Montreal Canadiens
Team Logo FOIL .07 .20
95 Max Pacioretty ILL .10 .25
96 Shea Weber STAR .07 .20
97 Alex Galchenyuk STAR .05 .15
98 Carey Price STAR .20 .50
99 Carey Price .20 .50
100 Andrew Shaw .05 .15
101 Jeff Petry .10 .25
102 Shea Weber .07 .20
103 Alex Galchenyuk .05 .15
104 Brendan Gallagher .10 .25
105 Max Pacioretty .10 .25
106 Tomas Plekanec .05 .15
107 Jonathan Drouin .07 .20
108 New Jersey Devils
Team Logo FOIL .07 .20
109 Cory Schneider ILL .10 .25
110 Taylor Hall STAR .10 .25
111 Kyle Palmieri STAR .07 .20
112 Travis Zajac STAR .05 .15
113 Cory Schneider .10 .25
114 Andy Greene .05 .15
115 John Moore .05 .15
116 Brian Boyle .05 .15
117 Marcus Johansson .07 .20
118 Taylor Hall .10 .25
119 Adam Henrique .07 .20
120 Kyle Palmieri .07 .20
121 Travis Zajac .05 .15
122 New York Islanders
Team Logo FOIL .07 .20
123 Anders Lee ILL .10 .25
124 Nick Leddy STAR .05 .15
125 John Tavares STAR .15 .40
126 Thomas Greiss STAR .07 .20
127 Thomas Greiss .07 .20
128 Johnny Boychuk .07 .20
129 Nick Leddy .05 .15
130 Jordan Eberle .10 .25
131 Josh Bailey .07 .20
132 Andrew Ladd .05 .15
133 Anders Lee .10 .25
134 Brock Nelson .10 .25
135 John Tavares .15 .40
136 New York Rangers
Team Logo FOIL .07 .20
137 Henrik Lundqvist ILL .25 .60
138 Ryan McDonagh STAR .05 .15
139 Chris Kreider STAR .12 .30
140 J.T. Miller STAR .12 .30
141 Henrik Lundqvist .25 .60
142 Ryan McDonagh .05 .15
143 Brady Skjei .07 .20
144 Kevin Hayes .07 .20
145 Chris Kreider .12 .30
146 J.T. Miller .12 .30
147 Rick Nash .10 .25
148 Kevin Shattenkirk .05 .15
149 Mats Zuccarello .10 .25
150 Ottawa Senators Team Logo FOIL .07 .20
151 Erik Karlsson ILL .12 .30
152 Kyle Turris STAR .10 .25
153 Mark Stone STAR .12 .30
154 Mike Hoffman STAR .05 .15
155 Craig Anderson .07 .20
156 Erik Karlsson .12 .30
157 Jean-Gabriel Pageau .05 .15
158 Dion Phaneuf .07 .20
159 Derick Brassard .05 .15
160 Mike Hoffman .05 .15
161 Bobby Ryan .07 .20
162 Mark Stone .12 .30
163 Kyle Turris .10 .25
164 Philadelphia Flyers
Team Logo FOIL .07 .20
165 Jakub Voracek ILL .07 .20
166 Shayne Gostisbehere STAR .10 .25
167 Claude Giroux STAR .10 .25
168 Wayne Simmonds STAR .12 .30
169 Brian Elliott .07 .20
170 Michal Neuvirth .07 .20
171 Shayne Gostisbehere .10 .25
172 Ivan Provorov .07 .20
173 Sean Couturier .07 .20
174 Claude Giroux .10 .25
175 Jori Lehtera .05 .15
176 Wayne Simmonds .12 .30
177 Jakub Voracek .07 .20
178 Pittsburgh Penguins
Team Logo FOIL .07 .20
179 Evgeni Malkin ILL .20 .50
180 Phil Kessel STAR .10 .25
181 Sidney Crosby STAR .40 1.00
182 Conor Sheary STAR .10 .25
183 Matt Murray .15 .40
184 Kris Letang .12 .30
185 Justin Schultz .10 .25
186 Jake Guentzel .15 .40
187 Sidney Crosby .40 1.00
188 Patric Hornqvist .05 .15
189 Phil Kessel .10 .25
190 Evgeni Malkin .20 .50
191 Conor Sheary .10 .25
192 Tampa Bay Lightning
Team Logo FOIL .07 .20
193 Nikita Kucherov ILL .20 .50
194 Victor Hedman STAR .12 .30
195 Tyler Johnson STAR .05 .15
196 Steven Stamkos STAR .20 .50
197 Andrei Vasilevskiy .15 .40
198 Victor Hedman .12 .30
199 Anton Stralman .07 .20
200 Ryan Callahan .05 .15
201 Alex Killorn .05 .15
202 Tyler Johnson .05 .15
203 Nikita Kucherov .20 .50
204 Brayden Point .12 .30
205 Steven Stamkos .20 .50
206 Toronto Maple Leafs
Team Logo FOIL .07 .20
207 Frederik Andersen ILL .12 .30
208 Auston Matthews STAR .40 1.00
209 Nazem Kadri STAR .12 .30
210 Mitch Marner STAR .15 .40
211 Frederik Andersen .12 .30
212 Jake Gardiner .05 .15
213 Morgan Rielly .10 .25
214 Tyler Bozak .05 .15
215 Nazem Kadri .12 .30
216 Mitch Marner .15 .40
217 Auston Matthews .40 1.00
218 William Nylander .20 .50
219 James van Riemsdyk .07 .20
220 Washington Capitals
Team Logo FOIL .07 .20
221 Braden Holtby ILL .12 .30
222 Evgeny Kuznetsov STAR .12 .30
223 Nicklas Backstrom STAR .10 .25
224 Alex Ovechkin STAR .40 1.00
225 Braden Holtby .12 .30
226 John Carlson .10 .25
227 Matt Niskanen .07 .20
228 Nicklas Backstrom .10 .25
229 Andre Burakovsky .05 .15
230 Dmitry Orlov .10 .25
231 Evgeny Kuznetsov .12 .30
232 T.J. Oshie .10 .25
233 Alex Ovechkin .40 1.00
234 Anaheim Ducks Team Logo FOIL .07 .20
235 Ryan Kesler ILL .10 .25
236 Corey Perry STAR .15 .40
237 Rickard Rakell STAR .07 .20
238 Ryan Getzlaf STAR .10 .25
239 John Gibson .10 .25
240 Cam Fowler .10 .25
241 Hampus Lindholm .05 .15
242 Sami Vatanen .05 .15
243 Ryan Getzlaf .10 .25
244 Ryan Kesler .10 .25
245 Corey Perry .15 .40
246 Rickard Rakell .07 .20
247 Jakob Silfverberg .05 .15
248 Arizona Coyotes Team Logo FOIL .07 .20
249 Oliver Ekman-Larsson ILL .10 .25
250 Tobias Rieder STAR .05 .15
251 Alex Goligoski STAR .07 .20
252 Max Domi STAR .10 .25
253 Louis Domingue .05 .15
254 Antti Raanta .10 .25
255 Oliver Ekman-Larsson .10 .25
256 Alex Goligoski .07 .20
257 Jakob Chychrun .10 .25
258 Max Domi .10 .25
259 Christian Dvorak .07 .20
260 Derek Stepan .05 .15
261 Tobias Rieder .05 .15
262 Calgary Flames Team Logo FOIL .07 .20
263 Sean Monahan ILL .05 .15
264 Mikael Backlund STAR .07 .20
265 Mark Giordano STAR .10 .25
266 Johnny Gaudreau STAR .15 .40
267 Mike Smith .10 .25
268 TJ Brodie .07 .20
269 Mark Giordano .10 .25
270 Dougie Hamilton .07 .20
271 Mikael Backlund .07 .20
272 Troy Brouwer .05 .15
273 Johnny Gaudreau .15 .40
274 Sean Monahan .05 .15
275 Matthew Tkachuk .20 .50
276 Chicago Blackhawks
Team Logo FOIL .07 .20
277 Duncan Keith ILL .07 .20
278 Jonathan Toews STAR .15 .40
279 Patrick Kane STAR .20 .50
280 Corey Crawford STAR .12 .30
281 Corey Crawford .12 .30
282 Duncan Keith .07 .20
283 Brent Seabrook .05 .15
284 Artem Anisimov .05 .15
285 Ryan Hartman .05 .15
286 Patrick Kane .20 .50
287 Brandon Saad .07 .20
288 Richard Panik .05 .15
289 Jonathan Toews .15 .40
290 Colorado Avalanche
Team Logo FOIL .07 .20
291 Mikko Rantanen ILL .25 .60

292 Nathan MacKinnon STAR .40 1.00
293 Gabriel Landeskog STAR .12 .30
294 Matt Duchene STAR .10 .25
295 Semyon Varlamov .10 .25
296 Jonathan Bernier .07 .20
297 Tyson Barrie .05 .15
298 Francois Beauchemin .05 .15
299 Erik Johnson .05 .15
300 Matt Duchene .10 .25
301 Gabriel Landeskog .12 .30
302 Nathan MacKinnon .40 1.00
303 Mikko Rantanen .25 .60
304 Dallas Stars Team Logo FOIL .07 .20
305 John Klingberg ILL .10 .25
306 Tyler Seguin STAR .12 .30
307 Jason Spezza STAR .10 .25
308 Jamie Benn STAR .10 .25
309 Ben Bishop .07 .20
310 Kari Lehtonen .07 .20
311 Alexander Radulov .10 .25
312 John Klingberg .10 .25
313 Jamie Benn .10 .25
314 Marc Methot .05 .15
315 Antoine Roussel .05 .15
316 Tyler Seguin .12 .30
317 Jason Spezza .10 .25
318 Edmonton Oilers Team Logo FOIL .07 .20
319 Connor McDavid ILL .50 1.25
320 Leon Draisaitl STAR .30 .75
321 Oscar Klefbom STAR .07 .20
322 Cam Talbot STAR .10 .25
323 Cam Talbot .10 .25
324 Oscar Klefbom .07 .20
325 Adam Larsson .10 .25
326 Andrej Sekera .05 .15
327 Leon Draisaitl .30 .75
328 Ryan Nugent-Hopkins .12 .30
329 Milan Lucic .10 .25
330 Connor McDavid .50 1.25
331 Patrick Maroon .07 .20
332 Los Angeles Kings Team Logo FOIL .07 .20
333 Drew Doughty ILL .12 .30
334 Jeff Carter STAR .07 .20
335 Tyler Toffoli STAR .10 .25
336 Tanner Pearson STAR .07 .20
337 Jonathan Quick .12 .30
338 Drew Doughty .12 .30
339 Alec Martinez .05 .15
340 Jake Muzzin .10 .25
341 Dustin Brown .10 .25
342 Jeff Carter .07 .20
343 Anze Kopitar .15 .40
344 Tanner Pearson .07 .20
345 Tyler Toffoli .10 .25
346 Minnesota Wild Team Logo FOIL .07 .20
347 Mikael Granlund ILL .07 .20
348 Ryan Suter STAR .07 .20
349 Devan Dubnyk STAR .07 .20
350 Zach Parise STAR .10 .25
351 Devan Dubnyk .07 .20
352 Jared Spurgeon .10 .25
353 Ryan Suter .07 .20
354 Mikael Granlund .07 .20
355 Mikko Koivu .07 .20
356 Nino Niederreiter .05 .15
357 Zach Parise .10 .25
358 Eric Staal .12 .30
359 Jason Zucker .10 .25
360 Nashville Predators Team Logo FOIL .07 .20
361 Roman Josi ILL .10 .25
362 P.K. Subban STAR .12 .30
363 Viktor Arvidsson STAR .05 .15
364 Filip Forsberg STAR .15 .40
365 Pekka Rinne .10 .25
366 Ryan Ellis .07 .20
367 Roman Josi .10 .25
368 P.K. Subban .12 .30
369 Viktor Arvidsson .05 .15
370 Calle Jarnkrok .07 .20
371 Filip Forsberg .15 .40
372 Ryan Johansen .07 .20
373 Mattias Ekholm .07 .20
374 San Jose Sharks Team Logo FOIL .07 .20
375 Martin Jones ILL .07 .20
376 Brent Burns STAR .10 .25
377 Joe Pavelski STAR .12 .30
378 Logan Couture STAR .12 .30
379 Martin Jones .07 .20
380 Brent Burns .10 .25
381 Marc-Edouard Vlasic .05 .15
382 Logan Couture .12 .30
383 Tomas Hertl .10 .25
384 Melker Karlsson .05 .15
385 Joe Pavelski .12 .30
386 Joe Thornton .15 .40
387 Joel Ward .07 .20
388 St. Louis Blues Team Logo FOIL .07 .20
389 Alex Pietrangelo ILL .07 .20
390 Vladimir Tarasenko STAR .12 .30
391 Jaden Schwartz STAR .12 .30
392 Jake Allen STAR .10 .25
393 Jake Allen .10 .25
394 Jay Bouwmeester .05 .15
395 Colton Parayko .05 .15
396 Alex Pietrangelo .07 .20
397 Robby Fabbri .05 .15
398 Jaden Schwartz .12 .30
399 Paul Stastny .07 .20
400 Alexander Steen .05 .15
401 Vladimir Tarasenko .12 .30
402 Vancouver Canucks Team Logo FOIL .07 .20
403 Henrik Sedin ILL .12 .30
404 Daniel Sedin STAR .12 .30
405 Bo Horvat STAR .12 .30
406 Alexander Edler STAR .05 .15
407 Jacob Markstrom .10 .25
408 Alexander Edler .05 .15
409 Christopher Tanev .05 .15
410 Sven Baertschi .05 .15
411 Loui Eriksson .05 .15
412 Bo Horvat .12 .30
413 Daniel Sedin .12 .30
414 Henrik Sedin .12 .30
415 Brandon Sutter .05 .15
416 Vegas Golden Knights Team Logo FOIL .07 .20
417 James Neal ILL .05 .15
418 Reilly Smith STAR .10 .25
419 Marc-Andre Fleury STAR .20 .50
420 Jonathan Marchessault STAR .12 .30
421 Marc-Andre Fleury .20 .50
422 Shea Theodore .12 .30
423 Jason Garrison .05 .15
424 Cody Eakin .05 .15
425 Oscar Lindberg .07 .20
426 Jonathan Marchessault .12 .30
427 James Neal .05 .15
428 David Perron .07 .20
429 Reilly Smith .10 .25
430 Winnipeg Jets Team Logo FOIL .07 .20
431 Jacob Trouba ILL .07 .20
432 Mark Scheifele STAR .15 .40
433 Blake Wheeler STAR .10 .25
434 Patrik Laine STAR .12 .30
435 Steve Mason .07 .20
436 Dustin Byfuglien .10 .25
437 Jacob Trouba .07 .20
438 Nikolaj Ehlers .10 .25
439 Patrik Laine .12 .30
440 Bryan Little .07 .20
441 Mathieu Perreault .05 .15
442 Mark Scheifele .15 .40
443 Blake Wheeler .10 .25
444 Centennial Classic Auston Matthews .40 1.00
445 Centennial Classic Photo puzzle 1 .07 .20
446 Centennial Classic Photo puzzle 2 .07 .20
447 Winter Classic Photo puzzle 1 .07 .20
448 Winter Classic Photo puzzle 2 .07 .20
449 Winter Classic Vladimir Tarasenko .12 .30
450 Stadium Series Jake Guentzel .15 .40
451 Stadium Series Photo puzzle 1 .07 .20
452 Stadium Series Photo puzzle 2 .07 .20
453 Connor McDavid Fastest Skater '17 ASG .50 1.25
454 2017 NHL All-Star Game Logo .07 .20
455 Four Line Challenge Winner Pacific Division .07 .20
456 Sidney Crosby Most Accurate Shooter .40 1.00
457 Wayne Simmonds All-Star MVP .12 .30
458 Shea Weber Hardest Shot .07 .20
459 Patrik Laine .12 .30
460 P.K. Subban .12 .30
461 Tyler Seguin .12 .30
462 Vladimir Tarasenko .12 .30
463 Jonathan Toews .15 .40
464 Jeff Carter .07 .20
465 Johnny Gaudreau .15 .40
466 Bo Horvat .12 .30
467 Connor McDavid .50 1.25
468 Joe Pavelski .12 .30
469 Erik Karlsson .12 .30
470 Carey Price .20 .50
471 Nikita Kucherov .20 .50
472 Auston Matthews .40 1.00
473 Vincent Trocheck .10 .25
474 Cam Atkinson .10 .25
475 Justin Faulk .07 .20
476 Braden Holtby .12 .30
477 Sidney Crosby .40 1.00
478 John Tavares .15 .40
479 Chicago Blackhawks vs. Nashville Predators .07 .20
480 Minnesota Wild vs. St. Louis Blues .07 .20
481 Anaheim Ducks vs. Calgary Flames .07 .20
482 Edmonton Oilers vs. San Jose Sharks .07 .20
483 St. Louis Blues vs. Nashville Predators .07 .20
484 Anaheim Ducks vs. Edmonton Oilers .07 .20
485 Anaheim Ducks vs. Nashville Predators .07 .20
486 Pittsburgh Penguins vs. Ottawa Senators .07 .20
487 Ottawa Senators vs. New York Rangers .07 .20
488 Washington Capitals vs. Pittsburgh Penguins .07 .20
489 Montreal Canadiens vs. New York Rangers .07 .20
490 Ottawa Senators vs. Boston Bruins .07 .20
491 Washington Capitals vs. Toronto Maple Leafs .07 .20
492 Pittsburgh Penguins vs. Columbus Blue Jackets .07 .20
493 Game 1 .07 .20
494 Game 2 .07 .20
495 Game 3 .07 .20
496 Game 4 .07 .20
497 Game 5 .07 .20
498 Game 6 .07 .20
499 Conn Smythe Trophy .07 .20
500 Sidney Crosby Conn Smythe Trophy Winner .40 1.00
501 Stanley Cup .07 .20
502 2017 Stanley Cup Champions Logo Left Side .07 .20
503 2017 Stanley Cup Champions Logo Right Side .07 .20
504 Pittsburgh Penguins Team Photo Left Side .07 .20
505 Pittsburgh Penguins Team Photo Right Side .07 .20
506 NHL 100th Anniversary Logo Top Left .07 .20
507 NHL 100th Anniversary Logo Top Right .07 .20
508 NHL 100th Anniversary Logo Bottom Left .07 .20
509 NHL 100th Anniversary Logo Bottom Right .07 .20

2018-19 Panini Stickers

1 Panini Knight Logo .07 .20
2 Hart Trophy Winner Taylor Hall .07 .20
3 Art Ross Trophy Winner Connor McDavid .50 1.25
4 Rocket Richard Trophy Winner Alex Ovechkin .07 .20
5 Vezina Trophy Winner Pekka Rinne .10 .25
6 Norris Trophy Winner Victor Hedman .12 .30
7 Selke Trophy Winner Anze Kopitar .15 .40
8 Calder Trophy Winner Mathew Barzal .12 .30
9 Lady Byng Trophy Winner William Karlsson .12 .30
10 Masterton Trophy Winner Brian Boyle .07 .20
11 Boston Bruins Logo .07 .20
12 STAR PLAYER Patrice Bergeron .12 .30
13 ILLUSTRATED PLAYER David Pastrnak .25 .60
14 STAR PLAYER Brad Marchand .20 .50
15 Tuukka Rask .12 .30
16 Zdeno Chara .10 .25
17 Torey Krug .07 .20
18 Charlie McAvoy .12 .30
19 Patrice Bergeron .12 .30
20 David Pastrnak .25 .60
21 Brad Marchand .20 .50
22 David Krejci .10 .25
23 Danton Heinen .07 .20
24 David Backes .05 .15
25 Jake DeBrusk .10 .25
26 Ryan Donato .15 .40
27 Buffalo Sabres Logo .07 .20
28 STAR PLAYER Kyle Okposo .05 .15
29 ILLUSTRATED PLAYER Jack Eichel .15 .40
30 STAR PLAYER Rasmus Ristolainen .05 .15
31 Carter Hutton .07 .20
32 Rasmus Ristolainen .05 .15
33 Zach Bogosian .07 .20
34 Marco Scandella .05 .15
35 Nathan Beaulieu .05 .15
36 Jack Eichel .15 .40
37 Conor Sheary .10 .25
38 Kyle Okposo .05 .15
39 Jason Pominville .05 .15
40 Zemgus Girgensons .07 .20
41 Sam Reinhart .20 .50
42 Casey Mittelstadt .20 .50
43 Carolina Hurricanes Logo .07 .20
44 STAR PLAYER Sebastian Aho .15 .40
45 ILLUSTRATED PLAYER Jordan Staal .07 .20
46 STAR PLAYER Teuvo Teravainen .10 .25
47 Scott Darling .07 .20
48 Brett Pesce .05 .15
49 Justin Faulk .07 .20
50 Jaccob Slavin .07 .20
51 Dougie Hamilton .07 .20
52 Sebastian Aho .15 .40
53 Jordan Staal .07 .20
54 Jeff Skinner .12 .30
55 Teuvo Teravainen .10 .25
56 Justin Williams .07 .20
57 Micheal Ferland .05 .15
58 Victor Rask .05 .15
59 Columbus Blue Jackets Logo .07 .20
60 STAR PLAYER Artemi Panarin .20 .50
61 ILLUSTRATED PLAYER Sergei Bobrovsky .15 .40
62 STAR PLAYER Seth Jones .10 .25
63 Sergei Bobrovsky .15 .40
64 Seth Jones .10 .25
65 David Savard .05 .15
66 Zach Werenski .15 .40
67 Artemi Panarin .20 .50
68 Nick Foligno .07 .20
69 Alexander Wennberg .05 .15
70 Cam Atkinson .10 .25
71 Pierre-Luc Dubois .12 .30
72 Josh Anderson .07 .20
73 Oliver Bjorkstrand .07 .20
74 Boone Jenner .10 .25
75 Detroit Red Wings Logo .07 .20
76 STAR PLAYER Dylan Larkin .12 .30
77 ILLUSTRATED PLAYER Henrik Zetterberg .12 .30
78 STAR PLAYER Anthony Mantha .07 .20
79 Jimmy Howard .12 .30
80 Trevor Daley .07 .20
81 Danny DeKeyser .07 .20
82 Jonathan Ericsson .05 .15
83 Niklas Kronwall .07 .20
84 Henrik Zetterberg .12 .30
85 Dylan Larkin .12 .30
86 Gustav Nyquist .05 .15
87 Justin Abdelkader .07 .20
88 Frans Nielsen .05 .15
89 Anthony Mantha .07 .20
90 Andreas Athanasiou .07 .20
91 Florida Panthers Logo .07 .20
92 STAR PLAYER Aleksander Barkov .15 .40
93 ILLUSTRATED PLAYER Roberto Luongo .15 .40
94 STAR PLAYER Aaron Ekblad .12 .30
95 Roberto Luongo .15 .40
96 James Reimer .10 .25
97 Aaron Ekblad .12 .30
98 Keith Yandle .05 .15
99 Mike Matheson .07 .20
100 Mark Pysyk .07 .20
101 Aleksander Barkov .15 .40
102 Jonathan Huberdeau .12 .30
103 Vincent Trocheck .10 .25
104 Evgenii Dadonov .05 .15
105 Nick Bjugstad .05 .15
106 Jamie McGinn .07 .20
107 Montreal Canadiens Logo .07 .20
108 STAR PLAYER Brendan Gallagher .10 .25
109 ILLUSTRATED PLAYER Carey Price .20 .50
110 STAR PLAYER Max Pacioretty .10 .25
111 Carey Price .20 .50
112 Karl Alzner .05 .15
113 Victor Mete .05 .15
114 Jeff Petry .10 .25
115 Shea Weber .10 .25
116 Paul Byron .05 .15
117 Phillip Danault .10 .25
118 Jonathan Drouin .07 .20
119 Max Domi .10 .25
120 Brendan Gallagher .10 .25
121 Max Pacioretty .10 .25
122 Andrew Shaw .05 .15
123 New Jersey Devils Logo .07 .20
124 STAR PLAYER Taylor Hall .10 .25
125 ILLUSTRATED PLAYER Brian Boyle .07 .20
126 STAR PLAYER Nico Hischier .15 .40
127 Keith Kinkaid .05 .15
128 Cory Schneider .10 .25
129 Will Butcher .07 .20
130 Andy Greene .05 .15
131 Damon Severson .05 .15
132 Sami Vatanen .05 .15
133 Brian Boyle .07 .20
134 Taylor Hall .10 .25
135 Travis Zajac .05 .15
136 Kyle Palmieri .07 .20
137 Marcus Johansson .07 .20
138 Nico Hischier .15 .40
139 New York Islanders Logo .07 .20
140 STAR PLAYER Anders Lee .07 .20
141 ILLUSTRATED PLAYER Mathew Barzal .12 .30
142 STAR PLAYER Josh Bailey .07 .20
143 Thomas Greiss .07 .20
144 Johnny Boychuk .07 .20
145 Nick Leddy .05 .15
146 Scott Mayfield .05 .15
147 Josh Bailey .07 .20
148 Mathew Barzal .12 .30
149 Anthony Beauvillier .05 .15
150 Casey Cizikas .05 .15
151 Jordan Eberle .10 .25
152 Andrew Ladd .05 .15
153 Anders Lee .07 .20
154 Cal Clutterbuck .05 .15
155 New York Rangers Logo .07 .20
156 STAR PLAYER Mika Zibanejad .12 .30
157 ILLUSTRATED PLAYER Mats Zuccarello .10 .25
158 STAR PLAYER Henrik Lundqvist .25 .60
159 Henrik Lundqvist .25 .60
160 Kevin Shattenkirk .05 .15
161 Brady Skjei .07 .20
162 Marc Staal .05 .15
163 Neal Pionk .10 .25
164 Pavel Buchnevich .07 .20
165 Mika Zibanejad .12 .30
166 Chris Kreider .12 .30
167 Mats Zuccarello .10 .25
168 Jesper Fast .05 .15
169 Kevin Hayes .07 .20
170 Filip Chytil .07 .20
171 Ottawa Senators Logo .07 .20
172 STAR PLAYER Matt Duchene .10 .25
173 ILLUSTRATED PLAYER Craig Anderson .07 .20
174 STAR PLAYER Mark Stone .12 .30
175 Craig Anderson .07 .20
176 Cody Ceci .05 .15
177 Erik Karlsson .12 .30
178 Thomas Chabot .10 .25
179 Bobby Ryan .07 .20
180 Jean-Gabriel Pageau .05 .15
181 Mark Stone .12 .30
182 Matt Duchene .10 .25
183 Tom Pyatt .07 .20
184 Ryan Dzingel .07 .20
185 Marian Gaborik .10 .25
186 Zack Smith .05 .15
187 Philadelphia Flyers Logo .07 .20
188 STAR PLAYER Claude Giroux .10 .25
189 ILLUSTRATED PLAYER Sean Couturier .07 .20
190 STAR PLAYER Shayne Gostisbehere .10 .25
191 Brian Elliott .07 .20
192 Michal Neuvirth .07 .20
193 Andrew MacDonald .05 .15
194 Ivan Provorov .07 .20
195 Shayne Gostisbehere .10 .25
196 Claude Giroux .10 .25
197 Jakub Voracek .07 .20
198 Michael Raffl .07 .20
199 Nolan Patrick .10 .25
200 Sean Couturier .07 .20
201 Travis Konecny .10 .25
202 Wayne Simmonds .10 .25
203 Pittsburgh Penguins Logo .07 .20
204 STAR PLAYER Evgeni Malkin .20 .50
205 ILLUSTRATED PLAYER Phil Kessel .10 .25
206 STAR PLAYER Sidney Crosby .40 1.00
207 Matt Murray .10 .25
208 Brian Dumoulin .05 .15
209 Justin Schultz .07 .20
210 Kris Letang .12 .30
211 Olli Maatta .05 .15
212 Derick Brassard .05 .15
213 Evgeni Malkin .20 .50
214 Jake Guentzel .15 .40
215 Patric Hornqvist .05 .15
216 Phil Kessel .10 .25
217 Sidney Crosby .40 1.00
218 Bryan Rust .10 .25
219 Tampa Bay Lightning Logo .07 .20
220 STAR PLAYER Nikita Kucherov .20 .50
221 ILLUSTRATED PLAYER Victor Hedman .12 .30
222 STAR PLAYER Steven Stamkos .20 .50
223 Andrei Vasilevskiy .15 .40
224 Victor Hedman .12 .30
225 Ryan McDonagh .10 .25
226 Mikhail Sergachev .07 .20
227 Alex Killorn .05 .15
228 Brayden Point .12 .30
229 Nikita Kucherov .20 .50
230 Ondrej Palat .07 .20
231 Steven Stamkos .20 .50
232 Tyler Johnson .05 .15
233 Yanni Gourde .07 .20
234 J.T. Miller .12 .30
235 Toronto Maple Leafs Logo .07 .20
236 STAR PLAYER Mitch Marner .15 .40
237 ILLUSTRATED PLAYER Auston Matthews .40 1.00
238 STAR PLAYER Frederik Andersen .12 .30
239 Frederik Andersen .12 .30
240 Jake Gardiner .05 .15
241 Morgan Rielly .10 .25
242 Nikita Zaitsev .07 .20
243 Auston Matthews .40 1.00
244 Nazem Kadri .12 .30
245 Mitch Marner .15 .40
246 Patrick Marleau .10 .25
247 William Nylander .20 .50
248 John Tavares .15 .40
249 Connor Brown .07 .20
250 Zach Hyman .15 .40
251 Washington Capitals Logo .07 .20
252 STAR PLAYER Alex Ovechkin .40 1.00
253 ILLUSTRATED PLAYER T.J. Oshie .10 .25
254 STAR PLAYER Evgeny Kuznetsov .12 .30
255 Braden Holtby .12 .30
256 Brett Connolly .05 .15
257 John Carlson .10 .25
258 Matt Niskanen .07 .20
259 Dmitry Orlov .10 .25
260 Alex Ovechkin .40 1.00
261 Evgeny Kuznetsov .12 .30
262 Nicklas Backstrom .10 .25
263 T.J. Oshie .10 .25
264 Andre Burakovsky .05 .15
265 Tom Wilson .10 .25
266 Lars Eller .05 .15
267 Anaheim Ducks Logo .07 .20
268 STAR PLAYER Rickard Rakell .07 .20
269 ILLUSTRATED PLAYER Cam Fowler .10 .25
270 STAR PLAYER Ryan Getzlaf .10 .25
271 John Gibson .10 .25
272 Cam Fowler .10 .25
273 Hampus Lindholm .10 .25
274 Josh Manson .05 .15
275 Andrew Cogliano .05 .15
276 Ryan Getzlaf .10 .25
277 Adam Henrique .07 .20
278 Ondrej Kase .05 .15
279 Ryan Kesler .10 .25
280 Corey Perry .15 .40
281 Rickard Rakell .07 .20
282 Jakob Silfverberg .05 .15
283 Arizona Coyotes Logo .07 .20
284 STAR PLAYER Clayton Keller .12 .30
285 ILLUSTRATED PLAYER Derek Stepan .05 .15
286 STAR PLAYER Oliver Ekman-Larsson .10 .25
287 Darcy Kuemper .10 .25
288 Antti Raanta .10 .25
289 Jakob Chychrun .10 .25
290 Jason Demers .07 .20
291 Alex Goligoski .05 .15
292 Oliver Ekman-Larsson .10 .25
293 Brendan Perlini .05 .15
294 Christian Dvorak .07 .20
295 Clayton Keller .12 .30
296 Derek Stepan .05 .15
297 Alex Galchenyuk .05 .15
298 Christian Fischer .05 .15
299 Calgary Flames Logo .07 .20
300 STAR PLAYER Sean Monahan .05 .15
301 ILLUSTRATED PLAYER Mark Giordano .10 .25
302 STAR PLAYER Johnny Gaudreau .15 .40
303 Mike Smith .07 .20
304 TJ Brodie .07 .20
305 Mark Giordano .10 .25
306 Michael Stone .07 .20
307 Travis Hamonic .07 .20
308 Mikael Backlund .07 .20
309 Troy Brouwer .05 .15
310 Sam Bennett .15 .40
311 Michael Frolik .07 .20
312 Johnny Gaudreau .15 .40
313 Sean Monahan .05 .15
314 Matthew Tkachuk .20 .50
315 Chicago Blackhawks Logo .07 .20
316 STAR PLAYER Patrick Kane .20 .50
317 ILLUSTRATED PLAYER Jonathan Toews .15 .40
318 STAR PLAYER Alex DeBrincat .12 .30
319 Corey Crawford .07 .20
320 Cam Ward .10 .25
321 Duncan Keith .07 .20
322 Connor Murphy .05 .15
323 Jan Rutta .05 .15
324 Brent Seabrook .05 .15
325 Artem Anisimov .05 .15
326 Alex DeBrincat .12 .30
327 Patrick Kane .20 .50
328 Brandon Saad .07 .20
329 Nick Schmaltz .07 .20
330 Jonathan Toews .15 .40
331 Colorado Avalanche Logo .07 .20
332 STAR PLAYER Mikko Rantanen .25 .60
333 ILLUSTRATED PLAYER Nathan MacKinnon .40 1.00
334 STAR PLAYER Gabriel Landeskog .12 .30
335 Semyon Varlamov .10 .25
336 Philipp Grubauer .10 .25
337 Tyson Barrie .05 .15
338 Samuel Girard .05 .15
339 Erik Johnson .05 .15
340 Nikita Zadorov .05 .15
341 J.T. Compher .05 .15
342 Alexander Kerfoot .07 .20
343 Gabriel Landeskog .12 .30
344 Nathan MacKinnon .40 1.00
345 Mikko Rantanen .25 .60
346 Carl Soderberg .05 .15
347 Dallas Stars Logo .07 .20
348 STAR PLAYER Jamie Benn .10 .25
349 ILLUSTRATED PLAYER Alexander Radulov .10 .25
350 STAR PLAYER Tyler Seguin .12 .30
351 Ben Bishop .07 .20
352 John Klingberg .10 .25
353 Marc Methot .05 .15
354 Esa Lindell .07 .20
355 Jamie Benn .10 .25
356 Radek Faksa .07 .20
357 Martin Hanzal .05 .15
358 Mattias Janmark .05 .15
359 Alexander Radulov .10 .25
360 Blake Comeau .05 .15
361 Tyler Seguin .12 .30
362 Jason Spezza .10 .25
363 Edmonton Oilers Logo .07 .20
364 STAR PLAYER Connor McDavid .50 1.25
365 ILLUSTRATED PLAYER Ryan Nugent-Hopkins .12 .30
366 STAR PLAYER Leon Draisaitl .30 .75
367 Cam Talbot .10 .25
368 Al Montoya .07 .20
369 Oscar Klefbom .07 .20
370 Adam Larsson .10 .25
371 Darnell Nurse .07 .20
372 Kris Russell .05 .15
373 Leon Draisaitl .30 .75
374 Milan Lucic .10 .25
375 Connor McDavid .50 1.25
376 Ryan Nugent-Hopkins .12 .30
377 Ryan Strome .10 .25
378 Pontus Aberg .05 .15
379 Los Angeles Kings Logo .07 .20
380 STAR PLAYER Anze Kopitar .15 .40
381 ILLUSTRATED PLAYER Dustin Brown .10 .25
382 STAR PLAYER Drew Doughty .12 .30
383 Jonathan Quick .12 .30
384 Drew Doughty .12 .30
385 Alec Martinez .07 .20
386 Jake Muzzin .10 .25
387 Dion Phaneuf .07 .20
388 Dustin Brown .10 .25
389 Jeff Carter .07 .20
390 Adrian Kempe .10 .25
391 Anze Kopitar .15 .40
392 Trevor Lewis .05 .15
393 Tanner Pearson .07 .20
394 Tyler Toffoli .10 .25
395 Minnesota Wild Logo .07 .20
396 STAR PLAYER Eric Staal .10 .25
397 ILLUSTRATED PLAYER Ryan Suter .07 .20
398 STAR PLAYER Mikael Granlund .07 .20
399 Devan Dubnyk .07 .20
400 Jonas Brodin .05 .15
401 Matt Dumba .07 .20
402 Jared Spurgeon .10 .25
403 Ryan Suter .07 .20
404 Charlie Coyle .05 .15
405 Mikael Granlund .07 .20
406 Mikko Koivu .07 .20
407 Nino Niederreiter .05 .15
408 Zach Parise .10 .25
409 Eric Staal .10 .25
410 Jason Zucker .10 .25
411 Nashville Predators Logo .07 .20
412 STAR PLAYER P.K. Subban .12 .30
413 ILLUSTRATED PLAYER Filip Forsberg .15 .40
414 STAR PLAYER Pekka Rinne .10 .25
415 Pekka Rinne .10 .25
416 Ryan Ellis .07 .20
417 Mattias Ekholm .07 .20
418 Roman Josi .10 .25
419 P.K. Subban .12 .30
420 Viktor Arvidsson .05 .15
421 Nick Bonino .05 .15
422 Kevin Fiala .07 .20
423 Filip Forsberg .15 .40
424 Ryan Johansen .07 .20
425 Craig Smith .05 .15
426 Kyle Turris .07 .20
427 San Jose Sharks Logo .07 .20
428 STAR PLAYER Logan Couture .12 .30
429 ILLUSTRATED PLAYER Joe Pavelski .12 .30
430 STAR PLAYER Brent Burns .10 .25
431 Martin Jones .07 .20
432 Justin Braun .07 .20
433 Brent Burns .10 .25
434 Marc-Edouard Vlasic .05 .15
435 Logan Couture .12 .30
436 Tomas Hertl .10 .25
437 Kevin Labanc .05 .15
438 Timo Meier .10 .25
439 Joe Pavelski .12 .30
440 Chris Tierney .05 .15
441 Evander Kane .10 .25
442 Joe Thornton .15 .40
443 St. Louis Blues Logo .07 .20
444 STAR PLAYER Vladimir Tarasenko .12 .30
445 ILLUSTRATED PLAYER Brayden Schenn .10 .25
446 STAR PLAYER Alex Pietrangelo .07 .20
447 Jake Allen .10 .25
448 Ryan O'Reilly .10 .25
449 Jay Bouwmeester .05 .15
450 Vince Dunn .07 .20
451 Colton Parayko .07 .20
452 Alex Pietrangelo .07 .20
453 David Perron .07 .20
454 Dmitrij Jaskin .05 .15
455 Brayden Schenn .10 .25
456 Jaden Schwartz .12 .30
457 Alexander Steen .05 .15
458 Vladimir Tarasenko .12 .30
459 Vancouver Canucks Logo .07 .20
460 STAR PLAYER Brock Boeser .07 .20
461 ILLUSTRATED PLAYER Alexander Edler .05 .15
462 STAR PLAYER Bo Horvat .12 .30
463 Jacob Markstrom .10 .25
464 Anders Nilsson .05 .15
465 Michael Del Zotto .07 .20
466 Alexander Edler .05 .15
467 Erik Gudbranson .05 .15
468 Christopher Tanev .05 .15
469 Sven Baertschi .07 .20
470 Brock Boeser .12 .30
471 Loui Eriksson .05 .15
472 Sam Gagner .05 .15
473 Bo Horvat .12 .30
474 Brandon Sutter .05 .15
475 Vegas Golden Knights Logo .07 .20
476 STAR PLAYER William Karlsson .12 .30
477 ILLUSTRATED PLAYER Jonathan Marchessault .12 .30
478 STAR PLAYER Marc-Andre Fleury .20 .50
479 Marc-Andre Fleury .20 .50
480 Deryk Engelland .07 .20
481 Colin Miller .05 .15
482 Nate Schmidt .07 .20
483 Shea Theodore .12 .30
484 Erik Haula .05 .15
485 William Karlsson .12 .30
486 Jonathan Marchessault .12 .30
487 Paul Stastny .07 .20
488 Cody Eakin .05 .15
489 Reilly Smith .10 .25
490 Alex Tuch .10 .25
491 Winnipeg Jets Logo .07 .20
492 STAR PLAYER Blake Wheeler .10 .25
493 ILLUSTRATED PLAYER Patrik Laine .12 .30
494 STAR PLAYER Connor Hellebuyck .20 .50
495 Connor Hellebuyck .20 .50
496 Dustin Byfuglien .10 .25
497 Tyler Myers .05 .15
498 Jacob Trouba .07 .20
499 Kyle Connor .15 .40
500 Nikolaj Ehlers .10 .25
501 Patrik Laine .12 .30
502 Bryan Little .05 .15
503 Mathieu Perreault .05 .15
504 Mark Scheifele .15 .40
505 Dmitry Kulikov .05 .15
506 Blake Wheeler .07 .20
507 NHL100 Classic - Carey Price .07 .20
508 NHL100 Classic Jean-Gabriel Pageau (Left Half) .05 .15
509 NHL100 Classic Jean-Gabriel Pageau (Right Half) .05 .15
510 NHL100 Classic Erik Karlsson .12 .30
511 Winter Classic Kevin Hayes .07 .20
512 Winter Classic J.T. Miller (Left Half) .12 .30
513 Winter Classic J.T. Miller (Right Half) .12 .30
514 Winter Classic Rasmus Ristolainen .05 .15
515 Stadium Series Nazem Kadri .12 .30
516 Stadium Series Alex Ovechkin (Left Half) .40 1.00
517 Stadium Series Alex Ovechkin (Right Half) .40 1.00

518 Stadium Series Nicklas Backstrom .10 .25
519 Fastest Skater Connor McDavid .50 1.25
520 Puck Control Relay Johnny Gaudreau .15 .40
521 Passing Challenge Alex Pietrangelo .07 .20
522 Save Streak Marc-Andre Fleury .20 .50
523 Most Accurate Shooter Brock Boeser .12 .30
524 NHL All-Star MVP Brock Boeser .12 .30
525 Hardest Shot Alex Ovechkin .40 1.00
526 Patrick Kane .20 .50
527 P.K. Subban .12 .30
528 Nathan MacKinnon .40 1.00
529 Pekka Rinne .10 .25
530 Blake Wheeler .10 .25
531 Brock Boeser .12 .30
532 Drew Doughty .12 .30
533 Johnny Gaudreau .15 .40
534 Connor McDavid .50 1.25
535 Rickard Rakell .07 .20
536 Jack Eichel .15 .40
537 Steven Stamkos .20 .50
538 Nikita Kucherov .20 .50
539 Brad Marchand .20 .50
540 Carey Price .20 .50
541 Sidney Crosby .40 1.00
542 Claude Giroux .10 .25
543 Kris Letang .12 .30
544 Alex Ovechkin .40 1.00
545 John Tavares .15 .40
546 Nashville Predators vs. Colorado Avalanche .07 .20
547 Winnipeg Jets vs. Minnesota Wild .07 .20
548 Vegas Golden Knights vs. Los Angeles Kings .07 .20
549 Anaheim Ducks vs. San Jose Sharks .07 .20
550 Nashville Predators vs. Winnipeg Jets .07 .20
551 Vegas Golden Knights vs. San Jose Sharks .07 .20
552 Vegas Golden Knights vs. Winnipeg Jets .07 .20
553 Tampa Bay Lightning vs. Washington Capitals .07 .20
554 Tampa Bay Lightning vs. Boston Bruins .07 .20
555 Washington Capitals vs. Pittsburgh Penguins .07 .20
556 Tampa Bay Lightning vs. New Jersey Devils .07 .20
557 Boston Bruins vs. Toronto Maple Leafs .07 .20
558 Washington Capitals vs. Columbus Blue Jackets .07 .20
559 Pittsburgh Penguins vs. Philadelphia Flyers .07 .20
560 Game 1 .07 .20
561 Game 2 .07 .20
562 Game 3 .07 .20
563 Game 4 .07 .20
564 Game 5 .07 .20
565 2018 Stanley Cup Champions Logo Left Side .07 .20
566 2018 Stanley Cup Champions Logo Right Side .07 .20
567 Washington Capitals Team Photo Left Side .07 .20
568 Washington Capitals Team Photo Right Side .07 .20
569 Conn Smythe Trophy Winner Alex Ovechkin .07 .20
570 Conn Smythe Trophy .07 .20
571 Stanley Cup .07 .20
572 Stanley Cup Top Left .07 .20
573 Stanley Cup Top Right .07 .20
574 Stanley Cup Bottom Left .07 .20
575 Stanley Cup Bottom Right .07 .20

2011-12 Panini Team Colors Toronto Fall Expo

1 Phil Kessel 1.25 3.00
2 Dion Phaneuf 1.00 2.50

2011-12 Panini Titanium

1 Jonathan Toews .60 1.50
2 Rick Nash .40 1.00
3 Jimmy Howard .50 1.25
4 Taylor Hall .40 1.00
5 Carey Price .75 2.00
6 Zach Parise .40 1.00
7 Claude Giroux .40 1.00
8 Alex Ovechkin 1.50 4.00
9 Marc-Andre Fleury .75 2.00
10 Brian Elliott .30 .75
11 Phil Kessel .40 1.00
12 Henrik Sedin .50 1.25
13 Teemu Selanne .75 2.00
14 Patrick Kane .75 2.00
15 Ryan Miller .40 1.00
16 Jose Theodore .40 1.00
17 Tyler Seguin .50 1.25
18 Loui Eriksson .25 .60
19 Anze Kopitar .60 1.50
20 Cal Clutterbuck .25 .60
21 Dustin Byfuglien .40 1.00
22 Brad Richards .40 1.00
23 Al Montoya .25 .60
24 Luke Adam .30 .75
25 Cam Ward .40 1.00
26 Shane Doan .30 .75
27 Patrick Marleau .40 1.00
28 Dion Phaneuf .30 .75
29 Ray Emery .30 .75
30 Milan Hejduk .30 .75
31 Zdeno Chara .40 1.00
32 Miikka Kiprusoff .40 1.00
33 Jason Pominville .25 .60
34 Johan Franzen .30 .75
35 Jordan Eberle .40 1.00
36 Mikko Koivu .30 .75
37 Marian Gaborik .40 1.00
38 Jaromir Jagr 1.25 3.00
39 Stephen Weiss .30 .75
40 Logan Couture .50 1.25
41 Jonathan Quick .50 1.25
42 Nicklas Lidstrom .25 .60
43 Evander Kane .40 1.00
44 Daniel Sedin .50 1.25
45 Martin Brodeur 1.00 2.50
46 Shea Weber .30 .75
47 Kris Versteeg .25 .60
48 Joffrey Lupul .25 .60
49 Blake Wheeler .40 1.00
50 Nicklas Backstrom .40 1.00
51 Patrick Sharp .40 1.00
52 Kari Lehtonen .30 .75
53 Tim Thomas .40 1.00
54 Corey Perry .60 1.50
55 Ryan O'Reilly .40 1.00
56 Daniel Alfredsson .40 1.00
57 Kris Letang .50 1.25
58 Jonas Gustavsson .40 1.00
59 Tomas Vokoun .30 .75
60 Jarome Iginla .50 1.25
61 Jeff Skinner .50 1.25
62 Matt Duchene .40 1.00
63 Matt Moulson .25 .60
64 Vincent Lecavalier .40 1.00
65 Henrik Lundqvist 1.00 2.50
66 Dany Heatley .30 .75
67 Henrik Zetterberg .50 1.25
68 Milan Lucic .40 1.00
69 Ondrej Pavelec .40 1.00
70 Jamie Benn .40 1.00
71 Evgeni Malkin .75 2.00
72 Derek Stepan .25 .60
73 Ilya Bryzgalov .40 1.00
74 Michael Cammalleri .30 .75
75 Nikolai Khabibulin .30 .75
76 P.K. Subban .50 1.25
77 Thomas Vanek .30 .75
78 Marian Hossa .40 1.00
79 Ryan Kesler .40 1.00
80 Joe Thornton .60 1.50
81 Ryan Getzlaf .40 1.00
82 Ilya Kovalchuk .40 1.00
83 James Neal .25 .60
84 John Tavares .60 1.50
85 Pavel Datsyuk .60 1.50
86 Patrice Bergeron .50 1.25
87 Roberto Luongo .60 1.50
88 Josh Harding .40 1.00
89 Jeff Carter .30 .75
90 Eric Staal .50 1.25
91 Steven Stamkos .75 2.00
92 Jean-Sebastien Giguere .40 1.00
93 Ales Hemsky .30 .75
94 Mike Smith .40 1.00
95 T.J. Oshie .40 1.00
96 Jason Spezza .40 1.00
97 Pekka Rinne .40 1.00
98 Rene Bourque .25 .60
99 Martin St. Louis .40 1.00
100 Sidney Crosby 1.50 4.00
101 Mika Zibanejad/93 RC 30.00 80.00
102 Ryan Nugent-Hopkins/93 RC 100.00 200.00
103 Gabriel Landeskog/92 RC 60.00 120.00
104 Cade Fairchild/82 RC 10.00 25.00
105 Tomas Vincour/81 RC 12.00 30.00
106 Dmitry Orlov/81 RC 30.00 80.00
107 Cam Talbot/81 RC 30.00 80.00
108 Brayden McNabb/81 RC 12.00 30.00
109 Corey Tropp/78 RC 12.00 30.00
110 Devante Smith-Pelly/77 RC 15.00 40.00
111 Scott Timmins/75 RC 20.00 40.00
112 Peter Holland/74 RC 12.00 30.00
113 Alexei Emelin/74 RC 12.00 30.00
114 Louis Leblanc/71 RC 20.00 50.00
115 Mike Murphy/70 RC 15.00 40.00
116 Mike Hoffman/68 RC 30.00 60.00
117 Joakim Andersson/63 RC 12.00 30.00
118 Carl Hagelin/62 RC 90.00 150.00
119 Frederic St-Denis/62 RC 12.00 30.00
120 Raphael Diaz/61 RC 12.00 30.00
121 Aaron Palushaj/60 RC 12.00 30.00
122 Roman Josi/59 RC 40.00 100.00
123 Kris Fredheim/59 RC 15.00 40.00
124 Carl Sneep/59 RC 15.00 40.00
125 David Savard/58 RC 15.00 40.00
126 Anton Lander/57 RC 15.00 40.00
127 Gabriel Bourque/57 RC 15.00 40.00
128 Teemu Hartikainen/56 RC 15.00 40.00
129 Mark Scheifele/55 RC 50.00 100.00
130 Zack Kassian/54 RC 20.00 50.00
131 Tim Erixon/53 RC 15.00 40.00
132 Roman Horak/51 RC 15.00 40.00
133 Jake Gardiner/51 RC 25.00 60.00
134 Cody Eakin/50 RC 25.00 60.00
135 Ryan Ellis/49 RC 15.00 40.00
136 Greg Nemisz/48 RC 15.00 40.00
137 Carl Klingberg/48 RC 15.00 40.00
138 Brendon Nash/47 RC 15.00 40.00
139 Yann Sauve/47 RC 30.00 60.00
140 Simon Despres/47 RC 15.00 40.00
141 Stefan Elliott/46 RC 20.00 50.00
142 Joe Vitale/46 RC 15.00 40.00
143 Patrick Wiercioch/46 RC 15.00 40.00
144 Kevin Marshall/45 RC 15.00 40.00
145 Anders Nilsson/45 RC 15.00 40.00
146 Erik Gudbranson/44 RC 20.00 50.00
147 Calvin de Haan/44 RC 15.00 40.00
148 Marc-Andre Bourdon/43 RC 15.00 40.00
149 Brandon Saad/43 RC 50.00 100.00
150 Bill Sweatt/41 RC 15.00 40.00
151 Brad Malone/42 RC 15.00 40.00
152 Stu Bickel/41 RC 15.00 40.00
153 David Ullstrom/41 RC 15.00 40.00
154 Robert Bortuzzo/41 RC 15.00 40.00
155 Allen York/41 RC 20.00 50.00
156 Matt Frattin/39 RC 20.00 50.00
157 Paul Postma/38 RC 15.00 40.00
158 Brian Strait/37 RC 20.00 50.00
159 Leland Irving/37 RC 15.00 40.00
160 Jimmy Hayes/39 RC 20.00 50.00
161 Zac Rinaldo/36 RC 15.00 40.00
162 Keith Kinkaid/35 RC 20.00 50.00
163 Harri Sateri/35 RC 40.00 80.00
164 David McIntyre/34 RC 20.00 50.00
165 Tomas Kubalik/33 RC 25.00 60.00
166 T.J. Brennan/33 RC 20.00 50.00
167 Colten Teubert/33 RC 20.00 50.00
168 Joe Colborne/32 RC 60.00 100.00
169 Eddie Lack/31 RC 20.00 50.00
170 Ben Scrivens/30 RC 40.00 80.00
171 Harry Zolnierczyk/29 RC 20.00 50.00
172 Justin Faulk/28 RC 30.00 80.00
173 Hugh Jessiman/28 RC 15.00 40.00
174 Slava Voynov/26 RC 75.00 150.00
175 Erik Gustafsson/26 RC 30.00 80.00
178 Matt Read/24 RC 125.00 200.00
179 Erik Condra/22 RC 40.00 80.00
180 Colton Sceviour/22 RC 20.00 50.00
181 Ben Holmstrom/22 RC 75.00 150.00
182 Andy Miele/21 RC 30.00 60.00
183 Brett Bulmer/19 RC 30.00 60.00
184 Ryan Johansen/19 RC 50.00 100.00
185 Marcus Kruger/16 RC 40.00 80.00
186 Craig Smith/15 RC 30.00 60.00
187 Blake Geoffrion/15 RC 60.00 120.00
194 Cody Hodgson/19 RC 200.00 350.00

2011-12 Panini Titanium Spectrum Ruby

*RUBY/99: 5X TO 12X BASIC CARDS
50 Nicklas Backstrom 4.00 10.00

2011-12 Panini Titanium Spectrum

104 Cade Fairchild/96 6.00 15.00
105 Tomas Vincour/100 8.00 20.00
106 Dmitry Orlov/55 25.00 60.00
107 Cam Talbot/100 20.00 50.00
108 Brayden McNabb/66 10.00 25.00
109 Corey Tropp/89 8.00 20.00
110 Devante Smith-Pelly/42 12.00 30.00
111 Scott Timmins/100 8.00 20.00
112 Peter Holland/15 15.00 40.00
113 Alexei Emelin/84 8.00 20.00
114 Louis Leblanc/18 60.00 120.00
115 Mike Murphy/100 8.00 20.00
116 Mike Hoffman/100 30.00 80.00
117 Joakim Andersson/88 8.00 20.00
118 Carl Hagelin/100 12.00 30.00
119 Frederic St-Denis/100 8.00 20.00
120 Raphael Diaz/100 8.00 20.00
121 Aaron Palushaj/44 10.00 25.00
122 Roman Josi/38 25.00 60.00
123 Kris Fredheim/100 8.00 20.00
124 Carl Sneep/32 10.00 25.00
125 David Savard/94 8.00 20.00
126 Anton Lander/40 10.00 25.00
127 Gabriel Bourque/100 8.00 20.00
128 Teemu Hartikainen/100 8.00 20.00
131 Tim Erixon/23 12.00 30.00
132 Roman Horak/100 10.00 25.00
133 Jake Gardiner/17 25.00 60.00
134 Cody Eakin/85 25.00 50.00
136 Greg Nemisz/25 12.00 30.00
137 Carl Klingberg/34 10.00 25.00
138 Brendon Nash/100 8.00 20.00
139 Yann Sauve/41 10.00 25.00
140 Simon Despres/30 10.00 25.00
141 Stefan Elliott/49 10.00 25.00
142 Joe Vitale/100 8.00 20.00
143 Patrick Wiercioch/42 10.00 25.00
144 Kevin Marshall/41 15.00 40.00
145 Anders Nilsson/62 8.00 20.00
148 Marc-Andre Bourdon/67 8.00 20.00
149 Brandon Saad/43 25.00 60.00
150 Bill Sweatt/38 10.00 25.00
151 Brad Malone/100 8.00 20.00
152 Stu Bickel/100 8.00 20.00
153 David Ullstrom/100 8.00 20.00
154 Robert Bortuzzo/78 8.00 20.00
155 Allen York/100 10.00 25.00
156 Matt Frattin/99 8.00 20.00
157 Paul Postma/100 8.00 20.00
158 Brian Strait/65 10.00 25.00
159 Leland Irving/26 12.00 30.00
160 Jimmy Hayes/80 10.00 25.00
161 Zac Rinaldo/100 8.00 20.00
162 Keith Kinkaid/100 8.00 20.00
163 Harri Sateri/100 10.00 25.00
164 David McIntyre/100 8.00 20.00
165 Tomas Kubalik/100 8.00 20.00
166 T.J. Brennan/31 10.00 25.00
168 Joe Colborne/16 15.00 40.00
169 Eddie Lack/100 8.00 20.00
170 Ben Scrivens/100 8.00 20.00
171 Harry Zolnierczyk/100 8.00 20.00
172 Justin Faulk/37 15.00 40.00
174 Slava Voynov/32 10.00 25.00
175 Erik Gustafsson/100 10.00 25.00
176 Stephane Da Costa/100 8.00 20.00
177 Cameron Gaunce/50 8.00 20.00
178 Matt Read/100 10.00 25.00
179 Erik Condra/100 8.00 20.00
180 Colton Sceviour/100 8.00 20.00
181 Ben Holmstrom/100 8.00 20.00
182 Andy Miele/100 8.00 20.00
183 Brett Bulmer/39 10.00 25.00
185 Marcus Kruger/100 12.00 30.00
186 Craig Smith/98 10.00 25.00
187 Blake Geoffrion/56 10.00 25.00
188 Colin Greening/100 8.00 20.00
189 Adam Henrique/82 20.00 50.00
192 Gustav Nyquist/100 20.00 50.00
193 Cam Atkinson/100 20.00 50.00
195 Jonathon Blum/23 12.00 30.00
196 David Rundblad/17 15.00 40.00
198 John Moore/21 12.00 30.00
199 Brendan Smith/27 40.00 80.00
200 Mikko Koskinen/31 12.00 30.00

2011-12 Panini Titanium Draft Day Autographs

1 Ryan Nugent-Hopkins/25 75.00 150.00
2 Gabriel Landeskog/25 20.00 50.00
3 Adam Larsson/99 12.00 30.00
4 Mika Zibanejad/99 12.00 30.00
5 Mark Scheifele/99 25.00 60.00
6 Sean Couturier/99 12.00 30.00
7 Brandon Saad/99 12.00 30.00
8 Taylor Hall/25 25.00 60.00
9 Tyler Seguin/25 60.00 120.00
10 Erik Gudbranson/99 8.00 20.00
11 Ryan Johansen/99 20.00 50.00
12 Brett Connolly/99 6.00 15.00
14 Alexander Burmistrov/99 8.00 20.00
15 Justin Faulk/99 10.00 25.00
16 Brett Bulmer/99 6.00 15.00
17 Devante Smith-Pelly/99 8.00 20.00
18 John Tavares/25 40.00 80.00
19 Victor Hedman/99 8.00 20.00
20 Matt Duchene/99 10.00 25.00
21 Evander Kane/99 10.00 25.00
22 Brayden Schenn/99 10.00 25.00
23 Oliver Ekman-Larsson/99 10.00 25.00
24 Nazem Kadri/99 12.00 30.00
25 Magnus Paajarvi/25 12.00 30.00
26 Calvin de Haan/99 8.00 20.00
27 Zack Kassian/99 8.00 20.00
28 Peter Holland/99 6.00 15.00
29 David Rundblad/99 8.00 20.00
30 Louis Leblanc/99 12.00 30.00
31 John Moore/99 6.00 15.00
32 Tim Erixon/99 6.00 15.00
33 Jordan Caron/99 10.00 25.00
34 Simon Despres/99 15.00 40.00
35 Steven Stamkos/25 30.00 80.00
36 Drew Doughty/25 25.00 50.00
37 Alex Pietrangelo/99 12.00 30.00
38 Luke Schenn/99 10.00 25.00
39 Cody Hodgson/25 40.00 80.00
40 Tyler Myers/99 6.00 15.00
41 Colten Teubert/99 6.00 15.00
42 Joe Colborne/99 6.00 15.00
43 Jake Gardiner/99 10.00 25.00
44 Jordan Eberle/25 40.00 80.00
45 Mattias Tedenby/99 6.00 15.00
46 Greg Nemisz/99 6.00 15.00
47 Tyler Ennis/99 8.00 20.00
48 Thomas McCollum/99 10.00 25.00
50 James van Riemsdyk/99 8.00 20.00

2011-12 Panini Titanium Four Star Memorabilia

*PRIME/25: .6X TO 1.5X BASIC JSY/75
1 Prry/Selan/Gtzlf/Fowlr/25 15.00 40.00
2 Lndqvst/Rchrds/Gbrk/Staal 20.00 50.00
3 Miller/Pminvlle/Adam/Vanek 8.00 20.00
4 Koptr/Rchrds/Dghty/Cliffrd 15.00 40.00
5 Datsk/Zetter/Hwrd/Hlmstrm 10.00 25.00
6 Brvsky/Prngr/Brre/vanRiems 12.00 30.00
7 Mrchnd/Thoms/Char/Lucic 12.00 30.00
8 Malkn/Fleury/Kendy/Letng 15.00 40.00
9 Reimr/Kessl/Phanf/Grbvsk 10.00 25.00
10 Ovchk/Nvirth/Semn/Jhasn 30.00 80.00
11 Toews/Sharp/Seabrk/Hoss 12.00 30.00
12 RNH/Ebrle/Khabi/Hmsky 15.00 40.00
13 Karlsn/Alfrdsn/Spezz/Folg 10.00 25.00
14 Iginla/Glncrs/Grdno/Bwmster 10.00 25.00
15 Dorsett/Prust/Neil/Ott 5.00 12.00
16 Parise/Pavlski/Kslr/Callhn 10.00 25.00
17 Kiprsff/Rinne/Bckstrm/Rask 10.00 25.00
20 RNH/Lndskg/Larsn/Ziban 15.00 40.00

2011-12 Panini Titanium Game Worn Gear

*PATCH/15-25: 1X TO 2.5X BASIC JSY
1 Vincent Lecavalier 4.00 10.00
2 Tyler Myers 4.00 10.00
3 Tyler Kennedy 2.50 6.00
4 Tuukka Rask 5.00 12.00
5 Trevor Daley 2.50 6.00
6 Tobias Enstrom 2.50 6.00
7 Tim Thomas 4.00 10.00
8 Thomas Vanek 3.00 8.00
9 Teemu Selanne 8.00 20.00
10 T.J. Galiardi 3.00 8.00
11 Steve Ott 2.50 6.00
12 Sidney Crosby 15.00 40.00
13 Shea Weber 3.00 8.00
14 Shawn Horcoff 2.50 6.00
15 Shane Doan 3.00 8.00
16 Sergei Bobrovsky 5.00 12.00
17 Sean Avery 4.00 10.00
18 Scott Gomez 3.00 8.00
19 Sam Gagner 2.50 6.00
20 Ryane Clowe 4.00 10.00
21 Ryan O'Reilly 4.00 10.00
22 Calvin de Haan 3.00 8.00
23 Ryan Miller 4.00 10.00
24 Ryan Kesler 4.00 10.00
25 Ryan Getzlaf 4.00 10.00
26 Rick Nash 4.00 10.00
27 Philip Larsen 2.50 6.00
28 Phil Kessel 4.00 10.00
29 Peter Regin 2.50 6.00
30 Pekka Rinne 4.00 10.00
31 Pavel Datsyuk 6.00 15.00
32 Paul Stastny 3.00 8.00
33 Paul Gaustad 2.50 6.00
34 Patrik Elias 4.00 10.00
35 Patrick Sharp 4.00 10.00
36 Patrick Kane 8.00 20.00
37 Patrice Bergeron 5.00 12.00
38 Nikolai Kulemin 2.50 6.00
39 Niklas Backstrom 4.00 10.00
40 Nicklas Backstrom 4.00 10.00
41 Nick Spaling 2.50 6.00
42 Nick Bonino 2.50 6.00
43 Nathan Horton 4.00 10.00
44 Milan Michalek 2.50 6.00
45 Milan Hejduk 3.00 8.00
46 Mikko Koivu 3.00 8.00
47 Mike Richards 3.00 8.00
48 Mike Green 3.00 8.00
49 Matt Duchene 4.00 10.00
50 Mats Zuccarello 4.00 10.00
51 Mark Giordano 4.00 10.00
52 Marian Gaborik 4.00 10.00
53 Marc-Andre Fleury 5.00 12.00
54 Loui Eriksson 2.50 6.00
56 Lars Eller 2.50 6.00
57 Kyle Okposo 2.50 6.00
58 Kris Letang SP 10.00 25.00
59 Keith Yandle 2.50 6.00
60 Kari Lehtonen 3.00 8.00
61 Jordan Staal 3.00 8.00
62 Jordan Eberle 5.00 12.00
63 Jonathan Toews SP 40.00 80.00
64 Jonathan Quick 5.00 12.00
65 Jonathan Bernier 3.00 8.00
66 Jonas Hiller 3.00 8.00
67 Jonas Gustavsson 4.00 10.00
68 Johan Franzen 3.00 8.00
69 Joe Thornton 6.00 15.00
70 Joe Pavelski 5.00 12.00
71 Jody Shelley 3.00 8.00
72 Jimmy Howard 5.00 12.00
73 Jason Spezza 4.00 10.00
74 Jamie Benn 4.00 10.00
75 James van Riemsdyk 3.00 8.00
76 James Neal 2.50 6.00
77 Henrik Lundqvist 10.00 25.00
78 Evgeni Malkin 8.00 20.00
79 Derek Stepan 2.50 6.00
80 Danny Briere 5.00 12.00
81 Corey Perry 6.00 15.00
82 Carey Price 8.00 20.00
83 Brent Seabrook 2.50 6.00
84 Brenden Morrow 3.00 8.00
85 Brad Richards 4.00 10.00
86 Brad Marchand 8.00 20.00
87 Anze Kopitar 6.00 15.00
88 Alex Ovechkin 15.00 40.00
89 Alexander Semin 4.00 10.00
90 Ales Hemsky 3.00 8.00
91 Alex Pietrangelo 3.00 8.00
92 Andrew Ladd 5.00 12.00
93 Brandon Dubinsky 2.50 6.00
94 Craig Anderson 4.00 10.00
95 David Backes 2.50 6.00
96 Jay Bouwmeester 2.50 6.00
97 Jeff Deslauriers 2.50 6.00
98 Joe Mullen 3.00 8.00
99 Nick Palmieri 3.00 8.00
100 Ryan McDonagh 2.50 6.00

2011-12 Panini Titanium Game Worn Gear Prime

*PRIME/50: .6X TO 1.5X BASIC INSERTS
*PRIME/25: .8X TO 2X BASIC INSERTS
30 Pekka Rinne/50 6.00 15.00
63 Jonathan Toews/50 10.00 25.00

2011-12 Panini Titanium Game Worn Gear Autographs

*PRIME/50: .6X TO 1.5X JSY AU/75-100
*PRIME/50: .5X TO 1.2X JSY AU/50
*PRIME/50: .4X TO 1X JSY AU/25
*PRIME/25: .8X TO 2X JSY AU/75-100
*PRIME/20-25: .6X TO 1.5X JSY AU/35-51
*PRIME/20-25: .5X TO 1.2X JSY AU/25
1 Vincent Lecavalier/50 10.00 25.00
4 Tuukka Rask/100 10.00 25.00
7 Tim Thomas/25 15.00 40.00
8 Thomas Vanek/50 8.00 20.00
13 Shea Weber/100 8.00 20.00
16 Sergei Bobrovsky/85 8.00 20.00
18 Scott Gomez/100 6.00 15.00
19 Sam Gagner/100 8.00 20.00
21 Ryan O'Reilly/50 10.00 25.00
22 Calvin de Haan/100 6.00 15.00
23 Ryan Miller/50 10.00 25.00
24 Ryan Kesler/50 12.00 30.00
27 Philip Larsen/100 5.00 12.00
28 Phil Kessel/75 8.00 20.00
30 Pekka Rinne/25 12.00 30.00
31 Pavel Datsyuk/100 10.00 25.00
34 Patrik Elias/25 12.00 30.00
38 Nikolai Kulemin/100 5.00 12.00
39 Niklas Backstrom/25 10.00 25.00
43 Nathan Horton/50 10.00 25.00
49 Matt Duchene/25 12.00 30.00
50 Mats Zuccarello/100 8.00 20.00
51 Mark Giordano/100 8.00 20.00
52 Marian Gaborik/25 12.00 30.00
54 Loui Eriksson/49 6.00 15.00
56 Lars Eller/100 5.00 12.00
57 Kyle Okposo/75 5.00 12.00
58 Kris Letang/50 12.00 30.00
61 Jordan Staal/100 6.00 15.00
62 Jordan Eberle/75 8.00 20.00
65 Jonathan Bernier/100 6.00 15.00
66 Jonas Hiller/75 6.00 15.00
67 Jonas Gustavsson/75 8.00 20.00
71 Jody Shelley/50 12.00 30.00
72 Jimmy Howard/100 12.00 30.00
74 Jamie Benn/25 15.00 40.00
75 James van Riemsdyk/100 6.00 15.00
76 James Neal/50 6.00 15.00
77 Henrik Lundqvist/25 30.00 80.00
79 Derek Stepan/25 8.00 20.00
80 Danny Briere/50 10.00 25.00
81 Corey Perry/50 15.00 40.00
82 Carey Price/50 20.00 50.00
84 Brenden Morrow/75 5.00 12.00
86 Brad Marchand/75 10.00 25.00
88 Alex Ovechkin/25 30.00 80.00
90 Ales Hemsky/100 6.00 15.00
91 Alex Pietrangelo/100 6.00 15.00
92 Andrew Ladd/32 6.00 15.00
93 Brandon Dubinsky/100 5.00 12.00
94 Craig Anderson/51 10.00 25.00
95 David Backes/42 6.00 15.00
96 Jay Bouwmeester/35 8.00 20.00
97 Jeff Deslauriers/100 5.00 12.00
98 Joe Mullen/100 6.00 15.00
99 Nick Palmieri/100 6.00 15.00
100 Ryan McDonagh/100 8.00 20.00

2011-12 Panini Titanium Game Worn Gear Autographs Patch

*PATCH AU/15: 1X TO 2.5X JSY AU/75-100
*PATCH AU/15: .8X TO 2X JSY AU/35-51
*PATCH AU/15: .6X TO 1.5X JSY AU/25
69 Joe Thornton/15 30.00 60.00
78 Evgeni Malkin/15 40.00 80.00

2011-12 Panini Titanium Game Worn Gear Dual Memorabilia

*PATCH/15: 1X TO 2.5X BASIC DUAL
*PATCH/15: .8X TO 2X DUAL/50
*PRIME/37-50: .8X TO 2X DUAL/100-300
*PRIME/25: 1X TO 2.5X DUAL/100-300
*PRIME/25: .8X TO 2X DUAL/50
1 B.Ryan/C.Fowler/300 5.00 12.00
2 T.Selanne/S.Koivu/50 10.00 25.00
3 M.Lucic/S.Thornton/150 5.00 12.00
4 L.Adam/P.Kaleta/300 4.00 10.00
5 D.Stafford/T.Vanek/300 4.00 10.00
6 M.Kiprusoff/J.Bouwmeester/300 5.00 12.00
7 D.Keith/B.Seabrook/50 5.00 12.00
8 E.Johnson/B.Yip/300 3.00 8.00
9 D.Brassard/D.Dorsett/300 3.00 8.00
10 B.Holtby/M.Neuvirth/300 10.00 25.00
11 R.Malone/B.Connolly/300 4.00 10.00
12 B.Prust/B.Boyle/300 3.00 8.00
13 E.Karlsson/N.Foligno/300 6.00 15.00
14 T.Wandell/P.Larsen/300 3.00 8.00
15 R.O'Reilly/B.Yip/300 5.00 12.00
16 M.Grabovski/N.Kulemin/300 3.00 8.00
17 I.Kovalchuk/T.Zajac/300 5.00 12.00
18 J.Staal/T.Kennedy/300 6.00 15.00
19 B.Laich/M.Knuble/300 3.00 8.00
20 A.Burrows/K.Bieksa/300 4.00 10.00
21 V.Lecavalier/D.Tyrell/300 5.00 12.00
22 P.Marleau/T.Mitchell/300 5.00 12.00
23 M.Boedker/K.Yandle/300 3.00 8.00
24 D.Briere/K.Timonen/300 3.00 8.00
25 D.Doughty/J.Johnson/300 5.00 12.00
26 H.Lundqvist/C.Crawford 8.00 20.00
27 R.Miller/J.Quick/300 6.00 15.00
28 M.Brodeur/J.Reimer/300 12.00 30.00
29 M.Kiprusoff/T.Rask/300 6.00 15.00
30 N.Khabibulin/S.Varlamov/300 5.00 12.00
31 C.Neil/D.Dorsett/300 3.00 8.00
32 Z.Chara/T.Myers/300 5.00 12.00
33 G.Parros/C.Perry/300 8.00 20.00
34 P.Sharp/M.Hossa/100 5.00 12.00
35 G.Landeskog/P.Mueller/300 4.00 10.00
36 T.Enstrom/A.Kulda/300 5.00 12.00
37 B.Hull/B.Smith/300 10.00 25.00
38 J.Pominville/J.Leopold/300 3.00 8.00
39 J.Nieuwendyk/J.Hedberg/300 4.00 10.00
40 S.Varlamov/M.Neuvirth/300 6.00 15.00
41 D.Krejci/P.Bergeron/300 6.00 15.00
42 J.Thornton/M.Vlasic/300 5.00 12.00
43 D.Kulikov/E.Gudbranson/300 4.00 10.00
44 J.Blum/C.Wilson/300 4.00 10.00
45 B.Wheeler/B.Little/300 5.00 12.00
46 J.Eberle/R.Whitney/100 6.00 15.00
47 L.Eller/J.Gorges/300 3.00 8.00
48 G.Campbell/M.Bartkowski/300 3.00 8.00
49 K.Lehtonen/E.Belfour/300 5.00 12.00
50 C.de Haan/T.Hamonic/300 4.00 10.00

2011-12 Panini Titanium Game Worn Gear Dual Memorabilia Prime

11 R.Malone/B.Connolly/50 8.00 20.00

2011-12 Panini Titanium Hat Tricks Memorabilia

*PATCH/15: .6X TO 2X BASIC JSY/199
*PRIME/15-25: .6X TO 1.5X BASIC JSY/199
1 Gaborik/Anisimov/Avery 6.00 15.00
2 Kopitar/Johnson/Brown 10.00 25.00
3 Burmistrov/Enstrom/Bogosian 8.00 20.00
4 Vokoun/Green/Backstrom 6.00 15.00
5 Sedin/Raymond/Hansen 8.00 20.00
6 Kiprusoff/Nemisz/Karlsson 6.00 15.00
7 Duchene/Yip/Galiardi 6.00 15.00
8 Johansen/Dorsett/Brassard 6.00 15.00
9 Koivu/Backstrom/Cltterbck 6.00 15.00
10 Cammalleri/Gorges/Gomez 5.00 12.00
11 Weber/Suter/Fisher 5.00 12.00
12 Lindros/Brodeur/Jagr 20.00 50.00
13 Price/Lundqvist/Thomas 15.00 40.00
14 Hull/Modano/Belfour 12.00 30.00
15 de Haan/DiPietro/Okposo 5.00 12.00
16 Daugavins/Spezza/Alfredsson 6.00 15.00
17 Pronger/Hartnell/van Riems 6.00 15.00
18 Stamkos/Tyrell/Connolly 8.00 20.00
19 Staal/Despres/Neal 5.00 12.00
20 Richards/Dubinsky/Staal 6.00 15.00
21 Shanahan/Howard/Datsyuk 15.00 40.00
22 Henrique/Kruger/Palushaj 6.00 15.00
23 Joseph/Fuhr/Giguere 10.00 25.00
24 Neely/Middleton/Vachon 10.00 25.00
25 Boychuk/McBain/Faulk 8.00 20.00
26 Lehtonen/Eriksson/Wandell 5.00 12.00
27 Messier/Del Zotto/Erixon 12.00 30.00
28 Kessel/Schenn/Orr 6.00 15.00
29 Yzerman/Zetterbrg/Lidstrm 15.00 40.00
30 Nugnt-Hop/de Hn/Johnsn 10.00 25.00

2011-12 Panini Titanium Hat Tricks Memorabilia Prime

4 Vokoun/Green/Backstrom 10.00 25.00
18 Stamkos/Tyrell/Connolly 12.00 30.00

2011-12 Panini Titanium Hat Tricks Memorabilia Patch

4 Vokoun/Green/Backstrom 12.00 30.00

2011-12 Panini Titanium Home Sweaters Memorabilia Autographs

*PRIME/25: .6X TO 1.5X BASIC JSY AU
1 Dobby Ryan/100 8.00 20.00
2 Brad Marchand/100 20.00 50.00
3 Nathan Gerbe/100 6.00 15.00
4 Henrik Karlsson/78 8.00 20.00
5 Jamie McBain/100 6.00 15.00
6 Denis Savard/100 12.00 30.00
7 Erik Johnson/100 6.00 15.00
9 John Moore/100 8.00 20.00
10 Ryan Johansen/100 10.00 25.00
11 Philip Larsen/100 8.00 20.00
12 Luc Robitaille/100 15.00 40.00
13 Pavel Datsyuk/100 15.00 40.00
14 Adam Graves/100 10.00 25.00
15 Nikolai Khabibulin/100 10.00 25.00
16 Grant Fuhr/100 20.00 50.00
17 Ryan Ellis/100 10.00 25.00
18 Adam Larsson/100 10.00 25.00
19 Travis Zajac/75 8.00 20.00
20 Calvin de Haan/100 10.00 25.00
21 Henrik Lundqvist/100 20.00 40.00
22 David Rundblad/100 8.00 20.00
23 Mika Zibanejad/100 25.00 60.00
24 Jakub Voracek/40 10.00 25.00
25 Vincent Lecavalier/100 10.00 25.00
26 Michal Neuvirth/100 10.00 25.00
28 Cody Hodgson/100 12.00 30.00
29 Gabriel Landeskog/100 25.00 60.00
30 Ryan Nugent-Hopkins/100 30.00 80.00

2011-12 Panini Titanium Marks of Honour Autographs

3 Stan Mikita/25 15.00 40.00
4 Scott Niedermayer/25 12.00 30.00
5 Ron Francis/25 15.00 40.00
6 Phil Esposito/25 20.00 40.00
7 Peter Stastny/25 10.00 25.00
9 Pat LaFontaine/25 15.00 40.00
10 Mike Bossy/25 12.00 30.00
15 Joe Sakic/25 30.00 60.00
16 Jean Beliveau/25 25.00 50.00
18 Felix Potvin/25 25.00 50.00
20 Curtis Joseph/25 15.00 40.00

2011-12 Panini Titanium New Wave Autographs

1 Drayson Bowman 4.00 10.00
2 Adam Henrique 10.00 25.00
3 Adam McQuaid 4.00 10.00
4 Craig Smith 6.00 15.00
5 Cody Eakin 6.00 15.00
6 Alex Urbom 4.00 10.00
7 Ben Scrivens 4.00 10.00
8 Blake Geoffrion 4.00 10.00
9 Louis Leblanc 4.00 10.00
10 Anders Lindback 5.00 12.00
11 Brandon Yip 4.00 10.00
12 Raphael Diaz 4.00 10.00
13 Slava Voynov 4.00 10.00
14 Zack Kassian 5.00 12.00
15 Carl Gunnarsson 4.00 10.00
16 Chris Vande Velde 5.00 12.00
17 Dale Weise 5.00 12.00
18 Dwight King 4.00 10.00
19 Adam Larsson SP 8.00 20.00
20 Justin Faulk 6.00 15.00
21 Mark Scheifele 15.00 40.00
22 Jared Cowen 5.00 12.00
23 Ryan Nugent-Hopkins 60.00 120.00
24 Gabriel Landeskog SP 20.00 50.00
25 Jay Rosehill 4.00 10.00
26 Taylor Hall 10.00 25.00
27 Timo Pielmeier 5.00 12.00
28 Travis Hamonic 5.00 12.00
29 Aaron Palushaj 4.00 10.00
30 Joe Vitale 4.00 10.00
31 Nick Bonino 4.00 10.00
32 David Rundblad 4.00 10.00
33 Robert Bortuzzo 4.00 10.00
34 Joe Colborne 4.00 10.00
35 Justin DiBenedetto 4.00 10.00
36 Justin Falk 4.00 10.00
37 Ryan McDonagh 5.00 12.00
38 Viktor Stalberg 4.00 10.00
39 J.P. Anderson 5.00 12.00
40 Tyler Seguin SP 40.00 80.00
41 Cody Hodgson 6.00 15.00
42 Brendon Nash 4.00 10.00
43 Calvin de Haan 4.00 10.00
44 Jonas Gustavsson 5.00 12.00
45 John McCarthy 4.00 10.00
46 Brad Marchand SP 15.00 30.00
47 Cameron Gaunce 3.00 8.00
48 Brandon Saad 12.00 30.00
49 Jonathon Blum 4.00 10.00
50 Cory Emmerton 5.00 12.00

2011-12 Panini Titanium Quad Memorabilia

1 Ryan Callahan/25 10.00 25.00
2 Milan Michalek/15 10.00 25.00
3 Milan Lucic/25 15.00 40.00
4 Ilya Kovalchuk/25 15.00 40.00
5 Shea Weber/25 12.00 30.00
6 Derek Roy/25 10.00 25.00
7 David Legwand/25 12.00 30.00
8 Shawn Horcoff/25 10.00 25.00
9 Ryan O'Reilly/25 15.00 40.00
10 Tim Thomas/25 15.00 40.00
11 Henrik Zetterberg/25 20.00 50.00
12 Dmitry Kulikov/25 10.00 25.00
13 John Carlson/25 15.00 40.00
14 Michael Cammalleri/25 12.00 30.00
15 Johan Franzen/25 12.00 30.00
16 Erik Johnson/25 10.00 25.00
17 Miikka Kiprusoff/25 15.00 40.00
18 Tyler Myers/25 10.00 25.00
19 Zdeno Chara/25 15.00 40.00
20 Kris Letang/25 20.00 50.00
21 Joe Pavelski/25 20.00 50.00
24 Phil Kessel/25 15.00 40.00
25 Ryan Kesler/25 15.00 40.00
26 Michal Neuvirth/25 12.00 30.00
29 Nicklas Lidstrom/25 10.00 25.00
30 Mike Richards/25 12.00 30.00
31 Brad Richards/25 15.00 40.00
32 Tuukka Rask/25 20.00 50.00
33 Jason Pominville/25 10.00 25.00
34 T.J. Galiardi/25 12.00 30.00
35 Jamie Benn/25 15.00 40.00
36 Kyle Okposo/25 10.00 25.00
37 Adam Larsson/25 15.00 40.00
38 Jason Spezza/25 15.00 40.00
39 Chris Pronger/25 15.00 40.00
40 Shane Doan/25 12.00 30.00
41 Patrick Marleau/25 15.00 40.00
42 Ryan Malone/25 10.00 25.00
44 Daniel Alfredsson/25 15.00 40.00
45 James van Riemsdyk/25 12.00 30.00
46 Drew Doughty/25 20.00 50.00
47 Nicklas Backstrom/25 15.00 40.00
49 Antti Niemi/25 12.00 30.00
50 Jonathan Quick/25 20.00 50.00

2011-12 Panini Titanium Reserve Autographs

1 Adam Henrique 12.00 30.00
2 Brandon Yip 4.00 10.00
3 Antoine Vermette 4.00 10.00
4 Anze Kopitar 10.00 25.00
5 Bobby Clarke 20.00 40.00
6 Manon Rheaume 20.00 40.00
7 Grant Clitsome 4.00 10.00
8 Brayden Schenn 6.00 15.00
9 Brenden Morrow 5.00 12.00
10 Cam Fowler 6.00 15.00
11 Cam Ward 6.00 15.00
12 Carey Price 15.00 30.00

13 Cody Hodgson 12.00 30.00
14 Corey Perry 10.00 25.00
15 Craig Anderson 6.00 15.00
16 Alex Ovechkin 30.00 80.00
17 Curtis Joseph 12.00 30.00
18 Daniel Sedin 8.00 20.00
19 Dany Heatley 5.00 12.00
20 David Backes 4.00 10.00
21 David Krejci 10.00 25.00
22 Devin Setoguchi 5.00 12.00
23 Dustin Brown 6.00 15.00
24 Gabriel Landeskog 12.00 30.00
25 James van Riemsdyk 5.00 12.00
26 Jonas Hiller 5.00 12.00
27 Marty Turco 6.00 15.00
28 Kevin Dineen 6.00 15.00
29 Marian Gaborik 6.00 15.00
31 Mark Messier SP 20.00 50.00
32 Martin Brodeur 40.00 80.00
33 Matt Hackett 5.00 12.00
34 Nathan Horton 6.00 15.00
35 Nazem Kadri 8.00 20.00
36 Nikolai Khabibulin 8.00 20.00
37 P.K. Subban 8.00 20.00
38 Patrice Bergeron SP 20.00 40.00
39 Patrick Wiercioch 5.00 12.00
40 Ryan Nugent-Hopkins 25.00 60.00
41 Sam Gagner 6.00 15.00
42 Sean Couturier 10.00 25.00
43 Steve Ott 4.00 10.00
44 Steven Stamkos SP 30.00 60.00
45 Mike Bossy 10.00 25.00
46 Teddy Purcell 4.00 10.00
47 Tuukka Rask 10.00 25.00
48 Kris Russell 6.00 15.00
49 Tyler Seguin SP 40.00 80.00
50 Zack Kassian 5.00 12.00

2011-12 Panini Titanium Road Sweaters Memorabilia Autographs

*PRIME/15: .6X TO 1.5X BASIC AU/50
*PRIME/15: .5X TO 1.2X BASIC AU/25
1 Alexander Burmistrov/50 10.00 25.00
2 Brandon Dubinsky/50 8.00 20.00
3 Cam Fowler/50 12.00 30.00
5 David Backes/50 8.00 20.00
6 Drew Doughty/50 10.00 25.00
7 Dustin Brown/50 15.00 40.00
8 Jaroslav Halak/50 12.00 30.00
9 Joe Vitale/50 10.00 25.00
10 Jonas Hiller/50 10.00 25.00
11 Jonathan Bernier/50 10.00 25.00
13 Marc Staal/50 8.00 20.00
14 Marian Gaborik/50 12.00 30.00
15 Mason Raymond/50 10.00 25.00
16 Matt Frattin/50 10.00 25.00
17 Matt Read/50 15.00 40.00
18 Michael Cammalleri/50 10.00 25.00
20 Michael Del Zotto/25 10.00 25.00
21 Nicklas Lidstrom/50 15.00 40.00
22 Carey Price/25 30.00 80.00
23 Patrick Marleau/50 12.00 30.00
24 Rick Nash/50 12.00 30.00
25 Ryan Ellis/50 12.00 30.00
26 Ryan Miller/50 15.00 40.00
27 Sean Couturier/50 15.00 40.00
28 Thomas Vanek/50 8.00 20.00
29 Zac Dalpe/25 10.00 25.00
30 Zack Kassian/50 15.00 40.00

2011-12 Panini Titanium Rookie Dual Signatures

1 Nugent-Hopkins/A.Lander 50.00 120.00
2 G.Landeskog/S.Elliott 25.00 50.00
3 S.Couturier/H.Zolnierczyk 20.00 50.00
4 M.Read/Z.Rinaldo EXCH 15.00 40.00
5 D.Smith-Pelly/P.Holland 10.00 25.00
6 Z.Kassian/B.McNabb 10.00 25.00
7 G.Nemisz/R.Horak 8.00 20.00
8 B.Saad/M.Kruger 15.00 40.00
9 R.Johansen/C.Atkinson 25.00 60.00
10 T.Vincour/C.Sceviour 10.00 25.00
11 Nugent-Hopkins/C.Teubert 40.00 100.00
12 E.Gudbranson/S.Timmins 10.00 25.00
14 L.Leblanc/A.Emelin 8.00 20.00
15 C.Smith/J.Blum 10.00 25.00
16 B.Geoffrion/R.Josi 10.00 25.00
17 A.Henrique/A.Larsson 20.00 40.00
19 C.Hagelin/T.Erixon 15.00 40.00
20 M.Zibanejad/C.Greening 25.00 60.00
21 A.Miele/D.Rundblad 10.00 25.00
22 B.Scrivens/B.Holmstrom 10.00 25.00
23 S.Despres/J.Vitale 15.00 40.00
24 J.Colborne/M.Frattin 8.00 20.00
25 C.Hodgson/G.Landeskog 25.00 50.00
26 D.Orlov/C.Eakin 20.00 50.00
27 M.Scheifele/C.Klingberg 10.00 25.00
28 J.Gardiner/S.Voynov 12.00 30.00
29 R.Diaz/A.Palushaj 8.00 20.00
30 B.Smith/G.Nyquist 15.00 40.00

2011-12 Panini Titanium Rookie Reserve Dual Memorabilia Autographs

*PATCH AU/15: 1X TO 2.5X JSY AU/90-100
*PRIME AU/21-25: .8X TO 2X JSY AU/90-100
1 Ryan Nugent-Hopkins/100 25.00 60.00
2 Sean Couturier/100 15.00 40.00
3 Adam Henrique/100 25.00 50.00
4 Craig Smith/100 10.00 25.00
5 Matt Read/100 15.00 40.00
6 Adam Larsson/100 12.00 30.00
7 Marcus Kruger/90 12.00 30.00
8 Gabriel Landeskog/100 20.00 50.00
9 Ryan Johansen/100 12.00 30.00
10 Cody Hodgson/100 10.00 25.00
11 Jake Gardiner/100 12.00 30.00
12 Brett Connolly/100 8.00 20.00
13 Zack Kassian/100 12.50 30.00
14 Simon Despres/100 8.00 20.00
15 Brendan Smith/100 8.00 20.00
16 Joe Colborne/100 12.00 30.00
17 Calvin de Haan/100 8.00 20.00
18 Greg Nemisz/100 8.00 20.00
19 Tim Erixon/100 8.00 20.00
20 David Rundblad/100 10.00 25.00
21 Louis Leblanc/100 15.00 40.00

22 Devante Smith-Pelly/100 10.00 25.00
23 Ben Scrivens/100 8.00 20.00
24 Cody Eakin/100 12.00 30.00
25 Erik Gudbranson/100 6.00 15.00

2011-12 Panini Titanium Six Star Memorabilia

1 Anze Kopitar/25 30.00 80.00
2 Ryan Miller/25 20.00 50.00
3 Henrik Lundqvist/25 50.00 125.00
4 Henrik Zetterberg/25 25.00 60.00
5 Corey Perry/25 30.00 80.00
6 Derek Stepan/25 12.00 30.00
7 Zdeno Chara/25 20.00 50.00
8 Nicklas Backstrom/25 20.00 50.00
9 Sidney Crosby/25 50.00 120.00
10 Ryan Getzlaf/25 20.00 50.00
12 Paul Stastny/25 15.00 40.00
13 Ed Belfour/25 20.00 50.00
14 Nicklas Lidstrom/25 12.00 30.00
15 Sam Gagner/25 12.00 30.00
16 Bernie Nicholls/25 15.00 40.00
18 Travis Hamonic/25 40.00 100.00
19 Jimmy Howard/25 25.00 60.00
20 Mario Lemieux/25 60.00 120.00
21 Steven Stamkos/25 40.00 100.00
22 Daniel Sedin/25 25.00 60.00
23 Mike Green/25 15.00 40.00
24 Steve Yzerman/25 50.00 125.00
25 Joe Pavelski/25 25.00 60.00

2011-12 Panini Titanium Third Sweaters Memorabilia Autographs

1 Sidney Crosby/25 75.00 150.00
2 Henrik Lundqvist/25 30.00 60.00
3 Tim Thomas/25 25.00 50.00
4 Alex Ovechkin/25 40.00 100.00
5 Joe Thornton/25 25.00 60.00
8 Saku Koivu/25 20.00 40.00
9 Martin St. Louis/24 15.00 40.00
10 Jarome Iginla/25 20.00 40.00
12 Steven Stamkos/25 40.00 80.00
13 Ryan Miller/25 25.00 50.00
14 Ryan Nugent-Hopkins/25 75.00 150.00
15 Henrik Sedin/25 20.00 50.00

2012-13 Panini Titanium Game Worn Gear

*PATCH/25: 1X TO 2.5X BASIC JSY
*PRIME/50: .8X TO 2X BASIC JSY
*PRIME/20-25: 1X TO 2.5X BASIC JSY
GGAA Artem Anisimov 2.50 6.00
GGAB Alexander Burmistrov SP 4.00 10.00
GGAC Andrew Cogliano 2.50 6.00
GGAK Andrei Kostitsyn 3.00 8.00
GGAM Andrei Markov 2.50 6.00
GGAM1 Al MacInnis 5.00 12.00
GGAM2 Alec Martinez 3.00 8.00
GGAN Antti Niemi 3.00 8.00
GGAO Alex Ovechkin 15.00 40.00
GGBB Brent Burns 4.00 10.00
GGBB1 Brian Boucher 3.00 8.00
GGBB2 Brian Boyle 2.50 6.00
GGBD Brandon Dubinsky 2.50 6.00
GGBE1 Ben Eager 2.50 6.00
GGBE2 Brian Elliott 3.00 8.00
GGBH Brett Hull 8.00 20.00
GGBJ Barret Jackman 2.50 6.00
GGBP Brandon Prust 3.00 8.00
GGBR Brad Richards 4.00 10.00
GGBS Brendan Shanahan 4.00 10.00
GGCA1 Colby Armstrong 3.00 8.00
GGCA2 Craig Anderson 4.00 10.00
GGCC Chris Chelios 4.00 10.00
GGCM Chris Mason 3.00 8.00
GGCS1 Chris Stewart 3.00 8.00
GGCS2 Cory Schneider 4.00 10.00
GGDA Daniel Alfredsson 4.00 10.00
GGDB1 Danny Briere 4.00 10.00
GGDB2 David Backes 2.50 6.00
GGDD Drew Doughty 5.00 12.00
GGDG Dan Girardi 2.50 6.00
GGDL David Legwand 3.00 8.00
GGDP1 Dion Phaneuf 3.00 8.00
GGDP2 Dustin Penner 3.00 8.00
GGDR Derek Roy 2.50 6.00
GGDS1 Daniel Sedin 5.00 12.00
GGDS2 Derek Stepan 2.50 6.00
GGDS3 Drew Stafford 2.50 6.00
GGDT Dana Tyrell 2.50 6.00
GGED Evgeny Dadonov 2.50 6.00
GGEK1 Erik Karlsson 5.00 12.00
GGEK2 Evander Kane 4.00 10.00
GGEL Eric Lindros 5.00 12.00
GGGH1 Gordie Howe SP 15.00 40.00
GGGL Gabriel Landeskog SP 6.00 15.00
GGGP George Parros 3.00 8.00
GGHL Henrik Lundqvist 10.00 25.00
GGHZ Henrik Zetterberg 5.00 12.00
GGJB Jamie Benn 4.00 10.00
GGJC Jeff Carter 3.00 8.00
GGJH Jaroslav Halak 4.00 10.00
GGJH1 Jimmy Howard 5.00 12.00
GGJH2 Johan Hedberg 3.00 8.00
GGJJ Jaromir Jagr 12.00 30.00
GGJM Jay McClement 2.50 6.00
GGJN1 James Neal 2.50 6.00
GGJN2 Joe Nieuwendyk 3.00 8.00
GGJP Jason Pominville 2.50 6.00
GGJQ Jonathan Quick 5.00 12.00
GGRE James Reimer 4.00 10.00
GGJS Jordan Staal 3.00 8.00
GGJS1 Jarret Stoll 3.00 8.00
GGJS2 Jason Spezza 4.00 10.00
GGJT Joe Thornton 6.00 15.00
GGJV James van Riemsdyk 3.00 8.00
GGJW Justin Williams 3.00 8.00
GGKP Keith Primeau 3.00 8.00
GGKT Kimmo Timonen 2.50 6.00
GGKY Keith Yandle 2.50 6.00
GGLR Luc Robitaille 4.00 10.00
GGMG1 Marian Gaborik 4.00 10.00
GGMG2 Mikhail Grabovski 4.00 10.00
GGMH Marian Hossa 4.00 10.00
GGMK Mikko Koivu 3.00 8.00
GGML1 Michael Leighton 3.00 8.00
GGML2 Milan Lucic 4.00 10.00
GGMM1 Milan Michalek 2.50 6.00
GGMM2 Matt Moulson 2.50 6.00
GGRD Matt Read SP 4.00 10.00
GGMR2 Mike Richards 3.00 8.00
GGMS Marc Staal 2.50 6.00
GGNB Nicklas Backstrom 4.00 10.00
GGNK Nikolai Khabibulin 4.00 10.00
GGPB Paul Bissonnette 3.00 8.00
GGPD Pavel Datsyuk 6.00 15.00
GGPM Peter Mueller 2.50 6.00
GGRI Brad Richards 4.00 10.00
GGRL Roberto Luongo 6.00 15.00
GGRN2 Rick Nash 4.00 10.00
GGRR Robyn Regehr 2.50 6.00
GGRV Rogie Vachon SP 8.00 20.00
GGRW Ryan Whitney 2.50 6.00
GGSC1 Sidney Crosby 8.00 20.00
GGCO Sean Couturier SP 4.00 10.00
GGSH Scott Hartnell 2.50 6.00
GGSS Steven Stamkos 8.00 20.00
GGSW Shea Weber 3.00 8.00
GGTM Torrey Mitchell 2.50 6.00
GGTS Tyler Seguin 5.00 12.00
GGTV Tomas Vokoun 3.00 8.00
GGTZ Travis Zajac 2.50 6.00

2012-13 Panini Titanium Metallic Marks

2 Andrew Desjardins B 3.00 8.00
3 Andrew Shaw B 3.00 8.00
4 Brandon Mashinter B 3.00 8.00
5 Brandon McMillan B 3.00 8.00
6 Brayden McNabb B 5.00 12.00
8 Brett Connolly B 3.00 8.00
9 Brett MacLean B 3.00 8.00
10 Cameron Gaunce B 3.00 8.00
11 Carl Hagelin B 3.00 8.00
12 Cody Eakin B 3.00 8.00
13 Colby Cohen B 3.00 8.00
14 Colten Teubert B 3.00 8.00
15 Colton Sceviour B 3.00 8.00
16 Corey Tropp B 4.00 10.00
17 Dana Tyrell B 3.00 8.00
18 David Rundblad B 4.00 10.00
19 Derick Brassard B 3.00 8.00
20 Gabriel Bourque B 4.00 10.00
22 Gustav Nyquist B 3.00 8.00
24 Harry Zolnierczyk B 3.00 8.00
25 Jacob Markstrom B 5.00 12.00
26 Jake Gardiner B SP 3.00 8.00
27 Jeff Skinner B SP 6.00 15.00
29 John McCarthy B 3.00 8.00
30 John Moore B 3.00 8.00
31 Jon Matsumoto B 3.00 8.00
33 Jonathan Bernier B 4.00 10.00
34 Jordan Caron B 5.00 12.00
35 Justin DiBenedetto B 3.00 8.00
36 Justin Falk B 3.00 8.00
37 Keith Aulie B 3.00 8.00
38 Lance Bouma B 3.00 8.00
39 Louis Leblanc B SP 3.00 8.00
40 Luca Caputi B 3.00 8.00
41 Magnus Paajarvi B 4.00 10.00
42 Matt Bartkowski B 3.00 8.00
44 Nino Niederreiter B 3.00 8.00
45 Oliver Ekman-Larsson B 5.00 12.00
46 Raphael Diaz B 3.00 8.00
48 Roman Josi B 5.00 12.00
49 Ryan Ellis B 3.00 8.00
50 Scott Timmins B 3.00 8.00
51 Slava Voynov B 5.00 12.00
52 Stefan Elliott B 4.00 10.00
53 T.J. Brennan B 3.00 8.00
54 Tim Erixon B 3.00 8.00
55 Tomas Kubalik B 3.00 8.00
57 Tommy Wingels B 3.00 8.00
58 Tyler Bozak B 3.00 8.00
59 Zac Dalpe B 3.00 8.00
61 Jean Beliveau S 5.00 12.00
62 Teemu Selanne S 10.00 25.00
63 Don Cherry S SP 15.00 40.00
64 Al Secord S 4.00 10.00
65 Steve Mason S 4.00 10.00
66 Brad Richards S 5.00 12.00
67 Brenden Morrow S 4.00 10.00
68 Corey Perry S 8.00 20.00
69 Henrik Sedin S 6.00 15.00
70 Victor Hedman S 6.00 15.00
71 Joe Thornton S 8.00 20.00
72 Kris Letang S 3.00 8.00
73 Logan Couture S 6.00 15.00
75 Niklas Backstrom S 4.00 10.00
76 P.K. Subban S 6.00 15.00
77 Rick Nash S 5.00 12.00
78 Roberto Luongo S SP 8.00 20.00
79 Ryan Miller S 5.00 12.00
80 Sam Gagner S SP 3.00 8.00
81 Tim Thomas S SP 5.00 12.00
82 Tyler Seguin S 6.00 15.00
83 Vincent Lecavalier S 5.00 12.00
84 Zach Parise S 5.00 12.00
85 Martin St. Louis S 5.00 12.00
86 Brendan Shanahan G 5.00 12.00
87 Joe Sakic G 10.00 25.00
88 John Tavares G 8.00 20.00
89 Patrick Roy G 12.00 30.00
90 Bobby Hull G 10.00 25.00
91 Martin Brodeur G 12.00 30.00
92 Ray Bourque G 8.00 20.00
94 Nicklas Lidstrom G 5.00 12.00
95 Eric Lindros G 25.00 60.00
96 Gordie Howe P 60.00 150.00
97 Mario Lemieux P 40.00 100.00
98 Mark Messier P 25.00 60.00
99 Steve Yzerman P 40.00 100.00
100 Sidney Crosby P 80.00 200.00

2012-13 Panini Titanium Rookies

1 Max Sauve/74 5.00 12.00
2 Mat Clark/73 6.00 15.00
3 Kris Foucault/72 5.00 12.00
4 Jordan Nolan/71 5.00 12.00
5 Michael Hutchinson/70 10.00 25.00
6 Robert Mayer/65 12.00 30.00
7 Travis Turnbull/65 5.00 12.00
8 Tyler Cuma/65 5.00 12.00
9 Lane MacDermid/64 6.00 15.00
10 Mark Stone/60 20.00 50.00
11 Carter Camper/58 5.00 12.00
12 Aaron Ness/55 5.00 12.00
13 Casey Cizikas/53 6.00 15.00
14 Brandon Bollig/52 5.00 12.00
15 Philippe Cornet/51 6.00 15.00
16 Cody Goloubef/48 8.00 20.00
17 Ryan Hamilton/48 8.00 20.00
18 Chay Genoway/47 8.00 20.00
19 Colby Robak/47 8.00 20.00
20 Dalton Prout/47 8.00 20.00
21 Sven Baertschi/47 12.00 30.00
22 Torey Krug/47 30.00 80.00
23 Matt Donovan/46 10.00 25.00
24 Tyson Barrie/41 25.00 60.00
25 Jussi Rynnas/40 8.00 20.00
26 Ryan Garbutt/40 8.00 20.00
27 Carter Ashton/37 8.00 20.00
28 Chet Pickard/37 10.00 25.00
29 Gabriel Dumont/37 10.00 25.00
30 Matt Watkins/50 5.00 12.00
31 Tyson Sexsmith/37 8.00 20.00
32 Jake Allen/34 25.00 60.00
33 Jakob Silfverberg/33 15.00 40.00
34 Shawn Hunwick/31 8.00 20.00
35 Akim Aliu/29 12.00 30.00
36 Andrew Joudrey/23 12.00 30.00
37 Michael Stone/29 12.00 30.00
38 Brandon Manning/23 12.00 30.00
39 Jeremy Welsh/23 12.00 30.00
40 Chris Kreider/20 75.00 150.00
41 J.T. Brown/19 12.00 30.00
42 Mike Connolly/18 12.00 30.00
43 Reilly Smith/18 30.00 80.00
44 Jason Zucker/16 25.00 60.00
45 Riley Sheahan/15 15.00 40.00
46 Scott Glennie/15 12.00 30.00

2012-13 Panini Titanium Rookies Gold

1 Max Sauve/47 8.00 20.00
2 Mat Clark/37 10.00 25.00
3 Kris Foucault/100 4.00 10.00
4 Jordan Nolan/100 4.00 10.00
5 Michael Hutchinson/100 6.00 15.00
6 Robert Mayer/100 12.00 30.00
7 Travis Turnbull/100 4.00 10.00
8 Tyler Cuma/23 10.00 25.00
9 Lane MacDermid/100 5.00 12.00
10 Mark Stone/100 15.00 40.00
11 Carter Camper/100 4.00 10.00
12 Aaron Ness/40 8.00 20.00
13 Casey Cizikas/92 5.00 12.00
14 Brandon Bollig/100 4.00 10.00
15 Philippe Cornet/100 5.00 12.00
16 Cody Goloubef/37 8.00 20.00
17 Ryan Hamilton/100 5.00 12.00
18 Chay Genoway/100 4.00 10.00
19 Colby Robak/46 8.00 20.00
20 Dalton Prout/100 4.00 10.00
22 Torey Krug/100 50.00 120.00
23 Matt Donovan/96 5.00 12.00
24 Tyson Barrie/64 15.00 40.00
25 Jussi Rynnas/100 4.00 10.00
26 Ryan Garbutt/100 4.00 10.00
27 Carter Ashton/29 10.00 25.00
28 Chet Pickard/18 12.00 30.00
29 Gabriel Dumont/100 5.00 12.00
30 Matt Watkins/100 4.00 10.00
31 Tyson Sexsmith/91 4.00 10.00
32 Jake Allen/34 25.00 60.00
33 Jakob Silfverberg/39 15.00 40.00
34 Shawn Hunwick/100 4.00 10.00
35 Akim Aliu/56 6.00 15.00
36 Andrew Joudrey/100 5.00 12.00
37 Michael Stone/69 6.00 15.00
38 Brandon Manning/100 5.00 12.00
39 Jeremy Welsh/100 5.00 12.00
40 Chris Kreider/19 75.00 150.00
41 J.T. Brown/100 5.00 12.00
42 Mike Connolly/100 5.00 12.00
43 Reilly Smith/69 15.00 40.00
44 Jason Zucker/59 12.00 30.00
45 Riley Sheahan/21 15.00 40.00
48 Brenden Dillon/100 5.00 12.00

2013-14 Panini Titanium

1 Adam Henrique .30 .75
2 Alex Ovechkin 1.50 4.00
3 Alex Pietrangelo .30 .75
4 Andrew Ladd .25 .60
5 Anze Kopitar .60 1.50
6 Ben Bishop .30 .75
7 Bobby Ryan .30 .75
8 Braden Holtby .50 1.25
9 Brayden Schenn .40 1.00
10 Brian Elliott .30 .75
11 Cal Clutterbuck .25 .60
12 Cam Ward .40 1.00
13 Carey Price .75 2.00
14 Clarke MacArthur .25 .60
15 Claude Giroux .40 1.00
16 Cody Hodgson .25 .60
17 Corey Crawford .50 1.25
18 Corey Perry .60 1.50
19 Cory Schneider .40 1.00
20 Craig Anderson .40 1.00
21 Daniel Alfredsson .40 1.00
22 Daniel Sedin .50 1.25
23 David Backes .25 .60
24 David Perron .30 .75
25 Derick Brassard .25 .60
26 Devin Setoguchi .30 .75
27 Dion Phaneuf .30 .75
28 Drew Doughty .50 1.25
29 Duncan Keith .30 .75
30 Dustin Brown .40 1.00
31 Dustin Byfuglien .40 1.00
32 Ed Jovanovski .25 .60
33 Eric Staal .50 1.25
34 Erik Karlsson .50 1.25
35 Evgeni Malkin .75 2.00
36 Gabriel Landeskog .50 1.25
37 Henrik Lundqvist 1.00 2.50
38 Henrik Sedin .50 1.25
39 Henrik Zetterberg .50 1.25
40 Jacob Markstrom .40 1.00
41 Jakob Silfverberg .25 .60
42 James van Riemsdyk .30 .75
43 Jamie Benn .40 1.00
44 Jarome Iginla .50 1.25
45 Jaromir Jagr 1.25 3.00
46 Jason Spezza .40 1.00
47 Jeff Skinner .50 1.25
48 Joe Pavelski .50 1.25
49 Joe Thornton .60 1.50
50 John Tavares .60 1.50
51 Jonas Hiller .30 .75
52 Jonathan Bernier .30 .75
53 Jonathan Quick .50 1.25
54 Jonathan Toews .60 1.50
55 Jordan Eberle .40 1.00
56 Kari Lehtonen .30 .75
57 Kris Versteeg .25 .60
58 Logan Couture .50 1.25
59 Loui Eriksson .25 .60
60 Marc-Andre Fleury .75 2.00
61 Marcus Foligno .30 .75
62 Marian Gaborik .40 1.00
63 Martin Brodeur 1.00 2.50
64 Matt Duchene .40 1.00
65 Matt Stajan .25 .60
66 Max Pacioretty .40 1.00
67 Michael Grabner .30 .75
68 Karri Ramo .30 .75
69 Mikael Backlund .30 .75
70 Mike Fisher .25 .60
71 Mike Smith .40 1.00
72 Nathan Horton .40 1.00
73 Nicklas Backstrom .40 1.00
74 Niklas Backstrom .30 .75
75 Oliver Ekman-Larsson .40 1.00
76 P.K. Subban .50 1.25
77 Patrick Kane .75 2.00
78 Pavel Datsyuk .60 1.50
79 Pekka Rinne .40 1.00
80 Phil Kessel .40 1.00
81 Rick Nash .40 1.00
82 Roberto Luongo .60 1.50
83 Ryan Getzlaf .40 1.00
84 Ryan Miller .40 1.00
85 Ryan Nugent-Hopkins .50 1.25
86 Ryan Suter .30 .75
87 Semyon Varlamov .40 1.00
88 Sergei Bobrovsky .60 1.50
89 Shane Doan .30 .75
90 Shea Weber .30 .75
91 Sidney Crosby 1.50 4.00
92 Stephen Weiss .30 .75
93 Steven Stamkos .75 2.00
94 Taylor Hall .40 1.00
95 Tuukka Rask .50 1.25
96 Tyler Seguin .50 1.25
97 Valtteri Filppula .25 .60
98 Vincent Lecavalier .40 1.00
99 Zach Parise .40 1.00
100 Zdeno Chara .40 1.00
101 Vladimir Tarasenko/91 RC 15.00 40.00
102 Cory Conacher/89 RC 4.00 10.00
103 John Muse/80 RC 6.00 15.00
104 Matt Tennyson/80 RC 4.00 10.00
105 Eric Selleck/76 RC 5.00 12.00
106 Radko Gudas/75 RC 6.00 15.00
107 Ondrej Palat/74 RC 10.00 25.00
108 Brett Bellemore/73 RC 5.00 12.00
109 Tyler Toffoli/73 RC 12.00 30.00
110 Igor Bobkov/72 RC 5.00 12.00
111 Nicolas Blanchard/72 RC 5.00 12.00
112 Alex Petrovic/72 RC 5.00 12.00
113 Joonas Rask/72 RC 4.00 10.00
114 Richard Panik/71 RC 6.00 15.00
115 Tanner Pearson/70 RC 6.00 15.00
116 Jamie Tardif/68 RC 4.00 10.00
117 Rickard Rakell/67 RC 6.00 15.00
118 Emerson Etem/65 RC 6.00 15.00
119 Brian Flynn/65 RC 5.00 12.00
120 Danny DeKeyser/65 RC 8.00 20.00
121 Nail Yakupov/64 RC 12.00 30.00
122 Mikael Granlund/64 RC 10.00 25.00
123 Greg Pateryn/64 RC 6.00 15.00
124 Victor Bartley/64 RC 5.00 12.00
125 Charlie Coyle/63 RC 10.00 25.00
126 Tyler Johnson/63 RC 8.00 20.00
127 Mark Arcobello/62 RC 6.00 15.00
128 Michael Caruso/62 RC 4.00 10.00
129 Eric Gryba/62 RC 5.00 12.00
130 Andrej Sustr/62 RC 4.00 10.00
131 Steve Oleksy/61 RC 6.00 15.00
132 Max Reinhart/59 RC 6.00 15.00
133 Dave Dziurzynski/59 RC 5.00 12.00
134 Ben Hanowski/58 RC 5.00 12.00
135 Chris Terry/58 RC 4.00 10.00
136 Patrick Bordeleau/58 RC 6.00 15.00
137 Christian Thomas/58 RC 5.00 12.00
138 Derek Grant/57 RC 5.00 12.00
139 Taylor Beck/56 RC 5.00 12.00
140 Ryan Stanton/18 RC 6.00 15.00
141 Nick Petrecki/54 RC 4.00 10.00
142 Mark Pysyk/53 RC 6.00 15.00
144 Jonathan Rheault/52 RC 4.00 10.00
145 Austin Watson/52 RC 5.00 12.00
146 Matt Irwin/52 RC 5.00 12.00
147 Ryan Spooner/51 RC 6.00 15.00
148 Daniel Bang/50 RC 5.00 12.00
149 Michal Jordan/47 RC 4.00 10.00
150 Johan Larsson/22 RC 8.00 20.00
152 Leo Komarov/47 RC 6.00 15.00
153 Carter Bancks/46 RC 5.00 12.00
154 Kevin Henderson/46 RC 5.00 12.00
155 Nicklas Jensen/46 RC 5.00 12.00
156 Sami Vatanen/45 RC 6.00 15.00
157 Jordan Schroeder/45 RC 6.00 15.00
158 Cameron Schilling/45 RC 4.00 10.00
159 Jean-Gabriel Pageau/44 RC 6.00 15.00
160 Chris Brown/44 RC 4.00 10.00
161 Michael Sgarbossa/43 RC 6.00 15.00
162 Sean Collins/43 RC 5.00 12.00
163 Tom Wilson/43 RC 12.00 30.00
164 Mark Cundari/42 RC 4.00 10.00
165 Shawn Lalonde/42 RC 6.00 15.00
166 Quinton Howden/42 RC 5.00 12.00
167 Jarred Tinordi/42 RC 6.00 15.00
168 Jason Akeson/42 RC 5.00 12.00
169 Cristopher Nilstorp/41 RC 5.00 12.00
170 Nathan Beaulieu/40 RC 4.00 10.00
171 Ben Street/38 RC 5.00 12.00
172 Oliver Lauridsen/38 RC 5.00 12.00
173 Jonathan Marchessault/36 RC 15.00 40.00
174 Jeff Zatkoff/36 RC 6.00 15.00
175 Darcy Kuemper/35 RC 12.00 30.00
176 Calvin Heeter/35 RC 5.00 12.00
177 Carl Soderberg/34 RC 6.00 15.00
178 Petr Mrazek/34 RC 12.00 30.00
179 Matthew Konan/34 RC 6.00 15.00
180 Eric Gelinas/32 RC 6.00 15.00
181 Edward Pasquale/32 RC 4.00 10.00
182 Frederik Andersen/31 RC 15.00 40.00
183 Calvin Pickard/31 RC 8.00 20.00
184 Eric Hartzell/31 RC 6.00 15.00
185 Philipp Grubauer/31 RC 15.00 40.00
186 Viktor Fasth/30 RC 6.00 15.00
187 Sami Aittokallio/30 RC 6.00 15.00
188 Joe Cannata/30 RC 5.00 12.00
189 Brock Nelson/29 RC 12.00 30.00
190 Dougie Hamilton/27 RC 10.00 25.00
191 Nick Bjugstad/27 RC 8.00 20.00
192 Alex Galchenyuk/27 RC 15.00 40.00
193 Anders Lee/27 RC 10.00 25.00
194 Dmitrij Jaskin/26 RC 6.00 15.00
195 Frank Corrado/26 RC 4.00 10.00
196 Mikhail Grigorenko/25 RC 4.00 10.00
197 Jonas Brodin/25 RC 8.00 20.00
198 Zach Redmond/25 RC 5.00 12.00
200 Brian Lashoff/23 RC 5.00 12.00
201 Scott Laughton/21 RC 8.00 20.00
202 Antoine Roussel/21 RC 6.00 15.00
203 Justin Schultz/19 RC 6.00 15.00
204 Beau Bennett/19 RC 8.00 20.00
205 Alex Killorn/17 RC 10.00 25.00
227 Anton Belov/77 RC 6.00 15.00
228 Will Acton/41 RC 5.00 12.00
229 Luke Gazdic/20 RC 5.00 12.00
230 Joakim Nordstrom/42 RC 5.00 12.00
231 Connor Carrick/58 RC 5.00 12.00
232 Michael Latta/46 RC 5.00 12.00
233 Nathan MacKinnon/29 RC 30.00 80.00
234 Zemgus Girgensons/28 RC 10.00 25.00
235 Rasmus Ristolainen/55 RC 10.00 25.00
237 Sean Monahan/23 RC 10.00 25.00
239 Justin Fontaine/52 RC 6.00 15.00
240 Aleksander Barkov/16 RC 20.00 50.00
241 Valeri Nichushkin/43 RC 12.00 30.00
242 Jesper Fast/31 RC 6.00 15.00
243 Lucas Lessio/51 RC 4.00 10.00
244 Matt Nieto/83 RC 5.00 12.00
245 Tomas Hertl/48 RC 12.00 30.00
246 Boone Jenner/38 RC 12.00 30.00
247 Ryan Murray/27 RC 6.00 15.00
248 Morgan Rielly/44 RC 15.00 40.00
249 Matt Dumba/55 RC 4.00 10.00
250 Hampus Lindholm/47 RC 10.00 25.00
251 Alex Grant/51 RC 4.00 10.00
252 Kevan Miller/86 RC 5.00 12.00
253 Nikita Zadorov/61 RC 4.00 10.00
254 Christopher Breen/43 RC 5.00 12.00
255 Reto Berra/20 RC 6.00 15.00
256 Chad Billins/41 RC 5.00 12.00
257 Antti Raanta/31 RC 12.00 30.00
258 Michael Chaput/39 RC 4.00 10.00
259 Kevin Connauton/23 RC 5.00 12.00
260 Xavier Ouellet/61 RC 6.00 15.00
261 Luke Glendening/41 RC 6.00 15.00
262 Adam Almquist/53 RC 4.00 10.00
263 Tyler Pitlick/68 RC 6.00 15.00
264 Taylor Fedun/81 RC 8.00 20.00
265 Martin Marincin/85 RC 5.00 12.00
266 Linden Vey/57 RC 4.00 10.00
267 Martin Jones/31 RC 10.00 25.00
268 Erik Haula/56 RC 8.00 20.00
269 Johan Gustafsson/31 RC 8.00 20.00
270 Patrick Holland/82 RC 10.00 25.00
271 Michael Bournival/49 RC 6.00 15.00
272 Magnus Hellberg/45 RC 6.00 15.00
273 Marek Mazanec/39 RC 6.00 15.00
274 Jon Merrill/34 RC 6.00 15.00
276 Jason Missiaen/31 RC 6.00 15.00
278 Jordan Szwarz/29 RC 6.00 15.00
280 Jayson Megna/59 RC 6.00 15.00
281 Zach Sill/38 RC 6.00 15.00
282 Brian Gibbons/49 RC 6.00 15.00
283 Freddie Hamilton/75 RC 6.00 15.00
284 Dmitry Korobov/24 RC 6.00 15.00
285 Nikita Kucherov/86 RC 40.00 100.00
286 Spencer Abbott/56 RC 5.00 12.00
287 Josh Leivo/32 RC 5.00 12.00
288 David Broll/46 RC 6.00 15.00
289 Jamie Devane/59 RC 5.00 12.00
290 Jerry D'Amigo/29 RC 6.00 15.00
291 Elias Lindholm/16 RC 15.00 40.00
292 Darren Archibald/49 RC 5.00 12.00
293 Nate Schmidt/88 RC 5.00 12.00
294 Patrick Wey/56 RC 5.00 12.00
295 Ben Chiarot/63 RC 6.00 15.00
296 John Albert/70 RC 5.00 12.00
297 Kent Simpson/40 RC 4.00 10.00
299 Dylan McIlrath/42 RC 4.00 10.00
300 Ryan Strome/18 RC 10.00 25.00
302 Tomas Jurco/26 RC 8.00 20.00
303 Philip Samuelsson/55 RC 4.00 10.00
304 Eric O'Dell/58 RC 4.00 10.00
305 Craig Cunningham/61 RC 5.00 12.00
306 David Warsofsky/79 RC 6.00 15.00
307 Niklas Svedberg/72 RC 12.00 30.00
308 Zach Trotman/42 RC 6.00 15.00
309 Conor Allen/37 RC 5.00 12.00
310 Joacim Eriksson/30 RC 6.00 15.00
311 Julian Melchiori/71 RC 4.00 10.00
312 Eriah Hayes/76 RC 6.00 15.00
313 Brad Hunt/59 RC 5.00 12.00
314 Alexey Marchenko/47 RC 5.00 12.00
315 Justin Florek/57 RC 15.00 40.00
317 John Gibson/36 RC 15.00 40.00

2013-14 Panini Titanium Draft Position

*1-100 VETS/62-100: 4X TO 10X BASIC CARD
*1-100 VETS/39-57: 5X TO 12X BASIC CARD
*1-100 VETS/20-33: 6X TO 15X BASIC CARD
*1-100 VETS/10-19: 8X TO 20X BASIC CARD
17 Corey Crawford/52 6.00 15.00
102 Cory Conacher/100 4.00 10.00
109 Tyler Toffoli/47 15.00 40.00
120 Danny DeKeyser/100 8.00 20.00
123 Greg Pateryn/100 6.00 15.00
126 Tyler Johnson/100 12.00 30.00
127 Mark Arcobello/100 6.00 15.00
147 Ryan Spooner/45 8.00 20.00
152 Leo Komarov/100 6.00 15.00
174 Jeff Zatkoff/74 6.00 15.00
175 Darcy Kuemper/100 8.00 20.00
177 Carl Soderberg/49 8.00 20.00
178 Petr Mrazek/100 12.00 30.00
182 Frederik Andersen/87 15.00 40.00
185 Philipp Grubauer/100 15.00 40.00
186 Viktor Fasth/100 6.00 15.00
194 Dmitrij Jaskin/41 8.00 20.00
203 Justin Schultz/43 8.00 20.00
215 Alex Chiasson/38 8.00 20.00
218 Brendan Gallagher/100 20.00 50.00
232 Michael Latta/72 10.00 25.00
239 Justin Fontaine/100 6.00 15.00
242 Jesper Fast/100 6.00 15.00
244 Matt Nieto/47 6.00 15.00

2013-14 Panini Titanium Jersey Number

*1-100 VETS/61-93: 4X TO 10X BASIC CARD
*1-100 VETS/39-57: 5X TO 12X BASIC CARD
*1-100 VETS/20-35: 6X TO 15X BASIC CARD
*1-100 VETS/10-19: 8X TO 20X BASIC CARD
17 Corey Crawford/50 6.00 15.00
73 Nicklas Backstrom/19 8.00 20.00

2013-14 Panini Titanium Four Star Memorabilia

4SBY Brandon Yip/25 4.00 10.00
4SDK Duncan Keith/25 5.00 12.00
4SEM Evgeni Malkin/25 12.00 30.00
4SHZ Henrik Zetterberg/25 8.00 20.00
4SJG Josh Gorges/25 5.00 12.00
4SJT John Tavares/25 10.00 25.00
4SKS Kevin Shattenkirk/25 4.00 10.00
4SMM Mark Messier/25 12.00 30.00
4SPK Patrick Kane/25 12.00 30.00
4SRG Ryan Getzlaf/25 6.00 15.00
4SSG Sam Gagner/25 4.00 10.00
4SST Shawn Thornton/25 4.00 10.00
4SSW Shea Weber/25 5.00 12.00
4SAHE Ales Hemsky/25 4.00 10.00
4SAKO Anze Kopitar/25 10.00 25.00
4SCST Chris Stewart/25 5.00 12.00
4SDKR David Krejci/25 6.00 15.00
4SJEN Jhonas Enroth/25 6.00 15.00
4SJMC Jay McClement/25 4.00 10.00
4SJSP Jason Spezza/25 6.00 15.00
4SKTI Kimmo Timonen/25 4.00 10.00
4SOPV Ondrej Pavelec/25 6.00 15.00
4SRBL Rob Blake/25 6.00 15.00

2013-14 Panini Titanium Game Worn Gear

*PATCH/25: .8X TO 2X BASIC JSY
*PATCH/25: .6X TO 1.5X BASIC JSY SP
*PRIME/50: .6X TO 1.5X BASIC JSY
*PRIME/30-50: .5X TO 1.2X BASIC JSY SP
GGAAN Artem Anisimov 1.25 3.00
GGAF Adam Foote 1.25 3.00
GGASE Alexander Semin 2.00 5.00
GGAV Antoine Vermette 1.25 3.00
GGBCA Brian Campbell SP 1.25 3.00
GGBDU Brandon Dubinsky 1.25 3.00
GGBJ Barret Jackman 1.25 3.00
GGBM Brenden Morrow 1.50 4.00
GGBR Bobby Ryan 1.50 4.00
GGBS Brendan Shanahan 2.00 5.00
GGBSE Brent Seabrook 1.25 3.00
GGCF Cam Fowler 2.00 5.00
GGCGX Claude Giroux SP 2.00 5.00
GGCP Carey Price 4.00 10.00
GGCSM Craig Smith 1.25 3.00
GGDA Dave Andreychuk 2.00 5.00
GGDBR Daniel Briere 2.00 5.00
GGDBY Dustin Byfuglien 2.00 5.00
GGDL David Legwand 1.50 4.00
GGDP David Perron 1.50 4.00
GGDRS Drew Stafford 1.25 3.00
GGDS Daniel Sedin 2.50 6.00
GGDSM Derek Smith 1.25 3.00
GGDST Derek Stepan 1.25 3.00
GGDSY Darryl Sydor 1.25 3.00
GGEK Erik Karlsson 2.50 6.00
GGET Eric Tangradi 1.25 3.00
GGFB Francois Beauchemin 1.25 3.00
GGGH Gordie Howe SP 12.00 30.00
GGHL Henrik Lundqvist 5.00 12.00
GGHS Henrik Sedin 2.50 6.00
GGJBA Josh Bailey 1.50 4.00
GGJLC John LeClair 2.00 5.00
GGJLU Joffrey Lupul SP 1.25 3.00
GGJPO Jason Pominville 1.25 3.00
GGJRE James Reimer 2.00 5.00
GGJS Joe Sakic SP 4.00 10.00
GGJTO Jonathan Toews SP 3.00 8.00
GGJVR James van Riemsdyk 1.50 4.00
GGKC Kyle Clifford 1.25 3.00
GGKD Kaspars Daugavins 1.25 3.00
GGKJS Kjell Samuelsson 1.25 3.00
GGKL Kari Lehtonen 1.50 4.00
GGKO Kyle Okposo 1.25 3.00
GGKP Keith Primeau 1.50 4.00
GGKS Kevin Shattenkirk 1.25 3.00
GGLAI Brooks Laich 1.25 3.00
GGLE Loui Eriksson 1.25 3.00
GGLEI Michael Leighton 1.50 4.00
GGLU Roberto Luongo SP 3.00 8.00
GGMB Martin Brodeur SP 5.00 12.00
GGMBA Mikael Backlund 1.50 4.00
GGMBI Martin Biron 1.50 4.00
GGMDZ Michael Del Zotto 1.25 3.00
GGMEV Marc-Edouard Vlasic 1.25 3.00
GGMHZ Martin Hanzal 1.25 3.00
GGMK Miikka Kiprusoff 2.00 5.00
GGMLO Matthew Lombardi 1.25 3.00
GGMM Mark Messier SP 4.00 10.00
GGMMS Marty McSorley 1.50 4.00
GGMN Michal Neuvirth 1.50 4.00
GGMRI Mike Richards SP 1.50 4.00
GGMSA Mikael Samuelsson 1.25 3.00
GGMSL Martin St. Louis 2.00 5.00
GGNKU Nikolai Kulemin SP 1.25 3.00
GGNL Nicklas Lidstrom 2.00 5.00

GGOPV Ondrej Pavelec 2.00 5.00
GGOVI Alex Ovechkin SP 8.00 20.00
GGPAS Paul Stastny 1.50 4.00
GGPBG Patrik Berglund 1.25 3.00
GGPC Paul Coffey 2.00 5.00
GGPF Pat Falloon 1.25 3.00
GGPM Patrick Marleau 2.00 5.00
GGPR Patrick Roy SP 5.00 12.00
GGPS Patrick Sharp 2.00 5.00
GGPT Pierre Turgeon 1.50 4.00
GGRBL Rob Blake 2.00 5.00
GGRE Ray Emery 1.50 4.00
GGRF Ron Francis 2.50 6.00
GGRM Ryan Miller 2.00 5.00
GGROR Ryan O'Reilly 2.00 5.00
GGSBE Steve Bernier 1.25 3.00
GGSC Sidney Crosby 8.00 20.00
GGSCL Scott Clemmensen 1.50 4.00
GGSD Shane Doan 1.50 4.00
GGSGR Stu Grimson 1.25 3.00
GGSH Shawn Horcoff 1.25 3.00
GGSK Saku Koivu 2.00 5.00
GGSS Steven Stamkos SP 4.00 10.00
GGSVA Semyon Varlamov 2.00 5.00
GGSW Shea Weber 1.50 4.00
GGSY Steve Yzerman SP 5.00 12.00
GGTD Trevor Daley 1.25 3.00
GGTJO T.J. Oshie 2.00 5.00
GGTM Torrey Mitchell 1.25 3.00
GGTR Tuukka Rask 2.50 6.00
GGTZ Travis Zajac 1.25 3.00
GGZP Zach Parise 2.00 5.00
GGVLE Ville Leino 1.50 4.00
GGZRI Zac Rinaldo 1.50 4.00

2013-14 Panini Titanium Game Worn Gear Autographs

*PRIME/25: .8X TO 2X JSY AU/75-100
*PRIME/25: .6X TO 1.5X JSY AU/50
GADB David Backes/100 5.00 12.00
GADD Drew Doughty/50 10.00 25.00
GADS Daniel Sedin/50 10.00 25.00
GAGL Gabriel Landeskog/50 10.00 25.00
GAJQ Jonathan Quick/50 10.00 25.00
GAJR Jeremy Roenick/25 12.00 30.00
GAMP Max Pacioretty /100 8.00 20.00
GANG Nathan Gerbe/75 5.00 12.00
GANH Nathan Horton/75 8.00 20.00
GAPM Patrick Marleau/50 8.00 20.00
GASK Saku Koivu/50 8.00 20.00
GATZ Travis Zajac/100 5.00 12.00
GAVH Victor Hedman/50 10.00 25.00
GAVL Vincent Lecavalier/25 8.00 20.00
GAZC Zdeno Chara/50 8.00 20.00
GAAMI Al MacInnis/50 10.00 25.00
GACGX Claude Giroux/50 8.00 20.00
GACPR Chris Pronger/100 8.00 20.00
GACSM Craig Smith/50 5.00 12.00
GACWI Colin Wilson/100 6.00 15.00
GADDU Devan Dubnyk /100 6.00 15.00
GADKR David Krejci/75 8.00 20.00
GADPH Dion Phaneuf/50 6.00 15.00
GADRS Drew Stafford/100 5.00 12.00
GADUB Dustin Brown/50 8.00 20.00
GAEVK Evander Kane/100 8.00 20.00
GAJBE Jonathan Bernier/100 6.00 15.00
GAJHA Jaroslav Halak/50 8.00 20.00
GAJHI Jonas Hiller/100 6.00 15.00
GAJHO Jimmy Howard/50 10.00 25.00
GAJSG Jean-Sebastien Giguere/50 8.00 20.00
GAJTO Jonathan Toews/25 25.00 60.00
GAJVI Joe Vitale/100 5.00 12.00
GAJVR James van Riemsdyk/100 6.00 15.00
GAMBO Mikkel Boedker/100 5.00 12.00
GAMRE Matt Read/100 5.00 12.00
GANBA Niklas Backstrom/100 6.00 15.00
GAPRF Patrice Bergeron/50 10.00 25.00
GAPEL Patrik Elias/50 8.00 20.00
GAPRI Pekka Rinne/50 8.00 20.00
GARBA Rod Brind'Amour/50 6.00 15.00
GARIB Richard Bachman/100 6.00 15.00
GARNH Ryan Nugent-Hopkins/50 10.00 25.00
GASVA Semyon Varlamov/100 8.00 20.00
GATEN Tyler Ennis/100 5.00 12.00
GATVA Thomas Vanek/75 6.00 15.00

2013-14 Panini Titanium Game Worn Gear Dual Memorabilia

*PATCH/15: 1X TO 2.5X DUAL JSY/300
*PRIME/50: .6X TO 1.5X DUAL JSY/300
*PRIME/25: .8X TO 2X DUAL JSY/300
*PRIME/25: .6X TO 1.5X DUAL JSY/100
GDAS K.Alzner/M.Staal/300 1.50 4.00
GDBB Berglund/Backstrom/300 2.50 6.00
GDBF D.Byfuglien/E.Fehr/300 2.50 6.00
GDBK Burrows/R.Kesler/300 2.50 6.00
GDBL Bobrovsky/Lundqvist/300 6.00 15.00
GDBM P.Bure/M.Messier/100 5.00 12.00
GDBR M.Boedker/D.Roy/300 1.50 4.00
GDBS Brodeur/Schneider/300 6.00 15.00
GDCO Clutterbuck/Okposo/300 1.50 4.00
GDCR J.Carter/M.Richards/300 2.00 5.00
GDCV S.Voynov/P.Coffey/300 2.50 6.00
GDDG Dubinsky/M.Gaborik/300 1.50 4.00
GDEL B.Laich/M.Erat/300 1.50 4.00
GDEM L.Eller/A.Markov/300 1.50 4.00
GDES L.Eriksson/T.Seguin/300 3.00 8.00
GDFM Falloon/P.Marleau/300 2.50 6.00
GDGL Getzlaf/Lombardi/300 2.50 6.00
GDGS Glencross/Stajan/300 1.50 4.00
GDHE R.Hextall/R.Emery/300 2.50 6.00
GDHJ Holtby/M.Johansson/300 3.00 8.00
GDHS M.Hossa/P.Sharp/300 2.50 6.00
GDIP A.Iafrate/D.Phaneuf/300 2.00 5.00
GDJH R.Jones/A.Hemsky/300 1.50 4.00
GDJJ E.Johnson/J.Johnson/300 1.50 4.00
GDJL Josefson/A.Larsson/300 2.50 6.00
GDKH Kronwall/Hedman/300 3.00 8.00
GDKH T.Kerr/S.Hartnell/300 2.00 5.00
GDLD M.Lucic/M.Duchene/300 2.50 6.00
GDLH P.Larsen/S.Horcoff/300 1.50 4.00
GDMA R.Miller/L.Adam/300 2.50 6.00
GDMD E.Malkin/P.Datsyuk/300 5.00 12.00
GDMS MacInnis/Shattnkirk/300 3.00 8.00
GDNYR B.Boyle/McDonagh/300 1.50 4.00
GDOD R.O'Reilly/S.Downie/300 2.50 6.00
GDOT Ovechkin/J.Tavares/100 10.00 25.00
GDPB Primeau/Brind'Amour/300 2.00 5.00
GDPC C.Price/C.Crawford/300 5.00 12.00
GDPS Z.Parise/D.Stepan/300 2.50 6.00
GDQH J.Quick/J.Howard/300 3.00 8.00
GDRC C.Crawford/T.Rask/300 3.00 8.00
GDRJ Reaves/B.Jackman/300 1.50 4.00
GDSF N.Spaling/M.Fisher/300 1.50 4.00
GDSG J.Sakic/M.Goulet/300 5.00 12.00
GDSK M.St. Louis/P.Kane/300 5.00 12.00
GDSS P.Subban/R.Suter/100 3.00 8.00
GDTB P.Bergeron/J.Toews/100 4.00 10.00
GDVN Varlamov/Nabokov/300 2.50 6.00
GDYH K.Yandle/M.Hanzal/300 1.50 4.00
GDZA Zetterberg/Alfredsson/300 3.00 8.00

2013-14 Panini Titanium Home Sweaters Memorabilia Autographs

*PRIME/15-25: .8X TO 2X JSY AU/75-100
*PRIME/15-25: .6X TO 1.5X JSY AU/50
HSAG Alex Galchenyuk/100 20.00 50.00
HSAH Adam Henrique/100 6.00 15.00
HSAK Alex Killorn/100 12.00 30.00
HSANP Anthony Peluso/100 8.00 20.00
HSBE Brian Elliott/100 8.00 20.00
HSBG Brendan Gallagher/100 15.00 40.00
HSBRI Brad Richards/50 10.00 25.00
HSBSC Brayden Schenn/50 12.00 30.00
HSCB Chris Brown/100 5.00 12.00
HSCC Cory Conacher/100 5.00 12.00
HSJE Jordan Eberle/50 10.00 25.00
HSJH Jonathan Huberdeau/100 12.00 30.00
HSJRE James Reimer/50 10.00 25.00
HSJSD Jordan Schroeder/100 8.00 20.00
HSMAR Mark Arcobello/100 8.00 20.00
HSMGR Mikael Granlund/100 8.00 20.00
HSMH Marian Hossa/75 20.00 40.00
HSPK Patrick Kane/50 30.00 60.00
HSRM Ryan Miller/50 10.00 25.00
HSSCO Sean Couturier/100 6.00 15.00
HSSMA Stefan Matteau/100 6.00 15.00
HSTP Tanner Pearson/100 10.00 25.00

2013-14 Panini Titanium Metallic Marks

MM1 Ben Holmstrom B 3.00 8.00
MM2 Jaden Schwartz B 6.00 15.00
MM3 Justin DiBenedetto B 3.00 8.00
MM4 Chris Kreider B SP 6.00 15.00
MM5 Brandon Manning B 3.00 8.00
MM6 David Rundblad B 4.00 10.00
MM7 Stefan Elliott B 4.00 10.00
MM8 Teddy Purcell B 3.00 8.00
MM9 Daniel Cleary B SP 5.00 12.00
MM10 Philip McRae B 3.00 8.00
MM11 Evan Brophey B 3.00 8.00
MM12 Scott Timmins B 3.00 8.00
MM13 Sven Baertschi B 4.00 10.00
MM14 Valtteri Filppula B SP 3.00 8.00
MM15 Jakob Silfverberg B 3.00 8.00
MM16 Mike Connolly B 4.00 10.00
MM17 Troy Brouwer B 3.00 8.00
MM18 Antoine Vermette B 3.00 8.00
MM19 Nino Niederreiter B 3.00 8.00
MM20 Akim Aliu B 3.00 8.00
MM23 Roman Josi B 5.00 12.00
MM25 Reilly Smith B 5.00 12.00
MM26 Mikhail Grabovski B SP 3.00 8.00
MM28 Riley Sheahan B 3.00 8.00
MM29 Corey Tropp B 3.00 8.00
MM30 Colten Teubert B 3.00 8.00
MM31 Joe Finley B 3.00 8.00
MM33 Chay Genoway B 5.00 12.00
MM34 Jason Zucker B 5.00 12.00
MM35 Tyson Barrie B 5.00 12.00
MM36 Marcus Kruger B SP 5.00 12.00
MM37 Max Sauve B 3.00 8.00
MM39 Maxime Macenauer B 3.00 8.00
MM41 Anders Nilsson B 3.00 8.00
MM42 Philippe Cornet B 3.00 8.00
MM43 Lane MacDermid B 4.00 10.00
MM44 Brayden McNabb B 3.00 8.00
MM45 Riley Nash B 3.00 8.00
MM46 Matt Donovan B 3.00 8.00
MM47 Mark Stone B 6.00 15.00
MM48 Matt Fraser B SP 3.00 8.00
MM49 Brenden Dillon B 3.00 8.00
MM50 Zac Rinaldo B 4.00 10.00
MM51 Ryan Hamilton B 3.00 8.00
MM52 Shawn Hunwick B 3.00 8.00
MM54 Cory Emmerton B 3.00 8.00
MM55 Colin Wilson B 3.00 8.00
MM57 Tim Erixon B 3.00 8.00
MM59 Carter Camper B 3.00 8.00
MM61 Jay Bouwmeester S/100* 3.00 8.00
MM62 Dany Heatley S/100* 3.00 8.00
MM63 Dan Boyle S/100* 3.00 8.00
MM64 Vincent Lecavalier S/25* 5.00 12.00
MM65 Dion Phaneuf S/100* 4.00 10.00
MM66 Semyon Varlamov S/100* 5.00 12.00
MM67 Chris Pronger S/100* 5.00 12.00
MM68 Daniel Briere S/100* 3.00 8.00
MM69 Brandon Dubinsky S/100* 3.00 8.00
MM70 Joe Thornton S/25* 8.00 20.00
MM71 Tyler Ennis S/100* 3.00 8.00
MM72 Chris Chelios S/100* 5.00 12.00
MM73 Bill Ranford S/100* 3.00 8.00
MM74 Jamie Benn S/100* 5.00 12.00
MM75 Eric Staal S/100* 6.00 15.00
MM76 Matt Moulson S/100* 3.00 8.00
MM77 Bobby Ryan S/100* 4.00 10.00
MM78 Jonathan Bernier S/100* 4.00 10.00
MM79 Taylor Hall S/100* 5.00 12.00
MM81 Nick Foligno S/100* 4.00 10.00
MM82 Brandon Saad S/100* 4.00 10.00
MM83 Matt Duchene S/100* 5.00 12.00
MM84 Michael Grabner S/100* 4.00 10.00
MM85 Phil Kessel S/100* 5.00 12.00

2013-14 Panini Titanium Milestone Goal Scorer Jerseys

*PRIME/15-25: .6X TO 1.5X BASIC JSY/50-100
MIBN Bernie Nicholls/50 5.00 12.00
MIBS Brendan Shanahan/100 5.00 12.00
MIBSY Mike Bossy/75 5.00 12.00
MICN Cam Neely/100 5.00 12.00
MICPE Corey Perry/100 8.00 20.00
MIDM Dennis Maruk/75 5.00 12.00
MIEM Evgeni Malkin/100 6.00 15.00
MIJI Jarome Iginla/100 8.00 20.00
MIJJ Jaromir Jagr/75 10.00 25.00
MIJN Joe Nieuwendyk/100 4.00 10.00
MIJR Jeremy Roenick/100 8.00 20.00
MIJS Joe Sakic/100 10.00 25.00
MILM Lanny McDonald/75 5.00 12.00
MILR Luc Robitaille/75 5.00 12.00
MIMHE Milan Hejduk/100 6.00 15.00
MIML Mario Lemieux/25 12.00 30.00
MIMO Mike Modano/100 8.00 20.00
MIOV Alex Ovechkin/75 20.00 50.00
MIPB Pavel Bure/75 8.00 20.00
MISC Sidney Crosby/100 20.00 50.00
MISS Steven Stamkos/75 10.00 25.00
MISY Steve Yzerman/75 12.00 30.00
MITMU Teemu Selanne/50 12.00 30.00
MIVL Vincent Lecavalier/100 5.00 12.00

2013-14 Panini Titanium Road Sweaters Memorabilia Autographs

*PRIME/15: .6X TO 1.5X JSY AU/50
*PRIME/15: .5X TO 1.2X JSY AU/25
RSAR Antoine Roussel/50 8.00 20.00
RSAW Austin Watson/50 6.00 15.00
RSBN Brock Nelson/50 15.00 40.00
RSFA Frederik Andersen/50 20.00 50.00
RSHS Henrik Sedin/25 10.00 25.00
RSJP Joe Pavelski/50 10.00 25.00
RSJQ Jonathan Quick/25 10.00 25.00
RSNY Nail Yakupov/25 20.00 50.00
RSPD Pavel Datsyuk/25 12.00 30.00
RSQH Quinton Howden/50 6.00 15.00
RSTW Tom Wilson/50 15.00 40.00
RSVF Viktor Fasth/50 8.00 20.00
RSCGX Claude Giroux/25 12.00 30.00
RSCPE Corey Perry/25 12.00 30.00
RSDDK Danny DeKeyser/50 10.00 25.00
RSJTO Jonathan Toews/25 25.00 60.00
RSMIK Mikhail Grigorenko/50 5.00 12.00
RSMRX Max Reinhart/50 8.00 20.00
RSPKS P.K. Subban/50 10.00 25.00
RSTHI Thomas Hickey/50 6.00 15.00
RSTMG Tye McGinn/50 8.00 20.00

2013-14 Panini Titanium Rookie Dual Signatures

RDBOS C.Soderberg/D.Hamilton 15.00 40.00
RDBUF M.Pysyk/M.Grigorenko 8.00 20.00
RDCGY M.Reinhart/B.Street 6.00 15.00
RDCOL M.Sgarbossa/C.Pickard 10.00 25.00
RDDAL J.Campbell/C.Nilstorp 20.00 50.00
RDDET D.DeKeyser/P.Mrazek 15.00 40.00
RDDUK S.Vatanen/V.Fasth 8.00 20.00
RDFLA M.Caruso/J.Huberdeau 12.00 30.00
RDFLY S.Laughton/T.McGinn 10.00 25.00
RDLAK T.Pearson/T.Toffoli 15.00 40.00
RDNJD H.Pesonen/S.Matteau 6.00 15.00
RDNSH A.Watson/F.Forsberg 25.00 60.00
RDPAN N.Bjugstad/Q.Howden 10.00 25.00
RDPHI J.Akeson/O.Lauridsen 8.00 20.00
RDSJS M.Irwin/N.Petrecki 6.00 15.00
RDSTR A.Chiasson/A.Roussel 8.00 20.00
RDTBL R.Panik/R.Gudas 8.00 20.00
RDWLD M.Granlund/D.Kuemper 15.00 40.00
RDWPG Z.Redmond/A.Peluso 6.00 15.00
RDWSH T.Wilson/P.Grubauer 15.00 40.00

2013-14 Panini Titanium Rookie Four Star Memorabilia

R4AB Aleksander Barkov/25 12.00 30.00
R4AG Alex Galchenyuk/25 10.00 25.00
R4BB Beau Bennett/25 5.00 12.00
R4BG Brendan Gallagher/25 10.00 25.00
R4CC Cory Conacher/25 2.50 6.00
R4DH Dougie Hamilton/25 6.00 15.00
R4EE Emerson Etem/25 4.00 10.00
R4FF Filip Forsberg/25 12.00 30.00
R4JH Jonathan Huberdeau/25 10.00 25.00
R4JO Jamie Oleksiak/25 3.00 8.00
R4JSD Jordan Schroeder/25 4.00 10.00
R4JUS Justin Schultz/25 4.00 10.00
R4MIK Mikhail Grigorenko/25 2.50 6.00
R4NMK Nathan MacKinnon/25 20.00 50.00
R4NY Nail Yakupov/25 8.00 20.00
R4RMP Ryan Murphy/25 4.00 10.00
R4SJ Seth Jones/25 8.00 20.00
R4SM Sean Monahan/25 6.00 15.00
R4SMA Stefan Matteau/25 4.00 10.00
R4TMG Tye McGinn/25 4.00 10.00
R4TP Tanner Pearson/25 4.00 10.00
R4TW Tom Wilson/25 8.00 20.00
R4VN Valeri Nichushkin/25 8.00 20.00
R4VT Vladimir Tarasenko/25 10.00 25.00

2013-14 Panini Titanium Rookie Gear

RGAB Aleksander Barkov 6.00 15.00
RGAG Alex Galchenyuk 6.00 15.00
RGAR Antoine Roussel 2.00 5.00
RGBG Brendan Gallagher 5.00 12.00
RGCC Cody Ceci 1.50 4.00
RGCM Connor Murphy 1.50 4.00
RGDH Dougie Hamilton 3.00 8.00
RGFA Frederik Andersen 5.00 12.00
RGFC Frank Corrado 1.25 3.00
RGJH Jonathan Huberdeau 5.00 12.00
RGNJ Nicklas Jensen 1.50 4.00
RGNY Nail Yakupov 6.00 15.00
RGNZ Nikita Zadorov 1.25 3.00
RGOM Olli Maatta 3.00 8.00
RGPG Philipp Grubauer 4.00 10.00
RGRS Ryan Strome 3.00 8.00
RGSJ Seth Jones 3.00 8.00
RGSL Scott Laughton 2.50 6.00
RGTP Tanner Pearson 2.00 5.00
RGTT Tyler Toffoli 4.00 10.00
RGTW Tom Wilson 4.00 10.00
RGVN Valeri Nichushkin 4.00 10.00
RGVT Vladimir Tarasenko 5.00 12.00
RGZG Zemgus Girgensons 3.00 8.00
RGBJE Boone Jenner 4.00 10.00
RGBNE Brock Nelson 4.00 10.00
RGDMI Dylan McIlrath 1.25 3.00
RGELI Elias Lindholm 5.00 12.00
RGHLI Hampus Lindholm 3.00 8.00
RGJAS Jared Staal 1.50 4.00
RGJME Jon Merrill 2.00 5.00
RGJNO Joakim Nordstrom 1.50 4.00
RGJTM J.T. Miller 5.00 12.00
RGJTR Jacob Trouba 5.00 12.00
RGJUS Justin Schultz 2.00 5.00
RGMDB Matt Dumba 1.25 3.00
RGMGR Mikael Granlund 3.00 8.00
RGMKK Michael Kostka 1.50 4.00
RGMMZ Marek Mazanec 2.00 5.00
RGNMK Nathan MacKinnon 10.00 25.00
RGRBE Reto Berra 2.00 5.00
RGRLY Morgan Rielly 5.00 12.00
RGRMP Ryan Murphy 2.00 5.00
RGRMR Ryan Murray 3.00 8.00
RGRSP Ryan Spooner 2.00 5.00
RGSMA Stefan Matteau 1.50 4.00
RGSMO Sean Monahan 5.00 12.00
RGTHE Tomas Hertl 4.00 10.00
RGTJU Tomas Jurco 2.50 6.00

2013-14 Panini Titanium Rookie Gear Patch

RANMK Nathan MacKinnon 40.00 80.00

2013-14 Panini Titanium Rookie Gear Autographs

*PRIME AU/25: .6X TO 1.5X JSY AU/100
*PATCH AU/15: .8X TO 2X JSY AU/100
RAAB Aleksander Barkov 15.00 40.00
RAAG Alex Galchenyuk 20.00 50.00
RAAR Antoine Roussel 5.00 12.00
RABG Brendan Gallagher 12.00 30.00
RABJE Boone Jenner 10.00 25.00
RABNE Brock Nelson 10.00 25.00
RACM Connor Murphy 4.00 10.00
RADH Dougie Hamilton 8.00 20.00
RADMI Dylan McIlrath 3.00 8.00
RAELI Elias Lindholm 12.00 30.00
RAFA Frederik Andersen 12.00 30.00
RAFC Frank Corrado 3.00 8.00
RAHLI Hampus Lindholm 8.00 20.00
RAJAS Jared Staal 4.00 10.00
RAJH Jonathan Huberdeau 12.00 30.00
RAJME Jon Merrill 5.00 12.00
RAJNO Joakim Nordstrom 4.00 10.00
RAJTR Jacob Trouba 8.00 20.00
RAJUS Justin Schultz 5.00 12.00
RAMDB Matt Dumba 3.00 8.00
RAMIG Mikael Granlund 8.00 20.00
RAMKK Michael Kostka 4.00 10.00
RAMMZ Marek Mazanec 5.00 12.00
RANJ Nicklas Jensen 4.00 10.00
RANMK Nathan MacKinnon 50.00 100.00
RANY Nail Yakupov 12.00 30.00
RANZ Nikita Zadorov 3.00 8.00
RAOM Olli Maatta 10.00 25.00
RAPG Philipp Grubauer 12.00 30.00
RARBE Reto Berra 5.00 12.00
RARLY Morgan Rielly 12.00 30.00
RARMR Ryan Murray 8.00 20.00
RARS Ryan Strome 8.00 20.00
RARSP Ryan Spooner 5.00 12.00
RASJ Seth Jones 10.00 25.00
RASL Scott Laughton 6.00 15.00
RASMA Stefan Matteau 4.00 10.00
RASMO Sean Monahan 8.00 20.00
RATHE Tomas Hertl 10.00 25.00
RATJU Tomas Jurco 6.00 15.00
RATP Tanner Pearson 6.00 15.00
RATT Tyler Toffoli 10.00 25.00
RATW Tom Wilson 10.00 25.00

2013-14 Panini Titanium Rookie Reserve Memorabilia Autographs

RRAG Alex Galchenyuk/50 10.00 25.00
RRAW Austin Watson/100 3.00 8.00
RRBG Brendan Gallagher/100 10.00 25.00
RRDH Dougie Hamilton/50 6.00 15.00
RRJB Jonas Brodin/100 6.00 15.00
RRJC Jack Campbell/100 6.00 15.00
RRJH Jonathan Huberdeau/50 10.00 25.00
RRNM Nathan MacKinnon/100 20.00 50.00
RRNY Nail Yakupov/50 8.00 20.00
RRSJ Seth Jones/100 8.00 20.00
RRSM Sean Monahan/100 8.00 20.00
RRTP Tanner Pearson/100 4.00 10.00
RRTW Tom Wilson/100 8.00 20.00
RRVN Valeri Nichushkin/100 8.00 20.00
RRAP Anthony Peluso/100 2.50 6.00
RRCSO Carl Soderberg/100 4.00 10.00
RRDDK Danny DeKeyser/100 5.00 12.00
RRDSH Drew Shore/100 3.00 8.00
RRJTM J.T. Miller/100 10.00 25.00
RRMGR Mikael Granlund/100 6.00 15.00
RRMIK Mikhail Grigorenko/100 2.50 6.00
RRSMA Stefan Matteau/100 3.00 8.00
RRTHI Thomas Hickey/100 3.00 8.00

2013-14 Panini Titanium Rookie Six Star Memorabilia

R6CSO Carl Soderberg 12.00 30.00
R6AB Aleksander Barkov 25.00 60.00
R6AG Alex Galchenyuk 20.00 50.00
R6AK Alex Killorn 12.00 30.00
R6AR Antoine Roussel 8.00 20.00
R6AW Austin Watson 6.00 15.00
R6BF Brian Flynn 6.00 15.00
R6BLA Brian Lashoff 6.00 15.00
R6COY Charlie Coyle 12.00 30.00
R6IB Igor Bobkov 6.00 15.00
R6JH Jonathan Huberdeau 20.00 50.00
R6JTI Jarred Tinordi 8.00 20.00
R6MI Matt Irwin 6.00 15.00
R6MIK Mikhail Grigorenko 5.00 12.00
R6NMK Nathan MacKinnon 30.00 80.00
R6NY Nail Yakupov 15.00 40.00
R6PG Philipp Grubauer 15.00 40.00
R6RCV Roman Cervenka 6.00 15.00
R6RMP Ryan Murphy 8.00 20.00
R6RR Rickard Rakell 8.00 20.00
R6SJ Seth Jones 15.00 40.00
R6SM Sean Monahan 12.00 30.00
R6TH Tomas Hertl 15.00 40.00
R6VN Valeri Nichushkin 15.00 40.00
R6VT Vladimir Tarasenko 20.00 50.00

2013-14 Panini Titanium Rookie Trio Signatures

RTANA Fsth/Bobkv/Andersn/25 25.00 60.00
RTDAL Chson/Oleksk/Cmpbll/25 25.00 60.00
RTDET Lshff/DeKey/Mrazek/25 12.00 30.00
RTFLA Huber/Shore/Hwdn/25 20.00 50.00
RTRK1 Gllghr/Hberd/Grigrnk/25 20.00 50.00

2013-14 Panini Titanium Rookie Jumbos

J1 Nathan MacKinnon 6.00 15.00
J2 Seth Jones 2.50 6.00
J3 Aleksander Barkov 4.00 10.00
J4 Nail Yakupov 5.00 12.00
J5 Alex Galchenyuk 5.00 12.00
J6 Jonathan Huberdeau 3.00 8.00
J7 Vladimir Tarasenko 3.00 8.00
J8 Dougie Hamilton 2.00 5.00
J9 Brendan Gallagher 3.00 8.00
J10 Filip Forsberg 2.00 5.00

2013-14 Panini Titanium Six Star Memorabilia

6SBEN Jamie Benn/25 15.00 40.00
6SBSE Brent Seabrook/25 10.00 25.00
6SCKU Chris Kunitz/25 15.00 40.00
6SCPE Corey Perry/25 25.00 60.00
6SGRN Mike Green/25 12.00 30.00
6SHL Henrik Lundqvist/25 40.00 100.00
6SIL Igor Larionov/25 20.00 50.00
6SJE Jordan Eberle/25 15.00 40.00
6SJFC Jeff Carter/25 12.00 30.00
6SJQ Jonathan Quick/25 20.00 50.00
6SJS Joe Sakic/25 30.00 80.00
6SML Mario Lemieux/25 60.00 150.00
6SMRI Mike Richards/25 12.00 30.00
6SPAS Paul Stastny/25 12.00 30.00
6SPS Patrick Sharp/25 15.00 40.00
6SRB Ray Bourque/15 30.00 80.00
6SRC Ryan Callahan/25 12.00 30.00
6SRN Rick Nash/25 15.00 40.00
6SSC Sidney Crosby/25 60.00 150.00
6SSHA Scott Hartnell/25 10.00 25.00
6STPL Tomas Plekanec/25 12.00 30.00
6STR Tuukka Rask/25 20.00 50.00

2013-14 Panini Titanium Team Building Quad Jerseys

*PRIME/25: .6X TO 1.5X QUAD JSY/100
TBANA Perry/Fwlr/Etem/Rakll 10.00 25.00
TBBOS Brgrn/Luc/Hmltn/Spnr 8.00 20.00
TBBUF Enrth/Grig/Adam/Ennis 8.00 20.00
TBCHI Keith/Crwfd/Tws/Kane 12.00 30.00
TBCOL Ststny/Dchn/Lnds/Pck 8.00 20.00
TBDAL Ben/Oleksk/Cmpbl/Dley 10.00 25.00
TBDET Frnzn/Hwrd/Dtsyk/Ztrb 6.00 15.00
TBEDM Dbnk/Hall/RNH/Yakpv 12.00 30.00
TBFLA Bjgstd/Hwd/Hbrd/Shre 6.00 15.00
TBLAK Qck/Toff/Prsn/Dghty 10.00 25.00
TBMON Prce/Sbn/Gllgh/Glchn 12.00 30.00
TBNJD Brdr/Lrsn/Mtteau/Zajc 15.00 40.00
TBNSH Hrngst/Rne/Wtsn/Lgw 6.00 15.00
TBNYI Nlsn/Bley/Tvres/Okpso 12.00 30.00
TBNYR Lndqvt/Staal/Stpn/Mllr 15.00 40.00
TBOTT Gryba/Krlsn/Spzz/Neil 8.00 20.00
TBPHI Ctrier/Rnldo/Girx/Lghtn 8.00 20.00
TBPHX Bdkr/Brwn/Doan/Hnzl 5.00 12.00
TBPIT Dsprs/Mlkn/Flry/Bnnt 8.00 20.00
TBSJS Ptrck/Mrlu/Vlsic/Pvlski 8.00 20.00
TBSTL Bcks/Osh/Trsnk/Jckm 10.00 25.00
TBTBL Kllrn/Stmks/Panik/Tyrll 8.00 20.00
TBVAN Edler/Sedins/Schroeder 8.00 20.00
TBWPG Lttl/E.Kne/Rdmnd/Psql 6.00 15.00
TBWSH Jhnsn/Ovch/Wlsn/Grbr 15.00 40.00

2013-14 Panini Titanium Third Sweaters Memorabilia Autographs

TSDH Dougie Hamilton/25 15.00 40.00
TSDJ Dmitrij Jaskin/25 10.00 25.00
TSGL Gabriel Landeskog/25 10.00 25.00
TSIB Igor Bobkov/25 8.00 20.00
TSKL Kris Letang/25 12.00 30.00
TSNM Nathan MacKinnon/25 50.00 125.00
TSNP Nick Petrecki/25 6.00 15.00
TSPM Patrick Marleau/25 10.00 25.00
TSRK Ryan Kesler/25 10.00 25.00
TSSV Sami Vatanen/25 8.00 20.00
TSTH Taylor Hall/25 10.00 25.00
TSCVP Calvin Pickard/25 12.00 30.00
TSJEN Jhonas Enroth/25 10.00 25.00
TSJTM J.T. Miller/25 25.00 60.00
TSMAF Marc-Andre Fleury/25 20.00 50.00
TSMDU Matt Duchene/25 10.00 25.00
TSRNH Ryan Nugent-Hopkins/25 12.00 30.00
TSRSP Ryan Spooner/25 10.00 25.00
TSSVA Semyon Varlamov/25 10.00 25.00

2013-14 Panini Titanium Three Star Selections Autographs

3GHL Henrik Lundqvist/25 40.00 100.00
3GJHO Jimmy Howard/50 15.00 40.00
3GJQ Jonathan Quick/50 12.00 30.00
3GJRE James Reimer/50 10.00 25.00
3GMB Martin Brodeur/25 30.00 60.00
3GMS Mike Smith/50 10.00 25.00
3GPRI Pekka Rinne/50 10.00 25.00
3GRM Ryan Miller/50 10.00 25.00
3RAG Alex Galchenyuk/50 15.00 40.00
3RBG Brendan Gallagher/100 8.00 20.00
3RDDK Danny DeKeyser/100 8.00 20.00
3RDH Dougie Hamilton/100 8.00 20.00
3RFF Filip Forsberg/100 10.00 25.00
3RMGR Mikael Granlund/100 8.00 15.00
3RNY Nail Yakupov/50 10.00 25.00
3RTW Tom Wilson/100 8.00 20.00
3SAH Adam Henrique/50 10.00 25.00
3SGL Gabriel Landeskog/50 15.00 40.00
3SJI Jarome Iginla/50 10.00 25.00
3SJP Joe Pavelski/25 8.00 20.00
3SJT John Tavares/50 20.00 50.00
3SLE Loui Eriksson/50 8.00 20.00
3SPD Pavel Datsyuk/50 25.00 50.00
3SRNH Ryan Nugent-Hopkins/50 15.00 40.00
3STS Tyler Seguin/50 15.00 40.00

2013-14 Panini Titanium Retail

COMP.SET w/o RC's (100) 12.00 30.00
*1-100 VETS: .3X TO .8X HOBBY
17 Corey Crawford .40 1.00
73 Nicklas Backstrom .30 .75
101 Vladimir Tarasenko RC 8.00 20.00
102 Cory Conacher RC 2.00 5.00
103 John Muse RC 3.00 8.00
104 Matt Tennyson RC 2.00 5.00
105 Eric Selleck RC 2.50 6.00
106 Radko Gudas RC 3.00 8.00
107 Ondrej Palat RC 5.00 12.00
108 Brett Bellemore RC 2.50 6.00
109 Tyler Toffoli RC 8.00 20.00
110 Igor Bobkov RC 2.50 6.00
111 Nicolas Blanchard RC 2.50 6.00
112 Alex Petrovic RC 2.50 6.00
113 Joonas Rask RC 2.00 5.00
114 Richard Panik RC 3.00 8.00
115 Tanner Pearson RC 3.00 8.00
116 Jamie Tardif RC 2.00 5.00
117 Rickard Rakell RC 3.00 8.00
118 Emerson Etem RC 3.00 8.00
119 Brian Flynn RC 2.50 6.00
120 Danny DeKeyser RC 4.00 10.00
121 Nail Yakupov RC 6.00 15.00
122 Mikael Granlund RC 5.00 12.00
123 Greg Pateryn RC 3.00 8.00
124 Victor Bartley RC 2.50 6.00
125 Charlie Coyle RC 5.00 12.00
126 Tyler Johnson RC 4.00 10.00
127 Mark Arcobello RC 3.00 8.00
128 Michael Caruso RC 2.50 6.00
129 Eric Gryba RC 2.50 6.00
130 Andrej Sustr RC 2.00 5.00
131 Steve Oleksy RC 3.00 8.00
132 Max Reinhart RC 3.00 8.00
133 Dave Dziurzynski RC 2.50 6.00
134 Ben Hanowski RC 2.50 6.00
135 Chris Terry RC 2.00 5.00
136 Patrick Bordeleau RC 3.00 8.00
137 Christian Thomas RC 2.50 6.00
138 Derek Grant RC 2.00 5.00
139 Taylor Beck RC 2.50 6.00
140 Ryan Stanton RC 2.50 6.00
141 Nick Petrecki RC 2.00 5.00
142 Mark Pysyk RC 3.00 8.00
143 Michael Kostka RC 2.50 6.00
144 Jonathan Rheault RC 2.50 6.00
145 Austin Watson RC 2.00 5.00
146 Matt Irwin RC 2.50 6.00
147 Ryan Spooner RC 3.00 8.00
148 Daniel Bang RC 2.50 6.00
149 Michal Jordan RC 2.00 5.00
150 Johan Larsson RC 4.00 10.00
151 J.T. Miller RC 8.00 20.00
152 Leo Komarov RC 3.00 8.00
153 Carter Bancks RC 2.50 6.00
154 Kevin Henderson RC 2.50 6.00
155 Nikitas Jensen RC 2.50 6.00
156 Sami Vatanen RC 3.00 8.00
157 Jordan Schroeder RC 2.50 6.00
158 Cameron Schilling RC 2.00 5.00
159 Jean-Gabriel Pageau RC 3.00 8.00
160 Chris Brown RC 2.00 5.00
161 Michael Sgarbossa RC 2.00 5.00
162 Sean Collins RC 2.50 6.00
163 Tom Wilson RC 6.00 15.00
164 Mark Cundari RC 2.00 5.00
165 Shawn Lalonde RC 2.00 5.00
166 Quinton Howden RC 2.50 6.00
167 Jarred Tinordi RC 2.50 6.00
168 Jason Akeson RC 2.50 6.00
169 Cristopher Nilstorp RC 2.50 6.00
170 Nathan Beaulieu RC 2.50 6.00
171 Ben Street RC 2.50 6.00
172 Oliver Lauridsen RC 2.50 6.00
173 Jonathan Marchessault RC 8.00 20.00
174 Jeff Zatkoff RC 3.00 8.00
175 Darcy Kuemper RC 4.00 10.00
176 Calvin Heeter RC 2.50 6.00
177 Carl Soderberg RC 3.00 8.00
178 Petr Mrazek RC 6.00 15.00
179 Matthew Konan RC 3.00 8.00
180 Eric Hartzell RC 3.00 8.00
181 Edward Pasquale RC 2.00 5.00
182 Frederik Andersen RC 8.00 20.00
183 Calvin Pickard RC 4.00 10.00
184 Eric Hartzell RC 2.00 5.00
185 Philipp Grubauer RC 8.00 20.00
186 Viktor Fasth RC 3.00 8.00
187 Sami Aittokallio RC 3.00 8.00
188 Joe Cannata RC 2.50 6.00
189 Brock Nelson RC 6.00 15.00
190 Dougie Hamilton RC 5.00 12.00
191 Nick Bjugstad RC 4.00 10.00
192 Alex Galchenyuk RC 8.00 20.00
193 Anders Lee RC 5.00 12.00
194 Dmitrij Jaskin RC 3.00 8.00
195 Frank Corrado RC 2.00 5.00
196 Mikhail Grigorenko RC 2.00 5.00
197 Jonas Brodin RC 4.00 10.00
198 Zach Redmond RC 2.50 6.00
199 Damien Brunner RC 2.50 6.00
200 Brian Lashoff RC 2.50 6.00
201 Scott Laughton RC 4.00 10.00
202 Antoine Roussel RC 3.00 8.00
203 Justin Schultz RC 3.00 8.00
204 Beau Bennett RC 4.00 10.00
205 Alex Killorn RC 5.00 12.00
206 Harri Pesonen RC 2.50 6.00
207 Drew Shore RC 2.50 6.00
208 Stefan Matteau RC 2.50 6.00
209 Tye McGinn RC 3.00 8.00
210 Drew LeBlanc RC 2.50 6.00
211 Thomas Hickey RC 2.50 6.00
212 Anthony Peluso RC 2.50 6.00
213 Jared Staal RC 2.50 6.00
214 Steven Pinizzotto RC 3.00 8.00
215 Alex Chiasson RC 3.00 8.00
216 Matt Anderson RC 2.00 5.00
217 Jonathan Huberdeau RC 8.00 20.00
218 Brendan Gallagher RC 8.00 20.00
219 Roman Cervenka RC 2.50 6.00
220 Filip Forsberg RC 10.00 25.00
221 Mark Barberio RC 2.00 5.00
222 Ryan Murphy RC 3.00 8.00
223 Chad Ruhwedel RC 2.00 5.00
224 Jamie Oleksiak RC 2.50 6.00
225 Jack Campbell RC 8.00 20.00
226 Jacob Trouba RC 8.00 20.00
227 Anton Belov RC 2.50 6.00
228 Will Acton RC 2.50 6.00
229 Luke Gazdic RC 2.50 6.00
230 Joakim Nordstrom RC 2.50 6.00
231 Connor Carrick RC 2.50 6.00
232 Michael Latta RC 2.50 6.00
233 Nathan MacKinnon RC 15.00 40.00
234 Zemgus Girgensons RC 5.00 12.00
235 Rasmus Ristolainen RC 5.00 12.00
236 Seth Jones RC 6.00 15.00
237 Sean Monahan RC 5.00 12.00
238 Olli Maatta RC 5.00 12.00
239 Justin Fontaine RC 3.00 8.00
240 Aleksander Barkov RC 10.00 25.00
241 Valeri Nichushkin RC 6.00 15.00
242 Jesper Fast RC 3.00 8.00
243 Lucas Lessio RC 2.00 5.00
244 Matt Nieto RC 2.50 6.00
245 Tomas Hertl RC 6.00 15.00
246 Boone Jenner RC 6.00 15.00
247 Ryan Murray RC 3.00 8.00
248 Morgan Rielly RC 8.00 20.00
249 Matt Dumba RC 2.00 5.00
250 Hampus Lindholm RC 5.00 12.00

2013-14 Panini Titanium Retail Red

*1-100 VETS/199: 2.5X TO 6X RETAIL
*101-250 ROOKIE/99: .6X TO 1.5X RETAIL/299
17 Corey Crawford 2.50 6.00
73 Nicklas Backstrom 2.00 5.00

2013-14 Panini Titanium Titanium Reserve Autographs

TRAA Akim Aliu 4.00 10.00
TRAJO Andrew Joudrey 4.00 10.00
TRAK Alex Killorn 10.00 25.00
TRANE Aaron Ness 4.00 10.00
TRANL Anton Lander 4.00 10.00
TRANP Anthony Peluso 4.00 10.00
TRAP Alex Pietrangelo SP 5.00 12.00
TRBES Ben Smith 5.00 12.00
TRBL Brian Leetch SP 5.00 12.00
TRBM Brenden Morrow SP 5.00 12.00
TRBMA Brandon Manning 4.00 10.00
TRBN Bernie Nicholls SP 5.00 12.00
TRBSM Brendan Smith 4.00 10.00
TRBWR Johnny Bower SP 6.00 15.00
TRCB Chris Brown 4.00 10.00
TRCCI Casey Cizikas 4.00 10.00
TRCGR Colin Greening SP 4.00 10.00
TRCJ Curtis Joseph SP 8.00 20.00
TRCK Chris Kreider SP 8.00 20.00
TRCNI Cristopher Nilstorp 5.00 12.00
TRCP Carey Price SP 12.00 30.00
TRCS Cory Schneider SP 6.00 15.00
TRCSO Carl Soderberg 6.00 15.00
TRDGR Derek Grant 5.00 12.00
TRDR Derek Roy SP 4.00 10.00
TREH Eric Hartzell 6.00 15.00
TRERS Eric Staal SP 8.00 20.00
TRFA Frederik Andersen 15.00 40.00
TRFF Filip Forsberg 20.00 50.00
TRFP Felix Potvin SP 10.00 25.00
TRGH Gordie Howe SP 100.00 200.00
TRGL Gabriel Landeskog SP 8.00 20.00
TRHP Harri Pesonen 5.00 12.00
TRJAM Jonathan Marchessault 15.00 40.00
TRJAS Jared Staal 5.00 12.00
TRJB Jonas Brodin 8.00 20.00
TRJHY Jimmy Hayes 4.00 10.00
TRJMO Jeremy Morin 5.00 12.00
TRJO Jamie Oleksiak 5.00 12.00
TRJS Joe Sakic SP 12.00 30.00
TRJSD Jordan Schroeder 6.00 15.00
TRJVR James van Riemsdyk SP 5.00 12.00
TRLE Loui Eriksson SP 4.00 10.00
TRLP Lennart Petrell 4.00 10.00
TRMAS Marc Staal SP 4.00 10.00
TRML Mario Lemieux SP 30.00 80.00
TRMPY Mark Pysyk 6.00 15.00
TRMXN Max Neinhart 6.00 15.00
TRMXT Maxime Talbot SP 4.00 10.00
TRNP Nick Petrecki 4.00 10.00
TROVI Alex Ovechkin SP 25.00 60.00
TRRCL Ryane Clowe SP 4.00 10.00
TRRH Ryan Hamilton 4.00 10.00
TRRIB Richard Bachman 5.00 12.00
TRRJO Roman Josi 6.00 15.00
TRRNH Ryan Nugent-Hopkins SP 8.00 20.00
TRRR Rickard Rakell 6.00 15.00
TRSE Stefan Elliott 5.00 12.00
TRSGO Scott Gomez SP 5.00 12.00
TRSTM Steve Mason SP 5.00 12.00
TRSV Sami Vatanen 6.00 15.00
TRTMG Tye McGinn 6.00 15.00
TRTVA Thomas Vanek SP 5.00 12.00
TRZK Zack Kassian 4.00 10.00

2011-12 Panini Toronto Fall Expo

1 Alex Ovechkin 2.50 6.00
2 Steven Stamkos 1.25 3.00
3 Tim Thomas .60 1.50
4 Sidney Crosby 2.50 6.00
5 Nicklas Lidstrom .40 1.00
6 Corey Perry .60 1.50
7 Ryan Nugent-Hopkins 8.00 20.00
8 Gabriel Landeskog 2.00 5.00
9 Adam Larsson .75 2.00
HOF1 Doug Gilmour 1.00 2.50
HOF2 Joe Nieuwendyk .60 1.50
HOF3 Ed Belfour .75 2.00

2012-13 Panini Toronto Fall Expo

COMPLETE SET (25)
COMP.SET w/o RC's (15)
1 Sidney Crosby .75 2.00
2 Alex Ovechkin .75 2.00
3 Tyler Seguin .60 1.50
4 Martin Brodeur .75 2.00
5 Phil Kessel .75 2.00
6 Carey Price .75 2.00
7 Jarome Iginla .60 1.50
8 Henrik Sedin .60 1.50
9 Daniel Sedin .60 1.50
10 Steven Stamkos .75 2.00
11 Claude Giroux .75 2.00
12 Ryan Nugent-Hopkins 1.00 2.50
13 Gabriel Landeskog .75 2.00
14 Adam Henrique .60 1.50
15 John Tavares .75 2.00

2012-13 Panini Toronto Fall Expo

16 Jakob Silfverberg RR 1.00 2.50
17 Tyson Barrie RR 1.00 2.50
18 Jordan Nolan RR 1.00 2.50
19 Carter Ashton RR 1.25 3.00
20 Sven Baertschi RR 1.25 3.00
21 Jaden Schwartz RR 1.25 3.00
22 Reilly Smith RR 1.00 2.50
23 Chet Pickard RR 1.00 2.50
24 Chris Kreider RR 2.00 5.00
25 Jake Allen RR 1.00 2.50

2013-14 Panini Toronto Fall Expo Hot Rookies

*LAVA FLOW: 1.2X TO 3X BASIC INSERTS
HK1 Austin Watson .40 1.00
HK2 Brock Nelson 1.00 2.50
HK3 Jamie Oleksiak .40 1.00
HK4 Beau Bennett .60 1.50
HK5 Charlie Coyle .75 2.00
HK6 Ryan Spooner .50 1.25
HK7 Ryan Murphy .50 1.25
HK8 Scott Laughton .60 1.50
HK9 Mikhail Grigorenko .30 .75
HK10 Christian Thomas .40 1.00
HK11 Cory Conacher .30 .75
HK12 Nicklas Jensen .40 1.00
HK13 Petr Mrazek 1.00 2.50
HK14 Tanner Pearson .50 1.25
HK15 Tom Wilson 1.00 2.50
HK16 Justin Schultz .50 1.25

2011-12 Panini Toronto Spring Expo

COMPLETE SET (10) 12.50 25.00
1 Tim Thomas .60 1.50
2 Evgeni Malkin 1.25 3.00
3 Phil Kessel .60 1.50
4 Henrik Lundqvist 1.50 4.00
5 Steven Stamkos 1.25 3.00
6 Claude Giroux .60 1.50
7 Pavel Datsyuk 1.00 2.50
8 Jonathan Toews 1.00 2.50
9 Alex Ovechkin SP 6.00 15.00
10 Sidney Crosby SP 6.00 15.00

2011-12 Panini Toronto Spring Expo Legends

COMPLETE SET (4) 4.00 10.00
MVP1 Gordie Howe 2.50 6.00
MVP2 Ray Bourque 1.25 3.00
MVP3 Joe Sakic 1.50 4.00
MVP4 Brett Hull 1.50 4.00

2011-12 Panini Toronto Spring Expo Rookie Patch Autographs

BS Brendan Smith/50* 12.50 25.00
EG Erik Gudbranson/50* 6.00 15.00
JB Jonathon Blum/24* 6.00 15.00
RE Ryan Ellis/25* 15.00 30.00
RJ Ryan Johansen/50* 8.00 20.00
SD Simon Despres/25* 15.00 30.00
ZK Zack Kassian/79* 6.00 15.00
CDH Calvin de Haan/50* 6.00 15.00

2011-12 Panini Toronto Spring Expo Rookies

COMPLETE SET (8) 20.00 50.00
RC1 Ryan Nugent-Hopkins 8.00 20.00
RC2 Gabriel Landeskog 3.00 8.00
RC3 Adam Larsson 1.25 3.00
RC4 Adam Henrique 2.50 6.00
RC5 Jake Gardiner 1.50 4.00
RC6 Sean Couturier 2.00 5.00
RC7 Matt Read 1.25 3.00
RC8 Cody Hodgson 1.50 4.00

2011-12 Panini Toronto Spring Expo Tools of the Trade

COMPLETE SET (5) 25.00 50.00
AS Daniel Sedin 5.00 12.00
BC Alex Ovechkin 6.00 15.00
FS Michael Grabner 3.00 8.00
HS Zdeno Chara 4.00 10.00
MVP Patrick Sharp 4.00 10.00

2013-14 Panini Toronto Spring Expo Autographs

BS Brendan Shanahan 8.00 20.00
CC Connor Carrick 10.00 25.00
JC Jack Campbell 3.00 8.00
LM Lanny McDonald 5.00 12.00
MM Mark Messier 12.00 30.00
MP Max Pacioretty 5.00 12.00
PR Patrick Roy 30.00 60.00
RL Roberto Luongo 4.00 10.00

2013-14 Panini Toronto Spring Expo Priority Signings 5x7

RS Ryan Strome 4.00 10.00
SM Sean Monahan 4.00 10.00

1993-94 Panthers Team Issue

COMPLETE SET (8) 4.80 12.00
1 Joe Cirella .60 1.50
2 Tom Fitzgerald .60 1.50
3 Mike Foligno .60 1.50
4 Paul Laus .75 2.00
5 Bill Lindsay .60 1.50
6 Andrei Lomakin .60 1.50
7 Scott Mellanby .75 2.00
8 Brent Severyn .60 1.50

1994-95 Panthers Boston Market

COMPLETE SET (28) 4.00 10.00
1 Stu Barnes .20 .50
2 Jesse Belanger .20 .50
3 Brian Benning .20 .50
4 Keith Brown .20 .50
5 Joe Cirella .20 .50
6 Jeff Daniels .20 .50
7 Tom Fitzgerald .20 .50
8 Mark Fitzpatrick .20 .50
9 Mike Hough .20 .50
10 Jody Hull .20 .50
11 Bob Kudelski .20 .50
12 Paul Laus .20 .50
13 Bill Lindsay .20 .50
14 Andrei Lomakin .20 .50
15 Dave Lowry .20 .50
16 Scott Mellanby .20 .50
17 Randy Moller .20 .50
18 Gord Murphy .20 .50
19 Rob Niedermayer .20 .50
20 Brent Severyn .20 .50
21 Brian Skrudland .20 .50
22 Geoff Smith .20 .50
23 John Vanbiesbrouck .30 .75
24 Roger Neilson .20 .50
25 Craig Ramsay .20 .50
26 Lindy Ruff .20 .50
27 Billy Smith .20 .50
28 The Panther .08 .25

1994-95 Panthers Pop-ups

COMPLETE SET (5) 4.00 10.00
1 Brian Skrudland .60 1.50
2 John Vanbiesbrouck 1.25 3.00
3 Scott Mellanby .60 1.50
4 Stu Barnes .60 1.50
5 Jesse Belanger .60 1.50

1995-96 Panthers Boston Market

COMPLETE SET (32) 4.00 10.00
1 Stu Barnes .20 .50
2 Jesse Belanger .20 .50
3 Terry Carkner .20 .50
4 Radek Dvorak .20 .50
5 Tom Fitzgerald .20 .50
6 Mark Fitzpatrick .20 .50
7 Johan Garpenlov .20 .50
8 Mike Hough .20 .50
9 Jody Hull .20 .50
10 Ed Jovanovski .20 .50
11 Bob Kudelski .20 .50
12 Paul Laus .20 .50
13 Bill Lindsay .20 .50
14 Dave Lowry .20 .50
15 Scott Mellanby .20 .50
16 Gord Murphy .20 .50
17 David Nemirovsky .20 .50
18 Rob Niedermayer .20 .50
19 Brian Skrudland .20 .50
20 Geoff Smith .20 .50
21 Robert Svehla .20 .50
22 Magnus Svensson .20 .50
23 John Vanbiesbrouck .30 .75
24 Rhett Warrener .20 .50
25 Jason Woolley .20 .50
26 Doug MacLean .20 .50
27 Lindy Ruff .20 .50
28 Duane Sutter .20 .50
29 Billy Smith .20 .50
30 Boston Market .08 .25
31 Stanley C. Panther .08 .25
32 Boston Market .08 .25

1999-00 Panthers Cigna

COMPLETE SET (36) 6.00 15.00
1 Dan Boyle .40 1.00
2 Pavel Bure 2.00 5.00
3 Radek Dvorak .20 .50
4 Dwayne Hay .20 .50
5 Bret Hedican .20 .50
6 John Jakopin .20 .50
7 Ryan Johnson .20 .50
8 Trevor Kidd .30 .75
9 Viktor Kozlov .30 .75
10 Filip Kuba .20 .50
11 Oleg Kvasha .20 .50
12 Paul Laus .20 .50
13 Scott Mellanby .20 .50
14 Rob Niedermayer .30 .75
15 Ivan Novoseltsev .20 .50
16 Mark Parrish .40 1.00
17 Lance Pitlick .20 .50
18 Ray Sheppard .30 .75
19 Mikhail Shtalenkov .20 .50
20 Denis Shvidki .20 .50
21 Todd Simpson .20 .50
22 Jaroslav Spacek .20 .50
23 Cam Stewart .20 .50
24 Robert Svehla .20 .50
25 Chris Wells .20 .50
26 Ray Whitney .40 1.00
27 Mike Wilson .20 .50
28 Peter Worrell .20 .50
29 Terry Murray CO .08 .25
30 Slavomir Lener ACO .08 .25
31 Billy Smith ACO .08 .25
32 Bryan Murray GM .08 .25
33 2000 Schedule .08 .25
34 Chuck Fletcher AGM .08 .25
35 Stanley C. Panther .08 .25
36 William Torrey PRES .08 .25

2000-01 Panthers Team Issue

COMPLETE SET (32) 10.00 25.00
1 Bill Torrey CO .04 .10
2 Chuck Fletcher GM .04 .10
3 Duane Sutter CO .10 .25
4 Panther MASCOT .04 .10
5 Slavomir Lener TR .04 .10
6 Billy Smith CO .40 1.00
7 Roberto Luongo 2.00 5.00
8 Lance Pitlick .20 .50
9 Paul Laus .40 1.00
10 Bret Hedican .20 .50
11 Mike Wilson .20 .50
12 Peter Worrell .60 1.50
13 Len Barrie .20 .50
14 Pavel Bure 2.00 5.00
15 Olli Jokinen .30 .75
16 Vaclav Prospal .20 .50
17 Ray Whitney .20 .50
18 John Jakopin .20 .50
19 Mike Sillinger .20 .50
20 Greg Adams .20 .50
21 Marcus Nilsson .20 .50
22 Serge Payer .20 .50
23 Todd Simpson .20 .50
24 Robert Svehla .20 .50
25 Viktor Kozlov .30 .75
26 Dan Boyle .20 .50
27 Scott Mellanby .20 .50
28 Anders Eriksson .20 .50
29 Trevor Kidd .30 .75
30 Ivan Novoseltsev .30 .75
31 Rob Niedermayer .20 .50
32 Lance Ward .20 .50

2003-04 Panthers Team Issue

COMPLETE SET (18) 8.00 20.00
1 Mathieu Biron .20 .50
2 Jay Bouwmeester .40 1.00
3 Valeri Bure .20 .50
4 Matt Cullen .20 .50
5 Niklas Hagman .20 .50
6 Darcy Hordichuk .40 1.00
7 Nathan Horton 1.50 4.00
8 Kristian Huselius .30 .75
9 Olli Jokinen .40 1.00
10 Viktor Kozlov .20 .50
11 Roberto Luongo 1.25 3.00
12 Eric Messier .20 .50
13 Branislav Mezei .20 .50
14 Lyle Odelein .20 .50
15 Mikael Samuelsson .20 .50
16 Pavel Trnka .20 .50
17 Mike Van Ryn .20 .50
18 Stephen Weiss .40 1.00

1943-48 Parade Sportive

COMPLETE SET 1250.00 2500.00
1 George Allen 12.50 25.00
2 Aldege(Bazz) Bastien 12.50 25.00
3 Bobby Bauer
Milt Schmidt
Woody Dumart 25.00 50.00
4 Joe Benoit 12.50 25.00
5 Paul Bibeault 12.50 25.00
6 Emile(Butch) Bouchard (2) 20.00 40.00
7 Butch Bouchard
Leo Lamoureux
Bill Durnan 20.00 40.00
8 Toe Blake 25.00 50.00
9 Lionel Bouvrette (2) 12.50 25.00
10 Frank Brimsek 20.00 40.00
11 Turk Broda (2) 25.00 50.00
12 Eddie Bruneteau 12.50 25.00
13 Modere Bruneteau (2) 12.50 25.00
14 Jean Claude Campeau 12.50 25.00
15 J.P. Campeau 12.50 25.00
16 Bob Carse 12.50 25.00
17 Joe Carveth 20.00 40.00
18 Denys Casavant (2) 12.50 25.00
19 Murph Chamberlain 12.50 25.00
20 Bill Cowley 12.50 25.00
21 Floyd Curry 12.50 25.00
22 Tony Demers (2) 12.50 25.00
23 Connie Dion 12.50 25.00
24 Bill Durnan (2) 20.00 40.00
25 Normand Dussault (2) 12.50 25.00
26 Frank Eddolls 12.50 25.00
27 Johnny Gagnon 12.50 25.00
28 Bob Fillion (2) 12.50 25.00
29 Johnny Gagnon
Aurel Joliat
Howie Morenz 12.50 25.00
30 Armand Gaudreault (2) 12.50 25.00
31 Fernand Gauthier (2) 12.50 25.00
32 Fernand Gauthier
Buddy O'Connor
Dutch Hiller 12.50 25.00
33 Jean-Paul Gladu (2) 12.50 25.00
34 Leo Gravelle 12.50 25.00
35 Glen Harmon (2) 12.50 25.00
36 Doug Harvey 20.00 40.00
37 Jerry Heffernan
Buddy O'Connor
Pete Morin 12.50 25.00
38 (Sugar) Jim Henry 15.00 30.00
39 Dutch Hiller (2) 12.50 25.00
40 Rosario Joanette 12.50 25.00
41 Michael Karakas (2) 12.50 25.00
42 Elmer Lach 25.00 50.00
43 Ernest Laforce 12.50 25.00
44 Leo Lamoureux 12.50 25.00
45 Edgar Laprade 12.50 25.00
46 Hal Laycoe 12.50 25.00
47 Roger Leger 12.50 25.00
48 Jacques Locas (2) 12.50 25.00
49 Harry Lumley 20.00 40.00
50 Fernand Mageau 12.50 25.00
51 Georges Mantha (2) 12.50 25.00
52 Jean Marois 12.50 25.00
53 Mike McMahon 12.50 25.00
54 Gerry McNeil 12.50 25.00
55 Pierre(Pete) Morin 12.50 25.00
56 Ken Mosdell 12.50 25.00
57 Bill Mosienko
Max Bentley
Doug Bentley 20.00 40.00
58 Buddy O'Connor 12.50 25.00
59 Gerry Plamondon 12.50 25.00
60 Robert(Bob) Pepin 12.50 25.00
61 Jimmy Peters 12.50 25.00
62 Jerry Plamondon 12.50 25.00
63 Paul Raymond 12.50 25.00
64 Billy Reay 15.00 30.00
65 John Quilty 12.50 25.00
66 Kenny Reardon 15.00 30.00
67 Maurice Richard (2) 37.50 75.00
68 Maurice Richard
Elmer Lach
Toe Blake 25.00 50.00
69 Howie(Rip) Riopelle 12.50 25.00
70 Gaye Stewart 12.50 25.00
71 Phil Watson 15.00 30.00
72 Montreal Canadiens
Team Photo 1943-44 12.50 25.00
73 Montreal Canadiens
Team Photo 1944-45 12.50 25.00
74 Montreal Canadiens
Team Photo 1945-46 12.50 25.00
75 Montreal Canadiens
Team Photo 1946-47 12.50 25.00

1997-98 Paramount

1 Guy Hebert .12 .30
2 Paul Kariya .15 .40
3 Espen Knutsen RC .15 .40
4 Dmitri Mironov .12 .30
5 Steve Rucchin .12 .30
6 Tomas Sandstrom .10 .25
7 Teemu Selanne .30 .75
8 Scott Young .12 .30
9 Ray Bourque .25 .60
10 Jim Carey .10 .25
11 Anson Carter .10 .25
12 Ted Donato .10 .25
13 Dave Ellett .10 .25
14 Dimitri Khristich .12 .30
15 Sergei Samsonov .12 .30
16 Joe Thornton .25 .60
17 Matthew Barnaby .10 .25
18 Jason Dawe .12 .30
19 Dominik Hasek .25 .60
20 Brian Holzinger .12 .30
21 Michael Peca .12 .30
22 Derek Plante .12 .30
23 Erik Rasmussen .12 .30
24 Miroslav Satan .10 .25
25 Steve Begin RC .10 .25
26 Andrew Cassels .10 .25
27 Chris Dingman RC .15 .40
28 Theo Fleury .20 .50
29 Jonas Hoglund .12 .30
30 Jarome Iginla .20 .50
31 Rick Tabaracci .12 .30
32 German Titov .10 .25
33 Kevin Dineen .12 .30
34 Nelson Emerson .12 .30
35 Trevor Kidd .10 .25
36 Stephen Leach .10 .25
37 Keith Primeau .12 .30
38 Steven Rice .12 .30
39 Gary Roberts .12 .30
40 Tony Amonte .12 .30
41 Chris Chelios .15 .40
42 Daniel Cleary .12 .30
43 Eric Daze .10 .25
44 Jeff Hackett .10 .25
45 Sergei Krivokrasov .10 .25
46 Ethan Moreau .10 .25
47 Alexei Zhamnov .10 .25
48 Adam Deadmarsh .10 .25
49 Peter Forsberg .30 .75
50 Valeri Kamensky .12 .30
51 Jari Kurri .15 .40
52 Claude Lemieux .12 .30
53 Sandis Ozolinsh .10 .25
54 Patrick Roy .40 1.00
55 Joe Sakic .30 .75
56 Ed Belfour .15 .40
57 Derian Hatcher .12 .30
58 Jamie Langenbrunner .12 .30
59 Jere Lehtinen .12 .30
60 Mike Modano .25 .60
61 Joe Nieuwendyk .12 .30
62 Darryl Sydor .10 .25
63 Pat Verbeek .12 .30
64 Anders Eriksson .12 .30
65 Sergei Fedorov .25 .60
66 Vyacheslav Kozlov .12 .30
67 Nicklas Lidstrom .15 .40
68 Darren McCarty .12 .30
69 Chris Osgood .15 .40
70 Brendan Shanahan .15 .40
71 Steve Yzerman .40 1.00
72 Jason Arnott .12 .30
73 Boyd Devereaux .12 .30
74 Mike Grier .12 .30
75 Curtis Joseph .20 .50
76 Andrei Kovalenko .10 .25
77 Ryan Smyth .12 .30
78 Doug Weight .15 .40
79 Dave Gagner .10 .25
80 Ed Jovanovski .10 .25
81 Scott Mellanby .12 .30
82 Kirk Muller .10 .25
83 Rob Niedermayer .10 .25
84 Ray Sheppard .12 .30
85 Esa Tikkanen .10 .25
86 John Vanbiesbrouck .15 .40
87 Rob Blake .15 .40
88 Stephane Fiset .12 .30
89 Garry Galley .10 .25
90 Olli Jokinen RC .20 .50
91 Luc Robitaille .15 .40
92 Jozef Stumpel .10 .25
93 Shayne Corson .12 .30
94 Vincent Damphousse .12 .30
95 Saku Koivu .15 .40
96 Andy Moog .15 .40
97 Mark Recchi .20 .50
98 Stephane Richer .10 .25
99 Brian Savage .10 .25
100 Dave Andreychuk .15 .40
101 Martin Brodeur .40 1.00
102 Doug Gilmour .20 .50
103 Bobby Holik .10 .25
104 John MacLean .10 .25
105 Brian Rolston .12 .30
106 Bryan Berard .10 .25
107 Todd Bertuzzi .15 .40
108 Travis Green .12 .30
109 Zigmund Palffy .15 .40
110 Robert Reichel .12 .30
111 Tommy Salo .10 .25
112 Bryan Smolinski .12 .30
113 Christian Dube .12 .30
114 Adam Graves .10 .25
115 Wayne Gretzky 1.00 2.50
116 Alexei Kovalev .12 .30
117 Pat LaFontaine .15 .40
118 Brian Leetch .12 .30
119 Mike Richter .15 .40
120 Brian Skrudland .10 .25
121 Kevin Stevens .12 .30
122 Daniel Alfredsson .15 .40
123 Radek Bonk .10 .25
124 Alexandre Daigle .10 .25
125 Marian Hossa RC .20 .50
126 Igor Kravchuk .10 .25
127 Chris Phillips .12 .30
128 Damian Rhodes .12 .30
129 Alexei Yashin .12 .30
130 Rod Brind'Amour .15 .40
131 Chris Gratton .10 .25
132 Ron Hextall .15 .40
133 John LeClair .15 .40
134 Eric Lindros .25 .60
135 Janne Niinimaa .12 .30
136 Vaclav Prospal RC .12 .30
137 Garth Snow .12 .30
138 Dainius Zubrus .12 .30
139 Mike Gartner .20 .50
140 Brad Isbister .12 .30
141 Nikolai Khabibulin .15 .40
142 Jeremy Roenick .25 .60
143 Cliff Ronning .10 .25
144 Keith Tkachuk .15 .40
145 Rick Tocchet .10 .25
146 Oleg Tverdovsky .12 .30
147 Tom Barrasso .12 .30
148 Ron Francis .20 .50
149 Kevin Hatcher .10 .25
150 Jaromir Jagr .50 1.25
151 Darius Kasparaitis .12 .30
152 Alexei Morozov .12 .30
153 Petr Nedved .15 .40
154 Ed Olczyk .10 .25
155 Jim Campbell .10 .25
156 Kelly Chase .10 .25
157 Geoff Courtnall .10 .25
158 Grant Fuhr .25 .60
159 Brett Hull .30 .75
160 Joe Murphy .12 .30
161 Pierre Turgeon .12 .30
162 Tony Twist .12 .30
163 Shawn Burr .10 .25
164 Jeff Friesen .12 .30
165 Tony Granato .10 .25
166 Viktor Kozlov .12 .30
167 Patrick Marleau .15 .40
168 Stephane Matteau .10 .25
169 Owen Nolan .15 .40
170 Mike Vernon .12 .30
171 Dino Ciccarelli .15 .40
172 Karl Dykhuis .10 .25
173 Roman Hamrlik .10 .25
174 Daymond Langkow .10 .25
175 Mikael Renberg .12 .30
176 Alexander Selivanov .10 .25
177 Paul Ysebaert .12 .30
178 Sergei Berezin .12 .30
179 Wendel Clark .25 .60
180 Glenn Healy .10 .25
181 Derek King .12 .30
182 Alyn McCauley .12 .30
183 Felix Potvin .25 .60
184 Martin Prochazka RC .12 .30
185 Mats Sundin .15 .40
186 Pavel Bure .15 .40
187 Martin Gelinas .10 .25
188 Trevor Linden .15 .40
189 Kirk McLean .12 .30
190 Mark Messier .30 .75
191 Lubomir Vaic RC .12 .30
192 Mattias Ohlund .12 .30
193 Peter Bondra .15 .40
194 Dale Hunter .12 .30
195 Joe Juneau .10 .25
196 Olaf Kolzig .15 .40
197 Steve Konowalchuk .12 .30
198 Adam Oates .15 .40
199 Bill Ranford .12 .30
200 Jaroslav Svejkovsky .12 .30
P60 Mike Modano PROMO .25 .60

1997-98 Paramount Copper

*COPPER: 1X TO 2.5X BASIC CARDS
*COPPER ROOKIE STAR: .4X TO 1X RC

1997-98 Paramount Dark Gray

*DARK GRAY: 1X TO 2.5X BASIC CARDS
*GRAY ROOKIE STAR: .4X TO 1X RC

1997-98 Paramount Emerald Green

*GREEN: 1X TO 2.5X BASIC CARDS
*GREEN ROOKIE STAR: .4X TO 1X RC

1997-98 Paramount Ice Blue

*ICE BLUE: 12X TO 30X BASIC CARDS
*ICE BLUE ROOKIE STAR: 5X TO 12X RC

1997-98 Paramount Red

*RED: 1X TO 2.5X BASIC CARDS
*RED ROOKIE STAR: .4X TO 1X RC

1997-98 Paramount Silver

*SILVER: 1X TO 2.5X BASIC CARDS
*SILVER ROOKIE STAR: .4X TO 1X RC

1997-98 Paramount Big Numbers Die-Cuts

COMPLETE SET (20) 25.00 50.00
1 Paul Kariya .75 2.00
2 Teemu Selanne .75 2.00
3 Joe Thornton 2.00 5.00
4 Dominik Hasek 1.50 4.00
5 Peter Forsberg 2.00 5.00
6 Patrick Roy 4.00 10.00
7 Joe Sakic 2.00 5.00
8 Sergei Fedorov 1.25 3.00
9 Brendan Shanahan .75 2.00
10 Steve Yzerman 4.00 10.00
11 John Vanbiesbrouck .60 1.50
12 Martin Brodeur 2.50 6.00
13 Doug Gilmour .75 2.00
14 Wayne Gretzky 5.00 12.00
15 Eric Lindros 1.25 3.00
16 Keith Tkachuk .75 2.00
17 Jaromir Jagr 1.25 3.00
18 Brett Hull 1.00 2.50
19 Pavel Bure 1.00 2.50
20 Mark Messier .75 2.00

1997-98 Paramount Canadian Greats

COMPLETE SET (12) 15.00 30.00
1 Paul Kariya .60 1.50
2 Joe Thornton 1.50 4.00
3 Jarome Iginla .75 2.00
4 Patrick Roy 4.00 10.00
5 Joe Sakic 1.25 3.00
6 Brendan Shanahan .60 1.50
7 Steve Yzerman 3.00 8.00
8 Ryan Smyth .50 1.25
9 Martin Brodeur 2.50 6.00
10 Wayne Gretzky 5.00 12.00
11 Eric Lindros 1.00 2.50
12 Mark Messier .60 1.50

1997-98 Paramount Glove Side Laser Cuts

COMPLETE SET (20) 25.00 60.00
1 Guy Hebert 2.00 5.00
2 Dominik Hasek 4.00 10.00
3 Trevor Kidd 2.00 5.00
4 Jeff Hackett 2.00 5.00
5 Patrick Roy 10.00 25.00
6 Ed Belfour 2.50 6.00
7 Chris Osgood 2.00 5.00
8 Curtis Joseph 2.50 6.00
9 John Vanbiesbrouck 2.00 5.00
10 Andy Moog 2.00 5.00
11 Martin Brodeur 6.00 15.00
12 Tommy Salo 2.00 5.00
13 Mike Richter 2.50 6.00
14 Ron Hextall 2.00 5.00
15 Garth Snow 2.00 5.00
16 Nikolai Khabibulin 2.00 5.00
17 Tom Barrasso 2.00 5.00
18 Grant Fuhr 2.00 5.00
19 Mike Vernon 2.00 5.00
20 Felix Potvin 3.00 8.00

1997-98 Paramount Photoengravings

COMPLETE SET (20) 8.00 20.00
1 Paul Kariya .60 1.50
2 Teemu Selanne .60 1.50
3 Joe Thornton 1.50 4.00
4 Dominik Hasek 1.25 3.00
5 Peter Forsberg 1.50 4.00
6 Patrick Roy 3.00 8.00
7 Joe Sakic 1.25 3.00
8 Mike Modano 1.00 2.50
9 Brendan Shanahan .60 1.50
10 Steve Yzerman 3.00 8.00
11 John Vanbiesbrouck .50 1.25
12 Saku Koivu .60 1.50
13 Wayne Gretzky 4.00 10.00
14 John LeClair .60 1.50
15 Eric Lindros .60 1.50
16 Keith Tkachuk .60 1.50
17 Jaromir Jagr 1.00 2.50
18 Brett Hull .75 2.00
19 Pavel Bure .60 1.50
20 Mark Messier .60 1.50

1998-99 Paramount

*COPPER: .8X TO 2X BASIC CARDS
*EMERALD: .8X TO 2X BASIC CARDS
*SILVER: .8X TO 2X BASIC CARDS
*HOLOELECTRIC: 8X TO 20X BASIC CARDS
1 Travis Green .10 .25
2 Guy Hebert .12 .30
3 Paul Kariya .15 .40
4 Josef Marha .10 .25
5 Steve Rucchin .10 .25
6 Tomas Sandstrom .10 .25
7 Teemu Selanne .30 .75
8 Jason Allison .12 .30
9 Per Axelsson .10 .25
10 Ray Bourque .25 .60
11 Anson Carter .12 .30
12 Byron Dafoe .12 .30
13 Ted Donato .10 .25
14 Dave Ellett .12 .30
15 Dimitri Khristich .10 .25
16 Sergei Samsonov .12 .30
17 Matthew Barnaby .10 .25
18 Michal Grosek .10 .25
19 Dominik Hasek .25 .60
20 Brian Holzinger .10 .25
21 Michael Peca .10 .25
22 Miroslav Satan .12 .30
23 Vaclav Varada .10 .25
24 Dixon Ward .12 .30
25 Alexei Zhitnik .10 .25
26 Andrew Cassels .10 .25
27 Theo Fleury .20 .50
28 Jarome Iginla .20 .50
29 Marty McInnis .10 .25
30 Derek Morris .10 .25
31 Michael Nylander .12 .30
32 Cory Stillman .10 .25
33 Rick Tabaracci .10 .25
34 Kevin Dineen .10 .25
35 Nelson Emerson .10 .25
36 Martin Gelinas .10 .25
37 Sami Kapanen .10 .25
38 Trevor Kidd .10 .25
39 Robert Kron .10 .25
40 Jeff O'Neill .10 .25
41 Keith Primeau .12 .30
42 Gary Roberts .10 .25
43 Tony Amonte .12 .30
44 Chris Chelios .15 .40
45 Paul Coffey .15 .40
46 Eric Daze .12 .30
47 Doug Gilmour .20 .50
48 Jeff Hackett .10 .25
49 Jean-Yves Leroux .12 .30
50 Eric Weinrich .10 .25
51 Alexei Zhamnov .10 .25
52 Craig Billington .10 .25
53 Adam Deadmarsh .10 .25
54 Adam Foote .10 .25
55 Peter Forsberg .30 .75
56 Valeri Kamensky .10 .25
57 Claude Lemieux .12 .30
58 Eric Messier .10 .25
59 Sandis Ozolinsh .10 .25
60 Patrick Roy .40 1.00
61 Joe Sakic .30 .75
62 Ed Belfour .15 .40
63 Derian Hatcher .10 .25
64 Brett Hull .30 .75
65 Jamie Langenbrunner .10 .25
66 Jere Lehtinen .12 .30
67 Juha Lind .10 .25
68 Mike Modano .25 .60
69 Joe Nieuwendyk .12 .30
70 Darryl Sydor .10 .25
71 Roman Turek .10 .25
72 Sergei Zubov .12 .30
73 Anders Eriksson .10 .25
74 Sergei Fedorov .25 .60
75 Kevin Hodson .10 .25
76 Vyacheslav Kozlov .10 .25
77 Igor Larionov .15 .40
78 Nicklas Lidstrom .20 .50
79 Darren McCarty .10 .25
80 Larry Murphy .12 .30
81 Chris Osgood .15 .40
82 Brendan Shanahan .15 .40
83 Steve Yzerman .40 1.00
84 Kelly Buchberger .10 .25
85 Mike Grier .10 .25
86 Bill Guerin .15 .40
87 Roman Hamrlik .10 .25
88 Todd Marchant .10 .25
89 Dean McAmmond .10 .25
90 Boris Mironov .10 .25
91 Janne Niinimaa .10 .25
92 Ryan Smyth .12 .30
93 Doug Weight .15 .40
94 Dino Ciccarelli .15 .40
95 Dave Gagner .10 .25
96 Ed Jovanovski .12 .30
97 Viktor Kozlov .12 .30
98 Paul Laus .12 .30
99 Scott Mellanby .10 .25
100 Robert Svehla .10 .25
101 Ray Whitney .10 .25
102 Rob Blake .15 .40
103 Russ Courtnall .10 .25
104 Stephane Fiset .12 .30
105 Glen Murray .12 .30
106 Yanic Perreault .10 .25
107 Luc Robitaille .15 .40
108 Jamie Storr .12 .30
109 Jozef Stumpel .10 .25
110 Vladimir Tsyplakov .10 .25
111 Shayne Corson .12 .30
112 Vincent Damphousse .12 .30
113 Saku Koivu .15 .40
114 Vladimir Malakhov .10 .25
115 Dave Manson .10 .25
116 Mark Recchi .20 .50
117 Martin Rucinsky .10 .25
118 Brian Savage .10 .25
119 Jocelyn Thibault .12 .30
120 Blair Atcheynum .10 .25
121 Andrew Brunette .12 .30
122 Mike Dunham .12 .30
123 Tom Fitzgerald .12 .30
124 Sergei Krivokrasov .10 .25
125 Denny Lambert .12 .30
126 Jay More .10 .25
127 Mikhail Shtalenkov .10 .25
128 Darren Turcotte .12 .30
129 Scott Walker .12 .30
130 Dave Andreychuk .15 .40
131 Jason Arnott .12 .30
132 Martin Brodeur .40 1.00
133 Patrik Elias .15 .40
134 Bobby Holik .10 .25
135 Randy McKay .12 .30
136 Scott Niedermayer .15 .40
137 Krzysztof Oliwa .10 .25
138 Sheldon Souray RC .20 .50
139 Scott Stevens .15 .40
140 Bryan Berard .12 .30
141 Mariusz Czerkawski .10 .25
142 Jason Dawe .10 .25
143 Kenny Jonsson .10 .25
144 Trevor Linden .15 .40
145 Zigmund Palffy .15 .40
146 Rich Pilon .10 .25
147 Robert Reichel .10 .25
148 Tommy Salo .12 .30
149 Bryan Smolinski .10 .25
150 Dan Cloutier .12 .30
151 Adam Graves .10 .25
152 Wayne Gretzky 1.00 2.50
153 Alexei Kovalev .12 .30
154 Pat LaFontaine .15 .40
155 Brian Leetch .12 .30
156 Mike Richter .15 .40
157 Ulf Samuelsson .12 .30
158 Kevin Stevens .12 .30
159 Niklas Sundstrom .10 .25
160 Daniel Alfredsson .15 .40
161 Magnus Arvedson .10 .25
162 Andreas Dackell .10 .25
163 Igor Kravchuk .10 .25
164 Shawn McEachern .10 .25
165 Chris Phillips .10 .25
166 Damian Rhodes .15 .40
167 Ron Tugnutt .10 .25
168 Alexei Yashin .12 .30
169 Rod Brind'Amour .15 .40
170 Alexandre Daigle .10 .25
171 Eric Desjardins .12 .30
172 Colin Forbes .10 .25
173 Chris Gratton .12 .30
174 Ron Hextall .15 .40
175 Trent Klatt .10 .25
176 John LeClair .15 .40
177 Eric Lindros .25 .60
178 John Vanbiesbrouck .15 .40
179 Dainius Zubrus .10 .25
180 Dallas Drake .10 .25
181 Brad Isbister .10 .25
182 Nikolai Khabibulin .15 .40
183 Teppo Numminen .10 .25
184 Jeremy Roenick .25 .60
185 Cliff Ronning .10 .25
186 Keith Tkachuk .15 .40
187 Rick Tocchet .12 .30
188 Oleg Tverdovsky .15 .40
189 Stu Barnes .10 .25
190 Tom Barrasso .12 .30
191 Kevin Hatcher .10 .25
192 Jaromir Jagr .50 1.25
193 Darius Kasparaitis .10 .25
194 Alexei Morozov .10 .25
195 Fredrik Olausson .10 .25
196 Jiri Slegr .10 .25
197 Martin Straka .10 .25
198 Jim Campbell .10 .25
199 Kelly Chase .10 .25
200 Craig Conroy .10 .25
201 Geoff Courtnall .12 .30
202 Pavol Demitra .20 .50

203 Grant Fuhr .25 .60
204 Al MacInnis .20 .50
205 Jamie McLennan .12 .30
206 Chris Pronger .15 .40
207 Pierre Turgeon .12 .30
208 Tony Twist .10 .25
209 Jeff Friesen .10 .25
210 Tony Granato .10 .25
211 Patrick Marleau .15 .40
212 Stephane Matteau .10 .25
213 Marty McSorley .12 .30
214 Owen Nolan .15 .40
215 Marco Sturm .10 .25
216 Mike Vernon .12 .30
217 Karl Dykhuis .10 .25
218 Sandy McCarty .10 .25
219 Mikael Renberg .12 .30
220 Stephane Richer .10 .25
221 Alexander Selivanov .10 .25
222 Paul Ysebaert .10 .25
223 Rob Zamuner .10 .25
224 Sergei Berezin .12 .30
225 Tie Domi .12 .30
226 Mike Johnson .10 .25
227 Curtis Joseph .20 .50
228 Derek King .10 .25
229 Igor Korolev .10 .25
230 Mathieu Schneider .10 .25
231 Mats Sundin .15 .40
232 Todd Bertuzzi .15 .40
233 Donald Brashear .10 .25
234 Pavel Bure .15 .40
235 Arturs Irbe .12 .30
236 Mark Messier .30 .75
237 Alexander Mogilny .12 .30
238 Mattias Ohlund .10 .25
239 Dave Scatchard .10 .25
240 Garth Snow .12 .30
241 Brian Bellows .10 .25
242 Peter Bondra .15 .40
243 Jeff Brown .10 .25
244 Sergei Gonchar .10 .25
245 Calle Johansson .10 .25
246 Joe Juneau .10 .25
247 Olaf Kolzig .15 .40
248 Steve Konowalchuk .10 .25
249 Adam Oates .15 .40
250 Richard Zednik .10 .25
NNO Martin Brodeur SAMPLE .40 1.00

1998-99 Paramount Ice Blue

*ICE BLUE: 6X TO 15X BASIC CARDS

1998-99 Paramount Glove Side Laser Cuts

1 Guy Hebert 2.00 5.00
2 Byron Dafoe 2.00 5.00
3 Dominik Hasek 4.00 10.00
4 Trevor Kidd 1.50 4.00
5 Jeff Hackett 1.50 4.00
6 Patrick Roy 6.00 15.00
7 Ed Belfour 2.50 6.00
8 Chris Osgood 2.50 6.00
9 Mike Dunham 2.00 5.00
10 Martin Brodeur 6.00 15.00
11 Tommy Salo 2.00 5.00
12 Mike Richter 2.50 6.00
13 Damian Rhodes 2.50 6.00
14 Ron Hextall 2.50 6.00
15 Nikolai Khabibulin 2.50 6.00
16 Tom Barrasso 2.00 5.00
17 Grant Fuhr 4.00 10.00
18 Mike Vernon 2.00 5.00
19 Curtis Joseph 3.00 8.00
20 Olaf Kolzig 2.50 6.00

1998-99 Paramount Hall of Fame Bound

*PROOF/20: 1X TO 2.5X BASIC INSERTS
1 Teemu Selanne 4.00 10.00
2 Dominik Hasek 3.00 8.00
3 Peter Forsberg 4.00 10.00
4 Patrick Roy 5.00 12.00
5 Steve Yzerman 5.00 12.00
6 Martin Brodeur 5.00 12.00
7 Wayne Gretzky 12.00 30.00
8 Eric Lindros 3.00 8.00
9 Jaromir Jagr 6.00 15.00
10 Mark Messier 4.00 10.00

1998-99 Paramount Ice Galaxy

COMPLETE SET (10) 100.00 200.00
SILVER/50: .8X TO 2X BRONZE/140*
1 Paul Kariya 6.00 15.00
2 Peter Forsberg 8.00 20.00
3 Patrick Roy 15.00 40.00
4 Joe Sakic 6.00 15.00
5 Steve Yzerman 15.00 40.00
6 Martin Brodeur 10.00 25.00
7 Wayne Gretzky 25.00 60.00
8 Alexei Yashin 4.00 10.00
9 Eric Lindros 8.00 20.00
10 Curtis Joseph 6.00 15.00

1998-99 Paramount Special Delivery Die-Cuts

1 Paul Kariya .60 1.50
2 Teemu Selanne 1.25 3.00
3 Sergei Samsonov .50 1.25
4 Peter Forsberg 1.25 3.00
5 Joe Sakic 1.25 3.00
6 Mike Modano 1.00 2.50
7 Sergei Fedorov 1.00 2.50
8 Brendan Shanahan .60 1.50
9 Steve Yzerman 1.50 4.00
10 Saku Koivu .60 1.50
11 Zigmund Palffy .60 1.50
12 Wayne Gretzky 4.00 10.00
13 John LeClair .60 1.50
14 Eric Lindros 1.00 2.50
15 Keith Tkachuk .60 1.50
16 Jaromir Jagr 2.00 5.00
17 Mats Sundin .60 1.50
18 Pavel Bure .60 1.50
19 Mark Messier 1.25 3.00
20 Peter Bondra .60 1.50

1998-99 Paramount Team Checklists Die-Cuts

1 Teemu Selanne 1.25 3.00
2 Sergei Samsonov .50 1.25
3 Dominik Hasek 1.00 2.50
4 Theo Fleury .75 2.00
5 Keith Primeau .50 1.25
6 Chris Chelios .60 1.50
7 Patrick Roy 1.50 4.00
8 Mike Modano 1.00 2.50
9 Steve Yzerman 1.50 4.00
10 Ryan Smyth .50 1.25
11 Dino Ciccarelli .60 1.50
12 Rob Blake .60 1.50
13 Saku Koivu .60 1.50
14 Tom Fitzgerald .50 1.25
15 Martin Brodeur 1.50 4.00
16 Zigmund Palffy .60 1.50
17 Wayne Gretzky 4.00 10.00
18 Alexei Yashin .50 1.25
19 Eric Lindros 1.00 2.50
20 Keith Tkachuk .60 1.50
21 Jaromir Jagr 2.00 5.00
22 Grant Fuhr 1.00 2.50
23 Patrick Marleau .60 1.50
24 Rob Zamuner .40 1.00
25 Mats Sundin .60 1.50
26 Mark Messier 1.25 3.00
27 Peter Bondra .60 1.50

1999-00 Paramount

1 Matt Cullen .05 .15
2 Guy Hebert .10 .25
3 Paul Kariya .10 .25
4 Marty McInnis .05 .15
5 Fredrik Olausson .05 .15
6 Steve Rucchin .05 .15
7 Ruslan Salei .05 .15
8 Teemu Selanne .20 .50
9 Jason Botterill .05 .15
10 Andrew Brunette .05 .15
11 Kelly Buchberger .05 .15
12 Matt Johnson .05 .15
13 Norm Maracle .05 .15
14 Damian Rhodes .05 .15
15 Steve Staios .05 .15
16 Jason Allison .07 .20
17 Ray Bourque .15 .40
18 Anson Carter .07 .20
19 Byron Dafoe .07 .20
20 Jonathan Girard .05 .15
21 Steve Heinze .05 .15
22 Dimitri Khristich .05 .15
23 Sergei Samsonov .07 .20
24 Joe Thornton .15 .40
25 Stu Barnes .07 .20
26 Curtis Brown .05 .15
27 Michal Grosek .05 .15
28 Dominik Hasek .15 .40
29 Michael Peca .07 .20
30 Geoff Sanderson .07 .20
31 Miroslav Satan .07 .20
32 Dixon Ward .07 .20
33 Jason Woolley .05 .15
34 Alexei Zhitnik .05 .15
35 Valeri Bure .05 .15
36 Rene Corbet .05 .15
37 Rico Fata .05 .15
38 Jean-Sebastien Giguere .10 .25
39 Phil Housley .07 .20
40 Jarome Iginla .12 .30
41 Derek Morris .05 .15
42 Steve Smith .05 .15
43 Cory Stillman .05 .15
44 Ron Francis .12 .30
45 Martin Gelinas .05 .15
46 Arturs Irbe .07 .20
47 Sami Kapanen .05 .15
48 Jeff O'Neill .05 .15
49 Keith Primeau .07 .20
50 Gary Roberts .05 .15
51 Shane Willis .05 .15
52 Tony Amonte .07 .20
53 Eric Daze .07 .20
54 J-P Dumont .07 .20
55 Doug Gilmour .12 .30
56 Dean McAmmond .05 .15
57 Boris Mironov .05 .15
58 Jocelyn Thibault .07 .20
59 Alexei Zhamnov .05 .15
60 Adam Deadmarsh .05 .15
61 Marc Denis .07 .20
62 Chris Drury .07 .20
63 Peter Forsberg .20 .50
64 Milan Hejduk .07 .20
65 Claude Lemieux .05 .15
66 Sandis Ozolinsh .05 .15
67 Patrick Roy .25 .60
68 Joe Sakic .20 .50
69 Ed Belfour .10 .25
70 Guy Carbonneau .05 .15
71 Derian Hatcher .07 .20
72 Brett Hull .20 .50
73 Jamie Langenbrunner .05 .15
74 Jere Lehtinen .07 .20
75 Mike Modano .15 .40
76 Joe Nieuwendyk .07 .20
77 Darryl Sydor .07 .20
78 Sergei Zubov .07 .20
79 Chris Chelios .10 .25
80 Sergei Fedorov .60 1.50
81 Vyacheslav Kozlov .05 .15
82 Igor Larionov .10 .25
83 Nicklas Lidstrom .10 .25
84 Darren McCarty .05 .15
85 Larry Murphy .07 .20
86 Chris Osgood .10 .25
87 Brendan Shanahan .10 .25
88 Steve Yzerman .25 .60
89 Josef Beranek .05 .15
90 Pat Falloon .07 .20
91 Mike Grier .05 .15
92 Bill Guerin .10 .25
93 Rem Murray .05 .15
94 Tom Poti .05 .15
95 Tommy Salo .07 .20
96 Ryan Smyth .07 .20
97 Doug Weight .10 .25
98 Pavel Bure .10 .25
99 Sean Burke .05 .15
100 Viktor Kozlov .05 .15
101 Oleg Kvasha .05 .15
102 Scott Mellanby .05 .15
103 Rob Niedermayer .05 .15
104 Marcus Nilsson .05 .15
105 Mark Parrish .05 .15
106 Ray Whitney .07 .20
107 Donald Audette .05 .15
108 Rob Blake .10 .25
109 Stephane Fiset .07 .20
110 Glen Murray .07 .20
111 Zigmund Palffy .10 .25
112 Jamie Storr .05 .15
113 Jozef Stumpel .05 .15
114 Benoit Brunet .05 .15
115 Shayne Corson .07 .20
116 Jeff Hackett .05 .15
117 Saku Koivu .10 .25
118 Trevor Linden .10 .25
119 Vladimir Malakhov .05 .15
120 Martin Rucinsky .05 .15
121 Igor Ulanov .05 .15
122 Dainius Zubrus .07 .20
123 Mike Dunham .05 .15
124 Tom Fitzgerald .05 .15
125 Greg Johnson .05 .15
126 Sergei Krivokrasov .05 .15
127 David Legwand .05 .15
128 Cliff Ronning .05 .15
129 Scott Walker .05 .15
130 Jason Arnott .07 .20
131 Martin Brodeur .25 .60
132 Patrik Elias .10 .25
133 Bobby Holik .05 .15
134 John Madden RC .60 1.50
135 Randy McKay .05 .15
136 Brendan Morrison .07 .20
137 Scott Niedermayer .10 .25
138 Brian Rolston .07 .20
139 Petr Sykora .07 .20
140 Eric Brewer .05 .15
141 Mariusz Czerkawski .05 .15
142 Kenny Jonsson .05 .15
143 Claude Lapointe .07 .20
144 Mats Lindgren .05 .15
145 Vladimir Orszagh RC .05 .15
146 Felix Potvin .15 .40
147 Mike Watt .05 .15
148 Theo Fleury .12 .30
149 Adam Graves .07 .20
150 Todd Harvey .05 .15
151 Valeri Kamensky .05 .15
152 Brian Leetch .07 .20
153 John MacLean .07 .20
154 Manny Malhotra .07 .20
155 Petr Nedved .05 .15
156 Mike Richter .10 .25
157 Kevin Stevens .05 .15
158 Daniel Alfredsson .10 .25
159 Magnus Arvedson .05 .15
160 Radek Bonk .05 .15
161 Andreas Dackell .05 .15
162 Marian Hossa .10 .25
163 Shawn McEachern .05 .15
164 Wade Redden .05 .15
165 Sami Salo .07 .20
166 Ron Tugnutt .07 .20
167 Alexei Yashin .07 .20
168 Rod Brind'Amour .10 .25
169 Eric Desjardins .07 .20
170 Keith Jones .05 .15
171 Daymond Langkow .07 .20
172 John LeClair .10 .25
173 Eric Lindros .15 .40
174 Mark Recchi .12 .30
175 Mikael Renberg .05 .15
176 John Vanbiesbrouck .10 .25
177 Greg Adams .05 .15
178 Dallas Drake .05 .15
179 Nikolai Khabibulin .07 .20
180 Jyrki Lumme .05 .15
181 Teppo Numminen .05 .15
182 Jeremy Roenick .15 .40
183 Mike Sullivan .05 .15
184 Keith Tkachuk .10 .25
185 Rick Tocchet .07 .20
186 Matthew Barnaby .05 .15
187 Tom Barrasso .07 .20
188 Jan Hrdina .05 .15
189 Jaromir Jagr .30 .75
190 Alexei Kovalev .07 .20
191 Ian Moran .05 .15
192 Martin Straka .05 .15
193 German Titov .05 .15
194 Craig Conroy .05 .15
195 Pavol Demitra .12 .30
196 Grant Fuhr .15 .40
197 Jochen Hecht RC .15 .40
198 Al MacInnis .12 .30
199 Ricard Persson .05 .15
200 Chris Pronger .10 .25
201 Pierre Turgeon .07 .20
202 Scott Young .05 .15
203 Vincent Damphousse .07 .20
204 Jeff Friesen .07 .20
205 Alexander Korolyuk .05 .15
206 Patrick Marleau .10 .25
207 Owen Nolan .10 .25
208 Mike Ricci .05 .15
209 Steve Shields .07 .20
210 Marco Sturm .05 .15
211 Ron Sutter .05 .15
212 Mike Vernon .07 .20
213 Karel Betik RC .05 .15
214 Dan Cloutier .07 .20
215 Jassen Cullimore .05 .15
216 Colin Forbes .05 .15
217 Chris Gratton .05 .15
218 Pavel Kubina .05 .15
219 Vincent Lecavalier .10 .25
220 Darcy Tucker .05 .15
221 Bryan Berard .05 .15
222 Sergei Berezin .07 .20
223 Tie Domi .07 .20
224 Mike Johnson .07 .20
225 Curtis Joseph .12 .30
226 Derek King .05 .15
227 Igor Korolev .05 .15
228 Yanic Perreault .05 .15
229 Steve Sullivan .05 .15
230 Mats Sundin .10 .25
231 Steve Thomas .05 .15
232 Adrian Aucoin .05 .15
233 Donald Brashear .05 .15
234 Ed Jovanovski .07 .20
235 Mark Messier .20 .50
236 Alexander Mogilny .07 .20
237 Bill Muckalt .05 .15
238 Markus Naslund .10 .25
239 Mattias Ohlund .05 .15
240 Garth Snow .07 .20
241 Brian Bellows .07 .20
242 Peter Bondra .10 .25
243 Jan Bulis .05 .15
244 Sergei Gonchar .05 .15
245 Olaf Kolzig .10 .25
246 Steve Konowalchuk .05 .15
247 Andrei Nikolishin .05 .15
248 Adam Oates .10 .25
249 Alexei Tezikov RC .10 .25
250 Richard Zednik .05 .15
251 Patrik Stefan RC .10 .25
252 Jonathan Girard AG .05 .15
253 Maxim Afinogenov AG .05 .15
254 Byron Ritchie AG .05 .15
255 Alex Tanguay AG .07 .20
256 Brenden Morrow AG .10 .25
257 Yuri Butsayev AG .05 .15
258 Ivan Novoseltsev AG .12 .30
259 Frantisek Kaberle AG .05 .15
260 Richard Lintner AG .05 .15
261 Tim Connolly AG .05 .15
263 Jason Doig AG .05 .15
264 Mike Fisher AG .10 .25
266 Stan Neckar AG .05 .15
267 Andrew Ference AG .05 .15
268 Paul Mara AG .05 .15
269 Steve Kariya AG .10 .25

1999-00 Paramount Copper

*COPPER: 2X TO 5X BASIC CARDS

1999-00 Paramount Emerald

*EMERALD: 2X TO 5X BASIC CARDS

1999-00 Paramount Gold

*GOLD: 2.5X TO 6X BASIC CARDS

1999-00 Paramount Holographic Emerald

*HOLO.EMERALD: 25X TO 60X BASIC CARDS

1999-00 Paramount Holographic Gold

*HOLO.GOLD: 10X TO 25X BASIC CARDS

1999-00 Paramount Holographic Silver

*HOLO.SILVER: 20X TO 50X BASIC CARDS

1999-00 Paramount Ice Blue

*ICE BLUE: 15X TO 40X BASIC CARDS

1999-00 Paramount Premiere Date

*PREM.DATE: 30X TO 80X BASIC CARDS

1999-00 Paramount Red

*RED: .6X TO 1.5X BASIC CARDS

1999-00 Paramount Glove Side Net Fusions

COMPLETE SET (20) 50.00 100.00
1 Guy Hebert 2.00 5.00
2 Byron Dafoe 2.00 5.00
3 Dominik Hasek 5.00 12.00
4 Arturs Irbe 2.00 5.00
5 Jocelyn Thibault 2.00 5.00
6 Patrick Roy 12.50 30.00
7 Ed Belfour 2.50 6.00
8 Chris Osgood 2.00 5.00
9 Tommy Salo 2.00 5.00
10 Jeff Hackett 2.00 5.00
11 Martin Brodeur 6.00 15.00
12 Felix Potvin 2.50 6.00
13 Mike Richter 2.50 6.00
14 Ron Tugnutt 2.00 5.00
15 John Vanbiesbrouck 2.00 5.00
16 Nikolai Khabibulin 2.00 5.00
17 Tom Barrasso 2.00 5.00
18 Grant Fuhr 2.00 5.00
19 Curtis Joseph 2.50 6.00
20 Olaf Kolzig 2.00 5.00

1999-00 Paramount Hall of Fame Bound

COMPLETE SET (10) 75.00 150.00
*PROOFS/35: 1.2X TO 3X BASIC INSERTS
1 Paul Kariya 5.00 12.00
2 Ray Bourque 8.00 20.00
3 Dominik Hasek 8.00 20.00
4 Peter Forsberg 10.00 25.00
5 Patrick Roy 15.00 40.00
6 Steve Yzerman 15.00 40.00
7 Martin Brodeur 12.50 30.00
8 Eric Lindros 5.00 12.00
9 Jaromir Jagr 6.00 15.00
10 Mark Messier 5.00 12.00

1999-00 Paramount Ice Advantage

COMPLETE SET (20) 20.00 40.00
1 Paul Kariya .60 1.50
2 Teemu Selanne .60 1.50
3 Dominik Hasek 1.25 3.00
4 Jarome Iginla .75 2.00
5 Peter Forsberg 1.50 4.00
6 Patrick Roy 3.00 8.00
7 Joe Sakic 1.25 3.00
8 Joe Nieuwendyk .50 1.25
9 Brendan Shanahan .60 1.50
10 Steve Yzerman 3.00 8.00
11 Doug Weight .50 1.25
12 Pavel Bure .60 1.50
13 Jeff Hackett .50 1.25
14 Martin Brodeur 1.50 4.00
15 Marian Hossa .60 1.50
16 Eric Lindros .60 1.50
17 Jaromir Jagr 1.00 2.50
18 Curtis Joseph .60 1.50
19 Mats Sundin .60 1.50
20 Mark Messier .60 1.50

1999-00 Paramount Ice Alliance

COMPLETE SET (28) 20.00 40.00
1 Paul Kariya .60 1.50
2 Damian Rhodes .50 1.25
3 Ray Bourque 1.00 2.50
4 Dominik Hasek 1.50 4.00
5 Jarome Iginla .75 2.00
6 Keith Primeau .50 1.25
7 Tony Amonte .50 1.25
8 Patrick Roy 3.00 8.00
9 Mike Modano 1.00 2.50
10 Steve Yzerman 3.00 8.00
11 Bill Guerin .50 1.25
12 Pavel Bure .60 1.50
13 Luc Robitaille .50 1.25
14 Jeff Hackett .50 1.25
15 Cliff Ronning .50 1.25
16 Martin Brodeur 1.50 4.00
17 Felix Potvin .60 1.50
18 Brian Leetch .50 1.25
19 Alexei Yashin .50 1.25
20 Eric Lindros .60 1.50
21 Keith Tkachuk .60 1.50
22 Jaromir Jagr 1.00 2.50
23 Pierre Turgeon .50 1.25
24 Vincent Damphousse .50 1.25
25 Vincent Lecavalier .60 1.50
26 Curtis Joseph .60 1.50
27 Mark Messier .60 1.50
28 Peter Bondra .50 1.25

1999-00 Paramount Personal Best

COMPLETE SET (36) 30.00 60.00
1 Paul Kariya .75 2.00
2 Teemu Selanne .75 2.00
3 Ray Bourque 1.25 3.00
4 Sergei Samsonov .40 1.00
5 Dominik Hasek 1.50 4.00
6 Michael Peca .40 1.00
7 Tony Amonte .40 1.00
8 Chris Drury .40 1.00
9 Peter Forsberg 2.00 5.00
10 Patrick Roy 4.00 10.00
11 Joe Sakic 1.50 4.00
12 Ed Belfour .75 2.00
13 Brett Hull 1.00 2.50
14 Mike Modano 1.25 3.00
15 Joe Nieuwendyk .40 1.00
16 Sergei Fedorov 1.50 4.00
17 Brendan Shanahan .75 2.00
18 Steve Yzerman 4.00 10.00
19 Pavel Bure .75 2.00
20 Saku Koivu .75 2.00
21 Martin Brodeur 2.00 5.00
22 Theo Fleury .40 1.00
23 Mike Richter .75 2.00
24 Alexei Yashin .40 1.00
25 John LeClair .75 2.00
26 Eric Lindros .75 2.00
27 Mark Recchi .40 1.00
28 John Vanbiesbrouck .40 1.00
29 Jeremy Roenick 1.00 2.50
30 Keith Tkachuk .75 2.00
31 Jaromir Jagr 1.25 3.00
32 Pavol Demitra .40 1.00
33 Vincent Lecavalier .75 2.00
34 Curtis Joseph .75 2.00
35 Mats Sundin .75 2.00
36 Mark Messier .75 2.00

2000-01 Paramount

COMPLETE SET (252) 20.00 40.00
1 Antti Aalto .10 .25
2 Maxim Balmochnykh .10 .25
3 Matt Cullen .10 .25
4 Guy Hebert .12 .30
5 Paul Kariya .15 .40
6 Steve Rucchin .10 .25
7 Teemu Selanne .30 .75
8 Oleg Tverdovsky .10 .25
9 Donald Audette .12 .30
10 Andrew Brunette .10 .25
11 Shean Donovan .10 .25
12 Scott Fankhouser .10 .25
13 Ray Ferraro .10 .25
14 Damian Rhodes .10 .25
15 Patrik Stefan .12 .30
16 Jason Allison .12 .30
17 Anson Carter .12 .30
18 Byron Dafoe .12 .30
19 John Grahame .10 .25
20 Brian Rolston .10 .25
21 Sergei Samsonov .12 .30
22 Don Sweeney .10 .25
23 Joe Thornton .25 .60
24 Maxim Afinogenov .10 .25
25 Stu Barnes .10 .25
26 Martin Biron .12 .30
27 Curtis Brown .10 .25
28 Doug Gilmour .20 .50
29 Chris Gratton .10 .25
30 Dominik Hasek .25 .60
31 Michael Peca .12 .30
32 Miroslav Satan .12 .30
33 Fred Brathwaite .12 .30
34 Valeri Bure .12 .30
35 Phil Housley .12 .30
36 Jarome Iginla .20 .50
37 Oleg Saprykin .10 .25
38 Marc Savard .10 .25
39 Cory Stillman .10 .25
40 Clarke Wilm .10 .25
41 Rod Brind'Amour .15 .40
42 Ron Francis .20 .50
43 Arturs Irbe .12 .30
44 Sami Kapanen .12 .30
45 Jeff O'Neill .10 .25
46 Dave Tanabe .10 .25
47 Glen Wesley .10 .25
48 Tony Amonte .12 .30
49 Michal Grosek .10 .25
50 Dean McAmmond .10 .25
51 Boris Mironov .10 .25
52 Michael Nylander .10 .25
53 Steve Sullivan .10 .25
54 Jocelyn Thibault .12 .30
55 Alexei Zhamnov .12 .30
56 Ray Bourque .25 .60
57 Adam Deadmarsh .12 .30
58 Chris Drury .12 .30
59 Adam Foote .12 .30
60 Peter Forsberg .30 .75
61 Milan Hejduk .12 .30
62 Patrick Roy .40 1.00
63 Joe Sakic .30 .75
64 Martin Skoula .12 .30
65 Alex Tanguay .12 .30
66 Kevyn Adams .10 .25
67 Serge Aubin RC .12 .30
68 Marc Denis .12 .30
69 Ted Drury .10 .25
70 Steve Heinze .10 .25
71 Lyle Odelein .10 .25
72 Ron Tugnutt .12 .30
73 Ed Belfour .15 .40
74 Derian Hatcher .12 .30
75 Brett Hull .30 .75
76 Jamie Langenbrunner .12 .30
77 Jere Lehtinen .12 .30
78 Roman Lyashenko .10 .25
79 Mike Modano .25 .60
80 Brenden Morrow .12 .30
81 Joe Nieuwendyk .12 .30
82 Sergei Zubov .12 .30
83 Chris Chelios .15 .40
84 Mathieu Dandenault .10 .25
85 Sergei Fedorov .25 .60
86 Martin Lapointe .12 .30
87 Nicklas Lidstrom .15 .40
88 Chris Osgood .15 .40
89 Brendan Shanahan .15 .40
90 Pat Verbeek .12 .30
91 Jesse Wallin .10 .25
92 Ken Wregget .12 .30
93 Steve Yzerman .40 1.00
94 Mike Grier .10 .25
95 Bill Guerin .15 .40
96 Todd Marchant .10 .25
97 Tom Poti .10 .25
98 Tommy Salo .12 .30
99 Alexander Selivanov .10 .25
100 Ryan Smyth .12 .30
101 Doug Weight .15 .40
102 Pavel Bure .15 .40
103 Brad Ference .10 .25
104 Trevor Kidd .10 .25
105 Viktor Kozlov .12 .30
106 Scott Mellanby .10 .25
107 Ivan Novoseltsev .10 .25
108 Robert Svehla .10 .25
109 Ray Whitney .10 .25
110 Rob Blake .15 .40
111 Stephane Fiset .12 .30
112 Glen Murray .10 .25
113 Zigmund Palffy .15 .40
114 Luc Robitaille .15 .40
115 Bryan Smolinski .12 .30
116 Jamie Storr .10 .25
117 Jozef Stumpel .10 .25
118 Manny Fernandez .10 .25
119 Sergei Krivokrasov .10 .25
120 Jamie McLennan .12 .30
121 Jeff Nielsen .10 .25
122 Sean O'Donnell .10 .25
123 Jeff Odgers .10 .25
124 Scott Pellerin .10 .25
125 Jeff Hackett .10 .25
126 Saku Koivu .15 .40
127 Trevor Linden .10 .25
128 Patrick Poulin .10 .25
129 Mike Ribeiro .10 .25
130 Martin Rucinsky .10 .25
131 Brian Savage .10 .25
132 Jose Theodore .15 .40
133 Dainius Zubrus .10 .25
134 Mike Dunham .10 .25
135 Greg Johnson .10 .25
136 David Legwand .15 .40
137 Cliff Ronning .10 .25
138 Rob Valicevic .10 .25
139 Tomas Vokoun .12 .30
140 Vitali Yachmenev .10 .25
141 Jason Arnott .12 .30
142 Martin Brodeur .40 1.00
143 Patrik Elias .15 .40
144 Scott Gomez .12 .30
145 John Madden .12 .30
146 Alexander Mogilny .12 .30
147 Scott Niedermayer .15 .40
148 Brian Rafalski .10 .25
149 Scott Stevens .15 .40
150 Petr Sykora .12 .30
151 Colin White RC .10 .25
152 Tim Connolly .10 .25
153 Mariusz Czerkawski .10 .25
154 Brad Isbister .10 .25
155 Jason Krog .10 .25
156 Claude Lapointe .10 .25
157 Bill Muckalt .10 .25
158 Steve Valiquette RC .12 .30
159 Radek Dvorak .12 .30
160 Theo Fleury .20 .50
161 Adam Graves .12 .30
162 Jan Hlavac .12 .30
163 Brian Leetch .12 .30
164 Sylvain Lefebvre .10 .25
165 Mark Messier .30 .75
166 Petr Nedved .12 .30
167 Mike Richter .15 .40
168 Mike York .10 .25
169 Daniel Alfredsson .15 .40
170 Magnus Arvedson .10 .25
171 Radek Bonk .12 .30
172 Marian Hossa .15 .40
173 Jani Hurme RC .60 1.50
174 Patrick Lalime .12 .30
175 Shawn McEachern .12 .30
176 Vaclav Prospal .10 .25
177 Brian Boucher .12 .30
178 Andy Delmore .10 .25
179 Eric Desjardins .12 .30
180 Simon Gagne .15 .40
181 Daymond Langkow .10 .25
182 John LeClair .15 .40
183 Eric Lindros .25 .60
184 Keith Primeau .12 .30
185 Mark Recchi .20 .50
186 Rick Tocchet .12 .30
187 Shane Doan .12 .30
188 Robert Esche .10 .25
189 Travis Green .10 .25
190 Trevor Letowski .10 .25
191 Stanislav Neckar .10 .25
192 Teppo Numminen .10 .25
193 Jeremy Roenick .25 .60
194 Keith Tkachuk .15 .40
195 Jean-Sebastien Aubin .12 .30
196 Matthew Barnaby .10 .25
197 Jan Hrdina .10 .25
198 Jaromir Jagr .50 1.25
199 Alexei Kovalev .12 .30
200 Robert Lang .10 .25
201 John Slaney .10 .25
202 Martin Straka .12 .30
203 Lubos Bartecko .10 .25
204 Pavol Demitra .20 .50
205 Michal Handzus .10 .25
206 Al MacInnis .20 .50
207 Jamal Mayers .10 .25
208 Chris Pronger .15 .40
209 Roman Turek .12 .30
210 Pierre Turgeon .12 .30
211 Scott Young .10 .25
212 Vincent Damphousse .12 .30
213 Jeff Friesen .10 .25
214 Patrick Marleau .15 .40
215 Owen Nolan .15 .40
216 Mike Ricci .10 .25
217 Steve Shields .10 .25
218 Brad Stuart .12 .30
219 Dan Cloutier .12 .30
220 Brian Holzinger .10 .25
221 Mike Johnson .10 .25
222 Vincent Lecavalier .15 .40
223 Fredrik Modin .10 .25
224 Petr Svoboda .10 .25
225 Todd Warriner .10 .25
226 Nikolai Antropov .12 .30
227 Sergei Berezin .10 .25
228 Tie Domi .12 .30
229 Jeff Farkas .10 .25
230 Curtis Joseph .20 .50
231 Tomas Kaberle .10 .25
232 Yanic Perreault .10 .25
233 Mats Sundin .15 .40
234 Steve Thomas .10 .25
235 Darcy Tucker .10 .25
236 Todd Bertuzzi .12 .30
237 Andrew Cassels .10 .25
238 Ed Jovanovski .12 .30
239 Steve Kariya .10 .25
240 Markus Naslund .15 .40
241 Mattias Ohlund .10 .25
242 Felix Potvin .25 .60
243 Peter Bondra .15 .40
244 Sergei Gonchar .10 .25
245 Jeff Halpern .10 .25
246 Olaf Kolzig .15 .40
247 Steve Konowalchuk .10 .25
248 Adam Oates .15 .40
249 Chris Simon .10 .25
250 Richard Zednik .10 .25
251 Daniel Sedin .20 .50
252 Henrik Sedin .20 .50

2000-01 Paramount Copper

*VETS: 1.5X TO 4X BASIC CARDS
165 Mark Messier 1.25 3.00

2000-01 Paramount Gold

*GOLD: 2X TO 5X BASIC CARDS
165 Mark Messier 2.00 5.00

2000-01 Paramount HoloGold

*HOLOGOLD/74: 10X TO 25X BASIC CARDS
165 Mark Messier 10.00 25.00

2000-01 Paramount HoloSilver

*HOLOSILVER/74: 10X TO 25X BASIC CARDS
165 Mark Messier 10.00 25.00

2000-01 Paramount Ice Blue

*BLUE/50: 15X TO 40X BASIC CARDS
165 Mark Messier 15.00 40.00

2000-01 Paramount Premiere Date

*PREM.DATE/45: 20X TO 50X BASIC CARDS
165 Mark Messier 20.00 50.00

2000-01 Paramount Epic Scope

COMPLETE SET (20) 30.00 60.00
1 Paul Kariya 1.00 2.50
2 Teemu Selanne 1.00 2.50
3 Dominik Hasek 2.00 5.00
4 Ray Bourque 2.00 5.00
5 Peter Forsberg 2.50 6.00
6 Patrick Roy 5.00 12.00
7 Joe Sakic 2.00 5.00
8 Brett Hull 1.25 3.00
9 Mike Modano 1.50 4.00
10 Brendan Shanahan 1.00 2.50
11 Steve Yzerman 5.00 12.00
12 Pavel Bure 1.00 2.50
13 Martin Brodeur 2.50 6.00
14 Scott Gomez .75 2.00
15 Brian Boucher .75 2.00
16 John LeClair 1.00 2.50
17 Jaromir Jagr 1.50 4.00
18 Vincent Lecavalier 1.00 2.50
19 Curtis Joseph 1.00 2.50
20 Mats Sundin 1.00 2.50

2000-01 Paramount Freeze Frame

COMPLETE SET (36) 50.00 100.00
1 Paul Kariya 1.25 3.00
2 Teemu Selanne 1.25 3.00
3 Doug Gilmour 1.25 3.00
4 Dominik Hasek 2.50 6.00

5 Valeri Bure .40 1.00
6 Tony Amonte 1.00 2.50
7 Ray Bourque 2.50 6.00
8 Peter Forsberg 3.00 8.00
9 Joe Sakic 2.50 6.00
10 Patrick Roy 6.00 15.00
11 Ed Belfour 1.25 3.00
12 Brett Hull 1.50 4.00
13 Mike Modano 2.00 5.00
14 Sergei Fedorov 2.50 6.00
15 Brendan Shanahan 1.25 3.00
16 Steve Yzerman 6.00 15.00
17 Doug Weight 1.00 2.50
18 Pavel Bure 1.25 3.00
19 Luc Robitaille 1.00 2.50
20 Saku Koivu 1.25 3.00
21 Martin Brodeur 3.00 8.00
22 Scott Gomez .40 1.00
23 Tim Connolly .40 1.00
24 Marian Hossa 1.25 3.00
25 Brian Boucher 1.25 3.00
26 John LeClair 1.25 3.00
27 Mark Recchi 1.00 2.50
28 Jaromir Jagr 2.00 5.00
29 Jeremy Roenick 1.50 4.00
30 Chris Pronger 1.00 2.50
31 Roman Turek 1.00 2.50
32 Owen Nolan 1.00 2.50
33 Vincent Lecavalier 1.25 3.00
34 Mats Sundin 1.25 3.00
35 Curtis Joseph 1.25 3.00
36 Olaf Kolzig 1.00 2.50

2000-01 Paramount Game Used Sticks

1 Ron Francis/165 10.00 25.00
2 Ray Bourque/190 12.00 30.00
3 Adam Deadmarsh/200 10.00 25.00
4 Chris Drury/205 10.00 25.00
5 Joe Sakic/190 10.00 25.00
6 Martin Skoula/200 10.00 25.00
7 Alex Tanguay/200 10.00 25.00
8 Ed Belfour/205 15.00 40.00
9 Chris Chelios/165 12.50 30.00
10 Chris Osgood/205 10.00 25.00
11 Doug Weight/165 10.00 25.00
12 Luc Robitaille/185 10.00 25.00
13 Alexander Mogilny/155 8.00 20.00
14 Theo Fleury/190 10.00 25.00
15 Eric Lindros/190 12.50 30.00
16 Al MacInnis/165 10.00 25.00
17 Curtis Joseph/150 12.50 30.00

2000-01 Paramount Jersey and Patches

1 Jarome Iginla 60.00 125.00
2 Tony Amonte 40.00 100.00
3 Ray Bourque 75.00 150.00
4 Joe Sakic 60.00 125.00
5 Darryl Sydor 40.00 100.00
6 Saku Koivu 25.00 60.00
7 John Vanbiesbrouck 50.00 100.00
8 Eric Desjardins 40.00 100.00
9 Shane Doan 40.00 100.00
10 Olaf Kolzig 40.00 100.00

2000-01 Paramount Glove Side Net Fusions

COMPLETE SET (20) 50.00 100.00
*PLATINUM/25: 2.5X TO 6X BASIC INSERTS
1 Byron Dafoe 2.00 5.00
2 Martin Biron 2.00 5.00
3 Dominik Hasek 5.00 12.00
4 Fred Brathwaite 2.00 5.00
5 Arturs Irbe 2.00 5.00
6 Jocelyn Thibault 2.00 5.00
7 Patrick Roy 12.50 30.00
8 Ed Belfour 2.50 6.00
9 Chris Osgood 2.00 5.00
10 Tommy Salo 2.00 5.00
11 Jose Theodore 3.00 8.00
12 Martin Brodeur 6.00 15.00
13 Mike Richter 2.50 6.00
14 Brian Boucher 2.00 5.00
15 Jean-Sebastien Aubin 2.00 5.00
16 Roman Turek 2.00 5.00
17 Steve Shields 2.00 5.00
18 Curtis Joseph 2.50 6.00
19 Felix Potvin 2.50 6.00
20 Olaf Kolzig 2.00 5.00

2000-01 Paramount Hall of Fame Bound

COMPLETE SET (10) 75.00 150.00
*PROOF/25: 1.2X TO 3X BASIC INSERTS
1 Paul Kariya 5.00 12.00
2 Dominik Hasek 8.00 20.00
3 Ray Bourque 8.00 20.00
4 Patrick Roy 15.00 40.00
5 Brett Hull 10.00 25.00
6 Steve Yzerman 15.00 40.00
7 Pavel Bure 6.00 15.00
8 Martin Brodeur 12.50 30.00
9 John LeClair 5.00 12.00
10 Jaromir Jagr 6.00 15.00

2000-01 Paramount Sub Zero

*GOLD/99: .8X TO 2X BASIC INSERTS
1 Paul Kariya 4.00 10.00
2 Peter Forsberg 6.00 15.00
3 Patrick Roy 15.00 40.00
4 Brendan Shanahan 4.00 10.00
5 Steve Yzerman 12.00 30.00
6 Pavel Bure 4.00 10.00
7 Martin Brodeur 10.00 25.00
8 Jaromir Jagr 6.00 15.00
9 Curtis Joseph 4.00 10.00
10 Mats Sundin 4.00 10.00

1951-52 Parkhurst

1 Elmer Lach 600.00 1500.00
2 Paul Meger RC 300.00 800.00
3 Butch Bouchard RC 300.00 800.00
4 Maurice Richard RC 4000.00 10000.00
5 Bert Olmstead RC 150.00 400.00
6 Bud MacPherson RC 150.00 400.00
7 Tom Johnson RC 80.00 200.00
8 Paul Masnick RC 40.00 100.00
9 Calum Mackay RC 60.00 150.00
10 Doug Harvey RC 800.00 2000.00
11 Ken Mosdell RC 100.00 250.00
12 Floyd Curry RC 40.00 100.00
13 Billy Reay RC 125.00 300.00
14 Bernie Geoffrion RC 500.00 1200.00
15 Gerry McNeil RC 250.00 600.00
16 Dick Gamble RC 150.00 400.00
17 Gerry Couture RC 100.00 250.00
18 Ross Robert Lowe RC 80.00 200.00
19 Jim Henry RC 125.00 300.00
20 Victor Ivan Lynn RC 50.00 125.00
21 Walter Kyle RC 40.00 100.00
22 Ed Sandford RC 40.00 100.00
23 John Henderson RC 80.00 200.00
24 Dunc Fisher RC 125.00 300.00
25 Hal Laycoe RC 60.00 150.00
26 Bill Quackenbush RC 125.00 300.00
27 George Sullivan RC 100.00 250.00
28 Woody Dumart 60.00 150.00
29 Milt Schmidt 150.00 400.00
30 Adam Brown RC 125.00 300.00
31 Pentti Lund RC 150.00 400.00
32 Ray Barry RC 50.00 125.00
33 Ed Kryznowski UER RC 80.00 200.00
34 Johnny Peirson RC 80.00 200.00
35 Lorne Ferguson RC 50.00 125.00
36 Clare Raglan RC 40.00 100.00
37 Bill Gadsby RC 250.00 600.00
38 Al Dewsbury RC 60.00 150.00
39 George Clare Martin RC 60.00 150.00
40 Gus Bodnar RC 100.00 250.00
41 Jim Peters RC 80.00 200.00
42 Bep Guidolin RC 125.00 300.00
43 George Gee RC 80.00 200.00
44 Jim McFadden RC 80.00 200.00
45 Fred Hucul RC 125.00 300.00
46 Lee Fogolin RC 40.00 100.00
47 Harry Lumley RC 200.00 500.00
48 Doug Bentley RC 125.00 300.00
49 Bill Mosienko RC 200.00 500.00
50 Roy Conacher 100.00 250.00
51 Pete Babando RC 125.00 300.00
52 B.Barilko/G.McNeil IA 600.00 1500.00
53 Jack Stewart 80.00 200.00
54 Marty Pavelich RC 80.00 200.00
55 Red Kelly RC 300.00 800.00
56 Ted Lindsay RC 500.00 1200.00
57 Glen Skov RC 150.00 400.00
58 Benny Woit RC 80.00 200.00
59 Tony Leswick RC 80.00 200.00
60 Fred Glover RC 125.00 300.00
61 Terry Sawchuk RC 1500.00 4000.00
62 Vic Stasiuk RC 100.00 250.00
63 Alex Delvecchio RC 250.00 600.00
64 Sid Abel 125.00 300.00
65 Metro Prystai RC 125.00 300.00
66 Gordie Howe RC 10000.00 25000.00
67 Bob Goldham RC 80.00 200.00
68 Marcel Pronovost RC 200.00 500.00
69 Leo Reise Jr. RC 150.00 400.00
70 Harry Watson RC 125.00 300.00
71 Danny Lewicki RC 80.00 200.00
72 Howie Meeker RC 150.00 400.00
73 Gus Mortson RC 80.00 200.00
74 Joe Klukay RC 50.00 125.00
75 Turk Broda 250.00 600.00
76 Al Rollins RC 100.00 250.00
77 Bill Juzda RC 30.00 80.00
78 Ray Timgren RC 100.00 250.00
79 Hugh Bolton RC 150.00 400.00
80 Fern Flaman RC 125.00 300.00
81 Max Bentley 250.00 600.00
82 Jim Thomson RC 80.00 200.00
83 Fleming Mackell RC 40.00 100.00
84 Sid Smith RC 60.00 150.00
85 Cal Gardner RC 80.00 200.00
86 Teeder Kennedy RC 250.00 600.00
87 Tod Sloan RC 50.00 125.00
88 Bob Solinger RC 50.00 125.00
89 Frank Eddolls RC 60.00 150.00
90 Jack Evans RC 80.00 200.00
91 Hy Buller RC 40.00 100.00
92 Steve Kraftcheck RC 80.00 200.00
93 Don Raleigh RC 80.00 200.00
94 Allan Stanley RC 150.00 400.00
95 Paul Ronty RC 80.00 200.00
96 Edgar Laprade RC 100.00 250.00
97 Nick Mickoski RC 100.00 250.00
98 Jack McLeod RC 60.00 150.00
99 Gaye Stewart RC 100.00 250.00
100 Wally Hergesheimer RC 80.00 200.00
101 Ed Kullman RC 50.00 125.00
102 Ed Slowinski RC 60.00 150.00
103 Reg Sinclair RC 100.00 250.00
104 Chuck Rayner RC 125.00 300.00
105 Jim Conacher RC 100.00 250.00

1952-53 Parkhurst

1 Maurice Richard 800.00 2000.00
2 Billy Reay 30.00 80.00
3 Boom Boom Geoffrion UER 200.00 500.00
4 Paul Meger 80.00 200.00
5 Dick Gamble 30.00 80.00
6 Elmer Lach 25.00 60.00
7 Floyd Curry 40.00 100.00
8 Ken Mosdell 15.00 40.00
9 Tom Johnson 60.00 150.00
10 Dickie Moore RC 150.00 400.00
11 Bud MacPherson 12.00 30.00
12 Gerry McNeil 80.00 200.00
13 Butch Bouchard 20.00 50.00
14 Doug Harvey 125.00 300.00
15 John McCormack RC 30.00 80.00
16 Pete Babando 50.00 125.00
17 Al Dewsbury 40.00 100.00
18 Ed Kullman 20.00 50.00
19 Ed Slowinski 10.00 25.00
20 Wally Hergesheimer 15.00 40.00
21 Allan Stanley 25.00 60.00
22 Chuck Rayner 40.00 100.00
23 Steve Kraftcheck 100.00 250.00
24 Paul Ronty 12.00 30.00
25 Gaye Stewart 12.00 30.00
26 Fred Hucul 15.00 40.00
27 Bill Mosienko 60.00 150.00
28 Jim Morrison RC 100.00 250.00
29 Ed Kryznowski 20.00 50.00
30 Cal Gardner 80.00 200.00
31 Al Rollins 25.00 60.00
32 Enio Sclisizzi RC 40.00 100.00
33 Pete Conacher RC 20.00 50.00
34 Leo Boivin RC 150.00 400.00
35 Jim Peters 30.00 80.00
36 George Gee 25.00 60.00
37 Gus Bodnar 25.00 60.00
38 Jim McFadden 10.00 25.00
39 Gus Mortson 15.00 40.00
40 Fred Glover 10.00 25.00
41 Gerry Couture 30.00 80.00
42 Howie Meeker 80.00 200.00
43 Jim Thomson 40.00 100.00
44 Teeder Kennedy 40.00 100.00
45 Sid Smith 50.00 125.00
46 Harry Watson 25.00 60.00
47 Fern Flaman 30.00 80.00
48 Tod Sloan 15.00 40.00
49 Leo Reise Jr. 40.00 100.00
50 Bob Solinger 20.00 50.00
51 George Armstrong RC 300.00 800.00
52 Dollard St.Laurent RC 25.00 60.00
53 Alex Delvecchio 125.00 300.00
54 Gord Hannigan RC 40.00 100.00
55 Lee Fogolin 40.00 100.00
56 Bill Gadsby 60.00 150.00
57 Herb Dickenson RC 30.00 80.00
58 Tim Horton RC 2000.00 5000.00
59 Harry Lumley 80.00 200.00
60 Metro Prystai 30.00 80.00
61 Marcel Pronovost 40.00 100.00
62 Benny Woit 50.00 125.00
63 Glen Skov 20.00 50.00
64 Bob Goldham 60.00 150.00
65 Tony Leswick 12.00 30.00
66 Marty Pavelich 15.00 40.00
67 Red Kelly 60.00 150.00
68 Bill Quackenbush 40.00 100.00
69 Ed Sandford 12.00 30.00
70 Milt Schmidt 25.00 60.00
71 Hal Laycoe 20.00 50.00
72 Woody Dumart 25.00 60.00
73 Zellio Toppazzini RC 40.00 100.00
74 Jim Henry 20.00 50.00
75 Joe Klukay 25.00 60.00
76 Dave Creighton RC 40.00 100.00
77 Jack McIntyre RC 20.00 50.00
78 Johnny Peirson 25.00 60.00
79 George Sullivan 50.00 125.00
80 Real Chevrefils RC 25.00 60.00
81 Leo Labine RC 40.00 100.00
82 Fleming Mackell 25.00 60.00
83 Pentti Lund 30.00 80.00
84 Bob Armstrong RC 30.00 80.00
85 Warren Godfrey RC 60.00 150.00
86 Terry Sawchuk 200.00 500.00
87 Ted Lindsay 150.00 400.00
88 Gordie Howe 1200.00 3000.00
89 Johnny Wilson RC 40.00 100.00
90 Vic Stasiuk 15.00 40.00
91 Larry Zeidel RC 12.00 30.00
92 Larry Wilson RC 50.00 125.00
93 Bert Olmstead 80.00 200.00
94 Ron Stewart RC 60.00 150.00
95 Max Bentley 20.00 50.00
96 Rudy Migay RC 25.00 60.00
97 Jack Stoddard RC 10.00 25.00
98 Hy Buller 20.00 50.00
99 Don Raleigh UER 12.00 30.00
100 Edgar Laprade 50.00 125.00
101 Nick Mickoski 60.00 150.00
102 Jack McLeod UER
(Robert on back) 40.00 100.00
103 Jim Conacher 20.00 50.00
104 Reg Sinclair 40.00 100.00
105 Bob Hassard RC 40.00 100.00

1953-54 Parkhurst

1 Harry Lumley 250.00 600.00
2 Sid Smith 60.00 150.00
3 Gord Hannigan 15.00 40.00
4 Bob Hassard 15.00 40.00
5 Tod Sloan 15.00 40.00
6 Leo Boivin 15.00 40.00
7 Teeder Kennedy 60.00 150.00
8 Jim Thomson 30.00 80.00
9 Ron Stewart 25.00 60.00
10 Eric Nesterenko RC 25.00 60.00
11 George Armstrong 40.00 100.00
12 Harry Watson 25.00 60.00
13 Tim Horton 150.00 400.00
14 Fern Flaman 40.00 100.00
15 Jim Morrison 20.00 50.00
16 Bob Solinger 40.00 100.00
17 Rudy Migay 20.00 50.00
18 Dick Gamble 15.00 40.00
19 Bert Olmstead 40.00 100.00
20 Eddie Mazur RC 25.00 60.00
21 Paul Meger 100.00 250.00
22 Bud MacPherson 30.00 80.00
23 Dollard St.Laurent 15.00 40.00
24 Maurice Richard 800.00 2000.00
25 Gerry McNeil 80.00 200.00
26 Doug Harvey 80.00 200.00
27 Jean Beliveau RC 1500.00 4000.00
28 Dickie Moore UER 50.00 125.00
29 Bernie Geoffrion 80.00 200.00
30 E.Lach/M.Richard 80.00 200.00
31 Elmer Lach 30.00 80.00
32 Butch Bouchard 30.00 80.00
33 Ken Mosdell 12.00 30.00
34 John McCormack 15.00 40.00
35 Floyd Curry 15.00 40.00
36 Earl Reibel RC 25.00 60.00
37 Al Arbour RC UER 30.00 80.00
38 Bill Dineen RC UER 40.00 100.00
39 Vic Stasiuk 20.00 50.00
40 Red Kelly 40.00 100.00
41 Marcel Pronovost 20.00 50.00
42 Metro Prystai 15.00 40.00
43 Tony Leswick 15.00 40.00
44 Marty Pavelich 25.00 60.00
45 Benny Woit 15.00 40.00
46 Terry Sawchuk 200.00 500.00
47 Alex Delvecchio 80.00 200.00
48 Glen Skov 25.00 60.00
49 Bob Goldham 15.00 40.00
50 Gordie Howe 500.00 1200.00
51 Johnny Wilson 20.00 50.00
52 Ted Lindsay 80.00 200.00
53 Gump Worsley RC 250.00 600.00
54 Jack Evans 40.00 100.00
55 Max Bentley 30.00 80.00
56 Andy Bathgate RC 125.00 300.00
57 Harry Howell RC 50.00 125.00
58 Hy Buller 25.00 60.00
59 Chuck Rayner 30.00 80.00
60 Jack Stoddard 20.00 50.00
61 Ed Kullman 25.00 60.00
62 Nick Mickoski 20.00 50.00
63 Paul Ronty 20.00 50.00
64 Allan Stanley 25.00 60.00
65 Leo Reise Jr. 20.00 50.00
66 Aldo Guidolin RC 20.00 50.00
67 Wally Hergesheimer 30.00 80.00
68 Don Raleigh 15.00 40.00
69 Jim Peters 15.00 40.00
70 Pete Conacher 15.00 40.00
71 Fred Hucul 20.00 50.00
72 Lee Fogolin 25.00 60.00
73 Larry Zeidel 20.00 50.00
74 Larry Wilson 20.00 50.00
75 Gus Bodnar 25.00 60.00
76 Bill Gadsby 25.00 60.00
77 Jim McFadden 20.00 50.00
78 Al Dewsbury 15.00 40.00
79 Clare Raglan 15.00 40.00
80 Bill Mosienko 30.00 80.00
81 Gus Mortson 20.00 50.00
82 Al Rollins 60.00 150.00
83 George Gee 15.00 40.00
84 Gerry Couture 25.00 60.00
85 Dave Creighton 20.00 50.00
86 Jim Henry 25.00 60.00
87 Hal Laycoe 20.00 50.00
88 Johnny Peirson UER 20.00 50.00
89 Real Chevrefils 25.00 60.00
90 Ed Sandford 15.00 40.00
91A Fleming Mackell No Bio 20.00 50.00
91B Fleming Mackell Full Bio 150.00 400.00
92 Milt Schmidt 40.00 100.00
93 Leo Labine 25.00 60.00
94 Joe Klukay 15.00 40.00
95 Warren Godfrey 20.00 50.00
96 Woody Dumart 30.00 80.00
97 Frank Martin RC 15.00 40.00
98 Jerry Toppazzini RC 20.00 50.00
99 Cal Gardner 15.00 40.00
100 Bill Quackenbush 60.00 150.00

1954-55 Parkhurst

1 Gerry McNeil 125.00 300.00
2 Dickie Moore 125.00 300.00
3 Jean Beliveau 250.00 600.00
4 Eddie Mazur 20.00 50.00
5 Bert Olmstead 15.00 40.00
6 Butch Bouchard 12.00 30.00
7 Maurice Richard 200.00 500.00
8 Bernie Geoffrion 40.00 100.00
9 John McCormack 25.00 60.00
10 Tom Johnson 25.00 60.00
11 Calum Mackay 40.00 100.00
12 Ken Mosdell 25.00 60.00
13 Paul Masnick 25.00 60.00
14 Doug Harvey 40.00 100.00
15 Floyd Curry 15.00 40.00
16 Harry Lumley 25.00 60.00
17 Harry Watson 40.00 100.00
18 Jim Morrison 15.00 40.00
19 Eric Nesterenko 15.00 40.00
20 Fern Flaman 20.00 50.00
21 Rudy Migay 12.00 30.00
22 Sid Smith 12.00 30.00
23 Ron Stewart 25.00 60.00
24 George Armstrong 25.00 60.00
25 Earl Balfour RC 15.00 40.00
26 Leo Boivin 60.00 150.00
27 Gord Hannigan 25.00 60.00
28 Bob Bailey RC 15.00 40.00
29 Teeder Kennedy 20.00 50.00
30 Tod Sloan 40.00 100.00
31 Tim Horton 125.00 300.00
32 Jim Thomson 20.00 50.00
33 Terry Sawchuk 125.00 300.00
34 Marcel Pronovost 20.00 50.00
35 Metro Prystai 30.00 80.00
36 Alex Delvecchio 25.00 60.00
37 Earl Reibel 15.00 40.00
38 Benny Woit 15.00 40.00
39 Bob Goldham 60.00 150.00
40 Glen Skov 50.00 125.00
41 Gordie Howe 300.00 800.00
42 Red Kelly 40.00 100.00
43 Marty Pavelich 15.00 40.00
44 Johnny Wilson 40.00 100.00
45 Tony Leswick 30.00 80.00
46 Ted Lindsay 40.00 100.00
47 Keith Allen RC 50.00 125.00
48 Bill Dineen 30.00 80.00
49 Jim Henry 30.00 80.00
50 Fleming Mackell 40.00 100.00
51 Bill Quackenbush 15.00 40.00
52 Hal Laycoe 25.00 60.00
53 Cal Gardner 30.00 80.00
54 Joe Klukay 25.00 60.00
55 Bob Armstrong 25.00 60.00
56 Warren Godfrey 30.00 80.00
57 Doug Mohns RC 40.00 100.00
58 Dave Creighton 25.00 60.00
59 Milt Schmidt 40.00 100.00
60 Johnny Peirson 12.00 30.00
61 Leo Labine 30.00 80.00
62 Gus Bodnar 20.00 50.00
63 Real Chevrefils 15.00 40.00
64 Ed Sandford 30.00 80.00
65 Johnny Bower UER RC 200.00 500.00
66 Paul Ronty 25.00 60.00
67 Leo Reise Jr. 12.00 30.00
68 Don Raleigh 30.00 80.00
69 Bob Chrystal RC 30.00 80.00
70 Harry Howell 30.00 80.00
71 Wally Hergesheimer 12.00 30.00
72 Jack Evans 151.00 40.00
73 Camille Henry RC 15.00 40.00
74 Dean Prentice RC 20.00 50.00
75 Nick Mickoski 20.00 50.00
76 Ron Murphy RC 15.00 40.00
77 Al Rollins 40.00 100.00
78 Al Dewsbury 12.00 30.00
79 Lou Jankowski RC 25.00 60.00
80 George Gee 15.00 40.00
81 Gus Mortson 15.00 40.00
82 Fred Sasakamoose RC 125.00 300.00
83 Ike Hildebrand RC 15.00 40.00
84 Lee Fogolin 20.00 50.00
85 Larry Wilson 15.00 40.00
86 Pete Conacher 15.00 40.00
87 Bill Gadsby 30.00 80.00
88 Jack McIntyre 15.00 40.00
89 Floyd Curry 30.00 80.00
90 Alex Delvecchio 20.00 50.00
91 R.Kelly/H.Lumley 30.00 80.00
92 Lumley/Howe/Stewart 50.00 125.00
93 H.Lumley/R.Murphy 40.00 100.00
94 P.Meger/J.Morrison 40.00 100.00
95 D.Harvey/E.Nesterenko 50.00 125.00
96 T.Sawchuk/T.Kennedy 30.00 80.00
97 Plante/B.Bouchard/Reibel 30.00 80.00
98 J.Plante/Harvey/Sloan 100.00 250.00
99 J.Plante/T.Kennedy 80.00 200.00
100 T.Sawchuk/B.Geoffrion 80.00 200.00

1955-56 Parkhurst

1 Harry Lumley 400.00 1000.00
2 Sid Smith 40.00 100.00
3A Tim Horton COR 200.00 500.00
4 George Armstrong 80.00 200.00
5 Ron Stewart 60.00 150.00
6 Joe Klukay 25.00 60.00
7 Marc Reaume RC 60.00 150.00
8 Jim Morrison 25.00 60.00
9 Parker MacDonald RC 20.00 50.00
10 Tod Sloan 60.00 150.00
11 Jim Thomson 20.00 50.00
12 Rudy Migay 20.00 50.00
13 Brian Cullen RC 20.00 50.00
14 Hugh Bolton 20.00 50.00
15 Eric Nesterenko 60.00 150.00
16 Larry Cahan RC 25.00 60.00
17 Willie Marshall RC 25.00 60.00
18 Dick Duff RC 100.00 400.00
19 Jack Caffery RC 40.00 100.00
20 Billy Harris RC 30.00 80.00
21 Lorne Chabot OTG 20.00 50.00
22 Harvey Jackson OTG 80.00 200.00
23 Turk Broda OTG 40.00 100.00
24 Joe Primeau OTG 30.00 80.00
25 Gordie Drillon OTG 20.00 50.00
26 Chuck Conacher OTG 40.00 100.00
27 Sweeney Schriner OTG 30.00 80.00
28 Syl Apps OTG 50.00 125.00
29 Teeder Kennedy OTG 50.00 125.00
30 Ace Bailey OTG 50.00 125.00
31 Babe Pratt OTG 40.00 100.00
32 Harold Cotton OTG 30.00 80.00
33 King Clancy CO 150.00 400.00
34 Hap Day 40.00 100.00
35 Don Marshall RC 30.00 80.00
36 Jackie LeClair RC 40.00 100.00
37 Maurice Richard 150.00 400.00
38 Dickie Moore 50.00 125.00
39 Ken Mosdell 40.00 100.00
40 Floyd Curry 20.00 50.00
41 Calum Mackay 40.00 100.00
42 Bert Olmstead 60.00 150.00
43 Bernie Geoffrion 80.00 200.00
44 Jean Beliveau 200.00 500.00
45 Doug Harvey 50.00 125.00
46 Butch Bouchard 20.00 50.00
47 Bud MacPherson 20.00 50.00
48 Dollard St.Laurent 20.00 50.00
49 Tom Johnson 30.00 80.00
50 Jacques Plante RC 2000.00 5000.00
51 Paul Meger 40.00 100.00
52 Gerry McNeil 50.00 125.00
53 Jean-Guy Talbot RC 40.00 100.00
54 Bob Turner RC 40.00 100.00
55 Newsy Lalonde OTG 50.00 125.00
56 Georges Vezina OTG 125.00 300.00
57 Howie Morenz OTG 100.00 250.00
58 Aurel Joliat OTG 60.00 150.00
59 George Hainsworth OTG 40.00 100.00
60 Sylvio Mantha OTG 40.00 100.00
61 Battleship Leduc OTG 40.00 100.00
62 Babe Siebert OTG UER 50.00 125.00
63 Bill Durnan OTG RC 125.00 300.00
64 Ken Reardon OTG 40.00 100.00
65 Johnny Gagnon OTG 25.00 60.00
66 Billy Reay OTG 20.00 50.00
67 Toe Blake CO 60.00 150.00
68 Frank Selke MG 125.00 300.00
69 Hugh Beats Hodge 20.00 50.00
70 Lumley Stops BoomBoom 60.00 150.00
71 J.Plante Is Protected 40.00 100.00
72 Rocket Roars Through 80.00 200.00
73 Richard Tests Lumley 60.00 150.00
74 Beliveau Bats Puck 30.00 80.00
75 Nesterenko/Smith/Plante 40.00 100.00
76 Curry/Lumley/Morrison 40.00 100.00
77 Sloan/MacD/Harvey/Beliv 60.00 150.00
78 Montreal Forum 200.00 500.00
79 Maple Leaf Gardens 250.00 600.00

1955-56 Parkhurst Quaker Oats

1 Harry Lumley 400.00 700.00
2 Sid Smith 20.00 60.00
3 Tim Horton 350.00 600.00
4 George Armstrong 75.00 200.00
5 Ron Stewart 15.00 40.00
6 Joe Klukay 15.00 40.00
7 Marc Reaume RC 15.00 40.00
8 Jim Morrison 15.00 40.00
9 Parker MacDonald RC 15.00 40.00
10 Tod Sloan 20.00 60.00
11 Jim Thomson 15.00 40.00
12 Rudy Migay 15.00 40.00
13 Brian Cullen RC 30.00 80.00
14 Hugh Bolton 15.00 40.00
15 Eric Nesterenko 20.00 60.00
16 Larry Cahan RC 20.00 60.00
17 Willie Marshall RC 15.00 40.00
18 Dick Duff RC 150.00 300.00
19 Jack Caffery RC 15.00 40.00
20 Billy Harris RC 30.00 80.00
21 Lorne Chabot OTG 40.00 100.00
22 Harvey Jackson OTG 60.00 150.00
23 Turk Broda OTG 150.00 300.00
24 Joe Primeau OTG 30.00 80.00
25 Gordie Drillon OTG 30.00 80.00
26 Chuck Conacher OTG 30.00 80.00
27 Sweeney Schriner OTG 30.00 80.00
28 Syl Apps OTG 30.00 80.00
29 Teeder Kennedy OTG 40.00 100.00
30 Ace Bailey OTG 50.00 125.00
31 Babe Pratt OTG 20.00 60.00
32 Harold Cotton OTG 20.00 60.00
33 King Clancy CO 75.00 200.00
34 Hap Day 30.00 80.00
35 Don Marshall RC 40.00 100.00
36 Jackie LeClair RC 20.00 60.00
37 Maurice Richard 500.00 750.00
38 Dickie Moore 60.00 150.00
39 Ken Mosdell 20.00 60.00
40 Floyd Curry 20.00 60.00
41 Calum Mackay 15.00 40.00
42 Bert Olmstead 20.00 60.00
43 Boom Boom Geoffrion 125.00 250.00
44 Jean Beliveau 400.00 700.00
45 Doug Harvey 125.00 250.00
46 Butch Bouchard 20.00 60.00
47 Bud MacPherson 15.00 40.00
48 Dollard St.Laurent 20.00 60.00
49 Tom Johnson 30.00 80.00
50 Jacques Plante RC 2000.00 3500.00
51 Paul Meger 20.00 60.00
52 Gerry McNeil 40.00 100.00
53 Jean-Guy Talbot RC 30.00 80.00
54 Bob Turner RC 15.00 40.00
55 Newsy Lalonde OTG 50.00 125.00
56 Georges Vezina OTG 150.00 300.00
57 Howie Morenz OTG 150.00 300.00
58 Aurel Joliat OTG 50.00 125.00
59 George Hainsworth OTG 125.00 250.00
60 Sylvio Mantha OTG 20.00 60.00
61 Battleship Leduc OTG 20.00 60.00
62 Babe Siebert OTG UER
(Misspelled Seibert
on both sides 30.00 80.00
63 Bill Durnan OTG RC 50.00 125.00
64 Ken Reardon OTG 50.00 125.00
65 Johnny Gagnon OTG 20.00 60.00
66 Billy Reay OTG 20.00 60.00
67 Toe Blake CO 40.00 100.00
68 Frank Selke MG 20.00 60.00
69 Hugh Beats Hodge 20.00 60.00
70 Lum Stops BoomBoom 50.00 125.00
71 J.Plante Is Protected 75.00 200.00
72 Rocket Roars Through 75.00 200.00
73 Richard Tests Lumley 75.00 200.00
74 Beliveau Bats Puck 60.00 150.00
75 Nester
Smith
Plante 75.00 200.00
76 Curry
Lumley
Morrison 30.00 80.00
77 Sloan
MacDonald
Harvey
Beliveau 60.00 150.00
78 Montreal Forum 500.00 750.00
79 Maple Leaf Gardens 500.00 750.00

1957-58 Parkhurst

M1 Doug Harvey 100.00 250.00
M2 Bernie Geoffrion 80.00 200.00
M3 Jean Beliveau 150.00 400.00
M4 Henri Richard RC 1200.00 3000.00
M5 Maurice Richard 250.00 600.00
M6 Tom Johnson 10.00 25.00
M7 André Pronovost RC 15.00 40.00
M8 Don Marshall 30.00 80.00
M9 Jean-Guy Talbot 8.00 20.00
M10 Dollard St.Laurent 8.00 20.00
M11 Phil Goyette RC 15.00 40.00
M12 Claude Provost RC 20.00 50.00
M13 Bob Turner 8.00 20.00
M14 Dickie Moore 25.00 60.00
M15 Jacques Plante 200.00 500.00
M16 Toe Blake CO 20.00 50.00
M17 Charlie Hodge RC 60.00 150.00
M18 Marcel Bonin 15.00 40.00
M19 Bert Olmstead 10.00 25.00
M20 Floyd Curry 15.00 40.00
M21 Len Broderick IA RC 15.00 40.00
M22 Brian Cullen scores 8.00 20.00
M23 Broderick/Harvey IA 15.00 40.00
M24 Geoffrion/Chadwick IA 20.00 50.00
M25 Olmstead/Chadwick IA 15.00 40.00
T1 George Armstrong 200.00 500.00
T2 Ed Chadwick RC 80.00 200.00
T3 Dick Duff 50.00 125.00
T4 Bob Pulford RC 200.00 500.00
T5 Tod Sloan 80.00 200.00
T6 Rudy Migay 20.00 50.00
T7 Ron Stewart 10.00 25.00
T8 Gerry James RC 10.00 25.00
T9 Brian Cullen 15.00 40.00
T10 Sid Smith 8.00 20.00
T11 Jim Morrison 8.00 20.00
T12 Marc Reaume 8.00 20.00
T13 Hugh Bolton 15.00 40.00
T14 Pete Conacher 15.00 40.00
T15 Billy Harris 8.00 20.00
T16 Mike Nykoluk RC 8.00 20.00
T17 Frank Mahovlich RC 1000.00 2500.00
T18 Ken Girard RC 8.00 20.00
T19 Al MacNeil RC 8.00 20.00
T20 Bob Baun RC 40.00 100.00
T21 Barry Cullen RC 15.00 40.00
T22 Tim Horton 80.00 200.00
T23 Gary Collins RC 8.00 20.00
T24 Gary Aldcorn RC 8.00 20.00
T25 Billy Reay CO 15.00 40.00

1958-59 Parkhurst

1 Bob Pulford IA 30.00 80.00
2 Henri Richard 80.00 200.00
3 Andre Pronovost 20.00 50.00
4 Billy Harris 25.00 60.00
5 Albert Langlois RC 20.00 50.00
6 Noel Price RC 8.00 20.00
7 G.Armstrong/Johnson IA 12.00 30.00
8 Dickie Moore 15.00 40.00
9 Toe Blake CO 25.00 60.00
10 Tom Johnson 10.00 25.00
11 J.Plante/G.Armstrong 20.00 50.00
12 Ed Chadwick 15.00 40.00
13 Bob Nevin RC 20.00 50.00
14 Ron Stewart 10.00 25.00
15 Bob Baun 15.00 40.00
16 Ralph Backstrom RC 40.00 100.00
17 Charlie Hodge 50.00 125.00
18 Gary Aldcorn 25.00 60.00
19 Willie Marshall 8.00 20.00
20 Marc Reaume 12.00 30.00
21 Jacques Plante IA 20.00 50.00
22 Jacques Plante 100.00 250.00
23 Allan Stanley UER 20.00 50.00
24 Ian Cushenan RC 40.00 100.00
25 Billy Reay CO 20.00 50.00
26 Jacques Plante IA 25.00 60.00
27 Bert Olmstead 15.00 40.00
28 Bernie Geoffrion 80.00 200.00
29 Dick Duff 10.00 25.00
30 Ab McDonald RC 8.00 20.00
31 Barry Cullen 15.00 40.00
32 Marcel Bonin 30.00 80.00
33 Frank Mahovlich 125.00 300.00
34 Jean Beliveau 125.00 300.00
35 Jacques Plante IA 40.00 60.00
36 Brian Cullen Shoots 10.00 25.00
37 Steve Kraftcheck 25.00 60.00
38 Maurice Richard 250.00 600.00
39 Jacques Plante IA 40.00 60.00
40 Bob Turner 12.00 30.00
41 Jean-Guy Talbot 30.00 80.00
42 Tim Horton 40.00 100.00
43 Claude Provost 10.00 25.00
44 Don Marshall 30.00 80.00
45 Bob Pulford 20.00 50.00
46 Johnny Bower UER 60.00 150.00
47 Phil Goyette 10.00 25.00
48 George Armstrong 15.00 40.00
49 Doug Harvey 40.00 100.00
50 Brian Cullen 15.00 40.00

1959-60 Parkhurst

1 Canadiens On Guard
Jacques Plante
Tom Johnson
Phil Goyette 40.00 100.00
2 Maurice Richard 250.00 600.00
3 Carl Brewer RC 30.00 80.00
4 Phil Goyette 30.00 80.00
5 Ed Chadwick 12.00 30.00
6 Jean Beliveau 125.00 300.00
7 George Armstrong 12.00 30.00
8 Doug Harvey 40.00 100.00
9 Billy Harris 30.00 80.00
10 Tom Johnson 20.00 50.00
11 Marc Reaume 10.00 25.00
12 Marcel Bonin 10.00 25.00
13 Johnny Wilson 10.00 25.00
14 Dickie Moore 25.00 60.00
15 Punch Imlach CO RC 20.00 60.00
16 Charlie Hodge 30.00 80.00
17 Larry Regan 12.00 30.00
18 Claude Provost 12.00 30.00
19 Gerry Ehman RC 10.00 25.00
20 Ab McDonald 10.00 25.00
21 Bob Baun 10.00 25.00
22 Ken Reardon VP 10.00 25.00
23 Tim Horton 80.00 200.00
24 Frank Mahovlich 80.00 200.00
25 Johnny Bower IA 15.00 40.00
26 Ron Stewart 20.00 50.00
27 Toe Blake CO 25.00 60.00
28 Bob Pulford 15.00 40.00
29 Ralph Backstrom 10.00 25.00
30 Action Around the Net 12.00 30.00
31 Bill Hicke RC 10.00 25.00
32 Johnny Bower 30.00 80.00
33 Bernie Geoffrion 25.00 60.00
34 Ted Hampson RC 15.00 40.00
35 Andre Pronovost 20.00 50.00
36 Stafford Smythe CHC 10.00 25.00
37 Don Marshall 10.00 25.00
38 Dick Duff 12.00 30.00
39 Henri Richard 80.00 200.00
40 Bert Olmstead 10.00 25.00
41 Jacques Plante 100.00 250.00
42 Noel Price 10.00 25.00
43 Bob Turner 20.00 50.00
44 Allan Stanley 25.00 60.00
45 Albert Langlois 12.00 30.00
46 Officials Intervene 12.00 30.00
47 Frank Selke MD 30.00 80.00
48 Gary Edmundson RC 10.00 25.00
49 Jean-Guy Talbot 10.00 25.00
50 King Clancy AGM 25.00 60.00

1960-61 Parkhurst

COMMON CARD 6.00 15.00
SEMISTARS 8.00 20.00
UNLISTED STARS 10.00 25.00
1 Tim Horton 125.00 300.00
2 Frank Mahovlich 30.00 80.00
3 Johnny Bower 40.00 100.00
4 Bert Olmstead 15.00 40.00
5 Gary Edmundson 10.00 25.00
6 Ron Stewart 8.00 20.00
7 Gerry James 20.00 50.00
8 Gerry Ehman 8.00 20.00
9 Red Kelly 15.00 40.00
10 Dave Creighton 6.00 15.00
11 Bob Baun 8.00 20.00
12 Dick Duff 10.00 25.00
13 Larry Regan 8.00 20.00
14 Johnny Wilson 8.00 20.00
15 Billy Harris 8.00 20.00
16 Allan Stanley 25.00 60.00
17 George Armstrong 20.00 50.00
18 Carl Brewer 8.00 20.00
19 Bob Pulford 8.00 20.00
20 Gordie Howe 150.00 400.00
21 Val Fonteyne RC 8.00 20.00
22 Murray Oliver RC 8.00 20.00
23 Sid Abel CO 10.00 25.00
24 Jack McIntyre 8.00 20.00
25 Marc Reaume 25.00 60.00

26 Norm Ullman 20.00 50.00
27 Brian Smith RC 8.00 20.00
28 Gerry Melnyk UER RC 8.00 20.00
29 Marcel Pronovost 12.00 30.00
30 Warren Godfrey 8.00 20.00
31 Terry Sawchuk 60.00 150.00
32 Barry Cullen 8.00 20.00
33 Gary Aldcorn 8.00 20.00
34 Pete Goegan 8.00 20.00
35 Len Lunde 8.00 20.00
36 Alex Delvecchio 12.00 30.00
37 John McKenzie RC 40.00 100.00
38 Dickie Moore 10.00 25.00
39 Albert Langlois 8.00 20.00
40 Bill Hicke 8.00 20.00
41 Ralph Backstrom 12.00 30.00
42 Don Marshall 15.00 40.00
43 Bob Turner 15.00 40.00
44 Tom Johnson 8.00 20.00
45 Maurice Richard 200.00 500.00
46 Bernie Geoffrion 30.00 80.00
47 Henri Richard 40.00 100.00
48 Doug Harvey 40.00 100.00
49 Jean Beliveau 80.00 200.00
50 Phil Goyette 10.00 25.00
51 Marcel Bonin 8.00 20.00
52 Jean-Guy Talbot 12.00 30.00
53 Jacques Plante 125.00 300.00
54 Claude Provost 8.00 20.00
55 Andre Pronovost 10.00 25.00
56 Hicke/McDonald/Backstrom 12.00 30.00
57 Marsh/H.Richard/Moore 25.00 60.00
58 Provost/Pronovost/Goyette 8.00 20.00
59 Boom/Marshall/Beliveau 40.00 100.00
60 Ab McDonald 8.00 20.00
61 Jim Morrison 40.00 100.00

1961-62 Parkhurst

COMMON CARD 6.00 15.00
SEMISTARS 8.00 20.00
UNLISTED STARS 10.00 25.00
1 Tim Horton 80.00 200.00
2 Frank Mahovlich 50.00 125.00
3 Johnny Bower 50.00 125.00
4 Bert Olmstead 8.00 20.00
5 Dave Keon RC 400.00 1000.00
6 Ron Stewart 8.00 20.00
7 Eddie Shack 25.00 60.00
8 Bob Pulford 20.00 50.00
9 Red Kelly 10.00 25.00
10 Bob Nevin 20.00 50.00
11 Bob Baun 15.00 40.00
12 Dick Duff 10.00 25.00
13 Larry Keenan RC 8.00 20.00
14 Larry Hillman 8.00 20.00
15 Billy Harris 8.00 20.00
16 Allan Stanley 8.00 20.00
17 George Armstrong 8.00 20.00
18 Carl Brewer 8.00 20.00
19 Howie Glover RC 8.00 20.00
20 Gordie Howe 150.00 400.00
21 Val Fonteyne 8.00 20.00
22 Al Johnson RC 8.00 20.00
23 Pete Goegan 8.00 20.00
24 Len Lunde 8.00 20.00
25 Alex Delvecchio 40.00 100.00
26 Norm Ullman 15.00 40.00
27 Bill Gadsby 8.00 20.00
28 Ed Litzenberger 8.00 20.00
29 Marcel Pronovost 25.00 60.00
30 Warren Godfrey 12.00 30.00
31 Terry Sawchuk 60.00 150.00
32 Vic Stasiuk 8.00 20.00
33 Leo Labine 8.00 20.00
34 John McKenzie 8.00 20.00
35 Bernie Geoffrion 30.00 80.00
36 Dickie Moore 15.00 40.00
37 Albert Langlois 8.00 20.00
38 Bill Hicke 12.00 30.00
39 Ralph Backstrom 8.00 20.00
40 Don Marshall 8.00 20.00
41 Bob Turner 8.00 20.00
42 Tom Johnson 8.00 20.00
43 Henri Richard 60.00 150.00
44 Wayne Connelly RC 8.00 20.00
45 Jean Beliveau 100.00 250.00
46 Phil Goyette 20.00 50.00
47 Marcel Bonin 12.00 30.00
48 Jean-Guy Talbot 15.00 40.00
49 Jacques Plante 80.00 200.00
50 Claude Provost 8.00 20.00
51 Andre Pronovost UER 15.00 40.00

1962-63 Parkhurst

COMMON CARD 5.00 12.00
SEMISTARS 6.00 15.00
UNLISTED STARS 8.00 20.00
1 Billy Harris 30.00 80.00
2 Dick Duff 12.00 30.00
3 Bob Baun 20.00 50.00
4 Frank Mahovlich 25.00 60.00
5 Red Kelly 10.00 25.00
6 Ron Stewart 10.00 25.00
7 Tim Horton 40.00 100.00
8 Carl Brewer 20.00 50.00
9 Allan Stanley 20.00 50.00
10 Bob Nevin 6.00 15.00
11 Bob Pulford 20.00 50.00
12 Ed Litzenberger 6.00 15.00
13 George Armstrong 12.00 30.00
14 Eddie Shack 12.00 30.00
15 Dave Keon 15.00 40.00
16 Johnny Bower 40.00 100.00
17 Larry Hillman 6.00 15.00
18 Frank Mahovlich 25.00 60.00
19 Hank Bassen RC 12.00 30.00
20 Gerry Odrowski RC 6.00 15.00
21 Norm Ullman 20.00 50.00
22 Vic Stasiuk 6.00 15.00
23 Bruce MacGregor RC 12.00 30.00
24 Claude Laforge 12.00 30.00
25 Bill Gadsby 15.00 40.00
26 Leo Labine 6.00 15.00
27 Val Fonteyne 8.00 20.00
28 Howie Glover 10.00 25.00
29 Marc Boileau RC 8.00 20.00
30 Gordie Howe 100.00 250.00
31 Gordie Howe 100.00 250.00
32 Alex Delvecchio 20.00 50.00
33 Marcel Pronovost 6.00 15.00
34 Sid Abel CO 6.00 15.00
35 Len Lunde 5.00 15.00
36 Warren Godfrey 6.00 15.00
37 Phil Goyette 10.00 25.00
38 Henri Richard 40.00 100.00
39 Jean Beliveau 80.00 200.00
40 Bill Hicke 20.00 50.00
41 Claude Provost 12.00 30.00
42 Dickie Moore 8.00 20.00
43 Don Marshall 8.00 20.00
44 Ralph Backstrom 6.00 15.00
45 Marcel Bonin 8.00 20.00
46 Gilles Tremblay RC 12.00 30.00
47 Bobby Rousseau RC 12.00 30.00
48 Bernie Geoffrion 12.00 30.00
49 Jacques Plante 80.00 200.00
50 Tom Johnson 10.00 25.00
51 Jean-Guy Talbot 8.00 20.00
52 Lou Fontinato 6.00 15.00
53 Bernie Geoffrion 12.00 30.00
54 J.C.Tremblay RC 25.00 60.00
NNO Zip Entry Game Card 60.00 150.00
NNO Checklist Card 100.00 250.00

1963-64 Parkhurst

COMMON CARD 5.00 12.00
SEMISTARS 6.00 15.00
UNLISTED STARS 8.00 20.00
1 Allan Stanley 15.00 40.00
2 Don Simmons 8.00 20.00
3 Red Kelly 10.00 25.00
4 Dick Duff 8.00 20.00
5 Johnny Bower 20.00 50.00
6 Ed Litzenberger 8.00 20.00
7 Kent Douglas RC 12.00 30.00
8 Carl Brewer 8.00 20.00
9 Eddie Shack 15.00 40.00
10 Bob Nevin 10.00 25.00
11 Billy Harris 8.00 20.00
12 Bob Pulford 8.00 20.00
13 George Armstrong 8.00 20.00
14 Ron Stewart 8.00 20.00
15 John MacMillan RC 8.00 20.00
16 Tim Horton 25.00 60.00
17 Frank Mahovlich 20.00 50.00
18 Bob Baun 8.00 20.00
19 Punch Imlach ACO/GM 15.00 40.00
20 King Clancy ACO 12.00 30.00
21 Gilles Tremblay 8.00 20.00
22 Jean-Guy Talbot 10.00 25.00
23 Henri Richard 20.00 50.00
24 Ralph Backstrom 8.00 20.00
25 Bill Hicke 8.00 20.00
26 Red Berenson RC 12.00 30.00
27 Jacques Laperriere RC 20.00 50.00
28 Jean Gauthier RC 8.00 20.00
29 Bernie Geoffrion 20.00 50.00
30 Jean Beliveau 60.00 150.00
31 J.C.Tremblay 8.00 20.00
32 Terry Harper RC 15.00 40.00
33 John Ferguson RC 25.00 60.00
34 Toe Blake CO 15.00 40.00
35 Bobby Rousseau 10.00 25.00
36 Claude Provost 10.00 25.00
37 Marc Reaume 10.00 25.00
38 Dave Balon 8.00 20.00
39 Gump Worsley 12.00 30.00
40 Cesare Maniago RC 20.00 50.00
41 Bruce MacGregor 12.00 30.00
42 Alex Faulkner RC 150.00 400.00
43 Pete Goegan 12.00 30.00
44 Parker MacDonald 8.00 20.00
45 Andre Pronovost 8.00 20.00
46 Marcel Pronovost 8.00 20.00
47 Bob Dillabough RC 12.00 30.00
48 Larry Jeffrey RC 8.00 20.00
49 Ian Cushenan 12.00 30.00
50 Alex Delvecchio 10.00 25.00
51 Hank Ciesla 8.00 20.00
52 Norm Ullman 10.00 25.00
53 Terry Sawchuk 50.00 125.00
54 Ron Ingram RC 8.00 20.00
55 Gordie Howe 250.00 600.00
56 Billy McNeil 8.00 20.00
57 Floyd Smith RC 8.00 20.00
58 Vic Stasiuk 8.00 20.00
59 Bill Gadsby 8.00 20.00
60 Doug Barkley RC 8.00 20.00
61 Allan Stanley 8.00 20.00
62 Don Simmons 15.00 40.00
63 Red Kelly 10.00 25.00
64 Dick Duff 12.00 30.00
65 Johnny Bower 20.00 50.00
66 Ed Litzenberger 8.00 20.00
67 Kent Douglas 8.00 20.00
68 Carl Brewer 8.00 20.00
69 Eddie Shack 15.00 40.00
70 Bob Nevin 8.00 20.00
71 Billy Harris 8.00 20.00
72 Bob Pulford 12.00 30.00
73 George Armstrong 8.00 20.00
74 Ron Stewart 8.00 20.00
75 Dave Keon 25.00 60.00
76 Tim Horton 15.00 40.00
77 Frank Mahovlich 15.00 40.00
78 Bob Baun 8.00 20.00
79 Punch Imlach ACO/GM 10.00 25.00
80 Gilles Tremblay 8.00 20.00
81 Jean-Guy Talbot 8.00 20.00
82 Henri Richard 25.00 60.00
83 Ralph Backstrom 12.00 30.00
84 Bill Hicke 8.00 20.00
85 Red Berenson RC 12.00 30.00
86 Jacques Laperriere RC 30.00 80.00
87 Jean Gauthier RC 15.00 40.00
88 Bernie Geoffrion 12.00 30.00
89 Jean Beliveau 25.00 60.00
90 J.C.Tremblay 8.00 20.00
91 Terry Harper RC 10.00 25.00
92 John Ferguson RC 20.00 50.00
93 Toe Blake CO 12.00 30.00
94 Bobby Rousseau 12.00 30.00
95 Claude Provost 8.00 20.00
96 Marc Reaume 10.00 25.00
97 Dave Balon 8.00 20.00
98 Gump Worsley 20.00 50.00
99 Cesare Maniago RC 40.00 100.00

1991-92 Parkhurst

*FRENCH: .5X TO 1.25X PARKHURST
1 Matt DelGuidice RC .20 .50
2 Ken Hodge Jr. .15 .40
3 Vladimir Ruzicka .15 .40
4 Craig Janney .15 .40
5 Glen Wesley .15 .40
6 Stephen Leach .15 .40
7 Garry Galley .15 .40
8 Andy Moog .20 .50
9 Ray Bourque .30 .75
10 Brad May .15 .40
11 Donald Audette .15 .40
12 Alexander Mogilny .15 .40
13 Randy Wood .15 .40
14 Daren Puppa .15 .40
15 Doug Bodger .15 .40
16 Pat LaFontaine .20 .50
17 Dave Andreychuk .20 .50
18 Dale Hawerchuk .25 .60
19 Mike Ramsey .15 .40
20 Tomas Forslund RC .20 .50
21 Robert Reichel .40 1.00
22 Theo Fleury .15 .40
23 Joe Nieuwendyk .15 .40
24 Gary Roberts .15 .40
25 Gary Suter .12 .30
26 Doug Gilmour .25 .60
27 Mike Vernon .15 .40
28 Al MacInnis .25 .60
29 Jeremy Roenick .30 .75
30 Ed Belfour .50 1.25
31 Steve Smith .20 .50
32 Chris Chelios .20 .50
33 Dirk Graham .15 .40
34 Steve Larmer .15 .40
35 Brent Sutter .15 .40
36 Michel Goulet .15 .40
37 Nicklas Lidstrom RC .75 2.00
38 Sergei Fedorov .30 .75
39 Tim Cheveldae .15 .40
40 Kevin Miller .15 .40
41 Ray Sheppard .15 .40
42 Paul Ysebaert .15 .40
43 Jimmy Carson .15 .40
44 Steve Yzerman .60 1.50
45 Shawn Burr .15 .40
46 Vladimir Konstantinov RC .50 1.25
47 Josef Beranek RC .20 .50
48 Vincent Damphousse .15 .40
49 Dave Manson .15 .40
50 Scott Mellanby .15 .40
51 Kevin Lowe .15 .40
52 Joe Murphy .15 .40
53 Bill Ranford .15 .40
54 Craig Simpson .12 .30
55 Esa Tikkanen .15 .40
56 Michel Picard RC .20 .50
57 Geoff Sanderson RC .20 .50
58 Kay Whitmore .15 .40
59 John Cullen .15 .40
60 Rob Brown .15 .40
61 Zarley Zalapski .15 .40
62 Brad Shaw .12 .30
63 Mikael Andersson .15 .40
64 Pat Verbeek .15 .40
65 Peter Ahola RC .20 .50
66 Tony Granato .12 .30
67 Dave Taylor .15 .40
68 Luc Robitaille .20 .50
69 Marty McSorley .15 .40
70 Tomas Sandstrom .15 .40
71 Kelly Hrudey .15 .40
72 Jari Kurri .15 .40
73 Wayne Gretzky 1.25 3.00
74 Larry Robinson .20 .50
75 Derian Hatcher .15 .40
76 Ulf Dahlen .15 .40
77 Jon Casey .15 .40
78 Dave Gagner .15 .40
79 Brian Bellows .15 .40
80 Neal Broten .15 .40
81 Mike Modano .40 1.00
82 Brian Propp .15 .40
83 Bobby Smith .15 .40
84 John LeClair RC .50 1.25
85 Eric Desjardins .20 .50
86 Shayne Corson .15 .40
87 Stephan Lebeau .15 .40
88 Mathieu Schneider .15 .40
89 Kirk Muller .12 .30
90 Patrick Roy .50 1.25
91 Sylvain Turgeon .15 .40
92 Guy Carbonneau .15 .40
93 Denis Savard .20 .50
94 Scott Niedermayer .20 .50
95 Tom Chorske .15 .40
96 Slava Fetisov .15 .40
97 Kevin Todd RC .20 .50
98 Chris Terreri .15 .40
99 David Maley .15 .40
100 Stephane Richer .15 .40
101 Claude Lemieux .15 .40
102 Scott Stevens .20 .50
103 Peter Stastny .15 .40
104 David Volek .15 .40
105 Steve Thomas .15 .40
106 Pierre Turgeon .15 .40
107 Glenn Healy .20 .50
108 Derek King .12 .30
109 Uwe Krupp .15 .40
110 Ray Ferraro .15 .40
111 Pat Flatley .15 .40
112 Tom Kurvers .15 .40
113 Adam Creighton .15 .40
114 Tony Amonte RC .50 1.25
115 John Ogrodnick .15 .40
116 Doug Weight RC .50 1.25
117 Mike Richter .20 .50
118 Darren Turcotte .15 .40
119 Brian Leetch .15 .40
120 James Patrick .15 .40
121 Mark Messier .40 1.00
122 Mike Gartner .25 .60
123 Mike Ricci .12 .30
124 Rod Brind'Amour .15 .40
125 Steve Duchesne .12 .30
126 Ron Hextall .20 .50
127 Brad Jones .15 .40
128 Pelle Eklund .15 .40
129 Rick Tocchet .15 .40
130 Mark Howe .20 .50
131 Andrei Lomakin .15 .40
132 Jaromir Jagr .60 1.50
133 Jim Paek RC .20 .50
134 Mark Recchi .25 .60
135 Kevin Stevens .15 .40
136 Phil Bourque .15 .40
137 Mario Lemieux .75 2.00
138 Bob Errey .15 .40
139 Tom Barrasso .15 .40
140 Paul Coffey .20 .50
141 Joe Mullen .15 .40
142 Kip Miller .15 .40
143 Owen Nolan .20 .50
144 Mats Sundin .20 .50
145 Mikhail Tatarinov .15 .40
146 Bryan Fogarty .15 .40
147 Stephane Morin .15 .40
148 Joe Sakic .60 1.50
149 Ron Tugnutt .15 .40
150 Mike Hough .15 .40
151 Nelson Emerson .15 .40
152 Curtis Joseph .25 .60
153 Brendan Shanahan .20 .50
154 Paul Cavallini .15 .40
155 Adam Oates .20 .50
156 Jeff Brown .15 .40
157 Brett Hull .40 1.00
158 Ron Sutter .15 .40
159 Dave Christian .12 .30
160 Pat Falloon .15 .40
161 Pat MacLeod RC .20 .50
162 Jarmo Myllys .15 .40
163 Wayne Presley .15 .40
164 Perry Anderson .15 .40
165 Kelly Kisio .15 .40
166 Brian Mullen .15 .40
167 Brian Lawton .15 .40
168 Doug Wilson .15 .40
169 Rob Pearson RC .20 .50
170 Wendel Clark .30 .75
171 Brian Bradley .15 .40
172 Dave Ellett .15 .40
173 Gary Leeman .15 .40
174 Peter Zezel .12 .30
175 Grant Fuhr .30 .75
176 Bob Rouse .15 .40
177 Glenn Anderson .15 .40
178 Petr Nedved .15 .40
179 Trevor Linden .20 .50
180 Jyrki Lumme .15 .40
181 Kirk McLean .15 .40
182 Cliff Ronning .12 .30
183 Greg Adams .15 .40
184 Doug Lidster .15 .40
185 Sergio Momesso .15 .40
186 Geoff Courtnall .15 .40
187 Dave Babych .15 .40
188 Peter Bondra .20 .50
189 Dimitri Khristich .15 .40
190 Randy Burridge .15 .40
191 Kevin Hatcher .15 .40
192 Mike Ridley .15 .40
193 Dino Ciccarelli .15 .40
194 Al Iafrate .15 .40
195 Dale Hunter .15 .40
196 Mike Liut .12 .30
197 Rod Langway .15 .40
198 Russell Romaniuk RC .20 .50
199 Bob Essensa .15 .40
200 Teppo Numminen .15 .40
201 Darrin Shannon .15 .40
202 Pat Elynuik .15 .40
203 Fredrik Olausson .15 .40
204 Ed Olczyk .15 .40
205 Phil Housley .15 .40
206 Troy Murray .15 .40
207 Wayne Gretzky 1000 1.25 3.00
208 Bryan Trottier 1000 .20 .50
209 Peter Stastny 1000 .15 .40
210 Jari Kurri 1000 .15 .40
211 Denis Savard 1000 .20 .50
212 Paul Coffey 1000 .20 .50
213 Mark Messier 1000 .40 1.00
214 Dave Taylor 1000 .15 .40
215 Michel Goulet 1000 .15 .40
216 Dale Hawerchuk 1000 .25 .60
217 Bobby Smith 1000 .15 .40
218 Ed Belfour LL .50 1.25
219 Brett Hull LL .40 1.00
220 Patrick Roy AS .50 1.25
221 Ray Bourque AS .30 .75
222 Wayne Gretzky AS 1.25 3.00
223 Jari Kurri AS .15 .40
224 Luc Robitaille AS .20 .50
225 Paul Coffey AS .20 .50
226 Bob Carpenter .15 .40
227 Gord Murphy .15 .40
228 Don Sweeney .12 .30
229 Glen Murray RC .20 .50
230 Ted Donato RC .20 .50
231 Jozef Stumpel RC .20 .50
232 Stephen Heinze RC .20 .50
233 Adam Oates .20 .50
234 Joe Juneau RC .20 .50
235 Gord Hynes RC .20 .50
236 Tony Tanti .15 .40
237 Petr Svoboda .15 .40
238 Bob Corkum .12 .30
239 Ken Sutton RC .20 .50
240 Tom Draper RC .20 .50
241 Grant Ledyard .15 .40
242 Christian Ruuttu .15 .40
243 Brad Miller .15 .40
244 Clint Malarchuk .15 .40
245 Trent Yawney .15 .40
246 Craig Berube .15 .40
247 Sergei Makarov .15 .40
248 Alexander Godynyuk RC .20 .50
249 Paul Ranheim .20 .50
250 Jeff Reese .15 .40
251 Chris Lindberg RC .20 .50
252 Michel Petit .15 .40
253 Joel Otto .15 .40
254 Gary Leeman .15 .40
255 Ray LeBlanc RC .20 .50
256 Jocelyn Lemieux .15 .40
257 Igor Kravchuk RC .20 .50
258 Rob Brown .15 .40
259 Stephane Matteau .15 .40
260 Mike Hudson .15 .40
261 Keith Brown .15 .40
262 Karl Dykhuis .15 .40
263 Dominik Hasek RC 2.00 5.00
264 Brian Noonan .12 .30
265 Yves Racine .15 .40
266 Slava Kozlov RC .20 .50
267 Martin Lapointe .15 .40
268 Steve Chiasson .15 .40
269 Gerard Gallant .12 .30
270 Brent Fedyk .15 .40
271 Brad McCrimmon .15 .40
272 Bob Probert .20 .50
273 Alan Kerr .15 .40
274 Luke Richardson .15 .40
275 Kelly Buchberger .15 .40
276 Craig MacTavish .15 .40
277 Ron Tugnutt .15 .40
278 Bernie Nicholls .15 .40
279 Anatoli Semenov .15 .40
280 Petr Klima .15 .40
281 Louie DeBrusk RC .20 .50
282 Norm Maciver RC .20 .50
283 Martin Gelinas .15 .40
284 Randy Cunneyworth .15 .40
285 Andrew Cassels .15 .40
286 Peter Sidorkiewicz .15 .40
287 Steve Konroyd .15 .40
288 Murray Craven .15 .40
289 Randy Ladouceur .15 .40
290 Bobby Holik .20 .50
291 Adam Burt .15 .40
292 Corey Millen RC .20 .50
293 Rob Blake .20 .50
294 Mike Donnelly RC .20 .50
295 Kyosti Karjalainen RC .20 .50
296 John McIntyre .15 .40
297 Paul Coffey .20 .50
298 Charlie Huddy .15 .40
299 Bob Kudelski .12 .30
300 Todd Elik .15 .40
301 Mike Craig .15 .40
302 Marc Bureau .15 .40
303 Jim Johnson .15 .40
304 Mark Tinordi .15 .40
305 Gaetan Duchesne .12 .30
306 Darcy Wakaluk RC .20 .50
307 Sylvain Lefebvre .15 .40
308 Russ Courtnall .15 .40
309 Patrice Brisebois .12 .30
310 Mike McPhee .15 .40
311 Mike Keane .12 .30
312 J.J. Daigneault .12 .30
313 Gilbert Dionne RC .20 .50
314 Brian Skrudland .15 .40
315 Brent Gilchrist .15 .40
316 Laurie Boschman .15 .40
317 Ken Daneyko .15 .40
318 Eric Weinrich .20 .50
319 Alexei Kasatonov .12 .30
320 Craig Billington RC .20 .50
321 Claude Vilgrain .15 .40
322 Bruce Driver .15 .40
323 Alexander Semak RC .20 .50
324 Valeri Zelepukin RC .20 .50
325 Rob DiMaio .15 .40
326 Scott Lachance RC .20 .50
327 Marty McInnis RC .20 .50
328 Joe Reekie .15 .40
329 Daniel Marois .15 .40
330 Wayne McBean .12 .30
331 Jeff Norton .15 .40
332 Benoit Hogue .15 .40
333 Tie Domi .15 .40
334 Sergei Nemchinov .15 .40
335 Randy Gilhen .15 .40
336 Paul Broten .12 .30
337 Kris King .15 .40
338 John Vanbiesbrouck .20 .50
339 Adam Graves .15 .40
340 Joe Cirella .15 .40
341 Jeff Beukeboom .15 .40
342 Terry Carkner .15 .40
343 Mark Freer RC .20 .50
344 Corey Foster RC .20 .50
345 Mark Pederson .15 .40
346 Kimbi Daniels RC .20 .50
347 Mark Recchi .25 .60
348 Kevin Dineen .15 .40
349 Kerry Huffman .12 .30
350 Garry Galley .15 .40
351 Dan Quinn .15 .40
352 Troy Loney .12 .30
353 Ron Francis .25 .60
354 Rick Tocchet .15 .40
355 Shawn McEachern RC .50 1.25
356 Kjell Samuelsson .15 .40
357 Ken Wreggett .15 .40
358 Larry Murphy .15 .40
359 Ken Priestlay .15 .40
360 Bryan Trottier .20 .50
361 Ulf Samuelsson .15 .40
362 Valeri Kamensky RC .50 1.25
363 Stephane Fiset .12 .30
364 Alexei Gusarov RC .15 .40
365 Greg Paslawski .15 .40
366 Martin Rucinsky RC .15 .40
367 Curtis Leschyshyn .15 .40
368 Jacques Cloutier .15 .40
369 Craig Wolanin .15 .40
370 Claude Lapointe RC .15 .40
371 Adam Foote RC .40 1.00
372 Rich Sutter .15 .40
373 Lee Norwood .12 .30
374 Garth Butcher .15 .40
375 Philippe Bozon RC .20 .50
376 Dave Lowry .15 .40
377 Darin Kimble .15 .40
378 Craig Janney .15 .40
379 Bob Bassen .15 .40
380 Rick Zombo .15 .40
381 Perry Berezan .15 .40
382 Neil Wilkinson .15 .40
383 Mike Sullivan RC .20 .50
384 David Bruce RC .20 .50
385 Johan Garpenlov .15 .40
386 Jeff Odgers RC .20 .50
387 Jay More RC .20 .50
388 Dean Evason .15 .40
389 Dale Craigwell .12 .30
390 Darryl Shannon RC .20 .50
391 Dimitri Mironov .15 .40
392 Kent Manderville .12 .30
393 Todd Gill .15 .40
394 Rick Wamsley .12 .30
395 Joe Sacco RC .20 .50
396 Doug Gilmour .25 .60
397 Mike Bullard .15 .40
398 Felix Potvin .40 1.00
399 Guy Larose RC .20 .50
400 Tom Fergus .12 .30
401 Ryan Walter .15 .40
402 Troy Gamble .12 .30
403 Robert Dirk .15 .40
404 Pavel Bure .20 .50
405 Jim Sandlak .15 .40
406 Igor Larionov .15 .40
407 Gerald Diduck .15 .40
408 Todd Krygier .15 .40
409 Tim Bergland .15 .40
410 Calle Johansson .15 .40
411 Nick Kypreos .15 .40
412 Michal Pivonka .15 .40
413 Brad Schlegel RC .20 .50
414 Kelly Miller .15 .40
415 John Druce .15 .40
416 Don Beaupre .15 .40
417 Alan May .15 .40
418 Randy Carlyle .15 .40
419 Stu Barnes .15 .40
420 Mike Eagles .15 .40
421 Igor Ulanov RC .20 .50
422 Evgeny Davydov RC .20 .50
423 Shawn Cronin .15 .40
424 Keith Tkachuk RC .20 .50
425 Luciano Borsato RC .20 .50
426 Stephane Beauregard .12 .30
427 Mike Lalor .15 .40
428 Michel Goulet 500 .15 .40
429 Wayne Gretzky 500 1.25 3.00
430 Mike Gartner 500 .25 .60
431 Bryan Trottier 500 .20 .50
432 Brett Hull LL .40 1.00
433 Wayne Gretzky LL 3.00 8.00
434 Steve Yzerman LL .60 1.50
435 Paul Ysebaert LL .15 .40
436 Gary Roberts LL .15 .40
437 Dave Andreychuk LL .20 .50
438 Brian Leetch LL .15 .40
439 Jeremy Roenick LL .30 .75
440 Kirk McLean LL .15 .40
441 Tim Cheveldae LL .15 .40
442 Patrick Roy LL .50 1.25
443 Tony Amonte RL .50 1.25
444 Kevin Todd RL .20 .50
445 Nicklas Lidstrom RL .75 2.00
446 Pavel Bure RL .20 .50
447 Gilbert Dionne RL .20 .50
448 Tom Draper RL .20 .50
449 Dominik Hasek RL .60 1.50
450 Dominic Roussel RL RC .20 .50
451 Checklist .12 .30
452 Trent Klatt XRC 1.25 3.00
453 Bill Guerin XRC 3.00 8.00
454 Ray Whitney XRC 2.00 5.00
455 Boston/Adams winner .12 .30
456 Pittsburgh/Patrick .15 .40
457 Chicago/Norris .15 .40
458 Edmonton/Smythe .15 .40
459 Pittsburgh/Wales .75 2.00
460 Chicago/Capbell .15 .40
461 Pittsburgh/Stanley Cup .60 1.50
462 Pavel Bure AW .20 .50
463 Patrick Roy AW .50 1.25
464 Brian Leetch AW .15 .40
465 Wayne Gretzky AW 1.25 3.00
466 Guy Carbonneau AW .15 .40
467 Mario Lemieux AW 5.00 12.00
468 Mark Messier AW 3.00 8.00
469 Ray Bourque AW 3.00 8.00
470 Patrick Roy AS 3.00 8.00
471 Brian Leetch AS 2.00 5.00
472 Ray Bourque AS 2.50 6.00
473 Kevin Stevens AS 2.00 5.00
474 Brett Hull AS 4.00 10.00
475 Mark Messier AS .40 1.00
SC Santa Claus .60 1.50
P1 Doug Gilmour PROMO 1.25 3.00
P2 Robert Reichel PROMO 1.25 3.00

1991-92 Parkhurst PHC

*FRENCH: .5X TO 1.25X BASIC INSERTS
PHC1 Gordie Howe 1.00 2.50
PHC2 Alex Delvecchio .30 .75
PHC3 Ken Hodge Jr. .25 .60
PHC4 Robert Kron .25 .60
PHC5 Sergei Fedorov .50 1.25
PHC6 Brett Hull .60 1.50
PHC7 Mario Lemieux 1.25 3.00
PHC8 Brian Leetch
Mark Messier .60 1.50
PHC9 Terry Sawchuk .25 .60

1992-93 Parkhurst Previews

PV1 Paul Ysebaert .60 1.50
PV2 Sean Burke .75 2.00
PV3 Gilbert Dionne .60 1.50
PV4 Ken Hammond .60 1.50
PV5 Grant Fuhr .75 2.00

1992-93 Parkhurst

1 Ray Bourque .15 .40
2 Joe Juneau .05 .15
3 Andy Moog .10 .25
4 Adam Oates .10 .25
5 Vladimir Ruzicka .05 .15
6 Glen Wesley .05 .15
7 Dmitri Kvartalnov RC .05 .15
8 Ted Donato .05 .15
9 Glen Murray .07 .20
10 Dave Andreychuk .10 .25
11 Dale Hawerchuk .12 .30
12 Pat LaFontaine .10 .25
13 Alexander Mogilny .07 .20
14 Richard Smehlik RC .05 .15
15 Keith Carney RC .20 .50
16 Philippe Boucher .05 .15
17 Viktor Gordijuk RC .05 .15
18 Donald Audette .07 .20
19 Theo Fleury .15 .40
20 Al MacInnis .12 .30
21 Joe Nieuwendyk .07 .20
22 Gary Roberts .05 .15
23 Gary Suter .05 .15
24 Mike Vernon .07 .20
25 Sergei Makarov .05 .15
26 Robert Reichel .05 .15
27 Chris Lindberg .05 .15
28 Ed Belfour .10 .25
29 Chris Chelios .10 .25
30 Steve Larmer .05 .15
31 Jeremy Roenick .15 .40
32 Steve Smith .05 .15
33 Brent Sutter .05 .15
34 Christian Ruuttu .05 .15
35 Igor Kravchuk .05 .15
36 Sergei Krivokrasov .05 .15
37 Tim Cheveldae .05 .15
38 Mike Sillinger .05 .15
39 Sergei Fedorov .15 .40
40 Slava Kozlov .07 .20
41 Bob Probert .10 .25
42 Nicklas Lidstrom .07 .20
43 Paul Ysebaert .05 .15
44 Steve Yzerman .25 .60
45 Dino Ciccarelli .07 .20
46 Esa Tikkanen .05 .15
47 Dave Manson .05 .15
48 Craig MacTavish .05 .15
49 Bernie Nicholls .07 .20
50 Bill Ranford .07 .20
51 Craig Simpson .05 .15
52 Scott Mellanby .05 .15
53 Shayne Corson .07 .20
54 Petr Klima .05 .15
55 Murray Craven .05 .15
56 Eric Weinrich .05 .15
57 Sean Burke .07 .20
58 Pat Verbeek .05 .15
59 Zarley Zalapski .05 .15
60 Patrick Poulin .05 .15
61 Robert Petrovicky RC .05 .15
62 Geoff Sanderson .07 .20
63 Paul Coffey .10 .25
64 Robert Lang RC .05 .15
65 Wayne Gretzky .60 1.50
66 Kelly Hrudey .07 .20
67 Jari Kurri .10 .25
68 Luc Robitaille .10 .25
69 Darryl Sydor .05 .15
70 Jim Hiller RC .05 .15
71 Alexei Zhitnik .05 .15
72 Derian Hatcher .05 .15
73 Jon Casey .05 .15
74 Richard Matvichuk RC .07 .20
75 Mike Modano .25 .60
76 Mark Tinordi .05 .15
77 Todd Elik .05 .15
78 Russ Courtnall .05 .15
79 Tommy Sjodin RC .05 .15
80 Eric Desjardins .07 .20
81 Gilbert Dionne .05 .15
82 Stephan Lebeau .05 .15
83 Kirk Muller .05 .15
84 Patrick Roy .25 .60
85 Denis Savard .10 .25
86 Vincent Damphousse .07 .20
87 Brian Bellows .07 .20
88 Ed Ronan RC .05 .15
89 Claude Lemieux .05 .15
90 John MacLean .07 .20
91 Stephane Richer .07 .20
92 Scott Stevens .10 .25
93 Chris Terreri .07 .20
94 Kevin Todd .05 .15
95 Scott Niedermayer .10 .25
96 Bobby Holik .07 .20
97 Bill Guerin RC .20 .50
98 Ray Ferraro .05 .15
99 Mark Fitzpatrick .07 .20
100 Derek King .05 .15
101 Uwe Krupp .05 .15
102 Darius Kasparaitis .05 .15
103 Pierre Turgeon .07 .20
104 Benoit Hogue .05 .15
105 Scott Lachance .05 .15
106 Marty McInnis .05 .15
107 Tony Amonte .07 .20
108 Mike Gartner .12 .30
109 Alexei Kovalev .07 .20
110 Brian Leetch .07 .20
111 Mark Messier .20 .50
112 Mike Richter .10 .25
113 James Patrick .05 .15
114 Sergei Nemchinov .05 .15
115 Doug Weight .20 .50
116 Mark Lamb .05 .15
117 Norm Maciver .05 .15
118 Mike Peluso .07 .20
119 Jody Hull .05 .15
120 Peter Sidorkiewicz .05 .15
121 Sylvain Turgeon .05 .15
122 Laurie Boschman .05 .15
123 Brad Marsh .07 .20
124 Neil Brady .05 .15
125 Brian Benning .05 .15
126 Rod Brind'Amour .05 .15
127 Kevin Dineen .05 .15
128 Eric Lindros .15 .40
129 Dominic Roussel .07 .20
130 Mark Recchi .12 .30
131 Brent Fedyk .05 .15
132 Greg Paslawski .05 .15
133 Dimitri Yushkevich RC .05 .15

134 Tom Barrasso .07 .20
135 Jaromir Jagr .20 .50
136 Mario Lemieux .40 1.00
137 Larry Murphy .07 .20
138 Kevin Stevens .07 .20
139 Rick Tocchet .07 .20
140 Martin Straka RC .20 .50
141 Ron Francis .12 .30
142 Shawn McEachern .05 .15
143 Steve Duchesne .05 .15
144 Ron Hextall .10 .25
145 Owen Nolan .10 .25
146 Mike Ricci .05 .15
147 Joe Sakic .20 .50
148 Mats Sundin .10 .25
149 Martin Rucinsky .05 .15
150 Andrei Kovalenko RC .15 .40
151 Dave Karpa RC .05 .15
152 Nelson Emerson .05 .15
153 Brett Hull .20 .50
154 Craig Janney .07 .20
155 Curtis Joseph .12 .30
156 Brendan Shanahan .10 .25
157 Vitali Prokhorov RC .05 .15
158 Igor Korolev RC .05 .15
159 Philippe Bozon .05 .15
160 Ray Whitney RC .15 .40
161 Pat Falloon .05 .15
162 Jeff Hackett .07 .20
163 Brian Lawton .07 .20
164 Sandis Ozolinsh .05 .15
165 Neil Wilkinson .05 .15
166 Kelly Kisio .07 .20
167 Doug Wilson .07 .20
168 Dale Craigwell .05 .15
169 Mikael Andersson .05 .15
170 Wendell Young .07 .20
171 Rob Zamuner RC .07 .20
172 Adam Creighton .05 .15
173 Roman Hamrlik RC .20 .50
174 Brian Bradley .05 .15
175 Rob Ramage .05 .15
176 Chris Kontos RC .05 .15
177 Stan Drulia RC .05 .15
178 Glenn Anderson .07 .20
179 Wendel Clark .15 .40
180 John Cullen .05 .15
181 Dave Ellett .05 .15
182 Grant Fuhr .15 .40
183 Doug Gilmour .12 .30
184 Kent Manderville .05 .15
185 Joe Sacco .05 .15
186 Nikolai Borschevsky RC .05 .15
187 Felix Potvin .20 .50
188 Pavel Bure .10 .25
189 Geoff Courtnall .05 .15
190 Trevor Linden .10 .25
191 Jyrki Lumme .05 .15
192 Kirk McLean .05 .15
193 Cliff Ronning .05 .15
194 Dixon Ward RC .07 .20
195 Greg Adams .05 .15
196 Jiri Slegr .05 .15
197 Don Beaupre .07 .20
198 Kevin Hatcher .05 .15
199 Brad Schlegel .05 .15
200 Mike Ridley .05 .15
201 Calle Johansson .05 .15
202 Steve Konowalchuk RC .07 .20
203 Al Iafrate .07 .20
204 Peter Bondra .10 .25
205 Pat Elynuik .05 .15
206 Keith Tkachuk .10 .25
207 Bob Essensa .07 .20
208 Phil Housley .07 .20
209 Teemu Selanne .20 .50
210 Alexei Zhamnov .07 .20
211 Evgeny Davydov .05 .15
212 Fredrik Olausson .05 .15
213 Ed Olczyk .05 .15
214 Thomas Steen .05 .15
215 Darius Kasparaitis .05 .15
216 Nikolai Borschevsky IRS .05 .15
217 Teemu Selanne IRS .20 .50
218 Alexander Mogilny IRS .07 .20
219 Sergei Fedorov IRS .15 .40
220 Jaromir Jagr IRS .20 .50
221 Mats Sundin IRS .10 .25
222 Dmitri Kvartalnov IRS .05 .15
223 Andrei Kovalenko IRS .15 .40
224 Tommy Sjodin IRS .05 .15
225 Alexei Kovalev IRS .07 .20
226 Evgeny Davydov .05 .15
227 Robert Lang IRS .05 .15
228 Valeri Zelepukin SPH .05 .15
229 Doug Weight .20 .50
230 Valeri Kamensky SPH .05 .15
231 Donald Audette .07 .20
232 Nelson Emerson SPH .05 .15
233 Pat Falloon SPH .05 .15
234 Pavel Bure SPH .10 .25
235 Tony Amonte SPH .07 .20
236 Sergei Nemchinov SPH .05 .15
237 Gilbert Dionne SPH .05 .15
238 Kevin Todd .05 .15
239 Nicklas Lidstrom SPH .07 .20
240 Brad May .05 .15
241 Stephen Leach .05 .15
242 Dave Poulin .05 .15
243 Grigori Panteleyev RC .05 .15
244 Don Sweeney .05 .15
245 John Blue RC .07 .20
246 C.J.Young RC .05 .15
247 Stephen Heinze .05 .15
248 Cam Neely .10 .25
249 David Reid .05 .15
250 Grant Fuhr .15 .40
251 Bob Sweeney .05 .15
252 Rob Ray .05 .15
253 Doug Bodger .05 .15
254 Ken Sutton .05 .15
255 Yuri Khmylev RC .05 .15
256 Mike Ramsey .05 .15
257 Brad May .05 .15
258 Brent Ashton .05 .15
259 Joel Otto .05 .15
260 Paul Ranheim .05 .15
261 Kevin Dahl RC .05 .15
262 Trent Yawney .07 .20
263 Roger Johansson .07 .20
264 Jeff Reese .05 .15
265 Ron Stern .07 .20
266 Brian Skrudland .07 .20
267 Bryan Marchment .07 .20
268 Stephane Matteau .05 .15
269 Frantisek Kucera .07 .20
270 Jim Waite .07 .20
271 Dirk Graham .05 .15
272 Michel Goulet .07 .20
273 Joe Murphy .05 .15
274 Keith Brown .07 .20
275 Jocelyn Lemieux .05 .15
276 Paul Coffey .10 .25
277 Keith Primeau .07 .20
278 Vincent Riendeau .07 .20
279 Mark Howe .10 .25
280 Ray Sheppard .05 .15
281 Jim Hiller .05 .15
282 Steve Chiasson .05 .15
283 Vladimir Konstantinov .10 .25
284 Brian Benning .05 .15
285 Kevin Todd .05 .15
286 Zdeno Ciger .05 .15
287 Brian Glynn .05 .15
288 Shaun Van Allen .07 .20
289 Brad Werenka RC .07 .20
290 Ron Tugnutt .07 .20
291 Igor Kravchuk .05 .15
292 Todd Elik .05 .15
293 Terry Yake .05 .15
294 Michael Nylander RC .05 .15
295 Yvon Corriveau .05 .15
296 Frank Pietrangelo .07 .20
297 Nick Kypreos .05 .15
298 Andrew Cassels .05 .15
299 Steve Konroyd .07 .20
300 Allen Pedersen .05 .15
301 Tony Granato .05 .15
302 Rob Blake .07 .20
303 Robb Stauber .07 .20
304 Marty McSorley .07 .20
305 Lonnie Loach RC .05 .15
306 Corey Millen .05 .15
307 Dave Taylor .07 .20
308 Jimmy Carson .05 .15
309 Warren Rychel RC .05 .15
310 Ulf Dahlen .07 .20
311 Dave Gagner .07 .20
312 Brad Berry RC .07 .20
313 Neal Broten .07 .20
314 Mike Craig .07 .20
315 Darcy Wakaluk .07 .20
316 Shane Churla .07 .20
317 Trent Klatt RC .07 .20
318 Mike Keane .05 .15
319 Mathieu Schneider .05 .15
320 Patrice Brisebois .05 .15
321 Andre Racicot .07 .20
322 Mario Roberge .07 .20
323 Gary Leeman .05 .15
324 Jean-Jacques Daigneault .05 .15
325 Lyle Odelein .07 .20
326 John LeClair .10 .25
327 Valeri Zelepukin .05 .15
328 Bernie Nicholls .07 .20
329 Alexander Semak .07 .20
330 Craig Billington .07 .20
331 Randy McKay .07 .20
332 Ken Daneyko .07 .20
333 Bruce Driver .07 .20
334 Slava Fetisov .07 .20
335 Dennis Vaske .05 .15
336 Brad Dalgarno .07 .20
337 Jeff Norton .05 .15
338 Steve Thomas .05 .15
339 Vladimir Malakhov .05 .15
340 David Volek .05 .15
341 Glenn Healy .07 .20
342 Patrick Flatley .07 .20
343 Travis Green RC .07 .20
344 Corey Hirsch RC .10 .25
345 Darren Turcotte .05 .15
346 Adam Graves .07 .20
347 Steven King RC .05 .15
348 Kevin Lowe .07 .20
349 John Vanbiesbrouck .10 .25
350 Ed Olczyk .05 .15
351 Sergei Zubov RC .15 .40
352 Brad Shaw .05 .15
353 Jamie Baker .05 .15
354 Mark Freer .05 .15
355 Darcy Loewen .05 .15
356 Darren Rumble RC .05 .15
357 Bob Kudelski .07 .20
358 Ken Hammond .07 .20
359 Daniel Berthiaume .07 .20
360 Josef Beranek .05 .15
361 Greg Hawgood .05 .15
362 Terry Carkner .07 .20
363 Vyatcheslav Butsayev RC .05 .15
364 Garry Galley .05 .15
365 Andre Faust RC .07 .20
366 Ryan McGill RC .05 .15
367 Tommy Soderstrom RC .07 .20
368 Joe Mullen .07 .20
369 Ulf Samuelsson .05 .15
370 Mike Needham RC .05 .15
371 Ken Wregget .07 .20
372 Dave Tippett .07 .20
373 Kjell Samuelsson .05 .15
374 Bob Errey .07 .20
375 Jim Paek .05 .15
376 Bill Lindsay RC .05 .15
377 Valeri Kamensky .05 .15
378 Stephane Fiset .07 .20
379 Steven Finn .05 .15
380 Mike Hough .05 .15
381 Scott Pearson .07 .20
382 Kerry Huffman .05 .15
383 Scott Young .05 .15
384 Stephane Quintal .07 .20
385 Bret Hedican RC .07 .20
386 Guy Hebert RC .15 .40
387 Vitali Karamnov RC .05 .15
388 Doug Crossman .07 .20
389 Ron Sutter .05 .15
390 Garth Butcher .07 .20
391 Basil McRae .05 .15
392 Dean Evason .05 .15
393 Doug Zmolek RC .05 .15
394 Jay More .05 .15
395 Mike Sullivan .05 .15
396 Arturs Irbe .07 .20
397 Johan Garpenlov .05 .15
398 Jeff Odgers .05 .15
399 Jaroslav Otevrel RC .07 .20
400 Marc Bureau .07 .20
401 Bob Beers .05 .15
402 Rob DiMaio .05 .15
403 Steve Kasper .05 .15
404 Pat Jablonski .07 .20
405 John Tucker .05 .15
406 Shawn Chambers .05 .15
407 Mike Hartman .05 .15
408 Danton Cole .07 .20
409 Dave Andreychuk .10 .25
410 Peter Zezel .05 .15
411 Mike Krushelnyski .05 .15
412 Daren Puppa .07 .20
413 Ken Baumgartner .05 .15
414 Rob Pearson .05 .15
415 Mike Foligno .07 .20
416 Sylvain Lefebvre .05 .15
417 Dimitri Mironov .05 .15
418 Petr Nedved .07 .20
419 Gerald Diduck .07 .20
420 Anatoli Semenov .05 .15
421 Sergio Momesso .05 .15
422 Gino Odjick .05 .15
423 Kay Whitmore .07 .20
424 Dave Babych .07 .20
425 Robert Dirk .07 .20
426 Reggie Savage .05 .15
427 Keith Jones RC .10 .25
428 Dimitri Khristich .05 .15
429 Jason Woolley RC .05 .15
430 Jim Hrivnak .07 .20
431 Sylvain Cote .07 .20
432 Michal Pivonka .05 .15
433 Rod Langway .07 .20
434 Tie Domi .07 .20
435 Sergei Bautin RC .05 .15
436 Darrin Shannon .05 .15
437 John Druce .05 .15
438 Teppo Numminen .07 .20
439 Luciano Borsato .07 .20
440 Igor Ulanov .05 .15
441 Mike O'Neill RC .07 .20
442 Kris King .07 .20
443 Roman Hamrlik IRS .20 .50
444 Steve Smith .05 .15
445 Jari Kurri .10 .25
446 Ulf Samuelsson .05 .15
447 Sergei Nemchinov IRS .05 .15
448 Tommy Soderstrom IRS .07 .20
449 Petr Nedved IRS .07 .20
450 Peter Sidorkiewicz .05 .15
451 Nicklas Lidstrom IRS .07 .20
452 Philippe Bozon IRS .05 .15
453 Uwe Krupp .05 .15
454 Steve Thomas .07 .20
455 Owen Nolan IRS .10 .25
456 Steve Yzerman AS .25 .60
457 Chris Chelios .10 .25
458 Paul Coffey AS .07 .20
459 Brett Hull AS .20 .50
460 Pavel Bure AS .10 .25
461 Ed Belfour AS .10 .25
462 Mario Lemieux AS .40 1.00
463 Patrick Roy AS .25 .60
464 Ray Bourque AS .15 .40
465 Jaromir Jagr AS .20 .50
466 Kevin Stevens AS .05 .15
467 Brian Leetch AS .07 .20
468 Bobby Clarke FLYER .15 .40
469 Bill Barber .07 .20
470 Bernie Parent FLYER .12 .30
471 Reggie Leach .07 .20
472 Rick MacLeish .07 .20
473 Dave Schultz .07 .20
474 Joe Watson .07 .20
475 Bobby Taylor .07 .20
476 Orest Kindrachuk .07 .20
477 Bob Kelly .05 .15
478 Bill Clement .07 .20
479 Ed Van Impe .07 .20
480 Fred Shero .07 .20
481 Bryan Smolinski RC .07 .20
482 Sergei Zholtok .07 .20
483 Matthew Barnaby RC .07 .20
484 Gary Shuchuk .07 .20
485 Guy Carbonneau .07 .20
486 Oleg Petrov RC .05 .15
487 Sean Hill RC .05 .15
488 Jesse Belanger RC .07 .20
489 Paul DiPietro .07 .20
490 Rich Pilon .05 .15
491 Greg Parks .07 .20
492 Jeff Daniels .07 .20
493 Denny Felsner RC .07 .20
494 Mike Eastwood RC .07 .20
495 Murray Craven .07 .20
496 Vincent Damphousse .07 .20
497 Grant Fuhr .15 .40
498 Mario Lemieux SCP .40 1.00
499 Ray Ferraro .07 .20
500 Teemu Selanne SCP .20 .50
501 Luc Robitaille SCP .10 .25
502 Doug Gilmour SCP .12 .30
503 Curtis Joseph SCP .12 .30
504 Kirk Muller .05 .15
505 Glenn Healy .07 .20
506 Pavel Bure SCP .10 .25
507 Felix Potvin SCP .20 .50
508 Guy Carbonneau .07 .20
509 Wayne Gretzky SCP .60 1.50
510 Patrick Roy SCP .25 .60

1992-93 Parkhurst Emerald Ice

COMPLETE SET (480) 60.00 120.00
COMP.SERIES 1 (240) 30.00 80.00
COMP.SERIES 2 (240) 40.00 80.00
COMP.FINAL UPDATE (30) 12.50 25.00
*VETS: 2X TO 5X BASIC CARDS
*ROOKIES: 1.2X TO 3X BASIC CARDS
*UPDATE: 1.2X TO 3X BASIC CARDS

1992-93 Parkhurst Cherry Picks

COMPLETE SET (21) 25.00 50.00
CP1 Doug Gilmour 1.50 4.00
CP2 Jeremy Roenick 2.50 6.00
CP3 Brent Sutter 1.00 2.50
CP4 Mark Messier 1.50 4.00
CP5 Kirk Muller 1.25 3.00
CP6 Eric Lindros 2.00 5.00
CP7 Dale Hunter 1.00 2.50
CP8 Gary Roberts 1.00 2.50
CP9 Bob Probert 1.25 3.00
CP10 Brendan Shanahan 2.00 5.00
CP11 Wendel Clark 1.25 3.00
CP12 Rick Tocchet 1.00 2.50
CP13 Owen Nolan 1.25 3.00
CP14 Cam Neely 1.50 4.00
CP15 Dave Manson 1.00 2.50
CP16 Chris Chelios 1.50 4.00
CP17 Marty McSorley UER 1.25 3.00
CP18 Scott Stevens 1.25 3.00
CP19 John Blue 1.00 2.50
CP20 Ron Hextall 1.50 4.00
CP1993 Doug Gilmour 5.00 12.00
AU Don Cherry AU 40.00 80.00
CL Don Cherry CL 8.00 20.00
NNO Don Cherry RDMP 15.00 40.00

1992-93 Parkhurst Cherry Picks Sheet

1 Dale Hunter
Dave Manson
Doug Gilmour
Gary Roberts
Chris Chelios
Jeremy Roenick
Bob Probert
Marty McSorley
B.Sutter
Brenden Shanahan
Don Cherry
Mark Messier
Wendel Clark
Kirk Muller
Rick Tocchet
Scott Stevens
Eric Lindros
Owen Nolan
John Blue
Ron Hextall 4.00 10.00

1992-93 Parkhurst Parkie Reprints

COMPLETE SET (36) 75.00 150.00
*PROMO: .4X TO 1X BASIC INSERT
PR1 Jacques Plante 3.00 8.00
PR2 Terry Sawchuk 3.00 8.00
PR3 Johnny Bower 2.50 6.00
PR4 Gump Worsley 2.50 6.00
PR5 Harry Lumley 2.50 6.00
PR6 Turk Broda 2.50 6.00
PR7 Jim Henry 1.50 4.00
PR8 Al Rollins 2.00 5.00
PR9 Bill Gadsby 2.00 5.00
PR10 Red Kelly 2.00 5.00
PR11 Allan Stanley 1.50 4.00
PR12 Bob Baun 2.00 5.00
PR13 Carl Brewer 1.50 4.00
PR14 Doug Harvey 2.50 6.00
PR15 Harry Howell 2.00 5.00
PR16 Tim Horton 2.00 5.00
PR17 George Armstrong 1.50 4.00
PR18 Ralph Backstrom 1.50 4.00
PR19 Alex Delvecchio 2.50 6.00
PR20 Bill Mosienko 1.50 4.00
PR21 Dave Keon 2.00 5.00
PR22 Andy Bathgate 2.00 5.00
PR23 Milt Schmidt 2.00 5.00
PR24 Dick Duff 2.00 5.00
PR25 Norm Ullman 2.00 5.00
PR26 Dickie Moore 2.00 5.00
PR27 Jerry Toppazzini 1.50 4.00
PR28 Henri Richard 2.50 6.00
PR29 Frank Mahovlich 2.50 6.00
PR30 Jean Beliveau 3.00 8.00
PR31 Ted Lindsay 2.50 6.00
PR32 Bernie Geoffrion 2.50 6.00
CL1 Parkies Checklist 1 1.50 4.00
CL2 Parkies Checklist 2 1.50 4.00
CL3 Parkies Checklist 3 1.50 4.00
CL4 Parkies Checklist 4 1.50 4.00
AU Don Cherry Parkie AU 50.00 100.00
NNO D.Cherry Parkie 101 2.50 6.00

1992-93 Parkhurst Arena Tour Sheets

1 Calgary Flames
Olympic 2.50 6.00
2 Edmonton Oilers
Northla 2.50 6.00
3 Quebec Nordiques
Colisee de Quebec, April 6 1993
Bill Lindsay
Ron Hextall
Valeri Kamensky
Kerry Huffman
Mats Sundin
Joe Sakic 2.50 6.00
4 Vancouver Canucks
Pacif 4.00 10.00
5 Montreal Canadiens
The 6.00 15.00
6 Toronto Maple Leafs
Maple Leaf Gardens
April 13& 5.00 12.00
7 Ottawa Senators
Ottawa 2.50 6.00
8 Winnipeg Jets
Winnipeg 2.50 6.00

1992-93 Parkhurst Parkie Sheets

1 Goalies
(7000 sheets issued) 6.00 15.00
2 Defensemen
(3000 sheets issued) 8.00 20.00
3 Forwards
Wingers
(7000 sheets issued) 6.00 15.00
4 Forwards
Centers
(3000 sheets issued) 8.00 20.00
5 Stanley Cup Update
(1000 sheets issued) 8.00 20.00

1992-93 Parkhurst Parkie Sheets Promo

*1-5 PROMO SHEET: .2X TO .5X NUMBERED SHEET
6 Maple Leafs vs. Canadiens 3.00 8.00

1993-94 Parkhurst

1 Steven King .10 .25
2 Sean Hill .10 .25
3 Anatoli Semenov .10 .25
4 Garry Valk .10 .25
5 Todd Ewen .10 .25
6 Bob Corkum .10 .25
7 Tim Sweeney .10 .25
8 Patrick Carnback RC .15 .40
9 Troy Loney .10 .25
10 Cam Neely .15 .40
11 Adam Oates .15 .40
12 Jon Casey .12 .30
13 Don Sweeney .10 .25
14 Ray Bourque .25 .60
15 Jozef Stumpel .10 .25
16 Glen Murray .12 .30
17 Glen Wesley .10 .25
18 Fred Knipscheer RC .10 .25
19 Craig Simpson .10 .25
20 Richard Smehlik .10 .25
21 Alexander Mogilny .12 .30
22 Grant Fuhr .25 .60
23 Dale Hawerchuk .20 .50
24 Philippe Boucher .10 .25
25 Scott Thomas RC .15 .40
26 Donald Audette .10 .25
27 Brad May .12 .30
28 Theo Fleury .10 .25
29 Andrei Trefilov .10 .25
30 Sandy McCarthy .10 .25
31 Joe Nieuwendyk .12 .30
32 Paul Ranheim .10 .25
33 Kelly Kisio .10 .25
34 Joel Otto .10 .25
35 Ted Drury .10 .25
36 Al MacInnis .20 .50
37 Kevin Todd .10 .25
38 Joe Murphy .10 .25
39 Christian Ruuttu .10 .25
40 Steve Dubinsky RC .15 .40
41 Stephane Matteau .10 .25
42 Ivan Droppa RC .10 .25
43 Jocelyn Lemieux .10 .25
44 Ed Belfour .15 .40
45 Chris Chelios .15 .40
46 Derian Hatcher .10 .25
47 Andy Moog .15 .40
48 Trent Klatt .10 .25
49 Mike Modano .25 .60
50 Paul Cavallini .10 .25
51 Mike McPhee .10 .25
52 Brent Gilchrist .10 .25
53 Russ Courtnall .10 .25
54 Neal Broten .12 .30
55 Steve Chiasson .10 .25
56 Paul Coffey .15 .40
57 Slava Kozlov .12 .30
58 Sergei Fedorov .25 .60
59 Tim Cheveldae .15 .40
60 Dino Ciccarelli .15 .40
61 Dallas Drake RC .15 .40
62 Nicklas Lidstrom .15 .40
63 Martin Lapointe .10 .25
64 Dean McAmmond .10 .25
65 Igor Kravchuk .10 .25
66 Shjon Podein RC .15 .40
67 Bill Ranford .12 .30
68 Brad Werenka .10 .25
69 Doug Weight .12 .30
70 Ian Herbers RC .10 .25
71 Todd Elik .10 .25
72 Steven Rice .10 .25
73 John Vanbiesbrouck .15 .40
74 Alexander Godynyuk .10 .25
75 Brian Skrudland .10 .25
76 Jody Hull .10 .25
77 Brent Severyn RC .15 .40
78 Evgeny Davydov .10 .25
79 Dave Lowry .10 .25
80 Scott Levins RC .15 .40
81 Scott Mellanby .12 .30
82 Dan Keczmer .10 .25
83 Michael Nylander .10 .25
84 Jim Sandlak .10 .25
85 Brian Propp .10 .25
86 Geoff Sanderson .12 .30
87 Mike Lenarduzzi RC .10 .25
88 Zarley Zalapski .10 .25
89 Robert Petrovicky .10 .25
90 Robert Kron .10 .25
91 Luc Robitaille .15 .40
92 Alexei Zhitnik .10 .25
93 Tony Granato .10 .25
94 Rob Blake .12 .30
95 Gary Shuchuk .10 .25
96 Darryl Sydor .10 .25
97 Kelly Hrudey .12 .30
98 Warren Rychel .10 .25
99 Wayne Gretzky 1.00 2.50
100 Patrick Roy .40 1.00
101 Gilbert Dionne .10 .25
102 Eric Desjardins .12 .30
103 Peter Popovic RC .10 .25
104 Vincent Damphousse .12 .30
105 Patrice Brisebois .10 .25
106 Pierre Sevigny .10 .25
107 John LeClair .15 .40
108 Paul DiPietro .10 .25
109 Alexander Semak .10 .25
110 Claude Lemieux .10 .25
111 Scott Niedermayer .15 .40
112 Chris Terreri .12 .30
113 Stephane Richer .12 .30
114 Scott Stevens .15 .40
115 John MacLean .12 .30
116 Scott Pellerin RC .15 .40
117 Bernie Nicholls .12 .30
118 Ron Hextall .15 .40
119 Derek King .10 .25
120 Scott Lachance .10 .25
121 Scott Scissons .10 .25
122 Darius Kasparaitis .10 .25
123 Ray Ferraro .10 .25
124 Steve Thomas .10 .25
125 Vladimir Malakhov .10 .25
126 Travis Green .12 .30
127 Mark Messier .30 .75
128 Sergei Nemchinov .10 .25
129 Mike Richter .15 .40
130 Alexei Kovalev .12 .30
131 Brian Leetch .12 .30
132 Tony Amonte .12 .30
133 Sergei Zubov .12 .30
134 Adam Graves .10 .25
135 Esa Tikkanen .10 .25
136 Sylvain Turgeon .10 .25
137 Norm Maciver .15 .40
138 Craig Billington .12 .30
139 Dmitri Filiminov .10 .25
140 Pavol Demitra .20 .50
141 Brian Glynn .10 .25
142 Darrin Madeley RC .15 .40
143 Radek Hamr RC .15 .40
144 Robert Burakovsky RC .15 .40
145 Dimitri Yushkevich .10 .25
146 Claude Boivin .10 .25
147 Pelle Eklund .10 .25
148 Brent Fedyk .10 .25
149 Mark Recchi .20 .50
150 Tommy Soderstrom .12 .30
151 Vyacheslav Butsayev .10 .25
152 Rod Brind'Amour .15 .40
153 Josef Beranek .10 .25
154 Jaromir Jagr .50 1.25
155 Ulf Samuelsson .10 .25
156 Martin Straka .10 .25
157 Tom Barrasso .12 .30
158 Kevin Stevens .12 .30
159 Joe Mullen .12 .30
160 Ron Francis .20 .50
161 Marty McSorley .10 .25
162 Larry Murphy .12 .30
163 Owen Nolan .15 .40
164 Stephane Fiset .12 .30
165 Dave Karpa .10 .25
166 Martin Gelinas .10 .25
167 Andrei Kovalenko .10 .25
168 Steve Duchesne .10 .25
169 Joe Sakic .30 .75
170 Martin Rucinsky .10 .25
171 Chris Simon RC .15 .40
172 Brendan Shanahan .15 .40
173 Jeff Brown .10 .25
174 Phil Housley .12 .30
175 Curtis Joseph .20 .50
176 Jim Montgomery RC .15 .40
177 Bret Hedican .10 .25
178 Kevin Miller .10 .25
179 Philippe Bozon .10 .25
180 Brett Hull .30 .75
181 Jimmy Waite .12 .30
182 Ray Whitney .10 .25
183 Pat Falloon .10 .25
184 Tom Pederson .10 .25
185 Igor Larionov .10 .25
186 Jody Wood RC .15 .40
187 Sandis Ozolinsh .10 .25
188 Sergei Makarov .10 .25
189 Rob Gaudreau RC .15 .40
190 Roman Hamrlik .10 .25
191 Stan Drulia .10 .25
192 Pat Jablonski .10 .25
193 Denis Savard .15 .40
194 Rob Zamuner .10 .25
195 Petr Klima .10 .25
196 Rob Dimaio .10 .25
197 Chris Kontos .10 .25
198 Mikael Andersson .10 .25
199 Drake Berehowsky .10 .25
200 Dave Andreychuk .15 .40
201 Glenn Anderson .12 .30
202 Felix Potvin .30 .75
203 Nikolai Borschevsky .10 .25
204 Kent Manderville .10 .25
205 Dave Ellett .10 .25
206 Peter Zezel .10 .25
207 Ken Baumgartner .10 .25
208 Murray Craven .10 .25
209 Dixon Ward .10 .25
210 Cliff Ronning .10 .25
211 Pavel Bure .15 .40
212 Sergio Momesso .10 .25
213 Kirk McLean .12 .30
214 Jiri Slegr .10 .25
215 Trevor Linden .15 .40
216 Geoff Courtnall .10 .25
217 Al Iafrate .10 .25
218 Mike Ridley .10 .25
219 Enrico Ciccone .10 .25
220 Dimitri Khristich .10 .25
221 Kevin Hatcher .10 .25
222 Peter Bondra .15 .40
223 Steve Konowalchuk .10 .25
224 Pat Elynuik .10 .25
225 Don Beaupre .12 .30
226 Stu Barnes .10 .25
227 Fredrik Olausson .10 .25
228 Keith Tkachuk .15 .40
229 Mike Eagles .10 .25
230 Tie Domi .12 .30
231 Teppo Numminen .10 .25
232 Arto Blomsten .10 .25
233 Teemu Selanne .30 .75
234 Bob Essensa .12 .30
235 Teemu Selanne SPH .30 .75
236 Eric Lindros SPH .25 .60
237 Felix Potvin SPH .30 .75
238 Alexei Kovalev SPH .12 .30
239 Vladimir Malakhov SPH .10 .25
240 Scott Niedermayer SPH .15 .40
241 Joe Juneau SPH .10 .25
242 Shawn McEachern SPH .10 .25
243 Alexei Zhamnov SPH .12 .30
244 Alexandre Daigle PKP .12 .30
245 Markus Naslund PKP .15 .40
246 Rob Niedermayer PKP .12 .30
247 Jocelyn Thibault RC .15 .40
248 Brent Gretzky PKP RC .15 .40
249 Chris Pronger PKP .15 .40
250 Chris Gratton PKP .12 .30
251 Mikael Renberg PKP .15 .40
252 Jarkko Varvio PKP .10 .25
253 Micah Aivazoff PKP RC .15 .40
254 Alexei Yashin PKP .12 .30
255 German Titov PKP RC .15 .40
256 Mattias Norstrom PKP RC .15 .40
257 Michal Sykora PKP RC .15 .40
258 Roman Oksiuta PKP RC .15 .40
259 Bryan Smolinski PKP .10 .25
260 Alexei Kudashov PKP RC .15 .40
261 Jason Arnott PKP RC .30 .75
262 Aaron Ward PKP RC .15 .40
263 Vesa Vitakoski PKP RC .15 .40
264 Boris Mironov PKP .10 .25
265 Darren McCarty PKP RC .25 .60
266 Vlastimil Kroupa PKP RC .15 .40
267 Denny Felsner PKP .10 .25
268 Milos Holan PKP RC .15 .40
269 Alex Karpovtsev PKP .10 .25
270 Greg Johnson PKP .10 .25
271 Terry Yake .10 .25
272 Bill Houlder .10 .25
273 Joe Sacco .10 .25
274 Myles O'Connor .10 .25
275 Mark Ferner RC .10 .25
276 Alexei Kasatanov .10 .25
277 Stu Grimson .10 .25
278 Shaun Van Allen .10 .25
279 Guy Hebert .12 .30
280 Joe Juneau .10 .25
281 Sergei Zholtok .10 .25
282 Daniel Marois .10 .25
283 Ted Donato .10 .25
284 Cam Stewart RC .15 .40
285 Stephen Leach .10 .25
286 Darren Banks .10 .25
287 Dmitri Kvartalnov .10 .25
288 Paul Stanton .10 .25
289 Pat LaFontaine .15 .40
290 Bob Sweeney .10 .25
291 Craig Muni .10 .25
292 Sergei Petrenko .10 .25
293 Derek Plante RC .15 .40
294 Wayne Presley .10 .25
295 Mark Astley RC .15 .40
296 Matthew Barnaby .12 .30
297 Randy Wood .10 .25
298 Kevin Dahl .10 .25
299 Gary Suter .10 .25
300 Robert Reichel .10 .25
301 Mike Vernon .12 .30
302 Gary Roberts .10 .25
303 Ronnie Stern .10 .25
304 Michel Petit .10 .25
305 Wes Walz .10 .25
306 Brad Miller RC .10 .25
307 Patrick Poulin .10 .25
308 Brent Sutter .10 .25
309 Jeremy Roenick .25 .60
310 Steve Smith .10 .25
311 Eric Weinrich .10 .25
312 Jeff Hackett .10 .25
313 Michel Goulet .10 .25
314 Jeff Shantz RC .15 .40
315 Neil Wilkinson .10 .25
316 Shane Churla .10 .25
317 Dave Gagner .12 .30
318 Chris Tancill .10 .25
319 Dean Evason .10 .25
320 Mark Tinordi .10 .25
321 Grant Ledyard .10 .25
322 Ulf Dahlen .10 .25
323 Mike Craig .10 .25
324 Paul Broten .10 .25
325 Vladimir Konstantinov .12 .30
326 Steve Yzerman .40 1.00
327 Keith Primeau .12 .30
328 Shawn Burr .10 .25
329 Chris Osgood RC 1.00 2.50
330 Ray Sheppard .12 .30
331 Mike Sillinger .10 .25
332 Terry Carkner .10 .25
333 Bob Probert .15 .40
334 Adam Bennett .15 .40
335 Dave Manson .10 .25
336 Zdeno Ciger .10 .25
337 Louie DeBrusk .10 .25
338 Shayne Corson .12 .30
339 Vladimir Vujtek .10 .25
340 Tyler Wright .10 .25
341 Ilya Byakin RC .15 .40
342 Craig MacTavish .10 .25
343 Brian Benning .10 .25
344 Mark Fitzpatrick .10 .25
345 Gord Murphy .10 .25
346 Jesse Belanger .10 .25
347 Joe Cirella .10 .25
348 Tom Fitzgerald .10 .25
349 Andrei Lomakin .10 .25
350 Bill Lindsay .10 .25
351 Len Barrie .10 .25
352 Frank Pietrangelo .12 .30
353 Pat Verbeek .10 .25
354 Jim Storm .10 .25
355 Mark Janssens .10 .25
356 Darren Turcotte .10 .25
357 Jim McKenzie .10 .25
358 Brad McCrimmon .10 .25
359 Andrew Cassels .10 .25
360 James Patrick .10 .25
361 Bob Jay RC .15 .40
362 Tomas Sandstrom .10 .25
363 Pat Conacher .10 .25
364 Shawn McEachern .10 .25

1992-93 Parkhurst Emerald Ice

365 Jari Kurri .15 .40
366 Dominic Lavoie .10 .25
367 Dave Taylor .10 .25
368 Jimmy Carson .10 .25
369 Mike Donnelly .10 .25
370 Lyle Odelein .10 .25
371 Brian Bellows .12 .30
372 Guy Carbonneau .10 .25
373 Mathieu Schneider .10 .25
374 Stephan Lebeau .10 .25
375 Benoit Brunet .10 .25
376 Kevin Haller .10 .25
377 J.J. Daigneault .10 .25
378 Kirk Muller .10 .25
379 Jason Smith RC .10 .25
380 Martin Brodeur .40 1.00
381 Corey Millen .10 .25
382 Bill Guerin .15 .40
383 Valeri Zelepukin .10 .25
384 Tom Chorske .10 .25
385 Bobby Holik .10 .25
386 Jaroslav Modry RC .15 .40
387 Ken Daneyko .10 .25
388 Uwe Krupp .10 .25
389 Pierre Turgeon .12 .30
390 Marty McInnis .10 .25
391 Patrick Flatley .10 .25
392 Tom Kurvers .10 .25
393 Brad Dalgarno .10 .25
394 Steve Junker RC .15 .40
395 David Volek .10 .25
396 Benoit Hogue .10 .25
397 Zigmund Palffy .10 .25
399 Joby Messier RC .15 .40
400 Mike Gartner .20 .50
401 Joey Kocur .10 .25
402 Ed Olczyk .10 .25
403 Doug Lidster .10 .25
404A Greg Gilbert .10 .25
404B Steve Larmer UER
(Should be 398) .12 .30
405 Glenn Healy .12 .30
406 Dennis Vial .10 .25
407 Darcy Loewen .10 .25
408 Bob Kudelski .10 .25
409 Hank Lammens RC .10 .25
410 Jarmo Kekalainen .10 .25
411 Darren Rumble .10 .25
412 Francois Leroux .10 .25
413 Troy Mallette .10 .25
414 Bill Huard RC .15 .40
415 Ryan McGill .10 .25
416 Eric Lindros .25 .60
417 Dominic Roussel .12 .30
418 Jason Bowen RC .15 .40
419 Andre Faust .10 .25
420 Stewart Malgunas RC .15 .40
421 Kevin Dineen .10 .25
422 Yves Racine .10 .25
423 Garry Galley .10 .25
424 Doug Brown .10 .25
425 Mario Lemieux .60 1.50
426 Ladislav Karabin RC .15 .40
427 Grant Jennings .10 .25
428 Rick Tocchet .12 .30
429 Jeff Daniels .10 .25
430 Peter Taglianetti .10 .25
431 Bryan Trottier .15 .40
432 Kjell Samuelsson .10 .25
433 Rene Corbet RC .15 .40
434 Iain Fraser RC .15 .40
435 Mats Sundin .15 .40
436 Curtis Leschyshyn .10 .25
437 Claude LaPointe .10 .25
438 Valeri Kamensky .12 .30
439 Mike Ricci .10 .25
440 Chris Lindberg .10 .25
441 Alexei Gusarov .10 .25
442 Tom Tilley .10 .25
443 Craig Janney .12 .30
444 Vitali Karamnov .10 .25
445 Bob Bassen .10 .25
446 Igor Korolev .10 .25
447 Kevin Miehm .10 .25
448 Tony Hrkac .10 .25
449 Garth Butcher .10 .25
450 Vitali Prokhorov .10 .25
451 Arturs Irbe .12 .30
452 Jay More .10 .25
453 Bob Errey .10 .25
454 Mike Sullivan .10 .25
455 Jeff Norton .10 .25
456 Gaetan Duchesne .10 .25
457 Doug Zmolek .10 .25
458 Mike Rathje .10 .25
459 Jamie Baker .10 .25
460 Joe Reekie .10 .25
461 Mark Bureau .10 .25
462 John Tucker .10 .25
463 Bill McDougall RC .15 .40
464 Danton Cole .10 .25
465 Brian Bradley .10 .25
466 Jason Lafreniere .10 .25
467 Donald Dufresne .10 .25
468 Daren Puppa .10 .25
469 Doug Gilmour .20 .50
470 Damian Rhodes RC .15 .40
471 Matt Martin RC .15 .40
472 Bill Berg .10 .25
473 John Cullen .10 .25
474 Rob Pearson .10 .25
475 Wendel Clark .25 .60
476 Mark Osborne .10 .25
477 Dmitri Mironov .10 .25
478A Kay Whitmore .10 .25
478B Kris King UER
(Should be 498) .10 .25
479 Shawn Antoski .10 .25
480 Greg Adams .10 .25
481 Dave Babych .10 .25
482 John McIntyre .10 .25
483 Jyrki Lumme .10 .25
484 Jose Charbonneau RC .15 .40
485 Gino Odjick .10 .25
486 Dana Murzyn .10 .25
487 Michal Pivonka .10 .25
488 Dave Poulin .10 .25
489 Sylvain Cote .10 .25
490 Pat Peake .10 .25
491 Kelly Miller .10 .25
492 Randy Burridge .10 .25
493 Kevin Kaminski RC .10 .25
494 John Slaney .10 .25
495 Keith Jones .10 .25
496 Harijs Vitolinsh .10 .25
497 Nelson Emerson .10 .25
499 Darrin Shannon .10 .25
500 Stephane Quintal .10 .25
501 Luciano Borsato .10 .25
502 Thomas Steen .10 .25
503 Alexei Zhamnov .12 .30
504 Paul Ysebaert .10 .25
505 Jeff Friesen RC .15 .40
506 Niklas Sundstrom .10 .25
507 Nick Stajduhar RC .15 .40
508 Jamie Storr RC .15 .40
509 Valeri Bure RC .15 .40
510 Jason Bonsignore RC .15 .40
511 Mats Lindgren RC .15 .40
512 Yanick Dube RC .15 .40
513 Todd Harvey RC .15 .40
514 Ladislav Prokupek RC .10 .25
515 Tomas Vlasak RC .10 .25
516 Josef Marha RC .10 .25
517 Tomas Blazek RC .10 .25
518 Zdenek Nedved RC .10 .25
519 Jaroslav Miklenda RC .15 .40
520 Janne Niinimaa RC .10 .25
521 Saku Koivu .15 .40
522 Tommi Miettinen RC .10 .25
523 Tuomas Gronman .10 .25
524 Jani Nikko RC .10 .25
525 Jouni Vauhkonen .10 .25
526 Nikolai Tsulygin .10 .25
527 Vadim Sharifjanov .12 .30
528 Valeri Bure RC .15 .40
529 Alex Kharlamov RC .15 .40
530 Nikolai Zavarukhin RC .10 .25
531 Oleg Tverdovsky RC .15 .40
532 Sergei Kondrashkin RC .10 .25
533 Evgeni Riabchikov RC .10 .25
534 Mats Lindgren RC .15 .40
535 Kenny Jonsson .10 .25
536 Edvin Frylen RC .15 .40
537 Mathias Johansson RC .10 .25
538 Johan Davidsson RC .10 .25
539 Mikael Hakansson RC .10 .25
540 Anders Eriksson RC .10 .25

1993-94 Parkhurst Emerald Ice

*VETS: 2.5X TO 6X BASIC CARDS
*ROOKIES: 1.5X TO 4X BASIC CARDS

1993-94 Parkhurst Calder Candidates

*GOLD: .6X TO 1.5X SILVER INSERTS
C1 Alexandre Daigle .40 1.00
C2 Chris Pronger 1.50 4.00
C3 Chris Gratton .40 1.00
C4 Rob Niedermayer .40 1.00
C5 Markus Naslund .40 1.00
C6 Jason Arnott 1.00 2.50
C7 Pierre Sevigny .40 1.00
C8 Jarkko Varvio .40 1.00
C9 Dean McAmmond .40 1.00
C10 Alexei Yashin .40 1.00
C11 Philippe Boucher .40 1.00
C12 Mikael Renberg .40 1.00
C13 Chris Simon .40 1.00
C14 Bryan Smolinski .40 1.00
C15 Jesse Belanger .40 1.00
C16 Jocelyn Thibault .75 2.00
C17 Chris Osgood .40 1.00
C18 Derek Plante .40 1.00
C19 Iain Fraser .40 1.00
C20 Vesa Viitakoski .40 1.00

1993-94 Parkhurst Cherry's Playoff Heroes

COMPLETE SET (20) 15.00 40.00
D1 Wayne Gretzky 3.00 8.00
D2 Mario Lemieux 2.50 6.00
D3 Al MacInnis .40 1.00
D4 Mark Messier .60 1.50
D5 Dino Ciccarelli .40 1.00
D6 Dale Hunter .40 1.00
D7 Grant Fuhr .75 2.00
D8 Paul Coffey .60 1.50
D9 Doug Gilmour .50 1.25
D10 Patrick Roy 6.00 10.00
D11 Alexandre Daigle .40 1.00
D12 Chris Gratton .40 1.00
D13 Chris Pronger .50 1.25
D14 Felix Potvin 1.00 2.50
D15 Eric Lindros .75 2.00
D16 Maurice Richard 2.50 6.00
D17 Gordie Howe 2.00 5.00
D18 Henri Richard .50 1.25
D19 Reggie Leach .40 1.00
D20 Don Cherry CL 1.00 2.50

1993-94 Parkhurst East/West Stars

COMPLETE SET (20) 15.00 35.00
COMP.EAST SERIES (10) 6.00 15.00
COMP.WEST SERIES (10) 8.00 20.00
E1 Eric Lindros .60 1.50
E2 Mario Lemieux 2.50 6.00
E3 Alexandre Daigle .20 .50
E4 Patrick Roy 2.50 6.00
E5 Rob Niedermayer .30 .75
E6 Chris Gratton .30 .75
E7 Alexei Yashin .20 .50
E8 Pat LaFontaine .40 1.00
E9 Joe Sakic 1.00 2.50
E10 Pierre Turgeon .30 .75
W1 Wayne Gretzky 3.00 8.00
W2 Pavel Bure .60 1.50
W3 Teemu Selanne .60 1.50
W4 Doug Gilmour .30 .75
W5 Steve Yzerman 2.50 6.00
W6 Jeremy Roenick .60 1.50
W7 Brett Hull .60 1.50
W8 Jason Arnott .60 1.50
W9 Felix Potvin 1.00 2.50
W10 Sergei Fedorov .75 2.00

1993-94 Parkhurst First Overall

COMPLETE SET (10) 8.00 20.00
F1 Alexandre Daigle .30 .75
F2 Roman Hamrlik .50 1.25
F3 Eric Lindros .75 2.00
F4 Owen Nolan .50 1.25
F5 Mats Sundin .75 2.00
F6 Mike Modano 1.25 3.00
F7 Pierre Turgeon .50 1.25
F8 Joe Murphy .30 .75
F9 Wendel Clark .50 1.25
F10 Mario Lemieux 4.00 10.00

1993-94 Parkhurst Parkie Reprints

COMPLETE SET (40) 25.00 60.00
PR33 Gordie Howe 2.50 6.00
PR34 Tim Horton 1.25 3.00
PR35 B.Barilko/McNeil 1.25 3.00
PR36 E.Lach/M.Richard 2.00 5.00
PR37 Terry Sawchuk 1.50 4.00
PR38 George Armstrong 1.00 2.50
PR39 William Harris 1.00 2.50
PR40 Doug Harvey 1.25 3.00
PR41 Gump Worsley 1.25 3.00
PR42 Gordie Howe 2.50 6.00
PR43 Jacques Plante 1.25 3.00
PR44 Frank Mahovlich 1.25 3.00
PR45 Fern Flaman 1.00 2.50
PR46 Bernie Geoffrion 1.50 4.00
PR47 Toe Blake CO 1.00 2.50
PR48 Maurice Richard 1.50 4.00
PR49 Ted Lindsay 1.00 2.50
PR50 Camille Henry 1.00 2.50
PR51 Gordie Howe 2.50 6.00
PR52 Jean-Guy Talbot 1.00 2.50
PR53 Terry Sawchuk 1.50 4.00
PR54 Warren Godfrey 1.00 2.50
PR55 Tom Johnson 1.00 2.50
PR56 Bert Olmstead 1.00 2.50
PR57 Cal Gardner 1.00 2.50
PR58 Red Kelly 1.25 3.00
PR59 Phil Goyette 1.00 2.50
PR60 Gordie Howe 2.50 6.00
PR61 Lou Fontinato 1.00 2.50
PR62 Bill Dineen 1.00 2.50
PR63 Maurice Richard 1.25 3.00
PR64 Vic Stasiuk 1.00 2.50
PR65 Marcel Pronovost 1.00 2.50
PR66 Ed Litzenberger 1.00 2.50
PR67 Dave Keon 1.25 3.00
PR68 Dollard St. Laurent 1.00 2.50
CL5 Parkies Checklist 5 .75 2.00
CL6 Parkies Checklist 6 .75 2.00
CL7 Parkies Checklist 7 .75 2.00
CL8 Parkies Checklist 8 .75 2.00

1993-94 Parkhurst Parkie Reprints Case Inserts

COMPLETE SET (12) 25.00 60.00
COMP.SERIES 1 SET (6) 12.50 30.00
COMP.SERIES 2 SET (6) 12.50 30.00
DPR1 Gordie Howe 6.00 15.00
DPR2 Milt Schmidt 2.50 6.00
DPR3 Tim Horton 3.00 8.00
DPR4 Al Rollins 2.50 6.00
DPR5 Maurice Richard 4.00 10.00
DPR6 Harry Howell 2.50 6.00
DPR7 Gordie Howe 6.00 15.00
DPR8 Johnny Bower 4.00 10.00
DPR9 Dean Prentice 2.50 6.00
DPR10 Leo Labine 2.50 6.00
DPR11 Harry Watson 3.00 8.00
DPR12 Dickie Moore 3.00 8.00

1993-94 Parkhurst USA/Canada Gold

COMPLETE SET (10) 10.00 25.00
G1 Wayne Gretzky 3.00 8.00
G2 Mario Lemieux 2.50 6.00
G3 Eric Lindros .50 1.25
G4 Brett Hull .60 1.50
G5 Rob Niedermayer .30 .75
G6 Alexandre Daigle .20 .50
G7 Pavel Bure .50 1.25
G8 Teemu Selanne .50 1.25
G9 Patrick Roy 2.50 6.00
G10 Doug Gilmour .30 .75

1994 Parkhurst Missing Link

COMPLETE SET (180) 20.00 35.00
1 Jerry Toppazzini .02 .10
2 Fern Flaman .15 .40
3 Fleming MacKell .02 .10
4 Leo Labine .07 .20
5 John Peirson .05 .15
6 Don McKenney .02 .10
7 Bob Armstrong .02 .10
8 Real Chevrefils .02 .10
9 Vic Stasiuk .05 .15
10 Cal Gardner .02 .10
11 Leo Boivin .15 .40
12 Jack Caffery .02 .10
13 Bob Beckett RC .02 .10
14 Jack Bionda .02 .10
15 Claude Pronovost RC .15 .40
16 Larry Regan .02 .10
17 Terry Sawchuk 1.00 2.50
18 Doug Mohns .07 .20
19 Marcel Bonin .05 .15
20 Allan Stanley .20 .50
21 Milt Schmidt CO .20 .50
22 Al Dewsbury .02 .10
23 Glen Skov .05 .15
24 Ed Litzenberger .05 .15
25 Nick Mickoski .02 .10
26 Walter Hergesheimer .02 .10
27 Jack McIntyre .02 .10
28 Al Rollins .20 .50
29 Hank Ciesla .02 .10
30 Gus Mortson .02 .10
31 Elmer Vasko .05 .15
32 Pierre Pilote .20 .50
33 Ron Ingram .02 .10
34 Frank Martin .02 .10
35 Forbes Kennedy .07 .20
36 Harry Watson .05 .15
37 Eddie Kachur RC .02 .10
38 Hec Lalande .02 .10
39 Eric Nesterenko .07 .20
40 Ben Woit .02 .10
41 Ken Mosdell .05 .15
42 Tommy Ivan CO RC .15 .40
43 Gordie Howe 1.50 4.00
44 Ted Lindsay .20 .50
45 Norm Ullman .20 .50
46 Glenn Hall .40 1.00
47 Billy Dea .02 .10
48 Bill McNeill .02 .10
49 Earl Reibel .05 .15
50 Bill Dineen .07 .20
51 Warren Godfrey .05 .15
52 Red Kelly .20 .50
53 Marty Pavelich .02 .10
54 Lorne Ferguson .02 .10
55 Larry Hillman .05 .15
56 John Bucyk .20 .50
57 Metro Prystai .02 .10
58 Marcel Pronovost .20 .50
59 Alex Delvecchio .20 .50
60 Murray Costello RC .02 .10
61 Al Arbour .20 .50
62 Bucky Hollingworth .02 .10
63 Jim Skinner CO RC .02 .10
64 Jean Beliveau .75 2.00
65 Maurice Richard 1.00 2.50
66 Henri Richard .20 .50
67 Doug Harvey .20 .50
68 BoomBoom Geoffrion .30 .75
69 Dollard St. Laurent .08 .25
70 Dickie Moore .20 .50
71 Bert Olmstead .08 .25
72 Jacques Plante 1.00 2.50
73 Claude Provost .15 .40
74 Phil Goyette .05 .15
75 Andre Pronovost .05 .15
76 Don Marshall .08 .25
77 Ralph Backstrom .07 .20
78 Floyd Curry .07 .20
79 Tom Johnson .20 .50
80 Jean Guy Talbot .07 .20
81 Bob Turner .02 .10
82 Connie Broden RC .02 .10
83 Jackie Leclair .02 .10
84 Toe Blake CO .30 .75
85 Frank Selke MD .20 .50
86 George Sullivan .02 .10
87 Larry Cahan .02 .10
88 Jean Guy Gendron .02 .10
89 Bill Gadsby .20 .50
90 Andy Bathgate .20 .50
91 Dean Prentice .02 .10
92 Gump Worsley .40 1.00
93 Lou Fontinato .05 .15
94 Gerry Foley .02 .10
95 Larry Popein .05 .15
96 Harry Howell .20 .50
97 Andy Hebenton .02 .10
98 Danny Lewicki .02 .10
99 Dave Creighton .02 .10
100 Camille Henry .02 .10
101 Jack Evans .02 .10
102 Ron Murphy .02 .10
103 Johnny Bower .30 .75
104 Parker MacDonald .02 .10
105 Bronco Horvath .07 .20
106 Bruce Cline RC .02 .10
107 Ivan Irwin .02 .10
108 Phil Watson CO .02 .10
109 Sid Smith .02 .10
110 Ron Stewart .02 .10
111 Rudy Migay .02 .10
112 Tod Sloan .05 .15
113 Bob Pulford .20 .50
114 Marc Reaume .05 .15
115 Jim Morrison .05 .15
116 Ted Kennedy .20 .50
117 Gerry James .07 .20
118 Brian Cullen .02 .10
119 Jim Thomson .02 .10
120 Barry Cullen .02 .10
121 Al MacNeil .05 .15
122 Gary Aldcorn .02 .10
123 Bob Baun .20 .50
124 Hugh Bolton .02 .10
125 George Armstrong .20 .50
126 Dick Duff .20 .50
127 Tim Horton .75 2.00
128 Ed Chadwick .02 .10
129 Billy Harris .15 .40
130 Mike Nykoluk .02 .10
131 Noel Price .02 .10
132 Ken Girard .02 .10
133 Howie Meeker .20 .50
134 Hap Day CO .08 .25
135 Jacques Plante AS .40 1.00
136 Doug Harvey AS .20 .50
137 Bill Gadsby AS .20 .50
138 Jean Beliveau AS .30 .75
139 Maurice Richard AS .40 1.00
140 Ted Lindsay AS .15 .40
141 Glenn Hall AS .20 .50
142 Red Kelly AS .20 .50
143 Tom Johnson AS .20 .50
144 Tod Sloan AS .05 .15
145 Gordie Howe AS .60 1.50
146 Bert Olmstead AS .08 .25
147 Earl Reibel AW
Lady Byng .02 .10
148 Doug Harvey AW
Norris .20 .50
149 Jean Beliveau AW .30 .75
150 Jean Beliveau AW .30 .75
151 Jacques Plante AW .40 1.00
152 Glenn Hall AW .20 .50
153 Sawchuk Picks Pocket .40 1.00
154 Action Shot .08 .25
155 Action Shot .08 .25
156 Beliveau Draws Crowd .30 .75
157 Beliveau in Close .30 .75
158 Leafs Besiege Hall .08 .25
159 Hall Makes The Save .08 .25
160 Howe Notches Another .60 1.50
161 Plante Stands Guard .40 1.00
162 Howe Outhustles Habs .60 1.50
163 Plante's Flying Save .40 1.00
164 Canadien's Big Line .08 .25
165 Gump Stops Leafs .08 .25
166 Action Shot .08 .25
167 Sawchuk Foils Duff .40 1.00
168 Sawchuk In Action .40 1.00
169 Vic Stasiuk SL .05 .15
170 George Sullivan SL .05 .15
171 Gordie Howe SL .60 1.50
172 Jean Beliveau SL .30 .75
173 Andy Bathgate SL .20 .50
174 Tod Sloan SL .05 .15
175 Stanley Cup .08 .25
176 Stanley Cup .08 .25
177 Stanley Cup .08 .25
178 Stanley Cup .08 .25
179 Checklist 1 .02 .10
180 Checklist 2 .02 .10

1994 Parkhurst Missing Link Autographs

1 Gordie Howe 75.00 150.00
2 Maurice Richard 100.00 200.00
3 Bernie Geoffrion 40.00 80.00
4 Gump Worsley 40.00 100.00
5 Jean Beliveau 75.00 150.00
6 Frank Mahovlich 25.00 60.00

1994 Parkhurst Missing Link Future Stars

COMPLETE SET (6) 30.00 70.00
FS1 Carl Brewer 3.00 8.00
FS2 Dave Keon 5.00 12.00
FS3 Stan Mikita 6.00 15.00
FS4 Eddie Shack 5.00 12.00
FS5 Frank Mahovlich 6.00 15.00
FS6 Charlie Hodge 5.00 12.00

1994 Parkhurst Missing Link Pop-Ups

COMPLETE SET (12) 125.00 200.00
P1 Howie Morenz 20.00 50.00
P2 George Hainsworth 12.00 30.00
P3 Georges Vezina 20.00 50.00
P4 King Clancy 15.00 40.00
P5 Syl Apps 12.00 30.00
P6 Turk Broda 12.00 30.00
P7 Eddie Shore 25.00 50.00
P8 Bill Cook 10.00 25.00
P9 Woody Dumart 10.00 25.00
P10 Lester Patrick 12.00 30.00
P11 Doug Bentley 10.00 25.00
P12 Earl Seibert 10.00 25.00

1994 Parkhurst Tall Boys

COMPLETE SET (180) 10.00 12.00
1 John Bucyk .15 .40
2 Murray Oliver .02 .10
3 Ted Green .05 .15
4 Tom Williams .02 .10
5 Dean Prentice .02 .10
6 Ed Westfall .02 .10
7 Orland Kurtenbach .02 .10
8 Reg Fleming .02 .10
9 Leo Boivin .05 .15
10 Bob McCord .02 .10
11 Bob Leiter .02 .10
12 Tom Johnson .08 .25
13 Bob Woytowich .02 .10
14 Ab McDonald .02 .10
15 Ed Johnston .08 .25
16 Forbes Kennedy .05 .15
17 Murray Balfour .02 .10
18 Wayne Cashman .05 .15
19 Don Awrey .02 .10
20 Gary Dornhoefer .05 .15
21 Ron Schock .02 .10
22 Milt Schmidt .20 .50
23 Ken Wharram .05 .15
24 Chico Maki .02 .10
25 Bobby Hull .75 2.00
26 Stan Mikita .30 .75
27 Doug Mohns .05 .15
28 Denis DeJordy .07 .20
29 Phil Esposito .20 .50
30 Elmer Vasko .05 .15
31 Pierre Pilote .08 .25
32 Glenn Hall .30 .75
33 Eric Nesterenko .02 .10
34 Doug Robinson .02 .10
35 Matt Ravlich .02 .10
36 John McKenzie .05 .15
37 Fred Stanfield .02 .10
38 Doug Jarrett .02 .10
39 Dennis Hull .07 .20
40 Al MacNeil .02 .10
41 Wayne Hillman .02 .10
42 Bill Hay .05 .15
43 Billy Reay .02 .10
44 Parker MacDonald .02 .10
45 Floyd Smith .02 .10
46 Gordie Howe 1.00 2.50
47 Bruce MacGregor .02 .10
48 Ron Murphy .02 .10
49 Doug Barkley .02 .10
50 Paul Henderson .05 .15
51 Pit Martin .05 .15
52 Al Langlois .02 .10
53 Roger Crozier .08 .25
54 Bill Gadsby .08 .25
55 Marcel Pronovost .15 .40
56 Alex Delvecchio .15 .40
57 Gary Bergman .02 .10
58 Norm Ullman .15 .40
59 Larry Jeffrey .02 .10
60 Lowell MacDonald .02 .10
61 Pete Goegan .02 .10
62 Andre Pronovost .05 .15
63 Warren Godfrey .02 .10
64 Ted Lindsay .15 .40
65 Sid Abel .15 .40
66 John Ferguson .05 .15
67 Henri Richard .20 .50
68 Dave Balon .02 .10
69 Noel Picard .02 .10
70 Claude Provost .05 .15
71 Claude Larose .02 .10
72 Jacques Laperriere .08 .25
73 Ralph Backstrom .05 .15
74 J.C. Tremblay .05 .15
75 Yvan Cournoyer .15 .40
76 Jean-Guy Talbot .05 .15
77 Gilles Tremblay .02 .10
78 Ted Harris .02 .10
79 Jim Roberts .02 .10
80 Red Berenson .05 .15
81 Gump Worsley .30 .75
82 Charlie Hodge .08 .25
83 Terry Harper .02 .10
84 Bobby Rousseau .02 .10
85 Jean Beliveau .60 1.50
86 Bill Hicke .02 .10
87 Toe Blake .20 .50
88 Don Marshall .05 .15
89 Jean Ratelle .15 .40
90 Vic Hadfield .02 .10
91 Earl Ingarfield .02 .10
92 Harry Howell .15 .40
93 Rod Seiling .02 .10
94 Dave Richardson .02 .10
95 Val Fonteyne .02 .10
96 Lou Angotti .02 .10
97 Arnie Brown .02 .10
98 Don Johns .02 .10
99 Jim Mikol .02 .10
100 Jacques Plante .75 2.00
101 Maurice Paille .05 .15
102 Jim Neilson .02 .10
103 Bob Nevin .02 .10
104 Rod Gilbert .15 .40
105 Phil Goyette .02 .10
106 Dick Duff .08 .25
107 Camille Henry .02 .10
108 Red Sullivan .02 .10
109 Kent Douglas .02 .10
110 Bob Pulford .05 .15
111 Dave Keon .20 .50
112 Don McKenney .02 .10
113 Pete Stemkowski .02 .10
114 Carl Brewer .05 .15
115 Allan Stanley .08 .25
116 Dickie Moore .15 .40
117 Eddie Shack .20 .50
118 Larry Hillman .02 .10
119 Terry Sawchuk .75 2.00
120 Bob Baun .08 .25
121 Brit Selby .02 .10
122 George Armstrong .20 .50
123 Jim Pappin .02 .10
124 Andy Bathgate .15 .40
125 Ron Ellis .02 .10
126 Billy Harris .05 .15
127 Red Kelly .07 .20
128 Ron Stewart .02 .10
129 Johnny Bower .20 .50
130 Frank Mahovlich .20 .50
131 Tim Horton .60 1.50
132 King Clancy .15 .40
133 Glenn Hall AS .20 .50
134 Pierre Pilote AS .08 .25
135 Tim Horton AS .30 .75
136 Bobby Hull AS .40 1.00
137 Ken Wharram AS .05 .15
138 Stan Mikita AS .20 .50
139 Charlie Hodge AS .05 .15
140 Jacques Laperriere AS .05 .15
141 Elmer Vasko AS .02 .10
142 Jean Beliveau AS .30 .75
143 Frank Mahovlich AS .15 .40
144 Gordie Howe AS .60 1.50
145 Pierre Pilote .08 .25
146 Jean Beliveau TW .30 .75
147 Stan Mikita TW .15 .40
148 Charlie Hodge .08 .25
149 Jacques Laperriere .08 .25
150 Ken Wharram .05 .15
151 1964 All Star Game .05 .15
152 Ratelle Invades Crease .08 .25
153 Center Ice Action .05 .15
154 G.Howe
T.Sawchuk IA .60 1.50
155 All Eyes on the Puck .05 .15
156 Terry Sawchuk IA .40 1.00
157 Crozier Makes The
Stretch .05 .15
158 Crozier Plays
Center Field .08 .25
159 Jean Beliveau IA .30 .75
160 Montreal's Speedy
Rookie .05 .15
161 Laperriere Wins Race .05 .15
162 Ellis Robbed by Habs .05 .15
163 Terry Sawchuk IA .40 1.00
164 Eddie Shack IA .15 .40
165 G.Hall
R.Kelly IA .20 .50
166 Hall Holds His
Ground .15 .40
167 Johnston Freezes
Action .05 .15
168 Ellis Robbed By
Johnston .05 .15
169 Murray Oliver LL .02 .10
170 Stan Mikita LL .20 .50
171 Gordie Howe LL .60 1.50
172 Jean Beliveau LL .30 .75
173 Phil Goyette LL .02 .10
174 Andy Bathgate LL .08 .25
175 Stanley Cup
Semi-Finals .02 .10
176 Stanley Cup
Semi-Finals .02 .10
177 G.Howe
T.Sawchuk SCF .60 1.50
178 Stanley Cup .08 .25
179 Checklist 1 .02 .10
180 Checklist 2 .02 .10

1994 Parkhurst Tall Boys Autographs

COMPLETE SET (6) 350.00 500.00
A1 Rod Gilbert 25.00 50.00
A2 Yvan Cournoyer 40.00 60.00
A3 Bobby Hull 40.00 100.00
A4 Phil Esposito 60.00 100.00
A5 Gordie Howe 75.00 150.00
A6 Dave Keon 50.00 80.00

1994 Parkhurst Tall Boys Future Stars

COMPLETE SET (6) 40.00 80.00
FS1 Jacques Lemaire 7.50 15.00
FS2 Gerry Cheevers 12.00 25.00
FS3 Ken Hodge 4.00 10.00
FS4 Bernie Parent 6.00 15.00
FS5 Rogatien Vachon 7.50 15.00
FS6 Derek Sanderson 10.00 20.00

1994 Parkhurst Tall Boys Greats

COMPLETE SET (12) 175.00 250.00
1 Ace Bailey 15.00 30.00
2 Alex Levinsky 6.00 15.00
3 Babe Pratt 6.00 15.00
4 Elmer Lach 6.00 15.00
5 Maurice Richard 25.00 40.00
6 Bill Durnan 15.00 30.00
7 Frank Brimsek 15.00 30.00
8 Dit Clapper 8.00 20.00
9 Tiny Thompson 15.00 30.00
10 Bun Cook 6.00 15.00
11 Ching Johnson 8.00 20.00
12 Lionel Conacher 15.00 30.00

1994 Parkhurst Tall Boys Mail-Ins

COMPLETE SET (18) 20.00 50.00
AS1 Roger Crozier 1.00 2.50
AS2 Pierre Pilote .75 2.00
AS3 Jacques Laperriere .75 2.00
AS4 Norm Ullman 1.00 2.50
AS5 Bobby Hull 4.00 10.00
AS6 Claude Provost .40 1.00
SL1 John Bucyk 1.00 2.50
SL2 Stan Mikita 1.50 4.00
SL3 Norm Ullman 1.00 2.50
SL4 Claude Provost .40 1.00
SL5 Rod Gilbert 1.00 2.50
SL6 Frank Mahovlich 1.50 4.00
TW1 Pierre Pilote .75 2.00
TW2 Bobby Hull 4.00 10.00
TW3 Stan Mikita 1.50 4.00
TW4 Terry Sawchuk
Johnny Bo 3.00 8.00
TW5 Roger Crozier 1.00 2.50
TW6 Bobby Hull 4.00 10.00

1994-95 Parkhurst

1 Anatoli Semenov .05 .15
2 Stephan Lebeau .05 .15
3 Stu Grimson .05 .15
4 Mikhail Shtalenkov RC .05 .15
5 Troy Loney .05 .15
6 Sean Hill .05 .15
7 Patrik Carnback .05 .15
8 John Lilley .05 .15
9 Tim Sweeney .05 .15
10 Maxim Bets .05 .15
11 Cam Neely .10 .25
12 Bryan Smolinski .05 .15
13 Ray Bourque .15 .40
14 Vincent Riendeau .05 .15
15 Al Iafrate .05 .15
16 Andrew McKim RC .05 .15
17 Glen Wesley .05 .15
18 Daniel Marois .05 .15
19 Jozef Stumpel .05 .15
20 Mariusz Czerkawski RC .10 .25
21 Alexander Mogilny .07 .20
22 Yuri Khmylev .05 .15
23 Donald Audette .05 .15
24 Dominik Hasek .15 .40
25 Randy Wood .05 .15
26 Brad May .05 .15
27 Wayne Presley .05 .15
28 Richard Smehlik .05 .15
29 Dale Hawerchuk .12 .30
30 Rob Ray .05 .15
31 Zarley Zalapski .05 .15
32 Michael Nylander .07 .20
33 Joe Nieuwendyk .07 .20
34 Robert Reichel .05 .15
35 Al MacInnis .12 .30
36 Andrei Trefilov .05 .15
37 Guy Larose .05 .15
38 Wes Walz .05 .15
39 Michel Petit .05 .15
40 James Patrick .05 .15
41 Ed Belfour .10 .25
42 Christian Ruuttu .05 .15
43 Eric Weinrich .05 .15
44 Joe Murphy .05 .15
45 Chris Chelios .10 .25
46 Jeff Shantz .05 .15
47 Gary Suter .05 .15
48 Paul Ysebaert .05 .15
49 Ivan Droppa .05 .15
50 Keith Carney .05 .15
51 Andy Moog .10 .25
52 Russ Courtnall .05 .15
53 Neal Broten .07 .20
54 Mike Craig .05 .15
55 Brent Gilchrist .05 .15
56 Pelle Eklund .05 .15
57 Richard Matvichuk .05 .15
58 Dave Gagner .07 .20
59 Mark Tinordi .05 .15
60 Paul Broten .05 .15
61 Nicklas Lidstrom .10 .25
62 Shawn Burr .05 .15
63 Paul Coffey .10 .25
64 Bob Essensa .05 .15
65 Dino Ciccarelli .07 .20
66 Slava Kozlov .05 .15
67 Keith Primeau .07 .20
68 Steve Chiasson .05 .15
69 Terry Carkner .05 .15
70 Martin Lapointe .05 .15
71 Bob Probert .10 .25
72 Bill Ranford .07 .20
73 Scott Thornton .05 .15
74 Doug Weight .07 .20
75 Shayne Corson .07 .20
76 Zdeno Ciger .05 .15
77 Adam Bennett .05 .15
78 Scott Pearson .05 .15
79 Brent Grieve RC .05 .15

80 Gordon Mark RC .05 .15
81 Shjon Podein .05 .15
82 Geoff Smith .05 .15
83 Bob Kudelski .05 .15
84 Andrei Lomakin .05 .15
85 Scott Mellanby .07 .20
86 Jesse Belanger .05 .15
87 Mark Fitzpatrick .07 .20
88 Peter Andersson .05 .15
89 Jody Hull .05 .15
90 Brent Severyn .05 .15
91 Jim Sandlak .05 .15
92 Pat Verbeek .07 .20
93 Ted Crowley .05 .15
94 Robert Petrovicky .05 .15
95 Geoff Sanderson .07 .20
96 Ted Drury .05 .15
97 Andrew Cassels .05 .15
98 Igor Chibirev .05 .15
99 Kevin Smyth .05 .15
100 Alexander Godynyuk .05 .15
101 Alexei Zhitnik .07 .20
102 Dixon Ward .05 .15
103 Wayne Gretzky .60 1.50
104 Jari Kurri .07 .20
105 Rob Blake .10 .25
106 Marty McSorley .07 .20
107 Pat Conacher .05 .15
108 Kevin Todd .05 .15
109 Robb Stauber .05 .15
110 Keith Redmond .07 .20
111 John LeClair .10 .25
112 Brian Bellows .07 .20
113 Patrick Roy .25 .60
114 Les Kuntar RC .05 .15
115 Vincent Damphousse .07 .20
116 Patrice Brisebois .05 .15
117 Pierre Sevigny .05 .15
118 Eric Desjardins .07 .20
119 Oleg Petrov .05 .15
120 Kevin Haller .05 .15
121 Christian Proulx RC .05 .15
122 Corey Millen .05 .15
123 Jaroslav Modry .05 .15
124 Valeri Zelepukin .05 .15
125 John MacLean .07 .20
126 Martin Brodeur .25 .60
127 Bill Guerin .10 .25
128 Bobby Holik .05 .15
129 Claude Lemieux .10 .25
130 Jason Smith .07 .20
131 Ken Daneyko .05 .15
132 Derek King .05 .15
133 Darius Kasparaitis .05 .15
134 Ray Ferraro .05 .15
135 Pierre Turgeon .07 .20
136 Ron Hextall .10 .25
137 Travis Green .07 .20
138 Joe Day .05 .15
139 David Volek .05 .15
140 Scott Lachance .05 .15
141 Dennis Vaske .05 .15
142 Alexei Kovalev .07 .20
143 Brian Noonan .05 .15
144 Sergei Zubov .07 .20
145 Craig MacTavish .05 .15
146 Steve Larmer .07 .20
147 Adam Graves .05 .15
148 Jeff Beukeboom .05 .15
149 Corey Hirsch .07 .20
150 Stephane Matteau .05 .15
151 Brian Leetch .07 .20
152 Mattias Norstrom .05 .15
153 Sylvain Turgeon .05 .15
154 Norm Maciver .05 .15
155 Scott Levins .05 .15
156 Derek Mayer .05 .15
157 Dave McLlwain .05 .15
158 Craig Billington .07 .20
159 Claude Boivin .05 .15
160 Troy Mallette .05 .15
161 Evgeny Davydov .05 .15
162 Dmitri Filimonov .05 .15
163 Dimitri Yushkevich .05 .15
164 Rob Zettler .05 .15
165 Mark Recchi .12 .30
166 Josef Beranek .05 .15
167 Rod Brind'Amour .07 .20
168 Yves Racine .05 .15
169 Dominic Roussel .07 .20
170 Brent Fedyk .05 .15
171 Bob Wilkie RC .05 .15
172 Kevin Dineen .05 .15
173 Shawn McEachern .05 .15
174 Jaromir Jagr .30 .75
175 Tomas Sandstrom .05 .15
176 Ron Francis .12 .30
177 Kevin Stevens .07 .20
178 Jim McKenzie .05 .15
179 Larry Murphy .07 .20
180 Joe Mullen .07 .20
181 Greg Hawgood .05 .15
182 Tom Barrasso .07 .20
183 Ulf Samuelsson .05 .15
184 Bob Bassen .05 .15
185 Mats Sundin .10 .25
186 Mike Ricci .05 .15
187 Iain Fraser .05 .15
188 Garth Butcher .07 .20
189 Jocelyn Thibault .07 .20
190 Valeri Kamensky .07 .20
191 Martin Rucinsky .05 .15
192 Ron Sutter .05 .15
193 Rene Corbet .05 .15
194 Reggie Savage .05 .15
195 Alexei Kasatonov .05 .15
196 Brendan Shanahan .10 .25
197 Phil Housley .07 .20
198 Jim Montgomery .05 .15
199 Curtis Joseph .12 .30
200 Craig Janney .07 .20
201 David Roberts .07 .20
202 Dave Mackey .05 .15
203 Peter Stastny .07 .20
204 Terry Hollinger RC .07 .20
205 Steve Duchesne .05 .15
206 Vitali Prokhorov .05 .15
207 Rob Gaudreau .05 .15
208 Sandis Ozolinsh .05 .15
209 Johan Garpenlov .05 .15
210 Todd Elik .05 .15
211 Sergei Makarov .05 .15
212 Jean-Francois Quintin .05 .15
213 Vyacheslav Butsayev .05 .15
214 Jimmy Waite .05 .15
215 Ulf Dahlen .05 .15
216 Andrei Nazarov .05 .15
217 Denis Savard .10 .25
218 Brent Gretzky .05 .15
219 Petr Klima .05 .15
220 Chris Gratton .05 .15
221 Brian Bradley .05 .15
222 Adam Creighton .05 .15
223 Shawn Chambers .05 .15
224 Rob Zamuner .05 .15
225 Daren Puppa .07 .20
226 Mikael Andersson .05 .15
227 Dave Ellett .05 .15
228 Mike Gartner .12 .30
229 Felix Potvin .15 .40
230 Yanic Perreault .05 .15
231 Nikolai Borschevsky .05 .15
232 Dmitri Mironov .05 .15
233 Todd Gill .05 .15
234 Eric Lacroix RC .10 .25
235 Kent Manderville .05 .15
236 Chris Govedaris .05 .15
237 Frank Bialowas RC .05 .15
238 Kirk McLean .07 .20
239 Jimmy Carson .05 .15
240 Geoff Courtnall .05 .15
241 Trevor Linden .10 .25
242 Murray Craven .05 .15
243 Bret Hedican .05 .15
244 Jeff Brown .05 .15
245 Mike Peca .07 .20
246 Yevgeny Namestnikov .05 .15
247 Nathan Lafayette .05 .15
248 Shawn Antoski .05 .15
249 Sergio Momesso .10 .25
250 Mike Ridley .05 .15
251 Peter Bondra .10 .25
252 Dimitri Khristich .05 .15
253 Dave Poulin .05 .15
254 Dale Hunter .05 .15
255 Rick Tabaracci .07 .20
256 Kelly Miller .05 .15
257 John Slaney .05 .15
258 Todd Krygier .05 .15
259 Kevin Hatcher .05 .15
260 Alexei Zhamnov .07 .20
261 Dallas Drake .05 .15
262 Dave Manson .05 .15
263 Thomas Steen .05 .15
264 Keith Tkachuk .10 .25
265 Russ Romaniuk .05 .15
266 Michal Grosek RC .05 .15
267 Nelson Emerson .05 .15
268 Michael O'Neill RC .05 .15
269 Kris King .05 .15
270 Teppo Numminen .05 .15
271 Jason Arnott RS .07 .20
272 Mikael Renberg RS .07 .20
273 Alexei Yashin RS .10 .25
274 Chris Pronger RS .10 .25
275 Jocelyn Thibault RS .07 .20
276 Bryan Smolinski RS .07 .20
277 Derek Plante RS .05 .15
278 Martin Brodeur RS .25 .60
279 Jim Dowd .05 .15
280 Iain Fraser .05 .15
281 Pat Peake .05 .15
282 Chris Gratton RS .05 .15
283 Chris Osgood RS .15 .40
284 Jesse Belanger .05 .15
285 Alexandre Daigle RS .05 .15
286 Robert Lang .05 .15
287 Markus Naslund .10 .25
288 Trevor Kidd .07 .20
289 Jeff Shantz .05 .15
290 Jaroslav Modry .05 .15
291 Oleg Petrov .05 .15
292 Scott Levins .05 .15
293 Jozef Stumpel .05 .15
294 Rob Niedermayer RS .07 .20
295 Brent Gretzky .05 .15
296 Mario Lemieux PB .40 1.00
297 Pavel Bure PB .10 .25
298 Brendan Shanahan PB .10 .25
299 Steve Yzerman PB .25 .60
300 Teemu Selanne PB .20 .50
301 Eric Lindros PB .15 .40
302 Jeremy Roenick PB .15 .40
303 Dave Andreychuk .10 .25
304 Ray Bourque PB .15 .40
305 Sergei Fedorov PB .15 .40
306 Wayne Gretzky PB .60 1.50
307 Adam Graves PB .07 .20
308 Mike Modano PB .15 .40
309 Brett Hull PB .15 .40
310 Pat LaFontaine PB .10 .25
311 Adam Oates PB .10 .25
312 Patrick Roy PB .25 .60
313 Doug Gilmour PB .12 .30
314 Jaromir Jagr PB .30 .75
315 Mark Recchi PB .12 .30

1994-95 Parkhurst Gold

*GOLD: 3X TO 8X BASIC

1994-95 Parkhurst Crash the Game Green

COMPLETE SET (28) 20.00 40.00
*GOLD: .2X TO .5X GREEN
*BLUE: .4X TO 1X GREEN
*RED: .4X TO 1X GREEN
H1 Stephan Lebeau .25 .60
H2 Ray Bourque .60 1.50
H3 Pat LaFontaine .60 1.50
H4 Joe Nieuwendyk .30 .75
H5 Jeremy Roenick .40 1.00
H6 Mike Modano .50 1.25
H7 Sergei Fedorov .75 2.00
H8 Jason Arnott .30 .75
H9 John Vanbiesbrouck .40 1.00
H10 Geoff Sanderson .25 .60
H11 Wayne Gretzky 2.50 6.00
H12 Patrick Roy 2.00 5.00
H13 Scott Stevens .30 .75
H14 Pierre Turgeon .30 .75
H15 Adam Graves .30 .75
H16 Alexei Yashin .30 .75
H17 Eric Lindros .75 2.00
H18 Mario Lemieux 2.00 5.00
H19 Joe Sakic .75 2.00
H20 Brett Hull .50 1.25
H21 Sandis Ozolinsh .30 .75
H22 Chris Gratton .25 .60
H23 Doug Gilmour .40 1.00
H24 Pavel Bure 1.00 2.50
H25 Joe Juneau .30 .75
H26 Teemu Selanne .40 1.00
H27 Mark Messier
Eastern 1.25 3.00
H28 Wayne Gretzky
Western 4.00 10.00

1994-95 Parkhurst Vintage

V1 Dominik Hasek .25 .60
V2 Mike Modano .25 .60
V3 Shayne Corson .12 .30
V4 Kirk Muller .10 .25
V5 Mike Richter .15 .40
V6 Mario Lemieux .60 1.50
V7 Sandis Ozolinsh .10 .25
V8 Dave Ellett .10 .25
V9 Dave Manson .10 .25
V10 Terry Yake .10 .25
V11 Craig Simpson .10 .25
V12 Paul Cavallini .10 .25
V13 John Vanbiesbrouck .15 .40
V14 Gilbert Dionne .10 .25
V15 Brian Leetch .12 .30
V16 Martin Straka .10 .25
V17 Curtis Joseph .20 .50
V18 Pavel Bure .15 .40
V19 Garry Valk .10 .25
V20 Theo Fleury .15 .40
V21 Brent Gilchrist .10 .25
V22 Rob Niedermayer .12 .30
V23 Vincent Damphousse .12 .30
V24 Alexei Kovalev .12 .30
V25 Rick Tocchet .12 .30
V26 Steve Duchesne .10 .25
V27 Jiri Slegr .10 .25
V28 Patrick Carnback .10 .25
V29 Gary Roberts .10 .25
V30 Derian Hatcher .10 .25
V31 Jesse Belanger .10 .25
V32 Mathieu Schneider .10 .25
V33 Mark Messier .30 .75
V34 Joe Sakic .30 .75
V35 Brett Hull .30 .75
V36 Martin Gelinas .10 .25
V37 Maxim Bets .10 .25
V38 Joel Otto .10 .25
V39 Sergei Fedorov .25 .60
V40 Chris Pronger .15 .40
V41 Scott Stevens .15 .40
V42 Alexandre Daigle .10 .25
V43 Owen Nolan .15 .40
V44 Petr Nedved .15 .40
V45 Jeff Brown .10 .25
V46 Adam Oates .15 .40
V47 Robert Reichel .10 .25
V48 Slava Kozlov .12 .30
V49 Geoff Sanderson .12 .30
V50 Stephane Richer .12 .30
V51 Sylvain Turgeon .10 .25
V52 Mike Ricci .10 .25
V53 Roman Hamrlik .10 .25
V54 Kevin Hatcher .10 .25
V55 Mariusz Czerkawski .12 .30
V56 Tony Amonte .12 .30
V57 Steve Yzerman .40 1.00
V58 Andrew Cassels .10 .25
V59 Claude Lemieux .10 .25
V60 Derek Mayer .10 .25
V61 Jocelyn Thibault .12 .30
V62 Brent Gretzky .10 .25
V63 Pat Peake .10 .25
V64 Cam Neely .15 .40
V65 Jeremy Roenick .25 .60
V66 Keith Primeau .15 .40
V67 Luc Robitaille .15 .40
V68 Steve Thomas .10 .25
V69 Eric Lindros .25 .60
V70 Pat Falloon .10 .25
V71 Brian Bradley .10 .25
V72 Kelly Miller .10 .25
V73 Pat LaFontaine .15 .40
V74 Gary Suter .10 .25
V75 Bill Ranford .15 .40
V76 Tony Granato .10 .25
V77 Vladimir Malakhov .10 .25
V78 Mikael Renberg .12 .30
V79 Arturs Irbe .12 .30
V80 Doug Gilmour .20 .50
V81 Teemu Selanne .30 .75
V82 Dale Hawerchuk .20 .50
V83 Eric Weinrich .10 .25
V84 Jason Arnott .12 .30
V85 Rob Blake .15 .40
V86 Ray Ferraro .10 .25
V87 Garry Galley .10 .25
V88 Igor Larionov .15 .40
V89 Dave Andreychuk .15 .40
V90 Dallas Drake .10 .25

1996 Parkhurst Beehive Promos

COMMON BOBBY ORR 4.00 10.00
COMMON GORDIE HOWE 3.00 8.00

2001-02 Parkhurst

1 Paul Kariya .20 .50
2 Patrik Stefan .15 .40
3 Jeremy Roenick .30 .75
4 Patrick Roy .50 1.25
5 Jarome Iginla .25 .60
6 Jeff O'Neill .15 .40
7 Sergei Samsonov .15 .40
8 Peter Forsberg .40 1.00
9 Scott Gomez .15 .40
10 Mike Modano .30 .75
11 Brendan Shanahan .20 .50
12 Jean-Sebastien Giguere .20 .50
13 Pavel Bure .20 .50
14 Zigmund Palffy .20 .50
15 Marian Gaborik .20 .50
16 Pavol Demitra .25 .60
17 Alexei Kovalev .15 .40
18 Patrik Elias .20 .50
19 Keith Tkachuk .20 .50
20 Mats Sundin .20 .50
21 Marian Hossa .20 .50
22 Mark Recchi .25 .60
23 John Madden .15 .40
24 Mario Lemieux .75 2.00
25 Teemu Selanne .40 1.00
26 Joe Sakic .40 1.00
27 Brad Richards .20 .50
28 Brian Leetch .15 .40
29 Markus Naslund .20 .50
30 Peter Bondra .20 .50
31 Steve Yzerman .50 1.25
32 Michael Peca .15 .40
33 Bill Guerin .20 .50
34 Jaromir Jagr .60 1.50
35 Alexei Yashin .15 .40
36 Theo Fleury .25 .60
37 Al MacInnis .25 .60
38 Milan Hejduk .15 .40
39 Martin Biron .15 .40
40 Brad Isbister .12 .30
41 Nicklas Lidstrom .20 .50
42 Rick DiPietro .15 .40
43 Roberto Luongo .30 .75
44 Tim Connolly .12 .30
45 Manny Fernandez .12 .30
46 Scott Niedermayer .20 .50
47 David Legwand .15 .40
48 Petr Sykora .12 .30
49 Ryan Smyth .15 .40
50 Mark Messier .40 1.00
51 Dave Tanabe .12 .30
52 Keith Primeau .15 .40
53 Teppo Numminen .12 .30
54 Milan Kraft .12 .30
55 Owen Nolan .20 .50
56 Alexander Mogilny .15 .40
57 Brent Johnson .15 .40
58 Curtis Joseph .25 .60
59 Felix Potvin .30 .75
60 Olaf Kolzig .20 .50
61 Eric Lindros .30 .75
62 Pierre Turgeon .15 .40
63 Martin Straka .12 .30
64 Maxim Afinogenov .12 .30
65 Oleg Saprykin .12 .30
66 Shane Willis .12 .30
67 Brett Hull .40 1.00
68 Alex Tanguay .15 .40
69 Marc Denis .15 .40
70 Ed Belfour .20 .50
71 Roman Cechmanek .15 .40
72 Tommy Salo .15 .40
73 Rob Blake .20 .50
74 Jose Theodore .20 .50
75 Henrik Sedin .25 .60
76 Tony Amonte .15 .40
77 Scott Hartnell .12 .30
78 Brian Rafalski .12 .30
79 Joe Thornton .30 .75
80 Patrick Marleau .20 .50
81 Daniel Alfredsson .20 .50
82 Simon Gagne .20 .50
83 Patrick Lalime .15 .40
84 Johan Hedberg .15 .40
85 Adam Oates .15 .40
86 Chris Pronger .20 .50
87 Vincent Lecavalier .20 .50
88 Tomas Kaberle .12 .30
89 Daniel Sedin .25 .60
90 Martin Lapointe .12 .30
91 Chris Drury .15 .40
92 Dominik Hasek .30 .75
93 Evgeni Nabokov .15 .40
94 Ed Jovanovski .15 .40
95 John LeClair .20 .50
96 Sergei Fedorov .30 .75
97 Martin Havlat .15 .40
98 Martin Brodeur .50 1.25
99 Jason Arnott .15 .40
100 Mike Comrie .15 .40
101 Petr Nedved .15 .40
102 Ray Ferraro .12 .30
103 Miroslav Satan .15 .40
104 Rod Brind'Amour .20 .50
105 Ron Tugnutt .15 .40
106 Oleg Tverdovsky .12 .30
107 Anson Carter .15 .40
108 Wes Walz .12 .30
109 Andrei Markov .20 .50
110 Mike Dunham .15 .40
111 Eric Desjardins .15 .40
112 Radek Dvorak .12 .30
113 Pavel Kubina .12 .30
114 Gary Roberts .15 .40
115 Andrew Cassels .12 .30
116 Vitali Vishnevski .12 .30
117 Byron Dafoe .15 .40
118 Chris Gratton .12 .30
119 Marc Savard .12 .30
120 Shawn McEachern .12 .30
121 Jocelyn Thibault .15 .40
122 Joe Nieuwendyk .15 .40
123 Janne Niinimaa .12 .30
124 Shane Doan .15 .40
125 Willie Mitchell .12 .30
126 Glen Murray .15 .40
127 Scott Walker .12 .30
128 Geoff Sanderson .12 .30
129 Kenny Jonsson .12 .30
130 Radek Bonk .12 .30
131 Brad Stuart .12 .30
132 Scott Young .12 .30
133 Brendan Morrison .15 .40
134 Sergei Gonchar .12 .30
135 Jonathan Girard .12 .30
136 Arturs Irbe .15 .40
137 Chris Herperger .12 .30
138 Brenden Morrow .15 .40
139 Sergei Zubov .15 .40
140 Lubomir Visnovsky .12 .30
141 Aaron Miller .12 .30
142 Ossi Vaananen .12 .30
143 Saku Koivu .20 .50
144 Sean Burke .12 .30
145 Darryl Sydor .12 .30
146 Chris Chelios .20 .50
147 Brian Savage .12 .30
148 Wade Redden .12 .30
149 Derian Hatcher .12 .30
150 Igor Larionov .20 .50
151 Steve Sullivan .12 .30
152 Michal Handzus .12 .30
153 Ron Francis .25 .60
154 David Vyborny .12 .30
155 Manny Legace .15 .40
156 Jeff Friesen .12 .30
157 Jeff Hackett .15 .40
158 Marian Cisar .12 .30
159 Mike York .12 .30
160 Nikolai Antropov .12 .30
161 Trevor Linden .20 .50
162 Bryan Smolinski .12 .30
163 Janne Laukkanen .12 .30
164 Dan Cloutier .15 .40
165 Scott Stevens .20 .50
166 Jani Hurme .15 .40
167 Fredrik Modin .12 .30
168 Steven Reinprecht .12 .30
169 Kevyn Adams .12 .30
170 Richard Zednik .15 .40
171 Viktor Kozlov .12 .30
172 Cliff Ronning .12 .30
173 Mariusz Czerkawski .12 .30
174 Todd Bertuzzi .20 .50
175 Vincent Damphousse .15 .40
176 Roman Hamrlik .12 .30
177 Sandis Ozolinsh .12 .30
178 Mike Richter .20 .50
179 Stu Barnes .15 .40
180 Patric Kjellberg .12 .30
181 Tomas Holmstrom .12 .30
182 Sergei Brylin .12 .30
183 Magnus Arvedson .12 .30
184 Sami Kapanen .12 .30
185 Niklas Sundstrom .15 .40
186 Todd Marchant .12 .30
187 Mark Parrish .12 .30
188 Adam Foote .15 .40
189 Peter Schaefer .12 .30
190 Mike Ricci .12 .30
191 Alexei Zhamnov .12 .30
192 Dainius Zubrus .12 .30
193 Espen Knutsen .12 .30
194 Shean Donovan .12 .30
195 Bobby Holik .15 .40
196 Tom Poti .15 .40
197 Marcus Ragnarsson .12 .30
198 Jozef Stumpel .12 .30
199 Martin Rucinsky .12 .30
200 Matt Davidson RC .12 .30
201 Jan Bulis .12 .30
202 Matt Pettinger .12 .30
203 Rob Zamuner .12 .30
204 Chris Osgood .20 .50
205 Dan Hinote .12 .30
206 Travis Green .12 .30
207 Joe Juneau .12 .30
208 Mikael Renberg .12 .30
209 Zdeno Ciger .12 .30
210 Jochen Hecht .12 .30
211 Jan Hlavac .12 .30
212 Jeff Halpern .12 .30
213 Tom Barrasso .15 .40
214 Bill Muckalt .12 .30
215 Luc Robitaille .20 .50
216 Jason Wiemer .12 .30
217 Deron Quint .12 .30
218 Jyrki Lumme .12 .30
219 Andreas Dackell .12 .30
220 Tomi Kallio .12 .30
221 Roman Turek .15 .40
222 Taylor Pyatt .12 .30
223 Richard Jackman .15 .40
224 Michael Nylander .12 .30
225 Brian Pothier RC .12 .30
226 Slava Kozlov .15 .40
227 Kim Johnsson .12 .30
228 J-P Dumont .12 .30
229 Marty Reasoner .12 .30
230 Dimitri Kalinin .12 .30
231 Damian Rhodes .15 .40
232 Jason Allison .12 .30
233 Doug Weight .20 .50
234 Yanic Perreault .12 .30
235 Eric Daze .15 .40
236 Brian Campbell .12 .30
237 Valeri Bure .12 .30
238 Adam Deadmarsh .15 .40
239 Robert Reichel .12 .30
240 Anders Eriksson .12 .30
241 Nikolai Khabibulin .20 .50
242 Sean O'Donnell .12 .30
243 Bob Essensa .15 .40
244 Josef Vasicek .12 .30
245 Donald Audette .12 .30
246 Steve Heinze .12 .30
247 Bryan Berard .15 .40
248 Ville Nieminen .12 .30
249 Eric Weinrich .12 .30
250 Adam Graves .15 .40
251 Jesse Boulerice 1.25 3.00
252 Marko Kiprusoff 1.25 3.00
253 Ivan Ciernik RC 1.25 3.00
254 Pavel Datsyuk RC 12.00 30.00
255 Jaroslav Bednar RC 1.25 3.00
256 Andreas Salomonsson RC 1.25 3.00
257 Mike Ribeiro 1.25 3.00
258 Darcy Hordichuk 1.25 3.00
259 Chris Neil RC 1.50 4.00
260 Rostislav Klesla 1.25 3.00
261 Kristian Huselius RC 2.00 5.00
262 Brian Sutherby RC 1.25 3.00
263 Jiri Dopita RC 1.25 3.00
264 Radek Martinek RC 1.25 3.00
265 Barrett Heisten 1.25 3.00
266 Krystofer Kolanos RC 1.25 3.00
267 Pascal Dupuis RC 2.00 5.00
268 Andreas Lilja 1.25 3.00
269 Chris Mason 1.25 3.00
270 Mathieu Garon 1.50 4.00
271 Andrew Raycroft 1.50 4.00
272 Jeff Jillson RC 1.25 3.00
273 Jiri Bicek 1.25 3.00
274 Niklas Hagman RC 1.50 4.00
275 Pavel Brendl 1.25 3.00
276 Stephen Peat 1.25 3.00
277 Sascha Goc 1.25 3.00
278 Nick Boynton 1.25 3.00
279 Timo Parssinen RC 1.50 4.00
280 Mika Noronen 1.25 3.00
281 Scott Clemmensen RC 1.25 3.00
282 Dan Blackburn RC 1.50 4.00
283 Nikita Alexeev RC 1.25 3.00
284 Vaclav Nedorost RC 1.25 3.00
285 Ilja Bryzgalov RC 3.00 8.00
286 Dany Heatley 1.50 4.00
287 Niko Kapanen RC 2.00 5.00
288 Rick Berry 1.25 3.00
289 Mark Bell 1.25 3.00
290 Kamil Piros RC 1.25 3.00
291 Maxime Ouellet 2.00 5.00
292 Kris Beech 1.25 3.00
293 Miikka Kiprusoff 2.00 5.00
294 Martti Jarventie 1.25 3.00
295 Ilya Kovalchuk RC 6.00 15.00
296 Nick Schultz RC 1.25 3.00
297 Bryan Allen 1.25 3.00
298 Josef Boumedienne RC 1.25 3.00
299 Jason Williams 1.25 3.00
300 Daniel Tjarnqvist 1.25 3.00
301 Frederic Cassivi RC .50 1.25
302 Mark Hartigan RC .50 1.25
303 Pasi Nurminen RC .50 1.25
304 Ivan Huml RC .50 1.25
305 Zdenek Kutlak RC .50 1.25
306 Ales Kotalik RC 1.00 2.50
307 Jukka Hentunen RC .50 1.25
308 Erik Cole RC 1.00 2.50
309 Tyler Arnason RC .60 1.50
310 Jaroslav Obsut RC .50 1.25
311 Riku Hahl RC .50 1.25
312 Martin Spanhel RC .50 1.25
313 Andrej Nedorost RC .50 1.25
314 Ty Conklin RC .75 2.00
315 Jason Chimera RC .50 1.25
316 Kyle Rossiter RC .50 1.25
317 Lukas Krajicek RC .50 1.25
318 Stephen Weiss RC 1.25 3.00
319 Tony Virta RC .50 1.25
320 Marcel Hossa RC .75 2.00
321 Olivier Michaud RC .75 2.00
322 Henrik Tallinder RC .50 1.25
323 Martin Erat RC .60 1.50
324 Nathan Perrott RC .50 1.25
325 Pavel Skrbek RC .50 1.25
326 Robert Schnabel RC .50 1.25
327 Christian Berglund .60 1.50
328 Stanislav Gron RC .50 1.25
329 Raffi Torres RC .75 2.00
330 Mikael Samuelsson RC .60 1.50
331 Chris Bala RC .50 1.25
332 Josh Langfeld RC .50 1.25
333 Martin Prusek RC .50 1.25
334 Sean Avery RC .50 1.25
335 Neil Little RC .50 1.25
336 Tomas Divisek RC .60 1.50
337 Vaclav Pletka RC .50 1.25
338 Guillaume Lefebvre RC .50 1.25
339 Branko Radivojevic RC .50 1.25
340 Trent Hunter RC 1.00 2.50
341 Jan Lasak RC .50 1.25
342 Tom Kostopoulos RC .50 1.25
343 Hannes Hyvonen RC .50 1.25
344 Shane Endicott RC .50 1.25
345 Evgeny Konstantinov RC .50 1.25
346 Martin Cibak RC .50 1.25
347 Karel Pilar RC .50 1.25
348 Sebastien Centomo RC .50 1.25
349 Mike Farrell RC .50 1.25
350 Sebastien Charpentier RC .50 1.25
351 Radim Vrbata .12 .30
352 Andy McDonald .12 .30
353 J.P. Vigier .12 .30
354 Donald Brashear .12 .30
355 Adrian Aucoin .12 .30
356 Stephane Richer .12 .30
357 Byron Ritchie .12 .30
358 Sergei Berezin .12 .30
359 Cliff Ronning .12 .30
360 Tony Hrkac .12 .30
361 Andre Roy .12 .30
362 Shjon Podein .12 .30
363 Andrei Nazarov .12 .30
364 Marty McInnis .15 .40
365 Petr Tenkrat .12 .30
366 Trevor Letowski .12 .30
367 Randy Robitaille .12 .30
368 Kim Johnsson .12 .30
369 Jozef Stumpel .12 .30
370 P.J. Stock .12 .30
371 Dean McAmmond .12 .30
372 Steve Thomas .12 .30
373 Darius Kasparaitis .12 .30
374 Mike Sillinger .12 .30
375 Jason Arnott .15 .40
376 Alex Auld .12 .30
377 Mike York .12 .30
378 Pierre Dagenais .12 .30
379 Andrew Brunette .12 .30
380 Sergei Zholtok .12 .30
381 Donald Audette .12 .30
382 Doug Gilmour .25 .60
383 Andy Delmore .12 .30
384 Martin Rucinsky .12 .30
385 Jamie Langenbrunner .12 .30
386 Joe Nieuwendyk .15 .40
387 John Vanbiesbrouck .20 .50
388 Shawn Bates .12 .30
389 Jonathan Barnaby .12 .30
390 Pavel Bure .20 .50
391 Tom Poti .12 .30
392 Zdeno Chara .20 .50
393 Adam Oates .20 .50
394 Marty Murray .12 .30
395 Brian Savage .12 .30
396 Daniil Markov .12 .30
397 Tom Barrasso .15 .40
398 Jan Hlavac .12 .30
399 Trevor Linden .20 .50
400 Ivan Ciernik .12 .30

2001-02 Parkhurst Gold

*GOLD/50: 4X TO 10X BASIC CARDS

2001-02 Parkhurst Silver

*SILVER/500: 1.5X TO 4X BASIC CARDS

2001-02 Parkhurst Autographs

PA1 Frank Mahovlich/20 40.00 100.00
PA2 Glenn Hall/90 15.00 40.00
PA3 Jean Beliveau/60 20.00 50.00
PA4 Frank Mahovlich/20 40.00 100.00
PA5 Henri Richard/90 20.00 50.00
PA6 Jean Beliveau/60 20.00 50.00
PA7 Milt Schmidt/90 12.00 30.00
PA8 Elmer Lach/90 12.00 30.00
PA9 Woody Dumart/20 40.00 100.00
PA10 Chuck Rayner/90 10.00 25.00
PA11 Henri Richard/90 20.00 50.00
PA12 Gordie Howe/20 100.00 250.00
PA13 Phil Esposito/20 25.00 60.00
PA14 Bernie Geoffrion/60 20.00 50.00
PA15 Dollard St.Laurent/90 12.00 30.00
PA16 Dickie Moore/90 12.00 30.00
PA17 Jean-Guy Talbot/90 12.00 30.00
PA18 Bill Gadsby/90 12.00 30.00
PA19 Lanny McDonald/80 12.00 30.00
PA20 Gilbert Perreault/60 15.00 40.00
PA21 Johnny Bucyk/90 15.00 40.00
PA22 Dale Hawerchuk/80 20.00 50.00
PA23 Mike Gartner/80 20.00 50.00
PA24 Johnny Bower/90 15.00 40.00
PA25 Butch Bouchard/90 12.00 30.00
PA26 Gordie Howe/20 100.00 250.00
PA27 Jean Beliveau/60 20.00 50.00
PA28 Guy Lafleur/60 20.00 50.00
PA29 Mike Bossy/80 15.00 40.00
PA30 Bryan Trottier/80 15.00 40.00
PA31 Marcel Dionne/60 20.00 50.00
PA32 Jari Kurri/80 15.00 40.00
PA33 Gerry Cheevers/90 15.00 40.00
PA34 Dino Ciccarelli/90 15.00 40.00
PA35 Stan Mikita/60 25.00 60.00
PA36 Gordie Howe/20 100.00 250.00
PA37 Tony Esposito/60 25.00 60.00
PA38 Gump Worsley/90 20.00 50.00
PA39 Ted Lindsay/90 15.00 40.00
PA40 Red Kelly/90 15.00 40.00
PA41 Joe Watson/90 12.00 30.00
PA42 Bobby Clarke/90 25.00 60.00
PA43 Dave Schultz/90 15.00 40.00
PA44 Tiger Williams/90 10.00 25.00
PA45 Serge Savard/90 15.00 40.00
PA46 Jacques Laperriere/90 12.00 30.00
PA47 Peter Mahovlich/90 12.00 30.00
PA48 Denis Potvin/90 15.00 40.00
PA49 Cam Neely/90 15.00 40.00
PA50 Ron Hextall/90 15.00 40.00
PA51 Steve Shutt/90 15.00 40.00
PA52 Yvan Cournoyer/90 15.00 40.00
PA53 Bill Barber/90 12.00 30.00
PA54 Reggie Leach/90 12.00 30.00
PA55 Dennis Hull/90 12.00 30.00
PA56 Bernie Parent/90 20.00 50.00
PA57 Bob Nystrom/90 12.00 30.00
PA58 Guy Lapointe/90 12.00 30.00
PA59 Larry Robinson/90 15.00 40.00

2001-02 Parkhurst 500 Goal Scorers

PGS1 Bobby Hull/30 30.00 80.00
PGS2 Gordie Howe/30 50.00 125.00
PGS3 Marcel Dionne/30 20.00 50.00
PGS4 Phil Esposito/30 25.00 60.00
PGS5 Mike Gartner/80 20.00 50.00
PGS6 Mark Messier/30 30.00 80.00
PGS7 Steve Yzerman/30 40.00 100.00
PGS8 Brett Hull/30 30.00 80.00
PGS9 Mario Lemieux/30 60.00 150.00
PGS10 Dino Ciccarelli/80 15.00 40.00
PGS11 Jari Kurri/80 15.00 40.00
PGS12 Luc Robitaille/30 15.00 40.00
PGS13 Mike Bossy/30 15.00 40.00
PGS14 Dave Andreychuk/80 15.00 40.00
PGS15 Guy Lafleur/30 20.00 50.00
PGS16 John Bucyk/80 15.00 40.00
PGS17 Maurice Richard/80 30.00 80.00
PGS18 Stan Mikita/80 25.00 60.00
PGS19 Frank Mahovlich/80 15.00 40.00
PGS20 Bryan Trottier/80 15.00 40.00
PGS21 Dale Hawerchuk/80 20.00 50.00
PGS22 Gilbert Perreault/80 20.00 50.00
PGS23 Jean Beliveau/80 20.00 50.00
PGS24 Pat Verbeek/80 12.00 30.00
PGS25 Michel Goulet/80 12.00 30.00
PGS26 Joe Mullen/80 12.00 30.00
PGS27 Lanny McDonald/80 12.00 30.00
NNO Ron Francis/25 20.00 50.00
NNO Brendan Shanahan/25 15.00 40.00

2001-02 Parkhurst He Shoots He Scores Points

1 Jean Beliveau 1 pt. .20 .50
2 Doug Harvey 1 pt. .20 .50
3 Tim Horton 1 pt. .20 .50
4 Bobby Hull 1 pt. .30 .75
5 Ted Lindsay 1 pt. .20 .50
6 Stan Mikita 1 pt. .30 .75
7 Jacques Plante 1 pt. .25 .60
8 Chris Pronger 1 pt. .20 .50
9 Terry Sawchuk 1 pt. .25 .60
10 Mats Sundin 1 pt. .20 .50
11 Martin Brodeur 2 pt. .50 1.25
12 Peter Forsberg 2 pt. .40 1.00
13 Patrick Roy 2 pt. 1.00 2.50
14 Joe Sakic 2 pt. .40 1.00
15 Steve Yzerman 2 pt. .75 2.00
16 Paul Kariya 2 pt. .25 .60
17 Pavel Bure 3 pt. .25 .60
18 Gordie Howe 3 pt. .75 2.00

19 Mario Lemieux 3 pt. 1.00 2.50
20 Rocket Richard 3 pt. .30 .75

2001-02 Parkhurst Heroes Dual Jerseys

H1 J.Beliveau/V.Lecavalier 20.00 50.00
H2 G.Howe/S.Yzerman 40.00 100.00
H3 T.Sawchuk/P.Roy 25.00 60.00
H4 R.Richard/P.Bure 30.00 80.00
H5 P.Esposito/J.Thornton 15.00 40.00
H6 G.Lafleur/P.Kariya 25.00 60.00
H7 D.Harvey/B.Leetch 15.00 40.00
H8 S.Mikita/J.Sakic 20.00 50.00
H9 J.Plante/M.Brodeur 25.00 60.00
H10 T.Lindsay/O.Nolan 20.00 50.00
H11 V.Tretiak/E.Belfour 30.00 80.00
H12 T.Horton/S.Stevens 15.00 40.00
H13 Bo.Hull/Br.Hull 25.00 60.00
H14 G.Perreault/M.Lemieux 25.00 60.00
H15 H.Richard/S.Gomez 15.00 40.00
H16 B.Gadsby/C.Pronger 15.00 40.00

2001-02 Parkhurst Jerseys

PJ1 Mario Lemieux 25.00 60.00
PJ2 Milan Hejduk 6.00 15.00
PJ3 Vincent Lecavalier 6.00 15.00
PJ4 Mats Sundin 8.00 20.00
PJ5 Mark Recchi 6.00 15.00
PJ6 Mark Messier 8.00 20.00
PJ7 Peter Bondra 8.00 20.00
PJ8 Jeff Friesen 6.00 15.00
PJ9 Scott Gomez 6.00 15.00
PJ10 Daniel Alfredsson 6.00 15.00
PJ11 Nicklas Lidstrom 8.00 20.00
PJ12 Daniel Sedin 6.00 15.00
PJ13 Peter Forsberg 10.00 25.00
PJ14 Ron Francis 6.00 15.00
PJ15 Joe Sakic 15.00 40.00
PJ16 Mike Modano 12.00 30.00
PJ17 Patrik Stefan 6.00 15.00
PJ18 Steve Yzerman 20.00 50.00
PJ19 Pavel Bure 8.00 20.00
PJ20 Al MacInnis 6.00 15.00
PJ21 Joe Thornton 12.00 30.00
PJ22 John LeClair 8.00 20.00
PJ23 Owen Nolan 6.00 15.00
PJ24 Paul Kariya 8.00 20.00
PJ25 Tony Amonte 6.00 15.00
PJ26 Zigmund Palffy 6.00 15.00
PJ27 Brian Leetch 6.00 15.00
PJ28 Scott Stevens 6.00 15.00
PJ29 Sergei Gonchar 6.00 15.00
PJ30 Chris Drury 6.00 15.00
PJ31 Fredrik Modin 6.00 15.00
PJ32 Alexei Zhamnov 6.00 15.00
PJ33 Curtis Joseph 6.00 15.00
PJ34 Patrik Elias 6.00 15.00
PJ35 Roberto Luongo 8.00 20.00
PJ36 Darren McCarty 6.00 15.00
PJ37 Saku Koivu 8.00 20.00
PJ38 Patrick Roy 20.00 50.00
PJ39 Brendan Shanahan 8.00 20.00
PJ40 Chris Pronger 6.00 15.00
PJ41 Martin Straka 6.00 15.00
PJ42 Chris Chelios 8.00 20.00
PJ43 Theo Fleury 6.00 15.00
PJ44 Roman Cechmanek 6.00 15.00
PJ45 Viktor Kozlov 6.00 15.00
PJ46 Martin Brodeur 20.00 50.00
PJ47 Radek Bonk 6.00 15.00
PJ48 Byron Dafoe 6.00 15.00
PJ49 Adam Foote 6.00 15.00
PJ50 Eric Daze 6.00 15.00
PJ51 Ed Belfour 8.00 20.00
PJ52 Milan Kraft 6.00 15.00
PJ53 Arturs Irbe 6.00 15.00
PJ54 Alex Tanguay 6.00 15.00
PJ55 Sergei Fedorov 8.00 20.00
PJ56 Mike Richter 8.00 20.00
PJ57 Marian Hossa 8.00 20.00
PJ58 Joe Nieuwendyk 6.00 15.00
PJ59 Keith Primeau 6.00 15.00
PJ60 Olaf Kolzig 6.00 15.00

2001-02 Parkhurst Jersey and Stick

PSJ1 Steve Yzerman 25.00 60.00
PSJ2 Pavel Bure 10.00 25.00
PSJ3 Mats Sundin 10.00 25.00
PSJ4 Paul Kariya 10.00 25.00
PSJ5 Patrick Roy 30.00 80.00
PSJ6 Chris Pronger 8.00 20.00
PSJ7 Ed Belfour 10.00 25.00
PSJ8 Martin Brodeur 25.00 60.00
PSJ9 Sergei Fedorov 10.00 25.00
PSJ10 Marian Hossa 10.00 25.00
PSJ11 Olaf Kolzig 8.00 20.00
PSJ12 Vincent Lecavalier 8.00 20.00
PSJ13 Joe Sakic 20.00 50.00
PSJ14 Peter Forsberg 20.00 50.00
PSJ15 Mark Recchi 8.00 20.00
PSJ16 Al MacInnis 8.00 20.00
PSJ17 Roman Cechmanek 8.00 20.00
PSJ18 John LeClair 10.00 25.00
PSJ19 Byron Dafoe 8.00 20.00
PSJ20 Joe Thornton 15.00 40.00

2001-02 Parkhurst Milestones

M1 Chris Osgood 6.00 15.00
M2 Martin Brodeur 15.00 40.00
M3 Jaromir Jagr 10.00 25.00
M4 Jaromir Jagr 10.00 25.00
M5 Ed Belfour 6.00 15.00
M6 Brian Leetch 6.00 15.00
M7 Luc Robitaille 6.00 15.00
M8 Jaromir Jagr 10.00 25.00
M9 Mark Recchi 6.00 15.00
M10 Curtis Joseph 8.00 20.00
M11 Dominik Hasek 12.00 30.00
M12 Mark Messier 12.00 30.00
M13 Scott Stevens 6.00 15.00
M14 Steve Yzerman 20.00 50.00
M15 Doug Gilmour 6.00 15.00
M16 Martin Brodeur 15.00 40.00
M17 Steve Yzerman 20.00 50.00
M18 Patrick Roy 20.00 50.00
M19 Ray Bourque 12.00 30.00
M19U Luc Robitaille 8.00 20.00
M20 Mario Lemieux 15.00 40.00
M20U Brett Hull 8.00 20.00
M21 Ray Bourque 12.00 30.00
M21U Mario Lemieux 15.00 40.00
M22 Jeremy Roenick 10.00 25.00
M22U Steve Yzerman 15.00 40.00
M23 Joe Nieuwendyk 6.00 15.00
M24 Ron Francis 5.00 12.00
M25 Brendan Shanahan 8.00 20.00
M26 Pavel Bure 8.00 20.00
M27 Alexander Mogilny 5.00 12.00
M28 Peter Bondra 5.00 12.00
M29 Mats Sundin 5.00 12.00
M30 Mark Recchi 5.00 12.00
M31 Mike Modano 10.00 25.00
M32 Teemu Selanne 8.00 20.00
M33 Steve Yzerman 15.00 40.00
M34 Adam Oates 5.00 12.00
M35 Mark Messier 8.00 20.00
M36 Mario Lemieux 20.00 50.00
M37 Patrick Roy 15.00 40.00
M38 Dominik Hasek 10.00 25.00
M39 Patrick Roy 20.00 50.00
M40 Ed Belfour 6.00 15.00
M41 Curtis Joseph 8.00 20.00
M42 Mike Richter 6.00 15.00
M43 Martin Brodeur 20.00 50.00
M44 Ron Francis 5.00 12.00
M45 Adam Oates 5.00 12.00
M46 Brett Hull 10.00 25.00
M47 Joe Sakic 12.00 30.00
M48 Al MacInnis 5.00 12.00
M49 Jaromir Jagr 8.00 20.00
M50 Theo Fleury 8.00 20.00
M51 Brendan Shanahan 6.00 15.00
M52 Jeremy Roenick 8.00 20.00

2001-02 Parkhurst Reprints

1 Gordie Howe 4.00 10.00
2 Maurice Richard 2.50 6.00
3 Bernie Geoffrion BC 2.50 6.00
4 Bill Mosienko BC 1.50 4.00
5 Terry Sawchuk 2.50 6.00
6 Woody Dumart BC 1.50 4.00
7 Doug Harvey 2.00 5.00
8 Frank Mahovlich BC 2.50 6.00
9 Jean Beliveau BC 3.00 8.00
10 Jacques Plante 2.50 6.00
11 Jean-Guy Talbot 2.00 5.00
12 Gordie Howe BC 4.00 10.00
13 Terry Sawchuk BC 2.50 6.00
14 Maurice Richard 2.50 6.00
15 Harry Lumley 2.00 5.00
16 Jean Beliveau 3.00 8.00
17 Red Kelly BC 2.00 5.00
18 Bernie Geoffrion 2.50 6.00
19 Dickie Moore 2.00 5.00
20 Dollard St. Laurent 1.50 4.00
21 Terry Sawchuk BC 2.50 6.00
22 Harry Lumley BC 2.00 5.00
23 Woody Dumart 1.50 4.00
24 Tim Horton 2.00 5.00
25 George Hainsworth 2.00 5.00
26 Johnny Bower BC 2.50 6.00
27 Doug Harvey 2.00 5.00
28 Bill Gadsby 2.00 5.00
29 Dickie Moore 2.00 5.00
30 Gordie Howe BC 4.00 10.00
31 Red Kelly BC 2.00 5.00
32 Bernie Geoffrion 2.50 6.00
33 Jean Beliveau BC 3.00 8.00
34 Jacques Plante 2.50 6.00
35 Henri Richard BC 2.50 6.00
36 Chuck Rayner 1.50 4.00
37 Henri Richard 2.50 6.00
38 Frank Mahovlich 2.50 6.00
39 Bill Gadsby BC 2.00 5.00
40 Bernie Geoffrion BC 2.50 6.00
41 Doug Harvey 2.00 5.00
42 Maurice Richard BC 2.50 6.00
43 Georges Vezina 2.50 6.00
44 Jean-Guy Talbot BC 2.00 5.00
45 Terry Sawchuk 2.50 6.00
46 Terry Sawchuk 2.50 6.00
47 Jacques Plante 2.50 6.00
48 Frank Mahovlich BC 2.50 6.00
49 Bill Gadsby BC 2.00 5.00
50 Butch Bouchard 1.50 4.00
51 Bernie Geoffrion BC 2.50 6.00
52 Dollard St. Laurent 1.50 4.00
53 Red Kelly BC 2.00 5.00
54 Red Kelly 2.00 5.00
55 Johnny Bower 2.50 6.00
56 Henri Richard 2.50 6.00
57 Bernie Geoffrion BC 2.50 6.00
58 Gordie Howe
Harry Lumley BC 3.00 8.00
59 Chuck Rayner 1.50 4.00
60 Red Kelly BC 2.00 5.00
61 Dickie Moore 2.00 5.00
62 Bernie Geoffrion BC 2.50 6.00
63 Butch Bouchard 1.50 4.00
64 Frank Mahovlich 2.50 6.00
65 Doug Harvey 2.00 5.00
66 Jacques Plante 2.50 6.00
67 Tim Horton BC 2.00 5.00
68 Dollard St. Laurent 1.50 4.00
69 Bernie Geoffrion 2.50 6.00
70 Butch Bouchard 1.50 4.00
71 Gordie Howe 4.00 10.00
72 Milt Schmidt 2.00 5.00
73 Butch Bouchard BC 1.50 4.00
74 Henri Richard 2.50 6.00
75 Tim Horton 2.00 5.00
76 Gordie Howe 4.00 10.00
77 Dickie Moore 2.00 5.00
78 Elmer Lach BC 2.00 5.00
79 Bernie Geoffrion 2.50 6.00
80 Jean Beliveau BC 3.00 8.00
81 Bill Gadsby 2.00 5.00
82 Jean Beliveau BC 3.00 8.00
83 Bill Gadsby BC 2.00 5.00
84 Henri Richard BC 2.50 6.00
85 Jacques Plante
Ted Sloan 2.50 6.00
86 Frank Mahovlich 2.50 6.00
87 Terry Sawchuk BC 2.50 6.00
88 Maurice Richard 2.50 6.00
89 Tim Horton 2.00 5.00
90 Ted Lindsay 2.50 6.00
91 Johnny Bower BC 2.50 6.00
92 Maurice Richard 2.50 6.00
93 Red Kelly 2.00 5.00
94 Dickie Moore BC 2.00 5.00
95 Bill Gadsby 2.00 5.00
96 Ted Lindsay BC 2.50 6.00
97 Tim Horton BC 2.00 5.00
98 Bernie Geoffrion 2.50 6.00
99 Woody Dumart 1.50 4.00
100 Doug Harvey 2.00 5.00
101 Frank Mahovlich 2.50 6.00
102 Dickie Moore 2.00 5.00
103 Tim Horton BC 2.00 5.00
104 Harry Lumley 2.00 5.00
105 Butch Bouchard BC 1.50 4.00
106 Turk Broda 2.00 5.00
107 Jean Beliveau 4.00 10.00
108 Maurice Richard 2.50 6.00
109 Red Kelly BC 2.00 5.00
110 Jean Beliveau BC 3.00 8.00
111 Jean-Guy Talbot 2.00 5.00
112 Terry Sawchuk
Bernie Geoffrion BC 2.50 6.00
113 Tim Horton 2.00 5.00
114 Dollard St. Laurent BC 1.50 4.00
115 Doug Harvey 2.00 5.00
116 Gump Worsley 2.50 6.00
117 Milt Schmidt 2.00 5.00
118 Jean Beliveau BC 3.00 8.00
119 Tim Horton BC 2.00 5.00
120 Dickie Moore BC 2.00 5.00
121 Doug Harvey 2.00 5.00
122 Henri Richard 2.50 6.00
123 Milt Schmidt BC 2.00 5.00
124 Frank Mahovlich 2.50 6.00
125 Johnny Bower 2.50 6.00
126 Ted Lindsay 2.50 6.00
127 Tim Horton BC 2.00 5.00
128 Jacques Plante 2.50 6.00
129 Jean-Guy Talbot 2.00 5.00
130 Jean Beliveau 3.00 8.00
131 Doug Harvey 2.00 5.00
132 Gump Worsley BC 2.50 6.00
133 Terry Sawchuk 2.50 6.00
134 Frank Mahovlich 2.50 6.00
135 Bill Mosienko 1.50 4.00
136 Jean Beliveau BC 3.00 8.00
137 Tim Horton BC 2.00 5.00
138 Jacques Plante 2.50 6.00
139 Johnny Bower 2.50 6.00
140 Gordie Howe 4.00 10.00
141 Chuck Rayner BC 1.50 4.00
142 Henri Richard 2.50 6.00
143 Gump Worsley BC 2.50 6.00
144 Red Kelly 2.00 5.00
145 Dickie Moore 2.00 5.00
146 Frank Mahovlich 2.50 6.00
147 Henri Richard BC 2.50 6.00
148 Johnny Bower 2.50 6.00
149 Red Kelly 2.00 5.00
150 Bill Gadsby BC 2.00 5.00

2001-02 Parkhurst Sticks

PS1 Mario Lemieux 25.00 60.00
PS2 Milan Hejduk 8.00 20.00
PS3 Vincent Lecavalier 8.00 20.00
PS4 Mats Sundin 8.00 20.00
PS5 Mark Recchi 6.00 15.00
PS6 Mark Messier 8.00 20.00
PS7 Peter Bondra 6.00 15.00
PS8 Jeff Friesen 6.00 15.00
PS9 Scott Gomez 5.00 12.00
PS10 Daniel Alfredsson 6.00 15.00
PS11 Nicklas Lidstrom 8.00 20.00
PS12 Daniel Sedin 6.00 15.00
PS13 Peter Forsberg 15.00 40.00
PS14 Ron Francis 6.00 15.00
PS15 Joe Sakic 15.00 40.00
PS16 Mike Modano 12.50 30.00
PS17 Patrik Stefan 6.00 15.00
PS18 Steve Yzerman 25.00 60.00
PS19 Pavel Bure 8.00 20.00
PS20 Al MacInnis 5.00 12.00
PS21 Joe Thornton 12.50 30.00
PS22 John LeClair 8.00 20.00
PS23 Owen Nolan 6.00 15.00
PS24 Paul Kariya 8.00 20.00
PS25 Tony Amonte 8.00 20.00
PS26 Zigmund Palffy 6.00 15.00
PS27 Brian Leetch 6.00 15.00
PS28 Scott Stevens 6.00 15.00
PS29 Sergei Gonchar 6.00 15.00
PS30 Chris Drury 6.00 15.00
PS31 Martin Brodeur 20.00 50.00
PS32 Chris Chelios 6.00 15.00
PS33 Rob Blake 6.00 15.00
PS34 Teemu Selanne 8.00 20.00
PS35 Pavol Demitra 6.00 15.00
PS36 Markus Naslund 8.00 20.00
PS37 Alex Tanguay 6.00 15.00
PS38 Keith Primeau 6.00 15.00
PS39 Olaf Kolzig 6.00 15.00
PS40 Sergei Fedorov 12.50 30.00
PS41 Brad Richards 6.00 15.00
PS42 Adam Oates 6.00 15.00
PS43 Darren McCarty 10.00 25.00
PS44 Adam Foote 6.00 15.00
PS45 Sandis Ozolinsh 6.00 15.00
PS46 Chris Pronger 6.00 15.00
PS47 Jason Arnott 6.00 15.00
PS48 Keith Tkachuk 8.00 20.00
PS49 Sergei Samsonov 6.00 15.00
PS50 Kenny Jonsson 6.00 15.00
PS51 Gary Roberts 6.00 15.00
PS52 Marian Hossa 8.00 20.00
PS53 Brendan Shanahan 8.00 20.00
PS54 Patrick Roy 20.00 50.00
PS55 Pierre Turgeon 6.00 15.00
PS56 Roman Turek 6.00 15.00
PS57 Doug Weight 6.00 15.00
PS58 Jaromir Jagr 12.50 30.00
PS59 Brett Hull 10.00 25.00
PS60 Dominik Hasek 15.00 40.00
PS61 Luc Robitaille 6.00 15.00
PS62 Eric Lindros 8.00 20.00
PS63 Stan Mikita 15.00 40.00
PS64 Guy Lafleur 12.00 30.00
PS65 Lanny McDonald 12.50 30.00
PS66 Jari Kurri 15.00 40.00
PS67 Jeremy Roenick 10.00 25.00
PS68 Rick DiPietro 6.00 15.00
PS69 Joe Nieuwendyk 6.00 15.00
PS70 Alexander Mogilny 6.00 15.00

2001-02 Parkhurst Teammates

T1 Shanahan/Yzerman/Lidstrom 75.00 150.00
T2 Kraft/Aubin/Lemieux 20.00 50.00
T3 Fleury/Messier/Leetch 20.00 50.00
T4 Dafoe/Thornton/Allison 15.00 40.00
T5 Foote/Sakic/Drury 20.00 50.00
T6 Kolzig/Gonchar/Bondra 20.00 50.00
T7 Joseph/Sundin/Kaberle 20.00 50.00
T8 Roy/Forsberg/Hejduk 40.00 100.00
T9 Thibault/Amonte/Daze 12.00 30.00
T10 Luongo/Bure/Kozlov 20.00 50.00
T11 Biron/Satan/Zhitnik 12.00 30.00
T12 Belfour/Modano/Sydor 15.00 40.00
T13 Cechmanek/Recchi/LeClair 12.00 30.00
T14 Brodeur/Stevens/Elias 30.00 80.00
T15 Holik/Gomez/Arnott 12.00 30.00
T16 Hossa/Alfredsson/Bonk 12.00 30.00
T17 D.Sedin/Naslund/Bertuzzi 15.00 40.00
T18 Francis/Irbe/Ozolinsh 15.00 40.00
T19 Samsonov/Thornton/Guerin 15.00 40.00
T20 Ozolinsh/V.Bure/Luongo 10.00 25.00
T21 Turco/Modano/Belfour 20.00 50.00
T22 Sakic/Roy/Drury 20.00 50.00
T23 Yzerman/Shanahan/Hasek 30.00 80.00
T24 Lindros/Leetch/Messier 15.00 40.00
T25 Selanne/Hurme/Kapanen 10.00 25.00
T26 Sundin/Salo/Naslund 10.00 25.00
T27 Jagr/Hasek/Kaberle 25.00 60.00
T28 Yzerman/Lemieux/Brodeur 40.00 100.00

2001-02 Parkhurst Vintage Memorabilia

PV1 Rocket Richard GJ/90 60.00 150.00
PV4 Jacques Plante GJ/90 30.00 80.00
PV5 Jacques Plante Glove/90 30.00 80.00
PV8 Jacques Plante Stick/90 30.00 80.00
PV9 Bill Gadsby Glove/90 15.00 40.00
PV10 Doug Harvey GJ/90 15.00 40.00
PV13 Gordie Howe GJ/40 50.00 120.00
PV16 Bill Mosienko Pants/90 15.00 40.00
PV17 Jean Beliveau GJ/90 30.00 60.00
PV20 Turk Broda Glove/90 25.00 60.00
PV21 Tim Horton Pants/90 20.00 50.00
PV22 Henri Richard GJ/90 15.00 40.00
PV24 Chuck Rayner Glove/90 30.00 80.00
PV25 Terry Sawchuk Glove/90 30.00 80.00
PV26 Terry Sawchuk Pad/90 30.00 80.00
PV27 Terry Sawchuk GJ/90 30.00 80.00
PV28 Ted Lindsay GJ/90 15.00 40.00
PV30 Johnny Bower Pad/90 12.00 30.00

2001-02 Parkhurst World Class Jerseys

*EMBLEM/20: 1X TO 2.5X JSY/80
*NUMBER/20: 1X TO 2.5X JSY/80
WCJ1 Steve Yzerman 25.00 60.00
WCJ2 Teemu Selanne 8.00 20.00
WCJ3 Olaf Kolzig 10.00 25.00
WCJ4 Zigmund Palffy 10.00 25.00
WCJ5 Peter Forsberg 15.00 40.00
WCJ6 Mike Modano 12.50 30.00
WCJ7 Jaromir Jagr 15.00 40.00
WCJ8 Alexei Yashin 10.00 25.00

2001-02 Parkhurst Waving the Flag

1 Mario Lemieux 6.00 15.00
2 Joe Sakic 2.00 5.00
3 Steve Yzerman 5.00 12.00
4 Paul Kariya 1.00 2.50
5 Curtis Joseph 1.00 2.50
6 Martin Brodeur 2.50 6.00
7 Eric Lindros 1.00 2.50
8 Chris Pronger .75 2.00
9 Jaromir Jagr 1.50 4.00
10 Milan Hejduk 1.00 2.50
11 Dominik Hasek 2.00 5.00
12 Martin Havlat .75 2.00
13 Teemu Selanne 1.00 2.50
14 Jani Hurme .75 2.00
15 Miikka Kiprusoff .75 2.00
16 Sami Kapanen .75 2.00
17 Mats Sundin 1.00 2.50
18 Nicklas Lidstrom 1.00 2.50
19 Tommy Salo .75 2.00
20 Kristian Huselius .75 2.00
21 Jeremy Roenick 1.25 3.00
22 Doug Weight .75 2.00
23 Tony Amonte .75 2.00
24 Brian Leetch .75 2.00
25 Mike Modano 1.50 4.00
26 Brett Hull 1.25 3.00
27 John LeClair 1.00 2.50
28 Keith Tkachuk 1.00 2.50
29 Alexei Yashin .75 2.00
30 Pavel Bure 1.00 2.50
31 Nikolai Khabibulin 1.00 2.50
32 Darius Kasparaitis .75 2.00

2001-02 Parkhurst Beckett Promos

*PROMO: .4X TO 1X BASIC CARDS

2002-03 Parkhurst

COMP.SET w/o SP's (200) 15.00 40.00
1 Rod Brind'Amour .30 .75
2 Alexei Kovalev .25 .60
3 Brad Richards .30 .75
4 Milan Hnilicka .25 .60
5 Arturs Irbe .25 .60
6 Al MacInnis .40 1.00
7 Pavel Bure .30 .75
8 Patrick Lalime .25 .60
9 Vincent Damphousse .25 .60
10 Bates Battaglia .20 .50
11 Evgeni Nabokov .25 .60
12 Glen Murray .25 .60
13 Chris Osgood .30 .75
14 Pierre Turgeon .25 .60
15 Scott Stevens .30 .75
16 Daniel Briere .25 .60
17 Patrik Stefan .25 .60
18 Pavol Demitra .40 1.00
19 Mark Parrish .20 .50
20 Jason Allison .25 .60
21 Jaromir Jagr 1.00 2.50
22 Mike Modano .50 1.25
23 Mark Messier .60 1.50
24 Ilya Kovalchuk .40 1.00
25 Teemu Selanne .60 1.50
26 Marty Turco .30 .75
27 Keith Tkachuk .30 .75
28 Simon Gagne .30 .75
29 Brent Johnson .25 .60
30 Anson Carter .25 .60
31 Jeff Jillson .20 .50
32 Gary Roberts .20 .50
33 Mike Richter .30 .75
34 Martin Lapointe .25 .60
35 Todd Bertuzzi .30 .75
36 Valeri Bure .25 .60
37 Marian Hossa .30 .75
38 Eric Daze .20 .50
39 Nikolai Khabibulin .30 .75
40 Miikka Kiprusoff .30 .75
41 Kevin Weekes .25 .60
42 Mark Recchi .40 1.00
43 Dan Cloutier .25 .60
44 Keith Primeau .25 .60
45 Alex Tanguay .25 .60
46 Ed Jovanovski .25 .60
47 Roberto Luongo .50 1.25
48 Saku Koivu .30 .75
49 Chris Drury .30 .75
50 Olaf Kolzig .30 .75
51 Dan Blackburn .25 .60
52 Erik Cole .20 .50
53 Darcy Tucker .20 .50
54 Chris Chelios .30 .75
55 Pavel Datsyuk .50 1.25
56 Mike Comrie .30 .75
57 Paul Kariya .30 .75
58 Eric Lindros .50 1.25
59 Martin Havlat .25 .60
60 Scott Niedermayer .25 .60
61 Krys Kolanos .20 .50
62 Rostislav Klesla .20 .50
63 Jocelyn Thibault .25 .60
64 Mike Dunham .25 .60
65 Shane Doan .25 .60
66 John LeClair .30 .75
67 Tommy Salo .25 .60
68 Doug Gilmour .40 1.00
69 Johan Hedberg .30 .75
70 Brett Hull .60 1.50
71 Alexander Mogilny .25 .60
72 Chris Pronger .30 .75
73 Sergei Fedorov .50 1.25
74 David Legwand .25 .60
75 Kristian Huselius .25 .60
76 Manny Fernandez .25 .60
77 Vincent Lecavalier .30 .75
78 Rick DiPietro .25 .60
79 Mike Peca .25 .60
80 Ryan Smyth .25 .60
81 Brian Rolston .25 .60
82 Brian Leetch .25 .60
83 Steve Sullivan .25 .60
84 Scott Gomez .25 .60
85 Adam Foote .20 .50
86 Scott Hartnell .20 .50
87 Alexei Zhamnov .25 .60
88 Marc Denis .25 .60
89 Joe Nieuwendyk .25 .60
90 Brad Stuart .20 .50
91 Patrik Elias .25 .60
92 Mats Sundin .30 .75
93 Joe Thornton .50 1.25
94 Brendan Shanahan .30 .75
95 Daniel Alfredsson .30 .75
96 Martin Brodeur .75 2.00
97 Jarome Iginla .40 1.00
98 Peter Bondra .30 .75
99 Peter Forsberg .60 1.50
100 Steve Yzerman .75 2.00
101 Alexei Yashin .25 .60
102 Patrick Roy .75 2.00
103 Markus Naslund .30 .75
104 Jeremy Roenick .50 1.25
105 Darius Kasparaitis .25 .60
106 Curtis Joseph .40 1.00
107 Marian Gaborik .30 .75
108 Bill Guerin .25 .60
109 Joe Sakic .60 1.50
110 Adam Oates .30 .75
111 Owen Nolan .30 .75
112 Rob Blake .30 .75
113 Nicklas Lidstrom .30 .75
114 Joe Thornton .50 1.25
115 Mario Lemieux 1.25 3.00
116 Sergei Gonchar .25 .60
117 Bobby Holik .20 .50
118 Sandis Ozolinsh .20 .50
119 Steven Reinprecht .20 .50
120 Jeff O'Neill .20 .50
121 Radek Bonk .20 .50
122 Milan Hejduk .30 .75
123 Zigmund Palffy .30 .75
124 Luc Robitaille .30 .75
125 Dany Heatley .30 .75
126 Doug Weight .30 .75
127 Fredrik Modin .20 .50
128 Ron Francis .40 1.00
129 Roman Turek .30 .75
130 Adam Deadmarsh .25 .60
131 Sami Kapanen .20 .50
132 Sergei Samsonov .20 .50
133 Jeff Friesen .20 .50
134 Martin St. Louis .30 .75
135 Phil Housley .20 .50
136 Mark Bell .20 .50
137 Felix Potvin .50 1.25
138 Ed Belfour .30 .75
139 Martin Biron .25 .60
140 Alyn McCauley .30 .75
141 Miroslav Satan .30 .75
142 Jan Hrdina .20 .50
143 Ron Tugnutt .20 .50
144 Steve Shields .20 .50
145 Cliff Ronning .20 .50
146 Wade Redden .20 .50
147 Patrick Marleau .30 .75
148 Tony Amonte .25 .60
149 Byron Dafoe .25 .60
150 Roman Cechmanek .25 .60
151 Martin Straka .25 .60
152 Sergei Zubov .25 .60
153 Maxim Afinogenov .20 .50
154 Brian Boucher .25 .60
155 Jason Arnott .25 .60
156 Oleg Tverdovsky .20 .50
157 Daymond Langkow .25 .60
158 Andrew Brunette .20 .50
159 Brian Rafalski .20 .50
160 Mike York .20 .50
161 Richard Zednik .20 .50
162 Radim Vrbata .20 .50
163 Tim Connolly .20 .50
164 Jamie Storr .25 .60
165 Henrik Sedin .40 1.00
166 Sean Burke .20 .50
167 Daniel Sedin .40 1.00
168 Jason Smith .20 .50
169 Stephen Weiss .30 .75
170 Bryan McCabe .20 .50
171 Theo Fleury .40 1.00
172 Jean-Sebastien Giguere .30 .75
173 Espen Knutsen .20 .50
174 Mika Noronen .25 .60
175 Michael Nylander .20 .50
176 Yanic Perreault .30 .75
177 Donald Brashear .20 .50
178 Denis Arkhipov .20 .50
179 Adrian Aucoin .20 .50
180 Tie Domi .25 .60
181 Andrew Cassels .20 .50
182 Eric Brewer .20 .50
183 Trevor Linden .30 .75
184 Brendan Witt .20 .50
185 Robert Lang .20 .50
186 Brendan Morrison .25 .60
187 Mike Fisher .25 .60
188 Alexei Morozov .20 .50
189 Martin Erat .20 .50
190 Jeff Hackett .25 .60
191 Mariusz Czerkawski .25 .60
192 Olli Jokinen .30 .75
193 Brad Isbister .20 .50
194 Niklas Hagman .20 .50
195 Jere Lehtinen .30 .75
196 Igor Larionov .30 .75
197 Curtis Brown .20 .50
198 Ray Whitney .25 .60
199 Grant Marshall .20 .50
200 Craig Conroy .20 .50
201 P-M Bouchard RC 2.50 6.00
202 Rick Nash RC 10.00 25.00
203 Dennis Seidenberg RC 2.50 6.00
204 Jay Bouwmeester RC 5.00 12.00
205 Stanislav Chistov RC 1.50 4.00
206 Jared Aulin RC 1.50 4.00
207 Ivan Majesky RC 1.50 4.00
208 Chuck Kobasew RC 2.00 5.00
209 Jordan Leopold RC 2.50 6.00
210 Ryan Miller RC 10.00 25.00
211 Ales Hemsky RC 6.00 15.00
212 Patrick Sharp RC 5.00 12.00
213 Kari Haakana RC 1.50 4.00
214 Dmitri Bykov RC 1.50 4.00
215 Pascal Leclaire RC 2.00 5.00
216 Henrik Zetterberg RC 10.00 25.00
217 Alexander Frolov RC 4.00 10.00
218 Steve Eminger RC 1.50 4.00
219 Scottie Upshall RC 2.00 5.00
220 Tom Koivisto RC 1.50 4.00
221 Shaone Morrisonn RC 1.50 4.00
222 Ron Hainsey RC 1.50 4.00
223 Martin Gerber RC 2.50 6.00
224 Adam Hall RC 1.50 4.00
225 Lasse Pirjeta RC 1.50 4.00
226 Anton Volchenkov RC 1.50 4.00
227 Craig Andersson RC 5.00 12.00
228 Rickard Wallin RC 1.50 4.00
229 Alexander Svitov RC 1.50 4.00
230 Alexei Smirnov RC 2.00 5.00
231 Jeff Taffe RC 1.50 4.00
232 Mikael Tellqvist RC 1.50 4.00
233 Radovan Somik RC 1.50 4.00
234 Dick Tarnstrom RC 1.50 4.00
235 Steve Ott RC 1.50 4.00
236 Brooks Orpik RC 1.50 4.00
237 Eric Bertrand RC 1.50 4.00
238 Sylvain Blouin RC 1.50 4.00
239 Greg Koehler RC 1.50 4.00
240 Stephane Veilleux RC 1.50 4.00
241 Curtis Sanford RC 2.50 6.00
242 Carlo Colaiacovo RC 2.50 6.00
243 Patrick Boileau RC 1.50 4.00
244 Tim Thomas RC 6.00 15.00
245 Mike Cammalleri RC 5.00 12.00
246 Levente Szuper RC 2.50 6.00
247 Jason Spezza RC 10.00 25.00
248 Cody Rudkowsky RC 1.50 4.00
249 Eric Godard RC 1.50 4.00
250 Valeri Kharlamov RC 5.00 12.00

2002-03 Parkhurst Bronze

*1-200 VETS/100: 4X TO 10X BASIC CARDS
*201-250 ROOKIE/100: .5X TO 1.2X BASIC RC
23 Mark Messier 6.00 15.00

2002-03 Parkhurst Silver

*1-200 VETS/50: 6X TO 15X BASIC CARDS
*201-250 ROOKIE/50: .8X TO 2X BASIC RC

2002-03 Parkhurst College Ranks

CR1 Chris Drury 2.50 6.00
CR2 Erik Cole 2.50 6.00
CR3 Keith Tkachuk 3.00 8.00
CR4 Rick DiPietro 3.00 8.00
CR5 Rob Blake 3.00 8.00
CR6 Adam Oates 2.50 6.00
CR7 Chris Chelios 3.00 8.00
CR8 Brett Hull 3.00 8.00
CR9 Paul Kariya 2.50 6.00
CR10 Tony Amonte 2.50 6.00
CR11 Doug Weight 2.50 6.00
CR12 Dany Heatley 4.00 10.00
CR13 Steven Reinprecht 1.50 4.00
CR14 Curtis Joseph 3.00 8.00
CR15 Anson Carter 1.50 4.00
CR16 Mike Dunham 1.50 4.00
CR17 Mike Richter 3.00 8.00
CR18 Ed Belfour 3.00 8.00

2002-03 Parkhurst College Ranks Jerseys

CRM1 Chris Drury 8.00 20.00
CRM2 Erik Cole 6.00 15.00
CRM3 Keith Tkachuk 8.00 20.00
CRM4 Rick DiPietro 8.00 20.00
CRM5 Rob Blake 6.00 15.00
CRM6 Adam Oates 8.00 20.00
CRM7 Chris Chelios 8.00 20.00
CRM8 Brett Hull 10.00 25.00
CRM9 Paul Kariya 8.00 20.00
CRM10 Tony Amonte 8.00 20.00
CRM11 Doug Weight 6.00 15.00
CRM12 Dany Heatley 8.00 20.00
CRM13 Steven Reinprecht 5.00 12.00
CRM14 Curtis Joseph 8.00 20.00
CRM15 Anson Carter 5.00 12.00
CRM16 Mike Dunham 5.00 12.00
CRM17 Mike Richter 8.00 20.00
CRM18 Ed Belfour 8.00 20.00

2002-03 Parkhurst Franchise Players Jerseys

FP1 Paul Kariya 8.00 20.00
FP2 Ilya Kovalchuk 12.50 30.00
FP3 Joe Thornton 15.00 40.00
FP4 Miroslav Satan 8.00 20.00
FP5 Jarome Iginla 15.00 40.00
FP6 Jeff O'Neill 8.00 20.00
FP7 Eric Daze 8.00 20.00
FP8 Patrick Roy 25.00 60.00
FP9 Rostislav Klesla 8.00 20.00
FP10 Mike Modano 10.00 25.00
FP11 Steve Yzerman 20.00 50.00
FP12 Mike Comrie 8.00 20.00
FP13 Roberto Luongo 10.00 25.00
FP14 Zigmund Palffy 8.00 20.00
FP15 Marian Gaborik 15.00 40.00
FP16 Jose Theodore 12.50 30.00
FP17 Scott Hartnell 8.00 20.00
FP18 Martin Brodeur 20.00 50.00
FP19 Alexei Yashin 8.00 20.00
FP20 Pavel Bure 8.00 20.00
FP21 Marian Hossa 8.00 20.00
FP22 Simon Gagne 8.00 20.00
FP23 Daniel Briere 8.00 20.00
FP24 Mario Lemieux 25.00 60.00
FP25 Chris Pronger 8.00 20.00
FP26 Owen Nolan 8.00 20.00
FP27 Nikolai Khabibulin 8.00 20.00
FP28 Mats Sundin 8.00 20.00
FP29 Markus Naslund 8.00 20.00
FP30 Jaromir Jagr 12.50 30.00

2002-03 Parkhurst Hardware

COMMON CARD 1.50 4.00
A1 Eric Lindros/96 2.00 5.00
A2 Jarome Iginla/95 2.50 6.00
A3 Jaromir Jagr/98 2.00 5.00
A4 Joe Sakic/97 2.00 5.00
A5 Markus Naslund/82 1.50 4.00
A6 Pavel Bure/94 2.00 5.00
A7 Peter Forsberg/83 2.00 5.00
A8 Mario Lemieux/88 5.00 12.00
A9 Mats Sundin/98 2.00 5.00
A10 Wild card/87 1.50 4.00
C1 Chuck Kobasew/95 1.50 4.00
C2 Henrik Zetterberg/78 4.00 10.00
C3 Alexander Svitov/94 1.50 4.00
C4 Jay Bouwmeester/92 2.00 5.00
C5 Jordan Leopold/95 1.50 4.00
C6 Ron Hainsey/96 1.50 4.00
C7 Rick Nash/81 4.00 10.00
C8 Stanislav Chistov/94 1.50 4.00
C9 Stephen Weiss/96 1.50 4.00
C10 Wild card/85 1.50 4.00
H1 Eric Lindros/92 2.00 5.00
H2 Jarome Iginla/88 2.50 6.00
H3 Jaromir Jagr/85 2.00 5.00
H4 Joe Sakic/82 2.00 5.00
H5 Jose Theodore/91 2.00 5.00
H6 Markus Naslund/78 1.50 4.00
H7 Pavel Bure/91 2.00 5.00
H8 Peter Forsberg/73 4.00 10.00
H9 Mario Lemieux/92 5.00 12.00
H10 Wildcard/85 1.50 4.00
N1 Nicklas Lidstrom/85 3.00 8.00
N2 Sergei Gonchar/95 1.50 4.00
N3 Rob Blake/93 1.50 4.00
N4 Ed Jovanovski/96 1.50 4.00
N5 Brian Rafalski/99 1.50 4.00
N6 Bryan McCabe/98 1.50 4.00
N7 Chris Chelios/95 2.00 5.00
N8 Adrian Aucoin/97 1.50 4.00
N9 Brian Leetch/96 2.00 5.00
N10 Wild card/77 1.50 4.00
P1 Eric Lindros/94 2.00 5.00
P2 Jarome Iginla/96 2.50 6.00
P3 Jaromir Jagr/88 2.00 5.00
P4 Joe Sakic/89 2.00 5.00
P5 Markus Naslund/79 3.00 8.00
P6 Pavel Bure/98 2.00 5.00
P7 Peter Forsberg/81 4.00 10.00
P8 Mario Lemieux/88 5.00 12.00
P9 Mats Sundin/93 2.00 5.00
P10 Wild card/77 1.50 4.00
V1 Curtis Joseph/96 2.00 5.00
V2 Evgeni Nabokov/95 1.50 4.00
V3 Jose Theodore/95 2.00 5.00
V4 Martin Brodeur/72 4.00 10.00
V5 Mike Richter/97 2.00 5.00
V6 Patrick Lalime/93 2.00 5.00
V7 Patrick Roy/86 4.00 10.00
V8 Roberto Luongo/97 2.50 6.00
V9 Olaf Kolzig/98 2.00 5.00
V10 Wildcard/86 1.50 4.00

2002-03 Parkhurst Heroes Jerseys

NH1 I.Kovalchuk/V.Kharlamov 15.00 40.00
NH2 J.Thornton/S.Yzerman 15.00 40.00
NH3 J.Iginla/M.Messier 15.00 40.00

NH4 S.Yzerman/B.Trottier 30.00 60.00
NH5 S.Gagne/M.Lemieux 25.00 50.00
NH6 E.Lindros/M.Messier 15.00 40.00
NH7 M.Lemieux/G.Lafleur 30.00 60.00
NH8 R.Nash/M.Sundin 20.00 50.00
NH9 C.Pronger/A.MacInnis 12.00 30.00
NH10 J.Bouwmeester/S.Yzerman 25.00 50.00
NH11 D.Heatley/B.Hull 15.00 40.00
NH12 S.Weiss/P.Forsberg 15.00 40.00

2002-03 Parkhurst He Shoots He Scores Points

1 Martin Brodeur 1pt. .40 1.00
2 Peter Forsberg 1pt. .40 1.00
3 Mark Messier 1pt. .40 1.00
4 Owen Nolan 1 pt. .40 1.00
5 Jeremy Roenick 1 pt. .40 1.00
6 Patrick Roy 1 pt. .40 1.00
7 Joe Sakic 1 pt. .40 1.00
8 Brendan Shanahan 1 pt. .40 1.00
9 Mats Sundin 1 pt. .40 1.00
10 Jose Theodore 1 pt. .40 1.00
11 Joe Thornton 1 pt. .40 1.00
12 Pavel Bure 2 pt. .40 1.00
13 Jaromir Jagr 2 pt. .40 1.00
14 Paul Kariya 2 pt. .40 1.00
15 Eric Lindros 2 pt. .40 1.00
16 Mike Modano 2 pt. .40 1.00
17 Steve Yzerman 2 pt. .40 1.00
18 Jarome Iginla 3 pt. .40 1.00
19 Ilya Kovalchuk 3 pt. .40 1.00
20 Mario Lemieux 3 pt. .40 1.00

2002-03 Parkhurst Jerseys

GJ1 Mario Lemieux 15.00 40.00
GJ2 Jose Theodore 8.00 20.00
GJ3 Brian Leetch 6.00 15.00
GJ4 Jaromir Jagr 10.00 25.00
GJ5 Steve Yzerman 15.00 40.00
GJ6 Eric Daze 6.00 15.00
GJ7 Saku Koivu 8.00 20.00
GJ8 John LeClair 8.00 20.00
GJ9 Jeff O'Neill 5.00 12.00
GJ10 Gary Roberts 6.00 15.00
GJ11 Al MacInnis 6.00 15.00
GJ12 Marian Gaborik 8.00 20.00
GJ13 Teemu Selanne 8.00 20.00
GJ14 Alexander Mogilny 6.00 15.00
GJ15 Eric Lindros 10.00 25.00
GJ16 Milan Hejduk 8.00 20.00
GJ17 Zigmund Palffy 6.00 15.00
GJ18 Luc Robitaille 6.00 15.00
GJ19 Ilya Kovalchuk 8.00 20.00
GJ20 Rostislav Klesla 6.00 15.00
GJ21 Mark Messier 8.00 20.00
GJ22 Ron Francis 6.00 15.00
GJ23 Chris Pronger 6.00 15.00
GJ24 Dany Heatley 8.00 20.00
GJ25 Mark Recchi 6.00 15.00
GJ26 Doug Weight 6.00 15.00
GJ27 Alex Tanguay 6.00 15.00
GJ28 Sergei Fedorov 10.00 25.00
GJ29 Todd Bertuzzi 6.00 15.00
GJ30 Sami Kapanen 5.00 12.00
GJ31 Sergei Samsonov 6.00 15.00
GJ32 Jeremy Roenick 10.00 25.00
GJ33 Mike Modano 8.00 20.00
GJ34 Joe Sakic 12.50 30.00
GJ35 Pavel Bure 10.00 25.00
GJ36 Paul Kariya 8.00 20.00
GJ37 Owen Nolan 6.00 15.00
GJ38 Rob Blake 6.00 15.00
GJ39 Nicklas Lidstrom 10.00 25.00
GJ40 Joe Thornton 8.00 20.00
GJ41 Brendan Shanahan 8.00 20.00
GJ42 Daniel Alfredsson 6.00 15.00
GJ43 Martin Brodeur 15.00 40.00
GJ44 Jarome Iginla 8.00 20.00
GJ45 Peter Bondra 6.00 15.00
GJ46 Peter Forsberg 8.00 20.00
GJ47 Mats Sundin 8.00 20.00
GJ48 Alexei Yashin 6.00 15.00
GJ49 Patrick Roy 15.00 40.00
GJ50 Markus Naslund 6.00 15.00
GJ51 Jay Bouwmeester 6.00 15.00
GJ52 Jason Spezza 8.00 20.00
GJ53 Stephen Weiss 5.00 12.00
GJ54 Ron Hainsey 6.00 15.00
GJ55 Jordan Leopold 5.00 12.00
GJ56 Chuck Kobasew 5.00 12.00
GJ57 Rick Nash 12.50 30.00
GJ58 Scottie Upshall 6.00 15.00

2002-03 Parkhurst Magnificent Inserts

MI1 2000-01 Season Jersey 30.00 80.00
MI2 1985-86 Season Jersey 30.00 80.00
MI3 2002 All-Star Game Jersey 30.00 80.00
MI4 1987 Canada Cup Jersey 30.00 80.00
MI5 Dual Jersey 50.00 125.00

2002-03 Parkhurst Mario's Mates

MM1 M.Lemieux/P.Roy 50.00 120.00
MM2 M.Lemieux/S.Yzerman 25.00 60.00
MM3 M.Lemieux/J.Jagr 30.00 80.00
MM4 M.Lemieux/M.Brodeur 50.00 120.00
MM5 M.Lemieux/E.Lindros 40.00 100.00
MM6 M.Lemieux/R.Francis 30.00 80.00
MM7 M.Lemieux/M.Sundin 25.00 60.00
MM8 M.Lemieux/J.Sakic 60.00 150.00
MM9 M.Lemieux/P.Kariya 30.00 80.00
MM10 M.Lemieux/J.Theodore 25.00 60.00

2002-03 Parkhurst Milestones

MS1 Jeremy Roenick 12.50 30.00
MS2 Martin Brodeur 15.00 40.00
MS3 Ed Belfour 10.00 25.00
MS4 Mike Richter 10.00 25.00
MS5 Jaromir Jagr 12.50 30.00
MS6 Vincent Damphousse 10.00 25.00
MS7 Ron Francis 10.00 25.00
MS8 Mats Sundin 10.00 25.00
MS9 Peter Forsberg 12.50 35.00
MS10 Pavel Bure 10.00 25.00
MS11 Patrick Roy/33 30.00 80.00

2002-03 Parkhurst Patented Power Jerseys

PP1 M.Lemieux/B.Shanahan 25.00 60.00
PP2 S.Yzerman/M.Sundin 40.00 100.00
PP3 J. Jagr/T.Selanne 25.00 60.00
PP4 P.Kariya/J.Roenick 15.00 40.00
PP5 J.Sakic/M.Modano 15.00 40.00
PP6 P.Bure/D.Heatley 15.00 40.00
PP7 P.Forsberg/S.Fedorov 20.00 50.00
PP8 E.Lindros/T.Bertuzzi 20.00 50.00
PP9 I.Kovalchuk/M.Messier 20.00 50.00
PP10 B.Hull/J.Thornton 15.00 40.00

2002-03 Parkhurst Reprints

151 Floyd Curry 1.50 4.00
152 Billy Reay 1.50 4.00
153 Jim Henry 1.50 4.00
154 Ed Sandford 1.50 4.00
155 Pentti Lund 1.50 4.00
156 Al Dewsbury 1.50 4.00
157 Gerry McNeil 2.00 5.00
158 Jack Stewart 1.50 4.00
159 Alex Delvecchio 2.50 6.00
160 Sid Abel 2.00 5.00
161 Ray Timgren 2.00 5.00
162 Ed Kullman 1.50 4.00
163 Billy Reay 1.50 4.00
164 Floyd Curry 1.50 4.00
165 Al Dewsbury 1.50 4.00
166 Allan Stanley 2.00 5.00
167 Paul Ronty 1.50 4.00
168 Gaye Stewart 1.50 4.00
169 Al Rollins 2.00 5.00
170 Leo Boivin 2.00 5.00
171 George Gee 2.00 5.00
172 Ted Kennedy 2.50 6.00
173 Alex Delvecchio 2.50 6.00
174 Marcel Pronovost 2.00 5.00
175 Leo Boivin 2.00 5.00
176 Ted Kennedy 2.50 6.00
177 Ron Stewart 2.00 5.00
178 Bud MacPherson 1.50 4.00
179 Marcel Pronovost 2.00 5.00
180 Alex Delvecchio 2.50 6.00
181 Max Bentley 2.00 5.00
182 Andy Bathgate 2.00 5.00
183 Harry Howell 2.00 5.00
184 Allan Stanley 2.00 5.00
185 Ed Sandford 1.50 4.00
186 Bill Quackenbush 2.00 5.00
187 Eddie Mazur 1.50 4.00
188 Floyd Curry 1.50 4.00
189 Eric Nesterenko 1.50 4.00
190 Ron Stewart 2.00 5.00
191 Leo Boivin 2.00 5.00
192 Ted Kennedy 2.50 6.00
193 Alex Delvecchio 2.50 6.00
194 Bob Armstrong 2.00 5.00
195 Paul Ronty 1.50 4.00
196 Camille Henry 1.50 4.00
197 Al Rollins 2.00 5.00
198 Al Dewsbury 1.50 4.00
199 Netminders nightmare 2.00 5.00
200 Ron Stewart 2.00 5.00
201 Dick Duff 2.00 5.00
202 Lorne Chabot 2.00 5.00
203 Busher Jackson 2.00 5.00
204 Joe Primeau 2.00 5.00
205 Harold Cotton 1.50 4.00
206 King Clancy 2.00 5.00
207 Hap Day 2.00 5.00
208 Newsy Lalonde 2.00 5.00
209 Albert Leduc 1.50 4.00
210 Babe Siebert 1.50 4.00
211 Toe Blake 2.00 5.00
212 Claude Provost 2.00 5.00
213 Toe Blake 2.00 5.00
214 Charlie Hodge 2.00 5.00
215 Floyd Curry 1.50 4.00
216 Len Broderick 1.50 4.00
217 Ed Chadwick 2.00 5.00
218 George Armstrong 2.00 5.00
219 Dick Duff 2.00 5.00
220 Ron Stewart 2.00 5.00
221 Billy Harris 1.50 4.00
222 Bob Baun 2.00 5.00
223 Billy Reay 1.50 4.00
224 Billy Harris 1.50 4.00
225 Toe Blake 2.00 5.00
226 Bob Nevin 1.50 4.00
227 Bob Baun 2.00 5.00
228 Charlie Hodge 2.00 5.00
229 Allan Stanley 2.00 5.00
230 Billy Reay 1.50 4.00
231 Dick Duff 2.00 5.00
232 Marcel Bonin 1.50 4.00
233 Claude Provost 2.00 5.00
234 Canadiens on guard 2.00 5.00
235 Elmer Lach
Maurice Richard 2.50 6.00
236 Billy Harris 1.50 4.00
237 Punch Imlach 2.00 5.00
238 Charlie Hodge 2.00 5.00
239 Bob Baun 2.00 5.00
240 Ron Stewart 2.00 5.00
241 Toe Blake 2.00 5.00
242 Action around the net 1.50 4.00
243 Officials intervene 2.00 5.00
244 Frank Selke 2.00 5.00
245 King Clancy 2.00 5.00
246 Ron Stewart 2.00 5.00
247 Bob Baun 2.00 5.00
248 Dick Duff 2.00 5.00
249 Billy Harris 1.50 4.00
250 Allan Stanley 2.00 5.00
251 Jacques Plante 2.50 6.00
252 Sid Abel 2.00 5.00
253 Norm Ullman 2.50 6.00
254 Marcel Pronovost 2.00 5.00
255 Alex Delvecchio 2.50 6.00
256 Marcel Bonin 1.50 4.00
257 Claude Provost 2.00 5.00
258 Ron Stewart 2.00 5.00
259 Bob Nevin 1.50 4.00
260 Bob Baun 2.00 5.00
261 Dick Duff 2.00 5.00
262 Billy Harris 1.50 4.00
263 Allan Stanley 2.00 5.00
264 Maurice Richard 3.00 8.00
265 Alex Delvecchio 2.50 6.00
266 Norm Ullman 2.50 6.00
267 Ed Litzenberger 1.50 4.00
268 Marcel Pronovost 2.00 5.00
269 Marcel Bonin 1.50 4.00
270 Billy Harris 1.50 4.00
271 Dick Duff 2.00 5.00
272 Bob Baun 2.00 5.00
273 Maurice Richard 3.00 8.00
274 Allan Stanley 2.00 5.00
275 Bob Nevin 1.50 4.00
276 Ed Litzenberger 1.50 4.00
277 Norm Ullman 2.50 6.00
278 Alex Delvecchio 2.50 6.00
279 Marcel Pronovost 2.00 5.00
280 Sid Abel 2.00 5.00
281 Claude Provost 2.00 5.00
282 J.C. Tremblay 2.00 5.00
283 Allan Stanley 2.00 5.00
284 Ed Litzenberger 1.50 4.00
285 Rocket Roars Through 2.50 6.00
286 Bob Nevin 1.50 4.00
287 Jacques Laperriere 2.00 5.00
288 J.C. Tremblay 2.00 5.00
289 John Ferguson 1.50 4.00
290 Toe Blake 2.00 5.00
291 Marcel Pronovost 2.00 5.00
292 Alex Delvecchio 2.50 6.00
293 Allan Stanley 2.00 5.00
294 Dick Duff 2.00 5.00
295 Maurice Richard 3.00 8.00
296 Ron Stewart 2.00 5.00
297 J.C. Tremblay 2.00 5.00
298 John Ferguson 1.50 4.00
299 Toe Blake 2.00 5.00
300 Bill Quackenbush 2.00 5.00

2002-03 Parkhurst Stick and Jerseys

*STK/JSY: .5X TO 1.25X JSY HI

2002-03 Parkhurst Teammates

TT1 Lindros/Leetch/Bure 12.50 30.00
TT2 LeClair/Recchi/Gagne 12.50 30.00
TT3 Sundin/Mogilny/Roberts 12.50 30.00
TT4 Yzerman/Shanahan/Fedorov 40.00 100.00
TT5 Brodeur/Stevens/Elias 20.00 50.00
TT6 Potvin/Palffy/Allison 15.00 40.00
TT7 Koivu/Theodore/Rivet 12.50 30.00
TT8 Thornton/Samsonov/McLaren 12.50 30.00
TT9 Kovalchuk/Heatley/Stefan 15.00 40.00
TT10 Dunham/Legwand/Hartnell 12.50 30.00
TT11 Alfredsson/Havlat/Hossa 15.00 40.00
TT12 Satan/Connolly/Dumont 12.50 30.00
TT13 Daze/Thibault/Zhamnov 12.50 30.00
TT14 Lemieux/Hedberg/Kovalev 30.00 80.00
TT15 Nolan/Selanne/Nabokov 12.50 30.00
TT16 Pronger/MacInnis/Weight 12.50 30.00
TT17 Jagr/Kolzig/Bondra 15.00 40.00
TT18 Cloutier/Bertuzzi/Naslund 12.50 30.00
TT19 Forsberg/Sakic/Roy 25.00 60.00
TT20 Burke/Briere/Numminen 12.50 30.00

2002-03 Parkhurst Vintage Memorabilia

VM1 John Bucyk 12.00 30.00
VM2 Gilbert Perreault 15.00 40.00
VM3 Bobby Hull 20.00 50.00
VM4 Stan Mikita 20.00 50.00
VM6 Jari Kurri 12.00 30.00
VM7 Jean Beliveau 25.00 50.00
VM8 Doug Harvey 12.00 30.00
VM9 Guy Lafleur 12.00 30.00
VM10 Frank Mahovlich 15.00 40.00
VM11 Henri Richard 15.00 40.00
VM12 Maurice Richard 30.00 80.00
VM13 Tiny Thompson 15.00 40.00
VM14 Bernie Parent 30.00 80.00
VM15 Tim Horton 15.00 40.00
VM17 Vladislav Tretiak 25.00 60.00
VM18 Gerry Cheevers 15.00 40.00
VM19 Ted Kennedy 20.00 50.00
VM20 Bill Gadsby 15.00 40.00

2002-03 Parkhurst Vintage Teammates

VT1 B.Hull/D.Hull 20.00 50.00
VT2 P.Esposito/Giacomin 15.00 40.00
VT3 Bucyk/G.Cheevers 15.00 40.00
VT4 Savard/Robinson 30.00 60.00
VT5 T.Esposito/Mikita 30.00 60.00
VT6 Sawchuk/S.Abel 20.00 40.00
VT7 Mahovlich/Mahovlich 20.00 40.00
VT8 Beliveau/D.Harvey 20.00 50.00
VT9 Lafleur/H.Richard 20.00 50.00
VT10 Trottier/M.Bossy 20.00 50.00
VT11 Potvin/B.Nystrom 15.00 40.00
VT12 Clarke/B.Barber 15.00 40.00
VT13 Parent/D.Schultz 25.00 60.00
VT14 T.Horton/R.Kelly 40.00 100.00
VT15 Kharlamov/Tretiak 50.00 100.00
VT16 Mosienko/H.Lumley 15.00 40.00
VT17 Delvecchio/Crozier 15.00 40.00
VT18 Bailey/K.Clancy 20.00 50.00
VT19 Shore/Thompson 20.00 50.00
VT20 McDonald/Williams 15.00 40.00

2005-06 Parkhurst

COMPLETE SET (700) 60.00 120.00
1 Andy McDonald .25 .60
2 Teemu Selanne .60 1.50
3 Scott Niedermayer .30 .75
4 Joffrey Lupul .20 .50
5 Todd Marchant .20 .50
6 Chris Kunitz .30 .75
7 Jean-Sebastien Giguere .30 .75
8 Samuel Pahlsson .20 .50
9 Jonathan Hedstrom .20 .50
10 Ilja Bryzgalov .30 .75
11 Jeff Friesen .20 .50
12 Rob Niedermayer .25 .60
13 Francois Beauchemin .20 .50
14 Vitaly Vishnevski .20 .50
15 Ruslan Salei .20 .50
16 Todd Fedoruk .20 .50
17 Dustin Penner RC 1.00 2.50
18 Ilya Kovalchuk .30 .75
19 Marc Savard .20 .50
20 Marian Hossa .30 .75
21 Vyacheslav Kozlov .20 .50
22 Peter Bondra .30 .75
23 Jaroslav Modry .20 .50
24 Greg de Vries .20 .50
25 Niclas Havelid .20 .50
26 Patrik Stefan .20 .50
27 Serge Aubin .20 .50
28 Andy Sutton .20 .50
29 Kari Lehtonen .25 .60
30 Garnet Exelby .20 .50
31 Michael Garnett .20 .50
32 Bobby Holik .20 .50
33 Scott Mellanby .20 .50
34 Patrice Bergeron .40 1.00
35 Brad Boyes .25 .60
36 Tim Thomas .30 .75
37 Glen Murray .25 .60
38 Marco Sturm .20 .50
39 Wayne Primeau .20 .50
40 Brad Stuart .20 .50
41 Andrew Raycroft .25 .60
42 P.J. Axelsson .20 .50
43 Brian Leetch .25 .60
44 Travis Green .20 .50
45 David Tanabe .20 .50
46 Nick Boynton .20 .50
47 Hal Gill .20 .50
48 Josh Langfeld .20 .50
49 Tom Fitzgerald .20 .50
50 Ales Kotalik .20 .50
51 Maxim Afinogenov .20 .50
52 Chris Drury .25 .60
53 Tim Connolly .20 .50
54 Ryan Miller .30 .75
55 Brian Campbell .25 .60
56 Jochen Hecht .20 .50
57 Teppo Numminen .20 .50
58 Martin Biron .25 .60
59 Derek Roy .20 .50
60 Mike Grier .20 .50
61 Paul Gaustad .20 .50
62 Daniel Briere .30 .75
63 Jason Pominville .20 .50
64 Jay McKee .20 .50
65 J.P. Dumont .20 .50
66 Henrik Tallinder .20 .50
67 Jarome Iginla .40 1.00
68 Daymond Langkow .20 .50
69 Kristian Huselius .20 .50
70 Tony Amonte .25 .60
71 Andrew Ference .20 .50
72 Chuck Kobasew .20 .50
73 Miikka Kiprusoff .30 .75
74 Robyn Regehr .20 .50
75 Roman Hamrlik .20 .50
76 Darren McCarty .20 .50
77 Stephane Yelle .20 .50
78 Chris Simon .20 .50
79 Jordan Leopold .20 .50
80 Rhett Warrener .20 .50
81 Shean Donovan .20 .50
82 Marcus Nilson .20 .50
83 Mike LeClerc .20 .50
84 Eric Staal .40 1.00
85 Cory Stillman .25 .60
86 Erik Cole .20 .50
87 Justin Williams .25 .60
88 Rod Brind`Amour .30 .75
89 Martin Gerber .25 .60
90 Doug Weight .30 .75
91 Ray Whitney .25 .60
92 Matt Cullen .20 .50
93 Frantisek Kaberle .20 .50
94 Bret Hedican .20 .50
95 Oleg Tverdovsky .20 .50
96 Kevyn Adams .20 .50
97 Aaron Ward .20 .50
98 Mark Recchi .40 1.00
99 Glen Wesley .20 .50
100 Josef Vasicek .20 .50
101 Brandon Bochenski RC 1.00 2.50
102 Kyle Calder .20 .50
103 Mark Bell .20 .50
104 Martin Lapointe .20 .50
105 Pavel Vorobiev .20 .50
106 Nikolai Khabibulin .30 .75
107 Craig Anderson .30 .75
108 Matthew Barnaby .20 .50
109 Radim Vrbata .20 .50
110 Rene Bourque RC 1.00 2.50
111 Eric Daze .25 .60
112 Tuomo Ruutu .30 .75
113 Adrian Aucoin .20 .50
114 Jim Vandermeer .20 .50
115 Milan Bartovic .20 .50
116 Curtis Brown .20 .50
117 Alex Tanguay .30 .75
118 Joe Sakic .60 1.50
119 Marek Svatos .25 .60
120 Jose Theodore .30 .75
121 Andrew Brunette .20 .50
122 Milan Hejduk .25 .60
123 John-Michael Liles .20 .50
124 Rob Blake .30 .75
125 Pierre Turgeon .25 .60
126 Ian Laperriere .20 .50
127 Antti Laaksonen .20 .50
128 Patrice Brisebois .20 .50
129 Brett Clark .20 .50
130 Karlis Skrastins .20 .50
131 Brett McLean .20 .50
132 Dan Hinote .20 .50
133 Steve Konowalchuk .20 .50
134 David Vyborny .20 .50
135 Nikolai Zherdev .20 .50
136 Bryan Berard .20 .50
137 Rick Nash .30 .75
138 Sergei Fedorov .50 1.25
139 Jan Hrdina .20 .50
140 Duvie Westcott .20 .50
141 Manny Malhotra .25 .60
142 Marc Denis .25 .60
143 Jason Chimera .20 .50
144 Trevor Letowski .20 .50
145 Adam Foote .20 .50
146 Rostislav Klesla .20 .50
147 Dan Fritsche .20 .50
148 Pascal LeClaire .25 .60
149 Jody Shelley .20 .50
150 Jaroslav Balastik RC .60 1.50
151 Johan Hedberg .25 .60
152 Trevor Daley .20 .50
153 Jon Klemm .20 .50
154 Willie Mitchell .20 .50
155 Steve Ott .20 .50
156 Antti Miettinen .20 .50
157 Niko Kapanen .20 .50
158 Stu Barnes .20 .50
159 Philippe Boucher .20 .50
160 Bill Guerin .30 .75
161 Jason Arnott .25 .60
162 Mike Modano .50 1.25
163 Marty Turco .30 .75
164 Brenden Morrow .25 .60
165 Sergei Zubov .25 .60
166 Jere Lehtinen .25 .60
167 Pavel Datsyuk .50 1.25
168 Henrik Zetterberg .40 1.00
169 Manny Legace .30 .75
170 Nicklas Lidstrom .30 .75
171 Brendan Shanahan .30 .75
172 Jason Williams .20 .50
173 Steve Yzerman .75 2.00
174 Mathieu Schneider .20 .50
175 Robert Lang .20 .50
176 Tomas Holmstrom .25 .60
177 Mikael Samuelsson .20 .50
178 Chris Osgood .30 .75
179 Kris Draper .40 1.00
180 Kirk Maltby .20 .50
181 Chris Chelios .30 .75
182 Johan Franzen RC 1.50 4.00
183 Brett Lebda RC .60 1.50
184 Jiri Fischer .20 .50
185 Shawn Horcoff .20 .50
186 Ty Conklin .25 .60
187 Ales Hemsky .25 .60
188 Jarret Stoll .25 .60
189 Ryan Smyth .25 .60
190 Chris Pronger .30 .75
191 Jaroslav Spacek .20 .50
192 Raffi Torres .20 .50
193 Jussi Markkanen .20 .50
194 Marc-Andre Bergeron .20 .50
195 Fernando Pisani .20 .50
196 Michael Peca .25 .60
197 Jason Smith .20 .50
198 Dwayne Roloson .25 .60
199 Georges Laraque .25 .60
200 Sergei Samsonov .25 .60
201 Olli Jokinen .30 .75
202 Roberto Luongo .50 1.25
203 Nathan Horton .30 .75
204 Joe Nieuwendyk .25 .60
205 Jozef Stumpel .20 .50
206 Jay Bouwmeester .20 .50
207 Gary Roberts .20 .50
208 Chris Gratton .20 .50
209 Martin Gelinas .20 .50
210 Stephen Weiss .20 .50
211 Mike Van Ryn .20 .50
212 Jamie McLennan .20 .50
213 Lukas Krajicek .20 .50
214 Jon Sim .20 .50
215 Sean Hill .20 .50
216 Juraj Kolnik .20 .50
217 Pavol Demitra .40 1.00
218 Mathieu Garon .25 .60
219 Lubomir Visnovsky .20 .50
220 Craig Conroy .20 .50
221 Alexander Frolov .20 .50
222 Mike Cammalleri .30 .75
223 Derek Armstrong .20 .50
224 Joe Corvo .20 .50
225 Eric Belanger .20 .50
226 Sean Avery .20 .50
227 Luc Robitaille .30 .75
228 Dustin Brown .30 .75
229 Jeremy Roenick .50 1.25
230 Jason Labarbera .25 .60
231 Mattias Norstrom .20 .50
232 Mark Parrish .20 .50
233 Brian Rolston .25 .60
234 Pierre-Marc Bouchard .30 .75
235 Manny Fernandez .20 .50
236 Marian Gaborik .30 .75
237 Randy Robitaille .20 .50
238 Todd White .20 .50
239 Alexandre Daigle .20 .50
240 Wes Walz .20 .50
241 Marc Chouinard .20 .50
242 Martin Skoula .20 .50
243 Filip Kuba .20 .50
244 Nick Schultz .20 .50
245 Kurtis Foster .20 .50
246 Derek Boogaard RC 1.50 4.00
247 Brent Burns .30 .75
248 Pascal Dupuis .20 .50
249 Saku Koivu .30 .75
250 David Aebischer .25 .60
251 Alex Kovalev .25 .60
252 Michael Ryder .25 .60
253 Mike Ribeiro .20 .50
254 Andrei Markov .30 .75
255 Jan Bulis .20 .50
256 Craig Rivet .20 .50
257 Steve Begin .20 .50
258 Sheldon Souray .20 .50
259 Tomas Plekanec .20 .50
260 Richard Zednik .20 .50
261 Cristobal Huet .25 .60
262 Francis Bouillon .20 .50
263 Chris Higgins .20 .50
264 Radek Bonk .20 .50
265 Niklas Sundstrom .20 .50
266 Pierre Dagenais .20 .50
267 Mathieu Dandenault .20 .50
268 Paul Kariya .30 .75
269 Tomas Vokoun .25 .60
270 Steve Sullivan .20 .50
271 Yanic Perreault .20 .50
272 Mike Sillinger .20 .50
273 Kimmo Timonen .20 .50
274 Marek Zidlicky .20 .50
275 Scott Hartnell .20 .50
276 Martin Erat .20 .50
277 Dan Hamhuis .25 .60
278 Adam Hall .20 .50
279 Scottie Upshall .20 .50
280 David Legwand .25 .60
281 Darcy Hordichuk .20 .50
282 Vernon Fiddler .20 .50
283 Scott Walker .20 .50
284 Brendan Witt .20 .50
285 Brian Gionta .20 .50
286 Scott Gomez .25 .60
287 Martin Brodeur .75 2.00
288 Jamie Langenbrunner .20 .50
289 Brian Rafalski .25 .60
290 Sergei Brylin .20 .50
291 Patrik Elias .30 .75
292 John Madden .20 .50
293 Viktor Kozlov .20 .50
294 Scott Clemmensen .20 .50
295 Grant Marshall .20 .50
296 Jay Pandolfo .20 .50
297 Richard Matvichuk .20 .50
298 Erik Rasmussen .20 .50
299 Colin White .20 .50
300 Paul Martin .20 .50
301 Alexei Yashin .25 .60
302 Miroslav Satan .25 .60
303 Mike York .20 .50
304 Jason Blake .20 .50
305 Robert Nilsson RC 1.00 2.50
306 Trent Hunter .20 .50
307 Alexei Zhitnik .20 .50
308 Eric Godard .20 .50
309 Rick DiPietro .25 .60
310 Arron Asham .20 .50
311 Denis Grebeshkov .20 .50
312 John Erskine .20 .50
313 Radek Martinek .20 .50
314 Garth Snow .25 .60
315 Shawn Bates .20 .50
316 Sean Bergenheim .20 .50
317 Jaromir Jagr 1.00 2.50
318 Martin Straka .20 .50
319 Michael Nylander .20 .50
320 Martin Rucinsky .20 .50
321 Kevin Weekes .25 .60
322 Petr Sykora .25 .60
323 Steve Rucchin .20 .50
324 Jason Ward .20 .50
325 Michal Rozsival .20 .50
326 Fedor Tyutin .20 .50
327 Marek Malik .20 .50
328 Tom Poti .20 .50
329 Dominic Moore .20 .50
330 Darius Kasparaitis .20 .50
331 Jed Ortmeyer .20 .50
332 Marcel Hossa .20 .50
333 Dominik Hasek .50 1.25
334 Daniel Alfredsson .30 .75
335 Dany Heatley .25 .60
336 Jason Spezza .30 .75
337 Wade Redden .20 .50
338 Peter Schaefer .20 .50
339 Bryan Smolinski .20 .50
340 Mike Fisher .20 .50
341 Zdeno Chara .30 .75
342 Chris Neil .20 .50
343 Antoine Vermette .25 .60
344 Ray Emery .30 .75
345 Patrick Eaves RC 1.00 2.50
346 Vaclav Varada .20 .50
347 Martin Havlat .30 .75
348 Chris Phillips .20 .50
349 Tyler Arnason .20 .50
350 Antero Niittymaki .25 .60
351 Simon Gagne .30 .75
352 Peter Forsberg .60 1.50
353 Mike Knuble .20 .50
354 Michal Handzus .25 .60
355 Joni Pitkanen .20 .50
356 Sami Kapanen .20 .50
357 Kim Johnsson .20 .50
358 Mike Rathje .20 .50
359 Eric Desjardins .25 .60
360 Derian Hatcher .20 .50
361 Robert Esche .25 .60
362 Brian Savage .20 .50
363 Chris Therien .20 .50
364 Keith Primeau .25 .60
365 Petr Nedved .20 .50
366 Donald Brashear .20 .50
367 Curtis Joseph .40 1.00
368 Ladislav Nagy .20 .50
369 Shane Doan .25 .60
370 Mike Comrie .25 .60
371 Mike Johnson .20 .50
372 Paul Mara .20 .50
373 Geoff Sanderson .20 .50
374 Steven Reinprecht .20 .50
375 Dave Scatchard .20 .50
376 Oleg Saprykin .20 .50
377 Zbynek Michalek .20 .50
378 Boyd Devereaux .20 .50
379 Fredrik Sjostrom .20 .50
380 Mike Ricci .20 .50
381 Tyson Nash .20 .50
382 Derek Morris .20 .50
383 Niklas Nordgren RC 1.00 2.50
384 Sergei Gonchar .20 .50
385 Marc-Andre Fleury .60 1.50
386 John LeClair .30 .75
387 Richard Jackman .20 .50
388 Ryan Malone .20 .50
389 Sebastien Caron .20 .50
390 Mario Lemieux 1.25 3.00
391 Brooks Orpik .20 .50
392 Konstantin Koltsov .20 .50
393 Erik Christensen RC .60 1.50
394 Josef Melichar .20 .50
395 Jocelyn Thibault .25 .60
396 Tomas Surovy .20 .50
397 Andre Roy .20 .50
398 Jani Rita .20 .50
399 Vesa Toskala .25 .60
400 Joe Thornton .50 1.25
401 Patrick Marleau .30 .75
402 Jonathan Cheechoo .25 .60
403 Evgeni Nabokov .25 .60
404 Nils Ekman .20 .50
405 Tom Preissing .20 .50
406 Milan Michalek .20 .50
407 Alyn McCauley .20 .50
408 Scott Thornton .20 .50
409 Kyle McLaren .20 .50
410 Scott Hannan .20 .50
411 Marcel Goc .25 .60
412 Grant Stevenson RC .60 1.50
413 Christian Ehrhoff .20 .50
414 Mark Smith .20 .50
415 Scott Young .20 .50
416 Petr Cajanek .20 .50
417 Dean McAmmond .20 .50
418 Curtis Sanford .25 .60
419 Keith Tkachuk .30 .75
420 Dallas Drake .20 .50
421 Jamal Mayers .20 .50
422 Jeff Hoggan RC .60 1.50
423 Christian Backman .20 .50
424 Barret Jackman .20 .50
425 Mark Rycroft .20 .50
426 Jay McClement RC .60 1.50
427 Patrick Lalime .25 .60
428 Kevin Dallman RC .75 2.00
429 Dennis Wideman RC .60 1.50
430 Brad Richards .30 .75
431 Vaclav Prospal .20 .50
432 John Grahame .20 .50
433 Vincent Lecavalier .30 .75
434 Martin St. Louis .30 .75
435 Dan Boyle .20 .50
436 Fredrik Modin .20 .50
437 Ruslan Fedotenko .20 .50
438 Pavel Kubina .20 .50
439 Darryl Sydor .20 .50
440 Sean Burke .20 .50
441 Tim Taylor .20 .50
442 Cory Sarich .20 .50
443 Nolan Pratt .20 .50
444 Rob DiMaio .20 .50
445 Paul Ranger RC .60 1.50
446 Ryan Craig RC .60 1.50
447 Mats Sundin .30 .75
448 Ed Belfour .30 .75
449 Bryan McCabe .20 .50
450 Jason Allison .25 .60
451 Tomas Kaberle .20 .50
452 Darcy Tucker .25 .60
453 Kyle Wellwood .25 .60
454 Jeff O`Neill .20 .50
455 Alexei Ponikarovsky .20 .50
456 Eric Lindros .50 1.25
457 Chad Kilger .20 .50
458 Mikael Tellqvist .25 .60
459 Staffan Kronwall RC .60 1.50
460 Nik Antropov .25 .60
461 Matt Stajan .20 .50
462 Tie Domi .25 .60
463 Luke Richardson .20 .50
464 Alexander Khavanov .20 .50
465 Markus Naslund .30 .75
466 Daniel Sedin .40 1.00
467 Henrik Sedin .40 1.00
468 Todd Bertuzzi .30 .75
469 Alexander Auld .20 .50
470 Brendan Morrison .20 .50
471 Anson Carter .25 .60
472 Sami Salo .20 .50
473 Ed Jovanovski .25 .60
474 Nolan Baumgartner .20 .50
475 Mattias Ohlund .20 .50
476 Dan Cloutier .25 .60
477 Jarkko Ruutu .20 .50
478 Bryan Allen .20 .50
479 Ryan Kesler .30 .75
480 Matt Cooke .20 .50
481 Trevor Linden .30 .75
482 Mika Noronen .25 .60
483 Brooks Laich .20 .50
484 Dainius Zubrus .20 .50
485 Olaf Kolzig .30 .75
486 Matt Pettinger .20 .50
487 Jeff Halpern .20 .50
488 Brian Willsie .20 .50
489 Brent Johnson .20 .50
490 Chris Clark .20 .50
491 Brian Sutherby .20 .50
492 Jamie Heward .20 .50
493 Ben Clymer .20 .50
494 Bryan Muir .20 .50
495 Mathieu Biron .20 .50
496 Shaone Morrisonn .20 .50
497 Matt Bradley .20 .50
498 Mike Green RC 1.25 3.00
499 Rico Fata .20 .50
500 Gordie Howe 1.00 2.50
501 Scott Niedermayer CPT .30 .75
502 Scott Mellanby CPT .20 .50
503 Vincent Lecavalier CPT .30 .75
504 Chris Drury CPT .25 .60
505 Jarome Iginla CPT .40 1.00
506 Rod Brind`Amour CPT .30 .75
507 Adrian Aucoin CPT .20 .50
508 Joe Sakic CPT .60 1.50
509 Adam Foote CPT .20 .50
510 Mike Modano CPT .50 1.25
511 Steve Yzerman CPT .75 2.00
512 Jason Smith CPT .20 .50
513 Olli Jokinen CPT .30 .75
514 Mattias Norstrom CPT .20 .50
515 Saku Koivu CPT .30 .75
516 Greg Johnson CPT .20 .50
517 Alexei Yashin CPT .25 .60
518 Daniel Alfredsson CPT .30 .75
519 Keith Primeau CPT .25 .60
520 Shane Doan CPT .25 .60
521 Patrick Marleau CPT .30 .75
522 Dallas Drake CPT .20 .50
523 Mats Sundin CPT .30 .75
524 Markus Naslund CPT .30 .75
525 Jeff Halpern CPT .20 .50
526 Sidney Crosby CPT 3.00 8.00
527 Brian Leetch CPT .25 .60
528 Jaromir Jagr CPT 1.00 2.50
529 Wes Walz CPT .20 .50
530 Patrik Elias CPT .30 .75

531 Anaheim Mighty Ducks .20 .50
532 Atlanta Thrashers .20 .50
533 Boston Bruins .20 .50
534 Buffalo Sabres .20 .50
535 Calgary Flames .20 .50
536 Carolina Hurricanes .20 .50
537 Chicago Blackhawks .20 .50
538 Colorado Colorado Avalanche .20 .50
539 Columbus Blue Jackets .20 .50
540 Dallas Stars .20 .50
541 Detroit Red Wings .20 .50
542 Edmonton Oilers .20 .50
543 Florida Panthers .20 .50
544 Los Angeles Kings .20 .50
545 Minnesota Wild .20 .50
546 Montreal Canadiens .20 .50
547 Nashville Predators .20 .50
548 New Jersey Devils .20 .50
549 New York Islanders .20 .50
550 New York Rangers .20 .50
551 Ottawa Senators .20 .50
552 Philadelphia Flyers .20 .50
553 Phoenix Coyotes .20 .50
554 Pittsburgh Penguins .20 .50
555 San Jose Sharks .20 .50
556 St. Louis Blues .20 .50
557 Tampa Bay Lightning .20 .50
558 Toronto Maple Leafs .20 .50
559 Vancouver Canucks .20 .50
560 Washington Capitals .20 .50
561 Martin Brodeur NS 1.50 4.00
562 Roberto Luongo NS .50 1.25
563 Marty Turco NS .30 .75
564 Rob Blake NS .30 .75
565 Adam Foote NS .20 .50
566 Chris Pronger NS .30 .75
567 Wade Redden NS .20 .50
568 Robyn Regehr NS .20 .50
569 Todd Bertuzzi NS .30 .75
570 Shane Doan NS .25 .60
571 Kris Draper NS .40 1.00
572 Simon Gagne NS .30 .75
573 Dany Heatley NS .25 .60
574 Jarome Iginla NS .40 1.00
575 Vincent Lecavalier NS .30 .75
576 Rick Nash NS .30 .75
577 Brad Richards NS .30 .75
578 Joe Sakic NS .60 1.50
579 Ryan Smyth NS .25 .60
580 Martin St. Louis NS .30 .75
581 Joe Thornton NS .50 1.25
582 Jay Bouwmeester NS .20 .50
583 Bryan McCabe NS .20 .50
584 Ed Jovanovski NS .25 .60
585 Scott Niedermayer NS .30 .75
586 Sidney Crosby HL 3.00 8.00
587 Sidney Crosby HL 3.00 8.00
588 Alexander Ovechkin HL 12.00 30.00
589 Ed Belfour HL .30 .75
590 Mario Lemieux HL 1.25 3.00
591 Joe Thornton HL .50 1.25
592 Teemu Selanne HL .60 1.50
593 Sidney Crosby HL 3.00 8.00
594 Jaromir Jagr HL 1.00 2.50
595 Luc Robitaille HL .30 .75
596 Manny Legace HL .30 .75
597 Alexander Ovechkin HL 12.00 30.00
598 Daniel Alfredsson HL .30 .75
599 Henrik Lundqvist HL 2.50 6.00
600 Alexander Ovechkin HL 12.00 30.00
601 Ryan Getzlaf RC 2.50 6.00
602 Corey Perry RC 3.00 8.00
603 Braydon Coburn RC 1.00 2.50
604 Jim Slater RC .75 2.00
605 Andrew Alberts RC .60 1.50
606 Hannu Toivonen RC 1.00 2.50
607 Milan Jurcina RC .75 2.00
608 Jordan Sigalet RC .60 1.50
609 Ben Walter RC .60 1.50
610 Thomas Vanek RC 2.00 5.00
611 Daniel Paille RC 1.00 2.50
612 Dion Phanouf RC 1.50 4.00
613 Eric Nystrom RC .75 2.00
614 Cam Ward RC 1.50 4.00
615 Andrew Ladd RC 1.25 3.00
616 Brent Seabrook RC 2.00 5.00
617 Cam Barker RC .75 2.00
618 Corey Crawford RC 3.00 8.00
619 Peter Budaj RC 1.25 3.00
620 Wojtek Wolski RC .75 2.00
621 Brad Richardson RC 1.00 2.50
622 Gilbert Brule RC 1.00 2.50
623 Alexandre Picard RC .60 1.50
624 Jussi Jokinen RC 1.00 2.50
625 Jim Howard RC 2.50 6.00
626 Kyle Quincey RC .75 2.00
627 Valtteri Filppula RC 1.25 3.00
628 Matt Greene RC .60 1.50
629 Jean-Francois Jacques RC .60 1.50
630 Rostislav Olesz RC .75 2.00
631 Anthony Stewart RC .75 2.00
632 Rob Globke RC .60 1.50
633 George Parros RC .60 1.50
634 Mikko Koivu RC 1.25 3.00
635 Yann Danis RC .75 2.00
636 Alexander Perezhogin RC .75 2.00
637 Maxim Lapierre RC 1.00 2.50
638 Andrei Kostitsyn RC 1.25 3.00
639 Ryan Suter RC 1.25 3.00
640 Zach Parise RC 2.50 6.00
641 Barry Tallackson RC .75 2.00
642 Jeff Tambellini RC .60 1.50
643 Chris Campoli RC .60 1.50
644 Jeremy Colliton RC .60 1.50
645 Bruno Gervais RC .60 1.50
646 Henrik Lundqvist RC 5.00 12.00
647 Petr Prucha RC 1.00 2.50
648 Al Montoya RC 1.00 2.50
649 Patrick Eaves 1.00 2.50
650 Andrej Meszaros RC .75 2.00
651 Christoph Schubert RC .60 1.50
652 Mike Richards RC 2.00 5.00
653 Jeff Carter RC 1.50 4.00
654 R.J. Umberger RC 1.00 2.50
655 Ben Eager RC .75 2.00
656 Keith Ballard RC .75 2.00
657 Sidney Crosby RC 12.00 30.00
658 Maxime Talbot RC 1.00 2.50
659 Ryan Whitney RC 1.00 2.50
660 Colby Armstrong RC 1.00 2.50
661 Ryane Clowe RC 1.25 3.00
662 Steve Bernier RC 1.00 2.50
663 Dimitri Patzold RC .60 1.50
664 Lee Stempniak RC 1.00 2.50
665 Evgeny Artyukhin RC .75 2.00
666 Jay Harrison RC .75 2.00
667 Alexander Steen RC 1.50 4.00
668 Kevin Bieksa RC 1.50 4.00
669 Alexander Ovechkin RC 80.00 200.00
670 Tomas Fleischmann RC 1.00 2.50
671 Jean-Sebastien Giguere TC .30 .75
672 Ilya Kovalchuk TC .30 .75
673 Patrice Bergeron TC .40 1.00
674 Ryan Miller TC .30 .75
675 Jarome Iginla TC .40 1.00
676 Eric Staal TC .40 1.00
677 Nikolai Khabibulin TC .30 .75
678 Joe Sakic TC .60 1.50
679 Rick Nash TC .30 .75
680 Mike Modano TC .50 1.25
681 Steve Yzerman TC .75 2.00
682 Chris Pronger TC .30 .75
683 Roberto Luongo TC .50 1.25
684 Luc Robitaille TC .30 .75
685 Marian Gaborik TC .30 .75
686 Saku Koivu TC .30 .75
687 Paul Kariya TC .30 .75
688 Martin Brodeur TC .75 2.00
689 Alexei Yashin TC .25 .60
690 Jaromir Jagr TC 1.00 2.50
691 Dominik Hasek TC .50 1.25
692 Peter Forsberg TC .60 1.50
693 Shane Doan TC .25 .60
694 Sidney Crosby TC 3.00 8.00
695 Joe Thornton TC .50 1.25
696 Keith Tkachuk TC .30 .75
697 Vincent Lecavalier TC .30 .75
698 Mats Sundin TC .30 .75
699 Markus Naslund TC .30 .75
700 Alexander Ovechkin TC 12.00 30.00

2005-06 Parkhurst Facsimile Auto Parallel

*STARS: 3X TO 8X BASE CARDS
*SUBSET CARDS: 1.5X TO 4X
*RCs: 2X TO 4X BASE CARDS
526 Sidney Crosby CPT 25.00 60.00
586 Sidney Crosby HL 25.00 60.00
587 Sidney Crosby HL 25.00 60.00
593 Sidney Crosby HL 25.00 60.00
652 Mike Richards 10.00 25.00
657 Sidney Crosby 60.00 120.00
669 Alexander Ovechkin 200.00 500.00
694 Sidney Crosby TC 25.00 60.00

2005-06 Parkhurst Signatures

AL Andrew Alberts 5.00 12.00
AB Adam Berkhoel 5.00 12.00
AK Andrei Kostitsyn 6.00 15.00
AL Andrew Ladd 8.00 20.00
AM Andrei Meszaros 3.00 8.00
AM Al Montoya 6.00 15.00
AN Antero Niittymaki 8.00 20.00
AO Alexander Ovechkin SP 200.00 500.00
AP Alexandre Picard SP 6.00 15.00
BA Milan Bartovic 3.00 8.00
BB Brad Boyes 3.00 8.00
BC Braydon Coburn 5.00 12.00
BE Ben Eager 5.00 12.00
BL Brett Lebda 5.00 12.00
BO Brandon Bochenski 5.00 12.00
BS Brent Seabrook 6.00 15.00
BT Barry Tallackson 5.00 12.00
BU Peter Budaj 6.00 15.00
BW Ben Walter 3.00 8.00
CC Chris Campoli 3.00 8.00
CK Chuck Kobasew 3.00 8.00
CS Christoph Schubert 3.00 8.00
CT Chris Thorburn 3.00 8.00
DD Daniel Briere 6.00 15.00
DE Derek Boogaard 6.00 15.00
DK Duncan Keith 12.00 30.00
DL David Leneveu 5.00 12.00
DP Dimitri Patzold 5.00 12.00
DW Dwayne Roloson 6.00 15.00
EA Evgeny Artyukhin 3.00 8.00
FP Fernando Pisani 6.00 15.00
GP George Parros 3.00 8.00
HO Marcel Hossa SP 10.00 25.00
JF Johan Franzen 12.00 30.00
JH Jeff Halpern 3.00 8.00
JH Jim Howard 10.00 25.00
JI Jarome Iginla SP 30.00 60.00
JJ Jussi Jokinen SP 10.00 25.00
JL Jason Labarbera 3.00 8.00
JS Jim Slater 5.00 12.00
JS Jordan Sigalet 6.00 15.00
JT Jeff Tambellini 3.00 8.00
JV Josef Vasicek 3.00 8.00
JW Jeff Woywitka 3.00 8.00
KC Kyle Calder 3.00 8.00
KN Kevin Nastiuk 5.00 12.00
KO Mikko Koivu 6.00 15.00
KQ Kyle Quincey 3.00 8.00
IL Ian Laperriere 5.00 12.00
LI John-Michael Liles 6.00 15.00
LS Lee Stempniak SP 8.00 20.00
MA Maxim Afinogenov SP 12.00 30.00
MB Martin Biron 6.00 15.00
MC Mike Cammalleri 8.00 20.00
MG Marian Gaborik SP 30.00 60.00
MH Michal Handzus 12.00 30.00
MJ Milan Jurcina SP 8.00 20.00
ML Maxim Lapierre 6.00 15.00
MM Milan Michalek SP 8.00 20.00
MR Mike Richards SP 30.00 60.00
MS Marc Savard 3.00 8.00
MT Mikael Tellqvist 6.00 15.00
NA Nik Antropov SP 10.00 25.00
NN Niklas Nordgren 3.00 8.00
OJ Olli Jokinen SP 10.00 25.00
OK Ole-Kristian Tollefson 3.00 8.00
OK Olaf Kolzig 6.00 15.00
PB Pierre-Marc Bouchard 3.00 8.00
PE Patrick Eaves 6.00 15.00
PN Petteri Nokelainen 3.00 8.00
PP Petr Prucha SP 10.00 25.00
PS Philippe Sauve 4.00 10.00
RC Ryan Craig 5.00 12.00
RE Robert Esche SP 10.00 25.00
RF Ruslan Fedotenko 3.00 8.00
RG Ryan Getzlaf SP 25.00 50.00
RH Ryan Hollweg 5.00 12.00
RM Ryan Malone 6.00 15.00
RN Robert Nilsson 5.00 12.00
RO Rostislav Olesz 5.00 12.00
SB Steve Bernier 6.00 15.00
SC Sidney Crosby SP 600.00 900.00
SH Scott Hartnell 3.00 8.00
TB Todd Bertuzzi SP 25.00 50.00
TC Ty Conklin 3.00 8.00
TF Tomas Fleischmann 5.00 12.00
TG Tim Gleason 3.00 8.00
TS Timofei Shishkanov 3.00 8.00
WI Brad Winchester 5.00 12.00
YD Yann Danis 6.00 15.00
ZM Zbynek Michalek 3.00 8.00
ZP Zach Parise 12.00 30.00

2005-06 Parkhurst True Colors

TCANA Anaheim Ducks 30.00 80.00
TCATL Atlanta Thrashers 30.00 80.00
TCBOS Boston Bruins 30.00 80.00
TCBUF Buffalo Sabres 25.00 60.00
TCCAR Carolina Hurricanes 25.00 60.00
TCCGY Calgary Flames 40.00 100.00
TCCHI Chicago Blackhawks 30.00 80.00
TCCLB Columbus Blue Jackets 40.00 100.00
TCCOL Colorado Avalanche 20.00 50.00
TCDAL Dallas Stars 25.00 60.00
TCDET Detroit Red Wings 40.00 100.00
TCEDM Edmonton Oilers 40.00 100.00
TCFLA Florida Panthers 25.00 60.00
TCLAK Los Angeles Kings 25.00 60.00
TCMIN Minnesota Wild 30.00 80.00
TCMTL Montreal Canadiens 30.00 80.00
TCNJD New Jersey Devils 40.00 100.00
TCNSH Nashville Predators 30.00 80.00
TCNYI New York Islanders SP 75.00 150.00
TCNYR New York Rangers 30.00 80.00
TCOTT Ottawa Senators 30.00 80.00
TCPHI Philadelphia Flyers 40.00 100.00
TCPHX Phoenix Coyotes 25.00 60.00
TCPIT Pittsburgh Penguins 40.00 100.00
TCSJS San Jose Sharks 30.00 80.00
TCSTL St. Louis Blues 20.00 50.00
TCTBL Tampa Bay Lightning 25.00 60.00
TCTOR Toronto Maple Leafs 30.00 80.00
TCVAN Vancouver Canucks 25.00 60.00
TCWAS Washington Capitals 50.00 125.00
TCCHDE Detroit/Chicago 40.00 100.00
TCDECO Colorado/Detroit 50.00 100.00
TCEDCA Edmonton/Calgary 40.00 100.00
TCFLTB Tampa Bay/Florida 30.00 80.00
TCMIDA Dallas/Minnesota 30.00 80.00
TCMOBO Boston/Montreal 40.00 100.00
TCNJNY Rangers/New Jersey 40.00 100.00
TCNYNY Rangers/Islanders 40.00 100.00
TCOTTO Ottawa/Toronto 40.00 100.00
TCPHPI Philadelphia/Pittsburgh 75.00 125.00
TCSJLA Los Angeles/San Jose 40.00 100.00
TCTOMO Toronto/Montreal 25.00 40.00

2006-07 Parkhurst

COMPLETE SET (250) 75.00 200.00
COMP.SET w/o SPs (160) 10.00 25.00
1 Ron MacLean .30 .75
2 John Anderson .20 .50
3 Al Arbour .25 .60
4 Lou Fontinato .20 .50
5 Grant Fuhr .50 1.25
6 Bill Gadsby .30 .75
7 Danny Gare .20 .50
8 Ed Giacomin .50 1.25
9 Andy Bathgate .25 .60
10 Bob Baun .30 .75
11 Don Beaupre .25 .60
12 Barry Beck .20 .50
13 Jean Beliveau .30 .75
14 Rod Gilbert .25 .60
15 Clark Gillies .30 .75
16 Doug Gilmour .40 1.00
17 Danny Grant .20 .50
18 Ron Greschner .20 .50
19 Bob Bourne .20 .50
20 Mike Bossy .30 .75
21 Johnny Bower .30 .75
22 Scotty Bowman .60 1.50
23 Stu Grimson .20 .50
24 Richard Brodeur .25 .60
25 Aaron Broten .20 .50
26 Neal Broten .20 .50
27 Dale Hawerchuk .40 1.00
28 Johnny Bucyk .30 .75
29 Paul Henderson .25 .60
30 Ron Hextall .30 .75
31 Rejean Houle .20 .50
32 Harry Howell .25 .60
33 Gerry Cheevers .30 .75
34 Don Cherry 1.00 2.50
35 Kelly Hrudey .25 .60
36 Bobby Hull .60 1.50
37 Dino Ciccarelli .30 .75
38 Wendel Clark .50 1.25
39 Bobby Clarke .50 1.25
40 Dale Hunter .25 .60
41 Dick Irvin .20 .50
42 Tom Johnson .25 .60
43 Mike Keenan .20 .50
44 J.P. Kelly .20 .50
45 Red Kelly .30 .75
46 John Davidson .30 .75
47 Kelly Kisio .20 .50
48 Marcel Dionne .40 1.00
49 Joey Kocur .20 .50
50 Kevin Dineen .20 .50
51 Jari Kurri .30 .75
52 Elmer Lach .25 .60
53 Ron Duguay .25 .60
54 Ron Ellis .20 .50
55 Guy Lafleur .40 1.00
56 Phil Esposito .50 1.25
57 Tony Esposito .30 .75
58 Bernie Federko .25 .60
59 Rod Langway .25 .60
60 Edgar Laprade .20 .50
61 Pierre Larouche .20 .50
62 Mike Foligno .20 .50
63 Reed Larson .20 .50
64 Reggie Leach .20 .50
65 Rejean Lemelin .20 .50
66 Ted Lindsay .30 .75
67 Mike Liut .20 .50
68 Al MacInnis .40 1.00
69 Clint Malarchuk .25 .60
70 Cesare Maniago .25 .60
71 Butch Bouchard .25 .60
72 Brian McFarlane .20 .50
73 Marty McSorley .25 .60
74 Howie Meeker .20 .50
75 Gilles Meloche .30 .75
76 Barry Melrose .25 .60
77 Ray Bourque .50 1.25
78 Brian Mullen .20 .50
79 Joe Mullen .25 .60
80 Cam Neely .30 .75
81 Eric Nesterenko .20 .50
82 Bernie Nicholls .25 .60
83 Kent Nilsson .20 .50
84 Ulf Nilsson .20 .50
85 Adam Oates .30 .75
86 John Ogrodnick .20 .50
87 Willie O'Ree .40 1.00
88 Terry O'Reilly .20 .50
89 Bobby Orr 1.00 2.50
90 Greg Millen .25 .60
91 Jim Pappin .20 .50
92 Bernie Parent .40 1.00
93 Brad Park .25 .60
94 Jim Peplinski .20 .50
95 Gilbert Perreault .30 .75
96 Pete Peeters .25 .60
97 Pierre Pilote .25 .60
98 Willi Plett .20 .50
99 Wayne Cashman .20 .50
100 Denis Potvin .30 .75
101 Bob Probert .30 .75
102 Marcel Pronovost .25 .60
103 Rob Ramage .20 .50
104 Mike Krushelnyski .20 .50
105 Pokey Reddick .25 .60
106 Larry Robinson .30 .75
107 Reijo Ruotsalainen .20 .50
108 Jim Rutherford .25 .60
109 Borje Salming .30 .75
110 Milt Schmidt .30 .75
111 Jim Schoenfeld .20 .50
112 Dave Schultz .25 .60
113 Dave Semenko .20 .50
114 Eddie Shack .25 .60
115 Claude Lemieux .25 .60
116 Darryl Sittler .40 1.00
117 Dickie Moore .20 .50
118 Bobby Smith .20 .50
119 Clint Smith .25 .60
120 Anton Stastny .20 .50
121 Marian Stastny .20 .50
122 Peter Stastny .25 .60
123 Thomas Steen .20 .50
124 Scott Stevens .30 .75
125 Brent Sutter .20 .50
126 Duane Sutter .20 .50
127 Darryl Sutter .20 .50
128 J.P. Parise .20 .50
129 Ron Sutter .30 .75
130 Brian Sutter .20 .50
131 Walt Tkaczuk .20 .50
132 Denis Savard .30 .75
133 Frank Udvari .20 .50
134 Gump Worsley .30 .75
135 Doug Jarvis .20 .50
136 Jacques Lemaire .25 .60
137 Peter McNab .20 .50
138 Rick Middleton .25 .60
139 Mike Rogers .20 .50
140 Mats Naslund .20 .50
141 Jim Neilson .20 .50
142 Don Metz .20 .50
143 Pat LaFontaine .30 .75
144 Gordie Howe 1.00 2.50
145 Patrick Roy .75 2.00
146 Garry Unger .20 .50
147 Larry Murphy .25 .60
148 Rick Vaive .30 .75
149 Tiger Williams .20 .50
150 Mario Lemieux 1.25 3.00
151 Michel Dion .25 .60
152 Bill Dineen .20 .50
153 Gary Dornhoefer .20 .50
154 Hakan Loob .20 .50
155 Craig MacTavish .25 .60
156 Allan Stanley .20 .50
157 Marc Tardif .20 .50
158 Ryan Walter .20 .50
159 Zigmund Palffy .30 .75
160 Wilf Paiement .20 .50
161 Milt Schmidt 1.50 4.00
162 Johnny Bucyk 1.50 4.00
163 Ray Bourque 2.50 6.00
164 Terry O'Reilly 1.00 2.50
165 Jim Schoenfeld 1.00 2.50
166 Danny Gare .60 1.50
167 Gilbert Perreault 1.00 2.50
168 Mike Foligno .60 1.50
169 Jim Peplinski .60 1.50
170 Pierre Pilote .75 2.00
172 Denis Savard 1.00 2.50
173 Bill Gadsby 1.00 2.50
174 Marc Tardif .60 1.50
175 Peter Stastny .75 2.00
176 J.P. Parise .60 1.50
177 Ted Lindsay 1.00 2.50
178 Red Kelly 1.00 2.50
179 Gordie Howe 2.50 6.00
180 Danny Grant .60 1.50
181 Reed Larson .60 1.50
182 Wayne Cashman .60 1.50
183 Craig MacTavish .75 2.00
184 Doug Wilson .75 2.00
185 Marcel Dionne 1.25 3.00
186 Butch Bouchard .75 2.00
187 Jean Beliveau 1.00 2.50
188 Wilf Paiement .60 1.50
189 Scott Stevens 1.00 2.50
190 Clark Gillies 1.00 2.50
191 Denis Potvin 1.00 2.50
192 Brent Sutter .60 1.50
193 Allan Stanley .60 1.50
194 Andy Bathgate .75 2.00
195 Brad Park .75 2.00
196 Phil Esposito 1.50 4.00
197 Barry Beck .60 1.50
198 Ron Greschner .60 1.50
199 Kelly Kisio .60 1.50
200 Bobby Clarke 1.50 4.00
201 Ron Sutter 1.00 2.50
202 Dale Hawerchuk 1.25 3.00
203 Thomas Steen .60 1.50
204 Mario Lemieux 2.50 6.00
205 Al Arbour .75 2.00
206 Brian Sutter .60 1.50
207 Bernie Federko .75 2.00
208 Scott Stevens 1.00 2.50
209 Darryl Sittler 1.25 3.00
210 Rick Vaive 1.00 2.50
211 Rob Ramage .60 1.50
212 Wendel Clark 1.50 4.00
213 Doug Gilmour 1.25 3.00
214 Kevin Dineen .60 1.50
215 Rod Langway .75 2.00
216 Dale Hunter .75 2.00
217 Adam Oates 1.00 2.50
218 Walt Tkaczuk .60 1.50
219 Harry Howell .75 2.00
220 Rob Ramage .60 1.50
221 Clint Smith .75 2.00
222 Doug Gilmour 1.25 3.00
223 Mike Rogers .60 1.50
224 Pat LaFontaine 1.00 2.50
225 Neal Broten .60 1.50
226 Al MacInnis 1.25 3.00
227 Kevin Dineen .60 1.50
228 Joey Kocur .60 1.50
229 Tiger Williams .60 1.50
230 Tiger Williams .60 1.50
231 Dale Hunter .75 2.00
232 Marty McSorley .75 2.00
233 Bob Probert 1.00 2.50
234 Stu Grimson .60 1.50
235 Dave Schultz .75 2.00
236 Bill Gadsby 1.00 2.50
237 Lou Fontinato .60 1.50
238 Joey Kocur .60 1.50
239 Ted Lindsay 1.00 2.50
240 Dave Semenko .60 1.50
241 Gary Dornhoefer .60 1.50
242 Pierre Pilote .75 2.00
243 Clark Gillies 1.00 2.50
244 Terry O'Reilly .60 1.50
245 Wendel Clark 1.50 4.00
246 Willi Plett .60 1.50
247 Wilf Paiement .60 1.50
248 Tiger Williams .60 1.50
249 Marty McSorley .75 2.00
250 Bob Probert 1.00 2.50

2006-07 Parkhurst Autographs

2 John Anderson 8.00 20.00
3 Al Arbour 8.00 20.00
4 Lou Fontinato 10.00 25.00
5 Grant Fuhr 10.00 25.00
6 Bill Gadsby 12.00 30.00
7 Danny Gare SP 12.00 30.00
8 Ed Giacomin 8.00 20.00
9 Andy Bathgate 6.00 15.00
10 Bob Baun 15.00 40.00
11 Don Beaupre 6.00 15.00
12 Barry Beck 4.00 10.00
13 Jean Beliveau SP 200.00 300.00
14 Rod Gilbert SP 60.00 100.00
15 Clark Gillies 8.00 20.00
16 Doug Gilmour 60.00 120.00
17 Danny Grant 6.00 15.00
18 Ron Greschner 6.00 15.00
19 Bob Bourne 4.00 10.00
20 Mike Bossy 30.00 75.00
21 Johnny Bower 20.00 50.00
22 Scotty Bowman SP 150.00 250.00
23 Stu Grimson 5.00 12.00
24 Richard Brodeur 4.00 10.00
25 Aaron Broten 4.00 10.00
26 Neal Broten 8.00 20.00
27 Dale Hawerchuk 10.00 25.00
28 Johnny Bucyk SP 60.00 120.00
29 Paul Henderson 10.00 25.00
30 Ron Hextall 12.00 30.00
31 Rejean Houle 8.00 20.00
32 Harry Howell 5.00 12.00
33 Gerry Cheevers 8.00 20.00
34 Don Cherry 15.00 40.00
35 Kelly Hrudey 5.00 12.00
36 Bobby Hull 30.00 80.00
37 Dino Ciccarelli 8.00 20.00
38 Wendel Clark 20.00 40.00
39 Bobby Clarke 12.00 30.00
40 Dale Hunter 10.00 25.00
41 Dick Irvin 8.00 20.00
42 Tom Johnson 30.00 80.00
43 Mike Keenan 8.00 20.00
44 J.P. Kelly 12.00 30.00
45 Red Kelly 6.00 15.00
46 John Davidson 8.00 20.00
47 Kelly Kisio 6.00 15.00
48 Marcel Dionne 10.00 25.00
49 Joey Kocur 30.00 80.00
50 Kevin Dineen 8.00 20.00
51 Jari Kurri 8.00 20.00
52 Elmer Lach 15.00 40.00
53 Ron Duguay 6.00 15.00
54 Ron Ellis 8.00 20.00
55 Guy Lafleur 15.00 40.00
56 Phil Esposito 25.00 60.00
57 Tony Esposito 20.00 50.00
58 Bernie Federko 5.00 12.00
59 Rod Langway 4.00 10.00
60 Edgar Laprade 20.00 50.00
61 Pierre Larouche 6.00 15.00
62 Mike Foligno 4.00 10.00
63 Reed Larson 8.00 20.00
64 Reggie Leach 8.00 20.00
66 Ted Lindsay 8.00 20.00
67 Mike Liut 6.00 15.00
68 Al MacInnis 6.00 15.00
69 Clint Malarchuk 8.00 20.00
70 Cesare Maniago 10.00 25.00
71 Butch Bouchard 30.00 80.00
72 Brian McFarlane 6.00 15.00
73 Marty McSorley 6.00 15.00
74 Howie Meeker 10.00 25.00
75 Gilles Meloche 6.00 15.00
76 Barry Melrose 6.00 15.00
77 Ray Bourque SP 60.00 100.00
78 Brian Mullen 4.00 10.00
79 Joe Mullen 5.00 12.00
80 Cam Neely 12.00 30.00
81 Eric Nesterenko 10.00 25.00
82 Bernie Nicholls 4.00 10.00
84 Ulf Nilsson 6.00 15.00
85 Adam Oates 8.00 20.00
86 John Ogrodnick 6.00 15.00
87 Willie O'Ree 12.00 30.00
88 Terry O'Reilly 15.00 40.00
89 Bobby Orr 60.00 120.00
90 Greg Millen 5.00 12.00
91 Jim Pappin 10.00 25.00
92 Bernie Parent 10.00 25.00
93 Brad Park 5.00 12.00
94 Jim Peplinski 10.00 25.00
95 Gilbert Perreault 12.00 30.00
96 Pete Peeters 6.00 15.00
97 Pierre Pilote 8.00 20.00
98 Willi Plett 4.00 10.00
100 Denis Potvin 6.00 15.00
101 Bob Probert 15.00 40.00
102 Marcel Pronovost 10.00 25.00
103 Rob Ramage 4.00 10.00
104 Mike Krushelnyski 4.00 10.00
106 Larry Robinson 10.00 25.00
107 Reijo Ruotsalainen 4.00 10.00
108 Jim Rutherford 10.00 25.00
109 Borje Salming 10.00 25.00
110 Milt Schmidt 12.00 30.00
111 Jim Schoenfeld 6.00 15.00
112 Dave Schultz 6.00 15.00
113 Dave Semenko 15.00 40.00
114 Eddie Shack 8.00 20.00
115 Claude Lemieux 8.00 20.00
116 Darryl Sittler 15.00 40.00
118 Bobby Smith 5.00 12.00
119 Clint Smith 30.00 60.00
120 Anton Stastny 6.00 15.00
121 Marian Stastny 6.00 15.00
122 Peter Stastny 10.00 25.00
123 Thomas Steen 4.00 10.00
124 Scott Stevens 30.00 60.00
125 Brent Sutter 4.00 10.00
126 Duane Sutter 5.00 12.00
127 Darryl Sutter 5.00 12.00
128 J.P. Parise 4.00 10.00
130 Brian Sutter 8.00 20.00
131 Walt Tkaczuk 6.00 15.00
132 Denis Savard SP 30.00 60.00
133 Frank Udvari 8.00 20.00
135 Doug Jarvis 8.00 20.00
136 Jacques Lemaire 8.00 20.00
137 Peter McNab 10.00 25.00
138 Rick Middleton 10.00 25.00
139 Mike Rogers 5.00 12.00
140 Mats Naslund 6.00 15.00
141 Jim Neilson 6.00 15.00
143 Pat LaFontaine 8.00 20.00
144 Gordie Howe 60.00 120.00
146 Garry Unger 12.00 30.00
148 Rick Vaive 6.00 15.00
149 Tiger Williams 12.00 30.00
150 Mario Lemieux SP 300.00 800.00
151 Michel Dion 15.00 40.00
152 Bill Dineen 12.00 30.00
153 Gary Dornhoefer 4.00 10.00
154 Hakan Loob 5.00 12.00
155 Craig MacTavish 6.00 15.00
156 Allan Stanley 10.00 25.00
157 Marc Tardif 12.00 30.00
158 Ryan Walter 4.00 10.00
160 Wilf Paiement 4.00 10.00
161 Milt Schmidt CAP 12.00 30.00
162 Johnny Bucyk CAP SP 125.00 250.00
163 Ray Bourque CAP SP 100.00 175.00
164 Terry O'Reilly CAP 12.00 30.00
165 Jim Schoenfeld CAP 8.00 20.00
166 Danny Gare CAP 12.00 30.00
167 Gilbert Perreault CAP 15.00 40.00
168 Mike Foligno CAP 4.00 10.00
169 Jim Peplinski CAP 12.00 30.00
170 Pierre Pilote CAP 15.00 40.00
171 Darryl Sutter CAP 15.00 40.00
172 Denis Savard CAP 50.00 100.00
173 Bill Gadsby CAP 12.00 30.00
174 Marc Tardif CAP 10.00 25.00
175 Peter Stastny CAP 25.00 60.00
176 J.P. Parise CAP 10.00 25.00
177 Ted Lindsay CAP 12.00 30.00
178 Red Kelly CAP 12.00 30.00
179 Gordie Howe CAP 100.00 175.00
180 Danny Grant CAP 8.00 20.00
181 Reed Larson CAP 6.00 15.00
183 Craig MacTavish CAP 5.00 12.00
185 Marcel Dionne CAP 40.00 70.00
186 Butch Bouchard CAP 25.00 60.00
187 Jean Beliveau CAP SP 25.00 50.00
188 Wilf Paiement CAP 12.00 30.00
189 Scott Stevens CAP 15.00 40.00
190 Clark Gillies CAP 10.00 25.00
191 Denis Potvin CAP 12.00 30.00
192 Brent Sutter CAP 10.00 25.00
193 Allan Stanley CAP 12.00 30.00
194 Andy Bathgate CAP 8.00 20.00
195 Brad Park CAP 8.00 20.00
196 Phil Esposito CAP 25.00 60.00
197 Barry Beck CAP 10.00 25.00
198 Ron Greschner CAP 8.00 20.00
199 Kelly Kisio CAP 12.00 30.00
200 Bobby Clarke CAP 30.00 60.00
201 Ron Sutter CAP 10.00 25.00
202 Dale Hawerchuk CAP 20.00 50.00
203 Thomas Steen CAP 10.00 25.00
205 Al Arbour CAP 12.00 30.00
206 Brian Sutter CAP 6.00 15.00
207 Bernie Federko CAP 10.00 25.00
208 Scott Stevens CAP SP 25.00 60.00
209 Darryl Sittler CAP 25.00 60.00
210 Rick Vaive CAP 25.00 50.00
211 Rob Ramage CAP 10.00 25.00
212 Wendel Clark CAP 50.00 100.00
213 Doug Gilmour CAP 12.00 30.00
215 Rod Langway CAP 10.00 25.00
216 Dale Hunter CAP 8.00 20.00
217 Adam Oates CAP 12.00 30.00
219 Harry Howell CAP 20.00 40.00
221 Clint Smith CAP 25.00 60.00
222 Doug Gilmour CAP EXCH 15.00 40.00
223 Mike Rogers CAP 20.00 50.00
225 Neal Broten CAP 12.00 30.00
226 Al MacInnis CAP 20.00 50.00
227 Kevin Dineen CAP 15.00 40.00
228 Joey Kocur ENF 20.00 50.00
229 Tiger Williams ENF EXCH 12.00 30.00
230 Tiger Williams ENF 25.00 50.00
231 Dale Hunter ENF 12.00 30.00
232 Marty McSorley ENF 25.00 50.00
233 Bob Probert ENF 30.00 60.00
234 Stu Grimson ENF 10.00 25.00
235 Dave Schultz ENF 20.00 50.00
236 Bill Gadsby ENF 20.00 50.00
238 Joey Kocur ENF 20.00 50.00
239 Ted Lindsay ENF 15.00 40.00
240 Dave Semenko ENF 15.00 40.00
241 Gary Dornhoefer ENF 15.00 30.00
242 Pierre Pilote ENF 20.00 40.00
243 Clark Gillies ENF 6.00 15.00
244 Terry O'Reilly ENF 20.00 50.00
245 Wendel Clark ENF 12.00 30.00
246 Willi Plett ENF 8.00 20.00
247 Wilf Paiement ENF 15.00 40.00
248 Tiger Williams ENF 15.00 40.00
249 Marty McSorley ENF 25.00 50.00
250 Bob Probert ENF 20.00 50.00

2006-07 Parkhurst Autographs Dual

DAAB A.Arbour/S.Bowman SP 60.00 100.00
DABB N.Broten/A.Broten 60.00 125.00
DABG M.Bossy/C.Gillies 40.00 80.00
DABL B.Bouchard/E.Lach 75.00 150.00
DABM J.Beliveau/D.Moore SP 150.00 300.00
DABO G.Cheevers/B.Park 50.00 100.00
DACL B.Clarke/R.Leach 90.00 150.00
DACP B.Clarke/B.Parent 50.00 100.00
DADN M.Dionne/B.Nicholls 25.00 60.00
DADR D.Savard/R.Vaive 25.00 60.00
DAEB P.Esposito/J.Bucyk 60.00 125.00
DAEE P.Esposito/T.Esposito 30.00 80.00
DAES R.Ellis/E.Shack 25.00 60.00
DAFM B.Federko/J.Mullen 30.00 80.00
DAGB R.Greschner/B.Beck 30.00 80.00
DAGC G.Fuhr/C.MacTavish 50.00 125.00
DAHE B.Hull/T.Esposito 50.00 100.00
DAHL G.Howe/T.Lindsay SP 100.00 200.00
DAHP B.Hull/J.Pappin 25.00 60.00
DAIM D.Irvin/B.McFarlane 15.00 40.00
DALD M.Liut/K.Dineen 40.00 80.00
DALK T.Lindsay/R.Kelly 50.00 100.00
DALL G.Lafleur/J.Lemaire 75.00 150.00
DAMB G.Meloche/D.Beaupre 75.00 150.00
DAMM J.Mullen/B.Mullen 40.00 80.00
DAMP M.McSorley/B.Probert 100.00 175.00
DANO C.Neely/A.Oates 25.00 60.00
DAOB B.Orr/R.Bourque SP 250.00 400.00
DAOL J.Ogrodnick/R.Larson 40.00 80.00
DAOM T.O'Reilly/P.McNab 20.00 50.00
DAPF G.Perreault/M.Foligno 25.00 60.00
DAPG G.Perreault/D.Gare 75.00 150.00
DAPK B.Probert/J.Kocur 25.00 60.00
DAPM P.Peeters/R.Middleton 20.00 50.00
DAPP J.Peplinski/W.Plett 25.00 60.00
DARP L.Robinson/D.Potvin 25.00 60.00
DASB M.Schmidt/J.Bucyk 60.00 100.00
DASD D.Schultz/G.Dornhoefer 40.00 80.00
DAST1 P.Stastny/A.Stastny 40.00 100.00
DAST2 P.Stastny/M.Stastny 25.00 60.00
DASU1 D.Sutter/D.Sutter 25.00 60.00
DASV D.Sittler/R.Vaive 40.00 80.00
DATB T.Williams/R.Brodeur 40.00 80.00
DAWS T.Williams/D.Semenko 75.00 125.00

1995-96 Parkhurst '66-67 Prototypes

COMPLETE SET (5) 6.00 15.00
16 Gerry Cheevers 1.25 3.00
42 Gordie Howe 4.00 10.00
125 Jean Beliveau Stan Mikita AS 1.50 4.00
128 Jacques Laperriere Norris Trophy Winner .30 .75
144 Bob Nevin .30 .75

1995-96 Parkhurst '66-67

COMPLETE SET (150) 12.50 25.00
1 Pit Martin .05 .15
2 Ron Stewart .05 .15
3 Joe Watson .02 .10
4 Ed Westfall .02 .10
5 John Bucyk .08 .25
6 Ted Green .05 .15
7 Bobby Orr 2.50 5.00
8 Bob Woytowich .02 .10
9 Murray Oliver .02 .10
10 John McKenzie .05 .15
11 Tom Williams .02 .10
12 Don Awrey .02 .10
13 Ron Schock .02 .10
14 Bernie Parent .40 1.00
15 Ron Murphy .02 .10
16 Gerry Cheevers .40 1.00
17 Gilles Marotte .02 .10
18 Ed Johnston .05 .15
19 Derek Sanderson .40 1.00
20 Wayne Connelly .02 .10
21 Bobby Hull 1.25 3.00
22 Matt Ravlich .02 .10
23 Ken Hodge .05 .15
24 Stan Mikita .60 1.50
25 Fred Stanfield .02 .10
26 Eric Nesterenko .05 .15

27 Doug Jarrett .02 .10
28 Lou Angotti .02 .10
29 Ken Wharram .02 .10
30 Bill Hay .02 .10
31 Glenn Hall .60 1.50
32 Chico Maki .02 .10
33 Phil Esposito .60 1.50
34 Pierre Pilote .08 .25
35 Doug Mohns .02 .10
36 Ed Van Impe .02 .10
37 Dennis Hull .05 .15
38 Pat Stapleton .02 .10
39 Denis DeJordy .02 .10
40 Paul Henderson .20 .50
41 Gary Bergman .02 .10
42 Gordie Howe 1.50 4.00
43 Bob McCord .02 .10
44 Andy Bathgate .08 .25
45 Norm Ullman .08 .25
46 Peter Mahovlich .05 .15
47 Ted Hampson .02 .10
48 Leo Boivin .08 .25
49 Bruce MacGregor .02 .10
50 Ab McDonald .05 .15
51 Dean Prentice .02 .10
52 Floyd Smith .02 .10
53 Alex Delvecchio .08 .25
54 Pete Goegan .02 .10
55 Parker MacDonald .02 .10
56 Roger Crozier .05 .15
57 Val Fonteyne .02 .10
58 Henri Richard .40 1.00
59 John Ferguson .05 .15
60 Yvan Cournoyer .08 .25
61 Claude Provost .05 .15
62 Dave Balon .02 .10
63 Ted Harris .02 .10
64 Ralph Backstrom .05 .15
65 Jacques Laperriere .08 .25
66 Terry Harper .05 .15
67 J.C. Tremblay .05 .15
68 Jean Guy Talbot .05 .15
69 Claude Larose .05 .15
70 Charlie Hodge .05 .15
71 Gilles Tremblay .02 .10
72 Jim Roberts .02 .10
73 Jean Beliveau .60 1.50
74 Serge Savard .10 .25
75 Rogatien Vachon .30 .75
76 Lorne Worsley .60 1.50
77 Bobby Rousseau .05 .15
78 Dick Duff .05 .15
79 Rod Gilbert .08 .25
80 Harry Howell .08 .25
81 Jim Neilson .02 .10
82 Don Marshall .02 .10
83 Reg Fleming .02 .10
84 Wayne Hillman .02 .10
85 Bob Nevin .02 .10
86 Arnie Brown .02 .10
87 Earl Ingarfield .02 .10
88 Jean Ratelle .08 .25
89 Bernie Geoffrion .40 1.00
90 Orland Kurtenbach .02 .10
91 Bill Hicke .02 .10
92 Red Berenson .05 .15
93 Ed Giacomin .08 .25
94 Al MacNeil .02 .10
95 Rod Seiling .02 .10
96 Doug Robinson .02 .10
97 Cesare Maniago .05 .15
98 Vic Hadfield .02 .10
99 Phil Goyette .02 .10
100 Dave Keon .08 .25
101 Mike Walton .02 .10
102 Frank Mahovlich .60 1.50
103 Tim Horton .60 1.50
104 Larry Hillman .02 .10
105 Kent Douglas .02 .10
106 Ron Ellis .02 .10
107 Jim Pappin .02 .10
108 Marcel Pronovost .08 .25
109 Red Kelly .08 .25
110 Allan Stanley .08 .25
111 Brit Selby .02 .10
112 Pete Stemkowski .02 .10
113 Eddie Shack .40 1.00
114 Bob Pulford .08 .25
115 Larry Jeffrey .02 .10
116 George Armstrong .08 .25
117 Bob Baun .10 .25
118 Bruce Gamble .02 .10
119 Johnny Bower .60 1.50
120 Terry Sawchuk .75 2.00
121 Hall/Worsley AS .30 .75
122 Laperriere/Stanley AS .05 .15
123 Pilote/Stapleton AS .05 .15
124 Hull/Mahovlich AS .40 1.00
125 Mikita/Beliveau AS .30 .75
126 Howe/Rousseau AS .60 1.50
127 Alex Delvecchio TW .05 .15
128 Jacques Laperriere TW .05 .15
129 Bobby Hull TW .60 1.50
130 Bobby Hull TW .60 1.50
131 Worsley/Hodge TW .20 .50
132 Brit Selby .02 .10
133 All-Stars Eye Richard .05 .15
134 Boston's Young Stars .05 .15
135 Gump Stumps Golden Jet .05 .15
136 Ellis Beats Crozier .05 .15
137 Habs Protect Rogie .05 .15
138 Phil Fills The Crease .05 .15
139 All Hands On Deck .05 .15
140 Murray Oliver L .02 .10
141 Bobby Hull LL .60 1.50
142 Gordie Howe LL .75 2.00
143 Bobby Rousseau L .02 .10
144 Bob Nevin L .02 .10
145 Mahovlich
Pulford L .08 .25
146 Stanley Cup Playoffs Semifinals .05 .15
147 Stanley Cup Playoffs Semifinals .05 .15
148 Stanley Cup Playoffs Finals .05 .15
149 Checklist .02 .10
150 Checklist .02 .10

1995-96 Parkhurst '66-67 Bobby Orr Super Rookie

COMMON ORR (SR1-SR5) 5.00 12.00
COMMON ORR AU/500 100.00 200.00
COMMON ORR JUMBO 6.00 15.00

1995-96 Parkhurst '66-67 Coins

COMPLETE SET (120) 90.00 175.00
1 Pit Martin .40 1.00
2 Ron Stewart .40 1.00
3 Joe Watson .25 .60
4 Ed Westfall .25 .60
5 John Bucyk .60 1.50
6 Ted Green .40 1.00
7 Bobby Orr 5.00 10.00
8 Bob Woytowich .25 .60
9 Murray Oliver .25 .60
10 John McKenzie .40 1.00
11 Tom Williams .25 .60
12 Don Awrey .25 .60
13 Ron Schock .25 .60
14 Bernie Parent 1.25 3.00
15 Ron Murphy .25 .60
16 Gerry Cheevers 1.25 3.00
17 Gilles Marotte .25 .60
18 Ed Johnston .40 1.00
19 Derek Sanderson 1.25 3.00
20 Wayne Connelly .25 .60
21 Bobby Hull 3.00 6.00
22 Matt Ravlich .25 .60
23 Ken Hodge .40 1.00
24 Stan Mikita 1.50 4.00
25 Fred Stanfield .25 .60
26 Eric Nesterenko .40 1.00
27 Doug Jarrett .25 .60
28 Lou Angotti .25 .60
29 Ken Wharram .25 .60
30 Bill Hay .25 .60
31 Glenn Hall 1.50 4.00
32 Chico Maki .25 .60
33 Phil Esposito 1.50 4.00
34 Pierre Pilote .60 1.50
35 Doug Mohns .25 .60
36 Ed Van Impe .25 .60
37 Dennis Hull .40 1.00
38 Pat Stapleton .25 .60
39 Denis DeJordy .25 .60
40 Paul Henderson 5.00 10.00
41 Gary Bergman .25 .60
42 Gordie Howe 4.00 8.00
43 Bob McCord .25 .60
44 Andy Bathgate .60 1.50
45 Norm Ullman .60 1.50
46 Peter Mahovlich .40 1.00
47 Ted Hampson .25 .60
48 Leo Boivin .60 1.50
49 Bruce MacGregor .25 .60
50 Ab McDonald .40 1.00
51 Dean Prentice .25 .60
52 Floyd Smith .25 .60
53 Alex Delvecchio .60 1.50
54 Pete Goegan .25 .60
55 Parker MacDonald .25 .60
56 Roger Crozier .40 1.00
57 Val Fonteyne .25 .60
58 Henri Richard 1.25 3.00
59 John Ferguson .40 1.00
60 Yvan Cournoyer .60 1.50
61 Claude Provost .40 1.00
62 Dave Balon .25 .60
63 Ted Harris .25 .60
64 Ralph Backstrom .40 1.00
65 Jacques Laperriere .60 1.50
66 Terry Harper .40 1.00
67 J.C. Tremblay .40 1.00
68 Jean Guy Talbot .40 1.00
69 Claude Larose .40 1.00
70 Charlie Hodge .40 1.00
71 Gilles Tremblay .25 .60
72 Jim Roberts .25 .60
73 Jean Beliveau 1.50 4.00
74 Serge Savard .60 1.50
75 Rogatien Vachon 1.25 3.00
76 Lorne Worsley 1.50 4.00
77 Bobby Rousseau .40 1.00
78 Dick Duff .40 1.00
79 Rod Gilbert .60 1.50
80 Harry Howell .60 1.50
81 Jim Neilson .25 .60
82 Don Marshall .25 .60
83 Reg Fleming .25 .60
84 Wayne Hillman .25 .60
85 Bob Nevin .25 .60
86 Arnie Brown .25 .60
87 Earl Ingarfield .25 .60
88 Jean Ratelle .60 1.50
89 Bernie Geoffrion 1.25 3.00
90 Orland Kurtenbach .25 .60
91 Bill Hicke .25 .60
92 Red Berenson .40 1.00
93 Ed Giacomin .60 1.50
94 Al MacNeil .25 .60
95 Rod Seiling .25 .60
96 Doug Robinson .25 .60
97 Cesare Maniago .40 1.00
98 Vic Hadfield .25 .60
99 Phil Goyette .25 .60
100 Dave Keon .60 1.50
101 Mike Walton .25 .60
102 Frank Mahovlich 1.50 4.00
103 Tim Horton 1.50 4.00
104 Larry Hillman .25 .60
105 Kent Douglas .25 .60
106 Ron Ellis .25 .60
107 Jim Pappin .25 .60
108 Marcel Pronovost .60 1.50
109 Red Kelly .60 1.50
110 Allan Stanley .60 1.50
111 Brit Selby .25 .60
112 Pete Stemkowski .25 .60
113 Eddie Shack 1.25 3.00
114 Bob Pulford .60 1.50
115 Larry Jeffrey .25 .60
116 George Armstrong .60 1.50
117 Bob Baun .40 1.00
118 Bruce Gamble .25 .60
119 Johnny Bower 1.50 4.00
120 Terry Sawchuk 2.50 5.00
B01 Bobby Orr Black Coin 4.00 10.00
B02 Bobby Orr Black Coin 4.00 10.00
B03 Bobby Orr Black Coin 4.00 10.00
B04 Bobby Orr Black Coin 4.00 10.00
B05 Bobby Orr Black Coin 4.00 10.00
GH1 Gordie Howe Black Coin 3.00 8.00
GH2 Gordie Howe Black Coin 3.00 8.00
GH3 Gordie Howe Black Coin 3.00 8.00
GH4 Gordie Howe Black Coin 3.00 8.00
GH5 Gordie Howe Black Coin 3.00 8.00

1995-96 Parkhurst '66-67 Gordie Howe Mr. Hockey

COMMON HOWE 5.00 12.00
COMMON HOWE AU/500 50.00 100.00
COMMON HOWE JUMBO 6.00 15.00

2011-12 Parkhurst Champions

COMPLETE SET (160) 50.00 120.00
COMP.SET w/o SPs (100) 12.00 30.00
1 Wayne Gretzky 1.50 4.00
2 Gordie Howe .75 2.00
3 Bobby Orr 1.00 2.50
4 Mario Lemieux 1.00 2.50
5 Patrick Roy .60 1.50
6 Bobby Hull .50 1.25
7 Jean Beliveau .25 .60
8 Mark Messier .50 1.25
9 Guy Lafleur .30 .75
10 Ray Bourque .40 1.00
11 Phil Esposito .40 1.00
12 Stan Mikita .30 .75
13 Mike Bossy .25 .60
14 Denis Potvin .25 .60
15 Ted Lindsay .25 .60
16 Bobby Clarke .40 1.00
17 Brett Hull .50 1.25
18 Red Kelly .25 .60
19 Larry Robinson .25 .60
20 Jari Kurri .25 .60
21 Marcel Dionne .30 .75
22 Johnny Bucyk .25 .60
23 Gilbert Perreault .25 .60
24 Eric Lindros .40 1.00
25 Joe Sakic .50 1.25
26 Peter Stastny .20 .50
27 Grant Fuhr .40 1.00
28 Andy Bathgate .25 .60
29 Cam Neely .25 .60
30 Claude Lemieux .20 .50
31 Tony Esposito .25 .60
32 Luc Robitaille .25 .60
33 Denis Savard .25 .60
34 Darryl Sittler .30 .75
35 Steve Shutt .25 .60
36 Borje Salming .25 .60
37 Ron Francis .30 .75
38 Milt Schmidt .20 .50
39 Dale Hawerchuk .30 .75
40 Doug Gilmour .30 .75
41 Dino Ciccarelli .25 .60
42 Johnny Bower .25 .60
43 Glenn Anderson .20 .50
44 Adam Oates .25 .60
45 Clark Gillies .25 .60
46 Guy Carbonneau .25 .60
47 Ron Hextall .25 .60
48 Igor Larionov .25 .60
49 Rogie Vachon .30 .75
50 Alex Delvecchio .25 .60
51 Wendel Clark .40 1.00
52 Neal Broten .20 .50
53 Joe Mullen .20 .50
54 Brad Park .20 .50
55 Richard Brodeur .25 .60
56 Bill Ranford .25 .60
57 Reggie Leach .20 .50
58 Bernie Federko .20 .50
59 Terry O'Reilly .20 .50
60 Harry Howell .20 .50
61 Bill Barber .25 .60
62 Anton Stastny .15 .40
63 Rick MacLeish .20 .50
64 Ken Morrow .15 .40
65 Tony Twist .15 .40
66 Wilf Paiement .20 .50
67 Doug Wilson .20 .50
68 Dave Schultz .25 .60
69 Ken Hodge .20 .50
70 Thomas Steen .15 .40
71 Duane Sutter .15 .40
72 Mike Liut .15 .40
73 Bernie Nicholls .20 .50
74 Brent Sutter .15 .40
75 Dave Taylor .20 .50
76 Ron Sutter .20 .50
77 Rejean Lemelin .15 .40
78 Steve Larmer .20 .50
79 Don Beaupre .20 .50
80 Darryl Sutter .20 .50
81 Mark Howe .25 .60
82 Russ Courtnall .15 .40
83 Tony Tanti .15 .40
84 Tim Kerr .15 .40
85 Mike Foligno .20 .50
86 Marty McSorley .20 .50
87 Danny Gare .20 .50
88 Basil McRae .15 .40
89 Brian Sutter .20 .50
90 Rich Sutter .20 .50
91 Stan Smyl .15 .40
92 Al Iafrate .20 .50
93 Jim Neilson .15 .40
94 Pat Stapleton .15 .40
95 Mike Gartner .30 .75
96 Rick Middleton .40 1.00
97 Willi Plett .20 .50
98 Gilles Villemure .20 .50
99 Wayne Gretzky 1.50 4.00
100 Gordie Howe .75 2.00
101 Wayne Gretzky WIRE 3.00 8.00
102 Mario Lemieux WIRE 2.00 5.00
103 Gordie Howe WIRE 1.50 4.00
104 Bobby Orr WIRE 2.00 5.00
105 Brett Hull WIRE 1.00 2.50
106 Mark Messier WIRE 1.00 2.50
107 Patrick Roy WIRE 1.25 3.00
108 Luc Robitaille WIRE .50 1.25
109 Marcel Dionne WIRE .60 1.50
110 Bobby Clarke WIRE .75 2.00
111 Ray Bourque WIRE .75 2.00
112 Denis Potvin WIRE .50 1.25
113 Red Kelly WIRE .50 1.25
114 Phil Esposito WIRE .75 2.00
115 Johnny Bower WIRE .50 1.25
116 Mike Bossy WIRE .50 1.25
117 Ted Lindsay WIRE .50 1.25
118 Larry Robinson WIRE .50 1.25
119 Jean Beliveau WIRE .50 1.25
120 Wendel Clark WIRE .75 2.00
121 Robnsn/Hawrchk WIRE 1.25 3.00
122 B.Park/B.Barber WIRE 1.00 2.50
123 W.Gretzky/G.Howe WIRE 6.00 15.00
124 M.Messier/J.Kurri WIRE 2.00 5.00
125 G.Howe/J.Bower WIRE 3.00 8.00
126 B.Hull/S.Mikita WIRE 2.00 5.00
127 T.Lindsay/G.Howe WIRE 3.00 8.00
128 T.Esposito/B.Orr WIRE 4.00 10.00
129 Esposito/Clarke/Orr WIRE 4.00 10.00
130 Esposito/Bucyk/Orr WIRE 4.00 10.00
131 Wayne Gretzky R 4.00 10.00
132 Bobby Orr R 2.50 6.00
133 Gordie Howe R 2.00 5.00
134 Mario Lemieux R 2.50 6.00
135 Brett Hull R 1.25 3.00
136 Patrick Roy R 1.50 4.00
137 Mark Messier R 1.25 3.00
138 Guy Lafleur R .75 2.00
139 Stan Mikita R .75 2.00
140 Mike Bossy R .60 1.50
141 Bobby Hull R 1.25 3.00
142 Bobby Clarke R 1.00 2.50
143 Ray Bourque R 1.00 2.50
144 Dale Hawerchuk R .75 2.00
145 Cam Neely R .60 1.50
146 Rogie Vachon R .75 2.00
147 Peter Stastny R .50 1.25
148 Darryl Sittler R .75 2.00
149 Eric Lindros R 1.00 2.50
150 Gilbert Perreault R .60 1.50
151 Patrick Roy R BW 4.00 10.00
152 Bobby Orr R BW 6.00 15.00
153 Guy Lafleur R BW 2.00 5.00
154 Phil Esposito R BW 2.50 6.00
155 Mark Messier R BW 3.00 8.00
156 Jean Beliveau R BW 1.50 4.00
157 Bobby Hull R BW 3.00 8.00
158 Gordie Howe R BW 5.00 12.00
159 Mario Lemieux R BW 6.00 15.00
160 Wayne Gretzky R BW 10.00 25.00

2011-12 Parkhurst Champions Autographs

1 Wayne Gretzky C EXCH 250.00 600.00
2 Gordie Howe C 75.00 150.00
3 Bobby Orr D 60.00 120.00
4 Mario Lemieux A 150.00 250.00
5 Patrick Roy A 150.00 250.00
6 Bobby Hull A 60.00 100.00
7 Jean Beliveau A 150.00 250.00
8 Mark Messier A 75.00 135.00
9 Guy Lafleur A 40.00 80.00
10 Ray Bourque A 125.00 200.00
11 Phil Esposito A 125.00 200.00
12 Stan Mikita A 75.00 135.00
13 Mike Bossy A 100.00 175.00
14 Denis Potvin B 15.00 40.00
15 Ted Lindsay C 10.00 25.00
16 Bobby Clarke C 30.00 60.00
17 Brett Hull A 175.00 300.00
18 Red Kelly B 25.00 50.00
19 Larry Robinson B 20.00 40.00
20 Jari Kurri C 15.00 30.00
21 Marcel Dionne B 25.00 50.00
22 Johnny Bucyk B 30.00 60.00
23 Gilbert Perreault C 25.00 50.00
25 Joe Sakic A 75.00 150.00
26 Peter Stastny C 10.00 25.00
27 Grant Fuhr A 60.00 100.00
28 Andy Bathgate B 10.00 25.00
29 Cam Neely B 15.00 40.00
30 Claude Lemieux D 5.00 12.00
31 Tony Esposito A 60.00 100.00
32 Luc Robitaille B 30.00 60.00
33 Denis Savard B 15.00 30.00
34 Darryl Sittler C 12.00 30.00
35 Steve Shutt B 30.00 60.00
36 Borje Salming B 12.00 30.00
37 Ron Francis A 125.00 225.00
38 Milt Schmidt E 5.00 12.00
39 Dale Hawerchuk C 12.00 30.00
40 Doug Gilmour C 8.00 20.00
41 Dino Ciccarelli C 12.50 30.00
42 Johnny Bower C 15.00 40.00
43 Glenn Anderson B 6.00 15.00
44 Adam Oates E 6.00 15.00
45 Clark Gillies C 6.00 15.00
46 Guy Carbonneau E 6.00 15.00
47 Ron Hextall B 25.00 60.00
48 Igor Larionov A 125.00 200.00
49 Rogie Vachon A 30.00 60.00
50 Alex Delvecchio D 8.00 20.00
51 Wendel Clark A 90.00 150.00
52 Neal Broten C 10.00 25.00
53 Joe Mullen B 5.00 12.00
54 Brad Park C 5.00 12.00
55 Richard Brodeur D 6.00 15.00
56 Bill Ranford D 6.00 15.00
57 Reggie Leach F 5.00 12.00
58 Bernie Federko C 10.00 25.00
59 Terry O'Reilly C 12.00 30.00
60 Harry Howell D 5.00 12.00
61 Bill Barber F 6.00 15.00
62 Anton Stastny C 4.00 10.00
63 Rick MacLeish F 5.00 12.00
64 Ken Morrow D 4.00 10.00
65 Tony Twist F 6.00 15.00
66 Wilf Paiement E 5.00 12.00
67 Doug Wilson F 5.00 12.00
68 Dave Schultz C 12.00 30.00
69 Ken Hodge F 5.00 12.00
70 Thomas Steen D 4.00 10.00
71 Duane Sutter E 4.00 10.00
72 Mike Liut D 6.00 15.00
73 Bernie Nicholls F 5.00 12.00
74 Brent Sutter E 4.00 10.00
75 Dave Taylor D 5.00 12.00
76 Ron Sutter E 5.00 12.00
77 Rejean Lemelin F 4.00 10.00
78 Steve Larmer D 6.00 15.00
79 Don Beaupre F 5.00 12.00
80 Darryl Sutter E 5.00 12.00
81 Mark Howe F 6.00 15.00
82 Russ Courtnall F 6.00 15.00
83 Tony Tanti C 12.00 30.00
84 Tim Kerr F 4.00 10.00
85 Mike Foligno E 5.00 12.00
86 Marty McSorley D 5.00 12.00
87 Danny Gare F 5.00 12.00
88 Basil McRae F 4.00 10.00
89 Brian Sutter E 5.00 12.00
90 Rich Sutter E 5.00 12.00
91 Stan Smyl E EXCH 4.00 10.00
92 Al Iafrate F 5.00 12.00
93 Jim Neilson E 4.00 10.00
94 Pat Stapleton F 4.00 10.00
95 Mike Gartner F 8.00 20.00
96 Rick Middleton A 60.00 120.00
97 Willi Plett D 5.00 12.00
98 Gilles Villemure F 5.00 12.00
99 Wayne Gretzky A EXCH 250.00 600.00
100 Gordie Howe A 100.00 200.00
101 Wayne Gretzky H WIRE 300.00 800.00
102 Mario Lemieux G WIRE 125.00 250.00
103 Gordie Howe I WIRE 100.00 175.00
104 Bobby Orr I WIRE 100.00 200.00
105 Brett Hull G WIRE 50.00 100.00
106 Mark Messier G WIRE 75.00 150.00
107 Patrick Roy G WIRE 125.00 250.00
108 Luc Robitaille I WIRE 30.00 80.00
109 Marcel Dionne H WIRE 40.00 80.00
110 Bobby Clarke I WIRE 40.00 80.00
111 Ray Bourque H WIRE 40.00 100.00
112 Denis Potvin H WIRE 50.00 100.00
113 Red Kelly I WIRE 25.00 60.00
114 Phil Esposito G WIRE 40.00 80.00
115 Johnny Bower I WIRE 40.00 80.00
116 Mike Bossy H WIRE 40.00 100.00
117 Ted Lindsay I WIRE 30.00 60.00
118 Larry Robinson H WIRE 30.00 60.00
119 Jean Beliveau G WIRE 150.00 250.00
120 Wendel Clark WIRE EXCH 50.00 100.00
122 B.Park/B.Barber WIRE K 125.00 250.00
123 Gretzky/Howe WIRE K EX 500.00 1200.00
124 Messier/Kurri WIRE K EX 200.00 400.00
125 G.Howe/J.Bower WIRE K 200.00 400.00
126 B.Hull/S.Mikita WIRE K 100.00 200.00
127 Lindsay/G.Howe WIRE K 200.00 400.00
128 T.Esposito/B.Orr WIRE K 250.00 500.00
130 Esposito/Bucyk/Orr WIRE J 250.00 400.00
131 Wayne Gretzky R M EXCH 300.00 800.00
132 Bobby Orr R N 150.00 300.00
134 Mario Lemieux R L 125.00 200.00
135 Brett Hull R L 50.00 100.00
136 Patrick Roy R M 100.00 175.00
137 Mark Messier R M 60.00 120.00
138 Guy Lafleur R M 50.00 100.00
139 Stan Mikita R M 40.00 80.00
140 Mike Bossy R M 30.00 60.00
141 Bobby Hull R M 30.00 60.00
142 Bobby Clarke R M 30.00 60.00
143 Ray Bourque R M 40.00 80.00
144 Dale Hawerchuk R N 25.00 50.00
145 Cam Neely R M 25.00 50.00
146 Rogie Vachon R N 12.00 30.00
147 Peter Stastny R N 25.00 60.00
148 Darryl Sittler R N 15.00 40.00
149 Eric Lindros R N 150.00 250.00
150 Gilbert Perreault R N 15.00 40.00
151 Patrick Roy R BW 175.00 300.00
152 Bobby Orr R BW 175.00 300.00
154 Phil Esposito R BW 200.00 350.00
156 Jean Beliveau R BW 150.00 250.00
157 Bobby Hull R BW 100.00 175.00
158 Gordie Howe R BW 175.00 300.00
160 Wayne Gretzky R BW 300.00 800.00

2011-12 Parkhurst Champions Champ's Fossils and Artifacts

NNO Redemption Card 75.00 135.00

2011-12 Parkhurst Champions Champ's Mini

COMPLETE SET (57) 40.00 100.00
COMP.SET w/o SPs (45) 12.00 30.00
*1-45 GREEN BACK: 1.2X TO 3X BASIC INSERT
*46-57 GREEN BACK: .6X TO 1.5X BASIC SP
*1-45 PARKHURST: 8X TO 20X BASIC INSERTS
1 Georges Vezina .30 .75
2 Denis Savard .30 .75
3 Stan Mikita .40 1.00
4 Adam Oates .30 .75
5 Alex Delvecchio .30 .75
6 Eric Lindros .50 1.25
7 Gump Worsley .30 .75
8 Don Cherry .30 .75
9 Andy Bathgate .30 .75
10 Borje Salming .30 .75
11 Clark Gillies .30 .75
12 Dale Hawerchuk .40 1.00
13 Denis Potvin .30 .75
14 Howie Morenz .25 .60
15 Duane Sutter .20 .50
16 Gilbert Perreault .30 .75
17 Jari Kurri .30 .75
18 Cam Neely .30 .75
19 Larry Robinson .30 .75
20 Marcel Dionne .40 1.00
21 Red Kelly .30 .75
22 Scotty Bowman .30 .75
23 Rogie Vachon .40 1.00
24 Ted Lindsay .30 .75
25 Terry O'Reilly .25 .60
26 Doug Gilmour .40 1.00
27 Johnny Bucyk .30 .75
28 Luc Robitaille .30 .75
29 Tony Esposito .30 .75
30 Steve Shutt .30 .75
31 King Clancy .25 .60
32 Mark Howe .30 .75
33 Darryl Sittler .40 1.00
34 Eddie Shore .25 .60
35 Igor Larionov .30 .75
36 Ron Francis .40 1.00
37 Willie O'Ree .40 1.00
38 Wendel Clark .50 1.25
39 Ron Hextall .30 .75
40 Glenn Anderson .25 .60
41 Joe Sakic .60 1.50
42 Ray Bourque .50 1.25
43 Peter Stastny .25 .60
44 Johnny Bower .30 .75
45 Grant Fuhr .50 1.25
46 Bobby Hull SP 5.00 12.00
47 Patrick Roy SP 6.00 15.00
48 Mark Messier SP 5.00 12.00
49 Brett Hull SP 5.00 12.00
50 Bobby Orr SP 10.00 25.00
51 Phil Esposito SP 4.00 10.00
52 Bobby Clarke SP 4.00 10.00
53 Mario Lemieux SP 10.00 25.00
54 Guy Lafleur SP 3.00 8.00
55 Mike Bossy SP 2.50 6.00
56 Gordie Howe SP 8.00 20.00
57 Wayne Gretzky SP 8.00 20.00

2011-12 Parkhurst Champions Champ's Mini Signatures

2 Denis Savard 15.00 40.00
3 Stan Mikita 15.00 30.00
4 Adam Oates 6.00 15.00
5 Alex Delvecchio 6.00 15.00
8 Don Cherry 12.00 30.00
9 Andy Bathgate 12.00 30.00
10 Borje Salming 12.00 30.00
11 Clark Gillies 6.00 15.00
12 Dale Hawerchuk 8.00 20.00
13 Denis Potvin 6.00 15.00
15 Duane Sutter 4.00 10.00
16 Gilbert Perreault 6.00 15.00
17 Jari Kurri 6.00 15.00
18 Cam Neely 6.00 15.00
19 Larry Robinson 6.00 15.00
20 Marcel Dionne 10.00 25.00
21 Red Kelly 6.00 15.00
22 Scotty Bowman 25.00 50.00
23 Rogie Vachon 8.00 20.00
24 Ted Lindsay 8.00 20.00
25 Terry O'Reilly 5.00 12.00
26 Doug Gilmour 20.00 40.00
27 Johnny Bucyk 6.00 15.00
28 Luc Robitaille 15.00 30.00
29 Tony Esposito 30.00 60.00
30 Steve Shutt 10.00 25.00
32 Mark Howe 6.00 15.00
33 Darryl Sittler 10.00 25.00
35 Igor Larionov 50.00 100.00
36 Ron Francis 15.00 40.00
37 Willie O'Ree 8.00 20.00
38 Wendel Clark EXCH 10.00 25.00
39 Ron Hextall 12.00 30.00
40 Glenn Anderson 5.00 12.00
41 Joe Sakic 40.00 80.00
42 Ray Bourque 40.00 80.00
43 Peter Stastny 6.00 15.00
44 Johnny Bower 10.00 25.00
45 Grant Fuhr EXCH 40.00 80.00
47 Patrick Roy SP 75.00 125.00
48 Mark Messier SP 75.00 125.00
49 Brett Hull SP 75.00 125.00
50 Bobby Orr SP 100.00 200.00
51 Phil Esposito SP 30.00 60.00
52 Bobby Clarke SP 30.00 60.00
53 Mario Lemieux SP 75.00 150.00
54 Guy Lafleur SP 60.00 120.00
55 Mike Bossy SP 20.00 40.00
56 Gordie Howe SP 90.00 150.00
57 Wayne Gretzky SP EXCH 250.00 600.00

2022-23 Parkhurst Champions

1 Andre Burakovsky .30 .75
2 Drew Doughty .60 1.50
3 Jeff Carter .40 1.00
4 Sean Couturier .40 1.00
5 Kyle Okposo .30 .75
6 Robin Lehner .40 1.00
7 Mika Zibanejad .60 1.50
8 Ivan Provorov .40 1.00
9 Phillip Danault .50 1.25
10 Phil Kessel .50 1.25
11 Tyler Seguin .60 1.50
12 Cam Fowler .50 1.25
13 David Perron .40 1.00
14 Matt Duchene .50 1.25
15 Bo Horvat .60 1.50
16 John Carlson .50 1.25
17 Tage Thompson .60 1.50
18 Mikhail Sergachev .40 1.00
19 Jared Spurgeon .50 1.25
20 Carter Verhaeghe .50 1.25
21 Logan Couture .60 1.50
22 David Pastrnak 1.25 3.00
23 Elias Pettersson .75 2.00
24 Ryan Donato .40 1.00
25 Alex Tuch .50 1.25
26 Torey Krug .40 1.00
27 Travis Konecny .50 1.25
28 Matt Dumba .30 .75
29 Tanner Pearson .50 1.25
30 Jordan Binnington .75 2.00
31 Jakob Chychrun .50 1.25
32 Adrian Kempe .50 1.25
33 Ondrej Kase .30 .75
34 Clayton Keller .60 1.50
35 Shea Theodore .60 1.50
36 Patrik Laine .60 1.50
37 Noah Dobson .60 1.50
38 Aaron Ekblad .60 1.50
39 Josh Norris .50 1.25
40 Reilly Smith .50 1.25
41 Jonathan Toews .75 2.00
42 Filip Forsberg .75 2.00
43 Jamie Benn .50 1.25
44 Joel Farabee .50 1.25
45 Mattias Ekholm .40 1.00
46 Adam Henrique .40 1.00
47 Alexander Wennberg .30 .75
48 Andrew Mangiapane .50 1.25
49 Jeff Skinner .50 1.25
50 Joel Eriksson Ek .40 1.00
51 Braden Holtby .60 1.50
52 Jaccob Slavin .40 1.00
53 Evan Rodrigues .40 1.00
54 Evgeny Kuznetsov .60 1.50
55 Nico Hischier .75 2.00
56 Ryan Strome .50 1.25
57 Bryan Rust .50 1.25
58 Nicklas Backstrom .50 1.25
59 Jake DeBrusk .50 1.25
60 Zach Werenski .75 2.00
61 Sonny Milano .40 1.00
62 Connor Brown .40 1.00
63 Pierre Engvall .30 .75
64 Alex Pietrangelo .40 1.00
65 Evan Bouchard .60 1.50
66 T.J. Oshie .50 1.25
67 Chandler Stephenson .40 1.00
68 Mikael Granlund .40 1.00
69 Vincent Trocheck .50 1.25
70 Ondrej Palat .40 1.00
71 Seth Jones .50 1.25
72 Neal Pionk .30 .75
73 Dylan Larkin .60 1.50
74 Casey Mittelstadt .50 1.25
75 Oliver Bjorkstrand .40 1.00
76 Juuse Saros .60 1.50
77 P.K. Subban .60 1.50
78 Tyson Barrie .30 .75
79 Filip Hronek .30 .75
80 Dmitry Orlov .50 1.25
81 Ryan Hartman .30 .75
82 Erik Karlsson .60 1.50
83 Jonathan Quick .60 1.50
84 Mackenzie Blackwood .50 1.25
85 Darnell Nurse .40 1.00
86 Colin White .40 1.00
87 Pavel Buchnevich .40 1.00
88 Alex Kerfoot .40 1.00
89 Brandon Hagel .40 1.00
90 Anthony Duclair .40 1.00
91 Kevin Hayes .40 1.00
92 Paul Stastny .40 1.00
93 Nick Schmaltz .40 1.00
94 Alex DeBrincat .60 1.50
95 Jaden Schwartz .40 1.00
96 Oliver Wahlstrom .30 .75
97 Andreas Johnsson .40 1.00
98 Alex Killorn .30 .75
99 Jonathan Drouin .40 1.00
100 Dominik Kubalik .50 1.25
101 Mark Scheifele .75 2.00
102 Sam Reinhart 1.00 2.50
103 Conor Garland .40 1.00
104 Claude Giroux .50 1.25
105 Drake Batherson .50 1.25
106 Nick Suzuki 1.00 2.50
107 Mats Zuccarello .50 1.25
108 Colton Parayko .40 1.00
109 Joe Pavelski .60 1.50
110 Cam Talbot .50 1.25
111 Jordan Eberle .50 1.25
112 Zach Hyman .75 2.00
113 John Gibson .50 1.25
114 Taylor Hall .50 1.25
115 Anze Kopitar .75 2.00
116 Tyler Bertuzzi .40 1.00
117 Tomas Hertl .50 1.25
118 Cam Atkinson .50 1.25
119 Pierre-Luc Dubois .40 1.00
120 Jesper Bratt .50 1.25
121 Carey Price 1.00 2.50
122 Patrick Kane 1.00 2.50
123 Elias Lindholm .50 1.25
124 Mathew Barzal .60 1.50
125 Thomas Chabot .50 1.25
126 Jason Robertson .75 2.00
127 Connor Hellebuyck 1.00 2.50
128 Tyler Toffoli .50 1.25
129 Kevin Fiala .40 1.00
130 Samuel Girard .30 .75
131 Teuvo Teravainen .50 1.25
132 Charlie Coyle .50 1.25
133 Tom Wilson .50 1.25
134 Jack Roslovic .30 .75
135 Nikolaj Ehlers .50 1.25
136 Brendan Gallagher .50 1.25
137 Roope Hintz .60 1.50
138 Brent Burns .50 1.25
139 Jonathan Marchessault .60 1.50
140 Robert Thomas .50 1.25
141 Josh Anderson .40 1.00
142 Jesse Puljujarvi .50 1.25
143 Josh Bailey .40 1.00
144 Dougie Hamilton .40 1.00
145 Alex Nedeljkovic .40 1.00
146 Ryan O'Reilly .50 1.25
147 Martin Necas .75 2.00
148 Pius Suter .40 1.00
149 Carter Hart .50 1.25
150 Marc-Andre Fleury 1.00 2.50
151 Brock Boeser .60 1.50
152 Jake Oettinger .75 2.00
153 Ilya Sorokin .75 2.00
154 Sean Monahan .30 .75
155 Boone Jenner .50 1.25
156 Troy Terry .40 1.00
157 Jared McCann .40 1.00
158 Anthony Cirelli .40 1.00
159 Elvis Merzlikins .50 1.25
160 Philipp Grubauer .50 1.25
161 Miro Heiskanen .60 1.50
162 Ilya Samsonov .50 1.25
163 Alexander Barabanov .30 .75
164 Shayne Gostisbehere .50 1.25
165 Tim Stutzle .60 1.50
166 Yanni Gourde .40 1.00
167 Dylan Strome .60 1.50
168 Mike Smith .30 .75
169 Jack Hughes 1.25 3.00
170 Kirby Dach .50 1.25
171 Victor Olofsson .50 1.25
172 John Klingberg .50 1.25
173 Brock Nelson .50 1.25
174 Victor Soderstrom .30 .75
175 Dylan Cozens .50 1.25
176 Connor McMichael .50 1.25
177 Jean-Gabriel Pageau .30 .75
178 Ryan McLeod .30 .75

Card	Low	High
179 Anders Lee	.40	1.00
180 Adam Fox	.60	1.50
181 Aleksander Barkov	.75	2.00
182 Alex Ovechkin	2.00	5.00
183 Andrei Svechnikov	.60	1.50
184 Andrei Vasilevskiy	.75	2.00
185 Brad Marchand	1.00	2.50
186 Brady Tkachuk	.75	2.00
187 Brayden Point	.60	1.50
188 Cale Makar	1.25	3.00
189 Jeff Petry	.50	1.25
190 Connor McDavid	2.50	6.00
191 Devon Toews	.40	1.00
192 Igor Shesterkin	1.00	2.50
193 J.T. Miller	.60	1.50
194 Jack Campbell	.50	1.25
195 Jacob Markstrom	.50	1.25
196 Jake Guentzel	.75	2.00
197 John Tavares	.75	2.00
198 Andrew Copp	.30	.75
199 Ryan Nugent-Hopkins	.60	1.50
200 Auston Matthews	2.00	5.00
201 Jonathan Huberdeau	.60	1.50
202 Kirill Kaprizov	1.50	4.00
203 Kris Letang	.60	1.50
204 Kyle Connor	.75	2.00
205 Leon Draisaitl	1.50	4.00
206 Mark Stone	.60	1.50
207 Matthew Tkachuk	1.00	2.50
208 Nathan MacKinnon	2.00	5.00
209 Quinn Hughes	1.25	3.00
210 Roman Josi	.50	1.25
211 Sergei Bobrovsky	.75	2.00
212 Sidney Crosby	2.00	5.00
213 Steven Stamkos	1.00	2.50
214 Thatcher Demko	.60	1.50
215 Tristan Jarry	.50	1.25
216 Brayden Schenn	.50	1.25
217 Lucas Raymond	.75	2.00
218 Trevor Zegras	.50	1.25
219 Moritz Seider	.60	1.50
220 Cole Caufield	1.00	2.50
221 Anton Lundell	.50	1.25
222 Michael Bunting	.50	1.25
223 Dawson Mercer	.60	1.50
224 Jamie Drysdale	.40	1.00
225 Jonathan Dahlen	.30	.75
226 Seth Jarvis	.60	1.50
227 Quinton Byfield	.60	1.50
228 Alex Newhook	.40	1.00
229 Spencer Knight	.50	1.25
230 Philip Tomasino	.30	.75
231 Cole Sillinger	.40	1.00
232 Alex Iafallo	.30	.75
233 Jeremy Swayman	.75	2.00
234 Artemi Panarin	1.00	2.50
235 Charlie McAvoy	.60	1.50
236 Mitch Marner	.75	2.00
237 Darcy Kuemper	.50	1.25
238 Karel Vejmelka	.30	.75
239 Evgeni Malkin	1.00	2.50
240 Frederik Andersen	.60	1.50
241 Gabriel Landeskog	.60	1.50
242 Alexis Lafreniere	.75	2.00
243 Cole Perfetti	.50	1.25
244 William Karlsson	.60	1.50
245 Johnny Gaudreau	.75	2.00
246 Jordan Kyrou	.50	1.25
247 Tanner Jeannot	.30	.75
248 Morgan Rielly	.50	1.25
249 Mikko Rantanen	1.25	3.00
250 Chris Kreider	.60	1.50
251 Rasmus Dahlin	.60	1.50
252 Nazem Kadri	.60	1.50
253 Nikita Kucherov	1.00	2.50
254 Patrice Bergeron	.60	1.50
255 Sebastian Aho	.75	2.00
256 Timo Meier	.50	1.25
257 Victor Hedman	.60	1.50
258 Vladimir Tarasenko	.60	1.50
259 William Nylander	1.00	2.50
260 Josh Morrissey	.60	1.50
261 Samuel Fagemo RC	.50	1.25
262 Braden Schneider RC	1.00	2.50
263 Fredrik Karlstrom RC	.50	1.25
264 Bobby Brink RC	.60	1.50
265 Brandon Biro RC	1.00	2.50
266 Jakub Galvas RC	.60	1.50
267 Isaac Ratcliffe RC	.60	1.50
268 Mads Sogaard RC	.75	2.00
269 Noah Cates RC	.60	1.50
270 Jonathan Kovacevic UER RC	.60	1.50
271 Alex Vlasic RC	.50	1.25
272 Zack Hayes RC	.50	1.25
273 Jack LaFontaine RC	.60	1.50
274 Thomas Bordeleau RC	.60	1.50
275 Carson Meyer RC	.50	1.25
276 Adam Raska RC	.60	1.50
277 Matias Maccelli RC	1.00	2.50
278 Mark Kastelic RC	.50	1.25
279 Dylan Samberg RC	.60	1.50
280 Pyotr Kochetkov RC	1.25	3.00
281 Nikita Okhotiuk RC	.50	1.25
282 Erik Kallgren RC	.60	1.50
283 Marc McLaughlin RC	.60	1.50
284 Nick Blankenburg RC	.50	1.25
285 Mitchell Chaffee RC	.50	1.25
286 Reilly Walsh RC	.60	1.50
287 Ronnie Attard RC	.60	1.50
288 Brayden Tracey RC	.50	1.25
289 Kaedan Korczak RC	.50	1.25
290 Vladislav Kolyachonok RC	.50	1.25
291 Trey Fix-Wolansky RC	.60	1.50
292 Michael Eyssimont RC	.60	1.50
293 Ben Meyers RC	.60	1.50
294 Filip Hallander RC	.60	1.50
295 Jack McBain RC	.60	1.50
296 Jordan Spence RC	.60	1.50
297 Nick Abruzzese RC	.60	1.50
298 Chase Pearson RC	.50	1.25
299 Valtteri Puustinen RC	.50	1.25
300 Jordan Harris RC	.75	2.00
301 Juraj Slafkovsky SP RC	4.00	10.00
302 Samuel Poulin SP RC	1.00	2.50
303 Brandt Clarke SP RC	1.50	4.00
304 Elmer Soderblom SP RC	1.50	4.00
305 Andrei Kuzmenko SP RC	1.50	4.00
306 Shane Wright SP RC	2.00	5.00
307 Simon Holmstrom SP RC	.75	2.00
308 Oskar Olausson SP RC	.75	2.00
309 Arber Xhekaj SP RC	1.50	4.00
310 David Jiricek SP RC	1.50	4.00
311 Lukas Dostal SP RC	1.50	4.00
312 Dylan Guenther SP RC	2.00	5.00
313 Jonatan Berggren SP RC	1.25	3.00
314 Jake Sanderson SP RC	2.00	5.00
315 Kaiden Guhle SP RC	1.50	4.00
316 Wyatt Johnston SP RC	3.00	8.00
317 Dylan Holloway SP RC	1.50	4.00
318 Lukas Reichel SP RC	1.50	4.00
319 Jacob Perreault SP RC	.75	2.00
320 Marco Rossi SP RC	2.00	5.00
321 Kent Johnson SP RC	1.50	4.00
322 Jack Quinn SP RC	1.25	3.00
323 Matty Beniers SP RC	2.00	5.00
324 Matt Boldy SP RC	2.50	6.00
325 Owen Power SP RC	1.50	4.00
326 Wayne Gretzky SP	8.00	20.00
327 Ray Bourque SP	2.00	5.00
328 Mark Messier SP	2.50	6.00
329 Jaromir Jagr SP	4.00	10.00
330 Steve Yzerman SP	3.00	8.00
331 Dominik Hasek SP	2.00	5.00
332 Martin Brodeur SP	3.00	8.00
333 Jacques Plante SP	1.25	3.00
334 Peter Forsberg SP	2.50	6.00
335 Peter Bondra SP	1.25	3.00
336 Lanny McDonald SP	1.25	3.00
337 Doug Gilmour SP	1.50	4.00
338 Paul Coffey SP	1.25	3.00
339 Bobby Clarke SP	2.00	5.00
340 Bobby Orr SP	5.00	12.00
341 Patrick Roy SP	3.00	8.00
342 Brett Hull SP	2.50	6.00
343 Stan Mikita SP	1.25	3.00
344 Tim Horton SP	2.00	5.00
345 Gordie Howe SP	4.00	10.00
346 Jean Beliveau SP	1.25	3.00
347 Teemu Selanne SP	2.50	6.00
348 Marcel Dionne SP	1.50	4.00
349 Mario Lemieux SP	5.00	12.00
350 Phil Esposito SP	2.00	5.00

2022-23 Parkhurst Champions Color Variation

*COLOR 1-300: .6X TO 1.5X BASIC
*COLOR 301-350: .75X TO 2X BASIC

2022-23 Parkhurst Champions Gold Rainbow

*GOLD 1-300: .75X TO 2X BASIC
*GOLD SP RC: 1X TO 2.5X BASIC
*GOLD LEG: 1.2X TO 3X BASIC

2022-23 Parkhurst Champions Rainbow

*RNBW 1-300: .5X TO 1.2X BASIC
*RNBW 301-350: .6X TO 1.5X BASIC

2022-23 Parkhurst Champions Red

*RED/51: 2.5X TO 6X BASIC

2022-23 Parkhurst Champions Silver

*SILVER: .5X TO 1.2X BASIC

2022-23 Parkhurst Champions 50s Flashbacks

*GOLD: .5X TO 1.2X BASIC

Card	Low	High
FB1 Color TV Introduced	1.25	3.00
FB2 Electricity from Nuclear Power	1.25	3.00
FB3 Harry Truman 33rd President	2.00	5.00
FB4 The Great Flood of Kansas	1.25	3.00
FB5 Laysan Albatross is Hatched	1.25	3.00
FB6 Banana Cream Pie	1.25	3.00
FB7 Coast to Coast Direct Dialing	1.25	3.00
FB8 Leidse Astronomers	1.25	3.00
FB9 1st North Pole Jet Crossing	1.25	3.00
FB10 United Nations Publishes Stamps	1.25	3.00
FB11 Video Tape Recorder Invented	1.25	3.00
FB12 Power Steering Invented	1.25	3.00
FB13 Gordie Howe wins Art Ross Trophy	2.00	5.00
FB14 X-Ray Machine	1.25	3.00
FB15 Gallon of Gas $0.27	1.25	3.00

2022-23 Parkhurst Champions 51 Retros

*BLUE: .5X TO 1.2X BASIC

Card	Low	High
R1 Sam Reinhart	4.00	10.00
R2 Cale Makar	5.00	12.00
R3 Tyler Bertuzzi	1.50	4.00
R4 Jeremy Swayman	3.00	8.00
R5 Yanni Gourde	1.50	4.00
R6 Tom Wilson	2.00	5.00
R7 Mathew Barzal	2.50	6.00
R8 J.T. Miller	2.50	6.00
R9 Carter Hart	2.00	5.00
R10 Anze Kopitar	3.00	8.00
R11 Patrick Kane	4.00	10.00
R12 Sean Durzi	1.25	3.00
R13 Josh Norris	2.00	5.00
R14 Joe Pavelski	2.50	6.00
R15 Mark Scheifele	3.00	8.00
R16 Tim Stutzle	2.50	6.00
R17 Lucas Raymond	3.00	8.00
R18 Trevor Zegras	2.00	5.00
R19 Eeli Tolvanen	2.00	5.00
R20 Miro Heiskanen	2.50	6.00
R21 Sidney Crosby	8.00	20.00
R22 Elias Lindholm	2.00	5.00
R23 Pierre-Luc Dubois	1.50	4.00
R24 Nick Suzuki	4.00	10.00
R25 Jason Robertson	3.00	8.00
R26 Brad Marchand	4.00	10.00
R27 Josh Anderson	1.50	4.00
R28 Tristan Jarry	2.00	5.00
R29 Josh Morrissey	2.50	6.00
R30 Aleksander Barkov	3.00	8.00
R31 Mats Zuccarello	2.00	5.00
R32 Jared McCann	1.50	4.00
R33 Boone Jenner	2.00	5.00
R34 Dylan Cozens	2.00	5.00
R35 Alex Iafallo	1.25	3.00
R36 Torey Krug	1.50	4.00
R37 Gabriel Landeskog	2.50	6.00
R38 Robert Thomas	2.00	5.00
R39 Jesse Puljujarvi	2.00	5.00
R40 Seth Jarvis	2.50	6.00
R41 Brock Nelson	2.00	5.00
R42 Michael Bunting	2.00	5.00
R43 Andrew Copp	1.25	3.00
R44 Drake Batherson	2.00	5.00
R45 Brent Burns	2.00	5.00
R46 Troy Terry	1.50	4.00
R47 Alex Ovechkin	8.00	20.00
R48 Tanner Jeannot	1.25	3.00
R49 Jonathan Marchessault	2.50	6.00
R50 Karel Vejmelka	1.25	3.00
R51 Marco Rossi	5.00	12.00
R52 Matty Beniers	5.00	12.00
R53 Jacob Perreault	2.00	5.00
R54 Lukas Reichel	4.00	10.00
R55 Jack Quinn	3.00	8.00
R56 Matt Boldy	6.00	15.00
R57 Owen Power	4.00	10.00
R58 Kent Johnson	4.00	10.00
R59 Mark Kastelic	1.50	4.00
R60 Braden Schneider	3.00	8.00
R61 Marc McLaughlin	2.00	5.00
R62 Alex Vlasic	1.50	4.00
R63 Samuel Fagemo	1.50	4.00
R64 Isaac Ratcliffe	2.00	5.00
R65 Kaedan Korczak	1.50	4.00
R66 Dylan Samberg	2.00	5.00
R67 Mads Sogaard	2.50	6.00
R68 Jordan Spence	2.00	5.00
R69 Thomas Bordeleau	2.00	5.00
R70 Pyotr Kochetkov	4.00	10.00
R71 Dylan Holloway	4.00	10.00
R72 Nick Abruzzese	2.00	5.00
R73 Bobby Brink	2.00	5.00
R74 Jack McBain	2.00	5.00
R75 Jordan Harris	2.50	6.00
R76 Lukas Dostal	4.00	10.00
R77 Reilly Walsh	2.00	5.00
R78 Matias Maccelli	3.00	8.00
R79 Trey Fix-Wolansky	2.00	5.00
R80 Erik Kallgren	2.00	5.00
R81 Paul Coffey	2.00	5.00
R82 Doug Wilson	1.50	4.00
R83 Ron Hextall	2.00	5.00
R84 Marcel Dionne	2.50	6.00
R85 Saku Koivu	2.00	5.00
R86 Brett Hull	4.00	10.00
R87 Martin Brodeur	5.00	12.00
R88 Shayne Corson	1.50	4.00
R89 Cliff Ronning	1.25	3.00
R90 Peter Bondra	2.00	5.00
R91 Peter Forsberg	4.00	10.00
R92 Lanny McDonald	2.00	5.00
R93 John Vanbiesbrouck	2.00	5.00
R94 Jonathan Cheechoo	1.50	4.00
R95 Mike Gartner	2.50	6.00
R96 Wayne Gretzky	12.00	30.00
R97 Jarome Iginla	2.50	6.00
R98 Bobby Orr	8.00	20.00
R99 Bob Bourne	1.25	3.00
R100 Bernie Nicholls	1.50	4.00

2022-23 Parkhurst Champions 51 Retros Gold Rainbow

*GOLD/51: 1.2X TO 3X BASIC

Card	Low	High
R2 Cale Makar	25.00	60.00
R24 Nick Suzuki	25.00	60.00
R25 Jason Robertson	20.00	50.00
R47 Alex Ovechkin	60.00	150.00
R96 Wayne Gretzky	150.00	400.00

2022-23 Parkhurst Champions 51 Retros Wrapper Back

*WRAPPER: .6X TO 1.5X BASIC

Card	Low	High
R96 Wayne Gretzky	60.00	150.00

2022-23 Parkhurst Champions 51 Retros Autographs

Card	Low	High
R1 Sam Reinhart	20.00	50.00
R4 Jeremy Swayman	20.00	50.00
R5 Yanni Gourde	8.00	20.00
R9 Carter Hart	10.00	25.00
R12 Sean Durzi	6.00	15.00
R13 Josh Norris	10.00	25.00
R14 Joe Pavelski	20.00	50.00
R16 Tim Stutzle	12.00	30.00
R17 Lucas Raymond	15.00	40.00
R20 Miro Heiskanen	12.00	30.00
R24 Nick Suzuki	20.00	50.00
R26 Brad Marchand SP	20.00	50.00
R28 Tristan Jarry	10.00	25.00
R30 Aleksander Barkov	15.00	40.00
R31 Mats Zuccarello	10.00	25.00
R32 Jared McCann	8.00	20.00
R33 Boone Jenner	10.00	25.00
R34 Dylan Cozens	10.00	25.00
R35 Alex Iafallo	6.00	15.00
R36 Torey Krug	8.00	20.00
R37 Gabriel Landeskog SP	20.00	50.00
R38 Robert Thomas	10.00	25.00
R42 Michael Bunting SP	10.00	25.00
R44 Drake Batherson	10.00	25.00
R45 Brent Burns SP	10.00	25.00
R47 Alex Ovechkin SP	150.00	400.00
R48 Tanner Jeannot	6.00	15.00
R49 Jonathan Marchessault	12.00	30.00
R50 Karel Vejmelka	6.00	15.00
R51 Marco Rossi SP	25.00	60.00
R52 Matty Beniers SP	25.00	60.00
R53 Jacob Perreault SP	10.00	25.00
R54 Lukas Reichel SP	20.00	50.00
R55 Jack Quinn SP	15.00	40.00
R56 Matt Boldy SP	30.00	80.00
R57 Owen Power SP	20.00	50.00
R58 Kent Johnson SP	20.00	50.00
R59 Mark Kastelic	8.00	20.00
R60 Braden Schneider	15.00	40.00
R61 Marc McLaughlin	10.00	25.00
R62 Alex Vlasic	8.00	20.00
R63 Samuel Fagemo	8.00	20.00
R64 Isaac Ratcliffe	10.00	25.00
R65 Kaedan Korczak	8.00	20.00
R66 Dylan Samberg	10.00	25.00
R67 Mads Sogaard	12.00	30.00
R68 Jordan Spence	10.00	25.00
R69 Thomas Bordeleau	10.00	25.00
R70 Pyotr Kochetkov	20.00	50.00
R71 Dylan Holloway	20.00	50.00
R72 Nick Abruzzese	10.00	25.00
R73 Bobby Brink	10.00	25.00
R74 Jack McBain	10.00	25.00
R75 Jordan Harris	12.00	30.00
R76 Lukas Dostal	20.00	50.00
R77 Reilly Walsh	10.00	25.00
R78 Matias Maccelli	15.00	40.00
R79 Trey Fix-Wolansky	10.00	25.00
R80 Erik Kallgren	10.00	25.00
R84 Marcel Dionne	40.00	100.00
R91 Peter Forsberg	60.00	150.00
R93 John Vanbiesbrouck	25.00	60.00
R94 Jonathan Cheechoo	10.00	25.00
R95 Mike Gartner	15.00	40.00

2022-23 Parkhurst Champions All Star Legends

Card	Low	High
AS1 Wayne Gretzky	60.00	150.00
AS2 Gordie Howe	30.00	80.00
AS3 Bobby Orr	40.00	100.00
AS4 Mario Lemieux	40.00	100.00
AS5 Mike Bossy	10.00	25.00
AS6 Teemu Selanne	20.00	50.00
AS7 Steve Yzerman	25.00	60.00
AS8 Bobby Hull	20.00	50.00
AS9 Guy Lafleur	12.00	30.00
AS10 Jaromir Jagr	30.00	80.00
AS11 Stan Mikita	10.00	25.00
AS12 Mark Messier	20.00	50.00
AS13 Phil Esposito	15.00	40.00
AS14 Marcel Dionne	12.00	30.00
AS15 Paul Coffey	10.00	25.00
AS16 Ray Bourque	15.00	40.00
AS17 Martin Brodeur	25.00	60.00
AS18 Brian Leetch	8.00	20.00
AS19 Pat LaFontaine	10.00	25.00
AS20 Patrick Roy	25.00	60.00

2022-23 Parkhurst Champions Autographs

Card	Low	High
102 Sam Reinhart	12.00	30.00
105 Drake Batherson	6.00	15.00
106 Nick Suzuki SP	12.00	30.00
107 Mats Zuccarello	6.00	15.00
108 Colton Parayko SP	5.00	12.00
109 Joe Pavelski	8.00	20.00
111 Jordan Eberle	6.00	15.00
112 Zach Hyman	10.00	25.00
117 Tomas Hertl	6.00	15.00
118 Cam Atkinson	6.00	15.00
125 Thomas Chabot	6.00	15.00
127 Connor Hellebuyck	12.00	30.00
128 Tyler Toffoli	6.00	15.00
131 Teuvo Teravainen	6.00	15.00
132 Charlie Coyle	6.00	15.00
135 Nikolaj Ehlers	6.00	15.00
136 Brendan Gallagher	6.00	15.00
137 Roope Hintz SP	8.00	20.00
143 Josh Bailey	5.00	12.00
145 Alex Nedeljkovic	5.00	12.00
148 Pius Suter	5.00	12.00
149 Carter Hart SP	6.00	15.00
150 Marc-Andre Fleury SP	50.00	125.00
152 Jake Oettinger SP	10.00	25.00
155 Boone Jenner	6.00	15.00
157 Jared McCann	5.00	12.00
159 Elvis Merzlikins	6.00	15.00
160 Philipp Grubauer	6.00	15.00
163 Alexander Barabanov	4.00	10.00
165 Tim Stutzle SP	8.00	20.00
166 Yanni Gourde	5.00	12.00
168 Mike Smith	4.00	10.00
169 Jack Hughes SP	15.00	40.00
171 Victor Olofsson	6.00	15.00
173 Brock Nelson SP	6.00	15.00
175 Dylan Cozens	6.00	15.00
177 Jean-Gabriel Pageau	4.00	10.00
178 Ryan McLeod	4.00	10.00
179 Anders Lee	5.00	12.00
181 Aleksander Barkov	10.00	25.00
182 Alex Ovechkin	100.00	250.00
183 Andrei Svechnikov SP	8.00	20.00
184 Andrei Vasilevskiy SP	10.00	25.00
185 Brad Marchand SP	20.00	50.00
186 Brady Tkachuk SP	10.00	25.00
193 J.T. Miller	8.00	20.00
195 Jacob Markstrom	6.00	15.00
200 Auston Matthews SP	80.00	200.00
201 Jonathan Huberdeau	8.00	20.00
203 Kris Letang	8.00	20.00
204 Kyle Connor SP	10.00	25.00
205 Leon Draisaitl SP	30.00	80.00
206 Mark Stone	8.00	20.00
207 Matthew Tkachuk SP	12.00	30.00
209 Quinn Hughes	15.00	40.00
215 Tristan Jarry	6.00	15.00
216 Brayden Schenn	6.00	15.00
217 Lucas Raymond SP	15.00	40.00
221 Anton Lundell	6.00	15.00
222 Michael Bunting	6.00	15.00
226 Seth Jarvis	8.00	20.00
227 Quinton Byfield	8.00	20.00
231 Cole Sillinger SP	5.00	12.00
232 Alex Iafallo	4.00	10.00
233 Jeremy Swayman	10.00	25.00
237 Darcy Kuemper	6.00	15.00
238 Karel Vejmelka	4.00	10.00
241 Gabriel Landeskog SP	8.00	20.00
242 Alexis Lafreniere	10.00	25.00
243 Cole Perfetti	6.00	15.00
245 Johnny Gaudreau	10.00	25.00
246 Jordan Kyrou	6.00	15.00
247 Tanner Jeannot	4.00	10.00
256 Timo Meier	6.00	15.00
261 Samuel Fagemo	5.00	12.00
262 Braden Schneider	10.00	25.00
263 Fredrik Karlstrom	5.00	12.00
264 Bobby Brink	6.00	15.00
267 Isaac Ratcliffe	6.00	15.00
268 Mads Sogaard	8.00	20.00
269 Noah Cates	6.00	15.00
271 Alex Vlasic	5.00	12.00
272 Zack Hayes	5.00	12.00
274 Thomas Bordeleau	6.00	15.00
277 Matias Maccelli	10.00	25.00
278 Mark Kastelic	5.00	12.00
279 Dylan Samberg	6.00	15.00
280 Pyotr Kochetkov	12.00	30.00
281 Nikita Okhotiuk	5.00	12.00
282 Erik Kallgren	6.00	15.00
283 Marc McLaughlin	6.00	15.00
284 Nick Blankenburg	5.00	12.00
286 Reilly Walsh	6.00	15.00
287 Ronnie Attard	6.00	15.00
288 Brayden Tracey	5.00	12.00
289 Kaedan Korczak	5.00	12.00
290 Vladislav Kolyachonok	5.00	12.00
291 Trey Fix-Wolansky	6.00	15.00
292 Michael Eyssimont	6.00	15.00
293 Ben Meyers	6.00	15.00
294 Filip Hallander	6.00	15.00
295 Jack McBain	6.00	15.00
296 Jordan Spence	6.00	15.00
297 Nick Abruzzese	6.00	15.00
298 Chase Pearson	5.00	12.00
299 Valtteri Puustinen	5.00	12.00
300 Jordan Harris	8.00	20.00
301 Juraj Slafkovsky SP	100.00	250.00
302 Samuel Poulin SP	8.00	20.00
303 Brandt Clarke SP	12.00	30.00
304 Elmer Soderblom SP	12.00	30.00
305 Andrei Kuzmenko SP	12.00	30.00
306 Shane Wright SP	15.00	40.00
308 Oskar Olausson SP	6.00	15.00
309 Arber Xhekaj SP	12.00	30.00
310 David Jiricek SP	12.00	30.00
311 Lukas Dostal SP	12.00	30.00
312 Dylan Guenther SP	15.00	40.00
313 Jonatan Berggren SP	10.00	25.00
314 Jake Sanderson SP	15.00	40.00
315 Kaiden Guhle SP	12.00	30.00
316 Wyatt Johnston SP	25.00	60.00
317 Dylan Holloway SP	12.00	30.00
318 Lukas Reichel SP	12.00	30.00
319 Jacob Perreault SP	6.00	15.00
320 Marco Rossi SP	15.00	40.00
321 Kent Johnson SP	12.00	30.00
322 Jack Quinn SP	10.00	25.00
323 Matty Beniers SP	15.00	40.00
324 Matt Boldy SP	20.00	50.00
325 Owen Power SP	12.00	30.00
327 Ray Bourque SP	30.00	80.00
328 Mark Messier SP	12.00	30.00
331 Dominik Hasek SP	60.00	150.00
332 Martin Brodeur SP	15.00	40.00
334 Peter Forsberg SP	12.00	30.00
335 Peter Bondra SP	6.00	15.00
336 Lanny McDonald SP	6.00	15.00
337 Doug Gilmour SP	8.00	20.00
341 Patrick Roy SP	15.00	40.00
347 Teemu Selanne SP	12.00	30.00
348 Marcel Dionne SP	8.00	20.00
349 Mario Lemieux SP	125.00	300.00

2022-23 Parkhurst Champions Autographs Blue

*BLUE: .6X TO 1.5X BASIC

Card	Low	High
321 Kent Johnson/25	80.00	200.00

2022-23 Parkhurst Champions Jerseys

Card	Low	High
101 Mark Scheifele	6.00	15.00
102 Sam Reinhart	8.00	20.00
103 Conor Garland	3.00	8.00
104 Claude Giroux	4.00	10.00
105 Drake Batherson	4.00	10.00
106 Nick Suzuki	8.00	20.00
107 Mats Zuccarello	4.00	10.00
108 Colton Parayko	3.00	8.00
109 Joe Pavelski	5.00	12.00
111 Jordan Eberle	4.00	10.00
112 Zach Hyman	6.00	15.00
113 John Gibson	4.00	10.00
114 Taylor Hall	4.00	10.00
115 Anze Kopitar	6.00	15.00
116 Tyler Bertuzzi	3.00	8.00
117 Tomas Hertl	4.00	10.00
118 Cam Atkinson	4.00	10.00
120 Jesper Bratt	4.00	10.00
121 Carey Price	8.00	20.00
122 Patrick Kane	8.00	20.00
123 Elias Lindholm	4.00	10.00
124 Mathew Barzal	5.00	12.00
125 Thomas Chabot	4.00	10.00
126 Jason Robertson	6.00	15.00
127 Connor Hellebuyck	8.00	20.00
128 Tyler Toffoli	4.00	10.00
129 Kevin Fiala	3.00	8.00
130 Samuel Girard	2.50	6.00
131 Teuvo Teravainen	4.00	10.00
132 Charlie Coyle	4.00	10.00
133 Tom Wilson	4.00	10.00
134 Jack Roslovic	2.50	6.00
135 Nikolaj Ehlers	4.00	10.00
136 Brendan Gallagher	4.00	10.00
137 Roope Hintz	5.00	12.00
138 Brent Burns	4.00	10.00
139 Jonathan Marchessault	5.00	12.00
140 Robert Thomas	4.00	10.00
141 Josh Anderson	3.00	8.00
142 Jesse Puljujarvi	4.00	10.00
143 Josh Bailey	3.00	8.00
144 Dougie Hamilton	3.00	8.00
145 Alex Nedeljkovic	3.00	8.00
146 Ryan O'Reilly	4.00	10.00
147 Martin Necas	6.00	15.00
149 Carter Hart	4.00	10.00
150 Marc-Andre Fleury	8.00	20.00
151 Brock Boeser	5.00	12.00
152 Jake Oettinger	6.00	15.00
153 Ilya Sorokin	6.00	15.00
154 Sean Monahan	2.50	6.00
155 Boone Jenner	4.00	10.00
156 Troy Terry	3.00	8.00
157 Jared McCann	3.00	8.00
159 Elvis Merzlikins	4.00	10.00
160 Philipp Grubauer	4.00	10.00
161 Miro Heiskanen	5.00	12.00
163 Alexander Barabanov	2.50	6.00
164 Shayne Gostisbehere	4.00	10.00
165 Tim Stutzle	5.00	12.00
166 Yanni Gourde	3.00	8.00
168 Mike Smith	2.50	6.00
169 Jack Hughes	10.00	25.00
170 Kirby Dach	4.00	10.00
171 Victor Olofsson	4.00	10.00
172 John Klingberg	4.00	10.00
173 Brock Nelson	4.00	10.00
175 Dylan Cozens	4.00	10.00
176 Connor McMichael	4.00	10.00
177 Jean-Gabriel Pageau	2.50	6.00
179 Anders Lee	3.00	8.00
180 Adam Fox	5.00	12.00
181 Aleksander Barkov	6.00	15.00
182 Alex Ovechkin	15.00	40.00
183 Andrei Svechnikov	5.00	12.00
184 Andrei Vasilevskiy	6.00	15.00
185 Brad Marchand	8.00	20.00
186 Brady Tkachuk	6.00	15.00
187 Brayden Point	5.00	12.00
188 Cale Makar	10.00	25.00
189 Jeff Petry	4.00	10.00
190 Connor McDavid	20.00	50.00
191 Devon Toews	3.00	8.00
192 Igor Shesterkin	8.00	20.00
193 J.T. Miller	5.00	12.00
195 Jacob Markstrom	4.00	10.00
196 Jake Guentzel	6.00	15.00
197 John Tavares	6.00	15.00
199 Ryan Nugent-Hopkins	5.00	12.00
200 Auston Matthews	15.00	40.00
201 Jonathan Huberdeau	5.00	12.00
202 Kirill Kaprizov	12.00	30.00
203 Kris Letang	5.00	12.00
204 Kyle Connor	6.00	15.00
205 Leon Draisaitl	12.00	30.00
206 Mark Stone	5.00	12.00
207 Matthew Tkachuk	8.00	20.00
208 Nathan MacKinnon	15.00	40.00
209 Quinn Hughes	10.00	25.00
210 Roman Josi	4.00	10.00
211 Sergei Bobrovsky	6.00	15.00
212 Sidney Crosby	15.00	40.00
213 Steven Stamkos	8.00	20.00
214 Thatcher Demko	5.00	12.00
215 Tristan Jarry	4.00	10.00
216 Brayden Schenn	4.00	10.00
217 Lucas Raymond	6.00	15.00
218 Trevor Zegras	4.00	10.00
219 Moritz Seider	5.00	12.00
220 Cole Caufield	8.00	20.00
221 Anton Lundell	4.00	10.00
222 Michael Bunting	4.00	10.00
223 Dawson Mercer	5.00	12.00
224 Jamie Drysdale	3.00	8.00
226 Seth Jarvis	5.00	12.00
227 Quinton Byfield	5.00	12.00
228 Alex Newhook	3.00	8.00
229 Spencer Knight	4.00	10.00
230 Philip Tomasino	2.50	6.00
231 Cole Sillinger	3.00	8.00
233 Jeremy Swayman	6.00	15.00
234 Artemi Panarin	8.00	20.00
235 Charlie McAvoy	5.00	12.00
236 Mitch Marner	6.00	15.00
237 Darcy Kuemper	4.00	10.00
238 Karel Vejmelka	2.50	6.00
239 Evgeni Malkin	8.00	20.00
240 Frederik Andersen	5.00	12.00
241 Gabriel Landeskog	5.00	12.00
242 Alexis Lafreniere	6.00	15.00
243 Cole Perfetti	4.00	10.00
244 William Karlsson	5.00	12.00
245 Johnny Gaudreau	6.00	15.00
246 Jordan Kyrou	4.00	10.00
247 Tanner Jeannot	2.50	6.00
248 Morgan Rielly	4.00	10.00
249 Mikko Rantanen	10.00	25.00
250 Chris Kreider	5.00	12.00
251 Rasmus Dahlin	5.00	12.00
252 Nazem Kadri	5.00	12.00
253 Nikita Kucherov	8.00	20.00
254 Patrice Bergeron	5.00	12.00
255 Sebastian Aho	6.00	15.00
256 Timo Meier	4.00	10.00
257 Victor Hedman	5.00	12.00
258 Vladimir Tarasenko	5.00	12.00
259 William Nylander	8.00	20.00
260 Josh Morrissey	5.00	12.00
261 Samuel Fagemo	3.00	8.00
262 Braden Schneider	6.00	15.00
263 Fredrik Karlstrom	3.00	8.00
264 Bobby Brink	4.00	10.00
267 Isaac Ratcliffe	4.00	10.00
268 Mads Sogaard	5.00	12.00
269 Noah Cates	4.00	10.00
271 Alex Vlasic	3.00	8.00
272 Zack Hayes	3.00	8.00
274 Thomas Bordeleau	4.00	10.00
277 Matias Maccelli	6.00	15.00
278 Mark Kastelic	3.00	8.00
279 Dylan Samberg	4.00	10.00
280 Pyotr Kochetkov	8.00	20.00
281 Nikita Okhotiuk	3.00	8.00
282 Erik Kallgren	4.00	10.00
283 Marc McLaughlin	4.00	10.00
284 Nick Blankenburg	3.00	8.00
286 Reilly Walsh	4.00	10.00
287 Ronnie Attard	4.00	10.00
288 Brayden Tracey	3.00	8.00
289 Kaedan Korczak	3.00	8.00
290 Vladislav Kolyachonok	3.00	8.00
291 Trey Fix-Wolansky	4.00	10.00
292 Michael Eyssimont	4.00	10.00
293 Ben Meyers	4.00	10.00
294 Filip Hallander	4.00	10.00
295 Jack McBain	4.00	10.00
296 Jordan Spence	4.00	10.00
297 Nick Abruzzese	4.00	10.00
298 Chase Pearson	3.00	8.00
299 Valtteri Puustinen	3.00	8.00
300 Jordan Harris	5.00	12.00
301 Juraj Slafkovsky SP	20.00	50.00
302 Samuel Poulin SP	5.00	12.00
303 Brandt Clarke SP	8.00	20.00
304 Elmer Soderblom SP	8.00	20.00
305 Andrei Kuzmenko SP	8.00	20.00
306 Shane Wright SP	10.00	25.00
307 Simon Holmstrom SP	4.00	10.00
309 Arber Xhekaj SP	8.00	20.00
310 David Jiricek SP	8.00	20.00
311 Lukas Dostal SP	8.00	20.00
312 Dylan Guenther SP	10.00	25.00
313 Jonatan Berggren SP	6.00	15.00
314 Jake Sanderson SP	10.00	25.00
315 Kaiden Guhle SP	8.00	20.00
316 Wyatt Johnston SP	15.00	40.00
317 Dylan Holloway SP	8.00	20.00
318 Lukas Reichel SP	8.00	20.00
319 Jacob Perreault SP	4.00	10.00
320 Marco Rossi SP	10.00	25.00
321 Kent Johnson SP	8.00	20.00
322 Jack Quinn SP	6.00	15.00
323 Matty Beniers SP	10.00	25.00
324 Matt Boldy SP	12.00	30.00
325 Owen Power SP	8.00	20.00
327 Ray Bourque SP	6.00	15.00
329 Jaromir Jagr SP	12.00	30.00
330 Steve Yzerman SP	10.00	25.00
332 Martin Brodeur SP	10.00	25.00
334 Peter Forsberg SP	8.00	20.00
338 Paul Coffey SP	4.00	10.00
341 Patrick Roy SP	10.00	25.00
342 Brett Hull SP	8.00	20.00
347 Teemu Selanne SP	8.00	20.00
349 Mario Lemieux SP	15.00	40.00

2022-23 Parkhurst Champions Jukebox Heroes

*GOLD: .6X TO 1.5X BASIC

Card	Low	High
JH1 Alex Ovechkin	4.00	10.00
JH2 Connor McDavid	5.00	12.00
JH3 Nathan MacKinnon	4.00	10.00
JH4 Kirill Kaprizov	3.00	8.00
JH5 Sidney Crosby	4.00	10.00
JH6 Auston Matthews	4.00	10.00
JH7 Jack Hughes	2.50	6.00
JH8 Jonathan Huberdeau	1.25	3.00
JH9 Leon Draisaitl	3.00	8.00
JH10 Miro Heiskanen	1.25	3.00
JH11 Sebastian Aho	1.50	4.00
JH12 Patrick Kane	2.00	5.00
JH13 Brad Marchand	2.00	5.00
JH14 Matthew Tkachuk	2.00	5.00
JH15 Lucas Raymond	1.50	4.00
JH16 Brady Tkachuk	1.50	4.00
JH17 Cole Caufield	2.00	5.00
JH18 Quinn Hughes	2.50	6.00
JH19 Jason Robertson	1.50	4.00
JH20 Nikita Kucherov	2.00	5.00

2022-23 Parkhurst Champions Jukebox Heroes Autographs

Card	Low	High
JH2 Connor McDavid/25	125.00	300.00
JH8 Jonathan Huberdeau/25	30.00	80.00
JH10 Miro Heiskanen/25	30.00	80.00
JH13 Brad Marchand/25	50.00	125.00
JH15 Lucas Raymond/25	40.00	100.00
JH18 Quinn Hughes/25	60.00	150.00

2022-23 Parkhurst Champions MEM-orable Booklet Rookie Autographs

Card	Low	High
MBRABO Matt Boldy	150.00	400.00
MBRAJQ Jack Quinn	80.00	200.00
MBRAKJ Kent Johnson	100.00	250.00
MBRAMB Matty Beniers	250.00	600.00
MBRAMM Marc McLaughlin	50.00	125.00
MBRAOP Owen Power	100.00	250.00
MBRAPK Pyotr Kochetkov	100.00	250.00

2022-23 Parkhurst Champions Patches

Card	Low	High
101 Mark Scheifele/25	20.00	50.00
102 Sam Reinhart AU/25	40.00	100.00
103 Conor Garland/25	10.00	25.00
105 Drake Batherson AU/25	20.00	50.00
106 Nick Suzuki AU/25	40.00	100.00
107 Mats Zuccarello AU/25	20.00	50.00
108 Colton Parayko/25	10.00	25.00
109 Joe Pavelski AU/25	25.00	60.00
111 Jordan Eberle/25	12.00	30.00
112 Zach Hyman/25	20.00	50.00
113 John Gibson AU/25	20.00	50.00
114 Taylor Hall/25	12.00	30.00
115 Anze Kopitar AU/25	30.00	80.00
116 Tyler Bertuzzi/25	10.00	25.00
117 Tomas Hertl/25	12.00	30.00
118 Cam Atkinson AU/25	20.00	50.00
120 Jesper Bratt/25	12.00	30.00
121 Carey Price AU/25	40.00	100.00
122 Patrick Kane/25	25.00	60.00
123 Elias Lindholm/25	12.00	30.00
124 Mathew Barzal/25	15.00	40.00
125 Thomas Chabot/25	12.00	30.00
127 Connor Hellebuyck AU/25	40.00	100.00
128 Tyler Toffoli AU/25	20.00	50.00
130 Samuel Girard/25	8.00	20.00
131 Teuvo Teravainen AU/25	20.00	50.00
132 Charlie Coyle AU/25	20.00	50.00
133 Tom Wilson/25	12.00	30.00
134 Jack Roslovic/25	8.00	20.00
135 Nikolaj Ehlers AU/25	20.00	50.00
136 Brendan Gallagher AU/25	20.00	50.00
137 Roope Hintz/25	15.00	40.00
139 Jonathan Marchessault AU/25	25.00	60.00
140 Robert Thomas/25	12.00	30.00
141 Josh Anderson/25	10.00	25.00
142 Jesse Puljujarvi/25	12.00	30.00
143 Josh Bailey AU/25	15.00	40.00
144 Dougie Hamilton/25	10.00	25.00
145 Alex Nedeljkovic AU/25	15.00	40.00
146 Ryan O'Reilly/25	12.00	30.00
147 Martin Necas/25	20.00	50.00
149 Carter Hart AU/25	20.00	50.00
150 Marc-Andre Fleury AU/25	40.00	100.00
151 Brock Boeser AU/25	25.00	60.00
152 Jake Oettinger AU/25	30.00	80.00
153 Ilya Sorokin/25	20.00	50.00
155 Boone Jenner/25	12.00	30.00
156 Troy Terry AU/25	15.00	40.00
157 Jared McCann/25	10.00	25.00
159 Elvis Merzlikins AU/25	20.00	50.00
160 Philipp Grubauer/25	12.00	30.00
161 Miro Heiskanen AU/25	25.00	60.00
163 Alexander Barabanov AU/25	12.00	30.00
164 Shayne Gostisbehere/25	12.00	30.00
165 Tim Stutzle AU/25	25.00	60.00
166 Yanni Gourde/25	10.00	25.00

169 Jack Hughes/25 30.00 80.00
171 Victor Olofsson/25 12.00 30.00
173 Brock Nelson/25 12.00 30.00
175 Dylan Cozens/25 12.00 30.00
176 Connor McMichael/25 12.00 30.00
177 Jean-Gabriel Pageau/25 8.00 20.00
179 Anders Lee AU/25 15.00 40.00
180 Adam Fox/25 15.00 40.00
181 Aleksander Barkov AU/25 30.00 80.00
182 Alex Ovechkin AU/25 125.00 300.00
183 Andrei Svechnikov AU/25 25.00 60.00
184 Andrei Vasilevskiy AU/25 30.00 80.00
185 Brad Marchand AU/25 40.00 100.00
186 Brady Tkachuk AU/25 30.00 80.00
187 Brayden Point/25 15.00 40.00
188 Cale Makar AU/25 50.00 125.00
190 Connor McDavid AU/25 300.00 800.00
191 Devon Toews/25 10.00 25.00
192 Igor Shesterkin/25 25.00 60.00
195 Jacob Markstrom AU/25 20.00 50.00
196 Jake Guentzel AU/25 30.00 80.00
197 John Tavares AU/25 30.00 80.00
200 Auston Matthews AU/25 200.00 500.00
202 Kirill Kaprizov/25 40.00 100.00
203 Kris Letang AU/25 25.00 60.00
204 Kyle Connor AU/25 30.00 80.00
205 Leon Draisaitl AU/25 60.00 150.00
206 Mark Stone AU/25 25.00 60.00
208 Nathan MacKinnon/25 50.00 125.00
209 Quinn Hughes AU/25 50.00 125.00
210 Roman Josi AU/25 20.00 50.00
212 Sidney Crosby AU/25 250.00 600.00
215 Tristan Jarry/25 12.00 30.00
216 Brayden Schenn/25 12.00 30.00
217 Lucas Raymond AU/25 30.00 80.00
221 Anton Lundell/25 12.00 30.00
222 Michael Bunting/25 12.00 30.00
223 Dawson Mercer AU/25 25.00 60.00
227 Quinton Byfield AU/25 25.00 60.00
229 Spencer Knight AU/25 20.00 50.00
230 Philip Tomasino AU/25 12.00 30.00
231 Cole Sillinger AU/25 15.00 40.00
233 Jeremy Swayman AU/25 30.00 80.00
234 Artemi Panarin/25 25.00 60.00
235 Charlie McAvoy/25 15.00 40.00
236 Mitch Marner/25 20.00 50.00
238 Karel Vejmelka/25 8.00 20.00
239 Evgeni Malkin/25 25.00 60.00
240 Frederik Andersen/25 15.00 40.00
241 Gabriel Landeskog AU/25 25.00 60.00
242 Alexis Lafreniere AU/25 30.00 80.00
243 Cole Perfetti AU/25 20.00 50.00
244 William Karlsson AU/25 25.00 60.00
246 Jordan Kyrou AU/25 20.00 50.00
247 Tanner Jeannot AU/25 12.00 30.00
248 Morgan Rielly/25 12.00 30.00
249 Mikko Rantanen AU/25 50.00 120.00
250 Chris Kreider/25 15.00 40.00
253 Nikita Kucherov AU/25 40.00 100.00
254 Patrice Bergeron/25 15.00 40.00
255 Sebastian Aho AU/25 30.00 80.00
256 Timo Meier AU/25 20.00 50.00
260 Andrew Copp/25 8.00 20.00
261 Samuel Fagemo AU/35 15.00 40.00
262 Braden Schneider AU/35 30.00 80.00
263 Fredrik Karlstrom AU/35 15.00 40.00
264 Bobby Brink AU/35 20.00 50.00
267 Isaac Ratcliffe AU/35 20.00 50.00
268 Mads Sogaard AU/35 25.00 60.00
269 Noah Cates AU/35 20.00 50.00
271 Alex Vlasic AU/35 15.00 40.00
272 Zack Hayes AU/35 15.00 40.00
274 Thomas Bordeleau AU/35 20.00 50.00
277 Matias Maccelli AU/35 30.00 80.00
278 Mark Kastelic AU/35 15.00 40.00
279 Dylan Samberg AU/35 20.00 50.00
280 Pyotr Kochetkov AU/35 40.00 100.00
281 Nikita Okhotiuk AU/35 15.00 40.00
282 Erik Kallgren AU/35 20.00 50.00
283 Marc McLaughlin AU/35 20.00 50.00
284 Nick Blankenburg AU/35 15.00 40.00
286 Reilly Walsh AU/35 20.00 50.00
287 Ronnie Attard AU/35 20.00 50.00
288 Brayden Tracey AU/35 15.00 40.00
289 Kaedan Korczak AU/35 15.00 40.00
290 Vladislav Kolyachonok AU/35 15.00 40.00
291 Trey Fix-Wolansky AU/35 20.00 50.00
292 Michael Eyssimont AU/35 20.00 50.00
293 Ben Meyers AU/35 20.00 50.00
294 Filip Hallander AU/35 20.00 50.00
295 Jack McBain AU/35 20.00 50.00
297 Nick Abruzzese AU/35 20.00 50.00
298 Chase Pearson AU/35 15.00 40.00
299 Valtteri Puustinen AU/35 15.00 40.00
300 Jordan Harris AU/35 25.00 60.00
302 Samuel Poulin AU/35 25.00 60.00
303 Brandt Clarke AU/35 40.00 100.00
304 Elmer Soderblom AU/35 40.00 100.00
305 Andrei Kuzmenko AU/35 40.00 100.00
306 Shane Wright AU/35 50.00 125.00
307 Simon Holmstrom AU/35 20.00 50.00
309 Arber Xhekaj AU/35 40.00 100.00
310 David Jiricek AU/35 40.00 100.00
311 Lukas Dostal AU/35 40.00 100.00
312 Dylan Guenther AU/35 50.00 125.00
313 Jonatan Berggren AU/35 30.00 80.00
314 Jake Sanderson AU/35 50.00 125.00
315 Kaiden Guhle AU/35 40.00 100.00
316 Wyatt Johnston AU/35 150.00 400.00
317 Dylan Holloway AU/35 40.00 100.00
318 Lukas Reichel AU/35 40.00 100.00
319 Jacob Perreault AU/35 20.00 50.00
320 Marco Rossi AU/35 50.00 125.00
321 Kent Johnson AU/35 40.00 100.00
322 Jack Quinn AU/35 30.00 80.00
323 Matty Beniers AU/35 50.00 125.00
324 Matt Boldy AU/35 60.00 150.00
325 Owen Power AU/35 40.00 100.00

2022-23 Parkhurst Champions Tomorrow's Riches

*GOLD: .6X TO 1.5X BASIC
TR1 Trevor Zegras 1.25 3.00
TR2 Cole Caufield 2.50 6.00
TR3 Jeremy Swayman 2.00 5.00
TR4 Moritz Seider 1.50 4.00
TR5 Mason McTavish 1.25 3.00
TR6 Tanner Jeannot .75 2.00
TR7 William Eklund 1.50 4.00
TR8 Matt Boldy 4.00 10.00
TR9 Quinton Byfield 1.50 4.00
TR10 Spencer Knight 1.25 3.00
TR11 Kent Johnson 2.50 6.00
TR12 Jack Quinn 2.00 5.00
TR13 Jamie Drysdale 1.00 2.50
TR14 Alex Newhook 1.00 2.50
TR15 Dawson Mercer 1.50 4.00
TR16 Alex Turcotte .75 2.00
TR17 Lucas Raymond 2.00 5.00
TR18 Seth Jarvis 1.50 4.00
TR19 Philip Tomasino .75 2.00
TR20 Cole Perfetti 1.25 3.00
TR21 Cole Sillinger 1.00 2.50
TR22 Marco Rossi 3.00 8.00
TR23 Alexander Holtz 1.25 3.00
TR24 Cam York .75 2.00
TR25 Vasily Podkolzin .75 2.00
TR26 Lukas Reichel 2.50 6.00
TR27 Owen Power 2.50 6.00
TR28 Matty Beniers 3.00 8.00
TR29 Anton Lundell 1.25 3.00
TR30 Braden Schneider 2.00 5.00

2022-23 Parkhurst Champions Tomorrow's Riches Autographs

TR3 Jeremy Swayman 15.00 40.00
TR5 Mason McTavish 10.00 25.00
TR6 Tanner Jeannot 6.00 15.00
TR7 William Eklund 12.00 30.00
TR8 Matt Boldy 30.00 80.00
TR9 Quinton Byfield 12.00 30.00
TR11 Kent Johnson 20.00 50.00
TR12 Jack Quinn 15.00 40.00
TR15 Dawson Mercer 12.00 30.00
TR16 Alex Turcotte 6.00 15.00
TR17 Lucas Raymond 15.00 40.00
TR20 Cole Perfetti 10.00 25.00
TR21 Cole Sillinger 8.00 20.00
TR22 Marco Rossi 25.00 60.00
TR23 Alexander Holtz 10.00 25.00
TR25 Vasily Podkolzin 6.00 15.00
TR26 Lukas Reichel 20.00 50.00
TR27 Owen Power 20.00 50.00
TR28 Matty Beniers 25.00 60.00
TR29 Anton Lundell 10.00 25.00
TR30 Braden Schneider 15.00 40.00

2022-23 Parkhurst Champions Wire Images

*GOLD: .5X TO 1.2X BASIC
WI1 Ryan Donato .75 2.00
WI2 Alexis Lafreniere 1.50 4.00
WI3 Jordan Eberle 1.00 2.50
WI4 Igor Shesterkin 2.00 5.00
WI5 Marc McLaughlin 1.00 2.50
WI6 Carey Price 2.00 5.00
WI7 Lucas Raymond 1.50 4.00
WI8 Moritz Seider 1.25 3.00
WI9 Seth Jarvis 1.25 3.00
WI10 Miro Heiskanen 1.25 3.00
WI11 Matthew Tkachuk 2.00 5.00
WI12 Jake Guentzel 1.50 4.00
WI13 Brad Marchand 2.00 5.00
WI14 Sean Durzi .60 1.50
WI15 Matt Boldy 3.00 8.00
WI16 Jason Robertson 1.50 4.00
WI17 Sidney Crosby 4.00 10.00
WI18 Timo Meier 1.00 2.50
WI19 Alex Ovechkin 4.00 10.00
WI20 Jonathan Huberdeau 1.25 3.00
WI21 Kirill Kaprizov 3.00 8.00
WI22 Artemi Panarin 2.00 5.00
WI23 Marc-Andre Fleury 2.00 5.00
WI24 Tanner Jeannot .60 1.50
WI25 Cale Makar 2.50 6.00
WI26 Connor McDavid 5.00 12.00
WI27 Jack Hughes 2.50 6.00
WI28 Claude Giroux 1.00 2.50
WI29 Steven Stamkos 2.00 5.00
WI30 Patrice Bergeron 1.25 3.00
WI31 Auston Matthews 4.00 10.00
WI32 Andrei Vasilevskiy 1.50 4.00
WI33 Trevor Zegras 1.00 2.50
WI34 Mitch Marner 1.50 4.00
WI35 Artturi Lehkonen .75 2.00

2023-24 Parkhurst Champions

1 Connor McDavid 2.50 6.00
2 Dylan Cozens .50 1.25
3 Miro Heiskanen .60 1.50
4 Joe Pavelski .60 1.50
5 Mika Zibanejad .60 1.50
6 Aleksander Barkov .75 2.00
7 Tim Stutzle .60 1.50
8 Owen Power .50 1.25
9 Matt Boldy .75 2.00
10 Ivan Miroshnichenko RC .75 2.00
11 Adam Fox .60 1.50
12 Jake Oettinger .75 2.00
13 Artemi Panarin 1.00 2.50
14 William Eklund .60 1.50
15 Filip Gustavsson .50 1.25
16 Simon Nemec RC 1.00 2.50
17 Tristen Robins RC .50 1.25
18 Zach Hyman .75 2.00
19 Mikko Rantanen 1.25 3.00
20 Dylan Guenther .60 1.50
21 Jamie Drysdale .40 1.00
22 Kent Johnson .50 1.25
23 Mark Stone .60 1.50
24 Jake Neighbours .50 1.25
25 Alex Tuch .50 1.25
26 Bo Horvat .60 1.50
27 Matthew Tkachuk 1.00 2.50
28 J.T. Miller .60 1.50
29 Alex Newhook .40 1.00
30 Bowen Byram .60 1.50
31 Colton Parayko .40 1.00
32 Philipp Grubauer .50 1.25
33 Logan Thompson .60 1.50
34 Leon Draisaitl 1.50 4.00
35 Tage Thompson .60 1.50
36 Jonathan Marchessault .60 1.50
37 John Beecher RC 1.00 2.50
38 Nick Suzuki 1.00 2.50
39 Nico Hischier .75 2.00
40 Ryan O'Reilly .50 1.25
41 Cole McWard RC .50 1.25
42 John Tavares .75 2.00
43 Lukas Rousek RC .40 1.00
44 Mario Ferraro .30 .75
45 K'Andre Miller .40 1.00
46 Cole Sillinger .40 1.00
47 JJ Peterka .50 1.25
48 Lukas Reichel .50 1.25
49 Matt Duchene .50 1.25
50 Hunter McKown RC .50 1.25
51 Brandt Clarke .50 1.25
52 Ross Colton .40 1.00
53 Brock Nelson .50 1.25
54 Cale Makar 1.25 3.00
55 Jet Greaves RC .75 2.00
56 Auston Matthews 2.00 5.00
57 Jacob Markstrom .50 1.25
58 Clayton Keller .60 1.50
59 Timo Meier .50 1.25
60 Fraser Minten RC 1.00 2.50
61 Ryan Strome .50 1.25
62 Andrei Kuzmenko .50 1.25
63 Tomas Hertl .50 1.25
64 Roope Hintz .60 1.50
65 Justin Sourdif RC .50 1.25
66 Josh Morrissey .60 1.50
67 Jared McCann .40 1.00
68 Arber Xhekaj .50 1.25
69 Alex Laferriere RC .75 2.00
70 Yanni Gourde .40 1.00
71 Brady Tkachuk .75 2.00
72 Drake Batherson .50 1.25
73 Roman Josi .50 1.25
74 John Gibson .50 1.25
75 Jake Livingstone RC .50 1.25
76 Andrei Svechnikov .60 1.50
77 Jonatan Berggren .40 1.00
78 Samuel Bolduc RC .50 1.25
79 Jonathan Huberdeau .60 1.50
80 David Perron .40 1.00
81 Chandler Stephenson .40 1.00
82 Nikolaj Ehlers .50 1.25
83 Juuse Saros .60 1.50
84 Michael Kesselring RC .50 1.25
85 Bryan Rust .50 1.25
86 Connor Zary RC 1.00 2.50
87 Henry Thrun RC .50 1.25
88 Tyler Toffoli .50 1.25
89 Mason McTavish .50 1.25
90 Ryan Nugent-Hopkins .60 1.50
91 Mats Zuccarello .50 1.25
92 Matthew Kessel RC .40 1.00
93 Isak Rosen RC .50 1.25
94 Cole Perfetti .50 1.25
95 Kirill Marchenko .60 1.50
96 Blake Coleman .40 1.00
97 Gabe Vilardi .50 1.25
98 Robert Thomas .50 1.25
99 Brent Burns .50 1.25
100 Sebastian Aho .75 2.00
101 Sidney Crosby 2.00 5.00
102 Darcy Kuemper .50 1.25
103 Noah Dobson .60 1.50
104 Michael Bunting .50 1.25
105 Jiri Patera RC .75 2.00
106 Seth Jarvis .60 1.50
107 Bobby McMann RC .75 2.00
108 Carter Hart .50 1.25
109 Brad Marchand 1.00 2.50
110 Trevor Zegras .50 1.25
111 Chris Kreider .60 1.50
112 Ryan Reaves .40 1.00
113 Dylan Strome .60 1.50
114 Valeri Nichushkin .50 1.25
115 Quinn Hughes 1.25 3.00
116 MacKenzie Weegar .40 1.00
117 Tyler Bertuzzi .40 1.00
118 Ryan Graves .30 .75
119 Jakob Chychrun .50 1.25
120 Jesper Bratt .50 1.25
121 Andre Burakovsky .30 .75
122 Brayden Point .60 1.50
123 Evander Kane .50 1.25
124 Patrik Laine .60 1.50
125 Ivan Provorov .40 1.00
126 Jordan Binnington .75 2.00
127 J.T. Compher .30 .75
128 Jack Hughes 1.25 3.00
129 Evgeni Malkin 1.00 2.50
130 Andrei Vasilevskiy .75 2.00
131 Joel Farabee .50 1.25
132 Victor Hedman .60 1.50
133 Sergei Bobrovsky .75 2.00
134 Adin Hill .50 1.25
135 Cole Caufield 1.00 2.50
136 Alex Ovechkin 2.00 5.00
137 Jack Eichel .75 2.00
138 Connor Hellebuyck 1.00 2.50
139 Taylor Hall .50 1.25
140 Quinton Byfield .60 1.50
141 Brock Boeser .60 1.50
142 Owen Tippett .30 .75
143 Matias Maccelli .40 1.00
144 Troy Terry .40 1.00
145 Nazem Kadri .60 1.50
146 Pierre-Luc Dubois .40 1.00
147 Wyatt Johnston 1.00 2.50
148 Ondrej Palat .40 1.00
149 Nathan MacKinnon 2.00 5.00
150 Nikita Kucherov 1.00 2.50
151 Erik Karlsson .60 1.50
152 Ilya Sorokin .75 2.00
153 Alex DeBrincat .60 1.50
154 Matty Beniers .60 1.50
155 Igor Shesterkin 1.00 2.50
156 Brandon Saad .40 1.00
157 Kyle Connor .75 2.00
158 Drew Doughty .50 1.25
159 Pavel Buchnevich .40 1.00
160 William Nylander 1.00 2.50
161 Rasmus Dahlin .60 1.50
162 Tom Wilson .50 1.25
163 Brandon Hagel .40 1.00
164 Stuart Skinner .60 1.50
165 Travis Konecny .50 1.25
166 Steven Stamkos 1.00 2.50
167 Mark Scheifele .75 2.00
168 Martin Necas .75 2.00
169 David Pastrnak 1.25 3.00
170 Jared Spurgeon .50 1.25
171 Nick Schmaltz .40 1.00
172 Evan Bouchard .60 1.50
173 Charlie McAvoy .60 1.50
174 Johnny Gaudreau .75 2.00
175 Rasmus Ristolainen .30 .75
176 Mattias Ekholm .40 1.00
177 Jeff Skinner .50 1.25
178 Michael Matheson .30 .75
179 Aaron Ekblad .60 1.50
180 T.J. Oshie .50 1.25
181 John Klingberg .50 1.25
182 Anze Kopitar .75 2.00
183 Joonas Korpisalo .50 1.25
184 Filip Forsberg .75 2.00
185 William Karlsson .60 1.50
186 Nick Bjugstad .30 .75
187 Brandon Montour .60 1.50
188 Jaccob Slavin .40 1.00
189 Morgan Rielly .50 1.25
190 Mathew Barzal .60 1.50
191 Ivan Barbashev .40 1.00
192 Sam Bennett .75 2.00
193 Radko Gudas .30 .75
194 Linus Ullmark .50 1.25
195 Lucas Raymond .75 2.00
196 Sam Reinhart 1.00 2.50
197 Carter Verhaeghe .50 1.25
198 Jake Guentzel .75 2.00
199 Elias Pettersson .75 2.00
200 Mitch Marner .75 2.00
201 Adrian Kempe .50 1.25
202 Moritz Seider .60 1.50
203 Jake DeBrusk .50 1.25
204 Thatcher Demko .60 1.50
205 Jordan Eberle .50 1.25
206 Elias Lindholm .50 1.25
207 Charlie Coyle .50 1.25
208 Dylan Larkin .60 1.50
209 Juraj Slafkovsky 1.00 2.50
210 Dawson Mercer .60 1.50
211 Pierre Engvall .30 .75
212 Alexandar Georgiev .50 1.25
213 Kris Letang .60 1.50
214 Kirill Kaprizov 1.50 4.00
215 Tristan Jarry .50 1.25
216 Frederik Andersen .60 1.50
217 Thomas Novak .30 .75
218 Ryan Hartman .30 .75
219 Vince Dunn .40 1.00
220 Seth Jones .50 1.25
221 Connor Bedard SP RC 15.00 40.00
222 Luke Hughes SP RC 2.50 6.00
223 Aidan McDonough SP RC .60 1.50
224 Yaroslav Askarov SP RC 2.00 5.00
225 Tye Kartye SP RC 1.25 3.00
226 Simon Edvinsson SP RC 1.50 4.00
227 Will Cuylle SP RC 1.25 3.00
228 Leo Carlsson SP RC 2.50 6.00
229 Ridly Greig SP RC 1.25 3.00
230 Brock Faber SP RC 2.00 5.00
231 Marco Kasper SP RC 2.00 5.00
232 Adam Fantilli SP RC 2.50 6.00
233 Luke Evangelista SP RC 1.25 3.00
234 Pavel Mintyukov SP RC 1.25 3.00
235 Owen Beck SP RC 1.25 3.00
236 Logan Cooley SP RC 2.50 6.00
237 Matthew Coronato SP RC 1.25 3.00
238 Leevi Merilainen SP RC .75 2.00
239 Devon Levi SP RC 2.00 5.00
240 Kevin Korchinski SP RC 1.25 3.00
241 Sean Farrell SP RC .75 2.00
242 Matthew Poitras SP RC 1.50 4.00
243 Jakob Pelletier SP RC 1.00 2.50
244 Danil Gushchin SP RC .75 2.00
245 Dustin Wolf SP RC 2.50 6.00
246 Zach Benson SP RC 1.25 3.00
247 William Dufour SP RC .60 1.50
248 Matt Savoie SP RC 1.50 4.00
249 Matthew Knies SP RC 3.00 8.00
250 Tyson Foerster SP RC 1.50 4.00
251 Dale Hawerchuk SP 2.00 5.00
252 Bernie Parent SP 2.00 5.00
253 Bobby Orr SP 6.00 15.00
254 Gordie Howe SP 5.00 12.00
255 Vincent Damphousse SP 1.25 3.00
256 Todd Bertuzzi SP 1.25 3.00
257 Martin Brodeur SP 4.00 10.00
258 Borje Salming SP 1.50 4.00
259 Brett Hull SP 3.00 8.00
260 Brian Leetch SP 1.25 3.00
261 Chris Chelios SP 1.50 4.00
262 Glenn Hall SP 1.50 4.00
263 Jean Ratelle SP 1.25 3.00
264 Eric Lindros SP 2.50 6.00
265 Joe Nieuwendyk SP 1.25 3.00
266 Marian Hossa SP 1.50 4.00
267 Maurice Richard SP 3.00 8.00
268 Mario Lemieux SP 6.00 15.00
269 Mats Sundin SP 1.50 4.00
270 Mike Gartner SP 2.00 5.00
271 Mike Modano SP 2.50 6.00
272 Patrick Roy SP 4.00 10.00
273 Paul Coffey SP 1.50 4.00
274 Mark Messier SP 3.00 8.00
275 Pete Mahovlich SP 1.50 4.00
276 Joe Sakic SP 3.00 8.00
277 Peter Stastny SP 1.25 3.00
278 Pierre Turgeon SP 1.25 3.00
279 Tony Esposito SP 1.50 4.00
280 Wayne Gretzky SP 10.00 25.00

2023-24 Parkhurst Champions Color Variation

*COLOR VAR: .8X TO 2X BASIC

2023-24 Parkhurst Champions Gold Rainbow

*GOLD RNBW: 1X TO 2.5X BASIC
221 Connor Bedard SP 80.00 200.00

2023-24 Parkhurst Champions Rainbow

*RAINBOW: .6X TO 1.5X BASIC

2023-24 Parkhurst Champions Red

*RED/52: 2.5X TO 6X BASIC
*RED LEG/52: 2X TO 5X BASIC

2023-24 Parkhurst Champions Silver

*SILVER: .5X TO 1.2X BASIC

2023-24 Parkhurst Champions '52 Retros

*ALBUM: .6X TO 1.5X BASIC
*GOLD RNBW/52: 1.2X TO 3X BASIC
R1 Connor McDavid 10.00 25.00
R2 Matthew Tkachuk 4.00 10.00
R3 Jason Robertson 3.00 8.00
R4 Jacob Markstrom 2.00 5.00
R5 Elias Pettersson 3.00 8.00
R6 Moritz Seider 2.50 6.00
R7 Kyle Connor 3.00 8.00
R8 Erik Karlsson 2.50 6.00
R9 Aleksander Barkov 3.00 8.00
R10 Igor Shesterkin 4.00 10.00
R11 Auston Matthews 8.00 20.00
R12 Ilya Sorokin 3.00 8.00
R13 Brad Marchand 4.00 10.00
R14 Anze Kopitar 3.00 8.00
R15 David Pastrnak 5.00 12.00
R16 Mark Stone 2.50 6.00
R17 Taylor Hall 2.00 5.00
R18 Tim Stutzle 2.50 6.00
R19 Robert Thomas 2.00 5.00
R20 Jordan Kyrou 2.00 5.00
R21 Rasmus Dahlin 2.50 6.00
R22 Quinn Hughes 5.00 12.00
R23 Pierre-Luc Dubois 1.50 4.00
R24 Cole Caufield 4.00 10.00
R25 Cale Makar 5.00 12.00
R26 Connor Hellebuyck 4.00 10.00
R27 Juuse Saros 2.50 6.00
R28 Sidney Crosby 8.00 20.00
R29 Timo Meier 2.00 5.00
R30 Jack Eichel 3.00 8.00
R31 Dylan Larkin 2.50 6.00
R32 Leon Draisaitl 6.00 15.00
R33 Clayton Keller 2.50 6.00
R34 Jake Oettinger 3.00 8.00
R35 Brent Burns 2.00 5.00
R36 Kirill Kaprizov 6.00 15.00
R37 Evgeni Malkin 4.00 10.00
R38 Mitch Marner 3.00 8.00
R39 Alex Ovechkin 8.00 20.00
R40 Matty Beniers 2.50 6.00
R41 Trevor Zegras 2.00 5.00
R42 Brady Tkachuk 3.00 8.00
R43 Mika Zibanejad 2.50 6.00
R44 Sebastian Aho 3.00 8.00
R45 Patrik Laine 2.50 6.00
R46 Jack Hughes 5.00 12.00
R47 Nick Suzuki 4.00 10.00
R48 Nathan MacKinnon 8.00 20.00
R49 Nazem Kadri 2.50 6.00
R50 Travis Konecny 2.00 5.00
R51 Luke Hughes 6.00 15.00
R52 Vincent Iorio 2.00 5.00
R53 Samuel Bolduc 2.00 5.00
R54 Hunter McKown 2.00 5.00
R55 Tyson Foerster 4.00 10.00
R56 William Dufour 1.50 4.00
R57 Owen Beck 3.00 8.00
R58 Matthew Knies 8.00 20.00
R59 Ridly Greig 3.00 8.00
R60 Jiri Patera 3.00 8.00
R61 Yaroslav Askarov 5.00 12.00
R62 Akito Hirose 1.50 4.00
R63 Wyatt Kaiser 2.00 5.00
R64 Sean Farrell 2.00 5.00
R65 Dustin Wolf 6.00 15.00
R66 Luke Evangelista 3.00 8.00
R67 Jakob Pelletier 2.50 6.00
R68 Joona Koppanen 1.50 4.00
R69 Egor Afanasyev 2.00 5.00
R70 Stanislav Svozil 1.50 4.00
R71 Danil Gushchin 2.00 5.00
R72 Brock Faber 5.00 12.00
R73 Nikita Nesterenko 2.00 5.00
R74 Simon Edvinsson 4.00 10.00
R75 Marco Kasper 5.00 12.00
R76 Will Cuylle 3.00 8.00
R77 Matthew Coronato 3.00 8.00
R78 Luke Philp 2.00 5.00
R79 Vincent Desharnais 2.50 6.00
R80 Connor Bedard 40.00 100.00
R81 Maurice Richard 4.00 10.00
R82 Gordie Howe 6.00 15.00
R83 Bobby Orr 8.00 20.00
R84 Bobby Clarke 3.00 8.00
R85 Cam Neely 2.00 5.00
R86 Jari Kurri 2.00 5.00
R87 Mario Lemieux 8.00 20.00
R88 Patrick Roy 5.00 12.00
R89 Rogie Vachon 2.00 5.00
R90 Jean Beliveau 2.00 5.00
R91 Doug Gilmour 2.50 6.00
R92 Rod Gilbert 2.00 5.00
R93 Mike Bossy 2.00 5.00
R94 Eric Lindros 3.00 8.00
R95 Jacques Plante 2.00 5.00
R96 Steve Yzerman 5.00 12.00
R97 Tony Esposito 2.00 5.00
R98 Ted Lindsay 2.00 5.00
R99 Marcel Dionne 2.50 6.00
R100 Wayne Gretzky 12.00 30.00

2023-24 Parkhurst Champions '52 Retros Autographs

R2 Matthew Tkachuk SP 25.00 60.00
R4 Jacob Markstrom 12.00 30.00
R5 Elias Pettersson SP 20.00 50.00
R9 Aleksander Barkov 20.00 50.00
R12 Ilya Sorokin 20.00 50.00
R13 Brad Marchand SP 25.00 60.00
R16 Mark Stone 15.00 40.00
R19 Robert Thomas 12.00 30.00
R26 Connor Hellebuyck 25.00 60.00
R27 Juuse Saros 15.00 40.00
R34 Jake Oettinger 20.00 50.00
R38 Mitch Marner SP 20.00 50.00
R42 Brady Tkachuk SP 20.00 50.00
R46 Jack Hughes SP 30.00 80.00
R47 Nick Suzuki 25.00 60.00
R51 Luke Hughes SP 40.00 100.00
R52 Vincent Iorio 12.00 30.00
R53 Samuel Bolduc 12.00 30.00
R55 Tyson Foerster 25.00 60.00
R56 William Dufour 10.00 25.00
R57 Owen Beck 20.00 50.00
R58 Matthew Knies SP 50.00 125.00
R59 Ridly Greig 20.00 50.00
R60 Jiri Patera 20.00 50.00
R61 Yaroslav Askarov 30.00 80.00
R62 Akito Hirose 10.00 25.00
R63 Wyatt Kaiser 12.00 30.00
R64 Sean Farrell 12.00 30.00
R65 Dustin Wolf 40.00 100.00
R66 Luke Evangelista SP 20.00 50.00
R67 Jakob Pelletier 15.00 40.00
R68 Joona Koppanen 10.00 25.00
R70 Stanislav Svozil 10.00 25.00
R72 Brock Faber 30.00 80.00
R73 Nikita Nesterenko 12.00 30.00
R74 Simon Edvinsson 25.00 60.00
R75 Marco Kasper 30.00 80.00
R77 Matthew Coronato 20.00 50.00
R78 Luke Philp 12.00 30.00
R79 Vincent Desharnais 15.00 40.00

2023-24 Parkhurst Champions Autographs

2 Dylan Cozens 6.00 15.00
3 Miro Heiskanen 8.00 20.00
4 Joe Pavelski 8.00 20.00
7 Tim Stutzle SP 8.00 20.00
8 Owen Power 6.00 15.00
10 Ivan Miroshnichenko 10.00 25.00
12 Jake Oettinger 10.00 25.00
15 Filip Gustavsson 6.00 15.00
17 Tristen Robins 6.00 15.00
19 Mikko Rantanen SP 15.00 40.00
20 Dylan Guenther 8.00 20.00
23 Mark Stone 8.00 20.00
24 Jake Neighbours 6.00 15.00
25 Alex Tuch 6.00 15.00
27 Matthew Tkachuk SP 12.00 30.00
29 Alex Newhook 5.00 12.00
30 Bowen Byram 8.00 20.00
31 Colton Parayko 5.00 12.00
32 Philipp Grubauer 6.00 15.00
33 Logan Thompson 8.00 20.00
35 Tage Thompson 8.00 20.00
36 Jonathan Marchessault 8.00 20.00
37 John Beecher 12.00 30.00
38 Nick Suzuki 12.00 30.00
39 Nico Hischier 10.00 25.00
40 Ryan O'Reilly SP 6.00 15.00
41 Cole McWard 6.00 15.00
43 Lukas Rousek 5.00 12.00
44 Mario Ferraro 4.00 10.00
45 K'Andre Miller 5.00 12.00
46 Cole Sillinger 5.00 12.00
47 JJ Peterka 6.00 15.00
48 Lukas Reichel 6.00 15.00
51 Brandt Clarke 6.00 15.00
52 Ross Colton 5.00 12.00
53 Brock Nelson 6.00 15.00
54 Cale Makar SP 15.00 40.00
55 Jet Greaves 10.00 25.00
57 Jacob Markstrom 6.00 15.00
60 Fraser Minten 12.00 30.00
61 Ryan Strome 6.00 15.00
62 Andrei Kuzmenko 6.00 15.00
63 Tomas Hertl 6.00 15.00
64 Roope Hintz 8.00 20.00
65 Justin Sourdif 6.00 15.00
66 Josh Morrissey 8.00 20.00
67 Jared McCann SP 5.00 12.00
68 Arber Xhekaj 6.00 15.00
69 Alex Laferriere 10.00 25.00
71 Brady Tkachuk SP 10.00 25.00
72 Drake Batherson 6.00 15.00
73 Roman Josi 6.00 15.00
74 John Gibson 6.00 15.00
75 Jake Livingstone 6.00 15.00
76 Andrei Svechnikov 8.00 20.00
77 Jonatan Berggren 5.00 12.00
78 Samuel Bolduc 6.00 15.00
79 Jonathan Huberdeau 8.00 20.00
80 David Perron 5.00 12.00
81 Chandler Stephenson 5.00 12.00
83 Juuse Saros 8.00 20.00
84 Michael Kesselring 6.00 15.00
86 Connor Zary 12.00 30.00
87 Henry Thrun 6.00 15.00
88 Tyler Toffoli 6.00 15.00
89 Mason McTavish 6.00 15.00
90 Ryan Nugent-Hopkins 8.00 20.00
92 Matthew Kessel 5.00 12.00
93 Isak Rosen 6.00 15.00
94 Cole Perfetti 6.00 15.00
95 Kirill Marchenko 8.00 20.00
97 Gabe Vilardi 6.00 15.00
98 Robert Thomas 6.00 15.00
104 Michael Bunting 6.00 15.00
105 Jiri Patera 10.00 25.00
106 Seth Jarvis 8.00 20.00
107 Bobby McMann 10.00 25.00
109 Brad Marchand 12.00 30.00
221 Connor Bedard 200.00 500.00
222 Luke Hughes SP 20.00 50.00
223 Aidan McDonough 5.00 12.00
224 Yaroslav Askarov 15.00 40.00
225 Tye Kartye 10.00 25.00
226 Simon Edvinsson 12.00 30.00
228 Leo Carlsson 20.00 50.00
229 Ridly Greig 10.00 25.00
230 Brock Faber 15.00 40.00
231 Marco Kasper 15.00 40.00
232 Adam Fantilli 20.00 50.00
233 Luke Evangelista 10.00 25.00
234 Pavel Mintyukov 10.00 25.00
235 Owen Beck 10.00 25.00
236 Logan Cooley 25.00 60.00
237 Matthew Coronato 10.00 25.00
238 Leevi Merilainen 6.00 15.00
239 Devon Levi 15.00 40.00
240 Kevin Korchinski 10.00 25.00
241 Sean Farrell 6.00 15.00
242 Matthew Poitras 12.00 30.00
243 Jakob Pelletier 8.00 20.00
245 Dustin Wolf 20.00 50.00
246 Zach Benson 10.00 25.00
247 William Dufour 5.00 12.00
248 Matt Savoie 12.00 30.00
249 Matthew Knies 25.00 60.00
250 Tyson Foerster 12.00 30.00
257 Martin Brodeur 60.00 150.00
261 Chris Chelios 30.00 80.00

2023-24 Parkhurst Champions Burnin' Rubber

*GOLD/349: .8X TO 2X BASIC
BR1 Nathan MacKinnon 4.00 10.00
BR2 Matty Beniers 1.25 3.00
BR3 Dylan Larkin 1.25 3.00
BR4 J.T. Miller 1.25 3.00
BR5 Connor McDavid 5.00 12.00
BR6 Jordan Kyrou 1.00 2.50
BR7 Mathew Barzal 1.25 3.00
BR8 Peyton Krebs .75 2.00
BR9 Kevin Fiala .75 2.00
BR10 Cale Makar 2.50 6.00
BR11 Alex Tuch 1.00 2.50
BR12 Alex DeBrincat 1.25 3.00
BR13 Tim Stutzle 1.25 3.00
BR14 Dylan Cozens 1.00 2.50
BR15 Jack Eichel 1.50 4.00
BR16 Shane Pinto .75 2.00
BR17 Johnny Gaudreau 1.50 4.00
BR18 Kyle Connor 1.50 4.00
BR19 Jordan Eberle 1.00 2.50
BR20 Matthew Tkachuk 2.00 5.00
BR21 Nikita Kucherov 2.00 5.00
BR22 Andrei Svechnikov 1.25 3.00
BR23 Mitch Marner 1.50 4.00
BR24 Kirill Kaprizov 3.00 8.00
BR25 Quinn Hughes 2.50 6.00
BR26 Taylor Raddysh .75 2.00
BR27 Cole Perfetti 1.00 2.50
BR28 Jonathan Marchessault 1.25 3.00
BR29 Wyatt Johnston 2.00 5.00
BR30 Sidney Crosby 4.00 10.00

2023-24 Parkhurst Champions Daddy-O Flows

*GOLD/349: .5X TO 1.2X BASIC
DF1 Jack Hughes 4.00 10.00
DF2 Mika Zibanejad 2.00 5.00
DF3 Owen Power 1.50 4.00
DF4 Mason McTavish 1.50 4.00
DF5 Clayton Keller 2.00 5.00
DF6 Brandon Tanev 1.25 3.00
DF7 William Nylander 3.00 8.00
DF8 Kyle Connor 2.50 6.00
DF9 Brent Burns 1.50 4.00
DF10 Arber Xhekaj 1.50 4.00
DF11 Kris Letang 2.00 5.00
DF12 Blake Coleman 1.25 3.00
DF13 Alex Tuch 1.50 4.00
DF14 Robert Thomas 1.50 4.00
DF15 William Karlsson 2.00 5.00
DF16 Joel Eriksson Ek 1.25 3.00
DF17 Johnny Gaudreau 2.50 6.00
DF18 Tyler Bertuzzi 1.25 3.00
DF19 Tyler Toffoli 1.50 4.00
DF20 Jaromir Jagr 5.00 12.00

2023-24 Parkhurst Champions Daddy-O Flows Autographs

DF1 Jack Hughes 40.00 100.00
DF3 Owen Power 15.00 40.00
DF4 Mason McTavish 15.00 40.00
DF13 Alex Tuch 15.00 40.00
DF14 Robert Thomas 15.00 40.00
DF15 William Karlsson 20.00 50.00
DF16 Joel Eriksson Ek 12.00 30.00
DF19 Tyler Toffoli 15.00 40.00

2023-24 Parkhurst Champions Goal Driven

*GOLD/349: .6X TO 1.5X BASIC
GD1 Auston Matthews 4.00 10.00
GD2 Bo Horvat 1.25 3.00
GD3 Sidney Crosby 4.00 10.00
GD4 Jack Hughes 2.50 6.00
GD5 Steven Stamkos 2.00 5.00
GD6 Matty Beniers 1.25 3.00
GD7 Alex Ovechkin 4.00 10.00
GD8 Bowen Byram 1.25 3.00
GD9 Evan Bouchard 1.25 3.00
GD10 Chandler Stephenson .75 2.00
GD11 Mark Stone 1.25 3.00
GD12 Leon Draisaitl 3.00 8.00
GD13 Seth Jarvis 1.25 3.00
GD14 Jamie Drysdale .75 2.00
GD15 Cale Makar 2.50 6.00
GD16 Colton Parayko .75 2.00
GD17 David Pastrnak 2.50 6.00
GD18 Roope Hintz 1.25 3.00
GD19 Adam Fox 1.25 3.00
GD20 Aaron Ekblad 1.25 3.00
GD21 Jonathan Huberdeau 1.25 3.00
GD22 Juraj Slafkovsky 2.00 5.00
GD23 Timo Meier 1.00 2.50
GD24 Mikko Rantanen 2.50 6.00
GD25 David Perron .75 2.00
GD26 Dylan Guenther 1.25 3.00
GD27 Quinn Hughes 2.50 6.00
GD28 Rasmus Dahlin 1.25 3.00
GD29 Moritz Seider 1.25 3.00
GD30 Filip Gustavsson 1.00 2.50
GD31 Evgeny Kuznetsov 1.25 3.00
GD32 Tage Thompson 1.25 3.00
GD33 Anze Kopitar 1.50 4.00
GD34 Andrei Vasilevskiy 1.50 4.00
GD35 Connor McDavid 5.00 12.00

2023-24 Parkhurst Champions Goal Driven Autographs

GD8 Bowen Byram 12.00 30.00
GD10 Chandler Stephenson 8.00 20.00
GD11 Mark Stone 12.00 30.00
GD13 Seth Jarvis 12.00 30.00
GD16 Colton Parayko 8.00 20.00
GD18 Roope Hintz 12.00 30.00
GD21 Jonathan Huberdeau 12.00 30.00

GD25 David Perron 8.00 20.00
GD26 Dylan Guenther 12.00 30.00
GD30 Filip Gustavsson 10.00 25.00
GD32 Tage Thompson 12.00 30.00
GD34 Andrei Vasilevskiy SP 30.00 80.00

2023-24 Parkhurst Champions Jerseys

*PATCH/25: 1.2X TO 3X BASIC
1 Connor McDavid 12.00 30.00
2 Dylan Cozens 2.50 6.00
3 Miro Heiskanen 3.00 8.00
4 Joe Pavelski 3.00 8.00
5 Mika Zibanejad 3.00 8.00
6 Aleksander Barkov 4.00 10.00
7 Tim Stutzle 3.00 8.00
8 Owen Power 2.50 6.00
9 Matt Boldy 4.00 10.00
10 Ivan Miroshnichenko 4.00 10.00
11 Adam Fox 3.00 8.00
12 Jake Oettinger 4.00 10.00
13 Artemi Panarin 5.00 12.00
14 William Eklund 3.00 8.00
15 Filip Gustavsson 2.50 6.00
16 Simon Nemec 5.00 12.00
17 Tristen Robins 2.50 6.00
18 Zach Hyman 4.00 10.00
19 Mikko Rantanen 6.00 15.00
20 Dylan Guenther 3.00 8.00
21 Jamie Drysdale 2.00 5.00
22 Kent Johnson 2.50 6.00
23 Mark Stone 3.00 8.00
25 Alex Tuch 2.50 6.00
26 Bo Horvat 3.00 8.00
27 Matthew Tkachuk 5.00 12.00
28 J.T. Miller 3.00 8.00
29 Alex Newhook 2.00 5.00
30 Bowen Byram 3.00 8.00
31 Colton Parayko 2.00 5.00
32 Philipp Grubauer 2.50 6.00
34 Leon Draisaitl 8.00 20.00
35 Tage Thompson 3.00 8.00
36 Jonathan Marchessault 3.00 8.00
37 John Beecher 5.00 12.00
38 Nick Suzuki 5.00 12.00
39 Nico Hischier 4.00 10.00
40 Ryan O'Reilly 2.50 6.00
41 Cole McWard 2.50 6.00
42 John Tavares 4.00 10.00
43 Lukas Rousek 2.50 6.00
44 Mario Ferraro 1.50 4.00
45 K'Andre Miller 2.00 5.00
46 Cole Sillinger 2.00 5.00
47 JJ Peterka 2.50 6.00
50 Hunter McKown 2.50 6.00
53 Brock Nelson 2.50 6.00
54 Cale Makar 6.00 15.00
55 Jet Greaves 4.00 10.00
56 Auston Matthews 10.00 25.00
57 Jacob Markstrom 2.50 6.00
58 Clayton Keller 3.00 8.00
59 Timo Meier 2.50 6.00
60 Fraser Minten 5.00 12.00
61 Ryan Strome 2.50 6.00
62 Andrei Kuzmenko 2.50 6.00
63 Tomas Hertl 2.50 6.00
64 Roope Hintz 3.00 8.00
65 Justin Sourdif 2.50 6.00
66 Josh Morrissey 3.00 8.00
67 Jared McCann 2.00 5.00
69 Alex Laferriere 4.00 10.00
71 Brady Tkachuk 4.00 10.00
72 Drake Batherson 2.50 6.00
73 Roman Josi 2.50 6.00
74 John Gibson 2.50 6.00
75 Jake Livingstone 2.50 6.00
76 Andrei Svechnikov 3.00 8.00
78 Samuel Bolduc 2.50 6.00
79 Jonathan Huberdeau 3.00 8.00
80 David Perron 2.00 5.00
81 Chandler Stephenson 2.00 5.00
82 Nikolaj Ehlers 2.50 6.00
83 Juuso Parssinen 3.00 8.00
84 Michael Kesselring 2.50 6.00
85 Bryan Rust 2.50 6.00
86 Connor Zary 5.00 12.00
87 Henry Thrun 2.50 6.00
88 Tyler Toffoli 2.50 6.00
89 Mason McTavish 2.50 6.00
90 Ryan Nugent-Hopkins 3.00 8.00
91 Mats Zuccarello 2.50 6.00
92 Matthew Kessel 2.00 5.00
93 Isak Rosen 2.50 6.00
94 Cole Perfetti 2.50 6.00
95 Kirill Marchenko 3.00 8.00
96 Blake Coleman 2.00 5.00
97 Gabe Vilardi 2.50 6.00
98 Robert Thomas 2.50 6.00
99 Brent Burns 2.50 6.00
100 Sebastian Aho 4.00 10.00
101 Sidney Crosby 10.00 25.00
102 Darcy Kuemper 2.50 6.00
103 Noah Dobson 3.00 8.00
104 Michael Bunting 2.50 6.00
105 Jiri Patera 4.00 10.00
106 Seth Jarvis 3.00 8.00
107 Bobby McMann 4.00 10.00
109 Brad Marchand 5.00 12.00
110 Trevor Zegras 2.50 6.00
222 Luke Hughes 8.00 20.00
223 Aidan McDonough 2.00 5.00
224 Yaroslav Askarov 6.00 15.00
225 Tye Kartye 4.00 10.00
226 Simon Edvinsson 5.00 12.00
227 Will Cuylle 4.00 10.00
228 Leo Carlsson 8.00 20.00
229 Ridly Greig 4.00 10.00
230 Brock Faber 6.00 15.00
231 Marco Kasper 6.00 15.00
232 Adam Fantilli 8.00 20.00
233 Luke Evangelista 4.00 10.00
234 Pavel Mintyukov 4.00 10.00
235 Owen Beck 4.00 10.00
236 Logan Cooley 10.00 25.00
237 Matthew Coronato 4.00 10.00
238 Leevi Merilainen 2.50 6.00
239 Devon Levi 6.00 15.00
240 Kevin Korchinski 4.00 10.00
241 Sean Farrell 2.50 6.00
242 Matthew Poitras 5.00 12.00
243 Jakob Pelletier 3.00 8.00
244 Danil Gushchin 2.50 6.00
245 Dustin Wolf 8.00 20.00
246 Zach Benson 4.00 10.00
247 William Dufour 2.00 5.00
248 Matt Savoie 5.00 12.00
249 Matthew Knies 10.00 25.00
250 Tyson Foerster 5.00 12.00
255 Vincent Damphousse 3.00 8.00
257 Martin Brodeur 10.00 25.00
258 Borje Salming 4.00 10.00
259 Brett Hull 8.00 20.00
261 Chris Chelios 4.00 10.00
262 Glenn Hall 4.00 10.00
264 Eric Lindros 6.00 15.00
265 Joe Nieuwendyk 3.00 8.00
266 Marian Hossa 4.00 10.00
268 Mario Lemieux 15.00 40.00
269 Mats Sundin 4.00 10.00
272 Patrick Roy 10.00 25.00
273 Paul Coffey 4.00 10.00
278 Pierre Turgeon 3.00 8.00
279 Tony Esposito 4.00 10.00

2023-24 Parkhurst Champions Legendary Captains

LC1 Connor McDavid 80.00 200.00
LC2 Alex Ovechkin 60.00 150.00
LC3 Sidney Crosby 60.00 150.00
LC4 Patrice Bergeron 20.00 50.00
LC5 Nick Suzuki 30.00 80.00
LC6 Steven Stamkos 30.00 80.00
LC7 Mark Stone 20.00 50.00
LC8 John Tavares 25.00 60.00
LC9 Denis Potvin 15.00 40.00
LC10 Ray Bourque 25.00 60.00
LC11 Steve Yzerman 40.00 100.00
LC12 Joe Sakic 30.00 80.00
LC13 Mark Messier 30.00 80.00
LC14 Mats Sundin 15.00 40.00
LC15 Jean Beliveau 15.00 40.00

2023-24 Parkhurst Champions Premium Relics

1 Connor McDavid AU/25 300.00 800.00
2 Dylan Cozens AU/25 15.00 40.00
4 Joe Pavelski AU/25 20.00 50.00
6 Aleksander Barkov AU/25 25.00 60.00
8 Owen Power AU/25 15.00 40.00
10 Ivan Miroshnichenko AU/35 25.00 60.00
12 Jake Oettinger AU/25 25.00 60.00
15 Filip Gustavsson AU/25 15.00 40.00
17 Tristen Robins AU/35 15.00 40.00
20 Dylan Guenther AU/25 20.00 50.00
23 Mark Stone AU/25 20.00 50.00
25 Alex Tuch AU/25 15.00 40.00
27 Matthew Tkachuk AU/25 30.00 80.00
30 Bowen Byram AU/25 20.00 50.00
31 Colton Parayko AU/25 12.00 30.00
35 Tage Thompson AU/25 20.00 50.00
36 Jonathan Marchessault AU/25 20.00 50.00
37 John Beecher AU/35 30.00 80.00
38 Nick Suzuki AU/25 30.00 80.00
39 Nico Hischier AU/25 25.00 60.00
40 Ryan O'Reilly AU/25 15.00 40.00
41 Cole McWard AU/35 15.00 40.00
43 Lukas Rousek AU/35 12.00 30.00
44 Mario Ferraro AU/25 10.00 25.00
45 K'Andre Miller AU/25 12.00 30.00
46 Cole Sillinger AU/25 12.00 30.00
53 Brock Nelson AU/25 15.00 40.00
55 Jet Greaves AU/35 25.00 60.00
56 Auston Matthews AU/25 200.00 500.00
57 Jacob Markstrom AU/25 15.00 40.00
60 Fraser Minten AU/35 30.00 80.00
61 Ryan Strome AU/25 15.00 40.00
62 Andrei Kuzmenko AU/25 15.00 40.00
63 Tomas Hertl AU/25 15.00 40.00
64 Roope Hintz AU/25 20.00 50.00
65 Justin Sourdif AU/35 15.00 40.00
66 Josh Morrissey AU/25 20.00 50.00
67 Jared McCann AU/25 12.00 30.00
69 Alex Laferriere AU/35 25.00 60.00
71 Brady Tkachuk AU/25 25.00 60.00
74 John Gibson AU/25 15.00 40.00
75 Jake Livingstone AU/35 15.00 40.00
76 Andrei Svechnikov AU/25 20.00 50.00
78 Samuel Bolduc AU/35 15.00 40.00
79 Jonathan Huberdeau AU/25 20.00 50.00
81 Chandler Stephenson AU/25 12.00 30.00
83 Juuse Saros AU/25 20.00 50.00
86 Connor Zary AU/35 30.00 80.00
87 Henry Thrun AU/35 15.00 40.00
89 Mason McTavish AU/25 15.00 40.00
90 Ryan Nugent-Hopkins AU/25 20.00 50.00
92 Matthew Kessel AU/35 12.00 30.00
93 Isak Rosen AU/35 15.00 40.00
94 Cole Perfetti AU/25 15.00 40.00
95 Kirill Marchenko AU/25 20.00 50.00
96 Blake Coleman AU/25 12.00 30.00
98 Robert Thomas AU/25 15.00 40.00
105 Jiri Patera AU/35 25.00 60.00
106 Seth Jarvis AU/25 20.00 50.00
107 Bobby McMann AU/35 25.00 60.00
109 Brad Marchand AU/25 30.00 80.00
221 Connor Bedard AU/35 500.00 1200.00
222 Luke Hughes AU/35 50.00 125.00
223 Aidan McDonough AU/35 12.00 30.00
224 Yaroslav Askarov AU/35 40.00 100.00
225 Tye Kartye AU/35 25.00 60.00
226 Simon Edvinsson AU/35 30.00 80.00
228 Leo Carlsson AU/35 50.00 125.00
229 Ridly Greig AU/35 25.00 60.00
230 Brock Faber AU/35 40.00 100.00
231 Marco Kasper AU/35 40.00 100.00
232 Adam Fantilli AU/35 50.00 125.00
233 Luke Evangelista AU/35 25.00 60.00
234 Pavel Mintyukov AU/35 25.00 60.00
235 Owen Beck AU/35 25.00 60.00
236 Logan Cooley AU/35 50.00 125.00
237 Matthew Coronato AU/35 25.00 60.00
238 Leevi Merilainen AU/35 15.00 40.00
239 Devon Levi AU/35 40.00 100.00
240 Kevin Korchinski AU/35 25.00 60.00
241 Sean Farrell AU/35 15.00 40.00
242 Matthew Poitras AU/35 30.00 80.00
243 Jakob Pelletier AU/35 20.00 50.00
245 Dustin Wolf AU/35 50.00 125.00
246 Zach Benson AU/35 25.00 60.00
247 William Dufour AU/35 12.00 30.00
248 Matt Savoie AU/35 30.00 80.00
249 Matthew Knies AU/35 60.00 150.00
250 Tyson Foerster AU/35 30.00 80.00

2023-24 Parkhurst Champions Wire Images

*GOLD/349: .5X TO 1.2X BASIC
WI1 Connor McDavid 5.00 12.00
WI2 Luke Hughes 3.00 8.00
WI3 Kirill Kaprizov 3.00 8.00
WI4 Juuse Saros 1.25 3.00
WI5 Brad Marchand 2.00 5.00
WI6 Auston Matthews 4.00 10.00
WI7 Brady Tkachuk 1.50 4.00
WI8 Elias Pettersson 1.50 4.00
WI9 Ilya Sorokin 1.50 4.00
WI10 Kent Johnson 1.00 2.50
WI11 Jason Robertson 1.50 4.00
WI12 Dawson Mercer 1.25 3.00
WI13 Devon Levi 2.50 6.00
WI14 Matthew Knies 4.00 10.00
WI15 Leon Draisaitl 3.00 8.00

2024-25 Parkhurst Champions

1 Jeremy Swayman .75 2.00
2 Dmitri Voronkov .30 .75
3 Luke Hughes .75 2.00
4 Tim Stutzle .60 1.50
5 Evan Bouchard .60 1.50
6 Leo Carlsson .75 2.00
7 Brock Faber .60 1.50
8 Roope Hintz .60 1.50
9 Anders Lee .40 1.00
10 Shea Theodore .60 1.50
11 Darren Raddysh .30 .75
12 Matt Boldy .75 2.00
13 Jonatan Berggren .40 1.00
14 Nick Suzuki 1.00 2.50
15 Sam Reinhart 1.00 2.50
16 Alexis Lafreniere .75 2.00
17 Charlie Lindgren .40 1.00
18 Alexandre Texier .30 .75
19 Troy Terry .40 1.00
20 Michael Bunting .50 1.25
21 Devon Toews .40 1.00
22 Matthew Knies 1.00 2.50
23 Kevin Fiala .40 1.00
24 Samuel Ersson .50 1.25
25 Kent Johnson .50 1.25
26 Mason Marchment .40 1.00
27 Arber Xhekaj .50 1.25
28 Nino Niederreiter .30 .75
29 Petr Mrazek .40 1.00
30 Mats Zuccarello .50 1.25
31 Fabian Zetterlund .30 .75
32 Artturi Lehkonen .40 1.00
33 Brandt Clarke .50 1.25
34 Pavel Mintyukov .40 1.00
35 Dylan Holloway .50 1.25
36 John Gibson .50 1.25
37 Andrei Svechnikov .60 1.50
38 Vince Dunn .40 1.00
39 Jacob Middleton .30 .75
40 Martin Necas .75 2.00
41 Connor Hellebuyck 1.00 2.50
42 Zach Benson .40 1.00
43 Nick Foligno .30 .75
44 Anton Lundell .50 1.25
45 Robert Thomas .50 1.25
46 Alex Tuch .50 1.25
47 Connor Zary .50 1.25
48 Kaiden Guhle .50 1.25
49 Joey Daccord .50 1.25
50 Teuvo Teravainen .50 1.25
51 Mikko Rantanen 1.25 3.00
52 Cole Perfetti .50 1.25
53 Boone Jenner .50 1.25
54 Jonathan Quick .60 1.50
55 Kevin Korchinski .40 1.00
56 Matthew Poitras .50 1.25
57 Simon Nemec .60 1.50
58 Tyson Foerster .50 1.25
59 Jake Oettinger .75 2.00
60 Kirill Marchenko .60 1.50
61 Jacob Trouba .40 1.00
62 Andrei Kuzmenko .50 1.25
63 Casey Mittelstadt .50 1.25
64 Thomas Novak .30 .75
65 Travis Sanheim .30 .75
66 Peyton Krebs .40 1.00
67 Andrew Copp .30 .75
68 Kris Letang .60 1.50
69 JJ Peterka .50 1.25
70 Marc-Andre Fleury 1.00 2.50
71 Shane Wright .60 1.50
72 Ryan Strome .50 1.25
73 Ukko-Pekka Luukkonen .40 1.00
74 Stuart Skinner .60 1.50
75 Cole Sillinger .40 1.00
76 Jaccob Slavin .40 1.00
77 Samuel Montembeault .50 1.25
78 William Karlsson .60 1.50
79 Brandon Carlo .40 1.00
80 Samuel Girard .30 .75
81 Colton Parayko .40 1.00
82 Blake Coleman .40 1.00
83 Thomas Harley .50 1.25
84 Thatcher Demko .60 1.50
85 Frank Vatrano .40 1.00
86 Roman Josi .50 1.25
87 Bowen Byram .60 1.50
88 Carter Verhaeghe .50 1.25
89 Seth Jarvis .60 1.50
90 Filip Gustavsson .50 1.25
91 Tristan Jarry .50 1.25
92 Trent Frederic .30 .75
93 Jean-Gabriel Pageau .30 .75
94 Dylan Cozens .50 1.25
95 Miro Heiskanen .60 1.50
96 Drake Batherson .50 1.25
97 Pavel Zacha .40 1.00
98 Trevor Moore .30 .75
99 Adin Hill .50 1.25
100 Jalen Chatfield .30 .75
101 Evander Kane .50 1.25
102 Mika Zibanejad .60 1.50
103 Matty Beniers .60 1.50
104 Rasmus Dahlin .60 1.50
105 Jordan Binnington .75 2.00
106 Drew Doughty .50 1.25
107 Tyler Toffoli .50 1.25
108 Lucas Raymond .75 2.00
109 Brock Nelson .50 1.25
110 Sam Bennett .75 2.00
111 Brayden Point .60 1.50
112 Brent Burns .50 1.25
113 Igor Shesterkin 1.00 2.50
114 Ryan O'Reilly .50 1.25
115 Chandler Stephenson .40 1.00
116 Bryan Rust .50 1.25
117 Aaron Ekblad .60 1.50
118 Claude Giroux .50 1.25
119 Trevor Zegras .50 1.25
120 Jordan Kyrou .50 1.25
121 Brendan Gallagher .50 1.25
122 Patrick Kane 1.00 2.50
123 William Nylander 1.00 2.50
124 Joel Eriksson Ek .40 1.00
125 Taylor Hall .50 1.25
126 Sergei Bobrovsky .75 2.00
127 Ryan Nugent-Hopkins .60 1.50
128 Ilya Sorokin .75 2.00
129 Erik Karlsson .60 1.50
130 Brandon Hagel .40 1.00
131 Vincent Trocheck .50 1.25
132 Tomas Hertl .50 1.25
133 Matt Duchene .50 1.25
134 Josh Morrissey .60 1.50
135 Darcy Kuemper .50 1.25
136 J.T. Miller .60 1.50
137 Owen Power .50 1.25
138 Ondrej Palat .40 1.00
139 Jake Neighbours .50 1.25
140 Mark Stone .60 1.50
141 Evgeni Malkin 1.00 2.50
142 Phillip Danault .50 1.25
143 Logan Cooley .75 2.00
144 Frederik Andersen .60 1.50
145 Chris Kreider .60 1.50
146 Juraj Slafkovsky 1.00 2.50
147 Timo Meier .50 1.25
148 Tyler Seguin .60 1.50
149 Josh Norris .50 1.25
150 Dustin Wolf .75 2.00
151 Brock Boeser .60 1.50
152 Jonathan Marchessault .60 1.50
153 Thomas Chabot .50 1.25
154 Charlie McAvoy .60 1.50
155 Noah Dobson .60 1.50
156 Evan Rodrigues .40 1.00
157 Shane Pinto .40 1.00
158 Elvis Merzlikins .50 1.25
159 John Tavares .75 2.00
160 Steven Stamkos 1.00 2.50
161 Alex Vlasic .30 .75
162 Nico Hischier .75 2.00
163 Pierre-Luc Dubois .40 1.00
164 Owen Tippett .30 .75
165 Jamie Benn .50 1.25
166 Dougie Hamilton .40 1.00
167 Philipp Grubauer .50 1.25
168 Seth Jarvis .60 1.50
169 Alex Newhook .40 1.00
170 Elias Lindholm .50 1.25
171 Zach Hyman .75 2.00
172 Jake Sanderson .60 1.50
173 Valeri Nichushkin .50 1.25
174 Andrei Vasilevskiy .75 2.00
175 Tom Wilson .50 1.25
176 Juuse Saros .60 1.50
177 Dylan Strome .60 1.50
178 Nazem Kadri .60 1.50
179 Logan Couture .60 1.50
180 Charlie Coyle .50 1.25
181 Jakob Chychrun .50 1.25
182 Quinton Byfield .60 1.50
183 Mark Scheifele .75 2.00
184 Christopher Tanev .30 .75
185 Adam Fox .60 1.50
186 Linus Ullmark .50 1.25
187 Alexandar Georgiev .50 1.25
188 Marco Rossi .60 1.50
189 K'Andre Miller .40 1.00
190 Jesper Bratt .50 1.25
191 Jake Guentzel .75 2.00
192 Victor Hedman .60 1.50
193 Brandon Montour .60 1.50
194 Alexander Holtz .50 1.25
195 Moritz Seider .60 1.50
196 Morgan Rielly .50 1.25
197 Luke Evangelista .40 1.00
198 Jamie Drysdale .40 1.00
199 Adrian Kempe .50 1.25
200 Bo Horvat .60 1.50
201 Jason Robertson .75 2.00
202 Jared McCann .40 1.00
203 Aleksander Barkov .75 2.00
204 Anze Kopitar .75 2.00
205 Jack Eichel .75 2.00
206 Connor Bedard 1.50 4.00
207 Brady Tkachuk .75 2.00
208 Alex DeBrincat .60 1.50
209 Leon Draisaitl 1.50 4.00
210 Auston Matthews 2.00 5.00
211 Tage Thompson .60 1.50
212 Quinn Hughes 1.25 3.00
213 Matthew Tkachuk 1.00 2.50
214 Artemi Panarin 1.00 2.50
215 Alex Ovechkin 2.00 5.00
216 MacKenzie Weegar .40 1.00
217 Cole Caufield 1.00 2.50
218 Mathew Barzal .60 1.50
219 Brad Marchand 1.00 2.50
220 Nathan MacKinnon 2.00 5.00
221 Sidney Crosby 2.00 5.00
222 Elias Pettersson .75 2.00
223 David Pastrnak 1.25 3.00
224 Filip Forsberg .75 2.00
225 Nikita Kucherov 1.00 2.50
226 Jacob Markstrom .50 1.25
227 Kyle Connor .75 2.00
228 Dylan Larkin .60 1.50
229 Adam Fantilli .75 2.00
230 Kirill Kaprizov 1.50 4.00
231 Clayton Keller .60 1.50
232 Sebastian Aho .75 2.00
233 William Eklund .60 1.50
234 Jack Hughes 1.25 3.00
235 Cale Makar 1.25 3.00
236 Travis Konecny .50 1.25
237 Wyatt Johnston 1.00 2.50
238 Mason McTavish .50 1.25
239 Mitch Marner .75 2.00
240 Connor McDavid 2.50 6.00
241 Cutter Gauthier RC 2.00 5.00
242 Justin Brazeau RC .75 2.00
243 Bradly Nadeau RC 1.25 3.00
244 Seamus Casey RC 1.00 2.50
245 Macklin Celebrini RC 8.00 20.00
246 Lane Hutson RC 6.00 15.00
247 Scott Morrow RC 1.00 2.50
248 Shakir Mukhamadullin RC 1.00 2.50
249 Samuel Honzek RC .75 2.00
250 Sam Colangelo RC .75 2.00
251 Brennan Othmann RC 1.25 3.00
252 Luca Del Bel Belluz RC .75 2.00
253 Marat Khusnutdinov RC .75 2.00
254 Mavrik Bourque RC 1.50 4.00
255 Will Smith RC 2.50 6.00
256 Jesper Wallstedt RC 2.00 5.00
257 Brad Lambert RC 1.00 2.50
258 Adam Klapka RC .75 2.00
259 Ethan Del Mastro RC .75 2.00
260 Matvei Michkov RC 6.00 15.00
261 Zach Dean RC .75 2.00
262 Joshua Roy RC 1.25 3.00
263 Logan Mailloux RC 1.25 3.00
264 Zachary Bolduc RC 1.50 4.00
265 Conor Geekie RC 1.50 4.00
266 Logan Stankoven RC 2.00 5.00
267 Jackson Blake RC 1.50 4.00
268 Josh Doan RC 1.25 3.00
269 Akil Thomas RC .75 2.00
270 Calum Ritchie RC 1.00 2.50
271 Jett Luchanko RC 1.50 4.00
272 Brendan Brisson RC 1.00 2.50
273 Frank Nazar RC 2.50 6.00
274 Olen Zellweger RC 1.50 4.00
275 Rutger McGroarty RC 1.50 4.00
276 Matt Rempe RC 1.50 4.00
277 Liam Ohgren RC 1.50 4.00
278 Gavin Brindley RC .75 2.00
279 Phil Kemp RC .75 2.00
280 Ivan Fedotov RC 1.50 4.00
281 Patrick Roy 3.00 8.00
282 Joe Thornton 2.00 5.00
283 Mark Messier 2.50 6.00
284 Lanny McDonald 1.25 3.00
285 Howie Morenz 1.25 3.00
286 Brian Leetch 1.00 2.50
287 Gordie Howe 4.00 10.00
288 Ron Hextall 1.25 3.00
289 Marian Hossa 1.25 3.00
290 Paul Coffey 1.25 3.00
291 Jean Ratelle 1.00 2.50
292 Mike Modano 2.00 5.00
293 Bobby Orr 5.00 12.00
294 Mario Lemieux 5.00 12.00
295 Rob Blake 1.25 3.00
296 Steve Yzerman 3.00 8.00
297 Frank Mahovlich 1.25 3.00
298 Martin Brodeur 3.00 8.00
299 Wayne Gretzky 8.00 20.00
300 Mike Richter 1.25 3.00

2024-25 Parkhurst Champions Baby Blue Border

*BLUE/25: 3X TO 8X BASIC
*BLUE/25: 2.5X TO 6X BASIC

2024-25 Parkhurst Champions Blank Back

*BLANK: 1.2X TO 3X BASIC
*BLANK LEG: 1X TO 2.5X BASIC
245 Macklin Celebrini 40.00 100.00
246 Lane Hutson 40.00 100.00
255 Will Smith 25.00 60.00
260 Matvei Michkov 40.00 100.00

2024-25 Parkhurst Champions Rainbow Foil Board

*RAINBOW: .6X TO 1.5X BASIC
255 Will Smith 10.00 25.00
260 Matvei Michkov 12.00 30.00

2024-25 Parkhurst Champions Shell Pink Border

*PINK/99: 1.2X TO 3X BASIC
*PINK RC/LEG: 1X TO 2.5X BASIC
245 Macklin Celebrini 80.00 200.00
246 Lane Hutson 50.00 125.00
255 Will Smith 20.00 50.00
260 Matvei Michkov 50.00 125.00

2024-25 Parkhurst Champions Silver

*SILVER: .5X TO 1.2X BASIC

2024-25 Parkhurst Champions '53-54 Retros

*GUM BACK: .5X TO 1.2X BASIC
1 Curtis Joseph 2.50 6.00
2 Bryan Trottier 2.00 5.00
3 Auston Matthews 8.00 20.00
4 Tiger Williams 1.25 3.00
5 Kevin Fiala 1.50 4.00
6 Owen Tippett 1.25 3.00
7 Macklin Celebrini 20.00 60.00
8 Cale Makar 5.00 12.00
9 Olen Zellweger 4.00 10.00
10 Sergei Bobrovsky 3.00 8.00
11 Ted Lindsay 2.00 5.00
12 Mitch Marner 3.00 8.00
13 Kent Johnson 2.00 5.00
14 Filip Forsberg 3.00 8.00
15 Serge Savard 2.00 5.00
16 Clayton Keller 2.50 6.00
17 Patrick Kane 4.00 10.00
18 Cutter Gauthier 5.00 12.00
19 Quinn Hughes 5.00 12.00
20 Sebastian Aho 3.00 8.00
21 Mathew Barzal 2.50 6.00
22 Conor Geekie 4.00 10.00
23 Carter Verhaeghe 2.00 5.00
24 Tim Stutzle 2.50 6.00
25 Guy Lafleur 2.50 6.00
26 Rasmus Dahlin 2.50 6.00
27 Zach Dean 2.00 5.00
28 Samuel Honzek 2.00 5.00
29 Nathan MacKinnon 8.00 20.00
30 C.Caufield/N.Suzuki 4.00 10.00
31 Leon Draisaitl 6.00 15.00
32 Brady Tkachuk 3.00 8.00
33 Frank Nazar 6.00 15.00
34 Nazem Kadri 2.50 6.00
35 Mikael Granlund 1.50 4.00
36 Teemu Selanne 4.00 10.00
37 Artemi Panarin 4.00 10.00
38 Connor Bedard 6.00 15.00
39 Juraj Slafkovsky 4.00 10.00
40 Logan Stankoven 5.00 12.00
41 Luke Hughes 3.00 8.00
42 Lane Hutson 15.00 40.00
43 Bradly Nadeau 3.00 8.00
44 Juuse Saros 2.50 6.00
45 Willie O'Ree 2.50 6.00
46 Matty Beniers 2.50 6.00
47 Jett Luchanko 4.00 10.00
48 Jason Robertson 3.00 8.00
49 Matvei Michkov 12.00 30.00
50 Kirill Kaprizov 6.00 15.00
51 Travis Konecny 2.00 5.00
52 Josh Doan 3.00 8.00
53 Tage Thompson 2.50 6.00
54 Terry Sawchuk 2.00 5.00
55 Jared McCann 1.50 4.00
56 Alex Ovechkin 8.00 20.00
57 Zachary Bolduc 4.00 10.00
58 Jack Eichel 3.00 8.00
59 Rutger McGroarty 4.00 10.00
60 Kris Letang 2.50 6.00
61 Bobby Hull 4.00 10.00
62 Sid Abel 2.00 5.00
63 Blake Coleman 1.50 4.00
64 Robert Thomas 2.00 5.00
65 Mats Sundin 2.00 5.00
66 Adam Fantilli 3.00 8.00
67 John Carlson 2.00 5.00
68 Jean Beliveau 2.00 5.00
69 Logan Mailloux 3.00 8.00
70 Stan Mikita 2.00 5.00
71 Nikita Kucherov 4.00 10.00
72 Liam Ohgren 4.00 10.00
73 Igor Shesterkin 4.00 10.00
74 Johnny Bower 2.00 5.00
75 Josh Morrissey 2.50 6.00
76 Andrei Vasilevskiy 3.00 8.00
77 Rogie Vachon 2.00 5.00
78 Seamus Casey 2.50 6.00
79 Sidney Crosby 8.00 20.00
80 Will Smith 6.00 15.00
81 Mason McTavish 2.00 5.00
82 Ed Belfour 2.00 5.00
83 Charlie Conacher 2.00 5.00
84 Mark Stone 2.50 6.00
85 Wayne Gretzky 12.00 30.00
86 Jack Hughes 5.00 12.00
87 Mavrik Bourque 4.00 10.00
88 David Pastrnak 5.00 12.00
89 Darryl Sittler 2.00 5.00
90 Connor McDavid 10.00 25.00

2024-25 Parkhurst Champions '53-54 Retros Rainbow Foil

*RAINBOW/53: 1.2X TO 3X BASIC
80 Will Smith 40.00 100.00

2024-25 Parkhurst Champions '53-54 Retros Autographs

2 Bryan Trottier/25 15.00 40.00
9 Olen Zellweger/25 30.00 80.00
18 Cutter Gauthier/25 40.00 100.00
23 Carter Verhaeghe/25 15.00 40.00
24 Tim Stutzle/25 20.00 50.00
27 Zach Dean/25 15.00 40.00
28 Samuel Honzek/25 15.00 40.00
32 Brady Tkachuk/25 25.00 60.00
33 Frank Nazar/25 50.00 125.00
35 Mikael Granlund/25 12.00 30.00
41 Luke Hughes/25 25.00 60.00
44 Juuse Saros/25 20.00 50.00
51 Travis Konecny/25 15.00 40.00
53 Tage Thompson/25 20.00 50.00
55 Jared McCann/25 12.00 30.00
57 Zachary Bolduc/25 30.00 80.00
60 Kris Letang/25 20.00 50.00
63 Blake Coleman/25 12.00 30.00
64 Robert Thomas/25 15.00 40.00
69 Logan Mailloux/25 25.00 60.00
72 Liam Ohgren/25 30.00 80.00
81 Mason McTavish/25 15.00 40.00
87 Mavrik Bourque/25 30.00 80.00

2024-25 Parkhurst Champions Atom Squad

AS1 Connor Bedard 3.00 8.00
AS2 Connor McDavid 5.00 12.00
AS3 Nikita Kucherov 2.00 5.00
AS4 Alex Ovechkin 4.00 10.00
AS5 Sidney Crosby 4.00 10.00
AS6 Nathan MacKinnon 4.00 10.00
AS7 David Pastrnak 2.50 6.00
AS8 Kirill Kaprizov 3.00 8.00
AS9 Quinn Hughes 2.50 6.00
AS10 Jack Hughes 2.50 6.00

2024-25 Parkhurst Champions Autographs

6 Leo Carlsson 12.00 30.00
9 Anders Lee 6.00 15.00
11 Darren Raddysh 5.00 12.00
13 Jonatan Berggren 6.00 15.00
15 Sam Reinhart SP 15.00 40.00
17 Charlie Lindgren 6.00 15.00
18 Alexandre Texier 5.00 12.00
21 Devon Toews 6.00 15.00
28 Nino Niederreiter 5.00 12.00
29 Petr Mrazek 6.00 15.00
36 John Gibson 8.00 20.00
38 Vince Dunn 6.00 15.00
39 Jacob Middleton 5.00 12.00
40 Martin Necas 12.00 30.00
42 Zach Benson 6.00 15.00
43 Nick Foligno 5.00 12.00
45 Robert Thomas SP 12.00 30.00
46 Alex Tuch 8.00 20.00
49 Joey Daccord 8.00 20.00
50 Teuvo Teravainen 8.00 20.00
52 Cole Perfetti 8.00 20.00
56 Matthew Poitras 8.00 20.00
60 Kirill Marchenko 10.00 25.00
61 Jacob Trouba 5.00 12.00
63 Casey Mittelstadt 8.00 20.00
65 Travis Sanheim 5.00 12.00
66 Peyton Krebs 6.00 15.00
67 Andrew Copp 5.00 12.00
68 Kris Letang SP 10.00 25.00
70 Marc-Andre Fleury SP 15.00 40.00
71 Shane Wright SP 10.00 25.00
72 Ryan Strome 8.00 20.00
73 Ukko-Pekka Luukkonen 6.00 15.00
75 Cole Sillinger 6.00 15.00
76 Jaccob Slavin 6.00 15.00
78 William Karlsson 10.00 25.00
80 Samuel Girard 5.00 12.00
81 Colton Parayko 6.00 15.00
82 Blake Coleman 6.00 15.00
83 Thomas Harley 8.00 20.00
85 Frank Vatrano 6.00 15.00
88 Carter Verhaeghe 8.00 20.00
89 Seth Jarvis SP 10.00 25.00
90 Filip Gustavsson 8.00 20.00
91 Tristan Jarry 8.00 20.00
92 Trent Frederic 5.00 12.00
93 Jean-Gabriel Pageau 5.00 12.00
96 Drake Batherson 8.00 20.00
97 Pavel Zacha 6.00 15.00
98 Trevor Moore 5.00 12.00
207 Brady Tkachuk 12.00 30.00
214 Artemi Panarin 15.00 40.00
221 Sidney Crosby SP 150.00 400.00
222 Elias Pettersson 12.00 30.00
225 Nikita Kucherov 20.00 50.00
226 Jacob Markstrom 8.00 20.00
227 Kyle Connor 12.00 30.00
230 Kirill Kaprizov 50.00 125.00
233 William Eklund 10.00 25.00
235 Cale Makar SP 50.00 125.00
236 Travis Konecny 8.00 20.00
238 Mason McTavish 8.00 20.00
241 Cutter Gauthier 20.00 50.00
242 Justin Brazeau 8.00 20.00
245 Macklin Celebrini SP 250.00 600.00
246 Lane Hutson 125.00 300.00
248 Shakir Mukhamadullin 10.00 25.00
249 Samuel Honzek 8.00 20.00
250 Sam Colangelo 8.00 20.00
254 Mavrik Bourque 15.00 40.00
255 Will Smith 80.00 200.00
256 Jesper Wallstedt 20.00 50.00
258 Adam Klapka 8.00 20.00
260 Matvei Michkov 80.00 200.00
263 Logan Mailloux 12.00 30.00
266 Logan Stankoven 20.00 50.00
273 Frank Nazar 40.00 100.00
274 Olen Zellweger 15.00 40.00
276 Matt Rempe 15.00 40.00
277 Liam Ohgren 15.00 40.00
279 Phil Kemp 8.00 20.00
282 Joe Thornton 12.00 30.00
284 Lanny McDonald 8.00 20.00
286 Brian Leetch 6.00 15.00
288 Ron Hextall 8.00 20.00
289 Marian Hossa SP 8.00 20.00
291 Jean Ratelle 6.00 15.00
292 Mike Modano SP 12.00 30.00
295 Rob Blake 8.00 20.00

2024-25 Parkhurst Champions Autographs Blue

*BLUE: .6X TO 1.5X BASIC
14 Nick Suzuki/25 40.00 100.00
15 Sam Reinhart/25 40.00 100.00
17 Charlie Lindgren/49 15.00 40.00
41 Connor Hellebuyck/25 40.00 100.00
49 Joey Daccord/49 15.00 40.00

2024-25 Parkhurst Champions Crease Lightning

CL1 Jeremy Swayman 2.50 6.00
CL2 Dominik Hasek 2.50 6.00
CL3 Igor Shesterkin 3.00 8.00
CL4 Jacob Markstrom 1.50 4.00
CL5 Darcy Kuemper 1.50 4.00
CL6 Grant Fuhr 2.50 6.00
CL7 Sergei Bobrovsky 2.50 6.00
CL8 Terry Sawchuk 1.50 4.00
CL9 Connor Hellebuyck 3.00 8.00
CL10 Samuel Montembeault 1.50 4.00
CL11 Jake Oettinger 2.50 6.00
CL12 Ukko-Pekka Luukkonen 1.25 3.00
CL13 Thatcher Demko 2.00 5.00
CL14 Bernie Parent 2.00 5.00
CL15 Juuse Saros 2.00 5.00
CL16 Linus Ullmark 1.50 4.00
CL17 Ilya Sorokin 2.50 6.00
CL18 Tony Esposito 1.50 4.00
CL19 Alexandar Georgiev 1.50 4.00
CL20 Adin Hill 1.50 4.00
CL21 John Gibson 1.50 4.00
CL22 Andrei Vasilevskiy 2.50 6.00
CL23 Martin Brodeur 4.00 10.00
CL24 Marc-Andre Fleury 3.00 8.00
CL25 Charlie Lindgren 1.25 3.00
CL26 Jacques Plante 1.50 4.00
CL27 Jordan Binnington 2.50 6.00
CL28 Jonathan Quick 2.00 5.00
CL29 Ed Belfour 1.50 4.00
CL30 Stuart Skinner 2.00 5.00

2024-25 Parkhurst Champions In Full Color Lenticulars

FC1 David Pastrnak 20.00 50.00
FC2 Nathan MacKinnon 30.00 80.00
FC3 Nikita Kucherov 15.00 40.00
FC4 Artemi Panarin 15.00 40.00
FC5 Auston Matthews 30.00 80.00
FC6 Quinn Hughes 20.00 50.00

FC7 Nick Suzuki 15.00 40.00
FC8 Connor McDavid 40.00 100.00
FC9 Jack Eichel 12.00 30.00
FC10 Sebastian Aho 12.00 30.00
FC11 Elias Pettersson 12.00 30.00
FC12 Aleksander Barkov 12.00 30.00
FC13 Leon Draisaitl 25.00 60.00
FC14 Marc-Andre Fleury 15.00 40.00
FC15 Alex Ovechkin 30.00 80.00
FC16 Sidney Crosby 30.00 80.00
FC17 Cale Makar 20.00 50.00
FC18 Jack Hughes 20.00 50.00
FC19 Connor Bedard 25.00 60.00
FC20 Andrei Vasilevskiy 12.00 30.00

2024-25 Parkhurst Champions Jerseys

201 Jason Robertson 5.00 12.00
202 Jared McCann 2.50 6.00
203 Aleksander Barkov 5.00 12.00
204 Anze Kopitar 5.00 12.00
205 Jack Eichel 5.00 12.00
206 Connor Bedard 10.00 25.00
207 Brady Tkachuk 5.00 12.00
208 Alex DeBrincat 4.00 10.00
209 Leon Draisaitl 10.00 25.00
210 Auston Matthews 12.00 30.00
211 Tage Thompson 4.00 10.00
212 Quinn Hughes 8.00 20.00
213 Matthew Tkachuk 6.00 15.00
214 Artemi Panarin 6.00 15.00
215 Alex Ovechkin 12.00 30.00
216 MacKenzie Weegar 2.50 6.00
217 Cole Caufield 6.00 15.00
218 Mathew Barzal 4.00 10.00
219 Brad Marchand 6.00 15.00
220 Nathan MacKinnon 12.00 30.00
221 Sidney Crosby 12.00 30.00
222 Elias Pettersson 5.00 12.00
223 David Pastrnak 8.00 20.00
224 Filip Forsberg 5.00 12.00
225 Nikita Kucherov 6.00 15.00
227 Kyle Connor 5.00 12.00
228 Dylan Larkin 4.00 10.00
229 Adam Fantilli 5.00 12.00
230 Kirill Kaprizov 10.00 25.00
231 Clayton Keller 4.00 10.00
232 Sebastian Aho 5.00 12.00
233 William Eklund 4.00 10.00
234 Jack Hughes 8.00 20.00
235 Cale Makar 8.00 20.00
236 Travis Konecny 3.00 8.00
237 Wyatt Johnston 6.00 15.00
238 Mason McTavish 3.00 8.00
239 Mitch Marner 5.00 12.00
240 Connor McDavid 15.00 40.00
241 Cutter Gauthier 8.00 20.00
242 Justin Brazeau 3.00 8.00
243 Bradly Nadeau 5.00 12.00
244 Seamus Casey 4.00 10.00
245 Macklin Celebrini 15.00 40.00
246 Lane Hutson 15.00 40.00
247 Scott Morrow 4.00 10.00
248 Shakir Mukhamadullin 4.00 10.00
249 Samuel Honzek 3.00 8.00
250 Sam Colangelo 3.00 8.00
251 Brennan Othmann 5.00 12.00
252 Luca Del Bel Belluz 3.00 8.00
254 Mavrik Bourque 6.00 15.00
255 Will Smith 10.00 25.00
256 Jesper Wallstedt 8.00 20.00
258 Adam Klapka 3.00 8.00
259 Ethan Del Mastro 3.00 8.00
260 Matvei Michkov 12.00 30.00
261 Zach Dean 3.00 8.00
262 Joshua Roy 5.00 12.00
263 Logan Mailloux 5.00 12.00
264 Zachary Bolduc 6.00 15.00
265 Conor Geekie 6.00 15.00
266 Logan Stankoven 8.00 20.00
267 Jackson Blake 6.00 15.00
268 Josh Doan 5.00 12.00
269 Akil Thomas 3.00 8.00
272 Brendan Brisson 4.00 10.00
273 Frank Nazar 10.00 25.00
274 Olen Zellweger 6.00 15.00
275 Rutger McGroarty 6.00 15.00
276 Matt Rempe 6.00 15.00
277 Liam Ohgren 6.00 15.00
278 Gavin Brindley 3.00 8.00
279 Phil Kemp 3.00 8.00
280 Ivan Fedotov 6.00 15.00
282 Joe Thornton 5.00 12.00
286 Brian Leetch 2.50 6.00
289 Marian Hossa 3.00 8.00
300 Mike Richter 3.00 8.00

2024-25 Parkhurst Champions Patches

204 Anze Kopitar/25 8.00 20.00
205 Jack Eichel/25 8.00 20.00
207 Brady Tkachuk/25 8.00 20.00
213 Matthew Tkachuk/25 10.00 25.00
214 Artemi Panarin/25 10.00 25.00
217 Cole Caufield/25 10.00 25.00
219 Brad Marchand/25 10.00 25.00
221 Sidney Crosby/25 20.00 50.00
223 David Pastrnak/25 12.00 30.00
224 Filip Forsberg/25 8.00 20.00
227 Kyle Connor/25 8.00 20.00
232 Sebastian Aho/25 8.00 20.00
239 Mitch Marner/25 8.00 20.00
241 Cutter Gauthier AU/25 40.00 100.00
246 Lane Hutson AU/25 250.00 600.00
247 Scott Morrow AU/25 20.00 50.00
248 Shakir Mukhamadullin AU/25 20.00 50.00
249 Samuel Honzek AU/25 15.00 40.00
250 Sam Colangelo AU/25 15.00 40.00
254 Mavrik Bourque AU/25 30.00 80.00
256 Jesper Wallstedt AU/25 40.00 100.00
258 Adam Klapka AU/25 15.00 40.00
261 Zach Dean AU/25 15.00 40.00
263 Logan Mailloux AU/25 25.00 60.00
264 Zachary Bolduc AU/25 30.00 80.00
266 Logan Stankoven AU/25 40.00 100.00
269 Akil Thomas AU/25 15.00 40.00
273 Frank Nazar AU/25 50.00 125.00
274 Olen Zellweger AU/25 30.00 80.00
276 Matt Rempe AU/25 30.00 80.00
277 Liam Ohgren AU/25 30.00 80.00
279 Phil Kemp AU/25 15.00 40.00
280 Ivan Fedotov AU/25 30.00 80.00

2024-25 Parkhurst Champions Retro-Active Lenticulars

RA1 T.Sawchuk/A.Vasilevskiy 20.00 50.00
RA2 J.Plante/M.Fleury 25.00 60.00
RA3 G.Howe/A.Ovechkin 50.00 125.00
RA4 F.Mahovlich/A.Matthews 50.00 125.00
RA5 M.Messier/C.McDavid 50.00 125.00
RA6 T.Lindsay/M.Tkachuk 25.00 60.00
RA7 J.Beliveau/C.Caufield 25.00 60.00
RA8 B.Hull/N.Kucherov 25.00 60.00
RA9 T.Horton/B.Burns 20.00 50.00
RA10 S.Mikita/C.Bedard 30.00 80.00
RA11 B.Orr/C.Makar 50.00 125.00
RA12 M.Lemieux/S.Crosby 50.00 125.00

2024-25 Parkhurst Champions Saturday Night Standouts

SS1 Nick Suzuki 2.00 5.00
SS2 Artemi Panarin 2.00 5.00
SS3 Auston Matthews 4.00 10.00
SS4 Bo Horvat 1.25 3.00
SS5 Victor Hedman 1.25 3.00
SS6 Brock Boeser 1.25 3.00
SS7 Cale Makar 2.50 6.00
SS8 Kyle Connor 1.50 4.00
SS9 Dylan Larkin 1.25 3.00
SS10 Elias Pettersson 1.50 4.00
SS11 Erik Karlsson 1.25 3.00
SS12 Evan Bouchard 1.25 3.00
SS13 Jason Robertson 1.50 4.00
SS14 Cole Caufield 2.00 5.00
SS15 Steven Stamkos 2.00 5.00
SS16 Lucas Raymond 1.50 4.00
SS17 Matt Boldy 1.50 4.00
SS18 Matthew Tkachuk 2.00 5.00
SS19 Nathan MacKinnon 4.00 10.00
SS20 Alex Ovechkin 4.00 10.00
SS21 Patrick Kane 2.00 5.00
SS22 Sidney Crosby 4.00 10.00
SS23 Leon Draisaitl 3.00 8.00
SS24 Brad Marchand 2.00 5.00
SS25 William Nylander 2.00 5.00

2024-25 Parkhurst Champions Shake Rattle and Roll

SRR1 Jamie Benn 1.00 2.50
SRR2 Nico Hischier 1.50 4.00
SRR3 Brad Marchand 2.00 5.00
SRR4 Roope Hintz 1.25 3.00
SRR5 Aleksander Barkov 1.50 4.00
SRR6 J.T. Miller 1.25 3.00
SRR7 Auston Matthews 4.00 10.00
SRR8 Sebastian Aho 1.50 4.00
SRR9 Mark Stone 1.25 3.00
SRR10 Troy Terry .75 2.00
SRR11 Nick Suzuki 2.00 5.00
SRR12 Zach Hyman 1.50 4.00
SRR13 Ryan O'Reilly 1.00 2.50
SRR14 Sean Couturier .75 2.00
SRR15 Carter Verhaeghe 1.00 2.50
SRR16 Mitch Marner 1.50 4.00
SRR17 Filip Forsberg 1.50 4.00
SRR18 Anze Kopitar 1.50 4.00
SRR19 Travis Konecny 1.00 2.50
SRR20 Elias Lindholm 1.00 2.50

2024-25 Parkhurst Champions You Wouldn't Believe

YB1 Glenn Hall 1.50 4.00
YB2 Wayne Gretzky 8.00 20.00
YB3 Sabres/Flyers 1.50 4.00
YB4 Kings/Rangers 1.50 4.00
YB5 Detroit Red Wings 1.50 4.00
YB6 Buffalo Sabres 1.50 4.00
YB7 Ron Hextall 1.50 4.00
YB8 Jacques Plante 1.50 4.00
YB9 Florida Panthers 1.50 4.00
YB10 Mike Sillinger 1.00 2.50
YB11 Patrick Roy 4.00 10.00
YB12 Bobby Orr 5.00 12.00
YB13 Chris Kontos 1.00 2.50
YB14 Peter Forsberg 3.00 8.00
YB15 Darryl Sittler 1.50 4.00

1995-96 Parkhurst International

1 Patrik Carnback .07 .20
2 Milos Holan .07 .20
3 Paul Kariya .12 .30
4 Guy Hebert .10 .25
5 Garry Valk .07 .20
6 Mikhail Shtalenkov .07 .20
7 Randy Ladouceur .07 .20
8 Shaun Van Allen .07 .20
9 Oleg Tverdovsky .12 .30
10 Kevin Stevens .10 .25
11 Ray Bourque .20 .50
12 Cam Neely .12 .30
13 Jozef Stumpel .07 .20
14 Blaine Lacher .10 .25
15 Alexei Kasatonov .07 .20
16 Adam Oates .12 .30
17 Ted Donato .07 .20
18 Mariusz Czerkawski .07 .20
19 Alexei Zhitnik .07 .20
20 Pat LaFontaine .12 .30
21 Garry Galley .07 .20
22 Scott Pearson .07 .20
23 Yuri Khmylev .07 .20
24 Jason Dawe .07 .20
25 Robb Stauber .07 .20
26 Wayne Primeau .07 .20
27 Brian Holzinger XRC .25 .60
28 German Titov .10 .25
29 Theo Fleury .15 .40
30 Phil Housley .10 .25
31 Zarley Zalapski .07 .20
32 Rick Tabaracci .10 .25
33 Joe Nieuwendyk .10 .25
34 Michael Nylander .07 .20
35 Trevor Kidd .10 .25
36 Dean Evason .07 .20
37 Bernie Nicholls .10 .25
38 Chris Chelios .12 .30
39 Gary Suter .07 .20
40 Denis Savard .12 .30
41 Ed Belfour .10 .25
42 Patrick Poulin .07 .20
43 Steve Smith .07 .20
44 Jeff Hackett .10 .25
45 Eric Daze .25 .60
46 Joe Sakic .25 .60
47 John Slaney .07 .20
48 Valeri Kamensky .10 .25
49 Owen Nolan .12 .30
50 Uwe Krupp .10 .25
51 Andrei Kovalenko .07 .20
52 Janne Laukkanen .07 .20
53 Jocelyn Thibault .10 .25
54 Adam Deadmarsh .07 .20
55 Mike Modano .20 .50
56 Kevin Hatcher .10 .25
57 Mike Donnelly .07 .20
58 Derian Hatcher .10 .25
59 Andy Moog .12 .30
60 Jamie Langenbrunner .07 .20
61 Shane Churla .07 .20
62 Todd Harvey .07 .20
63 Manny Fernandez .07 .20
64 Nicklas Lidstrom .12 .30
65 Vyacheslav Kozlov .10 .25
66 Paul Coffey .12 .30
67 Chris Osgood .12 .30
68 Slava Fetisov .10 .25
69 Vladimir Konstantinov .10 .25
70 Steve Yzerman .30 .75
71 Aaron Ward .07 .20
72 Keith Primeau .10 .25
73 Jason Arnott .10 .25
74 Igor Kravchuk .07 .20
75 Boris Mironov .07 .20
76 David Oliver .07 .20
77 Kelly Buchberger .07 .20
78 Bill Ranford .10 .25
79 Zdeno Ciger .10 .25
80 Jason Bonsignore .07 .20
81 Louie DeBrusk .10 .25
82 Rob Niedermayer .10 .25
83 Magnus Svensson .10 .25
84 Robert Svehla .07 .20
85 John Vanbiesbrouck .12 .30
86 Stu Barnes .07 .20
87 Jesse Belanger .07 .20
88 Mark Fitzpatrick .10 .25
89 Jason Woolley .07 .20
90 Johan Garpenlov .07 .20
91 Geoff Sanderson .07 .20
92 Robert Kron .07 .20
93 Darren Turcotte .07 .20
94 Andrei Nikolishin .07 .20
95 Steven Rice .07 .20
96 Sean Burke .07 .20
97 Brendan Shanahan .12 .30
98 Glen Wesley .07 .20
99 Marek Malik .07 .20
100 Wayne Gretzky .75 2.00
101 Robert Lang .07 .20
102 Jari Kurri .12 .30
103 Kelly Hrudey .10 .25
104 Jamie Storr .10 .25
105 Marty McSorley .10 .25
106 Rob Blake .10 .25
107 Eric LaCroix .07 .20
108 Dimitri Khristich .07 .20
109 Pierre Turgeon .10 .25
110 Vincent Damphousse .10 .25
111 Peter Popovic .07 .20
112 Brian Savage .07 .20
113 Patrick Roy .30 .75
114 Valeri Bure .07 .20
115 Vladimir Malakhov .07 .20
116 Benoit Brunet .07 .20
117 Stephane Quintal .10 .25
118 Stephane Richer .10 .25
119 Sergei Brylin .07 .20
120 Neal Broten .10 .25
121 Scott Stevens .12 .30
122 Martin Brodeur .30 .75
123 John MacLean .10 .25
124 Bill Guerin .12 .30
125 Bobby Holik .07 .20
126 Tommy Albelin .07 .20
127 Tommy Soderstrom .10 .25
128 Tommy Salo .20 .50
129 Kirk Muller .10 .25
130 Mathieu Schneider .07 .20
131 Zigmund Palffy .12 .30
132 Derek King .10 .25
133 Brett Lindros .07 .20
134 Marty McInnis .07 .20
135 Alexander Semak .07 .20
136 Mark Messier .25 .60
137 Adam Graves .10 .25
138 Mike Richter .12 .30
139 Alexei Kovalev .10 .25
140 Luc Robitaille .12 .30
141 Sergei Nemchinov .07 .20
142 Alexander Karpovtsev .07 .20
143 Mattias Norstrom .10 .25
144 Brian Leetch .10 .25
145 Martin Straka .07 .20
146 Sylvain Turgeon .07 .20
147 Radek Bonk .07 .20
148 Stanislav Neckar .07 .20
149 Pavol Demitra .15 .40
150 Alexandre Daigle .07 .20
151 Alexei Yashin .10 .25
152 Don Beaupre .10 .25
153 Steve Duchesne .07 .20
154 Eric Lindros .20 .50
155 Kjell Samuelsson .07 .20
156 Chris Therien .07 .20
157 John LeClair .12 .30
158 Rod Brind'Amour .12 .30
159 Ron Hextall .12 .30
160 Patrik Juhlin .07 .20
161 Mikael Renberg .10 .25
162 Joel Otto .07 .20
163 Markus Naslund .12 .30
164 Ron Francis .15 .40
165 Jaromir Jagr .40 1.00
166 Tomas Sandstrom .10 .25
167 Ken Wregget .10 .25
168 Bryan Smolinski .07 .20
169 Richard Park .12 .30
170 Mario Lemieux .50 1.25
171 Norm Maciver .10 .25
172 Brett Hull .25 .60
173 Esa Tikkanen .07 .20
174 Shayne Corson .10 .25
175 Chris Pronger .12 .30
176 Ian Laperriere .07 .20
177 Jon Casey .10 .25
178 Al MacInnis .15 .40
179 David Roberts .07 .20
180 Dale Hawerchuk .15 .40
181 Michal Sykora .07 .20
182 Jeff Friesen .07 .20
183 Ray Whitney .10 .25
184 Igor Larionov .07 .20
185 Sandis Ozolinsh .07 .20
186 Andrei Nazarov .10 .25
187 Viktor Kozlov .10 .25
188 Arturs Irbe .10 .25
189 Wade Flaherty .10 .25
190 Brian Bradley .10 .25
191 Paul Ysebaert .07 .20
192 John Tucker .07 .20
193 Jason Wiemer .07 .20
194 Alexander Selivanov .10 .25
195 Daren Puppa .10 .25
196 Mikael Andersson .10 .25
197 Petr Klima .07 .20
198 Roman Hamrlik .07 .20
199 Doug Gilmour .15 .40
200 Damian Rhodes .10 .25
201 Mats Sundin .12 .30
202 Todd Gill .07 .20
203 Kenny Jonsson .12 .30
204 Felix Potvin .20 .50
205 Tie Domi .10 .25
206 Mike Gartner .15 .40
207 Larry Murphy .10 .25
208 Josef Beranek .07 .20
209 Trevor Linden .12 .30
210 Russ Courtnall .07 .20
211 Roman Oksiuta .07 .20
212 Alexander Mogilny .10 .25
213 Kirk McLean .10 .25
214 Mike Ridley .07 .20
215 Jyrki Lumme .07 .20
216 Bret Hedican .07 .20
217 Keith Jones .10 .25
218 Calle Johansson .07 .20
219 Kelly Miller .07 .20
220 Olaf Kolzig .12 .30
221 Joe Juneau .07 .20
222 Sylvain Cote .07 .20
223 Dale Hunter .10 .25
224 Mark Tinordi .07 .20
225 Sergei Gonchar .07 .20
226 Alexei Zhamnov .12 .30
227 Igor Korolev .07 .20
228 Teppo Numminen .07 .20
229 Craig Martin .07 .20
230 Nikolai Khabibulin .10 .25
231 Michal Grosek .07 .20
232 Teemu Selanne .25 .60
233 Dave Manson .07 .20
234 Tim Cheveldae .10 .25
235 Esa Tikkanen .07 .20
236 Dominik Hasek II .20 .50
237 Peter Forsberg II .25 .60
238 Sergei Fedorov II .20 .50
239 Jari Kurri .12 .30
240 Tommy Soderstrom .10 .25
241 Alexei Zhamnov II .12 .30
242 Alexei Yashin II .10 .25
243 Mikael Renberg II .10 .25
244 Jaromir Jagr II .40 1.00
245 Ulf Dahlen .07 .20
246 Alexander Mogilny II .10 .25
247 Mats Sundin II .12 .30
248 Pavel Bure II .12 .30
249 Slava Fetisov .10 .25
250 Teemu Selanne II .25 .60
251 Arturs Irbe .10 .25
252 Nicklas Lidstrom .12 .30
253 Aki Berg .12 .30
254 Zdenek Nedved .07 .20
255 Chad Kilger .12 .30
256 Bryan McCabe .12 .30
257 Daniel Alfredsson XRC .60 1.50
258 Brendan Witt .12 .30
259 Jeff O'Neill .12 .30
260 Radek Dvorak .15 .40
261 Niklas Sundstrom .12 .30
262 Kyle McLaren .07 .20
263 Saku Koivu .12 .30
264 Todd Bertuzzi .15 .40
265 Jere Lehtinen .10 .25
266 Vitali Yachmenev .12 .30
267 Shane Doan .40 1.00
268 Marko Kiprusoff .10 .25
269 Deron Quint .10 .25
270 Daymond Langkow XRC .12 .30
271 Alex Hicks .07 .20
272 Steve Rucchin .10 .25
273 David Karpa .07 .20
274 Mike Sillinger .07 .20
275 Teemu Selanne .25 .60
276 Todd Krygier .07 .20
277 Valeri Karpov .07 .20
278 Peter Douris .07 .20
279 Team Checklist .05 .15
280 Shawn McEachern .07 .20
281 Dave Reid .07 .20
282 Bill Ranford .10 .25
283 Don Sweeney .07 .20
284 Stephen Leach .07 .20
285 Craig Billington .10 .25
286 Clayton Beddoes .10 .25
287 Rick Tocchet .10 .25
288 Team Checklist .05 .15
289 Brad May .07 .20
290 Mike Peca .10 .25
291 Dominik Hasek .20 .50
292 Donald Audette .10 .25
293 Randy Burridge .07 .20
294 Derek Plante .07 .20
295 Martin Biron XRC .25 .60
296 Andrei Trefilov .07 .20
297 Team Checklist .05 .15
298 Steve Chiasson .07 .20
299 Cory Stillman .07 .20
300 Mike Sullivan .10 .25
301 Gary Roberts .07 .20
302 Pavel Torgajev .07 .20
303 James Patrick .07 .20
304 Corey Millen .07 .20
305 Ed Ward .10 .25
306 Team Checklist .05 .15
307 Jeremy Roenick .20 .50
308 Mike Prokopec .07 .20
309 Joe Murphy .07 .20
310 Eric Weinrich .07 .20
311 Tony Amonte .10 .25
312 Bob Probert .12 .30
313 Murray Craven .07 .20
314 Sergei Krivokrasov .07 .20
315 Team Checklist .05 .15
316 Peter Forsberg .25 .60
317 Stephane Fiset .10 .25
318 Mike Ricci .07 .20
319 Claude Lemieux .12 .30
320 Sandis Ozolinsh .07 .20
321 Sylvain Lefebvre .07 .20
322 Scott Young .07 .20
323 Patrick Roy .30 .75
324 Team Checklist .05 .15
325 Brent Fedyk .07 .20
326 Brent Gilchrist .07 .20
327 Greg Adams .07 .20
328 Richard Matvichuk .10 .25
329 Joe Nieuwendyk .10 .25
330 Benoit Hogue .07 .20
331 Darcy Wakaluk .07 .20
332 Guy Carbonneau .12 .30
333 Team Checklist .05 .15
334 Mike Vernon .10 .25
335 Mathieu Dandenault .25 .60
336 Igor Larionov .07 .20
337 Sergei Fedorov .20 .50
338 Greg Johnson .07 .20
339 Dino Ciccarelli .10 .25
340 Martin Lapointe .07 .20
341 Darren McCarty .07 .20
342 Team Checklist .05 .15
343 Joaquin Gage .10 .25
344 Jiri Slegr .07 .20
345 Mariusz Czerkawski .07 .20
346 Doug Weight .12 .30
347 Todd Marchant .07 .20
348 Miroslav Satan XRC .15 .40
349 Jeff Norton .07 .20
350 Curtis Joseph .15 .40
351 Team Checklist .05 .15
352 Tom Fitzgerald .07 .20
353 Jody Hull .07 .20
354 Terry Carkner .07 .20
355 Scott Mellanby .10 .25
356 Bill Lindsay .07 .20
357 Gord Murphy .07 .20
358 Brian Skrudland .07 .20
359 David Nemirovsky .10 .25
360 Team Checklist .05 .15
361 Paul Ranheim .07 .20
362 Jason Muzzatti .10 .25
363 Glen Featherstone .07 .20
364 Andrew Cassels .07 .20
365 Jeff Brown .10 .25
366 Kevin Dineen .10 .25
367 Nelson Emerson .07 .20
368 Gerald Diduck .07 .20
369 Team Checklist .05 .15
370 Kevin Stevens .10 .25
371 Darryl Sydor .10 .25
372 Yanic Perreault .07 .20
373 Arto Blomsten .07 .20
374 Kevin Todd .07 .20
375 Byron Dafoe .10 .25
376 Tony Granato .07 .20
377 Vladimir Tsyplakov XRC .25 .60
378 Team Checklist .05 .15
379 Martin Rucinsky .07 .20
380 Patrice Brisebois .07 .20
381 Lyle Odelein .07 .20
382 Andrei Kovalenko .07 .20
383 Mark Recchi .15 .40
384 Jocelyn Thibault .10 .25
385 Turner Stevenson .07 .20
386 Pat Jablonski .07 .20
387 Team Checklist .05 .15
388 Scott Niedermayer .12 .30
389 Corey Schwab XRC .25 .60
390 Steve Thomas .10 .25
391 Valeri Zelepukin .07 .20
392 Shawn Chambers .07 .20
393 Jocelyn Lemieux .10 .25
394 Brian Rolston .10 .25
395 Denis Pederson .07 .20
396 Team Checklist .05 .15
397 Martin Straka .07 .20
398 Niclas Andersson .10 .25
399 Wendel Clark .20 .50
400 Travis Green .10 .25
401 Chris Marinucci .10 .25
402 Darius Kasparaitis .07 .20
403 Patrick Flatley .07 .20
404 Jamie McLennan .07 .20
405 Team Checklist .05 .15
406 Glenn Healy .10 .25
407 Pat Verbeek .10 .25
408 Ian Laperriere .07 .20
409 Ray Ferraro .07 .20
410 Jeff Beukeboom .07 .20
411 Ulf Samuelsson .07 .20
412 Doug Lidster .07 .20
413 Bruce Driver .07 .20
414 Team Checklist .05 .15
415 Antti Tormanen .07 .20
416 Sean Hill .07 .20
417 Damian Rhodes .10 .25
418 Jaroslav Modry .07 .20
419 Mike Bales .07 .20
420 Trent McCleary .10 .25
421 Randy Cunneyworth .07 .20
422 Ted Drury .07 .20
423 Team Checklist .05 .15
424 Pat Falloon .07 .20
425 Garth Snow .10 .25
426 Shjon Podein .07 .20
427 Petr Svoboda .07 .20
428 Eric Desjardins .10 .25
429 Anatoli Semenov .10 .25
430 Kevin Haller .07 .20
431 Rob Dimaio .07 .20
432 Team Checklist .05 .15
433 Chris Joseph .07 .20
434 Sergei Zubov .10 .25
435 Tom Barrasso .10 .25
436 Chris Tamer .07 .20
437 Dmitri Mironov .07 .20
438 Petr Nedved .10 .25
439 Neil Wilkinson .07 .20
440 Glen Murray .10 .25
441 Team Checklist .05 .15
442 J.J. Daigneault .07 .20
443 Grant Fuhr .20 .50
444 Adam Creighton .07 .20
445 Brian Noonan .07 .20
446 Stephane Matteau .07 .20
447 Roman Vopat .07 .20
448 Geoff Courtnall .07 .20
449 Wayne Gretzky .75 2.00
450 Team Checklist .05 .15
451 Chris Terreri .10 .25
452 Ulf Dahlen .07 .20
453 Owen Nolan .12 .30
454 Doug Bodger .07 .20
455 Craig Janney .07 .20
456 Ville Peltonen .07 .20
457 Ray Sheppard .10 .25
458 Shean Donovan .07 .20
459 Team Checklist .05 .15
460 Jeff Reese .07 .20
461 Shawn Burr .07 .20
462 Chris Gratton .07 .20
463 John Cullen .07 .20
464 Bill Houlder .07 .20
465 J.C. Bergeron .10 .25
466 Brian Bellows .10 .25
467 Drew Bannister .10 .25
468 Team Checklist .05 .15
469 Dimitri Yushkevich .07 .20
470 Dave Andreychuk .12 .30
471 Dave Gagner .07 .20
472 Todd Warriner .10 .25
473 Sergio Momesso .07 .20
474 Kirk Muller .10 .25
475 Dave Ellett .07 .20
476 Ken Baumgartner .07 .20
477 Team Checklist .05 .15
478 Esa Tikkanen .07 .20
479 Cliff Ronning .07 .20
480 Martin Gelinas .07 .20
481 Brian Loney .07 .20
482 Pavel Bure .12 .30
483 Corey Hirsch .10 .25
484 Scott Walker .07 .20
485 Jim Dowd .07 .20
486 Team Checklist .05 .15
487 Michal Pivonka .07 .20
488 Pat Peake .07 .20
489 Martin Gendron .10 .25
490 Peter Bondra .12 .30
491 Nolan Baumgartner .07 .20
492 Jim Carey .10 .25
493 Steve Konowalchuk .10 .25
494 Jason Allison .10 .25
495 Team Checklist .05 .15
496 Oleg Tverdovsky .12 .30
497 Craig Mills .07 .20
498 Darren Turcotte .07 .20
499 Norm Maciver .10 .25
500 Chad Kilger PN .12 .30
501 Keith Tkachuk .12 .30
502 Kris King .07 .20
503 Dallas Drake .07 .20
504 Team Checklist .05 .15
505 Saku Koivu PN .12 .30
506 Vitali Yachmenev PN .12 .30
507 Daniel Alfredsson PN .60 1.50
508 Radek Dvorak .15 .40
509 Miroslav Satan .15 .40
510 Aki Berg PN .12 .30
511 Valeri Bure .07 .20
512 Petr Sykora PN .30 .75
513 Andrei Vasilyev PN .07 .20
514 Niklas Sundstrom .12 .30
515 Viktor Kozlov .10 .25
516 Sami Kapanen .10 .25
517 Anders Myrvold .10 .25
518 Jere Lehtinen .10 .25
519 Marcus Ragnarsson XRC .15 .40
520 Stefan Ustorf .07 .20
521 Ville Peltonen .07 .20
522 Antti Tormanen PN .07 .20
523 Petr Sykora .30 .75
524 Scott Bailey XRC .15 .40
525 Kevin Hodson XRC .25 .60
526 Landon Wilson .07 .20
527 Aaron Gavey .07 .20
528 Darren Langdon XRC .25 .60
529 Jason Doig .12 .30
530 Marty Murray .12 .30
531 Marcus Ragnarsson .15 .40
532 Peter Ferraro .10 .25
533 Grant Marshall .07 .20
534 Mike Wilson XRC .25 .60
535 Rory Fitzpatrick .10 .25
536 Ed Jovanovski .12 .30
537 Eric Fichaud .10 .25
538 Stefan Ustorf .07 .20
539 Stephane Yelle .10 .25
540 Ethan Moreau XRC .25 .60
NNO1 M.Renberg AU/2500 5.00 12.00
NNO2 T.Selanne AU/2500 30.00 80.00
NNO3 M.Brodeur AU/1500 25.00 60.00
NNO4 S.Koivu AU/1500 12.00 30.00
NNO5 Saku Koivu Jumbo 1.50 4.00
NNO6 Saku Koivu Jumbo AU 10.00 25.00

1995-96 Parkhurst International Emerald Ice

*1-270 VETS: 2X TO 5X BASIC CARDS
*1-270 XRCs: 1.5X TO 4X BASIC XRC
*271-540 VETS: 2X TO 5X BASIC CARDS
*271-540 XRCs: 1.5X TO 4X BASIC XRC

1995-96 Parkhurst International All-Stars

COMPLETE SET (6) 6.00 15.00
1 D.Hasek/A.Irbe 1.00 2.50
2 N.Lidstrom/S.Ozolinsh 3.00 8.00
3 S.Zubov/A.Zhitnik .40 1.00
4 S.Fedorov/P.Forsberg 1.25 3.00
5 J.Jagr/T.Selanne 1.00 2.50
6 M.Sundin/M.Renberg 3.00 8.00

1995-96 Parkhurst International Crown Collection Silver Series 1

COMPLETE SET (16) 12.00 30.00
*GOLD: 1.2X TO 3X SILVER
1 Eric Lindros .50 1.25
2 Felix Potvin .50 1.25
3 Mario Lemieux 2.50 6.00
4 Paul Kariya .50 1.25
5 Pavel Bure .50 1.25
6 Wayne Gretzky 4.00 10.00
7 Mikael Renberg .30 .75
8 Paul Coffey .50 1.25
9 Teemu Selanne .50 1.25
10 Brett Hull .60 1.50
11 Martin Brodeur 1.25 3.00
12 Doug Gilmour .30 .75
13 Peter Forsberg 1.25 3.00
14 Sergei Fedorov .75 2.00
15 Saku Koivu .50 1.25
16 Jim Carey .30 .75

1995-96 Parkhurst International Crown Collection Silver Series 2

COMPLETE SET (16) 10.00 25.00
*GOLD: 1.2X TO 3X SILVER
1 Jaromir Jagr .75 2.00
2 Patrick Roy 2.50 6.00
3 Alexander Mogilny .30 .75
4 Paul Kariya .50 1.25
5 Dominik Hasek 1.00 2.50
6 Peter Forsberg 1.25 3.00
7 Mark Messier .50 1.25
8 Mats Sundin .50 1.25
9 Ray Bourque .75 2.00
10 Wayne Gretzky 4.00 10.00
11 Eric Lindros .50 1.25
12 John Vanbiesbrouck .30 .75
13 Chris Chelios .50 1.25
14 Brian Leetch .30 .75
15 Daniel Alfredsson 1.25 3.00
16 Eric Daze .30 .75

1995-96 Parkhurst International Goal Patrol

COMPLETE SET (12) 10.00 25.00
1 Martin Brodeur 3.00 8.00
2 Felix Potvin 1.25 3.00
3 Patrick Roy 4.00 10.00
4 Dominik Hasek 2.50 6.00
5 Jim Carey .75 2.00
6 Ed Belfour 1.25 3.00
7 John Vanbiesbrouck .75 2.00
8 Trevor Kidd .75 2.00
9 Bill Ranford .75 2.00
10 Arturs Irbe .75 2.00
11 Kirk McLean .75 2.00
12 Mike Richter 1.25 3.00

1995-96 Parkhurst International NHL All-Stars

COMPLETE SET (6) 10.00 25.00
1 M.Lemieux/W.Gretzky 6.00 15.00
2 J.Jagr/B.Hull 1.25 3.00
3 B.Shanahan/P.Bure 2.50 6.00
4 S.Stevens/C.Chelios 2.50 6.00
5 R.Bourque/P.Coffey 1.50 4.00
6 M.Brodeur/E.Belfour 3.00 8.00

1995-96 Parkhurst International Parkie's Trophy Picks

COMPLETE SET (54) 40.00 80.00
PP1 Eric Lindros 1.25 3.00
PP2 Mario Lemieux 3.00 8.00
PP3 Sergei Fedorov 1.25 3.00
PP4 Peter Forsberg 1.50 4.00
PP5 John Vanbiesbrouck .75 2.00
PP6 Mark Messier 1.00 2.50
PP7 Jaromir Jagr 1.50 4.00
PP8 Joe Sakic 2.00 5.00
PP9 Grant Fuhr .75 2.00
PP10 Eric Lindros 1.25 3.00
PP11 Mario Lemieux 3.00 8.00
PP12 Mark Messier 1.00 2.50
PP13 Peter Forsberg 1.50 4.00
PP14 Jaromir Jagr 1.50 4.00
PP15 Paul Kariya 1.00 2.50
PP16 Joe Sakic 4.00 10.00
PP17 Teemu Selanne 1.00 2.50
PP18 Alexander Mogilny .60 1.50
PP19 Paul Coffey 1.00 2.50
PP20 Chris Chelios 1.00 2.50
PP21 Brian Leetch .60 1.50
PP22 Ray Bourque 1.00 2.50
PP23 Larry Murphy .40 1.00
PP24 Nicklas Lidstrom 1.00 2.50
PP25 Roman Hamrlik .40 1.00
PP26 Gary Suter .40 1.00
PP27 Sergei Zubov .40 1.00
PP28 Dominik Hasek 1.50 4.00
PP29 John Vanbiesbrouck .75 2.00
PP30 Chris Osgood .60 1.50
PP31 Mike Richter 1.00 2.50
PP32 Martin Brodeur 2.00 5.00
PP33 Ron Hextall .75 2.00
PP34 Grant Fuhr 1.00 2.50
PP35 Patrick Roy 3.00 8.00
PP36 Jim Carey .40 1.00
PP37 Vitali Yachmenev .40 1.00
PP38 Daniel Alfredsson .60 1.50
PP39 Saku Koivu 1.00 2.50
PP40 Eric Daze .40 1.00
PP41 Marcus Ragnarsson .40 1.00

PP42 Ed Jovanovski .40 1.00
PP43 Petr Sykora .40 1.00
PP44 Todd Bertuzzi 1.00 2.50
PP45 Radek Dvorak .40 1.00
PP46 Paul Kariya 1.00 2.50
PP47 Ron Francis .60 1.50
PP48 Alexander Mogilny .60 1.50
PP49 Pat LaFontaine 1.00 2.50
PP50 Pierre Turgeon .40 1.00
PP51 Teemu Selanne 1.00 2.50
PP52 Sergei Fedorov 1.25 3.00
PP53 Adam Oates .60 1.50
PP54 Brett Hull 1.25 3.00

1995-96 Parkhurst International Trophy Winners

COMPLETE SET (6) 3.00 8.00
1 Eric Lindros .50 1.25
2 Jaromir Jagr .75 2.00
3 Peter Forsberg 1.25 3.00
4 Paul Coffey .50 1.25
5 Dominik Hasek 1.00 2.50
6 Ron Francis .30 .75

2003-04 Parkhurst Original Six Boston

COMPLETE SET (100) 15.00 40.00
1 P.J. Axelsson .15 .40
2 Michal Grosek .15 .40
3 Nick Boynton .15 .40
4 Jeff Jillson .15 .40
5 Felix Potvin .40 1.00
6 Patrick Leahy XRC .40 1.00
7 Joe Thornton .60 1.50
8 Ted Donato .15 .40
9 Hal Gill .15 .40
10 Jonathan Girard .15 .40
11 Rob Zamuner .15 .40
12 Shoane Morrisonn .15 .40
13 Martin Samuelsson .15 .40
14 Doug Doull XRC .15 .40
15 Ivan Huml .15 .40
16 Mike Knuble .15 .40
17 Kris Vernarsky .15 .40
18 Patrice Bergeron XRC 3.00 8.00
19 Sergei Zinovjev XRC .40 1.00
20 Martin Lapointe .15 .40
21 Dan McGillis .15 .40
22 Sandy McCarthy .15 .40
23 Glen Murray .15 .40
24 P.J. Stock .15 .40
25 Sean O'Donnell .15 .40
26 Andrew Raycroft .40 1.00
27 Brian Rolston .15 .40
28 Sergei Samsonov .40 1.00
29 Ian Moran .15 .40
30 Travis Green .15 .40
31 Adam Oates .40 1.00
32 Cam Neely .75 2.00
33 Jason Allison .15 .40
34 Dit Clapper .40 1.00
35 Fern Flaman .15 .40
36 John Bucyk .40 1.00
37 Milt Schmidt .40 1.00
38 Brad Park .40 1.00
39 Terry O'Reilly .40 1.00
40 Wayne Cashman .40 1.00
41 Ray Bourque .75 2.00
42 Allan Stanley .15 .40
43 Bernie Parent .60 1.50
44 Derek Sanderson .40 1.00
45 Bobby Orr 1.50 4.00
46 Tiny Thompson .60 1.50
47 Eddie Shore 1.00 2.50
48 Frank Brimsek .40 1.00
49 Jean Ratelle .40 1.00
50 Ken Hodge .40 1.00
51 Lionel Hitchman .15 .40
52 Phil Esposito .60 1.50
53 Rick Middleton .40 1.00
54 Terry Sawchuk .60 1.50
55 Woody Dumart .15 .40
56 Gerry Cheevers .60 1.50
57 Andy Moog .40 1.00
58 Byron Dafoe .40 1.00
59 Anson Carter .15 .40
60 Bill Guerin .40 1.00
61 Frank Brimsek .40 1.00
62 Bobby Orr 1.50 4.00
63 Eddie Shore 1.00 2.50
64 Dit Clapper .40 1.00
65 Cam Neely .75 2.00
66 Phil Esposito .60 1.50
67 Milt Schmidt .40 1.00
68 Johnny Bucyk .40 1.00
69 Woody Dumart .15 .40
70 Ray Bourque .75 2.00
71 Joe Thornton .60 1.50
72 Dit Clapper .40 1.00
73 Ray Bourque .75 2.00
74 Fern Flaman .15 .40
75 Johnny Bucyk .40 1.00
76 Milt Schmidt .40 1.00
77 Rick Middleton .40 1.00
78 Terry O'Reilly .40 1.00
79 Wayne Cashman .40 1.00
80 Lionel Hitchman .15 .40
81 Bobby Orr 1.50 4.00
82 Johnny Bucyk .40 1.00
83 Phil Esposito .60 1.50
84 Frank Brimsek .40 1.00
85 Fern Flaman .15 .40
86 Gerry Cheevers .60 1.50
87 Dit Clapper .40 1.00
88 Woody Dumart .15 .40
89 Eddie Shore 1.00 2.50
90 Milt Schmidt .40 1.00
91 Bobby Orr 1.50 4.00
92 Johnny Bucyk .40 1.00
93 Terry O'Reilly .40 1.00
94 Ray Bourque .75 2.00
95 Cam Neely .75 2.00
96 Phil Esposito .60 1.50
97 Bobby Orr 1.50 4.00
98 Cam Neely .75 2.00
99 Phil Esposito .60 1.50
100 Ray Bourque .75 2.00

2003-04 Parkhurst Original Six Boston Autographs

1 Ray Bourque/30 75.00 175.00
2 Johnny Bucyk/90 25.00 60.00
3 Wayne Cashman/85 25.00 60.00
4 Gerry Cheevers/90 50.00 125.00
5 Phil Esposito/55 75.00 175.00
6 Fern Flaman/85 30.00 80.00
7 Ken Hodge/90 25.00 60.00
8 Stan Jonathan/85 20.00 50.00
9 Rick Middleton/90 20.00 50.00
10 Andy Moog/90 25.00 60.00
11 Cam Neely/90 40.00 80.00
12 Terry O'Reilly/95 50.00 100.00
13 Bobby Orr/30 350.00 600.00
14 Bernie Parent/90 20.00 50.00
15 Brad Park/90 25.00 50.00
16 Jean Ratelle/90 30.00 60.00
17 Derek Sanderson/90 40.00 80.00
18 Milt Schmidt/85 30.00 80.00

2003-04 Parkhurst Original Six Boston Inserts

COMPLETE SET (17) 30.00 60.00
B1 Eddie Shore 2.00 5.00
B2 Milt Schmidt 1.25 3.00
B3 Dit Clapper 1.25 3.00
B4 Phil Esposito 2.00 5.00
B5 Johnny Bucyk 1.25 3.00
B6 Bobby Orr 3.00 8.00
B7 Eddie Shore 2.00 5.00
B8 Phil Esposito 2.00 5.00
B9 Milt Schmidt 1.25 3.00
B10 Phil Esposito 2.00 5.00
B11 Bobby Orr 3.00 8.00
B12 Ray Bourque 2.50 6.00
B13 Derek Sanderson 1.25 3.00
B14 Tiny Thompson 2.00 5.00
B15 Frank Brimsek 1.25 3.00
B16 Joe Thornton 2.00 5.00
B17 Ray Bourque 2.50 6.00

2003-04 Parkhurst Original Six Boston Memorabilia

BM1 Brian Rolston 8.00 20.00
BM2 Sergei Samsonov 6.00 15.00
BM3 Martin Lapointe 6.00 15.00
BM4 Don Sweeny 6.00 15.00
BM5 Nick Boynton 6.00 15.00
BM6 Joe Thornton 20.00 50.00
BM7 Jeff Hackett 6.00 15.00
BM8 Ivan Huml 6.00 15.00
BM9 Steve Shields 8.00 20.00
BM10 Glen Murray 6.00 15.00
BM11 Shaone Morrisonn 6.00 15.00
BM12 Bryan Berard 8.00 20.00
BM13 Mike Knuble 6.00 15.00
BM14 Bryan Berard J/S 12.00 30.00
BM15 Sergei Samsonov J/S 15.00 40.00
BM16 Joe Thornton J/S/50 30.00 80.00
BM17 Jeff Hackett J/S 8.00 20.00
BM18 Steve Shields J/S 15.00 40.00
BM20 S.Samsonov/50 Glove 12.00 30.00
BM22 Gilles Gilbert/50 15.00 40.00
BM23 Gerry Cheevers/50 Pad 30.00 80.00
BM25 Eddie Shore/60 Pants 20.00 50.00
BM27 John Bucyk J 20.00 50.00
BM28 Gerry Cheevers J 20.00 50.00
BM29 Andy Moog J 20.00 50.00
BM30 Gilles Gilbert J 20.00 50.00
BM31 Jason Allison J 15.00 40.00
BM32 Cam Neely J 30.00 80.00
BM33 Phil Esposito J 20.00 50.00
BM34 Adam Oates J 25.00 60.00
BM35 Phil Esposito/30 S 20.00 50.00
BM36 Ray Bourque/50 S 30.00 80.00
BM38 Gerry Cheevers/50 S 15.00 40.00
BM40 Cam Neely/20 RN J 75.00 150.00
BM41 Mario Lemieux SS 15.00 40.00
BM42 Ron Francis SS 6.00 15.00
BM43 Joe Sakic SS 12.50 30.00
BM44 Brett Hull SS 8.00 20.00
BM45 Jaromir Jagr SS 8.00 20.00
BM46 Mike Modano SS 8.00 20.00
BM47 Teemu Selanne SS 10.00 25.00
BM48 Pavel Bure SS 6.00 15.00
BM49 Paul Kariya SS 8.00 20.00
BM50 Peter Forsberg SS 10.00 25.00
BM51 G.Cheevers/F.Potvin 20.00 50.00
BM52 P.Esposito/J.Thornton 25.00 60.00
BM53 B.Orr/R.Bourque 75.00 150.00
BM54 J.Bucyk/G.Murray 20.00 50.00
BM55 T.O'Reilly/C.Neely 25.00 60.00
BM56 T.Thompson/B.Parent 30.00 80.00
BM57 Bobby Orr J 100.00 200.00
BM58 Bobby Orr/50 100.00 200.00
BM59 Bobby Orr/50 S 100.00 200.00
BM61 Felix Potvin 12.00 30.00
BM62 Andrew Raycroft 15.00 40.00
BM63 Felix Potvin J/S 25.00 60.00
BM64 Ray Bourque/50 15.00 40.00
BM65 Brad Park/50 J 20.00 50.00
BM66 Ray Bourque/50 J 20.00 50.00
BM67 Terry O'Reilly/50 J 20.00 50.00

2003-04 Parkhurst Original Six Chicago

COMPLETE SET 15.00 40.00
1 Tyler Arnason .40 1.00
2 Mark Bell .15 .40
3 Deron Quint .15 .40
4 Kyle Calder .15 .40
5 Bryan Berard .15 .40
6 Eric Daze .40 1.00
7 Jason Strudwick .15 .40
8 Nathan Dempsey .15 .40
9 Jon Klemm .15 .40
10 Igor Korolev .15 .40
11 Pavel Vorobiev XRC .75 2.00
12 Scott Nichol .15 .40
13 Alexander Karpovtsev .15 .40
14 Tuomo Ruutu XRC 1.25 3.00
15 Ville Nieminen .15 .40
16 Steve McCarthy .15 .40
17 Igor Radulov .15 .40
18 Alexei Zhamnov .15 .40
19 Burke Henry .15 .40
20 Craig Andersson .40 1.00
21 Steve Passmore .40 1.00
22 Lasse Kukkonen XRC .75 2.00
23 Steve Poapst .15 .40
24 Michael Leighton .40 1.00
25 Shawn Thornton .15 .40
26 Brett McLean .15 .40
27 Steve Sullivan .15 .40
28 Jocelyn Thibault .40 1.00
29 Travis Moen XRC .75 2.00
30 Ryan Vandenbussche .15 .40
31 Chris Chelios .50 1.25
32 Dominik Hasek .75 2.00
33 Jeremy Roenick .60 1.50
34 Ed Belfour .50 1.25
35 Doug Gilmour .40 1.00
36 Charlie Gardiner .40 1.00
37 Howie Morenz .60 1.50
38 Steve Larmer .40 1.00
39 Dirk Graham .15 .40
40 Ken Wharram .40 1.00
41 Pat Stapleton .15 .40
42 Pierre Pilote .40 1.00
43 Bobby Hull 1.25 3.00
44 Tony Amonte .40 1.00
45 Stan Mikita .60 1.50
46 Dennis Hull .60 1.50
47 Denis Savard .75 2.00
48 Doug Wilson .15 .40
49 Bobby Orr 1.50 3.50
50 Glenn Hall .75 2.00
51 Harry Lumley .50 1.25
52 Bill Mosienko .50 1.25
53 Ken Hodge .40 1.00
54 Michel Goulet .50 1.25
55 Keith Magnuson .75 2.00
56 Ted Lindsay .50 1.25
57 Bill Gadsby .40 1.00
58 Darren Pang .50 1.25
59 Tony Esposito .75 2.00
60 Phil Esposito .75 2.00
61 Glenn Hall .75 2.00
62 Ed Belfour .50 1.25
63 Charlie Gardiner .40 1.00
64 Tony Esposito .75 2.00
65 Stan Mikita .60 1.50
66 Bobby Hull 1.25 3.00
67 Pierre Pilote .40 1.00
68 Doug Wilson .15 .40
69 Chris Chelios .50 1.25
70 Ken Wharram .40 1.00
71 Alexei Zhamnov .15 .40
72 Chris Chelios .50 1.25
73 Doug Gilmour .40 1.00
74 Bill Gadsby .40 1.00
75 Denis Savard .75 2.00
76 Tony Amonte .40 1.00
77 Dirk Graham .15 .40
78 Stan Mikita .60 1.50
79 Ed Litzenberger .40 1.00
80 Pierre Pilote .40 1.00
81 Denis Savard .75 2.00
82 Johnny Bower .40 1.00
83 Stan Mikita .60 1.50
84 Bill Mosienko .50 1.25
85 Glenn Hall .75 2.00
86 Bobby Hull 1.25 3.00
87 Phil Esposito .75 2.00
88 Tony Esposito .75 2.00
89 Bill Gadsby .40 1.00
90 Michel Goulet .50 1.25
91 Bobby Hull 1.25 3.00
92 Stan Mikita .60 1.50
93 Stan Mikita .60 1.50
94 Tony Esposito .75 2.00
95 Bobby Hull 1.25 3.00
96 Denis Savard .75 2.00
97 Tony Esposito 1.25 3.00
98 Ed Belfour .50 1.25
99 Chris Chelios .50 1.25
100 Steve Larmer .40 1.00

2003-04 Parkhurst Original Six Chicago Autographs

1 Phil Esposito/55 50.00 100.00
2 Tony Esposito/85 30.00 60.00
3 Michel Goulet/90 20.00 50.00
4 Dirk Graham/90 15.00 40.00
5 Glenn Hall/85 50.00 125.00
6 Ken Hodge/89 20.00 50.00
7 Bobby Hull/75 50.00 100.00
8 Steve Larmer/85 40.00 80.00
9 Ted Lindsay/90 25.00 60.00
10 Eddie Litzenberger/90 20.00 50.00
11 Keith Magnuson/99 40.00 80.00
12 Stan Mikita/80 20.00 50.00
13 Darren Pang/99 15.00 40.00
14 Pierre Pilote/85 20.00 50.00
15 Denis Savard/90 25.00 60.00
16 Ken Wharram/90 25.00 60.00
17 Doug Wilson/90 25.00 60.00

2003-04 Parkhurst Original Six Chicago Inserts

COMPLETE SET (16) 30.00 60.00
C1 Stan Mikita 2.00 5.00
C2 Bobby Hull 2.00 5.00
C3 Tony Esposito 2.00 5.00
C4 Glenn Hall 1.50 4.00
C5 Denis Savard 1.50 4.00
C6 Bobby Hull 2.00 5.00
C7 Ed Belfour 1.50 4.00
C8 Tony Esposito 2.00 5.00
C9 Glenn Hall 1.50 4.00
C10 Tony Esposito 2.00 5.00
C11 Stan Mikita 2.00 5.00
C12 Bobby Hull 2.00 5.00
C13 Pierre Pilote 1.50 4.00
C14 Charlie Gardiner 1.50 4.00
C15 Jeremy Roenick 2.00 5.00
C16 Denis Savard 1.50 4.00

2003-04 Parkhurst Original Six Chicago Memorabilia

CM1 Jocelyn Thibault/100* 10.00 25.00
CM2 Steve Sullivan/100* 10.00 25.00
CM3 Eric Daze/100* 6.00 15.00
CM4 Alexei Zhamnov/100* 6.00 15.00
CM5 Mark Bell/100* 6.00 15.00
CM6 Steve McCarthy/100* 6.00 15.00
CM7 Tyler Arnason/100* 6.00 15.00
CM8 Steve Passmore/100* 10.00 25.00
CM9 Ryan Vandenbussche/100* 6.00 15.00
CM10 Jocelyn Thibault/80* J/S 20.00 50.00
CM11 Steve Sullivan/80* J/S 15.00 40.00
CM12 Eric Daze/80* J/S 12.50 30.00
CM13 Alexei Zhamnov/80* J/S 12.50 30.00
CM14 Jocelyn Thibault/50 30.00 80.00
CM16 Bill Mosienko/20* Pants 15.00 40.00
CM17 Chuck Gardiner/20* Pad 20.00 40.00
CM18 Harry Lumley/20* 30.00 60.00
CM20 Ed Belfour/100* J 15.00 40.00
CM21 Jeremy Roenick/100* J 12.50 30.00
CM22 Tony Amonte/100* J 12.50 30.00
CM23 Bill Mosienko/60* J 25.00 60.00
CM24 Michel Goulet/100* J 12.50 30.00
CM25 Bobby Hull/50* J 25.00 60.00
CM26 Dennis Hull/60* J 15.00 40.00
CM27 Glenn Hall/50* J 20.00 50.00
CM28 Tony Esposito/50* J 25.00 60.00
CM29 Harry Lumley/50* J 20.00 50.00
CM30 Stan Mikita/50* J 25.00 60.00
CM31 Bobby Hull/50* S 25.00 60.00
CM32 Tony Esposito/60* S 25.00 60.00
CM33 Glenn Hall/60* S 15.00 40.00
CM34 Michel Goulet/70* S 10.00 25.00
CM35 Tony Amonte/70* S 10.00 25.00
CM36 Jeremy Roenick/70* S 10.00 25.00
CM37 Stan Mikita/20* RN 25.00 50.00
CM38 Bobby Hull/20* RN 60.00 120.00
CM41 Mario Lemieux/100* SS 15.00 40.00
CM42 Ron Francis/100* SS 8.00 20.00
CM43 Joe Sakic/100* SS 8.00 20.00
CM44 Brett Hull/100* SS 8.00 20.00
CM45 Jaromir Jagr/100* SS 8.00 20.00
CM46 Mike Modano/100* SS 8.00 20.00
CM47 Teemu Selanne/100* SS 10.00 25.00
CM48 Pavel Bure/100* SS 6.00 15.00
CM49 Paul Kariya/100* SS 8.00 20.00
CM50 Peter Forsberg/100* SS 10.00 25.00
CM51 G.Hall/T.Esposito/100* 12.50 30.00
CM52 B.Hull/J.Roenick/100* 20.00 50.00
CM53 S.Mikita/T.Amonte/100* 15.00 40.00
CM54 H.Lumley/J.Thibault/100* 12.50 30.00
CM55 M.Goulet/E.Daze/100* 15.00 40.00
CM56 B.Mosienko/S.Sullivan/100* 12.50 30.00
CM57 F.Brimsek/E.Belfour/100* 12.50 30.00
CM58 D.Hull/A.Zhamnov/100* 15.00 40.00
CM59 Chris Chelios/100* J 15.00 40.00
CM60 Jeff Hackett/100* J 15.00 40.00
CM61 Bob Probert/100* J 20.00 50.00
CM62 Denis Savard/100* J 20.00 50.00

2003-04 Parkhurst Original Six Detroit

COMPLETE SET (100) 15.00 40.00
1 Mathieu Schneider .15 .40
2 Chris Chelios .40 1.00
3 Mathieu Dandenault .15 .40
4 Pavel Datsyuk .60 1.50
5 Boyd Devereaux .15 .40
6 Kris Draper .15 .40
7 Jason Woolley .15 .40
8 Mark Mowers .15 .40
9 Ray Whitney .15 .40
10 Jiri Fischer .15 .40
11 Tomas Holmstrom .15 .40
12 Brett Hull .60 1.50
13 Curtis Joseph .50 1.25
14 Jamie Rivers .15 .40
15 Dominik Hasek .75 2.00
16 Henrik Zetterberg .60 1.50
17 Steve Thomas .15 .40
18 Manny Legace .40 1.00
19 Nicklas Lidstrom .60 1.50
20 Kirk Maltby .15 .40
21 Darren McCarty .15 .40
22 Jiri Hudler XRC 1.50 4.00
23 Brendan Shanahan .50 1.25
24 Marc Lamothe .40 1.00
25 Derian Hatcher .15 .40
26 Jason Williams .30 .75
27 Steve Yzerman 2.00 4.00
28 Michel Picard .15 .40
29 Derek King .15 .40
30 Dmitri Bykov .15 .40
31 Bob Probert .40 1.00
32 Chris Osgood .40 1.00
33 Mike Vernon .40 1.00
34 Adam Oates .40 1.00
35 Terry Sawchuk .50 1.25
36 Alex Delvecchio .50 1.25
37 Danny Gare .15 .40
38 Marcel Dionne .50 1.25
39 Mickey Redmond .40 1.00
40 Ted Lindsay .40 1.00
41 Sid Abel .40 1.00
42 Red Kelly .40 1.00
43 Reed Larson .15 .40
44 Ebbie Goodfellow .15 .40
45 Bill Gadsby .40 1.00
46 Dino Ciccarelli .40 1.00
47 Glenn Hall .50 1.25
48 John Bucyk .50 1.25
49 Brad Smith .40 1.00
50 Norm Ullman .40 1.00
51 Marcel Pronovost .15 .40
52 Roger Crozier .50 1.25
53 Brad Park .50 1.25
54 Keith Primeau .40 1.00
55 Adam Graves .40 1.00
56 Ed Giacomin .50 1.25
57 Pat Verbeek .40 1.00
58 Harry Lumley .40 1.00
59 Gary Bergman .15 .40
60 Gerard Gallant .15 .40
61 Terry Sawchuk AS .50 1.25
62 Glenn Hall AS .50 1.25
63 Red Kelly AS .40 1.00
64 Nicklas Lidstrom AS .60 1.50
65 Marcel Pronovost AS .15 .40
66 Ted Lindsay AS .40 1.00
67 Sid Abel AS .40 1.00
68 Steve Yzerman AS .75 2.00
69 Brendan Shanahan AS .50 1.25
70 Alex Delvecchio AS .50 1.25
71 Steve Yzerman C .75 2.00
72 Alex Delvecchio C .50 1.25
73 Danny Gare C .15 .40
74 Marcel Dionne C .50 1.25
75 Mickey Redmond C .40 1.00
76 Ted Lindsay C .40 1.00
77 Sid Abel C .40 1.00
78 Red Kelly C .40 1.00
79 Reed Larson C .15 .40
80 Ebbie Goodfellow C .15 .40
81 Sid Abel E .40 1.00
82 Alex Delvecchio E .50 1.25
83 Ed Giacomin E .50 1.25
84 Red Kelly E .40 1.00
85 Ted Lindsay E .40 1.00
86 Marcel Pronovost E .15 .40
87 Terry Sawchuk E .50 1.25
88 Norm Ullman E .40 1.00
89 Bill Gadsby E .40 1.00
90 Glenn Hall E .50 1.25
91 Steve Yzerman FL .75 2.00
92 Steve Yzerman FL .75 2.00
93 Steve Yzerman FL .75 2.00
94 Terry Sawchuk FL .50 1.25
95 Terry Sawchuk FL .50 1.25
96 Steve Yzerman FL .75 2.00
97 Sergei Fedorov FL .30 .75
98 Nicklas Lidstrom FL .60 1.50
99 Marcel Dionne FL .50 1.25
100 Alex Delvecchio FL .50 1.25

2003-04 Parkhurst Original Six Detroit Autographs

OSNU Norm Ullman/85 15.00 40.00
OSMP Marcel Pronovost/88 20.00 50.00
OSDG Danny Gare/90 15.00 40.00
OSRL Reed Larson/98 15.00 40.00
OSBG Bill Gadsby/90 15.00 40.00
OSBS Brad Smith/90 15.00 40.00
OSDC Dino Ciccarelli/85 20.00 50.00
OSAD Alex Delvecchio/90 25.00 60.00
OSMD Marcel Dionne/75 15.00 40.00
OSGH Glenn Hall/80 30.00 80.00
OSGG Gerard Gallant/90 15.00 40.00
OSRK Red Kelly/80 25.00 60.00
OSTL Ted Lindsay/90 25.00 60.00
OSJB John Bucyk/80 25.00 60.00

2003-04 Parkhurst Original Six Detroit Inserts

COMPLETE SET (18) 30.00 60.00
D1 Terry Sawchuk 2.00 5.00
D2 Ted Lindsay 1.50 4.00
D3 Alex Delvecchio 2.00 5.00
D4 Sid Abel 1.50 4.00
D5 Ted Lindsay 1.50 4.00
D6 Sid Abel 1.50 4.00
D7 Terry Sawchuk 2.00 5.00
D8 Red Kelly 1.50 4.00
D9 Glenn Hall 2.00 5.00
D10 Roger Crozier 2.00 5.00
D11 Alex Delvecchio 2.00 5.00
D12 Red Kelly 1.50 4.00
D13 Nicklas Lidstrom 2.00 5.00
D14 Steve Yzerman 3.00 8.00
D15 Steve Yzerman 3.00 8.00
D16 Keith Primeau 1.50 4.00
D17 Marcel Dionne 2.00 5.00
D18 Martin Lapointe 1.50 4.00

2003-04 Parkhurst Original Six Detroit Memorabilia

DM1 Nicklas Lidstrom 10.00 25.00
DM2 Brendan Shanahan 10.00 25.00
DM3 Sergei Fedorov 15.00 40.00
DM4 Luc Robitaille 12.00 30.00
DM5 Steve Yzerman 20.00 50.00
DM6 Manny Legace 10.00 25.00
DM7 Mathieu Dandenault 6.00 15.00
DM8 Jiri Fischer 10.00 25.00
DM9 Darren McCarty 12.00 30.00
DM10 Pavel Datsyuk 12.00 30.00
DM11 Brett Hull 12.00 30.00
DM12 Igor Larionov 15.00 40.00
DM13 Chris Chelios 12.00 30.00
DM14 Nicklas Lidstrom J/S 15.00 40.00
DM15 Steve Yzerman J/S 40.00 80.00
DM16 Luc Robitaille J/S 15.00 40.00
DM17 Brendan Shanahan J/S 15.00 40.00
DM18 Sergei Fedorov J/S 20.00 50.00
DM19 Brett Hull J/S 15.00 40.00
DM20 Sergei Fedorov Glove 60.00 120.00
DM24 Roger Crozier/20 Pad 100.00 200.00
DM26 Sid Abel/40 J 40.00 100.00
DM27 Dino Ciccarelli/60 J 20.00 50.00
DM28 Alex Delvecchio/60 J 12.00 30.00
DM30 Ted Lindsay/20 J 20.00 50.00
DM31 Chris Osgood/80 J 12.50 30.00
DM32 Keith Primeau/80 J 12.50 30.00
DM33 Roger Crozier/50 J 12.50 30.00
DM35 Dino Ciccarelli/60 S 12.00 30.00
DM36 Ed Giacomin/60 S 25.00 60.00
DM38 A.Delvecchio/20 RN J 75.00 150.00
DM41 Mario Lemieux SS 15.00 40.00
DM42 Ron Francis SS 6.00 15.00
DM43 Joe Sakic SS 10.00 25.00
DM44 Brett Hull SS 10.00 25.00
DM45 Jaromir Jagr SS 8.00 20.00
DM46 Mike Modano SS 8.00 20.00
DM47 Teemu Selanne SS 10.00 25.00
DM48 Pavel Bure SS 6.00 15.00
DM49 Paul Kariya SS 8.00 20.00
DM50 Peter Forsberg SS 10.00 25.00
DM51 T.Lindsay/B.Hull 15.00 40.00
DM52 T.Sawchuk/D.Hasek 30.00 80.00
DM53 S.Abel/S.Yzerman 25.00 60.00
DM54 A.Delvecchio/B.Shanahan 20.00 50.00
DM55 D.Ciccarelli/P.Datsyuk 20.00 50.00
DM56 R.Crozier/C.Osgood 15.00 40.00
DM57 Henrik Zetterberg 10.00 25.00
DM58 Dominik Hasek 15.00 40.00
DM59 Manny Legace 12.50 30.00
DM60 Henrik Zetterberg J/S 25.00 60.00
DM61 Pavel Datsyuk J/S 25.00 60.00
DM62 Dominik Hasek J/S 20.00 50.00
DM63 Mike Vernon/100 J 15.00 40.00

2003-04 Parkhurst Original Six Montreal

COMPLETE SET (100) 15.00 40.00
COMP. SET w/o SP's
1 Tomas Plekanec XRC .15 .40
2 Jose Theodore .50 .13
3 Ron Hainsey .15 .40
4 Patrice Brisebois .15 .40
5 Jan Bulis .15 .40
6 Niklas Sundstrom .15 .40
7 Steve Begin .15 .40
8 Andreas Dackell .15 .40
9 Karl Dykhuis .15 .40
10 Michael Ryder .50 1.25
11 Jason Ward .15 .40
12 Benoit Gratton .15 .40
13 Chistopher Higgins XRC .40 1.00
14 Craig Rivet .15 .40
15 Marcel Hossa .30 .75
16 Joe Juneau .15 .40
17 Chad Kilger .15 .40
18 Saku Koivu .50 1.25
19 Sheldon Souray .15 .40
20 Andrei Markov .15 .40
21 Olivier Michaud .15 .40
22 Mathieu Garon .15 .40
23 Yanic Perreault .15 .40
24 Francis Bouillon .15 .40
25 Mike Ribeiro .15 .40
26 Stephane Quintal .15 .40
27 Richard Zednik .15 .40
28 Darren Langdon .15 .40
29 Mike Komisarek .15 .40
30 Pierre Dagenais .15 .40
31 Chris Chelios .50 1.25
32 John LeClair .50 1.25
33 Mark Recchi .40 1.00
34 Rejean Houle .15 .40
35 Howie Morenz .40 1.00
36 Jacques Laperriere .15 .40
37 Elmer Lach .40 1.00
38 Yvan Cournoyer .50 1.25
39 Larry Robinson .50 1.25
40 Serge Savard .50 1.25
41 Butch Bouchard .15 .40
42 Guy Lafleur 1.00 2.50
43 Henri Richard .50 1.25
44 Jean Beliveau .50 1.25
45 Maurice Richard 1.50 4.00
46 Toe Blake .50 1.25
47 Guy Lapointe .15 .40
48 Gump Worsley .75 2.00
49 Patrick Roy 1.50 4.00
50 Rogie Vachon .40 1.00
51 Bill Durnan .40 1.00
52 John Ferguson .40 1.00
53 Georges Vezina 1.25 3.00
54 Denis Savard .40 1.00
55 Doillard St-Laurent .15 .40
56 Jean-Guy Talbot .15 .40
57 Steve Shutt .40 1.00
58 Frank Mahovlich .50 1.25
59 Jacques Plante 1.00 2.50
60 Dickie Moore .40 1.00
61 Howie Morenz .40 1.00
62 Maurice Richard 1.50 4.00
63 Jean Beliveau .50 1.25
64 Elmer Lach .40 1.00
65 Henri Richard .50 1.25
66 Doug Harvey .50 1.25
67 Jacques Plante 1.00 2.50
68 Larry Robinson .50 1.25
69 Patrick Roy 1.50 4.00
70 Guy Lafleur 1.00 2.50
71 Saku Koivu .50 1.25
72 Butch Bouchard .15 .40
73 Vincent Damphousse .15 .40
74 Henri Richard .50 1.25
75 Jean Beliveau .50 1.25
76 Maurice Richard 1.50 4.00
77 Newsy Lalonde .15 .40
78 Yvan Cournoyer .50 1.25
79 Doug Harvey .50 1.25
80 Serge Savard .50 1.25
81 Howie Morenz .40 1.00
82 Georges Vezina 1.25 3.00
83 Elmer Lach .40 1.00
84 Maurice Richard 1.50 4.00
85 Jean Beliveau .50 1.25
86 Yvan Cournoyer .50 1.25
87 Doug Harvey .50 1.25
88 Guy Lafleur 1.00 2.50
89 Larry Robinson .50 1.25
90 Henri Richard .40 1.00
91 Henri Richard .40 1.00
92 Maurice Richard 1.50 4.00
93 Guy Lafleur 1.00 2.50
94 Guy Lafleur 1.00 2.50
95 Jacques Plante 1.00 2.50
96 Steve Shutt .40 1.00
97 Jean Beliveau .50 1.25
98 Larry Robinson .50 1.25
99 Patrick Roy 2.00 5.00
100 Maurice Richard 1.50 4.00

2003-04 Parkhurst Original Six Montreal Autographs

1 Jean Beliveau/85 75.00 125.00
2 Butch Bouchard/85 20.00 50.00
3 Yvan Cournoyer/85 25.00 60.00
4 John Ferguson/90 20.00 50.00
5 Charlie Hodge/85 25.00 60.00
6 Rejean Houle/85 20.00 50.00
7 Elmer Lach/90 25.00 60.00
8 Guy Lafleur/85 40.00 80.00
9 Jacques Laperriere/85 20.00 50.00
10 Frank Mahovlich/90 25.00 60.00
11 Dickie Moore/85 20.00 50.00
12 Henri Richard/85 25.00 60.00
13 Larry Robinson/85 40.00 100.00
14 Denis Savard/90 20.00 50.00
15 Serge Savard/85 25.00 60.00
16 Steve Shutt/85 20.00 50.00
17 Jean-Guy Talbot/85 20.00 50.00
18 Gump Worsley/40 75.00 150.00

2003-04 Parkhurst Original Six Montreal Inserts

COMPLETE SET (16) 25.00 50.00
M1 Jacques Plante 2.00 5.00
M2 Doug Harvey 1.50 4.00
M3 Jean Beliveau 1.50 4.00
M4 Maurice Richard 3.00 8.00
M5 Henri Richard 1.50 4.00
M6 Howie Morenz 1.50 4.00
M7 Guy Lafleur 2.00 5.00
M8 Jean Beliveau 2.00 5.00
M9 Jacques Plante 2.00 5.00
M10 Howie Morenz 1.50 4.00
M11 Doug Harvey 1.50 4.00
M12 Elmer Lach 1.50 4.00
M13 Bill Durnan 1.50 4.00
M14 Patrick Roy 3.00 8.00
M15 Saku Koivu 1.50 4.00
M16 Guy Lafleur 2.00 5.00

2003-04 Parkhurst Original Six Montreal Memorabilia

MM1 Jose Theodore 12.50 30.00
MM2 Niklas Sundstrom 6.00 15.00
MM3 Stephane Quintal 6.00 15.00
MM4 Jan Bulis 6.00 15.00
MM5 Saku Koivu 10.00 25.00
MM6 Craig Rivet 6.00 15.00
MM7 Mathieu Garon 10.00 25.00
MM8 Yanic Perreault 8.00 20.00
MM9 Chad Kilger 8.00 20.00
MM10 Marcel Hossa 10.00 25.00
MM11 Jose Theodore J/S 25.00 60.00
MM12 Stephane Quintal J/S 12.50 30.00
MM13 Saku Koivu J/S 25.00 60.00
MM14 Jose Theodore/80 20.00 50.00
MM15 Patrick Roy/80 Pad 25.00 60.00
MM16 Dickie Moore/70 J 30.00 80.00
MM18 Guy Lafleur/80 J 30.00 80.00
MM19 Doug Harvey/60 20.00 50.00
MM20 Charlie Hodge/50 Glove 20.00 50.00
MM21 Newsy Lalonde/60 30.00 80.00
MM22 Aurel Joliat/50 J 30.00 80.00
MM23 Henri Richard/60 J 20.00 50.00
MM24 Jean Beliveau/60 J 20.00 50.00
MM25 Doug Harvey/60 J 20.00 50.00
MM26 Guy Lafleur/50 J 20.00 50.00
MM27 Gump Worsley/70 J 20.00 50.00
MM30 Patrick Roy/80 J 25.00 60.00
MM32 Jean Beliveau/60 S 25.00 60.00
MM33 Guy Lafleur/50 S 30.00 80.00
MM34 Jacques Plante/60 S 30.00 80.00
MM41 Mario Lemieux SS 15.00 40.00
MM42 Ron Francis SS 6.00 15.00
MM43 Joe Sakic SS 12.50 30.00
MM44 Brett Hull SS 10.00 25.00
MM45 Jaromir Jagr SS 8.00 20.00
MM46 Mike Modano SS 8.00 20.00
MM47 Teemu Selanne SS 6.00 15.00
MM48 Pavel Bure SS 6.00 15.00
MM49 Paul Kariya SS 8.00 20.00
MM50 Peter Forsberg SS 10.00 25.00
MM51 J.Plante/P.Roy 50.00 120.00
MM52 H.Richard/S.Koivu 30.00 80.00
MM53 D.Harvey/L.Robinson 15.00 40.00
MM54 G.Worsley/J.Theodore 40.00 100.00
MM55 J.Beliveau/J.LeClair 15.00 40.00
MM56 A.Joliat/G.Lafleur 50.00 100.00
MM57 Mike Komisarek/100 J 10.00 25.00
MM58 Ron Hainsey/100 J 10.00 25.00
MM59 Guy Lapointe/80 J 20.00 50.00
MM60 Serge Savard/100 J 20.00 50.00
MM61 Steve Shutt/100 J 20.00 50.00
MM62 Peter Mahovlich/100 J 20.00 50.00
MM63 Jacques Plante/100 J 30.00 60.00

2003-04 Parkhurst Original Six New York

COMPLETE SET (100) 15.00 40.00
1 Matthew Barnaby .15 .40
2 Alex Kovalev .40 1.00
3 Dan Blackburn .40 1.00
4 Pavel Bure .50 1.25
5 Anson Carter .40 1.00
6 Jussi Markkanen .40 1.00
7 Jamie Lundmark .15 .40
8 Boris Mironov .15 .40
9 Joel Bouchard .15 .40
10 Dale Purinton .15 .40
11 Bobby Holik .15 .40
12 Dan Lacouture .15 .40
13 Mike Dunham .40 1.00
14 Greg de Vries .15 .40
15 Darius Kasparaitis .15 .40
16 Dominic Moore XRC .15 .40
17 Martin Rucinsky .15 .40
18 Brian Leetch .75 2.00
19 Pascal Rheaume .15 .40
20 Eric Lindros .50 1.25
21 Jan Hlavac .15 .40
22 Chris Simon .15 .40
23 Vladimir Malakhov .15 .40
24 Jed Ortmeyer XRC .15 .40
25 Mark Messier 1.50 4.00
26 Jason Labarbera .15 .40
27 Phil Osaer XRC .15 .40
28 Petr Nedved .15 .40
29 Tom Poti .15 .40
30 Jason MacDonald XRC .15 .40
31 Adam Graves .15 .40
32 Doug Weight .40 1.00
33 Tony Amonte .40 1.00
34 Ed Giacomin .60 1.50
35 Mike Gartner 1.50 3.00
36 Phil Esposito 1.50 4.00
37 Dan Cloutier .40 1.00
38 Ron Greschner .40 1.00
39 Luc Robitaille .40 1.00
40 Andy Bathgate .40 1.00
41 Frank Boucher .40 1.00
42 Brad Park .50 1.25
43 Ron Duguay .40 1.00
44 Bill Gadsby .40 1.00
45 Harry Howell .40 1.00
46 Ching Johnson .40 1.00
47 Doug Harvey .50 1.25
48 Guy Lafleur 1.50 3.00
49 John Davidson .60 1.50

50 Jean Ratelle .50 1.25
51 Mike Richter .75 2.00
52 John Vanbiesbrouck .40 1.00
53 Chuck Rayner .40 1.00
54 Lou Fontinato .15 .40
55 Rod Gilbert .50 1.25
56 Lester Patrick .50 1.25
57 Vic Hadfield .50 1.25
58 Walt Tkaczuk .15 .40
59 Gump Worsley .75 2.00
60 Bun Cook .40 1.00
61 Mark Messier 1.50 4.00
62 Brian Leetch .75 2.00
63 Phil Esposito 1.50 4.00
64 Ed Giacomin .60 1.50
65 Brad Park .50 1.25
66 Jean Ratelle .50 1.25
67 Pat Verbeek .15 .40
68 Barry Beck .15 .40
69 Rod Gilbert .50 1.25
70 Chuck Rayner .40 1.00
71 Mark Messier 1.50 4.00
72 Brian Leetch .75 2.00
73 Vic Hadfield .50 1.25
74 Phil Esposito 1.50 4.00
75 Ron Greschner .40 1.00
76 Walt Tkaczuk .15 .40
77 Harry Howell .40 1.00
78 Andy Bathgate .40 1.00
79 Barry Beck .15 .40
80 Brad Park .50 1.25
81 Brad Park .50 1.25
82 Ed Giacomin .60 1.50
83 Jean Ratelle .50 1.25
84 Phil Esposito 1.50 4.00
85 Rod Gilbert .50 1.25
86 Harry Howell .40 1.00
87 Chuck Rayner .40 1.00
88 Ching Johnson .40 1.00
89 Bill Cook .75 2.00
90 Andy Bathgate .40 1.00
91 Rod Gilbert .50 1.25
92 Harry Howell .40 1.00
93 Brian Leetch .75 2.00
94 Mike Richter .75 2.00
95 Ed Giacomin .60 1.50
96 Jean Ratelle .50 1.25
97 Brad Park .50 1.25
98 Mark Messier 1.50 4.00
99 Brian Leetch .75 2.00
100 Adam Graves .15 .40

2003-04 Parkhurst Original Six New York Autographs

1 Andy Bathgate/80 20.00 50.00
2 John Davidson/90 15.00 40.00
3 Ron Duguay/90 15.00 40.00
4 Phil Esposito/55 25.00 60.00
5 Lou Fontinato/95 15.00 40.00
6 Ed Giacomin/90 30.00 80.00
7 Rod Gilbert/85 30.00 80.00
8 Ron Greschner/95 15.00 40.00
9 Vic Hadfield/90 15.00 40.00
10 Harry Howell/95 15.00 40.00
11 Guy Lafleur/80 30.00 80.00
12 Brad Park/90 20.00 50.00
13 Jean Ratelle/90 20.00 50.00
14 Allan Stanley/85 20.00 50.00
15 Walt Tkaczuk/90 15.00 40.00
16 Gump Worsley/80 25.00 60.00

2003-04 Parkhurst Original Six New York Inserts

COMPLETE SET (16) 25.00 60.00
N1 Rod Gilbert 1.50 4.00
N2 Ed Giacomin 2.00 5.00
N3 Frank Boucher 1.50 4.00
N4 Rod Gilbert 1.50 4.00
N5 Phil Esposito 3.00 8.00
N6 Gump Worsley 2.00 5.00
N7 Ed Giacomin 2.00 5.00
N8 Doug Harvey 1.50 4.00
N9 Mark Messier 3.00 8.00
N10 Jean Ratelle 1.50 4.00
N11 Andy Bathgate 1.50 4.00
N12 Brian Leetch 2.00 5.00
N13 Chuck Rayner 1.50 4.00
N14 Brian Leetch 1.50 4.00
N15 Alex Kovalev 1.50 4.00
N16 Brad Park 1.50 4.00

2003-04 Parkhurst Original Six New York Memorabilia

NM1 Mike Dunham/100* 10.00 25.00
NM2 Brian Leetch/100* 15.00 40.00
NM3 Eric Lindros/100* 10.00 25.00
NM4 Mark Messier 10.00 25.00
NM5 Tom Poti/100* 6.00 15.00
NM6 Pavel Bure/100* 10.00 25.00
NM7 Mike Richter/100* 12.50 30.00
NM8 Dan Blackburn/100* 6.00 15.00
NM9 Darius Kasparaitis/100* 6.00 15.00
NM10 Bobby Holik/100* 6.00 15.00
NM11 Vladimir Malakhov/100* 6.00 15.00
NM12 Jamie Lundmark/100* 6.00 15.00
NM13 Brian Leetch J-S/80* 15.00 40.00
NM14 Eric Lindros J-S/80* 15.00 40.00
NM15 Mark Messier J-S/80* 30.00 80.00
NM16 Mike Richter J-S/80* 20.00 50.00
NM17 Pavel Bure J-S/80* 15.00 40.00
NM18 Dan Blackburn J-S/80* 12.50 30.00
NM19 Mike Dunham J-S/80* 15.00 40.00
NM20 Eric Lindros/30* 15.00 40.00
NM21 Terry Sawchuk/20* 40.00 80.00
NM22 Jacques Plante/20* 40.00 80.00
NM23 Bill Gadsby/20* 25.00 50.00
NM24 Doug Harvey/20* 40.00 80.00
NM27 Theo Fleury/50* J 10.00 25.00
NM28 Bryan Berard/60* J 10.00 25.00
NM29 Marcel Dionne/60* J 12.50 30.00
NM30 Ed Giacomin/50* J 30.00 80.00
NM31 Phil Esposito/50* J 15.00 40.00
NM32 Rod Gilbert/50* J 25.00 60.00
NM33 Jean Ratelle/50* J 25.00 60.00
NM34 Emile Francis/60* S 15.00 40.00
NM35 Gilles Villemure/60* S 15.00 40.00
NM36 Ed Giacomin/20* S 50.00 100.00
NM37 Phil Esposito/20* S 40.00 80.00
NM38 Johnny Bower/20* S 75.00 150.00
NM41 Mario Lemieux SS/100* 15.00 40.00
NM42 Ron Francis SS/100* 6.00 15.00
NM43 Joe Sakic SS/100* 10.00 25.00
NM44 Brett Hull SS/100* 8.00 20.00
NM45 Jaromir Jagr SS/100* 8.00 20.00
NM46 Mike Modano SS/100* 8.00 20.00
NM47 Teemu Selanne SS/100* 10.00 25.00
NM48 Pavel Bure SS/100* 6.00 15.00
NM49 Paul Kariya SS/100* 8.00 20.00
NM50 Peter Forsberg SS/100* 10.00 25.00
NM51 E.Giacomin/D.Blackburn 30.00 80.00
NM52 P.Esposito/E.Lindros 20.00 50.00
NM53 M.Dionne/A.Kovalev 12.50 30.00
NM54 J.Ratelle/M.Messier 40.00 100.00
NM55 R.Gilbert/P.Bure 12.50 30.00
NM56 Alex Kovalev/100 J 12.50 30.00
NM57 Alex Kovalev/100 J/S 12.50 30.00
NM58 Anson Carter/100 J 12.50 30.00
NM59 John Davidson/100 S 15.00 40.00
NM60 Marcel Dionne/100 S 12.50 30.00
NM61 Adam Graves/100 S 8.00 20.00
NM62 Sergei Zubov/100 J 8.00 20.00
NM63 Dan Cloutier/100 J 12.50 30.00

2003-04 Parkhurst Original Six Toronto

COMPLETE SET (100) 15.00 40.00
1 Nikolai Antropov .15 .40
2 Wade Belak .30 .75
3 Ed Belfour .40 1.00
4 Aki Berg .15 .40
5 Maxim Kondratiev XRC 1.25 3.00
6 Owen Nolan .30 .75
7 Nathan Perrott .15 .40
8 Tie Domi .40 1.00
9 Matt Stajan XRC 1.50 4.00
10 Ken Klee .15 .40
11 Bryan Marchment .15 .40
12 Jamie Hodson .15 .40
13 Carlo Colaiacovo .15 .40
14 Tomas Kaberle .15 .40
15 Joe Nieuwendyk .40 1.00
16 Bryan McCabe .15 .40
17 Ric Jackman .15 .40
18 Alexander Mogilny .40 1.00
19 Karel Pilar .15 .40
20 Alexei Ponikarovsky .15 .40
21 Robert Reichel .15 .40
22 Mikael Renberg .15 .40
23 Gary Roberts .15 .40
24 Mats Sundin .40 1.00
25 Mikael Tellqvist .30 .75
26 Darcy Tucker .15 .40
27 Aaron Gavey .15 .40
28 Josh Holden .15 .40
29 Trevor Kidd .40 1.00
30 Tom Fitzgerald .15 .40
31 Charlie Conacher .40 1.00
32 Doug Gilmour .40 1.00
33 Felix Potvin .40 1.00
34 Vincent Damphousse .40 1.00
35 Terry Sawchuk .75 2.00
36 Tiger Williams .75 2.00
37 Wendel Clark .60 1.50
38 Teeder Kennedy .40 1.00
39 Syl Apps .40 1.00
40 Hap Day .15 .40
41 Rick Vaive .15 .40
42 Curtis Joseph .40 1.00
43 Darryl Sittler .40 1.00
44 Bill Barilko .60 1.50
45 Bobby Baun .40 1.00
46 Borje Salming .40 1.00
47 Harry Lumley .40 1.00
48 Dick Duff .40 1.00
49 Mike Palmateer 1.00 2.50
50 Norm Ullman .40 1.00
51 Frank Mahovlich .40 1.00
52 Red Kelly .40 1.00
53 Sid Smith .40 1.00
54 Mike Gartner .60 1.50
55 Dave Andreychuk .15 .40
56 Johnny Bower 1.50 4.00
57 Turk Broda .60 1.50
58 Tim Horton 1.25 3.50
59 King Clancy .40 1.00
60 Ace Bailey .60 1.50
61 Mats Sundin .40 1.00
62 Doug Gilmour .40 1.00
63 Borje Salming .40 1.00
64 Lanny McDonald .40 1.00
65 Darryl Sittler .60 2.00
66 King Clancy .40 1.00
67 Turk Broda .60 1.50
68 Felix Potvin .40 1.00
69 Tim Horton 1.25 3.50
70 Sid Smith .40 1.00
71 Mats Sundin .40 1.00
72 Doug Gilmour .40 1.00
73 Wendel Clark .60 1.50
74 Teeder Kennedy .40 1.00
75 Syl Apps .40 1.00
76 Hap Day .15 .40
77 Rick Vaive .15 .40
78 Charlie Conacher .40 1.00
79 Darryl Sittler .60 2.00
80 Sid Smith .40 1.00
81 Ace Bailey .60 1.50
82 Johnny Bower 1.50 4.00
83 Turk Broda .60 1.50
84 Tim Horton 1.25 3.50
85 Red Kelly .40 1.00
86 Frank Mahovlich .40 1.00
87 Borje Salming .40 1.00
88 Marcel Pronovost .75 2.00
89 King Clancy .40 1.00
90 Syl Apps .40 1.00
91 Darryl Sittler .60 2.00
92 Tim Horton 1.25 3.50
93 Darryl Sittler .60 2.00
94 Borje Salming .40 1.00
95 Turk Broda .60 1.50
96 Rick Vaive .15 .40
97 Doug Gilmour .40 1.00
98 Frank Mahovlich .40 1.00
99 Wendel Clark .60 1.50
100 Ed Belfour .40 1.00

2003-04 Parkhurst Original Six Toronto Autographs

COMMON CARD (1-16) 20.00 50.00
1 Bobby Baun/85 30.00 80.00
2 Johnny Bower/90 25.00 60.00
3 Wendel Clark/90 30.00 80.00
4 Dick Duff/85 25.00 60.00
5 Red Kelly/90 25.00 60.00
6 Ted Kennedy/85 25.00 60.00
7 Frank Mahovlich/85 25.00 60.00
8 Eddie Shack/85 25.00 60.00
9 Darryl Sittler/95 25.00 60.00
10 Sid Smith/95 40.00 100.00
11 Ron Stewart/85 25.00 60.00
12 Rick Vaive/95 20.00 50.00
13 Tiger Williams/90 20.00 50.00
14 Mike Palmateer/95 25.00 60.00
15 Mike Gartner/85 25.00 60.00
16 Borje Salming/85 30.00 80.00

2003-04 Parkhurst Original Six Toronto Inserts

COMPLETE SET (17) 30.00 60.00
T1 Bill Barilko 2.00 5.00
T2 Ace Bailey 2.00 5.00
T3 Tim Horton 3.00 8.00
T4 Syl Apps 1.50 4.00
T5 Ted Kennedy 2.00 5.00
T6 Frank Mahovlich 3.00 8.00
T7 Ted Kennedy 2.00 5.00
T8 Red Kelly 2.00 5.00
T9 Ace Bailey 2.00 5.00
T10 Charlie Conacher 2.00 5.00
T11 Syl Apps 1.50 4.00
T12 Turk Broda 2.00 5.00
T13 Terry Sawchuk 2.00 5.00
T14 Johnny Bower 2.50 6.00
T15 Darryl Sittler 1.50 4.00
T16 Wendel Clark 3.00 8.00
T17 Lanny McDonald 1.50 4.00

2003-04 Parkhurst Original Six Toronto Memorabilia

TM1 Mats Sundin 15.00 40.00
TM2 Gary Roberts 10.00 25.00
TM3 Bryan McCabe 8.00 20.00
TM4 Darcy Tucker 10.00 25.00
TM5 Nik Antropov 10.00 25.00
TM6 Tomas Kaberle 10.00 25.00
TM7 Alexander Mogilny 10.00 25.00
TM8 Tie Domi 10.00 25.00
TM9 Ed Belfour 12.50 30.00
TM10 Owen Nolan 8.00 20.00
TM11 Carlo Colaiacovo 6.00 15.00
TM12 Robert Svehla 6.00 15.00
TM13 Trevor Kidd 10.00 25.00
TM14 Mats Sundin J/S 15.00 40.00
TM15 Alexander Mogilny J/S 12.50 30.00
TM16 Darcy Tucker J/S 12.50 30.00
TM17 Bryan McCabe J/S 12.50 30.00
TM18 Tomas Kaberle J/S 15.00 40.00
TM19 Gary Roberts J/S 12.50 30.00
TM24 Tim Horton/60 Pants 40.00 100.00
TM25 Wendel Clark/30 20.00 50.00
TM27 Borje Salming/80 15.00 40.00
TM30 Lanny McDonald/60 J 20.00 50.00
TM31 Tiger Williams/60 J 15.00 40.00
TM32 Curtis Joseph/60 J 20.00 50.00
TM33 Frank Mahovlich/50 S 25.00 60.00
TM34 Johnny Bower/50 S 25.00 60.00
TM36 Mats Sundin/50 25.00 50.00
TM41 Mario Lemieux SS 15.00 40.00
TM42 Ron Francis SS 6.00 15.00
TM43 Joe Sakic SS 10.00 25.00
TM44 Brett Hull SS 8.00 20.00
TM45 Jaromir Jagr SS 8.00 20.00
TM46 Mike Modano SS 8.00 20.00
TM47 Teemu Selanne SS 8.00 20.00
TM48 Pavel Bure SS 6.00 15.00
TM49 Paul Kariya SS 8.00 20.00
TM50 Peter Forsberg SS 10.00 25.00
TM51 T.Horton/W.Clark 30.00 80.00
TM52 R.Kelly/O.Nolan 15.00 40.00
TM53 L.McDonald/A.Mogilny 15.00 40.00
TM54 T.Williams/T.Domi 20.00 50.00
TM55 D.Sittler/M.Sundin 30.00 80.00
TM56 M.Gartner/G.Roberts 15.00 40.00
TM57 B.Salming/B.McCabe 15.00 40.00
TM58 R.Vaive/D.Tucker 15.00 40.00
TM59 Felix Potvin/100 J 15.00 40.00
TM60 Wendel Clark/100 J 20.00 50.00
TM61 Mike Gartner/100 J 15.00 40.00
TM62 Rick Vaive/100 J 15.00 40.00
TM63 Mike Gartner/80 S 15.00 40.00

2002-03 Parkhurst Retro

COMP.SET w/o SP's (200) 20.00 50.00
1 Mario Lemieux 1.25 3.00
2 Jarome Iginla .40 1.00
3 Jaromir Jagr 1.00 2.50
4 Alexei Kovalev .25 .60
5 Todd Bertuzzi .30 .75
6 Joe Thornton .50 1.25
7 Jason Allison .25 .60
8 Markus Naslund .30 .75
9 Eric Lindros .50 1.25
10 Keith Tkachuk .30 .75
11 Adam Oates .30 .75
12 Mike Modano .50 1.25
13 Pavel Bure .30 .75
14 Ron Francis .40 1.00
15 Joe Sakic .60 1.50
16 Brendan Shanahan .30 .75
17 Alexei Yashin .25 .60
18 Patrick Roy .75 2.00
19 Dwayne Roloson .20 .50
20 Pavol Demitra .40 1.00
21 Sergei Samsonov .25 .60
22 Steve Yzerman .75 2.00
23 Mats Sundin .30 .75
24 Peter Bondra .30 .75
25 Daniel Alfredsson .30 .75
26 Jeremy Roenick .50 1.25
27 Zigmund Palffy .30 .75
28 Ray Whitney .25 .60
29 Sami Kapanen .20 .50
30 Alexei Zhamnov .25 .60
31 Radek Bonk .25 .60
32 Eric Daze .20 .50
33 Tommy Salo .25 .60
34 Marian Gaborik .30 .75
35 Alexander Mogilny .25 .60
36 Glen Murray .25 .60
37 Patrik Elias .30 .75
38 Simon Gagne .30 .75
39 Ryan Smyth .25 .60
40 Bill Guerin .30 .75
41 Jeff Oneill .20 .50
42 Miroslav Satan .30 .75
43 Adam Deadmarsh .20 .50
44 Sergei Fedorov .50 1.25
45 Owen Nolan .30 .75
46 Tony Amonte .25 .60
47 Doug Weight .30 .75
48 Marian Hossa .30 .75
49 Mark Parrish .20 .50
50 Theo Fleury .40 1.00
51 Steven Reinprecht .20 .50
52 Dany Heatley .25 .60
53 Sergei Gonchar .25 .60
54 Ilya Kovalchuk .40 1.00
55 Brett Hull .60 1.50
56 Daniel Briere .25 .60
57 Brad Richards .30 .75
58 Brendan Morrison .25 .60
59 Steve Sullivan .20 .50
60 Mike York .20 .50
61 Nicklas Lidstrom .30 .75
62 Michael Peca .25 .60
63 Mark Recchi .40 1.00
64 Daymond Langkow .25 .60
65 Tyler Arnason .30 .75
66 Rob Blake .30 .75
67 Mike Comrie .30 .75
68 Felix Potvin .50 1.25
69 Brian Rolston .25 .60
70 Martin Brodeur .75 2.00
71 Anson Carter .25 .60
72 Roberto Luongo .50 1.25
73 Joe Nieuwendyk .25 .60
74 Dean McAmmond .20 .50
75 Niko Kapanen .25 .60
76 Jan Hrdina .20 .50
77 Vincent Damphousse .25 .60
78 Jozef Stumpel .20 .50
79 Milan Hejduk .25 .60
80 Stu Barnes .20 .50
81 Pierre Turgeon .25 .60
82 Marty Turco .30 .75
83 Bryan McCabe .20 .50
84 Gary Roberts .20 .50
85 Martin Havlat .25 .60
86 Kyle Calder .20 .50
87 Paul Kariya .30 .75
88 Martin Straka .25 .60
89 Yanic Perreault .20 .50
90 Brian Boucher .25 .60
91 Darcy Tucker .20 .50
92 Mike Ricci .20 .50
93 Keith Primeau .25 .60
94 Bobby Holik .20 .50
95 Chris Osgood .30 .75
96 Brian Leetch .25 .60
97 Teemu Selanne .60 1.50
98 Alex Tanguay .25 .60
99 Rod Brind'Amour .30 .75
100 Petr Sykora .25 .60
101 Jere Lehtinen .30 .75
102 Kevin Weekes .25 .60
103 Jason Arnott .25 .60
104 Al MacInnis .40 1.00
105 Scott Gomez .25 .60
106 Byron Dafoe .25 .60
107 Evgeni Nabokov .25 .60
108 Sandis Ozolinsh .20 .50
109 John LeClair .30 .75
110 Mike Dunham .25 .60
111 Manny Fernandez .20 .50
112 Johan Hedberg .30 .75
113 Chris Pronger .30 .75
114 Fredrik Modin .20 .50
115 Rostislav Klesla .20 .50
116 Manny Legace .30 .75
117 Teppo Numminen .20 .50
118 Shane Doan .25 .60
119 Martin Biron .25 .60
120 Luc Robitaille .30 .75
121 Igor Larionov .30 .75
122 Doug Gilmour .40 1.00
123 Roman Cechmanek .25 .60
124 Marc Savard .20 .50
125 Scott Stevens .30 .75
126 Steve Rucchin .20 .50
127 Olaf Kolzig .30 .75
128 Ed Jovanovski .25 .60
129 Petr Nedved .20 .50
130 Valeri Bure .25 .60
131 J-P Dumont .20 .50
132 Jocelyn Thibault .25 .60
133 Martin Lapointe .25 .60
134 Tomas Kaberle .20 .50
135 Jose Theodore .30 .75
136 Bates Battaglia .20 .50
137 Chris Drury .30 .75
138 Patrick Lalime .25 .60
139 Derek Morris .20 .50
140 Sean Burke .20 .50
141 Radek Dvorak .25 .60
142 Ladislav Nagy .20 .50
143 Oleg Petrov .20 .50
144 Kristian Huselius .20 .50
145 Mark Messier .60 1.50
146 Curtis Joseph .40 1.00
147 Tim Connolly .20 .50
148 Arturs Irbe .25 .60
149 Espen Knutsen .20 .50
150 Ed Belfour .30 .75
151 Jaroslav Modry .20 .50
152 Dan Cloutier .25 .60
153 Jeff Friesen .20 .50
154 Janne Niinimaa .20 .50
155 Nikolai Khabibulin .30 .75
156 Justin Williams .25 .60
157 Kyle McLaren .20 .50
158 Sergei Zubov .25 .60
159 Brian Savage .20 .50
160 Chris Chelios .30 .75
161 Roman Hamrlik .20 .50
162 Scott Niedermayer .30 .75
163 Danny Markov .20 .50
164 Marc Denis .25 .60
165 Scott Hartnell .20 .50
166 Roman Turek .30 .75
167 Brenden Morrow .25 .60
168 David Legwand .25 .60
169 Henrik Sedin .40 1.00
170 Oleg Tverdovsky .20 .50
171 Peter Forsberg .60 1.50
172 Vincent Lecavalier .30 .75
173 Pavel Datsyuk .50 1.25
174 Dan Blackburn .25 .60
175 Adam Foote .20 .50
176 Joe Juneau .20 .50
177 Mike Richter .30 .75
178 Shawn Bates .20 .50
179 Erik Cole .20 .50
180 Jean-Sebastien Giguere .30 .75
181 Saku Koivu .30 .75
182 Zdeno Chara .30 .75
183 Stephen Weiss .30 .75
184 Robert Svehla .20 .50
185 Patrick Stefan .25 .60
186 Robert Lang .20 .50
187 Olli Jokinen .30 .75
188 Pavel Brendl .20 .50
189 Brent Johnson .25 .60
190 Boris Mironov .20 .50
191 Tomas Vokoun .25 .60
192 Darius Kasparaitis .20 .50
193 Martin St. Louis .30 .75
194 Radim Vrbata .20 .50
195 Jeff Hackett .25 .60
196 Nik Antropov .25 .60
197 Craig Conroy .20 .50
198 Nick Boynton .20 .50
199 Richard Zednik .20 .50
200 Vaclav Prospal .20 .50
201 P-M Bouchard RC 3.00 8.00
202 Rick Nash RC 15.00 40.00
203 Dennis Seidenberg RC 3.00 8.00
204 Jay Bouwmeester RC 6.00 15.00
205 Stanislav Chistov RC 2.00 5.00
206 Pascal Leclaire RC 2.50 6.00
207 Jared Aulin RC 2.00 5.00
208 Chuck Kobasew RC 2.50 6.00
209 Jordan Leopold RC 3.00 8.00
210 Steve Ott RC 2.00 5.00
211 Ales Hemsky RC 8.00 20.00
212 Matt Walker RC 2.00 5.00
213 Tomas Malec RC 2.00 5.00
214 Dmitri Bykov RC 2.00 5.00
215 Michael Leighton RC 3.00 8.00
216 Henrik Zetterberg RC 20.00 50.00
217 Alexander Frolov RC 5.00 12.00
218 Steve Eminger RC 2.00 5.00
219 Scottie Upshall RC 2.50 6.00
220 Rickard Wallin RC 2.00 5.00
221 Alexei Semenov RC 2.00 5.00
222 Ron Hainsey RC 2.00 5.00
223 Martin Gerber RC 3.00 8.00
224 Adam Hall RC 2.00 5.00
225 Ray Emery RC 6.00 15.00
226 Anton Volchenkov RC 2.00 5.00
227 Levente Szuper RC 3.00 8.00
228 Carlo Colaiacovo RC 3.00 8.00
229 Alexander Svitov RC 2.00 5.00
230 Alexei Smirnov RC 2.50 6.00
231 Jeff Taffe RC 2.00 5.00
232 Mikael Tellqvist RC 2.00 5.00
233 Ari Ahonen RC 2.00 5.00
234 Martin Samuelsson RC 2.00 5.00
235 Shaone Morrisonn RC 2.00 5.00
236 Craig Andersson RC 8.00 20.00
237 Jim Fahey RC 2.00 5.00
238 Brooks Orpik RC 2.00 5.00
239 Mike Komisarek RC 3.00 8.00
240 Frederic Cloutier RC 2.00 5.00
241 Curtis Sanford RC 3.00 8.00
242 Jim Vandermeer RC 2.00 5.00
243 Paul Manning RC 2.00 5.00
244 Kris Vernarsky RC 2.00 5.00
245 Dany Sabourin RC 2.00 5.00
246 Mike Cammalleri RC 6.00 15.00
247 Jason Spezza RC 12.00 30.00
248 Cristobal Huet RC 4.00 10.00
249 Ryan Miller RC 12.00 30.00
250 Dick Tarnstrom RC 2.00 5.00

2002-03 Parkhurst Retro Minis

*1-200 VETS: 1.2X TO 3X BASIC CARDS
*201-250 ROOKIE: .3X TO .8X BASIC RC
145 Mark Messier 2.00 5.00

2002-03 Parkhurst Retro Back In Time

1 1951-52 Parkhurst 25.00 60.00
2 1952-53 Parkhurst 25.00 60.00
3 1953-54 Parkhurst 25.00 60.00
4 1954-55 Parkhurst 25.00 60.00
5 1955-56 Parkhurst 25.00 60.00
6 1957-58 Parkhurst 25.00 60.00
7 1958-89 Parkhurst 25.00 60.00
8 1959-60 Parkhurst 25.00 60.00
9 1960-61 Parkhurst 25.00 60.00
10 1961-62 Parkhurst 25.00 60.00
11 1962-63 Parkhurst 25.00 60.00
12 1962-63 Parkhurst 25.00 60.00
13 1962-63 Parkhurst 25.00 60.00
14 1963-64 Parkhurst 25.00 60.00
15 1963-64 Parkhurst 25.00 60.00

2002-03 Parkhurst Retro Franchise Players Jerseys

RF1 Paul Kariya 8.00 20.00
RF2 Dany Heatley 10.00 25.00
RF3 Joe Thornton 12.50 30.00
RF4 Miroslav Satan 8.00 20.00
RF5 Jarome Iginla 12.50 30.00
RF6 Ron Francis 8.00 20.00
RF7 Jocelyn Thibault 8.00 20.00
RF8 Rick Nash 12.50 30.00
RF9 Joe Sakic 15.00 40.00
RF10 Mike Modano 10.00 25.00
RF11 Steve Yzerman 15.00 40.00
RF12 Mike Comrie 8.00 20.00
RF13 Roberto Luongo 12.50 30.00
RF14 Jason Allison 8.00 20.00
RF15 Marian Gaborik 12.50 30.00
RF16 Jose Theodore 12.50 30.00
RF17 David Legwand 8.00 20.00
RF18 Martin Brodeur 15.00 40.00
RF19 Mike Peca 8.00 20.00
RF20 Pavel Bure 8.00 20.00
RF21 Marian Hossa 8.00 20.00
RF22 Jeremy Roenick 10.00 25.00
RF23 Daniel Briere 8.00 20.00
RF24 Mario Lemieux 20.00 50.00
RF25 Teemu Selanne 8.00 20.00
RF26 Chris Pronger 8.00 20.00
RF27 Vincent Lecavalier 8.00 20.00
RF28 Mats Sundin 8.00 20.00
RF29 Markus Naslund 8.00 20.00
RF30 Jaromir Jagr 12.50 30.00

2002-03 Parkhurst Retro He Shoots He Scores Points

1 Marian Gaborik 1 pt. .20 .50
2 Dany Heatley 1 pt. .20 .50
3 Marian Hossa 1 pt. .20 .50
4 Mike Modano 1 pt. .20 .50
5 Rick Nash 1 pt. .20 .50
6 Brendan Shanahan 1 pt. .20 .50
7 Joe Thornton 1 pt. .20 .50
8 Marty Turco 1 pt. .20 .50
9 Ed Belfour 2 pts. .20 .50
10 Martin Brodeur 2 pts. .20 .50
11 Pavel Bure 2 pts. .20 .50
12 Peter Forsberg 2 pts. .20 .50
13 Jaromir Jagr 2 pts. .20 .50
14 Paul Kariya 2 pts. .20 .50
15 Ilya Kovalchuk 2 pts. .20 .50
16 Eric Lindros 2 pts. .20 .50
17 Joe Sakic 2 pts. .20 .50
18 Mario Lemieux 3 pts. .20 .50
19 Patrick Roy 3 pts. .20 .50
20 Steve Yzerman 3 pts. .20 .50

2002-03 Parkhurst Retro Hopefuls

CH1 Tyler Arnason 12.50 30.00
CH2 Rick Nash 25.00 60.00
CH3 Ryan Miller 15.00 40.00
CH4 Niko Kapanen 10.00 25.00
CH5 Alexander Frolov 12.50 30.00
CH6 Stanislav Chistov 12.50 30.00
CH7 Barret Jackman 12.50 30.00
CH8 Jay Bouwmeester 12.50 30.00
HH1 Mario Lemieux 25.00 60.00
HH2 Joe Thornton 12.50 30.00
HH3 Markus Naslund 12.50 30.00
HH4 Marty Turco 12.50 30.00
HH5 Nicklas Lidstrom 12.50 30.00
HH6 Marian Gaborik 15.00 40.00
HH7 Marian Hossa 12.50 30.00
HH8 Jaromir Jagr 15.00 40.00
NH1 Nicklas Lidstrom 12.50 30.00
NH2 Rob Blake 12.50 30.00
NH3 Adam Foote 12.50 30.00
NH4 Al MacInnis 12.50 30.00
NH5 Sergei Zubov 10.00 25.00
NH6 Ed Jovanovski 10.00 25.00
NH7 Tomas Kaberle 10.00 25.00
NH8 Derian Hatcher 10.00 25.00
RR1 Jaromir Jagr 15.00 40.00
RR2 Marian Hossa 12.50 30.00
RR3 Mats Sundin 12.50 30.00
RR4 Marian Gaborik 15.00 40.00
RR5 Markus Naslund 10.00 25.00
RR6 Ilya Kovalchuk 20.00 50.00
RR7 Joe Thornton 12.50 30.00
RR8 Milan Hejduk 10.00 25.00
VH1 Ed Belfour 15.00 40.00
VH2 Marty Turco 10.00 25.00
VH3 Martin Brodeur 20.00 50.00
VH4 Patrick Lalime 10.00 25.00
VH5 Jean-Sebastien Giguere 10.00 25.00
VH6 Jocelyn Thibault 10.00 25.00
VH7 Patrick Roy 20.00 50.00
VH8 Nikolai Khabibulin 10.00 25.00

2002-03 Parkhurst Retro Jerseys

RJ1 Patrick Roy 12.00 30.00
RJ2 Mike Modano 8.00 20.00
RJ3 Peter Forsberg 10.00 25.00
RJ4 Mark Messier 8.00 20.00
RJ5 Brett Hull 10.00 25.00
RJ6 Martin Brodeur 12.50 30.00
RJ7 Joe Thornton 10.00 25.00
RJ8 Ed Belfour 8.00 20.00
RJ9 Pavel Bure 8.00 20.00
RJ10 Rick Nash 12.50 30.00
RJ11 Marty Turco 6.00 15.00
RJ12 Jay Bouwmeester 6.00 15.00
RJ13 Jason Spezza 10.00 30.00
RJ14 Jaromir Jagr 8.00 20.00
RJ15 Mario Lemieux 15.00 40.00
RJ16 Markus Naslund 8.00 20.00
RJ17 Brendan Shanahan 8.00 20.00
RJ18 Paul Kariya 8.00 20.00
RJ19 Roberto Luongo 10.00 25.00
RJ20 Joe Sakic 12.50 30.00
RJ21 Mats Sundin 8.00 20.00
RJ22 Steve Yzerman 12.50 30.00
RJ23 Dany Heatley 8.00 20.00
RJ24 Jose Theodore 8.00 20.00
RJ25 John LeClair 8.00 20.00
RJ26 Marian Hossa 8.00 20.00
RJ27 Eric Lindros 8.00 20.00
RJ28 Sergei Fedorov 8.00 20.00
RJ29 Todd Bertuzzi 8.00 20.00
RJ30 Sergei Samsonov 6.00 15.00
RJ31 Jeremy Roenick 8.00 20.00
RJ32 Nicklas Lidstrom 8.00 20.00
RJ33 Bill Guerin 6.00 15.00
RJ34 Chris Pronger 6.00 15.00
RJ35 Saku Koivu 8.00 20.00
RJ36 Marian Gaborik 8.00 20.00
RJ37 Ilya Kovalchuk 8.00 20.00
RJ38 Jocelyn Thibault 6.00 15.00
RJ39 Vincent Lecavalier 6.00 15.00
RJ40 Teemu Selanne 8.00 20.00

2002-03 Parkhurst Retro Jersey and Sticks

*JSY/STK: .6X TO 1.5X JSY CARD HI

2002-03 Parkhurst Retro Magnificent Inserts

MI1 Mario Lemieux 2000-01 Season 30.00 80.00
MI2 Mario Lemieux 1985-86 Season 30.00 80.00
MI3 Mario Lemieux 2002 All-Star 30.00 80.00
MI4 Mario Lemieux 1987 Canada Cup 30.00 80.00
MI5 Mario Lemieux Dual Jersey 50.00 125.00

2002-03 Parkhurst Retro Memorabilia

RM1 Mario Lemieux/50 15.00 40.00
RM2 Joe Sakic/50 12.50 30.00
RM3 Joe Thornton/60 12.50 30.00
RM4 Marian Hossa/50 10.00 25.00
RM5 Nicklas Lidstrom/50 10.00 25.00
RM6 Patrick Roy/50 15.00 40.00
RM7 Jose Theodore/50 12.50 30.00
RM8 Mario Lemieux/30 25.00 60.00
RM9 Martin Brodeur/50 15.00 40.00
RM10 Dany Heatley/50 12.50 30.00
RM11 Ilya Kovalchuk/60 12.50 30.00
RM12 Marty Turco/50 10.00 25.00
RM13 Sergei Fedorov/50 10.00 25.00
RM14 Steve Yzerman/50 20.00 50.00
RM15 Jason Spezza/60 12.50 30.00
RM16 Pavel Bure/50 10.00 25.00
RM17 Peter Forsberg/50 12.50 30.00
RM18 Brendan Shanahan/50 10.00 25.00
RM19 Joe Thornton/30 15.00 40.00
RM20 Mike Modano/60 10.00 25.00
RM21 Nikolai Khabibulin/30 10.00 25.00
RM22 Jaromir Jagr/60 10.00 25.00
RM23 Joe Sakic/50 12.50 30.00
RM24 Mats Sundin/50 10.00 25.00
RM25 Saku Koivu/60 10.00 25.00
RM26 Jay Bouwmeester/60 12.50 30.00
RM27 Paul Kariya/60 10.00 25.00
RM28 Rick Nash/50 12.50 30.00
RM29 Mario Lemieux/50 15.00 40.00
RM30 Brett Hull/30 12.50 30.00

2002-03 Parkhurst Retro Nicknames

RN1 Frank Brimsek/35* 20.00 40.00
RN2 Henri Richard/40* 20.00 50.00
RN3 Ed Giacomin/40* 20.00 50.00
RN4 Bobby Hull/35* 20.00 50.00
RN5 Bernie Geoffrion/20* 30.00 80.00
RN6 Gerry Cheevers/50* 12.00 30.00
RN7 Johnny Bucyk/40* 20.00 50.00
RN8 Johnny Bower/40* 20.00 50.00
RN9 Gump Worsley/40* 30.00 80.00
RN10 Glenn Hall/40* 15.00 40.00
RN11 Red Kelly/40* 15.00 40.00
RN12 F.Mahvlch/P.Mahvlch/40* 40.00 80.00
RN13 Ace Bailey/20* 60.00 120.00
RN14 King Clancy/20* 30.00 60.00
RN15 Roy Worters/20* 15.00 40.00
RN16 Stan Mikita/50* 15.00 40.00
RN17 Rocket Richard/20* 50.00 100.00
RN18 Turk Broda/20* 12.00 30.00
RN19 Tony Esposito/35* 20.00 50.00
RN20 Jean Beliveau/35* 40.00 80.00
RN21 Jacques Plante/35* 30.00 80.00
RN22 Steve Yzerman/65* 15.00 40.00
RN23 Brett Hull/65* 15.00 40.00
RN24 Patrick Roy/65* 20.00 50.00
RN25 Felix Potvin/65* 15.00 40.00
RN26 Teemu Selanne/65* 12.00 30.00
RN27 Olaf Kolzig/65* 12.00 30.00
RN28 Pavel Bure/65* 12.00 30.00
RN29 Eric Lindros/65* 12.00 30.00
RN30 Mario Lemieux/65* 30.00 80.00

2003-04 Parkhurst Rookie

1 Steve Yzerman 4.00 10.00
2 Joe Sakic 3.00 8.00
3 Jeremy Roenick 2.50 6.00
4 Brian Leetch 1.25 3.00
5 Andrew Raycroft 1.25 3.00
6 Dan Cloutier 1.25 3.00
7 Marty Turco 1.50 4.00
8 Owen Nolan 1.50 4.00
9 Joe Thornton 2.50 6.00
10 Marian Gaborik 1.50 4.00
11 Mario Lemieux 6.00 15.00
12 Zigmund Palffy 1.50 4.00
13 Vincent Lecavalier 1.50 4.00
14 Sean Burke 1.00 2.50
15 Miikka Kiprusoff 1.50 4.00
16 Dominik Hasek 2.50 6.00
17 Nikolai Khabibulin 1.50 4.00
18 Ed Belfour 1.50 4.00
19 Ilya Kovalchuk 1.50 4.00
20 Marian Hossa 1.50 4.00
21 Tommy Salo 1.25 3.00
22 Keith Tkachuk 1.50 4.00
23 Alex Kovalev 1.25 3.00
24 Michael Ryder 1.25 3.00
25 Steve Sullivan 1.00 2.50
26 Martin St-Louis 1.50 4.00
27 Al MacInnis 2.00 5.00
28 Sergei Gonchar 1.00 2.50
29 Jaromir Jagr 5.00 12.00
30 Ron Francis 2.00 5.00
31 Henrik Zetterberg 2.00 5.00
32 Paul Kariya 1.50 4.00
33 Robert Lang 1.00 2.50
34 Nicklas Lidstrom 1.50 4.00
35 Sergei Fedorov 2.50 6.00
36 Jarome Iginla 2.00 5.00
37 Bill Guerin 1.50 4.00
38 Jose Theodore 1.50 4.00
39 Roberto Luongo 2.50 6.00
40 Alex Tanguay 1.25 3.00
41 Peter Forsberg 3.00 8.00
42 Mike Modano 2.50 6.00
43 Dwayne Roloson 1.25 3.00
44 Martin Brodeur 4.00 10.00
45 Dany Heatley 1.25 3.00

46 Rick Nash 1.50 4.00
47 Jason Spezza 1.50 4.00
48 Chris Pronger 1.50 4.00
49 Brett Hull 3.00 8.00
50 Markus Naslund 1.50 4.00
51 Curtis Joseph 2.00 5.00
52 Olaf Kolzig 1.50 4.00
53 Peter Bondra 1.50 4.00
54 Eric Lindros 2.50 6.00
55 Mats Sundin 1.50 4.00
56 Patrick Roy 4.00 10.00
57 Ray Bourque 4.00 10.00
58 Terry Sawchuk 3.00 8.00
59 Maurice Richard 5.00 12.00
60 Bobby Orr 10.00 25.00
61 Bartovic RC/Pominville RC 6.00 15.00
62 McDonell RC/A.Johnson RC 3.00 8.00
63 Hutchinson RC/L.Pivko RC 2.50 6.00
64 Gernander RC/P.Osaer RC 2.50 6.00
65 R.Mrozik RC/J.Pollock RC 2.50 6.00
66 S.Meyer RC/D.Verot RC 3.00 8.00
67 M.Yeats RC/D.Zinger RC 2.50 6.00
68 J.DiPenta RC/J. Olson RC 3.00 8.00
69 Rourke RC/J.MacMillan RC 3.00 8.00
70 Underhill RC/D.Salficky RC 3.00 8.00
71 Vauclair RC/Z.Michalek RC 2.50 6.00
72 M.Hussey RC/M.Stutzel RC 2.50 6.00
73 B.Lampman RC/T.Pock RC 3.00 8.00
74 G.Mink RC/R.Tvrdon RC 2.50 6.00
75 MacDonald RC/Morrison RC 3.00 8.00
76 Pandolfo RC/G.Mauldin RC 3.00 8.00
77 J.Yablonski RC/C.Larose RC 3.00 8.00
78 C.Brandner RC/E.Perrin RC 3.00 8.00
79 Michal Barinka RC 2.50 6.00
80 Erik Westrum RC 2.50 6.00
81 Gavin Morgan RC 3.00 8.00
82 Matt Ellison RC 2.50 6.00
83 Seamus Kotyk RC 2.50 6.00
84 Andy Chiodo RC 2.50 6.00
85 Mikko Luoma RC 2.50 6.00
86 Jed Ortmeyer RC 2.50 6.00
87 Brad Boyes RC 4.00 10.00
88 Robert Scuderi RC 3.00 8.00
89 Nolan Schaefer RC 2.50 6.00
90 Colton Orr RC 3.00 8.00
91 Travis Moen RC 3.00 8.00
92 Fred Meyer RC 2.50 6.00
93 Joe Motzko RC 2.50 6.00
94 Ryan Barnes RC 2.50 6.00
95 Rob Skrlac RC 2.50 6.00
96 Quintin Laing RC 2.50 6.00
97 Mikhail Kuleshov RC 2.50 6.00
98 Adam Munro RC 2.50 6.00
99 Wade Dubielewicz RC 2.50 6.00
100 Matt Keith RC 2.50 6.00
101 Steve McLaren RC 2.50 6.00
102 Tim Jackman RC 3.00 8.00
103 Doug Doull RC 2.50 6.00
104 Lawrence Nycholat RC 3.00 8.00
105 Aleksander Suglobov RC 2.50 6.00
106 Martin Strbak RC 3.00 8.00
107 Lasse Kukkonen RC 2.50 6.00
108 Gregory Campbell RC 2.50 6.00
109 Tony Martensson RC 2.50 6.00
110 Carl Corazzini RC 2.50 6.00
111 Mike Green RC 3.00 8.00
112 Nathan Robinson RC 2.50 6.00
113 Brent Krahn RC 2.50 6.00
114 Mike Smith RC 8.00 20.00
115 Mike Stuart RC 2.50 6.00
116 Karl Stewart RC 2.50 6.00
117 Jason MacDonald RC 2.50 6.00
118 Brooks Laich RC 4.00 10.00
119 Tom Preissing RC 3.00 8.00
120 Mikhail Yakubov RC 2.50 6.00
121 Benoit Dusablon RC 2.50 6.00
122 Nathan Smith RC 2.50 6.00
123 Goran Bezina RC 2.50 6.00
124 Dan Ellis RC 3.00 8.00
125 Pat Rissmiller RC 3.00 8.00
126 Owen Fussey RC 2.50 6.00
127 Miko Bichai RC 2.50 6.00
128 Matt Murley RC 3.00 8.00
129 Wade Brookbank RC 3.00 8.00
130 Randy Jones RC 2.50 6.00
131 Fedor Tyutin JSY RC 4.00 10.00
132 Niklas Kronwall JSY RC 8.00 20.00
133 Boyd Kane JSY RC 4.00 10.00
134 Sergei Zinovjev JSY RC 4.00 10.00
135 Mark Popovic JSY RC 5.00 12.00
136 Sean Bergenheim JSY RC 5.00 12.00
137 Ryan Kesler JSY RC 15.00 40.00
138 Christian Ehrhoff JSY RC 5.00 12.00
139 Peter Sejna JSY RC 5.00 12.00
140 Denis Grebeshkov JSY RC 4.00 10.00
141 Tuomas Pihlman JSY RC 5.00 12.00
142 A. Niittymaki JSY RC 10.00 25.00
143 Patrick Leahy JSY RC 5.00 12.00
144 Rastislav Stana JSY RC 6.00 15.00
145 Grant McNeill JSY RC 4.00 10.00
146 Cody McCormick JSY RC 5.00 12.00
147 Boyd Gordon JSY RC 5.00 12.00
148 Garth Murray JSY RC 5.00 12.00
149 Trevor Daley JSY RC 6.00 15.00
150 M. Svatos JSY RC 8.00 20.00
151 Esa Pirnes JSY RC 4.00 10.00
152 Garrett Burnett JSY RC 4.00 10.00
153 Tony Salmelainen JSY RC 4.00 10.00
154 John Pohl JSY RC 4.00 10.00
155 Dominic Moore JSY RC 4.00 10.00
156 Fredrik Sjostrom AU RC 10.00 25.00
157 Jozef Balej AU RC 6.00 15.00
158 Jiri Hudler AU RC 15.00 40.00
159 Joffrey Lupul AU RC 15.00 40.00
160 Tomas Plekanec AU RC 20.00 50.00
161 Kyle Wellwood AU RC 10.00 25.00
162 Peter Sarno AU RC 6.00 15.00
163 Pavel Vorobiev AU RC 8.00 20.00
164 Andrew Peters AU RC 8.00 20.00
165 Jeff Hamilton AU RC 6.00 15.00
166 Darryl Bootland AU RC 8.00 20.00
167 Noah Clarke AU RC 6.00 15.00
168 Matthew Spiller AU RC 8.00 20.00
169 Milan Michalek AU RC 12.00 30.00
170 Doug Lynch AU RC 6.00 15.00
171 Timofei Shishkanov AU RC 6.00 15.00
172 Maxim Kondratiev AU RC 6.00 15.00
173 Chris Kunitz AU RC 12.00 30.00
174 Jordin Tootoo AU RC 12.00 30.00
175 Anton Babchuk AU RC 6.00 15.00
176 Eric Staal JSY AU RC 40.00 100.00
177 Dan Fritsche JSY AU RC 10.00 25.00
178 J. Pitkanen JSY AU RC 15.00 40.00
179 Tim Gleason JSY AU RC 12.00 30.00
180 C. Higgins JSY AU RC 20.00 50.00
181 N.Horton JSY AU RC 25.00 60.00
182 Marek Zidlicky JSY AU RC 10.00 25.00
183 Antti Miettinen JSY AU RC 15.00 40.00
184 P.Bergeron JSY AU RC 100.00 250.00
185 R. Malone JSY AU RC 20.00 50.00
186 M. Lombardi JSY AU RC 12.00 30.00
187 Dan Hamhuis JSY AU RC 12.00 30.00
188 J-M Liles JSY AU RC 12.00 30.00
189 David Hale JSY AU RC 10.00 25.00
190 T.Ruutu JSY AU RC 15.00 40.00
191 Derek Roy JSY AU RC 15.00 40.00
192 Paul Martin JSY AU RC 12.00 30.00
193 K.Lehtonen JSY AU RC 60.00 150.00
194 Dustin Brown JSY AU RC 25.00 60.00
195 A. Vermette JSY AU RC 20.00 50.00
196 A. Semin JSY AU RC 25.00 60.00
197 Brent Burns JSY AU RC 30.00 80.00
198 Matt Stajan JSY AU RC 15.00 40.00
199 Nik Zherdev JSY AU RC 20.00 50.00
200 M.Fleury JSY AU RC 75.00 175.00

2003-04 Parkhurst Rookie All-Rookie Jerseys

ART1 Andrew Raycroft 6.00 15.00
ART2 Paul Martin 6.00 15.00
ART3 Joni Pitkanen 6.00 15.00
ART4 Eric Staal 10.00 25.00
ART5 Michael Ryder 10.00 25.00
ART6 Ryan Malone 6.00 15.00
ART7 Philippe Sauve 6.00 15.00
ART8 Dan Hamhuis 6.00 15.00
ART9 John-Michael Liles 6.00 15.00
ART10 Tuomo Ruutu 6.00 15.00
ART11 Nikolai Zherdev 8.00 20.00
ART12 Joffrey Lupul 6.00 15.00

2003-04 Parkhurst Rookie Before the Mask

BTM1 Roy Worters 12.50 30.00
BTM2 Frank Brimsek 12.50 30.00
BTM3 Harry Lumley 12.50 30.00
BTM4 Gump Worsley 12.50 30.00
BTM5 Johnny Bower 12.50 30.00
BTM6 Jacques Plante 20.00 50.00
BTM7 Tiny Thompson 12.50 30.00
BTM8 Charlie Gardiner 12.50 30.00
BTM9 Bill Durnan 12.50 30.00
BTM10 George Hainsworth 20.00 50.00
BTM11 Terry Sawchuk 20.00 50.00
BTM12 Glenn Hall 12.50 30.00
BTM13 Ed Giacomin 12.50 30.00
BTM14 Roger Crozier 12.50 30.00
BTM15 Chuck Rayner 12.50 30.00
BTM16 Turk Broda 15.00 40.00

2003-04 Parkhurst Rookie Calder Candidates

CMC1 Eric Staal 8.00 20.00
CMC2 Michael Ryder 8.00 20.00
CMC3 Marc-Andre Fleury 12.50 30.00
CMC4 Patrice Bergeron 8.00 20.00
CMC5 Ryan Malone 6.00 15.00
CMC6 Joffrey Lupul 6.00 15.00
CMC7 Andrew Raycroft 6.00 15.00
CMC8 Mathew Lombardi 6.00 15.00
CMC9 Joni Pitkanen 6.00 15.00
CMC10 Nikolai Zherdev 6.00 15.00
CMC11 Jordin Tootoo 8.00 20.00
CMC12 Matt Stajan 6.00 15.00
CMC13 Nathan Horton 8.00 20.00
CMC14 Tuomo Ruutu 6.00 15.00
CMC15 Derek Roy 6.00 15.00

2003-04 Parkhurst Rookie High Expectations Jerseys

HE1 Ilya Kovalchuk 10.00 25.00
HE2 Rick Nash 10.00 25.00
HE3 Wendel Clark 10.00 25.00
HE4 Mario Lemieux 15.00 40.00
HE5 Guy Lafleur 8.00 20.00
HE6 Gilbert Perreault 10.00 25.00
HE7 Denis Potvin 8.00 20.00
HE8 Mike Modano 10.00 25.00
HE9 Mats Sundin 8.00 20.00
HE10 Joe Thornton 12.50 30.00
HE11 Rick DiPietro 8.00 20.00
HE12 Marc-Andre Fleury 12.50 30.00
HE13 Vincent Lecavalier 8.00 20.00
HE14 Owen Nolan 8.00 20.00

2003-04 Parkhurst Rookie Jerseys

GJ1 Mario Lemieux 15.00 40.00
GJ2 Ilya Kovalchuk 10.00 25.00
GJ3 Joe Thornton 12.00 30.00
GJ4 Bill Guerin 6.00 15.00
GJ5 Jason Spezza 6.00 15.00
GJ6 Peter Forsberg 10.00 25.00
GJ7 Brian Leetch 6.00 15.00
GJ8 Milan Hejduk 6.00 15.00
GJ9 Evgeni Nabokov 6.00 15.00
GJ10 Martin St. Louis 6.00 15.00
GJ11 Rick Nash 6.00 15.00
GJ12 Steve Yzerman 15.00 40.00
GJ13 Pavel Datsyuk 6.00 15.00
GJ14 Henrik Zetterberg 8.00 20.00
GJ15 Joe Sakic 12.00 30.00
GJ16 Jeremy Roenick 10.00 25.00
GJ17 Martin Brodeur 15.00 40.00
GJ18 Mats Sundin 6.00 15.00
GJ19 Keith Tkachuk 6.00 15.00
GJ20 Mike Modano 10.00 25.00
GJ21 Dany Heatley 8.00 20.00
GJ22 Roberto Luongo 10.00 25.00
GJ23 Markus Naslund 6.00 15.00
GJ24 Jose Theodore 8.00 20.00
GJ25 Dominik Hasek 12.00 30.00
GJ26 Paul Kariya 6.00 15.00
GJ27 Teemu Selanne 8.00 20.00
GJ28 Marian Hossa 6.00 15.00
GJ29 Marian Gaborik 10.00 25.00
GJ30 Sergei Fedorov 8.00 20.00
GJ31 Mark Messier 12.50 30.00
GJ32 Jarome Iginla 10.00 25.00
GJ33 Brendan Shanahan 8.00 20.00
GJ34 Ed Belfour 8.00 20.00
GJ35 Curtis Joseph 8.00 20.00
GJ36 Zdeno Chara 8.00 20.00
GJ37 Vincent Lecavalier 8.00 20.00
GJ38 Brett Hull 10.00 25.00
GJ39 Nicklas Lidstrom 8.00 20.00
GJ40 Marty Turco 6.00 15.00
GJ41 Patrick Roy 15.00 40.00
GJ42 Bobby Clarke 10.00 25.00
GJ43 Lanny McDonald 6.00 15.00
GJ44 Marcel Dionne 6.00 15.00
GJ45 Gilbert Perreault 8.00 20.00
GJ46 Ray Bourque 12.00 30.00
GJ47 Mike Bossy 6.00 15.00
GJ48 Vladislav Tretiak 20.00 50.00
GJ49 Bobby Orr 40.00 100.00
GJ50 Cam Neely 8.00 20.00

2003-04 Parkhurst Rookie Jersey and Sticks

*JSY/STKS: .6X TO 1.5X JSY
SJ6 Marc-Andre Fleury 20.00 50.00
SJ7 Eric Lindros 12.50 30.00
SJ15 Chris Pronger 10.00 25.00
SJ21 Andrew Raycroft 12.50 30.00

2003-04 Parkhurst Rookie Records Jerseys

RRE1 Teemu Selanne 8.00 20.00
RRE2 Teemu Selanne 8.00 20.00
RRE3 Luc Robitaille 8.00 20.00
RRE4 Joe Nieuwendyk 8.00 20.00
RRE5 Brian Leetch 8.00 20.00
RRE6 Tony Esposito 12.50 30.00
RRE7 Patrick Lalime 8.00 20.00
RRE8 Terry Sawchuk 20.00 40.00

2003-04 Parkhurst Rookie Retro Rookies

RR1 Mike Modano 10.00 25.00
RR2 Peter Forsberg 12.50 30.00
RR3 Joe Sakic 12.50 30.00
RR4 Patrick Roy 20.00 40.00
RR5 Jaromir Jagr 10.00 25.00
RR6 Rob Blake 8.00 20.00
RR7 Brett Hull 10.00 25.00
RR8 Roberto Luongo 10.00 25.00
RR9 Brian Leetch 8.00 20.00
RR10 Jeremy Roenick 10.00 25.00
RR11 Mats Sundin 8.00 20.00
RR12 Ed Belfour 8.00 20.00
RR13 Curtis Joseph 8.00 20.00
RR14 Sergei Fedorov 10.00 25.00
RR15 Paul Kariya 8.00 20.00
RR16 Mark Messier 10.00 25.00
RR17 Al MacInnis 8.00 20.00
RR18 Felix Potvin 12.00 30.00
RR19 Eric Lindros 10.00 25.00
RR20 Teemu Selanne 15.00 40.00

2003-04 Parkhurst Rookie Road to the NHL Jerseys

RNJ1 Nick Schultz 6.00 15.00
RNJ2 Jason Spezza 12.50 30.00
RNJ3 Rick Nash 12.50 30.00
RNJ4 Dustin Brown 6.00 15.00
RNJ5 Jay Bouwmeester 6.00 15.00
RNJ6 Jose Theodore 10.00 25.00
RNJ7 Barret Jackman 6.00 15.00
RNJ8 Dany Heatley 10.00 25.00
RNJ9 Eric Staal 12.50 30.00
RNJ10 Scottie Upshall 6.00 15.00
RNJ11 Derek Roy 6.00 15.00
RNJ12 Dan Blackburn 6.00 15.00
RNJ13 Tim Gleason 6.00 15.00
RNJ14 Ron Hainsey 6.00 15.00
RNJ15 Mathieu Garon 6.00 15.00
RNJ16 Steve Ott 8.00 20.00
RNJ17 Dan Hamhuis 6.00 15.00

2003-04 Parkhurst Rookie Rookie Emblems

RE1 Patrice Bergeron 15.00 40.00
RE2 Fedor Tyutin 3.00 8.00
RE3 Joffrey Lupul 8.00 20.00
RE4 Antti Miettinen 5.00 12.00
RE5 Nathan Horton 8.00 20.00
RE6 Dustin Brown 8.00 20.00
RE7 Tim Gleason 4.00 10.00
RE8 Chris Higgins 6.00 15.00
RE9 Jordin Tootoo 6.00 15.00
RE10 Dan Hamhuis 4.00 10.00
RE11 David Hale 3.00 8.00
RE12 Garth Murray 4.00 10.00
RE13 Paul Martin 4.00 10.00
RE14 Sean Bergenheim 4.00 10.00
RE15 Joni Pitkanen 5.00 12.00
RE16 John Pohl 3.00 8.00
RE17 Libor Pivko 3.00 8.00
RE18 Marek Svatos 6.00 15.00
RE19 Dan Fritsche 3.00 8.00
RE20 Denis Grebeshkov 3.00 8.00
RE21 Antero Niittymaki 8.00 20.00
RE22 Tuomo Ruutu 5.00 12.00
RE23 Kari Lehtonen 12.00 30.00
RE24 Dominic Moore 3.00 8.00
RE25 Tony Salmelainen 3.00 8.00
RE26 Christian Ehrhoff 4.00 10.00
RE27 Trevor Daley 5.00 12.00
RE28 Nikolai Zherdev 6.00 15.00
RE29 Mark Popovic 4.00 10.00
RE30 Peter Sejna 4.00 10.00
RE31 Derek Roy 5.00 12.00
RE32 Trent Hunter 3.00 8.00
RE33 Cody McCormick 4.00 10.00
RE34 John-Michael Liles 4.00 10.00
RE35 Matthew Lombardi 4.00 10.00
RE36 Marek Zidlicky 3.00 8.00
RE37 Ryan Malone 6.00 15.00
RE38 Niklas Kronwall 6.00 15.00
RE39 Rastislav Stana 5.00 12.00
RE40 Andrew Raycroft 4.00 10.00
RE41 Alexander Semin 10.00 25.00
RE42 Andrew Peters 4.00 10.00
RE43 Brent Burns 10.00 25.00
RE44 Matt Stajan 5.00 12.00
RE45 Antoine Vermette 6.00 15.00
RE46 Michael Ryder 4.00 10.00
RE47 Ryan Kesler 12.00 30.00
RE48 Eric Staal 15.00 40.00
RE49 Patrick Leahy 4.00 10.00
RE50 Marc-Andre Fleury 20.00 50.00

2003-04 Parkhurst Rookie Rookie Jerseys

RJ1 Patrice Bergeron 10.00 25.00
RJ2 Fedor Tyutin 6.00 15.00
RJ3 Joffrey Lupul 6.00 15.00
RJ4 Antti Miettinen 6.00 15.00
RJ5 Nathan Horton 8.00 20.00
RJ6 Dustin Brown 8.00 20.00
RJ7 Tim Gleason 6.00 15.00
RJ8 Chris Higgins 6.00 15.00
RJ9 Jordin Tootoo 8.00 20.00
RJ10 Dan Hamhuis 6.00 15.00
RJ11 David Hale 6.00 15.00
RJ12 Garth Murray 6.00 15.00
RJ13 Paul Martin 6.00 15.00
RJ14 Sean Bergenheim 6.00 15.00
RJ15 Joni Pitkanen 6.00 15.00
RJ16 John Pohl 6.00 15.00
RJ17 Libor Pivko 6.00 15.00
RJ18 Marek Svatos 6.00 15.00
RJ19 Dan Fritsche 6.00 15.00
RJ20 Denis Grebeshkov 6.00 15.00
RJ21 Antero Niittymaki 8.00 20.00
RJ22 Tuomo Ruutu 6.00 15.00
RJ23 Kari Lehtonen 10.00 25.00
RJ24 Dominic Moore 6.00 15.00
RJ25 Tony Salmelainen 6.00 15.00
RJ26 Christian Ehrhoff 6.00 15.00
RJ27 Trevor Daley 6.00 15.00
RJ28 Nikolai Zherdev 8.00 20.00
RJ29 Mark Popovic 6.00 15.00
RJ30 Peter Sejna 6.00 15.00
RJ31 Derek Roy 6.00 15.00
RJ32 Trent Hunter 6.00 15.00
RJ33 Cody McCormick 6.00 15.00
RJ34 John-Michael Liles 6.00 15.00
RJ35 Matthew Lombardi 6.00 15.00
RJ36 Marek Zidlicky 6.00 15.00
RJ37 Ryan Malone 6.00 15.00
RJ38 Niklas Kronwall 8.00 20.00
RJ39 Rastislav Stana 6.00 15.00
RJ40 Andrew Raycroft 8.00 20.00
RJ41 Alexander Semin 8.00 20.00
RJ42 Andrew Peters 6.00 15.00
RJ43 Brent Burns 6.00 15.00
RJ44 Matt Stajan 6.00 15.00
RJ45 Antoine Vermette 6.00 15.00
RJ46 Michael Ryder 8.00 20.00
RJ47 Ryan Kesler 6.00 15.00
RJ48 Eric Staal 10.00 25.00
RJ49 Patrick Leahy 6.00 15.00
RJ50 Marc-Andre Fleury 12.50 30.00

2003-04 Parkhurst Rookie ROYalty Jerseys

VR1 Dany Heatley 12.50 30.00
VR2 Martin Brodeur 20.00 50.00
VR3 Peter Forsberg 15.00 40.00
VR4 Daniel Alfredsson 10.00 25.00
VR5 Teemu Selanne 10.00 25.00
VR6 Sergei Samsonov 10.00 25.00
VR7 Ray Bourque 15.00 40.00
VR8 Brian Leetch 10.00 25.00
VR9 Mario Lemieux 25.00 60.00
VR10 Bobby Orr 30.00 80.00
VR11 Terry Sawchuk 15.00 40.00
VR12 Jacques Laperriere 10.00 25.00
VR13 Gilbert Perreault 10.00 25.00
VR14 Bryan Trottier 10.00 25.00
VR15 Denis Potvin 10.00 25.00
VR16 Roger Crozier 10.00 25.00
VR17 Pavel Bure 10.00 25.00
VR18 Ed Belfour 10.00 25.00
VR19 Glenn Hall 10.00 25.00
VR20 Evgeni Nabokov 10.00 25.00
VR21 Frank Brimsek 10.00 25.00
VR22 Mike Bossy 12.50 30.00
VR23 Luc Robitaille 10.00 25.00
VR24 Scott Gomez 10.00 25.00
VR25 Bernie Geoffrion 12.50 30.00
VR26 Gump Worsley 10.00 25.00
VR27 Joe Nieuwendyk 10.00 25.00
VR28 Tony Esposito 12.50 30.00

2003-04 Parkhurst Rookie Teammates Jerseys

RT1 M.Lemieux/M.Fleury 15.00 40.00
RT2 S.Fedorov/J.Lupul 10.00 25.00
RT3 M.Sundin/M.Stajan 12.50 30.00
RT4 R.Nash/N.Zherdev 12.50 30.00
RT5 M.Modano/T.Daley 8.00 20.00
RT6 J.Bouwmeester/N.Horton 10.00 25.00
RT7 A.Frolov/D.Brown 8.00 20.00
RT8 J.Spezza/A.Vermette 10.00 25.00
RT9 J.Roenick/J.Pitkanen 8.00 20.00
RT10 J.Sakic/C.McCormick 10.00 25.00
RT11 J.Thornton/P.Bergeron 12.50 30.00
RT12 P.Forsberg/M.Svatos 12.50 30.00
RT13 D.Legwand/J.Tootoo 10.00 25.00
RT14 K.Tkachuk/P.Sejna 8.00 20.00
RT15 S.Stevens/P.Martin 8.00 20.00
RT16 J.Theodore/M.Ryder 12.50 30.00
RT17 R.Blake/J.Michael Liles 8.00 20.00
RT18 J.Iginla/M.Lombardi 10.00 25.00
RT19 M.Satan/D.Roy 8.00 20.00
RT20 S.Koivu/C.Higgins 8.00 20.00
RT21 M.Messier/D.Moore 12.50 30.00
RT22 J.Thibault/T.Ruutu 8.00 20.00

1994-95 Parkhurst SE

*GOLD: 1X TO 2.5X BASIC INSERTS
SE1 Guy Hebert .07 .20
SE2 Bob Corkum .05 .15
SE3 Randy Ladouceur .07 .20
SE4 Tom Kurvers .05 .15
SE5 Joe Sacco .05 .15
SE6 Valeri Karpov .05 .15
SE7 Garry Valk .05 .15
SE8 Paul Kariya .10 .25
SE9 Alexei Kasatonov .05 .15
SE10 Sergei Zholtok .05 .15
SE11 Glen Murray .07 .20
SE12 David Reid .05 .15
SE13 Adam Oates .10 .25
SE14 Ted Donato .05 .15
SE15 Don Sweeney .05 .15
SE16 Philippe Boucher .05 .15
SE17 Bob Sweeney .05 .15
SE18 Pat LaFontaine .10 .25
SE19 Derek Plante .05 .15
SE20 Jason Dawe .05 .15
SE21 Petr Svoboda .05 .15
SE22 Craig Simpson .05 .15
SE23 Viktor Gordiouk .07 .20
SE24 Trevor Kidd .07 .20
SE25 Todd Hlushko .07 .20
SE26 German Titov .05 .15
SE27 Gary Roberts .05 .15
SE28 Theo Fleury .10 .25
SE29 Cory Stillman .05 .15
SE30 Phil Housley .07 .20
SE31 Joel Otto .05 .15
SE32 Patrick Poulin .05 .15
SE33 Christian Soucy .07 .20
SE34 Karl Dykhuis .07 .20
SE35 Jeremy Roenick .15 .40
SE36 Tony Amonte .07 .20
SE37 Sergei Krivokrasov .05 .15
SE38 Bernie Nicholls .07 .20
SE39 Todd Harvey .05 .15
SE40 Jarkko Varvio .05 .15
SE41 Shane Churla .05 .15
SE42 Paul Cavallini .05 .15
SE43 Trent Klatt .05 .15
SE44 Darcy Wakaluk .07 .20
SE45 Derian Hatcher .05 .15
SE46 Dean Evason .05 .15
SE47 Mike Modano .15 .40
SE48 Greg Johnson .05 .15
SE49 Ray Sheppard .07 .20
SE50 Sergei Fedorov .15 .40
SE51 Bob Rouse .05 .15
SE52 Mike Vernon .07 .20
SE53 Vladimir Konstantinov .07 .20
SE54 Chris Osgood .15 .40
SE55 Steve Yzerman .25 .60
SE56 Jason York .05 .15
SE57 Boris Mironov .05 .15
SE58 Igor Kravchuk .05 .15
SE59 Jason Arnott .07 .20
SE60 David Oliver .05 .15
SE61 Todd Marchant .05 .15
SE62 Dean McAmmond .05 .15
SE63 Brian Skrudland .05 .15
SE64 Tom Fitzgerald .05 .15
SE65 Brian Benning .05 .15
SE66 Stu Barnes .05 .15
SE67 John Vanbiesbrouck .10 .25
SE68 Rob Niedermayer .07 .20
SE69 Jimmy Carson .05 .15
SE70 Mark Janssens .05 .15
SE71 Sean Burke .07 .20
SE72 Andrei Nikolishin .05 .15
SE73 Chris Pronger .10 .25
SE74 Jeff Reese .05 .15
SE75 Darren Turcotte .05 .15
SE76 Robert Kron .05 .15
SE77 Kevin Brown .10 .25
SE78 Robert Lang .05 .15
SE79 Rick Tocchet .07 .20
SE80 Jamie Storr .07 .20
SE81 Kelly Hrudey .07 .20
SE82 Darryl Sydor .05 .15
SE83 Tony Granato .05 .15
SE84 Warren Rychel .05 .15
SE85 Gary Shuchuk .07 .20
SE86 Peter Popovic .05 .15
SE87 Valeri Bure .05 .15
SE88 Kirk Muller .05 .15
SE89 Lyle Odelein .07 .20
SE90 Brian Savage .05 .15
SE91 Gilbert Dionne .05 .15
SE92 Mathieu Schneider .05 .15
SE93 Jim Montgomery .05 .15
SE94 Chris Terreri .07 .20
SE95 Scott Niedermayer .10 .25
SE96 Bob Carpenter .07 .20
SE97 Scott Stevens .10 .25
SE98 Jim Dowd .05 .15
SE99 Brian Rolston .07 .20
SE100 Stephane Richer .07 .20
SE101 Mick Vukota .07 .20
SE102 Steve Thomas .05 .15
SE103 Patrick Flatley .05 .15
SE104 Marty McInnis .05 .15
SE105 Rich Pilon .07 .20
SE106 Benoit Hogue .05 .15
SE107 Zigmund Palffy .07 .20
SE108 Vladimir Malakhov .05 .15
SE109 Brett Lindros .05 .15
SE110 Mike Richter .10 .25
SE111 Greg Gilbert .05 .15
SE112 Kevin Lowe .05 .15
SE113 Mark Messier .20 .50
SE114 Alexander Karpovtsev .05 .15
SE115 Sergei Nemchinov .05 .15
SE116 Petr Nedved .07 .20
SE117 Glenn Healy .07 .20
SE118 Dave Archibald .05 .15
SE119 Alexandre Daigle .05 .15
SE120 Darrin Madeley .05 .15
SE121 Pavol Demitra .12 .30
SE122 Brad Shaw .05 .15
SE123 Alexei Yashin .10 .25
SE124 Sean Hill .05 .15
SE125 Vladislav Boulin .10 .25
SE126 Kevin Haller .05 .15
SE127 Chris Therien .05 .15
SE128 Garry Galley .05 .15
SE129 Mikael Renberg .07 .20
SE130 Ron Hextall .10 .25
SE131 Eric Lindros .15 .40
SE132 Craig MacTavish .05 .15
SE133 Patrik Juhlin .05 .15
SE134 Martin Straka .05 .15
SE135 Doug Brown .05 .15
SE136 Markus Naslund .10 .25
SE137 Luc Robitaille .10 .25
SE138 Kjell Samuelsson .05 .15
SE139 Ken Wregget .07 .20
SE140 John Cullen .05 .15
SE141 Peter Taglianetti .05 .15
SE142 Janne Laukkanen .07 .20
SE143 Owen Nolan .10 .25
SE144 Adam Deadmarsh .05 .15
SE145 Dave Karpa .05 .15
SE146 Wendel Clark .15 .40
SE147 Joe Sakic .20 .50
SE148 Alexei Gusarov .07 .20
SE149 Peter Forsberg .20 .50
SE150 Kevin Miller .05 .15
SE151 Denny Felsner .05 .15
SE152 Al MacInnis .12 .30
SE153 Philippe Bozon .07 .20
SE154 Brett Hull .20 .50
SE155 Guy Carbonneau .05 .15
SE156 Igor Korolev .05 .15
SE157 Esa Tikkanen .05 .15
SE158 Jon Casey .07 .20
SE159 Viktor Kozlov .05 .15
SE160 Mike Rathje .05 .15
SE161 Bob Errey .05 .15
SE162 Arturs Irbe .07 .20
SE163 Ray Whitney .05 .15
SE164 Igor Larionov .05 .15
SE165 Pat Falloon .05 .15
SE166 Jeff Friesen .05 .15
SE167 Vlastimil Kroupa .05 .15
SE168 Chris Joseph .05 .15
SE169 Danton Cole .05 .15
SE170 John Tucker .05 .15
SE171 Roman Hamrlik .05 .15
SE172 Jason Wiemer .05 .15
SE173 Kenny Jonsson .05 .15
SE174 Eric Fichaud XRC .10 .25
SE175 Mats Sundin .10 .25
SE176 Doug Gilmour .12 .30
SE177 Drake Berehowsky .05 .15
SE178 Mike Ridley .05 .15
SE179 Jamie Macoun .05 .15
SE180 Alexei Kudashov .05 .15
SE181 Bill Berg .05 .15
SE182 Dave Andreychuk .10 .25
SE183 Mike Eastwood .05 .15
SE184 Martin Gelinas .05 .15
SE185 Greg Adams .05 .15
SE186 Gino Odjick .05 .15
SE187 Pavel Bure .10 .25
SE188 Cliff Ronning .05 .15
SE189 Jiri Slegr .05 .15
SE190 Jyrki Lumme .05 .15
SE191 Jassen Cullimore .05 .15
SE192 Steve Konowalchuk .05 .15
SE193 Sylvain Cote .05 .15
SE194 Jason Allison .07 .20
SE195 Sergei Gonchar .05 .15
SE196 Pat Peake .05 .15
SE197 Calle Johansson .05 .15
SE198 Joe Juneau .05 .15
SE199 Jeff Nelson .05 .15
SE200 Luciano Borsato .05 .15
SE201 Teemu Selanne .20 .50
SE202 Tie Domi .07 .20
SE203 Tim Cheveldae .07 .20
SE204 Darrin Shannon .05 .15
SE205 Ravil Gusmanov .05 .15
SE206 Todd Harvey .05 .15
SE207 Ed Jovanovski XRC .15 .40
SE208 Jason Allison .07 .20
SE209 Bryan McCabe .05 .15
SE210 Dan Cloutier XRC .15 .40
SE211 Ladislav Kohn XRC .10 .25
SE212 Marek Malik XRC .05 .15
SE213 Jan Hlavac XRC .15 .40
SE214 Petr Cajanek XRC .15 .40
SE215 Jussi Markkanen XRC .75 2.00
SE216 Jere Karalahti XRC .10 .25
SE217 Janne Niinimaa .10 .25
SE218 Kimmo Timonen .07 .20
SE219 Mikko Helisten XRC .10 .25
SE220 Niko Halttunen XRC .10 .25
SE221 Tommi Miettinen .07 .20
SE222 Veli-Pekka Nutikka XRC .10 .25
SE223 Timo Salonen XRC .10 .25
SE224 Tommi Sova XRC .10 .25
SE225 Jussi Tarvainen XRC .10 .25
SE226 Tommi Rajamaki XRC .07 .20
SE227 Antti Aalto XRC .07 .20
SE228 Alexander Korolyuk XRC .10 .25
SE229 Vitali Yachmenev .10 .25
SE230 Nicolai Zavaroukhine .10 .25
SE231 Vadim Epantchinsev .07 .20
SE232 Dmitri Klevakin .07 .20
SE233 Anders Eriksson .07 .20
SE234 Anders Soderberg .07 .20
SE235 Per Svartvadet XRC .10 .25
SE236 Johan Davidsson .10 .25
SE237 Niklas Sundstrom .10 .25
SE238 J. Andersson-Junkka XRC .10 .25
SE239 Dick Tarnstrom XRC .10 .25
SE240 P.J. Axelsson XRC .10 .25
SE241 Frederik Johansson .10 .25
SE242 Peter Strom .10 .25
SE243 Mattias Ohlund .15 .40
SE244 Jesper Mattsson .07 .20
SE245 Jonas Forsberg .07 .20
SE246 Adam Deadmarsh .05 .15
SE247 Deron Quint .05 .15
SE248 Jamie Langenbrunner .07 .20
SE249 Richard Park .05 .15
SE250 Bryan Berard XRC .15 .40
SE251 David Belitski XRC .10 .25
SE252 Mike McBain XRC .10 .25
SE253 Hugh Hamilton XRC .10 .25
SE254 Jason Doig XRC .10 .25
SE255 Xavier Delisle XRC .10 .25
SE256 Wade Redden XRC .15 .40
SE257 Jeff Ware XRC .10 .25
SE258 Christian Dube XRC .10 .25
SE259 Louis-Phil.Sevigny XRC .10 .25
SE260 Jarome Iginla XRC 4.00 10.00
SE261 Daniel Briere XRC 4.00 10.00
SE262 Justin Kurtz XRC .10 .25
SE263 Marc Savard XRC .10 .25
SE264 Alyn McCauley XRC .10 .25
SE265 Brad Mehalko XRC .10 .25
SE266 Jeffrey Ambrosio XRC .10 .25
SE267 Todd Norman XRC .10 .25
SE268 Brian Scott XRC .10 .25
SE269 Brad Larsen XRC .10 .25
SE270 J-S Giguere XRC 2.50 6.00
NNO Wayne Gretzky Large .60 1.50

1994-95 Parkhurst SE Euro-Stars

COMPLETE SET (20) 8.00 20.00
ES1 Peter Forsberg 2.50 6.00
ES2 Mats Sundin .60 1.50
ES3 Mikael Renberg .30 .75
ES4 Niklas Lidstrom .60 1.50
ES5 Mariusz Czerkawski .15 .40
ES6 Ulf Dahlen .15 .40
ES7 Kjell Samuelsson .15 .40
ES8 Jyrki Lumme .15 .40
ES9 Jari Kurri .30 .75
ES10 Teppo Numminen .15 .40
ES11 Esa Tikkanen .15 .40
ES12 Christian Ruuttu .15 .40
ES13 Teemu Selanne .60 1.50
ES14 Alexander Mogilny .30 .75
ES15 Pavel Bure .60 1.50
ES16 Sergei Fedorov 1.00 2.50
ES17 Arturs Irbe .30 .75
ES18 Alexei Kovalev .15 .40
ES19 Dominik Hasek 1.25 3.00
ES20 Jaromir Jagr 1.00 2.50

1994-95 Parkhurst SE Vintage

COMPLETE SET (45) 15.00 40.00
1 Paul Kariya .60 1.50
2 Dino Ciccarelli .20 .50
3 Patrick Roy 3.00 8.00
4 Markus Naslund .60 1.50
5 Trevor Linden .40 1.00
6 Valeri Karpov .20 .50
7 Pat Verbeek .20 .50
8 Martin Brodeur 1.50 4.00
9 Kevin Stevens .20 .50
10 Kirk McLean .40 1.00
11 Stephan Lebeau .20 .50
12 Scott Niedermayer .20 .50
13 Peter Bondra .40 1.00
14 Ed Belfour .60 1.50
15 Paul Coffey .60 1.50
16 Chris Gratton .20 .50
17 Joe Juneau .40 1.00
18 Ray Bourque .60 1.50
19 Sergei Krivokrasov .20 .50
20 Wayne Gretzky 4.00 10.00
21 Alexei Yashin .20 .50
22 Al Iafrate .20 .50
23 Doug Weight .40 1.00
24 Jari Kurri .20 .50
25 Rod Brind'Amour .40 1.00
26 Bryan Smolinski .20 .50
27 Darius Kasparaitis .20 .50
28 Mark Recchi .20 .50
29 Mike Gartner .40 1.00
30 Russ Courtnall .20 .50
31 Pierre Turgeon .40 1.00
32 Felix Potvin .60 1.50
33 Nelson Emerson .20 .50
34 Alexander Mogilny .40 1.00
35 Bob Kudelski .20 .50
36 Brett Lindros .20 .50
37 Mats Sundin .60 1.50
38 Keith Tkachuk .60 1.50
39 Derek Plante .20 .50
40 Oleg Petrov .20 .50
41 Adam Graves .20 .50
42 Jaromir Jagr 1.00 2.50
43 Viktor Kozlov .20 .50
44 Nathan Lafayette .20 .50
45 Alexei Zhamnov .40 1.00

2003-04 Parkhurst Toronto Spring Expo Rookie Preview

PRP1 Marc-Andre Fleury 40.00 100.00
PRP2 Jordin Tootoo 15.00 40.00
PRP3 Joni Pitkanen 10.00 25.00
PRP4 Fedor Tyutin 8.00 20.00
PRP5 Derek Roy 15.00 40.00
PRP6 Nathan Horton 15.00 40.00
PRP7 Eric Staal 25.00 60.00
PRP8 Patrice Bergeron 25.00 60.00
PRP9 Dustin Brown 10.00 25.00
PRP10 Dan Hamhuis 10.00 25.00
PRP11 Tim Gleason 8.00 20.00
PRP12 Rastislav Stana 8.00 20.00
PRP13 Matt Stajan 15.00 40.00
PRP14 Matthew Lombardi 8.00 20.00
PRP15 Nikolai Zherdev 20.00 50.00
PRP16 Tuomo Ruutu 20.00 50.00
PRP17 Ryan Malone 15.00 40.00
PRP18 Antoine Vermette 8.00 20.00
PRP19 Kari Lehtonen 30.00 80.00
PRP20 Alexander Semin 20.00 50.00

2016-17 Parkhurst

1 Corey Perry .40 1.00
2 Ryan Kesler .25 .60
3 John Gibson .25 .60
4 Jakob Silfverberg .15 .40
5 Sami Vatanen .20 .50
6 Cam Fowler .25 .60
7 Rickard Rakell .20 .50
8 Jonathan Bernier .20 .50
9 Hampus Lindholm .15 .40
10 Ryan Getzlaf .25 .60
11 Nick Ritchie .15 .40
12 Oliver Ekman-Larsson .25 .60
13 Anthony Duclair .20 .50
14 Max Domi .25 .60
15 Connor Murphy .15 .40
16 Tobias Rieder .15 .40
17 Martin Hanzal .20 .50
18 Mike Smith .25 .60
19 Alex Goligoski .15 .40
20 Shane Doan .20 .50
21 Jamie McGinn .20 .50
22 Jordan Martinook .15 .40
23 David Krejci .25 .60
24 David Backes .15 .40
25 Brad Marchand .50 1.25
26 Zdeno Chara .25 .60

27 Ryan Spooner .20 .50
28 Torey Krug .20 .50
29 Matt Beleskey .20 .50
30 Patrice Bergeron .30 .75
31 Tuukka Rask .30 .75
32 David Pastrnak .60 1.50
33 Jimmy Hayes .15 .40
34 Ryan O'Reilly .25 .60
35 Sam Reinhart .50 1.25
36 Brian Gionta .15 .40
37 Evander Kane .25 .60
38 Zemgus Girgensons .20 .50
39 Rasmus Ristolainen .15 .40
40 Jack Eichel .40 1.00
41 Tyler Ennis .15 .40
42 Cody Franson .15 .40
43 Matt Moulson .15 .40
44 Kyle Okposo .15 .40
45 Sean Monahan .15 .40
46 Mark Giordano .25 .60
47 Mikael Backlund .20 .50
48 T.J. Brodie .20 .50
49 Dougie Hamilton .20 .50
50 Johnny Gaudreau .40 1.00
51 Dennis Wideman .15 .40
52 Sam Bennett .40 1.00
53 Brian Elliott .20 .50
54 Alex Chiasson .20 .50
55 Troy Brouwer .15 .40
56 Victor Rask .15 .40
57 Elias Lindholm .25 .60
58 Noah Hanifin .25 .60
59 Justin Faulk .20 .50
60 Jeff Skinner .30 .75
61 Joakim Nordstrom .15 .40
62 Ron Hainsey .20 .50
63 Cam Ward .25 .60
64 Jay McClement .15 .40
65 Andrej Nestrasil .20 .50
66 Teuvo Teravainen .25 .60
67 Artem Anisimov .15 .40
68 Artemi Panarin .50 1.25
69 Duncan Keith .20 .50
70 Patrick Kane .50 1.25
71 Brent Seabrook .15 .40
72 Corey Crawford .30 .75
73 Niklas Hjalmarsson .15 .40
74 Marian Hossa .25 .60
75 Jonathan Toews .40 1.00
76 Marcus Kruger .15 .40
77 Brian Campbell .20 .50
78 Matt Duchene .25 .60
79 Gabriel Landeskog .30 .75
80 Nathan MacKinnon 1.00 2.50
81 Carl Soderberg .15 .40
82 Tyson Barrie .15 .40
83 Jarome Iginla .30 .75
84 Francois Beauchemin .20 .50
85 Mikhail Grigorenko .15 .40
86 Semyon Varlamov .25 .60
87 Erik Johnson .15 .40
88 Blake Comeau .15 .40
89 Cam Atkinson .25 .60
90 Brandon Saad .20 .50
91 Brandon Dubinsky .15 .40
92 Scott Hartnell .15 .40
93 Alexander Wennberg .15 .40
94 Nick Foligno .20 .50
95 Seth Jones .25 .60
96 Ryan Murray .15 .40
97 Boone Jenner .25 .60
98 Sergei Bobrovsky .40 1.00
99 Jack Johnson .15 .40
100 Jamie Benn .25 .60
101 Jason Spezza .25 .60
102 John Klingberg .25 .60
103 Patrick Sharp .20 .50
104 Valeri Nichushkin .25 .60
105 Antoine Roussel .15 .40
106 Ales Hemsky .20 .50
107 Johnny Oduya .20 .50
108 Antti Niemi .20 .50
109 Kari Lehtonen .20 .50
110 Tyler Seguin .30 .75
111 Henrik Zetterberg .30 .75
112 Mike Green .20 .50
113 Gustav Nyquist .15 .40
114 Justin Abdelkader .20 .50
115 Andreas Athanasiou .25 .60
116 Tomas Tatar .15 .40
117 Frans Nielsen .15 .40
118 Niklas Kronwall .20 .50
119 Petr Mrazek .25 .60
120 Dylan Larkin .30 .75
121 Danny DeKeyser .15 .40
122 Leon Draisaitl .75 2.00
123 Jordan Eberle .25 .60
124 Ryan Nugent-Hopkins .30 .75
125 Connor McDavid 1.25 3.00
126 Andrej Sekera .15 .40
127 Oscar Klefbom .40 1.00
128 Nail Yakupov .15 .40
129 Adam Larsson .25 .60
130 Milan Lucic .20 .50
131 Benoit Pouliot .20 .50
132 Cam Talbot .25 .60
133 Aaron Ekblad .30 .75
134 Aleksander Barkov .40 1.00
135 Jonathan Huberdeau .30 .75
136 Jussi Jokinen .25 .60
137 Vincent Trocheck .25 .60
138 Reilly Smith .25 .60
139 Alex Petrovic .15 .40
140 Jaromir Jagr .75 2.00
141 Nick Bjugstad .15 .40
142 Roberto Luongo .40 1.00
143 Keith Yandle .15 .40
144 Anze Kopitar .40 1.00
145 Jeff Carter .20 .50
146 Tyler Toffoli .25 .60
147 Jake Muzzin .25 .60
148 Dustin Brown .25 .60
149 Drew Doughty .30 .75
150 Jonathan Quick .30 .75
151 Marian Gaborik .25 .60
152 Alec Martinez .15 .40
153 Nick Shore .15 .40
154 Tanner Pearson .20 .50
155 Mikko Koivu .20 .50
156 Ryan Suter .20 .50
157 Charlie Coyle .25 .60
158 Jason Pominville .15 .40
159 Jason Zucker .25 .60
160 Zach Parise .25 .60
161 Mikael Granlund .20 .50
162 Eric Staal .30 .75
163 Nino Niederreiter .15 .40
164 Jonas Brodin .15 .40
165 Devan Dubnyk .20 .50
166 Max Pacioretty .25 .60
167 Alex Galchenyuk .15 .40
168 Tomas Plekanec .15 .40
169 Brendan Gallagher .25 .60
170 Andrei Markov .15 .40
171 Nathan Beaulieu .15 .40
172 David Desharnais .15 .40
173 Sven Andrighetto .20 .50
174 Andrew Shaw .15 .40
175 Carey Price .50 1.25
176 Shea Weber .20 .50
177 Filip Forsberg .40 1.00
178 Roman Josi .25 .60
179 James Neal .15 .40
180 Calle Jarnkrok .20 .50
181 Mike Ribeiro .15 .40
182 Ryan Johansen .20 .50
183 Colin Wilson .25 .60
184 Craig Smith .15 .40
185 P.K. Subban .30 .75
186 Mattias Ekholm .20 .50
187 Pekka Rinne .25 .60
188 Kyle Palmieri .20 .50
189 Adam Henrique .20 .50
190 Cory Schneider .25 .60
191 Travis Zajac .15 .40
192 Michael Cammalleri .20 .50
193 Taylor Hall .25 .60
194 Damon Severson .15 .40
195 Reid Boucher .15 .40
196 Devante Smith-Pelly .20 .50
197 Jon Merrill .15 .40
198 Sergei Kalinin .15 .40
199 Nick Leddy .15 .40
200 John Tavares .40 1.00
201 Anders Lee .25 .60
202 Johnny Boychuk .20 .50
203 Brock Nelson .25 .60
204 Jason Chimera .15 .40
205 Casey Cizikas .15 .40
206 Cal Clutterbuck .15 .40
207 Thomas Greiss .20 .50
208 Andrew Ladd .15 .40
209 Jaroslav Halak .25 .60
210 Henrik Lundqvist .60 1.50
211 Mats Zuccarello .25 .60
212 Marc Staal .15 .40
213 Derek Stepan .15 .40
214 J.T. Miller .30 .75
215 Chris Kreider .30 .75
216 Ryan McDonagh .15 .40
217 Oscar Lindberg .15 .40
218 Mika Zibanejad .30 .75
219 Kevin Hayes .20 .50
220 Rick Nash .25 .60
221 Mark Stone .30 .75
222 Bobby Ryan .20 .50
223 Mike Hoffman .15 .40
224 Chris Wideman .15 .40
225 Jean-Gabriel Pageau .15 .40
226 Kyle Turris .20 .50
227 Cody Ceci .15 .40
228 Erik Karlsson .30 .75
229 Derick Brassard .15 .40
230 Craig Anderson .25 .60
231 Dion Phaneuf .20 .50
232 Wayne Simmonds .30 .75
233 Brayden Schenn .25 .60
234 Jakub Voracek .20 .50
235 Sean Couturier .20 .50
236 Shayne Gostisbehere .25 .60
237 Michael Raffl .15 .40
238 Radko Gudas .15 .40
239 Matt Read .20 .50
240 Steve Mason .20 .50
241 Claude Giroux .25 .60
242 Michal Neuvirth .20 .50
243 Evgeni Malkin .50 1.25
244 Phil Kessel .25 .60
245 Patric Hornqvist .15 .40
246 Nick Bonino .15 .40
247 Chris Kunitz .25 .60
248 Olli Maatta .15 .40
249 Trevor Daley .20 .50
250 Carl Hagelin .15 .40
251 Sidney Crosby 1.00 2.50
252 Matt Murray .40 1.00
253 Kris Letang .30 .75
254 Brent Burns .25 .60
255 Joe Pavelski .30 .75
256 Patrick Marleau .25 .60
257 Tomas Hertl .25 .60
258 Joel Ward .20 .50
259 Logan Couture .30 .75
260 Joe Thornton .40 1.00
261 Mikkel Boedker .15 .40
262 Marc-Edouard Vlasic .15 .40
263 Martin Jones .20 .50
264 Joonas Donskoi .15 .40
265 Kevin Shattenkirk .15 .40
266 Jaden Schwartz .30 .75
267 David Perron .20 .50
268 Alexander Steen .15 .40
269 Alex Pietrangelo .20 .50
270 Robby Fabbri .15 .40
271 Paul Stastny .20 .50
272 Jori Lehtera .15 .40
273 Colton Parayko .20 .50
274 Jake Allen .25 .60
275 Vladimir Tarasenko .30 .75
276 Tyler Johnson .15 .40
277 Jonathan Drouin .20 .50
278 Alex Killorn .15 .40
279 Victor Hedman .30 .75
280 Steven Stamkos .50 1.25
281 Ondrej Palat .20 .50
282 Vladislav Namestnikov .15 .40
283 Nikita Kucherov .50 1.25
284 Ryan Callahan .15 .40
285 Ben Bishop .20 .50
286 Anton Stralman .20 .50
287 Nazem Kadri .30 .75
288 Colin Greening .20 .50
289 Leo Komarov .15 .40
290 James van Riemsdyk .20 .50
291 Morgan Rielly .25 .60
292 Jake Gardiner .15 .40
293 Tyler Bozak .15 .40
294 Matt Martin .15 .40
295 Roman Polak .15 .40
296 Frederik Andersen .30 .75
297 Milan Michalek .15 .40
298 Daniel Sedin .30 .75
299 Bo Horvat .30 .75
300 Henrik Sedin .30 .75
301 Alexandre Burrows .15 .40
302 Jannik Hansen .15 .40
303 Sven Baertschi .15 .40
304 Ben Hutton .25 .60
305 Jake Virtanen .30 .75
306 Erik Gudbranson .15 .40
307 Ryan Miller .25 .60
308 Loui Eriksson .15 .40
309 John Carlson .25 .60
310 Alexander Ovechkin 1.00 2.50
311 T.J. Oshie .25 .60
312 Nicklas Backstrom .25 .60
313 Evgeny Kuznetsov .30 .75
314 Justin Williams .20 .50
315 Andre Burakovsky .15 .40
316 Matt Niskanen .20 .50
317 Lars Eller .15 .40
318 Karl Alzner .15 .40
319 Braden Holtby .30 .75
320 Jacob Trouba .20 .50
321 Mark Scheifele .40 1.00
322 Drew Stafford .15 .40
323 Nikolaj Ehlers .25 .60
324 Bryan Little .20 .50
325 Blake Wheeler .25 .60
326 Tyler Myers .15 .40
327 Marko Dano .15 .40
328 Adam Lowry .20 .50
329 Connor Hellebuyck .50 1.25
330 Dustin Byfuglien .25 .60
331 Brendan Leipsic RC 1.00 2.50
332 Ryan Pulock RC 1.25 3.00
333 Tom Kuhnhackl RC 1.00 2.50
334 Tobias Lindberg RC 2.00 5.00
335 Alan Quine RC 1.25 3.00
336 Chase De Leo RC 1.25 3.00
337 Pontus Aberg RC 1.50 4.00
338 Steven Santini RC 1.00 2.50
339 Nikita Soshnikov RC .75 2.00
340 Kasperi Kapanen RC 2.00 5.00
341 Oliver Kylington RC 1.00 2.50
342 Miles Wood RC 1.00 2.50
343 Jason Dickinson RC 1.00 2.50
344 Josh Morrissey RC 3.00 8.00
345 Charlie Lindgren RC 2.00 5.00
346 Justin Bailey RC 1.25 3.00
347 Connor Brown RC 2.00 5.00
348 Nic Dowd RC 1.00 2.50
349 Trevor Carrick RC 1.25 3.00
350 William Nylander RC 5.00 12.00
351 Oliver Bjorkstrand RC 1.50 4.00
352 Stephen Johns RC 1.00 2.50
353 Nick Paul RC 1.50 4.00
354 Sergey Tolchinsky RC 1.00 2.50
355 Chris Bigras RC 1.00 2.50
356 Mike Reilly RC 1.00 2.50
357 J.C. Lipon RC 1.25 3.00
358 Dominik Simon RC 1.00 2.50
359 Frederik Gauthier RC 1.00 2.50
360 Sonny Milano RC 1.50 4.00
361 Hudson Fasching RC 1.25 3.00
362 Michael Matheson RC 1.25 3.00
363 Zach Hyman RC 4.00 10.00
364 Evan Rodrigues RC 2.00 5.00
365 Anthony Mantha RC 2.50 6.00
366 Pavel Zacha RC 2.00 5.00
367 Ivan Provorov RC 2.00 5.00
368 Nick Sorensen RC 1.25 3.00
369 Artturi Lehkonen RC 1.50 4.00
370 Auston Matthews RC 8.00 20.00
371 Tyler Motte RC 1.25 3.00
372 Brayden Point RC 3.00 8.00
373 Zach Werenski RC 4.00 10.00
374 Travis Konecny RC 2.50 6.00
375 Patrik Laine RC 3.00 8.00
376 Pavel Buchnevich RC 2.00 5.00
377 Nick Schmaltz RC 1.50 4.00
378 Danton Heinen RC 1.00 2.50
379 Thomas Chabot RC 2.50 6.00
380 Mikhail Sergachev RC 2.00 5.00
381 Jimmy Vesey RC 2.00 5.00
382 Anthony Beauvillier RC 1.25 3.00
383 Christian Dvorak RC 1.50 4.00
384 Jesse Puljujarvi RC 2.50 6.00
385 Matthew Tkachuk RC 5.00 12.00
386 Sebastian Aho RC 4.00 10.00
387 Mathew Barzal RC 4.00 10.00
388 Jakob Chychrun RC 2.50 6.00
389 Lawson Crouse RC 1.00 2.50
390 Mitch Marner RC 4.00 10.00
391 Brandon Carlo RC 2.00 5.00
392 Zach Sanford RC 1.25 3.00
393 Joel Eriksson Ek RC 2.00 5.00
394 Gustav Forsling RC 2.50 6.00
395 Dylan Strome RC 3.00 8.00
396 Kyle Connor RC 4.00 10.00
397 Jamie Benn CL .40 1.00
398 Connor McDavid CL 2.00 5.00
399 Sidney Crosby CL 1.50 4.00
400 Auston Matthews CL 2.50 6.00

2016-17 Parkhurst Black

*VETS: 1.25X TO 3X BASIC CARDS
*ROOKIES: 1.5X TO 4X BASIC CARDS
72 Corey Crawford 2.00 5.00
277 Jonathan Drouin 1.25 3.00
312 Nicklas Backstrom 1.50 4.00
313 Evgeny Kuznetsov 2.00 5.00
370 Auston Matthews 80.00 150.00

2016-17 Parkhurst All Star Favorites

AS1 Sidney Crosby 8.00 20.00
AS2 Patrick Kane 4.00 10.00
AS3 Jamie Benn 2.00 5.00
AS4 Erik Karlsson 2.50 6.00
AS5 Brent Burns 2.00 5.00
AS6 Drew Doughty 2.50 6.00
AS7 Vladimir Tarasenko 2.50 6.00
AS8 John Tavares 3.00 8.00
AS9 Claude Giroux 2.00 5.00
AS10 Alexander Ovechkin 8.00 20.00

2016-17 Parkhurst Letter On The Sweater

LS1 Henrik Zetterberg 2.50 6.00
LS2 Zdeno Chara 2.00 5.00
LS3 Shane Doan 1.50 4.00
LS4 Jonathan Toews 3.00 8.00
LS5 Henrik Sedin 2.50 6.00
LS6 Sidney Crosby 8.00 20.00
LS7 Alexander Ovechkin 8.00 20.00
LS8 Jamie Benn 2.00 5.00

2016-17 Parkhurst Protectors Of The Net

DN1 Carey Price 4.00 10.00
DN2 Braden Holtby 2.50 6.00
DN3 Jonathan Quick 2.50 6.00
DN4 Cory Schneider 2.00 5.00
DN5 Henrik Lundqvist 5.00 12.00
DN6 Corey Crawford 2.50 6.00
DN7 Tuukka Rask 2.50 6.00
DN8 Pekka Rinne 2.00 5.00

2016-17 Parkhurst Rookie Parade

RP1 William Nylander 20.00 50.00
RP2 Pavel Zacha 8.00 20.00
RP3 Justin Bailey 5.00 12.00
RP4 Sonny Milano 6.00 15.00
RP5 Anthony Mantha 10.00 25.00
RP6 Kasperi Kapanen 8.00 20.00
RP7 Miles Wood 4.00 10.00
RP8 Josh Morrissey 12.00 30.00
RP9 Jason Dickinson 4.00 10.00
RP10 Brendan Leipsic 4.00 10.00
RP11 Charlie Lindgren 8.00 20.00
RP12 Hudson Fasching 5.00 12.00
RP13 Connor Brown 8.00 20.00
RP14 Oliver Kylington 4.00 10.00
RP15 Ryan Pulock 5.00 12.00
RP16 Daniel Altshuller 4.00 10.00
RP17 Trevor Carrick 5.00 12.00
RP18 Sergey Tolchinsky 4.00 10.00
RP19 Michael Matheson 5.00 12.00
RP20 Tom Kuhnhackl 4.00 10.00
RP21 Dylan Strome 12.00 30.00
RP22 Ivan Provorov 8.00 20.00
RP23 Matthew Tkachuk 20.00 50.00
RP24 Jimmy Vesey 8.00 20.00
RP25 Patrik Laine 12.00 30.00
RP26 Travis Konecny 10.00 25.00
RP27 Kyle Connor 15.00 40.00
RP28 Zach Werenski 15.00 40.00
RP29 Mikhail Sergachev 8.00 20.00
RP30 Jesse Puljujarvi 10.00 25.00
RP31 Mathew Barzal 15.00 40.00
RP32 Mitch Marner 15.00 40.00
RP33 Auston Matthews 30.00 80.00

2016-17 Parkhurst Rookie Parade Blue

RP20 Tom Kuhnhackl AU E 20.00 50.00

2016-17 Parkhurst Tis The Season

TS1 Carey Price 15.00 40.00
TS2 John Tavares 12.00 30.00
TS3 Steven Stamkos 15.00 40.00
TS4 Jonathan Toews 12.00 30.00
TS5 Henrik Lundqvist 20.00 50.00
TS6 Henrik Zetterberg 10.00 25.00
TS7 Connor McDavid 40.00 100.00
TS8 Sidney Crosby 30.00 80.00
TS9 Drew Doughty 10.00 25.00
TS10 Patrice Bergeron 10.00 25.00
TS11 Henrik Sedin 10.00 25.00
TS12 Alex Ovechkin 30.00 80.00
TS13 Mark Messier 15.00 40.00
TS14 Mike Bossy 8.00 20.00
TS15 Patrick Roy 20.00 50.00
TS16 Doug Gilmour 10.00 25.00
TS17 Bobby Orr 30.00 80.00
TS18 Wayne Gretzky 50.00 125.00

2016-17 Parkhurst Top 25

TOP1 Jonathan Toews 3.00 8.00
TOP2 Henrik Zetterberg 2.50 6.00
TOP3 Brent Burns 2.00 5.00
TOP4 Alexander Ovechkin 8.00 20.00
TOP5 Evgeni Malkin 4.00 10.00
TOP6 Nikita Kucherov 4.00 10.00
TOP7 David Krejci 2.00 5.00
TOP8 Drew Doughty 2.50 6.00
TOP9 John Tavares 3.00 8.00
TOP10 Sidney Crosby 8.00 20.00
TOP11 Carey Price 4.00 10.00
TOP12 Jamie Benn 2.00 5.00
TOP13 Anze Kopitar 3.00 8.00
TOP14 Corey Perry 3.00 8.00
TOP15 Pekka Rinne 2.00 5.00
TOP16 Patrick Kane 4.00 10.00
TOP17 Joe Pavelski 2.50 6.00
TOP18 Nathan MacKinnon 8.00 20.00
TOP19 Steven Stamkos 4.00 10.00
TOP20 Max Pacioretty 2.00 5.00
TOP21 Connor McDavid 10.00 25.00
TOP22 Erik Karlsson 2.50 6.00
TOP23 Ryan Getzlaf 2.00 5.00
TOP24 Vladimir Tarasenko 2.50 6.00
TOP25 Tyler Seguin 2.50 6.00

017-18 Parkhurst Priority Signings

PSAB Anders Bjork/50 10.00 25.00
PSAD Alex DeBrincat/50 20.00 50.00
PSAF Alex Formenton/50 8.00 20.00
PSAK Adrian Kempe/75 15.00 40.00
PSAK Alex Kerfoot/50 15.00 40.00
PSAL Artturi Lehkonen/75 6.00 15.00
PSAN Alexander Nylander/50 12.00 30.00
PSAT Alex Tuch/40 20.00 50.00
PSBB Brock Boeser/50 80.00 150.00
PSBL Brendan Lemieux/75 8.00 20.00
PSBR Bobby Ryan/25 6.00 15.00
PSBS Brady Skjei/25 6.00 15.00
PSBU Will Butcher/50 10.00 25.00
PSCA Cam Atkinson/25 8.00 20.00
PSCD Chris DiDomenico/75 6.00 15.00
PSCF Christian Fischer/50 10.00 25.00
PSCH Carl Hagelin/25 5.00 12.00
PSCK Clayton Keller/75 20.00 50.00
PSCW Colin White/50 10.00 25.00
PSDB David Backes/25 5.00 12.00
PSDG Denis Gurianov/75 20.00 50.00
PSEC J.T. Compher/50 8.00 20.00
PSEK Evander Kane/25 8.00 20.00
PSES Evgeny Svechnikov/75 15.00 40.00
PSJB Jesper Bratt/50 15.00 40.00
PSJG Jon Gillies/75 8.00 20.00
PSJH Josh Ho-Sang/50 10.00 25.00
PSJM Josh Morrissey/25 10.00 25.00
PSJM Jake Muzzin/50 8.00 20.00
PSJR Jack Roslovic/50 10.00 25.00
PSKT Kyle Turris/25 8.00 20.00
PSKY Kailer Yamamoto/50 20.00 50.00
PSLE Anders Lee/25 8.00 20.00
PSLK Luke Kunin/50 8.00 20.00
PSMA Jacob Markstrom/25 15.00 40.00
PSMB Madison Bowey/75 5.00 12.00
PSMG Mikael Granlund/50 6.00 15.00
PSMM Mitch Marner/25 30.00 80.00
PSMS Mark Stone/25 10.00 25.00
PSMV Mike Vecchione/75 6.00 15.00
PSNE Nikolaj Ehlers/25 8.00 20.00
PSNS Nikita Scherbak/50 10.00 25.00
PSOM Olli Maatta/25 5.00 12.00
PSPD Phillip Danault/50 8.00 20.00
PSPD Pierre-Luc Dubois/50 12.00 30.00
PSRH Robert Hagg/50 8.00 20.00
PSRN Ryan Nugent-Hopkins/25 10.00 25.00
PSST Shea Theodore/25 10.00 25.00
PSTH Tage Thompson/50 20.00 50.00
PSTJ Tyson Jost/50 15.00 40.00
PSTP Tucker Poolman/75 6.00 15.00
PSTS Troy Stecher/25 15.00 40.00
PSTS Travis Sanheim/50 8.00 20.00
PSTT Teuvo Teravainen/25 8.00 20.00
PSVH Ville Husso/75 10.00 25.00
PSVM Victor Mete/50 8.00 20.00
PSVS Vadim Shipachyov/75 10.00 25.00
PSWN William Nylander/25 15.00 40.00

2017-18 Parkhurst

*RED.VET: 1X TO 2.5X BASIC CARDS
*RED.RC: .6X TO 1.5X BASIC CARDS
*BLACK.VET: 1.5X TO 4X BASIC CARDS
*BLACK.RC: 1X TO 2.5X BASIC CARDS
1 Ryan Getzlaf .25 .60
2 Corey Perry .40 1.00
3 Ryan Kesler .25 .60
4 Jakob Silfverberg .15 .40
5 Cam Fowler .25 .60
6 Sami Vatanen .15 .40
7 John Gibson .25 .60
8 Rickard Rakell .20 .50
9 Derek Stepan .15 .40
10 Oliver Ekman-Larsson .25 .60
11 Max Domi .25 .60
12 Christian Dvorak .20 .50
13 Jakob Chychrun .25 .60
14 Antti Raanta .25 .60
15 Alex Goligoski .20 .50
16 Dylan Strome .30 .75
17 David Backes .15 .40
18 Brad Marchand .50 1.25
19 David Krejci .25 .60
20 Patrice Bergeron .30 .75
21 Torey Krug .20 .50
22 Tuukka Rask .30 .75
23 David Pastrnak .60 1.50
24 Zdeno Chara .25 .60
25 Jack Eichel .40 1.00
26 Rasmus Ristolainen .15 .40
27 Sam Reinhart .50 1.25
28 Jason Pominville .15 .40
29 Kyle Okposo .15 .40
30 Ryan O'Reilly .25 .60
31 Evander Kane .25 .60
32 Robin Lehner .20 .50
33 Sean Monahan .15 .40
34 Dougie Hamilton .20 .50
35 Mike Smith .25 .60
36 Matthew Tkachuk .50 1.25
37 Travis Hamonic .20 .50
38 Mark Giordano .25 .60
39 Mikael Backlund .20 .50
40 Johnny Gaudreau .40 1.00
41 Jeff Skinner .30 .75
42 Victor Rask .15 .40
43 Jordan Staal .20 .50
44 Justin Williams .20 .50
45 Noah Hanifin .25 .60
46 Sebastian Aho .40 1.00
47 Justin Faulk .20 .50
48 Scott Darling .20 .50
49 Duncan Keith .20 .50
50 Patrick Sharp .20 .50
51 Jonathan Toews .40 1.00
52 Artem Anisimov .15 .40
53 Brent Seabrook .15 .40
54 Brandon Saad .20 .50
55 Corey Crawford .30 .75
56 Patrick Kane .50 1.25
57 Tyson Barrie .15 .40
58 Gabriel Landeskog .30 .75
59 Mikko Rantanen .60 1.50
60 Nathan MacKinnon 1.00 2.50
61 Semyon Varlamov .25 .60
62 Erik Johnson .15 .40
63 Nail Yakupov .15 .40
64 Blake Comeau .15 .40
65 Artemi Panarin .50 1.25
66 Zach Werenski .40 1.00
67 Alexander Wennberg .15 .40
68 Nick Foligno .20 .50
69 Sergei Bobrovsky .40 1.00
70 Cam Atkinson .25 .60
71 Seth Jones .25 .60
72 Boone Jenner .25 .60
73 Martin Hanzal .20 .50
74 Jason Spezza .25 .60
75 Jamie Benn .25 .60
76 Radek Faksa .20 .50
77 Alexander Radulov .25 .60
78 Ben Bishop .20 .50
79 Marc Methot .15 .40
80 Tyler Seguin .30 .75
81 Anthony Mantha .20 .50
82 Andreas Athanasiou .25 .60
83 Dylan Larkin .30 .75
84 Trevor Daley .20 .50
85 Henrik Zetterberg .30 .75
86 Gustav Nyquist .15 .40
87 Tomas Tatar .15 .40
88 Jim Howard .30 .75
89 Leon Draisaitl .75 2.00
90 Connor McDavid 1.25 3.00
91 Ryan Nugent-Hopkins .30 .75
92 Milan Lucic .25 .60
93 Oscar Klefbom .20 .50
94 Andrej Sekera .15 .40
95 Patrick Maroon .20 .50
96 Cam Talbot .25 .60
97 Aleksander Barkov .40 1.00
98 Jonathan Huberdeau .30 .75
99 Roberto Luongo .40 1.00
100 Checklist Card .15 .40
101 Aaron Ekblad .30 .75
102 Vincent Trocheck .25 .60
103 Keith Yandle .15 .40
104 Jason Demers .15 .40
105 Radim Vrbata .15 .40
106 Anze Kopitar .40 1.00
107 Tanner Pearson .20 .50
108 Jeff Carter .20 .50
109 Jonathan Quick .30 .75
110 Drew Doughty .30 .75
111 Dustin Brown .25 .60
112 Tyler Toffoli .25 .60
113 Alec Martinez .15 .40
114 Mikael Granlund .20 .50
115 Ryan Suter .20 .50
116 Eric Staal .30 .75
117 Charlie Coyle .25 .60
118 Nino Niederreiter .15 .40
119 Mikko Koivu .20 .50
120 Devan Dubnyk .20 .50
121 Zach Parise .25 .60
122 Max Pacioretty .25 .60
123 Shea Weber .20 .50
124 Jonathan Drouin .20 .50
125 Carey Price .50 1.25
126 Paul Byron .20 .50
127 Jeff Petry .25 .60
128 Alex Galchenyuk .15 .40
129 Karl Alzner .15 .40
130 P.K. Subban .30 .75
131 Filip Forsberg .40 1.00
132 Roman Josi .25 .60
133 Pekka Rinne .25 .60
134 Ryan Johansen .20 .50
135 Viktor Arvidsson .15 .40
136 Ryan Ellis .20 .50
137 Mattias Ekholm .20 .50
138 Nick Bonino .15 .40
139 Cory Schneider .25 .60
140 Marcus Johansson .20 .50
141 Taylor Hall .25 .60
142 Adam Henrique .20 .50
143 Andy Greene .15 .40
144 Kyle Palmieri .20 .50
145 Pavel Zacha .20 .50
146 Travis Zajac .15 .40
147 Josh Bailey .20 .50
148 Anders Lee .25 .60
149 Nick Leddy .15 .40
150 John Tavares .40 1.00
151 Jordan Eberle .25 .60
152 Andrew Ladd .15 .40
153 Thomas Greiss .20 .50
154 Brock Nelson .25 .60
155 Mats Zuccarello .25 .60
156 J.T. Miller .30 .75
157 Chris Kreider .30 .75
158 Ryan McDonagh .15 .40
159 Brady Skjei .20 .50
160 Henrik Lundqvist .60 1.50
161 Kevin Shattenkirk .15 .40
162 Rick Nash .25 .60
163 Mike Hoffman .15 .40
164 Dion Phaneuf .20 .50
165 Kyle Turris .25 .60
166 Mark Stone .30 .75
167 Jean-Gabriel Pageau .15 .40
168 Bobby Ryan .20 .50
169 Craig Anderson .25 .60
170 Erik Karlsson .30 .75
171 Wayne Simmonds .30 .75
172 Shayne Gostisbehere .25 .60
173 Ivan Provorov .20 .50
174 Jakub Voracek .20 .50
175 Sean Couturier .20 .50
176 Claude Giroux .25 .60
177 Travis Konecny .25 .60
178 Brian Elliott .20 .50
179 Evgeni Malkin .50 1.25
180 Sidney Crosby 1.00 2.50
181 Matt Murray .40 1.00
182 Jake Guentzel .40 1.00
183 Phil Kessel .25 .60
184 Kris Letang .30 .75
185 Justin Schultz .25 .60
186 Patric Hornqvist .15 .40
187 Conor Sheary .25 .60
188 Joe Thornton .40 1.00
189 Joe Pavelski .30 .75
190 Brent Burns .25 .60
191 Martin Jones .20 .50
192 Logan Couture .30 .75
193 Marc-Edouard Vlasic .15 .40
194 Tomas Hertl .25 .60
195 Joel Ward .20 .50
196 Colton Parayko .20 .50
197 Jake Allen .25 .60
198 Alexander Steen .15 .40
199 Jaden Schwartz .30 .75
200 Checklist Card .15 .40
201 Paul Stastny .20 .50
202 Vladimir Tarasenko .30 .75
203 Alex Pietrangelo .20 .50
204 Robby Fabbri .15 .40
205 Alex Killorn .15 .40
206 Andrei Vasilevskiy .40 1.00
207 Nikita Kucherov .50 1.25
208 Victor Hedman .30 .75
209 Ondrej Palat .20 .50
210 Steven Stamkos .50 1.25
211 Brayden Point .30 .75
212 Tyler Johnson .15 .40
213 Patrick Marleau .25 .60
214 William Nylander .50 1.25
215 Frederik Andersen .30 .75
216 Mitch Marner .40 1.00
217 Nazem Kadri .30 .75
218 Morgan Rielly .25 .60
219 James van Riemsdyk .20 .50
220 Auston Matthews 1.00 2.50
221 Troy Stecher .15 .40
222 Henrik Sedin .30 .75
223 Jacob Markstrom .25 .60
224 Bo Horvat .30 .75
225 Daniel Sedin .30 .75
226 Sven Baertschi .15 .40
227 Sam Gagner .15 .40
228 Loui Eriksson .15 .40
229 Jonathan Marchessault .30 .75
230 Marc-Andre Fleury .50 1.25
231 James Neal .15 .40
232 Reilly Smith .25 .60
233 Oscar Lindberg .20 .50
234 Shea Theodore .30 .75
235 David Perron .20 .50
236 Nate Schmidt .20 .50
237 T.J. Oshie .25 .60
238 Nicklas Backstrom .25 .60
239 Braden Holtby .30 .75
240 Alexander Ovechkin 1.00 2.50
241 Evgeny Kuznetsov .30 .75
242 John Carlson .25 .60
243 Matt Niskanen .20 .50
244 Andre Burakovsky .15 .40
245 Bryan Little .20 .50
246 Blake Wheeler .25 .60
247 Dustin Byfuglien .25 .60
248 Steve Mason .20 .50
249 Jacob Trouba .20 .50
250 Mark Scheifele .40 1.00
251 Nikolaj Ehlers .25 .60
252 Patrik Laine .30 .75
253 Alexander Nylander RC 1.25 3.00
254 Josh Ho-Sang RC 1.00 2.50
255 Adrian Kempe RC 1.50 4.00
256 Ivan Barbashev RC 1.00 2.50
257 Christian Fischer RC 1.00 2.50
258 Tyson Jost RC 1.50 4.00
259 Colin White RC 1.00 2.50
260 Jon Gillies RC .75 2.00
261 J.T. Compher RC .75 2.00
262 Mike Vecchione RC .60 1.50
263 Nikita Scherbak RC 1.00 2.50
264 Riley Barber RC .75 2.00
265 Jonny Brodzinski RC .75 2.00
266 Jordan Schmaltz RC 1.00 2.50
267 Vladislav Kamenev RC .75 2.00
268 Jakob Forsbacka-Karlsson RC .75 2.00
269 Gabriel Carlsson RC .60 1.50
270 Brock Boeser RC 2.00 5.00
271 Denis Gurianov RC 2.00 5.00
272 Alex Tuch RC 2.00 5.00
273 Jack Roslovic RC 1.00 2.50
274 Charlie McAvoy RC 2.00 5.00
275 Clayton Keller RC 2.00 5.00
276 Nicolas Kerdiles RC .75 2.00
277 Eric Comrie RC .60 1.50
278 Marcus Sorensen RC .60 1.50
279 Jake Dotchin RC .60 1.50
280 Evgeny Svechnikov RC 1.50 4.00
281 Carter Rowney RC .60 1.50
282 Jesper Bratt RC 1.50 4.00
283 Will Butcher RC 1.00 2.50
284 Nathan Walker RC .75 2.00
285 Nolan Patrick RC 1.50 4.00
286 Kailer Yamamoto RC 2.00 5.00
287 Anders Bjork RC 1.00 2.50
288 Alex DeBrincat RC 2.00 5.00
289 Owen Tippett RC 1.50 4.00
290 Nico Hischier RC 2.50 6.00
291 Filip Chytil RC .75 2.00
292 Martin Necas RC 2.50 6.00
293 Jake DeBrusk RC 2.00 5.00
294 Victor Mete RC .75 2.00
295 Pierre-Luc Dubois RC 1.25 3.00
296 Calle Rosen RC .75 2.00
297 Logan Brown RC .75 2.00
298 Luke Kunin RC .75 2.00
299 Vadim Shipachyov RC 1.00 2.50
300 Checklist Card RC .15 .40

2017-18 Parkhurst Blow The Horn

BH1 Connor McDavid 2.50 6.00
BH2 Evgeni Malkin 1.00 2.50
BH3 Patrick Kane 1.00 2.50
BH4 Vladimir Tarasenko .60 1.50
BH5 Alexander Ovechkin 2.00 5.00
BH6 Auston Matthews 2.00 5.00
BH7 Patrik Laine .60 1.50
BH8 Nikita Kucherov 1.00 2.50
BH9 Brad Marchand 1.00 2.50
SH10 Sidney Crosby 2.00 5.00

2017-18 Parkhurst East Vs. West

E1 Sidney Crosby 2.50 6.00
E2 Auston Matthews 2.50 6.00
E3 Victor Hedman .75 2.00
E4 Erik Karlsson .75 2.00
E5 Alexander Ovechkin 2.50 6.00
E6 Brad Marchand 1.25 3.00
E7 Evgeni Malkin 1.25 3.00
E8 Carey Price 1.25 3.00
W1 Connor McDavid 3.00 8.00
W2 Patrick Kane 1.25 3.00
W3 Brent Burns .60 1.50
W4 P.K. Subban .75 2.00
W5 Patrik Laine .75 2.00
W6 Drew Doughty .75 2.00
W7 Jonathan Toews 1.00 2.50
W8 Vladimir Tarasenko .75 2.00

2017-18 Parkhurst Parkhurst International

PI1 Sidney Crosby 1.50 4.00
PI2 Connor McDavid 2.00 5.00
PI3 Wayne Gretzky 2.50 6.00
PI4 Patrick Kane .75 2.00
PI5 Auston Matthews 1.50 4.00
PI6 Mike Modano .60 1.50
PI7 Evgeni Malkin .75 2.00
PI8 Alexander Ovechkin 1.50 4.00
PI9 Pavel Bure .40 1.00
PI10 Erik Karlsson .50 1.25
PI11 Henrik Zetterberg .50 1.25
PI12 Nicklas Lidstrom .40 1.00
PI13 Mikael Granlund .30 .75
PI14 Pekka Rinne .40 1.00
PI15 Teemu Selanne .75 2.00
PI16 Jakub Voracek .30 .75
PI17 David Krejci .40 1.00
PI18 Dominik Hasek .60 1.50
PI19 Leon Draisaitl 1.25 3.00
PI20 Thomas Greiss .30 .75
PI21 Dennis Seidenberg .25 .60
PI22 Roman Josi .40 1.00
PI23 Nino Niederreiter .25 .60
PI24 Mark Streit .30 .75

2017-18 Parkhurst Prominent Prospects

*GREEN/399: .75X TO 2X BASIC INSERTS
*RED/199: 1.25X TO 3X BASIC INSERTS
*GOLD/99: 2X TO 5X BASIC INSERTS
PP1 Brock Boeser 1.50 4.00
PP2 Nikita Scherbak .75 2.00
PP3 Colin White .75 2.00
PP4 Christian Fischer .75 2.00
PP5 Josh Ho-Sang .75 2.00
PP6 Alexander Nylander 1.00 2.50
PP7 Evgeny Svechnikov 1.25 3.00
PP8 Jack Roslovic .75 2.00
PP9 Ivan Barbashev .75 2.00
PP10 Clayton Keller 1.50 4.00
PP11 Tyson Jost 1.25 3.00
PP12 Jon Gillies .60 1.50
PP13 Adrian Kempe 1.25 3.00
PP14 Alex Tuch 1.50 4.00
PP15 Charlie McAvoy 1.50 4.00
PP16 Nico Hischier 2.00 5.00
PP17 Alex DeBrincat 1.50 4.00
PP18 Kailer Yamamoto 1.50 4.00
PP19 Owen Tippett 1.25 3.00
PP20 Pierre-Luc Dubois 1.00 2.50
PP21 Filip Chytil .60 1.50
PP22 Logan Brown .60 1.50
PP23 Vadim Shipachyov .75 2.00
PP24 Will Butcher .75 2.00
PP25 Nolan Patrick 1.25 3.00

2017-18 Parkhurst Seeing Stars

*RED: .75X TO 2X BASIC INSERTS
*BLUE: 1.5X TO 4X BASIC INSERTS
SS1 Sidney Crosby 1.50 4.00
SS2 Patrick Kane .75 2.00
SS3 Henrik Zetterberg .50 1.25
SS4 Brad Marchand .75 2.00
SS5 Auston Matthews 1.50 4.00
SS6 Carey Price .75 2.00
SS7 Henrik Lundqvist 1.00 2.50
SS8 Evgeni Malkin .75 2.00
SS9 Alexander Ovechkin 1.50 4.00
SS10 Connor McDavid 2.00 5.00

2018-19 Parkhurst

1 Auston Matthews 1.00 2.50
2 Brad Marchand .50 1.25
3 Johnny Gaudreau .40 1.00
4 Taylor Hall .25 .60
5 Patrick Kane .50 1.25
6 Jack Eichel .40 1.00
7 Nathan MacKinnon 1.00 2.50
8 Derek Stepan .15 .40
9 Ryan Kesler .25 .60
10 P.K. Subban .30 .75
11 Victor Rask .15 .40
12 Henrik Zetterberg .30 .75
13 Sergei Bobrovsky .40 1.00
14 Jonathan Huberdeau .30 .75
15 Connor McDavid 1.25 3.00
16 Drew Doughty .30 .75
17 Eric Staal .25 .60
18 Evgeni Malkin .50 1.25
19 Jamie Benn .25 .60
20 Carey Price .50 1.25
21 Jake Allen .25 .60
22 Mathew Barzal .30 .75
23 Wayne Simmonds .25 .60
24 Joe Pavelski .30 .75
25 Alexander Ovechkin 1.00 2.50
26 Mika Zibanejad .30 .75
27 Bobby Ryan .20 .50
28 Erik Haula .15 .40
29 Patrik Laine .30 .75
30 Brock Boeser .30 .75
31 Steven Stamkos .50 1.25
32 Alex DeBrincat .30 .75
33 Aleksander Barkov .40 1.00
34 Jake DeBrusk .25 .60
35 Leon Draisaitl .75 2.00
36 Sean Monahan .15 .40
37 Devan Dubnyk .20 .50
38 Tyler Toffoli .25 .60
39 Kyle Palmieri .20 .50
40 Claude Giroux .25 .60
41 Tyson Barrie .15 .40
42 Kyle Okposo .15 .40
43 Frans Nielsen .15 .40
44 Ryan Johansen .20 .50
45 Braden Holtby .30 .75
46 Brendan Perlini .15 .40
47 Jordan Eberle .25 .60
48 Alexander Steen .15 .40
49 Kevin Shattenkirk .15 .40
50 Marc-Andre Fleury .50 1.25
51 Marian Gaborik .25 .60
52 Connor Brown .20 .50
53 Andrew Cogliano .15 .40
54 Jordan Staal .20 .50
55 Nikolaj Ehlers .25 .60
56 Loui Eriksson .15 .40
57 Alexander Radulov .25 .60
58 Cam Atkinson .25 .60
59 Victor Hedman .30 .75
60 Jonathan Drouin .20 .50
61 Patric Hornqvist .15 .40
62 Evander Kane .25 .60
63 Andrew Ladd .15 .40
64 Brayden Point .30 .75
65 Patrick Marleau .25 .60
66 Filip Forsberg .40 1.00
67 Will Butcher .20 .50
68 Tomas Tatar .15 .40
69 Dustin Byfuglien .25 .60
70 Nikita Kucherov .50 1.25
71 Colin White .15 .40
72 Jakub Voracek .20 .50
73 Colin Miller .15 .40
74 Jaden Schwartz .30 .75
75 Tyler Johnson .15 .40
76 Alex Goligoski .20 .50
77 Joonas Donskoi .15 .40
78 Jake Virtanen .20 .50
79 T.J. Oshie .25 .60
80 Artturi Lehkonen .20 .50
81 Mats Zuccarello .25 .60
82 Milan Lucic .20 .50
83 Zach Parise .25 .60
84 Bo Horvat .30 .75
85 Connor Hellebuyck .50 1.25
86 Matthew Tkachuk .50 1.25
87 Teuvo Teravainen .25 .60
88 Reilly Smith .25 .60
89 Erik Johnson .15 .40
90 Jake Muzzin .25 .60
91 Justin Abdelkader .20 .50
92 Nazem Kadri .30 .75
93 Brandon Saad .20 .50
94 Aaron Ekblad .30 .75
95 Max Pacioretty .25 .60
96 Jason Spezza .25 .60
97 John Gibson .25 .60
98 Brandon Dubinsky .15 .40
99 Kyle Turris .20 .50
100 Frederik Andersen .30 .75
101 Josh Bailey .20 .50
102 John Klingberg .25 .60
103 Brent Seabrook .15 .40
104 Tyson Jost .20 .50
105 Craig Anderson .20 .50
106 David Pastrnak .60 1.50
107 Sean Couturier .20 .50
108 Zack Smith .15 .40
109 Olli Maatta .15 .40
110 Checklist Card .15 .40
111 Rasmus Ristolainen .15 .40
112 Marc-Edouard Vlasic .15 .40
113 Mikael Granlund .20 .50
114 Brayden Schenn .25 .60
115 Ryan Nugent-Hopkins .30 .75
116 Evgeny Kuznetsov .30 .75
117 Christian Fischer .15 .40
118 Andreas Athanasiou .20 .50
119 Anze Kopitar .40 1.00
120 Travis Konecny .25 .60
121 Justin Williams .20 .50
122 Ben Bishop .20 .50
123 Chris Kreider .30 .75
124 Viktor Arvidsson .15 .40
125 Artemi Panarin .50 1.25
126 Brandon Sutter .15 .40
127 Dustin Brown .25 .60
128 Torey Krug .20 .50
129 Hampus Lindholm .15 .40
130 Jonathan Marchessault .30 .75
131 Andrew Shaw .15 .40
132 Mikael Backlund .20 .50
133 Nino Niederreiter .15 .40
134 Boone Jenner .25 .60
135 Matt Duchene .25 .60
136 Niklas Hjalmarsson .15 .40
137 Blake Wheeler .25 .60
138 Jason Pominville .15 .40
139 Nick Leddy .15 .40
140 Nicklas Backstrom .25 .60
141 Nick Schmaltz .20 .50
142 Shayne Gostisbehere .25 .60
143 Bryan Rust .25 .60
144 Bryan Little .15 .40
145 Tyler Seguin .30 .75
146 Vladislav Namestnikov .15 .40
147 Sam Gagner .15 .40
148 T.J. Brodie .20 .50
149 Sebastian Aho .40 1.00
150 Vladimir Tarasenko .30 .75
151 Brendan Gallagher .25 .60
152 Timo Meier .25 .60
153 Nick Bonino .15 .40
154 Mikko Rantanen .60 1.50
155 Marcus Johansson .20 .50
156 Nick Foligno .20 .50
157 Dylan Larkin .30 .75
158 Michael Matheson .20 .50
159 Cam Fowler .25 .60
160 William Karlsson .30 .75
161 Brett Pesce .15 .40
162 Thomas Chabot .25 .60
163 Ryan Strome .25 .60
164 Christian Dvorak .20 .50
165 Corey Crawford .20 .50
166 Charlie McAvoy .30 .75
167 Ryan Suter .20 .50
168 Johnny Boychuk .20 .50
169 Jeff Carter .20 .50
170 Mitch Marner .40 1.00
171 John Carlson .25 .60
172 Brayden McNabb .15 .40
173 Pavel Buchnevich .20 .50
174 Kyle Connor .40 1.00
175 Cam Talbot .25 .60
176 Sven Baertschi .20 .50
177 Brock Nelson .25 .60
178 Shea Weber .25 .60
179 Alexander Wennberg .15 .40
180 William Nylander .50 1.25
181 Ivan Provorov .20 .50
182 Mark Giordano .25 .60
183 Martin Jones .20 .50
184 Martin Hanzal .15 .40
185 Colton Parayko .20 .50
186 Jesper Bratt .25 .60
187 Alex Tuch .25 .60
188 Jakob Silfverberg .15 .40
189 Jared Spurgeon .25 .60
190 Andrei Vasilevskiy .40 1.00
191 Anthony Mantha .20 .50
192 Tanner Pearson .20 .50
193 Alex Pietrangelo .20 .50
194 Justin Faulk .20 .50
195 Roberto Luongo .40 1.00
196 Roman Josi .25 .60
197 Morgan Rielly .25 .60
198 Alex Kerfoot .20 .50
199 Duncan Keith .20 .50
200 Sidney Crosby 1.00 2.50
201 Joe Thornton .40 1.00
202 Pavel Zacha .20 .50
203 Tomas Plekanec .15 .40
204 Sam Bennett .40 1.00
205 Oliver Ekman-Larsson .25 .60
206 Sam Reinhart .50 1.25
207 Rickard Rakell .20 .50
208 Tuukka Rask .30 .75
209 Radek Faksa .20 .50
210 Pekka Rinne .25 .60
211 Jaccob Slavin .20 .50
212 J.T. Compher .15 .40
213 Charlie Coyle .25 .60
214 Anthony Beauvillier .15 .40
215 Nolan Patrick .25 .60
216 Oscar Klefbom .20 .50
217 Pierre-Luc Dubois .20 .50
218 Mark Stone .30 .75
219 Nico Hischier .40 1.00
220 Checklist Card .15 .40
221 Tyler Bozak .15 .40
222 Mike Green .20 .50
223 Lars Eller .15 .40
224 Carter Hutton .20 .50
225 Jake Guentzel .40 1.00
226 Paul Stastny .20 .50
227 Artem Anisimov .15 .40
228 Charles Hudon .20 .50
229 David Perron .20 .50
230 Josh Morrissey .30 .75
231 Mike Hoffman .15 .40
232 Jimmy Vesey .20 .50
233 Vincent Trocheck .25 .60
234 Sami Vatanen .15 .40
235 Ondrej Palat .20 .50
236 Mattias Ekholm .20 .50
237 Danton Heinen .20 .50
238 James van Riemsdyk .20 .50
239 Colin Wilson .20 .50
240 John Tavares .40 1.00
241 Adam Larsson .25 .60
242 Michael Frolik .20 .50
243 Cal Clutterbuck .15 .40
244 Blake Coleman .20 .50
245 Matt Murray .25 .60
246 Michael Grabner .15 .40
247 Tomas Hertl .25 .60
248 J.T. Miller .30 .75
249 Jason Zucker .25 .60
250 Henrik Lundqvist .60 1.50
251 Danny DeKeyser .15 .40
252 Dougie Hamilton .20 .50
253 Adam Henrique .20 .50
254 Adrian Kempe .25 .60
255 Marc Staal .15 .40
256 Cory Schneider .25 .60
257 Seth Jones .25 .60
258 Patrik Berglund .15 .40
259 Andre Burakovsky .15 .40
260 Mark Scheifele .40 1.00
261 Max Domi .25 .60
262 Jonathan Quick .30 .75
263 Chris Kunitz .20 .50
264 Jean-Gabriel Pageau .15 .40
265 Patrice Bergeron .30 .75
266 Nick Bjugstad .15 .40
267 Nikita Zaitsev .20 .50
268 Michael Del Zotto .25 .60
269 Ryan McDonagh .15 .40
270 James Neal .15 .40
271 Alex Killorn .15 .40
272 Kris Letang .30 .75
273 Jeff Skinner .30 .75
274 Jesse Puljujarvi .25 .60
275 Ryan Getzlaf .25 .60
276 Justin Schultz .20 .50
277 Matt Niskanen .20 .50
278 Craig Smith .15 .40
279 Kevin Hayes .20 .50
280 Zdeno Chara .25 .60
281 Alexander Edler .15 .40
282 Alex Galchenyuk .15 .40
283 Ryan O'Reilly .25 .60
284 Carl Soderberg .15 .40
285 Logan Couture .30 .75
286 Stephen Johns .15 .40
287 Antoine Roussel .15 .40
288 Travis Zajac .15 .40
289 Matt Dumba .15 .40
290 Phil Kessel .25 .60
291 Mikkel Boedker .15 .40
292 Mathieu Perreault .15 .40
293 Niklas Kronwall .20 .50
294 Leo Komarov .15 .40
295 Gabriel Landeskog .30 .75
296 Michael Raffl .20 .50
297 Conor Sheary .25 .60
298 Devante Smith-Pelly .20 .50
299 Ilya Kovalchuk .20 .50
300 Jonathan Toews .40 1.00
301 Kris Russell .15 .40
302 David Backes .15 .40
303 Evgenii Dadonov .15 .40
304 Zach Werenski .40 1.00
305 Corey Perry .40 1.00
306 Noah Hanifin .25 .60
307 Clayton Keller .30 .75
308 Gustav Nyquist .15 .40
309 Brent Burns .25 .60
310 Checklist Card .15 .40
311 Alexander Ovechkin 1.00 2.50
312 Sidney Crosby 1.00 2.50
313 Auston Matthews 1.00 2.50
314 Erik Karlsson .30 .75
315 Carey Price .50 1.25
316 John Tavares .40 1.00
317 Steven Stamkos .50 1.25
318 Jack Eichel .40 1.00
319 Kris Letang .30 .75
320 Braden Holtby .30 .75
321 Connor McDavid 1.25 3.00
322 Patrick Kane .50 1.25
323 Brock Boeser .30 .75
324 Brent Burns .25 .60
325 Pekka Rinne .25 .60
326 Nathan MacKinnon 1.00 2.50
327 Anze Kopitar .40 1.00
328 Johnny Gaudreau .40 1.00
329 P.K. Subban .30 .75
330 Marc-Andre Fleury .50 1.25
331 Elias Pettersson RC 2.50 6.00
332 Ryan Donato RC 1.25 3.00
333 Dylan Sikura RC 1.00 2.50
334 Miro Heiskanen RC 2.00 5.00
335 Lias Andersson RC 1.25 3.00
336 Michael Rasmussen RC 1.00 2.50
337 Troy Terry RC 1.25 3.00
338 Robert Thomas RC 1.50 4.00
339 Jaret Anderson-Dolan RC .60 1.50
340 Rasmus Dahlin RC 2.00 5.00
341 Kristian Vesalainen RC 1.00 2.50
342 Evan Bouchard RC 2.00 5.00
343 Michael Dal Colle RC .75 2.00
344 Maxim Mamin RC .75 2.00
345 Noah Juulsen RC .75 2.00
346 Rourke Chartier RC .60 1.50
347 Travis Dermott RC 1.25 3.00
348 Mikhail Vorobyev RC .60 1.50
349 Zach Aston-Reese RC 1.25 3.00
350 Andrei Svechnikov RC 2.00 5.00
351 Max Lajoie RC 1.25 3.00
352 Dennis Cholowski RC .75 2.00
353 Maxime Comtois RC .75 2.00
354 Anthony Cirelli RC 1.25 3.00
355 Dillon Dube RC 1.00 2.50
356 Isac Lundestrom RC .60 1.50
357 Dominik Kahun RC .75 2.00
358 Roope Hintz RC 2.00 5.00
359 Ethan Bear RC 1.25 3.00
360 Jesperi Kotkaniemi RC 1.50 4.00
361 Jordan Greenway RC .75 2.00
362 Oskar Lindblom RC 1.25 3.00
363 Mathieu Joseph RC 1.00 2.50
364 Brett Howden RC 1.00 2.50
365 Austin Wagner RC .60 1.50
366 Tomas Hyka RC .75 2.00
367 Antti Suomela RC .60 1.50
368 Sami Niku RC .60 1.50
369 Eeli Tolvanen RC 1.50 4.00
370 Brady Tkachuk RC 2.50 6.00
371 Christoffer Ehn RC .60 1.50
372 Jordan Kyrou RC 1.50 4.00
373 Andreas Johnsson RC 1.00 2.50
374 Henri Jokiharju RC .60 1.50
375 Warren Foegele RC .75 2.00
376 Juuso Valimaki RC .75 2.00
377 Henrik Borgstrom RC 1.25 3.00
378 Sam Steel RC .75 2.00
379 Adam Gaudette RC 1.25 3.00
380 Casey Mittelstadt RC 1.50 4.00

2018-19 Parkhurst Ice Ambassadors

IA1 Sidney Crosby 2.00 5.00
IA2 Auston Matthews 2.00 5.00
IA3 Steven Stamkos 1.00 2.50
IA4 Henrik Lundqvist 1.25 3.00
IA5 Connor McDavid 2.50 6.00
IA6 Jonathan Toews .75 2.00
IA7 Marc-Andre Fleury 1.00 2.50
IA8 Anze Kopitar .75 2.00
IA9 Alexander Ovechkin 2.00 5.00
IA10 Carey Price 1.00 2.50

2018-19 Parkhurst Original 6

O61 Maurice Richard 1.25 3.00
O62 Carey Price 1.25 3.00
O63 Artturi Lehkonen .50 1.25
O64 Tim Horton 1.00 2.50
O65 Morgan Rielly .60 1.50
O66 Auston Matthews 2.50 6.00
O67 Johnny Bucyk .60 1.50
O68 Patrice Bergeron .75 2.00
O69 Jake DeBrusk .60 1.50
O610 Alex Delvecchio .60 1.50
O611 Henrik Zetterberg .75 2.00
O612 Anthony Mantha .50 1.25
O613 Stan Mikita .60 1.50
O614 Jonathan Toews 1.00 2.50
O615 Alex DeBrincat .75 2.00
O616 Andy Bathgate .50 1.25
O617 Henrik Lundqvist 1.50 4.00
O618 Pavel Buchnevich .50 1.25

2018-19 Parkhurst Parkhurst Permits

PA1 Alexander Ovechkin 3.00 8.00
PA2 Sidney Crosby 3.00 8.00
PA3 Johnny Gaudreau 1.25 3.00
PA4 Nikita Kucherov 1.50 4.00
PA5 Jonathan Toews 1.25 3.00
PA6 Marc-Andre Fleury 1.50 4.00
PA7 Artemi Panarin 1.50 4.00
PA8 Brent Burns .75 2.00
PA9 Patrik Laine 1.00 2.50
PA10 Vladimir Tarasenko 1.00 2.50
PA11 Roman Josi .75 2.00
PA12 Auston Matthews 3.00 8.00
PA13 Evgeni Malkin 1.50 4.00
PA14 Tomas Tatar .50 1.25
PA15 Brock Boeser 1.00 2.50
PA16 Taylor Hall .75 2.00
PA17 Blake Wheeler .75 2.00
PA18 P.K. Subban 1.00 2.50
PA19 Anze Kopitar 1.25 3.00
PA20 Tuukka Rask 1.00 2.50
PA21 Leon Draisaitl 2.50 6.00
PA22 Nico Hischier 1.25 3.00
PA23 Jesperi Kotkaniemi 1.50 4.00
PA24 Elias Pettersson 2.50 6.00
PA25 Rasmus Dahlin 2.00 5.00

2018-19 Parkhurst Prominent Prospects Autographs

PP1 Elias Pettersson A 50.00 125.00
PP2 Casey Mittelstadt A 30.00 80.00
PP3 Miro Heiskanen A 40.00 100.00
PP4 Eeli Tolvanen B 30.00 80.00
PP5 Andrei Svechnikov A 40.00 100.00
PP6 Evan Bouchard B 40.00 100.00
PP7 Jordan Greenway C 15.00 40.00
PP8 Jordan Kyrou B 30.00 80.00
PP9 Sam Steel C 15.00 40.00
PP10 Henrik Borgstrom C 25.00 60.00
PP11 Michael Rasmussen B 20.00 50.00
PP12 Travis Dermott C 25.00 60.00
PP13 Dillon Dube B 20.00 50.00
PP14 Troy Terry C 4.00 10.00
PP16 Adam Gaudette B 25.00 60.00
PP17 Brady Tkachuk A 50.00 125.00
PP18 Michael Dal Colle C 15.00 40.00
PP19 Lias Andersson A 25.00 60.00
PP20 Ryan Donato A 25.00 60.00
PP21 Robert Thomas B 30.00 80.00
PP22 Zach Aston-Reese C 25.00 60.00
PP24 Dylan Sikura C 20.00 50.00

2018-19 Parkhurst View from the Ice

VI1 Connor McDavid 3.00 8.00
VI2 Jamie Benn .60 1.50
VI3 Jonathan Toews 1.00 2.50
VI4 Claude Giroux .60 1.50
VI5 Vladimir Tarasenko .75 2.00
VI6 Carey Price 1.25 3.00
VI7 William Karlsson .75 2.00
VI8 Zdeno Chara .60 1.50
VI9 Brock Boeser .75 2.00
VI10 Alexander Ovechkin 2.50 6.00
VI11 Connor Hellebuyck 1.25 3.00
VI12 Henrik Zetterberg .75 2.00
VI13 Jeff Carter .50 1.25
VI14 Evgeni Malkin 1.25 3.00
VI15 Mikko Rantanen 1.50 4.00
VI16 Aaron Ekblad .75 2.00
VI17 Taylor Hall .60 1.50
VI18 Auston Matthews 2.50 6.00

2019-20 Parkhurst

*SILVER.VETS: .6X TO 1.5X BASIC CARDS
*SILVER.SP: .6X TO 1.5X BASIC CARDS
*SILVER.RC: .5X TO 1.25X BASIC CARDS
*GOLD.VETS: .8X TO 2X BASIC CARDS
*GOLD.SP: .8X TO 2X BASIC CARDS
*GOLD.RC: .6X TO 1.5X BASIC CARDS
1 Sidney Crosby 1.00 2.50
2 Jeff Skinner .25 .60
3 Pierre-Luc Dubois .20 .50
4 Zach Parise .25 .60
5 Teuvo Teravainen .25 .60
6 Keith Yandle .15 .40
7 Bo Horvat .30 .75
8 J.T. Compher .15 .40
9 Roman Josi .25 .60
10 Patrick Kane .50 1.25
11 Reilly Smith .25 .60
12 Brock Boeser .30 .75
13 Nolan Patrick .25 .60
14 William Karlsson .30 .75
15 Sean Couturier .20 .50
16 Timo Meier .25 .60
17 Ryan Johansen .20 .50
18 Jonathan Marchessault .30 .75
19 Evander Kane .25 .60
20 Jake Guentzel .40 1.00
21 Brayden Schenn .25 .60
22 Mikael Granlund .20 .50
23 Brock Nelson .25 .60
24 Jakub Voracek .20 .50
25 Pekka Rinne .25 .60
26 Brett Pesce .15 .40
27 Jonathan Drouin .20 .50
28 Oliver Ekman-Larsson .25 .60
29 Duncan Keith .20 .50
30 Max Domi .25 .60
31 Adam Larsson .20 .50
32 Evgeny Kuznetsov .30 .75
33 Ryan Kesler .25 .60
34 Brandon Montour .30 .75
35 Ryan Getzlaf .25 .60
36 Torey Krug .20 .50
37 Jason Zucker .25 .60
38 Adam Henrique .20 .50
39 Philipp Grubauer .25 .60
40 Elias Lindholm .25 .60
41 Jordan Binnington .40 1.00
42 Corey Crawford .25 .60
43 Jaccob Slavin .20 .50
44 Cam Fowler .25 .60
45 Morgan Rielly .25 .60
46 Ilya Kovalchuk .25 .60
47 Paul Stastny .20 .50
48 Aleksander Barkov .40 1.00
49 Rasmus Ristolainen .15 .40
50 Elias Pettersson .40 1.00
51 Alex DeBrincat .30 .75
52 Noah Hanifin .25 .60
53 Kris Russell .15 .40
54 Mitch Marner .40 1.00
55 Mark Stone .30 .75
56 Filip Forsberg .40 1.00
57 Miro Heiskanen .30 .75
58 Tyson Jost .20 .50
59 Casey Mittelstadt .25 .60
60 Jonathan Huberdeau .30 .75
61 Nino Niederreiter .15 .40
62 Dylan Strome .30 .75
63 Nick Leddy .15 .40
64 Roberto Luongo .40 1.00
65 Evgenii Dadonov .15 .40
66 Pavel Buchnevich .20 .50
67 Travis Zajac .15 .40
68 Dustin Brown .25 .60
69 Chris Kreider .30 .75
70 Logan Couture .30 .75
71 John Klingberg .25 .60
72 Sam Reinhart .50 1.25
73 Aaron Ekblad .30 .75
74 Shea Weber .25 .60
75 Brayden Point .30 .75
76 Nate Schmidt .20 .50
77 Seth Jones .25 .60
78 Eric Staal .25 .60
79 Anders Lee .20 .50
80 Nick Bjugstad .15 .40
81 Derek Stepan .15 .40
82 Sebastian Aho .40 1.00
83 Anze Kopitar .40 1.00
84 Travis Hamonic .15 .40
85 John Carlson .25 .60
86 Josh Morrissey .30 .75
87 Jordan Eberle .25 .60
88 Michael Grabner .20 .50
89 Ben Bishop .20 .50
90 Sean Monahan .15 .40
91 Robert Thomas .25 .60
92 Colin White .15 .40
93 Mikhail Sergachev .20 .50
94 Ivan Provorov .20 .50
95 Cam Atkinson .25 .60
96 Brendan Gallagher .25 .60
97 Josh Bailey .20 .50
98 Auston Matthews 1.00 2.50
99 Ryan Suter .20 .50
100 Connor McDavid 1.25 3.00
101 Alec Martinez .15 .40
102 Will Butcher .20 .50
103 Mathew Barzal .30 .75
104 Tomas Tatar .15 .40
105 Ryan Nugent-Hopkins .30 .75
106 Filip Chytil .20 .50
107 Nicklas Backstrom .25 .60
108 Nick Schmaltz .20 .50
109 Craig Anderson .20 .50
110 Andrei Vasilevskiy .40 1.00
111 Jeff Carter .20 .50
112 Matt Dumba .15 .40
113 Braden Holtby .30 .75
114 Kyle Palmieri .20 .50
115 Kyle Connor .40 1.00
116 Jordan Greenway .15 .40
117 Brady Skjei .20 .50
118 Casey Cizikas .15 .40
119 Thomas Chabot .25 .60
120 Matthew Tkachuk .50 1.25
121 Cory Schneider .25 .60
122 Frank Vatrano .20 .50
123 Jordan Staal .20 .50
124 Conor Sheary .25 .60
125 Victor Hedman .30 .75
126 Esa Lindell .20 .50
127 James van Riemsdyk .20 .50
128 Boone Jenner .25 .60
129 Chris Tierney .20 .50
130 Patrice Bergeron .30 .75
131 Kasperi Kapanen .20 .50
132 Sven Baertschi .15 .40
133 Alexander Wennberg .15 .40
134 Tyler Toffoli .25 .60
135 Mark Giordano .25 .60
136 Devan Dubnyk .20 .50
137 Claude Giroux .25 .60
138 Samuel Girard .15 .40
139 Kyle Turris .20 .50
140 Alexander Radulov .25 .60
141 Andreas Athanasiou .20 .50
142 Ryan Ellis .20 .50
143 Brady Tkachuk .40 1.00
144 Jaden Schwartz .30 .75
145 David Krejci .25 .60
146 Hampus Lindholm .15 .40
147 Ryan Pulock .20 .50
148 Jesper Bratt .25 .60
149 T.J. Oshie .25 .60
150 Jamie Benn .25 .60
151 Marc-Edouard Vlasic .15 .40
152 Oscar Klefbom .25 .60
153 Vincent Hinostroza .15 .40
154 Anthony Mantha .20 .50
155 Nikolaj Ehlers .25 .60
156 Bobby Ryan .20 .50
157 Mikko Koskinen .15 .40
158 Dmitry Orlov .25 .60
159 Dylan Larkin .30 .75
160 Darnell Nurse .20 .50
161 Mikko Koivu .20 .50
162 Connor Hellebuyck .50 1.25
163 Viktor Arvidsson .15 .40
164 Lars Eller .15 .40
165 Marc-Andre Fleury .50 1.25
166 Mikael Backlund .20 .50
167 Tom Wilson .25 .60
168 Brent Seabrook .15 .40
169 Jim Howard .30 .75
170 Zdeno Chara .25 .60
171 Dustin Byfuglien .25 .60
172 Martin Jones .20 .50
173 Nikita Kucherov .50 1.25
174 Vincent Trocheck .25 .60
175 Tuukka Rask .30 .75
176 Lias Andersson .20 .50
177 Jonathan Quick .30 .75
178 Sam Bennett .40 1.00
179 Bryan Rust .25 .60
180 Tomas Hertl .25 .60
181 Frederik Andersen .30 .75
182 Jakob Silfverberg .15 .40
183 Zach Werenski .40 1.00
184 Andrei Svechnikov .30 .75
185 Mika Zibanejad .30 .75
186 Troy Stecher .15 .40
187 Jakob Chychrun .25 .60
188 Jake Muzzin .25 .60
189 Yanni Gourde .20 .50
190 Nico Hischier .40 1.00
191 Alexander Edler .15 .40
192 Alex Pietrangelo .20 .50
193 Carl Hagelin .15 .40
194 Matt Murray .25 .60
195 Drew Doughty .30 .75
196 Jason Dickinson .15 .40
197 Jesperi Kotkaniemi .25 .60
198 Erik Karlsson .30 .75
199 Tyler Bertuzzi .20 .50
200 Ryan O'Reilly .25 .60
201 Charlie McAvoy .30 .75
202 Ryan McDonagh .15 .40
203 William Nylander .50 1.25
204 Colton Parayko .20 .50
205 Clayton Keller .30 .75
206 Dougie Hamilton .20 .50
207 Nick Foligno .20 .50
208 Rickard Rakell .20 .50
209 Patric Hornqvist .15 .40
210 Gabriel Landeskog .30 .75
211 John Tavares .40 1.00
212 John Gibson .25 .60
213 Alex Tuch .25 .60
214 Niklas Hjalmarsson .15 .40
215 Rasmus Dahlin .30 .75
216 Frans Nielsen .15 .40
217 Kris Letang .30 .75
218 Michael Frolik .20 .50
219 Carter Hart .25 .60
220 Patrik Laine .30 .75
221 Sergei Bobrovsky SP .60 1.50
222 Matt Duchene SP .40 1.00
223 Ben Chiarot SP .25 .60
224 Kevin Hayes SP .30 .75
225 Carl Soderberg SP .25 .60
226 Jacob Trouba SP .30 .75
227 Tyler Myers SP .25 .60
228 Joe Pavelski SP .50 1.25
229 Phil Kessel SP .40 1.00
230 Calvin de Haan SP .25 .60
231 Jake Gardiner SP .25 .60
232 James Neal SP .25 .60
233 Mats Zuccarello SP .40 1.00
234 Tyson Barrie SP .25 .60
235 Alex Galchenyuk SP .25 .60
236 Kevin Shattenkirk SP .25 .60
237 Neal Pionk SP .25 .60
238 Nazem Kadri SP .50 1.25
239 Gustav Nyquist SP .25 .60
240 Artemi Panarin SP .75 2.00
241 Leon Draisaitl SP 1.25 3.00
242 Johnny Gaudreau SP .60 1.50
243 Mikko Rantanen SP 1.00 2.50
244 Alexander Ovechkin SP 1.50 4.00
245 Brad Marchand SP .75 2.00
246 David Pastrnak SP 1.00 2.50
247 Carey Price SP .75 2.00
248 Jack Eichel SP .60 1.50
249 Mark Scheifele SP .60 1.50
250 P.K. Subban SP .50 1.25
251 Steven Stamkos SP .75 2.00
252 Taylor Hall SP .40 1.00
253 Nathan MacKinnon SP 1.50 4.00
254 Vladimir Tarasenko SP .50 1.25
255 Blake Wheeler SP .40 1.00
256 Evgeni Malkin SP .75 2.00
257 Henrik Lundqvist SP 1.00 2.50
258 Tyler Seguin SP .50 1.25
259 Brent Burns SP .40 1.00
260 Jonathan Toews SP .60 1.50
261 Sidney Crosby SP 1.50 4.00
262 Erik Karlsson SP .50 1.25
263 Claude Giroux SP .40 1.00
264 Marc-Andre Fleury SP .75 2.00
265 Auston Matthews SP 1.50 4.00
266 Drew Doughty SP .50 1.25
267 Nikita Kucherov SP .75 2.00
268 Patrick Kane SP .75 2.00
269 John Tavares SP .60 1.50
270 Connor McDavid SP 2.00 5.00
271 Alexandre Texier RC .75 2.00
272 Max Jones RC .75 2.00
273 Max Veronneau RC .60 1.50
274 Zach Senyshyn RC .75 2.00
275 Cale Makar RC 4.00 10.00
276 Victor Olofsson RC 1.50 4.00
277 Joakim Nygard RC .60 1.50
278 Dennis Gilbert RC .60 1.50
279 Jimmy Schuldt RC .60 1.50
280 Filip Zadina RC 1.25 3.00
281 Philippe Myers RC .60 1.50
282 Karson Kuhlman RC .75 2.00
283 Carter Verhaeghe RC 1.25 3.00
284 Nico Sturm RC .60 1.50
285 Mario Ferraro RC .60 1.50
286 Kevin Boyle RC .75 2.00
287 Vitaly Abramov RC .75 2.00
288 Adam Johnson RC .60 1.50
289 Joel L'Esperance RC .75 2.00
290 Quinn Hughes RC 4.00 10.00
291 Dante Fabbro RC .75 2.00
292 Rudolfs Balcers RC .75 2.00
293 Ryan Kuffner RC .60 1.50
294 Conor Timmins RC .75 2.00
295 Carsen Twarynski RC .60 1.50
296 Erik Brannstrom RC .75 2.00
297 Josh Teves RC .60 1.50
298 Tobias Bjornfot RC .75 2.00
299 Carl Grundstrom RC .75 2.00
300 Kaapo Kakko RC 1.25 3.00
301 Taro Hirose RC .75 2.00
302 Cody Glass RC 1.25 3.00
303 Ville Heinola RC 1.00 2.50
304 Mackenzie MacEachern RC .75 2.00
305 Dominik Kubalik RC 1.50 4.00
306 Jacob Middleton RC .60 1.50
307 William Borgen RC .60 1.50
308 Kaden Fulcher RC .75 2.00
309 Kole Sherwood RC .75 2.00

310 Ryan Poehling RC 1.25 3.00
311 Barrett Hayton RC 1.50 4.00
312 Nick Suzuki RC 3.00 8.00
313 Teddy Blueger RC .75 2.00
314 Blake Lizotte RC .75 2.00
315 Rasmus Sandin RC 1.25 3.00
316 Josh Currie RC .60 1.50
317 Noah Dobson RC 2.00 5.00
318 Guillaume Brisebois RC .75 2.00
319 Nikita Gusev RC 1.25 3.00
320 Jack Hughes RC 4.00 10.00

2019-20 Parkhurst Hail Storm

*GOLD: .8X TO 2X BASIC INSERTS
HS1 Sidney Crosby 1.50 4.00
HS2 Nikita Kucherov .75 2.00
HS3 Vladimir Tarasenko .50 1.25
HS4 Brad Marchand .75 2.00
HS5 Patrick Kane .75 2.00
HS6 Brent Burns .40 1.00
HS7 Henrik Lundqvist 1.00 2.50
HS8 Claude Giroux .40 1.00
HS9 Dylan Larkin .50 1.25
HS10 Auston Matthews 1.50 4.00
HS11 P.K. Subban .50 1.25
HS12 Alexander Ovechkin 1.50 4.00
HS13 Nathan MacKinnon 1.50 4.00
HS14 Johnny Gaudreau .60 1.50
HS15 Blake Wheeler .40 1.00
HS16 John Tavares .60 1.50
HS17 Steven Stamkos .75 2.00
HS18 Elias Pettersson .60 1.50
HS19 Carey Price .75 2.00
HS20 Connor McDavid 2.00 5.00

2019-20 Parkhurst Parkies

PK1 Connor McDavid 2.00 5.00
PK2 Jonathan Marchessault .50 1.25
PK3 Jonathan Drouin .30 .75
PK4 Seth Jones .40 1.00
PK5 Joe Pavelski .50 1.25
PK6 Patrick Kane .75 2.00
PK7 Cale Makar 2.00 5.00
PK8 Alexander Ovechkin 1.50 4.00
PK9 Carter Hart .40 1.00
PK10 Nikita Kucherov .75 2.00
PK11 Pierre-Luc Dubois .30 .75
PK12 Mark Stone .50 1.25
PK13 Brady Skjei .30 .75
PK14 Marc-Andre Fleury .75 2.00
PK15 Cam Atkinson .40 1.00
PK16 Sebastian Aho .60 1.50
PK17 Brayden Point .50 1.25
PK18 Dylan Larkin .50 1.25
PK19 Filip Zadina .60 1.50
PK20 Sidney Crosby 1.50 4.00
PK21 Timo Meier .40 1.00
PK22 Jack Eichel .60 1.50
PK23 Nico Hischier .60 1.50
PK24 Kyle Turris .30 .75
PK25 John Klingberg .40 1.00
PK26 Mitch Marner .60 1.50
PK27 Elias Pettersson .60 1.50
PK28 Max Domi .40 1.00
PK29 Ryan Poehling .60 1.50
PK30 John Tavares .60 1.50
PK31 Jacob Trouba .30 .75
PK32 Leon Draisaitl 1.25 3.00
PK33 Alexander Radulov .40 1.00
PK34 Artemi Panarin .75 2.00
PK35 Matt Murray .40 1.00
PK36 Anders Lee .30 .75
PK37 Jake Guentzel .60 1.50
PK38 Brock Boeser .50 1.25
PK39 Quinn Hughes 2.00 5.00
PK40 Auston Matthews 1.50 4.00

2019-20 Parkhurst Prominent Prospects Autographs Gold

PP1 Jack Hughes 50.00 125.00
PP2 Erik Brannstrom 10.00 25.00
PP3 Max Jones 10.00 25.00
PP5 Ryan Poehling 15.00 40.00
PP6 Ilya Mikheyev 15.00 40.00
PP7 Emil Bemstrom 10.00 25.00
PP8 Taro Hirose 10.00 25.00
PP9 Vitaly Abramov 10.00 25.00
PP10 Cale Makar 50.00 125.00
PP11 Victor Olofsson 20.00 50.00
PP12 Noah Dobson 25.00 60.00
PP13 Trent Frederic 10.00 25.00
PP14 Adam Fox 25.00 60.00
PP15 Filip Zadina 15.00 40.00
PP16 Brady Keeper 10.00 25.00
PP17 Alexandre Texier 10.00 25.00
PP18 Carl Grundstrom 10.00 25.00
PP20 Quinn Hughes 50.00 125.00
PP21 Nick Suzuki 40.00 100.00
PP22 Philippe Myers 8.00 20.00
PP23 Nikita Gusev 15.00 40.00
PP24 Dante Fabbro 10.00 25.00
PP25 Cody Glass 15.00 40.00

2019-20 Parkhurst View From The Ice

*GOLD: .8X TO 2X BASIC INSERTS
V1 Auston Matthews 1.50 4.00
V2 Nikita Kucherov .75 2.00
V3 Alexander Ovechkin 1.50 4.00
V4 Johnny Gaudreau .60 1.50
V5 Brad Marchand .75 2.00
V6 Patrick Kane .75 2.00
V7 P.K. Subban .50 1.25
V8 Brent Burns .40 1.00
V9 Drew Doughty .50 1.25
V10 Sidney Crosby 1.50 4.00
V11 Nathan MacKinnon 1.50 4.00
V12 Mark Scheifele .60 1.50
V13 Vladimir Tarasenko .50 1.25
V14 Carey Price .75 2.00
V15 Connor McDavid 2.00 5.00

2020-21 Parkhurst

1 Alexander Steen .15 .40
2 Andrei Vasilevskiy .40 1.00
3 Will Butcher .20 .50
4 Quinn Hughes .60 1.50
5 Teuvo Teravainen .25 .60
6 William Karlsson .30 .75
7 Andrew Cogliano .15 .40
8 Nick Schmaltz .20 .50
9 Anthony Cirelli .20 .50
10 Patric Hornqvist .15 .40
11 Ondrej Palat .25 .60
12 Lars Eller .15 .40
13 Yanni Gourde .20 .50
14 Adam Henrique .20 .50
15 Ryan Getzlaf .25 .60
16 Aaron Ekblad .30 .75
17 Blake Wheeler .25 .60
18 Christian Dvorak .20 .50
19 Paul Stastny .20 .50
20 David Krejci .25 .60
21 Derek Stepan .15 .40
22 Jordan Eberle .25 .60
23 Oliver Ekman-Larsson .25 .60
24 Darnell Nurse .20 .50
25 Noel Acciari .15 .40
26 Tyler Johnson .15 .40
27 Rudolfs Balcers .15 .40
28 Brayden Point .30 .75
29 Jaccob Slavin .20 .50
30 Jordan Staal .20 .50
31 Nikita Gusev .20 .50
32 Bo Horvat .30 .75
33 Jakob Silfverberg .15 .40
34 Ivan Provorov .20 .50
35 Filip Zadina .20 .50
36 Rickard Rakell .20 .50
37 Adrian Kempe .25 .60
38 Sebastian Aho .40 1.00
39 Alex Goligoski .20 .50
40 Evgeny Kuznetsov .30 .75
41 Matt Dumba .15 .40
42 Jeff Skinner .25 .60
43 Nick Leddy .15 .40
44 David Backes .15 .40
45 Mikael Backlund .20 .50
46 Joel Farabee .25 .60
47 Alex Killorn .15 .40
48 Colin White .15 .40
49 Jake Guentzel .40 1.00
50 Valtteri Filppula .15 .40
51 Marcus Foligno .20 .50
52 Tom Wilson .25 .60
53 Jack Hughes .60 1.50
54 Travis Konecny .25 .60
55 Josh Morrissey .30 .75
56 Kyle Okposo .15 .40
57 Tanner Pearson .25 .60
58 Ryan Suter .20 .50
59 T.J. Oshie .25 .60
60 Jared Spurgeon .25 .60
61 Denis Gurianov .30 .75
62 Tyler Myers .15 .40
63 Colton Parayko .20 .50
64 Vincent Trocheck .25 .60
65 Nikolaj Ehlers .25 .60
66 Hampus Lindholm .15 .40
67 Andrei Svechnikov .30 .75
68 Kyle Connor .40 1.00
69 Dougie Hamilton .20 .50
70 Lawson Crouse .15 .40
71 Phillip Danault .25 .60
72 William Nylander .50 1.25
73 Mark Stone .30 .75
74 Sean Couturier .20 .50
75 Mike Reilly .15 .40
76 Jakub Vrana .25 .60
77 Martin Necas .40 1.00
78 Josh Archibald .15 .40
79 Rasmus Ristolainen .15 .40
80 Jeff Petry .25 .60
81 Phil Kessel .25 .60
82 Shea Theodore .30 .75
83 Jonathan Quick .30 .75
84 Neal Pionk .15 .40
85 Kasperi Kapanen .20 .50
86 Dylan Strome .30 .75
87 Jakub Voracek .20 .50
88 Richard Panik .15 .40
89 Ryan Donato .20 .50
90 Miles Wood .15 .40
91 Brayden Schenn .25 .60
92 Nino Niederreiter .15 .40
93 Samuel Girard .15 .40
94 Givani Smith .15 .40
95 Anthony Beauvillier .15 .40
96 Eric Staal .25 .60
97 Logan Couture .30 .75
98 Bryan Rust .25 .60
99 Jonathan Marchessault .30 .75
100 Tyler Bertuzzi .20 .50
101 Damon Severson .15 .40
102 Michael Matheson .15 .40
103 Tuukka Rask .30 .75
104 Leo Komarov .15 .40
105 Marcus Johansson .20 .50
106 James van Riemsdyk .20 .50
107 Dustin Brown .25 .60
108 Nick Suzuki .50 1.25
109 Pavel Buchnevich .20 .50
110 Thomas Chabot .25 .60
111 Filip Hronek .15 .40
112 John Gibson .25 .60
113 Connor Hellebuyck .50 1.25
114 Joel Armia .15 .40
115 David Rittich .20 .50
116 Reilly Smith .25 .60
117 Victor Olofsson .25 .60
118 Darren Helm .15 .40
119 Justin Abdelkader .20 .50
120 Robert Thomas .25 .60
121 Joonas Donskoi .15 .40
122 Jean-Gabriel Pageau .15 .40
123 Artem Anisimov .15 .40
124 Tomas Hertl .25 .60
125 Duncan Keith .20 .50
126 Keith Yandle .15 .40
127 Oscar Klefbom .25 .60
128 Kevin Fiala .20 .50
129 Andrew Copp .15 .40
130 Pavel Zacha .20 .50
131 Nazem Kadri .30 .75
132 Alex Chiasson .20 .50
133 Colton Sceviour .15 .40
134 Sam Reinhart .50 1.25
135 Pierre-Luc Dubois .20 .50
136 Travis Zajac .15 .40
137 Matt Niskanen .20 .50
138 J.T. Miller .30 .75
139 J.T. Compher .15 .40
140 Brett Connolly .15 .40
141 Kaapo Kakko .20 .50
142 Tomas Tatar .15 .40
143 Mark Giordano .25 .60
144 Mikko Koskinen .15 .40
145 Ryan Nugent-Hopkins .30 .75
146 Alex Kerfoot .20 .50
147 Derek Ryan .15 .40
148 Seth Jones .25 .60
149 Gabriel Landeskog .30 .75
150 Brandon Tanev .20 .50
151 P.K. Subban .30 .75
152 Jonathan Bernier .20 .50
153 Jason Zucker .25 .60
154 Igor Shesterkin .50 1.25
155 Ben Bishop .20 .50
156 Frank Vatrano .20 .50
157 Anders Lee .20 .50
158 Ben Chiarot .15 .40
159 Sam Steel .20 .50
160 Sergei Bobrovsky .40 1.00
161 Frederik Andersen .30 .75
162 Cam Fowler .25 .60
163 Blake Lizotte .15 .40
164 Zack Kassian .15 .40
165 Joel Eriksson Ek .20 .50
166 Matt Duchene .25 .60
167 Nikita Zaitsev .15 .40
168 Kyle Palmieri .20 .50
169 Charlie Coyle .25 .60
170 Alex Iafallo .15 .40
171 Tyler Bozak .15 .40
172 Sean Monahan .15 .40
173 Marc-Edouard Vlasic .15 .40
174 John Klingberg .25 .60
175 Ryan Johansen .20 .50
176 Ryan Ellis .20 .50
177 Kevin Hayes .20 .50
178 Gustav Nyquist .15 .40
179 Loui Eriksson .15 .40
180 Connor Brown .20 .50
181 Darcy Kuemper .25 .60
182 Elvis Merzlikins .25 .60
183 Conor Garland .20 .50
184 Brock Nelson .25 .60
185 Evander Kane .25 .60
186 Bobby Ryan .20 .50
187 Chris Wagner .15 .40
188 Jeff Carter .20 .50
189 David Perron .20 .50
190 Zach Parise .25 .60
191 Cam Atkinson .25 .60
192 Alexander Radulov .25 .60
193 Elias Lindholm .25 .60
194 Anthony Duclair .20 .50
195 Adam Fox .30 .75
196 Sean Kuraly .15 .40
197 Miro Heiskanen .30 .75
198 Kyle Turris .20 .50
199 Dominik Kubalik .25 .60
200 Jaden Schwartz .30 .75
201 Zach Werenski .40 1.00
202 Viktor Arvidsson .15 .40
203 Noah Hanifin .25 .60
204 John Marino .25 .60
205 Joe Pavelski .30 .75
206 Ondrej Kase .15 .40
207 Josh Bailey .20 .50
208 Kirby Dach .25 .60
209 Jacob Trouba .20 .50
210 Tony DeAngelo .15 .40
211 Colin Miller .15 .40
212 Charlie McAvoy .30 .75
213 Mats Zuccarello .25 .60
214 Oliver Bjorkstrand .20 .50
215 Alexander Edler .15 .40
216 Rocco Grimaldi .15 .40
217 Timo Meier .25 .60
218 Nick Bonino .15 .40
219 Jamie Benn .25 .60
220 Chris Kreider .30 .75
221 Connor McDavid SP 2.00 5.00
222 Nathan MacKinnon SP 1.50 4.00
223 Patrick Kane SP .75 2.00
224 Leon Draisaitl SP 1.25 3.00
225 Kris Letang SP .50 1.25
226 Nico Hischier SP .60 1.50
227 Ryan O'Reilly SP .40 1.00
228 Elias Pettersson SP .60 1.50
229 Victor Hedman SP .50 1.25
230 David Pastrnak SP 1.00 2.50
231 Jason Spezza SP .40 1.00
232 Brad Marchand SP .75 2.00
233 Brent Burns SP .40 1.00
234 Patrik Laine SP .50 1.25
235 Drew Doughty SP .50 1.25
236 Alex DeBrincat SP .50 1.25
237 Rasmus Dahlin SP .50 1.25
238 Pekka Rinne SP .40 1.00
239 Marc-Andre Fleury SP .75 2.00
240 Mikko Rantanen SP 1.00 2.50
241 Tyler Seguin SP .50 1.25
242 Morgan Rielly SP .40 1.00
243 Nicklas Backstrom SP .40 1.00
244 Max Pacioretty SP .40 1.00
245 Filip Forsberg SP .60 1.50
246 Vladimir Tarasenko SP .50 1.25
247 Brendan Gallagher SP .40 1.00
248 Shea Weber SP .40 1.00
249 Clayton Keller SP .50 1.25
250 Brady Tkachuk SP .60 1.50
251 Jordan Binnington SP .60 1.50
252 Roman Josi SP .40 1.00
253 Cale Makar SP 1.00 2.50
254 Mitch Marner SP .60 1.50
255 Brock Boeser SP .50 1.25
256 Mark Scheifele SP .60 1.50
257 Aleksander Barkov SP .60 1.50
258 Jack Eichel SP .60 1.50
259 Carter Hart SP .40 1.00
260 Jonathan Huberdeau SP .50 1.25
261 Matthew Tkachuk SP .75 2.00
262 Anze Kopitar SP .60 1.50
263 Dylan Larkin SP .50 1.25
264 Erik Karlsson SP .50 1.25
265 Evgeni Malkin SP .75 2.00
266 Mathew Barzal SP .50 1.25
267 John Carlson SP .40 1.00
268 Claude Giroux SP .40 1.00
269 Johnny Gaudreau SP .60 1.50
270 Jonathan Toews SP .60 1.50
271 Steven Stamkos SP .75 2.00
272 Patrice Bergeron SP .50 1.25
273 John Tavares SP .60 1.50
274 Artemi Panarin SP .75 2.00
275 Mika Zibanejad SP .50 1.25
276 Nikita Kucherov SP .75 2.00
277 Carey Price SP .75 2.00
278 Auston Matthews SP 1.50 4.00
279 Alex Ovechkin SP 1.50 4.00
280 Sidney Crosby SP 1.50 4.00
281 Josh Norris RC 1.50 4.00
282 Liam Foudy RC 1.00 2.50
283 Jason Robertson RC 2.50 6.00
284 Martin Kaut RC 1.00 2.50
285 Morgan Geekie RC 1.00 2.50
286 Nicolas Beaudin RC 1.00 2.50
287 Alexis Lafreniere RC 3.00 8.00
288 Bowen Byram RC 2.00 5.00
289 Alexander Alexeyev RC .75 2.00
290 Brandon Hagel RC 1.25 3.00
291 Calvin Thurkauf RC .75 2.00
292 Matiss Kivlenieks RC 1.25 3.00
293 Connor McMichael RC 1.50 4.00
294 Philip Broberg RC 1.00 2.50
295 Vitali Kravtsov RC 2.00 5.00
296 Nick Robertson RC 1.50 4.00
297 Alexander True RC .75 2.00
298 Peyton Krebs RC 1.50 4.00
299 Thomas Harley RC 1.50 4.00
300 Ty Dellandrea RC 1.00 2.50
301 Dylan Coghlan RC 1.00 2.50
302 Pavel Francouz RC 1.25 3.00
303 Victor Soderstrom RC .75 2.00
304 Kieffer Bellows RC .75 2.00
305 Mikey Anderson RC 1.00 2.50
306 Lucas Carlsson RC .75 2.00
307 Michael DiPietro RC 1.25 3.00
308 Gabe Vilardi RC 1.50 4.00
309 Timothy Liljegren RC 1.00 2.50
310 Tyler Benson RC 1.00 2.50
311 Steve Yzerman 1.00 2.50
312 Martin Brodeur 1.00 2.50
313 Teemu Selanne .75 2.00
314 Dominik Hasek .60 1.50
315 Bobby Hull 1.00 2.50
316 Glenn Hall .40 1.00
317 Jarome Iginla .50 1.25
318 Guy Lafleur .50 1.25
319 Cam Neely .40 1.00
320 Brett Hull .75 2.00
321 Mats Sundin .40 1.00
322 Pat LaFontaine .40 1.00
323 Nicklas Lidstrom .40 1.00
324 Ron Hextall .40 1.00
325 Phil Esposito .60 1.50
326 Joe Sakic .75 2.00
327 Peter Forsberg .75 2.00
328 Mark Messier .75 2.00
329 Jaromir Jagr 1.25 3.00
330 Wayne Gretzky 2.50 6.00

2020-21 Parkhurst Gold

*GOLD: .75X TO 2X BASIC
*SP/LEG.GOLD: .75X TO 2X BASIC
*RC.GOLD: .6X TO 1.5X BASIC

2020-21 Parkhurst Silver

*SILVER: .6X TO 1.5X BASIC
*SP/LEG.SILVER: .6X TO 1.5X BASIC
*RC.SILVER: .5X TO 1.25X BASIC

2020-21 Parkhurst Encore

*GOLD: .75X TO 2X BASIC
E1 Quinn Hughes 1.25 3.00
E2 Cale Makar 1.25 3.00
E3 Rasmus Sandin .40 1.00
E4 Victor Olofsson .50 1.25
E5 Dominik Kubalik .50 1.25
E6 Adam Fox .60 1.50
E7 Nick Suzuki 1.00 2.50
E8 Jack Hughes 1.25 3.00
E9 Ilya Mikheyev .40 1.00
E10 Kirby Dach .50 1.25

2020-21 Parkhurst Encore Autographs

E1 Quinn Hughes 25.00 60.00
E3 Rasmus Sandin 8.00 20.00
E4 Victor Olofsson 10.00 25.00
E5 Dominik Kubalik 10.00 25.00
E6 Adam Fox 12.00 30.00
E7 Nick Suzuki 20.00 50.00
E10 Kirby Dach 10.00 25.00

2020-21 Parkhurst Parkies

PK1 Dylan Larkin .60 1.50
PK2 Ryan O'Reilly .50 1.25
PK3 John Gibson .50 1.25
PK4 Miro Heiskanen .60 1.50
PK5 Carter Hart .50 1.25
PK6 Andrei Svechnikov .60 1.50
PK7 Jakub Vrana .50 1.25
PK8 Andrei Vasilevskiy .75 2.00
PK9 Brady Tkachuk .75 2.00
PK10 Brendan Gallagher .50 1.25
PK11 Aleksander Barkov .75 2.00
PK12 Mark Scheifele .75 2.00
PK13 Matthew Tkachuk 1.00 2.50
PK14 Gabe Vilardi 1.00 2.50
PK15 Liam Foudy .60 1.50

2020-21 Parkhurst Prominent Prospects

PP1 Gabe Vilardi .75 2.00
PP2 Liam Foudy .60 1.50
PP3 Timothy Liljegren .60 1.50
PP4 Jason Robertson 1.50 4.00
PP5 Tyler Benson .60 1.50
PP6 Kieffer Bellows .50 1.25
PP7 Martin Kaut .60 1.50
PP8 Morgan Geekie .60 1.50
PP9 Brandon Hagel .75 2.00
PP10 Matiss Kivlenieks .75 2.00
PP11 Mikey Anderson .60 1.50
PP12 Jake Evans .60 1.50
PP13 Egor Korshkov .40 1.00
PP14 Lucas Carlsson .50 1.25
PP15 Jani Hakanpaa .40 1.00
PP16 Shane Bowers .50 1.25
PP17 Josh Norris 1.00 2.50
PP18 Alexander Alexeyev .50 1.25
PP19 Thomas Harley 1.00 2.50
PP20 Ty Dellandrea .60 1.50
PP21 Peyton Krebs 1.00 2.50
PP22 Nick Robertson 1.00 2.50
PP23 Victor Soderstrom .50 1.25
PP24 Bowen Byram 1.25 3.00
PP25 Alexis Lafreniere 2.00 5.00

2020-21 Parkhurst Prominent Prospects Autographs Gold

PP2 Liam Foudy E 10.00 25.00
PP3 Timothy Liljegren B 10.00 25.00
PP4 Jason Robertson E 25.00 60.00
PP5 Tyler Benson D 10.00 25.00
PP6 Kieffer Bellows E 8.00 20.00
PP7 Martin Kaut C 10.00 25.00
PP8 Morgan Geekie D 10.00 25.00
PP10 Matiss Kivlenieks D 12.00 30.00
PP11 Mikey Anderson D 10.00 25.00
PP12 Jake Evans D 10.00 25.00
PP14 Lucas Carlsson E 8.00 20.00
PP16 Shane Bowers D 8.00 20.00
PP20 Ty Dellandrea E 10.00 25.00
PP21 Peyton Krebs C 15.00 40.00
PP22 Nick Robertson C 15.00 40.00
PP24 Bowen Byram B 20.00 50.00

2021-22 Parkhurst

*BRONZE: .5X TO 1.25X BASIC CARDS
*SILVER: .6X TO 1.5X BASIC CARDS
*GOLD.RC: .75X TO 2X BASIC CARDS
*FX: 1X TO 2.5X BASIC CARDS
1 Alexis Lafreniere .40 1.00
2 Nick Suzuki .50 1.25
3 Andre Burakovsky .15 .40
4 Kirby Dach .25 .60
5 Mats Zuccarello .25 .60
6 William Nylander .50 1.25
7 Mika Zibanejad .30 .75
8 Adam Pelech .15 .40
9 Drew Doughty .30 .75
10 Dylan Cozens .25 .60
11 Travis Konecny .25 .60
12 Drake Batherson .25 .60
13 Vladimir Tarasenko .30 .75
14 Andrei Svechnikov .30 .75
15 Erik Karlsson .30 .75
16 Ondrej Palat .20 .50
17 Jeff Petry .25 .60
18 K'Andre Miller .20 .50
19 Jonathan Marchessault .30 .75
20 Jakob Chychrun .25 .60
21 T.J. Oshie .25 .60
22 Jonathan Quick .30 .75
23 Zack Kassian .15 .40
24 Patrik Laine .30 .75
25 Pierre-Luc Dubois .20 .50
26 Brett Pesce .15 .40
27 Pavel Zacha .20 .50
28 Anthony Duclair .20 .50
29 Adrian Kempe .25 .60
30 Elias Lindholm .25 .60
31 Elvis Merzlikins .25 .60
32 Seth Jones .25 .60
33 John Marino .25 .60
34 Zach Werenski .40 1.00
35 Logan Couture .30 .75
36 Justin Holl .15 .40
37 Mikael Granlund .20 .50
38 Jonathan Toews .40 1.00
39 Alex Killorn .15 .40
40 Victor Olofsson .25 .60
41 Jack Roslovic .15 .40
42 William Karlsson .30 .75
43 Sean Couturier .20 .50
44 Alex Iafallo .15 .40
45 Brayden Schenn .25 .60
46 Jordan Staal .20 .50
47 Mattias Ekholm .20 .50
48 Nico Hischier .40 1.00
49 Charlie Coyle .25 .60
50 J.T. Compher .15 .40
51 Brock Nelson .25 .60
52 Bo Horvat .30 .75
53 Cam Talbot .25 .60
54 Jeff Skinner .25 .60
55 Robby Fabbri .15 .40
56 Josh Bailey .20 .50
57 Ryan Dzingel .20 .50
58 Milan Lucic .20 .50
59 Connor Brown .20 .50
60 Artturi Lehkonen .20 .50
61 Thomas Chabot .25 .60
62 Ryan Getzlaf .25 .60
63 Jean-Gabriel Pageau .15 .40
64 Dylan Strome .30 .75
65 Miles Wood .15 .40
66 Bryan Rust .25 .60
67 Adam Henrique .20 .50
68 Neal Pionk .15 .40
69 Danny DeKeyser .15 .40
70 Shea Theodore .30 .75
71 T.J. Brodie .15 .40
72 Jamie Benn .25 .60
73 Tristan Jarry .25 .60
74 Matthew Tkachuk .50 1.25
75 Nino Niederreiter .15 .40
76 Connor Hellebuyck .50 1.25
77 James van Riemsdyk .20 .50
78 Mike Smith .15 .40
79 Evander Kane .25 .60
80 Teuvo Teravainen .25 .60
81 Anton Khudobin .25 .60
82 J.T. Miller .30 .75
83 Filip Forsberg .40 1.00
84 Eric Robinson .20 .50
85 Kris Letang .30 .75
86 Clayton Keller .30 .75
87 Devon Toews .20 .50
88 Adam Erne .15 .40
89 Kevin Shattenkirk .15 .40
90 Mackenzie Blackwood .25 .60
91 Andrew Mangiapane .25 .60
92 Ryan Strome .25 .60
93 Ryan Hartman .15 .40
94 Morgan Rielly .25 .60
95 Rasmus Andersson .20 .50
96 Anthony Cirelli .20 .50
97 Alexander Radulov .25 .60
98 Patric Hornqvist .15 .40
99 Brendan Gallagher .25 .60
100 Marcus Foligno .20 .50
101 Vincent Trocheck .25 .60
102 Oscar Klefbom .25 .60
103 Christian Fischer .15 .40
104 Justin Schultz .20 .50
105 Ilya Lyubushkin .15 .40
106 Kevin Labanc .15 .40
107 Aaron Ekblad .30 .75
108 Kevin Hayes .20 .50
109 Nick Paul .15 .40
110 Philipp Kurashev .20 .50
111 Adam Lowry .20 .50
112 Tyler Myers .15 .40
113 P.K. Subban .30 .75
114 Tyson Barrie .15 .40
115 Charlie McAvoy .30 .75
116 Dylan Larkin .30 .75
117 Tom Wilson .25 .60
118 Jakub Vrana .20 .50
119 David Perron .20 .50
120 Jakob Silfverberg .15 .40
121 Filip Chytil .20 .50
122 Anthony Beauvillier .15 .40
123 Timo Meier .25 .60
124 Brayden Point .30 .75
125 Craig Smith .15 .40
126 Jake Muzzin .25 .60
127 Alex Pietrangelo .20 .50
128 Dominik Kubalik .25 .60
129 Jason Zucker .25 .60
130 Barrett Hayton .25 .60
131 Lars Eller .15 .40
132 Cal Petersen .15 .40
133 Thatcher Demko .30 .75
134 Boone Jenner .25 .60
135 Torey Krug .20 .50
136 Casey Mittelstadt .25 .60
137 Semyon Varlamov .25 .60
138 Filip Zadina .20 .50
139 Ty Smith .25 .60
140 MacKenzie Weegar .20 .50
141 Evan Bouchard .30 .75
142 Brandon Hagel .20 .50
143 Kasperi Kapanen .20 .50
144 Jordan Kyrou .25 .60
145 Joel Farabee .25 .60
146 Anders Lee .20 .50
147 Marco Scandella .15 .40
148 Alexandre Texier .15 .40
149 Jared Spurgeon .25 .60
150 Ilya Mikheyev .20 .50
151 Ryan Pulock .20 .50
152 Thomas Greiss .20 .50
153 Chris Kreider .30 .75
154 Jonathan Drouin .20 .50
155 Eeli Tolvanen .25 .60
156 Evan Bouchard .30 .75
157 Ryan Lindgren .15 .40
158 Rickard Rakell .20 .50
159 Reilly Smith .25 .60
160 Jaccob Slavin .20 .50
161 Carter Hart .25 .60
162 Mikhail Sergachev .20 .50
163 Taylor Hall .25 .60
164 Ilya Sorokin .40 1.00
165 Mikael Backlund .20 .50
166 John Klingberg .25 .60
167 Tyson Jost .20 .50
168 Nikolaj Ehlers .25 .60
169 Jesse Puljujarvi .25 .60
170 Jake DeBrusk .25 .60
171 Vladislav Namestnikov .15 .40
172 Max Domi .25 .60
173 Patrice Bergeron .30 .75
174 Esa Lindell .20 .50
175 Darnell Nurse .20 .50
176 Martin Necas .40 1.00
177 Chandler Stephenson .20 .50
178 Cam Fowler .25 .60
179 Alex Tuch .25 .60
180 Blake Wheeler .25 .60
181 Nick Schmaltz .20 .50
182 Josh Morrissey .30 .75
183 Tomas Hertl .25 .60
184 Dylan DeMelo .15 .40
185 Sergei Bobrovsky .40 1.00
186 Kaapo Kakko .20 .50
187 Sean Monahan .15 .40
188 Dustin Brown .25 .60
189 Tim Stutzle .30 .75
190 Troy Terry .20 .50
191 Yegor Sharangovich .25 .60
192 Dmitry Orlov .25 .60
193 Matt Dumba .20 .50
194 Jordan Binnington .40 1.00
195 Tyler Seguin .30 .75
196 Juuse Saros .30 .75
197 Marc-Edouard Vlasic .15 .40
198 Alex Kerfoot .20 .50
199 Josh Anderson .20 .50
200 Gabe Vilardi .25 .60
201 Joonas Korpisalo .25 .60
202 Conor Sheary .25 .60
203 Justin Faulk .20 .50
204 Denis Gurianov .30 .75
205 Patrick Maroon .15 .40
206 Johan Larsson .20 .50
207 Conor Garland .20 .50
208 Filip Hronek .15 .40
209 Victor Rask .25 .60
210 Nils Hoglander .20 .50
211 Colton Parayko .20 .50
212 Robert Thomas .25 .60
213 Jesper Fast .15 .40
214 Kailer Yamamoto .25 .60
215 Evgeny Kuznetsov .30 .75
216 Radim Simek .15 .40
217 Nazem Kadri .30 .75
218 Alexander Romanov .20 .50
219 Roope Hintz .30 .75
220 Josh Norris .25 .60
221 Tyler Toffoli .25 .60
222 Miro Heiskanen .30 .75
223 Johnny Gaudreau .40 1.00
224 Brady Tkachuk .40 1.00
225 Carter Verhaeghe .25 .60
226 Ryan Nugent-Hopkins .30 .75
227 Brock Boeser .30 .75
228 Kyle Connor .40 1.00
229 Mathew Barzal .30 .75
230 Gabriel Landeskog .30 .75
231 Roman Josi .25 .60
232 Jack Hughes .60 1.50
233 Oliver Bjorkstrand .20 .50
234 Joe Pavelski .30 .75
235 Claude Giroux .25 .60
236 Robin Lehner .20 .50
237 Kevin Fiala .20 .50
238 Andrei Vasilevskiy .40 1.00
239 Sebastian Aho .40 1.00
240 John Carlson .25 .60
241 John Gibson .25 .60
242 Phil Kessel .25 .60
243 Victor Hedman .30 .75
244 Brent Burns .25 .60
245 Matt Duchene .25 .60
246 Adam Fox .30 .75
247 Anze Kopitar .40 1.00
248 Evgeni Malkin .50 1.25
249 Steven Stamkos .50 1.25
250 Patrick Marleau .20 .50
251 Alex DeBrincat .30 .75
252 Jack Eichel .40 1.00
253 Brad Marchand .50 1.25
254 Max Pacioretty .25 .60
255 Quinn Hughes .60 1.50
256 Aleksander Barkov .40 1.00
257 Cale Makar .60 1.50
258 Mark Scheifele .40 1.00
259 Mark Stone .30 .75
260 Ryan O'Reilly .25 .60
261 Mikko Rantanen .60 1.50
262 Nicklas Backstrom .25 .60
263 Jonathan Huberdeau .30 .75
264 Kirill Kaprizov .75 2.00
265 Jonathan Marchessault .30 .75
266 Elias Pettersson .40 1.00
267 Carey Price .50 1.25
268 Jake Guentzel .40 1.00
269 Mitch Marner .40 1.00
270 Artemi Panarin .50 1.25
271 John Tavares .40 1.00
272 Leon Draisaitl .75 2.00
273 Nikita Kucherov .50 1.25
274 Patrick Kane .50 1.25
275 David Pastrnak .60 1.50
276 Alex Ovechkin 1.00 2.50
277 Nathan MacKinnon 1.00 2.50
278 Auston Matthews 1.00 2.50
279 Sidney Crosby 1.00 2.50
280 Connor McDavid 1.25 3.00
281 William Eklund RC 2.00 5.00
282 Lucas Raymond RC 2.50 6.00
283 Anton Lundell RC 1.50 4.00
284 Moritz Seider RC 2.00 5.00
285 Philip Tomasino RC 1.00 2.50
286 Brett Murray RC .75 2.00
287 Sampo Ranta RC .75 2.00
288 Cole Perfetti RC 1.50 4.00
289 Mike Hardman RC .75 2.00
290 Rasmus Kupari RC .75 2.00
291 Parker Kelly RC .75 2.00
292 Ross Colton RC 1.00 2.50
293 Mattias Samuelsson RC .75 2.00
294 Arttu Ruotsalainen RC .75 2.00
295 Taylor Raddysh RC 1.25 3.00
296 Ukko-Pekka Luukkonen RC 1.25 3.00
297 Radim Zohorna RC .75 2.00
298 Cam York RC .75 2.00
299 Vasily Podkolzin RC 1.00 2.50
300 Cole Sillinger RC 1.25 3.00
301 Tanner Laczynski RC .75 2.00
302 Jacob Bryson RC .75 2.00
303 Frederic Allard RC .75 2.00
304 Tanner Jeannot RC .75 2.00
305 Adam Ruzicka RC .75 2.00
306 Wyatt Kalynuk RC .75 2.00
307 Ivan Prosvetov RC .75 2.00
308 Tyce Thompson RC .75 2.00
309 Oskar Steen RC 1.00 2.50
310 Joey Keane RC .60 1.50
311 Wade Allison RC .75 2.00
312 Matthew Phillips RC .75 2.00
313 Zac Jones RC 1.00 2.50
314 David Farrance RC .75 2.00
315 Jesse Ylonen RC .75 2.00
316 Filip Gustavsson RC 1.50 4.00
317 Kole Lind RC 1.00 2.50
318 Jacob Bernard-Docker RC .75 2.00
319 Jamie Drysdale RC 1.25 3.00
320 Calen Addison RC .75 2.00
321 Shane Pinto RC 1.25 3.00
322 Morgan Barron RC .60 1.50
323 Grigori Denisenko RC 1.00 2.50
324 Joe Veleno RC 1.00 2.50
325 Jeremy Swayman RC 2.50 6.00
326 Alex Newhook RC 1.25 3.00
327 Spencer Knight RC 1.50 4.00
328 Trevor Zegras RC 1.50 4.00
329 Quinton Byfield RC 2.00 5.00
330 Cole Caufield RC 3.00 8.00

2021-22 Parkhurst Family Tradition
*BLUE: .6X TO 1.5X BASIC INSERTS
*GOLD: 1.25X TO 3X BASIC INSERTS
FT1 Brett Hull .75 2.00
FT2 Brandon Sutter .30 .75
FT3 Quinn Hughes 1.25 3.00
FT4 William Nylander 1.00 2.50
FT5 Andrei Svechnikov .60 1.50
FT6 Brady Tkachuk .75 2.00
FT7 Ron Hextall .50 1.25
FT8 P.K. Subban .60 1.50
FT9 Phil Esposito .75 2.00
FT10 Jordan Staal .40 1.00

2021-22 Parkhurst Ice in Their Veins
*BLUE: .6X TO 1.5X BASIC CARDS
*GOLD: 1.25X TO 3X BASIC INSERTS
IV1 Connor McDavid 2.50 6.00
IV2 Steven Stamkos 1.00 2.50
IV3 Sidney Crosby 2.00 5.00
IV4 Alex Ovechkin 2.00 5.00
IV5 Leon Draisaitl 1.50 4.00
IV6 Auston Matthews 2.00 5.00
IV7 Nathan MacKinnon 2.00 5.00
IV8 John Tavares .75 2.00
IV9 David Pastrnak 1.25 3.00
IV10 Carey Price 1.00 2.50
IV11 Artemi Panarin 1.00 2.50
IV12 Elias Pettersson .75 2.00
IV13 Mark Scheifele .75 2.00
IV14 Marc-Andre Fleury 1.00 2.50
IV15 Jack Eichel .75 2.00

2021-22 Parkhurst Parkies Blue
PK1 Cam Talbot 10.00 25.00
PK3 Devon Toews 8.00 20.00
PK5 Boone Jenner 10.00 25.00
PK6 Spencer Knight 20.00 50.00
PK8 Miro Heiskanen 12.00 30.00
PK11 Victor Olofsson 10.00 25.00
PK13 Jordan Staal 8.00 20.00
PK14 Brock Boeser 12.00 30.00
PK15 Cale Makar 25.00 60.00
PK17 Jean-Gabriel Pageau 6.00 15.00
PK18 Zach Hyman 15.00 40.00
PK20 Ross Colton 12.00 30.00
PK21 John Gibson 10.00 25.00
PK22 Mark Stone 12.00 30.00
PK23 Jeremy Swayman 80.00 200.00
PK24 Joe Pavelski 12.00 30.00

2021-22 Parkhurst Prominent Prospects
*PURPLE/99: .6X TO 1.5X BASIC INSERTS
*BLUE/25: 1.25X TO 3X BASIC INSERTS
PP1 Cole Caufield 2.00 5.00
PP2 Quinton Byfield 1.25 3.00
PP3 Spencer Knight 1.00 2.50
PP4 Wyatt Kalynuk .50 1.25
PP5 Jake Leschyshyn .50 1.25
PP6 Jacob Bryson .50 1.25
PP7 Vasily Podkolzin .60 1.50
PP8 Filip Gustavsson 1.00 2.50
PP9 Philip Tomasino .60 1.50
PP10 Ross Colton .60 1.50
PP11 Anton Lundell 1.00 2.50
PP12 Lucas Raymond 1.50 4.00
PP13 Cam York .50 1.25
PP14 Moritz Seider 1.25 3.00
PP15 Jamie Drysdale .75 2.00
PP16 Cole Perfetti 1.00 2.50
PP17 Trevor Zegras 1.00 2.50
PP18 Jesse Ylonen .50 1.25
PP19 Taylor Raddysh .75 2.00
PP20 Jeremy Swayman 1.50 4.00
PP21 Grigori Denisenko .60 1.50
PP22 Benoit-Olivier Groulx .50 1.25
PP23 Nils Lundkvist .50 1.25
PP24 Calen Addison .50 1.25
PP25 Alex Newhook .75 2.00

2021-22 Parkhurst Prominent Prospects Gold
PP1 Cole Caufield 50.00 125.00
PP2 Quinton Byfield 30.00 80.00
PP3 Spencer Knight 25.00 60.00
PP4 Wyatt Kalynuk 12.00 30.00
PP6 Jacob Bryson 12.00 30.00
PP8 Filip Gustavsson 25.00 60.00
PP9 Philip Tomasino 15.00 40.00
PP11 Anton Lundell 25.00 60.00
PP12 Lucas Raymond 40.00 100.00
PP14 Moritz Seider 30.00 80.00
PP15 Jamie Drysdale 20.00 50.00
PP16 Cole Perfetti 25.00 60.00
PP19 Taylor Raddysh 20.00 50.00
PP20 Jeremy Swayman 40.00 100.00
PP21 Grigori Denisenko 15.00 40.00
PP22 Benoit-Olivier Groulx 12.00 30.00
PP23 Nils Lundkvist 12.00 30.00
PP24 Calen Addison 12.00 30.00
PP25 Alex Newhook 20.00 50.00

2022-23 Parkhurst Bronze Border
1 John Gibson .30 .75
2 Erik Haula .20 .50
3 Taylor Raddysh .25 .60
4 Darcy Kuemper .30 .75
5 John Klingberg .30 .75
6 Mikko Koskinen .20 .50
7 Ryan Hartman .20 .50
8 Alexandre Carrier .20 .50
9 Oliver Wahlstrom .20 .50
10 Colin White .25 .60
11 Jeff Carter .25 .60
12 Pavel Buchnevich .25 .60
13 John Tavares .50 1.25
14 Tanner Pearson .30 .75
15 Nicklas Backstrom .30 .75
16 Cam Fowler .30 .75
17 Jeff Skinner .30 .75
18 Jaccob Slavin .25 .60
19 Nazem Kadri .40 1.00
20 Dylan Larkin .40 1.00
21 Sam Reinhart .60 1.50
22 Jared Spurgeon .30 .75
23 Matt Duchene .30 .75
24 Josh Bailey .25 .60
25 Thomas Chabot .30 .75
26 Erik Karlsson .40 1.00
27 Brandon Saad .25 .60
28 Jack Campbell .30 .75
29 Evgenii Dadonov .20 .50
30 Mark Scheifele .50 1.25
31 Jeremy Swayman .50 1.25
32 Sean Monahan .20 .50
33 Mikko Rantanen .75 2.00
34 Roope Hintz .40 1.00
35 Jesse Puljujarvi .30 .75
36 Viktor Arvidsson .20 .50
37 Josh Anderson .25 .60
38 P.K. Subban .40 1.00
39 Josh Norris .30 .75
40 Kris Letang .40 1.00
41 Morgan Geekie .20 .50
42 Alex Killorn .20 .50
43 Brock Boeser .40 1.00
44 Conor Sheary .30 .75
45 Charlie Coyle .30 .75
46 Andrew Mangiapane .30 .75
47 Dylan Strome .40 1.00
48 Miro Heiskanen .40 1.00
49 Tyson Barrie .20 .50
50 Phillip Danault .30 .75
51 Rem Pitlick .20 .50
52 Dawson Mercer .40 1.00
53 Jacob Trouba .25 .60
54 Kasperi Kapanen .25 .60
55 Jared McCann .25 .60
56 Brayden Point .40 1.00
57 J.T. Miller .40 1.00
58 Dmitry Orlov .30 .75
59 Charlie McAvoy .40 1.00
60 Mikael Backlund .25 .60
61 Jonathan Toews .50 1.25
62 Jamie Benn .30 .75
63 Ryan Nugent-Hopkins .40 1.00
64 Quinton Byfield .40 1.00
65 Chris Wideman .20 .50
66 Jesper Bratt .30 .75
67 Barclay Goodrow .20 .50
68 Tristan Jarry .30 .75
69 Jaden Schwartz .25 .60
70 Victor Hedman .40 1.00
71 Oliver Ekman-Larsson .20 .50
72 Vitek Vanecek .30 .75
73 Shayne Gostisbehere .30 .75
74 Jacob Markstrom .30 .75
75 Seth Jones .30 .75
76 Boone Jenner .30 .75
77 Darnell Nurse .25 .60
78 Anton Lundell .30 .75
79 Jake Evans .20 .50
80 Yegor Sharangovich .30 .75
81 Ryan Strome .30 .75
82 Evgeni Malkin .60 1.50
83 Jordan Eberle .30 .75
84 Nikita Kucherov .60 1.50
85 Thatcher Demko .40 1.00
86 Chandler Stephenson .25 .60
87 Nick Schmaltz .25 .60
88 Elias Lindholm .30 .75
89 Dominik Kubalik .30 .75
90 Oliver Bjorkstrand .25 .60
91 Alex Nedeljkovic .25 .60
92 Anthony Duclair .25 .60
93 Brendan Gallagher .30 .75
94 Tomas Tatar .20 .50
95 Mika Zibanejad .40 1.00
96 Kevin Hayes .25 .60
97 Philipp Grubauer .30 .75
98 David Perron .30 .75
99 Michael Bunting .30 .75
100 Jonathan Marchessault .40 1.00
101 Blake Wheeler .30 .75
102 Lawson Crouse .20 .50
103 Victor Olofsson .30 .75
104 Seth Jarvis .40 1.00
105 Juuse Saros .40 1.00
106 Michael Rasmussen .20 .50
107 Claude Giroux .30 .75
108 Jeff Petry .30 .75
109 Dougie Hamilton .25 .60
110 Chris Kreider .40 1.00
111 James van Riemsdyk .25 .60
112 James Reimer .25 .60
113 Ivan Barbashev .25 .60
114 Mark Giordano .30 .75
115 Shea Theodore .40 1.00
116 Pierre-Luc Dubois .30 .75
117 Casey Mittelstadt .30 .75
118 Dylan Cozens .30 .75
119 Martin Necas .50 1.25
120 Jack Roslovic .20 .50
121 Robby Fabbri .20 .50
122 Carter Verhaeghe .30 .75
123 Joel Eriksson Ek .25 .60
124 Mackenzie Blackwood .30 .75
125 Adam Fox .40 1.00
126 Sean Couturier .25 .60
127 Alexander Barabanov .20 .50
128 Robert Thomas .30 .75
129 Alex Kerfoot .25 .60
130 Robin Lehner .25 .60
131 Nikolaj Ehlers .30 .75
132 Adam Henrique .25 .60
133 Jake DeBrusk .30 .75
134 Rasmus Andersson .25 .60
135 Andre Burakovsky .25 .60
136 Jake Oettinger .50 1.25
137 Zach Hyman .50 1.25
138 Cal Petersen .20 .50
139 Tanner Jeannot .20 .50
140 Brock Nelson .30 .75
141 Drake Batherson .30 .75
142 Bryan Rust .30 .75
143 Ryan Donato .25 .60
144 Corey Perry .50 1.25
145 Conor Garland .25 .60
146 Connor McMichael .30 .75
147 Jamie Drysdale .25 .60
148 Craig Smith .20 .50
149 Tyler Toffoli .30 .75
150 Devon Toews .25 .60
151 Tyler Seguin .40 1.00
152 Evan Bouchard .40 1.00
153 Alex Iafallo .20 .50
154 Mikael Granlund .40 1.00
155 Adam Pelech .20 .50
156 Connor Brown .25 .60
157 Evan Rodrigues .25 .60
158 Adam Larsson .30 .75
159 Anthony Cirelli .25 .60
160 Bo Horvat .40 1.00
161 Evgeny Kuznetsov .40 1.00
162 Taylor Hall .30 .75
163 Noah Hanifin .30 .75
164 Gabriel Landeskog .40 1.00
165 Ryan Suter .25 .60
166 Evander Kane .30 .75
167 Drew Doughty .40 1.00
168 Mike Hoffman .20 .50
169 Ilya Sorokin .50 1.25
170 Shane Pinto .25 .60
171 Zach Parise .30 .75
172 Alexander Wennberg .20 .50
173 Ondrej Palat .25 .60
174 Vasily Podkolzin .20 .50
175 T.J. Oshie .30 .75
176 Kevin Shattenkirk .20 .50
177 Tage Thompson .40 1.00
178 Frederik Andersen .40 1.00
179 Valeri Nichushkin .30 .75
180 Tyler Bertuzzi .25 .60
181 Sergei Bobrovsky .50 1.25
182 Marc-Andre Fleury .60 1.50
183 Philip Tomasino .20 .50
184 Jean-Gabriel Pageau .20 .50
185 Nikita Zaitsev .20 .50
186 Brent Burns .30 .75
187 Brayden Schenn .30 .75
188 William Nylander .60 1.50
189 Ross Colton .25 .60
190 Lars Eller .20 .50
191 Jakob Chychrun .30 .75
192 Alex Tuch .30 .75
193 Vincent Trocheck .30 .75
194 Jakub Voracek .25 .60
195 Pius Suter .20 .50
196 Aaron Ekblad .40 1.00
197 Marcus Foligno .25 .60
198 Ryan Johansen .25 .60
199 Noah Dobson .40 1.00
200 Joel Farabee .30 .75
201 Logan Couture .40 1.00
202 Ville Husso .20 .50
203 Morgan Rielly .30 .75
204 Mark Stone .40 1.00
205 Cole Perfetti .30 .75
206 Phil Kessel .30 .75
207 Kyle Okposo .20 .50
208 Teuvo Teravainen .30 .75
209 Zach Werenski .50 1.25
210 Filip Hronek .20 .50
211 Mason Marchment .25 .60
212 Mats Zuccarello .30 .75
213 Colton Sissons .30 .75
214 Alexis Lafreniere .50 1.25
215 Carter Hart .30 .75
216 Nick Bonino .30 .75
217 Ryan O'Reilly .30 .75
218 Jonathan Dahlen .20 .50
219 Alex Pietrangelo .25 .60
220 Connor Hellebuyck .60 1.50
221 Patrice Bergeron .60 1.50
222 Aleksander Barkov .50 1.25
223 Nico Hischier .50 1.25
224 Jake Guentzel .50 1.25
225 Max Pacioretty .25 .60
226 Troy Terry .30 .75
227 Alex DeBrincat .40 1.00
228 Cole Caufield .60 1.50
229 Travis Konecny .30 .75
230 Mitch Marner .50 1.25
231 Rasmus Dahlin .40 1.00
232 Adrian Kempe .30 .75
233 Anders Lee .25 .60
234 Tomas Hertl .30 .75
235 John Carlson .30 .75
236 Matthew Tkachuk .60 1.50
237 Anze Kopitar .50 1.25
238 Igor Shesterkin .60 1.50
239 Yanni Gourde .25 .60
240 Kyle Connor .50 1.25
241 Clayton Keller .40 1.00
242 Joe Pavelski .40 1.00
243 Filip Forsberg .50 1.25
244 Cam Atkinson .30 .75
245 Elias Pettersson .50 1.25
246 Andrei Svechnikov .40 1.00
247 Kevin Fiala .25 .60
248 Brady Tkachuk .50 1.25
249 Vladimir Tarasenko .40 1.00
250 Brad Marchand .60 1.50
251 Trevor Zegras .30 .75
252 Cale Makar .75 2.00
253 Leon Draisaitl 1.00 2.50
254 Mathew Barzal .40 1.00
255 Andrei Vasilevskiy .50 1.25
256 David Pastrnak .75 2.00
257 Patrik Laine .40 1.00
258 Jonathan Huberdeau .40 1.00
259 Artemi Panarin .60 1.50
260 Steven Stamkos .60 1.50
261 Johnny Gaudreau .60 1.50
262 Jason Robertson .50 1.25
263 Kirill Kaprizov 1.00 2.50
264 Tim Stutzle .40 1.00
265 Auston Matthews 1.25 3.00
266 Sebastian Aho .40 1.00
267 Lucas Raymond .50 1.25
268 Nick Suzuki .60 1.50
269 Sidney Crosby 1.25 3.00
270 Quinn Hughes .50 1.25
271 Patrick Kane .60 1.50
272 Moritz Seider .40 1.00
273 Roman Josi .30 .75
274 Timo Meier .30 .75
275 Jack Eichel .50 1.25
276 Nathan MacKinnon 1.25 3.00
277 Connor McDavid 1.50 4.00
278 Jack Hughes .75 2.00
279 Jordan Kyrou .30 .75
280 Alex Ovechkin 1.25 3.00
281 Jacob Perreault 1.00 2.50
282 Matias Maccelli 1.50 4.00
283 Samuel Fagemo .75 2.00
284 Brandt Clarke 2.00 5.00
285 Fredrik Karlstrom .75 2.00
286 Lukas Reichel 2.00 5.00
287 Andrei Kuzmenko 2.00 5.00
288 Jordan Spence 1.00 2.50
289 Noah Cates 1.00 2.50
290 Alex Vlasic .75 2.00
291 Kaedan Korczak .75 2.00
292 Erik Kallgren 1.00 2.50
293 Marc McLaughlin 1.00 2.50
294 Brayden Tracey .75 2.00
295 Kent Johnson 2.00 5.00
296 Dylan Guenther 2.50 6.00
297 Valtteri Puustinen .75 2.00
298 Jack Quinn 1.50 4.00
299 Braden Schneider 1.50 4.00
300 Elmer Soderblom 2.00 5.00
301 Nick Abruzzese 1.00 2.50
302 Nikita Okhotiuk .75 2.00
303 Mark Kastelic .75 2.00
304 Matt Boldy 3.00 8.00
305 Reilly Walsh 1.00 2.50
306 Shane Wright 2.50 6.00
307 Isaac Ratcliffe .75 2.00
308 Juraj Slafkovsky 5.00 12.00
309 Pyotr Kochetkov 2.00 5.00
310 Vladislav Kolyachonok .75 2.00
311 Trey Fix-Wolansky 1.00 2.50
312 Dylan Samberg 1.00 2.50
313 Lukas Dostal 2.00 5.00
314 Jake Sanderson 2.50 6.00
315 Linus Sandin .75 2.00
316 Marco Rossi 2.50 6.00
317 Chase Pearson .75 2.00
318 Mads Sogaard 1.25 3.00
319 Jordan Harris 1.25 3.00
320 Dylan Holloway 2.00 5.00
321 Thomas Bordeleau 1.00 2.50
322 Carson Meyer .75 2.00
323 Cole Reinhardt 1.00 2.50
324 Filip Hallander 1.00 2.50
325 Wyatt Johnston 4.00 10.00
326 Ben Meyers 1.00 2.50
327 Owen Power 2.00 5.00
328 Matty Beniers 2.50 6.00
329 Bobby Brink 1.00 2.50
330 Jack McBain 1.00 2.50

2022-23 Parkhurst Gold Foil
*GOLD: 2X TO 5X BRONZE
*GOLD RC: 1X TO 2.5X BRONZE

2022-23 Parkhurst Parkies
*RED: 1X TO 2.5X BASIC
PK1 Matty Beniers 1.50 4.00
PK2 William Karlsson .75 2.00
PK3 Elias Lindholm .60 1.50
PK4 Tyler Bertuzzi .50 1.25
PK5 Tim Stutzle .75 2.00
PK6 Thatcher Demko .75 2.00
PK7 Taylor Hall .60 1.50
PK8 Samuel Girard .40 1.00
PK9 Sam Bennett 1.00 2.50
PK10 Michael Bunting .60 1.50
PK11 Juuse Saros .75 2.00
PK12 Kris Letang .75 2.00
PK13 Cam Talbot .60 1.50
PK14 Josh Anderson .50 1.25
PK15 Jacob Perreault .60 1.50
PK16 Jack Campbell .60 1.50
PK17 Igor Shesterkin 1.25 3.00
PK18 Drake Batherson .60 1.50
PK19 Dawson Mercer .75 2.00
PK20 Connor McDavid 3.00 8.00
PK21 Cole Sillinger .50 1.25
PK22 Brock Nelson .60 1.50
PK23 Brandon Duhaime .40 1.00
PK24 Kent Johnson 1.25 3.00
PK25 Alex Newhook .50 1.25

2022-23 Parkhurst Parkies Autographs Blue
PK1 Matty Beniers 25.00 60.00
PK2 William Karlsson 12.00 30.00
PK4 Tyler Bertuzzi 8.00 20.00
PK5 Tim Stutzle 12.00 30.00
PK8 Samuel Girard 6.00 15.00
PK9 Sam Bennett 15.00 40.00
PK10 Michael Bunting 10.00 25.00
PK11 Juuse Saros 12.00 30.00
PK12 Kris Letang 12.00 30.00
PK13 Cam Talbot 10.00 25.00
PK15 Jacob Perreault 10.00 25.00
PK17 Igor Shesterkin 20.00 50.00
PK18 Drake Batherson 10.00 25.00
PK19 Dawson Mercer 12.00 30.00
PK20 Connor McDavid 200.00 500.00
PK21 Cole Sillinger 8.00 20.00
PK22 Brock Nelson 10.00 25.00
PK23 Brandon Duhaime 6.00 15.00
PK24 Kent Johnson 20.00 50.00
PK25 Alex Newhook 8.00 20.00

2022-23 Parkhurst Prominent Prospects
*BLUE/25: 4X TO 10X BASIC
PP1 Matt Boldy 1.50 4.00
PP2 Jacob Perreault .50 1.25
PP3 Jack Quinn .75 2.00
PP4 Marco Rossi 1.25 3.00
PP5 Brayden Tracey .40 1.00
PP6 Vladislav Kolyachonok .40 1.00
PP7 Kent Johnson 1.00 2.50
PP8 Lukas Reichel 1.00 2.50
PP9 Trey Fix-Wolansky .50 1.25
PP10 Samuel Fagemo .40 1.00
PP11 Braden Schneider .75 2.00
PP12 Isaac Ratcliffe .50 1.25
PP13 Kaedan Korczak .40 1.00
PP14 Dylan Samberg .50 1.25
PP15 Alex Vlasic .40 1.00
PP16 Owen Power 1.00 2.50
PP17 Matty Beniers 1.25 3.00
PP18 Declan Chisholm .50 1.25
PP19 Thomas Bordeleau .50 1.25
PP20 Jordan Spence .50 1.25
PP21 Pyotr Kochetkov 1.00 2.50
PP22 Nathan Smith .40 1.00
PP23 Filip Hallander .50 1.25
PP24 Jack McBain .50 1.25
PP25 Jack LaFontaine .50 1.25

2022-23 Parkhurst Retro Achievements
A1 Sidney Crosby 4.00 10.00
A2 Nathan MacKinnon 4.00 10.00
A3 Matt Boldy 3.00 8.00
A4 Leon Draisaitl 3.00 8.00
A5 Kyle Connor 1.50 4.00
A6 Matthew Tkachuk 2.00 5.00
A7 Jonathan Huberdeau 1.25 3.00
A8 Igor Shesterkin 2.00 5.00
A9 Connor McDavid 5.00 12.00
A10 Auston Matthews 4.00 10.00
A11 Alex Ovechkin 4.00 10.00
A12 Owen Power 2.00 5.00
A13 Matty Beniers 2.50 6.00
A14 Jack Quinn 1.50 4.00
A15 Kent Johnson 2.00 5.00

2022-23 Parkhurst Sizzling Shots
*RED: .6X TO 1.5X BASIC
SS1 Steven Stamkos 1.25 3.00
SS2 Sidney Crosby 2.50 6.00
SS3 Sebastian Aho 1.00 2.50
SS4 Patrick Kane 1.25 3.00
SS5 Moritz Seider .75 2.00
SS6 Mikko Rantanen 1.50 4.00
SS7 Kirill Kaprizov 2.00 5.00
SS8 Jonathan Huberdeau .75 2.00
SS9 Johnny Gaudreau 1.00 2.50
SS10 Jason Robertson 1.00 2.50
SS11 Kyle Connor 1.00 2.50
SS12 David Pastrnak 1.50 4.00
SS13 Connor McDavid 3.00 8.00
SS14 Auston Matthews 2.50 6.00
SS15 Alex Ovechkin 2.50 6.00

2022-23 Parkhurst You're Next
YN1 T.Bertuzzi/L.Raymond 1.00 2.50
YN2 N.MacKinnon/A.Newhook 2.50 6.00
YN3 P.Kane/L.Reichel 1.25 3.00
YN4 L.Draisaitl/D.Holloway 2.00 5.00
YN5 K.Kaprizov/M.Boldy 2.00 5.00
YN6 T.Seguin/J.Robertson 1.00 2.50
YN7 R.Dahlin/O.Power 1.25 3.00
YN8 C.Kreider/A.Lafreniere 1.00 2.50
YN9 S.Bobrovsky/S.Knight 1.00 2.50
YN10 S.Aho/S.Jarvis 1.00 2.50

2023-24 Parkhurst Silver
1 Trevor Zegras .30 .75
2 Troy Terry .25 .60
3 Cam Fowler .30 .75
4 Mason McTavish .30 .75
5 Frank Vatrano .25 .60
6 Ryan Strome .30 .75
7 Adam Henrique .25 .60
8 John Gibson .30 .75
9 Jakob Silfverberg .20 .50
10 Leo Carlsson 3.00 8.00
11 Clayton Keller .40 1.00
12 Nick Schmaltz .25 .60
13 Matias Maccelli .25 .60
14 Lawson Crouse .20 .50
15 Barrett Hayton .30 .75
16 Travis Boyd .20 .50
17 J.J. Moser .20 .50
18 Karel Vejmelka .20 .50
19 Sean Durzi .20 .50
20 Logan Cooley 3.00 8.00
21 David Pastrnak .75 2.00
22 Brad Marchand .60 1.50
23 Linus Ullmark .30 .75
24 Pavel Zacha .25 .60
25 Matthew Poitras 2.00 5.00
26 Hampus Lindholm .20 .50
27 Charlie McAvoy .40 1.00
28 Jake DeBrusk .30 .75
29 Jeremy Swayman .50 1.25
30 Joona Koppanen .75 2.00
31 Tage Thompson .40 1.00
32 Rasmus Dahlin .40 1.00
33 Owen Power .30 .75
34 Dylan Cozens .30 .75
35 Jeff Skinner .30 .75
36 Alex Tuch .30 .75
37 Victor Olofsson .30 .75
38 Jack Quinn .25 .60
39 Casey Mittelstadt .30 .75
40 Devon Levi 2.50 6.00
41 Jonathan Huberdeau .40 1.00
42 Elias Lindholm .30 .75
43 Nazem Kadri .40 1.00
44 Mikael Backlund .25 .60
45 Rasmus Andersson .25 .60
46 MacKenzie Weegar .25 .60
47 Andrew Mangiapane .30 .75
48 Blake Coleman .25 .60
49 Noah Hanifin .30 .75
50 Matthew Coronato 1.50 4.00
51 Dustin Wolf 3.00 8.00
52 Sebastian Aho .50 1.25
53 Brent Burns .30 .75
54 Seth Jarvis .40 1.00
55 Martin Necas .40 1.00
56 Andrei Svechnikov .40 1.00
57 Brett Pesce .20 .50
58 Brady Skjei .20 .50
59 Jesperi Kotkaniemi .30 .75
60 Teuvo Teravainen .30 .75
61 Taylor Raddysh .25 .60
62 Seth Jones .30 .75
63 Boris Katchouk .20 .50
64 Lukas Reichel .30 .75
65 Kevin Korchinski 1.50 4.00
66 Connor Murphy .25 .60
67 Tyler Johnson .20 .50
68 Andreas Athanasiou .25 .60
69 David Gust 1.00 2.50
70 Connor Bedard 6.00 15.00
71 Cale Makar .75 2.00
72 Nathan MacKinnon 1.25 3.00
73 Mikko Rantanen .75 2.00
74 Samuel Girard .20 .50
75 Alexandar Georgiev .30 .75
76 J.T. Compher .20 .50
77 Valeri Nichushkin .30 .75
78 Artturi Lehkonen .25 .60
79 Devon Toews .25 .60
80 Bowen Byram .40 1.00
81 Cole Sillinger .25 .60
82 Kent Johnson .30 .75
83 Johnny Gaudreau .50 1.25
84 Patrik Laine .40 1.00
85 Boone Jenner .30 .75
86 Jack Roslovic .20 .50
87 Kirill Marchenko .40 1.00
88 Elvis Merzlikins .30 .75
89 Adam Fantilli 3.00 8.00
90 Stanislav Svozil .75 2.00
91 Jason Robertson .50 1.25
92 Jamie Benn .30 .75
93 Joe Pavelski .40 1.00
94 Roope Hintz .40 1.00
95 Miro Heiskanen .40 1.00
96 Tyler Seguin .40 1.00
97 Wyatt Johnston .60 1.50
98 Mason Marchment .25 .60
99 Ty Dellandrea .20 .50
100 Matt Murray 1.00 2.50
101 Lucas Raymond .50 1.25
102 Moritz Seider .40 1.00
103 Dylan Larkin .40 1.00
104 Joe Veleno .25 .60
105 Andrew Copp .20 .50
106 David Perron .25 .60
107 Ville Husso .20 .50
108 Jonatan Berggren .25 .60
109 Marco Kasper 2.50 6.00
110 Simon Edvinsson 2.00 5.00
111 Connor McDavid 1.50 4.00
112 Leon Draisaitl 1.00 2.50
113 Ryan Nugent-Hopkins .40 1.00
114 Darnell Nurse .25 .60
115 Zach Hyman .50 1.25
116 Evander Kane .30 .75
117 Warren Foegele .20 .50
118 Evan Bouchard .40 1.00
119 Jack Campbell .30 .75
120 Vincent Desharnais 1.25 3.00
121 Matthew Tkachuk .60 1.50
122 Aleksander Barkov .50 1.25
123 Evan Rodrigues .25 .60
124 Anton Lundell .30 .75
125 Aaron Ekblad .40 1.00
126 Sergei Bobrovsky .50 1.25
127 Carter Verhaeghe .30 .75
128 Sam Bennett .50 1.25
129 Brandon Montour .40 1.00
130 Mackie Samoskevich 1.50 4.00
131 Anze Kopitar .50 1.25
132 Kevin Fiala .25 .60
133 Adrian Kempe .30 .75
134 Drew Doughty .30 .75
135 Arthur Kaliyev .30 .75
136 Mikey Anderson .25 .60
137 Quinton Byfield .40 1.00
138 Viktor Arvidsson .20 .50
139 Phillip Danault .30 .75
140 Pheonix Copley .20 .50
141 Kirill Kaprizov 1.00 2.50
142 Matt Boldy .50 1.25
143 Mats Zuccarello .30 .75
144 Joel Eriksson Ek .25 .60
145 Calen Addison .20 .50
146 Frederick Gaudreau .20 .50
147 Ryan Hartman .20 .50
148 Marc-Andre Fleury .60 1.50
149 Jared Spurgeon .30 .75
150 Brock Faber 2.50 6.00
151 Cole Caufield .60 1.50
152 Nick Suzuki .60 1.50
153 Kirby Dach .30 .75
154 Jordan Harris .30 .75
155 Juraj Slafkovsky .60 1.50
156 Brendan Gallagher .30 .75
157 Owen Beck 1.50 4.00
158 Josh Anderson .25 .60
159 Sean Farrell 1.00 2.50
160 Joel Teasdale 1.00 2.50
161 Roman Josi .30 .75
162 Ryan O'Reilly .30 .75
163 Thomas Novak .20 .50
164 Juuso Parssinen .20 .50
165 Ryan McDonagh .20 .50
166 Filip Forsberg .50 1.25
167 Cody Glass .25 .60
168 Tyson Barrie .20 .50
169 Luke Evangelista 1.50 4.00
170 Yaroslav Askarov 2.50 6.00
171 Jack Hughes .75 2.00
172 Dawson Mercer .40 1.00
173 Nico Hischier .50 1.25
174 Dougie Hamilton .25 .60
175 Jesper Bratt .30 .75
176 Tomas Tatar .20 .50
177 Timo Meier .30 .75
178 Ondrej Palat .25 .60
179 Vitek Vanecek .30 .75
180 Luke Hughes 3.00 8.00
181 Mathew Barzal .40 1.00
182 Brock Nelson .30 .75
183 Anders Lee .25 .60
184 Oliver Wahlstrom .20 .50
185 Noah Dobson .40 1.00
186 Bo Horvat .40 1.00
187 Kyle Palmieri .25 .60
188 Jean-Gabriel Pageau .20 .50
189 Ilya Sorokin .50 1.25
190 William Dufour .75 2.00
191 Artemi Panarin .60 1.50
192 Adam Fox .40 1.00
193 Chris Kreider .40 1.00
194 Mika Zibanejad .40 1.00
195 Alexis Lafreniere .50 1.25
196 Vincent Trocheck .30 .75
197 K'Andre Miller .25 .60
198 Jacob Trouba .25 .60
199 Igor Shesterkin .60 1.50
200 Will Cuylle 1.50 4.00
201 Tim Stutzle .40 1.00
202 Shane Pinto .25 .60
203 Brady Tkachuk .50 1.25
204 Claude Giroux .30 .75
205 Thomas Chabot .30 .75
206 Josh Norris .30 .75
207 Jake Sanderson .40 1.00
208 Drake Batherson .30 .75
209 Tyler Kleven 1.00 2.50
210 Ridly Greig 1.50 4.00
211 Travis Konecny .30 .75
212 Noah Cates .20 .50
213 Carter Hart .30 .75
214 Owen Tippett .20 .50
215 Joel Farabee .30 .75
216 Morgan Frost .25 .60
217 Scott Laughton .20 .50
218 Wade Allison .20 .50
219 Elliot Desnoyers 1.00 2.50
220 Tyson Foerster 2.00 5.00
221 Sidney Crosby 1.25 3.00
222 Evgeni Malkin .60 1.50
223 Jake Guentzel .50 1.25
224 Pierre-Olivier Joseph .20 .50
225 Rickard Rakell .25 .60
226 Tristan Jarry .30 .75
227 Bryan Rust .30 .75
228 Jeff Carter .25 .60
229 Kris Letang .40 1.00
230 Jonathan Gruden 1.00 2.50
231 Logan Couture .40 1.00
232 Tomas Hertl .30 .75
233 Alexander Barabanov .20 .50
234 Kevin Labanc .20 .50
235 Nico Sturm .20 .50
236 William Eklund .40 1.00
237 Matt Benning .20 .50
238 Oskar Lindblom .25 .60
239 Tristen Robins 1.00 2.50
240 Danil Gushchin 1.00 2.50
241 Jordan Eberle .30 .75
242 Matty Beniers .40 1.00
243 Jared McCann .25 .60
244 Vince Dunn .25 .60
245 Yanni Gourde .25 .60
246 Daniel Sprong .20 .50
247 Oliver Bjorkstrand .25 .60
248 Jaden Schwartz .25 .60
249 Alexander Wennberg .20 .50
250 Tye Kartye 1.50 4.00
251 Jordan Kyrou .30 .75
252 Pavel Buchnevich .25 .60
253 Brayden Schenn .30 .75
254 Robert Thomas .30 .75
255 Justin Faulk .25 .60
256 Brandon Saad .25 .60
257 Torey Krug .25 .60
258 Colton Parayko .25 .60
259 Jordan Binnington .50 1.25
260 Matthew Kessel .75 2.00
261 Steven Stamkos .60 1.50
262 Andrei Vasilevskiy .50 1.25
263 Nikita Kucherov .60 1.50
264 Brayden Point .40 1.00
265 Victor Hedman .40 1.00
266 Brandon Hagel .25 .60
267 Anthony Cirelli .25 .60
268 Mikhail Sergachev .25 .60
269 Nick Paul .20 .50
270 Tanner Jeannot .20 .50
271 Auston Matthews 1.25 3.00
272 Mitch Marner .50 1.25
273 William Nylander .60 1.50
274 John Tavares .50 1.25
275 Ryan Reaves .25 .60
276 Morgan Rielly .30 .75
277 Ilya Samsonov .30 .75
278 Calle Jarnkrok .20 .50
279 Bobby McMann 1.50 4.00
280 Matthew Knies 4.00 10.00
281 Elias Pettersson .50 1.25
282 J.T. Miller .40 1.00
283 Quinn Hughes .75 2.00
284 Andrei Kuzmenko .30 .75
285 Brock Boeser .40 1.00
286 Conor Garland .25 .60
287 Thatcher Demko .40 1.00
288 Dakota Joshua .20 .50
289 Aidan McDonough .75 2.00
290 Akito Hirose .75 2.00
291 Jack Eichel .50 1.25
292 Mark Stone .40 1.00
293 Jonathan Marchessault .40 1.00
294 Adin Hill .30 .75
295 Chandler Stephenson .25 .60
296 Ivan Barbashev .25 .60
297 Alex Pietrangelo .25 .60
298 William Karlsson .40 1.00
299 Shea Theodore .40 1.00
300 Jiri Patera 1.50 4.00
301 Alex Ovechkin 1.25 3.00
302 Dylan Strome .40 1.00
303 Evgeny Kuznetsov .40 1.00
304 T.J. Oshie .30 .75
305 Sonny Milano .25 .60
306 John Carlson .30 .75
307 Nicklas Backstrom .30 .75
308 Matthew Phillips .20 .50
309 Tom Wilson .30 .75
310 Vincent Iorio 1.00 2.50
311 Kyle Connor .50 1.25
312 Josh Morrissey .40 1.00
313 Mark Scheifele .50 1.25
314 Mason Appleton .20 .50

315 Gabe Vilardi .30 .75
316 Nikolaj Ehlers .30 .75
317 Connor Hellebuyck .60 1.50
318 Cole Perfetti .30 .75
319 Neal Pionk .20 .50
320 Nate Schmidt .20 .50
321 Rasmus Dahlin .40 1.00
322 Nikita Kucherov .60 1.50
323 Leon Draisaitl 1.00 2.50
324 Nick Suzuki .60 1.50
325 Andrei Vasilevskiy .50 1.25
326 Kirill Kaprizov 1.00 2.50
327 Nathan MacKinnon 1.25 3.00
328 Cale Makar .75 2.00
329 Jason Robertson .50 1.25
330 Connor McDavid 1.50 4.00

2023-24 Parkhurst Gold

*GOLD: .6X TO 1.5X SILVER

2023-24 Parkhurst Patterned Foil

*PAT FOIL: .8X TO 2X SILVER
*PAT FOIL RC: .6X TO 1.5X SILVER
70 Connor Bedard 15.00 40.00

2023-24 Parkhurst Patterned Foil Gold

*PAT GOLD: 2X TO 5X SILVER
*PAT GOLD RC: .8X TO 2X SILVER

2023-24 Parkhurst Patterned Foil Red

*PAT RED/25: 4X TO 10X SILVER
*PAT RED RC: 1.5X TO 4X SILVER

2023-24 Parkhurst Pink

*PINK/50: 2X TO 5X SILVER
*PINK RC/50: 1X TO 2.5X SILVER

2023-24 Parkhurst Last Line of Defense

*RED: .8X TO 2X BASIC
*PINK/50: 1.5X TO 4X BASIC
LD1 Ville Husso .60 1.50
LD2 Alexandar Georgiev 1.00 2.50
LD3 Ilya Sorokin 1.50 4.00
LD4 Devon Levi 2.50 6.00
LD5 Adin Hill 1.00 2.50
LD6 Dustin Wolf 3.00 8.00
LD7 Igor Shesterkin 2.00 5.00
LD8 Jake Oettinger 1.50 4.00
LD9 Carter Hart 1.00 2.50
LD10 John Gibson 1.00 2.50
LD11 Connor Hellebuyck 2.00 5.00
LD12 Logan Thompson 1.25 3.00
LD13 Jeremy Swayman 1.50 4.00
LD14 Vitek Vanecek 1.00 2.50
LD15 Tristan Jarry 1.00 2.50
LD16 Juuse Saros 1.25 3.00
LD17 Jake Allen 1.00 2.50
LD18 Jordan Binnington 1.50 4.00
LD19 Stuart Skinner 1.25 3.00
LD20 Linus Ullmark 1.00 2.50
LD21 Yaroslav Askarov 2.50 6.00
LD22 Ilya Samsonov 1.00 2.50
LD23 Andrei Vasilevskiy 1.50 4.00
LD24 Marc-Andre Fleury 2.00 5.00
LD25 Sergei Bobrovsky 1.50 4.00

2023-24 Parkhurst Like a Boss

*RED: .8X TO 2X BASIC
*PINK/50: 2.5X TO 6X BASIC
LB1 Connor McDavid 3.00 8.00
LB2 Sidney Crosby 2.50 6.00
LB3 David Pastrnak 1.50 4.00
LB4 Kirill Kaprizov 2.00 5.00
LB5 Kyle Connor 1.00 2.50
LB6 Elias Pettersson 1.00 2.50
LB7 Cole Caufield 1.25 3.00
LB8 Auston Matthews 2.50 6.00
LB9 Cale Makar 1.50 4.00
LB10 Jack Hughes 1.50 4.00
LB11 Artemi Panarin 1.25 3.00
LB12 Mathew Barzal .75 2.00
LB13 Travis Konecny .60 1.50
LB14 Nikita Kucherov 1.25 3.00
LB15 Matthew Tkachuk 1.25 3.00
LB16 Tage Thompson .75 2.00
LB17 Tim Stutzle .75 2.00
LB18 Lucas Raymond 1.00 2.50
LB19 Jordan Kyrou .60 1.50
LB20 Tyler Toffoli .60 1.50
LB21 Jonathan Marchessault .75 2.00
LB22 Anze Kopitar 1.00 2.50
LB23 Matty Beniers .75 2.00
LB24 Erik Karlsson .75 2.00
LB25 Trevor Zegras .60 1.50

2023-24 Parkhurst Parkies

*RED: .8X TO 2X BASIC
*PINK/50: 1.5X TO 4X BASIC
P1 Jack Eichel 1.00 2.50
P2 Moritz Seider .75 2.00
P3 Adam Fox .75 2.00
P4 Rasmus Dahlin .75 2.00
P5 Walker Duehr .50 1.25
P6 Matty Beniers .75 2.00
P7 Johnny Gaudreau 1.00 2.50
P8 Mikko Rantanen 1.50 4.00
P9 Lucas Raymond 1.00 2.50
P10 Steven Stamkos 1.25 3.00
P11 Nikita Kucherov 1.25 3.00
P12 Nick Suzuki 1.25 3.00
P13 Simon Edvinsson 1.25 3.00
P14 Cole Caufield 1.25 3.00
P15 Trevor Zegras .60 1.50
P16 Jason Robertson 1.00 2.50
P17 Nathan MacKinnon 2.50 6.00
P18 Connor McDavid 3.00 8.00
P19 Owen Power .60 1.50
P20 Brad Marchand 1.25 3.00
P21 Lukas Rousek .60 1.50
P22 Mark Stone .75 2.00
P23 Auston Matthews 2.50 6.00
P24 Luke Hughes 2.00 5.00
P25 J.T. Miller .75 2.00
P26 Alexis Lafreniere 1.00 2.50
P27 Andrei Kuzmenko .60 1.50
P28 Matt Boldy 1.00 2.50
P29 Devon Levi 1.50 4.00
P30 Tim Stutzle .75 2.00
P31 Tye Kartye 1.00 2.50
P32 Mitch Marner 1.00 2.50
P33 Samuel Bolduc .60 1.50
P34 Nick Swaney .60 1.50
P35 Sidney Crosby 2.50 6.00
P36 Kirill Kaprizov 2.00 5.00
P37 Evgeni Malkin 1.25 3.00
P38 Adam Ginning .60 1.50
P39 Yaroslav Askarov 1.50 4.00
P40 Troy Terry .50 1.25
P41 Clayton Keller .75 2.00
P42 Mark Scheifele 1.00 2.50
P43 Marco Kasper 1.50 4.00
P44 David Pastrnak 1.50 4.00
P45 Leon Draisaitl 2.00 5.00
P46 Alex Ovechkin 2.50 6.00
P47 Matthew Coronato 1.00 2.50
P48 Matthew Tkachuk 1.25 3.00
P49 Kevin Fiala .50 1.25
P50 Matthew Knies 2.50 6.00

2023-24 Parkhurst Parkies Autographs Blue

P1 Jack Eichel 15.00 40.00
P5 Walker Duehr 8.00 20.00
P6 Matty Beniers 12.00 30.00
P7 Johnny Gaudreau 15.00 40.00
P8 Mikko Rantanen 25.00 60.00
P13 Simon Edvinsson 20.00 50.00
P18 Connor McDavid 200.00 500.00
P19 Owen Power 10.00 25.00
P21 Lukas Rousek 10.00 25.00
P22 Mark Stone 12.00 30.00
P23 Auston Matthews 40.00 100.00
P24 Luke Hughes 30.00 80.00
P27 Andrei Kuzmenko 10.00 25.00
P28 Matt Boldy 15.00 40.00
P31 Tye Kartye 15.00 40.00
P33 Samuel Bolduc 10.00 25.00
P34 Nick Swaney 10.00 25.00
P38 Adam Ginning 10.00 25.00
P39 Yaroslav Askarov 25.00 60.00
P40 Troy Terry 8.00 20.00
P43 Marco Kasper 25.00 60.00
P45 Leon Draisaitl 40.00 100.00
P46 Alex Ovechkin 40.00 100.00
P47 Matthew Coronato 15.00 40.00
P50 Matthew Knies 40.00 100.00

2023-24 Parkhurst Prominent Prospects

*PURPLE/99: 1.2X TO 3X BASIC
*BLUE/25: 4X TO 10X BASIC
PPAF Adam Fantilli 1.50 4.00
PPAH Akito Hirose .40 1.00
PPAM Aidan McDonough .40 1.00
PPBF Brock Faber 1.25 3.00
PPBM Bobby McMann .75 2.00
PPBS Billy Sweezey .50 1.25
PPCB Connor Bedard 6.00 15.00
PPCO Logan Cooley 2.00 5.00
PPDG David Gust .50 1.25
PPDL Devon Levi 1.25 3.00
PPDW Dustin Wolf 1.50 4.00
PPFM Fraser Minten 1.00 2.50
PPGU Danil Gushchin .50 1.25
PPHM Hunter McKown .50 1.25
PPHU Hugh McGing .50 1.25
PPJG Jonathan Gruden .50 1.25
PPJK Joona Koppanen .40 1.00
PPJP Jiri Patera .75 2.00
PPJS Justin Sourdif .75 2.00
PPKA Marco Kasper 1.25 3.00
PPKE Michael Kesselring .50 1.25
PPKK Kevin Korchinski .75 2.00
PPKN Matthew Knies 2.00 5.00
PPLC Leo Carlsson 1.50 4.00
PPLE Luke Evangelista .75 2.00
PPLH Luke Hughes 1.50 4.00
PPLM Leevi Merilainen .50 1.25
PPLP Luke Philp .50 1.25
PPLR Lukas Rousek .50 1.25
PPMA Matthew Kessel .40 1.00
PPMC Matthew Coronato .75 2.00
PPMK Milos Kelemen .50 1.25
PPMM Matt Murray .50 1.25
PPMP Matthew Poitras 1.00 2.50
PPNN Nikita Nesterenko .50 1.25
PPOB Owen Beck .75 2.00
PPOE Olle Eriksson Ek .50 1.25
PPPE Jakob Pelletier .60 1.50
PPPM Pavel Mintyukov .75 2.00
PPRG Ridly Greig .75 2.00
PPSE Simon Edvinsson 1.00 2.50
PPSF Sean Farrell .50 1.25
PPSM Mackie Samoskevich .75 2.00
PPTF Tyson Foerster 1.00 2.50
PPTK Tye Kartye .75 2.00
PPVD Vincent Desharnais .60 1.50
PPVI Vincent Iorio .50 1.25
PPWD William Dufour .40 1.00
PPYA Yaroslav Askarov 1.25 3.00
PPZB Zach Benson .75 2.00

2023-24 Parkhurst Prominent Prospects Green

*GREEN/150: .8X TO 2X BASIC
PPCB Connor Bedard 25.00 60.00

2023-24 Parkhurst Prominent Prospects Orange

*ORANGE: .5X TO 1.2X BASIC
PPCB Connor Bedard 15.00 40.00

2023-24 Parkhurst Prominent Prospects Autographs Gold

PPAF Adam Fantilli 15.00 40.00
PPAH Akito Hirose 4.00 10.00
PPAM Aidan McDonough 4.00 10.00
PPBF Brock Faber 12.00 30.00
PPBM Bobby McMann 8.00 20.00
PPBS Billy Sweezey 5.00 12.00
PPCB Connor Bedard 200.00 500.00
PPCO Logan Cooley 15.00 40.00
PPDG David Gust 5.00 12.00
PPDL Devon Levi 12.00 30.00
PPDW Dustin Wolf 15.00 40.00
PPFM Fraser Minten 10.00 25.00
PPGU Danil Gushchin 5.00 12.00
PPHM Hunter McKown 5.00 12.00
PPHU Hugh McGing 5.00 12.00
PPJG Jonathan Gruden 5.00 12.00
PPJK Joona Koppanen 4.00 10.00
PPJP Jakob Pelletier 6.00 15.00
PPJS Justin Sourdif 5.00 12.00
PPKE Milos Kelemen 5.00 12.00
PPKK Kevin Korchinski 8.00 20.00
PPKN Matthew Knies 20.00 50.00
PPLC Leo Carlsson 15.00 40.00
PPLE Luke Evangelista 8.00 20.00
PPLH Luke Hughes 15.00 40.00
PPLM Leevi Merilainen 5.00 12.00
PPLP Luke Philp 5.00 12.00
PPLR Lukas Rousek 4.00 10.00
PPMA Matthew Kessel 4.00 10.00
PPMC Matthew Coronato 8.00 20.00
PPMI Michael Kesselring 5.00 12.00
PPMK Marco Kasper 12.00 30.00
PPMM Matt Murray 5.00 12.00
PPMP Matthew Poitras 10.00 25.00
PPNN Nikita Nesterenko 5.00 12.00
PPOB Owen Beck 8.00 20.00
PPOE Olle Eriksson Ek 5.00 12.00
PPPA Jiri Patera 8.00 20.00
PPPM Pavel Mintyukov 8.00 20.00
PPRG Ridly Greig 8.00 20.00
PPSE Simon Edvinsson 10.00 25.00
PPSF Sean Farrell 5.00 12.00
PPSM Mackie Samoskevich 15.00 40.00
PPTF Tyson Foerster 10.00 25.00
PPTK Tye Kartye 8.00 20.00
PPVD Vincent Desharnais 6.00 15.00
PPVI Vincent Iorio 5.00 12.00
PPWD William Dufour 4.00 10.00
PPYA Yaroslav Askarov 12.00 30.00
PPZB Zach Benson 8.00 20.00

2023-24 Parkhurst Tis the Season

TS1 Owen Beck 10.00 25.00
TS2 Noah Cates 4.00 10.00
TS3 K'Andre Miller 5.00 12.00
TS4 Devon Levi 15.00 40.00
TS5 Matias Maccelli 5.00 12.00
TS6 Taylor Raddysh 5.00 12.00
TS7 Matthew Knies 25.00 60.00
TS8 Bryan Rust 6.00 15.00
TS9 Shane Pinto 5.00 12.00
TS10 Jordan Eberle 6.00 15.00
TS11 Gabe Vilardi 6.00 15.00
TS12 Evan Bouchard 8.00 20.00
TS13 Alex Newhook 5.00 12.00
TS14 Peyton Krebs 5.00 12.00
TS15 Anton Lundell 6.00 15.00
TS16 Noah Dobson 8.00 20.00
TS17 Sonny Milano 5.00 12.00
TS18 Wyatt Johnston 12.00 30.00

1971-72 Penguins Postcards

COMPLETE SET (22) 20.00 40.00
1 Syl Apps 1.25 2.50
2 Les Binkley 1.25 2.50
3 Dave Burrows 1.00 2.00
4 Darryl Edestrand .75 1.50
5 Roy Edwards 1.00 2.00
6 Val Fonteyne .75 1.50
7 Nick Harbaruk .75 1.50
8 Bryan Hextall 2.00 4.00
9 Sheldon Kannegiesser .75 1.50
10 Red Kelly CO 2.00 4.00
11 Bob Leiter .75 1.50
12 Keith McCreary .75 1.50
13 Joe Noris .75 1.50
14 Greg Polis .75 1.50
15 Jean Pronovost 2.00 4.00
16 Rene Robert 1.25 2.50
17 Jim Rutherford 1.25 2.50
18 Ken Schinkel .75 1.50
19 Ron Schock 1.00 2.00
20 Bryan Watson 1.00 2.00
21 Bob Woytowich .75 1.50
22 Title Card .75 1.50

1974-75 Penguins Postcards

COMPLETE SET (22) 15.00 30.00
1 Syl Apps 1.25 2.50
2 Chuck Arnason .75 1.50
3 Dave Burrows 1.00 2.00
4 Colin Campbell 1.25 2.50
5 Nelson Debenedet .75 1.50
6 Steve Durbano .75 1.50
7 Vic Hadfield 1.00 2.00
8 Gary Inness 1.00 2.00
9 Bob(B.J.) Johnson .75 1.50
10 Rick Kehoe 1.25 2.50
11 Bob Kelly .75 1.50
12 Jean-Guy Lagace .75 1.50
13 Ron Lalonde .75 1.50
14 Pierre Larouche 2.50 5.00
15 Lowell MacDonald 1.00 2.00
16 Dennis Owchar .75 1.50
17 Bob Paradise .75 1.50
18 Kelly Pratt .75 1.50
19 Jean Pronovost 1.00 2.00
20 Ron Schock 1.00 2.00
21 Ron Stackhouse 1.00 2.00
22 Barry Williams .75 1.50

1977-78 Penguins Puck Bucks

COMPLETE SET (18) 12.50 25.00
1 Denis Herron 1.50 3.00
3 Ron Stackhouse 1.00 2.00
4 Dave Burrows .75 1.50
6 Colin Campbell 1.25 2.50
7 Russ Anderson .75 1.50
9 Blair Chapman .75 1.50
10 Pierre Larouche 1.50 3.00
12 Greg Malone 1.00 2.00
14 Wayne Bianchin .75 1.50
17 Rick Kehoe 1.50 3.00
18 Lowell MacDonald 1.00 2.00
19 Jean Pronovost 1.25 2.50
23 Jim Hamilton .75 1.50
25 Dennis Owchar .75 1.50
26 Syl Apps 1.00 2.00
27 Mike Corrigan .75 1.50
29 Dunc Wilson 1.00 2.00
NNO Johnny Wilson CO .50 1.00

1983-84 Penguins Coke

COMPLETE SET (19) 10.00 25.00
1 Pat Boutette .60 1.50
2 Andy Brickley .40 1.00
3 Mike Bullard .75 2.00
4 Ted Bulley .40 1.00
5 Rod Buskas .40 1.00
6 Randy Carlyle .75 2.00
7 Michel Dion .75 2.00
8 Bob Errey .75 2.00
9 Ron Flockhart .60 1.50
10 Steve Gatzos .40 1.00
11 Jim Hamilton .40 1.00
12 Dave Hannan .40 1.00
13 Denis Herron 1.00 2.50
14 Troy Loney .40 1.00
15 Bryan Maxwell .40 1.00
16 Marty McSorley 2.00 5.00
17 Norm Schmidt .40 1.00
18 Mark Taylor .40 1.00
19 Greg Tebbutt .40 1.00

1983-84 Penguins Heinz Photos

COMPLETE SET (22) 10.00 25.00
1 Paul Baxter .60 1.50
2 Pat Boutette .60 1.50
3 Randy Boyd .40 1.00
4 Mike Bullard .75 2.00
5 Randy Carlyle .75 2.00
6 Marc Chorney .40 1.00
7 Michel Dion .75 2.00
8 Bill Gardner .40 1.00
9 Pat Graham .40 1.00
10 Anders Hakansson .40 1.00
11 Dave Hannan .40 1.00
12 Denis Herron 1.00 2.50
13 Greg Hotham .40 1.00
14 Stan Jonathan .60 1.50
15 Rick Kehoe 1.00 2.50
16 Peter Lee .75 2.00
17 Greg Malone .60 1.50
18 Kevin McClelland .60 1.50
19 Ron Meighan .40 1.00
20 Doug Shedden .40 1.00
21 Andre St. Laurent .40 1.00
22 Rich Sutter .60 1.50

1984-85 Penguins Heinz Photos

COMPLETE SET (22) 10.00 25.00
1 Pat Boutette .60 1.50
2 Andy Brickley .40 1.00
3 Mike Bullard .75 2.00
4 Rod Buskas .40 1.00
5 Randy Carlyle .75 2.00
6 Michel Dion .75 2.00
7 Bob Errey .60 1.50
8 Ron Flockhart .60 1.50
9 Greg Fox .40 1.00
10 Steve Gatzos .40 1.00
11 Denis Herron 1.00 2.50
12 Greg Hotham .40 1.00
13 Rick Kehoe .75 2.00
14 Bryan Maxwell .60 1.50
15 Marty McSorley 2.00 5.00
16 Tom O'Regan .40 1.00
17 Gary Rissling .40 1.00
18 Roberto Romano .60 1.50
19 Tom Roulston .40 1.00
20 Rocky Saganiuk .40 1.00
21 Doug Shedden .60 1.50
22 Mark Taylor .40 1.00

1986-87 Penguins Kodak

COMPLETE SET (26) 20.00 50.00
1 Bob Berry CO .20 .50
2 Mike Blaisdell 26 .40 1.00
3 Doug Bodger 3 .40 1.00
4 Rod Buskas 7 .30 .75
5 John Chabot 9 .30 .75
6 Randy Cunneyworth 15 .30 .75
7 Ron Duguay 10 .40 1.00
8 Bob Errey 12 .40 1.00
9 Dan Frawley 28 .30 .75
10 Dave Hannan 32 .30 .75
11 Randy Hillier 23 .30 .75
12 Jim Johnson 6 .30 .75
13 Kevin Lavallee 16 .30 .75
14 Mario Lemieux 66 6.00 15.00
15 Willy Lindstrom 19 .30 .75
16 Moe Mantha 20 .30 .75
17 Gilles Meloche 27 .40 1.00
18 Dan Quinn 14 .40 1.00
19 Jim Roberts CO .20 .50
20 Roberto Romano 30 .40 1.00
21 Terry Ruskowski 8 .40 1.00
22 Norm Schmidt 25 .30 .75
23 Craig Simpson 18 .60 1.50
24 Ville Siren 5 .30 .75
25 Warren Young 35 .40 1.00
NNO Team Photo .75 2.00

1987-88 Penguins Masks

COMPLETE SET (10) 8.00 20.00
1 Doug Bodger .40 1.00
2 Randy Cunneyworth .40 1.00
3 Bob Errey .40 1.00
4 Dan Frawley .40 1.00
5 Jim Johnson .40 1.00
6 Mario Lemieux 4.00 10.00
7 Gilles Meloche .75 2.00
8 Dan Quinn .40 1.00
9 Craig Simpson .75 2.00
10 Ville Siren .40 1.00

1987-88 Penguins Kodak

COMPLETE SET (26) 14.00 35.00
1 Doug Bodger 3 .30 .75
2 Rob Brown 44 .40 1.00
3 Rod Buskas 7 .30 .75
4 Jock Callander 36 .30 .75
5 Paul Coffey 77 .75 2.00
6 Randy Cunneyworth 15 .30 .75
7 Chris Dahlquist 4 .30 .75
8 Bob Errey 12 .30 .75
9 Dan Frawley 28 .30 .75
10 Steve Guenette 30 .40 1.00
11 Randy Hillier 23 .30 .75
12 Dave Hunter 20 .30 .75
13 Jim Johnson 6 .30 .75
14 Mark Kachowski 26 .30 .75
15 Chris Kontos 14 .30 .75
16 Mario Lemieux 66 6.00 15.00
17 Troy Loney 24 .30 .75
18 Dwight Mathiasen 34 .30 .75
19 Dave McLlwain 19 .30 .75
20 Gilles Meloche 27 .40 1.00
21 Dan Quinn 10 .40 1.00
22 Pat Riggin 1 .40 1.00
23 Charlie Simmer 16 .40 1.00
24 Ville Siren 5 .30 .75
25 Wayne Van Dorp .30 .75
NNO Large Team Photo 1.50 4.00

1989-90 Penguins Coke/Elby's

COMPLETE SET (5) 4.80 12.00
1 Phil Bourque .20 .50
2 Rob Brown .30 .75
3 Mario Lemieux 4.00 10.00
4 Kevin Stevens .75 2.00
5 Zarley Zalapski .30 .75

1989-90 Penguins Foodland

COMPLETE SET (15) 8.00 20.00
1 Rob Brown .30 .75
2 Jim Johnson .20 .50
3 Zarley Zalapski .30 .75
4 Paul Coffey .75 2.00
5 Phil Bourque .20 .50
6A Dan Quinn .30 .75
6B Gilbert Delorme SP .75 2.00
7 Kevin Stevens .75 2.00
8 Bob Errey .20 .50
9 John Cullen .30 .75
10 Mario Lemieux 4.00 10.00
11 Randy Hillier .20 .50
12 Jay Caufield .20 .50
13A Andrew McBain .20 .50
13B Troy Loney SP .75 2.00
14 Wendell Young .30 .75
15 Tom Barrasso .40 1.00

1990-91 Penguins Foodland

COMPLETE SET (15) 12.00 30.00
1 Phil Bourque 29 .08 .25
2 Paul Coffey 77 .40 1.00
3 Randy Hillier 23 .08 .25
4 Barry Pederson 10 .15 .40
5 Tom Barrasso 35 .30 .75
6 Mark Recchi 8 .75 2.00
7 Bob Johnson CO .75 2.00
8 Joe Mullen 7 .30 .75
9 Kevin Stevens 25 .60 1.50
10 John Cullen 11 .15 .40
11 Jaromir Jagr 68 10.00 25.00
12 Zarley Zalapski 33 .15 .40
13 Mario Lemieux 66 3.00 8.00
14 Tony Tanti 9 .08 .25
15 Bryan Trottier 19 .30 .75

1991-92 Penguins Coke/Elby's

COMPLETE SET (24) 10.00 25.00
1 Wendell Young .30 .75
2 Jim Paek .20 .50
3 Grant Jennings .20 .50
5 Ulf Samuelsson .40 1.00
7 Joe Mullen .40 1.00
8 Mark Recchi .75 2.00
10 Ron Francis 1.00 2.50
16 Jay Caufield .20 .50
18 Ken Priestlay .20 .50
19 Bryan Trottier .40 1.00
20 Jamie Leach .20 .50
22 Paul Stanton .20 .50
24 Troy Loney .20 .50
25 Kevin Stevens .40 1.00
28 Gord Roberts .20 .50
29 Phil Bourque .20 .50
32 Peter Taglianetti .20 .50
40 Frank Pietrangelo .30 .75
43 Jeff Daniels .20 .50
55 Larry Murphy .40 1.00
66 Mario Lemieux 2.50 6.00
68 Jaromir Jagr 3.00 8.00
NNO Scotty Bowman CO .40 1.00

1991-92 Penguins Foodland

COMPLETE SET (15) 8.00 20.00
1 Jim Paek .20 .50
2 Ulf Samuelsson .30 .75
3 Ron Francis .75 2.00
4 Mario Lemieux 3.00 8.00
5 Rick Tocchet .40 1.00
6 Joe Mullen .40 1.00
7 Troy Loney .20 .50
8 Kevin Stevens .30 .75
9 Tom Barrasso .40 1.00
10 Larry Murphy .30 .75
11 Jaromir Jagr 3.00 8.00
12 Bryan Trottier .40 1.00
13 Paul Stanton .20 .50
14 Peter Taglianetti .20 .50
15 Phil Bourque .20 .50

1991-92 Penguins Foodland Coupon Stickers

COMPLETE SET (12) 6.00 15.00
1 Bryan Trottier .30 .75
2 Joe Mullen .30 .75
3 Larry Murphy .30 .75
4 Tom Barrasso .30 .75
5 Ron Francis .60 1.50
6 Ulf Samuelsson .30 .75
7 Jaromir Jagr 2.50 6.00
8 Mario Lemieux 2.50 6.00
9 Kevin Stevens .30 .75
10 Mark Recchi .40 1.00
11 Paul Coffey .60 1.50
12 Frank Pietrangelo .30 .75

1992-93 Penguins Coke/Clark

COMPLETE SET (26) 10.00 25.00
1 Tom Barrasso .40 1.00
2 Scotty Bowman CO .60 1.50
3 Jay Caufield .20 .50
4 Jeff Daniels .20 .50
5 Bob Errey .20 .50
6 Bryan Fogarty .20 .50
7 Ron Francis .75 2.00
8 Jaromir Jagr 2.50 6.00
9 Grant Jennings .20 .50
10 Mario Lemieux 2.50 6.00
11 Troy Loney .20 .50
12 Shawn McEachern .40 1.00
13 Joe Mullen .40 1.00
14 Larry Murphy .40 1.00
15 Mike Needham .20 .50
16 Jim Paek .20 .50
17 Kjell Samuelsson .20 .50
18 Ulf Samuelsson .30 .75
19 Paul Stanton .20 .50
20 Mike Stapleton .20 .50
21 Kevin Stevens .30 .75
22 Martin Straka .40 1.00
23 Dave Tippett .20 .50
24 Rick Tocchet .50 1.25
25 Ken Wregget .50 1.25
26 Penguins Mascot .08 .25

1992-93 Penguins Foodland

COMPLETE SET (18) 6.00 15.00
1 Mario Lemieux 2.00 5.00
2 Bob Errey .20 .50
3 Jaromir Jagr 1.25 3.00
4 Rick Tocchet .40 1.00
5 Tom Barrasso .40 1.00
6 Joe Mullen .30 .75
7 Ron Francis .75 2.00
8 Troy Loney .20 .50
9 Shawn McEachern .20 .50
10 Larry Murphy .30 .75
11 Jim Paek .20 .50
12 Ulf Samuelsson .20 .50
13 Paul Stanton .20 .50
14 Kjell Samuelsson .20 .50
15 Kevin Stevens .30 .75
16 Dave Tippett .20 .50
17 Martin Straka .40 1.00
18 Penguins Mascot .08 .25

1992-93 Penguins Foodland Coupon Stickers

COMPLETE SET (12) 6.00 15.00
1 Tom Barrasso W2 .40 1.00
2 Ron Francis W1 .60 1.50
3 Jaromir Jagr W4 2.00 5.00
4 Mario Lemieux W2 2.50 6.00
5 Troy Loney W2 .20 .50
6 Shawn McEachern W4 .20 .50
7 Joe Mullen W3 .30 .75
8 Larry Murphy W4 .30 .75
9 Jim Paek W1 .20 .50
10 Ulf Samuelsson W3 .20 .50
11 Kevin Stevens W1 .30 .75
12 Rick Tocchet W3 .40 1.00

1993-94 Penguins Foodland

COMPLETE SET (25) 6.00 15.00
1 Mario Lemieux 1.50 4.00
2 Grant Jennings .15 .40
3 Ulf Samuelsson .20 .50
4 Rick Tocchet .30 .75
5 Marty McSorley .30 .75
6 Rick Kehoe ACO .08 .25
7 Doug Brown .15 .40
8 Martin Straka .30 .75
9 Jim Paek .15 .40
10 Ken Wregget .30 .75
11 Jeff Daniels .15 .40
12 Bryan Trottier .30 .75
13 Larry Murphy .30 .75
14 Ron Francis .40 1.00
15 Mike Needham .15 .40
16 Mike Ramsey .15 .40
17 Kevin Stevens .20 .50
18 Kjell Samuelsson .15 .40
19 Ed Johnston .08 .25
20 Markus Naslund .20 .50
21 Mike Stapleton .15 .40
22 Peter Taglianetti .15 .40
23 Jaromir Jagr .75 2.00
24 Tom Barrasso .30 .75
25 Joe Mullen .20 .50

1994-95 Penguins Foodland

COMPLETE SET (25) 4.80 12.00
1 Grant Jennings .10 .30
2 Greg Hawgood .10 .30
3 Shawn McEachern .20 .50
4 Len Barrie .10 .30
5 Ulf Samuelsson .20 .50
6 Joe Mullen .20 .50
7 John Cullen .20 .50
8 Mike Hudson .10 .30
9 Ron Francis .40 1.00
10 Tomas Sandstrom .20 .50
11 Eddie Johnston CO .08 .25
12 Chris Tamer .10 .30
13 Francois Leroux .10 .30
14 Luc Robitaille .40 1.00
15 Markus Naslund .20 .50
16 Ken Wregget .20 .50
17 Chris Joseph .10 .30
18 Peter Taglianetti .10 .30
19 Kevin Stevens .20 .50
20 Jim McKenzie .10 .30
21 Kjell Samuelsson .10 .30
22 Tom Barrasso .20 .50
23 Jaromir Jagr 1.50 4.00
24 Larry Murphy .30 .75
25 Martin Straka .10 .30

1995-96 Penguins Foodland

COMPLETE SET (25) 4.00 10.00
1 Ron Francis .40 1.00
2 Glen Murray .08 .25
3 Chris Wells .08 .25
4 Markus Naslund .10 .30
5 Jaromir Jagr 1.25 3.00
6 Francois Leroux .08 .25
7 Richard Park .08 .25
8 Norm Maciver .08 .25
9 Ken Wregget .20 .50
10 Tom Barrasso .20 .50
11 Rick Kehoe .08 .25
12 Sergei Zubov .20 .50
13 Joe Dziedzic .08 .25
14 Ed Patterson .08 .25
15 Tomas Sandstrom .10 .30
16 Dave Roche .08 .25
17 Petr Nedved .20 .50
18 Chris Tamer .08 .25
19 Chris Joseph .08 .25
20 Ian Moran .08 .25
21 Iceburgh (Mascot) .02 .10
22 Ed Johnston CO .08 .25
23 Mario Lemieux 1.50 4.00
24 Bryan Smolinski .10 .30
25 Dmitri Mironov .10 .30

1996-97 Penguins Tribune-Review

COMPLETE SET (8) 12.00 30.00
1 Ron Francis 1.50 4.00
2 Joe Mullen .75 2.00
3 Ulf Samuelsson .75 2.00
4 Bryan Trottier 1.25 3.00
5 Tom Barrasso .75 2.00
6 Kevin Stevens 1.25 3.00
7 Jaromir Jagr 3.00 8.00
8 Mario Lemieux 4.00 10.00

1997-98 Penguins USPS Lineup Cards

COMPLETE SET (?) 3.00 8.00
NNO Darius Kasparaitis .75 2.00
NNO Jaromir Jagr 2.00 5.00
NNO Ron Francis .75 2.00

1980-81 Pepsi-Cola Caps

COMPLETE SET (140) 100.00 200.00
1 Dan Bouchard .75 2.00
2 Guy Chouinard .75 2.00
3 Bill Clement .75 2.00
4 Randy Holt .60 1.50
5 Ken Houston .60 1.50
6 Kevin Lavallee .60 1.50
7 Don Lever .60 1.50
8 Bob MacMillan .60 1.50
9 Brad Marsh 1.00 2.50
10 Bob Murdoch .60 1.50
11 Kent Nilsson .75 2.00
12 Willi Plett .75 2.00
13 Jim Peplinski .75 2.00
14 Pekka Rautakillio .60 1.50
15 Paul Reinhart .75 2.00
16 Pat Riggin .75 2.00
17 Phil Russell .60 1.50
18 Brad Smith .60 1.50
19 Eric Vail .60 1.50
20 Bert Wilson .60 1.50
21 Glenn Anderson 1.50 4.00
22 Curt Brackenbury .60 1.50
23 Brett Callighen .60 1.50
24 Paul Coffey 7.50 15.00
25 Lee Fogolin .60 1.50
26 Matti Hagman .60 1.50
27 John Hughes .60 1.50
28 Dave Hunter .60 1.50
29 Jari Kurri 4.00 8.00
30 Ron Low .75 2.00
31 Kevin Lowe 1.00 2.50
32 Dave Lumley .60 1.50
33 Blair MacDonald .60 1.50
34 Mark Messier 12.50 25.00
35 Ed Mio .75 2.00
36 Don Murdoch .60 1.50
37 Pat Price .60 1.50
38 Dave Semenko .75 2.00
39 Risto Siltanen .60 1.50
40 Stan Weir .60 1.50
41 Keith Acton .60 1.50
42 Brian Engblom .60 1.50
43 Bob Gainey 1.25 3.00
44 Gaston Gingras .60 1.50
45 Denis Herron .75 2.00
46 Rejean Houle .60 1.50
47 Doug Jarvis .60 1.50
48 Yvon Lambert .60 1.50
49 Rod Langway 1.25 3.00
50 Guy Lapointe .75 2.00
51 Pierre Larouche 1.00 2.50
52 Pierre Mondou .60 1.50
53 Mark Napier .75 2.00
54 Chris Nilan 1.00 2.50
55 Doug Risebrough .60 1.50
56 Larry Robinson 1.50 4.00
57 Serge Savard .75 2.00
58 Steve Shutt 1.25 3.00
59 Mario Tremblay .75 2.00
60 Doug Wickenheiser .60 1.50
61 Serge Bernier .60 1.50
62 Kim Clackson .75 2.00
63 Real Cloutier .60 1.50
64 Andre Dupont .60 1.50
65 Robbie Florek .75 2.00
66 Michel Goulet 2.50 5.00
67 Jamie Hislop .60 1.50
68 Dale Hoganson .60 1.50
69 Dale Hunter 1.50 4.00
70 Pierre Lacroix .60 1.50
71 Garry Lariviere .60 1.50
72 Rich Leduc .60 1.50
73 John Paddock .75 2.00
74 Michel Plasse .75 2.00
75 Jacques Richard .60 1.50
76 Anton Stastny .75 2.00
77 Peter Stastny 3.00 6.00
78 Mark Tardif .75 2.00
79 Wally Weir .60 1.50
80 John Wensink .75 2.00
81 John Anderson .60 1.50
82 Laurie Boschman .60 1.50
83 Jiri Crha .75 2.00
84 Bill Derlago .60 1.50
85 Vitezslav Duris .60 1.50
86 Ron Ellis .75 2.00
87 Dave Farrish .60 1.50
88 Stewart Gavin .75 2.00

89 Pat Hickey .60 1.50
90 Dan Maloney .75 2.00
91 Terry Martin .60 1.50
92 Barry Melrose .75 2.00
93 Wilf Paiement .75 2.00
94 Robert Picard .60 1.50
95 Jim Rutherford 1.00 2.50
96 Rocky Saganiuk .60 1.50
97 Borje Salming 1.25 3.00
98 David Shand .60 1.50
99 Ian Turnbull .75 2.00
100 Rick Vaive 1.00 2.50
101 Brent Ashton .60 1.50
102 Ivan Boldirev .60 1.50
103 Per-Olov Brasar .60 1.50
104 Richard Brodeur 1.00 2.50
105 Jerry Butler .60 1.50
106 Colin Campbell .75 2.00
107 Curt Fraser .60 1.50
108 Thomas Gradin .75 2.00
109 Dennis Kearns .60 1.50
110 Rick Lanz .60 1.50
111 Lars Lindgren .60 1.50
112 Dave Logan .60 1.50
113 Mario Marois .60 1.50
114 Kevin McCarthy .60 1.50
115 Gerald Minor .60 1.50
116 Darcy Rota .60 1.50
117 Bobby Schmautz .60 1.50
118 Stan Smyl .75 2.00
119 Harold Snepsts 1.00 2.50
120 Tiger Williams 1.00 2.50
121 Dave Babych .75 2.00
122 Al Cameron .60 1.50
123 Scott Campbell .60 1.50
124 Dave Christian .75 2.00
125 Jude Drouin .60 1.50
126 Norm Dupont .60 1.50
127 Dan Geoffrion .60 1.50
128 Pierre Hamel .60 1.50
129 Barry Legge .60 1.50
130 Willy Lindstrom .60 1.50
131 Barry Long .60 1.50
132 Kris Manery .60 1.50
133 Jimmy Mann .75 2.00
134 Moe Mantha .60 1.50
135 Markus Mattsson .75 2.00
136 Doug Smail .75 2.00
137 Don Spring .60 1.50
138 Anders Steen .60 1.50
139 Peter Sullivan .60 1.50
140 Ron Wilson .60 1.50
NNO Plastic Circular Display 40.00 80.00

2007-08 Pepsi

COMPLETE SET (32) 25.00 50.00
1 Sidney Crosby 4.00 10.00
2 Joe Sakic 2.00 5.00
3 Nicklas Lidstrom 1.25 3.00
4 Saku Koivu 1.25 3.00
5 Daniel Alfredsson 1.25 3.00
6 Vincent Lecavalier 1.25 3.00
7 Mats Sundin 1.25 3.00
8 Patrice Bergeron 1.50 4.00
9 Rick Nash 1.25 3.00
10 Marian Gaborik 1.25 3.00
11 Jaromir Jagr 4.00 10.00
12 Simon Gagne 1.25 3.00
13 Doug Weight 1.25 3.00
14 Duncan Keith 1.00 2.50
15 Jay Bouwmeester .75 2.00
16 Rob Blake 1.25 3.00
17 Shea Weber 1.00 2.50
18 Ed Jovanovski 1.00 2.50
19 Ryan Miller 1.25 3.00
20 Miikka Kiprusoff 1.25 3.00
21 Marty Turco 1.25 3.00
22 Dwayne Roloson 1.00 2.50
23 Martin Brodeur 2.50 6.00
24 Rick DiPietro 1.00 2.50
25 Roberto Luongo 2.00 5.00
26 Jean-Sebastien Giguere 1.25 3.00
27 Ilya Kovalchuk 1.25 3.00
28 Cam Ward 1.25 3.00
29 Evgeni Malkin 2.00 5.00
30 Joe Thornton 2.00 5.00
31 Alexander Ovechkin 4.00 10.00
32 Sidney Crosby 4.00 10.00

2007-08 Pepsi 3x5 Stanley Cup Champion

COMPLETE SET (7) 6.00 15.00
1 Jean-Sebastien Giguere 1.00 2.50
2 Patrik Elias 1.00 2.50
3 Nicklas Lidstrom 1.00 2.50
4 Rob Brind' Amour 1.00 2.50
5 Chris Drury .75 2.00
6 Ryan Getzlaf 1.00 2.50
7 Mark Messier 2.00 5.00

1972-73 Philadelphia Blazers

COMPLETE SET (3) 15.00 30.00
1 Danny Lawson 5.00 10.00
2 Bernie Parent 10.00 20.00
3 Ron Plumb 5.00 10.00

1974-75 Phoenix Roadrunners WHA Pins

COMPLETE SET (9) 20.00 40.00
1 Bob Barlow 2.00 4.00
2 Cam Connor 2.00 4.00
3 Michel Cormier 2.00 4.00
4 Robbie Ftorek 6.00 12.00
5 Dave Gorman 2.00 4.00
6 John Hughes 2.00 4.00
7 Murray Koegan 2.00 4.00
8 Dennis Sobchuk 2.00 4.00
9 Howie Young 2.00 4.00

1975-76 Phoenix Roadrunners WHA

COMPLETE SET (22) 25.00 50.00
1 Serge Beaudoin 1.00 2.00
2 Jim Boyd 1.00 2.00
3 Jim Clarke 1.00 2.00
4 Cam Connors 1.00 2.00
5 Michel Cormier 1.00 2.00
6 Barry Dean 1.00 2.00
7 Robbie Ftorek 7.50 15.00
8 Dave Gorman 1.50 3.00
9 John Gray 1.00 2.00
10 Del Hall 1.00 2.00
11 Ron Huston 1.00 2.00
12 Murray Keogan 1.00 2.00
13 Gary Kurt 1.00 2.00
14 Garry Lariviere 1.00 2.00
15 Al McLeod 1.00 2.00
16 Peter NcNamee 1.00 2.00
17 John Migneault 1.00 2.00
18 Lauri Mononen 1.00 2.00
19 Jim Niekamp 1.00 2.00
20 Jack Norris 1.00 2.00
21 Pekka Rautakallio 2.00 4.00
22 Ron Serafini 1.00 2.00

1976-77 Phoenix Roadrunners WHA

COMPLETE SET (18) 25.00 50.00
1 Serge Beaudoin 1.00 2.00
2 Michel Cormier 1.00 2.00
3 Robbie Ftorek 7.50 15.00
4 Del Hall 1.00 2.00
5 Clay Hebenton 1.00 2.00
6 Andre Hinse 1.00 2.00
7 Mike Hobin 1.00 2.00
8 Frank Hughes 1.00 2.00
9 Ron Huston 1.00 2.00
10 Gary Kurt 1.00 2.00
11 Garry Lariviere 1.00 2.00
12 Bob Liddington 1.00 2.00
13 Lauri Mononen 1.00 2.00
14 Jim Niekamp 1.00 2.00
15 Pekka Rautakallio 2.00 4.00
16 Seppo Repo 2.00 4.00
17 Jerry Rollins 1.00 2.00
18 Juhani Tamminen 2.00 4.00

1991-92 Pinnacle

1 Mario Lemieux .60 1.50
2 Trevor Linden .15 .40
3 Kirk Muller .10 .25
4 Phil Housley .12 .30
5 Mike Modano .30 .75
6 Adam Oates .15 .40
7 Tom Kurvers .12 .30
8 Doug Bodger .12 .30
9 Rod Brind'Amour .12 .30
10 Mats Sundin .15 .40
11 Gary Suter .10 .25
12 Glenn Anderson .12 .30
13 Doug Wilson .12 .30
14 Stephane Richer .12 .30
15 Ray Bourque .25 .60
16 Adam Graves .12 .30
17 Luc Robitaille .15 .40
18 Steve Smith .15 .40
19 Uwe Krupp .12 .30
20 Rick Tocchet .12 .30
21 Tim Cheveldae .12 .30
22 Kay Whitmore .12 .30
23 Kelly Miller .12 .30
24 Esa Tikkanen .12 .30
25 Pat LaFontaine .15 .40
26 James Patrick .12 .30
27 Daniel Marois .12 .30
28 Denis Savard .15 .40
29 Steve Larmer .12 .30
30 Pierre Turgeon .12 .30
31 Gary Leeman .12 .30
32 Mike Ricci .10 .25
33 Troy Murray .12 .30
34 Sergio Momesso .12 .30
35 Marty McSorley .12 .30
36 Paul Ysebaert .12 .30
37 Gary Roberts .12 .30
38 Miko Hudoon .12 .30
39 Kelly Hrudey .12 .30
40 Dale Hunter .12 .30
41 Brendan Shanahan .15 .40
42 Steve Duchesne .10 .25
43 Pat Verbeek .12 .30
44 Tom Barrasso .12 .30
45 Scott Mellanby .12 .30
46 Stephen Leach .12 .30
47 Darren Turcotte .12 .30
48 Jari Kurri .12 .30
49 Michel Petit .12 .30
50 Mark Messier .30 .75
51 Terry Carkner .12 .30
52 Tim Kerr .10 .25
53 Jaromir Jagr .50 1.25
54 Joe Nieuwendyk .12 .30
55 Randy Burridge .12 .30
56 Robert Reichel .30 .75
57 Craig Janney .12 .30
58 Chris Chelios .15 .40
59 Bryan Fogarty .12 .30
60 Christian Ruuttu .12 .30
61 Steve Bozek .12 .30
62 Dave Manson .12 .30
63 Bruce Driver .12 .30
64 Mike Ramsey .12 .30
65 Bobby Holik .15 .40
66 Bob Essensa .12 .30
67 Pat Flatley .12 .30
68 Wayne Presley .12 .30
69 Mike Bullard .12 .30
70 Claude Lemieux .12 .30
71 Dave Gagner .12 .30
72 Jeff Brown .12 .30
73 Eric Desjardins .15 .40
74 Fredrik Olausson .12 .30
75 Steve Yzerman .50 1.25
76 Tony Granato .10 .25
77 Adam Burt .12 .30
78 Cam Neely .15 .40
79 Brent Sutter .12 .30
80 Dale Hawerchuk .20 .50
81 Scott Stevens .15 .40
82 Adam Creighton .12 .30
83 Brian Hayward .12 .30
84 Dan Quinn .12 .30
85 Garth Butcher .12 .30
86 Shawn Burr .12 .30
87 Peter Bondra .15 .40
88 Brad Shaw .10 .25
89 Eric Weinrich .15 .40
90 Brian Bradley .12 .30
91 Vincent Damphousse .12 .30
92 Doug Gilmour .20 .50
93 Martin Gelinas .12 .30
94 Mike Ridley .12 .30
95 Ron Sutter .12 .30
96 Mark Osborne .12 .30
97 Mikhail Tatarinov .12 .30
98 Bob McGill .12 .30
99 Bob Carpenter .12 .30
100 Wayne Gretzky 1.00 2.50
101 Slava Fetisov .12 .30
102 Shayne Corson .12 .30
103 Clint Malarchuk .12 .30
104 Randy Wood .12 .30
105 Curtis Joseph .20 .50
106 Cliff Ronning .10 .25
107 Derek King .10 .25
108 Neil Wilkinson .12 .30
109 Michel Goulet .12 .30
110 Zarley Zalapski .12 .30
111 Dave Ellett .12 .30
112 Glen Wesley .12 .30
113 Bob Kudelski .10 .25
114 Jamie Macoun .12 .30
115 John MacLean .12 .30
116 Steve Thomas .12 .30
117 Pat Elynuik .12 .30
118 Ron Hextall .15 .40
119 Jeff Hackett .12 .30
120 Jeremy Roenick .25 .60
121 John Vanbiesbrouck .15 .40
122 Dave Andreychuk .15 .40
123 Ray Ferraro .12 .30
124 Ron Tugnutt .12 .30
125 John Cullen .12 .30
126 Andy Moog .15 .40
127 Ed Belfour .40 1.00
128 Dino Ciccarelli .12 .30
129 Brian Bellows .12 .30
130 Guy Carbonneau .12 .30
131 Kevin Hatcher .12 .30
132 Mike Vernon .12 .30
133 Kevin Miller .12 .30
134 Pelle Eklund .12 .30
135 Brian Mullen .12 .30
136 Brian Leetch .12 .30
137 Daren Puppa .12 .30
138 Steven Finn .10 .25
139 Stephan Lebeau .12 .30
140 Gord Murphy .12 .30
141 Rob Brown .12 .30
142 Ken Daneyko .12 .30
143 Larry Murphy .12 .30
144 Jon Casey .12 .30
145 John Ogrodnick .12 .30
146 Benoit Hogue .12 .30
147 Mike McPhee .12 .30
148 Don Beaupre .12 .30
149 Kjell Samuelsson .12 .30
150 Joe Sakic .50 1.25
151 Mark Recchi .20 .50
152 Ulf Dahlen .12 .30
153 Dean Evason .12 .30
154 Keith Brown .12 .30
155 Ray Sheppard .12 .30
156 Owen Nolan .15 .40
157 Sergei Fedorov .25 .60
158 Kirk McLean .12 .30
159 Petr Klima .12 .30
160 Brian Skrudland .12 .30
161 Neal Broten .12 .30
162 Dimitri Khristich .12 .30
163 Alexander Mogilny .12 .30
164 Mike Richter .15 .40
165 Daniel Berthiaume .12 .30
166 Teppo Numminen .12 .30
167 Ron Francis .20 .50
168 Grant Fuhr .25 .60
169 Mike Liut .10 .25
170 Bill Ranford .12 .30
171 Garry Galley .12 .30
172 Jeff Norton .12 .30
173 Jimmy Carson .12 .30
174 Peter Zezel .10 .25
175 Patrick Roy .40 1.00
176 Joe Mullen .12 .30
177 Murray Craven .12 .30
178 Tomas Sandstrom .12 .30
179 Joel Otto .12 .30
180 Steve Konroyd .12 .30
181 Vladimir Ruzicka .12 .30
182 Paul Cavallini .12 .30
183 Bob Probert .15 .40
184 Brian Propp .12 .30
185 Glenn Healy .15 .40
186 Paul Coffey .15 .40
187 Jan Erixon .12 .30
188 Kevin Lowe .12 .30
189 Doug Lidster .12 .30
190 Theo Fleury .12 .30
191 Kevin Stevens .12 .30
192 Petr Nedved .12 .30
193 Ed Olczyk .12 .30
194 Mike Hough .12 .30
195 Rod Langway .12 .30
196 Craig Simpson .10 .25
197 Petr Svoboda .12 .30
198 David Volek .12 .30
199 Mark Tinordi .12 .30
200 Brett Hull .30 .75
201 Rob Blake .15 .40
202 Mike Gartner .20 .50
203 Ken Hodge Jr. .12 .30
204 Murray Baron .12 .30
205 Gerard Gallant .10 .25
206 Joe Murphy .12 .30
207 Al Iafrate .12 .30
208 Larry Robinson .15 .40
209 Mathieu Schneider .12 .30
210 Bobby Smith .12 .30
211 Gerald Diduck .12 .30
212 Luke Richardson .12 .30
213 Rob Zettler .12 .30
214 Brad McCrimmon .12 .30
215 Craig MacTavish .12 .30
216 Gino Cavallini .12 .30
217 Craig Wolanin .12 .30
218 Greg Adams .12 .30
219 Mike Craig .12 .30
220 Al MacInnis .20 .50
221 Sylvain Cote .12 .30
222 Bob Sweeney .10 .25
223 Dave Snuggerud .10 .25
224 Randy Ladouceur .12 .30
225 Charlie Huddy .12 .30
226 Sylvain Turgeon .12 .30
227 Phil Bourque .12 .30
228 Rob Ramage .12 .30
229 Jeff Beukeboom .12 .30
230 Alexei Gusarov RC .12 .30
231 Kelly Kisio .12 .30
232 Calle Johansson .12 .30
233 Yves Racine .12 .30
234 Peter Sidorkiewicz .12 .30
235 Jim Johnson .12 .30
236 Brent Gilchrist .12 .30
237 Jyrki Lumme .12 .30
238 Randy Gilhen .12 .30
239 Ken Baumgartner .10 .25
240 Joey Kocur .10 .25
241 Bryan Trottier .15 .40
242 Todd Krygier .12 .30
243 Darrin Shannon .12 .30
244 Dave Christian .10 .25
245 Stephane Morin .12 .30
246 Kevin Dineen .12 .30
247 Chris Terreri .12 .30
248 Craig Ludwig .12 .30
249 Dave Taylor .12 .30
250 Wendel Clark .25 .60
251 David Shaw .12 .30
252 Paul Ranheim .15 .40
253 Mark Hunter .12 .30
254 Russ Courtnall .12 .30
255 Alexei Kasatonov .10 .25
256 Randy Moller .12 .30
257 Bob Errey .12 .30
258 Curtis Leschyshyn .12 .30
259 Rick Zombo .12 .30
260 Dana Murzyn .12 .30
261 Dirk Graham .12 .30
262 Craig Muni .12 .30
263 Geoff Courtnall .12 .30
264 Todd Elik .12 .30
265 Mike Keane .10 .25
266 Peter Stastny .12 .30
267 Ulf Samuelsson .12 .30
268 Rich Sutter .12 .30
269 Mike Krushelnyski .12 .30
270 Dave Babych .12 .30
271 Sergei Makarov .12 .30
272 David Maley .12 .30
273 Normand Rochefort .12 .30
274 Gordie Roberts .12 .30
275 Thomas Steen .12 .30
276 Dave Lowry .12 .30
277 Michal Pivonka .12 .30
278 Todd Gill .12 .30
279 Paul MacDermid .12 .30
280 Brent Ashton .12 .30
281 Randy Hillier .12 .30
282 Frank Musil .12 .30
283 Geoff Smith .12 .30
284 John Tonelli .12 .30
285 Joe Reekie .12 .30
286 Greg Paslawski .12 .30
287 Perry Berezan .12 .30
288 Randy Carlyle .12 .30
289 Chris Nilan .10 .25
290 Patrik Sundstrom .12 .30
291 Garry Valk .12 .30
292 Mike Foligno .15 .40
293 Igor Larionov .12 .30
294 Jim Sandlak .12 .30
295 Tom Chorske .12 .30
296 Claude Loiselle .12 .30
297 Mark Howe .15 .40
298 Steve Chiasson .12 .30
299 Mike Donnelly RC .15 .40
300 Bernie Nicholls .12 .30
301 Tony Amonte RC .40 1.00
302 Brad May .12 .30
303 Josef Beranek RC .15 .40
304 Rob Pearson RC .15 .40
305 Andrei Lomakin .12 .30
306 Kip Miller .12 .30
307 Kevin Haller RC .15 .40
308 Kevin Todd RC .15 .40
309 Geoff Sanderson RC .15 .40
310 Doug Weight RC .40 1.00
311 Vladimir Konstantinov RC .40 1.00
312 Peter Ahola RC .15 .40
313 Claude Lapointe RC .12 .30
314 Nelson Emerson .12 .30
315 Pavel Bure .15 .40
316 Jim Waite .12 .30
317 Sergei Nemchinov .12 .30
318 Alexander Godynyuk RC .15 .40
319 Stu Barnes .12 .30
320 Nicklas Lidstrom RC 1.00 2.50
321 Darryl Sydor .12 .30
322 John LeClair RC .40 1.00
323 Arturs Irbe .12 .30
324 Russ Romaniuk RC .15 .40
325 Ken Sutton RC .15 .40
326 Bob Beers .10 .25
327 Michel Picard RC .15 .40
328 Derian Hatcher .12 .30
329 Pat Falloon .12 .30
330 Donald Audette .12 .30
331 Pat Jablonski RC .12 .30
332 Corey Foster RC .15 .40
333 Tomas Forslund RC .15 .40
334 Steven Rice .12 .30
335 Marc Bureau .12 .30
336 Kimbi Daniels RC .15 .40
337 Adam Foote RC .30 .75
338 Dan Kordic RC .12 .30
339 Link Gaetz .12 .30
340 Valeri Kamensky RC .40 1.00
341 Tom Draper RC .15 .40
342 Jayson More RC .15 .40
343 Dominic Roussel RC .15 .40
344 Jim Paek RC .15 .40
345 Felix Potvin .30 .75
346 Dan Lambert RC .12 .30
347 Louie DeBrusk RC .15 .40
348 Jamie Baker RC .12 .30
349 Scott Niedermayer .15 .40
350 Paul DiPietro RC .12 .30
351 Chris Winnes RC .12 .30
352 Mark Greig .12 .30
353 Luciano Borsato RC .15 .40
354 Valeri Zelepukin RC .15 .40
355 Martin Lapointe .12 .30
356 Brett Hull GW .30 .75
357 Steve Larmer GW .12 .30
358 Theo Fleury GW .12 .30
359 Jeremy Roenick GW .25 .60
360 Mark Recchi GW .20 .50
361 Brad Marsh .15 .40
362 Kris King .12 .30
363 Doug Brown .12 .30
364 Carey Wilson .12 .30
365 Eric Lindros .25 .60
366 Kevin Dineen GG .12 .30
367 John Vanbiesbrouck GG .15 .40
368 Ray Bourque GG .25 .60
369 Doug Wilson GG .12 .30
370 Keith Brown GG .12 .30
371 Kevin Lowe GG .12 .30
372 Kelly Miller GG .12 .30
373 Dave Taylor GG .12 .30
374 Guy Carbonneau GG .12 .30
375 Tim Hunter GG .12 .30
376 Brett Hull TECH .30 .75
377 Paul Coffey TECH .15 .40
378 Adam Oates TECH .15 .40
379 Andy Moog TECH .15 .40
380 Mario Lemieux TECH .60 1.50
381 J.Sakic/W.Gretzky 1.00 2.50
382 R.Blake/L.Robinson .15 .40
383 D.Weight/S.Yzerman .50 1.25
384 M.Richter/B.Parent .15 .40
385 L.Robitaille/M.Dionne .20 .50
386 E.Olczyk/B.Clarke .12 .30
387 P.Roy/R.Vachon .40 1.00
388 E.Belfour/T.Esposito .40 1.00
389 M.Sundin/M.Naslund .15 .40
390 T.Amonte/M.Messier .40 1.00
391 J.Cullen/R.Cullen .12 .30
392 G.Suter/B.Orr .60 1.50
393 R.Zombo/G.Resch .12 .30
394 T.Krygier/G.Perreault .12 .30
395 J.Druce/B.Gainey .12 .30
396 Bob Carpenter SL .12 .30
397 Clint Malarchuk SL .12 .30
398 Jim Kyte SL .12 .30
399 Al MacInnis SL .20 .50
400 Ed Belfour SL .40 1.00
401 Brad Marsh SL .15 .40
402 Brian Benning SL .12 .30
403 Larry Robinson SL .15 .40
404 Craig Ludwig SL .12 .30
405 Pat Flatley SL .12 .30
406 Gary Nylund SL .12 .30
407 Kjell Samuelsson SL .12 .30
408 Dan Quinn SL .12 .30
409 Garth Butcher SL .12 .30
410 Rick Zombo SL .12 .30
411 Paul Cavallini SL .12 .30
412 Link Gaetz SL .12 .30
413 Dave Hannan SL .12 .30
414 Peter Zezel SL .10 .25
415 Randy Gregg SL .12 .30
416 Pat Elynuik SL .12 .30
417 Rod Buskas SL .12 .30
418 Mark Howe SL .15 .40
419 Don Sweeney .10 .25
420 Mark Hardy .12 .30

1991-92 Pinnacle French

*FRENCH: .4X TO 1X BASIC PINNACLE

1991-92 Pinnacle B

COMPLETE SET (12) 60.00 120.00
*FRENCH: SAME VALUE
B1 Patrick Roy 8.00 20.00
B2 Ray Bourque 6.00 15.00
B3 Brian Leetch 4.00 10.00
B4 Kevin Stevens 2.50 6.00
B5 Mario Lemieux 15.00 30.00
B6 Cam Neely 4.00 10.00
B7 Bill Ranford 3.00 8.00
B8 Al MacInnis 3.00 8.00
B9 Chris Chelios 4.00 10.00
B10 Luc Robitaille 3.00 8.00
B11 Wayne Gretzky 12.00 30.00
B12 Brett Hull 5.00 12.00

1992-93 Pinnacle American Promo Panel

1 Promo Sheet
91 Andy Moog
Boston Bruins/36 Nelso 1.25 3.00

1992-93 Pinnacle Canadian Promo Panels

COMPLETE SET (3) 2.50 6.00
1 Promo Panel
Bure
Iafrate
Recchi
S.Stevens 1.25 3.00
2 Promo Panel
Brian Bradley
Tampa Bay Lightning# .75 2.00
3 Promo Panel
Doug Gilmour
Toronto Maple Leafs/ .75 2.00

1992-93 Pinnacle

*FRENCH: .4X TO 1X BASIC CARDS
1 Mark Messier .25 .60
2 Ray Bourque .20 .50
3 Gary Roberts .07 .20
4 Bill Ranford .10 .25
5 Gilbert Dionne .07 .20
6 Owen Nolan .12 .30
7 Pat LaFontaine .12 .30
8 Nicklas Lidstrom .10 .25
9 Pat Falloon .07 .20
10 Jeremy Roenick .20 .50
11 Kevin Hatcher .07 .20
12 Cliff Ronning .07 .20
13 Jeff Brown .10 .25
14 Kevin Dineen .07 .20
15 Brian Leetch .10 .25
16 Eric Desjardins .10 .25
17 Derek King .07 .20
18 Mark Tinordi .07 .20
19 Kelly Hrudey .10 .25
20 Sergei Fedorov .20 .50
21 Mike Ramsey .07 .20
22 Michel Goulet .10 .25
23 Joe Murphy .07 .20
24 Mark Fitzpatrick .10 .25
25 Cam Neely .12 .30
26 Rod Brind'Amour .07 .20
27 Neil Wilkinson .07 .20
28 Greg Adams .07 .20
29 Thomas Steen .07 .20
30 Calle Johansson .07 .20
31 Joe Nieuwendyk .10 .25
32 Rob Blake .10 .25
33 Darren Turcotte .07 .20
34 Derian Hatcher .07 .20
35 Mikhail Tatarinov .07 .20
36 Nelson Emerson .07 .20
37 Tim Cheveldae .07 .20
38 Donald Audette .10 .25
39 Brent Sutter .07 .20
40 Adam Oates .12 .30
41 Luke Richardson .10 .25
42 Jon Casey .07 .20
43 Guy Carbonneau .10 .25
44 Patrick Flatley .10 .25
45 Brian Benning .07 .20
46 Curtis Leschyshyn .10 .25
47 Trevor Linden .12 .30
48 Don Beaupre .10 .25
49 Troy Murray .07 .20
50 Paul Coffey .12 .30
51 Frank Musil .10 .25
52 Doug Wilson .10 .25
53 Pat Elynuik .07 .20
54 Curtis Joseph .15 .40
55 Tony Amonte .10 .25
56 Bob Probert .12 .30
57 Steve Smith .07 .20
58 Dave Andreychuk .12 .30
59 Vladimir Ruzicka .07 .20
60 Jari Kurri .12 .30
61 Denis Savard .12 .30
62 Benoit Hogue .07 .20
63 Terry Carkner .10 .25
64 Valeri Kamensky .07 .20
65 Jyrki Lumme .07 .20
66 Al Iafrate .10 .25
67 Paul Ranheim .07 .20
68 Ulf Dahlen .07 .20
69 Tony Granato .07 .20
70 Phil Housley .10 .25
71 Brian Lawton .10 .25
72 Garth Butcher .10 .25
73 Steve Leach .07 .20
74 Steve Larmer .07 .20
75 Mike Richter .12 .30
76 Vladimir Konstantinov .12 .30
77 Alexander Mogilny .10 .25
78 Craig MacTavish .07 .20
79 Mathieu Schneider .07 .20
80 Mark Recchi .15 .40
81 Gerald Diduck .10 .25
82 Peter Bondra .12 .30
83 Al MacInnis .15 .40
84 Bob Kudelski .10 .25
85 Dave Gagner .10 .25
86 Uwe Krupp .07 .20
87 Randy Carlyle .10 .25
88 Eric Lindros .20 .50
89 Rob Zettler .07 .20
90 Mats Sundin .12 .30
91 Andy Moog .12 .30
92 Keith Brown .10 .25
93 Paul Ysebaert .07 .20
94 Mike Gartner .15 .40
95 Kelly Buchberger .07 .20
96 Dominic Roussel .10 .25
97 Doug Bodger .07 .20
98 Mike Donnelly .07 .20
99 Mike Craig .07 .20
100 Brett Hull .25 .60
101 Robert Reichel .07 .20
102 Jeff Norton .10 .25
103 Garry Galley .07 .20
104 Dale Hunter .10 .25
105 Jeff Hackett .10 .25
106 Darrin Shannon .07 .20
107 Craig Wolanin .07 .20
108 Adam Graves .07 .20
109 Chris Chelios .12 .30
110 Pavel Bure .12 .30
111 Kirk Muller .07 .20
112 Jeff Beukeboom .07 .20
113 Mike Hough .10 .25
114 Brendan Shanahan .12 .30
115 Randy Burridge .07 .20
116 Dave Poulin .07 .20
117 Petr Svoboda .10 .25
118 Ed Belfour .12 .30
119 Ray Sheppard .07 .20
120 Bernie Nicholls .10 .25
121 Glenn Healy .10 .25
122 Johan Garpenlov .07 .20
123 Mike Lalor .10 .25
124 Brad McCrimmon .07 .20
125 Theo Fleury .20 .50
126 Randy Gilhen .07 .20
127 Petr Nedved .10 .25
128 Steve Thomas .10 .25
129 Rick Zombo .07 .20
130 Patrick Roy .30 .75
131 Rod Langway .10 .25
132 Gord Murphy .10 .25
133 Randy Wood .07 .20
134 Mike Hudson .07 .20
135 Gerard Gallant .07 .20
136 Brian Glynn .07 .20
137 Jim Johnson .10 .25
138 Corey Millen .07 .20
139 Daniel Marois .07 .20
140 James Patrick .07 .20
141 Claude Lapointe .07 .20
142 Bobby Smith .10 .25
143 Charlie Huddy .10 .25
144 Murray Baron .07 .20
145 Ed Olczyk .07 .20
146 Dimitri Khristich .07 .20
147 Doug Lidster .10 .25
148 Perry Berezan .07 .20
149 Pelle Eklund .10 .25
150 Joe Sakic .25 .60
151 Michal Pivonka .07 .20
152 Joey Kocur .07 .20
153 Patrice Brisebois .07 .20
154 Ray Ferraro .07 .20
155 Mike Modano .30 .75
156 Marty McSorley .10 .25
157 Norm Maciver .07 .20
158 Sergei Nemchinov .07 .20
159 David Bruce .07 .20
160 Kelly Miller .07 .20
161 Alexei Gusarov .07 .20
162 Andrei Lomakin .07 .20
163 Sergio Momesso .07 .20
164 Mike Keane .07 .20
165 Pierre Turgeon .10 .25
166 Martin Gelinas .07 .20
167 Chris Dahlquist .10 .25
168 Kris King .07 .20
169 Dean Evason .07 .20
170 Mike Ridley .07 .20
171 Shawn Burr .07 .20
172 Dana Murzyn .07 .20
173 Dirk Graham .07 .20
174 Trent Yawney .10 .25
175 Luc Robitaille .12 .30
176 Randy Moller .07 .20
177 Vincent Riendeau .10 .25
178 Brian Propp .07 .20
179 Don Sweeney .07 .20
180 Stephane Matteau .07 .20
181 Garry Valk .07 .20
182 Sylvain Cote .10 .25
183 Dave Snuggerud .07 .20
184 Gary Leeman .07 .20
185 John Druce .07 .20
186 John Vanbiesbrouck .12 .30
187 Geoff Courtnall .07 .20
188 David Volek .07 .20
189 Doug Weight .25 .60
190 Bob Essensa .10 .25
191 Jan Erixon .10 .25
192 Geoff Smith .07 .20
193 Dave Christian .07 .20
194 Brian Noonan .07 .20
195 Gary Suter .07 .20
196 Craig Janney .10 .25
197 Brad May .07 .20
198 Gaetan Duchesne .07 .20
199 Adam Creighton .07 .20
200 Wayne Gretzky .75 2.00
201 Dave Babych .10 .25
202 Fredrik Olausson .07 .20
203 Bob Bassen .07 .20
204 Todd Krygier .10 .25
205 Grant Ledyard .07 .20
206 Michel Petit .07 .20
207 Todd Elik .07 .20
208 Josef Beranek .07 .20
209 Neal Broten .10 .25
210 Jim Sandlak .07 .20
211 Kevin Haller .07 .20
212 Paul Broten .07 .20
213 Mark Pederson .07 .20
214 John McIntyre .07 .20
215 Teppo Numminen .07 .20
216 Ken Sutton .07 .20
217 Ronnie Stern .10 .25
218 Luciano Borsato .07 .20
219 Claude Loiselle .07 .20
220 Mark Hardy .10 .25
221 Joe Juneau .07 .20
222 Keith Tkachuk .12 .30
223 Scott Lachance .07 .20
224 Glen Murray .10 .25
225 Igor Kravchuk .07 .20
226 Evgeny Davydov .07 .20
227 Ray Whitney RC .20 .50
228 Bret Hedican RC .10 .25
229 Keith Carney RC .25 .60
230 Slava Kozlov .10 .25
231 Drake Berehowsky .07 .20
232 Cam Neely SL .12 .30
233 Doug Gilmour SL .15 .40
234 Randy Wood SL .07 .20
235 Luke Richardson SL .10 .25
236 Eric Lindros SL .20 .50
237 Dale Hunter SL .10 .25
238 Pat Falloon SL .07 .20
239 Dean Kennedy SL .10 .25
240 Uwe Krupp SL .07 .20
241 S.Niedermayer/S.Yzerman .30 .75
242 Gary Roberts IDOL (Lanny McDonald) .07 .20
243 Peter Ahola IDOL (Jari Kurri) .12 .30
244 Scott Lachance IDOL (Mark Howe) .12 .30
245 R.Pearson/M.Bossy .12 .30
246 Kirk McLean IDOL (Bernie Parent) .15 .40
247 Dmitri Mironov IDOL (Viacheslav Fetisov) .07 .20
248 Brendan Shanahan IDOL (Darryl Sittler) .15 .40
249 P.Nedved/W.Gretzky .75 2.00
250 Todd Ewen IDOL (Clark Gillies .12 .30
251 Luc Robitaille GG .12 .30
252 Mark Tinordi GG .07 .20
253 Kris King GG .07 .20
254 Pat LaFontaine GG .12 .30
255 Ryan Walter GG .10 .25
256 Jeremy Roenick GW .20 .50

257 Brett Hull GW	.25	.60
258 Steve Yzerman GW	.30	.75
259 Claude Lemieux GW	.07	.20
260 Mike Modano GW	.30	.75
261 Vincent Damphousse GW	.10	.25
262 Tony Granato GW	.07	.20
263 Andy Moog MASK	.12	.30
264 Curtis Joseph MASK	.15	.40
265 Ed Belfour MASK	.12	.30
266 Brian Hayward MASK	.07	.20
267 Grant Fuhr MASK	.20	.50
268 Don Beaupre MASK	.10	.25
269 Tim Cheveldae MASK	.07	.20
270 Mike Richter MASK	.12	.30
271 Zarley Zalapski	.07	.20
272 Kevin Todd	.07	.20
273 Dave Ellett	.07	.20
274 Chris Terreri	.10	.25
275 Jaromir Jagr	.25	.60
276 Wendel Clark	.20	.50
277 Bobby Holik	.10	.25
278 Bruce Driver	.07	.20
279 Doug Gilmour	.15	.40
280 Scott Stevens	.12	.30
281 Murray Craven	.07	.20
282 Rick Tocchet	.10	.25
283 Peter Zezel	.07	.20
284 Claude Lemieux	.07	.20
285 John Cullen	.07	.20
286 Valeri Zelepukin	.07	.20
287 Rob Pearson	.07	.20
288 Kevin Stevens	.10	.25
289 Alexei Kasatonov	.07	.20
290 Todd Gill	.07	.20
291 Randy Ladouceur	.07	.20
292 Larry Murphy	.10	.25
293 Tom Chorske	.10	.25
294 Jamie Macoun	.10	.25
295 Sean Burke	.10	.25
296 Ulf Samuelsson	.07	.20
297 Eric Weinrich	.07	.20
298 Tom Barrasso	.10	.25
299 Slava Fetisov	.07	.20
300 Mario Lemieux	.50	1.25
301 Grant Fuhr	.20	.50
302 Zdeno Ciger	.07	.20
303 Ron Francis	.15	.40
304 Scott Niedermayer	.12	.30
305 Mark Osborne	.07	.20
306 Kjell Samuelsson	.10	.25
307 Geoff Sanderson	.10	.25
308 Paul Stanton	.07	.20
309 Frank Pietrangelo	.10	.25
310 Bob Errey	.10	.25
311 Dino Ciccarelli	.10	.25
312 Gordie Roberts	.10	.25
313 Kevin Miller	.07	.20
314 Mike Ricci	.07	.20
315 Bob Carpenter	.10	.25
316 Dale Hawerchuk	.15	.40
317 Christian Ruuttu	.07	.20
318 Mike Vernon	.10	.25
319 Paul Cavallini	.07	.20
320 Steve Duchesne	.07	.20
321 Craig Simpson	.07	.20
322 Mark Howe	.12	.30
323 Shayne Corson	.10	.25
324 Tom Kurvers	.07	.20
325 Brian Bellows	.10	.25
326 Glen Wesley	.07	.20
327 Daren Puppa	.10	.25
328 Joel Otto	.07	.20
329 Jimmy Carson	.07	.20
330 Kirk McLean	.07	.20
331 Rob Brown	.07	.20
332 Yves Racine	.07	.20
333 Brian Mullen	.07	.20
334 Dave Manson	.07	.20
335 Sergei Makarov	.07	.20
336 Esa Tikkanen	.07	.20
337 Russ Courtnall	.07	.20
338 Kevin Lowe	.10	.25
339 Steve Chiasson	.07	.20
340 Ron Hextall	.12	.30
341 Stephan Lebeau	.07	.20
342 Mike McPhee	.07	.20
343 David Shaw	.10	.25
344 Petr Klima	.07	.20
345 Tomas Sandstrom	.10	.25
346 Scott Mellanby	.07	.20
347 Brian Skrudland	.10	.25
348 Pat Verbeek	.07	.20
349 Vincent Damphousse	.10	.25
350 Steve Yzerman	.30	.75
351 John MacLean	.10	.25
352 Steve Konroyd	.10	.25
353 Phil Bourque	.07	.20
354 Ken Daneyko	.07	.20
355 Glenn Anderson	.10	.25
356 Ken Wregget	.10	.25
357 Brent Gilchrist	.07	.20
358 Bob Rouse	.10	.25
359 Peter Stastny	.10	.25
360 Joe Mullen	.10	.25
361 Stephane Richer	.10	.25
362 Kelly Kisio	.10	.25
363 Keith Acton	.10	.25
364 Felix Potvin	.25	.60
365 Martin Lapointe	.07	.20
366 Ron Tugnutt	.10	.25
367 Dave Taylor	.10	.25
368 Tim Kerr	.07	.20
369 Carey Wilson	.10	.25
370 Greg Paslawski	.07	.20
371 Peter Sidorkiewicz	.07	.20
372 Brad Shaw	.07	.20
373 Sylvain Turgeon	.07	.20
374 Mark Lamb	.07	.20
375 Laurie Boschman	.07	.20
376 Mark Osiecki	.10	.25
377 Doug Smail	.07	.20
378 Brad Marsh	.10	.25
379 Mike Peluso	.10	.25
380 Steve Weeks	.07	.20
381 Wendell Young	.10	.25
382 Joe Reekie	.07	.20
383 Peter Taglianetti	.10	.25
384 Mikael Andersson	.07	.20
385 Marc Bergevin	.10	.25
386 Anatoli Semenov	.07	.20
387 Brian Bradley	.07	.20
388 Michel Mongeau	.10	.25
389 Rob Ramage	.07	.20
390 Ken Hodge Jr.	.07	.20
391 Richard Matvichuk RC	.10	.25
392 Alexei Zhitnik	.07	.20
393 Richard Smehlik RC	.07	.20
394 Dimitri Yushkevich RC	.07	.20
395 Andrei Kovalenko RC	.20	.50
396 Vladimir Vujtek RC	.07	.20
397 Nikolai Borschevsky RC	.07	.20
398 Vitali Karamnov RC	.07	.20
399 Jim Hiller RC	.07	.20
400 Michael Nylander RC	.07	.20
401 Tommy Sjodin RC	.07	.20
402 Robert Petrovicky RC	.07	.20
403 Alexei Kovalev	.10	.25
404 Vitali Prokhorov RC	.07	.20
405 Dmitri Kvartalnov RC	.07	.20
406 Teemu Selanne	.25	.60
407 Darius Kasparaitis	.07	.20
408 Roman Hamrlik RC	.25	.60
409 Vladimir Malakhov	.07	.20
410 Sergei Krivokrasov	.07	.20
411 Robert Lang RC	.07	.20
412 Jozef Stumpel	.07	.20
413 Denny Felsner RC	.10	.25
414 Rob Zamuner RC	.10	.25
415 Jason Woolley RC	.07	.20
416 Alexei Zhamnov	.10	.25
417 Igor Korolev RC	.07	.20
418 Patrick Poulin	.07	.20
419 Dmitri Mironov	.07	.20
420 Shawn McEachern	.07	.20

1992-93 Pinnacle Team 2000

*FRENCH: 1X TO 1.25X BASIC CARDS

1 Eric Lindros	.30	.75
2 Mike Modano	.50	1.25
3 Nicklas Lidstrom	.15	.40
4 Tony Amonte	.15	.40
5 Felix Potvin	.40	1.00
6 Scott Lachance	.12	.30
7 Mats Sundin	.20	.50
8 Pavel Bure	.20	.50
9 Eric Desjardins	.15	.40
10 Owen Nolan	.20	.50
11 Dominic Roussel	.15	.40
12 Scott Niedermayer	.20	.50
13 Slava Kozlov	.15	.40
14 Patrick Poulin	.12	.30
15 Jaromir Jagr	.40	1.00
16 Rob Blake	.15	.40
17 Pierre Turgeon	.15	.40
18 Rod Brind'Amour	.12	.30
19 Joe Juneau	.12	.30
20 Tim Cheveldae	.12	.30
21 Joe Sakic	.40	1.00
22 Kevin Todd	.12	.30
23 Rob Pearson	.12	.30
24 Trevor Linden	.20	.50
25 Dimitri Khristich	.12	.30
26 Pat Falloon	.12	.30
27 Jeremy Roenick	.30	.75
28 Alexander Mogilny	.15	.40
29 Gilbert Dionne	.12	.30
30 Sergei Fedorov	.30	.75

1992-93 Pinnacle Team Pinnacle

*FRENCH: .4X TO 1X BASIC INSERTS

1 M.Richter/E.Belfour	2.50	6.00
2 R.Bourque/C.Chelios	2.00	5.00
3 B.Leeth/P.Coffey	3.00	8.00
4 K.Stevens/P.Bure	2.50	6.00
5 E.Lindros/W.Gretzky	4.00	10.00
6 J.Jagr/B.Hull	3.00	8.00

1992-93 Pinnacle Eric Lindros

COMPLETE SET (30)	4.80	12.00
1 St. Michael's Buzzers	.30	.75
2 Detroit Compuware	.20	.50
3 Oshawa Generals (Skatin	.20	.50
4 Oshawa Generals (Red je	.20	.50
5 Oshawa Generals (Passin	.20	.50
6 Oshawa Generals (Slidin	.20	.50
7 Memorial Cup	.20	.50
8 World Junior Championsh	.20	.50
9 World Junior Championsh	.20	.50
10 World Junior Championship	.40	1.00
11 Canada Cup	.40	1.00
12 Canada Cup	.20	.50
13 Canadian National Team (In action& black eye vis	.40	1.00
14 Canadian National Team (White jersey& arms raise	.40	1.00
15 Canadian National Team	.20	.50
16 Canadian National Team	.20	.50
17 First-Round Draft Pick	.20	.50
18 Trade To Philadelphia	.20	.50
19 Happy Flyer	.20	.50
20 Preseason Action (White	.20	.50
21 Preseason Action (Black	.20	.50
22 Regular Season Debut	.20	.50
23 First NHL Goal	.20	.50
24 Winning Home Debut	.20	.50
25 First NHL Hat Trick	.20	.50
26 Playing Golf	.20	.50
27 Backyard Fun	.20	.50
28 Fan Favorite	.20	.50
29 Welcome To Philly	.20	.50
30 Philly Hero	.40	1.00

1993-94 Pinnacle I Samples

COMPLETE SET (6)	1.50	4.00
1 Tony Amonte	.10	.30
2 Tom Barrasso	.02	.10
3 Joe Juneau	.08	.25
4 Eric Lindros	.75	2.00
5 Teemu Selanne	.60	1.50
6 Mats Sundin	.20	.50

1993-94 Pinnacle II Samples

COMPLETE SEALED SET (11)	4.00	10.00
275 Brian Leetch	.01	.05
280 Guy Carbonneau	.01	.05
300 Pat LaFontaine	.01	.05
320 Pavel Bure	.08	.25
340 Terry Yake	.01	.05
341 Brian Benning	.01	.05
0 World Jr. Championship	.30	.75
NF9 Alexander Mogilny	1.25	3.00
SR1 Alexandre Daigle	.20	.50
NNO Ad Card	.20	.50
NNO Winner Card	.60	1.50

1993-94 Pinnacle

1 Eric Lindros	.25	.60
2 Mats Sundin	.15	.40
3 Tom Barrasso	.12	.30
4 Teemu Selanne	.30	.75
5 Joe Juneau	.10	.25
6 Tony Amonte	.12	.30
7 Bob Probert	.15	.40
8 Chris Kontos	.10	.25
9 Geoff Sanderson	.12	.30
10 Alexander Mogilny	.12	.30
11 Kevin Lowe	.10	.25
12 Nikolai Borschevsky	.10	.25
13 Dale Hunter	.10	.25
14 Gary Suter	.10	.25
15 Curtis Joseph	.20	.50
16 Mark Tinordi	.10	.25
17 Doug Weight	.12	.30
18 Benoit Hogue	.10	.25
19 Tommy Soderstrom	.12	.30
20 Pat Falloon	.10	.25
21 Jyrki Lumme	.10	.25
22 Brian Bellows	.12	.30
23 Alexei Zhitnik	.10	.25
24 Dirk Graham	.10	.25
25 Scott Stevens	.15	.40
26 Adam Foote	.10	.25
27 Mike Gartner	.20	.50
28 Dallas Drake RC	.15	.40
29 Ulf Samuelsson	.10	.25
30 Cam Neely	.15	.40
31 Sean Burke	.10	.25
32 Petr Svoboda	.10	.25
33 Keith Tkachuk	.15	.40
34 Roman Hamrlik	.10	.25
35 Robert Reichel	.10	.25
36 Igor Kravchuk	.10	.25
37 Mathieu Schneider	.10	.25
38 Bob Kudelski	.10	.25
39 Jeff Brown	.10	.25
40 Mike Modano	.25	.60
41 Rob Gaudreau RC	.15	.40
42 Dave Andreychuk	.15	.40
43 Trevor Linden	.15	.40
44 Dimitri Khristich	.10	.25
45 Joe Murphy	.10	.25
46 Rob Blake	.12	.30
47 Alexander Semak	.10	.25
48 Ray Ferraro	.10	.25
49 Curtis Leschyshyn	.10	.25
50 Mark Recchi	.20	.50
51 Sergei Nemchinov	.10	.25
52 Larry Murphy	.12	.30
53 Steve Heinze	.10	.25
54 Sergei Fedorov	.25	.60
55 Gary Roberts	.10	.25
56 Alexei Zhamnov	.12	.30
57 Derian Hatcher	.10	.25
58 Kelly Buchberger	.10	.25
59 Eric Desjardins	.12	.30
60 Brian Bradley	.10	.25
61 Patrick Poulin	.10	.25
62 Scott Lachance	.10	.25
63 Johan Garpenlov	.10	.25
64 Sylvain Turgeon	.10	.25
65 Grant Fuhr	.25	.60
66 Garth Butcher	.10	.25
67 Michal Pivonka	.10	.25
68 Todd Gill	.10	.25
69 Cliff Ronning	.10	.25
70 Steve Smith	.10	.25
71 Bobby Holik	.10	.25
72 Garry Galley	.10	.25
73 Steve Leach	.10	.25
74 Ron Francis	.20	.50
75 Jari Kurri	.15	.40
76 Alexei Kovalev	.12	.30
77 Dave Gagner	.12	.30
78 Steve Duchesne	.10	.25
79 Theo Fleury	.10	.25
80 Paul Coffey	.15	.40
81 Bill Ranford	.12	.30
82 Doug Bodger	.10	.25
83 Nick Kypreos	.10	.25
84 Darius Kasparaitis	.10	.25
85 Vincent Damphousse	.12	.30
86 Arturs Irbe	.12	.30
87 Shawn Chambers	.10	.25
88 Murray Craven	.10	.25
89 Rob Pearson	.10	.25
90 Kevin Hatcher	.10	.25
91 Brent Sutter	.10	.25
92 Teppo Numminen	.10	.25
93 Shawn Burr	.10	.25
94 Valeri Zelepukin	.10	.25
95 Ron Sutter	.10	.25
96 Craig MacTavish	.10	.25
97 Dominic Roussel	.12	.30
98 Nicklas Lidstrom	.15	.40
99 Adam Graves	.10	.25
100 Doug Gilmour	.20	.50
101 Frank Musil	.10	.25
102 Ted Donato	.10	.25
103 Andrew Cassels	.10	.25
104 Vladimir Malakhov	.10	.25
105 Shawn McEachern	.10	.25
106 Petr Nedved	.10	.25
107 Calle Johansson	.10	.25
108 Rich Sutter	.10	.25
109 Evgeny Davydov	.10	.25
110 Mike Ricci	.10	.25
111 Scott Niedermayer	.15	.40
112 John LeClair	.15	.40
113 Darryl Sydor	.10	.25
114 Paul DiPietro	.10	.25
115 Stephane Fiset	.12	.30
116 Christian Ruuttu	.10	.25
117 Doug Zmolek	.10	.25
118 Bob Sweeney	.10	.25
119 Brent Fedyk	.10	.25
120 Norm Maciver	.10	.25
121 Rob Zamuner	.10	.25
122 Brian Mullen	.10	.25
123 Trent Yawney	.10	.25
124 David Shaw	.10	.25
125 Mark Messier	.30	.75
126 Kevin Miller	.10	.25
127 Dino Ciccarelli	.12	.30
128 Derek King	.10	.25
129 Scott Young	.10	.25
130 Craig Janney	.12	.30
131 Jamie Macoun	.10	.25
132 Geoff Courtnall	.10	.25
133 Bob Essensa	.12	.30
134 Ken Daneyko	.10	.25
135 Mike Ridley	.10	.25
136 Stephan Lebeau	.10	.25
137 Tony Granato	.10	.25
138 Kay Whitmore	.10	.25
139 Luke Richardson	.10	.25
140 Jeremy Roenick	.25	.60
141 Brad May	.12	.30
142 Sandis Ozolinsh	.10	.25
143 Stephane Richer	.12	.30
144 John Tucker	.10	.25
145 Luc Robitaille	.15	.40
146 Dimitri Yushkevich	.10	.25
147 Sean Hill	.10	.25
148 John Vanbiesbrouck	.15	.40
149 Kevin Stevens	.12	.30
150 Patrick Roy	.40	1.00
151 Owen Nolan	.15	.40
152 Richard Smehlik	.10	.25
153 Ray Sheppard	.12	.30
154 Ed Olczyk	.10	.25
155 Al MacInnis	.20	.50
156 Sergei Zubov	.12	.30
157 Wendel Clark	.25	.60
158 Kirk McLean	.12	.30
159 Thomas Steen	.10	.25
160 Pierre Turgeon	.12	.30
161 Dmitri Kvartalnov	.10	.25
162 Brian Noonan	.10	.25
163 Mike McPhee	.10	.25
164 Peter Bondra	.15	.40
165 Bernie Nicholls	.12	.30
166 Michael Nylander	.10	.25
167 Guy Hebert	.12	.30
168 Scott Mellanby	.12	.30
169 Bob Bassen	.10	.25
170 Rod Brind'Amour	.12	.30
171 Andrei Kovalenko	.10	.25
172 Mike Donnelly	.10	.25
173 Steve Thomas	.10	.25
174 Rick Tocchet	.12	.30
175 Steve Yzerman	.40	1.00
176 Dixon Ward	.10	.25
177 Randy Wood	.10	.25
178 Dean Kennedy	.10	.25
179 Joel Otto	.10	.25
180 Kirk Muller	.10	.25
181 Chris Chelios	.15	.40
182 Richard Matvichuk	.10	.25
183 John MacLean	.12	.30
184 Joe Kocur	.10	.25
185 Adam Oates	.15	.40
186 Bob Beers	.10	.25
187 Ron Tugnutt	.12	.30
188 Brian Skrudland	.10	.25
189 Al Iafrate	.10	.25
190 Felix Potvin	.30	.75
191 David Reid	.10	.25
192 Jim Johnson	.10	.25
193 Kevin Haller	.10	.25
194 Steve Chiasson	.10	.25
195 Jaromir Jagr	.50	1.25
196 Martin Rucinsky	.10	.25
197 Sergei Bautin	.10	.25
198 Joe Nieuwendyk	.12	.30
199 Gilbert Dionne	.10	.25
200 Brett Hull	.30	.75
201 Yuri Khmylev	.10	.25
202 Todd Elik	.10	.25
203 Patrick Flatley	.10	.25
204 Martin Straka	.10	.25
205 Brendan Shanahan	.15	.40
206 Mark Beaufait RC	.15	.40
207 Mike Lenarduzzi RC	.10	.25
208 Chris LiPuma	.10	.25
209 Andre Faust	.10	.25
210 Ben Hankinson RC	.10	.25
211 Darrin Madeley RC	.15	.40
212 Oleg Petrov	.10	.25
213 Philippe Boucher	.10	.25
214 Tyler Wright	.10	.25
215 Jason Bowen RC	.15	.40
216 Matthew Barnaby	.12	.30
217 Bryan Smolinski	.10	.25
218 Dan Keczmer	.10	.25
219 Chris Simon RC	.15	.40
220 Corey Hirsch	.12	.30
221 Mario Lemieux AW	.60	1.50
222 Teemu Selanne AW	.30	.75
223 Chris Chelios AW	.15	.40
224 Ed Belfour AW	.15	.40
225 Pierre Turgeon AW	.12	.30
226 Doug Gilmour AW	.20	.50
227 Ed Belfour AW	.15	.40
228 Patrick Roy AW	.40	1.00
229 Dave Poulin AW	.10	.25
230 Mario Lemieux AW	.60	1.50
231 Mike Vernon HH	.12	.30
232 Vincent Damphousse HH	.12	.30
233 Chris Chelios HH	.15	.40
234 Cliff Ronning HH	.10	.25
235 Mark Howe HH	.15	.40
236 Alexandre Daigle	.10	.25
237 Wayne Gretzky NT	1.00	2.50
238 Mark Messier NT	.30	.75
239 Dino Ciccarelli	.12	.30
240 Joe Mullen	.12	.30
241 Mike Gartner	.20	.50
242 Mike Richter	.15	.40
243 Pat Verbeek	.10	.25
244 Valeri Kamensky	.12	.30
245 Nelson Emerson	.10	.25
246 James Patrick	.10	.25
247 Greg Adams	.10	.25
248 Ulf Dahlen	.10	.25
249 Shayne Corson	.12	.30
250 Ray Bourque	.25	.60
251 Claude Lemieux	.10	.25
252 Kelly Hrudey	.12	.30
253 Patrice Brisebois	.10	.25
254 Mark Howe	.15	.40
255 Ed Belfour	.15	.40
256 Pelle Eklund	.10	.25
257 Zarley Zalapski	.10	.25
258 Sylvain Cote	.10	.25
259 Uwe Krupp	.10	.25
260 Dale Hawerchuk	.20	.50
261 Alexei Gusarov	.10	.25
262 Dave Ellett	.10	.25
263 Tomas Sandstrom	.10	.25
264 Vladimir Konstantinov	.12	.30
265 Paul Ranheim	.10	.25
266 Darrin Shannon	.10	.25
267 Chris Terreri	.12	.30
268 Russ Courtnall	.10	.25
269 Don Sweeney	.10	.25
270 Kevin Todd	.10	.25
271 Brad Shaw	.10	.25
272 Adam Creighton	.10	.25
273 Dana Murzyn	.10	.25
274 Donald Audette	.10	.25
275 Brian Leetch	.12	.30
276 Kevin Dineen	.10	.25
277 Bruce Driver	.10	.25
278 Jim Paek	.10	.25
279 Esa Tikkanen	.10	.25
280 Guy Carbonneau	.10	.25
281 Eric Weinrich	.10	.25
282 Tim Cheveldae	.12	.30
283 Bryan Marchment	.10	.25
284 Kelly Miller	.10	.25
285 Jimmy Carson	.10	.25
286 Terry Carkner	.10	.25
287 Mike Sullivan	.10	.25
288 Joe Reekie	.10	.25
289 Bob Rouse	.10	.25
290 Joe Sakic	.30	.75
291 Gerald Diduck	.10	.25
292 Don Beaupre	.12	.30
293 Kjell Samuelsson	.10	.25
294 Claude Lapointe	.10	.25
295 Tie Domi	.12	.30
296 Charlie Huddy	.10	.25
297 Peter Zezel	.10	.25
298 Craig Muni	.10	.25
299 Rick Tabaracci	.10	.25
300 Pat LaFontaine	.15	.40
301 Lyle Odelein	.10	.25
302 Jocelyn Lemieux	.10	.25
303 Craig Ludwig	.10	.25
304 Marc Bergevin	.10	.25
305 Bill Guerin	.15	.40
306 Rick Zombo	.10	.25
307 Steven Finn	.10	.25
308 Gino Odjick	.10	.25
309 Jeff Beukeboom	.10	.25
310 Mario Lemieux	.60	1.50
311 J.J. Daigneault	.10	.25
312 Vincent Riendeau	.10	.25
313 Adam Burt	.10	.25
314 Mike Craig	.10	.25
315 Bret Hedican	.10	.25
316 Kris King	.10	.25
317 Sylvain Lefebvre	.10	.25
318 Troy Murray	.10	.25
319 Gordie Roberts	.10	.25
320 Pavel Bure	.15	.40
321 Marc Bureau	.10	.25
322 Randy McKay	.10	.25
323 Mark Lamb	.10	.25
324 Brian Mullen	.10	.25
325 Ken Wregget	.10	.25
326 Stephane Quintal	.10	.25
327 Robert Dirk	.10	.25
328 Mike Krushelnyski	.10	.25
329 Mikael Andersson	.10	.25
330 Paul Stanton	.10	.25
331 Phil Bourque	.10	.25
332 Andre Racicot	.10	.25
333 Brad Dalgarno	.10	.25
334 Neal Broten	.12	.30
335 John Blue	.12	.30
336 Ken Sutton	.10	.25
337 Greg Paslawski	.10	.25
338 Robb Stauber	.10	.25
339 Mike Keane	.10	.25
340 Terry Yake	.10	.25
341 Brian Benning	.10	.25
342 Brian Propp	.10	.25
343 Frank Pietrangelo	.12	.30
344 Stephane Matteau	.10	.25
345 Steven King	.10	.25
346 Joe Cirella	.10	.25
347 Andy Moog	.15	.40
348 Paul Ysebaert	.10	.25
349 Petr Klima	.10	.25
350 Corey Millen	.10	.25
351 Phil Housley	.12	.30
352 Craig Billington	.12	.30
353 Jeff Norton	.10	.25
354 Neil Wilkinson	.10	.25
355 Doug Lidster	.10	.25
356 Steve Larmer	.12	.30
357 Jon Casey	.12	.30
358 Brad McCrimmon	.10	.25
359 Alexei Kasatonov	.10	.25
360 Andrei Lomakin	.10	.25
361 Daren Puppa	.10	.25
362 Sergei Makarov	.10	.25
363 Dave Manson	.10	.25
364 Jim Sandlak	.10	.25
365 Glenn Healy	.12	.30
366 Martin Gelinas	.10	.25
367 Igor Larionov	.10	.25
368 Anatoli Semenov	.10	.25
369 Mark Fitzpatrick	.10	.25
370 Paul Cavallini	.10	.25
371 Jimmy Waite	.12	.30
372 Yves Racine	.10	.25
373 Jeff Hackett	.10	.25
374 Marty McSorley	.12	.30
375 Scott Pearson	.10	.25
376 Ron Hextall	.15	.40
377 Gaetan Duchesne	.10	.25
378 Jamie Baker	.10	.25
379 Troy Loney	.10	.25
380 Gord Murphy	.10	.25
381 Peter Sidorkiewicz	.10	.25
382 Pat Elynuik	.10	.25
383 Glen Wesley	.10	.25
384 Dean Evason	.10	.25
385 Mike Peluso	.10	.25
386 Darren Turcotte	.10	.25
387 Dave Poulin	.10	.25
388 John Cullen	.10	.25
389 Randy Ladouceur	.10	.25
390 Tom Fitzgerald	.10	.25
391 Denis Savard	.15	.40
392 Fredrik Olausson	.10	.25
393 Sergio Momesso	.10	.25
394 Mike Ramsey	.10	.25
395 Kelly Kisio	.10	.25
396 Craig Simpson	.10	.25
397 Slava Fetisov	.10	.25
398 Glenn Anderson	.12	.30
399 Michel Goulet	.10	.25
400 Wayne Gretzky	1.00	2.50
401 Stu Grimson	.10	.25
402 Mike Hough	.10	.25
403 Dominik Hasek	.25	.60
404 Gerard Gallant	.10	.25
405 Greg Gilbert	.10	.25
406 Vladimir Ruzicka	.10	.25
407 Jim Hrivnak	.10	.25
408 Dave Lowry	.10	.25
409 Todd Ewen	.10	.25
410 Bob Errey	.10	.25
411 Bryan Trottier	.15	.40
412 Dave Taylor	.10	.25
413 Grant Ledyard	.10	.25
414 Chris Dahlquist	.10	.25
415 Brent Gilchrist	.10	.25
416 Geoff Smith	.10	.25
417 Jiri Slegr	.10	.25
418 Randy Burridge	.10	.25
419 Sergei Krivokrasov	.10	.25
420 Keith Primeau	.12	.30
421 Robert Kron	.10	.25
422 Keith Brown	.10	.25
423 David Volek	.10	.25
424 Josef Beranek	.10	.25
425 Wayne Presley	.10	.25
426 Stu Barnes	.10	.25
427 Milos Holan RC	.15	.40
428 Jeff Shantz	.10	.25
429 Brent Gretzky RC	.15	.40
430 Jarkko Varvio	.10	.25
431 Chris Osgood RC	1.00	2.50
432 Aaron Ward RC	.15	.40
433 Jason Smith RC	.10	.25
434 Cam Stewart RC	.15	.40
435 Derek Plante RC	.15	.40
436 Pat Peake	.10	.25
437 Alexander Karpovtsev	.10	.25
438 Jim Montgomery RC	.15	.40
439 Rob Niedermayer	.12	.30
440 Jocelyn Thibault RC	.15	.40
441 Jason Arnott RC	.30	.75
442 Mike Rathje	.10	.25
443 Chris Gratton	.12	.30
444 Vesa Viitakoski RC	.15	.40
445 Alexei Kudashov RC	.15	.40
446 Pavol Demitra	.20	.50
447 Ted Drury	.10	.25
448 Rene Corbet RC	.15	.40
449 Markus Naslund	.15	.40
450 Dmitri Filimonov	.10	.25
451 Roman Oksiuta RC	.15	.40
452 Michal Sykora RC	.15	.40
453 Greg Johnson	.10	.25
454 Mikael Renberg	.15	.40
455 Alexei Yashin	.12	.30
456 Chris Pronger	.15	.40
457 Manny Fernandez RC	.15	.40
458 Jamie Storr RC	.15	.40
459 Chris Armstrong RC	.15	.40
460 Drew Bannister RC	.10	.25
461 Joel Bouchard RC	.15	.40
462 Bryan McCabe RC	.15	.40
463 Nick Stajduhar RC	.15	.40
464 Brent Tully	.12	.30
465 Brendan Witt RC	.15	.40
466 Jason Allison RC	.15	.40
467 Jason Botterill RC	.15	.40
468 Curtis Bowen RC	.15	.40
469 Anson Carter RC	.15	.40
470 Brandon Convery RC	.15	.40
471 Yanick Dube RC	.15	.40
472 Jeff Friesen RC	.15	.40
473 Aaron Gavey RC	.15	.40
474 Martin Gendron RC	.12	.30
475 Rick Girard RC	.15	.40
476 Todd Harvey RC	.15	.40
477 Marty Murray RC	.15	.40
478 Mike Peca RC	.15	.40
479 Aaron Ellis RC	.15	.40
480 Toby Kvalevog RC	.15	.40
481 Jon Coleman RC	.15	.40
482 Ashlin Halfnight RC	.10	.25
483 Jason McBain RC	.15	.40
484 Chris O'Sullivan RC	.15	.40
485 Deron Quint RC	.15	.40
486 Blake Sloan RC	.10	.25
487 David Wilkie RC	.15	.40
488 Kevyn Adams RC	.15	.40
489 Jason Bonsignore RC	.15	.40
490 Andy Brink RC	.10	.25
491 Adam Deadmarsh	.10	.25
492 John Emmons	.10	.25
493 Kevin Hilton RC	.15	.40
494 Jason Karmanos RC	.10	.25
495 Bob Lachance RC	.15	.40
496 Jam.Langenbrunner RC	.15	.40
497 Jay Pandolfo RC	.15	.40
498 Richard Park RC	.15	.40
499 Ryan Sittler	.10	.25
500 John Varga RC	.15	.40
501 Valeri Bure RC	.15	.40
502 Maxim Bets RC	.10	.25
503 Vadim Sharifjanov	.12	.30
504 Alex.Kharlamov RC	.10	.25
505 Pavel Desyatkov RC	.10	.25
506 Oleg Tverdovsky RC	.15	.40
507 Nikolai Tsulygin	.10	.25
508 Evgeni Ryabchikov RC	.10	.25
509 Sergei Brylin RC	.15	.40
510 Maxim Sushinski RC	.10	.25
511 Sergei Kondrashkin RC	.10	.25
512 Wayne Gretzky HL SP	1.00	2.50
AU1 Alexandre Daigle AU	12.00	30.00
AU2 Eric Lindros AU	12.00	30.00
NNO Eric/Brett Lindros	1.50	4.00
NNO Lindros Redempt.Exp.	.25	.60

1993-94 Pinnacle Canadian

COMPLETE SET (511)	12.00	30.00
COMP.SERIES 1 (236)	6.00	15.00
COMP.SERIES 2 (275)	6.00	15.00

*CANADIAN: .4X TO 1X BASIC CARDS

1 Eric Lindros	1.00	2.50
2 Mats Sundin	.15	.40
3 Tom Barrasso	.05	.15
4 Teemu Selanne	.40	1.00
5 Joe Juneau	.15	.40
6 Tony Amonte	.02	.10
7 Bob Probert	.02	.10
8 Chris Kontos	.04	.10
9 Geoff Sanderson	.02	.10
10 Alexander Mogilny	.15	.40
11 Kevin Lowe	.04	.10
12 Nikolai Borschevsky	.04	.10
13 Dale Hunter	.02	.10
14 Gary Suter	.02	.10
15 Curtis Joseph	.10	.30
16 Mark Tinordi	.04	.10
17 Doug Weight	.02	.10
18 Benoit Hogue	.04	.10
19 Tommy Soderstrom	.02	.10
20 Pat Falloon	.04	.10
21 Jyrki Lumme	.04	.10
22 Brian Bellows	.02	.10
23 Alexei Zhitnik	.02	.10
24 Dirk Graham	.04	.10
25 Scott Stevens	.02	.10
26 Adam Foote	.04	.10
27 Mike Gartner	.05	.15
28 Dallas Drake RC	.07	.20
29 Ulf Samuelsson	.04	.10
30 Cam Neely	.10	.30
31 Sean Burke	.05	.15
32 Petr Svoboda	.04	.10
33 Keith Tkachuk	.15	.40
34 Roman Hamrlik	.02	.10
35 Robert Reichel	.02	.10
36 Igor Kravchuk	.04	.10
37 Mathieu Schneider	.04	.10
38 Bob Kudelski	.04	.10
39 Jeff Brown	.02	.10
40 Mike Modano	.10	.30
41 Rob Gaudreau RC	.04	.10
42 Dave Andreychuk	.05	.15
43 Trevor Linden	.05	.15
44 Dimitri Khristich	.04	.10
45 Joe Murphy	.02	.10
47 Alexander Semak	.04	.10
48 Ray Ferraro	.02	.10
49 Curtis Leschyshyn	.04	.10
50 Mark Recchi	.08	.25
51 Sergei Nemchinov	.04	.10
52 Larry Murphy	.05	.15
53 Steve Heinze	.04	.10
54 Sergei Fedorov	.40	1.00
55 Gary Roberts	.02	.10
56 Alexei Zhamnov	.20	.50
57 Derian Hatcher	.04	.10
58 Kelly Buchberger	.04	.10
60 Brian Bradley	.04	.10
61 Patrick Poulin	.04	.10
62 Scott Lachance	.04	.10
63 Johan Garpenlov	.04	.10
64 Sylvain Turgeon	.04	.10
65 Grant Fuhr	.05	.15
66 Garth Butcher	.04	.10
67 Michal Pivonka	.04	.10
68 Todd Gill	.04	.10
69 Cliff Ronning	.04	.10
70 Steve Smith	.04	.10
71 Bobby Holik	.04	.10
72 Garry Galley	.04	.10
73 Steve Leach	.04	.10
74 Ron Francis	.05	.15
75 Jari Kurri	.05	.15
76 Alexei Kovalev	.15	.40
77 Dave Gagner	.02	.10
78 Steve Duchesne	.02	.10
79 Theo Fleury	.05	.15
80 Paul Coffey	.07	.20
81 Bill Ranford	.05	.15
82 Doug Bodger	.04	.10
83 Nick Kypreos	.04	.10
84 Darius Kasparaitis	.04	.10
85 Vincent Damphousse	.02	.10
86 Arturs Irbe	.20	.50
87 Shawn Chambers	.04	.10
88 Murray Craven	.04	.10
89 Rob Pearson	.04	.10
90 Kevin Hatcher	.02	.10
91 Brent Sutter	.02	.10
92 Teppo Numminen	.04	.10
93 Shawn Burr	.04	.10
94 Valeri Zelepukin	.04	.10
95 Ron Sutter	.04	.10
96 Craig MacTavish	.04	.10
97 Dominic Roussel	.02	.10
98 Nicklas Lidstrom	.02	.10
99 Adam Graves	.08	.25
100 Doug Gilmour	.10	.30
101 Frank Musil	.04	.10

102 Ted Donato .04 .10
103 Andrew Cassels .04 .10
104 Vladimir Malakhov .02 .10
105 Shawn McEachern .04 .10
106 Petr Nedved .02 .10
107 Calle Johansson .04 .10
108 Rich Sutter .04 .10
109 Evgeny Davydov .04 .10
110 Mike Ricci .02 .10
111 Scott Niedermayer .02 .10
112 John LeClair .15 .40
113 Darryl Sydor .04 .10
114 Paul DiPietro .04 .10
115 Stephane Fiset .05 .15
116 Christian Ruuttu .04 .10
117 Doug Zmolek .04 .10
118 Bob Sweeney .04 .10
119 Brent Fedyk .04 .10
120 Norm Maciver .04 .10
121 Rob Zamuner .04 .10
122 Brian Mullen .05 .15
123 Trent Yawney .04 .10
124 David Shaw .04 .10
125 Mark Messier .07 .20
126 Kevin Miller .04 .10
127 Dino Ciccarelli .05 .15
128 Derek King .04 .10
129 Scott Young .04 .10
130 Craig Janney .02 .10
131 Jamie Macoun .04 .10
132 Geoff Courtnall .02 .10
133 Bob Essensa .02 .10
134 Ken Daneyko .04 .10
135 Mike Ridley .02 .10
136 Stephan Lebeau .04 .10
137 Tony Granato .04 .10
138 Kay Whitmore .02 .10
139 Luke Richardson .04 .10
140 Jeremy Roenick .30 .75
141 Brad May .04 .10
142 Sandis Ozolinsh .02 .10
143 Stephane Richer .02 .10
144 John Tucker .04 .10
145 Luc Robitaille .07 .20
146 Dimitri Yushkevich .04 .10
147 Sean Hill .04 .10
148 John Vanbiesbrouck .05 .15
149 Kevin Stevens .08 .25
150 Patrick Roy .40 1.00
151 Owen Nolan .02 .10
152 Richard Smehlik .04 .10
153 Ray Sheppard .02 .10
154 Ed Olczyk .04 .10
155 Al MacInnis .05 .15
156 Sergei Zubov .20 .50
157 Wendel Clark .05 .15
158 Kirk McLean .05 .15
159 Thomas Steen .04 .10
160 Pierre Turgeon .10 .30
161 Dmitri Kvartalnov .04 .10
162 Brian Noonan .04 .10
163 Mike McPhee .04 .10
164 Peter Bondra .02 .10
165 Bernie Nicholls .05 .15
166 Michael Nylander .04 .10
167 Guy Hebert .07 .20
168 Scott Mellanby .04 .10
169 Bob Bassen .04 .10
170 Rod Brind'Amour .05 .15
171 Andrei Kovalenko .04 .10
172 Mike Donnelly .04 .10
173 Steve Thomas .02 .10
174 Rick Tocchet .05 .15
175 Steve Yzerman .20 .50
176 Dixon Ward .04 .10
177 Randy Wood .04 .10
178 Dean Kennedy .04 .10
179 Joel Otto .04 .10
180 Kirk Muller .02 .10
181 Chris Chelios .05 .15
182 Richard Matvichuk .04 .10
183 John MacLean .02 .10
184 Joe Kocur .04 .10
185 Adam Oates .07 .20
186 Bob Beers .04 .10
187 Ron Tugnutt .02 .10
188 Brian Skrudland .04 .10
189 Al Iafrate .02 .10
190 Felix Potvin .40 1.00
191 David Reid .04 .10
192 Jim Johnson .04 .10
193 Kevin Haller .04 .10
194 Steve Chiasson .04 .10
195 Jaromir Jagr .40 1.00
196 Martin Rucinsky .04 .10
197 Sergei Bautin .04 .10
198 Joe Nieuwendyk .05 .15
199 Gilbert Dionne .04 .10
200 Brett Hull .30 .75
201 Yuri Khmylev .04 .10
202 Todd Elik .04 .10
203 Patrick Flatley .04 .10
204 Martin Straka .02 .10
205 Brendan Shanahan .15 .40
206 Mark Beaufait RC .04 .10
207 Mike Lenarduzzi RC .02 .10
208 Chris LiPuma .04 .10
209 Andre Faust .04 .10
210 Ben Hankinson RC .04 .10
211 Darrin Madeley RC .02 .10
212 Oleg Petrov .04 .10
213 Philippe Boucher .04 .10
214 Tyler Wright .04 .10
215 Jason Bowen RC .04 .10
216 Matthew Barnaby .04 .10
217 Bryan Smolinski .15 .40
218 Dan Keczmer .04 .10
219 Chris Simon RC .07 .20
220 Corey Hirsch .02 .10
221 Mario Lemieux AW .15 .40
222 Teemu Selanne AW .15 .40
223 Chris Chelios AW .02 .10
224 Ed Belfour AW .05 .15
225 Pierre Turgeon AW .05 .15
226 Doug Gilmour AW .07 .20
227 Ed Belfour AW .05 .15
228 Patrick Roy AW .15 .40
229 Dave Poulin AW .04 .10
230 Mario Lemieux AW .15 .40
231 Mike Vernon HH .02 .10
232 Vincent Damphousse HH .02 .10
233 Chris Chelios HH .02 .10
234 Cliff Ronning HH .04 .10
235 Mark Howe HH .02 .10
236 Alexandre Daigle .20 .50
237 Wayne Gretzky NT .60 1.50
238 Mark Messier NT .08 .25
239 Dino Ciccarelli .04 .10
240 Joe Mullen .05 .15
241 Mike Gartner .05 .15
242 Mike Richter .08 .25
243 Pat Verbeek .02 .10
244 Valeri Kamensky .04 .10
245 Nelson Emerson .04 .10
246 James Patrick .04 .10
247 Greg Adams .04 .10
248 Ulf Dahlen .04 .10
249 Shayne Corson .02 .10
250 Ray Bourque .07 .20
251 Claude Lemieux .02 .10
252 Kelly Hrudey .05 .15
253 Patrice Brisebois .04 .10
254 Mark Howe .02 .10
255 Ed Belfour .15 .40
256 Pelle Eklund .04 .10
257 Zarley Zalapski .04 .10
258 Sylvain Cote .04 .10
259 Uwe Krupp .04 .10
260 Dale Hawerchuk .05 .15
261 Alexei Gusarov .04 .10
262 Dave Ellett .04 .10
263 Tomas Sandstrom .02 .10
264 Vladimir Konstantinov .04 .10
265 Paul Ranheim .04 .10
266 Darrin Shannon .04 .10
267 Chris Terreri .02 .10
268 Russ Courtnall .02 .10
269 Don Sweeney .04 .10
270 Kevin Todd .04 .10
271 Brad Shaw .04 .10
272 Adam Creighton .04 .10
273 Dana Murzyn .04 .10
274 Donald Audette .04 .10
275 Brian Leetch .08 .25
276 Kevin Dineen .04 .10
277 Bruce Driver .04 .10
278 Jim Paek .04 .10
279 Esa Tikkanen .02 .10
280 Guy Carbonneau .02 .10
281 Eric Weinrich .04 .10
282 Tim Cheveldae .02 .10
283 Bryan Marchment .04 .10
284 Kelly Miller .04 .10
285 Jimmy Carson .04 .10
286 Terry Carkner .04 .10
287 Mike Sullivan .04 .10
288 Joe Reekie .04 .10
289 Bob Rouse .04 .10
290 Joe Sakic .15 .40
291 Gerald Diduck .04 .10
292 Don Beaupre .02 .10
293 Kjell Samuelsson .04 .10
294 Claude Lapointe .04 .10
296 Charlie Huddy .04 .10
297 Peter Zezel .04 .10
298 Craig Muni .04 .10
299 Rick Tabaracci .02 .10
300 Pat LaFontaine .07 .20
301 Lyle Odelein .04 .10
302 Jocelyn Lemieux .04 .10
303 Craig Ludwig .04 .10
304 Marc Bergevin .04 .10
305 Bill Guerin .04 .10
306 Rick Zombo .04 .10
307 Steven Finn .04 .10
308 Gino Odjick .04 .10
309 Jeff Beukeboom .04 .10
310 Mario Lemieux .40 1.00
311 J.J. Daigneault .04 .10
312 Vincent Riendeau .02 .10
313 Adam Burt .04 .10
314 Mike Craig .04 .10
315 Bret Hedican .04 .10
316 Kris King .04 .10
317 Sylvain Lefebvre .04 .10
318 Troy Murray .04 .10
319 Gordie Roberts .04 .10
320 Pavel Bure .60 1.50
321 Marc Bureau .04 .10
322 Randy McKay .04 .10
323 Mark Lamb .04 .10
324 Brian Mullen .02 .10
325 Ken Wregget .02 .10
326 Stephane Quintal .04 .10
327 Robert Dirk .04 .10
328 Mike Krushelnyski .04 .10
329 Mikael Andersson .04 .10
330 Paul Stanton .04 .10
331 Phil Bourque .04 .10
332 Andre Racicot .02 .10
333 Brad Dalgarno .04 .10
334 Neal Broten .02 .10
335 John Blue .02 .10
336 Ken Sutton .04 .10
337 Greg Paslawski .04 .10
338 Robb Stauber .02 .10
339 Mike Keane .04 .10
340 Terry Yake .04 .10
341 Brian Benning .04 .10
342 Brian Propp .02 .10
343 Frank Pietrangelo .02 .10
344 Stephane Matteau .04 .10
345 Steven King .04 .10
346 Joe Cirella .04 .10
347 Andy Moog .05 .15
348 Paul Ysebaert .04 .10
349 Petr Klima .04 .10
350 Corey Millen .04 .10
351 Phil Housley .02 .10
352 Craig Billington .02 .10
353 Jeff Norton .04 .10
354 Neil Wilkinson .04 .10
355 Doug Lidster .04 .10
356 Steve Larmer .05 .15
357 Jon Casey .02 .10
358 Brad McCrimmon .04 .10
359 Alexei Kasatonov .04 .10
360 Andrei Lomakin .04 .10
361 Daren Puppa .05 .15
362 Sergei Makarov .05 .15
363 Dave Manson .04 .10
364 Jim Sandlak .04 .10
365 Glenn Healy .02 .10
366 Martin Gelinas .04 .10
367 Igor Larionov .02 .10
368 Anatoli Semenov .04 .10
369 Mark Fitzpatrick .02 .10
370 Paul Cavallini .04 .10
371 Jimmy Waite .02 .10
372 Yves Racine .04 .10
373 Jeff Hackett .02 .10
374 Marty McSorley .02 .10
375 Scott Pearson .04 .10
376 Ron Hextall .02 .10
377 Gaetan Duchesne .04 .10
378 Jamie Baker .04 .10
379 Troy Loney .04 .10
380 Gord Murphy .04 .10
381 Peter Sidorkiewicz .02 .10
382 Pat Elynuik .04 .10
383 Glen Wesley .04 .10
384 Dean Evason .04 .10
385 Mike Peluso .04 .10
386 Darren Turcotte .04 .10
387 Dave Poulin .04 .10
388 John Cullen .04 .10
389 Randy Ladouceur .04 .10
390 Tom Fitzgerald .04 .10
391 Denis Savard .05 .15
392 Fredrik Olausson .04 .10
393 Sergio Momesso .04 .10
394 Mike Ramsey .04 .10
395 Kelly Kisio .04 .10
396 Craig Simpson .04 .10
397 Slava Fetisov .02 .10
398 Glenn Anderson .02 .10
399 Michel Goulet .05 .15
400 Wayne Gretzky .75 2.00
401 Stu Grimson .04 .10
402 Mike Hough .04 .10
403 Dominik Hasek .20 .50
404 Gerard Gallant .04 .10
405 Greg Gilbert .04 .10
406 Vladimir Ruzicka .04 .10
407 Jim Hrivnak .02 .10
408 Dave Lowry .04 .10
409 Todd Ewen .04 .10
410 Bob Errey .04 .10
411 Bryan Trottier .05 .15
412 Dave Taylor .05 .15
413 Grant Ledyard .04 .10
414 Chris Dahlquist .04 .10
415 Brent Gilchrist .04 .10
416 Geoff Smith .04 .10
417 Jiri Slegr .04 .10
418 Randy Burridge .04 .10
419 Sergei Krivokrasov .02 .10
420 Keith Primeau .05 .15
421 Robert Kron .04 .10
422 Keith Brown .04 .10
423 David Volek .04 .10
424 Josef Beranek .04 .10
425 Wayne Presley .04 .10
426 Stu Barnes .04 .10
427 Milos Holan RC .07 .20
428 Jeff Shantz .04 .10
429 Brent Gretzky RC .10 .30
430 Jarkko Varvio .04 .10
431 Chris Osgood RC .25 .60
432 Aaron Ward RC .04 .10
433 Jason Smith RC .04 .10
434 Cam Stewart RC .04 .10
435 Derek Plante RC .08 .25
436 Pat Peake .04 .10
437 Alexander Karpovtsev .04 .10
438 Jim Montgomery RC .04 .10
439 Rob Niedermayer .15 .40
440 Jocelyn Thibault RC .30 .75
441 Jason Arnott RC .75 2.00
442 Mike Rathje .04 .10
443 Chris Gratton .15 .40
444 Vesa Viitakoski RC .04 .10
445 Alexei Kudashov RC .04 .10
447 Ted Drury .04 .10
448 Rene Corbet RC .04 .10
449 Markus Naslund .04 .10
450 Dmitri Filimonov .04 .10
451 Roman Oksiuta RC .08 .25
452 Michal Sykora RC .07 .20
453 Greg Johnson .04 .10
454 Mikael Renberg .30 .75
456 Chris Pronger .15 .40
457 Emmanuel Fernandez RC .25 .60
458 Jamie Storr RC .75 2.00
459 Chris Armstrong RC .05 .15
460 Drew Bannister RC .05 .15
461 Joel Bouchard RC .05 .15
462 Bryan McCabe RC .15 .40
463 Nick Stajduhar RC .10 .30
464 Brent Tully .05 .15
465 Brendan Witt RC .15 .40
466 Jason Allison RC .30 .75
467 Jason Botterill RC .15 .40
468 Curtis Bowen RC .05 .15
469 Anson Carter RC .08 .25
470 Brandon Convery RC .08 .25
471 Yanick Dube RC .15 .40
472 Jeff Friesen RC 1.00 2.50
473 Aaron Gavey RC .20 .50
474 Martin Gendron RC .15 .40
475 Rick Girard RC .05 .15
476 Todd Harvey RC .50 1.25
477 Marty Murray RC .30 .75
478 Mike Peca RC .15 .40
479 Aaron Ellis RC .05 .15
480 Toby Kvalevog RC .05 .15
481 Jon Coleman RC .05 .15
482 Ashlin Halfnight RC .05 .15
483 Jason McBain RC .05 .15
484 Chris O'Sullivan RC .07 .20
485 Deron Quint RC .15 .40
486 Blake Sloan RC .05 .15
487 David Wilkie RC .15 .40
488 Kevyn Adams RC .20 .50
489 Jason Bonsignore RC .30 .75
490 Andy Brink RC .05 .15
491 Adam Deadmarsh .15 .40
492 John Emmons .05 .15
493 Kevin Hilton RC .15 .40
494 Jason Karmanos RC .05 .15
495 Bob Lachance RC .05 .15
496 Jamie Langenbrunner RC .20 .50
497 Jay Pandolfo RC .05 .15
498 Richard Park RC .30 .75
499 Ryan Sittler .05 .15
500 John Varga RC .15 .40
501 Valeri Bure RC .40 1.00
502 Maxim Bets RC .08 .25
503 Vadim Sharifjanov .08 .25
504 Alexander Kharlamov RC .25 .60
505 Pavel Desyatkov RC .05 .15
506 Oleg Tverdovsky RC .50 1.25
507 Nikolai Tsulygin .05 .15
508 Evgeni Ryabchikov RC .15 .40
509 Sergei Brylin RC .15 .40
510 Maxim Sushinski RC .05 .15
511 Sergei Kondrashkin RC .07 .20
NNO Brett/Eric Lindros CDN 3.00 8.00

1993-94 Pinnacle All-Stars

COMPLETE INSERT SET (45) 5.00 10.00
COMP.MAIL-IN SET (5) 10.00 25.00
1 Craig Billington .07 .20
2 Zarley Zalapski .05 .15
3 Kevin Lowe .05 .15
4 Scott Stevens .08 .25
5 Pierre Turgeon .08 .25
6 Mark Recchi .08 .25
7 Kirk Muller .05 .15
8 Mike Gartner .08 .25
9 Adam Oates .08 .25
10 Brad Marsh .05 .15
11 Pat LaFontaine .08 .25
12 Peter Bondra .08 .25
13 Joe Sakic .20 .50
14 Rick Tocchet .08 .25
15 Kevin Stevens .08 .25
16 Steve Duchesne .05 .15
17 Peter Sidorkiewicz .08 .25
18 Patrick Roy .50 1.25
19 Al Iafrate .05 .15
20 Jaromir Jagr .15 .40
21 Ray Bourque .08 .25
22 Alexander Mogilny .08 .25
23 Steve Chiasson .05 .15
24 Garth Butcher .05 .15
25 Phil Housley .07 .20
26 Chris Chelios .08 .25
27 Randy Carlyle .05 .15
28 Mike Modano .15 .40
29 Gary Roberts .05 .15
30 Kelly Kisio .05 .15
31 Pavel Bure .08 .25
32 Teemu Selanne .08 .25
33 Brian Bradley .05 .15
34 Brett Hull .10 .30
35 Jari Kurri .08 .25
36 Steve Yzerman .50 1.25
37 Luc Robitaille .08 .25
38 Dave Manson .05 .15
39 Jeremy Roenick .10 .30
40 Mike Vernon .08 .25
41 Jon Casey .08 .25
42 Ed Belfour .08 .25
43 Paul Coffey .08 .25
44 Doug Gilmour .08 .25
45 Wayne Gretzky .60 1.50
46 Mike Gartner 1.50 4.00
47 Al Iafrate 1.50 4.00
48 Ray Bourque 6.00 15.00
49 Jon Casey 1.50 4.00
50 Campbell Conf. 2.00 5.00

1993-94 Pinnacle Captains

COMPLETE SET (27) 40.00 100.00
*CANADIAN: .4X TO 1X BASIC INSERTS
1 Troy Loney .75 2.00
2 Ray Bourque 2.50 6.00
3 Pat LaFontaine 1.25 3.00
4 Joe Nieuwendyk 1.25 3.00
5 Dirk Graham .75 2.00
6 Mark Tinordi .75 2.00
7 Steve Yzerman 6.00 15.00
8 Craig MacTavish .75 2.00
9 Brian Skrudland .75 2.00
10 Pat Verbeek .75 2.00
11 Wayne Gretzky 8.00 20.00
12 Guy Carbonneau .75 2.00
13 Scott Stevens .75 2.00
14 Pat Flatley .75 2.00
15 Mark Messier 2.50 6.00
16 Mark Lamb .75 2.00
17 Kevin Dineen .75 2.00
18 Mario Lemieux 8.00 20.00
19 Joe Sakic 5.00 12.00
20 Brett Hull 2.50 6.00
21 Bob Errey .75 2.00
22 M.Bergevin
D.Savard .75 2.00
23 Wendel Clark 1.25 3.00
24 Trevor Linden 1.25 3.00
25 Kevin Hatcher .75 2.00
26 Keith Tkachuk 1.25 3.00
27 Checklist Card 2.00 5.00

1993-94 Pinnacle Expansion

COMPLETE SET (6) 5.00 10.00
1 J.Vanbiesbrouck
G.Hebert 1.25 3.00
2 G.Murphy
R.Ladouceur .75 2.00
3 J.Cirella
S.Hill .75 2.00
4 D.Lowry
T.Loney .75 2.00
5 B.Skrudland
T.Yake .75 2.00
6 S.Mellanby
S.King .75 2.00

1993-94 Pinnacle Masks

COMPLETE SET (10) 30.00 80.00
1 Grant Fuhr 4.00 10.00
2 Mike Vernon 4.00 10.00
3 Robb Stauber 4.00 10.00
4 Dominic Roussel 4.00 10.00
5 Pat Jablonski 4.00 10.00
6 Stephane Fiset 4.00 10.00
7 Wendell Young 4.00 10.00
8 Ron Hextall 4.00 10.00
9 John Vanbiesbrouck 4.00 10.00
10 Peter Sidorkiewicz 4.00 10.00

1993-94 Pinnacle Nifty Fifty

1 Introductory CL 2.00 5.00
2 Alexander Mogilny .50 1.25
3 Teemu Selanne 1.00 2.50
4 Mario Lemieux 4.00 10.00
5 Luc Robitaille .50 1.25
6 Pavel Bure 1.25 3.00
7 Pierre Turgeon .50 1.25
8 Steve Yzerman 3.00 8.00
9 Kevin Stevens .30 .75
10 Brett Hull 2.00 5.00
11 Dave Andreychuk .50 1.25
12 Pat LaFontaine 1.00 2.50
13 Mark Recchi .50 1.25
14 Brendan Shanahan 1.00 2.50
15 Jeremy Roenick 1.00 2.50

1993-94 Pinnacle Super Rookies

COMPLETE SET (9) 2.00 5.00
*CANADIAN: .4X TO 1X BASIC INSERTS
1 Alexandre Daigle .20 .50
2 Chris Pronger .60 1.50
3 Chris Gratton .20 .50
4 Rob Niedermayer .20 .50
5 Alexei Yashin .20 .50
6 Mikael Renberg .20 .50
7 Jason Arnott .60 1.50
8 Markus Naslund .40 1.00
9 Pat Peake .20 .50

1993-94 Pinnacle Team Pinnacle

COMPLETE SET (12) 50.00 100.00
COMP.SERIES 1 (6) 30.00 60.00
COMP.SERIES 2 (6) 20.00 40.00
*CANADIAN: .5X TO 1.2X BASIC INSERTS
1 P.Roy/E.Belfour 8.00 20.00
2 B.Leetch/C.Chelios 6.00 15.00
3 S.Stevens/A.MacInnis 4.00 10.00
4 K.Stevens/L.Robitaille 3.00 8.00
5 M.Lemieux/W.Gretzky 15.00 40.00
6 J.Jagr/B.Hull 5.00 12.00
7 T.Barrasso/K.McLean 5.00 12.00
8 R.Bourque/P.Coffey 4.00 10.00
9 A.Iafrate/P.Housley 4.00 10.00
10 V.Damphousse/P.Bure 4.00 10.00
11 E.Lindros/J.Roenick 5.00 12.00
12 A.Mogilny/T.Selanne 5.00 12.00

1993-94 Pinnacle Team 2001

*CANADIAN: .4X TO 1X BASIC
1 Eric Lindros 1.50 4.00
2 Alexander Mogilny .60 1.50
3 Pavel Bure 1.50 4.00
4 Joe Juneau .50 1.25
5 Felix Potvin 1.50 4.00
6 Nicklas Lidstrom .75 2.00
7 Alexei Kovalev .60 1.50
8 Patrick Poulin .50 1.25
9 Shawn McEachern .50 1.25
10 Teemu Selanne 1.50 4.00
11 Rod Brind'Amour .60 1.50
12 Jaromir Jagr 2.00 5.00
13 Pierre Turgeon .60 1.50
14 Scott Niedermayer .75 2.00
15 Mats Sundin .75 2.00
16 Trevor Linden .75 2.00
17 Mike Modano 1.25 3.00
18 Roman Hamrlik .50 1.25
19 Tony Amonte .60 1.50
20 Jeremy Roenick 1.25 3.00
21 Scott Lachance .50 1.25
22 Mike Ricci .50 1.25
23 Dimitri Khristich .50 1.25
24 Sergei Fedorov 1.25 3.00
25 Joe Sakic 1.50 4.00
26 Pat Falloon .50 1.25
27 Mathieu Schneider .50 1.25
28 Owen Nolan .75 2.00
29 Brendan Shanahan .75 2.00
30 Mark Recchi 1.00 2.50

1993-94 Pinnacle Daigle Entry Draft

1 Alexandre Daigle 4.00 10.00

1994-95 Pinnacle I Hobby Samples

COMPLETE SEALED SET (10) 1.00 2.50
1 Eric Lindros
Philadelph .40 1.00
2 Alexandre Daigle
Ottawa .07 .20
3 Mike Modano
Dallas Star .20 .50
4 Vincent Damphousse
Mont .02 .10
5 Dave Andreychuk
Toronto .02 .10
6 Curtis Joseph
St. Louis .10 .30
7 Joe Juneau
Washington C .02 .10
246 Mariusz Czerkawski
Bost .01 .05
BR1 Al Iafrate
Boston Bruin .08 .25
NNO Title Card .20 .50

1994-95 Pinnacle

1 Eric Lindros .30 .75
2 Alexandre Daigle .12 .30
3 Mike Modano .30 .75
4 Vincent Damphousse .15 .40
5 Dave Andreychuk .20 .50
6 Curtis Joseph .25 .60
7 Joe Juneau .12 .30
8 Trevor Linden .20 .50
9 Rob Blake .20 .50
10 Mike Richter .20 .50
11 Chris Pronger .20 .50
12 Robert Reichel .12 .30
13 Bryan Smolinski .12 .30
14 Ray Sheppard .15 .40
15 Guy Hebert .15 .40
16 Tony Amonte .15 .40
17 Richard Smehlik .12 .30
18 Doug Weight .15 .40
19 Chris Gratton .12 .30
20 Tom Barrasso .15 .40
21 Brian Skrudland .12 .30
22 Sandis Ozolinsh .12 .30
23 Bill Guerin .20 .50
24 Curtis Leschyshyn .12 .30
25 Teemu Selanne .40 1.00
26 Darius Kasparaitis .12 .30
27 Garry Galley .12 .30
28 Alexei Yashin .20 .50
29 Mark Tinordi .12 .30
30 Patrick Roy .50 1.25
31 Mike Gartner .25 .60
32 Brendan Shanahan .20 .50
33 Sylvain Cote .12 .30
34 Jeff Brown .12 .30
35 Jari Kurri .15 .40
36 Sergei Zubov .15 .40
37 Pat Verbeek .15 .40
38 Theo Fleury .20 .50
39 Al Iafrate .12 .30
40 Keith Primeau .15 .40
41 Bobby Dollas .12 .30
42 Ed Belfour .20 .50
43 Dale Hawerchuk .25 .60
44 Shayne Corson .15 .40
45 Danton Cole .12 .30
46 Ulf Samuelsson .12 .30
47 Stu Barnes .12 .30
48 Ulf Dahlen .12 .30
49 Valeri Zelepukin .12 .30
50 Joe Sakic .40 1.00
51 Dave Manson .12 .30
52 Steve Thomas .12 .30
53 Mark Recchi .25 .60
54 Dave McLlwain .12 .30
55 Derian Hatcher .12 .30
56 Mathieu Schneider .12 .30
57 Bill Berg .12 .30
58 Petr Nedved .15 .40
59 Dimitri Khristich .12 .30
60 Kirk McLean .15 .40
61 Marty McSorley .15 .40
62 Adam Graves .12 .30
63 Geoff Sanderson .15 .40
64 Frank Musil .12 .30
65 Cam Neely .20 .50
66 Nicklas Lidstrom .20 .50
67 Stephan Lebeau .12 .30
68 Joe Murphy .12 .30
69 Yuri Khmylev .12 .30
70 Zdeno Ciger .12 .30
71 Daren Puppa .15 .40
72 Ron Francis .25 .60
73 Scott Mellanby .15 .40
74 Igor Larionov .12 .30
75 Scott Niedermayer .20 .50
76 Owen Nolan .20 .50
77 Teppo Numminen .12 .30
78 Pierre Turgeon .15 .40
79 Mikael Renberg .15 .40
80 Norm Maciver .12 .30
81 Paul Cavallini .12 .30
82 Kirk Muller .12 .30
83 Felix Potvin .30 .75
84 Craig Janney .15 .40
85 Dale Hunter .12 .30
86 Jyrki Lumme .12 .30
87 Alexei Zhitnik .15 .40
88 Steve Larmer .15 .40
89 Jocelyn Lemieux .12 .30
90 Joe Nieuwendyk .15 .40
91 Don Sweeney .12 .30
92 Slava Kozlov .15 .40
93 Tim Sweeney .12 .30
94 Chris Chelios .20 .50
95 Derek Plante .12 .30
96 Igor Kravchuk .12 .30
97 Shawn Chambers .12 .30
98 Jaromir Jagr .60 1.50
99 Jeff Norton .12 .30
100 John Vanbiesbrouck .20 .50
101 John MacLean .15 .40
102 Stephane Fiset .15 .40
103 Keith Tkachuk .20 .50
104 Vladimir Malakhov .12 .30
105 Mike McPhee .12 .30
106 Eric Desjardins .15 .40
107 Alexei Kovalev .15 .40
108 Steve Duchesne .12 .30
109 Peter Zezel .12 .30
110 Randy Burridge .12 .30
111 Jason Bowen .12 .30
112 Phil Bourque .12 .30
113 Cliff Ronning .12 .30
114 Sean Burke .15 .40
115 Gary Roberts .12 .30
116 Vladimir Konstantinov .15 .40
117 Brent Sutter .15 .40
118 Tony Granato .12 .30
119 Garry Valk .12 .30
120 Adam Oates .20 .50
121 Arturs Irbe .15 .40
122 Jesse Belanger .12 .30
123 Roman Hamrlik .12 .30
124 Jason Arnott .15 .40
125 Alexander Mogilny .15 .40
126 Bruce Driver .12 .30
127 Shawn McEachern .12 .30
128 Andrei Kovalenko .12 .30
129 Benoit Hogue .12 .30
130 Tim Cheveldae .15 .40
131 Brian Noonan .12 .30
132 Lyle Odelein .15 .40
133 Russ Courtnall .12 .30
134 Peter Stastny .15 .40
135 Doug Gilmour .25 .60
136 Pat Peake .12 .30
137 Gary Suter .12 .30
138 Paul Ranheim .12 .30
139 Troy Murray .12 .30
140 Pavel Bure .20 .50
141 Gord Murphy .12 .30
142 Michael Nylander .15 .40
143 Craig Muni .12 .30
144 Bob Corkum .12 .30
145 Martin Brodeur .50 1.25
146 Ted Donato .12 .30
147 Alexei Zhamnov .15 .40
148 Josef Beranek .12 .30
149 Joe Mullen .15 .40
150 Sergei Fedorov .30 .75
151 Mike Keane .12 .30
152 Sergei Makarov .12 .30
153 Marty McInnis .12 .30
154 Steven Rice .12 .30
155 Brian Leetch .15 .40
156 Chris Joseph .12 .30
157 Darcy Wakaluk .15 .40
158 Kelly Miller .12 .30
159 Jim Montgomery .12 .30
160 Nikolai Borschevsky .12 .30
161 Darren Turcotte .12 .30
162 Brad Shaw .12 .30
163 Mark Lamb .12 .30
164 Alexei Gusarov .15 .40
165 Jeremy Roenick .30 .75
166 Stephane Richer .15 .40
167 German Titov .12 .30
168 Rob Niedermayer .15 .40
169 Glen Murray .15 .40
170 Mario Lemieux .75 2.00
171 Thomas Steen .12 .30
172 Ron Tugnutt .15 .40
173 Pat Falloon .12 .30
174 Esa Tikkanen .12 .30
175 Dominik Hasek .30 .75
176 Patrick Flatley .12 .30
177 Gino Odjick .12 .30
178 Charlie Huddy .12 .30
179 Dave Poulin .12 .30
180 Darren McCarty .12 .30
181 Todd Gill .12 .30
182 Tom Chorske .12 .30
183 Marc Bergevin .12 .30
184 Dave Lowry .12 .30
185 Brent Gilchrist .12 .30
186 Eric Weinrich .12 .30
187 Ted Drury .12 .30
188 Boris Mironov .12 .30
189 Patrik Carnback .12 .30
190 Ray Bourque .30 .75
191 Patrice Brisebois .12 .30
192 Bob Errey .12 .30
193 Scott Lachance .12 .30
194 Brad May .12 .30
195 Jeff Beukeboom .12 .30
196 James Patrick .12 .30
197 Doug Brown .12 .30
198 Dana Murzyn .12 .30
199 Chris Osgood .30 .75
200 Wayne Gretzky 1.25 3.00
201 Bob Carpenter .15 .40
202 Evgeny Davydov .12 .30
203 Oleg Petrov .12 .30
204 Grant Ledyard .12 .30
205 Jocelyn Thibault .15 .40
206 Bill Houlder .12 .30
207 Tom Fitzgerald .12 .30
208 Dominic Roussel .15 .40
209 Dave Ellett .12 .30
210 Frank Kucera .12 .30
211 Steve Smith .12 .30
212 Vincent Riendeau .12 .30
213 Scott Pearson .12 .30
214 John Slaney .12 .30
215 Larry Murphy .15 .40
216 Travis Green .15 .40
217 Joel Otto .12 .30
218 Randy Wood .12 .30
219 Gaetan Duchesne .12 .30
220 Sergei Nemchinov .12 .30
221 Terry Carkner .12 .30
222 Randy McKay .12 .30
223 Mike Donnelly .12 .30
224 J.J. Daigneault .12 .30
225 Dallas Drake .12 .30
226 John Tucker .12 .30
227 Dimitri Yushkevich .12 .30
228 Mike Stapleton .15 .40
229 Dmitri Mironov .12 .30
230 Ken Wregget .15 .40
231 Claude Lapointe .12 .30
232 Joe Sacco .12 .30
233 Craig Ludwig .12 .30
234 David Reid .12 .30
235 Rich Sutter .12 .30
236 Mark Fitzpatrick .15 .40
237 Jim Storm .15 .40
238 Brad Dalgarno .12 .30
239 Dixon Ward .12 .30
240 Greg Adams .12 .30
241 Dino Ciccarelli .15 .40
242 Vlastimil Kroupa .12 .30
243 Joe Kocur .12 .30
244 Donald Audette .12 .30
245 Trent Yawney .12 .30
246 Mariusz Czerkawski RC .20 .50
247 Jason Allison .15 .40
248 Brian Savage .12 .30
249 Fred Knipscheer .12 .30
250 Jamie McLennan .15 .40
251 Aaron Gavey .12 .30
252 Jeff Friesen .12 .30
253 Adam Deadmarsh .12 .30
254 Jamie Storr .15 .40
255 Brian Rolston .15 .40
256 Zigmund Palffy .15 .40
257 Brett Lindros .12 .30
258 Denis Tsygurov RC .20 .50
259 Chris Tamer RC .12 .30
260 Mike Peca .15 .40

261 Oleg Tverdovsky .15 .40
262 Todd Harvey .12 .30
263 Yan Kaminsky .12 .30
264 Kenny Jonsson .12 .30
265 Paul Kariya .20 .50
266 Peter Forsberg .40 1.00
267 Atlantic Division Checklist .05 .15
268 Northeast Division Checklist .05 .15
269 Central Division Checklist .05 .15
270 Pacific Division Checklist .05 .15
271 Steve Yzerman .50 1.25
272 John LeClair .20 .50
273 Rod Brind'Amour .15 .40
274 Ron Hextall .20 .50
275 Todd Elik .12 .30
276 Geoff Courtnall .12 .30
277 Kjell Samuelsson .12 .30
278 Brian Bradley .12 .30
279 Darrin Shannon .12 .30
280 Mike Ricci .12 .30
281 Peter Bondra .20 .50
282 Terry Yake .12 .30
283 Patrick Poulin .12 .30
284 Bob Kudelski .12 .30
285 Bill Ranford .15 .40
286 Alexander Godynyuk .12 .30
287 Claude Lemieux .20 .50
288 S.Turgeon/P. Kane 15.00 40.00
289 Kevin Miller .12 .30
290 Brian Bellows .15 .40
291 Murray Craven .12 .30
292 Kelly Hrudey .15 .40
293 Neal Broten .15 .40
294 Craig Simpson .12 .30
295 Mark Howe .20 .50
296 Johan Garpenlov .12 .30
297 Jamie Macoun .12 .30
298 Steve Leach .12 .30
299 Kevin Stevens .15 .40
300 Mark Messier .40 1.00
301 Paul Ysebaert .12 .30
302 Derek King .12 .30
303 Fredrik Olausson .12 .30
304 John Druce .15 .40
305 Calle Johansson .12 .30
306 Kelly Kisio .12 .30
307 Sergio Momesso .20 .50
308 Joe Cirella .12 .30
309 Tommy Soderstrom .15 .40
310 Scott Stevens .20 .50
311 Petr Klima .12 .30
312 Steven Finn .12 .30
313 Tomas Sandstrom .12 .30
314 Ray Ferraro .12 .30
315 Andy Moog .20 .50
316 Ray Whitney .12 .30
317 Dirk Graham .12 .30
318 Shawn Burr .12 .30
319 Andrew Cassels .12 .30
320 Craig Billington .15 .40
321 Wayne Presley .12 .30
322 Anatoli Semenov .12 .30
323 Michal Pivonka .12 .30
324 Martin Gelinas .12 .30
325 Nelson Emerson .12 .30
326 Brent Fedyk .12 .30
327 Bob Bassen .12 .30
328 Darryl Sydor .12 .30
329 Stephane Matteau .12 .30
330 Ken Daneyko .12 .30
331 Mikhail Shtalenkov RC .12 .30
332 Kelly Buchberger .12 .30
333 Mike Hough .12 .30
334 Dave Gagner .15 .40
335 Chris Terreri .15 .40
336 Robert Kron .12 .30
337 Andrei Lomakin .12 .30
338 Kevin Lowe .12 .30
339 Steve Konroyd .12 .30
340 Denis Savard .20 .50
341 Steve Heinze .12 .30
342 Zarley Zalapski .12 .30
343 Valeri Kamensky .15 .40
344 Tie Domi .15 .40
345 Kevin Hatcher .12 .30
346 Dean Evason .12 .30
347 Bobby Holik .12 .30
348 Steve Konowalchuk .12 .30
349 Rob Gaudreau .12 .30
350 Pat LaFontaine .20 .50
351 Joe Reekie .12 .30
352 Martin Straka .12 .30
353 Dave Babych .12 .30
354 Geoff Smith .12 .30
355 Don Beaupre .15 .40
356 Adam Burt .12 .30
357 Doug Bodger .12 .30
358 Dean McAmmond .12 .30
359 Gerald Diduck .12 .30
360 Rob DiMaio .12 .30
361 Scott Young .12 .30
362 Alexander Semak .12 .30
363 Mike Rathje .12 .30
364 Alexander Karpovtsev .12 .30
365 Trevor Kidd .15 .40
366 Jason Dawe .12 .30
367 Vitali Prokhorov .12 .30
368 Keith Brown .12 .30
369 Bret Hedican .12 .30
370 Markus Naslund .20 .50
371 Rick Tocchet .15 .40
372 Guy Carbonneau .12 .30
373 Kevin Haller .12 .30
374 Bob Rouse .12 .30
375 Rob Pearson .12 .30
376 Steve Chiasson .12 .30
377 Mike Vernon .15 .40
378 Keith Jones .12 .30
379 Sylvain Lefebvre .12 .30
380 Tom Kurvers .12 .30
381 Pat Elynuik .12 .30
382 Uwe Krupp .12 .30
383 Ron Sutter .12 .30
384 Mike Ridley .12 .30
385 Wendel Clark .30 .75
386 Mats Sundin .20 .50
387 Al MacInnis .25 .60
388 Glen Wesley .12 .30
389 Jim Paek .12 .30
390 Rudy Poeschek .15 .40
391 Yves Racine .12 .30
392 Craig MacTavish .12 .30
393 Jon Casey .15 .40
394 Garth Butcher .15 .40
395 Sean Hill .12 .30
396 Troy Loney .12 .30
397 John Cullen .12 .30
398 Alexei Kasatonov .12 .30
399 Mike Craig .12 .30
400 Luc Robitaille .20 .50
401 Randy Moller .12 .30
402 Chris Dahlquist .12 .30
403 Pat Conacher .12 .30
404 Bob Probert .20 .50
405 Robert Dirk .12 .30
406 Randy Cunneyworth .12 .30
407 Bryan Marchment .15 .40
408 Nick Kypreos .12 .30
409 Doug Lidster .12 .30
410 Phil Housley .15 .40
411 Bob Sweeney .12 .30
412 Mike Ramsey .12 .30
413 Robert Lang .12 .30
414 Brian Benning .12 .30
415 Greg Gilbert .12 .30
416 Martin Rucinsky .12 .30
417 Jason Smith .15 .40
418 Jozef Stumpel .12 .30
419 Bob Beers .12 .30
420 Ed Olczyk .12 .30
421 Grant Fuhr .30 .75
422 Gilbert Dionne .12 .30
423 Mike Peluso .12 .30
424 Petr Svoboda .12 .30
425 Corey Millen .12 .30
426 Kevin Dineen .12 .30
427 Brad McCrimmon .12 .30
428 Bob Essensa .12 .30
429 Paul Coffey .20 .50
430 Glenn Healy .15 .40
431 Luke Richardson .12 .30
432 Adam Foote .12 .30
433 Paul Broten .12 .30
434 Christian Ruuttu .12 .30
435 David Shaw .12 .30
436 Jimmy Carson .12 .30
437 Ken Sutton .12 .30
438 Kay Whitmore .12 .30
439 Jim Dowd .12 .30
440 Jim Johnson .12 .30
441 Kirk Maltby .12 .30
442 Trent Klatt .12 .30
443 Paul DiPietro .12 .30
444 Rick Tabaracci .15 .40
445 Craig Wolanin .12 .30
446 Dave Hannan .12 .30
447 Rick Zombo .12 .30
448 Tom Pederson .12 .30
449 Martin LaPointe .12 .30
450 Brett Hull .40 1.00
451 Mikael Andersson .12 .30
452 Benoit Brunet .12 .30
453 Nathan Lafayette .12 .30
454 Kent Manderville .12 .30
455 Todd Krygier .12 .30
456 Dennis Vaske .12 .30
457 Peter Popovic .12 .30
458 Jeff Shantz .12 .30
459 Darrin Madeley .12 .30
460 Rene Corbet .12 .30
461 Alexandre Daigle IB .12 .30
462 Martin Brodeur IB .50 1.25
463 Jason Arnott IB .15 .40
464 Mikael Renberg IB .15 .40
465 Alexei Yashin IB .20 .50
466 Chris Pronger IB .20 .50
467 Mariusz Czerkawski IB .20 .50
468 Chris Gratton IB .12 .30
469 Rob Niedermayer IB .15 .40
470 Bryan Smolinski IB .12 .30
471 Chris Osgood IB .30 .75
472 Derek Plante IB .12 .30
473 Brian Rolston IB .15 .40
474 Jason Allison IB .15 .40
475 Jamie Storr IB .15 .40
476 Kenny Jonsson IB .12 .30
477 Viktor Kozlov IB .12 .30
478 Brett Lindros IB .12 .30
479 Peter Forsberg IB .40 1.00
480 Paul Kariya IB .20 .50
481 Viktor Kozlov .12 .30
482 Michal Grosek RC .12 .30
483 Maxim Bets .12 .30
484 Jason Wiemer RC .12 .30
485 Janne Laukkanen .15 .40
486 Valeri Karpov RC .12 .30
487 Andrei Nikolishhin .12 .30
488 Dan Plante RC .12 .30
489 Mattias Norstrom .12 .30
490 David Oliver RC .12 .30
491 Todd Simon RC .12 .30
492 Valeri Bure .12 .30
493 Eric Fichaud RC .20 .50
494 Cory Stillman RC .12 .30
495 Chris Therien .12 .30
496 Matt Johnson RC .12 .30
497 Joby Messier .12 .30
498 Slava Butsayev .12 .30
499 Bernie Nicholls .15 .40
500 Mark Osborne .12 .30
501 Stephane Quintal .12 .30
502 Jamie Baker .12 .30
503 Todd Ewen .12 .30
504 Dan Quinn .15 .40
505 Peter Taglianetti .12 .30
506 Chris Simon .12 .30
507 Jay Wells .12 .30
508 Tommy Albelin .12 .30
509 Warren Rychel .12 .30
510 Brent Hughes .12 .30
511 Greg Johnson .12 .30
512 Stu Grimson .12 .30
513 Iain Fraser .12 .30
514 Rob Ray .12 .30
515 Craig Berube .12 .30
516 Shane Churla .12 .30
517 Checklist .05 .15
518 Checklist .05 .15
519 Checklist .05 .15
520 Checklist .05 .15
521 Jamie Storr .15 .40
522 Dan Cloutier RC .30 .75
523 Bryan McCabe .12 .30
524 Ed Jovanovski RC .30 .75
525 Nolan Baumgartner RC .20 .50
526 Jamie Rivers RC .20 .50
527 Wade Redden RC .30 .75
528 Lee Sorochan RC .20 .50
529 Eric Daze RC .30 .75
530 Jason Allison .15 .40
531 Alexandre Daigle .12 .30
532 Jeff Friesen .12 .30
533 Todd Harvey .12 .30
534 Jeff O'Neill RC .15 .40
535 Ryan Smyth RC .60 1.50
536 Marty Murray .15 .40
537 Darcy Tucker RC .30 .75
538 Denis Pederson RC .15 .40
539 Shean Donovan RC .20 .50
540 Larry Courville RC .20 .50
MVPC Pavel Bure 12.00 30.00
MVPU Dominik Hasek 8.00 20.00

1994-95 Pinnacle Artist's Proofs

*VETS: 12X TO 30X BASIC CARDS
*ROOKIES: 4X TO 10X BASIC CARDS
200 Wayne Gretzky 60.00 150.00
288 S. Turgeon/P. Kane 20.00 50.00

1994-95 Pinnacle Rink Collection

*VETS: 4X TO 10X BASIC CARDS
*ROOKIES: 2X TO 5X BASIC CARDS
288 S. Turgeon/P. Kane 30.00 80.00

1994-95 Pinnacle Boomers

COMPLETE SET (18) 15.00 40.00
BR1 Al Iafrate .60 1.50
BR2 Vladimir Malakhov .60 1.50
BR3 Al MacInnis 1.00 2.50
BR4 Chris Chelios 2.00 5.00
BR5 Mike Modano 3.00 8.00
BR6 Brendan Shanahan 2.00 5.00
BR7 Ray Bourque 3.00 8.00
BR8 Geoff Sanderson 1.00 2.50
BR9 Brett Hull 2.50 6.00
BR10 Rob Blake 1.00 2.50
BR11 Steve Thomas .60 1.50
BR12 Cam Neely 2.00 5.00
BR13 Pavel Bure 2.00 5.00
BR14 Stephane Richer 1.00 2.50
BR15 Teemu Selanne 2.00 5.00
BR16 Eric Lindros 2.00 5.00
BR17 Alexander Mogilny 1.00 2.50
BR18 Rick Tocchet 1.00 2.50

1994-95 Pinnacle Gamers

COMPLETE SET (18) 20.00 50.00
GR1 Teemu Selanne 2.00 5.00
GR2 Pat LaFontaine 1.25 3.00
GR3 Sergei Fedorov 2.00 5.00
GR4 Pavel Bure 2.00 5.00
GR5 Jaromir Jagr 3.00 8.00
GR6 Alexandre Daigle .75 2.00
GR7 Kirk Muller .75 2.00
GR8 Mike Modano 2.00 5.00
GR9 Mark Messier 2.00 5.00
GR10 Brendan Shanahan 2.00 5.00
GR11 Doug Gilmour .75 2.00
GR12 Rick Tocchet .75 2.00
GR13 Wendel Clark .75 2.00
GR14 Jeremy Roenick 2.00 5.00
GR15 Adam Graves .75 2.00
GR16 Eric Lindros 2.00 5.00
GR17 Cam Neely 2.00 5.00
GR18 Keith Tkachuk 1.25 3.00

1994-95 Pinnacle Goaltending Greats

COMPLETE SET (18) 40.00 80.00
GT1 Dominik Hasek 3.00 8.00
GT2 Mike Richter 2.50 6.00
GT3 John Vanbiesbrouck 1.50 4.00
GT4 Ed Belfour 3.00 8.00
GT5 Patrick Roy 8.00 20.00
GT6 Bill Ranford 1.50 4.00
GT7 Martin Brodeur 5.00 12.00
GT8 Felix Potvin 3.00 8.00
GT9 Arturs Irbe 1.50 4.00
GT10 Mike Vernon 1.50 4.00
GT11 Kirk McLean 1.50 4.00
GT12 Sean Burke 1.50 4.00
GT13 Curtis Joseph 2.50 6.00
GT14 Andy Moog 1.50 4.00
GT15 Daren Puppa 1.50 4.00
GT16 Chris Osgood 1.50 4.00
GT17 Tom Barrasso 1.50 4.00
GT18 Jocelyn Thibault 1.50 4.00

1994-95 Pinnacle Masks

COMPLETE SET (10) 100.00 200.00
MA1 Patrick Roy 25.00 50.00
MA2 John Vanbiesbrouck 10.00 25.00
MA3 Kelly Hrudey 10.00 25.00
MA4 Guy Hebert 8.00 20.00
MA5 Rick Tabaracci 8.00 20.00
MA6 Ron Hextall 10.00 25.00
MA7 Trevor Kidd 8.00 20.00
MA8 Andy Moog 10.00 25.00
MA9 Jimmy Waite 8.00 20.00
MA10 Curtis Joseph 10.00 25.00

1994-95 Pinnacle Northern Lights

COMPLETE SET (18) 15.00 40.00
NL1 Patrick Roy 5.00 12.00
NL2 Kirk Muller .75 2.00
NL3 Vincent Damphousse .75 2.00
NL4 Joe Sakic 2.50 6.00
NL5 Wendel Clark 1.25 3.00
NL6 Alexandre Daigle .75 2.00
NL7 Alexei Yashin .75 2.00
NL8 Doug Gilmour 1.25 3.00
NL9 Felix Potvin 2.50 6.00
NL10 Mats Sundin 1.50 4.00
NL11 Teemu Selanne 1.50 4.00
NL12 Keith Tkachuk 1.25 3.00
NL13 Bill Ranford 1.25 3.00
NL14 Jason Arnott .75 2.00
NL15 Theo Fleury .75 2.00
NL16 Gary Roberts .75 2.00
NL17 Pavel Bure 1.50 4.00
NL18 Trevor Linden 1.25 3.00

1994-95 Pinnacle Rookie Team Pinnacle

COMPLETE SET (12) 15.00 40.00
1 C.Hirsch/J.Storr 1.00 2.50
2 M.Norstrom/O.Tverdovsky 1.00 2.50
3 D.Tsygurov/J.Laukkanen 1.00 2.50
4 C.Tamer/K.Jonsson 1.00 2.50
5 Z.Palffy/V.Kozlov 2.00 5.00
6 R.Corbet/M.Bets 1.00 2.50
7 J.Allison/J.Friesen 2.00 5.00
8 B.Rolston/M.Peca 2.00 5.00
9 P.Forsberg/P.Kariya 8.00 20.00
10 B.Savage/T.Harvey 1.00 2.50
11 B.Lindros/V.Karpov 1.00 2.50
12 M.Czerkawski/S.Krivokrasov 1.00 2.50

1994-95 Pinnacle Team Pinnacle

COMPLETE SET (12) 75.00 150.00
*DUFEX BACK: .4X TO 1X BASIC INSERTS
TP1 F.Potvin/P.Roy 8.00 20.00
TP2 C.Joseph/M.Richter 5.00 12.00
TP3 C.Chelios/R.Bourque 4.00 10.00
TP4 B.Leetch/R.Blake 6.00 15.00
TP5 S.Stevens/P.Coffey 6.00 15.00
TP6 B.Shanahan/A.Graves 10.00 25.00
TP7 L.Robitaille/K.Stevens 4.00 10.00
TP8 S.Fedorov/E.Lindros 8.00 20.00
TP9 W.Gretzky/M.Messier 10.00 25.00
TP10 D.Gilmour/M.Lemieux 8.00 20.00
TP11 B.Hull/J.Jagr 5.00 12.00
TP12 P.Bure/C.Neely 8.00 20.00

1994-95 Pinnacle World Edition

COMPLETE SET (18) 15.00 40.00
WE1 Teemu Selanne 1.00 2.50
WE2 Doug Gilmour .60 1.50
WE3 Jeremy Roenick 1.00 2.50
WE4 Ulf Dahlen .40 1.00
WE5 Sergei Fedorov 1.00 2.50
WE6 Dominik Hasek 2.00 5.00
WE7 Jari Kurri .60 1.50
WE8 Mario Lemieux 4.00 10.00
WE9 Mike Modano 1.00 2.50
WE10 Mikael Renberg .40 1.00
WE11 Sandis Ozolinsh .40 1.00
WE12 Alexei Kovalev .40 1.00
WE13 Robert Reichel .40 1.00
WE14 Eric Lindros 1.00 2.50
WE15 Brian Leetch 1.00 2.50
WE16 Nicklas Lidstrom 1.00 2.50
WE17 Alexei Yashin .40 1.00
WE18 Petr Nedved .40 1.00

1995-96 Pinnacle

1 Pavel Bure .10 .25
2 Paul Kariya .10 .25
3 Adam Oates .10 .25
4 Garry Galley .05 .15
5 Mark Messier .20 .50
6 Theo Fleury .12 .30
7 Alexandre Daigle .05 .15
8 Joe Murphy .05 .15
9 Eric Lindros .15 .40
10 Kevin Hatcher .07 .20
11 Jaromir Jagr .30 .75
12 Owen Nolan .10 .25
13 Ulf Dahlen .05 .15
14 Paul Coffey .10 .25
15 Brett Hull .20 .50
16 Jason Arnott .07 .20
17 Paul Ysebaert .05 .15
18 Jesse Belanger .05 .15
19 Mats Sundin .10 .25
20 Darren Turcotte .05 .15
21 Dale Hunter .07 .20
22 Jari Kurri .10 .25
23 Alexei Zhamnov .10 .25
24 Mark Recchi .12 .30
25 Dallas Drake .05 .15
26 John MacLean .07 .20
27 Keith Jones .07 .20
28 Mathieu Schneider .05 .15
29 Jeff Brown .07 .20
30 Patrick Flatley .05 .15
31 Dave Andreychuk .10 .25
32 Bill Guerin .10 .25
33 Chris Gratton .05 .15
34 Pierre Turgeon .07 .20
35 Stephane Richer .07 .20
36 Marty McSorley .07 .20
37 Craig Janney .05 .15
38 Geoff Sanderson .05 .15
39 Ron Francis .12 .30
40 Stu Barnes .05 .15
41 Mikael Renberg .07 .20
42 David Oliver .05 .15
43 Radek Bonk .05 .15
44 Sergei Fedorov .15 .40
45 Adam Graves .07 .20
46 Uwe Krupp .07 .20
47 Mike Richter .10 .25
48 Todd Harvey .05 .15
49 Stanislav Neckar .05 .15
50 Chris Chelios .10 .25
51 John LeClair .10 .25
52 German Titov .07 .20
53 Garth Butcher .05 .15
54 Pat LaFontaine .10 .25
55 Jeff Friesen .05 .15
56 Ray Bourque .15 .40
57 Esa Tikkanen .05 .15
58 Steve Rucchin .07 .20
59 Roman Hamrlik .07 .20
60 Oleg Tverdovsky .10 .25
61 Doug Gilmour .12 .30
62 Jocelyn Lemieux .07 .20
63 Roman Oksiuta .05 .15
64 Alexei Zhitnik .05 .15
65 Sylvain Cote .05 .15
66 Paul Kruse .05 .15
67 Teppo Numminen .05 .15
68 Gary Suter .05 .15
69 Darrin Shannon .05 .15
70 Derian Hatcher .07 .20
71 Sergei Gonchar .05 .15
72 Adam Deadmarsh .05 .15
73 Jyrki Lumme .05 .15
74 Dino Ciccarelli .07 .20
75 Mike Gartner .12 .30
76 Todd Marchant .05 .15
77 Jason Wiemer .05 .15
78 Scott Mellanby .07 .20
79 Al MacInnis .12 .30
80 Glen Wesley .05 .15
81 Igor Larionov .05 .15
82 Eric Lacroix .05 .15
83 Mike Keane .05 .15
84 Vincent Damphousse .07 .20
85 Robert Kron .05 .15
86 Scott Stevens .10 .25
87 Don Beaupre .07 .20
88 Zigmund Palffy .10 .25
89 Kevin Lowe .07 .20
90 Tommy Soderstrom .07 .20
91 Glenn Healy .07 .20
92 Randy McKay .05 .15
93 Sean Hill .05 .15
94 Brian Savage .05 .15
95 Ron Hextall .10 .25
96 Darryl Sydor .07 .20
97 Tom Barrasso .07 .20
98 Andrei Nikolishin .05 .15
99 Viktor Kozlov .07 .20
100 Rob Niedermayer .07 .20
101 Wayne Gretzky .60 1.50
102 Shaun Van Allen .05 .15
103 Dave Manson .05 .15
104 Donald Audette .07 .20
105 Daren Puppa .07 .20
106 Jeremy Roenick .15 .40
107 Ken Wregget .07 .20
108 Mike Modano .15 .40
109 Rod Brind'Amour .10 .25
110 Eric Desjardins .07 .20
111 Pat Verbeek .07 .20
112 Jeff Beukeboom .05 .15
113 John Druce .07 .20
114 Andy Moog .10 .25
115 Turner Stevenson .05 .15
116 Alexander Selivanov .07 .20
117 Neal Broten .07 .20
118 Nikolai Khabibulin .07 .20
119 Claude Lemieux .10 .25
120 Sergei Brylin .05 .15
121 Bob Corkum .05 .15
122 Kelly Hrudey .07 .20
123 Jason Dawe .05 .15
124 Sean Burke .05 .15
125 Dave Gagner .05 .15
126 Kirk Maltby .07 .20
127 Ian Laperriere .05 .15
128 Slava Kozlov .07 .20
129 Vladimir Konstantinov .07 .20
130 Kenny Jonsson .10 .25
131 Sylvain Lefebvre .05 .15
132 Kirk McLean .07 .20
133 Brian Leetch .07 .20
134 Olaf Kolzig .10 .25
135 Patrick Poulin .05 .15
136 Tim Cheveldae .07 .20
137 Gary Roberts .05 .15
138 Jim Carey .07 .20
139 Dominik Hasek .15 .40
140 Josef Beranek .05 .15
141 Don Sweeney .05 .15
142 Felix Potvin .15 .40
143 Guy Hebert .07 .20
144 Guy Carbonneau .10 .25
145 Mikhail Shtalenkov .05 .15
146 Kevin Miller .07 .20
147 Blaine Lacher .07 .20
148 Craig MacTavish .05 .15
149 Derek Plante .05 .15
150 Kevin Dineen .07 .20
151 Trevor Kidd .07 .20
152 Sergei Nemchinov .05 .15
153 Ed Belfour .07 .20
154 Sergei Krivokrasov .05 .15
155 Mike Rathje .07 .20
156 Mike Donnelly .05 .15
157 David Roberts .05 .15
158 Jocelyn Thibault .07 .20
159 Tie Domi .07 .20
160 Chris Osgood .10 .25
161 Martin Gelinas .05 .15
162 Scott Thornton .07 .20
163 Bob Rouse .05 .15
164 Randy Wood .05 .15
165 Chris Therien .05 .15
166 Steven Rice .05 .15
167 Scott Lachance .05 .15
168 Petr Svoboda .05 .15
169 Patrick Roy .25 .60
170 Norm Maciver .07 .20
171 Todd Gill .05 .15
172 Brian Rolston .07 .20
173 Wade Flaherty RC .07 .20
174 Valeri Bure .05 .15
175 Mark Fitzpatrick .07 .20
176 Darren McCarty .05 .15
177 Ken Daneyko .05 .15
178 Yves Racine .05 .15
179 Murray Craven .05 .15
180 Nicklas Lidstrom .10 .25
181 Gord Murphy .05 .15
182 Eric Weinrich .05 .15
183 Todd Krygier .05 .15
184 Cliff Ronning .05 .15
185 Mariusz Czerkawski .05 .15
186 Benoit Hogue .05 .15
187 Richard Smehlik .07 .20
188 Jeff Norton .05 .15
189 Steve Chiasson .05 .15
190 Andrei Nazarov .07 .20
191 Steve Smith .05 .15
192 Mario Lemieux .40 1.00
193 Trent Klatt .05 .15
194 Valeri Zelepukin .05 .15
195 Adam Foote .07 .20
196 Lyle Odelein .05 .15
197 Keith Primeau .07 .20
198 Rob Blake .07 .20
199 Dave Lowry .05 .15
200 Adam Burt .05 .15
201 Martin Gendron .07 .20
202 Tommy Salo RC .15 .40
203 Eric Daze .20 .50
204 Ryan Smyth .07 .20
205 Brian Holzinger RC .20 .50
206 Chris Marinucci RC .07 .20
207 Jason Bonsignore .05 .15
208 Craig Johnson .05 .15
209 Steve Larouche RC .05 .15
210 Chris McAlpine RC .07 .20
211 Shean Donovan .05 .15
212 Cory Stillman .05 .15
213 Craig Darby .05 .15
214 Philippe DeRouville .07 .20
215 Kevin Brown .07 .20
216 Manny Fernandez .05 .15
217 Radim Bicanek .07 .20
218 Craig Conroy RC .07 .20
219 Todd Warriner .07 .20
220 Richard Park .10 .25
221 Checklist .05 .15
222 Checklist .05 .15
223 Checklist .05 .15
224 Checklist .05 .15
225 Checklist .05 .15

1995-96 Pinnacle Artist's Proofs

*VETS: 12X TO 30X BASIC CARDS
*ROOKIES: 4X TO 10X BASIC CARDS

1995-96 Pinnacle Rink Collection

*VETS: 4X TO 10X BASIC CARDS
*ROOKIES: 2X TO 5X BASIC CARDS

1995-96 Pinnacle Clear Shots

1 Martin Brodeur 5.00 12.00
2 Brett Hull 4.00 10.00
3 Paul Kariya 2.00 5.00
4 Eric Lindros 3.00 8.00
5 Cam Neely 2.00 5.00
6 Doug Gilmour 2.50 6.00
7 Sergei Fedorov 3.00 8.00
8 Peter Forsberg 4.00 10.00
9 Wayne Gretzky 12.00 30.00
10 Patrick Roy 5.00 12.00
11 Jaromir Jagr 6.00 15.00
12 Pavel Bure 2.00 5.00
13 Mario Lemieux 8.00 20.00
14 Pierre Turgeon 1.50 4.00
15 Dominik Hasek 3.00 8.00

1995-96 Pinnacle First Strike

COMPLETE SET (15) 10.00 20.00
1 Mark Messier .40 1.00
2 Wayne Gretzky 2.50 6.00
3 Doug Gilmour .20 .50
4 Patrick Roy 2.00 5.00
5 Cam Neely .40 1.00
6 Brian Leetch .20 .50
7 Ed Belfour .40 1.00
8 Wendel Clark .20 .50
9 Chris Chelios .40 1.00
10 Claude Lemieux .10 .30
11 Peter Forsberg .75 2.00
12 Brett Hull .50 1.25
13 Mario Lemieux 2.00 5.00
14 Dominik Hasek .75 2.00
15 Theo Fleury .10 .30

1995-96 Pinnacle Full Contact

COMPLETE SET (12) 5.00 12.00
1 Cam Neely .30 .75
2 Scott Stevens .30 .75
3 Owen Nolan .20 .50
4 Jeremy Roenick .50 1.25
5 Brendan Shanahan .20 .50
6 Chris Chelios .30 .75
7 Brett Lindros .20 .50
8 Jason Arnott .20 .50
9 Tie Domi .20 .50
10 Mark Tinordi .20 .50
11 Keith Tkachuk .30 .75
12 Mark Messier .40 1.00

1995-96 Pinnacle Global Gold

1 Pavel Bure 2.50 6.00
2 Jaromir Jagr 3.00 8.00
3 Mats Sundin 1.00 2.50
4 Jari Kurri .75 2.00
5 Mikael Renberg .75 2.00
6 Radek Bonk .20 .50
7 Sergei Fedorov 2.00 5.00
8 Uwe Krupp .20 .50
9 German Titov .20 .50
10 Esa Tikkanen .75 2.00
11 Oleg Tverdovsky .20 .50
12 Teppo Numminen .20 .50
13 Jyrki Lumme .20 .50
14 Zigmund Palffy 1.00 2.50
15 Tommy Soderstrom .75 2.00
16 Viktor Kozlov .75 2.00
17 Alexander Selivanov .20 .50
18 Sergei Brylin .20 .50
19 Dominik Hasek 2.00 5.00
20 Sergei Nemchinov .20 .50
21 Petr Svoboda .20 .50
22 Valeri Bure .75 2.00
23 Nicklas Lidstrom 1.00 2.50
24 Mariusz Czerkawski .75 2.00
25 Valeri Zelepukin .20 .50

1995-96 Pinnacle Masks

COMPLETE SET (10) 60.00 120.00
1 Blaine Lacher 4.00 10.00
2 Martin Brodeur 15.00 40.00
3 Jim Carey 4.00 10.00
4 Felix Potvin 10.00 25.00
5 Andy Moog 4.00 10.00
6 Mike Vernon 5.00 12.00
7 Mark Fitzpatrick 8.00 20.00
8 Ron Hextall 5.00 12.00
9 Sean Burke 5.00 12.00
10 Jocelyn Thibault 10.00 25.00

1995-96 Pinnacle Roaring 20s

COMPLETE SET (20) 20.00 50.00
1 Eric Lindros 1.25 3.00
2 Paul Kariya 1.00 2.50
3 Martin Brodeur 3.00 8.00
4 Jeremy Roenick 1.50 4.00
5 Mike Modano 1.50 4.00
6 Sergei Fedorov 1.50 4.00
7 Mats Sundin 1.00 2.50
8 Pavel Bure 1.25 3.00
9 Jim Carey .60 1.50
10 Felix Potvin 2.50 6.00
11 Alexei Zhamnov .60 1.50
12 Mikael Renberg .60 1.50
13 Jaromir Jagr 2.00 5.00
14 Peter Bondra .60 1.50
15 Peter Forsberg 2.00 5.00
16 John LeClair .60 1.50
17 Joe Sakic 2.50 6.00
18 Brendan Shanahan 1.25 3.00
19 Teemu Selanne 1.25 3.00
20 Pierre Turgeon .60 1.50

1995-96 Pinnacle FANtasy

COMPLETE SET (30) 15.00 40.00
1 Cam Neely .40 1.00
2 Ray Bourque 1.25 3.00
3 Alexandre Daigle .10 .30
4 Mariusz Czerkawski .10 .25
5 Adam Oates .40 1.00
6 Brendan Shanahan .75 2.00
7 Arturs Irbe .40 1.00
8 Mario Lemieux 3.00 8.00
9 Theo Fleury .40 1.00
10 Patrick Roy 3.00 8.00
11 Roman Hamrlik .20 .50
12 Pavel Bure 1.25 3.00
13 Wayne Gretzky 4.00 10.00
14 Mike Modano .75 2.00
15 Teemu Selanne .75 2.00
16 John Vanbiesbrouck .40 1.00
17 Dominik Hasek .75 2.00
18 Mark Messier .75 2.00
19 Martin Brodeur 1.25 3.00
20 Jim Carey .20 .50
21 Wendel Clark .20 .50
22 Jason Arnott .20 .50
23 Jeremy Roenick .60 1.50
24 Brett Hull .75 2.00
25 Peter Forsberg 1.25 3.00
26 Paul Kariya 2.00 5.00
27 Eric Lindros 1.25 3.00
28 Kevin Stevens .10 .30
29 Felix Potvin .40 1.00
30 Sergei Fedorov .75 2.00
31 Travis Roy Bobby Orr SP 8.00 20.00

1996-97 Pinnacle

1 Wayne Gretzky 1.25 3.00
2 Mark Messier .40 1.00
3 Kevin Hatcher .12 .30
4 Scott Stevens .20 .50
5 Derek Plante .12 .30
6 Theo Fleury .40 1.00
7 Brian Rolston .15 .40
8 Teppo Numminen .12 .30
9 Adam Graves .12 .30
10 Jason Dawe .12 .30
11 Sergei Nemchinov .12 .30
12 Jeff Brown .12 .30
13 Alexei Zhamnov .15 .40
14 Paul Coffey .20 .50
15 Kevin Miller .12 .30
16 Mike Vernon .15 .40
17 Brian Bradley .12 .30
18 Jeff Friesen .12 .30
19 Phil Housley .15 .40
20 Ray Whitney .12 .30
21 Sergei Fedorov .30 .75
22 Pierre Turgeon .15 .40
23 Rick Tocchet .15 .40
24 Uwe Krupp .12 .30
25 Steve Yzerman .50 1.25
26 Tom Chorske .12 .30
27 Pat LaFontaine .20 .50
28 Nicklas Lidstrom .25 .60
29 Ray Ferraro .12 .30
30 Brian Noonan .12 .30
31 Dino Ciccarelli .20 .50
32 Rob Niedermayer .15 .40
33 Stephane Richer .15 .40
34 Chris Chelios .20 .50
35 Mike Gartner .25 .60
36 German Titov .12 .30
37 Sean Burke .12 .30
38 Robert Svehla .12 .30
39 Dave Gagner .20 .50
40 Sergei Gonchar .12 .30
41 Bernie Nicholls .15 .40
42 Yanic Perreault .12 .30
43 Adam Deadmarsh .12 .30
44 Dale Hawerchuk .25 .60
45 Alexei Kovalev .15 .40
46 Esa Tikkanen .12 .30
47 Valeri Kamensky .15 .40
48 Craig Janney .15 .40
49 John LeClair .20 .50
50 Radek Bonk .12 .30
51 David Oliver .12 .30
52 Todd Harvey .12 .30
53 Steve Thomas .12 .30
54 Tony Amonte .15 .40
55 Mikael Renberg .15 .40
56 Brendan Shanahan .20 .50
57 Tom Fitzgerald .12 .30
58 Chris Pronger .20 .50
59 Donald Audette .12 .30
60 Nelson Emerson .12 .30
61 Joe Mullen .15 .40
62 Marty McInnis .12 .30
63 Martin Rucinsky .12 .30
64 Mark Recchi .25 .60

65 Vladimir Konstantinov .15 .40
66 Rick Tabaracci .15 .40
67 Marty McSorley .15 .40
68 Pat Verbeek .12 .30
69 Garry Galley .12 .30
70 Travis Green .15 .40
71 Chris Tancill .12 .30
72 Vincent Damphousse .15 .40
73 Benoit Hogue .12 .30
74 Igor Larionov .20 .50
75 Russ Courtnall .12 .30
76 Mike Hough .12 .30
77 Alexander Selivanov .12 .30
78 Peter Forsberg .40 1.00
79 Petr Klima .12 .30
80 Adam Creighton .12 .30
81 Dave Lowry .12 .30
82 Andrew Cassels .12 .30
83 Martin Gelinas .12 .30
84 Bob Probert .20 .50
85 Calle Johansson .15 .40
86 Mario Lemieux .75 2.00
87 Alexander Mogilny .15 .40
88 Guy Hebert .15 .40
89 Bill Ranford .15 .40
90 Kirk McLean .15 .40
91 Kenny Jonsson .12 .30
92 Martin Brodeur .50 1.25
93 Keith Jones .12 .30
94 Ed Belfour .20 .50
95 Tom Barrasso .15 .40
96 Felix Potvin .30 .75
97 Daren Puppa .15 .40
98 Jeremy Roenick .30 .75
99 Chris Osgood UER .20 .50
100 Zigmund Palffy .20 .50
101 Ron Hextall .20 .50
102 Jaromir Jagr .60 1.50
103 Chris Terreri .15 .40
104 Shayne Corson .15 .40
105 Jim Carey .20 .50
106 Dominik Hasek .30 .75
107 Eric Lindros .30 .75
108 Petr Nedved .15 .40
109 Peter Bondra .20 .50
110 Jeff Hackett .15 .40
111 Trevor Linden .20 .50
112 Mike Richter .20 .50
113 Claude Lemieux .12 .30
114 Keith Tkachuk .20 .50
115 Pat Falloon .12 .30
116 Brent Fedyk .12 .30
117 Todd Marchant .12 .30
118 Jason Arnott .15 .40
119 Zarley Zalapski .12 .30
120 Kelly Hrudey .15 .40
121 Alexei Yashin .15 .40
122 Sergei Zubov .15 .40
123 Rod Brind'Amour .20 .50
124 Mathieu Schneider .12 .30
125 Bryan Smolinski .12 .30
126 Scott Mellanby .12 .30
127 Doug Gilmour .25 .60
128 Brett Hull .40 1.00
129 Vyacheslav Kozlov .12 .30
130 Adam Oates .20 .50
131 Steve Konowalchuk .12 .30
132 Robert Kron .12 .30
133 Alexandre Daigle .12 .30
134 Brian Savage .12 .30
135 Stu Barnes .12 .30
136 Cam Neely .20 .50
137 Steve Rucchin .12 .30
138 Patrick Roy .50 1.25
139 Roman Oksiuta .12 .30
140 Greg Johnson .12 .30
141 Chris Gratton .15 .40
142 Jocelyn Thibault .15 .40
143 Ron Francis .25 .60
144 Mats Sundin .20 .50
145 Oleg Tverdovsky .12 .30
146 Geoff Courtnall .12 .30
147 Kirk Muller .12 .30
148 Zdeno Ciger .12 .30
149 John MacLean .15 .40
150 Damian Rhodes .15 .40
151 Michael Nylander .12 .30
152 Andrei Kovalenko .12 .30
153 Al MacInnis .25 .60
154 Mike Modano .30 .75
155 Teemu Selanne .40 1.00
156 Tomas Sandstrom .12 .30
157 Bobby Dollas .12 .30
158 Doug Weight .20 .50
159 Sandis Ozolinsh .12 .30
160 Joe Juneau .12 .30
161 Nikolai Khabibulin .15 .40
162 Murray Craven .12 .30
163 Cliff Ronning .12 .30
164 Curtis Joseph .25 .60
165 Darren Turcotte .12 .30
166 Andy Moog .20 .50
167 Mariusz Czerkawski .12 .30
168 Keith Primeau .15 .40
169 Eric Desjardins .15 .40
170 Bill Guerin .20 .50
171 Glenn Anderson .15 .40
172 Mike Ridley .12 .30
173 Michal Pivonka .12 .30
174 Trevor Kidd .12 .30
175 Pavel Bure .20 .50
176 Todd Gill .12 .30
177 Dave Andreychuk .20 .50
178 Roman Hamrlik .12 .30
179 Andrei Nikolishin .12 .30
180 Alexei Zhitnik .12 .30
181 Grant Fuhr .30 .75
182 Dave Reid .12 .30
183 Joe Nieuwendyk .15 .40
184 Paul Kariya .20 .50
185 Jyrki Lumme .12 .30
186 Owen Nolan .20 .50
187 Geoff Sanderson .12 .30
188 Alexander Semak .12 .30
189 Larry Murphy .15 .40
190 Dimitri Khristich .15 .40
191 Shane Churla .12 .30
192 Bill Lindsay .12 .30
193 Brian Leetch .15 .40
194 Greg Adams .12 .30
195 Gary Suter .12 .30
196 Wendel Clark .30 .75
197 Scott Young .12 .30
198 Randy Burridge .12 .30
199 Ray Bourque .30 .75
200 Joe Murphy .12 .30
201 Joe Sakic .40 1.00
202 Saku Koivu .20 .50
203 John Vanbiesbrouck .20 .50
204 Ed Jovanovski .15 .40
205 Daniel Alfredsson .20 .50
206 Vitali Yachmenev .12 .30
207 Marcus Ragnarsson .12 .30
208 Todd Bertuzzi .20 .50
209 Valeri Bure .12 .30
210 Jeff O'Neill .12 .30
211 Corey Hirsch .15 .40
212 Eric Daze .15 .40
213 David Sacco .12 .30
214 Jan Vopat .12 .30
215 Scott Bailey .12 .30
216 Jamie Rivers .12 .30
217 Jose Theodore .25 .60
218 Peter Ferraro .12 .30
219 Anders Eriksson .12 .30
220 Wayne Primeau .12 .30
221 Denis Pederson .12 .30
222 Jay McKee RC .12 .30
223 Sean Pronger .12 .30
224 Martin Biron RC .25 .60
225 Marek Malik .12 .30
226 Steve Sullivan RC .15 .40
227 Curtis Brown .12 .30
228 Eric Fichaud .15 .40
229 Jan Caloun RC .20 .50
230 Niklas Sundblad .12 .30
231 Steve Staios RC .20 .50
232 Steve Washburn RC .20 .50
233 Chris Ferraro .12 .30
234 Marko Kiprusoff .12 .30
235 Larry Courville .12 .30
236 David Nemirovsky .12 .30
237 Ralph Intranuovo .12 .30
238 Kevin Hodson RC .20 .50
239 Ethan Moreau RC .20 .50
240 Daymond Langkow .15 .40
241 Brandon Convery .12 .30
242 Cale Hulse .12 .30
243 Zdenek Nedved .12 .30
244 Tommy Salo .15 .40
245 Nolan Baumgartner .12 .30
246 Patrick Labrecque .12 .30
247 Jamie Langenbrunner .12 .30
248 Pavel Bure CL .20 .50
249 Peter Forsberg CL .40 1.00
250 Teemu Selanne CL .40 1.00

1996-97 Pinnacle Artist's Proofs
*VETS: 12X TO 30X BASIC CARDS
*ROOKIES: 4X TO 10X

1996-97 Pinnacle Foil
*VETS: .6X TO 1.5X BASIC CARDS
*ROOKIES: .2X TO .5X
2 Mark Messier .30 .75

1996-97 Pinnacle Premium Stock
*VETS: 1.2X TO 3X BASIC CARDS
*ROOKIES: .4X TO 1X BASIC CARDS
2 Mark Messier .60 1.50

1996-97 Pinnacle Rink Collection
*RINK: 1.5X TO 4X BASIC

1996-97 Pinnacle By The Numbers
COMPLETE SET (15) 25.00 50.00
*PREM.STOCK: 1X TO 2.5X BASIC INSERTS
1 Teemu Selanne 1.50 4.00
2 Brendan Shanahan 1.50 4.00
3 Sergei Fedorov 2.00 5.00
4 Ed Jovanovski 1.00 2.50
5 Doug Weight 1.00 2.50
6 Brett Hull 2.00 5.00
7 Doug Gilmour 1.00 2.50
8 Jaromir Jagr 2.50 6.00
9 Wayne Gretzky 10.00 25.00
10 Daniel Alfredsson 1.50 4.00
11 Eric Daze 1.00 2.50
12 Mark Messier 1.50 4.00
13 Jocelyn Thibault 1.50 4.00
14 Eric Lindros 2.00 5.00
15 Pavel Bure 1.50 4.00
P1 Teemu Selanne PROMO 1.50 4.00
P11 Eric Daze PROMO 1.50 4.00
P16 Brett Hull PROMO 2.00 5.00

1996-97 Pinnacle Masks
COMPLETE SET (10) 60.00 125.00
*DIE CUTS: .6X TO 1.5X BASIC CARDS
1 Patrick Roy 15.00 40.00
2 Jim Carey 6.00 15.00
3 John Vanbiesbrouck 8.00 20.00
4 Martin Brodeur 10.00 25.00
5 Jocelyn Thibault 5.00 12.00
6 Ron Hextall 6.00 15.00
7 Nikolai Khabibulin 6.00 15.00
8 Stephane Fiset 5.00 12.00
9 Mike Richter 6.00 15.00
10 Kelly Hrudey 5.00 12.00

1996-97 Pinnacle Team Pinnacle
1 W.Gretzky/J.Sakic 8.00 20.00
2 M.Lemieux/P.Forsberg 6.00 15.00
3 E.Lindros/J.Roenick 4.00 10.00
4 M.Messier/D.Weight 4.00 10.00
5 B.Shanahan/P.Kariya 4.00 10.00
6 J.Jagr/B.Hull 5.00 12.00
7 E.Jovanovski/P.Coffey 4.00 10.00
8 J.Vanbiesbrouck/P.Roy 6.00 15.00
9 M.Brodeur/C.Osgood 5.00 12.00
10 S.Koivu/E.Daze 4.00 10.00

1996-97 Pinnacle Trophies
COMPLETE SET (10) 30.00 80.00
1 Mario Lemieux 12.00 30.00
2 Paul Kariya 10.00 25.00
3 Sergei Fedorov 5.00 12.00
4 Daniel Alfredsson 3.00 8.00
5 Jim Carey 1.50 4.00
6 C.Osgood
M.Vernon 6.00 15.00
7 Kris King 1.50 4.00
8 Chris Chelios 3.00 8.00
9 Joe Sakic 8.00 20.00
10 Colorado Avalanche 6.00 15.00

1997-98 Pinnacle
1 Espen Knutsen RC .15 .40
2 Juha Lind RC .15 .40
3 Erik Rasmussen .12 .30
4 Olli Jokinen RC .20 .50
5 Chris Phillips .12 .30
6 Alexei Morozov .12 .30
7 Chris Dingman RC .15 .40
8 Mattias Ohlund .12 .30
9 Sergei Samsonov .12 .30
10 Daniel Cleary .12 .30
11 Terry Ryan .10 .25
12 Patrick Marleau .15 .40
13 Boyd Devereaux .12 .30
14 Donald MacLean .15 .40
15 Marc Savard .10 .25
16 Magnus Arvedson .15 .40
17 Marian Hossa RC .20 .50
18 Alyn McCauley .12 .30
19 Vaclav Prospal RC .12 .30
20 Brad Isbister .12 .30
21 Robert Dome RC .10 .25
22 Kevyn Adams .10 .25
23 Joe Thornton .25 .60
24 Jan Bulis RC .12 .30
25 Jaroslav Svejkovsky .12 .30
26 Saku Koivu .15 .40
27 Mark Messier .30 .75
28 Dominik Hasek .25 .60
29 Patrick Roy .40 1.00
30 Jaromir Jagr .50 1.25
31 Jarome Iginla .20 .50
32 Joe Sakic .30 .75
33 Jeremy Roenick .25 .60
34 Chris Osgood .15 .40
35 Brett Hull .30 .75
36 Mike Vernon .12 .30
37 John Vanbiesbrouck .15 .40
38 Ray Bourque .25 .60
39 Doug Gilmour .20 .50
40 Keith Tkachuk .20 .50
41 Pavel Bure .15 .40
42 Sean Burke .10 .25
43 Martin Brodeur .40 1.00
44 Damian Rhodes .12 .30
45 Geoff Sanderson .12 .30
46 Bill Ranford .12 .30
47 Kevin Hodson .12 .30
48 Eric Lindros .25 .60
49 Owen Nolan .15 .40
50 Mats Sundin .15 .40
51 Ed Belfour .12 .30
52 Stephane Fiset .12 .30
53 Paul Kariya .15 .40
54 Doug Weight .15 .40
55 Mike Richter .15 .40
56 Zigmund Palffy .12 .30
57 John LeClair .15 .40
58 Alexander Mogilny .15 .40
59 Tommy Salo .10 .25
60 Trevor Kidd .10 .25
61 Jason Arnott .12 .30
62 Adam Oates .15 .40
63 Garth Snow .12 .30
64 Rob Blake .15 .40
65 Chris Chelios .15 .40
66 Eric Fichaud .12 .30
67 Wayne Gretzky 1.00 2.50
68 Dino Ciccarelli .15 .40
69 Pat LaFontaine .15 .40
70 Andy Moog .15 .40
71 Steve Yzerman .40 1.00
72 Jeff Hackett .10 .25
73 Peter Forsberg .30 .75
74 Arturs Irbe .12 .30
75 Pierre Turgeon .12 .30
76 Tom Barrasso .12 .30
77 Sergei Fedorov .25 .60
78 Ron Francis .20 .50
79 Mike Dunham .12 .30
80 Brendan Shanahan .12 .30
81 Grant Fuhr .25 .60
82 Jamie Storr .12 .30
83 Jim Carey .10 .25
84 Daren Puppa .12 .30
85 Vincent Damphousse .12 .30
86 Teemu Selanne .30 .75
87 Dwayne Roloson .12 .30
88 Kirk McLean .12 .30
89 Olaf Kolzig .15 .40
90 Guy Hebert .12 .30
91 Mike Modano .25 .60
92 Brian Leetch .15 .40
93 Curtis Joseph .20 .50
94 Nikolai Khabibulin .15 .40
95 Felix Potvin .25 .60
96 Ken Wregget .10 .25
97 Steve Shields RC .15 .40
98 Jocelyn Thibault .12 .30
99 Ron Tugnutt .15 .40
100 Ron Hextall .15 .40
101 Mike Peca .12 .30
102 Donald Audette .12 .30
103 Theo Fleury .20 .50
104 Mark Recchi .20 .50
105 Dainius Zubrus .12 .30
106 Trevor Linden .15 .40
107 Joe Juneau .10 .25
108 Matthew Barnaby .10 .25
109 Keith Primeau .12 .30
110 Joe Nieuwendyk .12 .30
111 Rod Brind'Amour .15 .40
112 Daymond Langkow .15 .40
113 Ed Jovanovski .10 .25
114 Adam Deadmarsh .10 .25
115 Scott Niedermayer .15 .40
116 Al MacInnis .20 .50
117 Slava Kozlov .12 .30
118 Jere Lehtinen .12 .30
119 Jeff Friesen .12 .30
120 Alexei Kovalev .12 .30
121 Eric Daze .10 .25
122 Mariusz Czerkawski .10 .25
123 Alexei Zhamnov .10 .25
124 Petr Nedved .15 .40
125 Dmitri Mironov .10 .25
126 Alexei Yashin .12 .30
127 Todd Marchant .10 .25
128 Sandis Ozolinsh .12 .30
129 Igor Larionov .12 .30
130 Jim Campbell .10 .25
131 Dave Andreychuk .15 .40
132 Glen Wesley .10 .25
133 Rem Murray .10 .25
134 Steve Sullivan .12 .30
135 Miroslav Satan .12 .30
136 Bill Guerin .15 .40
137 Mike Gartner .20 .50
138 Jozef Stumpel .10 .25
139 Darryl Sydor .10 .25
140 Darcy Tucker .15 .40
141 Robert Svehla .12 .30
142 Steve Duchesne .10 .25
143 Kevin Stevens .10 .25
144 Mikael Renberg .12 .30
145 Bryan Berard .10 .25
146 Ray Ferraro .10 .25
147 Jason Allison .12 .30
148 Tony Amonte .12 .30
149 Luc Robitaille .15 .40
150 Mathieu Schneider .12 .30
151 Steve Rucchin .12 .30
152 Brian Savage .10 .25
153 Paul Coffey .15 .40
154 Jeff O'Neill .12 .30
155 Daniel Alfredsson .12 .30
156 Dave Gagner .10 .25
157 Rob Niedermayer .10 .25
158 Scott Stevens .15 .40
159 Alexandre Daigle .10 .25
160 Stephane Richer .10 .25
161 Harry York .10 .25
162 Sergei Berezin .12 .30
163 Claude Lemieux .12 .30
164 Ray Sheppard .12 .30
165 Bernie Nicholls .12 .30
166 Oleg Tverdovsky .10 .25
167 Travis Green .10 .25
168 Martin Gelinas .10 .25
169 Derek Plante .10 .25
170 Gary Roberts .12 .30
171 Kevin Hatcher .10 .25
172 Martin Rucinsky .12 .30
173 Pat Verbeek .12 .30
174 Adam Graves .10 .25
175 Roman Hamrlik .10 .25
176 Darren McCarty .12 .30
177 Mike Grier .12 .30
178 Andrew Cassels .10 .25
179 Dimitri Khristich .10 .25
180 Tomas Sandstrom .10 .25
181 Peter Bondra .15 .40
182 Derian Hatcher .12 .30
183 Chris Gratton .10 .25
184 John MacLean .10 .25
185 Wendel Clark .25 .60
186 Valeri Kamensky .12 .30
187 Tony Granato .10 .25
188 Vladimir Vorobiev RC .12 .30
189 Ethan Moreau .10 .25
190 Kirk Muller .10 .25
191 Peter Forsberg SM .30 .75
192 Wayne Gretzky SM 1.00 2.50
193 Jaromir Jagr SM .50 1.25
194 Mark Messier SM .30 .75
195 Brian Leetch SM .15 .40
196 John LeClair SM .15 .40
197 Jeremy Roenick SM .25 .60
198 Checklist .02 .10
199 Checklist .02 .10
200 Checklist .02 .10
NNO John Vanbiesbrouck 3x5 PROMO .15 .40
NNO Paul Kariya 3x5 PROMO .15 .40

1997-98 Pinnacle Artist's Proofs
*ART.PROOF: 12X TO 30X BASIC CARDS

1997-98 Pinnacle Rink Collection
*RINK COLL.: 4X TO 10X BASIC CARDS

1997-98 Pinnacle Epix Game Orange
COMPLETE SET (24) 40.00 100.00
*PURPLE: .6X TO 1.5X ORANGE
*EMERALD: 1.2X TO 3X ORANGE
1 Wayne Gretzky 8.00 20.00
2 John Vanbiesbrouck .75 2.00
3 Joe Sakic 2.00 5.00
4 Alexei Yashin .75 2.00
5 Sergei Fedorov 1.50 4.00
6 Keith Tkachuk .75 2.00
7 Patrick Roy 6.00 15.00
8 Martin Brodeur 3.00 8.00
9 Steve Yzerman 6.00 15.00
10 Saku Koivu .75 2.00
11 Felix Potvin .75 2.00
12 Mark Messier 1.25 3.00
13 Eric Lindros 1.25 3.00
14 Peter Forsberg 2.50 6.00
15 Teemu Selanne 1.25 3.00
16 Brendan Shanahan 1.25 3.00
17 Curtis Joseph 1.25 3.00
18 Brett Hull 1.50 4.00
19 Paul Kariya 1.25 3.00
20 Jaromir Jagr 2.00 5.00
21 Pavel Bure 1.25 3.00
22 Dominik Hasek 2.00 5.00
23 John LeClair .75 2.00
24 Doug Gilmour .75 2.00

1997-98 Pinnacle Epix Moment Orange
COMPLETE SET (24) 100.00 200.00
*PURPLE: .6X TO 1.5X ORANGE
*EMERALD: 1.2X TO 3X ORANGE
1 Wayne Gretzky 20.00 50.00
2 John Vanbiesbrouck 2.00 5.00
3 Joe Sakic 6.00 15.00
4 Alexei Yashin 2.00 5.00
5 Sergei Fedorov 4.00 10.00
6 Keith Tkachuk 2.00 5.00
7 Patrick Roy 15.00 40.00
8 Martin Brodeur 10.00 25.00
9 Steve Yzerman 12.00 30.00
10 Saku Koivu 3.00 8.00
11 Felix Potvin 3.00 8.00
12 Mark Messier 3.00 8.00
13 Eric Lindros 3.00 8.00
14 Peter Forsberg 8.00 20.00
15 Teemu Selanne 3.00 8.00
16 Brendan Shanahan 3.00 8.00
17 Curtis Joseph 3.00 8.00
18 Brett Hull 4.00 10.00
19 Paul Kariya 3.00 8.00
20 Jaromir Jagr 5.00 12.00
21 Pavel Bure 3.00 8.00
22 Dominik Hasek 6.00 15.00
23 John LeClair 2.00 5.00
24 Doug Gilmour 2.00 5.00

1997-98 Pinnacle Epix Play Orange
COMPLETE SET (24) 40.00 80.00
*PURPLE: .6X TO 1.5X ORANGE
*EMERALD: 1.2X TO 3X ORANGE
1 Wayne Gretzky 8.00 20.00
2 John Vanbiesbrouck .60 1.50
3 Joe Sakic 1.50 4.00
4 Alexei Yashin .60 1.50
5 Sergei Fedorov 1.25 3.00
6 Keith Tkachuk .75 2.00
7 Patrick Roy 4.00 10.00
8 Martin Brodeur 2.00 5.00
9 Steve Yzerman 4.00 10.00
10 Saku Koivu .75 2.00
11 Felix Potvin .75 2.00
12 Mark Messier .75 2.00
13 Eric Lindros .75 2.00
14 Peter Forsberg 2.00 5.00
15 Teemu Selanne .75 2.00
16 Brendan Shanahan .75 2.00
17 Curtis Joseph .75 2.00
18 Brett Hull 1.00 2.50
19 Paul Kariya .75 2.00
20 Jaromir Jagr 1.25 3.00
21 Pavel Bure .75 2.00
22 Dominik Hasek 1.50 4.00
23 John LeClair .75 2.00
24 Doug Gilmour .60 1.50

1997-98 Pinnacle Epix Season Orange
COMPLETE SET (24) 75.00 150.00
*PURPLE: .6X TO 1.5X ORANGE
*EMERALD: 1.2X TO 3X ORANGE
1 Wayne Gretzky 10.00 25.00
2 John Vanbiesbrouck 1.50 4.00
3 Joe Sakic 5.00 12.00
4 Alexei Yashin 1.50 4.00
5 Sergei Fedorov 3.00 8.00
6 Keith Tkachuk 1.50 4.00
7 Patrick Roy 8.00 20.00
8 Martin Brodeur 7.50 15.00
9 Steve Yzerman 8.00 20.00
10 Saku Koivu 2.50 6.00
11 Felix Potvin 3.00 8.00
12 Mark Messier 2.50 6.00
13 Eric Lindros 2.50 6.00
14 Peter Forsberg 6.00 15.00
15 Teemu Selanne 2.50 6.00
16 Brendan Shanahan 2.50 6.00
17 Curtis Joseph 2.50 6.00
18 Brett Hull 3.00 8.00
19 Paul Kariya 2.50 6.00
20 Jaromir Jagr 4.00 10.00
21 Pavel Bure 3.00 8.00
22 Dominik Hasek 4.00 10.00
23 John LeClair 1.50 4.00
24 Doug Gilmour 1.50 4.00

1997-98 Pinnacle Masks
COMPLETE SET (10) 75.00 150.00
*JUMBOS: .4X TO 1X BASIC INSERTS
*PROMOS: .15X TO .4X BASIC INSERTS
1 John Vanbiesbrouck 4.00 10.00
2 Mike Richter 4.00 10.00
3 Martin Brodeur 10.00 25.00
4 Curtis Joseph 5.00 12.00
5 Patrick Roy 10.00 25.00
6 Guy Hebert 3.00 8.00
7 Jeff Hackett 2.50 6.00
8 Garth Snow 3.00 8.00
9 Nikolai Khabibulin 4.00 10.00
10 Grant Fuhr 6.00 15.00

1997-98 Pinnacle Masks Die Cuts
*DIE CUT: .5X TO 1.2X BASIC INSERTS

1997-98 Pinnacle Team Pinnacle
*MIRROR: 1X TO 2.5X BASIC INSERTS
*WHITE FRONT PARALLEL: .4X TO 1X
1 M.Brodeur/P.Roy 8.00 20.00
2 D.Hasek/C.Joseph 5.00 12.00
3 B.Leetch/C.Chelios 3.00 8.00
4 W.Gretzky/P.Kariya 20.00 50.00
5 E.Lindros/M.Messier 6.00 15.00
6 J.Jagr/K.Tkachuk 10.00 25.00
7 S.Koivu/P.Forsberg 6.00 15.00
8 J.LeClair/B.Shanahan 3.00 8.00
9 D.Gilmour/S.Yzerman 8.00 20.00
10 J.Vanbiesbrouck/C.Osgood 3.00 8.00

2010-11 Pinnacle
*AP.VETS: 3X TO 8X BASIC CARDS
*AP. ROOKIES: .6X TO 1.5X BASE
1 Nicklas Backstrom .20 .50
2 Mike Green .15 .40
3 Michal Neuvirth .15 .40
4 Karl Alzner .12 .30
5 David Steckel .12 .30
6 Eric Fehr .12 .30
7 Alex Ovechkin .75 2.00
8 Ryan Kesler .20 .50
9 Roberto Luongo .30 .75
10 Mason Raymond .12 .30
11 Henrik Sedin .25 .60
12 Dan Hamhuis .12 .30
13 Daniel Sedin .25 .60
14 Alexandre Burrows .12 .30
15 Tyler Bozak .12 .30
16 Tomas Kaberle .12 .30
17 Phil Kessel .20 .50
18 Nikolai Kulemin .12 .30
19 Kris Versteeg .12 .30
20 Jonas Gustavsson .25 .60
21 Dion Phaneuf .15 .40
22 Vincent Lecavalier .20 .50
23 Victor Hedman .25 .60
24 Steven Stamkos .40 1.00
25 Simon Gagne .20 .50
26 Martin St. Louis .20 .50
27 Dan Ellis .15 .40
28 T.J. Oshie .20 .50
29 Jaroslav Halak .20 .50
30 David Perron .15 .40
31 David Backes .12 .30
32 Cam Janssen .12 .30
33 B.J. Crombeen .12 .30
34 Torrey Mitchell .12 .30
35 Ryane Clowe .12 .30
36 Patrick Marleau .20 .50
37 Joe Thornton .30 .75
38 Joe Pavelski .25 .60
39 Dany Heatley .15 .40
40 Antero Niittymaki .15 .40
41 Zbynek Michalek .12 .30
42 Sidney Crosby .75 2.00
43 Max Talbot .12 .30
44 Marc-Andre Fleury .40 1.00
45 Jordan Staal .15 .40
46 Evgeni Malkin .40 1.00
47 Vernon Fiddler .12 .30
48 Shane Doan .15 .40
49 Scottie Upshall .12 .30
50 Ray Whitney .15 .40
51 Paul Bissonnette .12 .30
52 Lee Stempniak .12 .30
53 Ilya Bryzgalov .15 .40
54 Ville Leino .15 .40
55 Sean O'Donnell .12 .30
56 Mike Richards .15 .40
57 Jeff Carter .15 .40
58 Danny Briere .20 .50
59 Claude Giroux .20 .50
60 Chris Pronger .20 .50
61 Sergei Gonchar .12 .30
62 Pascal Leclaire .15 .40
63 Nick Foligno .15 .40
64 Jason Spezza .20 .50
65 Daniel Alfredsson .20 .50
66 Brian Elliott .15 .40
67 Alex Kovalev .15 .40
68 Sean Avery .15 .40
69 Ryan Callahan .12 .30
70 Michael Del Zotto .12 .30
71 Martin Biron .12 .30
72 Marian Gaborik .12 .30
73 Henrik Lundqvist .50 1.25
74 Matt Moulson .15 .40
75 Kyle Okposo .15 .40
76 Josh Bailey .15 .40
77 John Tavares .30 .75
78 Dwayne Roloson .15 .40
79 Zach Parise .20 .50
80 Travis Zajac .12 .30
81 Patrik Elias .20 .50
82 Martin Brodeur .50 1.25
83 Ilya Kovalchuk .20 .50
84 Steve Sullivan .12 .30
85 Shea Weber .15 .40
86 Pekka Rinne .20 .50
87 Patric Hornqvist .12 .30
88 Matthew Lombardi .12 .30
89 Joel Ward .12 .30
90 Cody Franson .12 .30
91 Tomas Plekanec .12 .30
92 Scott Gomez .15 .40
93 Michael Cammalleri .20 .50
94 Josh Gorges .12 .30
95 Carey Price .40 1.00
96 Brian Gionta .12 .30
97 Andrei Kostitsyn .15 .40
98 Niklas Backstrom .15 .40
99 Mikko Koivu .20 .50
100 Matt Cullen .12 .30
101 Jose Theodore .20 .50
102 Pierre-Marc Bouchard .20 .50
103 Andrew Brunette .12 .30
104 Brent Burns .20 .50
105 Wayne Simmonds .25 .60
106 Ryan Smyth .15 .40
107 Jonathan Quick .25 .60
108 Jack Johnson .12 .30
109 Dustin Brown .20 .50
110 Drew Doughty .25 .60
111 Anze Kopitar .30 .75
112 Tomas Vokoun .15 .40
113 Steve Bernier .12 .30
114 Radek Dvorak .12 .30
115 Keaton Ellerby .12 .30
116 David Booth .12 .30
117 Bryan McCabe .12 .30
118 Shawn Horcoff .12 .30
119 Sam Gagner .12 .30
120 Ryan Whitney .12 .30
121 Nikolai Khabibulin .15 .40
122 Kurtis Foster .12 .30
123 Dustin Penner .12 .30
124 Ales Hemsky .15 .40
125 Todd Bertuzzi .15 .40
126 Pavel Datsyuk .30 .75
127 Nicklas Lidstrom .20 .50
128 Mike Modano .30 .75
129 Johan Franzen .15 .40
130 Jimmy Howard .25 .60
131 Henrik Zetterberg .25 .60
132 Tom Wandell .12 .30
133 Steve Ott .12 .30
134 Kari Lehtonen .15 .40
135 Loui Eriksson .12 .30
136 James Neal .12 .30
137 Brenden Morrow .15 .40
138 Adam Burish .12 .30
139 Mathieu Garon .15 .40
140 Rick Nash .20 .50
141 R.J. Umberger .12 .30
142 Nikita Filatov .12 .30
143 Jakub Voracek .15 .40
144 Derek Dorsett .12 .30
145 Antoine Vermette .12 .30
146 T.J. Galiardi .15 .40
147 Paul Stastny .15 .40
148 Milan Hejduk .15 .40
149 Matt Duchene .20 .50
150 John-Michael Liles .12 .30
151 Craig Anderson .20 .50
152 Chris Stewart .15 .40
153 Patrick Sharp .20 .50
154 Patrick Kane .40 1.00
155 Niklas Hjalmarsson .12 .30
156 Marian Hossa .20 .50
157 Jonathan Toews .30 .75
158 Duncan Keith .15 .40
159 Corey Crawford .25 .60
160 Tuomo Ruutu .15 .40
161 Tim Gleason .12 .30
162 Jussi Jokinen .12 .30
163 Eric Staal .25 .60
164 Cam Ward .20 .50
165 Brandon Sutter .12 .30
166 Rene Bourque .12 .30
167 Olli Jokinen .15 .40
168 Niklas Hagman .12 .30
169 Miikka Kiprusoff .20 .50
170 Jay Bouwmeester .12 .30
171 Jarome Iginla .25 .60
172 Alex Tanguay .12 .30
173 Tyler Myers .12 .30
174 Tyler Ennis .12 .30
175 Tim Connolly .12 .30
176 Thomas Vanek .15 .40
177 Ryan Miller .20 .50
178 Nathan Gerbe .12 .30
179 Derek Roy .12 .30
180 Tim Thomas .20 .50
181 Shawn Thornton .12 .30
182 Patrice Bergeron .25 .60
183 Nathan Horton .15 .40
184 Milan Lucic .20 .50
185 Mark Recchi .25 .60
186 Marc Savard .12 .30
187 Tobias Enstrom .12 .30
188 Ondrej Pavelec .12 .30
189 Nik Antropov .15 .40
190 Niklas Bergfors .15 .40
191 Evander Kane .20 .50
192 Dustin Byfuglien .20 .50
193 Chris Mason .15 .40
194 Teemu Selanne .40 1.00
195 Saku Koivu .20 .50
196 Ryan Getzlaf .20 .50
197 Lubomir Visnovsky .12 .30
198 George Parros .15 .40
199 Corey Perry .30 .75
200 Bobby Ryan .15 .40
201 Jordan Eberle RC 3.00 8.00
202 Nazem Kadri RC 4.00 10.00
203 Tyler Seguin RC 4.00 10.00
204 Brayden Schenn RC 3.00 8.00
205 Travis Hamonic RC 1.50 4.00
206 Sergei Bobrovsky RC 5.00 12.00
207 Alexander Burmistrov RC 1.25 3.00
208 Nino Niederreiter RC 2.00 5.00
209 Nick Leddy RC 1.50 4.00
210 Luke Adam RC 1.25 3.00
211 Jordan Caron RC 1.50 4.00
212 Taylor Hall RC 3.00 8.00
213 Jacob Josefson RC 1.25 3.00
214 Kyle Clifford RC 1.50 4.00
215 Jared Spurgeon RC 3.00 8.00
216 Patrice Cormier RC 1.25 3.00
217 Steven Kampfer RC 2.00 5.00
218 P.K. Subban RC 4.00 10.00
219 Magnus Paajarvi RC 1.50 4.00
220 Evan Brophey RC 1.25 3.00
221 Kevin Poulin RC 1.50 4.00
222 Linus Omark RC 1.50 4.00
223 Jeff Skinner RC 3.00 8.00
224 Nathan Lawson RC 1.25 3.00
225 Marcus Johansson RC 2.00 5.00
226 Brandon Pirri RC 1.25 3.00
227 Brandon McMillan RC 1.25 3.00
228 Nick Holden RC 1.25 3.00
229 Richard Bachman RC 1.50 4.00
230 Anders Lindback RC 1.25 3.00
231 Alexander Vasyunov RC 1.25 3.00
232 Cam Fowler RC 3.00 8.00
233 Ben Smith RC 1.50 4.00
234 Dana Tyrell RC 1.25 3.00
235 Ryan Reaves RC 1.50 4.00
236 Alex Urbom RC 1.25 3.00
237 Kyle Palmieri RC 2.50 6.00
238 Mark Dekanich RC 1.25 3.00
239 Matt Kassian RC 1.25 3.00
240 Jonas Holos RC 1.25 3.00
241 Rob Klinkhammer RC 1.25 3.00
242 Jamie Arniel RC 1.25 3.00
243 Justin Braun RC 1.25 3.00
244 Keith Aulie RC 1.25 3.00
245 Kevin Shattenkirk RC 2.50 6.00
246 Johan Harju RC 1.25 3.00
247 Stefan Della Rovere RC 1.25 3.00
248 Evgeny Grachev RC 1.25 3.00
249 Eric Wellwood RC 1.50 4.00
250 Jeremy Morin RC 1.25 3.00
251 Mattias Tedenby AU RC 4.00 10.00
252 Brayden Irwin AU RC 4.00 10.00
253 Bobby Butler AU RC 4.00 10.00
254 Ian Cole AU RC 4.00 10.00
255 Derek Stepan AU/199 RC 12.00 30.00
256 Jake Muzzin AU RC 10.00 25.00
257 Jared Cowen AU RC 4.00 10.00
258 John McCarthy AU RC 4.00 10.00
259 Dustin Tokarski AU RC 4.00 10.00
260 Nick Bonino AU RC 5.00 12.00
261 Justin Mercier AU RC 4.00 10.00

262 Maxim Noreau AU RC 3.00 8.00
263 Mats Zuccarello AU RC 12.00 30.00
264 Jacob Markstrom AU RC 20.00 40.00
265 Robin Lehner AU RC 8.00 20.00
266 Jamie McBain AU RC 4.00 10.00
267 Ryan McDonagh AU RC 15.00 30.00
268 Tomas Tatar AU RC 10.00 25.00
269 Zach Hamill AU RC 4.00 10.00
270 Philip Larsen AU RC 4.00 10.00

2010-11 Pinnacle Artists Proofs

159 Corey Crawford 2.00 5.00
218 P.K. Subban 15.00 40.00
223 Jeff Skinner 15.00 40.00

2010-11 Pinnacle Rink Collection

*1-200 VETS: 2.5X TO 6X BASIC CARDS
*201-250 ROOKIES: .5X TO 1.2X
159 Corey Crawford 2.00 5.00
212 Taylor Hall 12.00 30.00
218 P.K. Subban 12.00 30.00
223 Jeff Skinner 12.00 30.00

2010-11 Pinnacle Chemistry On Canvas

1 A.Ovechkin/N.Backstrom 4.00 10.00
2 R.Getzlaf/C.Perry 1.50 4.00
3 S.Stamkos/M.St. Louis 2.00 5.00
4 D.Krejci/M.Lucic 1.00 2.50
5 N.Lidstrom/B.Rafalski 1.00 2.50
6 H.Sedin/D.Sedin 1.25 3.00
7 P.Stastny/C.Stewart .75 2.00
8 J.Thornton/D.Heatley 1.50 4.00
9 B.Richards/L.Eriksson 1.00 2.50
10 T.Selanne/S.Koivu 2.00 5.00
11 D.Alfredsson/J.Spezza 1.00 2.50
12 D.Keith/B.Seabrook .75 2.00
13 H.Zetterberg/P.Datsyuk 1.50 4.00
14 M.Richards/C.Giroux 1.00 2.50
15 M.Koivu/A.Brunette 1.00 2.50
16 J.Tavares/M.Moulson 1.50 4.00
17 B.Gionta/S.Gomez .75 2.00
18 A.Kopitar/R.Smyth 1.50 4.00

2010-11 Pinnacle City Lights Materials

*PRIME/25: .8X TO 2X BASIC JSY
1 Sidney Crosby 8.00 20.00
2 Brian Elliott 1.50 4.00
3 Zdeno Chara 2.00 5.00
4 Anze Kopitar 3.00 8.00
5 Christian Hanson 1.25 3.00
6 Jordan Staal 1.50 4.00
7 Dustin Penner 1.25 3.00
8 Peter Regin 1.50 4.00
9 Miikka Kiprusoff 2.00 5.00
10 Tobias Enstrom 1.25 3.00
11 Ryan Malone 1.25 3.00
12 Paul Stastny 1.50 4.00
13 Daniel Sedin 2.50 6.00
14 Mikael Samuelsson 1.25 3.00
15 Zach Bogosian 1.50 4.00
16 Jarome Iginla 2.50 6.00
17 Mason Raymond 1.25 3.00
18 Nik Antropov 1.50 4.00
19 Jeff Deslauriers 1.25 3.00
20 Tuukka Rask 2.50 6.00
21 Steve Ott 1.25 3.00
22 Chris Pronger 2.00 5.00
23 Ryan Suter 1.50 4.00
24 Tomas Vokoun 1.50 4.00
25 Ryan Smyth 1.50 4.00
26 Stephen Weiss 1.50 4.00
27 Jonas Gustavsson 2.50 6.00
28 Mike Green 1.50 4.00
29 Rene Bourque 1.25 3.00
30 Darcy Hordichuk 1.25 3.00
31 Erik Karlsson 2.50 6.00
32 Mike Smith 2.00 5.00
33 Loui Eriksson 1.25 3.00
34 Pekka Rinne 2.00 5.00
35 Cory Schneider 2.00 5.00
36 Vincent Lecavalier 2.00 5.00
37 James van Riemsdyk 1.50 4.00
38 Mike Fisher 1.25 3.00
39 Fredrik Sjostrom 1.25 3.00
40 Martin St. Louis 2.00 5.00
41 Alex Tanguay 1.25 3.00
42 Andrew Bodnarchuk 1.50 4.00
43 Ilya Kovalchuk 2.00 5.00
44 Brad Richards 2.00 5.00
45 Mikael Backlund 1.50 4.00
46 Patric Hornqvist 1.25 3.00
47 Roberto Luongo 3.00 8.00
48 Steve Downie 1.25 3.00
49 Cody Bass 1.50 4.00
50 Jannik Hansen 1.50 4.00
51 Matt Zaba 2.00 5.00
52 Henrik Zetterberg/299 2.50 6.00
53 Victor Hedman 2.50 6.00
54 Wade Belak 1.50 4.00
55 Martin Erat 1.25 3.00
56 Shawn Thornton 1.25 3.00
57 Nicklas Bergfors/199 1.50 4.00
58 Evander Kane 2.00 5.00
59 Evan Oberg 2.00 5.00
60 Jamie Langenbrunner/399 1.25 3.00
61 Mike Brodeur 1.50 4.00
62 Karl Alzner 1.25 3.00
63 Maxim Lapierre 1.25 3.00
64 Ilya Bryzgalov 1.50 4.00
65 Travis Zajac/99 2.50 6.00
66 Milan Hejduk 1.50 4.00
67 Jason Spezza/399 2.00 5.00
68 Jamie Benn 2.50 6.00
69 Wayne Simmonds/99 3.00 8.00
70 Joe Thornton 3.00 8.00
71 James Neal 1.25 3.00
72 Evgeni Malkin 4.00 10.00
73 Craig Anderson 2.00 5.00
74 Marian Gaborik 2.00 5.00
75 Steve Mason/399 1.50 4.00
76 Jordin Tootoo/99 2.50 6.00
77 John Tavares/99 3.00 8.00
78 Mikkel Boedker 1.25 3.00
79 Luke Schenn 2.00 5.00
80 Jeff Carter 1.50 4.00
81 Jared Cowen 1.50 4.00
82 Zach Hamill 1.50 4.00
83 Nazem Kadri 5.00 12.00
84 Kevin Shattenkirk 3.00 8.00
85 Jeff Skinner 4.00 10.00
86 Magnus Paajarvi 2.00 5.00
87 Tyler Seguin 5.00 12.00
88 Taylor Hall 3.00 8.00
89 Jordan Eberle/499 4.00 10.00
90 Brayden Schenn 4.00 10.00
91 Ryan Getzlaf/99 2.00 5.00
92 Kari Lehtonen 1.50 4.00
93 Marc Staal 1.25 3.00
94 Shane Doan/99 1.50 4.00
95 Matt Moulson/99 1.50 4.00
96 Henrik Sedin/499 2.50 6.00
97 Scott Hartnell 1.25 3.00
98 Shea Weber 1.50 4.00
99 Andy Greene/99 1.25 3.00
100 Colton Orr 1.25 3.00

2010-11 Pinnacle City Lights Signatures

1 Sidney Crosby/35 30.00 80.00
2 Brian Elliott/100 5.00 12.00
3 Zdeno Chara/100 6.00 15.00
4 Anze Kopitar/100 10.00 25.00
5 Christian Hanson/100 4.00 10.00
6 Jordan Staal/100 5.00 12.00
7 Dustin Penner/100 4.00 10.00
8 Peter Regin/100 5.00 12.00
11 Ryan Malone/100 4.00 10.00
12 Paul Stastny/100 5.00 12.00
13 Daniel Sedin/100 8.00 20.00
14 Mikael Samuelsson/100 4.00 10.00
15 Zach Bogosian/100 5.00 12.00
16 Jarome Iginla/100 8.00 20.00
17 Mason Raymond/100 4.00 10.00
19 Jeff Deslauriers/100 4.00 10.00
20 Tuukka Rask/100 8.00 20.00
21 Steve Ott/100 4.00 10.00
22 Chris Pronger/100 6.00 15.00
23 Ryan Suter/100 5.00 12.00
24 Tomas Vokoun/100 5.00 12.00
25 Ryan Smyth/100 5.00 12.00
26 Stephen Weiss/100 5.00 12.00
27 Jonas Gustavsson/100 8.00 20.00
28 Mike Green/100 5.00 12.00
29 Rene Bourque/100 4.00 10.00
31 Erik Karlsson/100 8.00 20.00
32 Mike Smith/100 6.00 15.00
33 Loui Eriksson/100 4.00 10.00
34 Pekka Rinne/100 6.00 15.00
35 Cory Schneider/100 6.00 15.00
36 Vincent Lecavalier/100 6.00 15.00
37 James van Riemsdyk/100 5.00 12.00
38 Mike Fisher/60 4.00 10.00
40 Martin St. Louis/100 6.00 15.00
41 Alex Tanguay/100 4.00 10.00
43 Ilya Kovalchuk/100 6.00 15.00
44 Brad Richards/100 6.00 15.00
45 Mikael Backlund/100 5.00 12.00
46 Patric Hornqvist/100 4.00 10.00
48 Steve Downie/100 4.00 10.00
54 Wade Belak/100 5.00 12.00
56 Shawn Thornton/100 4.00 10.00
58 Evander Kane/100 6.00 15.00
61 Mike Brodeur/100 5.00 12.00
62 Karl Alzner/100 4.00 10.00
64 Ilya Bryzgalov/50 5.00 12.00
65 Travis Zajac/100 4.00 10.00
66 Milan Hejduk/100 5.00 12.00
67 Jason Spezza/100 6.00 15.00
68 Jamie Benn/100 8.00 20.00
69 Wayne Simmonds/100 8.00 20.00
70 Joe Thornton/97 10.00 25.00
71 James Neal/100 4.00 10.00
72 Evgeni Malkin/100 12.00 30.00
73 Craig Anderson/100 6.00 15.00
74 Marian Gaborik/100 6.00 15.00
75 Steve Mason/100 5.00 12.00
76 Jordin Tootoo/100 5.00 12.00
77 John Tavares/100 10.00 25.00
78 Mikkel Boedker/100 4.00 10.00
79 Luke Schenn/100 6.00 15.00
80 Jeff Carter/100 5.00 12.00
81 Jared Cowen/100 5.00 12.00
82 Zach Hamill/100 5.00 12.00
83 Nazem Kadri/100 15.00 40.00
84 Kevin Shattenkirk/100 10.00 25.00
85 Jeff Skinner/100 12.00 30.00
86 Magnus Paajarvi/100 6.00 15.00
87 Tyler Seguin/100 15.00 40.00
88 Taylor Hall/100 12.00 30.00
89 Jordan Eberle/100 12.00 30.00
90 Brayden Schenn/100 12.00 30.00
91 Ryan Getzlaf/100 6.00 15.00
92 Kari Lehtonen/100 5.00 12.00
93 Marc Staal/100 4.00 10.00
94 Shane Doan/100 5.00 12.00
95 Matt Moulson/100 5.00 12.00
96 Henrik Sedin/75 8.00 20.00
98 Shea Weber/100 5.00 12.00
99 Andy Greene/95 4.00 10.00
100 Colton Orr/100 4.00 10.00

2010-11 Pinnacle Pantheon

1 Pavel Datsyuk 4.00 10.00
2 Daniel Alfredsson 2.50 6.00
3 Jonathan Toews 4.00 10.00
4 Nicklas Lidstrom 2.50 6.00
5 Zach Parise 2.50 6.00
6 Martin St. Louis 2.50 6.00
7 Patrick Marleau 2.50 6.00
8 Henrik Sedin 3.00 8.00
9 Mikko Koivu 2.50 6.00
10 Jean Beliveau 2.50 6.00
11 Joe Nieuwendyk 2.00 5.00
12 Joe Sakic 5.00 12.00
13 Rick Middleton 2.50 6.00
14 Brian Leetch 2.00 5.00
15 Dale Hawerchuk 3.00 8.00
16 Ed Giacomin 4.00 10.00
17 Denis Savard 2.50 6.00
18 Gilbert Perreault 2.50 6.00

2010-11 Pinnacle Pencraft

1 Jaroslav Halak/100 8.00 20.00
2 Martin Brodeur/50 20.00 50.00
3 Mike Richards/50 6.00 15.00
4 Marian Gaborik/50 8.00 20.00
5 Ryan Miller/50 8.00 20.00
6 Ryan Getzlaf/50 8.00 20.00
7 Sidney Crosby/50 30.00 80.00
8 Teemu Selanne/50 15.00 40.00
9 Chris Pronger/50 8.00 20.00
10 Cam Janssen/100 5.00 12.00
11 Brandon Sutter/100 5.00 12.00
12 Artem Anisimov/100 5.00 12.00
13 Jeff Carter/50 6.00 15.00
14 Patrick Kane/50 15.00 40.00
15 John Tavares/50 12.00 30.00
16 Shane Doan/100 6.00 15.00
17 Thomas Vanek/100 6.00 15.00
18 Rich Peverley/100 8.00 20.00
19 Tomas Vokoun/50 6.00 15.00
20 Marc-Andre Fleury/50 15.00 40.00
21 Joe Thornton/50 12.00 30.00
22 Kari Lehtonen/50 6.00 15.00
23 Jonathan Quick/100 10.00 25.00
24 Dion Phaneuf/50 6.00 15.00
25 Doug Gilmour/50 10.00 25.00
26 Derek Sanderson/50 8.00 20.00
27 Brian Leetch/50 6.00 15.00
28 Bobby Hull/50 15.00 40.00
29 Stan Mikita/50 10.00 25.00
30 Yvan Cournoyer/50 8.00 20.00
31 Richard Brodeur/100 8.00 20.00
32 Reggie Lemelin/50 5.00 12.00
33 Ken Linseman/100 8.00 20.00
34 Jean Beliveau/50 25.00 60.00
35 Keith Primeau/50 6.00 15.00

2010-11 Pinnacle Rookie Team Pinnacle Signatures

1 T.Hall/T.Seguin 100.00 200.00
2 J.Eberle/M.Paajarvi 50.00 100.00
3 J.Skinner/N.Kadri 50.00 100.00
4 C.Fowler/N.Leddy 20.00 40.00
5 P.Subban/O.Ekman-Larsson 60.00 150.00
6 R.Lehner/S.Bobrovsky 20.00 50.00

2010-11 Pinnacle Saving Face

COMPLETE SET (13) 20.00 50.00
1 Curtis McElhinney 1.25 3.00
2 Ondrej Pavelec 2.00 5.00
3 Tim Thomas 2.00 5.00
5 Cam Ward 2.00 5.00
6 Corey Crawford 2.50 6.00
9 Jonathan Quick 2.50 6.00
10 Jose Theodore 2.00 5.00
11 Carey Price 4.00 10.00
12 Martin Brodeur 5.00 12.00
14 Marc-Andre Fleury 4.00 10.00
15 Cory Schneider 2.00 5.00
16 Michal Neuvirth 1.50 4.00
18 Nikolai Khabibulin 1.50 4.00

2010-11 Pinnacle Team Pinnacle

COMPLETE SET (12) 50.00 100.00
1 M.Richards/P.Datsyuk 8.00 20.00
2 A.Ovechkin/D.Sedin 12.00 30.00
3 M.Gaborik/P.Kane 6.00 15.00
4 M.Green/D.Keith 2.50 6.00
5 C.Pronger/D.Doughty 4.00 10.00
6 R.Miller/I.Bryzgalov 3.00 8.00
7 H.Sedin/S.Stamkos 6.00 15.00
8 H.Zetterberg/M.Lucic 4.00 10.00
9 C.Perry/M.St. Louis 5.00 12.00
10 N.Lidstrom/T.Myers 3.00 8.00
11 S.Weber/Z.Chara 3.00 8.00
12 M.Brodeur/J.Quick 8.00 20.00

2010-11 Pinnacle Threads

*PRIME/25: .5X TO 1.2X BASIC/499
*PRIME/25: .4X TO 1X BASIC/50
AA Artem Anisimov 3.00 8.00
AH Ales Hemsky 4.00 10.00
AK Andrei Kostitsyn 4.00 10.00
AK Anze Kopitar/50 10.00 25.00
AV Antoine Vermette 3.00 8.00
BC Blake Comeau 3.00 8.00
BER Nicklas Bergfors 4.00 10.00
BL Bryan Little/50 6.00 15.00
BM Brenden Morrow 4.00 10.00
BP Benoit Pouliot 3.00 8.00
BR Bobby Ryan 4.00 10.00
BS Brayden Schenn 6.00 15.00
CA Craig Anderson 5.00 12.00
CC Cal Clutterbuck 3.00 8.00
CE Christian Ehrhoff 3.00 8.00
CG Claude Giroux 5.00 12.00
CP Corey Perry/50 10.00 25.00
DB Danny Briere 5.00 12.00
DB Dustin Brown 5.00 12.00
DK Duncan Keith 4.00 10.00
DK Dmitry Kulikov 4.00 10.00
DK David Krejci 5.00 12.00
DR Derek Roy 3.00 8.00
DWN Steve Downie 3.00 8.00
EF Eric Fehr 3.00 8.00
HL Henrik Lundqvist/50 15.00 40.00
HZ Henrik Zetterberg/50 8.00 20.00
IB Ilya Bryzgalov 4.00 10.00
JB Jamie Benn 6.00 15.00
JB Jay Bouwmeester 3.00 8.00
JE Jordan Eberle 6.00 15.00
JI Jarome Iginla 6.00 15.00
JP Joe Pavelski/400 6.00 15.00
JR James van Riemsdyk 4.00 10.00
JS Jordan Staal 4.00 10.00
JS Jason Spezza 5.00 12.00
JS Jeff Skinner 6.00 15.00
JT Jordin Tootoo 4.00 10.00
JT Joe Thornton/50 10.00 25.00
KA Karl Alzner 3.00 8.00
KL Kristopher Letang 6.00 15.00
KO Kyle Okposo 3.00 8.00
LE Loui Eriksson 3.00 8.00
MD Michael Del Zotto 4.00 10.00
MF Mike Fisher 3.00 8.00
MF Michael Frolik 3.00 8.00
MF Marc-Andre Fleury/50 12.00 30.00
MG Marian Gaborik/50 6.00 15.00
MK Miikka Kiprusoff/50 6.00 15.00
ML Milan Lucic 5.00 12.00
MM Matt Moulson 4.00 10.00
MP Magnus Paajarvi/50 3.00 8.00
MR Mason Raymond 3.00 8.00
MS Marc Staal 3.00 8.00
MZ Mats Zuccarello 20.00 50.00
NA Nik Antropov 4.00 10.00
NB Niklas Backstrom 5.00 12.00
NK Nikolai Kulemin 3.00 8.00
PA Pascal Leclaire 4.00 10.00
PB Patrice Bergeron 6.00 15.00
PD Pavel Datsyuk/50 10.00 25.00
PE Patrik Elias 5.00 12.00
PLL Pierre-Luc Letourneau-Leblond 3.00 8.00
PM Peter Mueller 4.00 10.00
PR Pekka Rinne/50 6.00 15.00
PS Patrick Sharp 5.00 12.00
PS Paul Stastny/50 5.00 12.00
RB Rene Bourque 3.00 8.00
RC Ryan Callahan 3.00 8.00
RG Ryan Getzlaf 5.00 12.00
RM Ryan Malone 3.00 8.00
RM Ryan Miller 5.00 12.00
RO Ryan O'Reilly/50 8.00 20.00
RS Ryan Smyth 4.00 10.00
SC Sidney Crosby/50 25.00 60.00
SD Shane Doan 4.00 10.00
SG Sam Gagner 3.00 8.00
SM Steve Mason 4.00 10.00
SO Steve Ott/50 4.00 10.00
SU Ryan Suter 4.00 10.00
SW Shea Weber/50 5.00 12.00
TB Tyler Bozak/50 4.00 10.00
TE Tobias Enstrom 3.00 8.00
TG T.J. Galiardi 4.00 10.00
THO Tomas Holmstrom 3.00 8.00
TH Taylor Hall/50 6.00 15.00
TR Tuukka Rask/50 12.00 30.00
TS Tyler Seguin/50 8.00 20.00
TT Tim Thomas 6.00 15.00
TV Tomas Vokoun 4.00 10.00
TZ Travis Zajac 3.00 8.00
VL Vincent Lecavalier 5.00 12.00
VO Jakub Voracek 4.00 10.00
WS Wayne Simmonds 6.00 15.00

2010-11 Pinnacle Tough Times

COMPLETE SET (12) 10.00 25.00
BK Bob Kelly 1.00 2.50
AD Andre Dupont 2.00 5.00
BS Bobby Schmautz 1.25 3.00
BW Bryan Watson 1.50 4.00
DP Dennis Polonich 1.25 3.00
DS Dave Schultz 1.50 4.00
JK Jerry Korab 2.50 6.00
JW John Wensink 1.00 2.50
NF Nick Fotiu 2.00 5.00
TO Terry O'Reilly 1.25 3.00
TW Tiger Williams 1.00 2.50
WP Willi Plett 1.25 3.00

2010-11 Pinnacle Tough Times Autographs

BK Bob Kelly 6.00 15.00
AD Andre Dupont 12.00 30.00
BS Bobby Schmautz 8.00 20.00
BW Bryan Watson 12.00 30.00
DP Dennis Polonich 8.00 20.00
DS Dave Schultz 10.00 25.00
JK Jerry Korab 15.00 40.00
JW John Wensink 6.00 15.00
NF Nick Fotiu 12.00 30.00
TO Terry O'Reilly 12.00 30.00
TW Tiger Williams 6.00 15.00
WP Willi Plett 8.00 20.00

2011-12 Pinnacle

COMP.SET w/o RC's (250) 20.00 40.00
1 Roberto Luongo .40 1.00
2 Dan Hamhuis .20 .50
3 Kevin Bieksa .20 .50
4 Taylor Hall .25 .60
5 Nicklas Lidstrom .15 .40
6 Shea Weber .20 .50
7 Jeff Carter .20 .50
8 Alex Ovechkin 1.00 2.50
9 Zach Parise .25 .60
10 Corey Perry .40 1.00
11 Saku Koivu .25 .60
12 Jarome Iginla .30 .75
13 Pavel Datsyuk .40 1.00
14 Alexandre Burrows .15 .40
15 Ryan Getzlaf .25 .60
16 Derick Brassard .15 .40
17 Milan Lucic .25 .60
18 Nathan Horton .25 .60
19 Tyler Seguin .30 .75
20 Chris Pronger .25 .60
21 James van Riemsdyk .20 .50
22 Daniel Sedin .30 .75
23 Milan Hejduk .20 .50
24 Martin Havlat .20 .50
25 Chris Stewart .20 .50
26 Martin St. Louis .25 .60
27 Alex Pietrangelo .20 .50
28 Claude Giroux .25 .60
29 Steve Ott .15 .40
30 Tim Thomas .25 .60
31 Carey Price .50 1.25
32 Niklas Backstrom .25 .60
33 Zdeno Chara .25 .60
34 Miikka Kiprusoff .25 .60
35 Jimmy Howard .30 .75
36 Dave Bolland .20 .50
37 Patrice Bergeron .30 .75
38 Derek Roy .15 .40
39 Logan Couture .30 .75
40 Henrik Zetterberg .30 .75
41 Jaroslav Halak .25 .60
42 David Backes .15 .40
43 Kyle Clifford .15 .40
44 Mark Letestu .20 .50
45 Jonathan Bernier .20 .50
46 David Krejci .25 .60
47 Andrei Kostitsyn .20 .50
48 Danny Briere .25 .60
49 Rich Peverley .25 .60
50 Corey Crawford .30 .75
51 Valtteri Filppula .15 .40
52 Mike Green .20 .50
53 Jeff Skinner .30 .75
54 David Jones .15 .40
55 Nick Schultz .15 .40
56 Nicklas Backstrom .25 .60
57 Tyler Myers .15 .40
58 Kris Letang .30 .75
59 Tomas Vokoun .20 .50
60 Jose Theodore .25 .60
61 Rick Nash .25 .60
62 Michal Neuvirth .20 .50
63 Brad Marchand .50 1.25
64 Joffrey Lupul .15 .40
65 Brad Richards .25 .60
66 Rene Bourque .15 .40
67 Mattias Tedenby .15 .40
68 Jaromir Jagr .75 2.00
69 Magnus Paajarvi .20 .50
70 Mikko Koivu .20 .50
71 Evgeni Malkin .50 1.25
72 Ilya Bryzgalov .25 .60
73 Curtis Glencross .15 .40
74 Sergei Kostitsyn .15 .40
75 Jay Bouwmeester .15 .40
76 P.K. Subban .30 .75
77 Victor Hedman .30 .75
78 Mike Richards .20 .50
79 Andrei Markov .15 .40
80 Nik Antropov .20 .50
81 Phil Kessel .25 .60
82 Anze Kopitar .40 1.00
83 Karl Alzner .15 .40
84 Mikhail Grabovski .15 .40
85 Jason Pominville .15 .40
86 Daymond Langkow .15 .40
87 Sidney Crosby 1.00 2.50
88 Patrick Kane .50 1.25
89 Danny Cleary .25 .60
90 Ian White .20 .50
91 Steven Stamkos .50 1.25
92 Andy McDonald .20 .50
93 Johan Franzen .20 .50
94 Ryan Smyth .20 .50
95 Justin Williams .20 .50
96 Pierre-Marc Bouchard .25 .60
97 Drew Doughty .30 .75
98 Brandon Dubinsky .15 .40
99 Derek Stepan .15 .40
100 Ville Leino .20 .50
101 Steve Mason .20 .50
102 Duncan Keith .20 .50
103 Marc Methot .15 .40
104 Vincent Lecavalier .25 .60
105 Mark Giordano .25 .60
106 Andy Greene .15 .40
107 Paul Martin .15 .40
108 Teemu Selanne .50 1.25
109 Matt Duchene .25 .60
110 Patrick Sharp .25 .60
111 Daniel Alfredsson .25 .60
112 Eric Staal .30 .75
113 Daniel Carcillo .15 .40
114 Jordan Eberle .25 .60
115 Andrew Brunette .15 .40
116 Eric Fehr .15 .40
117 Ilya Kovalchuk .25 .60
118 R.J. Umberger .15 .40
119 Joe Thornton .40 1.00
120 Alexander Steen .15 .40
121 Brooks Laich .15 .40
122 Cal Clutterbuck .15 .40
123 Dustin Brown .25 .60
124 Ryan Callahan .15 .40
125 Chris Neil .15 .40
126 Patrik Elias .25 .60
127 Manny Malhotra .20 .50
128 Alexander Semin .25 .60
129 Marc-Andre Fleury .50 1.25
130 Martin Brodeur .60 1.50
131 Antti Niemi .20 .50
132 Kari Lehtonen .20 .50
133 Henrik Sedin .30 .75
134 James Reimer .25 .60
135 Nikolai Khabibulin .20 .50
136 Drew Stafford .15 .40
137 Ryan O'Reilly .25 .60
138 Brayden Schenn .25 .60
139 Matt Beleskey .15 .40
140 Alex Tanguay .15 .40
141 Jakub Voracek .20 .50
142 Steve Sullivan .15 .40
143 David Steckel .15 .40
144 Evgeni Nabokov .20 .50
145 Wayne Simmonds .30 .75
146 John-Michael Liles .15 .40
147 Cam Janssen .15 .40
148 Matthew Lombardi .15 .40
149 Travis Zajac .15 .40
150 Antoine Vermette .15 .40
151 Brian Campbell .15 .40
152 Shawn Horcoff .15 .40
153 Erik Cole .15 .40
154 Joe Corvo .15 .40
155 Ed Jovanovski .15 .40
156 James Wisniewski .15 .40
157 Devin Setoguchi .20 .50
158 David Desharnais .15 .40
159 Patrik Berglund .15 .40
160 Marc Staal .15 .40
161 Mike Ribeiro .15 .40
162 Tomas Fleischmann .15 .40
163 Tyler Ennis .15 .40
164 Kris Versteeg .15 .40
165 Steve Downie .15 .40
166 Jason Spezza .25 .60
167 Anthony Stewart .15 .40
168 Shane Doan .20 .50
169 Cam Ward .25 .60
170 Ray Whitney .20 .50
171 Nick Foligno .20 .50
172 Henrik Lundqvist .60 1.50
173 Brenden Morrow .20 .50
174 T.J. Oshie .25 .60
175 Scottie Upshall .15 .40
176 Ryan Malone .15 .40
177 Milan Michalek .15 .40
178 Tuomo Ruutu .20 .50
179 Martin Hanzal .15 .40
180 Andrew Ladd .15 .40
181 Marian Hossa .25 .60
182 Paul Stastny .20 .50
183 Mike Fisher .15 .40
184 Matt Moulson .15 .40
185 Jamie Benn .25 .60
186 David Booth .15 .40
187 Semyon Varlamov .25 .60
188 Brent Burns .25 .60
189 Mike Santorelli .15 .40
190 Zack Smith .15 .40
191 Brandon Sutter .15 .40
192 Radim Vrbata .15 .40
193 Evander Kane .25 .60
194 Jean-Sebastien Giguere .25 .60
195 Jordin Tootoo .20 .50
196 John Tavares .40 1.00
197 Michael Ryder .15 .40
198 Craig Anderson .25 .60
199 Tomas Kaberle .15 .40
200 Kyle Turris .15 .40
201 Jonas Hiller .20 .50
202 Mark Streit .15 .40
203 Dion Phaneuf .20 .50
204 Cam Fowler .25 .60
205 Dan Girardi .15 .40
206 Ryan Whitney .15 .40
207 Matt Cullen .15 .40
208 Joe Pavelski .30 .75
209 Bobby Ryan .20 .50
210 Marian Gaborik .25 .60
211 Jordan Staal .20 .50
212 Patrick Marleau .25 .60
213 Michael Cammalleri .20 .50
214 Tomas Plekanec .15 .40
215 Dany Heatley .20 .50
216 Teddy Purcell .15 .40
217 Ryan Kesler .25 .60
218 James Neal .15 .40
219 Jonathan Toews .40 1.00
220 Ryan Suter .20 .50
221 Brian Gionta .15 .40
222 Dan Boyle .15 .40
223 Linus Omark .25 .60
224 Blake Wheeler .25 .60
225 Pekka Rinne .25 .60
226 Thomas Vanek .20 .50
227 Rick DiPietro .20 .50
228 Mike Smith .25 .60
229 Ryane Clowe .15 .40
230 Ryan Miller .25 .60
231 Ondrej Pavelec .25 .60
232 Josh Bailey .20 .50
233 Dustin Byfuglien .25 .60
234 Matt Halischuk .15 .40
235 Dwayne Roloson .20 .50
236 Sheldon Souray .15 .40
237 Alexander Burmistrov .20 .50
238 Keith Yandle .15 .40
239 Matt Carkner .20 .50
240 Michael Grabner .20 .50
241 Bryan Little .25 .60
242 Kyle Okposo .15 .40
243 Tim Gleason .15 .40
244 Erik Johnson .15 .40
245 Raffi Torres .15 .40
246 Al Montoya .15 .40
247 Jack Johnson .15 .40
248 Martin Erat .15 .40
249 Loui Eriksson .15 .40
250 Tim Thomas .25 .60
251 Blake Geoffrion RC 1.00 2.50
252 Ben Scrivens RC 1.00 2.50
253 Patrick Wiercioch RC 1.00 2.50
254 Matt Frattin RC 1.00 2.50
255 Brett Connolly RC 1.00 2.50
256 Tomas Vincour RC 1.00 2.50
257 Brendon Nash RC 1.00 2.50
258 Erik Condra RC 1.00 2.50
259 Zac Rinaldo RC 1.00 2.50
260 Devante Smith-Pelly RC 1.25 3.00
261 David Savard RC 1.00 2.50
262 Brandon Saad RC 2.00 5.00
263 Erik Gudbranson RC 1.25 3.00
264 Raphael Diaz RC 1.00 2.50
265 Jonathon Blum RC 1.00 2.50
266 Adam Henrique RC 2.50 6.00
267 Maxime Macenauer RC 1.00 2.50
268 Justin Faulk RC 1.50 4.00
269 Cam Atkinson RC 2.50 6.00
270 Roman Horak RC 1.00 2.50
271 Anton Lander RC 1.00 2.50
272 Brett Bulmer RC 1.00 2.50
273 Alexei Emelin RC 1.00 2.50
274 Craig Smith RC 1.25 3.00
275 Adam Larsson RC 1.25 3.00
276 Stephane Da Costa RC 1.00 2.50
277 Colin Greening RC 1.00 2.50
278 Matt Read RC 3.00 8.00
279 Joe Vitale RC 1.00 2.50
280 Harri Sateri RC 1.00 2.50
281 Tim Erixon AU RC 8.00 20.00
282 Cody Hodgson AU RC 10.00 25.00
283 Joe Colborne AU RC 6.00 15.00
284 Nugent-Hopkins AU SP RC 20.00 50.00
285 Gabriel Landeskog AU RC 15.00 40.00
286 Mika Zibanejad AU RC 10.00 25.00
287 Mark Scheifele AU RC 25.00 60.00
288 Ryan Johansen AU RC 8.00 20.00
289 Sean Couturier AU RC 12.00 30.00
290 Jake Gardiner AU RC 8.00 20.00
291 Iiro Tarkki RC 1.50 4.00
292 Jeremy Smith RC 1.50 4.00
293 Pierre-Cedric Labrie RC 1.25 3.00
294 Dylan Olsen RC 1.50 4.00
295 Andrew Shaw RC 3.00 8.00
296 Colten Teubert RC 1.25 3.00
297 Greg Rallo RC 1.50 4.00
298 Jarod Palmer RC 1.25 3.00
299 Joe Finley RC 1.25 3.00
300 Stu Bickel RC 1.25 3.00
301 John Moore RC 1.25 3.00
302 Anders Nilsson RC 1.25 3.00
303 Brayden McNabb RC 1.25 3.00
304 David Ullstrom RC 1.25 3.00
305 Eddie Lack RC 1.25 3.00
306 Brian Foster RC 1.50 4.00
307 David McIntyre RC 1.25 3.00
308 Roman Josi RC 3.00 8.00
309 Keith Kinkaid RC 1.25 3.00
310 Peter Holland RC 1.25 3.00
311 Chad Rau RC 1.25 3.00
312 Kevin Marshall RC 1.25 3.00
313 Marc-Andre Bourdon RC 1.25 3.00
314 T.J. Brennan RC 1.25 3.00
315 Stefan Elliott RC 1.25 3.00
316 Corey Tropp RC 1.25 3.00
317 Brendan Smith RC 1.25 3.00
318 Slava Voynov RC 1.25 3.00
319 Dmitry Orlov RC 3.00 8.00
320 Matt Fraser RC 1.50 4.00
321 Allen York RC 1.50 4.00
322 Leland Irving RC 1.25 3.00
323 Harry Zolnierczyk RC 1.25 3.00
324 Frederic St-Denis RC 1.25 3.00
325 Gabriel Bourque RC 1.25 3.00
326 Jimmy Hayes RC 1.50 4.00
327 Riley Nash RC 1.25 3.00
328 Mike Murphy RC 1.25 3.00
329 Carl Sneep RC 1.25 3.00
330 Ryan Ellis RC 1.25 3.00
331 David Rundblad RC 1.25 3.00
332 Cody Eakin RC 2.00 5.00
333 Zack Kassian RC 1.50 4.00
334 Louis Leblanc RC 1.25 3.00
335 Andy Miele RC 1.25 3.00
336 Marcus Foligno RC 2.00 5.00
337 Joakim Andersson RC 1.25 3.00
338 Gustav Nyquist RC 3.00 8.00
339 Carl Hagelin RC 2.00 5.00
340 Calvin de Haan RC 1.25 3.00
341 Jordie Benn RC 1.25 3.00
342 Brad Malone RC 1.25 3.00
343 Derek Whitmore RC 1.50 4.00
344 Greg Nemisz RC 1.25 3.00
345 Ryan Russell RC 1.50 4.00
346 Lennart Petrell RC 1.50 4.00
347 Mark Borowiecki RC 1.50 4.00
348 Cade Fairchild RC 1.00 2.50
349 Mike Angelidis RC 1.50 4.00
350 Yann Sauve RC 1.25 3.00
351 Carl Klingberg RC 1.25 3.00
352 Tomas Kundratek RC 1.50 4.00
353 Andre Petersson RC 1.50 4.00
354 Simon Despres RC 1.25 3.00
355 Erik Gustafsson RC 1.50 4.00
356 Robert Bortuzzo RC 1.25 3.00
357 Mike Hoffman RC 5.00 12.00
358 Bill Sweatt RC 1.25 3.00
359 Paul Postma RC 1.25 3.00
360 Marcus Kruger RC 2.00 5.00
361 Lance Bouma RC 1.25 3.00
362 Warren Peters RC 1.50 4.00
363 Aaron Palushaj RC 1.25 3.00
364 Milan Kytnar RC 1.50 4.00
365 Kris Fredheim RC 1.25 3.00

2011-12 Pinnacle Rink Collection

*1-250 VETS: 2.5X TO 6X BASIC CARDS
50 Corey Crawford 2.00 5.00
56 Nicklas Backstrom 1.50 4.00

2011-12 Pinnacle Black

1 Sidney Crosby 25.00 60.00
2 Steven Stamkos 12.00 30.00
3 Alex Ovechkin 25.00 60.00
4 Carey Price 12.00 30.00
5 Tim Thomas 8.00 20.00
6 Martin Brodeur 15.00 40.00
7 Jonathan Toews 10.00 25.00
8 Roberto Luongo 10.00 25.00
9 Jeff Skinner 8.00 20.00
10 Joe Sakic 12.00 30.00
11 Patrick Roy 15.00 40.00
12 Mario Lemieux 25.00 60.00
13 Mark Messier 10.00 25.00
14 Steve Yzerman 12.00 30.00

2011-12 Pinnacle Breakthrough

COMPLETE SET (20) 15.00 30.00
1 Ryan Kesler 1.00 2.50
2 Corey Perry 1.50 4.00
3 Claude Giroux 1.00 2.50
4 Corey Crawford 1.25 3.00
5 Jeff Skinner 1.25 3.00
6 David Backes .60 1.50
7 Ryane Clowe .60 1.50
8 Clarke MacArthur .60 1.50
9 Keith Yandle .60 1.50
10 Milan Lucic 1.00 2.50
11 Nikolai Kulemin .60 1.50
12 Jamie Benn 1.00 2.50
13 Logan Couture 1.25 3.00
14 James van Riemsdyk .75 2.00
15 Brad Marchand 2.00 5.00
16 Andrew Ladd .60 1.50
17 David Krejci 1.00 2.50
18 Michael Grabner .75 2.00
19 James Reimer 1.25 3.00
20 Loui Eriksson .60 1.50

2011-12 Pinnacle Canvas Creations

1 Sidney Crosby 8.00 20.00
2 Martin Brodeur 5.00 12.00
3 Patrick Kane 4.00 10.00
4 Pavel Datsyuk 3.00 8.00
5 Alex Ovechkin 8.00 20.00
6 Carey Price 4.00 10.00
7 Claude Giroux 2.00 5.00
8 Jordan Eberle 2.00 5.00
9 Roberto Luongo 3.00 8.00
10 Tim Thomas 2.00 5.00
11 Evgeni Malkin 4.00 10.00
12 Rick Nash 2.00 5.00
13 James Reimer 2.50 6.00
14 Mike Richards 1.50 4.00
15 Marian Gaborik 2.00 5.00
16 Steven Stamkos 4.00 10.00
17 Logan Couture 2.50 6.00
18 Jarome Iginla 2.50 6.00

2011-12 Pinnacle Captains

1 Jonathan Toews 4.00 10.00
2 Nicklas Lidstrom 1.50 4.00
3 Joe Thornton 4.00 10.00
4 Alex Ovechkin 10.00 25.00
5 Henrik Sedin 3.00 8.00

6 Zdeno Chara 2.50 6.00
7 Sidney Crosby 10.00 25.00
8 Daniel Alfredsson 2.50 6.00
9 Dion Phaneuf 2.00 5.00
10 Vincent Lecavalier 2.50 6.00
11 Brian Gionta 1.50 4.00
12 Shane Doan 2.00 5.00
13 Andrew Ladd 1.50 4.00
14 Rick Nash 2.50 6.00
15 Shea Weber 2.00 5.00
16 Eric Staal 3.00 8.00
17 Jarome Iginla 3.00 8.00
18 Ryan Getzlaf 2.50 6.00
19 Mikko Koivu 2.00 5.00
20 Shawn Horcoff 1.50 4.00

2011-12 Pinnacle Fans of the Game

1 Michelle Beadle 1.50 4.00
2 Heidi Androl 1.50 4.00
3 Dave Hanson 2.00 5.00
4 Jeff Carlson 1.50 4.00
5 Steve Carlson 1.50 4.00
6 Jonathan Davis 1.50 4.00
7 Alyssa Milano 1.50 4.00
8 Jaime Pressly 1.50 4.00

2011-12 Pinnacle Fans of the Game Autographs

1 Michelle Beadle 15.00 40.00
2 Heidi Androl 6.00 15.00
3 Dave Hanson 12.00 30.00
4 Jeff Carlson 12.00 30.00
5 Steve Carlson 6.00 15.00
6 Jonathan Davis 60.00 150.00
7 Alyssa Milano 100.00 250.00

2011-12 Pinnacle Foundation Tandems East

1 T.Seguin/T.Thomas 1.00 2.50
2 R.Miller/T.Ennis .75 2.00
3 E.Staal/J.Skinner 1.25 3.00
4 C.Price/P.Subban 2.00 5.00
5 M.Brodeur/Z.Parise 2.50 6.00
6 H.Lundqvist/D.Stepan 2.50 6.00
7 C.Giroux/B.Schenn 1.00 2.50
8 S.Crosby/M.Letestu 4.00 10.00
9 S.Stamkos/V.Lecavalier 2.00 5.00
10 J.Carlson/A.Ovechkin 3.00 8.00

2011-12 Pinnacle Foundation Tandems West

1 C.Fowler/R.Getzlaf .75 2.00
2 J.Toews/M.Kruger 1.25 3.00
3 P.Stastny/M.Duchene .75 2.00
4 R.Nash/J.Moore .75 2.00
5 P.Datsyuk/T.Tatar 1.25 3.00
6 J.Eberle/T.Hall .75 2.00
7 A.Pietrangelo/J.Halak .75 2.00
8 J.Thornton/L.Couture 1.25 3.00
9 C.Hodgson/R.Luongo .75 2.00
10 G.Nemisz/J.Iginla 1.00 2.50

2011-12 Pinnacle Game Night Materials

*PRIME/30-50: .6X TO 1.5X BASIC JSY
1 Sidney Crosby 8.00 20.00
2 Alex Ovechkin 8.00 20.00
3 Carey Price 8.00 20.00
4 Zdeno Chara 4.00 10.00
5 Bobby Butler 3.00 8.00
6 Tyler Seguin 5.00 12.00
7 Matt Carkner 3.00 8.00
8 Tim Thomas 4.00 10.00
9 Tyler Myers 2.50 6.00
10 Jarome Iginla 5.00 12.00
11 Patrick Kane 8.00 20.00
12 Pavel Datsyuk 6.00 15.00
13 Jeff Carter 3.00 8.00
14 Bobby Ryan 3.00 8.00
15 Nathan Horton 4.00 10.00
16 Anze Kopitar 6.00 15.00
17 Curtis Glencross 2.50 6.00
18 Marian Gaborik 4.00 10.00
19 Kevin Bieksa 3.00 8.00
20 Corey Perry 6.00 15.00
21 Stephane Da Costa 3.00 8.00
22 Ryan Kesler 4.00 10.00
23 David Backes 2.50 6.00
24 Taylor Hall 4.00 10.00
25 Shawn Thornton 2.50 6.00
26 Jamie Benn 4.00 10.00
27 Ondrej Pavelec 4.00 10.00
28 Scott Hartnell 2.50 6.00
29 Cam Fowler 4.00 10.00
30 Pekka Rinne 4.00 10.00
31 Logan Couture 5.00 12.00
32 P.K. Subban 5.00 12.00
33 Ryan Suter 3.00 8.00
34 Niklas Backstrom 4.00 10.00
35 Drew Doughty 5.00 12.00
36 Dustin Byfuglien 4.00 10.00
37 Henrik Sedin 5.00 12.00
38 Claude Giroux 4.00 10.00
39 Marc-Andre Fleury 8.00 20.00
40 Dany Heatley 3.00 8.00
41 Henrik Lundqvist 4.00 10.00
42 Jeff Skinner 5.00 12.00
43 Mike Richards 3.00 8.00
44 Dion Phaneuf 3.00 8.00
45 Ryan Smyth 3.00 8.00
46 Zac Dalpe 2.50 6.00
47 Patrick Marleau 4.00 10.00
48 Paul Stastny 3.00 8.00
49 Vincent Lecavalier 4.00 10.00
50 Martin St. Louis 4.00 10.00

2011-12 Pinnacle Game Night Signatures

1 Sidney Crosby/25* 60.00 120.00
2 Alex Ovechkin/50* 30.00 80.00
3 Carey Price/25* 15.00 40.00
5 Bobby Butler/75* 6.00 15.00
6 Tyler Seguin/25* 30.00 60.00
8 Tim Thomas/25* 15.00 30.00
9 Tyler Myers/35* 6.00 15.00
10 Jarome Iginla/75* 10.00 25.00
11 Patrick Kane/75* 20.00 40.00
12 Pavel Datsyuk/50* 10.00 25.00
13 Jeff Carter/50* 6.00 15.00
14 Bobby Ryan/75* 6.00 15.00
15 Nathan Horton/50* 8.00 20.00
17 Curtis Glencross/75* 5.00 12.00
20 Corey Perry/75* 12.00 30.00
21 Stephane Da Costa/75* 6.00 15.00
22 Ryan Kesler/50* 12.00 30.00
25 Shawn Thornton/20* 25.00 50.00
26 Jamie Benn/75* 8.00 20.00
27 Ondrej Pavelec/75* 8.00 20.00
29 Cam Fowler/75* 8.00 20.00
31 Logan Couture/75* 10.00 25.00
32 P.K. Subban/75* 15.00 40.00
34 Niklas Backstrom/75* 8.00 20.00
35 Drew Doughty/35* 12.00 30.00
37 Henrik Sedin/25* 12.00 30.00
38 Claude Giroux/50* 8.00 20.00
39 Marc-Andre Fleury/75* 15.00 30.00
41 Henrik Lundqvist/50* 15.00 30.00
42 Jeff Skinner/75* 10.00 25.00
44 Dion Phaneuf/25* 12.00 30.00
45 Ryan Smyth/75* 6.00 15.00
47 Patrick Marleau/75* 8.00 20.00
49 Vincent Lecavalier/35* 10.00 25.00

2011-12 Pinnacle Ice Breakers Autographs

302 Anders Nilsson 6.00 15.00
305 Eddie Lack 6.00 15.00
308 Roman Josi 15.00 40.00
310 Peter Holland 6.00 15.00
317 Brendan Smith 6.00 15.00
318 Slava Voynov 6.00 15.00
323 Harry Zolnierczyk 6.00 15.00
326 Jimmy Hayes 8.00 20.00
330 Ryan Ellis 6.00 15.00
331 David Rundblad 6.00 15.00
332 Cody Eakin 10.00 25.00
333 Zack Kassian 8.00 20.00
335 Andy Miele 6.00 15.00
338 Gustav Nyquist 15.00 40.00
339 Carl Hagelin 10.00 25.00
340 Calvin de Haan 6.00 15.00
344 Greg Nemisz 6.00 15.00
351 Carl Klingberg 6.00 15.00
354 Simon Despres 6.00 15.00
361 Lance Bouma 6.00 15.00

2011-12 Pinnacle Pantheon

1 Steven Stamkos 12.00 30.00
2 Tim Thomas 10.00 25.00
3 Alex Ovechkin 25.00 60.00
4 Corey Perry 10.00 25.00
5 Daniel Sedin 8.00 20.00
6 Sidney Crosby 25.00 60.00
7 Carey Price 12.00 30.00
9 Jarome Iginla 8.00 20.00
10 Claude Giroux 25.00 50.00

2011-12 Pinnacle Revolution

1 P.K. Subban 2.00 5.00
2 Jeff Skinner 2.00 5.00
3 Alex Ovechkin 6.00 15.00
4 Steven Stamkos 3.00 8.00
5 Sidney Crosby 6.00 15.00
6 Milan Lucic 1.50 4.00
7 Dustin Byfuglien 1.50 4.00
8 Tyler Ennis 1.00 2.50
9 James Reimer 1.50 4.00
10 Henrik Lundqvist 4.00 10.00

2011-12 Pinnacle Starting Six Threads

*1-10 PRIME/50: .6X TO 1.5X BASIC JSY/199
1 Thms/Chr/Brg/Lcic/Hrtn/Brtk 20.00 40.00
2 Hmh/Sdin/Ehr/Sdn/Brrw/Lng 12.00 30.00
3 Mrkv/Gnta/Kst/Prc/Cam/Sbn 10.00 25.00
4 Klm/Rmr/Phnf/Kssl/Grbv/Sch 12.00 30.00
5 Flry/Mlkn/Stl/Neal/Letng/Strt 12.00 30.00
6 Alzn/Smn/Ovc/Bck/Crls/Nvlh 15.00 40.00
7 Lpld/Mlr/Pmvl/Ry/Myrs/Ennis 8.00 20.00
8 Glbrt/Wht/Khb/Hmsk/Hll/Ebrl 10.00 25.00
9 Mrl/Clwe/Thrn/Byle/Nmi/Brns 12.00 30.00
10 Dbn/Stl/Gbrk/Clhn/DlZt/Lndq 10.00 25.00
11 Predators/137* 6.00 15.00
12 Kings/200* 12.00 30.00
13 Ducks/200* 15.00 30.00
14 Blackhawks/25* 40.00 80.00
15 Avalanche/200* 12.00 30.00
16 Stars/50* 15.00 30.00
17 Oilers/200* 10.00 25.00
18 Wild/200* 10.00 25.00
19 Devils/200* 20.00 50.00
20 Senators/200* 12.00 30.00
21 Flyers/100* 20.00 40.00
22 Red Wings/200* 8.00 20.00
23 Hurricanes/100* 10.00 25.00
24 Blue Jackets/200* 15.00 40.00
25 Islanders/200* 6.00 15.00
26 Tws/Grx/Ebr/Kth/Prn/Prc/100* 12.00 30.00
27 Bck/Kne/Rch/Str/Yndl/Thm 15.00 40.00
28 Sdn Br./Alfrd/Krlsn/Lds/Lnd 12.00 30.00
29 Kvu/Slne/Flpp/Tim/Kth/Kip 15.00 40.00
30 Jgr/Ert/Mclk/Krjc/Kbrl/Nvr 12.00 30.00
31 Dtsk/Ov/Kvl/Gnch/Voy/Khb 12.00 30.00
32 Nl/Spz/Kss/Piet/Dn/Hwrd 12.00 30.00
33 Hrtn/Stm/StL/Dgty/Zot/Nie 12.00 30.00
34 Ctr/Hnrq/Smt/Jhn/Emln/Yrk 12.00 30.00
35 Jhn/Smt/Krg/Sav/Emln/Scr 20.00 50.00
36 Adm/RNH/Ctr/Voy/Els/Scr 12.00 30.00
37 Lnd/Hnrq/Rd/Grd/Flk/Yrk 12.00 30.00
38 Hag/Grn/Frt/Dz/Lrsn/Yrk 6.00 15.00
39 Hnrq/Rd/Grn/Svr/Grd/Scr 10.00 25.00
40 RNH/Lnd/Hds/Voy/Els/Yrk 8.00 20.00

2011-12 Pinnacle Team Pinnacle

1 H.Sedin/S.Stamkos 4.00 10.00
2 M.St. Louis/C.Perry 3.00 8.00
3 D.Sedin/A.Ovechkin 8.00 20.00
4 Z.Chara/N.Lidstrom 2.50 6.00
5 T.Thomas/R.Luongo 3.00 8.00
6 S.Crosby/J.Toews 5.00 12.00
7 J.Iginla/C.Giroux 2.50 6.00
8 M.Lucic/H.Zetterberg 2.50 6.00
9 S.Weber/P.Subban 4.00 10.00
10 P.Rinne/C.Price 4.00 10.00

2011-12 Pinnacle Threads

*PATCH/15-25: .8X TO 2X BASIC JSY
*PRIME/50: .6X TO 1.5X BASIC JSY
1 Corey Perry 6.00 15.00
2 Eric Staal 5.00 12.00
3 Thomas Vanek 3.00 8.00
4 Mark Giordano 4.00 10.00
5 Sidney Crosby 15.00 40.00
6 Alex Ovechkin 10.00 25.00
7 Anze Kopitar 6.00 15.00
8 Martin St. Louis 4.00 10.00
9 Daniel Alfredsson 4.00 10.00
10 John Tavares 6.00 15.00
11 Patrick Roy 10.00 25.00
12 Dion Phaneuf 3.00 8.00
13 Joe Thornton 6.00 15.00
14 Matt Duchene 4.00 10.00
15 Nicklas Lidstrom 2.50 6.00
16 Ryan Getzlaf 4.00 10.00
17 Jason Spezza 4.00 10.00
18 Henrik Zetterberg 5.00 12.00
19 Jonathan Toews 6.00 15.00
20 Milan Lucic 4.00 10.00
21 Alexandre Burrows 2.50 6.00
22 Nazem Kadri 5.00 12.00
23 Sergei Kostitsyn 2.50 6.00
24 Mike Green 3.00 8.00
25 Steve Ott 2.50 6.00
26 Jonas Gustavsson 4.00 10.00
27 Rene Bourque 2.50 6.00
28 Kris Letang 5.00 12.00
29 Rick DiPietro 3.00 8.00
30 Taylor Hall 4.00 10.00
31 Trevor Daley 2.50 6.00
32 Ales Hemsky 3.00 8.00
33 Andrei Markov 2.50 6.00
34 Antti Niemi 3.00 8.00
35 Barret Jackman 2.50 6.00
36 Brad Marchand 8.00 20.00
37 Brandon McMillan 2.50 6.00
38 Marc-Andre Fleury 8.00 20.00
39 Magnus Paajarvi 3.00 8.00
40 Luke Schenn 4.00 10.00
41 Loui Eriksson 2.50 6.00
42 Linus Omark 4.00 10.00
43 Kris Versteeg 2.50 6.00
44 Keith Yandle 2.50 6.00
45 Tim Thomas 4.00 10.00
46 Tom Wandell 2.50 6.00
47 Tomas Tatar 2.50 6.00
48 Zdeno Chara 4.00 10.00
49 Cal Clutterbuck 2.50 6.00
50 Brian Gionta 2.50 6.00
51 Brian Boyle 2.50 6.00
52 Brent Seabrook 2.50 6.00
53 Colin Wilson 3.00 8.00
54 Shea Weber 3.00 8.00
55 Derek Stepan 2.50 6.00
56 Erik Johnson 2.50 6.00
57 Evgeni Malkin 8.00 20.00
58 Devan Dubnyk 3.00 8.00
59 Drew Doughty 5.00 12.00
60 Dustin Tokarski 4.00 10.00
61 Mattias Tedenby 2.50 6.00
62 Ryan McDonagh 2.50 6.00
63 Rick Nash 4.00 10.00
64 Henrik Lundqvist 10.00 25.00
65 Alexander Burmistrov 3.00 8.00
66 Jamie McBain 2.50 6.00
67 Jordan Leopold 2.50 6.00
68 Milan Michalek 2.50 6.00
69 Nathan Gerbe 2.50 6.00
70 Jordan Staal 3.00 8.00
71 Niklas Backstrom 4.00 10.00
72 Patrik Elias 4.00 10.00
73 Scott Gomez 3.00 8.00
74 Tomas Vokoun 3.00 8.00
75 Travis Zajac 2.50 6.00
76 Zach Hamill 3.00 8.00
77 Duncan Keith 5.00 12.00
78 Dustin Brown 4.00 10.00
79 Craig Anderson 4.00 10.00
80 Claude Giroux 4.00 10.00
81 Carey Price 8.00 20.00
82 Chris Pronger 4.00 10.00
83 George Parros 3.00 8.00
84 Henrik Sedin 6.00 15.00
85 Ilya Kovalchuk 4.00 10.00
86 James Neal 2.50 6.00
87 Jason Pominville 2.50 6.00
88 Logan Couture 5.00 12.00
89 Marc Staal 2.50 6.00
90 P.K. Subban 6.00 15.00

2011-12 Pinnacle Tough Times

1 Wendel Clark 2.50 6.00
3 Rob Ray 1.00 2.50
4 Bruce Shoebottom 1.00 2.50
5 Marty McSorley 1.25 3.00
8 Gino Odjick 1.00 2.50
10 Shane Churla 1.00 2.50

2011-12 Pinnacle Tough Times Autographs

1 Wendel Clark 15.00 40.00
3 Rob Ray 5.00 12.00
4 Bruce Shoebottom 5.00 12.00
5 Marty McSorley 6.00 15.00
8 Gino Odjick SP 12.00 30.00
10 Shane Churla 5.00 12.00

2011-12 Pinnacle Winter Classic

1 Ryan Miller GO 1.25 3.00
2 Jonathan Toews GO 2.00 5.00
3 Marian Hossa GO 1.25 3.00
4 Alex Ovechkin GO 4.00 10.00
5 Tim Thomas GO 1.25 3.00
PF1 Chris Pronger 1.25 3.00
PF2 Claude Giroux 1.25 3.00
PF3 Ilya Bryzgalov 1.25 3.00
PF4 Jaromir Jagr 4.00 10.00
PF5 Sean Couturier 3.00 8.00
WC1 Tim Thomas 1.25 3.00
WC2 Gabriel Landeskog 5.00 12.00
WC3 Ryan Nugent-Hopkins 12.50 30.00
WC4 Steven Stamkos 2.50 6.00
WC5 Alex Ovechkin 5.00 12.00
NYR1 Brad Richards 1.25 3.00
NYR2 Derek Stepan .75 2.00
NYR3 Henrik Lundqvist 3.00 8.00
NYR4 Marian Gaborik 1.25 3.00
NYR5 Tim Erixon 1.00 2.50

2011-12 Pinnacle All Star Game

COMPLETE SET (10) 10.00 20.00
1 Daniel Alfredsson .40 1.00
2 Nicklas Lidstrom .40 1.00
3 Jaromir Jagr .40 1.00
4 Alex Ovechkin 1.25 3.00
5 Sidney Crosby 1.50 3.50
6 Tim Thomas .75 2.00
7 Ryan Nugent-Hopkins 1.50 4.00
8 Mika Zibanejad 1.25 3.00
9 Gabriel Landeskog 1.50 3.50
ML Mario Lemieux 1.00 2.50

1997-98 Pinnacle Collector's Club Team Pinnacle

COMPLETE SET (10) 40.00 80.00
H1 Wayne Gretzky 8.00 20.00
H2 Patrick Roy 6.00 15.00
H3 Eric Lindros 3.00 8.00
H4 Paul Kariya 5.00 12.00
H5 Peter Forsberg 5.00 12.00
H6 John Vanbiesbrouck 2.00 5.00
H7 Martin Brodeur 6.00 15.00
H8 Steve Yzerman 6.00 15.00
H9 Jaromir Jagr 4.00 10.00
H10 Mark Messier 3.00 8.00
NNO Wayne Gretzky PROMO 10.00 25.00
NNO Peter Forsberg PROMO 6.00 15.00

1997-98 Pinnacle Certified

1 Dominik Hasek .30 .75
2 Patrick Roy .50 1.25
3 Martin Brodeur .50 1.25
4 Chris Osgood .20 .50
5 Andy Moog .20 .50
6 John Vanbiesbrouck .20 .50
7 Steve Shields RC .20 .50
8 Mike Vernon .15 .40
9 Ed Belfour .20 .50
10 Grant Fuhr .30 .75
11 Felix Potvin .30 .75
12 Bill Ranford .15 .40
13 Mike Richter .20 .50
14 Stephane Fiset .15 .40
15 Jim Carey .15 .40
16 Nikolai Khabibulin .20 .50
17 Ken Wregget .12 .30
18 Curtis Joseph .25 .60
19 Guy Hebert .15 .40
20 Damian Rhodes .15 .40
21 Trevor Kidd .12 .30
22 Daren Puppa .15 .40
23 Patrick Lalime .15 .40
24 Tommy Salo .12 .30
25 Sean Burke .15 .40
26 Jocelyn Thibault .15 .40
27 Kirk McLean .15 .40
28 Garth Snow .15 .40
29 Ron Tugnutt .20 .50
30 Jeff Hackett .15 .40
31 Eric Lindros .30 .75
32 Peter Forsberg .40 1.00
33 Mike Modano .30 .75
34 Paul Kariya .20 .50
35 Jaromir Jagr .60 1.50
36 Brian Leetch .15 .40
37 Keith Tkachuk .20 .50
38 Steve Yzerman .50 1.25
39 Teemu Selanne .40 1.00
40 Bryan Berard .12 .30
41 Ray Bourque .30 .75
42 Theo Fleury .25 .60
43 Mark Messier .40 1.00
44 Saku Koivu .20 .50
45 Pavel Bure .20 .50
46 Peter Bondra .20 .50
47 Dave Gagner .12 .30
48 Ed Jovanovski .12 .30
49 Adam Oates .20 .50
50 Joe Sakic .40 1.00
51 Doug Gilmour .25 .60
52 Jim Campbell .12 .30
53 Mats Sundin .20 .50
54 Derian Hatcher .15 .40
55 Jarome Iginla .25 .60
56 Sergei Fedorov .30 .75
57 Keith Primeau .15 .40
58 Mark Recchi .25 .60
59 Owen Nolan .20 .50
60 Alexander Mogilny .15 .40
61 Brendan Shanahan .20 .50
62 Pierre Turgeon .15 .40
63 Joe Juneau .12 .30
64 Steve Rucchin .12 .30
65 Jeremy Roenick .30 .75
66 Doug Weight .20 .50
67 Valeri Kamensky .15 .40
68 Tony Amonte .15 .40
69 Dave Andreychuk .20 .50
70 Brett Hull .40 1.00
71 Wendel Clark .30 .75
72 Vincent Damphousse .15 .40
73 Mike Grier .12 .30
74 Chris Chelios .20 .50
75 Nicklas Lidstrom .20 .50
76 Joe Nieuwendyk .15 .40
77 Rob Blake .15 .40
78 Alexei Yashin .15 .40
79 Ryan Smyth .15 .40
80 Pat LaFontaine .15 .40
81 Jeff Friesen .15 .40
82 Ray Ferraro .12 .30
83 Steve Sullivan .12 .30
84 Chris Gratton .12 .30
85 Mike Gartner .25 .60
86 Kevin Hatcher .12 .30
87 Ted Donato .12 .30
88 German Titov .12 .30
89 Sandis Ozolinsh .12 .30
90 Ray Sheppard .15 .40
91 John MacLean .12 .30
92 Luc Robitaille .20 .50
93 Rod Brind'Amour .20 .50
94 Zigmund Palffy .20 .50
95 Petr Nedved .20 .50
96 Adam Graves .12 .30
97 Jozef Stumpel .12 .30
98 Alexandre Daigle .12 .30
99 Mike Peca .15 .40
100 Wayne Gretzky 1.25 3.00
101 Alexei Zhamnov .12 .30
102 Paul Coffey .20 .50
103 Oleg Tverdovsky .15 .40
104 Trevor Linden .20 .50
105 Dino Ciccarelli .20 .50
106 Andrei Kovalenko .12 .30
107 Scott Mellanby .15 .40
108 Bryan Smolinski .15 .40
109 Bernie Nicholls .15 .40
110 Derek Plante .15 .40
111 Pat Verbeek .15 .40
112 Adam Deadmarsh .12 .30
113 Martin Gelinas .12 .30
114 Daniel Alfredsson .20 .50
115 Scott Stevens .20 .50
116 Dainius Zubrus .15 .40
117 Kirk Muller .12 .30
118 Brian Holzinger .15 .40
119 John LeClair .20 .50
120 Al MacInnis .25 .60
121 Ron Francis .25 .60
122 Eric Daze .12 .30
123 Travis Green .15 .40
124 Jason Arnott .15 .40
125 Geoff Sanderson .15 .40
126 Dimitri Khristich .15 .40
127 Sergei Berezin .15 .40
128 Jeff O'Neill .15 .40
129 Claude Lemieux .15 .40
130 Andrew Cassels .12 .30
NNO CHECKLIST 1 .07 .20
NNO CHECKLIST 2 .07 .20

1997-98 Pinnacle Certified Red

*RED: 1.2X TO 3X BASIC CARDS

1997-98 Pinnacle Certified Mirror Blue

*MIRROR BLUE: 6X TO 15X BASIC CARDS

1997-98 Pinnacle Certified Mirror Gold

*MIRROR GOLD: 12X TO 30X BASIC CARDS
100 Wayne Gretzky 75.00 150.00

1997-98 Pinnacle Certified Mirror Red

*MIRROR RED: 4X TO 10X BASIC CARDS

1997-98 Pinnacle Certified Team

COMPLETE SET (20) 75.00 150.00
*GOLD TEAM/300: 2X TO 5X BASIC INSERTS
*GT PROMOS: .2X TO .5X BASIC INSERTS
1 Martin Brodeur 5.00 12.00
2 Patrick Roy 10.00 25.00
3 John Vanbiesbrouck 1.25 3.00
4 Dominik Hasek 4.00 10.00
5 Chris Chelios 2.00 5.00
6 Brian Leetch 2.00 5.00
7 Wayne Gretzky 12.50 30.00
8 Eric Lindros 2.00 5.00
9 Paul Kariya 2.00 5.00
10 Peter Forsberg 5.00 12.00
11 Keith Tkachuk 2.00 5.00
12 Mark Messier 2.00 5.00
13 Steve Yzerman 10.00 25.00
14 Jaromir Jagr 3.00 8.00
15 Mats Sundin 2.00 5.00
16 Teemu Selanne 2.00 5.00
17 Brendan Shanahan 2.00 5.00
18 Saku Koivu 2.00 5.00
19 Brett Hull 2.50 6.00
20 John LeClair 2.00 5.00

1997-98 Pinnacle Certified Rookie Redemption

COMPLETE SET (12) 25.00 50.00
*GOLD: 2X TO 5X BASIC INSERTS
*MIRROR GOLD: 8X TO 20X BASIC INSERTS
A Joe Thornton 5.00 12.00
B Chris Phillips 1.50 4.00
C Patrick Marleau 4.00 10.00
D Sergei Samsonov 1.50 4.00
E Daniel Cleary 1.50 4.00
F Olli Jokinen 2.50 6.00
G Alyn McCauley 1.50 4.00
H Alexei Morozov 1.50 4.00
I Brad Isbister 1.50 4.00
J Boyd Devereaux 1.50 4.00
K Espen Knutsen 1.50 4.00
L Marc Savard 1.50 4.00

1997-98 Pinnacle Certified Summit Silver

COMMON CARD (1-5) 4.00 10.00
NNO P.Henderson SIL AU/200 30.00 60.00
NNO P.Henderson BLK AU/700 20.00 50.00
NNO P.Henderson GLD AU/100 75.00 200.00

1996-97 Pinnacle Fantasy

FC1 Ray Bourque 1.00 2.50
FC2 Paul Coffey .40 1.00
FC3 Eric Lindros 1.50 4.00
FC4 Mario Lemieux 3.00 8.00
FC5 Wayne Gretzky 4.00 10.00
FC6 Mark Messier 1.00 2.50
FC7 Jaromir Jagr 1.50 4.00
FC8 Brendan Shanahan 1.50 4.00
FC9 John Vanbiesbrouck .60 1.50
FC10 Mike Richter .60 1.50
FC11 Chris Chelios .60 1.50
FC12 Nicklas Lidstrom .20 .50
FC13 Sergei Fedorov 1.50 4.00
FC14 Pavel Bure 1.50 4.00
FC15 Peter Forsberg 2.50 6.00
FC16 Brett Hull 1.00 2.50
FC17 Joe Sakic 1.50 4.00
FC18 Owen Nolan .40 1.00
FC19 Patrick Roy 3.00 8.00
FC20 Ed Belfour .60 1.50
NNO1 Kelly Hrudey 10.00 25.00
NNO2 Kelly Hrudey FOIL 15.00 40.00
NNO3 Kelly Hrudey Offer Card 40.00 100.00

1997-98 Pinnacle Inside

COMPLETE SET (190) 20.00 40.00
1 Brendan Shanahan .25 .60
2 Dominik Hasek .50 1.25
3 Wayne Gretzky 1.50 4.00
4 Eric Lindros .25 .60
5 Keith Tkachuk .25 .60
6 Jaromir Jagr .40 1.00
7 Martin Brodeur .60 1.50
8 Peter Forsberg .60 1.50
9 Chris Osgood .20 .50
10 Paul Kariya .25 .60
11 Pavel Bure .25 .60
12 Brett Hull .30 .75
13 Saku Koivu .25 .60
14 Zigmund Palffy .20 .50
15 Mike Modano .40 1.00
16 Ray Bourque .40 1.00
17 Jarome Iginla .30 .75
18 Chris Chelios .25 .60
19 John Vanbiesbrouck .20 .50
20 Brian Leetch .25 .60
21 Mats Sundin .25 .60
22 Ron Hextall .20 .50
23 Stephane Fiset .20 .50
24 Steve Yzerman 1.25 3.00
25 Curtis Joseph .25 .60
26 Daniel Alfredsson .25 .60
27 Owen Nolan .20 .50
28 Adam Oates .20 .50
29 Corey Hirsch .20 .50
30 Sean Burke .20 .50
31 Eric Fichaud .20 .50
32 Ken Wregget .20 .50
33 Dainius Zubrus .25 .60
34 Alexander Mogilny .20 .50
35 Bill Ranford .20 .50
36 Vincent Damphousse .07 .20
37 Patrick Roy 1.25 3.00
38 Teemu Selanne .25 .60
39 Pat LaFontaine .25 .60
40 Theo Fleury .07 .20
41 Jeff Hackett .07 .20
42 Sergei Fedorov .40 1.00
43 Jocelyn Thibault .20 .50
44 Nikolai Khabibulin .20 .50
45 Daren Puppa .20 .50
46 Felix Potvin .25 .60
47 Andy Moog .20 .50
48 Doug Weight .20 .50
49 Tommy Salo .20 .50
50 Mark Messier .25 .60
51 Grant Fuhr .20 .50
52 Ron Francis .20 .50
53 Tony Amonte .20 .50
54 Joe Sakic .50 1.25
55 Jason Arnott .20 .50
56 Jose Theodore .30 .75
57 Alexei Yashin .07 .20
58 John LeClair .25 .60
59 Jeremy Roenick .30 .75
60 Kirk McLean .20 .50
61 Arturs Irbe .20 .50
62 Jim Carey .20 .50
63 Jean-Sebastien Giguere .20 .50
64 Marc Denis .20 .50
65 Damian Rhodes .20 .50
66 Jim Campbell .07 .20
67 Patrick Lalime .20 .50
68 Garth Snow .20 .50
69 Marcel Cousineau .20 .50
70 Guy Hebert .20 .50
71 Rob Blake .20 .50
72 Tomas Vokoun RC .25 .60
73 Doug Gilmour .20 .50
74 Ed Belfour .25 .60
75 Parris Duffus RC .07 .20
76 Mike Fountain .07 .20
77 Steve Shields RC .25 .60
78 Geoff Sanderson .07 .20
79 Roman Turek .20 .50
80 Bryan Berard .20 .50
81 Mike Richter .25 .60
82 Ron Tugnutt .20 .50
83 Peter Bondra .20 .50
84 Mike Vernon .20 .50
85 Mike Grier .07 .20
86 Ed Jovanovski .20 .50
87 Trevor Kidd .20 .50
88 Eric Daze .20 .50
89 Wendel Clark .20 .50
90 Checklist (1-190) .07 .20
91 Nicklas Lidstrom .25 .60
92 Rod Brind'Amour .20 .50
93 Hnat Domenichelli .07 .20
94 Rem Murray .07 .20
95 Scott Niedermayer .07 .20
96 Martin Rucinsky .07 .20
97 Mike Gartner .20 .50
98 Kevin Hatcher .07 .20
99 Daymond Langkow .20 .50
100 Jamie Langenbrunner .07 .20
101 Ted Donato .07 .20
102 Steve Sullivan .07 .20
103 Martin Gelinas .07 .20
104 Adam Graves .07 .20
105 Donald Audette .07 .20
106 Andrew Cassels .07 .20
107 Alexei Zhamnov .07 .20
108 Kirk Muller .07 .20
109 Alexandre Daigle .07 .20
110 Chris Gratton .07 .20
111 Andrew Brunette .07 .20
112 Mark Recchi .20 .50
113 Jari Kurri .20 .50
114 Valeri Kamensky .20 .50
115 Joe Nieuwendyk .20 .50
116 Slava Kozlov .07 .20
117 Steve Kelly .07 .20
118 Dave Andreychuk .20 .50
119 Mikael Renberg .20 .50
120 Sergei Berezin .20 .50
121 Jeff Friesen .07 .20
122 Pierre Turgeon .07 .20
123 Vladimir Vorobiev RC .07 .20
124 Dimitri Khristich .07 .20
125 Jaroslav Svejkovsky .20 .50
126 Vladimir Konstantinov .20 .50
127 Jozef Stumpel .07 .20
128 Mike Peca .20 .50
129 Jonas Hoglund .07 .20
130 Travis Green .07 .20
131 Bill Guerin .20 .50
132 Oleg Tverdovsky .07 .20
133 Petr Nedved .20 .50
134 Dino Ciccarelli .20 .50
135 Brian Savage .07 .20
136 Steve Duchesne .07 .20
137 Sandis Ozolinsh .07 .20
138 Derian Hatcher .07 .20
139 Ray Sheppard .07 .20
140 Brian Bellows .07 .20
141 Paul Brousseau .07 .20
142 Tony Granato .07 .20
143 Vaclav Prospal RC .25 .60
144 Vitali Yachmenev .07 .20
145 John MacLean .07 .20
146 Igor Larionov .07 .20
147 Jason Allison .07 .20
148 Derek Plante .07 .20
149 Jeff O'Neill .07 .20
150 Trevor Linden .20 .50
151 Joe Juneau .20 .50
152 Brandon Convery .07 .20
153 Kevin Stevens .20 .50
154 Scott Stevens .20 .50
155 Niklas Sundstrom .07 .20
156 Claude Lemieux .07 .20
157 Pat Verbeek .07 .20
158 Mariusz Czerkawski .07 .20
159 Robert Svehla .07 .20
160 Paul Coffey .25 .60
161 Al MacInnis .20 .50
162 Roman Hamrlik .20 .50
163 Brian Holzinger .07 .20
164 Cory Stillman .07 .20
165 Scott Mellanby .07 .20
166 Todd Warriner .07 .20
167 Terry Ryan .07 .20
168 Luc Robitaille .20 .50
169 Ed Olczyk .07 .20
170 Adam Deadmarsh .07 .20
171 Anson Carter .20 .50
172 Mike Knuble RC .07 .20
173 Cliff Ronning .07 .20
174 Rick Tocchet .20 .50
175 Chris Pronger .20 .50
176 Matthew Barnaby .07 .20
177 Andrei Kovalenko .07 .20
178 Bryan Smolinski .07 .20
179 Janne Niinimaa .07 .20
180 Ray Ferraro .07 .20
181 Dave Gagner .07 .20
182 Rob Niedermayer .07 .20
183 Vadim Sharifijanov .07 .20
184 Ethan Moreau .07 .20
185 Bernie Nicholls .07 .20
186 Jean-Yves Leroux RC .07 .20
187 Jere Lehtinen .07 .20
188 Steve Rucchin .07 .20
189 Keith Primeau .07 .20
190 Red Wings Champs CL .20 .50

1997-98 Pinnacle Inside Coach's Collection

*COACH COLL.: 3X TO 8X BASIC CARDS

1997-98 Pinnacle Inside Executive Collection

*EXEC.COLL.: 8X TO 20X BASIC CARDS

1997-98 Pinnacle Inside Stand Up Guys

COMPLETE SET (20) 15.00 30.00
*PROMOS: .4X TO 1X BASIC INSERTS
1A/B M.Vernon/T.Barasso .60 1.50
1C/D M.Vernon/T.Barasso .60 1.50
2A/B J.Vanbiesbrck./M.Brodeur 2.00 5.00
2C/D J.Vanbiesbrck./M.Brodeur 2.00 5.00
3A/B J.Thibault/J.Carey .60 1.50
3C/D J.Thibault/J.Carey .60 1.50
4A/B G.Snow/M.Cousineau .60 1.50
4C/D G.Snow/M.Cousineau .60 1.50
5A/B P.Roy/E.Fichaud 4.00 10.00
5C/D P.Roy/E.Fichaud 4.00 10.00
6A/B P.Lalime/G.Fuhr .60 1.50
6C/D P.Lalime/G.Fuhr .60 1.50
7A/B O.Kolzig/J.Hackett .60 1.50
7C/D O.Kolzig/J.Hackett .60 1.50
8A/B T.Kidd/G.Hebert .60 1.50
8C/D T.Kidd/G.Hebert .60 1.50
9A/B N.Khabibulin/C.Hirsch .60 1.50
9C/D N.Khabibulin/C.Hirsch .60 1.50
10A/B C.Joseph/K.Hrudey .60 1.50
10C/D C.Joseph/K.Hrudey .60 1.50

1997-98 Pinnacle Inside Stoppers

COMPLETE SET (24) 30.00 60.00
1 Patrick Roy 8.00 20.00
2 John Vanbiesbrouck 1.00 2.50
3 Dominik Hasek 3.00 8.00
4 Martin Brodeur 4.00 10.00
5 Mike Richter 1.50 4.00
6 Guy Hebert 1.00 2.50
7 Jim Carey 1.00 2.50
8 Jeff Hackett 1.00 2.50
9 Roman Turek 1.00 2.50
10 Kevin Hodson 1.00 2.50
11 Mike Vernon 1.00 2.50
12 Curtis Joseph 1.50 4.00
13 Jean-Sebastien Giguere 1.00 2.50
14 Jose Theodore 2.00 5.00
15 Jocelyn Thibault 1.00 2.50
16 Nikolai Khabibulin 1.00 2.50
17 Garth Snow 1.00 2.50
18 Ron Hextall 1.00 2.50
19 Steve Shields 1.00 2.50
20 Grant Fuhr 1.00 2.50
21 Felix Potvin 1.50 4.00
22 Marcel Cousineau 1.00 2.50
23 Bill Ranford 1.00 2.50
24 Ed Belfour 1.50 4.00

1997-98 Pinnacle Inside Track

COMPLETE SET (30) 75.00 200.00
1 Wayne Gretzky 10.00 25.00
2 Patrick Roy 10.00 25.00
3 Eric Lindros 3.00 8.00
4 Paul Kariya 3.00 8.00

5 Peter Forsberg 4.00 10.00
6 Martin Brodeur 6.00 15.00
7 John Vanbiesbrouck 2.00 5.00
8 Joe Sakic 5.00 12.00
9 Steve Yzerman 10.00 25.00
10 Jaromir Jagr 4.00 10.00
11 Teemu Selanne 3.00 8.00
12 Pavel Bure 3.00 8.00
13 Sergei Fedorov 3.00 8.00
14 Brendan Shanahan 3.00 8.00
15 Dominik Hasek 5.00 12.00
16 Saku Koivu 2.00 5.00
17 Jocelyn Thibault 1.00 2.50
18 Mark Messier 2.00 5.00
19 Brett Hull 4.00 10.00
20 Felix Potvin 4.00 10.00
21 Curtis Joseph 3.00 8.00
22 Zigmund Palffy 2.00 5.00
23 Mats Sundin 3.00 8.00
24 Keith Tkachuk 3.00 8.00
25 John LeClair 3.00 8.00
26 Mike Richter 3.00 8.00
27 Alexander Mogilny 2.00 5.00
28 Jarome Iginla 4.00 10.00
29 Mike Grier 1.00 2.50
30 Dainius Zubrus 1.00 2.50

1997-98 Pinnacle Inside Cans

COMPLETE SET (24) 8.00 20.00
*GOLD CANS: 2.5X TO 6X BASIC CAN
1 Brendan Shanahan .15 .40
2 Jaromir Jagr .30 .75
3 Saku Koivu .15 .40
4 Mats Sundin .15 .40
5 Mike Vernon .20 .50
6 John LeClair .15 .40
7 Keith Tkachuk .15 .40
8 Joe Sakic .30 .75
9 Steve Yzerman .60 1.50
10 Eric Lindros .15 .40
11 Guy Hebert .20 .50
12 Patrick Roy .75 2.00
13 Pavel Bure .15 .40
14 Jocelyn Thibault .20 .50
15 Paul Kariya .40 1.00
16 Peter Forsberg .40 1.00
17 Martin Brodeur .40 1.00
18 Wayne Gretzky 1.00 2.50
19 Teemu Selanne .30 .75
20 John Vanbiesbrouck .20 .50
21 Mark Messier .15 .40
22 Mike Richter .15 .40
23 Brett Hull .20 .50
24 Curtis Joseph .15 .40

1997-98 Pinnacle Inside Promos

1 Brendan Shanahan PROMO .40 1.00
7 Martin Brodeur/250 .75 2.00
8 Peter Forsberg PROMO .75 2.00
10 Paul Kariya/250 .75 2.00
70 Guy Hebert PROMO .40 1.00
84 Mike Vernon PROMO .40 1.00

1997 Pinnacle Mario's Moments

COMPLETE SET (18) 10.00 25.00
COMMON CARD (1-18) .60 1.50
*GOLD: 2X to 5X BASIC CARDS
NNO Mario Lemieux AUTO 60.00 120.00

1996-97 Pinnacle Mint

COMP.DIE CUT SET (30) 10.00 25.00
1 Mario Lemieux 1.25 3.00
2 Dominik Hasek .50 1.25
3 Eric Lindros .50 1.25
4 Jaromir Jagr 1.00 2.50
5 Paul Kariya .30 .75
6 Peter Forsberg .60 1.50
7 Pavel Bure .30 .75
8 Sergei Fedorov .50 1.25
9 Saku Koivu .30 .75
10 Daniel Alfredsson .30 .75
11 Joe Sakic .60 1.50
12 Steve Yzerman .75 2.00
13 Teemu Selanne .60 1.50
14 Brett Hull .60 1.50
15 Jeremy Roenick .50 1.25
16 Mark Messier .60 1.50
17 Mats Sundin .30 .75
18 Brendan Shanahan .30 .75
19 Keith Tkachuk .30 .75
20 Paul Coffey .30 .75
21 Patrick Roy .75 2.00
22 Chris Chelios .30 .75
23 Martin Brodeur .75 2.00
24 Felix Potvin .50 1.25
25 Chris Osgood .30 .75
26 John Vanbiesbrouck .30 .75
27 Jocelyn Thibault .25 .60
28 Jim Carey .30 .75
29 Jarome Iginla .40 1.00
30 Jim Campbell .20 .50
P3A Eric Lindros Bronze Promo 1.50 4.00
P3B Eric Lindros Die-Cut Promo .50 1.25

1996-97 Pinnacle Mint Bronze

*BRONZE: 1X TO 2X BASIC CARDS

1996-97 Pinnacle Mint Gold

*GOLD: 4X TO 10X BASIC

1996-97 Pinnacle Mint Silver

*SILVER: 4X TO 10X BASIC CARDS

1996-97 Pinnacle Mint Coins Brass

COMP.BRASS SET (30) 12.00 30.00
*NICKEL: 2X TO 5X BRASS
*GOLD PLATED: 5X TO 12X BRASS
1 Mario Lemieux 1.50 4.00
2 Dominik Hasek .60 1.50
3 Eric Lindros .75 2.00
4 Jaromir Jagr 1.00 2.50
5 Paul Kariya 1.25 3.00
6 Peter Forsberg .75 2.00
7 Pavel Bure .75 2.00
8 Sergei Fedorov .60 1.50
9 Saku Koivu .30 .75
10 Daniel Alfredsson .25 .60
11 Joe Sakic .60 1.50
12 Steve Yzerman 1.00 2.50
13 Teemu Selanne .60 1.50
14 Brett Hull .40 1.00
15 Jeremy Roenick .30 .75
16 Mark Messier .40 1.00
17 Mats Sundin .30 .75
18 Brendan Shanahan .50 1.25
19 Keith Tkachuk .30 .75
20 Paul Coffey .30 .75
21 Patrick Roy 1.50 4.00
22 Chris Chelios .30 .75
23 Martin Brodeur .75 2.00
24 Felix Potvin .30 .75
25 Chris Osgood .30 .75
26 John Vanbiesbrouck .30 .75
27 Jocelyn Thibault .25 .60
28 Jim Carey .25 .60
29 Jarome Iginla .25 .60
30 Jim Campbell .25 .60

1997-98 Pinnacle Mint

1 Eric Lindros .15 .40
2 Paul Kariya .15 .40
3 Peter Forsberg .40 1.00
4 John Vanbiesbrouck .10 .30
5 Steve Yzerman .75 2.00
6 Brendan Shanahan .15 .40
7 Teemu Selanne .15 .40
8 Dominik Hasek .30 .75
9 Jarome Iginla .20 .50
10 Mats Sundin .15 .40
11 Patrick Roy .75 2.00
12 Joe Sakic .30 .75
13 Mark Messier .15 .40
14 Sergei Fedorov .25 .60
15 Saku Koivu .15 .40
16 Martin Brodeur .40 1.00
17 Pavel Bure .15 .40
18 Wayne Gretzky 1.00 2.50
19 Brian Leetch .10 .30
20 John LeClair .15 .40
21 Keith Tkachuk .15 .40
22 Jaromir Jagr .25 .60
23 Brett Hull .20 .50
24 Curtis Joseph .15 .40
25 Jaroslav Svejkovsky .07 .20
26 Sergei Samsonov .10 .30
27 Alexei Morozov .07 .20
28 Alyn McCauley .07 .20
29 Joe Thornton .25 .60
30 Vaclav Prospal RC .10 .30
P3 Peter Forsberg PROMO 3.00 8.00

1997-98 Pinnacle Mint Bronze

*BRONZE: .8X TO 2X BASIC CARDS

1997-98 Pinnacle Mint Gold Team

*GOLD TEAM: 10X TO 25X BASIC CARDS

1997-98 Pinnacle Mint Silver Team

*SILVER TEAM: 5X TO 12X BASIC CARDS

1997-98 Pinnacle Mint Coins Brass

COMP.BRASS SET (30) 30.00 60.00
*BRASS PROOF/500: 6X TO 15X BRASS
*NICKEL SILVER: 2X TO 5X BRASS
*NICKEL PROOF: 10X TO 25X BRASS
*GOLD PLATED: 10X TO 25X BRASS
*GOLD PLT PROOF/100: 25X TO 60X BRASS
1 Eric Lindros .75 2.00
2 Paul Kariya 1.25 3.00
3 Peter Forsberg .75 2.00
4 John Vanbiesbrouck .30 .75
5 Steve Yzerman 1.00 2.50
6 Brendan Shanahan .50 1.25
7 Teemu Selanne .60 1.50
8 Dominik Hasek .60 1.50
9 Jarome Iginla .25 .60
10 Mats Sundin .30 .75
11 Patrick Roy 1.50 4.00
12 Joe Sakic .60 1.50
13 Mark Messier .40 1.00
14 Sergei Fedorov .60 1.50
15 Saku Koivu .30 .75
16 Martin Brodeur .75 2.00
17 Pavel Bure .75 2.00
18 Wayne Gretzky 2.50 5.00
19 Brian Leetch .30 .75
20 John LeClair .50 1.25
21 Keith Tkachuk .30 .75
22 Jaromir Jagr 1.00 2.50
23 Brett Hull .40 1.00
24 Curtis Joseph .40 1.00
25 Jaroslav Svejkovsky .25 .60
26 Sergei Samsonov .30 .75
27 Alexei Morozov .25 .60
28 Alyn McCauley .25 .60
29 Joe Thornton .30 .75
30 Vaclav Prospal .25 .60

1997-98 Pinnacle Mint Minternational

COMPLETE SET (6) 15.00 30.00
1 Eric Lindros 6.00 15.00
2 Peter Forsberg 4.00 10.00
3 Brett Hull 2.00 5.00
4 Teemu Selanne 2.50 6.00
5 Dominik Hasek 3.00 8.00
6 Pavel Bure 2.50 6.00

1997-98 Pinnacle Mint Minternational Coins

COMPLETE SET (6) 30.00 60.00
1 Eric Lindros 8.00 20.00
2 Peter Forsberg 8.00 20.00
3 Brett Hull 3.00 8.00
4 Teemu Selanne 5.00 12.00
5 Dominik Hasek 5.00 12.00
6 Pavel Bure 6.00 12.00

2011 Pinnacle NHL Draft

COMPLETE SET (6) 8.00 20.00
1 Alex Ovechkin 1.00 2.50
2 Steven Stamkos 1.00 2.50
4 Tyler Seguin 1.25 3.00
5 Mario Lemieux .75 2.00
6 Mark Messier .75 2.00

2011 Pinnacle NHL Draft Minnesota

COMPLETE SET (6) 6.00 12.00
1 Martin Havlat .75 2.00
2 Mikko Koivu .75 2.00
3 Niklas Backstrom 1.00 2.50
4 Cal Clutterbuck 1.00 2.50
5 Mike Modano 1.25 3.00
6 Dino Ciccarelli 1.00 2.50

2012 Pinnacle NHL Draft Pittsburgh

COMPLETE SET (7) 6.00 12.00
1 Sidney Crosby 2.00 5.00
2 Evgeni Malkin 1.00 2.50
3 Marc-Andre Fleury .60 1.50
4 James Neal .50 1.25
5 Kris Letang .50 1.25
6 Jordan Staal .50 1.25
7 Simon Despres .50 1.25
NNO Checklist .30 .75

1996 Pinnacle Bobby Orr Autograph

NNO Bobby Orr 100.00 200.00

1997-98 Pinnacle Power Pack Blow-Ups

1 Eric Lindros 1.00 2.50
2 Paul Kariya 1.25 3.00
3 Joe Thornton .40 1.00
4 Dominik Hasek .60 1.50
5 Patrick Roy 1.50 4.00
6 Keith Tkachuk .30 .75
7 Martin Brodeur .75 2.00
8 Brett Hull .40 1.00
9 Mark Messier .40 1.00
10 Saku Koivu .30 .75
11 Jaromir Jagr 1.00 2.50
12 Joe Sakic .60 1.50
13 John Vanbiesbrouck .30 .75
14 Pavel Bure .75 2.00
15 Jarome Iginla .40 1.00
16 Mats Sundin .30 .75
17 Wayne Gretzky 2.00 5.00
18 Steve Yzerman 1.00 2.50
19 Peter Forsberg .75 2.00
20 Brendan Shanahan .60 1.50
21 Sergei Fedorov .60 1.50
22 Curtis Joseph .40 1.00
23 John LeClair .40 1.00
24 Teemu Selanne .60 1.50
P2 Paul Kariya PROMO 1.25 3.00
P13 John Vanbiesbrouck PROMO .60 1.50

1997-98 Pinnacle Tins

COMPLETE SET (10) 6.00 15.00
1 Martin Brodeur 1.25 3.00
2 Grant Fuhr .40 1.00
3 Jeff Hackett .40 1.00
4 Guy Hebert .40 1.00
5 Curtis Joseph .40 1.00
6 Nikolai Khabibulin .40 1.00
7 Mike Richter .50 1.25
8 Patrick Roy 2.00 5.00
9 Garth Snow .40 1.00
10 John Vanbiesbrouck .75 2.00

1997-98 Pinnacle Totally Certified Platinum Blue

*PLAT.BLUE: .8X TO 2X PLAT.RED

1997-98 Pinnacle Totally Certified Platinum Gold

*PLAT.GOLD: 6X TO 15X PLAT.RED

1997-98 Pinnacle Totally Certified Platinum Red

COMPLETE SET (130) 100.00 250.00
1 Dominik Hasek 5.00 10.00
2 Patrick Roy 12.50 25.00
3 Martin Brodeur 6.00 12.00
4 Chris Osgood 1.50 4.00
5 Andy Moog 1.50 4.00
6 John Vanbiesbrouck 1.50 4.00
7 Steve Shields RC 2.00 5.00
8 Mike Vernon 1.50 4.00
9 Ed Belfour 2.00 5.00
10 Grant Fuhr 1.50 4.00
11 Felix Potvin 2.00 5.00
12 Bill Ranford 1.50 4.00
13 Mike Richter 2.00 5.00
14 Stephane Fiset 1.25 3.00
15 Jim Carey 1.50 4.00
16 Nikolai Khabibulin 1.50 4.00
17 Ken Wregget 1.25 3.00
18 Curtis Joseph 2.00 5.00
19 Guy Hebert 1.50 4.00
20 Damian Rhodes 1.50 4.00
21 Trevor Kidd 1.50 4.00
22 Daren Puppa 1.25 3.00
23 Patrick Lalime 1.50 4.00
24 Tommy Salo 1.50 4.00
25 Sean Burke 1.25 3.00
26 Jocelyn Thibault 1.50 4.00
27 Kirk McLean 1.50 4.00
28 Garth Snow 1.50 4.00
29 Ron Tugnutt 1.50 4.00
30 Jeff Hackett 1.25 3.00
31 Eric Lindros 1.50 4.00
32 Peter Forsberg 5.00 10.00
33 Mike Modano 3.00 6.00
34 Paul Kariya 1.50 4.00
35 Jaromir Jagr 2.50 6.00
36 Brian Leetch 1.50 4.00
37 Keith Tkachuk 1.50 4.00
38 Steve Yzerman 10.00 20.00
39 Teemu Selanne 1.50 4.00
40 Bryan Berard 1.25 3.00
41 Ray Bourque 2.50 5.00
42 Theo Fleury .75 2.00
43 Mark Messier 2.00 5.00
44 Saku Koivu 1.50 4.00
45 Pavel Bure 2.00 5.00
46 Peter Bondra 1.25 3.00
47 Dave Gagner .75 2.00
48 Ed Jovanovski 1.25 3.00
49 Adam Oates 1.25 3.00
50 Joe Sakic 4.00 8.00
51 Doug Gilmour 1.25 3.00
52 Jim Campbell .75 2.00
53 Mats Sundin 1.50 4.00
54 Derian Hatcher .75 2.00
55 Jarome Iginla 2.00 5.00
56 Sergei Fedorov 2.50 6.00
57 Keith Primeau .75 2.00
58 Mark Recchi 1.25 3.00
59 Owen Nolan 1.25 3.00
60 Alexander Mogilny 1.25 3.00
61 Brendan Shanahan 2.00 5.00
62 Pierre Turgeon 1.25 3.00
63 Joe Juneau 1.25 3.00
64 Steve Rucchin .75 2.00
65 Jeremy Roenick 2.00 5.00
66 Doug Weight 1.25 3.00
67 Valeri Kamensky 1.25 3.00
68 Tony Amonte 1.25 3.00
69 Dave Andreychuk .75 2.00
70 Brett Hull 2.50 5.00
71 Wendel Clark 1.25 3.00
72 Vincent Damphousse .75 2.00
73 Mike Grier .75 2.00
74 Chris Chelios 1.50 4.00
75 Nicklas Lidstrom 1.50 4.00
76 Joe Nieuwendyk 1.25 3.00
77 Rob Blake 1.25 3.00
78 Alexei Yashin .75 2.00
79 Ryan Smyth .75 2.00
80 Pat Lafontaine 1.50 4.00
81 Jeff Friesen .75 2.00
82 Ray Ferraro .75 2.00
83 Steve Sullivan .75 2.00
84 Chris Gratton 1.25 3.00
85 Mike Gartner 1.25 3.00
86 Kevin Hatcher .75 2.00
87 Ted Donato .75 2.00
88 German Titov .75 2.00
89 Sandis Ozolinsh .75 2.00
90 Ray Sheppard .75 2.00
91 John MacLean .75 2.00
92 Luc Robitaille 1.25 3.00
93 Rod Brind'Amour 1.25 3.00
94 Zigmund Palffy 1.25 3.00
95 Petr Nedved 1.25 3.00
96 Adam Graves .75 2.00
97 Jozef Stumpel 1.25 3.00
98 Alexandre Daigle .75 2.00
99 Mike Peca .75 2.00
100 Wayne Gretzky 12.50 25.00
101 Alexei Zhamnov .75 2.00
102 Paul Coffey 1.50 4.00
103 Oleg Tverdovsky .75 2.00
104 Trevor Linden 1.25 3.00
105 Dino Ciccarelli .75 2.00
106 Andrei Kovalenko .75 2.00
107 Scott Mellanby .75 2.00
108 Bryan Smolinski .75 2.00
109 Bernie Nicholls .75 2.00
110 Derek Plante .75 2.00
111 Pat Verbeek .75 2.00
112 Adam Deadmarsh .75 2.00
113 Martin Gelinas .75 2.00
114 Daniel Alfredsson 1.25 3.00
115 Scott Stevens .75 2.00
116 Dainius Zubrus 2.50 6.00
117 Kirk Muller .75 2.00
118 Brian Holzinger .75 2.00
119 John LeClair 2.00 5.00
120 Al MacInnis 1.25 3.00
121 Ron Francis 1.25 3.00
122 Eric Daze 1.25 3.00
123 Travis Green .75 2.00
124 Jason Arnott .75 2.00
125 Geoff Sanderson 1.25 3.00
126 Dimitri Khristich .75 2.00
127 Sergei Berezin .75 2.00
128 Jeff O'Neill .75 2.00
129 Claude Lemieux .75 2.00
130 Andrew Cassels .75 2.00
82P Ray Ferraro PROMO .40 1.00
106P Andrei Kovalenko PROMO .40 1.00

1997-98 Pinnacle Totally Certified Platinum Gold Mirror

*MIRROR GOLD/25: 12X TO 30X PLAT.RED

1997-98 Pinnacle Hockey Night in Canada

COMPLETE SET (13) 30.00 75.00
1 Steve Armitage 1.25 3.00
2 Don Cherry 20.00 50.00
3 Bob Cole 2.00 5.00
4 Chris Cuthbert 1.25 3.00
5 John Garrett 2.00 5.00
6 Dick Irvin, Jr. 4.00 10.00
7 Ron Maclean 4.00 10.00
8 Greg Millen 1.25 3.00
9 Harry Neale 2.00 5.00
10 Scott Oake 1.25 3.00
11 Scott Russell 1.25 3.00
12 John Shannon .75 2.00
13 Don Whittman 1.25 3.00

1995-96 Playoff One on One

1 Guy Hebert .12 .30
2 Paul Kariya .15 .40
3 Mike Sillinger .10 .25
4 Oleg Tverdovsky .15 .40
5 Ray Bourque .25 .60
6 Alexei Kasatonov .10 .25
7 Blaine Lacher .12 .30
8 Cam Neely .15 .40
9 Adam Oates .15 .40
10 Kevin Stevens .12 .30
11 Donald Audette .12 .30
12 Dominik Hasek .25 .60
13 Pat LaFontaine .15 .40
14 Alexei Zhitnik .10 .25
15 Steve Chiasson .10 .25
16 Theo Fleury .20 .50
17 Phil Housley .12 .30
18 Joe Nieuwendyk .12 .30
19 Gary Roberts .10 .25
20 German Titov .12 .30
21 Ed Belfour .12 .30
22 Chris Chelios .15 .40
23 Bernie Nicholls .12 .30
24 Jeremy Roenick .25 .60
25 Peter Forsberg .30 .75
26 Sylvain Lefebvre .10 .25
27 Owen Nolan .15 .40
28 Joe Sakic .30 .75
29 Jocelyn Thibault .12 .30
30 Dave Gagner .10 .25
31 Mike Modano .25 .60
32 Andy Moog .15 .40
33 Paul Coffey .15 .40
34 Sergei Fedorov .25 .60
35 Keith Primeau .12 .30
36 Ray Sheppard .12 .30
37 Jason Arnott .12 .30
38 David Oliver .10 .25
39 Mike Stapleton .10 .25
40 Jesse Belanger .10 .25
41 Paul Laus .10 .25
42 Rob Niedermayer .12 .30
43 Brian Skrudland .10 .25
44 John Vanbiesbrouck .15 .40
45 Sean Burke .10 .25
46 Andrew Cassels .10 .25
47 Brendan Shanahan .15 .40
48 Rob Blake .12 .30
49 Tony Granato .10 .25
50 Wayne Gretzky 1.00 2.50
51 Marty McSorley .12 .30
52 Jamie Storr .12 .30
53 Vincent Damphousse .12 .30
54 Mark Recchi .20 .50
55 Patrick Roy .40 1.00
56 Pierre Turgeon .12 .30
57 Martin Brodeur .40 1.00
58 Bill Guerin .15 .40
59 Scott Niedermayer .15 .40
60 Stephane Richer .12 .30
61 Scott Stevens .15 .40
62 Patrick Flatley .10 .25
63 Brett Lindros .10 .25
64 Mathieu Schneider .10 .25
65 Kirk Muller .12 .30
66 Adam Graves .12 .30
67 Alexei Kovalev .12 .30
68 Brian Leetch .12 .30
69 Mike Richter .15 .40
70 Pat Verbeek .12 .30
71 Luc Robitaille .15 .40
72 Radek Bonk .10 .25
73 Alexandre Daigle .10 .25
74 Alexei Yashin .12 .30
75 Eric Desjardins .12 .30
76 Eric Lindros .25 .60
77 Ron Francis .20 .50
78 Jaromir Jagr .50 1.25
79 Mario Lemieux .60 1.50
80 Ken Wregget .12 .30
81 Francois Leroux .10 .25
82 Pat Falloon .10 .25
83 Jeff Friesen .10 .25
84 Arturs Irbe .12 .30
85 Igor Larionov .10 .25
86 Shayne Corson .12 .30
87 Geoff Courtnall .10 .25
88 Steve Duchesne .10 .25
89 Brett Hull .30 .75
90 Al MacInnis .20 .50
91 Brian Bellows .12 .30
92 Chris Gratton .10 .25
93 Dave Andreychuk .15 .40
94 Tie Domi .12 .30
95 Mike Gartner .20 .50
96 Doug Gilmour .20 .50
97 Larry Murphy .12 .30
98 Felix Potvin .25 .60
99 Mats Sundin .15 .40
100 Pavel Bure .15 .40
101 Kirk McLean .12 .30
102 Alexander Mogilny .12 .30
103 Christian Ruuttu .12 .30
104 Jim Carey .12 .30
105 Joe Juneau .10 .25
106 Jason Allison .12 .30
107 Teppo Numminen .10 .25
108 Teemu Selanne .30 .75
109 Keith Tkachuk .15 .40
110 Alexei Zhamnov .15 .40
111 Patrik Carnback .10 .25
112 Bobby Dollas .10 .25
113 Guy Hebert .12 .30
114 Paul Kariya .15 .40
115 Shaun Van Allen .10 .25
116 Ray Bourque .25 .60
117 Mariusz Czerkawski .10 .25
118 Todd Elik .10 .25
119 Blaine Lacher .12 .30
120 Cam Neely .15 .40
121 Adam Oates .15 .40
122 Dave Reid .10 .25
123 Kevin Stevens .12 .30
124 Garry Galley .10 .25
125 Dominik Hasek .25 .60
126 Brian Holzinger .30 .75
127 Pat LaFontaine .15 .40
128 Mike Peca .12 .30
129 Phil Housley .12 .30
130 Paul Kruse .10 .25
131 Ronnie Stern .10 .25
132 Zarley Zalapski .10 .25
133 Patrick Poulin .10 .25
134 Bob Probert .15 .40
135 Jeremy Roenick .25 .60
136 Adam Deadmarsh .10 .25
137 Peter Forsberg .30 .75
138 Andrei Kovalenko .10 .25
139 Joe Sakic .30 .75
140 Derian Hatcher .12 .30
141 Grant Ledyard .10 .25
142 Mike Modano .25 .60
143 Paul Coffey .15 .40
144 Sergei Fedorov .25 .60
145 Vladimir Konstantinov .12 .30
146 Nicklas Lidstrom .15 .40
147 Steve Yzerman .40 1.00
148 Igor Kravchuk .10 .25
149 Kirk Maltby .12 .30
150 Boris Mironov .10 .25
151 Bill Ranford .12 .30
152 Stu Barnes .10 .25
153 Jesse Belanger .10 .25
154 Scott Mellanby .12 .30
155 Adam Burt .10 .25
156 Steven Rice .10 .25
157 Brendan Shanahan .15 .40
158 Glen Wesley .10 .25
159 Wayne Gretzky .60 1.50
160 Darryl Sydor .12 .30
161 Rick Tocchet .12 .30
162 Benoit Brunet .10 .25
163 J.J. Daigneault .10 .25
164 Saku Koivu .15 .40
165 Lyle Odelein .10 .25
166 Patrick Roy .40 1.00
167 Scott Stevens .15 .40
168 Valeri Zelepukin .10 .25
169 Steve Thomas .12 .30
170 Dennis Vaske .10 .25
171 Brett Lindros .10 .25
172 Zigmund Palffy .15 .40
173 Ray Ferraro .10 .25
174 Brian Leetch .12 .30
175 Mark Messier .30 .75
176 Ulf Samuelsson .10 .25
177 Don Beaupre .12 .30
178 Alexandre Daigle .10 .25
179 Steve Larouche .10 .25
180 Scott Levins .10 .25
181 Ron Hextall .15 .40
182 Eric Lindros .25 .60
183 Mikael Renberg .12 .30
184 Kjell Samuelsson .10 .25
185 Jaromir Jagr .50 1.25
186 Mario Lemieux .60 1.50
187 Sergei Zubov .12 .30
188 Bryan Smolinski .10 .25
189 Dmitri Mironov .10 .25
190 Ulf Dahlen .10 .25
191 Arturs Irbe .12 .30
192 Craig Janney .10 .25
193 Sandis Ozolinsh .10 .25
194 Jon Casey .12 .30
195 Brett Hull .30 .75
196 Esa Tikkanen .10 .25
197 Brian Bradley .12 .30
198 Daren Puppa .12 .30
199 Alexander Selivanov .12 .30
200 Rob Zamuner .10 .25
201 Ken Baumgartner .10 .25
202 Doug Gilmour .20 .50
203 Kenny Jonsson .15 .40
204 Felix Potvin .25 .60
205 Randy Wood .10 .25
206 Jeff Brown .12 .30
207 Pavel Bure .15 .40
208 Trevor Linden .15 .40
209 Alexander Mogilny .12 .30
210 Roman Oksiuta .10 .25
211 Cliff Ronning .10 .25
212 Peter Bondra .15 .40
213 Jim Carey .12 .30
214 Pat Peake .10 .25
215 Mark Tinordi .10 .25
216 Mike Eastwood .10 .25
217 Nelson Emerson .10 .25
218 Dave Manson .10 .25
219 Teemu Selanne .30 .75
220 Keith Tkachuk .15 .40
221 Bob Corkum R .10 .25
222 Peter Douris R .10 .25
223 Paul Kariya URB .15 .40
224 Todd Krygier URS .10 .25
225 Mike Sillinger R .10 .25
226 Ray Bourque URB .25 .60
227 Fred Knipscheer R .10 .25
228 Cam Neely URB .15 .40
229 Adam Oates URB .15 .40
230 Jason Dawe R .10 .25
231 Yuri Khmylev R .10 .25
232 Bob Sweeney URS .10 .25
233 Trevor Kidd R .12 .30
234 Eric Daze R .30 .75
235 Tony Amonte R .12 .30
236 Jeremy Roenick URB .25 .60
237 Denis Savard R .15 .40
238 Gary Suter R .10 .25
239 Peter Forsberg URS .30 .75
240 Curtis Leschyshyn R .10 .25
241 Owen Nolan URB .15 .40
242 Joe Sakic URS .30 .75
243 Valeri Kamensky R .12 .30
244 Claude Lemieux R .15 .40
245 Bob Bassen R .10 .25
246 Shane Churla R .10 .25
247 Todd Harvey R .10 .25
248 Kevin Hatcher URS .12 .30
249 Richard Matvichuk R .12 .30
250 Mike Modano URB .25 .60
251 Dino Ciccarelli R .12 .30
252 Paul Coffey URS .15 .40
253 Sergei Fedorov URS .25 .60
254 Vyacheslav Kozlov R .12 .30
255 Mike Vernon R .12 .30
256 Jason Bonsignore R .10 .25
257 Dean McAmmond R .10 .25
258 Bill Ranford R .12 .30
259 Doug Weight URB .15 .40
260 Bob Kudelski R .10 .25
261 Dave Lowry R .10 .25
262 Gord Murphy R .10 .25
263 Rob Niedermayer URS .12 .30
264 Frantisek Kucera R .10 .25
265 Paul Ranheim R .10 .25
266 Geoff Sanderson URS .10 .25
267 Darren Turcotte R .10 .25
268 Pat Conacher R .10 .25
269 Wayne Gretzky URB 1.00 2.50
270 Kelly Hrudey R .12 .30
271 Jari Kurri R .15 .40
272 Patrice Brisebois R .10 .25
273 Vladimir Malakhov R .10 .25
274 Patrick Roy URB .40 1.00
275 Martin Brodeur URB .40 1.00
276 Neal Broten R .12 .30
277 Sergei Brylin R .10 .25
278 John MacLean R .12 .30
279 Wendel Clark R .25 .60
280 Travis Green R .12 .30
281 Scott Lachance URS .10 .25
282 Tommy Salo R .25 .60
283 Brian Leetch URB .12 .30
284 Mark Messier URB .30 .75
285 Sergei Nemchinov R .10 .25
286 Luc Robitaille URS .15 .40
287 Sean Hill R .10 .25
288 Jim Paek URS .10 .25
289 Martin Straka R .10 .25
290 Sylvain Turgeon R .10 .25
291 Rod Brind'Amour URS .15 .40
292 Kevin Haller R .10 .25
293 John LeClair R .15 .40
294 Eric Lindros URB .25 .60
295 Joel Otto R .10 .25
296 Chris Therien R .10 .25
297 Jaromir Jagr URS .50 1.25
298 Mario Lemieux URB .60 1.50
299 Glen Murray R .12 .30
300 Petr Nedved R .12 .30
301 Jamie Baker R .10 .25
302 Arturs Irbe URB .12 .30
303 Jayson More R .10 .25
304 Ray Whitney R .12 .30
305 Geoff Courtnall URS .10 .25
306 Dale Hawerchuk R .20 .50
307 Brett Hull URB .30 .75
308 Ian Laperriere R .10 .25
309 Chris Pronger R .15 .40
310 Roman Hamrlik R .10 .25
311 Petr Klima URS .10 .25
312 John Tucker R .10 .25
313 Paul Ysebaert URB .10 .25
314 Ken Baumgartner R .10 .25
315 Doug Gilmour URB .20 .50
316 Pavel Bure URB .15 .40
317 Bret Hedican R .10 .25
318 Alexander Mogilny URS .12 .30
319 Mike Ridley R .10 .25
320 Peter Bondra R .15 .40
321 Sylvain Cote R .10 .25
322 Dale Hunter R .12 .30
323 Keith Jones URS .12 .30
324 Kelly Miller R .10 .25
325 Tim Cheveldae R .12 .30
326 Dallas Drake R .10 .25
327 Igor Korolev R .10 .25
328 Teppo Numminen R .10 .25
329 Teemu Selanne URB .30 .75
330 Alexei Zhamnov URS .15 .40

1996-97 Playoff One on One

COMPLETE SET (110) 80.00 200.00
331 Mike Sillinger C .02 .10
332 Oleg Tverdovsky C .07 .20
333 Kevin Stevens C .02 .10
334 Joe Nieuwendyk C .07 .20
335 Owen Nolan C .08 .25
336 Jocelyn Thibault C .07 .20
337 Dave Gagner C .02 .10
338 Ray Sheppard C .02 .10
339 Jesse Belanger C .02 .10
340 Tony Granato C .02 .10
341 Daniel Alfredsson C .07 .20
342 Stephane Richer C .02 .10
343 Mathieu Schneider C .02 .10
344 Kirk Muller C .02 .10
345 Arturs Irbe C .08 .25
346 Igor Larionov C .02 .10
347 Steve Duchesne C .02 .10
348 Dave Andreychuk C .02 .10
349 Mike Gartner C .07 .20
350 Teppo Numminen C .02 .10
351 Keith Tkachuk C .20 .50
352 Mike Modano C .20 .50
353 Paul Kariya C .30 .75
354 German Titov C .02 .10
355 Bernie Nicholls C .02 .10
356 Doug Gilmour C .20 .50
357 Peter Forsberg C .30 .75
358 David Oliver C .02 .10
359 Pat Verbeek C .02 .10
360 Ron Francis C .07 .20
361 Pat Falloon C .02 .10
362 Jeff Friesen C .07 .20
363 Todd Krygier C .02 .10
364 Felix Potvin C .20 .50
365 Shane Churla C .02 .10
366 Steve Yzerman C .40 1.00
367 Kelly Hrudey C .02 .10
368 Mariusz Czerkawski U .07 .20
369 Patrick Poulin U .05 .15
370 Chris Chelios U .40 1.00
371 Ray Bourque U .75 2.00
372 Igor Kravchuk U .05 .15
373 Kirk Maltby U .05 .15
374 Bill Ranford U .07 .20
375 Darryl Sydor U .05 .15
376 Rick Tocchet U .07 .20
377 J.J. Daigneault U .05 .15
378 Chris Osgood U .40 1.00
379 Zigmund Palffy U .20 .50
380 Ray Ferraro U .05 .15
381 Don Beaupre U .07 .20
382 Andy Moog U .20 .50
383 Sergei Zubov U .07 .20
384 Craig Janney U .05 .15
385 Sandis Ozolinsh U .07 .20
386 Dave Reid U .05 .15
387 Scott Mellanby U .07 .20
388 Saku Koivu U .40 1.00
389 Bryan Smolinski U .07 .20
390 Alexander Selivanov U .05 .15
391 Peter Bondra U .20 .50
392 Esa Tikkanen U .07 .20
393 Ken Baumgartner U .05 .15
394 Ed Belfour U .40 1.00
395 Randy Wood U .05 .15
396 Jeff Brown U .05 .15
397 Roman Oksiuta U .05 .15
398 Cliff Ronning U .05 .15
399 Mike Eastwood U .05 .15
400 Nelson Emerson U .05 .15
401 Dave Manson U .05 .15
402 Jamie Baker U .05 .15
403 Ian Laperriere U .05 .15
404 Petr Klima U .05 .15

405 Dallas Drake R .07 .20
406 Tim Cheveldae R .20 .50
407 Igor Korolev R .07 .20
408 Kevin Hatcher R .07 .20
409 Dale Hawerchuk R .40 1.00
410 Martin Straka R .30 .75
411 Wendel Clark R .75 2.00
412 Jari Kurri R .75 2.00
413 Darren Turcotte R .07 .20
414 Yuri Khmylev R .07 .20
415 Bob Corkum R .07 .20
416 Roman Hamrlik R .30 .75
417 Jayson More R .07 .20
418 Travis Green R .30 .75
419 Dean McAmmond R .07 .20
420 Valeri Kamensky R .20 .50
421 Jason Dawe R .07 .20
422 Alexander Mogilny R .75 2.00
423 Keith Jones R .07 .20
424 Mark Messier R 3.00 8.00
425 John Vanbiesbrouck R 2.00 5.00
426 Jim Carey R .40 1.00
427 Brett Hull R 4.00 10.00
428 Teemu Selanne UR 6.00 15.00
429 Phil Housley UR 2.00 5.00
430 Wayne Gretzky UR 20.00 50.00
431 Patrick Roy UR 15.00 40.00
432 Joe Sakic UR 8.00 20.00
433 Jaromir Jagr UR 8.00 20.00
434 Doug Weight UR 2.00 5.00
435 Rob Niedermayer UR 2.00 5.00
436 Mario Lemieux UR 15.00 40.00
437 Sergei Fedorov UR 6.00 15.00
438 Pavel Bure UR 6.00 15.00
439 Eric Lindros UR 6.00 15.00
440 Martin Brodeur UR 8.00 20.00

2010-11 Playoff Contenders

COMP.SET w/o SPs (100) 10.00 25.00
1 Corey Perry .60 1.50
2 Nicklas Bergfors .30 .75
3 Derek Roy .25 .60
4 Eric Staal .50 1.25
5 Patrick Kane .75 2.00
6 Mathieu Garon .30 .75
7 Pavel Datsyuk .60 1.50
8 Ryan Whitney .25 .60
9 Drew Doughty .50 1.25
10 Matt Cullen .25 .60
11 Matthew Lombardi .25 .60
12 John Tavares .60 1.50
13 Sean Avery .30 .75
14 Claude Giroux .40 1.00
15 Kristopher Letang .50 1.25
16 Patrick Marleau .40 1.00
17 David Backes .25 .60
18 Vincent Lecavalier .40 1.00
19 Phil Kessel .40 1.00
20 Henrik Sedin .50 1.25
21 Ryan Getzlaf .40 1.00
22 Tim Thomas .40 1.00
23 Thomas Vanek .30 .75
24 Brandon Sutter .25 .60
25 Matt Duchene .40 1.00
26 Brad Richards .40 1.00
27 Nicklas Lidstrom .40 1.00
28 Ales Hemsky .30 .75
29 Jonathan Quick .50 1.25
30 Carey Price .75 2.00
31 Ilya Kovalchuk .40 1.00
32 Dwayne Roloson .30 .75
33 Jason Spezza .40 1.00
34 Jeff Carter .30 .75
35 Evgeni Malkin .75 2.00
36 Joe Thornton .60 1.50
37 Jaroslav Halak .40 1.00
38 Mike Smith .40 1.00
39 Roberto Luongo .60 1.50
40 Alex Ovechkin 1.50 4.00
41 Teemu Selanne .75 2.00
42 Milan Lucic .40 1.00
43 Jarome Iginla .50 1.25
44 Cam Ward .40 1.00
45 Chris Stewart .30 .75
46 Loui Eriksson .25 .60
47 Henrik Zetterberg .50 1.25
48 David Booth .25 .60
49 Ryan Smyth .30 .75
50 Tomas Plekanec .25 .60
51 Zach Parise .40 1.00
52 Brandon Dubinsky .25 .60
53 Daniel Alfredsson .40 1.00
54 Mike Richards .30 .75
55 Brent Johnson .30 .75
56 Joe Pavelski .50 1.25
57 T.J. Oshie .40 1.00
58 Jean-Sebastien Giguere .40 1.00
59 Alexandre Burrows .25 .60
60 John Carlson .40 1.00
61 Andrew Ladd .25 .60
62 Nathan Horton .30 .75
63 Miikka Kiprusoff .40 1.00
64 Duncan Keith .30 .75
65 Derick Brassard .25 .60
66 Steve Ott .25 .60
67 Jimmy Howard .50 1.25
68 Tomas Vokoun .30 .75
69 Mikko Koivu .30 .75
70 Michael Cammalleri .40 1.00
71 Martin Brodeur 1.00 2.50
72 Henrik Lundqvist 1.00 2.50
73 Chris Neil .25 .60
74 Ville Leino .30 .75
75 Sidney Crosby 1.50 4.00
76 Dany Heatley .30 .75
77 Martin St. Louis .40 1.00
78 Jonas Gustavsson .50 1.25
79 Cory Schneider .40 1.00
80 Michal Neuvirth .30 .75
81 Evander Kane .40 1.00
82 Ryan Miller .40 1.00
83 Rene Bourque .25 .60
84 Jonathan Toews .60 1.50
85 Rick Nash .40 1.00
86 Todd Bertuzzi .30 .75
87 Nikolai Khabibulin .30 .75
88 Anze Kopitar .60 1.50
89 Niklas Backstrom .40 1.00
90 Pekka Rinne .40 1.00
91 Josh Bailey .30 .75
92 Ryan Callahan .25 .60
93 Chris Pronger .40 1.00
94 Zbynek Michalek .25 .60
95 Ryane Clowe .25 .60
96 Alex Steen .25 .60
97 Steven Stamkos .75 2.00
98 Mikhail Grabovski .25 .60
99 Daniel Sedin .50 1.25
100 Nicklas Backstrom .40 1.00
101 Paul Coffey 1.50 4.00
102 Stan Mikita 2.00 5.00
103 Trevor Linden 1.50 4.00
104 Darryl Sittler 2.00 5.00
105 Rod Gilbert 1.50 4.00
106 Reggie Lemelin 1.00 2.50
107 Patrick Roy 4.00 10.00
108 Mario Lemieux 6.00 15.00
109 Luc Robitaille 1.50 4.00
110 Joe Sakic 3.00 8.00
111 Kelly Hrudey 1.25 3.00
112 Steve Yzerman 4.00 10.00
113 Johnny Bower 1.50 4.00
114 Joe Nieuwendyk 1.25 3.00
115 Gerry Cheevers 1.50 4.00
116 Cam Fowler AU SP RC EXCH 10.00 25.00
117 Kyle Palmieri AU RC 8.00 20.00
118 Alexander Burmistrov AU RC 4.00 10.00
119 Jordan Caron AU RC 5.00 12.00
120 Tyler Seguin AU SP RC 25.00 60.00
121 Zach Hamill AU RC 4.00 10.00
122 Luke Adam AU RC 4.00 10.00
123 T.J. Brodie AU RC 5.00 12.00
124 Henrik Karlsson AU RC 4.00 10.00
125 Zac Dalpe AU RC 5.00 12.00
126 Jeff Skinner AU SP RC 10.00 25.00
127 Nick Leddy AU RC 5.00 12.00
128 Jeremy Morin AU RC 4.00 10.00
129 Evan Brophey AU RC 4.00 10.00
130 Brandon Yip AU RC 4.00 10.00
131 Mark Olver AU RC 4.00 10.00
132 Philip McRae AU RC 4.00 10.00
133 Kevin Shattenkirk AU RC 8.00 20.00
134 Jeff Penner AU SP RC 6.00 15.00
135 Taylor Hall AU SP RC 10.00 25.00
136 Magnus Paajarvi AU SP RC 20.00 50.00
137 Jordan Eberle AU SP RC 10.00 25.00
138 Jake Muzzin AU RC 10.00 25.00
139 Kyle Clifford AU RC 5.00 12.00
140 Brayden Schenn AU SP RC 10.00 25.00
141 Matt Kassian AU RC 4.00 10.00
142 P.K. Subban AU SP RC 20.00 50.00
143 Anders Lindback AU RC 4.00 10.00
144 Mark Dekanich AU RC 4.00 10.00
145 Jeff Frazee AU RC 6.00 15.00
146 Linus Omark AU RC 5.00 12.00
147 Matt Taormina AU RC 4.00 10.00
148 Jacob Josefson AU RC 4.00 10.00
149 Alexander Vasyunov AU RC 4.00 10.00
150 Nino Niederreiter AU RC 6.00 15.00
151 Derek Stepan AU RC 5.00 12.00
152 Evgeny Grachev AU RC 4.00 10.00
153 Robin Lehner AU RC 8.00 20.00
154 Sergei Bobrovsky AU RC 15.00 40.00
155 Eric Wellwood AU RC 5.00 12.00
156 Oliver Ekman-Larsson AU RC 10.00 25.00
157 Eric Tangradi AU RC 4.00 10.00
158 Mike Moore AU RC 4.00 10.00
159 Tommy Wingels AU RC 4.00 10.00
160 Ryan Reaves AU RC 5.00 12.00
161 Ian Cole AU RC 4.00 10.00
162 Dana Tyrell AU RC 4.00 10.00
163 Nazem Kadri AU SP RC 10.00 25.00
164 Korbinian Holzer AU RC 4.00 10.00
165 M.Johansson AU RC 6.00 15.00

2010-11 Playoff Contenders Playoff Tickets

*1-100 PLAYOFF TIX: 2X TO 5X BASE
*101-115 PLAYOFF TIX: .6X TO 1.5X BASE
*116-165 PLAYOFF TIX: .2X TO .5X BASE
100 Nicklas Backstrom 2.50 6.00
120 Tyler Seguin 12.00 30.00
121 Zach Hamill 5.00 12.00
126 Jeff Skinner 12.00 30.00
135 Taylor Hall 6.00 15.00
136 Magnus Paajarvi 3.00 8.00
137 Jordan Eberle 12.00 30.00
140 Brayden Schenn 6.00 15.00
142 P.K. Subban 15.00 40.00
157 Eric Tangradi 5.00 12.00
163 Nazem Kadri 6.00 15.00

2010-11 Playoff Contenders Against The Glass

COMPLETE SET (18) 15.00 40.00
1 Alex Ovechkin 6.00 15.00
2 Ryan Callahan 1.00 2.50
3 Dustin Brown 1.50 4.00
4 Troy Brouwer 1.00 2.50
5 Luke Schenn 1.50 4.00
6 Shea Weber 1.25 3.00
7 Ryan Getzlaf 1.50 4.00
8 Tuomo Ruutu 1.25 3.00
9 Steve Ott 1.00 2.50
10 Chris Neil 1.00 2.50
11 Michael Del Zotto 1.25 3.00
12 Dustin Byfuglien 1.50 4.00
13 Evander Kane 1.50 4.00
14 Drew Doughty 2.00 5.00
15 Jarome Iginla 2.00 5.00
16 James Neal 1.00 2.50
17 Tyler Myers 1.00 2.50
18 Bobby Ryan 1.25 3.00

2010-11 Playoff Contenders Against The Glass Autographs

1 Alex Ovechkin/25 30.00 80.00
2 Ryan Callahan 5.00 12.00
3 Dustin Brown 8.00 20.00
4 Troy Brouwer 8.00 20.00
5 Luke Schenn 8.00 20.00
6 Shea Weber 6.00 15.00
7 Ryan Getzlaf 8.00 20.00
8 Tuomo Ruutu 6.00 15.00
9 Steve Ott 5.00 12.00
10 Chris Neil 5.00 12.00
11 Michael Del Zotto 6.00 15.00
12 Dustin Byfuglien 8.00 20.00
13 Evander Kane 8.00 20.00
14 Drew Doughty 10.00 25.00
15 Jarome Iginla 10.00 25.00
16 James Neal 5.00 12.00
17 Tyler Myers 5.00 12.00
18 Bobby Ryan 6.00 15.00

2010-11 Playoff Contenders Awards Contenders

COMPLETE SET (20) 25.00 60.00
*GREEN/50: .6X TO 1.5X BASIC
*PURPLE/100: .5X TO 1.2X BASIC
1 Tim Thomas 1.50 4.00
2 Carey Price 3.00 8.00
3 Jimmy Howard 2.00 5.00
4 Jonathan Quick 2.00 5.00
5 Ondrej Pavelec 1.50 4.00
6 Nicklas Lidstrom 1.50 4.00
7 Drew Doughty 2.00 5.00
8 Kristopher Letang 2.00 5.00
9 John-Michael Liles 1.00 2.50
10 Zdeno Chara 1.50 4.00
11 Sidney Crosby 6.00 15.00
12 Patrick Sharp 1.50 4.00
13 Steven Stamkos 3.00 8.00
14 Daniel Sedin 2.00 5.00
15 Alex Ovechkin 6.00 15.00
16 Sidney Crosby 6.00 15.00
17 Steven Stamkos 3.00 8.00
18 Alexander Semin 1.50 4.00
19 Alex Ovechkin 6.00 15.00
20 Henrik Sedin 2.00 5.00

2010-11 Playoff Contenders Awards Contenders Autographs

1 Tim Thomas/50 20.00 50.00
2 Carey Price/50 25.00 60.00
3 Jimmy Howard/50 10.00 25.00
4 Jonathan Quick/50 12.00 30.00
5 Ondrej Pavelec/50 10.00 25.00
6 Nicklas Lidstrom/50 12.00 30.00
7 Drew Doughty/50 10.00 25.00
8 Kristopher Letang/50 25.00 60.00
9 John-Michael Liles/50 8.00 20.00
10 Zdeno Chara/50 10.00 25.00
12 Patrick Sharp/50 12.00 30.00
13 Steven Stamkos/25 30.00 60.00
14 Daniel Sedin/50 12.00 30.00
17 Steven Stamkos/25 25.00 60.00
18 Alexander Semin/50 8.00 20.00
20 Henrik Sedin/50 10.00 25.00

2010-11 Playoff Contenders Classic Tickets Autographs

101 Paul Coffey/25 12.00 30.00
102 Stan Mikita 15.00 40.00
103 Trevor Linden/25 25.00 60.00
104 Darryl Sittler 20.00 50.00
105 Rod Gilbert 15.00 40.00
106 Reggie Lemelin 12.00 30.00
111 Kelly Hrudey /50 6.00 15.00
113 Johnny Bower/25 20.00 50.00
114 Joe Nieuwendyk 6.00 15.00
115 Gerry Cheevers/25 15.00 40.00

2010-11 Playoff Contenders Draft Tandems

COMPLETE SET (20) 25.00 60.00
*GREEN/50: .6X TO 1.5X BASIC
*PURPLE/100: .5X TO 1.2X BASIC
1 M.Messier/R.Bourque 3.00 8.00
2 P.Coffey/D.Savard 1.50 4.00
3 G.Fuhr/D.Hawerchuk 2.50 6.00
4 P.LaFontaine/S.Yzerman 4.00 10.00
5 P.Roy/M.Lemieux 6.00 15.00
6 B.Leetch/A.Graves 1.25 3.00
7 B.Shanahan/J.Sakic 3.00 8.00
8 M.Modano/T.Linden 2.50 6.00
9 F.Potvin/M.Brodeur 4.00 10.00
10 R.Smyth/T.Holmstrom 1.25 3.00
11 J.Iginla/S.Doan 2.00 5.00
12 P.Marleau/J.Thornton 2.50 6.00
13 S.Gagne/V.Lecavalier 1.50 4.00
14 H.Sedin/D.Sedin 2.00 5.00
15 D.Roy/A.Hemsky 1.25 3.00
16 R.Nash/K.Lehtonen 1.50 4.00
17 M.Fleury/E.Staal 3.00 8.00
18 E.Malkin/A.Ovechkin 6.00 15.00
19 B.Ryan/J.Johnson 1.25 3.00
20 J.Toews/J.Staal 2.50 6.00

2010-11 Playoff Contenders Draft Tandems Autographs

2 P.Coffey/D.Savard 15.00 40.00
3 G.Fuhr/D.Hawerchuk 20.00 50.00
4 P.LaFontaine/S.Yzerman 40.00 100.00
6 B.Leetch/A.Graves 10.00 25.00
7 B.Shanahan/J.Sakic 60.00 120.00
8 M.Modano/T.Linden 60.00 120.00
9 F.Potvin/M.Brodeur 50.00 100.00
10 R.Smyth/T.Holmstrom 12.00 30.00
11 J.Iginla/S.Doan 15.00 40.00
12 P.Marleau/J.Thornton 20.00 50.00
13 S.Gagne/V.Lecavalier 12.00 30.00
14 H.Sedin/D.Sedin 20.00 50.00
15 D.Roy/A.Hemsky 10.00 25.00
16 R.Nash/K.Lehtonen 15.00 40.00
17 M.Fleury/E.Staal 25.00 60.00
18 E.Malkin/A.Ovechkin 100.00 200.00
19 B.Ryan/J.Johnson 10.00 25.00
20 J.Toews/J.Staal 20.00 50.00

2010-11 Playoff Contenders Leather Larceny

COMPLETE SET (18) 20.00 50.00
1 Cam Ward 2.00 5.00
2 Carey Price 4.00 10.00
3 Chris Mason 1.50 4.00
4 Craig Anderson 2.00 5.00
5 Dwayne Roloson 1.50 4.00
6 Henrik Lundqvist 5.00 12.00
7 Jaroslav Halak 2.00 5.00
8 Jonas Gustavsson 2.50 6.00
9 Jonas Hiller 1.50 4.00
10 Kari Lehtonen 1.50 4.00
11 Marc-Andre Fleury 4.00 10.00
12 Martin Brodeur 5.00 12.00
13 Mike Smith 2.00 5.00
14 Niklas Backstrom 2.00 5.00
15 Pekka Rinne 2.00 5.00
16 Ryan Miller 2.00 5.00
17 Steve Mason 1.50 4.00
18 Tim Thomas 2.00 5.00

2010-11 Playoff Contenders Leather Larceny Autographs

1 Cam Ward 15.00 40.00
2 Carey Price 15.00 40.00
3 Chris Mason 8.00 20.00
4 Craig Anderson 10.00 25.00
5 Dwayne Roloson 12.00 30.00
6 Henrik Lundqvist 25.00 60.00
7 Jaroslav Halak 15.00 40.00
8 Jonas Gustavsson 12.00 30.00
9 Jonas Hiller 8.00 20.00
10 Kari Lehtonen 8.00 20.00
11 Marc-Andre Fleury 15.00 40.00
13 Mike Smith 10.00 25.00
14 Niklas Backstrom 10.00 25.00
15 Pekka Rinne 10.00 25.00
16 Ryan Miller 15.00 40.00
17 Steve Mason 8.00 20.00
18 Tim Thomas 20.00 50.00

2010-11 Playoff Contenders Legendary Contenders

COMPLETE SET (20) 20.00 50.00
*GREEN/50: .6X TO 1.5X BASIC
*PURPLE/100: .5X TO 1.2X BASIC
1 Yvan Cournoyer 1.50 4.00
2 Phil Esposito 2.50 6.00
3 Rogie Vachon 2.00 5.00
4 Mike Bossy 1.50 4.00
5 Richard Brodeur 1.50 4.00
6 Mario Lemieux 6.00 15.00
7 Ken Hodge 1.25 3.00
8 Johnny Bucyk 1.50 4.00
9 Guy Lafleur 2.00 5.00
10 Charlie Hodge 1.25 3.00
11 Bryan Trottier 1.50 4.00
12 Bobby Clarke 2.50 6.00
13 Brett Hull 3.00 8.00
14 Bernie Parent 2.00 5.00
15 Glenn Hall 1.50 4.00
16 Henri Richard 1.50 4.00
17 Jeremy Roenick 2.50 6.00
18 Grant Fuhr 2.50 6.00
19 Tony Esposito 1.50 4.00
20 Terry O'Reilly 1.25 3.00

2010-11 Playoff Contenders Legendary Contenders Autographs

1 Yvan Cournoyer 15.00 40.00
2 Phil Esposito 12.00 30.00
3 Rogie Vachon 6.00 15.00
4 Mike Bossy 8.00 20.00
5 Richard Brodeur 8.00 20.00
6 Mario Lemieux 40.00 80.00
7 Ken Hodge 6.00 15.00
8 Johnny Bucyk 8.00 20.00
9 Guy Lafleur 40.00 80.00
10 Charlie Hodge 6.00 15.00
11 Bryan Trottier 8.00 20.00
12 Bobby Clarke 12.00 30.00
13 Brett Hull 15.00 40.00
14 Bernie Parent 12.00 30.00
17 Jeremy Roenick 12.00 30.00
18 Grant Fuhr 15.00 40.00
19 Tony Esposito 12.00 30.00
20 Terry O'Reilly 6.00 15.00

2010-11 Playoff Contenders Lottery Winners

COMPLETE SET (15) 20.00 50.00
*GREEN/50: .6X TO 1.5X BASIC
*PURPLE/100: .5X TO 1.2X BASIC
1 Alex Ovechkin 6.00 15.00
2 Jonathan Toews 2.50 6.00
3 Patrick Kane 3.00 8.00
4 Sidney Crosby 6.00 15.00
5 John Tavares 2.50 6.00
6 Steven Stamkos 3.00 8.00
7 Matt Duchene 1.50 4.00
8 Evander Kane 1.50 4.00
9 Jordan Staal 1.25 3.00
10 Zach Bogosian 1.25 3.00
11 Sam Gagner 1.00 2.50
12 James van Riemsdyk 1.25 3.00
13 Drew Doughty 2.00 5.00
14 Carey Price 3.00 8.00
15 Bobby Ryan 1.25 3.00

2010-11 Playoff Contenders Lottery Winners Autographs

1 Alex Ovechkin/25 40.00 100.00
2 Jonathan Toews 25.00 50.00
3 Patrick Kane 15.00 40.00
4 Sidney Crosby/25 100.00 200.00
5 John Tavares 12.00 30.00
6 Steven Stamkos 20.00 50.00
7 Matt Duchene 8.00 20.00
8 Evander Kane 8.00 20.00
9 Jordan Staal 10.00 25.00
10 Zach Bogosian 6.00 15.00
11 Sam Gagner 5.00 12.00
12 James van Riemsdyk 6.00 15.00
13 Drew Doughty 10.00 25.00
14 Carey Price 20.00 50.00
15 Bobby Ryan 6.00 15.00

2010-11 Playoff Contenders Perennial Contenders

COMPLETE SET (20) 25.00 60.00
*GREEN/50: .6X TO 1.5X BASIC
*PURPLE/100: .5X TO 1.2X BASIC
1 Nicklas Lidstrom 1.50 4.00
2 Joe Thornton 2.50 6.00
3 Roberto Luongo 2.50 6.00
4 Drew Doughty 2.00 5.00
5 Dany Heatley 1.25 3.00
6 Patrick Kane 3.00 8.00
7 Henrik Sedin 2.00 5.00
8 Jonathan Toews 2.50 6.00
9 Henrik Zetterberg 2.00 5.00
10 Jonathan Quick 2.00 5.00
11 Sidney Crosby 6.00 15.00
12 Mike Richards 1.25 3.00
13 Tomas Holmstrom 1.00 2.50
14 Alex Ovechkin 6.00 15.00
15 Zach Parise 1.50 4.00
16 Marc-Andre Fleury 3.00 8.00
17 Carey Price 3.00 8.00
18 Chris Pronger 1.50 4.00
19 Claude Giroux 1.50 4.00
20 Jordan Staal 1.25 3.00

2010-11 Playoff Contenders Perennial Contenders Autographs

1 Nicklas Lidstrom 12.00 30.00
2 Joe Thornton 12.00 30.00
4 Drew Doughty 10.00 25.00
5 Dany Heatley 6.00 15.00
6 Patrick Kane 15.00 40.00
7 Henrik Sedin 10.00 25.00
8 Jonathan Toews 12.00 30.00
10 Jonathan Quick 12.00 30.00
11 Sidney Crosby 75.00 150.00
12 Mike Richards 25.00 60.00
13 Tomas Holmstrom 12.00 30.00
14 Alex Ovechkin 40.00 100.00
15 Zach Parise 10.00 25.00
16 Marc-Andre Fleury 15.00 40.00
17 Carey Price 20.00 50.00
18 Chris Pronger 8.00 20.00
19 Claude Giroux 15.00 40.00
20 Jordan Staal 6.00 15.00

2010-11 Playoff Contenders Rookie of the Year Contenders

COMPLETE SET (15) 20.00 50.00
*GREEN/50: .6X TO 1.5X BASIC
*PURPLE/100: .5X TO 1.2X BASIC
1 Jeff Skinner 3.00 8.00
2 Derek Stepan 1.50 4.00
3 Jordan Eberle 3.00 8.00
4 Logan Couture 2.00 5.00
5 Tyler Ennis 1.00 2.50
6 Taylor Hall 3.00 8.00
7 John Carlson 1.50 4.00
8 Cam Fowler 3.00 8.00
9 Kevin Shattenkirk 2.50 6.00
10 Sergei Bobrovsky 5.00 12.00
11 Michal Neuvirth 1.25 3.00
12 Tyler Seguin 4.00 10.00
13 P.K. Subban 4.00 10.00
14 Mattias Tedenby 1.25 3.00
15 Jake Dowell 1.25 3.00

2010-11 Playoff Contenders Rookie of the Year Contenders Autographs

1 Jeff Skinner 20.00 50.00
2 Derek Stepan 10.00 25.00
3 Jordan Eberle 15.00 40.00
4 Logan Couture 5.00 12.00
5 Tyler Ennis 5.00 12.00
6 Taylor Hall 15.00 40.00
7 John Carlson 8.00 20.00
8 Cam Fowler 15.00 40.00
9 Kevin Shattenkirk 12.00 30.00
11 Michal Neuvirth 6.00 15.00
12 Tyler Seguin 20.00 50.00
13 P.K. Subban 30.00 80.00
14 Mattias Tedenby 6.00 15.00
15 Jake Dowell EXCH 6.00 15.00

2010-11 Playoff Contenders The Great Outdoors

COMPLETE SET (18) 20.00 50.00
1 Jose Theodore 1.50 4.00
2 Ryan Smyth 1.25 3.00
3 Sidney Crosby 6.00 15.00
4 Ryan Miller 1.50 4.00
5 Derek Roy 1.00 2.50
6 Jordan Staal 1.25 3.00
7 Pavel Datsyuk 2.50 6.00
8 Jonathan Toews 2.50 6.00
9 Marian Hossa 1.50 4.00
10 Dustin Byfuglien 1.50 4.00
11 Tim Thomas 1.50 4.00
12 Mark Recchi 2.00 5.00
13 Shawn Thornton 1.00 2.50
14 Michael Leighton 1.25 3.00
15 Jeff Carter 1.25 3.00
16 Evgeni Malkin 3.00 8.00
17 Alex Ovechkin 6.00 15.00
18 Mario Lemieux 6.00 15.00

2010-11 Playoff Contenders The Great Outdoors Autographs

1 Jose Theodore 8.00 20.00
2 Ryan Smyth 12.00 30.00
3 Sidney Crosby/25 100.00 200.00
4 Ryan Miller 12.00 30.00
5 Derek Roy 5.00 12.00
6 Jordan Staal 12.00 30.00
7 Pavel Datsyuk 15.00 40.00
8 Jonathan Toews 25.00 60.00
9 Marian Hossa 8.00 20.00
10 Dustin Byfuglien 8.00 20.00
11 Tim Thomas 20.00 50.00
12 Mark Recchi 15.00 40.00
13 Shawn Thornton 20.00 50.00
14 Evgeni Malkin 25.00 60.00
15 Jeff Carter 10.00 25.00
17 Alex Ovechkin/25 75.00 150.00
16 Michael Leighton 6.00 15.00
18 Mario Lemieux/25 75.00 150.00

1975-76 Popsicle

COMPLETE SET (18) 15.00 30.00
1 Chicago Blackhawks 1.00 2.00
2 St. Louis Blues 1.00 2.00
3 Boston Bruins 1.50 3.00
4 Montreal Canadiens 1.50 3.00
5 Vancouver Canucks 1.00 2.00
6 Washington Capitals 1.00 2.00
7 Atlanta Flames 1.50 3.00
8 Philadelphia Flyers 1.00 2.00
9 California Golden Seals 1.50 3.00
10 New York Islanders 1.00 2.00
11 Los Angeles Kings 1.00 2.00
12 Toronto Maple Leafs 1.50 3.00
13 Minnesota North Stars 1.00 2.00
14 Pittsburgh Penguins 1.00 2.00
15 New York Rangers 1.50 3.00
16 Detroit Red Wings 1.50 3.00
17 Buffalo Sabres 1.00 2.00
18 Kansas City Scouts 1.50 3.00

1976-77 Popsicle

COMPLETE SET (19) 20.00 40.00
1 Cleveland Barons 1.50 3.00
2 Chicago Blackhawks 1.50 3.00
3 St. Louis Blues 1.00 2.00
4 Boston Bruins 1.50 3.00
5 Montreal Canadiens 1.50 3.00
6 Vancouver Canucks 1.00 2.00
7 Washington Capitals 1.00 2.00
8 Atlanta Flames 1.50 3.00
9 Philadelphia Flyers 1.00 2.00
10 New York Islanders 1.00 2.00
11 Los Angeles Kings 1.00 2.00
12 Toronto Maple Leafs 1.50 3.00
13 Minnesota North Stars 1.00 2.00
14 Pittsburgh Penguins 1.00 2.00
15 New York Rangers 1.50 3.00
16 Detroit Red Wings 1.50 3.00
17 Colorado Rockies 1.50 3.00
18 Buffalo Sabres 1.00 2.00
19 Membership Card 1.50 3.00

1966-67 Post Cereal Box Backs

1 Gump Worsley 15.00 40.00
2 Bob Pulford 15.00 40.00
3 Glenn Hall 15.00 40.00

1967-68 Post Cereal Box Backs

1 Gordie Howe net in background 25.00 50.00
2 Gordie Howe no net 25.00 50.00
3 Harry Howell passing 10.00 20.00
4 Harry Howell kneeling 10.00 20.00
5 Jacques Laperriere net in background 10.00 20.00
6 Jacques Laperriere no net 10.00 20.00
7 Stan Mikita red jersey 15.00 30.00
8 Stan Mikita white jersey 15.00 30.00
9 Bobby Orr posed 25.00 50.00
10 Bobby Orr in action 25.00 50.00
11 Henri Richard with puck 12.50 25.00
12 Henri Richard no puck 12.50 25.00
13 Checklist 25.00 50.00

1967-68 Post Flip Books

COMPLETE SET (12) 100.00 200.00
1 Gump Worsley Johnny Bower 15.00 30.00
2 Rogatien Vachon Johnny Bower 17.50 35.00
3 J.C. Tremblay Tim Horton 12.50 25.00
4 Jacques Laperriere Marcel Pronovost 7.50 15.00
5 Henri Richard Frank Mahovlich 12.50 25.00
6 Dick Duff Dave Keon 10.00 20.00
7 Jean Beliveau Jim Pappin 15.00 30.00
8 Jean Beliveau Ron Ellis 15.00 30.00
9 Gilles Tremblay George Armstrong 10.00 20.00
10 J.C. Tremblay Pete Stemkowski 5.00 10.00
11 Ralph Backstrom Bob Pulford 7.50 15.00
12 Bobby Rousseau Wayne Hillman 5.00 10.00

1968-69 Post Marbles

COMPLETE SET (30) 250.00 500.00
1 Ralph Backstrom MC 4.00 8.00
2 Jean Beliveau MC 20.00 40.00
3 Johnny Bower TML 7.50 15.00
4 Wayne Carleton TML 4.00 8.00
5 Yvan Cournoyer MC 10.00 20.00
6 Ron Ellis TML 4.00 8.00
7 John Ferguson MC 4.00 8.00
8 Bruce Gamble TML 4.00 8.00
9 Terry Harper MC 4.00 8.00
10 Ted Harris MC 4.00 8.00
11 Paul Henderson TML 5.00 10.00
12 Tim Horton TML 20.00 40.00
13 Dave Keon TML 12.50 25.00
14 Jacques Laperriere MC 5.00 10.00
15 Jacques Lemaire MC 12.50 25.00
16 Murray Oliver TML 4.00 8.00
17 Mike Pelyk TML 4.00 8.00
18 Pierre Pilote TML 5.00 10.00
19 Marcel Pronovost TML 5.00 10.00
20 Bob Pulford TML 5.00 10.00
21 Henri Richard MC 10.00 20.00
22 Bobby Rousseau MC 4.00 8.00
23 Serge Savard MC 5.00 10.00
24 Floyd Smith TML 4.00 8.00
25 Gilles Tremblay MC 4.00 8.00
26 J.C. Tremblay MC 4.00 8.00
27 Norm Ullman TML 5.00 10.00
28 Rogatien Vachon MC 15.00 30.00
29 Mike Walton TML 4.00 8.00
30 Gump Worsley MC 10.00 20.00
xx Game Board 87.50 175.00

1970-71 Post Shooters

COMPLETE SET (16) 150.00 300.00
1 Bobby Orr 50.00 100.00
2 Paul Henderson 7.50 15.00
3 Dennis Hull 6.25 12.50
4 Johnny Bucyk 7.50 15.00
5 Ken Hodge 6.25 12.50
6 Ron Ellis 6.25 12.50
7 Jacques Laperriere 6.25 12.50
8 Jacques Lemaire 7.50 15.00
9 Frank Mahovlich 7.50 15.00
10 Peter Mahovlich 6.25 12.50
11 J.C. Tremblay 6.25 12.50
12 Orland Kurtenbach 5.00 10.00
13 Dale Tallon 5.00 10.00
14 Jean Ratelle 7.50 15.00
15 Ed Giacomin 10.00 20.00
16 Jacques Plante 20.00 40.00

1972-73 Post Action Transfers

COMPLETE SET (12) 125.00 250.00
1 Garry Unger Bobby Orr Defense 30.00 60.00
2 Red Berenson Dale Tallon In the Corner 7.50 15.00
3 Gary Dornhoeffer Wayne Cashman Face Off 7.50 15.00
4 Jim McKenny Ed Giacomin Power Save 10.00 20.00
5 Pat Quinn Keith Magnuson Power Play Goal 7.50 15.00
6 Paul Shmyr Rod Seiling Break Away 7.50 15.00
7 Danny Grant Jacques Plante Slap Shot 10.00 20.00
8 Syl Apps Jr. Serge Savard Rebound 10.00 20.00
9 Gump Worsley Gary Bergman Wrist Shot 12.50 25.00
10 Roger Crozier Ed Westfall Last Minute 10.00 20.00
11 Dennis Hull Orland Kurtenbach Goalmouth Scramble 7.50 15.00
12 Roger Vachon Yvan Cournoyer Chest Save 15.00 30.00

1981-82 Post Standups

COMPLETE SET (28) 20.00 50.00
1 Ray Bourque 3.00 8.00
2 Gilbert Perreault 1.00 2.50
3 Denis Savard 1.50 4.00
4 Dale McCourt .40 1.00
5 Bobby Smith .60 1.50
6 Mike Bossy 2.50 6.00
7 Bobby Clarke 1.50 4.00
8 Randy Carlyle .40 1.00
9 Mike Palmateer .75 2.00
10 Tiger Williams .60 1.50
11 Mark Howe .75 2.00
12 Marcel Dionne 1.25 3.00
13 Mike Liut .60 1.50
14 Barry Beck .40 1.00
15 Mark Messier 5.00 12.00
16 Larry Robinson 1.25 3.00
17 Real Cloutier .40 1.00
18 Borje Salming .75 2.00
19 Morris Lukowich .40 1.00
20 Brett Callighen .40 1.00
21 Rob Ramage .60 1.50
22 Wilf Paiement .40 1.00
23 Mario Tremblay .60 1.50
24 Robbie Florek .40 1.00
25 Stan Smyl .60 1.50
26 Dave Babych .40 1.00
27 Willi Plett .40 1.00
28 Kent Nilsson .75 2.00
xx Display Box 8.00 20.00

1982-83 Post Cereal Panels

COMPLETE SET (21) 30.00 80.00
1 Bruins
Rogie Vachon
Ray Bourque
Peter McNab
Steve Kasper
Wayne Cashman
Mike Gillis
Rick Middleton
Stan Jonathan
Mike O'Connell
Brad Park
Terry O'Reilly
Mike Milbury
Tom Fergus
Brad McCrimmon
Bruce Crowder
Larry Melnyk 2.50 6.00
2 Sabres
Don Edwards
Richie Dunn
John Van Boxmeer
Mike Ramsey
Dale McCourt
Tony McKegney
Craig Ramsay
Gilbert Perreault
Andre Savard
Yvon Lambert
Ric Seiling
Mike Foligno
J.Francois Sauve
Lindy Ruff
Bill Hajt
Larry Playfair 2.00 5.00
3 Flames
Mel Bridgman
Guy Chouinard
Denis Cyr
Jamie Hislop
Ken Houston
Kevin Lavallee
Gary McAdam
Lanny McDonald
Bob Murdoch
Kent Nilsson
Jim Peplinski

1982-83 Post Cereal Panels

Jim Peplinski
Willi Plett
Paul Reinhart
Pat Riggin
Phil Russell 2.00 5.00
4 Blackhawks
Greg Fox
Dave Hutchison
Terry Ruskowski
Reg Kerr
Tom Lysiak
Bill Gardner
Tim Higgins
Rich Preston
Denis Savard
Al Secord
Grant Mulvey
Doug Crossman
Doug Wilson
Rick Paterson
Ted Bulley
Tony Esposito 2.50 6.00
5 Red Wings
Jim Schoenfeld
John Barrett
Greg Smith
Willie Huber
Walt McKechnie
Paul Woods
Mark Kirton
Danny Gare
Vaclav Nedomansky
Mike Blaisdell
Greg Joly
Mark Osborne
Derek Smith
John Ogrodnick
Reed Larson
Bob Sauve 1.50 4.00
6 Oilers
Grant Fuhr
Lee Fogolin
Kevin Lowe
Garry Lariviere
Paul Coffey
Risto Siltanen
Glenn Anderson
Matti Hagman
Mark Messier
Dave Hunter
Pat Hughes
Jari Kurri
Brett Callighen
Dave Lumley
Dave Semenko
Wayne Gretzky 8.00 20.00
7 Whalers
Paul Shmyr
Ron Francis
Mark Howe
Blake Wesley
Garry Howatt
Jordy Douglas
Dave Keon
George Lyle
Blaine Stoughton
Doug Sulliman
Chris Kotsopoulos
Don Nachbaur
Warren Miller
Pierre Larouche
Greg Millen 2.00 5.00
8 Kings
Mario Lessard
Rick Chartraw
Jerry Korab
Larry Murphy
Charlie Simmer
Dean Hopkins
Marcel Dionne
John P.Kelly
Dave Taylor
Jim Fox
Mark Hardy
Steve Jensen
Doug Smith
Jay Wells
Dave Lewis
Steve Bozek 2.00 5.00
9 North Stars
Curt Giles
Fred Barrett
Craig Hartsburg
Brad Maxwell
K.E. Anderson
Gord Roberts
Tom McCarthy
Brad Palmer
Bobby Smith
Tim Young
Dino Ciccarelli
Gary Sargent
Al MacAdam
Steve Payne
Gilles Meloche
Steve Christoff 1.50 4.00
10 Canadiens
Brian Engblom
Pierre Mondou
Doug Risebrough
Guy Lafleur
Keith Acton
Mario Tremblay
Rod Langway
Larry Robinson
Mark Hunter
Doug Jarvis
Steve Shutt
Bob Gainey
Robert Picard
Craig Laughlin
Mark Napier
Richard Sevigny 3.00 8.00
11 Rockies
Brent Ashton
Dave Cameron
Joe Cirella
Dwight Foster
Mike Kitchen
Don Lever
Bob Lorimer
Bob MacMillan
Merlin Malinowski
Kevin Maxwell
Joe Micheletti
Joe Micheletti
Bobby Miller
Glenn Resch
Steve Tambellini
John Wensink 1.50 4.00
12 Islanders
Mike McEwen
Tomas Jonsson
Denis Potvin
Ken Morrow
Stefan Persson
Clark Gillies
Wayne Merrick
Bob Bourne
Bryan Trottier
Mike Bossy
Bob Nystrom
Dave Langevin
John Tonelli
Anders Kallur
Billy Smith
Butch Goring 3.00 8.00
13 Rangers
Tom Laidlaw
Barry Beck
Ron Greschner
Steve Vickers
Ron Duguay
Don Maloney
Mike Allison
Ed Johnstone 1.50 4.00
Nick Fotiu
Dave Maloney
Mike Rogers
Reijo Ruotsalainen
Steve Weeks
Andre Dore
Robbie Ftorek
Mark Pavelich 1.50 4.00
14 Flyers
Behn Wilson
Fred Arthur
Bill Barber
Brad Marsh
Reid Bailey
Darryl Sittler
Tim Kerr
Kenny Linseman
Bobby Clarke
Paul Holmgren
Jimmy Watson
Ilkka Sinisalo
Brian Propp
Reggie Leach
Glen Cochrane
Pete Peeters 2.50 6.00
15 Penguins
Pat Price
Ron Stackhouse
Paul Baxter
Peter Lee
George Ferguson
Greg Malone
Doug Shedden
Pat Boutette
Marc Chorney
Rick Kehoe
Gregg Sheppard
Paul Gardner
Mike Bullard
Pat Graham
Randy Carlyle
Michel Dion 1.50 4.00
16 Nordiques
John Garrett
Wally Weir
Normand Rochefort
Marc Tardif
Real Cloutier
Jere Gillis
Michel Goulet
Marian Stastny
Alain Cote
Anton Stastny
Mario Marois
Jacques Richard
Peter Stastny
Wilf Paiement
Andre Dupont
Dale Hunter 2.00 5.00
17 Blues
Mike Liut
Guy Lapointe
Larry Patey
Perry Turnbull
Wayne Babych
Brian Sutter
Jack Brownschidle
Ed Kea
Rick Lapointe
Blake Dunlop
Mike Zuke
Jorgen Pettersson
Bernie Federko
Bill Baker
Mike Crombeen
Jim Payese 1.50 4.00
18 Maple Leafs
Michel Larocque
Bob Manno
Bob McGill
Rocky Saganiuk
John Anderson
Fred Boimistruck
Walt Poddubny
Miroslav Frycer
Jim Benning
Stewart Gavin
Bill Derlago
Borje Salming
Rick Vaive
Normand Aubin
Terry Martin
Barry Melrose 2.00 5.00
19 Canucks
Doug Halward
Gary Lupul
Ivan Boldirev
Stan Smyl
Lars Lindgren
Darcy Rota
Ron Delorme
Ivan Hlinka
Tiger Williams
Thomas Gradin
Curt Fraser
Kevin McCarthy
Lars Molin
Harold Snepsts
Marc Crawford
Richard Brodeur 1.50 4.00
20 Capitals
Doug Hicks
Randy Holt
Rick Green
Darren Veitch
Ryan Walter
Bob Carpenter
Mike Gartner
Glen Currie
Gaetan Duchesne
Bengt Gustafsson
Greg Theberge
Dennis Maruk
Bob Gould
Terry Murray
Chris Valentine
Al Jensen 2.00 5.00
21 Jets
Bryan Maxwell
Tim Watters
Dale Hawerchuk
Scott Arniel
Morris Lukowich
Dave Christian
Tim Trimper
Paul MacLean
Serge Savard
Willy Lindstrom
Bengt Lundholm
Lucien DeBlois
Don Spring
Norm Dupont
Ed Staniowski
Dave Babych 2.00 5.00

1994-95 Post Box Backs

COMPLETE SET (25) 16.00 40.00
1 Tony Amonte
Chicago Bla .75 2.00
2 Jason Arnott
Edmonton O .60 1.50
3 Ray Bourque
Boston 1.25 3.00
4 Martin Brodeur
New Jers 1.25 3.00
5 Pavel Bure
Vancouver Ca 1.25 3.00
6 Chris Chelios
Chicago B .75 2.00
7 Geoff Courtnall
Vancouv .60 1.50
8 Russ Courtnall
Dallas S .60 1.50
9 Steve Duchesne
St. Loui .60 1.50
10 Sergei Fedorov
Detroit 1.25 3.00
11 Theo Fleury
Calgary .75 2.00
12 Doug Gilmour
Toronto Ma .75 2.00
13 Wayne Gretzky
Los Angel 4.00 10.00
14 Jari Kurri
Los Angeles .60 1.50
15 Eric Lindros
Philadelph 1.25 3.00
16 Marty McSorley
Los Ange .60 1.50
17 Alexander Mogilny
Buffa .60 1.50
18 Kirk Muller
Montreal Ca .60 1.50
19 Rob Niedermayer .60 1.50
20 Felix Potvin
Toronto Ma .75 2.00
21 Luc Robitaille
Pittsbur .75 2.00
22 Joe Sakic
Quebec Nordiq 1.50 4.00
23 Teemu Selanne
Winnipeg 1.25 3.00
24 Alexei Yashin
Ottawa Se .60 1.50
25 Title Card .40 1.00

1995-96 Post Upper Deck

COMPLETE FACTORY SET (26) 14.00 35.00
COMPLETE CELLO. BOX SET (24) 20.00 50.00
1 Ray Bourque .75 2.00
2 Martin Brodeur 1.50 4.00
3 Steve Duchesne .08 .25
4 Vincent Damphousse .20 .50
5 Eric Desjardins .08 .25
6 Eric Lindros 2.00 5.00
7 Joe Juneau .20 .50
8 Luc Robitaille .20 .50
9 Mark Recchi .20 .50
10 Patrick Roy 3.00 8.00
11 Brendan Shanahan 1.25 3.00
12 Scott Stevens .08 .25
13 Jason Arnott .20 .50
14 Trevor Linden .08 .25
15 Chris Chelios .60 1.50
16 Paul Coffey .60 1.50
17 Wayne Gretzky 4.00 10.00
18 Doug Gilmour .60 1.50
19 Kelly Hrudey .08 .25
20 Paul Kariya 2.50 6.00
21 Larry Murphy .08 .25
22 Felix Potvin .75 2.00
23 Keith Tkachuk .60 1.50
24 Rob Blake .08 .25
AU17 Wayne Gretzky AUTO (500) 300.00 800.00
NNO Title card .08 .25
NNO Checklist .08 .25

1996-97 Post Upper Deck

COMPLETE SET (24) 18.00 45.00
1 Ray Bourque .50 1.25
2 Chris Chelios .30 .75
3 Paul Coffey .30 .75
4 Vincent Damphousse .25 .60
5 Steve Duchesne .20 .50
6 Theo Fleury .60 1.50
7 Doug Gilmour .40 1.00
8 Wayne Gretzky 1.50 4.00
9 Curtis Joseph .40 1.00
10 Ed Jovanovski .25 .60
11 Paul Kariya .30 .75
12 Eric Lindros .50 1.25
13 Al MacInnis .40 1.00
14 Felix Potvin .50 1.25
15 Mark Recchi .40 1.00
16 Luc Robitaille .30 .75
17 Jeremy Roenick .50 1.25
18 Patrick Roy .75 2.00
19 Joe Sakic .60 1.50
20 Mathieu Schneider .20 .50
21 Brendan Shanahan .30 .75
22 Scott Stevens .30 .75
23 John Vanbiesbrouck .30 .75
24 Alexei Yashin .25 .60

1997 Post Pinnacle

COMPLETE SET (24) 12.00 30.00
1 Eric Lindros 1.00 2.50
2 Patrick Roy 1.50 4.00
3 Joe Sakic .60 1.50
4 Brian Leetch .30 .75
5 Mark Messier .40 1.00
6 Jason Arnott .25 .60
7 Paul Kariya 1.25 3.00
8 Martin Brodeur .75 2.00
9 Vincent Damphousse .25 .60
10 Steve Yzerman 1.00 2.50
11 Brett Hull .40 1.00
12 Chris Chelios .30 .75
13 Sergei Fedorov .60 1.50
14 Nicklas Lidstrom .25 .60
15 Sergei Berezin .15 .40
16 Dominik Hasek .60 1.50
17 Pavel Bure .75 2.00
18 Saku Koivu .30 .75
19 Teemu Selanne .60 1.50
20 Peter Forsberg .75 2.00
21 Jaromir Jagr 1.00 2.50
22 Peter Bondra .30 .75
23 Alexei Yashin .15 .40
24 Slava Fetisov .15 .40
NNO Eric Lindros AUTO/888 25.00 50.00

1998-99 Post

1 Wayne Gretzky 2.50 6.00
2 Martin Brodeur 1.00 2.50
3 Joe Nieuwendyk .30 .75
4 Rick Tocchet .30 .75
5 Theoren Fleury .50 1.25
6 Adam Oates .40 1.00
7 Mark Recchi .50 1.25
8 Eric Lindros .60 1.50
9 Steve Yzerman 1.00 2.50
10 Wade Redden .25 .60
11 Glen Murray .30 .75
12 Mike Johnson .25 .60
13 Kelly Buchberger .25 .60
14 Joe Sakic .75 2.00
15 Mark Messier .75 2.00
16 Keith Primeau .30 .75
17 Mike Vernon .30 .75
18 Chris Pronger .40 1.00
19 Mike Peca .25 .60
20 Dave Gagner .25 .60
21 Rob Zamuner .25 .60
22 Doug Gilmour .50 1.25
G1 Wayne Gretzky 2.50 6.00
G2 Wayne Gretzky 2.50 6.00
G3 Wayne Gretzky 2.50 6.00
G4 Wayne Gretzky 2.50 6.00
G5 Wayne Gretzky 2.50 6.00
G6 Wayne Gretzky 2.50 6.00

1999-00 Post Wayne Gretzky

COMPLETE SET (14) 12.00 30.00
COMMON CARD (1-14) 1.25 3.00

2012-13 Post Cereal CHL Goalies

17 Matt Murray .50 1.25
20 Garret Sparks .60 1.50

2013-14 Post Cereal CHL

COMPLETE SET (24) 8.00 20.00
1 Madison Bowey .30 .75
2 William Carrier .50 1.25
3 Laurent Dauphin .30 .75
4 Jean-Sebastien Dea .50 1.25
5 Mathew Dumba .30 .75
6 Aaron Ekblad 1.25 3.00
7 Adam Erne .50 1.25
8 Brendan Gaunce .40 1.00
9 Frederik Gauthier .50 1.25
10 Bo Horvat 1.00 2.50
11 Morgan Klimchuk .40 1.00
12 Curtis Lazar .50 1.25
13 Connor McDavid 5.00 12.00
14 Sean Monahan .75 2.00
15 Josh Morrissey .50 1.25
16 Darnell Nurse .60 1.50
17 Marc-Olivier Roy .50 1.25
18 Gabryel Paquin-Boudreau .40 1.00
19 Emile Poirier .50 1.25
20 Derrick Pouliot .60 1.50
21 Ryan Pulock .50 1.25
22 Nick Ritchie .50 1.25
23 Hunter Shinkaruk .60 1.50
24 Tom Wilson 1.00 2.50

2014-15 Post Cereal CHL

COMPLETE SET (24) 8.00 20.00
1 Aaron Ekblad 1.25 3.00
2 Alexis Vanier .30 .75
3 Anthony DeLuca .40 1.00
4 Brayden Point .60 1.50
5 Brendan Perlini .75 2.00
6 Brycen Martin .50 1.25
7 Connor McDavid 4.00 10.00
8 Daniel Sprong .75 2.00
9 Haydn Fleury .50 1.25
10 Ivan Barbashev .50 1.25
11 Jake Virtanen .60 1.50
12 Jayce Hawryluk .30 .75
13 Jeremy Roy .30 .75
14 Joe Hicketts .30 .75
15 Josh Ho-Sang .60 1.50
16 Michael Dal Colle .60 1.50
17 Nathan Noel .30 .75
18 Nicolas Petan .50 1.25
19 Nicolas Roy .50 1.25
20 Nikolaj Ehlers 1.00 2.50
21 Sam Bennett 1.25 3.00
22 Spencer Martin .60 1.50
23 Travis Konecny 1.00 2.50
24 Tristan Jarry .50 1.25

1993-94 PowerPlay

1 Stu Grimson .05 .15
2 Guy Hebert .07 .20
3 Sean Hill .05 .15
4 Bill Houlder .05 .15
5 Alexei Kasatonov .05 .15
6 Steven King .05 .15
7 Lonnie Loach .05 .15
8 Troy Loney .05 .15
9 Joe Sacco .05 .15
10 Anatoli Semenov .05 .15
11 Jarrod Skalde .05 .15
12 Tim Sweeney .05 .15
13 Ron Tugnutt .07 .20
14 Terry Yake .05 .15
15 Shaun Van Allen .05 .15
16 Ray Bourque .15 .40
17 Jon Casey .07 .20
18 Ted Donato .05 .15
19 Joe Juneau .05 .15
20 Dmitri Kvartalnov .05 .15
21 Steve Leach .05 .15
22 Cam Neely .10 .25
23 Adam Oates .10 .25
24 Don Sweeney .05 .15
25 Glen Wesley .05 .15
26 Doug Bodger .05 .15
27 Grant Fuhr .15 .40
28 Viktor Gordiouk .05 .15
29 Dale Hawerchuk .12 .30
30 Yuri Khmylev .05 .15
31 Pat LaFontaine .10 .25
32 Alexander Mogilny .07 .20
33 Richard Smehlik .05 .15
34 Bob Sweeney .05 .15
35 Randy Wood .05 .15
36 Theo Fleury .05 .15
37 Kelly Kisio .05 .15
38 Al MacInnis .12 .30
39 Joe Nieuwendyk .07 .20
40 Joel Otto .05 .15
41 Robert Reichel .05 .15
42 Gary Roberts .05 .15
43 Ronnie Stern .05 .15
44 Gary Suter .05 .15
45 Mike Vernon .07 .20
46 Ed Belfour .10 .25
47 Chris Chelios .10 .25
48 Karl Dykhuis .05 .15
49 Michel Goulet .05 .15
50 Dirk Graham .05 .15
51 Sergei Krivokrasov .05 .15
52 Steve Larmer .07 .20
53 Joe Murphy .05 .15
54 Jeremy Roenick .15 .40
55 Steve Smith .05 .15
56 Brent Sutter .05 .15
57 Neal Broten .07 .20
58 Russ Courtnall .05 .15
59 Ulf Dahlen .05 .15
60 Dave Gagner .07 .20
61 Derian Hatcher .05 .15
62 Trent Klatt .05 .15
63 Mike Modano .15 .40
64 Andy Moog .10 .25
65 Tommy Sjodin .05 .15
66 Mark Tinordi .05 .15
67 Tim Cheveldae .07 .20
68 Steve Chiasson .05 .15
69 Dino Ciccarelli .07 .20
70 Paul Coffey .10 .25
71 Dallas Drake RC .10 .25
72 Sergei Fedorov .15 .40
73 Vladimir Konstantinov .07 .20
74 Nicklas Lidstrom .10 .25
75 Keith Primeau .07 .20
76 Ray Sheppard .07 .20
77 Steve Yzerman .25 .60
78 Zdeno Ciger .05 .15
79 Shayne Corson .07 .20
80 Todd Elik .05 .15
81 Igor Kravchuk .05 .15
82 Craig MacTavish .05 .15
83 Dave Manson .05 .15
84 Shjon Podein RC .10 .25
85 Bill Ranford .07 .20
86 Steven Rice .05 .15
87 Doug Weight .07 .20
88 Doug Barrault RC .05 .15
89 Jesse Belanger .05 .15
90 Brian Benning .05 .15
91 Joe Cirella .05 .15
92 Mark Fitzpatrick .05 .15
93 Randy Gilhen .05 .15
94 Mike Hough .05 .15
95 Bill Lindsay .05 .15
96 Andrei Lomakin .05 .15
97 Dave Lowry .05 .15
98 Scott Mellanby .07 .20
99 Gord Murphy .05 .15
100 Brian Skrudland .05 .15
101 Milan Tichy RC .05 .15
102 John Vanbiesbrouck .10 .25
103 Sean Burke .05 .15
104 Andrew Cassels .05 .15
105 Nick Kypreos .05 .15
106 Michael Nylander .05 .15
107 Robert Petrovicky .05 .15
108 Patrick Poulin .05 .15
109 Geoff Sanderson .07 .20
110 Pat Verbeek .05 .15
111 Eric Weinrich .05 .15
112 Zarley Zalapski .05 .15
113 Rob Blake .07 .20
114 Jimmy Carson .05 .15
115 Tony Granato .05 .15
116 Wayne Gretzky .60 1.50
117 Kelly Hrudey .07 .20
118 Jari Kurri .10 .25
119 Shawn McEachern .05 .15
120 Luc Robitaille .10 .25
121 Tomas Sandstrom .05 .15
122 Darryl Sydor .05 .15
123 Alexei Zhitnik .05 .15
124 Brian Bellows .07 .20
125 Patrice Brisebois .05 .15
126 Guy Carbonneau .05 .15
127 Vincent Damphousse .07 .20
128 Eric Desjardins .07 .20
129 Mike Keane .05 .15
130 Stephan Lebeau .05 .15
131 Kirk Muller .05 .15
132 Lyle Odelein .05 .15
133 Patrick Roy .25 .60
134 Mathieu Schneider .05 .15
135 Bruce Driver .05 .15
136 Slava Fetisov .05 .15
137 Claude Lemieux .05 .15
138 John MacLean .07 .20
139 Bernie Nicholls .07 .20
140 Scott Niedermayer .10 .25
141 Stephane Richer .07 .20
142 Alexander Semak .05 .15
143 Scott Stevens .10 .25
144 Chris Terreri .07 .20
145 Valeri Zelepukin .05 .15
146 Patrick Flatley .05 .15
147 Ron Hextall .10 .25
148 Benoit Hogue .05 .15
149 Darius Kasparaitis .05 .15
150 Derek King .05 .15
151 Uwe Krupp .05 .15
152 Scott Lachance .05 .15
153 Vladimir Malakhov .05 .15
154 Steve Thomas .05 .15
155 Pierre Turgeon .07 .20
156 Tony Amonte .07 .20
157 Mike Gartner .12 .30
158 Adam Graves .05 .15
159 Alexei Kovalev .07 .20
160 Brian Leetch .07 .20
161 Joby Messier RC .10 .25
162 Mark Messier .20 .50
163 Sergei Nemchinov .05 .15
164 James Patrick .05 .15
165 Mike Richter .10 .25
166 Darren Turcotte .05 .15
167 Sergei Zubov .07 .20
168 Dave Archibald .05 .15
169 Craig Billington .07 .20
170 Bob Kudelski .05 .15
171 Mark Lamb .05 .15
172 Norm Maciver .05 .15
173 Darren Rumble .05 .15
174 Vladimir Ruzicka .05 .15
175 Brad Shaw .05 .15
176 Sylvain Turgeon .05 .15
177 Josef Beranek .05 .15
178 Rod Brind'Amour .07 .20
179 Kevin Dineen .05 .15
180 Pelle Eklund .05 .15
181 Brent Fedyk .05 .15
182 Garry Galley .05 .15
183 Eric Lindros .15 .40
184 Mark Recchi .12 .30
185 Tommy Soderstrom .07 .20
186 Dimitri Yushkevich .05 .15
187 Tom Barrasso .07 .20
188 Ron Francis .12 .30
189 Jaromir Jagr .30 .75
190 Mario Lemieux .40 1.00
191 Marty McSorley .07 .20
192 Joe Mullen .07 .20
193 Larry Murphy .07 .20
194 Ulf Samuelsson .05 .15
195 Kevin Stevens .07 .20
196 Rick Tocchet .07 .20
197 Steve Duchesne .05 .15
198 Stephane Fiset .07 .20
199 Valeri Kamensky .07 .20
200 Andrei Kovalenko .05 .15
201 Owen Nolan .10 .25
202 Mike Ricci .05 .15
203 Martin Rucinsky .05 .15
204 Joe Sakic .20 .50
205 Mats Sundin .10 .25
206 Scott Young .05 .15
207 Jeff Brown .05 .15
208 Garth Butcher .05 .15
209 Nelson Emerson .05 .15
210 Bret Hedican .05 .15
211 Brett Hull .20 .50
212 Craig Janney .07 .20
213 Curtis Joseph .12 .30
214 Igor Korolev .05 .15
215 Kevin Miller .05 .15
216 Brendan Shanahan .10 .25
217 Ed Courtenay .05 .15
218 Pat Falloon .05 .15
219 Johan Garpenlov .05 .15
220 Rob Gaudreau RC .10 .25
221 Arturs Irbe .07 .20
222 Sergei Makarov .05 .15
223 Jeff Norton .05 .15
224 Jeff Odgers .05 .15
225 Sandis Ozolinsh .05 .15
226 Tom Pederson .05 .15
227 Bob Beers .05 .15
228 Brian Bradley .05 .15
229 Shawn Chambers .05 .15
230 Gerard Gallant .05 .15
231 Roman Hamrlik .05 .15
232 Petr Klima .05 .15
233 Chris Kontos .05 .15
234 Daren Puppa .05 .15
235 John Tucker .05 .15
236 Rob Zamuner .05 .15
237 Glenn Anderson .07 .20
238 Dave Andreychuk .10 .25
239 Drake Berehowsky .05 .15
240 Nikolai Borschevsky .05 .15
241 Wendel Clark .15 .40
242 John Cullen .05 .15
243 Dave Ellett .05 .15
244 Doug Gilmour .12 .30
245 Dimitri Mironov .05 .15
246 Felix Potvin .20 .50
247 Greg Adams .05 .15
248 Pavel Bure .10 .25
249 Geoff Courtnall .05 .15
250 Gerald Diduck .05 .15
251 Trevor Linden .10 .25
252 Jyrki Lumme .05 .15
253 Kirk McLean .07 .20
254 Petr Nedved .05 .15
255 Cliff Ronning .05 .15
256 Jiri Slegr .05 .15
257 Dixon Ward .05 .15
258 Peter Bondra .10 .25
259 Sylvain Cote .05 .15
260 Pat Elynuik .05 .15
261 Kevin Hatcher .05 .15
262 Dale Hunter .05 .15
263 Al Iafrate .05 .15
264 Dimitri Khristich .05 .15
265 Michal Pivonka .05 .15
266 Mike Ridley .05 .15
267 Rick Tabaracci .05 .15
268 Sergei Bautin .05 .15
269 Evgeny Davydov .05 .15
270 Bob Essensa .07 .20
271 Phil Housley .07 .20
272 Teppo Numminen .05 .15
273 Fredrik Olausson .05 .15
274 Teemu Selanne .20 .50
275 Thomas Steen .05 .15
276 Keith Tkachuk .10 .25
277 Paul Ysebaert .05 .15
278 Alexei Zhamnov .07 .20
279 Checklist .05 .15
280 Checklist .05 .15
281 Patrick Carnback RC .10 .25
282 Bob Corkum .05 .15
283 Bobby Dollas .05 .15
284 Peter Douris .05 .15
285 Todd Ewen .05 .15
286 Garry Valk .05 .15
287 John Blue .07 .20
288 Glen Featherstone .05 .15
289 Steve Heinze .05 .15
290 David Reid .05 .15
291 Bryan Smolinski .05 .15
292 Cam Stewart RC .10 .25
293 Jozef Stumpel .05 .15
294 Sergei Zholtok .05 .15
295 Donald Audette .05 .15
296 Philippe Boucher .05 .15
297 Dominik Hasek .15 .40
298 Brad May .07 .20
299 Craig Muni .05 .15
300 Derek Plante RC .10 .25
301 Craig Simpson .05 .15
302 Scott Thomas RC .10 .25
303 Ted Drury .05 .15
304 Dan Keczmer RC .05 .15
305 Trevor Kidd .07 .20
306 Sandy McCarthy .05 .15
307 Frank Musil .05 .15
308 Michel Petit .05 .15
309 Paul Ranheim .05 .15
310 German Titov RC .10 .25
311 Andrei Trefilov .05 .15
312 Jeff Hackett .05 .15
313 Stephane Matteau .05 .15
314 Brian Noonan .05 .15
315 Patrick Poulin .05 .15
316 Jeff Shantz RC .05 .15
317 Rich Sutter .05 .15
318 Kevin Todd .05 .15
319 Eric Weinrich .05 .15
320 Dave Barr .05 .15
321 Paul Cavallini .05 .15
322 Mike Craig .05 .15
323 Dean Evason .05 .15
324 Brent Gilchrist .05 .15
325 Grant Ledyard .05 .15
326 Mike McPhee .05 .15
327 Darcy Wakaluk .05 .15
328 Terry Carkner .05 .15
329 Mark Howe .10 .25
330 Greg Johnson .05 .15
331 Slava Kozlov .07 .20
332 Martin Lapointe .05 .15
333 Darren McCarty RC .15 .40
334 Chris Osgood RC .60 1.50
335 Bob Probert .10 .25
336 Mike Sillinger .05 .15
337 Jason Arnott RC .20 .50
338 Bob Beers .05 .15
339 Fred Brathwaite RC .10 .25
340 Kelly Buchberger .05 .15
341 Ilya Byakin RC .05 .15
342 Fredrik Olausson .05 .15
343 Vladimir Vujtek .05 .15
344 Peter White RC .05 .15
345 Stu Barnes .05 .15
346 Mike Foligno .05 .15
347 Greg Hawgood .05 .15
348 Bob Kudelski .05 .15
349 Rob Niedermayer .07 .20
350 Igor Chibirev RC .05 .15
351 Robert Kron .05 .15
352 Bryan Marchment .05 .15
353 James Patrick .05 .15
354 Chris Pronger .10 .25

355 Jeff Reese .05 .15
356 Jim Storm RC .05 .15
357 Darren Turcotte .05 .15
358 Pat Conacher .05 .15
359 Mike Donnelly .05 .15
360 John Druce .05 .15
361 Charlie Huddy .05 .15
362 Warren Rychel .05 .15
363 Robb Stauber .05 .15
364 Dave Taylor .05 .15
365 Dixon Ward .05 .15
366 Benoit Brunet .05 .15
367 J.J. Daigneault .05 .15
368 Gilbert Dionne .05 .15
369 Paul DiPietro .05 .15
370 Kevin Haller .05 .15
371 Oleg Petrov .05 .15
372 Peter Popovic RC .10 .25
373 Ron Wilson .05 .15
374 Martin Brodeur .25 .60
375 Tom Chorske .05 .15
376 Jim Dowd RC .10 .25
377 David Emma .05 .15
378 Bobby Holik .05 .15
379 Corey Millen .05 .15
380 Jaroslav Modry RC .10 .25
381 Jason Smith RC .05 .15
382 Ray Ferraro .05 .15
383 Travis Green .07 .20
384 Tom Kurvers .05 .15
385 Marty McInnis .05 .15
386 Jamie McLennan RC .05 .15
387 Dennis Vaske .05 .15
388 Dave Volek .05 .15
389 Jeff Beukeboom .05 .15
390 Glenn Healy .07 .20
391 Alexander Karpovtsev .05 .15
392 Steve Larmer .07 .20
393 Kevin Lowe .05 .15
394 Ed Olczyk .05 .15
395 Esa Tikkanen .05 .15
396 Alexandre Daigle .05 .15
397 Evgeny Davydov .05 .15
398 Dmitri Filimonov .05 .15
399 Brian Glynn .05 .15
400 Darrin Madeley RC .10 .25
401 Troy Mallette .05 .15
402 Dave McLlwain .05 .15
403 Alexei Yashin .07 .20
404 Jason Bowen RC .05 .15
405 Jeff Finley .05 .15
406 Yves Racine .05 .15
407 Rob Ramage .05 .15
408 Mikael Renberg .10 .25
409 Dominic Roussel .07 .20
410 Dave Tippett .05 .15
411 Doug Brown .05 .15
412 Markus Naslund .10 .25
413 Pat Neaton RC .10 .25
414 Kjell Samuelsson .05 .15
415 Martin Straka .05 .15
416 Bryan Trottier .10 .25
417 Ken Wregget .05 .15
418 Adam Foote .05 .15
419 Iain Fraser RC .10 .25
420 Alexei Gusarov .05 .15
421 Dave Karpa .05 .15
422 Claude Lapointe .05 .15
423 Curtis Leschyshyn .05 .15
424 Mike McKee RC .05 .15
425 Garth Snow RC .05 .15
426 Jocelyn Thibault RC .10 .25
427 Phil Housley .07 .20
428 Jim Hrivnak .05 .15
429 Vitali Karamnov .05 .15
430 Basil McRae .05 .15
431 Jim Montgomery RC .10 .25
432 Vitali Prokhorov .05 .15
433 Gaetan Duchesne .05 .15
434 Todd Elik .05 .15
435 Bob Errey .05 .15
436 Igor Larionov .05 .15
437 Mike Rathje .05 .15
438 Jim Waite .07 .20
439 Ray Whitney .05 .15
440 Mikael Andersson .05 .15
441 Danton Cole .05 .15
442 Pat Elynuik .05 .15
443 Chris Gratton .07 .20
444 Pat Jablonski .05 .15
445 Chris Joseph .05 .15
446 Chris LiPuma RC .05 .15
447 Denis Savard .10 .25
448 Ken Baumgartner .05 .15
449 Todd Gill .05 .15
450 Sylvain Lefebvre .05 .15
451 Jamie Macoun .05 .15
452 Mark Osborne .05 .15
453 Rob Pearson .05 .15
454 Damian Rhodes RC .10 .25
455 Peter Zezel .05 .15
456 Dave Babych .05 .15
457 Jose Charbonneau RC .10 .25
458 Murray Craven .05 .15
459 Neil Eisenhut RC .10 .25
460 Dan Kesa RC .10 .25
461 Gino Odjick .05 .15
462 Kay Whitmore .05 .15
463 Don Beaupre .07 .20
464 Randy Burridge .05 .15
465 Calle Johansson .05 .15
466 Keith Jones .05 .15
467 Todd Krygier .05 .15
468 Kelly Miller .05 .15
469 Pat Peake .05 .15
470 Dave Poulin .05 .15
471 Luciano Borsato .05 .15
472 Nelson Emerson .05 .15
473 Randy Gilhen .05 .15
474 Boris Mironov .05 .15
475 Stephane Quintal .05 .15
476 Thomas Steen .05 .15
477 Igor Ulanov .07 .20
478 Adrian Aucoin RC .10 .25
479 Todd Brost RC .10 .25
480 Martin Gendron RC .07 .20
481 David Harlock .07 .20
482 Corey Hirsch .07 .20
483 Todd Hlushko RC .07 .20
484 Fabian Joseph RC .07 .20
485 Paul Kariya .40 1.00
486 Brett Lindros RC .15 .40
487 Ken Lovsin RC .07 .20
488 Jason Marshall .07 .20
489 Derek Mayer RC .05 .15
490 Petr Nedved .05 .15
491 Dwayne Norris RC .05 .15
492 Russ Romaniuk .05 .15
493 Brian Savage RC .10 .25
494 Trevor Sim RC .10 .25
495 Chris Therien RC .10 .25
496 Todd Warriner RC .10 .25
497 Craig Woodcroft RC .10 .25
498 Mark Beaufait RC .10 .25
499 Jim Campbell .07 .20
500 Ted Crowley RC .10 .25
501 Mike Dunham .07 .20
502 Chris Ferraro RC .07 .20
503 Peter Ferraro .07 .20
504 Brett Hauer RC .07 .20
505 Darby Hendrickson RC .07 .20
506 Chris Imes RC .07 .20
507 Craig Johnson RC .07 .20
508 Peter Laviolette RC .07 .20
509 Jeff Lazaro .07 .20
510 John Lilley RC .07 .20
511 Todd Marchant .07 .20
512 Ian Moran RC .07 .20
513 Travis Richards RC .07 .20
514 Barry Richter RC .07 .20
515 David Roberts RC .07 .20
516 Brian Rolston .07 .20
517 David Sacco RC .07 .20
518 Checklist .05 .15
519 Checklist .05 .15
520 Checklist .05 .15

1993-94 PowerPlay Gamebreakers

COMPLETE SET (10) 10.00 20.00
1 Sergei Fedorov .60 1.50
2 Doug Gilmour .20 .50
3 Wayne Gretzky 2.50 6.00
4 Curtis Joseph .40 1.00
5 Mario Lemieux 2.00 5.00
6 Eric Lindros .40 1.00
7 Felix Potvin .40 1.00
8 Jeremy Roenick .50 1.25
9 Patrick Roy 2.00 5.00
10 Steve Yzerman 2.00 5.00

1993-94 PowerPlay Global Greats

COMPLETE SET (10) 3.00 8.00
1 Pavel Bure .50 1.25
2 Sergei Fedorov .50 1.25
3 Jaromir Jagr .75 2.00
4 Jari Kurri .40 1.00
5 Alexander Mogilny .25 .60
6 Mikael Renberg .10 .30
7 Teemu Selanne .50 1.25
8 Mats Sundin .50 1.25
9 Esa Tikkanen .10 .30
10 Alexei Yashin .10 .30

1993-94 PowerPlay Netminders

COMPLETE SET (8) 10.00 25.00
1 Tom Barrasso .75 2.00
2 Ed Belfour 1.50 4.00
3 Grant Fuhr .75 2.00
4 Curtis Joseph 1.50 4.00
5 Felix Potvin 1.50 4.00
6 Bill Ranford .75 2.00
7 Patrick Roy 4.00 10.00
8 Tommy Soderstrom .75 2.00

1993-94 PowerPlay Point Leaders

COMPLETE SET (20) 8.00 20.00
1 Pavel Bure .40 1.00
2 Doug Gilmour .20 .50
3 Wayne Gretzky 2.00 5.00
4 Brett Hull .50 1.25
5 Jaromir Jagr .60 1.50
6 Joe Juneau .10 .30
7 Pat LaFontaine .20 .50
8 Mario Lemieux 1.50 4.00
9 Mark Messier .40 1.00
10 Alexander Mogilny .20 .50
11 Adam Oates .20 .50
12 Mark Recchi .20 .50
13 Luc Robitaille .20 .50
14 Jeremy Roenick .50 1.25
15 Joe Sakic .75 2.00
16 Teemu Selanne .40 1.00
17 Kevin Stevens .10 .30
18 Mats Sundin .40 1.00
19 Pierre Turgeon .20 .50
20 Steve Yzerman 1.50 4.00

1993-94 PowerPlay Rising Stars

COMPLETE SET (10) 4.00 10.00
1 Arturs Irbe .30 .75
2 Slava Kozlov .30 .75
3 Felix Potvin 2.00 5.00
4 Keith Primeau .30 .75
5 Robert Reichel .30 .75
6 Geoff Sanderson .30 .75
7 Martin Straka .30 .75
8 Keith Tkachuk .75 2.00
9 Alexei Zhamnov .30 .75
10 Sergei Zubov .40 1.00

1993-94 PowerPlay Rookie Standouts

COMPLETE SET (16) 3.00 8.00
1 Jason Arnott .40 1.00
2 Jesse Belanger .10 .30
3 Alexandre Daigle .10 .30
4 Iain Fraser .10 .30
5 Chris Gratton .10 .30
6 Boris Mironov .10 .30
7 Jaroslav Modry .10 .30
8 Rob Niedermayer .25 .60
9 Chris Osgood .75 2.00
10 Pat Peake .10 .30
11 Derek Plante .10 .30
12 Chris Pronger .75 2.00
13 Mikael Renberg .10 .30
14 Bryan Smolinski .10 .30
15 Jocelyn Thibault .40 1.00
16 Alexei Yashin .10 .30

1993-94 PowerPlay Second Year Stars

COMPLETE SET (12) 6.00 12.00
1 Rob Gaudreau .10 .25
2 Joe Juneau .20 .50
3 Darius Kasparaitis .10 .25
4 Dmitri Kvartalnov .10 .25
5 Eric Lindros .60 1.50
6 Vladimir Malakhov .10 .25
7 Shawn McEachern .10 .25
8 Felix Potvin .60 1.50
9 Patrick Poulin .10 .25
10 Teemu Selanne .60 1.50
11 Tommy Soderstrom .20 .50
12 Alexei Zhamnov .20 .50

1993-94 PowerPlay Slapshot Artists

COMPLETE SET (10) 8.00 20.00
1 Dave Andreychuk .40 1.00
2 Ray Bourque 1.50 4.00
3 Sergei Fedorov 1.25 3.00
4 Brett Hull 1.25 3.00
5 Al Iafrate .40 1.00
6 Brian Leetch .60 1.50
7 Al MacInnis .60 1.50
8 Mike Modano 1.50 4.00
9 Teemu Selanne 1.25 3.00
10 Brendan Shanahan 1.25 3.00

2017 PPG Paints Pittsburgh Penguins 50 Years

NNO1 Syl Apps 3.00 8.00
NNO2 Tom Barrasso 3.00 8.00
NNO3 Andy Bathgate 3.00 8.00
NNO4 Les Binkley 3.00 8.00
NNO5 Michel Briere 3.00 8.00
NNO6 Randy Carlyle 3.00 8.00
NNO7 Paul Coffey 3.00 8.00
NNO8 Sidney Crosby 6.00 15.00
NNO9 Marc-Andre Fleury 3.00 8.00
NNO10 Ron Francis 3.00 8.00
NNO11 Jaromir Jagr 3.00 8.00
NNO12 Darius Kasparaitis 3.00 8.00
NNO13 Rick Kehoe 3.00 8.00
NNO14 Phil Kessel 3.00 8.00
NNO15 Pierre Larouche 3.00 8.00
NNO16 Mario Lemieux 6.00 15.00
NNO17 Kris Letang 3.00 8.00
NNO18 Evgeni Malkin 3.00 8.00
NNO19 Joe Mullen 3.00 8.00
NNO20 Matt Murray 3.00 8.00
NNO21 Jean Pronovost 3.00 8.00
NNO22 Ulf Samuelsson 3.00 8.00
NNO23 Martin Straka 3.00 8.00
NNO24 Max Talbot 3.00 8.00
NNO25 Bryan Trottier 3.00 8.00

1998-99 Predators Team Issue

COMPLETE SET (25) 8.00 20.00
1 Blair Atcheynum .30 .75
2 Drake Berehowsky .30 .75
3 Sebastien Bordeleau .30 .75
4 Joel Bouchard .30 .75
5 Bob Boughner .40 1.00
6 Andrew Brunette .40 1.00
7 Patrick Cote .40 1.00
8 Mike Dunham .75 2.00
9 Eric Fichaud .40 1.00
10 Tom Fitzgerald .30 .75
11 Jamie Heward .30 .75
12 Greg Johnson .30 .75
13 Patric Kjellberg .30 .75
14 Sergei Krivokrasov .30 .75
15 Denny Lambert .30 .75
16 Jayson More .30 .75
17 Ville Peltonen .40 1.00
18 Cliff Ronning .40 1.00
19 John Slaney .30 .75
20 Kimmo Timonen .30 .75
21 Darren Turcotte .30 .75
22 Tomas Vokoun .60 1.50
23 Jan Vopat .30 .75
24 Scott Walker .40 1.00
25 Vitali Yachmenev .30 .75

2002-03 Predators Team Issue

1 Brent Gilchrist 1.25 3.00
2 Scott Hartnell 2.50 6.00
3 Greg Johnson 1.50 4.00
4 Domenic Pittis 1.25 3.00
5 Kimmo Timonen 1.50 4.00
6 Vitali Yachmenev 1.25 3.00

2010-11 Prestige Player of the Day

COMPLETE SET (7) 10.00 20.00
*GOLD/160: .6X TO 1.5X BASIC CARDS
PODAO Alex Ovechkin 2.50 6.00
PODJS Jeff Skinner 1.25 3.00
PODRM Ryan Miller .60 1.50
PODSC Sidney Crosby 2.50 6.00
PODSS Steven Stamkos 1.25 3.00
PODTH Taylor Hall 1.25 3.00
PODTS Tyler Seguin 1.50 4.00

2000-01 Private Stock

1 Guy Hebert .15 .40
2 Paul Kariya .20 .50
3 Teemu Selanne .40 1.00
4 Ray Ferraro .12 .30
5 Damian Rhodes .12 .30
6 Patrik Stefan .15 .40
7 Byron Dafoe .15 .40
8 Sergei Samsonov .15 .40
9 Joe Thornton .30 .75
10 Maxim Afinogenov .12 .30
11 Doug Gilmour .25 .60
12 Dominik Hasek .30 .75
13 Miroslav Satan .12 .30
14 Fred Brathwaite .15 .40
15 Valeri Bure .15 .40
16 Ron Francis .25 .60
17 Arturs Irbe .15 .40
18 Sami Kapanen .12 .30
19 Tony Amonte .15 .40
20 Jocelyn Thibault .15 .40
21 Alexei Zhamnov .15 .40
22 Ray Bourque .30 .75
23 Peter Forsberg .40 1.00
24 Milan Hejduk .15 .40
25 Patrick Roy .50 1.25
26 Joe Sakic .40 1.00
27 Marc Denis .15 .40
28 Ted Drury .12 .30
29 Geoff Sanderson .15 .40
30 Ed Belfour .20 .50
31 Brett Hull .40 1.00
32 Mike Modano .30 .75
33 Brenden Morrow .15 .40
34 Joe Nieuwendyk .15 .40
35 Sergei Fedorov .30 .75
36 Chris Osgood .20 .50
37 Brendan Shanahan .20 .50
38 Steve Yzerman .50 1.25
39 Tommy Salo .15 .40
40 Ryan Smyth .15 .40
41 Doug Weight .20 .50
42 Pavel Bure .20 .50
43 Trevor Kidd .12 .30
44 Viktor Kozlov .15 .40
45 Stephane Fiset .12 .30
46 Zigmund Palffy .20 .50
47 Luc Robitaille .20 .50
48 Manny Fernandez .12 .30
49 Sergei Krivokrasov .12 .30
50 Stacy Roest .12 .30
51 Saku Koivu .20 .50
52 Trevor Linden .20 .50
53 Jose Theodore .20 .50
54 Mike Dunham .12 .30
55 David Legwand .20 .50
56 Jason Arnott .15 .40
57 Martin Brodeur .50 1.25
58 Patrik Elias .20 .50
59 Scott Gomez .15 .40
60 Petr Sykora .15 .40
61 Tim Connolly .12 .30
62 Mariusz Czerkawski .12 .30
63 John Vanbiesbrouck .12 .30
64 Theo Fleury .25 .60
65 Brian Leetch .15 .40
66 Mark Messier .40 1.00
67 Mike Richter .15 .40
68 Daniel Alfredsson .20 .50
69 Radek Bonk .15 .40
70 Marian Hossa .20 .50
71 Brian Boucher .15 .40
72 Simon Gagne .20 .50
73 John LeClair .20 .50
74 Eric Lindros .30 .75
75 Nikolai Khabibulin .30 .75
76 Jeremy Roenick .30 .75
77 Keith Tkachuk .20 .50
78 Jean-Sebastien Aubin .15 .40
79 Jan Hrdina .12 .30
80 Jaromir Jagr .60 1.50
81 Martin Straka .15 .40
82 Pavol Demitra .25 .60
83 Al MacInnis .25 .60
84 Chris Pronger .20 .50
85 Roman Turek .15 .40
86 Pierre Turgeon .15 .40
87 Vincent Damphousse .15 .40
88 Jeff Friesen .12 .30
89 Owen Nolan .20 .50
90 Dan Cloutier .15 .40
91 Vincent Lecavalier .20 .50
92 Nikolai Antropov .15 .40
93 Curtis Joseph .25 .60
94 Mats Sundin .20 .50
95 Steve Kariya .12 .30
96 Markus Naslund .20 .50
97 Felix Potvin .30 .75
98 Jeff Halpern .12 .30
99 Olaf Kolzig .20 .50
100 Adam Oates .20 .50
101 Jonas Ronnqvist RC 3.00 8.00
102 Samuel Pahlsson 3.00 8.00
103 Andrew Raycroft RC 8.00 20.00
104 Eric Boulton RC 3.00 8.00
105 Dimitri Kalinin 3.00 8.00
106 Mika Noronen 3.00 8.00
107 Oleg Saprykin 3.00 8.00
108 Josef Vasicek RC 8.00 20.00
109 Shane Willis 3.00 8.00
110 Steven McCarthy 3.00 8.00
111 David Aebischer RC 6.00 15.00
112 Serge Aubin RC 4.00 10.00
113 Rostislav Klesla RC 8.00 20.00
114 David Vyborny 3.00 8.00
115 Tyler Bouck RC 3.00 8.00
116 Richard Jackman 3.00 8.00
117 Marty Turco RC 6.00 15.00
118 Dan Lacouture 3.00 8.00
119 Brian Swanson RC 3.00 8.00
120 Denis Shvidki 3.00 8.00
121 Eric Belanger RC 4.00 10.00
122 Steven Reinprecht RC 5.00 12.00
123 Lubomir Visnovsky RC 6.00 15.00
124 Manny Fernandez 3.00 8.00
125 Marian Gaborik RC 10.00 25.00
126 Filip Kuba 3.00 8.00
127 Maxim Sushinski 3.00 8.00
128 Andrei Markov 6.00 15.00
129 Scott Hartnell RC 8.00 20.00
130 Colin White RC 3.00 8.00
131 Taylor Pyatt 3.00 8.00
132 Martin Havlat RC 10.00 25.00
133 Jani Hurme RC 3.00 8.00
134 Karel Rachunek 3.00 8.00
135 Maxime Ouellet 5.00 12.00
136 Justin Williams RC 8.00 20.00
137 Robert Esche 3.00 8.00
138 Wyatt Smith 3.00 8.00
139 Ossi Vaananen RC 4.00 10.00
140 Brent Johnson 4.00 10.00
141 Ladislav Nagy 3.00 8.00
142 Mike Van Ryn 3.00 8.00
143 Bryce Salvador RC 4.00 10.00
144 Evgeni Nabokov 4.00 10.00
145 Alexander Kharitonov RC 3.00 8.00
146 Brad Richards 5.00 12.00
147 Petr Svoboda RC 4.00 10.00
148 Daniel Sedin 6.00 15.00
149 Henrik Sedin 6.00 15.00
150 Kris Beech 3.00 8.00
151 Rick DiPietro RC 6.00 15.00
152 Mario Lemieux 2.50 6.00

2000-01 Private Stock Gold

*GOLD.VET/75: 2X TO 5X BASIC
*GOLD.RC/75: .5X TO 1.2X BASIC
152 Mario Lemieux 40.00 100.00

2000-01 Private Stock Premiere Date

*1-100 VETS/60: 8X TO 20X BASIC CARDS
*101-152 SP VET/60 101-151: .6X TO 1.5X SP/155
*101-152 ROOK/60: .4X TO 1X SP RC/155
66 Mark Messier 10.00 25.00

2000-01 Private Stock Retail

*1-100 VETS: .4X TO 1X BASIC CARDS
*101-150 SP/230: .25X TO .6X SP/155
66 Mark Messier .50 1.25

2000-01 Private Stock Silver

*1-100 VETS/120: 5X TO 12X BASIC CARDS
*101-152 SP VET/120 101-151: .4X TO 1X SP/155
*101-152 ROOK/120: .3X TO .8X SP RC/155
66 Mark Messier 6.00 15.00

2000-01 Private Stock Artist's Canvas

1 Paul Kariya 1.50 4.00
2 Teemu Selanne 3.00 8.00
3 Joe Thornton 2.50 6.00
4 Maxim Afinogenov 1.00 2.50
5 Dominik Hasek 2.50 6.00
6 Peter Forsberg 3.00 8.00
7 Patrick Roy 4.00 10.00
8 Joe Sakic 3.00 8.00
9 Brett Hull 3.00 8.00
10 Mike Modano 2.50 6.00
11 Brendan Shanahan 1.50 4.00
12 Steve Yzerman 4.00 10.00
13 Pavel Bure 1.50 4.00
14 Martin Brodeur 4.00 10.00
15 Mark Messier 3.00 8.00
16 John LeClair 1.50 4.00
17 Jeremy Roenick 2.50 6.00
18 Jaromir Jagr 5.00 12.00
19 Vincent Lecavalier 1.50 4.00
20 Curtis Joseph 2.00 5.00

2000-01 Private Stock Extreme Action

1 Paul Kariya .75 2.00
2 Teemu Selanne 1.50 4.00
3 Dominik Hasek 1.25 3.00
4 Patrick Roy 2.00 5.00
5 Joe Sakic 1.50 4.00
6 Ed Belfour .75 2.00
7 Brett Hull 1.50 4.00
8 Mike Modano 1.25 3.00
9 Steve Yzerman 2.00 5.00
10 Luc Robitaille .75 2.00
11 Trevor Linden .75 2.00
12 Petr Sykora .60 1.50
13 Martin Brodeur 4.00 10.00
14 Tim Connolly .50 1.25
15 John LeClair .75 2.00
16 Eric Lindros 1.25 3.00
17 Jeremy Roenick 1.25 3.00
18 Jaromir Jagr 2.50 6.00
19 Vincent Lecavalier .75 2.00
20 Curtis Joseph 1.00 2.50

2000-01 Private Stock Game Gear

1 Guy Hebert J 3.00 8.00
2 Marty McInnis J 3.00 8.00
3 Teemu Selanne J 8.00 20.00
4 Shawn Bates J 2.50 6.00
5 Paul Coffey S 4.00 10.00
6 Paul Coffey J/S 4.00 10.00
7 Bill Guerin S 4.00 10.00
8 Sergei Samsonov J 3.00 8.00
9 Dominik Hasek S 6.00 15.00
10 Jay McKee J/S 2.50 6.00
11 Jarome Iginla J 5.00 12.00
12 Rod Brind'Amour S 4.00 10.00
13 Kevin Hatcher S 2.50 6.00
14 Sandis Ozolinsh S 2.50 6.00
15 Tony Amonte J 3.00 8.00
16 Eric Daze J 3.00 8.00
17 Alexei Zhamnov J 3.00 8.00
18 Ray Bourque J 6.00 15.00
19 Ray Bourque S 6.00 15.00
20 Greg DeVries J 2.50 6.00
21 Chris Dingman J 2.50 6.00
22 Chris Drury S 3.00 8.00
23 Adam Foote S 3.00 8.00
24 Peter Forsberg S 8.00 20.00
25 Peter Forsberg J/S 8.00 20.00
26 Eric Messier J 2.50 6.00
27 Aaron Miller J 2.50 6.00
28 Patrick Roy S 10.00 25.00
29 Joe Sakic J/S 8.00 20.00
30 Joe Sakic S 8.00 20.00
31 Martin Skoula S 3.00 8.00
32 Alex Tanguay S 3.00 8.00
33 Marc Denis S 3.00 8.00
34 Ed Belfour S 4.00 10.00
35 Derian Hatcher J 3.00 8.00
36 Derian Hatcher J 3.00 8.00
37 Jamie Langenbrunner J 3.00 8.00
38 Jere Lehtinen J 3.00 8.00
39 Mike Modano J 6.00 15.00
40 Darryl Sydor J 3.00 8.00
41 Darryl Sydor J 3.00 8.00
42 Sergei Zubov J 3.00 8.00
43 Chris Chelios S 4.00 10.00
44 Sergei Fedorov J 6.00 15.00
45 Nicklas Lidstrom J 4.00 10.00
46 Chris Osgood J 4.00 10.00
47 Brendan Shanahan J 4.00 10.00
48 Anson Carter J 3.00 8.00
49 Tommy Salo S 3.00 8.00
50 Doug Weight J 4.00 10.00
51 Olli Jokinen S 3.00 8.00
52 Roberto Luongo J 6.00 15.00
53 Scott Mellanby S 2.50 6.00
54 Rob Blake S 4.00 10.00
55 Zigmund Palffy S 4.00 10.00
56 Jeff Hackett J 2.50 6.00
57 Saku Koivu J 4.00 10.00
58 Trevor Linden S 4.00 10.00
59 Brian Savage S 2.50 6.00
60 Eric Weinrich S 2.50 6.00
61 Dainius Zubrus J 2.50 6.00
62 Cliff Ronning S 2.50 6.00
63 Bobby Holik J 2.50 6.00
64 Scott Niedermayer J 4.00 10.00
65 Petr Sykora J 3.00 8.00
66 Chris Terreri J 2.50 6.00
67 Zdeno Chara J 4.00 10.00
68 Tim Connolly S 2.50 6.00
69 Mariusz Czerkawski J 2.50 6.00
70 Claude LaPointe J 2.50 6.00
71 Mats Lindgren J 2.50 6.00
72 John Vanbiesbrouck J 4.00 10.00
73 Adam Graves S 3.00 8.00
74 Valeri Kamensky S 2.50 6.00
75 Brian Leetch J 3.00 8.00
76 Brian Leetch J/S 3.00 8.00
77 Mark Messier J 8.00 20.00
78 Mike Richter J 4.00 10.00
79 Mike Richter J 4.00 10.00
80 Andreas Dackell J 2.50 6.00
81 Eric Desjardins J 3.00 8.00
82 Daymond Langkow J 2.50 6.00
83 John LeClair J 4.00 10.00
84 Eric Lindros J 6.00 15.00
85 Eric Lindros S 6.00 15.00
86 Rick Tocchet S 3.00 8.00
87 Shane Doan J 3.00 8.00
88 Radoslav Suchy J 2.50 6.00
89 Jaromir Jagr J 12.00 30.00
90 Dallas Drake J 2.50 6.00
91 Vincent Damphousse J 3.00 8.00
92 Vincent Damphousse J/S 3.00 8.00
93 Vincent Lecavalier S 4.00 10.00
94 Petr Svoboda J 3.00 8.00
95 Shayne Corson J 3.00 8.00
96 Curtis Joseph S 5.00 12.00
97 Yanic Perreault S 2.50 6.00
98 Gary Roberts S 2.50 6.00
99 Mats Sundin J 4.00 10.00
100 Craig Berube S 2.50 6.00
101 Peter Bondra J 4.00 10.00
102 Sylvain Cote S 2.50 6.00
103 Ulf Dahlen J 2.50 6.00
104 Olaf Kolzig J/S 4.00 10.00
105 Adam Oates S 4.00 10.00

2000-01 Private Stock Game Gear Patches

*PATCH/17-417: .6X TO 1.5X BASIC INSERTS
1 Guy Hebert/164 5.00 12.00
2 Marty McInnis/156 5.00 12.00
3 Teemu Selanne/202 12.00 30.00
4 Shawn Bates/156 4.00 10.00
8 Sergei Samsonov/101 5.00 12.00
10 Jay McKee/161 4.00 10.00
11 Jarome Iginla/94 8.00 20.00
15 Tony Amonte/134 5.00 12.00
16 Eric Daze/177 5.00 12.00
17 Alexei Zhamnov/142 5.00 12.00
18 Ray Bourque/39 125.00 300.00
20 Greg DeVries/184 4.00 10.00
21 Chris Dingman/163 4.00 10.00
26 Eric Messier/121 4.00 10.00
27 Aaron Miller/202 4.00 10.00
35 Derian Hatcher/172 5.00 12.00
36 Derian Hatcher/184 5.00 12.00
37 Jamie Langenbrunner/178 5.00 12.00
38 Jere Lehtinen/151 5.00 12.00
39 Mike Modano/417 10.00 25.00
40 Darryl Sydor/41 15.00 40.00
41 Darryl Sydor/88 15.00 40.00
42 Sergei Zubov/220 5.00 12.00
44 Sergei Fedorov/175 10.00 25.00
45 Nicklas Lidstrom/193 6.00 15.00
46 Chris Osgood/143 6.00 15.00
47 Brendan Shanahan/17 25.00 60.00
48 Anson Carter/190 5.00 12.00
50 Doug Weight/162 6.00 15.00
52 Roberto Luongo/183 10.00 25.00
56 Jeff Hackett/149 4.00 10.00
57 Saku Koivu/28 60.00 150.00
61 Dainius Zubrus/172 4.00 10.00
63 Bobby Holik/144 4.00 10.00
64 Scott Niedermayer/119 6.00 15.00
65 Petr Sykora/247 5.00 12.00
66 Chris Terreri/149 4.00 10.00
67 Zdeno Chara/149 6.00 15.00
69 Mariusz Czerkawski/169 4.00 10.00
70 Claude LaPointe/137 4.00 10.00
71 Mats Lindgren/166 4.00 10.00
72 John Vanbiesbrouck/108 6.00 15.00
75 Brian Leetch/122 5.00 12.00
77 Mark Messier/67 20.00 50.00
78 Mike Richter/184 6.00 15.00
79 Mike Richter/193 6.00 15.00
80 Andreas Dackell/175 4.00 10.00
81 Eric Desjardins/20 12.00 30.00
82 Daymond Langkow/77 15.00 40.00
83 John LeClair/158 6.00 15.00
84 Eric Lindros 15.00 40.00
87 Shane Doan/92 15.00 40.00
88 Radoslav Suchy/125 4.00 10.00
89 Jaromir Jagr/388 20.00 50.00
90 Dallas Drake/180 4.00 10.00
94 Petr Svoboda/227 5.00 12.00
95 Shayne Corson/165 5.00 12.00
99 Mats Sundin/103 6.00 15.00
101 Peter Bondra/190 6.00 15.00
103 Ulf Dahlen/183 4.00 10.00

2000-01 Private Stock PS-2001 Action

1 Paul Kariya .50 1.25
2 Teemu Selanne 1.00 2.50
3 Sergei Samsonov .40 1.00
4 Joe Thornton .75 2.00
5 Maxim Afinogenov .30 .75
6 Doug Gilmour .60 1.50
7 Dominik Hasek .75 2.00
8 Ray Bourque .75 2.00
9 Chris Drury .40 1.00
10 Peter Forsberg 1.00 2.50
11 Milan Hejduk .40 1.00
12 Patrick Roy 1.25 3.00
13 Joe Sakic 1.00 2.50
14 Alex Tanguay .40 1.00
15 Marc Denis .40 1.00
16 Ed Belfour .50 1.25
17 Brett Hull 1.00 2.50
18 Mike Modano .75 2.00
19 Chris Chelios .50 1.25
20 Sergei Fedorov .75 2.00
21 Chris Osgood .50 1.25
22 Brendan Shanahan .50 1.25
23 Steve Yzerman 1.25 3.00
24 Doug Weight .50 1.25
25 Pavel Bure .50 1.25
26 Zigmund Palffy .50 1.25
27 Luc Robitaille .50 1.25
28 Saku Koivu .50 1.25
29 Jose Theodore .50 1.25
30 David Legwand .50 1.25
31 Martin Brodeur 1.25 3.00
32 Patrik Elias .50 1.25
33 Scott Gomez .40 1.00
34 Petr Sykora .40 1.00
35 Tim Connolly .30 .75
36 Theo Fleury .60 1.50
37 Brian Leetch .40 1.00
38 Mark Messier 1.00 2.50
39 Mike Richter .50 1.25
40 Marian Hossa .50 1.25
41 Brian Boucher .40 1.00
42 John LeClair .50 1.25
43 Eric Lindros .75 2.00
44 Jeremy Roenick .75 2.00
45 Keith Tkachuk .50 1.25
46 Jan Hrdina .30 .75
47 Jaromir Jagr 1.50 4.00
48 Martin Straka .40 1.00
49 Jeff Friesen .30 .75
50 Owen Nolan .50 1.25
51 Pavol Demitra .60 1.50
52 Chris Pronger .50 1.25
53 Pierre Turgeon .40 1.00
54 Vincent Lecavalier .50 1.25
55 Curtis Joseph .60 1.50
56 Mats Sundin .50 1.25
57 Steve Kariya .30 .75
58 Markus Naslund .50 1.25
59 Peter Bondra .50 1.25
60 Olaf Kolzig .50 1.25

2000-01 Private Stock PS-2001 New Wave

COMPLETE SET (26) 60.00 150.00
1 Patrik Stefan 2.50 6.00
2 Joe Thornton 5.00 12.00
3 Maxim Afinogenov 2.00 5.00
4 Sami Kapanen 2.00 5.00
5 Valeri Bure 2.50 6.00
6 Oleg Saprykin 2.00 5.00
7 Jocelyn Thibault 2.50 6.00
8 Milan Hejduk 2.50 6.00
9 Marc Denis 2.50 6.00
10 Brenden Morrow 2.50 6.00
11 Jose Theodore 3.00 8.00
12 David Legwand 3.00 8.00
13 Patrik Elias 3.00 8.00
14 Scott Gomez 2.50 6.00
15 Tim Connolly 2.00 5.00
16 Marian Hossa 3.00 8.00
17 Brian Boucher 2.50 6.00
18 Simon Gagne 3.00 8.00
19 Jean-Sebastien Aubin 2.50 6.00
20 Roman Turek 2.50 6.00
21 Jeff Friesen 2.00 5.00
22 Dan Cloutier 2.50 6.00
23 Vincent Lecavalier 3.00 8.00
24 Nikolai Antropov 2.50 6.00
25 Steve Kariya 2.00 5.00
26 Rick DiPietro 4.00 10.00

2000-01 Private Stock PS-2001 Rookies

1 Samuel Pahlsson 3.00 8.00
2 Andrew Raycroft 8.00 20.00
3 Dimitri Kalinin 3.00 8.00
4 Oleg Saprykin 3.00 8.00
5 Josef Vasicek 8.00 20.00
6 David Aebischer 6.00 15.00
7 David Vyborny 3.00 8.00
8 Marty Turco 6.00 15.00
9 Eric Belanger 4.00 10.00
10 Steven Reinprecht 5.00 12.00
11 Marian Gaborik 10.00 25.00
12 Andrei Markov 6.00 15.00
13 Colin White 3.00 8.00
14 Martin Havlat 10.00 25.00
15 Maxime Ouellet 5.00 12.00
16 Justin Williams 8.00 20.00
17 Wyatt Smith 3.00 8.00
18 Ossi Vaananen 4.00 10.00
19 Brent Johnson 4.00 10.00
20 Ladislav Nagy 3.00 8.00
21 Evgeni Nabokov 4.00 10.00
22 Alexander Kharitonov 3.00 8.00
23 Brad Richards 5.00 12.00
24 Daniel Sedin 6.00 15.00
25 Henrik Sedin 6.00 15.00
26 Rick DiPietro 6.00 15.00

2000-01 Private Stock PS-2001 Stars

1 Paul Kariya 3.00 8.00
2 Teemu Selanne 6.00 15.00
3 Sergei Samsonov 2.50 6.00
4 Dominik Hasek 5.00 12.00
5 Ray Bourque 5.00 12.00
6 Peter Forsberg 6.00 15.00
7 Patrick Roy 8.00 20.00
8 Joe Sakic 6.00 15.00
9 Brett Hull 6.00 15.00
10 Mike Modano 5.00 12.00

11 Sergei Fedorov 5.00 12.00
12 Brendan Shanahan 3.00 8.00
13 Steve Yzerman 8.00 20.00
14 Pavel Bure 3.00 8.00
15 Luc Robitaille 3.00 8.00
16 Saku Koivu 3.00 8.00
17 Martin Brodeur 8.00 20.00
18 Mark Messier 6.00 15.00
19 John LeClair 3.00 8.00
20 Eric Lindros 5.00 12.00
21 Jeremy Roenick 5.00 12.00
22 Jaromir Jagr 10.00 25.00
23 Pierre Turgeon 2.50 6.00
24 Curtis Joseph 4.00 10.00
25 Mats Sundin 3.00 8.00

2000-01 Private Stock Reserve

1 Paul Kariya 1.50 4.00
2 Teemu Selanne 3.00 8.00
3 Patrik Stefan 1.25 3.00
4 Dominik Hasek 2.50 6.00
5 Peter Forsberg 3.00 8.00
6 Patrick Roy 4.00 10.00
7 Joe Sakic 3.00 8.00
8 Mike Modano 2.50 6.00
9 Brendan Shanahan 1.50 4.00
10 Steve Yzerman 4.00 10.00
11 Pavel Bure 1.50 4.00
12 Saku Koivu 1.50 4.00
13 Scott Gomez 1.25 3.00
14 Martin Brodeur 4.00 10.00
15 Mark Messier 3.00 8.00
16 John LeClair 1.50 4.00
17 Eric Lindros 2.50 6.00
18 Jaromir Jagr 5.00 12.00
19 Vincent Lecavalier 1.50 4.00
20 Curtis Joseph 2.00 5.00

2001-02 Private Stock

1 Jeff Friesen .12 .30
2 Paul Kariya .20 .50
3 Milan Hnilicka .15 .40
4 Patrik Stefan .15 .40
5 Bill Guerin .20 .50
6 Sergei Samsonov .15 .40
7 Joe Thornton .30 .75
8 Martin Biron .15 .40
9 Tim Connolly .12 .30
10 J-P Dumont .12 .30
11 Jarome Iginla .25 .60
12 Marc Savard .12 .30
13 Roman Turek .15 .40
14 Ron Francis .25 .60
15 Arturs Irbe .15 .40
16 Jeff O'Neill .15 .40
17 Tony Amonte .15 .40
18 Steve Sullivan .12 .30
19 Jocelyn Thibault .15 .40
20 Rob Blake .20 .50
21 Chris Drury .15 .40
22 Milan Hejduk .15 .40
23 Patrick Roy .50 1.25
24 Joe Sakic .40 1.00
25 Alex Tanguay .15 .40
26 Espen Knutsen .12 .30
27 Ron Tugnutt .15 .40
28 Ed Belfour .20 .50
29 Mike Modano .30 .75
30 Joe Nieuwendyk .15 .40
31 Pierre Turgeon .15 .40
32 Sergei Fedorov .30 .75
33 Dominik Hasek .30 .75
34 Brett Hull .40 1.00
35 Nicklas Lidstrom .20 .50
36 Luc Robitaille .20 .50
37 Brendan Shanahan .20 .50
38 Steve Yzerman .50 1.25
39 Mike Comrie .15 .40
40 Tommy Salo .15 .40
41 Ryan Smyth .15 .40
42 Pavel Bure .20 .50
43 Roberto Luongo .30 .75
44 Jason Allison .15 .40
45 Zigmund Palffy .20 .50
46 Felix Potvin .30 .75
47 Manny Fernandez .12 .30
48 Marian Gaborik .20 .50
49 Yanic Perreault .12 .30
50 Brian Savage .12 .30
51 Jose Theodore .20 .50
52 Mike Dunham .15 .40
53 David Legwand .15 .40
54 Jason Arnott .15 .40
55 Martin Brodeur .50 1.25
56 Patrik Elias .20 .50
57 Scott Gomez .15 .40
58 Chris Osgood .20 .50
59 Michael Peca .15 .40
60 Alexei Yashin .15 .40
61 Theo Fleury .25 .60
62 Brian Leetch .15 .40
63 Eric Lindros .30 .75
64 Mark Messier .40 1.00
65 Mike Richter .20 .50
66 Daniel Alfredsson .20 .50
67 Martin Havlat .15 .40
68 Marian Hossa .20 .50
69 Patrick Lalime .15 .40
70 Roman Cechmanek .15 .40
71 Simon Gagne .20 .50
72 John LeClair .20 .50
73 Mark Recchi .25 .60
74 Jeremy Roenick .30 .75
75 Sean Burke .12 .30
76 Daymond Langkow .15 .40
77 Alexei Kovalev .15 .40
78 Mario Lemieux .75 2.00
79 Martin Straka .12 .30
80 Brent Johnson .15 .40
81 Chris Pronger .20 .50
82 Keith Tkachuk .20 .50
83 Doug Weight .20 .50
84 Patrick Marleau .20 .50
85 Evgeni Nabokov .15 .40
86 Owen Nolan .20 .50
87 Teemu Selanne .40 1.00
88 Vincent Lecavalier .20 .50
89 Brad Richards .20 .50
90 Curtis Joseph .25 .60
91 Alexander Mogilny .15 .40
92 Mats Sundin .20 .50
93 Dan Cloutier .15 .40
94 Markus Naslund .20 .50
95 Daniel Sedin .25 .60
96 Henrik Sedin .25 .60
97 Peter Bondra .20 .50
98 Jaromir Jagr .60 1.50
99 Olaf Kolzig .20 .50
100 Adam Oates .20 .50
101 Dany Heatley SP 3.00 8.00
102 Mark Bell SP 2.50 6.00
103 Rostislav Klesla SP 2.50 6.00
104 Jason Williams SP 2.50 6.00
105 Rick DiPietro SP 3.00 8.00
106 Pavel Brendl SP 2.50 6.00
107 Kris Beech SP 2.50 6.00
108 Johan Hedberg SP 3.00 8.00
109 Miikka Kiprusoff SP 4.00 10.00
110 Bryan Allen SP 2.50 6.00
111 Ilja Bryzgalov RC 6.00 15.00
112 Timo Parssinen RC 3.00 8.00
113 Ilya Kovalchuk RC 12.00 30.00
114 Kamil Piros RC 2.50 6.00
115 Brian Pothier RC 2.50 6.00
116 Jukka Hentunen RC 2.50 6.00
117 Erik Cole RC 5.00 12.00
118 Vaclav Nedorost RC 2.50 6.00
119 Niko Kapanen RC 4.00 10.00
120 Pavel Datsyuk RC 15.00 40.00
121 Jason Chimera RC 2.50 6.00
122 Niklas Hagman RC 3.00 8.00
123 Kristian Huselius RC 4.00 10.00
124 Jaroslav Bednar RC 2.50 6.00
125 Pascal Dupuis RC 4.00 10.00
126 Nick Schultz RC 2.50 6.00
127 Francis Belanger RC 3.00 8.00
128 Martin Erat RC 3.00 8.00
129 Scott Clemmensen RC 2.50 6.00
130 Radek Martinek RC 2.50 6.00
131 Dan Blackburn RC 3.00 8.00
132 Peter Smrek RC 2.50 6.00
133 Chris Neil RC 3.00 8.00
134 Jiri Dopita RC 2.50 6.00
135 David Cullen RC 2.50 6.00
136 Krystofer Kolanos RC 2.50 6.00
137 Jeff Jillson RC 2.50 6.00
138 Mark Rycroft RC 3.00 8.00
139 Nikita Alexeev RC 2.50 6.00
140 Brian Sutherby RC 2.50 6.00

2001-02 Private Stock Gold

*1-100 VETS/106: 5X TO 12X BASIC CARDS
*101-110 VETS/106: .5X TO 1.2X BASIC SP
*111-140 ROOKIE/106: .3X TO .8X RC

2001-02 Private Stock Premiere Date

*1-100 VETS/100: 5X TO 12X BASIC CARDS
*101-110 VETS/100: .5X TO 1.2X SP
*111-140 ROOKIES/100: .4X TO 1X RC

2001-02 Private Stock Retail

*1-100 VETS: .4X TO 1X HOBBY
*101-110 VETS: .3X TO .8X SP
*111-140 ROOKIE/450: .4X TO 1X HOB

2001-02 Private Stock Silver

*1-100 VETS/108: 5X TO 12X BASIC CARDS
*101-100 VETS/108: .5X TO 1.2X SP
*111-140 ROOKIES/108: .4X TO 1X RC

2001-02 Private Stock Game Gear

1 Jean-Sebastien Giguere 5.00 12.00
2 Paul Kariya 5.00 12.00
3 Mike Leclerc SP 3.00 8.00
4 Steve Rucchin 3.00 8.00
5 Oleg Tverdovsky 3.00 8.00
6 Ilya Kovalchuk STK/200 15.00 40.00
7 P.J. Axelsson 3.00 8.00
8 Byron Dafoe 5.00 12.00
9 Stu Barnes SP 3.00 8.00
10 J-P Dumont 3.00 8.00
11 Jay McKee SP 3.00 8.00
12 Rob Ray 3.00 8.00
13 Richard Smehlik SP 3.00 8.00
14 Craig Conroy 3.00 8.00
15 Jarome Iginla 6.00 15.00
16 Marc Savard 3.00 8.00
17 Roman Turek 5.00 12.00
18 Rod Brind'Amour STK/200 10.00 25.00
19 Jeff O'Neill STK/200 10.00 25.00
20 Tony Amonte 5.00 12.00
21 Kyle Calder 3.00 8.00
22 Eric Daze SP 3.00 8.00
23 Boris Mironov 3.00 8.00
24 Michael Nylander 3.00 8.00
25 Steve Sullivan 3.00 8.00
26 Jocelyn Thibault 5.00 12.00
27 Alexei Zhamnov 3.00 8.00
28 Chris Drury STK/200 10.00 25.00
29 Peter Forsberg SP 12.50 30.00
30 Patrick Roy SP 12.50 30.00
31 Joe Sakic 8.00 20.00
32 Grant Marshall SP 3.00 8.00
33 Blake Sloan SP 3.00 8.00
34 Ed Belfour 5.00 12.00
35 Derian Hatcher 3.00 8.00
36 Jamie Langenbrunner 3.00 8.00
37 Mike Modano 8.00 20.00
38 Joe Nieuwendyk 5.00 12.00
39 Darryl Sydor 3.00 8.00
40 Pierre Turgeon 5.00 12.00
41 Sergei Zubov 3.00 8.00
42 Dominik Hasek SP 12.50 30.00
43 Brett Hull SP 10.00 25.00
44 Brendan Shanahan 5.00 12.00
45 Steve Yzerman 10.00 25.00
46 Anson Carter SP 5.00 12.00
47 Jochen Hecht 3.00 8.00
48 Ryan Smyth SP 3.00 8.00
49 Valeri Bure SP 3.00 8.00
50 Robert Svehla 3.00 8.00
51 Aaron Miller 3.00 8.00
52 Felix Potvin SP 6.00 15.00
53 Jamie McLennan 3.00 8.00
54 Saku Koivu SP 5.00 12.00
55 Jose Theodore 6.00 15.00
56 Mike Dunham 5.00 12.00
57 Tom Fitzgerald 3.00 8.00
59 Cliff Ronning 3.00 8.00
60 Bobby Holik 3.00 8.00
61 Shawn Bates 3.00 8.00
62 Mariusz Czerkawski 3.00 8.00
63 Kenny Jonsson SP 3.00 8.00
64 Chris Osgood 5.00 12.00
66 Rico Fata 3.00 8.00
67 Eric Lindros SP 5.00 12.00
68 Petr Nedved 3.00 8.00
69 Mike Richter 5.00 12.00
70 Pavel Brendl 5.00 12.00
71 John LeClair SP 5.00 12.00
73 Sean Burke 5.00 12.00
74 Shane Doan 3.00 8.00
75 Jean-Sebastien Aubin 5.00 12.00
76 Jan Hrdina 3.00 8.00
77 Alexei Kovalev 5.00 12.00
78 Milan Kraft 5.00 12.00
79 Mario Lemieux SP 12.00 30.00
80 Ian Moran 3.00 8.00
81 Alexei Morozov 3.00 8.00
82 Wayne Primeau SP 3.00 8.00
83 Michal Rozsival 3.00 8.00
84 Kevin Stevens 3.00 8.00
85 Martin Straka 3.00 8.00
86 Fred Brathwaite 5.00 12.00
87 Mike Eastwood 3.00 8.00
88 Cory Stillman 3.00 8.00
89 Doug Weight SP 5.00 12.00
90 Scott Young 3.00 8.00
91 Vincent Damphousse SP 3.00 8.00
92 Teemu Selanne 5.00 12.00
93 Vincent Lecavalier SP 5.00 12.00
94 Tie Domi 5.00 12.00
95 Curtis Joseph SP 8.00 20.00
96 Robert Reichel STK/200 10.00 25.00
97 Mats Sundin 5.00 12.00
98 Andrew Cassels 3.00 8.00
99 Peter Bondra 5.00 12.00
100 Jaromir Jagr 8.00 20.00

2001-02 Private Stock Game Gear Patches

*PATCH: .6X TO 1.5X BSIC JERSEY
58 David Legwand 10.00 20.00
65 Alexei Yashin 6.00 15.00
72 Jeremy Roenick 12.50 25.00

2001-02 Private Stock Moments in Time

1 Dany Heatley 15.00 40.00
2 Ilya Kovalchuk 20.00 50.00
3 Vaclav Nedorost 15.00 40.00
4 Rostislav Klesla 10.00 25.00
5 Jaroslav Bednar 10.00 25.00
6 Rick DiPietro 10.00 25.00
7 Dan Blackburn 6.00 15.00
8 Pavel Brendl 10.00 25.00
9 Krystofer Kolanos 10.00 25.00
10 Johan Hedberg 10.00 25.00

2001-02 Private Stock PS-2002

1 Paul Kariya .40 1.00
2 Steve Shields .20 .50
3 Ray Ferraro .20 .50
4 Jason Allison .20 .50
5 Byron DaFoe .30 .75
6 Joe Thornton .60 1.50
7 Stu Barnes .20 .50
8 Martin Biron .30 .75
9 Miroslav Satan .30 .75
10 Jarome Iginla .50 1.25
11 Derek Morris .20 .50
12 Sami Kapanen .20 .50
13 Jeff O'Neill .20 .50
14 Eric Daze .30 .75
15 Jocelyn Thibault .30 .75
16 David Aebischer .30 .75
17 Chris Drury .30 .75
18 Peter Forsberg 1.00 2.50
19 Patrick Roy 2.00 5.00
20 Joe Sakic .75 2.00
21 Marc Denis .30 .75
22 Geoff Sanderson .20 .50
23 Ed Belfour .40 1.00
24 Mike Modano .60 1.50
25 Marty Turco .30 .75
26 Pat Verbeek .20 .50
27 Dominik Hasek .75 2.00
28 Brett Hull .50 1.25
29 Brendan Shanahan .60 1.50
30 Steve Yzerman 2.00 5.00
31 Mike Comrie .30 .75
32 Tommy Salo .30 .75
33 Ryan Smyth .20 .50
34 Pavel Bure .60 1.50
35 Roberto Luongo .50 1.25
36 Zigmund Palffy .30 .75
37 Felix Potvin .40 1.00
38 Marian Gaborik .75 2.00
39 Doug Gilmour .30 .75
40 Jeff Hackett .30 .75
41 Joe Juneau .20 .50
42 Cliff Ronning .20 .50
43 Jason Arnott .20 .50
44 Martin Brodeur 1.00 2.50
45 Michael Peca .20 .50
46 Alexei Yashin .20 .50
47 Zdeno Ciger .20 .50
48 Eric Lindros .60 1.50
49 Mark Messier .50 1.25
50 Petr Nedved .20 .50
51 Radek Bonk .20 .50
52 Martin Havlat .30 .75
53 Roman Cechmanek .30 .75
54 John LeClair .50 1.25
55 Jeremy Roenick .50 1.25
56 Sean Burke .30 .75
57 Shane Doan .20 .50
58 Robert Lang .20 .50
59 Mario Lemieux 2.50 6.00
60 Fred Brathwaite .30 .75
61 Chris Pronger .30 .75
62 Keith Tkachuk .40 1.00
63 Doug Weight .30 .75
64 Evgeni Nabokov .30 .75
65 Owen Nolan .30 .75
66 Teemu Selanne .40 1.00
67 Nikolai Khabibulin .40 1.00
68 Vincent Lecavalier .40 1.00
69 Brad Richards .30 .75
70 Curtis Joseph .40 1.00
71 Mats Sundin .40 1.00
72 Andrew Cassels .20 .50
73 Brendan Morrison .30 .75
74 Peter Bondra .40 1.00
75 Jaromir Jagr .60 1.50
76 Ilja Bryzgalov .30 .75
77 Timo Parssinen .20 .50
78 Erik Cole .50 1.25
79 Mark Bell .20 .50
80 Pavel Datsyuk 6.00 15.00
81 Jason Williams .20 .50
82 Jaroslav Bednar .20 .50
83 Scott Clemmensen .30 .75
84 Pavel Brendl .30 .75
85 Jiri Dopita .20 .50
86 Kris Beech .20 .50
87 Mark Rycroft .20 .50
88 Jeff Jillson .20 .50
89 Miikka Kiprusoff .30 .75
90 Nikita Alexeev .20 .50
91 Bryan Allen .20 .50
92 Brian Sutherby .20 .50
93 Dany Heatley SP 12.50 30.00
94 Ilya Kovalchuk SP 25.00 60.00
95 Vaclav Nedorost SP 12.50 30.00
96 Rostislav Klesla SP 12.50 30.00
97 Kristian Huselius SP 12.50 30.00
98 Martin Erat SP 12.50 30.00
99 Rick DiPietro SP 12.50 30.00
100 Dan Blackburn SP 12.50 30.00
101 Krystofer Kolanos SP 12.50 30.00
102 Johan Hedberg SP 12.50 30.00

2001-02 Private Stock Reserve

G1 Martin Biron 1.50 4.00
G2 Patrick Roy 8.00 20.00
G3 Ed Belfour 2.00 5.00
G4 Dominik Hasek 4.00 10.00
G5 Tommy Salo 1.50 4.00
G6 Roberto Luongo 3.00 8.00
G7 Martin Brodeur 5.00 12.00
G8 Roman Cechmanek 1.50 4.00
G9 Evgeni Nabokov 1.50 4.00
G10 Curtis Joseph 2.00 5.00
R1 Dany Heatley 6.00 15.00
R2 Ilya Kovalchuk 12.00 30.00
R3 Vaclav Nedorost 1.50 4.00
R4 Pavel Datsyuk 8.00 20.00
R5 Jaroslav Bednar 1.50 4.00
R6 Dan Blackburn 1.50 4.00
R7 Pavel Brendl 1.50 4.00
R8 Krys Kolanos 1.50 4.00
R9 Kris Beech 1.50 4.00
R10 Nikita Alexeev 1.50 4.00
S1 Paul Kariya 2.00 5.00
S2 Joe Thornton 3.00 8.00
S3 Joe Sakic 4.00 10.00
S4 Brendan Shanahan 2.00 5.00
S5 Steve Yzerman 8.00 20.00
S6 Mike Comrie 1.00 2.50
S7 Pavel Bure 2.50 6.00
S8 Zigmund Palffy 1.00 2.50
S9 Marian Gaborik 3.00 8.00
S10 Alexei Yashin 1.00 2.50
S11 Eric Lindros 2.00 5.00
S12 Martin Havlat 1.00 2.50
S13 John LeClair 1.00 2.50
S14 Jeremy Roenick 2.50 6.00
S15 Mario Lemieux 12.00 30.00
S16 Keith Tkachuk 1.00 2.50
S17 Teemu Selanne 2.00 5.00
S18 Vincent Lecavalier 2.00 5.00
S19 Mats Sundin 2.00 5.00
S20 Jaromir Jagr 3.00 8.00

2002-03 Private Stock Reserve

COMP.SET w/o SP's (100) 15.00 40.00
1 Jean-Sebastien Giguere .30 .75
2 Paul Kariya .30 .75
3 Petr Sykora .25 .60
4 Milan Hnilicka .25 .60
5 Patrik Stefan .25 .60
6 Glen Murray .25 .60
7 Brian Rolston .25 .60
8 Sergei Samsonov .25 .60
9 Steve Shields .25 .60
10 Martin Biron .25 .60
11 Tim Connolly .20 .50
12 J-P Dumont .20 .50
13 Craig Conroy .20 .50
14 Chris Drury .30 .75
15 Rod Brind'Amour .30 .75
16 Erik Cole .20 .50
17 Arturs Irbe .25 .60
18 Jeff O'Neill .20 .50
19 Mark Bell .20 .50
20 Eric Daze .20 .50
21 Jocelyn Thibault .25 .60
22 Alexei Zhamnov .25 .60
23 Rob Blake .30 .75
24 Peter Forsberg .60 1.50
25 Milan Hejduk .25 .60
26 Dean McAmmond .20 .50
27 Steven Reinprecht .20 .50
28 Alex Tanguay .25 .60
29 Radim Vrbata .20 .50
30 Andrew Cassels .20 .50
31 Espen Knutsen .20 .50
32 Ray Whitney .25 .60
33 Marty Turco .30 .75
34 Pierre Turgeon .25 .60
35 Chris Chelios .30 .75
36 Brett Hull .60 1.50
37 Brendan Shanahan .30 .75
38 Anson Carter .25 .60
39 Ryan Smyth .25 .60
40 Mike York .20 .50
41 Valeri Bure .25 .60
42 Kristian Huselius .20 .50
43 Stephen Weiss .30 .75
44 Jason Allison .25 .60
45 Adam Deadmarsh .20 .50
46 Zigmund Palffy .30 .75
47 Bryan Smolinski .25 .60
48 Andrew Brunette .20 .50
49 Manny Fernandez .20 .50
50 Cliff Ronning .20 .50
51 Mariusz Czerkawski .20 .50
52 Marcel Hossa .20 .50
53 Saku Koivu .30 .75
54 Yanic Perreault .20 .50
55 Richard Zednik .20 .50
56 Denis Arkhipov .20 .50
57 Mike Dunham .25 .60
58 Scott Hartnell .20 .50
59 Greg Johnson .20 .50
60 Christian Berglund .20 .50
61 Jeff Friesen .20 .50
62 Joe Nieuwendyk .25 .60
63 Chris Osgood .30 .75
64 Mark Parrish .20 .50
65 Dan Blackburn .25 .60
66 Pavel Bure .30 .75
67 Bobby Holik .20 .50
68 Brian Leetch .25 .60
69 Mike Richter .30 .75
70 Daniel Alfredsson .30 .75
71 Radek Bonk .25 .60
72 Martin Havlat .25 .60
73 Patrick Lalime .25 .60
74 John LeClair .30 .75
75 Jeremy Roenick .50 1.25
76 Tony Amonte .25 .60
77 Daniel Briere .25 .60
78 Sean Burke .20 .50
79 Johan Hedberg .30 .75
80 Alexei Kovalev .25 .60
81 Alexei Morozov .20 .50
82 Pavol Demitra .40 1.00
83 Barret Jackman .20 .50
84 Brent Johnson .25 .60
85 Doug Weight .30 .75
86 Vincent Damphousse .25 .60
87 Patrick Marleau .30 .75
88 Teemu Selanne .60 1.50
89 Scott Thornton .20 .50
90 Dave Andreychuk .30 .75
91 Vincent Lecavalier .30 .75
92 Alexander Mogilny .25 .60
93 Gary Roberts .20 .50
94 Darcy Tucker .20 .50
95 Dan Cloutier .25 .60
96 Brendan Morrison .25 .60
97 Markus Naslund .30 .75
98 Sergei Gonchar .25 .60
99 Olaf Kolzig .30 .75
100 Dainius Zubrus .20 .50
101 Adam Oates JSY/1225 4.00 10.00
102 Dany Heatley JSY/975 3.00 8.00
103 Ilya Kovalchuk JSY/725 5.00 12.00
104 Joe Thornton JSY/1475 6.00 15.00
105 Miroslav Satan JSY/510 4.00 10.00
106 Jarome Iginla JSY/1000 8.00 20.00
107 Roman Turek JSY/1475 4.00 10.00
108 Ron Francis JSY/1175 5.00 12.00
109 Theo Fleury JSY/1100 5.00 12.00
110 Patrick Roy JSY/475 10.00 25.00
111 Joe Sakic JSY/975 8.00 20.00
112 Marc Denis JSY/1175 3.00 8.00
113 Jason Arnott JSY/1475 3.00 8.00
114 Bill Guerin JSY/875 4.00 10.00
115 Mike Modano JSY/975 6.00 15.00
116 Sergei Fedorov JSY 6.00 15.00
117 Dominik Hasek JSY/1475 6.00 15.00
118 Curtis Joseph JSY/1475 5.00 12.00
119 Nicklas Lidstrom JSY/1475 4.00 10.00
120 Luc Robitaille JSY/1475 4.00 10.00
121 Steve Yzerman JSY/730 10.00 25.00
122 Mike Comrie JSY/1475 4.00 10.00
123 Tommy Salo JSY/1475 3.00 8.00
124 Roberto Luongo JSY/1475 6.00 15.00
125 Felix Potvin JSY/1250 6.00 15.00
126 Marian Gaborik JSY/1175 8.00 20.00
127 Jose Theodore JSY/1475 4.00 10.00
128 David Legwand JSY/1475 3.00 8.00
129 Martin Brodeur JSY/975 8.00 20.00
130 Patrik Elias JSY/1475 4.00 10.00
131 Michael Peca JSY/1475 3.00 8.00
132 Alexei Yashin JSY/1475 3.00 8.00
133 Eric Lindros JSY/1475 6.00 15.00
134 Marian Hossa JSY/1100 4.00 10.00
135 Roman Cechmanek JSY/1475 3.00 8.00
136 Simon Gagne JSY/1475 4.00 10.00
137 Daymond Langkow JSY/1175 3.00 8.00
138 Mario Lemieux JSY/531 15.00 40.00
139 Chris Pronger JSY/1475 4.00 10.00
140 Keith Tkachuk JSY/1475 4.00 10.00
141 Evgeni Nabokov JSY/1475 3.00 8.00
142 Owen Nolan JSY/1475 4.00 10.00
143 Nikolai Khabibulin JSY/1475 4.00 10.00
144 Brad Richards JSY/1475 4.00 10.00
145 Ed Belfour JSY/865 4.00 10.00
146 Mats Sundin JSY 8.00 20.00
147 Todd Bertuzzi JSY/1475 4.00 10.00
148 Peter Bondra JSY/1475 4.00 10.00
149 Jaromir Jagr JSY/1475 8.00 20.00
150 Robert Lang JSY/1475 2.50 6.00
151 Stanislav Chistov RC 8.00 20.00
152 Martin Gerber RC 12.00 30.00
153 Alexei Smirnov RC 10.00 25.00
154 Tim Thomas RC 40.00 80.00
155 Chuck Kobasew RC 10.00 25.00
156 Jordan Leopold RC 12.00 30.00
157 Rick Nash RC 75.00 150.00
158 Lasse Pirjeta RC 8.00 20.00
159 Dmitri Bykov RC 8.00 20.00
160 Henrik Zetterberg RC 60.00 120.00
161 Kari Haakana RC 8.00 20.00
162 Ales Hemsky RC 30.00 80.00
163 Jay Bouwmeester RC 25.00 60.00
164 Alexander Frolov RC 20.00 50.00
165 P-M Bouchard RC 12.00 30.00
166 Stephane Veilleux RC 8.00 20.00
167 Sylvain Blouin RC 8.00 20.00
168 Ron Hainsey RC 8.00 20.00
169 Adam Hall RC 8.00 20.00
170 Scottie Upshall RC 10.00 25.00
171 Ray Schultz RC 8.00 20.00
172 Mattias Weinhandl 8.00 20.00
173 Jason Spezza RC 75.00 150.00
174 Anton Volchenkov RC 8.00 20.00
175 Dennis Seidenberg RC 12.00 30.00
176 Patrick Sharp RC 25.00 50.00
177 Radovan Somik RC 8.00 20.00
178 Jeff Taffe RC 8.00 20.00
179 Dick Tarnstrom RC 8.00 20.00
180 Tom Koivisto RC 8.00 20.00
181 Curtis Sanford RC 12.00 30.00
182 Alexander Svitov RC 8.00 20.00
183 Carlo Colaiacovo RC 12.00 30.00
184 Steve Eminger RC 8.00 20.00
185 Alex Henry RC 10.00 25.00

2002-03 Private Stock Reserve Blue

*1-100 VETS/499: 1.2X TO 3X BASIC CARDS
*151-185 ROOKIE/250: .05X TO .15X HOB

2002-03 Private Stock Reserve Red

*1-100 VETS/50: 6X TO 15X BASIC CARDS
*101-150 JSY/50: .8X TO 2X BASIC JSY
*151-185 ROOKIE/50: .2X TO .5X BASIC RC

2002-03 Private Stock Reserve Retail

*1-100 VETS: .4X TO 1X BASIC CARDS
*101-150 JSY: .3X TO .8X BASIC JSY
COMMON ROOKIE/1550 1.00 2.50
ROOK.SEMISTARS/1550 1.25 3.00
ROOK.UNL.STARS/1550 1.50 4.00
154 Tim Thomas RC 4.00 10.00
157 Rick Nash RC 6.00 15.00
160 Henrik Zetterberg RC 10.00 25.00
162 Ales Hemsky RC 4.00 10.00
163 Jay Bouwmeester RC 3.00 8.00
164 Alexander Frolov RC 2.50 6.00
173 Jason Spezza RC 6.00 15.00
176 Patrick Sharp RC 3.00 8.00

2002-03 Private Stock Reserve Class Act

COMPLETE SET (10) 15.00 40.00
1 Stanislav Chistov 1.50 4.00
2 Alexei Smirnov 1.50 4.00
3 Ivan Huml 1.50 4.00
4 Chuck Kobasew 2.00 5.00
5 Tyler Arnason 1.50 4.00
6 Rick Nash 6.00 15.00
7 Henrik Zetterberg 6.00 15.00
8 Jay Bouwmeester 4.00 10.00
9 Stephen Weiss 2.00 5.00
10 Barret Jackman 1.50 4.00

2002-03 Private Stock Reserve Elite

COMPLETE SET (6) 15.00 40.00
1 Ilya Kovalchuk 2.50 6.00
2 Peter Forsberg 4.00 10.00
3 Patrick Roy 5.00 12.00
4 Steve Yzerman 5.00 12.00
5 Mario Lemieux 5.00 12.00
6 Jaromir Jagr 2.50 6.00

2002-03 Private Stock Reserve InCrease Security

COMPLETE SET (20) 15.00 30.00
1 Jean-Sebastien Giguere .75 2.00
2 Roman Turek .75 2.00
3 Arturs Irbe .75 2.00
4 Jocelyn Thibault .75 2.00
5 Patrick Roy 3.00 8.00
6 Marc Denis .75 2.00
7 Marty Turco .75 2.00
8 Curtis Joseph 1.25 3.00
9 Tommy Salo .75 2.00
10 Roberto Luongo 2.00 5.00
11 Felix Potvin .75 2.00
12 Jose Theodore 2.00 5.00
13 Martin Brodeur 2.50 6.00
14 Chris Osgood .75 2.00
15 Mike Richter 1.25 3.00
16 Roman Cechmanek .75 2.00
17 Sean Burke .75 2.00
18 Brent Johnson .75 2.00
19 Evgeni Nabokov .75 2.00
20 Ed Belfour 1.50 4.00

2002-03 Private Stock Reserve Moments in Time

COMPLETE SET (8) 10.00 25.00
1 Chuck Kobasew 2.00 5.00
2 Rick Nash 6.00 15.00
3 Jay Bouwmeester 3.00 8.00
4 Stephen Weiss 2.00 5.00
5 Alexander Frolov 2.00 5.00
6 Jamie Lundmark 1.50 4.00
7 Barret Jackman 1.50 4.00
8 Alexander Svitov 2.00 5.00

2002-03 Private Stock Reserve Patches

102 Dany Heatley/50 20.00 50.00
103 Ilya Kovalchuk/50 25.00 60.00
104 Joe Thornton/275 12.50 30.00
105 Miroslav Satan/275 10.00 25.00
106 Jarome Iginla/70 15.00 40.00
107 Roman Turek/90 10.00 25.00
109 Theo Fleury/275 10.00 25.00
112 Marc Denis/250 10.00 25.00
113 Jason Arnott/250 10.00 25.00
114 Bill Guerin/100 10.00 25.00
115 Mike Modano/150 15.00 40.00
116 Sergei Fedorov/150 15.00 40.00
119 Nicklas Lidstrom/275 12.50 30.00
122 Mike Comrie/125 10.00 25.00
123 Tommy Salo/275 10.00 25.00
124 Roberto Luongo/150 15.00 40.00
125 Felix Potvin/250 12.50 30.00
126 Marian Gaborik/100 15.00 40.00
127 Jose Theodore/50 15.00 40.00
128 David Legwand/250 10.00 25.00
129 Martin Brodeur/150 15.00 40.00
130 Patrik Elias/150 10.00 25.00
131 Michael Peca/250 10.00 25.00
133 Eric Lindros/250 12.50 30.00
134 Marian Hossa/250 12.50 30.00
135 Roman Cechmanek/250 10.00 25.00
136 Simon Gagne/200 12.50 30.00
137 Daymond Langkow/150 10.00 25.00
139 Chris Pronger/250 10.00 25.00
140 Keith Tkachuk/150 12.50 30.00
141 Evgeni Nabokov/200 10.00 25.00
142 Owen Nolan/250 10.00 25.00
143 Nikolai Khabibulin/275 12.50 30.00
144 Brad Richards/275 10.00 25.00
145 Ed Belfour/245 12.50 30.00
147 Todd Bertuzzi/275 12.50 30.00
148 Peter Bondra/275 10.00 25.00
150 Robert Lang/250 10.00 25.00

2003-04 Private Stock Reserve

COMP.SET w/o SP's (100) 15.00 40.00
1 Stanislav Chistov .20 .50
2 Jean-Sebastien Giguere .30 .75
3 Vaclav Prospal .20 .50
4 Petr Sykora .25 .60
5 Byron Dafoe .25 .60
6 Slava Kozlov .25 .60
7 Pasi Nurminen .25 .60
8 Marc Savard .20 .50
9 Mike Knuble .20 .50
10 Felix Potvin .50 1.25
11 Sergei Samsonov .25 .60
12 Daniel Briere .30 .75
13 Ales Kotalik .20 .50
14 Ryan Miller .30 .75
15 Blair Betts .20 .50
16 Chuck Kobasew .20 .50
17 Jordan Leopold .20 .50
18 Ron Francis .40 1.00
19 Jeff O'Neill .20 .50
20 Kevin Weekes .25 .60
21 Igor Radulov .20 .50
22 Jocelyn Thibault .25 .60
23 Alexei Zhamnov .25 .60
24 David Aebischer .25 .60
25 Rob Blake .30 .75
26 Andrew Cassels .20 .50
27 Rick Nash .30 .75
28 Geoff Sanderson .20 .50
29 Niko Kapanen .20 .50
30 Jere Lehtinen .25 .60
31 Steve Ott .20 .50
32 Pavel Datsyuk .50 1.25
33 Nicklas Lidstrom .30 .75
34 Dominik Hasek .50 1.25
35 Henrik Zetterberg .40 1.00
36 Ales Hemsky .30 .75
37 Georges Laraque .25 .60
38 Tommy Salo .25 .60
39 Mike York .20 .50
40 Jay Bouwmeester .20 .50
41 Valeri Bure .20 .50
42 Viktor Kozlov .20 .50
43 Roberto Luongo .50 1.25
44 Stephen Weiss .20 .50
45 Roman Cechmanek .25 .60
46 Adam Deadmarsh .20 .50
47 Alexander Frolov .25 .60
48 Pierre-Marc Bouchard .30 .75
49 Andrew Brunette .20 .50
50 Marian Gaborik .30 .75
51 Dwayne Roloson .25 .60
52 Mathieu Garon .20 .50
53 Marcel Hossa .20 .50
54 Yanic Perreault .20 .50
55 Mike Ribeiro .20 .50
56 Andreas Johansson .20 .50
57 Scottie Upshall .25 .60
58 Scott Walker .20 .50
59 Patrik Elias .30 .75
60 Jeff Friesen .20 .50
61 Jamie Langenbrunner .25 .60
62 Scott Stevens .30 .75
63 Jason Blake .20 .50
64 Oleg Kvasha .20 .50
65 Mark Parrish .20 .50
66 Garth Snow .25 .60
67 Mattias Weinhandl .20 .50
68 Mike Dunham .25 .60
69 Alex Kovalev .25 .60
70 Brian Leetch .25 .60
71 Mark Messier .60 1.50
72 Radek Bonk .25 .60
73 Vaclav Varada .20 .50
74 Todd White .20 .50
75 Simon Gagne .30 .75
76 John LeClair .30 .75
77 Mark Recchi .40 1.00
78 Shane Doan .25 .60
79 Mike Johnson .20 .50
80 Daymond Langkow .20 .50
81 Ladislav Nagy .20 .50
82 Sebastien Caron .25 .60
83 Alexei Morozov .20 .50
84 Brent Johnson .25 .60
85 Al MacInnis .40 1.00
86 Chris Pronger .30 .75
87 Keith Tkachuk .30 .75
88 Jonathan Cheechoo .25 .60
89 Vincent Damphousse .25 .60
90 Patrick Marleau .30 .75
91 Evgeni Nabokov .25 .60
92 Dave Andreychuk .30 .75
93 Dan Boyle .20 .50
94 Alexander Mogilny .25 .60
95 Owen Nolan .30 .75
96 Darcy Tucker .25 .60
97 Ed Jovanovski .25 .60
98 Trevor Linden .30 .75
99 Sergei Gonchar .20 .50
100 Olaf Kolzig .30 .75
101 Garrett Burnett RC 6.00 15.00
102 Joffrey Lupul RC 15.00 40.00
103 Joe DiPenta RC 8.00 20.00
104 Patrice Bergeron RC 30.00 80.00
105 Milan Bartovic RC 8.00 20.00
106 Andrew Peters RC 8.00 20.00
107 Brent Krahn RC 6.00 15.00
108 Eric Staal RC 30.00 80.00
109 Lasse Kukkonen RC 6.00 15.00
110 Travis Moen RC 8.00 20.00
111 Tuomo Ruutu RC 10.00 25.00
112 Pavel Vorobiev RC 8.00 20.00
113 Cody McCormick RC 8.00 20.00
114 Dan Fritsche RC 6.00 15.00
115 Kent McDonell RC 8.00 20.00

Card	Low	High
116 Trevor Daley RC	10.00	25.00
117 Antti Miettinen RC	10.00	25.00
118 Jiri Hudler RC	15.00	40.00
119 Nathan Horton RC	15.00	40.00
120 Dustin Brown RC	15.00	40.00
121 Tim Gleason RC	8.00	20.00
122 Esa Pirnes RC	6.00	15.00
123 Brent Burns RC	20.00	50.00
124 Chris Higgins RC	12.00	30.00
125 Dan Hamhuis RC	8.00	20.00
126 Jordin Tootoo RC	12.00	30.00
127 Marek Zidlicky RC	6.00	15.00
128 David Hale RC	6.00	15.00
129 Paul Martin RC	8.00	20.00
130 Sean Bergenheim RC	8.00	20.00
131 Antoine Vermette RC	12.00	30.00
132 Joni Pitkanen RC	10.00	25.00
133 Matthew Spiller RC	8.00	20.00
134 Marc-Andre Fleury RC	50.00	100.00
135 Matt Murley RC	8.00	20.00
136 Peter Sejna RC	8.00	20.00
137 Milan Michalek RC	12.00	30.00
138 Maxim Kondratiev RC	6.00	15.00
139 Matt Stajan RC	10.00	25.00
140 Boyd Gordon RC	8.00	20.00
141 Sergei Fedorov JSY	6.00	15.00
142 Dany Heatley JSY/700	3.00	8.00
143 Ilya Kovalchuk JSY/900	4.00	10.00
144 Glen Murray JSY	3.00	8.00
145 Joe Thornton JSY/900	6.00	15.00
146 Martin Biron JSY/1000	3.00	8.00
147 Chris Drury JSY	3.00	8.00
148 Miroslav Satan JSY/1000	3.00	8.00
149 Craig Conroy JSY	2.50	6.00
150 Jarome Iginla JSY	5.00	12.00
151 Erik Cole JSY	2.50	6.00
152 Eric Daze JSY	3.00	8.00
153 Theo Fleury JSY	5.00	12.00
154 Peter Forsberg JSY	8.00	20.00
155 Milan Hejduk JSY	3.00	8.00
156 Paul Kariya JSY	4.00	10.00
157 Patrick Roy JSY/99	15.00	40.00
158 Joe Sakic JSY/975	8.00	20.00
159 Teemu Selanne JSY	8.00	20.00
160 Marc Denis JSY	3.00	8.00
161 Rostislav Klesla JSY	2.50	6.00
162 Bill Guerin JSY	4.00	10.00
163 Mike Modano JSY/1000	6.00	15.00
164 Marty Turco JSY	4.00	10.00
165 Brett Hull JSY/750	8.00	20.00
166 Steve Yzerman JSY/900	10.00	25.00
167 Mike Comrie JSY	3.00	8.00
168 Ryan Smyth JSY	3.00	8.00
169 Olli Jokinen JSY/1000	4.00	10.00
170 Jason Allison JSY	3.00	8.00
171 Zigmund Palffy JSY/1000	4.00	10.00
172 Filip Kuba JSY/99	8.00	20.00
173 Saku Koivu JSY/1000	4.00	10.00
174 Jose Theodore JSY	4.00	10.00
175 Richard Zednik JSY/1000	2.50	6.00
176 David Legwand JSY	3.00	8.00
177 Tomas Vokoun JSY	3.00	8.00
178 Martin Brodeur JSY/750	10.00	25.00
179 Rick DiPietro JSY/900	3.00	8.00
180 Michael Peca JSY/900	3.00	8.00
181 Alexei Yashin JSY/750	3.00	8.00
182 Pavel Bure JSY/750	4.00	10.00
183 Eric Lindros JSY	6.00	15.00
185 Daniel Alfredsson JSY	4.00	10.00
186 Marian Hossa JSY	4.00	10.00
187 Patrick Lalime JSY	3.00	8.00
188 Bryan Smolinski JSY	2.50	6.00
189 Jason Spezza JSY/750	4.00	10.00
190 Tony Amonte JSY	3.00	8.00
191 Jeff Hackett JSY/1000	3.00	8.00
192 Jeremy Roenick JSY/500	6.00	15.00
193 Sean Burke JSY	2.50	6.00
194 Mario Lemieux JSY/99	10.00	25.00
195 Martin Straka JSY	2.50	6.00
196 Pavol Demitra JSY	5.00	12.00
197 Chris Osgood JSY	4.00	10.00
198 Doug Weight JSY	4.00	10.00
199 Nikolai Khabibulin JSY	4.00	10.00
200 Vincent Lecavalier JSY/500	4.00	10.00
201 Fredrik Modin JSY/600	2.50	6.00
202 Brad Richards JSY/750	4.00	10.00
203 Martin St. Louis JSY	4.00	10.00
204 Cory Stillman JSY/99	8.00	20.00
205 Ed Belfour JSY	4.00	10.00
206 Mats Sundin JSY	4.00	10.00
207 Todd Bertuzzi JSY	4.00	10.00
208 Dan Cloutier JSY	3.00	8.00
209 Brendan Morrison JSY/750	3.00	8.00
210 Markus Naslund JSY/950	4.00	10.00
211 Jaromir Jagr JSY	12.00	30.00
212 Robert Lang JSY/425	2.50	6.00

2003-04 Private Stock Reserve Blue

*1-100 VETS/350: 1.5X TO 4X BASIC CARDS
*101-140 ROOKIE/250: .1X TO .3X RC/99
*JERSEY/25: 1.2X TO 3X BASIC JSY
*JERSEY/25: .8X TO 2X JSY/99

Card	Low	High
71 Mark Messier	2.50	6.00

2003-04 Private Stock Reserve Patches

*PATCHES: 1.25X TO 3X BASE JSY

Card	Low	High
141 Sergei Fedorov	15.00	40.00
142 Dany Heatley/50	15.00	40.00
143 Ilya Kovalchuk/25	50.00	120.00
144 Glen Murray	10.00	25.00
145 Joe Thornton/50	20.00	50.00
146 Martin Biron	15.00	30.00
147 Chris Drury	15.00	30.00
148 Miroslav Satan	15.00	30.00
150 Jarome Iginla	12.50	30.00
152 Eric Daze	12.50	40.00
153 Theo Fleury	10.00	25.00
154 Peter Forsberg/70	20.00	50.00
155 Milan Hejduk	12.50	30.00
156 Paul Kariya	12.50	30.00
157 Patrick Roy	15.00	40.00
158 Joe Sakic	15.00	40.00
160 Marc Denis	15.00	30.00
162 Bill Guerin	12.50	40.00
163 Mike Modano	15.00	40.00
164 Marty Turco/50	12.50	40.00
165 Brett Hull	15.00	40.00
167 Mike Comrie/25	30.00	80.00
168 Ryan Smyth/25	15.00	40.00
169 Olli Jokinen	12.50	40.00
170 Jason Allison	10.00	25.00
171 Zigmund Palffy	15.00	30.00
172 Filip Kuba	12.50	30.00
173 Saku Koivu	12.50	30.00
174 Jose Theodore	15.00	40.00
175 Richard Zednik	10.00	25.00
176 David Legwand	12.50	40.00
177 Tomas Vokoun	15.00	30.00
178 Martin Brodeur	30.00	80.00
179 Rick DiPietro/200	15.00	40.00
180 Michael Peca	10.00	25.00
181 Alexei Yashin	10.00	25.00
182 Pavel Bure	12.50	30.00
183 Eric Lindros	12.50	30.00
185 Daniel Alfredsson	15.00	40.00
186 Marian Hossa	12.50	30.00
187 Patrick Lalime	12.50	40.00
189 Jason Spezza/25	15.00	40.00
190 Tony Amonte	10.00	25.00
191 Jeff Hackett	15.00	30.00
192 Jeremy Roenick	15.00	40.00
193 Sean Burke/65	15.00	40.00
194 Mario Lemieux	25.00	60.00
195 Martin Straka	10.00	25.00
197 Chris Osgood	15.00	40.00
198 Doug Weight	15.00	40.00
199 Nikolai Khabibulin	12.50	30.00
200 Vincent Lecavalier	12.50	30.00
201 Fredrik Modin	12.50	30.00
202 Brad Richards/25	25.00	60.00
203 Martin St. Louis	15.00	40.00
204 Cory Stillman	8.00	20.00
205 Ed Belfour	12.50	30.00
206 Mats Sundin/50	10.00	30.00
207 Todd Bertuzzi	12.50	30.00
208 Dan Cloutier	15.00	30.00
209 Brendan Morrison	12.50	40.00
210 Markus Naslund/75	12.50	30.00
211 Jaromir Jagr	20.00	50.00
212 Robert Lang	10.00	25.00

2003-04 Private Stock Reserve Red

*1-100 VETS/199: 2.5X TO 6X BASIC CARDS
*101-140 ROOKIE/225: .1X TO .3X RC/99
*JERSEY/50: .8X TO 2X BASIC JSY
*JERSEY/50: .5X TO 1.2X BASIC JSY/99

Card	Low	High
71 Mark Messier	4.00	10.00

2003-04 Private Stock Reserve Retail

*1-100 VETS: .4X TO 1X HOBBY
*101-140 ROOKIE/1299: .08X TO .2X HOBBY/99
*141-212 JERSEY: .6X TO 1.5X HOBBY
*141-212 JERSEY: .4X TO 1X JSY/99

Card	Low	High
71 Mark Messier	.60	1.50

2003-04 Private Stock Reserve Class Act

Card	Low	High
COMPLETE SET (12)	15.00	30.00
1 Joffrey Lupul	.60	1.50
2 Eric Staal	1.25	3.00
3 Tuomo Ruutu	.60	1.50
4 Nathan Horton	1.00	2.50
5 Dustin Brown	.60	1.50
6 Chris Higgins	.40	1.00
7 Jordin Tootoo	1.00	2.50
8 Joni Pitkanen	.60	1.50
9 Marc-Andre Fleury	2.00	5.00
10 Peter Sejna	.40	1.00
11 Milan Michalek	.40	1.00
12 Matt Stajan	.40	1.00

2003-04 Private Stock Reserve Increase Security

Card	Low	High
COMPLETE SET (16)	10.00	25.00
1 Jean-Sebastien Giguere	.75	2.00
2 Felix Potvin	.75	2.00
3 Ryan Miller	1.00	2.50
4 Jocelyn Thibault	.75	2.00
5 David Aebischer	.75	2.00
6 Marty Turco	.75	2.00
7 Dominik Hasek	1.50	4.00
8 Jose Theodore	1.00	2.50
9 Martin Brodeur	2.50	6.00
10 Rick DiPietro	.75	2.00
11 Patrick Lalime	.75	2.00
12 Sean Burke	.75	2.00
13 Marc-Andre Fleury	2.50	6.00
14 Evgeni Nabokov	.75	2.00
15 Nikolai Khabibulin	.75	2.00
16 Ed Belfour	.75	2.00

2003-04 Private Stock Reserve Moments in Time

Card	Low	High
COMPLETE SET (10)	20.00	40.00
UNLISTED STARS	1.00	2.50
1 Sergei Fedorov	1.00	2.50
2 Joe Thornton	1.25	3.00
3 Peter Forsberg	1.50	4.00
4 Paul Kariya	1.25	3.00
5 Joe Sakic	1.50	4.00
6 Mike Modano	1.25	3.00
7 Brett Hull	1.00	2.50
8 Steve Yzerman	2.00	5.00
9 Mario Lemieux	2.50	6.00
10 Todd Bertuzzi	.75	2.00

2003-04 Private Stock Reserve Rising Stock

Card	Low	High
COMPLETE SET (12)	10.00	20.00
1 Ilya Kovalchuk	1.00	2.50
2 Ales Kotalik	.40	1.00
3 Ryan Miller	.75	2.00
4 Chuck Kobasew	.40	1.00
5 Rick Nash	.75	2.00
6 Henrik Zetterberg	.75	2.00
7 Ales Hemsky	.50	1.25
8 Jay Bouwmeester	.40	1.00
9 Pierre-Marc Bouchard	.40	1.00
10 Marcel Hossa	.40	1.00
11 Jason Spezza	1.00	2.50
12 Barret Jackman	.40	1.00

1995-96 Pro Magnets

Card	Low	High
COMPLETE SET (130)	30.00	75.00
1 Ed Belfour	1.00	2.50
2 Chris Chelios	1.00	2.50
3 Joe Murphy	.50	1.25
4 Jeremy Roenick	1.00	2.50
5 Bernie Nicholls	.50	1.25
6 Brett Hull	1.00	2.50
7 Esa Tikkanen	.50	1.25
8 Chris Pronger	.50	1.25
9 Al MacInnis	.50	1.25
10 Geoff Courtnall	.50	1.25
11 Ray Bourque	1.50	4.00
12 Blaine Lacher	.60	1.50
13 Cam Neely	.75	2.00
14 Adam Oates	.75	2.00
15 Kevin Stevens	.50	1.25
16 Vincent Damphousse	.60	1.50
17 Mark Recchi	.75	2.00
18 Pierre Turgeon	.60	1.50
19 Valeri Bure	.50	1.25
20 Patrick Roy	3.00	8.00
21 Pavel Bure	1.50	4.00
22 Alexander Mogilny	.60	1.50
23 Trevor Linden	.75	2.00
24 Kirk McLean	.60	1.50
25 Cliff Ronning	.50	1.25
26 Jim Carey	.60	1.50
27 Dale Hunter	.50	1.25
28 Joe Juneau	.50	1.25
29 Jason Allison	.50	1.25
30 Brendan Witt	.50	1.25
31 John MacLean	.50	1.25
32 Scott Niedermayer	.50	1.25
33 Martin Brodeur	1.50	4.00
34 Stephane Richer	.50	1.25
35 Scott Stevens	.50	1.25
36 Patrik Carnback	.50	1.25
37 Guy Hebert	.60	1.50
38 Oleg Tverdovsky	.50	1.25
39 Paul Kariya	2.00	5.00
40 Garry Valk	.50	1.25
41 Theo Fleury	.75	2.00
42 German Titov	.50	1.25
43 Joe Nieuwendyk	.60	1.50
44 Gary Roberts	.50	1.25
45 Trevor Kidd	.50	1.25
46 Rod Brind'Amour	.50	1.25
47 Eric Lindros	1.50	4.00
48 Ron Hextall	.60	1.50
49 John LeClair	1.00	2.50
50 Mikael Renberg	.50	1.25
51 Patrick Flatley	.50	1.25
52 Kirk Muller	.50	1.25
53 Mathieu Schneider	.50	1.25
54 Wendel Clark	.50	1.25
55 Brett Lindros	.50	1.25
56 Tim Cheveldae	.50	1.25
57 Dallas Drake	.50	1.25
58 Teemu Selanne	1.25	3.00
59 Keith Tkachuk	.75	2.00
60 Alexei Zhamnov	.50	1.25
61 Rob Blake	.75	2.00
62 Wayne Gretzky	5.00	12.00
63 Jari Kurri	.50	1.25
64 Jamie Storr	.50	1.25
65 Rick Tocchet	.50	1.25
66 Brian Bradley	.50	1.25
67 Roman Hamrlik	.50	1.25
68 Rob Zamuner	.50	1.25
69 Paul Ysebaert	.50	1.25
70 Chris Gratton	.50	1.25
71 Dave Andreychuk	.50	1.25
72 Kenny Jonsson	.50	1.25
73 Doug Gilmour	.75	2.00
74 Felix Potvin	1.00	2.50
75 Mats Sundin	.75	2.00
76 Claude Lemieux	.50	1.25
77 Peter Forsberg	1.00	2.50
78 Mike Ricci	.50	1.25
79 Stephane Fiset	.60	1.50
80 Joe Sakic	1.50	4.00
81 Jason Arnott	.60	1.50
82 Jason Bonsignore	.50	1.25
83 Doug Weight	.50	1.25
84 Todd Marchant	.50	1.25
85 Bill Ranford	.50	1.25
86 Rob Niedermayer	.50	1.25
87 Jody Hull	.50	1.25
88 Bob Kudelski	.50	1.25
89 Scott Mellanby	.50	1.25
90 John Vanbiesbrouck	.75	2.00
91 Bryan Smolinski	.50	1.25
92 Mario Lemieux	3.00	8.00
93 Jaromir Jagr	1.50	4.00
94 Sergei Zubov	.50	1.25
95 Ron Francis	.60	1.50
96 Adam Graves	.50	1.25
97 Brian Leetch	.75	2.00
98 Mark Messier	1.00	2.50
99 Mike Richter	.75	2.00
100 Luc Robitaille	.60	1.50
101 Paul Coffey	.60	1.50
102 Sergei Fedorov	1.50	4.00
103 Nicklas Lidstrom	1.00	2.50
104 Ray Sheppard	.50	1.25
105 Steve Yzerman	3.00	8.00
106 Dominik Hasek	1.50	4.00
107 Alexei Zhitnik	.50	1.25
108 Yuri Khmylev	.50	1.25
109 Pat LaFontaine	.50	1.25
110 Donald Audette	.50	1.25
111 Radek Bonk	.50	1.25
112 Alexandre Daigle	.50	1.25
113 Steve Larouche	.50	1.25
114 Martin Straka	.50	1.25
115 Randy Cunneyworth	.50	1.25
116 Jeff Friesen	.50	1.25
117 Arturs Irbe	.60	1.50
118 Ulf Dahlen	.50	1.25
119 Craig Janney	.50	1.25
120 Pat Falloon	.50	1.25
121 Shane Churla	.50	1.25
122 Todd Harvey	.50	1.25
123 Derian Hatcher	.50	1.25
124 Mike Modano	1.00	2.50
125 Andy Moog	.60	1.50
126 Sean Burke	.50	1.25
127 Andrew Cassels	.50	1.25
128 Darren Turcotte	.50	1.25
129 Geoff Courtnall	.50	1.25
130 Brendan Shanahan	1.25	3.00

1995-96 Pro Magnets Iron Curtain

Card	Low	High
IC1 Ed Belfour	2.50	6.00
IC2 Martin Brodeur	3.00	8.00
IC3 Arturs Irbe	2.00	5.00
IC4 Mike Richter	2.00	5.00
IC5 Mike Vernon	2.00	5.00
IC6 Ron Hextall	2.50	6.00

1990-91 Pro Set

Card	Low	High
1 Brett Hull Promo	1.00	2.50
1 Ray Bourque ERR	.20	.50
1 Ray Bourque COR	.20	.50
2 Randy Burridge	.10	.25
3 Lyndon Byers RC	.10	.25
4 Bob Carpenter	.10	.25
5 John Carter RC	.10	.25
6 Dave Christian	.07	.20
7A Garry Galley ERR RC	.07	.20
7B Garry Galley COR RC	.07	.20
8 Craig Janney	.12	.30
9 Rejean Lemelin	.07	.20
10 Andy Moog	.12	.30
11 Cam Neely	.12	.30
12 Allen Pedersen	.07	.20
13 Dave Poulin	.12	.30
14 Brian Propp	.12	.30
15 Bob Sweeney	.07	.20
16 Glen Wesley	.10	.25
17A Dave Andreychuk ERR	.12	.30
17B Dave Andreychuk COR	.12	.30
18A Scott Arniel ERR	.07	.20
18B Scott Arniel COR	.07	.20
19 Doug Bodger	.10	.25
20 Mike Foligno	.10	.25
21A Phil Housley ERR	.10	.25
21B Phil Housley COR	.10	.25
22 Dean Kennedy RC	.07	.20
23 Uwe Krupp	.12	.30
24 Grant Ledyard RC	.12	.30
25 Clint Malarchuk	.10	.25
26 Alexander Mogilny RC	.40	1.00
27 Daren Puppa	.10	.25
28 Mike Ramsey	.07	.20
29 Christian Ruuttu	.10	.25
30 Dave Snuggerud RC	.10	.25
31 Pierre Turgeon	.10	.25
32 Rick Vaive	.10	.25
33 Theo Fleury	.15	.40
34 Doug Gilmour	.15	.40
35 Al MacInnis	.15	.40
36 Brian MacLellan	.10	.25
37 Jamie Macoun	.10	.25
38 Sergei Makarov RC	.25	.60
39A Brad McCrimmon ERR	.12	.30
39B Brad McCrimmon COR	.12	.30
40A Joe Mullen ERR	.10	.25
40B Joe Mullen COR	.10	.25
41 Dana Murzyn	.12	.30
42A Joe Nieuwendyk ERR	.10	.25
42B Joe Nieuwendyk COR	.10	.25
43 Joel Otto	.10	.25
44 Paul Ranheim RC	.12	.30
45 Gary Roberts	.12	.30
46 Gary Suter	.07	.20
47 Mike Vernon	.10	.25
48 Rick Wamsley	.12	.30
49 Keith Brown	.10	.25
50 Adam Creighton	.07	.20
51 Dirk Graham	.10	.25
52 Steve Konroyd	.07	.20
53A Steve Larmer ERR	.10	.25
53B Steve Larmer COR	.10	.25
54A Dave Manson ERR	.12	.30
54B Dave Manson COR	.12	.30
55A Bob McGill ERR	.07	.20
55B Bob McGill COR	.07	.20
56 Greg Millen	.10	.25
57A Troy Murray	.10	.25
57B Troy Murray	.10	.25
58 Jeremy Roenick RC	.40	1.00
59A Denis Savard	.12	.30
59B Denis Savard	.12	.30
60A Al Secord ERR	.07	.20
60B Al Secord COR	.07	.20
61A Duane Sutter ERR	.10	.25
61B Duane Sutter COR	.10	.25
62 Steve Thomas	.07	.20
63A Doug Wilson ERR	.10	.25
63B Doug Wilson COR	.10	.25
64 Trent Yawney	.12	.30
65 Dave Barr	.12	.30
66A Shawn Burr	.10	.25
67 Jimmy Carson	.10	.25
68 John Chabot	.12	.30
69 Steve Chiasson	.07	.20
70 Bernie Federko	.10	.25
71 Gerard Gallant	.07	.20
72 Glen Hanlon	.10	.25
73 Joey Kocur RC	.25	.60
74 Lee Norwood	.10	.25
75 Mike O'Connell	.10	.25
76 Bob Probert	.12	.30
77 Torrie Robertson	.07	.20
78 Daniel Shank RC	.12	.30
79 Steve Yzerman	.40	1.00
80 Rick Zombo RC	.12	.30
81 Glenn Anderson	.10	.25
82 Grant Fuhr	.20	.50
83 Martin Gelinas RC	.25	.60
84 Adam Graves RC	.25	.60
85 Charlie Huddy	.10	.25
86 Petr Klima	.07	.20
87A Jari Kurri ERR	.15	.40
87B Jari Kurri COR	.15	.40
88 Mark Lamb	.12	.30
89 Kevin Lowe	.12	.30
90 Craig MacTavish	.10	.25
91 Mark Messier	.25	.60
92 Craig Muni	.10	.25
93 Joe Murphy RC	.10	.25
94 Bill Ranford	.10	.25
95 Craig Simpson	.10	.25
96 Steve Smith	.10	.25
97 Esa Tikkanen	.10	.25
98 Mikael Andersson	.12	.30
99 Dave Babych	.07	.20
100 Yvon Corriveau RC	.10	.25
101 Randy Cunneyworth	.10	.25
102 Kevin Dineen	.12	.30
103 Dean Evason	.10	.25
104 Ray Ferraro	.10	.25
105 Ron Francis	.15	.40
106 Grant Jennings RC	.12	.30
107 Todd Krygier RC	.10	.25
108 Randy Ladouceur	.12	.30
109 Ulf Samuelsson	.12	.30
110 Brad Shaw RC	.10	.25
111 Dave Tippett	.10	.25
112 Pat Verbeek	.10	.25
113 Scott Young	.07	.20
114 Brian Benning	.10	.25
115 Steve Duchesne	.07	.20
116 Todd Elik RC	.12	.30
117A Tony Granato	.07	.20
118 Wayne Gretzky	.75	2.00
119 Kelly Hrudey	.07	.20
120 Steve Kasper	.07	.20
121A Mike Kushelnyski ERR	.12	.30
121B Mike Kushelnyski COR	.12	.30
122 Bob Kudelski RC	.10	.25
123 Tom Laidlaw	.12	.30
124 Marty McSorley	.10	.25
125 Larry Robinson	.12	.30
126 Luc Robitaille	.12	.30
127 Tomas Sandstrom	.12	.30
128 Dave Taylor	.12	.30
129A John Tonelli ERR	.10	.25
129B John Tonelli COR	.10	.25
130A Brian Bellows ERR	.10	.25
130B Brian Bellows COR ERR	.10	.25
131A Aaron Broten	.10	.25
132 Neal Broten	.07	.20
133 Jon Casey	.12	.30
134 Shawn Chambers	.10	.25
135 Shane Churla RC	.07	.20
136 Ulf Dahlen	.12	.30
137 Gaetan Duchesne	.12	.30
138 Dave Gagner	.12	.30
139 Stewart Gavin	.12	.30
140 Curt Giles	.10	.25
141 Basil McRae	.07	.20
142 Mike Modano RC	.40	1.00
143 Larry Murphy	.10	.25
144 Ville Siren RC	.10	.25
145 Mark Tinordi RC	.07	.20
146 Guy Carbonneau	.07	.20
147A Chris Chelios ERR	.12	.30
147B Chris Chelios COR	.12	.30
148 Shayne Corson	.10	.25
149 Russ Courtnall	.12	.30
150 Brian Hayward	.12	.30
151 Mike Keane RC	.07	.20
152 Stephan Lebeau RC	.10	.25
153 Claude Lemieux	.07	.20
154 Craig Ludwig	.12	.30
155 Mike McPhee	.10	.25
156 Stephane Richer	.12	.30
157 Patrick Roy	.30	.75
158 Mathieu Schneider RC	.10	.25
159 Brian Skrudland	.10	.25
160 Bobby Smith	.10	.25
161 Petr Svoboda	.10	.25
162 Tommy Albelin	.07	.20
163 Doug Brown	.10	.25
164 Sean Burke	.10	.25
165 Ken Daneyko	.07	.20
166 Bruce Driver	.12	.30
167A Slava Fetisov ERR RC	.25	.60
167B Slava Fetisov COR RC	.25	.60
168 Mark Johnson	.10	.25
169 Alexei Kasatonov RC	.12	.30
170 John MacLean	.10	.25
171A David Maley ERR RC	.12	.30
171B David Maley COR RC	.12	.30
172 Kirk Muller	.10	.25
173 Janne Ojanen RC	.12	.30
174 Brendan Shanahan	.12	.30
175A Peter Stastny ERR	.10	.25
175B Peter Stastny COR	.10	.25
176A Patrik Sundstrom ERR	.10	.25
176B Patrik Sundstrom COR	.10	.25
177 Sylvain Turgeon	.10	.25
178 Ken Baumgartner RC	.12	.30
179 Doug Crossman	.10	.25
180 Gerald Diduck	.10	.25
181 Mark Fitzpatrick RC	.10	.25
182 Pat Flatley	.12	.30
183 Glenn Healy RC	.25	.60
184 Alan Kerr	.10	.25
185 Derek King	.12	.30
186 Pat LaFontaine	.12	.30
187 Don Maloney	.12	.30
188 Hubie McDonough RC	.10	.25
189 Jeff Norton	.12	.30
190 Gary Nylund	.10	.25
191 Brent Sutter	.10	.25
192 Bryan Trottier	.12	.30
193 David Volek	.12	.30
194 Randy Wood	.07	.20
195 Jan Erixon	.12	.30
196 Mike Gartner	.15	.40
197 Ron Greschner	.07	.20
198A Miloslav Horava ERR RC	.10	.25
198B Miloslav Horava COR RC	.10	.25
199 Mark Janssens RC	.12	.30
200 Kelly Kisio	.10	.25
201 Brian Leetch	.15	.40
202 Randy Moller	.12	.30
203 Brian Mullen	.12	.30
204 Bernie Nicholls	.10	.25
205A Chris Nilan ERR	.07	.20
205B Chris Nilan COR	.07	.20
206 John Ogrodnick	.12	.30
207 James Patrick	.12	.30
208 Darren Turcotte RC	.10	.25
209 John Vanbiesbrouck	.12	.30
210 Carey Wilson	.10	.25
211 Mike Bullard	.10	.25
212 Terry Carkner	.10	.25
213 Jeff Chychrun RC	.10	.25
214 Murray Craven	.12	.30
215 Pelle Eklund	.07	.20
216 Ron Hextall	.12	.30
217 Mark Howe	.12	.30
218 Tim Kerr	.07	.20
219 Ken Linseman	.10	.25
220 Scott Mellanby	.12	.30
221 Gord Murphy	.12	.30
222 Kjell Samuelsson	.10	.25
223 Ilkka Sinisalo	.10	.25
224 Ron Sutter	.10	.25
225 Rick Tocchet	.12	.30
226 Ken Wregget	.12	.30
227 Tom Barrasso	.10	.25
228A Phil Bourque ERR	.10	.25
228B Phil Bourque COR	.10	.25
229 Rob Brown	.25	.60
230 Alain Chevrier	.10	.25
231 Paul Coffey	.12	.30
232 John Cullen	.12	.30
233 Gord Dineen	.10	.25
234 Bob Errey	.10	.25
235 Jim Johnson	.07	.20
236 Mario Lemieux	.50	1.25
237 Troy Loney RC	.12	.30
238 Barry Pederson	.10	.25
239 Mark Recchi RC	.40	1.00
240 Kevin Stevens RC	.25	.60
241 Tony Tanti	.10	.25
242 Zarley Zalapski	.10	.25
243 Joe Cirella	.07	.20
244 Lucien DeBlois	.10	.25
245A Marc Fortier ERR	.10	.25
245B Marc Fortier COR	.10	.25
246A P.Gillis ERR bloody nose	30.00	80.00
246B Paul Gillis COR	.10	.25
247 Mike Hough	.10	.25
248 Tony Hrkac	.07	.20
249 Jeff Jackson RC	.10	.25
250 Guy Lafleur	.15	.40
251 Curtis Leschyshyn RC	.10	.25
252 Claude Loiselle RC	.07	.20
253 Mario Marois	.10	.25
254 Tony McKegney	.07	.20
255 Ken McRae RC	.12	.30
256A Michel Petit ERR	.10	.25
256B Michel Petit COR	.10	.25
257 Joe Sakic	.40	1.00
258 Ron Tugnutt	.10	.25
259 Rod Brind'Amour RC	.25	.60
260 Jeff Brown	.12	.30
261 Gino Cavallini	.12	.30
262 Paul Cavallini	.10	.25
263 Brett Hull	.25	.60
264 Mike Lalor RC	.10	.25
265 Dave Lowry RC	.10	.25
266 Paul MacLean	.10	.25
267 Rick Meagher	.10	.25
268 Sergio Momesso RC	.10	.25
269 Adam Oates	.12	.30
270 Vincent Riendeau RC	.12	.30
271 Gordie Roberts	.07	.20
272 Rich Sutter	.12	.30
273 Steve Tuttle	.10	.25
274 Peter Zezel	.12	.30
275A Allan Bester ERR	.12	.30
275B Allan Bester COR	.12	.30
276 Wendel Clark	.20	.50
277 Brian Curran	.07	.20
278 Vin Damphousse	.10	.25
279A Tom Fergus ERR	.07	.20
279B Tom Fergus COR	.07	.20
280 Lou Franceschetti RC	.12	.30
281 Al Iafrate	.07	.20
282 Tom Kurvers	.12	.30
283 Gary Leeman	.10	.25
284 Daniel Marois	.10	.25
285 Brad Marsh	.10	.25
286 Ed Olczyk	.12	.30
287 Mark Osborne	.10	.25
288 Rob Ramage	.12	.30
289 Luke Richardson	.10	.25
290 Gilles Thibaudeau RC	.07	.20
291 Greg Adams	.07	.20
292 Jim Benning	.07	.20
293 Steve Bozek	.10	.25
294 Brian Bradley	.10	.25
295 Garth Butcher	.10	.25
296 Vladimir Krutov RC	.25	.60
297 Igor Larionov RC	.25	.60
298 Doug Lidster	.12	.30
299 Trevor Linden	.12	.30
300 Jyrki Lumme RC	.07	.20
301A Andrew McBain ERR	.10	.25
301B Andrew McBain COR	.10	.25
302 Kirk McLean	.07	.20
303 Dan Quinn	.10	.25
304 Paul Reinhart	.12	.30
305 Jim Sandlak	.12	.30
306 Petri Skriko	.12	.30
307 Don Beaupre	.07	.20
308 Dino Ciccarelli	.12	.30
309 Geoff Courtnall	.10	.25
310 John Druce RC	.12	.30
311 Kevin Hatcher	.10	.25
312 Dale Hunter	.12	.30
313 Calle Johansson	.12	.30
314 Rod Langway	.12	.30
315 Stephen Leach	.10	.25
316 Mike Liut	.07	.20
317 Alan May RC	.07	.20
318 Kelly Miller	.07	.20
319 Michal Pivonka RC	.10	.25
320A Mike Ridley ERR	.07	.20
320B Mike Ridley COR	.07	.20
321 Scott Stevens	.12	.30
322 John Tucker	.10	.25
323 Brent Ashton	.12	.30
324 Laurie Boschman	.10	.25
325 Randy Carlyle	.10	.25
326 Dave Ellett	.07	.20
327 Pat Elynuik	.10	.25
328 Bob Essensa RC	.20	.50
329 Paul Fenton	.12	.30
330A Dale Hawerchuk ERR	.15	.40
330B Dale Hawerchuk COR	.15	.40
331 Paul MacDermid	.10	.25
332A Moe Mantha	.12	.30
333 Dave McLlwain	.12	.30
334 Teppo Numminen RC	.25	.60
335A Fredrik Olausson ERR	.10	.25
335B Fredrik Olausson COR	.10	.25
336 Greg Paslawski	.10	.25
337 Al MacInnis AS	.15	.40
338 Mike Vernon AS	.10	.25
339 Kevin Lowe AS	.12	.30
340 Wayne Gretzky AS	.75	2.00
341 Luc Robitaille AS	.12	.30
342 Brett Hull AS	.25	.60
343 Joe Mullen AS	.10	.25
344 Joe Nieuwendyk AS	.10	.25
345 Steve Larmer AS	.10	.25
346 Doug Wilson AS	.10	.25
347 Steve Yzerman AS	.40	1.00
348A Jari Kurri AS ERR	.15	.40
348B Jari Kurri AS COR (includes ""Signed With"")	.15	.40
349 Mark Messier AS	.25	.60
350 Steve Duchesne AS	.07	.20
351 Mike Gartner AS	.15	.40
352 Bernie Nicholls AS	.10	.25
353 Paul Cavallini AS	.10	.25
354 Al Iafrate AS	.07	.20
355 Kirk McLean AS	.07	.20
356 Thomas Steen AS	.10	.25
357 Ray Bourque AS	.20	.50
358 Cam Neely AS	.12	.30
359 Patrick Roy AS	.30	.75
360 Brian Propp AS	.12	.30
361 Paul Coffey AS	.12	.30
362 Mario Lemieux AS	.50	1.25
363 Dave Andreychuk AS	.12	.30
364 Phil Housley AS	.10	.25
365 Daren Puppa AS	.10	.25
366 Pierre Turgeon AS	.10	.25
367 Ron Francis AS	.15	.40
368 Chris Chelios AS	.12	.30
369A Shayne Corson AS ERR	.10	.25
369B Shayne Corson AS COR	.10	.25
370 Stephane Richer AS	.12	.30
371 Kirk Muller AS	.10	.25
372 Pat LaFontaine AS	.12	.30
373 Brian Leetch AS	.15	.40
374 Rick Tocchet AS	.12	.30
375 Joe Sakic AS	.40	1.00
376 Kevin Hatcher AS	.10	.25
377 Bob Murdoch Adams	.07	.20
378 Brett Hull Byng	.25	.60
379 Sergei Makarov Calder	.25	.60
380 Kevin Lowe Clancy	.12	.30
381 Mark Messier Hart	.25	.60
382 Moog Lemelin Jennings	.12	.30
383 Gord Kluzak Mast	.07	.20
384 Ray Bourque Norris	.20	.50
385A Len Ceglarski Patrick ERR	.07	.20
385B Len Ceglarski Patrick COR	.07	.20
386 Mark Messier Pearson	.25	.60
387 Boston Bruins	.05	.15
388 Wayne Gretzky Ross	.75	2.00
389 Rick Meagher Selke	.10	.25
390 Bill Ranford Smythe	.10	.25
391 Patrick Roy Vezina	.30	.75
392 Edmonton Oilers	.05	.15
393 Boston Bruins	.05	.15
394 Wayne Gretzky LL	.75	2.00
395 Brett Hull LL UER	.25	.60
396 Sergei Makarov ROY	.25	.60
397 Mark Messier MVP	.25	.60
398 Mike Richter RLL	.40	1.00
399 Patrick Roy LL	.30	.75
400 Darren Turcotte RLL	.10	.25
401 Owen Nolan RC	.40	1.00
402 Petr Nedved RC	.12	.30
403 Phil Esposito HOF	.20	.50
404 Darryl Sittler HOF	.15	.40
405 Stan Mikita HOF	.15	.40
406 Andy Brickley	.07	.20
407 Peter Douris RC	.12	.30
408 Nevin Markwart	.07	.20
409 Chris Nilan	.07	.20
410 Stephane Quintal RC	.07	.20
411 Bruce Shoebottom RC	.07	.20
412 Don Sweeney RC	.12	.30
413 Jim Wiemer RC	.12	.30
414 Mike Hartman RC	.12	.30
415 Dale Hawerchuk	.15	.40
416 Benoit Hogue	.12	.30
417 Bill Houlder RC	.12	.30
418 Mikko Makela	.10	.25
419 Robert Ray RC	.12	.30
420 John Tucker	.10	.25
421 Jiri Hrdina RC	.10	.25
422 Mark Hunter	.07	.20
423 Tim Hunter RC	.10	.25
424 Roger Johansson RC	.12	.30
425 Frank Musil	.07	.20
426 Ric Nattress	.07	.20
427 Chris Chelios	.12	.30
428 Jacques Cloutier RC	.10	.25
429 Greg Gilbert	.07	.20
430 Michel Goulet UER (White position and number on front, not black)	.07	.20
431 Mike Hudson RC	.10	.25
432 Jocelyn Lemieux RC	.10	.25
433 Brian Noonan	.12	.30
434 Wayne Presley	.07	.20
435 Brent Fedyk RC	.12	.30
436 Rick Green	.12	.30
437 Marc Habscheid	.10	.25
438 Brad McCrimmon	.12	.30
439 Jeff Beukeboom RC	.10	.25
440 Dave Brown RC	.07	.20
441 Kelly Buchberger RC	.07	.20
442 Greg Hawgood	.10	.25
443 Chris Joseph RC	.07	.20
444 Ken Linseman	.10	.25
445 Eldon Reddick RC	.25	.60
446 Geoff Smith RC	.12	.30
447 Adam Burt RC	.10	.25

448 Sylvain Cote .07 .20
449 Paul Cyr .07 .20
450 Ed Kastelic RC .12 .30
451 Peter Sidorkiewicz .12 .30
452 Mike Tomlak RC .12 .30
453 Carey Wilson .10 .25
454 Daniel Berthiaume .10 .25
455 Scott Bjugstad .07 .20
456 Rod Buskas RC .12 .30
457 John McIntyre .10 .25
458 Tim Watters .07 .20
459 Perry Berezan RC .12 .30
460 Brian Propp .12 .30
461 Ilkka Sinisalo .10 .25
462 Doug Smail .10 .25
463 Bobby Smith .10 .25
464 Chris Dahlquist RC .12 .30
465 Neil Wilkinson RC .10 .25
466 J.J. Daigneault RC .07 .20
467 Eric Desjardins RC .25 .60
468 Gerald Diduck .10 .25
469 Donald Dufresne RC .07 .20
470A Todd Ewen ERR RC .07 .20
470B Todd Ewen COR RC .07 .20
471 Brent Gilchrist RC .10 .25
472 Sylvain Lefebvre RC .10 .25
473 Denis Savard .12 .30
474 Sylvain Turgeon .10 .25
475 Ryan Walter .12 .30
476 Laurie Boschman .10 .25
477 Pat Conacher RC .07 .20
478 Claude Lemieux .07 .20
479 Walt Poddubny .10 .25
480 Alan Stewart RC .12 .30
481 Chris Terreri RC .25 .60
482 Brad Dalgarno .07 .20
483 Dave Chyzowski RC .10 .25
484 Craig Ludwig .12 .30
485 Wayne McBean RC .07 .20
486 Rich Pilon RC .07 .20
487 Joe Reekie RC .07 .20
488 Mick Vukota RC .12 .30
489 Mark Hardy .07 .20
490 Jody Hull RC .12 .30
491 Kris King RC .12 .30
492 Troy Mallette RC .10 .25
493 Kevin Miller RC .12 .30
494 Normand Rochefort .07 .20
495 David Shaw .12 .30
496 Ray Sheppard .07 .20
497 Keith Acton .12 .30
498 Craig Berube RC .07 .20
499 Tony Horacek RC .07 .20
500 Normand Lacombe RC .07 .20
501 Jiri Latal RC .12 .30
502 Pete Peeters .07 .20
503 Derrick Smith RC .10 .25
504 Jay Caufield RC .07 .20
505 Peter Taglianetti .10 .25
506 Randy Gilhen RC .07 .20
507 Randy Hillier .12 .30
508 Joe Mullen .10 .25
509 Frank Pietrangelo RC .07 .20
510 Gordie Roberts .07 .20
511 Bryan Trottier .12 .30
512 Wendell Young RC .12 .30
513 Shawn Anderson RC .07 .20
514 Steven Finn RC .07 .20
515 Bryan Fogarty RC .07 .20
516 Mike Hough .10 .25
517 Darin Kimble .25 .60
518 Randy Velischek .07 .20
519 Craig Wolanin RC .10 .25
520 Bob Bassen RC .07 .20
521 Geoff Courtnall .10 .25
522 Robert Dirk RC .07 .20
523 Glen Featherstone RC .10 .25
524 Mario Marois .10 .25
525 Herb Raglan RC .07 .20
526 Cliff Ronning .07 .20
527 Harold Snepsts .07 .20
528 Scott Stevens .12 .30
529 Ron Wilson .07 .20
530 Aaron Broten .10 .25
531 Lucien DeBlois .10 .25
532 Dave Ellett .07 .20
533A Paul Fenton ERR .12 .30
533B Paul Fenton COR .12 .30
534 Todd Gill RC .07 .20
535 Dave Hannan .07 .20
536 John Kordic .25 .60
537 Mike Krushelnyski .12 .30
538 Kevin Maguire RC .07 .20
539 Michel Petit .10 .25
540 Jeff Reese RC .12 .30
541 David Reid RC .12 .30
542 Doug Shedden .07 .20
543 Dave Capuano RC .12 .30
544 Craig Coxe RC .10 .25
545 Kevan Guy RC .07 .20
546 Rob Murphy RC .12 .30
547 Robert Nordmark RC .10 .25
548 Stan Smyl .07 .20
549 Ronnie Stern RC .07 .20
550 Tim Bergland RC .10 .25
551 Nick Kypreos RC .12 .30
552 Mike Lalor RC .10 .25
553 Rob Murray RC .07 .20
554 Bob Rouse .07 .20
555 Dave Tippett .10 .25
556 Peter Zezel .12 .30
557 Scott Arniel .07 .20
558 Don Barber .10 .25
559 Shawn Cronin RC .07 .20
560 Gord Donnelly RC .07 .20
561 Doug Evans RC .12 .30
562 Phil Housley .10 .25
563 Ed Olczyk .12 .30
564 Mark Osborne .10 .25
565 Thomas Steen .10 .25
566 Boston Bruins Logo .05 .15
567 Buffalo Sabres Logo .05 .15
568 Calgary Flames Logo .05 .15
569 Chicago Blackhawks Logo .05 .15
570 Detroit Red Wings Logo .05 .15
571 Edmonton Oilers Logo .05 .15
572 Hartford Whalers Logo .05 .15
573A Los Angeles Kings Logo ERR .05 .15
573B Los Angeles Kings Logo COR .05 .15
574 Minn. North Stars Logo .05 .15
575 Montreal Canadiens Logo .10 .25
576 New Jersey Devils Logo .05 .15
577 New York Islanders Logo .05 .15
578 New York Rangers Logo .05 .15
579 Philadelphia Flyers Logo .05 .15
580 Pittsburgh Penguins Logo .05 .15
581 Quebec Nordiques Logo .05 .15
582 St. Louis Blues Logo .05 .15
583 Toronto Maple Leafs Logo .08 .20
584 Vancouver Canucks Logo .05 .15
585 Washington Capitals Logo .05 .15
586 Winnipeg Jets Logo .05 .15
587 Ken Hodge Jr. RC .12 .30
588 Vladimir Ruzicka RC .12 .30
589 Wes Walz RC .12 .30
590 Greg Brown RC .12 .30
591 Brad Miller .07 .20
592 Darrin Shannon RC .12 .30
593 Stephane Matteau RC .12 .30
594 Sergei Priakin RC .07 .20
595 Robert Reichel RC .12 .30
596 Ken Sabourin RC .07 .20
597 Tim Sweeney RC .12 .30
598 Ed Belfour RC .40 1.00
599 Frantisek Kucera RC .12 .30
600 Mike McNeil .07 .20
601 Mike Peluso RC .07 .20
602 Tim Cheveldae RC .10 .25
603 Per Djoos RC .12 .30
604 Sergei Fedorov RC .25 .60
605 Johan Garpenlov RC .12 .30
606 Keith Primeau RC .20 .50
607 Paul Ysebaert RC .10 .25
608 Anatoli Semenov RC .10 .25
609 Bobby Holik RC .12 .30
610 Kay Whitmore RC .10 .25
611 Rob Blake RC .20 .50
612 Francois Breault RC .07 .20
613 Mike Craig RC .12 .30
614 Jean-Claude Bergeron RC .12 .30
615 Andrew Cassels RC .07 .20
616 Tom Chorske RC .10 .25
617 Lyle Odelein RC .07 .20
618 Mark Pederson RC .12 .30
619 Zdeno Ciger .12 .30
620 Troy Crowder RC .07 .20
621 Jon Morris RC .07 .20
622 Eric Weinrich RC .12 .30
623 David Marcinyshyn RC .12 .30
624 Jeff Hackett RC .20 .50
625 Rob DiMaio RC .12 .30
626 Steven Rice RC .12 .30
627 Mike Richter RC .40 1.00
628 Dennis Vial RC .10 .25
629 Martin Hostak RC .12 .30
630 Pat Murray RC .12 .30
631 Mike Ricci RC .12 .30
632A Jaromir Jagr RC ERR .75 2.00
632B Jaromir Jagr RC COR .75 2.00
633 Paul Stanton RC .12 .30
634 Scott Gordon RC .07 .20
635 Owen Nolan .40 1.00
636 Mats Sundin RC .20 .50
637 John Tanner RC .12 .30
638 Curtis Joseph RC .40 1.00
639 Peter Ing RC .12 .30
640 Scott Thornton RC .07 .20
641 Troy Gamble RC .12 .30
642 Robert Kron RC .12 .30
643 Petr Nedved .12 .30
644 Adrien Plavsic RC .12 .30
645 Peter Bondra RC .20 .50
646 Jim Hrivnak RC .12 .30
647 Mikhail Tatarinov RC .07 .20
648 Stephane Beauregard RC .10 .25
649 Rick Tabaracci RC .07 .20
650 Mike Bossy CPL .12 .30
651 Bobby Clarke CPL .20 .50
652 Alex Delvecchio CPL .12 .30
653 Marcel Dionne CPL .15 .40
654 Gordie Howe CPL .40 1.00
655 Stan Mikita CPL .15 .40
656 Denis Potvin CPL .12 .30
657 Bobby Clarke HOF .20 .50
658 Alex Delvecchio HOF .12 .30
659 Tony Esposito HOF .07 .20
660 Gordie Howe HOF .40 1.00
661 Mike Milbury CO .07 .20
662 Rick Dudley CO .07 .20
663 Doug Risebrough CO .07 .20
664 Bryan Murray CO RC .07 .20
665 John Muckler CO RC .07 .20
666 Rick Ley CO .07 .20
667 Tom Webster CO .07 .20
668 Bob Gainey CO .07 .20
669 Pat Burns CO RC .25 .60
670 John Cunniff CO RC .07 .20
671 Al Arbour CO .07 .20
672 Roger Neilson CO RC .25 .60
673 Paul Holmgren CO .10 .25
674 Bob Johnson CO RC .25 .60
675 Dave Chambers CO RC .07 .20
676 Brian Sutter CO .07 .20
677 Tom Watt CO RC .07 .20
678 Bob McCammon CO .07 .20
679 Terry Murray CO .07 .20
680 Bob Murdoch CO .07 .20
681 Ron Asselstine OFF .07 .20
682 Wayne Bonney OFF .07 .20
683 Kevin Collins OFF .07 .20
684 Pat Dapuzzo OFF .07 .20
685 Ron Finn OFF .07 .20
686 Kerry Fraser OFF .07 .20
687 Gerard Gauthier OFF .07 .20
688 Terry Gregson OFF .07 .20
689 Bob Hodges OFF .07 .20
690 Ron Hoggarth OFF .07 .20
691 Don Koharski OFF .07 .20
692 Dan Marouelli OFF .07 .20
693 Danny McCourt OFF .07 .20
694 Bill McCreary OFF .07 .20
695 Denis Morel OFF .07 .20
696 Jerry Pateman OFF .07 .20
697 Ray Scapinello OFF .07 .20
698 Rob Shick OFF .07 .20
699 Paul Stewart OFF .07 .20
700 Leon Stickle OFF .07 .20
701 Andy van Hellemond OFF .07 .20
702 Mark Vines OFF .07 .20
703 Wayne Gretzky 2000th .75 2.00
704 Stanley Cup Champs .05 .15
705 The Puck-La Rondelle .05 .15
335C Fred Olausson .10 .25
NNO Stanley Cup Hologram 200.00 350.00

1990-91 Pro Set Player of the Month

COMPLETE SET (4) 8.00 20.00
P1 Tom Barrasso
POM December 1990 1.50 4.00
P2 Wayne Gretzky
POM January 1991 4.00 10.00
P3 Brett Hull
POM February 1991 2.50 6.00
NNO Pete Peeters
POM November 1990 1.50 4.00

1991-92 Pro Set Preview

COMPLETE SET (6) .60 1.50
151 Randy Wood NNO .08 .25
171 Gord Murphy NNO .08 .25
203 Craig Wolanin NNO .08 .25
229 David Reid NNO .08 .25
266 Bob Essensa NNO .08 .25
NNO Title Card .02 .10

1991-92 Pro Set

1 Glen Wesley .07 .20
2 Craig Janney .07 .20
3 Ken Hodge Jr. .07 .20
4 Randy Burridge .07 .20
5 Cam Neely .10 .25
6 Bob Sweeney .05 .15
7 Garry Galley .07 .20
8 Petri Skriko .05 .15
9 Ray Bourque .15 .40
10 Andy Moog UER .10 .25
11 Dave Christian .05 .15
12 Dave Poulin .07 .20
13 Jeff Lazaro RC .07 .20
14 Darrin Shannon .07 .20
15 Pierre Turgeon UER .07 .20
16 Alexander Mogilny .07 .20
17 Benoit Hogue UER
(Stats show two seasons
with Winnipeg .07 .20
18 Dave Snuggerud .05 .15
19 Doug Bodger UER .07 .20
20 Uwe Krupp .07 .20
21 Daren Puppa .07 .20
22 Christian Ruuttu .07 .20
23 Dave Andreychuk .10 .25
24 Dale Hawerchuk .12 .30
25 Mike Ramsey .07 .20
26 Rick Vaive .05 .15
27 Stephane Matteau .07 .20
28 Theo Fleury .07 .20
29 Joe Nieuwendyk .07 .20
30 Gary Roberts .07 .20
31 Paul Ranheim .10 .25
32 Gary Suter .05 .15
33 Al MacInnis .12 .30
34 Doug Gilmour .12 .30
35 Mike Vernon .07 .20
36 Carey Wilson .07 .20
37 Joel Otto .07 .20
38 Jamie Macoun .07 .20
39 Sergei Makarov .07 .20
40 Jeremy Roenick .15 .40
41 Dave Manson .07 .20
42 Adam Creighton .07 .20
43 Ed Belfour .25 .60
44 Wayne Presley .07 .20
45 Steve Thomas .07 .20
46 Troy Murray .07 .20
47 Bob McGill .07 .20
48 Chris Chelios .10 .25
49 Steve Larmer .07 .20
50 Michel Goulet .07 .20
51 Dirk Graham .07 .20
52 Doug Wilson .07 .20
53 Sergei Fedorov .15 .40
54 Yves Racine .07 .20
55 Jimmy Carson .07 .20
56 Johan Garpenlov .07 .20
57 Tim Cheveldae .07 .20
58 Shawn Burr .07 .20
59 Paul Ysebaert .07 .20
60 Kevin Miller .07 .20
61 Bob Probert .10 .25
62 Steve Yzerman .30 .75
63 Gerard Gallant .05 .15
64 Rick Zombo .07 .20
65 Dave Barr .07 .20
66 Martin Gelinas .07 .20
67 Adam Graves UER .07 .20
68 Joe Murphy .07 .20
69 Craig Simpson .05 .15
70 Bill Ranford .07 .20
71 Esa Tikkanen .07 .20
72 Petr Klima .07 .20
73 Steve Smith .10 .25
74 Mark Messier .20 .50
75 Glenn Anderson .07 .20
76 Kevin Lowe .07 .20
77 Craig MacTavish .07 .20
78 Grant Fuhr .15 .40
79 Bobby Holik .10 .25
80 Rob Brown .07 .20
81 Doug Houda .07 .20
82 Sylvain Cote .07 .20
83 Todd Krygier .07 .20
84 Dean Evason .07 .20
85 John Cullen .07 .20
86 Pat Verbeek .07 .20
87 Brad Shaw .05 .15
88 Paul Cyr UER .07 .20
89 Kevin Dineen .07 .20
90 Peter Sidorkiewicz .07 .20
91 Zarley Zalapski .07 .20
92 Rob Blake .10 .25
93 Jari Kurri UER .07 .20
94 Todd Elik .07 .20
95 Luc Robitaille .10 .25
96 Steve Duchesne .05 .15
97 Tomas Sandstrom .07 .20
98 Tony Granato .05 .15
99 Bob Kudelski .05 .15
100 Marty McSorley .07 .20
101 Wayne Gretzky .60 1.50
102 Kelly Hrudey .07 .20
103 Dave Taylor .07 .20
104 Larry Robinson .10 .25
105 Mike Modano .20 .50
106 Ulf Dahlen .07 .20
107 Mark Tinordi .07 .20
108 Dave Gagner .07 .20
109 Brian Bellows .07 .20
110 Gaetan Duchesne .05 .15
111 Jon Casey .07 .20
112 Neal Broten .07 .20
113 Brian Propp .07 .20
114 Curt Giles .10 .25
115 Bobby Smith .07 .20
116 Jim Johnson .07 .20
117 Doug Smail .07 .20
118 Eric Desjardins .10 .25
119 Mathieu Schneider .07 .20
120 Stephan Lebeau .07 .20
121 Mike Keane .05 .15
122 Stephane Richer .07 .20
123 Petr Svoboda .07 .20
124 J.J. Daigneault .05 .15
125 Patrick Roy .25 .60
126 Russ Courtnall .07 .20
127 Brian Skrudland .07 .20
128 Denis Savard .10 .25
129 Mike McPhee .07 .20
130 Guy Carbonneau .07 .20
131 Brendan Shanahan .10 .25
132 Sean Burke .10 .25
133 Eric Weinrich .10 .25
134 Kirk Muller .05 .15
135 Claude Lemieux .07 .20
136 John MacLean .07 .20
137 Chris Terreri .07 .20
138 Doug Brown .07 .20
139 Ken Daneyko .07 .20
140 Bruce Driver .07 .20
141 Patrik Sundstrom .07 .20
142 Slava Fetisov .07 .20
143 Peter Stastny .07 .20
144 Wayne McBean .05 .15
145 Bill Berg .07 .20
146 Derek King .05 .15
147 David Volek .07 .20
148 Jeff Norton .07 .20
149 Pat LaFontaine .10 .25
150 Gary Nylund .07 .20
151 Randy Wood .07 .20
152 Pat Flatley .07 .20
153 Glenn Healy .10 .25
154 Brent Sutter .07 .20
155 Craig Ludwig .07 .20
156 Ray Ferraro .07 .20
157 Troy Mallette .07 .20
158 Mark Janssens .07 .20
159 Brian Leetch UER .07 .20
160 Darren Turcotte .07 .20
161 Mike Richter .10 .25
162 Ray Sheppard .07 .20
163 Randy Moller .07 .20
164 James Patrick .07 .20
165 Brian Mullen UER .07 .20
166 Bernie Nicholls .07 .20
167 Mike Gartner .12 .30
168 Kelly Kisio UER .07 .20
169 John Ogrodnick .07 .20
170 Mike Ricci .05 .15
171 Gord Murphy .07 .20
172 Scott Mellanby .07 .20
173 Terry Carkner .07 .20
174 Derrick Smith .07 .20
175 Murray Craven .07 .20
176 Ron Hextall .10 .25
177 Rick Tocchet .07 .20
178 Ron Sutter .07 .20
179 Pelle Eklund .07 .20
180 Tim Kerr UER .05 .15
181 Kjell Samuelsson .07 .20
182 Mark Howe .10 .25
183 Jaromir Jagr .30 .75
184 Mark Recchi .12 .30
185 Kevin Stevens .07 .20
186 Tom Barrasso .07 .20
187 Bob Errey .07 .20
188 Ron Francis .12 .30
189 Phil Bourque .07 .20
190 Paul Coffey .10 .25
191 Joe Mullen .07 .20
192 Bryan Trottier .10 .25
193 Larry Murphy .07 .20
194 Mario Lemieux .40 1.00
195 Scott Young .07 .20
196 Owen Nolan .10 .25
197 Mats Sundin .10 .25
198 Curtis Leschyshyn .07 .20
199 Joe Sakic .30 .75
200 Bryan Fogarty .07 .20
201 Stephane Morin .07 .20
202 Ron Tugnutt .07 .20
203 Craig Wolanin .07 .20
204 Steven Finn .05 .15
205 Tony Hrkac .07 .20
206 Randy Velischek .07 .20
207 Alexei Gusarov RC .07 .20
208 Scott Pearson .07 .20
209 Dan Quinn .07 .20
210 Garth Butcher .07 .20
211 Rod Brind'Amour UER .07 .20
212 Jeff Brown .07 .20
213 Vincent Riendeau .07 .20
214 Paul Cavallini .07 .20
215 Brett Hull .20 .50
216 Scott Stevens .10 .25
217 Rich Sutter .07 .20
218 Gino Cavallini .07 .20
219 Adam Oates UER .10 .25
220 Ron Wilson .07 .20
221 Bob Bassen .07 .20
222 Peter Ing .07 .20
223 Daniel Marois .07 .20
224 Vincent Damphousse .07 .20
225 Wendel Clark .15 .40
226 Todd Gill .07 .20
227 Peter Zezel .05 .15
228 Bob Rouse .07 .20
229 David Reid .05 .15
230 Dave Ellett .07 .20
231 Gary Leeman .07 .20
232 Rob Ramage .07 .20
233 Mike Krushelnyski .07 .20
234 Tom Fergus .05 .15
235 Petr Nedved .07 .20
236 Trevor Linden .10 .25
237 Dave Capuano .07 .20
238 Troy Gamble .05 .15
239 Robert Kron UER .07 .20
240 Jyrki Lumme .07 .20
241 Cliff Ronning .05 .15
242 Sergio Momesso .07 .20
243 Greg Adams .07 .20
244 Tom Kurvers .07 .20
245 Geoff Courtnall .07 .20
246 Igor Larionov .07 .20
247 Doug Lidster UER .07 .20
248 Calle Johansson .07 .20
249 Kevin Hatcher .07 .20
250 Al Iafrate .07 .20
251 John Druce .07 .20
252 Michal Pivonka .07 .20
253 Stephen Leach .07 .20
254 Mike Ridley .07 .20
255 Mike Lalor .07 .20
256 Kelly Miller .07 .20
257 Don Beaupre .07 .20
258 Dino Ciccarelli .07 .20
259 Rod Langway .07 .20
260 Dimitri Khristich .07 .20
261 Teppo Numminen .07 .20
262 Pat Elynuik .07 .20
263 Danton Cole .05 .15
264 Fredrik Olausson UER .07 .20
265 Ed Olczyk .07 .20
266 Bob Essensa .07 .20
267 Phil Housley .07 .20
268 Shawn Cronin .07 .20
269 Paul MacDermid .07 .20
270 Mark Osborne .07 .20
271 Thomas Steen .07 .20
272 Brent Ashton .07 .20
273 Randy Carlyle .07 .20
274 Theo Fleury AS .07 .20
275 Al MacInnis AS .12 .30
276 Gary Suter AS .05 .15
277 Mike Vernon AS .07 .20
278 Chris Chelios AS .10 .25
279 Steve Larmer AS .07 .20
280 Jeremy Roenick AS .15 .40
281 Steve Yzerman AS .30 .75
282 Mark Messier AS .20 .50
283 Bill Ranford AS .07 .20
284 Steve Smith AS .10 .25
285 Wayne Gretzky AS .60 1.50
286 Luc Robitaille AS .10 .25
287 Tomas Sandstrom AS .07 .20
288 Dave Gagner AS .07 .20
289 Bobby Smith AS .07 .20
290 Brett Hull AS .20 .50
291 Adam Oates AS .10 .25
292 Scott Stevens AS .10 .25
293 Vincent Damphousse AS .07 .20
294 Trevor Linden AS .10 .25
295 Phil Housley AS .07 .20
296 Ray Bourque AS .15 .40
297 Dave Christian AS .05 .15
298 Garry Galley AS .07 .20
299 Andy Moog AS .10 .25
300 Cam Neely AS .10 .25
301 Uwe Krupp AS .07 .20
302 John Cullen AS .07 .20
303 Pat Verbeek AS .07 .20
304 Patrick Roy AS .25 .60
305 Denis Savard AS .10 .25
306 Brian Skrudland AS .07 .20
307 John MacLean AS .07 .20
308 Pat LaFontaine AS .10 .25
309 Brian Leetch AS .07 .20
310 Darren Turcotte AS .07 .20
311 Rick Tocchet AS .07 .20
312 Paul Coffey AS .10 .25
313 Mark Recchi AS .12 .30
314 Kevin Stevens AS .07 .20
315 Joe Sakic AS .30 .75
316 Kevin Hatcher AS .07 .20
317 Guy Lafleur AS .12 .30
318 Mario Lemieux Smythe .40 1.00
319 Pittsburgh Penguins UER .30 .75
320 Brett Hull Hart .20 .50
321 Ed Belfour Jennings
Vezina .25 .60
322 Ray Bourque
Norris .15 .40
323 Dirk Graham
Selke .07 .20
324 W.Gretzky Ross/Byng .60 1.50
325 Dave Taylor
King Clancy Trophy .07 .20
326 Brett Hull PS-POY .20 .50
327 Brian Hayward .07 .20
328 Neil Wilkinson UER .07 .20
329 Craig Coxe .05 .15
330 Rob Zettler .07 .20
331 Jeff Hackett .07 .20
332 Joe Malone .07 .20
333 Georges Vezina .07 .20
334 The Modern Arena .05 .15
335 Ace Bailey Benefit .07 .20
336 Howie Morenz .07 .20
337 The Punch Line .20 .50
338 The Kid Line .07 .20
339 Before the Zamboni .05 .15
340 Bill Barilko 4.00 10.00
341 Jacques Plante .07 .20
342 Arena Designs .05 .15
343 Terry Sawchuk .07 .20
344 Gordie Howe .30 .75
345 Guy Carbonneau .07 .20
346 Stephen Leach .07 .20
347 Peter Douris .07 .20
348 David Reid .05 .15
349 Bob Carpenter .07 .20
350 Stephane Quintal .07 .20
351 Barry Pederson .07 .20
352 Brent Ashton .07 .20
353 Vladimir Ruzicka .07 .20
354 Brad Miller .07 .20
355 Robert Ray .05 .15
356 Colin Patterson .07 .20
357 Gord Donnelly .07 .20
358 Pat LaFontaine .10 .25
359 Randy Wood .07 .20
360 Randy Hillier .07 .20
361 Robert Reichel .20 .50
362 Ronnie Stern .07 .20
363 Ric Nattress .07 .20
364 Tim Sweeney .07 .20
365 Marc Habscheid .07 .20
366 Tim Hunter .07 .20
367 Rick Wamsley .05 .15
368 Frank Musil .07 .20
369 Mike Hudson .07 .20
370 Steve Smith .10 .25
371 Keith Brown .07 .20
372 Greg Gilbert .07 .20
373 John Tonelli .07 .20
374 Brent Sutter .07 .20
375 Brad Lauer .07 .20
376 Alan Kerr .07 .20
377 Brad McCrimmon .07 .20
378 Brad Marsh .10 .25
379 Brent Fedyk .07 .20
380 Ray Sheppard .07 .20
381 Vincent Damphousse .07 .20
382 Craig Muni .07 .20
383 Scott Mellanby .07 .20
384 Geoff Smith .07 .20
385 Kelly Buchberger .07 .20
386 Bernie Nicholls .07 .20
387 Luke Richardson .07 .20
388 Peter Ing .07 .20
389 Dave Manson .07 .20
390 Mark Hunter .07 .20
391 Jim McKenzie RC .10 .25
392 Randy Cunneyworth .07 .20
393 Murray Craven .07 .20
394 Mikael Andersson .07 .20
395 Andrew Cassels .07 .20
396 Randy Ladouceur .07 .20
397 Marc Bergevin .07 .20
398 Brian Benning .07 .20
399 Mike Donnelly RC .10 .25
400 Charlie Huddy .07 .20
401 John McIntyre .07 .20
402 Jay Miller .07 .20
403 Randy Gilhen .07 .20
404 Stewart Gavin .07 .20
405 Mike Craig .07 .20
406 Brian Glynn .07 .20
407 Rob Ramage .07 .20
408 Chris Dahlquist .07 .20
409 Basil McRae .05 .15
410 Todd Elik .07 .20
411 Craig Ludwig .07 .20
412 Kirk Muller .05 .15
413 Shayne Corson .07 .20
414 Brent Gilchrist .07 .20
415 Mario Roberge .07 .20
416 Sylvain Turgeon .07 .20
417 Alain Cote .07 .20
418 Donald Dufresne .07 .20
419 Todd Ewen .07 .20
420 Stephane Richer .07 .20
421 David Maley .07 .20
422 Randy McKay .07 .20
423 Scott Stevens .10 .25
424 Jon Morris .07 .20
425 Claude Vilgrain .07 .20
426 Laurie Boschman .07 .20
427 Pat Conacher .07 .20
428 Tom Kurvers .07 .20
429 Joe Reekie .07 .20
430 Rob DiMaio .07 .20
431 Tom Fitzgerald .07 .20
432 Ken Baumgartner .05 .15
433 Pierre Turgeon .07 .20
434 Dave McLlwain .07 .20
435 Benoit Hogue .07 .20
436 Uwe Krupp .07 .20
437 Adam Creighton .07 .20
438 Steve Thomas .07 .20
439 Mark Messier .20 .50
440 Tie Domi .07 .20
441 Sergei Nemchinov .07 .20
442 Mark Hardy .07 .20
443 Adam Graves .07 .20
444 Jeff Beukeboom .07 .20
445 Kris King .07 .20
446 Tim Kerr .05 .15
447 John Vanbiesbrouck .10 .25
448 Steve Duchesne .05 .15
449 Steve Kasper .05 .15
450 Ken Wregget .07 .20
451 Kevin Dineen .07 .20
452 Dave Brown .05 .15
453 Rod Brind'Amour .07 .20
454 Jiri Latal .05 .15
455 Tony Horacek .07 .20
456 Brad Jones .07 .20
457 Paul Stanton .07 .20
458 Gordie Roberts .07 .20
459 Ulf Samuelsson .07 .20
460 Ken Priestlay .07 .20
461 Jiri Hrdina .07 .20
462 Mikhail Tatarinov .07 .20
463 Mike Hough .07 .20
464 Don Barber .07 .20
465 Greg Smyth RC .07 .20
466 Doug Smail .07 .20
467 Mike McNeill .07 .20
468 John Kordic .07 .20
469 Greg Paslawski .07 .20
470 Herb Raglan .07 .20
471 Dave Christian .05 .15
472 Murray Baron .07 .20
473 Curtis Joseph .12 .30
474 Rick Zombo .07 .20
475 Brendan Shanahan .10 .25
476 Ron Sutter .07 .20
477 Mario Marois .07 .20
478 Doug Wilson .07 .20
479 Kelly Kisio .07 .20
480 Bob McGill .07 .20
481 Perry Anderson .07 .20
482 Brian Lawton .07 .20
483 Neil Wilkinson .07 .20
484 Ken Hammond RC .07 .20
485 David Bruce RC .10 .25
486 Steve Bozek .07 .20
487 Perry Berezan .07 .20
488 Wayne Presley .07 .20
489 Brian Bradley .07 .20
490 Darryl Shannon .10 .25
491 Lucien DeBlois .07 .20
492 Michel Petit .07 .20
493 Claude Loiselle .07 .20
494 Grant Fuhr .15 .40
495 Craig Berube .07 .20
496 Mike Bullard .07 .20
497 Jim Sandlak .07 .20
498 Dana Murzyn .07 .20
499 Garry Valk .07 .20
500 Andrew McBain .07 .20
501 Kirk McLean .07 .20
502 Gerald Diduck .07 .20
503 Dave Babych .07 .20
504 Ryan Walter .07 .20
505 Gino Odjick .05 .15
506 Dale Hunter .07 .20
507 Tim Bergland .07 .20
508 Alan May .07 .20
509 Jim Hrivnak .07 .20
510 Randy Burridge .07 .20
511 Peter Bondra .10 .25
512 Sylvain Cote .07 .20
513 Nick Kypreos .07 .20
514 Troy Murray .07 .20
515 Darrin Shannon .07 .20
516 Bryan Erickson .07 .20
517 Petri Skriko .05 .15
518 Mike Eagles .07 .20
519 Mike Hartman .07 .20
520 Bob Beers .05 .15
521 Matt DelGuidice RC .10 .25
522 Chris Winnes .07 .20
523 Brad May .07 .20
524 Donald Audette .07 .20
525 Kevin Haller RC .10 .25
526 Martin Simard .07 .20
527 Tomas Forslund RC .10 .25
528 Mark Osiecki .07 .20
529 Dominik Hasek RC .30 .75
530 Jimmy Waite .07 .20
531 Nicklas Lidstrom RC .40 1.00
532 Martin Lapointe .07 .20
533 Vladimir Konstantinov RC .25 .60
534 Josef Beranek RC .10 .25
535 Louie DeBrusk RC .10 .25
536 Geoff Sanderson RC .10 .25
537 Mark Greig .07 .20
538 Michel Picard RC .10 .25
539 Chris Tancill RC .07 .20
540 Peter Ahola RC .10 .25
541 Francois Breault .07 .20
542 Darryl Sydor .07 .20
543 Derian Hatcher .07 .20
544 Marc Bureau .07 .20
545 John LeClair RC .25 .60
546 Paul DiPietro RC .07 .20
547 Scott Niedermayer .10 .25
548 Kevin Todd RC .10 .25
549 Doug Weight RC .25 .60
550 Tony Amonte RC .25 .60
551 Corey Foster RC .10 .25
552 Dominic Roussel RC .10 .25
553 Dan Kordic RC .07 .20
554 Jim Paek RC .10 .25
555 Kip Miller .07 .20
556 Claude Lapointe RC .07 .20
557 Nelson Emerson .07 .20
558 Pat Falloon .07 .20
559 Pat MacLeod RC .10 .25
560 Rick Lessard RC .07 .20
561 Link Gaetz .07 .20
562 Rob Pearson RC .10 .25
563 Alexander Godynyuk RC .10 .25
564 Pavel Bure .10 .25
565 Russell Romaniuk RC .10 .25
566 Stu Barnes .07 .20
567 Ray Bourque CAP .15 .40
568 Mike Ramsey CAP .07 .20
569 Joe Nieuwendyk CAP .07 .20
570 Dirk Graham CAP .07 .20
571 Steve Yzerman CAP .30 .75
572 Kevin Lowe CAP .07 .20
573 Randy Ladouceur CAP .07 .20
574 Wayne Gretzky CAP .60 1.50
575 Mark Tinordi CAP .07 .20
576 Guy Carbonneau CAP .07 .20
577 Bruce Driver CAP .07 .20
578 Pat Flatley CAP .07 .20
579 Mark Messier CAP .20 .50
580 Rick Tocchet CAP .07 .20
581 Mario Lemieux CAP .40 1.00
582 Mike Hough CAP .07 .20
583 Garth Butcher CAP .07 .20
584 Doug Wilson CAP .07 .20
585 Wendel Clark CAP .15 .40
586 Trevor Linden CAP .10 .25
587 Rod Langway CAP .07 .20
588 Troy Murray CAP .07 .20
589 Practicing Outdoors .05 .15
590 Shape Up .05 .15
591 Boston Bruins Cartoon .05 .15
592 Opening Night .05 .15
593 Rod Gilbert .07 .20
594 Phil Esposito .15 .40
595 Dale Tallon .07 .20
596 Gilbert Perreault .10 .25
597 Bernie Federko .07 .20
598 All-Star Game .05 .15

599 Patrick Roy LL .25 .60
600 Ed Belfour LL .25 .60
601 Don Beaupre LL .07 .20
602 Bob Essensa LL .07 .20
603 Kirk McLean UER LL .07 .20
604 Mike Gartner LL .12 .30
605 Jeremy Roenick LL .15 .40
606 Rob Brown LL .07 .20
607 Ulf Dahlen LL .07 .20
608 Paul Ysebaert LL .07 .20
609 Brad McCrimmon LL .07 .20
610 Nicklas Lidstrom LL .40 1.00
611 Kelly Miller LL .07 .20
612 Jim Kyte SMART .07 .20
613 Patrick Roy SMART .25 .60
614 Alan May SMART .07 .20
615 Kelly Miller SMART .07 .20
AU125 Patrick Roy AU/1000 40.00 100.00
AU501 Kirk McLean AU/500 20.00 50.00
AU599 Patrick Roy LL AU/1000 40.00 100.00
NNO 75th Anniv.HOLO/10,000 20.00 50.00

1991-92 Pro Set French

COMPLETE SET (615) 6.00 15.00
COMP.SERIES 1 (345) 3.00 8.00
COMP.SERIES 2 (270) 3.00 8.00
*FRENCH: .4X TO 1X BASIC PRO SET

1991-92 Pro Set CC

COMPLETE SET (9) 6.00 15.00
*FRENCH: .5X TO 1.2X BASIC INSERTS
CC1 Entry Draft .40 1.00
CC2 The Mask 2.00 5.00
CC3 Pat Falloon SP 3.00 8.00
CC4 Scott Niedermayer SP 3.00 8.00
CC5 Wayne Gretzky 2.00 5.00
CC6 Brett Hull .60 1.50
CC7 Adam Oates .50 1.25
CC8 Mark Recchi .60 1.50
CC9 John Cullen .40 1.00

1991-92 Pro Set Gazette

COMPLETE SET (2) 2.00 5.00
2 Patrick Roy
(Gazette Collectible) 1.25 3.00
SC1 Patrick Roy
(Special Collectible 1) 1.25 3.00

1991-92 Pro Set HOF Induction

COMPLETE SET (14) 30.00 75.00
1 Mike Bossy/1991 HOF Inductee 6.00 15.00
2 Denis Potvin/1991 HOF Inductee 5.00 12.00
3 Bob Pulford/1991 HOF Inductee 3.00 8.00
4 William Scott Bowman
1991 HOF Inductee 6.00 15.00
5 Neil P. Armstrong
1991 HOF Inductee 2.50 6.00
6 Clint Smith/1991 HOF Inductee 2.50 6.00
7 1903-04 Ottawa Silver
Seven 2.00 5.00
8 1905 Ottawa Silver
Seven 2.00 5.00
9 1909 Ottawa Senators 2.00 5.00
10 1911 Ottawa Senators 2.00 5.00
11 1920-21 Ottawa
Senators 2.00 5.00
12 1923 Ottawa Senators 2.00 5.00
13 1927 Ottawa Senators 2.00 5.00
14 Title Card
1991 Hockey Hall of Fame 2.00 5.00

1991-92 Pro Set Awards Special

AC1 Ed Belfour 12.00 30.00
AC2 Mike Richter 12.00 30.00
AC3 Patrick Roy 75.00 200.00
AC4 Wayne Gretzky 125.00 300.00
AC5 Joe Sakic 30.00 75.00
AC6 Brett Hull 25.00 60.00
AC7 Ray Bourque 25.00 60.00
AC8 Al MacInnis 6.00 15.00
AC9 Luc Robitaille 10.00 25.00
AC10 Sergei Fedorov 40.00 100.00
AC11 Ken Hodge Jr. .75 2.00
AC12 Dirk Graham .75 2.00
AC13 Steve Larmer 2.00 5.00
AC14 Esa Tikkanen 4.00 10.00
AC15 Chris Chelios 15.00 40.00
AC16 Dave Taylor 1.50 4.00
NNO Title Card .40 1.00

1991-92 Pro Set NHL Sponsor Awards

AC17 Kevin Dineen
Bud Light
NHL Man
of the Year Award 2.50 6.00
AC18 Brett Hull
NHL Pro Set Player
of the Year Award 25.00 60.00
AC19 Ed Belfour
Trico Goaltender Award 10.00 25.00
AC20 Theo Fleury
Alka-Seltzer
Plus Award 10.00 25.00
AC21 Marty McSorley
Alka-Seltzer
Plus Award 2.50 6.00
AC22 Mike Ilitch
Detroit Red Wings OWN
Lester Patrick Award 1.50 4.00
AC23 Rod Gilbert
Lester Patrick Award 2.50 6.00
NNO Title Card
1990-91 NHL
Sponsor Awards .40 1.00

1991-92 Pro Set Opening Night

COMPLETE SET (2) 3.00 8.00
NNO NHL 75th Anniversary
Opening Night 1.50 4.00
NNO 1991-92 Opening Night 1.50 4.00

1991-92 Pro Set Platinum PC

COMPLETE SET (20) 12.50 25.00
PC1 John Vanbiesbrouck .50 1.25
PC2 Pete Peeters .30 .75
PC3 Tom Barrasso .30 .75
PC4 Wayne Gretzky 2.00 5.00
PC5 Brett Hull .75 2.00
PC6 Kelly Hrudey .30 .75
PC7 Sergei Fedorov .75 2.00
PC8 Rob Blake .30 .75
PC9 Ken Hodge Jr. .20 .50
PC10 Eric Weinrich .20 .50
PC11 Mike Gartner .30 .75
PC12 Paul Coffey .50 1.25
PC13 Bobby Smith .30 .75
PC14 Wayne Gretzky 2.00 5.00
PC15 Michel Goulet .40 1.00
PC16 Mike Liut .30 .75
PC17 Brian Propp .20 .50
PC18 Denis Savard .30 .75
PC19 Bryan Trottier .40 1.00
PC20 Mark Messier .60 1.50

1991-92 Pro Set Platinum HOF 75th

COMPLETE SET (8) 3.00 8.00
145 Boston Bruins .02 .10
146 Chicago Blackhawks .02 .10
147 Detroit Red Wings .02 .10
148 Montreal Canadiens .02 .10
149 New York Rangers .02 .10
150 Toronto Maple Leafs .02 .10
NNO Title Card
(Blank back) 1.25 3.00
HHOF1 Hockey Hall of Fame 2.00 5.00

1991-92 Pro Set Player of the Month

COMPLETE SET (6) 28.00 70.00
P1 Kirk McLean 2.00 5.00
P2 Kevin Stevens 2.00 5.00
P3 Mario Lemieux 12.00 30.00
P4 Andy Moog 4.00 10.00
P5 Pat LaFontaine 4.00 10.00
P6 Luc Robitaille 4.00 10.00

1991-92 Pro Set Puck Candy Promos

COMPLETE SET (3) 1.50 4.00
1 Kirk McLean .40 1.00
2 Andy Moog .75 2.00
3 Pat Verbeek .40 1.00

1991-92 Pro Set Puck Candy

COMPLETE SET (30) 16.00 40.00
1 Ray Bourque .75 2.00
2 Andy Moog .30 .75
3 Doug Bodger .15 .40
4 Theo Fleury .30 .75
5 Al MacInnis .30 .75
6 Jeremy Roenick .60 1.50
7 Tim Cheveldae .15 .40
8 Steve Yzerman 1.50 4.00
9 Craig Simpson .15 .40
10 Pat Verbeek .15 .40
11 Wayne Gretzky 15.00 30.00
12 Luc Robitaille .30 .75
13 Brian Bellows .15 .40
14 Patrick Roy 3.00 8.00
15 Guy Carbonneau .15 .40
16 Peter Stastny .30 .75
17 Adam Creighton .15 .40
18 Glenn Healy .30 .75
19 Mark Messier .75 2.00
20 Rod Brind'Amour .30 .75
21 Paul Coffey .60 1.50
22 Tom Barasso .30 .75
23 Joe Sakic 1.25 3.00
24 Brett Hull .75 2.00
25 Adam Oates .30 .75
26 Kelly Kisio .15 .40
27 Grant Fuhr .30 .75
28 Kirk McLean .30 .75
29 Kevin Hatcher .15 .40
30 Phil Housley .15 .40

1991-92 Pro Set Rink Rat

COMPLETE SET (2) 3.00 8.00
RR1 Rink Rat 1.50 4.00
RR2 Rink Rat 1.50 4.00

1991-92 Pro Set St. Louis Midwest

COMPLETE SET (4) 4.00 10.00
1 Adam Oates 1.25 3.00
2 Paul Cavallini .40 1.00
3 Rick Meagher .40 1.00
4 Brett Hull 3.00 8.00

1992-93 Pro Set

1 Mario Lemieux PS-POY .40 1.00
2 Patrick Roy THN-POY .25 .60
3 Adam Oates .10 .25
4 Ray Bourque .15 .40
5 Vladimir Ruzicka .05 .15
6 Stephen Leach .05 .15
7 Andy Moog .10 .25
8 Cam Neely .10 .25
9 Dave Poulin .05 .15
10 Glen Wesley .05 .15
11 Gord Murphy .07 .20
12 Dale Hawerchuk .12 .30
13 Pat LaFontaine .10 .25
14 Tom Draper .05 .15
15 Dave Andreychuk .10 .25
16 Petr Svoboda .07 .20
17 Doug Bodger .05 .15
18 Donald Audette .07 .20
19 Alexander Mogilny .07 .20
20 Randy Wood .05 .15
21 Gary Roberts .05 .15
22 Al MacInnis .12 .30
23 Theo Fleury .15 .40
24 Sergei Makarov .05 .15
25 Mike Vernon .07 .20
26 Joe Nieuwendyk .07 .20
27 Gary Suter .05 .15
28 Joel Otto .05 .15
29 Paul Ranheim .05 .15
30 Jeremy Roenick .15 .40
31 Steve Larmer .05 .15
32 Michel Goulet .07 .20
33 Ed Belfour .10 .25
34 Chris Chelios .10 .25
35 Igor Kravchuk .05 .15
36 Brent Sutter .05 .15
37 Steve Smith .05 .15
38 Dirk Graham .05 .15
39 Steve Yzerman .25 .60
40 Sergei Fedorov .15 .40
41 Paul Ysebaert .05 .15
42 Nicklas Lidstrom .07 .20
43 Tim Cheveldae .05 .15
44 Vladimir Konstantinov .10 .25
45 Shawn Burr .05 .15
46 Bob Probert .10 .25
47 Ray Sheppard .05 .15
48 Kelly Buchberger .05 .15
49 Joe Murphy .05 .15
50 Norm Maciver .05 .15
51 Bill Ranford .07 .20
52 Bernie Nicholls .07 .20
53 Esa Tikkanen .05 .15
54 Scott Mellanby .05 .15
55 Dave Manson .05 .15
56 Craig Simpson .05 .15
57 John Cullen .05 .15
58 Pat Verbeek .05 .15
59 Zarley Zalapski .05 .15
60 Murray Craven .05 .15
61 Bobby Holik .07 .20
62 Steve Konroyd .07 .20
63 Geoff Sanderson .07 .20
64 Frank Pietrangelo .07 .20
65 Mikael Andersson UER .05 .15
66 Wayne Gretzky .60 1.50
67 Rob Blake .07 .20
68 Jari Kurri .10 .25
69 Marty McSorley .07 .20
70 Kelly Hrudey .07 .20
71 Paul Coffey .10 .25
72 Luc Robitaille .10 .25
73 Peter Ahola .05 .15
74 Tony Granato .05 .15
75 Derian Hatcher .05 .15
76 Mike Modano .25 .60
77 Dave Gagner .07 .20
78 Mark Tinordi .05 .15
79 Craig Ludwig .07 .20
80 Ulf Dahlen .05 .15
81 Bobby Smith .07 .20
82 Jon Casey .05 .15
83 Jim Johnson .07 .20
84 Denis Savard .10 .25
85 Patrick Roy .25 .60
86 Eric Desjardins .07 .20
87 Kirk Muller .05 .15
88 Guy Carbonneau .07 .20
89 Shayne Corson .07 .20
90 Brent Gilchrist .05 .15
91 Mathieu Schneider UER .05 .15
92 Gilbert Dionne .05 .15
93 Stephane Richer .07 .20
94 Kevin Todd .05 .15
95 Scott Stevens .10 .25
96 Slava Fetisov .05 .15
97 Chris Terreri .07 .20
98 Claude Lemieux .05 .15
99 Bruce Driver .05 .15
100 Peter Stastny .07 .20
101 Alexei Kasatonov .05 .15
102 Patrick Flatley .07 .20
103 Adam Creighton UER .05 .15
104 Pierre Turgeon .07 .20
105 Ray Ferraro .05 .15
106 Steve Thomas .07 .20
107 Mark Fitzpatrick .07 .20
108 Benoit Hogue .05 .15
109 Uwe Krupp .05 .15
110 Derek King .05 .15
111 Mark Messier .20 .50
112 Brian Leetch .07 .20
113 Mike Gartner .12 .30
114 Darren Turcotte .05 .15
115 Adam Graves .05 .15
116 Mike Richter .10 .25
117 Sergei Nemchinov .05 .15
118 Tony Amonte .07 .20
119 James Patrick .05 .15
120 Andrew McBain .07 .20
121 Rob Murphy .05 .15
122 Mike Peluso .07 .20
123 Sylvain Turgeon .05 .15
124 Brad Shaw .05 .15
125 Peter Sidorkiewicz .05 .15
126 Brad Marsh .07 .20
127 Mark Freer .05 .15
128 Marc Fortier .05 .15
129 Ron Hextall .10 .25
130 Claude Boivin .05 .15
131 Mark Recchi .12 .30
132 Rod Brind'Amour .05 .15
133 Mike Ricci .05 .15
134 Kevin Dineen .05 .15
135 Brian Benning .05 .15
136 Kerry Huffman .05 .15
137 Steve Duchesne .05 .15
138 Rick Tocchet .07 .20
139 Mario Lemieux .40 1.00
140 Kevin Stevens .07 .20
141 Jaromir Jagr .20 .50
142 Joe Mullen .07 .20
143 Ulf Samuelsson .05 .15
144 Ron Francis .12 .30
145 Tom Barrasso .07 .20
146 Larry Murphy .07 .20
147 Alexei Gusarov .05 .15
148 Valeri Kamensky .05 .15
149 Mats Sundin .10 .25
150 Joe Sakic .20 .50
151 Claude Lapointe .05 .15
152 Stephane Fiset .05 .15
153 Owen Nolan .10 .25
154 Mike Hough .07 .20
155 Greg Paslawski .05 .15
156 Brett Hull .20 .50
157 Craig Janney .07 .20
158 Jeff Brown .07 .20
159 Paul Cavallini .05 .15
160 Garth Butcher .07 .20
161 Nelson Emerson .05 .15
162 Ron Sutter .05 .15
163 Brendan Shanahan .10 .25
164 Curtis Joseph .12 .30
165 Doug Wilson .07 .20
166 Pat Falloon .05 .15
167 Kelly Kisio .07 .20
168 Neil Wilkinson .05 .15
169 Jay More .05 .15
170 David Bruce .05 .15
171 Jeff Hackett .07 .20
172 David Williams RC .05 .15
173 Brian Lawton .07 .20
174 Brian Bradley .05 .15
175 Jock Callander RC .07 .20
176 Basil McRae .05 .15
177 Rob Ramage .05 .15
178 Pat Jablonski .07 .20
179 Joe Reekie .05 .15
180 Doug Crossman .07 .20
181 Jim Benning .07 .20
182 Ken Hodge Jr. .05 .15
183 Grant Fuhr .15 .40
184 Doug Gilmour .12 .30
185 Glenn Anderson .07 .20
186 Dave Ellett .05 .15
187 Peter Zezel .05 .15
188 Jamie Macoun .07 .20
189 Wendel Clark .15 .40
190 Bob Halkidis .07 .20
191 Rob Pearson .05 .15
192 Pavel Bure .10 .25
193 Kirk McLean .05 .15
194 Sergio Momesso .05 .15
195 Cliff Ronning .05 .15
196 Jyrki Lumme .05 .15
197 Trevor Linden .10 .25
198 Geoff Courtnall .05 .15
199 Doug Lidster .07 .20
200 Dave Babych .07 .20
201 Michal Pivonka .05 .15
202 Dale Hunter .07 .20
203 Calle Johansson .05 .15
204 Kevin Hatcher .05 .15
205 Al Iafrate .07 .20
206 Don Beaupre .07 .20
207 Randy Burridge .05 .15
208 Dimitri Khristich .05 .15
209 Peter Bondra .10 .25
210 Teppo Numminen .05 .15
211 Bob Essensa .07 .20
212 Phil Housley .07 .20
213 Ed Olczyk .05 .15
214 Pat Elynuik .05 .15
215 Troy Murray .05 .15
216 Igor Ulanov .05 .15
217 Thomas Steen .05 .15
218 Darrin Shannon .05 .15
219 Joe Juneau .05 .15
220 Steve Heinze .05 .15
221 Ted Donato .05 .15
222 Glen Murray .07 .20
223 Keith Carney RC .20 .50
224 Dean McAmmond RC .05 .15
225 Slava Kozlov .07 .20
226 Martin Lapointe .05 .15
227 Patrick Poulin .05 .15
228 Darryl Sydor .05 .15
229 Trent Klatt RC .07 .20
230 Bill Guerin RC .20 .50
231 Jarrod Skalde .05 .15
232 Scott Niedermayer .10 .25
233 Marty McInnis .05 .15
234 Scott Lachance .05 .15
235 Dominic Roussel .07 .20
236 Eric Lindros .15 .40
237 Shawn McEachern .05 .15
238 Martin Rucinsky .05 .15
239 Bill Lindsay RC .05 .15
240 Bret Hedican RC .07 .20
241 Ray Whitney RC .15 .40
242 Felix Potvin .20 .50
243 Keith Tkachuk .10 .25
244 Evgeny Davydov .05 .15
245 Brett Hull LL .20 .50
246 Wayne Gretzky LL .60 1.50
247 Steve Yzerman LL .25 .60
248 Paul Ysebaert SL .05 .15
249 Dave Andreychuk SL .10 .25
250 Kirk McLean LL .05 .15
251 Tim Cheveldae SL .05 .15
252 Jeremy Roenick LL .15 .40
253 NHL Pro Set NR .05 .15
254 NHL Pro Set NR .05 .15
255 NHL Pro Set NR .05 .15
256 Mike Gartner MS .12 .30
257 Brian Propp MS .05 .15
258 Dave Taylor MS .07 .20
259 Bobby Smith MS .07 .20
260 Denis Savard MS .10 .25
261 Ray Bourque MS .15 .40
262 Joe Mullen MS .07 .20
263 John Tonelli MS .07 .20
264 Brad Marsh MS .07 .20
265 Randy Carlyle MS .07 .20
266 Mike Hough PS .07 .20
267 Bob Essensa PS .07 .20
268 Mike Lalor PS .07 .20
269 Terry Carkner PS .07 .20
270 Todd Krygier PS .07 .20
AU239 Kirk McLean AU/100 15.00 40.00

1992-93 Pro Set Award Winners

COMPLETE SET (5) 8.00 15.00
CC1 Mark Messier 1.00 2.50
CC2 Patrick Roy 4.00 10.00
CC3 Pavel Bure 1.00 2.50
CC4 Brian Leetch 1.00 2.50
CC5 Guy Carbonneau .40 1.00

1992-93 Pro Set Gold Team Leaders

COMPLETE SET (15) 10.00 25.00
1 Gary Roberts .20 .50
2 Jeremy Roenick 1.25 3.00
3 Steve Yzerman 2.00 5.00
4 Nicklas Lidstrom .75 2.00
5 Vincent Damphousse .40 1.00
6 Wayne Gretzky 3.00 8.00
7 Mike Modano 1.25 3.00
8 Brett Hull 1.25 3.00
9 Nelson Emerson .20 .50
10 Pat Falloon .20 .50
11 Doug Gilmour .40 1.00
12 Trevor Linden .40 1.00
13 Pavel Bure .75 2.00
14 Phil Housley .40 1.00
15 Luciano Borsato .20 .50

1992-93 Pro Set Rookie Goal Leaders

COMPLETE SET (12) 2.50 6.00
1 Tony Amonte .40 1.00
2 Pavel Bure 1.25 3.00
3 Donald Audette .20 .50
4 Pat Falloon .20 .50
5 Nelson Emerson .20 .50
6 Gilbert Dionne .20 .50
7 Kevin Todd .20 .50
8 Luciano Borsato .20 .50
9 Rob Pearson .20 .50
10 Valeri Zelepukin .20 .50
11 Geoff Sanderson .40 1.00
12 Claude Lapointe .20 .50

2021-22 Pro Set

PS01 Brett Hull .50 1.25
PS02 Eric Lindros .50 1.25
PS03 Gordie Howe 1.00 2.50
PS04 Guy Lafleur .40 1.00
PS05 Jaromir Jagr 1.00 2.50
PS06 Mario Lemieux 1.25 3.00
PS07 Mark Messier .60 1.50
PS08 Martin Brodeur .75 2.00
PS09 Pavel Bure .30 .75
PS10 Teemu Selanne .60 1.50

2021-22 Pro Set Red

*RED: .5X TO 1.25X BASIC

2021-22 Pro Set Yellow

*YELLOW: .5X TO 1.25X BASIC

2021-22 Pro Set Memorabilia

PSM01 Adam Oates 1.00 2.50
PSM02 Adam Oates 1.00 2.50
PSM03 Alexander Mogilny .75 2.00
PSM04 Alexei Kovalev .75 2.00
PSM05 Andy Moog 1.00 2.50
PSM06 Bernie Nicholls .75 2.00
PSM07 Bernie Parent 1.25 3.00
PSM08 Bill Guerin 1.00 2.50
PSM09 Bill Guerin 1.00 2.50
PSM10 Brett Hull 1.50 4.00
PSM11 Brett Hull 1.50 4.00
PSM12 Brian Leetch .75 2.00
PSM13 Brian Leetch .75 2.00
PSM14 Chris Chelios 1.00 2.50
PSM15 Chris Chelios 1.00 2.50
PSM16 Chris Osgood 1.00 2.50
PSM17 Curtis Joseph 1.25 3.00
PSM18 Curtis Joseph 1.25 3.00
PSM19 Dominik Hasek 1.50 4.00
PSM20 Dominik Hasek 1.50 4.00
PSM21 Doug Gilmour 1.25 3.00
PSM22 Ed Belfour 1.00 2.50
PSM23 Eric Lindros 1.50 4.00
PSM24 Eric Lindros 1.50 4.00
PSM25 Felix Potvin 1.50 4.00
PSM26 Felix Potvin 1.50 4.00
PSM27 Gilles Gilbert .75 2.00
PSM28 Grant Fuhr 1.50 4.00
PSM29 Grant Fuhr 1.50 4.00
PSM30 Igor Larionov 1.00 2.50
PSM31 Jaromir Jagr 3.00 8.00
PSM32 Jaromir Jagr 3.00 8.00
PSM33 Jeremy Roenick 1.50 4.00
PSM34 Jeremy Roenick 1.50 4.00
PSM35 Jocelyn Thibault .75 2.00
PSM36 Joe Sakic 2.00 5.00
PSM37 Joe Sakic 2.00 5.00
PSM38 John LeClair 1.00 2.50
PSM39 John Vanbiesbrouck 1.00 2.50
PSM40 Jose Theodore 1.00 2.50
PSM41 Lanny McDonald 1.00 2.50
PSM42 Larry Murphy .75 2.00
PSM43 Luc Robitaille 1.00 2.50
PSM44 Luc Robitaille 1.00 2.50
PSM45 Manny Fernandez .60 1.50
PSM46 Mario Lemieux 4.00 10.00
PSM47 Mario Lemieux 4.00 10.00
PSM48 Mark Messier 2.00 5.00
PSM49 Mark Messier 2.00 5.00
PSM50 Mark Recchi 1.00 2.50
PSM51 Martin Brodeur 2.50 6.00
PSM52 Martin Brodeur 2.50 6.00
PSM53 Mike Bossy 1.00 2.50
PSM54 Mike Modano 1.50 4.00
PSM55 Mike Modano 1.50 4.00
PSM56 Mike Richter 1.00 2.50
PSM57 Nicklas Lidstrom 1.00 2.50
PSM58 Olaf Kolzig 1.00 2.50
PSM59 Pat LaFontaine 1.00 2.50
PSM60 Patrick Lalime .75 2.00
PSM61 Paul Coffey 1.25 3.00
PSM62 Pavel Bure 1.00 2.50
PSM63 Pavel Bure 1.00 2.50
PSM64 Peter Forsberg 2.00 5.00
PSM65 Phil Esposito 1.50 4.00
PSM66 Phil Housley .75 2.00
PSM67 Raymond Bourque 1.50 4.00
PSM68 Raymond Bourque 1.50 4.00
PSM69 Saku Koivu 1.00 2.50
PSM70 Sergei Fedorov 1.50 4.00
PSM71 Sergei Fedorov 1.50 4.00
PSM72 Steve Yzerman 2.50 6.00
PSM73 Teemu Selanne 2.00 5.00
PSM74 Teemu Selanne 2.00 5.00
PSM75 Wendel Clark 1.50 4.00

1991 Pro Stars Posters

COMPLETE SET (3) 4.00 10.00
3 Wayne Gretzky 1.60 4.00

1987 Pro-Sport All-Stars

COMPLETE SET (17) 20.00 50.00
1 Larry Robinson 1.25 3.00
2 Guy Carbonneau .75 2.00
3 Chris Chelios 2.00 5.00
5 Mario Lemieux 4.00 10.00
6 Mike Bossy 1.50 4.00
7 Dale Hawerchuk 1.25 3.00
8 Joe Mullen 1.25 3.00
9 Rick Vaive .75 2.00
10 Wendel Clark 1.50 4.00
11 Michel Goulet 1.25 3.00
12 Peter Stastny 1.25 3.00
13 Mark Messier 2.50 6.00
14 Paul Coffey 2.00 5.00
15 Tony Tanti .75 2.00
16 Borje Salming 1.25 3.00
17 Chris Nilan .75 2.00
18 Mats Naslund 1.25 3.00

1983-84 Puffy Stickers

COMPLETE SET (25) 30.00 75.00
1 Doug Risebrough
Wayne Gretzky
Mats Naslund
Bill Derlago
Richard Brodeur
Dave Babych 6.00 15.00
2 Glenn Anderson
Larry Robinson
Rick Vaive
Stan Smyl
Scott Arniel
Don Edwards 1.50 4.00
3 Ryan Walter
Peter Ihnacak
Thomas Gradin
Morris Lukowich
Kent Nilsson
Paul Coffey 1.25 3.00
4 John Anderson
Tiger Williams
Brian Mullen
Steve Tambellini
Mark Messier
Guy Lafleur 2.50 6.00
5 Darcy Rota
Dale Hawerchuk
Paul Reinhart
Jari Kurri
Mario Tremblay
Mike Palmateer 1.25 3.00
6 Paul MacLean
Lanny McDonald
Ken Linseman
Steve Shutt
Borje Salming
Kevin McCarthy 1.50 4.00
7 Barry Pederson
Mike Foligno
Jim Fox
Don Lever
Bobby Clarke
Greg Malone 1.25 3.00
8 Gilbert Perreault
Charlie Simmer
Hector Marini
Mark Howe
Rick Kehoe
Jim Schoenfeld 1.25 3.00
9 Larry Murphy
Phil Russell
Bill Barber
Mike Bullard
Pete Peeters
John Van Boxmeer 1.25 3.00
10 Tapio Levo
Darryl Sittler
Paul Gardner
Rick Middleton
Real Cloutier
Bernie Nicholls 1.50 4.00
11 Brian Propp
Michel Dion
Ray Bourque
Dale McCourt
Marcel Dionne
Bob MacMillan 1.50 4.00
12 Randy Carlyle
Terry O'Reilly
Phil Housley
Dave Taylor
Glenn Resch
Behn Wilson 1.25 3.00
13 Tony Esposito
Ron Duguay
Pierre Larouche
Neal Broten
Peter Stastny
Blake Dunlop 1.50 4.00
14 Walt McKechnie
Risto Siltanen
Bobby Smith
Anton Stastny
Mike Liut
Doug Wilson 1.00 2.50
15 Blaine Stoughton
Dino Ciccarelli
Michel Goulet
Jorgen Pettersson
Tom Lysiak
Brad Park 1.25 3.00
16 Craig Hartsburg
Marian Stastny
Rob Ramage
Al Secord
John Ogrodnick
Greg Millen 1.00 2.50
17 Tony McKegney
Brian Sutter
Steve Larmer
Danny Gare
Mark Johnson
Brian Bellows 1.00 2.50
18 Bernie Federko
Denis Savard
Reed Larson
Ron Francis
Dennis Maruk
Dan Bouchard 1.25 3.00
19 Mike Bossy
Anders Hedberg
Rod Langway
Billy Smith
Reijo Ruotsalainen
Milan Novy 1.50 4.00
20 Barry Beck
Bob Carpenter
Clark Gillies
Rob McClanahan
Brian Engblom
Denis Potvin 1.25 3.00
21 Mike Gartner
John Tonelli
Willie Huber
Pat Riggin
Bryan Trottier
Don Maloney 1.50 4.00
22 Norris Division
Blackhawks logo
Red Wings logo
North Stars logo
Blues logo
Maple Leafs logo
NHL logo 2.00 5.00
23 Patrick Division
Devils logo
Islanders logo
Rangers logo
Flyers logo
Penguins logo
Capitals logo 2.00 5.00
24 Adams Division
Bruins logo
Sabres logo
Whalers logo
Canadiens logo
Nordiques logo
NHL logo 2.00 5.00
25 Smythe Division
Flames logo
Oilers logo
Kings logo
Canucks logo
Jets logo
NHL logo 2.00 5.00
xx Album 10.00 25.00

1938-39 Quaker Oats Photos

COMPLETE SET (30) 750.00 1500.00
1 Syl Apps 62.50 125.00
2 Toe Blake 125.00 250.00
3 Buzz Boll 25.00 50.00
4 Turk Broda 87.50 175.00
5 Walter Buswell 25.00 50.00
6 Herb Cain 30.00 60.00
7 Murph Chamberlain 25.00 50.00
8 Wilf Cude 30.00 60.00
9 Bob Davidson 25.00 50.00
10 Gordie Drillon 50.00 100.00
11 Paul Drouin 25.00 50.00
12 Stew Evans 25.00 50.00
13 James Fowler 25.00 50.00
14 Johnny Gagnon 25.00 50.00
15 Robert Gracie 25.00 50.00
16 Reg Hamilton 25.00 50.00
17 Paul Haynes 25.00 50.00
18 Foster Hewitt 50.00 100.00
19 Red Horner 50.00 100.00
20 Harvey(Busher) Jackson 75.00 125.00
21 Bingo Kampman 25.00 50.00
22 Pep Kelly 25.00 50.00
23 Rod Lorrain 25.00 50.00
24 George Mantha 25.00 50.00
25 Nick Metz 25.00 50.00
26 George Parsons 25.00 50.00
27 Babe Siebert 50.00 100.00
28 Bill Thoms 25.00 50.00
29 James Ward 25.00 50.00
30 Cy Wentworth 30.00 60.00

1945-54 Quaker Oats Photos

1A Syl Apps/Home Still,
CJS Apps auto. 15.00 30.00
1B Syl Apps/Home Still,
Syl Apps auto. 12.50 25.00
1C Syl Apps/Away With Stanley Cup 75.00150.00
2 George Armstrong/Home Action 12.50 25.00
3 Doug Baldwin/Home Still 50.00 100.00
4A Bill Barilko/Home Action/auto.
1/4-inch from border 12.50 25.00
4B Bill Barilko/Home Action/auto.
3/4-inch from border 12.50 25.00
4C Bill Barilko/Away Action 12.50 25.00
5 Baz Bastien/Home Still 62.50 125.00
6 Gordon Bell/Home Still 62.50 125.00
7A Max Bentley/Home Still 10.00 20.00
7B Max Bentley/Home
Dressing Room 75.00 150.00
7C Max Bentley/Away Action 10.00 20.00
8 Gus Bodnar/Home Still 20.00 40.00
9A Garth Boesch/Home Still,
closed B in auto. 7.50 15.00
9B Garth Boesch/Home Still,
open B in auto. 7.50 15.00
9C Garth Boesch/Away Action 50.00 100.00
10 Hugh Bolton/Home Action 6.00 12.00
11 Leo Boivin/Home Action 15.00 30.00
12A Turk Broda/Away Splits,
W.E. auto. 25.00 50.00
12B Turk Broda/Away Splits,
Turk auto. 20.00 40.00
12C Turk Broda/Away Action 20.00 40.00
13 Lorne Carr/Home Still 15.00 30.00
14 Les Costello/Home Still 15.00 30.00
15 Bob Davidson/Home Still 12.50 25.00
16A Bill Ezinicki/cropped
William auto., blue tint 10.00 20.00
16B Bill Ezinicki/entire William auto. 6.00 12.00
16C Bill Ezinicki/Home Still, Bill auto. 6.00 12.00
16D Bill Ezinicki/Away Action 6.00 12.00
17 Fernie Flaman/Home Action 7.50 15.00
18A Cal Gardner/Home Still 6.00 12.00
18B Cal Gardner/Away Action 6.00 12.00
19A Bob Goldham/sweeping G in auto. 6.0012.00
19B Bob Goldham/normal G,
entire blade 6.00 12.00
19C Bob Goldham/normal G,
blade cropped 75.00 150.00
20 Gord Hannigan/Home Action 15.00 30.00
21 Bob Hassard/Away Action 25.00 50.00
22 Mel Hill/Home Still 40.00 80.00
23 Tim Horton/Home Action 50.00 100.00
24A Bill Judza/Home Still 6.00 12.00
24B Bill Judza/Away Action 6.00 12.00
25A Ted Kennedy/Home Still,
blade in corner 25.00 50.00

Card	Low	High
25B Ted Kennedy/Home Still	25.00	50.00
25C Ted Kennedy/Home Still	50.00	100.00
25D Ted Kennedy Home Still, C on jersey	10.00	20.00
25E Ted Kennedy Home With Stanley Cup	87.50	175.00
25F Ted Kennedy/Away Action	10.00	20.00
26A Joe Klukay/Home Still	6.00	12.00
26B Joe Klukay/Away Action	6.00	12.00
27 Danny Lewicki/Home Action	7.50	15.00
28 Harry Lumley/Home Action	30.00	60.00
29A Vic Lynn/Home Still head 3/8-inch from border	6.00	12.00
29B Vic Lynn/Home Still head 1/8-inch from border	15.00	30.00
29C Vic Lynn/Away Action	6.00	12.00
30A Fleming Mackell/Home Still	6.00	12.00
30B Fleming Mackell/Away Action	7.50	15.00
31 Phil Maloney/Home Action	40.00	80.00
32 Frank Mathers/Home Still	20.00	40.00
33 Frank McCool/Home Still	62.50	125.00
34 John McCormick/Away Action	15.00	30.00
35A Howie Meeker/Home Still, large image	10.00	20.00
35B Howie Meeker/Home Still, small image	10.00	20.00
35C Howie Meeker/Away Action	10.00	20.00
36A Don Metz/Home, posed to right	6.00	12.00
36B Don Metz/Home, center pose, b&w tint	12.50	25.00
36C Don Metz/Home, center pose, blue tint	40.00	80.00
37A Nick Metz/Home Still, original stick	6.00	12.00
37B Nick Metz/Home Still	12.50	25.00
37C Nick Metz/Home Still	25.00	50.00
38 Rudy Migay/Home Action	30.00	60.00
39 Elwyn Morris/Home Still	40.00	80.00
40 Jim Morrison/Home Action	6.00	12.00
41A Gus Mortson/Home Still	6.00	12.00
41B Gus Mortson/Away Action	6.00	12.00
42 Eric Nesterenko/Home Action	40.00	80.00
43 Bud Poile/Home Still	15.00	30.00
44 Babe Pratt/Home Still	50.00	100.00
45 Al Rollins/Home Action	12.50	25.00
46 Dave Schriner/Home Still	30.00	60.00
47A Tod Sloan/Home Still	12.50	25.00
47B Tod Sloan/Home Action	6.00	12.00
48A Sid Smith/Home Still	12.50	25.00
48B Sid Smith/Away Action	6.00	12.00
49 Bob Solinger	15.00	30.00
50A Wally Stanowski/Home Still, entire blade	12.50	25.00
50B Wally Stanowski/Home Still, blade cropped	6.00	12.00
51A Gaye Stewart/Home Still	50.00	100.00
51B Gaye Stewart/Home Still, blue tint	6.00	12.00
52 Ron Stewart/Home Action	50.00	100.00
53 Harry Taylor/Home Still	7.50	15.00
54 Billy Taylor/Home Still	25.00	50.00
55 Cy Thomas/Home Still	25.00	50.00
56A Jim Thomson/Home Still, stick cropped	30.00	60.00
56B Jim Thomson/Home Still/stick touching border	6.00	12.00
56C Jim Thomson/Home Still stick away from border	30.00	60.00
56D Jim Thomson/Away Action	6.00	12.00
57A Ray Timgren/Home Still	7.50	15.00
57B Ray Timgren/Away Action	6.00	12.00
58A Harry Watson/Home Still, tape on stick	6.00	12.00
58B Harry Watson/Home Still, no tape visible	6.00	12.00
58C Harry Watson/Away Action	6.00	12.00
59 1947-49 Toronto Team Picture	30.00	60.00
60A Leafs Attack McNeil	87.50	175.00
60B Gardner attacks Harvey	100.00	200.00
60C Rollins, Judza stop Curry	100.00	200.00
60D McNeil Saves on Gardner	100.00	200.00
61 George Allen/Home Still	6.00	12.00
62 Jean Beliveau/Home Action	87.50	175.00
63 Joe Benoit/Home Still	10.00	20.00
64A Toe Blake/Hector Toe Blake auto.	75.00	150.00
64B Toe Blake/Toe Blake auto. above skates	10.00	20.00
64C Toe Blake/Toe Blake auto. below skate	10.00	20.00
65A Butch Bouchard/Home Still, entire skate	6.00	12.00
65B Butch Bouchard/Home Still, skate cropped	6.00	12.00
65C Butch Bouchard/Home Action	7.50	15.00
66 Todd Campeau/Home Still	6.00	12.00
67 Bob Carse/Home Still	6.00	12.00
68 Joe Carveth/Home Portrait	6.00	12.00
69A Murph Chamberlain/facing sideways, entire skates	10.00	20.00
69B Murph Chamberlain/Home Still	10.00	20.00
69C Murph Chamberlain/Home Still, facing forward	15.00	30.00
70 Gerry Couture/Away Action	6.00	12.00
71A Floyd Curry/Home Still	62.50	125.00
71B Floyd Curry/Home Action	6.00	12.00
72 Ed Dorohoy/Home Action	6.00	12.00
73A Bill Durnan/Home Still/stick handle cropped	12.50	25.00
73B Bill Durnan/Home Still	25.00	50.00
73C Bill Durnan/Home Still	87.50	175.00
73D Bill Durnan/Home Action	15.00	30.00
74A Norm Dussault/Home Portrait	6.00	12.00
74B Norm Dussault/Home Action	15.00	30.00
75 Frank Eddolls/Home Still	10.00	20.00
76A Bob Fillion/Home Still small image	25.00	50.00
76B Bob Fillion/Home Still	6.00	12.00
76C Bob Fillion/Home Still/test	12.50	25.00
76D Bob Fillion/Home Action {teststesttees/testst	6.00	12.00
77 Dick Gamble/Away Action	10.00	20.00
78 Bernie Geoffrion/Home Action	15.00	30.00
79A Leo Gravelle/Home Still	6.00	12.00
79B Leo Gravelle/Away Still	25.00	50.00
79C Leo Gravelle/Home Action	6.00	12.00
80A Glen Harmon/Home Still, entire puck	6.00	12.00
80B Glen Harmon/Home Still, no puck	6.00	12.00
80C Glen Harmon/Home Action	12.50	25.00
81A Doug Harvey/Home Still	12.50	25.00
81B Doug Harvey/Home Action	10.00	20.00
82 Dutch Hiller/Home Still	10.00	20.00
83 Bert Hirschfield/Home Action/Testtestestsetstset	10.00	20.00
84 Tom Johnson/Home Action/sdfsdfsdfsdfsdfsdfsdf	10.00	20.00
85 Vern Kaiser/Home Action	10.00	20.00
86A Elmer Lach/Home Still, stick in corner	10.00	20.00
86B Elmer Lach/Home Still, stick cropped	10.00	20.00
86C Elmer Lach/Home Still/stick 1/2-inch up from corner	40.00	80.00
86D Elmer Lach/Home Action	10.00	20.00
87A Leo Lamoureaux/Home Still, entire blade	12.50	25.00
87B Leo Lamoureaux/Home Still, blade cropped	10.00	20.00
88A Hal Laycoe/Home Portrait	50.00	100.00
88B Hal Laycoe/Home Action	6.00	12.00
89A Roger Leger/Home Still/light background	6.00	12.00
89B Roger Leger/Home Still dark background	6.00	12.00
89C Roger Leger/Home Action	25.00	50.00
90 Jacques Locas/Home Still	10.00	20.00
91 Ross Lowe/Away Action	10.00	20.00
92 Callum MacKay/Home Action	6.00	12.00
93 Murdo MacKay/Home Portrait	6.00	12.00
94 James MacPherson/Home Action	6.00	12.00
95 Paul Masnick/Home Action	6.00	12.00
96A John McCormick Home Action, vertical	50.00	100.00
96B John McCormick Home Action, horizontal	30.00	60.00
97 Mike McMahon/Home Still	50.00	100.00
98 Gerry McNeil/Home Action	12.50	25.00
99 Paul Meger/Home Action	7.50	15.00
100 Dickie Moore/Home Action	15.00	30.00
101A Ken Mosdell/Home Still, small image	6.00	12.00
101B Ken Mosdell/Home Still, large image/auto. croppe	25.00	50.00
101C Ken Mosdell/Home Still, large image/auto. not cr	25.00	50.00
101D Ken Mosdell/Home Action	6.00	12.00
102A Buddy O'Connor/Home Still, entire blade	20.00	40.00
102B Buddy O'Connor/Home Still, blade cropped	10.00	20.00
103 Bert Olmstead/Home Action	12.50	25.00
104A Jim Peters/Home Still, large image	6.00	12.00
104B Jim Peters/Home Still, small image	6.00	12.00
105 Gerry Plamondon/Home Action	7.50	15.00
106 Johnny Quilty/Home Portrait	7.50	15.00
107A Ken Reardon/Home Still, large image	10.00	20.00
107B Ken Reardon/Home Still, small image	15.00	30.00
107C Kenny Reardon/Home Action	10.00	20.00
108A Billy Reay/Home Still, large image/stick touchin	6.00	12.00
108B Billy Reay/Home Still, large image/stick away fr	6.00	12.00
108C Billy Reay/Home Still, small image	62.50	125.00
108D Billy Reay/Home Action	6.00	12.00
109A Maurice Richard/Home, screen background	150.00	300.00
109B Maurice Richard/Home, large image/auto. cropped	15.00	30.00
109C Maurice Richard/Home, large image/entire auto.	15.00	30.00
109D Maurice Richard/Home Action	30.00	60.00
110A Howie Riopelle/Home Still	10.00	20.00
110B Howie Riopelle/Home Action	10.00	20.00
111 George Robertson/Home Action	20.00	40.00
112 Dollard St. Laurent/Home Action	30.00	60.00
113 Grant Warwick/Home Action	40.00	80.00

1972-73 Whalers New England WHA

Card	Low	High
COMPLETE SET (15)	20.00	40.00
1 Mike Byers	1.00	2.00
2 Terry Caffery	1.00	2.00
3 John Cunniff	1.50	3.00
4 John Danby	1.00	2.00
5 Jim Dorey	1.50	3.00
6 Tom Earl	1.00	2.00
7 John French	1.00	2.00
8 Ted Green	2.50	5.00
9 Ric Jordan	1.00	2.00
10 Bruce Landon	1.00	2.00
11 Rick Ley	2.50	5.00
12 Larry Pleau	2.00	4.00
13 Brad Selwood	1.00	2.00
14 Tim Sheehy	1.00	2.00
15 Al Smith	2.50	5.00
16 Tom Webster	2.50	5.00
17 Tom Williams	2.00	4.00

1973-74 Quaker Oats WHA

Card	Low	High
COMPLETE SET (50)	137.50	275.00
1 Jim Wiste	2.50	5.00
2 Al Smith	3.00	6.00
3 Rosaire Paiement	2.50	5.00
4 Ted Hampson	2.00	4.00
5 Gavin Kirk	2.00	4.00
6 Andre Lacroix	3.00	6.00
7 John Schella	2.00	4.00
8 Gerry Cheevers	10.00	20.00
9 Norm Beaudin	2.00	4.00
10 Jim Harrison	2.00	4.00
11 Gerry Pinder	2.50	5.00
12 Bob Sicinski	2.00	4.00
13 Bryan Campbell	2.00	4.00
14 Murray Hall	2.00	4.00
15 Chris Bordeleau	2.50	5.00
16 Al Hamilton	3.00	6.00
17 Jimmy McLeod	2.00	4.00
18 Larry Pleau	2.50	5.00
19 Larry Lund	2.00	4.00
20 Bobby Sheehan	2.50	5.00
21 Jan Popiel	2.00	4.00
22 Andre Gaudette	2.00	4.00
23 Bob Charlebois	2.00	4.00
24 Gene Peacosh	2.00	4.00
25 Rick Ley	2.50	5.00
26 Larry Hornung	2.00	4.00
27 Gary Jarrett	2.00	4.00
28 Ted Taylor	2.00	4.00
29 Pete Donnelly	2.00	4.00
30 J.C. Tremblay	3.00	6.00
31 Jim Cardiff	2.00	4.00
32 Gary Veneruzzo	2.00	4.00
33 John French	2.00	4.00
34 Ron Ward	2.50	5.00
35 Wayne Connelly	2.50	5.00
36 Ron Buchanan	2.00	4.00
37 Ken Block	2.00	4.00
38 Alain Caron	2.00	4.00
39 Brit Selby	2.50	5.00
40 Guy Trottier	2.00	4.00
41 Ernie Wakely	3.00	6.00
42 J.P. LeBlanc	2.00	4.00
43 Michel Parizeau	2.00	4.00
44 Wayne Rivers	2.00	4.00
45 Reg Fleming	2.50	5.00
46 Don Herriman	2.00	4.00
47 Jim Dorey	2.00	4.00
48 Danny Lawson	3.00	6.00
49 Dick Paradise	2.00	4.00
50 Bobby Hull	30.00	60.00

1950 R423

Card	Low	High
1 Taffy Abel	12.50	25.00
2 George Allen	10.00	20.00
3 Syl Apps	12.50	25.00
4 Pete Backor	10.00	20.00
5 Baz Bastien	10.00	20.00
6 Bobby Bauer	10.00	20.00
7 Gordie Bell	10.00	20.00
8 Lin Bend	10.00	20.00
9 Paul Bibeault	10.00	20.00
10 Garth Boesch	10.00	20.00
11 Butch Bouchard	12.50	25.00
12 Frank Boucher	12.50	25.00
13 Adam Brown	10.00	20.00
14 Hal Brown	10.00	20.00
15 Mud Bruneteau	10.00	20.00
16 Frank Bull	10.00	20.00
17 Scotty Cameron	10.00	20.00
18 Joe Carveth	10.00	20.00
19 Murph Chamberlain	10.00	20.00
20 Dit Clapper	12.50	25.00
21 Mac Colville	10.00	20.00
22 Lionel Conacher	15.00	30.00
23 Bun Cook	10.00	20.00
24 Ernie Dickens	10.00	20.00
25 Cecil Dillon	10.00	20.00
26 Connie Dion	10.00	20.00
27 Gordie Drillon	10.00	20.00
28 Bill Ezinicki	10.00	20.00
29 Wilfy Field	10.00	20.00
30 Bob Fillion	10.00	20.00
31 Chuck Gardiner	10.00	20.00
32 George Gee	10.00	20.00
33 Gus Giesebrecht	10.00	20.00
34 Bob Goldham	10.00	20.00
35 Dutch Hiller	10.00	20.00
36 Dick Irvin	10.00	20.00
37 Aurel Joliat	12.50	25.00
38 Alex Kaleta	10.00	20.00
39 Mike Karakas	10.00	20.00
40 Ted Kennedy	15.00	30.00
41 Dave Kerr	12.50	25.00
42 Roger Leger	10.00	20.00
43 Carl Liscombe	10.00	20.00
44 Vic Lynn	10.00	20.00
45 Kilby MacDonald	10.00	20.00
46 Bucko McDonald	10.00	20.00
47 Howie Morenz	20.00	35.00
48 Gus Mortson	10.00	20.00
49 Ken Mosdell	10.00	20.00
50 Frank Nighbor	12.50	25.00
51 Lynn Patrick	12.50	25.00
52 Billy Reay	10.00	20.00
53 Leo Reise	10.00	20.00
54 Earl Babe Seibert	12.50	25.00
55 Clint Smith	10.00	20.00
56 Wally Stanowski	10.00	20.00
57 Gaye Stewart	10.00	20.00
58 Tiny Thompson	15.00	30.00
59 Roy Worters	12.50	25.00

1989-90 Rangers Marine Midland Bank

Card	Low	High
COMPLETE SET (30)	14.00	35.00
2 Brian Leetch	3.00	8.00
3 James Patrick	.30	.75
4 Ron Greschner	.40	1.00
5 Normand Rochefort	.20	.50
6 Miloslav Horava	.20	.50
8 Darren Turcotte	.30	.75
9 Bernie Nicholls	.40	1.00
11 Kelly Kisio	.30	.75
12 Kris King	.40	1.00
14 Mark Hardy	.20	.50
15 Mark Janssens	.20	.50
16 Ulf Dahlen	.30	.75
17 Carey Wilson	.20	.50
19 Brian Mullen	.30	.75
20 Jan Erixon	.20	.50
21 David Shaw	.20	.50
23 Corey Millen	.20	.50
24 Randy Moller	.20	.50
25 John Ogrodnick	.40	1.00
26 Troy Mallette	.20	.50
29 Rudy Poeschek	.40	1.00
30 Chris Nilan	.40	1.00
33 Bob Froese	.40	1.00
34 John Vanbiesbrouck	1.50	4.00
35 Mike Richter	3.00	8.00
37 Paul Broten	.20	.50
38 Jeff Bloemberg	.20	.50
44 Lindy Ruff	.20	.50
NNO Roger Neilson CO	.20	.50
NNO Rangers MasterCard	.02	.10

2002-03 Rangers Team Issue

Card	Low	High
1 Matthew Barnaby	.60	1.50
2 Dan Blackburn	.60	1.50
3 Pavel Bure	2.00	5.00
4 Ted Green ACO	.20	.50
5 Bobby Holik	.40	1.00
6 Dave Karpa	.40	1.00
7 Darius Kasparaitis	.40	1.00
8 Sylvain Lefebvre	.40	1.00
9 Vladimir Malakhov	.40	1.00
10 Sandy McCarthy	.60	1.50
11 Mark Messier	2.00	5.00
12 Terry O'Reilly ACO	.40	1.00
13 Mike Richter	.75	2.00
14 Jim Schoenfeld ACO	.20	.50

2003-04 Rangers Team Issue

Card	Low	High
COMPLETE SET (24)	15.00	30.00
1 Matthew Barnaby	.75	2.00
2 Dan Blackburn	.60	1.50
3 Anson Carter	.60	1.50
4 Greg deVries	.40	1.00
5 Mike Dunham	.60	1.50
6 Jan Hlavac	.40	1.00
7 Bobby Holik	.40	1.00
8 Darius Kasparaitis	.40	1.00
9 Alexei Kovalev	.40	1.00
10 Dan Lacouture	.40	1.00
11 Brian Leetch	.75	2.00
12 Eric Lindros	1.25	3.00
13 Jamie Lundmark	.40	1.00
14 Vladimir Malakhov	.40	1.00
15 Jussi Markkanen	.75	2.00
16 Mark Messier	.75	2.00
17 Boris Mironov	.40	1.00
18 Petr Nedved	.40	1.00
19 Tom Poti	.40	1.00
20 Dale Purinton	.75	2.00
21 Martin Rucinsky	.40	1.00
22 Glen Sather HCO	.20	.50
23 Chris Simon	.60	1.50
24 Glen Sather Tom Renney Terry O'Reilly Ted Green	.20	.50

1970-71 Red Wings Volpe Marathon Oil

Card	Low	High
COMPLETE SET (11)	40.00	80.00
1 Gary Bergman	2.50	5.00
2 Wayne Connelly	2.00	4.00
3 Alex Delvecchio	5.00	10.00
4 Roy Edwards	2.50	5.00
5 Gordie Howe	25.00	50.00
6 Bruce MacGregor	2.00	4.00
7 Frank Mahovlich	6.00	12.00
8 Dale Rolfe	2.00	4.00
9 Jim Rutherford	3.00	6.00
10 Garry Unger	2.50	5.00
11 Tom Webster	2.50	5.00

1971 Red Wings Citgo Tumblers

Card	Low	High
COMPLETE SET	100.00	200.00
1 Wayne Connelly	12.50	25.00
2 Alex Delvecchio	20.00	40.00
3 Don Edwards	10.00	20.00
4 Garry Unger	10.00	20.00
5 Gordie Howe	37.50	75.00
6 Frank Mahovlich	15.00	30.00

1973-74 Red Wings Team Issue

Card	Low	High
COMPLETE SET (18)	50.00	100.00
1 Ace Bailey	2.50	5.00
2 Red Berenson	4.00	8.00
3 Gary Bergman	2.50	5.00
4 Thommie Bergman	4.00	8.00
5 Guy Charron	2.50	5.00
6 Bill Collins	2.50	5.00
7 Denis Dejordy	4.00	8.00
8 Alex Delvecchio	7.50	15.00
9 Marcel Dionne	7.50	15.00
10 Gary Doak	2.50	5.00
11 Tim Ecclestone	2.50	5.00
12 Larry Johnston	2.50	5.00
13 Al Karlander	2.50	5.00
14 Brian Lavender	2.50	5.00
15 Nick Libett	2.50	5.00
16 Ken Murphy	2.50	5.00
17 Mickey Redmond	7.50	15.00
18 Ron Stackhouse	2.50	5.00

1973-75 Red Wings McCarthy Postcards

Card	Low	High
COMPLETE SET (15)	12.50	25.00
1 Garnet Bailey	1.00	2.00
2 Thommie Bergman	1.00	2.00
3 Henry Boucha	1.25	2.50
4 Guy Charron	1.00	2.00
5 Bill Collins	1.00	2.00
6 Doug Grant	1.00	2.00
7 Ted Harris	1.00	2.00
8 Bill Hogaboam	1.00	2.00
9 Brent Hughes	1.00	2.00
10 Pierre Jarry	1.00	2.00
11 Larry Johnston	1.00	2.00
12 Nick Libett	1.00	2.00
13 Tom Mellor	1.00	2.00
14 Doug Roberts	1.00	2.00
15 Ron Stackhouse	1.00	2.00

1979 Red Wings Postcards

Card	Low	High
COMPLETE SET (18)	7.50	15.00
1 Thommie Bergman	.38	.75
2 Dan Bolduc	.38	.75
3 Mike Foligno	.38	.75
4 Jean Hamel	.38	.75
5 Glen Hicks	.38	.75
6 Greg Joly	.38	.75
7 Willie Huber	.38	.75
8 Jim Korn	.38	.75
9 Dan Labraaten	.38	.75
10 Barry Long	.38	.75
11 Reed Larson	.38	.75
12 Dale McCourt	.38	.75
13 Vaclav Nedomansky	.38	.75
14 Jim Rutherford	.38	.75
15 Dennis Polonich	.38	.75
16 Errol Thompson	.38	.75
17 Rogie Vachon	.38	.75
18 Paul Woods	.38	.75

1981-82 Red Wings Oldtimers

Card	Low	High
COMPLETE SET (24)	10.00	25.00
1 Bob Johnson	.40	1.00
2 Ed Giacomin	.75	2.00
3 Gary Bergman	.40	1.00
4 Bill Gadsby	.40	1.00
5 Larry Johnston	.40	1.00
6 Jim Peters	.40	1.00
7 Bobby Kromm	.40	1.00
8 Marcel Pronovost	.75	2.00
9 Gerry Abel	.40	1.00
10 Bill Collins	.40	1.00
11 Billy Dea	.40	1.00
12 Nelson DeBenedet	.40	1.00
13 Alex Delvecchio	.75	2.00
14 Dennis Hextall	.60	1.50
15 Nick Libett	.40	1.00
16 Mickey Redmond	1.25	3.00
17 John Wilson	.40	1.00
18 Joe Klukay	.40	1.00
19 Art Skov	.40	1.00
20 Art Bouge	.40	1.00
21 Rollie Roulston	.40	1.00
22 Gordie Howe	2.00	5.00
23 Dr.C Boone	.40	1.00
24 Checklist	.40	1.00

1987-88 Red Wings Little Caesars

Card	Low	High
COMPLETE SET (30)	18.00	45.00
1 Brent Ashton	.40	1.00
2 Dave Barr	.40	1.00
3 Mel Bridgman	.40	1.00
4 Shawn Burr	.40	1.00
5 John Chabot	.40	1.00
6 Steve Chiasson	.60	1.50
7 Gilbert Delorme	.40	1.00
8 Jacques Demers CO	.75	2.00
9 Ron Duguay	.40	1.00
10 Dwight Foster	.40	1.00
11 Gerard Gallant	.40	1.00
12 Adam Graves	1.50	4.00
13 Doug Halward	.40	1.00
14 Glen Hanlon	.60	1.50
15 Tim Higgins	.40	1.00
16 Petr Klima	.60	1.50
17 Joe Kocur	.75	2.00
18 Lane Lambert	.40	1.00
19 Joe Murphy	.40	1.00
20 Lee Norwood	.40	1.00
21 Adam Oates	4.00	10.00
22 Mike O'Connell	.40	1.00
23 John Ogrodnick	.60	1.50
24 Bob Probert	2.00	5.00
25 Jeff Sharples	.40	1.00
26 Greg Smith	.40	1.00
27 Greg Stefan	.60	1.50
28 Darren Veitch	.40	1.00
29 Steve Yzerman	5.00	12.00
30 Rick Zombo	.40	1.00

1988-89 Red Wings Little Caesars

Card	Low	High
COMPLETE SET (24)	10.00	25.00
1 David Barr	.40	1.00
2 Shawn Burr	.40	1.00
3 John Chabot	.40	1.00
4 Steve Chiasson	.75	2.00
5 Gilbert Delorme	.40	1.00
6 Jacques Demers	.40	1.00
7 Gerard Gallant	.40	1.00
8 Adam Graves	.75	2.00
9 Doug Houda	.40	1.00
10 Glen Hanlon	.60	1.50
11 Kris King	.40	1.00
12 Petr Klima	.40	1.00
13 Joe Kocur	.60	1.50
14 Paul Maclean	.40	1.00
15 Jim Nill	.40	1.00
16 Lee Norwood	.40	1.00
17 Adam Oates	1.25	3.00
18 Mike O'Connell	.40	1.00
19 Jim Pavese	.40	1.00
20 Bob Probert	.75	2.00
21 Jeff Sharples	.40	1.00
22 Greg Stefan	.60	1.50
23 Steve Yzerman	2.50	6.00
24 Rick Zombo	.40	1.00

1989-90 Red Wings Little Caesars

Card	Low	High
COMPLETE SET (24)	10.00	25.00
1 Dave Barr	.40	1.00
2 Shawn Burr	.40	1.00
3 Jim Carson	.40	1.00
4 John Chabot	.40	1.00
5 Steve Chiasson	.40	1.00
6 Bernie Federko	.40	1.00
7 Gerard Gallant	.40	1.00
8 Marc Habscheid	.40	1.00
9 Glen Hanlon	.40	1.00
10 Doug Houda	.40	1.00
11 Joey Kocur	.40	1.00
12 Kevin McLelland	.40	1.00
13 Lee Norwood	.40	1.00
14 Mike O'Connell	.40	1.00
15 Borje Salming	.40	1.00
16 Greg Stefan	.40	1.00
17 Steve Yzerman	.40	1.00
18 Rick Zombo	.40	1.00
19 Jacques Demers CO	.40	1.00
20 Team Photo	.40	1.00
21 Mickey Redmond	.20	.50
22 Dave Lewis Phil Myre Jacques Demers Colin Campbell	.20	.50
23 Bruce Martin Paul Woods	.20	.50
24 Dave Strader Mickey Redmond	.20	.50

1990-91 Red Wings Little Caesars

Card	Low	High
COMPLETE SET (20)	16.00	40.00
1 Dave Barr	.40	1.00
2 Shawn Burr	.40	1.00
3 John Chabot	.40	1.00
4 Tim Cheveldae	.60	1.50
5 Per Djoos	.40	1.00
6 Bobby Dollas	.40	1.00
7 Sergei Fedorov	4.00	10.00
8 Brent Fedyk	.40	1.00
9 Johan Garpenlov	.40	1.00
10 Rick Green	.40	1.00
11 Sheldon Kennedy	.75	2.00
12 Kevin McClelland	.40	1.00
13 Brad McCrimmon	.40	1.00
14 Randy McKay	.40	1.00
15 Keith Primeau	1.50	4.00
16 Bob Probert	1.25	3.00
17 Steve Yzerman	2.00	5.00
18 Rick Zombo	.40	1.00
19 Bryan Murray CO	.40	1.00
20 Team Photo	.75	2.00

1991-92 Red Wings Little Caesars

Card	Low	High
COMPLETE SET (19)	16.00	40.00
1 Shawn Burr	.40	1.00
2 Jimmy Carson	.40	1.00
3 Steve Chiasson	.40	1.00
4 Sergei Fedorov	3.00	8.00
5 Gerard Gallant	.40	1.00
6 Johan Garpenlov	.40	1.00
7 Rick Green	.40	1.00
8 Marc Habscheid	.40	1.00
9 Sheldon Kennedy	.40	1.00
10 Martin Lapointe	.75	2.00
11 Nicklas Lidstrom	1.25	3.00
12 Brad McCrimmon	.40	1.00
13 Bryan Murray CO MG	.20	.50
14 Keith Primeau	.60	1.50
15 Bob Probert	1.25	3.00
16 Dennis Vial	.40	1.00
17 Paul Ysebaert	.40	1.00
18 Steve Yzerman	4.00	10.00
19 Team Card	.75	2.00

1996-97 Red Wings Detroit News/Free Press

Card	Low	High
COMPLETE SET (5)	8.00	20.00
1 D.McCarty K.Draper K.Maltby J.Kocur	1.50	4.00
2 Sergei Fedorov	2.50	6.00
3 Mike Vernon	1.50	4.00
4 Mike Vernon	1.50	4.00
5 Sergei Fedorov	2.50	6.00

1932 Reemstma Olympia

Card	Low	High
188 Dutch hockey player	10.00	20.00
191 USA vs. Canada	25.00	50.00

1936 Reemstma Olympia

Card	Low	High
30 Team Canada 6 3/4 x 4 3/4	20.00	40.00
31 Ice Hockey Spectators	20.00	40.00
32 Hockey Action Photo	20.00	40.00
33 Goalie making sliding save	20.00	40.00
34 Hockey Action Photo	20.00	40.00
35 Hockey Action Photo Canada player in crease	20.00	40.00
36 Team Canada Photo	20.00	40.00
37 Team USA Photo	20.00	40.00
38 Gustav Jaenecke	20.00	40.00
39 Teiji Homna Japan Goalie	20.00	40.00
40 Clearing the Ice	20.00	40.00

1997-98 Revolution

Card	Low	High
COMPLETE SET (150)	30.00	60.00
1 Guy Hebert	.30	.75
2 Paul Kariya	.40	1.00
3 Dmitri Mironov	.20	.50
4 Ruslan Salei	.20	.50
5 Teemu Selanne	.40	1.00
6 Jason Allison	.20	.50
7 Ray Bourque	.75	2.00
8 Byron Dafoe	.30	.75
9 Ted Donato	.20	.50
10 Dimitri Khristich	.20	.50
11 Joe Thornton	.60	1.50
12 Matthew Barnaby	.20	.50
13 Jason Dawe	.20	.50
14 Dominik Hasek	.75	2.00
15 Michael Peca	.20	.50
16 Miroslav Satan	.20	.50
17 Theo Fleury	.20	.50
18 Jarome Iginla	.50	1.25
19 Marty McInnis	.20	.50
20 Cory Stillman	.20	.50
21 Rick Tabaracci	.30	.75
22 Martin Gelinas	.20	.50
23 Sami Kapanen	.20	.50
24 Trevor Kidd	.30	.75
25 Keith Primeau	.20	.50
26 Gary Roberts	.20	.50
27 Tony Amonte	.30	.75
28 Chris Chelios	.40	1.00
29 Eric Daze	.30	.75
30 Jeff Hackett	.30	.75
31 Dmitri Nabokov	.20	.50
32 Peter Forsberg	1.00	2.50
33 Valeri Kamensky	.30	.75
34 Jari Kurri	.30	.75
35 Claude Lemieux	.20	.50
36 Eric Messier RC	.30	.75
37 Sandis Ozolinsh	.20	.50
38 Patrick Roy	1.50	4.00
39 Joe Sakic	.75	2.00
40 Ed Belfour	.40	1.00
41 Jamie Langenbrunner	.20	.50
42 Jere Lehtinen	.20	.50
43 Mike Modano	.60	1.50
44 Joe Nieuwendyk	.30	.75
45 Sergei Zubov	.20	.50
46 Slava Fetisov	.20	.50
47 Nicklas Lidstrom	.40	1.00
48 Darren McCarty	.20	.50
49 Larry Murphy	.20	.50
50 Chris Osgood	.30	.75
51 Brendan Shanahan	.40	1.00
52 Steve Yzerman	1.50	4.00
53 Roman Hamrlik	.30	.75
54 Bill Guerin	.30	.75
55 Curtis Joseph	.40	1.00
56 Ryan Smyth	.30	.75
57 Doug Weight	.30	.75
58 Dino Ciccarelli	.20	.50
59 Dave Gagner	.20	.50
60 Ed Jovanovski	.30	.75
61 Paul Laus	.20	.50
62 John Vanbiesbrouck	.30	.75
63 Ray Whitney	.20	.50
64 Russ Courtnall	.20	.50
65 Yanic Perreault	.20	.50
66 Luc Robitaille	.30	.75
67 Jozef Stumpel	.30	.75
68 Vladimir Tsyplakov	.20	.50
69 Shayne Corson	.20	.50
70 Vincent Damphousse	.20	.50
71 Saku Koivu	.40	1.00
72 Andy Moog	.30	.75
73 Mark Recchi	.30	.75
74 Jocelyn Thibault	.30	.75
75 Martin Brodeur	1.00	2.50
76 Patrik Elias RC	2.00	5.00
77 Doug Gilmour	.30	.75
78 Bobby Holik	.20	.50
79 Scott Niedermayer	.20	.50
80 Bryan Berard	.30	.75
81 Travis Green	.20	.50
82 Zigmund Palffy	.30	.75
83 Robert Reichel	.20	.50
84 Tommy Salo	.30	.75
85 Dan Cloutier	.20	.50
86 Adam Graves	.20	.50
87 Wayne Gretzky	2.00	5.00
88 Pat LaFontaine	.40	1.00
89 Brian Leetch	.40	1.00
90 Mike Richter	.40	1.00
91 Kevin Stevens	.30	.75
92 Daniel Alfredsson	.30	.75
93 Shawn McEachern	.20	.50
94 Damian Rhodes	.30	.75
95 Ron Tugnutt	.30	.75
96 Alexei Yashin	.20	.50
97 Rod Brind'Amour	.30	.75
98 Paul Coffey	.40	1.00
99 Alexandre Daigle	.20	.50
100 Chris Gratton	.30	.75
101 Ron Hextall	.30	.75
102 John LeClair	.40	1.00
103 Eric Lindros	.40	1.00
104 Dainius Zubrus	.40	1.00
105 Mike Gartner	.30	.75
106 Craig Janney	.20	.50
107 Nikolai Khabibulin	.30	.75
108 Jeremy Roenick	.50	1.25
109 Keith Tkachuk	.40	1.00
110 Stu Barnes	.20	.50
111 Tom Barrasso	.30	.75
112 Ron Francis	.30	.75
113 Jaromir Jagr	.60	1.50
114 Peter Skudra RC	.20	.50
115 Martin Straka	.20	.50
116 Blair Atcheynum RC	.20	.50
117 Jim Campbell	.20	.50
118 Geoff Courtnall	.20	.50
119 Steve Duchesne	.20	.50
120 Grant Fuhr	.30	.75
121 Brett Hull	.50	1.25
122 Pierre Turgeon	.30	.75
123 Jeff Friesen	.20	.50
124 John MacLean	.20	.50
125 Patrick Marleau	.30	.75
126 Owen Nolan	.30	.75
127 Marco Sturm RC	1.00	2.50
128 Mike Vernon	.30	.75
129 Daren Puppa	.30	.75
130 Mikael Renberg	.30	.75
131 Paul Ysebaert	.20	.50
132 Rob Zamuner	.20	.50
133 Wendel Clark	.30	.75
134 Tie Domi	.30	.75
135 Igor Korolev	.20	.50
136 Felix Potvin	.40	1.00
137 Mats Sundin	.40	1.00
138 Donald Brashear	.20	.50
139 Pavel Bure	.40	1.00
140 Sean Burke	.30	.75
141 Trevor Linden	.30	.75
142 Mark Messier	.40	1.00
143 Alexander Mogilny	.30	.75
144 Mattias Ohlund	.30	.75
145 Peter Bondra	.30	.75
146 Phil Housley	.20	.50
147 Dale Hunter	.20	.50
148 Joe Juneau	.30	.75
149 Olaf Kolzig	.30	.75
150 Adam Oates	.30	.75

1997-98 Revolution Copper

*VETS: 2X TO 8X BASIC CARDS
*ROOKIES: 1.5X TO 4X BASIC CARDS

1997-98 Revolution Emerald

*VETS: 3X TO 8X BASIC CARDS
*ROOKIES: 1.5X TO 4X BASIC CARDS

1997-98 Revolution Ice Blue

*VETS: 5X TO 12X BASIC CARDS
*ROOKIES: 2X TO 4X BASIC CARDS

1997-98 Revolution Red

*VETS: 3X TO 8X BASIC CARDS
*ROOKIES: 2X TO 4X BASIC CARDS

Card	Low	High
1 Guy Hebert	2.50	6.00
2 Paul Kariya	3.00	8.00
3 Dmitri Mironov	1.50	4.00
4 Ruslan Salei	1.50	4.00
5 Teemu Selanne	3.00	8.00
6 Jason Allison	1.50	4.00
7 Ray Bourque	6.00	15.00
8 Byron Dafoe	2.50	6.00
9 Ted Donato	1.50	4.00
10 Dimitri Khristich	1.50	4.00
11 Joe Thornton	5.00	12.00
12 Matthew Barnaby	1.50	4.00
13 Jason Dawe	1.50	4.00
14 Dominik Hasek	6.00	15.00
15 Michael Peca	1.50	4.00
16 Miroslav Satan	1.50	4.00
17 Theoren Fleury	1.50	4.00
18 Jarome Iginla	4.00	10.00
19 Marty McInnis	1.50	4.00
20 Cory Stillman	1.50	4.00
21 Rick Tabaracci	2.50	6.00

22 Martin Gelinas 1.50 4.00
23 Sami Kapanen 1.50 4.00
24 Trevor Kidd 2.50 6.00
25 Keith Primeau 1.50 4.00
26 Gary Roberts 1.50 4.00
27 Tony Amonte 2.50 6.00
28 Chris Chelios 3.00 8.00
29 Eric Daze 2.50 6.00
30 Jeff Hackett 2.50 6.00
31 Dmitri Nabokov 1.50 4.00
32 Peter Forsberg 8.00 20.00
33 Valeri Kamensky 2.50 6.00
34 Jari Kurri 2.50 6.00
35 Claude Lemieux 1.50 4.00
36 Eric Messier 2.00 5.00
37 Sandis Ozolinsh 1.50 4.00
38 Patrick Roy 12.00 30.00
39 Joe Sakic 6.00 15.00
40 Ed Belfour 3.00 8.00
41 Jamie Langenbrunner 1.50 4.00
42 Jere Lehtinen 1.50 4.00
43 Mike Modano 5.00 12.00
44 Joe Nieuwendyk 2.50 6.00
45 Sergei Zubov 1.50 4.00
46 Viacheslav Fetisov 1.50 4.00
47 Nicklas Lidstrom 3.00 8.00
48 Darren McCarty 1.50 4.00
49 Larry Murphy 1.50 4.00
50 Chris Osgood 2.50 6.00
51 Brendan Shanahan 3.00 8.00
52 Steve Yzerman 12.00 30.00
53 Roman Hamrlik 2.50 6.00
54 Bill Guerin 2.50 6.00
55 Curtis Joseph 3.00 8.00
56 Ryan Smyth 2.50 6.00
57 Doug Weight 2.50 6.00
58 Dino Ciccarelli 1.50 4.00
59 Dave Gagner 1.50 4.00
60 Ed Jovanovski 2.50 6.00
61 Paul Laus 1.50 4.00
62 John Vanbiesbrouck 2.50 6.00
63 Ray Whitney 1.50 4.00
64 Russ Courtnall 1.50 4.00
65 Yanic Perreault 1.50 4.00
66 Luc Robitaille 2.50 6.00
67 Jozef Stumpel 2.50 6.00
68 Vladimir Tsyplakov 1.50 4.00
69 Shayne Corson 1.50 4.00
70 Vincent Damphousse 1.50 4.00
71 Saku Koivu 3.00 8.00
72 Andy Moog 2.50 6.00
73 Mark Recchi 2.50 6.00
74 Jocelyn Thibault 2.50 6.00
75 Martin Brodeur 8.00 20.00
76 Patrik Elias 12.00 30.00
77 Doug Gilmour 2.50 6.00
78 Bobby Holik 1.50 4.00
79 Scott Niedermayer 1.50 4.00
80 Bryan Berard 2.50 6.00
81 Travis Green 1.50 4.00
82 Zigmund Palffy 2.50 6.00
83 Robert Reichel 1.50 4.00
84 Tommy Salo 2.50 6.00
85 Dan Cloutier 1.50 4.00
86 Adam Graves 1.50 4.00
87 Wayne Gretzky 15.00 40.00
88 Pat LaFontaine 3.00 8.00
89 Brian Leetch 3.00 8.00
90 Mike Richter 3.00 8.00
91 Kevin Stevens 2.50 6.00
92 Daniel Alfredsson 2.50 6.00
93 Shawn McEachern 1.50 4.00
94 Damian Rhodes 2.50 6.00
95 Ron Tugnutt 2.50 6.00
96 Alexei Yashin 1.50 4.00
97 Rod Brind'Amour 2.50 6.00
98 Paul Coffey 3.00 8.00
99 Alexandre Daigle 1.50 4.00
100 Chris Gratton 2.50 6.00
101 Ron Hextall 2.50 6.00
102 John LeClair 3.00 8.00
103 Eric Lindros 3.00 8.00
104 Dainius Zubrus 3.00 8.00
105 Mike Gartner 2.50 6.00
106 Craig Janney 1.50 4.00
107 Nikolai Khabibulin 2.50 6.00
108 Jeremy Roenick 4.00 10.00
109 Keith Tkachuk 3.00 8.00
110 Stu Barnes 1.50 4.00
111 Tom Barrasso 2.50 6.00
112 Ron Francis 2.50 6.00
113 Jaromir Jagr 5.00 12.00
114 Peter Skudra 1.25 3.00
115 Martin Straka 1.50 4.00
116 Blair Atcheynum 1.25 3.00
117 Jim Campbell 1.50 4.00
118 Geoff Courtnall 1.50 4.00
119 Steve Duchesne 1.50 4.00
120 Grant Fuhr 2.50 6.00
121 Brett Hull 4.00 10.00
122 Pierre Turgeon 2.50 6.00
123 Jeff Friesen 1.50 4.00
124 John MacLean 1.50 4.00
125 Patrick Marleau 2.50 6.00
126 Owen Nolan 2.50 6.00
127 Marco Sturm 6.00 15.00
128 Mike Vernon 2.50 6.00
129 Daren Puppa 2.50 6.00
130 Mikael Renberg 2.50 6.00
131 Paul Ysebaert 1.50 4.00
132 Rob Zamuner 1.50 4.00
133 Wendel Clark 2.50 6.00
134 Tie Domi 2.50 6.00
135 Igor Korolev 1.50 4.00
136 Felix Potvin 3.00 8.00
137 Mats Sundin 3.00 8.00
138 Donald Brashear 1.50 4.00
139 Pavel Bure 3.00 8.00
140 Sean Burke 2.50 6.00
141 Trevor Linden 2.50 6.00
142 Mark Messier 3.00 8.00
143 Alexander Mogilny 2.50 6.00
144 Mattias Ohlund 2.50 6.00
145 Peter Bondra 2.50 6.00
146 Phil Housley 1.50 4.00
147 Dale Hunter 1.50 4.00
148 Joe Juneau 2.50 6.00
149 Olaf Kolzig 2.50 6.00
150 Adam Oates 2.50 6.00

1997-98 Revolution Silver

*VETS: 3X TO 8X BASIC CARDS
*ROOKIES: 1.5X TO 4X BASIC CARDS

1997-98 Revolution 1998 All-Star Game Die-Cuts

COMPLETE SET (20) 40.00 80.00
1 Teemu Selanne 1.50 4.00
2 Ray Bourque 3.00 8.00
3 Dominik Hasek 3.00 8.00
4 Theo Fleury 1.25 3.00
5 Chris Chelios 1.50 4.00
6 Peter Forsberg 4.00 10.00
7 Patrick Roy 6.00 15.00
8 Joe Sakic 4.00 10.00
9 Ed Belfour 1.50 4.00
10 Mike Modano 2.50 6.00
11 Brendan Shanahan 1.50 4.00
12 Saku Koivu 1.50 4.00
13 Martin Brodeur 4.00 10.00
14 Wayne Gretzky 10.00 25.00
15 John LeClair 1.50 4.00
16 Eric Lindros 1.50 4.00
17 Jaromir Jagr 2.50 6.00
18 Pavel Bure 1.50 4.00
19 Mark Messier 1.50 4.00
20 Peter Bondra 1.25 3.00

1997-98 Revolution NHL Icons

COMPLETE SET (10) 30.00 60.00
1 Paul Kariya 1.50 4.00
2 Teemu Selanne 1.50 4.00
3 Peter Forsberg 4.00 10.00
4 Patrick Roy 6.00 15.00
5 Steve Yzerman 6.00 15.00
6 Martin Brodeur 4.00 10.00
7 Wayne Gretzky 8.00 20.00
8 Eric Lindros 1.50 4.00
9 Jaromir Jagr 2.50 6.00
10 Pavel Bure 1.50 4.00

1997-98 Revolution Return to Sender Die-Cuts

COMPLETE SET (20) 15.00 40.00
1 Guy Hebert 1.00 2.50
2 Byron Dafoe 1.00 2.50
3 Dominik Hasek 2.50 6.00
4 Jeff Hackett 1.00 2.50
5 Patrick Roy 5.00 12.00
6 Ed Belfour 1.25 3.00
7 Chris Osgood 1.00 2.50
8 Curtis Joseph 1.25 3.00
9 John Vanbiesbrouck 1.00 2.50
10 Andy Moog 1.00 2.50
11 Martin Brodeur 3.00 8.00
12 Tommy Salo 1.00 2.50
13 Mike Richter 1.25 3.00
14 Ron Hextall 1.00 2.50
15 Nikolai Khabibulin 1.00 2.50
16 Tom Barrasso 1.00 2.50
17 Grant Fuhr 1.00 2.50
18 Mike Vernon 1.00 2.50
19 Felix Potvin 1.25 3.00
20 Olaf Kolzig 1.00 2.50

1997-98 Revolution Team Checklist Laser Cuts

COMPLETE SET (26) 40.00 80.00
1 Paul Kariya 1.25 3.00
2 Joe Thornton 2.00 5.00
3 Michael Peca .60 1.50
4 Theo Fleury .60 1.50
5 Keith Primeau .60 1.50
6 Chris Chelios 1.25 3.00
7 Patrick Roy 5.00 12.00
8 Mike Modano 2.00 5.00
9 Steve Yzerman 4.00 10.00
10 Ryan Smyth 1.00 2.50
11 John Vanbiesbrouck 1.00 2.50
12 Jozef Stumpel 1.00 2.50
13 Saku Koivu 1.25 3.00
14 Martin Brodeur 3.00 8.00
15 Zigmund Palffy 1.00 2.50
16 Wayne Gretzky 6.00 15.00
17 Daniel Alfredsson 1.00 2.50
18 Eric Lindros 1.25 3.00
19 Keith Tkachuk 1.25 3.00
20 Jaromir Jagr 2.00 5.00
21 Brett Hull 1.50 4.00
22 Mike Vernon 1.00 2.50
23 Rob Zamuner .60 1.50
24 Mats Sundin 1.25 3.00
25 Pavel Bure 1.25 3.00
26 Peter Bondra 1.00 2.50

1998-99 Revolution

*RED/99: 1.5X TO 4X BASIC CARDS
*ICE/99: 3X TO 8X BASIC CARDS
1 Guy Hebert .20 .50
2 Paul Kariya .25 .60
3 Marty McInnis .15 .40
4 Steve Rucchin .15 .40
5 Teemu Selanne .50 1.25
6 Jason Allison .25 .60
7 Ray Bourque .40 1.00
8 Anson Carter .20 .50
9 Byron Dafoe .20 .50
10 Dimitri Khristich .15 .40
11 Sergei Samsonov .20 .50
12 Matthew Barnaby .15 .40
13 Michal Grosek .15 .40
14 Dominik Hasek .40 1.00
15 Michael Peca .15 .40
16 Miroslav Satan .20 .50
17 Dixon Ward .15 .40
18 Theo Fleury .30 .75
19 Jean-Sebastien Giguere .20 .50
20 Jarome Iginla .30 .75
21 Tyler Moss .15 .40
22 Cory Stillman .15 .40
23 Ron Francis .30 .75
24 Arturs Irbe .20 .50
25 Trevor Kidd .15 .40
26 Keith Primeau .20 .50
27 Ray Sheppard .15 .40
28 Tony Amonte .20 .50
29 Chris Chelios .25 .60
30 Eric Daze .20 .50
31 Doug Gilmour .30 .75
32 Jocelyn Thibault .20 .50
33 Adam Deadmarsh .15 .40
34 Chris Drury .20 .50
35 Peter Forsberg .50 1.25
36 Milan Hejduk RC .40 1.00
37 Claude Lemieux .20 .50
38 Patrick Roy .60 1.50
39 Joe Sakic .50 1.25
40 Ed Belfour .25 .60
41 Brett Hull .50 1.25
42 Jamie Langenbrunner .15 .40
43 Jere Lehtinen .20 .50
44 Mike Modano .40 1.00
45 Joe Nieuwendyk .20 .50
46 Darryl Sydor .15 .40
47 Sergei Fedorov .40 1.00
48 Nicklas Lidstrom .30 .75
49 Norm Maracle RC .20 .50
50 Darren McCarty .15 .40
51 Chris Osgood .25 .60
52 Brendan Shanahan .25 .60
53 Steve Yzerman .60 1.50
54 Bill Guerin .20 .50
55 Andrei Kovalenko .15 .40
56 Mikhail Shtalenkov .15 .40
57 Ryan Smyth .20 .50
58 Doug Weight .25 .60
59 Pavel Bure .25 .60
60 Sean Burke .15 .40
61 Dino Ciccarelli .25 .60
62 Viktor Kozlov .20 .50
63 Rob Niedermayer .15 .40
64 Mark Parrish RC .40 1.00
65 Rob Blake .25 .60
66 Stephane Fiset .20 .50
67 Olli Jokinen .20 .50
68 Luc Robitaille .25 .60
69 Pavel Rosa RC .15 .40
70 Jozef Stumpel .15 .40
71 Shayne Corson .20 .50
72 Vincent Damphousse .20 .50
73 Jeff Hackett .20 .50
74 Saku Koivu .25 .60
75 Mark Recchi .30 .75
76 Brian Savage .15 .40
77 Andrew Brunette .15 .40
78 Mike Dunham .20 .50
79 Sergei Krivokrasov .15 .40
80 Cliff Ronning .15 .40
81 Tomas Vokoun .20 .50
82 Jason Arnott .20 .50
83 Martin Brodeur .60 1.50
84 Patrik Elias .25 .60
85 Bobby Holik .15 .40
86 Brendan Morrison .25 .60
87 Felix Potvin .40 1.00
88 Trevor Linden .25 .60
89 Zigmund Palffy .25 .60
90 Tommy Salo .20 .50
91 Mike Watt .15 .40
92 Wayne Gretzky 1.50 4.00
93 Todd Harvey .15 .40
94 Brian Leetch .25 .60
95 Manny Malhotra .20 .50
96 Petr Nedved .15 .40
97 Mike Richter .25 .60
98 Daniel Alfredsson .25 .60
99 Marian Hossa .25 .60
100 Shawn McEachern .15 .40
101 Damian Rhodes .25 .60
102 Alexei Yashin .20 .50
103 Rod Brind'Amour .25 .60
104 Ron Hextall .25 .60
105 John LeClair .25 .60
106 Eric Lindros .40 1.00
107 John Vanbiesbrouck .25 .60
108 Dainius Zubrus .15 .40
109 Daniel Briere .20 .50
110 Nikolai Khabibulin .25 .60
111 Jeremy Roenick .40 1.00
112 Keith Tkachuk .25 .60
113 Rick Tocchet .20 .50
114 Jim Waite .15 .40
115 Jean-Sebastien Aubin RC .40 1.00
116 Stu Barnes .15 .40
117 Tom Barrasso .20 .50
118 Jaromir Jagr .75 2.00
119 Alexei Kovalev .20 .50
120 Martin Straka .15 .40
121 Pavol Demitra .30 .75
122 Grant Fuhr .40 1.00
123 Al MacInnis .30 .75
124 Chris Pronger .25 .60
125 Pierre Turgeon .20 .50
126 Jeff Friesen .15 .40
127 Patrick Marleau .25 .60
128 Owen Nolan .25 .60
129 Marco Sturm .15 .40
130 Mike Vernon .20 .50
131 Wendel Clark .40 1.00
132 Daren Puppa .20 .50
133 Vincent Lecavalier .50 1.25
134 Stephane Richer .15 .40
135 Rob Zamuner .15 .40
136 Tie Domi .20 .50
137 Mike Johnson .15 .40
138 Curtis Joseph .25 .60
139 Tomas Kaberle RC .30 .75
140 Mats Sundin .25 .60
141 Mark Messier .50 1.25
142 Alexander Mogilny .20 .50
143 Bill Muckalt RC .20 .50
144 Mattias Ohlund .15 .40
145 Garth Snow .20 .50
146 Peter Bondra .25 .60
147 Joe Juneau .15 .40
148 Olaf Kolzig .25 .60
149 Adam Oates .25 .60
150 Richard Zednik .15 .40
NNO Martin Brodeur SAMPLE .60 1.50

1998-99 Revolution All-Star Die Cuts

1 Tony Amonte .75 2.00
2 Ed Belfour 1.00 2.50
3 Peter Bondra 1.00 2.50
4 Ray Bourque 1.50 4.00
5 Martin Brodeur 2.50 6.00
6 Theo Fleury 1.25 3.00
7 Peter Forsberg 2.00 5.00
8 Wayne Gretzky 6.00 15.00
9 Dominik Hasek 1.50 4.00
10 Bobby Holik .60 1.50
11 Arturs Irbe .75 2.00
12 Jaromir Jagr 3.00 8.00
13 Paul Kariya 1.00 2.50
14 Nikolai Khabibulin 1.00 2.50
15 Sergei Krivokrasov .60 1.50
16 John LeClair 1.00 2.50
17 Nicklas Lidstrom 1.25 3.00
18 Eric Lindros 1.50 4.00
19 Al MacInnis 1.25 3.00
20 Mike Modano 1.50 4.00
21 Mattias Ohlund .60 1.50
22 Keith Primeau .75 2.00
23 Chris Pronger 1.00 2.50
24 Mark Recchi 1.25 3.00
25 Jeremy Roenick 1.50 4.00
26 Teemu Selanne 2.00 5.00
27 Brendan Shanahan 1.00 2.50
28 Mats Sundin 1.00 2.50
29 Keith Tkachuk 1.00 2.50
30 Alexei Yashin .75 2.00

1998-99 Revolution Chalk Talk Laser-Cuts

1 Paul Kariya 1.00 2.50
2 Teemu Selanne 2.00 5.00
3 Theo Fleury 1.25 3.00
4 Peter Forsberg 2.00 5.00
5 Joe Sakic 2.00 5.00
6 Brett Hull 2.00 5.00
7 Mike Modano 1.50 4.00
8 Sergei Fedorov 1.50 4.00
9 Brendan Shanahan 1.00 2.50
10 Steve Yzerman 2.50 6.00
11 Wayne Gretzky 6.00 15.00
12 Alexei Yashin .75 2.00
13 John LeClair 1.00 2.50
14 Eric Lindros 1.25 3.00
15 Keith Tkachuk 1.00 2.50
16 Jaromir Jagr 3.00 8.00
17 Vincent Lecavalier 2.00 5.00
18 Mats Sundin 1.00 2.50
19 Mark Messier 1.25 3.00
20 Peter Bondra 1.00 2.50

1998-99 Revolution NHL Icons

1 Paul Kariya 1.25 3.00
2 Dominik Hasek 2.00 5.00
3 Peter Forsberg 2.50 6.00
4 Patrick Roy 3.00 8.00
5 Mike Modano 2.00 5.00
6 Steve Yzerman 3.00 8.00
7 Martin Brodeur 3.00 8.00
8 Wayne Gretzky 8.00 20.00
9 Eric Lindros 2.00 5.00
10 Jaromir Jagr 5.00 12.00

1998-99 Revolution Showstoppers

1 Paul Kariya 1.25 3.00
2 Teemu Selanne 2.50 6.00
3 Ray Bourque 2.00 5.00
4 Dominik Hasek 2.00 5.00
5 Michael Peca .75 2.00
6 Theo Fleury 1.50 4.00
7 Tony Amonte 1.00 2.50
8 Chris Chelios 1.25 3.00
9 Doug Gilmour 1.50 4.00
10 Peter Forsberg 2.50 6.00
11 Patrick Roy 3.00 8.00
12 Joe Sakic 2.50 6.00
13 Ed Belfour 1.25 3.00
14 Brett Hull 2.50 6.00
15 Mike Modano 2.00 5.00
16 Sergei Fedorov 2.00 5.00
17 Brendan Shanahan 1.25 3.00
18 Steve Yzerman 3.00 8.00
19 Mark Parrish 2.00 5.00
20 Saku Koivu 1.25 3.00
21 Martin Brodeur 3.00 8.00
22 Zigmund Palffy 1.25 3.00
23 Wayne Gretzky 8.00 20.00
24 Alexei Yashin 1.00 2.50
25 John LeClair 1.25 3.00
26 Eric Lindros 2.00 5.00
27 John Vanbiesbrouck 1.25 3.00
28 Nikolai Khabibulin 1.25 3.00
29 Jeremy Roenick 2.00 5.00
30 Keith Tkachuk 1.25 3.00
31 Jaromir Jagr 4.00 10.00
32 Vincent Lecavalier 2.50 6.00
33 Curtis Joseph 1.50 4.00
34 Mats Sundin 1.25 3.00
35 Mark Messier 2.50 6.00
36 Peter Bondra 1.25 3.00

1998-99 Revolution Three Pronged Attack

COMPLETE SET (30) 15.00 30.00
*1-10 PARALLEL/99: 5X TO 12X BASIC INSERT
*11-20 PARALLEL/199: 3X TO 8X BASIC INSERT
*21-30 PARALLEL/299: 2X TO 5X BASIC INSERT
1 Matthew Barnaby .30 .75
2 Theo Fleury .30 .75
3 Chris Chelios .50 1.25
4 Darren McCarty .30 .75
5 Brendan Shanahan .50 1.25
6 Eric Lindros .50 1.25
7 Keith Tkachuk .50 1.25
8 Tony Twist .30 .75
9 Tie Domi .30 .75
10 Donald Brashear .30 .75
11 Dominik Hasek .75 2.00
12 Patrick Roy 1.25 3.00
13 Ed Belfour .50 1.25
14 Chris Osgood .40 1.00
15 Martin Brodeur 1.00 2.50
16 Mike Richter .50 1.25
17 John Vanbiesbrouck .40 1.00
18 Nikolai Khabibulin .40 1.00
19 Curtis Joseph .50 1.25
20 Olaf Kolzig .40 1.00
21 Paul Kariya .50 1.25
22 Teemu Selanne .50 1.25
23 Peter Forsberg 1.00 2.50
24 Joe Sakic .75 2.00
25 Mike Modano .30 .75
26 Steve Yzerman 1.25 3.00
27 Wayne Gretzky 1.50 4.00
28 John LeClair .50 1.25
29 Jaromir Jagr .60 1.50
30 Pavel Bure .50 1.25

1999-00 Revolution

1 Guy Hebert .30 .75
2 Paul Kariya .30 .75
3 Marty McInnis .20 .50
4 Teemu Selanne .60 1.50
5 Steve Rucchin .20 .50
6 Kelly Buchberger .20 .50
7 Ray Ferraro .20 .50
8 Damian Rhodes .20 .50
9 Johan Garpenlov .20 .50
10 Jason Allison .25 .60
11 Ray Bourque .50 1.25
12 Anson Carter .25 .60
13 Byron Dafoe .25 .60
14 Sergei Samsonov .25 .60
15 Joe Thornton .50 1.25
16 Martin Biron .25 .60
17 Curtis Brown .20 .50
18 Dominik Hasek .50 1.25
19 Michael Peca .25 .60
20 Miroslav Satan .20 .50
21 Dixon Ward .20 .50
22 Valeri Bure .20 .50
23 Fred Brathwaite .20 .50
24 Phil Housley .25 .60
25 Jarome Iginla .40 1.00
26 Cory Stillman .20 .50
27 Ron Francis .40 1.00
28 Arturs Irbe .25 .60
29 Sami Kapanen .20 .50
30 Keith Primeau .25 .60
31 Gary Roberts .20 .50
32 Tony Amonte .25 .60
33 J-P Dumont .25 .60
34 Doug Gilmour .40 1.00
35 Jocelyn Thibault .25 .60
36 Alexei Zhamnov .20 .50
37 Adam Deadmarsh .20 .50
38 Chris Drury .25 .60
39 Peter Forsberg .60 1.50
40 Milan Hejduk .25 .60
41 Claude Lemieux .25 .60
42 Patrick Roy .75 2.00
43 Joe Sakic .60 1.50
44 Ed Belfour .30 .75
45 Brett Hull .60 1.50
46 Jamie Langenbrunner .20 .50
47 Jere Lehtinen .20 .50
48 Mike Modano .50 1.25
49 Joe Nieuwendyk .25 .60
50 Chris Chelios .30 .75
51 Sergei Fedorov .50 1.25
52 Vyacheslav Kozlov .20 .50
53 Nicklas Lidstrom .30 .75
54 Chris Osgood .30 .75
55 Brendan Shanahan .30 .75
56 Steve Yzerman .75 2.00
57 Mike Grier .20 .50
58 Bill Guerin .30 .75
59 Tommy Salo .25 .60
60 Ryan Smyth .30 .75
61 Doug Weight .30 .75
62 Pavel Bure .30 .75
63 Sean Burke .20 .50
64 Viktor Kozlov .20 .50
65 Mark Parrish .20 .50
66 Ray Whitney .25 .60
67 Donald Audette .20 .50
68 Rob Blake .20 .50
69 Stephane Fiset .25 .60
70 Zigmund Palffy .30 .75
71 Luc Robitaille .30 .75
72 Jamie Storr .20 .50
73 Shayne Corson .25 .60
74 Jeff Hackett .20 .50
75 Saku Koivu .30 .75
76 Vladimir Malakhov .20 .50
77 Martin Rucinsky .20 .50
78 Mike Dunham .25 .60
79 Greg Johnson .20 .50
80 Sergei Krivokrasov .20 .50
81 Cliff Ronning .20 .50
82 Scott Walker .20 .50
83 Jason Arnott .25 .60
84 Martin Brodeur .75 2.00
85 Patrik Elias .30 .75
86 Bobby Holik .20 .50
87 Brendan Morrison .25 .60
88 Scott Niedermayer .30 .75
89 Petr Sykora .25 .60
90 Mariusz Czerkawski .20 .50
91 Kenny Jonsson .20 .50
92 Mats Lindgren .20 .50
93 Felix Potvin .50 1.25
94 Mike Watt .20 .50
95 Theo Fleury .40 1.00
96 Adam Graves .25 .60
97 Brian Leetch .25 .60
98 John MacLean .20 .50
99 Petr Nedved .20 .50
100 Mike Richter .30 .75
101 Magnus Arvedson .20 .50
102 Marian Hossa .30 .75
103 Shawn McEachern .30 .75
104 Ron Tugnutt .20 .50
105 Alexei Yashin .25 .60
106 Rod Brind'Amour .30 .75
107 Eric Lindros .50 1.25
108 John LeClair .50 1.25
109 Mark Recchi .25 .60
110 John Vanbiesbrouck .30 .75
111 Nikolai Khabibulin .25 .60
112 Teppo Numminen .20 .50
113 Jeremy Roenick .50 1.25
114 Keith Tkachuk .30 .75
115 Rick Tocchet .25 .60
116 Tom Barrasso .30 .75
117 Jan Hrdina .20 .50
118 Jaromir Jagr 1.00 2.50
119 Alexei Kovalev .25 .60
120 Martin Straka .30 .75
121 Pavol Demitra .40 1.00
122 Jochen Hecht RC .50 1.25
123 Al MacInnis .40 1.00
124 Chris Pronger .30 .75
125 Pierre Turgeon .25 .60
126 Vincent Damphousse .25 .60
127 Jeff Friesen .25 .60
128 Patrick Marleau .30 .75
129 Steve Shields .25 .60
130 Mike Vernon .25 .60
131 Chris Gratton .20 .50
132 Colin Forbes .20 .50
133 Vincent Lecavalier .30 .75
134 Darcy Tucker .20 .50
135 Sergei Berezin .20 .50
136 Tie Domi .25 .60
137 Mike Johnson .20 .50
138 Curtis Joseph .40 1.00
139 Derek King .20 .50
140 Mats Sundin .30 .75
141 Steve Thomas .20 .50
142 Mark Messier .60 1.50
143 Bill Muckalt .20 .50
144 Markus Naslund .30 .75
145 Mattias Ohlund .20 .50
146 Garth Snow .25 .60
147 Peter Bondra .30 .75
148 Sergei Gonchar .20 .50
149 Olaf Kolzig .30 .75
150 Adam Oates .30 .75

1999-00 Revolution Premiere Date

*PREM.DATE: 15X TO 40X BASIC CARDS

1999-00 Revolution Red

*RED: 4X TO 10X BASIC CARDS

1999-00 Revolution Shadow Series

*SHADOWS: 10X TO 25X BASIC CARDS

1999-00 Revolution Ice Sculptures

COMPLETE SET (10) 50.00 100.00
1 Paul Kariya 2.00 5.00
2 Dominik Hasek 4.00 10.00
3 Patrick Roy 10.00 25.00
4 Joe Sakic 4.00 10.00
5 Steve Yzerman 10.00 25.00
6 Pavel Bure 2.50 6.00
7 Martin Brodeur 5.00 12.00
8 Theo Fleury 2.00 5.00
9 Eric Lindros 3.00 8.00
10 Jaromir Jagr 3.00 8.00

1999-00 Revolution NHL Icons

COMPLETE SET (20) 30.00 80.00
1 Teemu Selanne 1.50 4.00
2 Ray Bourque 3.00 8.00
3 Dominik Hasek 3.00 8.00
4 Doug Gilmour 1.25 3.00
5 Peter Forsberg 4.00 10.00
6 Patrick Roy 6.00 15.00
7 Joe Sakic 3.00 8.00
8 Brett Hull 2.00 5.00
9 Mike Modano 2.50 6.00
10 Brendan Shanahan 1.50 4.00
11 Steve Yzerman 6.00 15.00
12 Martin Brodeur 4.00 10.00
13 John LeClair 1.50 4.00
14 Eric Lindros 1.50 4.00
15 John Vanbiesbrouck 1.25 3.00
16 Keith Tkachuk 1.50 4.00
17 Jaromir Jagr 2.50 6.00
18 Curtis Joseph 1.50 4.00
19 Mats Sundin 1.50 4.00
20 Mark Messier 1.50 4.00

1999-00 Revolution Ornaments

COMPLETE SET (20) 40.00 80.00
1 Paul Kariya 1.25 3.00
2 Teemu Selanne 1.50 4.00
3 Sergei Samsonov 1.00 2.50
4 Dominik Hasek 3.00 8.00
5 Jarome Iginla 1.50 4.00
6 Peter Forsberg 3.00 8.00
7 Patrick Roy 5.00 12.00
8 Ed Belfour 1.25 3.00
9 Mike Modano 2.50 6.00
10 Brendan Shanahan 1.25 3.00
11 Steve Yzerman 6.00 15.00
12 Pavel Bure 2.50 6.00
13 Martin Brodeur 4.00 10.00
14 John LeClair 1.25 3.00
15 Eric Lindros 2.50 6.00
16 Jaromir Jagr 2.50 6.00
17 Vincent Lecavalier 1.25 3.00
18 Curtis Joseph 1.25 3.00
19 Mats Sundin 1.25 3.00
20 Mark Messier 1.25 3.00

1999-00 Revolution Showstoppers

COMPLETE SET (36) 30.00 70.00
1 Paul Kariya 1.00 2.50
2 Teemu Selanne 1.00 2.50
3 Ray Bourque 1.50 4.00
4 Byron Dafoe .40 1.00
5 Dominik Hasek 1.50 4.00
6 Michael Peca .40 1.00
7 Tony Amonte .75 2.00
8 Chris Drury .75 2.00
9 Peter Forsberg 1.50 4.00
10 Patrick Roy 4.00 10.00
11 Joe Sakic 2.00 5.00
12 Ed Belfour 1.00 2.50
13 Brett Hull 1.00 2.50
14 Mike Modano 1.00 2.50
15 Joe Nieuwendyk .75 2.00
16 Sergei Fedorov 1.00 2.50
17 Brendan Shanahan 1.00 2.50
18 Doug Weight .40 1.00
19 Pavel Bure 1.00 2.50
20 Mark Parrish .40 1.00
21 Martin Brodeur 2.50 6.00
22 Felix Potvin 1.00 2.50
23 Mike Richter 1.00 2.50
24 Marian Hossa .75 2.00
25 Alexei Yashin .40 1.00
26 John LeClair .75 2.00
27 John Vanbiesbrouck 1.25 3.00
28 Jeremy Roenick 1.00 2.50
29 Keith Tkachuk .75 2.00
30 Pavol Demitra .40 1.00
31 Patrick Marleau .75 2.00
32 Vincent Lecavalier 1.00 2.50
33 Curtis Joseph 1.00 2.50
34 Mats Sundin .75 2.00
35 Mark Messier 1.00 2.50
36 Peter Bondra .40 1.00

1999-00 Revolution Top of the Line

1 Paul Kariya/99 12.00 30.00
2 Sergei Samsonov/99 10.00 25.00
3 Brendan Shanahan/99 12.00 30.00
4 Pavel Bure/99 12.00 30.00
5 Luc Robitaille/99 10.00 25.00
6 Marian Hossa/99 10.00 25.00
7 John LeClair/99 8.00 20.00
8 Keith Tkachuk/99 12.00 30.00
9 Pavol Demitra/99 8.00 20.00
10 Jeff Friesen/99 8.00 20.00
11 Chris Drury/199 4.00 10.00
12 Peter Forsberg/199 12.00 30.00
13 Joe Sakic/199 12.00 30.00
14 Steve Yzerman/199 25.00 60.00
15 Mike Modano/199 10.00 25.00
16 Joe Nieuwendyk/199 6.00 15.00
17 Alexei Yashin/199 4.00 10.00
18 Eric Lindros/199 5.00 12.00
19 Mats Sundin/199 6.00 15.00
20 Mark Messier/199 6.00 15.00
21 Teemu Selanne/299 4.00 10.00
22 Miroslav Satan/299 3.00 8.00
23 Jarome Iginla/299 6.00 15.00
24 Tony Amonte/299 3.00 8.00
25 Milan Hejduk/299 3.00 8.00
26 Brett Hull/299 6.00 15.00
27 Theo Fleury/299 3.00 8.00
28 Mark Recchi/299 3.00 8.00
29 Jaromir Jagr/299 8.00 20.00
30 Peter Bondra/299 3.00 8.00

1999-00 Revolution CSC Silver

*CSC SILVER: 20X TO 50X BASIC CARDS

2000-01 Revolution

*RED/99: 3X TO 8X BASIC CARDS
*BLUE/99: 3X TO 8X BASIC CARDS
1 Guy Hebert .20 .50
2 Paul Kariya .25 .60
3 Steve Rucchin .15 .40
4 Teemu Selanne .50 1.25
5 Andrew Brunette .15 .40
6 Ray Ferraro .15 .40
7 Damian Rhodes .15 .40
8 Patrik Stefan .20 .50
9 Anson Carter .20 .50
10 Byron Dafoe .20 .50
11 John Grahame .15 .40
12 Sergei Samsonov .20 .50
13 Joe Thornton .40 1.00
14 Maxim Afinogenov .15 .40
15 Martin Biron .20 .50
16 Doug Gilmour .30 .75
17 Dominik Hasek .40 1.00
18 Michael Peca .20 .50
19 Miroslav Satan .15 .40
20 Fred Brathwaite .20 .50
21 Valeri Bure .20 .50
22 Phil Housley .20 .50
23 Jarome Iginla .30 .75
24 Oleg Saprykin .15 .40
25 Rod Brind'Amour .25 .60
26 Ron Francis .30 .75
27 Arturs Irbe .20 .50
28 Sami Kapanen .15 .40
29 Tony Amonte .20 .50
30 Michal Grosek .15 .40
31 Steve Sullivan .15 .40
32 Jocelyn Thibault .20 .50
33 Alexei Zhamnov .20 .50
34 Ray Bourque .40 1.00
35 Chris Drury .20 .50
36 Peter Forsberg .50 1.25
37 Milan Hejduk .20 .50
38 Patrick Roy .60 1.50
39 Joe Sakic .50 1.25
40 Alex Tanguay .20 .50
41 Kevyn Adams .15 .40
42 Marc Denis .20 .50
43 Krzysztof Oliwa .15 .40
44 Geoff Sanderson .20 .50
45 Ed Belfour .25 .60
46 Brett Hull .50 1.25
47 Mike Modano .40 1.00
48 Brenden Morrow .20 .50
49 Joe Nieuwendyk .20 .50
50 Chris Chelios .25 .60
51 Sergei Fedorov .40 1.00
52 Nicklas Lidstrom .25 .60
53 Chris Osgood .25 .60
54 Brendan Shanahan .25 .60
55 Steve Yzerman .60 1.50
56 Bill Guerin .25 .60
57 Todd Marchant .15 .40
58 Tommy Salo .20 .50
59 Ryan Smyth .20 .50
60 Doug Weight .20 .50
61 Pavel Bure .25 .60
62 Trevor Kidd .15 .40
63 Viktor Kozlov .20 .50
64 Scott Mellanby .15 .40
65 Ray Whitney .20 .50
66 Rob Blake .25 .60
67 Stephane Fiset .15 .40
68 Zigmund Palffy .25 .60
69 Luc Robitaille .25 .60
70 Jamie Storr .15 .40
71 Manny Fernandez .15 .40
72 Jamie McLennan .15 .40
73 Sean O'Donnell .15 .40
74 Stacy Roest .15 .40
75 Jeff Hackett .15 .40

76 Saku Koivu .25 .60
77 Trevor Linden .25 .60
78 Martin Rucinsky .15 .40
79 Jose Theodore .25 .60
80 Mike Dunham .15 .40
81 David Gosselin RC .20 .50
82 David Legwand .25 .60
83 Cliff Ronning .15 .40
84 Jason Arnott .20 .50
85 Martin Brodeur .60 1.50
86 Patrik Elias .25 .60
87 Scott Gomez .20 .50
88 Scott Stevens .25 .60
89 Petr Sykora .20 .50
90 Tim Connolly .15 .40
91 Mariusz Czerkawski .15 .40
92 Brad Isbister .15 .40
93 Steve Valiquette RC .20 .50
94 Theo Fleury .30 .75
95 Adam Graves .20 .50
96 Brian Leetch .20 .50
97 Mark Messier .50 1.25
98 Petr Nedved .20 .50
99 Mike Richter .25 .60
100 Mike York .15 .40
101 Daniel Alfredsson .25 .60
102 Radek Bonk .20 .50
103 Marian Hossa .25 .60
104 Patrick Lalime .20 .50
105 Shawn McEachern .15 .40
106 Brian Boucher .20 .50
107 Eric Desjardins .20 .50
108 Simon Gagne .25 .60
109 John LeClair .25 .60
110 Eric Lindros .40 1.00
111 Mark Recchi .30 .75
112 Shane Doan .20 .50
113 Nikolai Khabibulin .40 1.00
114 Jeremy Roenick .40 1.00
115 Keith Tkachuk .25 .60
116 Jean-Sebastien Aubin .20 .50
117 Jan Hrdina .15 .40
118 Jaromir Jagr .75 2.00
119 Alexei Kovalev .20 .50
120 Martin Straka .20 .50
121 Pavol Demitra .30 .75
122 Michal Handzus .15 .40
123 Al MacInnis .30 .75
124 Chris Pronger .25 .60
125 Roman Turek .20 .50
126 Pierre Turgeon .20 .50
127 Vincent Damphousse .20 .50
128 Jeff Friesen .15 .40
129 Patrick Marleau .25 .60
130 Owen Nolan .25 .60
131 Steve Shields .15 .40
132 Dan Cloutier .20 .50
133 Mike Johnson .15 .40
134 Dieter Kochan RC .15 .40
135 Vincent Lecavalier .25 .60
136 Nikolai Antropov .20 .50
137 Tie Domi .20 .50
138 Jeff Farkas .15 .40
139 Curtis Joseph .30 .75
140 Mats Sundin .25 .60
141 Darcy Tucker .15 .40
142 Todd Bertuzzi .20 .50
143 Steve Kariya .15 .40
144 Markus Naslund .25 .60
145 Felix Potvin .40 1.00
146 Peter Bondra .25 .60
147 Jeff Halpern .15 .40
148 Olaf Kolzig .25 .60
149 Adam Oates .25 .60
150 Chris Simon .15 .40

2000-01 Revolution Premiere Date

*PREM.DATE/60: 5X TO 12X BASIC CARDS
97 Mark Messier 12.00 30.00

2000-01 Revolution Game-Worn Jerseys

*PATCH/50: .75X TO 2X BASIC JSY
1 Marty McInnis 2.50 6.00
2 Anson Carter 2.50 6.00
3 Jarome Iginla 4.00 10.00
4 Tony Amonte 2.50 6.00
5 Jamie Langenbrunner 2.50 6.00
6 Saku Koivu 3.00 8.00
7 Zdeno Chara 3.00 8.00
8 Brian Leetch 2.50 6.00
9 Andreas Dackell 2.00 5.00
10 Petr Svoboda 2.00 5.00

2000-01 Revolution HD NHL

COMPLETE SET (36) 30.00 60.00
1 Paul Kariya 1.00 2.50
2 Teemu Selanne 1.00 2.50
3 Patrik Stefan .50 1.25
4 Joe Thornton 1.50 4.00
5 Dominik Hasek 2.00 5.00
6 Jarome Iginla 1.25 3.00
7 Tony Amonte .75 2.00
8 Peter Forsberg 2.50 6.00
9 Milan Hejduk 1.00 2.50
10 Joe Sakic 2.00 5.00
11 Patrick Roy 5.00 12.00
12 Ed Belfour 1.00 2.50
13 Brett Hull 1.25 3.00
14 Sergei Fedorov 1.50 4.00
15 Brendan Shanahan 1.00 2.50
16 Pavel Bure 1.00 2.50
17 Zigmund Palffy .75 2.00
18 Luc Robitaille .75 2.00
19 Saku Koivu 1.00 2.50
20 Martin Brodeur 2.50 6.00
21 Patrik Elias .75 2.00
22 Scott Gomez .50 1.25
23 Marian Hossa 1.00 2.50
24 Brian Boucher 1.00 2.50
25 John LeClair 1.00 2.50
26 Mark Recchi .75 2.00
27 Jeremy Roenick 1.25 3.00
28 Keith Tkachuk 1.00 2.50
29 Chris Pronger .75 2.00
30 Roman Turek .75 2.00
31 Owen Nolan .75 2.00
32 Vincent Lecavalier 1.00 2.50
33 Nikolai Antropov .50 1.25
34 Mats Sundin 1.00 2.50
35 Curtis Joseph 1.00 2.50
36 Olaf Kolzig .75 2.00

2000-01 Revolution Ice Immortals

COMPLETE SET (20) 30.00 60.00
1 Paul Kariya 1.25 3.00
2 Teemu Selanne 1.25 3.00
3 Dominik Hasek 2.50 6.00
4 Ray Bourque 2.50 6.00
5 Peter Forsberg 3.00 8.00
6 Patrick Roy 6.00 15.00
7 Ed Belfour 1.25 3.00
8 Brett Hull 1.50 4.00
9 Mike Modano 2.00 5.00
10 Brendan Shanahan 1.25 3.00
11 Steve Yzerman 6.00 15.00
12 Pavel Bure 1.25 3.00
13 Martin Brodeur 3.00 8.00
14 Scott Gomez .60 1.50
15 John LeClair 1.25 3.00
16 Mark Recchi 1.00 2.50
17 Jeremy Roenick 1.50 4.00
18 Jaromir Jagr 2.00 5.00
19 Curtis Joseph 1.25 3.00
20 Olaf Kolzig 1.00 2.50

2000-01 Revolution NHL Game Gear

1 Peter Forsberg 15.00 40.00
2 Joe Sakic 15.00 40.00
3 Mike Modano 12.50 30.00
4 Sergei Fedorov 12.50 30.00
5 Nicklas Lidstrom 8.00 20.00
6 Steve Yzerman 20.00 50.00
7 Mark Messier 8.00 20.00
8 Nikolai Khabibulin 8.00 20.00
9 Jaromir Jagr 12.50 30.00
10 Peter Bondra 6.00 15.00

2000-01 Revolution NHL Icons

COMPLETE SET (20) 50.00 100.00
1 Paul Kariya 2.00 5.00
2 Teemu Selanne 1.50 4.00
3 Doug Gilmour 1.25 3.00
4 Dominik Hasek 3.00 8.00
5 Ray Bourque 3.00 8.00
6 Peter Forsberg 5.00 12.00
7 Patrick Roy 6.00 15.00
8 Joe Sakic 3.00 8.00
9 Brett Hull 2.00 5.00
10 Mike Modano 2.50 6.00
11 Brendan Shanahan 1.50 4.00
12 Steve Yzerman 6.00 15.00
13 Pavel Bure 2.00 5.00
14 Luc Robitaille 1.25 3.00
15 Martin Brodeur 4.00 10.00
16 John LeClair 2.00 5.00
17 Jaromir Jagr 2.50 6.00
18 Curtis Joseph 1.50 4.00
19 Mats Sundin 1.50 4.00
20 Olaf Kolzig 1.25 3.00

2000-01 Revolution Stat Masters

COMPLETE SET (30) 100.00 200.00
1 Teemu Selanne/99 6.00 15.00
2 Tony Amonte/99 5.00 12.00
3 Milan Hejduk/99 5.00 12.00
4 Brett Hull/99 6.00 15.00
5 Brendan Shanahan/99 5.00 12.00
6 Pavel Bure/99 5.00 12.00
7 Luc Robitaille/99 5.00 12.00
8 John LeClair/99 5.00 12.00
9 Jaromir Jagr/99 10.00 25.00
10 Owen Nolan/99 5.00 12.00
11 Martin Biron/199 2.50 6.00
12 Dominik Hasek/199 6.00 15.00
13 Patrick Roy/199 10.00 25.00
14 Ed Belfour/199 2.50 6.00
15 Jose Theodore/199 3.00 8.00
16 Martin Brodeur/199 6.00 15.00
17 Brian Boucher/199 2.50 6.00
18 Roman Turek/199 2.50 6.00
19 Curtis Joseph/199 2.50 6.00
20 Olaf Kolzig/199 2.50 6.00
21 Paul Kariya/299 5.00 12.00
22 Doug Gilmour/299 2.00 5.00
23 Ray Bourque/299 4.00 10.00
24 Joe Sakic/299 4.00 10.00
25 Mike Modano/299 3.00 8.00
26 Steve Yzerman/299 8.00 20.00
27 Scott Gomez/299 2.00 5.00
28 Mark Recchi/299 2.00 5.00
29 Mats Sundin/299 2.00 5.00
30 Adam Oates/299 2.00 5.00

2006-07 Rochester Americans

COMPLETE SET (25) 10.00 18.00
1 Craig Anderson .30 .75
2 David Booth .20 .50
3 Mike Card .20 .50
4 Adam Dennis .40 1.00
5 Mike Funk .20 .50
6 Rob Globke .40 1.00
7 Dylan Hunter .40 1.00
8 Greg Jacina .20 .50
9 Patrick Kaleta .20 .50
10 Kamil Kreps .20 .50
11 Drew Larman .20 .50
12 Martin Lojek .20 .50
13 Clarke MacArthur .40 1.00
14 Mark Mancari .40 1.00
15 Stefan Meyer .20 .50
16 Daniel Paille .40 1.00
17 Michael Ryan .40 1.00
18 Andrej Sekera .20 .50
19 Brandon Smith .20 .50
20 Janis Sprukts .20 .50
21 Drew Stafford .75 2.00
22 Anthony Stewart .30 .75
23 Marek Zagrapan .30 .75
24 Coaches .10 .25
NNO Cover Card .01 .01

1976-77 Rockies Puck Bucks

COMPLETE SET (20) 37.50 75.00
1 Ron Andruff 2.00 4.00
2 Chuck Arnason 2.00 4.00
3 Henry Boucha 2.50 5.00
4 Colin Campbell 3.00 6.00
5 Gary Croteau 2.00 4.00
6 Guy Delparte 2.00 4.00
7 Steve Durbano 2.50 5.00
8 Tom Edur 2.00 4.00
9 Doug Favell 3.00 6.00
10 Dave Hudson 2.00 4.00
11 Bryan Lefley 2.00 4.00
12 Roger Lemelin 2.00 4.00
13 Simon Nolet 2.00 4.00
14 Wilf Paiement 2.50 5.00
15 Michel Plasse 3.00 6.00
16 Tracy Pratt 2.00 4.00
17 Nelson Pyatt 2.00 4.00
18 Phil Roberto 2.00 4.00
19 Sean Shanahan 2.00 4.00
20 Larry Skinner 2.00 4.00

1979-80 Rockies Team Issue

COMPLETE SET (23) 20.00 40.00
1 Hardy Astrom 1.50 3.00
2 Doug Berry .75 1.50
3 Nick Beverley 1.00 2.00
4 Mike Christie .75 1.50
5 Gary Croteau 1.00 2.00
6 Lucien Deblois 1.00 2.00
7 Ron Delorme .75 1.50
8 Mike Gillis .75 1.50
9 Trevor Johansen .75 1.50
10 Mike Kitchen .75 1.50
11 Lanny McDonald 2.50 5.00
12 Mike McEwen .75 1.50
13 Bill McKenzie .75 1.50
14 Kevin Morrison .75 1.50
15 Bill Olesehuk .75 1.50
16 Randy Pierce .75 1.50
17 Michel Plasse 1.50 3.00
18 Joel Quenneville 1.00 2.00
19 Rob Ramage 2.50 5.00
20 Rene Robert 1.00 2.00
21 Don Saleski 1.00 2.00
22 Barry Smith 1.00 2.00
23 Jack Valiquette .75 1.50

1981-82 Rockies Postcards

COMPLETE SET (30) 14.00 35.00
1 Brent Ashton .75 2.00
2 Aaron Broten .40 1.00
3 Dave Cameron .40 1.00
4 Joe Cirella .75 2.00
5 Dwight Foster .40 1.00
6 Paul Gagne .40 1.00
7 Marshall Johnston CO .40 1.00
8 Veli-Pekka Ketola .60 1.50
9 Mike Kitchen .40 1.00
10 Rick Laferriere .40 1.00
11 Don Lever .60 1.50
12 Tapio Levo .40 1.00
13 Bob Lorimer .40 1.00
14 Bill MacMillan .40 1.00
15 Bob MacMillan VP .60 1.50
16 Merlin Malinowski .60 1.50
17 Bert Marshall GM .40 1.00
18 Kevin Maxwell .40 1.00
19 Joe Micheletti .75 2.00
20 Bobby Miller .40 1.00
21 Phil Myre .75 2.00
22 Graeme Nicolson .40 1.00
23 Jukka Porvari .40 1.00
24 Joel Quenneville .60 1.50
25 Rob Ramage 1.25 3.00
26 Glenn Resch 1.25 3.00
27 Steve Tambellini .60 1.50
28 Yvon Vautour .40 1.00
29 John Wensink .60 1.50
30 Title Card
(Team logo) .75 2.00

2010-11 Rookies and Stars Toronto Fall Expo Autographs

TH Taylor Hall 175.00 250.00

1952 Royal Desserts

COMPLETE SET (8) 6500.00 13000.00
1 Tony Leswick 300.00 750.00
2 Chuck Rayner 400.00 800.00
3 Edgar Laprade 300.00 750.00
4 Sid Abel 600.00 1200.00
5 Ted Lindsay 600.00 1200.00
6 Leo Reise Jr. 300.00 750.00
7 Red Kelly 600.00 1200.00
8 Gordie Howe 3000.00 6000.00

1971-72 Sabres Postcards

COMPLETE SET (22) 15.00 30.00
69 Punch Imlach CO 1.25 3.00
70 Roger Crozier 1.50 4.00
71 Jim Watson .75 2.00
72 Mike Robitaille .75 2.00
73 Tracy Pratt .75 2.00
74 Doug Barrie .75 2.00
75 Al Hamilton .75 2.00
76 Richard Martin 1.50 4.00
77 Dick Duff .75 2.00
78 Danny Lawson .75 2.00
79 Phil Goyette .75 2.00
80 Gil Perreault 3.00 6.00
81 Rod Zaine .75 2.00
82 Gerry Meehan .75 2.00
83 Ron Anderson .75 2.00
84 Floyd Smith .75 2.00
85 Kevin O'Shea .75 2.00
86 Steve Atkinson .75 2.00
87 Don Luce .75 2.00
88 Ray McKay .75 2.00
89 Eddie Shack 1.25 3.00
90 Dave Dryden 1.25 3.00

1972-73 Sabres Pepsi Pinback Buttons

COMPLETE SET (9) 25.00 50.00
1 Roger Crozier 2.50 5.00
2 Don Luce 2.00 4.00
3 Rick Martin (action) 2.50 5.00
4 Rick Martin (head) 2.50 5.00
5 Gilbert Perreault (action) 5.00 10.00
6 Gilbert Perreault (head) 5.00 10.00
7 Gilbert Perreault (action) 2.50 5.00
8 Jim Schoenfeld 2.50 5.00
9 French Connection 5.00 10.00

1972-73 Sabres Postcards

COMPLETE SET (20) 30.00 60.00
1 Steve Atkinson 1.00 2.00
2 Larry Carriere 1.00 2.00
3 Roger Crozier 4.00 8.00
4 Butch Deadmarsh 1.00 2.00
5 Dave Dryden 1.50 3.00
6 Larry Hillman 1.00 2.00
7 Tim Horton 5.00 10.00
8 Jim Lorentz 1.00 2.00
9 Don Luce 1.50 3.00
10 Richard Martin 3.00 6.00
11 Gerry Meehan 1.50 3.00
12 Larry Mickey 1.00 2.00
13 Gilbert Perreault 5.00 10.00
14 Tracy Pratt 1.50 3.00
15 Craig Ramsay 1.50 3.00
16 Rene Robert 1.50 3.00
17 Mike Robitaille 1.00 2.00
18 Jim Schoenfeld 3.00 6.00
19 Paul Terbenche 1.00 2.00
20 Randy Wyrozub 1.00 2.00

1973-74 Sabres Bells

COMPLETE SET (4) 15.00 30.00
1 Roger Crozier 4.00 8.00
2 Jim Lorentz 2.50 5.00
3 Richard Martin 4.00 8.00
4 Gilbert Perreault 6.00 12.00

1973-74 Sabres Postcards

COMPLETE SET (13) 20.00 40.00
1 Roger Crozier 2.00 4.00
2 Dave Dryden 2.00 4.00
3 Tim Horton 5.00 10.00
4 Jim Lorentz 1.00 2.00
5 Don Luce 1.25 2.50
6 Rick Martin 2.00 4.00
7 Gerry Meehan 1.50 3.00
8 Larry Mickey 1.00 2.00
9 Joe Noris 1.00 2.00
10 Gilbert Perreault 4.00 8.00
11 Mike Robitaille 1.00 2.00
12 Jim Schoenfeld 2.00 4.00
13 Paul Terbenche 1.00 2.00

1974-75 Sabres Postcards

COMPLETE SET (21) 30.00 60.00
1 Gary Bromley 2.00 4.00
2 Larry Carriere 1.00 2.00
3 Roger Crozier 4.00 8.00
4 Rick Dudley 2.00 4.00
5 Rocky Farr 1.00 2.00
6 Lee Fogolin 2.00 4.00
7 Danny Gare 2.00 4.00
8 Norm Gratton 1.00 2.00
9 Jocelyn Guevremont 1.00 2.00
10 Bill Hajt 1.00 2.00
11 Jerry Korab 2.00 4.00
12 Jim Lorentz 1.00 2.00
13 Don Luce 1.25 2.50
14 Richard Martin 2.00 4.00
15 Peter McNab 1.25 2.50
16 Larry Mickey 1.00 2.00
17 Gilbert Perreault 4.00 8.00
18 Craig Ramsay 1.50 3.00
19 Rene Robert 1.50 3.00
20 Jim Schoenfeld 2.00 4.00
21 Brian Spencer 2.50 5.00

1975-76 Sabres Linnett

COMPLETE SET (12) 15.00 30.00
1 Roger Crozier 2.00 4.00
2 Gerry Desjardins 1.50 3.00
3 Dave Dryden 1.50 3.00
4 Jim Lorentz 1.00 2.00
5 Don Luce 1.25 2.50
6 Richard Martin 2.00 4.00
7 Peter McNab 1.25 2.50
8 Gerry Meehan 1.00 2.00
9 Gilbert Perreault 4.00 8.00
10 Rene Robert 1.50 3.00
11 Jim Schoenfeld 2.00 4.00
12 Fred Stanfield 1.50 3.00

1976-77 Sabres Glasses

COMPLETE SET (4) 12.50 25.00
1 Jerry Korab 3.00 6.00
2 Rick Martin 3.00 6.00
3 Gilbert Perreault 3.00 6.00
4 Jim Schoenfeld 3.00 6.00

1979-80 Sabres Bells

COMPLETE SET (9) 10.00 20.00
1 Don Edwards 2.00 4.00
2 Danny Gare 1.25 2.50
3 Jerry Korab 1.00 2.00
4 Richard Martin 2.00 4.00
5 Tony McKegney 1.25 2.50
6 Craig Ramsay 1.00 2.00
7 Bob Sauve 2.00 4.00
8 Jim Schoenfeld 1.50 3.00
9 John Van Boxmeer 1.00 2.00

1979-80 Sabres Milk Panels

COMPLETE SET (4) 3.00 6.00
1 Don Edwards .50 1.00
2 Ric Seiling .50 1.00
3 Jerry Korab .50 1.00
4 Gil Perreault .50 1.00

1980-81 Sabres Milk Panels

COMPLETE SET (2) 15.00 30.00
4 Gilbert Perreault
Ric Seiling 10.00 20.00
8 Bob Sauve
Richard Martin 6.00 12.00

1981-82 Sabres Milk Panels

COMPLETE SET (17) 60.00 150.00
1 Craig Ramsay 4.00 10.00
2 John Van Boxmeer 4.00 10.00
3 Don Edwards 5.00 12.00
4 Gilbert Perreault 8.00 20.00
5 Alan Haworth 4.00 10.00
6 Jim Schoenfeld 6.00 15.00
7 Richie Dunn 4.00 10.00
8 Bob Sauve 5.00 12.00
9 Bill Hajt 4.00 10.00
10 Larry Playfair 4.00 10.00
11 Tony McKegney 5.00 12.00
12 Mike Ramsey 5.00 12.00
13 Andre Savard 4.00 10.00
14 Derek Smith 4.00 10.00
15 Ric Seiling 4.00 10.00
16 Yvon Lambert 4.00 10.00
17 Dale McCourt 4.00 10.00

1982-83 Sabres Milk Panels

COMPLETE SET (17) 60.00 150.00
2 1982-83 Home Schedule 6.00 15.00
3 Craig Ramsay 4.00 10.00
4 John Van Boxmeer 4.00 10.00
5 Lindy Ruff 4.00 10.00
6 Bob Sauve 5.00 12.00
7 Gilbert Perreault 8.00 20.00
8 Ric Seiling 4.00 10.00
9 Jacques Cloutier 5.00 12.00
10 Larry Playfair 4.00 10.00
11 Phil Housley 8.00 20.00
12 Mike Foligno 5.00 12.00
13 Tony McKegney 5.00 12.00
14 Dale McCourt 4.00 10.00
15 Mike Ramsey 4.00 10.00
16 Hannu Virta 4.00 10.00
17 Brent Peterson 4.00 10.00
18 Scott Bowman GM 8.00 20.00

1984-85 Sabres Blue Shield

COMPLETE SET (21) 40.00 100.00
1 Dave Andreychuk 8.00 20.00
2 Tom Barrasso 8.00 20.00
3 Adam Creighton 2.00 5.00
4 Paul Cyr 1.25 3.00
5 Malcolm Davis 1.25 3.00
6 Mike Foligno 2.00 5.00
7 Bill Hajt 1.25 3.00
8 Gilles Hamel 1.25 3.00
9 Phil Housley 4.00 10.00
10 Sean McKenna 1.25 3.00
11 Mike Moller 1.25 3.00
12 Gilbert Perreault 6.00 15.00
13 Brent Peterson 1.25 3.00
14 Larry Playfair 1.25 3.00
15 Craig Ramsay 2.00 5.00
16 Mike Ramsey 2.00 5.00
17 Lindy Ruff 2.00 5.00
18 Bob Sauve 2.00 5.00
19 Ric Seiling 1.25 3.00
20 John Tucker 2.00 5.00
21 Hannu Virta 1.25 3.00

1985-86 Sabres Blue Shield

COMPLETE SET (27) 16.00 40.00
1 Mikael Andersson .40 1.00
2 Dave Andreychuk 2.00 5.00
3 Tom Barrasso 1.25 3.00
4 Adam Creighton .40 1.00
5 Paul Cyr .40 1.00
6 Malcolm Davis .40 1.00
7 Steve Dykstra .40 1.00
8 Dave Fenyves .40 1.00
9 Mike Foligno .40 1.00
10 Bill Hajt .40 1.00
11 Bob Halkidis .40 1.00
12 Gilles Hamel .40 1.00
13 Phil Housley 1.25 3.00
14 Pat Hughes .40 1.00
15 Normand Lacombe .40 1.00
16 Chris Langevin .40 1.00
17 Sean McKenna .40 1.00
18 Gates Orlando .75 2.00
19 Gilbert Perreault 2.00 5.00
20 Larry Playfair .40 1.00
21 Daren Puppa 1.00 2.50
22 Craig Ramsay ACO .20 .50
23 Mike Ramsey .40 1.00
24 Lindy Ruff .40 1.00
25 Jim Schoenfeld CO SP 6.00 15.00
26 Ric Seiling .40 1.00
27 John Tucker .60 1.50
28 Hannu Virta .40 1.00

1985-86 Sabres Blue Shield Small

COMPLETE SET (27) 16.00 40.00
1 Mikael Andersson .40 1.00
2 Dave Andreychuk 1.50 4.00
3 Tom Barrasso .75 2.00
4 Adam Creighton .40 1.00
5 Paul Cyr .40 1.00
6 Malcolm Davis .40 1.00
7 Steve Dykstra .40 1.00
8 Dave Fenyves .40 1.00
9 Mike Foligno .40 1.00
10 Bill Hajt .40 1.00
11 Bob Halkidis .40 1.00
12 Gilles Hamel .40 1.00
13 Phil Housley .75 2.00
14 Pat Hughes .40 1.00
15 Normand Lacombe .40 1.00
16 Chris Langevin .40 1.00
17 Sean McKenna .40 1.00
18 Gates Orlando .60 1.50
19 Gilbert Perreault 1.50 4.00
20 Larry Playfair .40 1.00
21 Daren Puppa .75 2.00
22 Craig Ramsay ACO .20 .50
23 Mike Ramsey .40 1.00
24 Lindy Ruff .40 1.00
25 Jim Schoenfeld CO SP 4.00 10.00
26 Ric Seiling .40 1.00
27 John Tucker .60 1.50
28 Hannu Virta .40 1.00

1986-87 Sabres Blue Shield

COMPLETE SET (28) 12.00 30.00
1 Shawn Anderson .30 .75
2 Dave Andreychuk 2.50 6.00
3 Scott Arniel .30 .75
4 Tom Barrasso 1.25 3.00
5 Jacques Cloutier .40 1.00
6 Adam Creighton .40 1.00
7 Paul Cyr .30 .75
8 Steve Dykstra .30 .75
9 Dave Fenyves .30 .75
10 Mike Foligno .60 1.50
11 Clark Gillies .75 2.00
12 Bill Hajt .30 .75
13 Bob Halkidis .30 .75
14 Jim Hofford .30 .75
15 Phil Housley 1.00 2.50
16 Jim Korn .30 .75
17 Uwe Krupp .60 1.50
18 Tom Kurvers .30 .75
19 Norm Lacombe .30 .75
20 Gates Orlando .30 .75
21 Wilf Paiement .40 1.00
22 Gilbert Perreault 2.00 5.00
23 Daren Puppa 1.25 3.00
24 Mike Ramsey .40 1.00
25 Lindy Ruff .30 .75
26 Christian Ruuttu .30 .75
27 Doug Smith .30 .75
28 John Tucker .40 1.00

1986-87 Sabres Blue Shield Small

COMPLETE SET (28) 14.00 35.00
1 Shawn Anderson .30 .75
2 Dave Andreychuk 2.50 6.00
3 Scott Arniel .30 .75
4 Tom Barrasso 1.25 3.00
5 Jacques Cloutier .40 1.00
6 Adam Creighton .40 1.00
7 Paul Cyr .30 .75
8 Steve Dykstra .30 .75
9 Dave Fenyves .30 .75
10 Mike Foligno .60 1.50
11 Clark Gillies .75 2.00
12 Bill Hajt .30 .75
13 Bob Halkidis .30 .75
14 Jim Hofford .30 .75
15 Phil Housley 1.25 3.00
16 Jim Korn .30 .75
17 Uwe Krupp .60 1.50
18 Tom Kurvers .30 .75
19 Norm Lacombe .30 .75
20 Gates Orlando .30 .75
21 Wilf Paiement .40 1.00
22 Gilbert Perreault 2.00 5.00
23 Daren Puppa 1.25 3.00
24 Mike Ramsey .40 1.00
25 Lindy Ruff .30 .75
26 Christian Ruuttu .30 .75
27 Doug Smith .30 .75
28 John Tucker .40 1.00

1987-88 Sabres Blue Shield

COMPLETE SET (28) 10.00 25.00
1 Mikael Andersson 14 .30 .75
2 Dave Andreychuk 25 1.25 3.00
3 Scott Arniel 9 .30 .75
4 Tom Barrasso 30 .60 1.50
5 Jacques Cloutier 1 .40 1.00
6 Adam Creighton 38 .40 1.00
7 Mike Donnelly 16 .30 .75
8 Mike Foligno 17 .40 1.00
9 Clark Gillies 90 .40 1.00
10 Bob Halkidis 18 .30 .75
11 Mike Hartman 20 .30 .75
12 Ed Hospodar 24 .30 .75
13 Phil Housley 6 .60 1.50
14 Calle Johansson 3 .40 1.00
15 Uwe Krupp 40 .40 1.00
16 Jan Ludvig 36 .30 .75
17 Kevin Maguire 19 .30 .75
18 Mark Napier 65 .30 .75
19 Ken Priestlay 12 .30 .75
20 Daren Puppa 35 .60 1.50
21 Mike Ramsey 5 .40 1.00
22 Joe Reekie 27 .30 .75
23 Lindy Ruff 22 .30 .75
24 Christian Ruuttu 21 .40 1.00
25 Ray Sheppard 23 1.25 3.00
26 Doug Smith 15 .30 .75
27 John Tucker 7 .40 1.00
28 Pierre Turgeon 77 4.00 10.00

1987-88 Sabres Wonder Bread/Hostess

COMPLETE SET (31) 8.00 20.00
1 Mikael Andersson 14 .20 .50
2 Shawn Anderson 37 .20 .50
3 Dave Andreychuk 25 1.00 2.50
4 Scott Arniel 9 .20 .50
5 Tom Barrasso 30 .75 2.00
6 Jacques Cloutier 1 .30 .75
7 Adam Creighton 38 .30 .75
8 Steve Dykstra 4 .20 .50
9 Mike Foligno 17 .30 .75
10 Clark Gillies 90 .30 .75
11 Ed Hospodar 24 .20 .50
12 Phil Housley 6 .50 1.25
13 Calle Johansson 3 .30 .75
14 Uwe Krupp 40 .30 .75
15 Don Lever CO .20 .50
16 Bob Logan 26 .20 .50
17 Jan Ludvig 36 .20 .50
18 Kevin Maguire 19 .20 .50
19 Mark Napier 65 .30 .75
20 Daren Puppa 31 .60 1.50
21 Mike Ramsey 5 .30 .75
22 Joe Reekie 27 .30 .75
23 Lindy Ruff 22 .20 .50
24 Christian Ruuttu 21 .30 .75
25 Ted Sator CO .20 .50
26 Ray Sheppard 23 .75 2.00
27 Barry Smith CO .20 .50
28 Doug Smith 15 .20 .50
29 John Tucker 7 .30 .75
30 Pierre Turgeon 77 3.00 8.00
NNO Large Team Photo 1.25 3.00

1988-89 Sabres Blue Shield

COMPLETE SET (28) 10.00 25.00
1 Mikael Andersson 14 .20 .50
2 Dave Andreychuk 25 .60 1.50
3 Scott Arniel 9 .08 .25
4 Doug Bodger 8 .30 .75
5 Jacques Cloutier 1 .30 .75
6 Mike Donnelly 16 .20 .50
7 Mike Foligno 17 .30 .75
8 Bob Halkidis 18 .08 .25
9 Mike Hartman 20 .08 .25
10 Benoit Hogue 33 SP 1.25 3.00
11 Phil Housley 6 .40 1.00
12 Calle Johansson 3 .30 .75
13 Uwe Krupp 4 .30 .75
14 Jan Ludvig 36 SP .75 2.00
15 Kevin Maguire 19 .08 .25
16 Mark Napier 65 SP .75 2.00
17 Jeff Parker 29 .08 .25
18 Larry Playfair 27 .08 .25
19 Daren Puppa 31 .75 2.00
20 Mike Ramsey 5 .20 .50
21 Joe Reekie 55 SP .75 2.00
22 Lindy Ruff 22 .08 .25
23 Christian Ruuttu 21 .20 .50
24 Sabretooth Mascot .08 .25
25 Ray Sheppard 23 .60 1.50
26 John Tucker 7 .20 .50
27 Pierre Turgeon 77 2.50 6.00
28 Rick Vaive 12 .30 .75

1988-89 Sabres Wonder Bread/Hostess

COMPLETE SET (31) 8.00 20.00
1 Mikael Andersson 14 .20 .50
2 Dave Andreychuk 25 .60 1.50
3 Scott Arniel 9 .20 .50
4 Doug Bodger 8 .30 .75
5 Jacques Cloutier 1 .30 .75
6 Adam Creighton 38 .25 .60
7 Mike Foligno 17 .30 .75
8 Bob Halkidis 18 .20 .50
9 Mike Hartman 20 .20 .50
10 Benoit Hogue 33 .40 1.00
11 Phil Housley 6 .40 1.00
12 Calle Johansson 3 .30 .75
13 Uwe Krupp 4 .30 .75
14 Don Lever CO .20 .50
15 Jan Ludvig 36 .20 .50
16 Kevin Maguire 19 .20 .50
17 Brad Miller 44 .20 .50
18 Mark Napier 65 .20 .50
19 Jeff Parker 29 .20 .50
20 Larry Playfair 27 .20 .50
21 Daren Puppa 31 .75 2.00
22 Mike Ramsey 5 .20 .50
23 Joe Reekie 55 .20 .50
24 Lindy Ruff 22 .20 .50
25 Christian Ruuttu 21 .20 .50
26 Ted Sator CO .20 .50
27 Ray Sheppard 23 .60 1.50
28 Barry Smith CO .20 .50
29 John Tucker 7 .20 .50
30 Pierre Turgeon 77 2.50 6.00
xx Large Team Photo .40 1.00

1989-90 Sabres Blue Shield

COMPLETE SET (24) 8.00 20.00
1 Dave Andreychuk 25 .60 1.50
2 Scott Arniel 9 .20 .50
3 Doug Bodger 8 .20 .50
4 Mike Foligno 17 .30 .75
5 Mike Hartman 20 .20 .50
6 Benoit Hogue 33 .40 1.00
7 Phil Housley 6 .40 1.00
8 Dean Kennedy 26 .20 .50
9 Uwe Krupp 4 .30 .75
10 Grant Ledyard 3 .20 .50
11 Kevin Maguire 19 .20 .50
12 Clint Malarchuk 30 .30 .75
13 Alexander Mogilny 89 2.00 5.00
14 Jeff Parker 29 .20 .50
15 Larry Playfair 27 .20 .50
16 Ken Priestlay 56 .20 .50
17 Daren Puppa 31 .60 1.50
18 Mike Ramsey 5 .20 .50
19 Christian Ruuttu 21 .20 .50
20 Ray Sheppard 23 .40 1.00
21 Dave Snuggerud 18 .20 .50
22 Sabretooth Mascot .08 .25
23 Pierre Turgeon 77 1.25 3.00
24 Rick Vaive 22 .30 .75

1989-90 Sabres Campbell's

COMPLETE SET (28) 8.00 20.00
1 Shawn Anderson 37 .20 .50
2 Dave Andreychuk 25 .60 1.50
3 Scott Arniel 9 .20 .50
4 Doug Bodger 8 .20 .50
5 Rick Dudley CO .30 .75
6 Mike Foligno 17 .30 .75
7 Mike Hartman 20 .20 .50
8 Benoit Hogue 33 .40 1.00
9 Phil Housley 6 .40 1.00
10 Dean Kennedy 26 .20 .50
11 Uwe Krupp 4 .30 .75
12 Grant Ledyard 3 .20 .50
13 Kevin Maguire 19 .20 .50
14 Clint Malarchuk 39 .30 .75
15 Alexander Mogilny 89 2.00 5.00
16 Mark Napier 65 .20 .50
17 Jeff Parker 29 .20 .50
18 Larry Playfair 27 .20 .50
19 Daren Puppa 31 .60 1.50
20 Mike Ramsey 5 .20 .50
21 Robert Ray 32 .40 1.00
22 Christian Ruuttu 21 .20 .50
23 Ray Sheppard 23 .40 1.00
24 Dave Snuggerud 18 .20 .50
25 John Tortorella CO .20 .50
26 Pierre Turgeon 77 1.25 3.00
27 Rick Vaive 22 .30 .75
xx Large Team Photo .40 1.00

1990-91 Sabres Blue Shield

COMPLETE SET (26) 6.00 15.00
1 Dave Andreychuk 25 .30 .75
2 Donald Audette 28 .40 1.00
3 Doug Bodger 8 .20 .50
4 Greg Brown 9 .20 .50
5 Brian Curran 39 .20 .50
6 Lou Franceschetti 15 .20 .50
7 Mike Hartman 20 .20 .50
8 Dale Hawerchuk 10 .40 1.00
9 Benoit Hogue 33 .25 .60
10 Dean Kennedy 26 .20 .50
11 Uwe Krupp 4 .30 .75
12 Grant Ledyard 3 .20 .50
13 Mikko Makela 42 .20 .50
14 Clint Malarchuk 30 .30 .75
15 Alexander Mogilny 89 1.25 3.00
16 Daren Puppa 31 .40 1.00
17 Mike Ramsey 5 .20 .50
18 Robert Ray 32 .30 .75
19 Christian Ruuttu 21 .20 .50
20 Sabretooth Mascot .08 .25

21 Jiri Sejba 23 .20 .50
22 Dave Snuggerud 18 .20 .50
23 John Tucker 7 .20 .50
24 Pierre Turgeon 77 .60 1.50
25 Rick Vaive 22 .20 .50
26 Jay Wells 24 .20 .50

1990-91 Sabres Campbell's

COMPLETE SET (32) 6.00 15.00
1 Dave Andreychuk 25 .30 .75
2 Donald Audette 28 .40 1.00
3 Doug Bodger 8 .20 .50
4 Greg Brown 9 .20 .50
5 Bob Corkum 19 .20 .50
6 Rick Dudley CO .08 .25
7 Mike Foligno 17 .30 .75
8 Mike Hartman 20 .20 .50
9 Dale Hawerchuk 10 .40 1.00
10 Benoit Hogue 33 .25 .60
11 Dean Kennedy 26 .20 .50
12 Uwe Krupp 4 .30 .75
13 Grant Ledyard 3 .20 .50
14 Darcy Loewen 36 .20 .50
15 Mikko Makela 42 .20 .50
16 Clint Malarchuk 30 .30 .75
17 Brad Miller 44 .20 .50
18 Alexander Mogilny 89 1.25 3.00
19 Daren Puppa 31 .40 1.00
20 Mike Ramsey 5 .20 .50
21 Robert Ray 32 .30 .75
22 Christian Ruuttu 21 .20 .50
23 Jiri Sejba 23 .20 .50
24 Darrin Shannon 16 .20 .50
25 Dave Snuggerud 18 .20 .50
26 John Tortorella CO .08 .25
27 John Tucker 7 .20 .50
28 Pierre Turgeon 77 .60 1.50
29 Rick Vaive 22 .20 .50
30 John Van Boxmeer CO .08 .25
31 Jay Wells 24 .20 .50
xx Large Team Photo
(In street clothes) .40 1.00

1991-92 Sabres Blue Shield

COMPLETE SET (26) 6.00 15.00
1 Dave Andreychuk 25 .40 1.00
2 Donald Audette 28 .30 .75
3 Doug Bodger 8 .25 .60
4 Gord Donnelly 34 .20 .50
5 Tom Draper 35 .25 .60
6 Kevin Haller 7 .20 .50
7 Dale Hawerchuk 10 .60 1.50
8 Randy Hillier 23 .20 .50
9 Pat LaFontaine 16 1.25 3.00
10 Grant Ledyard 3 .20 .50
11 Clint Malarchuk 30 .30 .75
12 Brad May 27 .40 1.00
13 Brad Miller 44 .20 .50
14 Alexander Mogilny 89 .75 2.00
15 Colin Patterson 17 .20 .50
16 Daren Puppa 31 .40 1.00
17 Mike Ramsey 5 .20 .50
18 Robert Ray 32 .30 .75
19 Christian Ruuttu 21 .20 .50
20 Dave Snuggerud 18 .20 .50
21 Ken Sutton 41 .20 .50
22 Tony Tanti 19 .20 .50
23 Rick Vaive 22 .25 .60
24 Jay Wells 24 .20 .50
25 Randy Wood 15 .20 .50
26 Sabretooth (Mascot) .08 .25

1991-92 Sabres Pepsi/Campbell's

COMPLETE SET (29) 6.00 15.00
1 Dave Andreychuk 25 .40 1.00
2 Donald Audette 28 .30 .75
3 Doug Bodger 8 .25 .60
4 Gord Donnelly 34 .20 .50
5 Tom Draper 35 .25 .60
6 Kevin Haller 7 .20 .50
7 Dale Hawerchuk 10 .60 1.50
8 Randy Hillier 23 .20 .50
9 Pat LaFontaine 16 .75 2.00
10 Grant Ledyard 3 .20 .50
11 Clint Malarchuk 30 .30 .75
12 Brad May 27 .40 1.00
13 Brad Miller 44 .20 .50
14 Alexander Mogilny 89 1.25 3.00
15 Colin Patterson 17 .20 .50
16 Daren Puppa 31 .40 1.00
17 Mike Ramsey 5 .20 .50
18 Robert Ray 32 .30 .75
19 Christian Ruuttu 21 .20 .50
20 Dave Snuggerud 18 .20 .50
21 Ken Sutton 41 .20 .50
22 Tony Tanti 19 .20 .50
23 Rick Vaive 22 .20 .50
24 Jay Wells 24 .20 .50
25 Randy Wood 15 .20 .50
26 Sabretooth (Mascot) .08 .25
27 Team Logo .08 .25
28 NHL Logo .08 .25
xx Large Team Photo
(In street clothes) .40 1.00

1992-93 Sabres Blue Shield

COMPLETE SET (26) 6.00 15.00
1 Dave Andreychuk .30 .75
2 Donald Audette .30 .75
3 Doug Bodger .15 .40
4 Bob Corkum .15 .40
5 Gord Donnelly .15 .40
6 Dave Hannan .15 .40
7 Dominik Hasek 2.50 6.00
8 Dale Hawerchuk .40 1.00
9 Yuri Khmylev .15 .40
10 Pat LaFontaine .60 1.50
11 Grant Ledyard .15 .40
12 Brad May .20 .50
13 Alexander Mogilny .60 1.50
14 Randy Moller .15 .40
15 John Muckler CO .15 .40
16 Colin Patterson .15 .40
17 Wayne Presley .15 .40
18 Daren Puppa .30 .75
19 Mike Ramsey .15 .40
20 Rob Ray .30 .75
21 Richard Smehlik .15 .40
22 Ken Sutton .15 .40
23 Petr Svoboda .20 .50
24 Bob Sweeney .15 .40
25 Randy Wood .15 .40
26 Sabretooth (Mascot) .02 .10

1992-93 Sabres Jubilee Foods

COMPLETE SET (16) 4.80 12.00
1 Dave Andreychuk .30 .75
2 Doug Bodger .15 .40
3 Gord Donnelly
Rob Ray .40 1.00
4 Dominik Hasek
Daren Puppa 2.50 6.00
5 Dale Hawerchuk .40 1.00
6 Yuri Khmylev
Viktor Gordijuk .15 .40
7 Pat LaFontaine .60 1.50
8 Brad May .30 .75
9 Alexander Mogilny .60 1.50
10 Randy Moller
Ken Sutton .15 .40
11 Wayne Presley
Donald Audette .30 .75
12 Mike Ramsey .15 .40
13 Richard Smehlik
Bob Corkum .15 .40
14 Petr Svoboda .20 .50
15 Bob Sweeney .15 .40
16 Randy Wood .15 .40

1993-94 Sabres Limited Edition Team Issue

COMPLETE SET (4) 4.00 10.00
1 Doug Bodger .40 1.00
2 Dominik Hasek 2.00 5.00
3 Dale Hawerchuk .75 2.00
4 Alexander Mogilny 1.25 3.00

1993-94 Sabres Noco

COMPLETE SET (20) 4.80 12.00
1 Roger Crozier .25 .60
2 Rick Dudley .20 .50
3 Mike Foligno .20 .50
4 Grant Fuhr .40 1.00
5 Danny Gare .20 .50
6 Dominik Hasek 2.00 5.00
7 Dale Hawerchuk .30 .75
8 Tim Horton .75 2.00
9 Pat LaFontaine .50 1.25
10 Don Luce .20 .50
11 Rick Martin .30 .75
12 Brad May .25 .60
13 Alexander Mogilny .50 1.25
14 Gilbert Perreault .40 1.00
15 Craig Ramsay .20 .50
16 Mike Ramsey .20 .50
17 Rene Robert .25 .60
18 Sabretooth Mascot .15 .40
19 Jim Schoenfeld .30 .75
20 Knoxes Unveil
Sabres Uniform
Northrup Knox
Punc .15 .40

2002-03 Sabres Team Issue

COMPLETE SET (14) 10.00 20.00
1 Stu Barnes .75 2.00
2 Martin Biron .75 2.00
3 Eric Boulton .75 2.00
4 Brian Campbell .75 2.00
5 Tim Connolly .40 1.00
6 Jochen Hecht .75 2.00
7 Dmitri Kalinin .40 1.00
8 Adam Mair .75 2.00
9 Jay McKee .40 1.00
10 Mika Noronen .75 2.00
11 James Patrick .75 2.00
12 Taylor Pyatt .40 1.00
13 Rob Ray .75 2.00
14 Rhett Warrener .40 1.00

1974-75 San Diego Mariners WHA

COMPLETE SET (7) 20.00 40.00
1 Andre Lacroix 5.00 10.00
2 Mike Laughton 2.50 5.00
3 Brian Morenz 2.50 5.00
4 Kevin Morrison 2.50 5.00
5 Gene Peacosh 2.50 5.00
6 Ron Plumb 4.00 8.00
7 Craig Reichmuth 2.50 5.00

1976-77 San Diego Mariners WHA

COMPLETE SET (14) 20.00 40.00
1 Kevin Devine 1.25 2.50
2 Bob Dobek 1.25 2.50
3 Norm Ferguson 1.25 2.50
4 Brent Hughes 1.25 2.50
5 Randy Legge 1.25 2.50
6 Ken Lockett 1.25 2.50
7 Kevin Morrison 1.25 2.50
8 Joe Norris 1.25 2.50
9 Gerry Pinder 2.00 4.00
10 Brad Rhiness 1.25 2.50
11 Wayne Rivers 2.00 4.00
12 Paul Shmyr 1.50 3.00
13 Gary Veneruzzo 1.50 3.00
14 Ernie Wakely 2.50 5.00

1994 Santa Fe Hotel and Casino Manon Rheaume Postcard

NNO Manon Rheaume 2.00 5.00

1970-71 Sargent Promotions Stamps

COMPLETE SET (224) 325.00 650.00
1 Bobby Orr 62.50 125.00
2 Don Awrey .50 1.00
3 Derek Sanderson 5.00 10.00
4 Ted Green .63 1.25
5 Eddie Johnston 1.25 2.50
6 Wayne Carleton .50 1.00
7 Ed Westfall .75 1.50
8 Johnny Bucyk 2.50 5.00
9 John McKenzie .50 1.00
10 Ken Hodge 1.00 2.00
11 Rick Smith .50 1.00
12 Fred Stanfield .50 1.00
13 Garnet Bailey .50 1.00
14 Phil Esposito 10.00 20.00
15 Gerry Cheevers 5.00 10.00
16 Dallas Smith .50 1.00
17 Joe Daley 1.00 2.00
18 Ron Anderson .50 1.00
19 Tracy Pratt .50 1.00
20 Gerry Meehan .75 1.50
21 Reg Fleming .50 1.00
22 Al Hamilton .63 1.25
23 Gil Perreault 12.50 25.00
24 Skip Krake .50 1.00
25 Kevin O'Shea .50 1.00
26 Roger Crozier 1.50 3.00
27 Bill Inglis .50 1.00
28 Mike McMahon .50 1.00
29 Cliff Schmautz .50 1.00
30 Floyd Smith .50 1.00
31 Randy Wyrozub .50 1.00
32 Jim Watson .50 1.00
33 Tony Esposito 15.00 30.00
34 Doug Jarrett .50 1.00
35 Keith Magnuson .63 1.25
36 Dennis Hull 1.00 2.00
37 Cliff Koroll .50 1.00
38 Eric Nesterenko .75 1.50
39 Pit Martin .63 1.25
40 Lou Angotti .50 1.00
41 Jim Pappin .63 1.25
42 Gerry Pinder .63 1.25
43 Bobby Hull 25.00 50.00
44 Pat Stapleton .63 1.25
45 Gerry Desjardins 1.00 2.00
46 Chico Maki .63 1.25
47 Doug Mohns .63 1.25
48 Stan Mikita 10.00 20.00
49 Gary Bergman .63 1.25
50 Pete Stemkowski .63 1.25
51 Bruce MacGregor .50 1.00
52 Ron Harris .50 1.00
53 Billy Dea .50 1.00
54 Wayne Connelly .50 1.00
55 Dale Rolfe .50 1.00
56 Gordie Howe 40.00 80.00
57 Tom Webster .63 1.25
58 Al Karlander .50 1.00
59 Alex Delvecchio 2.50 5.00
60 Nick Libett .63 1.25
61 Garry Unger 1.00 2.00
62 Roy Edwards 1.00 2.00
63 Frank Mahovlich 5.00 10.00
64 Bob Baun 1.25 2.50
65 Dick Duff 1.00 2.00
66 Ross Lonsberry .50 1.00
67 Ed Joyal .50 1.00
68 Dale Hoganson .50 1.00
69 Eddie Shack 2.50 5.00
70 Real Lemieux .50 1.00
71 Matt Ravlich .50 1.00
72 Bob Pulford 1.50 3.00
73 Denis DeJordy 1.25 2.50
74 Larry Mickey .50 1.00
75 Bill Flett .50 1.00
76 Juha Widing .75 1.50
77 Jim Peters .63 1.25
78 Gilles Marotte .63 1.25
79 Larry Cahan .50 1.00
80 Howie Hughes .50 1.00
81 Cesare Maniago 1.25 2.50
82 Ted Harris .50 1.00
83 Tom Williams .50 1.00
84 Gump Worsley 5.00 10.00
85 Tom Reid .50 1.00
86 Murray Oliver .50 1.00
87 Charlie Burns .50 1.00
88 Jude Drouin .50 1.00
89 Walt McKechnie .50 1.00
90 Danny O'Shea .50 1.00
91 Barry Gibbs .50 1.00
92 Danny Grant .63 1.25
93 Bob Barlow .50 1.00
94 J.P. Parise .63 1.25
95 Bill Goldsworthy .75 1.50
96 Bobby Rousseau .63 1.25
97 Jacques Laperriere 1.00 2.00
98 Henri Richard 5.00 10.00
99 J.C. Tremblay .75 1.50
100 Rogie Vachon 4.00 8.00
101 Claude Larose .50 1.00
102 Pete Mahovlich .75 1.50
103 Jacques Lemaire 4.00 8.00
104 Bill Collins .50 1.00
105 Guy Lapointe 1.50 3.00
106 Mickey Redmond 2.50 5.00
107 Larry Pleau .63 1.25
108 Jean Beliveau 12.50 25.00
109 Yvan Cournoyer 4.00 8.00
110 Serge Savard 4.00 8.00
111 Terry Harper .63 1.25
112 Phil Myre 1.00 2.00
113 Syl Apps .63 1.25
114 Ted Irvine .50 1.00
115 Ed Giacomin 5.00 10.00
116 Arnie Brown .50 1.00
117 Walt Tkaczuk .63 1.25
118 Jean Ratelle 2.50 5.00
119 Dave Balon .50 1.00
120 Ron Stewart .50 1.00
121 Jim Neilson .50 1.00
122 Rod Gilbert 2.50 5.00
123 Bill Fairbairn .50 1.00
124 Brad Park 10.00 20.00
125 Tim Horton 7.50 15.00
126 Vic Hadfield .75 1.50
127 Bob Nevin .50 1.00
128 Rod Seiling .50 1.00
129 Gary Smith 1.25 2.50
130 Carol Vadnais .50 1.00
131 Bert Marshall .50 1.00
132 Earl Ingarfield .50 1.00
133 Dennis Hextall .63 1.25
134 Harry Howell 1.50 3.00
135 Wayne Muloin .50 1.00
136 Mike Laughton .50 1.00
137 Ted Hampson .50 1.00
138 Doug Roberts .50 1.00
139 Dick Mattiussi .50 1.00
140 Gary Jarrett .50 1.00
141 Gary Croteau .50 1.00
142 Norm Ferguson .50 1.00
143 Bill Hicke .50 1.00
144 Gerry Ehman .50 1.00
145 Ralph McSweyn .50 1.00
146 Bernie Parent 7.50 15.00
147 Brent Hughes .50 1.00
148 Bobby Clarke 20.00 40.00
149 Gary Dornhoefer .63 1.25
150 Simon Nolet .50 1.00
151 Garry Peters .50 1.00
152 Doug Favell 1.25 2.50
153 Jim Johnson .50 1.00
154 Andre Lacroix .75 1.50
155 Larry Hale .50 1.00
156 Joe Watson .50 1.00
157 Jean-Guy Gendron .50 1.00
158 Larry Hillman .50 1.00
159 Ed Van Impe .50 1.00
160 Wayne Hillman .50 1.00
161 Al Smith 1.00 2.00
162 Jean Pronovost .63 1.25
163 Bob Woytowich .50 1.00
164 Bryan Watson .63 1.25
165 Dean Prentice .75 1.50
166 Duane Rupp .50 1.00
167 Glen Sather 1.00 2.00
168 Keith McCreary .50 1.00
169 Jim Morrison .50 1.00
170 Ron Schock .50 1.00
171 Wally Boyer .50 1.00
172 Nick Harbaruk .50 1.00
173 Andy Bathgate 2.50 5.00
174 Ken Schinkel .50 1.00
175 Les Binkley 1.00 2.00
176 Val Fonteyne .50 1.00
177 Red Berenson .75 1.50
178 Ab McDonald .50 1.00
179 Jim Roberts .50 1.00
180 Frank St. Marseille .50 1.00
181 Ernie Wakely 1.25 2.50
182 Terry Crisp .63 1.25
183 Bob Plager .75 1.50
184 Barclay Plager .75 1.50
185 Chris Bordeleau .50 1.00
186 Gary Sabourin .50 1.00
187 Bill Plager .63 1.25
188 Tim Ecclestone .50 1.00
189 Jean-Guy Talbot .75 1.50
190 Noel Picard .50 1.00
191 Bob Wall .50 1.00
192 Jim Lorentz .50 1.00
193 Bruce Gamble 1.50 3.00
194 Jim Harrison .50 1.00
195 Paul Henderson 1.50 3.00
196 Brian Glennie .50 1.00
197 Jim Dorey .50 1.00
198 Rick Ley .63 1.25
199 Jacques Plante 12.50 25.00
200 Ron Ellis .75 1.50
201 Jim McKenny .50 1.00
202 Brit Selby .50 1.00
203 Mike Pelyk .50 1.00
204 Norm Ullman 2.50 5.00
205 Bill MacMillan .50 1.00
206 Mike Walton .63 1.25
207 Garry Monahan .50 1.00
208 Dave Keon 2.50 5.00
209 Pat Quinn 1.00 2.00
210 Wayne Maki .50 1.00
211 Charlie Hodge 1.25 2.50
212 Orland Kurtenbach .63 1.25
213 Paul Popiel .63 1.25
214 Dan Johnson .50 1.00
215 Dale Tallon .63 1.25
216 Ray Cullen .63 1.25
217 Bob Dillabough .50 1.00
218 Gary Doak .50 1.00
219 Andre Boudrias .75 1.50
220 Rosaire Paiement .63 1.25
221 Darryl Sly .50 1.00
222 George Gardner .50 1.00
223 Jim Wiste .50 1.00
224 Murray Hall .50 1.00
NNO Stamp Album
(Bobby Orr on cover) 17.50 35.00

1971-72 Sargent Promotions Stamps

COMPLETE SET (224) 225.00 450.00
1 Fred Stanfield .50 1.00
2 Ed Westfall .75 1.50
3 John McKenzie .50 1.00
4 Derek Sanderson 4.00 8.00
5 Rick Smith .50 1.00
6 Teddy Green .63 1.25
7 Phil Esposito 7.50 15.00
8 Ken Hodge 1.00 2.00
9 Johnny Bucyk 4.00 8.00
10 Bobby Orr 50.00 100.00
11 Dallas Smith .50 1.00
12 Mike Walton .63 1.25
13 Don Awrey .50 1.00
14 Unknown .50 1.00
15 Eddie Johnston 1.00 2.00
16 Gerry Cheevers 4.00 8.00
17 Gerry Meehan .75 1.50
18 Ron Anderson .50 1.00
19 Gilbert Perreault 6.00 12.00
20 Eddie Shack 2.00 4.00
21 Jim Watson .50 1.00
22 Kevin O'Shea .50 1.00
23 Al Hamilton .50 1.00
24 Dick Duff .75 1.50
25 Tracy Pratt .50 1.00
26 Don Luce .50 1.00
27 Roger Crozier 1.00 2.00
28 Doug Barrie .50 1.00
29 Mike Robitaille .50 1.00
30 Phil Goyette .50 1.00
31 Larry Keenan .50 1.00
32 Dave Dryden 1.00 2.00
33 Stan Mikita 6.00 12.00
34 Bobby Hull 20.00 40.00
35 Cliff Koroll .50 1.00
36 Chico Maki .63 1.25
37 Danny O'Shea .50 1.00
38 Lou Angotti .50 1.00
39 Andre Lacroix .63 1.25
40 Jim Pappin .50 1.00
41 Doug Jarrett .50 1.00
42 Pit Martin .63 1.25
43 Gary Smith 1.00 2.00
44 Tony Esposito 7.50 15.00
45 Pat Stapleton .50 1.00
46 Dennis Hull 1.00 2.00
47 Bill White .50 1.00
48 Keith Magnuson .63 1.25
49 Bill Collins .50 1.00
50 Bob Wall .50 1.00
51 Red Berenson .75 1.50
52 Mickey Redmond 1.50 3.00
53 Nick Libett .50 1.00
54 Gary Bergman .63 1.25
55 Alex Delvecchio 2.50 5.00
56 Tim Ecclestone .50 1.00
57 Arnie Brown .50 1.00
58 Ron Harris .50 1.00
59 Ab McDonald .50 1.00
60 Guy Charron .63 1.25
61 Al Smith 1.00 2.00
62 Joe Daley 1.00 2.00
63 Leon Rochefort .50 1.00
64 Ron Stackhouse .50 1.00
65A Larry Johnston .75 1.50
65B Juha Widing .50 1.00
66 Bob Pulford 1.00 2.00
67 Bill Flett .50 1.00
68 Rogie Vachon 2.50 5.00
69 Ross Lonsberry .50 1.00
70 Gilles Marotte .50 1.00
71 Harry Howell 1.00 2.00
72 Real Lemieux .50 1.00
73 Butch Goring .50 1.00
74 Ed Joyal .50 1.00
75 Larry Hillman .50 1.00
76 Lucien Grenier .50 1.00
77 Paul Curtis .50 1.00
78 Unknown .50 1.00
79 Unknown .50 1.00
80 Unknown .50 1.00
81 Jude Drouin .50 1.00
82 Tom Reid .50 1.00
83 J.P. Parise .63 1.25
84 Doug Mohns .63 1.25
85 Danny Grant .63 1.25
86 Bill Goldsworthy .75 1.50
87 Charlie Burns .50 1.00
88 Murray Oliver .50 1.00
89 Dean Prentice .75 1.50
90 Bob Nevin .63 1.25
91 Ted Harris .63 1.25
92 Cesare Maniago 1.00 2.00
93 Lou Nanne .63 1.25
94 Ted Hampton .50 1.00
95 Barry Gibbs .50 1.00
96 Gump Worsley 4.00 8.00
97 J.C. Tremblay .75 1.50
98 Guy Lapointe 1.00 2.00
99 Pete Mahovlich .75 1.50
100 Larry Pleau .63 1.25
101 Phil Myre 1.00 2.00
102 Yvan Cournoyer 2.50 5.00
103 Henri Richard 5.00 10.00
104 Frank Mahovlich 5.00 10.00
105 Jacques Lemaire 2.00 4.00
106 Claude Larose .50 1.00
107 Terry Harper .63 1.25
108 Jacques Laperriere 1.00 2.00
109 Phil Roberto .50 1.00
110 Serge Savard 2.00 4.00
111 Marc Tardif .63 1.25
112 Pierre Bouchard .63 1.25
113 Rod Gilbert 2.50 5.00
114 Jean Ratelle 2.50 5.00
115 Pete Stemkowski .50 1.00
116 Brad Park 4.00 8.00
117 Bobby Rousseau .50 1.00
118 Dale Rolfe .50 1.00
119 Rod Seiling .50 1.00
120 Walt Tkaczuk .50 1.00
121 Vic Hadfield .63 1.25
122 Jim Neilson .50 1.00
123 Bill Fairbairn .50 1.00
124 Bruce MacGregor .50 1.00
125 Dave Balon .50 1.00
126 Ted Irvine .50 1.00
127 Gilles Villemure 1.00 2.00
128 Ed Giacomin 4.00 8.00
129 Walt McKechnie .50 1.00
130 Tom Williams .50 1.00
131 Wayne Carleton .63 1.25
132 Gerry Pinder .50 1.00
133 Gary Croteau .50 1.00
134 Bert Marshall .50 1.00
135 Tom Webster .50 1.00
136 Norm Ferguson .50 1.00
137 Carol Vadnais .50 1.00
138 Gary Jarrett .50 1.00
139 Ernie Hicke .50 1.00
140 Paul Shmyr .50 1.00
141 Marshall Johnston .50 1.00
142 Don O'Donoghue .50 1.00
143 Joey Johnston .50 1.00
144 Dick Redmond .50 1.00
145 Simon Nolet .50 1.00
146 Wayne Hillman .50 1.00
147 Brent Hughes .50 1.00
148 Jim Johnson .50 1.00
149 Larry Mickey .50 1.00
150 Ed Van Impe .50 1.00
151 Gary Dornhoefer .63 1.25
152 Bobby Clarke 12.50 25.00
153 Jean-Guy Gendron .50 1.00
154 Larry Hale .50 1.00
155 Serge Bernier .50 1.00
156 Doug Favell 1.00 2.00
157 Bob Kelly .50 1.00
158 Joe Watson .50 1.00
159 Larry Brown .50 1.00
160 Bruce Gamble 1.00 2.00
161 Syl Apps .63 1.25
162 Ken Schinkel .50 1.00
163 Val Fonteyne .50 1.00
164 Bryan Watson .75 1.50
165 Bob Woytowich .50 1.00
166 Les Binkley 1.00 2.00
167 Roy Edwards 1.00 2.00
168 Jean Pronovost .63 1.25
169 Tim Horton 6.00 12.00
170 Ron Schock .50 1.00
171 Nick Harbaruk .50 1.00
172 Greg Polis .50 1.00
173 Bryan Hextall .63 1.25
174 Keith McCreary .50 1.00
175 Bill Hicke .50 1.00
176 Jim Rutherford 1.00 2.00
177 Gary Sabourin .50 1.00
178 Garry Unger 1.00 2.00
179 Terry Crisp .63 1.25
180 Noel Picard .50 1.00
181 Jim Roberts .50 1.00
182 Barclay Plager .75 1.50
183 Brit Selby .50 1.00
184 Frank St. Marseille .50 1.00
185 Ernie Wakely 1.00 2.00
186 Wayne Connelly .50 1.00
187 Chris Bordeleau .50 1.00
188 Bill Sutherland .50 1.00
189 Bob Plager .75 1.50
190 Bill Plager .63 1.25
191 George Morrison .50 1.00
192 Jim Lorentz .50 1.00
193 Norm Ullman 2.50 5.00
194 Jim McKenny .50 1.00
195 Rick Ley .50 1.00
196 Bob Baun 1.00 2.00
197 Mike Pelyk .50 1.00
198 Bill MacMillan .50 1.00
199 Garry Monahan .50 1.00
200 Paul Henderson 1.50 3.00
201 Jim Dorey .50 1.00
202 Jim Harrison .50 1.00
203 Ron Ellis .75 1.50
204 Darryl Sittler 3.00 6.00
205 Bernie Parent 2.50 5.00
206 Dave Keon 2.50 5.00
207 Brad Selwood .50 1.00
208 Don Marshall .50 1.00
209 Dale Tallon .63 1.25
210 Dan Johnson .50 1.00
211 Murray Hall .50 1.00
212 Paul Popiel .63 1.25
213 George Gardner .50 1.00
214 Gary Doak .50 1.00
215 Andre Boudrias .63 1.25
216 Orland Kurtenbach .63 1.25
217 Wayne Maki .50 1.00
218 Rosaire Paiement .63 1.25
219 Pat Quinn 1.00 2.00
220 Fred Speck .50 1.00
221 Barry Wilkins .50 1.00
222 Dunc Wilson 1.00 2.00
223 Ted Taylor .50 1.00
224 Mike Corrigan .50 1.00
NNO Stamp Album
(Bobby Orr on cover) 12.50 25.00

1972-73 Sargent Promotions Stamps

COMPLETE SET (224) 112.50 225.00
1 Lucien Grenier .25 .50
2 Phil Myre .50 1.00
3 Ernie Hicke .25 .50
4 Keith McCreary .25 .50
5 Bill MacMillan .25 .50
6 Pat Quinn .50 1.00
7 Bill Plager .38 .75
8 Noel Price .25 .50
9 Bob Leiter .25 .50
10 Randy Manery .25 .50
11 Bob Paradise .25 .50
12 Larry Romanchych .25 .50
13 Lew Morrison .25 .50
14 Dan Bouchard .50 1.00
15 Fred Stanfield .25 .50
16 Johnny Bucyk 1.50 3.00
17 Bobby Orr 20.00 40.00
18 Wayne Cashman .38 .75
19 Dallas Smith .25 .50
20 Ed Johnston .75 1.50
21 Phil Esposito 5.00 10.00
22 Ken Hodge .50 1.00
23 Don Awrey .25 .50
24 Mike Walton .25 .50
25 Carol Vadnais .25 .50
26 Doug Roberts .25 .50
27 Don Marcotte .25 .50
28 Garnet Bailey .25 .50
29 Gerry Meehan .25 .50
30 Tracy Pratt .25 .50
31 Gilbert Perreault 2.00 4.00
32 Roger Crozier 1.00 2.00
33 Don Luce .25 .50
34 Dave Dryden .50 1.00
35 Richard Martin .50 1.00
36 Jim Lorentz .25 .50
37 Tim Horton 4.00 8.00
38 Craig Ramsay .25 .50
39 Larry Hillman .25 .50
40 Steve Atkinson .25 .50
41 Jim Schoenfeld .38 .75
42 Rene Robert .38 .75
43 Walt McKechnie .25 .50
44 Marshall Johnston .25 .50
45 Joey Johnston .25 .50
46 Dick Redmond .25 .50
47 Bert Marshall .25 .50
48 Gary Croteau .25 .50
49 Marv Edwards .50 1.00
50 Gilles Meloche .50 1.00
51 Ivan Boldirev .25 .50
52 Stan Gilbertson .25 .50
53 Peter Laframboise .25 .50
54 Reggie Leach .50 1.00
55 Craig Patrick .50 1.00
56 Bob Stewart .25 .50
57 Keith Magnuson .38 .75
58 Doug Jarrett .25 .50
59 Cliff Koroll .25 .50
60 Chico Maki .25 .50
61 Gary Smith .50 1.00
62 Bill White .25 .50
63 Stan Mikita 3.00 6.00
64 Jim Pappin .25 .50
65 Lou Angotti .25 .50
66 Tony Esposito 4.00 8.00
67 Dennis Hull .50 1.00
68 Pit Martin .25 .50
69 Pat Stapleton .25 .50
70 Dan Maloney .25 .50
71 Bill Collins .25 .50
72 Arnie Brown .25 .50
73 Red Berenson .38 .75
74 Mickey Redmond 1.00 2.00
75 Nick Libett .25 .50
76 Alex Delvecchio 1.25 2.50
77 Ron Stackhouse .25 .50
78 Tim Ecclestone .25 .50
79 Gary Bergman .25 .50
80 Guy Charron .25 .50
81 Leon Rochefort .25 .50
82 Larry Johnston .25 .50
83 Andy Brown .25 .50
84 Henry Boucha .38 .75
85 Paul Curtis .25 .50
86 Jim Stanfield .25 .50
87 Rogatien Vachon 1.50 3.00
88 Ralph Backstrom .38 .75
89 Gilles Marotte .25 .50
90 Harry Howell .75 1.50
91 Real Lemieux .25 .50
92 Butch Goring .38 .75
93 Juha Widing .25 .50
94 Mike Corrigan .25 .50
95 Larry Brown .25 .50
96 Terry Harper .38 .75
97 Serge Bernier .25 .50
98 Bob Berry .25 .50
99 Tom Reid .25 .50
100 Jude Drouin .25 .50
101 Jean-Paul Parise .38 .75
102 Doug Mohns .38 .75
103 Danny Grant .38 .75
104 Bill Goldsworthy .50 1.00
105 Gump Worsley 2.50 5.00
106 Charlie Burns .25 .50
107 Murray Oliver .25 .50
108 Barry Gibbs .25 .50
109 Ted Harris .25 .50
110 Cesare Maniago 1.00 2.00
111 Lou Nanne .38 .75
112 Bob Nevin .25 .50
113 Guy Lapointe .75 1.50
114 Peter Mahovlich .38 .75
115 Jacques Lemaire 1.00 2.00
116 Pierre Bouchard .25 .50
117 Yvan Cournoyer 1.25 2.50
118 Marc Tardif .25 .50
119 Henri Richard 2.50 5.00
120 Frank Mahovlich 2.50 5.00
121 Jacques Laperriere .75 1.50
122 Claude Larose .25 .50
123 Serge Savard 1.00 2.00
124 Ken Dryden 10.00 20.00
125 Rejean Houle .38 .75
126 Jim Roberts .25 .50
127 Ed Westfall .38 .75
128 Terry Crisp .38 .75
129 Gerry Desjardins .50 1.00
130 Denis DeJordy .75 1.50
131 Billy Harris .25 .50
132 Brian Spencer .50 1.00
133 Germaine Gagnon UER .25 .50
134 David Hedson .25 .50
135 Lorne Henning .25 .50
136 Brian Marchinko .25 .50
137 Tom Miller .25 .50
138 Gerry Hart .25 .50
139 Bryan Lefley .25 .50
140 James Mair .25 .50
141 Rod Gilbert 1.25 2.50
142 Jean Ratelle 1.25 2.50
143 Pete Stemkowski .25 .50
144 Brad Park 1.50 3.00
145 Bobby Rousseau .25 .50
146 Dale Rolfe .25 .50
147 Ed Giacomin 1.50 3.00
148 Rod Seiling .25 .50
149 Walt Tkaczuk .25 .50
150 Bill Fairbairn .25 .50
151 Vic Hadfield .38 .75
152 Ted Irvine .25 .50
153 Bruce MacGregor .25 .50
154 Jim Neilson .25 .50
155 Brent Hughes .25 .50
156 Wayne Hillman .25 .50
157 Doug Favell .75 1.50
158 Simon Nolet .25 .50
159 Joe Watson .25 .50
160 Ed Van Impe .25 .50
161 Gary Dornhoefer .38 .75
162 Bobby Clarke 5.00 10.00
163 Bob Kelly .25 .50
164 Bill Flett .25 .50
165 Rick Foley .25 .50
166 Ross Lonsberry .25 .50
167 Rick MacLeish .50 1.00
168 Bill Clement .50 1.00
169 Syl Apps .38 .75
170 Ken Schinkel .25 .50
171 Nick Harbaruk .25 .50
172 Bryan Watson .38 .75
173 Bryan Hextall .38 .75
174 Roy Edwards .50 1.00
175 Jim Rutherford .75 1.50
176 Jean Pronovost .38 .75
177 Rick Kessell .25 .50
178 Greg Polis .25 .50
179 Ron Schock .25 .50
180 Duane Rupp .25 .50
181 Darryl Edestrand .25 .50
182 Dave Burrows .25 .50
183 Gary Sabourin .25 .50
184 Garry Unger .50 1.00
185 Noel Picard .25 .50
186 Bob Plager .38 .75
187 Barclay Plager .38 .75
188 Frank St. Marseille .25 .50
189 Danny O'Shea .25 .50

190 Kevin O'Shea .25 .50
191 Wayne Stephenson .50 1.00
192 Chris Evans .25 .50
193 Jacques Caron .25 .50
194 Andre Dupont .25 .50
195 Mike Murphy .25 .50
196 Jack Egers .25 .50
197 Norm Ullman 1.25 2.50
198 Jim McKenny .25 .50
199 Bob Baun .50 1.00
200 Mike Pelyk .25 .50
201 Ron Ellis .38 .75
202 Garry Monahan .25 .50
203 Paul Henderson 1.00 2.00
204 Darryl Sittler 1.75 3.50
205 Brian Glennie .25 .50
206 Dave Keon 1.25 2.50
207 Jacques Plante 5.00 10.00
208 Pierre Jarry .25 .50
209 Rick Kehoe .38 .75
210 Denis Dupere .25 .50
211 Dale Tallon .38 .75
212 Murray Hall .25 .50
213 Dunc Wilson .50 1.00
214 Andre Boudrias .38 .75
215 Orland Kurtenbach .38 .75
216 Wayne Maki .25 .50
217 Barry Wilkins .25 .50
218 Richard Lemieux .25 .50
219 Bobby Schmautz .25 .50
220 Dave Balon .25 .50
221 Robert Lalonde .25 .50
222 Jocelyn Guevremont .25 .50
223 Gregg Boddy .25 .50
224 Dennis Kearns .25 .50
NNO1 Stamp Album (Paul Hende 17.50 35.00
NNO2 Stamp Album Richard Martin 25.00 50.00
NNO3 Stamp Album (Bobby Orr 10.00 20.00

1990 Score Rookie/Traded

COMP.FACT.SET (110) 1.25 3.00
100T Eric Lindros .40 1.00

1990-91 Score Promos

1A Wayne Gretzky ERR (Catches left in cardback bio) 25.00 60.00
1B Wayne Gretzky COR (Shoots left in cardback bio) 10.00 25.00
10 Patrick Roy (kick save photo on front) 8.00 20.00
40 Gary Leeman .30 .75
100A Mark Messier ERR (Won Smythe in 1990) 6.00 15.00
100B Mark Messier COR (Won Smythe in 1984) 2.50 6.00
179 Jeremy Roenick 2.00 5.00
200 Ray Bourque 2.50 6.00

1990-91 Score

1 Wayne Gretzky 1.00 2.50
2 Mario Lemieux .60 1.50
3 Steve Yzerman .50 1.25
4 Cam Neely .15 .40
5 Al MacInnis .20 .50
6 Paul Coffey .15 .40
7 Brian Bellows .12 .30
8 Joe Sakic .50 1.25
9 Bernie Nicholls .12 .30
10 Patrick Roy .40 1.00
11 Doug Houda RC .15 .40
12 David Volek .15 .40
13 Esa Tikkanen .12 .30
14 Thomas Steen .12 .30
15 Chris Chelios .15 .40
16 Bob Carpenter .12 .30
17 Dirk Graham .12 .30
18 Garth Butcher .12 .30
19 Patrik Sundstrom .12 .30
20 Rod Langway .15 .40
21 Scott Young .10 .25
22 Ulf Dahlen .15 .40
23 Mike Ramsey .10 .25
24 Peter Zezel .15 .40
25 Ron Hextall .15 .40
26 Steve Duchesne .10 .25
27 Allan Bester .15 .40
28 Everett Sanipass RC .12 .30
29 Steve Konroyd .10 .25
30A Joe Nieuwendyk ERR .12 .30
30B Joe Nieuwendyk COR .12 .30
31A Brent Ashton ERR (No position on card front) .15 .40
31B Brent Ashton COR (LW on card front) .15 .40
32 Trevor Linden .15 .40
33 Mike Ridley .10 .25
34 Sean Burke .12 .30
35 Pat Verbeek .12 .30
36 Rob Ramage .15 .40
37 Kelly Kisio .12 .30
38 Craig Muni .12 .30
39 Brent Sutter .12 .30
40 Gary Leeman .12 .30
41 Jeff Brown .15 .40
42 Greg Millen .12 .30
43 Alexander Mogilny RC .50 1.25
44 Dale Hunter .15 .40
45 Randy Moller .15 .40
46 Peter Sidorkiewicz .15 .40
47 Terry Carkner .12 .30
48 Tony Granato .10 .25
49 Shawn Burr .12 .30
50 Dale Hawerchuk .20 .50
51A Don Sweeney RC .15 .40
52 Mike Vernon UER .12 .30
53 Kevin Stevens RC .30 .75
54 Bryan Fogarty RC .10 .25
55 Dan Quinn .12 .30
56 Murray Craven .15 .40
57 Shawn Chambers .15 .40
58 Craig Simpson .12 .30
59 Doug Crossman .12 .30
60 Daren Puppa .12 .30
61 Bobby Smith .12 .30
62 Slava Fetisov RC .30 .75
63 Gino Cavallini .15 .40
64 Jimmy Carson .12 .30
65 Dave Ellett .10 .25
66 Steve Thomas .10 .25
67 Mike Lalor RC .12 .30
68 Mike Liut .10 .25
69 Tom Laidlaw .15 .40
70 Ron Francis .20 .50
71 Sergei Makarov RC .30 .75
72 Randy Burridge .12 .30
73 Doug Lidster .15 .40
74 Mike Richter RC .50 1.25
75 Stephane Richer .15 .40
76 Randy Hillier .15 .40
77 Christian Ruuttu .12 .30
78 Marc Fortier .12 .30
79 Bill Ranford .12 .30
80 Rick Tocchet .15 .40
81 Fredrik Olausson .12 .30
82 Adam Creighton .10 .25
83 Sylvain Cote .10 .25
84 Brian Mullen .15 .40
85 Adam Oates .15 .40
86 Gary Nylund .12 .30
87 Tim Cheveldae RC .12 .30
88 Gary Suter .10 .25
89 John Tonelli .12 .30
90 Kevin Hatcher .12 .30
91 Guy Carbonneau .10 .25
92 Curtis Leschyshyn RC .12 .30
93 Kirk McLean .10 .25
94 Curt Giles .12 .30
95 Vincent Damphousse .12 .30
96 Peter Stastny .12 .30
97 Glen Wesley .12 .30
98 David Shaw .15 .40
99 Brad Shaw RC .12 .30
100 Mark Messier .30 .75
101 Rick Zombo RC .15 .40
102A Mark Fitzpatrick ERR RC .12 .30
102B Mark Fitzpatrick COR RC .12 .30
103 Rick Vaive .12 .30
104 Mark Osborne .12 .30
105 Rob Brown .30 .75
106 Gary Roberts .15 .40
107 Vincent Riendeau RC .15 .40
108 Dave Gagner .15 .40
109 Bruce Driver .15 .40
110 Pierre Turgeon .12 .30
111 Claude Lemieux .10 .25
112 Bob Essensa RC .25 .60
113 John Ogrodnick .15 .40
114 Glenn Anderson .12 .30
115 Kelly Hrudey .10 .25
116 Sylvain Turgeon .12 .30
117 Gord Murphy RC .15 .40
118 Craig Janney .15 .40
119 Randy Wood .10 .25
120 Mike Modano RC .50 1.25
121 Tom Barrasso .12 .30
122 Daniel Marois .12 .30
123 Igor Larionov RC .30 .75
124 Geoff Courtnall .60 1.50
125 Denis Savard .12 .30
126 Ron Tugnutt .12 .30
127 Mathieu Schneider RC .12 .30
128 Joel Otto .12 .30
129 Steve Smith .12 .30
130 Mike Gartner .20 .50
131 Rod Brind'Amour RC .30 .75
132 Jyrki Lumme RC .12 .30
133 Mike Foligno .15 .40
134 Ray Ferraro .12 .30
135 Steve Larmer .12 .30
136 Randy Carlyle .12 .30
137 Tony Tanti .12 .30
138 Jeff Chychrun RC .12 .30
139 Gerald Diduck .12 .30
140 Andy Moog .15 .40
141 Paul Gillis .12 .30
142 Tom Kurvers .12 .30
143 Bob Probert .15 .40
144 Neal Broten .10 .25
145 Phil Housley .12 .30
146 Brendan Shanahan .15 .40
147 Bob Rouse .10 .25
148 Russ Courtnall .15 .40
149 Normand Rochefort UER (RW, should be D) .10 .25
150 Luc Robitaille .15 .40
151 Curtis Joseph RC .50 1.25
152 Ulf Samuelsson .12 .30
153 Ron Sutter .12 .30
154 Petri Skriko .15 .40
155 Doug Gilmour .20 .50
156 Paul Fenton .15 .40
157 Jeff Norton .15 .40
158 Jari Kurri .20 .50
159 Rejean Lemelin .10 .25
160 Kirk Muller .12 .30
161 Keith Brown .12 .30
162 Aaron Broten UER .12 .30
163 Adam Graves RC .30 .75
164 v .15 .40
165 Craig Ludwig .15 .40
166 Dave Taylor .15 .40
167 Craig Wolanin RC .12 .30
168 Kelly Miller .10 .25
169 Uwe Krupp .15 .40
170 Kevin Lowe .15 .40
171 Wendel Clark .25 .60
172 Dave Babych .12 .30
173 Paul Reinhart .10 .25
174 Pat Flatley .12 .30
175 John Vanbiesbrouck .15 .40
176 Teppo Numminen RC .30 .75
177 Tim Kerr .15 .40
178 Ken Daneyko .10 .25
179 Jeremy Roenick RC .50 1.25
180 Gerard Gallant .12 .30
181 Allen Pederson .15 .40
182 Jon Casey .15 .40
183 Tomas Sandstrom .15 .40
184 Brad McCrimmon .15 .40
185 Paul Cavallini .12 .30
186 Mark Recchi RC .50 1.25
187 Michel Petit .12 .30
188 Scott Stevens .15 .40
189 Dave Andreychuk .15 .40
190 John MacLean .12 .30
191 Petr Svoboda .12 .30
192 Dave Tippett .12 .30
193 Dave Manson .12 .30
194 James Patrick .15 .40
195 Al Iafrate .10 .25
196 Doug Smail .12 .30
197 Kjell Samuelsson .12 .30
198 Brian Bradley .12 .30
199 Charlie Huddy .12 .30
200 Ray Bourque .25 .60
201 Joey Kocur RC .30 .75
202 Jim Johnson UER .10 .25
203 Paul MacLean .12 .30
204 Tim Watters .10 .25
205 Pat Elynuik .15 .40
206 Larry Murphy .12 .30
207 Claude Loiselle RC .10 .25
208 Joe Mullen .12 .30
209 Alexei Kasatonov RC .15 .40
210 Ed Olczyk .15 .40
211 Doug Bodger .12 .30
212 Kevin Dineen .15 .40
213 Shayne Corson .12 .30
214 Steve Chiasson .10 .25
215 Don Beaupre .10 .25
216 Jamie Macoun .10 .25
217 Dave Poulin .15 .40
218 Zarley Zalapski .12 .30
219 Brad Marsh .12 .30
220 Mark Howe .15 .40
221 Michel Goulet .10 .25
222 Hubie McDonough RC .12 .30
223 Frank Musil .10 .25
224 Sergio Momesso RC .12 .30
225 Brian Leetch .20 .50
226 Theo Fleury .20 .50
227 Mike Krushelnyski .15 .40
228 Glen Hanlon .12 .30
229 Mario Marois .12 .30
230 Dino Ciccarelli .15 .40
231A Dave McLlwain ERR (Shoots right) .15 .40
231B Dave McLlwain COR (Shoots left) .15 .40
232 Petr Klima .10 .25
233 Grant Ledyard RC .12 .30
234 Phil Bourque .12 .30
235 Rob Sweeney .10 .25
236 Luke Richardson .10 .25
237 Todd Krygier RC .12 .30
238 Brian Skrudland .12 .30
239 Chris Terreri RC .30 .75
240 Greg Adams .10 .25
241 Darren Turcotte RC .15 .40
242 Scott Mellanby .15 .40
243 Troy Murray .12 .30
244 Stewart Gavin .15 .40
245 Gordie Roberts .10 .25
246 John Druce RC .15 .40
247 Steve Kasper .10 .25
248 Paul Ranheim RC .12 .30
249 Greg Paslawski .12 .30
250 Pat LaFontaine .15 .40
251 Scott Arniel .10 .25
252 Bernie Federko .12 .30
253 Garry Galley RC .12 .30
254 Carey Wilson .12 .30
255 Bob Errey .10 .25
256 Tony Hrkac .10 .25
257 Andrew McBain .12 .30
258 Craig MacTavish .12 .30
259A Dean Evason ERR (Reversed negative) .12 .30
259B Dean Evason COR (photo is correct) .12 .30
260 Larry Robinson .15 .40
261 Basil McRae .10 .25
262 Stephan Lebeau RC .12 .30
263 Ken Wregget .15 .40
264 Greg Gilbert .10 .25
265 Ken Baumgartner RC .15 .40
266 Lou Franceschetti RC .15 .40
267 Rick Meagher .12 .30
268 Michal Pivonka RC .12 .30
269 Brian Propp .15 .40
270 Bryan Trottier .12 .30
271 Marty McSorley .12 .30
272 Jan Erixon .15 .40
273 Vladimir Krutov RC .30 .75
274 Dana Murzyn .15 .40
275 Grant Fuhr .25 .60
276 Randy Cunneyworth .12 .30
277 John Chabot .15 .40
278 Walt Poddubny .12 .30
279 Stephen Leach .12 .30
280 Doug Wilson .12 .30
281 Rich Sutter .15 .40
282 Stephane Beauregard RC .12 .30
283 John Carter RC .12 .30
284 Don Barber RC .12 .30
285 Tom Fergus .10 .25
286 Ilkka Sinisalo .12 .30
287 Kevin McClelland UER .12 .30
288 Troy Mallette RC .12 .30
289 Clint Malarchuk UER .12 .30
290 Guy Lafleur .20 .50
291 Bob Joyce .12 .30
292 Trent Yawney .15 .40
293 Joe Murphy RC .12 .30
294 Glenn Healy RC .30 .75
295 Dave Christian .10 .25
296 Paul MacDermid .12 .30
297 Todd Elik RC .12 .30
298 Wendell Young RC .15 .40
299 Dean Kennedy RC .12 .30
300 Brett Hull .30 .75
301 Keith Acton .15 .40
302 Yvon Corriveau RC .10 .25
303 Don Maloney .12 .30
304 Mark Tinordi RC .10 .25
305 Bob Kudelski RC .12 .30
306 Brian Benning .12 .30
307 Alan Kerr .12 .30
308 Pelle Eklund .10 .25
309 Calle Johansson .15 .40
310 David Maley RC .15 .40
311 Chris Nilan .10 .25
312 Patrick Roy AS1 .40 1.00
313 Ray Bourque AS1 .25 .60
314 Al MacInnis AS1 .20 .50
315 Mark Messier AS1 .30 .75
316 Luc Robitaille AS1 .15 .40
317 Brett Hull AS1 .30 .75
318 Daren Puppa AS2 .12 .30
319 Paul Coffey AS2 .15 .40
320 Doug Wilson AS2 .12 .30
321 Wayne Gretzky AS2 1.00 2.50
322 Brian Bellows AS2 .12 .30
323 Cam Neely AS2 .15 .40
324 Bob Essensa ART .25 .60
325 Brad Shaw ART .12 .30
326 Geoff Smith ART .12 .30
327 Mike Modano ART .50 1.25
328 Rod Brind'Amour ART .30 .75
329 Sergei Makarov ART .30 .75
330A Kip Miller Hob ERR RC (Score logo missing on front) .12 .30
330B Kip Miller Hob COR RC (Score logo appears on front) .12 .30
331 Edmonton Oilers Champs .30 .75
332 Paul Coffey Speed .15 .40
333 Mike Gartner Speed .20 .50
334 Al Iafrate Blaster .10 .25
335 Al MacInnis Blaster .20 .50
336 Wayne Gretzky Sniper 1.00 2.50
337 Mario Lemieux Sniper .60 1.50
338 Wayne Gretzky Magic 1.00 2.50
339 Steve Yzerman Magic .50 1.25
340 Cam Neely Banger .15 .40
341 Scott Stevens Banger .15 .40
342 Esa Tikkanen Shadow .12 .30
343 Jan Erixon Shadow .12 .30
344 Patrick Roy Stopper .40 1.00
345 Bill Ranford Stopper .12 .30
346 Brett Hull RB .30 .75
347 Wayne Gretzky RB 1.00 2.50
348 Jari Kurri LL .20 .50
349 Paul Cavallini LL .12 .30
350 Sergei Makarov RLL .30 .75
351 Brett Hull LL .30 .75
352 Wayne Gretzky LL 1.00 2.50
353 Wayne Gretzky LL 1.00 2.50
354 P.Roy/Liut LL .40 1.00
355 Gilbert Perreault HOF .15 .40
356 Bill Barber HOF .12 .30
357 Fern Flaman HOF .12 .30
358 Bill Ranford Smythe .12 .30
359 Rick Meagher Selke .12 .30
360 Mark Messier Hart .30 .75
361 Wayne Gretzky Ross 1.00 2.50
362 Sergei Makarov Calder .30 .75
363 Ray Bourque Norris .25 .60
364 Patrick Roy Vezina .40 1.00
365 Andy Moog Reggie Lemelin Jennings .15 .40
366 Brett Hull Byng .30 .75
367 Gord Kluzak Mast .10 .25
368 Boston/Washington UER .25 .60
369 Edmonton Chicago .12 .30
370 Adam Burt RC .12 .30
371 Troy Loney RC .15 .40
372 Dave Chyzowski RC .12 .30
373 Geoff Smith RC .15 .40
374 Stan Smyl .10 .25
375 Gaetan Duchesne .15 .40
376 Bob Murray .12 .30
377 Daniel Shank RC .12 .30
378 Tommy Albelin .10 .25
379 Perry Berezan RC .15 .40
380 Ken Linseman .12 .30
381 Stephane Matteau RC .15 .40
382 Mario Thyer RC .12 .30
383 Nelson Emerson RC .15 .40
384 Kory Kocur RC .12 .30
385 Bob Beers RC .12 .30
386 Jim Hrivnak RC .15 .40
387 Mark Pederson RC .15 .40
388 Jeff Hackett RC .25 .60
389 Eric Weinrich RC .15 .40
390 Steven Rice RC .15 .40
391 Stu Barnes RC .12 .30
392 Olaf Kolzig RC UER .15 .40
393 Francois Leroux RC .12 .30
394 Adrien Plavsic RC .15 .40
395 Michel Mongeau RC .15 .40
396 Rick Corriveau RC .12 .30
397 Wayne Doucet RC .12 .30
398 Mats Sundin RC .25 .60
399 Murray Baron RC .12 .30
400 Rick Bennett RC .12 .30
401 Jon Morris RC .10 .25
402 Kay Whitmore RC .12 .30
403 Peter Lappin RC .12 .30
404 Kris Draper RC .12 .30
405 Shayne Stevenson RC .12 .30
406 Paul Ysebaert RC .12 .30
407A Jim Waite ERR RC .15 .40
407B Jim Waite COR RC .15 .40
408 Cam Russell RC .12 .30
409 Kim Issel RC .12 .30
410 Darrin Shannon RC .15 .40
411 Link Gaetz RC .12 .30
412 Craig Fisher RC .15 .40
413 Bruce Hoffort RC .15 .40
414 Peter Ing RC .15 .40
415 Stephane Fiset RC .30 .75
416 Dominic Lavoie RC .12 .30
417 Steve Maltais RC .12 .30
418 Wes Walz RC .15 .40
419 Terry Yake RC .15 .40
420 Jamie Leach RC .12 .30
421 Rob Blake RC .25 .60
422 Andrew Cassels RC .10 .25
423 Marc Bureau RC .12 .30
424 Scott Allison RC .12 .30
425 Darryl Sydor RC .15 .40
426 Turner Stevenson RC .12 .30
427 Brad May RC .12 .30
428 Jaromir Jagr RC 2.50 6.00
429 Shawn Antoski RC .12 .30
430 Derian Hatcher RC .12 .30
431 Mark Greig RC .12 .30
432 Scott Scissons RC .12 .30
433 Mike Ricci RC .15 .40
434 Drake Berehowsky RC .12 .30
435 Owen Nolan RC .50 1.25
436 Keith Primeau RC .25 .60
437 Karl Dykhuis RC .12 .30
438 Trevor Kidd RC .12 .30
439 Martin Brodeur RC 2.50 6.00
440 Eric Lindros RC 2.00 5.00
B1 Eric Lindros Junior B Team 1.00 2.50
B2 Eric Lindros Regular Junior OHL 1.00 2.50
B3 Eric Lindros OHL All-Star 1.00 2.50
B4 Eric Lindros Oshawa Generals (Non-action pose; head shot with his gloves over his mouth) 1.00 2.50
B5 Eric Lindros Oshawa Generals (Non-action pose; shot from waist up& arms draped over hockey stick across his back) 1.00 2.50

1990-91 Score Canadian

*CANADIAN: .4X TO 1X BASIC SCORE

1990-91 Score Hottest/Rising Stars

1 Wayne Gretzky .75 2.00
2 Craig Simpson .10 .25
3 Brian Bellows .10 .25
4 Steve Yzerman .40 1.00
5 Bernie Nicholls .10 .25
6 Esa Tikkanen .10 .25
7 Joe Sakic .40 1.00
8 Thomas Steen .10 .25
9 Chris Chelios .10 .25
10 Patrik Sundstrom .10 .25
11 Rod Langway .10 .25
12 Scott Young .07 .20
13 Mike Ramsey .07 .20
14 Ron Hextall .10 .25
15 Steve Duchesne .07 .20
16 Trevor Linden .10 .25
17 Sean Burke .10 .25
18 Pat Verbeek .10 .25
19 Brent Sutter .10 .25
20 Gary Leeman .10 .25
21 Shawn Burr .10 .25
22 Dale Hawerchuk .15 .40
23 Mike Vernon .10 .25
24 Dan Quinn .10 .25
25 Patrick Roy .30 .75
26 Daren Puppa .12 .30
27 Gino Cavallini .12 .30
28 Jimmy Carson .10 .25
29 Dave Ellett .07 .20
30 Steve Thomas .07 .20
31 Jeremy Roenick .40 1.00
32 Mike Liut .07 .20
33 Mark Messier .25 .60
34 Mario Lemieux .50 1.25
35 Ray Bourque .20 .50
36 Al MacInnis .15 .40
37 Ron Francis .15 .40
38 Stephane Richer .12 .30
39 Bill Ranford .10 .25
40 Rick Tocchet .12 .30
41 Adam Oates .12 .30
42 Kevin Hatcher .10 .25
43 Guy Carbonneau .07 .20
44 Curtis Leschyshyn .10 .25
45 Joe Nieuwendyk .15 .40
46 Kirk McLean .07 .20
47 Vincent Damphousse .10 .25
48 Peter Stastny .10 .25
49 Rick Zombo .10 .25
50 Mark Fitzpatrick .10 .25
51 Rob Brown .25 .60
52 Dave Gagner .12 .30
53 Pierre Turgeon .10 .25
54 Glenn Anderson .10 .25
55 Kelly Hrudey .07 .20
56 Gord Murphy .12 .30
57 Glen Wesley .10 .25
58 Craig Janney .12 .30
59 Denis Savard .12 .30
60 Mike Gartner .15 .40
61 Steve Larmer .10 .25
62 Andy Moog .12 .30
63 Phil Housley .12 .30
64 Ulf Samuelsson .12 .30
65 Paul Coffey .15 .40
66 Luc Robitaille .15 .40
67 Cam Neely .12 .30
68 Doug Wilson .12 .30
69 Doug Gilmour .12 .30
70 Jeff Norton .12 .30
71 Kirk Muller .12 .30
72 Aaron Broten .12 .30
73 John Cullen .12 .30
74 Craig Ludwig .12 .30
75 Kevin Lowe .12 .30
76 John Vanbiesbrouck .12 .30
77 Tim Kerr .07 .20
78 Gerard Gallant .07 .20
79 Tomas Sandstrom .12 .30
80 Jon Casey .12 .30
81 Mark Recchi .40 1.00
82 Scott Stevens .12 .30
83 John MacLean .10 .25
84 James Patrick .12 .30
85 Al Iafrate .07 .20
86 Pat Elynuik .25 .60
87 Dave Andreychuk .12 .30
88 Joe Mullen .12 .30
89 Ed Olczyk .12 .30
90 Kevin Dineen .12 .30
91 Shayne Corson .12 .30
92 Mark Howe .12 .30
93 Brian Leetch .15 .40
94 Dino Ciccarelli .12 .30
95 Pat LaFontaine .12 .30
96 Guy Lafleur .15 .40
97 Mike Modano .40 1.00
98 Rod Brind'Amour .25 .60
99 Sergei Makarov .25 .60
100 Brett Hull .25 .60

1990-91 Score Rookie Traded

1T Denis Savard .15 .40
2T Dale Hawerchuk .20 .50
3T Phil Housley .12 .30
4T Chris Chelios .15 .40
5T Geoff Courtnall .12 .30
6T Peter Zezel .15 .40
7T Joe Mullen .12 .30
8T Craig Ludwig .15 .40
9T Claude Lemieux .10 .25
10T Bobby Holik RC .15 .40
11T Peter Ing .15 .40
12T Rod Buskas RC .15 .40
13T Tim Sweeney RC .15 .40
14T Don Barber .12 .30
15T Ray Ferraro .12 .30
16T Peter Taglianetti .12 .30
17T Johan Garpenlov RC .15 .40
18T Kevin Miller RC .15 .40
19T Frank Musil .10 .25
20T Sergei Fedorov RC .60 1.50
21T Aaron Broten .12 .30
22T Chris Nilan .10 .25
23T Gerald Diduck .12 .30
24T Marc Habscheid .12 .30
25T Glen Featherstone RC .12 .30
26T Mikko Makela .12 .30
27T Paul Stanton .15 .40
28T Mark Osborne .12 .30
29T Dave Tippett .12 .30
30T Robert Reichel RC .15 .40
31T Grant Jennings RC .15 .40
32T Troy Gamble .15 .40
33T Mark Janssens .15 .40
34T Brian Propp .15 .40
35T Donald Dufresne RC .10 .25
36T Martin Hostak RC .12 .30
37T Brad McCrimmon .15 .40
38T Dave Lowry RC .12 .30
39T Anatoli Semenov RC .12 .30
40T Scott Stevens .15 .40
41T Paul Broten .12 .30
42T Carey Wilson .12 .30
43T Troy Crowder RC .10 .25
44T Vladimir Ruzicka RC .15 .40
45T Rich Pilon .10 .25
46T John McIntyre RC .15 .40
47T Mike Krushelnyski .15 .40
48T Dave Snuggerud .12 .30
49T Bob McGill .10 .25
50T Petr Nedved RC .50 1.25
51T Ed Olczyk .15 .40
52T Doug Crossman .12 .30
53T Mikhail Tatarinov RC .10 .25
54T Michel Petit .12 .30
55T Frank Pietrangelo RC .10 .25
56T Brian MacLellan .12 .30
57T Paul Fenton .15 .40
58T Eric Desjardins RC .25 .60
59T Mike Craig RC .15 .40
60T Mike Ricci .15 .40
61T Harold Snepsts .10 .25
62T John Byce .12 .30
63T Laurie Boschman .12 .30
64T Randy Velischek .10 .25
65T Robert Kron .15 .40
66T Jocelyn Lemieux .12 .30
67T Dave Ellett .10 .25
68T Scott Arniel .10 .25
69T Doug Smail .12 .30
70T Jaromir Jagr 3.00 8.00
71T Peter Bondra RC .40 1.00
72T Paul Cyr .10 .25
73T Daniel Berthiaume .12 .30
74T Lee Norwood .12 .30
75T Bobby Smith .12 .30
76T Kris King RC .15 .40
77T Mark Hunter .10 .25
78T Brian Hayward .15 .40
79T Greg Hawgood .12 .30
80T Owen Nolan .50 1.25
81T Cliff Ronning .10 .25
82T Zdeno Ciger RC .15 .40
83T Gordie Roberts .10 .25
84T Rick Green .15 .40
85T Ken Hodge Jr. RC .15 .40
86T Derek King .15 .40
87T Brent Gilchrist RC .12 .30
88T Eric Lindros .75 2.00
89T Steve Bozek .12 .30
90T Keith Primeau .25 .60
91T Roger Johansson RC .12 .30
92T Wayne Presley .10 .25
93T Ilkka Sinisalo .12 .30
94T Mario Marois .15 .40
95T Ken Linseman .12 .30
96T Greg Brown RC .12 .30
97T Ray Sheppard .10 .25
98T Mike Lalor .12 .30
99T Normand Lacombe .10 .25
100T Mats Sundin .40 1.00
101T Jergus Baca RC .12 .30
102T Mike Keane RC .10 .25
103T Ed Belfour RC .50 1.25
104T Mark Hardy .10 .25
105T Dave Capuano RC .15 .40
106T Bryan Trottier .15 .40
107T Per Djoos RC .15 .40
108T Sylvain Turgeon .12 .30
109T David Reid .15 .40
110T W.Gretzky 2000th 1.00 2.50

1990-91 Score Young Superstars

1 Pierre Turgeon .12 .30
2 Brian Leetch .15 .40
3 Daniel Marois .10 .25
4 Peter Sidorkiewicz .12 .30
5 Rob Brown .25 .60
6 Theo Fleury .15 .40
7 Mats Sundin .20 .50
8 Glen Wesley .10 .25
9 Sergei Fedorov .25 .60
10 Joe Sakic .40 1.00
11 Sean Burke .10 .25
12 Dave Chyzowski .10 .25
13 Gord Murphy .12 .30
14 Scott Young .07 .20
15 Curtis Joseph .40 1.00
16 Darren Turcotte .10 .25
17 Kevin Stevens .25 .60
18 Mathieu Schneider .10 .25
19 Trevor Linden .12 .30
20 Mike Modano .40 1.00
21 Martin Gelinas .25 .60
22 Stephane Fiset .25 .60
23 Brendan Shanahan .12 .30
24 Jeremy Roenick .40 1.00
25 John Druce .12 .30
26 Alexander Mogilny .40 1.00
27 Mike Richter .40 1.00
28 Pat Elynuik .10 .25
29 Robert Reichel .12 .30
30 Craig Janney .12 .30
31 Rod Brind'Amour .25 .60
32 Mark Fitzpatrick .10 .25
33 Tony Granato .07 .20
34 Bobby Holik .12 .30
35 Mark Recchi .40 1.00
36 Owen Nolan .40 1.00
37 Petr Nedved .12 .30
38 Keith Primeau .20 .50
39 Mike Ricci .12 .30
40 Eric Lindros 3.00 8.00

1991 Score National Convention

COMPLETE SET (10) 6.00 15.00
*NCWA BACK: .4X TO 1X NATIONAL
1 Wayne Gretzky 2.00 5.00
2 Brett Hull .60 1.50
3 Ray Bourque .60 1.50
4 Al MacInnis .40 1.00
5 Luc Robitaille .40 1.00
6 Ed Belfour .60 1.50
7 Steve Yzerman 1.25 3.00
8 Cam Neely .40 1.00
9 Paul Coffey .40 1.00
10 Patrick Roy 1.50 4.00

1991 Score Fanfest

COMPLETE SET (10) 12.00 30.00
1 Wayne Gretzky 4.00 10.00
2 Brett Hull .75 2.00
3 Ray Bourque .75 2.00
4 Al MacInnis .60 1.50
5 Luc Robitaille .60 1.50
6 Ed Belfour .75 2.00
7 Steve Yzerman 2.00 5.00
8 Cam Neely .60 1.50
9 Paul Coffey .60 1.50
10 Patrick Roy 2.50 6.00

1991-92 Score American

1 Brett Hull .30 .75
2 Al MacInnis .20 .50
3 Luc Robitaille .15 .40
4 Pierre Turgeon .12 .30
5 Brian Leetch .12 .30
6 Cam Neely .15 .40
7 John Cullen .12 .30
8 Trevor Linden .15 .40
9 Rick Tocchet .12 .30
10 John Vanbiesbrouck .15 .40
11 Steve Smith .12 .30
12 Doug Smail .12 .30
13 Craig Ludwig .12 .30
14 Paul Fenton .12 .30
15 Dirk Graham .12 .30
16 Brad McCrimmon .12 .30
17 Dean Evason .12 .30
18 Fredrik Olausson .12 .30
19 Guy Carbonneau .12 .30
20 Kevin Hatcher .12 .30
21 Paul Ranheim .15 .40
22 Claude Lemieux .12 .30
23 Vincent Riendeau .12 .30
24 Garth Butcher .12 .30
25 Joe Sakic .50 1.25
26 Rick Vaive .10 .25
27 Rob Blake .15 .40
28 Mike Ricci .10 .25
29 Pat Flatley .12 .30
30 Bill Ranford .12 .30
31 Larry Murphy .12 .30
32 Bobby Smith .12 .30
33 Mike Krushelnyski .12 .30
34 Gerard Gallant .10 .25
35 Doug Wilson .12 .30
36 John Ogrodnick .12 .30
37 Mikhail Tatarinov .12 .30
38 Doug Crossman .12 .30
39 Mark Osborne .12 .30
40 Scott Stevens .15 .40
41 Ron Tugnutt .12 .30
42 Russ Courtnall .12 .30
43 Gord Murphy .12 .30
44 Greg Adams .12 .30
45 Christian Ruuttu .12 .30
46 Ken Daneyko .12 .30
47 Glenn Anderson .12 .30
48 Ray Ferraro .12 .30
49 Tony Tanti .12 .30
50 Ray Bourque .25 .60
51 Sergei Makarov .12 .30
52 Jim Johnson .12 .30
53 Troy Murray .12 .30
54 Shawn Burr .12 .30
55 Peter Ing .12 .30
56 Dale Hunter .12 .30
57 Tony Granato .10 .25
58 Curtis Leschyshyn .12 .30
59 Brian Mullen .12 .30
60 Ed Olczyk .12 .30
61 Mike Ramsey .12 .30
62 Dan Quinn .12 .30
63 Rich Sutter .12 .30
64 Terry Carkner .12 .30
65 Shayne Corson .12 .30
66 Peter Stastny .12 .30
67 Craig Muni .12 .30
68 Glenn Healy .15 .40

Card	Low	High
69 Phil Bourque	.12	.30
70 Pat Verbeek	.12	.30
71 Garry Galley	.12	.30
72 Dave Gagner	.12	.30
73 Bob Probert	.15	.40
74 Craig Wolanin	.12	.30
75 Patrick Roy	.40	1.00
76 Keith Brown	.12	.30
77 Gary Leeman	.12	.30
78 Brent Ashton	.12	.30
79 Randy Moller	.12	.30
80 Mike Vernon	.12	.30
81 Kelly Miller	.12	.30
82 Ulf Samuelsson	.12	.30
83 Todd Elik	.12	.30
84 Uwe Krupp	.12	.30
85 Rod Brind'Amour	.12	.30
86 Dave Capuano	.12	.30
87 Geoff Smith	.12	.30
88 David Volek	.12	.30
89 Bruce Driver	.12	.30
90 Andy Moog	.15	.40
91 Pelle Eklund	.12	.30
92 Joey Kocur	.10	.25
93 Mark Tinordi	.12	.30
94 Steve Thomas	.12	.30
95 Petr Svoboda	.12	.30
96 Joel Otto	.12	.30
97 Todd Krygier	.12	.30
98 Jaromir Jagr	.50	1.25
99 Mike Liut	.10	.25
100 Wayne Gretzky	1.00	2.50
101 Teppo Numminen	.12	.30
102 Randy Burridge	.12	.30
103 Michel Petit	.12	.30
104 Tony McKegney	.12	.30
105 Mathieu Schneider	.12	.30
106 Daren Puppa	.12	.30
107 Paul Cavallini	.12	.30
108 Tim Kerr	.10	.25
109 Kevin Lowe	.12	.30
110 Kirk Muller	.10	.25
111 Zarley Zalapski	.12	.30
112 Mike Hough	.12	.30
113 Ken Hodge Jr.	.12	.30
114 Grant Fuhr	.25	.60
115 Paul Coffey	.15	.40
116 Wendel Clark	.25	.60
117 Patrik Sundstrom	.12	.30
118 Kevin Dineen	.12	.30
119 Eric Desjardins	.15	.40
120 Mike Richter	.15	.40
121 Sergio Momesso	.12	.30
122 Tony Hrkac	.12	.30
123 Joe Reekie	.12	.30
124 Petr Nedved	.12	.30
125 Randy Carlyle	.12	.30
126 Kevin Miller	.12	.30
127 Rejean Lemelin	.10	.25
128 Dino Ciccarelli	.12	.30
129 Sylvain Cote	.12	.30
130 Mats Sundin	.15	.40
131 Eric Weinrich	.15	.40
132 Daniel Berthiaume	.12	.30
133 Keith Acton	.12	.30
134 Benoit Hogue	.12	.30
135 Mike Gartner	.20	.50
136 Petr Klima	.12	.30
137 Curt Giles	.15	.40
138 Scott Pearson	.12	.30
139 Luke Richardson	.12	.30
140 Steve Larmer	.12	.30
141 Ken Wregget	.12	.30
142 Frank Musil	.12	.30
143 Owen Nolan	.15	.40
144 Keith Primeau	.12	.30
145 Mark Recchi	.20	.50
146 Don Sweeney	.10	.25
147 Mike McPhee	.12	.30
148 Ken Baumgartner	.10	.25
149 Dave Lowry	.12	.30
150 Geoff Courtnall	.12	.30
151 Chris Terreri	.12	.30
152 Dave Manson	.12	.30
153 Bobby Holik	.15	.40
154 Bob Kudelski	.10	.25
155 Calle Johansson	.12	.30
156 Mark Hunter	.12	.30
157 Randy Gilhen	.12	.30
158 Yves Racine	.12	.30
159 Martin Gelinas	.12	.30
160 Brian Bellows	.12	.30
161 David Shaw	.12	.30
162 Bob Carpenter	.12	.30
163 Doug Brown	.12	.30
164 Ulf Dahlen	.12	.30
165 Denis Savard	.15	.40
166 Paul Ysebaert	.12	.30
167 Derek King	.10	.25
168 Igor Larionov	.12	.30
169 Bob Errey	.12	.30
170 Joe Nieuwendyk	.12	.30
171 Normand Rochefort	.12	.30
172 John Tonelli	.12	.30
173 David Reid	.10	.25
174 Tom Kurvers	.12	.30
175 Dimitri Khristich	.12	.30
176 Bob Sweeney	.10	.25
177 Rick Zombo	.12	.30
178 Troy Mallette	.12	.30
179 Bob Bassen	.12	.30
180 John Druce	.12	.30
181 Mike Craig	.12	.30
182 John McIntyre	.12	.30
183 Murray Baron	.12	.30
184 Slava Fetisov	.12	.30
185 Don Beaupre	.12	.30
186 Brian Benning	.12	.30
187 Dave Barr	.12	.30
188 Petri Skriko	.10	.25
189 Steve Konroyd	.12	.30
190 Steve Yzerman	.50	1.25
191 Jon Casey	.12	.30
192 Gary Nylund	.12	.30
193 Michal Pivonka	.12	.30
194 Alexei Kasatonov	.10	.25
195 Garry Valk	.12	.30
196 Darren Turcotte	.12	.30
197 Chris Nilan	.10	.25
198 Thomas Steen	.12	.30
199 Gary Roberts	.12	.30
200 Mario Lemieux	.60	1.50
201 Michel Goulet	.12	.30
202 Craig MacTavish	.12	.30
203 Peter Sidorkiewicz	.12	.30
204 Johan Garpenlov	.12	.30
205 Steve Duchesne	.10	.25
206 Dave Snuggerud	.10	.25
207 Kjell Samuelsson	.12	.30
208 Sylvain Turgeon	.12	.30
209 Al Iafrate	.12	.30
210 John MacLean	.12	.30
211 Brian Hayward	.12	.30
212 Cliff Ronning	.10	.25
213 Ray Sheppard	.12	.30
214 Dave Taylor	.12	.30
215 Doug Lidster	.12	.30
216 Peter Bondra	.15	.40
217 Marty McSorley	.12	.30
218 Doug Gilmour	.20	.50
219 Paul MacDermid	.12	.30
220 Jeremy Roenick	.25	.60
221 Wayne Presley	.12	.30
222 Jeff Norton	.12	.30
223 Brian Propp	.12	.30
224 Jimmy Carson	.12	.30
225 Tom Barrasso	.12	.30
226 Theo Fleury	.12	.30
227 Carey Wilson	.12	.30
228 Rod Langway	.12	.30
229 Bryan Trottier	.15	.40
230 James Patrick	.12	.30
231 Kelly Hrudey	.12	.30
232 Dave Poulin	.12	.30
233 Rob Ramage	.12	.30
234 Stephane Richer	.12	.30
235 Chris Chelios	.15	.40
236 Alexander Mogilny	.12	.30
237 Bryan Fogarty	.12	.30
238 Adam Oates	.15	.40
239 Ron Hextall	.15	.40
240 Bernie Nicholls	.12	.30
241 Esa Tikkanen	.12	.30
242 Jyrki Lumme	.12	.30
243 Brent Sutter	.12	.30
244 Gary Suter	.10	.25
245 Sean Burke	.15	.40
246 Rob Brown	.12	.30
247 Mike Modano	.30	.75
248 Kevin Stevens	.12	.30
249 Mike Lalor	.12	.30
250 Sergei Fedorov	.25	.60
251 Bob Essensa	.12	.30
252 Mark Howe	.15	.40
253 Craig Janney	.12	.30
254 Daniel Marois	.12	.30
255 Craig Simpson	.10	.25
256 Steve Kasper	.10	.25
257 Randy Velischek	.12	.30
258 Gino Cavallini	.12	.30
259 Dale Hawerchuk	.20	.50
260 Pat LaFontaine	.15	.40
261 Kirk McLean	.12	.30
262 Murray Craven	.12	.30
263 Robert Reichel	.30	.75
264 Jan Erixon	.12	.30
265 Adam Creighton	.12	.30
266 Mark Fitzpatrick	.12	.30
267 Ron Francis	.20	.50
268 Joe Mullen	.12	.30
269 Peter Zezel	.10	.25
270 Tomas Sandstrom	.12	.30
271 Phil Housley	.12	.30
272 Tim Cheveldae	.12	.30
273 Glen Wesley	.12	.30
274 Stephan Lebeau	.12	.30
275 Dave Ellett	.12	.30
276 Jeff Brown	.12	.30
277 Dave Andreychuk	.15	.40
278 Steven Finn	.10	.25
279 Scott Mellanby	.12	.30
280 Neal Broten	.12	.30
281 Randy Wood	.12	.30
282 Troy Gamble	.10	.25
283 Mike Ridley	.12	.30
284 Jamie Macoun	.12	.30
285 Mark Messier	.30	.75
286 Brendan Shanahan	.15	.40
287 Scott Young	.12	.30
288 Kelly Kisio	.12	.30
289 Brad Shaw	.10	.25
290 Ed Belfour	.40	1.00
291 Larry Robinson	.15	.40
292 Dave Christian	.10	.25
293 Steve Chiasson	.12	.30
294 Brian Skrudland	.12	.30
295 Pat Elynuik	.12	.30
296 Curtis Joseph	.20	.50
297 Doug Bodger	.12	.30
298 Ron Sutter	.12	.30
299 Joe Murphy	.12	.30
300 Vincent Damphousse	.12	.30
301 Cam Neely CC	.15	.40
302 Rick Tocchet CC	.12	.30
303 Scott Stevens CC	.15	.40
304 Ulf Samuelsson CC	.12	.30
305 Jeremy Roenick CC	.25	.60
306 The Hunter Brothers		
Dale Hunter		
Mark Hunter	.12	.30
307 The Broten Brothers		
Aaron Broten		
Neal Broten	.12	.30
308 The Cavallini Brothers		
Gino Cavallini		
Paul Cavallini	.12	.30
309 The Miller Brothers		
Kelly Miller		
Kevin Miller	.12	.30
310 Dennis Vaske TP	.12	.30
311 Rob Pearson RC	.15	.40
312 Jason Miller TP	.12	.30
313 John LeClair RC	.40	1.00
314 Bryan Marchment TP RC	.12	.30
315 Gary Shuchuk TP	.12	.30
316 Dominik Hasek RC	.50	1.25
317 Michel Picard TP RC	.15	.40
318 Corey Millen RC	.15	.40
319 Joe Sacco RC	.15	.40
320 Reggie Savage RC	.12	.30
321 Pat Murray TP	.12	.30
322 Myles O'Connor TP	.12	.30
323 Shawn Antoski TP	.12	.30
324 Geoff Sanderson RC	.15	.40
325 Chris Govedaris TP	.12	.30
326 Alexei Gusarov RC	.12	.30
327 Mike Sillinger TP	.12	.30
328 Bob Wilkie TP	.12	.30
329 Pat Jablonski RC	.12	.30
330 David Emma RC	.12	.30
331 Kirk Muller FP	.10	.25
332 Pat LaFontaine FP	.15	.40
333 Brian Leetch FP	.12	.30
334 Rick Tocchet FP	.12	.30
335 Mario Lemieux FP	.60	1.50
336 Joe Sakic FP	.50	1.25
337 Brett Hull FP	.30	.75
338 Vincent Damphousse FP	.12	.30
339 Trevor Linden FP	.15	.40
340 Kevin Hatcher FP	.12	.30
341 Pat Elynuik FP	.12	.30
342 Patrick Roy DT	.40	1.00
343 Brian Leetch DT	.12	.30
344 Ray Bourque DT	.25	.60
345 Luc Robitaille DT	.15	.40
346 Wayne Gretzky DT	1.00	2.50
347 Brett Hull DT	.30	.75
348 Ed Belfour ART	.40	1.00
349 Rob Blake ART	.15	.40
350 Eric Weinrich ART	.15	.40
351 Jaromir Jagr ART	.50	1.25
352 Sergei Fedorov ART	.25	.60
353 Ken Hodge Jr. ART	.12	.30
354 Eric Lindros ART	.25	.60
355 Eric Lindros Awards	.25	.60
356 Eric Lindros Number 1	.25	.60
357 Dana Murzyn	.12	.30
358 Adam Graves	.12	.30
359 Ken Linseman	.12	.30
360 Mike Keane	.10	.25
361 Stephane Morin	.12	.30
362 Grant Ledyard	.12	.30
363 Kris King	.12	.30
364 Paul Gillis	.12	.30
365 Chris Dahlquist	.12	.30
366 Paul Stanton	.12	.30
367 Jeff Hackett	.12	.30
368 Bob McGill	.12	.30
369 Neil Wilkinson	.12	.30
370 Rob Zettler	.12	.30
371 Brett Hull MOY	.30	.75
372 Paul Coffey 1000	.15	.40
373 Mark Messier 1000	.30	.75
374 Dave Taylor 1000	.12	.30
375 Michel Goulet 1000	.12	.30
376 Dale Hawerchuk 1000	.20	.50
377 The Turgeon Brothers		
Pierre Turgeon		
Sylvain Turgeon	.12	.30
378 The Sutter Brothers		
Rich Sutter		
Brian Sutter		
Ron Sutter	.12	.30
379 The Mullen Brothers		
Brian Mullen		
Joe Mullen	.12	.30
380 The Courtnall Brothers		
Geoff Courtnall		
Russ Courtnall	.12	.30
381 Trevor Kidd TP	.12	.30
382 Patrice Brisebois TP	.10	.25
383 Mark Greig TP	.12	.30
384 Kip Miller TP	.12	.30
385 Drake Berehowsky TP	.12	.30
386 Kevin Haller RC	.15	.40
387 Dave Gagnon TP	.12	.30
388 Jason Marshall TP	.12	.30
389 Donald Audette TP	.12	.30
390 Patrick Lebeau RC	.12	.30
391 Alexander Godynyuk TP	.15	.40
392 Jarrod Skalde TP RC	.12	.30
393 Ken Sutton RC	.15	.40
394 Sergei Kharin TP	.12	.30
395 Andre Racicot TP RC	.12	.30
396 Doug Weight RC	.40	1.00
397 Kevin Todd RC	.15	.40
398 Tony Amonte TP RC	.40	1.00
399 Kimbi Daniels TP	.15	.40
400 Jeff Daniels RC	.12	.30
401 Guy Lafleur	.20	.50
402 Guy Lafleur	.20	.50
403 Guy Lafleur	.20	.50
404 Brett Hull SL	.30	.75
405 Wayne Gretzky SL	1.00	2.50
406 Wayne Gretzky SL	1.00	2.50
407 Theo Fleury SL		
Marty McSorley SL	.12	.30
408 Sergei Fedorov SL	.25	.60
409 Al MacInnis SL	.20	.50
410 Ed Belfour SL	.40	1.00
411 Ed Belfour SL	.40	1.00
412 Brett Hull 50/50	.30	.75
413 Wayne Gretzky 700th	1.00	2.50
414 San Jose Sharks Logo	.10	.25
415 Ray Bourque FP	.25	.60
416 Pierre Turgeon FP	.12	.30
417 Al MacInnis FP	.20	.50
418 Jeremy Roenick FP	.25	.60
419 Steve Yzerman FP	.50	1.25
420 Mark Messier FP	.30	.75
421 John Cullen FP	.12	.30
422 Wayne Gretzky FP	1.00	2.50
423 Mike Modano FP	.30	.75
424 Patrick Roy FP	.40	1.00
425 Stanley Cup Champs	.60	1.50
426 Mario Lemieux Smythe	.60	1.50
427 Wayne Gretzky Ross	1.00	2.50
428 Brett Hull Hart	.30	.75
429 Ray Bourque Norris	.25	.60
430 Ed Belfour Calder	.40	1.00
431 Ed Belfour Vezina	.40	1.00
432 Dirk Graham Selke	.12	.30
433 Ed Belfour Jennings	.40	1.00
434 Wayne Gretzky Byng	1.00	2.50
435 Dave Taylor Masterton Tr.	.12	.30
436 Randy Ladouceur	.12	.30
437 Dave Tippett	.12	.30
438 Clint Malarchuk	.12	.30
439 Gordie Roberts	.12	.30
440 Frank Pietrangelo	.12	.30

1991-92 Score Canadian Bilingual

Card	Low	High
1 Brett Hull	.30	.75
2 Al MacInnis	.20	.50
3 Luc Robitaille	.15	.40
4 Pierre Turgeon	.12	.30
5 Brian Leetch	.12	.30
6 Cam Neely	.15	.40
7 John Cullen	.12	.30
8 Trevor Linden	.15	.40
9 Rick Tocchet	.12	.30
10 John Vanbiesbrouck	.15	.40
11 Steve Smith	.15	.40
12 Doug Smail	.12	.30
13 Craig Ludwig	.12	.30
14 Paul Fenton	.12	.30
15 Dirk Graham	.12	.30
16 Brad McCrimmon	.12	.30
17 Dean Evason	.12	.30
18 Fredrik Olausson	.12	.30
19 Guy Carbonneau	.12	.30
20 Kevin Hatcher	.12	.30
21 Paul Ranheim	.15	.40
22 Claude Lemieux	.12	.30
23 Vincent Riendeau	.12	.30
24 Garth Butcher	.12	.30
25 Joe Sakic	.50	1.25
26 Rick Vaive	.10	.25
27 Rob Blake	.15	.40
28 Mike Ricci	.10	.25
29 Pat Flatley	.12	.30
30 Bill Ranford	.12	.30
31 Larry Murphy	.12	.30
32 Bobby Smith	.12	.30
33 Mike Krushelnyski	.12	.30
34 Gerard Gallant	.10	.25
35 Doug Wilson	.12	.30
36 John Ogrodnick	.12	.30
37 Mikhail Tatarinov	.12	.30
38 Doug Crossman	.12	.30
39 Mark Osborne	.12	.30
40 Scott Stevens	.15	.40
41 Ron Tugnutt	.12	.30
42 Russ Courtnall	.12	.30
43 Gord Murphy	.12	.30
44 Greg Adams	.12	.30
45 Christian Ruuttu	.12	.30
46 Ken Daneyko	.12	.30
47 Glenn Anderson	.12	.30
48 Ray Ferraro	.12	.30
49 Tony Tanti	.12	.30
50 Ray Bourque	.25	.60
51 Sergei Makarov	.12	.30
52 Jim Johnson	.12	.30
53 Troy Murray	.12	.30
54 Shawn Burr	.12	.30
55 Peter Ing	.12	.30
56 Dale Hunter	.12	.30
57 Tony Granato	.10	.25
58 Curtis Leschyshyn	.12	.30
59 Brian Mullen	.12	.30
60 Ed Olczyk	.12	.30
61 Mike Ramsey	.12	.30
62 Dan Quinn	.12	.30
63 Rich Sutter	.12	.30
64 Terry Carkner	.12	.30
65 Shayne Corson	.12	.30
66 Peter Stastny	.12	.30
67 Craig Muni	.12	.30
68 Glenn Healy	.15	.40
69 Phil Bourque	.12	.30
70 Pat Verbeek	.12	.30
71 Garry Galley	.12	.30
72 Dave Gagner	.12	.30
73 Bob Probert	.15	.40
74 Craig Wolanin	.12	.30
75 Patrick Roy	.40	1.00
76 Keith Brown	.12	.30
77 Gary Leeman	.12	.30
78 Brent Ashton	.12	.30
79 Randy Moller	.12	.30
80 Mike Vernon	.12	.30
81 Kelly Miller	.12	.30
82 Ulf Samuelsson	.12	.30
83 Todd Elik	.12	.30
84 Uwe Krupp	.12	.30
85 Rod Brind'Amour	.12	.30
86 Dave Capuano	.12	.30
87 Geoff Smith	.12	.30
88 David Volek	.12	.30
89 Bruce Driver	.12	.30
90 Andy Moog	.15	.40
91 Pelle Eklund	.12	.30
92 Joey Kocur	.10	.25
93 Mark Tinordi	.12	.30
94 Steve Thomas	.12	.30
95 Petr Svoboda	.12	.30
96 Joel Otto	.12	.30
97 Todd Krygier	.12	.30
98 Jaromir Jagr	.50	1.25
99 Mike Liut	.10	.25
100 Wayne Gretzky	1.00	2.50
101 Teppo Numminen	.12	.30
102 Randy Burridge	.12	.30
103 Michel Petit	.12	.30
104 Tony McKegney	.12	.30
105 Mathieu Schneider	.12	.30
106 Daren Puppa	.12	.30
107 Paul Cavallini	.12	.30
108 Tim Kerr	.10	.25
109 Kevin Lowe	.12	.30
110 Kirk Muller	.10	.25
111 Zarley Zalapski	.12	.30
112 Mike Hough	.12	.30
113 Ken Hodge Jr.	.12	.30
114 Grant Fuhr	.25	.60
115 Paul Coffey	.15	.40
116 Wendel Clark	.25	.60
117 Patrik Sundstrom	.12	.30
118 Kevin Dineen	.12	.30
119 Eric Desjardins	.15	.40
120 Mike Richter	.15	.40
121 Sergio Momesso	.12	.30
122 Tony Hrkac	.12	.30
123 Joe Reekie	.12	.30
124 Petr Nedved	.12	.30
125 Randy Carlyle	.12	.30
126 Kevin Miller	.12	.30
127 Rejean Lemelin	.10	.25
128 Dino Ciccarelli	.12	.30
129 Sylvain Cote	.12	.30
130 Mats Sundin	.15	.40
131 Eric Weinrich	.15	.40
132 Daniel Berthiaume	.12	.30
133 Keith Acton	.12	.30
134 Benoit Hogue	.12	.30
135 Mike Gartner	.20	.50
136 Petr Klima	.12	.30
137 Curt Giles	.15	.40
138 Scott Pearson	.12	.30
139 Luke Richardson	.12	.30
140 Steve Larmer	.12	.30
141 Ken Wregget	.12	.30
142 Frank Musil	.12	.30
143 Owen Nolan	.15	.40
144 Keith Primeau	.12	.30
145 Mark Recchi	.20	.50
146 Don Sweeney	.10	.25
147 Mike McPhee	.12	.30
148 Ken Baumgartner	.10	.25
149 Dave Lowry	.12	.30
150 Geoff Courtnall	.12	.30
151 Chris Terreri	.12	.30
152 Dave Manson	.12	.30
153 Bobby Holik	.15	.40
154 Bob Kudelski	.10	.25
155 Calle Johansson	.12	.30
156 Mark Hunter	.12	.30
157 Randy Gilhen	.12	.30
158 Yves Racine	.12	.30
159 Martin Gelinas	.12	.30
160 Brian Bellows	.12	.30
161 David Shaw	.12	.30
162 Bob Carpenter	.12	.30
163 Doug Brown	.12	.30
164 Ulf Dahlen	.12	.30
165 Denis Savard	.15	.40
166 Paul Ysebaert	.12	.30
167 Derek King	.10	.25
168 Igor Larionov	.12	.30
169 Bob Errey	.12	.30
170 Joe Nieuwendyk	.12	.30
171 Normand Rochefort	.12	.30
172 John Tonelli	.12	.30
173 David Reid	.10	.25
174 Tom Kurvers	.12	.30
175 Dimitri Khristich	.12	.30
176 Bob Sweeney	.10	.25
177 Rick Zombo	.12	.30
178 Troy Mallette	.12	.30
179 Bob Bassen	.12	.30
180 John Druce	.12	.30
181 Mike Craig	.12	.30
182 John McIntyre	.12	.30
183 Murray Baron	.12	.30
184 Slava Fetisov	.12	.30
185 Don Beaupre	.12	.30
186 Brian Benning	.12	.30
187 Dave Barr	.12	.30
188 Petri Skriko	.10	.25
189 Steve Konroyd	.12	.30
190 Steve Yzerman	.50	1.25
191 Jon Casey	.12	.30
192 Gary Nylund	.12	.30
193 Michal Pivonka	.12	.30
194 Alexei Kasatonov	.10	.25
195 Garry Valk	.12	.30
196 Darren Turcotte	.12	.30
197 Chris Nilan	.10	.25
198 Thomas Steen	.12	.30
199 Gary Roberts	.12	.30
200 Mario Lemieux	.60	1.50
201 Michel Goulet	.12	.30
202 Craig MacTavish	.12	.30
203 Peter Sidorkiewicz	.12	.30
204 Johan Garpenlov	.12	.30
205 Steve Duchesne	.10	.25
206 Dave Snuggerud	.10	.25
207 Kjell Samuelsson	.12	.30
208 Sylvain Turgeon	.12	.30
209 Al Iafrate	.12	.30
210 John MacLean	.12	.30
211 Brian Hayward	.12	.30
212 Cliff Ronning	.10	.25
213 Ray Sheppard	.12	.30
214 Dave Taylor	.12	.30
215 Doug Lidster	.12	.30
216 Peter Bondra	.15	.40
217 Marty McSorley	.12	.30
218 Doug Gilmour	.20	.50
219 Paul MacDermid	.12	.30
220 Jeremy Roenick	.25	.60
221 Wayne Presley	.12	.30
222 Jeff Norton	.12	.30
223 Brian Propp	.12	.30
224 Jimmy Carson	.12	.30
225 Tom Barrasso	.12	.30
226 Theo Fleury	.12	.30
227 Carey Wilson	.12	.30
228 Rod Langway	.12	.30
229 Bryan Trottier	.15	.40
230 James Patrick	.12	.30
231 Dana Murzyn	.12	.30
232 Rick Wamsley	.10	.25
233 Dave McLlwain	.12	.30
234 Tom Fergus	.10	.25
235 Adam Graves	.12	.30
236 Jacques Cloutier	.12	.30
237 Gino Odjick	.10	.25
238 Andrew Cassels	.12	.30
239 Ken Linseman	.12	.30
240 Danton Cole	.10	.25
241 Dave Hannan	.12	.30
242 Stephane Matteau	.12	.30
243 Gerald Diduck	.12	.30
244 Rick Tabaracci	.12	.30
245 Sylvain Lefebvre	.12	.30
246 Bob Rouse	.12	.30
247 Charlie Huddy	.12	.30
248 Mike Foligno	.15	.40
249 Ric Nattress	.12	.30
250 Aaron Broten	.12	.30
251 Mike Keane	.10	.25
252 Steve Bozek	.12	.30
253 Jeff Beukeboom	.12	.30
254 Stephane Morin	.12	.30
255 Brian Bradley	.12	.30
256 Scott Arniel	.10	.25
257 Robert Kron	.12	.30
258 Anatoli Semenov	.12	.30
259 Brent Gilchrist	.12	.30
260 Jim Sandlak	.12	.30
261 Brett Hull MOY	.30	.75
262 Paul Coffey 1000 PTS	.15	.40
263 Mark Messier 1000 PTS	.30	.75
264 Dave Taylor 1000 PTS	.12	.30
265 Michel Goulet 1000 PTS	.12	.30
266 Dale Hawerchuk 1000 PTS	.20	.50
267 Turgeon Bros.	.12	.30
268 Sutter Bros.	.12	.30
269 Mullen Bros.	.12	.30
270 Courtnall Bros.	.12	.30
271 Trevor Kidd TP	.12	.30
272 Patrice Brisebois TP	.10	.25
273 Mark Greig TP	.12	.30
274 Kip Miller TP	.12	.30
275 Drake Berehowsky TP	.12	.30
276 Kevin Haller RC	.15	.40
277 Dave Gagnon TP	.12	.30
278 Jason Marshall TP	.12	.30
279 Donald Audette TP	.12	.30
280 Patrick Lebeau RC	.12	.30
281 Alexander Godynyuk TP	.15	.40
282 Jarrod Skalde TP RC	.12	.30
283 Ken Sutton RC	.15	.40
284 Sergei Kharin TP	.12	.30
285 Andre Racicot TP RC	.12	.30
286 Doug Weight RC	.40	1.00
287 Kevin Todd RC	.15	.40
288 Tony Amonte TP RC	.40	1.00
289 Kimbi Daniels TP	.15	.40
290 Jeff Daniels RC	.12	.30
291 Guy Lafleur	.20	.50
292 Guy Lafleur	.20	.50
293 Guy Lafleur	.20	.50
294 Brett Hull SL	.30	.75
295 Wayne Gretzky SL	1.00	2.50
296 Wayne Gretzky SL	.60	2.50
297 Theo Fleury		
Marty McSorley SL	.12	.30
298 Sergei Fedorov SL	.25	.60
299 Al MacInnis SL	.20	.50
300 Ed Belfour SL	.40	1.00
301 Ed Belfour SL	.40	1.00
302 Brett Hull 50/50	.30	.75
303 Wayne Gretzky 700th	.60	2.50
304 San Jose Sharks Logo	.05	.15
305 Cam Neely Crunch	.15	.40
306 Rick Tocchet Crunch	.12	.30
307 Scott Stevens Crunch	.15	.40
308 Ulf Samuelsson Crunch	.12	.30
309 Jeremy Roenick Crunch	.25	.60
310 Mark Messier FRAN	.30	.75
311 John Cullen FRAN	.12	.30
312 Wayne Gretzky FRAN	.60	2.50
313 Mike Modano FRAN	.30	.75
314 Patrick Roy FRAN	.40	1.00
315 Stanley Cup Champs	.60	1.50
316 Mario Lemieux Smythe	.60	1.50
317 Wayne Gretzky Ross	.60	2.50
318 Brett Hull Hart	.30	.75
319 Ray Bourque Norris	.25	.60
320 Ed Belfour Calder	.40	1.00
321 Ed Belfour Vezina	.40	1.00
322 Dirk Graham Selke	.12	.30
323 Ed Belfour Jennings	.40	1.00
324 Wayne Gretzky Byng	.60	2.50
325 Dave Taylor Masterton	.12	.30
326 Jeff Hackett	.12	.30
327 Bob McGill	.12	.30
328 Neil Wilkinson	.12	.30
329 Eric Lindros Draft	.25	.60
330 Eric Lindros Medals	.25	.60
331 Ray Bourque FP	.25	.60
332 Pierre Turgeon FP	.12	.30
333 Al MacInnis FP	.20	.50
334 Jeremy Roenick FP	.25	.60
335 Steve Yzerman FP	.50	1.25
336 Hunter Bros.	.12	.30
337 Broten Bros.	.12	.30
338 Cavallini Bros.	.12	.30
339 Miller Bros.	.12	.30
340 Dennis Vaske TP	.12	.30
341 Rob Pearson RC	.15	.40
342 Jason Miller TP	.12	.30
343 John LeClair RC	.40	1.00
344 Bryan Marchment TP RC	.12	.30
345 Gary Shuchuk TP	.12	.30
346 Dominik Hasek RC	.50	1.25
347 Michel Picard TP RC	.15	.40
348 Corey Millen RC	.15	.40
349 Joe Sacco RC	.15	.40
350 Reggie Savage RC	.12	.30
351 Pat Murray TP	.12	.30
352 Myles O'Connor TP	.12	.30
353 Shawn Antoski TP	.12	.30
354 Geoff Sanderson RC	.15	.40
355 Chris Govedaris TP	.12	.30
356 Alexei Gusarov RC	.12	.30
357 Mike Sillinger TP	.12	.30
358 Bob Wilkie TP	.12	.30
359 Pat Jablonski RC	.12	.30
360 Memorial Cup		
Spokane Chiefs	.05	.14
361 Kirk Muller FP	.10	.25
362 Pat LaFontaine FP	.15	.40
363 Brian Leetch FP	.12	.30
364 Rick Tocchet FP	.12	.30
365 Mario Lemieux FP	.60	1.50
366 Joe Sakic FP	.50	1.25
367 Brett Hull FP	.30	.75
368 Vincent Damphousse FP	.12	.30
369 Trevor Linden FP	.15	.40
370 Kevin Hatcher FP	.12	.30
371 Pat Elynuik FP	.12	.30
372 Patrick Roy DT	.40	1.00
373 Brian Leetch DT	.12	.30
374 Ray Bourque DT	.25	.60
375 Luc Robitaille DT	.15	.40
376 Wayne Gretzky DT	1.00	2.50
377 Brett Hull DT	.30	.75
378 Ed Belfour ART	.40	1.00
379 Rob Blake ART	.15	.40
380 Eric Weinrich ART	.15	.40
381 Jaromir Jagr ART	.50	1.25
382 Sergei Fedorov ART	.25	.60
383 Ken Hodge Jr. ART	.12	.30
384 Eric Lindros Art	.25	.60
385 E.Lindros/R.Pearson	.25	.60
386 Ottawa/Tampa Bay	.07	.20
387 Mick Vukota	.12	.30
388 Lou Franceschetti	.12	.30
389 Mike Hudson	.12	.30
390 Frantisek Kucera	.12	.30
391 Basil McRae	.10	.25
392 Donald Dufresne	.12	.30
393 Tommy Albelin	.10	.25
394 Normand Lacombe	.12	.30
395 Lucien DeBlois	.12	.30
396 Tony Twist RC	.10	.25
397 Rob Murphy	.10	.25
398 Ken Sabourin	.12	.30
399 Doug Evans	.10	.25
400 Walt Poddubny	.10	.25
401 Grant Ledyard	.12	.30
402 Kris King	.12	.30
403 Paul Gillis	.12	.30
404 Chris Dahlquist	.12	.30
405 Zdeno Ciger	.12	.30
406 Paul Stanton	.12	.30
407 Randy Ladouceur	.12	.30
408 Ronnie Stern	.12	.30
409 Dave Tippett	.12	.30
410 Jeff Reese	.12	.30
411 Vladimir Ruzicka	.12	.30
412 Brent Fedyk	.12	.30
413 Paul Cyr	.12	.30
414 Mike Eagles	.12	.30
415 Chris Joseph	.12	.30
416 Brad Marsh	.15	.40
417 Rich Pilon	.12	.30
418 Jiri Hrdina	.12	.30
419 Clint Malarchuk	.12	.30
420 Steven Rice	.12	.30
421 Mark Janssens	.12	.30
422 Gordie Roberts	.12	.30
423 Shawn Cronin	.12	.30
424 Randy Cunneyworth	.12	.30
425 Frank Pietrangelo	.12	.30
426 David Maley	.12	.30
427 Rod Buskas	.12	.30
428 Dennis Vial	.10	.25
429 Kelly Buchberger	.12	.30
430 Wes Walz	.12	.30
431 Dean Kennedy	.12	.30
432 Nick Kypreos	.12	.30
433 Stewart Gavin	.12	.30
434 Norm Maciver RC	.15	.40
435 Mark Pederson	.12	.30
436 Laurie Boschman	.12	.30
437 Stephane Quintal	.12	.30
438 Darrin Shannon	.12	.30
439 Trent Yawney	.12	.30
440 Gaetan Duchesne	.10	.25
441 Joe Cirella	.12	.30
442 Doug Houda	.12	.30
443 Dave Chyzowski	.10	.25
444 Derrick Smith	.12	.30
445 Jeff Lazaro	.12	.30
446 Brian Glynn	.12	.30
447 Jocelyn Lemieux	.12	.30
448 Peter Taglianetti	.10	.25
449 Adam Burt	.12	.30
450 Hubie McDonough	.12	.30
451 Kelly Hrudey	.12	.30
452 Dave Poulin	.12	.30
453 Mark Hardy	.12	.30
454 Mike Hartman	.12	.30
455 Chris Chelios	.15	.40
456 Alexander Mogilny	.12	.30
457 Bryan Fogarty	.12	.30
458 Adam Oates	.15	.40
459 Ron Hextall	.15	.40
460 Bernie Nicholls	.12	.30
461 Esa Tikkanen	.12	.30
462 Jyrki Lumme	.12	.30
463 Brent Sutter	.12	.30
464 Gary Suter	.10	.25
465 Sean Burke	.15	.40
466 Rob Brown	.12	.30
467 Mike Modano	.30	.75
468 Kevin Stevens	.12	.30
469 Mike Lalor	.12	.30
470 Sergei Fedorov	.25	.60
471 Bob Essensa	.12	.30
472 Mark Howe	.15	.40
473 Craig Janney	.12	.30
474 Daniel Marois	.12	.30
475 Craig Simpson	.10	.25
476 Marc Bureau	.12	.30
477 Randy Velischek	.12	.30
478 Gino Cavallini	.12	.30
479 Dale Hawerchuk	.20	.50
480 Pat LaFontaine	.15	.40
481 Kirk McLean	.12	.30
482 Murray Craven	.12	.30
483 Robert Reichel	.30	.75
484 Jan Erixon	.12	.30
485 Adam Creighton	.12	.30
486 Mark Fitzpatrick	.12	.30
487 Ron Francis	.20	.50
488 Joe Mullen	.12	.30
489 Peter Zezel	.10	.25
490 Tomas Sandstrom	.12	.30
491 Phil Housley	.12	.30
492 Tim Cheveldae	.12	.30
493 Glen Wesley	.12	.30
494 Stephan Lebeau	.12	.30
495 Dave Ellett	.12	.30

496 Jeff Brown .12 .30
497 Dave Andreychuk .15 .40
498 Steven Finn .10 .25
499 Mike Donnelly RC .15 .40
500 Neal Broten .12 .30
501 Randy Wood .12 .30
502 Troy Gamble .10 .25
503 Mike Ridley .12 .30
504 Jamie Macoun .12 .30
505 Mark Messier .30 .75
506 Moe Mantha .12 .30
507 Scott Young .12 .30
508 Robert Dirk .12 .30
509 Brad Shaw .10 .25
510 Ed Belfour .40 1.00
511 Larry Robinson .15 .40
512 Dale Kushner .12 .30
513 Steve Chiasson .12 .30
514 Brian Skrudland .12 .30
515 Pat Elynuik .12 .30
516 Curtis Joseph .20 .50
517 Doug Bodger .12 .30
518 Greg Brown .10 .25
519 Joe Murphy .12 .30
520 J.J. Daigneault .10 .25
521 Todd Gill .12 .30
522 Troy Loney .10 .25
523 Tim Watters .10 .25
524 Jody Hull .10 .25
525 Colin Patterson .12 .30
526 Darin Kimble .12 .30
527 Perry Berezan .12 .30
528 Lee Norwood .10 .25
529 Mike Peluso .12 .30
530 Wayne McBean .10 .25
531 Grant Jennings .12 .30
532 Claude Loiselle .12 .30
533 Ron Wilson .12 .30
534 Phil Sykes .12 .30
535 Jim Wiemer .12 .30
536 Herb Raglan .12 .30
537 Tim Hunter .12 .30
538 Mike Tomlak .12 .30
539 Greg Gilbert .12 .30
540 Jiri Latal .10 .25
541 Bill Berg .12 .30
542 Shane Churla .10 .25
543 Jay Miller .12 .30
544 Pete Peeters .10 .25
545 Alan May .12 .30
546 Mario Marois .12 .30
547 Jim Kyte .12 .30
548 Jon Morris .12 .30
549 Mikko Makela .12 .30
550 Nelson Emerson .12 .30
551 Doug Wilson .12 .30
552 Brian Mullen .12 .30
553 Kelly Kisio .12 .30
554 Brian Hayward .12 .30
555 Tony Hrkac .12 .30
556 Steve Bozek .12 .30
557 John Carter .12 .30
558 Neil Wilkinson .12 .30
559 Wayne Presley .12 .30
560 Bob McGill .12 .30
561 Craig Ludwig .12 .30
562 Mikhail Tatarinov .12 .30
563 Todd Elik .12 .30
564 Randy Burridge .12 .30
565 Tim Kerr .12 .30
566 Randy Gilhen .12 .30
567 John Tonelli .12 .30
568 Tom Kurvers .12 .30
569 Steve Duchesne .10 .25
570 Charlie Huddy .12 .30
571 Alan Kerr .12 .30
572 Shawn Chambers .10 .25
573 Rob Ramage .12 .30
574 Steve Kasper .10 .25
575 Scott Mellanby .12 .30
576 Stephen Leach .12 .30
577 Scott Niedermayer .15 .40
578 Craig Berube .12 .30
579 Greg Paslawski .12 .30
580 Randy Hillier .12 .30
581 Stephane Richer .12 .30
582 Brian MacLellan .12 .30
583 Marc Habscheid .12 .30
584 Dave Babych .12 .30
585 Troy Murray .12 .30
586 Ray Sheppard .12 .30
587 Glen Featherstone .10 .25
588 Brendan Shanahan .15 .40
589 Dave Christian .10 .25
590 Mike Bullard .12 .30
591 Ryan Walter .12 .30
592 Doug Smail .12 .30
593 Paul Fenton .12 .30
594 Adam Graves .12 .30
595 Scott Stevens .15 .40
596 Sylvain Cote .12 .30
597 Dave Barr .12 .30
598 Randy Gregg .12 .30
599 Allen Pedersen .10 .25
600 Jari Kurri .12 .30
601 Troy Mallette .12 .30
602 Troy Crowder .12 .30
603 Brad Jones .12 .30
604 Randy McKay .12 .30
605 Scott Thornton .12 .30
606 Bryan Marchment RC .12 .30
607 Andrew Cassels .12 .30
608 Grant Fuhr .25 .60
609 Vincent Damphousse .12 .30
610 Robert Ray .10 .25
611 Glenn Anderson .12 .30
612 Peter Ing .12 .30
613 Tom Chorske .12 .30
614 Kirk Muller .10 .25
615 Dan Quinn .10 .25
616 Murray Baron .12 .30
617 Sergei Nemchinov .12 .30
618 Rod Brind'Amour .12 .30
619 Ron Sutter .12 .30
620 Luke Richardson .12 .30
621 Nicklas Lidstrom RC .60 1.50
622 Ken Linseman .12 .30
623 Steve Smith .15 .40
624 Dave Manson .12 .30
625 Kay Whitmore .12 .30
626 Jeff Chychrun .10 .25
627 Russ Romaniuk RC .12 .30
628 Brad May .12 .30
629 Tomas Forslund RC .15 .40
630 Stu Barnes .12 .30
631 Darryl Sydor .12 .30
632 Jimmy Waite .12 .30
633 Peter Douris .12 .30
634 Dave Brown .10 .25
635 Mark Messier .30 .75
636 Neil Sheehy .12 .30
637 Todd Krygier .12 .30
638 Stephane Beauregard .10 .25
639 Barry Pederson .12 .30
640 Pat Falloon .12 .30
641 Dean Evason .12 .30
642 Jeff Hackett .12 .30
643 Rob Zettler .12 .30
644 David Bruce RC .15 .40
645 Pat MacLeod RC .15 .40
646 Craig Coxe .10 .25
647 Ken Hammond RC .12 .30
648 Brian Lawton .12 .30
649 Perry Anderson .12 .30
650 Kevin Evans .10 .25
651 Mike McHugh .12 .30
652 Mark Lamb .10 .25
653 Darcy Wakaluk RC .15 .40
654 Pat Conacher .12 .30
655 Martin Lapointe .12 .30
656 Derian Hatcher .12 .30
657 Bryan Erickson .12 .30
658 Ken Priestlay .12 .30
659 Vladimir Konstantinov RC .40 1.00
660 Andrei Lomakin .12 .30

1991-92 Score Canadian English

*CANADIAN ENGLISH: .4X TO 1X BASIC CARDS

1991-92 Score Bobby Orr

COMPLETE SET (6) 20.00 40.00
COMMON ORR (1-6) 3.00 8.00
AU Bobby Orr AU/2500* 200.00 500.00

1991-92 Score Eric Lindros

COMPLETE SET (3) 6.00 15.00
COMMON LINDROS (1-3) 2.00 5.00

1991-92 Score Hot Cards

1 Eric Lindros .60 1.50
2 Wayne Gretzky 3.00 8.00
3 Brett Hull 1.00 2.50
4 Sergei Fedorov .60 1.50
5 Mario Lemieux 2.50 6.00
6 Adam Oates .60 1.50
7 Theo Fleury .40 1.00
8 Jaromir Jagr 2.00 5.00
9 Ed Belfour .60 1.50
10 Jeremy Roenick .60 1.50

1991-92 Score Rookie Traded

1T Doug Wilson .12 .30
2T Brian Mullen .12 .30
3T Kelly Kisio .12 .30
4T Brian Hayward .12 .30
5T Tony Hrkac .12 .30
6T Steve Bozek .12 .30
7T John Carter .12 .30
8T Neil Wilkinson .12 .30
9T Wayne Presley .12 .30
10T Bob McGill .12 .30
11T Craig Ludwig .12 .30
12T Mikhail Tatarinov .12 .30
13T Todd Elik .10 .25
14T Randy Burridge .12 .30
15T Tim Kerr .10 .25
16T Randy Gilhen .12 .30
17T John Tonelli .12 .30
18T Tom Kurvers .12 .30
19T Steve Duchesne .10 .25
20T Charlie Huddy .12 .30
21T Adam Creighton .12 .30
22T Brent Ashton .12 .30
23T Rob Ramage .12 .30
24T Steve Kasper .10 .25
25T Scott Mellanby .12 .30
26T Stephen Leach .12 .30
27T Scott Niedermayer .15 .40
28T Craig Berube .12 .30
29T Greg Paslawski .12 .30
30T Randy Hillier .12 .30
31T Stephane Richer .12 .30
32T Brian MacLellan .12 .30
33T Marc Habscheid .12 .30
34T Dave Babych .12 .30
35T Troy Murray .12 .30
36T Ray Sheppard .12 .30
37T Glen Featherstone .10 .25
38T Brendan Shanahan .15 .40
39T Dave Christian .10 .25
40T Mike Bullard .12 .30
41T Ryan Walter .12 .30
42T Randy Wood .12 .30
43T Vincent Riendeau .12 .30
44T Adam Graves .12 .30
45T Scott Stevens .15 .40
46T Sylvain Cote .12 .30
47T Dave Barr .12 .30
48T Randy Gregg .12 .30
49T Pavel Bure .15 .40
50T Jari Kurri .12 .30
51T Steve Thomas .12 .30
52T Troy Crowder .12 .30
53T Brad Jones .12 .30
54T Randy McKay .12 .30
55T Scott Thornton .12 .30
56T Bryan Marchment .12 .30
57T Andrew Cassels .12 .30
58T Grant Fuhr .25 .60
59T Vincent Damphousse .12 .30
60T Rick Zombo .12 .30
61T Glenn Anderson .12 .30
62T Peter Ing .12 .30
63T Tom Chorske .12 .30
64T Kirk Muller .10 .25
65T Dan Quinn .10 .25
66T Murray Baron .12 .30
67T Sergei Nemchinov .12 .30
68T Rod Brind'Amour .12 .30
69T Ron Sutter .12 .30
70T Luke Richardson .12 .30
71T Nicklas Lidstrom RC .60 1.50
72T Petri Skriko .10 .25
73T Steve Smith .15 .40
74T Dave Manson .12 .30
75T Kay Whitmore .12 .30
76T Valeri Kamensky RC .40 1.00
77T Russ Romaniuk RC .15 .40
78T Brad May .12 .30
79T Tomas Forslund RC .15 .40
80T Stu Barnes .12 .30
81T Darryl Sydor .12 .30
82T Jimmy Waite .12 .30
83T Vladimir Ruzicka .12 .30
84T Dave Brown .10 .25
85T Mark Messier .30 .75
86T Neil Sheehy .12 .30
87T Todd Krygier .12 .30
88T Eric Lindros .25 .60
89T Nelson Emerson .12 .30
90T Pat Falloon .12 .30
91T Dean Evason .12 .30
92T Jeff Hackett .12 .30
93T Rob Zettler .12 .30
94T Perry Berezan .12 .30
95T Pat MacLeod RC .15 .40
96T Craig Coxe .10 .25
97T Ken Hammond RC .15 .40
98T Brian Lawton .12 .30
99T Perry Anderson .12 .30
100T Pat LaFontaine .15 .40
101T Pierre Turgeon .12 .30
102T Dave McLlwain .12 .30
103T Brent Sutter .12 .30
104T Uwe Krupp .12 .30
105T Martin Lapointe .12 .30
106T Derian Hatcher .12 .30
107T Darrin Shannon .12 .30
108T Benoit Hogue .12 .30
109T Vladimir Konstantinov RC .40 1.00
110T Andrei Lomakin .12 .30

1991-92 Score Kellogg's

COMPLETE SET (24) 14.00 35.00
1 Patrick Roy 3.00 8.00
2 Rick Tocchet .40 1.00
3 Wendel Clark .40 1.00
4 Mike Modano .75 2.00
5 Jeremy Roenick .60 1.50
6 Pierre Turgeon .40 1.00
7 Kevin Hatcher .20 .50
8 Brian Leetch .60 1.50
9 Mark Recchi .40 1.00
10 Andy Moog .40 1.00
11 Kevin Dineen .20 .50
12 Joe Sakic 1.25 3.00
13 John MacLean .20 .50
14 Steve Yzerman 2.00 5.00
15 Pat LaFontaine .40 1.00
16 Al MacInnis .40 1.00
17 Petr Klima .20 .50
18 Ed Olczyk .20 .50
19 Doug Wilson .20 .50
20 Trevor Linden .20 .50
21 Brett Hull .75 2.00
22 Rob Blake .20 .50
23 Dave Ellett .20 .50
24 Cornelius Rooster SP
Kellogg's mascot .75 2.00
NNO Card Binder 2.00 5.00

1991-92 Score Young Superstars

1 Sergei Fedorov .25 .60
2 Mike Richter .15 .40
3 Mats Sundin .15 .40
4 Theo Fleury .12 .30
5 John Cullen .12 .30
6 Dimitri Khristich .12 .30
7 Stephan Lebeau .12 .30
8 Rob Blake .15 .40
9 Ken Hodge Jr. .12 .30
10 Mike Ricci .10 .25
11 Trevor Linden .15 .40
12 Peter Ing .12 .30
13 Alexander Mogilny .12 .30
14 Martin Gelinas .12 .30
15 Chris Terreri .12 .30
16 Jeff Norton .12 .30
17 Bob Essensa .12 .30
18 Mark Tinordi .12 .30
19 Curtis Joseph .20 .50
20 Joe Sakic .50 1.25
21 Jeremy Roenick .25 .60
22 Mark Recchi .20 .50
23 Eric Desjardins .15 .40
24 Robert Reichel .30 .75
25 Tim Cheveldae .12 .30
26 Eric Weinrich .15 .40
27 Murray Baron .12 .30
28 Darren Turcotte .12 .30
29 Troy Gamble .10 .25
30 Eric Lindros .25 .60
31 Benoit Hogue .12 .30
32 Ed Belfour .40 1.00
33 Ron Tugnutt .12 .30
34 Pat Elynuik .12 .30
35 Mike Modano .30 .75
36 Bobby Holik .15 .40
37 Yves Racine .12 .30
38 Jaromir Jagr .50 1.25
39 Stephane Morin .12 .30
40 Kevin Miller .12 .30

1992-93 Score Canadian Promo Sheets

COMPLETE SET (2) 2.00 5.00
1 Promo Sheet 1
6. Pat LaFontaine
25. Kevin Stevens
2. Chris Chelios
16. Esa Tikkanen .75 2.00
2 Promo Sheet 2
5. Mike Richter
14. Pavel Bure
6. Pat LaFontaine
25. Kevin Stevens 1.50 4.00

1992-93 Score

1 Wayne Gretzky 1.00 2.50
2 Chris Chelios .15 .40
3 Joe Mullen .12 .30
4 Russ Courtnall .10 .25
5 Mike Richter .15 .40
6 Pat LaFontaine .15 .40
7 Mark Tinordi .10 .25
8 Claude Lemieux .10 .25
9 Jimmy Carson .10 .25
10 Cam Neely .15 .40
11 Al Iafrate .12 .30
12 Steve Thomas .12 .30
13 Fredrik Olausson .10 .25
14 Pavel Bure .15 .40
15 Doug Wilson .12 .30
16 Esa Tikkanen .10 .25
17 Gary Suter .10 .25
18 Murray Craven .10 .25
19 Garry Galley .10 .25
20 Grant Fuhr .25 .60
21 Craig Wolanin .10 .25
22 Paul Cavallini .10 .25
23 Eric Desjardins .12 .30
24 Joey Kocur .10 .25
25 Kevin Stevens .12 .30
26 Marty McSorley .12 .30
27 Dirk Graham .10 .25
28 Mike Ramsey .10 .25
29 Gord Murphy .12 .30
30 John MacLean .12 .30
31 Vladimir Konstantinov .15 .40
32 Neal Broten .12 .30
33 Dimitri Khristich .10 .25
34 Gerald Diduck .12 .30
35 Ken Baumgartner .10 .25
36 Darrin Shannon .10 .25
37 Steve Bozek .10 .25
38 Michel Petit .10 .25
39 Kevin Lowe .12 .30
40 Doug Gilmour .20 .50
41 Peter Sidorkiewicz .10 .25
42 Gino Cavallini .10 .25
43 Dan Quinn .12 .30
44 Steven Finn .10 .25
45 Larry Murphy .12 .30
46 Brent Gilchrist .10 .25
47 Daren Puppa .12 .30
48 Steve Smith .10 .25
49 Dave Taylor .10 .25
50 Mike Gartner .20 .50
51 Derian Hatcher .10 .25
52 Bob Probert .15 .40
53 Ken Daneyko .10 .25
54 Steve Leach .10 .25
55 Kelly Miller .10 .25
56 Jeff Norton .10 .25
57 Kelly Kisio .12 .30
58 Igor Larionov .12 .30
59 Paul MacDermid .12 .30
60 Mike Vernon .12 .30
61 Randy Ladouceur .10 .25
62 Luke Richardson .10 .25
63 Daniel Marois .10 .25
64 Mike Hough .10 .25
65 Garth Butcher .12 .30
66 Terry Carkner .12 .30
67 Mike Donnelly .10 .25
68 Keith Brown .12 .30
69 Mathieu Schneider .10 .25
70 Tom Barrasso .12 .30
71 Adam Graves .10 .25
72 Brian Propp .10 .25
73 Randy Wood .10 .25
74 Yves Racine .10 .25
75 Scott Stevens .15 .40
76 Chris Nilan .10 .25
77 Uwe Krupp .10 .25
78 Sylvain Cote .10 .25
79 Sergio Momesso .10 .25
80 Thomas Steen .10 .25
81 Craig Muni .10 .25
82 Jeff Hackett .12 .30
83 Frank Musil .12 .30
84 Mike Ricci .10 .25
85 Brad Shaw .10 .25
86 Ron Sutter .10 .25
87 Curtis Leschyshyn .10 .25
88 Jamie Macoun .10 .25
89 Brian Noonan .10 .25
90 Ulf Samuelsson .10 .25
91 Mike McPhee .10 .25
92 Charlie Huddy .10 .25
93 Tim Kerr .10 .25
94 Craig Ludwig .12 .30
95 Paul Ysebaert .10 .25
96 Brad May .10 .25
97 Slava Fetisov .10 .25
98 Todd Krygier .10 .25
99 Patrick Flatley .10 .25
100 Ray Bourque .25 .60
101 Petr Nedved .10 .25
102 Teppo Numminen .10 .25
103 Dean Evason .10 .25
104 Ron Hextall .15 .40
105 Josef Beranek .10 .25
106 Robert Reichel .10 .25
107 Mikhail Tatarinov .10 .25
108 Geoff Sanderson .12 .30
109 Dave Lowry .12 .30
110 Wendel Clark .25 .60
111 Corey Millen UER .10 .25
112 Brent Sutter .12 .30
113 Jaromir Jagr .30 .75
114 Petr Svoboda .12 .30
115 Sergei Nemchinov .10 .25
116 Tony Tanti .10 .25
117 Stewart Gavin .10 .25
118 Doug Brown .12 .30
119 Gerard Gallant .10 .25
120 Andy Moog .15 .40
121 John Druce .10 .25
122 Dave McLlwain .12 .30
123 Bob Essensa .12 .30
124 Doug Lidster .12 .30
125 Pat Falloon .12 .30
126 Kelly Buchberger .10 .25
127 Carey Wilson .12 .30
128 Bobby Holik .12 .30
129 Andrei Lomakin .10 .25
130 Bob Rouse .12 .30
131 Adam Foote .12 .30
132 Bob Bassen .10 .25
133 Brian Benning .10 .25
134 Greg Gilbert .12 .30
135 Paul Stanton .12 .30
136 Brian Skrudland .12 .30
137 Jeff Beukeboom .12 .30
138 Clint Malarchuk .10 .25
139 Mike Modano .40 1.00
140 Stephane Richer .12 .30
141 Brad McCrimmon .10 .25
142 Bob Carpenter .12 .30
143 Rod Langway .12 .30
144 Adam Creighton .10 .25
145 Ed Olczyk .10 .25
146 Greg Adams .10 .25
147 Jay More .10 .25
148 Scott Mellanby .10 .25
149 Paul Ranheim .10 .25
150 John Cullen .10 .25
151 Steve Duchesne .10 .25
152 Dave Ellett .10 .25
153 Mats Sundin .15 .40
154 Rick Zombo .10 .25
155 Kelly Hrudey .12 .30
156 Mike Hudson .10 .25
157 Bryan Trottier .15 .40
158 Shayne Corson .12 .30
159 Kevin Haller .10 .25
160 John Vanbiesbrouck .15 .40
161 Jim Johnson .12 .30
162 Kevin Todd .10 .25
163 Ray Sheppard .10 .25
164 Brent Ashton .10 .25
165 Peter Bondra .15 .40
166 David Volek .10 .25
167 Randy Carlyle .12 .30
168 Dana Murzyn .10 .25
169 Perry Berezan .10 .25
170 Vincent Damphousse .12 .30
171 Gary Leeman .10 .25
172 Steve Konroyd .12 .30
173 Pelle Eklund .10 .25
174 Peter Zezel .10 .25
175 Greg Paslawski .10 .25
176 Murray Baron .10 .25
177 Rob Blake .10 .25
178 Ed Belfour .15 .40
179 Mike Keane .10 .25
180 Mark Recchi .20 .50
181 Kris King .10 .25
182 Dave Snuggerud .10 .25
183 David Shaw .12 .30
184 Tom Chorske .12 .30
185 Steve Chiasson .10 .25
186 Don Sweeney .10 .25
187 Mike Ridley .12 .30
188 Glenn Healy .10 .25
189 Troy Murray .10 .25
190 Tom Fergus .10 .25
191 Rob Zettler .10 .25
192 Geoff Smith .10 .25
193 Joe Nieuwendyk .12 .30
194 Mark Hunter .10 .25
195 Kjell Samuelsson .12 .30
196 Todd Gill .10 .25
197 Doug Smail .10 .25
198 Dave Christian .10 .25
199 Tomas Sandstrom .12 .30
200 Jeremy Roenick .25 .60
201 Gordie Roberts .12 .30
202 Denis Savard .15 .40
203 James Patrick .10 .25
204 Dave Andreychuk .15 .40
205 Bobby Smith .10 .25
206 Valeri Zelepukin .10 .25
207 Shawn Burr .10 .25
208 Vladimir Ruzicka .10 .25
209 Calle Johansson .10 .25
210 Mark Fitzpatrick .12 .30
211 Dean Kennedy .10 .25
212 Dave Babych .10 .25
213 Wayne Presley .10 .25
214 Dave Manson .10 .25
215 Mikael Andersson .10 .25
216 Trent Yawney .12 .30
217 Mark Howe .15 .40
218 Mike Bullard .12 .30
219 Claude Lapointe .10 .25
220 Jeff Brown .12 .30
221 Bob Kudelski .10 .25
222 Michel Goulet .12 .30
223 Phil Bourque .10 .25
224 Darren Turcotte .10 .25
225 Kirk Muller .10 .25
226 Doug Bodger .10 .25
227 Dave Gagner .12 .30
228 Craig Billington .12 .30
229 Kevin Miller .10 .25
230 Glen Wesley .12 .30
231 Dale Hunter .12 .30
232 Tom Kurvers .10 .25
233 Pat Elynuik .10 .25
234 Geoff Courtnall .10 .25
235 Neil Wilkinson .10 .25
236 Bill Ranford .12 .30
237 Ronnie Stern .10 .25
238 Zarley Zalapski .10 .25
239 Kerry Huffman .10 .25
240 Joe Sakic .30 .75
241 Glenn Anderson .12 .30
242 Stephane Quintal .10 .25
243 Tony Granato .10 .25
244 Rob Brown .10 .25
245 Rick Tocchet .12 .30
246 Stephan Lebeau .10 .25
247 Mark Hardy .10 .25
248 Alexander Mogilny .12 .30
249 Jon Casey .10 .25
250 Adam Oates .15 .40
251 Bruce Driver .10 .25
252 Sergei Fedorov .25 .60
253 Michal Pivonka .10 .25
254 Cliff Ronning .10 .25
255 Derek King .10 .25
256 Luciano Borsato .10 .25
257 Paul Fenton .12 .30
258 Craig Berube .10 .25
259 Brian Bradley .10 .25
260 Craig Simpson .10 .25
261 Adam Burt .10 .25
262 Curtis Joseph .20 .50
263 Mark Pederson .10 .25
264 Alexei Gusarov .10 .25
265 Paul Coffey .15 .40
266 Steve Larmer .10 .25
267 Ron Francis .20 .50
268 Randy Gilhen .10 .25
269 Guy Carbonneau .12 .30
270 Chris Terreri .12 .30
271 Mike Craig .10 .25
272 Dale Hawerchuk .20 .50
273 Kevin Hatcher .10 .25
274 Ken Hodge Jr. .10 .25
275 Tim Cheveldae .10 .25
276 Benoit Hogue .10 .25
277 Marc Osborne .10 .25
278 Brian Mullen .10 .25
279 Robert Dirk .12 .30
280 Theo Fleury .25 .60
281 Martin Gelinas .10 .25
282 Pat Verbeek .12 .30
283 Mike Krushelnyski .10 .25
284 Kevin Dineen .10 .25
285 Craig Janney .12 .30
286 Owen Nolan .15 .40
287 Bob Errey .12 .30
288 Bryan Marchment .12 .30
289 Randy Moller .10 .25
290 Luc Robitaille .15 .40
291 Peter Stastny .12 .30
292 Ken Sutton .10 .25
293 Brad Marsh .10 .25
294 Chris Dahlquist .12 .30
295 Patrick Roy .40 1.00
296 Andy Brickley .10 .25
297 Randy Burridge .10 .25
298 Ray Ferraro .10 .25
299 Phil Housley .12 .30
300 Mark Messier .30 .75
301 David Bruce .10 .25
302 Al MacInnis .20 .50
303 Craig MacTavish .10 .25
304 Kay Whitmore .12 .30
305 Trevor Linden .15 .40
306 Steve Kasper .10 .25
307 Todd Elik .10 .25
308 Eric Weinrich .10 .25
309 Jocelyn Lemieux .10 .25
310 Peter Ahola .10 .25
311 J.J. Daigneault .10 .25
312 Colin Patterson .10 .25
313 Darcy Wakaluk .10 .25
314 Doug Weight .30 .75
315 Dave Barr .10 .25
316 Keith Primeau .12 .30
317 Bob Sweeney .10 .25
318 Jyrki Lumme .10 .25
319 Stu Barnes .10 .25
320 Don Beaupre .10 .25
321 Joe Murphy .10 .25
322 Gary Roberts .10 .25
323 Andrew Cassels .10 .25
324 Rod Brind'Amour .10 .25
325 Pierre Turgeon .10 .25
326 Claude Vilgrain .12 .30
327 Rich Sutter .10 .25
328 Claude Loiselle .12 .30
329 John Ogrodnick .10 .25
330 Ulf Dahlen .10 .25
331 Gilbert Dionne .10 .25
332 Joel Otto .10 .25
333 Rob Pearson .10 .25
334 Christian Ruuttu .10 .25
335 Brian Bellows .10 .25
336 Anatoli Semenov .10 .25
337 Brent Fedyk .12 .30
338 Gaetan Duchesne .12 .30
339 Randy McKay .12 .30
340 Bernie Nicholls .12 .30
341 Keith Acton .12 .30
342 John Tonelli .12 .30
343 Brian Lawton .12 .30
344 Ric Nattress .10 .25
345 Mike Eagles .10 .25
346 Frantisek Kucera .10 .25
347 John McIntyre .10 .25
348 Troy Loney .10 .25
349 Norm Maciver .10 .25
350 Brett Hull .30 .75
351 Rob Ramage .10 .25
352 Claude Boivin .10 .25
353 Paul Broten .10 .25
354 Stephane Fiset .10 .25
355 Garry Valk .10 .25
356 Basil McRae .10 .25
357 Alan May .10 .25
358 Grant Ledyard .10 .25
359 Dave Poulin .10 .25
360 Valeri Kamensky .10 .25
361 Brian Glynn .10 .25
362 Jan Erixon .10 .25
363 Mike Lalor .10 .25
364 Jeff Chychrun .10 .25
365 Ron Wilson .10 .25
366 Shawn Cronin .10 .25
367 Sylvain Turgeon .10 .25
368 Mike Liut .10 .25
369 Joe Cirella .10 .25
370 David Maley .10 .25
371 Lucien Deblois .10 .25
372 Per Djoos .10 .25
373 Dominik Hasek .25 .60
374 Laurie Boschman .10 .25
375 Brian Leetch .12 .30
376 Nelson Emerson .10 .25
377 Normand Rochefort .10 .25
378 Jacques Cloutier .10 .25
379 Jim Sandlak .10 .25
380 David Reid .10 .25
381 Gary Nylund .10 .25
382 Sergei Makarov .10 .25
383 Petr Klima .10 .25
384 Peter Douris .10 .25
385 Kirk McLean .10 .25
386 Bob McGill .10 .25
387 Ron Tugnutt .12 .30
388 Patrice Brisebois .10 .25
389 Tony Amonte .12 .30
390 Mario Lemieux .60 1.50
391 Nicklas Lidstrom .12 .30
392 Brendan Shanahan .15 .40
393 Donald Audette .12 .30
394 Alexei Kasatonov .10 .25
395 Dino Ciccarelli .12 .30
396 Vincent Riendeau .12 .30
397 Joe Reekie .10 .25
398 Jari Kurri .15 .40
399 Ken Wregget .12 .30
400 Steve Yzerman .40 1.00
401 Scott Niedermayer .15 .40
402 Stephane Beauregard .12 .30
403 Tim Hunter .10 .25
404 Marc Bergevin .12 .30
405 Sylvain Lefebvre .10 .25
406 Johan Garpenlov .10 .25
407 Tony Hrkac .10 .25
408 Tie Domi .12 .30
409 Martin Lapointe .10 .25
410 Darryl Sydor .10 .25
411 Brett Hull SL .30 .75
412 Wayne Gretzky SL 1.00 2.50
413 Mario Lemieux SL .60 1.50
414 Paul Ysebaert SL .10 .25
415 Tony Amonte SL .12 .30
416 Brian Leetch SL .12 .30
417 Tim Cheveldae SL .10 .25
418 Patrick Roy SL .40 1.00
419 Ray Bourque FP .25 .60
420 Pat LaFontaine FP .15 .40
421 Al MacInnis FP .20 .50
422 Jeremy Roenick FP .25 .60
423 Steve Yzerman FP .40 1.00
424 Bill Ranford FP .12 .30
425 John Cullen FP .12 .30
426 Wayne Gretzky FP 1.00 2.50
427 Mike Modano FP .40 1.00
428 Patrick Roy FP .40 1.00
429 Kevin Stevens FP .15 .40
430 Pierre Turgeon FP .12 .30
431 Mark Messier FP .30 .75
432 Eric Lindros FP .25 .60
433 Mario Lemieux FP .60 1.50
434 Joe Sakic FP .30 .75
435 Brett Hull FP .30 .75
436 Pat Falloon FP .10 .25
437 Grant Fuhr FP .25 .60
438 Trevor Linden FP .15 .40
439 Kevin Hatcher FP .10 .25
440 Phil Housley FP .12 .30
441 Paul Coffey SH .15 .40
442 Brett Hull HL .30 .75
443 Mike Gartner SH .20 .50
444 Michel Goulet SH .12 .30
445 Mike Gartner SH .20 .50
446 Bobby Smith SH .10 .25
447 Ray Bourque SH .25 .60
448 Mario Lemieux HL .60 1.50
449 Scott Lachance TP .10 .25
450 Keith Tkachuk .15 .40
451 Alexander Semak TP .10 .25
452 John Tanner TP .10 .25
453 Joe Juneau TP .12 .30
454 Igor Kravchuk TP .10 .25
455 Brent Thompson TP .12 .30
456 Evgeny Davydov TP .10 .25
457 Arturs Irbe TP .10 .25
458 Kent Manderville TP .10 .25
459 Shawn McEachern TP .10 .25
460 Guy Hebert RC .25 .60
461 Keith Carney TP RC .30 .75
462 Karl Dykhuis TP .30 .75
463 Bill Lindsay TP RC .12 .30
464 Dominic Roussel TP .12 .30
465 Marty McInnis TP .10 .25
466 Dale Craigwell TP .10 .25
467 Igor Ulanov TP .10 .25
468 Dmitri Mironov TP .10 .25
469 Dean McAmmond TP RC .10 .25
470 Bill Guerin TP RC .30 .75
471 Bret Hedican TP RC .12 .30
472 Felix Potvin .30 .75
473 Slava Kozlov TP .10 .25
474 Martin Rucinsky TP .10 .25
475 Ray Whitney TP RC .25 .60
476 Steve Heinze TP .10 .25
477 Brad Schlegel TP .10 .25
478 Patrick Poulin TP .10 .25
479 Ted Donato TP .10 .25
480 Martin Brodeur .40 1.00
481 Denny Felsner TP RC .12 .30
482 Trent Klatt TP RC .12 .30
483 Gord Hynes TP .12 .30
484 Glen Murray TP .12 .30
485 Chris Lindberg TP .10 .25
486 Ray LeBlanc TP .12 .30
487 Yanic Perreault TP RC .40 1.00
488 J.F.Quintin TP RC .10 .25
489 Patrick Roy DT .40 1.00
490 Ray Bourque DT .25 .60
491 Brian Leetch DT .12 .30
492 Kevin Stevens DT .12 .30
493 Mark Messier DT .30 .75
494 Jaromir Jagr DT .30 .75
495 Bill Ranford DT .12 .30
496 Al MacInnis DT .20 .50
497 Chris Chelios DT .15 .40
498 Luc Robitaille DT .15 .40
499 Jeremy Roenick DT .25 .60
500 Brett Hull DT .30 .75
501 Felix Potvin DT .30 .75
502 Nicklas Lidstrom DT .15 .40
503 Vladimir Konstantinov .15 .40
504 Pavel Bure DT .15 .40
505 Nelson Emerson DT .10 .25
506 Tony Amonte DT .12 .30
507 T.B.Lightning Logo .05 .15

508 Shawn Chambers .10 .25
509 Basil McRae .10 .25
510 Joe Reekie .10 .25
511 Wendell Young .12 .30
512 Ottawa Senators Logo .05 .15
513 Laurie Boschman .10 .25
514 Mark Lamb .10 .25
515 Peter Sidorkiewicz .10 .25
516 Sylvain Turgeon .10 .25
517 Bill Dineen
Kevin Dineen .10 .25
518 Stanley Cup
Champions .20 .50
519 Mario Lemieux AW .60 1.50
520 Ray Bourque AW .25 .60
521 Mark Messier AW .30 .75
522 Brian Leetch AW .12 .30
523 Pavel Bure AW .15 .40
524 Guy Carbonneau AW .12 .30
525 Wayne Gretzky AW 1.00 2.50
526 Mark Fitzpatrick AW .12 .30
527 Patrick Roy AW .40 1.00
528 Memorial Cup Kamloops .05 .15
529 Rick Tabaracci .10 .25
530 Tom Draper .10 .25
531 Adrien Plavsic .10 .25
532 Joe Sacco .10 .25
533 Mike Sullivan .10 .25
534 Zdeno Ciger .10 .25
535 Frank Pietrangelo .12 .30
536 Mike Peluso .12 .30
537 Jim Paek .12 .30
538 Dave Hannan .10 .25
539 David Williams RC .10 .25
540 Gino Odjick .10 .25
541 Yvon Corriveau .10 .25
542 Grant Jennings .10 .25
543 Stephane Matteau .10 .25
544 Pat Conacher .10 .25
545 Steven Rice .10 .25
546 Marc Habscheid .10 .25
547 Steve Weeks .10 .25
548A Jay Wells USA .15 .40
548C Maurice Richard CAN .30 .75
549A Mick Vukota USA .15 .40
549C Maurice Richard CAN .30 .75
550 Eric Lindros .25 .60
NNO E.Lindros Press Conf. 10.00 25.00

1992-93 Score Canadian

*CANADIAN: .4X TO 1X SCORE US

1992-93 Score Canadian Olympians

COMPLETE SET (13) 15.00 40.00
1 Eric Lindros 2.50 5.00
2 Joe Juneau 1.00 2.50
3 Dave Archibald 1.00 2.50
4 Randy Smith 1.00 2.50
5 Gord Hynes 1.00 2.50
6 Chris Lindberg 1.00 2.50
7 Jason Woolley 1.00 2.50
8 Fabian Joseph 1.00 2.50
9 Brad Schlegel 1.00 2.50
10 Kent Manderville 1.00 2.50
11 Adrien Plavsic 1.00 2.50
12 Trevor Kidd 1.00 2.50
13 Sean Burke 1.00 2.50
NNO1 Maurice Richard 2.00 5.00
NNO2 Maurice Richard 2.00 5.00
AU1 Maurice Richard AU/1250 80.00 150.00

1992-93 Score Sharp Shooters

COMPLETE SET (30) 5.00 12.00
*CANADIAN: .4X TO 1X US INSERTS
1 Gary Roberts .08 .25
2 Sergei Makarov .08 .25
3 Ray Ferraro .08 .25
4 Dale Hunter .40 1.00
5 Sergei Nemchinov .08 .25
6 Mike Ridley .08 .25
7 Gilbert Dionne .08 .25
8 Pat LaFontaine .50 1.25
9 Jimmy Carson .08 .25
10 Jeremy Roenick .60 1.50
11 Kelly Buchberger .08 .25
12 Owen Nolan .40 1.00
13 Igor Larionov .08 .25
14 Claude Vilgrain .08 .25
15 Derek King .08 .25
16 Greg Paslawski .08 .25
17 Bob Probert .40 1.00
18 Mark Recchi .40 1.00
19 Donald Audette .08 .25
20 Ray Sheppard .08 .25
21 Benoit Hogue .08 .25
22 Rob Brown .08 .25
23 Pat Elyniuk .08 .25
24 Petr Klima .08 .25
25 Pierre Turgeon .40 1.00
26 Corey Millen .08 .25
27 Dimitri Khristich .08 .25
28 Anatoli Semenov .08 .25
29 Kirk Muller .08 .25
30 Craig Simpson .08 .25

1992-93 Score USA Greats

COMPLETE SET (15) 15.00 40.00
1 Pat LaFontaine 1.50 4.00
2 Chris Chelios 1.50 4.00
3 Jeremy Roenick 1.50 4.00
4 Tony Granato 1.00 2.50
5 Mike Modano 2.00 5.00
6 Mike Richter 1.50 4.00
7 John Vanbiesbrouck 1.50 4.00
8 Brian Leetch 1.50 4.00
9 Joe Mullen 1.00 2.50
10 Kevin Stevens 1.00 2.50
11 Craig Janney 1.00 2.50
12 Brian Mullen 1.00 2.50
13 Kevin Hatcher 1.00 2.50
14 Kelly Miller 1.00 2.50
15 Ed Olczyk 1.00 2.50

1992-93 Score Young Superstars

COMP.FACT SET (40) 3.00 8.00
1 Eric Lindros 1.00 2.50
2 Tony Amonte .10 .30
3 Mats Sundin .20 .50
4 Jaromir Jagr 1.00 2.50
5 Sergei Fedorov .60 1.50
6 Gilbert Dionne .02 .10
7 Mark Recchi .10 .30
8 Alexander Mogilny .10 .30
9 Mike Richter .20 .50
10 Jeremy Roenick .20 .50
11 Nicklas Lidstrom .20 .50
12 Scott Lachance .02 .10
13 Nelson Emerson .02 .10
14 Pat Falloon .02 .10
15 Dimitri Khristich .02 .10
16 Trevor Linden .10 .30
17 Curtis Joseph .40 1.00
18 Rob Pearson .02 .10
19 Kevin Todd .02 .10
20 Joe Sakic .60 1.50
21 Tim Cheveldae .10 .30
22 Joe Juneau .10 .30
23 Vladimir Konstantinov .10 .30
24 Valeri Kamensky .10 .30
25 Ed Belfour .20 .50
26 Rod Brind'Amour .10 .30
27 Pierre Turgeon .10 .30
28 Eric Desjardins .10 .30
29 Keith Tkachuk .20 .50
30 Pavel Bure .75 2.00
31 Patrick Poulin .02 .10
32 Viacheslav Kozlov .10 .30
33 Scott Niedermayer .10 .30
34 Jyrki Lumme .02 .10
35 Paul Ysebaert .02 .10
36 Dominic Roussel .10 .30
37 Owen Nolan .10 .30
38 Rob Blake .10 .30
39 Felix Potvin .20 .50
40 Mike Modano .20 .50

1993-94 Score Promo Panel

587 Alexandre Daigle
(Gold .75 2.00

1993-94 Score Samples

COMPLETE SET (6) 1.50 4.00
1 Eric Lindros .75 2.00
2 Mike Gartner .20 .50
3 Steve Larmer .08 .25
4 Brian Bellows .08 .25
5 Felix Potvin .40 1.00
6 Pierre Turgeon .30 .75

1993-94 Score

*CANADIAN: .4X TO 1X BASIC CARDS
1 Eric Lindros .25 .60
2 Mike Gartner .20 .50
3 Steve Larmer .12 .30
4 Brian Bellows .12 .30
5 Felix Potvin .30 .75
6 Pierre Turgeon .12 .30
7 Joe Mullen .12 .30
8 Craig MacTavish .10 .25
9 Mats Sundin .15 .40
10 Pat Verbeek .10 .25
11 Andy Moog .15 .40
12 Dirk Graham .10 .25
13 Gary Suter .10 .25
14 Brent Fedyk .10 .25
15 Brad Shaw .10 .25
16 Benoit Hogue .10 .25
17 Cliff Ronning .10 .25
18 Mathieu Schneider .10 .25
19 Bernie Nicholls .12 .30
20 Vladimir Konstantinov .12 .30
21 Doug Bodger .10 .25
22 Peter Stastny .12 .30
23 Larry Murphy .12 .30
24 Darren Turcotte .10 .25
25 Doug Crossman .10 .25
26 Bob Essensa .12 .30
27 Kelly Kisio .10 .25
28 Nelson Emerson .10 .25
29 Ray Bourque .25 .60
30 Kelly Miller .10 .25
31 Peter Zezel .10 .25
32 Owen Nolan .15 .40
33 Sergei Makarov .10 .25
34 Stephane Richer .12 .30
35 Adam Graves .10 .25
36 Rob Ramage .10 .25
37 Ed Olczyk .10 .25
38 Jeff Hackett .10 .25
39 Ron Sutter .10 .25
40 Dale Hunter .10 .25
41 Nikolai Borschevsky .10 .25
42 Curtis Leschyshyn .10 .25
43 Mike Vernon .12 .30
44 Brent Sutter .10 .25
45 Rod Brind'Amour .12 .30
46 Sylvain Turgeon .10 .25
47 Kirk McLean .12 .30
48 Derek King .10 .25
49 Murray Craven .10 .25
50 Jaromir Jagr .50 1.25
51 Guy Carbonneau .10 .25
52 Tony Granato .10 .25
53 Mark Tinordi .10 .25
54 Brad McCrimmon .10 .25
55 Randy Wood .10 .25
56 Scott Young .10 .25
57 Jamie Baker .10 .25
58 Don Beaupre .12 .30
59 Bob Probert .15 .40
60 Ray Ferraro .10 .25
61 Alexei Kasatonov .10 .25
62 Corey Millen .10 .25
63 Scott Mellanby .12 .30
64 Brian Benning .10 .25
65 Doug Lidster .10 .25
66 Doug Gilmour .20 .50
67 Shawn McEachern .10 .25
68 Tim Cheveldae .12 .30
69 Jeff Norton .10 .25
70 Ed Belfour .15 .40
71 Thomas Steen .10 .25
72 Stephan Lebeau .10 .25
73 James Patrick .10 .25
74 Joel Otto .10 .25
75 Grant Fuhr .25 .60
76 Calle Johansson .10 .25
77 Donald Audette .10 .25
78 Geoff Courtnall .10 .25
79 Fredrik Olausson .10 .25
80 Dimitri Khristich .10 .25
81 John MacLean .12 .30
82 Dominic Roussel .12 .30
83 Ray Sheppard .12 .30
84 Christian Ruuttu .10 .25
85 Mike McPhee .10 .25
86 Adam Creighton .10 .25
87 Uwe Krupp .10 .25
88 Steve Leach .10 .25
89 Kevin Miller .10 .25
90 Charlie Huddy .10 .25
91 Mark Howe .15 .40
92 Sylvain Cote .10 .25
93 Anatoli Semenov .10 .25
94 Jeff Beukeboom .10 .25
95 Gord Murphy .10 .25
96 Rob Pearson .10 .25
97 Esa Tikkanen .10 .25
98 Dave Gagner .12 .30
99 Mike Richter .15 .40
100 Jari Kurri .15 .40
101 Chris Chelios .15 .40
102 Peter Sidorkiewicz .10 .25
103 Scott Lachance .10 .25
104 Zarley Zalapski .10 .25
105 Denis Savard .15 .40
106 Paul Coffey .15 .40
107 Ulf Dahlen .10 .25
108 Shayne Corson .12 .30
109 Jimmy Carson .10 .25
110 Petr Svoboda .10 .25
111 Scott Stevens .15 .40
112 Kevin Lowe .10 .25
113 Chris Kontos .10 .25
114 Evgeny Davydov .10 .25
115 Doug Wilson .12 .30
116 Curtis Joseph .20 .50
117 Trevor Linden .15 .40
118 Michal Pivonka .10 .25
119 Dave Ellett .10 .25
120 Mike Ricci .10 .25
121 Al MacInnis .20 .50
122 Kevin Dineen .10 .25
123 Norm Maciver .10 .25
124 Darius Kasparaitis .10 .25
125 Adam Oates .15 .40
126 Sean Burke .10 .25
127 Dave Manson .10 .25
128 Eric Desjardins .12 .30
129 Tomas Sandstrom .10 .25
130 Russ Courtnall .10 .25
131 Roman Hamrlik .10 .25
132 Teppo Numminen .10 .25
133 Pat Falloon .10 .25
134 Jyrki Lumme .10 .25
135 Joe Sakic .30 .75
136 Kevin Hatcher .10 .25
137 Wendel Clark .25 .60
138 Neil Wilkinson .10 .25
139 Craig Simpson .10 .25
140 Kelly Hrudey .12 .30
141 Steve Thomas .10 .25
142 Mike Modano .25 .60
143 Garry Galley .10 .25
144 Jim Johnson .10 .25
145 Rod Langway .10 .25
146 Bob Sweeney .10 .25
147 Gary Leeman .10 .25
148 Alexei Zhitnik .10 .25
149 Adam Foote .10 .25
150 Mark Recchi .20 .50
151 Ron Francis .20 .50
152 Ron Hextall .15 .40
153 Michel Goulet .10 .25
154 Vladimir Ruzicka .10 .25
155 Bill Ranford .12 .30
156 Mike Craig .10 .25
157 Vladimir Malakhov .10 .25
158 Nicklas Lidstrom .15 .40
159 Dale Hawerchuk .20 .50
160 Claude Lemieux .10 .25
161 Ulf Samuelsson .10 .25
162 John Vanbiesbrouck .15 .40
163 Patrice Brisebois .10 .25
164 Andrew Cassels .10 .25
165 Paul Ranheim .10 .25
166 Neal Broten .12 .30
167 Joe Reekie .10 .25
168 Derian Hatcher .10 .25
169 Don Sweeney .10 .25
170 Mike Keane .10 .25
171 Mark Fitzpatrick .10 .25
172 Paul Cavallini .10 .25
173 Garth Butcher .10 .25
174 Andrei Kovalenko .10 .25
175 Shawn Burr .10 .25
176 Mike Donnelly .10 .25
177 Glenn Healy .12 .30
178 Gilbert Dionne .10 .25
179 Mike Ramsey .10 .25
180 Glenn Anderson .12 .30
181 Pelle Eklund .10 .25
182 Kerry Huffman .10 .25
183 Johan Garpenlov .10 .25
184 Kjell Samuelsson .10 .25
185 Todd Elik .10 .25
186 Craig Janney .12 .30
187 Dmitri Kvartalnov .10 .25
188 Al Iafrate .10 .25
189 John Cullen .10 .25
190 Steve Duchesne .10 .25
191 Theo Fleury .10 .25
192 Steve Smith .10 .25
193 Jon Casey .12 .30
194 Jeff Brown .10 .25
195 Keith Tkachuk .15 .40
196 Greg Adams .10 .25
197 Mike Ridley .10 .25
198 Bobby Holik .10 .25
199 Joe Nieuwendyk .12 .30
200 Mark Messier .30 .75
201 Jim Hrivnak .10 .25
202 Patrick Poulin .10 .25
203 Alexei Kovalev .12 .30
204 Robert Reichel .10 .25
205 David Shaw .10 .25
206 Brent Gilchrist .10 .25
207 Craig Billington .12 .30
208 Bob Errey .10 .25
209 Dmitri Mironov .10 .25
210 Dixon Ward .10 .25
211 Rick Zombo .10 .25
212 Marty McSorley .12 .30
213 Geoff Sanderson .12 .30
214 Dino Ciccarelli .12 .30
215 Tony Amonte .12 .30
216 Dimitri Yushkevich .10 .25
217 Scott Niedermayer .15 .40
218 Sergei Nemchinov .10 .25
219 Steve Konroyd .10 .25
220 Patrick Flatley .10 .25
221 Steve Chiasson .10 .25
222 Alexander Mogilny .12 .30
223 Pat Elynuik .10 .25
224 Jamie Macoun .10 .25
225 Tom Barrasso .12 .30
226 Gaetan Duchesne .10 .25
227 Eric Weinrich .10 .25
228 Dave Poulin .10 .25
229 Slava Fetisov .10 .25
230 Brian Bradley .10 .25
231 Petr Nedved .10 .25
232 Phil Housley .12 .30
233 Terry Carkner .10 .25
234 Kirk Muller .10 .25
235 Brian Leetch .12 .30
236 Rob Blake .12 .30
237 Chris Terreri .12 .30
238 Brendan Shanahan .15 .40
239 Paul Ysebaert .10 .25
240 Jeremy Roenick .25 .60
241 Gary Roberts .10 .25
242 Petr Klima .10 .25
243 Glen Wesley .10 .25
244 Vincent Damphousse .12 .30
245 Luc Robitaille .15 .40
246 Dallas Drake RC .15 .40
247 Rob Gaudreau RC .15 .40
248 Tommy Sjodin .10 .25
249 Richard Smehlik .10 .25
250 Sergei Fedorov .25 .60
251 Steve Heinze .10 .25
252 Luke Richardson .10 .25
253 Doug Weight .12 .30
254 Martin Rucinsky .10 .25
255 Sergio Momesso .10 .25
256 Alexei Zhamnov .12 .30
257 Bob Kudelski .10 .25
258 Brian Skrudland .10 .25
259 Terry Yake .10 .25
260 Alexei Gusarov .10 .25
261 Sandis Ozolinsh .10 .25
262 Ted Donato .10 .25
263 Bruce Driver .10 .25
264 Yves Racine .10 .25
265 Mike Peluso .10 .25
266 Craig Muni .10 .25
267 Bob Carpenter .12 .30
268 Kevin Haller .10 .25
269 Brad May .12 .30
270 Joe Kocur .10 .25
271 Igor Korolev .10 .25
272 Troy Murray .10 .25
273 Daren Puppa .10 .25
274 Gordie Roberts .10 .25
275 Michel Petit .10 .25
276 Vincent Riendeau .10 .25
277 Robert Petrovicky .10 .25
278 Valeri Zelepukin .10 .25
279 Bob Bassen .10 .25
280 Darrin Shannon .10 .25
281 Dominik Hasek .25 .60
282 Craig Ludwig .10 .25
283 Lyle Odelein .10 .25
284 Alexander Semak .10 .25
285 Richard Matvichuk .10 .25
286 Ken Daneyko .10 .25
287 Jan Erixon .10 .25
288 Robert Dirk .10 .25
289 Laurie Boschman .10 .25
290 Greg Paslawski .10 .25
291 Rob Zamuner .10 .25
292 Todd Gill .10 .25
293 Neil Brady .10 .25
294 Murray Baron .10 .25
295 Peter Taglianetti .10 .25
296 Wayne Presley .10 .25
297 Paul Broten .10 .25
298 Dana Murzyn .10 .25
299 J.J. Daigneault .10 .25
300 Wayne Gretzky 1.00 2.50
301 Keith Acton .10 .25
302 Yuri Khmylev .10 .25
303 Frank Musil .10 .25
304 Bob Rouse .10 .25
305 Greg Gilbert .10 .25
306 Geoff Smith .10 .25
307 Adam Burt .10 .25
308 Phil Bourque .10 .25
309 Igor Kravchuk .10 .25
310 Steve Yzerman .40 1.00
311 Darryl Sydor .10 .25
312 Tie Domi .12 .30
313 Sergei Zubov .12 .30
314 Chris Dahlquist .10 .25
315 Patrick Roy .40 1.00
316 Mark Osborne .10 .25
317 Kelly Buchberger .10 .25
318 John LeClair .15 .40
319 Randy McKay .10 .25
320 Jody Hull .10 .25
321 Paul Stanton .10 .25
322 Steven Finn .10 .25
323 Rich Sutter .10 .25
324 Ray Whitney .10 .25
325 Kevin Stevens .12 .30
326 Valeri Kamensky .12 .30
327 Doug Zmolek .10 .25
328 Mikhail Tatarinov .10 .25
329 Ken Wregget .10 .25
330 Joe Juneau .10 .25
331 Teemu Selanne .30 .75
332 Trent Yawney .10 .25
333 Pavel Bure .15 .40
334 Jim Paek .10 .25
335 Brett Hull .30 .75
336 Tommy Soderstrom .12 .30
337 Grigori Panteleyev .10 .25
338 Kevin Todd .10 .25
339 Mark Janssens .10 .25
340 Rick Tocchet .12 .30
341 Wendell Young .10 .25
342 Cam Neely .15 .40
343 Dave Andreychuk .15 .40
344 Peter Bondra .15 .40
345 Pat LaFontaine .15 .40
346 Robb Stauber .10 .25
347 Brian Mullen .10 .25
348 Joe Murphy .10 .25
349 Pat Jablonski .10 .25
350 Mario Lemieux .60 1.50
351 Sergei Bautin .10 .25
352 Claude Lapointe .10 .25
353 Dean Evason .10 .25
354 John Tucker .10 .25
355 Drake Berehowsky .10 .25
356 Gerald Diduck .10 .25
357 Todd Krygier .10 .25
358 Adrien Plavsic .10 .25
359 Sylvain Lefebvre .10 .25
360 Kay Whitmore .10 .25
361 Sheldon Kennedy .10 .25
362 Kris King .10 .25
363 Marc Bergevin .10 .25
364 Keith Primeau .12 .30
365 Jimmy Waite .12 .30
366 Dean Kennedy .10 .25
367 Mike Krushelnyski .10 .25
368 Ron Tugnutt .12 .30
369 Bob Beers .10 .25
370 Randy Burridge .10 .25
371 David Reid .10 .25
372 Frantisek Kucera .10 .25
373 Scott Pellerin RC .15 .40
374 Brad Dalgarno .10 .25
375 Martin Straka .10 .25
376 Scott Pearson .10 .25
377 Arturs Irbe .12 .30
378 Jiri Slegr .10 .25
379 Stephane Fiset .12 .30
380 Stu Barnes .10 .25
381 Ric Nattress .10 .25
382 Steven King .10 .25
383 Michael Nylander .10 .25
384 Keith Brown .10 .25
385 Gino Odjick .10 .25
386 Bryan Marchment .10 .25
387 Mike Foligno .10 .25
388 Zdeno Ciger .10 .25
389 Dave Taylor .10 .25
390 Mike Sullivan .10 .25
391 Shawn Chambers .10 .25
392 Brad Marsh .10 .25
393 Mike Hough .10 .25
394 Jeff Reese .10 .25
395 Bill Guerin .15 .40
396 Greg Hawgood .10 .25
397 Jim Sandlak .10 .25
398 Stephane Matteau .10 .25
399 John Blue .12 .30
400 Tony Twist .10 .25
401 Luciano Borsato .10 .25
402 Gerard Gallant .10 .25
403 Rick Tabaracci .10 .25
404 Nick Kypreos .10 .25
405 Marty McInnis .10 .25
406 Craig Wolanin .10 .25
407 Mark Lamb .10 .25
408 Martin Gelinas .10 .25
409 Ronnie Stern .10 .25
410 Ken Sutton .10 .25
411 Brian Noonan .10 .25
412 Stephane Quintal .10 .25
413 Rob Zettler .10 .25
414 Gino Cavallini .10 .25
415 Mark Hardy .10 .25
416 Jay Wells .10 .25
417 Keith Jones .10 .25
418 Dave McLlwain .10 .25
419 Frank Pietrangelo .12 .30
420 Jocelyn Lemieux .10 .25
421 Slava Kozlov .12 .30
422 Randy Moller .10 .25
423 Kevin Dahl .10 .25
424 Shjon Podein RC .15 .40
425 Shane Churla .10 .25
426 Guy Hebert .12 .30
427 Mikael Andersson .10 .25
428 Robert Kron .10 .25
429 Mike Eagles .10 .25
430 Alan May .10 .25
431 Ron Wilson .10 .25
432 Darcy Wakaluk .10 .25
433 Rob Ray .10 .25
434 Brent Ashton .10 .25
435 Jason Woolley .10 .25
436 Basil McRae .10 .25
437 Andre Racicot .10 .25
438 Brad Werenka .10 .25
439 Josef Beranek .10 .25
440 Dave Christian .10 .25
441 Theo Fleury LBM .10 .25
442 Mark Recchi LBM .20 .50
443 Cliff Ronning LBM .10 .25
444 Tony Granato LBM .10 .25
445 John Vanbiesbrouck LBM .15 .40
446 Jari Kurri HL .15 .40
447 Mike Gartner HL .20 .50
448 Steve Yzerman HL .40 1.00
449 Glenn Anderson HL .12 .30
450 Iafrate
Cote
Hatcher .10 .25
451 Luc Robitaille HL .15 .40
452 Pittsburgh Penguins HL
17-Game Winning Streak .05 .15
453 Corey Hirsch TR .12 .30
454 Jesse Belanger TR .10 .25
455 Philippe Boucher TR .10 .25
456 Robert Lang TR .12 .30
457 Doug Darrault TR RC .10 .25
458 Steve Konowalchuk TR .10 .25
459 Oleg Petrov TR .10 .25
460 Niclas Andersson TR .10 .25
461 Milan Tichy RC .10 .25
462 Darrin Madeley TR RC .15 .40
463 Tyler Wright TR .10 .25
464 Sergei Krivokrasov TR .10 .25
465 Vladimir Vujtek .10 .25
466 Rick Knickle RC .12 .30
467 Gord Kruppke RC .12 .30
468 David Emma .10 .25
469 Scott Thomas RC .15 .40
470 Shawn Rivers RC .12 .30
471 Jason Bowen TR RC .15 .40
472 Bryan Smolinski TR .10 .25
473 Chris Simon TR RC .15 .40
474 Peter Ciavaglia RC .12 .30
475 Sergei Zholtok TR .10 .25
476 Radek Hamr RC .15 .40
477 T.Selanne
A.Mogilny SL .30 .75
478 Adam Oates SL .15 .40
479 Mario Lemieux SL .60 1.50
480 Mario Lemieux SL .60 1.50
481 Dave Andreychuk SL .15 .40
482 Phil Housley SL .12 .30
483 Tom Barrasso SL .12 .30
484 Felix Potvin SL .30 .75
485 Ed Belfour SL .15 .40
486 S.S.Marie Mem. Cup .05 .15
487 Canadiens Stanley Cup .05 .15
488 Mighty Ducks Logo .05 .15
489 Guy Hebert .12 .30
490 Sean Hill Ducks .10 .25
491 Florida Panthers Logo .05 .15
492 J.Vanbiesbrouck Panthers .15 .40
493 Tom Fitzgerald Panthers .10 .25
494 Paul DiPietro .10 .25
495 David Volek .10 .25
496 Alexandre Daigle SP .10 .25
497 Shawn McEachern .10 .25
498 Rich Sutter .10 .25
499 Evgeny Davydov .10 .25
500 Sean Hill .10 .25
501 John Vanbiesbrouck .15 .40
502 Guy Hebert .12 .30
503 Scott Mellanby .12 .30
504 Ron Tugnutt .12 .30
505 Brian Skrudland .10 .25
506 Nelson Emerson .10 .25
507 Kevin Todd .10 .25
508 Terry Carkner .10 .25
509 Stephane Quintal .10 .25
510 Paul Stanton .10 .25
511 Terry Yake .10 .25
512 Brian Benning .10 .25
513 Brian Propp .10 .25
514 Steven King .10 .25
515 Joe Cirella .10 .25
516 Andy Moog .15 .40
517 Paul Ysebaert .10 .25
518 Petr Klima .10 .25
519 Corey Millen .10 .25
520 Phil Housley .12 .30
521 Craig Billington .12 .30
522 Jeff Norton .10 .25
523 Neil Wilkinson .10 .25
524 Doug Lidster .10 .25
525 Steve Larmer .12 .30
526 Jon Casey .12 .30
527 Brad McCrimmon .10 .25
528 Alexei Kasatonov .10 .25
529 Andrei Lomakin .10 .25
530 Daren Puppa .10 .25
531 Sergei Makarov .10 .25
532 Jim Sandlak .10 .25
533 Glenn Healy .12 .30
534 Martin Gelinas .10 .25
535 Igor Larionov .10 .25
536 Anatoli Semenov .10 .25
537 Mark Fitzpatrick .10 .25
538 Paul Cavallini .10 .25
539 Jimmy Waite .12 .30
540 Yves Racine .10 .25
541 Jeff Hackett .10 .25
542 Marty McSorley .12 .30
543 Scott Pearson .10 .25
544 Ron Hextall .15 .40
545 Gaetan Duchesne .10 .25
546 Jamie Baker .10 .25
547 Troy Loney .10 .25
548 Gord Murphy .10 .25
549 Bob Kudelski .10 .25
550 Dean Evason .10 .25
551 Mike Peluso .10 .25
552 Dave Poulin .10 .25
553 Randy Ladouceur .10 .25
554 Tom Fitzgerald .10 .25
555 Denis Savard .15 .40
556 Kelly Kisio .10 .25
557 Craig Simpson .10 .25
558 Stu Grimson .10 .25
559 Mike Hough .10 .25
560 Gerard Gallant .10 .25
561 Greg Gilbert .10 .25
562 Vladimir Ruzicka .10 .25
563 Jim Hrivnak .10 .25
564 Dave Lowry .10 .25
565 Todd Ewen .10 .25
566 Bob Errey .10 .25
567 Bryan Trottier .15 .40
568 Grant Ledyard .10 .25
569 Keith Brown .10 .25
570 Darren Turcotte .10 .25
571 Patrick Poulin .10 .25
572 Jimmy Carson .10 .25
573 Eric Weinrich .10 .25
574 James Patrick .10 .25
575 Bob Beers .10 .25
576 Chris Joseph .10 .25
577 Bryan Marchment .10 .25
578 Bob Carpenter .12 .30
579 Craig Muni .10 .25
580 Pat Elynuik .10 .25
581 Todd Elik .10 .25
582 Doug Brown .10 .25
583 Dave McLlwain .10 .25
584 Dave Tippett .10 .25
585 Jesse Belanger .10 .25
586 Chris Pronger .15 .40
587 Alexandre Daigle .10 .25
588 Cam Stewart RC .15 .40
589 Derek Plante RC .15 .40
590 Pat Peake .10 .25
591 Alexander Karpovtsev .10 .25
592 Rob Niedermayer .12 .30
593 Jocelyn Thibault RC .15 .40
594 Jason Arnott RC .30 .75
595 Mike Rathje .10 .25
596 Chris Gratton .12 .30
597 Markus Naslund .15 .40
598 Dmitri Filimonov .10 .25
599 Andrei Trefilov .10 .25
600 Michal Sykora RC .15 .40
601 Greg Johnson .10 .25
602 Mikael Renberg .15 .40
603 Alexei Yashin .12 .30
604 Damian Rhodes RC .15 .40
605 Jeff Shantz RC .10 .25
606 Brent Gretzky RC .15 .40
607 Boris Mironov .10 .25
608 Ted Drury .10 .25
609 Chris Osgood RC 1.00 2.50
610 Jim Storm RC .10 .25
611 Dave Karpa .10 .25
612 Stewart Malgunas RC .15 .40
613 Jason Smith RC .10 .25
614 German Titov RC .15 .40
615 Patrick Carnback RC .15 .40
616 Jaroslav Modry RC .15 .40
617 Scott Levins RC .15 .40
618 Fred Brathwaite RC .15 .40
619 Ilya Byakin RC .10 .25
620 Jarkko Varvio .10 .25
621 Jim Montgomery RC .15 .40
622 Vesa Viitakoski RC .15 .40
623 Alexei Kudashov RC .15 .40
624 Pavol Demitra .20 .50
625 Iain Fraser RC .15 .40
626 Peter Popovic RC .15 .40
627 Kirk Maltby RC .15 .40
628 Garth Snow RC .10 .25
629 Peter White RC .10 .25
630 Mike McKee RC .10 .25
631 Darren McCarty RC .25 .60
632 Pat Neaton RC .15 .40
633 Sandy McCarthy .10 .25
634 Pierre Sevigny .10 .25
635 Matt Martin RC .15 .40
636 John Slaney .10 .25
637 Bob Corkum .10 .25
638 Mike Stapleton RC .12 .30
639 Bill Houlder .10 .25
640 Warren Rychel .10 .25
641 Garry Valk .10 .25
642 Greg Hawgood .10 .25
643 Randy Gilhen .10 .25
644 Stu Barnes .10 .25
645 Fredrik Olausson .10 .25
646 Geoff Smith .10 .25
647 Mike Foligno .10 .25
648 Martin Brodeur .40 1.00
649 Ryan McGill .10 .25
650 Jeff Reese .10 .25
651 Mike Sillinger .10 .25
652 Brent Severyn RC .15 .40
653 Rob Ramage .10 .25
654 Dixon Ward .10 .25
655 Danton Cole .10 .25
656 Viacheslav Butsayev .10 .25
657 Ron Wilson .10 .25
658 Paul Broten .10 .25
659 Mike Hudson .12 .30
660 Trevor Kidd .12 .30
661 Travis Green .12 .30
662 Wayne Gretzky 802 1.00 2.50
NNO A.Daigle Redemption .10 .25
NNO Eric Lindros AS SP 4.00 10.00

1993-94 Score Gold Rush

COMPLETE SET (166) 15.00 40.00
*VETS: 2.5X TO 6X BASIC CARDS
*ROOKIES: 1.2X TO 3X BASIC CARDS

1993-94 Score Canadian Gold

*CAN.GOLD: .75X TO 2X BASIC CARDS

1993-94 Score Dream Team

1 Tom Barrasso .50 1.25
2 Patrick Roy 1.50 4.00
3 Chris Chelios .60 1.50
4 Al MacInnis .75 2.00
5 Scott Stevens .60 1.50
6 Brian Leetch .50 1.25
7 Ray Bourque 1.00 2.50
8 Paul Coffey .60 1.50
9 Al Iafrate .40 1.00
10 Mario Lemieux 2.50 6.00
11 Wayne Gretzky 4.00 10.00
12 Eric Lindros 1.00 2.50
13 Pat LaFontaine .60 1.50
14 Joe Sakic 1.25 3.00
15 Pierre Turgeon .50 1.25
16 Steve Yzerman 1.50 4.00
17 Adam Oates .60 1.50
18 Brett Hull 1.25 3.00
19 Pavel Bure .60 1.50
20 Alexander Mogilny .50 1.25
21 Teemu Selanne 1.25 3.00
22 Steve Larmer .50 1.25
23 Kevin Stevens .50 1.25
24 Luc Robitaille .60 1.50

1993-94 Score Dynamic Duos Canadian

1 D.Gilmour/D.Andreychuk 1.50 4.00
2 T.Selanne/A.Zhamnov 2.50 6.00
3 A.Daigle/A.Yashin 1.00 2.50
4 G.Roberts/J.Nieuwendyk 1.00 2.50
5 J.Sakic/M.Sundin 2.50 6.00
6 B.Bellows/K.Muller 1.00 2.50
7 S.Corson/J.Arnott 2.50 6.00
8 M.Lemieux/K.Stevens 5.00 12.00
9 P.Turgeon/Derek King 1.00 2.50

1993-94 Score Dynamic Duos U.S.

DD1 M.Recchi/E.Lindros 2.00 5.00
DD2 LaFontaine/A.Mogilny 1.25 3.00
DD3 A.Oates/C.Neely 1.25 3.00
DD4 B.Hull/C.Janney 2.50 6.00
DD5 M.Messier/A.Graves 2.50 6.00
DD6 J.Roenick/J.Murphy 2.00 5.00
DD7 J.Kurri/W.Gretzky 5.00 12.00
DD8 S.Makarov/I.Larionov .75 2.00
DD9 S.Yzerman/S.Fedorov 3.00 8.00

1993-94 Score Franchise

1 Ray Bourque 1.25 3.00
2 Pat Lafontaine .75 2.00
3 Al MacInnis 1.00 2.50
4 Jeremy Roenick 1.25 3.00
5 Mike Modano 1.25 3.00
6 Steve Yzerman 2.00 5.00
7 Bill Ranford .60 1.50
8 Sean Burke .50 1.25
9 Wayne Gretzky 5.00 12.00
10 Patrick Roy 2.00 5.00
11 Scott Stevens .75 2.00
12 Pierre Turgeon .60 1.50
13 Brian Leetch .60 1.50
14 Peter Sidorkiewicz .50 1.25
15 Eric Lindros 1.25 3.00
16 Mario Lemieux 5.00 12.00
17 Joe Sakic 1.50 4.00
18 Brett Hull 1.50 4.00
19 Pat Falloon .50 1.25
20 Brian Bradley .50 1.25
21 Doug Gilmour 1.00 2.50
22 Pavel Bure .75 2.00
23 Kevin Hatcher .50 1.25
24 Teemu Selanne 1.50 4.00

1993-94 Score International Stars

COMPLETE SET (22) 8.00 20.00
*CANADIAN: .4X TO 1X BASIC INSERTS
1 Pavel Bure .75 2.00
2 Teemu Selanne .75 2.00
3 Sergei Fedorov 1.25 3.00
4 Peter Bondra .40 1.00
5 Tommy Soderstrom .20 .50
6 Robert Reichel .20 .50
7 Jari Kurri .75 2.00
8 Alexander Mogilny .40 1.00
9 Jaromir Jagr 1.25 3.00
10 Mats Sundin .75 2.00
11 Uwe Krupp .20 .50
12 Nikolai Borschevsky .20 .50
13 Ulf Dahlen .20 .50
14 Alexander Semak .20 .50
15 Michal Pivonka .20 .50
16 Sergei Nemchinov .20 .50
17 Darius Kasparaitis .20 .50
18 Sandis Ozolinsh .20 .50
19 Alexei Kovalev .40 1.00
20 Dimitri Khristich .20 .50
21 Tomas Sandstrom .20 .50
22 Petr Nedved .20 .50

1994-95 Score Samples

COMPLETE SEALED SET (12) 1.50 4.00
1 Eric Lindros Philadelph .20 .50
2 Pat LaFontaine Buffalo .01 .05
3 Wendel Clark Toronto Ma .01 .05
4 Cam Neely .01 .05
5 Larry Murphy Pittsburgh .01 .05
6 Patrick Poulin Chicago .01 .05
7 Bob Beers Edmonton Oile .01 .05
254 Jason Arnott Edmonton Oilers Young Stars .02 .10
CI3 Darius Kasparaitis New .75 2.00
TF16 Alexandre Daigle Ottawa .40 1.00
NNO Pro Debut Rookie Redemp .20 .50
NNO Title Card .01 .05

1994-95 Score

1 Eric Lindros .20 .50
2 Pat LaFontaine .12 .30
3 Wendel Clark .20 .50
4 Cam Neely .12 .30
5 Larry Murphy .10 .25
6 Patrick Poulin .07 .20
7 Bob Beers .07 .20
8 James Patrick .07 .20
9 Gino Odjick .07 .20
10 Arturs Irbe .10 .25
11 Darius Kasparaitis .07 .20
12 Peter Bondra .12 .30
13 Garth Butcher .10 .25
14 Sergei Nemchinov .07 .20
15 Doug Brown .07 .20
16 Anatoli Semenov .07 .20
17 Mike McPhee .07 .20
18 Joel Otto .07 .20
19 Dino Ciccarelli .10 .25
20 Marty McSorley .10 .25
21 Ron Tugnutt .10 .25
22 Scott Niedermayer .12 .30
23 John Tucker .07 .20
24 Norm Maciver .07 .20
25 Kevin Miller .07 .20
26 Garry Galley .07 .20
27 Ted Donato .07 .20
28 Bob Kudelski .07 .20
29 Craig Muni .07 .20
30 Nikolai Borschevsky .07 .20
31 Tom Barrasso .10 .25
32 Brent Sutter .10 .25
33 Igor Kravchuk .07 .20
34 Andrew Cassels .07 .20
35 Jyrki Lumme .07 .20
36 Sandis Ozolinsh .07 .20
37 Steve Thomas .07 .20
38 Dave Poulin .07 .20
39 Andrei Kovalenko .07 .20
40 Steve Larmer .10 .25
41 Nelson Emerson .07 .20
42 Guy Hebert .10 .25
43 Russ Courtnall .07 .20
44 Gary Suter .07 .20
45 Steve Chiasson .07 .20
46 Guy Carbonneau .07 .20
47 Rob Blake .12 .30
48 Roman Hamrlik .07 .20
49 Valeri Zelepukin .07 .20
50 Mark Recchi .15 .40
51 Darrin Madeley .07 .20
52 Steve Duchesne .07 .20
53 Brian Skrudland .07 .20
54 Craig Simpson .07 .20
55 Todd Gill .07 .20
56 Dirk Graham .07 .20
57 Joe Mullen .10 .25
58 Doug Weight .10 .25
59 Michael Nylander .10 .25
60 Kirk McLean .10 .25
61 Igor Larionov .07 .20
62 Vladimir Malakhov .07 .20
63 Kelly Miller .07 .20
64 Curtis Leschyshyn .07 .20
65 Thomas Steen .07 .20
66 Jeff Beukeboom .07 .20
67 Troy Loney .07 .20
68 Mark Tinordi .07 .20
69 Theo Fleury .12 .30
70 Slava Kozlov .10 .25
71 Tony Granato .07 .20
72 Daren Puppa .10 .25
73 Brian Bellows .10 .25
74 Bernie Nicholls .10 .25
75 Rick Zombo .07 .20
76 Brad Shaw .07 .20
77 Josef Beranek .07 .20
78 Dominik Hasek .20 .50
79 Steve Leach .07 .20
80 David Reid .07 .20
81 Dave Lowry .07 .20
82 Martin Straka .07 .20
83 Dave Ellett .07 .20
84 Sean Burke .10 .25
85 Craig MacTavish .07 .20
86 Cliff Ronning .07 .20
87 Bob Errey .07 .20
88 Marty McInnis .07 .20
89 Mats Sundin .12 .30
90 Randy Burridge .07 .20
91 Teppo Numminen .07 .20
92 Tony Amonte .10 .25
93 Terry Yake .07 .20
94 Paul Cavallini .07 .20
95 German Titov .07 .20
96 Vladimir Konstantinov .10 .25
97 Darryl Sydor .07 .20
98 Chris Joseph .07 .20
99 Corey Millen .07 .20
100 Brett Hull .25 .60
101 Don Sweeney .07 .20
102 Scott Mellanby .10 .25
103 Mathieu Schneider .07 .20
104 Brad May .07 .20
105 Dominic Roussel .10 .25
106 Jamie Macoun .07 .20
107 Bryan Marchment .10 .25
108 Shawn McEachern .07 .20
109 Murray Craven .07 .20
110 Eric Desjardins .10 .25
111 Jon Casey .10 .25
112 Mike Gartner .15 .40
113 Neal Broten .10 .25
114 Jari Kurri .10 .25
115 Bruce Driver .07 .20
116 Patrick Flatley .07 .20
117 Gord Murphy .07 .20
118 Dimitri Khristich .07 .20
119 Nicklas Lidstrom .12 .30
120 Al MacInnis .15 .40
121 Steve Smith .07 .20
122 Zdeno Ciger .07 .20
123 Tie Domi .10 .25
124 Joe Juneau .07 .20
125 Todd Elik .07 .20
126 Stephane Fiset .10 .25
127 Craig Janney .10 .25
128 Stephan Lebeau .07 .20
129 Richard Smehlik .07 .20
130 Mike Richter .12 .30
131 Danton Cole .07 .20
132 Rod Brind'Amour .10 .25
133 Dave Archibald .07 .20
134 Dana Murzyn .07 .20
135 Jaromir Jagr .40 1.00
136 Esa Tikkanen .07 .20
137 Rob Pearson .07 .20
138 Stu Barnes .07 .20
139 Frank Musil .07 .20
140 Ron Hextall .12 .30
141 Adam Oates .12 .30
142 Ken Daneyko .07 .20
143 Dale Hunter .07 .20
144 Geoff Sanderson .10 .25
145 Kelly Hrudey .10 .25
146 Kirk Muller .07 .20
147 Fredrik Olausson .07 .20
148 Derian Hatcher .07 .20
149 Ed Belfour .12 .30
150 Steve Yzerman .30 .75
151 Adam Foote .07 .20
152 Pat Falloon .07 .20
153 Shawn Chambers .07 .20
154 Alexei Zhamnov .10 .25
155 Brendan Shanahan .12 .30
156 Ulf Samuelsson .07 .20
157 Donald Audette .07 .20
158 Bob Corkum .07 .20
159 Joe Nieuwendyk .10 .25
160 Felix Potvin .20 .50
161 Geoff Courtnall .07 .20
162 Yves Racine .07 .20
163 Tom Fitzgerald .07 .20
164 Adam Graves .07 .20
165 Vincent Damphousse .10 .25
166 Pierre Turgeon .10 .25
167 Craig Billington .10 .25
168 Al Iafrate .07 .20
169 Darren Turcotte .07 .20
170 Joe Murphy .07 .20
171 Alexei Zhitnik .10 .25
172 John MacLean .10 .25
173 Andy Moog .12 .30
174 Shayne Corson .10 .25
175 Ray Sheppard .10 .25
176 Johan Garpenlov .07 .20
177 Ron Sutter .07 .20
178 Teemu Selanne .25 .60
179 Brian Bradley .07 .20
180 Ray Bourque .20 .50
181 Curtis Joseph .15 .40
182 Kevin Stevens .10 .25
183 Alexei Kasatonov .07 .20
184 Brian Leetch .10 .25
185 Doug Gilmour .15 .40
186 Gary Roberts .07 .20
187 Mike Keane .07 .20
188 Mike Modano .20 .50
189 Chris Chelios .12 .30
190 Pavel Bure .12 .30
191 Bob Essensa .07 .20
192 Dale Hawerchuk .15 .40
193 Scott Stevens .12 .30
194 Claude Lapointe .07 .20
195 Scott Lachance .07 .20
196 Gaetan Duchesne .07 .20
197 Kevin Dineen .07 .20
198 Doug Bodger .07 .20
199 Mike Ridley .07 .20
200 Alexander Mogilny .10 .25
201 Jamie Storr .10 .25
202 Jason Botterill .10 .25
203 Jeff Friesen .07 .20
204 Todd Harvey .07 .20
205 Brendan Witt .07 .20
206 Jason Allison .10 .25
207 Aaron Gavey .07 .20
208 Deron Quint .07 .20
209 Jason Bonsignore .12 .30
210 Richard Park .07 .20
211 Jamie Langenbrunner .10 .25
212 Vadim Sharifjanov .07 .20
213 Alexander Kharlamov .07 .20
214 Oleg Tverdovsky .10 .25
215 Valeri Bure .07 .20
216 Dane Jackson RC .07 .20
217 Josef Cierny RC .07 .20
218 Yevgeny Namestnikov .07 .20
219 Daniel Laperriere .07 .20
220 Fred Knipscheer .07 .20
221 Yan Kaminsky .07 .20
222 David Roberts .10 .25
223 Derek Mayer .07 .20
224 Jamie McLennan .10 .25
225 Kevin Smyth .07 .20
226 Todd Marchant .07 .20
227 Mariusz Czerkawski RC .12 .30
228 John Lilley .07 .20
229 Aaron Ward .07 .20
230 Brian Savage .07 .20
231 Jason Allison .10 .25
232 Maxim Bets .07 .20
233 Ted Crowley .07 .20
234 Todd Simon RC .07 .20
235 Zigmund Palffy .10 .25
236 Rene Corbet .07 .20
237 Mike Peca .10 .25
238 Dwayne Norris .07 .20
239 Andrei Nazarov .07 .20
240 David Sacco .07 .20
241 Wayne Gretzky HL .75 2.00
242 Mike Gartner .15 .40
243 Dino Ciccarelli .10 .25
244 Ron Francis .15 .40
245 Bernie Nicholls .10 .25
246 Dino Ciccarelli .10 .25
247 Brian Propp .07 .20
248 Alexandre Daigle YS .07 .20
249 Mikael Renberg YS .10 .25
250 Jocelyn Thibault YS .10 .25
251 Derek Plante YS .07 .20
252 Chris Pronger YS .12 .30
253 Alexei Yashin YS .12 .30
254 Jason Arnott YS .10 .25
255 Boris Mironov .07 .20
256 Chris Osgood YS .20 .50
257 Jesse Belanger .07 .20
258 Darren McCarty .07 .20
259 Trevor Kidd .10 .25
260 Oleg Petrov .07 .20
261 Mike Rathje .07 .20
262 John Slaney .07 .20
263 Anaheim Mighty Ducks Boston Bruins CL .05 .15
264 Buffalo Sabres Calgary Flames CL .05 .15
265 Chicago Blackhawks Dallas Stars CL .05 .15
266 Detroit Red Wings Edmonton Oilers CL .05 .15
267 Florida Panthers Hartford Whalers CL .05 .15
268 Los Angeles Kings Montreal Canadiens CL .05 .15
269 New Jersey Devils New York Islanders CL .05 .15
270 New York Rangers Ottawa Senators CL .05 .15
271 Philadelphia Flyers Pittsburgh Penguins CL .05 .15
272 Quebec Nordiques St.Louis Blues CL .05 .15
273 San Jose Sharks Tampa Bay Lightning CL .05 .15
274 Toronto Maple Leafs Vancouver Canucks CL .05 .15
275 Washington Capitals Winnipeg Jets CL .05 .15

1994-95 Score Gold Line

*VETS: 4X TO 10X BASIC CARDS
*ROOKIES: 2.5X TO 6X BASIC CARDS
*HOLE PUNCHED: .8X TO 2X BASIC GOLD

1994-95 Score Platinum

COMP.BLACKHAWKS (9) 15.00 30.00
COMP.BLUES (10) 15.00 30.00
COMP.BRUINS (11) 12.50 25.00
COMP.CANADIENS (10) 12.50 25.00
COMP.CANUCKS (11) 20.00 40.00
COMP.CAPITALS (10) 7.50 15.00
COMP.DEVILS (9) 7.50 15.00
COMP.FLAMES (10) 12.50 25.00
COMP.FLYERS (9) 30.00 60.00
COMP.ISLANDERS (11) 7.50 15.00
COMP.JETS (6) 12.50 25.00
COMP.KINGS (8) 50.00 75.00
COMP.LIGHTNING (7) 7.50 15.00
COMP.MAPLE LEAFS (11) 15.00 30.00
COMP.MIGHTY DUCKS (8) 7.50 15.00
COMP.NORDIQUES (11) 15.00 30.00
COMP.OILERS (10) 12.50 25.00
COMP.PANTHERS (8) 7.50 15.00
COMP.PENGUINS (10) 17.50 35.00
COMP.RANGERS (8) 15.00 30.00
COMP.RED WINGS (13) 20.00 40.00
COMP.SABRES (12) 10.00 20.00
COMP.SENATORS (8) 7.50 15.00
COMP.SHARKS (10) 10.00 20.00
COMP.STARS (8) 7.50 15.00
COMP.WHALERS (9) 7.50 15.00
*VETS: 20X TO 40X BASIC CARDS
*ROOKIES: 10X TO 20X BASIC CARDS

1994-95 Score Check It

CI1 Eric Lindros 8.00 20.00
CI2 Scott Stevens 5.00 12.00
CI3 Darius Kasparaitis 3.00 8.00
CI4 Kevin Stevens 4.00 10.00
CI5 Brendan Shanahan 5.00 12.00
CI6 Jeremy Roenick 8.00 20.00
CI7 Ulf Samuelsson 3.00 8.00
CI8 Cam Neely 5.00 12.00
CI9 Adam Graves 3.00 8.00
CI10 Kirk Muller 3.00 8.00
CI11 Rick Tocchet 4.00 10.00
CI12 Gary Roberts 3.00 8.00
CI13 Wendel Clark 8.00 20.00
CI14 Keith Tkachuk 5.00 12.00
CI15 Theo Fleury 5.00 12.00
CI16 Claude Lemieux 5.00 12.00
CI17 Chris Chelios 5.00 12.00
CI18 Pat Verbeek 4.00 10.00

1994-95 Score Dream Team

COMPLETE SET (24) 50.00 100.00
DT1 Patrick Roy 10.00 25.00
DT2 Felix Potvin 2.50 6.00
DT3 Ray Bourque 2.50 6.00
DT4 Brian Leetch 2.00 5.00
DT5 Scott Stevens 1.50 4.00
DT6 Paul Coffey 2.00 5.00
DT7 Al MacInnis 1.50 4.00
DT8 Chris Chelios 2.00 5.00
DT9 Adam Graves 1.25 3.00
DT10 Luc Robitaille 1.00 2.50
DT11 Dave Andreychuk 1.00 2.50
DT12 Sergei Fedorov 2.50 6.00
DT13 Doug Gilmour 1.50 4.00
DT14 Wayne Gretzky 6.00 15.00
DT15 Mario Lemieux 6.00 15.00
DT16 Mark Messier 2.50 6.00
DT17 Mike Modano 6.00 15.00
DT18 Jeremy Roenick 2.50 6.00
DT19 Eric Lindros 3.00 8.00
DT20 Steve Yzerman 4.00 10.00
DT21 Alexandre Daigle 1.00 2.50
DT22 Brett Hull 2.50 6.00
DT23 Cam Neely 2.50 6.00
DT24 Pavel Bure 2.50 6.00

1994-95 Score Franchise

COMPLETE SET (26) 75.00 200.00
TF1 Guy Hebert 4.00 10.00
TF2 Cam Neely 4.00 10.00
TF3 Pat LaFontaine 4.00 10.00
TF4 Theo Fleury 2.00 5.00
TF5 Jeremy Roenick 4.00 10.00
TF6 Mike Modano 4.00 10.00
TF7 Sergei Fedorov 5.00 12.00
TF8 Jason Arnott 2.00 5.00
TF9 John Vanbiesbrouck 2.00 5.00
TF10 Geoff Sanderson 2.00 5.00
TF11 Wayne Gretzky 15.00 40.00
TF12 Patrick Roy 10.00 25.00
TF13 Scott Stevens 2.00 5.00
TF14 Pierre Turgeon 2.00 5.00
TF15 Mark Messier 4.00 10.00
TF16 Alexandre Daigle 2.00 5.00
TF17 Eric Lindros 4.00 10.00
TF18 Mario Lemieux 10.00 25.00
TF19 Joe Sakic 6.00 15.00
TF20 Brett Hull 5.00 12.00
TF21 Arturs Irbe 2.00 5.00
TF22 Daren Puppa 2.00 5.00
TF23 Doug Gilmour 2.00 5.00
TF24 Pavel Bure 4.00 10.00
TF25 Joe Juneau 2.00 5.00
TF26 Teemu Selanne 4.00 10.00

1994-95 Score 90 Plus Club

1 Wayne Gretzky 4.00 10.00
2 Sergei Fedorov 1.00 2.50
3 Adam Oates .60 1.50
4 Doug Gilmour .75 2.00
5 Pavel Bure .60 1.50
6 Jeremy Roenick 1.00 2.50
7 Mark Recchi .75 2.00
8 Brendan Shanahan .60 1.50
9 Jaromir Jagr 2.00 5.00
10 Dave Andreyckuk .60 1.50
11 Brett Hull 1.25 3.00
12 Eric Lindros 1.00 2.50
13 Rod Brind'Amour .50 1.25
14 Pierre Turgeon .50 1.25
15 Ray Sheppard .50 1.25
16 Mike Modano 1.00 2.50
17 Robert Reichel .40 1.00
18 Ron Francis .75 2.00
19 Joe Sakic 1.25 3.00
20 Vincent Damphousse .50 1.25
21 Ray Bourque 1.00 2.50

1994-95 Score Team Canada

COMPLETE SET (24) 30.00 60.00
CT1 Paul Kariya 5.00 12.00
CT2 Petr Nedved 1.50 4.00
CT3 Todd Warriner 1.25 3.00
CT4 Corey Hirsch 1.50 4.00
CT5 Greg Johnson 1.25 3.00
CT6 Chris Kontos 1.25 3.00
CT7 Dwayne Norris 1.25 3.00
CT8 Brian Savage 1.50 4.00
CT9 Todd Hlushko 1.25 3.00
CT10 Fabian Joseph 1.25 3.00
CT11 Greg Parks 1.25 3.00
CT12 Jean Yves Roy 1.25 3.00
CT13 Mark Astley 1.25 3.00
CT14 Adrian Aucoin 1.25 3.00
CT15 David Harlock 1.25 3.00
CT16 Ken Lovsin 1.25 3.00
CT17 Derek Mayer 1.25 3.00
CT18 Brad Schlegel 1.25 3.00
CT19 Chris Therien 1.50 4.00
CT20 Manny Legace 2.00 5.00
CT21 Brad Werenka 1.25 3.00
CT22 Wally Schreiber 1.25 3.00
CT23 Allain Roy 1.25 3.00
CT24 Brett Lindros 1.25 3.00

1994-95 Score Top Rookie Redemption

COMPLETE SET (10) 20.00 40.00
1 Paul Kariya 8.00 20.00
2 Peter Forsberg 8.00 20.00
3 Brett Lindros 1.25 3.00
4 Oleg Tverdovsky 1.25 3.00
5 Jamie Storr 1.25 3.00
6 Kenny Jonsson 1.25 3.00
7 Brian Rolston 1.25 3.00
8 Jeff Friesen 1.25 3.00
9 Todd Harvey 1.25 3.00
10 Viktor Kozlov 1.25 3.00

1995-96 Score Promos

COMPLETE SEALED SET (9) .75 2.00
3 Chris Chelios .08 .25
8 Jason Arnott .02 .10
10 Mark Recchi .05 .15
19 Trevor Kidd .05 .15
25 Martin Brodeur .20 .50
33 Keith Tkachuk .15 .40
313 Jamie Linden .01 .05
3 Cam Neely Border Battle .40 1.00
NNO Ad Card .01 .05

1995-96 Score

*BLACKICE: 1.25X TO 3X BASIC CARDS
*BLACKICEAP: 12X TO 30X BASIC CARDS
1 Jaromir Jagr .40 1.00
2 Adam Graves .10 .25
3 Chris Chelios .12 .30
4 Felix Potvin .20 .50
5 Joe Sakic .25 .60
6 Chris Pronger .12 .30
7 Teemu Selanne .25 .60
8 Jason Arnott .10 .25
9 John LeClair .12 .30
10 Mark Recchi .15 .40
11 Rob Blake .10 .25
12 Kevin Hatcher .10 .25
13 Shawn Burr .07 .20
14 Brett Lindros .07 .20
15 Craig Janney .07 .20
16 Oleg Tverdovsky .12 .30
17 Blaine Lacher .10 .25
18 Alexandre Daigle .07 .20
19 Trevor Kidd .10 .25
20 Brendan Shanahan .12 .30
21 Alexander Mogilny .10 .25
22 Stu Barnes .07 .20
23 Jeff Brown .10 .25
24 Paul Coffey .12 .30
25 Martin Brodeur .30 .75
26 Darryl Sydor .10 .25
27 Steve Smith .07 .20
28 Ted Donato .07 .20
29 Bernie Nicholls .10 .25
30 Kenny Jonsson .12 .30
31 Peter Forsberg .25 .60
32 Sean Burke .07 .20
33 Keith Tkachuk .12 .30
34 Todd Marchant .07 .20
35 Mikael Renberg .10 .25
36 Vincent Damphousse .10 .25
37 Rick Tocchet .10 .25
38 Todd Harvey .07 .20
39 Chris Gratton .07 .20
40 Darius Kasparaitis .07 .20
41 Sergei Nemchinov .07 .20
42 Bob Corkum .07 .20
43 Bryan Smolinski .07 .20
44 Kevin Stevens .10 .25
45 Phil Housley .10 .25
46 Al MacInnis .15 .40
47 Alexei Zhitnik .07 .20
48 Rob Niedermayer .10 .25
49 Kirk McLean .10 .25
50 Mark Messier .25 .60
51 Nicklas Lidstrom .12 .30
52 Scott Niedermayer .12 .30
53 Peter Bondra .12 .30
54 Luc Robitaille .12 .30
55 Jeremy Roenick .20 .50
56 Mats Sundin .12 .30
57 Wendel Clark .20 .50
58 Todd Elik .07 .20
59 Dave Manson .07 .20
60 David Oliver .07 .20
61 Yuri Khmylev .07 .20
62 Sergei Krivokrasov .07 .20
63 Randy Wood .07 .20
64 Andy Moog .12 .30
65 Petr Klima .07 .20
66 Ray Ferraro .07 .20
67 Sandis Ozolinsh .07 .20
68 Joe Sacco .07 .20
69 Zarley Zalapski .07 .20
70 Ron Tugnutt .10 .25
71 German Titov .10 .25
72 Ian Laperriere .07 .20
73 Doug Gilmour .15 .40
74 Brian Skrudland .07 .20
75 Cliff Ronning .07 .20
76 Brian Savage .07 .20
77 John MacLean .10 .25
78 Jim Carey .10 .25
79 Alexei Kovalev .10 .25
80 Brian Rolston .10 .25
81 Shawn McEachern .07 .20
82 Gary Suter .07 .20
83 Owen Nolan .12 .30
84 Ray Whitney .10 .25
85 Alexei Zhamnov .12 .30
86 Shawn Chambers .07 .20
87 Ed Belfour .10 .25
88 Patrice Tardif .10 .25
89 Greg Adams .07 .20
90 Pierre Turgeon .10 .25
91 Jeff Friesen .07 .20
92 Marty McSorley .10 .25
93 Dave Gagner .07 .20
94 Guy Hebert .10 .25
95 Keith Jones .10 .25
96 Kirk Muller .10 .25
97 Gary Roberts .07 .20
98 Chris Therien .07 .20
99 Steve Duchesne .07 .20
100 Sergei Fedorov .20 .50
101 Donald Audette .10 .25
102 Jyrki Lumme .07 .20
103 Darrin Shannon .07 .20
104 Gord Murphy .07 .20
105 John Cullen .07 .20
106 Bill Guerin .12 .30
107 Dale Hunter .10 .25
108 Uwe Krupp .10 .25
109 Dave Andreychuk .12 .30
110 Joe Murphy .07 .20
111 Geoff Sanderson .07 .20
112 Garry Galley .07 .20
113 Ron Sutter .10 .25
114 Viktor Kozlov .10 .25
115 Jari Kurri .12 .30
116 Paul Ysebaert .07 .20
117 Vladimir Malakhov .07 .20
118 Josef Beranek .07 .20
119 Adam Oates .12 .30
120 Mike Modano .20 .50
121 Theo Fleury .15 .40
122 Pat Verbeek .10 .25
123 Esa Tikkanen .07 .20
124 Brian Leetch .10 .25
125 Paul Kariya .12 .30
126 Ken Wregget .10 .25
127 Ray Sheppard .10 .25
128 Jason Allison .10 .25
129 Dave Ellett .07 .20
130 Stephane Richer .10 .25
131 Jocelyn Thibault .10 .25
132 Martin Straka .07 .20
133 Tony Amonte .10 .25
134 Scott Mellanby .10 .25
135 Pavel Bure .12 .30
136 Andrew Cassels .07 .20
137 Ulf Dahlen .07 .20
138 Valeri Bure .07 .20
139 Teppo Numminen .07 .20
140 Mike Richter .12 .30
141 Rob Gaudreau .07 .20
142 Nikolai Khabibulin .10 .25
143 Mariusz Czerkawski .07 .20
144 Mark Tinordi .07 .20
145 Patrick Roy .30 .75
146 Steve Chiasson .07 .20
147 Mike Donnelly .07 .20
148 Patrice Brisebois .07 .20
149 Jason Wiemer .07 .20
150 Eric Lindros .20 .50
151 Dimitri Khristich .07 .20
152 Tom Barrasso .10 .25
153 Curtis Leschyshyn .07 .20
154 Robert Kron .07 .20
155 Jesse Belanger .07 .20
156 Brian Noonan .07 .20
157 Mike Peca .10 .25
158 Patrick Poulin .07 .20
159 Sergei Makarov .07 .20
160 Scott Stevens .12 .30
161 Sergio Momesso .07 .20
162 Todd Gill .07 .20
163 Don Sweeney .07 .20
164 Randy Burridge .07 .20
165 Slava Kozlov .10 .25
166 Shaun Van Allen .07 .20
167 Steven Rice .07 .20
168 Adam Deadmarsh .07 .20
169 Andrei Nikolishin .07 .20
170 Valeri Karpov .07 .20
171 Doug Bodger .07 .20
172 Corey Millen .07 .20
173 Mark Fitzpatrick .10 .25
174 Bob Errey .07 .20
175 Dan Quinn .10 .25
176 Vladimir Konstantinov .10 .25
177 Scott Lachance .07 .20
178 Jeff Norton .07 .20
179 Valeri Zelepukin .07 .20
180 Dmitri Mironov .07 .20
181 Pat Peake .07 .20
182 Dominic Roussel .07 .20
183 Sylvain Cote .07 .20
184 Pat Falloon .07 .20
185 Roman Hamrlik .07 .20
186 Joel Otto .07 .20
187 Ron Francis .15 .40
188 Sergei Zubov .10 .25
189 Arturs Irbe .10 .25
190 Radek Bonk .07 .20
191 John Tucker .07 .20
192 Sylvain Lefebvre .07 .20
193 Doug Brown .07 .20
194 Glen Wesley .07 .20
195 Ron Hextall .12 .30
196 Patrick Flatley .07 .20
197 Darcy Wakaluk .07 .20
198 Kelly Hrudey .10 .25
199 Ray Bourque .20 .50
200 Dominik Hasek .20 .50
201 Pat LaFontaine .12 .30
202 Chris Osgood .12 .30
203 Ulf Samuelsson .07 .20
204 Mike Gartner .15 .40
205 Stephane Fiset .10 .25
206 Mathieu Schneider .07 .20
207 Eric Desjardins .10 .25
208 Trevor Linden .12 .30
209 Cam Neely .12 .30
210 Daren Puppa .10 .25
211 Steve Larmer .10 .25
212 Tim Cheveldae .10 .25
213 Derek Plante .07 .20
214 Murray Craven .07 .20
215 Tommy Soderstrom .10 .25
216 Bob Bassen .07 .20
217 Marty McInnis .07 .20
218 Dave Lowry .07 .20
219 Mike Vernon .10 .25
220 Petr Nedved .10 .25
221 Yves Racine .07 .20
222 Dale Hawerchuk .15 .40
223 Wayne Presley .07 .20
224 Darren Turcotte .07 .20
225 Derian Hatcher .10 .25
226 Steve Thomas .10 .25
227 Stephane Matteau .07 .20
228 Grant Fuhr .20 .50
229 Joe Nieuwendyk .10 .25
230 Alexei Yashin .10 .25
231 Brian Bellows .10 .25
232 Brian Bradley .10 .25
233 Tony Granato .07 .20
234 Mike Ricci .07 .20
235 Brett Hull .25 .60
236 Mike Ridley .07 .20
237 Al Iafrate .10 .25
238 Derek King .10 .25
239 Bill Ranford .10 .25
240 Steve Yzerman .30 .75
241 John Vanbiesbrouck .12 .30
242 Russ Courtnall .07 .20
243 Chris Terreri .10 .25
244 Rod Brind'Amour .12 .30
245 Shayne Corson .10 .25
246 Don Beaupre .10 .25
247 Dino Ciccarelli .10 .25
248 Kevin Lowe .10 .25
249 Craig MacTavish .07 .20
250 Wayne Gretzky .75 2.00
251 Curtis Joseph .15 .40
252 Joe Mullen .10 .25
253 Andrei Kovalenko .07 .20
254 Igor Larionov .07 .20
255 Geoff Courtnall .07 .20
256 Joe Juneau .07 .20
257 Bruce Driver .07 .20
258 Michal Pivonka .07 .20
259 Nelson Emerson .07 .20
260 Larry Murphy .10 .25
261 Brent Gilchrist .07 .20
262 Benoit Hogue .07 .20
263 Doug Weight .12 .30
264 Keith Primeau .10 .25
265 Neal Broten .10 .25
266 Mike Keane .07 .20
267 Zigmund Palffy .12 .30
268 Valeri Kamensky .10 .25
269 Claude Lemieux .12 .30
270 Bryan Marchment .07 .20
271 Kelly Miller .07 .20
272 Brent Sutter .07 .20
273 Glenn Healy .10 .25
274 Sergei Brylin .07 .20
275 Tie Domi .10 .25
276 Norm Maciver .10 .25
277 Kevin Dineen .10 .25
278 Scott Young .07 .20
279 Tomas Sandstrom .10 .25
280 Guy Carbonneau .12 .30
281 Denis Savard .12 .30
282 Ed Olczyk .07 .20
283 Adam Creighton .07 .20
284 Tom Chorske .07 .20
285 Roman Oksiuta .07 .20
286 David Roberts .07 .20
287 Petr Svoboda .07 .20
288 Brad May .07 .20
289 Michael Nylander .07 .20
290 Jon Casey .10 .25
291 Philippe DeRouville .10 .25
292 Craig Johnson .07 .20
293 Chris McAlpine RC .10 .25
294 Ralph Intranuovo .07 .20
295 Richard Park .12 .30
296 Todd Warriner .10 .25
297 Craig Conroy RC .10 .25
298 Marek Malik .07 .20
299 Manny Fernandez .07 .20
300 Cory Stillman .07 .20
301 Kevin Brown .10 .25
302 Steve Larouche RC .07 .20
303 Chris Taylor .10 .25
304 Ryan Smyth .10 .25
305 Craig Darby .07 .20
306 Radim Bicanek .10 .25
307 Shean Donovan .07 .20
308 Jason Bonsignore .07 .20
309 Chris Marinucci RC .10 .25
310 Brian Holzinger RC .25 .60
311 Mike Torchia RC .10 .25
312 Eric Daze .25 .60
313 Jamie Linden .10 .25
314 Tommy Salo RC .20 .50
315 Martin Gendron .10 .25
316 Felix Potvin ST .20 .50
317 Jim Carey ST .10 .25
318 Ed Belfour ST .10 .25
319 Mike Vernon ST .10 .25
320 Sean Burke ST .07 .20
321 Mike Richter ST .12 .30
322 John Vanbiesbrouck ST .12 .30
323 Martin Brodeur ST .30 .75
324 Patrick Roy ST .30 .75
325 Dominik Hasek ST .20 .50

326 Checklist
Pacific Division .05 .15
327 Checklist
Central Division .05 .15
328 Checklist
Atlantic Division .05 .15
329 Checklist
Northeast Division .05 .15
330 Checklist - Chase .05 .15
AD4 Ron Hextall Contest Winner 2.50 5.00

1995-96 Score Border Battle

1 Pierre Turgeon .30 .75
2 Wayne Gretzky 2.50 6.00
3 Cam Neely .40 1.00
4 Joe Sakic .75 2.00
5 Doug Gilmour .50 1.25
6 Brett Hull .75 2.00
7 Pat LaFontaine .40 1.00
8 Joe Mullen .30 .75
9 Mike Modano .60 1.50
10 Jeremy Roenick .60 1.50
11 Pavel Bure .40 1.00
12 Alexei Zhamnov .40 1.00
13 Sergei Fedorov .60 1.50
14 Jaromir Jagr 1.25 3.00
15 Mats Sundin .40 1.00

1995-96 Score Check It

1 Eric Lindros 2.50 6.00
2 Owen Nolan 1.50 4.00
3 Brett Lindros 1.00 2.50
4 Chris Gratton 1.00 2.50
5 Chris Pronger 1.50 4.00
6 Adam Deadmarsh 1.00 2.50
7 Peter Forsberg 3.00 8.00
8 Derian Hatcher 1.25 3.00
9 Rob Blake 1.25 3.00
10 Jeff Friesen 1.00 2.50
11 Keith Tkachuk 1.50 4.00
12 Mike Ricci 1.00 2.50

1995-96 Score Dream Team

1 Wayne Gretzky 8.00 20.00
2 Sergei Fedorov 2.00 5.00
3 Eric Lindros 2.00 5.00
4 Mark Messier 2.50 6.00
5 Peter Forsberg 2.50 6.00
6 Doug Gilmour 1.50 4.00
7 Paul Kariya 1.25 3.00
8 Jaromir Jagr 4.00 10.00
9 Brett Hull 2.50 6.00
10 Pavel Bure 1.25 3.00
11 Patrick Roy 3.00 8.00
12 Jim Carey 1.00 2.50

1995-96 Score Golden Blades

1 Joe Sakic 2.50 6.00
2 Teemu Selanne 2.50 6.00
3 Alexander Mogilny 1.00 2.50
4 Peter Bondra 1.25 3.00
5 Paul Coffey 1.25 3.00
6 Mike Modano 2.00 5.00
7 Alexei Yashin 1.00 2.50
8 Pat LaFontaine 1.25 3.00
9 Paul Kariya 1.25 3.00
10 Peter Forsberg 2.50 6.00
11 Jeff Friesen .75 2.00
12 Steve Yzerman 3.00 8.00
13 Theo Fleury 1.50 4.00
14 Stephane Richer 1.00 2.50
15 Mark Messier 2.50 6.00
16 Mats Sundin 1.25 3.00
17 Brendan Shanahan 1.25 3.00
18 Mark Recchi 1.50 4.00
19 Jeremy Roenick 2.00 5.00
20 Jason Arnott 1.00 2.50

1995-96 Score Lamplighters

1 Wayne Gretzky 0.00 15.00
2 Pavel Bure 1.00 2.50
3 Cam Neely 1.00 2.50
4 Owen Nolan 1.00 2.50
5 Sergei Fedorov 1.50 4.00
6 Pierre Turgeon .75 2.00
7 Peter Bondra 1.00 2.50
8 Mikael Renberg .75 2.00
9 Luc Robitaille 1.00 2.50
10 Alexei Zhamnov 1.00 2.50
11 Brett Hull 2.00 5.00
12 Jaromir Jagr 3.00 8.00
13 Theo Fleury 1.25 3.00
14 Teemu Selanne 2.00 5.00
15 Eric Lindros 1.50 4.00

1996-97 Score Samples

COMPLETE SET (8) 3.00 8.00
1 Patrick Roy 1.00 2.50
10W Martin Brodeur WINNER .50 1.25
10GBW Martin Brodeur
Golden Blades WINNER .50 1.25
10 Martin Brodeur .50 1.25
16 Alexander Mogilny .20 .50
19 Brett Hull .25 .60
63 John Vanbiesbrouck .30 .75
77 Sergei Fedorov .40 1.00
236 Eric Daze .20 .50
238 Saku Koivu .20 .50

1996-97 Score

*AP: 8X TO 20X BASIC CARDS
1 Patrick Roy .30 .75
2 Brendan Shanahan .12 .30
3 Rob Niedermayer .10 .25
4 Jeff Friesen .07 .20
5 Teppo Numminen .07 .20
6 Mario Lemieux .50 1.25
7 Eric Lindros .20 .50
8 Paul Kariya .12 .30
9 Joe Sakic .25 .60
10 Martin Brodeur .30 .75
11 Mark Tinordi .07 .20
12 Theo Fleury .25 .60
13 Guy Hebert .10 .25
14 Dave Gagner .12 .30
15 Travis Green .10 .25
16 Alexander Mogilny .10 .25
17 Stephane Fiset .10 .25
18 Dominik Hasek .20 .50
19 Brett Hull .25 .60
20 Zdeno Ciger .07 .20
21 Pat Falloon .07 .20
22 Jyrki Lumme .07 .20
23 Rick Tabaracci .10 .25
24 Mark Messier .25 .60
25 Yanic Perreault .07 .20
26 Mark Recchi .15 .40
27 Alexander Selivanov .07 .20
28 Chris Terreri .07 .20
29 Jaromir Jagr .40 1.00
30 Ted Donato .07 .20
31 Scott Mellanby .10 .25
32 Geoff Courtnall .07 .20
33 Michal Pivonka .07 .20
34 Glenn Healy .10 .25
35 Pavel Bure .12 .30
36 Chris Chelios .12 .30
37 Nelson Emerson .07 .20
38 Petr Nedved .10 .25
39 Greg Adams .07 .20
40 Bill Ranford .10 .25
41 Wayne Gretzky .75 2.00
42 Wendel Clark .20 .50
43 Sandis Ozolinsh .07 .20
44 Dave Andreychuk .12 .30
45 Brian Bradley .07 .20
46 Sean Burke .07 .20
47 Keith Tkachuk .12 .30
48 Brad May .07 .20
49 Brent Gilchrist .07 .20
50 Vincent Damphousse .10 .25
51 Dale Hawerchuk .15 .40
52 Randy Burridge .07 .20
53 Ray Bourque .20 .50
54 Keith Primeau .10 .25
55 Jason Arnott .10 .25
56 Ron Francis .15 .40
57 Craig Janney .10 .25
58 Trevor Kidd .07 .20
59 Jason Dawe .07 .20
60 Steve Yzerman .30 .75
61 Alexei Kovalev .10 .25
62 Steve Duchesne .07 .20
63 John Vanbiesbrouck .12 .30
64 Steve Thomas .07 .20
65 Bernie Nicholls .10 .25
66 Alexandre Daigle .07 .20
67 Pat Peake .07 .20
68 Kelly Hrudey .10 .25
69 Owen Nolan .12 .30
70 Alexei Zhitnik .07 .20
71 Pierre Turgeon .10 .25
72 Mike Modano .20 .50
73 Slava Fetisov .07 .20
74 Jim Carey .12 .30
75 Larry Murphy .10 .25
76 Roman Oksiuta .07 .20
77 Sergei Fedorov .20 .50
78 Shayne Corson .10 .25
79 Michael Nylander .07 .20
80 Ron Hextall .12 .30
81 Adam Graves .07 .20
82 Tommy Soderstrom .10 .25
83 Robert Svehla .07 .20
84 Vladimir Konstantinov .10 .25
85 Jeff Hackett .10 .25
86 Todd Harvey .07 .20
87 Jeff Brown .07 .20
88 Bryan Smolinski .07 .20
89 Oleg Tverdovsky .10 .25
90 Curtis Joseph .15 .40
91 Grant Fuhr .20 .50
92 Rick Tocchet .10 .25
93 Adam Deadmarsh .07 .20
94 Pat Verbeek .07 .20
95 Doug Gilmour .15 .40
96 Jocelyn Thibault .10 .25
97 Radek Bonk .07 .20
98 Martin Gelinas .07 .20
99 Peter Forsberg .25 .60
100 Joe Murphy .07 .20
101 Dino Ciccarelli .12 .30
102 Rod Brind'Amour .12 .30
103 Kirk Muller .07 .20
104 Andy Moog .12 .30
105 Nikolai Khabibulin .10 .25
106 Mike Ricci .07 .20
107 Ray Ferraro .07 .20
108 Scott Niedermayer .12 .30
109 Russ Courtnall .07 .20
110 Dale Hunter .10 .25
111 Cam Neely .12 .30
112 Ray Sheppard .10 .25
113 Luc Robitaille .12 .30
114 Al MacInnis .15 .40
115 Mathieu Schneider .07 .20
116 Claude Lemieux .07 .20
117 Kevin Hatcher .07 .20
118 Daren Puppa .10 .25
119 Geoff Sanderson .10 .25
120 Zigmund Palffy .12 .30
121 Denis Savard .12 .30
122 Dimitri Khristich .07 .20
123 Ed Belfour .12 .30
124 Tom Barrasso .10 .25
125 Bob Rouse .07 .20
126 Tomas Sandstrom .07 .20
127 Roman Hamrlik .07 .20
128 Alexei Zhamnov .10 .25
129 Chris Osgood .12 .30
130 Rob Blake .12 .30
131 Garry Galley .07 .20
132 Greg Johnson .07 .20
133 Brian Skrudland .07 .20
134 Martin Rucinsky .07 .20
135 Steve Konowalchuk .07 .20
136 Damian Rhodes .10 .25
137 Jeremy Roenick .20 .50
138 Scott Stevens .12 .30
139 Pat LaFontaine .12 .30
140 Scott Young .07 .20
141 Benoit Hogue .07 .20
142 Paul Coffey .12 .30
143 John MacLean .10 .25
144 Joe Juneau .07 .20
145 Teemu Selanne .25 .60
146 Andrew Cassels .07 .20
147 Brian Savage .07 .20
148 Chris Gratton .10 .25
149 Corey Hirsch .10 .25
150 Mike Richter .12 .30
151 Shawn McEachern .07 .20
152 Joe Nieuwendyk .10 .25
153 Phil Housley .10 .25
154 Mike Gartner .15 .40
155 Kirk McLean .10 .25
156 Bob Probert .12 .30
157 Valeri Kamensky .10 .25
158 Vyacheslav Kozlov .07 .20
159 Eric Desjardins .10 .25
160 Mats Sundin .12 .30
161 John LeClair .12 .30
162 Adam Oates .12 .30
163 Cliff Ronning .07 .20
164 Mike Vernon .10 .25
165 German Titov .07 .20
166 Chris Pronger .12 .30
167 Norm Maciver .07 .20
168 Kenny Jonsson .07 .20
169 Tony Amonte .10 .25
170 Doug Weight .12 .30
171 Sergei Zubov .10 .25
172 Felix Potvin .20 .50
173 Trevor Linden .12 .30
174 Derek Plante .07 .20
175 Uwe Krupp .07 .20
176 Nicklas Lidstrom .15 .40
177 Mikael Renberg .10 .25
178 Igor Larionov .12 .30
179 Brian Leetch .10 .25
180 Stu Barnes .07 .20
181 Alexei Yashin .10 .25
182 Gary Suter .07 .20
183 Ken Wregget .10 .25
184 Mike Ridley .07 .20
185 Peter Bondra .12 .30
186 Steve Rucchin .07 .20
187 Jozef Stumpel .07 .20
188 Matthew Barnaby .07 .20
189 James Patrick .07 .20
190 Chris Simon .07 .20
191 Brent Fedyk .07 .20
192 Kris Draper .07 .20
193 David Oliver .07 .20
194 Dave Lowry .07 .20
195 Robert Kron .07 .20
196 Andrei Kovalenko .07 .20
197 Bill Guerin .12 .30
198 Ed Olczyk .07 .20
199 Yuri Khmylev .07 .20
200 Rob Ray .07 .20
201 Joe Mullen .10 .25
202 Petr Klima .07 .20
203 Todd Krygier .07 .20
204 Garth Snow .10 .25
205 Zarley Zalapski .07 .20
206 Ken Baumgartner .07 .20
207 Tony Twist .07 .20
208 Todd Gill .10 .25
209 Mike Peca .07 .20
210 Darcy Wakaluk .07 .20
211 Milos Holan .07 .20
212 Alexander Semak .07 .20
213 Jeff Reese .07 .20
214 Jon Casey .10 .25
215 Sandy McCarthy .07 .20
216 Curtis Leschyshyn .07 .20
217 Todd Marchant .07 .20
218 Bob Bassen .07 .20
219 Darren Turcotte .07 .20
220 David Reid .07 .20
221 Brian Bellows .10 .25
222 Jesse Belanger .07 .20
223 Bill Lindsay .07 .20
224 Lyle Odelein .07 .20
225 Keith Jones .07 .20
226 Sylvain Lefebvre .07 .20
227 Shaun Van Allen .07 .20
228 Dan Quinn .07 .20
229 Richard Matvichuk .07 .20
230 Craig MacTavish .07 .20
231 Craig Billington .07 .20
232 Stephane Richer .10 .25
233 Donald Audette .07 .20
234 Ulf Dahlen .07 .20
235 Steve Chiasson .07 .20
236 Eric Daze .10 .25
237 Petr Sykora .07 .20
238 Saku Koivu .12 .30
239 Ed Jovanovski .10 .25
240 Daniel Alfredsson .12 .30
241 Vitali Yachmenev .07 .20
242 Marcus Ragnarsson .07 .20
243 Cory Stillman .07 .20
244 Todd Bertuzzi .12 .30
245 Valeri Bure .07 .20
246 Jere Lehtinen .07 .20
247 Radek Dvorak .10 .25
248 Niclas Andersson .07 .20
249 Miroslav Satan .07 .20
250 Jeff O'Neill .07 .20
251 Nolan Baumgartner .07 .20
252 Roman Vopat .07 .20
253 Bryan McCabe .07 .20
254 Jamie Langenbrunner .07 .20
255 Chad Kilger .07 .20
256 Eric Fichaud .10 .25
257 Landon Wilson .07 .20
258 Kyle McLaren .07 .20
259 Aaron Gavey .07 .20
260 Byron Dafoe .10 .25
261 Grant Marshall .07 .20
262 Shane Doan .10 .25
263 Ralph Intranuovo .07 .20
264 Aki Berg .07 .20
265 Antti Tormanen .07 .20
266 Brian Holzinger .10 .25
267 Jose Theodore .15 .40
268 Ethan Moreau RC .12 .30
269 Niklas Sundstrom .07 .20
270 Brendan Witt .07 .20
271 Checklist (1-70) .01 .05
272 Checklist (71-140) .01 .05
273 Checklist (141-210) .01 .05
274 Checklist (211-275) .01 .05
275 Checklist (Chase Program) .01 .05

1996-97 Score Dealer's Choice Artist's Proofs

*SINGLES: 50X TO 100X BASIC CARDS

1996-97 Score Special Artist's Proofs

*SINGLES: 60X TO 120X BASIC CARDS

1996-97 Score Check It

COMPLETE SET (16) 15.00 30.00
1 Eric Lindros 2.00 5.00
2 Peter Forsberg 2.00 5.00
3 Keith Tkachuk 1.00 2.50
4 Cam Neely 2.50 6.00
5 Jeremy Roenick 1.50 4.00
6 Brendan Shanahan 1.50 4.00
7 Wendel Clark 1.50 4.00
8 Owen Nolan .60 1.50
9 Doug Gilmour .60 1.50
10 Trevor Linden .75 2.00
11 Saku Koivu .60 1.50
12 Ed Jovanovski .60 1.50
13 Theo Fleury .75 2.00
14 Doug Weight .60 1.50
15 Chris Chelios .60 1.50
16 Eric Daze .60 1.50

1996-97 Score Golden Blades

COMPLETE SET (275) 100.00 200.00
*SINGLES: 4X TO 10X BASIC CARDS

1996-97 Score Golden Blades Winners

*SINGLES: 5X TO 12X BASIC CARDS

1996-97 Score Golden Blades Winners Punched

*SINGLES: 5X TO 12X BASIC CARDS

1996-97 Score Dream Team

COMPLETE SET (12) 12.50 30.00
1 Eric Lindros .60 1.50
2 Paul Kariya .60 1.50
3 Joe Sakic 1.25 3.00
4 Peter Forsberg 1.50 4.00
5 Mark Messier .60 1.50
6 Mario Lemieux 3.00 8.00
7 Jaromir Jagr 1.00 2.50
8 Wayne Gretzky 4.00 10.00
9 Alexander Mogilny .25 .60
10 Pavel Bure .60 1.50
11 Sergei Fedorov .75 2.00
12 Patrick Roy 3.00 8.00

1996-97 Score Net Worth

COMPLETE SET (18) 10.00 20.00
1 Patrick Roy 2.00 5.00
2 Martin Brodeur 2.00 5.00
3 Jim Carey .40 1.00
4 Dominik Hasek 1.25 3.00
5 Ed Belfour .40 1.00
6 Chris Osgood .40 1.00
7 Curtis Joseph .40 1.00
8 John Vanbiesbrouck .40 1.00
9 Jocelyn Thibault .40 1.00
10 Stephane Fiset .40 1.00
11 Ron Hextall .40 1.00
12 Tom Barrasso .40 1.00
13 Daren Puppa .40 1.00
14 Mike Vernon .40 1.00
15 Bill Ranford .40 1.00
16 Corey Hirsch .40 1.00
17 Damian Rhodes .40 1.00
18 Nikolai Khabibulin .40 1.00

1996-97 Score Sudden Death

COMPLETE SET (15) 12.00 25.00
1 M.Brodeur/P.Turgeon .75 2.00
2 J.Carey/S.Yzerman 1.00 2.50
3 D.Hasek/B.Shanahan .40 1.00
4 E.Belfour/B.Hull .40 1.00
5 C.Osgood/J.Roenick .40 1.00
6 C.Joseph/P.Bure .40 1.00
7 J.Vanbiesbrouck/M.Lemieux 3.00 8.00
8 J.Thibault/A.Mogilny .40 1.00
9 M.Richter/J.Jagr .40 1.00
10 T.Barrasso/M.Messier .40 1.00
11 D.Puppa/J.Sakic .75 2.00
12 F.Potvin/W.Gretzky 4.00 10.00
13 C.Hirsch/P.Kariya .40 1.00
14 R.Hextall/S.Fedorov .40 1.00
15 N.Khabibulin/T.Selanne .40 1.00

1996-97 Score Superstitions

COMPLETE SET (13) 3.00 8.00
1 Teemu Selanne .30 .75
2 Doug Weight .25 .60
3 Mats Sundin .30 .75
4 Mike Modano .40 1.00
5 Felix Potvin .30 .75
6 Paul Coffey .30 .75
7 Ray Bourque .50 1.25
8 Chris Chelios .30 .75
9 Ron Hextall .25 .60
10 Alexander Selivanov .25 .60
11 Brett Hull .40 1.00
12 Mike Richter .30 .75
13 Scott Mellanby .25 .60

1997-98 Score

1 Sean Burke .07 .20
2 Chris Osgood .12 .30
3 Garth Snow .10 .25
4 Mike Vernon .10 .25
5 Grant Fuhr .20 .50
6 Guy Hebert .10 .25
7 Arturs Irbe .10 .25
8 Andy Moog .12 .30
9 Tommy Salo .07 .20
10 Nikolai Khabibulin .12 .30
11 Mike Richter .12 .30
12 Corey Hirsch .10 .25
13 Bill Ranford .10 .25
14 Jim Carey .07 .20
15 Jeff Hackett .07 .20
16 Damian Rhodes .10 .25
17 Tom Barrasso .10 .25
18 Daren Puppa .10 .25
19 Craig Billington .07 .20
20 Ed Belfour .12 .30
21 Mikhail Shtalenkov .10 .25
22 Glenn Healy .07 .20
23 Marcel Cousineau .10 .25
24 Kevin Hodson .10 .25
25 Olaf Kolzig .12 .30
26 Eric Fichaud .10 .25
27 Ron Hextall .12 .30
28 Rick Tabaracci .10 .25
29 Felix Potvin .20 .50
30 Martin Brodeur .30 .75
31 Curtis Joseph .15 .40
32 Ken Wregget .07 .20
33 Patrick Roy .30 .75
34 John Vanbiesbrouck .12 .30
34 John Vanbiesbrouck PROMO .12 .30
35 Stephane Fiset .10 .25
36 Roman Turek .10 .25
37 Trevor Kidd .07 .20
38 Dwayne Roloson .10 .25
39 Dominik Hasek .20 .50
40 Patrick Lalime .10 .25
41 Jocelyn Thibault .10 .25
42 Jose Theodore .12 .30
43 Kirk McLean .10 .25
44 Steve Shields RC .12 .30
45 Mike Dunham .10 .25
46 Jamie Storr .10 .25
47 Byron Dafoe .10 .25
48 Chris Terreri .07 .20
49 Ron Tugnutt .12 .30
50 Kelly Hrudey .10 .25
51 Vaclav Prospal RC .10 .25
52 Alyn McCauley .10 .25
53 Jaroslav Svejkovsky .10 .25
54 Joe Thornton .20 .50
55 Chris Dingman RC .12 .30
56 Vadim Sharifijanov .10 .25
57 Larry Courville .07 .20
58 Erik Rasmussen .10 .25
59 Sergei Samsonov .10 .25
60 Kevyn Adams .07 .20
61 Daniel Cleary .10 .25
62 Martin Prochazka RC .10 .25
63 Mattias Ohlund .10 .25
64 Juha Lind RC .12 .30
65 Olli Jokinen RC .15 .40
66 Espen Knutsen RC .12 .30
67 Marc Savard .07 .20
68 Hnat Domenichelli .10 .25
69 Warren Luhning RC .07 .20
70 Magnus Arvedson RC .12 .30
71 Chris Phillips .10 .25
72 Brad Isbister .10 .25
73 Boyd Devereaux .10 .25
74 Alexei Morozov .10 .25
75 Vladimir Vorobiev RC .12 .30
76 Steven Rice .10 .25
77 Tony Granato .07 .20
78 Lonny Bohonos .10 .25
79 Dave Gagner .07 .20
80 Brendan Shanahan .12 .30
81 Brett Hull .25 .60
82 Jaromir Jagr .40 1.00
83 Peter Forsberg .25 .60
84 Paul Kariya .12 .30
85 Mark Messier .25 .60
86 Steve Yzerman .30 .75
87 Keith Tkachuk .12 .30
88 Eric Lindros .20 .50
89 Ray Bourque .20 .50
90 Chris Chelios .12 .30
91 Sergei Fedorov .20 .50
92 Mike Modano .20 .50
93 Doug Gilmour .15 .40
94 Saku Koivu .12 .30
95 Mats Sundin .12 .30
96 Pavel Bure .12 .30
97 Theo Fleury .15 .40
98 Keith Primeau .10 .25
99 Wayne Gretzky .75 2.00
100 Doug Weight .12 .30
101 Alexandre Daigle .07 .20
102 Owen Nolan .12 .30
103 Peter Bondra .12 .30
104 Pat LaFontaine .12 .30
105 Kirk Muller .07 .20
106 Zigmund Palffy .12 .30
107 Jeremy Roenick .20 .50
108 John LeClair .12 .30
109 Derek Plante .10 .25
110 Geoff Sanderson .10 .25
111 Dimitri Khristich .10 .25
112 Vincent Damphousse .10 .25
113 Teemu Selanne .25 .60
114 Tony Amonte .10 .25
115 Dave Andreychuk .12 .30
116 Alexei Yashin .10 .25
117 Adam Oates .12 .30
118 Pierre Turgeon .10 .25
119 Dino Ciccarelli .12 .30
120 Ryan Smyth .10 .25
121 Ray Sheppard .10 .25
122 Jozef Stumpel .07 .20
123 Jarome Iginla .15 .40
124 Pat Verbeek .10 .25
125 Joe Sakic .25 .60
126 Brian Leetch .10 .25
127 Rod Brind'Amour .12 .30
128 Wendel Clark .20 .50
129 Alexander Mogilny .10 .25
130 Mark Recchi .15 .40
131 Daniel Alfredsson .12 .30
132 Ron Francis .15 .40
133 Martin Gelinas .07 .20
134 Andrew Cassels .07 .20
135 Joe Nieuwendyk .10 .25
136 Jason Arnott .10 .25
137 Bryan Berard .07 .20
138 Mikael Renberg .10 .25
139 Mike Gartner .15 .40
140 Joe Juneau .07 .20
141 John MacLean .07 .20
142 Adam Graves .07 .20
143 Petr Nedved .12 .30
144 Trevor Linden .12 .30
145 Sergei Berezin .10 .25
146 Adam Deadmarsh .07 .20
147 Jeff O'Neill .10 .25
148 Rob Blake .12 .30
149 Luc Robitaille .12 .30
150 Markus Naslund .12 .30
151 Ethan Moreau .07 .20
152 Martin Rucinsky .10 .25
153 Mike Grier .10 .25
154 Craig Janney .07 .20
155 John Cullen .07 .20
156 Alexei Kovalev .10 .25
157 Tony Twist .10 .25
158 Claude Lemieux .10 .25
159 Kevin Stevens .10 .25
160 Mathieu Schneider .10 .25
161 Randy Cunneyworth .07 .20
162 Darius Kasparaitis .10 .25
163 Joe Murphy .10 .25
164 Brandon Convery .07 .20
165 Janne Niinimaa .10 .25
166 Paul Coffey .12 .30
167 Daymond Langkow .07 .20
168 Chris Gratton .07 .20
169 Ray Ferraro .07 .20
170 Jeff Friesen .10 .25
171 Ted Donato .07 .20
172 Brian Holzinger .10 .25
173 Travis Green .10 .25
174 Sandis Ozolinsh .07 .20
175 Alexei Zhamnov .07 .20
176 Steve Rucchin .10 .25
177 Scott Mellanby .10 .25
178 Andrei Kovalenko .07 .20
179 Donald Audette .10 .25
180 Bernie Nicholls .10 .25
181 Jonas Hoglund .10 .25
182 Nicklas Lidstrom .12 .30
183 Bobby Holik .07 .20
184 Geoff Courtnall .07 .20
185 Steve Sullivan .10 .25
186 Valeri Kamensky .10 .25
187 Mike Peca .10 .25
188 Jere Lehtinen .10 .25
189 Robert Svehla .10 .25
190 Darren McCarty .10 .25
191 Brian Savage .07 .20
192 Harry York .10 .25
193 Eric Daze .07 .20
194 Niklas Sundstrom .10 .25
195 Oleg Tverdovsky .10 .25
196 Eric Desjardins .07 .20
197 German Titov .07 .20
198 Derian Hatcher .10 .25
199 Bill Guerin .12 .30
200 Rob Zamuner .07 .20
201 Dale Hunter .10 .25
202 Darcy Tucker .12 .30
203 Andreas Dackell .10 .25
204 Jason Dawe .10 .25
205 Brian Rolston .10 .25
206 Ed Olczyk .07 .20
207 Todd Warriner .10 .25
208 Mariusz Czerkawski .07 .20
209 Slava Kozlov .10 .25
210 Marty McInnis .07 .20
211 Jamie Langenbrunner .10 .25
212 Vitali Yachmenev .10 .25
213 Stephane Richer .07 .20
214 Roman Hamrlik .07 .20
215 Jim Campbell .07 .20
216 Matthew Barnaby .07 .20
217 Benoit Hogue .10 .25
218 Robert Reichel .10 .25
219 Tie Domi .10 .25
220 Steve Konowalchuk .10 .25
221 Radek Dvorak .10 .25
222 Kevin Hatcher .07 .20
223 Viktor Kozlov .10 .25
224 Scott Stevens .12 .30
225 Cory Stillman .10 .25
226 Anson Carter .07 .20
227 Rem Murray .07 .20
228 Vladimir Konstantinov .07 .20
229 Scott Niedermayer .12 .30
230 Steve Duchesne .07 .20
231 Valeri Bure .07 .20
232 Miroslav Satan .07 .20
233 Jason Allison .10 .25
234 Mark Fitzpatrick .07 .20
235 Ed Jovanovski .07 .20
236 Esa Tikkanen .07 .20
237 Stu Barnes .07 .20
238 Darryl Sydor .07 .20
239 Ulf Samuelsson .12 .30
240 Dmitri Mironov .10 .25
241 Bryan Smolinski .10 .25
242 Rob Ray .07 .20
243 Todd Marchant .10 .25
244 Cliff Ronning .07 .20
245 Alexander Selivanov .07 .20
246 Rick Tocchet .07 .20
247 Vladimir Malakhov .07 .20
248 Al MacInnis .15 .40
249 Dainius Zubrus .10 .25
250 Keith Jones .07 .20
251 Darren Turcotte .10 .25
252 Ulf Dahlen .07 .20
253 Rob Niedermayer .07 .20
254 J.J. Daigneault .10 .25
255 Michal Grosek .07 .20
256 Chris Therien .07 .20
257 Adam Foote .07 .20
258 Tomas Sandstrom .07 .20
259 Scott Lachance .10 .25
260 Paul Kariya SM .12 .30
261 Pavel Bure SM .12 .30
262 Mike Modano SM .20 .50
263 Steve Yzerman SM .30 .75
264 Sergei Fedorov SM .20 .50
265 Eric Lindros SM .20 .50
266 Dominik Hasek CL (1-66) .20 .50
267 Bryan Berard CL (67-132) .07 .20
268 Mike Peca CL (133-201) .10 .25
269 M.Brodeur
M.Dunham CL (202-270) .30 .75
270 Paul Kariya CL (inserts) .12 .30
82 Jaromir Jagr PROMO .40 1.00
83 Peter Forsberg PROMO .25 .60
84 Paul Kariya PROMO .12 .30
86 Steve Yzerman PROMO .30 .75
88 Eric Lindros PROMO .20 .50

1997-98 Score Artist's Proofs

*ART.PROOF: 25X TO 60X BASIC CARDS

1997-98 Score Golden Blades

*GOLDEN BLADES: 1.2X TO 3X BASIC CARDS

1997-98 Score Check It

COMPLETE SET (18) 5.00 12.00
COMMON CARD (1-18) .20 .50
SEMISTARS .15 .40
UNLISTED STARS .30 .75
1 Eric Lindros .75 2.00
2 Mark Recchi .20 .50
3 Brendan Shanahan .60 1.50
4 Keith Tkachuk .30 .75
5 John LeClair .30 .75
6 Doug Gilmour .20 .50
7 Jarome Iginla .50 1.25
8 Ryan Smyth .20 .50
9 Chris Chelios .30 .75
10 Mike Grier .10 .25
11 Vincent Damphousse .10 .25
12 Bryan Berard .20 .50
13 Jaromir Jagr .75 2.00
14 Mike Peca .10 .25
15 Dino Ciccarelli .10 .25
16 Rod Brind'Amour .20 .50
17 Owen Nolan .20 .50
18 Pat Verbeek .20 .50

1997-98 Score Net Worth

COMPLETE SET (18) 8.00 15.00
1 Guy Hebert .25 .60
2 Jim Carey .25 .60
3 Trevor Kidd .25 .60
4 Chris Osgood .25 .60
5 Curtis Joseph .40 1.00
6 Mike Richter .40 1.00
7 Damian Rhodes .25 .60
8 Garth Snow .25 .60
9 Nikolai Khabibulin .25 .60
10 Grant Fuhr .25 .60
11 Jocelyn Thibault .25 .60
12 Tommy Salo .25 .60
13 Patrick Roy 2.00 5.00
14 Martin Brodeur 1.00 2.50
15 John Vanbiesbrouck .25 .60
16 Felix Potvin .40 1.00
17 Dominik Hasek .75 2.00
18 Ed Belfour .40 1.00

1997-98 Score Avalanche

COMPLETE SET (20) 4.00 10.00
*PLATINUM: 1.2X TO 3X BASIC CARDS
*PREMIER: 3X TO 8X BASIC CARDS
1 Patrick Roy 1.50 4.00
2 Craig Billington .25 .60
3 Marc Denis .25 .60
4 Peter Forsberg 1.00 2.50
5 Jari Kurri .25 .60
6 Sandis Ozolinsh .25 .60
7 Valeri Kamensky .25 .60
8 Adam Deadmarsh .25 .60
9 Keith Jones .10 .30
10 Josef Marha .08 .25
11 Claude Lemieux .25 .60
12 Adam Foote .10 .30
13 Eric Lacroix .08 .25
14 Rene Corbet .08 .25
15 Uwe Krupp .08 .25
16 Sylvain Lefebvre .08 .25
17 Mike Ricci .25 .60
18 Joe Sakic .75 2.00
19 Stephane Yelle .08 .25
20 Yves Sarault .08 .25

1997-98 Score Blues

COMPLETE SET (20) 3.00 8.00
*PLATINUM: 1.2X TO 3X BASIC CARDS
*PREMIER: 3X TO 8X BASIC CARDS
1 Brett Hull .40 1.00
2 Pierre Turgeon .25 .60
3 Joe Murphy .08 .25
4 Jim Campbell .08 .25
5 Harry York .08 .25
6 Al MacInnis .25 .60
7 Chris Pronger .25 .60
8 Darren Turcotte .08 .25
9 Robert Petrovicky .08 .25
10 Tony Twist .30 .75
11 Grant Fuhr .25 .60
12 Scott Pellerin .08 .25
13 Jamie Rivers .10 .25
14 Chris McAlpine .08 .25
15 Geoff Courtnall .25 .60
16 Steve Duchesne .20 .50
17 Libor Zabransky .08 .25
18 Pavol Demitra .25 .60
19 Marc Bergevin .08 .25
20 Jamie McLennan .08 .25

1997-98 Score Bruins

COMPLETE SET (20) 2.50 6.00
*PLATINUM: 1.2X TO 3X BASIC CARDS
*PREMIER: 3X TO 8X BASIC CARDS
1 Shawn Bates .08 .25
2 Jim Carey .15 .40
3 Rob Tallas .08 .25
4 Ray Bourque .30 .75
5 Dimitri Khristich .08 .25
6 Ted Donato .08 .25
7 Jason Allison .25 .60
8 Anson Carter .15 .40
9 Rob Dimaio .08 .25
10 Steve Heinze .08 .25
11 Jean Yves Roy .08 .25
12 Randy Robitaille .08 .25
13 Byron Dafoe .30 .75
14 Sergei Samsonov .75 2.00
15 Ken Baumgartner .08 .25
16 Dave Ellett .08 .25
17 Joe Thornton .75 2.00
18 Jeff Odgers .08 .25
19 Kyle McLaren .08 .25
20 Don Sweeney .08 .25

1997-98 Score Canadiens

COMPLETE SET (20) 3.00 8.00
*PLATINUM: 1.2X TO 3X BASIC CARDS
*PREMIER: 3X TO 8X BASIC CARDS
1 Andy Moog .25 .60

2 Jocelyn Thibault .25 .60
3 Jose Theodore .25 .60
4 Vincent Damphousse .25 .60
5 Mark Recchi .25 .60
6 Brian Savage .08 .25
7 Saku Koivu .60 1.50
8 Stephane Richer .25 .60
9 Martin Rucinsky .08 .25
10 Valeri Bure .08 .25
11 Vladimir Malakhov .08 .25
12 Shayne Corson .25 .60
13 Darcy Tucker .08 .25
14 Sebastien Bordeleau .08 .25
15 Terry Ryan .08 .25
16 David Ling .08 .25
17 Dave Manson .08 .25
18 Benoit Brunet .08 .25
19 Marc Bureau .08 .25
20 Patrice Brisebois .08 .25

1997-98 Score Canucks

COMPLETE SET (20) 3.00 8.00
*PLATINUM: 1.2X TO 3X BASIC CARDS
*PREMIER: 3X TO 8X BASIC CARDS
1 Pavel Bure .60 1.50
2 Alexander Mogilny .25 .60
3 Mark Messier .40 1.00
4 Trevor Linden .25 .60
5 Martin Gelinas .08 .25
6 Mattias Ohlund .15 .40
7 Markus Naslund .08 .25
8 Jyrki Lumme .08 .25
9 Lonny Bohonos .08 .25
10 Kirk McLean .25 .60
11 Corey Hirsch .25 .60
12 Arturs Irbe .25 .60
13 Larry Courville .08 .25
14 Adrian Aucoin .08 .25
15 Grant Ledyard .08 .25
16 Gino Odjick .08 .25
17 Donald Brashear .08 .25
18 Brian Noonan .08 .25
19 David Roberts .08 .25
20 Dave Babych .08 .25

1997-98 Score Devils

COMPLETE SET (20) 3.00 8.00
*PLATINUM: 1.2X TO 3X BASIC CARDS
*PREMIER: 3X TO 8X BASIC CARDS
1 Doug Gilmour .30 .75
2 Bobby Holik .08 .25
3 Dave Andreychuk .25 .60
4 John MacLean .08 .25
5 Bill Guerin .08 .25
6 Brian Rolston .08 .25
7 Scott Niedermayer .08 .25
8 Scott Stevens .08 .25
9 Valeri Zelepukin .08 .25
10 Steve Thomas .08 .25
11 Denis Pederson .08 .25
12 Randy McKay .08 .25
13 Mike Dunham .25 .60
14 Petr Sykora .15 .40
15 Lyle Odelein .08 .25
16 Martin Brodeur .75 2.00
17 Vadim Sharifijanov .08 .25
18 Bob Carpenter .08 .25
19 Sergei Brylin .08 .25
20 Ken Daneyko .08 .25

1997-98 Score Flyers

COMPLETE SET (20) 4.00 10.00
*PLATINUM: 1.2X TO 3X BASIC CARDS
*PREMIER: 3X TO 8X BASIC CARDS
1 Ron Hextall .25 .60
2 Garth Snow .25 .60
3 Eric Lindros 1.25 3.00
4 John LeClair .60 1.50
5 Rod Brind'Amour .25 .60
6 Chris Gratton .15 .40
7 Eric Desjardins .08 .25
8 Trent Klatt .08 .25
9 Janne Niinimaa .25 .60
10 Luke Richardson .08 .25
11 Paul Coffey .30 .75
12 Dainius Zubrus .30 .75
13 Shjon Podein .08 .25
14 Joel Otto .08 .25
15 Chris Therien .08 .25
16 Pat Falloon .08 .25
17 Petr Svoboda .08 .25
18 Vaclav Prospal .30 .75
19 John Druce .08 .25
20 Daniel Lacroix .08 .25

1997-98 Score Maple Leafs

COMPLETE SET (20) 3.00 8.00
*PLATINUM: 1.2X TO 3X BASIC CARDS
*PREMIER: 3X TO 8X BASIC CARDS
1 Felix Potvin .30 .75
2 Glenn Healy .25 .60
3 Marcel Cousineau .25 .60
4 Mats Sundin .30 .75
5 Wendel Clark .25 .60
6 Sergei Berezin .25 .60
7 Steve Sullivan .08 .25
8 Tie Domi .10 .30
9 Todd Warriner .08 .25
10 Mathieu Schneider .08 .25
11 Mike Craig .08 .25
12 Darby Hendrickson .08 .25
13 Fredrik Modin .08 .25
14 Brandon Convery .08 .25
15 Kevyn Adams .08 .25
16 Dimitri Yushkevich .08 .25
17 Alyn McCauley .08 .25
18 Derek King .08 .25
19 Jamie Baker .08 .25
20 Martin Prochazka .08 .25

1997-98 Score Mighty Ducks

COMPLETE SET (20) 4.00 10.00
*PLATINUM: 1.2X TO 3X BASIC CARDS
*PREMIER: 3X TO 8X BASIC CARDS
1 Paul Kariya 1.25 3.00
2 Teemu Selanne .75 2.00
3 Steve Rucchin .08 .25
4 Dmitri Mironov .08 .25
5 Matt Cullen .08 .25
6 Kevin Todd .08 .25
7 Joe Sacco .08 .25
8 J.J. Daigneault .08 .25
9 Darren Van Impe .08 .25
10 Scott Young .08 .25
11 Ted Drury .08 .25
12 Tomas Sandstrom .08 .25
13 Warren Rychel .08 .25
14 Guy Hebert .25 .60
15 Shawn Antoski .08 .25
16 Mikhail Shtalenkov .25 .60
17 Peter Leboutillier .08 .25
18 Sean Pronger .08 .25
19 Dave Karpa .08 .25
20 Espen Knutsen .20 .50

1997-98 Score Penguins

COMPLETE SET (20) 3.60 9.00
*PLATINUM: 1.2X TO 3X BASIC CARDS
*PREMIER: 3X TO 8X BASIC CARDS
1 Tom Barrasso .08 .25
2 Ken Wregget .25 .60
3 Patrick Lalime .25 .60
4 Jaromir Jagr 1.00 2.50
5 Ron Francis .25 .60
6 Petr Nedved .25 .60
7 Ed Olczyk .08 .25
8 Kevin Hatcher .08 .25
9 Stu Barnes .08 .25
10 Darius Kasparaitis .08 .25
11 Greg Johnson .08 .25
12 Garry Valk .08 .25
13 Roman Oksiuta .08 .25
14 Dan Quinn .08 .25
15 Alex Hicks .08 .25
16 Robert Dome .08 .25
17 Dave Roche .08 .25
18 Alexei Morozov .25 .60
19 Rob Brown .08 .25
20 Domenic Pittis .08 .25

1997-98 Score Rangers

COMPLETE SET (20) 4.00 10.00
*PLATINUM: 1.2X TO 3X BASIC CARDS
*PREMIER: 3X TO 8X BASIC CARDS
1 Wayne Gretzky 2.00 5.00
2 Brian Leetch .30 .75
3 Mike Keane .08 .25
4 Adam Graves .25 .60
5 Niklas Sundstrom .08 .25
6 Kevin Stevens .08 .25
7 Alexei Kovalev .08 .25
8 Alexander Karpovtsev .08 .25
9 Bill Berg .08 .25
10 Pat Lafontaine .25 .60
11 Bruce Driver .08 .25
12 Pat Flatley .08 .25
13 Vladimir Vorobiev .08 .25
14 Christian Dube .08 .25
15 Ulf Samuelsson .08 .25
16 Mike Richter .30 .75
17 Jason Muzzatti .08 .25
18 Daniel Goneau .08 .25
19 Marc Savard .08 .25
20 Jeff Beukeboom .08 .25

1997-98 Score Red Wings

COMPLETE SET (20) 4.00 10.00
*PLATINUM: 1.2X TO 3X BASIC CARDS
*PREMIER: 3X TO 8X BASIC CARDS
1 Brendan Shanahan .60 1.50
2 Steve Yzerman 1.00 2.50
3 Sergei Fedorov .60 1.50
4 Nicklas Lidstrom .25 .60
5 Igor Larionov .15 .40
6 Darren McCarty .25 .60
7 Slava Kozlov .25 .60
8 Larry Murphy .25 .60
9 Vladimir Konstantinov .25 .60
10 Martin Lapointe .10 .30
11 Slava Fetisov .10 .30
12 Kris Draper .10 .30
13 Doug Brown .08 .25
14 Brent Gilchrist .08 .25
15 Kirk Maltby .08 .25
16 Tomas Holmstrom .08 .25
17 Chris Osgood .30 .75
18 Kevin Hodson .30 .75
19 Jamie Pushor .08 .25
20 Mike Knuble .25 .60

1997-98 Score Sabres

COMPLETE SET (20) 3.00 8.00
*PLATINUM: 1.2X TO 3X BASIC CARDS
*PREMIER: 3X TO 8X BASIC CARDS
1 Dominik Hasek .75 2.00
2 Steve Shields .25 .60
3 Dixon Ward .08 .25
4 Donald Audette .08 .25
5 Matthew Barnaby .08 .25
6 Randy Burridge .08 .25
7 Jason Dawe .08 .25
8 Michael Grosek .08 .25
9 Brian Holzinger .25 .60
10 Brad May .08 .25
11 Mike Peca .30 .75
12 Derek Plante .08 .25
13 Wayne Primeau .08 .25
14 Rob Ray .25 .60
15 Miroslav Satan .25 .60
16 Erik Rasmussen .08 .25
17 Jason Woolley .08 .25
18 Alexei Zhitnik .08 .25
19 Darryl Shannon .08 .25
20 Mike Wilson .08 .25

2010-11 Score

COMP.SET w/o SSPs (550) 40.00 80.00
COMP.SET w/o SPs (500) 15.00 40.00
COMP.R/T.FACT.SET (105) 20.00 40.00
COMP.ROOK/TRD SET (99) 12.00 30.00
1 Joe Sakic banner HL .40 1.00
2 Elmer Lach banner HL .15 .40
3 Emile Bouchard banner HL .20 .50
4 Phil Kessel HL .20 .50
5 Josh Bailey HL .15 .40
6 Cristobal Huet HL .20 .50
7 NHL heads overseas HL
Nicklas Lidstrom .20 .50
8 Martin Brodeur HL .50 1.25
9 B.Pouliot/G.Latendresse .15 .40
10 Michael Cammalleri HL .20 .50
11 Martin Brodeur HL .50 1.25
12 Marco Sturm HL .12 .30
13 Tim Thomas HL .20 .50
14 Roberto Luongo HL .30 .75
15 Ryan Miller HL .20 .50
16 Jonathan Toews HL .30 .75
17 Chris Chelios HL .20 .50
18 Dion Phaneuf HL .15 .40
19 Ilya Kovalchuk HL .20 .50
20 Alex Ovechkin HL .75 2.00
21 Shane Doan HL
Vern Fiddler .15 .40
22 Claude Giroux HL .20 .50
23 Keith Tkachuk HL .20 .50
24 Bobby Orr Statue HL .75 2.00
25 Sidney Crosby HL .75 2.00
26 Steven Stamkos HL .40 1.00
27 I.Bryzgalov/J.Quick .15 .40
28 Henrik Sedin HL .25 .60
29 Jordan Staal HL .15 .40
30 Marian Hossa HL .20 .50
31 Hawks capture Cup HL .40 1.00
32 Jonathan Toews HL .30 .75
33 Brent Sopel HL .12 .30
34 Rob Blake HL .20 .50
35 Scott Niedermayer HL .20 .50
36 Corey Perry .30 .75
37 Ryan Getzlaf .20 .50
38 Joffrey Lupul .12 .30
39 Saku Koivu .20 .50
40 George Parros .15 .40
41 Dan Sexton .15 .40
42 Ryan Carter .12 .30
43 Troy Bodie .12 .30
44 Matt Beleskey .15 .40
45 Teemu Selanne .40 1.00
46 Bobby Ryan .15 .40
47 Lubomir Visnovsky .12 .30
48 Luca Sbisa .15 .40
49 Jonas Hiller .15 .40
50 Curtis McElhinney .12 .30
51 Nik Antropov .15 .40
52 Evander Kane .20 .50
53 Todd White .12 .30
54 Dustin Byfuglien .20 .50
55 Bryan Little .20 .50
56 Niclas Bergfors .15 .40
57 Rich Peverley .20 .50
58 Chris Thorburn .12 .30
59 Ben Eager .12 .30
60 Ron Hainsey .12 .30
61 Tobias Enstrom .12 .30
62 Zach Bogosian .15 .40
63 Johnny Oduya .15 .40
64 Chris Mason .15 .40
65 Ondrej Pavelec .20 .50
66 Marc Savard .12 .30
67 Patrice Bergeron .25 .60
68 David Krejci .20 .50
69 Marco Sturm .12 .30
70 Milan Lucic .20 .50
71 Nathan Horton .15 .40
72 Mark Recchi .25 .60
73 Blake Wheeler .20 .50
74 Matt Hunwick .12 .30
75 Johnny Boychuk .15 .40
76 Zdeno Chara .20 .50
77 Mark Stuart .12 .30
78 Shawn Thornton .12 .30
79 Tuukka Rask .25 .60
80 Tim Thomas .20 .50
81 Thomas Vanek .15 .40
82 Jason Pominville .12 .30
83 Tim Connolly .12 .30
84 Derek Roy .12 .30
85 Jochen Hecht .12 .30
86 Paul Gaustad .12 .30
87 Drew Stafford .12 .30
88 Tyler Ennis .12 .30
89 Nathan Gerbe .12 .30
90 Patrick Kaleta .12 .30
91 Craig Rivet .12 .30
92 Tyler Myers .12 .30
93 Chris Butler .12 .30
94 Ryan Miller .20 .50
95 Jhonas Enroth .20 .50
96 Jarome Iginla .25 .60
97 Daymond Langkow .12 .30
98 Rene Bourque .12 .30
99 David Moss .12 .30
100 Curtis Glencross .12 .30
101 Niklas Hagman .12 .30
102 Olli Jokinen .15 .40
103 Matt Stajan .12 .30
104 Mikael Backlund .15 .40
105 Jay Bouwmeester .12 .30
106 Robyn Regehr .12 .30
107 Cory Sarich .12 .30
108 Mark Giordano .20 .50
109 Alex Tanguay .12 .30
110 Miikka Kiprusoff .20 .50
111 Eric Staal .25 .60
112 Tuomo Ruutu .15 .40
113 Erik Cole .12 .30
114 Sergei Samsonov .15 .40
115 Jussi Jokinen .12 .30
116 Chad LaRose .12 .30
117 Brandon Sutter .12 .30
118 Drayson Bowman .15 .40
119 Jiri Tlusty .12 .30
120 Tom Kostopoulos .12 .30
121 Zach Boychuk .15 .40
122 Joni Pitkanen .15 .40
123 Tim Gleason .12 .30
124 Cam Ward .20 .50
125 Justin Peters .15 .40
126 Marian Hossa .20 .50
127 Patrick Sharp .20 .50
128 Patrick Kane .40 1.00
129 Jonathan Toews .30 .75
130 Dave Bolland .15 .40
131 Troy Brouwer .12 .30
132 Viktor Stalberg .15 .40
133 Jack Skille .15 .40
134 Brent Seabrook .12 .30
135 Duncan Keith .15 .40
136 Niklas Hjalmarsson .12 .30
137 Jordan Hendry .12 .30
138 Brian Campbell .12 .30
139 Tomas Kopecky .15 .40
140 Marty Turco .20 .50
141 Paul Stastny .15 .40
142 Milan Hejduk .15 .40
143 Matt Duchene .20 .50
144 Peter Mueller .15 .40
145 Ryan O'Reilly .20 .50
146 T.J. Galiardi .15 .40
147 Adam Foote .12 .30
148 Chris Stewart .15 .40
149 Ryan Stoa .12 .30
150 Cody McLeod .12 .30
151 David Jones .12 .30
152 Scott Hannan .12 .30
153 Kyle Cumiskey .12 .30
154 Peter Budaj .15 .40
155 Craig Anderson .20 .50
156 Rick Nash .20 .50
157 Kristian Huselius .12 .30
158 R.J. Umberger .12 .30
159 Antoine Vermette .12 .30
160 Samuel Pahlsson .12 .30
161 Chris Clark .12 .30
162 Jakub Voracek .15 .40
163 Derick Brassard .12 .30
164 Derek Dorsett .12 .30
165 Mike Commodore .12 .30
166 Kris Russell .12 .30
167 Marc Methot .12 .30
168 Jan Hejda .12 .30
169 Steve Mason .15 .40
170 Mathieu Garon .15 .40
171 Brad Richards .20 .50
172 Brenden Morrow .15 .40
173 Loui Eriksson .12 .30
174 Steve Ott .12 .30
175 Jamie Benn .25 .60
176 James Neal .12 .30
177 Tom Wandell .12 .30
178 Brandon Segal .12 .30
179 Krys Barch .12 .30
180 Trevor Daley .12 .30
181 Stephane Robidas .12 .30
182 Mark Fistric .12 .30
183 Nicklas Grossman .12 .30
184 Raymond Sawada .12 .30
185 Kari Lehtonen .15 .40
186 Pavel Datsyuk .30 .75
187 Henrik Zetterberg .25 .60
188 Tomas Holmstrom .12 .30
189 Johan Franzen .15 .40
190 Valtteri Filppula .12 .30
191 Daniel Cleary .20 .50
192 Justin Abdelkader .15 .40
193 Mattias Ritola .12 .30
194 Drew Miller .12 .30
195 Mike Modano .30 .75
196 Nicklas Lidstrom .20 .50
197 Brian Rafalski .12 .30
198 Niklas Kronwall .15 .40
199 Jimmy Howard .25 .60
200 Chris Osgood .20 .50
201 Dustin Penner .12 .30
202 Sam Gagner .12 .30
203 Ales Hemsky .15 .40
204 Shawn Horcoff .12 .30
205 Zack Stortini .12 .30
206 Gilbert Brule .20 .50
207 Andrew Cogliano .12 .30
208 J-F Jacques .12 .30
209 Alex Plante .15 .40
210 Kurtis Foster .12 .30
211 Tom Gilbert .12 .30
212 Ryan Whitney .12 .30
213 Taylor Chorney .15 .40
214 Nikolai Khabibulin .15 .40
215 Jeff Deslauriers .12 .30
216 Stephen Weiss .15 .40
217 David Booth .12 .30
218 Cory Stillman .12 .30
219 Rostislav Olesz .12 .30
220 Michael Frolik .12 .30
221 Steve Reinprecht .12 .30
222 Michal Repik .12 .30
223 Shawn Matthias .12 .30
224 Byron Bitz .12 .30
225 Radek Dvorak .12 .30
226 Dmitry Kulikov .15 .40
227 Keaton Ellerby .12 .30
228 Dennis Wideman .12 .30
229 Tomas Vokoun .15 .40
230 Tyler Plante .12 .30
231 Anze Kopitar .30 .75
232 Ryan Smyth .15 .40
233 Dustin Brown .20 .50
234 Jarret Stoll .15 .40
235 Justin Williams .15 .40
236 Michal Handzus .15 .40
237 Wayne Simmonds .25 .60
238 Oscar Moller .15 .40
239 Alexei Ponikarovsky .12 .30
240 Matt Greene .12 .30
241 Drew Doughty .25 .60
242 Davis Drewiske .12 .30
243 Jack Johnson .12 .30
244 Jonathan Quick .25 .60
245 Jonathan Bernier .15 .40
246 Mikko Koivu .20 .50
247 Martin Havlat .15 .40
248 Pierre-Marc Bouchard .20 .50
249 Andrew Brunette .12 .30
250 Antti Miettinen .12 .30
251 Chuck Kobasew .12 .30
252 James Sheppard .12 .30
253 Cal Clutterbuck .12 .30
254 Guillaume Latendresse .15 .40
255 Colton Gillies .12 .30
256 Brent Burns .20 .50
257 Nick Schultz .12 .30
258 Greg Zanon .12 .30
259 Cam Barker .12 .30
260 Niklas Backstrom .20 .50
261 Scott Gomez .15 .40
262 Michael Cammalleri .20 .50
263 Brian Gionta .12 .30
264 Benoit Pouliot .12 .30
265 Andrei Kostitsyn .15 .40
266 Travis Moen .12 .30
267 Max Pacioretty .20 .50
268 Tom Pyatt .12 .30
269 Maxim Lapierre .12 .30
270 Josh Gorges .12 .30
271 Tomas Plekanec .12 .30
272 Lars Eller .12 .30
273 Hal Gill .12 .30
274 Andrei Markov .20 .50
275 Carey Price .40 1.00
276 Martin Erat .12 .30
277 Patric Hornqvist .12 .30
278 Colin Wilson .15 .40
279 Jordin Tootoo .15 .40
280 J.P. Dumont .12 .30
281 Steve Sullivan .12 .30
282 Joel Ward .12 .30
283 David Legwand .15 .40
284 Matthew Lombardi .12 .30
285 Shea Weber .15 .40
286 Ryan Suter .15 .40
287 Kevin Klein .12 .30
288 Cody Franson .12 .30
289 Pekka Rinne .20 .50
290 Matt Halischuk .15 .40
291 Ilya Kovalchuk .20 .50
292 Zach Parise .20 .50
293 Travis Zajac .12 .30
294 Jamie Langenbrunner .12 .30
295 Patrik Elias .20 .50
296 Brian Rolston .15 .40
297 Dainius Zubrus .12 .30
298 Pierre-Luc Letourneau-Leblond .12 .30
299 Andrew Peters .12 .30
300 Jason Arnott .15 .40
301 Colin White .12 .30
302 Bryce Salvador .12 .30
303 Andy Greene .12 .30
304 David Clarkson .12 .30
305 Martin Brodeur .50 1.25
306 John Tavares .30 .75
307 Matt Moulson .15 .40
308 Rob Schremp .12 .30
309 Trent Hunter .12 .30
310 Josh Bailey .15 .40
311 Kyle Okposo .12 .30
312 Doug Weight .20 .50
313 Blake Comeau .12 .30
314 Zenon Konopka .15 .40
315 Frans Nielsen .12 .30
316 Mark Streit .12 .30
317 Bruno Gervais .12 .30
318 Jack Hillen .12 .30
319 Dwayne Roloson .15 .40
320 Rick DiPietro .15 .40
321 Marian Gaborik .20 .50
322 Alexander Frolov .12 .30
323 Chris Drury .15 .40
324 Ryan Callahan .12 .30
325 Sean Avery .15 .40
326 Brandon Dubinsky .12 .30
327 Artem Anisimov .12 .30
328 Brian Boyle .12 .30
329 Wade Redden .12 .30
330 Matt Gilroy .12 .30
331 Michael Del Zotto .15 .40
332 Daniel Girardi .12 .30
333 Marc Staal .12 .30
334 Brandon Prust .12 .30
335 Henrik Lundqvist .50 1.25
336 Jason Spezza .20 .50
337 Daniel Alfredsson .20 .50
338 Milan Michalek .12 .30
339 Mike Fisher .12 .30
340 Chris Neil .12 .30
341 Chris Kelly .15 .40
342 Alex Kovalev .15 .40
343 Nick Foligno .15 .40
344 Peter Regin .15 .40
345 Sergei Gonchar .12 .30
346 Chris Phillips .12 .30
347 Erik Karlsson .25 .60
348 Matt Carkner .15 .40
349 Pascal Leclaire .15 .40
350 Brian Elliott .15 .40
351 Mike Richards .15 .40
352 Jeff Carter .15 .40
353 Nikolai Zherdev .12 .30
354 James van Riemsdyk .15 .40
355 Daniel Carcillo .12 .30
356 Kimmo Timonen .12 .30
357 Daniel Briere .20 .50
358 Scott Hartnell .12 .30
359 Claude Giroux .20 .50
360 Ville Leino .15 .40
361 Matt Carle .15 .40
362 Braydon Coburn .12 .30
363 Chris Pronger .20 .50
364 Brian Boucher .15 .40
365 Michael Leighton .15 .40
366 Wojtek Wolski .12 .30
367 Shane Doan .15 .40
368 Ray Whitney .15 .40
369 Radim Vrbata .12 .30
370 Scottie Upshall .12 .30
371 Vernon Fiddler .12 .30
372 Petr Prucha .12 .30
373 Martin Hanzal .12 .30
374 Mikkel Boedker .12 .30
375 Lee Stempniak .12 .30
376 Kurt Sauer .12 .30
377 Keith Yandle .12 .30
378 Ed Jovanovski .12 .30
379 Jason LaBarbera .15 .40
380 Ilya Bryzgalov .15 .40
381 Evgeni Malkin .40 1.00
382 Sidney Crosby .75 2.00
383 Jordan Staal .15 .40
384 Chris Kunitz .20 .50
385 Pascal Dupuis .12 .30
386 Max Talbot .12 .30
387 Mike Rupp .12 .30
388 Tyler Kennedy .12 .30
389 Matt Cooke .12 .30
390 Brooks Orpik .12 .30
391 Alex Goligoski .15 .40
392 Kristopher Letang .25 .60
393 Marc-Andre Fleury .40 1.00
394 Brent Johnson .15 .40
395 Paul Martin .12 .30
396 Joe Thornton .30 .75
397 Joe Pavelski .25 .60
398 Patrick Marleau .20 .50
399 Dany Heatley .15 .40
400 Ryane Clowe .12 .30
401 Devin Setoguchi .15 .40
402 Logan Couture .25 .60
403 Torrey Mitchell .12 .30
404 Marc-Edouard Vlasic .12 .30
405 Douglas Murray .12 .30
406 Dan Boyle .12 .30
407 Kent Huskins .12 .30
408 Jason Demers .12 .30
409 Antero Niittymaki .15 .40
410 Antti Niemi .15 .40
411 T.J. Oshie .20 .50
412 Patrik Berglund .12 .30
413 Andy McDonald .15 .40
414 Brad Boyes .12 .30
415 David Backes .12 .30
416 Alex Steen .12 .30
417 Jay McClement .12 .30
418 David Perron .15 .40
419 Matt D'Agostini .12 .30
420 Cam Janssen .12 .30
421 Erik Johnson .12 .30
422 Barret Jackman .12 .30
423 Alex Pietrangelo .15 .40
424 Jaroslav Halak .20 .50
425 Ty Conklin .15 .40
426 Vincent Lecavalier .20 .50
427 Steven Stamkos .40 1.00
428 Martin St. Louis .20 .50
429 Ryan Malone .12 .30
430 Steve Downie .12 .30
431 Blair Jones .12 .30
432 Teddy Purcell .12 .30
433 James Wright .12 .30
434 Dan Ellis .15 .40
435 Pavel Kubina .12 .30
436 Mattias Ohlund .12 .30
437 Victor Hedman .25 .60
438 Simon Gagne .20 .50
439 Matt Smaby .12 .30
440 Mike Smith .20 .50
441 Phil Kessel .20 .50
442 Tyler Bozak .12 .30
443 Mikhail Grabovski .12 .30
444 Colton Orr .12 .30
445 Kris Versteeg .12 .30
446 Christian Hanson .12 .30
447 Fredrik Sjostrom .12 .30
448 Luca Caputi .15 .40
449 Colby Armstrong .12 .30
450 Mike Komisarek .12 .30
451 Francois Beauchemin .12 .30
452 Dion Phaneuf .15 .40
453 Luke Schenn .20 .50
454 Jonas Gustavsson .25 .60
455 Jean-Sebastien Giguere .20 .50
456 Henrik Sedin .25 .60
457 Daniel Sedin .25 .60
458 Alexandre Burrows .12 .30
459 Mason Raymond .12 .30
460 Ryan Kesler .20 .50
461 Mikael Samuelsson .12 .30
462 Rick Rypien .20 .50
463 Sergei Shirokov .15 .40
464 Christian Ehrhoff .12 .30
465 Sami Salo .12 .30
466 Dan Hamhuis .15 .40
467 Darcy Hordichuk .12 .30
468 Keith Ballard .12 .30
469 Cory Schneider .20 .50
470 Roberto Luongo .30 .75
471 Alex Ovechkin .75 2.00
472 Alexander Semin .20 .50
473 Nicklas Backstrom .20 .50
474 Mike Knuble .12 .30
475 Brooks Laich .12 .30
476 Eric Fehr .12 .30
477 David Steckel .12 .30
478 Tomas Fleischmann .12 .30
479 Mathieu Perreault .12 .30
480 Mike Green .15 .40
481 Jeff Schultz .12 .30
482 John Carlson .20 .50
483 Karl Alzner .12 .30
484 Michal Neuvirth .15 .40
485 Semyon Varlamov .20 .50
486 Jaroslav Halak .20 .50
487 Brian Boucher .15 .40
488 Tuukka Rask .25 .60
489 Sidney Crosby .75 2.00
490 Joe Pavelski .25 .60
491 Marian Hossa .20 .50
492 Alexandre Burrows .12 .30
493 Jimmy Howard .25 .60
494 Jaroslav Halak .20 .50
495 Simon Gagne .20 .50
496 Patrick Marleau .20 .50
497 Dustin Byfuglien .20 .50
498 Michael Leighton .15 .40
499 Antti Niemi .15 .40
500 Jonathan Toews .30 .75
501 Nazem Kadri HR RC 2.00 5.00
502 Nick Johnson HR RC .50 1.25
503 Matt Martin HR RC 1.00 2.50
504 Jamie McBain HR RC .60 1.50
505 Nick Palmieri HR RC .60 1.50
506 Derek Smith HR RC .60 1.50
507 Brandon Yip HR RC .60 1.50
508 Justin Mercier HR RC .60 1.50
509 Evgeny Dadonov HR RC .75 2.00
510 Brad Thiessen HR RC .75 2.00
511 A.Pechurskiy HR RC .75 2.00
512 Dustin Kohn HR RC .60 1.50
513 Tomas Kana HR RC .60 1.50
514 Dustin Tokarski HR RC .60 1.50
515 Jerome Samson HR RC .60 1.50
516 Kyle Wilson HR RC .75 2.00
517 Arturs Kulda HR RC .60 1.50
518 Matt Zaba HR RC .75 2.00
519 P.K. Subban HR RC 5.00 12.00
520 Casey Wellman HR RC .60 1.50
521 Justin Falk HR RC .50 1.25
522 Cody Almond HR RC .60 1.50
523 Nick Bonino HR RC .75 2.00
524 Anton Klementyev HR RC .60 1.50
525 Nick Spaling HR RC .60 1.50
526 Brayden Irwin HR RC .60 1.50
527 Bobby Butler HR RC .60 1.50
528 Jeremy Duchesne HR RC .75 2.00
529 Andrew Bodnarchuk HR RC .60 1.50
530 J.Philippe Levasseur HR RC .60 1.50
531 Trevor Frischmon HR RC .60 1.50
532 Carter Hutton HR RC 1.50 4.00
533 Dylan Reese HR RC .60 1.50
534 Philip Larsen HR RC .60 1.50
535 Jared Cowen HR RC .60 1.50
536 Maxim Noreau HR RC .50 1.25
537 Jeff Penner HR RC 1.00 2.50
538 Eric Tangradi HR RC .60 1.50
539 Zach Hamill HR RC .60 1.50
540 James Wyman HR RC .60 1.50
541 Brock Trotter HR RC 1.25 3.00
542 Corey Elkins HR RC .50 1.25
543 Rich Clune HR RC .75 2.00
544 Evan Oberg HR RC .75 2.00
545 Bryan Pitton HR RC .75 2.00
546 John McCarthy HR RC .60 1.50
547 Marc-Andre Cliche HR RC .50 1.25
548 Maxime Fortunus HR RC .50 1.25
549 Adam McQuaid HR RC .75 2.00
550 Scott Jackson HR RC .60 1.50
551 Cam Fowler HR RC 8.00 20.00
552 Derek Stepan HR RC 8.00 20.00
553 Nino Niederreiter HR RC 12.00 30.00
554 Tyler Seguin HR RC 12.00 30.00
555 Magnus Paajarvi HR RC 8.00 20.00
556 Jordan Eberle HR RC 20.00 50.00
557 Brayden Schenn HR RC 12.00 30.00
558 Jeff Skinner HR RC 8.00 20.00
559 Taylor Hall HR RC 15.00 40.00
560 Taylor Hall 1.25 3.00
561 Tyler Seguin 1.50 4.00
562 Cam Fowler 1.25 3.00
563 Brayden Schenn 1.25 3.00
564 Jeff Skinner 1.25 3.00
565 Derek Stepan .60 1.50
566 Jordan Eberle 1.25 3.00
567 Magnus Paajarvi .60 1.50
568 Nino Niederreiter .75 2.00
569 Dustin Penner .12 .30
570 Jason Arnott .15 .40
571 Erik Johnson .12 .30
572 Chris Stewart .15 .40
573 Blake Wheeler .20 .50
574 Rich Peverley .20 .50
575 Craig Anderson .20 .50
576 Brian Elliott .15 .40
577 Peter Forsberg .40 1.00
578 Tomas Kaberle .12 .30
579 Ray Emery .15 .40
580 Dennis Wideman .12 .30
581 Bryan McCabe .12 .30
582 Mike Fisher .12 .30
583 Marco Sturm .12 .30
584 Alex Kovalev .15 .40
585 James Neal .12 .30
586 Kris Versteeg .12 .30
587 Michael Frolik .12 .30
588 Al Montoya .15 .40
589 Tomas Fleischmann .12 .30
590 Dwayne Roloson .15 .40
591 Joffrey Lupul .12 .30
592 James Wisniewski .12 .30
593 Michael Grabner .15 .40
594 Justin Braun RC .50 1.25
595 Zac Dalpe RC .60 1.50
596 Evgeny Dadonov .60 1.50
597 Jonas Holos RC .50 1.25
598 Jordan Caron RC .60 1.50
599 Alexander Burmistrov RC .50 1.25
600 Nick Leddy RC .60 1.50
601 Kevin Shattenkirk RC 1.00 2.50
602 Tomas Tatar RC 1.25 3.00
603 Anders Lindback RC .50 1.25
604 Andreas Engqvist RC .75 2.00
605 Luke Adam RC .50 1.25
606 Cory Emmerton RC .60 1.50
607 Linus Omark RC .60 1.50
608 Kyle Clifford RC .60 1.50
609 Jacob Markstrom RC 1.25 3.00
610 Mats Zuccarello RC 1.00 2.50
611 Jordan Pearce RC .75 2.00
612 Matt Calvert RC .75 2.00
613 Mattias Tedenby RC .50 1.25
614 Kevin Poulin RC .60 1.50
615 Patrice Cormier RC .60 1.50
616 Philip McRae RC .50 1.25
617 Sergei Bobrovsky RC 2.00 5.00
618 Travis Hamonic RC .60 1.50
619 Thomas McCollum RC .60 1.50
620 Jeff Frazee RC .75 2.00
621 Henrik Karlsson RC .50 1.25
622 Jan Mursak RC 1.00 2.50
623 Eric Wellwood RC .60 1.50
624 Jamie Arniel RC .50 1.25
625 Alex Stalock RC .50 1.25
626 Evgeny Grachev RC .50 1.25
627 Jacob Josefson RC .50 1.25
628 Jim O'Brien RC .60 1.50
629 Keith Aulie RC .50 1.25
630 Steven Kampfer RC .75 2.00
631 Robin Lehner RC 1.00 2.50
632 Ryan McDonagh RC 1.25 3.00
633 Jeremy Morin RC .50 1.25
634 Brandon McMillan RC .50 1.25
635 Chris Mueller RC .50 1.25
636 Richard Bachman RC .60 1.50
637 Stefan Della Rovere RC .50 1.25
638 Rhett Rakhshani RC .50 1.25
639 Oliver Ekman-Larsson RC .75 2.00
640 Matt Taormina RC .50 1.25
641 Marcus Johansson RC .75 2.00
642 Mike Moore RC .50 1.25
643 Dana Tyrell RC .50 1.25

644 Cedrick Desjardins RC .60 1.50
645 Chris Summers RC .50 1.25
646 Alexander Vasyunov RC .50 1.25
647 Ian Cole RC .50 1.25
648 Jake Muzzin RC 1.25 3.00
649 Marcel Mueller RC .60 1.50
650 Mark Dekanich RC .50 1.25
651 Brandon Pirri RC .50 1.25
652 Evan Brophey RC .50 1.25
653 Kyle Palmieri RC 1.00 2.50
654 Matt Bartkowski RC .60 1.50
655 Timo Pielmeier RC .60 1.50
656 Tommy Wingels RC .50 1.25
657 Paul Byron RC .60 1.50
658 Jeff Petry RC 1.00 2.50
659 Taro Tsujimoto SP 10.00 25.00

2010-11 Score Anniversary
*ANNIVERSARY 35-500: 5X TO 12X BASE
*ANN.ROOKIES 501-550: 1.2X TO 3X BASE
473 Nicklas Backstrom 2.50 6.00

2010-11 Score Glossy
*GLOSSY 1-500: 2X TO 5X BASE
*GLOSSY ROOKIES 501-550: .5X TO 1.2X BASE
473 Nicklas Backstrom 1.00 2.50

2010-11 Score Gold
*GOLD TRADED: 2.5X TO 6X BASE
*GOLD ROOKIES: .8X TO 2X BASE

2010-11 Score Canadian Greats
COMPLETE SET (20) 40.00 80.00
1 Sidney Crosby 6.00 15.00
2 Jonathan Toews 2.50 6.00
3 Mike Richards 1.25 3.00
4 Jarome Iginla 2.00 5.00
5 Martin Brodeur 4.00 10.00
6 Carey Price 3.00 8.00
7 Dany Heatley 1.25 3.00
8 Steve Yzerman 4.00 10.00
9 Corey Perry 2.50 6.00
10 Drew Doughty 2.00 5.00
11 Duncan Keith 1.25 3.00
12 John Tavares 2.50 6.00
13 Patrice Bergeron 2.00 5.00
14 Patrick Roy 4.00 10.00
15 Roberto Luongo 2.50 6.00
16 Ryan Smyth 1.25 3.00
17 Mario Lemieux 6.00 15.00
18 Scott Niedermayer 1.50 4.00
19 Vincent Lecavalier 1.50 4.00
20 Ryan Getzlaf 1.50 4.00

2010-11 Score Franchise
COMPLETE SET (30) 25.00 60.00
1 Ryan Getzlaf 1.25 3.00
2 Zach Bogosian 1.00 2.50
3 Tuukka Rask 1.50 4.00
4 Ryan Miller 1.25 3.00
5 Jarome Iginla 1.50 4.00
6 Eric Staal 1.50 4.00
7 Jonathan Toews 2.00 5.00
8 Matt Duchene 1.25 3.00
9 Rick Nash 1.25 3.00
10 James Neal .75 2.00
11 Pavel Datsyuk 2.00 5.00
12 Ales Hemsky 1.00 2.50
13 Tomas Vokoun 1.00 2.50
14 Drew Doughty 1.50 4.00
15 Mikko Koivu 1.25 3.00
16 Carey Price 2.50 6.00
17 Shea Weber 1.00 2.50
18 Zach Parise 1.25 3.00
19 Henrik Lundqvist 3.00 8.00
20 John Tavares 2.00 5.00
21 Daniel Alfredsson 1.25 3.00
22 Mike Richards 1.00 2.50
23 Ilya Bryzgalov 1.00 2.50
24 Sidney Crosby 5.00 12.00
25 Joe Thornton 2.00 5.00
26 Erik Johnson .75 2.00
27 Steven Stamkos 2.50 6.00
28 Jonas Gustavsson 1.50 4.00
29 H.Sedin/D.Sedin 1.50 4.00
30 Alex Ovechkin 5.00 12.00

2010-11 Score Net Cam
COMPLETE SET (20) 10.00 25.00
1 Ryan Miller 1.00 2.50
2 Martin Brodeur 2.50 6.00
3 Tuukka Rask 1.25 3.00
4 Roberto Luongo 1.50 4.00
5 Jimmy Howard 1.25 3.00
6 Jonas Gustavsson 1.25 3.00
7 Carey Price 2.00 5.00
8 Marc-Andre Fleury 2.00 5.00
9 Steve Mason .75 2.00
10 Cam Ward 1.00 2.50
11 Miikka Kiprusoff 1.00 2.50
12 Ilya Bryzgalov .75 2.00
13 Michael Leighton .75 2.00
14 Craig Anderson 1.00 2.50
15 Jonathan Quick 1.25 3.00
16 Pekka Rinne 1.00 2.50
17 Niklas Backstrom 1.00 2.50
18 Tomas Vokoun .75 2.00
19 Henrik Lundqvist 2.50 6.00
20 Antti Niemi .75 2.00

2010-11 Score Playoff Heroes
COMPLETE SET (25) 6.00 15.00
1 Joe Pavelski .75 2.00
2 Tuukka Rask .75 2.00
3 Michael Cammalleri .60 1.50
4 Sidney Crosby 2.50 6.00
5 Johan Franzen .50 1.25
6 Mike Richards .50 1.25
7 Jaroslav Halak .60 1.50
8 Joe Thornton 1.00 2.50
9 Antti Niemi .50 1.25
10 Michael Leighton .50 1.25
11 Simon Gagne .60 1.50
12 Daniel Briere .60 1.50
13 Mikael Samuelsson .40 1.00
14 Claude Giroux .60 1.50
15 Henrik Zetterberg .75 2.00
16 P.K. Subban 1.50 4.00
17 Marian Hossa .60 1.50
18 Ville Leino .50 1.25
19 Dustin Byfuglien .60 1.50
20 Brian Gionta .40 1.00
21 Mark Recchi .75 2.00
22 Chris Pronger .60 1.50
23 Duncan Keith .50 1.25
24 Patrick Kane 1.25 3.00
25 Jonathan Toews 1.00 2.50

2010-11 Score Signatures
49 Jonas Hiller/25* 6.00 15.00
54 Dustin Byfuglien/25* 8.00 20.00
57 Rich Peverley/25* 8.00 20.00
62 Zach Bogosian/25* 6.00 15.00
88 Tyler Ennis/25* 5.00 12.00
89 Nathan Gerbe/25* 5.00 12.00
94 Ryan Miller/25* 8.00 20.00
96 Jarome Iginla/25* 20.00 50.00
105 Jay Bouwmeester/25* 5.00 12.00
121 Zach Boychuk/25* 5.00 12.00
141 Paul Stastny/25* 12.00 30.00
143 Matt Duchene/25* 8.00 20.00
155 Craig Anderson/25* 8.00 20.00
159 Antoine Vermette/25* 5.00 12.00
172 Brenden Morrow/25* 6.00 15.00
179 Krys Barch/25* 5.00 12.00
185 Kari Lehtonen/25* 6.00 15.00
189 Johan Franzen/25* 8.00 20.00
205 Zack Stortini/25* 5.00 12.00
220 Michael Frolik/25* 8.00 20.00
232 Ryan Smyth/25* 6.00 15.00
245 Jonathan Bernier/25* 6.00 15.00
254 Guillaume Latendresse/25* 6.00 15.00
262 Michael Cammalleri/25* 8.00 20.00
263 Brian Gionta/25* 5.00 12.00
267 Max Pacioretty/25* 8.00 20.00
275 Carey Price/25* 40.00 80.00
277 Patric Hornqvist/25* 5.00 12.00
278 Colin Wilson/25* 10.00 25.00
293 Travis Zajac/25* 8.00 20.00
298 Pierre-Luc Letourneau-Leblond/25* 5.00 12.00
303 Andy Greene/25* 5.00 12.00
306 John Tavares/25* 12.00 30.00
307 Matt Moulson/25* 6.00 15.00
310 Josh Bailey/25* 6.00 15.00
321 Marian Gaborik/25* 8.00 20.00
327 Artem Anisimov/25* 5.00 12.00
337 Daniel Alfredsson/25* EXCH 10.00 25.00
339 Mike Fisher/25* 6.00 15.00
348 Matt Carkner/25* 6.00 15.00
350 Brian Elliott/25* 6.00 15.00
359 Claude Giroux/25* 8.00 20.00
364 Brian Boucher/25* 8.00 20.00
377 Keith Yandle/25* 5.00 12.00
383 Jordan Staal/25* 6.00 15.00
397 Joe Pavelski/25* 10.00 25.00
398 Patrick Marleau/25* 8.00 20.00
415 David Backes/25* 5.00 12.00
420 Cam Janssen/25* 15.00 40.00
428 Martin St. Louis/25* 8.00 20.00
430 Steve Downie/25* 12.00 30.00
438 Simon Gagne/25* 10.00 25.00
440 Mike Smith/25* 8.00 20.00
444 Colton Orr/25* 5.00 12.00
460 Ryan Kesler/25* 25.00 50.00
482 John Carlson/25* 8.00 20.00
501 Nazem Kadri 40.00 100.00
505 Nick Palmieri SP 6.00 15.00
507 Brandon Yip 4.00 10.00
508 Justin Mercier 4.00 10.00
510 Brad Thiessen 5.00 12.00
519 P.K. Subban/50* 40.00 100.00
523 Nick Bonino SP 8.00 20.00
525 Nick Spaling 4.00 10.00
526 Brayden Irwin 4.00 10.00
527 Bobby Butler SP 6.00 15.00
534 Philip Larsen SP 6.00 15.00
535 Jared Cowen SP 6.00 15.00
538 Eric Tangradi 4.00 10.00
539 Zach Hamill SP 6.00 15.00
540 James Wyman 4.00 10.00
549 Adam McQuaid SP 8.00 20.00
551 Cam Fowler 15.00 40.00
552 Derek Stepan 40.00 80.00
553 Nino Niederreiter 6.00 15.00
554 Tyler Seguin 30.00 80.00
555 Magnus Paajarvi 5.00 12.00
556 Jordan Eberle 50.00 120.00
557 Brayden Schenn 30.00 60.00
558 Jeff Skinner 20.00 50.00
559 Taylor Hall 50.00 120.00
560 Taylor Hall 75.00 150.00
561 Tyler Seguin 50.00 100.00
568 Nino Niederreiter 8.00 20.00
595 Zac Dalpe 6.00 15.00
597 Jonas Holos 15.00 40.00
598 Jordan Caron 6.00 15.00
601 Kevin Shattenkirk 10.00 25.00
606 Cory Emmerton 6.00 15.00
607 Linus Omark 8.00 20.00
609 Jacob Markstrom 12.00 30.00
612 Matt Calvert 8.00 20.00
613 Mattias Tedenby 5.00 12.00
617 Sergei Bobrovsky 20.00 50.00
618 Travis Hamonic 6.00 15.00
620 Jeff Frazee 6.00 15.00
622 Jan Mursak 15.00 40.00
631 Robin Lehner 10.00 25.00
632 Ryan McDonagh 8.00 20.00
635 Chris Mueller 5.00 12.00
638 Rhett Rakhshani 6.00 15.00
640 Matt Taormina 5.00 12.00
647 Ian Cole 5.00 12.00
649 Marcel Mueller 8.00 20.00
650 Mark Dekanich 6.00 15.00
651 Brandon Pirri 5.00 12.00
654 Matt Bartkowski 6.00 15.00
657 Paul Byron 8.00 20.00

2010-11 Score Snow Globe Die Cuts
COMPLETE SET (13) 15.00 40.00
1 Henrik Sedin 1.50 4.00
2 Alex Ovechkin 5.00 12.00
3 Martin Brodeur 3.00 8.00
4 Patrick Kane 2.50 6.00
5 Joe Thornton 2.00 5.00
6 Steven Stamkos 2.50 6.00
7 Henrik Zetterberg 1.50 4.00
8 Jarome Iginla 1.50 4.00
9 Roberto Luongo 2.00 5.00
10 Antti Niemi 1.00 2.50
11 Mike Richards 1.00 2.50
12 John Tavares 2.00 5.00
13 Jonas Gustavsson 1.50 4.00

2010-11 Score Sudden Death
COMPLETE SET (12) 15.00 40.00
1 Sidney Crosby 5.00 12.00
2 Jonathan Toews 2.00 5.00
3 Mike Modano 2.00 5.00
4 Anze Kopitar 2.00 5.00
5 Scott Niedermayer 1.25 3.00
6 Teemu Selanne 2.50 6.00
7 Zach Parise 1.25 3.00
8 Nicklas Backstrom 1.25 3.00
9 Steven Stamkos 2.50 6.00
10 Claude Giroux 1.25 3.00
11 Alex Ovechkin 5.00 12.00
12 Drew Doughty 1.50 4.00

2010-11 Score USA Greats
COMPLETE SET (20) 20.00 50.00
1 Patrick Kane 3.00 8.00
2 Zach Parise 1.50 4.00
3 Ryan Kesler 1.50 4.00
4 Scott Gomez 1.25 3.00
5 Paul Stastny 1.25 3.00
6 Erik Johnson 1.00 2.50
7 Brett Hull 3.00 8.00
8 Ryan Miller 1.50 4.00
9 Joe Pavelski 2.00 5.00
10 Jonathan Quick 2.00 5.00
11 Phil Kessel 1.50 4.00
12 Jack Johnson 1.00 2.50
13 Mike Modano 2.50 6.00
14 Peter Mueller 1.25 3.00
15 Craig Anderson 1.50 4.00
16 T.J. Oshie 1.50 4.00
17 Kyle Okposo 1.00 2.50
18 John Carlson 1.50 4.00
19 Pat LaFontaine 1.50 4.00
20 Bill Guerin 1.50 4.00

2010-11 Score All Star Game
1 Eric Staal 2.50 6.00
2 Alexander Ovechkin 8.00 20.00
3 Sidney Crosby 8.00 20.00
4 Steven Stamkos 4.00 10.00
5 Ryan Miller 2.00 5.00
6 Jeff Skinner HR 4.00 10.00
7 Taylor Hall HR 4.00 10.00
JS Jeff Skinner HL 4.00 10.00
SC Cam Ward HL 2.00 5.00

2010-11 Score Franchise All Star Game
ES Eric Staal 3.00 8.00

2010-11 Score Net Cam All Star Game
CW Cam Ward 2.50 6.00

2010-11 Score USA Greats All Star Game
PM Peter Mueller 2.00 5.00

2011-12 Score
COMP.SET w/o SP's (500) 15.00 40.00
1 Taylor Hall SH .20 .50
2 Jason Pominville SH .12 .30
3 Brandon Sutter SH .12 .30
4 Antti Niemi SH .15 .40
5 Radim Vrbata SH .12 .30
6 Daniel Alfredsson SH .20 .50
7 Nicklas Lidstrom SH .12 .30
8 Steven Stamkos SH .40 1.00
9 Sidney Crosby SH .75 2.00
10 Mario Lemieux SH .75 2.00
11 Eric Fehr SH .12 .30
12 Patrick Marleau SH .20 .50
13 Eric Staal SH .25 .60
14 P.K. Subban SH .25 .60
15 Zdeno Chara SH .20 .50
16 Matt Duchene SH .20 .50
17 Tim Thomas SH .20 .50
18 Logan Couture SH .25 .60
19 Rod Brind'Amour SH .15 .40
20 Shane Doan SH .15 .40
21 Martin Brodeur SH .50 1.25
22 Lanny McDonald SH .20 .50
23 Miikka Kiprusoff SH .20 .50
24 Roberto Luongo SH .30 .75
25 Henrik Lundqvist SH .50 1.25
26 Corey Perry SH .30 .75
27 Tim Stapleton SH .12 .30
28 Daniel Sedin SH .25 .60
29 Ryan Kesler SH .20 .50
30 Tim Thomas SH .20 .50
31 Joel Ward SH .12 .30
32 Mark Recchi SH .25 .60
33 Peter Forsberg SH .40 1.00
34 Doug Weight SH .15 .40
35 Brian Rafalski SH .12 .30
36 Bobby Ryan .15 .40
37 Corey Perry .30 .75
38 George Parros .15 .40
39 Ryan Getzlaf .20 .50
40 Saku Koivu .20 .50
41 Teemu Selanne .40 1.00
42 Jason Blake .12 .30
43 Brandon McMillan .12 .30
44 Matt Beleskey .12 .30
45 Cam Fowler .20 .50
46 Francois Beauchemin .12 .30
47 Lubomir Visnovsky .12 .30
48 Luca Sbisa .15 .40
49 Jonas Hiller .15 .40
50 Dan Ellis .15 .40
51 Brad Marchand .40 1.00
52 Chris Kelly .15 .40
53 David Krejci .20 .50
54 Gregory Campbell .12 .30
55 Milan Lucic .20 .50
56 Nathan Horton .20 .50
57 Patrice Bergeron .25 .60
58 Tyler Seguin .25 .60
59 Daniel Paille .12 .30
60 Shawn Thornton .12 .30
61 Zdeno Chara .20 .50
62 Dennis Seidenberg .12 .30
63 Johnny Boychuk .15 .40
64 Tim Thomas .20 .50
65 Tuukka Rask .25 .60
66 Brad Boyes .12 .30
67 Derek Roy .12 .30
68 Drew Stafford .12 .30
69 Jason Pominville .12 .30
70 Jochen Hecht .12 .30
71 Nathan Gerbe .12 .30
72 Patrick Kaleta .12 .30
73 Paul Gaustad .12 .30
74 Thomas Vanek .15 .40
75 Tyler Ennis .12 .30
76 Shaone Morrisonn .12 .30
77 Jordan Leopold .12 .30
78 Tyler Myers .12 .30
79 Ryan Miller .20 .50
80 Jhonas Enroth .20 .50
81 Alex Tanguay .12 .30
82 Curtis Glencross .12 .30
83 Jarome Iginla .25 .60
84 Matt Stajan .12 .30
85 Mikael Backlund .15 .40
86 Olli Jokinen .15 .40
87 David Moss .12 .30
88 Rene Bourque .12 .30
89 Tom Kostopoulos .12 .30
90 Tim Jackman .12 .30
91 Cory Sarich .12 .30
92 Jay Bouwmeester .12 .30
93 Mark Giordano .20 .50
94 Miikka Kiprusoff .20 .50
95 Henrik Karlsson .15 .40
96 Brandon Sutter .12 .30
97 Eric Staal .25 .60
98 Jeff Skinner .25 .60
99 Tuomo Ruutu .15 .40
100 Jussi Jokinen .12 .30
101 Chad LaRose .12 .30
102 Patrick Dwyer .12 .30
103 Drayson Bowman .12 .30
104 Jerome Samson .12 .30
105 Jiri Tlusty .12 .30
106 Tim Gleason .12 .30
107 Tomas Kaberle .12 .30
108 Jamie McBain .12 .30
109 Cam Ward .20 .50
110 Justin Peters .12 .30
111 Dave Bolland .15 .40
112 Jonathan Toews .30 .75
113 Marian Hossa .20 .50
114 Michael Frolik .12 .30
115 Patrick Kane .40 1.00
116 Patrick Sharp .20 .50
117 Bryan Bickell .12 .30
118 John Scott .12 .30
119 Andrew Brunette .12 .30
120 Rostislav Olesz .12 .30
121 Nick Leddy .12 .30
122 Duncan Keith .15 .40
123 Brent Seabrook .12 .30
124 Niklas Hjalmarsson .12 .30
125 Corey Crawford .25 .60
126 Matt Duchene .20 .50
127 Paul Stastny .15 .40
128 Ryan O'Reilly .20 .50
129 Milan Hejduk .15 .40
130 David Jones .12 .30
131 Daniel Winnik .12 .30
132 Jay McClement .12 .30
133 Cody McLeod .12 .30
134 Brandon Yip .12 .30
135 T.J. Galiardi .15 .40
136 Ryan O'Byrne .12 .30
137 Erik Johnson .12 .30
138 Kyle Quincey .12 .30
139 Semyon Varlamov .20 .50
140 Jean-Sebastien Giguere .20 .50
141 Antoine Vermette .12 .30
142 Derick Brassard .12 .30
143 Jeff Carter .15 .40
144 Matt Calvert .12 .30
145 R.J. Umberger .12 .30
146 Rick Nash .20 .50
147 Samuel Pahlsson .12 .30
148 Kristian Huselius .12 .30
149 James Wisniewski .12 .30
150 Grant Clitsome .12 .30
151 Marc Methot .12 .30
152 Fedor Tyutin .12 .30
153 Kris Russell .12 .30
154 Steve Mason .15 .40
155 Mark Dekanich .12 .30
156 Adam Burish .12 .30
157 Brenden Morrow .15 .40
158 Jamie Benn .20 .50
159 Loui Eriksson .12 .30
160 Steve Ott .12 .30
161 Tom Wandell .12 .30
162 Mike Ribeiro .12 .30
163 Krys Barch .12 .30
164 Michael Ryder .12 .30
165 Sheldon Souray .12 .30
166 Alex Goligoski .12 .30
167 Stephane Robidas .12 .30
168 Nicklas Grossman .12 .30
169 Kari Lehtonen .15 .40
170 Andrew Raycroft .12 .30
171 Pavel Datsyuk .30 .75
172 Henrik Zetterberg .25 .60
173 Johan Franzen .15 .40
174 Valtteri Filppula .15 .40
175 Daniel Cleary .12 .30
176 Jiri Hudler .15 .40
177 Todd Bertuzzi .12 .30
178 Tomas Holmstrom .12 .30
179 Darren Helm .12 .30
180 Justin Abdelkader .12 .30
181 Niklas Kronwall .12 .30
182 Brad Stuart .12 .30
183 Jakub Kindl .12 .30
184 Nicklas Lidstrom .12 .30
185 Jimmy Howard .25 .60
186 Ales Hemsky .15 .40
187 Shawn Horcoff .12 .30
188 Taylor Hall .20 .50
189 Sam Gagner .12 .30
190 Gilbert Brule .20 .50
191 Jordan Eberle .20 .50
192 Magnus Paajarvi .15 .40
193 Linus Omark .20 .50
194 Ryan Jones .15 .40
195 Ryan Smyth .15 .40
196 Tom Gilbert .12 .30
197 Ryan Whitney .12 .30
198 Ladislav Smid .12 .30
199 Nikolai Khabibulin .15 .40
200 Devan Dubnyk .15 .40
201 David Booth .12 .30
202 Michal Repik .12 .30
203 Stephen Weiss .12 .30
204 Evgeny Dadonov .15 .40
205 Jack Skille .15 .40
206 Tomas Fleischmann .12 .30
207 Kris Versteeg .12 .30
208 Scottie Upshall .12 .30
209 Ed Jovanovski .12 .30
210 Brian Campbell .12 .30
211 Dmitry Kulikov .12 .30
212 Mike Weaver .12 .30
213 Jason Garrison .12 .30
214 Jacob Markstrom .20 .50
215 Scott Clemmensen .15 .40
216 Anze Kopitar .30 .75
217 Simon Gagne .20 .50
218 Dustin Penner .12 .30
219 Jarret Stoll .15 .40
220 Justin Williams .15 .40
221 Dustin Brown .15 .40
222 Kevin Westgarth .12 .30
223 Kyle Clifford .12 .30
224 Mike Richards .15 .40
225 Scott Parse .12 .30
226 Drew Doughty .25 .60
227 Jack Johnson .12 .30
228 Matt Greene .12 .30
229 Jonathan Bernier .15 .40
230 Jonathan Quick .25 .60
231 Dany Heatley .15 .40
232 Pierre-Marc Bouchard .12 .30
233 Mikko Koivu .15 .40
234 Matt Cullen .12 .30
235 Guillaume Latendresse .15 .40
236 Eric Nystrom .12 .30
237 Cal Clutterbuck .12 .30
238 Kyle Brodziak .12 .30
239 Brad Staubitz .12 .30
240 Devin Setoguchi .12 .30
241 Nick Schultz .12 .30
242 Greg Zanon .12 .30
243 Marek Zidlicky .12 .30
244 Niklas Backstrom .20 .50
245 Josh Harding .20 .50
246 Scott Gomez .12 .30
247 Mike Cammalleri .15 .40
248 Brian Gionta .12 .30
249 Tomas Plekanec .12 .30
250 Travis Moen .12 .30
251 Lars Eller .12 .30
252 David Desharnais .25 .60
253 Andrei Kostitsyn .12 .30
254 Max Pacioretty .20 .50
255 Andrei Markov .15 .40
256 P.K. Subban .25 .60
257 Jaroslav Spacek .12 .30
258 Hal Gill .12 .30
259 Carey Price .40 1.00
260 Peter Budaj .15 .40
261 Colin Wilson .15 .40
262 Martin Erat .12 .30
263 Mike Fisher .12 .30
264 David Legwand .12 .30
265 Sergei Kostitsyn .12 .30
266 Nick Spaling .12 .30
267 Patric Hornqvist .12 .30
268 Jordin Tootoo .12 .30
269 Jerred Smithson .12 .30
270 Shea Weber .15 .40
271 Ryan Suter .12 .30
272 Kevin Klein .12 .30
273 Francis Bouillon .12 .30
274 Pekka Rinne .20 .50
275 Anders Lindback .15 .40
276 Ilya Kovalchuk .20 .50
277 Patrik Elias .20 .50
278 Travis Zajac .15 .40
279 Dainius Zubrus .12 .30
280 David Clarkson .12 .30
281 David Steckel .12 .30
282 Jacob Josefson .12 .30
283 Mattias Tedenby .12 .30
284 Rod Pelley .12 .30
285 Zach Parise .20 .50
286 Andy Greene .12 .30
287 Anton Volchenkov .12 .30
288 Colin White .12 .30
289 Martin Brodeur .50 1.25
290 Johan Hedberg .15 .40
291 John Tavares .30 .75
292 Matt Moulson .15 .40
293 Blake Comeau .12 .30
294 Pierre Parenteau .12 .30
295 Frans Nielsen .12 .30
296 Kyle Okposo .15 .40
297 Trevor Gillies .12 .30
298 Michael Grabner .15 .40
299 Josh Bailey .15 .40
300 Andrew MacDonald .12 .30
301 Mark Streit .12 .30
302 Mark Katic .12 .30
303 Travis Hamonic .12 .30
304 Al Montoya .15 .40
305 Rick DiPietro .15 .40
306 Marian Gaborik .20 .50
307 Wojtek Wolski .12 .30
308 Brad Richards .20 .50
309 Sean Avery .12 .30
310 Ruslan Fedotenko .12 .30
311 Derek Stepan .12 .30
312 Brandon Prust .12 .30
313 Mats Zuccarello-Aasen .20 .50
314 Erik Christensen .12 .30
315 Brandon Dubinsky .12 .30
316 Marc Staal .12 .30
317 Daniel Girardi .12 .30
318 Ryan McDonagh .12 .30
319 Henrik Lundqvist .50 1.25
320 Martin Biron .15 .40
321 Jason Spezza .20 .50
322 Daniel Alfredsson .20 .50
323 Milan Michalek .12 .30
324 Chris Neil .12 .30
325 Nick Foligno .15 .40
326 Zack Smith .12 .30
327 Peter Regin .12 .30
328 Jesse Winchester .12 .30
329 Brian Lee .15 .40
330 Sergei Gonchar .12 .30
331 Erik Karlsson .25 .60
332 Chris Phillips .12 .30
333 Matt Carkner .15 .40
334 Craig Anderson .12 .30
335 Alex Auld .15 .40
336 Daniel Briere .20 .50
337 Brayden Schenn .20 .50
338 Wayne Simmonds .25 .60
339 Scott Hartnell .12 .30
340 Andreas Nodl .12 .30
341 James van Riemsdyk .15 .40
342 Jakub Voracek .15 .40
343 Jody Shelley .15 .40
344 Claude Giroux .20 .50
345 Blair Betts .12 .30
346 Jaromir Jagr .60 1.50
347 Chris Pronger .20 .50
348 Kimmo Timonen .12 .30
349 Sergei Bobrovsky .30 .75
350 Ilya Bryzgalov .20 .50
351 Shane Doan .15 .40
352 Ray Whitney .15 .40
353 Lee Stempniak .12 .30
354 Martin Hanzal .12 .30
355 Taylor Pyatt .12 .30
356 Paul Bissonnette .12 .30
357 Mikkel Boedker .12 .30
358 Radim Vrbata .12 .30
359 Kyle Turris .12 .30
360 Keith Yandle .12 .30
361 Derek Morris .12 .30
362 Rostislav Klesla .12 .30
363 David Schlemko .12 .30
364 Mike Smith .12 .30
365 Jason LaBarbera .15 .40
366 Sidney Crosby .75 2.00
367 Evgeni Malkin .40 1.00
368 Jordan Staal .15 .40
369 Chris Kunitz .20 .50
370 James Neal .15 .40
371 Matt Cooke .12 .30
372 Mark Letestu .15 .40
373 Pascal Dupuis .12 .30
374 Tyler Kennedy .12 .30
375 Kristopher Letang .25 .60
376 Brooks Orpik .12 .30
377 Paul Martin .12 .30
378 Ben Lovejoy .12 .30
379 Marc-Andre Fleury .40 1.00
380 Brent Johnson .12 .30
381 Joe Pavelski .25 .60
382 Martin Havlat .15 .40
383 Patrick Marleau .20 .50
384 Ryane Clowe .12 .30
385 Joe Thornton .30 .75
386 Logan Couture .25 .60
387 Torrey Mitchell .12 .30
388 Benn Ferriero .12 .30
389 Brent Burns .20 .50
390 Dan Boyle .12 .30
391 Marc-Edouard Vlasic .12 .30
392 Doug Murray .12 .30
393 Jason Demers .12 .30
394 Antero Niittymaki .15 .40
395 Antti Niemi .15 .40
396 Andy McDonald .12 .30
397 Alexander Steen .15 .40
398 Chris Stewart .15 .40
399 David Backes .15 .40
400 David Perron .15 .40
401 Patrik Berglund .12 .30
402 Vladimir Sobotka .12 .30
403 T.J. Oshie .20 .50
404 B.J. Crombeen .12 .30
405 Alex Pietrangelo .15 .40
406 Carlo Colaiacovo .12 .30
407 Barret Jackman .12 .30
408 Kevin Shattenkirk .15 .40
409 Jaroslav Halak .12 .30
410 Ben Bishop .15 .40
411 Vincent Lecavalier .20 .50
412 Martin St. Louis .20 .50
413 Steven Stamkos .40 1.00
414 Teddy Purcell .12 .30
415 Adam Hall .12 .30
416 Steve Downie .12 .30
417 Ryan Malone .12 .30
418 Nate Thompson .12 .30
419 Dominic Moore .12 .30
420 Dana Tyrell .12 .30
421 Pavel Kubina .12 .30
422 Mattias Ohlund .12 .30
423 Victor Hedman .25 .60
424 Eric Brewer .12 .30
425 Dwayne Roloson .15 .40
426 Mathieu Garon .15 .40
427 Phil Kessel .20 .50
428 Joffrey Lupul .12 .30
429 Tyler Bozak .12 .30
430 Colby Armstrong .12 .30
431 Nazem Kadri .25 .60
432 Nikolai Kulemin .12 .30
433 Mikhail Grabovski .12 .30
434 Colton Orr .12 .30
435 Clarke MacArthur .12 .30
436 Dion Phaneuf .12 .30
437 Luke Schenn .20 .50
438 Keith Aulie .15 .40
439 Jonas Gustavsson .20 .50
440 James Reimer .20 .50
441 Daniel Sedin .25 .60
442 Henrik Sedin .25 .60
443 Ryan Kesler .20 .50
444 Mason Raymond .12 .30
445 Mikael Samuelsson .12 .30
446 Manny Malhotra .15 .40
447 Alexandre Burrows .12 .30
448 Maxim Lapierre .12 .30
449 Kevin Bieksa .15 .40
450 Dan Hamhuis .15 .40
451 Keith Ballard .12 .30
452 Sami Salo .12 .30
453 Alexander Edler .12 .30
454 Cory Schneider .20 .50
455 Roberto Luongo .30 .75
456 Alexander Ovechkin .75 2.00
457 Alexander Semin .20 .50
458 Marcus Johansson .15 .40
459 Nicklas Backstrom .20 .50
460 Brooks Laich .12 .30
461 Jay Beagle .12 .30
462 Jason Chimera .12 .30
463 Mike Knuble .12 .30
464 Matt Hendricks .12 .30
465 Mike Green .15 .40
466 Karl Alzner .12 .30
467 John Carlson .20 .50
468 Jeff Schultz .12 .30
469 Michal Neuvirth .15 .40
470 Braden Holtby .25 .60
471 Alexander Burmistrov .15 .40
472 Andrew Ladd .12 .30
473 Blake Wheeler .20 .50
474 Bryan Little .20 .50
475 Evander Kane .20 .50
476 Nik Antropov .15 .40
477 Patrice Cormier .12 .30
478 Chris Thorburn .12 .30
479 Jim Slater .12 .30
480 Tobias Enstrom .12 .30
481 Dustin Byfuglien .20 .50
482 Johnny Oduya .15 .40
483 Zach Bogosian .15 .40
484 Ondrej Pavelec .20 .50
485 Chris Mason .15 .40
486 Dwayne Roloson HL .15 .40
487 Michael Ryder HL .12 .30
488 Alexander Ovechkin HL .75 2.00
489 James van Riemsdyk HL .15 .40
490 Pekka Rinne HL .20 .50
491 Alexandre Burrows HL .12 .30
492 Pavel Datsyuk HL .30 .75
493 Joe Thornton HL .30 .75
494 Milan Lucic HL .20 .50
495 Vincent Lecavalier HL .20 .50
496 Antti Niemi HL .15 .40
497 Ryan Kesler HL .20 .50
498 Nathan Horton HL .20 .50
499 Daniel Sedin HL .25 .60
500 Brad Marchand HL .40 1.00
501 Paul Postma HR RC .60 1.50
502 Lance Bouma HR RC .60 1.50
503 Greg Nemisz HR RC .60 1.50
504 Marcus Kruger HR RC 1.00 2.50
505 Cameron Gaunce HR RC .50 1.25
506 John Moore HR RC .60 1.50
507 Tomas Kubalik HR RC .60 1.50
508 Colton Sceviour HR RC .60 1.50
509 Tomas Vincour HR RC .60 1.50
510 Chris Vande Velde HR RC 1.00 2.50
511 Teemu Hartikainen HR RC .60 1.50
512 Scott Timmins HR RC .60 1.50
513 Hugh Jessiman HR RC .60 1.50
514 Carson McMillan HR RC .75 2.00
515 Brendon Nash HR RC .60 1.50
516 Aaron Palushaj HR RC .60 1.50
517 Jonathon Blum HR RC .60 1.50
518 Blake Geoffrion HR RC .60 1.50
519 Mark Katic HR RC .60 1.50
520 Mikko Koskinen HR RC .75 2.00
521 Matt Campanale HR RC .60 1.50
522 Justin DiBenedetto HR RC .50 1.25
523 Colin Greening HR RC .60 1.50
524 Erik Condra HR RC .60 1.50
525 Andre Benoit HR RC .75 2.00
526 Roman Wick HR RC .75 2.00
527 Stephane Da Costa HR RC .60 1.50
528 Patrick Wiercioch HR RC .60 1.50
529 Erik Gustafsson HR RC .75 2.00
530 Ben Holmstrom HR RC .60 1.50
531 Brian Strait HR RC .75 2.00
532 Joe Vitale HR RC .60 1.50
533 Cody Hodgson HR RC 1.00 2.50
534 Yann Sauve HR RC .60 1.50
535 Cam Talbot HR RC 1.50 4.00
536 Carl Klingberg HR RC .60 1.50
537 Todd Ford HR RC .75 2.00
538 Ben Scrivens HR RC .60 1.50
539 Andrey Zubarev HR RC .75 2.00
540 Joe Colborne HR RC .60 1.50
541 Zac Rinaldo HR RC .60 1.50
542 Matt Frattin HR RC .60 1.50
543 Adam Henrique HR RC 1.50 4.00
544 Jamie Doornbosch HR RC .60 1.50
545 Shane Sims HR RC .60 1.50
546 Drew Bagnall HR RC .60 1.50
551 Nugent-Hopkins HR SP RC 10.00 25.00
552 Mika Zibanejad HR SP RC 10.00 25.00
553 G.Landeskog HR SP RC 8.00 20.00
554 Devante Smith-Pelly HR SP RC 4.00 10.00
555 Brandon Saad HR SP RC 6.00 15.00
556 Mark Scheifele HR SP RC 12.00 30.00
557 Sean Couturier HR SP RC 6.00 15.00
558 Brett Connolly HR SP RC 3.00 8.00
559 Tim Erixon HR SP RC 3.00 8.00
560 Jake Gardiner HR SP RC 5.00 12.00
561 Ryan Johansen HR SP RC 10.00 25.00
562 Adam Larsson HR SP RC 4.00 10.00
563 Justin Faulk HR SP RC 5.00 12.00
564 Erik Gudbranson HR SP RC 4.00 10.00
565 Matt Read HR SP RC 4.00 10.00
566 Alexei Emelin HR SP RC 5.00 12.00
567 Roman Horak HR SP RC 10.00 25.00
568 Craig Smith HR SP RC 6.00 15.00
569 Harri Sateri HR SP RC 10.00 25.00
570 Cam Atkinson HR SP RC 12.00 30.00
NNO Bruins Champs SP 40.00 80.00

2011-12 Score Black
*BLACK: 20X TO 50X BASE
125 Corey Crawford 12.00 30.00
459 Nicklas Backstrom 10.00 25.00

2011-12 Score Glossy
COMPLETE SET (500) 40.00 100.00
*GLOSSY: 1.2X TO 3X BASE
125 Corey Crawford .75 2.00
459 Nicklas Backstrom .60 1.50

2011-12 Score Gold
*1-500 VETERANS: 4X TO 10X BASIC CARDS
125 Corey Crawford 3.00 8.00
459 Nicklas Backstrom 2.50 6.00

2011-12 Score B
COMPLETE SET (10) 15.00 40.00
1 Marc-Andre Fleury 3.00 8.00
2 Martin Brodeur 4.00 10.00
3 Roberto Luongo 2.50 6.00
4 Carey Price 3.00 8.00
5 Alexander Ovechkin 6.00 15.00
6 Daniel Sedin 2.00 5.00
7 Steven Stamkos 3.00 8.00
8 Corey Perry 2.50 6.00
9 Taylor Hall 1.50 4.00
10 Sidney Crosby 6.00 15.00

2011-12 Score First Goal
COMPLETE SET (15) 15.00 40.00
1 Jeff Skinner 1.25 3.00
2 Taylor Hall 1.00 2.50
3 Erik Condra .75 2.00
4 Derek Stepan .60 1.50
5 Jordan Eberle 1.00 2.50
6 Cam Fowler 1.00 2.50
7 P.K. Subban 1.25 3.00
8 Blake Geoffrion .75 2.00
9 Cody Hodgson 1.25 3.00
10 David Desharnais .60 1.50
11 Linus Omark 1.00 2.50
12 Brad Marchand 2.00 5.00
13 Nino Niederreiter .60 1.50
14 Tomas Tatar .60 1.50
15 Marcus Johansson .75 2.00

2011-12 Score Franchise
COMP.SET wo SPs (30) 40.00 100.00
1 Corey Perry 2.00 5.00
2 Dustin Byfuglien 1.25 3.00
3 Tim Thomas 1.25 3.00
4 Ryan Miller 1.25 3.00
5 Jarome Iginla 1.50 4.00
6 Jeff Skinner 1.50 4.00
7 Patrick Kane 2.50 6.00
8 Matt Duchene 1.25 3.00
9 Rick Nash 1.25 3.00
10 Jamie Benn 1.25 3.00
11 Nicklas Lidstrom .75 2.00
12 Taylor Hall 1.25 3.00
13 Jacob Markstrom 1.25 3.00
14 Anze Kopitar 2.00 5.00
15 Mikko Koivu 1.00 2.50
16 Carey Price 2.50 6.00
17 Pekka Rinne 1.25 3.00
18 Martin Brodeur 3.00 8.00
19 John Tavares 2.00 5.00
20 Henrik Lundqvist 3.00 8.00
21 Daniel Alfredsson 1.25 3.00
22 Claude Giroux 1.25 3.00
23 Shane Doan 1.00 2.50
24 Sidney Crosby 5.00 12.00
25 Joe Thornton 2.00 5.00
26 David Backes .75 2.00
27 Steven Stamkos 2.50 6.00
28 Dion Phaneuf 1.00 2.50
29 Roberto Luongo 2.00 5.00
30 Alexander Ovechkin 5.00 12.00
31 Guy Lafleur SP 15.00 40.00
32 Mario Lemieux SP 20.00 40.00
33 Steve Yzerman SP 20.00 40.00
34 Dale Hawerchuk SP 20.00 40.00
35 Joe Sakic SP 12.50 25.00
36 Mark Messier SP 12.50 25.00

2011-12 Score Making An Entrance
COMPLETE SET (10) 10.00 25.00
1 Jamie Benn 1.00 2.50
2 Joe Thornton 1.50 4.00
3 Jordan Eberle 1.00 2.50
4 Alexander Ovechkin 4.00 10.00
5 Marc-Andre Fleury 2.00 5.00
6 Patrick Kane 2.00 5.00
7 Martin St. Louis 1.00 2.50
8 Nicklas Lidstrom .60 1.50
9 Carey Price 2.00 5.00
10 Miikka Kiprusoff 1.00 2.50

2011-12 Score Net Cam
COMPLETE SET (15) 12.00 30.00
1 Tim Thomas 1.00 2.50
2 Pekka Rinne 1.00 2.50
3 Roberto Luongo 1.50 4.00
4 Cam Ward 1.00 2.50
5 Carey Price 2.00 5.00
6 Miikka Kiprusoff 1.00 2.50
7 Jimmy Howard 1.25 3.00
8 Henrik Lundqvist 2.50 6.00
9 Ryan Miller 1.00 2.50
10 Michal Neuvirth .75 2.00
11 Antti Niemi .75 2.00
12 Martin Brodeur 2.50 6.00
13 Corey Crawford 1.25 3.00
14 James Reimer 1.00 2.50
15 Jonathan Quick 1.25 3.00

2011-12 Score NHL Shield Die Cuts
COMPLETE SET (10) 15.00 40.00
1 Pekka Rinne 1.25 3.00
2 Henrik Lundqvist 3.00 8.00
3 Nicklas Lidstrom .75 2.00
4 P.K. Subban 1.50 4.00
5 Jarome Iginla 1.50 4.00
6 Sidney Crosby 5.00 12.00
7 Alexander Ovechkin 5.00 12.00
8 Henrik Sedin 1.50 4.00
9 Steven Stamkos 2.50 6.00
10 Eric Staal 1.50 4.00

2011-12 Score Playoff Heroes
COMPLETE SET (10) 10.00 25.00
1 Michael Ryder .75 2.00
2 Joe Thornton 2.00 5.00
3 Alexandre Burrows .75 2.00
4 Kevin Bieksa 1.00 2.50
5 Nathan Horton 1.25 3.00
6 Ryan Kesler 1.25 3.00
7 Dwayne Roloson 1.00 2.50
8 Teddy Purcell .75 2.00
9 Patrice Bergeron 1.50 4.00
10 Roberto Luongo 2.00 5.00

2011-12 Score Signatures
38 George Parros 6.00 15.00
49 Jonas Hiller 6.00 15.00
50 Dan Ellis 6.00 15.00
56 Nathan Horton 8.00 20.00
58 Tyler Seguin 25.00 60.00
64 Tim Thomas EXCH 10.00 25.00
65 Tuukka Rask 12.00 25.00
74 Thomas Vanek 10.00 25.00
83 Jarome Iginla 20.00 40.00
88 Rene Bourque 10.00 25.00
97 Eric Staal 10.00 25.00
98 Jeff Skinner 15.00 40.00
99 Tuomo Ruutu 6.00 15.00
103 Drayson Bowman 5.00 12.00
134 Brandon Yip 5.00 12.00
135 T.J. Galiardi 6.00 15.00
137 Erik Johnson 5.00 12.00
139 Semyon Varlamov 8.00 20.00
144 Matt Calvert 5.00 12.00
146 Rick Nash 12.00 30.00
154 Steve Mason 12.00 30.00
158 Jamie Benn 8.00 20.00
159 Loui Eriksson 12.00 25.00
160 Steve Ott 5.00 12.00
163 Krys Barch 5.00 12.00
180 Justin Abdelkader 6.00 15.00
185 Jimmy Howard 10.00 25.00
188 Taylor Hall 20.00 40.00
192 Magnus Paajarvi 8.00 20.00
216 Anze Kopitar 20.00 40.00
217 Simon Gagne 10.00 25.00
224 Mike Richards 12.00 30.00
239 Brad Staubitz 8.00 20.00
254 Max Pacioretty 10.00 25.00
256 P.K. Subban 25.00 60.00
259 Carey Price 15.00 40.00
261 Colin Wilson 6.00 15.00
263 Mike Fisher 5.00 12.00
286 Andy Greene 5.00 12.00
289 Martin Brodeur 40.00 80.00
292 Matt Moulson 5.00 12.00
297 Trevor Gillies 5.00 12.00
306 Marian Gaborik 8.00 20.00
311 Derek Stepan 5.00 12.00
316 Marc Staal 5.00 12.00
331 Erik Karlsson 10.00 25.00
333 Matt Carkner 6.00 15.00
337 Brayden Schenn 8.00 20.00
338 Wayne Simmonds 10.00 25.00
342 Jakub Voracek 6.00 15.00
344 Claude Giroux 8.00 20.00
347 Chris Pronger 8.00 20.00
366 Sidney Crosby 60.00 120.00
367 Evgeni Malkin 20.00 40.00
385 Joe Thornton 10.00 25.00
389 Brent Burns 8.00 20.00
390 Dan Boyle 5.00 12.00
395 Antti Niemi 6.00 15.00
398 Chris Stewart 6.00 15.00
399 David Backes 5.00 12.00
403 T.J. Oshie 8.00 20.00
411 Vincent Lecavalier 25.00 50.00
413 Steven Stamkos 20.00 50.00
416 Steve Downie 8.00 20.00
425 Dwayne Roloson 6.00 15.00
434 Colton Orr 12.00 30.00
436 Dion Phaneuf 6.00 15.00
441 Daniel Sedin 15.00 40.00
445 Mikael Samuelsson 6.00 15.00
447 Alexandre Burrows 5.00 12.00
450 Dan Hamhuis 6.00 15.00
454 Cory Schneider 8.00 20.00
467 John Carlson 12.00 30.00
475 Evander Kane 8.00 20.00
481 Dustin Byfuglien 8.00 20.00
501 Paul Postma HR 6.00 15.00
503 Greg Nemisz HR 6.00 15.00
504 Marcus Kruger HR 10.00 25.00
505 Cameron Gaunce HR 5.00 12.00
506 John Moore HR 8.00 20.00
507 Tomas Kubalik HR 6.00 15.00
508 Colton Sceviour HR 6.00 15.00
509 Tomas Vincour HR 6.00 15.00
511 Teemu Hartikainen HR 6.00 15.00
512 Scott Timmins HR 6.00 15.00
513 Hugh Jessiman HR 6.00 15.00
516 Aaron Palushaj HR 6.00 15.00
517 Jonathon Blum HR 8.00 20.00
518 Blake Geoffrion HR 6.00 15.00
519 Mark Katic HR 6.00 15.00
520 Mikko Koskinen HR 8.00 20.00
522 Justin DiBenedetto HR 8.00 20.00
523 Colin Greening HR 6.00 15.00
524 Erik Condra HR 6.00 15.00
527 Stephane Da Costa HR 6.00 15.00
528 Patrick Wiercioch HR 6.00 15.00
529 Erik Gustafsson HR 8.00 20.00
530 Ben Holmstrom HR 6.00 15.00
531 Brian Strait HR 8.00 20.00
532 Joe Vitale HR 6.00 15.00
533 Cody Hodgson HR 15.00 40.00
534 Yann Sauve HR 6.00 15.00
535 Cam Talbot HR 15.00 40.00
536 Carl Klingberg HR 6.00 15.00
538 Ben Scrivens HR 10.00 25.00
540 Joe Colborne HR 20.00 50.00
541 Zac Rinaldo HR 6.00 15.00
542 Matt Frattin HR 6.00 15.00
543 Adam Henrique HR 30.00 60.00
546 Drew Bagnall HR 6.00 15.00
551 Ryan Nugent-Hopkins HR 200.00 400.00
552 Mika Zibanejad HR 15.00 40.00
554 Devante Smith-Pelly HR 8.00 20.00
555 Brandon Saad HR 15.00 40.00
556 Mark Scheifele HR 50.00 100.00
557 Sean Couturier HR 30.00 60.00
558 Brett Connolly HR 12.00 30.00
559 Tim Erixon HR 15.00 40.00
560 Jake Gardiner HR 20.00 50.00
561 Ryan Johansen HR 20.00 50.00
562 Adam Larsson HR 15.00 40.00
565 Matt Read HR 20.00 50.00

2011-12 Score Snow Globe Die Cuts
COMPLETE SET (10) 15.00 40.00
1 Daniel Sedin 2.50 6.00
2 Sidney Crosby 8.00 20.00
3 Ryan Kesler 2.00 5.00
4 Thomas Vanek 1.50 4.00
5 Anze Kopitar 3.00 8.00
6 Patrick Sharp 2.00 5.00
7 Matt Duchene 2.00 5.00
8 Jeff Skinner 2.50 6.00
9 Mikko Koivu 1.50 4.00
10 Logan Couture 2.50 6.00

2011-12 Score Sudden Death
COMPLETE SET (25) 15.00 40.00
1 Linus Omark 1.00 2.50
2 Alexander Ovechkin 4.00 10.00
3 Simon Gagne 1.00 2.50
4 Ryane Clowe .60 1.50
5 Patrick Marleau 1.00 2.50
6 P.K. Subban 1.25 3.00
7 Nazem Kadri 1.25 3.00
8 Mats Zuccarello-Aasen 1.00 2.50
9 Alexandre Burrows .60 1.50
10 Shea Weber .75 2.00
11 Ilya Kovalchuk 1.00 2.50
12 Lubomir Visnovsky .60 1.50
13 Bobby Ryan .75 2.00
14 Brandon Sutter .60 1.50
15 Ryan Callahan .60 1.50
16 Henrik Zetterberg 1.25 3.00
17 Alexander Steen .60 1.50
18 Jason Chimera .60 1.50
19 Tyler Ennis .60 1.50
20 John Tavares 1.50 4.00
21 Corey Perry 1.50 4.00
22 Steven Stamkos 2.00 5.00
23 Martin St. Louis 1.00 2.50
24 Jarome Iginla 1.25 3.00
25 Matt Duchene 1.00 2.50

2011-12 Score Supreme Team
COMPLETE SET (20) 25.00 60.00
1 Sidney Crosby 8.00 20.00
2 Steven Stamkos 4.00 10.00
3 Henrik Sedin 2.50 6.00
4 Jonathan Toews 3.00 8.00
5 Jeff Skinner 2.50 6.00
6 Pavel Datsyuk 3.00 8.00
7 Daniel Sedin 2.50 6.00
8 Alexander Ovechkin 8.00 20.00
9 Henrik Zetterberg 2.50 6.00
10 Milan Lucic 2.00 5.00
11 Corey Perry 3.00 8.00
12 Martin St. Louis 2.00 5.00
13 Claude Giroux 2.00 5.00
14 Patrick Kane 4.00 10.00
15 Nicklas Lidstrom 1.25 3.00
16 P.K. Subban 2.50 6.00
17 Drew Doughty 2.50 6.00
18 Tim Thomas 2.00 5.00
19 Roberto Luongo 3.00 8.00
20 Carey Price 4.00 10.00

2012-13 Score
1 Ryan Nugent-Hopkins SH .25 .60
2 Thomas Vanek SH .15 .40
3 Anze Kopitar SH .30 .75
4 Bobby Ryan SH .15 .40
5 Luke Adam SH .15 .40
6 Bernie Parent SH .25 .60
7 Mark Messier SH .40 1.00
8 Henrik Lundqvist SH .50 1.25
9 Brayden Schenn SH .20 .50
10 Pavel Datsyuk SH .30 .75
11 Carl Hagelin SH .12 .30
12 Patrick Kane SH .40 1.00
13 Jamie Benn SH .20 .50
14 Zdeno Chara SH .20 .50
15 Steven Stamkos SH .40 1.00
16 Marian Gaborik SH .20 .50
17 Tim Thomas SH .20 .50
18 Teemu Selanne SH .40 1.00
19 Jaromir Jagr SH .60 1.50
20 Ray Whitney SH .15 .40
21 Cam Ward SH .20 .50
22 Miikka Kiprusoff SH .20 .50
23 Daniel Alfredsson SH .20 .50
24 Marian Hossa SH .20 .50
25 Ilya Kovalchuk SH .20 .50
26 Jarome Iginla SH .25 .60
27 Evgeni Malkin SH .40 1.00
28 Steven Stamkos SH .40 1.00
29 Henrik Lundqvist SH .50 1.25
30 Martin Brodeur SH .50 1.25
31 Sam Gagner SH .12 .30
32 Jimmy Howard SH .25 .60
33 Nicklas Lidstrom SH .20 .50
34 Stephen Weiss SH .15 .40
35 Sidney Crosby SH .75 2.00
36 Cam Ward SH .20 .50
37 Nik Antropov SH .15 .40
38 Scott Niedermayer SH .20 .50
39 Steven Stamkos SH .40 1.00
40 Shane Doan SH .15 .40
41 Corey Perry .30 .75
42 Teemu Selanne .40 1.00
43 Saku Koivu .20 .50
44 Ryan Getzlaf .20 .50
45 Bobby Ryan .15 .40
46 Andrew Cogliano .12 .30
47 Jonas Hiller .15 .40
48 Cam Fowler .20 .50
49 Devante Smith-Pelly .15 .40
50 Sheldon Souray .12 .30
51 Francois Beauchemin .12 .30
52 Niklas Hagman .12 .30
53 Luca Sbisa .15 .40
54 Dan Ellis .15 .40
55 Nick Bonino .12 .30
56 Tyler Seguin .25 .60
57 Tim Thomas .20 .50
58 Zdeno Chara .20 .50
59 Patrice Bergeron .25 .60
60 David Krejci .20 .50
61 Milan Lucic .20 .50
62 Brad Marchand .40 1.00
63 Rich Peverley .20 .50
64 Tuukka Rask .25 .60
65 Shawn Thornton .12 .30
66 Nathan Horton .20 .50
67 Johnny Boychuk .15 .40
68 Chris Kelly .15 .40
69 Benoit Pouliot .12 .30
70 Gregory Campbell .12 .30
71 Ryan Miller .20 .50
72 Jason Pominville .12 .30
73 Drew Stafford .12 .30
74 Thomas Vanek .15 .40
75 Steve Ott .12 .30
76 Cody Hodgson .12 .30
77 Tyler Myers .12 .30
78 Tyler Ennis .12 .30
79 Jhonas Enroth .20 .50
80 Christian Ehrhoff .12 .30
81 Nathan Gerbe .12 .30
82 Luke Adam .15 .40
83 Corey Tropp .15 .40
84 Marcus Foligno .15 .40
85 Brayden McNabb .20 .50
86 Jarome Iginla .25 .60
87 Jay Bouwmeester .12 .30
88 Miikka Kiprusoff .20 .50
89 Jiri Hudler .15 .40
90 Alex Tanguay .15 .40
91 Curtis Glencross .12 .30
92 Lee Stempniak .12 .30
93 Michael Cammalleri .15 .40
94 Matt Stajan .12 .30
95 Leland Irving .15 .40
96 Blake Comeau .12 .30
97 Mark Giordano .20 .50
98 Mikael Backlund .15 .40
99 Greg Nemisz .12 .30
100 Tim Jackman .12 .30
101 Eric Staal .25 .60
102 Jordan Staal .15 .40
103 Tim Gleason .12 .30
104 Cam Ward .20 .50
105 Jussi Jokinen .12 .30
106 Jeff Skinner .25 .60
107 Jiri Tlusty .12 .30
108 Tuomo Ruutu .15 .40
109 Chad LaRose .12 .30
110 Justin Faulk .15 .40
111 Joe Corvo .12 .30
112 Jamie McBain .12 .30
113 Riley Nash .12 .30
114 Zach Boychuk .12 .30
115 Brian Boucher .15 .40
116 Jonathan Toews .30 .75
117 Patrick Sharp .20 .50
118 Duncan Keith .15 .40
119 Patrick Kane .40 1.00
120 Marian Hossa .20 .50
121 Corey Crawford .25 .60
122 Viktor Stalberg .12 .30
123 Dave Bolland .15 .40
124 Brandon Saad .15 .40
125 Brent Seabrook .12 .30
126 Nick Leddy .12 .30
127 Andrew Shaw .12 .30
128 Marcus Kruger .12 .30
129 Ray Emery .15 .40
130 Bryan Bickell .12 .30
131 Gabriel Landeskog .25 .60
132 Paul Stastny .15 .40
133 Milan Hejduk .15 .40
134 Matt Duchene .20 .50
135 Ryan O'Reilly .20 .50
136 David Jones .12 .30
137 Semyon Varlamov .20 .50
138 Erik Johnson .12 .30
139 Steve Downie .12 .30
140 P.A. Parenteau .12 .30
141 Cameron Gaunce .12 .30
142 Jamie McGinn .12 .30
143 Jean-Sebastien Giguere .20 .50
144 Peter Mueller .12 .30
145 Ryan Wilson .15 .40
146 Ryan Johansen .15 .40
147 Rick Nash .20 .50
148 Vinny Prospal .12 .30
149 R.J. Umberger .12 .30
150 Derick Brassard .12 .30
151 Derek Dorsett .12 .30
152 James Wisniewski .12 .30
153 Jack Johnson .12 .30
154 Nick Foligno .15 .40
155 Steve Mason .15 .40
156 John Moore .12 .30
157 Mark Letestu .15 .40
158 Sergei Bobrovsky .30 .75
159 Jared Boll .12 .30
160 Cam Atkinson .20 .50
161 Loui Eriksson .12 .30
162 Brenden Morrow .15 .40
163 Derek Roy .12 .30
164 Stephane Robidas .12 .30
165 Kari Lehtonen .15 .40
166 Jamie Benn .20 .50
167 Cody Eakin .12 .30
168 Richard Bachman .15 .40
169 Jaromir Jagr .60 1.50
170 Ray Whitney .15 .40
171 Alex Goligoski .12 .30
172 Trevor Daley .12 .30
173 Tomas Vincour .12 .30
174 Michael Ryder .12 .30
175 Colton Sceviour .12 .30
176 Pavel Datsyuk .30 .75
177 Nicklas Lidstrom .20 .50
178 Henrik Zetterberg .25 .60
179 Niklas Kronwall .15 .40
180 Jimmy Howard .25 .60
181 Valtteri Filppula .12 .30
182 Johan Franzen .15 .40
183 Jordin Tootoo .15 .40
184 Todd Bertuzzi .15 .40
185 Danny Cleary .20 .50
186 Brendan Smith .12 .30
187 Drew Miller .12 .30
188 Tomas Holmstrom .12 .30
189 Justin Abdelkader .15 .40
190 Gustav Nyquist .12 .30
191 Ryan Nugent-Hopkins .25 .60
192 Taylor Hall .20 .50
193 Jordan Eberle .20 .50
194 Shawn Horcoff .12 .30
195 Ales Hemsky .15 .40
196 Ryan Whitney .12 .30
197 Sam Gagner .12 .30
198 Ryan Smyth .15 .40
199 Devan Dubnyk .15 .40
200 Nikolai Khabibulin .20 .50
201 Ryan Jones .15 .40
202 Ben Eager .12 .30
203 Magnus Paajarvi .15 .40
204 Anton Lander .15 .40
205 Teemu Hartikainen .15 .40
206 Stephen Weiss .15 .40
207 Brian Campbell .12 .30
208 Tomas Kopecky .15 .40
209 Ed Jovanovski .12 .30
210 Jose Theodore .20 .50
211 Tomas Fleischmann .12 .30
212 Kris Versteeg .12 .30
213 Jacob Markstrom .20 .50
214 Sean Bergenheim .12 .30
215 Erik Gudbranson .12 .30
216 Dmitry Kulikov .12 .30
217 George Parros .15 .40
218 Krys Barch .12 .30
219 Wojtek Wolski .12 .30
220 Scott Clemmensen .15 .40
221 Anze Kopitar .30 .75
222 Dustin Brown .20 .50
223 Matt Greene .15 .40
224 Jonathan Quick .25 .60
225 Drew Doughty .25 .60
226 Justin Williams .15 .40
227 Mike Richards .15 .40
228 Simon Gagne .20 .50
229 Jeff Carter .15 .40
230 Jarret Stoll .15 .40
231 Jonathan Bernier .15 .40
232 Dustin Penner .15 .40
233 Slava Voynov .20 .50
234 Kyle Clifford .12 .30
235 Willie Mitchell .15 .40
236 Mikko Koivu .15 .40
237 Dany Heatley .15 .40
238 Matt Cullen .12 .30
239 Cal Clutterbuck .12 .30
240 Kyle Brodziak .12 .30
241 Devin Setoguchi .15 .40
242 Nick Johnson .15 .40
243 Niklas Backstrom .15 .40
244 Zach Parise .20 .50
245 Josh Harding .20 .50
246 Pierre-Marc Bouchard .20 .50
247 Ryan Suter .15 .40
248 Zenon Konopka .15 .40
249 Torrey Mitchell .12 .30
250 Matt Kassian .12 .30
251 Carey Price .40 1.00
252 Andrei Markov .12 .30
253 Brian Gionta .12 .30
254 Max Pacioretty .20 .50
255 Erik Cole .12 .30
256 David Desharnais .12 .30
257 P.K. Subban .25 .60
258 Tomas Plekanec .12 .30
259 Lars Eller .12 .30
260 Louis Leblanc .12 .30
261 Blake Geoffrion .20 .50
262 Brandon Prust .12 .30
263 Colby Armstrong .12 .30
264 Yannick Weber .12 .30
265 Alexei Emelin .12 .30
266 Pekka Rinne .20 .50
267 Chris Mason .15 .40
268 Shea Weber .15 .40
269 Martin Erat .12 .30
270 David Legwand .15 .40
271 Mike Fisher .12 .30
272 Sergei Kostitsyn .12 .30
273 Patric Hornqvist .12 .30
274 Ryan Ellis .12 .30
275 Craig Smith .12 .30
276 Nick Spaling .12 .30
277 Colin Wilson .15 .40
278 Andrei Kostitsyn .15 .40
279 Gabriel Bourque .15 .40
280 Roman Josi .20 .50
281 Martin Brodeur .50 1.25
282 Anton Volchenkov .12 .30
283 Patrik Elias .20 .50
284 Ilya Kovalchuk .20 .50
285 Adam Henrique .15 .40
286 David Clarkson .12 .30
287 Petr Sykora .15 .40
288 Dainius Zubrus .12 .30
289 Johan Hedberg .15 .40
290 Adam Larsson .20 .50
291 Alexei Ponikarovsky .12 .30
292 Mark Fayne .12 .30
293 Andy Greene .12 .30
294 Travis Zajac .12 .30
295 Jacob Josefson .12 .30
296 John Tavares .30 .75
297 Mark Streit .12 .30
298 Kyle Okposo .12 .30
299 Steve Staios .12 .30
300 Matt Moulson .12 .30
301 Anders Nilsson .12 .30
302 Frans Nielsen .12 .30
303 Michael Grabner .15 .40
304 Josh Bailey .15 .40
305 Evgeni Nabokov .15 .40
306 Travis Hamonic .15 .40
307 Eric Boulton .12 .30
308 Andrew MacDonald .12 .30
309 Calvin de Haan .12 .30
310 Rick DiPietro .15 .40
311 Henrik Lundqvist .50 1.25
312 Ryan Callahan .12 .30
313 Brad Richards .20 .50
314 Marian Gaborik .20 .50
315 Derek Stepan .12 .30
316 Michael Del Zotto .12 .30
317 Carl Hagelin .12 .30
318 Marc Staal .12 .30
319 Artem Anisimov .12 .30
320 Brandon Dubinsky .12 .30
321 Ryan McDonagh .12 .30
322 Dan Girardi .12 .30
323 Brian Boyle .12 .30
324 Taylor Pyatt .12 .30
325 Martin Biron .15 .40
326 Daniel Alfredsson .20 .50
327 Jason Spezza .20 .50
328 Erik Karlsson .25 .60
329 Chris Phillips .12 .30
330 Craig Anderson .20 .50
331 Milan Michalek .12 .30
332 Guillaume Latendresse .15 .40
333 Sergei Gonchar .12 .30
334 Colin Greening .12 .30
335 Mika Zibanejad .25 .60
336 Kyle Turris .12 .30
337 Jared Cowen .20 .50
338 Chris Neil .12 .30
339 Erik Condra .12 .30
340 Zack Smith .12 .30
341 Claude Giroux .20 .50
342 Scott Hartnell .12 .30
343 Brayden Schenn .20 .50
344 Danny Briere .20 .50
345 Jakub Voracek .15 .40
346 Wayne Simmonds .25 .60
347 Matt Read .15 .40
348 Chris Pronger .20 .50
349 Ilya Bryzgalov .20 .50
350 Sean Couturier .15 .40
351 Luke Schenn .20 .50
352 Zac Rinaldo .15 .40
353 Kimmo Timonen .12 .30
354 Max Talbot .12 .30
355 Eric Wellwood .12 .30
356 Shane Doan .15 .40
357 Keith Yandle .12 .30
358 Paul Bissonnette .12 .30
359 Martin Hanzal .12 .30
360 Mikkel Boedker .12 .30
361 Mike Smith .20 .50
362 Radim Vrbata .12 .30
363 David Rundblad .15 .40
364 Oliver Ekman-Larsson .20 .50
365 Rostislav Klesla .12 .30
366 Raffi Torres .12 .30
367 Antoine Vermette .12 .30
368 Daymond Langkow .12 .30
369 Andy Miele .12 .30
370 Michal Rozsival .12 .30
371 Sidney Crosby .75 2.00
372 Evgeni Malkin .40 1.00
373 Brandon Sutter .12 .30
374 Marc-Andre Fleury .40 1.00
375 Kris Letang .25 .60
376 James Neal .12 .30
377 Brooks Orpik .12 .30
378 Chris Kunitz .20 .50
379 Pascal Dupuis .12 .30
380 Steve Sullivan .12 .30
381 Tyler Kennedy .12 .30
382 Matt Cooke .12 .30
383 Joe Vitale .12 .30
384 Simon Despres .15 .40
385 Paul Martin .12 .30
386 Joe Thornton .30 .75
387 Patrick Marleau .20 .50
388 Dan Boyle .12 .30
389 Ryane Clowe .12 .30
390 Logan Couture .25 .60
391 Joe Pavelski .25 .60
392 Antti Niemi .15 .40
393 Brent Burns .20 .50
394 Martin Havlat .15 .40
395 Michal Handzus .12 .30
396 Adam Burish .12 .30
397 Marc-Edouard Vlasic .12 .30
398 Brad Winchester .12 .30
399 Andrew Desjardins .12 .30
400 T.J. Galiardi .15 .40
401 David Backes .12 .30
402 Alexander Steen .12 .30
403 Andy McDonald .15 .40
404 Brian Elliott .15 .40
405 Jaroslav Halak .20 .50
406 Alex Pietrangelo .15 .40
407 T.J. Oshie .20 .50
408 Barret Jackman .12 .30
409 Jamie Langenbrunner .12 .30
410 Kevin Shattenkirk .12 .30
411 David Perron .15 .40
412 Patrik Berglund .12 .30
413 Jason Arnott .15 .40
414 Chris Stewart .15 .40
415 Vladimir Sobotka .12 .30
416 Steven Stamkos .40 1.00
417 Martin St. Louis .20 .50
418 Vincent Lecavalier .20 .50
419 Eric Brewer .12 .30
420 Mattias Ohlund .12 .30
421 Teddy Purcell .12 .30
422 Ryan Malone .12 .30
423 Brett Connolly .12 .30
424 Victor Hedman .25 .60
425 Dwayne Roloson .15 .40
426 Anders Lindback .12 .30
427 Tom Pyatt .12 .30
428 J.T. Wyman .12 .30
429 Marc-Andre Bergeron .12 .30
430 Dana Tyrell .12 .30
431 Phil Kessel .20 .50
432 Dion Phaneuf .15 .40
433 Mikhail Grabovski .12 .30
434 Mike Komisarek .15 .40
435 Jake Gardiner .12 .30
436 Joffrey Lupul .12 .30
437 Tyler Bozak .12 .30
438 James van Riemsdyk .15 .40
439 James Reimer .20 .50
440 Cody Franson .12 .30
441 Clarke MacArthur .12 .30
442 Joe Colborne .15 .40
443 Tim Connolly .12 .30
444 Nazem Kadri .25 .60
445 Matt Frattin .15 .40
446 Henrik Sedin .25 .60
447 Daniel Sedin .25 .60
448 Ryan Kesler .20 .50
449 Cory Schneider .20 .50
450 Alexandre Burrows .12 .30
451 Kevin Bieksa .15 .40
452 Manny Malhotra .15 .40
453 Roberto Luongo .30 .75
454 Alexander Edler .12 .30
455 Zack Kassian .12 .30
456 Jannik Hansen .15 .40
457 Dan Hamhuis .15 .40
458 Maxim Lapierre .12 .30
459 Dale Weise .15 .40
460 Chris Higgins .12 .30
461 Alex Ovechkin .75 2.00
462 Nicklas Backstrom .20 .50
463 Brooks Laich .12 .30
464 Troy Brouwer .12 .30
465 Mike Knuble .12 .30
466 Alexander Semin .20 .50
467 Braden Holtby .25 .60
468 Mike Green .15 .40
469 Dmitry Orlov .20 .50
470 Marcus Johansson .15 .40
471 Mike Ribeiro .12 .30
472 Joel Ward .12 .30
473 John Carlson .20 .50
474 Mathieu Perreault .12 .30
475 Michal Neuvirth .15 .40
476 Evander Kane .20 .50
477 Dustin Byfuglien .20 .50
478 Blake Wheeler .20 .50
479 Andrew Ladd .12 .30
480 Mark Scheifele .30 .75
481 Tobias Enstrom .12 .30
482 Al Montoya .12 .30
483 Alexander Burmistrov .15 .40
484 Olli Jokinen .15 .40
485 Bryan Little .20 .50
486 Nik Antropov .15 .40
487 Zach Bogosian .15 .40
488 Ondrej Pavelec .20 .50
489 Kyle Wellwood .15 .40
490 Mark Stuart .12 .30
491 Evgeni Malkin AW .40 1.00
492 Evgeni Malkin AW .40 1.00
493 Henrik Lundqvist AW .50 1.25
494 Gabriel Landeskog AW .25 .60
495 Steven Stamkos AW .40 1.00
496 Erik Karlsson AW .25 .60
497 Brian Campbell AW .12 .30
498 Patrice Bergeron AW .25 .60
499 Jonathan Quick AW .25 .60
500 Jonathan Quick AW .25 .60
501 Philippe Cornet HR RC .40 1.00
502 Andrew Joudrey HR RC .40 1.00
503 Tyson Sexsmith HR RC .30 .75
504 Jakob Silfverberg HR RC .60 1.50
505 Tyson Barrie HR RC 1.00 2.50
506 Mike Connolly HR RC .40 1.00
507 Aaron Ness HR RC .30 .75
508 Jordan Nolan HR RC .30 .75
509 Colby Robak HR RC .30 .75
510 Kristopher Foucault HR RC .30 .75
511 Ryan Garbutt HR RC .30 .75
512 Michael Stone HR RC .40 1.00
513 Carter Camper HR RC .30 .75
514 Casey Cizikas HR RC .40 1.00
515 Brandon Bollig HR RC .30 .75
516 Lane MacDermid HR RC .40 1.00
517 Carter Ashton HR RC .30 .75
518 Sven Baertschi HR RC .50 1.25
519 Brandon Manning HR RC .40 1.00
520 Maxime Sauve HR RC .30 .75
521 Jaden Schwartz HR RC 1.00 2.50
522 Travis Turnbull HR RC .30 .75
523 Ryan Hamilton HR RC .30 .75
524 Jussi Rynnas HR RC .30 .75
525 Shawn Hunwick HR RC .30 .75
526 Reilly Smith HR RC 1.00 2.50
527 Cody Goloubef HR RC .30 .75
528 J.T. Brown HR RC .40 1.00
529 Mat Clark HR RC .40 1.00
530 Dalton Prout HR RC .30 .75
531 Torey Krug HR RC 1.00 2.50
532 Matt Donovan HR RC .40 1.00
533 Robert Mayer HR RC .50 1.25
534 Gabriel Dumont HR RC .40 1.00
535 Akim Aliu HR RC .40 1.00
536 Tyler Cuma HR RC .30 .75
537 Chet Pickard HR RC .40 1.00
538 Riley Sheahan HR RC .50 1.25
539 Jeremy Welsh HR RC .40 1.00
540 Chay Genoway HR RC .30 .75
541 Scott Glennie HR RC .40 1.00
542 Brenden Dillon HR RC .40 1.00
543 Chris Kreider HR RC 1.25 3.00
544 Jake Allen HR RC 1.00 2.50
545 Jason Zucker HR RC .75 2.00
546 Matt Watkins HR RC .30 .75
547 Michael Hutchinson HR RC .50 1.25
548 Mark Stone HR RC 1.25 3.00

2012-13 Score Black Ice
*VETS 1-500: 15X TO 40X BASIC CARDS
*ROOKIES 501-548: 4X TO 10X BASIC CARDS
121 Corey Crawford 5.00 12.00
462 Nicklas Backstrom 4.00 10.00

2012-13 Score Gold Rush
*VETS 1-500: 1.2X TO 3X BASIC CARDS
*ROOKIES 101-548: .6X TO 1.5X BASIC RC
121 Corey Crawford .75 2.00
462 Nicklas Backstrom .60 1.50
543 Chris Kreider HR 6.00 15.00

2012-13 Score Check It
C1 Cal Clutterbuck 2.50 6.00
C2 Zdeno Chara 4.00 10.00
C3 Alex Ovechkin 15.00 40.00
C4 Dion Phaneuf 3.00 8.00
C5 Jeremy Roenick 6.00 15.00
C6 Cam Neely 10.00 20.00
C7 Chris Pronger 4.00 10.00
C8 Dustin Brown 4.00 10.00
C9 Milan Lucic 4.00 10.00
C10 Niklas Kronwall 3.00 8.00
C11 Eric Lindros 4.00 10.00
C12 Steve Ott 3.00 8.00
C13 Ryan Callahan 2.50 6.00
C14 Matt Martin 2.50 6.00
C15 David Backes 2.50 6.00
C16 Luke Schenn 6.00 15.00
C17 Brendan Shanahan 4.00 10.00
C18 Dustin Byfuglien 4.00 10.00
C19 Wendel Clark 4.00 10.00
C20 Chris Neil 2.50 6.00

2012-13 Score First Goal
FG1 Matt Read .75 2.00
FG2 Gabriel Landeskog 1.25 3.00
FG3 Andrew Shaw .60 1.50
FG4 Ryan Nugent-Hopkins 1.25 3.00
FG5 Chris Kreider 2.50 6.00
FG6 Adam Henrique .75 2.00
FG7 Carl Hagelin .60 1.50
FG8 Craig Smith .60 1.50
FG9 Sean Couturier .75 2.00
FG10 Marcus Kruger .60 1.50
FG11 Ryan Johansen .75 2.00
FG12 Mark Scheifele 1.50 4.00
FG13 Sven Baertschi 1.00 2.50
FG14 Jake Gardiner .60 1.50
FG15 Slava Voynov 1.00 2.50
FG16 Brayden Schenn 1.00 2.50
FG17 Justin Faulk .75 2.00
FG18 Matt Frattin .75 2.00
FG19 Gabriel Bourque .75 2.00
FG20 Devante Smith-Pelly .75 2.00
FG21 Cam Atkinson 1.00 2.50
FG22 Marcus Foligno .75 2.00
FG23 Jared Cowen 1.00 2.50
FG24 Roman Josi 1.00 2.50

2012-13 Score Franchise
F1 Corey Perry 2.00 5.00
F2 Tyler Seguin 1.50 4.00
F3 Ryan Miller 1.25 3.00
F4 Jarome Iginla 1.50 4.00
F5 Eric Staal 1.50 4.00
F6 Jonathan Toews 2.00 5.00
F7 Matt Duchene 1.25 3.00
F8 Rick Nash 1.25 3.00
F9 Loui Eriksson .75 2.00
F10 Pavel Datsyuk 2.00 5.00
F11 Jordan Eberle 1.25 3.00
F12 Stephen Weiss 1.00 2.50
F13 Jonathan Quick 1.50 4.00
F14 Dany Heatley 1.00 2.50
F15 Max Pacioretty 1.25 3.00
F16 Pekka Rinne 1.25 3.00
F17 Ilya Kovalchuk 1.25 3.00
F18 John Tavares 2.00 5.00
F19 Henrik Lundqvist 3.00 8.00
F20 Jason Spezza 1.25 3.00
F21 Claude Giroux 1.25 3.00
F22 Keith Yandle .75 2.00
F23 Sidney Crosby 5.00 12.00
F24 Joe Thornton 2.00 5.00
F25 David Backes .75 2.00
F26 Steven Stamkos 2.50 6.00
F27 Phil Kessel 1.25 3.00
F28 Henrik Sedin 1.50 4.00
F29 Alex Ovechkin 5.00 12.00
F30 Dustin Byfuglien 1.25 3.00

2012-13 Score Franchise Original Six
OS1 Johnny Bucyk 1.00 2.50
OS2 Gordie Howe 3.00 8.00
OS3 Johnny Bower 1.00 2.50
OS4 Jean Beliveau 1.00 2.50
OS5 Ed Giacomin 1.00 2.50
OS6 Bobby Hull 2.00 5.00
FCL1 Hull/Howe/Bower 15.00 40.00
FCL2 Giac/Beliv/Bucyk 10.00 25.00

2012-13 Score Net Cam
COMPLETE SET (20) 12.50 25.00
NC1 Jonathan Quick 1.25 3.00
NC2 Henrik Lundqvist 2.50 6.00
NC3 Corey Crawford 1.25 3.00
NC4 Jimmy Howard 1.25 3.00
NC5 Brian Elliott .75 2.00
NC6 Tim Thomas 1.00 2.50
NC7 Carey Price 2.00 5.00
NC8 Mike Smith 1.00 2.50
NC9 Kari Lehtonen .75 2.00
NC10 Marc-Andre Fleury 2.00 5.00
NC11 Pekka Rinne 1.00 2.50
NC12 Roberto Luongo 1.50 4.00
NC13 Martin Brodeur 2.50 6.00
NC14 Antti Niemi .75 2.00
NC15 Cory Schneider 1.00 2.50
NC16 Jose Theodore 1.00 2.50
NC17 Ilya Bryzgalov 1.00 2.50
NC18 Braden Holtby 1.25 3.00
NC19 Ryan Miller 1.00 2.50
NC20 Miikka Kiprusoff 1.00 2.50

2012-13 Score Hot Rookie Autographs
503 Tyson Sexsmith 6.00 15.00
506 Mike Connolly 8.00 20.00
508 Jordan Nolan 15.00 40.00
515 Brandon Bollig 6.00 15.00
517 Carter Ashton 6.00 15.00
518 Sven Baertschi 10.00 25.00
520 Maxime Sauve 6.00 15.00
521 Jaden Schwartz 20.00 50.00
524 Jussi Rynnas 25.00 50.00
533 Robert Mayer 10.00 25.00
537 Chet Pickard 8.00 20.00
541 Scott Glennie 8.00 20.00
543 Chris Kreider 150.00 250.00
544 Jake Allen 20.00 50.00
548 Mark Stone 25.00 60.00

2012-13 Score Signatures
SSAA Artem Anisimov 4.00 10.00
SSAB Alexander Burmistrov 5.00 12.00
SSAE Andreas Engqvist 5.00 12.00
SSAL Anton Lander 5.00 12.00
SSAM Andy Miele 4.00 10.00
SSAS Alex Stalock 4.00 10.00
SSBB Bobby Butler 5.00 12.00
SSBHO Ben Holmstrom 6.00 15.00
SSBY Brandon Yip 4.00 10.00
SSCAR Daniel Carcillo 4.00 10.00
SSCC Cal Clutterbuck 4.00 10.00
SSCDH Calvin de Haan 4.00 10.00
SSCE Cody Eakin 4.00 10.00
SSCF Cam Fowler 6.00 15.00
SSCGR Colin Greening 4.00 10.00
SSCHM Chris Mason 5.00 12.00
SSCOW Jared Cowen 6.00 15.00
SSCSM Craig Smith 4.00 10.00
SSDD Derek Dorsett 4.00 10.00
SSDR Dwayne Roloson 5.00 12.00
SSEME Alexei Emelin 4.00 10.00
SSFAU Justin Faulk 5.00 12.00
SSFRO Michael Frolik 6.00 15.00
SSGN Gustav Nyquist 8.00 20.00
SSGRA Michael Grabner 5.00 12.00
SSHAY Jimmy Hayes 4.00 10.00
SSJAB Justin Abdelkader 5.00 12.00
SSJAG Jaromir Jagr SP 40.00 80.00
SSJB Justin Braun 5.00 12.00
SSJC Jeff Carter 5.00 12.00
SSJOS Roman Josi 6.00 15.00
SSKM Kenndal McArdle 4.00 10.00
SSLAC Eddie Lack 6.00 15.00
SSLAN Gabriel Landeskog SP 15.00 40.00
SSLAR Adam Larsson 6.00 15.00
SSLI Leland Irving SP 8.00 20.00
SSLID Nicklas Lidstrom SP 75.00 135.00
SSLL Louis Leblanc 4.00 10.00
SSMAC Clarke MacArthur 6.00 15.00
SSMAF Marc-Andre Fleury 12.00 30.00
SSMCN Brayden McNabb 6.00 15.00
SSMF Marcus Foligno 12.00 30.00
SSMG Mikhail Grabovski 4.00 10.00
SSMIT Torrey Mitchell 4.00 10.00
SSML Michael Leighton 6.00 15.00
SSMOU Matt Moulson 4.00 10.00
SSMP Max Pacioretty 6.00 15.00
SSNA Nik Antropov 5.00 12.00
SSNB Nick Bonino 4.00 10.00
SSNP Nick Palmieri 5.00 12.00
SSOE Oliver Ekman-Larsson 6.00 15.00
SSOP Ondrej Pavelec 6.00 15.00
SSORL Dmitry Orlov 6.00 15.00
SSOTT Steve Ott 4.00 10.00
SSPER David Perron 5.00 12.00
SSPHO Peter Holland 4.00 10.00
SSPK Phil Kessel 6.00 15.00
SSPL Philip Larsen 4.00 10.00
SSRBZ Robert Bortuzzo 4.00 10.00
SSRH Roman Horak 5.00 12.00
SSSAT Harri Sateri 5.00 12.00
SSSAV David Savard 4.00 10.00
SSSD Steve Downie 4.00 10.00
SSSW Stephen Weiss 5.00 12.00
SSTB Troy Brouwer 4.00 10.00
SSTG T.J. Galiardi 5.00 12.00
SSTOE Jonathan Toews SP 25.00 50.00
SSTRO Corey Tropp 5.00 12.00
SSVAR Semyon Varlamov 6.00 15.00
SSYS Yann Sauve 4.00 10.00
SSZB Zach Boychuk 4.00 10.00

2012-13 Score Team Future
TF1 Gabriel Landeskog 2.00 6.00
TF2 Ryan Nugent-Hopkins 2.00 5.00
TF3 Sean Couturier 1.25 3.00
TF4 Jake Gardiner 1.00 2.50
TF5 Adam Larsson 1.50 4.00
TF6 Richard Bachman 1.25 3.00
TF7 Carl Hagelin 1.00 2.50
TF8 Adam Henrique 1.25 3.00
TF9 Andrew Shaw 1.00 2.50
TF10 Ryan Ellis 1.00 2.50
TF11 Justin Faulk 1.25 3.00
TF12 Jake Allen 3.00 8.00

2012-13 Score Team Score
COMPLETE SET (12) 8.00 20.00
TS1 Pavel Datsyuk 1.50 4.00
TS2 Evgeni Malkin 2.00 5.00
TS3 Claude Giroux 1.00 2.50
TS4 Erik Karlsson 1.25 3.00
TS5 Zdeno Chara 1.00 2.50
TS6 Henrik Lundqvist 2.50 6.00
TS7 Daniel Sedin 1.25 3.00
TS8 Steven Stamkos 2.00 5.00
TS9 Phil Kessel 1.00 2.50
TS10 Shea Weber .75 2.00
TS11 Keith Yandle .60 1.50
TS12 Jonathan Quick 1.25 3.00

2013-14 Score
*BLACK VET: 8X TO 20X BASIC CARDS
*ROOKIES: 2.5X TO 6X BASIC CARDS
1 Bobby Ryan .12 .30
2 Jonas Hiller .12 .30
3 Ryan Getzlaf .15 .40
4 Corey Perry .25 .60
5 Teemu Selanne .30 .75
6 Cam Fowler .15 .40
7 Francois Beauchemin .10 .25
8 Sheldon Souray .10 .25
9 Saku Koivu .15 .40
10 Andrew Cogliano .10 .25
11 Luca Sbisa .12 .30
12 Daniel Winnik .10 .25
13 Kyle Palmieri .12 .30
14 Devante Smith-Pelly .12 .30
15 Bryan Allen .10 .25
16 Matt Beleskey .10 .25
17 Nick Bonino .10 .25
18 Matthew Lombardi .10 .25
19 Tyler Seguin .20 .50
20 Patrice Bergeron .20 .50
21 Zdeno Chara .15 .40
22 Milan Lucic .15 .40
23 Brad Marchand .30 .75
24 Tuukka Rask .20 .50
25 Nathan Horton .15 .40
26 David Krejci .15 .40
27 Rich Peverley .15 .40
28 Shawn Thornton .10 .25
29 Gregory Campbell .10 .25
30 Anton Khudobin .15 .40
31 Jaromir Jagr .50 1.25
32 Dennis Seidenberg .12 .30
33 Johnny Boychuk .12 .30
34 Daniel Paille .10 .25
35 Chris Kelly .10 .25
36 Adam McQuaid .10 .25
37 Andrew Ference .10 .25
38 Torey Krug .12 .30
39 Ryan Miller .15 .40
40 Thomas Vanek .12 .30
41 Drew Stafford .10 .25
42 Tyler Myers .10 .25
43 Cody Hodgson .12 .30
44 Nathan Gerbe .10 .25
45 Christian Ehrhoff .10 .25
46 Steve Ott .10 .25
47 Tyler Ennis .10 .25
48 Jhonas Enroth .15 .40
49 Ville Leino .12 .30
50 Patrick Kaleta .10 .25
51 Marcus Foligno .12 .30
52 Jochen Hecht .10 .25
53 Luke Adam .12 .30
54 John Scott .10 .25
55 Andrej Sekera .10 .25
56 Curtis Glencross .10 .25
57 Miikka Kiprusoff .15 .40
58 Mike Cammalleri .12 .30
59 Mikael Backlund .12 .30
60 Akim Aliu .10 .25
61 Alex Tanguay .10 .25
62 Sven Baertschi .12 .30
63 Roman Horak .12 .30
64 Mark Giordano .15 .40
65 Lee Stempniak .10 .25
66 Jiri Hudler .12 .30
67 Matt Stajan .10 .25
68 Dennis Wideman .10 .25
69 Cory Sarich .10 .25
70 Chris Butler .10 .25
71 T.J. Brodie .10 .25
72 Leland Irving .12 .30
73 Tim Jackman .10 .25
74 Eric Staal .20 .50
75 Cam Ward .15 .40
76 Chad LaRose .10 .25
77 Jeff Skinner .20 .50
78 Tuomo Ruutu .12 .30
79 Jordan Staal .12 .30
80 Alexander Semin .15 .40
81 Justin Faulk .12 .30
82 Jamie McBain .10 .25
83 Jeremy Welsh .10 .25
84 Joni Pitkanen .12 .30
85 Tim Gleason .10 .25
86 Jay Harrison .10 .25
87 Jiri Tlusty .10 .25
88 Joe Corvo .10 .25
89 Zac Dalpe .10 .25
90 Dan Ellis .10 .25
91 Jonathan Toews .25 .60
92 Patrick Kane .30 .75
93 Patrick Sharp .15 .40
94 Duncan Keith .12 .30
95 Marian Hossa .15 .40
96 Brent Seabrook .12 .30
97 Corey Crawford .20 .50
98 Nick Leddy .10 .25
99 Michael Frolik .10 .25
100 Viktor Stalberg .10 .25
101 Niklas Hjalmarsson .10 .25
102 Dave Bolland .10 .25
103 Brandon Saad .12 .30
104 Marcus Kruger .10 .25
105 Andrew Shaw .10 .25
106 Johnny Oduya .10 .25
107 Bryan Bickell .10 .25
108 Brandon Bollig .12 .30
109 Gabriel Landeskog .20 .50
110 Milan Hejduk .10 .25
111 Matt Duchene .15 .40
112 Paul Stastny .10 .25
113 Semyon Varlamov .15 .40
114 Erik Johnson .10 .25
115 David Jones .10 .25
116 P.A. Parenteau .10 .25
117 Greg Zanon .10 .25
118 Cody McLeod .10 .25
119 Jan Hejda .10 .25
120 Shane O'Brien .10 .25
121 Jamie McGinn .10 .25
122 Matt Hunwick .10 .25
123 Jean-Sebastien Giguere .15 .40
124 John Mitchell .10 .25
125 Mike Connolly .12 .30
126 Tyson Barrie .10 .25
127 Ryan O'Reilly .15 .40
128 R.J. Umberger .10 .25
129 Ryan Johansen .12 .30
130 Marian Gaborik .12 .30
131 Jack Johnson .10 .25
132 Vinny Prospal .10 .25
133 James Wisniewski .10 .25
134 Brandon Dubinsky .10 .25
135 Cam Atkinson .15 .40
136 Fedor Tyutin .10 .25
137 Nick Foligno .10 .25
138 Nikita Nikitin .10 .25
139 Artem Anisimov .10 .25
140 Tim Erixon .10 .25
141 Mark Letestu .12 .30
142 Michael Leighton .12 .30
143 Jared Boll .10 .25
144 Sergei Bobrovsky .25 .60
145 Loui Eriksson .10 .25
146 Ryan Garbutt .10 .25
147 Kari Lehtonen .12 .30
148 Jamie Benn .15 .40
149 Stephane Robidas .10 .25
150 Cody Eakin .10 .25
151 Alex Goligoski .10 .25
152 Lane MacDermid .12 .30
153 Trevor Daley .10 .25
154 Scott Glennie .12 .30
155 Philip Larsen .10 .25
156 Reilly Smith .15 .40
157 Brenden Dillon .12 .30
158 Ray Whitney .12 .30
159 Erik Cole .10 .25
160 Aaron Rome .10 .25
161 Jordie Benn .12 .30
162 Tom Wandell .10 .25
163 Pavel Datsyuk .25 .60
164 Henrik Zetterberg .20 .50
165 Jimmy Howard .20 .50
166 Niklas Kronwall .12 .30
167 Johan Franzen .12 .30
168 Valtteri Filppula .12 .30
169 Todd Bertuzzi .12 .30
170 Justin Abdelkader .12 .30
171 Jonathan Ericsson .10 .25
172 Daniel Cleary .15 .40
173 Mikael Samuelsson .10 .25
174 Kyle Quincey .10 .25
175 Ian White .12 .30
176 Damien Brunner RC .40 1.00
177 Jonas Gustavsson .12 .30
178 Patrick Eaves .10 .25
179 Brendan Smith .10 .25
180 Jordin Tootoo .12 .30
181 Jordan Eberle .15 .40
182 Taylor Hall .15 .40
183 Ryan Nugent-Hopkins .20 .50
184 Ryan Smyth .12 .30
185 Shawn Horcoff .10 .25
186 Sam Gagner .10 .25
187 Ryan Whitney .10 .25
188 Ales Hemsky .10 .25
189 Ladislav Smid .10 .25
190 Nick Schultz .10 .25
191 Devan Dubnyk .12 .30
192 Jeff Petry .15 .40
193 Eric Belanger .10 .25
194 Ben Eager .10 .25
195 Ryan Jones .12 .30
196 Mark Fistric .10 .25
197 Teemu Hartikainen .12 .30
198 Magnus Paajarvi .12 .30
199 Ed Jovanovski .12 .30
200 Brian Campbell .10 .25
201 Stephen Weiss .10 .25
202 Tomas Fleischmann .10 .25
203 Filip Kuba .10 .25
204 Kris Versteeg .10 .25
205 Dmitry Kulikov .10 .25
206 Peter Mueller .10 .25
207 Tomas Kopecky .12 .30
208 Mike Weaver .10 .25
209 Scottie Upshall .10 .25
210 George Parros .12 .30
211 Shawn Matthias .10 .25
212 Erik Gudbranson .10 .25
213 Marcel Goc .10 .25
214 Jack Skille .10 .25
215 Scott Clemmensen .12 .30
216 Jose Theodore .15 .40
217 Anze Kopitar .25 .60
218 Dustin Brown .15 .40
219 Jonathan Quick .20 .50
220 Drew Doughty .20 .50
221 Mike Richards .12 .30
222 Jeff Carter .12 .30
223 Justin Williams .12 .30
224 Rob Scuderi .10 .25
225 Jarret Stoll .10 .25
226 Jonathan Bernier .12 .30
227 Matt Greene .10 .25
228 Jordan Nolan .10 .25
229 Slava Voynov .10 .25
230 Dustin Penner .12 .30
231 Alec Martinez .10 .25
232 Trevor Lewis .10 .25
233 Kyle Clifford .10 .25
234 Keaton Ellerby .10 .25
235 Zach Parise .15 .40
236 Dany Heatley .10 .25
237 Mikko Koivu .12 .30
238 Ryan Suter .12 .30
239 Niklas Backstrom .10 .25
240 Pierre-Marc Bouchard .12 .30
241 Matt Cullen .10 .25
242 Tom Gilbert .10 .25
243 Devin Setoguchi .10 .25
244 Jared Spurgeon .12 .30
245 Cal Clutterbuck .10 .25
246 Kyle Brodziak .10 .25
247 Josh Harding .10 .25
248 Clayton Stoner .10 .25
249 Torrey Mitchell .10 .25
250 Zenon Konopka .10 .25
251 Mike Rupp .10 .25
252 Jason Pominville .10 .25
253 Carey Price .30 .75
254 Max Pacioretty .15 .40
255 Tomas Plekanec .10 .25
256 Andrei Markov .10 .25
257 Michael Ryder .10 .25
258 Brian Gionta .10 .25
259 P.K. Subban .20 .50
260 Raphael Diaz .10 .25
261 Rene Bourque .10 .25
262 David Desharnais .10 .25
263 Josh Gorges .10 .25
264 Ryan White .10 .25
265 Travis Moen .10 .25
266 Francis Bouillon .10 .25
267 Lars Eller .10 .25
268 Alexei Emelin .10 .25
269 Brandon Prust .10 .25
270 Tomas Kaberle .10 .25
271 Peter Budaj .10 .25
272 Shea Weber .10 .25
273 Pekka Rinne .10 .25
274 Mike Fisher .10 .25
275 Craig Smith .10 .25
276 Roman Josi .15 .40
277 Patric Hornqvist .12 .30
278 David Legwand .12 .30
279 Sergei Kostitsyn .10 .25
280 Kevin Klein .10 .25
281 Jonathon Blum .12 .30
282 Nick Spaling .10 .25
283 Colin Wilson .12 .30
284 Chris Mason .12 .30
285 Brandon Yip .10 .25
286 Paul Gaustad .10 .25
287 Hal Gill .10 .25
288 Gabriel Bourque .12 .30
289 Rich Clune .10 .25
290 Ilya Kovalchuk .15 .40
291 Adam Henrique .12 .30
292 Martin Brodeur .40 1.00
293 Patrik Elias .15 .40
294 Travis Zajac .12 .30
295 Adam Larsson .15 .40
296 Dainius Zubrus .10 .25
297 Anton Volchenkov .10 .25
298 Andy Greene .10 .25
299 Johan Hedberg .12 .30
300 David Clarkson .10 .25
301 Bryce Salvador .10 .25
302 Jacob Josefson .10 .25
303 Stephen Gionta .10 .25
304 Marek Zidlicky .10 .25
305 Henrik Tallinder .10 .25
306 Ryan Carter .10 .25
307 Steve Bernier .10 .25
308 John Tavares .25 .60
309 Matt Moulson .10 .25
310 Kyle Okposo .10 .25
311 Josh Bailey .12 .30
312 Michael Grabner .10 .25
313 Rick DiPietro .12 .30
314 Andrew MacDonald .10 .25
315 Frans Nielsen .10 .25
316 Travis Hamonic .10 .25
317 Evgeni Nabokov .15 .40
318 Mark Streit .10 .25
319 Brad Boyes .10 .25
320 David Ullstrom .10 .25
321 Lubomir Visnovsky .10 .25
322 Brian Strait .10 .25
323 Matt Martin .10 .25
324 Matt Carkner .10 .25
325 Colin McDonald .10 .25
326 Henrik Lundqvist .40 1.00
327 Ryane Clowe .10 .25
328 Brad Richards .15 .40
329 Rick Nash .15 .40
330 Ryan Callahan .10 .25
331 Marc Staal .10 .25
332 Ryan McDonagh .10 .25
333 Carl Hagelin .10 .25
334 Martin Biron .12 .30
335 Dan Girardi .10 .25
336 Derek Stepan .10 .25
337 Michael Del Zotto .10 .25
338 Chris Kreider .20 .50
339 Brian Boyle .10 .25
340 Derick Brassard .10 .25
341 Taylor Pyatt .10 .25
342 Darroll Powe .10 .25
343 Matt Gilroy .10 .25
344 Anton Stralman .10 .25
345 Erik Karlsson .20 .50
346 Daniel Alfredsson .15 .40
347 Jason Spezza .15 .40
348 Craig Anderson .15 .40
349 Milan Michalek .10 .25
350 Kyle Turris .10 .25
351 Sergei Gonchar .10 .25
352 Colin Greening .10 .25
353 Chris Neil .10 .25
354 Chris Phillips .10 .25
355 Erik Condra .10 .25
356 Zack Smith .10 .25
357 Marc Methot .10 .25
358 Mika Zibanejad .20 .50
359 Jakob Silfverberg .10 .25
360 Guillaume Latendresse .12 .30
361 Robin Lehner .12 .30
362 Jim O'Brien .10 .25
363 Claude Giroux .15 .40
364 Danny Briere .15 .40
365 Sean Couturier .12 .30
366 Kimmo Timonen .10 .25
367 Braydon Coburn .10 .25
368 Scott Hartnell .10 .25
369 Maxime Talbot .10 .25
370 Luke Schenn .15 .40
371 Wayne Simmonds .20 .50
372 Brayden Schenn .15 .40
373 Andrej Meszaros .10 .25
374 Jakub Voracek .12 .30
375 Ilya Bryzgalov .10 .25
376 Matt Read .10 .25
377 Nicklas Grossmann .10 .25
378 Steve Mason .12 .30
379 Ruslan Fedotenko .10 .25
380 Simon Gagne .15 .40
381 Shane Doan .12 .30
382 Keith Yandle .10 .25
383 Martin Hanzal .10 .25
384 Mike Smith .15 .40
385 Derek Morris .10 .25
386 Antoine Vermette .10 .25
387 Mikkel Boedker .10 .25
388 Radim Vrbata .10 .25
389 Zbynek Michalek .10 .25
390 Michael Stone .12 .30
391 Jason LaBarbera .12 .30
392 Boyd Gordon .10 .25
393 Oliver Ekman-Larsson .15 .40
394 Lauri Korpikoski .10 .25
395 Rostislav Klesla .10 .25
396 David Moss .10 .25
397 Paul Bissonnette .10 .25
398 Kyle Chipchura .10 .25
399 Sidney Crosby .60 1.50
400 Evgeni Malkin .25 .60
401 Marc-Andre Fleury .20 .50
402 James Neal .10 .25
403 Kris Letang .20 .50
404 Pascal Dupuis .10 .25
405 Chris Kunitz .15 .40
406 Brooks Orpik .10 .25
407 Tyler Kennedy .10 .25
408 Jarome Iginla .20 .50
409 Tomas Vokoun .12 .30
410 Brandon Sutter .10 .25
411 Matt Niskanen .12 .30
412 Craig Adams .10 .25
413 Matt Cooke .10 .25
414 Brenden Morrow .12 .30
415 Tanner Glass .10 .25
416 Simon Despres .12 .30
417 Joe Thornton .25 .60
418 Patrick Marleau .15 .40
419 Logan Couture .20 .50
420 Joe Pavelski .20 .50
421 Dan Boyle .10 .25
422 Antti Niemi .12 .30
423 Brent Burns .15 .40
424 Scott Hannan .10 .25
425 James Sheppard .10 .25
426 Martin Havlat .15 .40
427 Marc-Edouard Vlasic .10 .25
428 Adam Burish .10 .25
429 Brad Stuart .10 .25
430 Tommy Wingels .10 .25
431 T.J. Galiardi .12 .30
432 Scott Gomez .12 .30
433 Jason Demers .10 .25
434 Justin Braun .10 .25
435 Andrew Desjardins .10 .25
436 Thomas Greiss .12 .30
437 David Backes .12 .30
438 Alex Pietrangelo .10 .25
439 T.J. Oshie .15 .40
440 Kevin Shattenkirk .10 .25
441 Jake Allen .15 .40
442 Jaroslav Halak .15 .40
443 Alexander Steen .10 .25
444 Barret Jackman .10 .25
445 David Perron .12 .30
446 Patrik Berglund .10 .25
447 Andy McDonald .12 .30
448 Roman Polak .10 .25
449 Chris Stewart .12 .30
450 Vladimir Sobotka .10 .25
451 Kris Russell .10 .25
452 Jaden Schwartz .20 .50
453 Ryan Reaves .10 .25
454 Ian Cole .10 .25
455 Jay Bouwmeester .10 .25
456 Steven Stamkos .30 .75
457 Vincent Lecavalier .15 .40
458 Martin St. Louis .15 .40
459 Victor Hedman .20 .50
460 Ryan Malone .10 .25
461 Anders Lindback .10 .25
462 Ondrej Palat RC .75 2.00
463 Ben Bishop .12 .30
464 Teddy Purcell .10 .25
465 Sami Salo .10 .25
466 Tom Pyatt .10 .25
467 Nate Thompson .10 .25
468 Eric Brewer .10 .25
469 Benoit Pouliot .10 .25
470 Matthew Carle .12 .30
471 B.J. Crombeen .10 .25
472 Keith Aulie .10 .25
473 Dana Tyrell .10 .25
474 Mathieu Garon .12 .30
475 Dion Phaneuf .12 .30
476 Phil Kessel .15 .40
477 Joffrey Lupul .10 .25
478 James van Riemsdyk .12 .30
479 Tyler Bozak .10 .25
480 Clarke MacArthur .10 .25
481 Mikhail Grabovski .10 .25
482 Carl Gunnarsson .10 .25
483 Nikolai Kulemin .10 .25
484 Korbinian Holzer .10 .25
485 James Reimer .15 .40
486 Ben Scrivens .12 .30
487 John-Michael Liles .10 .25
488 Jay McClement .10 .25
489 Nazem Kadri .20 .50
490 Jake Gardiner .10 .25
491 Matt Frattin .10 .25
492 Cody Franson .12 .30
493 Colton Orr .10 .25
494 Henrik Sedin .20 .50
495 Daniel Sedin .20 .50
496 Ryan Kesler .15 .40
497 Alexandre Burrows .10 .25
498 Roberto Luongo .25 .60
499 Kevin Bieksa .10 .25
500 Cory Schneider .12 .30
501 Manny Malhotra .12 .30
502 Mason Raymond .10 .25
503 Dan Hamhuis .12 .30
504 Zack Kassian .10 .25
505 Keith Ballard .10 .25
506 Jannik Hansen .12 .30
507 Chris Higgins .10 .25
508 Alexander Edler .10 .25
509 Maxim Lapierre .10 .25
510 Jason Garrison .10 .25
511 David Booth .10 .25
512 Chris Tanev .10 .25
513 Derek Roy .10 .25
514 Alex Ovechkin .60 1.50
515 Mike Green .12 .30
516 Brooks Laich .10 .25
517 Nicklas Backstrom .15 .40
518 Marcus Johansson .12 .30
519 John Carlson .15 .40
520 Braden Holtby .20 .50
521 Mike Ribeiro .10 .25
522 Michal Neuvirth .12 .30
523 Karl Alzner .10 .25
524 Troy Brouwer .10 .25
525 Joel Ward .10 .25
526 Jason Chimera .10 .25
527 Jay Beagle .10 .25
528 Dmitry Orlov .10 .25
529 Eric Fehr .10 .25
530 Wojtek Wolski .10 .25
531 Tomas Kundratek .12 .30
532 Martin Erat .10 .25
533 Dustin Byfuglien .15 .40
534 Andrew Ladd .12 .30
535 Ondrej Pavelec .15 .40
536 Nik Antropov .12 .30
537 Evander Kane .15 .40
538 Zach Bogosian .12 .30
539 Blake Wheeler .15 .40
540 Mark Scheifele .25 .60
541 Bryan Little .15 .40
542 Olli Jokinen .12 .30
543 Alexander Burmistrov .12 .30
544 Tobias Enstrom .10 .25
545 Chris Thorburn .10 .25
546 Ron Hainsey .10 .25
547 Kyle Wellwood .12 .30
548 Al Montoya .10 .25
549 Jim Slater .10 .25
550 Mark Stuart .10 .25
551 Gtzlf/Prry/Prry/Fsth .25 .60
552 Rask/Mrchnd/Krjci/Lucic .30 .75
553 Vanek/Ott/Miller/Ennis .15 .40
554 Kprusff/Glncrss/Stmpnk/Jckmn.15 .40
555 Ward/Tlusty/Staal/Staal .20 .50
556 Toews/Kane/Bollig/Crwfrd .30 .75
557 Varlamov/McLd/Prnteau/Duchne.15 .40
558 Letestu/Tyutin/Boll/Bbrvsky .25 .60
559 Lhtnen/Glgski/Roussel/Erikssn.15 .40
560 Dtsyk/Zttrbrg/Tootoo/Howard .25 .60
561 Dubnyk/Hall/Brown/Yakupov .30 .75
562 Flschmnn/Parros/Mrkstrm/Kpcky.15 .40
563 Quick/Crtr/Kopitar/Ellerby .25 .60
564 Parise/Suter/Knpka/Backstrom .15 .40
565 Price/Sbbn/Prust/Ryder .30 .75
566 Weber/Clune/Rinne/Legwand .15 .40
567 Clarksn/Elias/Clarksn/Brodeur .40 1.00
568 Nabkv/Tavares/Mulsn/Martin .25 .60
569 Lndqvst/Nash/Stepan/Clowe .40 1.00
570 Turris/Gnchar/Neil/Andersn .15 .40
571 Voracek/Giroux/Rinaldo/Bryzglv.15 .40
572 Smith/Doan/Ekmn-Lrssn/Yandle.15 .40
573 Fleury/Kunitz/Crsby/Glass .60 1.50
574 Couture/Thrntn/Desjrdins/Niemi.25 .60
575 Stwrt/Reaves/Ellitt/Backes .12 .30
576 Bishp/Stamks/St. Louis/Crmbeen.30 .75
577 Kessel/Orr/Reimer/Kessel .15 .40
578 Burrws/Sedin/Schneider/Sestito.20 .50
579 Hltby/Ovechkn/Backstrm/Hndrcks.60 1.50
580 Ladd/Kane/Pavelec/Wheeler .15 .40
581 Los Angeles Kings SH .12 .30
582 Chicago Blackhawks SH .10 .30
583 Patrick Marleau SH .15 .40
584 Vincent Lecavalier SH .15 .40
585 Milan Hejduk SH .12 .30
586 Marian Hossa SH .15 .40
587 Jaromir Jagr SH .50 1.25
588 Martin Brodeur SH .40 1.00
589 Sidney Crosby SH .60 1.50
590 Teemu Selanne SH .30 .75
591 Alex Killorn HR RC .75 2.00
592 Sean Collins HR RC .40 1.00
593 Dave Dziurzynski HR RC .40 1.00
594 Derek Grant HR RC .40 1.00
595 Christian Thomas HR RC .40 1.00
596 Eddie Pasquale HR RC .30 .75
597 Beau Bennett HR RC .60 1.50
598 Tyler Toffoli HR RC 1.00 2.50
599 Calvin Pickard HR RC .60 1.50
600 Michal Jordan HR RC .30 .75
601 Darcy Kuemper HR RC 1.00 2.50
602 Anthony Peluso HR RC .30 .75
603 Richard Panik HR RC .50 1.25
604 Nathan Beaulieu HR RC .30 .75
605 Ryan Murphy HR RC .50 1.25
606 Mark Arcobello HR RC .50 1.25
607 Ryan Spooner HR RC .50 1.25
608 J.T. Miller HR RC 1.25 3.00
609 Charlie Coyle HR RC .75 2.00
610 Zach Redmond HR RC .40 1.00
611 Jonas Brodin HR RC .60 1.50
612 Jack Campbell HR RC 1.25 3.00
613 Jamie Tardif HR RC .30 .75
614 Jamie Oleksiak HR RC .40 1.00
615 Sami Vatanen HR RC .50 1.25
616 Michael Sgarbossa HR RC .50 1.25
617 Antoine Roussel HR RC .50 1.25
618 Matt Irwin HR RC .40 1.00
619 Philipp Grubauer HR RC 1.25 3.00
620 Patrick Bordeleau HR RC .50 1.25
621 Cory Conacher HR RC .30 .75
622 Rickard Rakell HR RC .50 1.25
623 Roman Cervenka HR RC .50 1.25
624 Brendan Gallagher HR RC 1.25 3.00
625 Viktor Fasth HR RC .50 1.25
626 Tye McGinn HR RC .50 1.25
627 Petr Mrazek HR RC 1.00 2.50
628 Michael Kostka HR RC .40 1.00
629 Jarred Tinordi HR RC .50 1.25
630 Filip Forsberg HR RC 1.50 4.00
631 Eric Gryba HR RC .40 1.00
632 Thomas Hickey HR RC .40 1.00
633 Drew Shore HR RC .40 1.00
634 Nick Petrecki HR RC .30 .75
635 Brian Lashoff HR RC .40 1.00
636 Christopher Nilstorp HR RC .40 1.00
637 Jordan Schroeder HR RC .50 1.25
638 Leo Komarov HR RC .50 1.25
639 Emerson Etem HR RC .50 1.25
640 Stefan Matteau HR RC .40 1.00
641 Quinton Howden HR RC .40 1.00
642 Justin Schultz HR RC .50 1.25
643 Mikhail Grigorenko HR RC .30 .75
644 Scott Laughton HR RC .60 1.50
645 Alex Galchenyuk HR RC 1.25 3.00
646 Dougie Hamilton HR RC .75 2.00
647 Vladimir Tarasenko HR RC 1.25 3.00
648 Jonathan Huberdeau HR RC 1.25 3.00
649 Mikael Granlund HR RC .75 2.00
650 Nail Yakupov HR RC 1.00 2.50
651 Jakob Silfverberg .10 .25
652 Loui Eriksson .10 .25
653 Matt Moulson .10 .25
654 Jarome Iginla .20 .50
655 Karri Ramo .10 .25
656 Nathan Gerbe .10 .25

657 Kris Versteeg .10 .25
658 Maxime Talbot .10 .25
659 Tyler Seguin .20 .50
660 Shawn Horcoff .10 .25
661 Daniel Alfredsson .15 .40
662 Stephen Weiss .12 .30
663 David Perron .12 .30
664 Ilya Bryzgalov .15 .40
665 Tim Thomas .15 .40
666 Jacob Markstrom .15 .40
667 Ben Scrivens .12 .30
668 Daniel Briere .15 .40
669 Jaromir Jagr .50 1.25
670 Cory Schneider .15 .40
671 Thomas Vanek .12 .30
672 Mats Zuccarello .15 .40
673 Bobby Ryan .12 .30
674 Clarke MacArthur .10 .25
675 Steve Downie .10 .25
676 Vincent Lecavalier .15 .40
677 Mike Ribeiro .10 .25
678 Jussi Jokinen .10 .25
679 Derek Roy .10 .25
680 Valtteri Filppula .10 .25
681 Dave Bolland .10 .25
682 Jonathan Bernier .12 .30
683 Mason Raymond .10 .25
684 David Clarkson .10 .25
685 Mikhail Grabovski .10 .25
686 Nathan MacKinnon HR RC 2.50 6.00
687 Aleksander Barkov HR RC 1.50 4.00
688 Seth Jones HR RC 1.00 2.50
689 Elias Lindholm HR RC 1.25 3.00
690 Sean Monahan HR RC .75 2.00
691 Valeri Nichushkin HR RC 1.00 2.50
692 Rasmus Ristolainen HR RC .75 2.00
693 Nikita Zadorov HR RC .30 .75
694 Ryan Murray HR RC .75 2.00
695 Morgan Rielly HR RC 1.25 3.00
696 Hampus Lindholm HR RC .75 2.00
697 Matt Dumba HR RC .30 .75
698 Jacob Trouba HR RC .75 2.00
699 Zemgus Girgensons HR RC .75 2.00
700 Tomas Hertl HR RC 1.00 2.50
701 Olli Maatta HR RC .75 2.00
702 Boone Jenner HR RC 1.00 2.50
703 Jon Merrill HR RC .50 1.25
704 Matt Nieto HR RC .40 1.00
705 Nikita Kucherov HR RC 8.00 20.00
706 Reto Berra HR RC .50 1.25
707 Joakim Nordstrom HR RC .40 1.00
708 Michael Bournival HR RC .50 1.25
709 Kevin Connauton HR RC .40 1.00
710 Xavier Ouellet HR RC .50 1.25
711 Magnus Hellberg HR RC .50 1.25
712 Marek Mazanec HR RC .50 1.25
713 Cody Ceci HR RC .40 1.00
714 Jesper Fast HR RC .50 1.25
715 Lucas Lessio HR RC .30 .75
716 Ryan Strome HR RC .75 2.00
717 Josh Leivo HR RC .40 1.00
718 Nicklas Jensen HR RC .40 1.00
719 Brock Nelson HR RC 1.00 2.50
720 Austin Watson HR RC .40 1.00
721 Frederik Andersen HR RC 1.25 3.00
722 Igor Bobkov HR RC .40 1.00
723 Alex Chiasson HR RC .50 1.25
724 Drew LeBlanc HR RC .30 .75
725 John Gibson HR RC 1.25 3.00
726 Johan Larsson HR RC .60 1.50
727 Max Reinhart HR RC .50 1.25
728 Mark Cundari HR RC .30 .75
729 Danny DeKeyser HR RC .60 1.50
730 Tyler Pitlick HR RC .50 1.25
731 Nick Bjugstad HR RC .60 1.50
732 Tanner Pearson HR RC .50 1.25
733 Tom Wilson HR RC 1.00 2.50
734 Jared Staal HR RC .40 1.00
735 Chris Brown HR RC .30 .75
736 Eric Hartzell HR RC .50 1.25
737 Taylor Beck HR RC .40 1.00
738 Anders Lee HR RC .75 2.00
739 Antti Raanta HR RC 1.00 2.50
740 Alex Petrovic HR RC .40 1.00
741 Mark Pysyk HR RC .50 1.25
742 Frank Corrado HR RC .30 .75
743 Joonas Rask HR RC .30 .75
744 Tomas Jurco HR RC .60 1.50
745 Radko Gudas HR RC .50 1.25
746 Jonathan Marchessault HR RC 1.25 3.00
747 Victor Bartley HR RC .40 1.00
748 Johan Gustafsson HR RC .60 1.50
749 Ben Street HR RC .40 1.00
750 Cameron Schilling HR RC .30 .75

2013-14 Score Gold

*VETS: 1.2X TO 3X BASIC CARDS
*ROOKIE: 1X TO 2.5X BASIC RC
*591-650 ROOKIE: .6X TO 1.5X BASIC RC
97 Corey Crawford .75 2.00
517 Nicklas Backstrom .60 1.50

2013-14 Score Red Back

*1-590 VETS: 15X TO 40X BASIC CARDS
*1-590 ROOKIES: 10X TO 25X BASIC RC
*591-650 ROOKIES: 4X TO 10X BASIC RC
97 Corey Crawford 10.00 25.00
517 Nicklas Backstrom 8.00 20.00

2013-14 Score Red Border

*1-590 VETS: 2X TO 5X BASIC CARDS
*1-590 ROOKIE: 1.5X TO 4X BASIC RC
*591-650 ROOKIE: 1.5X TO 4X BASIC RC
97 Corey Crawford 1.25 3.00
517 Nicklas Backstrom 1.00 2.50

2013-14 Score Check It

1 Brenden Dillon 1.25 3.00
2 Leo Komarov 2.00 5.00
3 Mark Fraser 1.25 3.00
4 Zac Rinaldo 1.50 4.00
5 Dougie Hamilton 3.00 8.00
6 Alexei Emelin 1.25 3.00
7 Ed Jovanovski 1.25 3.00
8 Milan Lucic 2.00 5.00
9 Brian Boyle 1.25 3.00
10 Steve Ott 1.25 3.00
11 Luke Schenn 2.00 5.00
12 Evander Kane 2.00 5.00
13 Shane Doan 1.50 4.00
14 Zdeno Chara 2.00 5.00
15 Chris Kunitz 2.00 5.00
16 Zack Kassian 1.25 3.00
17 Colin Greening 1.25 3.00
18 Matt Martin 1.25 3.00
19 Anton Volchenkov 1.25 3.00
20 Alex Ovechkin 8.00 20.00
21 Rob Blake 2.00 5.00
22 Denis Potvin 2.00 5.00
23 Cam Neely 2.00 5.00
24 Eric Lindros 3.00 8.00
25 Derian Hatcher 1.25 3.00

2013-14 Score First Goal

1 Nail Yakupov 4.00 10.00
2 Mikael Granlund 1.50 4.00
3 Vladimir Tarasenko 2.50 6.00
4 Jonathan Huberdeau 2.50 6.00
5 Mikhail Grigorenko .60 1.50
6 Mika Zibanejad 1.25 3.00
7 Alex Galchenyuk 4.00 10.00
8 Damien Brunner .75 2.00
9 Alex Killorn 1.50 4.00
10 Justin Schultz 1.00 2.50
11 Dougie Hamilton 1.50 4.00
12 Jason Zucker 1.00 2.50
13 Stefan Matteau 1.00 2.50
14 J.T. Miller 2.50 6.00
15 Brandon Saad 1.25 3.00
16 Brendan Gallagher 2.50 6.00
17 Drew Shore .75 2.00
18 Tye McGinn 1.00 2.50
19 Leo Komarov 1.00 2.50
20 Jordan Schroeder 1.25 3.00

2013-14 Score Franchise

1 Ryan Getzlaf 1.25 3.00
2 Zdeno Chara 1.25 3.00
3 Thomas Vanek 1.00 2.50
4 Miikka Kiprusoff 1.25 3.00
5 Jeff Skinner 1.50 4.00
6 Patrick Kane 2.50 6.00
7 Gabriel Landeskog 1.50 4.00
8 Jack Johnson .75 2.00
9 Kari Lehtonen 1.00 2.50
10 Henrik Zetterberg 1.50 4.00
11 Taylor Hall 1.25 3.00
12 Ed Jovanovski .75 2.00
13 Dustin Brown 1.25 3.00
14 Zach Parise 1.25 3.00
15 Carey Price 2.50 6.00
16 Shea Weber 1.00 2.50
17 Martin Brodeur 3.00 8.00
18 John Tavares 2.00 5.00
19 Rick Nash 1.25 3.00
20 Erik Karlsson 1.50 4.00
21 Sean Couturier 1.00 2.50
22 Mike Smith 1.25 3.00
23 Evgeni Malkin 2.50 6.00
24 Patrick Marleau 1.25 3.00
25 Alex Pietrangelo 1.00 2.50
26 Steven Stamkos 2.50 6.00
27 Dion Phaneuf 1.00 2.50
28 Daniel Sedin 1.50 4.00
29 Alex Ovechkin 5.00 12.00
30 Evander Kane 1.25 3.00

2013-14 Score Future Franchise

1 Nail Yakupov 3.00 8.00
2 Dougie Hamilton 2.50 6.00
3 Mikael Granlund 2.50 6.00
4 Jonathan Huberdeau 4.00 10.00
5 Vladimir Tarasenko 4.00 10.00
6 Alex Galchenyuk 4.00 10.00
7 Mikhail Grigorenko 1.00 2.50
8 Damien Brunner 1.25 3.00
9 Alex Killorn 2.50 6.00
10 Emerson Etem 1.50 4.00

2013-14 Score Hot Rookie Signatures

591 Alex Killorn 8.00 20.00
592 Sean Collins 4.00 10.00
593 Dave Dziurzynski 4.00 10.00
594 Derek Grant 4.00 10.00
595 Christian Thomas 4.00 10.00
596 Eddie Pasquale 3.00 8.00
597 Beau Bennett 8.00 20.00
598 Tyler Toffoli 6.00 15.00
599 Calvin Pickard 6.00 15.00
600 Michal Jordan 3.00 8.00
601 Darcy Kuemper 10.00 25.00
602 Anthony Peluso 3.00 8.00
603 Richard Panik 5.00 12.00
604 Nathan Beaulieu 3.00 8.00
605 Ryan Murphy SP 8.00 20.00
606 Mark Arcobello 5.00 12.00
607 Ryan Spooner 5.00 12.00
608 J.T. Miller SP 20.00 50.00
609 Charlie Coyle 8.00 20.00
610 Zach Redmond 4.00 10.00
611 Jonas Brodin SP 10.00 25.00
612 Jack Campbell SP 20.00 50.00
613 Jamie Tardif 3.00 8.00
614 Jamie Oleksiak 4.00 10.00
615 Sami Vatanen 5.00 12.00
616 Michael Sgarbossa 5.00 12.00
617 Antoine Roussel 5.00 12.00
618 Matt Irwin 4.00 10.00
619 Philipp Grubauer 12.00 30.00
620 Patrick Bordeleau 5.00 12.00
621 Cory Conacher 3.00 8.00
622 Rickard Rakell 5.00 12.00
623 Roman Cervenka 4.00 10.00
624 Brendan Gallagher SP 25.00 60.00
625 Viktor Fasth 5.00 12.00
626 Tye McGinn 5.00 12.00
627 Petr Mrazek 10.00 25.00
628 Michael Kostka 4.00 10.00
629 Jarred Tinordi 6.00 15.00
631 Eric Gryba 4.00 10.00
632 Thomas Hickey SP 6.00 15.00
633 Drew Shore 4.00 10.00
634 Nick Petrecki 3.00 8.00
635 Brian Lashoff 4.00 10.00
636 Christopher Nilstorp 4.00 10.00
637 Jordan Schroeder 5.00 12.00
638 Leo Komarov 5.00 12.00
639 Emerson Etem SP 10.00 25.00
640 Stefan Matteau SP 6.00 15.00
641 Quinton Howden 4.00 10.00
642 Justin Schultz SP 8.00 20.00
643 Mikhail Grigorenko SP 8.00 20.00
644 Scott Laughton 6.00 15.00
646 Dougie Hamilton SP 8.00 20.00
647 Vladimir Tarasenko SP 50.00 125.00
686 Nathan MacKinnon 50.00 125.00
687 Aleksander Barkov 15.00 40.00
688 Seth Jones 10.00 25.00
689 Elias Lindholm 12.00 30.00
690 Sean Monahan 8.00 20.00
691 Valeri Nichushkin 10.00 25.00
693 Nikita Zadorov 3.00 8.00
694 Ryan Murray 8.00 20.00
695 Morgan Rielly 12.00 30.00
696 Hampus Lindholm 8.00 20.00
697 Matt Dumba 3.00 8.00
698 Jacob Trouba 8.00 20.00
699 Zemgus Girgensons 8.00 20.00
700 Tomas Hertl 8.00 20.00
701 Olli Maatta 8.00 20.00
702 Boone Jenner 10.00 25.00
703 Jon Merrill 5.00 12.00
704 Matt Nieto 4.00 10.00
706 Reto Berra 5.00 12.00
708 Michael Bournival 5.00 12.00
709 Kevin Connauton 4.00 10.00
710 Xavier Ouellet 5.00 12.00
711 Magnus Hellberg 5.00 12.00
712 Marek Mazanec 5.00 12.00
713 Cody Ceci 4.00 10.00
714 Jesper Fast 5.00 12.00
715 Lucas Lessio 3.00 8.00
716 Ryan Strome 8.00 20.00
717 Josh Leivo 4.00 10.00
718 Nicklas Jensen 4.00 10.00
719 Brock Nelson 10.00 25.00
720 Austin Watson 4.00 10.00
721 Frederik Andersen 12.00 30.00
722 Igor Bobkov 4.00 10.00
723 Alex Chiasson 5.00 12.00
724 Drew LeBlanc 3.00 8.00
725 Carl Soderberg 5.00 12.00
726 Johan Larsson 6.00 15.00
727 Max Reinhart 5.00 12.00
728 Mark Cundari 3.00 8.00
729 Danny DeKeyser 6.00 15.00
730 Tyler Pitlick 5.00 12.00
731 Nick Bjugstad 6.00 15.00
732 Tanner Pearson 5.00 12.00
733 Tom Wilson 10.00 25.00
734 Jared Staal 4.00 10.00
735 Chris Brown 3.00 8.00
736 Eric Hartzell 5.00 12.00
737 Taylor Beck 4.00 10.00
738 Anders Lee 8.00 20.00
739 Antti Raanta 10.00 25.00
740 Alex Petrovic 4.00 10.00
741 Mark Pysyk 5.00 12.00
742 Frank Corrado 3.00 8.00
743 Joonas Rask 3.00 8.00
744 Tomas Jurco 6.00 15.00
745 Radko Gudas 5.00 12.00
746 Jonathan Marchessault 12.00 30.00
747 Victor Bartley 4.00 10.00
748 Johan Gustafsson 6.00 15.00
749 Ben Street 4.00 10.00
750 Cameron Schilling 3.00 8.00

2013-14 Score Net Cams

1 Anders Lindback .60 1.50
2 Devan Dubnyk .75 2.00
3 Henrik Lundqvist 2.50 6.00
4 Semyon Varlamov 1.00 2.50
5 Ondrej Pavelec 1.00 2.50
6 Corey Crawford 1.25 3.00
7 Tuukka Rask 1.25 3.00
8 James Reimer 1.00 2.50
9 Cory Schneider 1.00 2.50
10 Jonathan Quick 1.25 3.00
11 Michal Neuvirth .75 2.00
12 Carey Price 2.00 5.00
13 Ryan Miller 1.00 2.50
14 Craig Anderson 1.00 2.50
15 Ilya Bryzgalov 1.00 2.50
16 Niklas Backstrom .75 2.00
17 Pekka Rinne 1.00 2.50
18 Patrick Roy 2.50 6.00
19 Mike Richter 1.00 2.50
20 Martin Brodeur 2.50 6.00

2013-14 Score Signatures

SSAA Aaron Ness 3.00 8.00
SSAM Andy Miele 3.00 8.00
SSAMC Andy McDonald 4.00 10.00
SSAN Anders Nilsson 4.00 10.00
SSBM Brayden McNabb 3.00 8.00
SSBS Ben Scrivens 4.00 10.00
SSCC Carter Camper 4.00 10.00
SSCCL Cal Clutterbuck 3.00 8.00
SSCDH Calvin de Haan 3.00 8.00
SSCG Claude Giroux 15.00 40.00
SSCS Chris Summers SP 4.00 10.00
SSCT Colten Teubert 3.00 8.00
SSCW Casey Wellman 3.00 8.00
SSDC Daniel Cleary 5.00 12.00
SSDO Dmitry Orlov 5.00 12.00
SSDS David Savard 3.00 8.00
SSDT Dana Tyrell SP 4.00 10.00
SSEL Eddie Lack 4.00 10.00
SSGB Gabriel Bourque 4.00 10.00
SSGN Gustav Nyquist 3.00 8.00
SSGP George Parros 4.00 10.00
SSHZ Harry Zolnierczyk 3.00 8.00
SSJA Jamie Arniel 4.00 10.00
SSJB Jonathan Bernier 4.00 10.00
SSJC Jordan Caron 12.00 30.00
SSJD Jeremy Duchesne 4.00 10.00
SSJF Justin Falk SP 4.00 10.00
SSJG Jonas Gustavsson 4.00 10.00
SSJH Jimmy Hayes 5.00 12.00
SSJI Jarome Iginla 6.00 15.00
SSJJ Jaromir Jagr 25.00 60.00
SSJM Jamie McBain 3.00 8.00
SSJS Jaden Schwartz 6.00 15.00
SSJZ Jason Zucker 5.00 12.00
SSKA Keith Aulie SP 4.00 10.00
SSLC Luca Caputi SP 4.00 10.00
SSLK Linus Klasen 3.00 8.00
SSMC John McCarthy 3.00 8.00
SSMD Matt Donovan 3.00 8.00
SSMF Marcus Foligno 4.00 10.00
SSMFT Matt Frattin 4.00 10.00
SSMO Mark Olver 3.00 8.00
SSMR Mason Raymond 3.00 8.00
SSMS Mikael Samuelsson SP 5.00 12.00
SSNK Nazem Kadri 6.00 15.00
SSNKU Nikolai Kulemin 3.00 8.00
SSNP Nick Palmieri 5.00 12.00
SSPK Patrick Kane 20.00 50.00
SSPL Pascal Leclaire SP 5.00 12.00
SSPR Peter Regin SP 5.00 12.00
SSRB Robert Bortuzzo 3.00 8.00
SSRC Ryane Clowe 3.00 8.00
SSRH Roman Horak 4.00 10.00
SSRJ Ryan Johansen 4.00 10.00
SSRS Reilly Smith 5.00 12.00
SSRSM Ryan Smyth 4.00 10.00
SSSC Sean Couturier 4.00 10.00
SSSE Stefan Elliott 4.00 10.00
SSSG Stephen Gionta 3.00 8.00
SSSGO Scott Gomez 4.00 10.00
SSSGR Stu Grimson 5.00 12.00
SSSV Semyon Varlamov 8.00 20.00
SSTB Tyson Barrie 3.00 8.00
SSTE Tim Erixon 3.00 8.00
SSTH Travis Hamonic 3.00 8.00
SSTK Tomas Kubalik 5.00 12.00
SSTM Travis Morin 3.00 8.00
SSTR Torey Krug 10.00 25.00
SSTS Tyler Seguin 12.00 30.00
SSTSE Tyson Sexsmith 3.00 8.00
SSTT Tim Thomas 8.00 20.00
SSVS Viktor Stalberg 3.00 8.00
SSYS Yann Sauve 3.00 8.00
SSZH Zach Hamill SP 5.00 12.00

2013-14 Score Team Future

1 Nail Yakupov 5.00 12.00
2 Chris Kreider 2.00 5.00
3 Alex Galchenyuk 5.00 12.00
4 Emerson Etem 1.50 4.00
5 Dougie Hamilton 1.50 4.00
6 Justin Schultz 1.00 2.50
7 Jack Campbell 4.00 10.00
8 Ryan Murphy 1.50 4.00
9 Jaden Schwartz 2.00 5.00
10 Quinton Howden 1.25 3.00
11 Scott Laughton 2.00 5.00
12 Tyler Toffoli 3.00 8.00
13 Jamie Oleksiak 1.25 3.00
14 Charlie Coyle 2.50 6.00
15 Beau Bennett 2.00 5.00

2013-14 Score Team Score

1 Sidney Crosby 5.00 12.00
2 Jonathan Toews 2.00 5.00
3 Rick Nash 1.25 3.00
4 Claude Giroux 1.25 3.00
5 Alex Ovechkin 5.00 12.00
6 Henrik Zetterberg 1.50 4.00
7 Alex Pietrangelo 1.00 2.50
8 Erik Karlsson 1.50 4.00
9 Martin Brodeur 3.00 8.00
10 Jonathan Quick 1.50 4.00

2013-14 Score Team 8s Jerseys

ALB Flames/Oilers SP 15.00 40.00
ANA Anaheim Ducks 10.00 25.00
ATL Atlantic Division 12.00 30.00
ATL2 Atlantic Division 15.00 40.00
AVS Colorado Avalanche 10.00 25.00
BLU St. Louis Blues 10.00 25.00
BOMO Bruins/Canadiens 15.00 40.00
BOS Boston Bruins 12.00 30.00
CAL Calgary Flames 12.00 30.00
CAP Washington Capitals 10.00 25.00
CEN Central Division 15.00 40.00
CHI Chicago Blackhawks SP 15.00 40.00
DAL Dallas Stars 10.00 25.00
DAMI Stars/Wild 12.00 30.00
DET Detroit Red Wings SP 15.00 40.00
DEV New Jersey Devils SP 15.00 40.00
FLA Panthers/Lightning SP 12.00 30.00
FLY Philadelphia Flyers 15.00 40.00
FRW Ducks/Kings 12.00 30.00
HAB Montreal Canadiens 20.00 50.00
JET Winnipeg Jets SP 15.00 40.00
KNG Los Angeles Kings 10.00 25.00
LAK Los Angeles Kings SP 15.00 40.00
MIN Minnesota Wild 10.00 25.00
NAS Nashville Predators SP 15.00 40.00
NE Northeast Division 15.00 40.00
NJNY Devils/Rangers 12.00 30.00
NYI New York Islanders 10.00 25.00
NYR New York Rangers 10.00 25.00
OIL Edmonton Oilers 15.00 40.00
PA Flyers/Penguins 15.00 40.00
PAC Pacific Division 12.00 30.00
PICA Penguins/Capitals SP 15.00 40.00
PIT Pittsburgh Penguins SP 25.00 60.00
RAG New York Rangers 30.00 80.00
RK Rookies/Yak/Galch 20.00 50.00
RK2 Rookies/Laugh/Spoon 15.00 40.00
RVL Leafs/Canadiens SP 20.00 50.00
SAB Buffalo Sabres SP 15.00 40.00
SEN Ottawa Senators 10.00 25.00
SJS San Jose Sharks SP 15.00 40.00
SJVA Sharks/Canucks 20.00 50.00
STL St. Louis Blues 12.00 30.00
STNA Blues/Predators SP 12.00 30.00
STP Blues/Coyotes 12.00 30.00
TBL Tampa Bay Lightning SP 12.00 30.00
TOR Toronto Maple Leafs 15.00 40.00

2013-14 Score NHL Draft

COMPLETE SET (6) 5.00 10.00
1 Sidney Crosby 2.50 6.00
2 John Tavares 1.00 2.50
3 Henrik Lundqvist 1.50 4.00
4 Tyler Seguin .75 2.00
5 Alex Ovechkin 2.50 6.00
6 Eric Lindros 1.00 2.50

1967-68 Seals Team Issue

1 Bobby Baun 10.00 20.00
2 Ron Boehm 2.00 4.00
3 Wally Boyer 3.00 6.00
4 Charlie Burns 4.00 8.00
5 Larry Cahan 2.00 4.00
6 Alain Caron 2.00 4.00
7 Terry Clancy 2.00 4.00
8 Kent Douglas 4.00 8.00
9 Gerry Ehman 3.00 6.00
10 Autry Erickson 3.00 6.00
11 Billy Harris 3.00 6.00
12 Ron Harris 3.00 6.00
13 Bill Hicke 3.00 6.00
14 Charlie Hodge 7.50 15.00
15 Mike Laughton 2.00 4.00
16 Bob Lemieux 2.00 4.00
17 Gary Smith 6.00 12.00
18 George Swarbrick 3.00 6.00
19 Joe Szura 3.00 6.00

1992-93 Seasons Patches

COMPLETE SET (70) 60.00 150.00
1 Jeremy Roenick 1.25 3.00
2 Steve Larmer 1.00 2.50
3 Ed Belfour 1.25 3.00
4 Chris Chelios 1.25 3.00
5 Sergei Fedorov 1.25 3.00
6 Steve Yzerman 2.00 5.00
7 Tim Cheveldae .40 1.00
8 Bob Probert 1.00 2.50
9 Wayne Gretzky 4.00 10.00
10 Luc Robitaille 1.00 2.50
11 Tony Granato .40 1.00
12 Kelly Hrudey 1.00 2.50
13 Brett Hull 1.25 3.00
14 Curtis Joseph 1.25 3.00
15 Brendan Shanahan 1.25 3.00
16 Nelson Emerson .40 1.00
17 Ray Bourque 1.25 3.00
18 Joe Juneau 1.00 2.50
19 Andy Moog 1.00 2.50
20 Adam Oates 1.00 2.50
21 Patrick Roy 3.00 8.00
22 Grant Mulvey PROMO 8.00 20.00
23 Denis Savard 1.00 2.50
24 Gilbert Dionne .40 1.00
25 Kirk Muller 1.00 2.50
26 Mark Messier 1.25 3.00
27 Tony Amonte 1.00 2.50
28 Brian Leetch 1.25 3.00
29 Mike Richter 1.25 3.00
30 Trevor Linden 1.00 2.50
31 Pavel Bure 1.25 3.00
32 Cliff Ronning .40 1.00
33 Russ Courtnall .40 1.00
34 Mario Lemieux 3.00 8.00
35 Jaromir Jagr 2.00 5.00
36 Tom Barrasso 1.00 2.50
37 Rick Tocchet 1.00 2.50
38 Eric Lindros 2.00 5.00
39 Rod Brind'Amour 1.00 2.50
40 Dominic Roussel .40 1.00
41 Mark Recchi 1.00 2.50
42 Pat LaFontaine 1.00 2.50
43 Donald Audette .40 1.00
44 Pat Verbeek 1.00 2.50
45 John Cullen .40 1.00
46 Owen Nolan 1.00 2.50
47 Joe Sakic
Quebec Nordiq 1.25 3.00
48 Kevin Hatcher .40 1.00
49 Don Beaupre .40 1.00
50 Scott Stevens 1.00 2.50
51 Chris Terreri .40 1.00
52 Scott Lachance .40 1.00
53 Pierre Turgeon 1.00 2.50
54 Grant Fuhr 1.00 2.50
55 Doug Gilmour 1.25 3.00
56 Dave Manson .40 1.00
57 Bill Ranford 1.00 2.50
58 Troy Murray .40 1.00
59 Phil Housley .40 1.00
60 Al MacInnis 1.00 2.50
61 Mike Vernon 1.00 2.50
62 Pat Falloon .40 1.00
63 Doug Wilson 1.00 2.50
64 Jon Casey .40 1.00
65 Mike Modano 1.25 3.00
66 Kevin Stevens .40 1.00
67 Al Iafrate .40 1.00
68 Dale Hawerchuk 1.00 2.50
69 Igor Kravchuk .40 1.00
70 Wendel Clark 1.00 2.50
71 Kirk McLean 1.00 2.50

1993-94 Seasons Patches

COMPLETE SET (20) 24.00 60.00
1 Ed Belfour .60 1.50
2 Pavel Bure 1.25 3.00
3 Paul Coffey .60 1.50
4 Doug Gilmour .60 1.50
5 Wayne Gretzky 4.00 10.00
6 Brett Hull .75 2.00
7 Jaromir Jagr 2.00 5.00
8 Joe Juneau .40 1.00
9 Mario Lemieux 3.00 8.00
10 Eric Lindros 2.00 5.00
11 Shawn McEachern .40 1.00
12 Alexander Mogilny .50 1.25
13 Adam Oates .50 1.25
14 Felix Potvin 1.50 4.00
15 Jeremy Roenick .60 1.50
16 Patrick Roy 3.00 8.00
17 Joe Sakic 1.25 3.00
18 Teemu Selanne 1.25 3.00
19 Kevin Stevens .40 1.00
20 Steve Yzerman 2.00 5.00

1994-95 Select Promos

COMPLETE SEALED SET (9) .40 1.00
7 John Vanbiesbrouck
Flor .05 .15
90 Felix Potvin
Toronto Ma .05 .15
108 Stephane Richer
New Jer .01 .05
118 Dino Ciccarelli
Detroit .01 .05
128 Sylvain Cote
Washington .01 .05
142 Kevin Dineen
Philadelph .01 .05
194 Mattias Norstrom
New Yo .01 .05
YE1 Jamie Storr
Los Angeles .40 1.00
NNO Title Card .02 .10

1994-95 Select

1 Mark Messier .20 .50
2 Rick Tocchet .07 .20
3 Alexandre Daigle .05 .15
4 Owen Nolan .10 .25
5 Bill Ranford .07 .20
6 Dave Gagner .07 .20
7 John Vanbiesbrouck .10 .25
8 Sergei Makarov .05 .15
9 Derek King .05 .15
10 Sergei Fedorov .15 .40
11 Trevor Linden .10 .25
12 Don Beaupre .07 .20
13 Dave Manson .05 .15
14 Sergei Zubov .07 .20
15 Keith Primeau .07 .20
16 Joe Mullen .07 .20
17 Bernie Nicholls .07 .20
18 Ray Bourque .15 .40
19 Mike Ridley .05 .15
20 Wendel Clark .15 .40
21 Mats Sundin .10 .25
22 Alexander Mogilny .07 .20
23 Mathieu Schneider .05 .15
24 Brian Leetch .07 .20
25 Rob Niedermayer .07 .20
26 Donald Audette .05 .15
27 Doug Weight .07 .20
28 Al MacInnis .12 .30
29 Jeremy Roenick .15 .40
30 Mark Recchi .12 .30
31 Chris Chelios .10 .25
32 Luc Robitaille .10 .25
33 Dale Hunter .05 .15
34 Kelly Hrudey .07 .20
35 Steve Yzerman .25 .60
36 Martin Straka .05 .15
37 Arturs Irbe .07 .20
38 Mike Modano .15 .40
39 Cam Neely .10 .25
40 Igor Larionov .05 .15
41 Ray Ferraro .05 .15
42 Dale Hawerchuk .12 .30
43 Brian Bradley .05 .15
44 Joe Murphy .05 .15
45 Daren Puppa .07 .20
46 Pierre Turgeon .07 .20
47 Shayne Corson .07 .20
48 Adam Graves .05 .15
49 Craig Billington .07 .20
50 Derian Hatcher .05 .15
51 Alexei Zhamnov .07 .20
52 Dominik Hasek .15 .40
53 Ed Belfour .10 .25
54 Mike Vernon .07 .20
55 Bob Kudelski .05 .15
56 Ray Sheppard .07 .20
57 Pat LaFontaine .10 .25
58 Adam Oates .10 .25
59 Vincent Damphousse .07 .20
60 Jaromir Jagr .30 .75
61 Mikael Renberg .07 .20
62 Joe Sakic .20 .50
63 Sandis Ozolinsh .05 .15
64 Kirk McLean .07 .20
65 Stephan Lebeau .05 .15
66 Alexei Kovalev .07 .20
67 Ron Hextall .10 .25
68 Geoff Sanderson .07 .20
69 Doug Gilmour .12 .30
70 Russ Courtnall .05 .15
71 Jari Kurri .07 .20
72 Paul Coffey .10 .25
73 Claude Lemieux .10 .25
74 Teemu Selanne .20 .50
75 Keith Tkachuk .10 .25
76 Pat Verbeek .07 .20
77 Chris Gratton .05 .15
78 Martin Brodeur .25 .60
79 Guy Hebert .07 .20
80 Al Iafrate .05 .15
81 Glen Wesley .05 .15
82 Scott Stevens .10 .25
83 Wayne Gretzky .60 1.50
84 Ron Francis .12 .30
85 Scott Mellanby .07 .20
86 Joe Juneau .05 .15
87 Jason Arnott .07 .20
88 Tom Barrasso .07 .20
89 Peter Bondra .10 .25
90 Felix Potvin .15 .40
91 Brian Bellows .07 .20
92 Pavel Bure .10 .25
93 Grant Fuhr .15 .40
94 Andy Moog .10 .25
95 Mike Gartner .12 .30
96 Patrick Roy .25 .60
97 Brett Hull .20 .50
98 Rob Blake .10 .25
99 Dave Andreychuk .10 .25
100 Eric Lindros .15 .40
101 Scott Niedermayer .10 .25
102 Tim Cheveldae .07 .20
103 Slava Kozlov .07 .20
104 Dimitri Khristich .05 .15
105 Steve Thomas .05 .15
106 Kevin Stevens .07 .20
107 Kirk Muller .05 .15
108 Stephane Richer .07 .20
109 Theo Fleury .10 .25
110 Jeff Brown .05 .15
111 Chris Pronger .10 .25
112 Steve Larmer .07 .20
113 Eric Desjardins .07 .20
114 Mike Ricci .05 .15
115 Tony Amonte .07 .20
116 Pat Falloon .05 .15
117 Garry Galley .05 .15
118 Dino Ciccarelli .07 .20
119 Rod Brind'Amour .07 .20
120 Petr Nedved .07 .20
121 Curtis Joseph .12 .30
122 Cliff Ronning .05 .15
123 Ulf Dahlen .05 .15
124 Marty McSorley .07 .20
125 Nelson Emerson .05 .15
126 Brian Skrudland .05 .15
127 Sean Burke .07 .20
128 Sylvain Cote .05 .15
129 Brendan Shanahan .10 .25
130 Benoit Hogue .05 .15
131 Joe Nieuwendyk .07 .20
132 Bryan Smolinski .05 .15
133 Mike Richter .10 .25
134 Nicklas Lidstrom .10 .25
135 Alexei Yashin .10 .25
136 John MacLean .07 .20
137 Geoff Courtnall .05 .15
138 Robert Reichel .05 .15
139 Craig Janney .07 .20
140 Zarley Zalapski .05 .15
141 Andrew Cassels .05 .15
142 Kevin Dineen .05 .15
143 Larry Murphy .07 .20
144 Valeri Kamensky .07 .20
145 Steve Duchesne .05 .15
146 Phil Housley .07 .20
147 Gary Roberts .05 .15
148 Kevin Hatcher .05 .15
149 Bryan Berard RC .15 .40
150 Marty Reasoner RC .10 .25
151 Andrew Berenzweig RC .10 .25
152 Erik Rasmussen RC .10 .25
153 Luke Curtin RC .10 .25
154 Dan Lacouture RC .10 .25
155 Brian Boucher RC .10 .25
156 Wyatt Smith RC .10 .25
157 Maxim Kuznetsov RC .10 .25
158 Alexei Morozov RC .10 .25
159 Dmitri Nabokov RC .10 .25
160 Wade Redden RC .15 .40
161 Jason Doig RC .10 .25
162 Alyn McCauley RC .10 .25
163 Jeff Ware RC .10 .25
164 Brad Larsen RC .10 .25
165 Jarome Iginla RC 3.00 8.00
166 Christian Dube RC .10 .25
167 Mike McBain RC .10 .25
168 Todd Norman RC .10 .25
169 Oleg Tverdovsky .07 .20
170 Jamie Storr .07 .20
171 Jason Wiemer RC .05 .15
172 Kenny Jonsson .05 .15
173 Paul Kariya .10 .25
174 Viktor Kozlov .05 .15
175 Peter Forsberg .20 .50
176 Jeff Friesen .05 .15
177 Brian Rolston .07 .20
178 Brett Lindros .05 .15
179 Adam Deadmarsh .05 .15
180 Aaron Gavey .05 .15
181 Janne Laukkanen .07 .20
182 Todd Harvey .05 .15
183 Valeri Karpov RC .05 .15
184 Andrei Nikolishin .05 .15
185 Pavol Demitra .12 .30
186 Radek Bonk RC .05 .15
187 Valeri Bure .05 .15
188 Eric Fichaud RC .10 .25
189 Jamie McLennan .07 .20
190 Mariusz Czerkawski RC .10 .25
191 John Lilley .05 .15
192 Brian Savage .05 .15
193 Jason Allison .07 .20
194 Mattias Norstrom .05 .15
195 Todd Simon RC .05 .15
196 Zigmund Palffy .07 .20
197 Rene Corbet .05 .15
198 Mike Peca .07 .20
199 Checklist (1-100) .05 .15
200 Checklist (101-198) .05 .15
NNO Mike Modano Large .15 .40

1994-95 Select Gold

COMPLETE SET (200) 25.00 60.00
*VETS: 1X TO 2.5X BASIC CARDS
*ROOKIES: .75X TO 2X BASIC CARDS

1994-95 Select First Line

COMPLETE SET (12) 15.00 30.00
FL1 Patrick Roy 5.00 12.00
FL2 Ray Bourque 1.50 4.00
FL3 Brian Leetch .75 2.00
FL4 Brendan Shanahan .75 2.00
FL5 Eric Lindros .75 2.00
FL6 Pavel Bure .75 2.00
FL7 Mike Richter .75 2.00
FL8 Scott Stevens .50 1.25
FL9 Chris Chelios .75 2.00
FL10 Luc Robitaille .50 1.25
FL11 Wayne Gretzky 6.00 15.00
FL12 Brett Hull 1.25 3.00

1994-95 Select Youth Explosion

COMPLETE SET (12) 8.00 15.00
YE1 Jamie Storr .50 1.25
YE2 Oleg Tverdovsky .50 1.25
YE3 Janne Laukkanen .20 .50
YE4 Kenny Jonsson .20 .50
YE5 Paul Kariya .50 1.25
YE6 Viktor Kozlov .50 1.25
YE7 Peter Forsberg 2.50 6.00
YE8 Jason Allison .60 1.50
YE9 Jeff Friesen .20 .50
YE10 Brian Rolston .50 1.25
YE11 Mariusz Czerkawski .60 1.50
YE12 Brett Lindros .30 .75

1995-96 Select Certified Promos

COMPLETE SET (9) 12.00 30.00
5 Pavel Bure 6.00 15.00
12 Jim Carey .60 1.50
13 Paul Kariya 4.00 10.00
17 Mike Modano 1.25 3.00
19 Owen Nolan .75 2.00
43 Alexander Mogilny .75 2.00
68 Peter Forsberg 3.00 8.00

69 Felix Potvin .75 2.00
NNO Title Card .08 .25

1995-96 Select Certified

1 Mario Lemieux .60 1.50
2 Chris Chelios .15 .40
3 Scott Mellanby .12 .30
4 Brett Hull .30 .75
5 Theo Fleury .20 .50
6 Alexei Zhamnov .15 .40
7 Mats Sundin .15 .40
8 Mathieu Schneider .10 .25
9 Jason Arnott .12 .30
10 Mark Recchi .20 .50
11 Adam Oates .15 .40
12 Jim Carey .12 .30
13 Paul Kariya .15 .40
14 Mark Messier .30 .75
15 Eric Lindros .25 .60
16 Pavel Bure .15 .40
17 Mike Modano .25 .60
18 Pat LaFontaine .15 .40
19 Owen Nolan .15 .40
20 Roman Hamrlik .10 .25
21 Paul Coffey .15 .40
22 Alexandre Daigle .10 .25
23 Wayne Gretzky 1.00 2.50
24 Martin Brodeur .40 1.00
25 Ulf Dahlen .10 .25
26 Geoff Sanderson .10 .25
27 Brian Leetch .12 .30
28 Dave Andreychuk .15 .40
29 Sergei Fedorov .25 .60
30 Jocelyn Thibault .12 .30
31 Mikael Renberg .12 .30
32 Joe Nieuwendyk .12 .30
33 Craig Janney .10 .25
34 Ray Bourque .25 .60
35 Jari Kurri .15 .40
36 Alexei Yashin .12 .30
37 Keith Tkachuk .15 .40
38 Jaromir Jagr .50 1.25
39 Stephane Richer .12 .30
40 Trevor Kidd .12 .30
41 Kevin Hatcher .12 .30
42 Mike Vernon .12 .30
43 Alexander Mogilny .12 .30
44 John LeClair .15 .40
45 Joe Sakic .30 .75
46 Kevin Stevens .12 .30
47 Adam Graves .12 .30
48 Doug Gilmour .20 .50
49 Pierre Turgeon .12 .30
50 Joe Murphy .10 .25
51 Peter Bondra .15 .40
52 Ron Francis .20 .50
53 Luc Robitaille .15 .40
54 Mike Gartner .20 .50
55 Bill Ranford .12 .30
56 Jeff Friesen .10 .25
57 Cam Neely .15 .40
58 Daren Puppa .12 .30
59 Rod Brind'Amour .15 .40
60 Jeremy Roenick .25 .60
61 Brett Lindros .10 .25
62 Todd Harvey .10 .25
63 Kirk McLean .12 .30
64 Brendan Shanahan .15 .40
65 Kelly Hrudey .12 .30
66 Scott Stevens .15 .40
67 Sergei Zubov .12 .30
68 Peter Forsberg .30 .75
69 Felix Potvin .25 .60
70 Scott Niedermayer .15 .40
71 Keith Primeau .12 .30
72 Al MacInnis .20 .50
73 Mike Richter .15 .40
74 Rob Blake .12 .30
75 Vincent Damphousse .12 .30
76 Teemu Selanne .30 .75
77 Andy Moog .15 .40
78 Ron Hextall .15 .40
79 Oleg Tverdovsky .15 .40
80 Joe Juneau .10 .25
81 Patrick Roy .40 1.00
82 Wendel Clark .25 .60
83 Brian Bradley .12 .30
84 Curtis Joseph .20 .50
85 John Vanbiesbrouck .15 .40
86 Phil Housley .12 .30
87 Trevor Linden .15 .40
88 Alexei Kovalev .12 .30
89 Dominik Hasek .25 .60
90 Larry Murphy .12 .30
91 Arturs Irbe .12 .30
92 John MacLean .12 .30
93 Ed Belfour .12 .30
94 Steve Yzerman .40 1.00
95 Tom Barrasso .12 .30
96 Rob Niedermayer .12 .30
97 Dale Hawerchuk .20 .50
98 Rick Tocchet .12 .30
99 Claude Lemieux .15 .40
100 Sean Burke .10 .25
101 Shayne Corson .12 .30
102 Dino Ciccarelli .12 .30
103 Kirk Muller .12 .30
104 Don Beaupre .12 .30
105 Valeri Kamensky .12 .30
106 Markus Naslund .15 .40
107 Tomas Sandstrom .12 .30
108 Pat Verbeek .12 .30
109 Doug Weight .15 .40
110 Brian Holzinger RC .30 .75
111 Antti Tormanen .10 .25
112 Tommy Salo RC .25 .60
113 Jason Bonsignore .10 .25
114 Shane Doan RC .50 1.25
115 Robert Svehla RC .10 .25
116 Chad Kilger RC .15 .40
117 Saku Koivu .15 .40
118 Jeff O'Neill .15 .40
119 Brendan Witt .15 .40
120 Byron Dafoe .12 .30
121 Ryan Smyth .12 .30
122 Daniel Alfredsson RC .75 2.00
123 Todd Bertuzzi RC .20 .50
124 Daymond Langkow RC .15 .40
125 Miroslav Satan RC .20 .50
126 Bryan McCabe .15 .40
127 Aki Berg RC .15 .40
128 Cory Stillman .10 .25
129 Deron Quint .12 .30
130 Vitali Yachmenev .15 .40
131 Valeri Bure .10 .25
132 Eric Daze .30 .75
133 Radek Dvorak RC .20 .50
134 Landon Wilson RC .10 .25
135 Niklas Sundstrom .15 .40
136 Jamie Storr .12 .30
137 Ed Jovanovski .15 .40
138 Marcus Ragnarsson RC .20 .50
139 Kyle McLaren RC .10 .25
140 Sandy Moger .10 .25
141 Marty Murray .15 .40
142 Darby Hendrickson .10 .25
143 Corey Hirsch .12 .30
144 Petr Sykora RC .40 1.00

1995-96 Select Certified Mirror Gold

*VETS: 2X TO 5X BASIC CARDS
*ROOKIES: .8X TO 2X

1995-96 Select Certified Double Strike

COMPLETE SET (20) 15.00 40.00
*GOLD: 1X TO 2.5X BASIC INSERTS
1 Doug Gilmour .75 2.00
2 Ron Francis .75 2.00
3 Ray Bourque 1.50 4.00
4 Chris Chelios 1.25 3.00
5 Adam Oates .75 2.00
6 Mike Ricci .75 2.00
7 Jeremy Roenick 1.25 3.00
8 Jason Arnott .75 2.00
9 Brendan Shanahan 1.25 3.00
10 Joe Nieuwendyk .75 2.00
11 Trevor Linden .75 2.00
12 Mikael Renberg .75 2.00
13 Theo Fleury .75 2.00
14 Sergei Fedorov 1.50 4.00
15 Mark Messier 1.50 4.00
16 Keith Primeau .75 2.00
17 Keith Tkachuk 1.25 3.00
18 Scott Stevens .75 2.00
19 Claude Lemieux .75 2.00
20 Alexei Zhamnov .75 2.00

1995-96 Select Certified Future

COMPLETE SET (10) 15.00 30.00
1 Peter Forsberg 6.00 15.00
2 Jim Carey .75 2.00
3 Paul Kariya 2.00 5.00
4 Jocelyn Thibault 1.25 3.00
5 Saku Koivu 2.00 5.00
6 Brian Holzinger .75 2.00
7 Todd Harvey .75 2.00
8 Jeff O'Neill .75 2.00
9 Oleg Tverdovsky .75 2.00
10 Ed Jovanovski .75 2.00

1995-96 Select Certified Gold Team

COMPLETE SET (10) 50.00 125.00
1 Eric Lindros 3.00 8.00
2 Wayne Gretzky 12.00 30.00
3 Mario Lemieux 10.00 25.00
4 Jaromir Jagr 4.00 10.00
5 Pavel Bure 3.00 8.00
6 Brett Hull 3.00 8.00
7 Cam Neely 3.00 8.00
8 Joe Sakic 6.00 15.00
9 Martin Brodeur 6.00 15.00
10 Patrick Roy 10.00 25.00

1996-97 Select Certified

*VETS: 3X TO 8X BASIC
1 Eric Lindros .30 .75
2 Mike Modano .30 .75
3 Jocelyn Thibault .15 .40
4 Wayne Gretzky 1.25 3.00
5 Ray Bourque .30 .75
6 Martin Brodeur .50 1.25
7 Rob Niedermayer .15 .40
8 Stephane Fiset .15 .40
9 Pat LaFontaine .20 .50
10 Mario Lemieux .75 2.00
11 Ed Belfour .20 .50
12 Ron Francis .25 .60
13 Luc Robitaille .20 .50
14 Paul Kariya .20 .50
15 Doug Gilmour .25 .60
16 Joe Sakic .40 1.00
17 Nikolai Khabibulin .15 .40
18 Valeri Bure .12 .30
19 Brett Hull .40 1.00
20 Chris Osgood .20 .50
21 Trevor Kidd .12 .30
22 Kirk McLean .15 .40
23 Zigmund Palffy .20 .50
24 Keith Tkachuk .20 .50
25 Andy Moog .20 .50
26 Bill Guerin .20 .50
27 Chris Chelios .20 .50
28 Damian Rhodes .15 .40
29 Jim Carey .20 .50
30 Ed Jovanovski .15 .40
31 Felix Potvin .30 .75
32 Teemu Selanne .40 1.00
33 John LeClair .20 .50
34 Pavel Bure .20 .50
35 Grant Fuhr .30 .75
36 Mark Messier .40 1.00
37 Vincent Damphousse .15 .40
38 Jason Arnott .15 .40
39 Mike Richter .20 .50
40 Keith Primeau .15 .40
41 Steve Yzerman .50 1.25
42 Trevor Linden .20 .50
43 Jaromir Jagr .60 1.50
44 Sean Burke .12 .30
45 Alexei Zhitnik .12 .30
46 Dimitri Khristich .12 .30
47 Daniel Alfredsson .20 .50
48 Roman Hamrlik .12 .30
49 Pat Verbeek .12 .30
50 Doug Weight .20 .50
51 Adam Graves .12 .30
52 Michal Pivonka .12 .30
53 Claude Lemieux .12 .30
54 Scott Stevens .20 .50
55 Sergei Fedorov .30 .75
56 Owen Nolan .20 .50
57 Niklas Andersson .12 .30
58 Cory Stillman .12 .30
59 John Vanbiesbrouck .20 .50
60 Craig Janney .15 .40
61 Jeff Friesen .12 .30
62 Igor Larionov .20 .50
63 Ron Hextall .20 .50
64 Saku Koivu .20 .50
65 Wendel Clark .30 .75
66 Curtis Joseph .25 .60
67 Valeri Kamensky .15 .40
68 Adam Oates .20 .50
69 Daren Puppa .15 .40
70 Alexander Mogilny .15 .40
71 Corey Hirsch .15 .40
72 Brendan Shanahan .20 .50
73 Shayne Corson .15 .40
74 Dominik Hasek .30 .75
75 Theo Fleury .40 1.00
76 Brian Leetch .15 .40
77 Jeremy Roenick .30 .75
78 Peter Bondra .20 .50
79 Eric Daze .15 .40
80 Todd Bertuzzi .20 .50
81 Patrick Roy .50 1.25
82 Pierre Turgeon .15 .40
83 Alexei Yashin .15 .40
84 Scott Mellanby .15 .40
85 Mats Sundin .20 .50
86 Jari Kurri .20 .50
87 Kelly Hrudey .15 .40
88 Joe Nieuwendyk .15 .40
89 Paul Coffey .20 .50
90 Jeff O'Neill .12 .30
91 Kai Nurminen RC .20 .50
92 Anders Eriksson .12 .30
93 Jarome Iginla .25 .60
94 Anson Carter .15 .40
95 Christian Dube .12 .30
96 Harry York RC .20 .50
97 Tomas Holmstrom RC .60 1.50
98 Sergei Berezin RC .30 .75
99 Mattias Timander RC .20 .50
100 Wade Redden .12 .30
101 Mike Grier RC .25 .60
102 Jonas Hoglund .12 .30
103 Eric Fichaud .15 .40
104 Janne Niinimaa .20 .50
105 Tuomas Gronman .12 .30
106 Jim Campbell .12 .30
107 Daniel Goneau RC .20 .50
108 Patrick Lalime RC .60 1.50
109 Ruslan Salei RC .20 .50
110 Richard Zednik RC .25 .60
111 Chris O'Sullivan .12 .30
112 Fredrik Modin RC .20 .50
113 Brad Smyth RC .15 .40
114 Bryan Berard .20 .50
115 Jamie Langenbrunner .12 .30
116 Ethan Moreau RC .20 .50
117 Daymond Langkow .15 .40
118 Andreas Dackell RC .20 .50
119 Rem Murray RC .20 .50
120 Dainius Zubrus RC .25 .60
48P Roman Hamrlik PROMO .12 .30
60P Craig Janney PROMO .15 .40
65P Wendel Clark PROMO .30 .75

1996-97 Select Certified Artist's Proofs

*PROOF: 3X TO 8X BASIC

1996-97 Select Certified Blue

*VETS: 3X TO 8X BASIC
*ROOKIES: 1.5X TO 4X

1996-97 Select Certified Mirror Blue

*MIR.BLUE: 8X TO 20X BASIC

1996-97 Select Certified Mirror Gold

*MIR.GOLD: 12X TO 30X BASIC

1996-97 Select Certified Mirror Red

*MIR.RED: 5X TO 12X BASIC
36 Mark Messier 5.00 12.00

1996-97 Select Certified Red

*VETS: 2.5X TO 6X BASIC
*ROOKIES: 1.2X TO 3X

1996-97 Select Certified Cornerstones

COMPLETE SET (15) 30.00 80.00
1 Eric Lindros 2.50 6.00
2 Mario Lemieux 6.00 15.00
3 Jaromir Jagr 3.00 8.00
4 Wayne Gretzky 8.00 20.00
5 Mark Messier 2.50 6.00
6 Brett Hull 2.50 6.00
7 Pavel Bure 2.50 6.00
8 Saku Koivu 2.00 5.00
9 Joe Sakic 4.00 10.00
10 Keith Tkachuk 2.00 5.00
11 Paul Kariya 2.50 6.00
12 Teemu Selanne 2.50 6.00
13 Sergei Fedorov 2.50 6.00
14 Steve Yzerman 6.00 15.00
15 Peter Forsberg 3.00 8.00

1996-97 Select Certified Freezers

COMPLETE SET (15) 40.00 100.00
1 Martin Brodeur 6.00 15.00
2 Patrick Roy 10.00 25.00
3 Jim Carey 2.00 5.00
4 John Vanbiesbrouck 2.50 6.00
5 Dominik Hasek 4.00 10.00
6 Ed Belfour 2.50 6.00
7 Curtis Joseph 2.50 6.00
8 Felix Potvin 3.00 8.00
9 Daren Puppa 2.00 5.00
10 Chris Osgood 2.50 6.00
11 Mike Richter 2.50 6.00
12 Jocelyn Thibault 2.00 5.00
13 Ron Hextall 2.00 5.00
14 Nikolai Khabibulin 2.00 5.00
15 Damian Rhodes 2.00 5.00

2013-14 Select

*RED/35: 3X TO 8X BASIC INSERTS
*GREEN/25: 3X TO 8X BASIC INSERTS
1 Patrick Kane .75 2.00
2 Jonathan Toews .60 1.50
3 Corey Crawford .50 1.25
4 Duncan Keith .30 .75
5 Marian Hossa .40 1.00
6 Sidney Crosby 1.50 4.00
7 Evgeni Malkin .75 2.00
8 Kris Letang .50 1.25
9 James Neal .25 .60
10 Marc-Andre Fleury .75 2.00
11 Corey Perry .60 1.50
12 Ryan Getzlaf .40 1.00
13 Saku Koivu .40 1.00
14 Jonas Hiller .30 .75
15 Cam Fowler .40 1.00
16 Max Pacioretty .40 1.00
17 Carey Price .75 2.00
18 P.K. Subban .50 1.25
19 Brian Gionta .25 .60
20 David Desharnais .25 .60
21 Patrice Bergeron .50 1.25
22 Jarome Iginla .50 1.25
23 Zdeno Chara .40 1.00
24 Milan Lucic .40 1.00
25 Tuukka Rask .50 1.25
26 Alex Pietrangelo .30 .75
27 T.J. Oshie .40 1.00
28 David Backes .25 .60
29 Jaroslav Halak .40 1.00
30 Alexander Steen .25 .60
31 Jonathan Quick .50 1.25
32 Dustin Brown .40 1.00
33 Anze Kopitar .60 1.50
34 Drew Doughty .50 1.25
35 Mike Richards .30 .75
36 Henrik Sedin .50 1.25
37 Daniel Sedin .50 1.25
38 Roberto Luongo .60 1.50
39 Ryan Kesler .40 1.00
40 Alexandre Burrows .25 .60
41 Joffrey Lupul .25 .60
42 James Reimer .40 1.00
43 Dion Phaneuf .30 .75
44 Phil Kessel .40 1.00
45 Nazem Kadri .50 1.25
46 Alex Ovechkin 1.50 4.00
47 Braden Holtby .50 1.25
48 Mike Green .30 .75
49 Nicklas Backstrom .40 1.00
50 Brooks Laich .25 .60
51 Logan Couture .50 1.25
52 Patrick Marleau .40 1.00
53 Joe Thornton .60 1.50
54 Antti Niemi .30 .75
55 Dan Boyle .25 .60
56 Henrik Lundqvist 1.00 2.50
57 Rick Nash .40 1.00
58 Ryan Callahan .25 .60
59 Derick Brassard .25 .60
60 Marc Staal .25 .60
61 Jimmy Howard .50 1.25
62 Pavel Datsyuk .60 1.50
63 Henrik Zetterberg .50 1.25
64 Johan Franzen .30 .75
65 Niklas Kronwall .30 .75
66 Craig Anderson .40 1.00
67 Jason Spezza .40 1.00
68 Erik Karlsson .50 1.25
69 Bobby Ryan .30 .75
70 Mika Zibanejad .50 1.25
71 Zach Parise .40 1.00
72 Dany Heatley .30 .75
73 Mikko Koivu .30 .75
74 Ryan Suter .30 .75
75 Niklas Backstrom .30 .75
76 John Tavares .60 1.50
77 Matt Moulson .25 .60
78 Evgeni Nabokov .40 1.00
79 Travis Hamonic .25 .60
80 Michael Grabner .30 .75
81 Sergei Bobrovsky .60 1.50
82 Marian Gaborik .40 1.00
83 Jack Johnson .25 .60
84 Brandon Dubinsky .25 .60
85 Ryan Johansen .30 .75
86 Ondrej Pavelec .40 1.00
87 Dustin Byfuglien .40 1.00
88 Andrew Ladd .25 .60
89 Evander Kane .40 1.00
90 Blake Wheeler .40 1.00
91 Mike Smith .40 1.00
92 Shane Doan .30 .75
93 Keith Yandle .25 .60
94 Mikkel Boedker .25 .60
95 Oliver Ekman-Larsson .40 1.00
96 Claude Giroux .40 1.00
97 Vincent Lecavalier .40 1.00
98 Sean Couturier .30 .75
99 Luke Schenn .40 1.00
100 Steve Mason .30 .75
101 Jamie Benn .40 1.00
102 Tyler Seguin .50 1.25
103 Kari Lehtonen .30 .75
104 Brenden Dillon .25 .60
105 Erik Cole .25 .60
106 Martin Brodeur 1.00 2.50
107 Adam Larsson .40 1.00
108 Adam Henrique .30 .75
109 Patrik Elias .40 1.00
110 Cory Schneider .40 1.00
111 Cody Hodgson .25 .60
112 Thomas Vanek .30 .75
113 Ryan Miller .40 1.00
114 Steve Ott .25 .60
115 Christian Ehrhoff .25 .60
116 Sam Gagner .25 .60
117 Taylor Hall .40 1.00
118 Ryan Nugent-Hopkins .50 1.25
119 Jordan Eberle .40 1.00
120 Devan Dubnyk .30 .75
121 Jiri Hudler .30 .75
122 Mike Cammalleri .30 .75
123 Curtis Glencross .25 .60
124 Miikka Kiprusoff .40 1.00
125 Mark Giordano .40 1.00
126 Cam Ward .40 1.00
127 Eric Staal .50 1.25
128 Alexander Semin .40 1.00
129 Jiri Tlusty .25 .60
130 Jordan Staal .30 .75
131 Shea Weber .30 .75
132 Pekka Rinne .40 1.00
133 Mike Fisher .25 .60
134 Patric Hornqvist .25 .60
135 Colin Wilson .30 .75
136 Martin St. Louis .40 1.00
137 Steven Stamkos .75 2.00
138 Anders Lindback .25 .60
139 Victor Hedman .50 1.25
140 Ben Bishop .30 .75
141 Matt Duchene .40 1.00
142 Gabriel Landeskog .50 1.25
143 Erik Johnson .25 .60
144 Semyon Varlamov .40 1.00
145 P.A. Parenteau .25 .60
146 Jacob Markstrom .40 1.00
147 Tomas Fleischmann .25 .60
148 Brian Campbell .25 .60
149 Kris Versteeg .25 .60
150 Erik Gudbranson .25 .60
151 Mario Lemieux 1.50 4.00
152 Mark Messier .75 2.00
153 Brett Hull .75 2.00
154 Bobby Hull .75 2.00
155 Joe Sakic .75 2.00
156 Patrick Roy 1.00 2.50
157 Guy Lafleur .50 1.25
158 Pat LaFontaine .40 1.00
159 Al MacInnis .50 1.25
160 Stan Mikita .50 1.25
161 Bobby Clarke .60 1.50
162 Brendan Shanahan .40 1.00
163 Brian Leetch .30 .75
164 Bryan Trottier .40 1.00
165 Cam Neely .40 1.00
166 Chris Chelios .40 1.00
167 Ray Bourque .60 1.50
168 Darryl Sittler .50 1.25
169 Mike Richter .40 1.00
170 Bernie Parent .50 1.25
171 Steve Yzerman 1.00 2.50
172 Gordie Howe 1.25 3.00
173 Grant Fuhr .60 1.50
174 Guy Carbonneau .40 1.00
175 Igor Larionov .40 1.00
176 Jari Kurri .40 1.00
177 Jeremy Roenick .60 1.50
178 Trevor Linden .40 1.00
179 Luc Robitaille .40 1.00
180 Pavel Bure .40 1.00
181 Mike Bossy .40 1.00
182 Mike Modano .60 1.50
183 Paul Coffey .40 1.00
184 Peter Stastny .30 .75
185 Phil Esposito .60 1.50
186 Andrej Sustr RC .75 2.00
187 Steve Oleksy RC 1.25 3.00
188 Steven Pinizzotto RC 1.25 3.00
189 Anders Lee RC 2.00 5.00
190 Ben Hanowski RC 1.00 2.50
191 Drew LeBlanc RC .75 2.00
192 Daniel Bang RC 1.00 2.50
193 Chad Ruhwedel RC .75 2.00
194 Cameron Schilling RC .75 2.00
195 John Muse RC 1.25 3.00
196 Jean-Gabriel Pageau RC 1.25 3.00
197 Carter Bancks RC 1.00 2.50
198 Jason Akeson RC 1.00 2.50
199 Nicolas Blanchard RC 1.00 2.50
200 Matthew Konan RC 1.25 3.00
201 Jamie Tardif AU/399 RC 2.00 5.00
202 Brian Flynn AU/399 RC 2.50 6.00
203 Mark Cundari AU/399 RC 2.00 5.00
204 Michal Jordan AU/399 RC 2.00 5.00
205 Chris Terry AU/399 RC 2.00 5.00
206 Shawn Lalonde AU/399 RC 3.00 8.00
207 Ryan Stanton AU/399 RC 3.00 8.00
208 Drew Shore AU/399 RC 2.50 6.00
209 Greg Pateryn AU/399 RC 3.00 8.00
210 J.Rheault AU/399 RC 2.00 5.00
211 Oliver Lauridsen AU/399 RC 2.50 6.00
212 Jeff Zatkoff AU/399 RC 3.00 8.00
213 Matt Tennyson AU/399 RC 2.00 5.00
214 Tyler Johnson AU/399 RC 6.00 15.00
215 Ben Street AU/399 RC 2.50 6.00
216 P.Bordeleau AU/399 RC 3.00 8.00
217 M.Sgarbossa AU/399 RC 3.00 8.00
218 Sean Collins AU/399 RC 2.50 6.00
219 Brian Lashoff AU/99 RC 2.50 6.00
220 Mark Arcobello AU/399 RC 3.00 8.00
221 Michael Caruso AU/399 RC 2.00 5.00
222 Petr Mrazek AU/399 RC 6.00 15.00
223 D.Dziurzynski AU/399 RC 2.50 6.00
224 Harri Pesonen AU/399 RC 2.50 6.00
225 Victor Bartley AU/399 RC 2.50 6.00
226 Darcy Kuemper AU/399 RC 6.00 15.00
227 Richard Panik AU/399 RC 3.00 8.00
228 Derek Grant AU/399 RC 2.50 6.00
229 J.Marchessault AU/399 RC 8.00 20.00
230 M.Reinhart AU/399 RC 3.00 8.00
231 Taylor Beck AU/399 RC 2.50 6.00
232 Tye McGinn AU/399 RC 3.00 8.00
233 Antoine Roussel AU/399 RC 3.00 8.00
234 Eric Gryba AU/399 RC 2.50 6.00
235 Matt Irwin AU/399 RC 2.50 6.00
236 Ondrej Palat AU/399 RC 6.00 15.00
237 J.Schroeder AU/399 RC 3.00 8.00
238 Philipp Grubauer AU/399 RC 8.00 20.00
239 Zach Redmond AU/399 RC 2.50 6.00
240 Radko Gudas AU/399 RC 3.00 8.00
241 Viktor Fasth AU/399 RC 3.00 8.00
242 Carl Soderberg AU/399 RC 3.00 8.00
243 Mark Pysyk AU/399 RC 3.00 8.00
244 R.Cervenka AU/199 RC 2.50 6.00
245 Calvin Pickard AU/399 RC 4.00 10.00
246 Alex Petrovic AU/399 RC 2.50 6.00
247 Johan Larsson AU/399 RC 4.00 10.00
248 Joonas Rask AU/399 RC 2.00 5.00
249 Chris Brown AU/399 RC 2.00 5.00
250 Nick Petrecki AU/399 RC 2.00 5.00
251 Dmitrij Jaskin AU/399 RC 3.00 8.00
252 Alex Killorn AU/399 RC 5.00 12.00
253 Frank Corrado AU/399 RC 2.00 5.00
254 Anthony Peluso AU/399 RC 2.00 5.00
255 Stefan Matteau AU/399 RC 2.50 6.00
256 Thomas Hickey AU/399 RC 2.50 6.00
257 D.DeKeyser AU/399 RC 4.00 10.00
258 E.Pasquale AU/399 RC 2.00 5.00
259 C.Thomas AU/399 RC 2.50 6.00
260 Eric Hartzell AU/399 RC 3.00 8.00
261 Rickard Rakell AU/399 RC 3.00 8.00
262 Leo Komarov AU/299 RC 3.00 8.00
263 Sami Vatanen AU/399 RC 3.00 8.00
264 C.Nilstorp AU/399 RC 2.50 6.00
265 Mathew Dumba AU/399 RC 2.00 5.00
266 Jonas Brodin AU/399 RC 4.00 10.00
267 Michael Kostka AU/399 RC 2.50 6.00
268 Nicklas Jensen AU/399 RC 2.50 6.00
269 Emerson Etem AU/399 RC 3.00 8.00
270 Ryan Spooner AU/399 RC EXCH 3.00 8.00
271 Jamie Oleksiak AU/399 RC 2.50 6.00
272 Q.Howden AU/199 RC 2.50 6.00
273 Ryan Murphy AU/199 RC 3.00 8.00
274 Charlie Coyle AU/399 RC 5.00 12.00
275 Jarred Tinordi AU/399 RC 3.00 8.00
276 Austin Watson AU/399 RC 2.50 6.00
277 Brock Nelson AU/399 RC 6.00 15.00
278 Scott Laughton AU/99 RC 4.00 10.00
279 Beau Bennett AU/399 RC 4.00 10.00
280 F.Andersen AU/399 RC 10.00 25.00
281 Nathan Beaulieu AU/99 RC 2.00 5.00
282 J.T. Miller AU/399 RC 8.00 20.00
283 M.Grigorenko AU/399 RC 2.00 5.00
284 Nick Bjugstad AU/399 RC 4.00 10.00
285 Tanner Pearson AU/399 RC 3.00 8.00
286 Jared Staal AU/399 RC 2.50 6.00
287 Tom Wilson AU/399 RC 6.00 15.00
288 M.Granlund AU/399 RC 5.00 12.00
289 Justin Schultz AU/399 RC 3.00 8.00
290 Tyler Toffoli AU/399 RC 6.00 15.00
291 Jack Campbell AU/399 RC 8.00 20.00
292 Filip Forsberg AU/399 RC 10.00 25.00
293 Dougie Hamilton AU/399 RC 5.00 12.00
294 Alex Chiasson AU/399 RC 3.00 8.00
295 B.Gallagher AU/399 RC 8.00 20.00
296 Cory Conacher AU/399 RC 2.00 5.00
297 V.Tarasenko AU/399 RC 8.00 20.00
298 A.Galchenyuk AU/399 RC 8.00 20.00
299 J.Huberdeau AU/199 RC 8.00 20.00
300 Nail Yakupov AU/399 RC 6.00 15.00
301 N.MacKinnon AU/399 RC 15.00 40.00
302 Seth Jones AU/399 RC 6.00 15.00
303 V.Nichushkin AU/399 RC 6.00 15.00
304 Sean Monahan AU/399 RC 5.00 12.00
305 Tomas Hertl AU/399 RC 6.00 15.00
306 Boone Jenner AU/399 RC 6.00 15.00
307 Ryan Murray AU/399 RC 5.00 12.00
308 Morgan Rielly AU/399 RC 8.00 20.00
309 Jason Missiaen JSY AU RC 3.00 8.00
310 Michael Raffl JSY AU RC 2.50 6.00
311 Cody Ceci JSY AU RC 2.50 6.00
312 Johan Gustafsson JSY AU RC 4.00 10.00
313 Jacob Trouba JSY AU RC 5.00 12.00
314 Hampus Lindholm JSY AU RC 5.00 12.00
315 Zemgus Girgensons JSY AU RC 5.00 12.00
317 Nikita Zadorov JSY AU RC 2.00 5.00
318 Reto Berra JSY AU RC 3.00 8.00
319 Elias Lindholm JSY AU RC 8.00 20.00
320 Joakim Nordstrom JSY AU RC 2.50 6.00
321 Xavier Ouellet JSY AU RC 3.00 8.00
322 Aleksander Barkov JSY AU RC 10.00 25.00
323 Michael Dournival JSY AU RC 3.00 8.00
324 Marek Mazanec JSY AU RC 3.00 8.00
325 Jon Merrill JSY AU RC 3.00 8.00
326 Tomas Jurco JSY AU RC 4.00 10.00
327 Olli Maatta JSY AU RC 5.00 12.00
328 Matt Nieto JSY AU RC 2.50 6.00
329 Martin Jones JSY AU RC 5.00 12.00
331 Kevin Connauton JSY AU RC 2.50 6.00
332 Connor Murphy JSY AU RC 2.50 6.00
333 Ryan Strome JSY AU RC 5.00 12.00
334 Dylan McIlrath JSY AU RC 2.00 5.00
335 Jesper Fast JSY AU RC 3.00 8.00
336 Magnus Hellberg JSY AU RC 3.00 8.00
337 Lucas Lessio JSY AU RC 2.00 5.00
338 John Gibson JSY AU RC 8.00 20.00
339 Josh Leivo AU/299 RC 2.50 6.00
340 Joe Cannata AU/299 RC 2.50 6.00
341 Linden Vey AU/299 RC 2.00 5.00
342 Taylor Fedun AU/299 RC 4.00 10.00
343 Calvin Heeter AU/299 RC 2.50 6.00
344 Jordan Szwarz AU/299 RC 3.00 8.00
345 Mark Barberio AU/299 RC 2.00 5.00
346 Michael Latta AU/299 RC 2.50 6.00
347 Jamie Devane AU/299 RC 2.50 6.00
348 Freddie Hamilton AU/299 RC 3.00 8.00
349 Tyler Pitlick AU/299 RC 3.00 8.00
350 Jayson Megna AU/299 RC 3.00 8.00
351 Darcy Kuemper AU/299 RC 6.00 15.00
352 Kevin Henderson AU/299 RC 2.50 6.00
353 David Broll AU/299 RC 3.00 8.00
354 Jerry D'Amigo AU/299 RC 3.00 8.00
355 Antti Raanta AU/299 RC 6.00 15.00
356 Karl Stollery RC 1.00 2.50
357 Kevan Miller RC 1.00 2.50
358 Christopher Breen RC 1.00 2.50
359 Chad Billins RC 1.00 2.50
360 Brett Bellemore RC 1.00 2.50
361 Sami Aittokallio RC 1.25 3.00
362 Michael Chaput RC .75 2.00
363 Luke Glendening RC 1.25 3.00
364 Luke Gazdic RC 1.00 2.50
365 Anton Belov RC 1.25 3.00
366 Will Acton RC 1.00 2.50
367 Eric Selleck RC 1.00 2.50
368 Justin Fontaine RC 1.25 3.00
369 Patrick Holland RC 2.00 5.00
370 Matt Anderson RC .75 2.00
371 David Warsofsky RC 1.25 3.00
372 Zach Sill RC 1.25 3.00
373 Brian Gibbons RC 1.25 3.00
374 Dmitry Korobov RC 1.25 3.00
375 Spencer Abbott RC 1.00 2.50
376 Darren Archibald RC 1.00 2.50
377 Connor Carrick RC 1.00 2.50
378 Alex Grant RC .75 2.00
379 Antti Raanta RC 2.50 6.00
380 Eric Gelinas RC 1.25 3.00
381 Julian Melchiori RC .75 2.00
382 Nate Schmidt RC 1.00 2.50
383 Nicolas Blanchard RC 1.00 2.50
384 Ben Chiarot RC 1.25 3.00
385 Reid Boucher RC 1.25 3.00
386 Kent Simpson RC .75 2.00
387 Martin Marincin RC 1.00 2.50
388 Patrick Wey RC 1.00 2.50
389 John Albert RC 1.00 2.50
390 Erik Haula RC 1.50 4.00
391 Adam Almquist RC .75 2.00
392 Craig Cunningham RC 1.00 2.50
393 Eric O'Dell RC .75 2.00
394 Philip Samuelsson RC .75 2.00
395 Brian Dumoulin RC 1.25 3.00
396 Conor Allen RC 1.00 2.50
397 Joacim Eriksson RC 1.25 3.00
398 Zach Trotman RC 1.25 3.00
399 Niklas Svedberg RC 2.50 6.00
400 Brad Hunt RC 1.00 2.50
401 Alexey Marchenko RC 1.00 2.50
402 Justin Florek RC 3.00 8.00
403 Mike Sislo RC 1.25 3.00
404 Eriah Hayes RC 1.25 3.00
405 Kevin Klein .25 .60
406 Devan Dubnyk .30 .75
407 Matt Hendricks .25 .60
408 Derek Roy .25 .60
409 Mats Zuccarello .40 1.00
410 Andrew Ference .25 .60
411 Mike Santorelli .30 .75
412 Michael Ryder .25 .60
413 Tim Gleason .25 .60
414 Maxim Lapierre .25 .60
415 Ray Emery .30 .75
416 Michael Del Zotto .25 .60
417 Zac Dalpe .25 .60
418 Mathieu Perreault .25 .60
419 Cal Clutterbuck .25 .60
420 Taylor Pyatt .25 .60
421 Daniel Briere .40 1.00
422 Jonathan Bernier .30 .75
423 Mike Ribeiro .25 .60
424 Manny Malhotra .30 .75
425 Kris Versteeg .25 .60
426 Dustin Penner .30 .75
427 Tyler Kennedy .25 .60
428 Thomas Vanek .30 .75
429 Loui Eriksson .25 .60
430 Brenden Morrow .30 .75
431 Ben Scrivens .30 .75
432 Mason Raymond .25 .60
433 Mikhail Grabovski .25 .60
434 Daniel Carcillo .25 .60
435 Tim Thomas .40 1.00
436 Maxime Talbot .25 .60
437 Daniel Alfredsson .40 1.00
438 Shawn Horcoff .25 .60
439 Ryane Clowe .25 .60
440 Valtteri Filppula .25 .60
441 David Clarkson .25 .60
442 Ilya Bryzgalov .40 1.00
443 Nathan Gerbe .25 .60
444 Karri Ramo .30 .75
445 Reilly Smith .40 1.00
446 Nino Niederreiter .25 .60
447 Steve Downie .25 .60
448 Matt Moulson .25 .60
449 Stephen Weiss .30 .75
450 Nathan Horton .40 1.00
451 Devin Setoguchi .30 .75
452 David Perron .30 .75
453 Jaromir Jagr 1.25 3.00
454 Clarke MacArthur .25 .60
455 Jakob Silfverberg .25 .60

2013-14 Select Cracked Ice Toronto Spring Expo

*405-455 VETS: 1.2X TO 3X BASIC CARDS
*356-404 ROOKIES: .5X TO 1.2X BASIC RC

2013-14 Select Prizms

*VETS: 1.2X TO 3X BASIC CARDS
*ROOKIES: .5X TO 1.2X BASIC RC
*ROOK.AU/99: .5X TO 1.2X AU RC/299-399
*ROOK.AU/99: .4X TO 1X AU RC/99-199
49 Nicklas Backstrom 1.25 3.00
297 Vladimir Tarasenko AU 50.00 100.00

2013-14 Select Cornerstone

*PRIZM/25: 1.5X TO 4X BASIC INSERTS
C1 Sidney Crosby 3.00 8.00
C2 Alex Ovechkin 3.00 8.00
C3 Claude Giroux .75 2.00
C4 Milan Lucic .75 2.00
C5 Taylor Hall .75 2.00
C6 Nazem Kadri 1.00 2.50
C7 Steven Stamkos 1.50 4.00
C8 Pavel Datsyuk 1.25 3.00
C9 Jonathan Toews 1.25 3.00
C10 Gabriel Landeskog 1.00 2.50
C11 Oliver Ekman-Larsson .75 2.00
C12 Adam Henrique .60 1.50
C13 Eric Staal 1.00 2.50
C14 John Tavares 1.25 3.00
C15 Erik Karlsson 1.00 2.50
C16 Alex Pietrangelo .60 1.50
C17 Henrik Sedin 1.00 2.50
C18 Ryan Getzlaf .75 2.00
C19 Anze Kopitar 1.25 3.00
C20 Patrick Marleau .75 2.00
C21 Evander Kane .75 2.00
C22 Zach Parise .75 2.00
C23 Jonathan Huberdeau 2.00 5.00
C24 Max Pacioretty .75 2.00
C25 Thomas Vanek .60 1.50

2013-14 Select Double Strike

*PRIZM/25: 1.5X TO 4X BASIC INSERTS
DS1 David Backes .50 1.25
DS2 Patrice Bergeron 1.00 2.50
DS3 Dustin Brown .75 2.00
DS4 Ryan Callahan .50 1.25

DS5 Pavel Datsyuk 1.25 3.00
DS6 Marian Hossa .75 2.00
DS7 Jonathan Toews 1.25 3.00
DS8 Ryan Kesler .75 2.00
DS9 Doug Gilmour 1.00 2.50
DS10 Steve Yzerman 2.00 5.00
DS11 Zdeno Chara .75 2.00
DS12 Erik Karlsson 1.00 2.50
DS13 Duncan Keith .60 1.50
DS14 Niklas Kronwall .60 1.50
DS15 Kris Letang 1.00 2.50
DS16 Alex Pietrangelo .60 1.50
DS17 P.K. Subban 1.00 2.50
DS18 Shea Weber .60 1.50
DS19 Nicklas Lidstrom .75 2.00
DS20 Al MacInnis 1.00 2.50
DS21 Martin Brodeur 2.00 5.00
DS22 Mike Smith .75 2.00
DS23 Ed Belfour .75 2.00
DS24 Ron Hextall .75 2.00
DS25 Marty Turco .75 2.00

2013-14 Select Fire on Ice Rookies

*BLUE: .4X TO 1X BASIC INSERTS
*FALL EXPO/35: 1X TO 2.5X BASIC INSERTS
*PRIZM/35: 1X TO 2.5X BASIC INSERTS
*PRIZM BLUE/25: 1.2X TO 3X BASIC INSERTS
*PRIZM GREEN/25: 1.2X TO 3X BASIC INSERTS
*PRIZM RED/25: 1.2X TO 3X BASIC INSERTS
FR1 Emerson Etem 1.25 3.00
FR2 Viktor Fasth 1.25 3.00
FR3 Dougie Hamilton 2.00 5.00
FR4 Mikhail Grigorenko .75 2.00
FR5 Mark Cundari .75 2.00
FR6 Ryan Murphy 1.25 3.00
FR7 Calvin Pickard 1.50 4.00
FR8 Alex Chiasson 1.25 3.00
FR9 Jack Campbell 3.00 8.00
FR10 Damien Brunner 1.00 2.50
FR11 Danny DeKeyser 1.50 4.00
FR12 Justin Schultz 1.25 3.00
FR13 Nail Yakupov 2.50 6.00
FR14 Jonathan Huberdeau 3.00 8.00
FR15 Drew Shore 1.00 2.50
FR16 Nick Bjugstad 1.50 4.00
FR17 Tyler Toffoli 2.50 6.00
FR18 Jonas Brodin 1.50 4.00
FR19 Mikael Granlund 2.00 5.00
FR20 Alex Galchenyuk 3.00 8.00
FR21 Brendan Gallagher 3.00 8.00
FR22 Jarred Tinordi 1.25 3.00
FR23 Nathan Beaulieu .75 2.00
FR24 Austin Watson 1.00 2.50
FR25 Filip Forsberg 4.00 10.00
FR26 Thomas Hickey 1.00 2.50
FR27 J.T. Miller 3.00 8.00
FR28 Jean-Gabriel Pageau 1.25 3.00
FR29 Cory Conacher .75 2.00
FR30 Scott Laughton 1.50 4.00
FR31 Tye McGinn 1.25 3.00
FR32 Beau Bennett 1.50 4.00
FR33 Matt Irwin 1.00 2.50
FR34 Vladimir Tarasenko 3.00 8.00
FR35 Radko Gudas 1.25 3.00
FR36 Alex Killorn 2.00 5.00
FR37 Leo Komarov 1.25 3.00
FR38 Jordan Schroeder 1.25 3.00
FR39 Tom Wilson 2.50 6.00
FR40 Zach Redmond 1.00 2.50

2013-14 Select Fire on Ice Stars

*BLUE: .4X TO 1X BASIC INSERTS
*PRIZM/35: 1X TO 2.5X BASIC INSERTS
*PRIZM BLUE/25: 1.2X TO 3X BASIC INSERTS
*PRIZM GREEN/25: 1.2X TO 3X BASIC INSERTS
*FALL EXPO/35: 1X TO 2.5X BASIC INSERTS
*PRIZM RED/25: 1.2X TO 3X BASIC INSERTS
FS1 Corey Perry 3.00 8.00
FS2 Teemu Selanne 4.00 10.00
FS3 Patrice Bergeron 2.50 6.00
FS4 Tuukka Rask 2.50 6.00
FS5 Zdeno Chara 2.00 5.00
FS6 Ryan Miller 2.00 5.00
FS7 Mike Cammalleri 1.50 4.00
FS8 Eric Staal 2.50 6.00
FS9 Jonathan Toews 3.00 8.00
FS10 Patrick Kane 4.00 10.00
FS11 Gabriel Landeskog 2.50 6.00
FS12 Henrik Zetterberg 2.50 6.00
FS13 Pavel Datsyuk 3.00 8.00
FS14 Sam Gagner 1.25 3.00
FS15 Taylor Hall 2.00 5.00
FS16 Jonathan Quick 2.50 6.00
FS17 Anze Kopitar 3.00 8.00
FS18 Zach Parise 2.00 5.00
FS19 Carey Price 4.00 10.00
FS20 P.K. Subban 2.50 6.00
FS21 Shea Weber 1.50 4.00
FS22 Pekka Rinne 2.00 5.00
FS23 Martin Brodeur 5.00 12.00
FS24 John Tavares 3.00 8.00
FS25 Henrik Lundqvist 5.00 12.00
FS26 Erik Karlsson 2.50 6.00
FS27 Claude Giroux 2.00 5.00
FS28 Sidney Crosby 8.00 20.00
FS29 Evgeni Malkin 4.00 10.00
FS30 Logan Couture 2.50 6.00
FS31 Alex Pietrangelo 1.50 4.00
FS32 Steven Stamkos 4.00 10.00
FS33 Martin St. Louis 2.00 5.00
FS34 Vincent Lecavalier 2.00 5.00
FS35 Phil Kessel 2.00 5.00
FS36 Joffrey Lupul 1.25 3.00
FS37 Henrik Sedin 2.50 6.00
FS38 Daniel Sedin 2.50 6.00
FS39 Alex Ovechkin 8.00 20.00
FS40 Andrew Ladd 1.25 3.00

2013-14 Select Freezers

*PRIZM/25: 1.2X TO 3X BASIC INSERTS
F1 Mike Richter 2.00 5.00
F2 Curtis Joseph 2.50 6.00
F3 Patrick Roy 5.00 12.00
F4 Ron Hextall 2.00 5.00
F5 John Vanbiesbrouck 2.00 5.00
F6 Martin Brodeur 5.00 12.00
F7 Jonathan Quick 2.50 6.00
F8 Jimmy Howard 2.50 6.00
F9 Henrik Lundqvist 5.00 12.00
F10 James Reimer 2.00 5.00
F11 Tuukka Rask 2.50 6.00
F12 Cam Ward 2.00 5.00
F13 Pekka Rinne 2.00 5.00
F14 Ryan Miller 2.00 5.00
F15 Carey Price 4.00 10.00
F16 Marc-Andre Fleury 4.00 10.00
F17 Corey Crawford 2.50 6.00
F18 Cory Schneider 2.00 5.00
F19 Sergei Bobrovsky 3.00 8.00
F20 Jacob Markstrom 2.00 5.00
F21 Jake Allen 2.00 5.00
F22 Darcy Kuemper 4.00 10.00
F23 Petr Mrazek 4.00 10.00
F24 Jack Campbell 5.00 12.00
F25 Viktor Fasth 2.00 5.00

2013-14 Select Future

*PRIZM/25: 1.2X TO 3X BASIC INSERTS
SF1 Nazem Kadri 2.50 6.00
SF2 Alex Killorn 3.00 8.00
SF3 Jake Allen 2.00 5.00
SF4 Vladimir Tarasenko 2.50 6.00
SF5 Mika Zibanejad 2.50 6.00
SF6 Jean-Gabriel Pageau 2.00 5.00
SF7 Emerson Etem 2.00 5.00
SF8 Cory Conacher 1.25 3.00
SF9 Alex Galchenyuk 2.50 6.00
SF10 Brendan Gallagher 2.50 6.00
SF11 Mikael Granlund 1.50 4.00
SF12 Tyler Toffoli 2.00 5.00
SF13 Jonathan Huberdeau 2.50 6.00
SF14 Danny DeKeyser 1.25 3.00
SF15 J.T. Miller 2.50 6.00
SF16 Nail Yakupov 2.00 5.00
SF17 Justin Schultz 1.00 2.50
SF18 Alex Chiasson 1.00 2.50
SF19 Jack Campbell 5.00 12.00
SF20 Gabriel Landeskog 2.50 6.00
SF21 Brandon Saad 1.50 4.00
SF22 Filip Forsberg 3.00 8.00
SF23 Mikhail Grigorenko .60 1.50
SF24 Dougie Hamilton 1.50 4.00
SF25 Mark Scheifele 3.00 8.00

2013-14 Select Honored Selections

*PRIZM/25: 1.2X TO 3X BASIC INSERTS
*FALL EXPO/35: 1X TO 2.5X BASIC INSERTS
HS1 Phil Esposito 3.00 8.00
HS2 Lanny McDonald 2.00 5.00
HS3 Bobby Hull 4.00 10.00
HS4 Stan Mikita 2.50 6.00
HS5 Joe Sakic 4.00 10.00
HS6 Gordie Howe 6.00 15.00
HS7 Steve Yzerman 5.00 12.00
HS8 Mark Messier 4.00 10.00
HS9 Jari Kurri 2.50 6.00
HS10 Marcel Dionne 2.50 6.00
HS11 Jean Beliveau 2.00 5.00
HS12 Guy Lafleur 2.50 6.00
HS13 Patrick Roy 5.00 12.00
HS14 Mike Bossy 2.00 5.00
HS15 Denis Potvin 2.00 5.00
HS16 Bobby Clarke 3.00 8.00
HS17 Mario Lemieux 8.00 20.00
HS18 Brett Hull 4.00 10.00
HS19 Darryl Sittler 2.50 6.00
HS20 Pavel Bure 2.00 5.00

2013-14 Select Rookies Jersey Autographs

*PRIME/50: .8X TO 2X JSY AU/199
*PRIME/50: .6X TO 1.5X JSY AU/99
*PRIME PRZM/25: 1X TO 2.5X JSY AU/199
*PRIME PRZM/25: .8X TO 2X JSY AU/99
*PRIZM/99: .5X TO 1.2X JSY AU/199
*PRIZM/99: .4X TO 1X JSY AU/99
201 Jamie Tardif/199 3.00 8.00
202 Brian Flynn/199 4.00 10.00
204 Michal Jordan/199 3.00 8.00
208 Drew Shore/199 4.00 10.00
215 Ben Street/199 4.00 10.00
217 Michael Sgarbossa/199 5.00 12.00
219 Brian Lashoff/199 4.00 10.00
220 Mark Arcobello/199 5.00 12.00
221 Michael Caruso/199 3.00 8.00
222 Petr Mrazek/199 10.00 25.00
227 Richard Panik/199 5.00 12.00
230 Maxwell Reinhart/199 5.00 12.00
232 Tye McGinn/199 5.00 12.00
233 Antoine Roussel/199 5.00 12.00
234 Eric Gryba/199 4.00 10.00
235 Matt Irwin/199 4.00 10.00
237 Jordan Schroeder/199 5.00 12.00
238 Philipp Grubauer/199 12.00 30.00
239 Zach Redmond/199 4.00 10.00
241 Viktor Fasth/199 5.00 12.00
242 Carl Soderberg/199 10.00 25.00
244 Roman Cervenka/199 4.00 10.00
245 Calvin Pickard/199 6.00 15.00
247 Johan Larsson/199 6.00 15.00
249 Chris Brown/199 3.00 8.00
250 Nick Petrecki/199 3.00 8.00
251 Dmitrij Jaskin/199 5.00 12.00
252 Alex Killorn/199 8.00 20.00
254 Anthony Peluso/199 3.00 8.00
255 Stefan Matteau/199 4.00 10.00
256 Thomas Hickey/199 4.00 10.00
257 Danny DeKeyser/199 6.00 15.00
258 Edward Pasquale/199 3.00 8.00
259 Christian Thomas/199 4.00 10.00
260 Eric Hartzell/199 5.00 12.00
261 Rickard Rakell/199 5.00 12.00
262 Leo Komarov/199 5.00 12.00
263 Sami Vatanen/199 5.00 12.00
264 Cristopher Nilstorp/199 4.00 10.00
265 Mathew Dumba/199 3.00 8.00
266 Jonas Brodin/199 6.00 15.00
267 Michael Kostka/199 4.00 10.00
268 Nicklas Jensen/199 4.00 10.00
269 Emerson Etem/199 5.00 12.00
270 Ryan Spooner/199 5.00 12.00
271 Jamie Oleksiak/199 4.00 10.00
272 Quinton Howden/199 4.00 10.00
273 Ryan Murphy/199 8.00 20.00
274 Charlie Coyle/199 8.00 20.00
275 Jarred Tinordi/199 5.00 12.00
276 Austin Watson/199 6.00 15.00
277 Brock Nelson/199 8.00 20.00
278 Scott Laughton/199 6.00 15.00
279 Beau Bennett/199 6.00 15.00
280 Frederik Andersen/199 12.00 30.00
281 Nathan Beaulieu/199 3.00 8.00
282 J.T. Miller/199 12.00 30.00
283 Mikhail Grigorenko/199 10.00 25.00
284 Nick Bjugstad/199 6.00 15.00
285 Tanner Pearson/199 5.00 12.00
286 Jared Staal/199 4.00 10.00
287 Tom Wilson/199 10.00 25.00
288 Mikael Granlund/199 8.00 20.00
289 Justin Schultz/199 5.00 12.00
290 Tyler Toffoli/199 10.00 25.00
291 Jack Campbell/199 12.00 30.00
292 Filip Forsberg/199 12.00 30.00
293 Dougie Hamilton/199 12.00 30.00
294 Alex Chiasson/199 5.00 12.00
295 Brendan Gallagher/199 12.00 30.00
296 Cory Conacher/199 3.00 8.00
297 Vladimir Tarasenko/99 50.00 100.00
298 Alex Galchenyuk/199 20.00 50.00
299 Jonathan Huberdeau/199 15.00 30.00
300 Nail Yakupov/199 15.00 40.00
301 Nathan MacKinnon/199 100.00 250.00
302 Seth Jones/199 20.00 40.00
303 Valeri Nichuskin/199 10.00 25.00
304 Sean Monahan/199 25.00 50.00
305 Tomas Hertl/199 10.00 25.00
306 Boone Jenner/199 10.00 25.00
307 Ryan Murray/199 6.00 15.00
308 Morgan Rielly/199 12.00 30.00

2013-14 Select Signatures

*PRIZM/25: .6X TO 1.5X BASIC INSERTS
SIBB Brad Boyes SP 4.00 10.00
SIBS Brandon Saad SP 5.00 12.00
SICG Cameron Gaunce 4.00 10.00
SICV Chris Vande Velde 4.00 10.00
SIDO Dylan Olsen SP 4.00 10.00
SIDR Dwayne Roloson 4.00 10.00
SIDW Steve Downie SP 4.00 10.00
SIFY Jeff Petry 6.00 15.00
SIGO Gino Odjick SP 4.00 10.00
SIHM Ben Holmstrom 4.00 10.00
SIJC John Carlson 6.00 15.00
SILM Lane MacDermid EXCH 5.00 12.00
SIMH Matt Hackett 4.00 10.00
SIML Mark Letestu 5.00 12.00
SIMM Maxime Macenauer SP 4.00 10.00
SIMS Mike Santorelli 5.00 12.00
SIMX Max Sauve 4.00 10.00
SIOJ Ondrej Pavelec SP 6.00 15.00
SION Brendon Nash 4.00 10.00
SIOR Ryan O'Reilly 6.00 15.00
SIPH Patric Hornqvist 4.00 10.00
SIRC Roman Cervenka SP 5.00 12.00
SIRL Robin Lehner SP 5.00 12.00
SIRS Ryan Stoa 4.00 10.00
SITC Tyler Cuma SP 5.00 12.00
SITI Scott Timmins 4.00 10.00
SITK Torey Krug 5.00 12.00
SITP Timo Pielmeier 4.00 10.00
SITR Travis Turnbull 5.00 12.00
SIUM Thomas McCollum 5.00 12.00
SIWI Colin Wilson SP 5.00 12.00
SIYS Yann Sauve 4.00 10.00

2013-14 Select Stars Jersey Autographs

*PRIZM/20: .4X TO 1X JSY AU/25
STAG Alex Galchenyuk/25 20.00 50.00
STAM Al MacInnis/25 10.00 25.00
STAN Antti Niemi/25 6.00 15.00
STBB Beau Bennett/25 10.00 25.00
STBG Brendan Gallagher/25 20.00 50.00
STBH Brett Hull/25 15.00 40.00
STBR Bobby Ryan/25 6.00 15.00
STCA Craig Anderson/25 8.00 20.00
STCI David Krejci/25 8.00 20.00
STCP Carey Price/25 15.00 40.00
STCS Cory Schneider/25 8.00 20.00
STDB David Backes/25 5.00 12.00
STDH Dougie Hamilton/25 12.00 30.00
STDZ Michael Del Zotto/25 5.00 12.00
STFP Felix Potvin/25 12.00 30.00
STGL Gabriel Landeskog/25 10.00 25.00
STGX Claude Giroux/25 8.00 20.00
STHL Henrik Lundqvist/25 20.00 50.00
STIK Marian Gaborik/25 8.00 20.00
STJB Jonas Brodin/25 10.00 25.00
STJE Borje Salming/25 8.00 20.00
STJH Jonathan Huberdeau/25 20.00 50.00
STJS Joe Sakic/25 15.00 40.00
STJT John Tavares/25 12.00 30.00
STKP Keith Primeau/25 6.00 15.00
STLC Logan Couture/25 10.00 25.00
STMB Martin Brodeur/25 20.00 50.00
STNY Nail Yakupov/25 15.00 40.00
STOS Chris Chelios/25 8.00 20.00
STOV Alex Ovechkin/25 30.00 80.00
STPK Patrick Kane/25 15.00 40.00
STSO Carl Soderberg/25 8.00 20.00
STST Martin St. Louis/25 8.00 20.00
STSX Marc Staal/25 5.00 12.00
STSZ Justin Schultz/25 8.00 20.00
STTT Tyler Toffoli/25 15.00 40.00
STUD Marcel Dionne/25 10.00 25.00
STVR James van Riemsdyk/25 6.00 15.00
STVT Vladimir Tarasenko/25 20.00 50.00
STWS Jonathan Toews/25 12.00 30.00
STXB Jamie Benn/25 8.00 20.00
STXE Jhonas Enroth/25 8.00 20.00

2013-14 Select Youth Explosion Autographs

*PRIZM/25: .6X TO 1.5X BASIC AU
YEAK Alex Killorn SP 8.00 20.00
YEAL Anders Lee 8.00 20.00
YEAS Andrew Shaw EXCH 3.00 8.00
YECC Cory Conacher SP 3.00 8.00
YECO Colby Cohen 3.00 8.00
YECT Colten Teubert SP 3.00 8.00
YEDV Matt Donovan SP 3.00 8.00
YEFR Matt Fraser 3.00 8.00
YEHT Michael Hutchinson SP 3.00 8.00
YEJD Justin DiBenedetto 3.00 8.00
YEJS Jaden Schwartz SP 6.00 15.00
YEKK Keith Kinkaid SP 3.00 8.00
YEKO Mikhail Grigorenko SP 3.00 8.00
YELB Lance Bouma 3.00 8.00
YELI Leland Irving SP 4.00 10.00
YEMC Mike Connolly 4.00 10.00
YEMZ Mika Zibanejad SP 6.00 15.00
YENH Ryan Nugent-Hopkins SP 6.00 15.00
YEPC Philippe Cornet SP 3.00 8.00
YEPI Chet Pickard SP 3.00 8.00
YEPM Patrick Maroon 3.00 8.00
YERD Raphael Diaz SP 3.00 8.00
YERG Ryan Garbutt 3.00 8.00
YERH Ryan Hamilton 3.00 8.00
YESE Stefan Elliott 4.00 10.00
YETJ Tyler Johnson 10.00 25.00
YEWN J.T. Brown 3.00 8.00
YEZD Zac Dalpe 3.00 8.00

1992-93 Senators Team Issue

COMPLETE SET (15) 6.00 15.00
1 Jamie Baker .40 1.00
2 Daniel Berthiaume .60 1.50
3 Neil Brady .40 1.00
4 Ken Hammond .40 1.00
5 Dave Hannan .40 1.00
6 Jody Hull .40 1.00
7 Mark Lamb .40 1.00
8 Darcy Loewen .40 1.00
9 Norm Maciver .40 1.00
10 Brad Marsh .60 1.50
11 Andrew McBain .40 1.00
12 Mike Peluso .50 1.25
13 Darren Rumble .40 1.00
14 Brad Shaw .40 1.00
15 Sylvain Turgeon .40 1.00

1993-94 Senators Kraft Sheets

COMPLETE SET (27) 60.00 150.00
1 Dave Archibald/3500 2.00 5.00
2 Craig Billington/6500 2.50 6.00
3 Rick Bowness CO/6500 2.00 5.00
4 Robert Burakovsky/1500 3.00 8.00
5 Alexandre Daigle/6500 2.00 5.00
6 Pavol Demitra/1500 4.00 10.00
7 Gord Dineen/3500 2.00 5.00
8 Dmitri Filimonov/1500 3.00 8.00
9 Brian Glynn/1500 3.00 8.00
10 Bill Huard/1500 3.00 8.00
11 Jarmo Kekalainen/1500 3.00 8.00
12 Bob Kudelski/1500 3.00 8.00
13 Mark Lamb/1500 3.00 8.00
14 Darcy Loewen/3500 2.00 5.00
15 Norm Maciver/3500 2.00 5.00
16 Darrin Madeley/1500 3.00 8.00
17 Troy Mallette/3500 2.00 5.00
18 Brad Marsh/6500 3.00 8.00
19 Dave McLlwain/3500 2.00 5.00
20 Darren Rumble/1500 3.00 8.00
21 Vladimir Ruzicka/1500 3.00 8.00
22 Brad Shaw/6500 2.00 5.00
23 Graeme Townshend/1500 3.00 8.00
24 Sylvain Turgeon/6500 2.50 6.00
25 Dennis Vial/1500 3.00 8.00
26 Alexei Yashin/6500 2.00 5.00
27 Team Photo/12500 2.00 5.00
ALB Album 6.00 15.00
NNO Team Photo 2.00 5.00

1994-95 Senators Team Issue

COMPLETE SET (28) 6.00 15.00
1 Dave Archibald .20 .50
2 Don Beaupre .30 .75
3 Radim Bicanek .20 .50
4 Craig Billington .30 .75
5 Claude Boivin .20 .50
6 Radek Bonk .40 1.00
7 Phil Bourque .20 .50
8 Rick Bowness CO .20 .50
9 Randy Cunneyworth .20 .50
10 Chris Dahlquist .20 .50
11 Alexandre Daigle .40 1.00
12 Pat Elynuik .20 .50
13 Rob Gaudreau .20 .50
14 Sean Hill .20 .50
15 Bill Huard .20 .50
16 Kerry Huffman .20 .50
17 Scott Levins .20 .50
18 Norm Maciver .20 .50
19 Darrin Madeley .30 .75
20 Troy Mallette .20 .50
21 Brad Marsh CO .30 .75
22 Dave McLlwain .20 .50
23 Troy Murray .20 .50
24 Stanislav Neckar .25 .60
25 Jim Paek .20 .50
26 Sylvain Turgeon .20 .50
27 Dennis Vial .20 .50
28 Alexei Yashin .75 2.00

1995-96 Senators Team Issue

COMPLETE SET (24) 6.00 15.00
1 Daniel Alfredsson 1.25 3.00
2 Dave Archibald .20 .50
3 Mike Bales .25 .60
4 Don Beaupre .30 .75
5 Radek Bonk .25 .60
6 Tom Chorske .20 .50
7 Randy Cunneyworth .20 .50
8 Alexandre Daigle .20 .50
9 Ted Drury .20 .50
10 Steve Duchesne .25 .60
11 Rob Gaudreau .20 .50
12 Sean Hill .20 .50
13 Kerry Huffman .20 .50
14 Scott Levins .20 .50
15 Troy Mallette .20 .50
16 Brad Marsh .40 1.00
17 Trent McCleary .20 .50
18 Jaroslav Modry .20 .50
19 Frank Musil .20 .50
20 Stan Neckar .25 .60
21 Martin Straka .40 1.00
22 Antti Tormanen .20 .50
23 Dennis Vial .20 .50
24 Alexei Yashin .40 1.00

1996-97 Senators Pizza Hut

COMPLETE SET (32) 6.00 15.00
1 Daniel Alfredsson .75 2.00
2 Radek Bonk .30 .75
3 Tom Chorske .20 .50
4 Randy Cunneyworth .20 .50
5 Andreas Dackell .20 .50
6 Alexandre Daigle .20 .50
7 Steve Duchesne .30 .75
8 Bruce Gardiner .20 .50
9 Dave Hannan .20 .50
10 Sean Hill .20 .50
11 Denny Lambert .20 .50
12 Janne Laukkanen .30 .75
13 Jacques Martin CO .08 .25
14 Shawn Mceachern .20 .50
15 Frank Musil .20 .50
16 Phil Myre .20 .50
17 Stan Neckar .20 .50
18 Christer Olsson .20 .50
19 Perry Pearn ACO .08 .25
20 Lance Pitlick .20 .50
21 Craig Ramsay .20 .50
22 Wade Redden .40 1.00
23 Damian Rhodes .40 1.00
24 Ron Tugnutt .40 1.00
25 Shaun Van Allen .20 .50
26 Dennis Vial .20 .50
27 Alexei Yashin .40 1.00
28 Jason York .20 .50
29 Jason Zent .20 .50
30 Sergei Zholtok .20 .50

1998-99 Senators Team Issue

COMPLETE SET (26) 6.00 15.00
1 Daniel Alfredsson .40 1.00
2 Magnus Arvedson .20 .50
3 Bill Berg .20 .50
4 Radek Bonk .20 .50
5 Andreas Dackell .20 .50
6 Bruce Gardiner .20 .50
7 Marian Hossa .75 2.00
8 Andreas Johansson .20 .50
9 Igor Kravchuk .20 .50
10 Janne Laukkanen .20 .50
11 Jacques Martin CO .20 .50
12 Steve Martins .20 .50
13 Shawn McEachern .20 .50
14 Chris Murray .20 .50
15 Chris Phillips .20 .50
16 Lance Pitlick .20 .50
17 Vaclav Prospal .20 .50
18 Wade Redden .40 1.00
19 Damian Rhodes .30 .75
20 Sami Salo .20 .50
21 Patrick Traverse .20 .50
22 Ron Tugnutt .40 1.00
23 Shaun Van Allen .20 .50
24 Alexei Yashin .20 .50
25 Ottawa Senators .20 .50
26 Spartacat MASCOT .08 .25

1999-00 Senators Team Issue

COMPLETE SET (26) 8.00 20.00
1 Daniel Alfredsson .40 1.00
2 Magnus Arvedson .20 .50
3 Radek Bonk .30 .75
4 Andreas Dackell .20 .50
5 Kevin Dineen .20 .50
6 Mike Fisher .40 1.00
7 Bruce Gardiner .20 .50
8 Marian Hossa 2.00 5.00
9 Joe Juneau .20 .50
10 Igor Kravchuk .20 .50
11 Patrick Lalime .60 1.50
12 Janne Laukkanen .20 .50
13 Shawn McEachern .30 .75
14 Chris Phillips .30 .75
15 Vaclav Prospal .20 .50
16 Wade Redden .40 1.00
17 Andre Roy .20 .50
18 Sami Salo .20 .50
19 Patrick Traverse .20 .50
20 Ron Tugnutt .40 1.00
21 Shaun Van Allen .20 .50
22 Jason York .20 .50
23 Rob Zamuner .20 .50
24 Jacques Martin HCO .08 .25
25 Spartacat MASCOT .02 .10
26 Team Photo .20 .50

2000-01 Senators Team Issue

1 Daniel Alfredsson .40 1.00
2 Magnus Arvedson .20 .50
3 Radek Bonk .30 .75
4 Andreas Dackell .20 .50
5 Mike Fisher .30 .75
6 Colin Forbes .20 .50
7 Martin Havlat 1.60 4.00
8 Marian Hossa 2.00 5.00
9 Jani Hurme .60 1.50
10 Patrick Lalime .60 1.50
11 Jacques Martin CO .10 .25
12 Shawn McEachern .20 .50
13 Roger Neilson ACO .10 .25
14 Perry Pearn ACO .10 .25
15 Ricard Persson .20 .50
16 Chris Phillips .20 .50
17 Vaclav Prospal .20 .50
18 Karel Rachunek .20 .50
19 Wade Redden .30 .75
20 Jamie Rivers .20 .50
21 Andre Roy .30 .75
22 Sami Salo .20 .50
23 Spartacat MASCOT .04 .10
24 Alexei Yashin .40 1.00
25 Jason York .20 .50
26 Rob Zamuner .20 .50

2001-02 Senators Team Issue

COMPLETE SET (29) 5.00 12.00
1 Daniel Alfredsson .60 1.50
2 Magnus Arvedson .20 .50
3 Radek Bonk .20 .50
4 Zdeno Chara .60 1.50
5 Ivan Ciernik .30 .75
6 Mike Fisher .30 .75
7 Martin Havlat 1.25 3.00
8 Chris Herperger .20 .50
9 Shane Hnidy .20 .50
10 Marian Hossa .75 2.00
11 Jani Hurme .60 1.50
12 Don Jackson ACO .04 .10
13 Patrick Lalime .40 1.00
14 Curtis Leschyshyn .20 .50
15 Jacques Martin CO .04 .10
16 Shawn McEachern .20 .50
17 Bill Muckalt .20 .50
18 Chris Neil .40 1.00
19 Roger Neilson ACO .04 .10
20 Perry Pearn ACO .04 .10
21 Ricard Persson .20 .50
22 Chris Phillips .20 .50
23 Karel Rachunek .20 .50
24 Wade Redden .30 .75
25 Andre Roy .30 .75
26 Sami Salo .20 .50
27 Todd White .20 .50
28 SpartaCat .04 .10
29 Autograph Card .04 .10

2002-03 Senators Team Issue

COMPLETE SET (15) 12.00 20.00
1 Daniel Alfredsson .75 2.00
2 Magnus Arvedson .40 1.00
3 Radek Bonk .40 1.00
4 Zdeno Chara .60 1.50
5 Mike Fisher .60 1.50
6 Martin Havlat 1.25 3.00
7 Marian Hossa 1.25 3.00
8 Jody Hull .40 1.00
9 Patrick Lalime .60 1.50
10 Curtis Leschyshyn .40 1.00
11 Chris Neil .40 1.00
12 Chris Phillips .40 1.00
13 Martin Prusek .60 1.50
14 Wade Redden .60 1.50
15 Anton Volchenkov .40 1.00

2003-04 Senators Postcards

COMPLETE SET (28) 10.00 20.00
1 Brian Pothier .20 .50
2 Zdeno Chara .40 1.00
3 Chris Phillips .20 .50
4 Wade Redden .40 1.00
5 Curtis Leschyshyn .20 .50
6 Martin Havlat .60 1.50
7 Daniel Alfredsson .75 2.00
8 Mike Fisher .40 1.00
9 Radek Bonk .20 .50
10 Peter Schaefer .20 .50
11 Jody Hull .20 .50
12 Marian Hossa .60 1.50
13 Petr Schastlivy .20 .50
14 Bryan Smolinski .20 .50
15 Shaun Van Allen .20 .50
16 Karel Rachunek .20 .50
17 Anton Volchenkov .20 .50
18 Chris Neil .20 .50
19 Vaclav Varada .20 .50
20 Todd White .20 .50
21 Martin Prusek .30 .75
22 Shane Hnidy .20 .50
23 Jason Spezza 1.25 3.00
24 Patrick Lalime .40 1.00
25 Jacques Martin CO .10 .25
26 Don Jackson ACO .10 .25
27 Perry Pearn ACO .10 .25
28 Spartacat MASCOT .04 .10

2006-07 Senators Postcards

3 Daniel Alfredsson 1.25 3.00
4 Joe Corvo .40 1.00
5 Denis Hamel .40 1.00
6 Dany Heatley 1.25 3.00
7 Chris Kelly .40 1.00
8 Brian McGrattan .75 2.00
9 Andrei Meszaros .40 1.00
10 Chris Phillips .40 1.00
11 Jason Spezza 1.25 3.00
12 Peter Schaefer .40 1.00
13 Christoph Schubert .40 1.00
14 Wade Redden .75 2.00
15 Logo Card .10 .25

1972-73 7-Eleven Slurpee Cups WHA

COMPLETE SET (20) 125.00 250.00
1 Norm Beaudin 5.00 10.00
2 Chris Bordeleau 5.00 10.00
3 Carl Brewer 5.00 10.00
4 Wayne Carleton 6.00 12.00
5 Gerry Cheevers 12.50 25.00
6 Wayne Connelly 7.50 15.00
7 Jean-Guy Gendron 5.00 10.00
8 Ted Green 5.00 10.00
9 Al Hamilton 5.00 10.00
10 Jim Harrison 5.00 10.00
11 Bobby Hull 25.00 50.00
12 Andre Lacroix 6.00 12.00
13 Danny Lawson 5.00 10.00
14 John McKenzie 5.00 10.00
15 Jim Mcleod 5.00 10.00
16 Jack Norris 5.00 10.00
17 John Schella 5.00 10.00
18 J.C. Tremblay 7.50 15.00
19 Ron Ward 5.00 10.00
20 Jim Watson 5.00 10.00

1984-85 7-Eleven Discs

COMPLETE SET (60) 50.00 125.00
1 Ray Bourque 7 2.00 5.00
2 Rick Middleton 16 .60 1.50
3 Tom Barrasso 30 1.00 2.50
4 Gilbert Perreault 11 .75 2.00
5 Rejean Lemelin 31 .60 1.50
6 Lanny McDonald 9 1.00 2.50
7 Paul Reinhart 23 .40 1.00
8 Doug Risebrough 8 .40 1.00
9 Denis Savard 18 1.00 2.50
10 Al Secord 20 .40 1.00
11 Steve Yzerman 19 6.00 15.00
12 Tiger Williams 55 .60 1.50
13 Glenn Anderson 9 .75 2.00
14 Paul Coffey 7 2.00 5.00
15 Michel Goulet 16 .75 2.00
16 Wayne Gretzky 99 8.00 20.00
17 Charlie Huddy 22 .40 1.00
18 Pat Hughes 16 .40 1.00
19 Jari Kurri 17 1.25 3.00
20 Kevin Lowe 4 .40 1.00
21 Mark Messier 11 3.00 8.00
22 Ron Francis 10 1.50 4.00
23 Sylvain Turgeon 16 .40 1.00
24 Marcel Dionne 16 .75 2.00
25 Dave Taylor 18 .60 1.50
26 Brian Bellows 23 .40 1.00
27 Dino Ciccarelli 20 .60 1.50
28 Harold Snepsts 28 .60 1.50
29 Bob Gainey 23 .75 2.00
30 Larry Robinson 19 1.00 2.50
31 Mel Bridgman 18 .40 1.00
32 Chico Resch 1 .60 1.50
33 Mike Bossy 22 1.25 3.00
34 Bryan Trottier 19 1.00 2.50
35 Barry Beck 5 .40 1.00
36 Don Maloney 12 .40 1.00
37 Tim Kerr 12 .60 1.50
38 Darryl Sittler 27 1.00 2.50
39 Mike Bullard 22 .40 1.00
40 Rick Kehoe 17 .60 1.50
41 Peter Stastny 26 1.25 3.00
42 Bernie Federko 24 .60 1.50
43 Rob Ramage 5 .40 1.00
44 John Anderson 10 .40 1.00
45 Bill Derlago 19 .40 1.00
46 Gary Nylund 2 .40 1.00
47 Rick Vaive 22 .40 1.00
48 Richard Brodeur 35 .60 1.50
49 Gary Lupul 7 .40 1.00
50 Darcy Rota 18 .40 1.00
51 Stan Smyl 12 .60 1.50
52 Tony Tanti 9 .40 1.00
53 Mike Gartner 11 1.25 3.00
54 Rod Langway 5 .40 1.00
55 Scott Arniel 11 .40 1.00
56 Dave Babych 44 .40 1.00
57 Laurie Boschman 16 .40 1.00
58 Dale Hawerchuk 10 1.00 2.50
59 Paul MacLean 15 .40 1.00
60 Brian Mullen 19 .40 1.00
NNO Wayne Gretzky Large 10.00 25.00
NNO Paper Checklist Sheet 2.00 5.00

1985-86 7-Eleven Credit Cards

COMPLETE SET (25) 14.00 35.00
1 Ray Bourque and Rick Middleton .75 2.00
2 Tom Barrasso Gilbert Perreault .60 1.50
3 Paul Reinhart Lanny McDonald .40 1.00
4 Denis Savard Doug Wilson .60 1.50
5 Ron Duguay Steve Yzerman 3.00 8.00
6 Paul Coffey Jari Kurri 1.00 2.50
7 Ron Francis Mike Liut .75 2.00
8 Marcel Dionne Dave Taylor .50 1.25
9 Brian Bellows Dino Ciccarelli .60 1.50
10 Larry Robinson Guy Carbonneau .60 1.50
11 Mel Bridgman Chico Resch .30 .75
12 Mike Bossy Bryan Trottier 1.00 2.50
13 Reijo Ruotsalainen Barry Beck .30 .75
14 Tim Kerr Mark Howe .30 .75
15 Mario Lemieux Mike Bullard 8.00 20.00
16 Peter Stastny Michel Goulet 1.00 2.50
17 Rob Ramage Brian Sutter .30 .75
18 Rick Vaive Borje Salming .40 1.00
19 Patrik Sundstrom Stan Smyl .30 .75
20 Rod Langway Mike Gartner .50 1.25
21 Dale Hawerchuk Paul MacLean .40 1.00
22 Stanley Cup Winners .30 .75
23 Prince of Wales Trophy Winners .30 .75
24 Clarence S. Campbell Bowl Winners .30 .75
25 Title Card .08 .25

1991-92 Sharks Sports Action

COMPLETE SET (22) 4.00 10.00
1 Perry Anderson .20 .50
2 Perry Berezan .20 .50
3 Steve Bozek .20 .50
4 Dean Evason .20 .50
5 Pat Falloon .30 .75
6 Paul Fenton .20 .50
7 Link Gaetz .20 .50
8 Jeff Hackett .40 1.00
9 Ken Hammond .20 .50
10 Brian Hayward .30 .75
11 Tony Hrkac .20 .50
12 Kelly Kisio .25 .60
13 Brian Lawton .20 .50
14 Pat MacLeod .20 .50
15 Bob McGill .20 .50
16 Brian Mullen .20 .50
17 Jarmo Myllys .25 .60
18 Wayne Presley .20 .50
19 Neil Wilkinson .25 .60
20 Doug Wilson .40 1.00
21 Rob Zettler .20 .50
22 San Jose Sharks .30 .75

1997 Sharks Fleer All-Star Sheet

9 Sharks Complete Sheet
Doug Bodger Fleer Picks
Kelly Hrudey Metal Universe
Al Iafrate Metal Universe
Bernie Nicholls Metal Universe
Owen Nolan Fleer
Marcus Ragnarsson Fleer
Chris Terreri Fleer
Alexei Yegorov Fleer Picks 1.50 4.00

2001-02 Sharks Postcards
1 Adam Graves .75 2.00
2 Vincent Damphousse .40 1.00
3 Matt Bradley .40 1.00
4 Brad Stuart .40 1.00
5 Owen Nolan .75 2.00
6 Patrick Marleau .75 2.00
7 Gary Suter .40 1.00
8 Niklas Sundstrom .40 1.00
9 Marco Sturm .40 1.00
10 Mike Ricci .40 1.00
11 Marcus Ragnarsson .40 1.00
12 Scott Thornton .40 1.00
13 Scott Hannan .40 1.00
14 Todd Harvey .40 1.00
15 Bryan Marchment .40 1.00
16 Teemu Selanne 1.25 3.00

2002-03 Sharks Team Issue
COMPLETE SET 4.00 10.00
1 Vincent Damphousse .40 1.00
2 Adam Graves .40 1.00
3 Patrick Marleau .40 1.00
4 Evgeni Nabokov .75 2.00
5 Mike Rathje .40 1.00
6 Mike Ricci .40 1.00
7 Teemu Selanne 1.25 3.00
8 Marco Sturm .40 1.00

2003-04 Sharks Postcards
COMPLETE SET 5.00 12.00
1 Jonathan Cheechoo 1.25 3.00
2 Vincent Damphousse .40 1.00
3 Rob Davidson .40 1.00
4 Nils Ekman .40 1.00
5 Jim Fahey .40 1.00
6 Scott Hannan .40 1.00
7 Todd Harvey .40 1.00
8 Alexander Korolyuk .40 1.00
9 Patrick Marleau .75 2.00
10 Alyn McCauley .40 1.00
11 Kyle McLaren .40 1.00
12 Evgeni Nabokov .75 2.00
13 Tom Preissing .40 1.00
14 Wayne Primeau .40 1.00
15 Mike Rathje .40 1.00
16 Mike Ricci .40 1.00
17 Brad Stuart .40 1.00
18 Marco Sturm .40 1.00
19 Scott Thornton .40 1.00

1960-61 Shirriff Coins
COMPLETE SET (120) 250.00 500.00
1 Johnny Bower 5.00 10.00
2 Dick Duff 2.50 5.00
3 Carl Brewer 2.50 5.00
4 Red Kelly 5.00 10.00
5 Tim Horton 7.50 15.00
6 Allan Stanley 2.50 5.00
7 Bob Baun 2.50 5.00
8 Billy Harris 1.50 3.00
9 George Armstrong 3.00 6.00
10 Ron Stewart 1.50 3.00
11 Bert Olmstead 2.50 5.00
12 Frank Mahovlich 7.50 15.00
13 Bob Pulford 2.50 5.00
14 Gary Edmundson 1.50 3.00
15 Johnny Wilson 1.50 3.00
16 Larry Regan 1.50 3.00
17 Gerry James 2.00 4.00
18 Rudy Migay 1.50 3.00
19 Gerry Ehman 1.50 3.00
20 Punch Imlach CO 2.00 4.00
21 Jacques Plante 12.50 25.00
22 Dickie Moore 3.00 6.00
23 Don Marshall 1.50 3.00
24 Albert Langlois 1.50 3.00
25 Tom Johnson 2.50 5.00
26 Doug Harvey 5.00 10.00
27 Phil Goyette 1.50 3.00
28 Boom Boom Geoffrion 6.00 12.00
29 Marcel Bonin 1.50 3.00
30 Jean Beliveau 10.00 20.00
31 Ralph Backstrom 2.00 4.00
32 Andre Pronovost 1.50 3.00
33 Claude Provost 2.00 4.00
34 Henri Richard 7.50 15.00
35 Jean-Guy Talbot 2.00 4.00
36 J.C. Tremblay 2.00 4.00
37 Bob Turner 1.50 3.00
38 Bill Hicke 1.50 3.00
39 Charlie Hodge 4.00 8.00
40 Toe Blake CO 2.50 5.00
41 Terry Sawchuk 10.00 20.00
42 Gordie Howe 25.00 50.00
43 John McKenzie 1.50 3.00
44 Alex Delvecchio 5.00 10.00
45 Norm Ullman 3.00 6.00
46 Jack McIntyre 1.50 3.00
47 Barry Cullen 2.00 4.00
48 Val Fonteyne 1.50 3.00
49 Warren Godfrey 1.50 3.00
50 Pete Goegan 1.50 3.00
51 Gerry Melnyk 1.50 3.00
52 Marc Reaume 1.50 3.00
53 Gary Aldcorn 1.50 3.00
54 Len Lunde 1.50 3.00
55 Murray Oliver 1.50 3.00
56 Marcel Pronovost 2.50 5.00
57 Howie Glover 1.50 3.00
58 Gerry Odrowski 1.50 3.00
59 Parker MacDonald 1.50 3.00
60 Sid Abel CO 2.50 5.00
61 Glenn Hall 6.00 12.00
62 Ed Litzenberger 2.00 4.00
63 Bobby Hull 20.00 40.00
64 Tod Sloan 1.50 3.00
65 Murray Balfour 1.50 3.00
66 Pierre Pilote 2.50 5.00
67 Al Arbour 2.50 5.00
68 Earl Balfour 1.50 3.00
69 Eric Nesterenko 2.00 4.00
70 Ken Wharram 2.50 5.00
71 Stan Mikita 12.50 25.00
72 Ab McDonald 1.50 3.00
73 Elmer Vasko 2.00 4.00
74 Dollard St.Laurent 2.00 4.00
75 Ron Murphy 1.50 3.00
76 Jack Evans 1.50 3.00
77 Bill Hay 1.50 3.00
78 Reg Fleming 2.00 4.00
79 Cecil Hoekstra 1.50 3.00
80 Tommy Ivan CO 2.00 4.00
81 Jack McCartan 4.00 8.00
82 Red Sullivan 1.50 3.00
83 Camille Henry 2.00 4.00
84 Larry Popein 1.50 3.00
85 John Hanna 1.50 3.00
86 Harry Howell 2.50 5.00
87 Eddie Shack 5.00 10.00
88 Irv Spencer 1.50 3.00
89 Andy Bathgate 3.00 6.00
90 Bill Gadsby 2.50 5.00
91 Andy Hebenton 1.50 3.00
92 Earl Ingarfield 1.50 3.00
93 Don Johns 1.50 3.00
94 Dave Balon 1.50 3.00
95 Jim Morrison 1.50 3.00
96 Ken Schinkel 1.50 3.00
97 Lou Fontinato 1.50 3.00
98 Ted Hampson 1.50 3.00
99 Brian Cullen 2.00 4.00
100 Alf Pike CO 1.50 3.00
101 Don Simmons 2.50 5.00
102 Fern Flaman 2.50 5.00
103 Vic Stasiuk 2.00 4.00
104 Johnny Bucyk 5.00 10.00
105 Bronco Horvath 2.00 4.00
106 Doug Mohns 4.00 8.00
107 Leo Boivin 2.50 5.00
108 Don McKenney 1.50 3.00
109 Jean-Guy Gendron 1.50 3.00
110 Jerry Toppazzini 1.50 3.00
111 Dick Meissner 1.50 3.00
112 Autry Erickson 1.50 3.00
113 Jim Bartlett 1.50 3.00
114 Orval Tessier 2.00 4.00
115 Billy Carter 1.50 3.00
116 Dallas Smith 2.00 4.00
117 Leo Labine 1.50 3.00
118 Bob Armstrong 1.50 3.00
119 Bruce Gamble 2.50 5.00
120 Milt Schmidt CO 3.00 6.00

1961-62 Shirriff/Salada Coins
1 Cliff Pennington 1.25 3.00
2 Dallas Smith 2.00 5.00
3 Andre Pronovost 1.25 3.00
4 Charlie Burns 1.25 3.00
5 Leo Boivin 2.50 6.00
6 Don McKenney 1.25 3.00
7 Johnny Bucyk 4.00 10.00
8 Murray Oliver 1.25 3.00
9 Jerry Toppazzini 1.25 3.00
10 Doug Mohns 2.00 5.00
11 Don Head 2.00 5.00
12 Bob Armstrong 1.25 3.00
13 Pat Stapleton 2.00 5.00
14 Orland Kurtenbach 2.00 5.00
15 Dick Meissner 1.25 3.00
16 Ted Green 2.00 5.00
17 Tom Williams 1.25 3.00
18 Autry Erickson 1.25 3.00
19 Phil Watson CO 2.50 6.00
20 Ed Chadwick 2.50 6.00
21 Wayne Hillman 5.00 12.00
22 Stan Mikita 6.00 15.00
23 Eric Nesterenko 2.00 5.00
24 Reg Fleming 1.25 3.00
25 Bobby Hull 12.00 30.00
26 Elmer Vasko 1.25 3.00
27 Pierre Pilote 2.50 6.00
28 Chico Maki 2.00 5.00
29 Glenn Hall 5.00 12.00
30 Murray Balfour 1.25 3.00
31 Bronco Horvath 1.50 4.00
32 Ken Wharram 2.00 5.00
33 Ab McDonald 1.25 3.00
34 Bill Hay 1.25 3.00
35 Dollard St.Laurent 2.00 5.00
36 Ron Murphy 1.25 3.00
37 Bob Turner 1.25 3.00
38 Gerry Melnyk 1.25 3.00
39 Jack Evans 1.25 3.00
40 Rudy Pilous CO 2.50 6.00
41 Johnny Bower 5.00 12.00
42 Allan Stanley 3.00 8.00
43 Frank Mahovlich 5.00 12.00
44 Tim Horton 8.00 20.00
45 Carl Brewer 2.00 5.00
46 Bob Pulford 2.50 6.00
47 Bob Nevin 2.00 5.00
48 Eddie Shack 4.00 10.00
49 Red Kelly 4.00 10.00
50 Bob Baun 2.00 5.00
51 George Armstrong 3.00 8.00
52 Bert Olmstead 2.50 6.00
53 Dick Duff 2.00 5.00
54 Billy Harris 2.00 5.00
55 Larry Keenan 1.25 3.00
56 Johnny MacMillan 1.25 3.00
57 Punch Imlach CO 2.00 5.00
58 Dave Keon 8.00 20.00
59 Larry Hillman 1.25 3.00
60 Al Arbour 2.50 6.00
61 Sid Abel CO 2.50 6.00
62 Warren Godfrey 1.25 3.00
63 Vic Stasiuk 1.25 3.00
64 Leo Labine 1.25 3.00
65 Howie Glover 1.25 3.00
66 Gordie Howe 20.00 50.00
67 Val Fonteyne 1.25 3.00
68 Marcel Pronovost 2.50 6.00
69 Parker MacDonald 1.25 3.00
70 Alex Delvecchio 4.00 10.00
71 Ed Litzenberger 1.25 3.00
72 Al Johnson 1.25 3.00
73 Bruce MacGregor 1.25 3.00
74 Howie Young 1.25 3.00
75 Pete Goegan 1.25 3.00
76 Norm Ullman 3.00 8.00
77 Terry Sawchuk 12.00 30.00
78 Gerry Odrowski 1.25 3.00
79 Bill Gadsby 2.50 6.00
80 Hank Bassen 2.00 5.00
81 Doug Harvey 4.00 10.00
82 Earl Ingarfield 1.25 3.00
83 Pat Hannigan 1.25 3.00
84 Dean Prentice 2.00 5.00
85 Gump Worsley 5.00 12.00
86 Irv Spencer 1.25 3.00
87 Camille Henry 2.00 5.00
88 Andy Bathgate 3.00 8.00
89 Harry Howell 2.50 6.00
90 Andy Hebenton 1.25 3.00
91 Red Sullivan 1.25 3.00
92 Ted Hampson 1.25 3.00
93 Jean-Guy Gendron 1.25 3.00
94 Albert Langlois 1.25 3.00
95 Larry Cahan 1.25 3.00
96 Bob Cunningham 1.25 3.00
97 Vic Hadfield 2.00 5.00
98 Jean Ratelle 5.00 12.00
99 Ken Schinkel 1.25 3.00
100 Johnny Wilson 1.25 3.00
101 Toe Blake CO 2.50 6.00
102 Jean Beliveau 10.00 25.00
103 Don Marshall 1.25 3.00
104 Boom Boom Geoffrion 6.00 15.00
105 Claude Provost 2.00 5.00
106 Tom Johnson 2.50 6.00
107 Dickie Moore 4.00 10.00
108 Bill Hicke 1.25 3.00
109 Jean-Guy Talbot 2.00 5.00
110 Henri Richard 5.00 12.00
111 Lou Fontinato 1.50 4.00
112 Gilles Tremblay 1.25 3.00
113 Jacques Plante 10.00 25.00
114 Ralph Backstrom 2.00 5.00
115 Marcel Bonin 1.25 3.00
116 Phil Goyette 1.25 3.00
117 Bobby Rousseau 2.00 5.00
118 J.C. Tremblay 2.00 5.00
119 Al MacNeil 1.25 3.00
120 Jean Gauthier 1.25 3.00
S1 Boston Bruins Shield 30.00 80.00
S2 Chicago Blackhawks Shield 30.00 80.00
S3 Detroit Red Wings Shield 30.00 80.00
S4 Montreal Canadiens Shield 30.00 80.00
S5 New York Rangers Shield 30.00 80.00
S6 Toronto Maple Leafs Shield 30.00 80.00

1962-63 Shirriff Coins
1 Johnny Bower 4.00 10.00
2 Allan Stanley 3.00 8.00
3 Frank Mahovlich 8.00 20.00
4 Tim Horton 8.00 20.00
5 Carl Brewer 2.00 5.00
6 Bob Pulford 3.00 8.00
7 Bob Nevin 2.00 5.00
8 Eddie Shack 3.00 8.00
9 Red Kelly 3.00 8.00
10 George Armstrong 3.00 8.00
11 Bert Olmstead 2.50 6.00
12 Dick Duff 2.00 5.00
13 Billy Harris 1.50 4.00
14 Johnny MacMillan 1.50 4.00
15 Punch Imlach CO 2.00 5.00
16 Dave Keon 6.00 15.00
17 Larry Hillman 1.50 4.00
18 Ed Litzenberger 1.50 4.00
19 Bob Baun 2.50 6.00
20 Al Arbour 3.00 8.00
21 Ron Stewart 1.50 4.00
22 Don Simmons 2.50 6.00
23 Lou Fontinato 1.50 4.00
24 Gilles Tremblay 1.50 4.00
25 Jacques Plante 10.00 25.00
26 Ralph Backstrom 2.00 5.00
27 Marcel Bonin 1.50 4.00
28 Phil Goyette 1.50 4.00
29 Bobby Rousseau 2.00 5.00
30 J.C. Tremblay 2.00 5.00
31 Toe Blake CO 3.00 8.00
32 Jean Beliveau 8.00 20.00
33 Don Marshall 1.50 4.00
34 Boom Boom Geoffrion 5.00 12.00
35 Claude Provost 2.00 5.00
36 Tom Johnson 2.50 6.00
37 Dickie Moore 4.00 10.00
38 Bill Hicke 1.50 4.00
39 Jean-Guy Talbot 2.00 5.00
40 Al MacNeil 2.00 5.00
41 Henri Richard 6.00 15.00
42 Red Berenson 2.00 5.00
43 Jacques Plante AS 10.00 25.00
44 Jean-Guy Talbot AS 2.00 5.00
45 Doug Harvey AS 4.00 10.00
46 Stan Mikita AS 4.00 10.00
47 Bobby Hull AS 10.00 25.00
48 Andy Bathgate AS 3.00 8.00
49 Glenn Hall AS 4.00 10.00
50 Pierre Pilote AS 3.00 8.00
51 Carl Brewer AS 2.00 5.00
52 Dave Keon AS 6.00 15.00
53 Frank Mahovlich AS 6.00 15.00
54 Gordie Howe AS 15.00 40.00
55 Dave Keon Byng 6.00 15.00
56 Bobby Rousseau Calder 2.00 5.00
57 Bobby Hull Ross 10.00 25.00
58 Jacques Plante Vezina 10.00 25.00
59 Jacques Plante Hart 10.00 25.00
60 Doug Harvey Norris 4.00 10.00

1968-69 Shirriff Coins
1 Eddie Shack 8.00 20.00
2 Ed Westfall 8.00 20.00
3 Don Awrey 10.00 25.00
4 Gerry Cheevers 10.00 25.00
5 Bobby Orr 80.00 150.00
6 Johnny Bucyk 10.00 25.00
7 Derek Sanderson 10.00 25.00
8 Phil Esposito 15.00 40.00
9 Fred Stanfield 12.00 30.00
10 Ken Hodge 12.00 30.00
11 John McKenzie 10.00 25.00
12 Ted Green 12.00 30.00
13 Dallas Smith SP 60.00 150.00
14 Gary Doak SP 60.00 150.00
15 Glen Sather SP 60.00 150.00
16 Tom Williams SP 80.00 150.00
17 Bobby Hull 20.00 50.00
18 Pat Stapleton 12.00 30.00
19 Wayne Maki 10.00 25.00
20 Denis DeJordy 10.00 25.00
21 Ken Wharram 10.00 25.00
22 Pit Martin 10.00 25.00
23 Chico Maki 5.00 12.00
24 Doug Mohns 8.00 20.00
25 Stan Mikita 10.00 25.00
26 Doug Jarrett 15.00 40.00
27 Dennis Hull 11 SP 40.00 100.00
28 Dennis Hull 11 30.00 80.00
29 Matt Ravlich 10.00 25.00
30 Dave Dryden SP 40.00 100.00
31 Eric Nesterenko SP 60.00 150.00
32 Gilles Marotte SP 60.00 150.00
33 Jim Pappin SP 60.00 150.00
34 Gary Bergman 10.00 25.00
35 Roger Crozier 10.00 25.00
36 Peter Mahovlich 10.00 25.00
37 Alex Delvecchio 10.00 25.00
38 Dean Prentice 10.00 25.00
39 Kent Douglas 12.00 30.00
40 Roy Edwards 10.00 25.00
41 Bruce MacGregor 12.00 30.00
42 Garry Unger 10.00 25.00
43 Pete Stemkowski 8.00 20.00
44 Gordie Howe 30.00 80.00
45 Frank Mahovlich 8.00 20.00
46 Bob Baun SP 150.00 250.00
47 Brian Conacher SP 40.00 100.00
48 Jim Watson SP 200.00 300.00
49 Nick Libett SP 50.00 125.00
50 Real Lemieux 8.00 20.00
20 Ted Irvine 8.00 20.00
52 Bob Wall 5.00 12.00
53 Bill White 8.00 20.00
54 Gord Labossiere 8.00 20.00
55 Eddie Joyal 8.00 20.00
56 Lowell MacDonald 8.00 20.00
57 Bill Flett 8.00 20.00
58 Wayne Rutledge 8.00 20.00
59 Dave Amadio 10.00 25.00
60 Skip Krake SP 30.00 80.00
61 Doug Robinson SP 25.00 60.00
62 Wayne Connelly 8.00 20.00
63 Bob Woytowich 8.00 20.00
64 Andre Boudrias 8.00 20.00
65 Bill Goldsworthy 8.00 20.00
66 Cesare Maniago 8.00 20.00
67 Milan Marcetta 8.00 20.00
68 Bill Collins SP 7 40.00 100.00
69 Claude Larose SP 7 40.00 100.00
70 Parker MacDonald 6.00 15.00
71 Ray Cullen 6.00 15.00
72 Mike McMahon 8.00 20.00
73 Bob McCord SP 25.00 60.00
74 Larry Hillman SP 30.00 80.00
75 Gump Worsley 8.00 20.00
76 Rogatien Vachon 8.00 20.00
77 Ted Harris 10.00 25.00
78 Jacques Laperriere 8.00 20.00
79 J.C. Tremblay 10.00 25.00
80 Jean Beliveau 20.00 50.00
81 Gilles Tremblay 10.00 25.00
82 Ralph Backstrom 8.00 20.00
83 Bobby Rousseau 8.00 20.00
84 John Ferguson 8.00 20.00
85 Dick Duff 8.00 20.00
86 Terry Harper 8.00 20.00
87 Yvan Cournoyer 10.00 25.00
88 Jacques Lemaire 8.00 20.00
89 Henri Richard 8.00 20.00
90 Claude Provost SP 50.00 125.00
91 Serge Savard SP 80.00 150.00
92 Mickey Redmond SP 80.00 150.00
93 Rod Seiling 8.00 20.00
94 Jean Ratelle 8.00 20.00
95 Ed Giacomin 12.00 30.00
96 Reg Fleming 8.00 20.00
97 Phil Goyette 8.00 20.00
98 Arnie Brown 8.00 20.00
99 Don Marshall 5.00 12.00
100 Orland Kurtenbach 8.00 20.00
101 Bob Nevin 10.00 25.00
102 Rod Gilbert 8.00 20.00
103 Harry Howell 8.00 20.00
104 Jim Neilson 12.00 30.00
105 Vic Hadfield SP 150.00 400.00
106 Larry Jeffrey SP 200.00 350.00
107 Dave Balon SP 80.00 150.00
108 Ron Stewart SP 300.00 400.00
109 Gerry Ehman 12.00 30.00
110 John Brenneman 15.00 40.00
111 Ted Hampson 25.00 60.00
112 Billy Harris 20.00 50.00
113 George Swarbrick SP 5 50.00 100.00
114 Carol Vadnais SP 5 900.00 1500.00
115 Gary Smith 12.00 30.00
116 Charlie Hodge 12.00 30.00
117 Bert Marshall 6.00 15.00
118 Bill Hicke 12.00 30.00
119 Tracy Pratt 10.00 25.00
120 Gary Jarrett SP 800.00 1200.00
121 Howie Young SP 800.00 1200.00
122 Bernie Parent 15.00 40.00
123 John Miszuk 8.00 20.00
124 Ed Hoekstra SP 3 50.00 100.00
125 Allan Stanley SP 3 60.00 150.00
126 Gary Dornhoefer 8.00 20.00
127 Doug Favell 10.00 25.00
128 Andre Lacroix 10.00 25.00
129 Brit Selby 6.00 15.00
130 Don Blackburn 8.00 20.00
131 Leon Rochefort 15.00 40.00
132 Forbes Kennedy 15.00 40.00
133 Claude Laforge SP 150.00 250.00
134 Pat Hannigan SP 50.00 125.00
135 Ken Schinkel 8.00 20.00
136 Earl Ingarfield 8.00 20.00
137 Val Fonteyne 8.00 20.00
138 Noel Price 10.00 25.00
139 Andy Bathgate 10.00 25.00
140 Les Binkley 12.00 30.00
141 Leo Boivin 12.00 30.00
142 Paul Andrea 6.00 15.00
143 Dunc McCallum 12.00 30.00
144 Keith McCreary 8.00 20.00
145 Lou Angotti SP 100.00 250.00
146 Wally Boyer SP 150.00 250.00
147 Ron Schock 10.00 25.00
148 Bob Plager 10.00 25.00
149 Al Arbour 6.00 15.00
150 Red Berenson 8.00 20.00
151 Glenn Hall 10.00 25.00
152 Jim Roberts 6.00 15.00
153 Noel Picard 8.00 20.00
154 Barclay Plager 8.00 20.00
155 Larry Keenan 8.00 20.00
156 Terry Crisp 10.00 25.00
157 Gary Sabourin SP 60.00 150.00
158 Ab McDonald SP 60.00 150.00
159 George Armstrong 10.00 25.00
160 Wayne Carleton 10.00 25.00
161 Paul Henderson 30.00 80.00
162 Bob Pulford 8.00 20.00
163 Mike Walton 6.00 15.00
164 Johnny Bower 10.00 25.00
165 Ron Ellis 10.00 25.00
166 Mike Pelyk 10.00 25.00
167 Murray Oliver 8.00 20.00
168 Norm Ullman 8.00 20.00
169 Dave Keon 25.00 60.00
170 Floyd Smith 10.00 25.00
171 Marcel Pronovost 10.00 25.00
172 Tim Horton 30.00 80.00
173 Bruce Gamble 20.00 50.00
174 Jim McKenny SP 80.00 150.00
175 Mike Byers SP 60.00 150.00
176 Pierre Pilote SP 80.00 150.00

1995-96 SkyBox Impact Promo Panel
PAN Uncut Panel
Theo Fleury IQ
Blaine Lacher
Blaine Lacher D
Jeremy Roenick PP .75 2.00
1 Theo Fleury IQ .30 .75
2 Blaine Lacher .20 .50
3 Blaine Lacher D .20 .50
4 Jeremy Roenick PP .30 .75

1995-96 SkyBox Impact
COMPLETE SET (250) 6.00 15.00
1 Bobby Dollas .01 .05
2 Guy Hebert .02 .10
3 Paul Kariya .07 .20
4 Todd Krygier .01 .05
5 Oleg Tverdovsky .01 .05
6 Shaun Van Allen .01 .05
7 Ray Bourque .10 .30
8 Al Iafrate .02 .10
9 Blaine Lacher .02 .10
10 Joe Mullen .02 .10
11 Cam Neely .07 .20
12 Adam Oates .02 .10
13 Kevin Stevens .01 .05
14 Donald Audette .01 .05
15 Garry Galley .01 .05
16 Dominik Hasek .15 .40
17 Pat LaFontaine .07 .20
18 Derek Plante .01 .05
19 Alexei Zhitnik .01 .05
20 Steve Chiasson .01 .05
21 Theo Fleury .01 .05
22 Phil Housley .02 .10
23 Trevor Kidd .02 .10
24 Joe Nieuwendyk .02 .10
25 German Titov .01 .05
26 Zarley Zalapski .01 .05
27 Ed Belfour .07 .20
28 Chris Chelios .07 .20
29 Sergei Krivokrasov .01 .05
30 Joe Murphy .01 .05
31 Bernie Nicholls .01 .05
32 Patrick Poulin .01 .05
33 Jeremy Roenick .08 .25
34 Gary Suter .01 .05
35 Peter Forsberg .20 .50
36 Valeri Kamensky .02 .10
37 Claude Lemieux .01 .05
38 Curtis Leschyshyn .01 .05
39 Sandis Ozolinsh .01 .05
40 Mike Ricci .02 .10
41 Joe Sakic .15 .40
42 Jocelyn Thibault .07 .20
43 Bob Bassen .01 .05
44 Dave Gagner .01 .05
45 Todd Harvey .02 .10
46 Derian Hatcher .01 .05
47 Kevin Hatcher .01 .05
48 Mike Modano .10 .30
49 Andy Moog .07 .20
50 Dino Ciccarelli .02 .10
51 Paul Coffey .07 .20
52 Sergei Fedorov .10 .30
53 Vladimir Konstantinov .02 .10
54 Slava Kozlov .02 .10
55 Nicklas Lidstrom .07 .20
56 Chris Osgood .02 .10
57 Keith Primeau .01 .05
58 Steve Yzerman .40 1.00
59 Jason Arnott .01 .05
60 Curtis Joseph .07 .20
61 Igor Kravchuk .01 .05
62 Todd Marchant .01 .05
63 David Oliver .01 .05
64 Bill Ranford .02 .10
65 Doug Weight .02 .10
66 Stu Barnes .01 .05
67 Jesse Belanger .01 .05
68 Gord Murphy .01 .05
69 Magnus Svensson .01 .05
70 John Vanbiesbrouck .02 .10
71 Sean Burke .02 .10
72 Andrew Cassels .01 .05
73 Nelson Emerson .01 .05
74 Andrei Nikolishin .01 .05
75 Geoff Sanderson .01 .05
76 Brendan Shanahan .07 .20
77 Glen Wesley .01 .05
78 Rob Blake .02 .10
79 Wayne Gretzky .60 1.50
80 Dimitri Khristich .01 .05
81 Jari Kurri .07 .20
82 Darryl Sydor .02 .10
83 Rick Tocchet .02 .10
84 Vincent Damphousse .01 .05
85 Vladimir Malakhov .01 .05
86 Mark Recchi .02 .10
87 Patrick Roy .40 1.00
88 Brian Savage .01 .05
89 Pierre Turgeon .02 .10
90 Martin Brodeur .20 .50
91 Neal Broten .02 .10
92 Shawn Chambers .01 .05
93 John MacLean .02 .10
94 Randy McKay .01 .05
95 Scott Niedermayer .01 .05
96 Stephane Richer .02 .10
97 Scott Stevens .02 .10
98 Steve Thomas .02 .10
99 Wendel Clark .02 .10
100 Patrick Flatley .01 .05
101 Scott Lachance .01 .05
102 Brett Lindros .01 .05
103 Kirk Muller .01 .05
104 Tommy Salo RC .30 .75
105 Mathieu Schneider .01 .05
106 Dennis Vaske .01 .05
107 Ray Ferraro .01 .05
108 Adam Graves .01 .05
109 Alexei Kovalev .01 .05
110 Brian Leetch .02 .10
111 Mark Messier .07 .20
112 Mike Richter .07 .20
113 Luc Robitaille .02 .10
114 Ulf Samuelsson .01 .05
115 Pat Verbeek .01 .05
116 Don Beaupre .02 .10
117 Radek Bonk .01 .05
118 Alexandre Daigle .01 .05
119 Steve Duchesne .01 .05
120 Dan Quinn .01 .05
121 Martin Straka .01 .05
122 Alexei Yashin .01 .05
123 Rod Brind'Amour .02 .10
124 Eric Desjardins .02 .10
125 Ron Hextall .02 .10
126 John LeClair .07 .20
127 Eric Lindros .07 .20
128 Mikael Renberg .02 .10
129 Chris Therien .01 .05
130 Ron Francis .02 .10
131 Jaromir Jagr .10 .30
132 Mario Lemieux .40 1.00
133 Petr Nedved .02 .10
134 Tomas Sandstrom .01 .05
135 Bryan Smolinski .01 .05
136 Ken Wregget .02 .10
137 Sergei Zubov .01 .05
138 Shayne Corson .01 .05
139 Geoff Courtnall .01 .05
140 Dale Hawerchuk .07 .20
141 Brett Hull .08 .25
142 Ian Laperriere .01 .05
143 Al MacInnis .02 .10
144 Chris Pronger .07 .20
145 Esa Tikkanen .01 .05
146 Ulf Dahlen .01 .05
147 Jeff Friesen .01 .05
148 Arturs Irbe .02 .10
149 Craig Janney .01 .05
150 Owen Nolan .02 .10
151 Mike Rathje .01 .05
152 Ray Sheppard .01 .05
153 Brian Bradley .01 .05
154 Chris Gratton .01 .05
155 Roman Hamrlik .02 .10
156 Petr Klima .01 .05
157 Daren Puppa .02 .10
158 Dave Andreychuk .02 .10
160 Mike Gartner .02 .10
160 Todd Gill .01 .05
161 Doug Gilmour .02 .10
162 Kenny Jonsson .01 .05
163 Larry Murphy .02 .10
164 Felix Potvin .07 .20
165 Mats Sundin .07 .20
166 Jeff Brown .01 .05
167 Pavel Bure .07 .20
168 Russ Courtnall .01 .05
169 Trevor Linden .02 .10
170 Kirk McLean .02 .10
171 Alexander Mogilny .02 .10
172 Roman Oksiuta .01 .05
173 Mike Ridley .01 .05
174 Peter Bondra .02 .10
175 Jim Carey .02 .10
176 Sergei Gonchar .01 .05
177 Dale Hunter .02 .10
178 Calle Johansson .01 .05
179 Joe Juneau .01 .05
180 Michal Pivonka .01 .05
181 Nikolai Khabibulin .02 .10
182 Dave Manson .01 .05
183 Teppo Numminen .01 .05
184 Teemu Selanne .07 .20
185 Keith Tkachuk .07 .20
186 Darren Turcotte .01 .05
187 Alexei Zhamnov .02 .10
188 Chad Kilger RC .01 .05
189 Kyle McLaren RC .01 .05
190 Brian Holzinger RC .07 .20
191 Wayne Primeau RC .01 .05
192 Marty Murray .01 .05
193 Eric Daze .02 .10
194 Jon Klemm RC .01 .05
195 Jere Lehtinen .01 .05
196 Jason Bonsignore .01 .05
197 Miroslav Satan RC .30 .75
198 Ryan Smyth .02 .10
199 Tyler Wright .01 .05
200 Radek Dvorak RC .15 .40
201 Ed Jovanovski .07 .20
202 Jeff O'Neill .01 .05
203 Aki Berg RC .02 .10
204 Jamie Storr .02 .10
205 Vitali Yachmenev .01 .05
206 Saku Koivu .07 .20
207 Denis Pederson .01 .05
208 Todd Bertuzzi RC .50 1.25
209 Bryan McCabe .01 .05
210 Dan Plante .08 .25
211 Peter Ferraro .01 .05
212 Darren Langdon RC .01 .05
213 Niklas Sundstrom .01 .05
214 Daniel Alfredsson RC .30 .75
215 Garth Snow .02 .10
216 Ian Moran .01 .05
217 Richard Park .01 .05
218 Jamie Rivers .01 .05
219 Roman Vopat RC .01 .05
220 Marcus Ragnarsson RC .02 .10
221 Aaron Gavey .01 .05
222 Daymond Langkow RC .15 .40
223 Darby Hendrickson .01 .05
224 Martin Gendron .01 .05
225 Brendan Witt .01 .05
226 Shane Doan RC .25 .60
227 Deron Quint .01 .05
228 Jim Carey HH .01 .05
229 Peter Forsberg HH .10 .30
230 Paul Kariya HH .07 .20
231 David Oliver HH .01 .05
232 Blaine Lacher HH .02 .10
233 Todd Harvey HH .01 .05
234 Todd Marchant HH .01 .05
235 Jeff Friesen HH .01 .05
236 Oleg Tverdovsky HH .01 .05
237 Jason Arnott HH .01 .05
238 Cam Neely PP .02 .10
239 Keith Tkachuk PP .07 .20
240 Owen Nolan PP .02 .10
241 Keith Primeau PP .01 .05
242 Peter Bondra PP .02 .10
243 Jeremy Roenick PP .08 .25
244 John LeClair PP .07 .20
245 Mikael Renberg PP .02 .10
246 Dave Andreychuk PP .02 .10
247 Rick Tocchet PP .02 .10
248 Checklist Card .02 .10
249 Checklist Card .02 .10
250 Checklist Card .02 .10
NNO Blaine Lacher SkyMotion 4.00 10.00
NNO Blaine Lacher EXCH .02 .10

1995-96 SkyBox Impact Deflectors
COMPLETE SET (12) 6.00 15.00
1 Dominik Hasek 1.00 2.50
2 Jim Carey .25 .60
3 Felix Potvin .75 2.00
4 Sean Burke .25 .60
5 Blaine Lacher .25 .60
6 John Vanbiesbrouck .40 1.00
7 Jocelyn Thibault .40 1.00
8 Patrick Roy 2.00 5.00
9 Ed Belfour .40 1.00
10 Trevor Kidd .25 .60
11 Martin Brodeur 1.50 4.00
12 Kirk McLean .25 .60

1995-96 SkyBox Impact Countdown to Impact
COMPLETE SET (9) 12.00 30.00
1 Eric Lindros 1.50 4.00
2 Jaromir Jagr 2.50 5.00
3 Mario Lemieux 4.00 10.00
4 Wayne Gretzky 6.00 15.00
5 Mark Messier 1.50 4.00
6 Sergei Fedorov 1.50 4.00
7 Paul Kariya 1.50 4.00
8 Doug Gilmour 1.00 2.50
9 Pavel Bure 1.50 4.00

1995-96 SkyBox Impact Ice Quake
COMPLETE SET (15) 15.00 40.00
1 Jaromir Jagr 2.50 6.00
2 Brett Hull 1.50 4.00
3 Pavel Bure 1.00 2.50
4 Eric Lindros 1.00 2.50
5 Mark Messier 1.50 4.00
6 Wayne Gretzky 6.00 15.00
7 Mario Lemieux 5.00 12.00
8 Peter Forsberg 2.50 6.00
9 Sergei Fedorov 1.50 4.00
10 Cam Neely 1.00 2.50
11 Owen Nolan .40 1.00
12 Alexei Zhamnov .40 1.00
13 Theo Fleury .40 1.00
14 Luc Robitaille .40 1.00
15 Teemu Selanne 1.00 2.50

1995-96 SkyBox Impact NHL On Fox
COMPLETE SET (18) 2.00 5.00
1 Mariusz Czerkawski .20 .50
2 Roman Oksiuta .20 .50
3 David Oliver .20 .50
4 Adam Deadmarsh .20 .50
5 Denis Chasse .20 .50
6 Sergei Krivokrasov .20 .50
7 Ian Laperriere .20 .50
8 Chris Therien .20 .50
9 Brian Savage .20 .50
10 Todd Marchant .20 .50
11 Jeff O'Neill .20 .50
12 Brett Lindros .20 .50
13 Kenny Jonsson .20 .50
14 Manny Fernandez .40 1.00
15 Brian Holzinger .20 .50
16 Niklas Sundstrom .20 .50
17 Eric Daze .20 .50
18 Chad Kilger .20 .50

1996-97 SkyBox Impact
1 Guy Hebert .12 .30
2 Paul Kariya .15 .40
3 Roman Oksiuta .10 .25
4 Teemu Selanne .30 .75
5 Ray Bourque .25 .60
6 Kyle McLaren .10 .25
7 Adam Oates .15 .40
8 Bill Ranford .12 .30
9 Rick Tocchet .12 .30
10 Dominik Hasek .25 .60

11 Pat LaFontaine .15 .40
12 Mike Peca .10 .25
13 Theo Fleury .30 .75
14 Trevor Kidd .10 .25
15 German Titov .10 .25
16 Tony Amonte .12 .30
17 Ed Belfour .15 .40
18 Chris Chelios .15 .40
19 Eric Daze .12 .30
20 Gary Suter .10 .25
21 Alexei Zhamnov .12 .30
22 Peter Forsberg .30 .75
23 Valeri Kamensky .12 .30
24 Uwe Krupp .10 .25
25 Claude Lemieux .10 .25
26 Sandis Ozolinsh .10 .25
27 Patrick Roy .40 1.00
28 Joe Sakic .30 .75
29 Derian Hatcher .10 .25
30 Mike Modano .25 .60
31 Joe Nieuwendyk .12 .30
32 Sergei Zubov .12 .30
33 Paul Coffey .15 .40
34 Sergei Fedorov .25 .60
35 Vladimir Konstantinov .12 .30
36 Slava Kozlov .10 .25
37 Nicklas Lidstrom .20 .50
38 Chris Osgood .15 .40
39 Keith Primeau .12 .30
40 Steve Yzerman .40 1.00
41 Jason Arnott .12 .30
42 Curtis Joseph .20 .50
43 Doug Weight .15 .40
44 Radek Dvorak .12 .30
45 Ed Jovanovski .12 .30
46 Scott Mellanby .12 .30
47 Rob Niedermayer .12 .30
48 Ray Sheppard .12 .30
49 Robert Svehla .10 .25
50 John Vanbiesbrouck .15 .40
51 Jeff Brown .10 .25
52 Sean Burke .10 .25
53 Andrew Cassels .10 .25
54 Geoff Sanderson .12 .30
55 Brendan Shanahan .15 .40
56 Byron Dafoe .12 .30
57 Ray Ferraro .10 .25
58 Dimitri Khristich .10 .25
59 Vitali Yachmenev .10 .25
60 Valeri Bure .10 .25
61 Vincent Damphousse .12 .30
62 Saku Koivu .15 .40
63 Mark Recchi .20 .50
64 Martin Rucinsky .10 .25
65 Jocelyn Thibault .12 .30
66 Pierre Turgeon .12 .30
67 Dave Andreychuk .15 .40
68 Martin Brodeur .40 1.00
69 Bill Guerin .15 .40
70 Scott Niedermayer .15 .40
71 Scott Stevens .15 .40
72 Petr Sykora .10 .25
73 Steve Thomas .10 .25
74 Todd Bertuzzi .15 .40
75 Travis Green .12 .30
76 Kenny Jonsson .10 .25
77 Zigmund Palffy .15 .40
78 Adam Graves .10 .25
79 Wayne Gretzky 1.00 2.50
80 Alexei Kovalev .12 .30
81 Brian Leetch .12 .30
82 Mark Messier .30 .75
83 Mike Richter .15 .40
84 Ulf Samuelsson .10 .25
85 Niklas Sundstrom .10 .25
86 Daniel Alfredsson .15 .40
87 Radek Bonk .10 .25
88 Alexandre Daigle .10 .25
89 Steve Duchesne .10 .25
90 Damian Rhodes .12 .30
91 Alexei Yashin .12 .30
92 Rod Brind'Amour .15 .40
93 Eric Desjardins .12 .30
94 Dale Hawerchuk .20 .50
95 Ron Hextall .15 .40
96 John LeClair .15 .40
97 Eric Lindros .25 .60
98 Mikael Renberg .12 .30
99 Tom Barrasso .12 .30
100 Ron Francis .20 .50
101 Jaromir Jagr .50 1.25
102 Mario Lemieux .60 1.50
103 Petr Nedved .12 .30
104 Bryan Smolinski .10 .25
105 Nikolai Khabibulin .12 .30
106 Teppo Numminen .10 .25
107 Keith Tkachuk .15 .40
108 Jeremy Roenick .25 .60
109 Oleg Tverdovsky .12 .30
110 Shayne Corson .12 .30
111 Geoff Courtnall .10 .25
112 Grant Fuhr .25 .60
113 Brett Hull .30 .75
114 Al MacInnis .20 .50
115 Chris Pronger .15 .40
116 Jeff Friesen .10 .25
117 Owen Nolan .15 .40
118 Marcus Ragnarsson .10 .25
119 Chris Terreri .12 .30
120 Brian Bradley .10 .25
121 Chris Gratton .12 .30
122 Roman Hamrlik .10 .25
123 Daren Puppa .12 .30
124 Alexander Selivanov .10 .25
125 Wendel Clark .25 .60
126 Doug Gilmour .20 .50
127 Kirk Muller .10 .25
128 Larry Murphy .12 .30
129 Felix Potvin .25 .60
130 Mats Sundin .15 .40
131 Pavel Bure .15 .40
132 Russ Courtnall .10 .25
133 Trevor Linden .15 .40
134 Kirk McLean .12 .30
135 Alexander Mogilny .12 .30
136 Peter Bondra .15 .40
137 Jim Carey .15 .40
138 Sylvain Cote .10 .25
139 Sergei Gonchar .10 .25
140 Phil Housley .12 .30
141 Joe Juneau .10 .25
142 Michal Pivonka .10 .25
143 Brendan Witt .10 .25
144 Nolan Baumgartner .10 .25
145 Martin Biron RC .20 .50
146 Jason Bonsignore .10 .25
147 Andrew Brunette RC .20 .50
148 Jason Doig .10 .25
149 Peter Ferraro .10 .25
150 Eric Fichaud .12 .30
151 Ladislav Kohn .10 .25
152 Jamie Langenbrunner .10 .25
153 Daymond Langkow .12 .30
154 Jay McKee RC .10 .25
155 Marty Murray .10 .25
156 Wayne Primeau .10 .25
157 Jamie Pushor .10 .25
158 Jamie Rivers .10 .25
159 Jamie Storr .10 .25
160 Steve Sullivan RC .12 .30
161 Jose Theodore .20 .50
162 Roman Vopat .10 .25
163 Alexei Yegorov RC .15 .40
164 Daniel Alfredsson PP .15 .40
165 Niklas Andersson PP .10 .25
166 Todd Bertuzzi PP .15 .40
167 Valeri Bure PP .10 .25
168 Eric Daze PP .12 .30
169 Saku Koivu PP .15 .40
170 Miroslav Satan PP .10 .25
171 Petr Sykora PP .10 .25
172 Cory Stillman PP .10 .25
173 Vitali Yachmenev PP .10 .25
174 Checklist 1 .02 .10
175 Checklist 2 UER .02 .10
S1 John LeClair PROMO .10 .30

1996-97 SkyBox Impact BladeRunners

1 Brian Bradley .30 .75
2 Chris Chelios .50 1.25
3 Peter Forsberg 1.00 2.50
4 Ron Francis .60 1.50
5 Mike Gartner .60 1.50
6 Doug Gilmour .60 1.50
7 Phil Housley .40 1.00
8 Brett Hull 1.00 2.50
9 Valeri Kamensky .40 1.00
10 Pat LaFontaine .50 1.25
11 John LeClair .50 1.25
12 Claude Lemieux .30 .75
13 Nicklas Lidstrom .60 1.50
14 Mark Messier 1.00 2.50
15 Alexander Mogilny .40 1.00
16 Petr Nedved .40 1.00
17 Adam Oates .50 1.25
18 Zigmund Palffy .50 1.25
19 Jeremy Roenick .75 2.00
20 Teemu Selanne 1.00 2.50
21 Brendan Shanahan .50 1.25
22 Keith Tkachuk .50 1.25
23 Pierre Turgeon .40 1.00
24 Doug Weight .50 1.25
25 Steve Yzerman 1.25 3.00

1996-97 SkyBox Impact Countdown to Impact

1 Pavel Bure 1.00 2.50
2 Sergei Fedorov 1.50 4.00
3 Wayne Gretzky 6.00 15.00
4 Jaromir Jagr 3.00 8.00
5 Ed Jovanovski .75 2.00
6 Paul Kariya 1.00 2.50
7 Mario Lemieux 4.00 10.00
8 Eric Lindros 1.50 4.00
9 Patrick Roy 2.50 6.00
10 Joe Sakic 2.00 5.00

1996-97 SkyBox Impact NHL on Fox

COMPLETE SET (20) 5.00 12.00
1 Daniel Alfredsson .40 1.00
2 Todd Bertuzzi .40 1.00
3 Ray Bourque 1.25 3.00
4 Valeri Bure .20 .50
5 Chris Chelios .75 2.00
6 Paul Coffey .75 2.00
7 Eric Daze .20 .50
8 Eric Desjardins .20 .50
9 Sergei Gonchar .20 .50
10 Phil Housley .20 .50
11 Ed Jovanovski .20 .50
12 Vladimir Konstantinov .75 2.00
13 Saku Koivu .75 2.00
14 Brian Leetch .40 1.00
15 Larry Murphy .20 .50
16 Teppo Numminen .20 .50
17 Sandis Ozolinsh .20 .50
18 Marcus Ragnarsson .20 .50
19 Petr Sykora .20 .50
20 Vitali Yachmenev .20 .50

1996-97 SkyBox Impact VersaTeam

COMPLETE SET (10) 40.00 100.00
1 Pavel Bure 2.50 6.00
2 Sergei Fedorov 2.50 6.00
3 Peter Forsberg 4.00 10.00
4 Wayne Gretzky 12.00 25.00
5 Jaromir Jagr 4.00 10.00
6 Paul Kariya 2.50 6.00
7 Mario Lemieux 12.00 30.00
8 Eric Lindros 2.50 6.00
9 Joe Sakic 6.00 15.00
10 Teemu Selanne 2.50 6.00

1996-97 SkyBox Impact Zero Heroes

COMPLETE SET (10) 20.00 50.00
1 Ed Belfour 2.50 6.00
2 Sean Burke 1.25 3.00
3 Jim Carey 1.25 3.00
4 Dominik Hasek 4.00 10.00
5 Ron Hextall 2.50 6.00
6 Chris Osgood 2.50 6.00
7 Felix Potvin 2.50 6.00
8 Daren Puppa 1.25 3.00
9 Patrick Roy 10.00 25.00
10 John Vanbiesbrouck 2.50 6.00

1994-95 Slapshot Promos

COMPLETE SET (8) .75 2.00
1 David Belitski .20 .50
3 Bill McGuigan .08 .25
4 Todd Norman .08 .25
5 Steve Rice .08 .25
6 Jamie Rivers .20 .50
7 Sudbury's World Juniors# .40 1.00
8 Ad Card .01 .05

1995-96 Slapshot

COMPLETE SET (440) 20.00 50.00
1 Checklist .01 .05
2 Checklist .01 .05
3 Checklist .01 .05
4 Checklist .01 .05
5 David E. Branch .01 .05
6 Bert Templeton .01 .05
7 Chris George .01 .05
8 Chris Thompson .08 .25
9 Quade Lightbody .01 .05
10 Shane Delaronde .01 .05
11 Justin Robinson .01 .05
12 Shawn Frappier .01 .05
13 Lucio Nasato .08 .25
14 Jason Payne .01 .05
15 Jason Cannon .01 .05
16 Alexandre Volchkov .08 .25
17 Daniel Tkaczuk .20 .50
18 Gerry Lanigan .01 .05
19 Darrell Woodley .01 .05
20 Brian Barker .01 .05
21 Mauricio Alvarez .01 .05
22 Brock Boucher .01 .05
23 Jeff Cowan .15 .40
24 Jan Bulis .20 .50
25 Jeff Tetzlaff .01 .05
26 Caleb Ward .05 .15
27 Mike White .01 .05
28 Jeremy Miculinic .01 .05
29 Andrew Morrison .01 .05
30 Robert Dubois .01 .05
31 Kory Cooper .08 .25
32 Jason Gaggi .08 .25
33 Mike Van Volsen .01 .05
34 Paul McInness .01 .05
35 Harkie Stingh .01 .05
36 Robin Lacour .01 .05
37 Jamie Sokolsky .01 .05
38 Marc Dupuis .01 .05
39 Daniel Cleary .20 .50
40 David Peca .01 .05
41 Adam Robbins .01 .05
42 Steve Tracze .01 .05
43 James Boyd .01 .05
44 Jake Irsag .01 .05
45 Ryan Ready .01 .05
46 Walker McDonald .01 .05
47 Rob Guinn .01 .05
48 Rob Fitzgerald .01 .05
49 Joe Coombs .01 .05
50 Daniel Reja .01 .05
51 Joe Van Volsen .02 .10
52 Craig Mills .08 .25
53 Murray Hogg .01 .05
54 Andrei Shurupov .08 .25
55 Andrew Williamson .01 .05
56 Mike Minard .08 .25
57 Robert Esche .75 2.00
58 Lee Jinman .08 .25
59 Corey Neilson .07 .20
60 Troy Smith .01 .05
61 Mike Rucinski .07 .20
62 Colin Beardsmore .01 .05
63 Dan Pawlacyzk .01 .05
64 Scott Blair .01 .05
65 Mike Morrone .01 .05
66 Matt Ball .01 .05
67 Steve Dumonski .01 .05
68 Murray Sheehan .01 .05
69 Sean Haggerty .08 .25
70 Andrew Taylor .01 .05
71 Steve Wasylko .02 .10
72 Jan Vodrazka .01 .05
73 Dan Preston .01 .05
74 Jesse Boulerice .20 .50
75 Bryan Berard .30 .75
76 Nicolas Beaudoin .08 .25
77 Tom Buckley .02 .10
78 Mark Cadotte .07 .20
79 Greg Stephan .01 .05
80 Peter DeBoer .02 .10
81 Regan Stocco .01 .05
82 Andy Adams .08 .25
83 Brett Thompson .08 .25
84 Darryl McArthur .01 .05
85 Ryan Risidore .07 .20
86 Joel Cort .02 .10
87 Chris Hajt .08 .25
88 Bryan McKinney .01 .05
89 Dwayne Hay .20 .50
90 Andrew Clark .01 .05
91 Ryan Robichaud .01 .05
92 Mike Vellinga .01 .05
93 Jamie Wright .01 .05
94 Herbert Vasilijevs .01 .05
95 Dan Cloutier .75 2.00
96 Brian Wesenberg .08 .25
97 Michael Pittman .01 .05
98 Jeff Williams .01 .05
99 Todd Norman .08 .25
100 Brian Willsie .01 .05
101 Jason Jackman .07 .20
102 Mike Lankshear .05 .15
103 Andrew Long .07 .20
104 Nick Bootland .02 .10
105 E.J. McGuire .01 .05
106 Bujar Amidovski .20 .50
107 John Hultberg .08 .25
108 Eric Olsen .01 .05
109 Chris Allen .20 .50
110 Michael Tilson .01 .05
111 Jeff DaCosta .01 .05
112 Gord Walsh .01 .05
113 Matt Bradley .01 .05
114 Robert Mailloux .01 .05
115 Justin Davis .01 .05
116 Marc Moro .15 .40
117 Cail MacLean .01 .05
118 Jason Sands .01 .05
119 Matt Price .01 .05
120 Zdenek Skorepa .02 .10
121 Jason Morgan .01 .05
122 Mike Oliveira .08 .25
123 Colin Chaulk .01 .05
124 Dylan Taylor .01 .05
125 Kurt Johnston .01 .05
126 Bill Minkhorst .01 .05
127 Wes Swinson .08 .25
128 Adam Fleming .01 .05
129 Chris MacDonald .01 .05
130 Gary Agnew .01 .05
131 David Belitski .08 .25
132 Jarrett Rose .01 .05
133 Ryan Mougenel .01 .05
134 Rob Stanfield .01 .05
135 Duncan Fader .01 .05
136 Rob Maric .01 .05
137 Mark McMahon .01 .05
138 Serge Payer .01 .05
139 Paul Traynor .01 .05
140 Bogdan Rudenko .01 .05
141 Robert DeCiantis .05 .15
142 Andrew Dale .08 .25
143 Jeff Ambrosio .02 .10
144 Paul Doyle .07 .20
145 Bryan Duce .01 .05
146 Jason Byrnes .01 .05
147 Ryan Pepperall .08 .25
148 Wes Vander Wal .01 .05
149 Boyd Devereaux .20 .50
150 Keith Walsh .01 .05
151 Joe Birch .01 .05
152 Craig Nelson .01 .05
153 Brian Hayden .01 .05
154 Matt O'Dette .01 .05
155 Geoff Ward .01 .05
156 Frank Ivankovic .08 .25
157 Eoin McInerney .20 .50
158 Joel Dezainde .01 .05
159 Duncan Dalmao .01 .05
160 Brandon Sugden .20 .50
161 Jamie Wentzell .01 .05
162 Ryan Burgoyne .01 .05
163 Todd Crane .01 .05
164 Chad Cavanagh .01 .05
165 Andrew Fagan .01 .05
166 Ryan Gardner .01 .05
167 Kevin Boyd .01 .05
168 Kevin Barry .01 .05
169 Richard Pitirri .01 .05
170 Adam Colagiacomo .20 .50
171 Jason Brooks .01 .05
172 Justin McPolin .01 .05
173 Travis Riggin .01 .05
174 Steve Lowe .01 .05
175 Todd St. Louis .01 .05
176 Kevin Slota .01 .05
177 Ryan McKie .01 .05
178 Corey Isen .01 .05
179 Sasha Cucuz .01 .05
180 Tom Barrett .01 .05
181 Ken Carroll .01 .05
182 Ryan Penney .08 .25
183 Jay McKee .30 .75
184 Ryan Taylor .01 .05
185 Jeff Paul .01 .05
186 Jason Ward .20 .50
187 Jesse Black .02 .10
188 Steve Nimigon .07 .20
189 Chris Haskett .01 .05
190 Geoff Peters .08 .25
191 Ryan Cirillo .01 .05
192 David Froh .01 .05
193 Jeff Johnstone .01 .05
194 Shane Nash .07 .20
195 Jason Robinson .01 .05
196 Rich Vrataric .01 .05
197 Colin Pepperall .01 .05
198 Craig Jalbert .01 .05
199 Andrew Williamson .01 .05
200 Greg Tymchuk .01 .05
201 Chester Gallant .01 .05
202 Mike Perna .01 .05
203 Adam Nitel .20 .50
204 Dave Burkholder .01 .05
205 Chris Johnstone .01 .05
206 Elliott Faust .08 .25
207 Scott Roche .08 .25
208 Kam White .01 .05
209 Scott Atkins .01 .05
210 Luc Belliveau .01 .05
211 Jamie Vossen .01 .05
212 Ryan MacDonald .01 .05
213 Jim Midgley .01 .05
214 Steven Carpenter .01 .05
215 Jake Martel .01 .05
216 Alex Matvichuk .01 .05
217 Trevor Gallant .08 .25
218 Ryan Gillis .01 .05
219 Kris Cantu .01 .05
220 Mark Provenzano .01 .05
221 Brian Whitley .01 .05
222 Dustin Virag .01 .05
223 Lee Jinman .08 .25
224 Peter McCague .01 .05
225 Herb Bonvie .01 .05
226 Philippe Poirier .01 .05
227 Greg Labanski .01 .05
228 Milan Kostolny .08 .25
229 Ryan Power .01 .05
230 Shane Parker .01 .05
231 Travis Scott .08 .25
232 Tyrone Garner .08 .25
233 Marty Wilford .08 .25
234 Ole Anderson .01 .05
235 Ryan Tocher .01 .05
236 Nathan Perrott .30 .75
237 Brandon Coalter .01 .05
238 John Tripp .08 .25
239 Jay Legault .20 .50
240 Wayne Primeau .20 .50
241 Trevor Edgar .01 .05
242 Peter Hogan .01 .05
243 Warren Holmes .01 .05
244 Jason Metcalfe .01 .05
245 Mike Zanutto .01 .05
246 Jeff Ware .08 .25
247 Ian MacNeil .01 .05
248 Jan Snopek .07 .20
249 Kurt Walsh .01 .05
250 Marc Savard .30 .75
251 Darcy O'Shea .01 .05
252 Jason Sweitzer .01 .05
253 Ryan Lindsay .01 .05
254 Scott Seiling .01 .05
255 Stan Butler .08 .25
256 Tim Keyes .08 .25
257 Craig Hillier .08 .25
258 Craig Whynot .01 .05
259 David Bell .01 .05
260 Rich Bronila .01 .05
261 Roy Gray .01 .05
262 Nick Boynton .40 1.00
263 Mike Sim .08 .25
264 B.J. Johnston .01 .05
265 Niall Maynard .01 .05
266 Dan Tudin .08 .25
267 Jure Kovacavic .01 .05
268 Ben Gustavson .01 .05
269 Steve Zaryk .01 .05
270 Darren Debrie .01 .05
271 Troy Stonier .01 .05
272 David Nemirovsky .08 .25
273 Joel Trottier .08 .25
274 Mike Lavell .01 .05
275 Brian Campbell .20 .50
276 Chris Despatis .01 .05
277 Sean Blanchard .08 .25
278 Alyn McCauley .30 .75
279 Chris Pittman .07 .20
280 Daryl Rivers .01 .05
281 Brent Johnson .75 2.00
282 Shaun Gallant .01 .05
283 Shane Kenny .01 .05
284 Chris Biagini .01 .05
285 Jim Ensom .02 .10
286 Marek Babic .01 .05
287 Oleg Tsyrkunov .01 .05
288 Mike Loach .01 .05
289 Peter MacKellar .01 .05
290 Ryan Davis .01 .05
291 John Argiropoulos .01 .05
292 Jason Campbell .01 .05
293 Ryan Christie .20 .50
294 Dan Snyder .40 1.00
295 Steve Gallace .01 .05
296 Scott Seiling .01 .05
297 Jeremy Rebek .01 .05
298 Adam Mair .20 .50
299 Matt Osborne .01 .05
300 Mike Gelati .01 .05
301 Wayne Primeau .20 .50
302 Chris Wismer .01 .05
303 Larry Paleczny .08 .25
304 Kurt Walsh .01 .05
305 John Lovell .01 .05
306 Allan Hitchen .08 .25
307 Zac Bierk .20 .50
308 Mike Martone .01 .05
309 Jonathan Murphy .01 .05
310 Adrian Murray .01 .05
311 Rob Gifin .01 .05
312 Corey Crocker .08 .25
313 Cameron Mann .20 .50
314 Ryan Pawluk .01 .05
315 Jason MacMillan .01 .05
316 Shawn Thornton .40 1.00
317 Wade Dawe .01 .05
318 Eric Landry .01 .05
319 Steve Hogg .01 .05
320 Kevin Bolibruck .01 .05
321 Dave Duerden .08 .25
322 Mike Williams .01 .05
323 Andy Johnson .01 .05
324 Jaret Nixon .01 .05
325 Evgeny Korolev .08 .25
326 Matthew Lahey .01 .05
327 Ryan Schmidt .01 .05
328 Scott Barney .08 .25
329 Steve Jones .01 .05
330 Dave McQueen .01 .05
331 Jeff Salajko .08 .25
332 Patrick DesRochers .20 .50
333 Gerald Moriarity .01 .05
334 Allan Carr .01 .05
335 Tom Brown .01 .05
336 Andy Delmore .20 .50
337 Darren Mortier .01 .05
338 Aaron Brand .08 .25
339 Eric Boulton .40 1.00
340 Jonathan Sim .20 .50
341 Trevor Letowski .20 .50
342 Michael Hanson .01 .05
343 Todd Miller .01 .05
344 Brendan Yarema .01 .05
345 Brad Simms .01 .05
346 David Nemirovsky .08 .25
347 Jeff Brown .08 .25
348 Andrew Proskurnicki .01 .05
349 Wes Mason .08 .25
350 Scott Corbett .01 .05
351 Dave Bourque .01 .05
352 Sean Brown .20 .50
353 Marcin Snita .01 .05
354 Rich Brown .01 .05
355 Mark Hunter .01 .05
356 Michal Podolka .08 .25
357 Dan Cloutier .75 2.00
358 Cory Murphy .01 .05
359 Kevin Murnaghan .01 .05
360 Andre Payette .01 .05
361 Richard Uniacke .07 .20
362 Joe Seroski .05 .15
363 Joe Thornton 4.00 10.00
364 Ben Schust .01 .05
365 Peter Cava .01 .05
366 Darryl Green .01 .05
367 Trevor Tokarczyk .01 .05
368 Jeff Gies .01 .05
369 Rico Fata .20 .50
370 Brian Secord .01 .05
371 Scott Cherrey .05 .15
372 Brian Stacey .01 .05
373 Lee Cole .01 .05
374 Richard Jackman .20 .50
375 Jason Doyle .08 .25
376 Brian Stewart .02 .10
377 Blaine Fitzpatrick .01 .05
378 Robert Mulick .01 .05
379 Andy Adams .08 .25
380 Joe Paterson .01 .05
381 Dave MacDonald .08 .25
382 Stephan Valiquette .40 1.00
383 Tim Swartz .01 .05
384 Gregg Lalonde .01 .05
385 Tyson Flinn .01 .05
386 Ryan Sly .01 .05
387 Neal Martin .01 .05
388 Kevin Hansen .01 .05
389 Joe Lombardo .01 .05
390 Darryl Moxam .01 .05
391 Jeremy Adduono .05 .15
392 Ryan Shanahan .01 .05
393 Sean Venedam .05 .15
394 Andrew Dale .08 .25
395 Rob Butler .01 .05
396 Brian Scott .01 .05
397 Liam MacEachern .01 .05
398 Luc Gagne .01 .05
399 Richard Rochefort .01 .05
400 Noel Burkitt .01 .05
401 Simon Sherry .01 .05
402 Brad Domonsky .08 .25
403 Ron Newhook .15 .40
404 Serge Dunphy .01 .05
405 Todd Lalonde .01 .05
406 Ryan Gelinas .08 .25
407 Terry Joss .07 .20
408 Mike Martin .07 .20
409 Chris Van Dyk .07 .20
410 D.J. Smith .20 .50
411 Glenn Crawford .07 .20
412 Robert Blain .01 .05
413 Matt Masterson .01 .05
414 Adam Young .01 .05
415 Matt Cooke .40 1.00
416 Jeff Zehr .20 .50
417 Wes Ward .07 .20
418 Matt Elich .15 .40
419 Rob Shearer .15 .40
420 Dean Mando .01 .05
421 Chris Kerr .01 .05
422 Vladimir Kretchine .01 .05
423 Jeff Martin .01 .05
424 Valeri Svoboda .01 .05
425 Dave Geris .07 .20
426 Ryan Pawluk .01 .05
427 Ryan Shaver .01 .05
428 Cameron Kincaid .01 .05
429 Tim Findlay .08 .25
430 Tim Bryan .01 .05
431 Alexandre Volchkov .20 .50
432 Boyd Devereaux .40 1.00
433 Chris Allen .08 .25
434 Paul Doyle .07 .20
435 Wes Mason .08 .25
436 Chris Hajt .08 .25
437 Kurt Walsh .01 .05
438 Glenn Crawford .07 .20
439 Jeff Brown .08 .25
440 Geoff Peters .08 .25
NNO Zac Bierk autograph 2.00 5.00
NNO Jay McKee promo .20 .50
NNO Zac Bierk promo .20 .50
NNO Cameron Mann promo .20 .50
NNO Mike Martin promo .20 .50
NNO Nick Boynton promo .40 1.00
NNO Ryan Pepperall promo .20 .50
NNO Scott Roche promo .20 .50
NNO Sean Haggerty promo .20 .50
NNO Adam Colagiacomo promo .20 .50

1994-95 SP

1 Paul Kariya .25 .60
2 Oleg Tverdovsky .20 .50
3 Stephan Lebeau .15 .40
4 Bob Corkum .15 .40
5 Guy Hebert .20 .50
6 Ray Bourque .40 1.00
7 Blaine Lacher RC .20 .50
8 Adam Oates .25 .60
9 Cam Neely .25 .60
10 Mariusz Czerkawski RC .25 .60
11 Bryan Smolinski .15 .40
12 Pat LaFontaine .25 .60
13 Alexander Mogilny .20 .50
14 Dominik Hasek .40 1.00
15 Dale Hawerchuk .30 .75
16 Alexei Zhitnik .20 .50
17 Theo Fleury .25 .60
18 German Titov .15 .40
19 Phil Housley .20 .50
20 Joe Nieuwendyk .20 .50
21 Trevor Kidd .20 .50
22 Jeremy Roenick .40 1.00
23 Chris Chelios .25 .60
24 Ed Belfour .25 .60
25 Bernie Nicholls .20 .50
26 Tony Amonte .20 .50
27 Joe Murphy .15 .40
28 Mike Modano .40 1.00
29 Trent Klatt .15 .40
30 Dave Gagner .20 .50
31 Kevin Hatcher .15 .40
32 Andy Moog .25 .60
33 Sergei Fedorov .40 1.00
34 Steve Yzerman .60 1.50
35 Slava Kozlov .20 .50
36 Paul Coffey .25 .60
37 Keith Primeau .20 .50
38 Ray Sheppard .20 .50
39 Doug Weight .20 .50
40 Jason Arnott .20 .50
41 Bill Ranford .20 .50
42 Shayne Corson .20 .50
43 Stu Barnes .15 .40
44 John Vanbiesbrouck .25 .60
45 Johan Garpenlov .15 .40
46 Bob Kudelski .15 .40
47 Scott Mellanby .20 .50
48 Chris Pronger .25 .60
49 Darren Turcotte .15 .40
50 Andrew Cassels .15 .40
51 Sean Burke .20 .50
52 Geoff Sanderson .20 .50
53 Rob Blake .25 .60
54 Wayne Gretzky 1.50 4.00
54 Wayne Gretzky PROMO 1.50 4.00
55 Rick Tocchet .20 .50
56 Tony Granato .15 .40
57 Jari Kurri .20 .50
58 Vincent Damphousse .20 .50
59 Patrick Roy .60 1.50
60 Vladimir Malakhov .15 .40
61 Pierre Turgeon .20 .50
62 Mark Recchi .30 .75
63 Martin Brodeur .60 1.50
64 Stephane Richer .20 .50
65 John MacLean .20 .50
66 Scott Stevens .25 .60
67 Scott Niedermayer .25 .60
68 Kirk Muller .15 .40
69 Ray Ferraro .15 .40
70 Brett Lindros .15 .40
71 Steve Thomas .15 .40
72 Pat Verbeek .20 .50
73 Mark Messier .50 1.25
74 Brian Leetch .20 .50
75 Mike Richter .25 .60
76 Alexei Kovalev .20 .50
77 Adam Graves .15 .40
78 Sergei Zubov .20 .50
79 Alexei Yashin .25 .60
80 Radek Bonk RC .15 .40
81 Alexandre Daigle .15 .40
82 Don Beaupre .20 .50
83 Mikael Renberg .20 .50
84 Eric Lindros .40 1.00
85 John LeClair .25 .60
86 Rod Brind'Amour .20 .50
87 Ron Hextall .25 .60
88 Ken Wregget .20 .50
89 Jaromir Jagr .75 2.00
90 Tomas Sandstrom .15 .40
91 John Cullen .15 .40
92 Ron Francis .30 .75
93 Luc Robitaille .25 .60
94 Joe Sakic .50 1.25
95 Owen Nolan .25 .60
96 Peter Forsberg .50 1.25
97 Wendel Clark .40 1.00
98 Mike Ricci .15 .40
99 Stephane Fiset .20 .50
100 Brett Hull .50 1.25
101 Brendan Shanahan .25 .60
102 Curtis Joseph .30 .75
103 Esa Tikkanen .15 .40
104 Al MacInnis .30 .75
105 Arturs Irbe .20 .50
106 Ray Whitney .15 .40
107 Sergei Makarov .15 .40
108 Sandis Ozolinsh .15 .40
109 Craig Janney .20 .50
110 Petr Klima .15 .40
111 Chris Gratton .15 .40
112 Roman Hamrlik .15 .40
113 Alexander Selivanov RC .20 .50
114 Brian Bradley .15 .40
115 Doug Gilmour .30 .75
116 Mats Sundin .25 .60
117 Felix Potvin .40 1.00
118 Mike Ridley .15 .40
119 Dave Andreychuk .25 .60
120 Dmitri Mironov .15 .40
121 Pavel Bure .25 .60
122 Trevor Linden .25 .60
123 Jeff Brown .15 .40
124 Kirk McLean .20 .50
125 Geoff Courtnall .15 .40
126 Joe Juneau .15 .40
127 Dale Hunter .15 .40
128 Jim Carey RC .25 .60
129 Peter Bondra .25 .60
130 Dimitri Khristich .15 .40
131 Teemu Selanne .50 1.25
132 Keith Tkachuk .25 .60
133 Alexei Zhamnov .20 .50
134 Dave Manson .15 .40
135 Nelson Emerson .15 .40
136 Alexandre Daigle .15 .40
137 Jamie Storr .20 .50
138 Todd Harvey .15 .40
139 Wade Redden RC .40 1.00
140 Ed Jovanovski RC .40 1.00
141 Jamie Rivers RC .25 .60
142 Ryan Smyth RC .75 2.00
143 Jason Botterill .20 .50
144 Denis Pederson RC .20 .50
145 Jeff Friesen .15 .40
146 Dan Cloutier RC .40 1.00
147 Lee Sorochan RC .25 .60
148 Marty Murray .20 .50
149 Shean Donovan RC .25 .60
150 Larry Courville RC .25 .60
151 Jason Allison .20 .50
152 Jeff O'Neill RC .20 .50
153 Bryan McCabe .15 .40
154 Miloslav Guren RC .25 .60
155 Petr Buzek RC .25 .60
156 Tomas Blazek .25 .60
157 Josef Marha .25 .60
158 Jan Hlavac RC .40 1.00
159 Veli-Pekka Nutikka RC .25 .60
160 Kimmo Timonen .20 .50
161 Antti Aalto RC .20 .50
162 Janne Niinimaa .25 .60
163 Nikolai Zavarukhin .25 .60
164 Vadim Epantchinsev RC .20 .50
165 Alexander Korolyuk RC .25 .60
166 Dmitri Klevakin RC .20 .50
167 Vitali Yachmenev RC .25 .60
168 Niklas Sundstrom .25 .60

169 Anders Soderberg RC .20 .50
170 Anders Eriksson .20 .50
171 Jesper Mattsson RC .20 .50
172 Mattias Ohlund RC .40 1.00
173 Jason Bonsignore .25 .60
174 Bryan Berard RC .40 1.00
175 Richard Park .15 .40
176 Mike McBain RC .25 .60
177 Jason Doig RC .25 .60
178 Xavier Delisle RC .25 .60
179 Christian Dube RC .25 .60
180 Louis-Phil.Sevigny RC .25 .60
181 Jarome Iginla RC .75 2.00
182 Marc Savard RC .25 .60
183 Alyn McCauley RC .25 .60
184 Brad Mehalko RC .25 .60
185 Todd Norman RC .25 .60
186 Brian Scott RC .25 .60
187 Brad Larsen RC .25 .60
188 Jeff Ware RC .25 .60
189 Sergei Samsonov RC .25 .60
190 Andrei Petrunin RC .25 .60
191 Sean Haggerty RC .25 .60
192 Rory Fitzpatrick RC .25 .60
193 Deron Quint .15 .40
194 Jamie Langenbrunner .20 .50
195 Jeff Mitchell RC .20 .50
SP1 Wayne Gretzky 2500 1.50 4.00

1994-95 SP Die Cuts

1 Paul Kariya .60 1.50
2 Oleg Tverdovsky .50 1.25
3 Stephan Lebeau .40 1.00
4 Bob Corkum .40 1.00
5 Guy Hebert .50 1.25
6 Ray Bourque 1.00 2.50
7 Blaine Lacher .50 1.25
8 Adam Oates .60 1.50
9 Cam Neely .60 1.50
10 Mariusz Czerkawski .60 1.50
11 Bryan Smolinski .40 1.00
12 Pat LaFontaine .60 1.50
13 Alexander Mogilny .50 1.25
14 Dominik Hasek 1.00 2.50
15 Dale Hawerchuk .75 2.00
16 Alexei Zhitnik .50 1.25
17 Theo Fleury .60 1.50
18 German Titov .40 1.00
19 Phil Housley .50 1.25
20 Joe Nieuwendyk .50 1.25
21 Trevor Kidd .50 1.25
22 Jeremy Roenick 1.00 2.50
23 Chris Chelios .60 1.50
24 Ed Belfour .60 1.50
25 Bernie Nicholls .50 1.25
26 Tony Amonte .50 1.25
27 Joe Murphy .40 1.00
28 Mike Modano 1.00 2.50
29 Trent Klatt .40 1.00
30 Dave Gagner .50 1.25
31 Kevin Hatcher .40 1.00
32 Andy Moog .60 1.50
33 Sergei Fedorov 1.00 2.50
34 Steve Yzerman 1.50 4.00
35 Slava Kozlov .50 1.25
36 Paul Coffey .60 1.50
37 Keith Primeau .50 1.25
38 Ray Sheppard .50 1.25
39 Doug Weight .50 1.25
40 Jason Arnott .50 1.25
41 Bill Ranford .50 1.25
42 Shayne Corson .50 1.25
43 Stu Barnes .40 1.00
44 John Vanbiesbrouck .60 1.50
45 Johan Garpenlov .40 1.00
46 Bob Kudelski .40 1.00
47 Scott Mellanby .50 1.25
48 Chris Pronger .60 1.50
49 Darren Turcotte .40 1.00
50 Andrew Cassels .40 1.00
51 Sean Burke .50 1.25
52 Geoff Sanderson .50 1.25
53 Rob Blake .60 1.50
54 Wayne Gretzky 3.00 8.00
55 Rick Tocchet .50 1.25
56 Tony Granato .40 1.00
57 Jari Kurri .50 1.25
58 Vincent Damphousse .50 1.25
59 Patrick Roy 1.50 4.00
60 Vladimir Malakhov .40 1.00
61 Pierre Turgeon .50 1.25
62 Mark Recchi .75 2.00
63 Martin Brodeur 1.50 4.00
64 Stephane Richer .50 1.25
65 John MacLean .50 1.25
66 Scott Stevens .60 1.50
67 Scott Niedermayer .60 1.50
68 Kirk Muller .40 1.00
69 Ray Ferraro .40 1.00
70 Brett Lindros .40 1.00
71 Steve Thomas .40 1.00
72 Pat Verbeek .50 1.25
73 Mark Messier 1.25 3.00
74 Brian Leetch .50 1.25
75 Mike Richter .60 1.50
76 Alexei Kovalev .50 1.25
77 Adam Graves .40 1.00
78 Sergei Zubov .50 1.25
79 Alexei Yashin .60 1.50
80 Radek Bonk .40 1.00
81 Alexandre Daigle .40 1.00
82 Don Beaupre .50 1.25
83 Mikael Renberg .50 1.25
84 Eric Lindros 1.00 2.50
85 John LeClair .60 1.50
86 Rod Brind'Amour .50 1.25
87 Ron Hextall .60 1.50
88 Ken Wregget .50 1.25
89 Jaromir Jagr 2.00 5.00
90 Tomas Sandstrom .40 1.00
91 John Cullen .40 1.00
92 Ron Francis .75 2.00
93 Luc Robitaille .60 1.50
94 Joe Sakic 1.25 3.00
95 Owen Nolan .60 1.50
96 Peter Forsberg 1.25 3.00
97 Wendel Clark 1.00 2.50
98 Mike Ricci .40 1.00
99 Stephane Fiset .50 1.25
100 Brett Hull 1.25 3.00
101 Brendan Shanahan .60 1.50
102 Curtis Joseph .75 2.00
103 Esa Tikkanen .40 1.00
104 Al MacInnis .75 2.00
105 Arturs Irbe .50 1.25
106 Ray Whitney .40 1.00
107 Sergei Makarov .40 1.00
108 Sandis Ozolinsh .40 1.00
109 Craig Janney .50 1.25
110 Petr Klima .40 1.00
111 Chris Gratton .40 1.00
112 Roman Hamrlik .40 1.00
113 Alexander Selivanov .50 1.25
114 Brian Bradley .40 1.00
115 Doug Gilmour .75 2.00
116 Mats Sundin .60 1.50
117 Felix Potvin 1.00 2.50
118 Mike Ridley .40 1.00
119 Dave Andreychuk .60 1.50
120 Dmitri Mironov .40 1.00
121 Pavel Bure .60 1.50
122 Trevor Linden .60 1.50
123 Jeff Brown .40 1.00
124 Kirk McLean .50 1.25
125 Geoff Courtnall .40 1.00
126 Joe Juneau .40 1.00
127 Dale Hunter .40 1.00
128 Jim Carey .60 1.50
129 Peter Bondra .60 1.50
130 Dimitri Khristich .40 1.00
131 Teemu Selanne 1.25 3.00
132 Keith Tkachuk .60 1.50
133 Alexei Zhamnov .50 1.25
134 Dave Manson .40 1.00
135 Nelson Emerson .40 1.00
136 Alexandre Daigle .40 1.00
137 Jamie Storr .50 1.25
138 Todd Harvey .40 1.00
139 Wade Redden 1.00 2.50
140 Ed Jovanovski 1.00 2.50
141 Jamie Rivers .60 1.50
142 Ryan Smyth 2.50 6.00
143 Jason Botterill .50 1.25
144 Denis Pederson .50 1.25
145 Jeff Friesen .40 1.00
146 Dan Cloutier 1.00 2.50
147 Lee Sorochan .60 1.50
148 Marty Murray .50 1.25
149 Shean Donovan .60 1.50
150 Larry Courville .60 1.50
151 Jason Allison .50 1.25
152 Jeff O'Neill .50 1.25
153 Bryan McCabe .40 1.00
154 Miloslav Guren .60 1.50
155 Petr Buzek .60 1.50
156 Tomas Blazek .60 1.50
157 Josef Marha .60 1.50
158 Jan Hlavac 1.00 2.50
159 Veli-Pekka Nutikka .60 1.50
160 Kimmo Timonen .50 1.25
161 Antti Aalto .50 1.25
162 Janne Niinimaa .60 1.50
163 Nikolai Zavarukhin .60 1.50
164 Vadim Epantchinsev .50 1.25
165 Alexander Korolyuk .60 1.50
166 Dmitri Klevakin .50 1.25
167 Vitali Yachmenev .60 1.50
168 Niklas Sundstrom .60 1.50
169 Anders Soderberg .50 1.25
170 Anders Eriksson .50 1.25
171 Jesper Mattsson .50 1.25
172 Mattias Ohlund 1.00 2.50
173 Jason Bonsignore .60 1.50
174 Bryan Berard 1.00 2.50
175 Richard Park .40 1.00
176 Mike McBain .60 1.50
177 Jason Doig .60 1.50
178 Xavier Delisle .60 1.50
179 Christian Dube .60 1.50
180 Louis-Philippe .60 1.50
181 Jarome Iginla 2.50 6.00
182 Marc Savard .60 1.50
183 Alyn McCauley .60 1.50
184 Brad Mehalko .60 1.50
185 Todd Norman .60 1.50
186 Brian Scott .60 1.50
187 Brad Larsen .60 1.50
188 Jeffrey Ware .60 1.50
189 Sergei Samsonov .60 1.50
190 Andrei Petrunin .60 1.50
191 Sean Haggerty .60 1.50
192 Rory Fitzpatrick .60 1.50
193 Deron Quint .40 1.00
194 Jamie Langenbrunner .50 1.25
195 Jeff Mitchell .50 1.25

1994-95 SP Premier

COMPLETE SET (30) 20.00 40.00
*DIE CUT: 4X TO 8X BASIC INSERTS
1 Paul Kariya .60 1.50
2 Peter Forsberg 1.50 4.00
3 Viktor Kozlov .30 .75
4 Todd Marchant .30 .75
5 Oleg Tverdovsky .15 .40
6 Todd Harvey .15 .40
7 Kenny Jonsson .30 .75
8 Blaine Lacher .30 .75
9 Radek Bonk .40 1.00
10 Brett Lindros .15 .40
11 Valeri Bure .30 .75
12 Brian Rolston .15 .40
13 David Oliver .15 .40
14 Ian Laperriere .15 .40
15 Adam Deadmarsh .30 .75
16 Pavel Bure .60 1.50
17 Wayne Gretzky 3.00 8.00
18 Jeremy Roenick .75 2.00
19 Dominik Hasek 1.25 3.00
20 Ray Bourque .75 2.00
21 Doug Gilmour .30 .75
22 Teemu Selanne .60 1.50
23 Cam Neely .60 1.50
24 Sergei Fedorov 1.00 2.50
25 Bernie Nicholls .15 .40
26 Jaromir Jagr .75 2.00
27 Joe Sakic 1.50 4.00
28 Mark Messier .60 1.50
29 Brett Hull .75 2.00
30 Eric Lindros .60 1.50

1995-96 SP

COMPLETE SET (188) 20.00 40.00
1 Paul Kariya .25 .60
2 Teemu Selanne .25 .60
3 Guy Hebert .10 .30
4 Steve Rucchin .10 .30
5 Ray Bourque .40 1.00
6 Cam Neely .25 .60
7 Adam Oates .10 .30
8 Kyle McLaren RC .05 .15
9 Bill Ranford .10 .30
10 Shawn McEachern .05 .15
11 Don Sweeney .05 .15
12 Pat LaFontaine .25 .60
13 Dominik Hasek .50 1.25
14 Brian Holzinger RC .25 .60
15 Alexei Zhitnik .05 .15
16 Theo Fleury .05 .15
17 Cory Stillman .05 .15
18 German Titov .05 .15
19 Phil Housley .10 .30
20 Michael Nylander .05 .15
21 Trevor Kidd .10 .30
22 Eric Daze .10 .30
23 Chris Chelios .25 .60
24 Jeremy Roenick .30 .75
25 Gary Suter .05 .15
26 Bernie Nicholls .05 .15
27 Ed Belfour .25 .60
28 Tony Amonte .10 .30
29 Peter Forsberg .60 1.50
30 Patrick Roy 1.25 3.00
31 Joe Sakic .50 1.25
32 Sandis Ozolinsh .05 .15
33 Adam Deadmarsh .05 .15
34 Stephane Fiset .10 .30
35 Claude Lemieux .05 .15
36 Mike Modano .40 1.00
37 Kevin Hatcher .05 .15
38 Joe Nieuwendyk .10 .30
39 Todd Harvey .10 .30
40 Derian Hatcher .05 .15
41 Jere Lehtinen .10 .30
42 Nicklas Lidstrom .25 .60
43 Mathieu Dandenault .05 .15
44 Sergei Fedorov .40 1.00
45 Paul Coffey .25 .60
46 Steve Yzerman 1.25 3.00
47 Keith Primeau .05 .15
48 Chris Osgood .10 .30
49 Vyacheslav Kozlov .10 .30
50 Doug Weight .10 .30
51 Jason Arnott .05 .15
52 Miroslav Satan RC 1.00 2.50
53 Zdeno Ciger .05 .15
54 Curtis Joseph .25 .60
55 Scott Mellanby .05 .15
56 John Vanbiesbrouck .10 .30
57 Jody Hull .05 .15
58 Ed Jovanovski .25 .60
59 Radek Dvorak RC .40 1.00
60 Rob Niedermayer .10 .30
61 Andrew Cassels .05 .15
62 Brendan Shanahan .25 .60
63 Nelson Emerson .05 .15
64 Jeff O'Neill .05 .15
65 Sean Burke .10 .30
66 Wayne Gretzky PROMO 4.00 10.00
66 Wayne Gretzky UDA AU/500 150.00 400.00
66 Craig Johnson .05 .15
67 Dimitri Khristich .05 .15
68 Vitali Yachmenev .05 .15
69 Aki Berg RC .10 .30
70 Byron Dafoe .10 .30
71 Pierre Turgeon .10 .30
72 Mark Recchi .10 .30
73 Saku Koivu .25 .60
74 Valeri Bure .05 .15
75 Vincent Damphousse .05 .15
76 Jocelyn Thibault .25 .60
77 Patrice Brisebois .05 .15
78 John MacLean .10 .30
79 Martin Brodeur .60 1.50
80 Steve Thomas .10 .30
81 Scott Stevens .10 .30
82 Bill Guerin .10 .30
83 Petr Sykora RC 1.00 2.50
84 Scott Niedermayer .05 .15
85 Stephane Richer .10 .30
86 Zigmund Palffy .10 .30
87 Travis Green .10 .30
88 Todd Bertuzzi RC 2.00 5.00
89 Mathieu Schneider .05 .15
90 Eric Fichaud .10 .30
91 Bryan McCabe .05 .15
92 Mark Messier .25 .60
93 Pat Verbeek .05 .15
94 Brian Leetch .10 .30
95 Mike Richter .25 .60
96 Niklas Sundstrom .10 .30
97 Luc Robitaille .10 .30
98 Adam Graves .05 .15
99 Alexei Kovalev .05 .15
100 Daniel Alfredsson RC 2.00 5.00
101 Alexei Yashin .05 .15
102 Radek Bonk .05 .15
103 Alexandre Daigle .05 .15
104 Damian Rhodes .10 .30
105 Antti Tormanen .05 .15
106 Eric Lindros .25 .60
107 Mikael Renberg .10 .30
108 John LeClair .25 .60
109 Ron Hextall .10 .30
110 Rod Brind'Amour .10 .30
111 Joel Otto .05 .15
112 Eric Desjardins .10 .30
113 Mario Lemieux 1.25 3.00
114 Jaromir Jagr .40 1.00
115 Ron Francis .10 .30
116 Markus Naslund .25 .60
117 Sergei Zubov .05 .15
118 Tomas Sandstrom .05 .15
119 Tom Barrasso .10 .30
120 Richard Park .05 .15
121 Brett Hull .30 .75
122 Shayne Corson .05 .15
123 Dale Hawerchuk .25 .60
124 Chris Pronger .25 .60
125 Al MacInnis .10 .30
126 Grant Fuhr .25 .60
127 Wayne Gretzky 1.50 4.00
128 Geoff Courtnall .05 .15
129 Owen Nolan .10 .30
130 Ray Sheppard .05 .15
131 Chris Terreri .10 .30
132 Marcus Ragnarsson RC .10 .30
133 Jeff Friesen .05 .15
134 Doug Bodger .05 .15
135 Roman Hamrlik .10 .30
136 Petr Klima .05 .15
137 Daren Puppa .10 .30
138 Aaron Gavey .05 .15
139 Daymond Langkow RC .40 1.00
140 Alexander Selivanov .05 .15
141 Mats Sundin .25 .60
142 Kirk Muller .05 .15
143 Larry Murphy .10 .30
144 Doug Gilmour .10 .30
145 Darby Hendrickson .05 .15
146 Felix Potvin .25 .60
147 Kenny Jonsson .05 .15
148 Alexander Mogilny .10 .30
149 Pavel Bure .25 .60
150 Trevor Linden .10 .30
151 Corey Hirsch .10 .30
152 Kirk McLean .10 .30
153 Esa Tikkanen .05 .15
154 Cliff Ronning .05 .15
155 Peter Bondra .10 .30
156 Jim Carey .10 .30
157 Michal Pivonka .05 .15
158 Joe Juneau .05 .15
159 Dale Hunter .10 .30
160 Steve Konowalchuk .05 .15
161 Stefan Ustorf .05 .15
162 Brendan Witt .05 .15
163 Chad Kilger RC .05 .15
164 Keith Tkachuk .25 .60
165 Deron Quint .05 .15
166 Oleg Tverdovsky .05 .15
167 Alexei Zhamnov .10 .30
168 Igor Korolev .05 .15
169 Wade Redden .05 .15
170 Jarome Iginla .30 .75
171 Christian Dube .05 .15
172 Jason Podollan .05 .15
173 Alyn McCauley .10 .30
174 Nolan Baumgartner .05 .15
175 Jason Botterill .05 .15
176 Chris Phillips RC .30 .75
177 Dmitri Nabokov .10 .30
178 Andrei Petrunin .05 .15
179 Alexander Korolyuk .10 .30
180 Sergei Samsonov .60 1.50
181 Ilja Gorokhov RC .10 .30
182 Alexei Kolkunov RC .10 .30
183 Samuel Pahlsson RC .05 .15
184 Mattias Ohlund .05 .15
185 Marcus Nilsson RC .25 .60
186 Daniel Tjarnqvist RC .05 .15
187 Per Anton Lundstrom RC .05 .15
188 Fredrik Loven RC .05 .15
GC1 Wayne Gretzky 15.00 40.00
GC2 Sergei Samsonov 8.00 20.00

1995-96 SP Holoviews

*SPECIAL FX: 1.25X TO 3X BASIC INSERTS
FX1 Teemu Selanne .60 1.50
FX2 Paul Kariya .30 .75
FX3 Chris Chelios .30 .75
FX4 Peter Forsberg .60 1.50
FX5 Sergei Fedorov .50 1.25
FX6 Paul Coffey .30 .75
FX7 Steve Yzerman 2.50 6.00
FX8 Jason Arnott .25 .60
FX9 Doug Weight .30 .75
FX10 Wayne Gretzky 4.00 10.00
FX11 Vitali Yachmenev .30 .75
FX12 Martin Brodeur 1.25 3.00
FX13 Scott Stevens .30 .75
FX14 Mark Messier .60 1.50
FX15 Daniel Alfredsson 1.50 4.00
FX16 Eric Lindros .50 1.25
FX17 Mario Lemieux 2.50 6.00
FX18 Jaromir Jagr 1.00 2.50
FX19 Shayne Corson .25 .60
FX20 Pavel Bure .30 .75

1995-96 SP Stars Etoiles

COMPLETE SET (30) 25.00 50.00
*GOLD: 3X TO 6X BASIC INSERTS
E1 Paul Kariya .50 1.25
E2 Teemu Selanne .50 1.25
E3 Ray Bourque .75 2.00
E4 Cam Neely .50 1.25
E5 Pat LaFontaine .50 1.25
E6 Theo Fleury .60 1.50
E7 Jeremy Roenick .60 1.50
E8 Joe Sakic 1.00 2.50
E9 Patrick Roy 2.50 6.00
E10 Peter Forsberg 1.25 3.00
E11 Mike Modano .75 2.00
E12 Sergei Fedorov .75 2.00
E13 Paul Coffey .50 1.25
E14 Steve Yzerman 2.50 6.00
E15 Pierre Turgeon .25 .60
E16 Brendan Shanahan .50 1.25
E17 Wayne Gretzky 2.50 6.00
E18 Martin Brodeur 1.25 3.00
E19 Mark Messier .50 1.25
E20 Brian Leetch .25 .60
E21 Eric Lindros .50 1.25
E22 Mario Lemieux 2.50 6.00
E23 Jaromir Jagr .75 2.00
E24 Brett Hull .60 1.50
E25 Roman Hamrlik .25 .60
E26 Mats Sundin .50 1.25
E27 Felix Potvin .50 1.25
E28 Alexander Mogilny .25 .60
E29 Pavel Bure .50 1.25
E30 Keith Tkachuk .50 1.25

1996-97 SP

1 Paul Kariya .25 .60
2 Teemu Selanne .50 1.25
3 Jari Kurri .25 .60
4 Darren Van Impe .15 .40
5 Guy Hebert .20 .50
6 Steve Rucchin .15 .40
7 Ray Bourque .40 1.00
8 Kyle McLaren .15 .40
9 Bill Ranford .20 .50
10 Don Sweeney .15 .40
11 Adam Oates .25 .60
12 Rick Tocchet .20 .50
13 Ted Donato .15 .40
14 Curtis Brown .15 .40
15 Pat LaFontaine .25 .60
16 Derek Plante .15 .40
17 Dominik Hasek .40 1.00
18 Brian Holzinger .20 .50
19 Alexei Zhitnik .15 .40
20 Theo Fleury .50 1.25
21 Trevor Kidd .15 .40
22 Steve Chiasson .15 .40
23 Jarome Iginla .30 .75
24 German Titov .15 .40
25 Zarley Zalapski .15 .40
26 Eric Daze .20 .50
27 Chris Chelios .25 .60
28 Ed Belfour .25 .60
29 Gary Suter .15 .40
30 Alexei Zhamnov .20 .50
31 Ethan Moreau RC .25 .60
32 Tony Amonte .20 .50
33 Peter Forsberg .50 1.25
34 Joe Sakic .50 1.25
35 Patrick Roy .60 1.50
36 Adam Deadmarsh .15 .40
37 Mike Ricci .15 .40
38 Adam Foote .15 .40
39 Claude Lemieux .15 .40
40 Mike Modano .40 1.00
41 Pat Verbeek .15 .40
42 Todd Harvey .15 .40
43 Sergei Zubov .20 .50
44 Andy Moog .25 .60
45 Derian Hatcher .15 .40
46 Jamie Langenbrunner .15 .40
47 Steve Yzerman .60 1.50
48 Sergei Fedorov .40 1.00
49 Slava Kozlov .15 .40
50 Brendan Shanahan .25 .60
51 Chris Osgood .25 .60
52 Nicklas Lidstrom .30 .75
53 Vladimir Konstantinov .20 .50
54 Curtis Joseph .30 .75
55 Jason Arnott .20 .50
56 Ryan Smyth .20 .50
57 Doug Weight .25 .60
58 Andrei Kovalenko .15 .40
59 Mariusz Czerkawski .15 .40
60 Ed Jovanovski .20 .50
61 John Vanbiesbrouck .25 .60
62 Rob Niedermayer .20 .50
63 Robert Svehla .15 .40
64 Brian Skrudland .15 .40
65 Scott Mellanby .20 .50
66 Ray Sheppard .20 .50
67 Jeff O'Neill .15 .40
68 Keith Primeau .20 .50
69 Geoff Sanderson .20 .50
70 Sean Burke .15 .40
71 Kevin Dineen .15 .40
72 Andrew Cassels .15 .40
73 Kevin Stevens .20 .50
74 Rob Blake .25 .60
75 Ed Olczyk .15 .40
76 Mattias Norstrom .15 .40
77 Stephane Fiset .20 .50
78 Vitali Yachmenev .15 .40
79 Saku Koivu .25 .60
80 Valeri Bure .15 .40
81 Jocelyn Thibault .20 .50
82 David Wilkie .15 .40
83 Stephane Richer .20 .50
84 Shayne Corson .20 .50
85 Mark Recchi .30 .75
86 Martin Brodeur .60 1.50
87 Bobby Holik .15 .40
88 Petr Sykora .15 .40
89 Scott Stevens .25 .60
90 Scott Niedermayer .25 .60
91 Bill Guerin .25 .60
92 Eric Fichaud .20 .50
93 Kenny Jonsson .15 .40
94 Travis Green .20 .50
95 Derek King .15 .40
96 Todd Bertuzzi .25 .60
97 Zigmund Palffy .25 .60
98 Mark Messier .50 1.25
99 Wayne Gretzky 1.50 4.00
100 Mike Richter .25 .60
101 Brian Leetch .20 .50
102 Luc Robitaille .25 .60
103 Adam Graves .15 .40
104 Alexei Kovalev .20 .50
105 Radek Bonk .15 .40
106 Alexandre Daigle .15 .40
107 Daniel Alfredsson .25 .60
108 Alexei Yashin .20 .50
109 Andreas Dackell RC .25 .60
110 Damian Rhodes .20 .50
111 Petr Svoboda .15 .40
112 John LeClair .25 .60
113 Eric Desjardins .20 .50
114 Eric Lindros .40 1.00
115 Mikael Renberg .20 .50
116 Ron Hextall .25 .60
117 Dainius Zubrus RC .30 .75
118 Keith Tkachuk .25 .60
119 Jeremy Roenick .40 1.00
120 Nikolai Khabibulin .20 .50
121 Oleg Tverdovsky .20 .50
122 Teppo Numminen .15 .40
123 Mike Gartner .30 .75
124 Cliff Ronning .15 .40
125 Mario Lemieux 1.00 2.50
126 Jaromir Jagr .75 2.00
127 Ron Francis .30 .75
128 Petr Nedved .20 .50
129 Darius Kasparaitis .15 .40
130 Kevin Hatcher .15 .40
131 Joe Mullen .20 .50
132 Joe Murphy .15 .40
133 Grant Fuhr .40 1.00
134 Harry York RC .25 .60
135 Chris Pronger .25 .60
136 Brett Hull .50 1.25
137 Pierre Turgeon .20 .50
138 Owen Nolan .25 .60
139 Bernie Nicholls .20 .50
140 Tony Granato .15 .40
141 Kelly Hrudey .20 .50
142 Darren Turcotte .15 .40
143 Jeff Friesen .15 .40
144 Roman Hamrlik .15 .40
145 Chris Gratton .20 .50
146 Daymond Langkow .20 .50
147 Dino Ciccarelli .25 .60
148 Alexander Selivanov .15 .40
149 Brian Bradley .15 .40
150 Wendel Clark .40 1.00
151 Mats Sundin .25 .60
152 Doug Gilmour .30 .75
153 Felix Potvin .40 1.00
154 Larry Murphy .20 .50
155 Mathieu Schneider .15 .40
156 Kirk Muller .15 .40
157 Pavel Bure .25 .60
158 Alexander Mogilny .20 .50
159 Corey Hirsch .20 .50
160 Jyrki Lumme .15 .40
161 Russ Courtnall .15 .40
162 Mike Fountain RC .20 .50
163 Peter Bondra .25 .60
164 Jim Carey .25 .60
165 Sergei Gonchar .15 .40
166 Joe Juneau .15 .40
167 Phil Housley .20 .50
168 Jason Allison .20 .50
169 Ruslan Salei RC .25 .60
170 Mattias Timander RC .25 .60
171 Vaclav Varada RC .25 .60
172 Jonas Hoglund .15 .40
173 Jason Podollan .20 .50
174 Jose Theodore .30 .75
175 Roman Turek RC .25 .60
176 Anders Eriksson .15 .40
177 Mike Grier RC .30 .75
178 Rem Murray RC .25 .60
179 Per Gustafsson RC .25 .60
180 Jay Pandolfo UER .25 .60
181 Kai Nurminen RC .25 .60
182 Bryan Berard .25 .60
183 Christian Dube .15 .40
184 Daniel Goneau RC .25 .60
185 Wade Redden .15 .40
186 Janne Niinimaa .25 .60
187 Jim Campbell .15 .40
188 Sergei Berezin RC .40 1.00
P99 Wayne Gretzky PROMO 1.50 4.00

1996-97 SP Clearcut Winner

CW1 Wayne Gretzky 20.00 50.00
CW2 Saku Koivu 2.50 6.00
CW3 Mario Lemieux 10.00 25.00
CW4 Sergei Fedorov 3.00 8.00
CW5 Paul Kariya 2.50 6.00
CW6 Patrick Roy 10.00 25.00
CW7 Jeremy Roenick 3.00 8.00
CW8 Brendan Shanahan 2.50 6.00
CW9 John Vanbiesbrouck 2.00 5.00
CW10 Doug Weight 2.00 5.00
CW11 Mark Messier 2.50 6.00
CW12 Mats Sundin 2.50 6.00
CW13 Paul Coffey 2.00 5.00
CW14 Theo Fleury 4.00 10.00
CW15 Steve Yzerman 8.00 20.00
CW16 Pavel Bure 2.50 6.00
CW17 Adam Deadmarsh 1.00 2.50
CW18 Chris Chelios 2.00 5.00
CW19 Joe Sakic 8.00 20.00
CW20 Eric Daze 1.00 2.50

1996-97 SP Holoview Collection

COMPLETE SET (30) 20.00 50.00
HC1 Wayne Gretzky 6.00 15.00
HC2 Eric Daze .40 1.00
HC3 Doug Gilmour .60 1.50
HC4 Jason Arnott .60 1.50
HC5 Sergei Fedorov 1.50 4.00
HC6 Chris Chelios 1.00 2.50
HC7 Alexei Kovalev .60 1.50
HC8 Pat LaFontaine .40 1.00
HC9 Daniel Alfredsson .60 1.50
HC10 Chris Pronger .60 1.50
HC11 Jocelyn Thibault .60 1.50
HC12 Chris Gratton .40 1.00
HC13 Alexei Yashin .40 1.00
HC14 Peter Bondra .60 1.50
HC15 Saku Koivu 1.00 2.50
HC16 Valeri Bure .40 1.00
HC17 Joe Juneau .40 1.00
HC18 Tony Amonte 1.00 2.50
HC19 Brian Holzinger .40 1.00
HC20 Mats Sundin 1.00 2.50
HC21 Chris Osgood .60 1.50
HC22 Roman Hamrlik .40 1.00
HC23 Ray Bourque 2.00 5.00
HC24 Doug Weight .60 1.50
HC25 Mike Modano 1.50 4.00
HC26 Niklas Sundstrom .40 1.00
HC27 Mike Richter 1.00 2.50
HC28 Zigmund Palffy .60 1.50
HC29 Adam Oates .60 1.50
HC30 Dominik Hasek 2.00 5.00

1996-97 SP Inside Info

COMPLETE SET (8) 20.00 50.00
*GOLDS: 2X TO 5X BASIC INSERTS
IN1 Wayne Gretzky 10.00 25.00
IN2 Keith Tkachuk 2.00 5.00
IN3 Brendan Shanahan 2.50 6.00
IN4 Teemu Selanne 3.00 8.00
IN5 Ray Bourque 3.00 8.00
IN6 Joe Sakic 4.00 10.00
IN7 Felix Potvin 3.00 8.00
IN8 Steve Yzerman 6.00 15.00

1996-97 SP Game Film

COMPLETE SET (20) 40.00 100.00
GF1 Wayne Gretzky 15.00 40.00
GF2 Peter Forsberg 4.00 10.00
GF3 Patrick Roy 10.00 25.00
GF4 Brett Hull 3.00 8.00
GF5 Keith Tkachuk 1.00 2.50
GF6 Eric Lindros 3.00 8.00
GF7 Felix Potvin 3.00 8.00
GF8 John Vanbiesbrouck 1.50 4.00
GF9 Paul Kariya 3.00 8.00
GF10 Mark Messier 2.50 6.00
GF11 Ed Belfour 2.50 6.00
GF12 Alexander Mogilny 1.00 2.50
GF13 Jim Carey 1.50 4.00
GF14 Ed Jovanovski 1.00 2.50
GF15 Theo Fleury 1.50 4.00
GF16 Doug Gilmour 1.50 4.00
GF17 John LeClair 1.00 2.50
GF18 Pat LaFontaine 1.00 2.50
GF19 Paul Coffey 1.50 4.00
GF20 Daniel Alfredsson 1.50 4.00

1996-97 SP SPx Force

COMPLETE SET (5) 60.00 150.00
1 Lind./Lemieux/Forsb./Gretz. 100.00 250.00
2 Brett Hull
Jaromir Jagr
Pavel Bure
Teemu Selanne 100.00 250.00
3 Osgo./Hasek/Brod./Richt. 30.00 80.00
4 Eriks./Berard/Iginla/Berezin 15.00 40.00
5 Iginla/Jagr/Gretzky/Brodeur 100.00 250.00

1996-97 SP SPx Force Autographs

1 Wayne Gretzky AU 2000.00 5000.00
2 Jaromir Jagr AU 1250.00 3000.00
3 Martin Brodeur AU 500.00 1200.00
4 Jarome Iginla AU 300.00 800.00

2018-19 SP

*VETS: .8X TO 2X BASIC CARDS
COMMON BLUE RC .75 2.00
BLUE.RC.SEMI 1.00 2.50
BLUE.RC.UNL.STARS 1.25 3.00
1 Alexander Ovechkin 1.00 2.50
2 William Karlsson .30 .75
3 Brock Boeser .30 .75
4 Ryan O'Reilly .25 .60
5 Jonathan Toews .40 1.00
6 Evander Kane .25 .60
7 Sean Couturier .20 .50
8 Matt Duchene .25 .60
9 Kevin Shattenkirk .15 .40
10 Taylor Hall .25 .60
11 Mathew Barzal .30 .75
12 Filip Forsberg .40 1.00
13 Jonathan Drouin .20 .50
14 Eric Staal .25 .60
15 Nikita Kucherov .50 1.25
16 Jonathan Quick .30 .75
17 Vincent Trocheck .25 .60
18 John Klingberg .25 .60
19 Justin Williams .20 .50
20 Connor McDavid 1.25 3.00
21 Sean Monahan .15 .40
22 John Gibson .25 .60
23 Sergei Bobrovsky .40 1.00
24 Alex Galchenyuk .15 .40
25 Jack Eichel .40 1.00
26 Patric Hornqvist .15 .40
27 Jake DeBrusk .25 .60
28 Connor Hellebuyck .50 1.25
29 Mikko Rantanen .60 1.50
30 Anthony Mantha .20 .50
31 Auston Matthews 1.00 2.50
32 Evgeny Kuznetsov .30 .75
33 Brendan Gallagher .25 .60
34 Alex Tuch .25 .60
35 Steven Stamkos .50 1.25
36 Colton Parayko .20 .50
37 Tomas Hertl .25 .60
38 Nolan Patrick .25 .60
39 Pekka Rinne .25 .60
40 Patrick Kane .50 1.25
41 Aaron Ekblad .30 .75
42 Mark Stone .30 .75
43 Alexander Radulov .25 .60
44 Max Domi .25 .60
45 Anze Kopitar .40 1.00
46 Jake Guentzel .40 1.00
47 Pierre-Luc Dubois .20 .50
48 Will Butcher .20 .50
49 Leon Draisaitl .75 2.00
50 Henrik Lundqvist .60 1.50
51 John Carlson .25 .60
52 Jonathan Marchessault .30 .75
53 Brayden Schenn .25 .60
54 Bo Horvat .30 .75
55 Erik Karlsson .30 .75
56 Kyle Connor .40 1.00
57 Mitch Marner .40 1.00
58 Rickard Rakell .20 .50
59 Charlie McAvoy .30 .75
60 Johnny Gaudreau .40 1.00
61 Roberto Luongo .40 1.00
62 Vladimir Tarasenko .30 .75
63 Teuvo Teravainen .25 .60
64 Jake Gardiner .15 .40
65 Jamie Benn .25 .60
66 Alex Kerfoot .20 .50
67 Andrei Vasilevskiy .40 1.00
68 Clayton Keller .30 .75
69 Dylan Larkin .30 .75
70 Evgeni Malkin .50 1.25
71 Tom Wilson .25 .60
72 Alex DeBrincat .30 .75
73 Nico Hischier .40 1.00
74 Brent Burns .25 .60
75 Carey Price .50 1.25
76 Mikael Granlund .20 .50
77 Blake Wheeler .25 .60
78 Jeff Skinner .30 .75
79 Jeff Carter .20 .50
80 John Tavares .40 1.00

81 Artemi Panarin .50 1.25
82 Duncan Keith .20 .50
83 James van Riemsdyk .20 .50
84 Craig Anderson .20 .50
85 Nathan MacKinnon 1.00 2.50
86 Ryan Ellis .20 .50
87 Sidney Crosby 1.00 2.50
88 James Neal .15 .40
89 Brad Marchand .50 1.25
90 Marc-Andre Fleury .50 1.25
91 Zach Hyman .40 1.00
92 Mats Zuccarello .25 .60
93 Cam Talbot .25 .60
94 Anders Lee .20 .50
95 Dominik Hasek .40 1.00
96 Guy Lafleur .30 .75
97 Jarome Iginla .30 .75
98 Marcel Dionne .30 .75
99 Wayne Gretzky 1.50 4.00
100 Mark Messier .50 1.25
101 Elias Pettersson RC 6.00 15.00
102 Brett Howden RC 2.50 6.00
103 Dillon Dube RC 2.50 6.00
104 Evan Bouchard RC 5.00 12.00
105 Andrei Svechnikov RC 5.00 12.00
106 Dylan Sikura RC 2.50 6.00
107 Henrik Borgstrom RC 3.00 8.00
108 Jordan Kyrou RC 4.00 10.00
109 Maxime Comtois RC 2.00 5.00
110 Brady Tkachuk RC 6.00 15.00
111 Michael Dal Colle RC 2.00 5.00
112 Eeli Tolvanen RC 4.00 10.00
113 Isac Lundestrom RC 1.50 4.00
114 Dennis Cholowski RC 2.00 5.00
115 Ryan Donato RC 3.00 8.00
116 Ilya Samsonov RC 4.00 10.00
117 Carter Hart RC 4.00 10.00
118 Andreas Johnsson RC 2.50 6.00
119 Dominik Kahun RC 2.00 5.00
120 Rasmus Dahlin RC 5.00 12.00
121 Maxime Lajoie RC 3.00 8.00
122 Jordan Greenway RC 2.00 5.00
123 Michael Rasmussen RC 2.50 6.00
124 Dan Vladar RC 2.50 6.00
125 Miro Heiskanen RC 5.00 12.00
126 Jakub Zboril RC 3.00 8.00
127 Kristian Vesalainen RC 2.50 6.00
128 Drake Batherson RC 4.00 10.00
129 Jonas Siegenthaler RC 2.00 5.00
130 Jesperi Kotkaniemi RC 4.00 10.00
131 Warren Foegele RC 2.00 5.00
132 Travis Dermott RC 3.00 8.00
133 Juuso Valimaki RC 2.00 5.00
134 Sam Steel RC 2.00 5.00
135 Adam Gaudette RC 3.00 8.00
136 Noah Juulsen RC 2.00 5.00
137 Robert Thomas RC 4.00 10.00
138 Henri Jokiharju RC 1.50 4.00
139 Lias Andersson RC 3.00 8.00
140 Casey Mittelstadt RC 4.00 10.00

2018-19 SP Authentic Profiles

*BLUE: .5X TO 1.5X BASIC INSERTS
APAM Auston Matthews 5.00 12.00
APAO Alexander Ovechkin 5.00 12.00
APBB Brent Burns 1.25 3.00
APCM Connor McDavid 6.00 15.00
APCP Carey Price 2.50 6.00
APEM Evgeni Malkin 2.50 6.00
APES Eric Staal 1.25 3.00
APJE Jack Eichel 2.00 5.00
APJG Johnny Gaudreau 2.00 5.00
APJQ Jonathan Quick 1.50 4.00
APJT John Tavares 2.00 5.00
APMD Max Domi 1.25 3.00
APMF Marc-Andre Fleury 2.50 6.00
APMR Mikko Rantanen 3.00 8.00
APMS Mark Stone 1.50 4.00
APPK Patrick Kane 2.50 6.00
APPS P.K. Subban 1.50 4.00
APSC Sidney Crosby 5.00 12.00
APSS Steven Stamkos 2.50 6.00
APWK William Karlsson 1.50 4.00

2018-19 SP Authentic Profiles Jerseys

APAM Auston Matthews 8.00 20.00
APAO Alexander Ovechkin 8.00 20.00
APBB Brent Burns 2.00 5.00
APCM Connor McDavid 10.00 25.00
APCP Carey Price 4.00 10.00
APEM Evgeni Malkin 4.00 10.00
APES Eric Staal 2.00 5.00
APJE Jack Eichel 3.00 8.00
APJG Johnny Gaudreau 3.00 8.00
APJQ Jonathan Quick 2.50 6.00
APJT John Tavares 3.00 8.00
APMD Max Domi 2.00 5.00
APMF Marc-Andre Fleury 4.00 10.00
APMR Mikko Rantanen 5.00 12.00
APMS Mark Stone 2.50 6.00
APPK Patrick Kane 4.00 10.00
APPS P.K. Subban 2.50 6.00
APSC Sidney Crosby 8.00 20.00
APSS Steven Stamkos 4.00 10.00
APWK William Karlsson 2.50 6.00

2018-19 SP Authentic Profiles Signatures

APAM Auston Matthews A 60.00 150.00
APBB Brent Burns B 15.00 40.00
APCM Connor McDavid A 150.00 250.00
APCP Carey Price A 30.00 80.00
APEM Evgeni Malkin A 30.00 80.00
APES Eric Staal C 15.00 40.00
APJE Jack Eichel B 25.00 60.00
APJG Johnny Gaudreau A 25.00 60.00
APJT John Tavares A 25.00 60.00
APMD Max Domi B 15.00 40.00
APMF Marc-Andre Fleury B 30.00 80.00
APMR Mikko Rantanen C 40.00 100.00
APWK William Karlsson C 20.00 50.00

2018-19 SP Authentic Signatures

ASAD Anthony Duclair C 8.00 20.00
ASBG Brendan Gaunce C 6.00 15.00
ASBR Brett Ritchie C 6.00 15.00
ASCH Charles Hudon C 8.00 20.00
ASCM Connor McDavid A 150.00 250.00
ASDH Danton Heinen C 8.00 20.00
ASDP Derrick Pouliot C 6.00 15.00
ASJV Jimmy Vesey C 8.00 20.00
ASJW Jordan Weal C 6.00 15.00
ASLD Louis Domingue C 8.00 20.00
ASLW Lucas Wallmark C 6.00 15.00
ASMB Madison Bowey C 6.00 15.00
ASMM Mitch Marner B 15.00 40.00
ASMP Mark Pysyk C 8.00 20.00
ASMT Matthew Tkachuk C 20.00 50.00
ASNG Nikolay Goldobin C 8.00 20.00
ASOB Oliver Bjorkstrand C 8.00 20.00
ASPD Phillip Danault C 10.00 25.00
ASRF Radek Faksa C 8.00 20.00
ASRM Ryan Murray C 8.00 20.00
ASSL Scott Laughton C 6.00 15.00
ASTP Tanner Pearson C 8.00 20.00
ASYW Yannick Weber C 6.00 15.00

2018-19 SP Jerseys

101 Elias Pettersson 6.00 15.00
102 Brett Howden 2.50 6.00
103 Dillon Dube 2.50 6.00
104 Evan Bouchard 5.00 12.00
105 Andrei Svechnikov 5.00 12.00
106 Dylan Sikura 2.50 6.00
107 Henrik Borgstrom 3.00 8.00
108 Jordan Kyrou 4.00 10.00
109 Maxime Comtois 2.00 5.00
110 Brady Tkachuk 6.00 15.00
111 Michael Dal Colle 2.00 5.00
112 Eeli Tolvanen 4.00 10.00
113 Isac Lundestrom 1.50 4.00
114 Dennis Cholowski 2.00 5.00
115 Ryan Donato 3.00 8.00
116 Ilya Samsonov 4.00 10.00
117 Carter Hart 4.00 10.00
118 Andreas Johnsson 2.50 6.00
119 Dominik Kahun 2.00 5.00
120 Rasmus Dahlin 5.00 12.00
121 Maxime Lajoie 3.00 8.00
122 Jordan Greenway 2.00 5.00
123 Michael Rasmussen 2.50 6.00
124 Dan Vladar 2.50 6.00
125 Miro Heiskanen 5.00 12.00
126 Jakub Zboril 3.00 8.00
127 Kristian Vesalainen 2.50 6.00
128 Drake Batherson 4.00 10.00
129 Jonas Siegenthaler 2.00 5.00
130 Jesperi Kotkaniemi 4.00 10.00
131 Warren Foegele 2.00 5.00
132 Travis Dermott 3.00 8.00
133 Juuso Valimaki 2.00 5.00
134 Sam Steel 2.00 5.00
135 Adam Gaudette 3.00 8.00
136 Noah Juulsen 2.00 5.00
137 Robert Thomas 4.00 10.00
138 Henri Jokiharju 1.50 4.00
139 Lias Andersson 3.00 8.00
140 Casey Mittelstadt 4.00 10.00

2018-19 SP Signatures

101 Elias Pettersson A 60.00 150.00
102 Brett Howden C 12.00 30.00
103 Dillon Dube C 12.00 30.00
104 Evan Bouchard C 25.00 60.00
105 Andrei Svechnikov A 25.00 60.00
107 Henrik Borgstrom C 15.00 40.00
108 Jordan Kyrou C 20.00 50.00
109 Maxime Comtois B 10.00 25.00
110 Brady Tkachuk A 30.00 80.00
111 Michael Dal Colle C 10.00 25.00
112 Eeli Tolvanen A 20.00 50.00
113 Isac Lundestrom A 8.00 20.00
114 Dennis Cholowski B 10.00 25.00
116 Ilya Samsonov C 20.00 50.00
119 Dominik Kahun B 10.00 25.00
122 Jordan Greenway B 10.00 25.00
123 Michael Rasmussen B 12.00 30.00
124 Dan Vladar C 12.00 30.00
125 Miro Heiskanen B 25.00 60.00
126 Jakub Zboril C 15.00 40.00
127 Kristian Vesalainen A 12.00 30.00
128 Drake Batherson A 20.00 50.00
129 Jonas Siegenthaler B 10.00 25.00
130 Jesperi Kotkaniemi A 20.00 50.00
131 Warren Foegele B 10.00 25.00
132 Travis Dermott C 15.00 40.00
134 Sam Steel C 10.00 25.00
136 Noah Juulsen B 10.00 25.00
137 Robert Thomas B 20.00 50.00
138 Henri Jokiharju B 8.00 20.00
139 Lias Andersson A 15.00 40.00
140 Casey Mittelstadt A 20.00 50.00

2018-19 SP Signatures Gold

*GOLD/25: .6X TO 1.5X BASIC INSERTS
101 Elias Pettersson 80.00 200.00

2019-20 SP

1 Jonathan Marchessault .30 .75
2 Oliver Bjorkstrand .20 .50
3 Dougie Hamilton .20 .50
4 Logan Couture .30 .75
5 Morgan Rielly .25 .60
6 Dylan Strome .30 .75
7 Sean Monahan .15 .40
8 Tyler Bertuzzi .20 .50
9 Ben Bishop .20 .50
10 Carey Price .50 1.25
11 Tomas Hertl .25 .60
12 John Gibson .25 .60
13 William Karlsson .30 .75
14 Duncan Keith .20 .50
15 Sergei Bobrovsky .40 1.00
16 Marc-Andre Fleury .50 1.25
17 Jonathan Quick .30 .75
18 Evgeni Malkin .50 1.25
19 Connor McDavid 1.25 3.00
20 Anthony Mantha .20 .50
21 Brayden Point .30 .75
22 Matt Murray .25 .60
23 Jake Guentzel .40 1.00
24 Alex DeBrincat .30 .75
25 Brayden Schenn .25 .60
26 Torey Krug .20 .50
27 Eric Staal .25 .60
28 Nico Hischier .40 1.00
29 Jakub Vrana .25 .60
30 Brad Marchand .50 1.25
31 Aleksander Barkov .40 1.00
32 Kyle Turris .20 .50
33 Henrik Lundqvist .60 1.50
34 Anders Lee .20 .50
35 Dylan Larkin .30 .75
36 Pierre-Luc Dubois .20 .50
37 Leon Draisaitl .75 2.00
38 Joe Pavelski .30 .75
39 Tom Wilson .25 .60
40 Jonathan Toews .40 1.00
41 Bo Horvat .30 .75
42 Jake DeBrusk .25 .60
43 Brady Tkachuk .40 1.00
44 Joe Thornton .40 1.00
45 Brock Boeser .30 .75
46 Viktor Arvidsson .15 .40
47 Ryan O'Reilly .25 .60
48 Matt Dumba .15 .40
49 Drew Doughty .30 .75
50 Teuvo Teravainen .25 .60
51 Sidney Crosby 1.00 2.50
52 Steven Stamkos .50 1.25
53 Cam Atkinson .25 .60
54 Claude Giroux .25 .60
55 Thomas Chabot .25 .60
56 Patrick Kane .50 1.25
57 Tuukka Rask .30 .75
58 John Klingberg .25 .60
59 Miro Heiskanen .30 .75
60 Zach Werenski .40 1.00
61 Vincent Trocheck .25 .60
62 Jack Eichel .40 1.00
63 Brent Burns .25 .60
64 Jesperi Kotkaniemi .25 .60
65 Mark Stone .30 .75
66 Mark Scheifele .40 1.00
67 Seth Jones .25 .60
68 Connor Hellebuyck .50 1.25
69 Alex Tuch .25 .60
70 Auston Matthews 1.00 2.50
71 John Tavares .40 1.00
72 Artemi Panarin .50 1.25
73 Jonathan Drouin .20 .50
74 Matthew Tkachuk .50 1.25
75 Andrei Vasilevskiy .40 1.00
76 Sebastian Aho .40 1.00
77 Jeff Skinner .25 .60
78 Mikael Granlund .20 .50
79 Elias Pettersson .40 1.00
80 Jaccob Slavin .20 .50
81 Erik Karlsson .30 .75
82 Vladimir Tarasenko .30 .75
83 Oscar Klefbom .25 .60
84 Roman Josi .25 .60
85 Mitch Marner .40 1.00
86 Taylor Hall .25 .60
87 Jacob Trouba .20 .50
88 Phil Kessel .25 .60
89 Clayton Keller .30 .75
90 P.K. Subban .30 .75
91 Philipp Grubauer .25 .60
92 Mikko Rantanen .60 1.50
93 Mathew Barzal .30 .75
94 Carter Hart .25 .60
95 Blake Wheeler .25 .60
96 Andrei Svechnikov .30 .75
97 Nathan MacKinnon 1.00 2.50
98 Rasmus Dahlin .30 .75
99 Rickard Rakell .20 .50
100 Alex Ovechkin 1.00 2.50
101 Kaapo Kakko RC 2.00 5.00
102 Adam Boqvist RC 1.25 3.00
103 Joel Farabee RC 2.00 5.00
104 Igor Shesterkin RC 5.00 12.00
105 Erik Brannstrom RC 1.25 3.00
106 Filip Zadina RC 2.00 5.00
107 Kirby Dach RC 2.50 6.00
108 Cale Fleury RC 1.50 4.00
109 Elvis Merzlikins RC 2.50 6.00
110 Sam Lafferty RC 1.00 2.50
111 Ilya Mikheyev RC 2.00 5.00
112 Jesper Boqvist RC 1.00 2.50
113 Connor Clifton RC 1.25 3.00
114 Cale Makar RC 6.00 15.00
115 Joel L'Esperance RC 1.25 3.00
116 Victor Olofsson RC 2.50 6.00
117 Noah Dobson RC 3.00 8.00
118 Taro Hirose RC 1.25 3.00
119 Rasmus Sandin RC 2.00 5.00
120 Alexandre Texier RC 1.25 3.00
121 Oliver Wahlstrom RC 2.00 5.00
122 Trevor Moore RC 1.00 2.50
123 Dominik Kubalik RC 2.50 6.00
124 Nikita Gusev RC 2.00 5.00
125 Ryan Poehling RC 2.00 5.00
126 David Gustafsson RC 1.00 2.50
127 Karson Kuhlman RC 1.25 3.00
128 Tobias Bjornfot RC 1.25 3.00
129 Adam Fox RC 3.00 8.00
130 Barrett Hayton RC 2.50 6.00
131 Nick Suzuki RC 5.00 12.00
132 Ville Heinola RC 1.50 4.00
133 Cody Glass RC 2.00 5.00
134 Emil Bemstrom RC 1.25 3.00
135 Philippe Myers RC 1.00 2.50
136 Quinn Hughes RC 6.00 15.00
137 Dante Fabbro RC 1.25 3.00
138 Julien Gauthier RC 1.25 3.00
139 Nicolas Hague RC 1.25 3.00
140 Jack Hughes RC 6.00 15.00

2019-20 SP Blue

*BLUE: .5X TO 1.25X BASIC
*BLUE RC: .5X TO 1.25X BASIC RC

2019-20 SP Authentic Profiles

*BLUE: .5X TO 1.5X BASIC INSERTS*BLUE: .5X TO 1.5X BASIC
APAB Aleksander Barkov 2.00 5.00
APAD Alex DeBrincat 1.50 4.00
APAM Auston Matthews 5.00 12.00
APAP Artemi Panarin 2.50 6.00
APBB Ben Bishop 1.00 2.50
APBM Brad Marchand 2.50 6.00
APBO Brock Boeser 1.50 4.00
APCA Cam Atkinson 1.25 3.00
APCM Connor McDavid 6.00 15.00
APDL Dylan Larkin 1.50 4.00
APGU Jake Guentzel 2.00 5.00
APJD Jonathan Drouin 1.00 2.50
APJE Jack Eichel 2.00 5.00
APJG John Gibson 1.25 3.00
APMF Marc-Andre Fleury 2.50 6.00
APMS Mark Stone 1.50 4.00
APNH Nico Hischier 2.00 5.00
APSB Sergei Bobrovsky 2.00 5.00
APSC Sidney Crosby 5.00 12.00
APTC Thomas Chabot 1.25 3.00

2019-20 SP Authentic Profiles Jerseys

APAB Aleksander Barkov 3.00 8.00
APAD Alex DeBrincat 2.50 6.00
APAM Auston Matthews 8.00 20.00
APAP Artemi Panarin 4.00 10.00
APBB Ben Bishop 1.50 4.00
APBM Brad Marchand 4.00 10.00
APBO Brock Boeser 2.50 6.00
APCA Cam Atkinson 2.00 5.00
APCM Connor McDavid 10.00 25.00
APDL Dylan Larkin 2.50 6.00
APGU Jake Guentzel 3.00 8.00
APJD Jonathan Drouin 1.50 4.00
APJE Jack Eichel 3.00 8.00
APJG John Gibson 2.00 5.00
APMF Marc-Andre Fleury 12.00 30.00
APMS Mark Stone 2.50 6.00
APNH Nico Hischier 3.00 8.00
APSB Sergei Bobrovsky 3.00 8.00
APSC Sidney Crosby 8.00 20.00
APTC Thomas Chabot 2.00 5.00

2019-20 SP Jerseys

101 Kaapo Kakko 3.00 8.00
102 Adam Boqvist 2.00 5.00
103 Joel Farabee 3.00 8.00
104 Igor Shesterkin 20.00 50.00
105 Erik Brannstrom 2.00 5.00
106 Filip Zadina 3.00 8.00
107 Kirby Dach 4.00 10.00
109 Elvis Merzlikins 4.00 10.00
110 Sam Lafferty 1.50 4.00
111 Ilya Mikheyev 3.00 8.00
112 Jesper Boqvist 1.50 4.00
114 Cale Makar 10.00 25.00
115 Joel L'Esperance 2.00 5.00
116 Victor Olofsson 4.00 10.00
117 Noah Dobson 5.00 12.00
118 Taro Hirose 2.00 5.00
119 Rasmus Sandin 3.00 8.00
120 Alexandre Texier 2.00 5.00
121 Oliver Wahlstrom 3.00 8.00
122 Trevor Moore 1.50 4.00
123 Dominik Kubalik 4.00 10.00
124 Nikita Gusev 3.00 8.00
125 Ryan Poehling 3.00 8.00
126 David Gustafsson 1.50 4.00
127 Karson Kuhlman 2.00 5.00
128 Tobias Bjornfot 2.00 5.00
129 Adam Fox 5.00 12.00
130 Barrett Hayton 4.00 10.00
131 Nick Suzuki 8.00 20.00
132 Ville Heinola 2.50 6.00
133 Cody Glass 3.00 8.00
134 Emil Bemstrom 2.00 5.00
135 Philippe Myers 1.50 4.00
136 Quinn Hughes 10.00 25.00
137 Dante Fabbro 2.00 5.00
138 Julien Gauthier 2.00 5.00
139 Nicolas Hague 2.00 5.00
140 Jack Hughes 10.00 25.00

2020-21 SP

1 Elias Pettersson .40 1.00
2 Cale Makar .60 1.50
3 Victor Hedman .30 .75
4 Kyle Connor .40 1.00
5 Brent Burns .25 .60
6 Ryan Getzlaf .25 .60
7 Max Pacioretty .25 .60
8 Ryan O'Reilly .25 .60
9 Igor Shesterkin .50 1.25
10 Matthew Tkachuk .50 1.25
11 Keith Yandle .15 .40
12 Alex Ovechkin 1.00 2.50
13 Tyson Barrie .15 .40
14 Anthony Mantha .20 .50
15 Dylan Strome .30 .75
16 Brock Boeser .30 .75
17 Mark Stone .30 .75
18 Travis Konecny .25 .60
19 Ryan Nugent-Hopkins .30 .75
20 Aleksander Barkov .40 1.00
21 Pekka Rinne .25 .60
22 John Tavares .40 1.00
23 John Carlson .25 .60
24 Mathew Barzal .30 .75
25 Pierre-Luc Dubois .20 .50
26 John Klingberg .25 .60
27 Darcy Kuemper .25 .60
28 Carter Hart .25 .60
29 Sebastian Aho .40 1.00
30 Shea Theodore .30 .75
31 Patrice Bergeron .30 .75
32 Matt Murray .25 .60
33 Leon Draisaitl .75 2.00
34 Jake Guentzel .40 1.00
35 Brad Marchand .50 1.25
36 Dougie Hamilton .20 .50
37 Mark Scheifele .40 1.00
38 Evgeni Malkin .50 1.25
39 Josh Bailey .20 .50
40 Mitch Marner .40 1.00
41 Jack Hughes .60 1.50
42 Mark Giordano .25 .60
43 Alex Tuch .25 .60
44 Jonathan Drouin .20 .50
45 Colton Parayko .20 .50
46 Miro Heiskanen .30 .75
47 Nico Hischier .40 1.00
48 Sean Monahan .15 .40
49 Eric Staal .25 .60
50 David Pastrnak .60 1.50
51 Martin Jones .20 .50
52 Seth Jones .25 .60
53 Steven Stamkos .50 1.25
54 Nick Suzuki .50 1.25
55 Quinn Hughes .60 1.50
56 Nikita Kucherov .50 1.25
57 Victor Olofsson .25 .60
58 Auston Matthews 1.00 2.50
59 Teuvo Teravainen .25 .60
60 Patrick Kane .50 1.25
61 Ryan Suter .20 .50
62 Nick Schmaltz .20 .50
63 John Gibson .25 .60
64 Brayden Point .30 .75
65 Brendan Gallagher .25 .60
66 Bo Horvat .30 .75
67 Mats Zuccarello .25 .60
68 Tyler Seguin .30 .75
69 Tomas Hertl .25 .60
70 Philipp Grubauer .25 .60
71 Connor Hellebuyck .50 1.25
72 Roman Josi .25 .60
73 Ryan Dzingel .20 .50
74 Carey Price .50 1.25
75 Dominik Kubalik .25 .60
76 Sidney Crosby 1.00 2.50
77 Tom Wilson .25 .60
78 David Perron .20 .50
79 James van Riemsdyk .20 .50
80 Dylan Larkin .30 .75
81 Andrei Svechnikov .30 .75
82 Dustin Brown .25 .60
83 Artemi Panarin .50 1.25
84 Rasmus Dahlin .30 .75
85 Jordan Staal .20 .50
86 Yanni Gourde .20 .50
87 Mika Zibanejad .30 .75
88 Zach Werenski .40 1.00
89 Jonathan Huberdeau .30 .75
90 Connor McDavid 1.25 3.00
91 Jack Eichel .40 1.00
92 Anze Kopitar .40 1.00
93 Anders Lee .20 .50
94 Nathan MacKinnon 1.00 2.50
95 Zach Parise .25 .60
96 Kyle Palmieri .20 .50
97 Brady Tkachuk .40 1.00
98 Joe Pavelski .30 .75
99 Brayden Schenn .25 .60
100 Andrei Vasilevskiy .40 1.00
101 Alexis Lafreniere RC 4.00 10.00
102 Matiss Kivlenieks RC 1.50 4.00
103 Philipp Kurashev RC 1.50 4.00
104 Arthur Kaliyev RC 2.00 5.00
105 Liam Foudy RC 1.25 3.00
106 Peyton Krebs RC 2.00 5.00
107 Pierre-Olivier Joseph RC 1.25 3.00
108 Shane Bowers RC 1.00 2.50
109 Victor Soderstrom RC 1.00 2.50
110 Thomas Harley RC 2.00 5.00
111 Jason Robertson RC 3.00 8.00
112 Tim Stutzle RC 2.50 6.00
113 Sasha Chmelevski RC 1.00 2.50
114 Ty Smith RC 2.00 5.00
115 Cal Foote RC 1.50 4.00
116 Ilya Sorokin RC 3.00 8.00
117 Jani Hakanpaa RC .75 2.00
118 Nick Robertson RC 2.00 5.00
119 Alexander Romanov RC 1.50 4.00
120 Dylan Cozens RC 2.00 5.00
121 Aleksi Heponiemi RC 1.50 4.00
122 Tyler Benson RC 1.25 3.00
123 Gabe Vilardi RC 2.00 5.00
124 Ty Dellandrea RC 1.25 3.00
125 Timothy Liljegren RC 1.25 3.00
126 Nolan Foote RC 1.25 3.00
127 Connor McMichael RC 2.00 5.00
128 Kieffer Bellows RC 1.00 2.50
129 Kirill Kaprizov RC 5.00 12.00
130 K'Andre Miller RC 2.50 6.00
131 Pius Suter RC 1.50 4.00
132 Olli Juolevi RC 1.25 3.00
133 Nicolas Beaudin RC 1.25 3.00
134 Ian Mitchell RC 1.00 2.50
135 Josh Norris RC 2.00 5.00
136 Jake Oettinger RC 3.00 8.00
137 Vitali Kravtsov RC 2.50 6.00
138 Vitek Vanecek RC 2.00 5.00
139 Nils Hoglander RC 1.25 3.00
140 Bowen Byram RC 2.50 6.00

2020-21 SP Blue

*BLUE: .4X TO 1X BASIC
*BLUE RC: .4X TO 1X BASIC RC

2020-21 SP Gold

*GOLD: .5X TO 1.25X BASIC
129 Kirill Kaprizov 25.00 60.00

2020-21 SP Purple

*PURPLE: 1X TO 2.5X BASIC
129 Kirill Kaprizov 200.00 500.00

2020-21 SP Pyrotechnic Gold

*PYRO: 1X TO 2.5X BASIC
101 Alexis Lafreniere 40.00 100.00
129 Kirill Kaprizov 60.00 150.00

2020-21 SP Red

*RED: .6X TO 1.5X BASIC
129 Kirill Kaprizov 30.00 80.00

2020-21 SP Silver Spectum

*SILVER: .5X TO 1.25X BASIC

2020-21 SP Sphericity

*SPHERICITY: .75X TO 2X BASIC
129 Kirill Kaprizov 20.00 50.00

2020-21 SP Authentic Profiles

*BLUE: .5X TO 1.25X BASIC
*SPHERICITY: .6X TO 1.5X BASIC
*PYRO: .75X TO 2X BASIC
*SILVER/1299: .5X TO 1.25X BASIC
*GOLD/999: .6X TO 1.5X BASIC
*RED/799: .6X TO 1.5X BASIC
*PURPLE/99: 1X TO 2.5X BASIC
*GREEN/25: 2X TO 5X BASIC
AP1 Connor McDavid 3.00 8.00
AP2 Andrei Svechnikov .75 2.00
AP3 Connor Hellebuyck 1.25 3.00
AP5 Nico Hischier 1.00 2.50
AP6 Brock Boeser .75 2.00
AP7 Brad Marchand 1.25 3.00
AP8 Cale Makar 1.50 4.00
AP9 Sidney Crosby 2.50 6.00
AP10 Nick Suzuki 1.25 3.00
AP11 Teuvo Teravainen .60 1.50
AP12 Miro Heiskanen .75 2.00
AP13 Tomas Hertl .60 1.50
AP14 Mitch Marner 1.00 2.50
AP15 Roman Josi .60 1.50
AP16 Patrick Kane 1.25 3.00
AP17 Dylan Larkin .75 2.00
AP18 Aleksander Barkov 1.00 2.50
AP19 Carter Hart .60 1.50
AP20 Auston Matthews 2.50 6.00

2020-21 SP Jerseys

101 Alexis Lafreniere 8.00 20.00
102 Matiss Kivlenieks 3.00 8.00
103 Philipp Kurashev 3.00 8.00
104 Arthur Kaliyev 4.00 10.00
105 Liam Foudy 2.50 6.00
106 Peyton Krebs 4.00 10.00
107 Pierre-Olivier Joseph 2.50 6.00
108 Shane Bowers 2.00 5.00
109 Victor Soderstrom 2.00 5.00
110 Thomas Harley 4.00 10.00
111 Jason Robertson 6.00 15.00
112 Tim Stutzle 5.00 12.00
113 Sasha Chmelevski 2.00 5.00
114 Ty Smith 4.00 10.00
115 Cal Foote 3.00 8.00
116 Ilya Sorokin 6.00 15.00
117 Jani Hakanpaa 1.50 4.00
118 Nick Robertson 4.00 10.00
119 Alexander Romanov 3.00 8.00
120 Dylan Cozens 4.00 10.00
121 Aleksi Heponiemi 3.00 8.00
122 Tyler Benson 2.50 6.00
123 Gabe Vilardi 4.00 10.00
124 Ty Dellandrea 2.50 6.00
125 Timothy Liljegren 2.50 6.00
126 Nolan Foote 2.50 6.00
127 Connor McMichael 4.00 10.00
128 Kieffer Bellows 2.00 5.00
129 Kirill Kaprizov 25.00 60.00
130 K'Andre Miller 5.00 12.00
131 Pius Suter 3.00 8.00
132 Olli Juolevi 2.50 6.00
133 Nicolas Beaudin 2.50 6.00
134 Ian Mitchell 2.00 5.00
135 Josh Norris 4.00 10.00
136 Jake Oettinger 6.00 15.00
137 Vitali Kravtsov 5.00 12.00
138 Vitek Vanecek 4.00 10.00
139 Nils Hoglander 2.50 6.00
140 Bowen Byram 5.00 12.00

2020-21 SP Signatures

103 Philipp Kurashev 10.00 25.00
104 Arthur Kaliyev 12.00 30.00
105 Liam Foudy 8.00 20.00
106 Peyton Krebs 12.00 30.00
107 Pierre-Olivier Joseph 8.00 20.00
108 Shane Bowers 6.00 15.00
109 Victor Soderstrom 6.00 15.00
110 Thomas Harley 12.00 30.00
111 Jason Robertson 80.00 200.00
112 Tim Stutzle 15.00 40.00
113 Sasha Chmelevski 6.00 15.00
114 Ty Smith 12.00 30.00
115 Cal Foote 10.00 25.00
116 Ilya Sorokin 20.00 50.00
117 Jani Hakanpaa 5.00 12.00
118 Nick Robertson 12.00 30.00
119 Alexander Romanov 10.00 25.00
120 Dylan Cozens 12.00 30.00
124 Ty Dellandrea 8.00 20.00
125 Timothy Liljegren 8.00 20.00
126 Nolan Foote 8.00 20.00
127 Connor McMichael 12.00 30.00
128 Kieffer Bellows 6.00 15.00
130 K'Andre Miller 15.00 40.00
131 Pius Suter 10.00 25.00
132 Olli Juolevi 8.00 20.00
134 Ian Mitchell 6.00 15.00
136 Jake Oettinger 20.00 50.00
138 Vitek Vanecek 12.00 30.00
139 Nils Hoglander 8.00 20.00
140 Bowen Byram 15.00 40.00

2021-22 SP

1 Connor McDavid 1.25 3.00
2 Jonathan Huberdeau .30 .75
3 Patrik Laine .30 .75
4 Carey Price .50 1.25
5 Ryan Getzlaf .25 .60
6 Patrick Kane .50 1.25
7 Cam Talbot .25 .60
8 Eeli Tolvanen .25 .60
9 Drake Batherson .25 .60
10 David Pastrnak .60 1.50
11 Jacob Markstrom .25 .60
12 Jordan Binnington .40 1.00
13 Jakub Vrana .20 .50
14 Rasmus Dahlin .30 .75
15 Clayton Keller .30 .75
16 Mikko Rantanen .60 1.50
17 Brayden Point .30 .75
18 Claude Giroux .25 .60
19 Tristan Jarry .25 .60
20 Miro Heiskanen .30 .75
21 Tyler Toffoli .25 .60
22 Troy Terry .20 .50
23 Marc-Andre Fleury .50 1.25
24 Aleksander Barkov .40 1.00
25 Andrei Vasilevskiy .40 1.00
26 Tyler Bertuzzi .20 .50
27 Quinn Hughes .60 1.50
28 Sebastian Aho .40 1.00
29 Taylor Hall .25 .60
30 Jakub Voracek .20 .50
31 Ryan Nugent-Hopkins .30 .75
32 Dougie Hamilton .20 .50
33 William Nylander .50 1.25
34 William Karlsson .30 .75
35 Carter Hart .25 .60
36 Igor Shesterkin .50 1.25
37 Cal Petersen .15 .40
38 Alex Ovechkin 1.00 2.50
39 Nico Hischier .40 1.00
40 John Tavares .40 1.00
41 John Gibson .25 .60
42 Sergei Bobrovsky .40 1.00
43 Artemi Panarin .50 1.25
44 Tyler Seguin .30 .75
45 Ryan O'Reilly .25 .60
46 Brady Tkachuk .40 1.00
47 Jeff Petry .25 .60
48 Juuse Saros .30 .75
49 Jack Hughes .60 1.50
50 Nikita Kucherov .50 1.25
51 Joe Pavelski .30 .75
52 Leon Draisaitl .75 2.00
53 Martin Necas .40 1.00
54 Teuvo Teravainen .25 .60
55 Nick Suzuki .50 1.25
56 Elias Lindholm .25 .60
57 Tim Stutzle .30 .75
58 Josh Bailey .20 .50
59 Seth Jones .25 .60
60 Brad Marchand .50 1.25
61 Conor Garland .20 .50
62 Connor Hellebuyck .50 1.25
63 Jonathan Marchessault .30 .75
64 Victor Olofsson .25 .60
65 Elvis Merzlikins .25 .60
66 Brock Boeser .30 .75
67 Jakob Chychrun .25 .60
68 Max Pacioretty .25 .60
69 Alex DeBrincat .30 .75
70 Nikolaj Ehlers .25 .60
71 Mathew Barzal .30 .75
72 Brent Burns .25 .60
73 Mark Stone .30 .75
74 John Carlson .25 .60
75 Nathan MacKinnon 1.00 2.50
76 Jordan Eberle .25 .60
77 Kris Letang .30 .75
78 Victor Hedman .30 .75
79 Anders Lee .20 .50
80 Nicklas Backstrom .25 .60
81 Tomas Hertl .25 .60
82 Matthew Tkachuk .50 1.25
83 Roman Josi .25 .60
84 Anze Kopitar .40 1.00
85 Mark Giordano .25 .60
86 Mark Scheifele .40 1.00
87 Sidney Crosby 1.00 2.50
88 Auston Matthews 1.00 2.50
89 Kevin Fiala .20 .50
90 Jake Guentzel .40 1.00
91 Dylan Larkin .30 .75
92 Patrice Bergeron .30 .75
93 Philipp Grubauer .25 .60
94 Brayden Schenn .25 .60
95 Mitch Marner .40 1.00
96 Elias Pettersson .40 1.00
97 Kirill Kaprizov .75 2.00
98 Cam Atkinson .25 .60
99 Adam Fox .30 .75
100 Cale Makar .60 1.50
101 Trevor Zegras RC 2.00 5.00
102 Brandon Duhaime RC 1.00 2.50
103 Tanner Jeannot RC 1.00 2.50
104 Jeremy Swayman RC 3.00 8.00
105 Kole Lind RC 1.25 3.00
106 Dawson Mercer RC 2.50 6.00
107 Vasily Podkolzin RC 1.25 3.00
108 Cole Sillinger RC 1.50 4.00
109 Jacob Bernard-Docker RC 1.00 2.50
110 Spencer Knight RC 2.00 5.00
111 Logan Thompson RC 2.50 6.00
112 Jonathan Dahlen RC 1.00 2.50
113 Rasmus Kupari RC 1.00 2.50
114 Joe Veleno RC 1.25 3.00
115 Scott Perunovich RC 1.00 2.50
116 Cole Perfetti RC 2.00 5.00
117 Wade Allison RC 1.00 2.50
118 Moritz Seider RC 2.50 6.00
119 Taylor Raddysh RC 1.50 4.00
120 Karel Vejmelka RC 1.25 3.00
121 J.J. Peterka RC 2.00 5.00
122 Zac Jones RC 1.25 3.00
123 Anton Lundell RC 2.00 5.00
124 Cole Caufield RC 4.00 10.00
125 Radim Zohorna RC 1.00 2.50
126 Riley Damiani RC 1.00 2.50
127 Quinton Byfield RC 2.50 6.00
128 Alexander Holtz RC 1.50 4.00
129 Philip Tomasino RC 1.25 3.00
130 Jan Jenik RC 1.25 3.00
131 Aliaksei Protas RC 1.00 2.50
132 Lucas Raymond RC 3.00 8.00
133 Ukko-Pekka Luukkonen RC 1.50 4.00
134 Hendrix Lapierre RC 1.00 2.50
135 Alex Barre-Boulet RC 1.00 2.50
136 Jamie Drysdale RC 1.50 4.00
137 Alex Turcotte RC 1.25 3.00
138 Mike Hardman RC 1.00 2.50
139 Seth Jarvis RC 2.50 6.00
140 Alex Newhook RC 1.50 4.00

2021-22 SP Blue

*BLUE: .5X TO 1.2X BASIC

2021-22 SP Gold

*GOLD/399: 1X TO 2.5X BASIC

2021-22 SP Gold Patterned Foilboard

*GOLD.PATT: .75X TO 2X BASIC

2021-22 SP Green

*GREEN/25: 3X TO 8X BASIC

2021-22 SP Green Patterned Foilboard

*GREEN.PATT: 2.5X TO 6X BASIC

2021-22 SP Patterned Foilboard

*PATTERNED: .75X TO 2X BASIC

2021-22 SP Purple

*RED/99: 1.5X TO 4X BASIC

2021-22 SP Red

*RED/199: 1.2X TO 3X BASIC

2021-22 SP Silver Spectrum

*SILVER/599: .75X TO 2X BASIC

2021-22 SP Authentic Profiles
*BLUE: .5X TO 1.2X BASIC
*PATTERNED: .75X TO 2X BASIC
*PATT.GOLD: 1.5X TO 4X BASIC
*PATT.GREEN: 2X TO 5X BASIC
*SILVER/599: .6X TO 1.5X BASIC
*GOLD/399: .75X TO 2X BASIC
*RED/199: 1X TO 2.5X BASIC
*PURPLE/99: 1.2X TO 3X BASIC
*GREEN/25: 1.5X TO 4X BASIC
AP1 Conor Garland .60 1.50
AP2 Cam Talbot .75 2.00
AP3 Drake Batherson .75 2.00
AP4 Jesper Bratt .75 2.00
AP5 Troy Terry .60 1.50
AP6 Josh Anderson .60 1.50
AP7 Chandler Stephenson .60 1.50
AP8 Jason Robertson 1.25 3.00
AP9 Samuel Girard .50 1.25
AP10 Mike Smith .50 1.25
AP11 Anthony Beauvillier .50 1.25
AP12 Brent Burns .75 2.00
AP13 Kyle Connor 1.25 3.00
AP14 Joe Pavelski 1.00 2.50
AP15 Anthony Cirelli .60 1.50
AP16 Martin Necas 1.25 3.00
AP17 Tyler Bertuzzi .60 1.50
AP18 Sam Bennett 1.25 3.00
AP19 William Karlsson 1.00 2.50
AP20 Connor McDavid 4.00 10.00

2021-22 SP Authentic Profiles Jerseys
AP1 Conor Garland 1.50 4.00
AP2 Cam Talbot 2.00 5.00
AP3 Drake Batherson 2.00 5.00
AP4 Jesper Bratt 2.00 5.00
AP5 Troy Terry 1.50 4.00
AP6 Josh Anderson 1.50 4.00
AP7 Chandler Stephenson 1.50 4.00
AP8 Jason Robertson 3.00 8.00
AP10 Mike Smith 1.25 3.00
AP11 Anthony Beauvillier 1.25 3.00
AP12 Brent Burns 2.00 5.00
AP13 Kyle Connor 3.00 8.00
AP14 Joe Pavelski 2.50 6.00
AP16 Martin Necas 3.00 8.00
AP17 Tyler Bertuzzi 1.50 4.00
AP18 Sam Bennett 3.00 8.00
AP19 William Karlsson 2.50 6.00
AP20 Connor McDavid 10.00 25.00

2021-22 SP Authentic Profiles Signatures
AP1 Conor Garland 6.00 15.00
AP2 Cam Talbot 8.00 20.00
AP3 Drake Batherson 8.00 20.00
AP4 Jesper Bratt 8.00 20.00
AP8 Jason Robertson 30.00 80.00
AP10 Mike Smith 5.00 12.00
AP12 Brent Burns 8.00 20.00
AP13 Kyle Connor 12.00 30.00
AP14 Joe Pavelski 10.00 25.00
AP16 Martin Necas 12.00 30.00
AP17 Tyler Bertuzzi 6.00 15.00
AP18 Sam Bennett 12.00 30.00
AP19 William Karlsson 10.00 25.00
AP20 Connor McDavid 150.00 400.00

2021-22 SP Authentic Signatures
ASAT Alex Tuch 20.00 50.00
ASAV Andrei Vasilevskiy 15.00 40.00
ASBM Brad Marchand 20.00 50.00
ASBO Brock Boeser 12.00 30.00
ASCG Conor Garland 8.00 20.00
ASDC Dylan Cozens 12.00 30.00
ASJB Jesper Bratt 10.00 25.00
ASJG Jean-Gabriel Pageau 6.00 15.00
ASJP Joe Pavelski 12.00 30.00
ASKF Kevin Fiala 8.00 20.00
ASKL Kris Letang 12.00 30.00
ASMF Marc-Andre Fleury 40.00 100.00
ASMN Martin Necas 15.00 40.00
ASMT Matthew Tkachuk 20.00 50.00
ASTB Tyler Bertuzzi 8.00 20.00
ASZP Zach Parise 8.00 20.00

2021-22 SP Jerseys
101 Trevor Zegras 4.00 10.00
102 Brandon Duhaime 2.00 5.00
103 Tanner Jeannot 2.00 5.00
104 Jeremy Swayman 6.00 15.00
105 Kole Lind 2.50 6.00
106 Dawson Mercer 5.00 12.00
107 Vasily Podkolzin 2.50 6.00
109 Jacob Bernard-Docker 2.00 5.00
110 Spencer Knight 4.00 10.00
111 Logan Thompson 5.00 12.00
112 Jonathan Dahlen 2.00 5.00
113 Rasmus Kupari 2.00 5.00
114 Joe Veleno 2.50 6.00
115 Scott Perunovich 2.00 5.00
116 Cole Perfetti 4.00 10.00
117 Wade Allison 2.00 5.00
118 Moritz Seider 5.00 12.00
119 Taylor Raddysh 3.00 8.00
120 Karel Vejmelka 2.50 6.00
121 J.J. Peterka 4.00 10.00
122 Zac Jones 2.50 6.00
123 Anton Lundell 4.00 10.00
124 Cole Caufield 8.00 20.00
125 Radim Zohorna 2.00 5.00
126 Riley Damiani 2.00 5.00
127 Quinton Byfield 5.00 12.00
128 Alexander Holtz 3.00 8.00
129 Philip Tomasino 2.50 6.00
130 Jan Jenik 2.50 6.00
132 Lucas Raymond 6.00 15.00
133 Ukko-Pekka Luukkonen 3.00 8.00
134 Hendrix Lapierre 2.00 5.00
136 Jamie Drysdale 3.00 8.00
137 Alex Turcotte 2.50 6.00
138 Mike Hardman 2.00 5.00
139 Seth Jarvis 5.00 12.00
140 Alex Newhook 3.00 8.00

2021-22 SP Signatures
*GOLD/25: .6X TO 1.5X BASIC
101 Trevor Zegras 12.00 30.00
102 Brandon Duhaime 6.00 15.00
103 Tanner Jeannot 6.00 15.00
104 Jeremy Swayman 20.00 50.00
105 Kole Lind 8.00 20.00
106 Dawson Mercer 15.00 40.00
107 Vasily Podkolzin 8.00 20.00
108 Cole Sillinger 10.00 25.00
109 Jacob Bernard-Docker 6.00 15.00
110 Spencer Knight 12.00 30.00
112 Jonathan Dahlen 6.00 15.00
113 Rasmus Kupari 6.00 15.00
114 Joe Veleno 8.00 20.00
115 Scott Perunovich 6.00 15.00
116 Cole Perfetti 12.00 30.00
118 Moritz Seider 15.00 40.00
119 Taylor Raddysh 10.00 25.00
120 Karel Vejmelka 8.00 20.00
121 J.J. Peterka 12.00 30.00
122 Zac Jones 8.00 20.00
126 Riley Damiani 6.00 15.00
127 Quinton Byfield 15.00 40.00
128 Alexander Holtz 10.00 25.00
129 Philip Tomasino 8.00 20.00
130 Jan Jenik 8.00 20.00
131 Aliaksei Protas 6.00 15.00
133 Ukko-Pekka Luukkonen 10.00 25.00
134 Hendrix Lapierre 6.00 15.00
136 Jamie Drysdale 10.00 25.00
137 Alex Turcotte 8.00 20.00
138 Mike Hardman 6.00 15.00
139 Seth Jarvis 15.00 40.00
140 Alex Newhook 10.00 25.00

2022-23 SP
1 Leon Draisaitl .75 2.00
2 Kirill Kaprizov .75 2.00
3 Zach Werenski .40 1.00
4 Jamie Drysdale .20 .50
5 Aaron Ekblad .30 .75
6 Nick Schmaltz .20 .50
7 Jordan Eberle .25 .60
8 Alex Ovechkin 1.00 2.50
9 Clayton Keller .30 .75
10 Patrik Laine .30 .75
11 Jonathan Huberdeau .30 .75
12 Josh Bailey .20 .50
13 Alexis Lafreniere .40 1.00
14 Nick Suzuki .50 1.25
15 Anton Lundell .25 .60
16 Joe Pavelski .30 .75
17 Dawson Mercer .30 .75
18 Tim Stutzle .30 .75
19 Matthew Tkachuk .50 1.25
20 Sebastian Aho .40 1.00
21 Jason Robertson .40 1.00
22 Cole Caufield .50 1.25
23 Lucas Raymond .40 1.00
24 Dylan Cozens .25 .60
25 Jordan Kyrou .25 .60
26 Kevin Fiala .20 .50
27 Nikolaj Ehlers .25 .60
28 Timo Meier .25 .60
29 Nathan MacKinnon 1.00 2.50
30 James van Riemsdyk .20 .50
31 Carey Price .50 1.25
32 Seth Jarvis .30 .75
33 Brady Tkachuk .40 1.00
34 Auston Matthews 1.00 2.50
35 John Gibson .25 .60
36 Mats Zuccarello .25 .60
37 Andrei Svechnikov .30 .75
38 Alex DeBrincat .30 .75
39 Alex Nedeljkovic .20 .50
40 Elias Pettersson .40 1.00
41 Brandon Saad .20 .50
42 Vitek Vanecek .25 .60
43 Quinn Hughes .60 1.50
44 Marc-Andre Fleury .50 1.25
45 Arthur Kaliyev .25 .60
46 Trevor Zegras .25 .60
47 Jack Campbell .25 .60
48 Tomas Hertl .25 .60
49 Jeremy Swayman .40 1.00
50 Dylan Larkin .30 .75
51 Jared McCann .20 .50
52 Ryan Strome .25 .60
53 Moritz Seider .30 .75
54 Aleksander Barkov .40 1.00
55 Bo Horvat .30 .75
56 Mitch Marner .40 1.00
57 Evgeni Malkin .50 1.25
58 Kris Letang .30 .75
59 Roman Josi .25 .60
60 Elvis Merzlikins .25 .60
61 Adam Fox .30 .75
62 William Karlsson .30 .75
63 Brad Marchand .50 1.25
64 Philipp Grubauer .25 .60
65 Teuvo Teravainen .25 .60
66 Juuse Saros .30 .75
67 Artemi Panarin .50 1.25
68 Blake Coleman .20 .50
69 Jack Eichel .40 1.00
70 Mark Stone .30 .75
71 Ilya Sorokin .40 1.00
72 Tage Thompson .30 .75
73 Thatcher Demko .30 .75
74 Jonathan Quick .30 .75
75 Mathew Barzal .30 .75
76 Roope Hintz .30 .75
77 Victor Hedman .30 .75
78 Kirby Dach .25 .60
79 Michael Bunting .25 .60
80 Filip Forsberg .40 1.00
81 Kyle Connor .40 1.00
82 Cale Makar .60 1.50
83 Miro Heiskanen .30 .75
84 Tanner Jeannot .15 .40
85 Tom Wilson .25 .60
86 Jack Hughes .60 1.50
87 Sidney Crosby 1.00 2.50
88 Patrick Kane .50 1.25
89 Cam Atkinson .25 .60
90 Ryan O'Reilly .25 .60
91 Steven Stamkos .50 1.25
92 Gabriel Landeskog .30 .75
93 Anze Kopitar .40 1.00
94 Josh Norris .25 .60
95 Jonathan Toews .40 1.00
96 Jacob Markstrom .25 .60
97 Connor McDavid 1.25 3.00
98 John Tavares .40 1.00
99 Andrei Vasilevskiy .40 1.00
100 Igor Shesterkin .50 1.25
101 Shane Wright RC 4.00 10.00
102 Braden Schneider RC 2.50 6.00
103 David Jiricek RC 3.00 8.00
104 Jake Sanderson RC 4.00 10.00
105 Matty Beniers RC 4.00 10.00
106 Lukas Reichel RC 3.00 8.00
107 Elmer Soderblom RC 3.00 8.00
108 Jordan Harris RC 2.00 5.00
109 Andrei Kuzmenko RC 3.00 8.00
110 Owen Power RC 3.00 8.00
111 Kaiden Guhle RC 3.00 8.00
112 Wyatt Johnston RC 6.00 15.00
113 Arber Xhekaj RC 3.00 8.00
114 Jack Quinn RC 2.50 6.00
115 Juraj Slafkovsky RC 8.00 20.00
116 Dylan Holloway RC 3.00 8.00
117 Matias Maccelli RC 2.50 6.00
118 Jordan Spence RC 1.50 4.00
119 Ben Meyers RC 1.50 4.00
120 Lukas Dostal RC 3.00 8.00
121 Samuel Fagemo RC 1.25 3.00
122 Brayden Tracey RC 1.25 3.00
123 Dylan Guenther RC 4.00 10.00
124 Marco Rossi RC 4.00 10.00
125 Nick Abruzzese RC 1.50 4.00
126 Cole Koepke RC 1.50 4.00
127 Pyotr Kochetkov RC 3.00 8.00
128 Pavol Regenda RC 1.50 4.00
129 Nick Perbix RC 1.25 3.00
130 Kent Johnson RC 3.00 8.00
131 Dylan Samberg RC 1.50 4.00
132 Zack Hayes RC 1.25 3.00
133 Thomas Bordeleau RC 1.50 4.00
134 Aatu Raty RC 1.50 4.00
135 Mark Kastelic RC 1.25 3.00
136 Kaedan Korczak RC 1.25 3.00
137 Matt Boldy RC 5.00 12.00
138 Jonatan Berggren RC 2.50 6.00
139 Brandt Clarke RC 3.00 8.00
140 Samuel Poulin RC 2.00 5.00

2022-23 SP Blue
*BLUE: .5X TO 1.2X BASIC

2022-23 SP Gold
*GOLD/199: .6X TO 1.5X BASIC

2022-23 SP Green
*GREEN/25: 1.2X TO 3X BASIC

2022-23 SP Patterned Foilboard
*PAT FOIL: .6X TO 1.5X BASIC

2022-23 SP Patterned Foilboard Gold
*PAT FOIL GOLD: .75X TO 2X BASIC

2022-23 SP Patterned Foilboard Green
*PAT FOIL GREEN: 1X TO 2.5X BASIC

2022-23 SP Purple
*PURPLE/99: 1X TO 2.5X BASIC

2022-23 SP Red
*RED/149: .75X TO 2X BASIC

2022-23 SP Silver Spectrum
*SILVER/299: .5X TO 1.2X BASIC

2022-23 SP Authentic Profiles
*BLUE: .4X TO 1X BASIC
*SILVER/299: .5X TO 1.2X BASIC
*GOLD/199: .6X TO 1.5X BASIC
*RED/149: .75X TO 2X BASIC
*PURPLE/99: 1X TO 2.5X BASIC
*GREEN/25: 1.2X TO 3X BASIC
*PAT FOIL: 1.2X TO 3X BASIC
*PAT FOIL GOLD: 1.5X TO 4X BASIC
*PAT FOIL GREEN: 2X TO 5X BASIC
AP1 Connor McDavid 5.00 12.00
AP2 Sidney Crosby 4.00 10.00
AP3 Brad Marchand 2.00 5.00
AP4 Matthew Tkachuk 2.00 5.00
AP5 Jason Robertson 1.50 4.00
AP6 Anze Kopitar 1.50 4.00
AP7 Brady Tkachuk 1.50 4.00
AP8 Alex Ovechkin 4.00 10.00
AP9 Tim Stutzle 1.25 3.00
AP10 Andrei Vasilevskiy 1.50 4.00
AP11 Roman Josi 1.00 2.50
AP12 Marc-Andre Fleury 2.00 5.00
AP13 Alexis Lafreniere 1.50 4.00
AP14 Michael Bunting 1.00 2.50
AP15 Jack Eichel 1.50 4.00
AP16 Cale Makar 2.50 6.00
AP17 Auston Matthews 4.00 10.00
AP18 Jonathan Quick 1.25 3.00
AP19 Tage Thompson 1.25 3.00
AP20 Leon Draisaitl 3.00 8.00

2022-23 SP Authentic Profiles Jerseys
AP1 Connor McDavid 10.00 25.00
AP2 Sidney Crosby 8.00 20.00
AP3 Brad Marchand 4.00 10.00
AP4 Matthew Tkachuk 4.00 10.00
AP5 Jason Robertson 3.00 8.00
AP6 Anze Kopitar 3.00 8.00
AP7 Brady Tkachuk 3.00 8.00
AP8 Alex Ovechkin 8.00 20.00
AP9 Tim Stutzle 2.50 6.00
AP10 Andrei Vasilevskiy 3.00 8.00
AP11 Roman Josi 2.00 5.00
AP12 Marc-Andre Fleury 4.00 10.00
AP13 Alexis Lafreniere 3.00 8.00
AP14 Michael Bunting 2.00 5.00
AP15 Jack Eichel 3.00 8.00
AP16 Cale Makar 5.00 12.00
AP17 Auston Matthews 8.00 20.00
AP18 Jonathan Quick 2.50 6.00
AP19 Tage Thompson 2.50 6.00
AP20 Leon Draisaitl 6.00 15.00

2022-23 SP Authentic Profiles Signatures
AP1 Connor McDavid A 150.00 400.00
AP3 Brad Marchand C 20.00 50.00
AP4 Matthew Tkachuk C 20.00 50.00
AP7 Brady Tkachuk C 15.00 40.00
AP9 Tim Stutzle C 12.00 30.00
AP10 Andrei Vasilevskiy B 15.00 40.00
AP12 Marc-Andre Fleury B 20.00 50.00
AP13 Alexis Lafreniere C 15.00 40.00
AP14 Michael Bunting C 10.00 25.00
AP16 Cale Makar B 25.00 60.00
AP17 Auston Matthews A 40.00 100.00
AP18 Jonathan Quick B 12.00 30.00
AP19 Tage Thompson C 12.00 30.00
AP20 Leon Draisaitl B 30.00 80.00

2022-23 SP Jerseys
101 Shane Wright 6.00 15.00
102 Braden Schneider 4.00 10.00
103 David Jiricek 5.00 12.00
104 Jake Sanderson 6.00 15.00
105 Matty Beniers 6.00 15.00
106 Lukas Reichel 5.00 12.00
107 Elmer Soderblom 5.00 12.00
108 Jordan Harris 3.00 8.00
109 Andrei Kuzmenko 5.00 12.00
110 Owen Power 5.00 12.00
111 Kaiden Guhle 5.00 12.00
112 Wyatt Johnston 10.00 25.00
113 Arber Xhekaj 5.00 12.00
114 Jack Quinn 4.00 10.00
115 Juraj Slafkovsky 12.00 30.00
116 Dylan Holloway 5.00 12.00
117 Matias Maccelli 4.00 10.00
118 Jordan Spence 2.50 6.00
119 Ben Meyers 2.50 6.00
120 Lukas Dostal 5.00 12.00
121 Samuel Fagemo 2.00 5.00
122 Brayden Tracey 2.00 5.00
123 Dylan Guenther 6.00 15.00
124 Marco Rossi 6.00 15.00
125 Nick Abruzzese 2.50 6.00
126 Cole Koepke 2.50 6.00
127 Pyotr Kochetkov 5.00 12.00
128 Pavol Regenda 2.50 6.00
129 Nick Perbix 2.00 5.00
130 Kent Johnson 5.00 12.00
131 Dylan Samberg 2.50 6.00
132 Zack Hayes 2.00 5.00
133 Thomas Bordeleau 2.50 6.00
135 Mark Kastelic 2.00 5.00
136 Kaedan Korczak 2.00 5.00
137 Matt Boldy 8.00 20.00
138 Jonatan Berggren 4.00 10.00
139 Brandt Clarke 5.00 12.00
140 Samuel Poulin 3.00 8.00

2022-23 SP Signatures
*GOLD/25: .6X TO 1.5X BASIC
101 Shane Wright A 15.00 40.00
102 Braden Schneider B 10.00 25.00
104 Jake Sanderson B 15.00 40.00
105 Matty Beniers A 15.00 40.00
106 Lukas Reichel B 12.00 30.00
107 Elmer Soderblom B 12.00 30.00
108 Jordan Harris C 8.00 20.00
110 Owen Power A 12.00 30.00
111 Kaiden Guhle B 12.00 30.00
112 Wyatt Johnston B 25.00 60.00
113 Arber Xhekaj C 12.00 30.00
114 Jack Quinn B 10.00 25.00
115 Juraj Slafkovsky A 30.00 80.00
116 Dylan Holloway B 12.00 30.00
119 Ben Meyers C 6.00 15.00
120 Lukas Dostal B 12.00 30.00
121 Samuel Fagemo B 5.00 12.00
123 Dylan Guenther A 15.00 40.00
124 Marco Rossi A 15.00 40.00
125 Nick Abruzzese C 6.00 15.00
126 Cole Koepke C 6.00 15.00
127 Pyotr Kochetkov C 12.00 30.00
128 Pavol Regenda C 6.00 15.00
129 Nick Perbix C 5.00 12.00
130 Kent Johnson B 12.00 30.00
131 Dylan Samberg C 6.00 15.00
132 Zack Hayes C 5.00 12.00
133 Thomas Bordeleau B 6.00 15.00
134 Aatu Raty B 6.00 15.00
135 Mark Kastelic C 5.00 12.00
136 Kaedan Korczak C 5.00 12.00
138 Jonatan Berggren B 10.00 25.00
139 Brandt Clarke A 12.00 30.00
140 Samuel Poulin B 8.00 20.00

2023-24 SP
1 Connor McDavid 1.25 3.00
2 Sidney Crosby 1.00 2.50
3 Alex Ovechkin 1.00 2.50
4 Auston Matthews 1.00 2.50
5 Leon Draisaitl .75 2.00
6 Marc-Andre Fleury .40 1.00
7 Cale Makar .60 1.50
8 John Tavares .40 1.00
9 Igor Shesterkin .50 1.25
10 Tim Stutzle .30 .75
11 Brad Marchand .50 1.25
12 Andrei Vasilevskiy .40 1.00
13 Anze Kopitar .40 1.00
14 Matty Beniers .30 .75
15 Jack Eichel .40 1.00
16 Dylan Cozens .25 .60
17 Alexis Lafreniere .40 1.00
18 Cole Caufield .50 1.25
19 Jonathan Huberdeau .30 .75
20 Sebastian Aho .40 1.00
21 Andrei Svechnikov .30 .75
22 Juraj Slafkovsky .50 1.25
23 Brent Burns .25 .60
24 Mikko Rantanen .60 1.50
25 Joe Pavelski .30 .75
26 Aleksander Barkov .40 1.00
27 Matthew Tkachuk .50 1.25
28 Nick Suzuki .50 1.25
29 Nico Hischier .40 1.00
30 Tage Thompson .30 .75
31 Brady Tkachuk .40 1.00
32 Noah Cates .15 .40
33 Jake Guentzel .30 .75
34 Jonathan Quick .40 1.00
35 Jeremy Swayman .40 1.00
36 Jake Oettinger .40 1.00
37 Ilya Sorokin .40 1.00
38 Brock Boeser .30 .75
39 Roman Josi .25 .60
40 Clayton Keller .30 .75
41 Shane Pinto .20 .50
42 Miro Heiskanen .30 .75
43 Ryan Nugent-Hopkins .30 .75
44 Mark Stone .30 .75
45 Jonathan Marchessault .30 .75
46 J.T. Miller .30 .75
47 Kyle Connor .30 .75
48 Troy Terry .20 .50
49 Jacob Markstrom .25 .60
50 Teuvo Teravainen .25 .60
51 Seth Jarvis .30 .75
52 Zach Hyman .40 1.00
53 Kevin Fiala .20 .50
54 Mats Zuccarello .25 .60
55 Brendan Gallagher .25 .60
56 Timo Meier .25 .60
57 Brock Nelson .25 .60
58 Josh Norris .25 .60
59 Robert Thomas .25 .60
60 Jordan Kyrou .25 .60
61 Chandler Stephenson .20 .50
62 Evgeny Kuznetsov .30 .75
63 Cole Perfetti .25 .60
64 Matt Boldy .40 1.00
65 Kirby Dach .25 .60
66 Joel Eriksson Ek .20 .50
67 Torey Krug .20 .50
68 Anton Lundell .25 .60
69 Sam Reinhart .50 1.25
70 Juuse Saros .30 .75
71 Bo Horvat .30 .75
72 Jordan Eberle .25 .60
73 Roope Hintz .30 .75
74 Kent Johnson .25 .60
75 Matias Maccelli .20 .50
76 David Pastrnak .60 1.50
77 David Perron .20 .50
78 Patrik Laine .30 .75
79 Jack Hughes .60 1.50
80 Alex Tuch .25 .60
81 Mason McTavish .25 .60
82 Bowen Byram .30 .75
83 K'Andre Miller .20 .50
84 Steven Stamkos .50 1.25
85 Tristan Jarry .25 .60
86 David Jiricek .25 .60
87 Nathan MacKinnon 1.00 2.50
88 Nazem Kadri .30 .75
89 Philipp Grubauer .25 .60
90 Dylan Larkin .30 .75
91 Mathew Barzal .30 .75
92 Travis Konecny .25 .60
93 Trevor Zegras .25 .60
94 Nikolaj Ehlers .25 .60
95 Mikey Anderson .20 .50
96 Mitch Marner .40 1.00
97 Kirill Kaprizov .75 2.00
98 Elias Pettersson .40 1.00
99 Brayden Point .30 .75
100 Moritz Seider .30 .75
101 Connor Bedard RC 20.00 50.00
102 Logan Cooley RC 3.00 8.00
103 Devon Levi RC 2.50 6.00
104 Tyson Foerster RC 2.00 5.00
105 Justin Sourdif RC 1.00 2.50
106 Ridly Greig RC 1.50 4.00
107 Adam Fantilli RC 3.00 8.00
108 Wyatt Kaiser RC 1.00 2.50
109 Samuel Bolduc RC 1.00 2.50
110 Luke Hughes RC 3.00 8.00
111 Vincent Iorio RC 1.00 2.50
112 Luke Evangelista RC 1.50 4.00
113 Akito Hirose RC .75 2.00
114 Simon Edvinsson RC 2.00 5.00
115 Leo Carlsson RC 3.00 8.00
116 Dustin Wolf RC 3.00 8.00
117 Matt Savoie RC 2.00 5.00
118 Kevin Korchinski RC 1.50 4.00
119 Stanislav Svozil RC .75 2.00
120 Vincent Desharnais RC 1.25 3.00
121 Matthew Knies RC 4.00 10.00
122 Lukas Rousek RC .75 2.00
123 Sean Farrell RC 1.00 2.50
124 Pavel Mintyukov RC 1.50 4.00
125 Marco Kasper RC 2.50 6.00
126 William Dufour RC .75 2.00
127 Leevi Merilainen RC 1.00 2.50
128 Brock Faber RC 2.50 6.00
129 Matthew Poitras RC 2.00 5.00
130 Will Cuylle RC 1.50 4.00
131 Alex Laferriere RC 1.50 4.00
132 Matthew Coronato RC 1.50 4.00
133 Owen Beck RC 1.50 4.00
134 Jakob Pelletier RC 1.25 3.00
135 John Beecher RC 2.00 5.00
136 Fraser Minten RC 2.00 5.00
137 Tye Kartye RC 1.50 4.00
138 Danil Gushchin RC 1.00 2.50
139 Yaroslav Askarov RC 2.50 6.00
140 Zach Benson RC 1.50 4.00

2023-24 SP Blue
*BLUE: .5X TO 1.2X BASIC
101 Connor Bedard 10.00 25.00

2023-24 SP Green
*GREEN/25: 2.5X TO 6X BASIC

2023-24 SP Patterned Foilboard
*PAT FOIL: 1X TO 2.5X BASIC

2023-24 SP Patterned Foilboard Gold Tint
*PAT GOLD: 1.2X TO 3X BASIC
101 Connor Bedard 80.00 200.00

2023-24 SP Patterned Foilboard Green Tint
*PAT GRN: 1.5X TO 4X BASIC

2023-24 SP Purple
*PURPLE/99: 1.5X TO 4X BASIC

2023-24 SP Red
*RED/899: .5X TO 1.2X BASIC
101 Connor Bedard 40.00 100.00

2023-24 SP Authentic Profiles
*BLUE: .5X TO 1.2X BASIC
*RED/899: .5X TO 1.2X BASIC
*PURPLE/99: 1.2X TO 3X BASIC
*GREEN/25: 1.5X TO 4X BASIC
*PAT FOIL: 1.5X TO 4X BASIC
*PAT GOLD: 2X TO 5X BASIC
*PAT GREEN: 2.5X TO 6X BASIC
AP1 Connor McDavid 4.00 10.00
AP2 Alex Tuch .75 2.00
AP3 Jack Hughes 2.00 5.00
AP4 Dylan Larkin 1.00 2.50
AP5 Johnny Gaudreau 1.25 3.00
AP6 Matty Beniers 1.00 2.50
AP7 Adam Fox 1.00 2.50
AP8 Matt Boldy 1.25 3.00
AP9 John Tavares 1.25 3.00
AP10 Brendan Gallagher .75 2.00
AP11 Robert Thomas .75 2.00
AP12 Nikolaj Ehlers .75 2.00
AP13 Clayton Keller 1.00 2.50
AP14 Aleksander Barkov 1.25 3.00
AP15 Kevin Fiala .60 1.50
AP16 Bowen Byram 1.00 2.50
AP17 Roope Hintz 1.00 2.50
AP18 Mark Stone 1.00 2.50
AP19 Jake DeBrusk .75 2.00
AP20 Elias Pettersson 1.25 3.00

2023-24 SP Authentic Profiles Jerseys
AP1 Connor McDavid 10.00 25.00
AP2 Alex Tuch 2.00 5.00
AP3 Jack Hughes 5.00 12.00
AP4 Dylan Larkin 2.50 6.00
AP5 Johnny Gaudreau 3.00 8.00
AP6 Matty Beniers 2.50 6.00
AP7 Adam Fox 2.50 6.00
AP8 Matt Boldy 3.00 8.00
AP9 John Tavares 3.00 8.00
AP10 Brendan Gallagher 2.00 5.00
AP11 Robert Thomas 2.00 5.00
AP12 Nikolaj Ehlers 2.00 5.00
AP13 Clayton Keller 2.50 6.00
AP14 Aleksander Barkov 3.00 8.00
AP15 Kevin Fiala 1.50 4.00
AP16 Bowen Byram 2.50 6.00
AP17 Roope Hintz 2.50 6.00
AP18 Mark Stone 2.50 6.00
AP19 Jake DeBrusk 2.00 5.00
AP20 Elias Pettersson 3.00 8.00

2023-24 SP Authentic Profiles Signatures
AP1 Connor McDavid SP 150.00 400.00
AP2 Alex Tuch 10.00 25.00
AP5 Johnny Gaudreau SP 15.00 40.00
AP6 Matty Beniers 12.00 30.00
AP8 Matt Boldy 15.00 40.00
AP9 John Tavares SP 15.00 40.00
AP11 Robert Thomas 10.00 25.00
AP14 Aleksander Barkov 15.00 40.00
AP15 Kevin Fiala 8.00 20.00
AP16 Bowen Byram 12.00 30.00
AP17 Roope Hintz 12.00 30.00
AP18 Mark Stone 12.00 30.00
AP19 Jake DeBrusk 10.00 25.00

2023-24 SP Authentic Signatures
ASAL Anton Lundell SP 10.00 25.00
ASCM Connor McDavid SP 200.00 500.00
ASCP Colton Parayko SP 8.00 20.00
ASDH Dylan Holloway 10.00 25.00
ASDJ Dakota Joshua 6.00 15.00
ASDT Devon Toews SP 8.00 20.00
ASFE Mario Ferraro 6.00 15.00
ASHL Hendrix Lapierre 6.00 15.00
ASJC John Carlson SP 10.00 25.00
ASJZ Jason Zucker 10.00 25.00
ASKG Kaiden Guhle 10.00 25.00
ASKL Kris Letang SP 12.00 30.00
ASMK Mark Kastelic 8.00 20.00
ASMR Marco Rossi 12.00 30.00
ASRC Ross Colton 8.00 20.00
ASRR Ryan Reaves 8.00 20.00
ASTM Timo Meier SP 10.00 25.00
ASYS Yegor Sharangovich 10.00 25.00

2023-24 SP Jerseys
101 Connor Bedard 40.00 100.00
102 Logan Cooley 8.00 20.00
103 Devon Levi 6.00 15.00
104 Tyson Foerster 5.00 12.00
105 Justin Sourdif 2.50 6.00
106 Ridly Greig 4.00 10.00
107 Adam Fantilli 8.00 20.00
108 Wyatt Kaiser 2.50 6.00
109 Samuel Bolduc 2.50 6.00
110 Luke Hughes 8.00 20.00
111 Vincent Iorio 2.50 6.00
112 Luke Evangelista 4.00 10.00
113 Akito Hirose 2.00 5.00
114 Simon Edvinsson 5.00 12.00
115 Leo Carlsson 8.00 20.00
116 Dustin Wolf 8.00 20.00
117 Matt Savoie 5.00 12.00
118 Kevin Korchinski 4.00 10.00
119 Stanislav Svozil 2.00 5.00
120 Vincent Desharnais 3.00 8.00
121 Matthew Knies 10.00 25.00
122 Lukas Rousek 2.00 5.00
123 Sean Farrell 2.50 6.00
124 Pavel Mintyukov 4.00 10.00
125 Marco Kasper 6.00 15.00
126 William Dufour 2.00 5.00
127 Leevi Merilainen 2.50 6.00
128 Brock Faber 6.00 15.00
129 Matthew Poitras 5.00 12.00
130 Will Cuylle 4.00 10.00
131 Alex Laferriere 4.00 10.00
132 Matthew Coronato 4.00 10.00
133 Owen Beck 4.00 10.00
134 Jakob Pelletier 3.00 8.00
135 John Beecher 5.00 12.00
136 Fraser Minten 5.00 12.00
137 Tye Kartye 4.00 10.00
138 Danil Gushchin 2.50 6.00
139 Yaroslav Askarov 6.00 15.00
140 Zach Benson 4.00 10.00

2023-24 SP Signatures
*GOLD/25: .6X TO 1.5X BASIC
103 Devon Levi SP 15.00 40.00
104 Tyson Foerster 12.00 30.00
105 Justin Sourdif 6.00 15.00
106 Ridly Greig 10.00 25.00
108 Wyatt Kaiser 6.00 15.00
109 Samuel Bolduc 6.00 15.00
111 Vincent Iorio 6.00 15.00
112 Luke Evangelista SP 10.00 25.00
113 Akito Hirose 5.00 12.00
114 Simon Edvinsson SP 12.00 30.00
116 Dustin Wolf SP 20.00 50.00
117 Matt Savoie 12.00 30.00
118 Kevin Korchinski SP 10.00 25.00
119 Stanislav Svozil 5.00 12.00
122 Lukas Rousek 5.00 12.00
124 Pavel Mintyukov SP 10.00 25.00
125 Marco Kasper SP 15.00 40.00
126 William Dufour 5.00 12.00
127 Leevi Merilainen 6.00 15.00
129 Matthew Poitras 12.00 30.00
130 Will Cuylle 10.00 25.00
131 Alex Laferriere 10.00 25.00
132 Matthew Coronato 10.00 25.00
133 Owen Beck 10.00 25.00
136 Fraser Minten 12.00 30.00
137 Tye Kartye 10.00 25.00
138 Danil Gushchin 6.00 15.00
140 Zach Benson SP 10.00 25.00

2024-25 SP
1 Connor McDavid 1.25 3.00
2 Auston Matthews 1.00 2.50
3 Mitch Marner .40 1.00
4 Leon Draisaitl .75 2.00
5 Sidney Crosby 1.00 2.50
6 Alex Ovechkin 1.00 2.50
7 Marc-Andre Fleury .50 1.25
8 Jack Eichel .40 1.00
9 Brad Marchand .50 1.25
10 Connor Bedard .75 2.00
11 Kirill Kaprizov .75 2.00
12 Dylan Larkin .30 .75
13 Jack Hughes .60 1.50
14 Nikita Kucherov .50 1.25
15 Elias Pettersson .40 1.00
16 Cale Makar .60 1.50
17 Sam Reinhart .50 1.25
18 Josh Norris .25 .60
19 Brayden Schenn .25 .60
20 Logan Cooley .50 1.25
21 Brady Tkachuk .40 1.00
22 Ryan Nugent-Hopkins .30 .75
23 Roman Josi .25 .60
24 Alex DeBrincat .30 .75
25 Matthew Tkachuk .50 1.25
26 Mathew Barzal .30 .75
27 Tage Thompson .30 .75
28 Nick Suzuki .50 1.25
29 Leo Carlsson .40 1.00
30 Jake Oettinger .40 1.00
31 Sebastian Aho .40 1.00
32 Travis Konecny .25 .60
33 Seth Jarvis .30 .75
34 John Carlson .25 .60
35 Wyatt Johnston .50 1.25
36 Alexis Lafreniere .40 1.00
37 Kent Johnson .25 .60
38 Kris Letang .30 .75
39 Aleksander Barkov .40 1.00
40 Matt Boldy .40 1.00
41 Brock Nelson .25 .60
42 Jeremy Swayman .40 1.00
43 Miro Heiskanen .30 .75
44 Tim Stutzle .30 .75
45 Shane Wright .30 .75
46 Andrei Svechnikov .30 .75
47 Travis Sanheim .15 .40
48 Petr Mrazek .20 .50
49 Cole Sillinger .20 .50
50 Jake Sanderson .30 .75
51 Thomas Novak .15 .40
52 Jakob Pelletier .15 .40
53 Jared McCann .20 .50
54 Ilya Sorokin .40 1.00
55 Samuel Ersson .25 .60
56 Luke Evangelista .20 .50
57 Jack Quinn .20 .50
58 Braden Schneider .20 .50
59 Mason McTavish .25 .60
60 Kirill Marchenko .30 .75
61 Mikael Granlund .20 .50
62 Samuel Montembeault .25 .60
63 Jonathan Marchessault .30 .75
64 Charlie Lindgren .20 .50
65 Nick Schmaltz .20 .50
66 Nico Hischier .40 1.00
67 Oliver Bjorkstrand .20 .50
68 Kevin Hayes .20 .50
69 Alexander Holtz .25 .60
70 Aliaksei Protas .15 .40
71 William Eklund .30 .75
72 Jake Neighbours .25 .60
73 Cole Perfetti .25 .60
74 Kevin Korchinski .20 .50
75 Matt Coronato .20 .50
76 Cole Caufield .50 1.25
77 Adam Fantilli .40 1.00
78 David Pastrnak .60 1.50
79 Bryan Rust .25 .60
80 Matty Beniers .30 .75
81 Artemi Panarin .50 1.25
82 William Nylander .50 1.25
83 Kyle Connor .40 1.00
84 Nathan MacKinnon 1.00 2.50
85 Anze Kopitar .40 1.00
86 John Tavares .40 1.00
87 Clayton Keller .30 .75
88 Jason Robertson .40 1.00
89 Andrei Vasilevskiy .40 1.00
90 Quinn Hughes .60 1.50

91 Devon Toews	.20	.50
92 Moritz Seider	.30	.75
93 Igor Shesterkin	.50	1.25
94 Connor Hellebuyck	.50	1.25
95 Trevor Zegras	.25	.60
96 Trevor Moore	.15	.40
97 Quinton Byfield	.30	.75
98 Patrick Kane	.50	1.25
99 Rasmus Dahlin	.30	.75
100 Thatcher Demko	.30	.75
101 Josh Doan RC	1.50	4.00
102 Jesper Wallstedt RC	2.50	6.00
103 Brennan Othmann RC	1.50	4.00
104 Mavrik Bourque RC	2.00	5.00
105 Logan Stankoven RC	2.50	6.00
106 Olen Zellweger RC	2.00	5.00
107 Joshua Roy RC	1.50	4.00
108 Graeme Clarke RC	1.00	2.50
109 Zack Ostapchuk RC	1.00	2.50
110 Devin Cooley RC	1.00	2.50
111 Logan Morrison RC	1.00	2.50
112 Brendan Brisson RC	1.25	3.00
113 Akil Thomas RC	1.00	2.50
114 Mason Morelli RC	1.00	2.50
115 Matt Rempe RC	2.00	5.00
116 Shakir Mukhamadullin RC	1.25	3.00
117 Zachary Bolduc RC	1.50	4.00
118 Zach Dean RC	1.00	2.50
119 Gage Goncalves RC	1.25	3.00
120 Yan Kuznetsov RC	1.00	2.50
121 Landon Slaggert RC	1.00	2.50
122 Collin Graf RC	1.00	2.50
123 Arshdeep Bains RC	1.25	3.00
124 Cutter Gauthier RC	2.50	6.00
125 Bradly Nadeau RC	1.50	4.00
126 Frank Nazar RC	3.00	8.00
127 Justin Brazeau RC	1.00	2.50
128 Lane Hutson RC	12.00	30.00
129 Liam Ohgren RC	2.00	5.00
130 Marshall Rifai RC	1.00	2.50
131 Seamus Casey RC	1.25	3.00
132 Samuel Honzek RC	1.00	2.50
133 Rutger McGroarty RC	2.00	5.00
134 Maxim Tsyplakov RC	1.50	4.00
135 Macklin Celebrini RC	20.00	50.00
136 Will Smith RC	3.00	8.00
137 Matvei Michkov RC	15.00	40.00
138 Conor Geekie RC	1.50	4.00
139 Jett Luchanko RC	2.00	5.00
140 Nolan Allan RC	1.00	2.50

2024-25 SP Blue

*BLUE: .5X TO 1.2X BASIC

128 Lane Hutson	8.00	20.00
135 Macklin Celebrini	8.00	20.00
137 Matvei Michkov	8.00	20.00

2024-25 SP Green

*GREEN/25: 2.5X TO 6X BASIC

2024-25 SP Patterned Foilboard

*PAT FOIL: 1X TO 2.5X BASIC

2024-25 SP Patterned Foilboard Gold

*PAT FOIL GOLD: 1.5X TO 4X BASIC

2024-25 SP Red

*RED/99: 1.5X TO 4X BASIC

2024-25 SP Authentic Profiles

*BLUE: .5X TO 1.2X BASIC
*RED/49: 1.5X TO 4X BASIC
*PAT FOIL: 1.5X TO 4X BASIC
*PAT FOIL GOLD: 2X TO 5X BASIC

AP1 Connor McDavid	4.00	10.00
AP2 Cale Makar	2.00	5.00
AP3 Marc-Andre Fleury	1.50	4.00
AP4 Nathan MacKinnon	3.00	8.00
AP5 Sidney Crosby	3.00	8.00
AP6 Jack Hughes	2.00	5.00
AP7 Kirill Kaprizov	2.50	6.00
AP8 Connor Bedard	2.50	6.00
AP9 Alex Ovechkin	3.00	8.00
AP10 Shane Wright	1.00	2.50
AP11 Quinn Hughes	2.00	5.00
AP12 Kent Johnson	.75	2.00
AP13 Wyatt Johnston	1.50	4.00
AP14 Dylan Cozens	.75	2.00
AP15 Brad Marchand	1.50	4.00
AP16 Nikita Kucherov	1.50	4.00
AP17 Andrei Vasilevskiy	1.25	3.00
AP18 Elias Pettersson	1.25	3.00
AP19 Leon Draisaitl	2.50	6.00
AP20 Auston Matthews	3.00	8.00

2024-25 SP Authentic Profiles Jerseys

AP1 Connor McDavid	10.00	25.00
AP2 Cale Makar	5.00	12.00
AP3 Marc-Andre Fleury	4.00	10.00
AP4 Nathan MacKinnon	8.00	20.00
AP5 Sidney Crosby	8.00	20.00
AP6 Jack Hughes	5.00	12.00
AP7 Kirill Kaprizov	6.00	15.00
AP8 Connor Bedard	6.00	15.00
AP9 Alex Ovechkin	8.00	20.00
AP10 Shane Wright	2.50	6.00
AP11 Quinn Hughes	5.00	12.00
AP13 Wyatt Johnston	4.00	10.00
AP14 Dylan Cozens	2.00	5.00
AP15 Brad Marchand	4.00	10.00
AP16 Nikita Kucherov	4.00	10.00
AP17 Andrei Vasilevskiy	3.00	8.00
AP18 Elias Pettersson	3.00	8.00
AP19 Leon Draisaitl	6.00	15.00
AP20 Auston Matthews	8.00	20.00

2024-25 SP Authentic Profiles Signatures

AP1 Connor McDavid SP	150.00	400.00
AP2 Cale Makar SP	25.00	60.00
AP3 Marc-Andre Fleury SP	20.00	50.00
AP4 Nathan MacKinnon SP	40.00	100.00
AP5 Sidney Crosby SP	40.00	100.00
AP7 Kirill Kaprizov	30.00	80.00
AP8 Connor Bedard SP	30.00	80.00
AP9 Alex Ovechkin SP	40.00	100.00
AP10 Shane Wright	12.00	30.00
AP11 Quinn Hughes SP	25.00	60.00
AP13 Wyatt Johnston	20.00	50.00
AP14 Dylan Cozens	10.00	25.00
AP16 Nikita Kucherov SP	20.00	50.00
AP17 Andrei Vasilevskiy SP	15.00	40.00
AP18 Elias Pettersson SP	15.00	40.00
AP19 Leon Draisaitl SP	30.00	80.00
AP20 Auston Matthews SP	40.00	100.00

2024-25 SP Authentic Signatures

ASAB Aleksander Barkov SP	15.00	40.00
ASBS Brandon Saad	8.00	20.00
ASBT Brady Tkachuk SP	15.00	40.00
ASCA Leo Carlsson	15.00	40.00
ASCS Cole Sillinger	8.00	20.00
ASDT Devon Toews	8.00	20.00
ASFV Frank Vatrano	8.00	20.00
ASJC J.T. Compher	6.00	15.00
ASJN Jake Neighbours	10.00	25.00
ASJP JJ Peterka	10.00	25.00
ASJQ Jack Quinn	8.00	20.00
ASJV Joe Veleno	8.00	20.00
ASKK Kevin Korchinski	8.00	20.00
ASLC Logan Cooley	20.00	50.00
ASMT Matthew Tkachuk SP	20.00	50.00
ASPM Pavel Mintyukov	8.00	20.00
ASPZ Pavel Zacha	8.00	20.00
ASTB Tyler Bertuzzi	8.00	20.00
ASTN Thomas Novak	6.00	15.00

2024-25 SP Jerseys

101 Josh Doan	5.00	12.00
102 Jesper Wallstedt	8.00	20.00
103 Brennan Othmann	5.00	12.00
104 Mavrik Bourque	6.00	15.00
105 Logan Stankoven	8.00	20.00
106 Olen Zellweger	6.00	15.00
107 Joshua Roy	5.00	12.00
108 Graeme Clarke	3.00	8.00
109 Zack Ostapchuk	3.00	8.00
110 Devin Cooley	3.00	8.00
111 Logan Morrison	3.00	8.00
112 Brendan Brisson	4.00	10.00
113 Akil Thomas	3.00	8.00
114 Mason Morelli	3.00	8.00
115 Matt Rempe	6.00	15.00
116 Shakir Mukhamadullin	4.00	10.00
117 Zachary Bolduc	5.00	12.00
118 Zach Dean	3.00	8.00
119 Gage Goncalves	4.00	10.00
120 Yan Kuznetsov	3.00	8.00
122 Collin Graf	3.00	8.00
123 Arshdeep Bains	4.00	10.00
124 Cutter Gauthier	8.00	20.00
125 Bradly Nadeau	5.00	12.00
126 Frank Nazar	10.00	25.00
127 Justin Brazeau	3.00	8.00
128 Lane Hutson	40.00	100.00
129 Liam Ohgren	6.00	15.00
130 Marshall Rifai	3.00	8.00
131 Seamus Casey	4.00	10.00
133 Rutger McGroarty	6.00	15.00
135 Macklin Celebrini	40.00	100.00
136 Will Smith	10.00	25.00
137 Matvei Michkov	40.00	100.00
138 Conor Geekie	5.00	12.00

2024-25 SP Signatures

101 Josh Doan	10.00	25.00
102 Jesper Wallstedt SP	15.00	40.00
103 Brennan Othmann	10.00	25.00
104 Mavrik Bourque	12.00	30.00
105 Logan Stankoven SP	40.00	100.00
106 Olen Zellweger	12.00	30.00
107 Joshua Roy	10.00	25.00
108 Graeme Clarke	6.00	15.00
109 Zack Ostapchuk	6.00	15.00
110 Devin Cooley	6.00	15.00
111 Logan Morrison	6.00	15.00
112 Brendan Brisson	8.00	20.00
113 Akil Thomas	6.00	15.00
114 Mason Morelli	6.00	15.00
115 Matt Rempe	12.00	30.00
116 Shakir Mukhamadullin	8.00	20.00
117 Zachary Bolduc	10.00	25.00
118 Zach Dean	6.00	15.00
119 Gage Goncalves	8.00	20.00
120 Yan Kuznetsov	6.00	15.00
122 Collin Graf	6.00	15.00
123 Arshdeep Bains	8.00	20.00
124 Cutter Gauthier SP	40.00	100.00
125 Bradly Nadeau	10.00	25.00
126 Frank Nazar	20.00	50.00
127 Justin Brazeau	6.00	15.00
128 Lane Hutson SP	125.00	300.00
129 Liam Ohgren	12.00	30.00
130 Marshall Rifai	6.00	15.00
131 Seamus Casey	8.00	20.00
133 Rutger McGroarty	12.00	30.00
135 Macklin Celebrini SP	200.00	500.00
136 Will Smith	80.00	200.00
137 Matvei Michkov SP	150.00	400.00
138 Conor Geekie	10.00	25.00
139 Jett Luchanko	12.00	30.00
140 Nolan Allan	6.00	15.00

2024-25 SP Signatures Gold

*GOLD/25: .6X TO 1.5X BASIC

128 Lane Hutson	250.00	600.00
135 Macklin Celebrini	400.00	1000.00
137 Matvei Michkov	300.00	800.00

1997-98 SP Authentic

COMPLETE SET (198)	30.00	60.00
1 Teemu Selanne	.60	1.50
2 Sean Pronger	.20	.50
3 Joe Sacco	.25	.60
4 Tomas Sandstrom	.20	.50
5 Steve Rucchin	.25	.60
6 Paul Kariya	.30	.75
7 Ted Donato	.20	.50
8 Ray Bourque	.50	1.25
9 Tim Taylor	.25	.60
10 Jason Allison	.25	.60
11 Kyle McLaren	.20	.50
12 Dimitri Khristich	.25	.60
13 Jason Dawe	.25	.60
14 Dominik Hasek	.50	1.25
15 Miroslav Satan	.20	.50
16 Brian Holzinger	.25	.60
17 Alexei Zhitnik	.20	.50
18 Theo Fleury	.40	1.00
19 Cory Stillman	.25	.60
20 Jarome Iginla	.40	1.00
21 Sandy McCarthy	.20	.50
22 German Titov	.20	.50
23 Glen Wesley	.20	.50
24 Keith Primeau	.25	.60
25 Geoff Sanderson	.25	.60
26 Gary Roberts	.25	.60
27 Sami Kapanen	.25	.60
28 Jeff O'Neill	.25	.60
29 Tony Amonte	.25	.60
30 Chris Chelios	.30	.75
31 Eric Daze	.20	.50
32 Alexei Zhamnov	.20	.50
33 Chris Terreri	.20	.50
34 Sergei Krivokrasov	.20	.50
35 Joe Sakic	.60	1.50
36 Peter Forsberg	.60	1.50
37 Patrick Roy	.75	2.00
38 Claude Lemieux	.25	.60
39 Valeri Kamensky	.25	.60
40 Adam Deadmarsh	.20	.50
41 Sandis Ozolinsh	.20	.50
42 Jari Kurri	.30	.75
43 Mike Modano	.50	1.25
44 Ed Belfour	.30	.75
45 Derian Hatcher	.25	.60
46 Sergei Zubov	.25	.60
47 Jamie Langenbrunner	.25	.60
48 Jere Lehtinen	.25	.60
49 Joe Nieuwendyk	.25	.60
50 Vyacheslav Kozlov	.25	.60
51 Chris Osgood	.30	.75
52 Steve Yzerman	.75	2.00
53 Nicklas Lidstrom	.30	.75
54 Igor Larionov	.20	.50
55 Brendan Shanahan	.30	.75
56 Anders Eriksson	.25	.60
57 Darren McCarty	.25	.60
58 Doug Weight	.30	.75
59 Jason Arnott	.25	.60
60 Curtis Joseph	.40	1.00
61 Ryan Smyth	.25	.60
62 Dean McAmmond	.20	.50
63 Mike Grier	.25	.60
64 Kelly Buchberger	.25	.60
65 Ed Jovanovski	.20	.50
66 Ray Whitney	.25	.60
67 Rob Niedermayer	.20	.50
68 Scott Mellanby	.25	.60
69 John Vanbiesbrouck	.30	.75
70 Viktor Kozlov	.25	.60
71 Jozef Stumpel	.20	.50
72 Rob Blake	.30	.75
73 Garry Galley	.20	.50
74 Vladimir Tsyplakov	.25	.60
75 Yanic Perreault	.25	.60
76 Stephane Fiset	.25	.60
77 Luc Robitaille	.30	.75
78 Valeri Bure	.20	.50
79 Mark Recchi	.40	1.00
80 Saku Koivu	.30	.75
81 Andy Moog	.30	.75
82 Vincent Damphousse	.25	.60
83 Vladimir Malakhov	.20	.50
84 Shayne Corson	.25	.60
85 Scott Stevens	.30	.75
86 Bill Guerin	.30	.75
87 Martin Brodeur	.75	2.00
88 Doug Gilmour	.40	1.00
89 Bobby Holik	.20	.50
90 Petr Sykora	.20	.50
91 Zigmund Palffy	.30	.75
92 Bryan Berard	.20	.50
93 Tommy Salo	.20	.50
94 Travis Green	.25	.60
95 Kenny Jonsson	.25	.60
96 Todd Bertuzzi	.30	.75
97 Robert Reichel	.25	.60
98 Pat LaFontaine	.30	.75
99 Wayne Gretzky	2.00	5.00
100 Brian Leetch	.25	.60
101 Mike Richter	.30	.75
102 Alexei Kovalev	.25	.60
103 Adam Graves	.20	.50
104 Niklas Sundstrom	.25	.60
105 Alexei Yashin	.25	.60
106 Daniel Alfredsson	.30	.75
107 Alexandre Daigle	.20	.50
108 Wade Redden	.20	.50
109 Andreas Dackell	.25	.60
110 Shawn McEachern	.20	.50
111 Eric Lindros	.50	1.25
112 Chris Gratton	.20	.50
113 Paul Coffey	.30	.75
114 John LeClair	.30	.75
115 Rod Brind'Amour	.30	.75
116 Ron Hextall	.30	.75
117 Dainius Zubrus	.25	.60
118 Jeremy Roenick	.50	1.25
119 Keith Tkachuk	.30	.75
120 Nikolai Khabibulin	.30	.75
121 Rick Tocchet	.20	.50
122 Teppo Numminen	.20	.50
123 Craig Janney	.20	.50
124 Mike Gartner	.40	1.00
125 Jaromir Jagr	1.00	2.50
126 Ron Francis	.40	1.00
127 Kevin Hatcher	.20	.50
128 Robert Dome RC	.20	.50
129 Martin Straka	.20	.50
131 Owen Nolan	.30	.75
132 Bernie Nicholls	.25	.60
133 Mike Vernon	.25	.60
134 Jeff Friesen	.25	.60
135 Tony Granato	.20	.50
136 Mike Ricci	.20	.50
137 Jim Campbell	.20	.50
138 Brett Hull	.60	1.50
139 Chris Pronger	.30	.75
140 Al MacInnis	.40	1.00
141 Pierre Turgeon	.25	.60
142 Pavol Demitra	.40	1.00
143 Grant Fuhr	.50	1.25
144 Steve Duchesne	.20	.50
145 Daymond Langkow	.20	.50
146 Alexander Selivanov	.20	.50
147 Daren Puppa	.25	.60
148 Dino Ciccarelli	.30	.75
149 Roman Hamrlik	.20	.50
150 Mats Sundin	.30	.75
151 Felix Potvin	.50	1.25
152 Wendel Clark	.50	1.25
153 Sergei Berezin	.25	.60
154 Steve Sullivan	.25	.60
155 Alexander Mogilny	.25	.60
156 Pavel Bure	.30	.75
157 Mark Messier	.60	1.50
158 Bret Hedican	.20	.50
159 Kirk McLean	.25	.60
160 Trevor Linden	.30	.75
161 Dave Scatchard RC	.25	.60
162 Adam Oates	.30	.75
163 Joe Juneau	.20	.50
164 Peter Bondra	.30	.75
165 Bill Ranford	.25	.60
166 Sergei Gonchar	.20	.50
167 Calle Johansson	.25	.60
168 Phil Housley	.25	.60
169 Espen Knutsen RC	.30	.75
170 Pavel Trnka RC	.20	.50
171 Joe Thornton	.50	1.25
172 Sergei Samsonov	.25	.60
173 Erik Rasmussen	.25	.60
174 Tyler Moss RC	.25	.60
175 Derek Morris RC	.30	.75
176 Craig Mills	.20	.50
177 Daniel Cleary	.25	.60
178 Eric Messier RC	.30	.75
179 Kevin Hodson	.25	.60
180 Mike Knuble RC	.30	.75
181 Boyd Deveraux	.25	.60
182 Craig Millar RC	.25	.60
183 Kevin Weekes RC	2.50	6.00
184 Donald MacLean RC	.30	.75
185 Patrik Elias RC	3.00	8.00
186 Zdeno Chara RC	8.00	20.00
187 Chris Phillips	.25	.60
188 Vaclav Prospal RC	.25	.60
189 Brad Isbister	.25	.60
190 Alexei Morozov	.25	.60
191 Patrick Marleau	.30	.75
192 Marco Sturm RC	.30	.75
193 Brendan Morrison RC	2.00	5.00
194 Mike Johnson RC	.25	.60
195 Alyn McCauley	.25	.60
196 Mattias Ohlund	.25	.60
197 Richard Zednik	.25	.60
198 Jan Bulis RC	.30	.75
99 Wayne Gretzky PROMO	2.00	5.00

1997-98 SP Authentic Authentics

10 W.Gretzky 802 Card/184	25.00	50.00

1997-98 SP Authentic Icons

COMPLETE SET (40)	40.00	80.00

*EMBOSSED: .8X TO 2X BASIC INSERTS
*DIE CUT: 4X TO 10X BASIC INSERTS

I1 Pat LaFontaine	.75	2.00
I2 Brett Hull	1.00	2.50
I3 Chris Chelios	.75	2.00
I4 Joe Sakic	1.50	4.00
I5 John Vanbiesbrouck	.60	1.50
I6 Patrik Elias	.75	2.00
I7 Eric Lindros	1.25	3.00
I8 Jaromir Jagr	1.25	3.00
I9 Joe Thornton	1.50	4.00
I10 Brendan Shanahan	.75	2.00
I11 Paul Kariya	.75	2.00
I12 Peter Forsberg	2.00	5.00
I13 Ed Belfour	.75	2.00
I14 Martin Brodeur	2.00	5.00
I15 Alexei Morozov	.60	1.50
I16 Mark Messier	.75	2.00
I17 John LeClair	.75	2.00
I18 Luc Robitaille	.60	1.50
I19 Teemu Selanne	.75	2.00
I20 Theo Fleury	.25	.60
I21 Steve Yzerman	2.00	5.00
I22 Chris Phillips	.25	.60
I23 Keith Tkachuk	.75	2.00
I24 Patrick Roy	2.00	5.00
I25 Mark Recchi	.60	1.50
I26 Wayne Gretzky	3.00	8.00
I27 Dino Ciccarelli	.25	.60
I28 Ray Bourque	1.25	3.00
I29 Tony Amonte	.60	1.50
I30 Daniel Alfredsson	.60	1.50
I31 Saku Koivu	.75	2.00
I32 Doug Weight	.60	1.50
I33 Mats Sundin	.75	2.00
I34 Dominik Hasek	1.50	4.00
I35 Scott Stevens	.60	1.50
I36 Pavel Bure	.75	2.00
I37 Mike Modano	1.25	3.00
I38 Zigmund Palffy	.60	1.50
I39 Brian Leetch	.75	2.00
I40 Marco Sturm	.75	2.00

1997-98 SP Authentic Mark of a Legend

M1 Gordie Howe/112	125.00	250.00
M2 Billy Smith/560	10.00	25.00
M3 Cam Neely/560	15.00	40.00
M4 Bryan Trottier/560	12.00	30.00
M5 Bobby Hull/560	25.00	60.00
M6 Wayne Gretzky/560	150.00	400.00

1997-98 SP Authentic Sign of the Times

BB Bryan Berard	2.00	5.00
BH Brett Hull	15.00	40.00
BH Brian Holzinger	2.00	5.00
CC Chris Chelios	6.00	15.00
DM Darren McCarty	4.00	10.00
DW Doug Weight	4.00	10.00
DZ Dainius Zubrus	4.00	10.00
GF Grant Fuhr	8.00	20.00
GH Guy Hebert	4.00	10.00
JI Jarome Iginla	6.00	15.00
JS Jaroslav Svejkovsky	2.00	5.00
JLA Jamie Langenbrunner	4.00	10.00
JT Joe Thornton	10.00	25.00
JTH Jose Theodore	8.00	20.00
MB Martin Brodeur	30.00	80.00
MG Mike Grier	4.00	10.00
MS Mats Sundin	15.00	40.00
NK Nikolai Khabibulin	6.00	15.00
NL Nicklas Lidstrom	10.00	25.00
PB Peter Bondra	4.00	10.00
PR Patrick Roy	30.00	80.00
RB Ray Bourque	20.00	50.00
RN Rob Niedermayer	4.00	10.00
SB Sergei Berezin	2.00	5.00
SS Sergei Samsonov	4.00	10.00
SY Steve Yzerman	50.00	100.00
TA Tony Amonte	4.00	10.00
WG Wayne Gretzky	125.00	300.00
YP Yanic Perreault	4.00	10.00

1997-98 SP Authentic Tradition

T1 W.Gretzky/G.Howe/158	300.00	800.00
T2 P.Roy/B.Smith/333	40.00	100.00
T3 J.Thornton/C.Neely/352	25.00	60.00
T4 B.Berard/B.Trottier/352	8.00	20.00
T5 B.Hull/B.Hull/352	30.00	80.00
T6 R.Bourque/C.Neely/140	50.00	120.00

1998-99 SP Authentic

COMPLETE SET (135)	125.00	300.00
COMP.SET w/o SP's (90)	10.00	25.00
1 Paul Kariya	.30	.75
2 Teemu Selanne	.30	.75
3 Guy Hebert	.25	.60
4 Sergei Samsonov	.25	.60
5 Joe Thornton	.50	1.25
6 Jason Allison	.08	.25
7 Ray Bourque	.50	1.25
8 Dominik Hasek	.60	1.50
9 Michael Peca	.08	.25
10 Michal Grosek	.08	.25
11 Derek Morris	.08	.25
12 Theo Fleury	.08	.25
13 Jarome Iginla	.40	1.00
14 Ron Francis	.25	.60
15 Keith Primeau	.08	.25
16 Sami Kapanen	.08	.25
17 Tony Amonte	.25	.60
18 Doug Gilmour	.25	.60
19 Chris Chelios	.30	.75
20 Peter Forsberg	.75	2.00
21 Patrick Roy	1.00	2.50
22 Joe Sakic	.60	1.50
23 Adam Deadmarsh	.08	.25
24 Brett Hull	.40	1.00
25 Mike Modano	.50	1.25
26 Ed Belfour	.30	.75
27 Jere Lehtinen	.08	.25
28 Sergei Fedorov	.50	1.25
29 Brendan Shanahan	.30	.75
30 Chris Osgood	.25	.60
31 Steve Yzerman	1.50	4.00
32 Nicklas Lidstrom	.30	.75
33 Doug Weight	.25	.60
34 Bill Guerin	.25	.60
35 Tom Poti	.08	.25
36 Rob Niedermayer	.08	.25
37 Ed Jovanovski	.08	.25
38 Luc Robitaille	.25	.60
39 Rob Blake	.25	.60
40 Glen Murray	.08	.25
41 Saku Koivu	.30	.75
42 Mark Recchi	.25	.60
43 Vincent Damphousse	.08	.25
44 Mike Dunham	.25	.60
45 Sergei Krivokrasov	.08	.25
46 Andrew Brunette	.25	.60
47 Brendan Morrison	.25	.60
48 Martin Brodeur	1.00	2.50
49 Scott Stevens	.25	.60
50 Patrik Elias	.25	.60
51 Trevor Linden	.25	.60
52 Zigmund Palffy	.25	.60
53 Bryan Berard	.08	.25
54 Robert Reichel	.08	.25
55 Mike Richter	.30	.75
56 Wayne Gretzky	2.00	4.00
57 Brian Leetch	.25	.60
58 Wade Redden	.08	.25
59 Alexei Yashin	.08	.25
60 Daniel Alfredsson	.25	.60
61 Eric Lindros	.30	.75
62 John Vanbiesbrouck	.25	.60
63 John LeClair	.30	.75
64 Rod Brind'Amour	.25	.60
65 Jeremy Roenick	.40	1.00
66 Keith Tkachuk	.30	.75
67 Nikolai Khabibulin	.25	.60
68 German Titov	.08	.25
69 Martin Straka	.08	.25
70 Jaromir Jagr	.50	1.25
71 Chris Pronger	.25	.60
72 Al MacInnis	.25	.60
73 Pierre Turgeon	.25	.60
74 Pavol Demitra	.25	.60
75 Patrick Marleau	.10	.30
76 Jeff Friesen	.08	.25
77 Owen Nolan	.08	.25
78 Bill Ranford	.08	.25
79 Wendel Clark	.25	.60
80 Craig Janney	.08	.25
81 Mike Johnson	.08	.25
82 Curtis Joseph	.30	.75
83 Mats Sundin	.30	.75
84 Mattias Ohlund	.25	.60
85 Mark Messier	.30	.75
86 Pavel Bure	.30	.75
87 Olaf Kolzig	.25	.60
88 Peter Bondra	.25	.60
89 Joe Juneau	.25	.60
90 Adam Oates	.25	.60
91 Johan Davidsson	1.50	4.00
92 Rico Fata	1.50	4.00
93 Mike Maneluk RC	2.00	5.00
94 J-P Dumont	1.50	4.00
95 Milan Hejduk RC	8.00	20.00
96 Chris Drury	1.50	4.00
97 Mark Parrish RC	4.00	10.00
98 Oleg Kvasha RC	2.00	5.00
99 Josh Green RC	2.00	5.00
100 Olli Jokinen	1.50	4.00
101 Manny Malhotra	1.50	4.00
102 Eric Brewer	1.50	4.00
103 Mike Watt	1.50	4.00
104 Daniel Briere	6.00	15.00
105 Jean-Sebastien Aubin RC	4.00	10.00
106 Jan Hrdina RC	2.00	5.00
107 Marty Reasoner	1.50	4.00
108 Michal Handzus RC	4.00	10.00
109 Vincent Lecavalier	4.00	10.00
110 Tomas Kaberle RC	4.00	10.00
111 Bill Muckalt RC	2.00	5.00
112 Josh Holden	1.50	4.00
113 Matt Herr RC	2.00	5.00
114 Brian Finley RC	3.00	8.00
115 Maxime Ouellet RC	2.00	5.00
116 Kurtis Foster RC	2.00	5.00
117 Barret Jackman RC	4.00	10.00
118 Ross Lupaschuk RC	2.00	5.00
119 Steven McCarthy RC	2.00	5.00
120 Peter Reynolds RC	2.00	5.00
121 Bart Rushmer RC	2.00	5.00
122 Jonathon Zion RC	2.00	5.00
123 Kris Beech RC	3.00	8.00
124 Brandin Cote RC	2.00	5.00
125 Scott Kelman RC	2.00	5.00
126 Jamie Lundmark RC	3.00	8.00
127 Derek MacKenzie RC	2.00	5.00
128 Rory McDade RC	2.00	5.00
129 David Morisset RC	2.00	5.00
130 Mirko Murovic RC	2.00	5.00
131 Taylor Pyatt RC	4.00	10.00
132 Charlie Stephens	2.00	5.00
133 Kyle Wanvig RC	2.00	5.00
134 Krzystof Wieckowski RC	2.00	5.00
135 Michael Zigomanis RC	2.00	5.00

1998-99 SP Authentic Power Shift

*1-90 POWER SHIFT: 4X TO 10X BAIC CARDS
*91-135 POWER SHIFT: 1X TO 3X BASIC SP

1998-99 SP Authentic Authentics

6 R.Blake Puck/75	12.50	25.00
7 R.Blake Photo/100	12.50	25.00
8 C.Chelios Photo/75	30.00	60.00
9 C.Chelios Puck/75	30.00	60.00
10 W.Gretzky Puck/50	200.00	500.00
11 W.Gretzky Photo/50	200.00	500.00
12 B.Hull Puck/90	30.00	60.00
13 K.Tkachuk Photo/75	30.00	60.00
14 K.Tkachuk Puck/75	30.00	60.00
15 S.Yzerman Card/50	50.00	100.00
16 S.Yzerman 2-card	75.00	150.00
17 S.Yzerman '98 BD Card/50	75.00	150.00

1998-99 SP Authentic Sign of the Times

AD Adam Deadmarsh	2.00	5.00
AM Alexander Mogilny	8.00	20.00
AS Alex Selivanov	3.00	8.00
BB Bates Battaglia	2.00	5.00
BD Byron Dafoe	4.00	10.00
BF Brian Finley	2.00	5.00
BH Brett Hull	12.50	30.00
BJ Barret Jackman	8.00	20.00
CJ Curtis Joseph	8.00	20.00
CS Charlie Stephens	2.00	5.00
DA Daniel Alfredsson	6.00	15.00
DM David Morisset	2.00	5.00
DMA Derek Mackenzie	2.00	5.00
DW Doug Weight	5.00	12.00
EJ Ed Jovanovski	4.00	10.00
JA Jason Allison	2.00	5.00
JJ Joe Juneau	4.00	10.00
JS Jozef Stumpel	2.00	5.00
JT Joe Thornton	10.00	25.00
KB Kris Beech	2.00	5.00
KF Kurtis Foster	3.00	8.00
KT Keith Tkachuk	8.00	20.00
MAO Maxime Ouellet	3.00	8.00
MB Matthew Barnaby	2.00	5.00
MH Marian Hossa	8.00	20.00
MIM Mirko Murovic	2.00	5.00
MM Manny Malhotra	4.00	10.00
MMC Marty McSorley	5.00	12.00
MO Mattias Ohlund	2.00	5.00
MS Mats Sundin	20.00	50.00
MZ Michael Zigomanis	2.00	5.00
NL Nicklas Lidstrom	12.50	30.00
ON Owen Nolan	4.00	10.00
PB Pavel Bure	10.00	25.00
PBO Peter Bondra	4.00	10.00
PR Patrick Roy	30.00	80.00
PRE Peter Reynolds	2.00	5.00
RB Rob Blake	4.00	10.00
RL Ross Lupaschuk	2.00	5.00
RM Rory McDade	2.00	5.00
RN Rumun Ndur	2.00	5.00
RS Ryan Smyth	4.00	10.00
SG Sergei Gonchar	2.00	5.00
SK Scott Kelman	3.00	8.00
SM Steven McCarthy	2.00	5.00
SY Steve Yzerman	40.00	80.00
TH Tomas Holmstrom	5.00	12.00
TP Taylor Pyatt	5.00	12.00
VL Vincent Lecavalier	8.00	20.00
WG Wayne Gretzky	150.00	400.00

1998-99 SP Authentic Sign of the Times Gold

AM A.Mogilny/89	25.00	50.00
AS Alex Selivanov/29	12.50	30.00
BD Byron Dafoe/34	20.00	50.00
BF Brian Finley/100	10.00	25.00
BJ Barret Jackman/100	10.00	25.00
CJ Curtis Joseph/31	50.00	125.00
CS Charlie Stephens/100	6.00	15.00
DM David Morisset/100	6.00	15.00
DMA Derek Mackenzie/100	6.00	15.00
DW Doug Weight/39	25.00	50.00
EJ E.Jovanovski/55	25.00	50.00
JA Jason Allison/41	10.00	25.00
JJ Joe Juneau/49	10.00	25.00
KB Kris Beech/100	6.00	15.00
KF Kurtis Foster/100	6.00	15.00
MAO Maxime Ouellet/100	10.00	25.00
MB Matthew Barnaby/36	10.00	25.00
MIM Mirko Murovic/100	6.00	15.00
MMC Marty McSorley/33	10.00	25.00
MZ Michael Zigomanis/100	8.00	20.00
PR Patrick Roy/33	200.00	350.00
PRE Peter Reynolds/100	6.00	15.00
RL Ross Lupaschuk/100	6.00	15.00
RM Rory McDade/100	6.00	15.00
RN Rumun Ndur/40	10.00	25.00
RS Ryan Smyth/94	12.50	30.00
SG Sergei Gonchar/55	12.50	30.00
SK Scott Kelman/100	6.00	15.00
SM Steven McCarthy/100	6.00	15.00
TH Tomas Holmstrom/96	10.00	25.00
TP Taylor Pyatt/100	15.00	30.00
WG Wayne Gretzky/99	250.00	600.00

1998-99 SP Authentic Snapshots

COMPLETE SET (30)	30.00	60.00
SS1 Wayne Gretzky	4.00	10.00
SS2 Patrick Roy	3.00	8.00
SS3 Steve Yzerman	3.00	8.00
SS4 Brett Hull	.75	2.00
SS5 Jaromir Jagr	1.00	2.50
SS6 Peter Forsberg	1.50	4.00
SS7 Dominik Hasek	1.25	3.00
SS8 Paul Kariya	.60	1.50
SS9 Eric Lindros	.60	1.50
SS10 Teemu Selanne	.60	1.50
SS11 John LeClair	.60	1.50
SS12 Mike Modano	1.00	2.50
SS13 Martin Brodeur	1.50	4.00
SS14 Brendan Shanahan	.60	1.50
SS15 Ray Bourque	1.00	2.50
SS16 John Vanbiesbrouck	.50	1.25
SS17 Brian Leetch	.50	1.25
SS18 Vincent Lecavalier	4.00	10.00
SS19 Joe Sakic	1.25	3.00
SS20 Chris Drury	.75	2.00
SS21 Eric Brewer	1.00	2.50
SS22 Jeremy Roenick	.75	2.00
SS23 Mats Sundin	.60	1.50
SS24 Zigmund Palffy	.50	1.25
SS25 Keith Tkachuk	.60	1.50
SS26 Sergei Samsonov	.50	1.25
SS27 Curtis Joseph	.60	1.50
SS28 Peter Bondra	.50	1.25
SS29 Sergei Fedorov	1.00	2.50
SS30 Doug Gilmour	.50	1.25

1998-99 SP Authentic Stat Masters

COMPLETE SET (30)	200.00	400.00
S1 Brendan Shanahan/400	2.50	6.00
S2 Brett Hull/1000	3.00	8.00
S3 Dominik Hasek/200	10.00	25.00
S4 Doug Gilmour/1200	2.50	6.00
S5 Doug Weight/500	2.50	6.00
S6 Eric Lindros/115	8.00	20.00
S7 Jaromir Jagr/301	6.00	15.00
S8 Joe Sakic/900	3.00	8.00
S9 John LeClair/500	3.00	8.00
S10 John Vanbiesbrouck/306	2.50	6.00
S11 Keith Tkachuk/250	2.50	6.00
S12 Mark Messier/600	2.50	6.00
S13 Martin Brodeur/200	12.50	30.00
S14 Mike Modano/650	3.00	8.00
S15 Patrick Roy/400	10.00	25.00
S16 Paul Kariya/108	30.00	80.00
S17 Pavel Bure/500	2.50	6.00
S18 Peter Bondra/300	2.50	6.00
S19 Peter Forsberg/400	5.00	12.00
S20 Ray Bourque/1500	3.00	8.00
S21 Ron Francis/1500	2.50	6.00
S22 Sergei Fedorov/600	3.00	8.00
S23 Steve Yzerman/1500	5.00	12.00
S24 Steve Yzerman/900	6.00	15.00
S25 Steve Yzerman/500	10.00	25.00
S26 Teemu Selanne/300	2.50	6.00
S27 Vincent Lecavalier/1998	2.50	6.00
S28 Wayne Gretzky/92	75.00	200.00
S29 Wayne Gretzky/900	5.00	12.00
S30 Wayne Gretzky/2000	3.00	8.00

1999-00 SP Authentic

1 Paul Kariya	.30	.75
2 Teemu Selanne	.60	1.50
3 Guy Hebert	.30	.75
4 Ray Ferraro	.20	.50
5 Andrew Brunette	.20	.50
6 Joe Thornton	.50	1.25
7 Ray Bourque	.50	1.25
8 Sergei Samsonov	.25	.60
9 Michael Peca	.25	.60
10 Dominik Hasek	.50	1.25
11 Miroslav Satan	.25	.60
12 Maxim Afinogenov	.20	.50
13 Valeri Bure	.20	.50
14 Marc Savard	.20	.50
15 Fred Brathwaite	.20	.50
16 Ron Francis	.40	1.00
17 Arturs Irbe	.25	.60
18 Sami Kapanen	.20	.50
19 Tony Amonte	.25	.60
20 Steve Passmore RC	.25	.60
21 Doug Gilmour	.40	1.00
22 Milan Hejduk	.25	.60
23 Joe Sakic	.60	1.50
24 Patrick Roy	.75	2.00
25 Chris Drury	.25	.60
26 Peter Forsberg	.60	1.50
27 Mike Modano	.50	1.25
28 Brett Hull	.60	1.50
29 Ed Belfour	.30	.75
30 Steve Yzerman	.75	2.00
31 Chris Osgood	.30	.75
32 Brendan Shanahan	.30	.75
33 Sergei Fedorov	.50	1.25
34 Doug Weight	.30	.75
35 Bill Guerin	.30	.75
36 Alexander Selivanov	.20	.50
37 Pavel Bure	.30	.75
38 Trevor Kidd	.20	.50
39 Viktor Kozlov	.20	.50
40 Luc Robitaille	.30	.75
41 Zigmund Palffy	.30	.75
42 Rob Blake	.30	.75
43 Saku Koivu	.30	.75
44 Mike Ribeiro	.20	.50
45 Jose Theodore	.30	.75
46 David Legwand	.20	.50
47 Mike Dunham	.20	.50

48 Rob Valicevic RC .25 .60
49 Martin Brodeur .75 2.00
50 Claude Lemieux .25 .60
51 Scott Gomez .25 .60
52 Tim Connolly .20 .50
53 Roberto Luongo .50 1.25
54 Kenny Jonsson .20 .50
55 Mike Richter .30 .75
56 Theo Fleury .40 1.00
57 Mike York .20 .50
58 Brian Leetch .25 .60
59 Radek Bonk .20 .50
60 Marian Hossa .30 .75
61 Patrick Lalime .25 .60
62 Keith Primeau .25 .60
63 Eric Lindros .50 1.25
64 John LeClair .30 .75
65 Trevor Letowski .20 .50
66 Keith Tkachuk .30 .75
67 Jeremy Roenick .50 1.25
68 Jaromir Jagr 1.00 2.50
69 Alexei Kovalev .25 .60
70 Martin Straka .20 .50
71 Brad Stuart .25 .60
72 Steve Shields .25 .60
73 Owen Nolan .30 .75
74 Jeff Friesen .25 .60
75 Pavol Demitra .40 1.00
76 Roman Turek .25 .60
77 Pierre Turgeon .25 .60
78 Vincent Lecavalier .30 .75
79 Dan Cloutier .20 .50
80 Chris Gratton .20 .50
81 Mats Sundin .30 .75
82 Bryan Berard .20 .50
83 Curtis Joseph .40 1.00
84 Jonas Hoglund .20 .50
85 Mark Messier .60 1.50
86 Peter Schaefer .20 .50
87 Alexander Mogilny .25 .60
88 Olaf Kolzig .30 .75
89 Adam Oates .30 .75
90 Peter Bondra .30 .75
91 Patrik Stefan RC 1.50 4.00
92 Dean Sylvester RC 1.00 2.50
93 Scott Fankhouser RC 1.00 2.50
94 Brian Campbell RC 1.50 4.00
95 Byron Ritchie RC 1.00 2.50
96 John Grahame RC 1.25 3.00
97 Andre Savage RC 1.00 2.50
98 Oleg Saprykin RC 1.50 4.00
99 Kyle Calder RC 1.25 3.00
100 Dan Hinote RC 1.25 3.00
101 Jonathan Sim RC 1.50 4.00
102 Marc Rodgers RC 1.00 2.50
103 Paul Comrie RC 2.50 6.00
104 Ivan Novoseltsev RC 2.00 5.00
105 Jason Blake RC 1.25 3.00
106 Brian Rafalski RC 1.50 4.00
107 John Madden RC 1.50 4.00
108 Jason Krog RC 1.00 2.50
109 Jorgen Jonsson RC 1.00 2.50
110 Kim Johnsson RC 1.00 2.50
111 Mike Fisher RC 1.50 4.00
112 Michal Rozsival RC 1.00 2.50
113 Mika Alatalo RC 1.25 3.00
114 Tyson Nash RC 1.00 2.50
115 Ladislav Nagy RC 4.00 10.00
116 Jochen Hecht RC 2.50 6.00
117 Adam Mair RC 1.00 2.50
118 Nikolai Antropov RC 4.00 10.00
119 Steve Kariya RC 1.50 4.00
120 Jeff Halpern RC 1.00 2.50
121 Alexandre Volchkov RC 1.00 2.50
122 Pavel Brendl RC 2.50 6.00
123 Sheldon Keefe RC 1.50 4.00
124 Branislav Mezei RC 1.00 2.50
125 Milan Kraft RC 1.25 3.00
126 Kristian Kudroc RC 1.00 2.50
127 Jaroslav Kristek RC 1.25 3.00
128 Alexander Buturlin RC 1.25 3.00
129 Andrei Shefer RC 1.25 3.00
130 Brad Moran RC 1.00 2.50
131 Ryan Jardine RC 1.25 3.00
132 Brett Lysak RC 1.25 3.00
133 Michal Sivek RC 1.25 3.00
134 Luke Sellars RC 1.50 4.00
135 Brad Ralph RC 1.25 3.00

1999-00 SP Authentic Buyback Autographs

1 P.Bure 94SP/65 30.00 60.00
3 P.Bure 94UDSPI/60 30.00 60.00
10 P.Bure 98SPA/30 30.00 80.00
11 W.Gretzky 94SP/56 200.00 500.00
13 W.Gretzky 94UDSPI/16 250.00 600.00
19 W.Gretzky 98SPA/101 150.00 400.00
21 B.Hull 94SP/92 25.00 60.00
28 B.Hull 98SPA/100 25.00 60.00
30 M.Johnson 97SPA/25 8.00 20.00
31 M.Johnson 98SPA/300 5.00 12.00
32 C.Joseph 94SP/65 12.00 30.00
34 C.Joseph 94UDSPI/34 12.00 30.00
36 C.Joseph 96SP/29 12.00 30.00
37 C.Joseph 98SPA/200 8.00 20.00
39 J.LeClair 94SP/150 12.00 30.00
41 J.LeClair 96SP/130 15.00 40.00
42 J.LeClair 98SPA/100 20.00 50.00
43 Z.Palffy 94UDSPI/75 12.00 30.00
45 Z.Palffy 96SP/33 12.00 30.00
47 Z.Palffy 98SPA/100 8.00 20.00
48 L.Robitaille 93SPI/16 25.00 50.00
49 L.Robitaille 94SP/20 25.00 50.00
50 L.Robitaille 94SPDC/19 50.00 40.00
51 L.Robitaille 94UDSPI/60 15.00 40.00
53 L.Robitaille 98SPA/65 15.00 40.00
55 J.Roenick 94SP/70 25.00 60.00
57 J.Roenick 94UDSPI/40 40.00 60.00
60 J.Roenick 96SP/32 40.00 80.00
61 J.Roenick 98SPA/97 25.00 60.00
62 S.Samsonov 94SP/65 12.00 30.00
65 S.Samsonov 98SPA/255 8.00 20.00
67 S.Yzerman 94SP/65 50.00 100.00
69 S.Yzerman 98SPA/77 50.00 100.00

1999-00 SP Authentic Honor Roll

HR1 Paul Kariya .60 1.50
HR2 Patrick Roy 1.50 4.00
HR3 Steve Yzerman 1.50 4.00
HR4 Martin Brodeur 1.50 4.00
HR5 Eric Lindros 1.00 2.50
HR6 Jaromir Jagr 2.00 5.00

1999-00 SP Authentic Legendary Heroes

LH1 Wayne Gretzky 8.00 20.00
LH2 Bobby Orr 5.00 12.00
LH3 Gordie Howe 5.00 12.00
LH4 Maurice Richard 2.50 6.00
LH5 Bobby Hull 2.00 5.00

1999-00 SP Authentic Sign of the Times

SGO Scott Gomez 8.00 20.00
AT Alex Tanguay 8.00 20.00
BC Brian Campbell 10.00 25.00
BH Bobby Hull 15.00 40.00
BHU Brett Hull 20.00 50.00
BM Bill Muckalt 6.00 15.00
BO Bobby Orr 60.00 150.00
BS Brad Stuart 8.00 20.00
CJ Curtis Joseph 12.00 30.00
DL David Legwand 6.00 15.00
DT Dave Tanabe 6.00 15.00
HG Gordie Howe 60.00 150.00
JH Jochen Hecht 15.00 40.00
JL John LeClair 10.00 25.00
JR Jeremy Roenick 15.00 40.00
JST Jozef Stumpel 6.00 15.00
LR Luc Robitaille 10.00 25.00
MH Marian Hossa 10.00 25.00
MRC Maurice Richard 20.00 50.00
MRI Mike Ribeiro 6.00 15.00
OS Oleg Saprykin 10.00 25.00
PB Pavel Bure 10.00 25.00
PM Paul Mara 6.00 15.00
PS Patrik Stefan 10.00 25.00
SF Sergei Fedorov 15.00 40.00
SG Simon Gagne 10.00 25.00
SS Sergei Samsonov 8.00 20.00
SY Steve Yzerman 25.00 60.00
TC Tim Connolly 6.00 15.00
TF Theo Fleury 12.00 30.00
WG Wayne Gretzky 200.00 500.00
ZP Zigmund Palffy 10.00 25.00

1999-00 SP Authentic Sign of the Times Gold

*GOLD: .6X TO 1.5X BASIC AU
HG Gordie Howe 150.00 300.00
WG Wayne Gretzky 300.00 800.00

1999-00 SP Authentic Special Forces

SF1 Paul Kariya .60 1.50
SF2 Joe Sakic 1.25 3.00
SF3 Patrick Roy 1.50 4.00
SF4 Steve Yzerman 1.50 4.00
SF5 Mike Modano 1.00 2.50
SF6 Pavel Bure .60 1.50
SF7 Jaromir Jagr 2.00 5.00
SF8 Eric Lindros 1.00 2.50
SF9 Curtis Joseph .75 2.00
SF10 Steve Kariya .60 1.50

1999-00 SP Authentic Supreme Skill

SS1 Paul Kariya .60 1.50
SS2 Teemu Selanne 1.25 3.00
SS3 Peter Forsberg 1.25 3.00
SS4 Brett Hull 1.25 3.00
SS5 Sergei Fedorov 1.00 2.50
SS6 Pavel Bure .60 1.50
SS7 Martin Brodeur 1.50 4.00
SS8 Theo Fleury .75 2.00
SS9 John LeClair .60 1.50
SS10 Keith Tkachuk .60 1.50
SS11 Jaromir Jagr 2.00 5.00

1999-00 SP Authentic Tomorrow's Headliners

TH1 Patrik Stefan .60 1.50
TH2 Joe Thornton 1.00 2.50
TH3 Maxim Afinogenov .40 1.00
TH4 Milan Hejduk .50 1.25
TH5 David Legwand .40 1.00
TH6 Scott Gomez .50 1.25
TH7 Marian Hossa .60 1.50
TH8 Jochen Hecht 1.00 2.50
TH9 Vincent Lecavalier .60 1.50
TH10 Steve Kariya .60 1.50

2000-01 SP Authentic

1 Paul Kariya .30 .75
2 Jean-Sebastien Giguere .30 .75
3 Oleg Tverdovsky .20 .50
4 Patrik Stefan .25 .60
5 Donald Audette .25 .60
6 Damian Rhodes .20 .50
7 Joe Thornton .50 1.25
8 Jason Allison .25 .60
9 Bill Guerin .30 .75
10 Dominik Hasek .50 1.25
11 Maxim Afinogenov .20 .50
12 Doug Gilmour .40 1.00
13 Valeri Bure .25 .60
14 Marc Savard .20 .50
15 Jarome Iginla .40 1.00
16 Ron Francis .40 1.00
17 Jeff O'Neill .25 .60
18 Sandis Ozolinsh .20 .50
19 Steve Sullivan .20 .50
20 Tony Amonte .25 .60
21 Rob Blake .30 .75
22 Ray Bourque .50 1.25
23 Patrick Roy .75 2.00
24 Peter Forsberg .60 1.50
25 Joe Sakic .60 1.50
26 Ron Tugnutt .25 .60
27 Geoff Sanderson .25 .60
28 Ed Belfour .30 .75
29 Mike Modano .50 1.25
30 Brett Hull .60 1.50
31 Steve Yzerman .75 2.00
32 Brendan Shanahan .30 .75
33 Nicklas Lidstrom .30 .75
34 Sergei Fedorov .50 1.25
35 Doug Weight .30 .75
36 Ryan Smyth .25 .60
37 Tommy Salo .25 .60
38 Pavel Bure .30 .75
39 Ray Whitney .25 .60
40 Ivan Novoseltsev .20 .50
41 Adam Deadmarsh .20 .50
42 Zigmund Palffy .30 .75
43 Luc Robitaille .30 .75
44 Darby Hendrickson .20 .50
45 Manny Fernandez .20 .50
46 Jose Theodore .30 .75
47 Andrei Markov .40 1.00
48 Trevor Linden .30 .75
49 David Legwand .30 .75
50 Mike Dunham .20 .50
51 Cliff Ronning .20 .50
52 Scott Gomez .25 .60
53 Martin Brodeur .75 2.00
54 Jason Arnott .25 .60
55 Mark Messier .60 1.50
56 Theo Fleury .40 1.00
57 Brian Leetch .25 .60
58 Tim Connolly .20 .50
59 Brad Isbister .20 .50
60 Taylor Pyatt .20 .50
61 Alexei Yashin .25 .60
62 Marian Hossa .30 .75
63 Patrick Lalime .25 .60
64 John LeClair .30 .75
65 Simon Gagne .30 .75
66 Mark Recchi .40 1.00
67 Jeremy Roenick .50 1.25
68 Keith Tkachuk .30 .75
69 Shane Doan .25 .60
70 Jaromir Jagr 1.00 2.50
71 Alexei Kovalev .25 .60
72 Mario Lemieux 1.25 3.00
73 Owen Nolan .30 .75
74 Patrick Marleau .30 .75
75 Evgeni Nabokov .25 .60
76 Pierre Turgeon .25 .60
77 Chris Pronger .30 .75
78 Roman Turek .25 .60
79 Brad Richards .30 .75
80 Vincent Lecavalier .30 .75
81 Fredrik Modin UER Jagr Stats .20 .50
82 Mats Sundin .30 .75
83 Curtis Joseph .40 1.00
84 Gary Roberts .20 .50
85 Daniel Sedin .40 1.00
86 Henrik Sedin .40 1.00
87 Markus Naslund .30 .75
88 Peter Bondra .30 .75
89 Olaf Kolzig .30 .75
90 Adam Oates .30 .75
91 Petr Tenkrat RC 2.00 5.00
92 Andy McDonald RC 4.00 10.00
93 Brad Tapper RC 2.00 5.00
94 Andrew Raycroft RC 5.00 12.00
95 Lee Goren RC 2.00 5.00
96 Josef Vasicek RC 5.00 12.00
97 Reto Von Arx RC 2.50 6.00
98 David Aebischer RC 5.00 12.00
99 Ville Nieminen RC 2.00 5.00
100 Serge Aubin RC 2.50 6.00
101 Rostislav Klesla RC 4.00 10.00
102 Marty Turco RC 4.00 10.00
103 Tyler Bouck RC 2.00 5.00
104 Jason Williams RC 3.00 8.00
105 Shawn Horcoff RC 4.00 10.00
106 Mike Comrie RC 5.00 12.00
107 Eric Belanger RC 2.50 6.00
108 Steven Reinprecht RC 3.00 8.00
109 Lubomir Visnovsky RC 4.00 10.00
110 Marian Gaborik RC 15.00 40.00
111 Petr Bartos RC 2.50 6.00
112 Scott Hartnell RC 8.00 20.00
113 Chris Mason RC 4.00 10.00
114 Rick DiPietro RC 10.00 25.00
115 Martin Havlat RC 10.00 25.00
116 Jani Hurme RC 2.00 5.00
117 Petr Hubacek RC 2.00 5.00
118 Justin Williams RC 5.00 12.00
119 Roman Cechmanek RC 2.50 6.00
120 Ruslan Fedotenko RC 2.00 5.00
121 Roman Simicek RC 2.00 5.00
122 Mark Smith RC 2.00 5.00
123 Alexander Kharitonov RC 2.00 5.00
124 Alexei Ponikarovsky RC 3.00 8.00
125 Matt Pettinger RC 2.00 5.00
126 Zdenek Blatny RC 2.00 5.00
127 Damian Surma RC 2.00 5.00
128 Marc-Andre Thinel RC 2.00 5.00
129 Fedor Fedorov RC 2.50 6.00
130 Jason Jaspers RC 2.00 5.00
131 Jordan Krestanovich RC 2.00 5.00
132 Jeff Bateman RC 2.00 5.00
133 Marc Chouinard RC 2.00 5.00
134 Darcy Hordichuk RC 2.00 5.00
135 Bryan Adams RC 2.00 5.00
136 Jarno Kultanen RC 2.00 5.00
137 Eric Boulton RC 2.00 5.00
138 Ronald Petrovicky RC 2.00 5.00
139 Martin Brochu RC 2.00 5.00
140 Craig Adams RC 2.00 5.00
141 Chris Nielsen RC 2.00 5.00
142 Petteri Nummelin RC 2.00 5.00
143 Brian Swanson RC 2.00 5.00
144 Michel Riesen RC 2.50 6.00
145 Lance Ward RC 2.00 5.00
146 Travis Scott RC 2.50 6.00
147 Lubomir Sekeras RC 2.00 5.00
148 Eric Landry RC 2.00 5.00
149 Greg Classen RC 2.00 5.00
150 Sascha Goc RC 2.00 5.00
151 Mike Commodore RC 2.00 5.00
152 Johan Holmqvist RC 2.00 5.00
153 Vitali Yeremeyev RC 2.50 6.00
154 Tomas Kloucek RC 2.00 5.00
155 Dale Purinton RC 2.00 5.00
156 Shane Hnidy RC 2.00 5.00
157 Todd Fedoruk RC 2.00 5.00
158 Jean-Guy Trudel RC 2.00 5.00
159 Ossi Vaananen RC 2.50 6.00
160 Greg Andrusak RC 2.50 6.00
161 Alexander Khavanov RC 2.00 5.00
162 Bryce Salvador RC 2.50 6.00
163 Reed Low RC 2.00 5.00
164 Petr Svoboda RC 2.50 6.00
165 Brent Sopel RC 3.00 8.00

2000-01 SP Authentic Buyback Autographs

1 B.Orr 99SPALH/49 150.00 300.00
6 S.Samsonov 99SPA/184 8.00 20.00
10 M.Satan 99SPA/145 20.00 40.00
12 Bo.Hull 99SPALH/98 25.00 60.00
13 M.Hejduk 99SPA/200 10.00 25.00
14 M.Hejduk 99SPATH/143 12.50 30.00
16 R.Bourque 98SPA/24 75.00 200.00
17 R.Bourque 99SPA/122 20.00 50.00
18 M.Modano 94SP/61 20.00 50.00
23 M.Modano 98SPA/40 25.00 60.00
24 M.Modano 99SPA/168 12.50 30.00
25 M.Modano 99SPASF/155 12.50 30.00
35 Br.Hull 98SPA/16 25.00 60.00
36 Br.Hull 99SPA/119 20.00 50.00
39 P.Bure 96SP/16 90.00 150.00
43 P.Bure 99SPA/225 15.00 30.00
44 P.Bure 99SPASF/154 15.00 30.00
45 P.Bure 99SPASS/69 15.00 40.00
47 L.Robitaille 94SP/36 25.00 60.00
52 L.Robitaille 99SPA/97 15.00 40.00
53 M.Ribeiro 99SPA/117 12.50 30.00
54 D.Legwand 99SPA/214 6.00 15.00
55 D.Legwand 99SPATH/130 12.50 25.00
56 S.Gomez 99SPA/243 10.00 25.00
57 S.Gomez 99SPATH/157 12.50 30.00
59 P.Elias 98SPA/43 15.00 40.00
69 M.Messier 94SP/50 40.00 80.00
73 M.Messier 98SPA/26 50.00 100.00
74 M.Messier 99SPA/147 30.00 60.00
77 M.Richter 95SP/21 25.00 50.00
80 M.Richter 98SPA/48 15.00 30.00
81 M.Richter 99SPA/214 10.00 25.00
82 M.York 99SPA/212 8.00 20.00
88 J.LeClair 98SPA/100 8.00 20.00
89 J.LeClair 99SPA/207 8.00 20.00
90 J.LeClair 99SPASS/116 15.00 40.00
91 J.Roenick 99SPA/98 15.00 40.00
95 S.Shields 99SPA/195 6.00 15.00
97 C.Joseph 99SPA/187 20.00 40.00
98 C.Joseph 99SPASF/135 15.00 40.00
105 S.Yzerman 94SPPRE/34 50.00 125.00
112 S.Yzerman 99SPA/152 30.00 80.00
113 S.Yzerman 99SPASF/35 50.00 125.00

2000-01 SP Authentic Honor

COMPLETE SET (7) 8.00 20.00
SP1 Paul Kariya .60 1.50
SP2 Patrick Roy 1.50 4.00
SP3 Pavel Bure .60 1.50
SP4 Martin Brodeur 1.50 4.00
SP5 Mark Messier 1.25 3.00
SP6 Mario Lemieux 2.50 6.00
SP7 Jaromir Jagr 2.00 5.00

2000-01 SP Authentic Parents' Scrapbook

COMPLETE SET (7) 4.00 10.00
PS1 Paul Kariya .50 1.25
PS2 Joe Thornton .75 2.00
PS3 Mike Modano .75 2.00
PS4 Scott Gomez .40 1.00
PS5 Martin Brodeur 1.25 3.00
PS6 John LeClair .50 1.25
PS7 Vincent Lecavalier .50 1.25

2000-01 SP Authentic Power Skaters

COMPLETE SET (7) 20.00 40.00
P1 Bobby Orr 2.50 6.00
P2 Bobby Hull 1.25 3.00
P3 Gordie Howe 2.00 5.00
P4 Wayne Gretzky 4.00 10.00
P5 Wayne Gretzky 4.00 10.00
P6 Wayne Gretzky 4.00 10.00
P7 Wayne Gretzky 4.00 10.00

2000-01 SP Authentic Sign of the Times

AC Anson Carter 3.00 8.00
AE Anders Eriksson 3.00 8.00
AU Serge Aubin 3.00 8.00
BD Byron Dafoe 3.00 8.00
BH Bobby Hull 20.00 50.00
BI Martin Biron 3.00 8.00
BO Bobby Orr SP 75.00 150.00
BR Pavel Brendl 3.00 8.00
CJ Curtis Joseph 8.00 20.00
DG David Gosselin 3.00 8.00
DL David Legwand 3.00 8.00
DS Daniel Sedin 8.00 20.00
FP Felix Potvin 10.00 25.00
GH Gordie Howe 50.00 100.00
HA Martin Havlat 6.00 15.00
HS Henrik Sedin 8.00 20.00
IN Ivan Novoseltsev 3.00 8.00
JA Jean-Sebastien Aubin 3.00 8.00
JH Jani Hurme 3.00 8.00
JL John LeClair 8.00 20.00
JT Jose Theodore 10.00 25.00
LB Lubos Bartecko 8.00 20.00
LR Luc Robitaille 6.00 15.00
MB Martin Brodeur 25.00 60.00
MD Marc Denis 3.00 8.00
MG Marian Gaborik 15.00 30.00
MH Milan Hejduk SP 50.00 100.00
MK Milan Kraft 3.00 8.00
ML Mario Lemieux SP 150.00 300.00
MM Mark Messier SP 40.00 100.00
MO Mike Modano 10.00 25.00
MR Mike Richter 10.00 25.00
MS Miroslav Satan 3.00 8.00
MT Marty Turco 8.00 20.00
MY Mike York 3.00 8.00
NL Nicklas Lidstrom 10.00 25.00
PB Pavel Bure 10.00 25.00
PE Patrik Elias 4.00 10.00
PS Petr Sykora 3.00 8.00
RB Ray Bourque/19* 200.00 400.00
RD Rick DiPietro 8.00 20.00
RI Michel Riesen 3.00 8.00
RK Rostislav Klesla 3.00 8.00
RO Mike Ribeiro 4.00 10.00
RT Ron Tugnutt 4.00 10.00
SA Sergei Samsonov 6.00 15.00
SG Scott Gomez 4.00 10.00
SH Scott Hartnell 6.00 15.00
SR Steven Reinprecht 3.00 8.00
SS Steve Shields 3.00 8.00
SY Steve Yzerman 30.00 80.00
TS Tommy Salo 4.00 10.00
WG Wayne Gretzky SP 400.00 1000.00
DBS M.Brodeur/P.Sykora 40.00 80.00
DBN P.Bure/I.Novoseltsev 10.00 25.00
DBY P.Brendl/M.York 8.00 20.00
DEG P.Elias/S.Gomez 8.00 20.00
DHG G.Howe/W.Gretzky 1250.00 3000.00
DHH B.Hull/B.Hull 30.00 80.00
DLK M.Lemieux/M.Kraft 75.00 200.00
DMG M.Messier/W.Gretzky 500.00 1200.00
DOB B.Orr/R.Bourque 100.00 200.00
DSS D.Sedin/H.Sedin 25.00 60.00
DYL S.Yzerman/N.Lidstrom 100.00 200.00
TBGE Brodr/Gmez/Elias/25 100.00 200.00
TGMF Grtzky/Mesr/Fuhr/25 750.00 2000.00
THLY Hull/Lem/Yzerman/25 250.00 500.00
THOG Howe/Grtzky/Orr/25 1250.00 3000.00
TLMB LeClr/Modno/Bre/25 50.00 100.00

2000-01 SP Authentic Significant Stars

COMPLETE SET (7) 8.00 15.00
ST1 Peter Forsberg 1.25 3.00
ST2 Brett Hull .60 1.50
ST3 Steve Yzerman 2.50 6.00
ST4 Pavel Bure .60 1.50
ST5 Mark Messier .60 1.50
ST6 Jaromir Jagr .75 2.00
ST7 Mario Lemieux 3.00 8.00

2000-01 SP Authentic Special Forces

COMPLETE SET (7) 4.00 8.00
SF1 Teemu Selanne 1.00 2.50
SF2 Mike Modano .75 2.00
SF3 Brendan Shanahan .50 1.25
SF4 Pavel Bure .50 1.25
SF5 John LeClair .50 1.25
SF6 Keith Tkachuk .50 1.25
SF7 Jaromir Jagr 1.50 4.00

2000-01 SP Authentic Super Stoppers

COMPLETE SET (7) 4.00 8.00
SS1 Dominik Hasek .75 2.00
SS2 Patrick Roy 1.25 3.00
SS3 Ed Belfour .50 1.25
SS4 Martin Brodeur 1.25 3.00
SS5 Roman Turek .40 1.00
SS6 Curtis Joseph .60 1.50
SS7 Olaf Kolzig .50 1.25

2001-02 SP Authentic

COMP.SET w/o SP's (90) 20.00 40.00
1 Jeff Friesen .12 .30
2 Paul Kariya .20 .50
3 Dany Heatley .15 .40
4 Milan Hnilicka .15 .40
5 Bill Guerin .20 .50
6 Joe Thornton .30 .75
7 Sergei Samsonov .15 .40
8 Miroslav Satan .15 .40
9 Martin Biron .15 .40
10 J-P Dumont .12 .30
11 Jarome Iginla .25 .60
12 Roman Turek .15 .40
13 Craig Conroy .12 .30
14 Tony Amonte .15 .40
15 Steve Sullivan .12 .30
16 Joe Sakic .40 1.00
17 Milan Hejduk .15 .40
18 Patrick Roy .50 1.25
19 Rob Blake .20 .50
20 Chris Drury .15 .40
21 Ron Tugnutt .15 .40
22 Geoff Sanderson .12 .30
23 Mike Modano .30 .75
24 Ed Belfour .20 .50
25 Pierre Turgeon .15 .40
26 Brett Hull .40 1.00
27 Dominik Hasek .30 .75
28 Steve Yzerman .50 1.25
29 Sergei Fedorov .30 .75
30 Luc Robitaille .20 .50
31 Brendan Shanahan .20 .50
32 Tommy Salo .15 .40
33 Ryan Smyth .15 .40
34 Mike Comrie .15 .40
35 Pavel Bure .20 .50
36 Valeri Bure .12 .30
37 Roberto Luongo .30 .75
38 Jason Allison .15 .40
39 Zigmund Palffy .20 .50
40 Felix Potvin .30 .75
41 Manny Fernandez .12 .30
42 Marian Gaborik .20 .50
43 Jose Theodore .20 .50
44 Brian Savage .12 .30
45 David Legwand .15 .40
46 Mike Dunham .15 .40
47 Patrik Elias .20 .50
48 Martin Brodeur .50 1.25
49 Jason Arnott .15 .40
50 Scott Stevens .20 .50
51 Chris Osgood .20 .50
52 Alexei Yashin .15 .40
53 Mark Parrish .12 .30
54 Mark Messier .40 1.00
55 Eric Lindros .30 .75
56 Petr Nedved .15 .40
57 Marian Hossa .20 .50
58 Radek Bonk .12 .30
59 Daniel Alfredsson .20 .50
60 Jeremy Roenick .30 .75
61 John LeClair .20 .50
62 Keith Primeau .15 .40
63 Mark Recchi .25 .60
64 Roman Cechmanek .15 .40
65 Sean Burke .12 .30
66 Michal Handzus .12 .30
67 Shane Doan .15 .40
68 Mario Lemieux .75 2.00
69 Alexei Kovalev .15 .40
70 Johan Hedberg .15 .40
71 Teemu Selanne .40 1.00
72 Owen Nolan .20 .50
73 Evgeni Nabokov .15 .40
74 Vincent Damphousse .15 .40
75 Pavol Demitra .25 .60
76 Doug Weight .20 .50
77 Keith Tkachuk .20 .50
78 Chris Pronger .20 .50
79 Brad Richards .20 .50
80 Vincent Lecavalier .20 .50
81 Nikolai Khabibulin .20 .50
82 Curtis Joseph .25 .60
83 Mats Sundin .20 .50
84 Alexander Mogilny .15 .40
85 Markus Naslund .20 .50
86 Daniel Sedin .25 .60
87 Henrik Sedin .25 .60
88 Peter Bondra .20 .50
89 Olaf Kolzig .20 .50
90 Jaromir Jagr .60 1.50
91 Paul Kariya ATG 1.25 3.00
92 Ray Bourque ATG 2.00 5.00
93 Patrick Roy ATG 3.00 8.00
94 Joe Sakic ATG 2.50 6.00
95 Mike Modano ATG 2.00 5.00
96 Ed Belfour ATG 1.25 3.00
97 Steve Yzerman ATG 3.00 8.00
98 Dominik Hasek ATG 2.00 5.00
99 Gordie Howe ATG 4.00 10.00
100 Brett Hull ATG 2.50 6.00
101 Wayne Gretzky ATG 8.00 20.00
102 Martin Brodeur ATG 3.00 8.00
103 Mark Messier ATG 2.50 6.00
104 John LeClair ATG 1.25 3.00
105 Jeremy Roenick ATG 2.00 5.00
106 Mario Lemieux ATG 5.00 12.00
107 Teemu Selanne ATG 2.50 6.00
108 Al MacInnis ATG 1.50 4.00
109 Curtis Joseph ATG 1.50 4.00
110 Jaromir Jagr ATG 4.00 10.00
111 Dany Heatley FG 1.00 2.50
112 Mike Comrie FG 1.00 2.50
113 David Legwand FG 1.00 2.50
114 Justin Williams FG 1.00 2.50
115 Mike Van Ryn FG .75 2.00
116 Alex Tanguay FG 1.00 2.50
117 Manny Fernandez FG .75 2.00
118 Martin Havlat FG 1.00 2.50
119 Kris Beech FG .75 2.00
120 Nikolai Antropov FG .75 2.00
121 Patrik Stefan FG 1.00 2.50
122 Steven Reinprecht FG .75 2.00
123 Marian Gaborik FG 1.25 3.00
124 Pavel Brendl FG .75 2.00
125 Brad Stuart FG .75 2.00
126 Martin Biron FG 1.00 2.50
127 Eric Belanger FG .75 2.00
128 Rick DiPietro FG 1.00 2.50
129 Ladislav Nagy FG .75 2.00
130 Brad Richards FG 1.25 3.00
131 Ilja Bryzgalov RC 4.00 10.00
132 Timo Parssinen RC 2.00 5.00
133 Kevin Sawyer RC 1.50 4.00
134 Brian Pothier RC 1.50 4.00
135 Kamil Piros RC 1.50 4.00
136 Ivan Huml RC 1.50 4.00
137 Scott Nichol RC 1.50 4.00
138 Jukka Hentunen RC 1.50 4.00
139 Erik Cole RC 3.00 8.00
140 Casey Hankinson RC 1.50 4.00
141 Jaroslav Obsut RC 1.50 4.00
142 Jody Shelley RC 2.00 5.00
143 Matt Davidson RC 1.50 4.00
144 Niko Kapanen RC 2.50 6.00
145 Pavel Datsyuk RC 80.00 200.00
146 Ty Conklin RC 2.50 6.00
147 Sean Selmser RC 1.50 4.00
148 Jason Chimera RC 1.50 4.00
149 Andrej Podkonicky RC 1.50 4.00
150 Niklas Hagman RC 2.00 5.00
151 Jaroslav Bednar RC 1.50 4.00
152 Mike Matteucci RC 1.50 4.00
153 Pascal Dupuis RC 2.50 6.00
154 Francis Belanger RC 2.00 5.00
155 Martti Jarventie 1.50 4.00
156 Pavel Skrbek RC 1.50 4.00
157 Martin Erat RC 2.00 5.00
158 Andreas Salomonsson RC 1.50 4.00
159 Scott Clemmensen RC 1.50 4.00
160 Josef Boumedienne RC 1.50 4.00
161 Peter Smrek RC 1.50 4.00
162 Mikael Samuelsson RC 2.00 5.00
163 Radek Martinek RC 1.50 4.00
164 Joel Kwiatkowski RC 1.50 4.00
165 Ivan Ciernik RC 1.50 4.00
166 Chris Neil RC 2.00 5.00
167 Jiri Dopita RC 1.50 4.00
168 Vaclav Pletka RC 1.50 4.00
169 David Cullen RC 1.50 4.00
170 Jeff Jillson RC 1.50 4.00
171 Mark Rycroft RC 2.00 5.00
172 Nikita Alexeev RC 1.50 4.00
173 Ryan Tobler RC 2.00 5.00
174 Bob Wren RC 1.50 4.00
175 Ilya Kovalchuk AU RC 30.00 60.00
176 Vaclav Nedorost AU RC 4.00 10.00
177 Kristian Huselius AU RC 6.00 15.00
178 Dan Blackburn AU RC 5.00 12.00
179 Krys Kolanos AU RC 4.00 10.00
180 Raffi Torres AU RC 10.00 25.00
NNO Pavel Bure SAMPLE 1.00 2.50

2001-02 SP Authentic Limited

*1-90 VETS/150: 3X TO 8X BASIC CARDS
*91-130 ATG/FG/150: .8X TO 2X SP/3500
*131-174 ROOK/150: .4X TO 1X RK/900
*175-180 RK.AU/150: .6X TO 1.5X AU/900
145 Pavel Datsyuk 200.00 500.00
175 Ilya Kovalchuk 60.00 120.00

2001-02 SP Authentic Limited Gold

*1-90 VETS/25: 10X TO 25X BASIC CARDS
*91-130 ATG/FG/150: 2.5X TO 6X SP/3500
*131-174 ROOK/25: 1.2X TO 3X RK/900
*175-180 RK.AU/25: 1X TO 2.5X AU/900
145 Pavel Datsyuk 300.00 800.00
175 Ilya Kovalchuk 200.00 400.00

2001-02 SP Authentic Buybacks

6 C.Joseph 99UDMVPSC/31 40.00 100.00
7 D.Heatley 00UD/50 200.00 400.00
9 D.Weight 91UD/20 20.00 50.00
13 M.Biron 00BDGG/41 25.00 60.00
14 M.Brodeur 00UDLGJ/30 60.00 150.00
16 M.Comrie 00BD/37 30.00 80.00
17 M.Gaborik 00UD/32 50.00 125.00
18 M.Havlat 00UD/37 40.00 100.00
20 M.Modano 90UD/75 20.00 50.00
21 M.Turco 00UD/37 30.00 80.00
22 O.Kolzig 00BDGG/20 20.00 50.00
26 R.Bourque 99MVPSCGS/20 40.00 100.00
28 R.DiPietro 00UD/31 20.00 50.00
29 R.Brind'Amour 90UD/95 12.50 30.00
30 R.Klesla 00UD/46 15.00 40.00
31 S.Hartnell 00UD/84 12.50 30.00

2001-02 SP Authentic Jerseys

NNBP Bob Probert/1034 8.00 20.00
NNBS Brendan Shanahan/955 6.00 15.00
NNCC Chris Chelios/1181 5.00 12.00
NNEL Eric Lindros/659 6.00 15.00
NNJK Jari Kurri/601 10.00 25.00
NNJL John LeClair/627 5.00 12.00
NNJS Joe Sakic/1178 10.00 25.00
NNKP Keith Primeau/496 4.00 10.00
NNMC Sandy McCarthy/1252 4.00 10.00
NNMG Mike Gartner/102 12.50 30.00
NNML Mario Lemieux/648 10.00 25.00
NNMM Mark Messier/651 6.00 15.00
NNMO Mike Modano/900 5.00 12.00
NNMR Mark Recchi/1010 4.00 10.00
NNPK Paul Kariya/531 5.00 12.00
NNRB Ray Bourque/1169 6.00 15.00
NNRT Rick Tocchet/950 4.00 10.00
NNSS Scott Stevens/1434 4.00 10.00
NNSY Steve Yzerman/1614 10.00 25.00
NNTD Tie Domi/1620 4.00 10.00
PPBH Brett Hull/86 20.00 50.00
PPJJ Jaromir Jagr/87 20.00 50.00
PPJS Joe Sakic/54 25.00 60.00
PPLR Luc Robitaille/63 12.00 30.00
PPMB Martin Brodeur/43 25.00 60.00
PPML Mario Lemieux/38 75.00 150.00
PPPR Patrick Roy/52 15.00 40.00
PPRB Ray Bourque/77 25.00 60.00
PPTS Teemu Selanne/76 20.00 50.00
PPWG Wayne Gretzky/92 60.00 150.00

2001-02 SP Authentic Sign of the Times

AI Arturs Irbe 6.00 15.00
AK Alexei Kovalev 6.00 15.00
AM Al MacInnis 6.00 15.00
BG Bill Guerin 5.00 12.00
BO Bobby Orr 100.00 200.00
BR Martin Brodeur 40.00 100.00
BS Brent Sopel 4.00 10.00
CJ Curtis Joseph 10.00 25.00
DH Dany Heatley 12.00 30.00
DS Daniel Sedin 6.00 15.00
DW Doug Weight 6.00 15.00
EB Ed Belfour 10.00 25.00
FP Felix Potvin 12.00 30.00
GH Gordie Howe 75.00 150.00
HA Martin Havlat 5.00 12.00
HE Johan Hedberg 4.00 10.00
HO Marian Hossa 6.00 15.00
HS Henrik Sedin 8.00 20.00
IK Ilya Kovalchuk 15.00 40.00
JA Jason Allison 4.00 10.00
JH Jochen Hecht 4.00 10.00
JI Jarome Iginla 10.00 25.00
JL John LeClair 8.00 20.00
JN Jeff O'Neill 4.00 10.00
JT Joe Thornton 12.50 30.00
KP Keith Primeau 5.00 12.00
MB Martin Biron 4.00 10.00
MC Mike Comrie 4.00 10.00
MF Manny Fernandez 6.00 15.00
MG Marian Gaborik 10.00 25.00
MH Milan Hejduk 8.00 20.00
MK Milan Kraft 4.00 10.00
MM Mike Modano 10.00 25.00
MN Markus Naslund 8.00 20.00
MR Mike Ribeiro 5.00 12.00
OK Olaf Kolzig 5.00 12.00
PB Pavel Bure 10.00 25.00
PR Patrick Roy/33 125.00 250.00
PS Patrik Stefan 4.00 10.00
RB Rod Brind'Amour 5.00 12.00
RB Rob Blake 4.00 10.00
RD Rick DiPietro 6.00 15.00
RK Rostislav Klesla 4.00 10.00
RL Roberto Luongo 20.00 50.00
SG Simon Gagne 8.00 20.00
SH Scott Hartnell 6.00 15.00
SY Steve Yzerman 30.00 80.00
TA Tony Amonte 6.00 15.00
TS Tommy Salo 5.00 12.00
TS Teemu Selanne 10.00 25.00
VL Vincent Lecavalier 8.00 20.00
WG Wayne Gretzky 200.00 500.00
ZP Zigmund Palffy 6.00 15.00
TRL Trevor Letowski 4.00 10.00
BB M.Brodeur/E.Belfour/150 30.00 80.00
BL P.Bure/R.Luongo/150 12.50 30.00
CH M.Comrie/J.Hecht/150 10.00 25.00
DL R.DiPietro/R.Luongo/150 15.00 40.00
ET P.Esposito/Thornton/150 15.00 40.00
FG Fernandez/Gaborik/150 12.00 30.00
GO G.Howe/B.Orr/150 150.00 300.00
HH M.Havlat/M.Hossa/150 12.00 30.00
HS J.Hedberg/T.Salo/150 12.50 30.00
HT M.Hossa/J.Thornton/150 20.00 50.00
HY G.Howe/S.Yzerman/150 125.00 250.00
IH J.Iginla/M.Hejduk/150 15.00 40.00
LR J.LeClair/M.Recchi/150 10.00 25.00
PP Z.Palffy/F.Potvin/150 12.50 30.00
SS D.Sedin/H.Sedin/150 15.00 40.00
TL Thornton/Lecavalier/150 25.00 60.00
WM D.Weight/MacInnis/150 10.00 25.00
YA S.Yzerman/J.Allison/150 30.00 80.00
BKK Bure/Kvlchk/Kovalv/25 100.00 250.00
BOB Bourque/Orr/Blake/25 150.00 300.00

GWA Guerin/Weight/Amonte/25 30.00 80.00
HBB Hejduk/Bourque/Blake/25 100.00 250.00
HGY Howe/Gretzky/Yzer/25 750.00 2000.00
HHS Havlat/Hejduk/Sykora/25 40.00 100.00
JBB Joseph/Brodeur/Belfr/25 125.00 250.00
PHG Palffy/Hossa/Gaborik/25 60.00 150.00
SDP Salo/DiPietro/Potvin/25 40.00 100.00
SSN Sedin/Sedin/Naslund/25 40.00 100.00

2002-03 SP Authentic

COMP.SET w/o SP's (90) 15.00 40.00
1 Jean-Sebastien Giguere .30 .75
2 Paul Kariya .30 .75
3 Adam Oates .30 .75
4 Dany Heatley .25 .60
5 Ilya Kovalchuk .40 1.00
6 Joe Thornton .50 1.25
7 Sergei Samsonov .25 .60
8 Steve Shields .25 .60
9 Martin Biron .25 .60
10 Miroslav Satan .30 .75
11 Tim Connolly .20 .50
12 Jarome Iginla .40 1.00
13 Roman Turek .30 .75
14 Arturs Irbe .25 .60
15 Rod Brind'Amour .30 .75
16 Ron Francis .40 1.00
17 Alexei Zhamnov .25 .60
18 Eric Daze .20 .50
19 Jocelyn Thibault .25 .60
20 Chris Drury .30 .75
21 Joe Sakic .60 1.50
22 Patrick Roy .75 2.00
23 Peter Forsberg .60 1.50
24 Rob Blake .30 .75
25 Ray Whitney .25 .60
26 Marc Denis .25 .60
27 Rostislav Klesla .20 .50
28 Bill Guerin .25 .60
29 Marty Turco .30 .75
30 Mike Modano .50 1.25
31 Brendan Shanahan .30 .75
32 Brett Hull .60 1.50
33 Curtis Joseph .40 1.00
34 Nicklas Lidstrom .30 .75
35 Sergei Fedorov .50 1.25
36 Steve Yzerman .75 2.00
37 Mike Comrie .30 .75
38 Tommy Salo .25 .60
39 Anson Carter .25 .60
40 Roberto Luongo .50 1.25
41 Olli Jokinen .25 .60
42 Felix Potvin .50 1.25
43 Zigmund Palffy .30 .75
44 Jason Allison .25 .60
45 Manny Fernandez .20 .50
46 Marian Gaborik .30 .75
47 Jose Theodore .30 .75
48 Saku Koivu .30 .75
49 Yanic Perreault .20 .50
50 Tomas Vokoun .25 .60
51 David Legwand .25 .60
52 Scott Hartnell .20 .50
53 Martin Brodeur .75 2.00
54 Patrik Elias .30 .75
55 Jeff Friesen .20 .50
56 Alexei Yashin .25 .60
57 Chris Osgood .30 .75
58 Michael Peca .25 .60
59 Eric Lindros .50 1.25
60 Bobby Holik .20 .50
61 Pavel Bure .30 .75
62 Daniel Alfredsson .30 .75
63 Marian Hossa .30 .75
64 Patrick Lalime .25 .60
65 Jeremy Roenick .50 1.25
66 Roman Cechmanek .25 .60
67 Simon Gagne .30 .75
68 John LeClair .30 .75
69 Sean Burke .20 .50
70 Tony Amonte .25 .60
71 Daniel Briere .25 .60
72 Alexei Kovalev .25 .60
73 Mario Lemieux 1.25 3.00
74 Evgeni Nabokov .25 .60
75 Owen Nolan .30 .75
76 Teemu Selanne .60 1.50
77 Doug Weight .30 .75
78 Pavol Demitra .40 1.00
79 Keith Tkachuk .30 .75
80 Nikolai Khabibulin .30 .75
81 Vincent Lecavalier .30 .75
82 Alexander Mogilny .25 .60
83 Ed Belfour .30 .75
84 Mats Sundin .30 .75
85 Markus Naslund .30 .75
86 Ed Jovanovski .25 .60
87 Todd Bertuzzi .30 .75
88 Jaromir Jagr 1.00 2.50
89 Olaf Kolzig .30 .75
90 Peter Bondra .30 .75
91 Paul Kariya HT 1.25 3.00
92 Joe Thornton HT 2.00 5.00
93 Jarome Iginla HT 1.50 4.00
94 Joe Sakic HT 2.50 6.00
95 Peter Forsberg HT 2.50 6.00
96 Steve Yzerman HT 3.00 8.00
97 Brendan Shanahan HT 1.25 3.00
98 Brett Hull HT 2.50 6.00
99 Wayne Gretzky HT 8.00 20.00
100 Eric Lindros HT 2.00 5.00
101 Pavel Bure HT 1.25 3.00
102 Mario Lemieux HT 5.00 12.00
103 Keith Tkachuk HT 1.25 3.00
104 Todd Bertuzzi HT 1.25 3.00
105 Peter Bondra HT 1.25 3.00
106 Andy McDonald FG 1.50 4.00
107 Dany Heatley FG 1.25 3.00
108 Ilya Kovalchuk FG 2.00 5.00
109 Ivan Huml FG 1.00 2.50
110 Maxim Afinogenov FG 1.00 2.50
111 Jaroslav Svoboda FG 1.00 2.50
112 Kyle Calder FG 1.00 2.50
113 Radim Vrbata FG 1.00 2.50
114 Rostislav Klesla FG 1.00 2.50
115 Pavel Datsyuk FG 2.50 6.00
116 Mike Comrie FG 1.50 4.00
117 Marcus Nilsson FG 1.00 2.50
118 Kristian Huselius FG 1.00 2.50
119 Marian Gaborik FG 1.50 4.00
120 Mike Ribeiro FG 1.00 2.50
121 Scott Hartnell FG 1.00 2.50
122 Brian Gionta FG 1.00 2.50
123 Raffi Torres FG 1.00 2.50
124 Dan Blackburn FG 1.25 3.00
125 Tom Poti FG 1.00 2.50
126 Petr Schastlivy FG 1.00 2.50
127 Pavel Brendl FG 1.00 2.50
128 Brian Boucher FG 1.25 3.00
129 Ville Nieminen FG 1.00 2.50
130 Jeff Jillson FG 1.00 2.50
131 Justin Papineau FG 1.00 2.50
132 Brad Richards FG 1.50 4.00
133 Nikita Alexeev FG 1.00 2.50
134 Nikolai Antropov FG 1.25 3.00
135 Matt Pettinger FG 1.00 2.50
136 Martin Gerber RC 3.00 8.00
137 Tim Thomas RC 8.00 20.00
138 Micki Dupont RC 2.00 5.00
139 Shawn Thornton RC 2.50 6.00
140 Matt Henderson RC 2.00 5.00
141 Jeff Paul RC 2.00 5.00
142 Lasse Pirjeta RC 2.00 5.00
143 Dmitri Bykov RC 2.00 5.00
144 Alex Henry RC 2.50 6.00
145 Kari Haakana RC 2.00 5.00
146 Ivan Majesky RC 2.00 5.00
147 Sylvain Blouin RC 2.00 5.00
148 Stephane Veilleux RC 2.00 5.00
149 Greg Koehler RC 2.00 5.00
150 Ray Schultz RC 2.00 5.00
151 Tomi Pettinen RC 2.00 5.00
152 Eric Godard RC 2.00 5.00
153 Dennis Seidenberg RC 3.00 8.00
154 Radovan Somik RC 2.00 5.00
155 Patrick Sharp RC 6.00 15.00
156 Lynn Loyns RC 2.00 5.00
157 Tom Koivisto RC 2.00 5.00
158 Curtis Sanford RC 5.00 12.00
159 Cody Rudkowsky RC 2.00 5.00
160 Steve Eminger RC 2.00 5.00
161 Shaone Morrisonn RC 2.00 5.00
162 Anton Volchenkov RC 2.00 5.00
163 Carlo Colaiacovo RC 3.00 8.00
164 Rickard Wallin RC 2.00 5.00
165 Matt Walker RC 2.00 5.00
166 Ryan Miller RC 10.00 25.00
167 Levente Szuper RC 3.00 8.00
168 Tomas Malec RC 2.00 5.00
169 Jim Fahey RC 2.00 5.00
170 Jonathan Hedstrom RC 2.00 5.00
171 Michael Leighton RC 3.00 8.00
172 Dany Sabourin RC 2.00 5.00
173 Mike Cammalleri RC 8.00 20.00
174 Craig Andersson RC 6.00 15.00
175 Darren Haydar RC 2.00 5.00
176 Vernon Fiddler RC 2.50 6.00
177 Curtis Murphy RC 2.00 5.00
178 Jared Aulin RC 2.00 5.00
179 Ian MacNeil RC 2.00 5.00
180 Dick Tarnstrom RC 2.00 5.00
181 Alexei Smirnov AU RC 4.00 10.00
182 Stanislav Chistov AU RC 3.00 8.00
183 Chuck Kobasew AU RC 4.00 10.00
184 Rick Nash AU RC 20.00 50.00
185 Pascal LeClaire AU RC 4.00 10.00
186 Henrik Zetterberg AU RC 30.00 80.00
187 Jay Bouwmeester AU RC 10.00 25.00
188 Alexander Frolov AU RC 8.00 20.00
189 Ron Hainsey AU RC 3.00 8.00
190 Adam Hall AU RC 3.00 8.00
191 Jason Spezza AU RC 25.00 60.00
192 Jeff Taffe AU RC 3.00 8.00
193 Kurt Sauer AU RC 3.00 8.00
194 Alexander Svitov AU RC 4.00 10.00
195 Mikael Tellqvist AU RC 3.00 8.00
196 Jordan Leopold AU RC 5.00 12.00
197 Ales Hemsky AU RC 12.00 30.00
198 P-M Bouchard AU RC 5.00 12.00
199 Scottie Upshall AU RC 4.00 10.00
200 Brooks Orpik AU RC 3.00 8.00
201 Steve Ott AU RC 3.00 8.00
202 Igor Radulov RC 2.00 5.00
203 Alexei Semenov RC 3.00 8.00
204 Mike Komisarek RC 3.00 8.00
205 Tomas Surovy RC 2.00 5.00
206 Jason Bacashihua RC 2.50 6.00
207 Ray Emery RC 6.00 15.00
208 Fernando Pisani RC 2.00 5.00
209 Simon Gamache RC 2.00 5.00
210 Ari Ahonen RC 2.00 5.00
211 Brandon Reid RC 2.00 5.00
212 Ryan Bayda RC 2.00 5.00
213 Niko Dimitrakos RC 2.00 5.00
214 Rob Davison RC 2.00 5.00
215 Konstantin Koltsov RC 2.50 6.00
216 Jarret Stoll RC 8.00 20.00
217 Cristobal Huet RC 4.00 10.00
218 Jason King RC 3.00 8.00
219 Tomas Kurka RC 2.00 5.00

2002-03 SP Authentic UD Promos

*UD PROMO: .8X TO 2X BASIC CARDS
16 Ron Francis .75 2.00

2002-03 SP Authentic Sign of the Times

AF Alexander Frolov 12.00 30.00
AI Arturs Irbe 6.00 15.00
BB B.Orr/Bouwmeester/99 60.00 150.00
BE Pavel Brendl 5.00 12.00
BO Bobby Orr SP 50.00 125.00
BR P.Roy/R.Bourque/99 40.00 100.00
CI M.Comrie/J.Iginla/99 20.00 50.00
CJ Curtis Joseph SP 12.00 30.00
DH Dany Heatley 6.00 15.00
EC Erik Cole 5.00 12.00
EN Evgeni Nabokov SP 6.00 15.00
GB S.Gagne/P.Brendl/99 15.00 40.00
GC W.Gretzky/M.Comrie/99 200.00 500.00
GH Gordie Howe 50.00 125.00
GL S.Gagne/J.LeClair/99 15.00 40.00
GW W.Gretzky/G.Howe/99 600.00 1500.00
HE Ales Hemsky 20.00 50.00
HY S.Yzerman/G.Howe/99 80.00 200.00
HZ Henrik Zetterberg 30.00 80.00
JB Jay Bouwmeester 15.00 40.00
JI Jarome Iginla 10.00 25.00
JL John LeClair 8.00 20.00
JT Joe Thornton 12.00 30.00
JW Justin Williams 6.00 15.00
KA Kovalchuk/Afinogenov/99 20.00 50.00
KH Kovalchuk/D.Heatley/99 20.00 50.00
KN Nabokov/Khabibulin/99 15.00 40.00
LW J.Leclair/J.Williams/99 15.00 40.00
MA Maxim Afinogenov 5.00 12.00
MB Martin Brodeur SP 25.00 60.00
MC Mike Comrie 8.00 20.00
MF Manny Fernandez 5.00 12.00
MH Martin Havlat 6.00 15.00
MK Milan Kraft 5.00 12.00
MM M.Brodeur/M.Ouellet/99 40.00 100.00
MN Markus Naslund 8.00 20.00
NK Nikolai Khabibulin SP 8.00 20.00
OB B.Orr/R.Bourque/99 100.00 200.00
PB Pavel Bure 8.00 20.00
PR Patrick Roy 30.00 80.00
RB Ray Bourque 12.00 30.00
RN Rick Nash SP 25.00 60.00
SG Simon Gagne 8.00 20.00
SN Selanne/E.Nabokov/99 30.00 80.00
SP Jason Spezza 20.00 50.00
SS Sergei Samsonov 6.00 15.00
ST Thornton/Samsonov/99 25.00 60.00
SY Steve Yzerman 25.00 60.00
SZ Spezza/H.Zetterberg/99 30.00 80.00
TS Teemu Selanne 15.00 40.00
WG Wayne Gretzky 200.00 500.00
YZ Yzerman/Zetterberg/99 60.00 150.00
GHO Gretzky/Howe/Orr/25 750.00 2000.00
HCI Heatley/Comrie/Iginla/25 60.00 120.00
OBT Orr/Bourque/Thornton/25 150.00 300.00
SZB Spezza/Zetter/Bouwm/25 60.00 120.00
TSB Thorntn/Sams/Bourqe/25 50.00 125.00

2002-03 SP Authentic Signed Patches

*SINGLE COLOR: .25X TO .75X HI
PAF Alexander Frolov 25.00 60.00
PAH Ales Hemsky 25.00 60.00
PAS Alexander Svitov 12.00 30.00
PCK Chuck Kobasew 12.00 30.00
PHA Adam Hall 8.00 20.00
PHZ Henrik Zetterberg 150.00 300.00
PJB Jay Bouwmeester 15.00 40.00
PJL Jordan Leopold 15.00 40.00
PJS Jason Spezza 80.00 200.00
PPB P-M Bouchard 15.00 40.00
PRH Ron Hainsey 12.00 30.00
PRN Rick Nash 60.00 150.00
PSC Stanislav Chistov 8.00 20.00
PSM Alexei Smirnov 8.00 20.00
PSU Scottie Upshall 15.00 40.00

2002-03 SP Authentic Super Premium Jerseys

SPAM Alexei Morozov 3.00 8.00
SPBG Bill Guerin 4.00 10.00
SPBI Martin Biron 3.00 8.00
SPBL Brian Leetch 4.00 10.00
SPBS Brendan Shanahan 5.00 12.00
SPDB Daniel Briere 4.00 10.00
SPDH Dan Hinote 3.00 8.00
SPEJ Ed Jovanovski 4.00 10.00
SPJA Jason Allison 3.00 8.00
SPJI Jarome Iginla 6.00 15.00
SPJJ Jaromir Jagr 6.00 15.00
SPJR Jeremy Roenick 6.00 15.00
SPJS Joe Sakic 8.00 20.00
SPJT Joe Thornton 6.00 15.00
SPMB Martin Brodeur 10.00 25.00
SPMD Marc Denis 3.00 8.00
SPML Mario Lemieux 10.00 25.00
SPMM Mike Modano 6.00 15.00
SPMN Markus Naslund 5.00 12.00
SPMS Mats Sundin 5.00 12.00
SPOK Olaf Kolzig 4.00 10.00
SPPF Peter Forsberg 5.00 12.00
SPPK Paul Kariya 5.00 12.00
SPPR Patrick Roy 10.00 25.00
SPSF Sergei Fedorov 6.00 15.00
SPSG Simon Gagne 5.00 12.00
SPSS Sergei Samsonov 4.00 10.00
SPSY Steve Yzerman 8.00 20.00
SPTH Jose Theodore 5.00 12.00
SPZP Zigmund Palffy 4.00 10.00
DPDS C.Drury/J.Sakic 6.00 15.00
DPFR P.Forsberg/P.Roy 12.00 30.00
DPGL M.Lemieux/W.Gretzky 25.00 60.00
DPKJ O.Kolzig/J.Jagr 8.00 20.00
DPMG M.Modano/B.Guerin 6.00 15.00
DPRG J.Roenick/S.Gagne 8.00 20.00
DPST S.Samsonov/J.Thornton 8.00 20.00
DPTK J.Theodore/S.Koivu 10.00 25.00
DPYS S.Yzerman/B.Shanahan 8.00 20.00
TPGLY Lemieux/Gretzky/Yzerman 125.00 250.00
TPRBB Roy/Brodeur/Belfour 50.00 100.00
TPTBN Thornton/Bourque/Neely 40.00 80.00

2003-04 SP Authentic

COMP.SET w/o SP's (90) 15.00 30.00
1 Jean-Sebastien Giguere .30 .75
2 Sergei Fedorov .50 1.25
3 Stanislav Chistov .20 .50
4 Dany Heatley .25 .60
5 Ilya Kovalchuk .30 .75
6 Felix Potvin .50 1.25
7 Joe Thornton .50 1.25
8 Sergei Samsonov .25 .60
9 Chris Drury .25 .60
10 Daniel Briere .30 .75
11 Martin Biron .25 .60
12 Jarome Iginla .40 1.00
13 Roman Turek .25 .60
14 Jamie Storr .25 .60
15 Ron Francis .40 1.00
16 Alexei Zhamnov .25 .60
17 Jocelyn Thibault .25 .60
18 Tyler Arnason .25 .60
19 David Aebischer .25 .60
20 Joe Sakic .60 1.50
21 Paul Kariya .30 .75
22 Peter Forsberg .60 1.50
23 Marc Denis .25 .60
24 Rick Nash .30 .75
25 Todd Marchant .20 .50
26 Bill Guerin .30 .75
27 Marty Turco .30 .75
28 Mike Modano .50 1.25
29 Dominik Hasek .50 1.25
30 Henrik Zetterberg .40 1.00
31 Steve Yzerman .75 2.00
32 Ales Hemsky .30 .75
33 Raffi Torres .20 .50
34 Adam Oates .30 .75
35 Tommy Salo .25 .60
36 Jay Bouwmeester .20 .50
37 Olli Jokinen .25 .60
38 Roberto Luongo .50 1.25
39 Luc Robitaille .30 .75
40 Roman Cechmanek .25 .60
41 Zigmund Palffy .30 .75
42 Manny Fernandez .20 .50
43 Marian Gaborik .30 .75
44 Pierre-Marc Bouchard .30 .75
45 Jose Theodore .30 .75
46 Marcel Hossa .20 .50
47 Michael Ryder .25 .60
48 Saku Koivu .30 .75
49 David Legwand .25 .60
50 Tomas Vokoun .25 .60
51 Martin Brodeur .75 2.00
52 Patrik Elias .30 .75
53 Scott Gomez .25 .60
54 Scott Stevens .30 .75
55 Alexei Yashin .25 .60
56 Michael Peca .25 .60
57 Rick DiPietro .25 .60
58 Eric Lindros .50 1.25
59 Mark Messier .60 1.50
60 Mike Dunham .30 .75
61 Jason Spezza .30 .75
62 Marian Hossa .30 .75
63 Patrick Lalime .25 .60
64 Jeff Hackett .25 .60
65 Jeremy Roenick .50 1.25
66 Simon Gagne .30 .75
67 Mike Johnson .20 .50
68 Sean Burke .20 .50
69 Mario Lemieux 1.25 3.00
70 Martin Straka .20 .50
71 Evgeni Nabokov .25 .60
72 Patrick Marleau .30 .75
73 Vincent Damphousse .25 .60
74 Chris Osgood .30 .75
75 Doug Weight .30 .75
76 Keith Tkachuk .30 .75
77 Pavol Demitra .40 1.00
78 Nikolai Khabibulin .30 .75
79 Vincent Lecavalier .30 .75
80 Alexander Mogilny .25 .60
81 Ed Belfour .30 .75
82 Mats Sundin .30 .75
83 Owen Nolan .30 .75
84 Ed Jovanovski .25 .60
85 Jason King .20 .50
86 Markus Naslund .30 .75
87 Todd Bertuzzi .30 .75
88 Jaromir Jagr 1.00 2.50
89 Olaf Kolzig .30 .75
90 Peter Bondra .30 .75
91 Andrew Hutchinson RC 2.50 6.00
92 Phil Osaer RC 2.50 6.00
93 Boyd Kane RC 2.50 6.00
94 Brent Krahn RC 2.50 6.00
95 Cody McCormick RC 3.00 8.00
96 Christoph Brandner RC 3.00 8.00
97 Dan Fritsche RC 2.50 6.00
98 David Hale RC 2.50 6.00
99 Esa Pirnes RC 2.50 6.00
100 Libor Pivko RC 2.50 6.00
101 Greg Campbell RC 2.50 6.00
102 John-Michael Liles RC 3.00 8.00
103 Mikhail Yakubov RC 2.50 6.00
104 Marek Svatos RC 5.00 12.00
105 Marek Zidlicky RC 2.50 6.00
106 Nathan Robinson RC 2.50 6.00
107 Matthew Lombardi RC 3.00 8.00
108 Matthew Spiller RC 3.00 8.00
109 Matt Murley RC 3.00 8.00
110 Maxim Kondratiev RC 2.50 6.00
111 Ryan Kesler RC 10.00 25.00
112 Paul Martin RC 3.00 8.00
113 Ryan Malone RC 5.00 12.00
114 Tim Gleason RC 2.50 6.00
115 Tom Preissing RC 3.00 8.00
116 Fredrik Sjostrom RC 4.00 10.00
117 Tony Martensson RC 2.50 6.00
118 Aaron Johnson RC 2.50 6.00
119 Seamus Kotyk RC 2.50 6.00
120 Pat Rissmiller RC 3.00 8.00
121 Jeff Hamilton RC 2.50 6.00
122 Sergei Zinovjev RC 2.50 6.00
123 Julien Vauclair RC 2.50 6.00
124 Nikolai Zherdev RC 5.00 12.00
125 Brent Burns RC 8.00 20.00
126 John Pohl RC 2.50 6.00
127 Dominic Moore RC 2.50 6.00
128 Rastislav Stana RC 4.00 10.00
129 Gavin Morgan RC 3.00 8.00
130 Darryl Bootland RC 3.00 8.00
131 Trevor Daley RC 4.00 10.00
132 Peter Sarno RC 2.50 6.00
133 Jed Ortmeyer RC 2.50 6.00
134 Nathan Smith RC 2.50 6.00
135 Grant McNeill RC 2.50 6.00
136 Joffrey Lupul AU RC 15.00 30.00
137 Eric Staal AU RC 30.00 60.00
138 Pavel Vorobiev AU RC 6.00 15.00
139 Tuomo Ruutu AU RC 6.00 15.00
140 Antoine Vermette AU RC 8.00 20.00
141 Antti Miettinen AU RC 6.00 15.00
142 Boyd Gordon AU RC 6.00 15.00
143 Nathan Horton AU RC 10.00 25.00
144 Tony Salmelainen AU RC 4.00 10.00
145 Christian Ehrhoff AU RC 5.00 12.00
146 Patrice Bergeron AU RC 300.00 800.00
147 Dan Hamhuis AU RC 5.00 12.00
148 Jordin Tootoo AU RC 8.00 20.00
149 Joni Pitkanen AU RC 6.00 15.00
150 Dustin Brown AU RC 10.00 25.00
151 Chris Higgins AU RC 8.00 20.00
152 Sean Bergenheim AU RC 5.00 12.00
153 Marc-Andre Fleury AU RC 250.00 600.00
154 Jiri Hudler AU RC 10.00 25.00
155 Milan Michalek AU RC 8.00 20.00
156 Peter Sejna AU RC 5.00 12.00
157 Matt Stajan AU RC 6.00 15.00
158 Alexander Semin AU RC 12.00 30.00
159 Nikolas Kronwall RC 5.00 12.00
160 Derek Roy RC 4.00 10.00
161 Kyle Wellwood RC 4.00 10.00
162 Brad Boyes RC 4.00 10.00
163 Timofei Shishkanov RC 2.50 6.00
164 Jason Pominville RC 6.00 15.00
165 Aleksander Suglobov RC 2.50 6.00
166 Carl Corazzini RC 3.00 8.00

2003-04 SP Authentic Limited

*1-90 VETS/99: 4X TO 10X BASIC CARDS
*91-135 ROOKIE/50: .8X TO 2X
*136-158 ROOK.AU/50: .8X TO 2X
59 Mark Messier 6.00 15.00
137 Eric Staal AU 75.00 150.00
146 Patrice Bergeron AU 500.00 1200.00
153 Marc-Andre Fleury AU 500.00 1200.00

2003-04 SP Authentic 10th Anniversary

COMPLETE SET (20) 10.00 20.00
*LIMITED: 1X TO 2.5X
SP1 Wayne Gretzky 3.00 8.00
SP2 Patrick Roy 1.50 4.00
SP3 Steve Yzerman 1.50 4.00
SP4 Mario Lemieux 2.00 5.00
SP5 Teemu Selanne .50 1.25
SP6 Joe Sakic 1.00 2.50
SP7 Jaromir Jagr .75 2.00
SP8 Sergei Fedorov .40 1.00
SP9 Mike Modano .75 2.00
SP10 Brett Hull .60 1.50
SP11 Jason Spezza .50 1.25
SP12 Joe Thornton .75 2.00
SP13 Rick Nash .60 1.50
SP14 Marian Gaborik .40 1.00
SP15 Ales Hemsky .40 1.00
SP16 Marian Hossa .40 1.00
SP17 Jean-Sebastien Giguere .40 1.00
SP18 Martin Brodeur 1.25 3.00
SP19 Todd Bertuzzi .40 1.00
SP20 Markus Naslund .40 1.00

2003-04 SP Authentic Breakout Seasons

*LIMITED: .75X TO 2X
B1 Steve Yzerman 4.00 10.00
B2 Martin Brodeur 4.00 10.00
B3 Nicklas Lidstrom 1.00 2.50
B4 Joe Thornton 1.50 3.00
B5 Jeremy Roenick 1.00 2.50
B6 Todd Bertuzzi 1.00 2.50
B7 Markus Naslund 1.00 2.50
B8 Sergei Fedorov 1.00 2.50
B9 Chris Pronger .75 2.00
B10 Zigmund Palffy .75 2.00
B11 Marian Gaborik 1.00 2.50
B12 Jose Theodore 1.25 3.00
B13 Mike Modano 1.50 3.00
B14 Vincent Lecavalier 1.00 2.50
B15 Jean-Sebastien Giguere .75 2.00
B16 Keith Tkachuk 1.00 2.50
B17 Mats Sundin 1.00 2.50
B18 Paul Kariya 1.00 2.50
B19 Jarome Iginla 1.25 3.00
B20 Jaromir Jagr 1.50 4.00
B21 Dominik Hasek 1.50 4.00
B22 Teemu Selanne 1.00 2.50
B23 Jocelyn Thibault .75 2.00
B24 Alexei Yashin .75 2.00
B25 Ilya Kovalchuk 1.25 3.00
B26 Marian Hossa 1.00 2.50
B27 Ed Belfour 1.00 2.50
B28 Peter Forsberg 2.50 6.00
B29 Mario Lemieux 5.00 12.00
B30 Saku Koivu 1.00 2.50

2003-04 SP Authentic Foundations

*LIMITED: .6X TO 1.5X
F1 S.Fedorov/J.Giguere 2.00 8.00
F2 J.Thornton/S.Samsonov 2.00 5.00
F3 P.Kariya/T.Selanne 2.00 5.00
F4 P.Forsberg/J.Sakic 4.00 10.00
F5 S.Yzerman/D.Hasek 4.00 10.00
F6 T.Bertuzzi/M.Naslund 2.00 5.00
F7 M.Modano/M.Turco 2.00 5.00
F8 M.Brodeur/S.Stevens 4.00 10.00
F9 M.Sundin/E.Belfour 3.00 8.00
F10 S.Koivu/J.Theodore 2.00 5.00

2003-04 SP Authentic Honors

*LIMITED: 1X TO 2.5X
H1 Wayne Gretzky 5.00 12.00
H2 Wayne Gretzky 5.00 12.00
H3 Wayne Gretzky 5.00 12.00
H4 Gordie Howe 2.50 6.00
H5 Gordie Howe 2.50 6.00
H6 Gordie Howe 2.50 6.00
H7 Scotty Bowman 1.00 2.50
H8 Scotty Bowman 1.00 2.50
H9 Scotty Bowman 1.00 2.50
H10 Don Cherry 1.00 2.50
H11 Don Cherry 1.00 2.50
H12 Patrick Roy 3.00 10.00
H13 Patrick Roy 4.00 8.00
H14 Bobby Clarke .60 1.50
H15 Marcel Dionne .60 1.50
H16 Guy Lafleur .75 2.00
H17 Mario Lemieux 4.00 10.00
H18 Jason Spezza .75 2.00
H19 Jean-Sebastien Giguere .60 1.50
H20 Mike Modano 1.25 3.00
H21 Rick Nash .75 2.00
H22 Todd Bertuzzi .75 2.00
H23 Marian Gaborik 1.25 3.00
H24 Martin Brodeur 2.50 5.00
H25 Joe Thornton 1.25 3.00
H26 Ed Belfour .75 2.00
H27 Saku Koivu .75 2.00
H28 Steve Yzerman 3.00 8.00
H29 Markus Naslund .75 2.00
H30 Marian Hossa .75 2.00

2003-04 SP Authentic Sign of the Times

AF Alexander Frolov 4.00 10.00
AH Adam Hall 3.00 8.00
AS Alexei Smirnov 3.00 8.00
BC Bobby Clarke SP 15.00 40.00
BO Bobby Orr 60.00 150.00
CK Chuck Kobasew 3.00 8.00
DA David Aebischer 4.00 10.00
DC Don Cherry 20.00 50.00
EL Eric Lindros SP 30.00 80.00
GL Guy Lafleur SP 20.00 50.00
HZ Henrik Zetterberg 10.00 25.00
IK Ilya Kovalchuk 5.00 12.00
JI Jarome Iginla 6.00 15.00
JK Jari Kurri 8.00 20.00
JL Jordan Leopold 3.00 8.00
JN Joe Nieuwendyk 4.00 10.00
JP Joni Pitkanen 5.00 12.00
JR Jeremy Roenick 8.00 20.00
JS Jason Spezza 5.00 12.00
JT Jose Theodore 5.00 12.00
KL Eric Staal SP 15.00 40.00
LM Lanny McDonald 8.00 20.00
MB Martin Brodeur 25.00 60.00
MC Mike Comrie 4.00 10.00
MG Marian Gaborik 5.00 12.00
MH Gordie Howe 80.00 150.00
MT Mikael Tellqvist SP 4.00 10.00
MT Marty Turco 5.00 12.00
PE Phil Esposito SP 15.00 40.00
PL Pascal Leclaire 3.00 8.00
PR Patrick Roy SP 50.00 120.00
RN Rick Nash 5.00 12.00
SB Scotty Bowman SP 20.00 50.00
SC Stanislav Chistov 3.00 8.00
SF Sergei Fedorov 12.00 30.00
SG Curtis Joseph 8.00 20.00
SH Scott Hartnell 3.00 8.00
SK Saku Koivu SP 15.00 40.00
SM Stan Mikita 6.00 15.00
SS Sergei Samsonov 4.00 10.00
TB Todd Bertuzzi 5.00 12.00
TR Tuomo Ruutu 5.00 12.00
WG Wayne Gretzky 200.00 500.00
ZP Zigmund Palffy 5.00 12.00
AHY Ales Hemsky 5.00 12.00
JLC John LeClair 5.00 12.00
JSG Jean-Sebastien Giguere 5.00 12.00
JTH Joe Thornton 8.00 20.00
MAF Marc-Andre Fleury 50.00 125.00
MHA Marian Hossa 10.00 25.00
BL P.Bure/E.Lindros 30.00 80.00
CF S.Chistov/S.Fedorov 20.00 50.00
CH M.Comrie/A.Hemsky 12.00 30.00
CR B.Clarke/J.Roenick 20.00 50.00
ET P.Esposito/J.Thornton 20.00 50.00
FG S.Fedorov/J.Giguere 20.00 50.00
FS E.Staal/M.Fleury 50.00 125.00
GK W.Gretzky/J.Kurri 200.00 500.00
GR J.Giguere/P.Roy 30.00 80.00
HS M.Hossa/J.Spezza 12.00 30.00
IM J.Iginla/L.McDonald 20.00 50.00
NB M.Naslund/T.Bertuzzi 12.00 30.00
NL R.Nash/P.Leclaire 12.00 30.00
TK J.Theodore/S.Koivu 12.00 30.00
BCY S.Bowman/D.Cherry 40.00 100.00
BTG Bossy/Trott/Gillies 60.00 150.00
CRG Clarke/Roen/Gagne 30.00 80.00
GCF Gig/Chistov/Fedorov 30.00 80.00
GKF Gretzky/Kurri/Fuhr 400.00 1000.00
GMM Howe/Howe/Howe 400.00 500.00
GTS Gretzky/Thorn/Spezza 300.00 800.00
LFR Staal/Fleury/Ruutu 50.00 120.00
NSZ Nash/Spezz/Zetter 50.00 120.00
PAF Palffy/Aulin/Frolov 15.00 40.00
RGB Roy/Giguere/Brodeur 250.00 400.00

2003-04 SP Authentic Signed Patches

*SINGLE COLOR: .25X TO .75X
AM Antti Miettinen 15.00 40.00
AS Alexander Semin 60.00 120.00
CH Chris Higgins 20.00 50.00
DB Dustin Brown 75.00 150.00
DH Dan Hamhuis 20.00 50.00
ES Eric Staal 100.00 200.00
JH Jiri Hudler 25.00 60.00
JL Joffrey Lupul 40.00 80.00
JP Joni Pitkanen 25.00 60.00
JT Jordin Tootoo 60.00 120.00
MF Marc-Andre Fleury 600.00 1500.00
MS Matt Stajan 25.00 60.00
NH Nathan Horton 30.00 80.00
PB Patrice Bergeron 200.00 500.00
PS Peter Sejna 25.00 60.00
SB Sean Bergenheim 30.00 80.00
TR Tuomo Ruutu 25.00 60.00
TS Tony Salmelainen 25.00 60.00

2004-05 SP Authentic

COMPLETE SET (150) 20.00 50.00
COMP.SET w/o SP's (90) 8.00 20.00
1 Jean-Sebastien Giguere .30 .75
2 Joffrey Lupul .20 .50
3 Sergei Fedorov .50 1.25
4 Dany Heatley .25 .60
5 Ilya Kovalchuk .30 .75
6 Kari Lehtonen .40 1.00
7 Andrew Raycroft .25 .60
8 Joe Thornton .50 1.25
9 Patrice Bergeron .40 1.00
10 Glen Murray .25 .60
11 Mika Noronen .25 .60
12 Miroslav Satan .25 .60
13 Maxim Afinogenov .20 .50
14 Jarome Iginla .40 1.00
15 Matthew Lombardi .20 .50
16 Miikka Kiprusoff .30 .75
17 Eric Staal .40 1.00
18 Erik Cole .20 .50
19 Tyler Arnason .20 .50
20 Tuomo Ruutu .25 .60
21 David Aebischer .25 .60
22 Joe Sakic .60 1.50
23 Peter Forsberg .60 1.50
24 Milan Hejduk .25 .60
25 Alex Tanguay .25 .60
26 Rick Nash .30 .75
27 Nikolai Zherdev .25 .60
28 Mike Modano .50 1.25
29 Bill Guerin .30 .75
30 Marty Turco .30 .75
31 Manny Legace .25 .60
32 Pavel Datsyuk .50 1.25
33 Brendan Shanahan .30 .75
34 Steve Yzerman .75 2.00
35 Henrik Zetterberg .40 1.00
36 Jason Smith .20 .50
37 Ryan Smyth .25 .60
38 Ty Conklin .25 .60
39 Nathan Horton .30 .75
40 Roberto Luongo .50 1.25
41 Olli Jokinen .25 .60
42 Alexander Frolov .25 .60
43 Zigmund Palffy .30 .75
44 Marian Gaborik .30 .75
45 Manny Fernandez .20 .50
46 Michael Ryder .25 .60
47 Jose Theodore .30 .75
48 Saku Koivu .30 .75
49 Steve Sullivan .20 .50
50 Jordin Tootoo .20 .50
51 Tomas Vokoun .25 .60
52 Martin Brodeur .75 2.00
53 Patrik Elias .30 .75
54 Scott Stevens .30 .75
55 Eric Lindros .50 1.25
56 Mark Messier .60 1.50
57 Jaromir Jagr 1.00 2.50
58 Michael Peca .25 .60
59 Rick DiPietro .25 .60
60 Daniel Alfredsson .30 .75
61 Marian Hossa .30 .75
62 Jason Spezza .30 .75
63 Martin Havlat .30 .75
64 Dominik Hasek .50 1.25
65 Jeremy Roenick .50 1.25
66 Robert Esche .25 .60
67 Simon Gagne .30 .75
68 Brett Hull .60 1.50
69 Mike Comrie .25 .60
70 Shane Doan .25 .60
71 Marc-Andre Fleury .60 1.50
72 Mario Lemieux 1.25 3.00
73 Mark Recchi .40 1.00
74 Evgeni Nabokov .25 .60
75 Patrick Marleau .30 .75
76 Chris Pronger .30 .75
77 Doug Weight .30 .75
78 Keith Tkachuk .30 .75
79 Brad Richards .30 .75
80 Nikolai Khabibulin .30 .75
81 Martin St. Louis .30 .75
82 Vincent Lecavalier .30 .75
83 Owen Nolan .30 .75
84 Ed Belfour .30 .75
85 Mats Sundin .30 .75
86 Gary Roberts .20 .50
87 Ed Jovanovski .25 .60
88 Markus Naslund .30 .75
89 Trevor Linden .30 .75
90 Olaf Kolzig .30 .75
91 Brad Fast RC .75 2.00
92 Brennan Evans RC .75 2.00
93 Layne Ulmer RC .60 1.50
94 Mel Angelstad RC .60 1.50
95 Garret Stroshein RC .60 1.50
96 Marcel Goc RC 1.00 2.50
97 Sergei Fedorov AW 1.25 3.00
98 Dany Heatley AW .60 1.50
99 Joe Thornton AW 1.25 3.00
100 Glen Murray AW .60 1.50
101 Ilya Kovalchuk AW .75 2.00
102 Miroslav Satan AW .60 1.50
103 Jarome Iginla AW 1.00 2.50
104 Eric Daze AW .60 1.50
105 Paul Kariya AW .75 2.00
106 Peter Forsberg AW 1.50 4.00
107 Joe Sakic AW 1.50 4.00
108 Patrick Roy AW 2.00 5.00
109 Milan Hejduk AW .60 1.50
110 Mike Modano AW 1.25 3.00
111 Bill Guerin AW .75 2.00
112 Nicklas Lidstrom AW .75 2.00
113 Steve Yzerman AW 2.00 5.00
114 Brendan Shanahan AW .75 2.00
115 Martin St. Louis AW .75 2.00
116 Roberto Luongo AW 1.25 3.00
117 Zigmund Palffy AW .75 2.00
118 Luc Robitaille AW .75 2.00
119 Marian Gaborik AW .75 2.00
120 Saku Koivu AW .75 2.00
121 Jose Theodore AW .75 2.00
122 Martin Brodeur AW 2.00 5.00
123 Scott Niedermayer AW .75 2.00
124 Scott Stevens AW .75 2.00
125 Patrik Elias AW .75 2.00
126 Alexei Yashin AW .60 1.50
127 Pavel Bure AW .75 2.00
128 Jaromir Jagr AW 2.50 6.00
129 Wayne Gretzky AW 5.00 12.00
130 Dominik Hasek AW 1.25 3.00
131 Marian Hossa AW .75 2.00
132 Daniel Alfredsson AW .75 2.00
133 Jeremy Roenick AW 1.25 3.00
134 Keith Primeau AW .60 1.50
135 John LeClair AW .75 2.00
136 Tony Amonte AW .60 1.50
137 Brett Hull AW 1.50 4.00
138 Mario Lemieux AW 3.00 8.00
139 Vincent Damphousse AW .60 1.50
140 Keith Tkachuk AW .75 2.00
141 Doug Weight AW .75 2.00
142 Chris Pronger AW .75 2.00
143 Vincent Lecavalier AW .75 2.00
144 Nikolai Khabibulin AW .75 2.00
145 Mats Sundin AW .75 2.00
146 Ed Belfour AW .75 2.00
147 Joe Nieuwendyk AW .60 1.50
148 Brian Leetch AW .60 1.50
149 Markus Naslund AW .75 2.00
150 Olaf Kolzig AW .75 2.00

2004-05 SP Authentic Buyback Autographs
13 A.Raycroft 03Rookie Upd/51 12.00 30.00
15 Bo.Hull 04Leg Sig/38 25.00 60.00
26 C.Drury 03Rookie Upd/23 8.00 20.00
35 D.Briere 03RK Upd/48 15.00 40.00
36 D.Heatley 03Rookie Upd/15 20.00 40.00
41 D.Aebischer 03Rookie Upd/50 12.00 30.00
44 D.Weight 03Beehive Jsy/23 10.00 25.00
50 E.Jovanovski 02SPA Sup Prem/21 12.0030.00
55 E.Jovanovski 03Rookie Upd/55 10.00 25.00
58 Cheevers 04Leg Sig/45 20.00 50.00
59 Perreault 04Leg Sig/22 15.00 40.00
64 Zetterberg 03RK Upd/40 15.00 40.00
75 J.Spezza 03Rookie Upd/39 8.00 20.00
80 J.Bouwmeester 03Rookie Upd/48 10.00 25.00
84 Beliveau 04Leg Sig/49 30.00 60.00
93 Roenick 03RK Upd/20 20.00 50.00
100 Theodore 03RK Upd/29 30.00 80.00
104 L.McDonald 04Leg Sig/48 15.00 40.00
114 Mari.Hossa 03Rookie Upd/18 20.00 40.00
139 M.Turco 03RK Upd/35 15.00 40.00
147 M.Noronen 03Rookie Upd/35 10.00 25.00
153 M.Bossy 04Legend Sig/47 12.00 30.00
156 M.Ribeiro 03Rookie Upd/53 10.00 25.00
161 Khabibulin 03RK Upd/26 25.00 60.00
164 R.Leach 04Leg Sig/24 15.00 40.00
165 R.Robert 04Leg Sig/24 8.00 20.00
169 R.Nash 03RK Upd/41 15.00 40.00
173 Luongo 03RK Upd/45 15.00 40.00
174 R.Smyth 03Beehive Jsy/20 12.00 30.00
187 S.Mikita 04Leg Sig/30 10.00 25.00
192 S.Sullivan 02UD Speed Demon/20 10.00 25.00
193 S.Sullivan 03Rookie Upd/26 10.00 25.00
194 T.Esposito 04Leg Sig/18 20.00 40.00
200 Z.Palffy 03Rookie Upd/32 10.00 25.00

2004-05 SP Authentic Rookie Redemptions
RR1 Corey Perry 12.00 30.00
RR2 Braydon Coburn 4.00 10.00
RR3 Hannu Toivonen 4.00 10.00
RR4 Thomas Vanek 8.00 20.00
RR5 Dion Phaneuf 12.00 30.00
RR6 Cam Ward 10.00 25.00
RR7 Brent Seabrook 6.00 15.00
RR8 Wojtek Wolski 8.00 20.00
RR9 Gilbert Brule 4.00 10.00
RR10 Jussi Jokinen 5.00 12.00
RR11 Jim Howard 10.00 25.00
RR12 Brad Winchester 4.00 10.00
RR13 Rostislav Olesz 3.00 8.00
RR14 George Parros 4.00 10.00
RR15 Matt Foy 4.00 10.00
RR16 Alexander Perezhogin 3.00 8.00
RR17 Ryan Suter 6.00 15.00
RR18 Zach Parise 10.00 25.00
RR19 Robert Nilsson 4.00 10.00
RR20 Henrik Lundqvist 15.00 40.00
RR21 Andrej Meszaros 3.00 8.00
RR22 Jeff Carter 8.00 20.00
RR23 David Leneveu 3.00 8.00
RR24 Sidney Crosby 125.00 250.00
RR25 Ryane Clowe 6.00 15.00
RR26 Jeff Woywitka 4.00 10.00
RR27 Evgeny Artyukhin 5.00 12.00
RR28 Alexander Steen 6.00 15.00
RR29 Rob McVicar 3.00 8.00
RR30 Alexander Ovechkin 60.00 120.00
RR31 Peter Budaj 5.00 12.00
RR32 Rene Bourque 4.00 10.00
RR33 Duncan Keith 8.00 20.00
RR34 Lee Stempniak 5.00 12.00
RR35 Andrew Alberts 3.00 8.00
RR36 Milan Jurcina 3.00 8.00
RR37 Yann Danis 4.00 10.00
RR38 Keith Ballard 4.00 10.00
RR39 Eric Nystrom 4.00 10.00
RR40 Mike Richards 12.00 30.00
PP41 Kevin Nastiuk 3.00 8.00
PP42 Petteri Nokelainen 3.00 8.00
RR43 Chris Campoli 3.00 8.00
RR44 Andrew Wozniewski 3.00 8.00
RR45 Ryan Getzlaf 12.00 30.00
RR46 Maxime Talbot 4.00 10.00
RR47 Petr Prucha 5.00 12.00
RR48 Johan Franzen 6.00 15.00
RR49 Brandon Bochenski 3.00 8.00
RR50 Patrick Eaves 5.00 12.00
RR51 Jim Slater 3.00 8.00

2004-05 SP Authentic Rookie Review Autographed Patches
RRAB David Aebischer 20.00 50.00
RRAF Alexander Frolov 20.00 50.00
RRBR Martin Brodeur 60.00 120.00
RRCD Chris Drury 20.00 50.00
RRDA Daniel Briere 25.00 60.00
RRDB Dustin Brown 20.00 50.00
RRDL David Legwand 15.00 40.00
RRDW Doug Weight 15.00 40.00
RREJ Ed Jovanovski 12.00 30.00
RRHE Milan Hejduk 25.00 60.00
RRHV Martin Havlat 25.00 60.00
RRHZ Henrik Zetterberg 25.00 60.00
RRIG Jarome Iginla 50.00 125.00
RRIK Ilya Kovalchuk 25.00 60.00
RRJB Jay Bouwmeester 15.00 40.00
RRJK Jari Kurri 40.00 100.00
RRJL Joffrey Lupul 20.00 50.00
RRJR Jeremy Roenick 20.00 50.00
RRJT Joe Thornton 30.00 80.00
RRKL Kari Lehtonen 20.00 50.00
RRKP Keith Primeau 15.00 40.00
RRMA Maxim Afinogenov 15.00 40.00
RRMG Marian Gaborik 30.00 80.00
RRMH Marcel Hossa 15.00 40.00
RRMN Markus Naslund 20.00 50.00
RRMP Mark Parrish 20.00 50.00
RRMR Michael Ryder 20.00 50.00
RRMT Marty Turco 15.00 40.00
RRNS Nathan Smith 15.00 40.00
RRPB Patrice Bergeron/90 30.00 80.00
RRPS Philippe Sauve 15.00 40.00
RRRE Robert Esche 12.00 30.00
RRRL Roberto Luongo 30.00 80.00
RRRN Rick Nash 40.00 100.00
RRRS Ryan Smyth 15.00 40.00
RRSC Stanislav Chistov 15.00 40.00
RRSG Simon Gagne 15.00 40.00
RRSP Jason Spezza 30.00 80.00
RRSW Stephen Weiss 15.00 40.00
RRZC Zdeno Chara 20.00 50.00

2004-05 SP Authentic Sign of the Times
STAB David Aebischer 5.00 12.00
STAF Maxim Afinogenov 15.00 40.00
STAH Ales Hemsky 6.00 15.00
STAR Andrew Raycroft 6.00 15.00
STAT Alex Tanguay 6.00 15.00
STBA Milan Bartovic 4.00 10.00
STBB Brad Boyes 5.00 12.00
STBI Martin Biron 6.00 15.00
STBL Brian Leetch SP 30.00 80.00
STBM Brenden Morrow 6.00 15.00
STBO Scotty Bowman SP 30.00 80.00
STBR Brad Richards 8.00 20.00
STCD Chris Drury 5.00 12.00
STCH Chris Higgins 6.00 15.00
STCP Chris Pronger 6.00 15.00
STDB Daniel Briere 6.00 15.00
STDC Don Cherry 15.00 40.00
STDH Dany Heatley SP 15.00 40.00
STDL David Legwand 5.00 12.00
STDR Dwayne Roloson 6.00 15.00
STDU Dustin Brown 6.00 15.00
STDW Doug Weight SP 10.00 25.00
STEC Erik Cole 5.00 12.00
STEJ Ed Jovanovski 5.00 12.00
STES Eric Staal 12.00 30.00
STFL Marc-Andre Fleury 12.00 30.00
STFM Frank Mahovlich SP 30.00 80.00
STFR Alexander Frolov 4.00 10.00
STFS Fredrik Sjostrom 4.00 10.00
STGA Marian Gaborik 12.00 30.00
STGE Georges Laraque 4.00 10.00
STGH Gordie Howe 50.00 100.00
STGI Gilbert Perreault SP 30.00 80.00
STGL Guy Lafleur SP 75.00 150.00
STHA Dominik Hasek SP 20.00 50.00
STHO Nathan Horton 5.00 12.00
STHZ Henrik Zetterberg 15.00 40.00
STIK Ilya Kovalchuk 15.00 40.00
STJB Jay Bouwmeester 5.00 12.00
STJG Jean-Sebastien Giguere 6.00 15.00
STJI Jarome Iginla 15.00 40.00
STJL Joffrey Lupul 6.00 15.00
STJO Jose Theodore SP 15.00 40.00
STJR Jeremy Roenick 10.00 25.00
STJT Joe Thornton 12.50 30.00
STKL Kari Lehtonen 8.00 20.00
STKU Jari Kurri 10.00 25.00
STLE Manny Legace 4.00 10.00
STLM Lanny McDonald 8.00 20.00
STLN Ladislav Nagy 4.00 10.00
STLO Matthew Lombardi 4.00 10.00
STMA Marcel Hossa 4.00 10.00
STMB Martin Brodeur SP 75.00 150.00
STMH Milan Hejduk 8.00 20.00
STMJ Matt Stajan 5.00 12.00
STML John-Michael Liles 4.00 10.00
STMN Markus Naslund 6.00 15.00
STMO Brendan Morrison 5.00 12.00
STMP Michael Peca 5.00 12.00
STMT Marty Turco 6.00 15.00
STNK Nikolai Khabibulin 10.00 25.00
STNS Nathan Smith 4.00 10.00
STNZ Nikolai Zherdev 6.00 15.00
STPA Mark Parrish 4.00 10.00
STPB Patrice Bergeron 40.00 100.00
STPR Patrick Roy SP 150.00 300.00
STPS Philippe Sauve 4.00 10.00
STPW Peter Worrell 4.00 10.00
STRE Robert Esche 4.00 10.00
STRL Roberto Luongo 8.00 20.00
STRN Rick Nash 12.50 30.00
STRR Robyn Regehr 4.00 10.00
STRS Ryan Smyth 6.00 15.00
STRY Michael Ryder 6.00 15.00
STSC Stanislav Chistov 4.00 10.00
STSD Shane Doan 5.00 12.00
STSG Simon Gagne 8.00 20.00
STSK Saku Koivu 10.00 25.00
STSP Jason Spezza SP 25.00 50.00
STST Martin St. Louis 6.00 15.00
STSU Steve Sullivan 4.00 10.00
STSW Stephen Weiss 5.00 12.00
STTA Tyler Arnason 4.00 10.00
STTH Trent Hunter 4.00 10.00
STTU Tuomo Ruutu 6.00 15.00
STVL Vincent Lecavalier SP 125.00 250.00
STWG Wayne Gretzky SP 200.00 500.00
STZC Zdeno Chara 10.00 25.00
DSPR Perreault/Robert/25 25.00 60.00
DSAH Alfredsson/Hossa/100 12.00 30.00
DSBC Bowman/Cherry/25 60.00 120.00
DSBD M.Biron/C.Drury/100 10.00 25.00
DSBR Brodeur/Roy/25 150.00 300.00
DSBT Bossy/Trottier/25 50.00 125.00
DSCR R.Esche/J.Roenick/100 12.50 30.00
DSDS S.Doan/F.Sjostrom/100 10.00 25.00
DSEE T.Espo/P.Espo/25 75.00 125.00
DSFH G.Fuhr/G.Hall/25 50.00 100.00
DSHG Howe/Gretzky/25 500.00 1200.00
DSHH M.Hossa/M.Hossa/100 15.00 40.00
DSHS D.Hasek/J.Spezza/100 20.00 50.00
DSIR J.Iginla/R.Regehr/100 20.00 50.00
DSKL Khabibulin/R.Luongo/100 20.00 50.00
DSKN Kovalchuk/Lehtonen/100 20.00 50.00
DSLB B.Leetch/E.Belfour/100 25.00 60.00
DSLK St.Louis/Kovalchuk/100 30.00 80.00
DSLL St. Louis/Lecavalier/25 30.00 80.00
DSLW G.Laraque/P.Worrell/100 12.00 30.00
DSMJ M.Ryder/J.Theodore/100 12.00 30.00
DSMT B.Morrow/M.Turco/100 12.00 30.00
DSMZ Naslund/Zetterberg/100 15.00 40.00
DSNH C.Neely/G.Howe/25 75.00 150.00
DSNJ Naslund/Jovanvski/100 15.00 40.00
DSNK Nabokov/Khabablin/100 12.00 30.00
DSNZ R.Nash/N.Zherdev/100 20.00 50.00
DSPH M.Peca/T.Hunter/100 10.00 25.00
DSPM P.Bergeron/M.Ryder/100 15.00 40.00
DSPW C.Pronger/D.Weight/100 12.00 30.00
DSRA R.Smyth/A.Hemsky/100 15.00 40.00
DSRL Raycroft/Lehtonen/100 15.00 40.00
DSRP R.Bourque/C.Neely/100 30.00 80.00
DSRR M.Ryder/M.Ribeiro/100 12.00 30.00
DSRT Raycroft/J.Thornton/100 15.00 40.00
DSSH J.Spezza/M.Havlat/100 15.00 40.00
DSST E.Staal/J.Thornton/100 25.00 60.00
DSTN J.Thornton/C.Neely/100 20.00 50.00
DSWL S.Weiss/R.Luongo/100 15.00 40.00
TSBNT Bourq/Neely/Thorn 75.00 150.00
TSBTG Bossy/Trottier/Gillies 75.00 125.00
TSCLR Clarke/Leach/Roenick 75.00 150.00
TSGKF Gretzky/Kurri/Fuhr 500.00 1200.00
TSGRE Gagne/Roenick/Esche 30.00 80.00
TSHLK Heatly/Lehtnen/Kovlchk 75.00 150.00
TSHTA Hejduk/Tang/Aebischer 40.00 80.00
TSIKN Iginla/Kovalchuk/Nash 100.00 250.00
TSILN Iginla/St. Louis/Nash 75.00 150.00
TSKLL Khabi/Luongo/Lehton 50.00 125.00
TSLPJ Leetch/Pronger/Jovo 40.00 100.00
TSLRZ Lupul/Ruutu/Zherdev 25.00 60.00
TSLWH Luongo/Weiss/Horton 60.00 150.00
TSNSS Nash/Spezza/Staal 125.00 250.00
TSPBF Palffy/Brown/Frolov 25.00 60.00
TSRBT Raycroft/Belfour/Turco 50.00 120.00
TSRKR Ribeiro/Koivu/Ryder 50.00 100.00
TSRLB Roy/Luongo/Brodeur 250.00 500.00
TSSHZ Staal/Horton/Zherdev 50.00 100.00
TSTRB Thorntn/Raycrft/Brgrn 40.00 100.00
QSHRBG Bo.Hull/Robit/Bcyk/Gill 60.00 120.00
QSBBLK Berg/Brown/Lupul/Kslr 60.00 120.00
QSBDPB Beliv/Dnne/Perr/Bossy 90.00 150.00
QSBPBP Brqe/Prngr/Bouw/Pitk 60.00 120.00
QSBTCR Bcyk/Thrn/Chvrs/Rycr 50.00 100.00
QSFBRE Fuhr/Brod/Roy/T.Espo 175.00 300.00
QSFSHZ M.Flry/Staal/Hrtn/Zhrdv 50.00 100.00
QSGPRE Ggne/Prim/Rnick/Esch 60.00 120.00
QSGTDC Grzky/Thrn/Dnne/Clrk 300.00 800.00
QSHINS Hejd/Ignla/Nash/St.Lou 75.00 150.00
QSIKHL Iginl/Kbas/Hejduk/Liles 60.00 120.00
QSLKSN St.L/Koval/Hossa/Nasl 60.00 120.00
QSLRLK St.L/Rich/Lecav/Khab 75.00 150.00
QSMHCL Mikta/Bo.Hll/Clrke/Lch 75.00 150.00
QSNHKS Nash/Heat/Koval/Berg 75.00 150.00
QSTAHS Tang/Aebs/Hjdk/Sve 60.00 120.00
QSTPLS Thrnt/Prim/Lecav/Staal 75.00 150.00
QSVANC Nslnd/Mrrsn/Jovan/Kslr 50.00 100.00

2004-05 SP Authentic UD Promos
*UD PROMO: .8X TO 2X BASIC CARDS
1 Jean-Sebastien Giguere .60 1.50
2 Joffrey Lupul .40 1.00
3 Sergei Fedorov 1.00 2.50
4 Dany Heatley .50 1.25
5 Ilya Kovalchuk .60 1.50
6 Kari Lehtonen .75 2.00
7 Andrew Raycroft .50 1.25
8 Joe Thornton 1.00 2.50
9 Patrice Bergeron .75 2.00
10 Glen Murray .50 1.25
11 Mika Noronen .50 1.25
12 Miroslav Satan .50 1.25
13 Maxim Afinogenov .40 1.00
14 Jarome Iginla .75 2.00
15 Matthew Lombardi .40 1.00
16 Miikka Kiprusoff .60 1.50
17 Eric Staal .75 2.00
18 Erik Cole .40 1.00
19 Tyler Arnason .40 1.00
20 Tuomo Ruutu .50 1.25
21 David Aebischer .50 1.25
22 Joe Sakic 1.25 3.00
23 Peter Forsberg 1.25 3.00
24 Milan Hejduk .50 1.25
25 Alex Tanguay .50 1.25
26 Rick Nash .60 1.50
27 Nikolai Zherdev .50 1.25
28 Mike Modano 1.00 2.50
29 Bill Guerin .60 1.50
30 Marty Turco .60 1.50
31 Manny Legace .50 1.25
32 Pavel Datsyuk 1.00 2.50
33 Brendan Shanahan .60 1.50
34 Steve Yzerman 1.50 4.00
35 Henrik Zetterberg .75 2.00
36 Jason Smith .40 1.00
37 Ryan Smyth .50 1.25
38 Ty Conklin .50 1.25
39 Nathan Horton .60 1.50
40 Roberto Luongo 1.00 2.50
41 Olli Jokinen .50 1.25
42 Alexander Frolov .50 1.25
43 Zigmund Palffy .60 1.50
44 Marian Gaborik .60 1.50
45 Manny Fernandez .40 1.00
46 Michael Ryder .50 1.25
47 Jose Theodore .60 1.50
48 Saku Koivu .60 1.50
49 Steve Sullivan .40 1.00
50 Jordin Tootoo .40 1.00
51 Tomas Vokoun .50 1.25
52 Martin Brodeur 1.50 4.00
53 Patrik Elias .60 1.50
54 Scott Stevens .60 1.50
55 Eric Lindros 1.00 2.50
56 Mark Messier 1.25 3.00
57 Jaromir Jagr 2.00 5.00
58 Michael Peca .50 1.25
59 Rick DiPietro .50 1.25
60 Daniel Alfredsson .60 1.50
61 Marian Hossa .60 1.50
62 Jason Spezza .60 1.50
63 Martin Havlat .60 1.50
64 Dominik Hasek 1.00 2.50
65 Jeremy Roenick 1.00 2.50
66 Robert Esche .50 1.25
67 Simon Gagne .60 1.50
68 Brett Hull 1.25 3.00
69 Mike Comrie .50 1.25
70 Shane Doan .50 1.25
71 Marc-Andre Fleury 1.25 3.00
72 Mario Lemieux 2.50 6.00
73 Mark Recchi .75 2.00
74 Evgeni Nabokov .50 1.25
75 Patrick Marleau .60 1.50
76 Chris Pronger .60 1.50
77 Doug Weight .60 1.50
78 Keith Tkachuk .60 1.50
79 Brad Richards .60 1.50
80 Nikolai Khabibulin .60 1.50
81 Martin St. Louis .60 1.50
82 Vincent Lecavalier .60 1.50
83 Owen Nolan .60 1.50
84 Ed Belfour .60 1.50
85 Mats Sundin .60 1.50
86 Gary Roberts .40 1.00
87 Ed Jovanovski .50 1.25
88 Markus Naslund .60 1.50
89 Trevor Linden .60 1.50
90 Olaf Kolzig .60 1.50

2005-06 SP Authentic
COMP.SET w/o SP's (100) 12.50 30.00
1 Jean-Sebastien Giguere .40 1.00
2 Joffrey Lupul .25 .60
3 Teemu Selanne .75 2.00
4 Scott Niedermayer .40 1.00
5 Ilya Kovalchuk .40 1.00
6 Kari Lehtonen .30 .75
7 Marian Hossa .40 1.00
8 Sergei Samsonov .30 .75
9 Brian Leetch .30 .75
10 Andrew Raycroft .30 .75
11 Patrice Bergeron .50 1.25
12 Glen Murray .30 .75
13 Chris Drury .30 .75
14 Martin Biron .30 .75
15 Daniel Briere .40 1.00
16 Jarome Iginla .50 1.25
17 Miikka Kiprusoff .40 1.00
18 Doug Weight .40 1.00
19 Martin Gerber .30 .75
20 Eric Staal .50 1.25
21 Nikolai Khabibulin .40 1.00
22 Tuomo Ruutu .40 1.00
23 Eric Daze .30 .75
24 Joe Sakic .75 2.00
25 Alex Tanguay .40 1.00
26 Milan Hejduk .30 .75
27 David Aebischer .30 .75
28 Rob Blake .40 1.00
29 Rick Nash .40 1.00
30 Sergei Fedorov .60 1.50
31 Mike Modano .60 1.50
32 Marty Turco .40 1.00
33 Bill Guerin .40 1.00
34 Brendan Shanahan .40 1.00
35 Steve Yzerman 1.00 2.50
36 Henrik Zetterberg .50 1.25
37 Pavel Datsyuk .60 1.50
38 Gordie Howe 1.25 3.00
39 Chris Pronger .40 1.00
40 Michael Peca .30 .75
41 Ryan Smyth .30 .75
42 Wayne Gretzky 2.50 6.00
43 Roberto Luongo .60 1.50
44 Olli Jokinen .40 1.00
45 Luc Robitaille .40 1.00
46 Jeremy Roenick .60 1.50
47 Alexander Frolov .25 .60
48 Pavol Demitra .50 1.25
49 Marian Gaborik .40 1.00
50 Dwayne Roloson .30 .75
51 Jose Theodore .40 1.00
52 Saku Koivu .40 1.00
53 Mike Ribeiro .25 .60
54 Michael Ryder .30 .75
55 Paul Kariya .40 1.00
56 Tomas Vokoun .30 .75
57 Martin Brodeur 1.00 2.50
58 Patrik Elias .40 1.00
59 Scott Gomez .30 .75
60 Brian Gionta .25 .60
61 Miroslav Satan .30 .75
62 Alexei Yashin .30 .75
63 Rick DiPietro .30 .75
64 Mark Parrish .25 .60
65 Jaromir Jagr 1.25 3.00
66 Martin Straka .25 .60
67 Dominik Hasek .60 1.50
68 Dany Heatley .30 .75
69 Wade Redden .25 .60
70 Martin Havlat .40 1.00
71 Daniel Alfredsson .40 1.00
72 Jason Spezza .40 1.00
73 Peter Forsberg .75 2.00
74 Keith Primeau .30 .75
75 Simon Gagne .40 1.00
76 Robert Esche .30 .75
77 Shane Doan .30 .75
78 Curtis Joseph .50 1.25
79 Mario Lemieux 1.50 4.00
80 Zigmund Palffy .40 1.00
81 Mark Recchi .50 1.25
82 Jonathan Cheechoo .30 .75
83 Evgeni Nabokov .30 .75
84 Patrick Marleau .40 1.00
85 Joe Thornton .60 1.50
86 Barret Jackman .25 .60
87 Keith Tkachuk .40 1.00
88 Martin St. Louis .40 1.00
89 Vincent Lecavalier .40 1.00
90 Brad Richards .40 1.00
91 Sean Burke .25 .60
92 Eric Lindros .60 1.50
93 Mats Sundin .40 1.00
94 Ed Belfour .40 1.00
95 Matt Stajan .25 .60
96 Jason Allison .30 .75
97 Todd Bertuzzi .40 1.00
98 Markus Naslund .40 1.00
99 Brendan Morrison .25 .60
100 Olaf Kolzig .40 1.00
101 Mario Lemieux/999 8.00 20.00
102 Joe Sakic/999 4.00 10.00
103 Jaromir Jagr/999 6.00 15.00
104 Mike Modano/999 3.00 8.00
105 Dominik Hasek/999 3.00 8.00
106 Ilya Kovalchuk/999 2.00 5.00
107 Steve Yzerman/999 5.00 12.00
108 Nikolai Khabibulin/999 2.00 5.00
109 Joe Thornton/999 3.00 8.00
110 Jarome Iginla/999 2.50 6.00
111 Martin St. Louis/999 2.00 5.00
112 Paul Kariya/999 2.00 5.00
113 Martin Brodeur/999 5.00 12.00
114 Mats Sundin/999 2.00 5.00
115 Peter Forsberg/999 4.00 10.00
116 Jean-Sebastien Giguere/999 2.00 5.00
117 Marian Hossa/999 2.00 5.00
118 Alex Tanguay/999 2.00 5.00
119 Rick Nash/999 2.00 5.00
120 Jeremy Roenick/999 3.00 8.00
121 Dany Heatley/999 1.50 4.00
122 Brendan Shanahan/999 2.00 5.00
123 Jose Theodore/999 2.00 5.00
124 Patrik Elias/999 2.00 5.00
125 Curtis Joseph/999 2.50 6.00
126 Evgeni Nabokov/999 1.50 4.00
127 Vincent Lecavalier/999 2.00 5.00
128 Markus Naslund/999 2.00 5.00
129 Olaf Kolzig/999 2.00 5.00
130 Doug Weight/999 2.00 5.00
131 Ryan Getzlaf AU RC 25.00 60.00
132 Corey Perry AU RC 25.00 60.00
133 Braydon Coburn AU RC 6.00 15.00
134 Jim Slater AU RC 5.00 12.00
135 Hannu Toivonen AU RC 6.00 15.00
136 Andrew Alberts AU RC 4.00 10.00
137 Milan Jurcina AU RC 5.00 12.00
138 Kevin Dallman AU RC 5.00 12.00
139 Thomas Vanek AU RC 12.00 30.00
140 Dion Phaneuf AU RC 8.00 20.00
141 Eric Nystrom AU RC 5.00 12.00
142 Cam Ward AU RC 12.00 30.00
143 Kevin Nastiuk AU RC 4.00 10.00
144 Niklas Nordgren AU RC 6.00 15.00
145 Brent Seabrook AU RC 20.00 50.00
146 Cam Barker AU RC 25.00 60.00
147 Duncan Keith AU RC 60.00 150.00
148 Rene Bourque AU RC 6.00 15.00
149 Wojtek Wolski AU RC 6.00 15.00
150 Peter Budaj AU RC 8.00 20.00
151 Gilbert Brule AU RC 6.00 15.00
152 Jaroslav Balastik AU RC 4.00 10.00
153 Jussi Jokinen AU RC 6.00 15.00
154 Johan Franzen AU RC 10.00 25.00
155 Jim Howard AU RC 12.00 30.00
156 Brett Lebda AU RC 4.00 10.00
157 Brad Winchester AU RC 6.00 15.00
158 Rostislav Olesz AU RC 5.00 12.00
159 Anthony Stewart AU RC 5.00 12.00
160 George Parros AU RC 5.00 12.00
161 Matt Foy AU RC 4.00 10.00
162 Derek Boogaard AU RC 15.00 40.00
163 Alexander Perezhogin AU RC 5.00 12.00
164 Yann Danis AU RC 5.00 12.00
165 Raitis Ivanans AU RC 4.00 10.00
166 Ryan Suter AU RC 8.00 20.00
167 Zach Parise AU RC 15.00 40.00
168 Robert Nilsson AU RC 6.00 15.00
169 Petteri Nokelainen AU RC 4.00 10.00
170 Al Montoya AU RC 6.00 15.00
171 Henrik Lundqvist AU RC 125.00 300.00
172 Petr Prucha AU RC 4.00 10.00
173 Ryan Hollweg AU RC 4.00 10.00
174 Patrick Eaves AU RC 6.00 15.00
175 Brandon Bochenski AU RC 6.00 15.00
176 Andrej Meszaros AU RC 5.00 12.00
177 Jeff Carter AU RC 20.00 50.00
178 Mike Richards AU RC 10.00 25.00
179 David Leneveu AU RC 4.00 10.00
180 Keith Ballard AU RC 4.00 10.00
181 Sidney Crosby AU RC 4000.00 10000.00
182 Maxime Talbot AU RC 6.00 15.00
183 Josh Gorges AU RC 5.00 12.00
184 Ryane Clowe AU RC 8.00 20.00
185 Jay McClement AU RC 4.00 10.00
186 Jeff Hoggan AU RC 4.00 10.00
187 Jeff Woywitka AU RC 4.00 10.00
188 Alexander Steen AU RC 8.00 20.00
189 Andy Wozniewski AU RC 5.00 12.00
190 Alexander Ovechkin AU RC 2500.00 6000.00
191 Ryan Whitney AU RC 12.00 30.00
192 R.J. Umberger AU RC 6.00 15.00
193 Mikko Koivu AU RC 6.00 15.00
194 Steve Bernier AU RC 6.00 15.00
195 Timo Helbling AU RC 4.00 10.00
196 Ryan Craig AU RC 4.00 10.00
197 Valtteri Filppula AU RC 8.00 20.00
198 Daniel Paille AU RC 6.00 15.00
199 Danny Richmond AU RC 4.00 10.00
200 Maxim Lapierre AU RC 6.00 15.00
201 Barry Tallackson AU RC 5.00 12.00
202 Chris Campoli AU RC 4.00 10.00
203 Jeremy Colliton AU RC 4.00 10.00
204 Christoph Schubert AU RC 4.00 10.00
205 Kevin Bieksa AU RC 40.00 100.00
206 Jordan Sigalet AU RC 4.00 10.00
207 Adam Berkhoel AU RC 5.00 12.00
208 Erik Christensen AU RC 4.00 10.00
209 Ole-Kristian Tollefsen AU RC 5.00 12.00
210 Dimitri Patzold AU RC 4.00 10.00
211 Brad Richardson AU RC 6.00 15.00
212 Lee Stempniak AU RC 6.00 15.00
213 Andrei Kostitsyn AU RC 8.00 20.00
214 Evgeny Artyukhin AU RC 5.00 12.00
215 Ben Eager AU RC 5.00 12.00
216 Andrew Ladd AU RC 8.00 20.00
217 Jeff Tambellini AU RC 4.00 10.00
218 Kyle Quincey AU RC 5.00 12.00
219 Tomas Fleischmann AU RC 6.00 15.00
220 Jakub Klepis AU RC 4.00 10.00
221 Michael Wall RC 2.00 5.00
222 Zenon Konopka RC 1.50 4.00
223 Vojtech Polak RC 1.50 4.00
224 Martin St. Pierre RC 1.50 4.00
225 Steve Goertzen RC 1.50 4.00
226 Andrew Penner RC 2.00 5.00
227 Danny Syvret RC 1.50 4.00
228 Jeff Giuliano RC 2.00 5.00
229 Adam Hauser RC 2.00 5.00
230 Kyle Brodziak RC 1.50 4.00
231 Cam Janssen RC 2.00 5.00
232 Kevin Colley RC 2.00 5.00
233 Chris Holt RC 1.50 4.00
234 Greg Jacina RC 1.50 4.00
235 Yanick Lehoux RC 2.50 6.00
236 Brian McGrattan RC 1.50 4.00
237 Colin Hemingway RC 1.50 4.00
238 Paul Ranger RC 1.50 4.00
239 Gerald Coleman RC 1.50 4.00
240 Dennis Wideman RC 1.50 4.00
241 Junior Lessard RC 1.50 4.00
242 Matt Jones RC 1.50 4.00
243 Brian Eklund RC 2.00 5.00
244 Nick Tarnasky RC 1.50 4.00
245 Bruno Gervais RC 1.50 4.00
246 Staffan Kronwall RC 1.50 4.00
247 Dustin Penner RC 2.50 6.00
248 Kevin Klein RC 1.50 4.00
249 Rob McVicar RC 2.00 5.00
250 Eric Healey RC 2.00 5.00
251 Ben Guite RC 2.00 5.00
252 Nathan Paetsch RC 2.00 5.00
253 Jiri Novotny RC 2.00 5.00
254 Richie Regehr RC 1.50 4.00
255 Mark Giordano RC 3.00 8.00
256 Chad Larose RC 1.50 4.00
257 Corey Crawford RC 8.00 20.00
258 Vitaly Kolesnik RC 2.00 5.00
259 Geoff Platt RC 2.00 5.00
260 Matt Greene RC 1.50 4.00
261 Jean-Francois Jacques RC 1.50 4.00
262 Rob Globke RC 1.50 4.00
263 Petr Taticek RC 2.00 5.00
264 Petr Kanko RC 2.00 5.00
265 Matt Ryan RC 2.00 5.00
266 Connor James RC 2.00 5.00
267 Richard Petiot RC 2.00 5.00
268 Mark Streit RC 1.50 4.00
269 Jean-Philippe Cote RC 1.50 4.00
270 Jonathan Ferland RC 2.00 5.00
271 Pekka Rinne RC 8.00 20.00
272 Jason Ryznar RC 1.50 4.00
273 Josh Gratton RC 2.00 5.00
274 Alexandre Picard RC 1.50 4.00
275 Colby Armstrong RC 2.50 6.00
276 Grant Stevenson RC 1.50 4.00
277 Doug Murray RC 1.50 4.00
278 Chris Beckford-Tseu RC 2.00 5.00
279 Jon DiSalvatore RC 2.00 5.00
280 Mike Glumac RC 2.00 5.00
281 Darren Reid RC 1.50 4.00
282 Doug O'Brien RC 1.50 4.00
283 Jay Harrison RC 2.00 5.00
284 Rick Rypien RC 3.00 8.00
285 Alexandre Burrows RC 3.00 8.00
286 David Steckel RC 2.00 5.00
287 Mike Green RC 3.00 8.00
288 Ben Walter AU RC 4.00 10.00
289 Alexandre Picard AU RC 4.00 10.00
290 Chris Thorburn AU RC 5.00 12.00

2005-06 SP Authentic Limited
*1-100 VETS: 6X TO 15X BASIC CARDS
*101-130 VETS: 1.2X TO 3X BASIC CARDS
*131-220 ROOK.JSY AU: 1X TO 2.5X BASIC RC
*221-287 ROOKIES: 1.5X TO 4X BASIC RC
147 D.Keith PATCH AU 125.00 300.00
181 S.Crosby PATCH AU 5000.00 12000.00
190 A. Ovechkin PATCH AU 4000.00 10000.00

2005-06 SP Authentic Chirography
SPAR Andrew Raycroft 10.00 25.00
SPAT Alex Tanguay 10.00 25.00
SPAY Alexei Yashin 8.00 20.00
SPCP Chris Pronger 10.00 25.00
SPDH Dany Heatley 12.00 30.00
SPEB Ed Belfour 10.00 25.00
SPEN Evgeni Nabokov 10.00 25.00
SPHK Dominik Hasek 20.00 50.00
SPHV Martin Havlat 10.00 25.00
SPIK Ilya Kovalchuk 20.00 50.00
SPJG Jean-Sebastien Giguere 10.00 25.00
SPJI Jarome Iginla 15.00 40.00
SPJO Joe Thornton 25.00 50.00
SPJR Jeremy Roenick 20.00 50.00
SPJT Jose Theodore 12.00 30.00
SPMB Martin Brodeur 40.00 100.00
SPMG Marian Gaborik 20.00 50.00
SPMH Milan Hejduk 8.00 20.00
SPML Manny Legace 8.00 20.00
SPMM Mike Modano 15.00 40.00
SPMN Markus Naslund 10.00 25.00
SPOK Olaf Kolzig 12.00 30.00
SPPB Patrice Bergeron 10.00 25.00
SPRL Roberto Luongo 15.00 40.00
SPRN Rick Nash 15.00 40.00
SPSL Martin St. Louis 10.00 25.00
SPTV Tomas Vokoun 10.00 25.00
SPVL Vincent Lecavalier 25.00 60.00

2005-06 SP Authentic Marks of Distinction
MDAO Alexander Ovechkin 1000.00 2500.00
MDAR Andrew Raycroft 15.00 40.00
MDAT Alex Tanguay 20.00 50.00
MDAY Alexei Yashin 8.00 20.00
MDBL Brian Leetch 20.00 50.00
MDBO Ray Bourque 60.00 120.00
MDBR Brad Richards 25.00 60.00
MDCP Chris Pronger 20.00 50.00
MDDH Dany Heatley 25.00 60.00
MDDW Doug Weight 15.00 40.00
MDEB Ed Belfour 50.00 100.00
MDGH Gordie Howe 100.00 200.00
MDGL Guy Lafleur 50.00 125.00
MDHV Martin Havlat 12.00 30.00
MDIK Ilya Kovalchuk 30.00 80.00
MDJC Jonathan Cheechoo 30.00 60.00
MDJG Jean-Sebastien Giguere 20.00 40.00
MDJI Jarome Iginla 40.00 80.00
MDJO Joe Thornton 40.00 80.00
MDJR Jeremy Roenick 25.00 60.00
MDJS Jason Spezza 20.00 50.00
MDJT Jose Theodore 30.00 60.00
MDKL Kari Lehtonen 25.00 60.00
MDKP Keith Primeau 12.00 30.00
MDMD Marcel Dionne 30.00 60.00
MDMH Milan Hejduk 15.00 40.00
MDMM Mike Modano 30.00 60.00
MDMN Markus Naslund 15.00 40.00
MDPB Patrice Bergeron 80.00 200.00
MDPE Phil Esposito 30.00 60.00
MDPR Patrick Roy 100.00 200.00
MDRB Rob Blake 12.00 30.00
MDRL Roberto Luongo 50.00 100.00
MDRN Rick Nash 50.00 100.00
MDSG Simon Gagne 12.00 30.00
MDSK Saku Koivu 40.00 80.00
MDSL Martin St. Louis 20.00 50.00
MDSN Scott Niedermayer 15.00 40.00
MDVL Vincent Lecavalier 40.00 80.00

2005-06 SP Authentic Prestigious Pairings
PPBN Bourque/Neely/50 40.00 80.00
PPBP Blake/Pronger/100 15.00 40.00
PPCR Carter/Richards/100 15.00 40.00
PPDT Dionne/Taylor/100 25.00 60.00
PPEP Esche/Pitkanen/100 5.00 12.00
PPFK Fuhr/Kurri/50 25.00 60.00
PPGR Gaborik/Roloson/100 12.00 30.00
PPGS Lafleur/Koivu/50 25.00 60.00
PPHE Bo.Hull/T.Espo/50 60.00 150.00
PPHG Howe/Gretzky/50 300.00 800.00
PPHV Hasek/Vokoun/100 15.00 40.00
PPIS Iginla/St. Louis/50 20.00 50.00
PPKN Khabi./Nabokov/100 8.00 20.00
PPLH Legace/Howard/100 15.00 40.00
PPLK Lehtonen/Koval./100 15.00 40.00
PPLM Lundqvist/Montoya/100 15.00 40.00
PPLR Lecav./Richards/100 20.00 50.00
PPMB Miller/Biron/100 20.00 50.00
PPNL Naslund/Linden/100 20.00 50.00
PPNZ Nash/Zherdev/100 15.00 40.00
PPOS Olesz/Stewart/100 5.00 12.00
PPPG Perry/Getzlaf/100 20.00 50.00
PPPH Parrish/Hunter/100 5.00 12.00
PPPN Phan./Nyst./100 30.00 80.00
PPPO Phanf/Ovech/50 EXCH 400.00 1000.00
PPPV Perreault/Vanek/100 15.00 40.00
PPRA Ruutu/Arnason/100 5.00 12.00
PPRB Roy/Brodeur/50 125.00 250.00
PPRR Ryder/Ribeiro/100 8.00 20.00
PPTB Trottier/Bossy/50 15.00 40.00
PPTC Thornton/Cheech/100 25.00 60.00
PPTF Thibault/Fleury/100 12.00 30.00
PPTZ Turco/Zubov/100 8.00 20.00

2005-06 SP Authentic Rookie Authentics
RAAM Andrej Meszaros 8.00 20.00
RAAO Alexander Ovechkin 1000.00 2500.00
RAAP Alexander Perezhogin 8.00 20.00
RAAS Alexander Steen 10.00 25.00
RABC Braydon Coburn 8.00 20.00
RABS Brent Seabrook 8.00 20.00
RABW Brad Winchester 8.00 20.00
RACP Corey Perry 12.00 30.00
RACW Cam Ward 12.00 30.00
RAEN Eric Nystrom 8.00 20.00
RAGB Gilbert Brule 10.00 25.00
RAHL Henrik Lundqvist 60.00 150.00
RAHT Hannu Toivonen 8.00 20.00
RAJC Jeff Carter 10.00 25.00
RAJH Jim Howard 15.00 40.00
RAJJ Jussi Jokinen 8.00 20.00
RAJW Jeff Woywitka 8.00 20.00
RAKB Keith Ballard 8.00 20.00
RAMR Mike Richards 12.00 30.00
RARG Ryan Getzlaf 12.00 30.00
RARN Robert Nilsson 8.00 20.00
RARO Rostislav Olesz 10.00 25.00
RARS Ryan Suter 10.00 25.00
RAST Anthony Stewart 8.00 20.00
RATV Thomas Vanek 15.00 40.00
RAWW Wojtek Wolski 10.00 25.00
RAYD Yann Danis 8.00 20.00
RAZP Zach Parise 20.00 50.00

2005-06 SP Authentic Scripts to Success
SSAF Alexander Frolov 6.00 15.00
SSAH Ales Hemsky 6.00 15.00
SSAR Andrew Raycroft 6.00 15.00
SSCB Christian Backman 4.00 10.00
SSCC Carlo Colaiacovo 4.00 10.00
SSDB Dustin Brown 6.00 15.00
SSDF Dan Fritsche 4.00 10.00
SSES Eric Staal 12.00 30.00
SSFT Fedor Tyutin 4.00 10.00
SSHZ Henrik Zetterberg 10.00 25.00
SSJB Jay Bouwmeester 6.00 15.00
SSJC Jonathan Cheechoo 8.00 20.00
SSJL Jamie Lundmark 4.00 10.00
SSJM John-Michael Liles 4.00 10.00
SSJP Joni Pitkanen 4.00 10.00
SSJR Jani Rita 4.00 10.00
SSKL Kari Lehtonen 10.00 25.00
SSLU Joffrey Lupul 4.00 10.00
SSMF Marc-Andre Fleury 12.00 30.00
SSMH Marcel Hossa 4.00 10.00
SSMR Mike Ribeiro 4.00 10.00
SSMS Matt Stajan 5.00 12.00
SSPB Patrice Bergeron 12.00 30.00
SSPL Pascal Leclaire 4.00 10.00
SSPS Philippe Sauve 6.00 15.00
SSRK Ryan Kesler 6.00 15.00
SSRM Ryan Miller 12.00 30.00
SSRY Michael Ryder 8.00 20.00
SSTA Tyler Arnason 4.00 10.00
SSTR Tuomo Ruutu 10.00 25.00

2005-06 SP Authentic Sign of the Times
AF Alexander Frolov 3.00 8.00
AR Andrew Raycroft 4.00 10.00
AT Jason Arnott 4.00 10.00
AY Alexei Yashin 4.00 10.00
BL Brett Lebda 3.00 8.00
BO Derek Boogaard 8.00 20.00
BR Brian Rafalski 4.00 10.00
BW Jay Bouwmeester 3.00 8.00
CB Christian Backman 3.00 8.00
CC Carlo Colaiacovo 3.00 8.00
CO Craig Conroy 3.00 8.00
CP Chris Pronger SP 8.00 20.00
CS Cory Stillman 3.00 8.00
DB Dustin Brown 5.00 12.00
DC Dan Cloutier 4.00 10.00
DF Dan Fritsche 3.00 8.00
DH Dany Heatley SP 15.00 40.00
DK Duncan Keith 15.00 40.00
DW Doug Weight 5.00 12.00
ED Eric Daze 4.00 10.00
ES Eric Staal 8.00 20.00
FT Fedor Tyutin 3.00 8.00
GL Georges Laraque 4.00 10.00

GM Glen Murray SP	15.00	40.00
GP George Parros	3.00	8.00
HE Timo Helbling	3.00	8.00
HG Jeff Hoggan	3.00	8.00
HO Marcel Hossa	3.00	8.00
HV Martin Havlat	5.00	12.00
HZ Henrik Zetterberg	6.00	15.00
IL Ian Laperriere	3.00	8.00
JA Jani Rita	3.00	8.00
JB Jaroslav Balastik	3.00	8.00
JC Jonathan Cheechoo	4.00	10.00
JH Jochen Hecht	3.00	8.00
JI Jarome Iginla SP	20.00	50.00
JL Jamie Lundmark	3.00	8.00
JM John-Michael Liles	3.00	8.00
JO Jeff O'Neill	3.00	8.00
JP Joni Pitkanen	3.00	8.00
JR Jeremy Roenick SP	15.00	40.00
JS Jim Slater	4.00	10.00
JT Jocelyn Thibault	4.00	10.00
KD Kris Draper	6.00	15.00
KE Kevin Dallman	4.00	10.00
KH Kristian Huselius	3.00	8.00
KL Kari Lehtonen	4.00	10.00
KP Keith Primeau	4.00	10.00
KW Kevin Weekes	4.00	10.00
LU Joffrey Lupul	3.00	8.00
MA Marc-Andre Fleury	10.00	25.00
MB Matthew Barnaby	3.00	8.00
MG Martin Gerber	4.00	10.00
MR Mike Ribeiro	3.00	8.00
MS Matt Stajan	3.00	8.00
MT Maxime Talbot	5.00	12.00
MW Brenden Morrow	4.00	10.00
NN Niklas Nordgren	5.00	12.00
NY Michael Nylander	3.00	8.00
OS Chris Osgood	5.00	12.00
PB Patrice Bergeron	40.00	100.00
PL Pascal Leclaire	4.00	10.00
PM Pierre-Marc Bouchard	5.00	12.00
PS Philippe Sauve	4.00	10.00
RA Raitis Ivanans	3.00	8.00
RH Ryan Hollweg	3.00	8.00
RI Brad Richards	5.00	12.00
RK Ryan Kesler	5.00	12.00
RL Roberto Luongo SP	8.00	20.00
RM Ryan Miller	5.00	12.00
RN Rob Niedermayer	4.00	10.00
RO Dwayne Roloson	4.00	10.00
RS Ryan Smith	4.00	10.00
RY Michael Ryder	6.00	15.00
RZ Richard Zednik	3.00	8.00
SA Miroslav Satan	4.00	10.00
SB Sean Burke	3.00	8.00
SC Sidney Crosby	800.00	2000.00
SL Martin St. Louis SP	15.00	40.00
SN Scott Niedermayer	6.00	15.00
SP Jason Spezza	8.00	20.00
SS Sheldon Souray	3.00	8.00
ST Marco Sturm	3.00	8.00
SZ Sergei Zubov	4.00	10.00
TA Tyler Arnason	3.00	8.00
TG Tim Gleason	3.00	8.00
TH Trent Hunter	3.00	8.00
TL Trevor Linden	5.00	12.00
TP Tom Poti	3.00	8.00
TU Tuomo Ruutu	5.00	12.00
VL Vincent Lecavalier	6.00	15.00
VP Vaclav Prospal	3.00	8.00
WG Wayne Gretzky/15 SP	400.00	1000.00

2005-06 SP Authentic Sign of the Times Duals

DAS N.Antropov/M.Stajan	6.00	15.00
DBM P.Bergeron/G.Murray	30.00	80.00
DCS E.Cole/E.Staal	10.00	25.00
DDV C.Drury/T.Vanek	10.00	25.00
DGW M.Gerber/C.Ward	8.00	20.00
DHK M.Hossa/I.Kovalchuk	12.00	30.00
DKO O.Kolzig/A.Ovechkin	300.00	800.00
DKP S.Koivu/A.Perezhogin	12.00	30.00
DLO M.Legace/C.Osgood	10.00	25.00
DLP J.Lupul/C.Perry	8.00	20.00
DMA M.Modano/J.Arnott	10.00	25.00
DMC B.Morrison/D.Cloutier	6.00	15.00
DNB R.Nash/G.Brule	25.00	60.00
DNC E.Nabokov/Cheechoo	10.00	25.00
DNN Niedermayer Bros.	12.00	30.00
DPH M.Peca/A.Hemsky	6.00	15.00
DPR K.Primeau/M.Richards	10.00	25.00
DPS C.Pronger/R.Smyth	10.00	25.00
DRR J.Roenick/L.Robitaille	20.00	50.00
DRT A.Raycroft/H.Toivonen	6.00	15.00
DSH J.Spezza/D.Heatley	25.00	60.00
DSS T.Steen/A.Steen	10.00	25.00
DTD J.Theodore/Y.Danis	8.00	20.00
DWL K.Weekes/H.Lundqvist	80.00	200.00
DYS A.Yashin/M.Satan	6.00	15.00
DZF Zetterberg/J.Franzen	12.50	30.00

2006-07 SP Authentic

COMP.SET w/o SPs (100)	10.00	25.00
1 Alexander Ovechkin	1.25	3.00
2 Olaf Kolzig	.30	.75
3 Markus Naslund	.30	.75
4 Roberto Luongo	.50	1.25
5 Brendan Morrison	.20	.50
6 Mats Sundin	.30	.75
7 Michael Peca	.25	.60
8 Alexander Steen	.20	.50
9 Andrew Raycroft	.25	.60
10 Vincent Lecavalier	.30	.75
11 Martin St. Louis	.30	.75
12 Brad Richards	.30	.75
13 Doug Weight	.30	.75
14 Keith Tkachuk	.30	.75
15 Manny Legace	.25	.60
16 Joe Thornton	.50	1.25
17 Patrick Marleau	.30	.75
18 Jonathan Cheechoo	.25	.60
19 Vesa Toskala	.25	.60
20 Sidney Crosby	1.25	3.00
21 Marc-Andre Fleury	.60	1.50
22 Mark Recchi	.40	1.00
23 Mario Lemieux	1.25	3.00
24 Shane Doan	.25	.60
25 Jeremy Roenick	.50	1.25
26 Owen Nolan	.30	.75
27 Curtis Joseph	.40	1.00
28 Peter Forsberg	.60	1.50
29 Simon Gagne	.30	.75
30 Jeff Carter	.25	.60
31 Mike Richards	.25	.60
32 Jason Spezza	.30	.75
33 Daniel Alfredsson	.30	.75
34 Dany Heatley	.25	.60
35 Martin Gerber	.25	.60
36 Jaromir Jagr	1.00	2.50
37 Brendan Shanahan	.30	.75
38 Henrik Lundqvist	.75	2.00
39 Petr Prucha	.25	.60
40 Miroslav Satan	.25	.60
41 Rick DiPietro –	.25	.60
42 Alexei Yashin	.25	.60
43 Martin Brodeur	.75	2.00
44 Patrik Elias	.30	.75
45 Brian Gionta	.20	.50
46 Paul Kariya	.30	.75
47 Tomas Vokoun	.25	.60
48 Saku Koivu	.30	.75
49 Michael Ryder	.20	.50
50 Cristobal Huet	.25	.60
51 Chris Higgins	.20	.50
52 Pavol Demitra	.40	1.00
53 Marian Gaborik	.30	.75
54 Manny Fernandez	.20	.50
55 Wayne Gretzky	2.00	5.00
56 Rob Blake	.30	.75
57 Alexander Frolov	.20	.50
58 Ed Belfour	.30	.75
59 Olli Jokinen	.30	.75
60 Todd Bertuzzi	.30	.75
61 Ryan Smyth	.25	.60
62 Ales Hemsky	.25	.60
63 Joffrey Lupul	.20	.50
64 Gordie Howe	1.00	2.50
65 Henrik Zetterberg	.40	1.00
66 Dominik Hasek	.50	1.25
67 Pavel Datsyuk	.50	1.25
68 Nicklas Lidstrom	.30	.75
69 Marty Turco	.30	.75
70 Mike Modano	.50	1.25
71 Eric Lindros	.50	1.25
72 Rick Nash	.30	.75
73 Pascal LeClaire	.25	.60
74 Sergei Fedorov	.50	1.25
75 Joe Sakic	.60	1.50
76 Jose Theodore	.30	.75
77 Milan Hejduk	.25	.60
78 Marek Svatos	.20	.50
79 Martin Havlat	.20	.50
80 Tuomo Ruutu	.30	.75
81 Nikolai Khabibulin	.30	.75
82 Eric Staal	.40	1.00
83 Cam Ward	.30	.75
84 Rod Brind`Amour	.30	.75
85 Miikka Kiprusoff	.30	.75
86 Alex Tanguay	.20	.50
87 Jarome Iginla	.40	1.00
88 Dion Phaneuf	.25	.60
89 Ryan Miller	.30	.75
90 Chris Drury	.25	.60
91 Daniel Briere	.30	.75
92 Patrice Bergeron	.40	1.00
93 Brad Boyes	.20	.50
94 Zdeno Chara	.30	.75
95 Bobby Orr	1.25	3.00
96 Marian Hossa	.30	.75
97 Kari Lehtonen	.25	.60
98 Ilya Kovalchuk	.30	.75
99 Chris Pronger	.30	.75
100 Teemu Selanne	.60	1.50
101 Ales Hemsky N	.75	2.00
102 Alexander Frolov N	.60	1.50
103 Alexander Ovechkin N	4.00	10.00
104 Alexander Steen N	.60	1.50
105 Bobby Orr N	4.00	10.00
106 Brendan Shanahan N	1.00	2.50
107 Cam Ward N	1.00	2.50
108 Dany Heatley N	.75	2.00
109 Dion Phaneuf N	.75	2.00
110 Dominik Hasek N	1.50	4.00
111 Doug Weight N	1.00	2.50
112 Ed Belfour N	1.00	2.50
113 Eric Staal N	1.25	3.00
114 Gordie Howe N	3.00	8.00
115 Henrik Lundqvist N	2.50	6.00
116 Henrik Zetterberg N	1.25	3.00
117 Ilya Kovalchuk N	1.00	2.50
118 Jarome Iginla N	1.25	3.00
119 Jaromir Jagr N	3.00	8.00
120 Larry Robinson N	1.00	2.50
121 Jason Spezza N	1.00	2.50
122 Jay Bouwmeester N	.60	1.50
123 Jeremy Roenick N	1.50	4.00
124 Joe Sakic N	2.00	5.00
125 Joe Thornton N	1.50	4.00
126 Jonathan Cheechoo N	.75	2.00
127 Jose Theodore N	1.00	2.50
128 Kari Lehtonen N	.75	2.00
129 Marc-Andre Fleury N	2.00	5.00
130 Marian Gaborik N	1.00	2.50
131 Mario Lemieux N	4.00	10.00
132 Markus Naslund N	1.00	2.50
133 Martin Brodeur N	2.50	6.00
134 Scott Stevens N	1.00	2.50
135 Martin Havlat N	.60	1.50
136 Martin St. Louis N	1.00	2.50
137 Mats Sundin N	1.00	2.50
138 Michael Ryder N	.60	1.50
139 Miikka Kiprusoff N	1.00	2.50
140 Mike Modano N	1.50	4.00
141 Milan Hejduk N	.75	2.00
142 Nicklas Lidstrom N	1.00	2.50
143 Patrice Bergeron N	1.25	3.00
144 Patrick Roy N	2.50	6.00
145 Paul Kariya N	1.00	2.50
146 Peter Forsberg N	2.00	5.00
147 Bobby Clarke N	1.50	4.00
148 Ray Bourque N	1.50	4.00
149 Rick Nash N	1.00	2.50
150 Rob Blake N	1.00	2.50
151 Roberto Luongo N	1.50	4.00
152 Ryan Miller N	1.00	2.50
153 Saku Koivu N	1.00	2.50
154 Shane Doan N	.75	2.00
155 Sidney Crosby N	6.00	15.00
156 Simon Gagne N	1.00	2.50
157 Teemu Selanne N	2.00	5.00
158 Tomas Vokoun N	.75	2.00
159 Vincent Lecavalier N	1.00	2.50
160 Wayne Gretzky N	6.00	15.00
161 Ryan Shannon AU RC	4.00	10.00
162 Shane O'Brien AU RC	4.00	10.00
163 Phil Kessel AU RC	30.00	80.00
164 Mark Stuart AU RC	4.00	10.00
165 Matt Lashoff AU RC	4.00	10.00
166 Yan Stastny AU RC	4.00	10.00
167 Nate Thompson AU RC	4.00	10.00
168 Drew Stafford AU RC	6.00	15.00
169 Dustin Boyd AU RC	4.00	10.00
170 Brandon Prust AU RC	4.00	10.00
171 Dave Bolland AU RC	6.00	15.00
172 Michael Blunden AU RC	4.00	10.00
173 Dustin Byfuglien AU RC	10.00	25.00
174 Paul Stastny AU RC	10.00	25.00
175 Karri Ramo AU RC	4.00	10.00
176 Loui Eriksson AU RC	10.00	25.00
177 Tomas Kopecky AU RC	5.00	12.00
178 Ladislav Smid AU RC	4.00	10.00
179 M-A Pouliot AU RC	4.00	10.00
180 Niklas Grossman AU RC	10.00	25.00
181 Patrick Thoresen AU RC	4.00	10.00
182 Janis Sprukts AU RC	4.00	10.00
183 P.O'Sullivan AU RC	6.00	15.00
184 Anze Kopitar AU RC	100.00	250.00
185 K.Pushkarev AU RC	5.00	12.00
186 G.Latendresse AU RC	6.00	15.00
187 Shea Weber AU RC	15.00	40.00
188 A.Radulov AU RC	20.00	50.00
189 Travis Zajac AU RC	8.00	20.00
190 Jarkko Immonen AU RC	5.00	12.00
191 Nigel Dawes AU RC	4.00	10.00
192 Kelly Guard AU RC	5.00	12.00
193 Ryan Potulny AU RC	4.00	10.00
194 Benoit Pouliot AU RC	5.00	12.00
195 Keith Yandle AU RC	10.00	25.00
196 Evgeni Malkin AU RC	125.00	200.00
197 Noah Welch AU RC	4.00	10.00
198 Jordan Staal AU RC	8.00	20.00
199 Michel Ouellet AU RC	5.00	12.00
200 K.Letang AU RC	25.00	60.00
201 Matt Carle AU RC	4.00	10.00
202 M-E Vlasic AU RC	6.00	15.00
203 Roman Polak AU RC	5.00	12.00
204 Jeremy Williams AU RC	4.00	10.00
205 Ian White AU RC	5.00	12.00
206 Jesse Schultz AU RC	4.00	10.00
207 Brendan Bell AU RC	4.00	10.00
208 Luc Bourdon AU RC	6.00	15.00
209 Alexander Edler AU RC	6.00	15.00
210 Eric Fehr AU RC	6.00	15.00
211 Daren Machesney RC	2.00	5.00
212 Nathan McIver RC	2.00	5.00
213 Patrick Coulombe RC	2.00	5.00
214 Alexei Mikhnov RC	2.00	5.00
215 Kris Newbury RC	2.00	5.00
216 Blair Jones RC	2.00	5.00
217 Marek Schwarz RC	3.00	8.00
218 David Backes RC	8.00	20.00
219 Joe Pavelski RC	10.00	25.00
220 Patrick Fischer RC	2.00	5.00
221 Bill Thomas RC	2.00	5.00
222 Triston Grant RC	2.00	5.00
223 Lars Jonsson RC	2.00	5.00
224 David Printz RC	2.00	5.00
225 Jussi Timonen RC	2.50	6.00
226 Martin Houle RC	2.50	6.00
227 Josh Hennessy RC	2.00	5.00
228 Blake Comeau RC	3.00	8.00
229 Masi Marjamaki RC	2.00	5.00
230 Ben Ondrus RC	2.00	5.00
231 Fredrik Norrena RC	2.00	5.00
232 Johnny Oduya RC	3.00	8.00
233 Enver Lisin RC	2.00	5.00
234 Mikhail Grabovski RC	6.00	15.00
235 Mikko Lehtonen RC	2.50	6.00
236 Niklas Backstrom RC	4.00	10.00
237 Miroslav Kopriva RC	2.00	5.00
238 Benoit Pouliot RC	2.50	6.00
239 Peter Harrold RC	2.00	5.00
240 David Booth RC	2.50	6.00
241 Drew Larman RC	2.00	5.00
242 Jan Hejda RC	2.00	5.00
243 Jeff Deslauriers RC	2.00	5.00
244 Stefan Liv RC	2.00	5.00
245 Adam Burish RC	3.00	8.00
246 Michael Funk RC	2.00	5.00
247 Mike Card RC	2.00	5.00
248 Adam Dennis RC	2.00	5.00
249 Clarke MacArthur RC	2.50	6.00
250 David McKee RC	2.00	5.00

2006-07 SP Authentic Chirography

AF Alexander Frolov	8.00	20.00
AH Ales Hemsky	6.00	15.00
AK Anze Kopitar	25.00	60.00
BB Brad Boyes	4.00	10.00
CP Corey Perry	8.00	20.00
DH Dany Heatley	12.00	30.00
DR Dwayne Roloson	4.00	10.00
DT Darcy Tucker	8.00	20.00
EM Evgeni Malkin	30.00	80.00
ES Eric Staal	8.00	20.00
GE Martin Gerber	8.00	20.00
HA Dominik Hasek	15.00	40.00
HE Milan Hejduk	6.00	15.00
JC Jonathan Cheechoo	8.00	20.00
JI Jarome Iginla	20.00	50.00
JS Jordan Staal	15.00	40.00
KD Kris Draper	6.00	15.00
MC Mike Cammalleri	8.00	20.00
MF Marc-Andre Fleury	15.00	40.00
MG Marian Gaborik	12.00	30.00
MH Martin Havlat	6.00	15.00
MM Mike Modano	10.00	25.00
MP Michael Peca	8.00	20.00
MS Marek Svatos	6.00	15.00
MT Marty Turco	8.00	20.00
NL Nicklas Lidstrom	15.00	30.00
PE Patrik Elias	6.00	15.00
PM Patrick Marleau	8.00	20.00
PO Patrick O'Sullivan	12.00	30.00
PP Petr Prucha	4.00	10.00
RM Ryan Miller	15.00	40.00
RN Rick Nash	15.00	40.00
RS Matt Carle	6.00	15.00
SC Sidney Crosby EXCH	100.00	200.00
TV Tomas Vokoun	8.00	20.00

2006-07 SP Authentic Limited

*1-100 LIMITED: 4X TO 10X BASIC CARDS
*101-160 NOTABLES: 1.2X TO 3X
*161-210 ROOKIE PATCH AU: 1.2X TO 3X
*211-250 ROOKIES: 1.2X TO 3X

184 Anze Kopitar JSY AU	125.00	300.00
196 Evgeni Malkin JSY AU	250.00	400.00
198 Jordan Staal JSY AU	50.00	100.00
209 Alexander Edler JSY AU	30.00	80.00

2006-07 SP Authentic Sign of the Times

STAF Alexander Frolov	4.00	10.00
STAH Ales Hemsky	5.00	12.00
STAR Andrew Raycroft	5.00	12.00
STBG Brian Gionta	4.00	10.00
STBH Bobby Hull SP	12.00	30.00
STBO Bobby Orr	50.00	125.00
STBU Johnny Bucyk	10.00	25.00
STCA Colby Armstrong SP	10.00	25.00
STCP Corey Perry	10.00	25.00
STCW Cam Ward	6.00	15.00
STDC Don Cherry	15.00	40.00
STDH Dominik Hasek	20.00	50.00
STDP Dion Phaneuf	12.00	30.00
STDR Dwayne Roloson	5.00	12.00
STDS Denis Savard	6.00	15.00
STEL Patrik Elias	6.00	15.00
STEM Evgeni Malkin	25.00	60.00
STES Eric Staal	8.00	20.00
STGB Gilbert Brule	5.00	12.00
STGE Martin Gerber SP	5.00	12.00
STGH Gordie Howe	50.00	125.00
STGO Scott Gomez	5.00	12.00
STHE Dany Heatley	5.00	12.00
STHJ Milan Hejduk	5.00	12.00
STIB Ray Bourque SP	25.00	60.00
STJB Jean Beliveau SP EXCH	150.00	250.00
STJC Jonathan Cheechoo	5.00	12.00
STJE Jeff Carter	5.00	12.00
STJG Jean-Sebastien Giguere	6.00	15.00
STJI Jarome Iginla	8.00	20.00
STJK Jari Kurri	6.00	15.00
STJM Joe Mullen	5.00	12.00
STJS Jarret Stoll	5.00	12.00
STJT Jose Theodore	6.00	15.00
STJW Justin Williams	5.00	12.00
STKD Kris Draper	4.00	10.00
STLR Luc Robitaille SP	25.00	60.00
STMA Matt Carle	4.00	10.00
STMB Martin Brodeur	30.00	80.00
STMF Marc-Andre Fleury	15.00	40.00
STMH Martin Havlat	4.00	10.00
STMI Ryan Miller	6.00	15.00
STML Mario Lemieux SP	80.00	150.00
STMM Mike Modano	10.00	25.00
STMO Brenden Morrow	5.00	12.00
STMT Marty Turco	6.00	15.00
STNL Nicklas Lidstrom	6.00	15.00
STPB Pierre-Marc Bouchard SP	6.00	15.00
STPE Michael Peca	5.00	12.00
STPK Phil Kessel	12.00	30.00
STPM Patrick Marleau SP	6.00	15.00
STPP Petr Prucha SP	5.00	12.00
STRN Rick Nash	6.00	15.00
STRS Ryan Smyth	5.00	12.00
STRY Michael Ryder	4.00	10.00
STSB Steve Bernier	4.00	10.00
STSC Sidney Crosby	80.00	200.00
STSK Saku Koivu SP	6.00	15.00
STSV Marek Svatos	4.00	10.00
STTE Tony Esposito	15.00	40.00
STTV Tomas Vokoun	5.00	12.00
STVT Vesa Toskala	5.00	12.00
STWC Wendel Clark	12.00	30.00
STWG Wayne Gretzky	250.00	600.00
STWO Willie O'Ree SP	20.00	50.00

2006-07 SP Authentic Sign of the Times Duals

STAS G.Anderson/R.Smyth	10.00	25.00
STBE R.Ellis/J.Bower	12.00	30.00
STBG M.Bossy/C.Gillies	15.00	40.00
STBM R.Blake/L.Murphy	12.00	30.00
STBW M.Brodeur/C.Ward	30.00	80.00
STCB J.Cheechoo/S.Bernier	10.00	25.00
STCC B.Clarke/J.Carter	20.00	50.00
STCG D. Ciccarelli/M. Gaborik	12.00	30.00
STCT G.Cheevers/H.Toivonen	12.00	30.00
STDS S.Koivu/D.Savard	12.00	30.00
STDV M.Dionne/R.Vachon	20.00	50.00
STDW D.Gilmour/W.Clark	20.00	50.00
STEG P.Elias/B.Gionta	12.00	30.00
STET T.Esposito/M.Turco	12.00	30.00
STFK A.Frolov/A.Kopitar	15.00	40.00
STFM B.Federko/J.Mullen	10.00	25.00
STGL M.Lemieux/W.Gretzky SP	300.00	800.00
STGR G.Fuhr/R.Miller	15.00	40.00
STHA D.Aebischer/C.Huet	10.00	25.00
STHE D.Heatley/P.Eaves	10.00	25.00
STHK M.Havlat/N.Khabibulin	12.00	30.00
STHO B.Orr/G.Howe	150.00	300.00
STHS M.Hejduk/M.Svatos	10.00	25.00
STIT Iginla/Tanguay	15.00	40.00
STKB P.Bergeron/P.Kessel	50.00	125.00
STKL I.Kovalchuk/K.Lehtonen	12.00	30.00
STLB R.Luongo/R.Brodeur	20.00	50.00
STLG S.Gagne/R.Leach	12.00	30.00
STLM M.Lemieux/E.Malkin SP	100.00	200.00
STLR G.Lafleur/M.Ryder	15.00	40.00
STLS N.Lidstrom/B.Salming	20.00	50.00
STLT V.Lecavalier/J.Thornton	20.00	50.00
STMC G.Lafleur/L.Robinson	15.00	40.00
STMM M.Modano/B.Morrow	20.00	50.00
STMR M.Modano/M.Ribeiro	20.00	50.00
STNB R.Nash/G.Brule	12.00	30.00
STNK C.Neely/P.Kessel	25.00	60.00
STOB B.Orr/R.Bourque	80.00	150.00
STPJ P.Marleau/J.Cheechoo	12.00	30.00
STPP Z.Parise/J.Parise	12.00	30.00
STQC P.Stastny/P.Stastny	20.00	50.00
STRB P.Roy/M.Brodeur SP	100.00	200.00
STRL M.Ryder/G.Latendresse	12.00	30.00
STRP D.Potvin/L.Robinson	12.00	30.00
STRR D.Roloson/B.Ranford	12.00	30.00
STRT L.Robitaille/D.Taylor	12.00	30.00
STSA C.Armstrong/J.Staal	20.00	50.00
STSS E.Staal/J.Staal	20.00	50.00
STSW E.Staal/C.Ward	15.00	40.00
STVA Vokoun/Arnott	10.00	25.00
STVH T.Vokoun/D.Hasek	20.00	50.00
STWR S.Weber/A.Radulov	20.00	50.00

2006-07 SP Authentic Sign of the Times Triples

ST3BBK Boyes/Berg/Kessel	30.00	80.00
ST3BEK Ellis/Bower/Kelly	30.00	80.00
ST3COS Cheev/O'Reilly/Sand	15.00	40.00
ST3DBM Drury/Briere/Miller	15.00	40.00
ST3HNS Heatley/Nash/Staal	20.00	50.00
ST3HTS Hejduk/Theo/Svatos	15.00	40.00
ST3ITK Iginla/Tang/Kipper	20.00	50.00
ST3LFM Mario/Fleury/Malkin	200.00	300.00
ST3LGH Lemieux/Gretz/Howe	600.00	1500.00
ST3LHZ Lidstrom/Holm/Zetter	40.00	100.00
ST3LRS Lafleur/Shutt/Robin	20.00	50.00
ST3MTC Marleau/Thorn/Chee	25.00	60.00
ST3MTM Modano/Turco/Morr	30.00	80.00
ST3NLM Nasl/Luongo/Morris	25.00	60.00
ST3OBE Espo/Orr/Bourque	150.00	250.00
ST3PGB Parrish/Gabby/Bouch	15.00	40.00
ST3RBW Roy/Brodeur/Ward	100.00	250.00
ST3RHG Redden/Heats/Gerb	12.00	30.00
ST3RKH Higgins/Koivu/Ryder	15.00	40.00
ST3RPT Raycroft/Peca/Tuck	12.00	30.00
ST3SSH Smyth/Stoll/Hemsky	12.00	30.00
ST3SSS Stastnys	25.00	60.00
ST3WSW Williams/Staal/Ward	20.00	50.00
ST3SUT1 Sutter/Sutter/Sutter	20.00	50.00
ST3SUT2 Sutter/Sutter/Sutter	15.00	40.00

2007-08 SP Authentic

COMP.SET w/o SP's (100)	10.00	25.00
1 Daniel Briere	.30	.75
2 Simon Gagne	.30	.75
3 Jeff Carter	.25	.60
4 Alexander Ovechkin	1.25	3.00
5 Olaf Kolzig	.30	.75
6 Alexander Semin	.30	.75
7 Patrice Bergeron	.40	1.00
8 Marc Savard	.20	.50
9 Phil Kessel	.30	.75
10 Tomas Vokoun	.25	.60
11 Nathan Horton	.30	.75
12 Olli Jokinen	.25	.60
13 Eric Staal	.40	1.00
14 Cam Ward	.30	.75
15 Rod Brind`Amour	.30	.75
16 Saku Koivu	.30	.75
17 Michael Ryder	.20	.50
18 Guillaume Latendresse	.25	.60
19 Cristobal Huet	.25	.60
20 Mats Sundin	.30	.75
21 Vesa Toskala	.25	.60
22 Darcy Tucker	.25	.60
23 Alexander Steen	.20	.50
24 Rick DiPietro	.25	.60
25 Bill Guerin	.30	.75
26 Miroslav Satan	.25	.60
27 Vincent Lecavalier	.30	.75
28 Brad Richards	.30	.75
29 Martin St. Louis	.30	.75
30 Jaromir Jagr	1.00	2.50
31 Henrik Lundqvist	.75	2.00
32 Brendan Shanahan	.30	.75
33 Chris Drury	.25	.60
34 Sidney Crosby	1.25	3.00
35 Evgeni Malkin	.60	1.50
36 Marc-Andre Fleury	.60	1.50
37 Jordan Staal	.25	.60
38 Dany Heatley	.25	.60
39 Ray Emery	.25	.60
40 Jason Spezza	.30	.75
41 Daniel Alfredsson	.30	.75
42 Ilya Kovalchuk	.30	.75
43 Kari Lehtonen	.25	.60
44 Marian Hossa	.30	.75
45 Martin Brodeur	.75	2.00
46 Patrik Elias	.30	.75
47 Zach Parise	.30	.75
48 Ryan Miller	.30	.75
49 Thomas Vanek	.25	.60
50 Jason Pominville	.20	.50
51 Shane Doan	.25	.60
52 Ilya Bryzgalov	.30	.75
53 Ed Jovanovski	.25	.60
54 Anze Kopitar	.50	1.25
55 Rob Blake	.30	.75
56 Alexander Frolov	.20	.50
57 Martin Havlat	.30	.75
58 Nikolai Khabibulin	.30	.75
59 Tuomo Ruutu	.30	.75
60 Ales Hemsky	.25	.60
61 Joni Pitkanen	.20	.50
62 Dwayne Roloson	.25	.60
63 Rick Nash	.30	.75
64 Sergei Fedorov	.50	1.25
65 David Vyborny	.20	.50
66 Paul Kariya	.30	.75
67 Manny Legace	.25	.60
68 Keith Tkachuk	.30	.75
69 Joe Sakic	.60	1.50
70 Ryan Smyth	.25	.60
71 Paul Stastny	.25	.60
72 Milan Hejduk	.25	.60
73 Jarome Iginla	.40	1.00
74 Miikka Kiprusoff	.30	.75
75 Alex Tanguay	.25	.60
76 Dion Phaneuf	.25	.60
77 Marian Gaborik	.30	.75
78 Mikko Koivu	.25	.60
79 Niklas Backstrom	.30	.75
80 Mike Modano	.50	1.25
81 Marty Turco	.30	.75
82 Mike Ribeiro	.20	.50
83 Joe Thornton	.50	1.25
84 Jonathan Cheechoo	.25	.60
85 Patrick Marleau	.30	.75
86 Chris Mason	.25	.60
87 Alexander Radulov	.30	.75
88 Jason Arnott	.25	.60
89 Roberto Luongo	.50	1.25
90 Markus Naslund	.30	.75
91 Henrik Sedin	.40	1.00
92 Daniel Sedin	.40	1.00
93 Ryan Getzlaf	.30	.75
94 Jean-Sebastien Giguere	.30	.75
95 Doug Weight	.30	.75
96 Chris Pronger	.30	.75
97 Pavel Datsyuk	.50	1.25
98 Nicklas Lidstrom	.30	.75
99 Henrik Zetterberg	.40	1.00
100 Dominik Hasek	.50	1.25
101 Alexander Ovechkin NOT	5.00	12.00
102 Markus Naslund NOT	1.25	3.00
103 Roberto Luongo NOT	2.00	5.00
104 Frank Mahovlich NOT	1.25	3.00
105 Mats Sundin NOT	1.25	3.00
106 Martin St. Louis NOT	1.25	3.00
107 Vincent Lecavalier NOT	1.25	3.00
108 Paul Kariya NOT	1.25	3.00
109 Brad Boyes NOT	.75	2.00
110 Patrick Marleau NOT	1.25	3.00
111 Joe Thornton NOT	2.00	5.00
112 Evgeni Malkin NOT	2.50	6.00
113 Marc-Andre Fleury NOT	2.50	6.00
114 Mario Lemieux NOT	5.00	12.00
115 Sidney Crosby NOT	5.00	12.00
116 Shane Doan NOT	1.00	2.50
117 Bernie Parent NOT	1.50	4.00
118 Bobby Clarke NOT	2.00	5.00
119 Daniel Briere NOT	1.25	3.00
120 Ron Hextall NOT	1.25	3.00
121 Simon Gagne NOT	1.25	3.00
122 Dany Heatley NOT	1.00	2.50
123 Ray Emery NOT	1.00	2.50
124 Brendan Shanahan NOT	1.25	3.00
125 Jaromir Jagr NOT	4.00	10.00
126 Mark Messier NOT	2.50	6.00
127 Rick DiPietro NOT	1.00	2.50
128 Zach Parise NOT	1.25	3.00
129 Martin Brodeur NOT	3.00	8.00
130 Guy Lafleur NOT	1.50	4.00
131 Larry Robinson NOT	1.25	3.00
132 Saku Koivu NOT	1.25	3.00
133 Marian Gaborik NOT	1.25	3.00
134 Luc Robitaille NOT	1.25	3.00
135 Tomas Vokoun NOT	1.00	2.50
136 Grant Fuhr NOT	2.00	5.00
137 Jari Kurri NOT	1.25	3.00
138 Wayne Gretzky NOT	8.00	20.00
139 Henrik Zetterberg NOT	1.50	4.00
140 Dominik Hasek NOT	2.00	5.00
141 Gordie Howe NOT	4.00	10.00
142 Nicklas Lidstrom NOT	1.25	3.00
143 Mike Modano NOT	2.00	5.00
144 Rick Nash NOT	1.25	3.00
145 Paul Stastny NOT	1.00	2.50
146 Joe Sakic NOT	2.50	6.00
147 Bobby Hull NOT	2.50	6.00
148 Stan Mikita NOT	1.50	4.00
149 Tony Esposito NOT	1.25	3.00
150 Jarome Iginla NOT	1.50	4.00
151 Miikka Kiprusoff NOT	1.25	3.00
152 Gilbert Perreault NOT	1.25	3.00
153 Thomas Vanek NOT	1.00	2.50
154 Bobby Orr NOT	5.00	12.00
155 Johnny Bucyk NOT	1.25	3.00
156 Patrice Bergeron NOT	1.50	4.00
157 Phil Esposito NOT	2.00	5.00
158 Ray Bourque NOT	2.00	5.00
159 J-S Giguere NOT	1.25	3.00
160 Ryan Getzlaf NOT	1.25	3.00
161 Petteri Wirtanen RC	2.50	6.00
162 Kent Huskins RC	2.50	6.00
163 Mike Weber RC	2.50	6.00
164 Mark Mancari RC	2.50	6.00
165 Kris Russell RC	4.00	10.00
166 Matt Keetley RC	2.50	6.00
167 David Moss RC	4.00	10.00
168 Magnus Johansson RC	2.50	6.00
169 David Koci RC	2.50	6.00
170 Jeff Finger RC	2.50	6.00
171 Tomas Popperle RC	2.50	6.00
172 Chris Conner RC	2.50	6.00
173 Joel Lundqvist RC	2.50	6.00
174 Matt Ellis RC	3.00	8.00
175 Bryan Young RC	2.50	6.00
176 Liam Reddox RC	2.50	6.00
177 Jonathan Quick RC	100.00	200.00
178 Cal Clutterbuck RC	4.00	10.00
179 Sergei Kostitsyn RC	3.00	8.00
180 Ryan O'Byrne RC	4.00	10.00
181 Mark Fraser RC	2.50	6.00
182 Cody Bass RC	2.50	6.00
183 Riley Cote RC	3.00	8.00
184 Craig Weller RC	2.50	6.00
185 Daniel Winnik RC	3.00	8.00
186 Tyler Kennedy RC	2.50	6.00
187 Lukas Kaspar RC	2.50	6.00
188 Tomas Plihal RC	2.50	6.00
189 Mike Lundin RC	2.50	6.00
190 Chris Bourque RC	3.00	8.00
191 Jonas Hiller AU RC	6.00	15.00
192 Drew Miller AU RC	4.00	10.00
193 Bobby Ryan AU RC	8.00	20.00
194 Ryan Carter AU RC	3.00	8.00
195 Bryan Little AU RC	5.00	12.00
196 Brett Sterling AU RC	3.00	8.00
197 Tobias Enstrom AU RC	6.00	15.00
198 Ondrej Pavelec AU RC	6.00	15.00
199 Milan Lucic AU RC	15.00	40.00
200 David Krejci AU RC	20.00	50.00
201 Tuukka Rask AU RC	80.00	200.00
202 Curtis McElhinney AU RC	5.00	12.00
203 Jonathan Toews AU RC	150.00	225.00
204 Patrick Kane AU RC	350.00	600.00
205 Jaroslav Hlinka AU RC	4.00	10.00
206 Tyler Weiman AU RC	4.00	10.00
207 Jonathan Sigalet AU RC	3.00	8.00
208 Jared Boll AU RC	4.00	10.00
209 Marc Methot AU RC	3.00	8.00
210 Matt Niskanen AU RC	5.00	12.00
211 Tobias Stephan AU RC	4.00	10.00
212 Andrew Cogliano AU RC	4.00	10.00
213 Sam Gagner AU RC	6.00	15.00
214 Tom Gilbert AU RC	4.00	10.00
215 Rob Schremp AU RC	4.00	10.00
216 Cory Murphy AU RC	3.00	8.00
217 Stefan Meyer AU RC	4.00	10.00
218 Jack Johnson AU RC	4.00	10.00
219 Jonathan Bernier AU RC	15.00	40.00
220 Lauri Tukonen AU RC	3.00	8.00
221 Petr Kalus AU RC	3.00	8.00
222 James Sheppard AU RC	3.00	8.00
223 Jaroslav Halak AU RC	10.00	25.00
224 Kyle Chipchura AU RC	5.00	12.00
225 Carey Price AU RC	250.00	600.00
226 Ville Koistinen AU RC	3.00	8.00
227 Nicklas Bergfors AU RC	3.00	8.00
228 Andy Greene AU RC	4.00	10.00
229 Frans Nielsen AU RC	5.00	12.00
230 Ryan Callahan AU RC	6.00	15.00
231 Marc Staal AU RC	5.00	12.00
232 Brandon Dubinsky AU RC	6.00	15.00
233 Daniel Girardi AU RC	4.00	10.00
234 Brian Elliott AU RC	6.00	15.00
235 Nick Foligno AU RC	6.00	15.00
236 Ryan Parent AU RC	3.00	8.00
237 Peter Mueller AU RC	4.00	10.00
238 Martin Hanzal AU RC	4.00	10.00
239 Daniel Carcillo AU RC	4.00	10.00
240 Torrey Mitchell AU RC	4.00	10.00
241 Devin Setoguchi AU RC	5.00	12.00
242 Erik Johnson AU RC	5.00	12.00
243 David Perron AU RC	20.00	50.00
244 Steve Wagner AU RC	3.00	8.00
245 Matt Smaby AU RC	3.00	8.00
246 Anton Stralman AU RC	3.00	8.00
247 Jiri Tlusty AU RC	5.00	12.00
248 Jannik Hansen AU RC	4.00	10.00
249 Mason Raymond AU RC	5.00	12.00
250 Nicklas Backstrom AU RC	20.00	50.00

2007-08 SP Authentic Limited

*1-100 VETS: 1.5X TO 4X BASIC CARDS
*101-160 NOTABLE: .6X TO 1.5X
*161-190 ROOKIES: .8X TO 2X

177 Jonathan Quick	150.00	250.00
191 Jonas Hiller AU PATCH	20.00	50.00
192 Drew Miller AU PATCH	12.00	30.00
193 Bobby Ryan AU PATCH	25.00	60.00
194 Ryan Carter AU PATCH	10.00	25.00
195 Bryan Little AU PATCH	12.00	30.00
196 Brett Sterling AU PATCH	10.00	25.00
197 Tobias Enstrom AU PATCH	20.00	50.00
198 Ondrej Pavelec AU PATCH	25.00	60.00
199 Milan Lucic AU PATCH	75.00	150.00
200 David Krejci AU PATCH	50.00	125.00
202 Curtis McElhinney AU PATCH	15.00	40.00
203 Jonathan Toews AU PATCH	300.00	500.00
204 Patrick Kane AU PATCH	500.00	800.00
205 Jaroslav Hlinka AU PATCH	12.00	30.00
206 Tyler Weiman AU PATCH	12.00	30.00
207 Jonathan Sigalet AU PATCH	10.00	25.00
208 Jared Boll AU PATCH	12.00	30.00
209 Marc Methot AU PATCH	10.00	25.00
210 Matt Niskanen AU PATCH	15.00	40.00
211 Tobias Stephan AU PATCH	12.00	30.00
212 Andrew Cogliano AU PATCH	12.00	30.00
213 Sam Gagner AU PATCH	20.00	50.00
214 Tom Gilbert AU PATCH	12.00	30.00
215 Rob Schremp AU PATCH	12.00	30.00
218 Jack Johnson AU PATCH	12.00	30.00
219 Jonathan Bernier AU PATCH	40.00	100.00
220 Lauri Tukonen AU PATCH	10.00	25.00
221 Petr Kalus AU PATCH	10.00	25.00
222 James Sheppard AU PATCH	10.00	25.00
223 Jaroslav Halak AU PATCH	20.00	50.00
224 Kyle Chipchura AU PATCH	15.00	40.00
225 Carey Price AU PATCH	800.00	2000.00
226 Ville Koistinen AU PATCH	10.00	25.00
227 Nicklas Bergfors AU PATCH	10.00	25.00
228 Andy Greene AU PATCH	12.00	30.00
229 Frans Nielsen AU PATCH	15.00	40.00
230 Ryan Callahan AU PATCH	20.00	50.00
231 Marc Staal AU PATCH	15.00	40.00
232 B.Dubinsky AU PATCH	20.00	50.00
233 Daniel Girardi AU PATCH	12.00	30.00
234 Brian Elliott AU PATCH	20.00	50.00
235 Nick Foligno AU PATCH	20.00	50.00
236 Ryan Parent AU PATCH	10.00	25.00
237 Peter Mueller AU PATCH	12.00	30.00
238 Martin Hanzal AU PATCH	12.00	30.00
239 Daniel Carcillo AU PATCH	12.00	30.00
240 Torrey Mitchell AU PATCH	12.00	30.00
241 Devin Setoguchi AU PATCH	15.00	40.00
242 Erik Johnson AU PATCH	15.00	40.00
243 David Perron AU PATCH	30.00	80.00
244 Steve Wagner AU PATCH	10.00	25.00
245 Matt Smaby AU PATCH	10.00	25.00
246 Anton Stralman AU PATCH	10.00	25.00
247 Jiri Tlusty AU PATCH	15.00	40.00
248 Jannik Hansen AU PATCH	12.00	30.00
249 Mason Raymond AU PATCH	15.00	40.00
250 N.Backstrom AU PATCH	50.00	100.00

2007-08 SP Authentic Chirography

AO Alexander Ovechkin	40.00	100.00
AR Alexander Radulov	10.00	25.00
DH Dany Heatley	12.00	30.00
IK Ilya Kovalchuk	15.00	40.00
JG Jean-Sebastien Giguere	6.00	15.00
JI Jarome Iginla	12.00	30.00
JT Joe Thornton	12.50	30.00
MB Martin Brodeur	25.00	60.00
MG Marian Gaborik	8.00	20.00
MM Mike Modano	12.50	30.00
MN Markus Naslund	10.00	25.00
NL Nicklas Lidstrom	12.50	30.00
PB Patrice Bergeron	8.00	20.00
RM Ryan Miller	12.00	30.00
RN Rick Nash	12.00	30.00
SC Sidney Crosby	100.00	200.00
SD Shane Doan	10.00	25.00
SG Simon Gagne	10.00	25.00
SK Saku Koivu	10.00	25.00
VL Vincent Lecavalier	12.50	30.00

2007-08 SP Authentic Holoview FX

COMPLETE SET (42)	50.00	100.00
FX1 Alexander Ovechkin	5.00	12.00
FX2 Alexander Radulov	1.25	3.00

FX3 Patrick Kane 5.00 12.00
FX4 Brendan Shanahan 1.25 3.00
FX5 Dany Heatley 1.00 2.50
FX6 Dwayne Roloson 1.00 2.50
FX7 Eric Staal 1.50 4.00
FX8 Evgeni Malkin 2.50 6.00
FX9 Henrik Zetterberg 1.50 4.00
FX10 Ilya Kovalchuk 1.25 3.00
FX11 Jarome Iginla 1.50 4.00
FX12 Jaromir Jagr 4.00 10.00
FX13 Jason Spezza 1.25 3.00
FX14 Jean-Sebastien Giguere 1.25 3.00
FX15 Joe Sakic 2.50 6.00
FX16 Joe Thornton 2.00 5.00
FX17 Marian Gaborik 1.25 3.00
FX18 Markus Naslund 1.25 3.00
FX19 Martin Brodeur 3.00 8.00
FX20 Martin St. Louis 1.25 3.00
FX21 Marty Turco 1.25 3.00
FX22 Mats Sundin 1.25 3.00
FX23 Michael Ryder .75 2.00
FX24 Miikka Kiprusoff 1.25 3.00
FX25 Mike Modano 2.00 5.00
FX26 Nicklas Lidstrom 1.25 3.00
FX27 Patrice Bergeron 1.50 4.00
FX28 Patrick Marleau 1.25 3.00
FX29 Paul Kariya 1.25 3.00
FX30 Phil Kessel 1.25 3.00
FX31 Rick Nash 1.25 3.00
FX32 Roberto Luongo 2.00 5.00
FX33 Ryan Getzlaf 1.25 3.00
FX34 Ryan Smyth 1.00 2.50
FX35 Saku Koivu 1.25 3.00
FX36 Jonathan Toews 5.00 12.00
FX37 Sidney Crosby 5.00 12.00
FX38 Simon Gagne 1.25 3.00
FX39 Thomas Vanek 1.00 2.50
FX40 Carey Price 5.00 12.00
FX41 Vincent Lecavalier 1.25 3.00
FX42 Zach Parise 1.25 3.00

2007-08 SP Authentic Holoview FX Die Cuts

*DIE CUTS: .8X TO 2X BASIC

2007-08 SP Authentic Prestigious Pairings

PPCR J.Cheechoo/M.Ryder 8.00 20.00
PPDH D.Heatley/S.Doan 12.00 30.00
PPGS M.St. Louis/S.Gagne 8.00 20.00
PPGT J.Giguere/M.Turco 12.00 30.00
PPHG M.Gaborik/M.Hossa EXCH 8.00 20.00
PPIN J.Iginla/R.Nash 12.00 30.00
PPJJ E.Johnson/J.Johnson 12.00 30.00
PPKR Kovalchuk/Radulov EXCH 15.00 40.00
PPKS P.Stastny/A.Kopitar EXCH 12.00 30.00
PPLS Lidstrom/Salming EXCH 12.00 30.00
PPLT Thornton/Lecavalier EXCH 15.00 40.00
PPMM M.Modano/J.Mullen 12.00 30.00
PPOM A.Ovechkin/E.Malkin 75.00 150.00
PPRP C.Perry/M.Richards EXCH 12.00 30.00
PPTB P.Bergeron/A.Tanguay 8.00 20.00
PPVH D.Hasek/T.Vokoun EXCH 12.00 30.00
PPVL T.Vanek/G.Latendresse 12.00 30.00

2007-08 SP Authentic Rookie Review Autographed Patches

RRAK Anze Kopitar 30.00 80.00
RRAO Alexander Ovechkin 600.00 1500.00
RRAR Andrew Raycroft 15.00 40.00
RRAT Alex Tanguay 15.00 40.00
RRBL Brian Leetch 15.00 40.00
RRCD Chris Drury 15.00 40.00
RRCW Cam Ward 20.00 50.00
RRDC Dino Ciccarelli 20.00 50.00
RRDH Dale Hawerchuk 25.00 60.00
RREM Evgeni Malkin 50.00 100.00
RREN Evgeni Nabokov 15.00 40.00
RRHE Dany Heatley 20.00 50.00
RRJC Jonathan Cheechoo 15.00 40.00
RRJI Jarome Iginla 15.00 40.00
RRJP Joni Pitkanen 12.00 30.00
RRJT Joe Thornton 20.00 50.00
RRJW Justin Williams 15.00 40.00
RRKB Kevin Bieksa 15.00 40.00
RRKD Kris Draper 10.00 25.00
RRMG Marian Gaborik 20.00 50.00
RRMH Marian Hossa 20.00 50.00
RRMM Mike Modano 30.00 80.00
RRMR Mike Ribeiro 12.00 30.00
RRMS Marc Savard 12.00 30.00
RRMT Marty Turco 20.00 50.00
RRNL Nicklas Lidstrom 20.00 50.00
RRPB Patrice Bergeron 25.00 50.00
RRPS Paul Stastny 15.00 40.00
RRRB Ray Bourque 25.00 60.00
RRRN Rick Nash 20.00 50.00
RRSC Sidney Crosby 100.00 200.00
RRSG Scott Gomez 15.00 40.00
RRST Peter Stastny 15.00 40.00
RRTH Jose Theodore 20.00 50.00

2007-08 SP Authentic Sign of the Times

STAC Andrew Cogliano 5.00 12.00
STAF Alexander Frolov 4.00 10.00
STAK Anze Kopitar 10.00 25.00
STAM Andy McDonald 5.00 12.00
STAO Adam Oates 6.00 15.00
STAT Alex Tanguay 5.00 12.00
STBA Nicklas Backstrom 10.00 25.00
STBB Brad Boyes 4.00 10.00
STBC Bobby Clarke 10.00 25.00
STBE Steve Bernier 8.00 20.00
STBF Bernie Federko 5.00 12.00
STBG Brian Gionta 4.00 10.00
STBI Kevin Bieksa 5.00 12.00
STBL Bryan Little 5.00 12.00
STBO Bobby Orr SP 175.00 300.00
STBP Bob Probert 20.00 50.00
STBR Dustin Brown 6.00 15.00
STCG Clark Gillies 6.00 15.00
STCK Chuck Kobasew 4.00 10.00
STCP Carey Price 60.00 150.00
STDB Dustin Boyd 4.00 10.00
STDG Doug Gilmour 8.00 20.00
STDH Dominik Hasek 12.00 30.00
STDT Darcy Tucker 5.00 12.00
STDW Doug Wilson 5.00 12.00
STEJ Erik Johnson 8.00 20.00
STEM Evgeni Malkin 25.00 60.00
STER Loui Eriksson 6.00 15.00
STES Eric Staal 8.00 20.00
STFP Fernando Pisani 4.00 10.00
STGB Gilbert Brule 5.00 12.00
STGF Grant Fuhr 12.00 30.00
STGH Gordie Howe SP 75.00 150.00
STHL Hakan Loob 4.00 10.00
STJA Jason Arnott 5.00 12.00
STJB Jonathan Bernier 6.00 15.00
STJC Jonathan Cheechoo 8.00 20.00
STJG Jean-Sebastien Giguere 6.00 15.00
STJI Jarome Iginla 10.00 25.00
STJJ Jack Johnson 5.00 12.00
STJK Jari Kurri SP 25.00 60.00
STJP Joni Pitkanen 4.00 10.00
STJS Jordan Staal 15.00 40.00
STJT Jonathan Toews 50.00 100.00
STJW Justin Williams 5.00 12.00
STKA Petr Kalus 4.00 10.00
STKB Keith Ballard 4.00 10.00
STKD Kris Draper 4.00 10.00
STKE Ryan Kesler 6.00 15.00
STKH Kelly Hrudey 5.00 12.00
STLE Brian Leetch 8.00 20.00
STLM Lanny McDonald 6.00 15.00
STMB Martin Brodeur SP 60.00 120.00
STMC Mike Cammalleri 5.00 12.00
STMD Marcel Dionne 30.00 60.00
STMF Marc-Andre Fleury 15.00 40.00
STMG Marian Gaborik 6.00 15.00
STMH Marian Hossa 6.00 15.00
STML Mario Lemieux SP 175.00 300.00
STMM Mark Messier 30.00 80.00
STMN Markus Naslund 6.00 15.00
STMO Mike Modano 15.00 40.00
STMP Marc-Antoine Pouliot 4.00 10.00
STMR Michael Ryder 4.00 10.00
STMS Marc Savard 4.00 10.00
STMT Marty Turco 8.00 20.00
STNB Nicklas Backstrom 20.00 50.00
STNF Nick Foligno 10.00 25.00
STNG Niklas Grossman 4.00 10.00
STNO Fredrik Norrena 4.00 10.00
STNZ Nikolai Zherdev 4.00 10.00
STOV Alexander Ovechkin 200.00 500.00
STPK Patrick Kane 80.00 200.00
STPM Peter Mueller 5.00 12.00
STPO Patrick O'Sullivan 5.00 12.00
STPP Petr Prucha 4.00 10.00
STPR Brandon Prust 4.00 10.00
STPS Paul Stastny 5.00 12.00
STRA Andrew Raycroft 5.00 12.00
STRI Mike Richards 5.00 12.00
STRK Red Kelly 8.00 20.00
STRP Ryan Parent 8.00 20.00
STRS Rob Schremp 5.00 12.00
STRY Ryan Potulny 4.00 10.00
STSA Miroslav Satan 5.00 12.00
STSB Scotty Bowman 10.00 25.00
STSC Sidney Crosby SP 125.00 250.00
STSD Shane Doan 5.00 12.00
STSS Steve Shutt 5.00 12.00
STST Martin St. Louis 6.00 15.00
STTK Tomas Kopecky 5.00 12.00
STTV Tomas Vokoun 5.00 12.00
STVF Valtteri Filppula 4.00 10.00
STVL Vincent Lecavalier 10.00 25.00
STWG Wayne Gretzky SP 300.00 800.00

2007-08 SP Authentic Sign of the Times Duals

ST2AN Ovechkin/Backstrom 100.00 250.00
ST2BC B.Clarke/J.Bucyk 15.00 40.00
ST2BG M.Bossy/C.Gillies 15.00 40.00
ST2BK P.Bergeron/P.Kessel 15.00 40.00
ST2CB Cheechoo/Bernier 8.00 20.00
ST2CG Cogliano/Gagner 15.00 40.00
ST2CH B.Clarke/R.Hextall 20.00 50.00
ST2DH D.Heatley/S.Doan 10.00 25.00
ST2FK A.Frolov/A.Kopitar 8.00 20.00
ST2FR G.Fuhr/B.Ranford 20.00 50.00
ST2FS M.Fleury/J.Staal 25.00 60.00
ST2GS M.Gaborik/J.Sheppard 12.00 30.00
ST2HM G.Howe/M.Messier 100.00 200.00
ST2IT J.Iginla/A.Tanguay 15.00 40.00
ST2KL I.Kovalchuk/B.Little 12.00 30.00
ST2LH Lidstrom/Holmstrom 15.00 40.00
ST2LS Lecavalier/M.St. Louis 15.00 40.00
ST2MM M.Modano/B.Morrow 20.00 50.00
ST2MP A.McDonald/C.Perry 10.00 25.00
ST2MR E.Malkin/A.Radulov 25.00 60.00
ST2NB R.Nash/G.Brule 12.00 30.00
ST2NK M.Naslund/R.Kesler 12.00 30.00
ST2OB B.Orr/R.Bourque 150.00 300.00
ST2RL Ryder/Latendresse 10.00 25.00
ST2SS E.Staal/J.Staal 10.00 25.00
ST2TK J.Toews/P.Kane 100.00 200.00
ST2VS T.Vanek/D.Stafford 10.00 25.00
ST2VT V.Filppula/T.Kopecky 10.00 25.00
ST2WS P.Stastny/W.Wolski 10.00 25.00

2007-08 SP Authentic Sign of the Times Triples

ST3FMS Malkin/Fleury/Staal 100.00 200.00
ST3GPR Getzlaf/Perry/Ryan 60.00 120.00
ST3GRL Gagne/Richards/Lupul 40.00 80.00
ST3HLD Hasek/Lidstrom/Draper 60.00 120.00
ST3KJB Kopitar/Johnson/Bernier 175.00 300.00
ST3MRT Modano/Turco/Ribeiro 30.00 80.00
ST3MSS Sittler/Salming/Mahov 40.00 80.00
ST3MVS Miller/Vanek/Stafford 25.00 60.00
ST3NZB Nash/Brule/Zherdev 40.00 80.00
ST3OJK Ovech/Johnson/Kane 100.00 200.00
ST3PHP Roy/Brodeur/Price 125.00 250.00
ST3PRL Price/Ryder/Latend 75.00 150.00
ST3RGP Roloson/Gagner/Pitkanen 30.00 60.00
ST3SBK Bergeron/Kessel/Savard 40.00 80.00
ST3SSS Staal/Staal/Staal 125.00 250.00
ST3SWS Stastny/Wolski/Svatos 50.00 100.00

2008-09 SP Authentic

COMP.SET w/o SPs (100) 10.00 25.00
1 Zach Parise .30 .75
2 Wayne Gretzky 2.00 5.00
3 Vincent Lecavalier .30 .75
4 Vesa Toskala .40 1.00
5 Mike Cammalleri .25 .60
6 Tomas Vokoun .25 .60
7 Tomas Kaberle .20 .50
8 Thomas Vanek .25 .60
9 Simon Gagne .30 .75
10 Sidney Crosby 1.25 3.00
11 Sam Gagner .20 .50
12 Shane Doan .25 .60
13 Scott Niedermayer .30 .75
14 Saku Koivu .30 .75
15 Ryan Miller .30 .75
16 Ryan Getzlaf .30 .75
17 Rod Brind`Amour .30 .75
18 Roberto Luongo .50 1.25
19 Rick Nash .30 .75
20 Rick DiPietro .25 .60
21 Phil Kessel .30 .75
22 Peter Mueller .25 .60
23 Pavel Datsyuk .50 1.25
24 Paul Stastny .25 .60
25 Paul Kariya .30 .75
26 Patrik Elias .30 .75
27 Patrick Sharp .30 .75
28 Mikko Koivu .25 .60
29 Patrick Kane .60 1.50
30 Pascal Leclaire .25 .60
31 Olli Jokinen .25 .60
32 Nikolai Zherdev .20 .50
33 Niklas Backstrom .30 .75
34 Nicklas Lidstrom .30 .75
35 Nicklas Backstrom .30 .75
36 Nathan Horton .25 .60
37 Milan Hejduk .25 .60
38 Mike Richards .25 .60
39 Andrew Cogliano .20 .50
40 Mike Modano .50 1.25
41 Miikka Kiprusoff .30 .75
42 Mikhail Grabovski .20 .50
43 Marty Turco .30 .75
44 Martin St. Louis .30 .75
45 Martin Brodeur .75 2.00
46 Martin Biron .25 .60
47 Doug Weight .30 .75
48 Miroslav Satan .30 .75
49 Marian Hossa .30 .75
50 Marian Gaborik .30 .75
51 Marc-Andre Fleury .60 1.50
52 Marc Savard .20 .50
53 Kari Lehtonen .40 1.00
54 Jordan Staal .25 .60
55 Jonathan Toews .50 1.25
56 Jonathan Cheechoo .25 .60
57 Johan Franzen .25 .60
58 Joe Thornton .50 1.25
59 Joe Sakic .60 1.50
60 Jean-Sebastien Giguere .30 .75
61 Jason Spezza .30 .75
62 Jason Pominville .20 .50
63 Jason Arnott .25 .60
64 Jarome Iginla .40 1.00
65 Dustin Brown .30 .75
66 Ilya Kovalchuk .30 .75
67 Henrik Zetterberg .40 1.00
68 Henrik Sedin .40 1.00
69 Henrik Lundqvist .75 2.00
70 Tomas Plekanec .20 .50
71 Gordie Howe 1.00 2.50
72 Evgeni Nabokov .25 .60
73 Evgeni Malkin .60 1.50
74 Eric Staal .40 1.00
75 Dion Phaneuf .25 .60
76 Derek Roy .20 .50
77 Dany Heatley .25 .60
78 Daniel Sedin .40 1.00
79 Daniel Briere .30 .75
80 Daniel Alfredsson .30 .75
81 Dan Ellis .20 .50
82 Cristobal Huet .25 .60
83 Alexander Semin .30 .75
84 Teemu Selanne .60 1.50
85 Chris Osgood .30 .75
86 Chris Drury .25 .60
87 Carey Price .60 1.50
88 Cam Ward .30 .75
89 Markus Naslund .30 .75
90 Brian Campbell .25 .60
91 Brad Richards .30 .75
92 Brad Boyes .20 .50
93 Patrice Bergeron .40 1.00
94 Mats Sundin .30 .75
95 Anze Kopitar .50 1.25
96 Alexander Ovechkin 1.25 3.00
97 Alexander Frolov .20 .50
98 Alex Tanguay .20 .50
99 Alex Kovalev .25 .60
100 Ales Hemsky .25 .60
101 Alexander Ovechkin N 5.00 12.00
102 Bernie Parent N 1.50 4.00
103 Bobby Clarke N 2.00 5.00
104 Bobby Hull N 2.50 6.00
105 Bobby Orr N 5.00 12.00
106 Mike Bossy N 1.25 3.00
107 Carey Price N 2.50 6.00
108 Chris Chelios N 1.25 3.00
109 Daniel Briere N 1.25 3.00
110 Dany Heatley N 1.00 2.50
111 Evgeni Malkin N 2.50 6.00
112 Guy Carbonneau N 1.25 3.00
113 Gordie Howe N 4.00 10.00
114 Grant Fuhr N 2.00 5.00
115 Guy Lafleur N 1.50 4.00
116 Henrik Lundqvist N 3.00 8.00
117 Henrik Zetterberg N 1.50 4.00
118 Jarome Iginla N 1.50 4.00
119 Jason Spezza N 1.25 3.00
120 Jean-Sebastien Giguere N 1.25 3.00
121 Joe Sakic N 2.50 6.00
122 Joe Thornton N 2.00 5.00
123 Johnny Bucyk N 1.25 3.00
124 Jonathan Toews N 2.00 5.00
125 Luc Robitaille N 1.25 3.00
126 Marc-Andre Fleury N 2.50 6.00
127 Marian Gaborik N 1.25 3.00
128 Mario Lemieux N 5.00 12.00
129 Mark Messier N 2.50 6.00
130 Markus Naslund N 1.25 3.00
131 Martin Brodeur N 3.00 8.00
132 Martin St. Louis N 1.25 3.00
133 Keith Tkachuk N 1.25 3.00
134 Mike Modano N 2.00 5.00
135 Nicklas Lidstrom N 1.25 3.00
136 Patrick Kane N 2.50 6.00
137 Paul Kariya N 1.25 3.00
138 Peter Forsberg N 2.50 6.00
139 Phil Esposito N 2.00 5.00
140 Ray Bourque N 2.00 5.00
141 Rick DiPietro N 1.00 2.50
142 Rick Nash N 1.25 3.00
143 Jeremy Roenick N 2.00 5.00
144 Roberto Luongo N 2.00 5.00
145 Mike Richards N 1.00 2.50
146 Miikka Kiprusoff N 1.25 3.00
147 Ryan Miller N 1.25 3.00
148 Saku Koivu N 1.25 3.00
149 Shane Doan N 1.00 2.50
150 Sidney Crosby N 5.00 12.00
151 Simon Gagne N 1.25 3.00
152 Stan Mikita N 1.50 4.00
153 Teemu Selanne N 2.50 6.00
154 Patrick Roy N 3.00 8.00
155 Thomas Vanek N 1.00 2.50
156 Tomas Vokoun N 1.00 2.50
157 Tony Esposito N 1.25 3.00
158 Vincent Lecavalier N 1.25 3.00
159 Wayne Gretzky N 8.00 20.00
160 Zach Parise N 1.25 3.00
161 Adam Pardy RC 2.50 6.00
162 Matthew Halischuk RC 2.00 5.00
163 Karl Alzner RC 2.00 5.00
164 Brendan Mikkelson RC 2.00 5.00
165 Trevor Lewis RC 3.00 8.00
166 Michal Repik RC 3.00 8.00
167 Chris Porter RC 3.00 8.00
168 Brad Staubitz RC 2.50 6.00
169 Cam Paddock RC 2.00 5.00
170 Jonas Frogren RC 2.00 5.00
171 Ben Bishop RC 5.00 12.00
172 Ben Maxwell RC 3.00 8.00
173 Nathan Gerbe RC 3.00 8.00
174 Tim Kennedy RC 3.00 8.00
175 Jesse Winchester RC 2.00 5.00
176 Simeon Varlamov RC 6.00 15.00
177 John Mitchell RC 2.50 6.00
178 Max Pacioretty RC 6.00 15.00
179 Chris Stewart RC 3.00 8.00
180 Brett Festerling RC 2.50 6.00
181 Mike Brown RC 3.00 8.00
182 Kenndal McArdle RC 2.50 6.00
183 Cory Schneider RC 8.00 20.00
184 Derek Dorsett RC 4.00 10.00
185 Ryan Jones RC 3.00 8.00
186 Ty Wishart RC 2.50 6.00
187 Theo Peckham RC 2.50 6.00
188 Tom Cavanagh RC 2.50 6.00
189 Wayne Simmonds RC 5.00 12.00
190 Janne Pesonen RC 2.50 6.00
191 Luke Schenn AU RC 6.00 15.00
192 Zach Bogosian AU RC 6.00 15.00
193 Justin Abdelkader AU RC 8.00 20.00
194 Ryan Jones AU RC 5.00 12.00
195 Brandon Sutter AU RC 25.00 60.00
196 Derick Brassard AU RC 5.00 12.00
197 Marc-Andre Gragnani RC 2.50 6.00
198 James Neal AU RC 10.00 25.00
199 Colton Gillies AU RC 4.00 10.00
200 Kyle Okposo AU RC 6.00 15.00
201 Brian Boyle AU RC 4.00 10.00
202 Petr Vrana AU RC 3.00 8.00
203 Zach Boychuk AU RC 5.00 12.00
204 Kevin Porter RC 2.50 6.00
205 Patric Hornqvist AU RC 5.00 12.00
206 Nikita Filatov AU RC 15.00 40.00
207 Mark Fistric AU RC 4.00 10.00
208 Dan LaCosta RC 3.00 8.00
209 Steve Mason AU RC 8.00 20.00
210 Erik Ersberg AU RC 4.00 10.00
211 Ryan Stone AU RC 3.00 8.00
212 Jon Filewich AU RC 4.00 10.00
213 Tyler Plante RC 2.50 6.00
214 Matt D'Agostini AU RC 4.00 10.00
215 Adam Pineault RC 2.50 6.00
216 Shawn Matthias AU RC 5.00 12.00
217 Viktor Tikhonov AU RC 4.00 10.00
218 Nikolai Kulemin AU RC 5.00 12.00
219 Blake Wheeler AU RC 15.00 40.00
220 Mattias Ritola AU RC 4.00 10.00
221 Tom Sestito RC 3.00 8.00
222 Darren Helm AU RC 5.00 12.00
223 Danny Taylor RC 2.50 6.00
224 Josh Bailey AU RC 30.00 80.00
225 Luca Sbisa AU RC 3.00 8.00
226 Jamie McGinn AU RC 5.00 12.00
227 Andrew Ebbett RC 2.00 5.00
228 Boris Valabik RC 3.00 8.00
229 Oscar Moller AU RC 4.00 10.00
230 Jonathan Ericsson AU RC 5.00 12.00
231 Alex Pietrangelo AU RC 12.00 30.00
232 Robbie Earl AU RC 3.00 8.00
233 Ilya Zubov AU RC 4.00 10.00
234 Teddy Purcell AU RC 4.00 10.00
235 Justin Pogge RC 2.50 6.00
236 Brian Lee AU RC 4.00 10.00
237 Claude Giroux AU RC 40.00 100.00
238 Vladimir Mihalik AU RC 3.00 8.00
239 Patrik Berglund AU RC 4.00 10.00
240 Lauri Korpikoski AU RC 3.00 8.00
241 Michael Frolik AU RC 5.00 12.00
242 Alex Goligoski AU RC 6.00 15.00
243 T.J. Oshie AU RC 20.00 50.00
244 Drew Doughty AU RC 35.00 60.00
245 Mikkel Boedker AU RC 6.00 15.00
246 Kyle Turris AU RC 10.00 25.00
247 Steven Stamkos AU RC 200.00 500.00
248 Jakub Voracek AU RC 12.00 30.00
249 Fabian Brunnstrom AU RC 4.00 10.00
250 Andreas Nodl AU RC 3.00 8.00

2008-09 SP Authentic Limited

*1-100 VETS: 2X TO 5X BASIC CARDS
*101-160 NOTABLE: .8X TO 2X
*161-250 ROOKIES: .6X TO 1.5X
35 Nicklas Backstrom 1.50 4.00

2008-09 SP Authentic Holoview FX

COMPLETE SET (42) 60.00 120.00
FX43 Colton Gillies 1.00 2.50
FX44 Teemu Selanne 2.50 6.00
FX45 Ilya Kovalchuk 1.25 3.00
FX46 Marc Savard .75 2.00
FX47 Ryan Miller 1.25 3.00
FX48 Jarome Iginla 1.50 4.00
FX49 Dion Phaneuf 1.00 2.50
FX50 Eric Staal 1.50 4.00
FX51 Patrick Kane 2.50 6.00
FX52 Jonathan Toews 2.00 5.00
FX53 Paul Stastny 1.00 2.50
FX54 Rick Nash 1.25 3.00
FX55 Brenden Morrow 1.00 2.50
FX56 Brad Richards 1.25 3.00
FX57 Henrik Zetterberg 1.50 4.00
FX58 Marian Hossa 1.25 3.00
FX59 Nicklas Lidstrom 1.25 3.00
FX60 Shawn Horcoff .75 2.00
FX61 Sam Gagner .75 2.00
FX62 Fabian Brunnstrom 1.00 2.50
FX63 Anze Kopitar 2.00 5.00
FX64 Marian Gaborik 1.25 3.00
FX65 Saku Koivu 1.25 3.00
FX66 Carey Price 2.50 6.00
FX67 Steven Stamkos 5.00 12.00
FX68 Martin Brodeur 3.00 8.00
FX69 Rick DiPietro 1.00 2.50
FX70 Dany Heatley 1.00 2.50
FX71 Mike Richards 1.00 2.50
FX72 Peter Mueller 1.00 2.50
FX73 Evgeni Malkin 2.50 6.00
FX74 Marc-Andre Fleury 2.50 6.00
FX75 Sidney Crosby 5.00 12.00
FX76 Jonathan Cheechoo 1.00 2.50
FX77 Joe Thornton 2.00 5.00
FX78 Blake Wheeler 3.00 8.00
FX79 Vincent Lecavalier 1.25 3.00
FX80 Kyle Turris 2.00 5.00
FX81 Jakub Voracek 2.50 6.00
FX82 Roberto Luongo 2.00 5.00
FX83 Alexander Ovechkin 5.00 12.00
FX84 Nicklas Backstrom 1.25 3.00

2008-09 SP Authentic Holoview FX Die Cuts

*SINGLES: 1.2X TO 3X BASIC INSERTS
FX84 Nicklas Backstrom 4.00 10.00

2008-09 SP Authentic Limited Autographed Patches

191 Luke Schenn 20.00 50.00
192 Zach Bogosian 20.00 50.00
193 Justin Abdelkader 25.00 60.00
194 Ryan Jones 15.00 40.00
195 Brandon Sutter 40.00 80.00
196 Derick Brassard 15.00 40.00
198 James Neal 20.00 50.00
199 Colton Gillies 12.00 30.00
201 Brian Boyle 12.00 30.00
202 Petr Vrana 10.00 25.00
203 Zach Boychuk 15.00 40.00
205 Patric Hornqvist 15.00 40.00
206 Nikita Filatov 40.00 100.00
207 Mark Fistric 12.00 30.00
209 Steve Mason 25.00 60.00
210 Erik Ersberg 12.00 30.00
211 Ryan Stone 10.00 25.00
212 Jon Filewich 12.00 30.00
214 Matt D'Agostini 12.00 30.00
216 Shawn Matthias 15.00 40.00
217 Viktor Tikhonov 12.00 30.00
218 Nikolai Kulemin 15.00 40.00
219 Blake Wheeler 40.00 100.00
220 Mattias Ritola 12.00 30.00
222 Darren Helm 15.00 40.00
224 Josh Bailey 20.00 50.00
225 Luca Sbisa 10.00 25.00
226 Jamie McGinn 15.00 40.00
229 Oscar Moller 12.00 30.00
230 Jonathan Ericsson 15.00 40.00
231 Alex Pietrangelo 25.00 60.00
232 Robbie Earl 10.00 25.00
233 Ilya Zubov 12.00 30.00
234 Teddy Purcell 12.00 30.00
236 Brian Lee 12.00 30.00
237 Claude Giroux 125.00 250.00
238 Vladimir Mihalik 10.00 25.00
239 Patrik Berglund 12.00 30.00
240 Lauri Korpikoski 10.00 25.00
241 Michael Frolik 15.00 40.00
242 Alex Goligoski 20.00 50.00
243 T.J. Oshie 40.00 80.00
244 Drew Doughty 60.00 120.00
245 Mikkel Boedker 15.00 40.00
246 Kyle Turris 25.00 60.00
247 Steven Stamkos 500.00 1200.00
248 Jakub Voracek 15.00 40.00
249 Fabian Brunnstrom 12.00 30.00
250 Andreas Nodl 10.00 25.00

2008-09 SP Authentic Marks of Distinction

MDBH Bobby Hull 75.00 150.00
MDBO Bobby Orr 175.00 300.00
MDGH Gordie Howe 125.00 200.00
MDMB Martin Brodeur 100.00 200.00
MDMM Mark Messier 100.00 200.00
MDPR Patrick Roy 125.00 200.00
MDSC Sidney Crosby 100.00 200.00
MDWG Wayne Gretzky 250.00 600.00

2008-09 SP Authentic Penned Perfection

PPCP Carey Price 20.00 50.00
PPES Eric Staal 12.00 30.00
PPHZ Henrik Zetterberg 12.00 30.00
PPJG Jean-Sebastien Giguere 10.00 25.00
PPJI Jarome Iginla 12.00 30.00
PPJT Joe Thornton 15.00 40.00
PPMG Nicklas Backstrom 10.00 25.00
PPMN Markus Naslund 10.00 25.00
PPMR Mike Richards 40.00 80.00
PPNL Nicklas Lidstrom 20.00 50.00
PPPB Patrice Bergeron 12.00 30.00
PPPK Patrick Kane 20.00 50.00
PPPM Peter Mueller 8.00 20.00
PPRM Ryan Miller 10.00 25.00
PPRN Rick Nash 20.00 40.00
PPSK Saku Koivu 10.00 25.00
PPTO Jonathan Toews 15.00 40.00

2008-09 SP Authentic Rookie Review Autographed Patches

RRBM Brenden Morrow 10.00 25.00
RRCD Chris Drury 10.00 25.00
RRCP Carey Price 50.00 100.00
RRCW Cam Ward 12.00 30.00
RRDH Dany Heatley 10.00 25.00
RRDK Dominik Hasek 20.00 50.00
RREM Evgeni Malkin 25.00 60.00
RRES Eric Staal 15.00 40.00
RRHZ Henrik Zetterberg 15.00 40.00
RRJI Jarome Iginla 15.00 40.00
RRJS Jordan Staal 10.00 25.00
RRJT Jonathan Toews 40.00 80.00
RRMB Martin Brodeur 40.00 80.00
RRMF Marc-Andre Fleury 40.00 80.00
RRMH Marian Hossa 12.00 30.00
RRMM Mike Modano 15.00 40.00
RRMR Mike Richards 10.00 25.00
RRMT Marty Turco 12.00 30.00
RRNL Nicklas Lidstrom 25.00 50.00
RRPK Patrick Kane 30.00 80.00
RRPS Paul Stastny 10.00 25.00
RRRG Ryan Getzlaf 12.00 30.00
RRRM Ryan Miller 20.00 50.00
RRRN Rick Nash 12.00 30.00
RRSC Sidney Crosby 100.00 200.00
RRSG Scott Gomez 10.00 25.00
RRTH Joe Thornton 20.00 50.00
RRVL Vincent Lecavalier 20.00 50.00

2008-09 SP Authentic Sign of the Times

STAP Alex Pietrangelo 5.00 12.00
STBB Brian Boyle 2.50 6.00
STBD Mikkel Boedker 4.00 10.00
STBH Bobby Hull 25.00 60.00
STBO Ray Bourque 30.00 80.00
STBS Brandon Sutter 3.00 8.00
STCA Carey Price 30.00 60.00
STCW Cam Ward 5.00 12.00
STDC Daniel Carcillo 3.00 8.00
STDD Drew Doughty 8.00 20.00
STDH Darren Helm 3.00 8.00
STDS Drew Stafford 3.00 8.00
STEM Evgeni Malkin 20.00 50.00
STES Eric Staal 6.00 15.00
STFL Marc-Andre Fleury 15.00 40.00
STGH Gordie Howe 60.00 120.00
STHE T.J. Hensick 4.00 10.00
STHZ Henrik Zetterberg 20.00 50.00
STJF Jon Filewich 2.50 6.00
STJH Josh Harding 5.00 12.00
STJI Jarome Iginla 6.00 15.00
STJK Jari Kurri 8.00 20.00
STJM Joe Mullen 4.00 10.00
STJO Joe Thornton 15.00 40.00
STJT Jonathan Toews 25.00 50.00
STJV Jakub Voracek 12.50 25.00
STKA Patrick Kane 25.00 50.00
STKO Kyle Okposo 4.00 10.00
STKT Kyle Turris 5.00 12.00
STLS Luke Schenn 4.00 10.00
STMB Martin Brodeur 75.00 150.00
STMI Mike Iggulden 4.00 10.00
STMK Mike Richards 4.00 10.00
STOR Bobby Orr 75.00 150.00
STPK Phil Kessel 6.00 15.00
STRE Robbie Earl 2.00 5.00
STRM Ryan Miller 8.00 20.00
STRN Rick Nash 15.00 40.00
STRS Ryan Stone 2.00 5.00
STSA Denis Savard 5.00 12.00
STSC Sidney Crosby 75.00 150.00
STSH James Sheppard 3.00 8.00
STSM Steve Mason 12.00 30.00
STSS Steven Stamkos 60.00 150.00
STST Paul Stastny 4.00 10.00
STTE Tobias Enstrom 3.00 8.00
STTJ T.J. Oshie 12.00 30.00
STTV Tomas Vokoun 4.00 10.00
STVA Thomas Vanek 4.00 10.00
STVL Vincent Lecavalier 15.00 40.00
STWG Wayne Gretzky 250.00 600.00
STZB Zach Bogosian 4.00 10.00
STZH Zach Boychuk 3.00 8.00

2008-09 SP Authentic Sign of the Times Duals

ST2BF M.Brodeur/M.Fleury 40.00 80.00
ST2BM S.Mason/D.Brassard 10.00 25.00
ST2EE T.Esposito/P.Esposito 20.00 50.00
ST2GM W.Gretzky/M.Messier 300.00 800.00
ST2HT B.Hull/J.Toews 50.00 100.00
ST2HZ D.Heatley/I.Zubov 8.00 20.00
ST2KP K.Okposo/P.Kessel 12.00 30.00
ST2KS P.Kane/J.Skille 15.00 40.00
ST2KT S.Koivu/A.Tanguay 15.00 40.00
ST2LM M.Lemieux/E.Malkin 75.00 150.00
ST2LT J.Thornton/V.Lecavalier 15.00 40.00
ST2MT M.Modano/M.Turco 15.00 40.00
ST2OB B.Orr/R.Bourque 100.00 200.00
ST2PK C.Price/P.Kane 20.00 50.00
ST2PP P.Stastny/P.Stastny 15.00 40.00
ST2PT P.Mueller/K.Turris 25.00 60.00
ST2RC M.Richards/J.Carter 20.00 50.00
ST2RK L.Robitaille/J.Kurri 20.00 50.00
ST2SS J.Staal/M.Staal 8.00 20.00
ST2SW E.Staal/C.Ward 12.00 30.00
ST2ZH G.Howe/H.Zetterberg 60.00 120.00

2008-09 SP Authentic Sign of the Times Triples

ST3BTK Kane/Toews/Backstrm 100.00 175.00
ST3CHS Hextall/Clarke/Schultz 50.00 100.00
ST3GND Naslund/Gomez/Drury 50.00 100.00
ST3GNT Turco/Nabkv/Giguer 30.00 60.00
ST3IHN Heatley/Iginla/Nash 40.00 100.00
ST3KTH Koivu/Tanguy/Higgins 50.00 100.00
ST3LBC Bouchrd/Carbon/Lafler 40.00 100.00
ST3LBM Messier/Mario/Bourque 150.00 300.00
ST3MCT Mueller/Turris/Carcillo 20.00 40.00
ST3MRM Modano/Morrow/Rbero 25.00 60.00
ST3MSG Gilmour/Mahov/Salming 40.00 100.00
ST3OGH Gretzky/Howe/Orr 750.00 2000.00
ST3PMV Miller/Vanek/Pominvle 60.00 120.00
ST3RBP Roy/Brodeur/Price 100.00 200.00
ST3SSS Staal/Staal/Staal 40.00 80.00

2009-10 SP Authentic

1 Phil Kessel .30 .75
2 Luke Schenn .30 .75
3 Doug Weight .30 .75
4 Drew Doughty .40 1.00
5 Carey Price .60 1.50
6 Vincent Lecavalier .30 .75
7 Joe Thornton .50 1.25
8 Alexander Ovechkin 1.25 3.00
9 Steve Mason .25 .60
10 Dany Heatley .25 .60
11 Peter Mueller .25 .60
12 Henrik Zetterberg .40 1.00
13 Ryan Getzlaf .30 .75
14 Claude Giroux .30 .75
15 Tomas Vokoun .25 .60
16 Roberto Luongo .50 1.25
17 Ilya Kovalchuk .30 .75
18 Mike Richards .25 .60
19 Jonathan Toews .50 1.25
20 Marian Gaborik .30 .75
21 Mike Modano .50 1.25
22 Eric Staal .40 1.00
23 Pekka Rinne .30 .75
24 Miikka Kiprusoff .30 .75
25 Jason Pominville .20 .50
26 Paul Stastny .25 .60
27 Paul Kariya .30 .75
28 Mikko Koivu .30 .75
29 Marc-Andre Fleury .60 1.50
30 Martin Brodeur .75 2.00
31 Sam Gagner .20 .50
32 Nicklas Lidstrom .20 .50
33 Jakub Voracek .25 .60
34 Chris Pronger .30 .75
35 Marc Staal .20 .50
36 Kris Versteeg .20 .50
37 Martin St. Louis .30 .75
38 Olli Jokinen .25 .60
39 Martin Havlat .25 .60
40 Jason Spezza .30 .75
41 Chris Stewart .25 .60
42 Brad Richards .30 .75
43 Bryan Little .30 .75
44 Nikolai Khabibulin .30 .75
45 Derek Roy .20 .50
46 Bobby Ryan .25 .60
47 Scott Gomez .25 .60
48 Shea Weber .25 .60
49 Henrik Lundqvist .75 2.00
50 Johan Franzen .25 .60
51 Tim Thomas .30 .75
52 Patrick Marleau .30 .75
53 Evgeni Malkin .60 1.50
54 Anze Kopitar .50 1.25
55 Jeff Carter .25 .60
56 Mike Ribeiro .20 .50
57 Tomas Kaberle .20 .50
58 Shane Doan .25 .60
59 Zach Parise .30 .75
60 Alex Kovalev .25 .60
61 Rick Nash .30 .75
62 Mike Green .25 .60
63 Andrei Markov .30 .75
64 Marian Hossa .30 .75
65 Nathan Horton .30 .75
66 Daniel Sedin .40 1.00
67 Kyle Okposo .20 .50
68 Dion Phaneuf .25 .60
69 Cam Ward .30 .75
70 Milan Hejduk .25 .60
71 Blake Wheeler .30 .75
72 Patrik Berglund .20 .50
73 Ales Hemsky .25 .60
74 Kari Lehtonen .25 .60
75 Niklas Backstrom .30 .75
76 Thomas Vanek .25 .60
77 Scott Niedermayer .30 .75
78 Simon Gagne .30 .75
79 Steven Stamkos .60 1.50
80 Jason Arnott .25 .60
81 Chris Drury .25 .60
82 Pavel Datsyuk .50 1.25
83 Nikolai Kulemin .20 .50
84 Ryan Smyth .25 .60
85 Marty Turco .30 .75
86 Mike Cammalleri .25 .60
87 Sidney Crosby 1.25 3.00
88 Patrick Kane .60 1.50
89 Patrik Elias .30 .75
90 Devin Setoguchi .25 .60
91 Zdeno Chara .30 .75
92 Andrew Cogliano .20 .50
93 Josh Bailey .25 .60
94 Derick Brassard .20 .50
95 Daniel Alfredsson .30 .75
96 Jarome Iginla .40 1.00
97 Rod Brind`Amour .30 .75
98 Semyon Varlamov .30 .75
99 Henrik Sedin .40 1.00
100 Ryan Miller .30 .75
101 Alexander Ovechkin ESS 3.00 8.00
102 Bobby Hull ESS 1.50 4.00
103 Bobby Orr ESS 3.00 8.00
104 Bobby Ryan ESS .60 1.50
105 Bryan Little ESS .75 2.00
106 Cam Neely ESS .75 2.00
107 Cam Ward ESS .75 2.00
108 Carey Price ESS 1.50 4.00
109 Dany Heatley ESS .60 1.50
110 Drew Doughty ESS 1.00 2.50
111 Eric Staal ESS 1.00 2.50
112 Evgeni Malkin ESS 1.50 4.00
113 Gordie Howe ESS 2.50 6.00
114 Henrik Lundqvist ESS 2.00 5.00
115 Henrik Zetterberg ESS 1.00 2.50
116 Ilya Kovalchuk ESS .75 2.00
117 Jarome Iginla ESS 1.00 2.50
118 Jason Spezza ESS .75 2.00
119 Jean Beliveau ESS .75 2.00
120 Jeff Carter ESS .60 1.50
121 Joe Thornton ESS 1.25 3.00
122 Johan Franzen ESS .60 1.50
123 Jonathan Toews ESS 1.25 3.00
124 Luke Schenn ESS .75 2.00
125 Marc-Andre Fleury ESS 1.50 4.00
126 Marian Gaborik ESS .75 2.00

127 Marian Hossa ESS .75 2.00
128 Mario Lemieux ESS 3.00 8.00
129 Mark Messier ESS 1.50 4.00
130 Martin Brodeur ESS 2.00 5.00
131 Martin St. Louis ESS .75 2.00
132 Marty Turco ESS .75 2.00
133 Miikka Kiprusoff ESS .75 2.00
134 Mike Richards ESS .60 1.50
135 Mikko Koivu ESS .75 2.00
136 Nicklas Backstrom ESS .75 2.00
137 Niklas Backstrom ESS .75 2.00
138 Nikolai Khabibulin ESS .75 2.00
139 Patrick Kane ESS 1.50 4.00
140 Patrick Marleau ESS .75 2.00
141 Patrick Roy ESS 2.00 5.00
142 Paul Kariya ESS .75 2.00
143 Paul Stastny ESS .60 1.50
144 Pavel Datsyuk ESS 1.25 3.00
145 Rick Nash ESS .75 2.00
146 Roberto Luongo ESS 1.25 3.00
147 Ryan Getzlaf ESS .75 2.00
148 Ryan Miller ESS .75 2.00
149 Sam Gagner ESS .50 1.25
150 Shane Doan ESS .60 1.50
151 Shea Weber ESS .60 1.50
152 Sidney Crosby ESS 3.00 8.00
153 Steve Mason ESS .60 1.50
154 Steve Yzerman ESS 2.00 5.00
155 Thomas Vanek ESS .60 1.50
156 Tim Thomas ESS .75 2.00
157 Vincent Lecavalier ESS .75 2.00
158 Wayne Gretzky ESS 5.00 12.00
159 Zach Parise ESS .75 2.00
160 Zdeno Chara ESS .75 2.00
161 Lars Eller RC 3.00 8.00
162 Ryan Wilson RC 3.00 8.00
163 Aaron Gagnon RC 2.00 5.00
164 James Reimer RC 8.00 20.00
165 Anton Khudobin RC 5.00 12.00
166 Scott Parse RC 3.00 8.00
167 Mathieu Carle RC 3.00 8.00
168 Alexander Salak RC 2.50 6.00
169 Mario Bliznak RC 3.00 8.00
170 Steven Zalewski RC 2.50 6.00
171 Peter Olvecky RC 3.00 8.00
172 Tom Pyatt RC 3.00 8.00
173 Ryan O'Marra RC 2.00 5.00
174 Deryk Engelland RC 4.00 10.00
175 Mathieu Perreault RC 4.00 10.00
176 Francis Wathier RC 2.50 6.00
177 Philippe Dupuis RC 3.00 8.00
178 David Laliberte RC 2.50 6.00
179 Shaun Heshka RC 3.00 8.00
180 Teemu Laakso RC 2.00 5.00
181 Ryan White RC 4.00 10.00
182 Victor Oreskovich RC 2.50 6.00
183 Davis Drewiske RC 3.00 8.00
184 Ryan Vesce RC 2.50 6.00
185 Peter Regin RC 2.50 6.00
186 Bobby Sanguinetti RC 2.00 5.00
187 Tyson Strachan RC 2.00 5.00
188 Guillaume Desbiens RC 3.00 8.00
189 Mika Pyorala RC 2.50 6.00
190 Devan Dubnyk RC 5.00 12.00
191 Phil Oreskovic RC 3.00 8.00
192 Andreas Thuresson RC 2.50 6.00
193 Jakub Kindl RC 3.00 8.00
194 Drayson Bowman RC 3.00 8.00
195 Johan Backlund RC 3.00 8.00
196 Ryan Stoa RC 2.50 6.00
197 Braden Holtby RC 15.00 40.00
198 Keaton Ellerby RC 2.50 6.00
199 Matthew Corrente RC 2.50 6.00
200 Alexander Sulzer RC 2.00 5.00
201 John Tavares AU RC 150.00 250.00
202 Victor Hedman AU RC 80.00 200.00
203 Matt Duchene AU RC 15.00 40.00
204 Colin Wilson AU RC 5.00 12.00
205 Tyler Bozak AU RC 8.00 20.00
206 James van Riemsdyk AU RC 10.00 25.00
207 Evander Kane AU RC 12.00 30.00
208 Michael Grabner AU RC 5.00 12.00
209 Erik Karlsson AU RC 60.00 150.00
210 Matt Gilroy AU RC 5.00 12.00
211 Tyler Myers AU RC 8.00 20.00
212 Antti Niemi AU RC 8.00 20.00
213 Ville Leino AU RC 4.00 10.00
214 Yannick Weber AU RC 5.00 12.00
215 Jonas Gustavsson AU RC 6.00 15.00
216 Brian Salcido AU RC 3.00 8.00
217 Spencer Machacek AU RC 5.00 12.00
218 Chris Butler AU RC 5.00 12.00
219 Lars Eller AU 5.00 12.00
220 Benn Ferriero AU RC 5.00 12.00
221 Alec Martinez AU RC 6.00 15.00
222 Ryan O'Reilly AU RC 30.00 80.00
223 Jamie Benn AU RC 25.00 60.00
224 Byron Bitz AU RC 4.00 10.00
225 John Scott AU RC 5.00 12.00
226 Riku Helenius AU RC 5.00 12.00
227 Jesse Joensuu AU RC 4.00 10.00
228 Cody Franson AU RC 5.00 12.00
229 Matt Beleskey AU RC 4.00 10.00
230 Dmitry Kulikov AU RC 5.00 12.00
231 Michael Del Zotto AU RC 5.00 12.00
232 Ivan Vishnevskiy AU RC 3.00 8.00
233 Jhonas Enroth AU RC 6.00 15.00
234 Christian Hanson AU RC 5.00 12.00
235 Mikael Backlund AU RC 8.00 20.00
236 Michal Neuvirth AU RC 8.00 20.00
237 Ray Macias AU RC 4.00 10.00
238 Cal O'Reilly AU RC 4.00 10.00
239 Taylor Chorney AU RC 5.00 12.00
240 Oskars Bartulis AU RC 5.00 12.00
241 Mike Santorelli AU RC 5.00 12.00
242 Tom Wandell AU RC 20.00 50.00
243 Andrew MacDonald AU RC 3.00 8.00
244 Artem Anisimov AU RC 3.00 8.00
245 Matt Pelech AU RC 5.00 12.00
246 Peter Regin AU 4.00 10.00
247 Ryan O'Marra AU 3.00 8.00
248 Joel Rechlicz AU RC 3.00 8.00
249 Jason Demers AU RC 8.00 20.00
250 Sergei Shirokov AU RC 3.00 8.00
251 Jay Rosehill AU RC 5.00 12.00
252 Frazer McLaren AU RC 4.00 10.00
253 Michael Sauer AU RC 4.00 10.00
254 Kris Chucko AU RC 3.00 8.00
255 T.J. Galiardi AU RC 5.00 12.00
256 Luca Caputi AU RC 20.00 50.00
257 Viktor Stalberg AU RC 5.00 12.00
258 Perttu Lindgren AU RC 4.00 10.00
259 Logan Couture AU RC 15.00 40.00
260 Brad Marchand AU RC 125.00 300.00

2009-10 SP Authentic Limited Autographed Patches

201 John Tavares 200.00 400.00
202 Victor Hedman 120.00 300.00
203 Matt Duchene 125.00 250.00
204 Colin Wilson 12.00 25.00
205 Tyler Bozak 25.00 60.00
206 James van Riemsdyk 25.00 60.00
207 Evander Kane 60.00 120.00
208 Michael Grabner 15.00 40.00
209 Erik Karlsson 100.00 200.00
210 Matt Gilroy 15.00 40.00
211 Tyler Myers 25.00 60.00
212 Antti Niemi 75.00 150.00
213 Ville Leino 12.00 30.00
214 Yannick Weber 15.00 40.00
215 Jonas Gustavsson 20.00 50.00
216 Brian Salcido 10.00 25.00
217 Spencer Machacek 15.00 40.00
218 Chris Butler 10.00 25.00
219 Lars Eller 25.00 50.00
220 Benn Ferriero 15.00 40.00
221 Alec Martinez 20.00 50.00
222 Ryan O'Reilly 60.00 150.00
223 Jamie Benn 60.00 150.00
224 Byron Bitz 12.00 30.00
225 John Scott 50.00 120.00
226 Riku Helenius 15.00 40.00
227 Jesse Joensuu 12.00 30.00
228 Cody Franson 12.00 30.00
229 Matt Beleskey 12.00 30.00
230 Dmitry Kulikov 15.00 40.00
231 Michael Del Zotto 15.00 40.00
232 Ivan Vishnevskiy 10.00 25.00
233 Jhonas Enroth 15.00 40.00
234 Christian Hanson 15.00 40.00
235 Mikael Backlund 25.00 60.00
236 Michal Neuvirth 20.00 50.00
237 Ray Macias 12.00 30.00
238 Cal O'Reilly 12.00 30.00
240 Oskars Bartulis 15.00 40.00
241 Mike Santorelli 15.00 40.00
243 Andrew MacDonald 10.00 25.00
244 Artem Anisimov 10.00 25.00
245 Matt Pelech 15.00 40.00
247 Ryan O'Marra 10.00 25.00
248 Joel Rechlicz 10.00 25.00
249 Jason Demers 25.00 60.00
250 Sergei Shirokov 10.00 25.00
251 Jay Rosehill 15.00 40.00
252 Frazer McLaren 12.00 30.00
253 Michael Sauer 12.00 30.00
254 Kris Chucko 10.00 25.00
255 T.J. Galiardi 15.00 40.00
257 Viktor Stalberg 15.00 40.00
258 Perttu Lindgren 12.00 30.00
259 Logan Couture 50.00 100.00
260 Brad Marchand 200.00 500.00

2009-10 SP Authentic Chirography

AM Andrei Markov 8.00 20.00
AO Alexander Ovechkin 30.00 80.00
AZ Anze Kopitar 12.00 30.00
BR Bobby Ryan 6.00 15.00
CD Chris Drury 6.00 15.00
CG Claude Giroux 8.00 20.00
DE Derick Brassard 5.00 12.00
DS Devin Setoguchi 6.00 15.00
EN Evgeni Nabokov 6.00 15.00
ES Eric Staal 10.00 25.00
JS James Sheppard 5.00 12.00
JT Jonathan Toews 30.00 80.00
LS Luke Schenn 8.00 20.00
MF Marc-Andre Fleury 15.00 40.00
MM Mike Modano 12.00 30.00
MR Mike Ribeiro 5.00 12.00
PD Pavel Datsyuk 12.00 30.00
PK Phil Kessel 8.00 20.00
PM Peter Mueller 6.00 15.00
PS Paul Stastny 6.00 15.00
RI Mike Richards 6.00 15.00
RM Ryan Miller 8.00 20.00
SC Sidney Crosby 60.00 150.00
SM Steve Mason 6.00 15.00
SS Steven Stamkos 15.00 40.00
ST Jordan Staal 6.00 15.00
SW Shea Weber 6.00 15.00
TV Tomas Vokoun 6.00 15.00
VF Valtteri Filppula 5.00 12.00

2009-10 SP Authentic Holoview FX

COMPLETE SET (42) 75.00 150.00
FX1 Alexander Ovechkin 5.00 12.00
FX2 Anze Kopitar 2.00 5.00
FX3 Bobby Orr 5.00 12.00
FX4 Carey Price 2.50 6.00
FX5 Dany Heatley 1.00 2.50
FX6 Eric Staal 1.50 4.00
FX7 Evgeni Malkin 2.50 6.00
FX8 Gordie Howe 4.00 10.00
FX9 Henrik Zetterberg 1.50 4.00
FX10 Ilya Kovalchuk 1.25 3.00
FX11 Jarome Iginla 1.50 4.00
FX12 Jason Spezza 1.25 3.00
FX13 Jeff Carter 1.00 2.50
FX14 Joe Thornton 2.00 5.00
FX15 John Tavares 5.00 12.00
FX16 Jonathan Toews 2.00 5.00
FX17 Marc-Andre Fleury 2.50 6.00
FX18 Marian Gaborik 1.25 3.00
FX19 Mario Lemieux 5.00 12.00
FX20 Mark Messier 2.50 6.00
FX21 Martin Brodeur 3.00 8.00
FX22 Matt Duchene 2.50 6.00
FX23 Mike Modano 2.00 5.00
FX24 Mikko Koivu 1.25 3.00
FX25 Patrick Kane 2.50 6.00
FX26 Patrick Roy 3.00 8.00
FX27 Paul Kariya 1.25 3.00
FX28 Paul Stastny 1.00 2.50
FX29 Pavel Datsyuk 2.00 5.00
FX30 Phil Kessel 1.25 3.00
FX31 Rick Nash 1.25 3.00
FX32 Roberto Luongo 2.00 5.00
FX33 Ryan Getzlaf 1.25 3.00
FX34 Ryan Miller 1.25 3.00
FX35 Sam Gagner .75 2.00
FX36 Shane Doan 1.00 2.50
FX37 Sidney Crosby 5.00 12.00
FX38 Steve Yzerman 3.00 8.00
FX39 Tim Thomas 1.25 3.00
FX40 Victor Hedman 3.00 8.00
FX41 Vincent Lecavalier 1.25 3.00
FX42 Wayne Gretzky 8.00 20.00

2009-10 SP Authentic Holoview FX Die Cuts

*SINGLES: 1.5X TO 4X HOLOVIEW

2009-10 SP Authentic Marks of Distinction

MDAK Anze Kopitar 20.00 50.00
MDAO Alexander Ovechkin 50.00 125.00
MDBL Brian Lee 12.00 30.00
MDBO Zach Boychuk 10.00 25.00
MDBW Blake Wheeler 12.00 30.00
MDCP Carey Price 25.00 60.00
MDCW Cam Ward 12.00 30.00
MDDH Dany Heatley 10.00 25.00
MDES Eric Staal 15.00 40.00
MDGA Simon Gagne 12.00 30.00
MDHL Henrik Lundqvist 30.00 80.00
MDIK Ilya Kovalchuk 12.00 30.00
MDJA Jason Arnott 10.00 25.00
MDJB Josh Bailey 10.00 25.00
MDJC Jeff Carter 10.00 25.00
MDJI Jarome Iginla 15.00 40.00
MDJT Jonathan Toews 20.00 50.00
MDKA Karl Alzner 8.00 20.00
MDMB Martin Brodeur 30.00 80.00
MDMG Marian Gaborik 12.00 30.00
MDMS Martin St. Louis 12.00 30.00
MDMT Marty Turco 12.00 30.00
MDNL Nicklas Lidstrom 8.00 20.00
MDPD Pavel Datsyuk 20.00 50.00
MDSC Sidney Crosby 80.00 200.00
MDSD Shane Doan 10.00 25.00
MDSG Scott Gomez 10.00 25.00
MDSS Steven Stamkos 25.00 60.00
MDTH Joe Thornton 20.00 50.00
MDVO Tomas Vokoun 10.00 25.00
MDZB Zach Bogosian 10.00 25.00

2009-10 SP Authentic Prestigious Pairings

PPBC S.Bowman/D.Cherry 40.00 80.00
PPBS Stamkos/Brassard 20.00 50.00
PPCG J.Carter/Cl.Giroux 10.00 25.00
PPEG Elias/Gaborik 10.00 25.00
PPFS Staal/Fleury 20.00 50.00
PPGP Price/Gomez 20.00 50.00
PPHH Howe/Howe 50.00 100.00
PPIS Iginla/Staal 12.00 30.00
PPKK P.Kessel/P.Kane 20.00 50.00
PPLS N.Lidstrom/B.Salming 10.00 25.00
PPMR M.Modano/M.Ribeiro 15.00 40.00
PPMT K.Turris/P.Mueller 10.00 25.00
PPNB D.Brassard/R.Nash 15.00 40.00
PPOB Ovechkin/Backstrom 40.00 100.00
PPPB Berglund/Perron 15.00 40.00
PPRS D.Setoguchi/B.Ryan 12.00 30.00
PPTH Heatley/Thornton 15.00 40.00
PPTT Thornton/Toews 15.00 40.00
PPTW Ward/Turco 10.00 25.00
PPVS Lecavalier/Stamkos 20.00 50.00
PPYM Yzerman/Messier 60.00 120.00
PPZB N.Backstrom/H.Zetterberg 15.00 40.00

2009-10 SP Authentic Rookie Review Autographed Patches

RRAK Anze Kopitar/100 20.00 50.00
RRAM Al MacInnis/25 20.00 50.00
RRAO Alexander Ovechkin/25 60.00 150.00
RRBL Brian Leetch/25 10.00 25.00
RRCD Chris Drury/100 10.00 25.00
RRCN Cam Neely/25 15.00 40.00
RRCW Cam Ward/100 12.00 30.00
RRDG Doug Gilmour/100 15.00 40.00
RRDH Dany Heatley/25 10.00 25.00
RREM Evgeni Malkin/25 25.00 60.00
RRES Eric Staal/100 15.00 40.00
RRHL Henrik Lundqvist/100 30.00 80.00
RRHS Henrik Sedin/100 15.00 40.00
RRHZ Henrik Zetterberg/25 15.00 40.00
RRIK Ilya Kovalchuk/25 15.00 40.00
RRJA Jason Arnott/100 10.00 25.00
RRJC Jeff Carter/100 10.00 25.00
RRJD J.P. Dumont/100 8.00 20.00
RRJG Jean-Sebastian Giguere/100 12.00 30.00
RRJI Jarome Iginla/25 15.00 40.00
RRJT Joe Thornton/25 20.00 50.00
RRLM Lanny McDonald/100 12.00 30.00
RRLR Luc Robitaille/100 12.00 30.00
RRMG Marian Gaborik/25 12.00 30.00
RRMH Milan Hejduk/100 10.00 25.00
RRMM Mike Modano/100 20.00 50.00
RRMS Martin St. Louis/100 12.00 30.00
RRMT Marty Turco/100 12.00 30.00
RRMV Andrei Markov/100 12.00 30.00
RRNB Nicklas Backstrom/25 12.00 30.00
RRPD Pavel Datsyuk/100 20.00 50.00
RRPL Pascal Leclaire/100 12.00 30.00
RRPR Patrick Roy/25 60.00 150.00
RRPS Peter Stastny/100 10.00 25.00
RRRI Mike Ribeiro/100 8.00 20.00
RRRO Larry Robinson/25 12.00 30.00
RRRS Ryan Smyth/100 10.00 25.00
RRSG Scott Gomez/100 10.00 25.00
RRSI Simon Gagne/100 12.00 30.00
RRSS Steve Shutt/100 12.00 30.00
RRSY Steve Yzerman/25 30.00 80.00
RRTV Thomas Vanek/100 10.00 25.00
RRVL Vincent Lecavalier/25 12.00 30.00
RRVO Tomas Vokoun/100 10.00 25.00

2009-10 SP Authentic Sign of the Times

STAA Artem Anisimov A 4.00 10.00
STAC Andrew Cogliano 4.00 10.00
STAE Andrew Ebbett 4.00 10.00
STAK Anze Kopitar 10.00 25.00
STAL Andrew Ladd 4.00 10.00
STAO Adam Oates 6.00 15.00
STAP Alex Pietrangelo 5.00 12.00
STBA Mikael Backlund 10.00 25.00
STBH Bobby Hull 12.00 30.00
STBL Brian Leetch 5.00 12.00
STBM Ben Maxwell 5.00 12.00
STBO Bobby Orr 60.00 150.00
STBR Bobby Ryan 5.00 12.00
STBS Brandon Sutter 4.00 10.00
STBW Blake Wheeler C 6.00 15.00
STCG Colton Gillies 6.00 15.00
STCH Christian Hanson 6.00 15.00
STCP Carey Price 12.00 30.00
STDB David Backes 4.00 10.00
STDC Daniel Carcillo 4.00 10.00
STDH Dale Hawerchuk C 8.00 20.00
STDP Dion Phaneuf A 5.00 12.00
STDS Darryl Sutter 5.00 12.00
STDU Matt Duchene 12.00 30.00
STEE Erik Ersberg 5.00 12.00
STEJ Jhonas Enroth 8.00 20.00
STEK Evander Kane 12.00 30.00
STEN Eric Nystrom 5.00 12.00
STES Eric Staal 8.00 20.00
STFB Fabian Brunnstrom 5.00 12.00
STFO Nick Foligno 5.00 12.00
STGA Simon Gagne 6.00 15.00
STGU Jonas Gustavsson 8.00 20.00
STHL Henrik Lundqvist 15.00 40.00
STIK Ilya Kovalchuk A 6.00 15.00
STIV Ivan Vishnevskiy 4.00 10.00
STJA Jason Arnott 5.00 12.00
STJB Josh Bailey 5.00 12.00
STJD J.P. Dumont 4.00 10.00
STJE Jonathan Ericsson 4.00 10.00
STJG Jean-Sebastian Giguere A 6.00 15.00
STJH Josh Harding 6.00 15.00
STJI Jarome Iginla SP 8.00 20.00
STJJ Jack Johnson 4.00 10.00
STJK Jari Kurri B 6.00 15.00
STJS James Sheppard 4.00 10.00
STJT Jonathan Toews 15.00 40.00
STKA Karl Alzner 4.00 10.00
STLS Luke Schenn C 6.00 15.00
STMA Andrei Markov 6.00 15.00
STMG Marian Gaborik 6.00 15.00
STMI Mikkel Boedker 4.00 10.00
STML Maxim Lapierre 4.00 10.00
STMP Max Pacioretty 6.00 15.00
STMS Mark Streit 4.00 10.00
STMT Maxime Talbot 4.00 10.00
STNB Nicklas Backstrom 6.00 15.00
STNG Nathan Gerbe 5.00 12.00
STOM Oscar Moller 4.00 10.00
STOV Alexander Ovechkin 25.00 60.00
STPD Pavel Datsyuk 20.00 50.00
STPK Phil Kessel 6.00 15.00
STPM Peter Mueller 5.00 12.00
STRI Mike Richards 5.00 12.00
STRM Ryan Miller 6.00 15.00
STSC Sidney Crosby SP 60.00 150.00
STSG Scott Gomez 5.00 12.00
STSM Martin St. Louis 6.00 15.00
STSS Steven Stamkos 12.00 30.00
STST Jordan Staal 5.00 12.00
STSW Stephen Weiss B 4.00 10.00
STSY Steve Yzerman SP 60.00 150.00
STTA John Tavares 25.00 60.00
STTK Tim Kennedy 5.00 12.00
STTV Thomas Vanek 5.00 12.00
STTW Ty Wishart 5.00 12.00
STVF Valtteri Filppula 4.00 10.00
STVH Victor Hedman 15.00 40.00
STVL Ville Leino 5.00 12.00
STVO Tomas Vokoun C 5.00 12.00
STVR James van Riemsdyk 12.00 30.00
STWE Shea Weber 5.00 12.00
STZB Zach Bogosian C 5.00 12.00

2009-10 SP Authentic Sign of the Times Duals

ST2AW J.Arnott/C.Wilson 10.00 25.00
ST2BH J.Harding/N.Backstrom 10.00 25.00
ST2BL L.Sbisa/B.Salcido 10.00 25.00
ST2BO D.Backes/T.Oshie 10.00 25.00
ST2BW P.Bergeron/B.Wheeler 12.00 30.00
ST2DC M.Duchene/P.Stastny 20.00 50.00
ST2DM P.Mueller/S.Doan 8.00 20.00
ST2DW S.Weber/J.Dumont 8.00 20.00
ST2EO P.Esposito/B.Orr 60.00 150.00
ST2EZ E.Staal/Z.Boychuk 12.00 30.00
ST2FF M.Foligno/N.Foligno 8.00 20.00
ST2FK J.Kurri/G.Fuhr 15.00 40.00
ST2FL V.Filppula/V.Leino 8.00 20.00
ST2FM N.Filatov/M.Mayorov 8.00 20.00
ST2FV I.Vishnevskiy/M.Fistric 6.00 15.00
ST2GA M.Green/K.Alzner 8.00 20.00
ST2GG C.Gillies/C.Gillies 10.00 25.00
ST2GL M.Gaborik/H.Lundqvist 25.00 60.00
ST2GS L.Schenn/J.Gustavsson 12.00 30.00
ST2HB T.Bozak/C.Hanson 15.00 40.00
ST2HD A.Delvecchio/G.Howe 30.00 80.00
ST2HT J.Toews/B.Hull 50.00 125.00
ST2IB J.Iginla/M.Backlund 15.00 40.00
ST2JD D.Doughty/J.Johnson 12.00 30.00
ST2KM A.Kopitar/O.Moller 15.00 40.00
ST2LE J.Ericsson/N.Lidstrom 6.00 15.00
ST2LF N.Foligno/P.Leclaire 10.00 25.00
ST2LG S.Gomez/M.Lapierre 8.00 20.00
ST2LM B.Leetch/M.Messier 8.00 20.00
ST2LP M.Pacioretty/M.Lapierre 10.00 25.00
ST2MA A.Anisimov/M.Gaborik 10.00 25.00
ST2MM T.Myers/R.Miller 15.00 40.00
ST2MP C.Price/A.Markov 20.00 50.00
ST2MW A.Markov/Y.Weber 10.00 25.00
ST2NC K.Chucko/E.Nystrom 8.00 20.00
ST2NV M.Neuvirth/S.Varlamov 15.00 40.00
ST2NW C.Neely/B.Wheeler 10.00 25.00
ST2OC P.O'Sullivan/A.Cogliano 8.00 20.00
ST2OM A.Ovechkin/E.Malkin 60.00 150.00
ST2PP D.Phaneuf/M.Pelech 10.00 25.00
ST2RB M.Beleskey/B.Ryan 8.00 20.00
ST2RC D.Carcillo/M.Richards 8.00 20.00
ST2SB M.Streit/J.Bailey 8.00 20.00
ST2SG J.Sheppard/C.Gillies 10.00 25.00
ST2SM M.Stajan/J.Mitchell 6.00 15.00
ST2SS P.Stastny/P.Stastny 8.00 20.00
ST2ST S.Stamkos/M.St. Louis 20.00 50.00
ST2SU B.Sutter/B.Sutter 6.00 15.00
ST2TC L.Caputi/M.Talbot 10.00 25.00
ST2TS M.Talbot/J.Staal 8.00 20.00
ST2VB Z.Bogosian/B.Valabik 10.00 25.00
ST2VK T.Kennedy/T.Vanek 8.00 20.00
ST2VW T.Vokoun/S.Weiss 8.00 20.00
ST2YB Yzerman/Bowman 25.00 60.00

2009-10 SP Authentic Sign of the Times Triples

ST3ADO Arnott/Dumont/O'Reilly 8.00 20.00
ST3BBM Brnstrm/Moller/Backlnd 15.00 40.00
ST3BEM Brodeur/T.Espo/Mason 25.00 60.00
ST3BMM Leetch/M.Staal/Sauer 8.00 20.00
ST3CGR Richrds/Gagne/Clrk 15.00 40.00
ST3DOM Datsyk/Ovech/Malk 40.00 100.00
ST3FME Fuhr/Miller/Enroth 15.00 40.00
ST3GSP Paciorty/Gomz/Shutt 10.00 25.00
ST3LEE Lndqvst/Ersberg/Enroth 25.00 60.00
ST3LHD Lindsay/Howe/Delvec 30.00 80.00
ST3LPM Mason/Price/Leclar 20.00 50.00
ST3LSS Lecav/St.L/Stamkos 20.00 50.00
ST3LYG Gretz/Yzermn/Mario 400.00 1000.00
ST3LYR Yzermn/Leetch/Robit 25.00 60.00
ST3MRW Weber/Robsn/Markv 10.00 25.00
ST3RCG Richards/Carter/Giroux 10.00 25.00
ST3SBS E.Staal/Sutter/Boychuk 12.00 30.00
ST3YZH Howe/Yzermn/Zetter 150.00 250.00

2010-11 SP Authentic

COMP.SET w/o SPs (150) 12.00 30.00
1 Sidney Crosby 1.25 3.00
2 Ryan Kesler .30 .75
3 Phil Kessel .30 .75
4 Thomas Vanek .25 .60
5 James van Riemsdyk .25 .60
6 Tomas Holmstrom .20 .50
7 Tyler Myers .20 .50
8 Milan Hejduk .25 .60
9 Tomas Vokoun .25 .60
10 Paul Stastny .25 .60
11 Martin St. Louis .30 .75
12 Jeff Carter .25 .60
13 Ryan Miller .30 .75
14 John Tavares .50 1.25
15 Blake Wheeler .30 .75
16 Victor Hedman .40 1.00
17 Nicklas Backstrom .30 .75
18 Michael Frolik .20 .50
19 Derick Brassard .20 .50
20 Shea Weber .25 .60
21 Matt Duchene .30 .75
22 Mike Green .25 .60
23 Daniel Sedin .40 1.00
24 Jason Arnott .25 .60
25 Jakub Voracek .25 .60
26 Evander Kane .30 .75
27 Joe Pavelski .40 1.00
28 Patrice Bergeron .40 1.00
29 Claude Giroux .30 .75
30 Devin Setoguchi .25 .60
31 Alexander Ovechkin 1.25 3.00
32 Steven Stamkos .60 1.50
33 Jarome Iginla .40 1.00
34 Joe Thornton .50 1.25
35 Martin Brodeur .75 2.00
36 Rick Nash .30 .75
37 Jonathan Toews .50 1.25
38 Patrick Kane .60 1.50
39 Drew Doughty .40 1.00
40 Evgeni Malkin .60 1.50
41 Pavel Datsyuk .50 1.25
42 Shane Doan .25 .60
43 Nicklas Lidstrom .30 .75
44 Mike Richards .25 .60
45 Marc-Andre Fleury .60 1.50
46 Carey Price .60 1.50
47 Johan Franzen .25 .60
48 Ryan Getzlaf .30 .75
49 Jean-Sebastien Giguere .30 .75
50 Eric Lindros .50 1.25
51 Joe Sakic .60 1.50
52 Ray Bourque .50 1.25
53 Luc Robitaille .30 .75
54 Guy Lafleur .40 1.00
55 Cam Neely .30 .75
56 Chris Osgood .30 .75
57 Steve Yzerman .75 2.00
58 Mark Messier .60 1.50
59 Mario Lemieux 1.25 3.00
60 Wayne Gretzky 2.00 5.00
61 Vincent Lecavalier .30 .75
62 Jaroslav Halak .30 .75
63 Ilya Bryzgalov .25 .60
64 Mike Fisher .20 .50
65 Daniel Alfredsson .30 .75
66 Josh Bailey .25 .60
67 Patric Hornqvist .20 .50
68 Tomas Plekanec .20 .50
69 Andrew Brunette .20 .50
70 Alexander Semin .30 .75
71 Gilbert Brule .30 .75
72 Alexandre Burrows .20 .50
73 James Neal .20 .50
74 Craig Anderson .30 .75
75 Marty Turco .30 .75
76 Cam Ward .30 .75
77 Derek Roy .20 .50
78 Dustin Byfuglien .30 .75
79 Bobby Ryan .25 .60
80 Steve Mason .25 .60
81 Miikka Kiprusoff .30 .75
82 Tuukka Rask .40 1.00
83A Semyon Varlamov .30 .75
83B Corey Perry .50 1.25
85 Luke Schenn .30 .75
86 Ryan Smyth .25 .60
87 Andrei Markov .30 .75
88 Jamie Langenbrunner .20 .50
89 Henrik Lundqvist .75 2.00
90 Chris Pronger .30 .75
91 Dany Heatley .25 .60
92 Dan Boyle .20 .50
93 Mark Streit .20 .50
94 Teemu Selanne .60 1.50
95 Jussi Jokinen .20 .50
96 Zdeno Chara .30 .75
97 Jonas Hiller .25 .60
98 Patrick Sharp .30 .75
99 Roberto Luongo .50 1.25
100 Kari Lehtonen .25 .60
101 David Backes .20 .50
102 Chris Drury .25 .60
103 David Clarkson .20 .50
104 Jim Howard .40 1.00
105 Henrik Sedin .40 1.00
106 Dion Phaneuf .25 .60
107 Jonathan Quick .40 1.00
108 Scott Gomez .25 .60
109 Antoine Vermette .20 .50
110 Guillaume Latendresse .25 .60
111 Rene Bourque .20 .50
112 Eric Staal .40 1.00
113 Mike Smith .30 .75
114 Michael Leighton .25 .60
115 Marian Gaborik .30 .75
116 Patrick Marleau .30 .75
117 Andy McDonald .25 .60
118 Jason Spezza .30 .75
119 Mike Ribeiro .20 .50
120 Ales Hemsky .25 .60
121 Anze Kopitar .50 1.25
122 Loui Eriksson .20 .50
123 Brandon Sutter .20 .50
124 Sam Gagner .20 .50
125 Niklas Backstrom .30 .75
126 Nik Antropov .25 .60
127 Henrik Zetterberg .40 1.00
128 Dustin Penner .20 .50
129 Mikko Koivu .30 .75
130 Mike Modano .50 1.25
131 Marian Hossa .30 .75
132 Marc Savard .20 .50
133 Steve Sullivan .20 .50
134 Zach Parise .30 .75
135 Wojtek Wolski .20 .50
136 Mikael Samuelsson .20 .50
137 Brian Elliott .25 .60
138 Jordan Staal .25 .60
139 Brian Gionta .20 .50
140 Rick DiPietro .25 .60
141 Stephen Weiss .25 .60
142 Alex Tanguay .20 .50
143 Dustin Brown .30 .75
144 Brandon Dubinsky .20 .50
145 Erik Johnson .20 .50
146 J.P. Dumont .20 .50
147 Ville Leino .25 .60
148 Brad Richards .30 .75
149 Ilya Kovalchuk .30 .75
150 Pekka Rinne .30 .75
151 Milan Lucic ESS .75 2.00
152 Teemu Selanne ESS 1.50 4.00
153 Joe Sakic ESS 1.50 4.00
154 Jakub Voracek ESS .60 1.50
155 Lanny McDonald ESS .75 2.00
156 Dustin Penner ESS .50 1.25
157 Mike Modano ESS 1.25 3.00
158 Patrik Elias ESS .75 2.00
159 Guillaume Latendresse ESS .60 1.50
160 Guy Lafleur ESS 1.00 2.50
161 Daniel Alfredsson ESS .75 2.00
162 Phil Esposito ESS 1.25 3.00
163 Alexander Ovechkin ESS 3.00 8.00
164 Evgeni Malkin ESS 1.50 4.00
165 Pekka Rinne ESS .75 2.00
166 Mario Lemieux ESS 3.00 8.00
167 Tony Esposito ESS .75 2.00
168 Tyler Myers ESS .50 1.25
169 Nicklas Lidstrom ESS .75 2.00
170 Milan Hejduk ESS .60 1.50
171 Duncan Keith ESS .60 1.50
172 Mikko Koivu ESS .75 2.00
173 Brandon Dubinsky ESS .50 1.25
174 Martin Brodeur ESS 2.00 5.00
175 Bobby Clarke ESS 1.25 3.00
176 Jaroslav Halak ESS .75 2.00
177 Steven Stamkos ESS 1.50 4.00
178 Henrik Sedin ESS 1.00 2.50
179 Eric Staal ESS 1.00 2.50
180 Corey Perry ESS 1.25 3.00
181 Dan Boyle ESS .50 1.25
182 Chris Pronger ESS .75 2.00
183 Phil Kessel ESS .75 2.00
184 Mike Green ESS .60 1.50
185 Anze Kopitar ESS 1.25 3.00
186 Jonathan Toews ESS 1.25 3.00
187 Sidney Crosby ESS 3.00 8.00
188 Mike Cammalleri ESS .75 2.00
189 Ray Bourque ESS 1.25 3.00
190 Dustin Byfuglien ESS .75 2.00
191 Brad Richards ESS .75 2.00
192 Johan Franzen ESS .60 1.50
193 Patrice Bergeron ESS 1.00 2.50
194 Dustin Brown ESS .75 2.00
195 Matt Duchene ESS .75 2.00
196 Jean-Sebastien Giguere ESS .75 2.00
197 Alexandre Burrows ESS .50 1.25
198 Doug Gilmour ESS 1.00 2.50
199 Wayne Gretzky ESS 5.00 12.00
200 Steve Yzerman ESS 2.00 5.00
201 Ilya Bryzgalov ESS .60 1.50
202 Jussi Jokinen ESS .50 1.25
203 Gilbert Perreault ESS .75 2.00
204 Joe Thornton ESS 1.25 3.00
205 Mark Messier ESS 1.50 4.00
206 Rick Nash ESS .75 2.00
207 Patrick Roy ESS 2.00 5.00
208 Gordie Howe ESS 2.50 6.00
209 Matt Kassian RC 3.00 8.00
210 Linus Klasen RC 3.00 8.00
211 Jon Matsumoto RC 3.00 8.00
212 Mark Dekanich RC 3.00 8.00
213 Adam McQuaid RC 4.00 10.00
214 Tomas Tatar RC 8.00 20.00
215 Korbinian Holzer RC 3.00 8.00
216 Jonas Holos RC 3.00 8.00
217 Jeremy Morin RC 3.00 8.00
218 Ben Smith RC 4.00 10.00
219 Nick Holden RC 3.00 8.00
220 Brandon McMillan RC 3.00 8.00
221 Travis Hamonic RC 4.00 10.00
222 Mats Zuccarello-Aasen RC 6.00 15.00
223 Evgeny Dadonov RC 4.00 10.00
224 Linus Omark RC 4.00 10.00
225 Patrice Cormier RC 4.00 10.00
226 Nikita Nikitin RC 3.00 8.00
227 Mike Moore RC 3.00 8.00
228 Jake Muzzin RC 8.00 20.00
229 Marco Scandella RC 3.00 8.00
230 Brad Mills RC 3.00 8.00
231 Alexander Urbom RC 3.00 8.00
232 Matt Taormina RC 3.00 8.00
233 Matt Martin RC 5.00 12.00
234 Alexander Vasyunov RC 3.00 8.00
235 Mark Fayne RC 3.00 8.00
236 Olivier Magnan-Grenier RC 3.00 8.00
237 Stephen Gionta RC 4.00 10.00
238 Derek Smith RC 3.00 8.00
239 Robin Lehner RC 6.00 15.00
240 Justin Braun RC 3.00 8.00
241 Brett MacLean RC 4.00 10.00
242 Johan Harju RC 3.00 8.00
243 Ryan Reaves RC 4.00 10.00
244 Jim O'Brien RC 4.00 10.00
245 Keith Aulie RC 3.00 8.00
246 Nicholas Drazenovic RC 4.00 10.00
247 Ryan McDonagh RC 8.00 20.00
248 Brian Fahey RC 3.00 8.00
249 Marcus Johansson AU RC 8.00 20.00
250 Nazem Kadri AU RC 40.00 100.00
251 Dustin Tokarski AU RC 5.00 12.00
252 Dana Tyrell AU RC 5.00 12.00
253 Tommy Wingels AU RC 5.00 12.00
254 Eric Tangradi AU RC 5.00 12.00
255 Nick Johnson AU RC 4.00 10.00
256 A.Pechurski AU RC 6.00 15.00
257 Joe Fallon AU RC 5.00 12.00
258 O.Ekman-Larsson AU RC 8.00 20.00
259 Sergei Bobrovsky AU RC 50.00 125.00
260 Kaspars Daugavins AU RC 6.00 15.00
261 Jared Cowen AU RC 5.00 12.00
262 Derek Stepan AU RC 6.00 15.00
263 Evgeny Grachev AU RC 5.00 12.00
264 Nino Niederreiter AU RC 8.00 20.00
265 Dustin Kohn AU RC 5.00 12.00
266 Eric Wellwood AU RC 6.00 15.00
267 Nick Palmieri AU RC 5.00 12.00
268 Jacob Josefson AU RC 5.00 12.00
269 Anders Lindback AU RC 5.00 12.00
270 Nick Spaling AU RC 5.00 12.00
271 P.K. Subban AU RC 25.00 60.00
272 J.T. Wyman AU RC 5.00 12.00
273 Justin Falk AU RC 4.00 10.00
274 Cody Almond AU RC 5.00 12.00
275 Maxim Noreau AU RC 4.00 10.00
276 Casey Wellman AU RC 5.00 12.00
277 Brayden Schenn AU RC 12.00 30.00
278 Kyle Clifford AU RC 6.00 15.00
279 Magnus Paajarvi AU RC 6.00 15.00
280 Taylor Hall AU RC 30.00 80.00
281 Jordan Eberle AU RC 15.00 40.00
282 Alex Plante AU RC 5.00 12.00
283 Mattias Tedenby AU RC 5.00 12.00
284 Evan Brophey AU RC 5.00 12.00
285 Philip Larsen AU RC 5.00 12.00
286 Brandon Pirri AU RC 5.00 12.00
287 Luke Adam AU RC 5.00 12.00
288 K.Shattenkirk AU RC 10.00 25.00
289 Colby Cohen AU RC 5.00 12.00
290 Chad Kolarik AU RC 5.00 12.00
291 Mark Olver AU RC 5.00 12.00
292 Brandon Yip AU RC 5.00 12.00
293 Justin Mercier AU RC 5.00 12.00
294 Nick Leddy AU RC 6.00 15.00
295 Jeff Skinner AU RC 15.00 40.00
296 Jamie McBain AU RC 5.00 12.00
297 Zac Dalpe AU RC 6.00 15.00
298 Ian Cole AU RC 5.00 12.00
299 Henrik Karlsson AU RC 5.00 12.00
300 T.J. Brodie AU RC 5.00 12.00
301 Tyler Seguin AU RC 30.00 80.00
302 Zach Hamill AU RC 5.00 12.00
303 A.Bodnarchuk AU RC 5.00 12.00
304 Jordan Caron AU RC 6.00 15.00
305 A.Burmistrov AU RC 5.00 12.00
306 Arturs Kulda AU RC 5.00 12.00
307 Cam Fowler AU RC 12.00 30.00
308 Kyle Palmieri AU RC 10.00 25.00
309 T.McCollum AU RC 6.00 15.00
310 Jacob Markstrom AU RC 20.00 50.00

2010-11 SP Authentic Limited Autographed Patches

1 Sidney Crosby/100 75.00 150.00
2 Ryan Kesler/100 20.00 50.00
3 Phil Kessel/100 15.00 40.00
4 Thomas Vanek/100 15.00 40.00
5 James van Riemsdyk/100 20.00 50.00
6 Tomas Holmstrom/100 10.00 25.00
8 Milan Hejduk/100 12.00 30.00
9 Tomas Vokoun/100 12.00 30.00
10 Paul Stastny/100 12.00 30.00
11 Martin St. Louis/100 15.00 40.00
12 Jeff Carter/100 12.00 30.00
13 Ryan Miller/100 15.00 40.00
14 John Tavares/100 30.00 60.00
15 Blake Wheeler/100 15.00 40.00
16 Victor Hedman/100 20.00 50.00
17 Nicklas Backstrom/100 25.00 50.00
20 Shea Weber/100 12.00 30.00
22 Mike Green/100 20.00 50.00
27 Joe Pavelski/100 20.00 50.00
28 Patrice Bergeron/100 30.00 80.00
30 Devin Setoguchi/100 12.00 30.00
31 Alexander Ovechkin/25 125.00 225.00
32 Steven Stamkos/25 60.00 120.00
33 Jarome Iginla/25 40.00 100.00
34 Joe Thornton/25 50.00 125.00
36 Rick Nash/25 30.00 80.00
37 Jonathan Toews/25 60.00 120.00
38 Patrick Kane/25 40.00 100.00
40 Evgeni Malkin/25 50.00 100.00
41 Pavel Datsyuk/25 40.00 80.00
43 Nicklas Lidstrom/25 60.00 120.00

45 Marc-Andre Fleury/25 25.00 60.00
46 Carey Price/25 100.00 200.00
47 Johan Franzen/25 25.00 60.00
48 Ryan Getzlaf/25 25.00 60.00
50 Eric Lindros/25 125.00 250.00
51 Joe Sakic/25 100.00 200.00
52 Ray Bourque/25 125.00 250.00
53 Luc Robitaille/25 40.00 100.00
54 Guy Lafleur/25 60.00 125.00
55 Cam Neely/25 60.00 120.00
56 Chris Osgood/25 50.00 100.00
57 Steve Yzerman/25 150.00 250.00
58 Mark Messier/25 100.00 200.00
59 Mario Lemieux/25 100.00 200.00
60 Wayne Gretzky/25 500.00 1200.00
249 Marcus Johansson 50.00 100.00
250 Nazem Kadri 50.00 125.00
251 Dustin Tokarski 10.00 25.00
252 Dana Tyrell 12.00 30.00
253 Tommy Wingels 12.00 30.00
254 Eric Tangradi 12.00 30.00
255 Nick Johnson 12.00 30.00
256 Alexander Pechurski 15.00 40.00
257 Joe Fallon 12.00 30.00
258 Oliver Ekman-Larsson 20.00 50.00
259 Sergei Bobrovsky 60.00 150.00
260 Kaspars Daugavins 15.00 40.00
261 Jared Cowen 12.00 30.00
262 Derek Stepan 20.00 50.00
263 Evgeny Grachev 12.00 30.00
264 Nino Niederreiter 20.00 50.00
265 Dustin Kohn 12.00 30.00
266 Eric Wellwood 12.00 30.00
267 Nick Palmieri 12.00 30.00
268 Jacob Josefson 12.00 30.00
269 Anders Lindback 15.00 40.00
270 Nick Spaling 12.00 30.00
271 P.K. Subban 80.00 150.00
272 J.T. Wyman 12.00 30.00
273 Justin Falk 10.00 25.00
274 Cody Almond 10.00 25.00
275 Maxim Noreau 10.00 25.00
276 Casey Wellman 12.00 30.00
277 Brayden Schenn 40.00 100.00
278 Kyle Clifford 15.00 40.00
279 Magnus Paajarvi 15.00 40.00
280 Taylor Hall 100.00 200.00
281 Jordan Eberle 40.00 100.00
282 Alex Plante 12.00 30.00
283 Mattias Tedenby 12.00 30.00
284 Evan Brophey 12.00 30.00
285 Philip Larsen 12.00 30.00
286 Brandon Pirri 20.00 50.00
287 Luke Adam 25.00 60.00
288 Kevin Shattenkirk 20.00 50.00
289 Colby Cohen 12.00 30.00
290 Chad Kolarik 12.00 30.00
291 Mark Olver 12.00 30.00
292 Brandon Yip 12.00 30.00
293 Justin Mercier 12.00 30.00
294 Nick Leddy 20.00 50.00
295 Jeff Skinner 100.00 200.00
296 Jamie McBain 12.00 30.00
297 Zac Dalpe 15.00 40.00
298 Ian Cole 12.00 30.00
299 Henrik Karlsson 12.00 30.00
300 T.J. Brodie 12.00 30.00
301 Tyler Seguin 125.00 200.00
302 Zach Hamill 12.00 30.00
303 Andrew Bodnarchuk 12.00 30.00
304 Jordan Caron 20.00 50.00
305 Alexander Burmistrov 25.00 60.00
306 Arturs Kulda 30.00 80.00
307 Cam Fowler 20.00 50.00
308 Kyle Palmieri 25.00 60.00
309 Thomas McCollum 15.00 40.00
310 Jacob Markstrom 60.00 120.00

2010-11 SP Authentic Chirography

CAK Anze Kopitar 15.00 40.00
CCP Carey Price 20.00 50.00
CHL Henrik Lundqvist 25.00 60.00
CJC Jeff Carter 8.00 20.00
CJG Jean-Sebastien Giguere 10.00 25.00
CJI Jarome Iginla 12.00 30.00
CJP Joe Pavelski 12.00 30.00
CJT John Tavares 20.00 50.00
CJV James van Riemsdyk 8.00 20.00
CMH Marian Hossa 15.00 40.00
CMM Mike Modano 15.00 40.00
COV Alexander Ovechkin 60.00 120.00
CPD Pavel Datsyuk 15.00 40.00
CPK Patrick Kane 20.00 50.00
CRM Ryan Miller 15.00 40.00
CRN Rick Nash 15.00 40.00
CSC Sidney Crosby 75.00 150.00
CSS Steven Stamkos 40.00 100.00
CTH Joe Thornton 15.00 40.00
CTO Jonathan Toews 15.00 40.00

2010-11 SP Authentic Holoview FX

COMPLETE SET (42) 75.00 150.00
*DIE CUTS: 1.5X TO 4X BASIC INSERTS
FX1 Wayne Gretzky 8.00 20.00
FX2 Mikko Koivu 1.25 3.00
FX3 Gilbert Perreault 1.25 3.00
FX4 Bobby Orr 5.00 12.00
FX5 Rick Nash 1.25 3.00
FX6 Martin Brodeur 3.00 8.00
FX7 Henrik Zetterberg 1.50 4.00
FX8 Alexander Ovechkin 5.00 12.00
FX9 Gordie Howe 4.00 10.00
FX10 Daniel Briere 1.25 3.00
FX11 Mark Messier 2.50 6.00
FX12 David Perron 1.00 2.50
FX13 Dion Phaneuf 1.00 2.50
FX14 Thomas Vanek 1.00 2.50
FX15 Dustin Penner .75 2.00
FX16 Drew Doughty 1.50 4.00
FX17 Guy Lafleur 1.50 4.00
FX18 Eric Staal 1.50 4.00
FX19 Steve Yzerman 3.00 8.00
FX20 Nicklas Lidstrom 1.25 3.00
FX21 Henrik Lundqvist 3.00 8.00
FX22 Henrik Sedin 1.50 4.00
FX23 Mario Lemieux 5.00 12.00
FX24 Patrick Marleau 1.25 3.00
FX25 John Tavares 2.00 5.00
FX26 Ilya Kovalchuk 1.25 3.00
FX27 Brian Gionta .75 2.00
FX28 Evgeni Malkin 2.50 6.00
FX29 Mike Richards 1.00 2.50
FX30 Matt Duchene 1.25 3.00
FX31 Jarome Iginla 1.50 4.00
FX32 Bobby Ryan 1.00 2.50
FX33 Patrick Roy 3.00 8.00
FX34 Mike Ribeiro .75 2.00
FX35 Daniel Alfredsson 1.25 3.00
FX36 Jonathan Toews 2.00 5.00
FX37 Shane Doan 1.00 2.50
FX38 Steven Stamkos 2.50 6.00
FX39 Duncan Keith 1.00 2.50
FX40 Joe Pavelski 1.50 4.00
FX41 Martin St. Louis 1.25 3.00
FX42 Sidney Crosby 5.00 12.00

2010-11 SP Authentic Marks of Distinction

MDAO Alexander Ovechkin 60.00 120.00
MDBC Bobby Clarke 50.00 100.00
MDBO Bobby Orr 200.00 300.00
MDCN Cam Neely 15.00 40.00
MDCP Carey Price 50.00 100.00
MDEM Evgeni Malkin 50.00 100.00
MDGH Gordie Howe 125.00 250.00
MDGL Guy Lafleur 50.00 100.00
MDHL Henrik Lundqvist 40.00 100.00
MDJI Jarome Iginla 40.00 80.00
MDJT John Tavares 30.00 80.00
MDLR Luc Robitaille 30.00 80.00
MDMH Milan Hejduk 25.00 60.00
MDMI Mike Bossy 15.00 40.00
MDML Mario Lemieux 60.00 125.00
MDMM Mark Messier 40.00 80.00
MDPD Pavel Datsyuk 25.00 60.00
MDPE Phil Esposito 25.00 60.00
MDPK Patrick Kane 50.00 100.00
MDPR Patrick Roy 75.00 150.00
MDRH Ron Hextall 15.00 40.00
MDRM Ryan Miller 15.00 40.00
MDRN Rick Nash 25.00 60.00
MDSC Sidney Crosby 100.00 200.00
MDSS Steven Stamkos 30.00 80.00
MDTH Joe Thornton 25.00 60.00
MDTO Jonathan Toews 25.00 60.00
MDWG Wayne Gretzky 300.00 800.00

2010-11 SP Authentic Prestigious Pairings

PPBO J.Bucyk/B.Orr 60.00 120.00
PPBP D.Potvin/M.Bossy 20.00 40.00
PPEE P.Esposito/T.Esposito 30.00 60.00
PPEO P.Esposito/B.Orr 75.00 150.00
PPGB M.Green/N.Backstrom 30.00 80.00
PPGM M.Messier/W.Gretzky 250.00 600.00
PPHG W.Gretzky/G.Howe 300.00 800.00
PPHM B.Hull/S.Mikita 30.00 80.00
PPIN R.Nash/J.Iginla 25.00 60.00
PPLR G.Lafleur/L.Robinson 25.00 50.00
PPLY M.Lemieux/S.Yzerman 75.00 150.00
PPMS J.Staal/E.Malkin 15.00 40.00
PPOF C.Osgood/M.Fleury 20.00 50.00
PPOS A.Ovechkin/S.Stamkos 60.00 120.00
PPPV G.Perreault/T.Vanek 15.00 40.00
PPRB R.Bourque/P.Roy 60.00 120.00
PPRK L.Robitaille/J.Kurri 15.00 40.00
PPSD P.Stastny/M.Duchene 10.00 25.00
PPTK P.Kane/J.Toews 60.00 100.00
PPTP J.Thornton/J.Pavelski 15.00 40.00
PPTS J.Tavares/S.Stamkos 50.00 100.00
PPVP R.Vachon/C.Price 50.00 100.00

2010-11 SP Authentic Sign of the Times

SOTAB Alexander Burmistrov 5.00 12.00
SOTAC Andrew Cogliano 4.00 10.00
SOTAN Antti Niemi 5.00 12.00
SOTAO Alexander Ovechkin 50.00 125.00
SOTAT Alex Tanguay 4.00 10.00
SOTBA Josh Bailey 5.00 12.00
SOTBC Bobby Clarke 20.00 50.00
SOTBM Barry Melrose 5.00 12.00
SOTBN Brayden Schenn 12.00 30.00
SOTBO Bobby Orr 50.00 125.00
SOTBR Bobby Ryan 5.00 12.00
SOTBS Bobby Sanguinetti 4.00 10.00
SOTCA Jeff Carter 5.00 12.00
SOTCO Chris Osgood 6.00 15.00
SOTCP Carey Price 12.00 30.00
SOTCR Sidney Crosby SP 80.00 200.00
SOTCS Chris Stewart 5.00 12.00
SOTCW Cam Ward 6.00 15.00
SOTDG Doug Gilmour 8.00 20.00
SOTDH Dany Heatley 5.00 12.00
SOTDS Devin Setoguchi 5.00 12.00
SOTEK Evander Kane 6.00 15.00
SOTEL Eric Lindros 10.00 25.00
SOTEM Evgeni Malkin 12.00 30.00
SOTES Eric Staal 8.00 20.00
SOTET Eric Tangradi 5.00 12.00
SOTGH Gordie Howe 80.00 200.00
SOTGR Wayne Gretzky SP 300.00 800.00
SOTHE Milan Hejduk 5.00 12.00
SOTHL Henrik Lundqvist 15.00 40.00
SOTJA Jay Bouwmeester 4.00 10.00
SOTJB Jamie Benn 8.00 20.00
SOTJC Jared Cowen 5.00 12.00
SOTJE Jordan Eberle 12.00 30.00
SOTJF Johan Franzen 5.00 12.00
SOTJG Jean-Sebastien Giguere 6.00 15.00
SOTJH Jaroslav Halak 6.00 15.00
SOTJI Jarome Iginla 8.00 20.00
SOTJK Jari Kurri 6.00 15.00
SOTJM Jamie McBain 5.00 12.00
SOTJP Joe Pavelski 8.00 20.00
SOTJS Jack Skille 5.00 12.00
SOTJT Joe Thornton 12.00 30.00
SOTJV James van Riemsdyk 5.00 12.00
SOTLC Logan Couture 8.00 20.00
SOTLE Lars Eller 4.00 10.00
SOTLR Luc Robitaille 10.00 25.00
SOTMA Mario Lemieux SP 200.00 300.00
SOTMB Martin Brodeur 15.00 40.00
SOTMC Matthew Corrente 5.00 12.00
SOTMD Matt Duchene 6.00 15.00
SOTMF Marc-Andre Fleury 12.00 30.00
SOTMH Marian Hossa 6.00 15.00
SOTMJ Marcus Johansson 8.00 20.00
SOTML Mario Lemieux 60.00 150.00
SOTMM Mark Messier 40.00 100.00
SOTMO Mike Modano 10.00 25.00
SOTMP Magnus Paajarvi 6.00 15.00
SOTMR Mike Richards 5.00 12.00
SOTMS Marc Staal 4.00 10.00
SOTMT Marty Turco 6.00 15.00
SOTNB Nicklas Bergfors 5.00 12.00
SOTNL Nicklas Lidstrom 10.00 25.00
SOTNZ Nazem Kadri 15.00 40.00
SOTPB Patrice Bergeron 8.00 20.00
SOTPD Pavel Datsyuk 10.00 25.00
SOTPE Phil Esposito 15.00 40.00
SOTPK Patrick Kane 25.00 60.00
SOTPL Perttu Lindgren 4.00 10.00
SOTPM Peter Mueller 5.00 12.00
SOTPR Patrick Roy 50.00 125.00
SOTPS P.K. Subban 25.00 60.00
SOTRB Ray Bourque 25.00 60.00
SOTRE Ray Emery 5.00 12.00
SOTRI Brad Richards 6.00 15.00
SOTRK Ryan Kesler 6.00 15.00
SOTRM Ryan Miller 6.00 15.00
SOTRN Rick Nash 6.00 15.00
SOTRV Rogie Vachon 8.00 20.00
SOTSC Cory Schneider 6.00 15.00
SOTSH James Sheppard 4.00 10.00
SOTSI Sidney Crosby 60.00 150.00
SOTSK Jeff Skinner 12.00 30.00
SOTSN Derek Stepan 6.00 15.00
SOTSS Steven Stamkos 12.00 30.00
SOTTA John Tavares 10.00 25.00
SOTTE Tony Esposito 20.00 50.00
SOTTH Taylor Hall 12.00 30.00
SOTTK Tim Kennedy 4.00 10.00
SOTTM Tyler Myers 4.00 10.00
SOTTO Jonathan Toews 25.00 60.00
SOTTS Tyler Seguin 15.00 40.00
SOTTV Thomas Vanek 5.00 12.00
SOTVH Victor Hedman 8.00 20.00
SOTWG Wayne Gretzky 200.00 500.00
SOTWI Colin Wilson 5.00 12.00
SOTWS Wayne Simmonds 8.00 20.00
SOTZH Zach Hamill 5.00 12.00

2010-11 SP Authentic Sign of the Times Duals

ST2BB N.Bergfors/D.Byfuglien 8.00 20.00
ST2BG J.Giguere/M.Brodeur 60.00 120.00
ST2BH J.Halak/D.Backes 8.00 20.00
ST2BP P.Kessel/B.Salming 15.00 30.00
ST2BT A.Tanguay/J.Bouwmeester 5.00 12.00
ST2CM J.Cowen/J.McBain 6.00 15.00
ST2DA A.Pietrangelo/D.Backes 10.00 25.00
ST2DG D.Stepan/E.Grachev 8.00 20.00
ST2DH D.Doughty/V.Hedman 10.00 25.00
ST2DY M.Duchene/B.Yip 8.00 20.00
ST2ET M.Turco/T.Esposito 20.00 40.00
ST2FH R.Hextall/G.Fuhr 20.00 50.00
ST2GF J.Giguere/M.Fleury 20.00 50.00
ST2HE J.Eberle/T.Hall 100.00 175.00
ST2HH M.Howe/G.Howe 50.00 100.00
ST2HK M.Hossa/P.Kane 20.00 50.00
ST2HP J.Halak/C.Price 30.00 80.00
ST2IK J.Iginla/R.Kesler 10.00 25.00
ST2KP J.Kurri/M.Paajarvi 8.00 20.00
ST2LD P.Datsyuk/N.Lidstrom 40.00 80.00
ST2LF N.Lidstrom/J.Franzen 20.00 50.00
ST2LM E.Malkin/M.Lemieux 30.00 80.00
ST2MD M.Modano/P.Datsyuk 25.00 60.00
ST2NM R.Nash/S.Mason 15.00 40.00
ST2OG B.Orr/W.Gretzky 300.00 800.00
ST2OR B.Orr/B.Orr 150.00 250.00
ST2OV A.Ovechkin/S.Varlamov 60.00 120.00
ST2PK P.Kessel/D.Phaneuf 15.00 40.00
ST2PM C.Price/S.Mason 40.00 80.00
ST2PN P.Subban/N.Kadri 30.00 80.00
ST2PS P.Subban/C.Price 100.00 200.00
ST2PV G.Perreault/T.Vanek 10.00 25.00
ST2QN P.Stastny/G.Lafleur 25.00 60.00
ST2RP P.Roy/C.Price 75.00 150.00
ST2SC T.Seguin/J.Caron 20.00 50.00
ST2SD S.Crosby/S.Crosby 150.00 250.00
ST2SK J.Sakic/J.Sakic 125.00 250.00
ST2SS P.Stastny/P.Stastny 20.00 50.00
ST2TB J.Bailey/J.Tavares 15.00 40.00
ST2TM E.Malkin/M.Talbot 25.00 60.00
ST2TP J.Thornton/J.Pavelski 12.00 30.00
ST2TS J.Tavares/S.Stamkos 30.00 80.00
ST2TT J.Toews/J.Toews 40.00 80.00
ST2VB J.Bernier/R.Vachon 12.00 30.00
ST2WG D.Wilson/D.Gilmour 15.00 40.00
ST2COL J.Sakic/R.Bourque 125.00 250.00
ST2TBL S.Stamkos/S.Gagne 15.00 40.00

2010-11 SP Authentic Sign of the Times Triples

ST31ST Kane/Stamkos/Tavares 100.00 175.00
ST3CHI Toews/Kane/Turco 40.00 100.00
ST3EDM Hall/Eberle/Paajarvi 125.00 250.00
ST3GR8 Lemieux/Yzerman/Messier 100.00 175.00
ST3HOF Gretzky/Howe/Orr 750.00 2000.00
ST3MTL Price/Roy/Vachon 125.00 200.00
ST3TBL Lecav/Hedman/Stamkos 75.00 150.00
ST3TCF Getzlaf/Nash/Iginla 75.00 150.00
ST3IIHF Dionne/Clarke/Esposito 60.00 120.00
ST3ROOK Subban/Kadri/Cowen 125.00 250.00

2010-11 SP Authentic By The Letter Legend Last Name

LSC Sidney Crosby/180* 150.00 300.00

2011-12 SP Authentic

COMP.SET w/o RC's (150) 10.00 25.00
1 P.K. Subban .30 .75
2 Jordan Eberle .25 .60
3 Sam Gagner .15 .40
4 David Clarkson .15 .40
5 Brandon Dubinsky .15 .40
6 Tyler Ennis .15 .40
7 Derek Roy .15 .40
8 Chris Osgood .25 .60
9 Lars Eller .15 .40
10 Bobby Ryan .20 .50
11 Nick Foligno .20 .50
12 Logan Couture .30 .75
13 Jaroslav Halak .25 .60
14 Matt Duchene .25 .60
15 Devin Setoguchi .20 .50
16 Nicklas Backstrom .25 .60
17 Mike Modano .40 1.00
18 Alexander Ovechkin 1.00 2.50
19 Ryan Getzlaf .25 .60
20 Tuukka Rask .30 .75
21 Derick Brassard .15 .40
22 Patrice Bergeron .30 .75
23 Carey Price .50 1.25
24 Ryan Kesler .25 .60
25 Jonathan Toews .40 1.00
26 Nikolai Kulemin .15 .40
27 Taylor Hall .25 .60
28 Patrick Marleau .25 .60
29 Kari Lehtonen .20 .50
30 Sidney Crosby 1.00 2.50
31 Tyler Seguin .30 .75
32 Keith Yandle .15 .40
33 Martin Brodeur .60 1.50
34 Jakub Voracek .20 .50
35 Shea Weber .20 .50
36 Jarome Iginla .30 .75
37 Jay Bouwmeester .15 .40
38 Ryan Smyth .20 .50
39 Steven Stamkos .50 1.25
40 Craig Anderson .25 .60
41 Brad Richards .25 .60
42 Patrick Kane .50 1.25
43 Jordan Staal .20 .50
44 Jonas Hiller .20 .50
45 Nathan Horton .25 .60
46 Thomas Vanek .20 .50
47 Eric Staal .30 .75
48 Ryan Miller .25 .60
49 Trevor Linden .25 .60
50 Larry Robinson .25 .60
51 Bill Barber .25 .60
52 Bill Ranford .25 .60
53 Brad Park .20 .50
54 Brett Hull .50 1.25
55 Luc Robitaille .25 .60
56 Joe Sakic .50 1.25
57 Wayne Gretzky 1.50 4.00
58 Roberto Luongo .40 1.00
59 Brendan Shanahan .25 .60
60 Zach Parise .25 .60
61 Tim Thomas .25 .60
62 Tyler Myers .15 .40
63 Miikka Kiprusoff .25 .60
64 Tomas Holmstrom .15 .40
65 Colin Wilson .20 .50
66 Jim Howard .30 .75
67 Daniel Sedin .30 .75
68 Patrik Berglund .15 .40
69 Brent Burns .25 .60
70 Evander Kane .25 .60
71 Kevin Shattenkirk .15 .40
72 Vincent Lecavalier .25 .60
73 Mike Green .20 .50
74 Tomas Vokoun .20 .50
75 Chris Stewart .20 .50
76 Loui Eriksson .15 .40
77 Chris Pronger .25 .60
78 Alexandre Burrows .15 .40
79 Marc-Andre Fleury .50 1.25
80 Rick Nash .25 .60
81 Marcus Johansson .20 .50
82 Ilya Kovalchuk .25 .60
83 T.J. Oshie .25 .60
84 Dan Cleary .25 .60
85 Brenden Morrow .20 .50
86 Henrik Sedin .30 .75
87 Radim Vrbata .15 .40
88 Martin St. Louis .25 .60
89 John Tavares .40 1.00
90 Ilya Bryzgalov .25 .60
91 Ville Leino .20 .50
92 Dany Heatley .20 .50
93 Ondrej Pavelec .25 .60
94 Bobby Orr 1.00 2.50
95 Pekka Rinne .25 .60
96 Jeff Skinner .30 .75
97 Patrick Sharp .25 .60
98 Teemu Selanne .50 1.25
99 Antoine Vermette .15 .40
100 Dan Boyle .15 .40
101 David Jones .15 .40
102 James Neal .15 .40
103 Joe Thornton .40 1.00
104 Jose Theodore .25 .60
105 Matt Moulson .15 .40
106 Mike Ribeiro .15 .40
107 Mikko Koivu .20 .50
108 Stephen Weiss .20 .50
109 Zdeno Chara .25 .60
110 Ryan Suter .20 .50
111 Ryane Clowe .15 .40
112 Scott Gomez .20 .50
113 Semyon Varlamov .25 .60
114 Shane Doan .20 .50
115 Phil Kessel .25 .60
116 Ryan Callahan .15 .40
117 Steve Mason UER
(Allen York pictured on front) .20 .50
118 Daniel Alfredsson .25 .60
119 Niklas Backstrom .25 .60
120 Pavel Datsyuk .40 1.00
121 Josh Gorges .15 .40
122 Dion Phaneuf .20 .50
123 Henrik Zetterberg .30 .75
124 Magnus Paajarvi .20 .50
125 Luke Adam .20 .50
126 Cam Ward .25 .60
127 Corey Perry .40 1.00
128 Mark Giordano .25 .60
129 Brian Campbell .15 .40
130 Claude Giroux .25 .60
131 Dwayne Roloson .20 .50
132 James Reimer .25 .60
133 Johan Franzen .20 .50
134 Erik Karlsson .30 .75
135 Drew Doughty .30 .75
136 Jussi Jokinen .15 .40
137 Paul Stastny .20 .50
138 Marian Hossa .25 .60
139 Michael Grabner .20 .50
140 James van Riemsdyk .20 .50
141 Henrik Lundqvist .60 1.50
142 Nicklas Lidstrom .15 .40
143 Daniel Briere .25 .60
144 Anze Kopitar .40 1.00
145 Corey Crawford .30 .75
146 Erik Johnson .15 .40
147 Mike Richards .20 .50
148 Dustin Byfuglien .25 .60
149 Evgeni Malkin .50 1.25
150 Dustin Brown .25 .60
151 Corey Perry ESS 1.25 3.00
152 Bobby Orr ESS 3.00 8.00
153 Tim Thomas ESS .75 2.00
154 Ryan Miller ESS .75 2.00
155 Jarome Iginla ESS 1.00 2.50
156 Jeff Skinner ESS 1.00 2.50
157 Jonathan Toews ESS 1.25 3.00
158 Matt Duchene ESS .75 2.00
159 Jamie Benn ESS .75 2.00
160 Jim Howard ESS 1.00 2.50
161 Taylor Hall ESS .75 2.00
162 Anze Kopitar ESS 1.25 3.00
163 Mike Richards ESS .60 1.50
164 Mikko Koivu ESS .60 1.50
165 Carey Price ESS 1.50 4.00
166 P.K. Subban ESS 1.00 2.50
167 Zach Parise ESS .75 2.00
168 Ilya Kovalchuk ESS .75 2.00
169 Martin Brodeur ESS 2.00 5.00
170 John Tavares ESS 1.25 3.00
171 Wayne Gretzky ESS 5.00 12.00
172 Mark Messier ESS 1.50 4.00
173 Henrik Lundqvist ESS 2.00 5.00
174 Eric Lindros ESS 1.25 3.00
175 Jaromir Jagr ESS 2.50 6.00
176 Sidney Crosby ESS 3.00 8.00
177 Steven Stamkos ESS 1.50 4.00
178 Phil Kessel ESS .75 2.00
179 Roberto Luongo ESS 1.25 3.00
180 Alexander Ovechkin ESS 3.00 8.00
181 Peter Holland RC 2.50 6.00
182 Pat Maroon RC 2.50 6.00
183 Iiro Tarkki RC 3.00 8.00
184 Brayden McNabb RC 2.50 6.00
185 Marcus Foligno RC 4.00 10.00
186 Leland Irving RC 2.50 6.00
187 Andrew Shaw RC 6.00 15.00
188 Jimmy Hayes RC 3.00 8.00
189 Brad Malone RC 2.50 6.00
190 Ryan Russell RC 3.00 8.00
191 Matt Fraser RC 3.00 8.00
192 Brendan Smith RC 2.50 6.00
193 Milan Kytnar RC 3.00 8.00
194 Greg Rallo RC 3.00 8.00
195 Brian Foster RC 3.00 8.00
196 Jarod Palmer RC 2.50 6.00
197 Kris Fredheim RC 2.50 6.00
198 David McIntyre RC 2.50 6.00
199 Frederic St. Denis RC 2.50 6.00
200 Mattias Ekholm RC 8.00 20.00
201 Ryan Ellis RC 2.50 6.00
202 Roman Josi RC 6.00 15.00
203 Keith Kinkaid RC 2.50 6.00
204 David Ullstrom RC 2.50 6.00
205 Calvin de Haan RC 2.50 6.00
206 Mikko Koskinen RC 3.00 8.00
207 Anders Nilsson RC 2.50 6.00
208 Stu Bickel RC 2.50 6.00
209 Carl Hagelin RC 4.00 10.00
210 Andre Petersson RC 3.00 8.00
211 Erik Condra RC 2.50 6.00
212 Mark Borowiecki RC 3.00 8.00
213 Zac Rinaldo RC 2.50 6.00
214 Harry Zolnierczyk RC 2.50 6.00
215 Kevin Marshall RC 2.50 6.00
216 Marc-Andre Bourdon RC 2.50 6.00
217 Robert Bortuzzo RC 2.50 6.00
218 Carl Sneep RC 2.50 6.00
219 Cade Fairchild RC 2.00 5.00
220 Dmitry Orlov RC 6.00 15.00
221 Gustav Nyquist AU RC 12.00 30.00
222 Andy Miele AU RC 4.00 10.00
223 Colten Teubert AU RC 4.00 10.00
224 Cody Hodgson AU RC 6.00 15.00
225 Jake Gardiner AU RC 10.00 25.00
226 Carl Klingberg AU RC 4.00 10.00
227 Mika Zibanejad AU RC 40.00 100.00
228 Mark Scheifele AU RC 25.00 60.00
229 Aaron Palushaj AU RC 4.00 10.00
230 Adam Larsson AU RC 8.00 20.00
231 Matt Read AU RC 5.00 12.00
232 Matt Frattin AU RC 4.00 10.00
233 Blake Geoffrion AU RC 4.00 10.00
234 Smith-Pelly AU RC EXCH 12.00 30.00
235 Erik Gudbranson AU RC 8.00 20.00
236 Jonathon Blum AU RC 4.00 10.00
237 Anton Lander AU RC 10.00 25.00
238 Brandon Saad AU RC 12.00 30.00
239 Adam Henrique AU RC 8.00 20.00
240 Brett Connolly AU RC 4.00 10.00
241 Harri Sateri AU RC 4.00 10.00
242 Joe Colborne AU RC 4.00 10.00
243 Marcus Kruger AU RC 6.00 15.00
244 Greg Nemisz AU RC 4.00 10.00
245 Ryan Johansen AU RC 12.00 30.00
246 Sean Couturier AU RC 12.00 30.00
247 G.Landeskog AU RC 80.00 200.00
248 Ryan Nugent-Hopkins AU RC 30.00 80.00
249 Roman Horak AU RC 4.00 10.00
250 John Moore AU RC 4.00 10.00
251 Colin Greening AU RC 4.00 10.00
252 Cam Atkinson AU RC 10.00 25.00
253 T.Vincour AU RC EXCH 4.00 10.00
254 Yann Sauve AU RC 4.00 10.00
255 Alexei Emelin AU RC 4.00 10.00
256 Cody Eakin AU RC 6.00 15.00
257 Justin Faulk AU RC 6.00 15.00
258 Cameron Gaunce AU RC 3.00 8.00
259 Joe Vitale AU RC 4.00 10.00
260 Brendon Nash AU RC 4.00 10.00
261 Erik Gustafsson AU RC 5.00 12.00
262 Raphael Diaz AU RC 4.00 10.00
263 David Savard AU RC 4.00 10.00
264 Tim Erixon AU RC 4.00 10.00
265 Teemu Hartikainen AU RC 4.00 10.00
266 Ben Scrivens AU RC 8.00 20.00
267 Paul Postma AU RC 4.00 10.00
268 Craig Smith AU RC 5.00 12.00
269 Patrick Wiercioch AU RC 4.00 10.00
270 Alex Stalock AU 3.00 8.00
271 Brett Bulmer AU RC 4.00 10.00
272 Stephane Da Costa AU RC 4.00 10.00
273 Viatcheslav Voynov AU RC 4.00 10.00
274 Simon Despres AU RC 4.00 10.00
275 Louis Leblanc AU RC 4.00 10.00
276 Lance Bouma AU RC 4.00 10.00
277 Brian Strait AU RC 5.00 12.00
278 Ben Holmstrom AU RC 4.00 10.00
279 Zack Kassian AU RC 8.00 20.00
280 Lennart Petrell AU RC 5.00 12.00

2011-12 SP Authentic Chirography

CBM Brad Marchand 15.00 30.00
CBO Bobby Orr 60.00 120.00
CCG Claude Giroux 20.00 40.00
CCP Carey Price 20.00 50.00
CDP Dion Phaneuf 8.00 20.00
CDR Derek Roy 6.00 15.00
CES Eric Staal 12.00 30.00
CHL Henrik Lundqvist 30.00 60.00
CJE Jordan Eberle 25.00 60.00
CJP Joe Pavelski 12.00 30.00
CJS Jeff Skinner 20.00 40.00
CLC Logan Couture 12.00 30.00
CMD Matt Duchene 10.00 25.00
CNB Nicklas Backstrom 10.00 25.00
CNH Nathan Horton 10.00 25.00
CPK Patrick Kane 30.00 60.00
CPS P.K. Subban 12.00 30.00
CRK Ryan Kesler 15.00 40.00
CRM Ryan Miller 10.00 25.00
CSC Sidney Crosby 60.00 120.00
CSS Steven Stamkos 30.00 80.00
CTV Thomas Vanek 8.00 20.00

2011-12 SP Authentic Holoview FX

*DIE CUTS: 1.2X TO 3X BASIC INSERTS
RFX1 Devante Smith-Pelly 1.25 3.00
RFX2 Greg Nemisz 1.00 2.50
RFX3 Marcus Kruger 1.50 4.00
RFX4 Brandon Saad 2.00 5.00
RFX5 Gabriel Landeskog 3.00 8.00
RFX6 Ryan Johansen 3.00 8.00
RFX7 Ryan Nugent-Hopkins 10.00 25.00
RFX8 Teemu Hartikainen 1.00 2.50
RFX9 Anton Lander 1.00 2.50
RFX10 Lennart Petrell 1.25 3.00
RFX11 Erik Gudbranson 1.25 3.00
RFX12 Aaron Palushaj 1.00 2.50
RFX13 Craig Smith 1.25 3.00
RFX14 Jonathon Blum 1.00 2.50
RFX15 Blake Geoffrion 1.00 2.50
RFX16 Adam Henrique 2.50 6.00
RFX17 Adam Larsson 1.25 3.00
RFX18 Tim Erixon 1.00 2.50
RFX19 Mika Zibanejad 3.00 8.00
RFX20 David Rundblad 1.00 2.50
RFX21 Sean Couturier 2.00 5.00
RFX22 Matt Read 1.25 3.00
RFX23 Harri Sateri 1.00 2.50
RFX24 Brett Connolly 1.00 2.50
RFX25 Jake Gardiner 1.50 4.00
RFX26 Joe Colborne 1.00 2.50
RFX27 Matt Frattin 1.00 2.50
RFX28 Cody Hodgson 1.50 4.00
RFX29 Carl Klingberg 1.00 2.50
RFX30 Mark Scheifele 4.00 10.00

2011-12 SP Authentic Limited Patches

*ROOKIE AU/100: 1.2X TO 3X BASIC AU RC
1 P.K. Subban AU/100 20.00 50.00
2 Jordan Eberle AU/100 20.00 50.00
3 Sam Gagner AU/100 12.00 30.00
4 David Clarkson AU/100 10.00 25.00
6 Tyler Ennis AU/100 10.00 25.00
7 Derek Roy AU/100 10.00 25.00
8 Chris Osgood AU/100 15.00 40.00
9 Lars Eller AU/100 10.00 25.00
12 Logan Couture AU/100 12.00 30.00
13 Jaroslav Halak AU/100 15.00 40.00
14 Matt Duchene AU/100 20.00 50.00
15 Devin Setoguchi AU/100 10.00 25.00
16 Nicklas Backstrom AU/25 30.00 80.00
17 Mike Modano AU/25 40.00 100.00
18 Alexander Ovechkin AU/25 40.00 80.00
19 Ryan Getzlaf AU/25 30.00 80.00
20 Tuukka Rask AU/25 30.00 80.00
21 Derick Brassard AU/25 20.00 50.00
22 Patrice Bergeron AU/25 50.00 100.00
23 Carey Price AU/25 60.00 120.00
24 Ryan Kesler AU/25 25.00 60.00
25 Jonathan Toews AU/25 60.00 120.00
26 Nikolai Kulemin AU/25 20.00 50.00
27 Taylor Hall AU/25 75.00 150.00
28 Patrick Marleau AU/25 25.00 60.00
30 Sidney Crosby AU/25 100.00 175.00
31 Tyler Seguin AU/25 40.00 100.00
33 Martin Brodeur AU/25 EXCH 60.00 120.00
35 Jarome Iginla AU/25 25.00 60.00
37 Jay Bouwmeester AU/25 25.00 60.00
39 Steven Stamkos AU/25 75.00 150.00
41 Brad Richards AU/25 30.00 80.00
42 Patrick Kane AU/25 25.00 60.00
43 Jordan Staal AU/25 25.00 60.00
44 Jonas Hiller AU/25 25.00 60.00
45 Nathan Horton AU/25 25.00 60.00
46 Thomas Vanek AU/25 15.00 40.00
47 Eric Staal AU/25 20.00 50.00
48 Ryan Miller AU/25 30.00 80.00
49 Trevor Linden AU/25 50.00 100.00
50 Larry Robinson AU/25 30.00 80.00
51 Bill Barber AU/25 30.00 80.00
52 Bill Ranford AU/25 30.00 80.00
53 Brad Park AU/25 25.00 60.00
54 Brett Hull AU/25 40.00 100.00
56 Joe Sakic AU/25 50.00 100.00
58 Roberto Luongo/25 20.00 50.00
59 Brendan Shanahan/25 12.00 30.00
60 Zach Parise/25 12.00 30.00
240 Brett Connolly AU/100 12.00 30.00
247 Gabriel Landeskog AU/100 80.00 200.00
248 Ryan Nugent-Hopkins AU/100 100.00 200.00

2011-12 SP Authentic Marks of Distinction

MDBO Bobby Orr 125.00 250.00
MDBY Mike Bossy 25.00 50.00
MDCP Carey Price 30.00 80.00
MDDH Dale Hawerchuk 25.00 60.00
MDDR Derek Roy 10.00 25.00
MDGP Gilbert Perreault 15.00 40.00
MDHL Henrik Lundqvist 30.00 60.00
MDJI Jarome Iginla 20.00 50.00
MDJS Joe Sakic 40.00 80.00
MDJT Joe Thornton 25.00 50.00
MDML Mario Lemieux 100.00 200.00
MDMM Mark Messier 40.00 100.00
MDMN Markus Naslund 15.00 40.00
MDPK Patrick Kane 30.00 80.00
MDPS P.K. Subban 25.00 50.00
MDRF Ron Francis 20.00 50.00
MDRM Ryan Miller 12.00 30.00
MDSC Sidney Crosby 100.00 175.00
MDSS Steven Stamkos 50.00 100.00
MDTH Taylor Hall 50.00 100.00
MDTO Jonathan Toews 25.00 60.00
MDWG Wayne Gretzky EXCH 200.00 500.00

2011-12 SP Authentic Prestigious Pairings

PPBB D.Boyle/B.Burns 12.00 30.00
PPEH T.Hall/J.Eberle 50.00 100.00
PPES P.Subban/L.Eller 15.00 40.00
PPGL H.Lundqvist/M.Gaborik 30.00 80.00
PPGV C.Giroux/Van Riemsdyk 12.00 30.00
PPHF M.Hossa/M.Frolik 12.00 30.00
PPHH B.Hull/B.Hull 75.00 150.00
PPHM D.Hasek/R.Miller 30.00 60.00
PPHO B.Hull/A.Oates 60.00 120.00
PPKH C.Hodgson/R.Kesler 30.00 60.00
PPLF M.Lemieux/R.Francis 60.00 120.00
PPMM J.Moore/S.Mason 8.00 20.00
PPOR B.Orr/L.Robinson 80.00 150.00
PPPC J.Pavelski/L.Couture 15.00 40.00
PPRK L.Robitaille/J.Kurri 25.00 50.00
PPSL S.Stamkos/Lecavalier 50.00 100.00
PPTK J.Toews/P.Kane 50.00 125.00
PPVR T.Vanek/D.Roy 10.00 25.00

2011-12 SP Authentic Rookie Extended

COMPLETE SET (100) 30.00 80.00
R1 Peter Holland .75 2.00
R2 Iiro Tarkki 1.00 2.50
R3 Devante Smith-Pelly 1.00 2.50
R4 Pat Maroon .75 2.00
R5 Corey Tropp .75 2.00
R6 T.J. Brennan .75 2.00
R7 Cody Hodgson 1.25 3.00
R8 Lance Bouma .75 2.00
R9 Roman Horak .75 2.00
R10 Leland Irving .75 2.00
R11 Greg Nemisz .75 2.00
R12 Mike Murphy .75 2.00
R13 Justin Faulk 1.25 3.00
R14 Brandon Saad 1.50 4.00
R15 Marcus Kruger 1.25 3.00
R16 Cameron Gaunce .60 1.50
R17 Gabriel Landeskog 2.50 6.00
R18 David Savard .75 2.00
R19 Cam Atkinson 2.00 5.00
R20 Tomas Kubalik .75 2.00
R21 John Moore .75 2.00
R22 Allen York 1.00 2.50
R23 Ryan Johansen 2.50 6.00
R24 Tomas Vincour .75 2.00
R25 Colton Sceviour .75 2.00
R26 Gustav Nyquist 2.00 5.00
R27 Brendan Smith .75 2.00
R28 Chris Vande Velde 1.25 3.00
R29 Teemu Hartikainen .75 2.00
R30 Lennart Petrell 1.00 2.50
R31 Anton Lander .75 2.00
R32 Colten Teubert .75 2.00
R33 Ryan Nugent-Hopkins 3.00 8.00
R34 Scott Timmins .75 2.00
R35 Hugh Jessiman .75 2.00
R36 Bracken Kearns .75 2.00
R37 Erik Gudbranson 1.00 2.50
R38 Viatcheslav Voynov .75 2.00
R39 Brett Bulmer .75 2.00
R40 Chad Rau .75 2.00
R41 Carson McMillan 1.00 2.50
R42 Kris Fredheim .75 2.00
R43 Raphael Diaz .75 2.00
R44 Brendon Nash .75 2.00
R45 Aaron Palushaj .75 2.00
R46 Alexei Emelin .75 2.00
R47 Frederic St. Denis .75 2.00
R48 Louis Leblanc .75 2.00
R49 Blake Geoffrion .75 2.00
R50 Jonathon Blum .75 2.00
R51 Craig Smith 1.00 2.50
R52 Ryan Ellis .75 2.00
R53 Jeremy Smith 1.00 2.50
R54 Keith Kinkaid .75 2.00
R55 Adam Henrique 2.00 5.00
R56 Adam Larsson 1.00 2.50
R57 Shane Sims .75 2.00
R58 Calvin de Haan .75 2.00
R59 Mikko Koskinen 1.00 2.50
R60 Matt Campanale .75 2.00
R61 Anders Nilsson .75 2.00
R62 David Ullstrom .75 2.00
R63 Carl Hagelin 1.25 3.00
R64 Tim Erixon .75 2.00
R65 Andre Petersson 1.00 2.50
R66 Patrick Wiercioch .75 2.00
R67 Colin Greening .75 2.00
R68 Roman Wick 1.00 2.50
R69 Andre Benoit 1.00 2.50
R70 Stephane Da Costa .75 2.00
R71 Erik Condra .75 2.00
R72 Mika Zibanejad 2.50 6.00
R73 Ben Holmstrom .75 2.00
R74 Erik Gustafsson 1.00 2.50
R75 Matt Read 1.00 2.50

R76 Harry Zolnierczyk .75 2.00
R77 Zac Rinaldo .75 2.00
R78 Kevin Marshall .75 2.00
R79 Sean Couturier 1.50 4.00
R80 David Rundblad .75 2.00
R81 Simon Despres .75 2.00
R82 Joe Vitale .75 2.00
R83 Brian Strait 1.00 2.50
R84 Robert Bortuzzo .75 2.00
R85 Harri Sateri .75 2.00
R86 Pierre-Cedric Labrie .75 2.00
R87 Brett Connolly .75 2.00
R88 Mike Angelidis 1.00 2.50
R89 Matt Frattin .75 2.00
R90 Jake Gardiner 1.25 3.00
R91 Joe Colborne .75 2.00
R92 Yann Sauve .75 2.00
R93 Eddie Lack .75 2.00
R94 Zack Kassian 1.00 2.50
R95 Tomas Kundratek 1.00 2.50
R96 Cody Eakin 1.25 3.00
R97 Dmitry Orlov 2.00 5.00
R98 Paul Postma .75 2.00
R99 Carl Klingberg .75 2.00
R100 Mark Scheifele 3.00 8.00

2011-12 SP Authentic Sign of the Times

SOTAL Andrew Ladd E 2.50 6.00
SOTAM Andrei Markov C 6.00 15.00
SOTAN Antti Niemi C 5.00 12.00
SOTAO A.Ovechkin A EXCH 50.00 100.00
SOTAP Alex Pietrangelo B 6.00 15.00
SOTAS Alex Stalock B 4.00 10.00
SOTBB Bill Barber D 6.00 15.00
SOTBC Bobby Clarke A 25.00 60.00
SOTBL Jared Boll E 2.50 6.00
SOTBM Richard Bachman E 3.00 8.00
SOTBO Bobby Orr D 60.00 120.00
SOTBR Bill Ranford E 6.00 15.00
SOTBW Drayson Bowman E 3.00 8.00
SOTCE Cory Emmerton E 5.00 12.00
SOTCG Claude Giroux 20.00 40.00
SOTCH Cody Hodgson B 8.00 20.00
SOTCL Claude Lemieux D 6.00 15.00
SOTCN Brett Connolly D 3.00 8.00
SOTCO Cal O'Reilly E 2.50 6.00
SOTCS Cory Schneider E 6.00 15.00
SOTCU Sean Couturier E 10.00 25.00
SOTDB Dan Boyle C 4.00 10.00
SOTDG Daniel Girardi E 4.00 10.00
SOTDP Dion Phaneuf B 12.00 30.00
SOTDR Derek Roy C 4.00 10.00
SOTDS Dave Schultz C 8.00 20.00
SOTEB Jordan Eberle C 40.00 80.00
SOTEM Evgeni Malkin C 15.00 40.00
SOTES Eric Staal 5.00 12.00
SOTEW Eric Wellwood D 5.00 12.00
SOTHL Henrik Lundqvist B 30.00 60.00
SOTJB Josh Bailey D 3.00 8.00
SOTJD Jordan Staal A 8.00 20.00
SOTJE Jonathan Ericsson E 2.50 6.00
SOTJH Josh Harding E 4.00 10.00
SOTJK Jack Skille E 3.00 8.00
SOTJM John Moore B 5.00 12.00
SOTJO Jonathon Blum B 5.00 12.00
SOTJP J.P. Dumont E 2.50 6.00
SOTJS James Sheppard E 2.50 6.00
SOTJT Jonathan Toews A 40.00 80.00
SOTKA Keith Aulie E 3.00 8.00
SOTLC Luca Caputi E 2.50 6.00
SOTLE Brian Lee E 3.00 8.00
SOTLI Trevor Linden D 8.00 20.00
SOTLK Gabriel Landeskog B 20.00 50.00
SOTLO Logan Couture C 10.00 25.00
SOTMA Brett MacLean E 4.00 10.00
SOTMC Philip McRae E 3.00 8.00
SOTMD Michael Del Zotto D 5.00 12.00
SOTME Barry Melrose C 5.00 12.00
SOTMF Michael Frolik 2.50 6.00
SOTMH Matthew Halischuk E 2.50 6.00
SOTMK Jacob Markstrom C 12.50 25.00
SOTML Maxim Lapierre E 3.00 8.00
SOTMM Milan Michalek 2.50 6.00
SOTMS Matt Stajan D 4.00 10.00
SOTMU Peter Mueller D 4.00 10.00
SOTMX Ben Maxwell E 3.00 8.00
SOTNF Nick Foligno C 5.00 12.00
SOTNG Nicklas Grossman E 2.50 6.00
SOTNH Nathan Horton A 30.00 60.00
SOTPD Pavel Datsyuk A 30.00 60.00
SOTPK Patrick Kane B 20.00 50.00
SOTPL Pascal Leclaire D 3.00 8.00
SOTPM Patrick Marleau E 4.00 10.00
SOTPS P.K. Subban C 20.00 50.00
SOTRG Ryan Getzlaf D 5.00 12.00
SOTRJ Ryan Jones E 5.00 12.00
SOTRK Ryan Kesler C 8.00 20.00
SOTRM Ryan Miller B 8.00 20.00
SOTRNH Ryan Nugent-Hopkins D 20.00 50.00
SOTRO Mike Ribeiro 2.50 6.00
SOTRY Ryan O'Reilly E 4.00 10.00
SOTSB Sergei Bobrovsky E 5.00 12.00
SOTSC Sidney Crosby A 75.00 150.00
SOTSF Mark Scheifele D 12.00 30.00
SOTSG Sam Gagner B 10.00 25.00
SOTSK Sergei Kostitsyn 2.50 6.00
SOTSM Shawn Matthias A 15.00 30.00
SOTSS Steven Stamkos B 25.00 50.00
SOTSV Steve Mason B 10.00 25.00
SOTTG Tim Gleason E 2.50 6.00
SOTTH Taylor Hall B 20.00 50.00
SOTTM Thomas McCollum C 5.00 12.00
SOTTS Tyler Seguin B 20.00 50.00
SOTTV John Tavares B 20.00 40.00
SOTWC Wendel Clark B 15.00 30.00
SOTWG Wayne Gretzky A 250.00 600.00

2011-12 SP Authentic Sign of the Times Duals

SOT2BM B.Barber/R.MacLeish C 15.00 40.00
SOT2BP Pietrangelo/D.Backes D 12.00 30.00
SOT2BR B.Orr/R.Bourque A 125.00 200.00
SOT2CH Hodgson/J.Colborne B 40.00 80.00
SOT2CT Couture/J.Thornton B 30.00 60.00
SOT2DH S.Doan/M.Hanzal D 8.00 20.00
SOT2EA Ericsson/Abdelkader D 8.00 20.00
SOT2GE J.Eberle/S.Gagner 20.00 50.00
SOT2GG Wayne Gretzky dual 400.00 1000.00
SOT2GR R.Getzlaf/B.Ryan B 12.00 30.00
SOT2HC Hedman/B.Connolly B 15.00 40.00
SOT2HM T.Myers/R.Miller B 12.00 30.00
SOT2HS Heatley/Setoguchi B 10.00 25.00
SOT2JJ J.Markstrom/J.Skille D 10.00 25.00
SOT2JM J.Boll/J.Moore D 8.00 20.00
SOT2KK P.Kane/R.Kesler B 40.00 80.00
SOT2LD Lidstrom/P.Datsyuk B 25.00 60.00
SOT2LF P.Leclaire/N.Foligno D 8.00 20.00
SOT2MB P.Marleau/D.Boyle B 10.00 25.00
SOT2ME MacLean/Ekman-Larsson 10.00 25.00
SOT2MS Santorelli/S.Matthias D 6.00 15.00
SOT2MT S.Mikita/J.Toews 60.00 120.00
SOT2PK P.K. Subban Dual D 40.00 80.00
SOT2PS C.Price/P.Subban B 40.00 80.00
SOT2RB Ribeiro/Bachman 8.00 20.00
SOT2RL P.Roy/C.Lemieux A 125.00 250.00
SOT2RV D.Roy/T.Vanek C 12.00 30.00
SOT2RY Nugent-Hopkins Dual D 30.00 80.00
SOT2SH H.Sateri/A.Stalock C 15.00 30.00
SOT2SK Scheifele/C.Klingberg C 30.00 80.00
SOT2SM M.Stajan/B.Mikkelson D 6.00 15.00
SOT2SS S.Stamkos Dual D 60.00 120.00
SOT2TS S.Stamkos/J.Tavares D 50.00 100.00
SOTMYS Mystery Redemption 50.00 100.00

2011-12 SP Authentic Sign of the Times Triples

SOT3#1 Ngnt-Hp/Hall/Tavrs 125.00 250.00
SOT3BOS Orr/P.Espo/Bucyk 175.00 300.00
SOT3BUF R.Millr/Vank/Myers 20.00 50.00
SOT3CHI Toews/Hossa/Kane 125.00 200.00
SOT3EDM Eberle/Pjarvi/Hall 30.00 60.00
SOT3GR8 Lemx/Sakic/Mssr 150.00 250.00
SOT3PHI Girx/vn Riems/Schn 40.00 100.00
SOT3QGF Roy/Brodr/Giguere 150.00 250.00
SOT3SJS Thrntn/Mrlu/Coutre 40.00 80.00
SOT3CANR Ngnt-Hp/Hdgs/Schf 100.00 175.00
SOT3CAPS Ovchkn/Bckstrm/Carlsn 40.00 80.00
SOT3JETS Hwrchk/Doan/Kne 50.00 100.00
SOT3KING Gretzky/Kurri/Robit 250.00 600.00
SOT3USAR Lndskog/Ctrier/Cnolly 30.00 60.00

2011-12 SP Authentic Signature Stoppers

SSCP Carey Price 30.00 80.00
SSCW Cam Ward 15.00 40.00
SSHL Henrik Lundqvist 40.00 80.00
SSJH Jonas Hiller EXCH 20.00 50.00
SSMB Martin Brodeur 50.00 100.00
SSPR Pekka Rinne 15.00 40.00
SSRH Ron Hextall 25.00 60.00
SSRO Patrick Roy 75.00 150.00
SSSM Steve Mason 12.00 30.00
SSTV Tomas Vokoun 12.00 30.00

2012-13 SP Authentic

1 Carey Price .50 1.25
2 Claude Giroux .25 .60
3 Bobby Ryan .20 .50
4 Jaroslav Halak .25 .60
5 Jamie Benn .25 .60
6 James Neal .15 .40
7 Jordan Eberle .25 .60
8 Braden Holtby .30 .75
9 Adam Henrique .20 .50
10 Simon Gagne .25 .60
11 Brad Marchand .50 1.25
12 Gabriel Landeskog .30 .75
13 Sean Couturier .20 .50
14 Ryan Kesler .25 .60
15 Taylor Hall .25 .60
16 Pekka Rinne .25 .60
17 Milan Hejduk .20 .50
18 Ales Hemsky .20 .50
19 Derek Roy .15 .40
20 P.K. Subban .30 .75
21 Ryan Nugent-Hopkins .30 .75
22 Anze Kopitar .40 1.00
23 Patrice Bergeron .30 .75
24 Ed Belfour .25 .60
25 Dino Ciccarelli .25 .60
26 Drew Doughty .30 .75
27 Brett Hull .50 1.25
28 Alexander Ovechkin 1.00 2.50
29 Henrik Lundqvist .60 1.50
30 Evgeni Malkin .50 1.25
31 Pavel Datsyuk .40 1.00
32 Curtis Joseph .30 .75
33 Jordan Staal .20 .50
34 Ryan Getzlaf .25 .60
35 Ray Bourque .40 1.00
36 Doug Gilmour .30 .75
37 Eric Lindros .40 1.00
38 Mark Messier .50 1.25
39 Martin Brodeur .60 1.50
40 Jaromir Jagr .75 2.00
41 Joe Sakic .50 1.25
42 Mario Lemieux 1.00 2.50
43 Bryan Trottier .25 .60
44 Wayne Gretzky 1.50 4.00
45 Brendan Shanahan .25 .60
46 Henrik Zetterberg .30 .75
47 Zdeno Chara .25 .60
48 Jason Spezza .25 .60
49 Ilya Kovalchuk .25 .60
50 Zach Parise .25 .60
51 Bobby Orr 1.00 2.50
52 Andrew Shaw .15 .40
53 Devin Setoguchi .20 .50
54 Cam Ward .25 .60
55 Bobby Hull .50 1.25
56 Lars Eller .15 .40
57 Mark Scheifele .40 1.00
58 Jean Beliveau .25 .60
59 Carl Hagelin .15 .40
60 Bernie Parent .30 .75
61 Zack Kassian .15 .40
62 Saku Koivu .25 .60
63 Tony Esposito .25 .60
64 Ron Hextall .25 .60
65 Patrick Roy .60 1.50
66 Wendel Clark .40 1.00
67 Tyler Seguin .30 .75
68 Steve Mason .20 .50
69 Nicklas Backstrom .25 .60
70 Matt Read .20 .50
71 Oliver Ekman-Larsson .25 .60
72 Guy Lafleur .30 .75
73 Erik Karlsson .30 .75
74 Clark Gillies .25 .60
75 Brayden Schenn .25 .60
76 Dustin Byfuglien .25 .60
77 Gilbert Perreault .25 .60
78 Cam Fowler .25 .60
79 Alex Pietrangelo .20 .50
80 Bill Ranford .25 .60
81 Marc Staal .15 .40
82 Logan Couture .30 .75
83 Joe Thornton .40 1.00
84 Jonas Hiller .20 .50
85 Evander Kane .25 .60
86 Brad Park .20 .50
87 Brandon Dubinsky .15 .40
88 Doug Gilmour .30 .75
89 David Backes .15 .40
90 Alexander Burmistrov .20 .50
91 Andrew Ladd .15 .40
92 Derek Stepan .15 .40
93 Dany Heatley .20 .50
94 Antti Niemi .20 .50
95 Marian Hossa .25 .60
96 Steven Stamkos .50 1.25
97 Shane Doan .20 .50
98 Patric Hornqvist .15 .40
99 Magnus Paajarvi .20 .50
100 Dion Phaneuf .20 .50
101 Stephen Weiss .20 .50
102 Luc Robitaille .25 .60
103 Trevor Linden .25 .60
104 Marc-Andre Fleury .50 1.25
105 Kris Versteeg .15 .40
106 Paul Stastny .20 .50
107 Josh Gorges .20 .50
108 Nick Foligno .20 .50
109 Nikolai Kulemin .15 .40
110 Jean-Sebastien Giguere .25 .60
111 Tuukka Rask .30 .75
112 Mike Ribeiro .15 .40
113 John Tavares .40 1.00
114 Marcel Dionne .30 .75
115 Mike Bossy .25 .60
116 Kevin Shattenkirk .15 .40
117 Marian Gaborik .25 .60
118 Patrick Marleau .25 .60
119 Dale Hawerchuk .30 .75
120 Scott Niedermayer .25 .60
121 Jonathan Toews .40 1.00
122 Dominik Hasek .40 1.00
123 Nicklas Lidstrom .25 .60
124 Louis Leblanc .15 .40
125 Martin St. Louis .25 .60
126 Jeff Carter .20 .50
127 Cody Hodgson .15 .40
128 Peter Stastny .20 .50
129 Patrick Kane .50 1.25
130 Jonathan Quick .30 .75
131 Rick Nash .25 .60
132 Eric Staal .30 .75
133 Ryan Miller .25 .60
134 Tomas Vokoun .20 .50
135 Mikkel Boedker .15 .40
136 Markus Naslund .25 .60
137 Matt Duchene .25 .60
138 Jarome Iginla .30 .75
139 Luke Adam .20 .50
140 Dustin Brown .25 .60
141 Mike Richards .20 .50
142 Ryan Callahan .15 .40
143 James van Riemsdyk .20 .50
144 Shea Weber .20 .50
145 Phil Esposito .40 1.00
146 Jeff Skinner .30 .75
147 Nathan Horton .25 .60
148 Vincent Lecavalier .25 .60
149 Phil Kessel .25 .60
150 Sidney Crosby 1.00 2.50
151 Zdeno Chara AM .75 2.00
152 Bobby Orr AM 3.00 8.00
153 Tyler Seguin AM 1.00 2.50
154 Jeff Skinner AM 1.00 2.50
155 Jonathan Toews AM 1.25 3.00
156 Gabriel Landeskog AM 1.00 2.50
157 Ryan Nugent-Hopkins AM 1.00 2.50
158 Jordan Eberle AM .75 2.00
159 Sam Gagner AM .50 1.25
160 Taylor Hall AM .75 2.00
161 Ron Francis AM 1.00 2.50
162 Wayne Gretzky AM 5.00 12.00
163 Jonathan Quick AM 1.00 2.50
164 Dustin Brown AM .75 2.00
165 Drew Doughty AM 1.00 2.50
166 Anze Kopitar AM 1.25 3.00
167 Patrick Roy AM 2.00 5.00
168 Pekka Rinne AM .75 2.00
169 Martin Brodeur AM 2.00 5.00
170 Chris Kreider AM 2.00 5.00
171 Mats Sundin AM 1.25 3.00
172 Pavel Bure AM .75 2.00
173 Erik Karlsson AM 1.00 2.50
174 Sidney Crosby AM 3.00 8.00
175 Evgeni Malkin AM 1.50 4.00
176 James Neal AM .50 1.25
177 Mario Lemieux AM 3.00 8.00
178 Brett Hull AM 1.50 4.00
179 Cory Schneider AM .75 2.00
180 Alexander Ovechkin AM 3.00 8.00
181 Skc/Sndn/Bre/Ots AM 1.50 4.00
182 W.Gretzky/P.Roy AM 5.00 12.00
183 T.Hall/J.Eberle AM .75 2.00
184 M.Sundin/J.Sakic AM 1.50 4.00
185 B.Orr/P.Esposito AM 3.00 8.00
186 M.Lemieux/J.Jagr AM 2.00 5.00
187 Kreider/M.Brodeur AM 2.00 5.00
188 B.Hull/B.Hull AM 1.50 4.00
189 T.Hall/T.Seguin AM 1.00 2.50
190 J.Halak/Pietrangelo AM .75 2.00
191 Theoren Fleury TC 1.00 2.50
192 Brayden Schenn TC .75 2.00
193 Carey Price TC 1.50 4.00
194 Sidney Crosby TC 3.00 8.00
195 Adam Henrique TC .60 1.50
196 Jordan Eberle TC .75 2.00
197 Jeff Skinner TC 1.00 2.50
198 John Tavares TC 1.25 3.00
199 Bobby Orr TC 3.00 8.00
200 Mario Lemieux TC 3.00 8.00
201 P.K. Subban TC 1.00 2.50
202 Martin Brodeur TC 2.00 5.00
203 Joe Sakic TC 1.50 4.00
204 Jonathan Toews TC 1.25 3.00
205 Wayne Gretzky TC 5.00 12.00
206 J.Tavares/J.Eberle TC 1.25 3.00
207 P.Subban/J.Eberle TC 1.00 2.50
208 Gretzky/Lemieux TC 5.00 12.00
209 M.Lemieux/J.Sakic TC 2.00 5.00
210 Hodgson/Duchene TC .75 2.00
211 Maxime Sauve AU RC 2.50 6.00
212 Sven Baertschi AU RC 4.00 10.00
213 Akim Aliu AU RC 3.00 8.00
214 Brandon Bollig AU RC 2.50 6.00
215 Tyson Barrie AU RC 8.00 20.00
216 Cody Goloubef AU RC 15.00 40.00
217 Reilly Smith AU RC EXCH 8.00 20.00
218 Brenden Dillon AU RC 3.00 8.00
219 Scott Glennie AU RC 3.00 8.00
220 Riley Sheahan AU RC 4.00 10.00
221 Jordan Nolan AU RC 2.50 6.00
222 Jason Zucker AU RC 6.00 15.00
223 Tyler Cuma AU RC 2.50 6.00
224 Gabriel Dumont AU RC 3.00 8.00
225 Chet Pickard AU RC 3.00 8.00
226 Casey Cizikas AU RC 3.00 8.00
227 Chris Kreider AU RC 80.00 200.00
228 Jakob Silfverberg AU RC 5.00 12.00
229 Mark Stone AU RC 40.00 100.00
230 Michael Stone AU RC 3.00 8.00
231 Jake Allen AU RC 8.00 20.00
232 Jaden Schwartz AU RC 8.00 20.00
233 J.T. Brown AU RC 3.00 8.00
234 Carter Ashton AU RC 2.50 6.00
235 Jussi Rynnas AU RC 2.50 6.00

2012-13 SP Authentic 1994-95 SP Retro

SP1 Tyson Barrie 2.00 5.00
SP2 Jussi Rynnas .60 1.50
SP3 Mats Sundin 2.50 6.00
SP4 Pavel Bure 1.50 4.00
SP5 Jakob Silfverberg 1.25 3.00
SP6 Sven Baertschi 1.00 2.50
SP7 Evander Kane 1.50 4.00
SP8 Dale Hawerchuk 2.00 5.00
SP9 Mark Scheifele 1.50 4.00
SP10 Andrew Ladd 1.00 2.50
SP11 Alexander Ovechkin 6.00 15.00
SP12 Nicklas Backstrom 1.50 4.00
SP13 Braden Holtby 2.00 5.00
SP14 Cody Hodgson 1.00 2.50
SP15 Ryan Kesler 1.50 4.00
SP16 Cory Schneider 1.50 4.00
SP17 Trevor Linden 1.50 4.00
SP18 Phil Kessel 1.50 4.00
SP19 Dion Phaneuf 1.25 3.00
SP20 Vincent Lecavalier 1.50 4.00
SP21 Steven Stamkos 3.00 8.00
SP22 Jaroslav Halak 1.50 4.00
SP23 Brett Hull 3.00 8.00
SP24 Jaden Schwartz 2.00 5.00
SP25 Jake Allen 2.00 5.00
SP26 Antti Niemi 1.25 3.00
SP27 Patrick Marleau 1.50 4.00
SP28 Joe Thornton 2.50 6.00
SP29 Logan Couture 2.00 5.00
SP30 Jordan Staal 1.25 3.00
SP31 Evgeni Malkin 3.00 8.00
SP32 Mario Lemieux 6.00 15.00
SP33 Marc-Andre Fleury 3.00 8.00
SP34 Sidney Crosby 6.00 15.00
SP35 Paul Coffey 1.50 4.00
SP36 Eric Lindros 2.50 6.00
SP37 Bobby Clarke 2.50 6.00
SP38 Jaromir Jagr 5.00 12.00
SP39 Claude Giroux 1.50 4.00
SP40 Brayden Schenn 1.50 4.00
SP41 Sean Couturier 1.25 3.00
SP42 Dominik Hasek 2.50 6.00
SP43 Erik Karlsson 2.00 5.00
SP44 Ryan Callahan 1.00 2.50
SP45 Marian Gaborik 1.50 4.00
SP46 Henrik Lundqvist 4.00 10.00
SP47 Mark Messier 3.00 8.00
SP48 Chris Kreider 2.50 6.00
SP49 Bryan Trottier 1.50 4.00
SP50 John Tavares 2.50 6.00
SP51 Mike Bossy 1.50 4.00
SP52 Martin Brodeur 4.00 10.00
SP53 Pekka Rinne 1.50 4.00
SP54 Jean Beliveau 2.00 5.00
SP55 Carey Price 3.00 8.00
SP56 Larry Robinson 1.50 4.00
SP57 P.K. Subban 2.00 5.00
SP58 Guy Lafleur 2.50 6.00
SP59 Josh Gorges 1.25 3.00
SP60 Jeff Carter 1.25 3.00
SP61 Anze Kopitar 2.50 6.00
SP62 Mike Richards 1.25 3.00
SP63 Luc Robitaille 1.50 4.00
SP64 Drew Doughty 2.00 5.00
SP65 Dustin Brown 1.50 4.00
SP66 Jonathan Quick 2.00 5.00
SP67 Ron Francis 2.00 5.00
SP68 Ryan Nugent-Hopkins 2.00 5.00
SP69 Taylor Hall 1.50 4.00
SP70 Grant Fuhr 2.50 6.00
SP71 Jari Kurri 1.50 4.00
SP72 Jordan Eberle 1.50 4.00
SP73 Wayne Gretzky 5.00 12.00
SP74 Bill Ranford 1.50 4.00
SP75 Pavel Datsyuk 2.50 6.00
SP76 Nicklas Lidstrom 1.50 4.00
SP77 Johan Franzen 1.25 3.00
SP78 Riley Sheahan 1.50 4.00
SP79 Rick Nash 1.50 4.00
SP80 Joe Sakic 3.00 8.00
SP81 Patrick Roy 4.00 10.00
SP82 Matt Duchene 1.50 4.00
SP83 Paul Stastny 1.25 3.00
SP84 Gabriel Landeskog 2.00 5.00
SP85 Patrick Kane 3.00 8.00
SP86 Bobby Hull 3.00 8.00
SP87 Jonathan Toews 2.50 6.00
SP88 Ed Belfour 1.50 4.00
SP89 Jeff Skinner 2.00 5.00
SP90 Jarome Iginla 2.00 5.00
SP91 Thomas Vanek 1.25 3.00
SP92 Ryan Miller 1.50 4.00
SP93 Ray Bourque 2.50 6.00
SP94 Bobby Orr 6.00 15.00
SP95 Phil Esposito 2.50 6.00
SP96 Cam Neely 1.50 4.00
SP97 Brad Marchand 3.00 8.00
SP98 Tyler Seguin 2.00 5.00
SP99 Ryan Getzlaf 1.50 4.00
SP100 Jonas Hiller 1.25 3.00

2012-13 SP Authentic 1994-95 SP Retro Die Cut Autographs

SP1 Tyson Barrie C 15.00 40.00
SP2 Jussi Rynnas C 5.00 12.00
SP3 Mats Sundin A2 12.00 30.00
SP4 Pavel Bure B 8.00 20.00
SP5 Jakob Silfverberg C 10.00 25.00
SP6 Sven Baertschi C 8.00 20.00
SP8 Dale Hawerchuk 10.00 25.00
SP9 Mark Scheifele C2 12.00 30.00
SP10 Andrew Ladd C 5.00 12.00
SP11 Alexander Ovechkin A 50.00 125.00
SP13 Braden Holtby C2 10.00 25.00
SP14 Cody Hodgson C2 5.00 12.00
SP15 Ryan Kesler C 8.00 20.00
SP16 Cory Schneider C2 8.00 20.00
SP17 Trevor Linden B 8.00 20.00
SP18 Phil Kessel B2 8.00 20.00
SP19 Dion Phaneuf B2 6.00 15.00
SP22 Jaroslav Halak C2 8.00 20.00
SP23 Brett Hull A 15.00 40.00
SP24 Jaden Schwartz C 15.00 40.00
SP25 Jake Allen C 15.00 40.00
SP26 Antti Niemi C2 6.00 15.00
SP27 Patrick Marleau B2 8.00 20.00
SP28 Joe Thornton B 12.00 30.00
SP29 Logan Couture B 10.00 25.00
SP30 Jordan Staal C 6.00 15.00
SP31 Evgeni Malkin A2 15.00 40.00
SP32 Mario Lemieux A 30.00 80.00
SP33 Marc-Andre Fleury B2 15.00 40.00
SP34 Sidney Crosby A 60.00 150.00
SP35 Paul Coffey A 8.00 20.00
SP36 Eric Lindros A 12.00 30.00
SP37 Bobby Clarke B 12.00 30.00
SP38 Jaromir Jagr C 25.00 60.00
SP39 Claude Giroux B2 8.00 20.00
SP40 Brayden Schenn C 8.00 20.00
SP42 Dominik Hasek A 12.00 30.00
SP45 Marian Gaborik A2 8.00 20.00
SP47 Mark Messier A 15.00 40.00
SP48 Chris Kreider C 20.00 50.00
SP49 Bryan Trottier A 8.00 20.00
SP50 John Tavares C 12.00 30.00
SP51 Mike Bossy B 8.00 20.00
SP52 Martin Brodeur A 20.00 50.00
SP53 Pekka Rinne C2 8.00 20.00
SP54 Jean Beliveau A 8.00 20.00
SP55 Carey Price B 15.00 40.00
SP56 Larry Robinson B 8.00 20.00
SP57 P.K. Subban 10.00 25.00
SP58 Guy Lafleur B 10.00 25.00
SP59 Josh Gorges C2 6.00 15.00
SP60 Jeff Carter B2 6.00 15.00
SP61 Anze Kopitar B 12.00 30.00
SP62 Mike Richards A2 6.00 15.00
SP63 Luc Robitaille B 8.00 20.00
SP65 Dustin Brown B 8.00 20.00
SP66 Jonathan Quick B EXCH 10.00 25.00
SP67 Ron Francis A 10.00 25.00
SP68 Ryan Nugent-Hopkins A 10.00 25.00
SP69 Taylor Hall B EXCH 8.00 20.00
SP70 Grant Fuhr B2 12.00 30.00
SP71 Jari Kurri C2 8.00 20.00
SP72 Jordan Eberle B2 8.00 20.00
SP73 Wayne Gretzky A 250.00 600.00
SP74 Bill Ranford C 8.00 20.00
SP75 Pavel Datsyuk B2 12.00 30.00
SP76 Nicklas Lidstrom B 8.00 20.00
SP77 Johan Franzen C2 6.00 15.00
SP78 Riley Sheahan C 8.00 20.00
SP79 Rick Nash 8.00 20.00
SP80 Joe Sakic A 15.00 40.00
SP81 Patrick Roy A 20.00 50.00
SP82 Matt Duchene C2 8.00 20.00
SP83 Paul Stastny C2 6.00 15.00
SP84 Gabriel Landeskog C 10.00 25.00
SP85 Patrick Kane B EXCH 15.00 40.00
SP86 Bobby Hull B 15.00 40.00
SP87 Jonathan Toews A 12.00 30.00
SP88 Ed Belfour A 8.00 20.00
SP89 Jeff Skinner A 10.00 25.00
SP90 Jarome Iginla A 10.00 25.00
SP92 Ryan Miller A2 8.00 20.00
SP93 Ray Bourque A 12.00 30.00
SP94 Bobby Orr A 150.00 250.00
SP95 Phil Esposito A 12.00 30.00
SP96 Cam Neely B 8.00 20.00
SP97 Brad Marchand C2 15.00 40.00
SP98 Tyler Seguin A2 10.00 25.00
SP99 Ryan Getzlaf 8.00 20.00
SP100 Jonas Hiller C 6.00 15.00

2012-13 SP Authentic All-Time Chirography

ATCBH Bobby Hull 25.00 60.00
ATCBO Bobby Orr 100.00 250.00
ATCGP Gilbert Perreault 15.00 40.00
ATCJB Jean Beliveau 90.00 150.00
ATCWG Wayne Gretzky 300.00 800.00

2012-13 SP Authentic Buyback Autographs

79 S.Stamkos '09-10 SPA 30.00 60.00

2012-13 SP Authentic Chirography

SPCBM Brad Marchand 25.00 60.00
SPCCG Claude Giroux 12.00 30.00
SPCCP Carey Price 25.00 50.00
SPCDP Dion Phaneuf 10.00 25.00
SPCEK Erik Karlsson 15.00 40.00
SPCIK Ilya Kovalchuk 12.00 30.00
SPCJT Jonathan Toews 25.00 50.00
SPCMB Martin Brodeur 40.00 80.00
SPCSC Sidney Crosby 90.00 150.00
SPCTV John Tavares 25.00 60.00

2012-13 SP Authentic Limited Autographs

51 Bobby Orr C 30.00 80.00
52 Andrew Shaw C 5.00 12.00
54 Cam Ward B 8.00 20.00
55 Bobby Hull A 30.00 80.00
56 Lars Eller D 5.00 12.00
57 Mark Scheifele C 12.00 30.00
58 Jean Beliveau A 8.00 20.00
59 Carl Hagelin D 5.00 12.00
61 Zack Kassian D 5.00 12.00
62 Saku Koivu A 8.00 20.00
63 Tony Esposito A 8.00 20.00
64 Ron Hextall B 8.00 20.00
65 Patrick Roy B 50.00 125.00
66 Wendel Clark A 12.00 30.00
67 Tyler Seguin A 10.00 25.00
68 Steve Mason C 6.00 15.00
70 Matt Read C 6.00 15.00
72 Guy Lafleur A 10.00 25.00
74 Clark Gillies C 8.00 20.00
75 Brayden Schenn C 8.00 20.00
76 Dustin Byfuglien B
(inserted in 2015-16 SP Authentic) 8.00 20.00
77 Gilbert Perreault A 8.00 20.00
79 Alex Pietrangelo C 6.00 15.00
80 Bill Ranford C 8.00 20.00
81 Marc Staal C 5.00 12.00
82 Logan Couture A 10.00 25.00
83 Joe Thornton B 12.00 30.00
84 Jonas Hiller D 6.00 15.00
86 Brad Park C 6.00 15.00
87 Brandon Dubinsky C 5.00 12.00
88 Doug Gilmour A 10.00 25.00
89 David Backes B 5.00 12.00
91 Andrew Ladd D 5.00 12.00
92 Derek Stepan B
(inserted in 2015-16 SP Authentic) 5.00 12.00
93 Dany Heatley A 6.00 15.00
94 Antti Niemi C 6.00 15.00
97 Shane Doan C 6.00 15.00
99 Magnus Paajarvi C 6.00 15.00
100 Dion Phaneuf A 6.00 15.00
101 Stephen Weiss C 6.00 15.00
102 Luc Robitaille B 8.00 20.00
103 Trevor Linden A 8.00 20.00
104 Marc-Andre Fleury A 15.00 40.00
106 Paul Stastny B 6.00 15.00
107 Josh Gorges C 6.00 15.00
108 Nick Foligno D 6.00 15.00
109 Nikolai Kulemin D 5.00 12.00
110 Jean-Sebastien Giguere A 8.00 20.00
113 John Tavares B 12.00 30.00
114 Marcel Dionne A 10.00 25.00
115 Mike Bossy A 8.00 20.00
116 Kevin Shattenkirk C 5.00 12.00
117 Marian Gaborik A 8.00 20.00
118 Patrick Marleau A 8.00 20.00
119 Dale Hawerchuk A 10.00 25.00
121 Jonathan Toews B EXCH 25.00 60.00
122 Dominik Hasek A 12.00 30.00
123 Nicklas Lidstrom A 8.00 20.00
124 Louis Leblanc D 5.00 12.00
125 Martin St. Louis B 8.00 20.00
126 Jeff Carter B 6.00 15.00
127 Cody Hodgson C 5.00 12.00
128 Peter Stastny B 6.00 15.00
129 Patrick Kane A 60.00 150.00
130 Jonathan Quick A
(inserted in 2015-16 SP Authentic) 10.00 25.00
131 Rick Nash A 8.00 20.00
132 Eric Staal B 10.00 25.00
133 Ryan Miller C 8.00 20.00
135 Mikkel Boedker D 5.00 12.00
136 Markus Naslund A 8.00 20.00
137 Matt Duchene B 8.00 20.00
138 Jarome Iginla A 10.00 25.00
139 Luke Adam D 6.00 15.00
140 Dustin Brown A 8.00 20.00
141 Mike Richards B 6.00 15.00
143 James van Riemsdyk C 6.00 15.00
144 Shea Weber C 6.00 15.00
145 Phil Esposito A 12.00 30.00
146 Jeff Skinner B 10.00 25.00
149 Phil Kessel A 8.00 20.00
150 Sidney Crosby A 60.00 150.00
152 Bobby Orr AM A 200.00 400.00
153 Tyler Seguin AM B 10.00 25.00
154 Jeff Skinner AM B 10.00 25.00
155 Jonathan Toews AM A 60.00 150.00
156 Gabriel Landeskog AM B 10.00 25.00
157 Ryan Nugent-Hopkins AM A 10.00 25.00
158 Jordan Eberle AM B 8.00 20.00
159 Sam Gagner AM B 5.00 12.00
160 Taylor Hall AM A 8.00 20.00
161 Ron Francis AM A 10.00 25.00
162 Wayne Gretzky AM A 300.00 800.00
163 Jonathan Quick AM
(inserted in 2015-16 SP Authentic) 10.00 25.00
164 Dustin Brown AM B 8.00 20.00
166 Anze Kopitar AM A 12.00 30.00
167 Patrick Roy AM A 60.00 150.00
168 Pekka Rinne AM B 8.00 20.00
169 Martin Brodeur AM A 60.00 150.00
170 Chris Kreider AM B 20.00 50.00
171 Mats Sundin AM A 12.00 30.00
172 Pavel Bure AM A 8.00 20.00
173 Erik Karlsson AM B 10.00 25.00
174 Sidney Crosby AM A 60.00 150.00
175 Evgeni Malkin AM A 15.00 40.00
176 James Neal AM B 5.00 12.00
177 Mario Lemieux AM A 150.00 250.00
178 Brett Hull AM A 50.00 125.00
179 Cory Schneider AM B 8.00 20.00
180 Alexander Ovechkin AM A 60.00 150.00
181 Sakc/Sndn/Bre/Otes AM A 50.00 125.00
182 W.Gretzky/P.Roy AM 400.00 1000.00
183 T.Hall/J.Eberle AM B 8.00 20.00
184 J.Sakic/M.Sundin AM A 40.00 100.00
185 B.Orr/P.Esposito AM 100.00 250.00
186 M.Lemieux/J.Jagr AM 250.00 350.00
187 C.Kreider/M.Brodeur AM 25.00 60.00
188 B.Hull/B.Hull AM 150.00 300.00
190 J.Halak/Pietrangelo AM B 8.00 20.00
191 Theoren Fleury TC B 10.00 25.00
192 Brayden Schenn TC C 8.00 20.00
193 Carey Price TC B 30.00 80.00
194 Sidney Crosby TC A 60.00 150.00
195 Adam Henrique TC C 6.00 15.00
196 Jordan Eberle TC 8.00 20.00
197 Jeff Skinner TC C 10.00 25.00
198 John Tavares TC C 20.00 50.00
199 Bobby Orr TC C 60.00 150.00
200 Mario Lemieux TC A 60.00 150.00
201 P.K. Subban TC 10.00 25.00
202 Martin Brodeur TC A 60.00 150.00
203 Joe Sakic TC A 15.00 40.00
204 Jonathan Toews TC 30.00 80.00
205 Wayne Gretzky TC A 300.00 800.00
206 Tavares/J.Eberle TC EXCH 25.00 60.00
207 J.Eberle TC/P.Subban 10.00 25.00
208 W.Gretzky/M.Lemieux TC 400.00 1000.00
209 M.Lemieux/J.Sakic TC 80.00 200.00
210 C.Hodgson/Duchene TC 8.00 20.00

2012-13 SP Authentic Limited Autographed Patches

1 Carey Price AU/100 20.00 50.00
2 Claude Giroux/100 10.00 25.00
3 Bobby Ryan AU/100 8.00 20.00
6 James Neal AU/25 6.00 15.00
7 Jordan Eberle/25 15.00 40.00
8 Braden Holtby/25 12.00 30.00
9 Adam Henrique AU/25 8.00 20.00
10 Simon Gagne/100 10.00 25.00
11 Brad Marchand/100 20.00 50.00
12 Gabriel Landeskog/100 12.00 30.00
14 Ryan Kesler AU/100 10.00 25.00
15 Taylor Hall/100 10.00 25.00
16 Pekka Rinne/100 10.00 25.00
17 Milan Hejduk 12.00 30.00
18 Ales Hemsky/100 8.00 20.00
19 Derek Roy/25 6.00 15.00
20 P.K. Subban AU/100 12.00 30.00
22 Anze Kopitar AU/25 40.00 100.00
23 Patrice Bergeron/25 20.00 50.00
24 Ed Belfour AU/25 25.00 60.00
27 Brett Hull AU/25 30.00 80.00
28 Alexander Ovechkin AU/25 60.00 150.00
32 Curtis Joseph/25 30.00 80.00
34 Ryan Getzlaf AU/25
(inserted in 2015-16 SP Authentic) 10.00 25.00
35 Ray Bourque AU/25 30.00 80.00
56 Lars Eller AU/25 15.00 40.00
59 Carl Hagelin AU/25 6.00 15.00
64 Ron Hextall/25 25.00 60.00
70 Matt Read AU/25 8.00 20.00
75 Brayden Schenn AU/25 10.00 25.00
80 Bill Ranford AU/25 15.00 40.00
81 Marc Staal/25 6.00 15.00
104 Marc-Andre Fleury/25 20.00 50.00
107 Josh Gorges/25 12.00 30.00
117 Marian Gaborik/25 10.00 25.00
118 Patrick Marleau/25 10.00 25.00
136 Markus Naslund AU/25 12.00 30.00
137 Matt Duchene/25 10.00 25.00
141 Mike Richards/25 8.00 20.00
144 Shea Weber/25 8.00 20.00
211 Maxime Sauve AU/100 6.00 15.00
212 Sven Baertschi AU/100 10.00 25.00
213 Akim Aliu AU/100 8.00 20.00
214 Brandon Bollig AU/100 6.00 15.00
215 Tyson Barrie AU/100 20.00 50.00
217 Reilly Smith AU/100
(inserted in 2015-16 SP Authentic) 20.00 50.00
218 Brenden Dillon AU/100 8.00 20.00
219 Scott Glennie AU/100 8.00 20.00
220 Riley Sheahan AU/100 10.00 25.00
221 Jordan Nolan AU/100 6.00 15.00
222 Jason Zucker AU/100 15.00 40.00
223 Tyler Cuma AU/100 6.00 15.00
224 Gabriel Dumont AU/100 8.00 20.00
225 Chet Pickard AU/100 8.00 20.00
226 Casey Cizikas AU/100 8.00 20.00
227 Chris Kreider AU/100 25.00 60.00
228 Jakob Silfverberg AU/100 12.00 30.00
229 Mark Stone AU/100 60.00 150.00
230 Michael Stone AU/100 8.00 20.00
231 Jake Allen AU/100 20.00 50.00
232 Jaden Schwartz AU/100 20.00 50.00
233 J.T. Brown/100 8.00 20.00
234 Carter Ashton AU/100 6.00 15.00
235 Jussi Rynnas AU/100 6.00 15.00

2012-13 SP Authentic Marks of Distinction

MDBT Bryan Trottier 15.00 40.00
MDCP Carey Price 30.00 80.00
MDEL Eric Lindros 40.00 100.00
MDEM Evgeni Malkin 30.00 80.00
MDJE Jordan Eberle 15.00 40.00
MDJJ Jaromir Jagr 50.00 125.00
MDJS Joe Sakic 30.00 80.00
MDNL Nicklas Lidstrom 15.00 40.00
MDPK Patrick Kane 30.00 80.00
MDPV Pavel Bure 60.00 150.00
MDRN Ryan Nugent-Hopkins 20.00 50.00
MDSC Sidney Crosby 60.00 150.00
MDSU Mats Sundin 25.00 60.00
MDTH Taylor Hall 15.00 40.00
MDWG Wayne Gretzky 200.00 500.00

2012-13 SP Authentic Premier Chirography

PTCCK Chris Kreider 10.00 25.00
PTCJE Jordan Eberle 10.00 25.00
PTCJS Jeff Skinner 12.00 30.00
PTCSB Sven Baertschi 6.00 15.00
PTCSC Jaden Schwartz 12.00 30.00
PTCTH Taylor Hall 12.00 30.00
PTCTS Tyler Seguin 12.00 30.00

2012-13 SP Authentic Sign of the Times

SOTAA Akim Aliu C 5.00 12.00
SOTAH Adam Henrique B 5.00 12.00
SOTBM Brad Marchand B2 12.00 30.00
SOTBO Bobby Orr A 60.00 150.00
SOTBP Brad Park B 5.00 12.00
SOTBS Brayden Schenn TC B 6.00 15.00
SOTBT Bryan Trottier TC B 6.00 15.00
SOTBU Pavel Bure A 50.00 125.00
SOTBV Alexander Burmistrov C 5.00 12.00
SOTBW J.T. Brown C 5.00 12.00
SOTCA Carter Ashton TC C 4.00 10.00
SOTCC Casey Cizikas TC C 5.00 12.00

Card	Low	High
SOTCG Claude Giroux A2	60.00	150.00
SOTCH Cody Hodgson B2	4.00	10.00
SOTCK Chris Kreider B2	15.00	40.00
SOTCP Carey Price TC A	12.00	30.00
SOTCW Cam Ward TC B	6.00	15.00
SOTCY Carey Price A	60.00	150.00
SOTDB Dustin Brown B	6.00	15.00
SOTDD Devan Dubnyk C	5.00	12.00
SOTDH Calvin de Haan TC C	4.00	10.00
SOTEL Eric Lindros A	10.00	25.00
SOTFL Theoren Fleury A	8.00	20.00
SOTFY Theoren Fleury TC A	8.00	20.00
SOTGL Guy Lafleur A	8.00	20.00
SOTGO Michel Goulet B	5.00	12.00
SOTGR Wayne Gretzky TC A	250.00	600.00
SOTJA Jake Allen TC C	12.00	30.00
SOTJB Jean Beliveau A	6.00	15.00
SOTJE Jordan Eberle A2	6.00	15.00
SOTJJ Jaromir Jagr A	60.00	150.00
SOTJR Jussi Rynnas C	4.00	10.00
SOTJS Jakob Silfverberg C	8.00	20.00
SOTJZ Jason Zucker C	10.00	25.00
SOTLE Mario Lemieux TC A	60.00	150.00
SOTLI Eric Lindros TC A	10.00	25.00
SOTLR Luc Robitaille AS A	25.00	60.00
SOTMB Martin Brodeur A	15.00	40.00
SOTME Mark Messier TC A	50.00	125.00
SOTMF Marc-Andre Fleury A	30.00	80.00
SOTML Mario Lemieux A	60.00	150.00
SOTMM Mark Messier A	50.00	125.00
SOTMO Andy Moog B	6.00	15.00
SOTOR Bobby Orr TC A	60.00	150.00
SOTPC Paul Coffey A2	25.00	60.00
SOTPR Patrick Roy AS A	60.00	150.00
SOTPS P.K. Subban	8.00	20.00
SOTRA Bill Ranford B	6.00	15.00
SOTRE Ryan Ellis TC C	4.00	10.00
SOTRG Ryan Getzlaf A2	6.00	15.00
SOTRI Pekka Rinne B2	6.00	15.00
SOTRN Ryan Nugent-Hopkins (inserted in 2015-16 SP Authentic)	8.00	20.00
SOTRS Riley Sheahan C	6.00	15.00
SOTSC Sidney Crosby A	60.00	150.00
SOTSG Scott Glennie C	5.00	12.00
SOTSJ Jaden Schwartz TC C	12.00	30.00
SOTSK Jeff Skinner TC B	8.00	20.00
SOTSU Mats Sundin A2	10.00	25.00
SOTSZ Dave Schultz B2	6.00	15.00
SOTTB Tyson Barrie TC C	12.00	30.00
SOTTH Taylor Hall B2	6.00	15.00
SOTWG Wayne Gretzky A	250.00	600.00

2012-13 SP Authentic Sign of the Times Duals

Card	Low	High
ST2AS J.Allen/J.Schwartz C	25.00	60.00
ST2BG J.Benn/S.Glennie	12.00	30.00
ST2BK D.Brown/A.Kopitar B	20.00	50.00
ST2BW B.Orr/W.Gretzky A	400.00	1000.00
ST2EH T.Hall/J.Eberle B	12.00	30.00
ST2FC R.Francis/P.Coffey B	15.00	40.00
ST2FS M.Fleury/J.Staal B	25.00	60.00
ST2GJ G.Lafleur/J.Beliveau B	15.00	40.00
ST2HH Br.Hull/Bo.Hull B	25.00	60.00
ST2IN J.Iginla/R.Nash TC B	15.00	40.00
ST2JK Johansen/Kassian TC C	10.00	25.00
ST2KS P.Kane/A.Shaw B EXCH	25.00	60.00
ST2LC L.Leblanc/C.Cizikas TC C	10.00	25.00
ST2LL Mario Lemieux dual A	50.00	125.00
ST2ND J.Neal/S.Despres C	10.00	25.00
ST2OG B.Orr/W.Gretzky TC A	400.00	1000.00
ST2OH A.Ovechkin/B.Holtby C	50.00	120.00
ST2PC L.Couture/J.Pavelski C	15.00	40.00
ST2PP Carey Price dual B	25.00	60.00
ST2PS P.Subban/C.Price B	25.00	60.00
ST2RH P.Roy/D.Hasek A	30.00	80.00
ST2TT John Tavares dual C	20.00	50.00
SOT2EE J.Eborlo/J.Eborlo	12.00	30.00
SOT2SK D.Stepan/C.Kreider	30.00	80.00

2012-13 SP Authentic Sign of the Times Triples

Card	Low	High
SOT3BOS Mrchnd/Brgrn/Sgn	40.00	100.00
SOT3EDM Gretzky/Messier/Kurri	300.00	800.00
SOT3OIL RNH/Hall/Eberle	25.00	60.00
SOT3STL Schwartz/Allen/Ptrnglo	40.00	100.00
SOT3VAN Kesler/Schnder/Burrws	20.00	50.00
SOT3WJC Tavares/Eberle/Subban	30.00	80.00
SOT3BEES Orr/Bourque/Park	80.00	200.00
SOT3PITT Lemieux/Jagr/Francis	80.00	200.00
SOT3ROOK Kreidr/Schwrtz/Brtschi	50.00	125.00

2012-13 SP Authentic Signature Stoppers

Card	Low	High
SSAM Andy Moog	15.00	40.00
SSCP Carey Price	30.00	80.00
SSCS Cory Schneider	15.00	40.00
SSDH Dominik Hasek	25.00	60.00
SSEB Ed Belfour	15.00	40.00
SSJH Jaroslav Halak	15.00	40.00
SSJQ Jonathan Quick EXCH	20.00	50.00
SSMB Martin Brodeur	40.00	100.00
SSPR Pekka Rinne	15.00	40.00
SSRO Patrick Roy	40.00	100.00

2012-13 SP Authentic SPx Inserts

Card	Low	High
1 Teemu Selanne	2.50	6.00
2 Milan Lucic	1.25	3.00
3 Ryan Miller	1.25	3.00
4 Jarome Iginla	1.50	4.00
5 Jeff Skinner	1.50	4.00
6 Jonathan Toews	2.00	5.00
7 Jack Johnson	.75	2.00
8 Johan Franzen	1.00	2.50
9 Ryan Nugent-Hopkins	1.50	4.00
10 Wayne Gretzky	8.00	20.00
11 Stephen Weiss	1.00	2.50
12 Mike Richards	1.00	2.50
13 Jonathan Quick	1.50	4.00
14 Carey Price	2.50	6.00
15 Pekka Rinne	1.25	3.00
16 Ilya Kovalchuk	1.25	3.00
17 John Tavares	2.00	5.00
18 Marian Gaborik	1.25	3.00
19 Henrik Lundqvist	3.00	8.00
20 Jason Spezza	1.25	3.00
21 Claude Giroux	1.25	3.00
22 Eric Lindros	2.00	5.00
23 Evgeni Malkin	2.50	6.00
24 Sidney Crosby	5.00	12.00
25 Mario Lemieux	3.00	8.00
26 Antti Niemi	1.00	2.50
27 David Backes	.75	2.00
28 Steven Stamkos	2.50	6.00
29 Alexander Ovechkin	5.00	12.00
30 Ondrej Pavelec	1.25	3.00

2012-13 SP Authentic SPx Inserts Rookie Jersey Autographs

*PATCH/30: 1X TO 2.5X BASIC INSERTS

Card	Low	High
1 Maxime Sauve JSY AU/275	4.00	10.00
2 Akim Aliu JSY AU/275	5.00	12.00
3 Brandon Bollig JSY AU/275	4.00	10.00
4 Cody Goloubef JSY AU/275	4.00	10.00
7 Scott Glennie JSY AU/275	5.00	12.00
8 Riley Sheahan JSY AU/275	6.00	15.00
9 Jordan Nolan JSY AU/275	4.00	10.00
10 Jason Zucker JSY AU/275	10.00	25.00
11 Tyler Cuma JSY AU/275	4.00	10.00
12 Gabriel Dumont JSY AU/275	5.00	12.00
13 Chet Pickard JSY AU/275	5.00	12.00
14 Casey Cizikas JSY AU/275	5.00	12.00
15 Mark Stone JSY AU/275	15.00	40.00
16 Michael Stone JSY AU/275	5.00	12.00
17 J.T. Brown JSY AU/275	5.00	12.00
18 Sven Baertschi JSY AU/175	6.00	15.00
19 Tyson Barrie JSY AU/175	12.00	30.00
20 Chris Kreider JSY AU/175	15.00	40.00
21 Jakob Silfverberg JSY AU/175	8.00	20.00
22 Jake Allen JSY AU/175	12.00	30.00
23 Jaden Schwartz JSY AU/175	12.00	30.00
24 Carter Ashton JSY AU/175	4.00	10.00
25 Jussi Rynnas JSY AU/175	4.00	10.00

2013-14 SP Authentic

Card	Low	High
COMP.SET w/o RC's (200)	10.00	25.00
1 Jonas Hiller	.20	.50
2 Markus Naslund	.25	.60
3 Kris Letang	.30	.75
4 Jonathan Bernier	.20	.50
5 Steve Mason	.20	.50
6 Doug Wilson	.20	.50
7 David Backes	.15	.40
8 Chris Pronger	.25	.60
9 Chris Osgood	.25	.60
10 Alexandre Burrows	.15	.40
11 Jason Spezza	.25	.60
12 Shea Weber	.20	.50
13 Shane Doan	.20	.50
14 Tyler Seguin	.30	.75
15 Mikko Koivu	.20	.50
16 John LeClair	.25	.60
17 Gabriel Landeskog	.30	.75
18 Dustin Brown	.25	.60
19 Andrew Ladd	.15	.40
20 Ales Hemsky	.15	.40
21 Anze Kopitar	.40	1.00
22 Claude Giroux	.25	.60
23 Joe Sakic	.50	1.25
24 Dominik Hasek	.40	1.00
25 Theoren Fleury	.30	.75
26 Dion Phaneuf	.20	.50
27 Eric Staal	.30	.75
28 Corey Perry	.40	1.00
29 Joe Thornton	.40	1.00
30 Vincent Lecavalier	.25	.60
31 Taylor Hall	.25	.60
32 Ryan Nugent-Hopkins	.30	.75
33 Matt Duchene	.25	.60
34 Al MacInnis	.30	.75
35 Brett Hull	.50	1.25
36 Curtis Joseph	.30	.75
37 Doug Gilmour	.30	.75
38 Ed Belfour	.25	.60
39 Jonathan Toews	.40	1.00
40 Martin Brodeur	.60	1.50
41 Eric Lindros	.40	1.00
42 Luc Robitaille	.25	.60
43 Mats Sundin	.25	.60
44 Alexander Ovechkin	1.00	2.50
45 Patrick Roy	.60	1.50
46 Steve Yzerman	.60	1.50
47 Dominik Hasek	.40	1.00
48 Sidney Crosby	1.00	2.50
49 Mario Lemieux	1.00	2.50
50 Wayne Gretzky	1.50	4.00
51 Adam Henrique	.20	.50
52 Alex Pietrangelo	.20	.50
53 Alex Tanguay	.15	.40
54 Alexander Burmistrov	.20	.50
55 Andy Moog	.25	.60
56 Arturs Irbe	.20	.50
57 Bobby Clarke	.40	1.00
58 Bobby Hull	.50	1.25
59 Bobby Orr	1.00	2.50
60 Bobby Ryan	.20	.50
61 Brent Seabrook	.15	.40
62 Braden Holtby	.30	.75
63 Brayden Schenn	.25	.60
64 Brian Campbell	.15	.40
65 Carey Price	.50	1.25
66 Carl Hagelin	.15	.40
67 Chris Kunitz	.25	.60
68 Cody Franson	.15	.40
69 Cody Hodgson	.15	.40
70 Cory Schneider	.25	.60
71 Craig Anderson	.25	.60
72 Dany Heatley	.20	.50
73 David Clarkson	.15	.40
74 Derek Roy	.15	.40
75 Drew Doughty	.30	.75
76 Erik Karlsson	.30	.75
77 Evander Kane	.25	.60
78 Evgeni Malkin	.50	1.25
79 Evgeni Nabokov	.25	.60
80 Gilbert Perreault	.25	.60
81 Grant Fuhr	.40	1.00
82 Guy Lafleur	.30	.75
83 Henrik Lundqvist	.60	1.50
84 Ilya Kovalchuk	.25	.60
85 Jacob Markstrom	.25	.60
86 Jakub Voracek	.20	.50
87 James Neal	.15	.40
88 James Reimer	.25	.60
89 Jarome Iginla	.30	.75
90 Jaroslav Halak	.25	.60
91 Jason Spezza	.25	.60
92 Jean Beliveau	.25	.60
93 Jeff Carter	.20	.50
94 Jeff Skinner	.30	.75
95 Jiri Tlusty	.15	.40
96 Bill Barber	.25	.60
97 Joe Pavelski	.30	.75
98 John Tavares	.40	1.00
99 Jonas Hiller	.20	.50
100 Jordan Staal	.20	.50
101 Josh Harding	.25	.60
102 Kari Lehtonen	.20	.50
103 Keith Yandle	.15	.40
104 Kevin Shattenkirk	.15	.40
105 Lanny McDonald	.25	.60
106 Loui Eriksson	.15	.40
107 Luc Robitaille	.25	.60
108 Marian Gaborik	.25	.60
109 Marian Hossa	.25	.60
110 Mark Messier	.50	1.25
111 Martin St. Louis	.25	.60
112 Matt Duchene	.25	.60
113 Matt Moulson	.15	.40
114 Mike Modano	.40	1.00
115 Mike Ribeiro	.15	.40
116 Mike Richards	.20	.50
117 Mike Smith	.25	.60
118 Nazem Kadri	.30	.75
119 Bryan Bickell	.15	.40
120 Nicklas Lidstrom	.25	.60
121 Oliver Ekman-Larsson	.25	.60
122 Ondrej Pavelec	.25	.60
123 P.K. Subban	.30	.75
124 Patric Hornqvist	.15	.40
125 Patrick Kane	.50	1.25
126 Patrick Marleau	.25	.60
127 Paul Coffey	.25	.60
128 Paul Stastny	.20	.50
129 Pavel Datsyuk	.40	1.00
130 Pekka Rinne	.25	.60
131 Phil Kessel	.25	.60
132 Ray Bourque	.40	1.00
133 Rick Nash	.25	.60
134 Ryan Ellis	.20	.50
135 Ryan Johansen	.20	.50
136 Ryan Kesler	.25	.60
137 Ryan Suter	.20	.50
138 Scott Hartnell	.15	.40
139 Sergei Bobrovsky	.40	1.00
140 Stan Mikita	.30	.75
141 Steven Stamkos	.50	1.25
142 Ted Lindsay	.25	.60
143 Teddy Purcell	.15	.40
144 Teemu Selanne	.50	1.25
145 Thomas Vanek	.20	.50
146 Tomas Fleischmann	.15	.40
147 Tuukka Rask	.30	.75
148 Tyler Seguin	.30	.75
149 Zach Parise	.25	.60
150 Zdeno Chara	.25	.60
151 Viktor Fasth AM	.75	2.00
152 Patrice Bergeron AM	1.00	2.50
153 Ray Bourque AM	1.25	3.00
154 Bobby Orr AM	3.00	8.00
155 Tyler Seguin AM	1.00	2.50
156 Cody Hodgson AM	.50	1.25
157 Thomas Vanek AM	.60	1.50
158 Eric Staal AM	1.00	2.50
159 Patrick Sharp AM	.75	2.00
160 Jonathan Toews AM	1.25	3.00
161 Patrick Kane AM	1.50	4.00
162 Gabriel Landeskog AM	1.00	2.50
163 Patrick Roy AM	2.00	5.00
164 Brett Hull AM	1.50	4.00
165 Jordan Eberle AM	.75	2.00
166 Nail Yakupov AM	1.50	4.00
167 Taylor Hall AM	.75	2.00
168 Wayne Gretzky AM	5.00	12.00
169 Jonathan Huberdeau AM	2.00	5.00
170 Slava Voynov AM	.60	1.50
171 Jonathan Quick AM	1.00	2.50
172 Luc Robitaille AM	.75	2.00
173 Ryan Nugent-Hopkins AM	1.00	2.50
174 Anze Kopitar AM	1.25	3.00
175 Zach Parise AM	.75	2.00
176 Marcel Dionne AM	1.00	2.50
177 Beau Bennett AM	1.00	2.50
178 Brendan Gallagher AM	2.00	5.00
179 Pekka Rinne AM	.75	2.00
180 Jaromir Jagr AM	2.50	6.00
181 Cory Conacher AM	.50	1.25
182 Aleksander Barkov AM	2.50	6.00
183 Sidney Crosby AM	3.00	8.00
184 Tomas Hertl AM	1.50	4.00
185 Mario Lemieux AM	3.00	8.00
186 Mats Sundin AM	.75	2.00
187 Nazem Kadri AM	1.00	2.50
188 Pavel Bure AM	.75	2.00
189 Nathan MacKinnon AM	4.00	10.00
190 Alexander Ovechkin AM	3.00	8.00
191 MacKinnon/S.Jones AM	4.00	10.00
192 MacKinnon/A.Barkov AM	4.00	10.00
193 E.Staal/A.Ladd AM	1.00	2.50
194 Perry/Getzlaf/Penner AM	1.25	3.00
195 J.Toews/P.Sharp AM	1.25	3.00
196 E.Malkin/M.Lemieux AM	3.00	8.00
197 J.Toews/C.Crawford AM	1.25	3.00
198 Bergeron/Marchand AM	1.50	4.00
199 J.Quick/D.Penner AM	1.00	2.50
200 P.Kane/J.Toews AM	1.50	4.00
201 Edward Pasquale RC	1.25	3.00
202 Ryan Stanton RC	2.00	5.00
203 Jarred Tinordi RC	2.00	5.00
204 Jayson Megna RC	2.00	5.00
205 Jared Staal RC	1.50	4.00
206 Josh Leivo RC	1.50	4.00
207 Ryan Spooner RC	2.00	5.00
208 Eric Gryba RC	1.50	4.00
209 Drew Shore RC	1.50	4.00
210 Nathan Beaulieu RC	1.25	3.00
211 Jeff Zatkoff RC	2.00	5.00
212 Luke Gazdic RC	1.50	4.00
213 Cameron Schilling RC	1.25	3.00
214 Carl Soderberg RC	2.00	5.00
215 Patrick Bordeleau RC	2.00	5.00
216 Brian Dumoulin RC	2.00	5.00
217 Thomas Hickey RC	1.50	4.00
218 Mark Barberio RC	1.25	3.00
219 Reid Boucher RC	2.00	5.00
220 Anthony Peluso RC	1.25	3.00
221 Frank Corrado RC	1.25	3.00
222 Jon Merrill RC	2.00	5.00
223 Tom Wilson RC	4.00	10.00
224 Ondrej Palat RC	4.00	10.00
225 Xavier Ouellet RC	2.00	5.00
226 Patrick Holland RC	3.00	8.00
227 Spencer Abbott RC	1.50	4.00
228 Sami Aittokallio RC	2.00	5.00
229 Linden Vey RC	1.25	3.00
230 Mark Pysyk RC	2.00	5.00
231 Frederik Andersen RC	6.00	15.00
232 Ryan Strome RC	3.00	8.00
233 Nikita Zadorov RC	1.25	3.00
234 Rickard Rakell RC	2.00	5.00
235 John Gibson RC	5.00	12.00
236 Eric Gelinas RC	2.00	5.00
237 Matthew Irwin RC	1.50	4.00
238 Martin Jones RC	3.00	8.00
239 J.T. Miller RC	5.00	12.00
240 Johan Larsson RC	2.50	6.00
241 Philipp Grubauer RC	5.00	12.00
242 Tomas Jurco RC	2.50	6.00
243 Andrej Sustr RC	1.25	3.00
244 Antti Raanta RC	4.00	10.00
245 Cody Ceci RC	1.50	4.00
246 Victor Bartley RC	1.50	4.00
247 Antoine Roussel RC	2.00	5.00
248 Richard Panik RC	2.00	5.00
249 Tyler Johnson RC	4.00	10.00
250 Freddie Hamilton RC	2.00	5.00
251 J.Audy-Marchessault RC	10.00	25.00
252 Nick Bjugstad RC	2.50	6.00
253 Jerry D'Amigo RC	2.00	5.00
254 Jonas Brodin RC	2.50	6.00
255 Viktor Fasth RC	2.00	5.00
256 Austin Watson RC	1.50	4.00
257 Reto Berra RC	2.00	5.00
258 Tyler Pitlick RC	2.00	5.00
259 Martin Marincin RC	1.50	4.00
260 Darcy Kuemper RC	4.00	10.00
261 Brian Lashoff AU RC	4.00	10.00
262 Ryan Murphy AU RC EXCH	15.00	40.00
263 Damien Brunner AU RC	4.00	10.00
264 Petr Mrazek AU RC	12.00	30.00
265 Nail Yakupov AU RC	10.00	25.00
266 Max Reinhart AU RC	5.00	12.00
267 Tanner Pearson AU RC	5.00	12.00
268 Morgan Rielly AU RC	40.00	100.00
269 Filip Forsberg AU RC	25.00	60.00
270 Seth Jones AU RC	10.00	25.00
271 Valeri Nichushkin AU RC	25.00	60.00
272 Sean Monahan AU RC	8.00	20.00
273 Cory Conacher AU RC	3.00	8.00
274 Tyler Toffoli AU RC	20.00	50.00
275 Radko Gudas AU RC	5.00	12.00
276 V.Tarasenko AU RC EXCH	100.00	250.00
277 Alex Galchenyuk AU RC	12.00	30.00
278 Jesper Fast AU RC	5.00	12.00
279 J.Huberdeau AU RC	125.00	300.00
280 Jordan Schroeder AU RC	5.00	12.00
281 Justin Fontaine AU RC	5.00	12.00
282 Elias Lindholm AU RC	20.00	50.00
283 Justin Schultz AU RC	5.00	12.00
284 Alex Killorn AU RC	10.00	25.00
285 Mark Arcobello AU RC	5.00	12.00
286 Nicklas Jensen AU RC	4.00	10.00
287 Hampus Lindholm AU RC	8.00	20.00
288 Beau Bennett AU RC	6.00	15.00
289 Calvin Pickard AU RC	6.00	15.00
290 Matt Nieto AU RC EXCH	40.00	100.00
291 Connor Carrick AU RC	25.00	60.00
292 Emerson Etem AU RC	5.00	12.00
293 Charlie Coyle AU RC	8.00	20.00
294 Brock Nelson AU RC	10.00	25.00
295 Michael Bournival AU RC	5.00	12.00
296 John Gibson AU	40.00	100.00
297 Ryan Murray AU RC	8.00	20.00
298 Alex Chiasson AU RC	5.00	12.00
299 Boone Jenner AU RC	10.00	25.00
300 R.Ristolainen AU RC	8.00	20.00
301 Lucas Lessio AU RC	3.00	8.00
302 Joakim Nordstrom AU RC	4.00	10.00
303 Jack Campbell AU RC	40.00	100.00
304 Dougie Hamilton AU RC	8.00	20.00
305 Olli Maatta AU RC	8.00	20.00
306 Michael Latta AU RC	4.00	10.00
307 Danny DeKeyser AU RC	6.00	15.00
308 Tomas Hertl AU RC	15.00	40.00
309 Z.Girgensons AU RC	12.00	30.00
310 Scott Laughton AU RC	6.00	15.00
311 Will Acton AU RC	4.00	10.00
312 N.MacKinnon AU RC	800.00	2000.00
313 Jacob Trouba AU RC	8.00	20.00
314 Mathew Dumba AU RC	3.00	8.00
315 Mike Kostka AU RC	4.00	10.00
316 A.Barkov AU RC	80.00	200.00
317 Anton Belov AU RC	5.00	12.00
318 Brendan Gallagher AU RC	30.00	80.00
319 Mikael Granlund AU RC	8.00	20.00
320 Mikhail Grigorenko AU RC	15.00	40.00

2013-14 SP Authentic Limited

Card	Low	High
COMMON CARD/100	6.00	15.00
SEMISTARS	8.00	20.00
UNLISTED STARS	10.00	25.00
COMMON CARD/25	12.00	30.00
SEMISTARS	15.00	40.00
UNLISTED STARS	20.00	50.00
1 Jonas Hiller JSY AU/100	8.00	20.00
2 Markus Naslund JSY AU/100	10.00	25.00
3 Kris Letang JSY AU/100 (inserted in 2015-16 SP Authentic)	12.00	30.00
5 Steve Mason JSY AU/100	8.00	20.00
6 Doug Wilson JSY AU/100	15.00	40.00
7 David Backes JSY AU/100	8.00	20.00
8 Chris Pronger JSY AU/100	10.00	25.00
9 Chris Osgood JSY AU/100	10.00	25.00
11 Jason Spezza JSY AU/100	10.00	25.00
12 Shea Weber JSY AU/100 (inserted in 2015-16 SP Authentic)	8.00	20.00
14 Tyler Seguin JSY AU/100	12.00	30.00
15 Mikko Koivu JSY AU/100	8.00	20.00
16 John LeClair JSY AU/100	10.00	25.00
17 Gabriel Landeskog JSY AU/100 (inserted in 2015-16 SP Authentic)	12.00	30.00
18 Dustin Brown JSY AU/100	10.00	25.00
19 Andrew Ladd JSY AU/100	6.00	15.00
21 Anze Kopitar JSY AU/25	30.00	80.00
22 Claude Giroux JSY AU/25 (inserted in 2015-16 SP Authentic)	20.00	50.00
23 Joe Sakic JSY AU/25	40.00	100.00
24 Dominik Hasek JSY AU/25	30.00	80.00
25 Theoren Fleury JSY AU/25	25.00	60.00
26 Dion Phaneuf JSY AU/25	15.00	40.00
27 Eric Staal JSY AU/25	25.00	60.00
28 Corey Perry JSY AU/25	30.00	80.00
29 Joe Thornton JSY AU/25	30.00	80.00
33 Matt Duchene JSY AU/25 (inserted in 2015-16 SP Authentic)	20.00	50.00
34 Al MacInnis JSY AU/25	25.00	60.00
35 Brett Hull JSY AU/25	40.00	100.00
36 Curtis Joseph JSY AU/25	25.00	60.00
37 Doug Gilmour JSY AU/25	25.00	60.00
38 Ed Belfour JSY AU/25	20.00	50.00
39 Jonathan Toews JSY AU/25	30.00	80.00
40 Martin Brodeur JSY AU/25	50.00	125.00
51 Adam Henrique AU D	6.00	15.00
52 Alex Pietrangelo AU C	6.00	15.00
53 Alex Tanguay AU C	5.00	12.00
55 Andy Moog AU E	8.00	20.00
56 Arturs Irbe AU C	6.00	15.00
57 Bobby Clarke AU C	12.00	30.00
58 Bobby Hull AU A	15.00	40.00
59 Bobby Orr AU E	60.00	150.00
60 Bobby Ryan AU B	6.00	15.00
61 Brent Seabrook AU C	5.00	12.00
62 Braden Holtby AU D	10.00	25.00
63 Brayden Schenn AU C	8.00	20.00
65 Carey Price AU A	15.00	40.00
66 Carl Hagelin AU E	5.00	12.00
67 Chris Kunitz AU D	8.00	20.00
68 Cody Franson AU C	5.00	12.00
69 Cody Hodgson AU B (inserted in 2015-16 SP Authentic)	5.00	12.00
70 Cory Schneider AU E	8.00	20.00
72 Dany Heatley AU B	6.00	15.00
74 Derek Roy AU E	5.00	12.00
78 Evgeni Malkin AU B	15.00	40.00
80 Gilbert Perreault AU C	8.00	20.00
81 Grant Fuhr AU B	12.00	30.00
82 Guy Lafleur AU B	10.00	25.00
85 Jacob Markstrom AU E	8.00	20.00
87 James Neal AU D	5.00	12.00
89 Jarome Iginla AU B	10.00	25.00
90 Jaroslav Halak AU C	8.00	20.00
92 Jean Beliveau AU A	8.00	20.00
94 Jeff Skinner AU A	10.00	25.00
95 Jiri Tlusty AU E	5.00	12.00
96 Bill Barber AU E	8.00	20.00
97 Joe Pavelski AU D	10.00	25.00
98 John Tavares AU C	12.00	30.00
99 Jonas Hiller AU C	6.00	15.00
100 Jordan Staal AU C	6.00	15.00
101 Josh Harding AU E	8.00	20.00
104 Kevin Shattenkirk AU E	5.00	12.00
106 Loui Eriksson AU D	5.00	12.00
107 Luc Robitaille AU B	8.00	20.00
110 Mark Messier AU A	15.00	40.00
112 Matt Duchene AU C	8.00	20.00
114 Mike Modano AU B	12.00	30.00
117 Mike Smith AU D	8.00	20.00
119 Bryan Bickell AU E	5.00	12.00
120 Nicklas Lidstrom AU B	8.00	20.00
123 P.K. Subban AU A (inserted in 2015-16 SP Authentic)	10.00	25.00
124 Patric Hornqvist AU D	5.00	12.00
125 Patrick Kane AU A	15.00	40.00
126 Patrick Marleau AU B	8.00	20.00
127 Paul Coffey AU A	8.00	20.00
128 Paul Stastny AU C	6.00	15.00
130 Pekka Rinne AU A (inserted in 2015-16 SP Authentic)	8.00	20.00
131 Phil Kessel AU B	8.00	20.00
132 Ray Bourque AU A	12.00	30.00
133 Rick Nash AU B	8.00	20.00
134 Ryan Ellis AU E	6.00	15.00
136 Ryan Kesler AU C	8.00	20.00
137 Ryan Suter AU B (inserted in 2015-16 SP Authentic)	6.00	15.00
138 Scott Hartnell AU C	5.00	12.00
139 Sergei Bobrovsky AU D	12.00	30.00
140 Stan Mikita AU A	10.00	25.00
143 Teddy Purcell AU D	5.00	12.00
148 Tyler Seguin AU C	10.00	25.00
149 Zach Parise AU B	8.00	20.00
151 Viktor Fasth AM AU F	8.00	20.00
152 Patrice Bergeron AM AU B	10.00	25.00
153 Ray Bourque AM AU B	12.00	30.00
154 Bobby Orr AM AU D	60.00	150.00
155 Tyler Seguin AM AU C	10.00	25.00
156 Cody Hodgson AM AU E	5.00	12.00
158 Eric Staal AM AU B	10.00	25.00
159 Patrick Sharp AM AU A	8.00	20.00
160 Jonathan Toews AM AU A	12.00	30.00
161 Patrick Kane AM AU A	15.00	40.00
162 G.Landeskog AM AU E	10.00	25.00
163 Patrick Roy AM AU B	20.00	50.00
164 Brett Hull AM AU A	15.00	40.00
165 Jordan Eberle AM AU D	8.00	20.00
166 Nail Yakupov AM AU D	15.00	40.00
168 Wayne Gretzky AM AU C	250.00	600.00
169 J.Huberdeau AM AU F	20.00	50.00
172 Luc Robitaille AM AU B	8.00	20.00
173 Ryan Nugent-Hopkins AM AU B (inserted in 2015-16 SP Authentic)	10.00	25.00
174 Anze Kopitar AM AU C	12.00	30.00
175 Zach Parise AM AU C	8.00	20.00
176 Marcel Dionne AM AU B	10.00	25.00
177 Beau Bennett AM AU F	10.00	25.00
178 B.Gallagher AM AU F	20.00	50.00
179 Pekka Rinne AM AU B (inserted in 2015-16 SP Authentic)	8.00	20.00
180 Jaromir Jagr AM AU B	100.00	200.00
181 Cory Conacher AM AU E	5.00	12.00
182 A.Barkov AM AU F	25.00	60.00
184 Tomas Hertl AM AU F	15.00	40.00
185 Mario Lemieux AM AU A	30.00	80.00
186 Mats Sundin AM AU C	8.00	20.00
188 Pavel Bure AM AU A (inserted in 2015-16 SP Authentic)	8.00	20.00
189 MacKinnon AM AU D EXCH	40.00	100.00
190 A.Ovechkin AM AU A	50.00	125.00
191 MacKin/S.Jones AM AU	60.00	150.00
192 MacKin/A.Barkov AM AU	100.00	200.00
195 J.Toews/P.Sharp AM AU	12.00	30.00
196 E.Malkin/Lemieux AM AU	100.00	200.00
200 P.Kane/J.Toews AM AU	15.00	40.00
201 Edward Pasquale	5.00	12.00
202 Ryan Stanton	8.00	20.00
203 Jarred Tinordi	8.00	20.00
204 Jayson Megna	8.00	20.00
205 Jared Staal	6.00	15.00
206 Josh Leivo	6.00	15.00
207 Ryan Spooner	8.00	20.00
208 Eric Gryba	6.00	15.00
209 Drew Shore	6.00	15.00
210 Nathan Beaulieu	5.00	12.00
211 Jeff Zatkoff	8.00	20.00
212 Luke Gazdic	6.00	15.00
213 Cameron Schilling	5.00	12.00
214 Carl Soderberg	8.00	20.00
215 Patrick Bordeleau	8.00	20.00
216 Brian Dumoulin	8.00	20.00
217 Thomas Hickey	6.00	15.00
218 Mark Barberio	5.00	12.00
219 Reid Boucher	8.00	20.00
220 Anthony Peluso	5.00	12.00
221 Frank Corrado	5.00	12.00
222 Jon Merrill	8.00	20.00
223 Tom Wilson	15.00	40.00
224 Ondrej Palat	12.00	30.00
225 Xavier Ouellet	8.00	20.00
226 Patrick Holland	12.00	30.00
227 Spencer Abbott	6.00	15.00
228 Sami Aittokallio	8.00	20.00
229 Linden Vey	5.00	12.00
230 Mark Pysyk	8.00	20.00
231 Frederik Andersen	20.00	50.00
232 Ryan Strome	12.00	30.00
233 Nikita Zadorov	5.00	12.00
234 Rickard Rakell	8.00	20.00
235 John Gibson	20.00	50.00
236 Eric Gelinas	8.00	20.00
237 Matthew Irwin	6.00	15.00
238 Martin Jones	12.00	30.00
239 J.T. Miller	20.00	50.00
240 Johan Larsson	10.00	25.00
241 Philipp Grubauer	20.00	50.00
242 Tomas Jurco	10.00	25.00
243 Andrej Sustr	5.00	12.00
244 Antti Raanta	15.00	40.00
245 Cody Ceci	6.00	15.00
246 Victor Bartley	6.00	15.00
247 Antoine Roussel	8.00	20.00
248 Richard Panik	8.00	20.00
249 Tyler Johnson	15.00	40.00
250 Freddie Hamilton	8.00	20.00
251 Jonathan Audy-Marchessault	20.00	50.00
252 Nick Bjugstad	10.00	25.00
253 Jerry D'Amigo	8.00	20.00
254 Jonas Brodin	10.00	25.00
255 Viktor Fasth	8.00	20.00
256 Austin Watson	6.00	15.00
257 Reto Berra	8.00	20.00
258 Tyler Pitlick	8.00	20.00
259 Martin Marincin	6.00	15.00
260 Darcy Kuemper	15.00	40.00
261 Brian Lashoff JSY AU	8.00	20.00
262 Ryan Murphy JSY AU	10.00	25.00
263 Damien Brunner JSY AU	8.00	20.00
264 Petr Mrazek JSY AU	20.00	50.00
265 Nail Yakupov JSY AU	20.00	50.00
266 Max Reinhart JSY AU	10.00	25.00
267 Tanner Pearson JSY AU	10.00	25.00
268 Morgan Rielly JSY AU	100.00	250.00
269 Filip Forsberg JSY AU	30.00	80.00
270 Seth Jones JSY AU	20.00	50.00
271 Valeri Nichushkin JSY AU	60.00	150.00
272 Sean Monahan JSY AU	16.00	40.00
273 Cory Conacher JSY AU	6.00	15.00
274 Tyler Toffoli JSY AU	60.00	150.00
275 Radko Gudas JSY AU	10.00	25.00
276 Vladimir Tarasenko JSY AU	60.00	150.00
277 Alex Galchenyuk JSY AU	25.00	60.00
278 Jesper Fast JSY AU	10.00	25.00
279 Jonathan Huberdeau JSY AU	150.00	400.00
280 Jordan Schroeder JSY AU	10.00	25.00
281 Justin Fontaine JSY AU	10.00	25.00
282 Elias Lindholm JSY AU	40.00	100.00
283 Justin Schultz JSY AU	10.00	25.00
284 Alex Killorn JSY AU	15.00	40.00
285 Mark Arcobello JSY AU	10.00	25.00
286 Nicklas Jensen JSY AU	8.00	20.00
287 Hampus Lindholm JSY AU	15.00	40.00
288 Beau Bennett JSY AU	12.00	30.00
289 Calvin Pickard JSY AU	12.00	30.00
290 Matt Nieto JSY AU	8.00	20.00
291 Connor Carrick JSY AU	8.00	20.00
292 Emerson Etem JSY AU	10.00	25.00
293 Charlie Coyle JSY AU	15.00	40.00
294 Brock Nelson JSY AU	20.00	50.00
295 Michael Bournival JSY AU	10.00	25.00
296 John Gibson JSY AU (inserted in 2015-16 SP Authentic)	25.00	60.00
297 Ryan Murray JSY AU	15.00	40.00
298 Alex Chiasson JSY AU	10.00	25.00
299 Boone Jenner JSY AU	20.00	50.00
301 Lucas Lessio JSY AU	6.00	15.00
302 Joakim Nordstrom JSY AU	8.00	20.00
303 Jack Campbell JSY AU	60.00	150.00
304 Dougie Hamilton JSY AU	15.00	40.00
305 Olli Maatta JSY AU	15.00	40.00
306 Michael Latta JSY AU	8.00	20.00
307 Danny DeKeyser JSY AU	12.00	30.00
308 Tomas Hertl JSY AU	20.00	50.00
309 Z.Girgensons JSY AU	15.00	40.00
310 Scott Laughton JSY AU	12.00	30.00
311 Will Acton JSY AU	8.00	20.00
312 MacKinnon JSY AU EXCH	1000.00	2500.00
313 Jacob Trouba JSY AU	15.00	40.00
314 Mathew Dumba JSY AU	12.00	30.00
315 Mike Kostka JSY AU	8.00	20.00
316 Aleksander Barkov JSY AU	200.00	500.00
318 B.Gallagher JSY AU EXCH	40.00	100.00
319 Mikael Granlund JSY AU	15.00	40.00
320 M.Grigorenko JSY AU	6.00	15.00

2013-14 SP Authentic 1993-94 SP Retro

Card	Low	High
931 Bryan Bickell	1.00	2.50
932 Andy Moog	1.50	4.00
933 Bobby Orr	3.00	8.00
934 Brad Marchand	3.00	8.00
935 Tyler Seguin	2.00	5.00
936 Cody Hodgson	1.00	2.50
937 Jordan Staal	1.25	3.00
938 Jeff Skinner	2.00	5.00
939 Brent Seabrook	1.00	2.50
9310 Patrick Kane	3.00	8.00
9311 Jonathan Toews	2.50	6.00
9312 Joe Sakic	3.00	8.00
9313 Patrick Roy	2.50	6.00
9314 Peter Forsberg	3.00	8.00
9315 Gabriel Landeskog	2.00	5.00
9316 Steve Yzerman	4.00	10.00
9317 Ales Hemsky	1.00	2.50
9318 Ryan Nugent-Hopkins	2.00	5.00
9319 Taylor Hall	1.50	4.00
9320 Jordan Eberle	1.50	4.00
9321 Wayne Gretzky	4.00	10.00
9322 Devan Dubnyk	1.25	3.00
9323 Anze Kopitar	2.50	6.00
9324 Dustin Brown	1.50	4.00
9325 Jonathan Quick	2.00	5.00
9326 Ryan Suter	1.25	3.00
9327 Zach Parise	1.50	4.00
9328 Carey Price	3.00	8.00
9329 Rick Nash	1.50	4.00
9330 Pekka Rinne	1.50	4.00
9331 Martin Brodeur	4.00	10.00
9332 Adam Henrique	1.25	3.00
9333 John Tavares	2.50	6.00
9334 Erik Karlsson	2.00	5.00
9335 Scott Hartnell	1.00	2.50
9336 Claude Giroux	1.50	4.00
9337 Eric Lindros	2.50	6.00
9338 Paul Coffey	1.50	4.00
9339 Evgeni Malkin	3.00	8.00
9340 Mario Lemieux	6.00	15.00
9341 Kris Letang	2.00	5.00
9342 Sidney Crosby	3.00	8.00
9343 Arturs Irbe	1.25	3.00
9344 Patrick Marleau	1.50	4.00
9345 Jaroslav Halak	1.50	4.00
9346 Brett Hull	3.00	8.00
9347 Alex Pietrangelo	1.25	3.00
9348 Chris Pronger	1.50	4.00
9349 Steven Stamkos	3.00	8.00
9350 Mats Sundin	1.50	4.00
9351 Jonathan Bernier	1.25	3.00
9352 Phil Kessel	1.50	4.00
9353 Dion Phaneuf	1.25	3.00
9354 James van Riemsdyk	1.25	3.00
9355 Felix Potvin	2.50	6.00
9356 Pavel Bure	1.50	4.00
9357 Alexandre Burrows	1.00	2.50
9358 Cory Schneider	1.50	4.00
9359 Alexander Ovechkin	6.00	15.00
9360 Evander Kane	1.50	4.00

2013-14 SP Authentic 1993-94 SP Retro Autographs

Card	Low	High
931 Bryan Bickell D	4.00	10.00
932 Andy Moog D	6.00	15.00
933 Bobby Orr C	25.00	60.00
935 Tyler Seguin C	8.00	20.00
936 Cody Hodgson D	4.00	10.00
937 Jordan Staal C	5.00	12.00
938 Jeff Skinner D	8.00	20.00
939 Brent Seabrook D	4.00	10.00
9310 Patrick Kane A	12.00	30.00
9311 Jonathan Toews A	40.00	100.00
9312 Joe Sakic A	40.00	100.00
9313 Patrick Roy A	40.00	100.00
9314 Peter Forsberg A	30.00	80.00
9315 Gabriel Landeskog D	8.00	20.00
9316 Steve Yzerman A	15.00	40.00
9318 Ryan Nugent-Hopkins B (inserted in 2015-16 SP Authentic)	8.00	20.00
9320 Jordan Eberle A (inserted in 2015-16 SP Authentic)	6.00	15.00
9321 Wayne Gretzky A	300.00	800.00
9322 Devan Dubnyk D	5.00	12.00
9323 Anze Kopitar B	10.00	25.00
9324 Dustin Brown B	6.00	15.00
9326 Ryan Suter D	5.00	12.00
9327 Zach Parise B	6.00	15.00
9328 Carey Price A	50.00	125.00
9329 Rick Nash C	6.00	15.00
9330 Pekka Rinne B	6.00	15.00
9331 Martin Brodeur A	30.00	80.00
9332 Adam Henrique D	5.00	12.00
9333 John Tavares D	10.00	25.00
9335 Scott Hartnell B	4.00	10.00
9336 Claude Giroux C	6.00	15.00
9338 Paul Coffey C	6.00	15.00
9339 Evgeni Malkin B	12.00	30.00
9340 Mario Lemieux A	30.00	80.00
9341 Kris Letang B	8.00	20.00
9343 Arturs Irbe B	5.00	12.00
9344 Patrick Marleau B	6.00	15.00
9345 Jaroslav Halak D	6.00	15.00
9346 Brett Hull B	12.00	30.00
9347 Alex Pietrangelo D	5.00	12.00
9348 Chris Pronger B	6.00	15.00
9350 Mats Sundin A	40.00	100.00
9351 Jonathan Bernier B	5.00	12.00
9352 Phil Kessel B	6.00	15.00
9353 Dion Phaneuf C	5.00	12.00
9354 James van Riemsdyk D	5.00	12.00
9355 Felix Potvin B	10.00	25.00
9356 Pavel Bure A (inserted in 2015-16 SP Authentic)	6.00	15.00
9358 Cory Schneider B	6.00	15.00
9359 Alexander Ovechkin A	40.00	100.00

2013-14 SP Authentic 1993-94 SP Retro Premier Prospects

Card	Low	High
PP1 Cory Conacher	.50	1.25
PP2 Mikhail Grigorenko	.50	1.25
PP3 Aleksander Barkov	2.50	6.00
PP4 Vladimir Tarasenko	2.00	5.00
PP5 Dougie Hamilton	1.25	3.00
PP6 Boone Jenner	1.50	4.00
PP7 Charlie Coyle	1.25	3.00
PP8 Seth Jones	1.50	4.00
PP9 Elias Lindholm	2.00	5.00
PP10 Valeri Nichushkin	1.50	4.00

PP11 Nail Yakupov 1.50 4.00
PP12 Jonathan Huberdeau 2.00 5.00
PP13 Zemgus Girgensons 1.25 3.00
PP14 Jordan Schroeder .75 2.00
PP15 Justin Schultz .75 2.00
PP16 Ryan Murray 1.25 3.00
PP17 Tyler Toffoli 1.50 4.00
PP18 Tom Wilson 1.50 4.00
PP19 Hampus Lindholm 1.25 3.00
PP20 Jacob Trouba 1.25 3.00
PP21 Nathan MacKinnon 4.00 10.00
PP22 Connor Carrick .60 1.50
PP23 Brendan Gallagher 2.00 5.00
PP24 Rasmus Ristolainen 1.25 3.00
PP25 Morgan Rielly 2.00 5.00
PP26 Sean Monahan 1.25 3.00
PP27 Ryan Murphy .75 2.00
PP28 Damien Brunner .60 1.50
PP29 Alex Galchenyuk 2.00 5.00
PP30 Tomas Hertl 1.50 4.00

2013-14 SP Authentic 1993-94 SP Retro Premier Prospects Gold Autographs

PP1 Cory Conacher 4.00 10.00
PP2 Mikhail Grigorenko 4.00 10.00
PP3 Aleksander Barkov 12.00 30.00
PP4 Vladimir Tarasenko 12.00 30.00
PP5 Dougie Hamilton 12.00 30.00
PP6 Boone Jenner 8.00 20.00
PP7 Charlie Coyle 10.00 25.00
PP8 Seth Jones 12.00 30.00
PP9 Elias Lindholm 15.00 40.00
PP10 Valeri Nichushkin 12.00 30.00
PP11 Nail Yakupov 12.00 30.00
PP12 Jonathan Huberdeau 15.00 40.00
PP13 Zemgus Girgensons 10.00 25.00
PP14 Jordan Schroeder 4.00 10.00
PP15 Justin Schultz 6.00 15.00
PP16 Ryan Murray 8.00 20.00
PP17 Tyler Toffoli 12.00 30.00
PP18 Tom Wilson 8.00 20.00
PP19 Hampus Lindholm 10.00 25.00
PP20 Jacob Trouba 10.00 25.00
PP21 Nathan MacKinnon 60.00 150.00
PP22 Connor Carrick 5.00 12.00
PP23 Brendan Gallagher 15.00 40.00
PP25 Morgan Rielly 15.00 40.00
PP26 Sean Monahan 10.00 25.00
PP27 Ryan Murphy 6.00 15.00
PP28 Damien Brunner 4.00 10.00
PP29 Alex Galchenyuk 15.00 40.00
PP30 Tomas Hertl 15.00 40.00

2013-14 SP Authentic 1993-94 SP Retro Silver Skates

R1 Wayne Gretzky 6.00 15.00
R2 Mario Lemieux 4.00 10.00
R3 John Tavares 1.50 4.00
R4 Jordan Eberle 1.00 2.50
R5 Taylor Hall 1.00 2.50
R6 Rick Nash 1.00 2.50
R7 Ryan Nugent-Hopkins 1.25 3.00
R8 Gabriel Landeskog 1.25 3.00
R9 Bobby Orr 4.00 10.00
R10 Jonathan Bernier .75 2.00
R11 Sidney Crosby 4.00 10.00
R12 Jonathan Toews 1.50 4.00
R13 Joe Sakic 2.00 5.00
R14 Steve Yzerman 2.50 6.00
R15 Alexander Ovechkin 4.00 10.00
R16 Nail Yakupov 1.50 4.00
R17 Alex Galchenyuk 2.00 5.00
R18 Sean Monahan 1.25 3.00
R19 Jonathan Huberdeau 2.00 5.00
R20 Elias Lindholm 2.00 5.00
R21 Morgan Rielly 2.00 5.00
R22 Mikhail Grigorenko .50 1.25
R23 Nathan MacKinnon 4.00 10.00
R24 Tomas Hertl 1.50 4.00
R25 Justin Schultz .75 2.00
R26 Dougie Hamilton 1.25 3.00
R27 Aleksander Barkov 2.50 6.00
R28 Ryan Murray 1.25 3.00
R29 Valeri Nichushkin 1.50 4.00
R30 Seth Jones 1.50 4.00

2013-14 SP Authentic 1993-94 SP Retro Silver Skates Autographs

R1 Wayne Gretzky B 250.00 600.00
R2 Mario Lemieux A 50.00 125.00
R3 John Tavares B 12.00 30.00
R4 Jordan Eberle B
(inserted in 2015-16 SP Authentic) 8.00 20.00
R6 Rick Nash B 8.00 20.00
R7 Ryan Nugent-Hopkins A
(inserted in 2015-16 SP Authentic) 10.00 25.00
R8 Gabriel Landeskog B 10.00 25.00
R9 Bobby Orr B 100.00 200.00
R10 Jonathan Bernier B 6.00 15.00
R12 Jonathan Toews B 12.00 30.00
R13 Joe Sakic B 15.00 40.00
R14 Steve Yzerman B 20.00 50.00
R15 Alexander Ovechkin A 30.00 80.00
R16 Nail Yakupov 15.00 40.00
R17 Alex Galchenyuk 20.00 50.00
R18 Sean Monahan 12.00 30.00
R19 Jonathan Huberdeau 20.00 50.00
R20 Elias Lindholm 20.00 50.00
R21 Morgan Rielly 20.00 50.00
R22 Mikhail Grigorenko 5.00 12.00
R23 Nathan MacKinnon 40.00 100.00
R24 Tomas Hertl 15.00 40.00
R25 Justin Schultz 8.00 20.00
R26 Dougie Hamilton 12.00 30.00
R27 Aleksander Barkov 25.00 60.00
R28 Ryan Murray 12.00 30.00
R29 Valeri Nichushkin 15.00 40.00
R30 Seth Jones 15.00 40.00

2013-14 SP Authentic Chirography

CAO Alexander Ovechkin 50.00 125.00
CCG Claude Giroux 12.00 30.00
CCP Carey Price 25.00 60.00
CCS Cory Schneider 12.00 30.00
CDP Dion Phaneuf 10.00 25.00
CEM Evgeni Malkin 25.00 60.00
CGL Gabriel Landeskog 15.00 40.00
CJB Jonathan Bernier 10.00 25.00
CJE Jordan Eberle
(inserted in 2015-16 SP Authentic) 12.00 30.00
CJN James Neal 8.00 20.00
CJT Jonathan Toews 20.00 50.00
CJV James van Riemsdyk 10.00 25.00
CMB Martin Brodeur 30.00 80.00
CMK Mikko Koivu 10.00 25.00
CNH Ryan Nugent-Hopkins
(inserted in 2015-16 SP Authentic) 15.00 40.00
CPD Pavel Datsyuk 20.00 50.00
CPK Patrick Kane 25.00 60.00
CPR Pekka Rinne 12.00 30.00
CRG Ryan Getzlaf 12.00 30.00
CRN Rick Nash 12.00 30.00
CRS Ryan Suter 10.00 25.00
CTA John Tavares 20.00 50.00
CTS Tyler Seguin 15.00 40.00
CZP Zach Parise 12.00 30.00

2013-14 SP Authentic Marks of Distinction

MDAO Alexander Ovechkin 60.00 150.00
MDCP Carey Price 30.00 80.00
MDEM Evgeni Malkin 30.00 80.00
MDJB Jean Beliveau 15.00 40.00
MDJS Joe Sakic 30.00 80.00
MDJT Jonathan Toews 25.00 60.00
MDMK Mikko Koivu 12.00 30.00
MDML Mario Lemieux 60.00 150.00
MDMM Mark Messier 30.00 80.00
MDMS Mats Sundin 15.00 40.00
MDPB Pavel Bure
(inserted in 2015-16 SP Authentic) 15.00 40.00
MDPK Patrick Kane EXCH 30.00 80.00
MDPR Patrick Roy 40.00 100.00
MDRN Ryan Nugent-Hopkins
(inserted in 2015-16 SP Authentic) 20.00 50.00
MDSP Jason Spezza 15.00 40.00
MDTA John Tavares 25.00 60.00
MDWG Wayne Gretzky 250.00 600.00
MDZP Zach Parise 15.00 40.00

2013-14 SP Authentic Premier Chirography

PCAG Alex Galchenyuk 10.00 25.00
PCBB Beau Bennett 5.00 12.00
PCBE Nathan Beaulieu 10.00 25.00
PCBG Brendan Gallagher 10.00 25.00
PCCC Charlie Coyle 6.00 15.00
PCCO Cory Conacher 2.50 6.00
PCDB Damien Brunner 3.00 8.00
PCDH Dougie Hamilton 6.00 15.00
PCEE Emerson Etem 4.00 10.00
PCGR Mikael Granlund 6.00 15.00
PCJC Jack Campbell 10.00 25.00
PCJH Jonathan Huberdeau 20.00 50.00
PCJO Jamie Oleksiak 3.00 8.00
PCJS Justin Schultz 4.00 10.00
PCMG Mikhail Grigorenko 10.00 25.00
PCNB Nick Bjugstad 5.00 12.00
PCNY Nail Yakupov 8.00 20.00
PCPM Petr Mrazek 8.00 20.00
PCQH Quinton Howden 4.00 10.00
PCRS Ryan Spooner 6.00 15.00
PCSC Jordan Schroeder 5.00 12.00
PCSL Scott Laughton 5.00 12.00
PCSM Stefan Matteau 3.00 8.00
PCTT Tyler Toffoli 10.00 25.00
PCTW Tom Wilson 6.00 15.00
PCVF Viktor Fasth 4.00 10.00

2013-14 SP Authentic Sign of the Times

SOTAG Alex Goligoski E 4.00 10.00
SOTAI Arturs Irbe D 5.00 12.00
SOTAL Alex Galchenyuk C 15.00 40.00
SOTBN Brock Nelson E 12.00 30.00
SOTBO Bobby Orr C 25.00 60.00
SOTBS Brent Seabrook B 4.00 10.00
SOTCF Cody Franson C 4.00 10.00
SOTCK Chris Kreider B 8.00 20.00
SOTCO Charlie Coyle D 10.00 25.00
SOTCT Christian Thomas D 5.00 12.00
SOTDD Devan Dubnyk B 5.00 12.00
SOTDS Dave Schultz B 6.00 15.00
SOTHI Thomas Hickey E 5.00 12.00
SOTJB Jean Beliveau A 6.00 15.00
SOTJE Jordan Eberle C 6.00 15.00
SOTJN James Neal B
(inserted in 2015-16 SP Authentic) 4.00 10.00
SOTJP Jean-Gabriel Pageau D 6.00 15.00
SOTJS Jaden Schwartz C 8.00 20.00
SOTJT Joe Thornton A 10.00 25.00
SOTMG Michel Goulet B 5.00 12.00
SOTMI Mikhail Grigorenko D 4.00 10.00
SOTMS Mats Sundin A 6.00 15.00
SOTNB Nick Bjugstad E 8.00 20.00
SOTNY Nail Yakupov D 12.00 30.00
SOTOS Chris Osgood A 6.00 15.00
SOTPB Pavel Bure A
(inserted in 2015-16 SP Authentic) 6.00 15.00
SOTPI Calvin Pickard E 8.00 20.00
SOTPS Mark Pysyk D 6.00 15.00
SOTRE Ryan Ellis C 5.00 12.00
SOTRI Pekka Rinne B 6.00 15.00
SOTRM Ryan Murphy E 6.00 15.00
SOTRN Ryan Nugent-Hopkins B
(inserted in 2015-16 SP Authentic) 8.00 20.00
SOTSL Scott Laughton D 8.00 20.00
SOTTF Theoren Fleury A 15.00 40.00
SOTWG Wayne Gretzky B 200.00 500.00

2013-14 SP Authentic Sign of the Times Duals

SOT2AA A.Niemi/A.Irbe 25.00 60.00
SOT2GC M.Granlund/C.Coyle 20.00 50.00
SOT2GG Galchenyuk/Gallagher 30.00 80.00
SOT2GM W.Gretzky/M.Messier 250.00 600.00
SOT2JR S.Jones/M.Rielly 30.00 80.00
SOT2LM E.Lindholm/Monahan 30.00 80.00
SOT2LO B.Orr/N.Lidstrom 100.00 200.00
SOT2MF T.Fleury/A.MacInnis 15.00 40.00
SOT2MJ R.Murray/B.Jenner 25.00 60.00
SOT2MY MacKinnon/N.Yakupov 60.00 150.00
SOT2NH V.Nichushkin/T.Hertl 25.00 60.00
SOT2RS P.Roy/J.Sakic 30.00 80.00
SOT2SY N.Yakupov/J.Schultz 25.00 60.00
SOT2TB J.Trouba/A.Barkov 40.00 100.00

2014-15 SP Authentic

1 Dustin Brown .25 .60
2 Claude Giroux .25 .60
3 Mike Modano .40 1.00
4 Joe Sakic .50 1.25
5 Kyle Turris .25 .60
6 Logan Couture .30 .75
7 Olli Maatta .15 .40
8 Tyler Toffoli .25 .60
9 Adam Oates .25 .60
10 Joe Pavelski .30 .75
11 Mark Scheifele .40 1.00
12 Wayne Gretzky 1.50 4.00
13 Ryan Nugent-Hopkins .30 .75
14 Patrick Kane .50 1.25
15 Tyler Johnson .15 .40
16 Sidney Crosby 1.00 2.50
17 Carey Price .50 1.25
18 Tyler Seguin .30 .75
19 Shea Weber .20 .50
20 Patrick Roy .60 1.50
21 Vladimir Tarasenko .30 .75
22 James van Riemsdyk .20 .50
23 Sean Couturier .20 .50
24 Nick Bjugstad .15 .40
25 Chris Chelios .25 .60
26 Damien Brunner .15 .40
27 Mike Gartner .30 .75
28 Mats Zuccarello .25 .60
29 Jeremy Roenick .40 1.00
30 Ryan Miller .25 .60
31 Vincent Lecavalier .25 .60
32 Sergei Bobrovsky .40 1.00
33 Antti Niemi .20 .50
34 Mario Lemieux 1.00 2.50
35 Dustin Byfuglien .25 .60
36 Torey Krug .20 .50
37 Marian Gaborik .25 .60
38 Mark Messier .50 1.25
39 Jaromir Jagr .75 2.00
40 Teemu Selanne .50 1.25
41 John Tavares .40 1.00
42 Taylor Hall .25 .60
43 Patrick Sharp .25 .60
44 Frederik Andersen .30 .75
45 Max Pacioretty .25 .60
46 Jim Howard .30 .75
47 Kari Lehtonen .20 .50
48 Zach Parise .25 .60
49 John Gibson .25 .60
50 Filip Forsberg .40 1.00
51 Nathan MacKinnon 1.00 2.50
52 Evgeni Malkin .50 1.25
53 Cory Schneider .25 .60
54 Nicklas Lidstrom .25 .60
55 David Backes .15 .40
56 David Krejci .25 .60
57 Pavel Datsyuk .40 1.00
58 Alexander Ovechkin 1.00 2.50
59 Anze Kopitar .40 1.00
60 Eric Staal .30 .75
61 Patrik Berglund .15 .40
62 Mikhail Grigorenko .15 .40
63 Rob Brown .20 .50
64 Ryan O'Reilly .25 .60
65 Paul Stastny .20 .50
66 Devan Dubnyk .20 .50
67 Brian Leetch .20 .50
68 Johan Franzen .20 .50
69 Morgan Rielly .25 .60
70 Pekka Rinne .25 .60
71 Martin St. Louis .25 .60
72 P.A. Parenteau .15 .40
73 Ryan Strome .25 .60
74 Brandon Saad .20 .50
75 Jari Kurri .25 .60
76 Ryan Suter .20 .50
77 Mats Sundin .25 .60
78 Adam Henrique .20 .50
79 Denis Savard .25 .60
80 Patrik Elias .25 .60
81 Pierre Turgeon .20 .50
82 James Neal .15 .40
83 Colton Orr .15 .40
84 Matt Duchene .25 .60
85 Antti Raanta .25 .60
86 Trevor Linden .25 .60
87 Kyle Quincey .15 .40
88 Martin Jones .20 .50
89 Alex Galchenyuk .15 .40
90 Mike Liut .15 .40
91 Mike Richter .25 .60
92 Steven Stamkos .50 1.25
93 Henrik Lundqvist .60 1.50
94 Henrik Zetterberg .30 .75
95 Nicklas Backstrom .25 .60
96 Tomas Hertl .25 .60
97 Ryan Kesler .25 .60
98 Brad Marchand .50 1.25
99 Alec Martinez .15 .40
100 Phil Kessel .25 .60
101 Patrick Marleau .25 .60
102 Jacob Trouba .20 .50
103 Martin Brodeur .60 1.50
104 Ryan Getzlaf .25 .60
105 Craig Anderson .25 .60
106 Blake Wheeler .25 .60
107 Jakub Voracek .20 .50
108 Darryl Sittler .30 .75
109 P.K. Subban .30 .75
110 Drew Doughty .30 .75
111 Bobby Ryan .20 .50
112 Derek Stepan .15 .40
113 Kyle Okposo .15 .40
114 Tomas Tatar .15 .40
115 Patrice Bergeron .30 .75
116 Niklas Kronwall .20 .50
117 Zdeno Chara .25 .60
118 Chris Kreider .30 .75
119 Theoren Fleury .30 .75
120 Valeri Nichushkin .25 .60
121 Aleksander Barkov .40 1.00
122 Seth Jones .25 .60
123 Ben Scrivens .20 .50
124 Ondrej Palat .20 .50
125 Corey Perry .40 1.00
126 Gustav Nyquist .15 .40
127 Alexander Steen .15 .40
128 Alex Pietrangelo .20 .50
129 Bobby Orr 1.00 2.50
130 Tomas Plekanec .15 .40
131 Darcy Kuemper .25 .60
132 Jonathan Quick .30 .75
133 David Perron .20 .50
134 Chris Kunitz .25 .60
135 Ryan Johansen .20 .50
136 Brandon Dubinsky .15 .40
137 Ryan Murray .15 .40
138 T.J. Oshie .25 .60
139 Andrew Cogliano .15 .40
140 Jarome Iginla .30 .75
141 Ryan McDonagh .15 .40
142 Rick Nash .25 .60
143 Ben Bishop .20 .50
144 Steve Mason .20 .50
145 Charlie Coyle .25 .60
146 Tom Barrasso .25 .60
147 David Desharnais .15 .40
148 Justin Williams .20 .50
149 Jonathan Bernier .20 .50
150 Elias Lindholm .25 .60
151 Tomas Hertl AM .75 2.00
152 Mike Smith AM .75 2.00
153 Teemu Selanne AM 1.50 4.00
154 Justin Williams AM .60 1.50
155 Corey Crawford AM 1.00 2.50
156 Nathan MacKinnon AM 3.00 8.00
157 Seth Jones AM .75 2.00
158 John Gibson AM .75 2.00
159 Carey Price AM 1.50 4.00
160 Martin St. Louis AM .75 2.00
161 Jonathan Bernier AM .60 1.50
162 Andre Burakovsky AM 1.25 3.00
163 Sidney Crosby AM 3.00 8.00
164 Aleksander Barkov AM 1.25 3.00
165 Jonathan Drouin AM 1.50 4.00
166 Semyon Varlamov AM .75 2.00
167 Alec Martinez AM .50 1.25
168 Jonathan Toews AM 1.25 3.00
169 Mats Zuccarello AM .75 2.00
170 Henrik Lundqvist AM 2.00 5.00
171 Ekbld/Rnhrt/Drstl AM 5.00 12.00
172 J.Pavelski/P.Marleau AM 1.25 3.00
173 J.Benn/T.Seguin AM 1.25 3.00
174 D.Nurse/L.Draisaitl AM 5.00 12.00
175 J.Quick/A.Kopitar AM 1.50 4.00
176 T.Toffoli/T.Pearson AM 1.00 2.50
177 J.Sekac/S.Andrighetto AM 1.25 3.00
178 M.Modano/R.Blake AM 1.50 4.00
179 D.Stepan/R.Nash AM 1.00 2.50
180 D.Hasek/P.Forsberg AM 2.00 5.00
181 Bobby Orr ATM 3.00 8.00
182 Brian Leetch ATM .60 1.50
183 Mike Modano ATM 1.25 3.00
184 Wayne Gretzky ATM 5.00 12.00
185 Jonathan Toews ATM 1.25 3.00
186 John Vanbiesbrouck ATM .75 2.00
187 Mike Krushelnyski ATM .60 1.50
188 Steve Yzerman ATM 2.00 5.00
189 Teemu Selanne ATM 1.50 4.00
190 Chris Chelios ATM .75 2.00
191 Jaromir Jagr ATM 2.50 6.00
192 Arturs Irbe ATM .60 1.50
193 Paul Coffey ATM .75 2.00
194 Mike Bossy ATM .75 2.00
195 Jean Beliveau ATM .75 2.00
196 M.Messier/M.Richter ATM 2.50 6.00
197 C.Chelios/D.Hasek ATM 2.00 5.00
198 W.Gretzky/W.Gretzky ATM 8.00 20.00
199 M.Bossy/W.Gretzky ATM 8.00 20.00
200 G.Lafleur/M.Dionne ATM 1.50 4.00
201 Iiro Pakarinen RC 1.50 4.00
202 Sam Carrick RC 2.00 5.00
203 Brandon Davidson RC 2.00 5.00
204 Miikka Salomaki RC 2.00 5.00
205 Kristers Gudlevskis RC 2.00 5.00
206 Oscar Klefbom RC 4.00 10.00
207 Tyler Gaudet RC 1.50 4.00
208 Jyrki Jokipakka RC 2.00 5.00
209 Brody Sutter RC 1.25 3.00
210 Barclay Goodrow RC 2.00 5.00
211 Klas Dahlbeck RC 1.50 4.00
212 Joe Whitney RC 1.25 3.00
213 Joel Armia RC 2.00 5.00
214 John Persson RC 1.50 4.00
215 Nikita Nesterov RC 2.00 5.00
216 Phoenix Copley RC 2.50 6.00
217 Scott Darling RC 4.00 10.00
218 Joe Morrow RC 2.50 6.00
219 Christopher Gibson RC 3.00 8.00
220 Petteri Lindbohm RC 1.50 4.00
221 Jordan Binnington RC 15.00 40.00
222 Seth Helgeson RC 1.50 4.00
223 Mike Halmo RC 1.25 3.00
224 Max Friberg RC 1.50 4.00
225 Rob Zepp RC 3.00 8.00
226 Brandon Gormley RC 2.00 5.00
227 Jonathan Racine RC 2.00 5.00
228 Joey Hishon RC 2.50 6.00
229 Bill Arnold RC 1.50 4.00
230 Brendan Shinnimin RC 1.50 4.00
231 Tyler Graovac RC 1.50 4.00
232 Jordan Martinook RC 1.50 4.00
233 Scott Mayfield RC 1.50 4.00
234 Josh Jooris RC 2.00 5.00
235 Bobby Farnham RC 2.00 5.00
236 Cedric Paquette RC 2.00 5.00
237 Troy Grosenick RC 2.00 5.00
238 Bryan Rust RC 25.00 60.00
239 Landon Ferraro RC 1.25 3.00
240 Colin Smith RC 2.00 5.00
241 Dominik Uher RC 1.50 4.00
242 Scott Harrington RC 2.00 5.00
243 Bogdan Yakimov RC 2.00 5.00
244 Tyler Wotherspoon RC 2.00 5.00
245 Pierre-Edouard Bellemare RC 2.00 5.00
246 Petter Granberg RC 1.50 4.00
247 Adam Clendening RC 2.00 5.00
248 Johan Sundstrom RC 2.00 5.00
249 Chris Wagner RC 2.00 5.00
250 Brandon Defazio RC 1.50 4.00
251 John Klingberg RC 4.00 10.00
252 Nicolas Deschamps RC 2.00 5.00
253 Borna Rendulic RC 2.00 5.00
254 Tim Schaller RC 1.25 3.00
255 Andrey Makarov RC 2.00 5.00
256 Anton Forsberg RC 1.50 4.00
257 Scott Wilson RC 1.50 4.00
258 Andrew Agozzino RC 1.50 4.00
259 Cody Kunyk RC 1.25 3.00
260 Matt Lindblad RC 1.50 4.00
261 William Karlsson AU RC 20.00 50.00
262 Darnell Nurse AU RC 40.00 100.00
263 Jake McCabe AU RC 5.00 12.00
264 Patrick Brown AU RC 5.00 12.00
265 Joni Ortio AU RC 20.00 50.00
266 Mark Visentin AU RC 5.00 12.00
267 Corban Knight AU RC 5.00 12.00
268 Stuart Percy AU RC 5.00 12.00
269 Phillip Danault AU RC 12.00 30.00
270 Patrik Nemeth AU RC 5.00 12.00
271 Colton Sissons AU RC 5.00 12.00
272 Curtis McKenzie AU RC 4.00 10.00
273 Sam Reinhart AU RC 30.00 80.00
274 Melker Karlsson AU RC 5.00 12.00
275 Nicolas Deslauriers AU RC 5.00 12.00
276 Christian Folin AU RC 5.00 12.00
277 Leon Draisaitl AU RC 500.00 1000.00
278 Sven Andrighetto AU RC 20.00 50.00
279 Chris Tierney AU RC 15.00 40.00
280 Trevor van Riemsdyk AU RC 8.00 20.00
281 A.Hammond AU RC EXCH 8.00 20.00
282 David Pastrnak AU RC 250.00 600.00
283 Vincent Trocheck AU RC 10.00 25.00
284 T.Teravainen AU RC EXCH 15.00 40.00
285 Bo Horvat AU RC 30.00 80.00
286 A.Duclair AU RC EXCH 25.00 60.00
287 Damon Severson AU RC 5.00 12.00
288 Evgeny Kuznetsov AU RC 12.00 30.00
289 Rocco Grimaldi AU RC 5.00 12.00
290 Dennis Everberg AU RC 5.00 12.00
291 Alexander Wennberg AU RC 8.00 20.00
292 Derrick Pouliot AU RC 6.00 15.00
293 Ryan Sproul AU RC 5.00 12.00
294 Kevin Hayes AU RC 12.00 30.00
295 Jiri Sekac AU RC 4.00 10.00
296 V.Namestnikov AU RC EXCH 40.00 100.00
297 Tobias Rieder AU RC EXCH 25.00 60.00
298 Brandon Kozun AU RC 4.00 10.00
299 Shayne Gostisbehere AU RC 25.00 60.00
300 Marko Dano AU RC 5.00 12.00
301 Calle Jarnkrok AU RC EXCH 25.00 60.00
302 Seth Griffith AU RC EXCH 40.00 100.00
303 Griffin Reinhart AU RC 5.00 12.00
304 Alexander Khokhlachev AU RC 5.00 12.00
305 Laurent Brossoit AU RC 5.00 12.00
306 J.Gaudreau AU RC EXCH 125.00 300.00
307 Brett Ritchie AU RC 5.00 12.00
308 Markus Granlund AU RC 8.00 20.00
309 Aaron Ekblad AU RC 12.00 30.00
310 Andrei Vasilevskiy AU RC 150.00 400.00
311 Adam Lowry AU RC 8.00 20.00
312 Andre Burakovsky AU RC 12.00 30.00
313 Jonathan Drouin AU RC 50.00 120.00
314 Curtis Lazar AU RC 5.00 12.00
315 Mirco Mueller AU RC 5.00 12.00
316 Teemu Pulkkinen AU RC 6.00 15.00
317 Ty Rattie AU RC EXCH 20.00 50.00
318 Victor Rask AU RC 30.00 80.00
319 Kerby Rychel AU RC 4.00 10.00
320 Jori Lehtera AU RC 25.00 60.00

2014-15 SP Authentic Limited

1 Dustin Brown JSY AU/100 12.00 30.00
3 Mike Modano JSY AU/25 30.00 80.00
4 Joe Sakic JSY AU/25 EXCH 40.00 100.00
5 Kyle Turris JSY AU/100 12.00 30.00
6 Logan Couture JSY AU/25 25.00 60.00
7 Olli Maatta JSY AU/100 8.00 20.00
9 Adam Oates JSY AU/25 30.00 80.00
10 Joe Pavelski JSY AU/100 15.00 40.00
11 Mark Scheifele JSY AU/100 20.00 50.00
17 Carey Price JSY AU/25 40.00 100.00
18 Tyler Seguin JSY AU/25 25.00 60.00
19 Shea Weber JSY AU/25 15.00 40.00
22 James van Riemsdyk JSY AU/25 15.00 40.00
23 Sean Couturier JSY AU/100
(inserted in 2015-16 SP Authentic) 10.00 25.00
25 Chris Chelios JSY AU/25 30.00 80.00
27 Mike Gartner JSY AU/25 25.00 60.00
28 Mats Zuccarello JSY AU/100 15.00 40.00
29 Jeremy Roenick JSY AU/100 20.00 50.00
32 Sergei Bobrovsky JSY AU/25 30.00 80.00
36 Torey Krug JSY AU/100 10.00 25.00
37 Marian Gaborik JSY AU/100 12.00 30.00
45 Max Pacioretty JSY AU/25 20.00 50.00
46 Jim Howard JSY AU/100 15.00 40.00
47 Kari Lehtonen JSY AU/100 10.00 25.00
49 John Gibson JSY AU/100 12.00 30.00
51 MacKinnon JSY AU/25 EXCH 60.00 150.00
53 Cory Schneider JSY AU/25 20.00 50.00
55 David Backes JSY AU/100 8.00 20.00
57 Pavel Datsyuk JSY AU/25 40.00 100.00
58 Ovechkin JSY AU/25 EXCH 80.00 200.00
60 Eric Staal JSY AU/25 25.00 60.00
63 Rob Brown AU D 8.00 20.00
65 Paul Stastny AU B 8.00 20.00
66 Devan Dubnyk AU C 8.00 20.00
67 Brain Leetch AU B 8.00 20.00
68 Johan Franzen AU C 8.00 20.00
69 Morgan Rielly AU C 15.00 40.00
72 P.A. Parenteau AU D 6.00 15.00
73 Ryan Strome AU C 10.00 25.00
74 Brandon Saad AU C
(inserted in 2015-16 SP Authentic) 8.00 20.00
75 Jari Kurri AU C 10.00 25.00
76 Ryan Suter AU B 8.00 20.00
77 Mats Sundin AU A 25.00 60.00
79 Denis Savard AU B 10.00 25.00
81 Pierre Turgeon AU B 8.00 20.00
86 Trevor Linden AU B 10.00 25.00
87 Kyle Quincey AU D 6.00 15.00
89 Alex Galchenyuk AU C 6.00 15.00
90 Mike Liut AU B 6.00 15.00
96 Tomas Hertl AU D 10.00 25.00
97 Ryan Kesler AU B 10.00 25.00
101 Patrick Marleau AU B 10.00 25.00
103 Martin Brodeur AU A 40.00 100.00
108 Darryl Sittler AU A 15.00 40.00
119 Theoren Fleury AU B 15.00 40.00
120 Val Nichushkin AU C 10.00 25.00
122 Seth Jones AU C 10.00 25.00
129 Bobby Orr AU B 80.00 150.00
136 Brandon Dubinsky AU C 6.00 15.00
140 Jarome Iginla AU A 15.00 40.00
141 Ryan McDonagh AU C 6.00 15.00
142 Rick Nash AU B 10.00 25.00
145 Charlie Coyle AU D 10.00 25.00
146 Tom Barrasso AU B 8.00 20.00
149 Jonathan Bernier AU B 8.00 20.00
151 Tomas Hertl AM AU B 12.00 30.00
153 Teemu Selanne AM AU B 40.00 100.00
156 Nathan MacKinnon AM AU 40.00 100.00
157 Seth Jones AM AU B 10.00 25.00
158 John Gibson AM AU B 10.00 25.00
159 Carey Price AM AU B 40.00 100.00
161 J.Bernier AM AU B 12.00 30.00
162 A.Burakovsky AM AU B 15.00 40.00
163 Sidney Crosby AM AU A 250.00 350.00
164 A.Barkov AM AU B 10.00 25.00
165 J.Drouin AM AU B 20.00 50.00
168 J.Toews AM AU B 60.00 150.00
169 Mats Zuccarello AM AU
(inserted in 2015-16 SP Authentic) 10.00 25.00
171 Ekblad/S.Rein/Drais AM AU 50.00 120.00
172 J.Pavelski/P.Marteau AM AU 20.00 50.00
174 Nurse/L.Draisaitl AM AU 50.00 125.00
177 J.Sekac/S.Andrighetto AM AU 12.00 30.00
178 Modano/R.Blake AM AU 80.00 200.00
180 D.Hasek/P.Forsberg AM AU 40.00 100.00
181 Bobby Orr ATM AU 80.00 150.00
182 Brian Leetch ATM AU 8.00 20.00
183 Mike Modano ATM AU 25.00 60.00
184 Wayne Gretzky ATM AU 400.00 1000.00
185 Jonathan Toews ATM AU 60.00 150.00
186 J.Vanbiesbrouck ATM AU 10.00 25.00
187 Mike Krushelnyski ATM AU 8.00 20.00
188 Steve Yzerman ATM AU 50.00 120.00
189 Teemu Selanne ATM AU 60.00 150.00
190 Chris Chelios ATM AU 10.00 25.00
191 Jaromir Jagr ATM AU 50.00 120.00
192 Arturs Irbe ATM AU 8.00 20.00
193 Paul Coffey ATM AU 10.00 25.00
194 Mike Bossy ATM AU 10.00 25.00
197 Chelios/D.Hasek ATM AU 80.00 150.00
198 W.Gretzky dual ATM AU 300.00 800.00
199 Bossy/Gretzky ATM AU 250.00 600.00
200 Lafleur/Dionne ATM AU 40.00 100.00
201 Iiro Pakarinen 5.00 12.00
202 Sam Carrick 6.00 15.00
203 Brandon Davidson 6.00 15.00
204 Miikka Salomaki 6.00 15.00
205 Kristers Gudlevskis 6.00 15.00
206 Oscar Klefbom 25.00 60.00
207 Tyler Gaudet 5.00 12.00
208 Jyrki Jokipakka 6.00 15.00
209 Brody Sutter 4.00 10.00
210 Barclay Goodrow 6.00 15.00
211 Klas Dahlbeck 5.00 12.00
212 Joe Whitney 4.00 10.00
213 Joel Armia 6.00 15.00
214 John Persson 5.00 12.00
215 Nikita Nesterov 6.00 15.00
216 Phoenix Copley 8.00 20.00
217 Scott Darling 12.00 30.00
218 Joe Morrow 8.00 20.00
219 Christopher Gibson 10.00 25.00
220 Petteri Lindbohm 5.00 12.00
221 Jordan Binnington 20.00 50.00
222 Seth Helgeson 5.00 12.00
223 Mike Halmo 4.00 10.00
224 Max Friberg 5.00 12.00
225 Rob Zepp 10.00 25.00
226 Brandon Gormley 6.00 15.00
227 Jonathan Racine 6.00 15.00
228 Joey Hishon 8.00 20.00
229 Bill Arnold 5.00 12.00
230 Brendan Shinnimin 5.00 12.00
231 Tyler Graovac 5.00 12.00
232 Jordan Martinook 5.00 12.00
233 Scott Mayfield 5.00 12.00
234 Josh Jooris 6.00 15.00
235 Bobby Farnham 6.00 15.00
236 Cedric Paquette 6.00 15.00
237 Troy Grosenick 6.00 15.00
238 Bryan Rust 100.00 250.00
239 Landon Ferraro 4.00 10.00
240 Colin Smith 6.00 15.00
241 Dominik Uher 5.00 12.00
242 Scott Harrington 6.00 15.00
243 Bogdan Yakimov 6.00 15.00
244 Tyler Wotherspoon 6.00 15.00
245 Pierre-Edouard Bellemare 6.00 15.00
246 Petter Granberg 5.00 12.00
247 Adam Clendening 6.00 15.00
248 Johan Sundstrom 6.00 15.00
249 Chris Wagner 6.00 15.00
250 Brandon Defazio 5.00 12.00
251 John Klingberg 12.00 30.00
252 Nicolas Deschamps 6.00 15.00
253 Borna Rendulic 6.00 15.00
254 Tim Schaller 4.00 10.00
255 Andrey Makarov 6.00 15.00
256 Anton Forsberg 5.00 12.00
257 Scott Wilson 5.00 12.00
258 Andrew Agozzino 5.00 12.00
259 Cody Kunyk 4.00 10.00
260 Matt Lindblad 5.00 12.00
261 William Karlsson JSY AU/100 40.00 100.00
262 Darnell Nurse JSY AU/100 80.00 200.00
263 Jake McCabe JSY AU/100 12.00 30.00
264 Patrick Brown JSY AU/100 12.00 30.00
265 Joni Ortio JSY AU/100 15.00 40.00
266 Mark Visentin JSY AU/100 12.00 30.00
267 Corban Knight JSY AU/100 12.00 30.00
268 Stuart Percy JSY AU/100 12.00 30.00
269 Phillip Danault JSY AU/100 25.00 60.00
270 Patrik Nemeth JSY AU/100 12.00 30.00
271 Colton Sissons JSY AU/100 12.00 30.00
272 Curtis McKenzie JSY AU/100 10.00 25.00
273 Sam Reinhart JSY AU/100 150.00 400.00
275 N.Deslauriers JSY AU/100 12.00 30.00
277 L.Draisaitl JSY AU/100 EXCH 500.00 1200.00
279 Chris Tierney JSY AU/100 12.00 30.00
281 A.Hammond JSY AU/100 EXCH 20.00 50.00
282 D.Pastrnak JSY
AU/100 EXCH 600.00 1500.00
283 V.Trocheck JSY AU/100 25.00 60.00
284 T.Teravainen JSY AU/100 EXCH 20.00 50.00
285 Bo Horvat JSY AU/100 80.00 200.00
286 Anthony Duclair JSY AU/100 20.00 50.00
287 D.Severson JSY AU/100 12.00 30.00
288 E.Kuznetsov JSY AU/100 30.00 80.00
289 Rocco Grimaldi JSY AU/100 12.00 30.00
290 D.Everberg JSY AU/100 12.00 30.00
291 A.Wennberg JSY AU/100 20.00 50.00
293 Ryan Sproul JSY AU/100 12.00 30.00
294 Kevin Hayes JSY AU/100 30.00 80.00
295 Jiri Sekac JSY AU/100 10.00 25.00
296 Vladislav Namestnikov
JSY AU/100 20.00 50.00
297 Tobias Rieder JSY AU/100 12.00 30.00
298 Brandon Kozun JSY AU/100 10.00 25.00
299 S.Gostisbehere JSY AU/100 25.00 60.00
300 Marko Dano JSY AU/100 12.00 30.00
302 Seth Griffith JSY AU/100 15.00 40.00
303 G.Reinhart JSY AU/100 12.00 30.00
304 A.Khokhlachev JSY AU/100 12.00 30.00
305 Laurent Brossoit JSY AU/100 12.00 30.00
306 J.Gaudreau JSY AU/100 EXCH 200.00 500.00
309 Aaron Ekblad JSY AU/100 30.00 80.00
310 A.Vasilevskiy JSY AU/100 400.00 1000.00
311 Adam Lowry JSY AU/100 20.00 50.00
312 A.Burakovsky JSY AU/100 20.00 50.00
313 J.Drouin JSY AU/100 80.00 200.00
314 Curtis Lazar JSY AU/100 25.00 60.00
315 Mirco Mueller JSY AU/100 12.00 30.00
316 T.Pulkkinen JSY AU/100 15.00 40.00
317 Ty Rattie JSY AU/100 12.00 30.00
318 Victor Rask JSY AU/100 20.00 50.00
319 Kerby Rychel JSY AU/100 10.00 25.00
320 Jori Lehtera JSY AU/100 15.00 40.00

2014-15 SP Authentic '94-95 SP Retro

1 Marty McSorley 1.25 3.00
2 Ryan Miller 1.50 4.00
3 Ryan Kesler 1.50 4.00
4 Vincent Lecavalier 1.50 4.00
5 Scott Hartnell 1.00 2.50
6 Steve Larmer 1.25 3.00
7 Mark Messier 3.00 8.00
8 Bobby Clarke 2.50 6.00
9 David Krejci 1.50 4.00
10 Wayne Gretzky 10.00 25.00
11 Alec Martinez 1.00 2.50
12 Vincent Damphousse 1.25 3.00
13 Mike Gartner 2.00 5.00
14 Jeremy Roenick 2.50 6.00
15 Jamie Benn 1.50 4.00
16 Phil Esposito 2.50 6.00
17 Jari Kurri 1.50 4.00
18 Jarome Iginla 2.00 5.00
19 Olaf Kolzig 1.50 4.00
20 Patrick Sharp 1.50 4.00
21 Henrik Lundqvist 4.00 10.00
22 Roberto Luongo 2.50 6.00
23 Evgeni Malkin 3.00 8.00
24 Marian Hossa 1.50 4.00
25 Teemu Selanne 3.00 8.00
26 Joe Pavelski 2.00 5.00
27 Jaromir Jagr 5.00 12.00
28 Matt Duchene 1.50 4.00
29 John LeClair 1.50 4.00
30 Patrick Roy 4.00 10.00
31 Andy Moog 1.50 4.00
32 Bill Ranford 1.50 4.00
33 Sergei Bobrovsky 2.50 6.00
34 Jeff Skinner 2.00 5.00
35 Pete Peeters 1.25 3.00
36 Denis Savard 1.50 4.00
37 Richard Brodeur 1.50 4.00
38 Mario Lemieux 6.00 15.00
39 Felix Potvin 2.50 6.00
40 Pavel Datsyuk 2.50 6.00
41 Pierre Turgeon 1.25 3.00
42 Chris Chelios 1.50 4.00
43 Derek Stepan 1.00 2.50
44 Theoren Fleury 2.00 5.00
45 Carey Price 3.00 8.00
46 Gabriel Landeskog 2.00 5.00
47 Brian Bellows 1.25 3.00
48 John Tavares 2.50 6.00
49 Sean Monahan 1.00 2.50
50 Ryan Suter 1.25 3.00
51 Brendan Gallagher 1.50 4.00
52 Torey Krug 1.25 3.00
53 Mats Sundin 1.50 4.00
54 Johan Franzen 1.25 3.00
55 Guy Lafleur 2.00 5.00
56 Patrik Elias 1.50 4.00
57 Mike Liut 1.00 2.50
58 Ryan McDonagh 1.00 2.50
59 Joe Sakic 3.00 8.00
60 Henrik Zetterberg 2.00 5.00
61 Tom Barrasso 1.50 4.00
62 Dominik Hasek 2.50 6.00
63 Jakub Voracek 1.25 3.00
64 Bobby Orr 6.00 15.00
65 Jonathan Bernier 1.25 3.00
66 Jason Pominville 1.00 2.50
67 Logan Couture 2.00 5.00
68 Martin Brodeur 4.00 10.00
69 Brad Park 1.25 3.00
70 Jaroslav Halak 1.50 4.00
71 Brian Leetch 1.25 3.00
72 Jim Howard 2.00 5.00
73 Paul Stastny 1.25 3.00
74 Arturs Irbe 1.25 3.00
75 Sean Couturier 1.25 3.00
76 Rick Nash 1.50 4.00
77 Nicklas Lidstrom 1.50 4.00
78 Shea Weber 1.25 3.00
79 Tony Esposito 1.50 4.00
80 Brandon Dubinsky 1.00 2.50
81 Evgeny Kuznetsov 5.00 12.00
82 Sam Reinhart 8.00 20.00
83 Victor Rask 2.00 5.00
84 Teuvo Teravainen 4.00 10.00
85 Alexander Wennberg 3.00 8.00
86 David Pastrnak 12.00 30.00
87 Calle Jarnkrok 2.00 5.00
88 Aaron Ekblad 4.00 10.00
89 Curtis Lazar 2.00 5.00
90 Leon Draisaitl 10.00 25.00

91 Vincent Trocheck 4.00 10.00
92 Damon Severson 2.00 5.00
93 Griffin Reinhart 2.00 5.00
94 Anthony Duclair 3.00 8.00
95 Johnny Gaudreau 6.00 15.00
96 Vladislav Namestnikov 3.00 8.00
97 Andre Burakovsky 4.00 10.00
98 Jonathan Drouin 4.00 10.00
99 Jiri Sekac 1.50 4.00
100 Darnell Nurse 4.00 10.00

2014-15 SP Authentic '94-95 SP Retro Die Cut Autographs

1 Marty McSorley C 5.00 12.00
3 Ryan Kesler C 6.00 15.00
6 Steve Larmer C 5.00 12.00
7 Mark Messier B 12.00 30.00
9 David Krejci C 6.00 15.00
10 Wayne Gretzky A 250.00 600.00
12 Vincent Damphousse C 5.00 12.00
13 Mike Gartner C 8.00 20.00
14 Jeremy Roenick B 10.00 25.00
15 Jamie Benn C 6.00 15.00
16 Phil Esposito A 10.00 25.00
17 Jari Kurri B 6.00 15.00
18 Jarome Iginla A 8.00 20.00
23 Evgeni Malkin B 12.00 30.00
25 Teemu Selanne B 12.00 30.00
26 Joe Pavelski B 8.00 20.00
27 Jaromir Jagr A 40.00 100.00
30 Patrick Roy A 15.00 40.00
33 Sergei Bobrovsky C 10.00 25.00
35 Pete Peeters C 5.00 12.00
36 Denis Savard B 6.00 15.00
37 Richard Brodeur C 6.00 15.00
38 Mario Lemieux A 40.00 100.00
39 Felix Potvin C 10.00 25.00
41 Pierre Turgeon B 5.00 12.00
42 Chris Chelios B 6.00 15.00
44 Theoren Fleury B 8.00 20.00
45 Carey Price B 12.00 30.00
46 Gabriel Landeskog C 8.00 20.00
48 John Tavares C 10.00 25.00
49 Sean Monahan C 4.00 10.00
50 Ryan Suter B 5.00 12.00
52 Torey Krug C 5.00 12.00
53 Mats Sundin A 6.00 15.00
54 Johan Franzen C 5.00 12.00
57 Mike Liut C 4.00 10.00
58 Ryan McDonagh C 4.00 10.00
59 Joe Sakic A 12.00 30.00
61 Tom Barrasso C 6.00 15.00
62 Dominik Hasek A 10.00 25.00
64 Bobby Orr A 100.00 200.00
65 Jonathan Bernier C 5.00 12.00
67 Logan Couture C 8.00 20.00
68 Martin Brodeur B 15.00 40.00
69 Brad Park B 5.00 12.00
71 Brian Leetch B 5.00 12.00
72 Jim Howard C 8.00 20.00
73 Paul Stastny C 5.00 12.00
74 Arturs Irbe B 5.00 12.00
75 Sean Couturier C 5.00 12.00
76 Rick Nash B 6.00 15.00
77 Nicklas Lidstrom B 6.00 15.00
78 Shea Weber B 5.00 12.00
79 Tony Esposito A 6.00 15.00
80 Brandon Dubinsky C 4.00 10.00
81 Evgeny Kuznetsov B 15.00 40.00
82 Sam Reinhart A 25.00 60.00
83 Victor Rask 6.00 15.00
84 Teuvo Teravainen 10.00 25.00
85 Alexander Wennberg B 10.00 25.00
86 David Pastrnak 100.00 250.00
88 Aaron Ekblad B 15.00 40.00
89 Curtis Lazar B 6.00 15.00
90 Leon Draisaitl 30.00 80.00
91 Vincent Trocheck B 12.00 30.00
92 Damon Severson B 6.00 15.00
93 Griffin Reinhart A 6.00 15.00
94 Anthony Duclair 10.00 25.00
95 Johnny Gaudreau A 40.00 100.00
96 Vladislav Namestnikov 10.00 25.00
97 Andre Burakovsky A 10.00 25.00
98 Jonathan Drouin A 12.00 30.00
99 Jiri Sekac B 5.00 12.00
100 Darnell Nurse B 12.00 30.00

2014-15 SP Authentic Buyback Autographs

142 Nicklas Lidstrom '11-12 SPA/20 15.00 40.00

2014-15 SP Authentic Chirography

CAG Alex Galchenyuk 6.00 15.00
CEM Evgeni Malkin 20.00 50.00
CES Eric Staal 12.00 30.00
CGL Gabriel Landeskog 12.00 30.00
CJB Jonathan Bernier 8.00 20.00
CJJ Jaromir Jagr 30.00 80.00
CJT John Tavares 15.00 40.00
CJV James van Riemsdyk 8.00 20.00
CLC Logan Couture 12.00 30.00
CSW Shea Weber 8.00 20.00

2014-15 SP Authentic Marks of Distinction

MDBO Bobby Orr 80.00 200.00
MDGL Guy Lafleur 25.00 60.00
MDJB Jonathan Bernier 15.00 40.00
MDJJ Jaromir Jagr 60.00 150.00
MDJT John Tavares 30.00 80.00
MDMG Mike Gartner 25.00 60.00
MDMP Max Pacioretty 20.00 50.00
MDMS Mats Sundin 20.00 50.00
MDTE Tony Esposito 20.00 50.00
MDTO Jonathan Toews 30.00 80.00
MDWG Wayne Gretzky 250.00 600.00

2014-15 SP Authentic Premier Chirography

PCAE Aaron Ekblad 20.00 50.00
PCEK Evgeny Kuznetsov 20.00 50.00
PCGI John Gibson 8.00 20.00
PCJD Jonathan Drouin 15.00 40.00
PCJG Johnny Gaudreau 100.00 250.00
PCLD Leon Draisaitl 40.00 100.00
PCMR Morgan Rielly 8.00 20.00
PCNM Nathan MacKinnon 30.00 80.00
PCTR Ty Rattie 8.00 20.00
PCTT Teuvo Teravainen 12.00 30.00
PCVN Val Nichushkin 8.00 20.00

2014-15 SP Authentic Sign of the Times

SOTTAI Arturs Irbe D 5.00 12.00
SOTTBL Brian Leetch A 5.00 12.00
SOTTBO Bobby Orr A 100.00 200.00
SOTTBR Richard Brodeur C 6.00 15.00
SOTTCC Chris Chelios B 6.00 15.00
SOTTCF Cody Franson E 4.00 10.00
SOTTCN Cam Neely D 6.00 15.00
SOTTDD Devan Dubnyk E 5.00 12.00
SOTTDK David Krejci E 6.00 15.00
SOTTFP Felix Potvin D 10.00 25.00
SOTTJH Jim Howard E 8.00 20.00
SOTTJK Jari Kurri C 6.00 15.00
SOTTJS Joe Sakic A 12.00 30.00
SOTTJV James van Riemsdyk A 5.00 12.00
SOTTLC Logan Couture A 8.00 20.00
SOTTMK Mike Krushelnyski D 5.00 12.00
SOTTMS Mark Scheifele E 10.00 25.00
SOTTMZ Mats Zuccarello A 6.00 15.00
SOTTPG Philip Grubauer B 6.00 15.00
SOTTPS Paul Stastny A 5.00 12.00
SOTTPT Pierre Turgeon B 5.00 12.00
SOTTRB Rob Brown C 5.00 12.00
SOTTRS Ryan Strome A 6.00 15.00
SOTTSB Sergei Bobrovsky B 10.00 25.00
SOTTTK Torey Krug B 5.00 12.00
SOTTTL Trevor Linden B 6.00 15.00
SOTTWG Wayne Gretzky A 250.00 600.00

2014-15 SP Authentic Sign of the Times Duals

ST2DM M.Duchene/N.MacKinnon 30.00 80.00
ST2DN D.Nurse/L.Draisaitl 40.00 100.00
ST2ED J.Drouin/A.Ekblad 20.00 50.00
ST2FP M.Fleury/C.Price 40.00 100.00
ST2GA F.Andersen/J.Gibson 15.00 40.00
ST2KG W.Gretzky/J.Kurri 300.00 800.00
ST2LD P.Datsyuk/N.Lidstrom 25.00 60.00
ST2PC J.Pavelski/L.Couture 10.00 25.00
ST2PF F.Potvin/G.Fuhr 25.00 60.00
ST2PS R.Suter/Z.Parise 25.00 60.00
ST2RR S.Reinhart/G.Reinhart 30.00 80.00
ST2YL S.Yzerman/N.Lidstrom 80.00 150.00

2014-15 SP Authentic Sign of the Times Triples

ST3DEF Orr/Brqe/Prk 250.00 400.00
ST3GR8 Grtzky/Mssr/Lmx 500.00 1200.00
ST3LOS Kptr/Brwn/Tffli 80.00 150.00
ST3MIN Coyle/Granlund/Parise 30.00 80.00
ST3NYI Tvrs/Okpso/Strme 60.00 100.00

2015-16 SP Authentic

1 Alexander Ovechkin 1.00 2.50
2 Ryan Strome .25 .60
3 P.K. Subban .30 .75
4 Jim Howard .30 .75
5 Marian Gaborik .25 .60
6 Adam Henrique .20 .50
7 Gabriel Landeskog .30 .75
8 Chris Chelios .25 .60
9 Kari Lehtonen .20 .50
10 Nathan MacKinnon 1.00 2.50
11 Nazem Kadri .30 .75
12 Patrice Bergeron .30 .75
13 Bo Horvat .30 .75
14 Zemgus Girgensons .20 .50
15 Marc-Andre Fleury .50 1.25
16 Joe Pavelski .30 .75
17 Matt Duchene .25 .60
18 James van Riemsdyk .20 .50
19 Corey Crawford .30 .75
20 Rick Nash .25 .60
21 Frederik Andersen .30 .75
22 Tyler Seguin .30 .75
23 Roberto Luongo .40 1.00
24 Alex Galchenyuk .15 .40
25 Steve Mason .20 .50
26 Zach Parise .25 .60
27 Pavel Datsyuk .40 1.00
28 Logan Couture .30 .75
29 Anthony Duclair .20 .50
30 Taylor Hall .25 .60
31 Tomas Plekanec .15 .40
32 Tyler Johnson .15 .40
33 Justin Faulk .20 .50
34 Tuukka Rask .30 .75
35 Ryan Getzlaf .25 .60
36 Sergei Bobrovsky .40 1.00
37 Jonathan Quick .30 .75
38 Mike Hoffman .15 .40
39 Daniel Sedin .30 .75
40 Jakub Voracek .20 .50
41 Ondrej Pavelec .25 .60
42 Jordan Eberle .25 .60
43 Tyler Ennis .15 .40
44 Filip Forsberg .40 1.00
45 Oliver Ekman-Larsson .25 .60
46 Carey Price .50 1.25
47 Corey Perry .40 1.00
48 Claude Giroux .25 .60
49 Ben Bishop .20 .50
50 Dustin Byfuglien .25 .60
51 Loui Eriksson .15 .40
52 Jason Pominville .15 .40
53 David Krejci .25 .60
54 Chris Kreider .30 .75
55 Anze Kopitar .40 1.00
56 Jeff Skinner .30 .75
57 Jaden Schwartz .30 .75
58 John Carlson .25 .60
59 Max Pacioretty .25 .60
60 Jonathan Toews .40 1.00
61 Brent Burns .25 .60
62 Ryan Kesler .25 .60
63 John Tavares .40 1.00
64 Duncan Keith .20 .50
65 Jonathan Bernier .20 .50
66 Braden Holtby .30 .75
67 Jamie Benn .25 .60
68 Jiri Hudler .20 .50
69 David Backes .15 .40
70 Jaromir Jagr .75 2.00
71 Drew Doughty .30 .75
72 Aaron Ekblad .30 .75
73 Jason Spezza .25 .60
74 Jonas Hiller .20 .50
75 Ryan Nugent-Hopkins .30 .75
76 Henrik Lundqvist .60 1.50
77 Vladimir Tarasenko .30 .75
78 Steven Stamkos .50 1.25
79 Brandon Saad .20 .50
80 Johnny Gaudreau .40 1.00
81 Jaroslav Halak .25 .60
82 Ryan Miller .25 .60
83 Eric Staal .30 .75
84 Mikael Granlund .20 .50
85 Patrick Roy .60 1.50
86 Jarome Iginla .30 .75
87 Sidney Crosby 1.00 2.50
88 Patrick Kane .50 1.25
89 Phil Kessel .25 .60
90 Ryan O'Reilly .25 .60
91 Cory Schneider .25 .60
92 Tyler Toffoli .25 .60
93 Evgeni Malkin .50 1.25
94 Blake Wheeler .25 .60
95 Henrik Zetterberg .30 .75
96 Erik Karlsson .30 .75
97 Roman Josi .25 .60
98 Kyle Turris .20 .50
99 Pekka Rinne .25 .60
100 Devan Dubnyk .20 .50
101 Theoren Fleury 1.00 2.50
102 Bob Nystrom .60 1.50
103 Glenn Hall .75 2.00
104 Gerry Cheevers .75 2.00
105 Pierre Turgeon .60 1.50
106 Al MacInnis 1.00 2.50
107 Willi Plett .75 2.00
108 Doug Weight .75 2.00
109 Brian Leetch .60 1.50
110 Bob Bourne .50 1.25
111 Joe Sakic 1.50 4.00
112 Mike Modano 1.25 3.00
113 Bobby Orr 3.00 8.00
114 Bill Guerin .75 2.00
115 Luc Robitaille .75 2.00
116 Curtis Joseph 1.00 2.50
117 Glenn Anderson .60 1.50
118 Steve Yzerman 2.00 5.00
119 Bobby Hull 1.50 4.00
120 Lanny McDonald .75 2.00
121 Doug Gilmour 1.00 2.50
122 Bobby Clarke 1.25 3.00
123 Denis Savard .75 2.00
124 Mario Lemieux 3.00 8.00
125 Teemu Selanne 1.50 4.00
126 Martin Brodeur 2.00 5.00
127 Felix Potvin 1.25 3.00
128 Borje Salming .75 2.00
129 Peter Forsberg 1.50 4.00
130 Wayne Gretzky 5.00 12.00
131 Bobby Orr ATM 4.00 10.00
132 Darryl Sittler ATM 1.25 3.00
133 Guy Lafleur ATM 1.25 3.00
134 Willi Plett ATM 1.00 2.50
135 Wayne Gretzky ATM 6.00 15.00
136 Marcel Dionne ATM 1.25 3.00
137 Doug Gilmour ATM 1.25 3.00
138 Steve Yzerman ATM 2.50 6.00
139 Theoren Fleury ATM 1.25 3.00
140 Mike Gartner ATM 1.25 3.00
141 Cam Neely ATM 1.00 2.50
142 Felix Potvin ATM 1.50 4.00
143 John Tavares AM 1.50 4.00
144 Nikolaj Ehlers AM 2.00 5.00
145 Jason Spezza AM 1.00 2.50
146 Carey Price AM 2.00 5.00
147 Alexander Ovechkin AM 4.00 10.00
148 Ondrej Pavelec AM 1.00 2.50
149 Jamie Benn AM 1.00 2.50
150 Aaron Ekblad AM 1.25 3.00
151 Jaromir Jagr AM 3.00 8.00
152 Zach Parise AM 1.00 2.50
153 Connor McDavid AM 15.00 40.00
154 Dylan Larkin AM 3.00 8.00
155 W.Gretzky/M.Messier ATM 8.00 20.00
156 J.Sakic/P.Roy ATM 3.00 8.00
157 Lidstrom/Yzerman/Chelios ATM 3.00 8.00
158 A.Ovechkin/J.Toews AM 5.00 12.00
159 J.Toews/P.Sharp AM 2.00 5.00
160 C.McDavid/T.Hall AM RC 20.00 50.00
161 T.Selanne/C.Perry FI 15.00 40.00
162 P.Roy/C.Price FI 20.00 50.00
163 O.Ekman-Larsson/S.Doan FI 8.00 20.00
164 B.Orr/P.Bergeron FI 30.00 80.00
165 G.Perreault/T.Ennis FI 8.00 20.00
166 T.Fleury/J.Gaudreau FI 12.00 30.00
167 M.Liut/E.Staal FI 10.00 25.00
168 B.Hull/J.Toews FI 15.00 40.00
169 J.Sakic/G.Landeskog FI 15.00 40.00
170 R.Nash/N.Foligno FI 8.00 20.00
171 M.Modano/J.Benn FI 12.00 30.00
172 S.Yzerman/H.Zetterberg FI 20.00 50.00
173 W.Gretzky/C.McDavid FI 100.00 250.00
174 R.Luongo/A.Ekblad FI 12.00 30.00
175 M.Dionne/A.Kopitar FI 12.00 30.00
176 M.Koivu/Z.Parise FI 8.00 20.00
177 S.Weber/F.Forsberg FI 12.00 30.00
178 M.Brodeur/C.Schneider FI 20.00 50.00
179 M.Bossy/J.Tavares FI 12.00 30.00
180 M.Messier/H.Lundqvist FI 20.00 50.00
181 M.Hossa/E.Karlsson FI 10.00 25.00
182 B.Clarke/C.Giroux FI 12.00 30.00
183 M.Lemieux/E.Malkin FI 30.00 80.00
184 A.Irbe/J.Pavelski FI 10.00 25.00
185 B.Hull/V.Tarasenko FI 15.00 40.00
186 M.St. Louis/S.Stamkos FI 15.00 40.00
187 D.Gilmour/N.Kadri FI 10.00 25.00
188 M.Naslund/H.Sedin FI 10.00 25.00
189 M.Gartner/A.Ovechkin FI 30.00 80.00
190 A.Ladd/M.Scheifele FI 12.00 30.00
191A Jack Eichel RC 25.00 60.00
192 Michael Mersch RC 6.00 15.00
193 Taylor Leier RC 6.00 15.00
194 Joseph Blandisi RC 6.00 15.00
195 Gustav Olofsson RC 6.00 15.00
196 Chris Wideman RC 6.00 15.00
197 Jujhar Khaira RC 5.00 12.00
198 Sergei Kalinin RC 4.00 10.00
199 Alexandre Grenier RC 5.00 12.00
200 Juuse Saros RC 15.00 40.00
201 Phil Di Giuseppe RC 6.00 15.00
202 Tomas Nosek RC 6.00 15.00
203 Jaccob Slavin RC 10.00 25.00
204 Ryan Dzingel RC 4.00 10.00
205 Laurent Dauphin RC 6.00 15.00
206 Ryan Carpenter RC 6.00 15.00
207 Brett Pesce RC 5.00 12.00
208 Frank Vatrano RC 8.00 20.00
209 Bud Holloway RC 6.00 15.00
210 Shea Theodore RC 10.00 25.00
211 Slater Koekkoek RC 4.00 10.00
212 Stanislav Galiev RC 6.00 15.00
213 Joonas Korpisalo RC 12.00 30.00
214 Yanni Gourde RC 10.00 25.00
215 Garret Sparks RC 6.00 15.00
216 Daniel Carr RC 5.00 12.00
217 Louis Domingue RC 6.00 15.00
218 Christoph Bertschy RC 5.00 12.00
219 Petr Straka RC 4.00 10.00
220 Matt Murray AU RC 40.00 100.00
221 Chris Driedger RC 5.00 12.00
222 Adam Pelech RC 5.00 12.00
223 Mark Alt RC 4.00 10.00
224 Nick Shore RC 4.00 10.00
225 Connor Hellebuyck RC 25.00 60.00
226 Connor McDavid AU RC 5000.00 8000.00
227 Zachary Fucale AU RC 6.00 15.00
228 Josh Anderson AU RC 15.00 40.00
229 Antoine Bibeau AU RC 8.00 20.00
230 Nick Cousins AU RC 8.00 20.00
231 Henrik Samuelsson AU RC 5.00 12.00
232 Ryan Hartman AU RC 10.00 25.00
233 Matt Puempel AU RC 6.00 15.00
234 Emile Poirier AU RC 6.00 15.00
235 Malcolm Subban AU RC 25.00 60.00
236 Jacob de la Rose AU RC 8.00 20.00
237 Kevin Fiala AU RC 20.00 50.00
238 Sam Bennett AU RC 40.00 100.00
239 Shane Prince AU RC 5.00 12.00
240 Chandler Stephenson AU RC 15.00 40.00
241 Devin Shore AU RC 8.00 20.00
242 Max Domi AU RC 60.00 150.00
243 Kyle Baun AU RC 8.00 20.00
244 Ronalds Kenins AU RC 5.00 12.00
245 Jared McCann AU RC 10.00 25.00
246 Nicolas Petan AU RC 8.00 20.00
247 Viktor Arvidsson AU RC 8.00 20.00
248 Dylan DeMelo AU RC 6.00 15.00
249 Sergei Plotnikov AU RC 20.00 50.00
250 Robby Fabbri AU RC 10.00 25.00
251 Charles Hudon AU RC 8.00 20.00
252 Derek Forbort AU RC 6.00 15.00
253 Ben Hutton AU RC 8.00 20.00
254 Mike Condon AU RC 8.00 20.00
255 Matt O'Connor AU RC 6.00 15.00
256 Joonas Donskoi AU RC 8.00 20.00
257 Connor Brickley AU RC 6.00 15.00
258 Artemi Panarin AU RC 200.00 500.00
259 Stefan Noesen AU RC 5.00 12.00
260 Dylan Larkin AU RC 25.00 60.00
261 Hunter Shinkaruk AU RC 8.00 20.00
262 Anthony Stolarz AU RC 20.00 50.00
263 Radek Faksa AU RC 8.00 20.00
264 Sam Brittain AU RC 8.00 20.00
265 Noah Hanifin AU RC 12.00 30.00
266 Nikolay Goldobin AU RC 8.00 20.00
267 Brock McGinn AU RC 8.00 20.00
268 Colton Parayko AU RC 12.00 30.00
269 Nick Ritchie AU RC 8.00 20.00
270 Brady Skjei AU RC 40.00 100.00
271 Anton Slepyshev AU RC 5.00 12.00
272 Mattias Janmark AU RC 8.00 20.00
273 Linus Ullmark AU RC 15.00 40.00
274 Colin Miller AU RC 6.00 15.00
275 Oscar Lindberg AU RC 8.00 20.00
276 Mikko Rantanen AU RC 125.00 300.00
277 Jake Virtanen AU RC 10.00 25.00
278 Andreas Athanasiou AU RC 20.00 50.00
279 Vincent Hinostroza AU RC 5.00 12.00
280 Daniel Sprong AU RC 25.00 60.00
281 Andrew Copp AU RC 8.00 20.00
282 Mike McCarron AU RC 20.00 50.00
283 Brendan Gaunce AU RC 10.00 25.00
284 Jordan Weal AU RC 5.00 12.00
285 Nikolaj Ehlers AU RC 15.00 40.00
191B Jack Eichel AU XRC 150.00 400.00

2015-16 SP Authentic '95-96 SP Retro

R1 Corey Perry 2.50 6.00
R2 Oliver Ekman-Larsson 1.50 4.00
R3 Sean Monahan 1.00 2.50
R4 Jonathan Toews 2.50 6.00
R5 Nathan MacKinnon 6.00 15.00
R6 Jamie Benn 1.50 4.00
R7 Taylor Hall 1.50 4.00
R8 Anze Kopitar 2.50 6.00
R9 Zach Parise 1.50 4.00
R10 Roman Josi 1.50 4.00
R11 Joe Pavelski 2.00 5.00
R12 Jaden Schwartz 2.00 5.00
R13 Radim Vrbata 1.00 2.50
R14 Andrew Ladd 1.00 2.50
R15 David Pastrnak 4.00 10.00
R16 Zemgus Girgensons 1.25 3.00
R17 Jeff Skinner 2.00 5.00
R18 Brandon Saad 1.25 3.00
R19 Tomas Tatar 1.00 2.50
R20 Aaron Ekblad 2.00 5.00
R21 Alex Galchenyuk 1.00 2.50
R22 Cory Schneider 1.50 4.00
R23 John Tavares 2.50 6.00
R24 Rick Nash 1.50 4.00
R25 Erik Karlsson 2.00 5.00
R26 Jakub Voracek 1.25 3.00
R27 Sidney Crosby 6.00 15.00
R28 Tyler Johnson 1.00 2.50
R29 James van Riemsdyk 1.25 3.00
R30 Alexander Ovechkin 6.00 15.00
R31 Bobby Orr 15.00 40.00
R32 Dominik Hasek 6.00 15.00
R33 Guy Lafleur 5.00 12.00
R34 Joe Sakic 8.00 20.00
R35 Wayne Gretzky 25.00 60.00
R36 Connor McDavid 25.00 60.00
R37 Max Domi 4.00 10.00
R38 Sam Bennett 6.00 15.00
R39 Mike Condon 2.00 5.00
R40 Jared McCann 2.50 6.00
R41 Mikko Rantanen 10.00 25.00
R42 Artemi Panarin 8.00 20.00
R43 Jake Virtanen 2.50 6.00
R44 Daniel Sprong 2.50 6.00
R45 Zachary Fucale 1.50 4.00
R46 Noah Hanifin 3.00 8.00
R47 Malcolm Subban 3.00 8.00
R48 Sergei Plotnikov 1.25 3.00
R49 Emile Poirier 1.50 4.00
R50 Shane Prince 1.25 3.00
R51 Nick Ritchie 2.00 5.00
R52 Stanislav Galiev 2.00 5.00
R53 Oscar Lindberg 2.00 5.00
R54 Nikolay Goldobin 2.00 5.00
R55 Colton Parayko 3.00 8.00
R56 Kevin Fiala 2.50 6.00
R57 Robby Fabbri 2.50 6.00
R58 Nikolaj Ehlers 4.00 10.00
R59 Dylan Larkin 6.00 15.00
R60 Jack Eichel 8.00 20.00

2015-16 SP Authentic '95-96 SP Retro Gold Autographs

R3 Sean Monahan 5.00 12.00
R4 Jonathan Toews A 12.00 30.00
R6 Jamie Benn C 8.00 20.00
R7 Taylor Hall C 8.00 20.00
R8 Anze Kopitar B 12.00 30.00
R9 Zach Parise B 8.00 20.00
R11 Joe Pavelski C 10.00 25.00
R14 Andrew Ladd D 5.00 12.00
R16 Zemgus Girgensons D 6.00 15.00
R18 Brandon Saad D 6.00 15.00
R19 Tomas Tatar E 5.00 12.00
R20 Aaron Ekblad C 10.00 25.00
R21 Alex Galchenyuk D 5.00 12.00
R22 Cory Schneider E 8.00 20.00
R23 John Tavares B 12.00 30.00
R24 Rick Nash C 8.00 20.00
R26 Jakub Voracek C 6.00 15.00
R27 Sidney Crosby A 30.00 80.00
R28 Tyler Johnson E 5.00 12.00
R29 James Van Riemsdyk 6.00 15.00
R30 Alexander Ovechkin A 30.00 80.00
R31 Bobby Orr C 80.00 200.00
R32 Dominik Hasek B 30.00 80.00
R33 Guy Lafleur 30.00 80.00
R34 Joe Sakic B 30.00 80.00
R35 Wayne Gretzky A 100.00 250.00
R36 Connor McDavid A 250.00 500.00
R38 Sam Bennett A 25.00 60.00
R39 Mike Condon C 8.00 20.00
R40 Jared McCann C 10.00 25.00
R41 Mikko Rantanen 40.00 100.00
R43 Jake Virtanen A 10.00 25.00
R45 Zachary Fucale C 6.00 15.00
R46 Noah Hanifin 12.00 30.00
R49 Emile Poirier C 6.00 15.00
R50 Shane Prince B 5.00 12.00
R52 Stanislav Galiev C 8.00 20.00
R53 Oscar Lindberg C 8.00 20.00
R54 Nikolay Goldobin C 8.00 20.00
R55 Colton Parayko C 12.00 30.00
R56 Kevin Fiala B 10.00 25.00
R57 Robby Fabbri C 10.00 25.00
R58 Nikolaj Ehlers B 15.00 40.00
R59 Dylan Larkin B 25.00 60.00

2015-16 SP Authentic Authentic Moments Booklet Autographs

ABAH Andrew Hammond C 12.00 30.00
ABAO Alexander Ovechkin A 40.00 100.00
ABBB Ben Bishop C 8.00 20.00
ABBO Bobby Orr B 150.00 300.00
ABBS Borje Salming A 40.00 100.00
ABCM Connor McDavid A 300.00 600.00
ABCP Carey Price B 20.00 50.00
ABDG Doug Gilmour B 12.00 30.00
ABDL Dylan Larkin C 30.00 80.00
ABJB Jamie Benn B 10.00 25.00
ABJG Johnny Gaudreau B 15.00 40.00
ABJH Jiri Hudler C 8.00 20.00
ABJT John Tavares B 15.00 40.00
ABKT Kyle Turris C 8.00 20.00
ABMD Max Domi A 20.00 50.00
ABML Mario Lemieux A 80.00 200.00
ABRF Robby Fabbri C 12.00 30.00
ABRI Pekka Rinne B 10.00 25.00
ABSB Sam Bennett C 30.00 80.00
ABSC Sidney Crosby A 200.00 350.00
ABTJ Tyler Johnson C 6.00 15.00
ABWG Wayne Gretzky A 300.00 800.00

2015-16 SP Authentic Great White North Autographs

GWNAE Aaron Ekblad D 15.00 40.00
GWNBB Brent Burns D 12.00 30.00
GWNCM Connor McDavid A 400.00 800.00
GWNJT Jonathan Toews B 80.00 200.00
GWNKT Kyle Turris E 10.00 25.00
GWNMD Matt Duchene D 12.00 30.00
GWNNR Nick Ritchie 12.00 30.00
GWNRN Rick Nash C 15.00 40.00
GWNRS Ryan Strome E 12.00 30.00
GWNSR Sam Reinhart D 25.00 60.00
GWNTA John Tavares C 25.00 60.00
GWNTH Taylor Hall C 15.00 40.00
GWNTT Tyler Toffoli 12.00 30.00
GWNWG Wayne Gretzky A 400.00 1000.00

2015-16 SP Authentic Limited Patch Autographs

226 Connor McDavid/100 5000.00 12000.00
228 Josh Anderson/100 20.00 50.00
232 Ryan Hartman/100 20.00 50.00
238 Sam Bennett/100 60.00 150.00
250 Robby Fabbri/100 40.00 100.00
255 Matt O'Connor/100 20.00 50.00
258 Artemi Panarin/100 200.00 500.00
260 Dylan Larkin/100 250.00 400.00
263 Radek Faksa/100 30.00 80.00
276 Mikko Rantanen/100 250.00 600.00
277 Jake Virtanen/100 40.00 100.00
278 Andreas Athanasiou/100 60.00 120.00
282 Mike McCarron/100 40.00 100.00
285 Nikolaj Ehlers/100 40.00 100.00

2015-16 SP Authentic Marks of Distinction

MDAK Anze Kopitar 30.00 80.00
MDBB Ben Bishop 15.00 40.00
MDCM Connor McDavid 350.00 500.00
MDDD Devan Dubnyk 20.00 50.00
MDDL Dylan Larkin 150.00 300.00
MDJB Jamie Benn 30.00 80.00
MDJI Jarome Iginla 12.00 30.00
MDJJ Jaromir Jagr 100.00 200.00
MDJP Joe Pavelski 20.00 50.00
MDPD Pavel Datsyuk 25.00 60.00
MDRN Rick Nash 20.00 50.00
MDSC Sidney Crosby 150.00 300.00
MDTH Taylor Hall 12.00 30.00
MDTJ Tyler Johnson 15.00 40.00
MDTO Jonathan Toews 50.00 120.00
MDZG Zemgus Girgensons 10.00 25.00
MDZP Zach Parise 8.00 20.00

2015-16 SP Authentic Scripted Stoppers

SSAH Andrew Hammond D 8.00 20.00
SSAI Arturs Irbe D 8.00 20.00
SSCP Carey Price B 75.00 150.00
SSCS Cory Schneider C 12.00 30.00
SSDD Devan Dubnyk C 10.00 25.00
SSDH Dominik Hasek B 75.00 150.00
SSFP Felix Potvin C 20.00 50.00
SSMB Martin Brodeur B 75.00 150.00
SSSB Sergei Bobrovsky C 8.00 20.00
SSSM Steve Mason D 8.00 20.00

2015-16 SP Authentic Sign of the Times

SOTTAE Aaron Ekblad D 10.00 25.00
SOTTAG Alex Galchenyuk D 5.00 12.00
SOTTAH Andrew Hammond F 10.00 25.00
SOTTAK Anze Kopitar C 12.00 30.00
SOTTAL Andrew Ladd E 5.00 12.00
SOTTAO Alexander Ovechkin B 30.00 80.00
SOTTBB Brent Burns C 8.00 20.00
SOTTBO Bobby Orr A 80.00 150.00
SOTTBR Bobby Ryan D 6.00 15.00
SOTTBS Matt Beleskey F 5.00 12.00
SOTTCL Curtis Lazar F 5.00 12.00
SOTTCP Carey Price B 30.00 80.00
SOTTDH Dougie Hamilton E 6.00 15.00
SOTTDK David Krejci C 8.00 20.00
SOTTEM Evgeni Malkin B 15.00 40.00
SOTTGL Gabriel Landeskog D 10.00 25.00
SOTTJF Justin Faulk E 6.00 15.00
SOTTJH Jiri Hudler F 6.00 15.00
SOTTJJ Jaromir Jagr B 40.00 100.00
SOTTJL John LeClair D 8.00 20.00
SOTTJP Joe Pavelski D 10.00 25.00
SOTTJV Jakub Voracek D 6.00 15.00
SOTTKH Kevin Hayes F 6.00 15.00
SOTTKT Kyle Turris F 6.00 15.00
SOTTLA Guy Lafleur A 10.00 25.00
SOTTMB Martin Biron D 6.00 15.00
SOTTMH Mike Hoffman F 5.00 12.00
SOTTMM Matt Moulson F 5.00 12.00
SOTTMN Markus Naslund D 8.00 20.00
SOTTMS Mark Scheifele F 12.00 30.00
SOTTMT Marty Turco E 8.00 20.00
SOTTNK Nikita Kucherov E 15.00 40.00
SOTTNY Nail Yakupov E 5.00 12.00
SOTTPE Corey Perry C 12.00 30.00
SOTTPM Patrick Marleau C 8.00 20.00
SOTTRH Ron Hextall C 8.00 20.00
SOTTRM Ryan Miller C 8.00 20.00
SOTTRO Ryan O'Reilly B 8.00 20.00
SOTTSM Sean Monahan C 5.00 12.00
SOTTST Mark Stone F 10.00 25.00
SOTTTA Tomas Tatar F 5.00 12.00
SOTTTJ Tyler Johnson E 5.00 12.00
SOTTTK Torey Krug D 6.00 15.00
SOTTTT Tyler Toffoli C 8.00 20.00
SOTTWG Wayne Gretzky A 250.00 600.00
SOTTZG Zemgus Girgensons C 6.00 15.00

2015-16 SP Authentic Sign of the Times Duals

ST2GP A.Galchenyuk/C.Price 80.00 200.00
ST2HB S.Hartnell/S.Bobrovsky 10.00 25.00
ST2HM T.Hall/C.McDavid 250.00 600.00
ST2HS A.Henrique/C.Schneider 15.00 40.00
ST2JB B.Bishop/T.Johnson 12.00 30.00
ST2LA J.Lehtera/J.Allen 12.00 30.00
ST2LL A.Ladd/A.Lowry 15.00 40.00
ST2LT A.Lee/J.Tavares 15.00 40.00
ST2PC J.Pavelski/L.Couture 15.00 40.00
ST2TL D.Larkin/T.Tatar 30.00 80.00
ST2VB J.van Riemsdyk/J.Bernier 8.00 20.00
ST2VM J.Voracek/S.Mason 30.00 80.00

2015-16 SP Authentic Sign of the Times Rookies

SOTRAA Andreas Athanasiou/299 15.00 40.00
SOTRBG Brendan Gaunce/299 8.00 20.00
SOTRCH Charles Hudon/299 6.00 15.00
SOTRCM Connor McDavid/99 300.00 500.00
SOTRCP Colton Parayko/299 10.00 25.00
SOTRCS Chandler Stephenson/299 8.00 20.00
SOTRDL Dylan Larkin/99 100.00 200.00
SOTREP Emile Poirier/299 5.00 12.00
SOTRJD Joonas Donskoi/299 6.00 15.00
SOTRJM Jared McCann/299 8.00 20.00
SOTRJV Jake Virtanen/199 15.00 40.00
SOTRLU Linus Ullmark/299 12.00 30.00
SOTRMC Mike Condon/299 15.00 40.00
SOTRMI Colin Miller/299 5.00 12.00
SOTRMJ Mattias Janmark/299 6.00 15.00
SOTRMM Mike McCarron/299 12.00 30.00
SOTRMR Mikko Rantanen/199 30.00 80.00
SOTRNE Nikolaj Ehlers/99 20.00 50.00
SOTRNH Noah Hanifin/199 10.00 25.00
SOTROL Oscar Lindberg/199 6.00 15.00
SOTRRF Robby Fabbri/199 8.00 20.00
SOTRSB Sam Bennett/99 20.00 50.00
SOTRVA Viktor Arvidsson/299 6.00 15.00
SOTRVH Vincent Hinostroza/299 4.00 10.00
SOTRZF Zachary Fucale/299 15.00 40.00

2015-16 SP Authentic Sign of the Times Rookies Inscriptions

SOTRBG Brendan Gaunce Gauntlet/25 12.00 30.00
SOTRCH Charles Hudon Hudy/25 10.00 25.00
SOTRCP Colton Parayko Go Colts/25 15.00 40.00
SOTRCS Chandler Stephenson Stevie/25 12.00 30.00
SOTREP Emile Poirier Poirs/25 8.00 20.00
SOTRJD Joonas Donskoi Menn Sharks/25 10.00 25.00
SOTRJM Jared McCann Go Canucks/25 12.00 30.00
SOTRMC Mike Condon Condo/25 10.00 25.00
SOTRMI Colin Miller Millsie/25 8.00 20.00
SOTRMM Mike McCarron Mac Attack/25 12.00 30.00
SOTRVA Viktor Arvidsson Go Preds Go/25 10.00 25.00
SOTRVH Vincent Hinostroza Lets go Hawks/25 6.00 15.00
SOTRZF Zachary Fucale Fucs/25 8.00 20.00

2016-17 SP Authentic

1 Patrick Kane .50 1.25
2 Erik Karlsson .30 .75
3 Nathan MacKinnon 1.00 2.50
4 Kyle Okposo .15 .40
5 Aaron Ekblad .30 .75
6 Mika Zibanejad .30 .75
7 Taylor Hall .25 .60
8 Alexander Ovechkin 1.00 2.50
9 Matt Duchene .25 .60
10 Adam Henrique .20 .50
11 Anze Kopitar .40 1.00
12 Marian Gaborik .25 .60
13 Ryan Johansen .20 .50
14 Jamie Benn .25 .60
15 Nino Niederreiter .15 .40
16 Joe Pavelski .30 .75
17 Jaden Schwartz .30 .75
18 Derick Brassard .15 .40
19 Jonathan Toews .40 1.00
20 Brayden Schenn .25 .60
21 Derek Stepan .15 .40
22 Shayne Gostisbehere .25 .60
23 Sean Monahan .15 .40
24 Leon Draisaitl .75 2.00
25 Daniel Sedin .30 .75
26 Mark Stone .30 .75
27 Alex Galchenyuk .15 .40
28 Jake Muzzin .25 .60
29 Marc-Andre Fleury .50 1.25
30 Henrik Lundqvist .60 1.50
31 Carey Price .50 1.25
32 Joe Thornton .40 1.00
33 Evgeny Kuznetsov .30 .75
34 P.K. Subban .30 .75
35 Cory Schneider .25 .60
36 Evgeni Malkin .50 1.25
37 Corey Perry .40 1.00
38 Johnny Gaudreau .40 1.00
39 Steven Stamkos .50 1.25
40 Henrik Zetterberg .30 .75
41 Oliver Ekman-Larsson .25 .60
42 Nazem Kadri .30 .75
43 Jeff Skinner .30 .75
44 Artemi Panarin .50 1.25
45 Gabriel Landeskog .30 .75
46 Tyler Seguin .30 .75
47 Boone Jenner .25 .60
48 Max Domi .25 .60
49 Elias Lindholm .25 .60
50 Zach Parise .25 .60
51 Andrew Ladd .15 .40
52 David Krejci .25 .60
53 Blake Wheeler .25 .60
54 Ryan Getzlaf .25 .60
55 Robby Fabbri .15 .40
56 Artem Anisimov .15 .40
57 Mats Zuccarello .25 .60
58 Braden Holtby .30 .75
59 Roman Josi .25 .60
60 Jonathan Drouin .20 .50
61 Milan Lucic .20 .50
62 Ryan Spooner .20 .50
63 Victor Hedman .30 .75
64 Mike Hoffman .15 .40
65 Tom Wilson .25 .60
66 Filip Forsberg .40 1.00
67 Max Pacioretty .25 .60
68 Jaromir Jagr .75 2.00
69 Nikolaj Ehlers .25 .60
70 Mikkel Boedker .15 .40
71 Dylan Larkin .30 .75
72 Jiri Hudler .20 .50
73 Tyler Toffoli .25 .60
74 Tomas Tatar .15 .40
75 Matt Murray .40 1.00
76 Rickard Rakell .20 .50
77 Jonathan Quick .30 .75
78 Jarome Iginla .30 .75
79 Patrice Bergeron .30 .75
80 Jack Eichel .40 1.00
81 Brendan Gallagher .25 .60
82 Mikko Koivu .20 .50
83 Anthony Duclair .20 .50
84 Claude Giroux .25 .60
85 David Backes .15 .40
86 Nikita Kucherov .50 1.25
87 Sidney Crosby 1.00 2.50
88 Brent Burns .25 .60
89 Morgan Rielly .25 .60
90 Ryan O'Reilly .25 .60
91 John Tavares .40 1.00
92 Mark Scheifele .40 1.00
93 Sam Bennett .40 1.00
94 Vladimir Tarasenko .30 .75
95 Kris Letang .30 .75
96 Brandon Saad .20 .50
97 Connor McDavid 1.25 3.00
98 Loui Eriksson .15 .40
99 Shea Weber .20 .50
100 Corey Crawford .30 .75
101 Jaromir Jagr AM 4.00 10.00
102 Marian Hossa AM 1.25 3.00

103 Patrick Kane AM 2.50 6.00
104 Joe Thornton AM 2.00 5.00
105 Artemi Panarin AM 2.50 6.00
106 Connor McDavid AM 6.00 15.00
107 Henrik Lundqvist AM 3.00 8.00
108 Sidney Crosby AM 5.00 12.00
109 P.K. Subban AM 1.50 4.00
110 Carey Price AM 2.50 6.00
111 Auston Matthews AM 8.00 20.00
112 Jimmy Vesey AM 2.00 5.00
113 Mitch Marner AM 4.00 10.00
114 Patrik Laine AM 3.00 8.00
115 Wayne Gretzky AM 8.00 20.00
116 William Nylander FW AU RC 40.00 100.00
117 Charlie Lindgren FW AU RC 12.00 30.00
118 Oliver Bjorkstrand FW AU RC 10.00 25.00
119 Steven Santini FW AU RC 6.00 15.00
120 Connor Brown FW AU RC 12.00 30.00
121 Ryan Pulock FW AU RC 8.00 20.00
122 Dominik Simon FW AU RC 6.00 15.00
123 Esa Lindell FW AU RC 8.00 20.00
124 Anthony Mantha FW AU RC 25.00 60.00
125 Chris Bigras FW AU RC 6.00 15.00
126 Kasperi Kapanen FW RC 6.00 15.00
127 Oliver Kylington FW AU RC 6.00 15.00
128 Pontus Aberg FW AU RC 10.00 25.00
129 Hudson Fasching FW AU RC 8.00 20.00
130 Trevor Carrick FW AU RC 8.00 20.00
131 Sonny Milano FW AU RC 10.00 25.00
132 Mark McNeill FW AU RC 8.00 20.00
133 Tom Kuhnhackl FW AU RC 6.00 15.00
134 Pavel Zacha FW AU RC 12.00 30.00
135 Nikita Soshnikov FW AU RC 5.00 12.00
136 Sergey Tolchinsky FW AU RC 6.00 15.00
137 Mike Reilly FW AU RC 6.00 15.00
138 Jason Dickinson FW AU RC 6.00 15.00
139 Josh Morrissey FW AU RC 15.00 40.00
140 Justin Bailey FW AU RC 8.00 20.00
141 Brendan Leipsic FW AU RC 6.00 15.00
142 Oskar Sundqvist FW AU RC 8.00 20.00
143 Michael Matheson FW AU RC 8.00 20.00
144 Daniel Altshuller FW AU RC 6.00 15.00
145 Miles Wood FW AU RC 6.00 15.00
146 Auston Matthews FW AU RC 2000.005000.00
147 Patrik Laine FW AU RC 150.00 300.00
148 Mitch Marner FW AU RC 300.00 1500.00
149 Jesse Puljujarvi FW AU RC 60.00 150.00
150 Matthew Tkachuk FW AU RC 150.00 400.00
151 Dylan Strome FW AU RC 20.00 50.00
152 Jimmy Vesey FW AU RC 6.00 15.00
153 Ivan Provorov FW AU RC 12.00 30.00
154 Travis Konecny FW AU RC 20.00 50.00
155 Joel Eriksson Ek FW AU RC 15.00 40.00
156 Zach Werenski FW AU RC 30.00 80.00
157 Kyle Connor FW AU RC 80.00 200.00
158 Sebastian Aho FW AU RC 200.00 500.00
159 Anthony Beauvillier FW AU RC 8.00 20.00
160 Brayden Point FW AU RC 150.00 400.00
161 Christian Dvorak FW AU RC 10.00 25.00
162 Danton Heinen FW AU RC 6.00 15.00
163 Tyler Motte FW AU RC 8.00 20.00
164 Troy Stecher FW AU RC 8.00 20.00
165 Mikhail Sergachev FW AU RC 20.00 50.00
166 Timo Meier FW AU RC 15.00 40.00
167 Nick Baptiste FW AU RC 8.00 20.00
168 Gustav Forsling FW AU RC 20.00 50.00
169 Lawson Crouse FW AU RC 6.00 15.00
170 Mathew Barzal FW AU RC 80.00 200.00
171 Denis Malgin FW RC 6.00 15.00
172 Anthony DeAngelo FW AU RC 6.00 15.00
173 Thomas Chabot FW AU RC 15.00 40.00
174 Stephen Johns FW RC 6.00 15.00
175 Nick Schmaltz FW RC 10.00 25.00
176 Brandon Carlo FW AU RC 12.00 30.00
177 Artturi Lehkonen FW RC 10.00 25.00
178 Jakob Chychrun FW AU RC 15.00 40.00
179 Zach Sanford FW RC 8.00 20.00
180 Pavel Buchnevich FW AU RC 20.00 50.00
181 Kevin Labanc FW AU RC 8.00 20.00
182 Jake Guentzel FW AU RC 60.00 150.00
183 John Quenneville FW AU RC 8.00 20.00
184 Jakub Vrana FW AU RC 30.00 80.00
185 Thatcher Demko FW AU RC 100.00 250.00
186 Brendan Perlini FW AU RC 8.00 20.00
187 Tyler Bertuzzi FW AU RC
All cards inscribed 40.00 100.00
188 Brendan Guhle FW AU RC 8.00 20.00
189 A.J. Greer FW AU RC 8.00 20.00
190 Blake Speers FW AU RC 8.00 20.00
191 Troy Stecher FW AU RC 8.00 20.00
192 Nikita Tryamkin FW AU RC 6.00 15.00
193 Brandon Tanev FW AU RC 10.00 25.00
194 Brandon Montour FW AU RC 20.00 50.00
195 Nic Dowd FW AU RC 6.00 15.00
196 Zach Hyman FW AU RC 50.00 125.00
197 Tristan Jarry FW AU RC 20.00 50.00

2016-17 SP Authentic Future Watch Black

116 William Nylander 100.00 250.00
117 Charlie Lindgren 40.00 100.00
119 Steven Santini 20.00 50.00
121 Ryan Pulock 25.00 60.00
122 Dominik Simon 20.00 50.00
123 Esa Lindell 25.00 60.00
124 Anthony Mantha 50.00 125.00
127 Oliver Kylington 20.00 50.00
128 Pontus Aberg 30.00 80.00
129 Hudson Fasching 25.00 60.00
131 Sonny Milano 30.00 80.00
132 Mark McNeill 25.00 60.00
134 Pavel Zacha 40.00 100.00
135 Nikita Soshnikov 15.00 40.00
136 Sergey Tolchinsky 20.00 50.00
137 Mike Reilly 20.00 50.00
138 Jason Dickinson 20.00 50.00
139 Josh Morrissey 60.00 150.00
140 Justin Bailey 25.00 60.00
141 Brendan Leipsic 20.00 50.00
143 Michael Matheson 25.00 60.00
144 Daniel Altshuller 20.00 50.00
145 Miles Wood 20.00 50.00
146 Auston Matthews 150.00 400.00
147 Patrik Laine 60.00 150.00
148 Mitch Marner 80.00 200.00
149 Jesse Puljujarvi 50.00 125.00
150 Matthew Tkachuk 100.00 250.00
151 Dylan Strome 20.00 50.00

152 Jimmy Vesey 40.00 100.00
153 Ivan Provorov 40.00 100.00
155 Joel Eriksson Ek 40.00 100.00
156 Zach Werenski 80.00 200.00
157 Kyle Connor 80.00 200.00
159 Anthony Beauvillier 25.00 60.00
160 Brayden Point 60.00 150.00
161 Christian Dvorak 30.00 80.00
162 Danton Heinen 20.00 50.00
163 Tyler Motte 25.00 60.00
165 Mikhail Sergachev 40.00 100.00
166 Timo Meier 50.00 125.00
167 Nick Baptiste 25.00 60.00
168 Gustav Forsling 50.00 125.00
169 Lawson Crouse 20.00 50.00
170 Mathew Barzal 80.00 200.00
172 Anthony DeAngelo 20.00 50.00
173 Thomas Chabot 50.00 125.00
176 Brandon Carlo 40.00 100.00
178 Jakob Chychrun 50.00 125.00
180 Pavel Buchnevich 40.00 100.00
181 Kevin Labanc 25.00 60.00
182 Jake Guentzel 80.00 200.00

2016-17 SP Authentic Future Watch Inscribed Autographs

116 William Nylander
2/29/16 150.00 250.00
117 Charlie Lindgren
4/7/16 20.00 50.00
118 Oliver Bjorkstrand
3/17/16 15.00 40.00
119 Steven Santini
4/9/16 10.00 25.00
120 Connor Brown
3/17/16 20.00 50.00
121 Ryan Pulock
2/28/16 12.00 30.00
122 Dominik Simon
3/13/16 10.00 25.00
123 Esa Lindell
1/19/16 12.00 30.00
124 Anthony Mantha
3/15/16 60.00 150.00
125 Chris Bigras
1/14/16 10.00 25.00
127 Oliver Kylington
4/9/16 10.00 25.00
128 Pontus Aberg
5/3/16 15.00 40.00
129 Hudson Fasching
8/26/16 12.00 30.00
130 Trevor Carrick
3/15/16 12.00 30.00
133 Tom Kuhnhackl
11/9/16 10.00 25.00
134 Pavel Zacha
4/9/16 20.00 50.00
135 Nikita Soshnikov
Soshki 8.00 20.00
136 Sergey Tolchinsky
3/31/16 10.00 25.00
137 Mike Reilly
1/9/16 10.00 25.00
138 Jason Dickinson
4/7/16 10.00 25.00
140 Justin Bailey
2/11/16 12.00 30.00
142 Oskar Sundqvist
2/5/16 12.00 30.00
143 Michael Matheson
2/20/16 12.00 30.00
145 Miles Wood
4/9/16 10.00 25.00
146 Auston Matthews
10/12/16 2500.00 6000.00
147 Patrik Laine
10/13/16 200.00 350.00
148 Mitch Marner
10/12/16 600.00 1500.00
149 Jesse Puljujarvi
10/12/16 80.00 200.00
152 Jimmy Vesey
10/13/16 10.00 25.00
153 Ivan Provorov
10/14/16 20.00 50.00
154 Travis Konecny
10/14/16 30.00 80.00
155 Joel Eriksson Ek
10/22/16 20.00 50.00
156 Zach Werenski
10/13/16 100.00 250.00
157 Kyle Connor
10/13/16 100.00 250.00
159 Anthony Beauvillier
10/13/16 12.00 30.00
160 Brayden Point
10/13/16 200.00 500.00
161 Christian Dvorak
10/15/16 15.00 40.00
162 Danton Heinen
10/13/16 10.00 25.00
163 Tyler Motte
10/12/16 12.00 30.00
165 Mikhail Sergachev
10/13/16 30.00 80.00
166 Timo Meier
12/16/16 25.00 60.00
167 Nick Baptiste
10/18/16 12.00 30.00
168 Gustav Forsling
10/12/16 40.00 100.00
169 Lawson Crouse
10/15/16 10.00 25.00
172 Anthony DeAngelo
11/6/16 10.00 25.00
176 Brandon Carlo
10/13/16 20.00 50.00
178 Jakob Chychrun
10/15/16 30.00 80.00
185 Thatcher Demko
12/10/16 150.00 400.00
186 Brendan Perlini
12/15/16 30.00 80.00
188 Brendan Guhle
12/3/16 12.00 30.00
189 A.J. Greer
11/13/16 12.00 30.00

190 Blake Speers
10/13/16 12.00 30.00
191 Troy Stecher
10/25/16 12.00 30.00
192 Nikita Tryamkin
3/16/16 10.00 25.00
193 Brandon Tanev
4/5/16 15.00 40.00
196 Zach Hyman
2/28/16 150.00 400.00
197 Tristan Jarry
4/13/16 30.00 80.00

2016-17 SP Authentic Global Chirography

CZEDK David Krejci D 6.00 15.00
FINPL Patrik Laine C 150.00 250.00
NIRON Owen Nolan C 6.00 15.00
SVKMA Marian Gaborik C 6.00 15.00
SVKPB Peter Bondra D 6.00 15.00
SWEHZ Henrik Zetterberg B 8.00 20.00
USAAM Auston Matthews A 350.00 600.00
USAPA Pat LaFontaine C 6.00 15.00

2016-17 SP Authentic Great White North Autographs

GWNAL Andrew Ladd D 3.00 8.00
GWNAM Anthony Mantha D 10.00 25.00
GWNDS Dylan Strome C 12.00 30.00
GWNJB Jamie Benn A 12.00 30.00
GWNJT Joe Thornton A 15.00 40.00
GWNLR Luc Robitaille B 20.00 50.00
GWNMB Mike Bossy A 20.00 50.00
GWNMM Mitch Marner A 30.00 80.00
GWNRO Ryan O'Reilly D 5.00 12.00

2016-17 SP Authentic Limited Patch Autographs

*LIMITED/25: 40X TO 100X BASIC CARDS
*LIMITED/50: 30X TO 80X BASIC CARDS
FW/100: .75X TO 2X BASIC CARD
29 Marc-Andre Fleury/50 40.00 100.00
68 Jaromir Jagr/25 150.00 250.00
116 William Nylander FW/100 150.00 300.00
117 Charlie Lindgren FW/100 25.00 60.00
124 Anthony Mantha FW/100 80.00 150.00
146 Auston Matthews FW/100 600.00 1500.00
147 Patrik Laine FW/100 250.00 450.00
148 Mitch Marner FW/100 800.00 2000.00
149 Jesse Puljujarvi FW/100 60.00 150.00
158 Sebastian Aho FW/100 250.00 600.00
160 Brayden Point FW/100 120.00 300.00

2016-17 SP Authentic Marks of Distinction

MDCP Carey Price 40.00 100.00
MDHL Henrik Lundqvist 30.00 80.00
MDHZ Henrik Zetterberg 30.00 80.00
MDJT Jonathan Toews 30.00 80.00
MDMM Mitch Marner 125.00 300.00
MDPL Patrik Laine 150.00 250.00
MDTA John Tavares 25.00 60.00

2016-17 SP Authentic Sign of the Times

SOTTAH Adam Henrique D 4.00 10.00
SOTTAS Andrew Shaw D 3.00 8.00
SOTTBE Brian Elliott E 4.00 10.00
SOTTBO Peter Bondra D 5.00 12.00
SOTTCH Carl Hagelin D 3.00 8.00
SOTTCM Connor McDavid A 150.00 250.00
SOTTDB David Backes D 3.00 8.00
SOTTDS Darryl Sittler B 12.00 30.00
SOTTHL Henrik Lundqvist C 15.00 40.00
SOTTHZ Henrik Zetterberg B 12.00 30.00
SOTTJM Jake Muzzin E 5.00 12.00
SOTTJT Joe Thornton A 40.00 100.00
SOTTLD Leon Draisaitl D 15.00 40.00
SOTTLM Larry Murphy B 4.00 10.00
SOTTMM Matt Murray E 20.00 50.00
SOTTPL Pat LaFontaine C 5.00 12.00
SOTTRS Ryan Spooner E 4.00 10.00
SOTTSC Sidney Crosby 150.00 250.00
SOTTTL Trevor Linden B 5.00 12.00
SOTTVR Victor Rask E 3.00 8.00
SOTTWG Wayne Gretzky A 300.00 800.00
SOTTZP Zach Parise B 5.00 12.00
SOTTTO Jonathan Toews 15.00 40.00

2016-17 SP Authentic Sign of the Times Duals

ST2BL M.Bossy/P.LaFontaine 30.00 80.00
ST2LB T.Linden/P.Bure 200.00 300.00
ST2LP J.Puljujarvi/P.Laine 50.00 125.00
ST2RL M.Richter/H.Lundqvist 60.00 150.00
ST2RP P.Roy/C.Price 100.00 250.00
ST2ZL H.Zetterberg/N.Lidstrom 25.00 60.00

2016-17 SP Authentic Sign of the Times Inscribed

SOTTAH Adam Henrique
100 Career Goal/25 12.00 30.00
SOTTBE Brian Elliott
Moose/40 12.00 30.00
SOTTCH Carl Hagelin
2016 SC Champ/25 12.00 30.00
SOTTDB David Backes
Fear the Bear/25 8.00 20.00
SOTTJM Jake Muzzin
14 SC Champ/40 10.00 25.00
SOTTJT Joe Thornton
Jumbo Joe/25 30.00 80.00
SOTTLD Leon Draisaitl
Oilers Nation/40 20.00 50.00
SOTTMM Matt Murray
2016 SC Champ/25 30.00 80.00
SOTTVR Victor Rask
Go Okraner/40 12.00 30.00

2016-17 SP Authentic Sign of the Times Rookies

SOTRAM Anthony Mantha/99 12.00 30.00
SOTRAM Auston Matthews/35 300.00 800.00
SOTRBL Brendan Leipsic/199 5.00 12.00
SOTRDS Dylan Strome/199 15.00 40.00
SOTRHF Hudson Fasching/199 6.00 15.00
SOTRJD Jason Dickinson/199 5.00 12.00
SOTRJP Jesse Puljujarvi/99 12.00 30.00
SOTRJV Jimmy Vesey/199 10.00 25.00
SOTRKC Kyle Connor/199 25.00 60.00

SOTRMM Michael Matheson/199 6.00 15.00
SOTRMM Mitch Marner/199 150.00 400.00
SOTRNS Nikita Soshnikov/199 4.00 10.00
SOTRPL Patrik Laine/99 80.00 150.00
SOTRPZ Pavel Zacha/99 10.00 25.00
SOTRSM Sonny Milano/199 8.00 20.00
SOTRWN William Nylander/99 30.00 80.00

2016-17 SP Authentic Sign of the Times Rookies Inscribed

*INSRIBED: .6X TO 1.5X BASIC INSERTS
SOTRMM Mitch Marner
The 6ix/25 200.00 500.00

2016-17 SP Authentic Silver Skates

SSAG Alex Galchenyuk .50 1.25
SSAM Auston Matthews 5.00 12.00
SSAO Alexander Ovechkin 3.00 8.00
SSCM Connor McDavid 4.00 10.00
SSDS Dylan Strome 2.00 5.00
SSHL Henrik Lundqvist 2.00 5.00
SSHZ Henrik Zetterberg 1.00 2.50
SSJP Jesse Puljujarvi 1.50 4.00
SSJT Jonathan Toews 1.25 3.00
SSJV Jimmy Vesey 1.25 3.00
SSKC Kyle Connor 2.50 6.00
SSMA Anthony Mantha 1.50 4.00
SSMM Mitch Marner 2.50 6.00
SSMS Mikhail Sergachev 1.25 3.00
SSMT Matthew Tkachuk 3.00 8.00
SSPK Patrick Kane 1.50 4.00
SSPL Patrik Laine 2.00 5.00
SSPZ Pavel Zacha 1.25 3.00
SSRL Roberto Luongo 1.25 3.00
SSSA Sebastian Aho 2.50 6.00
SSSC Sidney Crosby 3.00 8.00
SSTA John Tavares 1.25 3.00
SSTK Travis Konecny 1.50 4.00
SSWN William Nylander 3.00 8.00
SSZW Zach Werenski 2.50 6.00

2016-17 SP Authentic Silver Skates Autographs

SSDS Dylan Strome/25 25.00 60.00
SSJP Jesse Puljujarvi/25 25.00 60.00
SSJV Jimmy Vesey/25 15.00 40.00
SSKC Kyle Connor/25 30.00 80.00
SSMA Anthony Mantha/25 20.00 50.00
SSMM Mitch Marner/25 125.00 300.00
SSMS Mikhail Sergachev/25 15.00 40.00
SSMT Matthew Tkachuk/25 40.00 100.00
SSPL Patrik Laine/25 25.00 60.00
SSPZ Pavel Zacha/25 15.00 40.00
SSSA Sebastian Aho/25 30.00 80.00
SSTK Travis Konecny/25 20.00 50.00
SSWN William Nylander/25 40.00 100.00
SSZW Zach Werenski/25 30.00 80.00

2016-17 SP Authentic Silver Skates Gold

SSAM Auston Matthews 20.00 50.00

2016-17 SP Authentic Spectrum Autographs

COMMON CARD 4.00 10.00
SEMISTARS 5.00 12.00
UNLISTED STARS 6.00 15.00
5 Aaron Ekblad B 5.00 12.00
7 Taylor Hall B 12.00 30.00
10 Adam Henrique C 5.00 12.00
11 Anze Kopitar B 25.00 60.00
12 Marian Gaborik B 6.00 15.00
14 Jamie Benn B 6.00 15.00
15 Nino Niederreiter D 4.00 10.00
16 Joe Pavelski B 15.00 40.00
20 Brayden Schenn C 6.00 15.00
24 Leon Draisaitl C 25.00 60.00
26 Mark Stone C 8.00 20.00
28 Jake Muzzin D 6.00 15.00
29 Marc-Andre Fleury B 25.00 60.00
30 Henrik Lundqvist A 60.00 150.00
31 Carey Price A 80.00 150.00
32 Joe Thornton A 15.00 40.00
35 Cory Schneider C 6.00 15.00
36 Evgeni Malkin A 40.00 100.00
40 Henrik Zetterberg B 20.00 50.00
46 Tyler Seguin A 20.00 50.00
47 Boone Jenner D 6.00 15.00
50 Zach Parise B 6.00 15.00
51 Andrew Ladd C 4.00 10.00
52 David Krejci C 6.00 15.00
55 Robby Fabbri D 4.00 10.00
56 Artem Anisimov D 4.00 10.00
62 Ryan Spooner D 5.00 12.00
64 Mike Hoffman C 4.00 10.00
65 Tom Wilson D 6.00 15.00
68 Jaromir Jagr A 80.00 150.00
69 Nikolaj Ehlers D 6.00 15.00
72 Jiri Hudler D 5.00 12.00
73 Tyler Toffoli C 6.00 15.00
75 Matt Murray D 10.00 25.00
78 Jarome Iginla A 20.00 50.00
85 David Backes B 4.00 10.00
86 Nikita Kucherov C 12.00 30.00
88 Brent Burns D 6.00 15.00
90 Ryan O'Reilly C 6.00 15.00
91 John Tavares B 10.00 25.00
92 Mark Scheifele D 10.00 25.00
98 Loui Eriksson C 4.00 10.00
101 Jaromir Jagr AM B 125.00 200.00
104 Joe Thornton AM C 8.00 20.00
107 Henrik Lundqvist AM B 50.00 120.00
112 Jimmy Vesey AM D 10.00 25.00
113 Mitch Marner AM C 60.00 150.00
114 Patrik Laine AM D 100.00 200.00

2016-17 SP Authentic Spectrum FX

S1 Patrick Kane 2.50 6.00
S2 Carey Price 2.50 6.00
S3 Johnny Gaudreau 2.00 5.00
S4 Steven Stamkos 2.50 6.00
S5 Connor McDavid 6.00 15.00
S6 Nathan MacKinnon 5.00 12.00
S7 Taylor Hall 1.25 3.00
S8 Jeff Skinner 1.50 4.00
S9 Mark Scheifele 2.00 5.00
S10 Alexander Ovechkin 5.00 12.00
S11 Erik Karlsson 1.50 4.00

S12 Jack Eichel 2.00 5.00
S13 Jonathan Quick 1.50 4.00
S14 Jamie Benn 1.25 3.00
S15 Sidney Crosby 5.00 12.00
S16 Shayne Gostisbehere 1.25 3.00
S17 David Pastrnak 3.00 8.00
S18 Brent Burns 1.25 3.00
S19 Jaromir Jagr 4.00 10.00
S20 John Tavares 2.00 5.00
S21 Max Domi 1.25 3.00
S22 Daniel Sedin 1.50 4.00
S23 P.K. Subban 1.50 4.00
S24 Brandon Saad 1.00 2.50
S25 Henrik Zetterberg 1.50 4.00
S26 Nazem Kadri 1.50 4.00
S27 Mikko Koivu 1.00 2.50
S28 Ryan Getzlaf 1.25 3.00
S29 Derek Stepan .75 2.00
S30 Vladimir Tarasenko 1.50 4.00
S31 Tyler Seguin 1.50 4.00
S32 Milan Lucic 1.00 2.50
S33 Tyler Toffoli 1.25 3.00
S34 Dylan Larkin 1.50 4.00
S35 Evgeni Malkin 2.50 6.00
S36 Nikita Kucherov 2.50 6.00
S37 Artemi Panarin 2.50 6.00
S38 Alex Galchenyuk .75 2.00
S39 Bobby Orr 5.00 12.00
S40 Wayne Gretzky 8.00 20.00
S41 Anthony DeAngelo FW 1.00 2.50
S42 Tyler Bertuzzi FW 4.00 10.00
S43 Jacob Larsson FW 4.00 10.00
S44 Artturi Lehkonen FW 3.00 8.00
S45 Brendan Guhle FW 2.50 6.00
S46 Kasperi Kapanen FW 4.00 10.00
S47 Oliver Bjorkstrand FW 3.00 8.00
S48 Tristan Jarry FW 5.00 12.00
S49 Michael Matheson FW 2.50 6.00
S50 Nick Schmaltz FW 3.00 8.00
S51 Julius Honka FW 2.50 6.00
S52 Zach Hyman FW 8.00 20.00
S53 Thatcher Demko FW 6.00 15.00
S54 Zach Sanford FW 2.50 6.00
S55 Jake Guentzel FW 8.00 20.00
S56 A.J. Greer FW 2.50 6.00
S57 Troy Stecher FW 2.50 6.00
S58 Josh Morrissey FW 6.00 15.00
S59 Thomas Chabot FW 5.00 12.00
S60 Ondrej Kase FW 2.50 6.00
S61 Denis Malgin FW 2.00 5.00
S62 Sonny Milano FW 3.00 8.00
S63 Nic Dowd FW 2.00 5.00
S64 Mark Jankowski FW 2.00 5.00
S65 Drake Caggiula FW 2.50 6.00
S66 John Quenneville FW 2.50 6.00
S67 Nikita Zaitsev FW 2.50 6.00
S68 Gustav Forsling FW 5.00 12.00
S69 Danton Heinen FW 2.00 5.00
S70 Brendan Leipsic FW 2.00 5.00
S71 Connor Brown FW 4.00 10.00
S72 Brandon Carlo FW 4.00 10.00
S73 Dylan Strome FW 6.00 15.00
S74 Anthony Beauvillier FW 2.50 6.00
S75 Lawson Crouse FW 2.00 5.00
S76 Kyle Connor FW 8.00 20.00
S77 Joel Eriksson Ek FW 4.00 10.00
S78 Sebastian Aho FW 8.00 20.00
S79 Pavel Buchnevich FW 4.00 10.00
S80 Mathew Barzal FW 8.00 20.00
S81 Christian Dvorak FW 2.50 6.00
S82 Brayden Point FW 6.00 15.00
S83 Tyler Motte FW 2.50 6.00
S84 Jakub Vrana FW 3.00 8.00
S85 Brendan Perlini FW 2.50 6.00
S86 Travis Konecny FW 5.00 12.00
S87 Pavel Zacha FW 4.00 10.00
S88 Kevin Labanc FW 2.50 6.00
S89 Jakob Chychrun FW 5.00 12.00
S90 Ivan Provorov FW 4.00 10.00
S91 Zach Werenski FW 8.00 20.00
S92 Anthony Mantha FW 5.00 12.00
S93 Mikhail Sergachev FW 4.00 10.00
S94 Matthew Tkachuk FW 10.00 25.00
S95 William Nylander FW 10.00 25.00
S96 Jimmy Vesey FW 4.00 10.00
S97 Jesse Puljujarvi FW 5.00 12.00
S98 Mitch Marner FW 25.00 60.00
S99 Patrik Laine FW 25.00 60.00
S100 Auston Matthews FWB 100.00 200.00

2016-17 SP Authentic Spectrum FX Gold

*FW/50: .75X TO 2X BASIC INSERTS
S80 Mathew Barzal FW 15.00 40.00
S98 Mitch Marner FW 60.00 150.00
S99 Patrik Laine FW 100.00 250.00
S100 Auston Matthews FW 150.00 300.00

2017-18 SP Authentic

1 Connor McDavid 1.25 3.00
2 Oliver Ekman-Larsson .25 .60
3 Cam Atkinson .25 .60
4 Jamie Benn .25 .60
5 Matt Murray .40 1.00
6 Mark Scheifele .40 1.00
7 Victor Hedman .30 .75
8 Wayne Simmonds .30 .75
9 Duncan Keith .40 1.00
10 Auston Matthews 1.00 2.50
11 Sebastian Aho .40 1.00
12 Ryan Kesler .25 .60
13 Johnny Gaudreau .40 1.00
14 P.K. Subban .30 .75
15 Patrik Laine .30 .75
16 Jason Pominville .15 .40
17 Jonathan Drouin .20 .50
18 David Pastrnak .60 1.50
19 Marcus Johansson .20 .50
20 John Tavares .40 1.00
21 Henrik Lundqvist .60 1.50
22 Joe Pavelski .30 .75
23 Brandon Saad .20 .50
24 Anthony Mantha .30 .75
25 Nathan MacKinnon 1.00 2.50
26 Jaden Schwartz .30 .75
27 Henrik Sedin .30 .75
28 Aleksander Barkov .40 1.00
29 Mikael Granlund .20 .50

30 Alexander Ovechkin 1.00 2.50
31 Marc-Andre Fleury .50 1.25
32 Mike Hoffman .15 .40
33 Leon Draisaitl .75 2.00
34 Christian Dvorak .20 .50
35 Patrick Marleau .25 .60
36 Jordan Eberle .25 .60
37 Alexander Wennberg .15 .40
38 Andrew Ladd .15 .40
39 Ryan O'Reilly .25 .60
40 Tyler Seguin .30 .75
41 Ivan Provorov .20 .50
42 Anze Kopitar .40 1.00
43 Logan Couture .30 .75
44 Matthew Tkachuk .50 1.25
45 Sidney Crosby 1.00 2.50
46 Max Pacioretty .25 .60
47 Tomas Tatar .15 .40
48 Gabriel Landeskog .30 .75
49 Jimmy Vesey .20 .50
50 Jonathan Toews .40 1.00
51 Corey Perry .40 1.00
52 Nick Bonino .15 .40
53 Reilly Smith .25 .60
54 Brad Marchand .50 1.25
55 Steven Stamkos .50 1.25
56 Erik Karlsson .30 .75
57 T.J. Oshie .25 .60
58 Noah Hanifin .25 .60
59 Bo Horvat .30 .75
60 Taylor Hall .25 .60
61 Roberto Luongo .40 1.00
62 Devan Dubnyk .20 .50
63 Jakub Voracek .20 .50
64 Jack Eichel .40 1.00
65 Jaromir Jagr .75 2.00
66 William Nylander .50 1.25
67 Colton Parayko .20 .50
68 Henrik Zetterberg .30 .75
69 Dustin Byfuglien .25 .60
70 Mikko Rantanen .60 1.50
71 Artemi Panarin .50 1.25
72 Kevin Shattenkirk .15 .40
73 Derek Stepan .15 .40
74 Mark Giordano .20 .50
75 Patrick Kane .50 1.25
76 Ryan Johansen .20 .50
77 Carey Price .50 1.25
78 Pavel Zacha .20 .50
79 Brent Burns .25 .60
80 Nino Niederreiter .15 .40
81 John Gibson .20 .50
82 Nikita Kucherov .50 1.25
83 Scott Darling .20 .50
84 Jeff Carter .20 .50
85 Jake Guentzel .40 1.00
86 Ben Bishop .20 .50
87 Evgeny Kuznetsov .30 .75
88 Vladimir Tarasenko .30 .75
89 Ryan Strome .25 .60
90 James Neal .15 .40
91 Mitch Marner .40 1.00
92 Phil Kessel .25 .60
93 Tuukka Rask .30 .75
94 Vincent Trocheck .25 .60
95 Conor Sheary .25 .60
96 Pavel Bure .25 .60
97 Mario Lemieux 1.00 2.50
98 Darryl Sittler .30 .75
99 Wayne Gretzky 1.50 4.00
100 Patrick Roy .60 1.50
101 Alexander Ovechkin AM 1.00 2.50
102 Sidney Crosby AM 1.00 2.50
103 Henrik Sedin AM .30 .75
104 Connor McDavid AM 1.25 3.00
105 Auston Matthews AM 1.00 2.50
106 Corey Perry AM .40 1.00
107 Colton Sissons AM .15 .40
108 Patrick Marleau AM .25 .60
109 Evgeni Malkin AM .50 1.25
110 Roberto Luongo AM .40 1.00
111 Leon Draisaitl AM .75 2.00
112 Joe Thornton AM .40 1.00
113 Detroit Red Wings AM .25 .60
114 Los Angeles Kings
Vancouver Canucks AM .25 .60
115 Nico Hischier AM .75 2.00
116 Charlie McAvoy FW
AU/949* RC 125.00 300.00
117 Jack Roslovic FW AU/949* RC 10.00 25.00
118 Adrian Kempe FW AU/949* RC 15.00 40.00
119 Alex Tuch FW AU/949* RC 20.00 50.00
120 Clayton Keller FW AU/949* RC 40.00 100.00
121 Jordan Schmaltz FW AU/949* RC 10.00 25.00
122 J.T. Compher FW AU/949* RC 8.00 20.00
123 Jon Gillies FW AU/949* RC 8.00 20.00
124 Riley Barber FW AU/949* RC 8.00 20.00
125 Brock Boeser FW AU/949* RC 100.00 250.00
126 Lucas Wallmark FW AU/949* RC 8.00 20.00
127 Jakob Forsbacka-Karlsson
FW AU/949* RC 8.00 20.00
128 Gabriel Carlsson FW AU/949* RC 6.00 15.00
129 Evgeny Svechnikov
FW AU/949* RC 15.00 40.00
130 Josh Ho-Sang FW AU/949* RC 10.00 25.00
131 Mike Vecchione FW AU/949* RC 6.00 15.00
132 Colin White FW AU/949* RC 10.00 25.00
133 Denis Gurianov FW AU/949* RC 20.00 50.00
134 Vladislav Kamenev
FW AU/949* RC 8.00 20.00
135 Tyson Jost FW AU/949* RC 15.00 40.00
136 Jonny Brodzinski FW AU/949* RC 8.00 20.00
137 Ivan Barbashev FW AU/949* RC 10.00 25.00
138 Nikita Scherbak FW AU/949* RC 10.00 25.00
139 Valentin Zykov FW AU/949* RC 8.00 20.00
140 Alexander Nylander
FW AU/949* RC 12.00 30.00
141 Samuel Morin FW AU/949* RC 5.00 12.00
142 Christian Fischer
FW AU/949* RC 10.00 25.00
143 Peter Cehlarik FW AU/949* RC 8.00 20.00
144 Nolan Patrick FW RC 15.00 40.00
145A Nico Hischier FW RC 8.00 20.00
145B Nico Hischier
FW AU/949* XRC 40.00 100.00
146 Anders Bjork FW AU/949* RC 10.00 25.00
147 Alex DeBrincat FW AU/949* RC 60.00 150.00

148 Haydn Fleury FW AU/949* RC 8.00 20.00
149 Alex Formenton FW AU/949* RC 8.00 20.00
150 Pierre-Luc Dubois
FW AU/949* RC 25.00 60.00
151 Owen Tippett FW AU/949* RC 15.00 40.00
152A Luke Kunin FW RC 8.00 20.00
152B Luke Kunin FW AU/949* XRC 4.00 10.00
153 Vince Dunn FW AU/949* RC 10.00 25.00
154 Christian Djoos FW AU/949* RC 8.00 20.00
155A Jake DeBrusk FW RC 20.00 50.00
155B Jake DeBrusk FW AU/949* XRC 15.00 40.00
156 Robert Hagg FW AU/949* RC 8.00 20.00
157 Michael Amadio FW AU/949* RC 8.00 20.00
158 Ville Husso FW AU/949* RC 10.00 25.00
159 Janne Kuokkanen
FW AU/949* RC 8.00 20.00
160 Kailer Yamamoto
FW AU/949* RC 20.00 50.00
161 Logan Brown FW RC 8.00 20.00
162 Jesper Bratt FW RC 15.00 40.00
163A Martin Necas FW RC 25.00 60.00
163B Martin Necas
FW AU/949* XRC 60.00 150.00
164 Tucker Poolman FW AU/949* RC 6.00 15.00
165 Victor Mete FW AU/949* RC 8.00 20.00
166 Remi Elie FW AU/949* RC 6.00 15.00
167 Madison Bowey FW RC 5.00 12.00
168A Calle Rosen FW RC 8.00 20.00
169 Tage Thompson
FW AU/949* RC 80.00 200.00
170 Will Butcher FW AU/949* RC 10.00 25.00
171 Filip Chlapik FW AU/949* RC 6.00 15.00
172 Ian McCoshen FW AU/949* RC 8.00 20.00
173 Alex Kerfoot FW AU/949* RC 15.00 40.00
174 Filip Chytil FW AU/949* RC 12.00 30.00
175 Nick Merkley FW AU/949* RC 8.00 20.00
176 Samuel Girard FW AU/949* RC 8.00 20.00
177 Nicolas Kerdiles FW AU/949* RC 8.00 20.00
178 Tim Heed FW AU/949* RC 8.00 20.00
179 Nathan Walker FW AU/949* RC 8.00 20.00
180 Brendan Lemieux FW AU/949* RC 8.00 20.00
181 Alex Nedeljkovic FW AU/949* RC 12.00 30.00
182 Andrew Mangiapane
FW AU/949* RC 80.00 200.00
183 Kalle Kossila FW AU/949* RC 8.00 20.00
184 Adin Hill FW AU/949* RC 40.00 100.00
185 Alexandre Carrier FW AU/949* RC 6.00 15.00
186 Andrew Poturalski
FW AU/949* RC 8.00 20.00
187 Roland McKeown
FW AU/949* RC 8.00 20.00
188 Kyle Capobianco FW RC 8.00 20.00
189 Christian Jaros FW RC 6.00 15.00
190 Jan Rutta FW RC 8.00 20.00
191 Kevin Roy FW RC 8.00 20.00
192 Alex Iafallo FW AU/949* RC 8.00 20.00

2017-18 SP Authentic '07-08 Retro Rookie Patch Autographs

RAB Anders Bjork 20.00 50.00
RAD Alex DeBrincat 100.00 250.00
RAT Alex Tuch 40.00 100.00
RBB Brock Boeser 40.00 100.00
RCF Christian Fischer 20.00 50.00
RCK Clayton Keller 40.00 100.00
RCM Charlie McAvoy 40.00 100.00
RFC Filip Chlapik 12.00 30.00
RHF Haydn Fleury 15.00 40.00
RJB Jesper Bratt 100.00 250.00
RJC J.T. Compher 15.00 40.00
RJH Josh Ho-Sang 20.00 50.00
RKY Kailer Yamamoto 40.00 100.00
RLK Luke Kunin 15.00 40.00
RMN Martin Necas 50.00 120.00
ROT Owen Tippett 30.00 80.00
RPD Pierre-Luc Dubois 25.00 60.00
RRH Robert Hagg 15.00 40.00
RTJ Tyson Jost 30.00 80.00
RTT Tage Thompson 60.00 150.00
RVD Vince Dunn 20.00 50.00
RVM Victor Mete 15.00 40.00
RWB Will Butcher 20.00 50.00

2017-18 SP Authentic '90-91 Retro Draft Picks

RDPAM Auston Matthews 6.00 15.00
RDPAO Alexander Ovechkin 6.00 15.00
RDPBB Brock Boeser 4.00 10.00
RDPCK Clayton Keller 4.00 10.00
RDPCM Connor McDavid 8.00 20.00
RDPEK Erik Karlsson 2.00 5.00
RDPJD Jonathan Drouin 1.25 3.00
RDPPL Patrik Laine 2.50 6.00
RDPSS Steven Stamkos 3.00 8.00
RDPTH Taylor Hall 1.50 4.00

2017-18 SP Authentic '90-91 Retro Draft Picks Autographs

RDPAO Alexander Ovechkin/25 100.00 200.00
RDPCK Clayton Keller/50 30.00 80.00
RDPCM Connor McDavid/25 300.00 400.00
RDPPL Patrik Laine/50 100.00 200.00

2017-18 SP Authentic Future Watch Inscribed Autographs

116 Charlie McAvoy/50* 150.00 400.00
119 Alex Tuch/50* 30.00 80.00
120 Clayton Keller/50* 100.00 200.00
125 Brock Boeser/50* 150.00 400.00
147 Alex DeBrincat/50* 150.00 400.00
150 Pierre-Luc Dubois/50* 100.00 250.00
169 Tage Thompson/50* 300.00 800.00
182 Andrew Mangiapane/50* 150.00 400.00
184 Adin Hill/50* 80.00 200.00

2017-18 SP Authentic Global Chirography

GERLD Leon Draisaitl A 25.00 60.00
NORAW Mats Zuccarello A 25.00 60.00
SLORP Richard Panik B 3.00 8.00
SWEVH Victor Hedman A 6.00 15.00
USACK Clayton Keller B 25.00 60.00
USAJV Jim Vanbiesbrouck A 25.00 60.00
USAPH Phil Housley B 4.00 10.00

2017-18 SP Authentic Great White North Signatures

GWNBB Bill Barber D 8.00 20.00
GWNJH Josh Ho-Sang E 6.00 15.00
GWNMD Marcel Dionne B 30.00 80.00

2016-17 SP Authentic Future Watch Black

GWNMM Matt Murray C 25.00 60.00
GWNSS Steven Stamkos A 100.00 200.00
GWNTJ Tyson Jost D 8.00 20.00

2017-18 SP Authentic Limited Autographs

1 Connor McDavid A 250.00 350.00
3 Cam Atkinson D 10.00 25.00
5 Matt Murray C 15.00 40.00
6 Mark Scheifele B 15.00 40.00
7 Victor Hedman B 12.00 30.00
8 Wayne Simmonds C 12.00 30.00
9 Duncan Keith B 8.00 20.00
11 Sebastian Aho D 15.00 40.00
12 Ryan Kesler C 10.00 25.00
15 Patrik Laine A 12.00 30.00
16 Jason Pominville D 6.00 15.00
17 Jonathan Drouin C 8.00 20.00
20 John Tavares A 15.00 40.00
21 Henrik Lundqvist A 25.00 60.00
22 Joe Pavelski B 12.00 30.00
24 Anthony Mantha D 8.00 20.00
30 Alexander Ovechkin A 40.00 100.00
31 Marc-Andre Fleury B 20.00 50.00
32 Mike Hoffman D 6.00 15.00
33 Leon Draisaitl B 30.00 80.00
34 Christian Dvorak D 8.00 20.00
37 Alexander Wennberg C 6.00 15.00
40 Tyler Seguin A 12.00 30.00
42 Anze Kopitar B 15.00 40.00
43 Logan Couture C 12.00 30.00
44 Matthew Tkachuk D 20.00 50.00
46 Max Pacioretty B 10.00 25.00
50 Jonathan Toews A 40.00 100.00
55 Steven Stamkos A 30.00 80.00
56 Erik Karlsson A 12.00 30.00
58 Noah Hanifin D 10.00 25.00
59 Bo Horvat C 12.00 30.00
60 Taylor Hall B 10.00 25.00
61 Roberto Luongo A 15.00 40.00
62 Devan Dubnyk C 8.00 20.00
67 Colton Parayko D 8.00 20.00
68 Henrik Zetterberg A 12.00 30.00
72 Kevin Shattenkirk D 6.00 15.00
75 Patrick Kane A 20.00 50.00
77 Carey Price A 20.00 50.00
78 Pavel Zacha D 8.00 20.00
82 Nikita Kucherov B 20.00 50.00
84 Jeff Carter B 8.00 20.00
85 Jake Guentzel C 15.00 40.00
88 Vladimir Tarasenko A 25.00 60.00
90 James Neal B 6.00 15.00
94 Vincent Trocheck C 10.00 25.00
95 Conor Sheary D 10.00 25.00
97 Mario Lemieux A 100.00 200.00
98 Darryl Sittler A 25.00 60.00
99 Wayne Gretzky A 250.00 600.00
100 Patrick Roy A 25.00 60.00
101 Alexander Ovechkin AM A 60.00 150.00
102 Sidney Crosby AM A 100.00 200.00
104 Connor McDavid AM 150.00 250.00
110 Roberto Luongo AM 15.00 40.00
111 Leon Draisaitl AM 30.00 80.00
112 Joe Thornton AM B 15.00 40.00

2017-18 SP Authentic Limited Patch Autographs

*PATCH/25-100: .6X TO 1.5X BASIC INSERTS
5 Matt Murray/25 40.00 100.00
15 Patrik Laine/25 150.00 250.00
20 John Tavares/25 50.00 125.00
22 Joe Pavelski/25 30.00 80.00
25 Nathan MacKinnon/25 60.00 150.00
33 Leon Draisaitl/50 25.00 60.00
40 Tyler Seguin/25 40.00 100.00
50 Jonathan Toews/25 50.00 125.00
55 Steven Stamkos/25 40.00 100.00
60 Taylor Hall/26 40.00 100.00
75 Patrick Kane/25 60.00 150.00
125 Brock Boeser FW/100 200.00 350.00
147 Alex DeBrincat FW/100 100.00 250.00
150 Pierre-Luc Dubois FW/100 80.00 200.00
162 Jesper Bratt FW/100 100.00 250.00
169 Tage Thompson FW/100 125.00 300.00

2017-18 SP Authentic Marks of Distinction

MDAK Anze Kopitar 25.00 60.00
MDCK Clayton Keller 100.00 200.00
MDVT Vladimir Tarasenko 30.00 80.00

2017-18 SP Authentic Rookie Year Milestones

RYMAE Aaron Ekblad .60 1.50
RYMAM Auston Matthews 2.00 5.00
RYMAO Alexander Ovechkin 2.00 5.00
RYMBR Martin Brodeur 1.25 3.00
RYMCM Connor McDavid 2.50 6.00
RYMDH Dale Hawerchuk .60 1.50
RYMDK Duncan Keith .40 1.00
RYMEB Ed Belfour .60 1.50
RYMEM Evgeni Malkin 1.00 2.50
RYMGL Gabriel Landeskog .60 1.50
RYMJG Jake Guentzel .75 2.00
RYMLM Larry Murphy .40 1.00
RYMMB Mike Bossy .50 1.25
RYMMD Marcel Dionne .60 1.50
RYMML Mario Lemieux 2.00 5.00
RYMMM Mike Modano .75 2.00
RYMNL Nicklas Lidstrom .50 1.25
RYMNM Nathan MacKinnon 2.00 5.00
RYMPB Pavel Bure .50 1.25
RYMPF Peter Forsberg 1.00 2.50
RYMPK Patrick Kane 1.00 2.50
RYMRB Ray Bourque .75 2.00
RYMSA Terry Sawchuk .40 1.00
RYMSC Sidney Crosby 2.00 5.00
RYMSM Steve Mason .40 1.00
RYMSY Steve Yzerman 1.25 3.00
RYMTB Tom Barrasso .40 1.00
RYMTE Tony Esposito .50 1.25
RYMTS Teemu Selanne 1.00 2.50
RYMWG Wayne Gretzky 3.00 8.00

2017-18 SP Authentic Rookie Year Milestones Autographs

RYMAE Aaron Ekblad/39 20.00 50.00
RYMCM Connor McDavid/16 300.00 400.00
RYMDK Duncan Keith/21 12.00 30.00
RYMJG Jake Guentzel/21 25.00 60.00
RYMLM Larry Murphy/60 12.00 30.00
RYMMD Marcel Dionne/49 20.00 50.00
RYMMM Mike Modano/29 25.00 60.00
RYMTB Tom Barrasso/26 12.00 30.00

2017-18 SP Authentic Sign of the Times

SOTTAN Craig Anderson F 5.00 12.00
SOTTCA Cam Atkinson G 5.00 12.00
SOTTCN Cam Neely B 5.00 12.00
SOTTCP Carey Price A 25.00 60.00
SOTTCS Conor Sheary G 5.00 12.00
SOTTDP Denis Potvin E 5.00 12.00
SOTTFP Felix Potvin E 8.00 20.00
SOTTGA Jake Gardiner B 3.00 8.00
SOTTGC Gerry Cheevers E 5.00 12.00
SOTTJC Jeff Carter C 4.00 10.00
SOTTJG Jake Guentzel D 8.00 20.00
SOTTJK Jari Kurri D 5.00 12.00
SOTTJP Jason Pominville C 3.00 8.00
SOTTJT Jacob Trouba G 4.00 10.00
SOTTKS Kevin Shattenkirk C 3.00 8.00
SOTTLC Logan Couture C 6.00 15.00
SOTTMF Marc-Andre Fleury B 60.00 150.00
SOTTMH Mike Hoffman G 3.00 8.00
SOTTML Mario Lemieux B 60.00 150.00
SOTTMR Mikko Rantanen F 12.00 30.00
SOTTMT Matthew Tkachuk G 10.00 25.00
SOTTNK Nikita Kucherov A 10.00 25.00
SOTTPA Colton Parayko F 4.00 10.00
SOTTPH Phil Housley D 4.00 10.00
SOTTPK Patrick Kane B 25.00 60.00
SOTTPL Patrik Laine B 25.00 60.00
SOTTPM Petr Mrazek G 5.00 12.00
SOTTPT Pierre Turgeon E 4.00 10.00
SOTTRE Ryan Ellis C 4.00 10.00
SOTTRH Ron Hextall E 5.00 12.00
SOTTRL Rod Langway G 5.00 12.00
SOTTRP Richard Panik G 3.00 8.00
SOTTSB Sergei Bobrovsky D 8.00 20.00
SOTTSI Charlie Simmer G 3.00 8.00
SOTTSS Steven Stamkos A 25.00 60.00
SOTTTA Tony Amonte F 4.00 10.00
SOTTTB Tom Barrasso D 4.00 10.00
SOTTTP Tanner Pearson G 4.00 10.00
SOTTVT Vincent Trocheck C 5.00 12.00
SOTTZH Zach Hyman G 8.00 20.00

2017-18 SP Authentic Sign of the Times Duals

ST2CS B.Clarke/D.Schultz 25.00 60.00
ST2DB A.Debrincat/B.Boeser 40.00 100.00
ST2KF C.Keller/C.Fischer 40.00 100.00
ST2LS P.Laine/M.Schiefele 25.00 60.00
ST2LV R.Luongo/J.Vanbiesbrouck 25.00 60.00
ST2MD C.McDavid/L.Draisaitl 80.00 200.00
ST2OS B.Orr/D.Sanderson 60.00 150.00
ST2PD M.Pacioretty/J.Drouin 15.00 40.00
ST2SK S.Stamkos/N.Kucherov 30.00 80.00

2017-18 SP Authentic Spectrum FX

S1 Auston Matthews 5.00 12.00
S2 Marc-Andre Fleury 2.50 6.00
S3 Phil Kessel 1.25 3.00
S4 Brandon Saad 1.00 2.50
S5 Alexander Ovechkin 5.00 12.00
S6 Kevin Shattenkirk .75 2.00
S7 Brent Burns 1.25 3.00
S8 Artemi Panarin 2.50 6.00
S9 Sean Couturier 1.00 2.50
S10 Carey Price 2.50 6.00
S11 Teuvo Teravainen 1.25 3.00
S12 Oliver Ekman-Larsson 1.25 3.00
S13 Ben Bishop 1.00 2.50
S14 Jack Eichel 2.00 5.00
S15 Jaromir Jagr 4.00 10.00
S16 Tomas Tatar .75 2.00
S17 Henrik Sedin 1.50 4.00
S18 Anze Kopitar 2.00 5.00
S19 Roberto Luongo 2.00 5.00
S20 Connor McDavid 6.00 15.00
S21 Gabriel Landeskog 1.50 4.00
S22 Corey Perry 2.00 5.00
S23 Nikita Kucherov 2.50 6.00
S24 Eric Staal 1.50 4.00
S25 Erik Karlsson 1.50 4.00
S26 Marcus Johansson 1.00 2.50
S27 Mitch Marner 2.00 5.00
S28 Johnny Gaudreau 2.00 5.00
S29 Leon Draisaitl 4.00 10.00
S30 P.K. Subban 1.50 4.00
S31 Tuukka Rask 1.50 4.00
S32 John Tavares 2.00 5.00
S33 William Karlsson 1.50 4.00
S34 Evgeny Kuznetsov 1.50 4.00
S35 Vladimir Tarasenko 1.50 4.00
S36 Patrik Laine 1.50 4.00
S37 Sidney Crosby 5.00 12.00
S38 Patrick Roy 3.00 8.00
S39 Mario Lemieux 5.00 12.00
S40 Wayne Gretzky 8.00 20.00
S41 Janne Kuokkanen FW 2.00 5.00
S42 Evgeny Svechnikov FW 4.00 10.00
S43 Nikita Scherbak FW 2.50 6.00
S44 J.T. Compher FW 2.00 5.00
S45 Calle Rosen FW 2.00 5.00
S46 Henrik Haapala FW 2.00 5.00
S47 Michael Amadio FW 2.00 5.00
S48 Alex Formenton FW 2.00 5.00
S49 Ivan Barbashev FW 2.50 6.00
S50 Jakob Forsbacka-Karlsson FW 2.00 5.00
S51 Denis Gurianov FW 5.00 12.00
S52 Eric Comrie FW 1.50 4.00
S53 Haydn Fleury FW 2.00 5.00
S54 Kevin Roy FW 2.00 5.00
S55 Ville Husso FW 2.50 6.00
S56 Samuel Girard FW 2.00 5.00
S57 Jake Dotchin FW 1.50 4.00
S58 Vince Dunn FW 2.50 6.00
S59 Alexandre Carrier FW 1.50 4.00
S60 John Hayden FW 1.50 4.00
S61 Lucas Wallmark FW 2.00 5.00
S62 Joakim Ryan FW 2.00 5.00
S63 Jon Gillies FW 2.00 5.00
S64 Christian Djoos FW 2.00 5.00
S65 Madison Bowey FW 1.25 3.00
S66 Samuel Blais FW 2.00 5.00
S67 Christian Jaros FW 1.50 4.00
S68 Travis Sanheim FW 2.00 5.00
S69 Andreas Borgman FW 2.00 5.00
S70 Carter Rowney FW 1.50 4.00
S71 Will Butcher FW 4.00 10.00
S72 Jake DeBrusk FW 8.00 20.00
S73 Adrian Kempe FW 6.00 15.00
S74 Logan Brown FW 3.00 8.00
S75 Alex Kerfoot FW 6.00 15.00
S76 Victor Mete FW 3.00 8.00
S77 Robert Hagg FW 3.00 8.00
S78 Jack Roslovic FW 4.00 10.00
S79 Filip Chytil FW 3.00 8.00
S80 Anders Bjork FW 4.00 10.00
S81 Alex Tuch FW 8.00 20.00
S82 Martin Necas FW 10.00 25.00
S83 Luke Kunin FW 3.00 8.00
S84 Colin White FW 4.00 10.00
S85 Owen Tippett FW 6.00 15.00
S86 Nick Merkley FW 3.00 8.00
S87 Josh Ho-Sang FW 4.00 10.00
S88 Tage Thompson FW 8.00 20.00
S89 Christian Fischer FW 4.00 10.00
S90 Jesper Bratt FW 6.00 15.00
S91 Nico Hischier FW 25.00 60.00
S92 Clayton Keller FW 20.00 50.00
S93 Charlie McAvoy FW 20.00 50.00
S94 Kailer Yamamoto FW 20.00 50.00
S95 Pierre-Luc Dubois FW 12.00 30.00
S96 Alex DeBrincat FW 20.00 50.00
S97 Alexander Nylander FW 12.00 30.00
S98 Tyson Jost FW 15.00 40.00
S99 Nolan Patrick FW 15.00 40.00

2018-19 SP Authentic

1 Alexander Ovechkin 1.00 2.50
2 William Karlsson .30 .75
3 Brock Boeser .30 .75
4 Ryan O'Reilly .25 .60
5 Jonathan Toews .40 1.00
6 Evander Kane .25 .60
7 Sean Couturier .20 .50
8 Matt Duchene .25 .60
9 Kevin Shattenkirk .15 .40
10 Taylor Hall .25 .60
11 Mathew Barzal .30 .75
12 Filip Forsberg .40 1.00
13 Jonathan Drouin .20 .50
14 Eric Staal .25 .60
15 Nikita Kucherov .50 1.25
16 Jonathan Quick .30 .75
17 Vincent Trocheck .25 .60
18 John Klingberg .25 .60
19 Justin Williams .20 .50
20 Connor McDavid 1.25 3.00
21 Sean Monahan .15 .40
22 John Gibson .25 .60
23 Sergei Bobrovsky .40 1.00
24 Alex Galchenyuk .15 .40
25 Jack Eichel .40 1.00
26 Patric Hornqvist .15 .40
27 Jake DeBrusk .25 .60
28 Connor Hellebuyck .50 1.25
29 Mikko Rantanen .60 1.50
30 Anthony Mantha .20 .50
31 Auston Matthews 1.00 2.50
32 Evgeny Kuznetsov .30 .75
33 Brendan Gallagher .25 .60
34 Alex Tuch .25 .60
35 Steven Stamkos .50 1.25
36 Colton Parayko .20 .50
37 Tomas Hertl .25 .60
38 Nolan Patrick .25 .60
39 Pekka Rinne .25 .60
40 Patrick Kane .50 1.25
41 Aaron Ekblad .30 .75
42 Mark Stone .30 .75
43 Alexander Radulov .25 .60
44 Max Domi .25 .60
45 Anze Kopitar .40 1.00
46 Jake Guentzel .40 1.00
47 Pierre-Luc Dubois .20 .50
48 Will Butcher .20 .50
49 Leon Draisaitl .75 2.00
50 Henrik Lundqvist .60 1.50
51 John Carlson .25 .60
52 Jonathan Marchessault .30 .75
53 Brayden Schenn .25 .60
54 Bo Horvat .30 .75
55 Erik Karlsson .30 .75
56 Kyle Connor .40 1.00
57 Mitch Marner .40 1.00
58 Rickard Rakell .20 .50
59 Charlie McAvoy .30 .75
60 Johnny Gaudreau .40 1.00
61 Roberto Luongo .40 1.00
62 Vladimir Tarasenko .30 .75
63 Teuvo Teravainen .25 .60
64 Jake Gardiner .15 .40
65 Jamie Benn .25 .60
66 Alex Kerfoot .20 .50
67 Andrei Vasilevskiy .40 1.00
68 Clayton Keller .30 .75
69 Dylan Larkin .30 .75
70 Evgeni Malkin .50 1.25
71 Tom Wilson .25 .60
72 Alex DeBrincat .30 .75
73 Nico Hischier .40 1.00
74 Brent Burns .25 .60
75 Carey Price .50 1.25
76 Mikael Granlund .20 .50
77 Blake Wheeler .25 .60
78 Jeff Skinner .30 .75
79 Jeff Carter .20 .50
80 John Tavares .40 1.00
81 Artemi Panarin .50 1.25
82 Duncan Keith .20 .50
83 James van Riemsdyk .20 .50
84 Craig Anderson .20 .50
85 Nathan MacKinnon 1.00 2.50
86 Ryan Ellis .20 .50
87 Sidney Crosby 1.00 2.50
88 James Neal .15 .40
89 Brad Marchand .50 1.25
90 Marc-Andre Fleury .50 1.25
91 Zach Hyman .40 1.00
92 Mats Zuccarello .25 .60
93 Cam Talbot .25 .60
94 Anders Lee .20 .50
95 Dominik Hasek .40 1.00
96 Guy Lafleur .30 .75
97 Jarome Iginla .30 .75
98 Marcel Dionne .30 .75
99 Wayne Gretzky 1.50 4.00
100 Mark Messier .50 1.25
101 William Karlsson AM .30 .75
102 Brock Boeser AM .30 .75
103 Connor McDavid AM 1.25 3.00
104 Patrick Kane AM .50 1.25
105 Jack Eichel AM .40 1.00
106 Roberto Luongo AM .40 1.00
107 Vegas Golden Knights AM .25 .60
108 Alexander Ovechkin AM 1.00 2.50
109 Rasmus Dahlin AM .60 1.50
110 Andrei Svechnikov AM .60 1.50
111 Morgan Rielly AM .25 .60
112 Nathan MacKinnon AM 1.00 2.50
113 Marc-Andre Fleury AM .50 1.25
114 Carey Price AM .50 1.25
115 Eric Staal AM .25 .60
116 Patrik Laine AM .30 .75
117 M.Messier/C.McDavid FI 20.00 50.00
118 C.Atkinson/A.Panarin FI 8.00 20.00
119 J.Iginla/J.Gaudreau FI 6.00 15.00
120 B.Orr/Z.Chara FI 15.00 40.00
121 R.Getzlaf/R.Rakell FI 4.00 10.00
122 P.Rinne/V.Arvidsson FI 4.00 10.00
123 K.Muller/N.Hischier FI 6.00 15.00
124 B.Clarke/N.Patrick FI 6.00 15.00
125 S.Crosby/E.Malkin FI 15.00 40.00
126 J.Thornton/T.Hertl FI 6.00 15.00
127 B.Wheeler/M.Scheifele FI 6.00 15.00
128 H.Lundqvist/M.Zibanejad FI 10.00 25.00
129 M.Koivu/J.Greenway FI 4.00 10.00
130 W.Gretzky/A.Kopitar FI 25.00 60.00
131 B.Hull/V.Tarasenko FI 8.00 20.00
132 S.Stamkos/N.Kucherov FI 8.00 20.00
133 P.Bure/B.Boeser FI 5.00 12.00
134 M.Bossy/M.Barzal FI 5.00 12.00
135 D.Sittler/A.Matthews FI 15.00 40.00
136 M.Stone/B.Tkachuk FI 5.00 12.00
137 P.Roy/C.Price FI 10.00 25.00
138 R.Luongo/A.Barkov FI 6.00 15.00
139 M.Modano/T.Seguin FI 8.00 20.00
140 A.Ovechkin/R.Langway FI 15.00 40.00
141 M.Fleury/A.Tuch FI 8.00 20.00
142 P.Forsberg/N.MacKinnon FI 15.00 40.00
143 R.Brind'Amour/A.Svechnikov FI 10.00 25.00
144 O.Ekman-Larsson/C.Keller FI 5.00 12.00
145 J.Toews/P.Kane FI 8.00 20.00
146 S.Yzerman/D.Larkin FI 10.00 25.00
147 D.Andreychuk/R.Dahlin FI 10.00 25.00
148 Casey Mittelstadt FW AU/949* RC 20.00 50.00
149 Anthony Cirelli FW AU/949* RC 25.00 60.00
150 Ryan Donato FW RC 8.00 20.00
151 Zach Aston-Reese FW AU/949* RC 12.00 30.00
152 Maxim Mamin FW RC 5.00 12.00
153 Noah Juulsen FW AU/949* RC 8.00 20.00
154 Blake Hillman FW AU/949* RC 8.00 20.00
155 Jordan Greenway FW AU/949* RC 8.00 20.00
156 Landon Bow FW AU/949* RC 6.00 15.00
157 Dominic Turgeon FW AU/949* RC 8.00 20.00
158 Samuel Montembeault FW AU/949* RC 15.00 40.00
159 Troy Terry FW AU/949* RC 20.00 50.00
160 Andreas Johnsson FW RC 6.00 15.00
161 Warren Foegele FW AU/949* RC 8.00 20.00
162 Morgan Klimchuk FW AU/949* RC 8.00 20.00
163 Zach Whitecloud FW AU/949* RC 6.00 15.00
164 Michael Dal Colle FW AU/949* RC 8.00 20.00
165 Eeli Tolvanen FW AU/949* RC 15.00 40.00
166 Ethan Bear FW AU/949* RC 12.00 30.00
167 Victor Ejdsell FW AU/949* RC 6.00 15.00
168 Spencer Foo FW AU/949* RC 6.00 15.00
169 Tomas Hyka FW AU/949* RC 8.00 20.00
170 Lias Andersson FW RC 8.00 20.00
171 Oskar Lindblom FW AU/949* RC 12.00 30.00
172 Dylan Gambrell FW AU/949* RC 8.00 20.00
173 Nicolas Roy FW AU/949* RC 5.00 12.00
174 Travis Dermott FW AU/949* RC 12.00 30.00
175 Henrik Borgstrom FW RC 8.00 20.00
176A Mackenzie Blackwood FW RC 10.00 25.00
177 Dylan Sikura FW AU/949* RC 10.00 25.00
178 Sami Niku FW AU/949* RC 6.00 15.00
179 Louie Belpedio FW AU/949* RC 6.00 15.00
180 Adam Gaudette FW AU/949* RC 12.00 30.00
181 Christian Wolanin FW RC 4.00 10.00
182 Marcus Pettersson FW AU/949* RC 8.00 20.00
183 Neal Pionk FW AU/949* RC 8.00 20.00
184 Mitch Reinke FW AU/949* RC 6.00 15.00
185 Carl Dahlstrom FW RC 4.00 10.00
186 John Gilmour FW AU/949* RC 5.00 12.00
187 Andrei Svechnikov FW AU/949* RC 125.00 300.00
188 Robert Thomas FW AU/949* RC 15.00 40.00
189 Elias Pettersson FW AU/949* RC 200.00 500.00
190 Jesperi Kotkaniemi FW AU/949* RC 15.00 40.00
191 Miro Heiskanen FW AU/949* RC 30.00 80.00
192 Kristian Vesalainen FW AU/949* RC 10.00 25.00
193 Henri Jokiharju FW AU/949* RC 6.00 15.00
194 Dillon Dube FW AU/949* RC 10.00 25.00
195 Maxime Lajoie FW AU/949* RC 12.00 30.00
196 Michael Rasmussen FW AU/949* RC 10.00 25.00
197 Isac Lundestrom FW AU/949* RC 6.00 15.00
198 Juuso Valimaki FW AU/949* RC 8.00 20.00
199 Evan Bouchard FW AU/949* RC 30.00 80.00
200 Brady Tkachuk FW AU/949* RC 80.00 200.00
201 Maxime Comtois FW RC 5.00 12.00
202 Brett Howden FW AU/949* RC 10.00 25.00
203 Antti Suomela FW AU/949* RC 6.00 15.00
204 Daniel Brickley FW AU/949* RC 8.00 20.00
205 Filip Hronek FW AU/949* RC 8.00 20.00
206 Jaret Anderson-Dolan FW AU/949* RC 6.00 15.00
207 Roope Hintz FW AU/949* RC 60.00 150.00
208 Jordan Kyrou FW AU/949* RC 60.00 150.00
209A Mathieu Joseph FW RC 6.00 15.00
210A Sam Steel FW RC 5.00 12.00
211A Jake Bean FW RC 5.00 12.00
212 Jeremy Lauzon FW AU/949* RC 10.00 25.00
213 Dennis Cholowski FW AU/949* RC 8.00 20.00
214 Dan Vladar FW AU/949* RC 10.00 25.00
215 Joey Anderson FW AU/949* RC 8.00 20.00
216 Cooper Marody FW AU/949* RC 8.00 20.00
217 Jakub Zboril FW AU/949* RC 12.00 30.00
218 Drake Batherson FW AU/949* RC 40.00 100.00
219 Michael McLeod FW RC 4.00 10.00
220 Ilya Samsonov FW RC 10.00 25.00
221 Austin Wagner FW AU/949* RC 6.00 15.00
222 Christoffer Ehn FW AU/949* RC 6.00 15.00
223 Jonas Siegenthaler FW AU/949* RC 8.00 20.00
224 Kiefer Sherwood FW AU/949* RC 6.00 15.00
225 Cal Petersen FW AU/949* RC 6.00 15.00
226 Brett Seney FW AU/949* RC 6.00 15.00
227 Carter Hart FW AU/949* RC 80.00 200.00
228 Joe Hicketts FW AU/949* RC 8.00 20.00
229 Par Lindholm FW AU/949* RC 8.00 20.00
230 Rasmus Dahlin FW RC 12.00 30.00
231 Dominik Kahun FW AU/949* RC 10.00 25.00
232 Conor Garland FW AU/949* RC 8.00 20.00
233 Jayce Hawryluk FW AU/949* RC 6.00 15.00
234 Mikhail Vorobyev FW AU/949* RC 6.00 15.00
235 Urho Vaakanainen FW AU/949* RC 15.00 40.00
236 Devon Toews FW RC 15.00 40.00
237 Mason Appleton FW RC 4.00 10.00
238 Lawrence Pilut FW RC 4.00 10.00

2018-19 SP Authentic '08-09 Retro Rookie Patch Autographs

RAS Andrei Svechnikov 125.00 300.00
RBH Brett Howden 60.00 150.00
RBT Brady Tkachuk 150.00 250.00
RCH Carter Hart 200.00 500.00
RCM Casey Mittelstadt 40.00 100.00
RDB Drake Batherson 60.00 150.00
RDS Dylan Sikura 60.00 150.00
REB Evan Bouchard 80.00 200.00
REP Elias Pettersson 400.00 1000.00
RET Eeli Tolvanen 150.00 250.00
RHJ Henri Jokiharju 30.00 80.00
RJG Jordan Greenway 60.00 150.00
RJK Jesperi Kotkaniemi 30.00 80.00
RKV Kristian Vesalainen 150.00 250.00
RMH Miro Heiskanen 200.00 300.00
RML Maxime Lajoie 30.00 80.00
RMR Michael Rasmussen 100.00 200.00
RRT Robert Thomas 150.00 250.00

2018-19 SP Authentic '99-00 Retro Draft Picks

RDPAM Anthony Mantha .60 1.50
RDPBT Brady Tkachuk 2.50 6.00
RDPEP Elias Pettersson 2.50 6.00
RDPJT Jonathan Toews 1.25 3.00
RDPMM Mitch Marner 1.25 3.00
RDPPM Patrick Marleau .75 2.00
RDPSC Sidney Crosby 3.00 8.00
RDPSM Sean Monahan .50 1.25
RDPVA Viktor Arvidsson .50 1.25
RDPVT Vladimir Tarasenko 1.00 2.50

2018-19 SP Authentic Future Watch Acetate

189 Elias Pettersson 250.00 400.00
230 Rasmus Dahlin 60.00 150.00

2018-19 SP Authentic Future Watch Inscriptions

*SINGLES: .75X TO 2X BASIC INSERTS
159 Troy Terry/50* 50.00 125.00
189 Elias Pettersson/50* 300.00 400.00
190 Jesperi Kotkaniemi/50* 30.00 80.00
191 Miro Heiskanen/50* 100.00 200.00
208 Jordan Kyrou/50* 125.00 300.00
227 Carter Hart/50* 150.00 400.00

2018-19 SP Authentic Limited Autographs

1 Alexander Ovechkin A 60.00 150.00
2 William Karlsson C 20.00 50.00
5 Jonathan Toews A 25.00 60.00
9 Kevin Shattenkirk E 10.00 25.00
14 Eric Staal D 15.00 40.00
17 Vincent Trocheck E 15.00 40.00
20 Connor McDavid A 250.00 350.00
21 Sean Monahan D 10.00 25.00
23 Sergei Bobrovsky D 25.00 60.00
25 Jack Eichel B 25.00 60.00
26 Patric Hornqvist D 10.00 25.00
28 Connor Hellebuyck D 30.00 80.00
29 Mikko Rantanen D 40.00 100.00
32 Evgeny Kuznetsov C 20.00 50.00
41 Aaron Ekblad D 20.00 50.00
45 Anze Kopitar B 25.00 60.00
46 Jake Guentzel D 25.00 60.00
48 Will Butcher E 12.00 30.00
50 Henrik Lundqvist B 40.00 100.00
52 Jonathan Marchessault D 20.00 50.00
53 Brayden Schenn D 15.00 40.00
62 Vladimir Tarasenko B 20.00 50.00
64 Jake Gardiner E 10.00 25.00
67 Andrei Vasilevskiy C 25.00 60.00
72 Alex DeBrincat E 20.00 50.00
73 Nico Hischier B 25.00 60.00
80 John Tavares A 25.00 60.00
84 Craig Anderson E 12.00 30.00
86 Ryan Ellis E 12.00 30.00
90 Marc-Andre Fleury B 30.00 80.00
91 Zach Hyman E 25.00 60.00
94 Anders Lee E 12.00 30.00
95 Dominik Hasek A 25.00 60.00
98 Marcel Dionne B 20.00 50.00
99 Wayne Gretzky A 250.00 600.00
100 Mark Messier A 30.00 80.00
101 William Karlsson AM C 20.00 50.00
105 Jack Eichel AM B 25.00 60.00
108 Alexander Ovechkin AM A 60.00 150.00
110 Andrei Svechnikov AM C 40.00 100.00
113 Marc-Andre Fleury AM B 30.00 80.00

2018-19 SP Authentic Limited Patch Autographs

*PATCH/25-100: .6X TO 1.5X BASIC INSERTS
25 Jack Eichel/25 150.00 300.00
159 Troy Terry FW/100 80.00 200.00
189 Elias Pettersson FW/100 600.00 700.00
190 Jesperi Kotkaniemi FW/100 50.00 125.00
218 Drake Batherson FW/100 125.00 300.00
227 Carter Hart FW/100 200.00 500.00

2018-19 SP Authentic Marks of Distinction

MDAM Auston Matthews 100.00 250.00
MDBB Brock Boeser 30.00 80.00
MDBM Brad Marchand 50.00 125.00
MDBO Bobby Orr 80.00 200.00
MDCA Casey Mittelstadt 15.00 40.00
MDCH Connor Hellebuyck 50.00 125.00
MDCM Connor McDavid 200.00 500.00
MDDH Dominik Hasek 80.00 200.00
MDDP Denis Potvin 20.00 50.00
MDDS Daniel Sedin 30.00 80.00
MDEK Evgeny Kuznetsov 30.00 80.00
MDEM Evgeni Malkin 50.00 125.00
MDEP Elias Pettersson 80.00 200.00
MDES Eric Staal 25.00 60.00
MDFP Felix Potvin 40.00 100.00
MDGL Guy Lafleur 30.00 80.00
MDHA Carter Hart 120.00 300.00
MDHL Henrik Lundqvist 60.00 150.00
MDHS Henrik Sedin 30.00 80.00
MDJT John Tavares 40.00 100.00
MDLD Leon Draisaitl 80.00 200.00
MDMB Martin Brodeur 60.00 150.00
MDMF Marc-Andre Fleury 50.00 125.00
MDPK Patrick Kane 50.00 125.00
MDRL Roberto Luongo 40.00 100.00
MDSB Scotty Bowman 25.00 60.00
MDSI Darryl Sittler 30.00 80.00
MDWO Willie O'Ree 40.00 100.00

2018-19 SP Authentic Rookie Year Milestones

RYMAD Alex DeBrincat .50 1.25
RYMAK Anze Kopitar .60 1.50
RYMBB Bill Barber .40 1.00
RYMBO Bobby Orr 1.50 4.00
RYMCK Clayton Keller .50 1.25
RYMGL Guy Lafleur .50 1.25
RYMHL Henrik Lundqvist 1.00 2.50
RYMIK Ilya Kovalchuk .30 .75
RYMJE Jack Eichel .60 1.50
RYMJK John Klingberg .40 1.00
RYMJS Joe Sakic .75 2.00
RYMMB Mathew Barzal .50 1.25
RYMMF Marc-Andre Fleury .75 2.00
RYMMG Mike Gartner .50 1.25
RYMMM Mark Messier .75 2.00
RYMMO Mike Modano .75 2.00
RYMMT Matthew Tkachuk .75 2.00
RYMNH Nico Hischier .60 1.50
RYMSC Sidney Crosby 1.50 4.00
RYMSS Steven Stamkos .75 2.00
RYMWG Wayne Gretzky 2.50 6.00

2018-19 SP Authentic Rookie Year Milestones Autographs

RYMAD Alex DeBrincat/52 20.00 50.00
RYMAK Anze Kopitar/41 25.00 60.00
RYMBB Bill Barber/64 15.00 40.00
RYMBO Bobby Orr/28 60.00 150.00
RYMHL Henrik Lundqvist/30 40.00 100.00
RYMJE Jack Eichel/24 40.00 100.00

2018-19 SP Authentic Sign of the Times 60's

ST60BB Bob Baun 8.00 20.00
ST60NU Norm Ullman 8.00 20.00

2018-19 SP Authentic Sign of the Times 80's

ST80DH Dale Hawerchuk C 20.00 50.00
ST80CF Grant Fuhr C 25.00 60.00
ST80JK Jari Kurri C 15.00 40.00
ST80LM Lanny McDonald B 15.00 40.00
ST80MB Mike Bossy B 15.00 40.00
ST80ML Mario Lemieux A 100.00 200.00
ST80MM Mark Messier A 100.00 200.00
ST80PC Paul Coffey B 15.00 40.00
ST80RH Ron Hextall C 15.00 40.00
ST80WG Wayne Gretzky B 200.00 500.00

2018-19 SP Authentic Sign of the Times 90's

ST90BH Brett Hull A 100.00 200.00
ST90CC Chris Chelios B 15.00 40.00
ST90DH Dominik Hasek A 100.00 200.00
ST90JV John Vanbiesbrouck C 15.00 40.00
ST90MM Mike Modano C 30.00 80.00
ST90PT Pierre Turgeon C 12.00 30.00
ST90RA Rod Brind'Amour C 15.00 40.00
ST90TA Tony Amonte C 12.00 30.00
ST90TB Tom Barrasso C 15.00 40.00

2018-19 SP Authentic Sign of the Times Duals

ST2BP M.Bossy/D.Potvin 15.00 40.00
ST2GH J.Guentzel/P.Hornqvist 25.00 60.00
ST2GM W.Gretzky/C.McDavid 200.00 500.00
ST2KM M.Fleury/J.Marchessault 30.00 80.00
ST2TS V.Tarasenko/B.Schenn 20.00 50.00

2018-19 SP Authentic Sign of the Times Rookies

SOTRAC Anthony Cirelli 15.00 40.00
SOTRAG Adam Gaudette 15.00 40.00
SOTRAS Andrei Svechnikov 25.00 60.00
SOTRBH Brett Howden 12.00 30.00
SOTRBO Evan Bouchard 25.00 60.00
SOTRBT Brady Tkachuk 30.00 80.00
SOTRCH Carter Hart 80.00 200.00
SOTRCM Casey Mittelstadt 20.00 50.00
SOTRDB Drake Batherson 20.00 50.00
SOTRDC Dennis Cholowski 10.00 25.00
SOTRDS Dylan Sikura 12.00 30.00
SOTREB Ethan Bear 15.00 40.00
SOTREP Elias Pettersson 100.00 200.00
SOTRET Eeli Tolvanen 20.00 50.00
SOTRHJ Henri Jokiharju 8.00 20.00
SOTRIL Isac Lundestrom 8.00 20.00
SOTRJG Jordan Greenway 10.00 25.00
SOTRJK Jesperi Kotkaniemi 20.00 50.00
SOTRJV Juuso Valimaki 10.00 25.00
SOTRKV Kristian Vesalainen 12.00 30.00
SOTRMC Michael Dal Colle 10.00 25.00
SOTRMH Miro Heiskanen 25.00 60.00
SOTRML Maxime Lajoie 15.00 40.00
SOTRMR Michael Rasmussen 12.00 30.00
SOTRNJ Noah Juulsen 10.00 25.00
SOTRRT Robert Thomas 20.00 50.00
SOTRSN Sami Niku 8.00 20.00
SOTRTD Travis Dermott 15.00 40.00
SOTRTT Troy Terry 15.00 40.00
SOTRWF Warren Foegele 10.00 25.00
SOTRZR Zach Aston-Reese 15.00 40.00

2018-19 SP Authentic Spectrum FX

S1 Alexander Ovechkin 4.00 10.00
S2 Brock Boeser 1.25 3.00
S3 Mikko Rantanen 2.50 6.00
S4 Taylor Hall 1.00 2.50
S5 Connor McDavid 5.00 12.00
S6 Nikita Kucherov 2.00 5.00
S7 Mitch Marner 1.50 4.00
S8 John Gibson 1.00 2.50
S9 Jack Eichel 1.50 4.00
S10 Jonathan Toews 1.50 4.00
S11 Henrik Lundqvist 2.50 6.00
S12 Evgeni Malkin 2.00 5.00
S13 Jamie Benn 1.00 2.50
S14 Nolan Patrick 1.00 2.50
S15 Steven Stamkos 2.00 5.00
S16 Dylan Larkin 1.25 3.00
S17 Max Domi 1.00 2.50
S18 Anze Kopitar 1.50 4.00
S19 Jake Guentzel 1.50 4.00
S20 Auston Matthews 4.00 10.00
S21 Andrei Vasilevskiy 1.50 4.00
S22 Mathew Barzal 1.25 3.00
S23 Johnny Gaudreau 1.50 4.00
S24 Vladimir Tarasenko 1.25 3.00
S25 Carey Price 2.00 5.00
S26 Erik Karlsson 1.25 3.00
S27 Patrick Kane 2.00 5.00
S28 Pekka Rinne 1.00 2.50
S29 Evgeny Kuznetsov 1.25 3.00
S30 Sidney Crosby 4.00 10.00
S31 John Tavares 1.50 4.00
S32 Nathan MacKinnon 4.00 10.00
S33 Blake Wheeler 1.00 2.50
S34 Marc-Andre Fleury 2.00 5.00
S35 Dominik Hasek 1.50 4.00
S36 Guy Lafleur 1.25 3.00
S37 Jarome Iginla 1.25 3.00
S38 Marcel Dionne 1.25 3.00
S39 Wayne Gretzky 6.00 15.00
S40 Mark Messier 2.00 5.00
S41 Christian Wolanin FW 1.50 4.00
S42 Isac Lundestrom FW 1.50 4.00
S43 Cal Petersen FW 1.50 4.00
S44 Noah Juulsen FW 2.00 5.00
S45 Dillon Dube FW 2.50 6.00
S46 Jeremy Lauzon FW 2.50 6.00
S47 Juuso Valimaki FW 2.00 5.00
S48 Jake Bean FW 2.00 5.00
S49 Dominik Kahun FW 2.00 5.00
S50 Adam Gaudette FW 3.00 8.00
S51 Sheldon Dries FW 1.50 4.00
S52 Alex Broadhurst FW 1.50 4.00
S53 Mackenzie Blackwood FW 4.00 10.00
S54 Filip Hronek FW 2.00 5.00
S55 Mathieu Joseph FW 2.50 6.00
S56 Cooper Marody FW 2.00 5.00
S57 Austin Wagner FW 1.50 4.00
S58 Michael McLeod FW 1.50 4.00
S59 Conor Garland FW 2.00 5.00
S60 Michael Dal Colle FW 2.00 5.00
S61 John Gilmour FW 1.25 3.00
S62 Warren Foegele FW 2.00 5.00
S63 Maxime Lajoie FW 3.00 8.00
S64 Oskar Lindblom FW 3.00 8.00
S65 Zach Aston-Reese FW 3.00 8.00
S66 Antti Suomela FW 1.50 4.00
S67 Neal Pionk FW 2.00 5.00
S68 Matt Luff FW 1.50 4.00
S69 Ethan Bear FW 3.00 8.00
S70 Zach Whitecloud FW 1.50 4.00
S71 Sam Steel FW 2.50 6.00
S72 Dylan Sikura FW 3.00 8.00
S73 Lias Andersson FW 4.00 10.00
S74 Troy Terry FW 4.00 10.00
S75 Ryan Donato FW 4.00 10.00
S76 Michael Rasmussen FW 3.00 8.00
S77 Evan Bouchard FW 6.00 15.00
S78 Robert Thomas FW 5.00 12.00
S79 Jordan Greenway FW 2.50 6.00
S80 Andreas Johnsson FW 3.00 8.00
S81 Dennis Cholowski FW 2.50 6.00
S82 Henri Jokiharju FW 2.00 5.00
S83 Brett Howden FW 3.00 8.00
S84 Jordan Kyrou FW 5.00 12.00
S85 Drake Batherson FW 5.00 12.00
S86 Anthony Cirelli FW 4.00 10.00
S87 Travis Dermott FW 4.00 10.00
S88 Maxime Comtois FW 2.50 6.00
S89 Kristian Vesalainen FW 3.00 8.00
S90 Ilya Samsonov FW 5.00 12.00
S91 Casey Mittelstadt FW 6.00 15.00
S92 Carter Hart FW 6.00 15.00
S93 Andrei Svechnikov FW 8.00 20.00
S94 Miro Heiskanen FW 8.00 20.00
S95 Jesperi Kotkaniemi FW 6.00 15.00
S96 Eeli Tolvanen FW 6.00 15.00
S97 Brady Tkachuk FW 10.00 25.00
S98 Henrik Borgstrom FW 5.00 12.00
S99 Rasmus Dahlin FW 8.00 20.00
S100 Elias Pettersson FW 10.00 25.00

2019-20 SP Authentic

1 Jonathan Marchessault .50 1.25
2 Oliver Bjorkstrand .30 .75
3 Dougie Hamilton .30 .75
4 Logan Couture .50 1.25
5 Morgan Rielly .40 1.00
6 Dylan Strome .50 1.25
7 Sean Monahan .25 .60
8 Tyler Bertuzzi .30 .75

9 Ben Bishop .30 .75
10 Carey Price .75 2.00
11 Tomas Hertl .40 1.00
12 John Gibson .40 1.00
13 William Karlsson .50 1.25
14 Duncan Keith .30 .75
15 Sergei Bobrovsky .60 1.50
16 Marc-Andre Fleury .75 2.00
17 Jonathan Quick .50 1.25
18 Evgeni Malkin .75 2.00
19 Connor McDavid 2.00 5.00
20 Anthony Mantha .30 .75
21 Brayden Point .50 1.25
22 Matt Murray .40 1.00
23 Jake Guentzel .60 1.50
24 Alex DeBrincat .50 1.25
25 Brayden Schenn .40 1.00
26 Torey Krug .30 .75
27 Eric Staal .40 1.00
28 Nico Hischier .60 1.50
29 Jakub Vrana .40 1.00
30 Brad Marchand .75 2.00
31 Aleksander Barkov .60 1.50
32 Kyle Turris .30 .75
33 Henrik Lundqvist 1.00 2.50
34 Anders Lee .30 .75
35 Dylan Larkin .50 1.25
36 Pierre-Luc Dubois .30 .75
37 Leon Draisaitl 1.25 3.00
38 Joe Pavelski .50 1.25
39 Tom Wilson .40 1.00
40 Jonathan Toews .60 1.50
41 Bo Horvat .50 1.25
42 Jake DeBrusk .40 1.00
43 Brady Tkachuk .60 1.50
44 Joe Thornton .60 1.50
45 Brock Boeser .50 1.25
46 Viktor Arvidsson .25 .60
47 Ryan O'Reilly .40 1.00
48 Matt Dumba .25 .60
49 Drew Doughty .50 1.25
50 Teuvo Teravainen .40 1.00
51 Sidney Crosby 1.50 4.00
52 Steven Stamkos .75 2.00
53 Cam Atkinson .40 1.00
54 Claude Giroux .40 1.00
55 Thomas Chabot .40 1.00
56 Patrick Kane .75 2.00
57 Tuukka Rask .50 1.25
58 John Klingberg .40 1.00
59 Miro Heiskanen .50 1.25
60 Zach Werenski .60 1.50
61 Vincent Trocheck .40 1.00
62 Jack Eichel .60 1.50
63 Brent Burns .40 1.00
64 Jesperi Kotkaniemi .40 1.00
65 Mark Stone .50 1.25
66 Mark Scheifele .60 1.50
67 Seth Jones .40 1.00
68 Connor Hellebuyck .75 2.00
69 Alex Tuch .40 1.00
70 Auston Matthews 1.50 4.00
71 John Tavares .60 1.50
72 Artemi Panarin .75 2.00
73 Jonathan Drouin .30 .75
74 Matthew Tkachuk .75 2.00
75 Andrei Vasilevskiy .60 1.50
76 Sebastian Aho .60 1.50
77 Jeff Skinner .40 1.00
78 Mikael Granlund .30 .75
79 Elias Pettersson .60 1.50
80 Jaccob Slavin .30 .75
81 Erik Karlsson .50 1.25
82 Vladimir Tarasenko .50 1.25
83 Oscar Klefbom .40 1.00
84 Roman Josi .40 1.00
85 Mitch Marner .60 1.50
86 Taylor Hall .40 1.00
87 Jacob Trouba .30 .75
88 Phil Kessel .40 1.00
89 Clayton Keller .50 1.25
90 P.K. Subban .50 1.25
91 Philipp Grubauer .40 1.00
92 Mikko Rantanen 1.00 2.50
93 Mathew Barzal .50 1.25
94 Carter Hart .40 1.00
95 Blake Wheeler .40 1.00
96 Andrei Svechnikov .50 1.25
97 Nathan MacKinnon 1.50 4.00
98 Rasmus Dahlin .50 1.25
99 Rickard Rakell .30 .75
100 Alex Ovechkin 1.50 4.00
101 Tuukka Rask AM .50 1.25
102 Sidney Crosby AM 1.50 4.00
103 Alex Ovechkin AM 1.50 4.00
104 Carey Price AM .75 2.00
105 Steven Stamkos AM .75 2.00
106 Nikita Kucherov AM .75 2.00
107 Ryan Poehling AM .60 1.50
108 Columbus Blue Jackets AM 1.00 2.50
109 Jordan Binnington AM .60 1.50
110 Alex Pietrangelo AM .30 .75
111 Jack Hughes AM 2.00 5.00
112 John Tavares AM .60 1.50
113 Cody Glass AM .60 1.50
114 Zdeno Chara AM .40 1.00
115 Connor McDavid AM 2.00 5.00
116 Henrik Lundqvist AM 1.00 2.50
117 J.Gibson/H.Lindholm FI 8.00 20.00
118 N.Schmaltz/C.Keller FI 8.00 20.00
119 D.Pastrnak/C.McAvoy FI 15.00 40.00
120 J.Eichel/R.Dahlin FI 15.00 40.00
121 M.Tkachuk/J.Gaudreau FI 12.00 30.00
122 A.Svechnikov/S.Aho FI 10.00 25.00
123 D.Strome/A.DeBrincat FI 12.00 30.00
124 N.MacKinnon/C.Makar FI 30.00 80.00
125 P.Dubois/Z.Werenski FI 12.00 30.00
126 M.Heiskanen/R.Hintz FI 12.00 30.00
127 D.Larkin/F.Zadina FI 15.00 40.00
128 C.McDavid/L.Draisaitl FI 30.00 80.00
129 A.Barkov/A.Ekblad FI 15.00 40.00
130 B.Lizotte/T.Bjornfot FI 15.00 40.00
131 M.Dumba/L.Kunin FI 12.00 30.00
132 N.Suzuki/R.Poehling FI 25.00 60.00
133 F.Forsberg/D.Fabbro FI 12.00 30.00
134 J.Hughes/N.Hischier FI 30.00 80.00
135 N.Dobson/O.Wahlstrom FI 8.00 20.00
136 K.Kakko/A.Fox FI 15.00 40.00
137 B.Tkachuk/T.Chabot FI 12.00 30.00
138 T.Konecny/I.Provorov FI 15.00 40.00
139 J.Guentzel/M.Murray FI 15.00 40.00
140 T.Meier/K.Labanc FI 12.00 30.00
141 S.Blais/V.Dunn FI 15.00 40.00
142 B.Point/M.Sergachev FI 15.00 40.00
143 A.Matthews/M.Marner FI 25.00 60.00
144 E.Pettersson/Q.Hughes FI 30.00 80.00
145 C.Glass/N.Hague FI 15.00 40.00
146 J.Vrana/I.Samsonov FI 15.00 30.00
147 P.Laine/V.Heinola FI 12.00 30.00
148 Jack Hughes FW AU/949* RC 250.00 600.00
149 Cale Makar FW AU/949* RC 600.00 1500.00
150 Kaden Fulcher FW AU/949* RC 8.00 20.00
151 Guillaume Brisebois FW AU/949* RC 8.00 20.00
152 Taro Hirose FW AU/949* RC 12.00 30.00
153 Riley Stillman FW AU/949* RC 8.00 20.00
154 Blake Lizotte FW AU/949* RC 8.00 20.00
155 Ryan Kuffner FW AU/949* RC 6.00 15.00
156 Max Veronneau FW AU/949* RC 6.00 15.00
157 Mackenzie MacEachern FW AU/949* RC 8.00 20.00
158 Joey Daccord FW AU/949* RC 15.00 40.00
159 Filip Zadina FW AU/949* RC 40.00 100.00
160 Carl Grundstrom FW AU/949* RC 8.00 20.00
161 Ryan Poehling FW AU/949* RC 12.00 30.00
162 Philippe Myers FW AU/949* RC 6.00 15.00
163 Quinn Hughes FW AU/949* RC 150.00 400.00
164 Brandon Gignac FW AU/949* RC 6.00 15.00
165 Nathan Bastian FW AU/949* RC 8.00 20.00
166 Nico Sturm FW AU/949* RC 6.00 15.00
167 Brady Keeper FW AU/949* RC 8.00 20.00
168 Zach Senyshyn FW AU/949* RC 8.00 20.00
169 Karson Kuhlman FW AU/949* RC 8.00 20.00
170 Zack MacEwen FW AU/949* RC 6.00 15.00
171 Ryan Lindgren FW AU/949* RC 8.00 20.00
172 Teddy Blueger FW AU/949* RC 12.00 30.00
173 Aleksi Saarela FW RC 8.00 20.00
174 Rem Pitlick FW AU/949* RC 8.00 20.00
175 Jimmy Schuldt FW AU/949* RC 6.00 15.00
176 Libor Hajek FW AU/949* RC 6.00 15.00
177 Kole Sherwood FW AU/949* RC 8.00 20.00
178 Joel L'Esperance FW AU/949* RC 8.00 20.00
179 Dante Fabbro FW AU/949* RC 8.00 20.00
180 Vitaly Abramov FW AU/949* RC 8.00 20.00
181 Victor Olofsson FW AU/949* RC 15.00 40.00
182 Alexandre Texier FW AU/949* RC 8.00 20.00
183 Trent Frederic FW AU/949* RC 8.00 20.00
184 Erik Brannstrom FW AU/949* RC 8.00 20.00
185 Max Jones FW AU/949* RC 8.00 20.00
186 Rudolfs Balcers FW AU/949* RC 8.00 20.00
187 Oliver Wahlstrom FW AU/949* RC 50.00 125.00
188 Tobias Bjornfot FW AU/949* RC 8.00 20.00
189 Ville Heinola FW AU/949* RC 10.00 25.00
190 Jesper Boqvist FW AU/949* RC 6.00 15.00
191 Elvis Merzlikins FW AU/949* RC 40.00 100.00
192 Nick Suzuki FW AU/949* RC 200.00 500.00
193 Noah Dobson FW AU/949* RC 10.00 25.00
194 Adam Fox FW AU/949* RC 150.00 400.00
195 Barrett Hayton FW AU/949* RC 15.00 40.00
196 Cody Glass FW AU/949* RC 12.00 30.00
197 Kaapo Kakko FW RC 12.00 30.00
198 Connor Clifton FW AU/949* RC 8.00 20.00
199 Kirby Dach FW AU/949* RC 50.00 125.00
200 Rasmus Sandin FW AU/949* RC 50.00 125.00
201 Cale Fleury FW RC 10.00 25.00
202 Martin Fehervary FW AU/949* RC 6.00 15.00
203 Danil Yurtaykin FW RC 6.00 15.00
204 Carter Verhaeghe FW RC 12.00 30.00
205 Dominik Kubalik FW AU/949* RC 30.00 80.00
206 Joakim Nygard FW RC 6.00 15.00
207 Matt Roy FW AU/949* RC 8.00 20.00
208 Lean Bergmann FW AU/949* RC 6.00 15.00
209 Kevin Stenlund FW RC 6.00 15.00
210 Mario Ferraro FW RC 6.00 15.00
211 Nicolas Hague FW AU/949* RC 8.00 20.00
212 Emil Bemstrom FW AU/949* RC 8.00 20.00
213 Ilya Mikheyev FW AU/949* RC 12.00 30.00
214 Nikita Gusev FW AU/949* RC 12.00 30.00
215 Julien Gauthier FW AU/949* RC 8.00 20.00
216 Joel Farabee FW AU/949* RC 80.00 200.00
217 Trevor Moore FW AU/949* RC 6.00 15.00
218 Sam Lafferty FW RC 6.00 15.00
219 Adam Boqvist FW AU/949* RC 8.00 20.00
220 German Rubtsov FW AU/949* RC 6.00 15.00
221 Alexander Volkov FW AU/949* RC 6.00 15.00
222 Conor Timmins FW RC 8.00 20.00
223 David Gustafsson FW RC 6.00 15.00
224 Givani Smith FW AU/949* RC 6.00 15.00
225 Joel Persson FW RC 6.00 15.00
226 Scott Sabourin FW RC 6.00 15.00
227 Yakov Trenin FW RC 6.00 15.00
228 Cameron Hughes FW RC 6.00 15.00
229 Gerald Mayhew FW RC 6.00 15.00
230 Jakob Lilja FW RC 6.00 15.00
231 C.J. Suess FW RC 6.00 15.00
232 Eetu Luostarinen FW AU/949* RC 8.00 20.00
233 J.C. Beaudin FW RC 8.00 20.00
234 Cole Bardreau FW RC 6.00 15.00
235 Joona Luoto FW RC 6.00 15.00
236 Nick Caamano FW RC 6.00 15.00
237 Jonathan Davidsson FW AU/949* RC 5.00 12.00
238 Rhett Gardner FW RC 6.00 15.00
239 Noah Gregor FW AU/949* RC 6.00 15.00
240 Nikolai Prokhorkin FW RC 6.00 15.00
241 John Marino FW AU/949* RC 30.00 80.00
242 Morgan Frost FW AU/949* RC 20.00 50.00
243 Dmytro Timashov FW RC 8.00 20.00
244 Cayden Primeau FW AU/949* RC 80.00 200.00
245 Jack Studnicka FW RC 8.00 20.00
246 Klim Kostin FW AU/949* RC 8.00 20.00
247 Otto Koivula FW RC 5.00 12.00
248 Jake Walman FW AU/949* RC 10.00 25.00
249 Rasmus Asplund FW AU/949* RC 6.00 15.00
250 Joachim Blichfeld FW AU/949* RC 8.00 20.00
251 Igor Shesterkin FW AU/949* RC 250.00 600.00

2019-20 SP Authentic '09-10 Retro Future Watch Autographs

RFWAAB Adam Boqvist 15.00 40.00
RFWAAF Adam Fox 125.00 300.00
RFWACM Cale Makar 300.00 800.00
RFWAEM Emil Bemstrom 15.00 40.00
RFWAFR Morgan Frost 25.00 60.00
RFWAFZ Filip Zadina 40.00 100.00
RFWAIM Ilya Mikheyev 25.00 60.00
RFWAJB Jesper Boqvist 12.00 30.00
RFWAJD Joey Daccord 30.00 80.00
RFWAJG Julien Gauthier 15.00 40.00
RFWAJH Jack Hughes 125.00 300.00
RFWAJS Jimmy Schuldt 12.00 30.00
RFWAKK Karson Kuhlman 15.00 40.00
RFWAKO Klim Kostin 15.00 40.00
RFWAKS Kole Sherwood 15.00 40.00
RFWAMJ Max Jones 15.00 40.00
RFWANH Nicolas Hague 15.00 40.00
RFWANS Nick Suzuki 60.00 150.00
RFWAPI Rem Pitlick 15.00 40.00
RFWAQH Quinn Hughes 80.00 200.00
RFWAST Nico Sturm 12.00 30.00
RFWAZM Zack MacEwen 12.00 30.00

2019-20 SP Authentic '09-10 Retro Future Watch Patch Autographs

09AF Adam Fox 300.00 800.00
09AT Alexandre Texier 20.00 50.00
09BH Barrett Hayton 40.00 100.00
09BL Blake Lizotte 20.00 50.00
09CG Cody Glass 30.00 80.00
09CM Cale Makar 600.00 1500.00
09IM Ilya Mikheyev 60.00 150.00
09JB Jesper Boqvist 12.00 30.00
09JH Jack Hughes 120.00 300.00
09KK Karson Kuhlman 20.00 50.00
09MF Morgan Frost 60.00 150.00
09ND Noah Dobson 50.00 125.00
09NG Nikita Gusev 30.00 80.00
09NH Nicolas Hague 20.00 50.00
09NS Nick Suzuki 150.00 400.00
09OW Oliver Wahlstrom 30.00 80.00
09PM Philippe Myers 15.00 40.00
09QH Quinn Hughes 200.00 500.00
09RS Rasmus Sandin 100.00 250.00
09TB Tobias Bjornfot 20.00 50.00

2019-20 SP Authentic '99-00 Retro Future Watch

RFW1 Jack Hughes 20.00 50.00
RFW2 Kirby Dach 12.00 30.00
RFW3 Cale Makar 30.00 80.00
RFW4 Cody Glass 10.00 25.00
RFW5 Rasmus Sandin 10.00 25.00
RFW6 Nick Suzuki 25.00 60.00
RFW7 Quinn Hughes 25.00 60.00
RFW8 Ryan Poehling 10.00 25.00
RFW9 Kaapo Kakko 10.00 25.00

2019-20 SP Authentic '99-00 Retro Sign of the Times

RSOTTBB Brent Burns B 15.00 40.00
RSOTTBI Ben Bishop C 5.00 12.00
RSOTTCM Connor McDavid A 100.00 250.00
RSOTTCN Cam Neely B 6.00 15.00
RSOTTDG Doug Gilmour A 8.00 20.00
RSOTTES Eric Staal D 6.00 15.00
RSOTTJP Joe Pavelski D 8.00 20.00
RSOTTMF Marc-Andre Fleury A 12.00 30.00
RSOTTSB Sergei Bobrovsky C 10.00 25.00

2019-20 SP Authentic '99-00 Retro Sign of the Times Rookies

RSOTTCG Cody Glass A 20.00 50.00
RSOTTFZ Filip Zadina B 20.00 50.00
RSOTTJH Jack Hughes A 60.00 150.00
RSOTTMA Cale Makar B 200.00 500.00
RSOTTMF Morgan Frost B 20.00 50.00
RSOTTNG Nikita Gusev B 20.00 50.00
RSOTTNS Nick Suzuki B 25.00 60.00
RSOTTQH Quinn Hughes A 60.00 150.00

2019-20 SP Authentic Authentic Winners

AWBO Bobby Orr 1.25 3.00
AWCJ Curtis Joseph .40 1.00
AWCM Connor McDavid 1.50 4.00
AWEM Evgeni Malkin .60 1.50
AWJH Jack Hughes 1.50 4.00
AWJL Jacques Lemaire .25 .60
AWJT Jonathan Toews .50 1.25
AWMM Mitch Marner .50 1.25
AWND Noah Dobson .75 2.00
AWWG Wayne Gretzky 2.00 5.00

2019-20 SP Authentic Authentic Winners Autographs

AWCJ Curtis Joseph/99 12.00 30.00
AWEM Evgeni Malkin/25 30.00 80.00
AWJH Jack Hughes/25 60.00 150.00
AWJL Jacques Lemaire/99 10.00 25.00
AWJT Jonathan Toews/25 20.00 50.00
AWMM Mitch Marner/25 25.00 60.00
AWND Noah Dobson/99 20.00 50.00

2019-20 SP Authentic Future Watch Inscriptions

*INSCRIPT: .75X TO 2X BASIC
149 Cale Makar/50* 1200.00 3000.00
150 Kaden Fulcher/50* 15.00 40.00
151 Guillaume Brisebois/50* 15.00 40.00
154 Blake Lizotte/50* 15.00 40.00
155 Ryan Kuffner/50* 12.00 30.00
156 Max Veronneau/50* 12.00 30.00
157 Mackenzie MacEachern/50* UER 15.00 40.00
158 Joey Daccord/50* 40.00 100.00
160 Carl Grundstrom/50* 15.00 40.00
163 Quinn Hughes/50* 200.00 500.00
165 Nathan Bastian/50* 15.00 40.00
166 Nico Sturm/50* 12.00 30.00
167 Brady Keeper/50* 15.00 40.00
168 Zach Senyshyn/50* 15.00 40.00
169 Karson Kuhlman/50* 15.00 40.00
170 Zack MacEwen/50* 12.00 30.00
171 Ryan Lindgren/50* 15.00 40.00
172 Teddy Blueger/50* 15.00 40.00
174 Rem Pitlick/50* 15.00 40.00
175 Jimmy Schuldt/50* 12.00 30.00
176 Libor Hajek/50* 12.00 30.00
177 Kole Sherwood/50* 15.00 40.00
180 Vitaly Abramov/50* 15.00 40.00
182 Alexandre Texier/50* 15.00 40.00
187 Oliver Wahlstrom/50* 80.00 200.00
188 Tobias Bjornfot/50* 15.00 40.00
189 Ville Heinola/50* 20.00 50.00
190 Jesper Boqvist/50* 12.00 30.00
191 Elvis Merzlikins/50* 30.00 80.00
193 Noah Dobson/50* 30.00 80.00
194 Adam Fox/50* 400.00 1000.00
195 Barrett Hayton/50* 30.00 80.00
196 Cody Glass/50* 25.00 60.00
198 Connor Clifton/50* 15.00 40.00
205 Dominik Kubalik/50* 80.00 200.00
207 Matt Roy/50* 15.00 40.00
208 Lean Bergmann/50* 12.00 30.00
211 Nicolas Hague/50* 15.00 40.00
212 Emil Bemstrom/50* 15.00 40.00
213 Ilya Mikheyev/50* 25.00 60.00
215 Julien Gauthier/50* 15.00 40.00
219 Adam Boqvist/50* 15.00 40.00
220 German Rubtsov/50* 12.00 30.00
221 Alexander Volkov/50* 12.00 30.00
224 Givani Smith/50* 12.00 30.00
232 Eetu Luostarinen/50* 15.00 40.00
237 Jonathan Davidsson/50* 10.00 25.00
239 Noah Gregor/50* 12.00 30.00
241 John Marino/50* 50.00 125.00
242 Morgan Frost/50* 40.00 100.00
244 Cayden Primeau/50* 100.00 250.00
246 Klim Kostin/50* 15.00 40.00
248 Jake Walman/50* 20.00 50.00
249 Rasmus Asplund/50* 12.00 30.00
250 Joachim Blichfeld/50* 15.00 40.00
251 Igor Shesterkin/50* 120.00 300.00

2019-20 SP Authentic Limited Autographs

6 Dylan Strome D 12.00 30.00
8 Tyler Bertuzzi D 8.00 20.00
9 Ben Bishop D 8.00 20.00
15 Sergei Bobrovsky C 15.00 40.00
16 Marc-Andre Fleury A 20.00 50.00
24 Alex DeBrincat D 12.00 30.00
27 Eric Staal C 10.00 25.00
31 Aleksander Barkov C 15.00 40.00
32 Kyle Turris D 8.00 20.00
34 Anders Lee D 8.00 20.00
36 Pierre-Luc Dubois D 8.00 20.00
38 Joe Pavelski C 12.00 30.00
39 Tom Wilson D 10.00 25.00
44 Joe Thornton A 15.00 40.00
55 Thomas Chabot Issued in '20-21 SPA 10.00 25.00
59 Miro Heiskanen C 12.00 30.00
63 Brent Burns B 10.00 25.00
64 Jesperi Kotkaniemi C 10.00 25.00
68 Connor Hellebuyck D 20.00 50.00
71 John Tavares A 15.00 40.00
78 Mikael Granlund D 8.00 20.00
91 Philipp Grubauer D 10.00 25.00
96 Andrei Svechnikov C 12.00 30.00
104 Carey Price AM A 80.00 200.00
111 Jack Hughes AM B 200.00 400.00
112 John Tavares AM A 60.00 150.00
113 Cody Glass AM C 20.00 50.00
115 Connor McDavid AM A 80.00 200.00

2019-20 SP Authentic Limited Patch Autographs

1 Jonathan Marchessault/50 30.00 80.00
2 Oliver Bjorkstrand/100 20.00 50.00
6 Dylan Strome/100 30.00 80.00
7 Sean Monahan/100 15.00 40.00
8 Tyler Bertuzzi/100 20.00 50.00
9 Ben Bishop/50 20.00 50.00
12 John Gibson/50 25.00 60.00
13 William Karlsson/100 30.00 80.00
16 Marc-Andre Fleury/25 50.00 125.00
22 Matt Murray/100 25.00 60.00
23 Jake Guentzel/50 40.00 100.00
24 Alex DeBrincat/50 30.00 80.00
27 Eric Staal/100 25.00 60.00
28 Nico Hischier/50 40.00 100.00
31 Aleksander Barkov/50 40.00 100.00
33 Henrik Lundqvist/25 60.00 150.00
34 Anders Lee/100 20.00 50.00
37 Leon Draisaitl/25 60.00 150.00
39 Tom Wilson/100 25.00 60.00
44 Joe Thornton/25 40.00 100.00
58 John Klingberg/50 25.00 60.00
59 Miro Heiskanen/100 30.00 80.00
62 Jack Eichel/50 40.00 100.00
63 Brent Burns/50 25.00 60.00
64 Jesperi Kotkaniemi/50 25.00 60.00
66 Mark Scheifele/25 40.00 100.00
68 Connor Hellebuyck/100 50.00 125.00
69 Alex Tuch/100 25.00 60.00
71 John Tavares/25 40.00 100.00
74 Matthew Tkachuk/50 50.00 125.00
75 Andrei Vasilevskiy/50 40.00 100.00
80 Jaccob Slavin/100 20.00 50.00
91 Philipp Grubauer/100 25.00 60.00
96 Andrei Svechnikov/100 30.00 80.00
148 Jack Hughes FW/100 125.00 300.00
149 Cale Makar FW/100 800.00 2000.00
150 Kaden Fulcher FW/100 25.00 60.00
151 Guillaume Brisebois FW/100 25.00 60.00
153 Riley Stillman FW/100 25.00 60.00
154 Blake Lizotte FW/100 25.00 60.00
155 Ryan Kuffner FW/100 20.00 50.00
156 Max Veronneau FW/100 20.00 50.00
157 Mackenzie MacEachern FW/100 25.00 60.00
158 Joey Daccord FW/100 50.00 125.00
159 Filip Zadina FW/100 125.00 300.00
160 Carl Grundstrom FW/100 25.00 60.00
161 Ryan Poehling FW/100 40.00 100.00
162 Philippe Myers FW/100 20.00 50.00
163 Quinn Hughes FW/100 200.00 500.00
164 Brandon Gignac FW/100 20.00 50.00
166 Nico Sturm FW/100 20.00 50.00
167 Brady Keeper FW/100 25.00 60.00
168 Zach Senyshyn FW/100 25.00 60.00
169 Karson Kuhlman FW/100 25.00 60.00
170 Zack MacEwen FW/100 20.00 50.00
171 Ryan Lindgren FW/100 25.00 60.00
172 Teddy Blueger FW/100 25.00 60.00
174 Rem Pitlick FW/100 25.00 60.00
175 Jimmy Schuldt FW/100 20.00 50.00
176 Libor Hajek FW/100 20.00 50.00
177 Kole Sherwood FW/100 25.00 60.00
178 Joel L'Esperance FW/100 25.00 60.00
180 Vitaly Abramov FW/100 25.00 60.00
181 Victor Olofsson FW/100 50.00 125.00
182 Alexandre Texier FW/100 25.00 60.00
183 Trent Frederic FW/100 25.00 60.00
187 Oliver Wahlstrom FW/100 80.00 200.00
188 Tobias Bjornfot FW/100 25.00 60.00
190 Jesper Boqvist FW/100 20.00 50.00
191 Elvis Merzlikins FW/100 50.00 125.00
192 Nick Suzuki FW/100 600.00 1500.00
193 Noah Dobson FW/100 30.00 80.00
194 Adam Fox FW/100 300.00 800.00
195 Barrett Hayton FW/100 50.00 125.00
196 Cody Glass FW/100 40.00 100.00
199 Kirby Dach FW/100 125.00 300.00
200 Rasmus Sandin FW/100 80.00 200.00
205 Dominik Kubalik FW/100 60.00 150.00
207 Matt Roy FW/100 25.00 60.00
208 Lean Bergmann FW/100 20.00 50.00
211 Nicolas Hague FW/100 25.00 60.00
212 Emil Bemstrom FW/100 25.00 60.00
213 Ilya Mikheyev FW/100 40.00 100.00
214 Nikita Gusev FW/100 40.00 100.00
215 Julien Gauthier FW/100 25.00 60.00
217 Trevor Moore FW/100 20.00 50.00
218 Sam Lafferty FW/100 20.00 50.00
242 Morgan Frost FW/100 40.00 100.00

2019-20 SP Authentic Marks of Distinction

MDJM Jonathan Marchessault 30.00 80.00
MDPD Pierre-Luc Dubois 12.00 30.00
MDQH Quinn Hughes 125.00 300.00

2019-20 SP Authentic Sign of the Times

SOTTAB Aleksander Barkov D 12.00 30.00
SOTTAD Alex DeBrincat D 10.00 25.00
SOTTAL Anders Lee E 6.00 15.00
SOTTAM Auston Matthews A 125.00 300.00
SOTTAR Alexander Radulov E 8.00 20.00
SOTTAT Alex Tuch E 8.00 20.00
SOTTAV Andrei Vasilevskiy D 12.00 30.00
SOTTBA Tyson Barrie F 5.00 12.00
SOTTBB Ben Bishop D 6.00 15.00
SOTTBH Bobby Hull A 20.00 50.00
SOTTBN Bernie Nicholls F 6.00 15.00
SOTTBR Bill Ranford E 6.00 15.00
SOTTBU Brent Burns B 8.00 20.00
SOTTCH Connor Hellebuyck D 15.00 40.00
SOTTCN Cam Neely C 8.00 20.00
SOTTCP Carey Price A 100.00 250.00
SOTTDG Doug Gilmour A 10.00 25.00
SOTTDN Darnell Nurse E 6.00 15.00
SOTTDS Dylan Strome D 10.00 25.00
SOTTED Evgenii Dadonov F 5.00 12.00
SOTTES Eric Staal D 8.00 20.00
SOTTGF Grant Fuhr C 12.00 30.00
SOTTGR Dirk Graham F 6.00 15.00
SOTTGU Jake Guentzel D 12.00 30.00
SOTTHL Henrik Lundqvist A 40.00 100.00
SOTTJE Jack Eichel B 12.00 30.00
SOTTJG John Gibson D 8.00 20.00
SOTTJI Jarome Iginla A 10.00 25.00
SOTTJJ Joe Thornton A 20.00 50.00
SOTTJK John Klingberg E 8.00 20.00
SOTTJM Jonathan Marchessault D 10.00 25.00
SOTTJP Joe Pavelski D 10.00 25.00
SOTTJS Jaccob Slavin F 6.00 15.00
SOTTJT John Tavares A 12.00 30.00
SOTTKL Kevin Labanc F 5.00 12.00
SOTTKM Kirk McLean E 6.00 15.00
SOTTKT Keith Tkachuk C 8.00 20.00
SOTTLD Leon Draisaitl D 25.00 60.00
SOTTMF Marc-Andre Fleury A 40.00 100.00
SOTTMG Mikael Granlund F 6.00 15.00
SOTTML Mike Liut F 5.00 12.00
SOTTMM Mike Modano B 12.00 30.00
SOTTMO Sean Monahan D 5.00 12.00
SOTTMT Matthew Tkachuk C 15.00 40.00
SOTTMU Matt Murray E 8.00 20.00
SOTTNH Nico Hischier B 12.00 30.00
SOTTOB Oliver Bjorkstrand F 6.00 15.00
SOTTPF Peter Forsberg A 60.00 150.00
SOTTPG Philipp Grubauer F 8.00 20.00
SOTTRD Ryan Dzingel F 6.00 15.00
SOTTRE Ryan Ellis 6.00 15.00
SOTTRH Ron Hextall D 8.00 20.00
SOTTRL Roberto Luongo B 12.00 30.00
SOTTSB Sergei Bobrovsky C 12.00 30.00
SOTTSC Sidney Crosby A 250.00 400.00
SOTTSM Mark Scheifele D 12.00 30.00
SOTTTC Thomas Chabot D 8.00 20.00
SOTTTR Jacob Trouba E 6.00 15.00
SOTTTU Kyle Turris F 6.00 15.00
SOTTTW Tom Wilson C 8.00 20.00
SOTTWC Wendel Clark A 12.00 30.00
SOTTWK William Karlsson E 10.00 25.00
SOTTYC Yvan Cournoyer C 8.00 20.00
SOTTYG Yanni Gourde E 6.00 15.00

2019-20 SP Authentic Sign of the Times 1980s

ST80AM Andy Moog C 15.00 40.00
ST80BN Bernie Nicholls C 12.00 30.00
ST80BR Bill Ranford C 12.00 30.00
ST80CC Chris Chelios B 15.00 40.00
ST80CN Cam Neely B 15.00 40.00
ST80DG Dirk Graham C 12.00 30.00
ST80KM Kirk McLean C 12.00 30.00
ST80LR Larry Robinson B 15.00 40.00
ST80ML Mike Liut C 10.00 25.00
ST80PT Pierre Turgeon B 12.00 30.00
ST80SB Scotty Bowman A 200.00 500.00
ST80WC Wendel Clark B 25.00 60.00

2019-20 SP Authentic Sign of the Times 1990s

ST90DG Doug Gilmour A 20.00 50.00
ST90DW Doug Weight B 15.00 40.00
ST90JL John LeClair B 15.00 40.00
ST90MM Mark Messier A 40.00 100.00
ST90MR Mark Recchi B 20.00 50.00
ST90RH Ron Hextall B 15.00 40.00
ST90SC Shayne Corson B 4.00 10.00
ST90WG Wayne Gretzky A 400.00 1000.00

2019-20 SP Authentic Sign of the Times 2000s

ST00BB Brent Burns B 15.00 40.00
ST00CO Carey Price A 100.00 250.00
ST00ES Eric Staal C 15.00 40.00
ST00JP Joe Pavelski C 20.00 50.00
ST00JT Joe Thornton A 25.00 60.00
ST00MB Martin Brodeur A 80.00 200.00
ST00MS Martin St. Louis B 15.00 40.00
ST00PM Patrick Marleau B 15.00 40.00
ST00PR Pekka Rinne B 15.00 40.00
ST00SG Scott Gomez C 12.00 30.00

2019-20 SP Authentic Sign of the Times Draft

SOTTDAB Aleksander Barkov C 25.00 60.00
SOTTDAD Alex DeBrincat C 20.00 50.00
SOTTDAM Auston Matthews 150.00 400.00
SOTTDBB Brent Burns B 15.00 40.00
SOTTDCM Connor McDavid A 80.00 200.00
SOTTDDB Dustin Brown C 15.00 40.00
SOTTDJI Jarome Iginla A 20.00 50.00
SOTTDJK Jesperi Kotkaniemi C 15.00 40.00
SOTTDJO Joe Thornton A 25.00 60.00
SOTTDKT Kyle Turris C 12.00 30.00
SOTTDMB Martin Brodeur A 80.00 200.00
SOTTDMH Miro Heiskanen B 20.00 50.00
SOTTDTW Tom Wilson B 15.00 40.00
SOTTDWC Wendel Clark B 25.00 60.00

2019-20 SP Authentic Sign of the Times Draft Inscriptions

SOTTDAB Aleksander Barkov/25 30.00 80.00
SOTTDAD Alex DeBrincat/25 25.00 60.00
SOTTDDB Dustin Brown/25 20.00 50.00
SOTTDJK Jesperi Kotkaniemi/25 20.00 50.00
SOTTDKT Kyle Turris/25 15.00 40.00

2019-20 SP Authentic Sign of the Times Draft Rookies

SOTTDFZ Filip Zadina C 12.00 30.00
SOTTDJH Jack Hughes A 60.00 150.00
SOTTDMA Cale Makar B 60.00 150.00
SOTTDMF Morgan Frost B 12.00 30.00

2019-20 SP Authentic Sign of the Times Draft Rookies Inscriptions

SOTTDFZ Filip Zadina/50 50.00 125.00
SOTTDMA Cale Makar/25 150.00 400.00
SOTTDMF Morgan Frost/25 60.00 150.00

2019-20 SP Authentic Sign of the Times Duals

ST2BB A.Barkov/S.Bobrovsky 30.00 80.00
ST2BT B.Burns/J.Thornton 30.00 80.00
ST2CG C.Chelios/D.Graham 20.00 50.00
ST2GC D.Gilmour/W.Clark 30.00 80.00
ST2HH B.Hull/G.Hall 50.00 125.00
ST2MR M.Messier/B.Ranford 40.00 100.00
ST2PB J.Pavelski/B.Bishop 25.00 60.00

2019-20 SP Authentic Sign of the Times Rookies

SOTRAF Adam Fox 100.00 250.00
SOTRAT Alexandre Texier 10.00 25.00
SOTRCC Connor Clifton 10.00 25.00
SOTRCG Cody Glass 15.00 40.00
SOTRCM Cale Makar 150.00 400.00
SOTRFZ Filip Zadina 15.00 40.00
SOTRGR Carl Grundstrom 10.00 25.00
SOTRIM Ilya Mikheyev 15.00 40.00
SOTRJB Jesper Boqvist 8.00 20.00
SOTRJG Julien Gauthier 10.00 25.00
SOTRJH Jack Hughes 50.00 125.00
SOTRKK Karson Kuhlman 10.00 25.00
SOTRKO Klim Kostin 10.00 25.00
SOTRMF Morgan Frost 15.00 40.00
SOTRNG Nikita Gusev 15.00 40.00
SOTRNS Nick Suzuki 50.00 125.00
SOTRQH Quinn Hughes 60.00 150.00

2019-20 SP Authentic SP Essentials

SPEAB Aleksander Barkov .75 2.00
SPEAD Alex DeBrincat .60 1.50
SPEAM Auston Matthews 2.00 5.00
SPEAP Artemi Panarin 1.00 2.50
SPEBB Brock Boeser .60 1.50
SPEBM Brad Marchand 1.00 2.50
SPECM Connor McDavid 2.50 6.00
SPECP Carey Price 1.00 2.50
SPEDP David Pastrnak 1.25 3.00
SPEJC John Carlson .50 1.25
SPEJE Jack Eichel .75 2.00
SPEJG John Gibson .50 1.25
SPEJK Jesperi Kotkaniemi .50 1.25
SPELD Leon Draisaitl 1.50 4.00
SPEMA Anthony Mantha .40 1.00
SPEMF Marc-Andre Fleury 1.00 2.50
SPEMH Miro Heiskanen .60 1.50
SPEMM Matt Murray .50 1.25
SPEMT Matthew Tkachuk 1.00 2.50
SPESC Sidney Crosby 2.00 5.00
SPETC Thomas Chabot .50 1.25

2019-20 SP Authentic SP Essentials Autographs

SPEAB Aleksander Barkov/99 15.00 40.00
SPEAD Alex DeBrincat/99 12.00 30.00
SPECP Carey Price/25 20.00 50.00
SPEJK Jesperi Kotkaniemi/99 25.00 60.00
SPEMF Marc-Andre Fleury/25 80.00 200.00
SPEMH Miro Heiskanen/99 12.00 30.00

2019-20 SP Authentic Spectrum FX

S1 Ryan O'Reilly 1.00 2.50
S2 Morgan Rielly 1.00 2.50
S3 Blake Wheeler 1.00 2.50
S4 Andrei Vasilevskiy 1.50 4.00
S5 John Gibson 1.00 2.50
S6 Leon Draisaitl 3.00 8.00
S7 Connor Hellebuyck 2.00 5.00
S8 Auston Matthews 4.00 10.00
S9 Carey Price 2.00 5.00
S10 Mark Stone 1.25 3.00
S11 Nathan MacKinnon 4.00 10.00
S12 Bo Horvat 1.25 3.00
S13 Brad Marchand 2.00 5.00
S14 Marc-Andre Fleury 2.00 5.00
S15 Mitch Marner 1.50 4.00
S16 Alex Ovechkin 4.00 10.00
S17 Dylan Larkin 1.25 3.00
S18 Jack Eichel 1.50 4.00
S19 Sidney Crosby 4.00 10.00
S20 Drew Doughty 1.25 3.00
S21 Andrei Svechnikov 1.25 3.00
S22 Brady Tkachuk 1.50 4.00
S23 Patrick Kane 2.00 5.00
S24 Evgeni Malkin 2.00 5.00
S25 Steven Stamkos 2.00 5.00
S26 Taylor Hall 1.00 2.50
S27 Pierre-Luc Dubois .75 2.00
S28 Connor McDavid 5.00 12.00
S29 Tuukka Rask 1.25 3.00
S30 Anthony Mantha .75 2.00
S31 Teuvo Teravainen 1.00 2.50
S32 John Tavares 1.50 4.00
S33 Mathew Barzal 1.25 3.00
S34 Artemi Panarin 2.00 5.00
S35 Rasmus Dahlin 1.25 3.00
S36 Brayden Point 1.25 3.00
S37 Mark Scheifele 1.50 4.00
S38 Aleksander Barkov 1.50 4.00
S39 Sean Monahan .60 1.50
S40 Elias Pettersson 1.50 4.00
S41 Jake Walman FW 1.50 4.00
S42 Dominik Kubalik FW 2.50 6.00
S43 Conor Timmins FW 1.25 3.00
S44 German Rubtsov FW 1.00 2.50
S45 Julien Gauthier FW 1.25 3.00
S46 Nikolai Prokhorkin FW 1.00 2.50
S47 Mario Ferraro FW 1.00 2.50
S48 John Marino FW 2.00 5.00
S49 Aleksi Saarela FW 1.25 3.00
S50 Trent Frederic FW 1.25 3.00
S51 Teddy Blueger FW 1.25 3.00
S52 Joey Daccord FW 2.50 6.00
S53 Rem Pitlick FW 1.25 3.00
S54 Max Jones FW 1.25 3.00
S55 Vitaly Abramov FW 1.25 3.00
S56 Karson Kuhlman FW 1.25 3.00
S57 Carl Grundstrom FW 1.25 3.00
S58 Jesper Boqvist FW 1.00 2.50
S59 Sam Lafferty FW 1.00 2.50
S60 Martin Fehervary FW 1.00 2.50
S61 Connor Clifton FW 1.25 3.00
S62 Alexander Volkov FW 1.00 2.50
S63 Blake Lizotte FW 1.25 3.00
S64 Philippe Myers FW 1.00 2.50
S65 Trevor Moore FW 1.00 2.50
S66 Ville Heinola FW 1.50 4.00
S67 Otto Koivula FW .75 2.00
S68 Tobias Bjornfot FW 1.25 3.00
S69 Emil Bemstrom FW 1.25 3.00
S70 Dmytro Timashov FW 1.25 3.00
S71 Igor Shesterkin FW 6.00 15.00
S72 Cale Fleury FW 2.00 5.00
S73 Taro Hirose FW 1.50 4.00
S74 Oliver Wahlstrom FW 2.50 6.00
S75 Klim Kostin FW 1.50 4.00
S76 Alexandre Texier FW 1.50 4.00
S77 Cayden Primeau FW 8.00 20.00
S78 Dante Fabbro FW 1.50 4.00
S79 Jack Studnicka FW 1.50 4.00
S80 Nicolas Hague FW 1.50 4.00
S81 Nikita Gusev FW 2.50 6.00
S82 Erik Brannstrom FW 1.50 4.00
S83 Ilya Mikheyev FW 2.50 6.00
S84 Barrett Hayton FW 3.00 8.00
S85 Adam Fox FW 4.00 10.00
S86 Joel Farabee FW 2.50 6.00
S87 Rasmus Sandin FW 2.50 6.00
S88 Adam Boqvist FW 1.50 4.00
S89 Noah Dobson FW 4.00 10.00
S90 Ryan Poehling FW 2.50 6.00
S91 Filip Zadina FW 4.00 10.00
S92 Morgan Frost FW 4.00 10.00
S93 Victor Olofsson FW 5.00 12.00
S94 Cody Glass FW 4.00 10.00
S95 Nick Suzuki FW 10.00 25.00
S96 Kirby Dach FW 5.00 12.00
S97 Quinn Hughes FW 12.00 30.00
S98 Cale Makar FW 20.00 50.00
S99 Kaapo Kakko FW 4.00 10.00
S100 Jack Hughes FW Bounty 25.00 60.00

2019-20 SP Authentic Spectrum FX Gold

*GOLD: 1.2X TO 3X BASIC
*GOLD RC: 4X TO 10X BASIC
S11 Nathan MacKinnon 15.00 40.00
S21 Andrei Svechnikov 15.00 40.00
S60 Martin Fehervary FW 12.00 30.00
S85 Adam Fox FW 25.00 60.00
S91 Filip Zadina FW 15.00 40.00
S92 Morgan Frost FW 15.00 40.00
S93 Victor Olofsson FW 15.00 40.00
S94 Cody Glass FW 15.00 40.00
S98 Cale Makar FW 40.00 100.00
S99 Kaapo Kakko FW 20.00 50.00
S100 Jack Hughes FW Bounty 125.00 300.00

2020-21 SP Authentic

*RED: .6X TO 1.5X BASIC CARDS
1 Elias Pettersson .60 1.50
2 Cale Makar 1.00 2.50
3 Victor Hedman .50 1.25
4 Kyle Connor .60 1.50
5 Brent Burns .40 1.00
6 Ryan Getzlaf .40 1.00
7 Max Pacioretty .40 1.00
8 Ryan O'Reilly .40 1.00
9 Igor Shesterkin .75 2.00
10 Matthew Tkachuk .75 2.00
11 Keith Yandle .25 .60
12 Alex Ovechkin 1.50 4.00
13 Tyson Barrie .25 .60
14 Anthony Mantha .30 .75
15 Dylan Strome .50 1.25
16 Brock Boeser .50 1.25
17 Mark Stone .50 1.25
18 Travis Konecny .40 1.00
19 Ryan Nugent-Hopkins .50 1.25
20 Aleksander Barkov .60 1.50

21 Pekka Rinne .40 1.00
22 John Tavares .60 1.50
23 John Carlson .40 1.00
24 Mathew Barzal .50 1.25
25 Pierre-Luc Dubois .30 .75
26 John Klingberg .40 1.00
27 Darcy Kuemper .40 1.00
28 Carter Hart .40 1.00
29 Sebastian Aho .60 1.50
30 Shea Theodore .50 1.25
31 Patrice Bergeron .50 1.25
32 Matt Murray .40 1.00
33 Leon Draisaitl 1.25 3.00
34 Jake Guentzel .60 1.50
35 Brad Marchand .75 2.00
36 Dougie Hamilton .30 .75
37 Mark Scheifele .60 1.50
38 Evgeni Malkin .75 2.00
39 Josh Bailey .30 .75
40 Mitch Marner .60 1.50
41 Jack Hughes 1.00 2.50
42 Mark Giordano .40 1.00
43 Alex Tuch .40 1.00
44 Jonathan Drouin .30 .75
45 Colton Parayko .30 .75
46 Miro Heiskanen .50 1.25
47 Nico Hischier .60 1.50
48 Sean Monahan .25 .60
49 Eric Staal .40 1.00
50 David Pastrnak 1.00 2.50
51 Martin Jones .30 .75
52 Seth Jones .40 1.00
53 Steven Stamkos .75 2.00
54 Nick Suzuki .75 2.00
55 Quinn Hughes 1.00 2.50
56 Nikita Kucherov .75 2.00
57 Victor Olofsson .40 1.00
58 Auston Matthews 1.50 4.00
59 Teuvo Teravainen .40 1.00
60 Patrick Kane .75 2.00
61 Ryan Suter .30 .75
62 Nick Schmaltz .30 .75
63 John Gibson .40 1.00
64 Brayden Point .50 1.25
65 Brendan Gallagher .40 1.00
66 Bo Horvat .50 1.25
67 Mats Zuccarello .40 1.00
68 Tyler Seguin .50 1.25
69 Tomas Hertl .40 1.00
70 Philipp Grubauer .40 1.00
71 Connor Hellebuyck .75 2.00
72 Roman Josi .40 1.00
73 Ryan Dzingel .30 .75
74 Carey Price .75 2.00
75 Dominik Kubalik .40 1.00
76 Sidney Crosby 1.50 4.00
77 Tom Wilson .40 1.00
78 David Perron .30 .75
79 James van Riemsdyk .30 .75
80 Dylan Larkin .50 1.25
81 Andrei Svechnikov .50 1.25
82 Dustin Brown .40 1.00
83 Artemi Panarin .75 2.00
84 Rasmus Dahlin .50 1.25
85 Jordan Staal .30 .75
86 Yanni Gourde .30 .75
87 Mika Zibanejad .50 1.25
88 Zach Werenski .60 1.50
89 Jonathan Huberdeau .50 1.25
90 Connor McDavid 2.00 5.00
91 Jack Eichel .60 1.50
92 Anze Kopitar .60 1.50
93 Anders Lee .30 .75
94 Nathan MacKinnon 1.50 4.00
95 Zach Parise .40 1.00
96 Kyle Palmieri .30 .75
97 Brady Tkachuk .60 1.50
98 Joe Pavelski .50 1.25
99 Brayden Schenn .40 1.00
100 Andrei Vasilevskiy .60 1.50
101 John Klingberg CM .40 1.00
102 Pekka Rinne CM .40 1.00
103 Quinn Hughes CM 1.00 2.50
104 Joe Thornton CM .60 1.50
105 Zach Parise CM .40 1.00
106 Tyler Toffoli CM .40 1.00
107 Alex Ovechkin CM 1.50 4.00
108 Connor McDavid CM 2.00 5.00
109 Brayden Point CM .50 1.25
110 Joe Pavelski CM .50 1.25
111 Steven Stamkos CM .75 2.00
112 Alexis Lafreniere CM 1.50 4.00
113 Kirill Kaprizov CM 2.00 5.00
114 Tim Stutzle CM 1.00 2.50
115 Bowen Byram CM 1.00 2.50
116 Auston Matthews CM 1.50 4.00
117 Sam Steel
Maxime Comtois FI 5.00 12.00
118 Victor Soderstrom
Barrett Hayton FI 6.00 15.00
119 Jake DeBrusk
Connor Clifton FI 6.00 15.00
120 Victor Olofsson
Dylan Cozens FI 12.00 30.00
121 Elias Lindholm
Rasmus Andersson FI 6.00 15.00
122 Teuvo Teravainen
Martin Necas FI 10.00 25.00
123 Kirby Dach
Dominik Kubalik FI 6.00 15.00
124 Mikko Rantanen
Bowen Byram FI 15.00 40.00
125 Seth Jones
Liam Foudy FI 8.00 20.00
126 Jake Oettinger
Ty Dellandrea FI 20.00 50.00
127 Anthony Mantha
Tyler Bertuzzi FI 5.00 12.00
128 Philip Broberg
Kailer Yamamoto FI 8.00 20.00
129 Jonathan Huberdeau
Owen Tippett FI 8.00 20.00
130 Arthur Kaliyev
Gabe Vilardi FI 12.00 30.00
131 Kirill Kaprizov
Kevin Fiala FI 30.00 80.00
132 Alexander Romanov
Jesperi Kotkaniemi FI 10.00 25.00
133 Roman Josi
Ryan Ellis FI 6.00 15.00
134 Mackenzie Blackwood
Ty Smith FI 12.00 30.00
135 Ilya Sorokin
Mathew Barzal FI 20.00 50.00
136 Alexis Lafreniere
Igor Shesterkin FI 25.00 60.00
137 Josh Norris
Tim Stutzle FI 15.00 40.00
138 Carter Hart
Joel Farabee FI 6.00 15.00
139 John Marino
Pierre-Olivier Joseph FI 8.00 20.00
140 Tomas Hertl
Evander Kane FI 6.00 15.00
141 Jordan Binnington
Robert Thomas FI 10.00 25.00
142 Andrei Vasilevskiy
Anthony Cirelli FI 10.00 25.00
143 William Nylander
Timothy Liljegren FI 12.00 30.00
144 Brock Boeser
Thatcher Demko FI 8.00 20.00
145 Peyton Krebs
Shea Theodore FI 12.00 30.00
146 Connor McMichael
Ilya Samsonov FI 12.00 30.00
147 Kyle Connor
Nikolaj Ehlers FI 10.00 25.00
148 Alexis Lafreniere RC 400.00 1000.00
149 Connor McMichael RC 40.00 100.00
150 Jani Hakanpaa RC 6.00 15.00
151 Nikolai Knyzhov RC 8.00 20.00
152 Egor Korshkov RC 6.00 15.00
153 Anthony Angello RC 8.00 20.00
154 Keegan Kolesar RC 8.00 20.00
155 Kieffer Bellows RC 8.00 20.00
156 Connor Ingram RC 8.00 20.00
157 Thomas Harley RC 15.00 40.00
158 Pavel Francouz RC 12.00 30.00
159 Dylan Coghlan RC 10.00 25.00
160 Jake Oettinger RC 25.00 60.00
161 Michael DiPietro RC 12.00 30.00
162 Josh Norris RC 15.00 40.00
163 Pierre-Olivier Joseph RC 10.00 25.00
164 Ty Dellandrea RC 10.00 25.00
165 Jake Evans RC 10.00 25.00
166 Gage Quinney RC 6.00 15.00
167 Peyton Krebs RC 60.00 150.00
168 Victor Soderstrom RC 8.00 20.00
169 Gustav Lindstrom RC 8.00 20.00
170 Jason Robertson RC 150.00 400.00
171 Martin Kaut RC 10.00 25.00
172 Alexander Yelesin RC 8.00 20.00
173 Nicolas Beaudin RC 10.00 25.00
174 Tyler Benson RC 10.00 25.00
175 Philipp Kurashev RC 12.00 30.00
176 Vitali Kravtsov RC 20.00 50.00
177 Philippe Maillet RC 8.00 20.00
178 Matiss Kivlenieks RC 12.00 30.00
179 Maxim Letunov RC 8.00 20.00
180 Alex Belzile RC 8.00 20.00
181 Vitek Vanecek RC 25.00 60.00
182 Ryan McLeod RC 8.00 20.00
183 Alec Regula RC 6.00 15.00
184 Brandon Hagel RC 12.00 30.00
185 Morgan Geekie RC 10.00 25.00
186 Mikhail Berdin RC 10.00 25.00
187 Alexander True RC 8.00 20.00
188 Nick Robertson RC 15.00 40.00
189 Olli Juolevi RC 10.00 25.00
190 Alexander Alexeyev RC 8.00 20.00
191 Jonas Johansson RC 10.00 25.00
192 Liam Foudy RC 10.00 25.00
193 Shane Bowers RC 8.00 20.00
194 Mikey Anderson RC 10.00 25.00
195 Timothy Liljegren RC 10.00 25.00
196 Gabe Vilardi RC 15.00 40.00
197 Bowen Byram RC 200.00 500.00
190 Kirill Kaprizov RC 000.00 2000.00
199 Ty Smith RC 15.00 40.00
200 John Leonard RC 8.00 20.00
201 Cal Foote RC 12.00 30.00
202 Mathias Brome RC 8.00 20.00
203 Ian Mitchell RC 8.00 20.00
204 Alexander Barabanov RC 10.00 25.00
205 Yegor Sharangovich RC 15.00 40.00
206 Alexander Romanov RC 12.00 30.00
207 Nils Hoglander RC 10.00 25.00
208 Dylan Cozens RC 125.00 300.00
209 K'Andre Miller RC 20.00 50.00
210 Pius Suter RC 12.00 30.00
211 Ilya Sorokin RC 125.00 300.00
212 Logan Stanley RC 10.00 25.00
213 Kevin Lankinen RC 15.00 40.00
214 Mikhail Maltsev RC 8.00 20.00
215 Arthur Kaliyev RC 15.00 40.00
216 Aleksi Heponiemi RC 12.00 30.00
217 Tim Stutzle RC 300.00 800.00
218 Calvin Thurkauf RC 8.00 20.00
219 Chase Priskie RC 8.00 20.00
220 Steven Lorentz RC 8.00 20.00
221 Lucas Carlsson RC 8.00 20.00
222 Reid Duke RC 10.00 25.00
223 Stuart Skinner RC 20.00 50.00
224 Cameron Hillis RC 8.00 20.00
225 Jack Rathbone RC 10.00 25.00
226 Joel Kiviranta RC 10.00 25.00
227 Drew O'Connor RC 10.00 25.00
228 Niko Mikkola RC 8.00 20.00
229 Gilles Senn RC 8.00 20.00
230 Mikko Lehtonen RC 8.00 20.00
231 Joel Hofer RC 10.00 25.00
232 Kevin Bahl RC 8.00 20.00

2020-21 SP Authentic '00-01 Retro

R1 Elias Pettersson 2.50 6.00
R2 Cale Makar 4.00 10.00
R3 Victor Hedman 2.00 5.00
R4 Kyle Connor 2.50 6.00
R5 Brent Burns 1.50 4.00
R6 Ryan Getzlaf 1.50 4.00
R7 Max Pacioretty 1.50 4.00
R8 Ryan O'Reilly 1.50 4.00
R9 Igor Shesterkin 3.00 8.00
R10 Matthew Tkachuk 3.00 8.00
R11 Keith Yandle 1.00 2.50
R12 Alex Ovechkin 6.00 15.00
R13 Tyson Barrie 1.00 2.50
R14 Anthony Mantha 1.25 3.00
R15 Dylan Strome 2.00 5.00
R16 Brock Boeser 2.00 5.00
R17 Mark Stone 2.00 5.00
R18 Travis Konecny 1.50 4.00
R19 Ryan Nugent-Hopkins 2.00 5.00
R20 Aleksander Barkov 2.50 6.00
R21 Pekka Rinne 1.50 4.00
R22 John Tavares 2.50 6.00
R23 John Carlson 1.50 4.00
R24 Mathew Barzal 2.00 5.00
R25 Pierre-Luc Dubois 1.25 3.00
R26 John Klingberg 1.50 4.00
R27 Darcy Kuemper 1.50 4.00
R28 Carter Hart 1.50 4.00
R29 Sebastian Aho 2.50 6.00
R30 Shea Theodore 2.00 5.00
R31 Patrice Bergeron 2.00 5.00
R32 Matt Murray 1.50 4.00
R33 Leon Draisaitl 5.00 12.00
R34 Jake Guentzel 2.50 6.00
R35 Brad Marchand 3.00 8.00
R36 Dougie Hamilton 1.25 3.00
R37 Mark Scheifele 2.50 6.00
R38 Evgeni Malkin 3.00 8.00
R39 Josh Bailey 1.25 3.00
R40 Mitch Marner 2.50 6.00
R41 Jack Hughes 4.00 10.00
R42 Mark Giordano 1.50 4.00
R43 Alex Tuch 1.50 4.00
R44 Jonathan Drouin 1.25 3.00
R45 Colton Parayko 1.25 3.00
R46 Miro Heiskanen 2.00 5.00
R47 Nico Hischier 2.50 6.00
R48 Sean Monahan 1.00 2.50
R49 Eric Staal 1.50 4.00
R50 David Pastrnak 4.00 10.00
R51 Martin Jones 1.25 3.00
R52 Seth Jones 1.50 4.00
R53 Steven Stamkos 3.00 8.00
R54 Nick Suzuki 3.00 8.00
R55 Quinn Hughes 4.00 10.00
R56 Nikita Kucherov 3.00 8.00
R57 Victor Olofsson 1.50 4.00
R58 Auston Matthews 6.00 15.00
R59 Teuvo Teravainen 1.50 4.00
R60 Patrick Kane 3.00 8.00
R61 Ryan Suter 1.25 3.00
R62 Nick Schmaltz 1.25 3.00
R63 John Gibson 1.50 4.00
R64 Brayden Point 2.00 5.00
R65 Brendan Gallagher 1.50 4.00
R66 Bo Horvat 2.00 5.00
R67 Mats Zuccarello 1.50 4.00
R68 Tyler Seguin 2.00 5.00
R69 Tomas Hertl 1.50 4.00
R70 Philipp Grubauer 1.50 4.00
R71 Connor Hellebuyck 3.00 8.00
R72 Roman Josi 1.50 4.00
R73 Ryan Dzingel 1.25 3.00
R74 Carey Price 3.00 8.00
R75 Dominik Kubalik 1.50 4.00
R76 Sidney Crosby 6.00 15.00
R77 Tom Wilson 1.50 4.00
R78 David Perron 1.25 3.00
R79 James van Riemsdyk 1.25 3.00
R80 Dylan Larkin 2.00 5.00
R81 Andrei Svechnikov 2.00 5.00
R82 Dustin Brown 1.50 4.00
R83 Artemi Panarin 3.00 8.00
R84 Rasmus Dahlin 2.00 5.00
R85 Jordan Staal 1.25 3.00
R86 Yanni Gourde 1.25 3.00
R87 Mika Zibanejad 2.00 5.00
R88 Zach Werenski 2.50 6.00
R89 Jonathan Huberdeau 2.00 5.00
R90 Connor McDavid 8.00 20.00
R91 Jack Eichel 2.50 6.00
R92 Anze Kopitar 2.50 6.00
R93 Anders Lee 1.25 3.00
R94 Nathan MacKinnon 6.00 15.00
R95 Zach Parise 1.50 4.00
R96 Kyle Palmieri 1.25 3.00
R97 Brady Tkachuk 2.50 6.00
R98 Joe Pavelski 2.00 5.00
R99 Brayden Schenn 1.50 4.00
R100 Andrei Vasilevskiy 2.50 6.00

2020-21 SP Authentic '00-01 Retro Autographs

RLE Anders Lee 6.00 15.00
RMG Mark Giordano 8.00 20.00
RPR Pekka Rinne 8.00 20.00

2020-21 SP Authentic '00-01 Retro Future Watch

RFW2 Pius Suter 4.00 10.00
RFW3 Tim Stutzle 6.00 15.00
RFW4 Victor Soderstrom 2.50 6.00
RFW5 Ilya Sorokin 8.00 20.00
RFW6 Bowen Byram 6.00 15.00
RFW7 Josh Norris 5.00 12.00
RFW8 Nick Robertson 5.00 12.00
RFW9 Arthur Kaliyev 5.00 12.00
RFW12 Liam Foudy 3.00 8.00
RFW13 Alexander Romanov 4.00 10.00
RFW14 Dylan Cozens 5.00 12.00
RFW15 Timothy Liljegren 3.00 8.00
RFW16 Kirill Kaprizov 12.00 30.00
RFW17 Gabe Vilardi 5.00 12.00
RFW18 Connor McMichael 5.00 12.00

2020-21 SP Authentic '00-01 Retro Future Watch Autographs

RAK Arthur Kaliyev 20.00 50.00
RBB Bowen Byram 80.00 200.00
RDC Dylan Cozens 80.00 200.00
RKK Kirill Kaprizov 600.00 1500.00
RNH Nils Hoglander 12.00 30.00
RPS Pius Suter 15.00 40.00
RTS Tim Stutzle 125.00 300.00

2020-21 SP Authentic '00-01 Retro Spectrum

*GOLD/100: .6X TO 1.5X BASIC INSERTS
R2 Cale Makar 12.00 30.00
R46 Miro Heiskanen 8.00 20.00
R58 Auston Matthews 30.00 80.00
R74 Carey Price 8.00 20.00
R76 Sidney Crosby 12.00 30.00
R80 Dylan Larkin 8.00 20.00
R91 Jack Eichel 6.00 15.00

2020-21 SP Authentic '10-11 Retro Future Watch Patch Autographs

RFWAPAR Alexander Romanov 80.00 200.00
RFWAPBB Bowen Byram 80.00 200.00
RFWAPCF Cal Foote 30.00 80.00
RFWAPDC Dylan Cozens 100.00 250.00
RFWAPJN Josh Norris 40.00 100.00
RFWAPJO Jake Oettinger 60.00 150.00
RFWAPKM K'Andre Miller 50.00 125.00
RFWAPKR Peyton Krebs 40.00 100.00
RFWAPLF Liam Foudy 25.00 60.00
RFWAPNB Nicolas Beaudin 25.00 60.00
RFWAPNH Nils Hoglander 25.00 60.00
RFWAPNR Nick Robertson 40.00 100.00
RFWAPOJ Olli Juolevi 25.00 60.00
RFWAPPJ Pierre-Olivier Joseph 25.00 60.00
RFWAPPK Philipp Kurashev 30.00 80.00
RFWAPSB Shane Bowers 20.00 50.00
RFWAPTD Ty Dellandrea 25.00 60.00
RFWAPTL Timothy Liljegren 25.00 60.00
RFWAPTS Tim Stutzle 50.00 125.00
RFWAPTY Ty Smith 40.00 100.00

2020-21 SP Authentic Chirography

CAF Adam Fox 10.00 25.00
CDA Phillip Danault 8.00 20.00
CJO Jake Oettinger 25.00 60.00
CKY Kailer Yamamoto 8.00 20.00
CMN Martin Necas 12.00 30.00
CPK Philipp Kurashev 12.00 30.00
CTS Tim Stutzle 50.00 125.00
CTT Teuvo Teravainen 8.00 20.00

2020-21 SP Authentic Immortal Ink

IIBO Bobby Orr 150.00 400.00
IIBS Billy Smith 40.00 100.00
IIDH Dominik Hasek 60.00 150.00
IIDS Darryl Sittler 50.00 125.00
IIGC Gerry Cheevers 40.00 100.00
IIMB Martin Brodeur 100.00 250.00
IIMR Mike Richter 40.00 100.00
IIPL Pat LaFontaine 40.00 100.00
IIPR Patrick Roy 100.00 250.00
IIWG Wayne Gretzky 500.00 1200.00
IIYC Yvan Cournoyer 40.00 100.00

2020-21 SP Authentic Limited Future Watch Patch Autographs

FWAPAA Alexander Alexeyev 15.00 40.00
FWAPAB Alex Belzile 15.00 40.00
FWAPAK Arthur Kaliyev 30.00 80.00
FWAPAL Alexis Lafreniere 800.00 2000.00
FWAPAN Anthony Angello 15.00 40.00
FWAPAR Alec Regula 12.00 30.00
FWAPBA Alexander Barabanov 20.00 50.00
FWAPBB Bowen Byram 40.00 100.00
FWAPBH Brandon Hagel 25.00 60.00
FWAPCF Cal Foote 25.00 60.00
FWAPCT Calvin Thurkauf 15.00 40.00
FWAPDC Dylan Cozens 200.00 500.00
FWAPGL Gustav Lindstrom 15.00 40.00
FWAPGQ Gage Quinney 12.00 30.00
FWAPIM Ian Mitchell 15.00 40.00
FWAPIS Ilya Sorokin 150.00 400.00
FWAPJE Jake Evans 20.00 50.00
FWAPJJ Jonas Johansson 20.00 50.00
FWAPJK Joel Kiviranta 20.00 50.00
FWAPJN Josh Norris 30.00 80.00
FWAPJO Jake Oettinger 50.00 125.00
FWAPJR Jason Robertson 600.00 1500.00
FWAPKA Kirill Kaprizov 2000.00 3000.00
FWAPKB Kieffer Bellows 15.00 40.00
FWAPKK Keegan Kolesar 15.00 40.00
FWAPKM K'Andre Miller 40.00 100.00
FWAPKU Philipp Kurashev 25.00 60.00
FWAPLC Lucas Carlsson 15.00 40.00
FWAPLF Liam Foudy 20.00 50.00
FWAPMA Mikey Anderson 20.00 50.00
FWAPMG Morgan Geekie 20.00 50.00
FWAPML Maxim Letunov 15.00 40.00
FWAPNB Nicolas Beaudin 20.00 50.00
FWAPNH Nils Hoglander 20.00 50.00
FWAPNK Nikolai Knyzhov 15.00 40.00
FWAPNR Nick Robertson 30.00 80.00
FWAPOJ Olli Juolevi 20.00 50.00
FWAPPF Pavel Francouz 25.00 60.00
FWAPPJ Pierre-Olivier Joseph 20.00 50.00
FWAPPK Peyton Krebs 30.00 80.00
FWAPPS Pius Suter 25.00 60.00
FWAPRD Reid Duke 20.00 50.00
FWAPRO Alexander Romanov 25.00 60.00
FWAPSB Shane Bowers 15.00 40.00
FWAPSL Steven Lorentz 15.00 40.00
FWAPSM Ty Smith 30.00 80.00
FWAPTB Tyler Benson 20.00 50.00
FWAPTD Ty Dellandrea 20.00 50.00
FWAPTL Timothy Liljegren 20.00 50.00
FWAPTR Alexander True 15.00 40.00
FWAPTS Tim Stutzle 600.00 1500.00
FWAPVV Vitek Vanecek 80.00 200.00
FWAPYS Yegor Sharangovich 30.00 80.00

2020-21 SP Authentic Limited Patch Autographs

LAMAM Anthony Mantha 12.00 30.00
LAMAS Andrei Svechnikov 20.00 50.00
LAMAT Alex Tuch 15.00 40.00
LAMAV Andrei Vasilevskiy 25.00 60.00
LAMBG Brendan Gallagher 15.00 40.00
LAMBH Bo Horvat 20.00 50.00
LAMBM Brad Marchand 30.00 80.00
LAMBO Brock Boeser 20.00 50.00
LAMBS Brayden Schenn 15.00 40.00
LAMBU Brent Burns 15.00 40.00
LAMCH Carter Hart 15.00 40.00
LAMCM Cale Makar 100.00 250.00
LAMDH Dougie Hamilton 12.00 30.00
LAMDP David Perron 12.00 30.00
LAMDS Dylan Strome 20.00 50.00
LAMEP Elias Pettersson 25.00 60.00
LAMGU Jake Guentzel 25.00 60.00
LAMHE Connor Hellebuyck 30.00 80.00
LAMHU Jonathan Huberdeau 20.00 50.00
LAMJB Josh Bailey 12.00 30.00
LAMJG John Gibson 15.00 40.00
LAMJH Jack Hughes 40.00 100.00
LAMJP Joe Pavelski 20.00 50.00
LAMJS Jordan Staal 12.00 30.00
LAMJT John Tavares 25.00 60.00
LAMKP Kyle Palmieri 12.00 30.00
LAMLD Leon Draisaitl 50.00 125.00
LAMMS Mark Scheifele 25.00 60.00
LAMMT Matthew Tkachuk 30.00 80.00
LAMNH Nico Hischier 25.00 60.00
LAMPA Colton Parayko 12.00 30.00
LAMPK Patrick Kane 30.00 80.00
LAMQH Quinn Hughes 40.00 100.00
LAMRN Ryan Nugent-Hopkins 20.00 50.00
LAMRO Ryan O'Reilly 15.00 40.00
LAMRS Ryan Suter 12.00 30.00
LAMTH Tomas Hertl 15.00 40.00
LAMTS Tyler Seguin 20.00 50.00
LAMTT Teuvo Teravainen 15.00 40.00
LAMWK William Karlsson 20.00 50.00
LAMYG Yanni Gourde 12.00 30.00
LAMZP Zach Parise 15.00 40.00

2020-21 SP Authentic Marks of Distinction

MDAL Alexis Lafreniere 300.00 800.00
MDAS Andrei Svechnikov 20.00 50.00
MDBB Bowen Byram 40.00 100.00
MDBH Bo Horvat 20.00 50.00
MDBM Brad Marchand 30.00 80.00
MDBU Brent Burns 15.00 40.00
MDCH Carter Hart 15.00 40.00
MDCM Cale Makar 200.00 500.00
MDDC Dylan Cozens 30.00 80.00
MDEP Elias Pettersson 25.00 60.00
MDHE Connor Hellebuyck 30.00 80.00
MDMC Connor McDavid 200.00 500.00
MDNH Nico Hischier 25.00 60.00
MDPK Peyton Krebs 30.00 80.00
MDRN Ryan Nugent-Hopkins 20.00 50.00
MDRO Ryan O'Reilly 15.00 40.00
MDTD Ty Dellandrea 20.00 50.00
MDTS Tyler Seguin 20.00 50.00

2020-21 SP Authentic Sign of the Times

*BLACK/5-49: X TO X BASIC INSERTS
SOTTAB Aleksander Barkov 12.00 30.00
SOTTAF Adam Fox 10.00 25.00
SOTTAG Andy Greene 5.00 12.00
SOTTAL Anders Lee 6.00 15.00
SOTTAM Anthony Mantha 6.00 15.00
SOTTAS Andrei Svechnikov 10.00 25.00
SOTTAT Alex Tuch 8.00 20.00
SOTTAU Auston Matthews 100.00 250.00
SOTTAV Andrei Vasilevskiy 12.00 30.00
SOTTBB Brent Burns 8.00 20.00
SOTTBI Paul Bissonnette 5.00 12.00
SOTTBM Brad Marchand 15.00 40.00
SOTTBO Brock Boeser 10.00 25.00
SOTTBS Brayden Schenn 8.00 20.00
SOTTBT Brady Tkachuk 12.00 30.00
SOTTCH Carter Hart 8.00 20.00
SOTTCM Connor McDavid 125.00 300.00
SOTTCP Colton Parayko 6.00 15.00
SOTTDH Dougie Hamilton 6.00 15.00
SOTTDK Dominik Kubalik 8.00 20.00
SOTTDP David Perron 6.00 15.00
SOTTDR David Rittich 6.00 15.00
SOTTDS Darryl Sittler 10.00 25.00
SOTTDU Pierre-Luc Dubois 6.00 15.00
SOTTDW Doug Weight 6.00 15.00
SOTTEP Elias Pettersson 12.00 30.00
SOTTES Eric Staal 8.00 20.00
SOTTFP Felix Potvin 12.00 30.00
SOTTGC Gerry Cheevers 8.00 20.00
SOTTGI Mark Giordano 8.00 20.00
SOTTHE Darren Helm 5.00 12.00
SOTTHI Nico Hischier 12.00 30.00
SOTTHO Bo Horvat 10.00 25.00
SOTTIS Ilya Samsonov 8.00 20.00
SOTTJB Josh Bailey 6.00 15.00
SOTTJG Jake Guentzel 12.00 30.00
SOTTJH Jonathan Huberdeau 10.00 25.00
SOTTJK John Klingberg 8.00 20.00
SOTTJM Josh Morrissey 10.00 25.00
SOTTJP Joe Pavelski 10.00 25.00
SOTTJS Jordan Staal 6.00 15.00
SOTTJV John Vanbiesbrouck 8.00 20.00
SOTTKT Keith Tkachuk 8.00 20.00
SOTTLD Leon Draisaitl 60.00 150.00
SOTTMA Marc Staal 5.00 12.00
SOTTMG Mike Gartner 10.00 25.00
SOTTMH Miro Heiskanen 10.00 25.00
SOTTMK Mark Stone 10.00 25.00
SOTTMR Mike Richter 8.00 20.00
SOTTMS Mark Scheifele 12.00 30.00
SOTTNF Nick Foligno 6.00 15.00
SOTTNH Niklas Hjalmarsson 5.00 12.00
SOTTNS Nick Suzuki 15.00 40.00
SOTTPB Peter Bondra 8.00 20.00
SOTTPD Phillip Danault 8.00 20.00
SOTTPE Phil Esposito 12.00 30.00
SOTTRD Ryan Dzingel 6.00 15.00
SOTTRH Roope Hintz 10.00 25.00
SOTTRM Manon Rheaume 20.00 50.00
SOTTRN Ryan Nugent-Hopkins 10.00 25.00
SOTTRO Ryan O'Reilly 8.00 20.00
SOTTSB Sergei Bobrovsky 12.00 30.00
SOTTSK Saku Koivu 8.00 20.00
SOTTSM Martin St. Louis 8.00 20.00
SOTTSR Sam Reinhart 15.00 40.00
SOTTST Shea Theodore 10.00 25.00
SOTTSY Steve Yzerman 20.00 50.00
SOTTTB Tyson Barrie 5.00 12.00
SOTTTH Tomas Hertl 8.00 20.00
SOTTTJ Tyler Johnson 5.00 12.00
SOTTTL Trevor Linden 8.00 20.00
SOTTTO Tyler Toffoli 8.00 20.00
SOTTTS Tyler Seguin 10.00 25.00
SOTTTT Teuvo Teravainen 8.00 20.00
SOTTVN Vladislav Namestnikov 5.00 12.00
SOTTYG Yanni Gourde 6.00 15.00
SOTTZP Zach Parise 8.00 20.00

2020-21 SP Authentic Sign of the Times 1980s

ST80AS Anton Stastny 6.00 15.00
ST80BS Billy Smith 8.00 20.00
ST80DS Darryl Sittler 10.00 25.00
ST80DW Doug Wilson 6.00 15.00
ST80GS Gary Suter 5.00 12.00
ST80HL Hakan Loob 5.00 12.00
ST80KM Ken Morrow 5.00 12.00
ST80MN Mats Naslund 5.00 12.00
ST80TK Tim Kerr 5.00 12.00

2020-21 SP Authentic Sign of the Times 1990s

ST90EL Eric Lindros 12.00 30.00
ST90FP Felix Potvin 12.00 30.00
ST90GF Grant Fuhr 12.00 30.00
ST90OK Olaf Kolzig 8.00 20.00
ST90PB Peter Bondra 8.00 20.00
ST90RR Rob Ray 5.00 12.00
ST90TL Trevor Linden 8.00 20.00
ST90TS Teemu Selanne 15.00 40.00
ST90WG Wayne Gretzky 100.00 250.00

2020-21 SP Authentic Sign of the Times 2000s

ST00AT Alex Tanguay 6.00 15.00
ST00CW Cam Ward 8.00 20.00
ST00HA Dominik Hasek 12.00 30.00
ST00HZ Henrik Zetterberg 10.00 25.00
ST00JB Jay Bouwmeester 5.00 12.00
ST00JC Jonathan Cheechoo 6.00 15.00
ST00JS Jason Spezza 8.00 20.00
ST00SG Simon Gagne 6.00 15.00
ST00SK Saku Koivu 8.00 20.00

2020-21 SP Authentic Sign of the Times 2010s

ST10AK Anze Kopitar 12.00 30.00
ST10AM Anthony Mantha 6.00 15.00
ST10BM Brad Marchand 15.00 40.00
ST10BO Brock Boeser 10.00 25.00
ST10BP Brayden Point 10.00 25.00
ST10CH Carter Hart 8.00 20.00
ST10CM Connor McDavid 125.00 300.00
ST10EP Elias Pettersson 12.00 30.00
ST10JT John Tavares 12.00 30.00
ST10MA Auston Matthews 200.00 500.00
ST10MS Mark Scheifele 12.00 30.00
ST10PK Patrick Kane 15.00 40.00
ST10RN Ryan Nugent-Hopkins 10.00 25.00
ST10SB Sergei Bobrovsky 12.00 30.00

2020-21 SP Authentic Sign of the Times Duals

ST2BP Elias Pettersson
Brock Boeser 30.00 80.00
ST2HS Mark Scheifele
Connor Hellebuyck 40.00 100.00
ST2KB Peter Bondra
Olaf Kolzig 80.00 200.00
ST2NY Kailer Yamamoto
Ryan Nugent-Hopkins 25.00 60.00
ST2SK Dylan Strome
Dominik Kubalik 25.00 60.00
ST2SS Gary Suter
Ryan Suter 15.00 40.00

2020-21 SP Authentic Spectrum FX

S1 David Pastrnak 2.50 6.00
S2 Roman Josi 1.00 2.50
S3 Victor Hedman 1.25 3.00
S4 Rasmus Dahlin 1.25 3.00
S5 Elias Pettersson 1.50 4.00
S6 Kyle Connor 1.50 4.00
S7 Mark Stone 1.25 3.00
S8 Mitch Marner 1.50 4.00
S9 Tyler Seguin 1.25 3.00
S10 Sidney Crosby 4.00 10.00
S11 John Carlson 1.00 2.50
S12 Nick Suzuki 2.00 5.00
S13 Matthew Tkachuk 2.00 5.00
S14 Sebastian Aho 1.50 4.00
S15 Auston Matthews 4.00 10.00
S16 Igor Shesterkin 2.00 5.00
S17 Cale Makar 2.50 6.00
S18 Mathew Barzal 1.25 3.00
S19 Quinn Hughes 2.50 6.00
S20 Leon Draisaitl 3.00 8.00
S21 Dylan Larkin 1.25 3.00
S22 Ryan O'Reilly 1.00 2.50
S23 Connor Hellebuyck 2.00 5.00
S24 Anze Kopitar 1.50 4.00
S25 Alex Ovechkin 4.00 10.00
S26 Jack Eichel 1.50 4.00
S27 Nico Hischier 1.50 4.00
S28 Jonathan Huberdeau 1.25 3.00
S29 Andrei Vasilevskiy 1.50 4.00
S30 Nathan MacKinnon 4.00 10.00
S31 Steven Stamkos 2.00 5.00
S32 Tuukka Rask 1.25 3.00
S33 Brady Tkachuk 1.50 4.00
S34 Pierre-Luc Dubois .75 2.00
S35 Artemi Panarin 2.00 5.00
S36 Connor McDavid 5.00 12.00
S37 Carter Hart 1.00 2.50
S38 Evgeni Malkin 2.00 5.00
S39 John Tavares 1.50 4.00
S40 Patrick Kane 2.00 5.00
S41 Jake Evans 3.00 8.00
S42 Artem Zub 2.50 6.00
S43 Matiss Kivlenieks 4.00 10.00
S44 Mikhail Berdin 3.00 8.00
S45 Martin Kaut 3.00 8.00
S46 Joel Kiviranta 3.00 8.00
S47 Alexander Barabanov 3.00 8.00
S48 Kevin Bahl 2.50 6.00
S49 Kevin Lankinen 5.00 12.00
S50 Sasha Chmelevski 2.50 6.00
S51 Morgan Geekie 3.00 8.00
S52 Pierre-Olivier Joseph 3.00 8.00
S53 Mathias Brome 2.50 6.00
S54 Jani Hakanpaa 2.00 5.00
S55 Kieffer Bellows 2.50 6.00
S56 Tyler Benson 3.00 8.00
S57 Michael DiPietro 4.00 10.00
S58 Dylan Coghlan 3.00 8.00
S59 Timothy Liljegren 3.00 8.00
S60 Joel Hofer 3.00 8.00
S61 Cal Foote 4.00 10.00
S62 Pavel Francouz 4.00 10.00
S63 Mikey Anderson 3.00 8.00
S64 Nicolas Beaudin 3.00 8.00
S65 John Leonard 2.50 6.00
S66 Philip Broberg 3.00 8.00
S67 Shane Bowers 2.50 6.00
S68 Yegor Sharangovich 5.00 12.00
S69 Alexander Alexeyev 2.50 6.00
S70 Jansen Harkins 2.50 6.00
S71 Ty Dellandrea 3.00 8.00
S72 Ian Mitchell 2.50 6.00
S73 Ty Smith 5.00 12.00
S74 Vitali Kravtsov 6.00 15.00
S75 Nolan Foote 3.00 8.00
S76 Thomas Harley 5.00 12.00
S77 Vitek Vanecek 5.00 12.00
S78 Pius Suter 4.00 10.00
S79 Nils Hoglander 3.00 8.00
S80 Jason Robertson 8.00 20.00
S81 Aleksi Heponiemi 4.00 10.00
S82 Victor Soderstrom 2.50 6.00
S83 Philipp Kurashev 4.00 10.00
S84 Gabe Vilardi 5.00 12.00
S85 Jake Oettinger 8.00 20.00
S86 Peyton Krebs 5.00 12.00
S87 K'Andre Miller 6.00 15.00
S88 Nick Robertson 5.00 12.00
S89 Liam Foudy 3.00 8.00
S90 Olli Juolevi 3.00 8.00
S91 Connor McMichael 5.00 12.00
S92 Dylan Cozens 5.00 12.00
S93 Tim Stutzle 6.00 15.00
S94 Alexander Romanov 4.00 10.00
S95 Kirill Kaprizov 12.00 30.00
S96 Ilya Sorokin 8.00 20.00
S97 Bowen Byram 6.00 15.00
S98 Josh Norris 5.00 12.00
S99 Arthur Kaliyev 5.00 12.00
S100 Alexis Lafreniere 10.00 25.00

2020-21 SP Authentic Top Performers

TPAL Alexis Lafreniere 5.00 12.00
TPAV Andrei Vasilevskiy 2.00 5.00
TPBH Brett Hull 2.50 6.00
TPBO Bobby Orr 5.00 12.00
TPEP Elias Pettersson 2.00 5.00
TPMH Miro Heiskanen 1.50 4.00
TPMM Mitch Marner 2.00 5.00
TPMS Mats Sundin 1.25 3.00
TPNR Nick Robertson 2.50 6.00
TPWG Wayne Gretzky 8.00 20.00

2020-21 SP Authentic Top Performers Autographs

TPAV Andrei Vasilevskiy 10.00 25.00
TPBH Brett Hull 30.00 80.00
TPMH Miro Heiskanen 8.00 20.00
TPMM Mitch Marner 10.00 25.00
TPMS Mats Sundin 15.00 40.00
TPNR Nick Robertson 12.00 30.00

2020-21 SP Authentic True Leaders

TLAB Aleksander Barkov 1.25 3.00
TLAK Anze Kopitar 1.25 3.00
TLAL Anders Lee .60 1.50
TLAO Alex Ovechkin 3.00 8.00
TLAP Alex Pietrangelo .60 1.50
TLBB Brent Burns .75 2.00
TLBH Bo Horvat 1.00 2.50
TLCG Claude Giroux .75 2.00
TLCM Connor McDavid 4.00 10.00
TLJE Jack Eichel 1.25 3.00
TLJK John Klingberg .75 2.00
TLJS Jordan Staal .60 1.50
TLMG Mark Giordano .75 2.00
TLNF Nick Foligno .60 1.50
TLPB Patrice Bergeron 1.00 2.50
TLRJ Roman Josi .75 2.00
TLRO Ryan O'Reilly .75 2.00
TLRS Ryan Suter .60 1.50
TLSC Sidney Crosby 3.00 8.00
TLSS Steven Stamkos 1.50 4.00
TLTA John Tavares 1.25 3.00

2020-21 SP Authentic True Leaders Autographs

TLAL Anders Lee/99 5.00 12.00
TLBB Brent Burns/25 6.00 15.00
TLJS Jordan Staal/99 5.00 12.00

2020-21 SP Authentic UD Authentics

UDAAS Andrei Svechnikov 12.00 30.00
UDAAV Andrei Vasilevskiy 15.00 40.00
UDABG Brendan Gallagher 10.00 25.00
UDABH Brett Hull 30.00 80.00
UDABM Brad Marchand 20.00 50.00
UDABP Brayden Point 12.00 30.00
UDACM Connor McDavid 125.00 300.00
UDADW Doug Wilson 8.00 20.00
UDAEL Eric Lindros 15.00 40.00
UDAEP Elias Pettersson 15.00 40.00
UDAJG Jake Guentzel 15.00 40.00
UDAJS Jaccob Slavin 8.00 20.00
UDAKT Keith Tkachuk 10.00 25.00
UDAKY Kailer Yamamoto 10.00 25.00
UDAMH Miro Heiskanen 12.00 30.00
UDAOK Olaf Kolzig 10.00 25.00
UDAPD Pierre-Luc Dubois 8.00 20.00
UDAPR Patrick Roy 25.00 60.00
UDARE Pekka Rinne 10.00 25.00
UDARN Ryan Nugent-Hopkins 12.00 30.00
UDARO Ryan O'Reilly 10.00 25.00
UDASB Sergei Bobrovsky 15.00 40.00
UDAST Shea Theodore 12.00 30.00
UDATT Teuvo Teravainen 10.00 25.00
UDAWG Wayne Gretzky 250.00 600.00

2021-22 SP Authentic

1 Connor McDavid 2.00 5.00
2 Jonathan Huberdeau .50 1.25
3 Patrik Laine .50 1.25
4 Carey Price .75 2.00
5 Ryan Getzlaf .40 1.00

6 Patrick Kane .75 2.00
7 Cam Talbot .40 1.00
8 Eeli Tolvanen .40 1.00
9 Drake Batherson .40 1.00
10 David Pastrnak 1.00 2.50
11 Jacob Markstrom .40 1.00
12 Jordan Binnington .60 1.50
13 Jakub Vrana .30 .75
14 Rasmus Dahlin .50 1.25
15 Clayton Keller .50 1.25
16 Mikko Rantanen 1.00 2.50
17 Brayden Point .50 1.25
18 Claude Giroux .40 1.00
19 Tristan Jarry .40 1.00
20 Miro Heiskanen .50 1.25
21 Tyler Toffoli .40 1.00
22 Troy Terry .30 .75
23 Marc-Andre Fleury .75 2.00
24 Aleksander Barkov .60 1.50
25 Andrei Vasilevskiy .60 1.50
26 Tyler Bertuzzi .30 .75
27 Quinn Hughes 1.00 2.50
28 Sebastian Aho .60 1.50
29 Taylor Hall .40 1.00
30 Jakub Voracek .30 .75
31 Ryan Nugent-Hopkins .50 1.25
32 Dougie Hamilton .30 .75
33 William Nylander .75 2.00
34 William Karlsson .50 1.25
35 Carter Hart .40 1.00
36 Igor Shesterkin .75 2.00
37 Cal Petersen .25 .60
38 Alex Ovechkin 1.50 4.00
39 Nico Hischier .60 1.50
40 John Tavares .60 1.50
41 John Gibson .40 1.00
42 Sergei Bobrovsky .60 1.50
43 Artemi Panarin .75 2.00
44 Tyler Seguin .50 1.25
45 Ryan O'Reilly .40 1.00
46 Brady Tkachuk .60 1.50
47 Jeff Petry .40 1.00
48 Juuse Saros .50 1.25
49 Jack Hughes 1.00 2.50
50 Nikita Kucherov .75 2.00
51 Joe Pavelski .50 1.25
52 Leon Draisaitl 1.25 3.00
53 Martin Necas .60 1.50
54 Teuvo Teravainen .40 1.00
55 Nick Suzuki .75 2.00
56 Elias Lindholm .40 1.00
57 Tim Stutzle .50 1.25
58 Josh Bailey .30 .75
59 Seth Jones .40 1.00
60 Brad Marchand .75 2.00
61 Conor Garland .30 .75
62 Connor Hellebuyck .75 2.00
63 Jonathan Marchessault .50 1.25
64 Victor Olofsson .40 1.00
65 Elvis Merzlikins .40 1.00
66 Brock Boeser .50 1.25
67 Jakob Chychrun .40 1.00
68 Max Pacioretty .40 1.00
69 Alex DeBrincat .50 1.25
70 Nikolaj Ehlers .40 1.00
71 Mathew Barzal .50 1.25
72 Brent Burns .40 1.00
73 Mark Stone .50 1.25
74 John Carlson .40 1.00
75 Nathan MacKinnon 1.50 4.00
76 Jordan Eberle .40 1.00
77 Kris Letang .50 1.25
78 Victor Hedman .50 1.25
79 Anders Lee .30 .75
80 Nicklas Backstrom .40 1.00
81 Tomas Hertl .40 1.00
82 Matthew Tkachuk .75 2.00
83 Roman Josi .40 1.00
84 Anze Kopitar .60 1.50
85 Mark Giordano .40 1.00
86 Mark Scheifele .60 1.50
87 Sidney Crosby 1.50 4.00
88 Auston Matthews 1.50 4.00
89 Kevin Fiala .30 .75
90 Jake Guentzel .60 1.50
91 Dylan Larkin .60 1.50
92 Patrice Bergeron .50 1.25
93 Philipp Grubauer .40 1.00
94 Brayden Schenn .40 1.00
95 Mitch Marner .60 1.50
96 Elias Pettersson .60 1.50
97 Kirill Kaprizov 1.25 3.00
98 Cam Atkinson .40 1.00
99 Adam Fox .50 1.25
100 Cale Makar 1.00 2.50
101 Cole Caufield
FW AU/949* RC 600.00 1500.00
102 Grigori Denisenko
FW AU/949* RC 10.00 25.00
103 Jeremy Swayman
FW AU/949* RC 125.00 300.00
104 Trevor Zegras FW AU/949* RC 300.00800.00
105 Ross Colton FW AU/949* RC 10.00 25.00
106 Cam York FW AU/949* RC 8.00 20.00
107 Jack Ahcan FW AU/949* RC 8.00 20.00
108 Lane Pederson FW RC 3.00 8.00
109 Radim Zohorna FW AU/949* RC 8.00 20.00
110 Shane Pinto FW AU/949* RC 12.00 30.00
111 Spencer Knight FW AU/949* RC 40.00100.00
112 Joe Veleno FW AU/949* RC 10.00 25.00
113 Wade Allison FW AU/949* RC 8.00 20.00
114 Ukko-Pekka Luukkonen
FW AU/949* RC 12.00 30.00
115 Morgan Barron FW AU/949* RC 6.00 15.00
116 Brett Murray FW AU/949* RC 8.00 20.00
117 David Farrance FW RC 3.00 8.00
118 Tyce Thompson FW AU/949* RC 8.00 20.00
119 Wyatt Kalynuk FW AU/949* RC 8.00 20.00
120 Logan Thompson
FW AU/949* RC 40.00 100.00
121 Alex Newhook FW AU/949* RC 12.00 30.00
122 Vasily Podkolzin FW AU/949* RC 30.0080.00
123 Matthew Phillips FW AU/949* RC 8.00 20.00
124 Alex Barre-Boulet
FW AU/949* RC 8.00 20.00
125 Mike Hardman FW AU/949* RC 8.00 20.00
126 Joey Keane FW RC 2.50 6.00
127 Jan Jenik FW AU/949* RC 10.00 25.00
128 Zac Jones FW AU/949* RC 10.00 25.00
129 Mattias Samuelsson
FW AU/949* RC 8.00 20.00
130 Rasmus Kupari FW AU/949* RC 8.00 20.00
131 Ivan Prosvetov FW AU/949* RC 8.00 20.00
132 Jamie Drysdale FW AU/949* RC 12.00 30.00
133 Calen Addison FW AU/949* RC 8.00 20.00
134 Jesse Ylonen FW AU/949* RC 8.00 20.00
135 Moritz Seider FW AU/949* RC 200.00500.00
136 Tanner Laczynski FW AU/949* RC 8.0020.00
137 Jonathan Dahlen FW RC 3.00 8.00
138 Jacob Bernard-Docker
FW AU/949* RC 8.00 20.00
139 Arttu Ruotsalainen FW RC 3.00 8.00
140 Parker Kelly FW AU/949* RC 8.00 20.00
141 Nils Lundkvist FW AU/949* RC 8.00 20.00
142 Sampo Ranta FW AU/949* RC 8.00 20.00
143 Philip Tomasino FW AU/949* RC 10.0025.00
144 Kole Lind FW AU/949* RC 10.00 25.00
145 Garrett Pilon FW AU/949* RC 10.00 25.00
146 Jake Neighbours FW AU/949* RC 15.0040.00
147 Jacob Bryson FW AU/949* RC 8.00 20.00
148 Filip Gustavsson FW AU/949* RC 15.0040.00
149 Lucas Raymond
FW AU/949* RC 125.00 300.00
150 Quinton Byfield
FW AU/949* RC 100.00 250.00
151 Alexander Holtz FW AU/949* RC 40.00100.00
152 J.J. Peterka FW AU/949* RC 60.00 150.00
153 Jasper Weatherby
FW AU/949* RC 8.00 20.00
154 Boris Katchouk FW AU/949* RC 6.00 15.00
155 Cole Perfetti FW AU/949* RC 40.00 100.00
156 Seth Jarvis FW AU/949* RC 60.00 150.00
157 Taylor Raddysh FW AU/949* RC 12.00 30.00
158 Paul Cotter FW AU/949* RC 8.00 20.00
159 Justus Annunen FW RC 4.00 10.00
160 Hendrix Lapierre FW AU/949* RC 8.00 20.00
161 Lassi Thomson FW AU/949* RC 8.00 20.00
162 Scott Perunovich FW AU/949* RC 8.00 20.00
163 Jake Leschyshyn FW AU/949* RC 8.00 20.00
164 Adam Beckman FW AU/949* RC 8.00 20.00
165 Alex Turcotte FW AU/949* RC 10.00 25.00
166 Yegor Chinakhov FW RC 5.00 12.00
167 Riley Damiani FW AU/949* RC 8.00 20.00
168 Brett Leason FW AU/949* RC 8.00 20.00
169 Ryan Merkley FW AU/949* RC 8.00 20.00
170 Karel Vejmelka FW AU/949* RC 10.00 25.00
171 Michael Bunting FW AU/949* RC 8.00 20.00
172 Thomas Novak FW RC 3.00 8.00
173 Jacob Peterson FW RC 3.00 8.00
174 Anton Lundell FW AU/949* RC 50.00 125.00
175 Gabriel Fortier FW AU/949* RC 8.00 20.00
176 Dawson Mercer
FW AU/949* RC 100.00 250.00
177 William Eklund FW AU/949* RC 50.00125.00
178 Egor Sokolov FW AU/949* RC 8.00 20.00
179 Oskar Steen FW AU/949* RC 10.00 25.00
180 Aliaksei Protas FW AU/949* RC 8.00 20.00
181 Brandon Duhaime
FW AU/949* RC 8.00 20.00
182 Mason McTavish
FW AU/949* RC 125.00 300.00
183 Pavel Dorofeyev FW AU/949* RC 10.0025.00
184 Benoit-Olivier Groulx
FW AU/949* RC 8.00 20.00
185 Justin Barron FW AU/949* RC 12.00 30.00
186 Robin Salo FW AU/949* RC 8.00 20.00
187 Sean Durzi FW AU/949* RC 8.00 20.00
188 Cole Sillinger FW AU/949* RC 40.00 100.00
189 Nico Daws FW AU/949* RC 12.00 30.00
190 Daniil Miromanov
FW AU/949* RC 8.00 20.00
191 Thomas Novak FW RC 3.00 8.00
192 Felix Sandstrom FW AU/949* RC 8.00 20.00
193 Cole Schwindt FW AU/949* RC 8.00 20.00
194 Jack Drury FW AU/949* RC 12.00 30.00
195 Riley Tufte FW AU/949* RC 8.00 20.00
196 Kasper Bjorkqvist
FW AU/949* RC 8.00 20.00
197 Daniil Tarasov FW RC 3.00 8.00
198 Tanner Jeannot FW AU/949* RC 8.00 20.00
199 Connor Dewar FW AU/949* RC 8.00 20.00

2021-22 SP Authentic Future Watch Inscriptions

*INSCRIPTIONS: 1X TO 2.5X BASIC
101 Cole Caufield/50* 1200.00 3000.00
111 Spencer Knight/50* 200.00 500.00
120 Logan Thompson/50* 150.00 400.00
122 Vasily Podkolzin/50* 100.00 250.00
150 Quinton Byfield/50* 150.00 400.00
152 John-Jason Peterka/50* 125.00 300.00
155 Cole Perfetti/50* 100.00 250.00
174 Anton Lundell/50* 100.00 250.00
176 Dawson Mercer/50* 200.00 500.00
177 William Eklund/50* 125.00 300.00
182 Mason McTavish/50* 250.00 600.00
188 Cole Sillinger/50* 125.00 300.00

2021-22 SP Authentic Limited Gold

*GOLD: 1.2X TO 3X RED
*GOLD FW: 1X TO 2.5X RED
101 Cole Caufield FW 100.00 250.00
104 Trevor Zegras FW 40.00 100.00
135 Moritz Seider FW 25.00 60.00
176 Dawson Mercer FW 15.00 40.00

2021-22 SP Authentic Limited Red

1 Connor McDavid 3.00 8.00
2 Jonathan Huberdeau .75 2.00
3 Patrik Laine .75 2.00
4 Carey Price 1.25 3.00
5 Ryan Getzlaf .60 1.50
6 Patrick Kane 1.25 3.00
7 Cam Talbot .60 1.50
8 Eeli Tolvanen .60 1.50
9 Drake Batherson .60 1.50
10 David Pastrnak 1.50 4.00
11 Jacob Markstrom .60 1.50
12 Jordan Binnington 1.00 2.50
13 Jakub Vrana .50 1.25
14 Rasmus Dahlin .75 2.00
15 Clayton Keller .75 2.00
16 Mikko Rantanen 1.50 4.00
17 Brayden Point .75 2.00
18 Claude Giroux .60 1.50
19 Tristan Jarry .60 1.50
20 Miro Heiskanen .75 2.00
21 Tyler Toffoli .60 1.50
22 Troy Terry .50 1.25
23 Marc-Andre Fleury 1.25 3.00
24 Aleksander Barkov 1.00 2.50
25 Andrei Vasilevskiy 1.00 2.50
26 Tyler Bertuzzi .50 1.25
27 Quinn Hughes 1.50 4.00
28 Sebastian Aho 1.00 2.50
29 Taylor Hall .60 1.50
30 Jakub Voracek .50 1.25
31 Ryan Nugent-Hopkins .75 2.00
32 Dougie Hamilton .50 1.25
33 William Nylander 1.25 3.00
34 William Karlsson .75 2.00
35 Carter Hart .60 1.50
36 Igor Shesterkin 1.25 3.00
37 Cal Petersen .40 1.00
38 Alex Ovechkin 2.50 6.00
39 Nico Hischier 1.00 2.50
40 John Tavares 1.00 2.50
41 John Gibson .60 1.50
42 Sergei Bobrovsky 1.00 2.50
43 Artemi Panarin 1.25 3.00
44 Tyler Seguin .75 2.00
45 Ryan O'Reilly .60 1.50
46 Brady Tkachuk 1.00 2.50
47 Jeff Petry .60 1.50
48 Juuse Saros .75 2.00
49 Jack Hughes 1.50 4.00
50 Nikita Kucherov 1.25 3.00
51 Joe Pavelski .75 2.00
52 Leon Draisaitl 2.00 5.00
53 Martin Necas 1.00 2.50
54 Teuvo Teravainen .60 1.50
55 Nick Suzuki 1.25 3.00
56 Elias Lindholm .60 1.50
57 Tim Stutzle .75 2.00
58 Josh Bailey .50 1.25
59 Seth Jones .60 1.50
60 Brad Marchand 1.25 3.00
61 Conor Garland .50 1.25
62 Connor Hellebuyck 1.25 3.00
63 Jonathan Marchessault .75 2.00
64 Victor Olofsson .60 1.50
65 Elvis Merzlikins .60 1.50
66 Brock Boeser .75 2.00
67 Jakob Chychrun .60 1.50
68 Max Pacioretty .60 1.50
69 Alex DeBrincat .75 2.00
70 Nikolaj Ehlers .60 1.50
71 Mathew Barzal .75 2.00
72 Brent Burns .60 1.50
73 Mark Stone .75 2.00
74 John Carlson .60 1.50
75 Nathan MacKinnon 2.50 6.00
76 Jordan Eberle .60 1.50
77 Kris Letang .75 2.00
78 Victor Hedman .75 2.00
79 Anders Lee .50 1.25
80 Nicklas Backstrom .60 1.50
81 Tomas Hertl .60 1.50
82 Matthew Tkachuk 1.25 3.00
83 Roman Josi .60 1.50
84 Anze Kopitar 1.00 2.50
85 Mark Giordano .60 1.50
86 Mark Scheifele 1.00 2.50
87 Sidney Crosby 2.50 6.00
88 Auston Matthews 2.50 6.00
89 Kevin Fiala .50 1.25
90 Jake Guentzel 1.00 2.50
91 Dylan Larkin .75 2.00
92 Patrice Bergeron .75 2.00
93 Philipp Grubauer .60 1.50
94 Brayden Schenn .60 1.50
95 Mitch Marner 1.00 2.50
96 Elias Pettersson 1.00 2.50
97 Kirill Kaprizov 2.00 5.00
98 Cam Atkinson .60 1.50
99 Adam Fox .75 2.00
100 Cale Makar 1.50 4.00
101 Cole Caufield FW 10.00 25.00
102 Grigori Denisenko FW 1.25 3.00
103 Jeremy Swayman FW 3.00 8.00
104 Trevor Zegras FW 2.00 5.00
105 Ross Colton FW 1.25 3.00
106 Cam York FW 1.00 2.50
107 Jack Ahcan FW 1.00 2.50
108 Lane Pederson FW 1.00 2.50
109 Radim Zohorna FW 1.00 2.50
110 Shane Pinto FW 1.50 4.00
111 Spencer Knight FW 2.00 5.00
112 Joe Veleno FW 1.00 2.50
113 Wade Allison FW 1.00 2.50
114 Ukko-Pekka Luukkonen FW 1.50 4.00
115 Morgan Barron FW .75 2.00
116 Brett Murray FW 1.00 2.50
117 David Farrance FW 1.00 2.50
118 Tyce Thompson FW 1.00 2.50
119 Wyatt Kalynuk FW 1.00 2.50
120 Logan Thompson FW 2.50 6.00
121 Alex Newhook FW 1.50 4.00
122 Vasily Podkolzin FW 1.25 3.00
123 Matthew Phillips FW 1.00 2.50
124 Alex Barre-Boulet FW 1.00 2.50
125 Mike Hardman FW 1.00 2.50
126 Joey Keane FW .75 2.00
127 Jan Jenik FW 1.25 3.00
128 Zac Jones FW 1.25 3.00
129 Mattias Samuelsson FW 1.00 2.50
130 Rasmus Kupari FW 1.00 2.50
131 Ivan Prosvetov FW 1.00 2.50
132 Jamie Drysdale FW 1.50 4.00
133 Calen Addison FW 1.00 2.50
134 Jesse Ylonen FW 1.00 2.50
135 Moritz Seider FW 2.50 6.00
136 Tanner Laczynski FW 1.00 2.50
137 Jonathan Dahlen FW 1.00 2.50
138 Jacob Bernard-Docker FW 1.00 2.50
139 Arttu Ruotsalainen FW 1.00 2.50
140 Parker Kelly FW 1.00 2.50
141 Nils Lundkvist FW 1.00 2.50
142 Sampo Ranta FW 1.00 2.50
143 Philip Tomasino FW 1.25 3.00
144 Kole Lind FW 1.25 3.00
145 Garrett Pilon FW 1.25 3.00
146 Jake Neighbours FW 2.00 5.00
147 Jacob Bryson FW 1.00 2.50
148 Filip Gustavsson FW 2.00 5.00
149 Lucas Raymond FW 3.00 8.00
150 Quinton Byfield FW 2.50 6.00
151 Alexander Holtz FW 1.50 4.00
152 J.J. Peterka FW 2.00 5.00
153 Jasper Weatherby FW 1.00 2.50
154 Boris Katchouk FW .75 2.00
155 Cole Perfetti FW 2.00 5.00
156 Seth Jarvis FW 2.50 6.00
157 Taylor Raddysh FW 1.50 4.00
158 Paul Cotter FW 1.00 2.50
159 Justus Annunen FW 1.25 3.00
160 Hendrix Lapierre FW 1.00 2.50
161 Lassi Thomson FW 1.00 2.50
162 Scott Perunovich FW 1.00 2.50
163 Jake Leschyshyn FW 1.00 2.50
164 Adam Beckman FW 1.00 2.50
165 Alex Turcotte FW 1.25 3.00
166 Yegor Chinakhov FW 1.50 4.00
167 Riley Damiani FW 1.00 2.50
168 Brett Leason FW 1.00 2.50
169 Ryan Merkley FW 1.25 3.00
170 Karel Vejmelka FW 1.25 3.00
171 Michael Bunting FW 1.00 2.50
172 Fabian Zetterlund FW 1.00 2.50
173 Jacob Peterson FW 1.00 2.50
174 Anton Lundell FW 2.00 5.00
175 Gabriel Fortier FW 1.00 2.50
176 Dawson Mercer FW 2.50 6.00
177 William Eklund FW 2.50 6.00
178 Egor Sokolov FW 1.00 2.50
179 Oskar Steen FW 1.25 3.00
180 Aliaksei Protas FW 1.00 2.50
181 Brandon Duhaime FW 1.00 2.50
182 Mason McTavish FW 2.00 5.00
183 Pavel Dorofeyev FW 1.25 3.00
184 Benoit-Olivier Groulx FW 1.00 2.50
185 Justin Barron FW 1.50 4.00
186 Robin Salo FW 1.00 2.50
187 Sean Durzi FW 1.00 2.50
188 Cole Sillinger FW 1.50 4.00
189 Nico Daws FW 1.50 4.00
190 Daniil Miromanov FW 1.00 2.50
191 Thomas Novak FW 1.00 2.50
192 Felix Sandstrom FW 1.00 2.50
193 Cole Schwindt FW 1.00 2.50
194 Jack Drury FW 1.50 4.00
195 Riley Tufte FW 1.00 2.50
196 Kasper Bjorkqvist FW 1.00 2.50
197 Daniil Tarasov FW 1.00 2.50
198 Tanner Jeannot FW 1.00 2.50
199 Connor Dewar FW 1.00 2.50
200 Lucas Raymond FW 3.00 8.00

2021-22 SP Authentic '01-02 Retro Autographs

01RAAB Anthony Beauvillier/199 6.00 15.00
01RAAC Andrew Copp/199 6.00 15.00
01RAAK Anze Kopitar/25 15.00 40.00
01RAAN Alex Nedeljkovic/199 8.00 20.00
01RAAT Alex Tuch/199 10.00 25.00
01RABA Josh Bailey/199 8.00 20.00
01RABB Brock Boeser/25 12.00 30.00
01RABE Tyler Bertuzzi/99 8.00 20.00
01RABM Brad Marchand/25 20.00 50.00
01RABN Brock Nelson/199 10.00 25.00
01RABU Brent Burns/25 10.00 25.00
01RABY Bowen Byram/99 12.00 30.00
01RACA Cam Atkinson/99 10.00 25.00
01RACH Connor Hellebuyck/25 20.00 50.00
01RACN Cam Neely/99 8.00 20.00
01RADB Drake Batherson/199 8.00 20.00
01RADV Dave Taylor/199 8.00 20.00
01RAET Eeli Tolvanen/199 10.00 25.00
01RAFH Filip Hronek/199 6.00 15.00
01RAGI John Gibson/25 10.00 25.00
01RAHI Roope Hintz/99 12.00 30.00
01RAHJ Henri Jokiharju/199 6.00 15.00
01RAJB Jesper Bratt/199 10.00 25.00
01RAJC Jack Campbell/199 10.00 25.00
01RAJE Jordan Eberle/99 10.00 25.00
01RAJG Jake Guentzel/25 15.00 40.00
01RAJH Jonathan Huberdeau/25 12.00 30.00
01RAJM Jonathan Marchessault/99 12.00 30.00
01RAJN Josh Norris/99 10.00 25.00
01RAJP Jeff Petry/99 10.00 25.00
01RAJT John Tavares/25 15.00 40.00
01RAJZ Jason Zucker/199 10.00 25.00
01RAKC Kyle Connor/25 15.00 40.00
01RAKF Kevin Fiala/199 8.00 20.00
01RALI Mike Liut/99 6.00 15.00
01RAMA Maxime Comtois/199 8.00 20.00
01RAMC Jared McCann/199 8.00 20.00
01RAMD Marcel Dionne/25 20.00 50.00
01RAMI Casey Mittelstadt/199 10.00 25.00
01RAMM Mike Modano/25 15.00 40.00
01RAMN Martin Necas/199 15.00 40.00
01RAMS Mike Smith/199 6.00 15.00
01RAMT Matthew Tkachuk/25 20.00 50.00
01RANH Nils Hoglander/99 8.00 20.00
01RAPA Joe Pavelski/99 12.00 30.00
01RAPG Philipp Grubauer/99 10.00 25.00
01RARB Ray Bourque/25 15.00 40.00
01RARH Ron Hextall/25 25.00 60.00
01RARO Jack Roslovic/199 6.00 15.00
01RARR Ryan Reaves/199 8.00 20.00
01RASG Samuel Girard/199 6.00 15.00
01RATF Theoren Fleury/25 10.00 25.00
01RATH Tomas Hertl/99 10.00 25.00
01RATJ Tristan Jarry/199 10.00 25.00
01RATO Tyler Toffoli/99 10.00 25.00
01RATS Tim Stutzle/25 12.00 30.00
01RATY Troy Terry/99 8.00 20.00
01RAVA John Vanbiesbrouck/25 50.00 125.00
01RAVL Vincent Lecavalier/25 10.00 25.00
01RAVO Victor Olofsson/99 10.00 25.00
01RAWK William Karlsson/99 12.00 30.00
01RAYG Yanni Gourde/199 8.00 20.00
01RAYS Yegor Sharangovich/199 10.00 25.00
01RAZP Zach Parise/25 10.00 25.00

2021-22 SP Authentic '01-02 Retro Future Watch

01FWAB Adam Beckman 2.50 6.00
01FWAH Alexander Holtz 4.00 10.00
01FWAL Anton Lundell 5.00 12.00
01FWAN Alex Newhook FW 4.00 10.00
01FWAP Aliaksei Protas 2.50 6.00
01FWAT Alex Turcotte 3.00 8.00
01FWBG Benoit-Olivier Groulx 2.50 6.00
01FWCC Cole Caufield 10.00 25.00
01FWCP Cole Perfetti 5.00 12.00
01FWCS Cole Sillinger 4.00 10.00
01FWCY Cam York 2.50 6.00
01FWDA Jonathan Dahlen 2.50 6.00
01FWDF David Farrance 2.50 6.00
01FWDM Dawson Mercer 6.00 15.00
01FWFG Filip Gustavsson 5.00 12.00
01FWGD Grigori Denisenko 3.00 8.00
01FWHL Hendrix Lapierre 2.50 6.00
01FWJD Jamie Drysdale 4.00 10.00
01FWJJ Jan Jenik 3.00 8.00
01FWJN Jake Neighbours 5.00 12.00
01FWJS Jeremy Swayman 8.00 20.00
01FWJV Joe Veleno 3.00 8.00
01FWKL Kole Lind 3.00 8.00
01FWLR Lucas Raymond 8.00 20.00
01FWMB J.J. Peterka 5.00 12.00
01FWMM Mason McTavish 5.00 12.00
01FWMP Matthew Phillips 2.50 6.00
01FWMR Tanner Jeannot 2.50 6.00
01FWMS Mattias Samuelsson 2.50 6.00
01FWNL Nils Lundkvist 2.50 6.00
01FWPI Shane Pinto 4.00 10.00
01FWPT Philip Tomasino 3.00 8.00
01FWQB Quinton Byfield 6.00 15.00
01FWRC Ross Colton 3.00 8.00
01FWRK Rasmus Kupari 2.50 6.00
01FWRM Ryan Merkley 3.00 8.00
01FWRS Robin Salo 2.50 6.00
01FWRT Riley Tufte 2.50 6.00
01FWRZ Radim Zohorna 2.50 6.00
01FWSE Moritz Seider 6.00 15.00
01FWSJ Seth Jarvis 6.00 15.00
01FWSK Spencer Knight 5.00 12.00
01FWSP Scott Perunovich 2.50 6.00
01FWSR Sampo Ranta 2.50 6.00
01FWTZ Trevor Zegras 5.00 12.00
01FWUL Ukko-Pekka Luukkonen 4.00 10.00
01FWVP Vasily Podkolzin 3.00 8.00
01FWWE William Eklund 6.00 15.00
01FWWK Wyatt Kalynuk 2.50 6.00
01FWYC Yegor Chinakhov 4.00 10.00

2021-22 SP Authentic '01-02 Retro Future Watch Limited

*LIMITED: .75X TO 2X BASIC
01FWCC Cole Caufield 60.00 150.00
01FWSE Moritz Seider 20.00 50.00
01FWTZ Trevor Zegras 25.00 60.00

2021-22 SP Authentic '01-02 Retro Future Watch Autographs

01FWAH Alexander Holtz 15.00 40.00
01FWCP Cole Perfetti 50.00 125.00
01FWCY Cam York 15.00 40.00
01FWFG Filip Gustavsson 40.00 100.00
01FWJJ Jan Jenik 12.00 30.00
01FWJS Jeremy Swayman 125.00 300.00
01FWMM Mason McTavish 80.00 200.00
01FWMP Matthew Phillips 15.00 40.00
01FWMS Mattias Samuelsson 10.00 25.00
01FWNL Nils Lundkvist 10.00 25.00
01FWPT Philip Tomasino 12.00 30.00
01FWRC Ross Colton 12.00 30.00
01FWRZ Radim Zohorna 10.00 25.00
01FWSK Spencer Knight 30.00 80.00
01FWSR Sampo Ranta 10.00 25.00

2021-22 SP Authentic '01-02 Retro Sign of the Times

SOTT1AC Anthony Cirelli E 8.00 20.00
SOTT1AG Andy Greene D 6.00 15.00
SOTT1AK Anze Kopitar B 15.00 40.00
SOTT1AL Anders Lee C 8.00 20.00
SOTT1BB Brent Burns C 10.00 25.00
SOTT1BG Brendan Gallagher E 10.00 25.00
SOTT1BM Brad Marchand B 20.00 50.00
SOTT1BR Rod Brind'Amour C 10.00 25.00
SOTT1CA Cam Atkinson E 8.00 20.00
SOTT1CG Conor Garland D 8.00 20.00
SOTT1CM Casey Mittelstadt E 10.00 25.00
SOTT1CN Cam Neely B 8.00 20.00
SOTT1CO Maxime Comtois E 8.00 20.00
SOTT1CT Cam Talbot E 10.00 25.00
SOTT1DB Drake Batherson E 10.00 25.00
SOTT1DH Dougie Hamilton C 8.00 20.00
SOTT1ET Eeli Tolvanen E 10.00 25.00
SOTT1IL Isac Lundestrom F 6.00 15.00
SOTT1JA Jake Allen E 10.00 25.00
SOTT1JB Jesper Bratt E 10.00 25.00
SOTT1JC Jack Campbell E 10.00 25.00
SOTT1JE Jordan Eberle D 10.00 25.00
SOTT1JM Jonathan Marchessault B 12.00 30.00
SOTT1JP Jeff Petry D 10.00 25.00
SOTT1JR Jack Roslovic F 6.00 15.00
SOTT1JT John Tavares A 15.00 40.00
SOTT1JZ Jason Zucker D 10.00 25.00
SOTT1KF Kevin Fiala C 8.00 20.00
SOTT1KY Keith Yandle E 6.00 15.00
SOTT1MA Jacob Markstrom F 10.00 25.00
SOTT1MC Jared McCann F 8.00 20.00
SOTT1MD Marcel Dionne C 12.00 30.00
SOTT1MN Martin Necas F 15.00 40.00
SOTT1MS Mike Smith F 6.00 15.00
SOTT1NH Nils Hoglander E 8.00 20.00
SOTT1NL Nicklas Lidstrom A 10.00 25.00
SOTT1PA Joe Pavelski C 12.00 30.00
SOTT1RB Ray Bourque A 15.00 40.00
SOTT1RD Ryan Dzingel F 8.00 20.00
SOTT1RH Ron Hextall B 8.00 20.00
SOTT1RO Ryan O'Reilly C 10.00 25.00
SOTT1RR Ryan Reaves F 8.00 20.00
SOTT1RT Robert Thomas C 10.00 25.00
SOTT1SG Samuel Girard F 6.00 15.00
SOTT1SR Sam Reinhart D 20.00 50.00
SOTT1ST Mark Stone C 20.00 50.00
SOTT1SW Sean Walker F 6.00 15.00
SOTT1TJ Tristan Jarry D 10.00 25.00
SOTT1TL Trevor Linden A 10.00 25.00
SOTT1TT Tyler Toffoli C 10.00 25.00
SOTT1VO Victor Olofsson D 10.00 25.00
SOTT1VV Vitek Vanecek F 10.00 25.00
SOTT1YG Yanni Gourde D 8.00 20.00
SOTT1ZP Zach Parise D 10.00 25.00

2021-22 SP Authentic '11-12 Retro Future Watch Autographs

RFWAAB Adam Beckman/99 10.00 25.00
RFWAAH Alexander Holtz/99 40.00 100.00
RFWAAL Anton Lundell/99 40.00 100.00
RFWAAN Alex Newhook/99 15.00 40.00
RFWAAP Aliaksei Protas/499 10.00 25.00
RFWAAT Alex Turcotte/99 12.00 30.00
RFWABA Alex Barre-Boulet/499 10.00 25.00
RFWABD Brandon Duhaime/499 10.00 25.00
RFWABG Benoit-Olivier Groulx/499 10.00 25.00
RFWABK Boris Katchouk/499 8.00 20.00
RFWABL Brett Leason/499 8.00 20.00
RFWABM Brett Murray/499 10.00 25.00
RFWABR Jacob Bryson/499 10.00 25.00
RFWABU Michael Bunting/99 10.00 25.00
RFWACA Calen Addison/499 10.00 25.00
RFWACC Cole Caufield/99 400.00 1000.00
RFWACP Cole Perfetti/99 60.00 150.00
RFWACS Cole Sillinger/99 15.00 40.00
RFWADM Daniil Miromanov/499 10.00 25.00
RFWADR Jamie Drysdale/99 15.00 40.00
RFWAES Egor Sokolov/499 10.00 25.00
RFWAFG Filip Gustavsson/99 20.00 50.00
RFWAFS Felix Sandstrom/499 10.00 25.00
RFWAFZ Fabian Zetterlund/499 10.00 25.00
RFWAGD Grigori Denisenko/99 12.00 30.00
RFWAGF Gabriel Fortier/499 10.00 25.00
RFWAGP Garrett Pilon/499 12.00 30.00
RFWAHL Hendrix Lapierre/99 10.00 25.00
RFWAIP Ivan Prosvetov/499 10.00 25.00
RFWAJA Jack Ahcan/499 10.00 25.00
RFWAJB Jacob Bernard-Docker/499 10.00 25.00
RFWAJD Jack Drury/499 15.00 40.00
RFWAJJ Jan Jenik/499 12.00 30.00
RFWAJL Jake Leschyshyn/499 10.00 25.00
RFWAJN Jake Neighbours/99 20.00 50.00
RFWAJP J.J. Peterka/99 30.00 80.00
RFWAJS Jeremy Swayman/99 125.00 300.00
RFWAJU Justin Barron/99 15.00 40.00
RFWAJV Joe Veleno/99 12.00 30.00
RFWAJW Jasper Weatherby/499 10.00 25.00
RFWAJY Jesse Ylonen/499 10.00 25.00
RFWAKB Kasper Bjorkqvist/499 10.00 25.00
RFWAKL Kole Lind/499 12.00 30.00
RFWAKV Karel Vejmelka/499 12.00 30.00
RFWALT Lassi Thomson/499 10.00 25.00
RFWAME Dawson Mercer/99 125.00 300.00
RFWAMM Mason McTavish/99 50.00 125.00
RFWAMO Morgan Barron/499 8.00 20.00
RFWAMP Matthew Phillips/499 10.00 25.00
RFWAMS Mattias Samuelsson/499 10.00 25.00
RFWAND Nico Daws/499 15.00 40.00
RFWANL Nils Lundkvist/499 10.00 25.00
RFWAOS Oskar Steen/499 10.00 25.00
RFWAPC Paul Cotter/499 10.00 25.00
RFWAPD Pavel Dorofeyev/499 12.00 30.00
RFWAPI Shane Pinto/499 15.00 40.00
RFWAPK Parker Kelly/499 10.00 25.00
RFWAPT Philip Tomasino/499 12.00 30.00
RFWAQB Quinton Byfield/99 200.00 500.00
RFWARC Ross Colton/499 12.00 30.00
RFWARK Rasmus Kupari/499 10.00 25.00
RFWARM Ryan Merkley/499 12.00 30.00
RFWARS Robin Salo/499 10.00 25.00
RFWART Riley Tufte/499 10.00 25.00
RFWARZ Radim Zohorna/499 10.00 25.00
RFWASC Cole Schwindt/499 10.00 25.00
RFWASD Sean Durzi/499 10.00 25.00
RFWASK Spencer Knight/99 60.00 150.00
RFWASP Scott Perunovich/499 10.00 25.00
RFWASR Sampo Ranta/499 10.00 25.00
RFWATH Logan Thompson/499 25.00 60.00
RFWATJ Tanner Jeannot/499 10.00 25.00
RFWATL Tanner Laczynski/499 10.00 25.00
RFWATR Taylor Raddysh/499 15.00 40.00
RFWATT Tyce Thompson/499 10.00 25.00
RFWAUL Ukko-Pekka Luukkonen/499 15.00 40.00
RFWAVP Vasily Podkolzin/99 30.00 80.00
RFWAWA Wade Allison/499 10.00 25.00
RFWAWE William Eklund/99 80.00 200.00
RFWAZJ Zac Jones/499 12.00 30.00

2021-22 SP Authentic '11-12 Retro Future Watch Patch Autographs

RFWAPAH Alexander Holtz/50 50.00 125.00
RFWAPAL Anton Lundell/99 60.00 150.00
RFWAPAN Alex Newhook/99 50.00 125.00
RFWAPAT Alex Turcotte/99 40.00 100.00
RFWAPBG Benoit-Olivier Groulx/99 30.00 80.00
RFWAPCC Cole Caufield/25 1000.00 2500.00
RFWAPCP Cole Perfetti/99 80.00 200.00
RFWAPCS Cole Sillinger/99 50.00 125.00
RFWAPCY Cam York/99 40.00 100.00
RFWAPDM Dawson Mercer/99 250.00 600.00
RFWAPJS Jeremy Swayman/99 300.00 800.00
RFWAPMM Mason McTavish/50 200.00 500.00
RFWAPNL Nils Lundkvist/99 30.00 80.00
RFWAPPT Philip Tomasino/99 40.00 100.00
RFWAPQB Quinton Byfield/25 150.00 400.00
RFWAPSP Shane Pinto/99 50.00 125.00
RFWAPVP Vasily Podkolzin/99 40.00 100.00

2021-22 SP Authentic Chirography

CAH Alexander Holtz B 12.00 30.00
CAN Alex Newhook B 12.00 30.00
CBG Brendan Gallagher B 8.00 20.00
CCA Cam Atkinson B 8.00 20.00
CCG Conor Garland B 6.00 15.00
CCH Connor Hellebuyck A 15.00 40.00
CCM Casey Mittelstadt C 8.00 20.00
CDB Drake Batherson B 8.00 20.00
CDH Dougie Hamilton A 6.00 15.00
CDS Dylan Strome C 10.00 25.00
CJD Jamie Drysdale B 10.00 25.00
CJG John Gibson A 8.00 20.00
CJN Jake Neighbours C 15.00 40.00
CJP Jeff Petry A 8.00 20.00
CJT John Tavares A 12.00 30.00
CJV Joe Veleno C 8.00 20.00
CKP Kyle Palmieri C 6.00 15.00
CKY Keith Yandle B 5.00 12.00
CMC Maxime Comtois B 6.00 15.00
CMH Miro Heiskanen A 10.00 25.00
CMM Mason McTavish C 30.00 80.00
CMS Mark Stone A 10.00 25.00
CNE Nikolaj Ehlers A 8.00 20.00
CNH Nils Hoglander C 6.00 15.00
CNL Nils Lundkvist C 8.00 20.00
CNO Josh Norris C 8.00 20.00
CNS Nick Suzuki A 15.00 40.00
CPE Cole Perfetti B 30.00 80.00
CPG Philipp Grubauer A 8.00 20.00
CRC Ross Colton C 10.00 25.00
CRS Ryan Suter A 6.00 15.00
CRT Robert Thomas C 8.00 20.00
CSB Sergei Bobrovsky A 12.00 30.00
CSK Spencer Knight A 15.00 40.00
CSP Scott Perunovich C 8.00 20.00
CSR Sam Reinhart C 15.00 40.00
CTB Tyler Bertuzzi A 6.00 15.00
CTH Tomas Hertl A 8.00 20.00
CTJ Tristan Jarry C 8.00 20.00
CTT Teuvo Teravainen A 8.00 20.00
CVO Victor Olofsson B 8.00 20.00
CVP Vasily Podkolzin C 10.00 25.00
CZP Zach Parise B 8.00 20.00

2021-22 SP Authentic Die Cuts

*BLUE: .6X TO 1.5X BASIC
*GREEN: 1X TO 2.5X BASIC
DC1 Connor McDavid 2.50 6.00
DC2 Lucas Raymond 1.50 4.00
DC3 Patrick Kane 1.00 2.50
DC4 Andrei Vasilevskiy .75 2.00
DC5 Nathan MacKinnon 2.00 5.00
DC6 Sebastian Aho .75 2.00
DC7 David Pastrnak 1.25 3.00
DC8 Mitch Marner .75 2.00
DC9 Alex Ovechkin 2.00 5.00
DC10 Cole Caufield 2.00 5.00
DC11 Max Pacioretty .50 1.25
DC12 Matthew Tkachuk 1.00 2.50
DC13 Connor Hellebuyck 1.00 2.50
DC14 Quinn Hughes 1.25 3.00
DC15 Nick Suzuki 1.00 2.50
DC16 Spencer Knight 1.00 2.50
DC17 Auston Matthews 2.00 5.00
DC18 Artemi Panarin 1.00 2.50
DC19 Moritz Seider 1.25 3.00
DC20 Brad Marchand 1.00 2.50
DC21 Leon Draisaitl 1.50 4.00
DC22 Quinton Byfield 1.25 3.00
DC23 Sidney Crosby 2.00 5.00
DC24 Jack Hughes 1.25 3.00
DC25 Kirill Kaprizov 1.50 4.00

2021-22 SP Authentic Future Icons

FI1 T.Terry/T.Zegras 2.00 5.00
FI2 C.Keller/J.Moser 1.25 3.00
FI3 J.Swayman/C.McAvoy 3.00 8.00
FI4 R.Dahlin/U.Luukkonen 1.50 4.00
FI5 A.Ruzicka/A.Mangiapane 1.00 2.50
FI6 S.Jarvis/A.Svechnikov 2.50 6.00
FI7 W.Kalynuk/P.Kurashev 1.00 2.50
FI8 A.Newhook/C.Makar 2.50 6.00
FI9 P.Laine/C.Sillinger 1.50 4.00
FI10 R.Tufte/R.Hintz 1.25 3.00
FI11 L.Raymond/M.Seider 3.00 8.00
FI12 K.Yamamoto/E.Bouchard 1.25 3.00
FI13 S.Knight/A.Lundell 2.00 5.00
FI14 Q.Byfield/G.Vilardi 2.50 6.00
FI15 K.Kaprizov/J.Greenway 3.00 8.00
FI16 C.Caufield/N.Suzuki 4.00 10.00
FI17 E.Tolvanen/J.Saros 1.25 3.00
FI18 D.Mercer/A.Holtz 2.50 6.00
FI19 I.Sorokin/O.Wahlstrom 1.50 4.00
FI20 A.Fox/N.Lundkvist 1.25 3.00
FI21 S.Pinto/J.Bernard-Docker 1.50 4.00
FI22 C.York/I.Provorov 1.00 2.50
FI23 B.Rust/T.Jarry 1.00 2.50
FI24 K.Lind/C.Driedger 1.25 3.00
FI25 W.Eklund/J.Dahlen 2.50 6.00
FI26 S.Perunovich/J.Kyrou 1.00 2.50
FI27 T.Raddysh/R.Colton 1.50 4.00
FI28 A.Matthews/J.Campbell 4.00 10.00
FI29 N.Hoglander/V.Podkolzin 1.25 3.00
FI30 J.Leschyshyn/L.Thompson 2.50 6.00
FI31 H.Lapierre/V.Vanecek 1.00 2.50
FI32 C.Perfetti/P.Dubois 2.00 5.00

2021-22 SP Authentic Future Icons Limited

*LIMITED/25: 1X TO 2.5X BASIC
FI16 Cole Caufield
Nick Suzuki 15.00 40.00

2021-22 SP Authentic Future Watch Patch Autographs

FWAPAB Adam Beckman 20.00 50.00
FWAPAH Alexander Holtz 100.00 250.00
FWAPAL Anton Lundell 125.00 300.00
FWAPAN Alex Newhook 80.00 200.00
FWAPAP Aliaksei Protas 20.00 50.00
FWAPAT Alex Turcotte 80.00 200.00
FWAPBA Morgan Barron 15.00 40.00
FWAPBK Boris Katchouk 15.00 40.00
FWAPBR Jacob Bryson 20.00 50.00
FWAPCA Calen Addison 40.00 100.00
FWAPCC Cole Caufield 1500.00 4000.00
FWAPCP Cole Perfetti 100.00 250.00
FWAPCS Cole Sillinger 80.00 200.00
FWAPCY Cam York 20.00 50.00
FWAPDM Dawson Mercer 150.00 400.00
FWAPDR Jamie Drysdale 125.00 300.00
FWAPGD Grigori Denisenko 40.00 100.00
FWAPGP Garrett Pilon 25.00 60.00
FWAPIP Ivan Prosvetov 20.00 50.00
FWAPJA Jack Ahcan 20.00 50.00
FWAPJB Jacob Bernard-Docker 20.00 50.00
FWAPJJ Jan Jenik 25.00 60.00
FWAPJL Jake Leschyshyn 20.00 50.00
FWAPJN Jake Neighbours 80.00 200.00
FWAPJS Jeremy Swayman 300.00 800.00
FWAPJV Joe Veleno 25.00 60.00
FWAPJW Jasper Weatherby 20.00 50.00
FWAPJY Jesse Ylonen 20.00 50.00
FWAPLP Lane Pederson 20.00 50.00
FWAPLT Logan Thompson 125.00 300.00
FWAPMH Mike Hardman 20.00 50.00

FWAPMM Mason McTavish 300.00 800.00
FWAPMP Matthew Phillips 20.00 50.00
FWAPMS Mattias Samuelsson 20.00 50.00
FWAPNL Nils Lundkvist 20.00 50.00
FWAPOS Oskar Steen 25.00 60.00
FWAPPD Pavel Dorofeyev 25.00 60.00
FWAPPI Shane Pinto 100.00 250.00
FWAPPK Parker Kelly 20.00 50.00
FWAPPT Philip Tomasino 80.00 200.00
FWAPQB Quinton Byfield 1500.00 4000.00
FWAPRC Ross Colton 25.00 60.00
FWAPRD Riley Damiani 20.00 50.00
FWAPRK Rasmus Kupari 20.00 50.00
FWAPRM Ryan Merkley 25.00 60.00
FWAPRT Riley Tufte 20.00 50.00
FWAPRZ Radim Zohorna 20.00 50.00
FWAPSJ Seth Jarvis 150.00 400.00
FWAPSK Spencer Knight 150.00 400.00
FWAPSP Scott Perunovich 20.00 50.00
FWAPSR Sampo Ranta 20.00 50.00
FWAPTL Tanner Laczynski 20.00 50.00
FWAPTR Taylor Raddysh 30.00 80.00
FWAPTT Tyce Thompson 20.00 50.00
FWAPTZ Trevor Zegras 1000.00 2500.00
FWAPUL Ukko-Pekka Luukkonen 60.00 150.00
FWAPWA Wade Allison 20.00 50.00
FWAPWE William Eklund 125.00 300.00
FWAPWK Wyatt Kalynuk 20.00 50.00
FWAPZJ Zac Jones 40.00 100.00

2021-22 SP Authentic Limited Autographs

2 Jonathan Huberdeau D 10.00 25.00
4 Carey Price A 15.00 40.00
7 Cam Talbot E 8.00 20.00
8 Eeli Tolvanen E 8.00 20.00
9 Drake Batherson E 8.00 20.00
11 Jacob Markstrom E 8.00 20.00
19 Tristan Jarry D 8.00 20.00
20 Miro Heiskanen E 10.00 25.00
21 Tyler Toffoli B 8.00 20.00
22 Troy Terry E 6.00 15.00
23 Marc-Andre Fleury C 15.00 40.00
24 Aleksander Barkov D 12.00 30.00
25 Andrei Vasilevskiy B 12.00 30.00
26 Tyler Bertuzzi D 6.00 15.00
34 William Karlsson E 10.00 25.00
37 Cal Petersen E 5.00 12.00
40 John Tavares B 12.00 30.00
41 John Gibson D 8.00 20.00
45 Ryan O'Reilly D 8.00 20.00
46 Brady Tkachuk D 12.00 30.00
47 Jeff Petry E 8.00 20.00
51 Joe Pavelski E 10.00 25.00
53 Martin Necas E 12.00 30.00
54 Teuvo Teravainen E 8.00 20.00
55 Nick Suzuki E 30.00 80.00
57 Tim Stutzle D 30.00 80.00
58 Josh Bailey E 6.00 15.00
60 Brad Marchand C 15.00 40.00
62 Connor Hellebuyck D 15.00 40.00
63 Jonathan Marchessault D 10.00 25.00
66 Brock Boeser D 10.00 25.00
70 Nikolaj Ehlers E 8.00 20.00
72 Brent Burns C 8.00 20.00
73 Mark Stone D 10.00 25.00
76 Jordan Eberle E 8.00 20.00
77 Kris Letang C 10.00 25.00
79 Anders Lee C 6.00 15.00
81 Tomas Hertl D 8.00 20.00
82 Matthew Tkachuk D 15.00 40.00
83 Roman Josi A 8.00 20.00
84 Anze Kopitar C 12.00 30.00
89 Kevin Fiala D 6.00 15.00
90 Jake Guentzel D 12.00 30.00
93 Philipp Grubauer E 8.00 20.00
98 Cam Atkinson D 8.00 20.00
100 Cale Makar C 20.00 50.00

2021-22 SP Authentic Limited Material Autographs

LAMAL Anders Lee/100 15.00 40.00
LAMAV Andrei Vasilevskiy/25 40.00 100.00
LAMBB Brent Burns/50 20.00 50.00
LAMBG Brendan Gallagher/50 20.00 50.00
LAMBM Brad Marchand/25 40.00 100.00
LAMBN Brock Nelson/100 20.00 50.00
LAMBO Brock Boeser/25 25.00 60.00
LAMBT Brady Tkachuk/50 30.00 80.00
LAMCA Cam Atkinson/50 20.00 50.00
LAMCH Connor Hellebuyck/50 40.00 100.00
LAMCM Cale Makar/25 50.00 125.00
LAMCO Maxime Comtois/100 15.00 40.00
LAMCT Cam Talbot/100 20.00 50.00
LAMDB Drake Batherson/100 20.00 50.00
LAMDH Dougie Hamilton/100 15.00 40.00
LAMDS Dylan Strome/100 25.00 60.00
LAMGI John Gibson/50 20.00 50.00
LAMHE Tomas Hertl/50 20.00 50.00
LAMJB Jesper Bratt/100 20.00 50.00
LAMJE Jordan Eberle/50 20.00 50.00
LAMJG Jake Guentzel/50 30.00 80.00
LAMJH Jonathan Huberdeau/50 25.00 60.00
LAMJP Jean-Gabriel Pageau/100 12.00 30.00
LAMJT John Tavares/25 30.00 80.00
LAMJZ Jason Zucker/100 20.00 50.00
LAMKC Kyle Connor/50 30.00 80.00
LAMKF Kevin Fiala/100 15.00 40.00
LAMKL Kris Letang/50 80.00 200.00
LAMMA Jacob Markstrom/100 20.00 50.00
LAMMG Mark Giordano/50 20.00 50.00
LAMMH Miro Heiskanen/50 25.00 60.00
LAMMI Casey Mittelstadt/100 20.00 50.00
LAMMN Martin Necas/100 30.00 80.00
LAMMT Matthew Tkachuk/25 60.00 150.00
LAMPA Joe Pavelski/50 25.00 60.00
LAMPE Jeff Petry/100 20.00 50.00
LAMPG Philipp Grubauer/50 20.00 50.00
LAMRO Ryan O'Reilly/25 20.00 50.00
LAMRT Robert Thomas/100 15.00 40.00
LAMSB Sergei Bobrovsky/50 30.00 80.00
LAMSR Sam Reinhart/100 40.00 100.00
LAMST Mark Stone/50 25.00 60.00
LAMTB Tyler Bertuzzi/50 15.00 40.00
LAMTH Shea Theodore/50 25.00 60.00
LAMTO Tyler Toffoli/50 20.00 50.00
LAMTT Teuvo Teravainen/50 20.00 50.00
LAMVO Victor Olofsson/100 20.00 50.00

2021-22 SP Authentic Marks of Distinction

MDAF Adam Fox 60.00 150.00
MDAH Alexander Holtz 15.00 40.00
MDAV Andrei Vasilevskiy 15.00 40.00
MDBB Brent Burns 10.00 25.00
MDBM Brad Marchand 20.00 50.00
MDBT Brady Tkachuk 15.00 40.00
MDCH Connor Hellebuyck 20.00 50.00
MDCM Cale Makar 25.00 60.00
MDDM Dawson Mercer 40.00 100.00
MDJH Jonathan Huberdeau 12.00 30.00
MDJP Joe Pavelski 12.00 30.00
MDJS Jeremy Swayman 60.00 150.00
MDJT John Tavares 25.00 60.00
MDKL Kris Letang 30.00 80.00
MDMC Connor McDavid 300.00 800.00
MDMT Matthew Tkachuk 20.00 50.00
MDQB Quinton Byfield 25.00 60.00
MDRO Ryan O'Reilly 10.00 25.00
MDSK Spencer Knight 20.00 50.00
MDWE William Eklund 40.00 100.00

2021-22 SP Authentic Pageantry

P1 Sidney Crosby 2.00 5.00
P2 Sebastian Aho .75 2.00
P3 Philipp Grubauer .50 1.25
P4 Andrei Vasilevskiy .75 2.00
P5 Roman Josi .50 1.25
P6 Brendan Gallagher .50 1.25
P7 Boone Jenner .50 1.25
P8 Nikolaj Ehlers .50 1.25
P9 Quinn Hughes 1.25 3.00
P10 John Gibson .50 1.25
P11 Kris Letang .60 1.50
P12 Leon Draisaitl 1.50 4.00
P13 Carey Price 1.00 2.50
P14 David Pastrnak 1.25 3.00
P15 Anders Lee .40 1.00
P16 Mitch Marner .75 2.00
P17 Sam Reinhart 1.00 2.50
P18 Brent Burns .50 1.25
P19 Dylan Larkin .60 1.50
P20 Tomas Hertl .50 1.25
P21 Tim Stutzle .60 1.50
P22 Igor Shesterkin 1.00 2.50
P23 Alex Ovechkin 2.00 5.00
P24 Cale Makar 1.25 3.00
P25 Mark Scheifele .75 2.00
P26 Nicklas Backstrom .50 1.25
P27 Patrice Bergeron .60 1.50
P28 Miro Heiskanen .60 1.50
P29 Max Pacioretty .50 1.25
P30 Auston Matthews 2.00 5.00
P31 Sean Monahan .30 .75
P32 Mark Stone .60 1.50
P33 Elias Pettersson .75 2.00
P34 Steven Stamkos 1.00 2.50
P35 Victor Olofsson .50 1.25
P36 Cam Atkinson .50 1.25
P37 Taylor Hall .50 1.25
P38 Anze Kopitar .75 2.00
P39 Jeff Petry .50 1.25
P40 Robin Lehner .40 1.00
P41 Phil Kessel .50 1.25
P42 Joe Pavelski .60 1.50
P43 Dougie Hamilton .40 1.00
P44 Patrick Kane 1.00 2.50
P45 Teuvo Teravainen .50 1.25
P46 Jonathan Huberdeau .60 1.50
P47 Ryan O'Reilly .50 1.25
P48 Kirill Kaprizov 1.50 4.00
P49 Jacob Markstrom .50 1.25
P50 Connor McDavid 2.50 6.00
P51 Alexander Holtz .75 2.00
P52 Quinton Byfield 1.25 3.00
P53 Cam York .50 1.25
P54 Vasily Podkolzin .60 1.50
P55 Trevor Zegras 1.00 2.50
P56 Nils Lundkvist .50 1.25
P57 Seth Jarvis 1.25 3.00
P58 Cole Sillinger .75 2.00
P59 Jonathan Dahlen .50 1.25
P60 Joe Veleno .60 1.50
P61 Alex Newhook .75 2.00
P62 Philip Tomasino .60 1.50
P63 Jeremy Swayman 1.50 4.00
P64 Ross Colton .60 1.50
P65 Grigori Denisenko .60 1.50
P66 Mason McTavish 1.00 2.50
P67 Calen Addison .50 1.25
P68 Lucas Raymond 1.50 4.00
P69 Cole Caufield 2.00 5.00
P70 Anton Lundell 1.00 2.50
P71 Shane Pinto .75 2.00
P72 William Eklund 1.25 3.00
P73 Hendrix Lapierre .50 1.25
P74 Moritz Seider 1.25 3.00
P75 Jamie Drysdale .75 2.00
P76 Scott Perunovich .50 1.25
P77 Wyatt Kalynuk .50 1.25
P78 Cole Perfetti 1.00 2.50
P79 Dawson Mercer 1.25 3.00
P80 Spencer Knight 1.00 2.50
P81 Wayne Gretzky 3.00 8.00
P82 Doug Gilmour .60 1.50
P83 Mark Messier 1.00 2.50
P84 Joe Sakic 1.00 2.50
P85 Mike Modano .75 2.00
P86 Phil Esposito .75 2.00
P87 Mike Bossy .50 1.25
P88 Marcel Dionne .60 1.50
P89 Paul Coffey .60 1.50

2021-22 SP Authentic Pageantry Autographs

P3 Philipp Grubauer C 10.00 25.00
P4 Andrei Vasilevskiy B 15.00 40.00
P5 Roman Josi C 10.00 25.00
P6 Brendan Gallagher E 10.00 25.00
P7 Boone Jenner E 10.00 25.00
P8 Nikolaj Ehlers D 10.00 25.00
P10 John Gibson E 10.00 25.00
P11 Kris Letang D 12.00 30.00
P12 Leon Draisaitl B 50.00 125.00
P13 Carey Price B 20.00 50.00
P15 Anders Lee D 8.00 20.00
P17 Sam Reinhart E 20.00 50.00
P18 Brent Burns C 10.00 25.00
P20 Tomas Hertl D 10.00 25.00
P21 Tim Stutzle D 40.00 100.00
P24 Cale Makar C 25.00 60.00
P28 Miro Heiskanen D 12.00 30.00
P32 Mark Stone C 12.00 30.00
P35 Victor Olofsson D 10.00 25.00
P36 Cam Atkinson E 10.00 25.00
P38 Anze Kopitar C 15.00 40.00
P39 Jeff Petry E 10.00 25.00
P42 Joe Pavelski D 12.00 30.00
P45 Teuvo Teravainen D 10.00 25.00
P46 Jonathan Huberdeau C 12.00 30.00
P47 Ryan O'Reilly D 10.00 25.00
P49 Jacob Markstrom C 10.00 25.00
P50 Connor McDavid B 250.00 600.00
P51 Alexander Holtz D 15.00 40.00
P52 Quinton Byfield A 25.00 60.00
P53 Cam York E 10.00 25.00
P54 Vasily Podkolzin C 12.00 30.00
P56 Nils Lundkvist D 10.00 25.00
P57 Seth Jarvis C 25.00 60.00
P58 Cole Sillinger D 15.00 40.00
P60 Joe Veleno E 12.00 30.00
P61 Alex Newhook C 15.00 40.00
P62 Philip Tomasino C 12.00 30.00
P63 Jeremy Swayman C 40.00 100.00
P64 Ross Colton E 12.00 30.00
P65 Grigori Denisenko C 12.00 30.00
P66 Mason McTavish E 20.00 50.00
P67 Calen Addison D 10.00 25.00
P69 Cole Caufield A 200.00 500.00
P70 Anton Lundell C 20.00 50.00
P71 Shane Pinto E 15.00 40.00
P72 William Eklund D 25.00 60.00
P73 Hendrix Lapierre E 10.00 25.00
P75 Jamie Drysdale C 15.00 40.00
P76 Scott Perunovich D 10.00 25.00
P77 Wyatt Kalynuk E 10.00 25.00
P78 Cole Perfetti C 20.00 50.00
P79 Dawson Mercer C 25.00 60.00
P80 Spencer Knight C 20.00 50.00
P83 Mark Messier B 20.00 50.00
P84 Joe Sakic B 20.00 50.00
P85 Mike Modano B 15.00 40.00
P88 Marcel Dionne D 12.00 30.00

2021-22 SP Authentic Sign of the Times

SOTTAB Anthony Beauvillier G 5.00 12.00
SOTTAC Anthony Cirelli G 6.00 15.00
SOTTAN Alex Nedeljkovic F 6.00 15.00
SOTTBB Bowen Byram F 10.00 25.00
SOTTBE Tyler Bertuzzi C 6.00 15.00
SOTTBG Brendan Gallagher C 8.00 20.00
SOTTBJ Boone Jenner F 8.00 20.00
SOTTBN Bernie Nicholls E 6.00 15.00
SOTTBQ Ray Bourque C 12.00 30.00
SOTTBR Brock Boeser C 10.00 25.00
SOTTBU Brent Burns C 8.00 20.00
SOTTCJ Calle Jarnkrok G 5.00 12.00
SOTTCM Casey Mittelstadt F 8.00 20.00
SOTTCO Maxime Comtois F 6.00 15.00
SOTTCP Andrew Copp G 5.00 12.00
SOTTCT Cam Talbot E 8.00 20.00
SOTTDB Drake Batherson E 8.00 20.00
SOTTDC Dylan Cozens G 8.00 20.00
SOTTDH Dany Heatley F 6.00 15.00
SOTTDS Dylan Strome D 10.00 25.00
SOTTDV Dave Taylor G 6.00 15.00
SOTTDW Doug Weight D 8.00 20.00
SOTTET Eeli Tolvanen E 8.00 20.00
SOTTFH Filip Hronek G 5.00 12.00
SOTTHE Tomas Hertl C 8.00 20.00
SOTTHJ Henri Jokiharju G 5.00 12.00
SOTTIL Isac Lundestrom G 5.00 12.00
SOTTJB Jesper Bratt G 8.00 20.00
SOTTJC Jack Campbell D 8.00 20.00
SOTTJE Jordan Eberle E 8.00 20.00
SOTTJG Jake Guentzel C 12.00 30.00
SOTTJH Jonathan Huberdeau D 10.00 25.00
SOTTJL John LeClair E 8.00 20.00
SOTTJM Jared McCann F 6.00 15.00
SOTTJN Josh Norris E 8.00 20.00
SOTTJO Jonathan Marchessault D 10.00 25.00
SOTTJP Jean-Gabriel Pageau F 5.00 12.00
SOTTJR Jack Roslovic F 5.00 12.00
SOTTJT John Tavares A 15.00 40.00
SOTTJZ Jason Zucker F 8.00 20.00
SOTTKC Kyle Connor D 12.00 30.00
SOTTKF Kevin Fiala D 6.00 15.00
SOTTMC Connor McDavid A 250.00 600.00
SOTTMF Marc-Andre Fleury B 15.00 40.00
SOTTMM Mike Modano B 30.00 80.00
SOTTMN Martin Necas E 12.00 30.00
SOTTMR Martin St. Louis B 8.00 20.00
SOTTMS Malcolm Subban G 6.00 15.00
SOTTMT Matthew Tkachuk C 15.00 40.00
SOTTNE Brock Nelson F 8.00 20.00
SOTTPA Joe Pavelski D 10.00 25.00
SOTTPB Paul Bissonnette F 5.00 12.00
SOTTPE Jeff Petry D 8.00 20.00
SOTTPF Peter Forsberg B 80.00 200.00
SOTTPK Peyton Krebs G 6.00 15.00
SOTTRB Rod Brind'Amour C 8.00 20.00
SOTTRH Ron Hextall D 8.00 20.00
SOTTRJ Roman Josi C 8.00 20.00
SOTTRP Roope Hintz F 10.00 25.00
SOTTRR Ryan Reaves G 6.00 15.00
SOTTRT Robert Thomas E 8.00 20.00
SOTTSG Samuel Girard G 5.00 12.00
SOTTSM Mike Smith G 5.00 12.00
SOTTST Mark Stone D 10.00 25.00
SOTTSW Sean Walker G 5.00 12.00
SOTTTF Theoren Fleury C 8.00 20.00
SOTTTJ Tristan Jarry D 8.00 20.00
SOTTTL Trevor Linden C 8.00 20.00
SOTTTO Tyler Toffoli C 8.00 20.00
SOTTTR Troy Terry E 6.00 15.00
SOTTTS Tim Stutzle D 30.00 80.00
SOTTTT Tony Twist F 5.00 12.00
SOTTVL Vincent Lecavalier E 8.00 20.00
SOTTVO Victor Olofsson E 8.00 20.00
SOTTVV Vitek Vanecek F 8.00 20.00
SOTTWG Wayne Gretzky A 200.00 500.00
SOTTWK William Karlsson E 10.00 25.00
SOTTWO Willie O'Ree D 15.00 40.00
SOTTYG Yanni Gourde E 20.00 50.00

2021-22 SP Authentic Sign of the Times 1990s

ST90BN Bernie Nicholls D 8.00 20.00
ST90CN Cam Neely B 20.00 50.00
ST90CR Cliff Ronning E 6.00 15.00
ST90KT Keith Tkachuk D 10.00 25.00
ST90PL Pat LaFontaine B 10.00 25.00
ST90RB Ray Bourque B 25.00 60.00
ST90TF Theoren Fleury B 10.00 25.00
ST90WC Wendel Clark D 25.00 60.00
ST90WG Wayne Gretzky A 200.00 500.00

2021-22 SP Authentic Sign of the Times 2000s

ST00BH Brett Hull B 100.00 250.00
ST00BM Brenden Morrow E 8.00 20.00
ST00DS Daniel Sedin B 80.00 200.00
ST00HS Henrik Sedin B 100.00 250.00
ST00JI Jarome Iginla B 50.00 125.00
ST00JS Joe Sakic A 20.00 50.00
ST00MM Mike Modano B 60.00 150.00
ST00RB Rod Brind'Amour C 10.00 25.00
ST00RS Ryan Suter C 8.00 20.00
ST00ZP Zach Parise C 10.00 25.00

2021-22 SP Authentic Sign of the Times 2010s

ST10AV Andrei Vasilevskiy B 15.00 40.00
ST10BG Brendan Gallagher C 10.00 25.00
ST10CH Connor Hellebuyck B 20.00 50.00
ST10JG John Gibson B 10.00 25.00
ST10KL Kris Letang B 12.00 30.00
ST10MH Miro Heiskanen B 12.00 30.00
ST10TB Tyler Bertuzzi C 8.00 20.00
ST10TH Tomas Hertl B 10.00 25.00

2021-22 SP Authentic Sign of the Times Rookies

SOTTRAL Anton Lundell A 20.00 50.00
SOTTRAN Alex Newhook A 15.00 40.00
SOTTRBG Benoit-Olivier Groulx B 10.00 25.00
SOTTRCC Cole Caufield A 500.00 1200.00
SOTTRCP Cole Perfetti A 20.00 50.00
SOTTRDM Dawson Mercer A 25.00 60.00
SOTTRJS Jeremy Swayman A 30.00 80.00
SOTTRPT Philip Tomasino B 12.00 30.00
SOTTRSK Spencer Knight B 20.00 50.00
SOTTRSP Scott Perunovich B 10.00 25.00
SOTTRTR Taylor Raddysh B 15.00 40.00
SOTTRVP Vasily Podkolzin B 12.00 30.00

2021-22 SP Authentic SP HoloFoil

HF1 Auston Matthews 20.00 50.00
HF2 Adam Fox 6.00 15.00
HF3 Matthew Tkachuk 10.00 25.00
HF4 Philipp Grubauer 5.00 12.00
HF5 Sidney Crosby 20.00 50.00
HF6 Brad Marchand 10.00 25.00
HF7 Andrei Vasilevskiy 8.00 20.00
HF8 Leon Draisaitl 15.00 40.00
HF9 Kirill Kaprizov 15.00 40.00
HF10 Sebastian Aho 8.00 20.00
HF11 Mark Stone 6.00 15.00
HF12 Patrick Kane 10.00 25.00
HF13 Alex Ovechkin 20.00 50.00
HF14 Cale Makar 12.00 30.00
HF15 Connor McDavid 25.00 60.00
HF16 Lucas Raymond 15.00 40.00
HF17 Cole Caufield 20.00 50.00
HF18 Trevor Zegras 10.00 25.00
HF19 Spencer Knight 10.00 25.00
HF20 Moritz Seider 12.00 30.00
HF21 Jaromir Jagr 15.00 40.00
HF22 Brett Hull 8.00 20.00
HF23 Patrick Roy 12.00 30.00
HF24 Bobby Orr 20.00 50.00
HF25 Wayne Gretzky 30.00 80.00

2021-22 SP Authentic Spectrum FX

S1 Connor McDavid 5.00 12.00
S2 Kirill Kaprizov 3.00 8.00
S3 Sebastian Aho 1.50 4.00
S4 Mark Stone 1.25 3.00
S5 Sidney Crosby 4.00 10.00
S6 Brad Marchand 2.00 5.00
S7 Cale Makar 2.50 6.00
S8 Claude Giroux 1.00 2.50
S9 Connor Hellebuyck 2.00 5.00
S10 Auston Matthews 4.00 10.00
S11 Aleksander Barkov 1.50 4.00
S12 Troy Terry .75 2.00
S13 Marc-Andre Fleury 2.00 5.00
S14 Jack Hughes 2.50 6.00
S15 Alex Ovechkin 4.00 10.00
S16 Mark Giordano 1.00 2.50
S17 Elias Lindholm 1.00 2.50
S18 Tyler Bertuzzi .75 2.00
S19 Victor Hedman 1.25 3.00
S20 Patrick Kane 2.00 5.00
S21 Nick Suzuki 2.00 5.00
S22 Anze Kopitar 1.50 4.00
S23 Artemi Panarin 2.00 5.00
S24 Brady Tkachuk 1.50 4.00
S25 Andrei Vasilevskiy 1.50 4.00
S26 Patrik Laine 1.25 3.00
S27 Brock Boeser 1.25 3.00
S28 Clayton Keller 1.25 3.00
S29 Logan Couture 1.25 3.00
S30 David Pastrnak 2.50 6.00
S31 Juuse Saros 1.25 3.00
S32 Rasmus Dahlin 1.25 3.00
S33 Andrei Svechnikov 1.25 3.00
S34 Kyle Connor 1.50 4.00
S35 Nathan MacKinnon 4.00 10.00
S36 Ryan O'Reilly 1.00 2.50
S37 Miro Heiskanen 1.25 3.00
S38 Mitch Marner 1.50 4.00
S39 Mathew Barzal 1.25 3.00
S40 Leon Draisaitl 3.00 8.00
S41 Calen Addison FW 2.50 6.00
S42 Ryan Merkley FW 3.00 8.00
S43 Karel Vejmelka FW 3.00 8.00
S44 Lassi Thomson FW 2.50 6.00
S45 Tyce Thompson FW 2.50 6.00
S46 Filip Gustavsson FW 5.00 12.00
S47 Yegor Chinakhov FW 4.00 10.00
S48 Nico Daws FW 4.00 10.00
S49 Logan Thompson FW 6.00 15.00
S50 Sean Durzi FW 2.50 6.00
S51 Parker Kelly FW 2.50 6.00
S52 Jasper Weatherby FW 2.50 6.00
S53 Jan Jenik FW 3.00 8.00
S54 Robin Salo FW 2.50 6.00
S55 Alex Barre-Boulet FW 2.50 6.00
S56 Jonathan Dahlen FW 2.50 6.00
S57 David Farrance FW 2.50 6.00
S58 Adam Beckman FW 2.50 6.00
S59 Jesse Ylonen FW 2.50 6.00
S60 Mike Hardman FW 2.50 6.00
S61 Egor Sokolov FW 2.50 6.00
S62 Wade Allison FW 2.50 6.00
S63 Radim Zohorna FW 2.50 6.00
S64 Matthew Phillips FW 2.50 6.00
S65 Jake Neighbours FW 5.00 12.00
S66 Jake Leschyshyn FW 2.50 6.00
S67 Kole Lind FW 3.00 8.00
S68 Wyatt Kalynuk FW 2.50 6.00
S69 Jacob Bernard-Docker FW 2.50 6.00
S70 Aliaksei Protas FW 2.50 6.00
S71 Ukko-Pekka Luukkonen FW 4.00 10.00
S72 Riley Tufte FW 2.50 6.00
S73 Rasmus Kupari FW 2.50 6.00
S74 Cam York FW 2.50 6.00
S75 Cole Sillinger FW 4.00 10.00
S76 Hendrix Lapierre FW 2.50 6.00
S77 Philip Tomasino FW 3.00 8.00
S78 Shane Pinto FW 4.00 10.00
S79 Nils Lundkvist FW 2.50 6.00
S80 Benoit-Olivier Groulx FW 2.50 6.00
S81 Scott Perunovich FW 2.50 6.00
S82 Joe Veleno FW 3.00 8.00
S83 Seth Jarvis FW 6.00 15.00
S84 Dawson Mercer FW 6.00 15.00
S85 Jamie Drysdale FW 4.00 10.00
S86 Vasily Podkolzin FW 3.00 8.00
S87 Ross Colton FW 3.00 8.00
S88 Alex Newhook FW 4.00 10.00
S89 Anton Lundell FW 5.00 12.00
S90 Jeremy Swayman FW 8.00 20.00
S91 William Eklund FW 6.00 15.00
S92 Alexander Holtz FW 4.00 10.00
S93 Lucas Raymond FW 8.00 20.00
S94 Spencer Knight FW 5.00 12.00
S95 Cole Perfetti FW 5.00 12.00
S96 Quinton Byfield FW 6.00 15.00
S97 Mason McTavish FW 5.00 12.00
S98 Moritz Seider FW 6.00 15.00
S99 Trevor Zegras FW 5.00 12.00
S100 Cole Caufield FW Bounty 80.00 200.00

2021-22 SP Authentic Spectrum FX Gold

*GOLD: 1.5X TO 4X BASIC
*GOLD.FW: 1X TO 2.5X BASIC
S1 Connor McDavid 40.00 100.00
S97 Mason McTavish FW 25.00 60.00
S98 Moritz Seider FW 30.00 80.00
S99 Trevor Zegras FW 40.00 100.00
S100 Cole Caufield FW 200.00 500.00

2021-22 SP Authentic Top Rookies

*BLUE: .6X TO 1.5X BASIC
*GREEN: .75X TO 2X BASIC
TR1 Cole Caufield 2.50 6.00
TR2 Alexander Holtz 1.00 2.50
TR3 Moritz Seider 1.50 4.00
TR4 Jacob Bernard-Docker .60 1.50
TR5 Benoit-Olivier Groulx .60 1.50
TR6 Nils Lundkvist .60 1.50
TR7 Cam York .60 1.50
TR8 Grigori Denisenko .75 2.00
TR9 William Eklund 1.50 4.00
TR10 Calen Addison .60 1.50
TR11 Vasily Podkolzin .75 2.00
TR12 Alex Newhook 1.00 2.50
TR13 Seth Jarvis 1.50 4.00
TR14 Shane Pinto 1.00 2.50
TR15 Philip Tomasino .75 2.00
TR16 Yegor Chinakhov 1.00 2.50
TR17 Quinton Byfield 1.50 4.00
TR18 Anton Lundell 1.25 3.00
TR19 Sampo Ranta .60 1.50
TR20 Mason McTavish 1.25 3.00
TR21 Filip Gustavsson 1.25 3.00
TR22 Jake Neighbours 1.25 3.00
TR23 Ukko-Pekka Luukkonen 1.00 2.50
TR24 Ross Colton .75 2.00
TR25 Spencer Knight 1.25 3.00
TR26 Hendrix Lapierre .60 1.50
TR27 Wade Allison .60 1.50
TR28 Jake Leschyshyn .60 1.50
TR29 Radim Zohorna .60 1.50
TR30 Zac Jones .75 2.00
TR31 Joe Veleno .75 2.00
TR32 Cole Sillinger 1.00 2.50
TR33 Cole Perfetti 1.25 3.00
TR34 Jonathan Dahlen .60 1.50
TR35 Adam Beckman .60 1.50
TR36 Alex Barre-Boulet .60 1.50
TR37 Riley Tufte .60 1.50
TR38 Matthew Phillips .60 1.50
TR39 Jamie Drysdale 1.00 2.50
TR40 Rasmus Kupari .60 1.50
TR41 Lucas Raymond 2.00 5.00
TR42 Jan Jenik .75 2.00
TR43 J.J. Peterka 1.25 3.00
TR44 Jeremy Swayman 2.00 5.00
TR45 Scott Perunovich .60 1.50
TR46 Dawson Mercer 1.50 4.00
TR47 David Farrance .60 1.50
TR48 Alex Turcotte .75 2.00
TR49 Wyatt Kalynuk .60 1.50
TR50 Trevor Zegras 1.25 3.00

2021-22 SP Authentic True Leaders

*BLUE: .5X TO 1.2X BASIC
*GREEN: .6X TO 1.5X BASIC
TL1 Connor McDavid 4.00 10.00
TL2 Brady Tkachuk 1.25 3.00
TL3 Mark Giordano .75 2.00
TL4 Gabriel Landeskog 1.00 2.50
TL5 John Tavares 1.25 3.00
TL6 Jonathan Toews 1.25 3.00
TL7 Ryan O'Reilly .75 2.00
TL8 Jared Spurgeon .75 2.00
TL9 Nico Hischier 1.25 3.00
TL10 Aleksander Barkov 1.25 3.00
TL11 Alex Ovechkin 3.00 8.00
TL12 Bo Horvat 1.00 2.50
TL13 Jamie Benn .75 2.00
TL14 Roman Josi .75 2.00
TL15 Claude Giroux .75 2.00
TL16 Dylan Larkin 1.00 2.50
TL17 Steven Stamkos 1.50 4.00
TL18 Mark Stone 1.00 2.50
TL19 Blake Wheeler .75 2.00
TL20 Ryan Getzlaf .75 2.00
TL21 Boone Jenner .75 2.00
TL22 Patrice Bergeron 1.00 2.50
TL23 Logan Couture 1.00 2.50
TL24 Anders Lee .60 1.50
TL25 Anze Kopitar 1.25 3.00

2021-22 SP Authentic UD Authentics Autographs

UDAAB Alexander Barabanov F 6.00 15.00
UDABB Bob Bourne E 10.00 25.00
UDABG Brendan Gallagher C 10.00 25.00
UDABI Billy Smith A 10.00 25.00
UDABM Brad Marchand B 20.00 50.00
UDABN Bernie Nicholls C 8.00 20.00
UDABR Rod Brind'Amour C 10.00 25.00
UDABU Brent Burns B 10.00 25.00
UDABY Bobby Smith F 10.00 25.00
UDACA Cam Atkinson C 10.00 25.00
UDACG Conor Garland D 8.00 20.00
UDACH Connor Hellebuyck B 20.00 50.00
UDACN Cam Neely C 8.00 20.00
UDACP Cal Petersen D 6.00 15.00
UDADB Drake Batherson E 10.00 25.00
UDADG Dirk Graham F 8.00 20.00
UDADO Dougie Hamilton C 8.00 20.00
UDADS Dylan Strome D 12.00 30.00
UDADW Doug Weight C 10.00 25.00
UDAET Eeli Tolvanen F 10.00 25.00
UDAGI Mark Giordano B 10.00 25.00
UDAHE Tomas Hertl C 10.00 25.00
UDAJB Josh Bailey E 8.00 20.00
UDAJC Jack Campbell E 10.00 25.00
UDAJG John Gibson C 10.00 25.00
UDAJI Jarome Iginla B 12.00 30.00
UDAJL John LeClair C 10.00 25.00
UDAJM Jared McCann F 8.00 20.00
UDAJP Joe Pavelski C 12.00 30.00
UDAJR Jack Roslovic F 6.00 15.00
UDAJS Joe Sakic B 20.00 50.00
UDAKF Kevin Fiala D 8.00 20.00
UDAKM Ken Morrow F 6.00 15.00
UDAKY Keith Yandle E 6.00 15.00
UDALE Anders Lee D 8.00 20.00
UDALM Lanny McDonald C 10.00 25.00
UDAMB Martin Brodeur B 25.00 60.00
UDAMD Marcel Dionne C 12.00 30.00
UDAMG Mike Gartner C 12.00 30.00
UDAML Mike Liut E 6.00 15.00
UDAMM Mike Modano B 15.00 40.00
UDAMN Martin Necas C 15.00 40.00
UDAMO Mattias Ohlund F 6.00 15.00
UDAMS Mark Stone B 12.00 30.00
UDAMT Matthew Tkachuk B 20.00 50.00
UDANH Nils Hoglander F 8.00 20.00
UDAPB Peter Bondra C 10.00 25.00
UDAPE Jeff Petry D 10.00 25.00
UDAPF Peter Forsberg B 60.00 150.00
UDAPG Philipp Grubauer C 10.00 25.00
UDAPL Pat LaFontaine C 10.00 25.00
UDARB Ray Bourque B 15.00 40.00
UDARD Ryan Dzingel F 8.00 20.00
UDARE Ryan Reaves F 8.00 20.00
UDARH Ron Hextall C 10.00 25.00
UDARR Rob Ray F 6.00 15.00
UDASC Shayne Corson D 8.00 20.00
UDASG Samuel Girard F 6.00 15.00
UDASI Darryl Sittler B 10.00 25.00
UDASK Saku Kuivu C 10.00 25.00
UDAST Tim Stutzle C 50.00 125.00
UDATB Tyler Bertuzzi C 8.00 20.00
UDATF Theoren Fleury C 10.00 25.00
UDATK Tim Kerr F 6.00 15.00
UDATL Trevor Linden C 10.00 25.00
UDATS Teemu Selanne A 20.00 50.00
UDATT Troy Terry D 8.00 20.00
UDAVA John Vanbiesbrouck D 10.00 25.00
UDAVN Vladislav Namestnikov F 6.00 15.00
UDAVO Victor Olofsson E 10.00 25.00
UDAWC Wendel Clark C 15.00 40.00
UDAWG Wayne Gretzky A 250.00 600.00
UDAWK William Karlsson D 12.00 30.00
UDAWO Willie O'Ree D 12.00 30.00
UDAZP Zach Parise E 10.00 25.00

2021-22 SP Authentic UD Authentics Patch Autographs

UDABM Brad Marchand/25 60.00 150.00
UDABU Brent Burns/25 15.00 40.00
UDACH Connor Hellebuyck/25 30.00 80.00
UDACM Connor McDavid/25 300.00 800.00
UDAHE Tomas Hertl/49 15.00 40.00
UDAJG John Gibson/49 15.00 40.00
UDAJP Joe Pavelski/49 20.00 50.00
UDAKF Kevin Fiala/49 12.00 30.00
UDAKL Kris Letang/49 80.00 200.00
UDALE Anders Lee/49 12.00 30.00
UDAMN Martin Necas/49 25.00 60.00
UDAMS Mark Stone/49 20.00 50.00
UDAPG Philipp Grubauer/49 15.00 40.00
UDASB Sergei Bobrovsky/49 30.00 80.00
UDATB Tyler Bertuzzi/49 12.00 30.00
UDAVO Victor Olofsson/49 15.00 40.00

2022-23 SP Authentic

1 Leon Draisaitl 1.25 3.00
2 Kirill Kaprizov 1.25 3.00
3 Zach Werenski .60 1.50
4 Jamie Drysdale .30 .75
5 Aaron Ekblad .50 1.25
6 Nick Schmaltz .30 .75
7 Jordan Eberle .40 1.00
8 Alex Ovechkin 1.50 4.00
9 Clayton Keller .50 1.25
10 Patrik Laine .50 1.25
11 Jonathan Huberdeau .50 1.25
12 Josh Bailey .30 .75
13 Alexis Lafreniere .60 1.50
14 Nick Suzuki .75 2.00
15 Anton Lundell .40 1.00
16 Joe Pavelski .50 1.25
17 Dawson Mercer .50 1.25
18 Tim Stutzle .50 1.25
19 Matthew Tkachuk .75 2.00
20 Sebastian Aho .60 1.50
21 Jason Robertson .60 1.50
22 Cole Caufield .75 2.00
23 Lucas Raymond .60 1.50
24 Dylan Cozens .40 1.00
25 Jordan Kyrou .40 1.00
26 Kevin Fiala .30 .75
27 Nikolaj Ehlers .40 1.00
28 Timo Meier .40 1.00
29 Nathan MacKinnon 1.50 4.00
30 James van Riemsdyk .30 .75
31 Carey Price .75 2.00
32 Seth Jarvis .50 1.25
33 Brady Tkachuk .60 1.50
34 Auston Matthews 1.50 4.00
35 John Gibson .40 1.00
36 Mats Zuccarello .40 1.00
37 Andrei Svechnikov .50 1.25
38 Alex DeBrincat .50 1.25
39 Alex Nedeljkovic .30 .75
40 Elias Pettersson .60 1.50
41 Brandon Saad .30 .75
42 Vitek Vanecek .40 1.00
43 Quinn Hughes 1.00 2.50
44 Marc-Andre Fleury .75 2.00
45 Arthur Kaliyev .40 1.00
46 Trevor Zegras .40 1.00
47 Jack Campbell .40 1.00
48 Tomas Hertl .40 1.00
49 Jeremy Swayman .60 1.50
50 Dylan Larkin .50 1.25
51 Jared McCann .30 .75
52 Ryan Strome .40 1.00
53 Moritz Seider .50 1.25
54 Aleksander Barkov .60 1.50
55 Bo Horvat .50 1.25
56 Mitch Marner .60 1.50
57 Evgeni Malkin .75 2.00
58 Kris Letang .50 1.25
59 Roman Josi .40 1.00
60 Elvis Merzlikins .40 1.00
61 Adam Fox .50 1.25
62 William Karlsson .50 1.25
63 Brad Marchand .75 2.00
64 Philipp Grubauer .40 1.00
65 Teuvo Teravainen .40 1.00
66 Juuse Saros .50 1.25
67 Artemi Panarin .75 2.00
68 Blake Coleman .30 .75
69 Jack Eichel .60 1.50
70 Mark Stone .50 1.25
71 Ilya Sorokin .60 1.50
72 Tage Thompson .50 1.25
73 Thatcher Demko .50 1.25
74 Jonathan Quick .50 1.25
75 Mathew Barzal .50 1.25
76 Roope Hintz .50 1.25
77 Victor Hedman .50 1.25
78 Kirby Dach .40 1.00
79 Michael Bunting .40 1.00
80 Filip Forsberg .60 1.50
81 Kyle Connor .60 1.50
82 Cale Makar 1.00 2.50
83 Miro Heiskanen .50 1.25
84 Tanner Jeannot .25 .60
85 Tom Wilson .40 1.00
86 Jack Hughes 1.00 2.50
87 Sidney Crosby 1.50 4.00
88 Patrick Kane .75 2.00
89 Cam Atkinson .40 1.00
90 Ryan O'Reilly .40 1.00
91 Steven Stamkos .75 2.00
92 Gabriel Landeskog .50 1.25
93 Anze Kopitar .60 1.50
94 Josh Norris .40 1.00
95 Jonathan Toews .60 1.50
96 Jacob Markstrom .40 1.00
97 Connor McDavid 2.00 5.00
98 John Tavares .60 1.50
99 Andrei Vasilevskiy .60 1.50
100 Igor Shesterkin .75 2.00
101 Matt Boldy FW AU/949* RC 125.00 300.00
102 Owen Power FW AU/949* RC 60.00 150.00
103 Matty Beniers FW AU/949* RC 80.00 200.00
104 Marco Rossi FW AU/949* RC 80.00 200.00
105 Kent Johnson FW AU/949* RC 40.00 100.00
106 Dylan Holloway FW AU/949* RC 40.00100.00
107 Lukas Reichel FW AU/949* RC 40.00 100.00
108 Jack Quinn FW AU/949* RC 80.00 200.00
109 Jacob Perreault FW RC 3.00 8.00
110 Brayden Tracey FW AU/949* RC 8.00 20.00
111 Alex Vlasic FW AU/949* RC 8.00 20.00
112 Dylan Samberg FW AU/949* RC 10.00 25.00
113 Lukas Dostal FW AU/949* RC 30.00 80.00
114 Jordan Spence FW AU/949* RC 10.00 25.00
115 Matias Maccelli FW AU/949* RC 40.00 100.00
116 Trey Fix-Wolansky FW AU/949* RC 10.00 25.00
117 Bobby Brink FW AU/949* RC 10.00 25.00
118 Isaac Ratcliffe FW AU/949* RC 10.00 25.00
119 Pyotr Kochetkov FW AU/949* RC 30.0080.00
120 Mads Sogaard FW AU/949* RC 12.00 30.00
121 Thomas Bordeleau FW AU/949* RC 10.00 25.00
122 Kaedan Korczak FW AU/949* RC 8.00 20.00
123 Jack McBain FW AU/949* RC 10.00 25.00
124 Jordan Harris FW AU/949* RC 12.00 30.00
125 Ronnie Attard FW AU/949* RC 10.00 25.00
126 Reilly Walsh FW AU/949* RC 10.00 25.00
127 Nick Abruzzese FW AU/949* RC 10.00 25.00
128 Fredrik Karlstrom FW AU/949* RC 8.0020.00
129 Erik Kallgren FW AU/949* RC 10.00 25.00
130 Marc McLaughlin FW AU/949* RC 10.00 25.00
131 Braden Schneider FW AU/949* RC 20.00 50.00
132 Samuel Fagemo FW RC 2.50 6.00

134 Kaiden Guhle FW AU/949* RC 60.00 150.00
135 Nathan Smith FW AU/949* RC 8.00 20.00
136 Mark Kastelic FW AU/949* RC 8.00 20.00
137 Chase Pearson FW AU/949* RC 8.00 20.00
138 Michael Eyssimont FW AU/949* RC 10.00 25.00
139 Hunter Drew FW AU/949* RC 10.00 25.00
140 Zack Hayes FW AU/949* RC 8.00 20.00
141 Valtteri Puustinen FW AU/949* RC 8.00 20.00
142 Andrei Kuzmenko FW AU/949* RC 80.00 200.00
143 Dylan Guenther FW AU/949* RC 50.00125.00
144 Jake Sanderson FW AU/949* RC 80.00 200.00
145 Samuel Poulin FW AU/949* RC 12.00 30.00
146 Wyatt Johnston FW AU/949* RC 150.00 400.00
147 Elmer Soderblom FW AU/949* RC 20.00 50.00
148 Brandt Clarke FW AU/949* RC 50.00 125.00
149 Juraj Slafkovsky FW AU/949* RC 125.00 300.00
150 Shane Wright FW AU/949* RC 80.00 200.00
151 David Jiricek FW AU/949* RC 40.00 100.00
152 Pavol Regenda FW AU/949* RC 10.00 25.00
153 Cole Koepke FW AU/949* RC 10.00 25.00
154 Arber Xhekaj FW AU/949* RC 40.00 100.00
155 Jakub Lauko FW RC 4.00 10.00
156 Nick Perbix FW AU/949* RC 8.00 20.00
157 Olle Lycksell FW AU/949* RC 10.00 25.00
158 Nils Aman FW AU/949* RC 10.00 25.00
159 Nikita Okhotiuk FW RC 2.50 6.00
160 Jake Christiansen FW AU/949* RC 10.00 25.00
161 Nick Blankenburg FW AU/949* RC 8.00 20.00
162 Jacob Moverare FW AU/949* RC 8.00 20.00
163 Ben Meyers FW AU/949* RC 10.00 25.00
164 Noah Cates FW AU/949* RC 10.00 25.00
165 Pontus Holmberg FW AU/949* RC 10.00 25.00
166 Vladislav Kolyachonok FW RC 2.50 6.00
167 Filip Roos FW AU/949* RC 8.00 20.00
168 Johnathan Kovacevic FW AU/949* RC 10.00 25.00
169 Hayden Hodgson FW AU/949* RC 8.0020.00
170 Matej Blumel FW RC 4.00 10.00
171 Jonatan Berggren FW AU/949* RC 25.00 60.00
172 Juuso Parssinen FW AU/949* RC 10.0025.00
173 Marcus Bjork FW AU/949* RC 10.00 25.00
174 Nikita Alexandrov FW AU/949* RC 10.00 25.00
175 Adam Raska FW RC 3.00 8.00
176 Bokondji Imama FW RC 2.50 6.00
177 Brandon Biro FW RC 5.00 12.00
178 Brayden Pachal FW RC 2.50 6.00
179 Carson Meyer FW RC 2.50 6.00
180 Cole Reinhardt FW RC 3.00 8.00
181 Declan Chisholm FW RC 3.00 8.00
182 Filip Kral FW RC 4.00 10.00
183 Jakub Galvas FW RC 3.00 8.00
184 Jeff Malott FW RC 3.00 8.00
185 Linus Hogberg FW RC 2.50 6.00
186 Linus Sandin FW RC 2.50 6.00
187 Mitchell Chaffee FW RC 2.50 6.00
188 Viktor Lodin FW RC 3.00 8.00
189 Tyler Tucker FW RC 3.00 8.00
190 Oskar Olausson FW AU/949* RC 10.0025.00
191 Lucas Johansen FW AU/949* RC 8.00 20.00
192 Simon Holmstrom FW RC 3.00 8.00
193 Anton Levtchi FW RC 3.00 8.00
194 Nick DeSimone FW AU/949* RC 10.00 25.00
195 Semyon Der-Arguchintsev FW RC 3.00 8.00
196 Jean-Luc Foudy FW AU/949* RC 10.0025.00
197 Kirill Marchenko FW AU/949* RC 40.00 100.00
198 William Bitten FW RC 3.00 8.00
199 Aatu Raty FW AU/949* RC 10.00 25.00

2022-23 SP Authentic Future Watch Acetate

101 Matt Boldy 40.00 100.00
102 Owen Power 25.00 60.00
103 Matty Beniers 30.00 80.00
104 Marco Rossi 30.00 80.00
105 Kent Johnson 25.00 60.00
106 Dylan Holloway 25.00 60.00
107 Lukas Reichel 25.00 60.00
108 Jack Quinn 20.00 50.00
109 Jacob Perreault 12.00 30.00
110 Brayden Tracey 10.00 25.00
111 Alex Vlasic 10.00 25.00
112 Dylan Samberg 12.00 30.00
113 Lukas Dostal 25.00 60.00
114 Jordan Spence 12.00 30.00
115 Matias Maccelli 20.00 50.00
116 Trey Fix-Wolansky 12.00 30.00
117 Bobby Brink 12.00 30.00
118 Isaac Ratcliffe 12.00 30.00
119 Pyotr Kochetkov 25.00 60.00
120 Mads Sogaard 15.00 40.00
121 Thomas Bordeleau 12.00 30.00
122 Kaedan Korczak 10.00 25.00
123 Jack McBain 12.00 30.00
124 Jordan Harris 15.00 40.00
125 Ronnie Attard 12.00 30.00
126 Reilly Walsh 12.00 30.00
127 Nick Abruzzese 12.00 30.00
128 Fredrik Karlstrom 10.00 25.00
129 Erik Kallgren 12.00 30.00
130 Marc McLaughlin 12.00 30.00
131 Braden Schneider 20.00 50.00
132 Samuel Fagemo 10.00 25.00
133 Filip Hallander 12.00 30.00
134 Wyatt Johnston 100.00 250.00
135 Nathan Smith 10.00 25.00
136 Mark Kastelic 10.00 25.00
137 Chase Pearson 10.00 25.00
138 Michael Eyssimont 12.00 30.00
139 Hunter Drew 12.00 30.00
140 Zack Hayes 10.00 25.00
141 Valtteri Puustinen 10.00 25.00
142 Andrei Kuzmenko 25.00 60.00
143 Dylan Guenther 80.00 200.00
144 Jake Sanderson 30.00 80.00
145 Elmer Soderblom 25.00 60.00
146 Kaiden Guhle 25.00 60.00
147 Samuel Poulin 15.00 40.00
148 Brandt Clarke 25.00 60.00
149 Juraj Slafkovsky 150.00 400.00
150 Shane Wright 30.00 80.00
151 David Jiricek 25.00 60.00
152 Pavol Regenda 12.00 30.00
153 Cole Koepke 12.00 30.00
154 Arber Xhekaj 25.00 60.00
155 Jakub Lauko 15.00 40.00
156 Nick Perbix 10.00 25.00
157 Olle Lycksell 12.00 30.00
158 Nils Aman 12.00 30.00
159 Nikita Okhotiuk 10.00 25.00
160 Jake Christiansen 12.00 30.00
161 Nick Blankenburg 10.00 25.00
162 Jacob Moverare 10.00 25.00
163 Ben Meyers 12.00 30.00
164 Noah Cates 12.00 30.00
165 Pontus Holmberg 12.00 30.00
166 Vladislav Kolyachonok 10.00 25.00
167 Filip Roos 10.00 25.00
168 Johnathan Kovacevic 12.00 30.00
169 Hayden Hodgson 10.00 25.00
170 Matej Blumel 15.00 40.00
171 Jonatan Berggren 20.00 50.00
172 Juuso Parssinen 12.00 30.00
173 Marcus Bjork 12.00 30.00
174 Nikita Alexandrov 12.00 30.00
175 Adam Raska 12.00 30.00
176 Bokondji Imama 10.00 25.00
177 Brandon Biro 20.00 50.00
178 Brayden Pachal 10.00 25.00
179 Carson Meyer 10.00 25.00
180 Cole Reinhardt 12.00 30.00
181 Declan Chisholm 12.00 30.00
182 Filip Kral 15.00 40.00
183 Jakub Galvas 12.00 30.00
184 Jeff Malott 12.00 30.00
185 Linus Hogberg 10.00 25.00
186 Linus Sandin 10.00 25.00
187 Mitchell Chaffee 10.00 25.00
188 Viktor Lodin 12.00 30.00
189 Tyler Tucker 12.00 30.00
190 Oskar Olausson 12.00 30.00
191 Lucas Johansen 10.00 25.00
192 Simon Holmstrom 12.00 30.00
193 James Hamblin 12.00 30.00
194 Nick DeSimone 12.00 30.00
195 Semyon Der-Arguchintsev 12.00 30.00
196 Jean-Luc Foudy 12.00 30.00
197 Kirill Marchenko 30.00 80.00
198 William Bitten 12.00 30.00
199 Aatu Raty 12.00 30.00

2022-23 SP Authentic Future Watch Inscriptions

*INSCRIPTIONS/50: .75X TO 2X BASIC
101 Matt Boldy/50* 300.00 800.00
102 Owen Power/50* 150.00 400.00
103 Matty Beniers/50* 500.00 1200.00
106 Dylan Holloway/50* 100.00 250.00
107 Lukas Reichel/50* 150.00 400.00
108 Jack Quinn/50* 125.00 300.00
113 Lukas Dostal/50* 125.00 300.00
115 Matias Maccelli/50* 125.00 300.00
119 Pyotr Kochetkov/50* 80.00 200.00
120 Mads Sogaard/50* 60.00 150.00
134 Kaiden Guhle/50* 150.00 400.00
144 Jake Sanderson/50* 250.00 600.00
146 Wyatt Johnston/50* 400.00 1000.00
147 Elmer Soderblom/50* 80.00 200.00
149 Juraj Slafkovsky/50* 400.00 1000.00
150 Shane Wright/50* 200.00 500.00
154 Arber Xhekaj/50* 80.00 200.00

2022-23 SP Authentic Limited Blue

*BLUE/399: .6X TO 1.5X RED

2022-23 SP Authentic Limited Gold

*GOLD/99: 1X TO 2.5X RED

2022-23 SP Authentic Limited Green

*GREEN/199: .75X TO 2X RED

2022-23 SP Authentic Limited Red

1 Leon Draisaitl 2.00 5.00
2 Kirill Kaprizov 2.00 5.00
3 Zach Werenski 1.00 2.50
4 Jamie Drysdale .50 1.25
5 Aaron Ekblad .75 2.00
6 Nick Schmaltz .50 1.25
7 Jordan Eberle .60 1.50
8 Alex Ovechkin 2.50 6.00
9 Clayton Keller .75 2.00
10 Patrik Laine .75 2.00
11 Jonathan Huberdeau .75 2.00
12 Josh Bailey .50 1.25
13 Alexis Lafreniere 1.00 2.50
14 Nick Suzuki 1.25 3.00
15 Anton Lundell .60 1.50
16 Joe Pavelski .75 2.00
17 Dawson Mercer .75 2.00
18 Tim Stutzle .75 2.00
19 Matthew Tkachuk 1.25 3.00
20 Sebastian Aho 1.00 2.50
21 Jason Robertson 1.00 2.50
22 Cole Caufield 1.25 3.00
23 Lucas Raymond 1.00 2.50
24 Dylan Cozens .60 1.50
25 Jordan Kyrou .60 1.50
26 Kevin Fiala .50 1.25
27 Nikolaj Ehlers .60 1.50
28 Timo Meier .60 1.50
29 Nathan MacKinnon 2.50 6.00
30 James van Riemsdyk .50 1.25
31 Carey Price 1.25 3.00
32 Seth Jarvis .75 2.00
33 Brady Tkachuk 1.00 2.50
34 Auston Matthews 2.50 6.00
35 John Gibson .60 1.50
36 Mats Zuccarello .60 1.50
37 Andrei Svechnikov .75 2.00
38 Alex DeBrincat .75 2.00
39 Alex Nedeljkovic .50 1.25
40 Elias Pettersson 1.00 2.50
41 Brandon Saad .50 1.25
42 Vitek Vanecek .60 1.50
43 Quinn Hughes 1.50 4.00
44 Marc-Andre Fleury 1.25 3.00
45 Arthur Kaliyev .60 1.50
46 Trevor Zegras .60 1.50
47 Jack Campbell .60 1.50
48 Tomas Hertl .60 1.50
49 Jeremy Swayman 1.00 2.50
50 Dylan Larkin .75 2.00
51 Jared McCann .50 1.25
52 Ryan Strome .60 1.50
53 Moritz Seider .75 2.00
54 Aleksander Barkov 1.00 2.50
55 Bo Horvat .75 2.00
56 Mitch Marner 1.00 2.50
57 Evgeni Malkin 1.25 3.00
58 Kris Letang .75 2.00
59 Roman Josi .60 1.50
60 Elvis Merzlikins .60 1.50
61 Adam Fox .75 2.00
62 William Karlsson .75 2.00
63 Brad Marchand 1.25 3.00
64 Philipp Grubauer .60 1.50
65 Teuvo Teravainen .60 1.50
66 Juuse Saros .75 2.00
67 Artemi Panarin 1.25 3.00
68 Blake Coleman .50 1.25
69 Jack Eichel 1.00 2.50
70 Mark Stone .75 2.00
71 Ilya Sorokin 1.00 2.50
72 Tage Thompson .75 2.00
73 Thatcher Demko .75 2.00
74 Jonathan Quick .75 2.00
75 Mathew Barzal .75 2.00
76 Roope Hintz .75 2.00
77 Victor Hedman .75 2.00
78 Kirby Dach .60 1.50
79 Michael Bunting .60 1.50
80 Filip Forsberg 1.00 2.50
81 Kyle Connor 1.00 2.50
82 Cale Makar 1.50 4.00
83 Miro Heiskanen .75 2.00
84 Tanner Jeannot .40 1.00
85 Tom Wilson .60 1.50
86 Jack Hughes 1.50 4.00
87 Sidney Crosby 2.50 6.00
88 Patrick Kane 1.25 3.00
89 Cam Atkinson .60 1.50
90 Ryan O'Reilly .60 1.50
91 Steven Stamkos 1.25 3.00
92 Gabriel Landeskog .75 2.00
93 Anze Kopitar 1.00 2.50
94 Josh Norris .60 1.50
95 Jonathan Toews 1.00 2.50
96 Jacob Markstrom .60 1.50
97 Connor McDavid 3.00 8.00
98 John Tavares 1.00 2.50
99 Andrei Vasilevskiy 1.00 2.50
100 Igor Shesterkin 1.25 3.00
101 Matt Boldy FW 3.00 8.00
102 Owen Power FW 2.00 5.00
103 Matty Beniers FW 2.50 6.00
104 Marco Rossi FW 2.50 6.00
105 Kent Johnson FW 2.00 5.00
106 Dylan Holloway FW 2.00 5.00
107 Lukas Reichel FW 2.00 5.00
108 Jack Quinn FW 1.50 4.00
109 Jacob Perreault FW 1.00 2.50
110 Brayden Tracey FW .75 2.00
111 Alex Vlasic FW .75 2.00
112 Dylan Samberg FW 1.00 2.50
113 Lukas Dostal FW 2.00 5.00
114 Jordan Spence FW 1.00 2.50
115 Matias Maccelli FW 1.50 4.00
116 Trey Fix-Wolansky FW 1.00 2.50
117 Bobby Brink FW 1.00 2.50
118 Isaac Ratcliffe FW 1.00 2.50
119 Pyotr Kochetkov FW 2.00 5.00
120 Mads Sogaard FW 1.25 3.00
121 Thomas Bordeleau FW 1.00 2.50
122 Kaedan Korczak FW .75 2.00
123 Jack McBain FW 1.00 2.50
124 Jordan Harris FW 1.25 3.00
125 Ronnie Attard FW 1.00 2.50
126 Reilly Walsh FW 1.00 2.50
127 Nick Abruzzese FW 1.00 2.50
128 Fredrik Karlstrom FW .75 2.00
129 Erik Kallgren FW 1.00 2.50
130 Marc McLaughlin FW 1.00 2.50
131 Braden Schneider FW 1.50 4.00
132 Samuel Fagemo FW .75 2.00
133 Filip Hallander FW 1.00 2.50
134 Wyatt Johnston FW 4.00 10.00
135 Nathan Smith FW .75 2.00
136 Mark Kastelic FW .75 2.00
137 Chase Pearson FW .75 2.00
138 Michael Eyssimont FW 1.00 2.50
139 Hunter Drew FW 1.00 2.50
140 Zack Hayes FW .75 2.00
141 Valtteri Puustinen FW .75 2.00
142 Andrei Kuzmenko FW 2.00 5.00
143 Dylan Guenther FW 2.50 6.00
144 Jake Sanderson FW 2.50 6.00
145 Elmer Soderblom FW 2.00 5.00
146 Kaiden Guhle FW 2.00 5.00
147 Samuel Poulin FW 1.25 3.00
148 Brandt Clarke FW 2.00 5.00
149 Juraj Slafkovsky FW 5.00 12.00
150 Shane Wright FW 2.50 6.00
151 David Jiricek FW 2.00 5.00
152 Pavol Regenda FW 1.00 2.50
153 Cole Koepke FW 1.00 2.50
154 Arber Xhekaj FW 2.00 5.00
155 Jakub Lauko FW 1.25 3.00
156 Nick Perbix FW .75 2.00
157 Olle Lycksell FW 1.00 2.50
158 Nils Aman FW 1.00 2.50
159 Nikita Okhotiuk FW .75 2.00
160 Jake Christiansen FW 1.00 2.50
161 Nick Blankenburg FW .75 2.00
162 Jacob Moverare FW .75 2.00
163 Ben Meyers FW 1.00 2.50
164 Noah Cates FW 1.00 2.50
165 Pontus Holmberg FW 1.00 2.50
166 Vladislav Kolyachonok FW .75 2.00
167 Filip Roos FW .75 2.00
168 Johnathan Kovacevic FW 1.00 2.50
169 Hayden Hodgson FW .75 2.00
170 Matej Blumel FW 1.25 3.00
171 Jonatan Berggren FW 1.50 4.00
172 Juuso Parssinen FW 1.00 2.50
173 Marcus Bjork FW 1.00 2.50
174 Nikita Alexandrov FW 1.00 2.50
175 Adam Raska FW 1.00 2.50
176 Bokondji Imama FW .75 2.00
177 Brandon Biro FW 1.50 4.00
178 Brayden Pachal FW .75 2.00
179 Carson Meyer FW .75 2.00
180 Cole Reinhardt FW 1.00 2.50
181 Declan Chisholm FW 1.00 2.50
182 Filip Kral FW 1.25 3.00
183 Jakub Galvas FW 1.00 2.50
184 Jeff Malott FW 1.00 2.50
185 Linus Hogberg FW .75 2.00
186 Linus Sandin FW .75 2.00
187 Mitchell Chaffee FW .75 2.00
188 Viktor Lodin FW 1.00 2.50
189 Tyler Tucker FW 1.00 2.50
190 Oskar Olausson FW 1.00 2.50
191 Lucas Johansen FW .75 2.00
192 Simon Holmstrom FW 1.00 2.50
193 James Hamblin FW 1.00 2.50
194 Nick DeSimone FW 1.00 2.50
195 Semyon Der-Arguchintsev FW 1.00 2.50
196 Jean-Luc Foudy FW 1.00 2.50
197 Kirill Marchenko FW 2.50 6.00
198 William Bitten FW 1.00 2.50
199 Aatu Raty FW 1.00 2.50
200 Matty Beniers FW 2.50 6.00

2022-23 SP Authentic '02-03 Retro Future Watch Autographs

RFWA2AK Andrei Kuzmenko/99 50.00 125.00
RFWA2AM Nils Aman/399 10.00 25.00
RFWA2AV Alex Vlasic/399 8.00 20.00
RFWA2AX Arber Xhekaj/399 20.00 50.00
RFWA2BB Bobby Brink/399 10.00 25.00
RFWA2BC Brandt Clarke/99 20.00 50.00
RFWA2BE Matty Beniers/99 60.00 150.00
RFWA2BM Ben Meyers/399 10.00 25.00
RFWA2BT Brayden Tracey/399 8.00 20.00
RFWA2CK Cole Koepke/399 10.00 25.00
RFWA2CP Chase Pearson/399 8.00 20.00
RFWA2DG Dylan Guenther/99 25.00 60.00
RFWA2DH Dylan Holloway/99 25.00 60.00
RFWA2DJ David Jiricek/99 20.00 50.00
RFWA2DS Dylan Samberg/399 10.00 25.00
RFWA2EK Erik Kallgren/399 10.00 25.00
RFWA2ES Elmer Soderblom/399 20.00 50.00
RFWA2FK Fredrik Karlstrom/399 8.00 20.00
RFWA2FR Filip Roos/399 8.00 20.00
RFWA2HD Hunter Drew/399 10.00 25.00
RFWA2HH Hayden Hodgson/399 8.00 20.00
RFWA2IR Isaac Ratcliffe/399 10.00 25.00
RFWA2JC Jake Christiansen/399 10.00 25.00
RFWA2JH Jordan Harris/399 12.00 30.00
RFWA2JK Johnathan Kovacevic/399 10.00 25.00
RFWA2JM Jack McBain/399 10.00 25.00
RFWA2JO Jordan Spence/399 10.00 25.00
RFWA2JQ Jack Quinn/99 25.00 60.00
RFWA2JS Jake Sanderson/99 25.00 60.00
RFWA2KG Kaiden Guhle/399 30.00 80.00
RFWA2KJ Kent Johnson/99 30.00 80.00
RFWA2KK Kaedan Korczak/399 8.00 20.00
RFWA2LD Lukas Dostal/399 20.00 50.00
RFWA2LR Lukas Reichel/99 20.00 50.00
RFWA2MA Matias Maccelli/399 15.00 40.00
RFWA2MB Matt Boldy/99 80.00 200.00
RFWA2ME Michael Eyssimont/399 10.00 25.00
RFWA2MK Mark Kastelic/399 8.00 20.00
RFWA2MM Marc McLaughlin/399 10.00 25.00
RFWA2MO Jacob Moverare/399 8.00 20.00
RFWA2MR Marco Rossi/99 60.00 150.00
RFWA2MS Mads Sogaard/399 12.00 30.00
RFWA2NA Nick Abruzzese/399 10.00 25.00
RFWA2NB Nick Blankenburg/399 8.00 20.00
RFWA2NC Noah Cates/399 10.00 25.00
RFWA2NP Nick Perbix/399 8.00 20.00
RFWA2NS Nathan Smith/399 8.00 20.00
RFWA2OP Owen Power/99 80.00 200.00
RFWA2PK Pyotr Kochetkov/399 20.00 50.00
RFWA2PR Pavol Regenda/399 10.00 25.00
RFWA2RA Ronnie Attard/399 10.00 25.00
RFWA2RW Reilly Walsh/399 10.00 25.00
RFWA2SL Juraj Slafkovsky/99 125.00 300.00
RFWA2SP Samuel Poulin/99 12.00 30.00
RFWA2SW Shane Wright/99 30.00 80.00
RFWA2TB Thomas Bordeleau/399 10.00 25.00
RFWA2TF Trey Fix-Wolansky/399 10.00 25.00
RFWA2VP Valtteri Puustinen/399 8.00 20.00
RFWA2WJ Wyatt Johnston/399 40.00 100.00
RFWA2ZH Zack Hayes/399 8.00 20.00

2022-23 SP Authentic '02-03 Retro Sign of the Times

RSOTTAB Aleksander Barkov D 15.00 40.00
RSOTTAG Adam Graves D 8.00 20.00
RSOTTAK Arthur Kaliyev F 10.00 25.00
RSOTTAM Auston Matthews B 40.00 100.00
RSOTTAN Alex Nedeljkovic F 8.00 20.00
RSOTTAT Cam Atkinson F 10.00 25.00
RSOTTBL Rob Blake D 10.00 25.00
RSOTTBM Brad Marchand C 20.00 50.00
RSOTTBR Martin Brodeur B 25.00 60.00
RSOTTCH Carter Hart D 10.00 25.00
RSOTTCP Cal Petersen F 6.00 15.00
RSOTTDB Drake Batherson F 10.00 25.00
RSOTTEB Evan Bouchard E 12.00 30.00
RSOTTED Evgenii Dadonov E 6.00 15.00
RSOTTEJ Jordan Eberle E 10.00 25.00
RSOTTEK Evgeny Kuznetsov E 12.00 30.00
RSOTTEM Elvis Merzlikins F 10.00 25.00
RSOTTGC Gerry Cheevers C 10.00 25.00
RSOTTGF Grant Fuhr C 15.00 40.00
RSOTTJE Jack Eichel C 15.00 40.00
RSOTTJH Jonathan Huberdeau C 12.00 30.00
RSOTTJK Jordan Kyrou D 10.00 25.00
RSOTTJO Jake Oettinger D 15.00 40.00
RSOTTJS Jeremy Swayman E 15.00 40.00
RSOTTKD Kirby Dach D 10.00 25.00
RSOTTKM K'Andre Miller E 8.00 20.00
RSOTTKT Keith Tkachuk D 10.00 25.00
RSOTTMA John Marino F 10.00 25.00
RSOTTMB Michael Bunting D 10.00 25.00
RSOTTMC Maxime Comtois F 8.00 20.00
RSOTTMF Marcus Foligno E 8.00 20.00
RSOTTNP Neal Pionk F 6.00 15.00
RSOTTNS Nick Schmaltz F 8.00 20.00
RSOTTPE Cole Perfetti D 10.00 25.00
RSOTTPK Peyton Krebs E 8.00 20.00
RSOTTPR Carey Price B 20.00 50.00
RSOTTRB Rod Brind'Amour D 10.00 25.00
RSOTTRF Ron Francis B 12.00 30.00
RSOTTRG Ryan Getzlaf C 10.00 25.00
RSOTTRM Rick Middleton E 10.00 25.00
RSOTTRS Ryan Strome F 10.00 25.00
RSOTTSK Spencer Knight C 10.00 25.00
RSOTTSM Sonny Milano F 8.00 20.00
RSOTTSR Sam Reinhart D 20.00 50.00
RSOTTTS Tim Stutzle C 12.00 30.00
RSOTTVV Vitek Vanecek E 10.00 25.00
RSOTTWG Wayne Gretzky A 200.00 500.00

2022-23 SP Authentic '12-13 Retro Future Watch Autographs

RFWAAB Nick Abruzzese/699 10.00 25.00
RFWAAK Andrei Kuzmenko/199 20.00 50.00
RFWAAM Nils Aman/699 10.00 25.00
RFWAAV Alex Vlasic/699 8.00 20.00
RFWAAX Arber Xhekaj/699 20.00 50.00
RFWABC Brandt Clarke/199 20.00 50.00
RFWABE Matty Beniers/199 40.00 100.00
RFWABJ Marcus Bjork/699 10.00 25.00
RFWABM Ben Meyers/699 10.00 25.00
RFWABO Thomas Bordeleau/699 10.00 25.00
RFWABR Bobby Brink/699 10.00 25.00
RFWABT Brayden Tracey/699 8.00 20.00
RFWACA Noah Cates/699 10.00 25.00
RFWACK Cole Koepke/699 10.00 25.00
RFWACP Chase Pearson/699 8.00 20.00
RFWADG Dylan Guenther/199 25.00 60.00
RFWADH Dylan Holloway/199 20.00 50.00
RFWADJ David Jiricek/199 20.00 50.00
RFWADS Dylan Samberg/699 10.00 25.00
RFWAEK Erik Kallgren/699 10.00 25.00
RFWAES Elmer Soderblom/699 20.00 50.00
RFWAFR Filip Roos/699 8.00 20.00
RFWAHD Hunter Drew/699 10.00 25.00
RFWAHH Hayden Hodgson/699 8.00 20.00
RFWAIR Isaac Ratcliffe/699 10.00 25.00
RFWAJA Jack McBain/699 10.00 25.00
RFWAJB Jonatan Berggren/699 15.00 40.00
RFWAJC Jake Christiansen/699 10.00 25.00
RFWAJF Jean-Luc Foudy/699 10.00 25.00
RFWAJH Jordan Harris/699 12.00 30.00
RFWAJK Johnathan Kovacevic/699 10.00 25.00
RFWAJO Jordan Spence/699 10.00 25.00
RFWAJQ Jack Quinn/199 15.00 40.00
RFWAJS Juraj Slafkovsky/199 80.00 200.00
RFWAKA Fredrik Karlstrom/699 8.00 20.00
RFWAKG Kaiden Guhle/199 20.00 50.00
RFWAKJ Kent Johnson/199 20.00 50.00
RFWAKK Kaedan Korczak/699 8.00 20.00
RFWAKM Kirill Marchenko/699 25.00 60.00
RFWALD Lukas Dostal/199 20.00 50.00
RFWALJ Lucas Johansen/699 8.00 20.00
RFWALR Lukas Reichel/199 20.00 50.00
RFWAMB Matt Boldy/199 60.00 150.00
RFWAME Michael Eyssimont/699 10.00 25.00
RFWAMK Mark Kastelic/699 8.00 20.00
RFWAMM Matias Maccelli/699 15.00 40.00
RFWAMO Jacob Moverare/699 8.00 20.00
RFWAMR Marco Rossi/199 30.00 80.00
RFWAMS Mads Sogaard/699 12.00 30.00
RFWANA Nikita Alexandrov/699 10.00 25.00
RFWANB Nick Blankenburg/699 8.00 20.00
RFWAND Nick DeSimone/699 10.00 25.00
RFWANP Nick Perbix/699 8.00 20.00
RFWANS Nathan Smith/699 8.00 20.00
RFWAOL Olle Lycksell/699 10.00 25.00
RFWAOO Oskar Olausson/699 10.00 25.00
RFWAOP Owen Power/199 40.00 100.00
RFWAPA Juuso Parssinen/699 10.00 25.00
RFWAPH Pontus Holmberg/699 10.00 25.00
RFWAPR Pavol Regenda/699 10.00 25.00
RFWARA Ronnie Attard/699 10.00 25.00
RFWARW Reilly Walsh/699 10.00 25.00
RFWASA Jake Sanderson/199 30.00 80.00
RFWASH Simon Holmstrom/699 10.00 25.00
RFWASP Samuel Poulin/699 12.00 30.00
RFWASW Shane Wright/199 40.00 100.00
RFWATF Trey Fix-Wolansky/699 10.00 25.00
RFWAVP Valtteri Puustinen/699 8.00 20.00
RFWAWB William Bitten/699 10.00 25.00
RFWAWJ Wyatt Johnston/699 40.00 100.00
RFWAZH Zack Hayes/699 8.00 20.00

2022-23 SP Authentic '12-13 Retro Future Watch Patch Autographs

RFWAAK Andrei Kuzmenko/100 125.00 300.00
RFWAAX Arber Xhekaj/100 60.00 150.00
RFWABC Brandt Clarke/50 100.00 250.00
RFWABE Matty Beniers/25 200.00 500.00
RFWABT Brayden Tracey/100 25.00 60.00
RFWADG Dylan Guenther/50 80.00 200.00
RFWADH Dylan Holloway/100 60.00 150.00
RFWAES Elmer Soderblom/100 60.00 150.00
RFWAJQ Jack Quinn/50 50.00 125.00
RFWAJS Jake Sanderson/50 80.00 200.00
RFWAKG Kaiden Guhle/100 125.00 300.00
RFWAKJ Kent Johnson/50 125.00 300.00
RFWALD Lukas Dostal/100 60.00 150.00
RFWAMB Matt Boldy/50 100.00 250.00
RFWAMS Mads Sogaard/100 40.00 100.00
RFWANA Nick Abruzzese/100 30.00 80.00
RFWAOP Owen Power/25 150.00 400.00
RFWASL Juraj Slafkovsky/25 150.00 400.00
RFWASP Samuel Poulin/100 40.00 100.00
RFWASW Shane Wright/25 200.00 500.00
RFWATB Thomas Bordeleau/100 30.00 80.00

2022-23 SP Authentic Chirography

CAB Aleksander Barkov B 12.00 30.00
CAE Aaron Ekblad B 10.00 25.00
CAG Adam Graves C 6.00 15.00
CAK Andrei Kuzmenko B 15.00 40.00
CAL Anton Lundell C 8.00 20.00
CAN Alex Nedeljkovic D 6.00 15.00
CAO Alex Ovechkin A 125.00 300.00
CBA Josh Bailey D 6.00 15.00
CBB Bobby Brink B 8.00 20.00
CBH Bo Horvat C 10.00 25.00
CBR Bryan Rust C 8.00 20.00
CBT Brayden Tracey B 6.00 15.00
CCA Cam Atkinson C 8.00 20.00
CCH Carter Hart C 20.00 50.00
CDH Dylan Holloway B 15.00 40.00
CDK Darcy Kuemper C 8.00 20.00
CEK Joel Eriksson Ek C 6.00 15.00
CES Elmer Soderblom C 15.00 40.00
CJB Jonatan Berggren B 12.00 30.00
CJG Jake Guentzel C 12.00 30.00
CJK Jordan Kyrou C 8.00 20.00
CJM John Marino D 8.00 20.00
CJS Jordan Spence B 8.00 20.00
CKR Peyton Krebs D 6.00 15.00
CKU Jari Kurri B 8.00 20.00
CLD Lukas Dostal B 15.00 40.00
CLM Lanny McDonald B 8.00 20.00
CMB Matty Beniers A 20.00 50.00
CMC Mason McTavish C 8.00 20.00
CMM Matias Maccelli B 12.00 30.00
CMS Martin St. Louis B 8.00 20.00
CNP Nick Perbix D 6.00 15.00
CSD Shane Doan B 6.00 15.00
CSM Sonny Milano D 6.00 15.00
CSO Mads Sogaard B 10.00 25.00
CST Mark Stone B 10.00 25.00
CSZ Sergei Zubov B 6.00 15.00
CTB Thomas Bordeleau B 8.00 20.00
CTH Shea Theodore C 10.00 25.00
CTK Torey Krug C 6.00 15.00
CTT Teuvo Teravainen B 8.00 20.00
CZW Zach Werenski C 12.00 30.00

2022-23 SP Authentic Collaborations

*BLUE: .6X TO 1.5X BASIC
*GREEN: 1X TO 2.5X BASIC
C1 C.McDavid/L.Draisaitl 2.50 6.00
C2 J.Pavelski/J.Robertson .75 2.00
C3 P.Kane/J.Toews 1.00 2.50
C4 A.Svechnikov/S.Aho .75 2.00
C5 C.Caufield/N.Suzuki 1.00 2.50
C6 J.Hughes/J.Bratt 1.25 3.00
C7 D.Pastrnak/P.Bergeron 1.25 3.00
C8 M.Scheifele/J.Morrissey .75 2.00
C9 J.Eichel/M.Stone .75 2.00
C10 N.MacKinnon/C.Makar 2.00 5.00
C11 O.Power/R.Dahlin 1.00 2.50
C12 M.Boldy/K.Kaprizov 1.50 4.00
C13 J.Gaudreau/P.Laine .75 2.00
C14 B.Tkachuk/T.Stutzle .75 2.00
C15 A.Panarin/A.Fox 1.00 2.50
C16 S.Stamkos/N.Kucherov 1.00 2.50
C17 T.Zegras/T.Terry .50 1.25
C18 B.Horvat/E.Pettersson .75 2.00
C19 A.Kopitar/A.Kempe .75 2.00
C20 R.Josi/F.Forsberg .75 2.00
C21 A.Matthews/M.Marner 2.00 5.00
C22 J.Kyrou/R.Thomas .50 1.25
C23 D.Larkin/D.Kubalik .60 1.50
C24 E.Karlsson/T.Meier .60 1.50
C25 J.Eberle/J.Schwartz .50 1.25

2022-23 SP Authentic Future Icons

FI1 J.Perreault/L.Dostal 2.00 5.00
FI2 C.Keller/D.Guenther 2.50 6.00
FI3 J.Swayman/C.McAvoy 1.50 4.00
FI4 O.Power/J.Quinn 2.00 5.00
FI5 A.Ruzicka/A.Mangiapane 1.00 2.50
FI6 J.Drury/S.Jarvis 1.25 3.00
FI7 L.Reichel/T.Raddysh 2.00 5.00
FI8 C.Makar/B.Byram 2.50 6.00
FI9 K.Johnson/J.Gaudreau 2.00 5.00
FI10 J.Robertson/W.Johnston 4.00 10.00
FI11 L.Raymond/J.Berggren 1.50 4.00
FI12 D.Holloway/E.Bouchard 2.00 5.00
FI13 M.Tkachuk/S.Knight 2.00 5.00
FI14 B.Clarke/G.Vilardi 2.00 5.00
FI15 K.Kaprizov/M.Boldy 3.00 8.00
FI16 J.Slafkovsky/C.Caufield 5.00 12.00
FI17 T.Jeannot/P.Tomasino .60 1.50
FI18 J.Hughes/D.Mercer 2.50 6.00
FI19 O.Wahlstrom/M.Barzal 1.25 3.00
FI20 A.Lafreniere/A.Fox 1.50 4.00
FI21 J.Sanderson/T.Stutzle 2.50 6.00
FI22 B.Brink/T.Konecny 1.00 2.50
FI23 S.Poulin/T.Jarry 1.25 3.00
FI24 M.Beniers/S.Wright 2.50 6.00
FI25 T.Meier/T.Hertl 1.00 2.50
FI26 R.Thomas/J.Kyrou 1.00 2.50
FI27 B.Hagel/M.Sergachev .75 2.00
FI28 A.Matthews/M.Marner 4.00 10.00
FI29 E.Pettersson/A.Kuzmenko 2.00 5.00
FI30 J.Eichel/S.Theodore 1.50 4.00
FI31 D.Strome/A.Protas 1.25 3.00
FI32 C.Perfetti/K.Connor 1.50 4.00

2022-23 SP Authentic Future Watch Patch Autographs

FWAPAK Andrei Kuzmenko 150.00 400.00
FWAPAM Nils Aman 20.00 50.00
FWAPAV Alex Vlasic 15.00 40.00
FWAPAX Arber Xhekaj 125.00 300.00
FWAPBB Bobby Brink 20.00 50.00
FWAPBC Brandt Clarke 125.00 300.00
FWAPBE Matty Beniers 150.00 400.00
FWAPBM Ben Meyers 20.00 50.00
FWAPBT Brayden Tracey 15.00 40.00
FWAPCK Cole Koepke 20.00 50.00
FWAPCP Chase Pearson 15.00 40.00
FWAPDG Dylan Guenther 125.00 300.00
FWAPDH Dylan Holloway 80.00 200.00
FWAPDJ David Jiricek 40.00 100.00
FWAPDS Dylan Samberg 20.00 50.00
FWAPEK Erik Kallgren 20.00 50.00
FWAPES Elmer Soderblom 40.00 100.00
FWAPFK Fredrik Karlstrom 15.00 40.00
FWAPIR Isaac Ratcliffe 20.00 50.00
FWAPJB Jonatan Berggren 80.00 200.00
FWAPJC Jake Christiansen 20.00 50.00
FWAPJH Jordan Harris 25.00 60.00
FWAPJK Johnathan Kovacevic 20.00 50.00
FWAPJM Jack McBain 20.00 50.00
FWAPJQ Jack Quinn 125.00 300.00
FWAPJS Jake Sanderson 150.00 400.00
FWAPKG Kaiden Guhle 125.00 300.00
FWAPKJ Kent Johnson 150.00 400.00
FWAPKK Kaedan Korczak 15.00 40.00
FWAPLD Lukas Dostal 80.00 200.00
FWAPLJ Lucas Johansen 15.00 40.00
FWAPLR Lukas Reichel 150.00 400.00
FWAPMB Matt Boldy 125.00 300.00
FWAPME Michael Eyssimont 20.00 50.00
FWAPMK Mark Kastelic 15.00 40.00
FWAPMM Matias Maccelli 150.00 400.00
FWAPMO Jacob Moverare 15.00 40.00
FWAPMR Marco Rossi 250.00 600.00
FWAPMS Mads Sogaard 80.00 200.00
FWAPNA Nick Abruzzese 20.00 50.00
FWAPNB Nick Blankenburg 15.00 40.00
FWAPNC Noah Cates 20.00 50.00
FWAPNP Nick Perbix 15.00 40.00
FWAPNS Nathan Smith 15.00 40.00
FWAPOL Olle Lycksell 20.00 50.00
FWAPOP Owen Power 150.00 400.00
FWAPPH Pontus Holmberg 20.00 50.00
FWAPPO Samuel Poulin 25.00 60.00
FWAPPR Pavol Regenda 20.00 50.00
FWAPRA Ronnie Attard 20.00 50.00
FWAPRW Reilly Walsh 20.00 50.00
FWAPSL Juraj Slafkovsky 300.00 800.00
FWAPSW Shane Wright 200.00 500.00
FWAPTB Thomas Bordeleau 20.00 50.00
FWAPTF Trey Fix-Wolansky 20.00 50.00
FWAPVP Valtteri Puustinen 15.00 40.00
FWAPWJ Wyatt Johnston 300.00 800.00
FWAPZH Zack Hayes 15.00 40.00

2022-23 SP Authentic Limited Autographs

3 Zach Werenski C 12.00 30.00
5 Aaron Ekblad B 10.00 25.00
7 Jordan Eberle C 8.00 20.00
8 Alex Ovechkin A 125.00 300.00
9 Clayton Keller C 10.00 25.00
12 Josh Bailey D 6.00 15.00
13 Alexis Lafreniere B 12.00 30.00
15 Anton Lundell C 8.00 20.00
18 Tim Stutzle B 25.00 60.00
25 Jordan Kyrou C 8.00 20.00
28 Timo Meier C 8.00 20.00
30 James van Riemsdyk C 6.00 15.00
31 Carey Price A 15.00 40.00
32 Seth Jarvis C 10.00 25.00
33 Brady Tkachuk C 12.00 30.00
34 Auston Matthews A 125.00 300.00
37 Andrei Svechnikov B 10.00 25.00
38 Alex DeBrincat C 10.00 25.00
39 Alex Nedeljkovic D 6.00 15.00
41 Brandon Saad D 6.00 15.00
43 Quinn Hughes C 20.00 50.00
44 Marc-Andre Fleury B 15.00 40.00
45 Arthur Kaliyev D 8.00 20.00
48 Tomas Hertl C 8.00 20.00
51 Jared McCann C 6.00 15.00
52 Ryan Strome C 8.00 20.00
54 Aleksander Barkov B 12.00 30.00
55 Bo Horvat C 10.00 25.00
60 Elvis Merzlikins D 8.00 20.00
62 William Karlsson C 10.00 25.00
63 Brad Marchand B 15.00 40.00
65 Teuvo Teravainen C 8.00 20.00
66 Juuse Saros C 10.00 25.00
68 Blake Coleman C 6.00 15.00
70 Mark Stone C 10.00 25.00
72 Tage Thompson C 10.00 25.00
78 Kirby Dach C 8.00 20.00
79 Michael Bunting C 8.00 20.00
84 Tanner Jeannot D 5.00 12.00
87 Sidney Crosby A 125.00 300.00
89 Cam Atkinson D 8.00 20.00
94 Josh Norris C 8.00 20.00
96 Jacob Markstrom C 8.00 20.00
97 Connor McDavid A 200.00 500.00

2022-23 SP Authentic Limited Material Autographs

3 Zach Werenski/50 30.00 80.00
4 Jamie Drysdale/100 15.00 40.00
5 Aaron Ekblad/50 25.00 60.00
6 Nick Schmaltz/100 15.00 40.00
9 Clayton Keller/100 25.00 60.00
11 Jonathan Huberdeau/50 25.00 60.00
12 Josh Bailey/100 15.00 40.00
13 Alexis Lafreniere/25 50.00 125.00
15 Anton Lundell/100 20.00 50.00
18 Tim Stutzle/50 25.00 60.00
20 Sebastian Aho/50 30.00 80.00
23 Lucas Raymond/50 30.00 80.00
25 Jordan Kyrou/50 20.00 50.00
28 Timo Meier/100 20.00 50.00
31 Carey Price/25 40.00 100.00
32 Seth Jarvis/50 50.00 125.00
33 Brady Tkachuk/50 30.00 80.00
37 Andrei Svechnikov/50 25.00 60.00
39 Alex Nedeljkovic/100 15.00 40.00
41 Brandon Saad/100 15.00 40.00
43 Quinn Hughes/50 80.00 200.00
45 Arthur Kaliyev/100 20.00 50.00
48 Tomas Hertl/100 20.00 50.00
51 Jared McCann/100 15.00 40.00
54 Aleksander Barkov/50 30.00 80.00
55 Bo Horvat/50 25.00 60.00
60 Elvis Merzlikins/100 20.00 50.00
63 Brad Marchand/25 40.00 100.00
65 Teuvo Teravainen/100 20.00 50.00
66 Juuse Saros/100 25.00 60.00
68 Blake Coleman/100 15.00 40.00
70 Mark Stone/50 25.00 60.00
72 Tage Thompson/100 25.00 60.00
76 Roope Hintz/50 25.00 60.00
78 Kirby Dach/100 20.00 50.00
79 Michael Bunting/100 20.00 50.00
89 Cam Atkinson/100 20.00 50.00
94 Josh Norris/100 20.00 50.00
96 Jacob Markstrom/50 20.00 50.00

2022-23 SP Authentic Marks of Distinction

MDAD Alex DeBrincat 20.00 50.00
MDAL Alexis Lafreniere 25.00 60.00
MDBB Brent Burns 15.00 40.00

MDBE Matty Beniers 60.00 150.00
MDBM Brad Marchand 30.00 80.00
MDBU Michael Bunting 15.00 40.00
MDJH Jonathan Huberdeau 20.00 50.00
MDJS Juraj Slafkovsky 80.00 200.00
MDMB Matt Boldy 50.00 125.00
MDOP Owen Power 30.00 80.00
MDRT Robert Thomas 15.00 40.00
MDSA Juuse Saros 20.00 50.00
MDSW Shane Wright 40.00 100.00
MDTT Tage Thompson 20.00 50.00

2022-23 SP Authentic Pageantry

*RED: .6X TO 1.5X BASIC
P1 Connor McDavid 2.50 6.00
P2 Tim Stutzle .60 1.50
P3 Carter Hart .50 1.25
P4 Tyler Toffoli .50 1.25
P5 Roman Josi .50 1.25
P6 Sidney Crosby 2.00 5.00
P7 Patrick Kane 1.00 2.50
P8 Alex Ovechkin 2.00 5.00
P9 Jack Eichel .75 2.00
P10 Kirill Kaprizov 1.50 4.00
P11 Anze Kopitar .75 2.00
P12 Elias Pettersson .75 2.00
P13 Alexis Lafreniere .75 2.00
P14 Jake Oettinger .75 2.00
P15 Artemi Panarin 1.00 2.50
P16 Joe Pavelski .60 1.50
P17 Jonathan Quick .60 1.50
P18 Jack Hughes 1.25 3.00
P19 Steven Stamkos 1.00 2.50
P20 Brent Burns .50 1.25
P21 Juuse Saros .60 1.50
P22 Cole Caufield 1.00 2.50
P23 Tage Thompson .60 1.50
P24 Mitch Marner .75 2.00
P25 Nick Suzuki 1.00 2.50
P26 Nikolaj Ehlers .50 1.25
P27 Yegor Sharangovich .50 1.25
P28 Matthew Tkachuk 1.00 2.50
P29 Leon Draisaitl 1.50 4.00
P30 Mark Stone .60 1.50
P31 Cam Atkinson .50 1.25
P32 Jonathan Huberdeau .60 1.50
P33 Miro Heiskanen .60 1.50
P34 Auston Matthews 2.00 5.00
P35 Cole Perfetti .50 1.25
P36 Robert Thomas .50 1.25
P37 Andrei Svechnikov .60 1.50
P38 Cale Makar 1.25 3.00
P39 David Pastrnak 1.25 3.00
P40 Anders Lee .40 1.00
P41 Evgeny Kuznetsov .60 1.50
P42 Alex DeBrincat .60 1.50
P43 Tristan Jarry .50 1.25
P44 Blake Coleman .40 1.00
P45 Aaron Ekblad .60 1.50
P46 Trevor Zegras .50 1.25
P47 Aleksander Barkov .75 2.00
P48 Moritz Seider .60 1.50
P49 Michael Bunting .50 1.25
P50 Andrei Vasilevskiy .75 2.00
P51 Mark Messier 1.00 2.50
P52 Ron Francis .60 1.50
P53 Grant Fuhr .75 2.00
P54 Adam Graves .40 1.00
P55 Bobby Hull 1.00 2.50
P56 Henrik Lundqvist 1.25 3.00
P57 Mike Modano .75 2.00
P58 Patrick Roy 1.25 3.00
P59 Bobby Orr 2.00 5.00
P60 Wayne Gretzky 3.00 8.00
P61 Juraj Slafkovsky 2.50 6.00
P62 Owen Power 1.00 2.50
P63 Matty Beniers 1.25 3.00
P64 Shane Wright 1.25 3.00
P65 Jonatan Berggren .75 2.00
P66 Brandt Clarke 1.00 2.50
P67 Kaiden Guhle 1.00 2.50
P68 Arber Xhekaj 1.00 2.50
P69 Matias Maccelli .75 2.00
P70 Braden Schneider .75 2.00
P71 Thomas Bordeleau .50 1.25
P72 Jack Quinn .75 2.00
P73 Lukas Reichel 1.00 2.50
P74 Matt Boldy 1.50 4.00
P75 Kent Johnson 1.00 2.50
P76 Zack Hayes .40 1.00
P77 Mads Sogaard .60 1.50
P78 Dylan Holloway 1.00 2.50
P79 Nathan Smith .40 1.00
P80 Pavol Regenda .50 1.25
P81 Andrei Kuzmenko 1.00 2.50
P82 Ben Meyers .50 1.25
P83 Mark Kastelic .40 1.00
P84 Pyotr Kochetkov 1.00 2.50
P85 David Jiricek 1.00 2.50
P86 Elmer Soderblom 1.00 2.50
P87 Brayden Tracey .40 1.00
P88 Jordan Spence .50 1.25
P89 Jordan Harris .60 1.50
P90 Nick Abruzzese .50 1.25

2022-23 SP Authentic Pageantry Autographs

P2 Tim Stutzle B 12.00 30.00
P3 Carter Hart C 10.00 25.00
P4 Tyler Toffoli C 10.00 25.00
P13 Alexis Lafreniere B 15.00 40.00
P14 Jake Oettinger B 15.00 40.00
P18 Jack Hughes A 25.00 60.00
P20 Brent Burns B 10.00 25.00
P21 Juuse Saros C 12.00 30.00
P23 Tage Thompson B 12.00 30.00
P30 Mark Stone B 12.00 30.00
P31 Cam Atkinson C 10.00 25.00
P32 Jonathan Huberdeau B 12.00 30.00
P35 Cole Perfetti C 10.00 25.00
P36 Robert Thomas C 10.00 25.00
P37 Andrei Svechnikov B 12.00 30.00
P40 Anders Lee D 8.00 20.00
P41 Evgeny Kuznetsov C 12.00 30.00
P42 Alex DeBrincat B 12.00 30.00
P43 Tristan Jarry C 10.00 25.00
P44 Blake Coleman D 8.00 20.00
P45 Aaron Ekblad B 12.00 30.00
P47 Aleksander Barkov C 15.00 40.00
P49 Michael Bunting C 10.00 25.00
P51 Mark Messier B 20.00 50.00
P52 Ron Francis B 12.00 30.00
P53 Grant Fuhr B 15.00 40.00
P54 Adam Graves B 8.00 20.00
P56 Henrik Lundqvist A 25.00 60.00
P57 Mike Modano B 15.00 40.00
P58 Patrick Roy A 25.00 60.00
P61 Juraj Slafkovsky B 50.00 125.00
P63 Matty Beniers B 25.00 60.00
P65 Jonatan Berggren C 15.00 40.00
P66 Brandt Clarke C 20.00 50.00
P67 Kaiden Guhle C 20.00 50.00
P68 Arber Xhekaj D 20.00 50.00
P69 Matias Maccelli D 15.00 40.00
P71 Thomas Bordeleau C 10.00 25.00
P72 Jack Quinn B 15.00 40.00
P73 Lukas Reichel C 20.00 50.00
P75 Kent Johnson B 20.00 50.00
P76 Zack Hayes E 8.00 20.00
P77 Mads Sogaard D 12.00 30.00
P78 Dylan Holloway C 20.00 50.00
P79 Nathan Smith D 8.00 20.00
P80 Pavol Regenda D 10.00 25.00
P81 Andrei Kuzmenko B 20.00 50.00
P82 Ben Meyers D 10.00 25.00
P83 Mark Kastelic E 8.00 20.00
P85 David Jiricek C 20.00 50.00
P86 Elmer Soderblom D 20.00 50.00
P87 Brayden Tracey D 8.00 20.00
P88 Jordan Spence D 10.00 25.00
P89 Jordan Harris D 12.00 30.00
P90 Nick Abruzzese E 10.00 25.00

2022-23 SP Authentic Sign of the Times

SOTTAB Adam Beckman F 5.00 12.00
SOTTAI Alex Iafallo F 5.00 12.00
SOTTAK Arthur Kaliyev F 8.00 20.00
SOTTAL Alexis Lafreniere A 12.00 30.00
SOTTAN Alex Nedeljkovic F 6.00 15.00
SOTTAP Aliaksei Protas F 5.00 12.00
SOTTAT Cam Atkinson E 8.00 20.00
SOTTBB Brent Burns C 8.00 20.00
SOTTBL Rob Blake C 8.00 20.00
SOTTBS Brandon Saad F 6.00 15.00
SOTTCC Charlie Coyle F 8.00 20.00
SOTTCH Carter Hart D 8.00 20.00
SOTTCJ Curtis Joseph B 10.00 25.00
SOTTCP Cole Perfetti D 8.00 20.00
SOTTCT Cam Talbot E 8.00 20.00
SOTTCW Chris Wideman F 5.00 12.00
SOTTDK Darcy Kuemper D 8.00 20.00
SOTTEB Evan Bouchard E 10.00 25.00
SOTTED Evgenii Dadonov E 5.00 12.00
SOTTEK Evgeny Kuznetsov D 10.00 25.00
SOTTEM Elvis Merzlikins E 8.00 20.00
SOTTES Egor Sokolov F 5.00 12.00
SOTTFL Marc-Andre Fleury A 15.00 40.00
SOTTFR Ron Francis A 10.00 25.00
SOTTGC Gerry Cheevers B 8.00 20.00
SOTTGE Morgan Geekie F 5.00 12.00
SOTTHL Hendrix Lapierre E 5.00 12.00
SOTTHO Bo Horvat C 10.00 25.00
SOTTJA Jake Allen F 8.00 20.00
SOTTJB Josh Bailey D 6.00 15.00
SOTTJE Joel Eriksson Ek F 6.00 15.00
SOTTJO John Marino F 8.00 20.00
SOTTJS Jaccob Slavin D 6.00 15.00
SOTTJV James van Riemsdyk D 6.00 15.00
SOTTKD Kirby Dach D 8.00 20.00
SOTTKF Kevin Fiala C 6.00 15.00
SOTTKK Kasperi Kapanen E 6.00 15.00
SOTTKL Kole Lind F 5.00 12.00
SOTTKM K'Andre Miller F 6.00 15.00
SOTTKT Keith Tkachuk C 8.00 20.00
SOTTLA Anton Lundell D 8.00 20.00
SOTTLE Anders Lee F 6.00 15.00
SOTTLR Luc Robitaille B 8.00 20.00
SOTTLU Henrik Lundqvist A 20.00 50.00
SOTTMA Mason Appleton F 5.00 12.00
SOTTMC Maxime Comtois F 6.00 15.00
SOTTMD Matt Duchene D 8.00 20.00
SOTTMF Marcus Foligno F 6.00 15.00
SOTTND Nico Daws F 6.00 15.00
SOTTNP Neal Pionk F 5.00 12.00
SOTTNR Nick Robertson F 8.00 20.00
SOTTPE Cal Petersen F 5.00 12.00
SOTTPK Peyton Krebs F 6.00 15.00
SOTTRB Rod Brind'Amour D 8.00 20.00
SOTTRF Robby Fabbri F 5.00 12.00
SOTTRK Rasmus Kupari D 5.00 12.00
SOTTRL Robin Lehner E 6.00 15.00
SOTTRM Ryan Merkley F 6.00 15.00
SOTTRR Ryan Reaves E 6.00 15.00
SOTTSB Sam Bennett C 12.00 30.00
SOTTSC Shayne Corson B 6.00 15.00
SOTTSH Shea Theodore D 10.00 25.00
SOTTSJ Seth Jarvis D 10.00 25.00
SOTTSP Scott Perunovich E 5.00 12.00
SOTTSR Sam Reinhart D 15.00 40.00
SOTTST Ryan Strome F 8.00 20.00
SOTTSZ Sergei Zubov B 6.00 15.00
SOTTTE Teuvo Teravainen D 8.00 20.00
SOTTTH Tage Thompson E 10.00 25.00
SOTTTK Torey Krug D 6.00 15.00
SOTTYS Yegor Sharangovich F 8.00 20.00
SOTTZW Zach Werenski D 12.00 30.00

2022-23 SP Authentic Sign of the Times Rookies

SOTTRAK Andrei Kuzmenko B 25.00 60.00
SOTTRAX Arber Xhekaj D 25.00 60.00
SOTTRBC Brandt Clarke D 25.00 60.00
SOTTRBE Matty Beniers A 60.00 150.00
SOTTRBM Ben Meyers D 12.00 30.00
SOTTRDG Dylan Guenther C 30.00 80.00
SOTTRDJ David Jiricek D 25.00 60.00
SOTTRES Elmer Soderblom D 25.00 60.00
SOTTRJQ Jack Quinn B 20.00 50.00
SOTTRJS Juraj Slafkovsky A 60.00 150.00
SOTTRKG Kaiden Guhle D 25.00 60.00
SOTTRKJ Kent Johnson C 25.00 60.00
SOTTRLR Lukas Reichel C 25.00 60.00
SOTTRMB Matt Boldy A 40.00 100.00
SOTTRMR Marco Rossi B 30.00 80.00
SOTTROP Owen Power A 25.00 60.00
SOTTRSA Jake Sanderson C 30.00 80.00
SOTTRSW Shane Wright A 30.00 80.00

2022-23 SP Authentic SP Curated Signatures

SPCAD Alex DeBrincat/99 10.00 25.00
SPCAE Aaron Ekblad/99 10.00 25.00
SPCAG Adam Graves/199 6.00 15.00
SPCAL Alexis Lafreniere/25 12.00 30.00
SPCAN Alex Nedeljkovic/199 6.00 15.00
SPCBH Bo Horvat/199 10.00 25.00
SPCBM Brad Marchand/25 15.00 40.00
SPCBS Brandon Saad/199 6.00 15.00
SPCBT Brady Tkachuk/99 12.00 30.00
SPCCA Cam Atkinson/199 8.00 20.00
SPCCC Charlie Coyle/199 8.00 20.00
SPCCH Carter Hart/99 8.00 20.00
SPCCP Cole Perfetti/199 8.00 20.00
SPCDK Darcy Kuemper/199 8.00 20.00
SPCED Evgenii Dadonov/199 5.00 12.00
SPCEJ Joel Eriksson Ek/199 6.00 15.00
SPCEK Evgeny Kuznetsov/99 10.00 25.00
SPCFA Robby Fabbri/199 5.00 12.00
SPCGF Grant Fuhr/99 12.00 30.00
SPCHL Henrik Lundqvist/25 50.00 125.00
SPCJH Jonathan Huberdeau/99 10.00 25.00
SPCJK Jordan Kyrou/99 8.00 20.00
SPCJM Jacob Markstrom/99 8.00 20.00
SPCJN Josh Norris/99 8.00 20.00
SPCJO Jake Oettinger/99 12.00 30.00
SPCJS Juuse Saros/99 10.00 25.00
SPCKA Arthur Kaliyev/199 8.00 20.00
SPCKK Kasperi Kapanen/199 6.00 15.00
SPCKM K'Andre Miller/199 6.00 15.00
SPCKT Keith Tkachuk/99 8.00 20.00
SPCLR Larry Robinson/25 8.00 20.00
SPCLU Anton Lundell/199 8.00 20.00
SPCMA John Marino/199 8.00 20.00
SPCMB Martin Brodeur/25 50.00 125.00
SPCMD Matt Duchene/99 8.00 20.00
SPCMF Marcus Foligno/199 6.00 15.00
SPCMG Matt Grzelcyk/199 6.00 15.00
SPCMM Mark Messier/25 30.00 80.00
SPCNP Neal Pionk/199 5.00 12.00
SPCPC Cal Petersen/199 5.00 12.00
SPCPE Jeff Petry/199 8.00 20.00
SPCPK Peyton Krebs/199 6.00 15.00
SPCRB Rob Blake/99 8.00 20.00
SPCRF Ron Francis/25 10.00 25.00
SPCRG Ryan Getzlaf/99 8.00 20.00
SPCRL Robin Lehner/199 6.00 15.00
SPCRM Rick Middleton/99 8.00 20.00
SPCRS Ryan Strome/199 8.00 20.00
SPCRT Robert Thomas/99 8.00 20.00
SPCSA Sebastian Aho/99 12.00 30.00
SPCSL Jaccob Slavin/199 6.00 15.00
SPCSR Sam Reinhart/199 15.00 40.00
SPCST Shea Theodore/199 10.00 25.00
SPCTE Teuvo Teravainen/99 8.00 20.00
SPCTH Tage Thompson/99 10.00 25.00
SPCTJ Tristan Jarry/199 8.00 20.00
SPCTM Timo Meier/199 8.00 20.00
SPCTS Tim Stutzle/99 10.00 25.00
SPCTT Tyler Toffoli/99 8.00 20.00
SPCUL Ukko-Pekka Luukkonen/199 6.00 15.00
SPCZW Zach Werenski/199 12.00 30.00

2022-23 SP Authentic SP Holofoils

HF1 Connor McDavid 25.00 60.00
HF2 Auston Matthews 20.00 50.00
HF3 Sidney Crosby 20.00 50.00
HF4 Cale Makar 12.00 30.00
HF5 David Pastrnak 12.00 30.00
HF6 Patrick Kane 10.00 25.00
HF7 Cole Caufield 10.00 25.00
HF8 Alex Ovechkin 20.00 50.00
HF9 Igor Shesterkin 10.00 25.00
HF10 Kirill Kaprizov 15.00 40.00
HF11 Trevor Zegras 5.00 12.00
HF12 Brad Marchand 10.00 25.00
HF13 Alexis Lafreniere 8.00 20.00
HF14 Michael Bunting 5.00 12.00
HF15 Steven Stamkos 10.00 25.00
HF16 Jack Hughes 12.00 30.00
HF17 Andrei Vasilevskiy 8.00 20.00
HF18 Mitch Marner 8.00 20.00
HF19 Artemi Panarin 10.00 25.00
HF20 Jack Eichel 8.00 20.00
HF21 Nikita Kucherov 10.00 25.00
HF22 Nick Suzuki 10.00 25.00
HF23 Erik Karlsson 6.00 15.00
HF24 Nathan MacKinnon 20.00 50.00
HF25 Matthew Tkachuk 10.00 25.00
HF26 Jason Robertson 8.00 20.00
HF27 Elias Pettersson 8.00 20.00
HF28 Tage Thompson 6.00 15.00
HF29 Mikko Rantanen 12.00 30.00
HF30 Matt Boldy 15.00 40.00
HF31 Matty Beniers 12.00 30.00
HF32 Owen Power 10.00 25.00
HF33 Juraj Slafkovsky 25.00 60.00
HF34 Shane Wright 12.00 30.00
HF35 Marco Rossi 12.00 30.00
HF36 Lukas Reichel 10.00 25.00
HF37 Jake Sanderson 12.00 30.00
HF38 Dylan Guenther 12.00 30.00
HF39 Brandt Clarke 10.00 25.00
HF40 Andrei Kuzmenko 10.00 25.00
HF41 Kaiden Guhle 10.00 25.00
HF42 Wyatt Johnston 20.00 50.00
HF43 Jonatan Berggren 8.00 20.00
HF44 Dylan Holloway 10.00 25.00
HF45 Kent Johnson 10.00 25.00
HF46 Samuel Poulin 6.00 15.00
HF47 David Jiricek 10.00 25.00
HF48 Elmer Soderblom 10.00 25.00
HF49 Jack Quinn 8.00 20.00
HF50 Braden Schneider 8.00 20.00

2022-23 SP Authentic Spectrum FX

S1 Connor McDavid 5.00 12.00
S2 Alex Ovechkin 4.00 10.00
S3 Sidney Crosby 4.00 10.00
S4 Patrick Kane 2.00 5.00
S5 Nathan MacKinnon 4.00 10.00
S6 David Pastrnak 2.50 6.00
S7 Jack Hughes 2.50 6.00
S8 Kirill Kaprizov 3.00 8.00
S9 Erik Karlsson 1.25 3.00
S10 Steven Stamkos 2.00 5.00
S11 Evgeni Malkin 2.00 5.00
S12 Artemi Panarin 2.00 5.00
S13 Nikita Kucherov 2.00 5.00
S14 Mitch Marner 1.50 4.00
S15 Elias Pettersson 1.50 4.00
S16 Johnny Gaudreau 1.50 4.00
S17 Mikko Rantanen 2.50 6.00
S18 Adam Fox 1.25 3.00
S19 Jamie Benn 1.00 2.50
S20 John Tavares 1.50 4.00
S21 Dylan Larkin 1.25 3.00
S22 Patrik Laine 1.25 3.00
S23 Jack Eichel 1.50 4.00
S24 Jason Robertson 1.50 4.00
S25 Leon Draisaitl 3.00 8.00
S26 Cale Makar 2.50 6.00
S27 Trevor Zegras 1.00 2.50
S28 Cole Caufield 2.00 5.00
S29 Nick Suzuki 2.00 5.00
S30 Igor Shesterkin 2.00 5.00
S31 Andrei Vasilevskiy 1.50 4.00
S32 Linus Ullmark 1.00 2.50
S33 Jake Oettinger 1.50 4.00
S34 Tage Thompson 1.25 3.00
S35 Jonathan Huberdeau 1.25 3.00
S36 J.T. Miller 1.25 3.00
S37 Matthew Tkachuk 2.00 5.00
S38 Brady Tkachuk 1.50 4.00
S39 Brad Marchand 2.00 5.00
S40 Quinn Hughes 2.50 6.00
S41 Jakub Lauko FW 3.00 8.00
S42 Nikita Alexandrov FW 2.50 6.00
S43 Cole Koepke FW 2.50 6.00
S44 Johnathan Kovacevic FW 2.50 6.00
S45 Alex Vlasic FW 2.00 5.00
S46 Vladislav Kolyachonok FW 2.00 5.00
S47 Jack McBain FW 2.50 6.00
S48 Dylan Samberg FW 2.50 6.00
S49 Erik Kallgren FW 2.50 6.00
S50 Nikita Okhotiuk FW 2.00 5.00
S51 Nils Aman FW 2.50 6.00
S52 Marcus Bjork FW 2.50 6.00
S53 Nick Perbix FW 2.00 5.00
S54 Pavol Regenda FW 2.50 6.00
S55 Filip Roos FW 2.00 5.00
S56 Nick Abruzzese FW 2.50 6.00
S57 Arber Xhekaj FW 5.00 12.00
S58 Mads Sogaard FW 3.00 8.00
S59 Isaac Ratcliffe FW 2.50 6.00
S60 Juuso Parssinen FW 2.50 6.00
S61 Pyotr Kochetkov FW 5.00 12.00
S62 Jordan Harris FW 3.00 8.00
S63 Reilly Walsh FW 2.50 6.00
S64 Jordan Spence FW 2.50 6.00
S65 Matias Maccelli FW 4.00 10.00
S66 Samuel Poulin FW 3.00 8.00
S67 Brayden Tracey FW 2.00 5.00
S68 Bobby Brink FW 2.50 6.00
S69 Thomas Bordeleau FW 2.50 6.00
S70 Brandt Clarke FW 5.00 12.00
S71 Elmer Soderblom FW 5.00 12.00
S72 Lukas Dostal FW 5.00 12.00
S73 Samuel Fagemo FW 2.00 5.00
S74 Jonatan Berggren FW 4.00 10.00
S75 Jacob Perreault FW 2.50 6.00
S76 Wyatt Johnston FW 10.00 25.00
S77 Braden Schneider FW 4.00 10.00
S78 Kaiden Guhle FW 5.00 12.00
S79 David Jiricek FW 5.00 12.00
S80 Andrei Kuzmenko FW 5.00 12.00
S81 Dylan Holloway FW 5.00 12.00
S82 Lukas Reichel FW 5.00 12.00
S83 Jack Quinn FW 4.00 10.00
S84 Owen Power FW 5.00 12.00
S85 Dylan Guenther FW 6.00 15.00
S86 Kent Johnson FW 5.00 12.00
S87 Jake Sanderson FW 6.00 15.00
S88 Shane Wright FW 6.00 15.00
S89 Matty Beniers FW 6.00 15.00
S90 Matt Boldy FW 8.00 20.00
S91 Juraj Slafkovsky FW 12.00 30.00

2022-23 SP Authentic Spectrum FX Gold

*GOLD/50: 2X TO 5X BASIC
*GOLD FW/50: 1.2X TO 3X BASIC

2022-23 SP Authentic Telemetry Autographs

TAL Anton Lundell D 8.00 20.00
TBC Brandt Clarke B 15.00 40.00
TBE Matty Beniers B 40.00 100.00
TBO Matt Boldy B 40.00 100.00
TBR Bryan Rust E 8.00 20.00
TDG Dylan Guenther B 20.00 50.00
TEK Evgeny Kuznetsov E 10.00 25.00
TES Elmer Soderblom B 15.00 40.00
TJD Jack Drury E 6.00 15.00
TJH Jonathan Huberdeau C 10.00 25.00
TJK Jordan Kyrou D 8.00 20.00
TJQ Jack Quinn B 12.00 30.00
TJS Jake Sanderson C 20.00 50.00
TKF Kevin Fiala D 6.00 15.00
TLE Anders Lee E 6.00 15.00
TMB Michael Bunting D 8.00 20.00
TMD Matt Duchene C 8.00 20.00
TMS Mark Stone C 10.00 25.00
TRL Robin Lehner E 6.00 15.00
TSL Juraj Slafkovsky A 60.00 150.00
TSR Sam Reinhart C 15.00 40.00
TTT Tyler Toffoli C 8.00 20.00

2022-23 SP Authentic Top Rookies

*BLUE: .6X TO 1.5X BASIC
*GREEN: .75X TO 2X BASIC
TR1 Matty Beniers 1.50 4.00
TR2 Matt Boldy 2.00 5.00
TR3 Dylan Guenther 1.50 4.00
TR4 Kaiden Guhle 1.25 3.00
TR5 Brandt Clarke 1.25 3.00
TR6 Kent Johnson 1.25 3.00
TR7 Marco Rossi 1.50 4.00
TR8 Jack Quinn 1.00 2.50
TR9 Jonatan Berggren 1.00 2.50
TR10 Andrei Kuzmenko 1.25 3.00
TR11 Samuel Fagemo .50 1.25
TR12 Jacob Perreault .60 1.50
TR13 Shane Wright 1.50 4.00
TR14 Thomas Bordeleau .60 1.50
TR15 Elmer Soderblom 1.25 3.00
TR16 Jordan Harris .75 2.00
TR17 Braden Schneider 1.00 2.50
TR18 Jordan Spence .60 1.50
TR19 Bobby Brink .60 1.50
TR20 Matias Maccelli 1.00 2.50
TR21 Wyatt Johnston 2.50 6.00
TR22 Nick Abruzzese .60 1.50
TR23 Brayden Tracey .50 1.25
TR24 Samuel Poulin .75 2.00
TR25 Mads Sogaard .75 2.00
TR26 Arber Xhekaj 1.25 3.00
TR27 Juraj Slafkovsky 3.00 8.00
TR28 Lukas Dostal 1.25 3.00
TR29 Pyotr Kochetkov 1.25 3.00
TR30 Isaac Ratcliffe .60 1.50
TR31 Johnathan Kovacevic .60 1.50
TR32 Lukas Reichel 1.25 3.00
TR33 Matej Blumel .75 2.00
TR34 Alex Vlasic .50 1.25
TR35 Kaedan Korczak .50 1.25
TR36 Dylan Samberg .60 1.50
TR37 Nikita Okhotiuk .50 1.25
TR38 Dylan Holloway 1.25 3.00
TR39 Owen Power 1.25 3.00
TR40 Jack McBain .60 1.50
TR41 Erik Kallgren .60 1.50
TR42 Juuso Parssinen .60 1.50
TR43 Pavol Regenda .60 1.50
TR44 Nikita Alexandrov .60 1.50
TR45 Aatu Raty .60 1.50
TR46 Marc McLaughlin .60 1.50
TR47 David Jiricek 1.25 3.00
TR48 Nick Perbix .50 1.25
TR49 Nathan Smith .50 1.25
TR50 Jake Sanderson 1.50 4.00

2022-23 SP Authentic True Leaders

*BLUE: .5X TO 1.2X BASIC
*GREEN: .6X TO 1.5X BASIC
TL1 Gabriel Landeskog 1.00 2.50
TL2 Steven Stamkos 1.50 4.00
TL3 Leon Draisaitl 2.50 6.00
TL4 Artemi Panarin 1.50 4.00
TL5 Auston Matthews 3.00 8.00
TL6 Roman Josi .75 2.00
TL7 Sidney Crosby 3.00 8.00
TL8 Evgeni Malkin 1.50 4.00
TL9 Connor McDavid 4.00 10.00
TL10 Mark Stone 1.00 2.50
TL11 Alex Ovechkin 3.00 8.00
TL12 Dylan Larkin 1.00 2.50
TL13 Nick Suzuki 1.50 4.00
TL14 Brady Tkachuk 1.25 3.00
TL15 Jacob Trouba .60 1.50
TL17 Jonathan Huberdeau 1.00 2.50
TL18 Nathan MacKinnon 3.00 8.00
TL19 Jack Hughes 2.00 5.00
TL20 Anze Kopitar 1.25 3.00
TL21 Ryan O'Reilly .75 2.00
TL22 Jonathan Toews 1.25 3.00
TL23 Patrice Bergeron 1.00 2.50
TL24 Anders Lee .60 1.50
TL25 Kyle Okposo .50 1.25

2022-23 SP Authentic UD Authentics Autographs

UDAAG Adam Graves D 8.00 20.00
UDAAH Alexander Holtz D 10.00 25.00
UDAAI Alex Iafallo F 6.00 15.00
UDAAL Anders Lee E 8.00 20.00
UDAAM Auston Matthews B 125.00 300.00
UDAAN Alex Nedeljkovic F 8.00 20.00
UDABC Blake Coleman E 8.00 20.00
UDABL Rob Blake C 10.00 25.00
UDABN Bernie Nicholls E 8.00 20.00
UDABR Bryan Rust E 10.00 25.00
UDACA Cam Atkinson F 10.00 25.00
UDACC Charlie Coyle F 10.00 25.00
UDACP Cal Petersen F 6.00 15.00
UDACS Cole Schwindt F 6.00 15.00
UDADB Drake Batherson E 10.00 25.00
UDADG Doug Gilmour C 12.00 30.00
UDADH Dany Heatley C 8.00 20.00
UDADI Marcel Dionne C 12.00 30.00
UDADP Denis Potvin C 10.00 25.00
UDADT Dave Taylor D 8.00 20.00
UDAED Evgenii Dadonov F 6.00 15.00
UDAEK Evgeny Kuznetsov E 12.00 30.00
UDAEM Elvis Merzlikins F 10.00 25.00
UDAGC Gerry Cheevers C 10.00 25.00
UDAGD Grigori Denisenko E 6.00 15.00
UDAHL Henrik Lundqvist B 60.00 150.00
UDAJB Josh Bailey F 8.00 20.00
UDAJD Jack Drury D 8.00 20.00
UDAJE Jack Eichel C 30.00 80.00
UDAJK Jari Kurri C 10.00 25.00
UDAJL John LeClair B 10.00 25.00
UDAJO Joel Eriksson Ek F 8.00 20.00
UDAJP Jeff Petry D 10.00 25.00
UDAJQ Jonathan Quick C 12.00 30.00
UDAJS Jeremy Swayman E 15.00 40.00
UDAJU Juuse Saros D 12.00 30.00
UDAKK Kasperi Kapanen F 8.00 20.00
UDAKM K'Andre Miller F 8.00 20.00
UDAKT Keith Tkachuk D 10.00 25.00
UDALR Larry Robinson B 10.00 25.00
UDAMA John Marino F 10.00 25.00
UDAMD Matt Duchene E 10.00 25.00
UDAMF Marcus Foligno F 8.00 20.00
UDAMJ Jonathan Marchessault E 12.00 30.00
UDAML Mario Lemieux B 80.00 200.00
UDAMO J.J. Moser F 6.00 15.00
UDANP Neal Pionk F 6.00 15.00
UDANS Nick Schmaltz E 8.00 20.00
UDAOE Jake Oettinger C 15.00 40.00
UDAPK Peyton Krebs D 8.00 20.00
UDARB Rod Brind'Amour C 10.00 25.00
UDARF Robby Fabbri F 6.00 15.00
UDARH Ron Hextall C 10.00 25.00
UDARM Rick Middleton D 10.00 25.00
UDARS Ryan Strome F 10.00 25.00
UDASM Sonny Milano F 8.00 20.00
UDASR Sam Reinhart E 20.00 50.00
UDAST Mark Stone E 12.00 30.00
UDASU Nick Suzuki C 40.00 100.00
UDATA Tanner Jeannot E 6.00 15.00
UDATJ Tristan Jarry D 10.00 25.00
UDATM Timo Meier E 10.00 25.00
UDATT Tony Twist E 6.00 15.00
UDAUL Ukko-Pekka Luukkonen F 8.00 20.00
UDAVV Vitek Vanecek F 10.00 25.00
UDAWE William Eklund E 12.00 30.00
UDAYS Yegor Sharangovich F 10.00 25.00

2022-23 SP Authentic UD Authentics Patch Autographs

UDAPAO Alex Ovechkin/25 300.00 800.00
UDAPDB Drake Batherson/49 15.00 40.00
UDAPDP Denis Potvin/25 15.00 40.00
UDAPEK Evgeny Kuznetsov/49 20.00 50.00
UDAPHL Henrik Lundqvist/25 125.00 300.00
UDAPJE Joel Eriksson Ek/49 12.00 30.00
UDAPJK Jari Kurri/49 15.00 40.00
UDAPJM Jacob Markstrom/49 15.00 40.00
UDAPJO Jake Oettinger/49 25.00 60.00
UDAPMD Matt Duchene/49 15.00 40.00
UDAPTJ Tristan Jarry/49 15.00 40.00
UDAPTM Timo Meier/49 15.00 40.00
UDAPUL Ukko-Pekka Luukkonen/49 12.00 30.00

2023-24 SP Authentic

1 Connor McDavid 2.00 5.00
2 Sidney Crosby 1.50 4.00
3 Alex Ovechkin 1.50 4.00
4 Auston Matthews 1.50 4.00
5 Leon Draisaitl 1.25 3.00
6 Marc-Andre Fleury .75 2.00
7 Cale Makar 1.00 2.50
8 John Tavares .60 1.50
9 Igor Shesterkin .75 2.00
10 Tim Stutzle .50 1.25
11 Brad Marchand .75 2.00
12 Andrei Vasilevskiy .60 1.50
13 Anze Kopitar .60 1.50
14 Matty Beniers .50 1.25
15 Jack Eichel .60 1.50
16 Dylan Cozens .40 1.00
17 Alexis Lafreniere .60 1.50
18 Cole Caufield .75 2.00
19 Jonathan Huberdeau .50 1.25
20 Sebastian Aho .60 1.50
21 Andrei Svechnikov .50 1.25
22 Juraj Slafkovsky .75 2.00
23 Brent Burns .40 1.00
24 Mikko Rantanen 1.00 2.50
25 Joe Pavelski .50 1.25
26 Aleksander Barkov .60 1.50
27 Matthew Tkachuk .75 2.00
28 Nick Suzuki .75 2.00
29 Nico Hischier .60 1.50
30 Tage Thompson .50 1.25
31 Brady Tkachuk .60 1.50
32 Noah Cates .25 .60
33 Jake Guentzel .60 1.50
34 Jonathan Quick .50 1.25
35 Jeremy Swayman .60 1.50
36 Jake Oettinger .60 1.50
37 Ilya Sorokin .60 1.50
38 Brock Boeser .50 1.25
39 Roman Josi .40 1.00
40 Clayton Keller .50 1.25
41 Shane Pinto .30 .75
42 Miro Heiskanen .50 1.25
43 Ryan Nugent-Hopkins .50 1.25
44 Mark Stone .50 1.25
45 Jonathan Marchessault .50 1.25
46 J.T. Miller .50 1.25
47 Kyle Connor .60 1.50
48 Troy Terry .30 .75
49 Jacob Markstrom .40 1.00
50 Teuvo Teravainen .40 1.00
51 Seth Jarvis .50 1.25
52 Zach Hyman .60 1.50
53 Kevin Fiala .30 .75
54 Mats Zuccarello .40 1.00
55 Brendan Gallagher .40 1.00
56 Timo Meier .40 1.00
57 Brock Nelson .40 1.00
58 Josh Norris .40 1.00
59 Robert Thomas .40 1.00
60 Jordan Kyrou .40 1.00
61 Chandler Stephenson .30 .75
62 Evgeny Kuznetsov .50 1.25
63 Cole Perfetti .40 1.00
64 Matt Boldy .60 1.50
65 Kirby Dach .40 1.00
66 Joel Eriksson Ek .30 .75
67 Torey Krug .30 .75
68 Anton Lundell .40 1.00
69 Sam Reinhart .75 2.00
70 Juuse Saros .50 1.25
71 Bo Horvat .50 1.25
72 Jordan Eberle .40 1.00
73 Roope Hintz .50 1.25
74 Kent Johnson .40 1.00
75 Matias Maccelli .30 .75
76 David Pastrnak 1.00 2.50
77 David Perron .30 .75
78 Patrik Laine .50 1.25
79 Jack Hughes 1.00 2.50
80 Alex Tuch .40 1.00
81 Mason McTavish .40 1.00
82 Bowen Byram .50 1.25
83 K'Andre Miller .30 .75
84 Steven Stamkos .75 2.00
85 Tristan Jarry .40 1.00
86 David Jiricek .40 1.00
87 Nathan MacKinnon 1.50 4.00
88 Nazem Kadri .50 1.25
89 Philipp Grubauer .40 1.00
90 Dylan Larkin .50 1.25
91 Mathew Barzal .50 1.25
92 Travis Konecny .40 1.00
93 Trevor Zegras .40 1.00
94 Nikolaj Ehlers .40 1.00
95 Mikey Anderson .30 .75
96 Mitch Marner .60 1.50
97 Kirill Kaprizov 1.25 3.00
98 Elias Pettersson .60 1.50
99 Brayden Point .50 1.25
100 Moritz Seider .50 1.25
101 Luke Hughes FW AU/949* RC 150.00 400.00
102 Ridly Greig FW AU/949* RC 25.00 60.00
103 Devon Levi FW AU/949* RC 80.00 200.00
104 Will Cuylle FW AU/949* RC 40.00 100.00
105 Marco Kasper FW AU/949* RC 50.00 125.00
106 Adam Fantilli FW AU/949* RC 150.00 400.00
107 Matthew Knies FW AU/949* RC 250.00 600.00
108 Matthew Coronato FW AU/949* RC 40.00 100.00
109 Brock Faber FW AU RC 150.00 400.00
110 Connor Bedard FW AU/949* RC 1500.00 4000.00
111 Dustin Wolf FW AU/949* RC 100.00 250.00
112 Sean Farrell FW AU/949* RC 10.00 25.00
113 Owen Beck FW AU/949* RC 30.00 80.00
114 Jakob Pelletier FW AU/949* RC 15.00 40.00
115 Tyson Foerster FW AU/949* RC 40.00 100.00
116 Yaroslav Askarov FW AU/949* RC 100.00 250.00
117 Luke Evangelista FW AU/949* RC 40.00 100.00
118 Hugh McGing FW AU/949* RC 10.00 25.00
119 Milos Kelemen FW AU/949* RC 10.00 25.00
120 Olle Eriksson Ek FW AU/949* RC 10.00 25.00
121 Walker Duehr FW AU/949* RC 8.00 20.00
122 Egor Afanasyev FW AU/949* RC 10.00 25.00
123 David Gust FW AU/949* RC 10.00 25.00
124 Lukas Rousek FW AU/949* RC 8.00 20.00
125 Matt Murray FW AU/949* RC 10.00 25.00
126 Samuel Bolduc FW AU/949* RC 10.00 25.00
127 Tye Kartye FW AU/949* RC 15.00 40.00
128 Billy Sweezey FW RC 3.00 8.00
129 Bobby McMann FW AU/949* RC 25.00 60.00
130 Matthew Kessel FW AU/949* RC 8.00 20.00
131 Akito Hirose FW AU/949* RC 8.00 20.00
132 Vincent Iorio FW AU/949* RC 10.00 25.00
133 Vincent Desharnais FW AU/949* RC 12.00 30.00
134 Jaxson Stauber FW AU/949* RC 10.00 25.00
135 Danil Gushchin FW AU RC 10.00 25.00
136 Nick Swaney FW AU/949* RC 10.00 25.00
137 Wyatt Kaiser FW AU/949* RC 10.00 25.00
138 Leevi Merilainen FW AU/949* RC 10.00 25.00
139 Tristen Robins FW AU/949* RC 10.00 25.00
140 Jonathan Gruden FW AU/949* RC 10.00 25.00
141 Joona Koppanen FW AU/949* RC 8.00 20.00
142 Luke Philp FW AU/949* RC 10.00 25.00
143 Elliot Desnoyers FW AU/949* RC 10.00 25.00
144 Aidan McDonough FW AU/949* RC 8.00 20.00
145 Jiri Patera FW AU/949* RC 15.00 40.00
146 Adam Ginning FW AU/949* RC 10.00 25.00
147 Nikita Nesterenko FW AU/949* RC 10.00 25.00
148 Arnaud Durandeau FW AU/949* RC 10.00 25.00
149 Jake Livingstone FW AU/949* RC 10.00 25.00
150 Cole Guttman FW AU/949* RC 10.00 25.00
151 Simon Edvinsson FW AU/949* RC 60.00 150.00
152 John Beecher FW AU/949* RC 30.00 80.00
153 Kevin Korchinski FW AU/949* RC 30.00 80.00
154 Mackie Samoskevich FW AU/949* RC 20.00 50.00
155 Jet Greaves FW AU/949* RC 15.00 40.00
156 Connor Zary FW AU/949* RC 40.00 100.00
157 Michael Kesselring FW AU/949* RC 10.00 25.00
158 Zach Benson FW AU/949* RC 30.00 80.00
159 Matt Savoie FW AU/949* RC 40.00 100.00
160 Henry Thrun FW AU/949* RC 10.00 25.00
161 Uvis Balinskis FW AU RC 10.00 25.00
162 Samuel Knazko FW AU/949* RC 10.00 25.00
163 Daemon Hunt FW RC 3.00 8.00
164 Matt Tomkins FW RC 3.00 8.00
165 Tyler Kleven FW AU/949* RC 10.00 25.00
166 Marc Del Gaizo FW RC 3.00 8.00
167 Cole McWard FW AU/949* RC 10.00 25.00
168 Fraser Minten FW AU/949* RC 40.00 100.00
169 Mason Lohrei FW RC 5.00 12.00
170 Jackson LaCombe FW AU/949* RC 10.00 25.00
171 Raphael Lavoie FW AU/949* RC 10.00 25.00
172 Hunter McKown FW AU/949* RC 10.00 25.00
173 Roby Jarventie FW RC 3.00 8.00
174 John Ludvig FW RC 3.00 8.00
175 Drew Helleson FW RC 3.00 8.00
176 Leo Carlsson FW AU/949* RC 150.00 400.00
177 Matthew Poitras FW AU/949* RC 50.00 125.00
178 Ryan Johnson FW RC 4.00 10.00
179 Nikolas Matinpalo FW RC 3.00 8.00
180 Stanislav Svozil FW AU/949* RC 8.00 20.00
181 Alex Laferriere FW AU/949* RC 60.00 150.00
182 Emil Andrae FW RC 3.00 8.00
183 Pavel Mintyukov FW AU/949* RC 40.00 100.00
184 Ryan Shea FW RC 3.00 8.00
185 Logan Cooley FW AU/949* RC 150.00 400.00
186 Ryan Winterton FW RC 3.00 8.00
187 Tristan Luneau FW RC 10.00 25.00
188 Ty Emberson FW RC 3.00 8.00
189 Justin Sourdif FW AU RC 10.00 25.00
190 William Dufour FW AU/949* RC 8.00 20.00
191 Simon Nemec FW AU/949* RC 40.00 100.00
192 Dmitri Voronkov FW RC 4.00 10.00
193 Isak Rosen FW AU/949* RC 10.00 25.00
194 Ryker Evans FW AU/949* RC 20.00 50.00
195 Jayden Struble FW RC 4.00 10.00
196 Ilya Solovyov FW AU/949* RC 10.00 25.00
197 Jiri Kulich FW AU RC 30.00 80.00
198 Ivan Miroshnichenko FW AU/949* RC 30.00 80.00
199 Martin Pospisil FW AU RC 15.00 40.00

2023-24 SP Authentic Future Watch Inscriptions

*INSCRIPTIONS/50: .8X TO 2X BASIC
104 Will Cuylle/50* 125.00 300.00
106 Adam Fantilli/50* 200.00 500.00
108 Matthew Coronato/50* 125.00 300.00
113 Owen Beck/50* 80.00 200.00
114 Jakob Pelletier/50* 40.00 100.00

127 Tye Kartye/50* 60.00 150.00
129 Bobby McMann/50* 100.00 250.00
159 Matt Savoie/50* 125.00 300.00
168 Fraser Minten/50* 125.00 300.00
191 Simon Nemec/50* 125.00 300.00

2023-24 SP Authentic Limited Blue

*BLUE/399: .6X TO 1.5X RED
110 Connor Bedard FW 60.00 150.00
200 Connor Bedard FW 60.00 150.00

2023-24 SP Authentic Limited Gold

*GOLD/99: 1X TO 2.5X RED
110 Connor Bedard FW 200.00 500.00
200 Connor Bedard FW 200.00 500.00

2023-24 SP Authentic Limited Green

*GREEN/199: .8X TO 2X RED
110 Connor Bedard FW 100.00 250.00
200 Connor Bedard FW 100.00 250.00

2023-24 SP Authentic Limited Red

1 Connor McDavid 3.00 8.00
2 Sidney Crosby 2.50 6.00
3 Alex Ovechkin 2.50 6.00
4 Auston Matthews 2.50 6.00
5 Leon Draisaitl 2.00 5.00
6 Marc-Andre Fleury 1.25 3.00
7 Cale Makar 1.50 4.00
8 John Tavares 1.00 2.50
9 Igor Shesterkin 1.25 3.00
10 Tim Stutzle .75 2.00
11 Brad Marchand 1.25 3.00
12 Andrei Vasilevskiy 1.00 2.50
13 Anze Kopitar 1.00 2.50
14 Matty Beniers .75 2.00
15 Jack Eichel 1.00 2.50
16 Dylan Cozens .60 1.50
17 Alexis Lafreniere 1.00 2.50
18 Cole Caufield 1.25 3.00
19 Jonathan Huberdeau .75 2.00
20 Sebastian Aho 1.00 2.50
21 Andrei Svechnikov .75 2.00
22 Juraj Slafkovsky 1.25 3.00
23 Brent Burns .60 1.50
24 Mikko Rantanen 1.50 4.00
25 Joe Pavelski .75 2.00
26 Aleksander Barkov 1.00 2.50
27 Matthew Tkachuk 1.25 3.00
28 Nick Suzuki 1.25 3.00
29 Nico Hischier 1.00 2.50
30 Tage Thompson .75 2.00
31 Brady Tkachuk 1.00 2.50
32 Noah Cates .40 1.00
33 Jake Guentzel 1.00 2.50
34 Jonathan Quick .75 2.00
35 Jeremy Swayman 1.00 2.50
36 Jake Oettinger 1.00 2.50
37 Ilya Sorokin 1.00 2.50
38 Brock Boeser .75 2.00
39 Roman Josi .60 1.50
40 Clayton Keller .75 2.00
41 Shane Pinto .50 1.25
42 Miro Heiskanen .75 2.00
43 Ryan Nugent-Hopkins .75 2.00
44 Mark Stone .75 2.00
45 Jonathan Marchessault .75 2.00
46 J.T. Miller .75 2.00
47 Kyle Connor 1.00 2.50
48 Troy Terry .50 1.25
49 Jacob Markstrom .60 1.50
50 Teuvo Teravainen .60 1.50
51 Seth Jarvis .75 2.00
52 Zach Hyman 1.00 2.50
53 Kevin Fiala .50 1.25
54 Mats Zuccarello .60 1.50
55 Brendan Gallagher .60 1.50
56 Timo Meier .60 1.50
57 Brock Nelson .60 1.50
58 Josh Norris .60 1.50
59 Robert Thomas .60 1.50
60 Jordan Kyrou .60 1.50
61 Chandler Stephenson .50 1.25
62 Evgeny Kuznetsov .75 2.00
63 Cole Perfetti .60 1.50
64 Matt Boldy 1.00 2.50
65 Kirby Dach .60 1.50
66 Joel Eriksson Ek .50 1.25
67 Torey Krug .50 1.25
68 Anton Lundell .60 1.50
69 Sam Reinhart 1.25 3.00
70 Juuse Saros .75 2.00
71 Bo Horvat .75 2.00
72 Jordan Eberle .60 1.50
73 Roope Hintz .75 2.00
74 Kent Johnson .60 1.50
75 Matias Maccelli .50 1.25
76 David Pastrnak 1.50 4.00
77 David Perron .50 1.25
78 Patrik Laine .75 2.00
79 Jack Hughes 1.50 4.00
80 Alex Tuch .60 1.50
81 Mason McTavish .60 1.50
82 Bowen Byram .75 2.00
83 K'Andre Miller .50 1.25
84 Steven Stamkos 1.25 3.00
85 Tristan Jarry .60 1.50
86 David Jiricek .60 1.50
87 Nathan MacKinnon 2.50 6.00
88 Nazem Kadri .75 2.00
89 Philipp Grubauer .60 1.50
90 Dylan Larkin .75 2.00
91 Mathew Barzal .75 2.00
92 Travis Konecny .60 1.50
93 Trevor Zegras .60 1.50
94 Nikolaj Ehlers .60 1.50
95 Mikey Anderson .50 1.25
96 Mitch Marner 1.00 2.50
97 Kirill Kaprizov 2.00 5.00
98 Elias Pettersson 1.00 2.50
99 Brayden Point .75 2.00
100 Moritz Seider .75 2.00
101 Luke Hughes FW 3.00 8.00
102 Ridly Greig FW 1.50 4.00
103 Devon Levi FW 2.50 6.00
104 Will Cuylle FW 1.50 4.00
105 Marco Kasper FW 2.50 6.00
106 Adam Fantilli FW 3.00 8.00
107 Matthew Knies FW 4.00 10.00
108 Matthew Coronato FW 1.50 4.00
109 Brock Faber FW 2.50 6.00
110 Connor Bedard FW 8.00 20.00
111 Dustin Wolf FW 3.00 8.00
112 Sean Farrell FW 1.00 2.50
113 Owen Beck FW 1.50 4.00
114 Jakob Pelletier FW 1.25 3.00
115 Tyson Foerster FW 2.00 5.00
116 Yaroslav Askarov FW 2.50 6.00
117 Luke Evangelista FW 1.50 4.00
118 Hugh McGing FW 1.00 2.50
119 Milos Kelemen FW 1.00 2.50
120 Olle Eriksson Ek FW 1.00 2.50
121 Walker Duehr FW .75 2.00
122 Egor Afanasyev FW 1.00 2.50
123 David Gust FW 1.00 2.50
124 Lukas Rousek FW .75 2.00
125 Matt Murray FW 1.00 2.50
126 Samuel Bolduc FW 1.00 2.50
127 Tye Kartye FW 1.50 4.00
128 Billy Sweezey FW 1.00 2.50
129 Bobby McMann FW 1.50 4.00
130 Matthew Kessel FW .75 2.00
131 Akito Hirose FW .75 2.00
132 Vincent Iorio FW 1.00 2.50
133 Vincent Desharnais FW 1.25 3.00
134 Jaxson Stauber FW 1.00 2.50
135 Danil Gushchin FW 1.00 2.50
136 Nick Swaney FW 1.00 2.50
137 Wyatt Kaiser FW 1.00 2.50
138 Leevi Merilainen FW 1.00 2.50
139 Tristen Robins FW 1.00 2.50
140 Jonathan Gruden FW 1.00 2.50
141 Joona Koppanen FW .75 2.00
142 Luke Philp FW 1.00 2.50
143 Elliot Desnoyers FW 1.00 2.50
144 Aidan McDonough FW .75 2.00
145 Jiri Patera FW 1.50 4.00
146 Adam Ginning FW 1.00 2.50
147 Nikita Nesterenko FW 1.00 2.50
148 Arnaud Durandeau FW 1.00 2.50
149 Jake Livingstone FW 1.00 2.50
150 Cole Guttman FW 1.00 2.50
151 Simon Edvinsson FW 2.00 5.00
152 John Beecher FW 2.00 5.00
153 Kevin Korchinski FW 1.50 4.00
154 Mackie Samoskevich FW 1.50 4.00
155 Jet Greaves FW 1.50 4.00
156 Connor Zary FW 2.00 5.00
157 Michael Kesselring FW 1.00 2.50
158 Zach Benson FW 1.50 4.00
159 Matt Savoie FW 2.00 5.00
160 Henry Thrun FW 1.00 2.50
161 Uvis Balinskis FW 1.00 2.50
162 Samuel Knazko FW 1.00 2.50
163 Daemon Hunt FW 1.00 2.50
164 Matt Tomkins FW 1.00 2.50
165 Tyler Kleven FW 1.00 2.50
166 Marc Del Gaizo FW 1.00 2.50
167 Cole McWard FW 1.00 2.50
168 Fraser Minten FW 2.00 5.00
169 Mason Lohrei FW 1.50 4.00
170 Jackson LaCombe FW 1.00 2.50
171 Raphael Lavoie FW 1.00 2.50
172 Hunter McKown FW 1.00 2.50
173 Roby Jarventie FW 1.00 2.50
174 John Ludvig FW 1.00 2.50
175 Drew Helleson FW 1.00 2.50
176 Leo Carlsson FW 3.00 8.00
177 Matthew Poitras FW 2.00 5.00
178 Ryan Johnson FW 1.25 3.00
179 Nikolas Matinpalo FW 1.00 2.50
180 Stanislav Svozil FW .75 2.00
181 Alex Laferriere FW 1.50 4.00
182 Emil Andrae FW 1.00 2.50
183 Pavel Mintyukov FW 1.50 4.00
184 Ryan Shea FW 1.00 2.50
185 Logan Cooley FW 3.00 8.00
186 Ryan Winterton FW 1.00 2.50
187 Tristan Luneau FW 1.00 2.50
188 Ty Emberson FW 1.00 2.50
189 Justin Sourdif FW 1.00 2.50
190 William Dufour FW .75 2.00
191 Simon Nemec FW 2.00 5.00
192 Dmitri Voronkov FW 1.25 3.00
193 Isak Rosen FW 1.00 2.50
194 Ryker Evans FW 1.25 3.00
195 Jayden Struble FW 1.25 3.00
196 Ilya Solovyov FW 1.00 2.50
197 Jiri Kulich FW 2.00 5.00
198 Ivan Miroshnichenko FW 1.50 4.00
199 Martin Pospisil FW 1.25 3.00
200 Connor Bedard FW 8.00 20.00

2023-24 SP Authentic '03-04 Retro Future Watch Autographs

RFWA21 William Dufour/399 6.00 15.00
RFWA24 Leevi Merilainen/399 8.00 20.00
RFWA25 Stanislav Svozil/399 6.00 15.00
RFWA26 Tye Kartye/399 12.00 30.00
RFWA27 Jackson LaCombe/399 8.00 20.00
RFWA28 Aidan McDonough/399 6.00 15.00
RFWA29 Arnaud Durandeau/399 8.00 20.00
RFWA210 Vincent Desharnais/399 10.00 25.00
RFWA211 Nikita Nesterenko/399 8.00 20.00
RFWA212 Akito Hirose/399 6.00 15.00
RFWA213 Elliot Desnoyers/399 8.00 20.00
RFWA214 Vincent Iorio/399 8.00 20.00
RFWA215 Tristen Robins/399 8.00 20.00
RFWA216 Wyatt Kaiser/399 8.00 20.00
RFWA219 Luke Philp/399 8.00 20.00
RFWA220 Matt Murray/399 8.00 20.00
RFWA221 Adam Ginning/399 8.00 20.00
RFWA222 Samuel Bolduc/399 8.00 20.00
RFWA223 Jake Livingstone/399 8.00 20.00
RFWA224 Henry Thrun/399 8.00 20.00
RFWA225 Tyler Kleven/399 8.00 20.00
RFWA226 Jet Greaves/399 12.00 30.00
RFWA227 Jiri Patera/399 12.00 30.00
RFWA228 Bobby McMann/399 15.00 40.00
RFWA229 David Gust/399 8.00 20.00
RFWA230 Cole Guttman/399 8.00 20.00
RFWA231 Joona Koppanen/399 6.00 15.00
RFWA232 Walker Duehr/399 6.00 15.00
RFWA233 Michael Kesselring/399 8.00 20.00
RFWA234 Nick Swaney/399 8.00 20.00
RFWA235 Jonathan Gruden/399 8.00 20.00
RFWA236 Egor Afanasyev/399 8.00 20.00
RFWA237 Hugh McGing/399 8.00 20.00
RFWA238 Milos Kelemen/399 8.00 20.00
RFWA239 Cole McWard/399 8.00 20.00
RFWA240 Matthew Kessel/399 6.00 15.00
RFWA241 Samuel Knazko/399 8.00 20.00
RFWA242 Jaxson Stauber/399 8.00 20.00
RFWA243 Olle Eriksson Ek/399 8.00 20.00
RFWA244 Billy Sweezey/399 8.00 20.00
RFWA245 Leo Carlsson/99 80.00 200.00
RFWA246 Connor Zary/99 40.00 100.00
RFWA247 Matthew Poitras/99 60.00 150.00
RFWA248 Zach Benson/99 20.00 50.00
RFWA249 Matt Savoie/99 25.00 60.00
RFWA250 Pavel Mintyukov/99 20.00 50.00
RFWA251 Connor Bedard/99 1200.00 3000.00
RFWA252 Matthew Coronato/399 15.00 40.00
RFWA253 Ridly Greig/99 20.00 50.00
RFWA254 Dustin Wolf/399 30.00 80.00
RFWA256 Will Cuylle/399 25.00 60.00
RFWA257 Marco Kasper/99 25.00 60.00
RFWA258 Sean Farrell/399 8.00 20.00
RFWA259 Tyson Foerster/99 30.00 80.00
RFWA260 Logan Cooley/99 80.00 200.00
RFWA261 Jakob Pelletier/399 10.00 25.00
RFWA262 Matthew Knies/99 80.00 200.00
RFWA263 Yaroslav Askarov/99 60.00 150.00
RFWA264 Simon Edvinsson/99 40.00 100.00
RFWA265 Devon Levi/99 60.00 150.00
RFWA267 Luke Evangelista/99 25.00 60.00
RFWA268 Adam Fantilli/99 80.00 200.00

2023-24 SP Authentic '03-04 Retro Sign of the Times

SOTT1AG Adam Graves SP 8.00 20.00
SOTT1AT Alex Tuch 10.00 25.00
SOTT1AV Andrei Vasilevskiy SP 15.00 40.00
SOTT1AX Arber Xhekaj 10.00 25.00
SOTT1BA Mikael Backlund 8.00 20.00
SOTT1BB Brent Burns SP 10.00 25.00
SOTT1BU Michael Bunting 10.00 25.00
SOTT1CC Chris Chelios SP 10.00 25.00
SOTT1CM Connor McDavid SP 200.00 500.00
SOTT1CN Cam Neely SP 10.00 25.00
SOTT1CP Colton Parayko 8.00 20.00
SOTT1CV Carter Verhaeghe 10.00 25.00
SOTT1DH Dany Heatley SP 8.00 20.00
SOTT1DT Dave Taylor 8.00 20.00
SOTT1FG Filip Gustavsson 10.00 25.00
SOTT1HA Dominik Hasek SP 15.00 40.00
SOTT1HC Connor Hellebuyck 20.00 50.00
SOTT1HE Tomas Hertl 10.00 25.00
SOTT1HU Jonathan Huberdeau 12.00 30.00
SOTT1IS Ilya Sorokin SP 30.00 80.00
SOTT1JA Jake Neighbours 10.00 25.00
SOTT1JP Joe Pavelski 12.00 30.00
SOTT1JS Juuse Saros 12.00 30.00
SOTT1JW Joseph Woll 12.00 30.00
SOTT1JY Jesse Ylonen 6.00 15.00
SOTT1JZ Jason Zucker 10.00 25.00
SOTT1KM K'Andre Miller 8.00 20.00
SOTT1KS Kiefer Sherwood 6.00 15.00
SOTT1LT Logan Thompson 12.00 30.00
SOTT1MA Mikey Anderson 8.00 20.00
SOTT1MB Matt Boldy 15.00 40.00
SOTT1MC Jared McCann 8.00 20.00
SOTT1MF Mario Ferraro 6.00 15.00
SOTT1ML Mario Lemieux SP 125.00 300.00
SOTT1MR Mikko Rantanen 25.00 60.00
SOTT1ND Noah Dobson 12.00 30.00
SOTT1NH Nico Hischier 15.00 40.00
SOTT1NP Nick Perbix 6.00 15.00
SOTT1PB Patrice Bergeron SP 40.00 100.00
SOTT1PK Peyton Krebs 8.00 20.00
SOTT1RB Ray Bourque SP 40.00 100.00
SOTT1RC Ross Colton 8.00 20.00
SOTT1RO Marco Rossi 12.00 30.00
SOTT1RT Robert Thomas 10.00 25.00
SOTT1SG Samuel Girard 6.00 15.00
SOTT1SW Jeremy Swayman 15.00 40.00
SOTT1TE Teuvo Teravainen SP 10.00 25.00
SOTT1TH Tyce Thompson 6.00 15.00
SOTT1TJ Tristan Jarry SP 10.00 25.00
SOTT1TK Torey Krug 8.00 20.00
SOTT1TT Tage Thompson 12.00 30.00
SOTT1WE William Eklund 12.00 30.00
SOTT1WG Wayne Gretzky SP 400.00 1000.00

2023-24 SP Authentic '13-14 Retro Future Watch Autographs

RFWAAD Arnaud Durandeau/699 10.00 25.00
RFWAAF Adam Fantilli/199 80.00 200.00
RFWAAG Adam Ginning/699 10.00 25.00
RFWAAH Akito Hirose/699 8.00 20.00
RFWAAL Alex Laferriere/699 15.00 40.00
RFWAAM Aidan McDonough/699 8.00 20.00
RFWABM Bobby McMann/699 15.00 40.00
RFWABS Billy Sweezey/699 10.00 25.00
RFWACA Leo Carlsson/199 80.00 200.00
RFWACB Connor Bedard/199 1500.00 4000.00
RFWACG Cole Guttman/699 10.00 25.00
RFWACM Cole McWard/699 10.00 25.00
RFWACZ Connor Zary/699 20.00 50.00
RFWADL Devon Levi/199 50.00 125.00
RFWADU William Dufour/699 8.00 20.00
RFWADW Dustin Wolf/199 50.00 125.00
RFWAEA Egor Afanasyev/699 10.00 25.00
RFWAED Elliot Desnoyers/699 10.00 25.00
RFWAFM Fraser Minten/699 20.00 50.00
RFWAGR Jonathan Gruden/699 10.00 25.00
RFWAGU David Gust/699 10.00 25.00
RFWAHT Henry Thrun/699 10.00 25.00
RFWAHU Hugh McGing/699 10.00 25.00
RFWAIS Ilya Solovyov/699 10.00 25.00
RFWAJB John Beecher/699 20.00 50.00
RFWAJG Jet Greaves/699 15.00 40.00
RFWAJK Joona Koppanen/699 8.00 20.00
RFWAJL Jake Livingstone/699 10.00 25.00
RFWAJP Jakob Pelletier/699 12.00 30.00
RFWAJS Jaxson Stauber/699 10.00 25.00
RFWAKA Marco Kasper/199 25.00 60.00
RFWAKE Matthew Kessel/699 8.00 20.00
RFWAKK Kevin Korchinski/199 15.00 40.00
RFWAKL Tyler Kleven/699 10.00 25.00
RFWAKM Milos Kelemen/699 10.00 25.00
RFWALA Jackson LaCombe/699 10.00 25.00
RFWALC Logan Cooley/199 80.00 200.00
RFWALE Luke Evangelista/199 15.00 40.00
RFWALM Leevi Merilainen/699 10.00 25.00
RFWALP Luke Philp/699 10.00 25.00
RFWAMC Matthew Coronato/199 20.00 50.00
RFWAMI Michael Kesselring/699 10.00 25.00
RFWAMK Matthew Knies/199 100.00 250.00
RFWAMM Matt Murray/699 10.00 25.00
RFWAMP Matthew Poitras/199 25.00 60.00
RFWAMS Matt Savoie/199 20.00 50.00
RFWANN Nikita Nesterenko/699 10.00 25.00
RFWANS Nick Swaney/699 10.00 25.00
RFWAOE Olle Eriksson Ek/699 10.00 25.00
RFWAPA Jiri Patera/699 15.00 40.00
RFWAPM Pavel Mintyukov/199 15.00 40.00
RFWARA Raphael Lavoie/699 10.00 25.00
RFWARG Ridly Greig/199 15.00 40.00
RFWASA Mackie Samoskevich/699 15.00 40.00
RFWASB Samuel Bolduc/699 10.00 25.00
RFWASE Simon Edvinsson/199 30.00 80.00
RFWASF Sean Farrell/699 10.00 25.00
RFWASK Samuel Knazko/699 10.00 25.00
RFWASS Stanislav Svozil/699 8.00 20.00
RFWATF Tyson Foerster/199 20.00 50.00
RFWATK Tye Kartye/699 15.00 40.00
RFWATL Tristan Luneau/699 10.00 25.00
RFWATR Tristen Robins/699 10.00 25.00
RFWAVD Vincent Desharnais/699 12.00 30.00
RFWAWC Will Cuylle/699 15.00 40.00
RFWAWD Walker Duehr/699 8.00 20.00
RFWAWK Wyatt Kaiser/699 10.00 25.00
RFWAYA Yaroslav Askarov/199 60.00 150.00
RFWAZB Zach Benson/199 15.00 40.00

2023-24 SP Authentic '13-14 Retro Future Watch Patch Autographs

101 Luke Hughes/25 200.00 500.00
102 Ridly Greig/50 50.00 125.00
103 Devon Levi/50 80.00 200.00
104 Will Cuylle/100 50.00 125.00
105 Marco Kasper/50 80.00 200.00
107 Matthew Knies/50 250.00 600.00
108 Matthew Coronato/100 50.00 125.00
109 Brock Faber/100 80.00 200.00
110 Connor Bedard/25 2500.00 6000.00
111 Dustin Wolf/100 125.00 300.00
112 Sean Farrell/100 30.00 80.00
114 Jakob Pelletier/100 40.00 100.00
115 Tyson Foerster/50 60.00 150.00
116 Yaroslav Askarov/100 80.00 200.00
117 Luke Evangelista/100 50.00 125.00
127 Tye Kartye/100 50.00 125.00
137 Wyatt Kaiser/100 30.00 80.00
138 Leevi Merilainen/100 30.00 80.00
147 Nikita Nesterenko/100 30.00 80.00
151 Simon Edvinsson/50 60.00 150.00
190 William Dufour/100 25.00 60.00

2023-24 SP Authentic Acetate Retro Future Watch

159 Troy Terry '18-19 8.00 20.00
178 Max Pacioretty '08-09 10.00 25.00
187 Andrei Svechnikov '18-19 25.00 60.00
188 Robert Thomas '18-19 10.00 25.00
189 Elias Pettersson '18-19 15.00 40.00
200 Brady Tkachuk '18-19 15.00 40.00
208 Jordan Kyrou '18-19 10.00 25.00
218 Drake Batherson '18-19 10.00 25.00
221 Jordan Binnington '14-15 15.00 40.00
224 Josh Bailey '08-09 8.00 20.00
230 Rasmus Dahlin '18-19 12.00 30.00
231 Alex Pietrangelo '08-09 8.00 20.00
237 Claude Giroux '08-09 10.00 25.00
244 Drew Doughty '08-09 10.00 25.00
247 Steven Stamkos '08-09 20.00 50.00
276 Vladimir Tarasenko '13-14 12.00 30.00
277 Leon Draisaitl '14-15 60.00 150.00
279 Jonathan Huberdeau '13-14 12.00 30.00
282 David Pastrnak '14-15 25.00 60.00
288 Evgeny Kuznetsov '14-15 12.00 30.00
296 John Gibson '13-14 10.00 25.00
308 Tomas Hertl '13-14 10.00 25.00
310 Andrei Vasilevskiy '14-15 15.00 40.00
312 Nathan MacKinnon '13-14 40.00 100.00
316 Aleksander Barkov '13-14 15.00 40.00

2023-24 SP Authentic Chirography

CAF Adam Fantilli SP 40.00 100.00
CAL Alexis Lafreniere SP 12.00 30.00
CAR Artturi Lehkonen 6.00 15.00
CBM Ben Meyers 5.00 12.00
CCA Cam Atkinson 8.00 20.00
CCC Connor Clifton 5.00 12.00
CCP Cole Perfetti 8.00 20.00
CCS Chandler Stephenson 6.00 15.00
CCV Carter Verhaeghe 8.00 20.00
CFV Frank Vatrano 6.00 15.00
CJE Jordan Eberle 8.00 20.00
CJG Jake Guentzel SP 12.00 30.00
CJP JJ Peterka 8.00 20.00
CKJ Kent Johnson SP 8.00 20.00
CKN Matthew Knies SP 60.00 150.00
CLC Logan Cooley SP 40.00 100.00
CLE Anders Lee 6.00 15.00
CLR Lukas Reichel 8.00 20.00
CLT Logan Thompson 10.00 25.00
CMC Matthew Coronato 12.00 30.00
CMK Marco Kasper SP 20.00 50.00
CMN Martin Necas SP 12.00 30.00
CMR Marco Rossi SP 10.00 25.00
CMT Matthew Tkachuk SP 15.00 40.00
CNC Noah Cates 5.00 12.00
CRT Robert Thomas SP 8.00 20.00
CSA Juuse Saros SP 10.00 25.00
CSE Simon Edvinsson SP 15.00 40.00
CSK Spencer Knight 8.00 20.00
CSP Shane Pinto 6.00 15.00
CTH Tomas Hertl 8.00 20.00
CTR Taylor Raddysh 6.00 15.00
CWE William Eklund 10.00 25.00

2023-24 SP Authentic Collaborations

*BLUE: .6X TO 1.5X BASIC
*GREEN: 1X TO 2.5X BASIC
C1 C.McDavid/L.Draisaitl 2.50 6.00
C2 D.Pastrnak/B.Marchand 1.25 3.00
C3 K.Korchinski/C.Bedard 3.00 8.00
C4 B.Coleman/N.Kadri .60 1.50
C5 A.Matthews/J.Tavares 2.00 5.00
C6 A.Kopitar/Q.Byfield .75 2.00
C7 N.MacKinnon/M.Rantanen 2.00 5.00
C8 D.Larkin/A.DeBrincat .60 1.50
C9 C.Keller/L.Cooley 1.50 4.00
C10 C.Caufield/J.Slafkovsky 1.00 2.50
C11 E.Pettersson/Q.Hughes 1.25 3.00
C12 P.Laine/A.Fantilli 1.50 4.00
C13 M.Beniers/J.McCann .60 1.50
C14 M.Heiskanen/J.Robertson .75 2.00
C15 J.Farabee/M.Frost .50 1.25
C16 V.Hedman/M.Sergachev .60 1.50
C17 M.Barzal/B.Horvat .60 1.50
C18 D.Cozens/Z.Benson .75 2.00
C19 T.Zegras/L.Carlsson 1.50 4.00
C20 E.Kuznetsov/T.Oshie .60 1.50
C21 E.Karlsson/K.Letang .60 1.50
C22 A.Panarin/C.Kreider 1.00 2.50
C23 T.Stutzle/C.Giroux .60 1.50
C24 J.Hughes/L.Hughes 1.50 4.00
C25 T.Hertl/W.Eklund .60 1.50

2023-24 SP Authentic Curated Signatures

SPCAL Alexis Lafreniere/25 30.00 80.00
SPCAN Mikey Anderson/299 6.00 15.00
SPCAR Aatu Raty/299 5.00 12.00
SPCAS Andrei Svechnikov/99 10.00 25.00
SPCAT Alex Tuch/99 8.00 20.00
SPCAV Andrei Vasilevskiy/25 20.00 50.00
SPCBC Brandt Clarke/99 8.00 20.00
SPCBE Matty Beniers/25 15.00 40.00
SPCBJ Boone Jenner/299 8.00 20.00
SPCBM Brad Marchand/25 20.00 50.00
SPCCD Connor Dewar/299 5.00 12.00
SPCCM Casey Mittelstadt/299 8.00 20.00
SPCCP Colton Parayko/99 6.00 15.00
SPCDG Dylan Guenther/99 10.00 25.00
SPCDM Dawson Mercer/99 10.00 25.00
SPCDP David Perron/299 6.00 15.00
SPCDT Devon Toews/299 6.00 15.00
SPCEK Joel Eriksson Ek/299 6.00 15.00
SPCFG Filip Gustavsson/99 8.00 20.00
SPCFR Filip Roos/299 5.00 12.00
SPCFV Frank Vatrano/299 6.00 15.00
SPCGV Gabe Vilardi/99 8.00 20.00
SPCIS Ilya Samsonov/99 8.00 20.00
SPCJA Jack McBain/299 5.00 12.00
SPCJE Jordan Eberle/99 8.00 20.00
SPCJH Jonathan Huberdeau/99 10.00 25.00
SPCJK Jordan Kyrou/25 15.00 40.00
SPCJM Jared McCann/99 6.00 15.00
SPCJN Jake Neighbours/99 8.00 20.00
SPCJP JJ Peterka/99 8.00 20.00
SPCJS Jake Sanderson/99 10.00 25.00
SPCJY Jesse Ylonen/299 5.00 12.00
SPCKH Kevin Hayes/299 6.00 15.00
SPCKJ Kent Johnson/99 8.00 20.00
SPCKM K'Andre Miller/99 6.00 15.00
SPCKS Kiefer Sherwood/299 5.00 12.00
SPCLR Lukas Reichel/99 8.00 20.00
SPCLT Logan Thompson/299 10.00 25.00
SPCMA Jacob Markstrom/99 8.00 20.00
SPCMB Mikael Backlund/299 6.00 15.00
SPCME Ben Meyers/299 5.00 12.00
SPCMF Mario Ferraro/299 5.00 12.00
SPCMJ Jacob Middleton/299 5.00 12.00
SPCMM Mason Marchment/299 6.00 15.00
SPCMR Marco Rossi/299 10.00 25.00
SPCMT Matthew Tkachuk/25 15.00 40.00
SPCND Noah Dobson/299 10.00 25.00
SPCNL Nils Lundkvist/299 5.00 12.00
SPCPA Juuso Parssinen/299 5.00 12.00
SPCPC Pheonix Copley/299 5.00 12.00
SPCPE Cole Perfetti/99 8.00 20.00
SPCPG Philipp Grubauer/299 8.00 20.00
SPCPJ Jeff Petry/299 8.00 20.00
SPCPK Peyton Krebs/299 6.00 15.00
SPCRC Ross Colton/299 6.00 15.00
SPCRH Roope Hintz/99 10.00 25.00
SPCRR Ryan Reaves/299 6.00 15.00
SPCSK Spencer Knight/299 8.00 20.00
SPCSO Ilya Sorokin/25 12.00 30.00
SPCSP Jared Spurgeon/299 8.00 20.00
SPCSR Sam Reinhart/99 15.00 40.00
SPCSW Jeremy Swayman/99 12.00 30.00
SPCTH Tyce Thompson/299 5.00 12.00
SPCTJ Tristan Jarry/99 8.00 20.00
SPCTR Taylor Raddysh/299 6.00 15.00
SPCTT Tage Thompson/99 10.00 25.00
SPCWJ Wyatt Johnston/99 15.00 40.00

2023-24 SP Authentic Evolve

*BLUE: .6X TO 1.5X BASIC
*GREEN: 1X TO 2.5X BASIC
E1 Connor McDavid 3.00 8.00
E2 Alex Tuch .60 1.50
E3 Tyler Bertuzzi .50 1.25
E4 Steven Stamkos 1.25 3.00
E5 Kevin Fiala .50 1.25
E6 Patrice Bergeron .75 2.00
E7 Vladimir Tarasenko .75 2.00
E8 Jared McCann .50 1.25
E9 Mattias Ekholm .50 1.25
E10 Tage Thompson .75 2.00
E11 Mats Zuccarello .60 1.50
E12 Tyler Toffoli .60 1.50
E13 Joe Pavelski .75 2.00
E14 Aleksander Barkov 1.00 2.50
E15 Sam Reinhart 1.25 3.00
E16 Matt Duchene .60 1.50
E17 J.T. Miller .75 2.00
E18 Timo Meier .60 1.50
E19 Bo Horvat .75 2.00
E20 Ryan O'Reilly .60 1.50
E21 Jack Eichel 1.00 2.50
E22 Carter Verhaeghe .60 1.50
E23 Jonathan Marchessault .75 2.00
E24 Erik Karlsson .75 2.00
E25 Patrick Kane 1.25 3.00

2023-24 SP Authentic Evolve Autographs

EAT Alex Tuch 10.00 25.00
ECM Connor McDavid SP 200.00 500.00
ECV Carter Verhaeghe 10.00 25.00
EJM Jared McCann 8.00 20.00
EJP Joe Pavelski 12.00 30.00
EKF Kevin Fiala 8.00 20.00
EMA Jonathan Marchessault 12.00 30.00
EPB Patrice Bergeron SP 80.00 200.00
ERO Ryan O'Reilly 10.00 25.00
ESR Sam Reinhart 20.00 50.00
ETM Timo Meier 10.00 25.00
ETT Tage Thompson SP 25.00 60.00

2023-24 SP Authentic Freshman Focus

*BLUE: .6X TO 1.5X BASIC
*GREEN: 1X TO 2.5X BASIC
FF1 Connor Bedard 5.00 12.00
FF2 Leo Carlsson 2.50 6.00
FF3 Fraser Minten 1.50 4.00
FF4 Simon Edvinsson 1.50 4.00
FF5 Devon Levi 2.00 5.00
FF6 Matthew Knies 3.00 8.00
FF7 Adam Fantilli 2.50 6.00
FF8 Hugh McGing .75 2.00
FF9 Kevin Korchinski 1.25 3.00
FF10 Luke Evangelista 1.25 3.00
FF11 Sean Farrell .75 2.00
FF12 Luke Hughes 2.50 6.00
FF13 Matt Murray .75 2.00
FF14 Tyson Foerster 1.50 4.00
FF15 Cole Guttman .75 2.00
FF16 Zach Benson 1.25 3.00
FF17 Aidan McDonough .60 1.50
FF18 Ridly Greig 1.25 3.00
FF19 Wyatt Kaiser .75 2.00
FF20 Michael Kesselring .75 2.00
FF21 Adam Ginning .75 2.00
FF22 Tyler Kleven .75 2.00
FF23 Yaroslav Askarov 2.00 5.00
FF24 Matthew Coronato 1.25 3.00
FF25 William Dufour .60 1.50
FF26 Brock Faber 2.00 5.00
FF27 Joona Koppanen .60 1.50
FF28 Walker Duehr .60 1.50
FF29 Nikita Nesterenko .75 2.00
FF30 Logan Cooley 2.50 6.00
FF31 Marco Kasper 2.00 5.00
FF32 Leevi Merilainen .75 2.00
FF33 Jackson LaCombe .75 2.00
FF34 Vincent Desharnais 1.00 2.50
FF35 Akito Hirose .60 1.50
FF36 Pavel Mintyukov 1.25 3.00
FF37 Lukas Rousek .60 1.50
FF38 Samuel Bolduc .75 2.00
FF39 Dustin Wolf 2.50 6.00
FF40 Matthew Poitras 1.50 4.00
FF41 Vincent Iorio .75 2.00
FF42 Stanislav Svozil .60 1.50
FF43 Jiri Patera 1.25 3.00
FF44 John Beecher 1.50 4.00
FF45 Owen Beck 1.25 3.00
FF46 Danil Gushchin .75 2.00
FF47 Will Cuylle 1.25 3.00
FF48 Jonathan Gruden .75 2.00
FF49 Tye Kartye 1.25 3.00
FF50 Jakob Pelletier 1.00 2.50

2023-24 SP Authentic Future Icon

FI1 Connor Bedard 50.00 125.00
FI2 Matthew Knies 10.00 25.00
FI3 Devon Levi 6.00 15.00
FI4 Ridly Greig 4.00 10.00
FI5 Tyson Foerster 5.00 12.00
FI6 Tye Kartye 4.00 10.00
FI7 Brock Faber 6.00 15.00
FI8 Danil Gushchin 2.50 6.00
FI9 Dustin Wolf 8.00 20.00
FI10 Adam Fantilli 8.00 20.00
FI11 Stanislav Svozil 2.00 5.00
FI12 Yaroslav Askarov 6.00 15.00
FI13 Leo Carlsson 8.00 20.00
FI14 Sean Farrell 2.50 6.00
FI15 Luke Hughes 8.00 20.00
FI16 Zach Benson 4.00 10.00
FI17 Jackson LaCombe 2.50 6.00
FI18 Jiri Patera 4.00 10.00
FI19 Connor Zary 5.00 12.00
FI20 Logan Cooley 8.00 20.00
FI21 Aidan McDonough 2.00 5.00
FI22 Jakob Pelletier 3.00 8.00
FI23 Vincent Desharnais 3.00 8.00
FI24 Will Cuylle 4.00 10.00
FI25 Marco Kasper 6.00 15.00
FI26 Vincent Iorio 2.50 6.00
FI27 William Dufour 2.00 5.00
FI28 Matthew Coronato 4.00 10.00
FI29 Owen Beck 4.00 10.00
FI30 Joona Koppanen 2.00 5.00
FI31 Luke Evangelista 4.00 10.00
FI32 Simon Edvinsson 5.00 12.00

2023-24 SP Authentic Future Watch Acetate

101 Luke Hughes 150.00 400.00
102 Ridly Greig 25.00 60.00
103 Devon Levi 60.00 150.00
104 Will Cuylle 25.00 60.00
105 Marco Kasper 40.00 100.00
106 Adam Fantilli 60.00 150.00
107 Matthew Knies 125.00 300.00
108 Matthew Coronato 25.00 60.00
109 Brock Faber 150.00 400.00
110 Connor Bedard 1200.00 3000.00
111 Dustin Wolf 60.00 150.00
112 Sean Farrell 15.00 40.00
113 Owen Beck 25.00 60.00
114 Jakob Pelletier 20.00 50.00
115 Tyson Foerster 30.00 80.00
116 Yaroslav Askarov 40.00 100.00
117 Luke Evangelista 60.00 150.00
121 Walker Duehr 12.00 30.00
124 Lukas Rousek 12.00 30.00
125 Matt Murray 15.00 40.00
126 Samuel Bolduc 15.00 40.00
127 Tye Kartye 25.00 60.00
131 Akito Hirose 12.00 30.00
132 Vincent Iorio 15.00 40.00
133 Vincent Desharnais 20.00 50.00
135 Danil Gushchin 15.00 40.00
138 Leevi Merilainen 15.00 40.00
145 Jiri Patera 25.00 60.00
151 Simon Edvinsson 40.00 100.00
152 John Beecher 30.00 80.00
153 Kevin Korchinski 25.00 60.00
154 Mackie Samoskevich 25.00 60.00
156 Connor Zary 30.00 80.00
157 Michael Kesselring 15.00 40.00
158 Zach Benson 40.00 100.00
159 Matt Savoie 30.00 80.00
168 Fraser Minten 80.00 200.00
169 Mason Lohrei 25.00 60.00
170 Jackson LaCombe 15.00 40.00
171 Raphael Lavoie 15.00 40.00
176 Leo Carlsson 80.00 200.00
177 Matthew Poitras 60.00 150.00
178 Ryan Johnson 20.00 50.00
180 Stanislav Svozil 12.00 30.00
181 Alex Laferriere 25.00 60.00
183 Pavel Mintyukov 25.00 60.00
188 Ty Emberson 15.00 40.00
189 Justin Sourdif 15.00 40.00
190 William Dufour 12.00 30.00

2023-24 SP Authentic Holofoil

HF1 Connor McDavid 15.00 40.00
HF2 Nikita Kucherov 6.00 15.00
HF3 Kirill Kaprizov 10.00 25.00
HF4 Moritz Seider 4.00 10.00
HF5 Connor Hellebuyck 6.00 15.00
HF6 John Tavares 5.00 12.00
HF7 Kirby Dach 3.00 8.00
HF8 David Pastrnak 8.00 20.00
HF9 Alex Ovechkin 12.00 30.00
HF10 Matty Beniers 4.00 10.00
HF11 Nick Schmaltz 2.50 6.00
HF12 Leon Draisaitl 10.00 25.00
HF13 Nathan MacKinnon 12.00 30.00
HF14 Ilya Sorokin 5.00 12.00
HF15 Mika Zibanejad 4.00 10.00
HF16 Sebastian Aho 5.00 12.00
HF17 Jack Eichel 5.00 12.00
HF18 Cole Caufield 6.00 15.00
HF19 Matthew Tkachuk 6.00 15.00
HF20 Jordan Kyrou 3.00 8.00
HF21 Cale Makar 8.00 20.00
HF22 Pierre-Luc Dubois 2.50 6.00
HF23 Trevor Zegras 3.00 8.00
HF24 Quinn Hughes 12.00 30.00
HF25 Auston Matthews 12.00 30.00
HF26 Jason Robertson 5.00 12.00
HF27 Rasmus Dahlin 4.00 10.00
HF28 Tim Stutzle 4.00 10.00
HF29 Timo Meier 3.00 8.00
HF30 Sidney Crosby 12.00 30.00
HF31 Connor Bedard 125.00 300.00
HF32 Brock Faber 8.00 20.00
HF33 Zach Benson 5.00 12.00
HF34 Kevin Korchinski 5.00 12.00
HF35 Simon Edvinsson 6.00 15.00
HF36 Matthew Knies 12.00 30.00
HF37 Owen Beck 5.00 12.00
HF38 Devon Levi 8.00 20.00
HF39 Adam Fantilli 10.00 25.00
HF40 Jakob Pelletier 4.00 10.00
HF41 Tyson Foerster 6.00 15.00
HF42 Logan Cooley 10.00 25.00
HF43 Matthew Coronato 5.00 12.00
HF44 Luke Hughes 10.00 25.00
HF45 Yaroslav Askarov 8.00 20.00
HF46 Pavel Mintyukov 5.00 12.00
HF47 Luke Evangelista 5.00 12.00
HF48 Dustin Wolf 10.00 25.00
HF49 Matthew Poitras 6.00 15.00
HF50 Ridly Greig 5.00 12.00

2023-24 SP Authentic Limited Autographs

4 Auston Matthews SP 125.00 300.00
6 Marc-Andre Fleury SP 15.00 40.00
10 Tim Stutzle SP 10.00 25.00
11 Brad Marchand SP 15.00 40.00
12 Andrei Vasilevskiy SP 12.00 30.00
14 Matty Beniers SP 10.00 25.00
17 Alexis Lafreniere SP 12.00 30.00
19 Jonathan Huberdeau 10.00 25.00
21 Andrei Svechnikov 10.00 25.00
22 Juraj Slafkovsky SP 15.00 40.00
23 Brent Burns SP 8.00 20.00
24 Mikko Rantanen SP 20.00 50.00
25 Joe Pavelski 10.00 25.00
27 Matthew Tkachuk 15.00 40.00
29 Nico Hischier 12.00 30.00
30 Tage Thompson 10.00 25.00
31 Brady Tkachuk SP 12.00 30.00
32 Noah Cates 5.00 12.00
33 Jake Guentzel SP 12.00 30.00
35 Jeremy Swayman SP 12.00 30.00
36 Jake Oettinger SP 12.00 30.00
37 Ilya Sorokin SP 12.00 30.00
38 Brock Boeser SP 10.00 25.00
41 Shane Pinto 6.00 15.00
42 Miro Heiskanen 10.00 25.00
44 Mark Stone 10.00 25.00
45 Jonathan Marchessault 10.00 25.00
47 Kyle Connor 12.00 30.00
48 Troy Terry 6.00 15.00
49 Jacob Markstrom 8.00 20.00
50 Teuvo Teravainen 8.00 20.00
53 Kevin Fiala 6.00 15.00
57 Brock Nelson 8.00 20.00
59 Robert Thomas 8.00 20.00
60 Jordan Kyrou 8.00 20.00
61 Chandler Stephenson 6.00 15.00
63 Cole Perfetti 8.00 20.00
64 Matt Boldy SP 12.00 30.00
66 Joel Eriksson Ek 6.00 15.00
67 Torey Krug 6.00 15.00
68 Anton Lundell SP 8.00 20.00
69 Sam Reinhart 15.00 40.00
70 Juuse Saros SP 10.00 25.00
72 Jordan Eberle 8.00 20.00
73 Roope Hintz 10.00 25.00
74 Kent Johnson 8.00 20.00
77 David Perron 6.00 15.00
80 Alex Tuch 8.00 20.00
83 K'Andre Miller 6.00 15.00
85 Tristan Jarry 8.00 20.00

Card	Low	High
89 Philipp Grubauer	8.00	20.00
92 Travis Konecny SP	8.00	20.00
95 Mikey Anderson	6.00	15.00
97 Kirill Kaprizov SP	25.00	60.00
98 Elias Pettersson SP	12.00	30.00

2023-24 SP Authentic Limited Patch Autographs

Card	Low	High
6 Marc-Andre Fleury/25	150.00	400.00
7 Cale Makar/25	200.00	500.00
11 Brad Marchand/25	40.00	100.00
12 Andrei Vasilevskiy/25	30.00	80.00
14 Matty Beniers/25	25.00	60.00
17 Alexis Lafreniere/50	50.00	125.00
19 Jonathan Huberdeau/50	25.00	60.00
21 Andrei Svechnikov/50	25.00	60.00
22 Juraj Slafkovsky/50	80.00	200.00
23 Brent Burns/50	20.00	50.00
24 Mikko Rantanen/50	50.00	125.00
25 Joe Pavelski/50	25.00	60.00
27 Matthew Tkachuk/50	40.00	100.00
28 Nick Suzuki/50	60.00	150.00
29 Nico Hischier/50	30.00	80.00
31 Brady Tkachuk/50	30.00	80.00
32 Noah Cates/50	12.00	30.00
33 Jake Guentzel/50	30.00	80.00
35 Jeremy Swayman/50	30.00	80.00
36 Jake Oettinger/50	30.00	80.00
37 Ilya Sorokin/50	60.00	150.00
38 Brock Boeser/50	25.00	60.00
41 Shane Pinto/50	15.00	40.00
42 Miro Heiskanen/50	25.00	60.00
44 Mark Stone/50	25.00	60.00
45 Jonathan Marchessault/50	25.00	60.00
47 Kyle Connor/100	30.00	80.00
48 Troy Terry/100	15.00	40.00
49 Jacob Markstrom/100	20.00	50.00
50 Teuvo Teravainen/100	20.00	50.00
53 Kevin Fiala/100	15.00	40.00
56 Timo Meier/100	20.00	50.00
57 Brock Nelson/100	20.00	50.00
59 Robert Thomas/100	20.00	50.00
60 Jordan Kyrou/100	20.00	50.00
61 Chandler Stephenson/100	15.00	40.00
63 Cole Perfetti/100	20.00	50.00
67 Torey Krug/100	15.00	40.00
68 Anton Lundell/100	20.00	50.00
69 Sam Reinhart/100	40.00	100.00
70 Juuse Saros/100	25.00	60.00
72 Jordan Eberle/100	20.00	50.00
73 Roope Hintz/100	25.00	60.00
74 Kent Johnson/100	20.00	50.00
101 Luke Hughes FW/100	300.00	800.00
102 Ridly Greig FW/100	50.00	125.00
103 Devon Levi FW/100	150.00	400.00
104 Will Cuylle FW/100	80.00	200.00
105 Marco Kasper FW/100	100.00	250.00
106 Adam Fantilli FW/100	200.00	500.00
107 Matthew Knies FW/100	400.00	1000.00
108 Matthew Coronato FW/100	60.00	150.00
109 Brock Faber FW/100	300.00	800.00
110 Connor Bedard FW/100	3000.00	8000.00
111 Dustin Wolf FW/100	200.00	500.00
112 Sean Farrell FW/100	20.00	50.00
114 Jakob Pelletier FW/100	25.00	60.00
115 Tyson Foerster FW/100	100.00	250.00
116 Yaroslav Askarov FW/100	250.00	600.00
117 Luke Evangelista FW/100	100.00	250.00
118 Hugh McGing FW/100	20.00	50.00
119 Milos Kelemen FW/100	20.00	50.00
120 Olle Eriksson Ek FW/100	20.00	50.00
121 Walker Duehr FW/100	15.00	40.00
122 Egor Afanasyev FW/100	20.00	50.00
125 Matt Murray FW/100	20.00	50.00
126 Samuel Bolduc FW/100	20.00	50.00
127 Tye Kartye FW/100	80.00	200.00
128 Billy Sweezey FW/100	20.00	50.00
129 Dobby McMann FW/100	100.00	250.00
130 Matthew Kessel FW/100	15.00	40.00
131 Akito Hirose FW/100	15.00	40.00
132 Vincent Iorio FW/100	20.00	50.00
133 Vincent Desharnais FW/100	30.00	80.00
134 Jaxson Stauber FW/100	20.00	50.00
136 Nick Swaney FW/100	20.00	50.00
137 Wyatt Kaiser FW/100	20.00	50.00
138 Leevi Merilainen FW/100	20.00	50.00
139 Tristen Robins FW/100	20.00	50.00
140 Jonathan Gruden FW/100	20.00	50.00
141 Joona Koppanen FW/100	15.00	40.00
143 Elliot Desnoyers FW/100	20.00	50.00
144 Aidan McDonough FW/100	15.00	40.00
145 Jiri Patera FW/100	30.00	80.00
146 Adam Ginning FW/100	20.00	50.00
147 Nikita Nesterenko FW/100	20.00	50.00
148 Arnaud Durandeau FW/100	20.00	50.00
149 Jake Livingstone FW/100	20.00	50.00
150 Cole Guttman FW/100	20.00	50.00
151 Simon Edvinsson FW/100	125.00	300.00
152 John Beecher FW/100	80.00	200.00
153 Kevin Korchinski FW/100	50.00	125.00
154 Mackie Samoskevich FW/100	30.00	80.00
155 Jet Greaves FW/100	30.00	80.00
156 Connor Zary FW/100	200.00	500.00
157 Michael Kesselring FW/100	20.00	50.00
158 Zach Benson FW/100	40.00	100.00
159 Matt Savoie FW/100	40.00	100.00
160 Henry Thrun FW/100	20.00	50.00
162 Samuel Knazko FW/100	20.00	50.00
165 Tyler Kleven FW/100	20.00	50.00
167 Cole McWard FW/100	20.00	50.00
168 Fraser Minten FW/100	100.00	250.00
171 Raphael Lavoie FW/100	20.00	50.00
176 Leo Carlsson FW/100	400.00	1000.00
177 Matthew Poitras FW/100	200.00	500.00
180 Stanislav Svozil FW/100	15.00	40.00
181 Alex Laferriere FW/100	150.00	400.00
183 Pavel Mintyukov FW/100	60.00	150.00
190 William Dufour FW/100	15.00	40.00

2023-24 SP Authentic Marks of Distinction

Card	Low	High
MDAT Alex Tuch	15.00	40.00
MDAV Andrei Vasilevskiy	25.00	60.00
MDBB Brock Boeser	20.00	50.00
MDCB Connor Bedard	800.00	2000.00
MDJE Jack Eichel	25.00	60.00
MDJO Jake Oettinger	25.00	60.00
MDKC Kyle Connor	25.00	60.00
MDLC Logan Cooley	60.00	150.00
MDMB Matty Beniers	20.00	50.00
MDMF Marc-Andre Fleury	50.00	125.00
MDMH Miro Heiskanen	20.00	50.00
MDMK Matthew Knies	300.00	800.00
MDMR Mikko Rantanen	40.00	100.00
MDMS Mark Stone	20.00	50.00
MDMT Matthew Tkachuk	30.00	80.00
MDRO Ryan O'Reilly	15.00	40.00
MDTF Tyson Foerster	30.00	80.00
MDTS Tim Stutzle	20.00	50.00
MDTT Tage Thompson	20.00	50.00

2023-24 SP Authentic Pageantry

*RED: .6X TO 1.5X BASIC

Card	Low	High
P1 Sidney Crosby	2.00	5.00
P2 Evan Bouchard	.60	1.50
P3 Andrei Svechnikov	.60	1.50
P4 Logan Thompson	.60	1.50
P5 Cale Makar	1.25	3.00
P6 Jonatan Berggren	.40	1.00
P7 Alexander Romanov	.40	1.00
P8 Evgenii Dadonov	.30	.75
P9 Kaiden Guhle	.50	1.25
P10 Philipp Grubauer	.50	1.25
P11 Adrian Kempe	.50	1.25
P12 Connor Dewar	.30	.75
P13 Nikolaj Ehlers	.50	1.25
P14 Zach Hyman	.75	2.00
P15 David Perron	.40	1.00
P16 John Carlson	.50	1.25
P17 Jared McCann	.40	1.00
P18 Mikko Rantanen	1.25	3.00
P19 Filip Roos	.30	.75
P20 Dawson Mercer	.60	1.50
P21 Filip Gustavsson	.50	1.25
P22 K'Andre Miller	.40	1.00
P23 Casey Mittelstadt	.50	1.25
P24 Bowen Byram	.60	1.50
P25 Colton Parayko	.40	1.00
P26 Brock Boeser	.60	1.50
P27 Mario Ferraro	.30	.75
P28 Tristan Jarry	.50	1.25
P29 Darnell Nurse	.40	1.00
P30 Mats Zuccarello	.50	1.25
P31 David Jiricek	.50	1.25
P32 Anton Lundell	.50	1.25
P33 Jacob Middleton	.30	.75
P34 Cole Sillinger	.40	1.00
P35 Nick Suzuki	1.00	2.50
P36 Brady Tkachuk	.75	2.00
P37 Dakota Joshua	.30	.75
P38 Chandler Stephenson	.40	1.00
P39 Mikey Anderson	.40	1.00
P40 J.T. Miller	.60	1.50
P41 Stuart Skinner	.60	1.50
P42 Grigori Denisenko	.30	.75
P43 Ryan Reaves	.40	1.00
P44 Jalen Chatfield	.30	.75
P45 Yanni Gourde	.40	1.00
P46 Mason Marchment	.40	1.00
P47 Connor Clifton	.30	.75
P48 Nick Perbix	.30	.75
P49 Peyton Krebs	.40	1.00
P50 Kyle Connor	.75	2.00
P51 Peter Forsberg	1.00	2.50
P52 Teemu Selanne	1.00	2.50
P53 Gerry Cheevers	.50	1.25
P54 Mike Modano	.75	2.00
P55 Andy Moog	.50	1.25
P56 Patrice Bergeron	.60	1.50
P57 Ryan Getzlaf	.50	1.25
P58 Marcel Dionne	.60	1.50
P59 Larry Robinson	.50	1.25
P60 Rogie Vachon	.50	1.25
P61 Connor Bedard	3.00	8.00
P62 Adam Fantilli	1.50	4.00
P63 Logan Cooley	1.50	4.00
P64 Matthew Knies	2.00	5.00
P65 Ridly Greig	.75	2.00
P66 Simon Edvinsson	1.00	2.50
P67 Pavel Mintyukov	.75	2.00
P68 Luke Hughes	1.50	4.00
P69 Tyson Foerster	1.00	2.50
P70 Yaroslav Askarov	1.25	3.00
P71 Devon Levi	1.25	3.00
P72 Will Cuylle	.75	2.00
P73 Akito Hirose	.40	1.00
P74 Danil Gushchin	.50	1.25
P75 Sean Farrell	.50	1.25
P76 Matthew Kessel	.40	1.00
P77 Dustin Wolf	1.50	4.00
P78 Leo Carlsson	1.50	4.00
P79 Tye Kartye	.75	2.00
P80 Lukas Rousek	.40	1.00
P81 Matthew Poitras	1.00	2.50
P82 Arnaud Durandeau	.50	1.25
P83 Matthew Coronato	.75	2.00
P84 William Dufour	.40	1.00
P85 Vincent Desharnais	.60	1.50
P86 Zach Benson	.75	2.00
P87 Owen Beck	.75	2.00
P88 Jakob Pelletier	.60	1.50
P89 Brock Faber	1.25	3.00
P90 Marco Kasper	1.25	3.00

2023-24 SP Authentic Pageantry Autographs

Card	Low	High
P3 Andrei Svechnikov	10.00	25.00
P4 Logan Thompson	10.00	25.00
P6 Jonatan Berggren	6.00	15.00
P9 Kaiden Guhle	8.00	20.00
P10 Philipp Grubauer	8.00	20.00
P12 Connor Dewar	5.00	12.00
P15 David Perron	6.00	15.00
P16 John Carlson	8.00	20.00
P17 Jared McCann	6.00	15.00
P18 Mikko Rantanen SP	20.00	50.00
P19 Filip Roos	5.00	12.00
P20 Dawson Mercer	10.00	25.00
P21 Filip Gustavsson	8.00	20.00
P22 K'Andre Miller	6.00	15.00
P23 Casey Mittelstadt	8.00	20.00
P25 Colton Parayko	6.00	15.00
P26 Brock Boeser SP	10.00	25.00
P27 Mario Ferraro	5.00	12.00
P28 Tristan Jarry	8.00	20.00
P33 Jacob Middleton	5.00	12.00
P34 Cole Sillinger	6.00	15.00
P36 Brady Tkachuk SP	12.00	30.00
P38 Chandler Stephenson	6.00	15.00
P39 Mikey Anderson	6.00	15.00
P43 Ryan Reaves	6.00	15.00
P46 Mason Marchment	6.00	15.00
P47 Connor Clifton	5.00	12.00
P48 Nick Perbix	5.00	12.00
P49 Peyton Krebs	6.00	15.00
P50 Kyle Connor SP	12.00	30.00
P53 Gerry Cheevers SP	8.00	20.00
P54 Mike Modano SP	12.00	30.00
P55 Andy Moog SP	8.00	20.00
P56 Patrice Bergeron SP	10.00	25.00
P57 Ryan Getzlaf SP	8.00	20.00
P58 Marcel Dionne SP	10.00	25.00
P59 Larry Robinson SP	8.00	20.00
P60 Rogie Vachon SP	8.00	20.00
P62 Adam Fantilli SP	30.00	80.00
P63 Logan Cooley SP	30.00	80.00
P64 Matthew Knies	40.00	100.00
P65 Ridly Greig	12.00	30.00
P66 Simon Edvinsson SP	15.00	40.00
P67 Pavel Mintyukov SP	12.00	30.00
P69 Tyson Foerster	15.00	40.00
P70 Yaroslav Askarov SP	20.00	50.00
P71 Devon Levi SP	20.00	50.00
P72 Will Cuylle	12.00	30.00
P73 Akito Hirose	6.00	15.00
P75 Sean Farrell SP	8.00	20.00
P76 Matthew Kessel	6.00	15.00
P77 Dustin Wolf SP	25.00	60.00
P78 Leo Carlsson SP	40.00	100.00
P79 Tye Kartye	12.00	30.00
P81 Matthew Poitras SP	15.00	40.00
P82 Arnaud Durandeau	8.00	20.00
P83 Matthew Coronato	12.00	30.00
P84 William Dufour	6.00	15.00
P85 Vincent Desharnais	10.00	25.00
P86 Zach Benson SP	12.00	30.00
P88 Jakob Pelletier	10.00	25.00
P90 Marco Kasper SP	20.00	50.00

2023-24 SP Authentic Sign of the Times

Card	Low	High
SOTTAL Anders Lee	6.00	15.00
SOTTAN Alex Newhook	6.00	15.00
SOTTAX Arber Xhekaj	8.00	20.00
SOTTBA Mikael Backlund	6.00	15.00
SOTTBM Ben Meyers	5.00	12.00
SOTTCA Cam Atkinson	8.00	20.00
SOTTCC Connor Clifton	5.00	12.00
SOTTCD Connor Dewar	5.00	12.00
SOTTCP Cal Petersen	5.00	12.00
SOTTCS Chandler Stephenson	6.00	15.00
SOTTDG Dylan Guenther	10.00	25.00
SOTTDP David Perron	6.00	15.00
SOTTDT Devon Toews	6.00	15.00
SOTTEB Jordan Eberle	8.00	20.00
SOTTFG Filip Gustavsson	8.00	20.00
SOTTFR Filip Roos	5.00	12.00
SOTTGV Gabe Vilardi	8.00	20.00
SOTTJE Joel Eriksson Ek	6.00	15.00
SOTTJH Jonathan Huberdeau	10.00	25.00
SOTTJJ JJ Peterka	8.00	20.00
SOTTJN Jake Neighbours	8.00	20.00
SOTTJP Jeff Petry	8.00	20.00
SOTTJS Juuse Saros	10.00	25.00
SOTTJW Joseph Woll	10.00	25.00
SOTTJY Jesse Ylonen	5.00	12.00
SOTTJZ Jason Zucker	8.00	20.00
SOTTKF Kevin Fiala	6.00	15.00
SOTTKK Kasperi Kapanen	6.00	15.00
SOTTKL Kevin Labanc	5.00	12.00
SOTTKM K'Andre Miller	6.00	15.00
SOTTKS Kiefer Sherwood	5.00	12.00
SOTTLR Lukas Reichel	8.00	20.00
SOTTLT Logan Thompson	10.00	25.00
SOTTLU Anton Lundell SP	8.00	20.00
SOTTMA Mikey Anderson	6.00	15.00
SOTTMB Michael Bunting	8.00	20.00
SOTTME Mason Marchment	6.00	15.00
SOTTMF Mario Ferraro	5.00	12.00
SOTTMH Miro Heiskanen	10.00	25.00
SOTTMI Jacob Middleton	5.00	12.00
SOTTMJ Jack McBain	5.00	12.00
SOTTMN Martin Necas	12.00	30.00
SOTTNC Noah Cates	5.00	12.00
SOTTNH Nico Hischier	12.00	30.00
SOTTNL Nils Lundkvist	5.00	12.00
SOTTNP Nick Perbix	5.00	12.00
SOTTPA Juuso Parssinen	5.00	12.00
SOTTPC Pheonix Copley	5.00	12.00
SOTTPE Cole Perfetti	8.00	20.00
SOTTPG Philipp Grubauer	8.00	20.00
SOTTPK Peyton Krebs	6.00	15.00
SOTTRC Ross Colton	6.00	15.00
SOTTRS Ryan Strome	8.00	20.00
SOTTSG Samuel Girard	5.00	12.00
SOTTSK Spencer Knight	8.00	20.00
SOTTSR Sam Reinhart	15.00	40.00
SOTTTE Troy Terry	6.00	15.00
SOTTTH Tyce Thompson	5.00	12.00
SOTTTK Torey Krug	6.00	15.00
SOTTTR Taylor Raddysh	6.00	15.00
SOTTTS Tim Stutzle SP	10.00	25.00
SOTTTT Teuvo Teravainen	8.00	20.00

2023-24 SP Authentic Sign of the Times Mystery Black

*MYS BLACK: 1X TO 2.5X BASIC

Card	Low	High
SOTTDG Dylan Guenther/25	30.00	80.00
SOTTDT Devon Toews/49	25.00	60.00
SOTTEB Jordan Eberle/49	40.00	100.00
SOTTJW Joseph Woll/49	30.00	80.00
SOTTMF Mario Ferraro/49	30.00	80.00
SOTTSK Spencer Knight/25	60.00	150.00
SOTTTE Troy Terry/25	20.00	50.00

2023-24 SP Authentic Sign of the Times Rookies

Card	Low	High
SOTTRAF Adam Fantilli SP	60.00	150.00
SOTTRCB Connor Bedard SP	800.00	2000.00
SOTTRDL Devon Levi	50.00	125.00
SOTTRDW Dustin Wolf	50.00	125.00
SOTTRJP Jakob Pelletier	15.00	40.00
SOTTRKN Matthew Knies	60.00	150.00
SOTTRLC Leo Carlsson SP	60.00	150.00
SOTTRMK Marco Kasper	30.00	80.00
SOTTRRG Ridly Greig	20.00	50.00
SOTTRSB Samuel Bolduc	12.00	30.00
SOTTRSE Simon Edvinsson	25.00	60.00
SOTTRTF Tyson Foerster	25.00	60.00
SOTTRWC Will Cuylle	20.00	50.00
SOTTRYA Yaroslav Askarov	30.00	80.00

2023-24 SP Authentic Spectrum FX

Card	Low	High
S1 Cale Makar	2.50	6.00
S2 Alex Ovechkin	4.00	10.00
S3 Kirill Kaprizov	3.00	8.00
S4 Tim Stutzle	1.25	3.00
S5 Johnny Gaudreau	1.50	4.00
S6 Nick Suzuki	2.00	5.00
S7 Elias Pettersson	1.50	4.00
S8 Jack Hughes	2.50	6.00
S9 Auston Matthews	4.00	10.00
S10 Cole Caufield	2.00	5.00
S11 Jordan Kyrou	1.00	2.50
S12 Adam Fox	1.25	3.00
S13 Mark Stone	1.25	3.00
S14 Sebastian Aho	1.50	4.00
S15 Ilya Sorokin	1.50	4.00
S16 Kyle Connor	1.50	4.00
S17 Matthew Tkachuk	2.00	5.00
S18 Brad Marchand	2.00	5.00
S19 Leon Draisaitl	3.00	8.00
S20 Quinton Byfield	1.25	3.00
S21 Seth Jones	1.00	2.50
S22 Nathan MacKinnon	4.00	10.00
S23 Jonathan Huberdeau	1.25	3.00
S24 Matty Beniers	1.25	3.00
S25 Connor McDavid	5.00	12.00
S26 Mitch Marner	1.50	4.00
S27 Steven Stamkos	2.00	5.00
S28 David Pastrnak	2.50	6.00
S29 Travis Konecny	1.00	2.50
S30 Filip Forsberg	1.50	4.00
S31 Nikita Kucherov	2.00	5.00
S32 Igor Shesterkin	2.00	5.00
S33 Dylan Larkin	1.25	3.00
S34 Wyatt Johnston	2.00	5.00
S35 Tage Thompson	1.25	3.00
S36 Jesper Bratt	1.00	2.50
S37 Tomas Hertl	1.00	2.50
S38 Trevor Zegras	1.00	2.50
S39 Clayton Keller	1.25	3.00
S40 Sidney Crosby	4.00	10.00
S41 Tye Kartye FW	4.00	10.00
S42 Vincent Desharnais FW	3.00	8.00
S43 Michael Kesselring FW	2.50	6.00
S44 Samuel Bolduc FW	2.50	6.00
S45 Akito Hirose FW	2.00	5.00
S46 William Dufour FW	2.00	5.00
S47 Jiri Patera FW	4.00	10.00
S48 Wyatt Kaiser FW	2.50	6.00
S49 Jonathan Gruden FW	2.50	6.00
S50 Bobby McMann FW	4.00	10.00
S51 Lukas Rousek FW	2.00	5.00
S52 John Beecher FW	5.00	12.00
S53 Jet Greaves FW	4.00	10.00
S54 Vincent Iorio FW	2.50	6.00
S55 Danil Gushchin FW	2.50	6.00
S56 Arnaud Durandeau FW	2.50	6.00
S57 Stanislav Svozil FW	2.00	5.00
S58 Joona Koppanen FW	2.00	5.00
S59 Matt Murray FW	2.50	6.00
S60 Elliot Desnoyers FW	2.50	6.00
S61 Cole Guttman FW	2.50	6.00
S62 Justin Sourdif FW	2.50	6.00
S63 Leevi Merilainen FW	2.50	6.00
S64 Sean Farrell FW	2.50	6.00
S65 Aidan McDonough FW	2.00	5.00
S66 Simon Nemec FW	5.00	12.00
S67 Kevin Korchinski FW	4.00	10.00
S68 Brock Faber FW	6.00	15.00
S69 Ridly Greig FW	4.00	10.00
S70 Owen Beck FW	4.00	10.00
S71 Yaroslav Askarov FW	6.00	15.00
S72 Pavel Mintyukov FW	4.00	10.00
S73 Luke Evangelista FW	4.00	10.00
S74 Matthew Coronato FW	4.00	10.00
S75 Simon Edvinsson FW	5.00	12.00
S76 Fraser Minten FW	5.00	12.00
S77 Marco Kasper FW	6.00	15.00
S78 Jakob Pelletier FW	3.00	8.00
S79 Will Cuylle FW	4.00	10.00
S80 Jackson LaCombe FW	2.50	6.00
S81 Dustin Wolf FW	8.00	20.00
S82 Matthew Poitras FW	5.00	12.00
S83 Matt Savoie FW	5.00	12.00
S84 Leo Carlsson FW	8.00	20.00
S85 Matthew Knies FW	10.00	25.00
S86 Devon Levi FW	6.00	15.00
S87 Adam Fantilli FW	8.00	20.00
S88 Luke Hughes FW	8.00	20.00
S89 Zach Benson FW	4.00	10.00
S90 Logan Cooley FW	8.00	20.00
S91 Connor Bedard FW	50.00	125.00
S92 Connor McDavid Bounty	50.00	125.00
S93 Alex Ovechkin Bounty	40.00	100.00
S94 Sidney Crosby Bounty	40.00	100.00
S95 Maurice Richard Bounty	20.00	50.00
S96 Patrick Roy Bounty	25.00	60.00
S97 Mario Lemieux Bounty	40.00	100.00
S98 Logan Cooley Bounty	30.00	80.00
S99 Adam Fantilli Bounty	30.00	80.00
S100 Connor Bedard Bounty	60.00	150.00

2023-24 SP Authentic Spectrum FX Gold

*GOLD: 2X TO 5X BASIC
*GOLD FW: 1.2X TO 3X BASIC
*GOLD BOUNTY: .8X TO 2X BASIC

Card	Low	High
S91 Connor Bedard FW	300.00	800.00
S96 Patrick Roy Bounty	60.00	150.00

2023-24 SP Authentic UD Authentics Autographs

Card	Low	High
UDAAD Alex DeBrincat	12.00	30.00
UDAAL Artturi Lehkonen	8.00	20.00
UDAAN Alex Newhook	8.00	20.00
UDAAR Aatu Raty	6.00	15.00
UDAAT Alex Tuch	10.00	25.00
UDAAV Andrei Vasilevskiy SP	15.00	40.00
UDAAX Arber Xhekaj	10.00	25.00
UDABC Brandt Clarke	10.00	25.00
UDABK Boris Katchouk	6.00	15.00
UDABM Brad Marchand SP	20.00	50.00
UDABO Matt Boldy	15.00	40.00
UDABT Brady Tkachuk	15.00	40.00
UDABU Brent Burns SP	10.00	25.00
UDACC Connor Clifton	6.00	15.00
UDACH Connor Hellebuyck	20.00	50.00
UDACP Colton Parayko	8.00	20.00
UDACS Cole Sillinger	8.00	20.00
UDACV Carter Verhaeghe	10.00	25.00
UDADM Dawson Mercer	12.00	30.00
UDAFG Filip Gustavsson	10.00	25.00
UDAIS Ilya Sorokin SP	15.00	40.00
UDAJK Jordan Kyrou	10.00	25.00
UDAJM Jared McCann	8.00	20.00
UDAJN Jake Neighbours	10.00	25.00
UDAJO Jake Oettinger	15.00	40.00
UDAJP Jeff Petry	10.00	25.00
UDAJS Jake Sanderson	12.00	30.00
UDAJU Juuse Saros	12.00	30.00
UDAKC Kyle Connor	15.00	40.00
UDAKG Kaiden Guhle	10.00	25.00
UDALT Logan Thompson	12.00	30.00
UDAMA Mikey Anderson	8.00	20.00
UDAMB Matty Beniers SP	12.00	30.00
UDAMC Connor McDavid SP	250.00	600.00
UDAMF Marc-Andre Fleury SP	20.00	50.00
UDAMH Miro Heiskanen	12.00	30.00
UDAMN Martin Necas	15.00	40.00
UDAMR Mikko Rantanen SP	25.00	60.00
UDAMS Mark Stone	12.00	30.00
UDAMT Matthew Tkachuk SP	20.00	50.00
UDAND Noah Dobson	12.00	30.00
UDANH Nico Hischier	15.00	40.00
UDAOP Owen Power SP	10.00	25.00
UDAPA Joe Pavelski	12.00	30.00
UDAPG Philipp Grubauer	10.00	25.00
UDAPI Shane Pinto	8.00	20.00
UDAQH Quinn Hughes	25.00	60.00
UDARC Ross Colton	8.00	20.00
UDARH Roope Hintz	12.00	30.00
UDART Robert Thomas	10.00	25.00
UDASJ Jared Spurgeon	10.00	25.00
UDASL Juraj Slafkovsky SP	30.00	80.00
UDASP Shane Pinto	8.00	20.00
UDASW Jeremy Swayman	15.00	40.00
UDATA Tage Thompson	12.00	30.00
UDATH Tomas Hertl	10.00	25.00
UDATS Tim Stutzle SP	12.00	30.00
UDATT Teuvo Teravainen	10.00	25.00
UDAWE William Eklund	12.00	30.00
UDAWJ Wyatt Johnston	30.00	80.00

2023-24 SP Authentic UD Authentics Patch Autographs

Card	Low	High
UDAPAL Alexis Lafreniere/49	25.00	60.00
UDAPAM Auston Matthews/25	150.00	400.00
UDAPAS Andrei Svechnikov/49	20.00	50.00
UDAPBT Brady Tkachuk/49	25.00	60.00
UDAPDH Dominik Hasek/25	25.00	60.00
UDAPHL Henrik Lundqvist/25	40.00	100.00
UDAPIS Ilya Sorokin/49	25.00	60.00
UDAPJH Jonathan Huberdeau/49	20.00	50.00
UDAPJP Joe Pavelski/49	20.00	50.00
UDAPJS Juraj Slafkovsky/49	80.00	200.00
UDAPJT Joe Thornton/49	25.00	60.00
UDAPMT Matthew Tkachuk/49	30.00	80.00
UDAPNS Nick Suzuki/49	50.00	125.00
UDAPRB Ray Bourque/25	25.00	60.00
UDAPSY Steve Yzerman/25	40.00	100.00
UDAPTT Tage Thompson/49	20.00	50.00

2000-01 SP Game Used

Card	Low	High
COMP.SET w/o SP's (60)	30.00	80.00
1 Paul Kariya	1.00	2.50
2 Teemu Selanne	2.00	5.00
3 Patrik Stefan	.75	2.00
4 Byron Dafoe	.75	2.00
5 Joe Thornton	1.50	4.00
6 Dominik Hasek	1.50	4.00
7 Maxim Afinogenov	.60	1.50
8 Valeri Bure	.75	2.00
9 Ron Francis	1.25	3.00
10 Arturs Irbe	.75	2.00
11 Tony Amonte	.75	2.00
12 Steve Sullivan	.60	1.50
13 Patrick Roy	2.50	6.00
14 Joe Sakic	2.00	5.00
15 Peter Forsberg	2.00	5.00
16 Ray Bourque	1.50	4.00
17 Ron Tugnutt	.75	2.00
18 Mike Modano	1.50	4.00
19 Brett Hull	2.00	5.00
20 Ed Belfour	1.00	2.50
21 Steve Yzerman	2.50	6.00
22 Brendan Shanahan	1.00	2.50
23 Sergei Fedorov	1.50	4.00
24 Nicklas Lidstrom	1.00	2.50
25 Doug Weight	1.00	2.50
26 Tommy Salo	.75	2.00
27 Pavel Bure	1.00	2.50
28 Trevor Kidd	.60	1.50
29 Luc Robitaille	1.00	2.50
30 Zigmund Palffy	1.00	2.50
31 Manny Fernandez	.60	1.50
32 Jose Theodore	1.00	2.50
33 Trevor Linden	1.00	2.50
34 Mike Dunham	.60	1.50
35 David Legwand	1.00	2.50
36 Martin Brodeur	2.50	6.00
37 Scott Gomez	.75	2.00
38 Tim Connolly	.60	1.50
39 John Vanbiesbrouck	1.00	2.50
40 Mike Richter	1.00	2.50
41 Mark Messier	2.00	5.00
42 Marian Hossa	1.00	2.50
43 Alexei Yashin	.75	2.00
44 Brian Boucher	.75	2.00
45 John LeClair	1.00	2.50
46 Jeremy Roenick	1.50	4.00
47 Keith Tkachuk	1.00	2.50
48 Jaromir Jagr	3.00	8.00
49 Mario Lemieux	4.00	10.00
50 Steve Shields	.60	1.50
51 Owen Nolan	1.00	2.50
52 Roman Turek	.75	2.00
53 Pavol Demitra	1.25	3.00
54 Vincent Lecavalier	1.00	2.50
55 Curtis Joseph	1.25	3.00
56 Mats Sundin	1.00	2.50
57 Daniel Sedin	1.25	3.00
58 Henrik Sedin	1.25	3.00
59 Olaf Kolzig	1.00	2.50
60 Chris Simon	.60	1.50
61 Jonas Ronnqvist RC	2.00	5.00
62 Andy McDonald RC	4.00	10.00
63 Andrew Raycroft RC	5.00	12.00
64 Josef Vasicek RC	5.00	12.00
65 David Aebischer RC	4.00	10.00
66 Rostislav Klesla RC	4.00	10.00
67 Marty Turco RC	6.00	15.00
68 Tyler Bouck RC	2.00	5.00
69 Steven Reinprecht RC	3.00	8.00
70 Marian Gaborik RC	8.00	20.00
71 Scott Hartnell RC	5.00	12.00
72 Greg Classen RC	2.00	5.00
73 Rick DiPietro RC	10.00	25.00
74 Jason LaBarbera RC	2.50	6.00
75 Martin Havlat RC	6.00	15.00
76 Jani Hurme RC	2.00	5.00
77 Roman Cechmanek RC	2.50	6.00
78 Ruslan Fedotenko RC	2.00	5.00
79 Justin Williams RC	5.00	12.00
80 Roman Simicek RC	2.00	5.00
81 Mark Smith RC	2.00	5.00
82 Matt Elich RC	2.50	6.00
83 Alexander Kharitonov RC	2.00	5.00
84 Fedor Fedorov RC	2.50	6.00
85 Marc-Andre Thinel RC	2.00	5.00
86 Zdenek Blatny RC	2.00	5.00
87 Jeff Bateman RC	2.00	5.00
88 Jason Jaspers RC	2.00	5.00
89 Jordan Krestanovich RC	2.00	5.00
90 Damian Surma RC	2.00	5.00

2000-01 SP Game Used Patch Cards

Card	Low	High
DFR P.Forsberg/P.Roy	75.00	200.00
DJL J.Jagr/M.Lemieux	125.00	300.00
DKG P.Kariya/W.Gretzky	150.00	300.00
DMG M.Messier/W.Gretzky	200.00	400.00
DOB B.Orr/R.Bourque	200.00	400.00
PBB Brian Boucher	20.00	50.00
PBH Brett Hull	30.00	80.00
PBO Bobby Orr	150.00	300.00
PGH Gordie Howe	50.00	120.00
PJJ Jaromir Jagr	30.00	80.00
PJL John LeClair	25.00	60.00
PJR Jeremy Roenick	30.00	80.00
PJS Joe Sakic	50.00	125.00
PKT Keith Tkachuk	25.00	60.00
PMB Martin Brodeur	60.00	150.00
PML Mario Lemieux	125.00	300.00
PMM Mark Messier	60.00	150.00
PMO Mike Modano	30.00	80.00
PMS Mats Sundin	20.00	50.00
PPB Pavel Bure	25.00	60.00
PPF Peter Forsberg	50.00	125.00
PPK Paul Kariya	25.00	60.00
PPR Patrick Roy	75.00	200.00
PRB Ray Bourque	50.00	125.00
PSF Sergei Fedorov	25.00	60.00
PSY Steve Yzerman	75.00	200.00
PTA Tony Amonte	20.00	50.00
PTS Teemu Selanne	30.00	80.00
PWG Wayne Gretzky	150.00	300.00

2000-01 SP Game Used Tools of the Game

*EXCL/350: .6X TO 1.5X BASIC

Card	Low	High
AM Al MacInnis	3.00	8.00
BB Brian Boucher	2.00	5.00
BD Byron Dafoe	2.00	5.00
BH Brett Hull	5.00	12.00
BL Brian Leetch	2.00	5.00
CO Chris Osgood	2.50	6.00
DL David Legwand	2.50	6.00
EL Eric Lindros	4.00	10.00
GH Gordie Howe	15.00	40.00
JJ Jaromir Jagr	6.00	15.00
JL John LeClair	2.50	6.00
JN Joe Nieuwendyk	2.00	5.00
JR Jeremy Roenick	4.00	10.00
JS Joe Sakic	5.00	12.00
KT Keith Tkachuk	2.50	6.00
MB Martin Brodeur	6.00	15.00
MH Michal Handzus	1.50	4.00
ML Mario Lemieux	10.00	25.00
MM Mark Messier	5.00	12.00
MO Mike Modano	4.00	10.00
MP Michael Peca	2.00	5.00
MR Mike Richter	2.50	6.00
MS Mats Sundin	2.50	6.00
NL Nicklas Lidstrom	2.50	6.00
PB Pavel Bure	2.50	6.00
PD Pavol Demitra	3.00	8.00
PF Peter Forsberg	5.00	12.00
PK Paul Kariya	2.50	6.00
PM Patrick Marleau	2.50	6.00
PR Patrick Roy	6.00	15.00
RB Ray Bourque	4.00	10.00
SF Sergei Fedorov	4.00	10.00
SO Sandis Ozolinsh	1.50	4.00
SS Sergei Samsonov	2.00	5.00
SY Steve Yzerman	6.00	15.00
TA Tony Amonte	2.00	5.00
TS Teemu Selanne	3.00	8.00
WG Wayne Gretzky	15.00	40.00

2000-01 SP Game Used Tools of the Game Combos

Card	Low	High
CBF P.Bure/S.Fedorov	20.00	50.00
CBR M.Brodeur/M.Richter	25.00	60.00
CDM P.Demitra/A.MacInnis	15.00	40.00
CGS D.Gilmour/M.Sundin	20.00	50.00
CGY S.Gomez/M.York	15.00	40.00
CHB B.Hull/E.Belfour	15.00	40.00
CHG G.Howe/W.Gretzky	75.00	150.00
CHP D.Hasek/M.Peca	15.00	40.00
CKS P.Kariya/T.Selanne	15.00	40.00
CLB B.Boucher/J.LeClair	15.00	40.00
CLG M.Lemieux/W.Gretzky	75.00	150.00
CLJ M.Lemieux/J.Jagr	50.00	120.00
CMG M.Messier/W.Gretzky	75.00	150.00
CMN M.Modano/J.Nieuwendyk	15.00	40.00
COL C.Osgood/N.Lidstrom	15.00	40.00
CRF P.Roy/P.Forsberg	25.00	60.00
CRT J.Roenick/K.Tkachuk	15.00	40.00
CSD B.Dafoe/S.Samsonov	15.00	40.00
CSH B.Shanahan/G.Howe	40.00	100.00
CSS J.Sakic/J.Sakic	40.00	100.00
CYH S.Yzerman/G.Howe	40.00	100.00

2000-01 SP Game Used Tools of the Game Autographed Bronze

*SILVER/100: .6X TO 1.5X BRONZE
*GOLD/25: .8X TO 2X BRONZE

Card	Low	High
ABR Brett Hull	20.00	50.00
AJL John LeClair	12.50	30.00
APB Pavel Bure	12.50	30.00
ARB Ray Bourque	25.00	60.00
ARL Roberto Luongo	20.00	50.00
ASG Scott Gomez	8.00	20.00
ASY Steve Yzerman	50.00	125.00
AWG Wayne Gretzky	200.00	500.00

2001-02 SP Game Used

Card	Low	High
COMPLETE SET (100)	125.00	250.00
COMP.SET w/o SP's (60)	30.00	80.00
1 Paul Kariya	1.00	2.50
2 Dany Heatley	.75	2.00
3 Joe Thornton	1.50	4.00
4 Bill Guerin	1.00	2.50
5 Miroslav Satan	.75	2.00
6 Roman Turek	.75	2.00
7 Jeff O'Neill	.75	2.00
8 Tony Amonte	.75	2.00
9 Rob Blake	1.00	2.50
10 Joe Sakic	2.00	5.00
11 Chris Drury	.75	2.00
12 Patrick Roy	2.50	6.00
13 Ron Tugnutt	.75	2.00
14 Mike Modano	1.50	4.00
15 Ed Belfour	1.00	2.50
16 Pierre Turgeon	.75	2.00
17 Brendan Shanahan	1.00	2.50
18 Steve Yzerman	2.50	6.00
19 Brett Hull	2.00	5.00
20 Dominik Hasek	1.50	4.00
21 Luc Robitaille	1.00	2.50
22 Mike Comrie	.75	2.00
23 Pavel Bure	1.00	2.50
24 Valeri Bure	.60	1.50
25 Adam Deadmarsh	.60	1.50
26 Zigmund Palffy	1.00	2.50
27 Marian Gaborik	1.00	2.50
28 Jose Theodore	1.00	2.50
29 Mike Dunham	.75	2.00
30 Patrik Elias	1.00	2.50
31 Martin Brodeur	2.50	6.00
32 Rick DiPietro	.75	2.00
33 Alexei Yashin	.75	2.00
34 Eric Lindros	1.50	4.00
35 Mark Messier	2.00	5.00
36 Marian Hossa	1.00	2.50
37 Radek Bonk	.60	1.50
38 John LeClair	1.00	2.50
39 Jeremy Roenick	1.50	4.00
40 Pavel Brendl	.60	1.50
41 Roman Cechmanek	.75	2.00
42 Sean Burke	.60	1.50
43 Mario Lemieux	4.00	10.00
44 Johan Hedberg	.75	2.00
45 Alexei Kovalev	.75	2.00
46 Teemu Selanne	2.00	5.00
47 Evgeni Nabokov	.75	2.00
48 Keith Tkachuk	1.00	2.50
49 Chris Pronger	1.00	2.50
50 Pavol Demitra	1.25	3.00
51 Doug Weight	1.00	2.50
52 Vincent Lecavalier	1.00	2.50
53 Curtis Joseph	1.25	3.00
54 Alexander Mogilny	.75	2.00
55 Mats Sundin	1.00	2.50
56 Markus Naslund	1.00	2.50
57 Daniel Sedin	1.25	3.00
58 Jaromir Jagr	3.00	8.00
59 Olaf Kolzig	1.00	2.50
60 Peter Bondra	1.00	2.50
61 Ilja Bryzgalov RC	5.00	12.00
62 Timo Parssinen RC	2.50	6.00
63 Kevin Sawyer RC	2.00	5.00
64 Brian Pothier RC	2.00	5.00
65 Kamil Piros RC	2.00	5.00
66 Ilya Kovalchuk RC	15.00	40.00
67 Zdenek Kutlak RC	2.00	5.00
68 Scott Nichol RC	2.00	5.00
69 Erik Cole RC	4.00	10.00
70 Jaroslav Obsut RC	2.00	5.00
71 Vaclav Nedorost RC	2.00	5.00
72 Mathieu Darche RC	3.00	8.00
73 Matt Davidson RC	2.00	5.00
74 Niko Kapanen RC	3.00	8.00
75 Pavel Datsyuk RC	30.00	80.00
76 Ty Conklin RC	3.00	8.00
77 Jason Chimera RC	2.00	5.00
78 Niklas Hagman RC	2.50	6.00
79 Kristian Huselius RC	3.00	8.00
80 Jaroslav Bednar RC	2.00	5.00
81 Nick Schultz RC	2.00	5.00
82 Travis Roche RC	2.00	5.00
83 Martin Erat RC	2.50	6.00
84 Scott Clemmensen RC	2.00	5.00
85 Josef Boumedienne RC	2.00	5.00
86 Raffi Torres RC	3.00	8.00
87 Radek Martinek RC	2.00	5.00
88 Dan Blackburn RC	2.50	6.00
89 Peter Smrek RC	2.00	5.00
90 Ivan Ciernik RC	2.00	5.00
91 Chris Neil RC	2.50	6.00
92 Vaclav Pletka RC	2.00	5.00
93 Jiri Dopita RC	2.00	5.00
94 Krys Kolanos RC	2.00	5.00
95 Jeff Jillson RC	2.00	5.00

96 Mark Rycroft RC 2.50 6.00
97 Ryan Tobler RC 2.50 6.00
98 Nikita Alexeev RC 2.00 5.00
99 Chris Corrinet RC 2.00 5.00
100 Brian Sutherby RC 2.00 5.00

2001-02 SP Game Used Authentic Fabric

*GOLD/300: .5X TO 1.2X BASIC JSY
*GOLD/50: .6X TO 1.5X BASIC JSY
AFAK Alexei Kovalev 3.00 8.00
AFBB Brian Boucher 3.00 8.00
AFBG Bill Guerin 3.00 8.00
AFBJ Brent Johnson 3.00 8.00
AFBN Radek Bonk 3.00 8.00
AFBS Brendan Shanahan 4.00 10.00
AFBU Pavel Bure SP 10.00 25.00
AFCO Chris Osgood 3.00 8.00
AFDH Dominik Hasek 6.00 15.00
AFEB Ed Belfour 4.00 10.00
AFFP Felix Potvin 5.00 12.00
AFGE Wayne Gretzky SP 20.00 50.00
AFGH Gordie Howe 15.00 40.00
AFGR Wayne Gretzky SP 20.00 50.00
AFJB Jaroslav Bednar 3.00 8.00
AFJD J-P Dumont 3.00 8.00
AFJH Jan Hlavac 3.00 8.00
AFJI Jarome Iginla 6.00 15.00
AFJJ Jaromir Jagr SP 12.50 30.00
AFJL John LeClair 4.00 10.00
AFJN Joe Nieuwendyk 3.00 8.00
AFJO Jose Theodore 6.00 15.00
AFJS Joe Sakic 6.00 15.00
AFJT Joe Thornton 10.00 25.00
AFKA Paul Kariya SP 15.00 40.00
AFKP Keith Primeau 3.00 8.00
AFLR Luc Robitaille 3.00 8.00
AFMA Maxim Afinogenov 3.00 8.00
AFMB Martin Brodeur 10.00 25.00
AFML Mario Lemieux 10.00 25.00
AFMM Mike Modano 5.00 12.00
AFMN Mika Noronen 3.00 8.00
AFMN Markus Naslund 4.00 10.00
AFMO Mike Modano SP 10.00 25.00
AFMR Mark Recchi 3.00 8.00
AFMS Miroslav Satan 3.00 8.00
AFMY Mike York 3.00 8.00
AFON Owen Nolan 3.00 8.00
AFPB Peter Bondra 4.00 10.00
AFPD Pavol Demitra 3.00 8.00
AFPF Peter Forsberg 6.00 15.00
AFPK Paul Kariya 4.00 10.00
AFPM Patrick Marleau 3.00 8.00
AFPR Patrick Roy 12.50 30.00
AFRB Ray Bourque 6.00 15.00
AFRD Radek Dvorak 3.00 8.00
AFRF Ruslan Fedotenko 3.00 8.00
AFRF Rico Fata 3.00 8.00
AFRL Robert Lang 3.00 8.00
AFSA Joe Sakic SP 12.50 30.00
AFSF Sergei Fedorov 5.00 12.00
AFSK Saku Koivu 4.00 10.00
AFSS Scott Stevens SP 10.00 25.00
AFSV Marc Savard 3.00 8.00
AFSY Steve Yzerman 10.00 25.00
AFTF Theo Fleury 5.00 12.00
AFTS Teemu Selanne SP 4.00 10.00
AFWG Wayne Gretzky SP 20.00 50.00
AFZP Zigmund Palffy 3.00 8.00
DFAB M.Afinogenov/M.Biron 6.00 15.00
DFBR M.Brodeur/P.Roy 30.00 80.00
DFDS J-P Dumont/M.Satan 6.00 15.00
DFFD T.Fleury/R.Dvorak 12.00 30.00
DFFS S.Fedorov/B.Shanahan 10.00 25.00
DFFS P.Forsberg/J.Sakic 15.00 40.00
DFIS J.Iginla/M.Savard 10.00 25.00
DFLB J.LeClair/B.Boucher 8.00 20.00
DFLG M.Lemieux/W.Gretzky 60.00 150.00
DFLK M.Lemieux/A.Kovalev 12.00 30.00
DFMB M.Modano/E.Belfour 8.00 20.00
DFNB M.Naslund/P.Bondra 10.00 25.00
DFPK Paul Kariya Dual 6.00 12.00
DFPL K.Primeau/J.LeClair 8.00 20.00
DFPP Z.Palffy/F.Potvin 15.00 40.00
DFPT F.Potvin/J.Theodore 20.00 50.00
DFRF M.Recchi/R.Fedotenko 10.00 25.00
DFTG J.Thornton/B.Guerin 15.00 40.00
DFYO S.Yzerman/C.Osgood 15.00 40.00
TFFSR Forsberg/Sakic/Roy 125.00 250.00
TFLKL Lemieux/Kovalev/Lang 125.00 200.00
TFLRP LeClair/Recchi/Primeau 30.00 80.00
TFMNB Modano/Nieuwy/Belfour 25.00 60.00
TFYSF Yzerman/Shanny/Fedorov 125.00 250.00

2001-02 SP Game Used Inked Sweaters

SCJ Curtis Joseph/50 20.00 50.00
SEB Ed Belfour/50 25.00 60.00
SGA Simon Gagne/50 20.00 50.00
SGH Gordie Howe/50 100.00 200.00
SJL John LeClair/50 15.00 40.00
SMB Martin Brodeur/50 75.00 150.00
SRB Ray Bourque/50 25.00 60.00
SSY Steve Yzerman/50 75.00 200.00
SWG Wayne Gretzky/50 300.00 800.00
ISAK Alexei Kovalev/100 10.00 25.00
ISCJ Curtis Joseph/100 15.00 40.00
ISHS Henrik Sedin/100 15.00 40.00
ISJI Jarome Iginla/100 25.00 60.00
ISJL John LeClair/100 15.00 40.00
ISJT Joe Thornton/100 40.00 80.00
ISMB Martin Brodeur/100 40.00 100.00
ISMB Martin Biron/100 5.00 12.00
ISMH Marian Hossa/100 12.00 30.00
ISMM Mike Modano/100 20.00 50.00
ISOK Olaf Kolzig/100 15.00 40.00
ISRB Ray Bourque/100 50.00 100.00
ISSG Simon Gagne/100 15.00 40.00
ISSY Steve Yzerman/100 75.00 150.00
ISVL Vincent Lecavalier/100 15.00 40.00
ISZP Zigmund Palffy/100 10.00 25.00

2001-02 SP Game Used Patches

PBI Martin Biron 10.00 25.00
PBO Peter Bondra 10.00 25.00
PBS Brendan Shanahan 15.00 40.00
PCJ Curtis Joseph 25.00 60.00
PEB Ed Belfour 20.00 50.00
PJH Jani Hurme 10.00 25.00
PJI Jarome Iginla 20.00 50.00
PJJ Jaromir Jagr 25.00 60.00
PJL John LeClair 10.00 25.00
PJS Joe Sakic 25.00 60.00
PJT Joe Thornton 15.00 40.00
PKP Keith Primeau 10.00 25.00
PMB Martin Brodeur 25.00 60.00
PMH Marian Hossa 15.00 40.00
PML Mario Lemieux 60.00 150.00
PMM Mike Modano 25.00 60.00
PMS Mats Sundin 15.00 40.00
POK Olaf Kolzig 15.00 40.00
PPB Pavel Bure 15.00 40.00
PPF Peter Forsberg 25.00 60.00
PPK Paul Kariya 15.00 40.00
PPR Patrick Roy 60.00 150.00
PPS Patrik Stefan 10.00 25.00
PSA Miroslav Satan 15.00 40.00
PSF Sergei Fedorov 20.00 50.00
PSG Simon Gagne 15.00 40.00
PSS Sergei Samsonov 15.00 40.00
PSY Steve Yzerman 40.00 100.00
PTA Tony Amonte 15.00 40.00
PWG Wayne Gretzky 75.00 150.00
CPAI T.Amonte/J.Iginla 30.00 80.00
CPBA P.Bondra/T.Amonte 20.00 50.00
CPBJ M.Brodeur/C.Joseph 75.00 200.00
CPGK S.Gagne/P.Kariya 20.00 50.00
CPHB J.Hurme/M.Brodeur 60.00 150.00
CPHH J.Hurme/M.Hossa 25.00 60.00
CPHL M.Hossa/J.LeClair 25.00 60.00
CPJB J.Jagr/P.Bondra 50.00 100.00
CPKB O.Kolzig/P.Bondra 30.00 80.00
CPKR O.Kolzig/P.Roy 75.00 200.00
CPKS P.Kariya/S.Samsonov 30.00 80.00
CPLJ M.Lemieux/J. Jagr 100.00 200.00
CPLP J.LeClair/K.Primeau 25.00 60.00
CPPG K.Primeau/S.Gagne 30.00 80.00
CPSB B.Shanahan/P.Bure 30.00 80.00
CPSJ M.Sundin/C.Joseph 20.00 50.00
CPSK M.Satan/P.Kariya 20.00 50.00
CPSR J.Sakic/P.Roy 150.00 350.00
CPSY B.Shanahan/S.Yzerman 75.00 150.00
CPYF S.Yzerman/S.Fedorov 75.00 200.00

2001-02 SP Game Used Patches Autographs

SPCJ Curtis Joseph 50.00 100.00
SPEB Ed Belfour 40.00 100.00
SPJI Jarome Iginla 30.00 80.00
SPJL John LeClair 25.00 60.00
SPJT Joe Thornton 25.00 60.00
SPKP Keith Primeau 25.00 60.00
SPMB Martin Brodeur 75.00 150.00
SPMB Martin Biron 30.00 80.00
SPMH Marian Hossa 30.00 80.00
SPOK Olaf Kolzig 30.00 80.00
SPPB Pavel Bure 30.00 80.00
SPPB Peter Bondra 30.00 80.00
SPPS Patrik Stefan 30.00 80.00
SPSG Simon Gagne 30.00 80.00
SPSS Sergei Samsonov 30.00 80.00
SPSY Steve Yzerman 75.00 200.00
SPTA Tony Amonte 30.00 80.00
SPTH Jose Theodore 40.00 100.00
SPTS Teemu Selanne 40.00 100.00
SPWG Wayne Gretzky 300.00 800.00

2001-02 SP Game Used Tools of the Game

TAC Anson Carter/100 12.50 30.00
TBB Brian Boucher/100 12.50 30.00
TBD Byron Dafoe/100 12.50 30.00
TCO Chris Osgood/100 12.50 30.00
TDA Byron Dafoe/100 12.50 30.00
TDF Byron Dafoe/100 12.50 30.00
TGF Grant Fuhr/100 15.00 40.00
TGP Gilbert Perreault/92 20.00 50.00
TJA Jaromir Jagr/100 15.00 40.00
TJF Jeff Friesen/100 8.00 20.00
TJH Johan Hedberg/100 10.00 25.00
TJJ Jaromir Jagr/100 15.00 40.00
TJT Joe Thornton/36 40.00 100.00
TLE John LeClair/100 10.00 25.00
TMM Mark Messier/100 12.50 30.00
TOK Olaf Kolzig/100 12.50 30.00
TPR Patrick Roy/100 30.00 80.00
TRA Bill Ranford/100 8.00 20.00
TRC Roman Cechmanek/100 12.50 30.00
TSA Sergei Samsonov/83 12.50 30.00
TSF Sergei Fedorov/100 12.50 30.00
TSS Sergei Samsonov/100 12.50 30.00
TSY Steve Yzerman/30 75.00 200.00
TTE Tony Esposito/100 15.00 40.00
TTH Jose Theodore/100 20.00 50.00
TWG Wayne Gretzky/71 100.00 250.00
CTCB R.Cechmanek/B.Boucher 20.00 50.00
CTCH R.Cechmanek/J.Hedberg 20.00 50.00
CTCS A.Carter/S.Samsonov 20.00 50.00
CTDB B.Dafoe/B.Boucher 20.00 50.00
CTDC B.Dafoe/G.Cheevers 20.00 50.00
CTEC T.Esposito/G.Cheevers 25.00 60.00
CTFC G.Fuhr/R.Cechmanek 20.00 50.00
CTFJ S.Fedorov/J.Friesen 20.00 50.00
CTFR S.Fedorov/P.Roy 50.00 100.00
CTHD J.Hedberg/B.Dafoe 20.00 50.00
CTKB O.Kolzig/B.Boucher 20.00 50.00
CTKT O.Kolzig/J.Theodore 20.00 50.00
CTLJ J.LeClair/J.Jagr 25.00 60.00
CTRC P.Roy/R.Cechmanek 25.00 60.00
CTRF P.Roy/G.Fuhr 30.00 80.00
CTRF B.Ranford/G.Fuhr 20.00 50.00
CTSF S.Samsonov/S.Fedorov 20.00 50.00
CTTD J.Theodore/B.Dafoe 20.00 50.00
TTDER Dafoe/Esposito/Roy 60.00 120.00
TTFCF Friesen/Carter/Fedorov 30.00 80.00
TTFSL Fedorov/Samsonov/LeClair 40.00 100.00
TTHCR Hedberg/Cheevers/Roy 60.00 150.00
TTKCH Kolzig/Cech/Hedberg 40.00 100.00
TTRBK Roy/Boucher/Kolzig 75.00 150.00
TTRFE Ranford/Fuhr/Esposito 40.00 100.00

2001-02 SP Game Used Tools of the Game Autographs

STBR Bill Ranford 20.00 50.00
STGF Grant Fuhr 20.00 50.00
STGP Gilbert Perrault 30.00 80.00
STJH Johan Hedberg 15.00 40.00
STJL John LeClair 12.00 30.00
STJT Jose Theodore 25.00 60.00
STJT Joe Thornton 25.00 60.00
STKP Keith Primeau 20.00 50.00
STLE John LeClair 15.00 40.00
STPB Peter Bondra 15.00 40.00
STRB Ray Bourque 40.00 100.00
STSA Sergei Samsonov 15.00 40.00
STSM Sergei Samsonov 15.00 40.00
STSY Steve Yzerman 60.00 120.00
STTS Teemu Selanne 20.00 50.00
SCBS R.Bourque/S.Samsonov 100.00 200.00
SCLT J.LeClair/J.Thornton 75.00 200.00
SCPS K.Primeau/S.Samsonov 25.00 60.00
SCPY K.Primeau/S.Yzerman 60.00 150.00
SCRF B.Ranford/G.Fuhr 40.00 100.00
SCRH B.Ranford/J.Hedberg 40.00 100.00
SCTY J.Thornton/S.Yzerman 125.00 250.00

2002-03 SP Game Used

COMP.SET w/o SP's (50) 60.00 125.00
1 Paul Kariya 1.00 2.50
2 Ilya Kovalchuk 1.25 3.00
3 Dany Heatley .75 2.00
4 Joe Thornton 1.50 4.00
5 Sergei Samsonov .75 2.00
6 Martin Biron .75 2.00
7 Jarome Iginla 1.25 3.00
8 Jeff O'Neill .60 1.50
9 Ron Francis 1.25 3.00
10 Eric Daze .60 1.50
11 Peter Forsberg 2.00 5.00
12 Joe Sakic 2.00 5.00
13 Patrick Roy 2.50 6.00
14 Marc Denis .75 2.00
15 Bill Guerin 1.00 2.50
16 Mike Modano 1.50 4.00
17 Steve Yzerman 2.50 6.00
18 Brendan Shanahan 1.00 2.50
19 Curtis Joseph 1.25 3.00
20 Mike Comrie 1.00 2.50
21 Roberto Luongo 1.50 4.00
22 Felix Potvin 1.50 4.00
23 Zigmund Palffy 1.00 2.50
24 Marian Gaborik 1.00 2.50
25 Jose Theodore 1.00 2.50
26 Saku Koivu 1.00 2.50
27 Mike Dunham .75 2.00
28 Martin Brodeur 2.50 6.00
29 Patrik Elias 1.00 2.50
30 Mike Peca .75 2.00
31 Alexei Yashin .75 2.00
32 Eric Lindros 1.50 4.00
33 Pavel Bure 1.00 2.50
34 Martin Havlat .75 2.00
35 Daniel Alfredsson 1.00 2.50
36 Simon Gagne 1.00 2.50
37 Jeremy Roenick 1.50 4.00
38 Sean Burke .60 1.50
39 Tony Amonte .75 2.00
40 Mario Lemieux 4.00 10.00
41 Owen Nolan 1.00 2.50
42 Evgeni Nabokov .75 2.00
43 Chris Pronger 1.00 2.50
44 Keith Tkachuk 1.00 2.50
45 Vincent Lecavalier 1.00 2.50
46 Mats Sundin 1.00 2.50
47 Ed Belfour 1.00 2.50
48 Markus Naslund 1.00 2.50
49 Olaf Kolzig 1.00 2.50
50 Jaromir Jagr 3.00 8.00
51 Gordie Howe AF 6.00 15.00
52 Mario Lemieux AF 8.00 20.00
53 Wayne Gretzky AF 12.00 30.00
54 Mario Lemieux AF 8.00 20.00
55 Wayne Gretzky AF 12.00 30.00
56 Vincent Damphousse AF 1.50 4.00
57 Brett Hull AF 4.00 10.00
58 Mike Richter AF 2.00 5.00
59 Ray Bourque AF 2.00 5.00
60 Mark Recchi AF 2.00 5.00
61 Teemu Selanne AF 4.00 10.00
62 Wayne Gretzky AF 12.00 30.00
63 Pavel Bure AF 2.00 5.00
64 Bill Guerin AF 2.00 5.00
65 Eric Daze AF 1.25 3.00
66 Alexei Smirnov RC 1.50 4.00
67 Stanislav Chistov RC 1.25 3.00
68 Martin Gerber RC 1.25 3.00
69 Kurt Sauer RC 1.25 3.00
70 Chuck Kobasew RC 1.50 4.00
71 Jordan Leopold RC 2.00 5.00
72 Jeff Paul RC 1.25 3.00
73 Rick Nash RC 12.50 30.00
74 Lasse Pirjeta RC 1.25 3.00
75 Henrik Zetterberg RC 10.00 25.00
76 Dmitri Bykov RC 1.25 3.00
77 Ales Hemsky RC 5.00 12.00
78 Jay Bouwmeester RC 4.00 10.00
79 Alexander Frolov RC 3.00 8.00
80 Sylvain Blouin RC 1.25 3.00
81 P-M Bouchard RC 2.00 5.00
82 Jason Spezza RC 10.00 25.00
83 Ron Hainsey RC 1.25 3.00
84 Adam Hall RC 1.25 3.00
85 Scottie Upshall RC 1.50 4.00
86 Anton Volchenkov RC 1.25 3.00
87 Dennis Seidenberg RC 2.00 5.00
88 Patrick Sharp RC 4.00 10.00
89 Jeff Taffe RC 1.25 3.00
90 Cody Rudkowsky RC 1.25 3.00
91 Tom Koivisto RC 1.25 3.00
92 Curtis Sanford RC 2.00 5.00
93 Alexander Svitov RC 1.25 3.00
94 Carlo Colaiacovo RC 2.00 5.00
95 Steve Eminger RC 1.25 3.00
96 Shaone Morrisonn RC 1.25 3.00
97 Ryan Miller RC 8.00 20.00
98 Levente Szuper RC 2.00 5.00
99 Mike Cammalleri RC 4.00 10.00
100 Stephane Veilleux RC 1.25 3.00
101 Darren Haydar RC 1.25 3.00
102 Lynn Loyns RC 1.25 3.00
103 Mikael Tellqvist RC 1.25 3.00

2002-03 SP Game Used Authentic Fabrics

AFAM Tony Amonte 3.00 8.00
AFAT Alex Tanguay 3.00 8.00
AFAY Alexei Yashin 3.00 8.00
AFBB Brian Boucher 3.00 8.00
AFBD Peter Bondra 3.00 8.00
AFBG Bill Guerin 3.00 8.00
AFBH Brett Hull 6.00 15.00
AFBI Martin Biron 3.00 8.00
AFBL Brian Leetch 3.00 8.00
AFBO Peter Bondra 3.00 8.00
AFBQ Ray Bourque 8.00 20.00
AFBS Brendan Shanahan 4.00 10.00
AFCD Chris Drury 3.00 8.00
AFCK Roman Cechmanek 3.00 8.00
AFDA Eric Daze 3.00 8.00
AFDB Donald Brashear 3.00 8.00
AFDR Chris Drury 3.00 8.00
AFED Eric Daze 3.00 8.00
AFFO Peter Forsberg 8.00 20.00
AFFP Felix Potvin 6.00 15.00
AFFV Sergei Fedorov 5.00 12.00
AFGI Jean-Sebastien Giguere 3.00 8.00
AFGM Glen Murray 3.00 8.00
AFGU Bill Guerin 3.00 8.00
AFGY Wayne Gretzky 25.00 60.00
AFHE Milan Hejduk 4.00 10.00
AFHO Marian Hossa 4.00 10.00
AFHU Brett Hull 5.00 12.00
AFIK Ilya Kovalchuk 8.00 20.00
AFJA Jason Allison 3.00 8.00
AFJF Jeff Friesen 3.00 8.00
AFJG Jean-Sebastien Giguere 3.00 8.00
AFJI Jarome Iginla 8.00 20.00
AFJJ Jaromir Jagr 6.00 15.00
AFJL John LeClair 4.00 10.00
AFJR Jeremy Roenick 6.00 15.00
AFJS Joe Sakic 8.00 20.00
AFJT Joe Thornton 6.00 15.00
AFJW Justin Williams 3.00 8.00
AFKA Paul Kariya 4.00 10.00
AFKK Ilya Kovalchuk 8.00 20.00
AFKO Alexei Kovalev 3.00 8.00
AFKP Keith Primeau 3.00 8.00
AFKV Alexei Kovalev 3.00 8.00
AFMB Martin Brodeur 15.00 40.00
AFMD Marc Denis 3.00 8.00
AFMH Marian Hossa 4.00 10.00
AFML Mario Lemieux 15.00 40.00
AFMM Mike Modano 5.00 12.00
AFMN Markus Naslund 4.00 10.00
AFMO Mike Modano 8.00 20.00
AFMR Mark Recchi 3.00 8.00
AFMS Mats Sundin 4.00 10.00
AFMT Mats Sundin 4.00 10.00
AFNA Markus Naslund 4.00 10.00
AFOK Olaf Kolzig 3.00 8.00
AFPB Pavel Bure 4.00 10.00
AFPD Pavol Demitra 3.00 8.00
AFPK Paul Kariya 4.00 10.00
AFPM Patrick Marleau 3.00 8.00
AFPR Patrick Roy 12.00 30.00
AFPU Keith Primeau 3.00 8.00
AFRB Ray Bourque 6.00 15.00
AFRC Roman Cechmanek 3.00 8.00
AFRO Jeremy Roenick 6.00 15.00
AFRW Ray Whitney 3.00 8.00
AFRY Patrick Roy 15.00 40.00
AFSA Miroslav Satan 3.00 8.00
AFSC Joe Sakic 10.00 25.00
AFSD Shane Doan 3.00 8.00
AFSF Sergei Fedorov 8.00 20.00
AFSH Steve Shields 3.00 8.00
AFSK Saku Koivu 4.00 10.00
AFSN Brendan Shanahan 4.00 10.00
AFSS Sergei Samsonov 3.00 8.00
AFSU Steve Sullivan 3.00 8.00
AFSV Sergei Samsonov 3.00 8.00
AFSY Steve Yzerman 15.00 40.00
AFTA Alex Tanguay 3.00 8.00
AFTH Jose Theodore 8.00 20.00
AFTT Jocelyn Thibault 3.00 8.00
AFWG Wayne Gretzky 25.00 60.00
AFZP Zigmund Palffy 4.00 10.00
CFCS T.Connolly/M.Satan 5.00 12.00
CFDT P.Demitra/K.Tkachuk 6.00 15.00
CFFO Peter Forsberg Dual 20.00 50.00
CFFP Felix Potvin Dual 8.00 20.00
CFGR Wayne Gretzky Dual 25.00 60.00
CFJB J.Jagr/P.Bondra 6.00 15.00
CFJJ Jaromir Jagr Dual 10.00 25.00
CFJS Joe Sakic Dual 12.50 30.00
CFLK M.Lemieux/P.Kariya 15.00 40.00
CFMO Mike Modano Dual 8.00 20.00
CFNB J.Nieuwendyk/M.Brodeur 10.00 25.00
CFSH B.Shanahan/B.Hull 6.00 15.00
CFTB J.Thibault/M.Brodeur 10.00 25.00
CFTK J.Theodore/S.Koivu 12.50 30.00
CFTL K.Tkachuk/J.LeClair 6.00 15.00
CFTS J.Thornton/S.Samsonov 6.00 15.00
CFWD D.Weight/P.Demitra 6.00 15.00
CFWG Wayne Gretzky Dual 30.00 80.00
CFYR S.Yzerman/L.Robitaille 10.00 25.00

2002-03 SP Game Used Authentic Fabrics Gold

*GOLD: .5X TO 1.25X BASIC JERSEYS

2002-03 SP Game Used First Rounder Patches

AD Adam Deadmarsh 15.00 40.00
AK Alexei Kovalev 15.00 40.00
AL Jason Allison 15.00 40.00
AT Alex Tanguay 15.00 40.00
AY Alexei Yashin 20.00 50.00
BB Brian Boucher 15.00 40.00
BG Bill Guerin 15.00 40.00
BI Martin Biron 15.00 40.00
BS Brendan Shanahan 20.00 50.00
CP Chris Pronger 15.00 40.00
DB Daniel Briere 15.00 40.00
DL David Legwand 15.00 40.00
EL Eric Lindros 25.00 60.00
GO Sergei Gonchar 15.00 40.00
IK Ilya Kovalchuk 25.00 60.00
JA Jason Arnott 15.00 40.00
JD J-P Dumont 15.00 40.00
JG Jean-Sebastien Giguere 15.00 40.00
JI Jarome Iginla 25.00 60.00
JJ Jaromir Jagr 30.00 80.00
JR Jeremy Roenick 30.00 80.00
JS Joe Sakic 40.00 100.00
JT Joe Thornton 30.00 80.00
JW Justin Williams 15.00 40.00
KK Krys Kolanos 15.00 40.00
KP Keith Primeau 15.00 40.00
KT Keith Tkachuk 25.00 60.00
MA Manny Malhotra 15.00 40.00
MB Martin Brodeur 40.00 100.00
MD Marc Denis 15.00 40.00
ML Mario Lemieux 60.00 150.00
MM Mike Modano 30.00 80.00
MN Markus Naslund 20.00 50.00
MS Mats Sundin 25.00 60.00
NO Mika Noronen 15.00 40.00
OK Olaf Kolzig 20.00 50.00
ON Owen Nolan 15.00 40.00
PF Peter Forsberg 30.00 80.00
PK Paul Kariya 20.00 50.00
PM Patrick Marleau 15.00 40.00
PS Patrik Stefan 15.00 40.00
RB Ray Bourque 40.00 100.00
RK Rostislav Klesla 15.00 40.00
RL Roberto Luongo 25.00 60.00
RT Raffi Torres 15.00 40.00
SD Shane Doan 15.00 40.00
SG Simon Gagne 20.00 50.00
SH Scott Hartnell 20.00 50.00
SK Saku Koivu 20.00 50.00
SS Sergei Samsonov 20.00 50.00
SY Steve Yzerman 75.00 150.00
TC Tim Connolly 15.00 40.00
TL Trevor Linden 15.00 40.00
TP Taylor Pyatt 15.00 40.00
TS Teemu Selanne 20.00 50.00
VL Vincent Lecavalier 25.00 60.00
BLA Dan Blackburn 15.00 40.00
BLE Brian Leetch 25.00 60.00

2002-03 SP Game Used Future Fabrics

FFAE David Aebischer 3.00 8.00
FFAT Alex Tanguay 3.00 8.00
FFBJ Brent Johnson 3.00 8.00
FFBM Brenden Morrow 3.00 8.00
FFCA Kyle Calder 3.00 8.00
FFDA Denis Arkhipov 3.00 8.00
FFDB Daniel Briere 3.00 8.00
FFEB Eric Belanger 3.00 8.00
FFHA Jeff Halpern 3.00 8.00
FFIB Ilja Bryzgalov 4.00 10.00
FFIK Ilya Kovalchuk 6.00 15.00
FFJG Jean-Sebastien Giguere 3.00 8.00
FFJH Jeff Halpern 3.00 8.00
FFKC Kyle Calder 3.00 8.00
FFKO Ilya Kovalchuk 6.00 15.00
FFMA Maxim Afinogenov 3.00 8.00
FFMB Mark Bell 3.00 8.00
FFME Martin Erat 3.00 8.00
FFMM Manny Malhotra 3.00 8.00
FFMP Matt Pettinger 3.00 8.00
FFMR Mike Ribeiro 3.00 8.00
FFMT Marty Turco 3.00 8.00
FFPB Pavel Brendl 3.00 8.00
FFRI Mike Ribeiro 3.00 8.00
FFRK Rostislav Klesla 3.00 8.00
FFSG Simon Gagne 4.00 10.00
FFSH Scott Hartnell 4.00 10.00
FFSR Steven Reinprecht 3.00 8.00
FFTC Tim Connolly 3.00 8.00
FFTP Taylor Pyatt 3.00 8.00
FFVN Ville Nieminen 3.00 8.00

2002-03 SP Game Used Future Fabrics Gold

*GOLD: .5X TO 1.25X BASIC JERSEY

2002-03 SP Game Used Piece of History

*GOLD/99: .6X TO 1.5X BASIC JSY/225
PHAD Adam Deadmarsh 3.00 8.00
PHAL Jason Allison 4.00 10.00
PHAM Tony Amonte 4.00 10.00
PHAT Alex Tanguay 4.00 10.00
PHAY Alexei Yashin 4.00 10.00
PHAZ Alexei Zhamnov 4.00 10.00
PHBD Peter Bondra 5.00 12.00
PHBH Brett Hull 10.00 25.00
PHBI Martin Biron 4.00 10.00
PHBL Brian Leetch 4.00 10.00
PHBO Peter Bondra 5.00 12.00
PHBQ Ray Bourque 8.00 20.00
PHBS Brendan Shanahan 5.00 12.00
PHCC Chris Chelios 5.00 12.00
PHCD Chris Drury 5.00 12.00
PHCJ Curtis Joseph 6.00 15.00
PHCK Roman Cechmanek 4.00 10.00
PHCL Claude Lemieux 5.00 12.00
PHDL David Legwand 4.00 10.00
PHDR Chris Drury 5.00 12.00
PHDU Mike Dunham 4.00 10.00
PHED Eric Daze 3.00 8.00
PHEK Espen Knutsen 3.00 8.00
PHEL Eric Lindros 8.00 20.00
PHFO Peter Forsberg 10.00 25.00
PHFP Felix Potvin 8.00 20.00
PHFV Sergei Fedorov 8.00 20.00
PHGO Sergei Gonchar 4.00 10.00
PHGU Bill Guerin 5.00 12.00
PHGY Wayne Gretzky 30.00 80.00
PHJA Jason Allison 4.00 10.00
PHJD J.P. Dumont 3.00 8.00
PHJG Jaromir Jagr 15.00 40.00
PHJI Jarome Iginla 6.00 15.00
PHJJ Jaromir Jagr 15.00 40.00
PHJL John LeClair 5.00 12.00
PHJN Joe Nieuwendyk 4.00 10.00
PHJO Jocelyn Thibault 4.00 10.00
PHJR Jeremy Roenick 8.00 20.00
PHJS Joe Sakic 10.00 25.00
PHJT Joe Thornton 8.00 20.00
PHKA Paul Kariya 5.00 12.00
PHKK Ilya Kovalchuk 6.00 15.00
PHKO Steve Konowalchuk 3.00 8.00
PHKP Keith Primeau 4.00 10.00
PHKU Saku Koivu 5.00 12.00
PHLM Nicklas Lidstrom 5.00 12.00
PHMB Martin Brodeur 10.00 25.00
PHMD Marc Denis 4.00 10.00
PHMH Milan Hejduk 4.00 10.00
PHML Mario Lemieux 20.00 50.00
PHMM Mike Modano 8.00 20.00
PHMN Markus Naslund 5.00 12.00
PHMO Mike Modano 8.00 20.00
PHMR Mark Recchi 6.00 15.00
PHMS Mats Sundin 5.00 12.00
PHMY Mike York 3.00 8.00
PHNA Markus Naslund 5.00 12.00
PHNL Nicklas Lidstrom 5.00 12.00
PHPB Pavel Bure 5.00 12.00
PHPF Peter Forsberg 10.00 25.00
PHPK Paul Kariya 5.00 12.00
PHPM Patrick Marleau 5.00 12.00
PHPR Patrick Roy 12.00 30.00
PHRB Ray Bourque 8.00 20.00
PHRC Roman Cechmanek 4.00 10.00
PHRK Jeremy Roenick 8.00 20.00
PHRO Rob Blake 5.00 12.00
PHRT Roman Turek 5.00 12.00
PHRY Patrick Roy 12.00 30.00
PHSA Marc Savard 3.00 8.00
PHSB Sean Burke 3.00 8.00
PHSC Joe Sakic 10.00 25.00
PHSF Sergei Fedorov 8.00 20.00
PHSG Simon Gagne 5.00 12.00
PHSH Brendan Shanahan 5.00 12.00
PHSK Saku Koivu 5.00 12.00
PHSS Sergei Samsonov 4.00 10.00
PHSU Mats Sundin 5.00 12.00
PHSV Sergei Samsonov 4.00 10.00
PHSY Steve Yzerman 12.00 30.00
PHTA Alex Tanguay 4.00 10.00
PHTC Tim Connolly 3.00 8.00
PHTH Jose Theodore 5.00 12.00
PHTS Teemu Selanne 10.00 25.00
PHTT Jocelyn Thibault 4.00 10.00
PHZP Zigmund Palffy 5.00 12.00

2002-03 SP Game Used Signature Style

AF Alexander Frolov 8.00 20.00
BO Bobby Orr 125.00 250.00
BR Pavel Brendl 5.00 12.00
CJ Curtis Joseph 12.00 30.00
DH Dany Heatley 10.00 25.00
EB Ed Belfour 15.00 40.00
EC Erik Cole 5.00 12.00
GH Gordie Howe 50.00 125.00
IK Ilya Kovalchuk 12.00 30.00
JI Jarome Iginla 10.00 25.00
JL John LeClair 5.00 12.00
JT Joe Thornton 12.00 30.00
JW Justin Williams 5.00 12.00
KH Kristian Huselius 5.00 12.00
MA Maxim Afinogenov 5.00 12.00
MB Martin Brodeur 40.00 100.00
MC Mike Comrie 5.00 12.00
MFO Manny Fernandez 5.00 12.00
MH Martin Havlat 5.00 12.00
MK Milan Kraft 6.00 12.00
NK Nikolai Khabibulin 8.00 20.00
PB Pavel Bure 8.00 20.00
PR Patrick Roy 50.00 125.00
RB Ray Bourque 20.00 50.00
SC Stanislav Chistov 6.00 15.00
SG Simon Gagne 6.00 15.00
SH Scott Hartnell 6.00 15.00
SP Jason Spezza 20.00 50.00
SS Sergei Samsonov 6.00 15.00
SY Steve Yzerman 30.00 80.00
TS Teemu Selanne 6.00 15.00
WG Wayne Gretzky 250.00 600.00

2002-03 SP Game Used Tools of the Game

AK Alexei Kovalev G 8.00 20.00
AM Alexander Mogilny G 8.00 20.00
BB Brian Boucher P 8.00 20.00
BD Byron Dafoe P 8.00 20.00
BE Ed Belfour P 12.50 30.00
BH Brett Hull G 15.00 40.00
BS Brendan Shanahan G 12.50 30.00
DH Dominik Hasek P 15.00 40.00
EB Ed Belfour G 12.50 30.00
JF Jeff Friesen G 8.00 20.00
JJ Jaromir Jagr G 12.00 30.00
JL John LeClair G 12.50 30.00
JR Jeremy Roenick G 12.50 30.00
JT Joe Thornton G 15.00 40.00
KP Keith Primeau G 8.00 20.00
KT Keith Tkachuk G 10.00 25.00
MD Marc Denis P 8.00 20.00
MS Mats Sundin G 12.50 30.00
OK Olaf Kolzig P 8.00 20.00
PB Peter Bondra G 8.00 20.00
PR Patrick Roy P 20.00 50.00
RC Roman Cechmanek P 8.00 20.00
RD Rick DiPietro P 8.00 20.00
RF Ron Francis G 8.00 20.00
RL Roberto Luongo P 15.00 40.00
SF Sergei Fedorov G 12.50 30.00
SH Steve Shields P 8.00 20.00
SS Sergei Samsonov G 8.00 20.00
TH Jose Theodore P 12.00 30.00
TS Teemu Selanne G 8.00 20.00

2003-04 SP Game Used

COMP.SET w/o SP's (50) 25.00 60.00
1 Jean-Sebastien Giguere 1.00 2.50
2 Sergei Fedorov 1.50 4.00
3 Dany Heatley .75 2.00
4 Ilya Kovalchuk 1.00 2.50
5 Joe Thornton 1.50 4.00
6 Sergei Samsonov .75 2.00
7 Chris Drury .75 2.00
8 Jarome Iginla 1.25 3.00
9 Ron Francis 1.25 3.00
10 Jocelyn Thibault .75 2.00
11 Joe Sakic 2.00 5.00
12 Peter Forsberg 2.00 5.00
13 Paul Kariya 1.00 2.50
14 Rick Nash 1.00 2.50
15 Marty Turco 1.00 2.50
16 Mike Modano 1.50 4.00
17 Steve Yzerman 2.50 6.00
18 Dominik Hasek 1.50 4.00
19 Ales Hemsky 1.00 2.50
20 Mike Comrie .75 2.00
21 Roberto Luongo 1.50 4.00
22 Zigmund Palffy 1.00 2.50
23 Marian Gaborik 1.00 2.50
24 Jose Theodore 1.00 2.50
25 Saku Koivu 1.00 2.50
26 Tomas Vokoun .75 2.00
27 Martin Brodeur 2.50 6.00
28 Alexei Yashin .75 2.00
29 Eric Lindros 1.50 4.00
30 Pavel Bure 1.00 2.50
31 Patrick Lalime .75 2.00
32 Marian Hossa 1.00 2.50
33 Jason Spezza 1.00 2.50
34 Simon Gagne 1.00 2.50
35 Jeremy Roenick 1.50 4.00
36 Sean Burke .60 1.50
37 Mario Lemieux 4.00 10.00
38 Niko Dimitrakos .60 1.50
39 Evgeni Nabokov .75 2.00
40 Al MacInnis 1.25 3.00
41 Keith Tkachuk 1.00 2.50
42 Chris Pronger 1.00 2.50
43 Nikolai Khabibulin 1.00 2.50
44 Vincent Lecavalier 1.00 2.50
45 Owen Nolan 1.00 2.50
46 Ed Belfour 1.00 2.50
47 Mats Sundin 1.00 2.50
48 Markus Naslund 1.00 2.50
49 Todd Bertuzzi 1.00 2.50
50 Jaromir Jagr 2.00 5.00
51 Jiri Hudler RC 5.00 12.00
52 Patrice Bergeron RC 10.00 25.00
53 Milan Bartovic RC 2.50 6.00
54 Matthew Lombardi RC 2.50 6.00
55 Lasse Kukkonen RC 2.00 5.00
56 Travis Moen RC 2.50 6.00
57 Marek Svatos RC 4.00 10.00
58 John-Michael Liles RC 2.50 6.00
59 Cody McCormick RC 2.50 6.00
60 Dan Fritsche RC 2.00 5.00
61 Antti Miettinen RC 3.00 8.00
62 Esa Pirnes RC 2.00 5.00
63 Tim Gleason RC 2.00 5.00
64 Brent Burns RC 6.00 15.00
65 Christoph Brandner RC 2.50 6.00
66 Chris Higgins RC 4.00 10.00
67 Dan Hamhuis RC 2.50 6.00
68 Marek Zidlicky RC 2.00 5.00
69 Wade Brookbank RC 2.50 6.00
70 David Hale RC 2.00 5.00
71 Paul Martin RC 2.50 6.00
72 Sean Bergenheim RC 2.50 6.00
73 Antoine Vermette RC 4.00 10.00
74 Matthew Spiller RC 2.50 6.00
75 Matt Murley RC 2.50 6.00
76 Christian Ehrhoff RC 2.50 6.00
77 Alexander Semin RC 6.00 15.00
78 Tom Preissing RC 2.50 6.00
79 Peter Sejna RC 2.50 6.00
80 Maxim Kondratiev RC 2.00 5.00
81 Matt Stajan RC 3.00 8.00
82 Boyd Gordon RC 2.50 6.00
83 Joffrey Lupul RC 15.00 40.00
84 Eric Staal RC 30.00 80.00
85 Tuomo Ruutu RC 10.00 25.00
86 Pavel Vorobiev RC 8.00 20.00
87 Nathan Horton RC 15.00 40.00
88 Dustin Brown RC 15.00 40.00
89 Jordin Tootoo RC 12.00 30.00
90 Joni Pitkanen RC 10.00 25.00
91 Marc-Andre Fleury RC 60.00 150.00
92 Milan Michalek RC 12.00 30.00
93 Joe Thornton JSY 8.00 20.00
94 Jason Blake JSY 3.00 8.00
95 Pavol Demitra JSY 6.00 15.00
96 Martin St. Louis JSY 5.00 12.00
97 Zigmund Palffy JSY 5.00 12.00
98 Sean Burke JSY 3.00 8.00
99 Todd Marchant JSY 3.00 8.00
100 Jarome Iginla JSY 6.00 15.00
101 Doug Weight JSY 5.00 12.00
102 Henrik Zetterberg JSY 6.00 15.00
103 Ilya Kovalchuk JSY 6.00 15.00
104 Alexei Yashin JSY 4.00 10.00
105 Mario Lemieux JSY 10.00 25.00
106 Milan Hejduk JSY 4.00 10.00
107 Martin Biron JSY 5.00 12.00
108 Tomas Vokoun JSY 4.00 10.00
109 Tommy Salo JSY 4.00 10.00
110 Anson Carter JSY 4.00 10.00
111 Nikolai Khabibulin JSY 5.00 12.00
112 Keith Tkachuk JSY 5.00 12.00
113 Martin Brodeur JSY 12.00 30.00
114 Steve Yzerman JSY 6.00 15.00
115 Jeremy Roenick JSY 8.00 20.00
116 Mike Modano JSY 8.00 20.00
117 Marian Hossa JSY 5.00 12.00
118 Paul Kariya JSY 5.00 12.00
119 Marty Turco JSY 5.00 12.00
120 Peter Forsberg JSY 8.00 20.00
121 Todd Bertuzzi JSY 5.00 12.00
122 David Aebischer JSY 4.00 10.00
123 Fedor Tyutin RC 2.00 5.00
124 John Pohl RC 2.00 5.00
125 Ryan Kesler RC 8.00 20.00
126 Fredrik Sjostrom RC 3.00 8.00
127 Aaron Johnson RC 2.00 5.00
128 Brad Boyes RC 3.00 8.00
129 Nikolai Zherdev RC 4.00 10.00
130 Tomas Plekanec RC 6.00 15.00

2003-04 SP Game Used Gold

*1-50 VETS/40: 2.5X TO 6X BASIC CARDS
*51-82 ROOKIES/40: .8X TO 2X RC/600
*83-92 ROOKIES/25: .4X TO 1X RC/99
*93-122 JERSEYS/30: .8X TO 2X BASIC JSY

2003-04 SP Game Used Authentic Fabrics

AFAF Alexander Frolov 5.00 12.00
AFEL Eric Lindros 6.00 15.00
AFHA Marcel Hossa 3.00 8.00
AFJG J-S Giguere 5.00 12.00
AFJI Jarome Iginla 10.00 25.00
AFJJ Jaromir Jagr 10.00 25.00
AFJR Jeremy Roenick 10.00 25.00
AFJS Jason Spezza 8.00 20.00

AFJT Joe Thornton 10.00 25.00
AFMH Marian Hossa 6.00 15.00
AFML Mario Lemieux 15.00 40.00
AFON Owen Nolan 5.00 12.00
AFPR Patrick Roy 15.00 40.00
AFPS Peter Sejna 3.00 8.00
AFRL Roberto Luongo 8.00 20.00
AFRN Rick Nash 12.50 30.00
AFSF Sergei Fedorov 10.00 25.00
AFSG Simon Gagne 6.00 15.00
AFSK Saku Koivu 5.00 12.00
AFTB Todd Bertuzzi 5.00 12.00
AFWG Wayne Gretzky 30.00 80.00
AFZP Zigmund Palffy 4.00 10.00
DFBJ R.Blake/E.Jovanovski 8.00 20.00
DFBL J.Bouwmeester/R.Luongo 15.00 40.00
DFBP M.Brodeur/P.Leclaire 15.00 40.00
DFBR M.Brodeur/P.Roy 25.00 60.00
DFBT Z.Palffy/A.Frolov 8.00 20.00
DFCM C.Drury/M.Satan 6.00 15.00
DFDS T.Domi/J.Shelley 8.00 20.00
DFFS P.Forsberg/J.Sakic 15.00 40.00
DFGR J.Giguere/P.Roy 15.00 40.00
DFGS W.Gretzky/J.Spezza 40.00 100.00
DFHC A.Hemsky/M.Comrie 8.00 20.00
DFHG G.Howe/W.Gretzky 50.00 125.00
DFHH M.Hossa/M.Hossa 10.00 25.00
DFHK D.Heatley/I.Kovalchuk 12.00 30.00
DFHL D.Hasek/N.Lidstrom 10.00 25.00
DFHY B.Hull/S.Yzerman 15.00 40.00
DFJB J.Jagr/P.Bondra 8.00 20.00
DFKF P.Kariya/P.Forsberg 12.00 30.00
DFKH S.Koivu/M.Hossa 8.00 20.00
DFKS P.Kariya/T.Selanne 8.00 20.00
DFLG M.Lemieux/W.Gretzky 50.00 125.00
DFLK G.Lafleur/S.Koivu 8.00 20.00
DFLP B.Leetch/T.Poti 8.00 20.00
DFMT M.Modano/M.Turco 15.00 40.00
DFNB M.Naslund/T.Bertuzzi 12.00 30.00
DFND R.Nash/M.Denis 8.00 20.00
DFNM R.Nash/T.Marchant 8.00 20.00
DFPC Z.Palffy/R.Cechmanek 6.00 15.00
DFRG J.Roenick/S.Gagne 8.00 20.00
DFSG S.Bowman/G.Lafleur 15.00 40.00
DFSH J.Spezza/M.Hossa 15.00 40.00
DFTK J.Theodore/S.Koivu 12.50 30.00
DFTM J.Thornton/G.Murray 8.00 20.00
DFVN V.Lecavalier/N.Khabibulin 8.00 20.00
DFWT D.Weight/K.Tkachuk 6.00 15.00
DFWY S.Yzerman/G.Howe 30.00 80.00
DFYP A.Yashin/M.Peca 6.00 15.00
DFZH H.Zetterberg/B.Hull 15.00 40.00
DFZT A.Zhamnov/J.Thibault 6.00 15.00
QARGL Amnte/Roen/Gags/LeC 25.00 60.00
QFSKS Frsbrg/Seln/Krya/Sakic 40.00 100.00
QKTHK Kvu/Thdre/Hsa/Kmisrk 30.00 80.00
QLGHL Lem/Gretz/Howe/Lafleur 150.00 350.00
QMGTM Modn/Grin/Trco/Morr 25.00 60.00
QNBJM Naslund/Bert/Jov/Morr 25.00 60.00
QRGBT Roy/J-S G/Brodr/Turco 60.00 150.00
QSAHL Spza/Alfrd/Hssa/Lalime 25.00 60.00
QSNBM Sndin/Nolan/Blfr/Mogil 25.00 60.00
QSNZH Spza/Nsh/Zettr/Hmsky 60.00 150.00
QYBHH Yzrm/Bowm/Hull/Hask 60.00 120.00

2003-04 SP Game Used Double Threads

DTAR D.Aebischer/P.Roy 40.00 100.00
DTBL J.Bouwmeester/R.Luongo 20.00 50.00
DTBR M.Brodeur/P.Roy 60.00 150.00
DTDS C.Drury/M.Satan 20.00 50.00
DTFS P.Forsberg/J.Sakic 20.00 50.00
DTKH S.Koivu/M.Hossa 20.00 50.00
DTKS P.Kariya/T.Selanne 20.00 50.00
DTLG M.Lemieux/W.Gretzky 75.00 150.00
DTLK V.Lecavalier/N.Khabibulin 20.00 50.00
DTLS V.Lecavalier/M.St. Louis 20.00 50.00
DTMG M.Modano/B.Guerin 20.00 50.00
DTMT M.Modano/M.Turco 20.00 50.00
DTNB M.Naslund/T.Bertuzzi 20.00 50.00
DTND R.Nash/M.Denis 25.00 60.00
DTNN R.Niedermayer/S.Niedermayer 25.00 60.00
DTPF Z.Palffy/A.Frolov 20.00 50.00
DTPK P.Kariya/P.Kariya 20.00 50.00
DTRA J.Roenick/T.Amonte 20.00 50.00
DTSB M.Sundin/E.Belfour 25.00 60.00
DTSF S.Fedorov/S.Fedorov 40.00 100.00
DTSH J.Spezza/M.Hossa 25.00 60.00
DTSN M.Sundin/O.Nolan 25.00 60.00
DTTM J.Thornton/G.Murray 20.00 50.00
DTTS J.Thornton/S.Samsonov 20.00 50.00
DTWG W.Gretzky/W.Gretzky 150.00 400.00
DTYZ S.Yzerman/H.Zetterberg 25.00 60.00
DTZT A.Zhamnov/J.Thibault 20.00 50.00

2003-04 SP Game Used Game Gear

GGBB Brian Boucher 6.00 15.00
GGBD Byron Dafoe 6.00 15.00
GGCJ Curtis Joseph 8.00 20.00
GGCO Chris Osgood 6.00 15.00
GGDH Dominik Hasek 12.50 30.00
GGGF Grant Fuhr 15.00 40.00
GGJF Jeff Friesen 6.00 15.00
GGJGR Jaromir Jagr 12.50 30.00
GGJH Johan Hedberg/36 6.00 15.00
GGJJ Jaromir Jagr 12.50 30.00
GGJT Jose Theodore 12.50 30.00
GGMB Martin Brodeur 15.00 40.00
GGMD Marc Denis 6.00 15.00
GGMS Mats Sundin 8.00 20.00
GGMT Marty Turco 6.00 15.00
GGOK Olaf Kolzig 6.00 15.00
GGPL Patrick Lalime 6.00 15.00
GGPR Patrick Roy 15.00 40.00
GGRC Roman Cechmanek 6.00 15.00
GGRD Rick DiPietro 6.00 15.00
GGRL Roberto Luongo 12.50 30.00
GGSAM Sergei Samsonov 6.00 15.00
GGSS Steve Shields 6.00 15.00
GGTS Teemu Selanne 8.00 20.00
GGTSA Tommy Salo 6.00 15.00

2003-04 SP Game Used Game Gear Combo

*COMBO: .5X TO 1.5X BASIC GEAR

2003-04 SP Game Used Limited Threads

*GOLD/21: .6X TO 1.5X BASIC JSY/75
LTAH Ales Hemsky 6.00 15.00
LTAK Ales Kotalik 6.00 15.00
LTAY Alexei Yashin 6.00 15.00
LTBG Bill Guerin 6.00 15.00
LTBL Brian Leetch 6.00 15.00
LTCD Chris Drury 6.00 15.00
LTDH Dany Heatley 10.00 25.00
LTDHA Dominik Hasek 12.50 30.00
LTG1 Wayne Gretzky 30.00 80.00
LTGL Guy Lafleur 12.50 30.00
LTIK Ilya Kovalchuk 10.00 25.00
LTJB Jay Bouwmeester 6.00 15.00
LTJBU Johnny Bucyk 6.00 15.00
LTJJ Jaromir Jagr 10.00 25.00
LTJS Jason Spezza 12.50 30.00
LTJSG Jean-Sebastien Giguere 6.00 15.00
LTJT Joe Thornton 12.50 30.00
LTJTH Jocelyn Thibault 6.00 15.00
LTLM Lanny McDonald 6.00 15.00
LTMB Mike Bossy 6.00 15.00
LTMH Gordie Howe 25.00 60.00
LTMHO Marian Hossa 6.00 15.00
LTMM Mike Modano 10.00 25.00
LTMN Markus Naslund 6.00 15.00
LTMS Mats Sundin 8.00 20.00
LTMT Marty Turco 6.00 15.00
LTPD Pavel Datsyuk 15.00 40.00
LTPF Peter Forsberg 15.00 40.00
LTPK Paul Kariya 6.00 15.00
LTPR Patrick Roy 20.00 60.00
LTRL Roberto Luongo 10.00 25.00
LTRN Rick Nash 10.00 25.00
LTSB Scotty Bowman 15.00 40.00
LTSF Sergei Fedorov 10.00 25.00
LTSU Scottie Upshall 6.00 15.00
LTSY Steve Yzerman 12.50 30.00
LTTA Tony Amonte 6.00 15.00
LTTB Todd Bertuzzi 6.00 15.00
LTTS Teemu Selanne 8.00 20.00
LTVL Vincent Lecavalier 8.00 20.00
LTWG Wayne Gretzky 30.00 80.00
LTWGR Wayne Gretzky 30.00 80.00

2003-04 SP Game Used Rookie Exclusives Autographs

RE1 Patrice Bergeron 20.00 50.00
RE2 Dustin Brown 15.00 30.00
RE3 Marc-Andre Fleury 125.00 300.00
RE4 Nathan Horton 15.00 40.00
RE5 Jiri Hudler 10.00 25.00
RE6 Joffrey Lupul 10.00 25.00
RE7 Joni Pitkanen 10.00 25.00
RE8 Tuomo Ruutu 15.00 40.00
RE9 Eric Staal 25.00 60.00
RE10 Jordin Tootoo 15.00 40.00

2003-04 SP Game Used Signers

SPSBO Bobby Orr 60.00 150.00
SPSCJ Curtis Joseph 6.00 15.00
SPSDA David Aebischer 6.00 15.00
SPSEL Eric Lindros 12.50 30.00
SPSGH Gordie Howe 30.00 80.00
SPSHA Marian Hossa 6.00 15.00
SPSHV Martin Havlat 6.00 15.00
SPSHZ Henrik Zetterberg 10.00 25.00
SPSJB Jaromir Jagr SP 25.00 50.00
SPSJI Jarome Iginla 10.00 25.00
SPSJR Jeremy Roenick 8.00 20.00
SPSJS Jason Spezza 8.00 20.00
SPSJT Joe Thornton 10.00 25.00
SPSMG Marian Gaborik 10.00 25.00
SPSMH Marcel Hossa 6.00 15.00
SPSMT Marty Turco 6.00 15.00
SPSPB Pavel Bure 6.00 15.00
SPSPR Patrick Roy SP 60.00 120.00
SPSRB Ray Bourque 15.00 40.00
SPSRL Roberto Luongo 12.50 30.00
SPSRN Rick Nash 12.50 30.00
SPSSF Sergei Fedorov 12.50 30.00
SPSTB Todd Bertuzzi 6.00 15.00
SPSWG Wayne Gretzky SP 150.00 400.00
SSJSG Jean-Sebastien Giguere 6.00 15.00

2005-06 SP Game Used

COMP.SET w/o SP's (100) 25.00 60.00
1 Jean-Sebastien Giguere 1.00 2.50
2 Teemu Selanne 2.00 5.00
3 Scott Niedermayer 1.00 2.50
4 Ilya Kovalchuk 1.00 2.50
5 Kari Lehtonen .75 2.00
6 Marian Hossa 1.00 2.50
7 Peter Bondra 1.00 2.50
8 Glen Murray .75 2.00
9 Brian Leetch .75 2.00
10 Andrew Raycroft .75 2.00
11 Patrice Bergeron 1.25 3.00
12 Chris Drury .75 2.00
13 Martin Biron .75 2.00
14 Maxim Afinogenov .60 1.50
15 Jarome Iginla 1.25 3.00
16 Miikka Kiprusoff 1.00 2.50
17 Tony Amonte .75 2.00
18 Erik Cole .60 1.50
19 Eric Staal 1.25 3.00
20 Nikolai Khabibulin 1.00 2.50
21 Tuomo Ruutu 1.00 2.50
22 Tyler Arnason .60 1.50
23 Joe Sakic 2.00 5.00
24 Milan Hejduk .75 2.00
25 Alex Tanguay .75 2.00
26 David Aebischer .75 2.00
27 Rob Blake 1.00 2.50
28 Rick Nash 1.00 2.50
29 Nikolai Zherdev .60 1.50
30 Sergei Fedorov 1.50 4.00
31 Mike Modano 1.50 4.00
32 Bill Guerin 1.00 2.50
33 Marty Turco 1.00 2.50
34 Brendan Shanahan 1.00 2.50
35 Steve Yzerman 2.50 6.00
36 Pavel Datsyuk 1.50 4.00
37 Henrik Zetterberg 1.25 3.00
38 Manny Legace 1.00 2.50
39 Ryan Smyth .75 2.00
40 Chris Pronger 1.00 2.50
41 Ty Conklin .75 2.00
42 Stephen Weiss .60 1.50
43 Joe Nieuwendyk .75 2.00
44 Roberto Luongo 1.50 4.00
45 Jeremy Roenick 1.50 4.00
46 Luc Robitaille 1.00 2.50
47 Pavol Demitra 1.25 3.00
48 Alexander Frolov .60 1.50
49 Marian Gaborik 1.00 2.50
50 Dwayne Roloson .75 2.00
51 Mike Ribeiro .60 1.50
52 Jose Theodore 1.00 2.50
53 Michael Ryder .75 2.00
54 Saku Koivu 1.00 2.50
55 Paul Kariya 1.00 2.50
56 Steve Sullivan .60 1.50
57 Tomas Vokoun .75 2.00
58 Martin Brodeur 2.50 6.00
59 Patrik Elias 1.00 2.50
60 Scott Gomez .75 2.00
61 Alexander Mogilny .75 2.00
62 Alexei Yashin .75 2.00
63 Miroslav Satan .75 2.00
64 Rick DiPietro .75 2.00
65 Mark Parrish .60 1.50
66 Kevin Weekes .75 2.00
67 Jaromir Jagr 3.00 8.00
68 Dany Heatley .75 2.00
69 Dominik Hasek 1.50 4.00
70 Jason Spezza 1.00 2.50
71 Martin Havlat 1.00 2.50
72 Peter Forsberg 2.00 5.00
73 Keith Primeau .75 2.00
74 Simon Gagne 1.00 2.50
75 Robert Esche .75 2.00
76 Shane Doan .75 2.00
77 Curtis Joseph 1.25 3.00
78 John LeClair 1.00 2.50
79 Mario Lemieux 4.00 10.00
80 Zigmund Palffy 1.00 2.50
81 Joe Thornton 1.50 4.00
82 Jonathan Cheechoo .75 2.00
83 Evgeni Nabokov .75 2.00
84 Patrick Marleau 1.00 2.50
85 Keith Tkachuk 1.00 2.50
86 Doug Weight 1.00 2.50
87 Martin St. Louis 1.00 2.50
88 Vincent Lecavalier 1.00 2.50
89 Brad Richards 1.00 2.50
90 Sean Burke .60 1.50
91 Mats Sundin 1.00 2.50
92 Ed Belfour 1.00 2.50
93 Eric Lindros 1.50 4.00
94 Jason Allison .75 2.00
95 Nik Antropov .75 2.00
96 Markus Naslund 1.00 2.50
97 Brendan Morrison .60 1.50
98 Todd Bertuzzi 1.00 2.50
99 Olaf Kolzig 1.00 2.50
100 Brendan Witt .60 1.50
101 Sidney Crosby RC 125.00 300.00
102 Brandon Bochenski RC 3.00 8.00
103 Rostislav Olesz RC 2.50 6.00
104 Jeff Hoggan RC 2.00 5.00
105 Brett Lebda RC 2.00 5.00
106 Brad Winchester RC 3.00 8.00
107 Wojtek Wolski RC 6.00 15.00
108 Patrick Eaves RC 3.00 8.00
109 Braydon Coburn RC 3.00 8.00
110 Yann Danis RC 2.50 6.00
111 Alexander Ovechkin RC 200.00 500.00
112 Peter Budaj RC 4.00 10.00
113 Jeff Carter RC 5.00 12.00
114 Duncan Keith RC 6.00 15.00
115 Mike Richards RC 8.00 20.00
116 Rene Bourque RC 3.00 8.00
117 Keith Ballard RC 2.50 6.00
118 Thomas Vanek RC 8.00 20.00
119 Robert Nilsson RC 3.00 8.00
120 Kevin Nastiuk RC 2.00 5.00
121 Jaroslav Balastik RC 2.00 5.00
122 Brent Seabrook RC 6.00 15.00
123 Maxime Talbot RC 3.00 8.00
124 Niklas Nordgren RC 3.00 8.00
125 David Leneveu RC 2.50 6.00
126 Eric Nystrom RC 2.50 6.00
127 Timo Helbling RC 2.00 5.00
128 George Parros RC 2.00 5.00
129 Lee Stempniak RC 3.00 8.00
130 Dion Phaneuf RC 10.00 25.00
131 Henrik Lundqvist RC 10.00 25.00
132 Cam Ward RC 5.00 12.00
133 Ryan Hollweg RC 2.00 5.00
134 Corey Perry RC 6.00 15.00
135 Matt Foy RC 2.00 5.00
136 Alexander Steen RC 5.00 12.00
137 Jim Slater RC 2.50 6.00
138 Ryan Suter RC 4.00 10.00
139 Gilbert Brule RC 3.00 8.00
140 Andrej Meszaros RC 3.00 8.00
141 Andrew Alberts RC 2.00 5.00
142 Zach Parise RC 8.00 20.00
143 Kevin Dallman RC 2.50 6.00
144 Chris Campoli RC 2.00 5.00
145 Johan Franzen RC 5.00 12.00
146 Jay McClement RC 2.00 5.00
147 Ryan Getzlaf RC 10.00 25.00
148 Alexander Perezhogin RC 2.50 6.00
149 Andrew Wozniewski RC 2.50 6.00
150 Jim Howard RC 8.00 20.00
151 Jeff Woywitka RC 2.00 5.00
152 Hannu Toivonen RC 3.00 8.00
153 Petteri Nokelainen RC 2.00 5.00
154 Jussi Jokinen RC 3.00 8.00
155 Ryane Clowe RC 4.00 10.00
156 Milan Jurcina RC 2.50 6.00
157 Mark Streit RC 2.00 5.00
158 Raitis Ivanans RC 2.00 5.00
159 Petr Prucha RC 3.00 8.00
160 Josh Gorges RC 2.50 6.00
161 Anthony Stewart RC 2.50 6.00
162 Alvaro Montoya RC 2.50 6.00
163 Paul Ranger RC 2.00 5.00
164 Chris Holt RC 2.00 5.00
165 Wade Skolney RC 2.00 5.00
166 Cam Barker RC 2.50 6.00
167 Adam Berkhoel RC 2.50 6.00
168 Kyle Brodziak RC 2.00 5.00
169 Brian McGrattan RC 2.00 5.00
170 Mikko Koivu RC 4.00 10.00
171 Derek Boogaard RC 5.00 12.00
172 Nick Tarnasky RC 2.00 5.00
173 Evgeny Artyukhin RC 2.50 6.00
174 Colin Hemingway RC 2.00 5.00
175 Michael Wall RC 2.50 6.00
176 Steve Goertzen RC 2.00 5.00
177 Junior Lessard RC 2.00 5.00
178 Vojtech Polak RC 2.00 5.00
179 Jakub Klepis RC 2.00 5.00
180 Jordan Sigalet RC 2.00 5.00
181 Steve Bernier RC 3.00 8.00
182 Dimitri Patzold RC 2.00 5.00
183 R.J. Umberger RC 3.00 8.00
184 Christoph Schubert RC 2.00 5.00
185 Staffan Kronwall RC 2.00 5.00
186 Ryan Whitney RC 3.00 8.00
187 Erik Christensen RC 2.00 5.00
188 Brian Eklund RC 2.50 6.00
189 Rob McVicar RC 2.50 6.00
190 Tomas Fleischmann RC 3.00 8.00
191 Zenon Konopka RC 2.00 5.00
192 Dustin Penner RC 3.00 8.00
193 Ben Walter RC 2.00 5.00
194 Daniel Paille RC 3.00 8.00
195 Chris Thorburn RC 2.50 6.00
196 Richie Regehr RC 2.00 5.00
197 Andrew Ladd RC 4.00 10.00
198 Chad Larose RC 2.00 5.00
199 Danny Richmond RC 2.00 5.00
200 Martin St. Pierre RC 2.00 5.00
201 Corey Crawford RC 10.00 25.00
202 Brad Richardson RC 3.00 8.00
203 Vitaly Kolesnik RC 2.50 6.00
204 Alexandre Picard RC 2.00 5.00
205 Ole-Kristian Tollefsen RC 2.50 6.00
206 Joakim Lindstrom RC 2.00 5.00
207 Kyle Quincey RC 2.50 6.00
208 Valtteri Filppula RC 4.00 10.00
209 Danny Syvret RC 2.00 5.00
210 Matt Greene RC 2.00 5.00
211 J-F Jacques RC 2.00 5.00
212 Greg Jacina RC 2.00 5.00
213 Rob Globke RC 2.00 5.00
214 Yanick Lehoux RC 3.00 8.00
215 Jeff Tambellini RC 2.50 6.00
216 Petr Kanko RC 2.00 5.00
217 Maxim Lapierre RC 3.00 8.00
218 J-P Cote RC 2.00 5.00
219 Andrei Kostitsyn RC 4.00 10.00
220 Kevin Klein RC 2.00 5.00
221 Pekka Rinne RC 8.00 20.00
222 Barry Tallackson RC 2.50 6.00
223 Jason Ryznar RC 2.00 5.00
224 Jeremy Colliton RC 2.00 5.00
225 Bruno Gervais RC 2.00 5.00
226 Stefan Ruzicka RC 2.00 5.00
227 Ben Eager RC 2.50 6.00
228 Alexandre Picard RC 2.00 5.00
229 Matt Jones RC 2.00 5.00
230 Colby Armstrong RC 3.00 8.00
231 Doug Murray RC 2.00 5.00
232 Grant Stevenson RC 2.00 5.00
233 Dennis Wideman RC 2.00 5.00
234 Doug O'Brien RC 2.00 5.00
235 Darren Reid RC 2.00 5.00
236 Ryan Craig RC 2.00 5.00
237 Jay Harrison RC 2.50 6.00
238 Tomas Mojzis RC 2.00 5.00
239 Kevin Bieksa RC 5.00 12.00
240 Mike Green RC 6.00 15.00

2005-06 SP Game Used Gold

*1-100 VETS/100: 1X TO 2.5X BASIC CARDS
*101-190 ROOK/25: 1.2X TO 3X BASIC RC
101 Sidney Crosby 200.00 350.00
111 Alexander Ovechkin 800.00 2000.00

2005-06 SP Game Used Authentic Fabrics

AFAD David Aebischer 3.00 8.00
AFAF Alexander Frolov 2.50 6.00
AFAR Andrew Raycroft 3.00 8.00
AFAT Alex Tanguay 4.00 10.00
AFAY Alexei Yashin 3.00 8.00
AFBE Daniel Briere 4.00 10.00
AFBG Bill Guerin 4.00 10.00
AFBL Rob Blake 4.00 10.00
AFBM Brendan Morrison 2.50 6.00
AFBO Mike Bossy 4.00 10.00
AFBR Martin Brodeur 8.00 20.00
AFBS Brendan Shanahan 4.00 10.00
AFCD Chris Drury 4.00 10.00
AFCJ Curtis Joseph 5.00 12.00
AFCN Cam Neely 5.00 12.00
AFCP Chris Pronger 4.00 10.00
AFDA Daniel Alfredsson 4.00 10.00
AFDB Dustin Brown 4.00 10.00
AFDC Dan Cloutier 3.00 8.00
AFDE Pavol Demitra 5.00 12.00
AFDH Dany Heatley 3.00 8.00
AFDW Doug Weight 4.00 10.00
AFEB Ed Belfour 4.00 10.00
AFGM Glen Murray 3.00 8.00
AFGS Scott Gomez 3.00 8.00
AFHA Dominik Hasek 6.00 15.00
AFHJ Milan Hejduk 3.00 8.00
AFHO Marian Hossa 4.00 10.00
AFHU Trent Hunter 2.50 6.00
AFHV Martin Havlat 4.00 10.00
AFHZ Henrik Zetterberg 5.00 12.00
AFIK Ilya Kovalchuk 4.00 10.00
AFJB Jay Bouwmeester 2.50 6.00
AFJC Jonathan Cheechoo 3.00 8.00
AFJF Jeff Friesen 2.50 6.00
AFJG Jean-Sebastien Giguere 4.00 10.00
AFJI Jarome Iginla 5.00 12.00
AFJJ Jaromir Jagr 12.00 30.00
AFJR Jeremy Roenick 6.00 15.00
AFJS Joe Sakic 8.00 20.00
AFJT Joe Thornton 6.00 15.00
AFKD Kris Draper 5.00 12.00
AFKL Kari Lehtonen 5.00 12.00
AFKP Keith Primeau 3.00 8.00
AFKT Keith Tkachuk 4.00 10.00
AFLE Manny Legace 4.00 10.00
AFMB Martin Biron 3.00 8.00
AFMD Marcel Dionne SP 6.00 15.00
AFMG Marian Gaborik 4.00 10.00
AFMI Mike Ribeiro 2.50 6.00
AFML Mario Lemieux 10.00 25.00
AFMM Mike Modano 6.00 15.00
AFMN Markus Naslund 4.00 10.00
AFMP Mark Parrish 2.50 6.00
AFMR Mark Recchi 5.00 12.00
AFMT Marty Turco 4.00 10.00
AFMW Brenden Morrow 3.00 8.00
AFNH Nathan Horton 4.00 10.00
AFNK Nikolai Khabibulin 4.00 10.00
AFNL Nicklas Lidstrom 4.00 10.00
AFNZ Nikolai Zherdev 2.50 6.00
AFOK Olaf Kolzig 4.00 10.00
AFPB Patrice Bergeron 5.00 12.00
AFPD Pavel Datsyuk 6.00 15.00
AFPE Patrik Elias 3.00 8.00
AFPF Peter Forsberg 8.00 20.00
AFPK Paul Kariya 4.00 10.00
AFPM Patrick Marleau 4.00 10.00
AFPR Patrick Roy 10.00 25.00
AFRB Ray Bourque 6.00 15.00
AFRD Rick DiPietro 3.00 8.00
AFRE Robert Esche 3.00 8.00
AFRI Brad Richards 4.00 10.00
AFRL Roberto Luongo 6.00 15.00
AFRN Rick Nash 4.00 10.00
AFRS Ryan Smyth 3.00 8.00
AFRY Michael Ryder 3.00 8.00
AFSA Miroslav Satan 3.00 8.00
AFSD Shane Doan 3.00 8.00
AFSF Sergei Fedorov 6.00 15.00
AFSG Simon Gagne 4.00 10.00
AFSK Saku Koivu 4.00 10.00
AFSP Jason Spezza 6.00 15.00
AFST Matt Stajan 2.50 6.00
AFSU Mats Sundin 4.00 10.00
AFSW Stephen Weiss 2.50 6.00
AFSY Steve Yzerman 8.00 20.00
AFTB Todd Bertuzzi 4.00 10.00
AFTC Ty Conklin 3.00 8.00
AFTH Jose Theodore 4.00 10.00
AFTP Tom Poti 2.50 6.00
AFTR Tuomo Ruutu 4.00 10.00
AFTV Tomas Vokoun 3.00 8.00
AFVL Vincent Lecavalier 4.00 10.00
AFZC Zdeno Chara 4.00 10.00
AFZP Zigmund Palffy 4.00 10.00

2005-06 SP Game Used Authentic Fabrics Autographs

AAFAE David Aebischer 10.00 25.00
AAFAF Alexander Frolov 8.00 20.00
AAFAR Andrew Raycroft 12.00 30.00
AAFAT Alex Tanguay 12.00 30.00
AAFAY Alexei Yashin 10.00 25.00
AAFBE Daniel Briere 12.00 30.00
AAFBL Rob Blake 12.00 30.00
AAFBM Brendan Morrison 8.00 20.00
AAFBO Mike Bossy 15.00 40.00
AAFCD Chris Drury 12.00 30.00
AAFCN Cam Neely 25.00 50.00
AAFCP Chris Pronger 12.00 30.00
AAFDA Daniel Alfredsson 15.00 40.00
AAFDB Dustin Brown 12.00 30.00
AAFDC Dan Cloutier 10.00 25.00
AAFDH Dany Heatley 15.00 40.00
AAFDW Doug Weight 12.00 30.00
AAFGM Glen Murray 10.00 25.00
AAFHA Dominik Hasek 20.00 50.00
AAFHJ Milan Hejduk 12.00 30.00
AAFHO Marian Hossa 12.00 30.00
AAFHU Trent Hunter 8.00 20.00
AAFHV Martin Havlat 12.00 30.00
AAFHZ Henrik Zetterberg 15.00 40.00
AAFIK Ilya Kovalchuk 15.00 40.00
AAFJB Jay Bouwmeester 8.00 20.00
AAFJC Jonathan Cheechoo 15.00 40.00
AAFJG Jean-Sebastien Giguere 12.00 30.00
AAFJI Jarome Iginla 12.00 30.00
AAFJR Jeremy Roenick 15.00 40.00
AAFJT Joe Thornton 15.00 40.00
AAFKD Kris Draper 10.00 25.00
AAFKL Kari Lehtonen 10.00 25.00
AAFKP Keith Primeau 10.00 25.00
AAFLE Manny Legace 10.00 25.00
AAFMB Martin Biron 10.00 25.00
AAFMD Marcel Dionne 12.00 30.00
AAFMI Mike Ribeiro 8.00 20.00
AAFMN Markus Naslund 12.00 30.00
AAFMP Mark Parrish 8.00 20.00
AAFMS Martin St. Louis 8.00 20.00
AAFMT Marty Turco 12.00 30.00
AAFMW Brenden Morrow 10.00 25.00
AAFNH Nathan Horton 10.00 25.00
AAFNZ Nikolai Zherdev 8.00 20.00
AAFOK Olaf Kolzig 12.00 30.00
AAFPB Patrice Bergeron 15.00 40.00
AAFRE Robert Esche 10.00 25.00
AAFRI Brad Richards 12.00 30.00
AAFRL Roberto Luongo 15.00 40.00
AAFRN Rick Nash 15.00 40.00
AAFRS Ryan Smyth 10.00 25.00
AAFRY Michael Ryder 10.00 25.00
AAFSA Miroslav Satan 10.00 25.00
AAFSD Shane Doan 10.00 25.00
AAFSG Simon Gagne 12.00 30.00
AAFSP Jason Spezza 15.00 40.00
AAFST Matt Stajan 8.00 20.00
AAFSW Stephen Weiss 8.00 20.00
AAFTB Todd Bertuzzi 12.00 30.00
AAFTC Ty Conklin 10.00 25.00
AAFTH Jose Theodore 12.00 30.00
AAFTP Tom Poti 8.00 20.00
AAFTR Tuomo Ruutu 12.00 30.00
AAFVL Vincent Lecavalier 15.00 40.00
AAFWG Wayne Gretzky 200.00 500.00
AAFZC Zdeno Chara 12.00 30.00

2005-06 SP Game Used Authentic Fabrics Dual

AH D.Alfredsson/D.Heatley 6.00 15.00
BB M.Biron/D.Briere 6.00 15.00
BF D.Brown/A.Frolov 6.00 15.00
BM E.Belfour/B.McCabe 6.00 15.00
BN M.Biron/M.Noronen 5.00 12.00
CO P.Roy/R.Bourque 15.00 40.00
DH S.Doan/B.Hull 12.00 30.00
DJ D.Heatley/J.Spezza 6.00 15.00
EB P.Elias/M.Brodeur 15.00 40.00
ER R.Esche/P.Forsberg 12.00 30.00
GH W.Gretzky/G.Howe 25.00 60.00
GK W.Gretzky/J.Kurri 30.00 80.00
GS J.Giguere/T.Selanne 12.00 30.00
HH D.Hasek/M.Havlat 10.00 25.00
HK M.Hossa/I.Kovalchuk 6.00 15.00
HL A.Hall/D.Legwand 5.00 12.00
HS T.Hunter/M.Satan 5.00 12.00
IK J.Iginla/M.Kiprusoff 8.00 20.00
IS J.Iginla/M.St.Louis 8.00 20.00
KK N.Khabibulin/M.Kiprusoff 6.00 15.00
KT S.Koivu/J.Theodore 6.00 15.00
KV P.Kariya/T.Vokoun 6.00 15.00
LN K.Lehtonen/M.Noronen 5.00 12.00
LS V.Lecavalier/M.St. Louis 6.00 15.00
MC P.Marleau/J.Cheechoo 6.00 15.00
MO M.Sundin/O.Nolan 6.00 15.00
MT M.Naslund/T.Bertuzzi 6.00 15.00
NB C.Neely/R.Bourque 10.00 25.00
NT R.Nash/J.Thornton 10.00 25.00
NY B.Trottier/M.Bossy 6.00 15.00
PB J.Thornton/P.Bergeron 10.00 25.00
PC C.Pronger/T.Conklin 6.00 15.00
PE J.Pitkanen/R.Esche 5.00 12.00
PG K.Primeau/S.Gagne 6.00 15.00
RA R.Torres/A.Hemsky 5.00 12.00
RB M.Ribeiro/P.Bergeron 8.00 20.00
RF D.Roloson/M.Fernandez 5.00 12.00
RR M.Ryder/M.Ribeiro 5.00 12.00
SA J.Spezza/D.Alfredsson 6.00 15.00
SB J.Sakic/R.Blake 12.00 30.00
SC R.Smyth/T.Conklin 5.00 12.00
SP D.Sittler/G.Perreault 8.00 20.00
SR P.Sauve/A.Raycroft 5.00 12.00
SS M.Stajan/E.Staal 8.00 20.00
TH A.Tanguay/M.Hejduk 6.00 15.00
TM M.Turco/M.Modano 10.00 25.00
WB P.Worrell/D.Brashear 4.00 10.00
WH S.Weiss/N.Horton 6.00 15.00
WT D.Weight/K.Tkachuk 6.00 15.00
YS S.Yzerman/B.Shanahan 15.00 40.00
ZD H.Zetterberg/K.Draper 8.00 20.00

2005-06 SP Game Used Authentic Fabrics Dual Autographs

BB M.Biron/D.Briere 20.00 50.00
CO P.Roy/R.Bourque 125.00 200.00
DJ D.Heatley/J.Spezza 40.00 100.00
DT M.Dionne/B.Trottier 20.00 50.00
GH W.Gretzky/G.Howe 400.00 1000.00
HH D.Hasek/M.Havlat 30.00 80.00
HK M.Hossa/I.Kovalchuk 25.00 60.00
HS T.Hunter/M.Satan 15.00 40.00
IS J.Iginla/M.St.Louis 20.00 50.00
KT S.Koivu/J.Theodore 30.00 80.00
LD G.Lafleur/M.Dionne 60.00 125.00
LN K.Lehtonen/M.Noronen 20.00 50.00
LS V.Lecavalier/M.St. Louis 40.00 100.00
MO M.Sundin/O.Nolan 30.00 80.00
MT M.Naslund/T.Bertuzzi 20.00 50.00
NB C.Neely/R.Bourque 75.00 150.00
NT R.Nash/J.Thornton 50.00 125.00
PB J.Thornton/P.Bergeron 25.00 60.00
PC C.Pronger/T.Conklin 20.00 50.00
PE J.Pitkanen/R.Esche 15.00 40.00
PG K.Primeau/S.Gagne 15.00 40.00
RB M.Ribeiro/P.Bergeron 15.00 40.00
RR M.Ryder/M.Ribeiro 15.00 40.00
SR P.Sauve/A.Raycroft 15.00 40.00
SS M.Stajan/E.Staal 25.00 60.00
TH A.Tanguay/M.Hejduk 25.00 60.00
TM M.Turco/M.Modano 20.00 50.00
WH S.Weiss/N.Horton 15.00 40.00

2005-06 SP Game Used Authentic Fabrics Gold

*GOLD/100: .8X TO 2X BASIC JSY
AFMD Marcel Dionne 8.00 20.00
AFWG Wayne Gretzky 40.00 100.00

2005-06 SP Game Used Authentic Fabrics Triple

ARS Alfredsson/Richards/St.Louis 40.00 80.00
BBP Bourque/Blake/Pronger 20.00 50.00
BBT Broduer/Belfour/Turco 30.00 80.00
BIS Brodeur/Iginla/St.Louis 60.00 125.00
BTR Brodeur/Theodore/Roy 75.00 150.00
CEA Conklin/Esche/Aebischer 20.00 50.00
CNP Chara/Niedermayer/Pronger 30.00 60.00
CRH Chara/Redden/Hasek 30.00 60.00
DBS Domi/Brashear/Simon 20.00 50.00
DKF Datsyuk/Kovalchuk/Fedorov 40.00 100.00
DLP Draper/Lehtinen/Peca 30.00 60.00
GLY Gretzky/Lemieux/Yzerman 175.00 300.00
GNP Gonchar/Niedermayer/Pronger 20.00 50.00
HJH Hasek/Jagr/Havlat 50.00 100.00
HND Hull/Nagy/Doan 20.00 50.00
INK Iginla/Nash/Kovalchuk 40.00 80.00
ISL Iginla/Shanahan/Linden 40.00 80.00
KNS Kovalchuk/Naslund/Stillman 20.00 50.00
KRT Kiprusoff/Roloson/Turco 40.00 80.00
KSK Kurri/Selanne/Koivu 60.00 125.00
MLR Modano/Linden/Roenick 30.00 80.00
NKL Noronen/Kiprusoff/Lehtonen 40.00 80.00
NPJ Nolan/Primeau/Jagr 30.00 60.00
NSL Nolan/Sundin/Lindros 25.00 60.00
PCS Pronger/Conklin/Smyth 20.00 50.00
RLA Raycroft/Lehtonen/Aebischer 30.00 60.00
SEL Sakic/Elias/Lang 25.00 60.00
SFI St.Louis/Forsberg/Iginla 30.00 80.00
SFN Sundin/Forsberg/Naslund 25.00 60.00
SHA St. Louis/Hossa/Alfredsson 20.00 50.00
SNI St.Louis/Naslund/Iginla 40.00 80.00
TBM Thornton/Bergeron/Murray 30.00 60.00
TSY Thornton/Sakic/Yzerman 50.00 100.00
VKL Vokoun/Kariya/Legwand 20.00 50.00
YSP Yashin/Satan/Parrish 30.00 60.00

2005-06 SP Game Used Authentic Fabrics Patches

*PATCH/75: 1.2X TO 3X BASIC JSY
APMD Marcel Dionne 12.00 30.00
APWG Wayne Gretzky 50.00 120.00

2005-06 SP Game Used Authentic Fabrics Autographs Patch

*PATCH/50: .6X TO 1.5X FABRIC AU/75
AAPWG Wayne Gretzky 250.00 600.00

2005-06 SP Game Used Authentic Fabrics Dual Patches

*DUAL PATCH/35: .8X TO 2X DUAL JSY
GH W.Gretzky/G.Howe 150.00 300.00
GK W.Gretzky/J.Kurri 100.00 250.00
GL W.Gretzky/M.Lemieux 150.00 300.00
LD Guy Lafleur/Marcel Dionne 20.00 50.00

2005-06 SP Game Used Auto Draft

ADAF Alexander Frolov/20 12.00 30.00
ADAL Daniel Alfredsson/133 8.00 20.00
ADAM Alvaro Montoya/29 25.00 60.00
ADAP A. Perezhogin/25 15.00 40.00
ADAS Alexander Steen/24 30.00 60.00
ADBR Brad Richards/64 10.00 25.00
ADBU Peter Budaj/63 15.00 40.00
ADBW Brad Winchester/35 12.00 30.00
ADBY Matthew Barnaby/83 6.00 15.00
ADCA Michael Cammalleri/49 12.00 30.00
ADCC Craig Conroy/123 5.00 12.00
ADCD Chris Drury/72 8.00 20.00
ADCP Corey Perry/28 25.00 60.00
ADCW Cam Ward/25 30.00 75.00
ADDA David Aebischer/161 6.00 15.00
ADDB Daniel Briere/24 15.00 40.00
ADDC Dan Cloutier/26 12.00 30.00
ADDF Dan Fristche/46 8.00 20.00
ADDK Duncan Keith/54 25.00 60.00
ADDL David Leneveu/46 10.00 25.00
ADDM Darren McCarty/46 8.00 20.00
ADEC Erik Cole/71 6.00 15.00
ADED Eric Daze/90 8.00 20.00
ADFT Fedor Tyutin/40 8.00 20.00
ADGL Georges Laraque/31 15.00 40.00
ADHE Jochen Hecht/49 8.00 20.00
ADHT Hannu Toivonen/29 20.00 50.00
ADHV Martin Havlat/26 25.00 60.00
ADJC Jonathan Cheechoo/29 25.00 60.00
ADJF Johan Franzen/97 15.00 40.00
ADJH Jim Howard/64 15.00 40.00
ADJJ Jussi Jokinen/192 8.00 20.00
ADJK Jari Kurri/69 15.00 40.00
ADJS Jim Slater/30 10.00 25.00
ADJT Jose Theodore/44 15.00 40.00
ADJV Josef Vasicek/91 6.00 15.00
ADJW Justin Williams/28 12.00 30.00
ADKD Kris Draper/62 12.00 30.00
ADKH Kristian Huselius/47 8.00 20.00
ADKW Kevin Weekes/41 10.00 25.00
ADLR Luc Robitaille/171 50.00 100.00
ADMA Maxim Afinogenov/69 6.00 15.00
ADMB Martin Brodeur/20 60.00 150.00
ADMC Jay McClement/57 6.00 15.00
ADMF Matt Foy/175 5.00 12.00
ADMH Milan Hejduk/87 8.00 20.00
ADMI Milan Bartovic/35 8.00 20.00
ADMJ Milan Jurcina/241 6.00 15.00
ADMN Markus Naslund/16 15.00 40.00
ADMR Mike Ribeiro/45 8.00 20.00
ADMS Matt Stajan/57 6.00 15.00
ADMW Brenden Morrow/25 12.00 30.00
ADNK Nikolai Khabibulin/204 8.00 20.00
ADNY Michael Nylander/59 6.00 15.00
ADPB Patrice Bergeron/45 30.00 60.00
ADPE Patrick Eaves/29 15.00 40.00
ADPR Patrick Roy/51 75.00 150.00
ADPS Philippe Sauve/38 10.00 25.00
ADRB Rob Blake/70 10.00 25.00
ADRE Robert Esche/139 6.00 15.00
ADRG Ryan Getzlaf/19 60.00 150.00
ADRI Mike Richards/24 50.00 100.00
ADRK Ryan Kesler/23 15.00 40.00
ADSB Sean Burke/24 10.00 25.00
ADSG Simon Gagne/22 30.00 60.00
ADSH Sheldon Souray/71 6.00 15.00
ADSK Saku Koivu/21 30.00 60.00
ADSS Steve Sullivan/233 5.00 12.00
ADSV Marc Savard/91 6.00 15.00
ADSZ Sergei Zubov/85 8.00 20.00
ADTA Tyler Arnason/183 5.00 12.00
ADTB Todd Bertuzzi/23 15.00 40.00
ADTG Tim Gleason/23 10.00 25.00
ADTH Trent Hunter/150 5.00 12.00
ADTP Tom Poti/59 6.00 15.00
ADTS Timofei Shishkanov/33 8.00 20.00
ADVP Vaclav Prospal/71 6.00 15.00
ADZC Zdeno Chara/56 10.00 25.00

2005-06 SP Game Used Awesome Authentics

*GOLD/25: .6X TO 1.5X BASIC JSY/75-100
AAAH Ales Hemsky 10.00 25.00
AAAR Andrew Raycroft 10.00 25.00
AAAT Alex Tanguay 12.00 30.00
AAAY Alexei Yashin 10.00 25.00
AABG Bill Guerin 12.00 30.00
AABI Martin Biron 10.00 25.00
AABM Bryan McCabe 8.00 20.00
AABR Brad Richards 12.00 30.00
AABS Brendan Shanahan 12.00 30.00
AACD Chris Drury 10.00 25.00
AACJ Curtis Joseph 15.00 40.00
AACP Chris Pronger 12.00 30.00
AADA Daniel Alfredsson 12.00 30.00
AADB Daniel Briere 12.00 30.00
AADC Dan Cloutier 10.00 25.00
AADH Dany Heatley 12.00 30.00
AADL David Legwand 10.00 25.00
AADU Dustin Brown 12.00 30.00
AADW Doug Weight 12.00 30.00
AAEB Ed Belfour 12.00 30.00
AAEL Eric Lindros 20.00 50.00
AAES Eric Staal 15.00 40.00
AAGM Glen Murray 10.00 25.00
AAHJ Milan Hejduk 10.00 25.00
AAHK Dominik Hasek/75 15.00 40.00
AAHV Martin Havlat 12.00 30.00
AAHZ Henrik Zetterberg 15.00 40.00
AAIK Ilya Kovalchuk 10.00 25.00
AAJB Jay Bouwmeester 8.00 20.00
AAJG Jean-Sebastien Giguere 12.00 30.00

AAJI Jarome Iginla 10.00 25.00
AAJJ Jaromir Jagr 15.00 40.00
AAJL John LeClair 12.00 30.00
AAJO Joe Thornton 12.00 30.00
AAJR Jeremy Roenick 10.00 25.00
AAJS Jason Spezza 10.00 25.00
AAJT Jocelyn Thibault 10.00 25.00
AAJW Justin Williams 10.00 25.00
AAKP Keith Primeau 10.00 25.00
AAKT Keith Tkachuk 12.00 30.00
AALN Ladislav Nagy 8.00 20.00
AALU Joffrey Lupul 8.00 20.00
AALX Mario Lemieux 25.00 60.00
AAMB Martin Brodeur 25.00 60.00
AAMF Manny Fernandez 8.00 20.00
AAMG Marian Gaborik 12.00 30.00
AAMK Miikka Kiprusoff 12.00 30.00
AAML Manny Legace 12.00 30.00
AAMM Mike Modano 10.00 25.00
AAMN Markus Naslund 12.00 30.00
AAMO Brendan Morrison 8.00 20.00
AAMP Mark Parrish 8.00 20.00
AAMS Matt Stajan 8.00 20.00
AAMT Marty Turco 12.00 30.00
AAMW Brenden Morrow 10.00 25.00
AANH Nathan Horton 12.00 30.00
AANK Nikolai Khabibulin 12.00 30.00
AANL Nicklas Lidstrom 12.00 30.00
AANZ Nikolai Zherdev 8.00 20.00
AAOK Olaf Kolzig 12.00 30.00
AAPB Patrice Bergeron 15.00 40.00
AAPE Patrik Elias 12.00 30.00
AAPF Peter Forsberg 12.00 30.00
AAPK Paul Kariya 12.00 30.00
AARA Brian Rafalski 10.00 25.00
AARB Rob Blake 12.00 30.00
AARD Rick DiPietro 10.00 25.00
AARE Mark Recchi 15.00 40.00
AARF Ruslan Fedotenko 8.00 20.00
AARL Roberto Luongo 12.00 30.00
AARN Rick Nash 10.00 25.00
AARO Robert Esche 10.00 25.00
AARS Ryan Smyth 10.00 25.00
AARY Michael Ryder 10.00 25.00
AARZ Richard Zednik 8.00 20.00
AASA Joe Sakic 12.00 30.00
AASD Shane Doan 10.00 25.00
AASF Sergei Fedorov/75 20.00 50.00
AASG Simon Gagne 12.00 30.00
AASK Saku Koivu 12.00 30.00
AASL Martin St. Louis 12.00 30.00
AASU Mats Sundin 12.00 30.00
AASY Steve Yzerman 25.00 60.00
AATC Ty Conklin 10.00 25.00
AATH Jose Theodore 10.00 25.00
AATR Tuomo Ruutu 12.00 30.00
AATS Teemu Selanne 25.00 60.00
AATV Tomas Vokoun 10.00 25.00
AAVL Vincent Lecavalier 12.00 30.00
AAWR Wade Redden 8.00 20.00
AAZP Zigmund Palffy 12.00 30.00

2005-06 SP Game Used Game Gear

GGAF Maxim Afinogenov 5.00 12.00
GGAK Alexei Kovalev 6.00 15.00
GGAM Alexander Mogilny 6.00 15.00
GGAO Alexander Ovechkin 125.00 300.00
GGAP Alexander Perezhogin 6.00 15.00
GGAR Andrew Raycroft 6.00 15.00
GGAS Alexander Steen 12.00 30.00
GGAT Alex Tanguay/45 10.00 25.00
GGBA Rod Brind'Amour 8.00 20.00
GGBE Patrice Bergeron 10.00 25.00
GGBG Bill Guerin 8.00 20.00
GGBL Rob Blake 8.00 20.00
GGBO Ray Bourque 12.00 30.00
GGBR Martin Brodeur 12.00 30.00
GGBS Billy Smith 5.00 12.00
GGBT Bryan Trottier 5.00 12.00
GGCB Cam Barker 6.00 15.00
GGCD Chris Drury 6.00 15.00
GGCE Christian Ehrhoff 5.00 12.00
GGCH Jonathan Cheechoo 6.00 15.00
GGCN Cam Neely 8.00 20.00
GGCP Chris Pronger 8.00 20.00
GGDB Daniel Briere 8.00 20.00
GGDH Dany Heatley 6.00 15.00
GGDL David Legwand 6.00 15.00
GGDP Dion Phaneuf 12.00 30.00
GGEN Eric Nystrom 6.00 15.00
GGES Eric Staal 10.00 25.00
GGGB Gilbert Brule 8.00 20.00
GGGL Guy Lafleur 10.00 25.00
GGHA Dominik Hasek 12.00 30.00
GGHL Henrik Lundqvist 30.00 80.00
GGHT Hannu Toivonen 6.00 15.00
GGHZ Henrik Zetterberg 10.00 25.00
GGIK Ilya Kovalchuk 8.00 20.00
GGJB Jean Beliveau 10.00 25.00
GGJC Jeff Carter 6.00 15.00
GGJF Jeff Friesen 5.00 12.00
GGJG Jean-Sebastien Giguere 8.00 20.00
GGJH Jim Howard 8.00 20.00
GGJI Jarome Iginla 10.00 25.00
GGJJ Jaromir Jagr 25.00 60.00
GGJO Joe Thornton 12.00 30.00
GGJP Joni Pitkanen 5.00 12.00
GGJR Jeremy Roenick 12.00 30.00
GGJS Jason Spezza 8.00 20.00
GGKP Keith Primeau 6.00 15.00
GGKT Keith Tkachuk 8.00 20.00
GGMA Paul Martin 5.00 12.00
GGMB Mike Bossy 8.00 20.00
GGML Mario Lemieux 12.00 30.00
GGMM Mike Modano 12.00 30.00
GGMR Mike Ribeiro 5.00 12.00
GGMT Marty Turco 8.00 20.00
GGOK Olaf Kolzig 8.00 20.00
GGOR Brooks Orpik 5.00 12.00
GGPB Peter Bondra 8.00 20.00
GGPE Corey Perry 6.00 15.00
GGPF Peter Forsberg 10.00 25.00
GGPK Paul Kariya 8.00 20.00
GGPM Pierre-Marc Bouchard 8.00 20.00
GGPS Philippe Sauve 6.00 15.00
GGRB Ray Bourque 12.00 30.00
GGRF Ruslan Fedotenko 5.00 12.00
GGRG Ryan Getzlaf 10.00 25.00
GGRI Mike Richards 6.00 15.00
GGRK Rostislav Klesla 5.00 12.00
GGRM Ryan Malone 5.00 12.00
GGRN Rick Nash 8.00 20.00
GGRT Raffi Torres 5.00 12.00
GGRY Michael Ryder 6.00 15.00
GGSA Joe Sakic 15.00 40.00
GGSC Sidney Crosby 50.00 125.00
GGSG Simon Gagne 8.00 20.00
GGSH Brendan Shanahan 8.00 20.00
GGSK Saku Koivu 8.00 20.00
GGST Anthony Stewart 6.00 15.00
GGSU Mats Sundin 8.00 20.00
GGSY Steve Yzerman 15.00 40.00
GGTH Trent Hunter 5.00 12.00
GGTV Thomas Vanek 8.00 20.00
GGWW Wojtek Wolski 8.00 20.00
GGYD Yann Danis 6.00 15.00
GGZP Zach Parise 10.00 25.00
GGBH2 Bobby Hull 12.00 30.00
GGGH1 Gordie Howe 12.00 30.00
GGGH2 Gordie Howe 12.00 30.00
GGPR1 Patrick Roy 15.00 40.00
GGPR2 Patrick Roy 20.00 50.00

2005-06 SP Game Used Heritage Classic Jerseys

*PATCH/25: .8X TO 2X BASIC JSY/100
HCBR Bill Ranford 8.00 20.00
HCBS Borje Salming 8.00 20.00
HCDG Doug Gilmour 10.00 25.00
HCDS Darryl Sittler 10.00 25.00
HCDW Tiger Williams 5.00 12.00
HCGF Grant Fuhr 12.00 30.00
HCKM Kirk Muller 5.00 12.00
HCLM Larry Murphy 6.00 15.00
HCMC Lanny McDonald 8.00 20.00
HCMK Mike Krushelnyski 5.00 12.00
HCPS Peter Stastny 6.00 15.00
HCRB Ray Bourque 10.00 20.00
HCRE Ron Ellis 5.00 12.00
HCRL Rod Langway 6.00 15.00
HCRV Rick Vaive 5.00 12.00
HCSS Steve Shutt 8.00 20.00
HCWC Wendel Clark 12.00 30.00

2005-06 SP Game Used Heritage Classic Jerseys Autographs

HCABR Bill Ranford 12.00 30.00
HCABS Borje Salming 12.00 30.00
HCADG Doug Gilmour 20.00 50.00
HCADS Darryl Sittler 15.00 40.00
HCADW Tiger Williams 8.00 20.00
HCAGF Grant Fuhr 15.00 40.00
HCAKM Kirk Muller 8.00 20.00
HCALM Larry Murphy 10.00 25.00
HCAMC Lanny McDonald 15.00 40.00
HCAMK Mike Krushelnyski 8.00 20.00
HCAPS Peter Stastny 10.00 25.00
HCARB Ray Bourque 20.00 50.00
HCARE Ron Ellis 10.00 25.00
HCARL Rod Langway 10.00 25.00
HCARV Rick Vaive 10.00 25.00
HCASS Steve Shutt 10.00 25.00
HCAWC Wendel Clark 20.00 50.00

2005-06 SP Game Used Oldtimer's Challenge Jerseys

*PATCH/25: .8X TO 2X BASIC JSY/100
OCBB Bob Bourne 4.00 10.00
OCBO Ray Bourque 10.00 25.00
OCBP Bob Probert 5.00 12.00
OCDB Doug Bodger 4.00 10.00
OCDG Doug Gilmour 10.00 25.00
OCDS Darryl Sittler 6.00 15.00
OCDW Tiger Williams 4.00 10.00
OCGA Glenn Anderson 4.00 10.00
OCGF Grant Fuhr 6.00 15.00
OCGL Guy Lafleur 5.00 12.00
OCGP Gilbert Perreault 4.00 10.00
OCKM Kirk Muller 4.00 10.00
OCMC Lanny McDonald 6.00 15.00
OCRB Richard Brodeur 4.00 10.00
OCSS Steve Shutt 4.00 10.00

2005-06 SP Game Used Oldtimer's Challenge Jerseys Autographs

OCABB Bob Bourne 10.00 25.00
OCABO Ray Bourque 20.00 50.00
OCABP Bob Probert 12.00 30.00
OCADB Doug Bodger 10.00 25.00
OCADG Doug Gilmour 20.00 50.00
OCADS Darryl Sittler 15.00 40.00
OCADW Tiger Williams 10.00 25.00
OCAGA Glenn Anderson 10.00 25.00
OCAGF Grant Fuhr 15.00 40.00
OCAGL Guy Lafleur 20.00 50.00
OCAGP Gilbert Perreault 10.00 25.00
OCAKM Kirk Muller 10.00 25.00
OCAMC Lanny McDonald 15.00 40.00
OCARB Richard Brodeur 10.00 25.00
OCASS Steve Shutt 10.00 25.00

2005-06 SP Game Used Rookie Exclusive Autographs

REAA Andrew Alberts 4.00 10.00
REAL Al Montoya 6.00 15.00
REAM Andrej Meszaros 5.00 12.00
REAO Alexander Ovechkin 1250.00 3000.00
REAP Alexander Perezhogin 5.00 12.00
REAS Alexander Steen 10.00 25.00
REAW Andrew Wozniewski 5.00 12.00
REBB Brandon Bochenski 6.00 15.00
REBC Braydon Coburn 6.00 15.00
REBL Brett Lebda 4.00 10.00
REBS Brent Seabrook 12.00 30.00
REBW Brad Winchester 6.00 15.00
RECB Cam Barker ERR 5.00 12.00
RECC Chris Campoli 4.00 10.00
RECP Corey Perry 15.00 40.00
RECW Cam Ward 20.00 50.00
REDK Duncan Keith 30.00 80.00
REDL David Leneveu 5.00 12.00
REDP Dion Phaneuf 12.50 30.00
REEN Eric Nystrom 5.00 12.00
REGB Gilbert Brule 6.00 15.00
REGP George Parros 4.00 10.00
REHL Henrik Lundqvist 25.00 60.00
REHT Hannu Toivonen 6.00 15.00
REJB Jaroslav Balastik 4.00 10.00
REJC Jeff Carter 8.00 20.00
REJF Johan Franzen 20.00 40.00
REJG Josh Gorges 5.00 12.00
REJH Jim Howard 15.00 40.00
REJJ Jussi Jokinen 6.00 15.00
REJM Jay McClement 4.00 10.00
REJS Jim Slater 5.00 12.00
REJW Jeff Woywitka 4.00 10.00
REKB Keith Ballard 5.00 12.00
REKD Kevin Dallman 5.00 12.00
REKN Kevin Nastiuk 4.00 10.00
RELS Lee Stempniak 6.00 15.00
REMF Matt Foy 4.00 10.00
REMJ Milan Jurcina 5.00 12.00
REMR Mike Richards 15.00 40.00
REMT Maxime Talbot 6.00 15.00
RENN Niklas Nordgren 6.00 15.00
REPB Peter Budaj 8.00 20.00
REPE Patrick Eaves 6.00 15.00
REPN Petteri Nokelainen 4.00 10.00
REPP Petr Prucha 6.00 15.00
RERB Rene Bourque 6.00 15.00
RERC Ryane Clowe 8.00 20.00
RERG Ryan Getzlaf 25.00 60.00
RERH Ryan Hollweg 4.00 10.00
RERI Raitis Ivanans 4.00 10.00
RERN Robert Nilsson 6.00 15.00
RERO Rostislav Olesz 5.00 12.00
RERS Ryan Suter 8.00 20.00
RESC Sidney Crosby 175.00 300.00
REST Anthony Stewart 5.00 12.00
RETV Thomas Vanek 20.00 50.00
REWW Wojtek Wolski 15.00 40.00
REYD Yann Danis 5.00 12.00
REZP Zach Parise 15.00 40.00

2005-06 SP Game Used SIGnificance

SAF Alexander Frolov 5.00 12.00
SAL Daniel Alfredsson 8.00 20.00
SAY Alexei Yashin 6.00 15.00
SBM Brendan Morrison 5.00 12.00
SBR Brad Richards 8.00 20.00
SCD Chris Drury 6.00 15.00
SCO Chris Osgood 8.00 20.00
SCP Chris Pronger 8.00 20.00
SCS Cory Stillman 6.00 15.00
SDA David Aebischer 6.00 15.00
SDB Dustin Brown 8.00 20.00
SDC Dan Cloutier 6.00 15.00
SDH Dany Heatley 6.00 15.00
SDL David Legwand 6.00 15.00
SDM Darren McCarty 5.00 12.00
SDR Dwayne Roloson 6.00 15.00
SEC Erik Cole 5.00 12.00
SED Eric Daze 6.00 15.00
SEJ Ed Jovanovski 6.00 15.00
SEN Evgeni Nabokov 6.00 15.00
SES Eric Staal 10.00 25.00
GH Gordie Howe 40.00 80.00
SGM Glen Murray 6.00 15.00
SHO Marian Hossa 8.00 20.00
SHZ Henrik Zetterberg 10.00 25.00
SIK Ilya Kovalchuk 15.00 40.00
SJA Jason Arnott 6.00 15.00
SJB Jay Bouwmeester 5.00 12.00
SJC Jonathan Cheechoo 6.00 15.00
SJI Jarome Iginla 10.00 25.00
SJL Joffrey Lupul 5.00 12.00
SJN Jocelyn Thibault 6.00 15.00
SJO Jeff O'Neill 5.00 12.00
SJP Joni Pitkanen 5.00 12.00
SJR Jeremy Roenick 12.00 30.00
SJS Jason Spezza 12.00 30.00
SJT Joe Thornton 15.00 40.00
SKD Kris Draper 10.00 25.00
SKP Keith Primeau 6.00 15.00
SMB Martin Brodeur 30.00 80.00
SMC Mike Cammalleri 8.00 20.00
SMH Martin Havlat 8.00 20.00
SML Manny Legace 8.00 20.00
SMN Markus Naslund 8.00 20.00
SMP Mark Parrish 5.00 12.00
SMR Michael Ryder 6.00 15.00
SMS Miroslav Satan 6.00 15.00
SMT Marty Turco 8.00 20.00
SMW Brenden Morrow 6.00 15.00
SNY Michael Nylander 5.00 12.00
SNZ Nikolai Zherdev 5.00 12.00
SOK Olaf Kolzig 8.00 20.00
SPB Patrice Bergeron 10.00 25.00
SPM Pierre-Marc Bouchard 8.00 20.00
SPR Patrick Roy 50.00 100.00
SPS Philippe Sauve 6.00 15.00
SRA Brian Rafalski 6.00 15.00
SRB Rob Blake 8.00 20.00
SRE Robert Esche 6.00 15.00
SRF Ruslan Fedotenko 5.00 12.00
SRL Roberto Luongo 12.00 30.00
SRM Ryan Miller 8.00 20.00
SRN Rick Nash 8.00 20.00
SRO Rob Niedermayer 6.00 15.00
SRS Ryan Smyth 6.00 15.00
SSB Sean Burke 5.00 12.00
SSD Shane Doan 6.00 15.00
SSL Martin St. Louis 8.00 20.00
SSN Scott Niedermayer 8.00 20.00
SSS Sheldon Souray 5.00 12.00
SSU Mats Sundin 8.00 20.00
SSW Stephen Weiss 5.00 12.00
SSZ Sergei Zubov 6.00 15.00
STA Tyler Arnason 5.00 12.00
STH Trent Hunter 5.00 12.00
STL Trevor Linden 8.00 20.00
SVL Vincent Lecavalier 8.00 20.00
SVP Vaclav Prospal 5.00 12.00
SZC Zdeno Chara 8.00 20.00

2005-06 SP Game Used SIGnificance Gold

*GOLD/25: .6X TO 1.5X BASIC AUTO
SGH Gordie Howe 75.00 175.00
SMB Martin Brodeur 75.00 150.00
SPR Patrick Roy 75.00 150.00

2005-06 SP Game Used SIGnificance Extra

BL M.Brodeur/R.Luongo 50.00 120.00
CR J.Cheechoo/M.Ryder 20.00 50.00
FB A.Frolov/D.Brown 12.50 30.00
GH G.Howe/W.Gretzky 400.00 1000.00
HH D.Heatley/M.Havlat 25.00 60.00
HK M.Hossa/I.Kovalchuk 25.00 60.00
IH J.Iginla/M.Hejduk 20.00 50.00
MS R.Miller/P.Sauve 15.00 40.00
MT B.Morrow/M.Turco 12.50 30.00
NM M.Naslund/B.Morrison 15.00 40.00
PE K.Primeau/R.Esche 12.50 30.00
RR M.Ryder/M.Ribeiro 12.00 30.00
SA M.Sundin/N.Antropov 15.00 40.00
SC R.Smyth/T.Conklin 12.00 30.00
SF M.St. Louis/R.Fedotenko 12.00 30.00
TA M.Turco/D.Aebischer 12.00 30.00
TB J.Thornton/P.Bergeron 25.00 50.00
WH S.Weiss/N.Horton 20.00 50.00
ZN N.Zherdev/R.Nash 20.00 50.00

2005-06 SP Game Used Significant Numbers

SNAF Alexander Frolov/24 10.00 25.00
SNAM Alvaro Montoya/29 15.00 40.00
SNAP A. Perezhogin/42 8.00 20.00
SNAY Alexei Yashin/79 10.00 25.00
SNBR Brian Rafalski/28 15.00 40.00
SNBU Peter Budaj/31 30.00 60.00
SNCB Cam Barker/25 ERR 25.00 60.00
SNCO Corey Perry/61 20.00 50.00
SNCP Chris Pronger/44 10.00 25.00
SNCW Cam Ward/30 25.00 60.00
SNDC Dan Cloutier/39 12.00 30.00
SNDL David Leneveu/30 15.00 40.00
SNDW Doug Weight/39 10.00 25.00
SNEA Patrick Eaves/44 8.00 20.00
SNEB Ed Belfour/20 40.00 100.00
SNED Eric Daze/55 8.00 20.00
SNEJ Ed Jovanovski/55 8.00 20.00
SNEN Eric Nystrom/23 15.00 40.00
SNGM Glen Murray/27 20.00 50.00
SNGP George Parros/57 8.00 20.00
SNHK Dominik Hasek/39 25.00 60.00
SNHL Henrik Lundqvist/30 50.00 120.00
SNHT Hannu Toivonen/33 12.00 30.00
SNHZ Henrik Zetterberg/40 15.00 40.00
SNJF Johan Franzen/39 12.00 30.00
SNJH Jim Howard/35 25.00 60.00
SNJJ Jussi Jokinen/36 10.00 25.00
SNJP Joni Pitkanen/44 8.00 20.00
SNJR Jeremy Roenick/97 12.00 30.00
SNJT Jose Theodore/61 15.00 40.00
SNJW Jeff Woywitka/29 12.00 30.00
SNKD Kris Draper/33 10.00 25.00
SNKL Kari Lehtonen/32 15.00 40.00
SNKP Keith Primeau/25 10.00 25.00
SNLR Luc Robitaille/20 15.00 40.00
SNMB Martin Brodeur/30 75.00 150.00
SNMH Milan Hejduk/23 10.00 25.00
SNMJ Milan Jurcina/62 8.00 20.00
SNMP Michael Peca/37 10.00 25.00
SNMS Miroslav Satan/81 8.00 20.00
SNMT Marty Turco/35 15.00 40.00
SNNA Nik Antropov/80 8.00 20.00
SNNI Robert Nilsson/21 12.00 30.00
SNNK Nikolai Khabibulin/53 15.00 40.00
SNON Jeff O'Neill/92 8.00 20.00
SNPB Patrice Bergeron/37 20.00 50.00
SNPE Phil Esposito/77 25.00 60.00
SNPM P-M Bouchard/96 8.00 20.00
SNPR Patrick Roy/33 75.00 150.00
SNRB Ray Bourque/77 25.00 60.00
SNRG Ryan Getzlaf/51 15.00 40.00
SNRN Rick Nash/61 20.00 50.00
SNRO Rostislav Olesz/85 6.00 15.00
SNRS Ryan Smyth/94 8.00 20.00
SNRY Michael Ryder/73 10.00 25.00
SNSC Sidney Crosby/87 200.00 350.00
SNSL Martin St. Louis/26 15.00 40.00
SNSM Ryan Suter/20 15.00 40.00
SNSN Scott Niedermayer/27 12.00 30.00
SNST Anthony Stewart/57 8.00 20.00
SNTB Todd Bertuzzi/44 15.00 40.00
SNTV Thomas Vanek/26 30.00 80.00
SNYD Yann Danis/75 8.00 20.00

2005-06 SP Game Used Statscriptions

STAF Alexander Frolov/79 10.00 25.00
STAH Ales Hemsky/64 10.00 25.00
STAR Andrew Raycroft/29 15.00 40.00
STAY Alexei Yashin/44 8.00 20.00
STBA Matthew Barnaby/43 8.00 20.00
STBG Bernie Geoffrion/50 30.00 80.00
STBH Bobby Hull/58 20.00 50.00
STBM Bryan McCabe/63 8.00 20.00
STBP Brad Park/57 6.00 15.00
STBR Brendan Morrison/71 6.00 15.00
STBT Bryan Trottier/50 8.00 20.00
STCB Christian Backman/18 10.00 25.00
STCC Craig Conroy/69 5.00 12.00
STCD Chris Drury/50 8.00 20.00
STCO Chris Osgood/45 8.00 20.00
STDA Daniel Alfredsson/37 15.00 40.00
STDB Dustin Brown/31 8.00 20.00
STDC Dan Cloutier/33 8.00 20.00
STDH Dany Heatley/41 15.00 40.00
STDL David Legwand/48 8.00 20.00
STDT Dave Taylor/47 6.00 15.00
STDW Doug Weight/79 10.00 25.00
STED Eric Daze/38 8.00 20.00
STES Eric Staal/81 12.00 30.00
STFT Fedor Tyutin/25 8.00 20.00
STGL Guy Lafleur/60 12.00 30.00
STGM Glen Murray/44 8.00 20.00
STHO Marcel Hossa/59 8.00 20.00
STHV Martin Havlat/31 15.00 40.00
STHZ Henrik Zetterberg/44 20.00 50.00
STIL Ian Laperriere/78 8.00 20.00
STJA Jason Arnott/68 6.00 15.00
STJB Jay Bouwmeester/82 6.00 15.00
STJC Jonathan Cheechoo/63 12.00 30.00
STJH Jochen Hecht/52 8.00 20.00
STJI Jarome Iginla/52 20.00 50.00
STJL Jamie Lundmark/29 8.00 20.00
STJM John-Michael Liles/79 5.00 12.00
STJO Jeff O'Neill/41 8.00 20.00
STJP Joni Pitkanen/71 6.00 15.00
STJS Jason Spezza/55 15.00 40.00
STJT Jocelyn Thibault/36 10.00 25.00
STJV Josef Vasicek/45 10.00 25.00
STKD Kris Draper/40 8.00 20.00
STKH Kristian Huselius/45 6.00 15.00
STKL Kari Lehtonen/30 20.00 50.00
STKP Keith Primeau/57 6.00 15.00
STKT Kimmo Timonen/55 6.00 15.00
STKW Kevin Weekes/66 6.00 15.00
STLM Larry Murphy/63 6.00 15.00
STLU Joffrey Lupul/34 10.00 25.00
STLU Roberto Luongo/25 20.00 50.00
STMA Marc-Andre Fleury/46 30.00 60.00
STMB Mike Bossy/69 10.00 25.00
STMD Marcel Dionne/59 12.00 30.00
STMG Martin Gerber/54 8.00 20.00
STMN Michael Nylander/64 8.00 20.00
STMR Mike Ribeiro/65 6.00 15.00
STMS Matt Stajan/27 12.00 30.00
STMT Marty Turco/37 12.00 30.00
STMW Brenden Morrow/48 6.00 15.00
STNA Nik Antropov/45 6.00 15.00
STNH Nathan Horton/55 6.00 15.00
STNZ Nikolai Zherdev/34 10.00 25.00
STOK Olaf Kolzig/41 20.00 50.00
STPB Patrice Bergeron/39 20.00 40.00
STPC Grant Fuhr/40 25.00 60.00
STPL Pascal Leclaire/62 8.00 20.00
STPM Pierre-Marc Bouchard/42 8.00 20.00
STPS Peter Stastny/47 10.00 25.00
STRA Brian Rafalski/52 8.00 20.00
STRB Rob Blake/68 8.00 20.00
STRF Ruslan Fedotenko/39 8.00 20.00
STRK Ryan Kesler/28 25.00 60.00
STRL Reggie Leach/61 8.00 20.00
STRM Ryan Miller/18 25.00 50.00
STRN Rob Niedermayer/61 8.00 20.00
STRS Ryan Smyth/39 12.00 30.00
STRV Rogie Vachon/33 12.00 30.00
STRY Michael Ryder/63 10.00 25.00
STRZ Richard Zednik/50 6.00 15.00
STSA Philippe Sauve/27 10.00 25.00
STSB Sean Burke/35 8.00 20.00
STSD Shane Doan/68 6.00 15.00
STSG Simon Gagne/66 10.00 25.00
STSL Martin St. Louis/38 12.00 30.00
STSN Scott Niedermayer/57 8.00 20.00
STST Marco Sturm/48 10.00 25.00
STSZ Sergei Zubov/79 6.00 15.00
STTA Tyler Arnason/55 8.00 20.00
STTE Tony Esposito/35 15.00 40.00
STTH Trent Hunter/51 6.00 15.00
STTL Trevor Linden/25 40.00 100.00
STTP Tom Poti/48 6.00 15.00
STTR Tuomo Ruutu/44 10.00 25.00
STVL Vincent Lecavalier/33 30.00 80.00
STVR Mike Van Ryn/37 10.00 25.00
STWC Wayne Cashman/30 8.00 20.00

2006-07 SP Game Used

COMPLETE SET w/o SPs (100) 50.00 100.00
1 Chris Pronger .75 2.00
2 Teemu Selanne 1.50 4.00
3 Jean-Sebastien Giguere .75 2.00
4 Ilya Kovalchuk .75 2.00
5 Kari Lehtonen .60 1.50
6 Marian Hossa .75 2.00
7 Patrice Bergeron 1.00 2.50
8 Brad Boyes .50 1.25
9 Hannu Toivonen .60 1.50
10 Bobby Orr 3.00 8.00
11 Ryan Miller .75 2.00
12 Chris Drury .60 1.50
13 Jarome Iginla 1.00 2.50
14 Miikka Kiprusoff .75 2.00
15 Alex Tanguay .50 1.25
16 Dion Phaneuf .60 1.50
17 Eric Staal 1.00 2.50
18 Cam Ward .75 2.00
19 Erik Cole .50 1.25
20 Rod Brind'Amour .75 2.00
21 Nikolai Khabibulin .75 2.00
22 Martin Havlat .50 1.25
23 Tuomo Ruutu .75 2.00
24 Joe Sakic 1.50 4.00
25 Jose Theodore .75 2.00
26 Milan Hejduk .60 1.50
27 Marek Svatos .50 1.25
28 Rick Nash .75 2.00
29 Sergei Fedorov 1.25 3.00
30 Pascal LeClaire .60 1.50
31 Mike Modano 1.25 3.00
32 Marty Turco .75 2.00
33 Eric Lindros 1.25 3.00
34 Gordie Howe 1.50 4.00
35 Henrik Zetterberg 1.00 2.50
36 Pavel Datsyuk 1.25 3.00
37 Dominik Hasek 1.25 3.00
38 Nicklas Lidstrom .75 2.00
39 Ales Hemsky .60 1.50
40 Ryan Smyth .60 1.50
41 Joffrey Lupul .50 1.25
42 Ed Belfour .75 2.00
43 Jay Bouwmeester .50 1.25
44 Todd Bertuzzi .75 2.00
45 Olli Jokinen .75 2.00
46 Wayne Gretzky 5.00 12.00
47 Alexander Frolov .50 1.25
48 Rob Blake .75 2.00
49 Marian Gaborik .75 2.00
50 Manny Fernandez .50 1.25
51 Pavol Demitra 1.00 2.50
52 Cristobal Huet .60 1.50
53 Patrick Roy 2.00 5.00
54 Michael Ryder .50 1.25
55 Saku Koivu .75 2.00
56 Alexei Kovalev .60 1.50
57 Paul Kariya .75 2.00
58 Tomas Vokoun .60 1.50
59 Jason Arnott .60 1.50
60 Martin Brodeur 2.00 5.00
61 Brian Gionta .50 1.25
62 Patrik Elias .75 2.00
63 Alexei Yashin .60 1.50
64 Miroslav Satan .60 1.50
65 Brendan Shanahan .75 2.00
66 Jaromir Jagr 2.50 6.00
67 Henrik Lundqvist 2.00 5.00
68 Dany Heatley .60 1.50
69 Martin Gerber .60 1.50
70 Daniel Alfredsson .75 2.00
71 Jason Spezza .75 2.00
72 Simon Gagne .75 2.00
73 Peter Forsberg 1.50 4.00
74 Jeff Carter .60 1.50
75 Joni Pitkanen .50 1.25
76 Shane Doan .60 1.50
77 Jeremy Roenick 1.25 3.00
78 Owen Nolan .75 2.00
79 Curtis Joseph 1.00 2.50
80 Sidney Crosby 3.00 8.00
81 Mario Lemieux 3.00 8.00
82 Marc-Andre Fleury 1.50 4.00
83 Mark Recchi 1.00 2.50
84 Joe Thornton 1.25 3.00
85 Patrick Marleau .75 2.00
86 Jonathan Cheechoo .60 1.50
87 Doug Weight .75 2.00
88 Keith Tkachuk .75 2.00
89 Vincent Lecavalier .75 2.00
90 Martin St. Louis .75 2.00
91 Brad Richards .75 2.00
92 Alexander Steen .50 1.25
93 Mats Sundin .75 2.00
94 Andrew Raycroft .60 1.50
95 Michael Peca .60 1.50
96 Markus Naslund .75 2.00
97 Roberto Luongo 1.25 3.00
98 Brendan Morrison .50 1.25
99 Alexander Ovechkin 3.00 8.00
100 Olaf Kolzig .75 2.00
101 Shane O'Brien RC 2.00 5.00
102 Ryan Shannon RC 2.00 5.00
103 Yan Stastny RC 2.00 5.00
104 Mark Stuart RC 2.00 5.00
105 Nate Thompson RC 2.00 5.00
106 Phil Kessel RC 5.00 12.00
107 Matt Lashoff RC 2.00 5.00
108 Dave Bolland RC 3.00 8.00
109 Michael Blunden RC 2.00 5.00
110 Dustin Byfuglien RC 5.00 12.00
111 Paul Stastny RC 5.00 12.00
112 Fredrik Norrena RC 2.00 5.00
113 Loui Eriksson RC 4.00 10.00
114 Tomas Kopecky RC 2.50 6.00
115 Alexei Mikhnov RC 2.00 5.00
116 Marc-Antoine Pouliot RC 2.00 5.00
117 Patrick Thoresen RC 2.00 5.00
118 Ladislav Smid RC 2.00 5.00
119 Janis Sprukts RC 2.00 5.00
120 Konstantin Pushkarev RC 2.50 6.00
121 Patrick O'Sullivan RC 3.00 8.00
122 Anze Kopitar RC 10.00 25.00
123 Benoit Pouliot RC 2.50 6.00
124 Miroslav Kopriva RC 2.00 5.00
125 Niklas Backstrom RC 4.00 10.00
126 Guillaume Latendresse RC 3.00 8.00
127 Alexander Radulov RC 4.00 10.00
128 Shea Weber RC 5.00 12.00
129 Mikko Lehtonen RC 2.50 6.00
130 Alex Brooks RC 2.00 5.00
131 John Oduya RC 3.00 8.00
132 Travis Zajac RC 4.00 10.00
133 Drew Stafford RC 3.00 8.00
134 Masi Marjamaki RC 2.00 5.00
135 Jarkko Immonen RC 2.50 6.00
136 Nigel Dawes RC 2.00 5.00
137 Alexei Kaigorodov RC 2.00 5.00
138 Lars Jonsson RC 2.00 5.00
139 Ryan Potulny RC 2.00 5.00
140 Triston Grant RC 2.00 5.00
141 Enver Lisin RC 2.00 5.00
142 Brandon Prust RC 2.00 5.00
143 Keith Yandle RC 5.00 12.00
144 Patrick Fischer RC 2.00 5.00
145 Noah Welch RC 2.00 5.00
146 Michel Ouellet RC 2.50 6.00
147 Jordan Staal RC 8.00 20.00
148 Kristopher Letang RC 8.00 20.00
149 Evgeni Malkin RC 15.00 40.00
150 Matt Carle RC 2.00 5.00
151 Marc-Edouard Vlasic RC 3.00 8.00
152 D.J. King RC 2.00 5.00
153 Roman Polak RC 2.50 6.00
154 Ben Ondrus RC 2.00 5.00
155 Brendan Bell RC 2.00 5.00
156 Ian White RC 2.50 6.00
157 Dustin Boyd RC 2.00 5.00
158 Luc Bourdon RC 3.00 8.00
159 Eric Fehr RC 3.00 8.00
160 Jonas Johansson RC 2.00 5.00

2006-07 SP Game Used Gold

*1-100 VETS: 2X TO 5X BASIC CARDS
*101-160 ROOKIES: 1X TO 2.5X BASIC RC

2006-07 SP Game Used Rainbow

*1-100 VETS: 4X TO 10X BASIC CARDS
*101-160 ROOKIES: 2X TO 5X BASIC RC
149 Evgeni Malkin 100.00 200.00

2006-07 SP Game Used Authentic Fabrics

AFAF Alexander Frolov 4.00 10.00
AFAH Ales Hemsky 5.00 12.00
AFAL Daniel Alfredsson 6.00 15.00
AFAO Alexander Ovechkin SP 15.00 40.00
AFAS Alexander Steen 4.00 10.00
AFAT Alex Tanguay 4.00 10.00
AFAY Alexei Yashin 5.00 12.00
AFBB Brad Boyes 4.00 10.00
AFBG Brian Gionta 4.00 10.00
AFBL Brian Leetch 5.00 12.00
AFBM Brenden Morrow 5.00 12.00
AFBO Pierre-Marc Bouchard 6.00 15.00
AFBR Brad Richards 6.00 15.00
AFBS Brendan Shanahan 6.00 15.00
AFCD Chris Drury 5.00 12.00
AFCJ Curtis Joseph 8.00 20.00
AFCS Curtis Sanford 5.00 12.00
AFCW Cam Ward 6.00 15.00
AFDA David Aebischer 5.00 12.00
AFDE Pavol Demitra 8.00 20.00
AFDH Dominik Hasek 8.00 20.00
AFDP Dion Phaneuf 4.00 10.00
AFDR Dwayne Roloson 5.00 12.00
AFDS Daniel Sedin 8.00 20.00
AFDW Doug Weight 6.00 15.00
AFEB Ed Belfour 6.00 15.00
AFEJ Ed Jovanovski 5.00 12.00
AFES Eric Staal 8.00 20.00
AFGA Simon Gagne 6.00 15.00
AFGR Gary Roberts 4.00 10.00
AFHE Dany Heatley 5.00 12.00
AFHL Henrik Lundqvist 15.00 40.00
AFHS Henrik Sedin 8.00 20.00
AFHT Hannu Toivonen 5.00 12.00
AFHZ Henrik Zetterberg 8.00 20.00
AFIK Ilya Kovalchuk SP 8.00 20.00
AFJB Jay Bouwmeester 4.00 10.00
AFJC Jeff Carter 5.00 12.00
AFJD J.P. Dumont 4.00 10.00
AFJI Jarome Iginla 8.00 20.00
AFJJ Jaromir Jagr SP 20.00 50.00
AFJL Jere Lehtinen 4.00 10.00
AFJN Joe Nieuwendyk 5.00 12.00
AFJP Joni Pitkanen 4.00 10.00
AFJS Joe Sakic 10.00 25.00
AFJT Joe Thornton 8.00 20.00
AFJW Jason Williams 4.00 10.00
AFLU Joffrey Lupul 4.00 10.00
AFMA Mark Recchi 8.00 20.00
AFMB Martin Brodeur SP 15.00 40.00
AFMC Mike Cammalleri 4.00 10.00
AFME Martin Erat 4.00 10.00
AFMF Manny Fernandez 4.00 10.00
AFMG Marian Gaborik 6.00 15.00
AFMH Milan Hejduk 5.00 12.00
AFMI Miroslav Satan 5.00 12.00
AFMM Mike Modano 8.00 20.00
AFMN Markus Naslund 6.00 15.00
AFMO Brendan Morrison 4.00 10.00
AFMP Michael Peca 5.00 12.00
AFMR Michael Ryder 4.00 10.00
AFMS Mats Sundin 6.00 15.00
AFNH Nathan Horton 6.00 15.00
AFNL Nicklas Lidstrom 6.00 15.00
AFOK Olaf Kolzig 6.00 15.00
AFPB Patrice Bergeron 8.00 20.00
AFPD Pavel Datsyuk 10.00 25.00
AFPE Patrik Elias 6.00 15.00
AFPF Peter Forsberg 10.00 25.00
AFPK Paul Kariya 5.00 12.00
AFPL Pascal LeClaire 5.00 12.00
AFPM Patrick Marleau 6.00 15.00
AFPS Patrik Stefan 4.00 10.00
AFPT Pierre Turgeon 5.00 12.00
AFRB Rob Blake 6.00 15.00
AFRD Rick DiPietro 5.00 12.00
AFRE Robert Esche 5.00 12.00
AFRF Ruslan Fedotenko 4.00 10.00
AFRG Ryan Getzlaf 6.00 15.00
AFRL Roberto Luongo 10.00 25.00
AFRM Ryan Malone 4.00 10.00
AFRN Rick Nash 6.00 15.00
AFRS Ryan Smyth 5.00 12.00
AFSC Sidney Crosby SP 40.00 80.00
AFSF Sergei Fedorov 10.00 25.00
AFSG Scott Gomez 5.00 12.00
AFSJ Matt Stajan 4.00 10.00
AFSK Saku Koivu 6.00 15.00
AFSM Martin St. Louis 6.00 15.00
AFSN Scott Niedermayer 6.00 15.00
AFSP Jason Spezza 6.00 15.00
AFSS Sergei Samsonov 5.00 12.00
AFST Jarret Stoll 5.00 12.00
AFSU Steve Sullivan 4.00 10.00
AFTA Tony Amonte 5.00 12.00
AFTH Tomas Holmstrom 5.00 12.00
AFTS Teemu Selanne 12.00 30.00
AFTT Tim Thomas 6.00 15.00
AFTV Tomas Vokoun 5.00 12.00
AFVL Vincent Lecavalier 6.00 15.00

2006-07 SP Game Used Authentic Fabrics Parallel

*PARALLEL 1X to 1.25X

2006-07 SP Game Used Authentic Fabrics Patches

*PATCHES: 2X to 4X HI BASE JERSEYS

2006-07 SP Game Used Authentic Fabrics Dual

AF2AB M.Afinogenov/D.Briere 6.00 15.00
AF2AH D.Aebischer/C.Huet 8.00 20.00
AF2AS J.Arnott/S.Sullivan 3.00 8.00
AF2BF R.Blake/A.Frolov 4.00 10.00
AF2BG M.Brodeur/B.Gionta 10.00 25.00
AF2BH J.Bouwmeester/N.Horton 3.00 8.00
AF2DG P.Demitra/M.Gaborik 6.00 15.00
AF2DM C.Drury/R.Miller 6.00 15.00
AF2FC P.Forsberg/J.Carter 6.00 15.00
AF2HK M.Havlat/N.Khabibulin 6.00 15.00
AF2HL A.Hemsky/J.Lupul 3.00 8.00
AF2HO D.Hasek/C.Osgood 10.00 25.00
AF2HS M.Hejduk/M.Svatos 3.00 8.00
AF2HZ T.Holmstrom/H.Zetterberg 8.00 20.00
AF2IK J.Iginla/M.Kiprusoff 10.00 25.00
AF2JL J.Jagr/H.Lundqvist 10.00 25.00
AF2KG S.Kapanen/S.Gagne 3.00 8.00
AF2KH M.Hossa/I.Kovalchuk 6.00 15.00
AF2KO O.Kolzig/A.Ovechkin 12.00 30.00
AF2KR S.Koivu/M.Ryder 4.00 10.00
AF2KV P.Kariya/T.Vokoun 6.00 15.00
AF2LC P.LeClaire/T.Conklin 3.00 8.00
AF2LJ J.Lehtinen/J.Jokinen 3.00 8.00
AF2LR V.Lecavalier/B.Richards 8.00 20.00
AF2ML M.Modano/E.Lindros 6.00 15.00
AF2MT P.Marleau/J.Thornton 8.00 20.00
AF2ND O.Nolan/S.Doan 4.00 10.00
AF2NF R.Nash/S.Fedorov 8.00 20.00
AF2NL M.Naslund/R.Luongo 6.00 15.00
AF2PB M.Parrish/P.Bouchard 3.00 8.00
AF2PT M.Peca/D.Tucker 4.00 10.00
AF2RC M.Recchi/S.Crosby 20.00 50.00
AF2RL G.Lapointe/L.Robinson 4.00 15.00
AF2SB M.Savard/P.Bergeron 6.00 15.00
AF2SC B.Stuart/Z.Chara 3.00 8.00
AF2SD M.Satan/R.DiPietro 4.00 10.00
AF2SH J.Spezza/D.Heatley 8.00 20.00
AF2SJ B.Shanahan/J.Jagr 10.00 25.00
AF2SP T.Selanne/C.Perry 6.00 15.00

AF2SS M.Sundin/A.Steen 6.00 15.00
AF2SW E.Staal/C.Ward 6.00 15.00
AF2TK A.Tanguay/C.Kobasew 4.00 10.00
AF2TM M.Turco/B.Morrow 4.00 10.00
AF2TP R.Torres/F.Pisani 3.00 8.00
AF2TS P.Turgeon/J.Sakic 8.00 20.00
AF2TT H.Toivonen/T.Thomas 4.00 10.00
AF2WB J.Williams/R.Brind'Amour 3.00 8.00
AF2WG D.Weight/B.Guerin 3.00 8.00

2006-07 SP Game Used Authentic Fabrics Dual Patches

*PATCHES: 2X to 4X DUAL JSY HI

2006-07 SP Game Used Authentic Fabrics Triple

AF3ANA Selan/Prong/Nied 20.00 50.00
AF3ATL Hossa/Kovy/Lehton 25.00 60.00
AF3BOS Boyes/Chara/Berg 20.00 50.00
AF3BUF Drury/Briere/Miller 25.00 60.00
AF3CAR Brind/Staal/Ward 20.00 50.00
AF3CGY Iggy/Tanguay/Kipper 30.00 80.00
AF3CHI Havlat/Ruutu/Khabi 15.00 40.00
AF3CLB LeClaire/Nash/Fedorov 25.00 60.00
AF3COL Sakic/Hejduk/Theo 40.00 100.00
AF3DAL Modano/Lind/Turco 25.00 60.00
AF3DET Hasek/Lidstrom/Zetty 40.00 100.00
AF3EDM Smyth/Rolo/Hemsky 15.00 40.00
AF3FLA Belfour/Bert/Bouw 20.00 50.00
AF3LAK Blake/Frolov/Cam 15.00 40.00
AF3MIN Demitra/Gabby/Bouch 20.00 50.00
AF3MTL Samson/Koivu/Ryder 30.00 80.00
AF3NAS Kariya/Vokoun/Arnott 20.00 50.00
AF3NJD Brodeur/Elias/Gionta 30.00 80.00
AF3NYI Satan/Yashin/DiPietro 20.00 50.00
AF3NYR Shanny/Jagr/Lundqvist 50.00 100.00
AF3OTT Alfred/Spezza/Heatley 25.00 60.00
AF3PHI Forsberg/Esche/Gagne 20.00 50.00
AF3PHX Joseph/Roenick/Doan 15.00 40.00
AF3PIT Recchi/Malone/Crosby 40.00 100.00
AF3SJS Marleau/Thorn/Chee 25.00 60.00
AF3STL Weight/Tkachuk/Leg 15.00 40.00
AF3TBL Lecav/Richards/St. Lou 30.00 80.00
AF3TOR Sundin/Raycroft/Steen 20.00 50.00
AF3VAN Naslund/Sedin/Sedin 25.00 60.00
AF3WAS Ovech/Kolzig/Zednik 30.00 80.00

2006-07 SP Game Used Inked Sweaters

ISAF Alexander Frolov 6.00 15.00
ISAH Ales Hemsky 8.00 20.00
ISAN Antero Niittymaki 10.00 25.00
ISAO Alexander Ovechkin SP 80.00 200.00
ISAR Andrew Raycroft 10.00 25.00
ISAY Alexei Yashin 6.00 15.00
ISBB Brad Boyes 6.00 15.00
ISBG Brian Gionta 6.00 15.00
ISBM Bryan McCabe 6.00 15.00
ISBS Borje Salming SP 15.00 30.00
ISCA Matt Carle 10.00 25.00
ISCH Chris Higgins 10.00 25.00
ISCN Cam Neely SP 25.00 60.00
ISCP Chris Pronger SP 15.00 40.00
ISCW Cam Ward 8.00 20.00
ISDA Dany Heatley 10.00 25.00
ISDB Daniel Briere 12.00 30.00
ISDH Dominik Hasek SP 40.00 80.00
ISDI Dion Phaneuf SP 25.00 60.00
ISDR Dwayne Roloson 10.00 25.00
ISDS Denis Savard SP 15.00 40.00
ISDT Darcy Tucker 10.00 25.00
ISEF Eric Fehr 6.00 15.00
ISEL Patrik Elias 8.00 20.00
ISES Eric Staal 12.00 30.00
ISFP Fernando Pisani 6.00 15.00
ISGE Martin Gerber 8.00 20.00
ISHA Martin Havlat 10.00 25.00
ISHE Milan Hejduk 8.00 20.00
ISHO Tomas Holmstrom 8.00 20.00
ISHT Hannu Toivonen 10.00 25.00
ISHU Cristobal Huet 10.00 25.00
ISIK Ilya Kovalchuk SP 25.00 60.00
ISIM Jarkko Immonen 8.00 20.00
ISJA Jason Arnott 6.00 15.00
ISJI Jarome Iginla SP 15.00 40.00
ISJL Joffrey Lupul 6.00 15.00
ISJP Joni Pitkanen 6.00 15.00
ISJS Jarret Stoll 6.00 15.00
ISJT Joe Thornton SP 25.00 60.00
ISJW Justin Williams 6.00 15.00
ISKD Kris Draper 6.00 15.00
ISKL Kari Lehtonen 10.00 25.00
ISKO Mikko Koivu 8.00 20.00
ISLN Ladislav Nagy 6.00 15.00
ISMA Al MacInnis SP 20.00 50.00
ISMB Martin Brodeur SP 60.00 150.00
ISMC Mike Cammalleri 8.00 20.00
ISMG Marian Gaborik 15.00 40.00
ISMI Ryan Miller 12.00 30.00
ISML Mario Lemieux SP 100.00 200.00
ISMM Milan Michalek 6.00 15.00
ISMO Mike Modano SP 20.00 50.00
ISMP Mark Parrish 6.00 15.00
ISMR Mike Ribeiro 6.00 15.00
ISMT Marty Turco 10.00 25.00
ISNL Nicklas Lidstrom SP 25.00 60.00
ISNZ Nikolai Zherdev 6.00 15.00
ISPB Pierre-Marc Bouchard 6.00 15.00
ISPE Michael Peca 6.00 15.00
ISPM Patrick Marleau 8.00 20.00
ISPO Marc-Antoine Pouliot 8.00 20.00
ISPP Petr Prucha 8.00 20.00
ISPR Patrick Roy SP 125.00 250.00
ISRG Ryan Getzlaf 10.00 25.00
ISRH Ron Hextall SP 20.00 50.00
ISRI Mike Richards 8.00 20.00
ISRN Rick Nash SP 25.00 60.00
ISRS Ryan Smyth 10.00 25.00
ISSA Marc Savard 8.00 20.00
ISSB Steve Bernier 8.00 20.00
ISSC Sidney Crosby 75.00 150.00
ISSG Scott Gomez 8.00 20.00
ISSK Saku Koivu SP 20.00 50.00
ISSV Marek Svatos 8.00 20.00
ISSW Shea Weber 10.00 25.00
ISTV Tomas Vokoun 10.00 25.00
ISVL Vincent Lecavalier SP 25.00 60.00
ISVT Vesa Toskala 10.00 25.00
ISWG Wayne Gretzky SP EXCH 250.00 600.00
ISWR Wade Redden 6.00 15.00
ISZC Zdeno Chara 6.00 15.00

2006-07 SP Game Used Inked Sweaters Patches

*PATCHES: 1.25X to 2X JSY HI
ISAF Alexander Frolov 12.00 30.00
ISAH Ales Hemsky 15.00 40.00
ISAN Antero Niittymaki 25.00 60.00
ISAR Andrew Raycroft 30.00 80.00
ISAY Alexei Yashin 12.00 30.00
ISBB Brad Boyes 12.00 30.00
ISBG Brian Gionta 12.00 30.00
ISBM Bryan McCabe 12.00 30.00
ISCA Matt Carle 20.00 50.00
ISCH Chris Higgins 20.00 50.00
ISCW Cam Ward 20.00 50.00
ISDA Dany Heatley 20.00 50.00
ISDB Daniel Briere 25.00 60.00
ISDR Dwayne Roloson 20.00 50.00
ISDT Darcy Tucker 20.00 50.00
ISEF Eric Fehr 12.00 30.00
ISEL Patrik Elias 15.00 40.00
ISES Eric Staal 20.00 50.00
ISFP Fernando Pisani 12.00 30.00
ISGE Martin Gerber 15.00 40.00
ISHA Martin Havlat 20.00 50.00
ISHE Milan Hejduk 15.00 40.00
ISHO Tomas Holmstrom 15.00 40.00
ISHT Hannu Toivonen 20.00 50.00
ISHU Cristobal Huet 30.00 80.00
ISIK Ilya Kovalchuk SP 60.00 100.00
ISIM Jarkko Immonen 15.00 40.00
ISJA Jason Arnott 12.00 30.00
ISJI Jarome Iginla SP 60.00 120.00
ISJL Joffrey Lupul 12.00 30.00
ISJP Joni Pitkanen 12.00 30.00
ISJS Jarret Stoll 12.00 30.00
ISJT Joe Thornton SP 125.00 200.00
ISJW Justin Williams 12.00 30.00
ISKD Kris Draper 15.00 40.00
ISKL Kari Lehtonen 20.00 50.00
ISKO Mikko Koivu 20.00 50.00
ISLN Ladislav Nagy 12.00 30.00
ISMC Mike Cammalleri 15.00 40.00
ISMG Marian Gaborik 30.00 80.00
ISMI Ryan Miller 25.00 60.00
ISMM Milan Michalek 12.00 30.00
ISMP Mark Parrish 12.00 30.00
ISMR Mike Ribeiro 12.00 30.00
ISMT Marty Turco 20.00 50.00
ISNZ Nikolai Zherdev 12.00 30.00
ISPB Pierre-Marc Bouchard 12.00 30.00
ISPM Patrick Marleau 15.00 40.00
ISPO Marc-Antoine Pouliot 15.00 40.00
ISPP Petr Prucha 15.00 40.00
ISRG Ryan Getzlaf 30.00 50.00
ISRI Mike Richards 15.00 40.00
ISRS Ryan Smyth 20.00 50.00
ISSA Marc Savard 15.00 40.00
ISSB Steve Bernier 15.00 40.00
ISSC Sidney Crosby 200.00 350.00
ISSG Scott Gomez 15.00 40.00
ISSV Marek Svatos 15.00 40.00
ISSW Shea Weber 20.00 50.00
ISTV Tomas Vokoun 15.00 40.00
ISVL Vincent Lecavalier SP 75.00 150.00
ISVT Vesa Toskala 25.00 60.00
ISWR Wade Redden 12.00 30.00
ISZC Zdeno Chara 12.00 30.00

2006-07 SP Game Used Inked Sweaters Dual

IS2AS J.Arnott/S.Sullivan 8.00 20.00
IS2BB B.Boyes/P.Bergeron 12.00 30.00
IS2CP G.Cheevers/R.Park 15.00 40.00
IS2DM C.Drury/R.Miller 15.00 40.00
IS2EG P.Elias/B.Gionta 10.00 25.00
IS2EP R.Esche/J.Pitkanen 8.00 20.00
IS2FC A.Frolov/M.Cammelleri 10.00 25.00
IS2FR G.Fuhr/B.Ranford 20.00 50.00
IS2GB M.Gaborik/P.Bouchard 20.00 50.00
IS2HA D.Aebischer/C.Huet 15.00 40.00
IS2HH M.Handzus/M.Havlat 8.00 20.00
IS2HO D.Hasek/C.Osgood 20.00 50.00
IS2HS J.Stoll/A.Hemsky 8.00 20.00
IS2HT M.Hejduk/J.Theodore 10.00 25.00
IS2IT J.Iginla/A.Tanguay 15.00 40.00
IS2KL I.Kovalchuk/K.Lehtonen 25.00 60.00
IS2KR S.Koivu/M.Ryder 12.00 30.00
IS2LP H.Lundqvist/P.Prucha 25.00 60.00
IS2LS N.Lidstrom/B.Salming 20.00 50.00
IS2MC P.Marleau/J.Cheechoo 15.00 40.00
IS2MM J.Mullen/A.MacInnis 12.00 30.00
IS2MS M.Savard/G.Murray 10.00 25.00
IS2MT M.Modano/M.Turco 12.00 30.00
IS2NH D.Heatley/R.Nash 20.00 50.00
IS2NM M.Naslund/B.Morrison 12.00 30.00
IS2OJ O.Jokinen/J.Bouwmeester 8.00 20.00
IS2PT M.Peca/D.Tucker 15.00 40.00
IS2RD J.Roenick/S.Doan 10.00 25.00
IS2RG W.Redden/M.Gerber 10.00 25.00
IS2RS A.Raycroft/A.Steen 15.00 40.00
IS2RT L.Robitaille/D.Taylor 25.00 60.00
IS2SD M.St. Louis/M.Denis 12.00 30.00
IS2SR R.Smyth/D.Roloson 12.00 30.00
IS2SW J.Williams/E.Staal 10.00 25.00
IS2SY M.Satan/A.Yashin 8.00 20.00
IS2VW T.Vokoun/S.Weber 12.00 30.00
IS2WP T.Williams/B.Probert 12.00 30.00
IS2WR D.Roloson/C.Ward 12.00 30.00
IS2ZH T.Holmstrom/H.Zetterberg 20.00 50.00

2006-07 SP Game Used Legendary Fabrics

LFBC Bobby Clarke/100 10.00 25.00
LFGH Gordie Howe/25 20.00 50.00
LFGL Guy Lafleur/100 8.00 20.00
LFJB Jean Beliveau/100 6.00 15.00
LFMB Mike Bossy/100 6.00 15.00
LFML Mario Lemieux/25 25.00 60.00
LFPE Phil Esposito/25 10.00 25.00
LFPR Patrick Roy/25 15.00 40.00
LFRB Ray Bourque/25 10.00 25.00
LFWG Wayne Gretzky/25 40.00 100.00

2006-07 SP Game Used Legendary Fabrics Autographs

LFBC Bobby Clarke 12.00 30.00
LFGH Gordie Howe 25.00 60.00
LFGL Guy Lafleur 10.00 25.00
LFJB Jean Beliveau 8.00 20.00
LFMB Mike Bossy 8.00 20.00
LFML Mario Lemieux SP 30.00 80.00
LFPE Phil Esposito SP 12.00 30.00
LFPR Patrick Roy SP 20.00 50.00
LFRB Ray Bourque SP 12.00 30.00
LFWG Wayne Gretzky SP EXCH 150.00 400.00

2006-07 SP Game Used Letter Marks

LMAF Alexander Frolov 10.00 25.00
LMAK Andrei Kostitsyn 12.00 30.00
LMAL Andrew Ladd 10.00 25.00
LMAN Antero Niittymaki 12.00 30.00
LMBB Brad Boyes 10.00 25.00
LMBG Brian Gionta 10.00 25.00
LMBM Brenden Morrow 12.00 30.00
LMBP Bernie Parent EXCH 20.00 50.00
LMBQ Ray Bourque 25.00 60.00
LMBR Bill Ranford EXCH 15.00 40.00
LMCG Clark Gillies 15.00 40.00
LMCH Cristobal Huet 12.00 30.00
LMCK Chuck Kobasew 10.00 25.00
LMCN Cam Neely 15.00 40.00
LMCW Cam Ward 15.00 40.00
LMDC Dino Ciccarelli EXCH 15.00 40.00
LMDP Denis Potvin 15.00 40.00
LMDR Dwayne Roloson 12.00 30.00
LMDS Denis Savard 15.00 40.00
LMDW Dave Williams 10.00 25.00
LMEC Erik Cole 10.00 25.00
LMEL Patrik Elias 15.00 40.00
LMEM Evgeni Malkin 60.00 150.00
LMES Eric Staal 20.00 50.00
LMFP Fernando Pisani 10.00 25.00
LMGC Gerry Cheevers 15.00 40.00
LMGL G.Latendresse EXCH 15.00 40.00
LMHA Dominik Hasek EXCH 25.00 60.00
LMHE Milan Hejduk 12.00 30.00
LMHO Gordie Howe 50.00 125.00
LMIK Ilya Kovalchuk EXCH 15.00 40.00
LMJA Jason Arnott 12.00 30.00
LMJC Jeff Carter 12.00 30.00
LMJI Jarome Iginla 20.00 50.00
LMJJ Jussi Jokinen 12.00 30.00
LMJL Joffrey Lupul 10.00 25.00
LMJP Joni Pitkanen 10.00 25.00
LMJT Jose Theodore 15.00 40.00
LMKD Kris Draper 10.00 25.00
LMLR Luc Robitaille 15.00 40.00
LMLU Roberto Luongo 25.00 60.00
LMMA Matt Carle 10.00 25.00
LMMB Martin Brodeur 40.00 100.00
LMMF Marc-Andre Fleury 30.00 80.00
LMMG Marian Gaborik 15.00 40.00
LMMI Mike Cammalleri 10.00 25.00
LMMM Mike Modano 25.00 60.00
LMMN Markus Naslund 15.00 40.00
LMMR Michael Ryder 10.00 25.00
LMMT Marty Turco 15.00 40.00
LMNL Nicklas Lidstrom 15.00 40.00
LMOJ Olli Jokinen 15.00 40.00
LMOR Bobby Orr 60.00 150.00
LMPE Michael Peca 12.00 30.00
LMPI P-M Bouchard 15.00 40.00
LMPK Phil Kessel 30.00 80.00
LMPM Patrick Marleau 15.00 40.00
LMPO Ryan Potulny 10.00 25.00
LMPP Petr Prucha 12.00 30.00
LMRH Ron Hextall 15.00 40.00
LMRI Mike Ribeiro 10.00 25.00
LMRL Reggie Leach EXCH 10.00 25.00
LMRM Mike Richards 12.00 30.00
LMRV Rogie Vachon 20.00 50.00
LMRY Ryan Miller 15.00 40.00
LMSB Steve Bernier 10.00 25.00
LMSC Sidney Crosby 100.00 200.00
LMSK Saku Koivu 15.00 40.00
LMSM Ryan Smyth 12.00 30.00
LMSV Marek Svatos 10.00 25.00
LMTH Tomas Holmstrom 12.00 30.00
LMTL Ted Lindsay 15.00 40.00
LMTO Terry O'Reilly 10.00 25.00
LMVA Thomas Vanek 12.00 30.00
LMWG Wayne Gretzky EXCH 250.00 600.00
LMZC Zdeno Chara 15.00 40.00

2006-07 SP Game Used Rookie Exclusives Autographs

REAB Adam Burish 10.00 25.00
REAE Alexander Edler 10.00 25.00
REAK Anze Kopitar 30.00 80.00
REAL Alex Brooks 6.00 15.00
REAR Alexander Radulov 12.00 30.00
REBB Brendan Bell 6.00 15.00
REBO Ben Ondrus 6.00 15.00
REBR Mike Brown 6.00 15.00
RECA Mike Card 6.00 15.00
REDB Dustin Byfuglien 15.00 40.00
REDL Drew Larman 6.00 15.00
REDS Drew Stafford 10.00 25.00
REDU Dustin Boyd 6.00 15.00
REEF Eric Fehr 10.00 25.00
REEM Evgeni Malkin 40.00 80.00
REGL Guillaume Latendresse 10.00 25.00
REIW Ian White 8.00 20.00
REJF Jean-Francois Racine 8.00 20.00
REJI Jarkko Immonen 8.00 20.00
REJS Jordan Staal 15.00 40.00
REJW Jeremy Williams 6.00 15.00
REKP Konstantin Pushkarev 8.00 20.00
REKY Keith Yandle 15.00 40.00
RELE Loui Eriksson 12.00 30.00
RELS Ladislav Smid 6.00 15.00
REMB Michael Blunden 6.00 15.00
REMC Matt Carle 6.00 15.00
REMM Masi Marjamaki 6.00 15.00
REMO Michel Ouellet 8.00 20.00
REMP Marc-Antoine Pouliot 6.00 15.00
REMS Mark Stuart 6.00 15.00
REMV Marc-Edouard Vlasic 10.00 25.00
REND Nigel Dawes 6.00 15.00
RENM Nathan McIver 6.00 15.00
RENO Fredrik Norrena 6.00 15.00
RENW Noah Welch 6.00 15.00
REPO Patrick O'Sullivan 10.00 25.00
REPK Phil Kessel 20.00 50.00
REPO Ryan Potulny 6.00 15.00
REPS Paul Stastny 15.00 40.00
REPT Patrick Thoresen 6.00 15.00
RERS Ryan Shannon 6.00 15.00
RESO Shane O'Brien 6.00 15.00
RESP Janis Sprukts 6.00 15.00
RESW Shea Weber 15.00 40.00
RETK Tomas Kopecky 8.00 20.00
RETZ Travis Zajac 12.00 30.00
REYS Yan Stastny 6.00 15.00

2006-07 SP Game Used SIGnificance

SAF Alexander Frolov 8.00 20.00
SAH Ales Hemsky 8.00 20.00
SAK Andrei Kostitsyn 6.00 15.00
SAL Andrew Ladd 8.00 20.00
SAM Al Montoya 8.00 20.00
SAN Antero Niittymaki 8.00 20.00
SBG Brian Gionta 8.00 20.00
SBM Bryan McCabe 6.00 15.00
SBN Bob Nystrom 6.00 15.00
SBR Daniel Briere 8.00 20.00
SCB Cam Barker 6.00 15.00
SCH Cristobal Huet 10.00 25.00
SCK Chuck Kobasew 6.00 15.00
SCN Cam Neely 12.00 30.00
SCW Cam Ward 10.00 25.00
SDB Dustin Brown 8.00 20.00
SDC Don Cherry 20.00 40.00
SDE Denis Savard 8.00 20.00
SDK Duncan Keith 8.00 20.00
SDP Denis Potvin 6.00 15.00
SDR Dwayne Roloson 6.00 15.00
SDS Derek Sanderson 8.00 20.00
SDT Dave Taylor 6.00 15.00
SEC Erik Cole 6.00 15.00
SEM Evgeni Malkin 40.00 80.00
SEN Eric Nystrom 6.00 15.00
SES Eric Staal 8.00 20.00
SFP Fernando Pisani 6.00 15.00
SGA Marian Gaborik 12.00 30.00
SGH Gordie Howe 50.00 100.00
SGL Guillaume Latendresse 10.00 25.00
SHI Chris Higgins 6.00 15.00
SHO Marcel Hossa 5.00 12.00
SHT Hannu Toivonen 6.00 15.00
SHZ Henrik Zetterberg 12.00 30.00
SIK Ilya Kovalchuk 15.00 40.00
SJA Jason Arnott 8.00 20.00
SJB Jay Bouwmeester 8.00 20.00
SJC Jeff Carter 8.00 20.00
SJP Joni Pitkanen 6.00 15.00
SJS Jarret Stoll 8.00 20.00
SKB Keith Ballard 6.00 15.00
SKD Kris Draper 8.00 20.00
SKL Kari Lehtonen 10.00 25.00
SKO Mikko Koivu 8.00 20.00
SLE Reggie Leach 8.00 20.00
SLN Ladislav Nagy 5.00 12.00
SMA Ryan Malone 6.00 15.00
SMB Martin Brodeur 40.00 100.00
SMC Mike Cammalleri 8.00 20.00
SMD Andy McDonald 6.00 15.00
SMG Martin Gerber 8.00 20.00
SMH Michal Handzus 5.00 12.00
SMM Milan Michalek 6.00 15.00
SMP Michael Peca 6.00 15.00
SMR Mike Richards 8.00 20.00
SMT Marty Turco 8.00 20.00
SNH Nathan Horton 8.00 20.00
SNZ Nikolai Zherdev 5.00 12.00
SPA Mark Parrish 5.00 12.00
SPB Pierre-Marc Bouchard 6.00 15.00
SPH Chris Phillips 5.00 12.00
SPP Petr Prucha 6.00 15.00
SRB Richard Brodeur 8.00 20.00
SRF Robert Esche 6.00 15.00
SRF Ruslan Fedotenko 5.00 12.00
SRH Ron Hextall 15.00 40.00
SRI Mike Ribeiro 5.00 12.00
SRK Rostislav Klesla 5.00 12.00
SRM Ryan Miller 20.00 50.00
SRN Rick Nash 10.00 25.00
SRS Ryan Smyth 6.00 15.00
SRV Rogie Vachon 15.00 40.00
SRW Ryan Whitney 5.00 12.00
SRY Michael Ryder 6.00 15.00
SSA Marc Savard 8.00 20.00
SSB Steve Bernier 6.00 15.00
SSC Sidney Crosby 100.00 200.00
SSV Marek Svatos 6.00 15.00
SSW Stephen Weiss 6.00 15.00
STH Tomas Holmstrom 6.00 15.00
STL Ted Lindsay 8.00 20.00
STO Terry O'Reilly 8.00 20.00
STU Darcy Tucker 8.00 20.00
STV Tomas Vokoun 8.00 20.00
SVA Thomas Vanek 10.00 25.00
SVF Valtteri Filppula 8.00 20.00
SVT Vesa Toskala 8.00 20.00
SWR Wade Redden 5.00 12.00
SZC Zdeno Chara 8.00 20.00

2007-08 SP Game Used

COMP.SET w/o SPs (100) 25.00 60.00
1 Alexander Ovechkin 3.00 8.00
2 Olaf Kolzig .75 2.00
3 Alexander Semin .75 2.00
4 Roberto Luongo 1.25 3.00
5 Markus Naslund .75 2.00
6 Henrik Sedin 1.00 2.50
7 Daniel Sedin 1.00 2.50
8 Mats Sundin .75 2.00
9 Vesa Toskala .60 1.50
10 Darcy Tucker .60 1.50
11 Alexander Steen .50 1.25
12 Martin St. Louis .75 2.00
13 Vincent Lecavalier .75 2.00
14 Brad Richards .75 2.00
15 Doug Weight .75 2.00
16 Keith Tkachuk .75 2.00
17 Paul Kariya .75 2.00
18 Joe Thornton 1.25 3.00
19 Jonathan Cheechoo .60 1.50
20 Evgeni Nabokov .60 1.50
21 Patrick Marleau .75 2.00
22 Jordan Staal .60 1.50
23 Sidney Crosby 3.00 8.00
24 Marc-Andre Fleury 1.50 4.00
25 Evgeni Malkin 1.50 4.00
26 Shane Doan .60 1.50
27 Ed Jovanovski .60 1.50
28 Simon Gagne .75 2.00
29 Daniel Briere .75 2.00
30 Jeff Carter .60 1.50
31 Jason Spezza .75 2.00
32 Daniel Alfredsson .75 2.00
33 Ray Emery .60 1.50
34 Dany Heatley .60 1.50
35 Jaromir Jagr 2.50 6.00
36 Henrik Lundqvist 2.00 5.00
37 Chris Drury .60 1.50
38 Bill Guerin .75 2.00
39 Rick DiPietro .60 1.50
40 Miroslav Satan .60 1.50
41 Martin Brodeur 2.00 5.00
42 Patrik Elias .75 2.00
43 Zach Parise .75 2.00
44 Chris Mason .60 1.50
45 Alexander Radulov .75 2.00
46 Jason Arnott .60 1.50
47 Saku Koivu .75 2.00
48 Cristobal Huet .60 1.50
49 Michael Ryder .50 1.25
50 Guillaume Latendresse .60 1.50
51 Marian Gaborik .75 2.00
52 Pierre-Marc Bouchard .75 2.00
53 Mikko Koivu .60 1.50
54 Anze Kopitar 1.25 3.00
55 Rob Blake .75 2.00
56 Alexander Frolov .50 1.25
57 Tomas Vokoun .60 1.50
58 Nathan Horton .75 2.00
59 Olli Jokinen .60 1.50
60 Dwayne Roloson .60 1.50
61 Ales Hemsky .60 1.50
62 Jarret Stoll .60 1.50
63 Pavel Datsyuk 1.25 3.00
64 Henrik Zetterberg 1.00 2.50
65 Nicklas Lidstrom .75 2.00
66 Dominik Hasek 1.25 3.00
67 Mike Modano 1.25 3.00
68 Marty Turco .75 2.00
69 Mike Ribeiro .50 1.25
70 Rick Nash .75 2.00
71 Sergei Fedorov 1.25 3.00
72 David Vyborny .50 1.25
73 Joe Sakic 1.50 4.00
74 Ryan Smyth .60 1.50
75 Milan Hejduk .60 1.50
76 Paul Stastny .60 1.50
77 Nikolai Khabibulin .75 2.00
78 Martin Havlat .75 2.00
79 Tuomo Ruutu .75 2.00
80 Eric Staal 1.00 2.50
81 Cam Ward .75 2.00
82 Justin Williams .60 1.50
83 Jarome Iginla 1.00 2.50
84 Alex Tanguay .60 1.50
85 Miikka Kiprusoff .75 2.00
86 Dion Phaneuf .60 1.50
87 Thomas Vanek .60 1.50
88 Ryan Miller .75 2.00
89 Jason Pominville .50 1.25
90 Drew Stafford .50 1.25
91 Patrice Bergeron 1.00 2.50
92 Manny Fernandez .50 1.25
93 Phil Kessel .75 2.00
94 Ilya Kovalchuk .75 2.00
95 Marian Hossa .75 2.00
96 Kari Lehtonen .60 1.50
97 Chris Pronger .75 2.00
98 Ryan Getzlaf .75 2.00
99 Jean-Sebastien Giguere .75 2.00
100 Scott Niedermayer .75 2.00
101 Jeff Schultz RC 5.00 12.00
102 Jamie Hunt RC 4.00 10.00
103 Mason Raymond RC 6.00 15.00
104 Jannik Hansen RC 5.00 12.00
105 Matt Smaby RC 4.00 10.00
106 Mike Lundin RC 4.00 10.00
107 Erik Johnson RC 6.00 15.00
108 David Perron RC 8.00 20.00
109 Steve Wagner RC 4.00 10.00
110 Torrey Mitchell RC 5.00 12.00
111 Tomas Plihal RC 4.00 10.00
112 Martin Hanzal RC 5.00 12.00
113 Craig Weller RC 4.00 10.00
114 Daniel Winnik RC 5.00 12.00
115 Daniel Carcillo RC 5.00 12.00
116 Ryan Parent RC 4.00 10.00
117 Stefan Meyer RC 5.00 12.00
118 Denis Tolpeko RC 4.00 10.00
119 Nathan Guenin RC 5.00 12.00
120 Riley Cote RC 5.00 12.00
121 Danny Bois RC 4.00 10.00
122 Nick Foligno RC 8.00 20.00
123 Brian Elliott RC 8.00 20.00
124 Marc Staal RC 6.00 15.00
125 Brandon Dubinsky RC 8.00 20.00
126 Ryan Callahan RC 8.00 20.00
127 Daniel Girardi RC 5.00 12.00
128 Frans Nielsen RC 6.00 15.00
129 Drew Fata RC 4.00 10.00
130 Nicklas Bergfors RC 4.00 10.00
131 Andy Greene RC 5.00 12.00
132 Mark Fraser RC 4.00 10.00
133 David Clarkson RC 4.00 10.00
134 Rod Pelley RC 4.00 10.00
135 Ville Koistinen RC 4.00 10.00
136 Rich Peverley RC 4.00 10.00
137 Kyle Chipchura RC 6.00 15.00
138 Jaroslav Halak RC 12.00 30.00
139 Duncan Milroy RC 4.00 10.00
140 Petr Kalus RC 4.00 10.00
141 Lauri Tukonen RC 4.00 10.00
142 Jonathan Bernier RC 8.00 20.00
143 Jack Johnson RC 5.00 12.00
144 Brady Murray RC 4.00 10.00
145 John Zeiler RC 4.00 10.00
146 Shay Stephenson RC 4.00 10.00
147 Joe Piskula RC 4.00 10.00
148 Gabe Gauthier RC 4.00 10.00
149 Martin Lojek RC 4.00 10.00
150 Cory Murphy RC 4.00 10.00
151 Rob Schremp RC 5.00 12.00
152 Andrew Cogliano RC 5.00 12.00
153 Tom Gilbert RC 5.00 12.00
154 Bryan Young RC 4.00 10.00
155 Zach Stortini RC 4.00 10.00
156 Sebastien Bisaillon RC 4.00 10.00
157 Matt Ellis RC 5.00 12.00
158 Matt Niskanen RC 6.00 15.00
159 Tobias Stephan RC 5.00 12.00
160 Joel Lundqvist RC 4.00 10.00
161 Chris Conner RC 4.00 10.00
162 Kris Russell RC 6.00 15.00
163 Tomas Popperle RC 4.00 10.00
164 Marc Methot RC 4.00 10.00
165 Jared Boll RC 5.00 12.00
166 Curtis Glencross RC 6.00 15.00
167 Tyler Weiman RC 5.00 12.00
168 Jaroslav Hlinka RC 5.00 12.00
169 Jeff Finger RC 4.00 10.00
170 Colin Fraser RC 4.00 10.00
171 Bryan Bickell RC 8.00 20.00
172 Magnus Johansson RC 4.00 10.00
173 Jonas Nordqvist RC 4.00 10.00
174 David Koci RC 4.00 10.00
175 Curtis McElhinney RC 6.00 15.00
176 Matt Keetley RC 4.00 10.00
177 David Moss RC 6.00 15.00
178 Tomi Maki RC 4.00 10.00
179 Mark Mancari RC 4.00 10.00
180 Patrick Kaleta RC 4.00 10.00
181 David Krejci RC 12.00 30.00
182 Milan Lucic RC 10.00 25.00
183 Jonathan Sigalet RC 4.00 10.00
184 Brett Sterling RC 4.00 10.00
185 Tobias Enstrom RC 6.00 15.00
186 Ondrej Pavelec RC 8.00 20.00
187 Drew Miller RC 5.00 12.00
188 Ryan Carter RC 4.00 10.00
189 Jonas Hiller RC 8.00 20.00
190 Kent Huskins RC 4.00 10.00
191 Nick Backstrom/99 RC 40.00 80.00
192 Peter Mueller/99 RC 12.00 30.00
193 Jiri Tlusty/99 RC 15.00 40.00
194 Carey Price/99 RC 60.00 150.00
195 J. Sheppard/99 RC 10.00 25.00
196 D. Setoguchi/99 RC 15.00 40.00
197 Sam Gagner/99 RC 20.00 50.00
198 J. Toews/99 RC 75.00 150.00
199 Patrick Kane/99 RC 100.00 200.00
200 Bryan Little/99 RC 15.00 40.00

2007-08 SP Game Used Gold

*1-100 GOLD/100: 2.5X TO 6X BASIC CARDS
*101-190 ROOK/50: .8X TO 2X BASIC RC
*1910-200 ROOKIE/50: .4X TO 1X BASIC RC
194 Carey Price 80.00 200.00
198 Jonathan Toews 60.00 120.00
199 Patrick Kane 50.00 100.00

2007-08 SP Game Used Spectrum

*SPEC (1-100): 3X TO 8X
*SPEC RCs (101-190): 1.2X TO 3X
*SPEC RCs (191-200): .6X TO1.5X
194 Carey Price 100.00 250.00
198 Jonathan Toews 75.00 150.00
199 Patrick Kane 60.00 120.00

2007-08 SP Game Used Authentic Fabrics

*PATCH/50: 1.5X TO 4X BASIC JSY
*RAINBOW/100: .8X TO 2X JSY
AFAK Alex Kovalev 4.00 10.00
AFAO Adam Oates 5.00 12.00
AFAR Alexander Radulov 5.00 12.00
AFAS Anton Stastny 3.00 8.00
AFAY Alexei Yashin 4.00 10.00
AFBB Bob Bourne 3.00 8.00
AFBG Bill Guerin 5.00 12.00
AFBI Bill Ranford 5.00 12.00
AFBM Brendan Morrison 3.00 8.00
AFBO Brad Boyes 3.00 8.00
AFBP Bob Probert 5.00 12.00
AFBR Brandon Bochenski 3.00 8.00
AFBS Billy Smith 5.00 12.00
AFBW Brendan Witt 3.00 8.00
AFCA Colby Armstrong 3.00 8.00
AFCC Chris Chelios 5.00 12.00
AFCD Chris Drury 4.00 10.00
AFCH Chris Higgins 3.00 8.00
AFCN Cam Neely 5.00 12.00
AFCO Mike Commodore 3.00 8.00
AFCW Cam Ward 5.00 12.00
AFDA Daniel Alfredsson 5.00 12.00
AFDG Doug Gilmour 6.00 15.00
AFDH Dale Hawerchuk 6.00 15.00
AFDL David Legwand 4.00 10.00
AFDR Dwayne Roloson 4.00 10.00
AFDW Doug Weight 5.00 12.00
AFEB Ed Belfour 5.00 12.00
AFEN Evgeni Nabokov 4.00 10.00
AFES Eric Staal 6.00 15.00
AFEV Evgeni Malkin 10.00 25.00
AFFM Frank Mahovlich 5.00 12.00
AFGF Grant Fuhr 8.00 20.00
AFGI Brian Gionta 3.00 8.00
AFGM Glen Murray 4.00 10.00
AFGR Gary Roberts 3.00 8.00
AFHE Dany Heatley 4.00 10.00
AFHL Henrik Lundqvist 12.00 30.00
AFHT Hannu Toivonen 4.00 10.00
AFIK Ilya Kovalchuk 5.00 12.00
AFJB Jay Bouwmeester 3.00 8.00
AFJC Jonathan Cheechoo 4.00 10.00
AFJG Jean-Sebastien Giguere 5.00 12.00
AFJI Jarome Iginla 6.00 15.00
AFJJ Jaromir Jagr 15.00 40.00
AFJL Joffrey Lupul 3.00 8.00
AFJO Joe Sakic 10.00 25.00
AFJP Joni Pitkanen 3.00 8.00
AFJS Jarret Stoll 4.00 10.00
AFJT Joe Thornton 8.00 20.00
AFJU Jussi Jokinen 3.00 8.00
AFJW Justin Williams 4.00 10.00
AFKL Kari Lehtonen 4.00 10.00
AFKO Anze Kopitar 8.00 20.00
AFKT Keith Tkachuk 5.00 12.00
AFLN Ladislav Nagy 3.00 8.00
AFLR Larry Robinson 5.00 12.00
AFMA Marc Savard 3.00 8.00
AFMB Martin Brodeur 12.00 30.00
AFMC Bryan McCabe 3.00 8.00
AFMF Manny Fernandez 3.00 8.00
AFMG Marian Gaborik 5.00 12.00
AFMH Marian Hossa 5.00 12.00
AFMK Mikko Koivu 4.00 10.00
AFML Manny Legace 4.00 10.00
AFMM Mike Modano 8.00 20.00
AFMN Markus Naslund 5.00 12.00
AFMO Brenden Morrow 4.00 10.00
AFMR Mike Ribeiro 3.00 8.00
AFMS Miroslav Satan 4.00 10.00
AFMT Marty Turco 5.00 12.00
AFON Owen Nolan 5.00 12.00
AFOV Alexander Ovechkin 8.00 20.00
AFPB Patrice Bergeron 6.00 15.00
AFPD Pavel Datsyuk 8.00 20.00
AFPE Patrik Elias 5.00 12.00
AFPR Patrick Roy 10.00 25.00
AFRA Andrew Raycroft 4.00 10.00
AFRB Brian Rafalski 4.00 10.00
AFRE Mark Recchi 6.00 15.00
AFRI Brad Richards 5.00 12.00
AFRL Roberto Luongo 8.00 20.00
AFRN Rick Nash 5.00 12.00
AFRS Ryan Smyth 4.00 10.00
AFRY Michael Ryder 3.00 8.00
AFSA Borje Salming 5.00 12.00
AFSC Sidney Crosby 8.00 20.00
AFSG Simon Gagne 5.00 12.00
AFSH Brendan Shanahan 5.00 12.00
AFSK Saku Koivu 5.00 12.00
AFSM Martin St. Louis 5.00 12.00
AFSN Scott Niedermayer 5.00 12.00
AFSP Jason Spezza 5.00 12.00
AFST Brad Stuart 3.00 8.00
AFSU Mats Sundin 5.00 12.00
AFSV Marek Svatos 3.00 8.00
AFTH Jose Theodore 5.00 12.00
AFTW Tiger Williams 3.00 8.00
AFVL Vincent Lecavalier 5.00 12.00

2007-08 SP Game Used Authentic Fabrics Duals

*PATCH/25: 1.2X TO 3X BASIC DUAL
AF2AD Tanguay/Phaneuf 3.00 8.00
AF2AH Alfredsson/Heatley 4.00 10.00
AF2AM Afinogenov/Miller 4.00 10.00
AF2BB E.Belfour/M.Brodeur 10.00 25.00
AF2BG M.Brodeur/B.Gionta 10.00 25.00
AF2BH Bouwmeester/Horton 4.00 10.00
AF2BK P.Bergeron/P.Kessel 5.00 12.00
AF2BL M.Brodeur/R.Luongo 10.00 25.00
AF2BW Brind'Amour/Ward 4.00 10.00
AF2CB J.Cheechoo/S.Bernier 3.00 8.00
AF2CM S.Crosby/E.Malkin 30.00 60.00
AF2CO S.Crosby/A.Ovechkin 30.00 60.00
AF2CR C.Chelios/B.Rafalski 4.00 10.00
AF2CS M.Commodore/E.Staal 5.00 12.00
AF2DD K.Draper/P.Datsyuk 6.00 15.00
AF2DG P.Demitra/M.Gaborik 5.00 12.00
AF2DS R.DiPietro/B.Smith 4.00 10.00
AF2EJ E.Staal/J.Staal 5.00 12.00
AF2FB Fernandez/Bergeron 5.00 12.00
AF2FR G.Fuhr/B.Ranford 6.00 15.00
AF2FS P.Forsberg/B.Salming 8.00 20.00
AF2FT Fernandez/Toivonen 3.00 8.00
AF2GB Gaborik/Bouchard 4.00 10.00
AF2GC S.Gagne/J.Carter 4.00 10.00
AF2GJ M.Green/M.Jurcina 3.00 8.00
AF2GK M.Gaborik/M.Koivu 4.00 10.00
AF2GL S.Gagne/J.Lupul 4.00 10.00
AF2GS B.Guerin/M.Satan 4.00 10.00
AF2HD D.Hasek/P.Datsyuk 6.00 15.00
AF2HK Hossa/Kovalchuk 4.00 10.00
AF2HL D.Hasek/N.Lidstrom 6.00 15.00
AF2IK J.Iginla/M.Kiprusoff 5.00 12.00
AF2JC J.Jagr/C.Drury 12.00 30.00
AF2JD J.Spezza/D.Heatley 4.00 10.00
AF2JH O.Jokinen/N.Horton 4.00 10.00
AF2JJ J.Sakic/J.Thornton 8.00 20.00
AF2JL J.Jagr/H.Lundqvist 12.00 30.00
AF2JP J.Jagr/P.Prucha 12.00 30.00
AF2JR J.Sakic/R.Smyth 8.00 20.00
AF2KB P.Kariya/B.Boyes 4.00 10.00
AF2KK S.Koivu/M.Koivu 4.00 10.00
AF2KT P.Kariya/K.Tkachuk 4.00 10.00
AF2LA D.Legwand/J.Arnott 3.00 8.00
AF2LB P.Leclaire/G.Brule 3.00 8.00
AF2LC Lemieux/Crosby 20.00 50.00
AF2LH M.Ryder/C.Huet 3.00 8.00
AF2LJ J.Lehtinen/J.Jokinen 2.50 6.00
AF2LM M.Lemieux/M.Messier 12.00 30.00
AF2LR D.Legwand/A.Radulov 4.00 10.00
AF2LZ Lidstrom/Zetterberg 5.00 12.00
AF2MA M.Sundin/A.Raycroft 4.00 10.00
AF2MB M.Sundin/B.Salming 4.00 10.00
AF2MC M.Ryder/C.Higgins 2.50 6.00
AF2MJ M.Modano/J.Mullen 6.00 15.00
AF2ML M.Sundin/A.Steen 4.00 10.00
AF2MM L.McDonald/J.Mullen 3.00 8.00
AF2MR M.Modano/M.Ribeiro 6.00 15.00
AF2MT Marleau/Thornton 6.00 15.00
AF2NB C.Neely/R.Bourque 6.00 15.00
AF2NG Niedermayer/Giguere 4.00 10.00
AF2NI O.Nolan/J.Iginla 5.00 12.00
AF2NK L.Nagy/A.Kopitar 6.00 15.00
AF2NL M.Naslund/R.Luongo 6.00 15.00
AF2NM Havlat/Khabibulin 4.00 10.00
AF2NO C.Neely/A.Oates 4.00 10.00
AF2OM A.Ovechkin/E.Malkin 15.00 40.00
AF2PB M.Parrish/P.Bouchard 4.00 10.00
AF2PM D.Phaneuf/A.MacInnis 5.00 12.00
AF2PV G.Perreault/T.Vanek 4.00 10.00
AF2RB P.Roy/M.Brodeur 12.00 30.00
AF2RH D.Roloson/A.Hemsky 3.00 8.00
AF2RR G.Roberts/M.Recchi 5.00 12.00
AF2SA S.Koivu/A.Kovalev 4.00 10.00
AF2SB B.Smith/B.Bourne 4.00 10.00
AF2SC M.Comrie/M.Satan 3.00 8.00
AF2SE H.Sedin/D.Sedin 5.00 12.00
AF2SF M.Sundin/P.Forsberg 8.00 20.00

AF2SH S.Samsonov/M.Havlat 4.00 10.00
AF2SL M.Legace/B.Boyes 3.00 8.00
AF2SM M.Savard/G.Murray 3.00 8.00
AF2SN Selanne/Niedermayer 8.00 20.00
AF2SP J.Stoll/F.Pisani 3.00 8.00
AF2SR S.Shutt/L.Robinson 4.00 10.00
AF2SS J.Sakic/P.Stastny 8.00 20.00
AF2ST J.Sakic/J.Theodore 8.00 20.00
AF2SW M.Svatos/W.Wolski 3.00 8.00
AF2TC Thornton/Cheechoo 6.00 15.00
AF2TM M.Turco/B.Morrow 4.00 10.00
AF2TO M.Stajan/A.Steen 2.50 6.00
AF2TP R.Torres/F.Pisani 2.50 6.00
AF2VB Lecavalier/B.Richards 4.00 10.00
AF2VC M.Naslund/M.Ohlund 4.00 10.00
AF2VJ T.Vokoun/O.Jokinen 3.00 8.00
AF2WK D.Wilson/D.Keith 3.00 8.00
AF2WS J.Williams/E.Staal 5.00 12.00
AF2WT D.Weight/K.Tkachuk 4.00 10.00
AF2ZF N.Zherdev/S.Fedorov 5.00 12.00

2007-08 SP Game Used Authentic Fabrics Triples

AF3AMV Afino/Miller/Vanek 25.00 50.00
AF3ASH Alfred/Spezza/Heatley 25.00 50.00
AF3BCC Blake/Calder/Cammi 12.00 30.00
AF3BEG Brodeur/Elias/Gionta 30.00 60.00
AF3BLK Brodeur/Luongo/Kip 25.00 60.00
AF3BPG Bertuzzi/Perry/Getzlaf 15.00 40.00
AF3BSW Brind/Staal/Ward 15.00 40.00
AF3CCW Commo/Cole/Williams 12.00 30.00
AF3CVP Connolly/Vanek/Paille 12.00 30.00
AF3DGK Demitra/Gabor/Koivu 12.00 30.00
AF3FBK Fernan/Berger/Kessel 25.00 50.00
AF3GBB Gagne/Briere/Biron 25.00 50.00
AF3GDH Gomez/Drury/Hollweg 25.00 50.00
AF3GSD Guerin/Satan/DiPietro 12.00 30.00
AF3HDD Hasek/Draper/Datsyuk 30.00 60.00
AF3HSB Hejduk/Svatos/Budaj 15.00 40.00
AF3ITK Iginla/Tanguay/Kipr 15.00 40.00
AF3JSP Jagr/Straka/Prucha 25.00 50.00
AF3KGO Kolzig/Green/Ovechkin 40.00 80.00
AF3KPK Kovalev/Perezh/Kostit 12.00 30.00
AF3KRK Koivu/Ryder/Kovalev 30.00 60.00
AF3KWT Kariya/Weight/Tkach 10.00 25.00
AF3LAR Legwand/Arnott/Radul 15.00 40.00
AF3LBS Legace/Boyes/Stemp 10.00 25.00
AF3LHZ Lidstrom/Holmstrom/Zett 20.00 50.00
AF3LNF Fedor/Leclaire/Nash 12.00 30.00
AF3LRC Lupul/Richards/Carter 10.00 25.00
AF3LRS Lecav/Richard/St. Lou 15.00 40.00
AF3MBC Michalek/Bernier/Carle 10.00 25.00
AF3MMM Lanny/Mullen/MacInnis 12.00 30.00
AF3MRT Modano/Ribeiro/Turco 12.00 30.00
AF3NMK Naslund/Morris/Kesler 15.00 40.00
AF3NRL Nolan/Regehr/Lombo 10.00 25.00
AF3PBM Parrish/Bouch/Moore 10.00 25.00
AF3REM Redden/Emery/Mesz 12.00 30.00
AF3RMA Recchi/Malone/Armstr 10.00 25.00
AF3SFA Sundin/Forsberg/Alfred 30.00 60.00
AF3SHR Sams/Havlat/Ruutu 12.00 30.00
AF3SKK Seabrook/Keith/Khabi 10.00 25.00
AF3SLT Sakic/Lecav/Thornton 25.00 50.00
AF3SMC Savard/Murray/Chara 15.00 40.00
AF3SMT Sundin/McCabe/Tosk 15.00 40.00
AF3SNG Selanne/Nied/Giggy 12.00 30.00
AF3SRH Stoll/Roloson/Hemsky 12.00 30.00
AF3SSJ Sakic/Shanahan/Jagr 15.00 40.00
AF3SSW Stajan/Steen/White 10.00 25.00
AF3STS Sakic/Theod/Smyth 15.00 40.00
AF3SWV Savard/Wilson/Vaive 10.00 25.00
AF3THP Torres/Horcoff/Pisani 10.00 25.00
AF3VJB Vokoun/Jokinen/Bouw 12.00 30.00
AF3VSB Vyborny/Shelley/Brule 10.00 25.00
AF3ZLM Zubov/Leht/Morrow 15.00 40.00

2007-08 SP Game Used Extra SIGnificance

XSAM A.Stastny/M.Stastny 25.00 50.00
XSBB K.Bieksa/L.Bourdon 25.00 50.00
XSBO S.Samsonov/R.Bourque 10.00 25.00
XSCC K.Calder/M.Cammalleri 10.00 25.00
XSDB B.Sutter/D.Sutter 12.00 30.00
XSGD S.Gomez/N.Dawes 12.00 30.00
XSGH W.Gretzky/G.Howe 250.00 600.00
XSHP A.Hemsky/J.Pitkanen 15.00 40.00
XSJP J.Johnson/R.Parent 10.00 25.00
XSKS R.Kesler/R.Shannon 20.00 50.00
XSMA R.Malone/C.Armstrong 20.00 40.00
XSMD Afinogenov/Stafford 10.00 25.00
XSMT M.Modano/M.Turco 20.00 50.00
XSMW M.Svatos/W.Wolski 12.00 30.00
XSPD P.Prucha/N.Dawes 12.00 30.00
XSRC M.Richards/J.Carter 30.00 60.00
XSRH M.Ryder/C.Huet 12.00 30.00
XSSR S.Bernier/R.Clowe 12.00 30.00
XSSW E.Staal/C.Ward 15.00 40.00
XSTC M.Talbot/E.Christensen 15.00 30.00
XSVP M.Vlasic/J.Pavelski 20.00 50.00
XSWC S.Weber/M.Carle 10.00 25.00
XSWL R.Whitney/K.Letang 12.00 30.00
XSWR S.Weber/A.Radulov 10.00 25.00
XSZB N.Zherdev/G.Brule 15.00 40.00

2007-08 SP Game Used Inked Sweaters

*PATCH/25: .5X TO 1.2X JSY AU/50
ISAF Alexander Frolov 8.00 20.00
ISAH Ales Hemsky 10.00 25.00
ISAK Andrei Kostitsyn 10.00 25.00
ISAR Alexander Radulov 12.00 30.00
ISAT Alex Tanguay 10.00 25.00
ISBB Brad Boyes 8.00 20.00
ISBF Bernie Federko 10.00 25.00
ISBG Brian Gionta 8.00 20.00
ISBM Brendan Morrison 8.00 20.00
ISBO Pierre-Marc Bouchard 12.00 30.00
ISBR Daniel Briere 12.00 30.00
ISCH Cristobal Huet 10.00 25.00
ISCK Chuck Kobasew 8.00 20.00
ISCP Corey Perry 20.00 50.00
ISCW Cam Ward 12.00 30.00
ISDB Dustin Brown 12.00 30.00
ISDH Dany Heatley 20.00 50.00
ISDP Dion Phaneuf 10.00 25.00
ISDR Dwayne Roloson 10.00 25.00
ISDW Doug Wilson 10.00 25.00
ISEM Evgeni Malkin 30.00 80.00
ISES Eric Staal 15.00 40.00
ISFP Fernando Pisani 8.00 20.00
ISGA Simon Gagne 12.00 30.00
ISGB Gilbert Brule 10.00 25.00
ISGE Martin Gerber 10.00 25.00
ISGL Guy Lafleur 30.00 80.00
ISGM Glen Murray 10.00 25.00
ISHE Milan Hejduk 10.00 25.00
ISHL Henrik Lundqvist 30.00 80.00
ISHT Hannu Toivonen 10.00 25.00
ISHU Trent Hunter 8.00 20.00
ISIW Ian White 8.00 20.00
ISJA Jason Arnott 10.00 25.00
ISJB Jay Bouwmeester 8.00 20.00
ISJC Jeff Carter 10.00 25.00
ISJG Jean-Sebastien Giguere 12.00 30.00
ISJI Jarome Iginla 15.00 40.00
ISJO Jonathan Cheechoo 10.00 25.00
ISJS Jarret Stoll 10.00 25.00
ISJT Jose Theodore 12.00 30.00
ISJW Justin Williams 10.00 25.00
ISKB Kevin Bieksa 10.00 25.00
ISKC Kyle Calder 8.00 20.00
ISKD Kris Draper 8.00 20.00
ISKL Kari Lehtonen 10.00 25.00
ISKO Anze Kopitar 20.00 50.00
ISLI John-Michael Liles 8.00 20.00
ISLN Ladislav Nagy 8.00 20.00
ISLS Ladislav Smid 8.00 20.00
ISMA Martin St. Louis 12.00 30.00
ISMB Martin Biron 10.00 25.00
ISMC Matt Carle 8.00 20.00
ISMF Marc-Andre Fleury 25.00 60.00
ISMG Marian Gaborik 12.00 30.00
ISMH Martin Havlat 12.00 30.00
ISMI Mike Richards 10.00 25.00
ISMJ Milan Jurcina 8.00 20.00
ISMM Mike Modano 20.00 50.00
ISMN Markus Naslund 12.00 30.00
ISMO Brenden Morrow 10.00 25.00
ISMP Marc-Antoine Pouliot 8.00 20.00
ISMR Michael Ryder 8.00 20.00
ISMS Marc Savard 8.00 20.00
ISMT Marty Turco 12.00 30.00
ISNH Nathan Horton 12.00 30.00
ISNL Nicklas Lidstrom 12.00 30.00
ISNZ Nikolai Zherdev 8.00 20.00
ISPB Patrice Bergeron 15.00 40.00
ISPE Patrik Elias 12.00 30.00
ISPK Phil Kessel 12.00 30.00
ISPL Pascal Leclaire 10.00 25.00
ISPP Petr Prucha 8.00 20.00
ISRA Andrew Raycroft 10.00 25.00
ISRE Robert Esche 10.00 25.00
ISRG Ryan Getzlaf 12.00 30.00
ISRI Mike Ribeiro 8.00 20.00
ISRK Ryan Kesler 12.00 30.00
ISRM Ryan Malone 8.00 20.00
ISRN Rick Nash 12.00 30.00
ISRY Ryan Miller 12.00 30.00
ISSA Miroslav Satan 10.00 25.00
ISSB Steve Bernier 8.00 20.00
ISSC Sidney Crosby 75.00 150.00
ISSD Shane Doan 10.00 25.00
ISSG Scott Gomez 10.00 25.00
ISSV Marek Svatos 8.00 20.00
ISSW Shea Weber 10.00 25.00
ISTF Tomas Fleischmann 8.00 20.00
ISTH Tomas Holmstrom 10.00 25.00
ISTV Tomas Vokoun 10.00 25.00
ISVL Vincent Lecavalier 12.00 30.00
ISWE Stephen Weiss 8.00 20.00
ISWW Wojtek Wolski 10.00 25.00
ISZP Zach Parise 12.00 30.00

2007-08 SP Game Used Inked Sweaters Dual

IS2CB Cheechoo/Bernier 12.00 30.00
IS2DA D.Roloson/A.Hemsky 12.00 30.00
IS2EG P.Elias/B.Gionta 15.00 40.00
IS2FK A.Frolov/A.Kopitar 25.00 60.00
IS2FM M.Fleury/E.Malkin 30.00 80.00
IS2GB M.Gaborik/P.Bouchard 15.00 40.00
IS2GC S.Gagne/J.Carter 15.00 40.00
IS2GH J.Giguere/D.Heatley 15.00 40.00
IS2GP S.Gomez/P.Prucha 12.00 30.00
IS2HL D.Hasek/N.Lidstrom 25.00 60.00
IS2HS M.Hejduk/M.Svatos 12.00 30.00
IS2IP J.Iginla/D.Phaneuf 20.00 50.00
IS2LT Lecavalier/Thornton 25.00 60.00
IS2MR M.Modano/M.Ribeiro 25.00 60.00
IS2MW R.Miller/C.Ward 15.00 40.00
IS2NM M.Naslund/B.Morrison 15.00 40.00
IS2OR A.Ovechkin/A.Radulov 60.00 150.00
IS2PG C.Perry/R.Getzlaf 25.00 60.00
IS2RB P.Roy/R.Bourque 40.00 100.00
IS2RH M.Ryder/C.Huet 12.00 30.00
IS2SB M.Savard/P.Bergeron 20.00 50.00
IS2SN M.St. Louis/R.Nash 15.00 40.00
IS2VH T.Vokoun/N.Horton 15.00 40.00
IS2WS J.Williams/E.Staal 20.00 50.00

2007-08 SP Game Used Legendary Fabrics

LFAM Al MacInnis 12.00 30.00
LFAO Adam Oates 10.00 25.00
LFBB Bob Bourne 6.00 15.00
LFBC Bobby Clarke 15.00 40.00
LFBN Bernie Nicholls 8.00 20.00
LFBP Bob Probert 10.00 25.00
LFBR Bill Ranford 10.00 25.00
LFBS Billy Smith 10.00 25.00
LFBU Johnny Bucyk 10.00 25.00
LFCN Cam Neely 10.00 25.00
LFDC Dino Ciccarelli 10.00 25.00
LFDE Denis Savard 10.00 25.00
LFDG Doug Gilmour 12.00 30.00
LFDH Dale Hawerchuk 12.00 30.00
LFDW Doug Wilson 8.00 20.00
LFFM Frank Mahovlich 10.00 25.00
LFGA Glenn Anderson 8.00 20.00
LFGF Grant Fuhr 15.00 40.00
LFGL Guy Lafleur 10.00 25.00
LFGP Gilbert Perreault 10.00 25.00
LFJM Joe Mullen 8.00 20.00
LFLM Lanny McDonald 10.00 25.00
LFLR Larry Robinson 10.00 25.00
LFML Mario Lemieux 20.00 40.00
LFMM Mark Messier 12.00 30.00
LFMU Larry Murphy 8.00 20.00
LFNY Bob Nystrom 6.00 15.00
LFPR Patrick Roy 20.00 40.00
LFPS Peter Stastny 8.00 20.00
LFRB Ray Bourque 12.00 30.00
LFRH Ron Hextall 8.00 20.00
LFRI Richard Brodeur 8.00 20.00
LFRO Luc Robitaille 8.00 20.00
LFRV Rogie Vachon 10.00 25.00
LFSA Borje Salming 10.00 25.00
LFSH Steve Shutt 8.00 20.00
LFSS Scott Stevens 10.00 25.00
LFTW Tiger Williams 6.00 15.00
LFWG Wayne Gretzky 20.00 50.00
LFZP Zigmund Palffy 10.00 25.00

2007-08 SP Game Used Legendary Fabrics Autographs

LAFAM Al MacInnis 20.00 50.00
LAFBB Bob Bourne 10.00 25.00
LAFBN Bernie Nicholls 12.00 30.00
LAFBS Billy Smith 15.00 40.00
LAFCN Cam Neely 20.00 50.00
LAFDC Dino Ciccarelli 15.00 40.00
LAFDG Doug Gilmour 20.00 50.00
LAFDH Dale Hawerchuk 20.00 50.00
LAFDW Doug Wilson 12.00 30.00
LAFFM Frank Mahovlich 25.00 60.00
LAFGA Glenn Anderson 12.00 30.00
LAFGF Grant Fuhr 15.00 40.00
LAFGP Gilbert Perreault 15.00 40.00
LAFJM Joe Mullen 12.00 30.00
LAFLR Larry Robinson 15.00 40.00
LAFML Mario Lemieux 75.00 150.00
LAFNY Bob Nystrom 12.00 30.00
LAFPR Patrick Roy 60.00 120.00
LAFPS Peter Stastny 12.00 30.00
LAFRB Ray Bourque 40.00 80.00
LAFRH Ron Hextall 15.00 40.00
LAFRI Richard Brodeur 12.00 30.00
LAFRO Luc Robitaille 15.00 40.00
LAFSA Borje Salming 15.00 40.00
LAFTW Tiger Williams 15.00 40.00
LAFWG Wayne Gretzky 150.00 400.00

2007-08 SP Game Used Legends Classic Jerseys

*PATCH/50: .8X TO 2X JSY/100
HGJAS Anton Stastny 4.00 10.00
HGJBB Bob Bourne 4.00 10.00
HGJBN Bernie Nicholls 5.00 12.00
HGJBR Bill Ranford 6.00 15.00
HGJBS Billy Smith 6.00 15.00
HGJBT Bryan Trottier 6.00 15.00
HGJDG Doug Gilmour 8.00 20.00
HGJDH Dale Hawerchuk 8.00 20.00
HGJDS Darryl Sittler 8.00 20.00
HGJGA Glenn Anderson 5.00 12.00
HGJGF Grant Fuhr 10.00 25.00
HGJHA Dale Hawerchuk 8.00 20.00
HGJJM Joe Mullen 5.00 12.00
HGJLM Lanny McDonald 6.00 15.00
HGJLR Larry Robinson 6.00 15.00
HGJMU Larry Murphy 5.00 12.00
HGJPS Peter Stastny 5.00 12.00
HGJRB Richard Brodeur 5.00 12.00
HGJRE Ron Ellis 4.00 10.00
HGJRV Rick Vaive 5.00 12.00
HGJSA Borje Salming 6.00 15.00
HGJSS Steve Shutt 5.00 12.00
HGJTW Tiger Williams 4.00 10.00
HGJWC Wendel Clark 10.00 25.00

2007-08 SP Game Used Legends Classic Jerseys Autographs

*PATCH AU/25: .8X TO 2X JSY AU/50
HGJAS Anton Stastny 8.00 20.00
HGJBB Bob Bourne 8.00 20.00
HGJBN Bernie Nicholls 10.00 25.00
HGJBR Bill Ranford 12.00 30.00
HGJBS Billy Smith 12.00 30.00
HGJBT Bryan Trottier 12.00 30.00
HGJDG Doug Gilmour 15.00 40.00
HGJDH Dale Hawerchuk 15.00 40.00
HGJDS Darryl Sittler 15.00 40.00
HGJGA Glenn Anderson 10.00 25.00
HGJGF Grant Fuhr 20.00 50.00
HGJHA Dale Hawerchuk 15.00 40.00
HGJJM Joe Mullen 10.00 25.00
HGJLM Lanny McDonald 12.00 30.00
HGJLR Larry Robinson 12.00 30.00
HGJMU Larry Murphy 10.00 25.00
HGJPS Peter Stastny 10.00 25.00
HGJRB Richard Brodeur 10.00 25.00
HGJRE Ron Ellis 8.00 20.00
HGJRV Rick Vaive 10.00 25.00
HGJSA Borje Salming 12.00 30.00
HGJSS Steve Shutt 10.00 25.00
HGJTW Tiger Williams 8.00 20.00
HGJWC Wendel Clark 8.00 20.00

2007-08 SP Game Used Letter Marks

LMAC A. Cogliano EXCH 15.00 40.00
LMAF Alexander Frolov 15.00 40.00
LMAH Ales Hemsky 25.00 60.00
LMAK Anze Kopitar 50.00 100.00
LMAM Al MacInnis 15.00 40.00
LMBC Bobby Clarke 50.00 80.00
LMBF Bernie Federko 15.00 40.00
LMBP Bernie Parent 50.00 100.00
LMBU Johnny Bucyk 25.00 60.00
LMCA M. Cammalleri EXCH 15.00 40.00
LMCG Clark Gillies 15.00 40.00
LMCN Cam Neely 40.00 80.00
LMCW Cam Ward 25.00 60.00
LMDP Denis Potvin 15.00 40.00
LMDW Doug Wilson 15.00 40.00
LMEM Evgeni Malkin 75.00 120.00
LMES Eric Staal 25.00 60.00
LMGH Gordie Howe 75.00 120.00
LMHE M. Hejduk EXCH 15.00 40.00
LMJB Jean Beliveau 40.00 80.00
LMJG Jean-Sebastien Giguere 15.00 40.00
LMJJ Jack Johnson 15.00 40.00
LMJK Jari Kurri 40.00 80.00
LMJS Jordan Staal 25.00 60.00
LMJT Jonathan Toews 100.00 200.00
LMKD Kris Draper 15.00 40.00
LMKE Phil Kessel 25.00 60.00
LMLA Guy Lafleur 50.00 100.00
LMMB Mike Bossy 60.00 80.00
LMMC Andy McDonald 15.00 40.00
LMMD Marcel Dionne 25.00 60.00
LMMF Marc-Andre Fleury 50.00 100.00
LMMS Milt Schmidt 15.00 40.00
LMMU Peter Mueller 20.00 50.00
LMPE Phil Esposito 40.00 80.00
LMPK Patrick Kane 75.00 150.00
LMPR Carey Price 80.00 200.00
LMRA Andrew Raycroft 15.00 40.00
LMRH Ron Hextall 50.00 100.00
LMRM Ryan Miller 25.00 60.00
LMRS Rob Schremp 25.00 60.00
LMSM Stan Mikita 25.00 60.00
LMTE Tony Esposito 100.00 200.00
LMTL Ted Lindsay 20.00 50.00
LMTO Terry O'Reilly 25.00 60.00
LMTV Tomas Vokoun 50.00 80.00
LMVL V. Lecavalier/25 EXCH 60.00 100.00
LMWG Wayne Gretzky 300.00 800.00

2007-08 SP Game Used Number Marks

NMAH Ales Hemsky 15.00 40.00
NMAK Anze Kopitar 25.00 60.00
NMAO Alexander Ovechkin 175.00 300.00
NMAR Andrew Raycroft 20.00 50.00
NMBC Bobby Clarke 75.00 150.00
NMBH Bobby Hull 40.00 100.00
NMBO Bobby Orr 200.00 400.00
NMBR Martin Brodeur 175.00 300.00
NMCA Jeff Carter 30.00 80.00
NMCW Cam Ward 15.00 40.00
NMDR Dwayne Roloson 15.00 40.00
NMEM Evgeni Malkin 100.00 200.00
NMES Eric Staal 25.00 60.00
NMGH Gordie Howe 125.00 250.00
NMGP Gilbert Perreault 30.00 80.00
NMHA Dominik Hasek 75.00 150.00
NMHL Henrik Lundqvist 75.00 150.00
NMJC Jonathan Cheechoo 30.00 80.00
NMJI Jarome Iginla 75.00 150.00
NMJJ J. Johnson EXCH 40.00 100.00
NMJK Jari Kurri 40.00 100.00
NMJS Jordan Staal 50.00 100.00
NMJT Jose Theodore 15.00 40.00
NMMB Mike Bossy 75.00 150.00
NMMC M. Cammalleri EXCH 20.00 50.00
NMMN Markus Naslund 15.00 40.00
NMMO Mike Modano 75.00 150.00
NMMR Michael Ryder 15.00 40.00
NMMS Martin St. Louis 25.00 60.00
NMMT Marty Turco 20.00 50.00
NMNL Nicklas Lidstrom 75.00 125.00
NMPE Patrik Elias 20.00 50.00
NMPK Phil Kessel 25.00 60.00
NMPS Paul Stastny 40.00 100.00
NMRA Alexander Radulov 40.00 100.00
NMRB R. Bourque EXCH 75.00 150.00
NMRM Ryan Miller 40.00 100.00
NMRN Rick Nash 75.00 150.00
NMSA Miroslav Satan 15.00 40.00
NMSC Sidney Crosby 200.00 400.00
NMSD Shane Doan 75.00 150.00
NMSG Simon Gagne 15.00 40.00
NMSV Marek Svatos 25.00 60.00
NMTE Tony Esposito 40.00 100.00
NMTH Joe Thornton 30.00 80.00
NMTV Tomas Vokoun 25.00 60.00
NMVL Vincent Lecavalier 40.00 100.00
NMWG Wayne Gretzky 300.00 800.00

2007-08 SP Game Used Rookie Exclusives Autographs

REAC Andrew Cogliano 8.00 20.00
REAG Andy Greene 8.00 20.00
REAS Anton Stralman 6.00 15.00
REBA Nicklas Backstrom 30.00 60.00
REBD Brandon Dubinsky 15.00 40.00
REBE Jonathan Bernier 12.00 30.00
REBL Bryan Little 8.00 20.00
REBR Bobby Ryan 15.00 40.00
REBS Brett Sterling 6.00 15.00
RECA Ryan Callahan 12.00 30.00
RECM Curtis McElhinney 10.00 25.00
RECP Carey Price 60.00 150.00
REDC Daniel Carcillo 8.00 20.00
REDG Daniel Girardi 8.00 20.00
REDK David Krejci 30.00 80.00
REDM Drew Miller 8.00 20.00
REDP David Perron 12.00 30.00
REDS Devin Setoguchi 10.00 25.00
REEJ Erik Johnson 10.00 25.00
REEL Brian Elliott 12.00 30.00
REFN Frans Nielsen 10.00 25.00
REHA Jaroslav Halak 10.00 25.00
REHL Jaroslav Hlinka 8.00 20.00
REJA Jannik Hansen 8.00 20.00
REJB Jared Boll 8.00 20.00
REJH Jonas Hiller 12.00 30.00
REJJ Jack Johnson 8.00 20.00
REJS Jonathan Sigalet 6.00 15.00
REJT Jonathan Toews 60.00 120.00
REKR Kris Russell 10.00 25.00
RELT Lauri Tukonen 6.00 15.00
REMA Matt Smaby 6.00 15.00
REME Matt Ellis 8.00 20.00
REMH Martin Hanzal 8.00 20.00
REML Milan Lucic 25.00 50.00
REMM Marc Methot 6.00 15.00
REMN Matt Niskanen 10.00 25.00
REMR Mason Raymond 10.00 25.00
REMS Marc Staal 10.00 25.00
REMU Cory Murphy 6.00 15.00
RENB Nicklas Bergfors 6.00 15.00
RENF Nick Foligno 12.00 30.00
REOP Ondrej Pavelec 12.00 30.00
REPA Ryan Parent 6.00 15.00
REPK Patrick Kane 50.00 100.00
REPM Peter Mueller 12.00 30.00
RERC Ryan Carter 6.00 15.00
RERP Rod Pelley 6.00 15.00
RERS Rob Schremp 8.00 20.00
RESG S. Gagner EXCH 15.00 40.00
RESH James Sheppard 6.00 15.00
RESM Stefan Meyer 8.00 20.00
RETE Tobias Enstrom 10.00 25.00
RETG Tom Gilbert 8.00 20.00
RETL Jiri Tlusty 10.00 25.00
RETM Torrey Mitchell 8.00 20.00
RETP Tomas Plihal 6.00 15.00
RETS Tobias Stephan 8.00 20.00
RETW Tyler Weiman 8.00 20.00

2007-08 SP Game Used SIGnificance

SAA Andrew Alberts 5.00 12.00
SAF Alexander Frolov 5.00 12.00
SAK Andrei Kostitsyn 6.00 15.00
SAM Al Montoya 6.00 15.00
SAO Adam Oates 8.00 20.00
SAR Alexander Radulov 12.00 30.00
SBB Brad Boyes 5.00 12.00
SBC Blake Comeau 5.00 12.00
SBG Brian Gionta 5.00 12.00
SBI Kevin Bieksa 6.00 15.00
SBM Barry Melrose 6.00 15.00
SBO David Booth 5.00 12.00
SBP Benoit Pouliot 5.00 12.00
SBW Ben Walter 5.00 12.00
SCA Colby Armstrong 5.00 12.00
SCB Christian Backman 5.00 12.00
SCH Chuck Kobasew 5.00 12.00
SCK Chris Kunitz 8.00 20.00
SCM Matt Carle 5.00 12.00
SCP Chris Phillips 5.00 12.00
SCR Craig MacTavish 5.00 12.00
SDA Daniel Briere 8.00 20.00
SDB Dustin Brown 8.00 20.00
SDK Duncan Keith 6.00 15.00
SDS Drew Stafford 5.00 12.00
SDW Doug Wilson 6.00 15.00
SEC Erik Christensen 5.00 12.00
SEF Eric Fehr 5.00 12.00
SFN Fredrik Norrena 5.00 12.00
SGH Gordie Howe 50.00 100.00
SHA Michal Handzus 6.00 15.00
SHL Hakan Loob 5.00 12.00
SIW Ian White 5.00 12.00
SJA Jason Arnott 6.00 15.00
SJG Josh Gorges 5.00 12.00
SJI Jarkko Immonen 5.00 12.00
SJM Jay McClement 5.00 12.00
SJP Joe Pavelski 10.00 25.00
SKB Keith Ballard 5.00 12.00
SKC Kyle Calder 5.00 12.00
SKD Kris Draper 5.00 12.00
SKH Kristian Huselius 5.00 12.00
SKL Rostislav Klesla 5.00 12.00
SKO Anze Kopitar 12.00 30.00
SKQ Kyle Quincey 5.00 12.00
SLA Pat LaFontaine 8.00 20.00
SLE Loui Eriksson 5.00 12.00
SLI John-Michael Liles 5.00 12.00
SLN Ladislav Nagy 5.00 12.00
SMA Maxim Afinogenov 5.00 12.00
SMB Martin Biron 6.00 15.00
SMC Andy McDonald 6.00 15.00
SMG Martin Gerber 6.00 15.00
SMH Marcel Hossa 5.00 12.00
SMI Mike Cammalleri 6.00 15.00
SMJ Milan Jurcina 5.00 12.00
SML Maxim Lapierre 5.00 12.00
SMN Markus Naslund 8.00 20.00
SMR Mike Richards 6.00 15.00
SMS Marek Svatos 5.00 12.00
SMT Maxime Talbot 5.00 12.00
SMV Marc-Edouard Vlasic 5.00 12.00
SNZ Nikolai Zherdev 5.00 12.00
SON Ben Ondrus 5.00 12.00
SPB Brandon Prust 5.00 12.00
SPE Corey Perry 12.00 30.00
SPI Pierre-Marc Bouchard 8.00 20.00
SPL Pascal Leclaire 6.00 15.00
SPO Patrick O'Sullivan 6.00 15.00
SPP Petr Prucha 5.00 12.00
SPR Bob Probert 8.00 20.00
SRB Rene Bourque 5.00 12.00
SRC Ryane Clowe 5.00 12.00
SRD Ron Duguay 15.00 40.00
SRG Ryan Getzlaf 8.00 20.00
SRK Red Kelly 8.00 20.00
SRL Rejean Lemelin 5.00 12.00
SRM Ryan Malone 5.00 12.00
SRP Ryan Potulny 5.00 12.00
SRW Ryan Whitney 6.00 15.00
SSB Steve Bernier 5.00 12.00
SSC Milt Schmidt 6.00 15.00
SSD Shane Doan 6.00 15.00
SSG Scott Gomez 6.00 15.00
SSI Sidney Crosby 100.00 200.00
SSS Sergei Samsonov 6.00 15.00
SST Mark Stuart 5.00 12.00
SSW Shea Weber 6.00 15.00
STH Tomas Holmstrom 6.00 15.00
STV Thomas Vanek 6.00 15.00
SVF Valtteri Filppula 5.00 12.00
SVO Tomas Vokoun 6.00 15.00
SWE Stephen Weiss 5.00 12.00
SWG Wayne Gretzky 150.00 400.00
SWW Wojtek Wolski 6.00 15.00
SYS Yan Stastny 5.00 12.00
SZP Zach Parise 12.00 30.00

2007-08 SP Game Used SIGnificant Numbers

SNAF Alexander Frolov/24 8.00 20.00
SNAR Alexander Radulov/47 12.00 30.00
SNAT Alex Tanguay/40 10.00 25.00
SNBB Brad Boyes/38 8.00 20.00
SNBC Bobby Clarke/16 20.00 50.00
SNBN Bob Nystrom/23 8.00 20.00
SNBR Bill Ranford/30 12.00 30.00
SNBS Borje Salming/21 12.00 30.00
SNCA Colby Armstrong/20 8.00 20.00
SNCW Cam Ward/30 12.00 30.00
SNDC Dino Ciccarelli/22 12.00 30.00
SNDG Doug Gilmour/93 15.00 40.00
SNDS Darryl Sittler/27 15.00 40.00
SNEM Evgeni Malkin/71 25.00 60.00
SNFM Frank Mahovlich/27 12.00 30.00
SNGB Gilbert Brule/17 10.00 25.00
SNGF Grant Fuhr/31 20.00 50.00
SNHA Dominik Hasek/39 20.00 50.00
SNHL Henrik Lundqvist/30 30.00 80.00
SNIK Ilya Kovalchuk/17 12.00 30.00
SNJA Jason Arnott/19 10.00 25.00
SNJE Jeff Carter/17 10.00 25.00
SNJG Jean-Sebastien Giguere/35 12.00 30.00
SNJK Jari Kurri/17 12.00 30.00
SNJS Jarret Stoll/16 10.00 25.00
SNJT Joe Thornton/19 20.00 50.00
SNKD Kris Draper/33 8.00 20.00
SNKL Kari Lehtonen/32 10.00 25.00
SNMB Martin Brodeur/30 30.00 80.00
SNMF Marc-Andre Fleury/29 25.00 60.00
SNMH Milan Hejduk/23 10.00 25.00
SNMN Markus Naslund/19 12.00 30.00
SNMR Michael Ryder/73 8.00 20.00
SNMS Marc Savard/71 8.00 20.00
SNMT Marty Turco/35 12.00 30.00
SNPB Patrice Bergeron/37 15.00 40.00
SNRH Ron Hextall/27 12.00 30.00
SNRI Mike Ribeiro/71 8.00 20.00
SNRM Ryan Miller/30 12.00 30.00
SNRN Rick Nash/61 12.00 30.00
SNSC Sidney Crosby/87 50.00 125.00
SNSD Shane Doan/19 10.00 25.00
SNSS Steve Shutt/22 10.00 25.00
SNST Martin St. Louis/26 12.00 30.00
SNTH Tomas Holmstrom/96 10.00 25.00
SNTJ Jose Theodore/60 12.00 30.00
SNTV Tomas Vokoun/29 10.00 25.00

2008-09 SP Game Used

COMP.SET w/o SPs (100) 30.00 60.00
1 Scott Niedermayer .75 2.00
2 Corey Perry 1.25 3.00
3 Chris Pronger .75 2.00
4 Ryan Getzlaf .75 2.00
5 Jean-Sebastien Giguere .75 2.00
6 Ilya Kovalchuk .75 2.00
7 Kari Lehtonen 1.00 2.50
8 Marc Savard .50 1.25
9 Bobby Orr 3.00 8.00
10 Michael Ryder .50 1.25
11 Phil Kessel .75 2.00
12 Thomas Vanek .60 1.50
13 Ryan Miller .75 2.00
14 Jason Pominville .50 1.25
15 Derek Roy .50 1.25
16 Jarome Iginla 1.00 2.50
17 Miikka Kiprusoff .75 2.00
18 Dion Phaneuf .60 1.50
19 Eric Staal 1.00 2.50
20 Cam Ward .75 2.00
21 Brian Campbell .60 1.50
22 Patrick Sharp .75 2.00
23 Jonathan Toews 1.25 3.00
24 Patrick Kane 1.50 4.00
25 Cristobal Huet .60 1.50
26 Patrick Roy 2.00 5.00
27 Joe Sakic 1.50 4.00
28 Milan Hejduk .60 1.50
29 Paul Stastny .60 1.50
30 Rick Nash .75 2.00
31 Pascal Leclaire .60 1.50
32 Brad Richards .75 2.00
33 Mike Modano 1.25 3.00
34 Marty Turco .75 2.00
35 Mike Ribeiro .50 1.25
36 Chris Osgood .75 2.00
37 Johan Franzen .60 1.50
38 Pavel Datsyuk 1.25 3.00
39 Henrik Zetterberg 1.00 2.50
40 Nicklas Lidstrom .75 2.00
41 Marian Hossa .75 2.00
42 Shawn Horcoff .50 1.25
43 Ales Hemsky .60 1.50
44 Tomas Vokoun .60 1.50
45 Nathan Horton .60 1.50
46 Gordie Howe 2.50 6.00
47 Wayne Gretzky 5.00 12.00
48 Anze Kopitar 1.25 3.00
49 Alexander Frolov .50 1.25
50 Brent Burns .75 2.00
51 Marian Gaborik .75 2.00
52 Pierre-Marc Bouchard .75 2.00
53 Niklas Backstrom .75 2.00
54 Alex Tanguay .50 1.25
55 Carey Price 1.50 4.00
56 Saku Koivu .75 2.00
57 Alex Kovalev .60 1.50
58 J.P. Dumont .50 1.25
59 Dan Ellis .50 1.25
60 Jason Arnott .60 1.50
61 Martin Brodeur 2.00 5.00
62 Patrik Elias .75 2.00
63 Zach Parise .75 2.00
64 Rick DiPietro .60 1.50
65 Nikolai Zherdev .50 1.25
66 Mark Messier 1.50 4.00
67 Brian Leetch .60 1.50
68 Henrik Lundqvist 2.00 5.00
69 Chris Drury .60 1.50
70 Jason Spezza .75 2.00
71 Daniel Alfredsson .75 2.00
72 Dany Heatley .60 1.50
73 Mike Richards .60 1.50
74 Martin Biron .60 1.50
75 Simon Gagne .75 2.00
76 Daniel Briere .75 2.00
77 Olli Jokinen .60 1.50
78 Shane Doan .60 1.50
79 Peter Mueller .60 1.50
80 Miroslav Satan .75 2.00
81 Mario Lemieux 3.00 8.00
82 Jordan Staal .60 1.50
83 Sidney Crosby 3.00 8.00
84 Marc-Andre Fleury 1.50 4.00
85 Evgeni Malkin 1.50 4.00
86 Rob Blake .75 2.00
87 Joe Thornton 1.25 3.00
88 Jonathan Cheechoo .60 1.50
89 Evgeni Nabokov .60 1.50
90 Brad Boyes .50 1.25
91 Paul Kariya .75 2.00
92 Martin St. Louis .75 2.00
93 Vincent Lecavalier .75 2.00
94 Mats Sundin .75 2.00
95 Vesa Toskala 1.00 2.50
96 Roberto Luongo 1.25 3.00
97 Henrik Sedin 1.00 2.50
98 Daniel Sedin 1.00 2.50
99 Nicklas Backstrom .75 2.00
100 Alexander Ovechkin 3.00 8.00
101 Adam Pineault RC 3.00 8.00
102 Alex Foster RC 3.00 8.00
103 Alex Goligoski RC 5.00 12.00
104 Andrew Ebbett RC 2.50 6.00
105 Andrew Murray RC 3.00 8.00
106 B.J. Crombeen RC 2.50 6.00
107 Boris Valabik RC 4.00 10.00
108 Brandon Nolan RC 3.00 8.00
109 Brian Boyle RC 3.00 8.00
110 Brian Lee RC 3.00 8.00
111 Chris Minard RC 4.00 10.00
112 Claude Giroux RC 10.00 25.00
113 Nikita Filatov RC 4.00 10.00
114 Cody McLeod RC 3.00 8.00
115 Colin Stuart RC 3.00 8.00
116 Corey Locke RC 3.00 8.00
117 Dan LaCosta RC 4.00 10.00
118 Danny Taylor RC 3.00 8.00
119 Darren Helm RC 4.00 10.00
120 Darryl Boyce RC 3.00 8.00
121 David Brine RC 2.50 6.00
122 Derick Brassard RC 4.00 10.00
123 Erik Ersberg RC 3.00 8.00
124 Garrett Stafford RC 4.00 10.00
125 Ilya Zubov RC 3.00 8.00
126 Jack Hillen RC 3.00 8.00
127 Jesse Winchester RC 2.50 6.00
128 Joe Jensen RC 4.00 10.00
129 Joey Mormina RC 3.00 8.00
130 Jon Filewich RC 3.00 8.00
131 Jonathan Ericsson RC 4.00 10.00
132 Jordan Hendry RC 3.00 8.00
133 Jordan LaVallee RC 4.00 10.00
134 Justin Abdelkader RC 6.00 15.00
135 Brandon Sutter RC 4.00 10.00
136 Kyle Greentree RC 4.00 10.00
137 Kyle Okposo RC 5.00 12.00
138 James Neal RC 8.00 20.00
139 Lauri Korpikoski RC 2.50 6.00
140 Marc-Andre Gragnani RC 3.00 8.00
141 Mark Fistric RC 3.00 8.00
142 Matt D'Agostini RC 3.00 8.00
143 Mattias Ritola RC 3.00 8.00
144 Mike Brown RC 4.00 10.00
145 Mike Iggulden RC 3.00 8.00
146 Mike Mole RC 3.00 8.00
147 Niklas Hjalmarsson RC 4.00 10.00
148 Pascal Pelletier RC 2.50 6.00
149 Luca Sbisa RC 2.50 6.00
150 Robbie Earl RC 2.50 6.00
151 Ryan Stone RC 2.50 6.00
152 Sami Lepisto RC 3.00 8.00
153 Shawn Matthias RC 4.00 10.00
154 Steve Mason RC 6.00 15.00
155 Colton Gillies RC 3.00 8.00
156 Michael Frolik RC 4.00 10.00
157 Nikolai Kulemin RC 4.00 10.00
158 T.J. Oshie RC 8.00 20.00
159 Patrik Berglund RC 3.00 8.00
160 Patric Hornqvist RC 4.00 10.00
161 Ryan Jones RC 4.00 10.00
162 Chris Porter RC 4.00 10.00
163 Viktor Tikhonov RC 3.00 8.00
164 Kevin Porter RC 3.00 8.00
165 Jonas Frogren RC 2.50 6.00
166 John Mitchell RC 3.00 8.00
167 Paul Bissonnette RC 5.00 12.00
168 Derek Dorsett RC 5.00 12.00
169 Janne Niskala RC 4.00 10.00
170 Vladimir Mihalik RC 2.50 6.00
171 Jared Ross RC 4.00 10.00
172 Wayne Simmonds RC 6.00 15.00
173 Adam Pardy RC 3.00 8.00
174 Dane Byers RC 3.00 8.00
175 Mitch Fritz RC 3.00 8.00
176 Zach Fitzgerald RC 4.00 10.00
177 Ben Bishop RC 6.00 15.00
178 Anssi Salmela RC 4.00 10.00
179 Andreas Nodl RC 2.50 6.00
180 Petr Vrana RC 2.50 6.00
181 Zach Boychuk RC 4.00 10.00
182 Nathan Oystrick RC 4.00 10.00
183 Oscar Moller RC 3.00 8.00
184 Teddy Purcell RC 3.00 8.00
185 Theo Peckham RC 3.00 8.00
186 Tim Conboy RC 3.00 8.00
187 Tim Ramholt RC 3.00 8.00
188 Tom Cavanagh RC 3.00 8.00
189 Tom Sestito RC 4.00 10.00
190 Tyler Plante RC 3.00 8.00
191 Mikkel Boedker RC 15.00 40.00
192 Kyle Turris RC 20.00 50.00
193 Fabian Brunnstrom RC 10.00 25.00
194 Jakub Voracek RC 15.00 40.00
195 Blake Wheeler RC 30.00 80.00
196 Luke Schenn RC 15.00 40.00
197 Zach Bogosian RC 15.00 40.00
198 Alex Pietrangelo RC 15.00 40.00
199 Drew Doughty RC 40.00 80.00
200 Steven Stamkos RC 100.00 175.00

2008-09 SP Game Used Gold

*GOLD (1-100): .8X TO 2X BASE
*GOLD (101-190): .5X TO 1.2X BASE
*GOLD (191-200): .2X TO .5X BASE
99 Nicklas Backstrom 1.50 4.00
192 Kyle Turris 30.00 80.00
200 Steven Stamkos 75.00 150.00

2008-09 SP Game Used Platinum

*PLATINUM (1-100): 2X TO 5X BASE
*PLATINUM (101-190): 1.2X TO 3X BASE
*GOLD (191-200): .3X TO .8X BASE
99 Nicklas Backstrom 4.00 10.00
200 Steven Stamkos 60.00 150.00

2008-09 SP Game Used Authentic Fabrics Duos

AF2AN V.Toskala/N.Antropov 6.00 15.00
AF2BG M.Brodeur/D.Gilmour 12.00 30.00
AF2BJ A.Kopitar/J.Johnson 8.00 20.00
AF2BL M.Brodeur/R.Luongo 12.00 30.00
AF2BM M.Brodeur/R.Miller 12.00 30.00
AF2BP M.Brodeur/C.Price 12.00 30.00

Card	Low	High
AF2BR M.Richards/D.Briere	5.00	12.00
AF2CM S.Crosby/E.Malkin	20.00	50.00
AF2CR C.Chelios/B.Rafalski	5.00	12.00
AF2CT E.Cole/T.Thomas	5.00	12.00
AF2CW E.Cole/G.Brule	3.00	8.00
AF2DB P.Demitra/S.Bernier	6.00	15.00
AF2DK S.Fedorov/I.Kovalchuk	8.00	20.00
AF2DM E.Malkin/R.Fedotenko	10.00	25.00
AF2DW J.Dumont/S.Weber	4.00	10.00
AF2ED J.Dumont/D.Legwand	4.00	10.00
AF2EE P.Esposito/T.Esposito	8.00	20.00
AF2EJ E.Staal/J.Staal	6.00	15.00
AF2EP Z.Parise/P.Elias	5.00	12.00
AF2FM E.Malkin/S.Fedorov	10.00	25.00
AF2FN M.Fleury/A.Niittymaki	6.00	15.00
AF2FO M.Fleury/C.Osgood	6.00	15.00
AF2FP T.Fleury/D.Phaneuf	6.00	15.00
AF2GB M.Gaborik/P.Bouchard	5.00	12.00
AF2GC S.Gagne/J.Carter	5.00	12.00
AF2GD S.Gomez/C.Drury	4.00	10.00
AF2GK M.Gaborik/M.Koivu	5.00	12.00
AF2GP Z.Parise/B.Gionta	5.00	12.00
AF2GW S.Gonchar/R.Whitney	5.00	12.00
AF2HF P.Forsberg/M.Hejduk	10.00	25.00
AF2HG S.Horcoff/S.Gagner	3.00	8.00
AF2HH M.Hossa/M.Hossa	5.00	12.00
AF2IK A.Kovalev/I.Kovalchuk	5.00	12.00
AF2JH S.Doan/O.Jokinen	4.00	10.00
AF2JJ J.Johnson/E.Johnson	3.00	8.00
AF2JM J.Staal/E.Johnson	10.00	25.00
AF2JP J.Sakic/P.Stastny	10.00	25.00
AF2JR J.Spezza/R.Nash	5.00	12.00
AF2KK S.Koivu/A.Kovalev	5.00	12.00
AF2KM I.Kovalchuk/E.Malkin	10.00	25.00
AF2KO A.Ovechkin/I.Kovalchuk	20.00	50.00
AF2KP P.Kariya/D.Perron	5.00	12.00
AF2KV S.Koivu/M.Koivu	5.00	12.00
AF2LA L.McDonald/A.MacInnis	6.00	15.00
AF2LB R.Luongo/S.Bernier	8.00	20.00
AF2LC M.Lemieux/S.Crosby	20.00	50.00
AF2LH N.Lidstrom/T.Holmstrom	5.00	12.00
AF2LI V.Lecavalier/M.Lundin	5.00	12.00
AF2LN H.Lundqvist/M.Naslund	12.00	30.00
AF2LS V.Lecavalier/M.St. Louis	5.00	12.00
AF2LT R.Luongo/M.Turco	8.00	20.00
AF2MG M.Modano/B.Guerin	8.00	20.00
AF2MJ J.Sakic/M.Svatos	10.00	25.00
AF2MM M.Gaborik/M.Hossa	5.00	12.00
AF2MP A.MacInnis/D.Phaneuf	6.00	15.00
AF2MS B.Salming/L.McDonald	5.00	12.00
AF2NH M.Naslund/T.Holmstrom	5.00	12.00
AF2NK E.Nabokov/M.Kiprusoff	5.00	12.00
AF2NL V.Lecavalier/R.Nash	5.00	12.00
AF2NS R.Nash/M.St. Louis	5.00	12.00
AF2OB A.Ovechkin/N.Backstrom	20.00	50.00
AF2OF A.Ovechkin/S.Fedorov	20.00	50.00
AF2PC D.Phaneuf/Z.Chara	5.00	12.00
AF2PG R.Getzlaf/Perry	8.00	20.00
AF2PS P.Sharp/B.Seabrook	5.00	12.00
AF2PZ M.Naslund/N.Zherdev	5.00	12.00
AF2RB P.Bouchard/M.Koivu	5.00	12.00
AF2RD L.Robitaille/M.Dionne	6.00	15.00
AF2RF P.Roy/P.Forsberg	12.00	30.00
AF2RJ R.Smyth/J.Spezza	5.00	12.00
AF2RN L.Robitaille/B.Nicholls	5.00	12.00
AF2SD M.Staal/C.Drury	4.00	10.00
AF2SF M.Sundin/P.Forsberg	10.00	25.00
AF2SG T.Selanne/R.Getzlaf	10.00	25.00
AF2SL M.Savard/M.Lucic	8.00	20.00
AF2SM S.Doan/P.Mueller	4.00	10.00
AF2SN M.Sundin/M.Naslund	5.00	12.00
AF2SS J.Sakic/R.Smyth	10.00	25.00
AF2TB M.Turco/P.Budaj	5.00	12.00
AF2TC J.Thornton/J.Cheechoo	8.00	20.00
AF2TL K.Lehtonen/V.Toskala	6.00	15.00
AF2TM V.Lecavalier/R.Malone	5.00	12.00
AF2TN J.Thornton/R.Nash	8.00	20.00
AF2TP J.Toews/C.Price	10.00	25.00
AF2TR T.Rask/V.Toskala	6.00	15.00
AF2TT T.Thomas/T.Rask	6.00	15.00
AF2VH D.Hasek/T.Vokoun	8.00	20.00
AF2WL W.Redden/H.Lundqvist	12.00	30.00
AF2ZC E.Malkin/H.Zetterberg	10.00	25.00
AF2ZD N.Zherdev/C.Drury	4.00	10.00
AF2ZF S.Fedorov/M.Afinogenov	8.00	20.00
AF2ZM Z.Parise/M.Modano	8.00	20.00

2008-09 SP Game Used Authentic Fabrics Duos Patches

Card	Low	High
AF2AN V.Toskala/N.Antropov	12.00	30.00
AF2BB D.Briere/P.Bergeron	12.00	30.00
AF2BG M.Brodeur/D.Gilmour	25.00	60.00
AF2BJ J.Johnson/A.Kopitar	15.00	40.00
AF2BK N.Backstrom/P.Kane	15.00	40.00
AF2BM R.Miller/M.Brodeur	25.00	60.00
AF2BP M.Brodeur/C.Price	20.00	50.00
AF2BR D.Briere/M.Richards	15.00	40.00
AF2CM S.Crosby/E.Malkin	40.00	100.00
AF2CR C.Chelios/B.Rafalski	10.00	25.00
AF2CT E.Cole/T.Thomas	10.00	25.00
AF2DK I.Kovalchuk/S.Fedorov	15.00	40.00
AF2ED J.Dumont/D.Legwand	8.00	20.00
AF2EE P.Esposito/T.Esposito	15.00	40.00
AF2EP P.Elias/Z.Parise	10.00	25.00
AF2FM S.Fedorov/E.Malkin	20.00	50.00
AF2FN A.Niittymaki/M.Fleury	20.00	50.00
AF2FO C.Osgood/M.Fleury	20.00	50.00
AF2GB M.Gaborik/P.Bouchard	10.00	25.00
AF2GC S.Gagne/J.Carter	10.00	25.00
AF2GD S.Gomez/C.Drury	8.00	20.00
AF2GK M.Gaborik/M.Koivu	10.00	25.00
AF2GP B.Gionta/Z.Parise	10.00	25.00
AF2HH M.Hossa/M.Hossa	10.00	25.00
AF2IK A.Kovalev/I.Kovalchuk	10.00	25.00
AF2JJ J.Johnson/E.Johnson	6.00	15.00
AF2JR J.Spezza/R.Nash	15.00	40.00
AF2KM I.Kovalchuk/E.Malkin	20.00	50.00
AF2KP P.Kariya/D.Perron	10.00	25.00
AF2KV S.Koivu/M.Koivu	10.00	25.00
AF2LA L.McDonald/A.MacInnis	12.00	30.00
AF2LB R.Luongo/S.Bernier	15.00	40.00
AF2LC M.Lemieux/S.Crosby	40.00	100.00
AF2LE K.Lehtonen/T.Enstrom	15.00	40.00
AF2LR J.Lehtinen/M.Ribeiro	6.00	15.00
AF2LS V.Lecavalier/M.St. Louis	10.00	25.00
AF2LT M.Turco/R.Luongo	15.00	40.00
AF2MJ J.Sakic/M.Svatos	20.00	50.00
AF2MM M.Hossa/M.Gaborik	15.00	30.00
AF2MP D.Phaneuf/A.MacInnis	12.00	30.00
AF2MS L.McDonald/B.Salming	10.00	25.00
AF2NH T.Holmstrom/M.Naslund	10.00	25.00
AF2NL V.Lecavalier/R.Nash	10.00	25.00
AF2NS M.St. Louis/R.Nash	10.00	25.00
AF2OB A.Ovechkin/N.Backstrom	40.00	100.00
AF2OF S.Fedorov/A.Ovechkin	40.00	100.00
AF2PA G.Perreault/M.Afinogenov	10.00	25.00
AF2PB P.Bergeron/P.Kessel	12.00	30.00
AF2PC Z.Chara/D.Phaneuf	10.00	25.00
AF2PG C.Perry/R.Getzlaf	15.00	40.00
AF2PS P.Sharp/B.Seabrook	8.00	20.00
AF2PZ M.Naslund/N.Zherdev	10.00	25.00
AF2RB P.Bouchard/M.Koivu	10.00	25.00
AF2RF P.Roy/P.Forsberg	25.00	60.00
AF2RJ J.Spezza/R.Smyth	10.00	25.00
AF2SA D.Stafford/M.Afinogenov	6.00	15.00
AF2SF M.Sundin/P.Forsberg	20.00	50.00
AF2SG T.Selanne/R.Getzlaf	20.00	50.00
AF2SL M.Savard/M.Lucic	15.00	40.00
AF2SM S.Doan/P.Mueller	8.00	20.00
AF2SN M.Sundin/M.Naslund	10.00	25.00
AF2SS J.Sakic/R.Smyth	20.00	50.00
AF2TC J.Thornton/J.Cheechoo	15.00	40.00
AF2TK J.Toews/P.Kane	20.00	50.00
AF2TL V.Toskala/K.Lehtonen	12.00	30.00
AF2TM V.Lecavalier/R.Malone	10.00	25.00
AF2TN J.Thornton/R.Nash	15.00	40.00
AF2TP J.Toews/C.Price	20.00	50.00
AF2TR V.Toskala/T.Rask	12.00	30.00
AF2VH T.Vokoun/D.Hasek	15.00	40.00
AF2WL W.Radden/H.Lundqvist	25.00	60.00
AF2ZF S.Fedorov/M.Afinogenov	12.00	30.00
AF2ZM M.Modano/Z.Parise	15.00	40.00

2008-09 SP Game Used Authentic Fabrics Trios

*PATCH/15: .6X TO 1.5X BASIC TRIO/25

Card	Low	High
AF3BEP Brodeur/Elias/Parise	20.00	50.00
AF3BKJ Kopitar/Johnson/Brown	12.00	30.00
AF3BLF Brodeur/Luongo/Fleury	20.00	50.00
AF3BLM Brodeur/Lundqvist/Miller	20.00	50.00
AF3BMG Backstrom/Gagner/Mueller	8.00	20.00
AF3BSS Brind/Staal/Samsnv	10.00	25.00
AF3CHO Hasek/Osgood/Chelios	12.00	30.00
AF3CTN Crosby/Toews/Nash	30.00	80.00
AF3DKO Ovech/Koval/Zherdev	30.00	80.00
AF3DWS Dumont/Weber/Sullivan	6.00	15.00
AF3GBR Richards/Briere/Gagne	8.00	20.00
AF3GGP Gaborik/Getzlaf/Parise	8.00	20.00
AF3GHC Gretzky/Howe/Crosby	50.00	125.00
AF3GND Gomez/Drury/Naslund	8.00	20.00
AF3HCG Horcoff/Cole/Gagner	5.00	12.00
AF3HEG Gaborik/Hossa/Elias	8.00	20.00
AF3HEW Hull/Esposito/Wilson	15.00	40.00
AF3HSW Smyth/Wolski/Hejduk	6.00	15.00
AF3KBJ Kariya/Johnson/Perron	8.00	20.00
AF3KOM Ovech/Malkin/Koval	15.00	40.00
AF3LBD Luongo/Bernier/Demitra	12.00	30.00
AF3LCM Lemieux/Crosby/Malkin	30.00	80.00
AF3LNZ Lndqvst/Naslnd/Zherdv	20.00	50.00
AF3LPG Lids/Phanf/Gonchar	8.00	20.00
AF3MFM McDld/Fleury/MacIn	10.00	25.00
AF3NGB Gaborik/Bouchard/Nolan	8.00	20.00
AF3OGB OvechBackstrm/Green	15.00	40.00
AF3RBP Roy/Brodeur/Price	20.00	50.00
AF3RTL Turco/Lehtinen/Ribeiro	8.00	20.00
AF3SFW Fleury/Sykora/Whitney	15.00	40.00
AF3SHF Sakic/Forsberg/Hejduk	15.00	40.00
AF3SKF Selanne/Kariya/Fedorov	15.00	40.00
AF3SKK Selanne/Koivu/Koivu	15.00	40.00
AF3SNF Sundin/Naslund/Frsbrg	15.00	40.00
AF3SNH Naslund/Sundin/Holstrm	8.00	20.00
AF3SPG Selanne/Getzlaf/Perry	15.00	40.00
AF3SSW Sakic/Smyth/Wolski	15.00	40.00
AF3TLM Lndqvst/Miller/Tskala	20.00	50.00
AF3TNC Thorn/Checho/Nabkv	12.00	30.00
AF3VKL Kolzig/Lehton/Vokoun	10.00	25.00
AF3ZLC Zetter/Lidstrom/Chelios	10.00	25.00

2008-09 SP Game Used Dual Authentic Fabrics

Card	Low	High
AFAM Andrei Markov	4.00	10.00
AFAN Antero Niittymaki	3.00	8.00
AFAO Alexander Ovechkin	15.00	40.00
AFAS Anton Stastny	2.50	6.00
AFBB Bob Bourne	2.50	6.00
AFBG Patrice Bergeron	5.00	12.00
AFBL Rob Blake	4.00	10.00
AFBN Bernie Nicholls	3.00	8.00
AFBQ Ray Bourque	6.00	15.00
AFBR Steve Bernier	2.50	6.00
AFBS Billy Smith	4.00	10.00
AFBZ Todd Bertuzzi	4.00	10.00
AFCC Chris Chelios	4.00	10.00
AFCH Jonathan Cheechoo	3.00	8.00
AFDB Doug Gilmour	5.00	12.00
AFDC Dino Ciccarelli	4.00	10.00
AFDE Pavol Demitra	5.00	12.00
AFDH Dominik Hasek	6.00	15.00
AFDL Darryl Sittler	5.00	12.00
AFDP Dion Phaneuf	3.00	8.00
AFDS Denis Savard	4.00	10.00
AFDW Doug Weight	4.00	10.00
AFEL Patrik Elias	4.00	10.00
AFEM Evgeni Malkin	8.00	20.00
AFES Eric Staal	5.00	12.00
AFGA Glenn Anderson	3.00	8.00
AFGN Simon Gagne	4.00	10.00
AFGP Gilbert Perreault	4.00	10.00
AFHK Roman Hamrlik	2.50	6.00
AFHL Henrik Lundqvist	10.00	25.00
AFHM Marian Hossa	4.00	10.00
AFHO Tomas Holmstrom	3.00	8.00
AFHW Dale Hawerchuk	5.00	12.00
AFIK Ilya Kovalchuk	4.00	10.00
AFJL Jere Lehtinen	2.50	6.00
AFJM Joe Mullen	3.00	8.00
AFJS Jordan Staal	3.00	8.00
AFJW Justin Williams	3.00	8.00
AFKL Kari Lehtonen	5.00	12.00
AFKM Mike Komisarek	2.50	6.00
AFKO Mikko Koivu	3.00	8.00
AFKV Saku Koivu	4.00	10.00
AFLG Roberto Luongo	6.00	15.00
AFLM Lanny McDonald	4.00	10.00
AFLR Larry Robinson	4.00	10.00
AFMA Maxim Afinogenov	2.50	6.00
AFMB Martin Brodeur	10.00	25.00
AFME Ryan Malone	2.50	6.00
AFMF Marc-Andre Fleury	8.00	20.00
AFMG Marian Gaborik	4.00	10.00
AFMH Milan Hejduk	3.00	8.00
AFMK Miikka Kiprusoff	4.00	10.00
AFMM Mike Modano	6.00	15.00
AFMN Manny Fernandez	2.50	6.00
AFMP Michael Peca	3.00	8.00
AFMR Mike Ribeiro	2.50	6.00
AFMS Marek Svatos	2.50	6.00
AFMT Marty Turco	4.00	10.00
AFNL Nicklas Lidstrom	4.00	10.00
AFNS Markus Naslund	4.00	10.00
AFNZ Nikolai Zherdev	2.50	6.00
AFOJ Olli Jokinen	3.00	8.00
AFPA Paul Kariya	4.00	10.00
AFPB Pierre-Marc Bouchard	4.00	10.00
AFPF Peter Forsberg	8.00	20.00
AFPK Phil Kessel	4.00	10.00
AFRB Richard Brodeur	3.00	8.00
AFRD Rod Brind'Amour	4.00	10.00
AFRE Ron Ellis	2.50	6.00
AFRF Ruslan Fedotenko	2.50	6.00
AFRG Ryan Getzlaf	4.00	10.00
AFRH Ron Hextall	4.00	10.00
AFRK Ryan Kesler	4.00	10.00
AFRL Rod Langway	3.00	8.00
AFRM Ryan Miller	4.00	10.00
AFRN Rick Nash	4.00	10.00
AFRO Patrick Roy	10.00	25.00
AFRS Ryan Smyth	3.00	8.00
AFRY Michael Ryder	2.50	6.00
AFSC Sidney Crosby	15.00	40.00
AFSD Shane Doan	3.00	8.00
AFSF Sergei Fedorov	6.00	15.00
AFSH Shawn Horcoff	2.50	6.00
AFSK Joe Sakic	8.00	20.00
AFSP Jason Spezza	4.00	10.00
AFSS Steve Shutt	4.00	10.00
AFST Miroslav Satan	4.00	10.00
AFSU Mats Sundin	4.00	10.00
AFSV Marc Savard	2.50	6.00
AFSY Peter Stastny	3.00	8.00
AFSZ Sergei Zubov	3.00	8.00
AFTH Tim Thomas	4.00	10.00
AFTR Tuukka Rask	5.00	12.00
AFTS Teemu Selanne	8.00	20.00
AFTW Tiger Williams	2.50	6.00
AFVL Vincent Lecavalier	4.00	10.00
AFVO Tomas Vokoun	3.00	8.00
AFVT Vesa Toskala	5.00	12.00
AFWB Shea Weber	3.00	8.00
AFZP Zach Parise	4.00	10.00

2008-09 SP Game Used Dual Authentic Fabrics Gold

*GOLD: .5X TO 1.2X BASE

2008-09 SP Game Used Dual Authentic Fabrics Platinum

*PLATINUM: .6X TO 1.5X BASE

2008-09 SP Game Used Extra SIGnificance

Card	Low	High
XSGBC Carcillo/Burish	10.00	25.00
XSGBE M.Brodeur/P.Elias	30.00	80.00
XSGBK P.Kane/N.Backstrom	25.00	60.00
XSGBM B.Dubinsky/M.Staal	8.00	20.00
XSGCG S.Gagner/A.Cogliano	8.00	20.00
XSGCH Hextall/Clarke	20.00	50.00
XSGCM P.Mueller/D.Carcillo	10.00	25.00
XSGDB Sittler/Salming	15.00	40.00
XSGDD B.Dubinsky/C.Drury	10.00	25.00
XSGDK Setoguchi/Letang	15.00	40.00
XSGDT Dionne/Taylor	15.00	40.00
XSGDV D.Cleary/V.Filppula	10.00	25.00
XSGEE T.Esposito/P.Esposito	20.00	50.00
XSGEJ E.Staal/J.Staal	15.00	40.00
XSGEM E.Lach/M.Schmidt	15.00	40.00
XSGES P.Esposito/D.Sanderson	12.00	30.00
XSGGB N.Backstrom/M.Green	12.00	30.00
XSGGS B.Smith/C.Gillies	12.00	30.00
XSGHD K.Draper/T.Holmstrom	10.00	25.00
XSGHG D.Heatley/M.Gerber	10.00	25.00
XSGHM H.Zetterberg/M.Hossa	15.00	40.00
XSGHP C.Price/J.Halak	25.00	60.00
XSGHS J.Harding/J.Sheppard	12.00	30.00
XSGIC J.Iginla/M.Cammalleri	15.00	40.00
XSGIK Kovalchuk/Lehtonen	15.00	40.00
XSGIP J.Iginla/D.Phaneuf	15.00	40.00
XSGJP J.Pominville/D.Paille	8.00	20.00
XSGKN K.Chipchura/N.Foligno	12.00	30.00
XSGKT K.Lehtonen/T.Enstrom	15.00	40.00
XSGLE Lidstrom/Enstrom	12.00	30.00
XSGLS Lecavalier/St. Louis	12.00	30.00
XSGMD Mancari/Paille	10.00	25.00
XSGMF T.Fleury/J.Mullen	15.00	40.00
XSGMG B.Gionta/M.Modano	20.00	50.00
XSGMH Miller/Harding	12.00	30.00
XSGMJ M.Staal/J.Staal	10.00	25.00
XSGMM Modano/Morrow	20.00	50.00
XSGMP Hejduk/Stastny	10.00	25.00
XSGMS Miller/Stafford	12.00	30.00
XSGNP E.Nabokov/D.Patzold	10.00	25.00
XSGNT N.Horton/T.Vokoun	10.00	25.00
XSGOB Ovechkin/Backstrom	50.00	120.00
XSGOM E.Malkin/A.Ovechkin	50.00	120.00
XSGPP P.Bergeron/P.Kessel	30.00	80.00
XSGPT Stastny/Hensick	10.00	25.00
XSGPV Vanek/Pominville	10.00	25.00
XSGRC M.Richards/J.Carter	10.00	25.00
XSGRK Raymond/Kesler	12.00	30.00
XSGRM B.Morrow/M.Ribeiro	10.00	25.00
XSGRT R.Clowe/T.Mitchell	8.00	20.00
XSGS2 Stastny/Stastny	10.00	25.00
XSGSH Smyth/Hejduk	10.00	25.00
XSGSS D.Sedin/H.Sedin	15.00	40.00
XSGST J.Tlusty/M.Stajan	8.00	20.00
XSGSW E.Staal/C.Ward	15.00	40.00
XSGTF Fleury/Talbot	25.00	60.00
XSGTH C.Higgins/A.Tanguay	8.00	20.00
XSGTK J.Toews/P.Kane	25.00	60.00
XSGTM Thornton/Michalek	20.00	50.00
XSGTP C.Price/J.Toews	25.00	60.00
XSGVP T.Vanek/D.Paille	10.00	25.00
XSGVW Ward/Vokoun	12.00	30.00
XSGZK S.Gagner/S.Kostitsyn	8.00	20.00

2008-09 SP Game Used Inked Sweaters Dual

Card	Low	High
INKBM M.Brodeur/R.Miller	40.00	100.00
INKBP M.Brodeur/C.Price	40.00	80.00
INKBV P.Budaj/T.Vokoun	12.00	30.00
INKFS M.Fleury/J.Staal	30.00	80.00
INKKM E.Malkin/I.Kovalchuk	50.00	100.00
INKLG W.Gretzky/M.Lemieux	300.00	800.00
INKLS Lecavalier/St. Louis	15.00	40.00
INKLZ N.Lidstrom/H.Zetterberg	20.00	50.00
INKMM Modano/Ribeiro	25.00	60.00
INKMT M.Modano/M.Turco	25.00	60.00
INKNZ Naslund/Zherdev	15.00	40.00
INKOB Ovechkin/Backstrom	60.00	150.00
INKSC Gomez/Drury	12.00	30.00
INKSH R.Smyth/M.Hejduk	12.00	30.00
INKSW C.Ward/E.Staal	20.00	50.00
INKTK P.Kane/J.Toews	30.00	80.00
INKZH H.Zetterberg/M.Hossa	20.00	50.00

2008-09 SP Game Used Letter Marks

Card	Low	High
LMBP Bob Probert	40.00	80.00
LMCA Daniel Carcillo	12.00	30.00
LMDS Denis Savard	20.00	50.00
LMEJ Erik Johnson	12.00	30.00
LMEM Evgeni Malkin	50.00	100.00
LMGC Guy Carbonneau	20.00	50.00
LMHS Henrik Sedin	25.00	60.00
LMJI Jarome Iginla	25.00	60.00
LMKT Kyle Turris	60.00	120.00
LMLR Luc Robitaille	20.00	50.00
LMMH Marian Hossa	20.00	50.00
LMMK Mike Knuble	12.00	30.00
LMMM Mark Messier	50.00	100.00
LMNH Nathan Horton	15.00	40.00
LMPK Phil Kessel	20.00	50.00
LMPS Paul Stastny	15.00	40.00
LMRG Ryan Getzlaf	20.00	50.00
LMRK Red Kelly	20.00	50.00
LMSC Sidney Crosby	125.00	250.00
LMSE Daniel Sedin	25.00	60.00
LMTV Thomas Vanek	20.00	50.00

2008-09 SP Game Used Letter Marks Nickname Edition

Card	Low	High
NEBH Bobby Hull	40.00	100.00
NEBN Bob Nystrom	12.00	30.00
NEDC Don Cherry	50.00	125.00
NEDG Doug Gilmour	25.00	60.00
NEDS Dave Schultz	20.00	50.00
NEEM Evgeni Malkin	30.00	80.00
NEEN Evgeni Nabokov	15.00	40.00
NEES Eddie Shack	15.00	40.00
NEGH Gordie Howe	100.00	175.00
NEJB Johnny Bucyk	20.00	50.00
NEJI Jarome Iginla	15.00	40.00
NELR Luc Robitaille	20.00	50.00
NEMF Marc-Andre Fleury	40.00	80.00
NEML Mario Lemieux	80.00	200.00
NEMM Mark Messier	75.00	150.00
NEMN Markus Naslund	20.00	50.00
NEMT Marty Turco	20.00	50.00
NETE Tony Esposito	50.00	100.00
NETO Terry O'Reilly	15.00	40.00

2008-09 SP Game Used Number Marks

Card	Low	High
NMAD Alex Delvecchio	25.00	60.00
NMBB Bob Baun	25.00	60.00
NMBC Bobby Clarke	40.00	100.00
NMBD Brandon Dubinsky	15.00	40.00
NMBN Bernie Nicholls	20.00	50.00
NMBO Pierre-Marc Bouchard	25.00	60.00
NMBR Bobby Ryan	20.00	50.00
NMBS Borje Salming	25.00	60.00
NMCB Cam Barker	15.00	40.00
NMCG Clark Gillies	25.00	60.00
NMCP Carey Price	50.00	125.00
NMDB Dan Boyle	15.00	40.00
NMDP Dustin Penner	20.00	50.00
NMDS Drew Stafford	15.00	40.00
NMES Eric Staal	30.00	80.00
NMGF Grant Fuhr	40.00	100.00
NMGL Guillaume Latendresse	15.00	40.00
NMJB Jonathan Bernier	20.00	50.00
NMJM Joe Mullen	20.00	50.00
NMJT Jonathan Toews	40.00	100.00
NMLM Lanny McDonald	25.00	60.00
NMMC Marty McSorley	25.00	60.00
NMMH Martin Havlat	25.00	60.00
NMMM Milan Michalek	15.00	40.00
NMMR Mike Ribeiro	15.00	40.00
NMPB Peter Budaj	20.00	50.00
NMPE Patrik Elias	25.00	60.00
NMPK Patrick Kane	50.00	125.00
NMPS Peter Stastny	20.00	50.00
NMRA Bill Ranford	25.00	60.00
NMRV Rogie Vachon	15.00	40.00
NMSB Steve Bernier	15.00	40.00
NMSE Devin Setoguchi/30	20.00	50.00
NMSS Steve Shutt	25.00	60.00
NMST Martin St. Louis	25.00	60.00
NMTF Theoren Fleury	30.00	80.00
NMTH Tomas Holmstrom	20.00	50.00

2008-09 SP Game Used Rookie Exclusive Autographs

Card	Low	High
REAE Andrew Ebbett	4.00	10.00
REAG Alex Goligoski	8.00	20.00
REAP Adam Pineault	5.00	12.00
REBB Brian Boyle	5.00	12.00
REBL Brian Lee	5.00	12.00
REBO Zach Boychuk	6.00	15.00
REBS Brandon Sutter	6.00	15.00
REBV Boris Valabik	6.00	15.00
REBW Blake Wheeler	15.00	40.00
RECG Claude Giroux	12.00	30.00
REDB Derick Brassard	6.00	15.00
REDD Drew Doughty	15.00	40.00
REDH Darren Helm	6.00	15.00
REDL Dan LaCosta	6.00	15.00
REEE Erik Ersberg	5.00	12.00
REFB Fabian Brunnstrom	5.00	12.00
REFR Jonas Frogren	4.00	10.00
REGI Colton Gillies	5.00	12.00
REIG Mike Iggulden	5.00	12.00
REIZ Ilya Zubov	5.00	12.00
REJA Justin Abdelkader	10.00	25.00
REJE Jonathan Ericsson	6.00	15.00
REJF Jon Filewich	5.00	12.00
REJM John Mitchell	5.00	12.00
REJN James Neal	12.00	30.00
REJV Jakub Voracek	12.00	30.00
REKO Kyle Okposo	8.00	20.00
REKP Kevin Porter	5.00	12.00
REKT Kyle Turris	10.00	25.00
RELK Lauri Korpikoski	4.00	10.00
RELS Luca Sbisa	4.00	10.00
REMA Steve Mason	10.00	25.00
REMB Mikkel Boedker	8.00	20.00
REMD Matt D'Agostini	5.00	12.00
REMF Mark Fistric	5.00	12.00
REMG Marc-Andre Gragnani	5.00	12.00
REMI Michael Frolik	6.00	15.00
REMR Mattias Ritola	5.00	12.00
RENF Nikita Filatov	6.00	15.00
RENK Nikolai Kulemin	6.00	15.00
RENO Nathan Oystrick	6.00	15.00
REOM Oscar Moller	5.00	12.00
REPB Patrik Berglund	5.00	12.00
REPH Patric Hornqvist	6.00	15.00
REPI Alex Pietrangelo	10.00	25.00
REPV Petr Vrana	4.00	10.00
RERE Robbie Earl	4.00	10.00
RERJ Ryan Jones	6.00	15.00
RERS Ryan Stone	4.00	10.00
RESC Luke Schenn	8.00	20.00
RESM Shawn Matthias	6.00	15.00
RESS Steven Stamkos	60.00	150.00
RETO T.J. Oshie	12.00	30.00
RETS Tom Sestito	6.00	15.00
REVM Vladimir Mihalik	4.00	10.00
REVT Viktor Tikhonov	5.00	12.00
REZB Zach Bogosian	8.00	20.00

2008-09 SP Game Used SIGnificance

Card	Low	High
SIGAC Andrew Cogliano	5.00	12.00
SIGAE Alexander Edler	5.00	12.00
SIGAO Alexander Ovechkin	30.00	80.00
SIGAT Alex Tanguay	5.00	12.00
SIGBB Bob Baun	8.00	20.00
SIGBD Brandon Dubinsky	5.00	12.00
SIGBE Jonathan Bernier	8.00	20.00
SIGBG Brian Gionta	5.00	12.00
SIGBM Brenden Morrow	6.00	15.00
SIGBO Brad Boyes	5.00	12.00
SIGCA Daniel Carcillo	5.00	12.00
SIGCB Cam Barker	5.00	12.00
SIGCD Chris Drury	6.00	15.00
SIGCI Dino Ciccarelli	6.00	15.00
SIGCK Chris Kunitz	8.00	20.00
SIGCP Carey Price	15.00	40.00
SIGCS Cory Stillman	5.00	12.00
SIGCW Cam Ward	8.00	20.00
SIGDA David Perron	6.00	15.00
SIGDB David Booth	8.00	20.00
SIGDC Dan Cleary	6.00	15.00
SIGDJ David Jones	5.00	12.00
SIGDP Daniel Paille	5.00	12.00
SIGDR Dwayne Roloson	6.00	15.00
SIGDS Daniel Sedin	10.00	25.00
SIGEJ Erik Johnson	5.00	12.00
SIGEM Evgeni Malkin	25.00	60.00
SIGES Eric Staal	10.00	25.00
SIGFN Fredrik Norrena	5.00	12.00
SIGGZ Scott Gomez	6.00	15.00
SIGHA Michal Handzus	6.00	15.00
SIGHE Milan Hejduk	6.00	15.00
SIGHI Jonas Hiller	6.00	15.00
SIGHO Tomas Holmstrom	6.00	15.00
SIGJC Jeff Carter	6.00	15.00
SIGJH Jaroslav Halak	8.00	20.00
SIGJI Jarome Iginla	10.00	25.00
SIGJJ Jack Johnson	5.00	12.00
SIGJL Joffrey Lupul	5.00	12.00
SIGJP Jason Pominville	5.00	12.00
SIGJS Jordan Staal	6.00	15.00
SIGJT Jiri Tlusty	6.00	12.00
SIGKA Petr Kalus	8.00	20.00
SIGKE Phil Kessel	8.00	20.00
SIGKL Kari Lehtonen	10.00	25.00
SIGKO Chuck Kobasew	5.00	12.00
SIGLE Kristopher Letang	15.00	40.00
SIGMC Bryan McCabe	5.00	12.00
SIGMF Marc-Andre Fleury	10.00	25.00
SIGMH Martin Havlat	8.00	20.00
SIGMI Ryan Miller	10.00	25.00
SIGMK Mike Knuble	5.00	12.00
SIGMR Mason Raymond	5.00	12.00
SIGMS Marco Sturm	8.00	20.00
SIGMT Maxime Talbot	5.00	12.00
SIGNB Nicklas Backstrom	12.00	30.00
SIGNZ Nikolai Zherdev	5.00	12.00
SIGPA Paul Stastny	6.00	15.00
SIGPB Pierre-Marc Bouchard	8.00	20.00
SIGPH Dion Phaneuf	6.00	15.00
SIGPK Patrick Kane	25.00	50.00
SIGPS Peter Stastny	6.00	15.00
SIGRM Ryan Malone	5.00	12.00
SIGRS Ryan Smyth	6.00	15.00
SIGSE Devin Setoguchi	6.00	15.00
SIGSG Sam Gagner	5.00	12.00
SIGSK Sergei Kostitsyn	5.00	12.00
SIGST Martin St. Louis	8.00	20.00
SIGTE Tobias Enstrom	5.00	12.00
SIGTH T.J. Hensick	6.00	15.00
SIGTO Jonathan Toews	12.00	30.00
SIGTR Tuukka Rask	10.00	25.00
SIGTV Thomas Vanek	6.00	15.00
SIGTZ Travis Zajac	5.00	12.00
SIGVO Tomas Vokoun	6.00	15.00

2008-09 SP Game Used SIGnificant Numbers Dual Swatches

Card	Low	High
SNBE Patrice Bergeron/37	15.00	40.00
SNBL Brian Lee/55	10.00	25.00
SNBS Borje Salming/21	12.00	30.00
SNBY Mike Bossy/22	12.00	30.00
SNCD Chris Drury/23	10.00	25.00
SNCP Carey Price/31	25.00	60.00
SNCW Cam Ward/30	12.00	30.00
SNDB Derick Brassard/16	12.00	30.00
SNDC Dino Ciccarelli/20	12.00	30.00
SNDP David Perron/57	10.00	25.00
SNDR Dwayne Roloson/35	10.00	25.00
SNEL Patrik Elias/26	12.00	30.00
SNFT Mark Fistric/28	10.00	25.00
SNGF Grant Fuhr/31	20.00	50.00
SNGX Claude Giroux/56	25.00	60.00
SNHE Milan Hejduk/23	10.00	25.00
SNHZ Henrik Zetterberg/40	15.00	40.00
SNIK Ilya Kovalchuk/17	12.00	30.00
SNJC Jeff Carter/17	10.00	25.00
SNJT Joe Thornton/19	20.00	50.00
SNKT Kyle Turris/91	20.00	50.00
SNKY Kyle Okposo/21	15.00	40.00
SNMB Martin Brodeur/30	30.00	80.00
SNMF Marc-Andre Fleury/29	25.00	60.00
SNMH Marian Hossa/81	12.00	30.00
SNMI Ryan Miller/30	12.00	30.00
SNML Milan Lucic/17	20.00	50.00
SNMN Markus Naslund/91	12.00	30.00
SNMR Michael Ryder/73	8.00	20.00
SNMS Steve Mason/30	20.00	50.00
SNMT Marty Turco/35	12.00	30.00
SNNB Nicklas Backstrom/19	12.00	30.00
SNNH Nathan Horton/16	10.00	25.00
SNPB Pierre-Marc Bouchard/96	12.00	30.00
SNPK Phil Kessel/81	12.00	30.00
SNPM Peter Mueller/88	10.00	25.00
SNPS Paul Stastny/26	10.00	25.00
SNRC Mike Richards/18	10.00	25.00
SNRI Mike Ribeiro/63	8.00	20.00
SNRS Ryan Smyth/94	10.00	25.00
SNSB Steve Bernier/18	8.00	20.00
SNSC Sidney Crosby/87	50.00	125.00
SNSL Martin St. Louis/26	12.00	30.00
SNSS Steve Shutt/22	12.00	30.00
SNTH Tomas Holmstrom/96	10.00	25.00
SNTO Jonathan Toews/19	20.00	50.00
SNTR Tuukka Rask/40	15.00	40.00
SNVO Tomas Vokoun/29	10.00	25.00

2008-09 SP Game Used SIGnificant Swatches

Card	Low	High
SSAG Alex Goligoski	12.00	30.00
SSAL Al MacInnis	12.00	30.00
SSAO Adam Oates	10.00	25.00
SSAP Adam Pineault	8.00	20.00
SSBB Bob Bourne	6.00	15.00
SSBL Brian Lee	8.00	20.00
SSBO Pierre-Marc Bouchard	10.00	25.00
SSBS Mike Bossy	10.00	25.00
SSBT Mark Fistric	8.00	20.00
SSBU Peter Budaj	8.00	20.00
SSBY Brian Boyle	8.00	20.00
SSCC Dino Ciccarelli	10.00	25.00
SSCD Chris Drury	8.00	20.00
SSCO Chris Osgood	10.00	25.00
SSCP Corey Perry	15.00	40.00
SSCS Cory Stillman	6.00	15.00
SSDA David Perron	8.00	20.00
SSDB Derick Brassard	10.00	25.00
SSDC Dino Ciccarelli	10.00	25.00
SSDG Doug Gilmour	12.00	30.00
SSDP Daniel Paille	6.00	15.00
SSDS Drew Stafford	6.00	15.00
SSDT Darcy Tucker	8.00	20.00
SSEJ Erik Johnson	6.00	15.00
SSEM Evgeni Malkin	20.00	50.00
SSES Eric Staal	12.00	30.00
SSGB Gilbert Brule	6.00	15.00
SSGC Guy Carbonneau	10.00	25.00
SSGH Gordie Howe	30.00	80.00
SSGP Gilbert Perreault	10.00	25.00
SSGX Claude Giroux	20.00	50.00
SSGZ Scott Gomez	8.00	20.00
SSIK Ilya Kovalchuk	10.00	25.00
SSIZ Ilya Zubov	8.00	20.00
SSJB Johnny Bucyk	10.00	25.00
SSJC Jeff Carter	8.00	20.00
SSJJ Jack Johnson	6.00	15.00
SSJK Jari Kurri	10.00	25.00
SSJO Joe Thornton	15.00	40.00
SSJS Jordan Staal	8.00	20.00
SSJT Jonathan Toews	15.00	40.00
SSKA Patrick Kane	20.00	50.00
SSKT Kyle Turris	15.00	40.00
SSLE Kristopher Letang	12.00	30.00
SSLM Lanny McDonald	10.00	25.00
SSLU Joffrey Lupul	6.00	15.00
SSMA Ryan Malone	6.00	15.00
SSMD Marcel Dionne	12.00	30.00
SSMG Marc-Andre Gragnani	8.00	20.00
SSMH Milan Hejduk	8.00	20.00
SSMI Mike Lundin	6.00	15.00
SSML Milan Lucic	15.00	40.00
SSMN Matt Niskanen	8.00	20.00
SSMO Brendan Morrison	6.00	15.00
SSMP Michael Peca	8.00	20.00
SSMR Mike Ribeiro	6.00	15.00
SSMT Marty Turco	10.00	25.00
SSNB Nicklas Backstrom	10.00	25.00
SSNH Nathan Horton	8.00	20.00
SSNZ Nikolai Zherdev	6.00	15.00
SSOK Kyle Okposo	12.00	30.00
SSOV Alexander Ovechkin	40.00	100.00
SSPB Patrice Bergeron	12.00	30.00
SSPE Patrik Elias	10.00	25.00
SSPH Chris Phillips	6.00	15.00
SSPK Phil Kessel	10.00	25.00
SSPM Peter Mueller	8.00	20.00
SSPO Denis Potvin	10.00	25.00
SSPR Carey Price	20.00	50.00
SSPS Paul Stastny	8.00	20.00
SSPT Peter Stastny	8.00	20.00
SSRB Richard Brodeur	8.00	20.00
SSRE Robbie Earl	6.00	15.00
SSRH Ron Hextall	10.00	25.00
SSRI Mike Richards	8.00	20.00
SSRK Ryan Kesler	10.00	25.00
SSRL Rod Langway	8.00	20.00
SSRM Ryan Miller	10.00	25.00
SSRN Ryan Stone	6.00	15.00
SSRV Rick Vaive	6.00	15.00
SSSB Steve Bernier	6.00	15.00
SSSG Sam Gagner	6.00	15.00
SSSH Shawn Matthias	10.00	25.00
SSST Matt Stajan	6.00	15.00
SSSV Steve Mason	15.00	40.00
SSSW Stephen Weiss	6.00	15.00
SSTF Theoren Fleury	12.00	30.00
SSTH Tomas Holmstrom	8.00	20.00
SSTR Tuukka Rask	12.00	30.00
SSVO Tomas Vokoun	8.00	20.00

2008-09 SP Game Used Team Marks

Card	Low	High
TMAM Al MacInnis	15.00	40.00
TMAO Alexander Ovechkin/25	100.00	200.00
TMBC Bobby Clarke	20.00	50.00
TMBF Bernie Federko	10.00	25.00
TMBO Bobby Orr	75.00	150.00
TMCN Cam Neely	12.00	30.00
TMCP Carey Price	50.00	100.00
TMCW Cam Ward	12.00	30.00
TMEL Patrik Elias	12.00	30.00
TMEM Evgeni Malkin	25.00	60.00
TMEN Evgeni Nabokov	10.00	25.00
TMES Eric Staal	15.00	40.00
TMGA Sam Gagner	8.00	20.00
TMGF Grant Fuhr	20.00	50.00
TMGH Gordie Howe	75.00	150.00
TMGP Gilbert Perreault	12.00	30.00
TMHE Dany Heatley	20.00	50.00
TMHS Henrik Sedin	15.00	40.00
TMJC Jeff Carter	10.00	25.00
TMJI Jarome Iginla	15.00	40.00
TMJK Jari Kurri	12.00	30.00
TMJM Joe Mullen	10.00	25.00
TMJT Jonathan Toews	20.00	50.00
TMLR Luc Robitaille	12.00	30.00
TMMB Martin Brodeur/25	50.00	100.00
TMME Mark Messier	50.00	100.00
TMMF Marc-Andre Fleury	25.00	60.00
TMMI Mike Bossy	12.00	30.00
TMMM Mike Modano	20.00	50.00
TMMN Markus Naslund	12.00	30.00
TMMS Martin St. Louis	12.00	30.00
TMNL Nicklas Lidstrom	12.00	30.00
TMPK Patrick Kane	25.00	60.00
TMPS Paul Stastny	15.00	40.00
TMRB Ray Bourque/25	50.00	100.00
TMRG Ryan Getzlaf	12.00	30.00
TMRL Rod Langway	12.00	30.00
TMRM Ryan Miller	12.00	30.00
TMRO Larry Robinson	12.00	30.00
TMSC Sidney Crosby	75.00	150.00
TMST Peter Stastny	20.00	50.00
TMTE Tony Esposito	30.00	80.00
TMTV Thomas Vanek	10.00	25.00

2008-09 SP Game Used Triple Authentic Fabrics

*GOLD/25: .6X TO 1.5X BASIC INSERTS

Card	Low	High
3AFAM Andrei Markov	6.00	15.00
3AFAO Adam Oates	6.00	15.00
3AFAS Anton Stastny	4.00	10.00
3AFBB Bob Bourne	4.00	10.00
3AFBL Rob Blake	6.00	15.00
3AFBN Brendan Morrison	4.00	10.00
3AFBO Pierre-Marc Bouchard	6.00	15.00
3AFBQ Ray Bourque	10.00	25.00
3AFBU Peter Budaj	5.00	12.00
3AFBY Billy Smith	6.00	15.00
3AFCA Carey Price	12.00	30.00
3AFCC Dino Ciccarelli	6.00	15.00
3AFCH Jonathan Cheechoo	5.00	12.00
3AFCJ Curtis Joseph	8.00	20.00
3AFCL David Clarkson	5.00	12.00
3AFCM Mike Commodore	4.00	10.00
3AFDC Dino Ciccarelli	6.00	15.00
3AFDG Doug Gilmour	8.00	20.00
3AFDH Dominik Hasek	10.00	25.00
3AFDP Dion Phaneuf	5.00	12.00
3AFDT Darcy Tucker	5.00	12.00
3AFEM Evgeni Malkin	12.00	30.00
3AFES Eric Staal	8.00	20.00
3AFFM Frank Mahovlich	6.00	15.00
3AFGA Simon Gagne	6.00	15.00
3AFGN Glenn Anderson	5.00	12.00
3AFHA Dale Hawerchuk	8.00	20.00
3AFHL Henrik Lundqvist	16.00	40.00
3AFHO Marian Hossa	6.00	15.00
3AFHR Trent Hunter	4.00	10.00
3AFJM Joe Mullen	5.00	12.00
3AFJT Jonathan Toews	10.00	25.00
3AFJW Justin Williams	5.00	12.00
3AFKA Paul Kariya	6.00	15.00
3AFKK Mike Komisarek	4.00	10.00
3AFKL Kari Lehtonen	8.00	20.00
3AFKO Mikko Koivu	5.00	12.00
3AFLA Rod Langway	5.00	12.00
3AFLG Robert Lang	4.00	10.00
3AFLM Lanny McDonald	6.00	15.00
3AFLT Brian Leetch	5.00	12.00
3AFLW Rod Langway	5.00	12.00
3AFMB Martin Brodeur	15.00	40.00
3AFMC Bryan McCabe	4.00	10.00
3AFMD Lanny McDonald	6.00	15.00
3AFME Ryan Malone	4.00	10.00
3AFMF Marc-Andre Fleury	12.00	30.00
3AFMG Marian Gaborik	6.00	15.00
3AFMH Milan Hejduk	5.00	12.00
3AFMK Miikka Kiprusoff	6.00	15.00
3AFMM Mike Modano	10.00	25.00
3AFMN Markus Naslund	6.00	15.00
3AFMR Michael Ryder	4.00	10.00
3AFMT Matt Carle	4.00	10.00
3AFMY Marty Turco	6.00	15.00
3AFNC Bernie Nicholls	5.00	12.00
3AFNL Nicklas Lidstrom	6.00	15.00
3AFNY Cam Neely	6.00	15.00
3AFNZ Nikolai Zherdev	4.00	10.00
3AFOK Olaf Kolzig	6.00	15.00
3AFOV Alexander Ovechkin	25.00	60.00
3AFPB Patrice Bergeron	8.00	20.00
3AFPE Gilbert Perreault	6.00	15.00
3AFPF Peter Forsberg	12.00	30.00
3AFPK Patrick Roy	15.00	40.00
3AFPM Patrick Marleau	6.00	15.00
3AFPT Peter Stastny	5.00	12.00
3AFRB Rod Brind'Amour	6.00	15.00
3AFRD Richard Brodeur	5.00	12.00
3AFRL Roberto Luongo	10.00	25.00
3AFRM Ryan Miller	6.00	15.00
3AFRN Rick Nash	6.00	15.00
3AFRV Rick Vaive	4.00	10.00
3AFRW Ryan Whitney	6.00	15.00

3AFRY Ryan Smyth 5.00 12.00
3AFSA Borje Salming 6.00 15.00
3AFSB Steve Bernier 4.00 10.00
3AFSC Sidney Crosby 20.00 50.00
3AFSF Sergei Fedorov 10.00 25.00
3AFSI Darryl Sittler 8.00 20.00
3AFSK Saku Koivu 6.00 15.00
3AFSL Steve Sullivan 5.00 12.00
3AFSS Sergei Samsonov 5.00 12.00
3AFST Jordan Staal 5.00 12.00
3AFSU Mats Sundin 6.00 15.00
3AFSV Steve Shutt 6.00 15.00
3AFSW Shea Weber 5.00 12.00
3AFTH Tomas Holmstrom 5.00 12.00
3AFTL Trevor Linden 6.00 15.00
3AFTP Tomas Plekanec 4.00 10.00
3AFTS Teemu Selanne 12.00 30.00
3AFTT Tim Thomas 6.00 15.00
3AFTU Tuomo Ruutu 6.00 15.00
3AFTW Tiger Williams 4.00 10.00
3AFVL Vincent Lecavalier 6.00 15.00
3AFVT Vesa Toskala 8.00 20.00
3AFWR Wade Redden 4.00 10.00
3AFWW Wojtek Wolski 5.00 12.00
3AFZP Zach Parise 6.00 15.00
3AFZV Sergei Zubov 5.00 12.00

2009-10 SP Game Used

1 Ryan Getzlaf .40 1.00
2 Teemu Selanne .75 2.00
3 Saku Koivu .40 1.00
4 Ilya Kovalchuk .40 1.00
5 Nik Antropov .30 .75
6 Bryan Little .40 1.00
7 Zdeno Chara .40 1.00
8 Tim Thomas .40 1.00
9 Marc Savard .25 .60
10 Milan Lucic .30 .75
11 Thomas Vanek .30 .75
12 Ryan Miller .40 1.00
13 Derek Roy .25 .60
14 Jason Pominville .25 .60
15 Jarome Iginla .50 1.25
16 Olli Jokinen .30 .75
17 Dion Phaneuf .30 .75
18 Miikka Kiprusoff .40 1.00
19 Eric Staal .50 1.25
20 Cam Ward .40 1.00
21 Rod Brind`Amour .40 1.00
22 Jonathan Toews .60 1.50
23 Patrick Kane .75 2.00
24 Marian Hossa .40 1.00
25 Brian Campbell .30 .75
26 Milan Hejduk .30 .75
27 Paul Stastny .30 .75
28 Craig Anderson .40 1.00
29 Rick Nash .40 1.00
30 Steve Mason .30 .75
31 Derick Brassard .25 .60
32 Mike Modano .60 1.50
33 Mike Ribeiro .25 .60
34 Marty Turco .40 1.00
35 Henrik Zetterberg .50 1.25
36 Pavel Datsyuk .60 1.50
37 Johan Franzen .30 .75
38 Nicklas Lidstrom .25 .60
39 Ales Hemsky .30 .75
40 Nikolai Khabibulin .40 1.00
41 Sam Gagner .25 .60
42 Andrew Cogliano .25 .60
43 Tomas Vokoun .30 .75
44 David Booth .25 .60
45 Michael Frolik .30 .75
46 Drew Doughty .50 1.25
47 Ryan Smyth .30 .75
48 Anze Kopitar .60 1.50
49 Mikko Koivu .40 1.00
50 Niklas Backstrom .40 1.00
51 Martin Havlat .30 .75
52 Carey Price .75 2.00
53 Scott Gomez .30 .75
54 Mike Cammalleri .30 .75
55 Andrei Markov .40 1.00
56 Pekka Rinne .40 1.00
57 Jason Arnott .30 .75
58 Shea Weber .30 .75
59 Martin Brodeur 1.00 2.50
60 Patrik Elias .40 1.00
61 Zach Parise .40 1.00
62 Kyle Okposo .25 .60
63 Doug Weight .40 1.00
64 Josh Bailey .30 .75
65 Henrik Lundqvist 1.00 2.50
66 Marian Gaborik .40 1.00
67 Chris Drury .30 .75
68 Jason Spezza .40 1.00
69 Daniel Alfredsson .40 1.00
70 Jonathan Cheechoo .30 .75
71 Mike Richards .30 .75
72 Jeff Carter .30 .75
73 Simon Gagne .40 1.00
74 Shane Doan .30 .75
75 Peter Mueller .30 .75
76 Ilya Bryzgalov .30 .75
77 Sidney Crosby 1.50 4.00
78 Evgeni Malkin .75 2.00
79 Marc-Andre Fleury .75 2.00
80 Jordan Staal .30 .75
81 Joe Thornton .60 1.50
82 Dany Heatley .30 .75
83 Patrick Marleau .40 1.00
84 Devin Setoguchi .30 .75
85 David Perron .30 .75
86 Paul Kariya .40 1.00
87 Patrik Berglund .25 .60
88 Steven Stamkos .75 2.00
89 Vincent Lecavalier .40 1.00
90 Martin St. Louis .40 1.00
91 Phil Kessel .40 1.00
92 Luke Schenn .40 1.00
93 Tomas Kaberle .25 .60
94 Roberto Luongo .60 1.50
95 Daniel Sedin .50 1.25
96 Henrik Sedin .50 1.25
97 Ryan Kesler .40 1.00
98 Alexander Ovechkin 1.50 4.00
99 Nicklas Backstrom .40 1.00
100 Mike Green .30 .75
101 Yannick Weber RC 2.50 6.00
102 Wes O'Neill RC 2.50 6.00
103 Ville Leino RC 2.00 5.00
104 Viktor Stalberg RC 2.50 6.00
105 Tyson Strachan RC 1.50 4.00
106 Tyler Myers RC 4.00 10.00
107 Troy Bodie RC 2.00 5.00
108 Tom Wandell RC 2.50 6.00
109 Tim Wallace RC 1.50 4.00
110 Teemu Laakso RC 1.50 4.00
111 Taylor Chorney RC 2.50 6.00
112 T.J. Galiardi RC 2.50 6.00
113 Spencer Machacek RC 2.50 6.00
114 Sergei Shirokov RC 1.50 4.00
115 Sean Collins RC 2.00 5.00
116 Sean Bentivoglio RC 2.00 5.00
117 Tyler Ennis RC 3.00 8.00
118 Ryan Wilson RC 2.50 6.00
119 Ryan Vesce RC 2.00 5.00
120 Ryan O'Reilly RC 5.00 12.00
121 Riley Armstrong RC 2.00 5.00
122 Riku Helenius RC 2.50 6.00
123 Ray Macias RC 2.00 5.00
124 Peter Regin RC 2.00 5.00
125 Perttu Lindgren RC 2.00 5.00
126 Daniel Larsson RC 2.00 5.00
127 Mike Santorelli RC 2.50 6.00
128 Mike McKenna RC 2.00 5.00
129 Mikael Backlund RC 4.00 10.00
130 Mika Pyorala RC 2.00 5.00
131 Michal Neuvirth RC 4.00 10.00
132 John Carlson RC 5.00 12.00
133 Michael Sauer RC 2.00 5.00
134 Michael Del Zotto RC 2.50 6.00
135 Matt Pelech RC 2.50 6.00
136 Matt Hendricks RC 2.00 5.00
137 Matt Gilroy RC 2.50 6.00
138 Matt Climie RC 2.00 5.00
139 Matt Beleskey RC 2.00 5.00
140 Luca Caputi RC 2.50 6.00
141 Logan Couture RC 5.00 12.00
142 Lars Eller RC 2.50 6.00
143 Kris Chucko RC 1.50 4.00
144 Kevin Westgarth RC 2.00 5.00
145 Kevin Quick RC 1.50 4.00
146 John Scott RC 2.50 6.00
147 John Negrin RC 2.50 6.00
148 Johan Backlund RC 2.50 6.00
149 Joel Rechlicz RC 1.50 4.00
150 Jhonas Enroth RC 3.00 8.00
151 Jesse Joensuu RC 2.00 5.00
152 Jay Rosehill RC 2.50 6.00
153 Jay Beagle RC 3.00 8.00
154 Jason Demers RC 4.00 10.00
155 Matthew Corrente RC 2.00 5.00
156 Jamie Fraser RC 2.00 5.00
157 James Reimer RC 6.00 15.00
158 Devan Dubnyk RC 4.00 10.00
159 Jaime Sifers RC 2.00 5.00
160 Ivan Vishnevskiy RC 1.50 4.00
161 Ilkka Pikkarainen RC 2.50 6.00
162 Geoff Kinrade RC 2.50 6.00
163 Frazer McLaren RC 2.00 5.00
164 Bobby Sanguinetti RC 1.50 4.00
165 Erik Karlsson RC 8.00 20.00
166 Dmitry Kulikov RC 2.50 6.00
167 Derek Peltier RC 1.50 4.00
168 Davis Drewiske RC 2.50 6.00
169 David Van Der Gulik RC 2.00 5.00
170 David Sloane RC 2.50 6.00
171 David Schlemko RC 2.00 5.00
172 Jakub Kindl RC 2.50 6.00
173 Colin Wilson RC 2.50 6.00
174 Cody Franson RC 2.50 6.00
175 Christian Hanson RC 2.50 6.00
176 Chris Durno RC 2.00 5.00
177 Cal O'Reilly RC 2.00 5.00
178 Byron Bitz RC 2.00 5.00
179 Bryan Rodney RC 2.00 5.00
180 Brian Salcido RC 1.50 4.00
181 Brandon Segal RC 2.00 5.00
182 Brad Marchand RC 12.00 30.00
183 Benn Ferriero RC 2.50 6.00
184 Ben Lovejoy RC 2.50 6.00
185 Artem Anisimov RC 1.50 4.00
186 Andrew MacDonald RC 1.50 4.00
187 Alexander Sulzer RC 1.50 4.00
188 Alec Martinez RC 3.00 8.00
189 Aaron MacKenzie RC 2.50 6.00
190 Aaron Gagnon RC 1.50 4.00
191 Jamie Benn RC/99 20.00 50.00
192 Victor Hedman RC/99 15.00 40.00
193 Tyler Bozak RC/99 10.00 25.00
194 Antti Niemi RC/99 10.00 25.00
195 Michael Grabner RC/99 6.00 15.00
196 Evander Kane RC/99 12.00 30.00
197 Jonas Gustavsson RC/99 8.00 20.00
198 James van Riemsdyk RC/99 12.00 30.00
199 Matt Duchene RC/99 12.00 30.00
200 John Tavares RC/99 25.00 60.00

2009-10 SP Game Used Gold

*GOLD 1-100: 1.2X TO 3X BASE
*GOLD ROOKIES 101-190: .5X TO 1.2X BASE
*GOLD ROOKIES 191-200: .25X TO.6X BASE
61 Zach Parise 2.50 6.00
99 Nicklas Backstrom 2.50 6.00
101 Yannick Weber 6.00 15.00
140 Luca Caputi 6.00 15.00
199 Matt Duchene 25.00 60.00
200 John Tavares 30.00 80.00

2009-10 SP Game Used Authentic Fabrics

*GOLD/100: .5X TO 1.2X BASIC JSY
*PATCH/35: 1X TO 2.5X BASIC JSY
AFAC Andrew Cogliano 2.50 6.00
AFAF Alexander Frolov 3.00 8.00
AFAM Andrei Markov 4.00 10.00
AFAO Adam Oates 4.00 10.00
AFAS Alexander Semin 4.00 10.00
AFBC Brian Campbell 3.00 8.00
AFBL Brian Leetch 3.00 8.00
AFBO David Booth 2.50 6.00
AFBW Blake Wheeler 4.00 10.00
AFCN Cam Neely 4.00 10.00
AFCP Carey Price 8.00 20.00
AFDD Drew Doughty 5.00 12.00
AFDE Derick Brassard 2.50 6.00
AFDG Doug Gilmour 5.00 12.00
AFDP Dion Phaneuf 3.00 8.00
AFDR Derek Roy 2.50 6.00
AFDS Daniel Sedin 5.00 12.00
AFDY Darcy Tucker 3.00 8.00
AFEM Evgeni Malkin 8.00 20.00
AFGF Grant Fuhr 6.00 15.00
AFGH Gordie Howe 12.00 30.00
AFGI Claude Giroux 4.00 10.00
AFGR Mike Green 3.00 8.00
AFGW Gump Worsley 6.00 15.00
AFHL Henrik Lundqvist 10.00 25.00
AFHS Henrik Sedin 5.00 12.00
AFHZ Henrik Zetterberg 5.00 12.00
AFIK Ilya Kovalchuk 4.00 10.00
AFJA Jason Arnott 3.00 8.00
AFJB Jay Bouwmeester 2.50 6.00
AFJC Jeff Carter 3.00 8.00
AFJD J.P. Dumont 2.50 6.00
AFJF Johan Franzen 3.00 8.00
AFJP Jason Pominville 2.50 6.00
AFJS Jason Spezza 4.00 10.00
AFJT Joe Thornton 6.00 15.00
AFJV Jakub Voracek 3.00 8.00
AFKE Phil Kessel 4.00 10.00
AFKM Mike Komisarek 3.00 8.00
AFLS Luke Schenn 4.00 10.00
AFMB Martin Brodeur 10.00 25.00
AFMC Mike Cammalleri 3.00 8.00
AFME Ryan Malone 2.50 6.00
AFMF Marc-Andre Fleury 8.00 20.00
AFMG Marian Gaborik 4.00 10.00
AFMK Miikka Kiprusoff 4.00 10.00
AFML Milan Lucic 3.00 8.00
AFMM Mike Modano 6.00 15.00
AFMR Mike Richards 3.00 8.00
AFMS Martin St. Louis 4.00 10.00
AFMT Marty Turco 4.00 10.00
AFNB Nicklas Backstrom 4.00 10.00
AFNF Nick Foligno 3.00 8.00
AFNH Nathan Horton 4.00 10.00
AFNL Nicklas Lidstrom 2.50 6.00
AFOV Alexander Ovechkin 15.00 40.00
AFPA Paul Stastny 3.00 8.00
AFPB Patrik Berglund 2.50 6.00
AFPD Pavel Datsyuk 6.00 15.00
AFPK Patrick Kane 8.00 20.00
AFPO Patrick O'Sullivan 3.00 8.00
AFPR Patrick Roy 10.00 25.00
AFRH Roman Hamrlik 2.50 6.00
AFRK Ryan Kesler 4.00 10.00
AFRL Roberto Luongo 6.00 15.00
AFRM Ryan Miller 4.00 10.00
AFRN Rick Nash 4.00 10.00
AFRS Ryan Smyth 3.00 8.00
AFSC Sidney Crosby 15.00 40.00
AFSG Sam Gagner 2.50 6.00
AFSK Saku Koivu 4.00 10.00
AFSM Steve Mason 3.00 8.00
AFSS Steven Stamkos 8.00 20.00
AFST Jordan Staal 3.00 8.00
AFSW Shea Weber 3.00 8.00
AFSY Steve Yzerman 10.00 25.00
AFTK Tomas Kaberle 2.50 6.00
AFTT Tim Thomas 4.00 10.00
AFTU Tuukka Rask 5.00 12.00
AFTV Thomas Vanek 3.00 8.00
AFVL Vincent Lecavalier 4.00 10.00
AFVO Tomas Vokoun 3.00 8.00
AFWG Wayne Gretzky 25.00 60.00
AFZP Zach Parise 4.00 10.00

2009-10 SP Game Used Authentic Fabrics Dual

AF2AA Frolov/Kopitar 8.00 20.00
AF2AD Arnott/Dumont 4.00 10.00
AF2AG Cogliano/Gagner 3.00 8.00
AF2AW Arnott/Weber 4.00 10.00
AF2BO Brown/O'Sullivan 5.00 12.00
AF2BP Brodeur/Parise 12.00 30.00
AF2BS Brind`Amour/Staal 6.00 15.00
AF2BV Brassard/Voracek 4.00 10.00
AF2CG Clark/Gilmour 8.00 20.00
AF2CM Crosby/Malkin 20.00 50.00
AF2CO Crosby/Ovechkin 20.00 50.00
AF2CT Campbell/Toews 8.00 20.00
AF2DB Doughty/Bogosian 6.00 15.00
AF2DH Sedin/Sedin 6.00 15.00
AF2DL Doan/Lombardi 4.00 10.00
AF2DR Smyth/Brown 5.00 12.00
AF2DW Dumont/Weber 4.00 10.00
AF2DZ Datsyuk/Zetterberg 8.00 20.00
AF2EC Staal/Ward 6.00 15.00
AF2EF Emery/Fleury 10.00 25.00
AF2FC Fleury/Crosby 20.00 50.00
AF2FK Fuhr/Kurri 8.00 20.00
AF2FS Fleury/Staal 10.00 25.00
AF2GC Gomez/Cammalleri 4.00 10.00
AF2GD Green/Doughty 6.00 15.00
AF2GK Gaborik/Kessel 5.00 12.00
AF2GM Gilmour/MacInnis 6.00 15.00
AF2HB Horton/Booth 5.00 12.00
AF2HD Holmstrom/Datsyuk 8.00 20.00
AF2HF Holmstrom/Franzen 4.00 10.00
AF2HH Hossa/Huet 5.00 12.00
AF2HM Hamrlik/Markov 5.00 12.00
AF2HW Redden/Lundqvist 12.00 30.00
AF2IK Iginla/Kiprusoff 6.00 15.00
AF2JC Carter/Giroux 5.00 12.00
AF2JD Bouwmeester/Phaneuf 4.00 10.00
AF2JI Jokinen/Iginla 6.00 15.00
AF2KL Kovalchuk/Lehtonen 5.00 12.00
AF2KP Kariya/Perron 5.00 12.00
AF2KR Luongo/Kiprusoff 8.00 20.00
AF2KS Kane/Stamkos 10.00 25.00
AF2LI Lecavalier/Iginla 6.00 15.00
AF2LN Neely/Lucic 5.00 12.00
AF2LR Luongo/Raymond 8.00 20.00
AF2LS Lidstrom/Salming 5.00 12.00
AF2LZ Lidstrom/Zetterberg 6.00 15.00
AF2MM Modano/Turco 8.00 20.00
AF2MR Modano/Richards 8.00 20.00
AF2MS McDonald/Sittler 6.00 15.00
AF2MW Svatos/Wolski 3.00 8.00
AF2NB Neely/Bourque 8.00 20.00
AF2NM Nash/Mason 5.00 12.00
AF2NV Nash/Voracek 5.00 12.00
AF2OB Ovechkin/Backstrom 12.00 30.00
AF2OM Ovechkin/Malkin 20.00 50.00
AF2PK Parise/Kane 10.00 25.00
AF2PM Price/Mason 10.00 25.00
AF2PP Stastny/Stastny 4.00 10.00
AF2PR Pominville/Roy 3.00 8.00
AF2RC Richards/Carter 4.00 10.00
AF2RD Sedin/Kesler 6.00 15.00
AF2RJ Pominville/Miller 5.00 12.00
AF2RL Roy/Luongo 12.00 30.00
AF2RR Luongo/Kesler 8.00 20.00
AF2RS Miller/Stafford 5.00 12.00
AF2RV Roy/Vanek 4.00 10.00
AF2SB Stoll/Brown 5.00 12.00
AF2SD Smyth/Doughty 6.00 15.00
AF2SR Shutt/Robinson 5.00 12.00
AF2SS Staal/Staal 6.00 15.00
AF2SW Svatos/Stastny 4.00 10.00
AF2TD Vanek/Stafford 4.00 10.00
AF2TL Kaberle/Schenn 5.00 12.00
AF2TM Thomas/Lucic 8.00 20.00
AF2TR Ryder/Thomas 5.00 12.00
AF2VH Vokoun/Horton 5.00 12.00
AF2VS Lecavalier/Stamkos 10.00 25.00
AF2WH Weiss/Horton 5.00 12.00
AF2YB Yzerman/Bowman 12.00 30.00
AF2YG Yzerman/Gretzky 30.00 80.00
AF2ZL Schenn/Bogosian 5.00 12.00

2009-10 SP Game Used Authentic Fabrics Dual Patches

*SINGLES: .8X TO 2X BASIC INSERTS
AF2DZ Datsyuk/Zetterberg 25.00 60.00
AF2KP Kariya/Perron 12.00 30.00
AF2NV Nash/Voracek 12.00 30.00

2009-10 SP Game Used Authentic Fabrics Triples

*PATCH/15: .6X TO 1.5X BASIC TRIPLE
AF3ADW Arntt/Dumnt/Webr 6.00 15.00
AF3ASF Alfred/Speza/Foligno 8.00 20.00
AF3BLM Brodeur/Lund/Miller 20.00 50.00
AF3BSO Brown/Stafford/Okposo 8.00 20.00
AF3BVM Brassard/Voracek/Mason 6.00 15.00
AF3CBP Brodeur/Prise/Clrksn 20.00 50.00
AF3CMS Crosby/Malkin/Staal 30.00 80.00
AF3COM Crosby/Ovech/Malkin 30.00 80.00
AF3DSB Doughty/Schenn/Bogosn 10.00 25.00
AF3DSS Demitra/Sedin/Sedin 15.00 40.00
AF3ERC Emery/Richards/Carter 6.00 15.00
AF3FBK Frolov/Brown/Kopitar 12.00 30.00
AF3FCM Fleury/Crosby/Malkin 30.00 80.00
AF3FGT Laraque/Brashear/Lucic 6.00 15.00
AF3GMP Gomez/Markov/Price 15.00 40.00
AF3HTK Hossa/Toews/Kane 15.00 40.00
AF3IKP Iginla/Kiprsff/Phneuf 10.00 25.00
AF3KKS Kabrle/Komis/Schenn 8.00 20.00
AF3KSM Kovlchk/Smin/Malkin 15.00 40.00
AF3LHN Lecav/Heatley/Nash 8.00 20.00
AF3LHZ Lidstrm/Homstrm/Ztter 10.00 25.00
AF3LKR Luongo/Keslr/Rymnd 12.00 30.00
AF3LMS Lecav/Malne/Stmkos 15.00 40.00
AF3LOD Lidstrm/Osgd/Datsyuk 12.00 30.00
AF3LSS Lecav/St.Louis/Stmkos 15.00 40.00
AF3MAH McDonld/Andersn/Hawerck 10.0025.00
AF3MMM McDnld/Mulln/McInnis 15.00 40.00
AF3MRT Modano/Ribeiro/Turco 12.00 30.00
AF3MSH McDnld/Shutt/Hawer 10.00 25.00
AF3MVS Miller/Vanek/Stafford 8.00 20.00
AF3NBV Nash/Brassard/Voracek 8.00 20.00
AF3OCG O'Sullivan/Cogliano/Gagner 6.00 15.00
AF3OGB Ovech/Green/Backs 20.00 50.00
AF3PHM Hamrlik/Markv/Pleknc 15.00 40.00
AF3PMC Markov/Camml/Pleknc 15.00 40.00
AF3PMV Pominville/Miller/Vanek 8.00 20.00
AF3PVS Pominvle/Vanek/Staffrd 6.00 15.00
AF3RBM Roy/Brodeur/Mason 20.00 50.00
AF3RCG Richards/Carter/Giroux 8.00 20.00
AF3RGL Redden/Gaboik/Lund 20.00 50.00
AF3RHD Luongo/Sedin/Sedin 12.00 30.00
AF3SBS Samsonov/Brind/Staal 10.00 25.00
AF3SGB Semin/Green/Backstrom 8.00 20.00
AF3SNT Spezza/Nash/Toews 12.00 30.00
AF3SOB Semin/Ovech/Backs 30.00 80.00
AF3SSK Sedin/Sedin/Kesler 30.00 80.00
AF3SSS Staal/Staal/Staal 10.00 25.00
AF3VHB Vokoun/Horton/Booth 8.00 20.00
AF3YGM Yzermn/Grtzky/Messr 50.00 125.00
AF3DROP Laraque/Komisarek/Lucic 6.00 15.00

2009-10 SP Game Used Extra SIGnificance

SIGTV Beliveau/Bouchard 30.00 60.00
XSGBO Oshie/Berglund 10.00 25.00
XSGBP Backes/Pietrangelo 15.00 40.00
XSGCG Cogliano/Gagner 6.00 15.00
XSGCS Price/Mason 30.00 80.00
XSGDZ Datsyuk/Zetterberg 30.00 60.00
XSGEE Esposito/Esposito 15.00 40.00
XSGEJ Staal/Staal 12.00 30.00
XSGFH Fuhr/Hawerchuk 15.00 40.00
XSGGB Green/Backstrom 10.00 25.00
XSGGK Kurri/Gretzky 150.00 400.00
XSGGL Gaborik/Lundqvist 25.00 60.00
XSGGS Schenn/Gustavsson 12.00 30.00
XSGGW Green/Weber 8.00 20.00
XSGHD Sedin/Sedin 25.00 50.00
XSGHR Ryan/Hiller 20.00 50.00
XSGIP Iginla/Phaneuf 12.00 30.00
XSGJB Johnson/Bernier 8.00 20.00
XSGJM Tavares/Duchene 40.00 100.00
XSGKJ Kessel/Gustavsson 12.00 30.00
XSGKO O'Reilly/Carcillo 8.00 20.00
XSGLD Lindsay/Delvecchio 20.00 40.00
XSGLM Lemieux/Malkin 75.00 150.00
XSGLS Lecavalier/Stamkos 20.00 50.00
XSGML Leetch/Messier 40.00 80.00
XSGMV Miller/Vanek 12.00 30.00
XSGOB Okposo/Bailey 8.00 20.00
XSGOE Ersberg/Moller 10.00 25.00
XSGOH Orr/Hull 125.00 200.00
XSGOK Kovalchuk/Ovechkin 60.00 120.00
XSGOM Ovechkin/Malkin 60.00 120.00
XSGRB Roy/Brodeur 75.00 150.00
XSGRM Markov/Robinson 10.00 25.00
XSGTK Toews/Kane 40.00 80.00
XSGYG Yzerman/Howe 100.00 200.00
XSGZM Zetterberg/Malkin 30.00 80.00

2009-10 SP Game Used Inked Sweaters

ISAC Andrew Cogliano 4.00 10.00
ISBW Blake Wheeler 6.00 15.00
ISCW Cam Ward 6.00 15.00
ISDC Matt Duchene 12.00 30.00
ISDD Drew Doughty 8.00 20.00
ISDP Dion Phaneuf 5.00 12.00
ISDS Daniel Sedin 8.00 20.00
ISDZ Michael Del Zotto 6.00 15.00
ISEK Evander Kane 12.00 30.00
ISGB Michael Grabner 6.00 15.00
ISGO Scott Gomez 5.00 12.00
ISGR Mike Green 5.00 12.00
ISGV Jonas Gustavsson 8.00 20.00
ISGX Claude Giroux 6.00 15.00
ISHL Henrik Lundqvist 15.00 40.00
ISHS Henrik Sedin 8.00 20.00
ISJA Jason Arnott 5.00 12.00
ISJC Jeff Carter 5.00 12.00
ISJD J.P. Dumont 5.00 12.00
ISJS Jordan Staal 5.00 12.00
ISJV Jakub Voracek 5.00 12.00
ISLS Luke Schenn 6.00 15.00
ISMF Marc-Andre Fleury 12.00 30.00
ISMG Marian Gaborik 6.00 15.00
ISNF Nick Foligno 5.00 12.00
ISNH Nathan Horton 6.00 15.00
ISNK Nikolai Khabibulin 6.00 15.00
ISNL Nicklas Lidstrom 4.00 10.00
ISPM Peter Mueller 5.00 12.00
ISPS Paul Stastny 5.00 12.00
ISSD Shane Doan 5.00 12.00
ISSG Sam Gagner 4.00 10.00
ISSM Steve Mason 5.00 12.00
ISST Steven Stamkos 12.00 30.00
ISSW Shea Weber 5.00 12.00
ISTA John Tavares 25.00 60.00
ISVO Tomas Vokoun 5.00 12.00
ISVR James van Riemsdyk 12.00 30.00

2009-10 SP Game Used Legends Classic

LCBB Bob Bourne 3.00 8.00
LCBS Billy Smith 5.00 12.00
LCDH Dale Hawerchuk 6.00 15.00
LCGA Glenn Anderson 4.00 10.00
LCLM Lanny McDonald 5.00 12.00
LCPS Peter Stastny 4.00 10.00
LCRL Rod Langway 4.00 10.00
LCSA Borje Salming 5.00 12.00
LCSS Steve Shutt 5.00 12.00
LCTW Tiger Williams 3.00 8.00

2009-10 SP Game Used Legends Classic Patches

*SINGLES: .6X TO 1.5X BASIC INSERTS

2009-10 SP Game Used Letter Marks

LMAA Artem Anisimov 10.00 25.00
LMAL Andrew Ladd 10.00 25.00
LMBO Mikkel Boedker 10.00 25.00
LMBR Bobby Ryan 12.00 30.00
LMBW Blake Wheeler 15.00 40.00
LMCG Claude Giroux 15.00 40.00
LMCH Christian Hanson 15.00 40.00
LMDB David Backes 40.00 80.00
LMDC Daniel Carcillo 25.00 60.00
LMDP Dion Phaneuf 12.00 30.00
LMGH Gordie Howe 50.00 120.00
LMIV Ivan Vishnevskiy 10.00 25.00
LMJA Justin Abdelkader 12.00 30.00
LMJC Jeff Carter 12.00 30.00
LMJE Jhonas Enroth 20.00 50.00
LMJI Jarome Iginla 20.00 50.00
LMJK Jari Kurri 15.00 40.00
LMJT Jonathan Toews 25.00 60.00
LMJV Jakub Voracek 12.00 30.00
LMKE Phil Kessel 15.00 40.00
LMLS Luke Schenn 15.00 40.00
LMMB Mikael Backlund 25.00 60.00
LMMG Mike Green 12.00 30.00
LMMP Max Pacioretty 15.00 40.00
LMMR Mike Richards 12.00 30.00
LMNB Nicklas Backstrom 15.00 40.00
LMNG Nathan Gerbe 12.00 30.00
LMPD Pavel Datsyuk 30.00 80.00
LMPK Patrick Kane 75.00 125.00
LMRM Ryan Miller 15.00 40.00
LMSM Steve Mason 12.00 30.00
LMSS Steven Stamkos 30.00 80.00
LMSY Steve Yzerman 75.00 150.00
LMTK Tyler Kennedy 15.00 40.00
LMTV Thomas Vanek 12.00 30.00
LMVL Ville Leino 12.00 30.00

2009-10 SP Game Used Marks of a Nation

MNAA Artem Anisimov 10.00 25.00
MNAF Marc-Andre Fleury 40.00 80.00
MNAK Anze Kopitar 25.00 60.00
MNBA Mikael Backlund 25.00 60.00
MNBH Bobby Hull 30.00 80.00
MNBL Brian Leetch 12.00 30.00
MNBO Bobby Orr 100.00 200.00
MNCP Carey Price 30.00 80.00
MNCW Cam Ward 15.00 40.00
MNDB David Backes 20.00 50.00
MNDP Dion Phaneuf 12.00 30.00
MNEM Evgeni Malkin 30.00 80.00
MNGH Gordie Howe 50.00 125.00
MNHZ Henrik Zetterberg 20.00 50.00
MNIV Ivan Vishnevskiy 12.00 30.00
MNJA Justin Abdelkader 12.00 30.00
MNJC Jeff Carter 12.00 30.00
MNJD J.P. Dumont 10.00 25.00
MNJI Jarome Iginla 20.00 50.00
MNJK Jari Kurri 15.00 40.00
MNJT Jonathan Toews 25.00 60.00
MNKE Phil Kessel 25.00 50.00
MNLC Luca Caputi 15.00 40.00
MNLS Luke Schenn 40.00 80.00
MNLV Vincent Lecavalier 15.00 40.00
MNMB Martin Brodeur 40.00 100.00
MNMG Mike Green 12.00 30.00
MNMH Marian Hossa 15.00 40.00
MNML Mario Lemieux 60.00 150.00
MNMM Mark Messier 40.00 100.00
MNMN Markus Naslund 15.00 40.00
MNMR Mike Richards 12.00 30.00
MNNB Nicklas Backstrom 15.00 40.00
MNNL Nicklas Lidstrom 40.00 80.00
MNPB Patrik Berglund 15.00 40.00
MNPD Pavel Datsyuk 40.00 80.00
MNPE Phil Esposito 25.00 60.00
MNPK Patrick Kane 30.00 80.00
MNPR Patrick Roy 60.00 120.00
MNRG Ryan Getzlaf 25.00 60.00
MNRH Riku Helenius 15.00 40.00
MNRM Ryan Miller 30.00 80.00
MNRN Rick Nash 25.00 60.00
MNSC Sidney Crosby 150.00 250.00
MNSD Shane Doan 12.00 30.00
MNSG Scott Gomez 12.00 30.00
MNSK Saku Koivu 40.00 80.00
MNSM Steve Mason 20.00 50.00
MNSS Steven Stamkos 30.00 80.00
MNSW Shea Weber 25.00 50.00
MNSY Steve Yzerman 125.00 200.00
MNTO T.J. Oshie 25.00 60.00
MNTV Thomas Vanek 20.00 50.00
MNVL Ville Leino 12.00 30.00
MNWG Wayne Gretzky 250.00 600.00
MNYW Yannick Weber 15.00 40.00

2009-10 SP Game Used Rookie Exclusives Autographs

REAA Artem Anisimov 4.00 10.00
REAM Alec Martinez 8.00 20.00
REAN Antti Niemi 10.00 25.00
REBA Mikael Backlund 10.00 25.00
REBB Byron Bitz 5.00 12.00
REBF Benn Ferriero 6.00 15.00
REBM Brad Marchand 40.00 100.00
REBS Brian Salcido 4.00 10.00
RECB Chris Butler 6.00 15.00
RECF Cody Franson 6.00 15.00
RECH Christian Hanson 6.00 15.00
RECO Cal O'Reilly 5.00 12.00
RECW Colin Wilson 6.00 15.00
REDE Michael Del Zotto 6.00 15.00
REDK Dmitry Kulikov 6.00 15.00
REEK Erik Karlsson 30.00 60.00
REFM Frazer McLaren 5.00 12.00
REGR Michael Grabner 6.00 15.00
REIV Ivan Vishnevskiy 4.00 10.00
REJB Jamie Benn 20.00 50.00
REJD Jason Demers 10.00 25.00
REJE Jhonas Enroth 8.00 20.00
REJG Jonas Gustavsson 40.00 80.00
REJJ Jesse Joensuu 5.00 12.00
REJR Jay Rosehill 6.00 15.00
REJS John Scott 6.00 15.00
REJT John Tavares 40.00 100.00
REJV James van Riemsdyk 12.00 30.00
REKA Evander Kane 12.00 30.00
REKC Kris Chucko 4.00 10.00
RELC Luca Caputi 6.00 15.00
RELG Logan Couture 12.00 30.00
REMA Andrew MacDonald 4.00 10.00
REMB Matt Beleskey 5.00 12.00
REMD Matt Duchene 15.00 40.00
REMG Matt Gilroy 6.00 15.00
REMH Matt Hendricks 5.00 12.00
REMN Michal Neuvirth 10.00 25.00
REMP Matt Pelech 6.00 15.00
REMS Michael Sauer 5.00 12.00
REPL Perttu Lindgren 5.00 12.00
REPR Peter Regin 5.00 12.00
RERE Joel Rechlicz 4.00 10.00
RERH Riku Helenius 6.00 15.00
RERM Ray Macias 5.00 12.00
RERO Ryan O'Reilly 12.00 30.00
RESA Mike Santorelli 6.00 15.00
RESM Spencer Machacek 6.00 15.00
RESS Sergei Shirokov 4.00 10.00
RETB Tyler Bozak 10.00 25.00
RETC Taylor Chorney 6.00 15.00
RETG T.J. Galiardi 6.00 15.00
RETM Tyler Myers 8.00 20.00
RETW Tom Wandell 6.00 15.00
REVH Victor Hedman 25.00 60.00
REVL Ville Leino 5.00 12.00
REVS Viktor Stalberg 6.00 15.00
REYW Yannick Weber 6.00 15.00

2009-10 SP Game Used SIGnificance

SIGAC Andrew Cogliano 5.00 12.00
SIGAK Anze Kopitar 12.00 30.00
SIGAO Alexander Ovechkin/25 50.00 120.00
SIGAP Alex Pietrangelo 6.00 15.00
SIGBA Josh Bailey 6.00 15.00
SIGBK Mikael Backlund 12.00 30.00
SIGBL Brian Leetch 10.00 25.00
SIGBO Bobby Orr/25 100.00 200.00
SIGBR Mikkel Boedker 5.00 12.00
SIGBW Blake Wheeler 8.00 20.00
SIGBZ Todd Bertuzzi 10.00 25.00
SIGCN Cam Neely 8.00 20.00
SIGCO Colton Gillies 8.00 20.00
SIGCP Carey Price 15.00 40.00
SIGDA Darren Helm 5.00 12.00
SIGDC Daniel Carcillo 5.00 12.00
SIGDD Drew Doughty 10.00 25.00
SIGDH Dale Hawerchuk 10.00 25.00
SIGDS Daniel Sedin 10.00 25.00
SIGDZ Michael Del Zotto 8.00 20.00
SIGEE Erik Ersberg 6.00 15.00
SIGEM Evgeni Malkin 12.00 30.00
SIGEN Evgeni Nabokov 6.00 15.00
SIGES Eric Staal 10.00 25.00
SIGGA Sam Gagner 5.00 12.00
SIGGB Gilbert Brule 10.00 25.00
SIGGH Gordie Howe/25 40.00 100.00
SIGGI Claude Giroux 8.00 20.00
SIGGP Gilbert Perreault 8.00 20.00
SIGGR Mike Green 6.00 15.00
SIGGV Jonas Gustavsson 10.00 25.00
SIGHK Jaroslav Halak 25.00 50.00
SIGHL Henrik Lundqvist 20.00 50.00
SIGHS Henrik Sedin 10.00 25.00
SIGHZ Henrik Zetterberg 10.00 25.00
SIGIV Ivan Vishnevskiy 5.00 12.00
SIGJA Justin Abdelkader 6.00 15.00
SIGJC Jeff Carter 6.00 15.00
SIGJD J.P. Dumont 5.00 12.00
SIGJE Jonathan Ericsson 5.00 12.00
SIGJM John-Michael Liles 5.00 12.00
SIGJN James Neal 5.00 12.00
SIGJS Jordan Staal 6.00 15.00
SIGJV Jakub Voracek 6.00 15.00
SIGKO Kyle Okposo 10.00 25.00
SIGKP Kevin Porter 5.00 12.00
SIGLC Luca Caputi 8.00 20.00
SIGLS Luke Schenn 8.00 20.00
SIGMA Steve Mason 6.00 15.00
SIGMB Martin Brodeur/25 30.00 80.00
SIGMD Matt Duchene 15.00 40.00
SIGMG Marian Gaborik 8.00 20.00
SIGMK Mike Knuble 20.00 50.00
SIGML Mario Lemieux/25 50.00 125.00
SIGMM Mark Messier/25 20.00 50.00
SIGNB Nicklas Backstrom 8.00 20.00
SIGNL Nicklas Lidstrom 5.00 12.00
SIGNV Michal Neuvirth 12.00 30.00
SIGOM Oscar Moller 5.00 12.00
SIGOR Terry O'Reilly 12.00 30.00
SIGPH Dion Phaneuf 6.00 15.00
SIGPN Dustin Penner 5.00 12.00
SIGPR Patrick Roy/25 30.00 80.00
SIGRA Mason Raymond 15.00 40.00
SIGRM Ryan Miller 15.00 40.00
SIGRN Rick Nash 8.00 20.00
SIGSC Sidney Crosby/25 75.00 150.00
SIGSE Devin Setoguchi 6.00 15.00
SIGSK Jack Skille 5.00 12.00
SIGST Steven Stamkos 15.00 40.00
SIGSW Shea Weber 6.00 15.00
SIGSY Steve Yzerman/25 75.00 150.00
SIGTA John Tavares 40.00 100.00
SIGTO Jonathan Toews 12.00 30.00
SIGTV Thomas Vanek 6.00 15.00
SIGTW Ty Wishart 6.00 15.00
SIGVR James van Riemsdyk 25.00 50.00
SIGWG Wayne Gretzky/25 150.00 400.00

2009-10 SP Game Used SIGnificant Numbers

SNAA Artem Anisimov/42 6.00 15.00
SNBA Mikael Backlund/60 15.00 40.00
SNBW Blake Wheeler/26 12.00 30.00
SNCP Carey Price/31 20.00 50.00
SNCW Cam Ward/30 10.00 25.00
SNDS Daniel Sedin/22 15.00 40.00
SNEM Evgeni Malkin/71 20.00 50.00
SNGB Michael Grabner/20 25.00 50.00
SNGF Grant Fuhr/31 15.00 40.00
SNGR Mike Green/52 8.00 20.00
SNHL Henrik Lundqvist/30 25.00 60.00
SNHS Henrik Sedin/33 12.00 30.00
SNHZ Henrik Zetterberg/40 12.00 30.00
SNIV Ivan Vishnevskiy/59 6.00 15.00
SNJA Jason Arnott/19 10.00 25.00
SNJD J.P. Dumont/71 6.00 15.00
SNJO Jonathan Toews/19 30.00 60.00
SNJP Jason Pominville/29 8.00 20.00
SNJT Joe Thornton/19 20.00 50.00
SNKE Phil Kessel/81 10.00 25.00
SNKO Kyle Okposo/21 12.00 30.00
SNLR Larry Robinson/19 12.00 30.00
SNMB Martin Brodeur/30 40.00 80.00
SNMF Marc-Andre Fleury/29 30.00 60.00
SNMR Mason Raymond/21 10.00 25.00
SNMT Marty Turco/35 10.00 25.00
SNNB Nicklas Backstrom/19 30.00 60.00
SNNF Nick Foligno/71 8.00 20.00
SNPK Patrick Kane/88 20.00 50.00
SNPR Patrick Roy/33 60.00 120.00
SNPS Paul Stastny/26 10.00 25.00
SNPT Peter Stastny/26 10.00 25.00
SNRB Ray Bourque/77 15.00 40.00
SNRI Mike Richards/18 10.00 25.00
SNRM Ryan Miller/30 10.00 25.00
SNRN Rick Nash/61 10.00 25.00
SNSC Sidney Crosby/87 75.00 150.00
SNSD Shane Doan/19 10.00 25.00
SNSG Sam Gagner/89 6.00 15.00
SNSS Steve Shutt/22 20.00 40.00
SNST Steven Stamkos/91 30.00 60.00
SNSY Steve Yzerman/19 40.00 80.00
SNTV Thomas Vanek/26 10.00 25.00
SNVO Tomas Vokoun/29 10.00 25.00
SNVR James van Riemsdyk/51 25.00 60.00
SNYW Yannick Weber/68 10.00 25.00

2010-11 SP Game Used

COMP.SET w/o SPs (100) 50.00 100.00
1 Ryan Getzlaf 1.00 2.50
2 Bobby Ryan .75 2.00
3 Jonas Hiller .75 2.00
4 Dustin Byfuglien 1.00 2.50
5 Evander Kane 1.00 2.50
6 Zdeno Chara 1.00 2.50
7 Tuukka Rask 1.25 3.00
8 Patrice Bergeron 1.25 3.00
9 Thomas Vanek .75 2.00
10 Ryan Miller 1.00 2.50
11 Tyler Myers .60 1.50
12 Rene Bourque .60 1.50
13 Jarome Iginla 1.25 3.00
14 Alex Tanguay .60 1.50
15 Miikka Kiprusoff 1.00 2.50
16 Eric Staal 1.25 3.00
17 Cam Ward 1.00 2.50
18 Jussi Jokinen .60 1.50
19 Jonathan Toews 1.50 4.00
20 Patrick Kane 2.00 5.00
21 Marian Hossa 1.00 2.50
22 Duncan Keith .75 2.00
23 Marty Turco 1.00 2.50
24 Matt Duchene 1.00 2.50
25 Paul Stastny .75 2.00
26 Craig Anderson 1.00 2.50
27 Rick Nash 1.00 2.50
28 Steve Mason .75 2.00
29 Jakub Voracek .75 2.00
30 Kari Lehtonen .75 2.00
31 Mike Ribeiro .60 1.50
32 Brad Richards 1.00 2.50
33 Jim Howard 1.25 3.00
34 Henrik Zetterberg 1.25 3.00
35 Pavel Datsyuk 1.50 4.00

36 Nicklas Lidstrom 1.00 2.50
37 Ales Hemsky .75 2.00
38 Sam Gagner .60 1.50
39 Dustin Penner .60 1.50
40 Stephen Weiss .75 2.00
41 Tomas Vokoun .75 2.00
42 Drew Doughty 1.25 3.00
43 Ryan Smyth .75 2.00
44 Anze Kopitar 1.50 4.00
45 Mikko Koivu 1.00 2.50
46 Niklas Backstrom 1.00 2.50
47 Guillaume Latendresse .75 2.00
48 Andrew Brunette .60 1.50
49 Tomas Plekanec .60 1.50
50 Carey Price 2.00 5.00
51 Scott Gomez .75 2.00
52 Mike Cammalleri 1.00 2.50
53 Brian Gionta .60 1.50
54 Pekka Rinne 1.00 2.50
55 Patric Hornqvist .60 1.50
56 Shea Weber .75 2.00
57 Martin Brodeur 2.50 6.00
58 Patrik Elias 1.00 2.50
59 Zach Parise 1.00 2.50
60 Ilya Kovalchuk 1.00 2.50
61 Rick DiPietro .75 2.00
62 Kyle Okposo .60 1.50
63 John Tavares 1.50 4.00
64 Henrik Lundqvist 2.50 6.00
65 Marian Gaborik 1.00 2.50
66 Chris Drury .75 2.00
67 Jason Spezza 1.00 2.50
68 Daniel Alfredsson 1.00 2.50
69 Chris Pronger 1.00 2.50
70 Mike Richards .75 2.00
71 Jeff Carter .75 2.00
72 Claude Giroux 1.00 2.50
73 Michael Leighton .75 2.00
74 Shane Doan .75 2.00
75 Wojtek Wolski .60 1.50
76 Ilya Bryzgalov .75 2.00
77 Sidney Crosby 4.00 10.00
78 Evgeni Malkin 2.00 5.00
79 Marc-Andre Fleury 2.00 5.00
80 Joe Thornton 1.50 4.00
81 Dany Heatley .75 2.00
82 Patrick Marleau 1.00 2.50
83 Devin Setoguchi .75 2.00
84 Jaroslav Halak 1.00 2.50
85 Patrik Berglund .60 1.50
86 Steven Stamkos 2.00 5.00
87 Vincent Lecavalier 1.00 2.50
88 Martin St. Louis 1.00 2.50
89 Dion Phaneuf .75 2.00
90 Phil Kessel 1.00 2.50
91 Luke Schenn 1.00 2.50
92 Jean-Sebastien Giguere 1.00 2.50
93 Roberto Luongo 1.50 4.00
94 Daniel Sedin 1.25 3.00
95 Henrik Sedin 1.25 3.00
96 Alexandre Burrows .60 1.50
97 Semyon Varlamov 1.00 2.50
98 Alexander Ovechkin 4.00 10.00
99 Nicklas Backstrom 1.00 2.50
100 Mike Green .75 2.00
101 Mattias Tedenby RC 2.50 6.00
102 Luke Adam RC 2.50 6.00
103 Evgeny Grachev RC 2.50 6.00
104 Mark Dekanich RC 2.50 6.00
105 Adam McQuaid RC 3.00 8.00
106 Jeff Penner RC 4.00 10.00
107 Brandon Pirri RC 2.50 6.00
108 Jonas Holos RC 2.50 6.00
109 Nikita Nikitin RC 2.50 6.00
110 Kyle Wilson RC 3.00 8.00
111 Maxime Fortunus RC 2.00 5.00
112 Marco Scandella RC 2.50 6.00
113 Kevin Shattenkirk RC 5.00 12.00
114 Ian Cole RC 2.50 6.00
115 Kyle Palmieri RC 5.00 12.00
116 Robin Lehner RC 5.00 12.00
117 Marc-Andre Cliche RC 2.00 5.00
118 Richard Clune RC 3.00 8.00
119 Corey Elkins RC 2.00 5.00
120 Jake Muzzin RC 6.00 15.00
121 Clayton Stoner RC 2.50 6.00
122 Nate Prosser RC 2.50 6.00
123 Alexander Urbom RC 2.50 6.00
124 Matt Taormina RC 2.50 6.00
125 Matt Martin RC 4.00 10.00
126 Matt Kassian RC 2.50 6.00
127 Michael Haley RC 2.50 6.00
128 Mark Flood RC 2.00 5.00
129 Keith Aulie RC 2.50 6.00
130 Derek Smith RC 2.50 6.00
131 Bobby Butler RC 2.50 6.00
132 Jeremy Duchesne RC 3.00 8.00
133 Jeremy Morin RC 2.50 6.00
134 John McCarthy RC 2.50 6.00
135 Ryan Reaves RC 3.00 8.00
136 Colby Cohen RC 2.50 6.00
137 Brayden Irwin RC 2.50 6.00
138 Guillaume Desbiens 3.00 8.00
139 Evan Oberg RC 3.00 8.00
140 Brian Fahey RC 2.50 6.00
141 Marcus Johansson RC 4.00 10.00
142 Dustin Tokarski RC 2.50 6.00
143 Dana Tyrell RC 2.50 6.00
144 Tommy Wingels RC 2.50 6.00
145 Eric Tangradi RC 2.50 6.00
146 Nick Johnson RC 2.00 5.00
147 Alexander Pechurski RC 3.00 8.00
148 Evan Brophey RC 2.50 6.00
149 Oliver Ekman-Larsson RC 4.00 10.00
150 Sergei Bobrovsky RC 10.00 25.00
151 Kaspars Daugavins RC 3.00 8.00
152 Jared Cowen RC 2.50 6.00
153 Matt Zaba RC 3.00 8.00
154 Nino Niederreiter RC 4.00 10.00
155 Dustin Kohn RC 2.50 6.00
156 Dylan Reese RC 2.50 6.00
157 Nick Palmieri RC 2.50 6.00
158 Jacob Josefson RC 2.50 6.00
159 Anders Lindback RC 2.50 6.00
160 Nick Spaling RC 2.50 6.00
161 J.T. Wyman RC 2.50 6.00
162 Justin Falk RC 2.00 5.00
163 Cody Almond RC 2.50 6.00
164 Maxim Noreau RC 2.00 5.00
165 Casey Wellman RC 2.50 6.00
166 Kyle Clifford RC 3.00 8.00
167 Alex Plante RC 2.50 6.00
168 Dean Arsene RC 2.50 6.00
169 Johan Motin RC 2.00 5.00
170 Philip Larsen RC 2.50 6.00
171 Raymond Sawada RC 2.00 5.00
172 Eric Wellwood RC 3.00 8.00
173 Tomas Kana RC 2.50 6.00
174 Grant Clitsome RC 2.50 6.00
175 Chad Kolarik RC 2.50 6.00
176 Mark Olver RC 2.50 6.00
177 Brandon Yip RC 2.50 6.00
178 Justin Mercier RC 2.50 6.00
179 Nick Leddy RC 3.00 8.00
180 Jamie McBain RC 2.50 6.00
181 Zac Dalpe RC 3.00 8.00
182 Jerome Samson RC 2.50 6.00
183 Henrik Karlsson RC 2.50 6.00
184 T.J. Brodie RC 2.50 6.00
185 Zach Hamill RC 2.50 6.00
186 Andrew Bodnarchuk RC 2.50 6.00
187 Jordan Caron RC 3.00 8.00
188 Arturs Kulda RC 2.50 6.00
189 Cam Fowler RC 6.00 15.00
190 Nick Bonino RC 3.00 8.00
191 Derek Stepan/99 RC 10.00 25.00
192 Alexander Burmistrov/99 RC 8.00 20.00
193 Jeff Skinner/99 RC 15.00 40.00
194 Brayden Schenn/99 RC 12.00 30.00
195 Jordan Eberle/99 RC 40.00 100.00
196 Magnus Paajarvi/99 RC 10.00 25.00
197 Nazem Kadri/99 RC 30.00 60.00
198 P.K. Subban/99 RC 50.00 120.00
199 Tyler Seguin/99 RC 60.00 100.00
200 Taylor Hall/99 RC 40.00 100.00

2010-11 SP Game Used Gold

*1-100 GOLD: 1X TO 2.5X BASE
*101-190 GOLD: .6X TO 1.5X BASE
*191-200 GOLD: .3X TO .8X BASE
99 Nicklas Backstrom 2.50 6.00

2010-11 SP Game Used Authentic Fabrics

*GOLD/60-100: .5X TO 1.2X BASIC JSY
AFAB Alexandre Burrows 2.50 6.00
AFAH Ales Hemsky 3.00 8.00
AFAK Anze Kopitar 6.00 15.00
AFAN Antti Niemi 3.00 8.00
AFAO Alexander Ovechkin 10.00 25.00
AFBA Nicklas Backstrom 4.00 10.00
AFBL Brian Leetch 3.00 8.00
AFBR Brad Richards 4.00 10.00
AFBS Borje Salming 4.00 10.00
AFCG Claude Giroux 4.00 10.00
AFCN Cam Neely 4.00 10.00
AFCP Carey Price 8.00 20.00
AFCW Cam Ward 4.00 10.00
AFDA Daniel Alfredsson 4.00 10.00
AFDB Dustin Byfuglien 4.00 10.00
AFDC Daniel Carcillo 2.50 6.00
AFDD Drew Doughty 5.00 12.00
AFDE Derick Brassard 2.50 6.00
AFDH Dany Heatley 3.00 8.00
AFDK Duncan Keith 3.00 8.00
AFDP Dion Phaneuf 3.00 8.00
AFDS Daniel Sedin 5.00 12.00
AFEK Evander Kane 4.00 10.00
AFEL Patrik Elias 4.00 10.00
AFEM Evgeni Malkin 8.00 20.00
AFFR Johan Franzen 3.00 8.00
AFGA Marian Gaborik 4.00 10.00
AFGF Grant Fuhr 6.00 15.00
AFHE Milan Hejduk 3.00 8.00
AFHL Henrik Lundqvist 10.00 25.00
AFHZ Henrik Zetterberg 5.00 12.00
AFIK Ilya Kovalchuk 4.00 10.00
AFJA Jason Arnott 3.00 8.00
AFJC Jeff Carter 3.00 8.00
AFJD J.P. Dumont 2.50 6.00
AFJG Jean-Sebastien Giguere 4.00 10.00
AFJI Jarome Iginla 5.00 12.00
AFJJ Jack Johnson 2.50 6.00
AFJL Jamie Langenbrunner 2.50 6.00
AFJO Joe Sakic 8.00 20.00
AFJP Joe Pavelski 5.00 12.00
AFJV James van Riemsdyk 3.00 8.00
AFKA Patrick Kane 8.00 20.00
AFKI Miikka Kiprusoff 4.00 10.00
AFLE Mario Lemieux 15.00 40.00
AFLS Luke Schenn 4.00 10.00
AFLU Loui Eriksson 2.50 6.00
AFMB Martin Brodeur 10.00 25.00
AFMC Mike Cammalleri 4.00 10.00
AFMD Matt Duchene 4.00 10.00
AFMG Mike Green 3.00 8.00
AFMH Marian Hossa 4.00 10.00
AFML Milan Lucic 4.00 10.00
AFMM Mark Messier 8.00 20.00
AFMR Mike Richards 3.00 8.00
AFMS Marc Savard 2.50 6.00
AFNB Niklas Backstrom 4.00 10.00
AFNK Nikolai Kulemin 2.50 6.00
AFNL Nicklas Lidstrom 4.00 10.00
AFOA Adam Oates 4.00 10.00
AFPB Patrice Bergeron 5.00 12.00
AFPD Pavel Datsyuk 6.00 15.00
AFPK Phil Kessel 4.00 10.00
AFPM Patrick Marleau 4.00 10.00
AFPR Patrick Roy 10.00 25.00
AFPS Paul Stastny 3.00 8.00
AFRB Rene Bourque 2.50 6.00
AFRG Ryan Getzlaf 4.00 10.00
AFRK Ryan Kesler 4.00 10.00
AFRL Roberto Luongo 6.00 15.00
AFRN Rick Nash 4.00 10.00
AFSC Sidney Crosby 8.00 20.00
AFSD Shane Doan 3.00 8.00
AFSH Patrick Sharp 4.00 10.00
AFSM Steve Mason 3.00 8.00
AFSP Jason Spezza 4.00 10.00
AFSS Steven Stamkos 8.00 20.00
AFST Martin St. Louis 4.00 10.00
AFTA John Tavares 6.00 15.00
AFVK Tomas Vokoun 3.00 8.00
AFVO Jakub Voracek 3.00 8.00
AFWG Wayne Gretzky 10.00 25.00
AFZP Zach Parise 4.00 10.00

2010-11 SP Game Used Authentic Fabrics Patches

*PATCH/35: 1X TO 2.5X BASIC JSY
AFBA Nicklas Backstrom 10.00 25.00
AFBS Borje Salming/20 20.00 50.00

2010-11 SP Game Used Authentic Fabrics Dual

*PATCH/25: .8X TO 2X DUAL
AF2AE J.Arnott/P.Elias 5.00 12.00
AF2AS D.Alfredsson/J.Spezza 5.00 12.00
AF2BK D.Brown/A.Kopitar 8.00 20.00
AF2BP Z.Parise/M.Brodeur 12.00 30.00
AF2CM S.Crosby/E.Malkin 15.00 40.00
AF2CO S.Crosby/A.Ovechkin 15.00 40.00
AF2CR Z.Chara/T.Rask 6.00 15.00
AF2CV J.van Riemsdyk/J.Carter 4.00 10.00
AF2DG M.Dionne/W.Gretzky 20.00 50.00
AF2DW J.Dumont/S.Weber 4.00 10.00
AF2GL M.Gaborik/H.Lundqvist 12.00 30.00
AF2GP J.Giguere/D.Phaneuf 5.00 12.00
AF2GV M.Green/S.Varlamov 5.00 12.00
AF2HD H.Sedin/D.Sedin 6.00 15.00
AF2HG M.Hossa/M.Gaborik 5.00 12.00
AF2HP A.Hemsky/D.Penner 4.00 10.00
AF2IB R.Bourque/J.Iginla 6.00 15.00
AF2JD J.Johnson/D.Doughty 6.00 15.00
AF2KB E.Kane/D.Byfuglien 5.00 12.00
AF2KK P.Kessel/N.Kulemin 5.00 12.00
AF2KM M.Messier/J.Kurri 10.00 25.00
AF2KR M.Kiprusoff/T.Rask 6.00 15.00
AF2LC S.Crosby/M.Lemieux 15.00 40.00
AF2LM R.Luongo/R.Miller 8.00 20.00
AF2LR M.Lucic/T.Rask 6.00 15.00
AF2LS S.Stamkos/V.Lecavalier 6.00 20.00
AF2MH P.Marleau/D.Heatley 5.00 12.00
AF2MN M.Koivu/N.Backstrom 5.00 12.00
AF2NB C.Neely/R.Bourque 8.00 20.00
AF2NV R.Nash/J.Voracek 5.00 12.00
AF2OB N.Backstrom/A.Ovechkin 8.00 20.00
AF2PD D.Keith/P.Kane 10.00 25.00
AF2PP C.Price/T.Plekanec 10.00 25.00
AF2PR R.Bourque/P.Roy 12.00 30.00
AF2RB P.Roy/M.Brodeur 12.00 30.00
AF2RG M.Richards/C.Giroux 5.00 12.00
AF2SD M.Duchene/P.Stastny 5.00 12.00
AF2SO A.Semin/A.Ovechkin 8.00 20.00
AF2SS M.St. Louis/S.Stamkos 8.00 20.00
AF2SW C.Ward/E.Staal 6.00 15.00
AF2SZ S.Crosby/Z.Parise 15.00 40.00
AF2TD J.Tavares/M.Duchene 10.00 25.00
AF2TK D.Keith/J.Toews 8.00 20.00
AF2TP J.Pavelski/J.Thornton 8.00 20.00
AF2WL L.Robitaille/W.Gretzky 20.00 50.00
AF2YD S.Yzerman/P.Datsyuk 10.00 25.00
AF2YL S.Yzerman/N.Lidstrom 10.00 25.00
AF2ZB H.Zetterberg/N.Backstrom 6.00 15.00

2010-11 SP Game Used Authentic Fabrics Triples

*PATCH/15: .6X TO 1.5X BASIC TRIPLE/25
AF3ANA Ryan/Getzlaf/Hiller 8.00 20.00
AF3ATL Antrpv/Kane/Byfugl 8.00 20.00
AF3BOS Bergrn/Chara/Rask 12.00 30.00
AF3CAL Brque/Kiprusoff/Iginla 10.00 25.00
AF3CAR Ruutu/Staal/Ward 10.00 25.00
AF3CBS Nash/Voracek/Mason 8.00 20.00
AF3CHI Keith/Toews/Kane 15.00 40.00
AF3COL Stastny/Hejduk/Duchn 8.00 20.00
AF3DAL Rchrds/Eriksson/Lehton 8.00 20.00
AF3DET Howard/Datsyuk/Zetter 15.00 40.00
AF3FLA Frolik/Weiss/Vokoun 6.00 15.00
AF3LAK Kopitar/Brown/Doughty 12.00 30.00
AF3MIN Koivu/Latend/Backstrm 8.00 20.00
AF3MON Price/Plekanec/Cammal 15.00 40.00
AF3NJD Kvalchk/Brdeur/Parise 20.00 50.00
AF3NSH Dumont/Weber/Rinne 8.00 20.00
AF3NYI DiPietro/Tavres/Okpso 15.00 40.00
AF3NYR Lundqvist/Gaborik/Drury 20.00 50.00
AF3OTT Alfrdssn/Gnchar/Spezza 8.00 20.00
AF3PHI Carter/Richards/van R 6.00 15.00
AF3PIT Crosby/Fleury/Malkin 30.00 80.00
AF3SJS Thrntn/Mrleau/Setgchi 12.00 30.00
AF3STL Johnsn/Berglnd/Backes 5.00 12.00
AF3TBL Lecav/St. Lou/Stamks 12.00 30.00
AF3TOR Giguere/Kessel/Phaneuf 15.00 40.00
AF3VAN Luongo/Sedin/Sedin 12.00 30.00
AF3WAS Ovech/Bckstrm/Varl 30.00 80.00

2010-11 SP Game Used Career Legacy

CL2BG Brian Gionta/40 4.00 10.00
CL2BL Brian Leetch/75 5.00 12.00
CL2JK Jari Kurri/75 6.00 15.00
CL2LM Lanny McDonald/75 6.00 15.00
CL2PE Phil Esposito/25 8.00 20.00
CL2PR Patrick Roy/75 15.00 40.00
CL2RB Ray Bourque/75 10.00 25.00
CL3DH Dany Heatley/35 10.00 25.00
CL3WG Wayne Gretzky/25 50.00 100.00

2010-11 SP Game Used Championship Marks

CMAL Andrew Ladd 50.00 100.00
CMAN Antti Niemi 50.00 100.00
CMJT Jonathan Toews 125.00 200.00
CMMH Marian Hossa 50.00 100.00
CMPK Patrick Kane 100.00 175.00
CMPS Patrick Sharp 30.00 60.00

2010-11 SP Game Used Extra SIGnificance

XSGBF M.Fleury/M.Brodeur 30.00 80.00
XSGBG M.Bossy/C.Gillies 12.00 30.00
XSGBM R.Miller/M.Brodeur 30.00 80.00
XSGBO B.Orr/R.Bourque 125.00 250.00
XSGBR M.Brodeur/P.Roy 75.00 150.00
XSGCG J.Carter/C.Giroux 12.00 30.00
XSGDT T.Seguin/D.Stepan 40.00 80.00
XSGEB P.Esposito/J.Bucyk 20.00 50.00
XSGEE T.Esposito/P.Esposito 30.00 80.00
XSGFM M.Fleury/E.Malkin 25.00 60.00
XSGGG Gustavsson/Giguere 15.00 40.00
XSGGH W.Gretzky/G.Howe 250.00 600.00
XSGHE T.Hall/J.Eberle 75.00 150.00
XSGHG M.Gaborik/M.Hossa 12.00 30.00
XSGHM D.Hasek/R.Miller 20.00 50.00
XSGHS D.Heatley/D.Setoguchi 10.00 25.00
XSGIB M.Backlund/J.Iginla 15.00 40.00
XSGIT J.Iginla/A.Tanguay 15.00 40.00
XSGJD J.Tavares/D.Stepan 50.00 100.00
XSGKO A.Ovechkin/I.Kovalchuk 60.00 120.00
XSGKS P.Subban/N.Kadri 40.00 100.00
XSGMS D.Savard/S.Mikita 15.00 40.00
XSGNM R.Nash/S.Mason 12.00 30.00
XSGOB A.Ovechkin/N.Backstrom 60.00 120.00
XSGOR L.Robinson/B.Orr 100.00 200.00
XSGPG J.Giguere/D.Phaneuf 12.00 30.00
XSGRB P.Bergeron/M.Ryder 15.00 40.00
XSGRC M.Richards/J.Carter 20.00 50.00
XSGRN T.Rask/A.Niemi 15.00 40.00
XSGSK A.Kopitar/R.Smyth 12.00 30.00
XSGTB J.Bailey/J.Tavares 20.00 50.00
XSGTD J.Tavares/M.Duchene 20.00 50.00
XSGYL N.Lidstrom/S.Yzerman 100.00 200.00

2010-11 SP Game Used Inked Sweaters

ISAO Alexander Ovechkin/15 50.00 120.00
ISBY Brandon Yip 6.00 15.00
ISCA Jeff Carter 6.00 15.00
ISDC Daniel Carcillo 5.00 12.00
ISDS Devin Setoguchi 6.00 15.00
ISEM Evgeni Malkin 20.00 50.00
ISET Eric Tangradi 6.00 15.00
ISGF Grant Fuhr 12.00 30.00
ISGU Jonas Gustavsson 12.00 30.00
ISHL Henrik Lundqvist 15.00 40.00
ISIK Ilya Kovalchuk 15.00 40.00
ISJC Jared Cowen 6.00 15.00
ISJF Johan Franzen 10.00 25.00
ISJG Jean-Sebastien Giguere 10.00 25.00
ISJI Jarome Iginla 10.00 25.00
ISJM Jamie McBain 6.00 15.00
ISJT John Tavares 15.00 40.00
ISJV Jakub Voracek 6.00 15.00
ISMB Martin Brodeur/15 40.00 80.00
ISMF Marc-Andre Fleury 12.00 30.00
ISMG Marian Gaborik 8.00 20.00
ISML Mario Lemieux/15 50.00 125.00
ISMM Mark Messier/15 25.00 60.00
ISMR Mike Richards 20.00 50.00
ISMS Martin St. Louis 8.00 20.00
ISNB Nicklas Backstrom 8.00 20.00
ISNH Nathan Horton 6.00 15.00
ISNK Nazem Kadri 15.00 40.00
ISNL Nicklas Lidstrom 12.00 30.00
ISPE Phil Esposito 15.00 40.00
ISPR Patrick Roy/15 40.00 80.00
ISPS Paul Stastny 6.00 15.00
ISRB Ray Bourque 12.00 30.00
ISRM Ryan Miller 12.00 30.00
ISRN Rick Nash 10.00 25.00
ISSC Sidney Crosby/15 60.00 120.00
ISVA James van Riemsdyk 6.00 15.00
ISWG Wayne Gretzky/15 200.00 500.00
ISYZ Steve Yzerman/15 30.00 80.00
ISZH Zach Hamill 6.00 15.00

2010-11 SP Game Used Letter Marks

LMAN Antti Niemi 12.00 30.00
LMAO Alexander Ovechkin 75.00 125.00
LMBS Brent Sutter 10.00 25.00
LMBY Brandon Yip 12.00 30.00
LMCS Chris Stewart 12.00 30.00
LMDS Devin Setoguchi 12.00 30.00
LMEK Evander Kane 15.00 40.00
LMET Eric Tangradi 12.00 30.00
LMIK Ilya Kovalchuk 20.00 50.00
LMJC Jared Cowen 12.00 30.00
LMJG Jonas Gustavsson 20.00 50.00
LMJI Jarome Iginla 15.00 40.00
LMJT John Tavares 25.00 60.00
LMJV James van Riemsdyk 12.00 30.00
LMLE Lars Eller 50.00 100.00
LMLR Luc Robitaille 15.00 40.00
LMMD Matt Duchene 15.00 40.00
LMML Mario Lemieux 60.00 120.00
LMNK Nazem Kadri 25.00 60.00
LMPK Patrick Kane 30.00 80.00
LMPS P.K. Subban 100.00 200.00
LMRK Ryan Kesler 30.00 80.00
LMSC Sidney Crosby 100.00 200.00
LMSG Sam Gagner 10.00 25.00
LMSS Steven Stamkos 60.00 120.00
LMSU Duane Sutter 10.00 25.00
LMTM Tyler Myers 10.00 25.00
LMTO Jonathan Toews 25.00 60.00
LMWC Wendel Clark 15.00 40.00

2010-11 SP Game Used Number Marks

NMAO Alexander Ovechkin 75.00 150.00
NMBC Bobby Clarke 25.00 60.00
NMBO Bobby Orr 200.00 350.00
NMEM Evgeni Malkin 50.00 120.00
NMJS Joe Sakic 40.00 100.00
NMJT John Tavares 30.00 80.00
NMJV James van Riemsdyk 20.00 50.00
NMMB Martin Brodeur 50.00 125.00
NMMD Matt Duchene 40.00 100.00
NMMR Mike Richards 40.00 100.00
NMPK Patrick Kane 40.00 100.00
NMSA Joe Sakic 40.00 100.00
NMSC Sidney Crosby 150.00 300.00
NMSS Steven Stamkos 60.00 120.00
NMSY Steve Yzerman 50.00 125.00
NMTO Jonathan Toews 50.00 100.00
NMWG Wayne Gretzky 300.00 800.00

2010-11 SP Game Used Retro Marks

RMBO Bobby Orr 100.00 200.00
RMGL Guy Lafleur 40.00 80.00
RMJS Joe Sakic 25.00 60.00
RMME Mark Messier 25.00 60.00
RMMM Mike Modano 25.00 60.00
RMPE Phil Esposito 15.00 40.00
RMSC Sidney Crosby 150.00 300.00

2010-11 SP Game Used Rookie Exclusives Autographs

REAB Alexander Burmistrov 12.00 30.00
REAK Arturs Kulda 5.00 12.00
REAL Anders Lindback 5.00 12.00
REBO Andrew Bodnarchuk 5.00 12.00
REBS Brayden Schenn 10.00 25.00
REBY Brandon Yip 10.00 25.00
RECA Cody Almond 5.00 12.00
RECO Jared Cowen 5.00 12.00
REDA Dean Arsene 5.00 12.00
REDR Dylan Reese 5.00 12.00
REDS Derek Stepan 20.00 50.00
REDT Dustin Tokarski 5.00 12.00
REEG Evgeny Grachev 5.00 12.00
REET Eric Tangradi 5.00 12.00
REGC Grant Clitsome 5.00 12.00
REHK Henrik Karlsson 5.00 12.00
REJC Jordan Caron 8.00 20.00
REJE Jordan Eberle 40.00 80.00
REJM Jamie McBain 5.00 12.00
REJO Johan Motin 4.00 10.00
REJS Jeff Skinner 15.00 40.00
REKC Kyle Clifford 6.00 15.00
REKD Kaspars Daugavins 6.00 15.00
REKS Kevin Shattenkirk 10.00 25.00
REMJ Marcus Johansson 10.00 25.00
REMN Maxim Noreau 4.00 10.00
REMO Mark Olver 5.00 12.00
REMP Magnus Paajarvi 6.00 15.00
REMT Mattias Tedenby 5.00 12.00
RENB Nick Bonino 6.00 15.00
RENJ Nick Johnson 4.00 10.00
RENK Nazem Kadri 12.50 30.00
RENL Nick Leddy 6.00 15.00
RENN Nino Niederreiter 8.00 20.00
RENP Nate Prosser 5.00 12.00
RENS Nick Spaling 5.00 12.00
REPA Nick Palmieri 5.00 12.00
REPE Alexander Pechurski 6.00 15.00
REPS P.K. Subban 30.00 80.00
RESB Sergei Bobrovsky 20.00 50.00
RETB T.J. Brodie 5.00 12.00
RETH Taylor Hall 50.00 120.00
RETS Tyler Seguin 30.00 60.00
RETW Tommy Wingels 5.00 12.00
RETY Dana Tyrell 5.00 12.00
REZD Zac Dalpe 6.00 15.00
REZH Zach Hamill 5.00 12.00

2010-11 SP Game Used SIGnificance

SIGAK Anze Kopitar 12.00 30.00
SIGAN Antti Niemi 6.00 15.00
SIGAO Alexander Ovechkin/15 40.00 100.00
SIGBA Mikael Backlund 6.00 15.00
SIGBL Brian Leetch 6.00 15.00
SIGBO Bobby Orr/15 100.00 200.00
SIGBS Brayden Schenn 15.00 40.00
SIGCA Jeff Carter 6.00 15.00
SIGCD Chris Drury 6.00 15.00
SIGCG Claude Giroux 8.00 20.00
SIGCN Cam Neely 15.00 40.00
SIGCP Carey Price 20.00 50.00
SIGCW Cam Ward 8.00 20.00
SIGDB Dan Boyle 5.00 12.00
SIGDD Drew Doughty 10.00 25.00
SIGDG Doug Gilmour 10.00 25.00
SIGDH Dany Heatley 6.00 15.00
SIGDP Dion Phaneuf 6.00 15.00
SIGEK Evander Kane 8.00 20.00
SIGEL Patrik Elias 8.00 20.00
SIGEM Evgeni Malkin 15.00 40.00
SIGEP Phil Esposito 12.00 30.00
SIGET Eric Tangradi 6.00 15.00
SIGGF Grant Fuhr 12.00 30.00
SIGGH Gordie Howe/15 60.00 120.00
SIGGL Guillaume Latendresse 6.00 15.00
SIGGU Jonas Gustavsson 10.00 25.00
SIGHE Milan Hejduk 6.00 15.00
SIGHL Henrik Lundqvist 20.00 50.00
SIGIK Ilya Kovalchuk 12.00 30.00
SIGIL Igor Larionov 8.00 20.00
SIGJB Josh Bailey 6.00 15.00
SIGJC Jared Cowen 6.00 15.00
SIGJD J.P. Dumont 5.00 12.00
SIGJE Jordan Eberle 15.00 40.00
SIGJG Jean-Sebastien Giguere 12.00 30.00
SIGJH Jonas Hiller 6.00 15.00
SIGJI Jarome Iginla 10.00 25.00
SIGJK Jari Kurri/15 12.00 30.00
SIGJS Jordan Staal 6.00 15.00
SIGJV James van Riemsdyk 6.00 15.00
SIGKE Phil Kessel 8.00 20.00
SIGLC Logan Couture 12.00 30.00
SIGLM Lanny McDonald 8.00 20.00
SIGLR Luc Robitaille 8.00 20.00
SIGLS Luke Schenn 8.00 20.00
SIGMB Martin Brodeur/15 30.00 60.00
SIGMF Marc-Andre Fleury 15.00 40.00
SIGMH Marian Hossa 10.00 25.00
SIGMM Mark Messier/15 40.00 80.00
SIGMP Magnus Paajarvi 8.00 20.00
SIGMR Mike Ribeiro 5.00 12.00
SIGMS Martin St. Louis 8.00 20.00
SIGNB Nicklas Backstrom 8.00 20.00
SIGNK Nazem Kadri 15.00 40.00
SIGNL Nicklas Lidstrom 10.00 25.00
SIGPB Patrice Bergeron 10.00 25.00
SIGPR Patrick Roy/15 60.00 120.00
SIGRG Ryan Getzlaf 8.00 20.00
SIGRI Mike Richards 6.00 15.00
SIGRM Ryan Miller 8.00 20.00
SIGRN Rick Nash 8.00 20.00
SIGRS Ryan Smyth 6.00 15.00
SIGSD Derek Stepan 8.00 20.00
SIGSE Devin Setoguchi 6.00 15.00
SIGSJ Jeff Skinner 30.00 80.00
SIGSK Saku Koivu 12.00 30.00
SIGSM Stan Mikita 12.00 30.00
SIGST Paul Stastny 6.00 15.00
SIGSW Shea Weber 6.00 15.00
SIGSY Steve Yzerman/15 60.00 120.00
SIGTA John Tavares 12.00 30.00
SIGTE Tony Esposito 15.00 40.00
SIGTH Taylor Hall 20.00 50.00
SIGTR Tuukka Rask 10.00 25.00
SIGTS Tyler Seguin 20.00 50.00
SIGTV Tomas Vokoun 6.00 15.00
SIGVH Victor Hedman 10.00 25.00
SIGVL Vincent Lecavalier 8.00 20.00
SIGWG Wayne Gretzky/15 250.00 600.00

2010-11 SP Game Used SIGnificant Numbers Autographs

SNAN Antti Niemi/31 8.00 20.00
SNBP Brad Park/22 15.00 40.00
SNBY Brandon Yip/59 15.00 40.00
SNCG Claude Giroux/28 25.00 60.00
SNCN Cam Neely/21 25.00 50.00
SNCO Jared Cowen/48 15.00 40.00
SNCP Carey Price/31 25.00 60.00
SNCW Cam Ward/30 10.00 25.00
SNEM Evgeni Malkin/71 25.00 60.00
SNET Eric Tangradi/56 8.00 20.00
SNGF Grant Fuhr/31 25.00 50.00
SNGI Jean-Sebastien Giguere/35 12.00 30.00
SNHL Henrik Lundqvist/30 25.00 60.00
SNJF Johan Franzen/93 10.00 25.00
SNJV James van Riemsdyk/21 25.00 50.00
SNKU Nikolai Kulemin/41 6.00 15.00
SNLR Luc Robitaille/20 25.00 50.00
SNMB Martin Brodeur/30 25.00 60.00
SNMF Marc-Andre Fleury/29 20.00 50.00
SNMH Milan Hejduk/23 15.00 40.00
SNMP Magnus Paajarvi/91 10.00 25.00
SNMS Martin St. Louis/26 12.00 30.00
SNNK Nazem Kadri/43 25.00 60.00
SNPE Patrik Elias/26 15.00 40.00
SNPK Phil Kessel/81 10.00 25.00
SNPS P.K. Subban/76 40.00 100.00
SNRM Ryan Miller/30 15.00 40.00
SNRN Rick Nash/61 12.00 30.00
SNSC Sidney Crosby/87 100.00 200.00
SNSD Derek Stepan/21 25.00 50.00
SNSS Steven Stamkos/91 30.00 80.00
SNST Paul Stastny/26 10.00 25.00
SNTA John Tavares/91 15.00 40.00
SNTE Tony Esposito/35 15.00 40.00
SNTR Tuukka Rask/40 12.00 30.00
SNTS Tyler Seguin/19 40.00 100.00
SNTV Thomas Vanek/26 10.00 25.00
SNVH Victor Hedman/77 12.00 30.00
SNVO Jakub Voracek/93 8.00 20.00
SNZH Zach Hamill/52 8.00 20.00

2010-11 SP Game Used Team Marks

TMAA Artem Anisimov 10.00 25.00
TMAO Adam Oates 25.00 60.00
TMBF Benn Ferriero 10.00 25.00
TMBO Bobby Orr 150.00 250.00
TMCD Chris Drury 12.00 30.00
TMCK Chris Kunitz 15.00 40.00
TMCN Cam Neely 40.00 100.00
TMCO Chris Osgood 15.00 40.00
TMDB Dan Boyle 10.00 25.00
TMDH Dany Heatley 12.00 30.00
TMDS Devin Setoguchi 12.00 30.00
TMEM Evgeni Malkin 30.00 80.00
TMET Eric Tangradi 12.00 30.00
TMGI Matt Gilroy 10.00 25.00
TMHL Henrik Lundqvist 40.00 100.00
TMJB Johnny Bucyk 25.00 60.00
TMJS Jordan Staal 12.00 30.00
TMJT Joe Thornton 20.00 50.00
TMLC Logan Couture 25.00 60.00
TMLR Luc Robitaille 15.00 40.00
TMMD Michael Del Zotto 10.00 25.00
TMMF Marc-Andre Fleury 30.00 80.00
TMMG Marian Gaborik 15.00 40.00
TMMS Michael Sauer 10.00 25.00
TMMT Maxime Talbot 25.00 60.00
TMNJ Nick Johnson 10.00 25.00
TMNL Nicklas Lidstrom 30.00 80.00
TMPD Pavel Datsyuk 20.00 50.00
TMPE Phil Esposito 25.00 60.00
TMRB Ray Bourque 25.00 60.00
TMSC Sidney Crosby 75.00 150.00
TMSY Steve Yzerman 50.00 100.00
TMTH Tomas Holmstrom 20.00 50.00
TMVF Valtteri Filppula 15.00 40.00

2011-12 SP Game Used

COMP.SET w/o RC's (100) 50.00 00.00
1 Ryan Getzlaf 1.00 2.50
2 Bobby Ryan .75 2.00
3 Jonas Hiller .75 2.00
4 Corey Perry 1.50 4.00
5 Zdeno Chara 1.00 2.50
6 Tim Thomas 1.00 2.50
7 David Krejci 1.00 2.50
8 Nathan Horton 1.00 2.50
9 Brad Marchand 2.00 5.00
10 Bobby Orr 4.00 10.00
11 Tyler Seguin 1.25 3.00
12 Thomas Vanek .75 2.00
13 Ryan Miller 1.00 2.50
14 Drew Stafford .60 1.50
15 Jarome Iginla 1.25 3.00
16 Miikka Kiprusoff 1.00 2.50
17 Eric Staal 1.25 3.00
18 Cam Ward 1.00 2.50
19 Jeff Skinner 1.25 3.00
20 Jonathan Toews 1.50 4.00
21 Patrick Kane 2.00 5.00
22 Marian Hossa 1.00 2.50
23 Matt Duchene 1.00 2.50
24 Paul Stastny .75 2.00
25 Rick Nash 1.00 2.50
26 Jeff Carter .75 2.00
27 Brenden Morrow .75 2.00
28 Jim Howard 1.25 3.00
29 Henrik Zetterberg 1.25 3.00
30 Pavel Datsyuk 1.50 4.00
31 Nicklas Lidstrom .60 1.50
32 Johan Franzen .75 2.00
33 Paul Coffey 1.00 2.50
34 Ales Hemsky .75 2.00
35 Jordan Eberle 1.00 2.50
36 Taylor Hall 1.00 2.50
37 Ryan Smyth .75 2.00
38 Wayne Gretzky 6.00 15.00
39 Tomas Fleischmann .60 1.50
40 Ron Francis 1.25 3.00
41 Drew Doughty 1.25 3.00
42 Anze Kopitar 1.50 4.00
43 Mike Richards .75 2.00
44 Mikko Koivu .75 2.00
45 Niklas Backstrom 1.00 2.50
46 Dany Heatley .75 2.00
47 Patrick Roy 2.50 6.00
48 Tomas Plekanec .60 1.50
49 Carey Price 2.00 5.00
50 P.K. Subban 1.25 3.00
51 Michael Cammalleri .75 2.00
52 Brian Gionta .60 1.50
53 Jean Beliveau 1.00 2.50
54 Pekka Rinne 1.00 2.50
55 Shea Weber .75 2.00
56 Martin Brodeur 2.50 6.00
57 Travis Zajac .60 1.50
58 Zach Parise 1.00 2.50
59 Ilya Kovalchuk 1.00 2.50
60 Michael Grabner .75 2.00
61 John Tavares 1.50 4.00
62 Mark Messier 2.00 5.00
63 Brad Richards 1.00 2.50
64 Henrik Lundqvist 2.50 6.00
65 Marian Gaborik 1.00 2.50
66 Craig Anderson 1.00 2.50
67 Jason Spezza 1.00 2.50
68 Daniel Alfredsson 1.00 2.50
69 Jaromir Jagr 3.00 8.00
70 Chris Pronger 1.00 2.50
71 Claude Giroux 1.00 2.50
72 Eric Lindros 1.50 4.00
73 Shane Doan .75 2.00
74 Mario Lemieux 4.00 10.00
75 Jordan Staal .75 2.00
76 Sidney Crosby 4.00 10.00
77 Evgeni Malkin 2.00 5.00
78 Marc-Andre Fleury 2.00 5.00
79 Joe Thornton 1.50 4.00
80 Patrick Marleau 1.00 2.50
81 Logan Couture 1.25 3.00
82 Jaroslav Halak 1.00 2.50
83 David Backes .60 1.50
84 Steven Stamkos 2.00 5.00
85 Vincent Lecavalier 1.00 2.50
86 Dwayne Roloson .75 2.00
87 James Reimer 1.00 2.50
88 Dion Phaneuf .75 2.00
89 Phil Kessel 1.00 2.50
90 Ryan Kesler 1.00 2.50
91 Roberto Luongo 1.50 4.00
92 Daniel Sedin 1.25 3.00
93 Henrik Sedin 1.25 3.00
94 Alexandre Burrows .60 1.50
95 Alexander Semin 1.00 2.50
96 Alexander Ovechkin 4.00 10.00
97 Nicklas Backstrom 1.00 2.50
98 Mike Green .75 2.00
99 Ondrej Pavelec 1.00 2.50
100 Evander Kane 1.00 2.50
101 Chris Vande Velde RC 4.00 10.00
102 Mark Katic RC 2.50 6.00
103 Cam Talbot RC 6.00 15.00
104 David Rundblad RC 2.50 6.00
105 Maxime Macenauer RC 2.50 6.00
106 Lance Bouma RC 2.50 6.00
107 Alex Stalock 2.00 5.00
108 Patrick Wiercioch RC 2.50 6.00
109 Craig Smith RC 3.00 8.00
110 Paul Postma RC 2.50 6.00
111 Ben Scrivens RC 2.50 6.00
112 Tim Erixon RC 2.50 6.00
113 David Savard RC 2.50 6.00
114 Raphael Diaz RC 2.50 6.00
115 Jean-Philippe Levasseur RC 2.50 6.00
116 Shane Sims RC 2.50 6.00
117 Simon Despres RC 2.50 6.00
118 Keith Kinkaid RC 2.50 6.00
119 Ben Holmstrom RC 2.50 6.00
120 Brett Bulmer RC 2.50 6.00
121 Teemu Hartikainen RC 2.50 6.00
122 Erik Gustafsson RC 3.00 8.00
123 Brendon Nash RC 2.50 6.00
124 Joe Vitale RC 2.50 6.00
125 Tomas Vincour RC 2.50 6.00
126 Cam Atkinson RC 6.00 15.00
127 Colin Greening RC 2.50 6.00
128 Roman Horak RC 2.50 6.00
129 Jonathon Blum RC 2.50 6.00
130 Blake Geoffrion RC 2.50 6.00
131 Matt Frattin RC 2.50 6.00
132 Matt Read RC 3.00 8.00
133 Aaron Palushaj RC 2.50 6.00
134 Carl Klingberg RC 2.50 6.00
135 Jake Gardiner RC 4.00 10.00
136 Scott Timmins RC 2.50 6.00
137 Justin DiBenedetto RC 2.00 5.00
138 Brandon Saad RC 5.00 12.00
139 Roman Wick RC 3.00 8.00
140 Mikko Koskinen RC 3.00 8.00
141 Tomas Kubalik RC 2.50 6.00
142 Drew Bagnall RC 2.50 6.00
143 John Moore RC 2.50 6.00
144 Devante Smith-Pelly RC 3.00 8.00
145 Colton Sceviour RC 2.50 6.00
146 Hugh Jessiman RC 2.50 6.00
147 Carson McMillan RC 3.00 8.00
148 Jamie Doornbosch RC 2.50 6.00
149 Matt Campanale RC 2.50 6.00
150 Andre Benoit RC 3.00 8.00
151 Brian Strait RC 3.00 8.00
152 Harry Zolnierczyk RC 2.50 6.00
153 Lennart Petrell RC 3.00 8.00
154 Zac Rinaldo RC 2.50 6.00
155 Todd Ford RC 3.00 8.00
156 Viatcheslav Voynov RC 2.50 6.00
157 Stephane Da Costa RC 2.50 6.00
158 Cameron Gaunce RC 2.00 5.00
159 Justin Faulk RC 4.00 10.00
160 Erik Condra RC 2.50 6.00
161 Alexei Emelin RC 2.50 6.00
162 Yann Sauve RC 2.50 6.00
163 Greg Nemisz RC 2.50 6.00
164 Marcus Kruger RC 4.00 10.00
165 Joe Colborne RC 2.50 6.00
166 Harri Sateri RC 2.50 6.00
167 Adam Henrique RC 5.00 12.00
168 Anton Lander RC 2.50 6.00
169 Bracken Kearns RC 2.50 6.00
170 Allen York RC 3.00 8.00
171 Andy Miele RC 2.50 6.00
172 Ryan Thang RC 2.00 5.00
173 Pat Maroon RC 2.50 6.00

174 Cody Eakin RC 4.00 10.00
175 Gustav Nyquist RC 6.00 15.00
176 Corey Tropp RC 2.50 6.00
177 Peter Holland RC 2.50 6.00
178 Robert Bortuzzo RC 2.50 6.00
179 Colten Teubert RC 2.50 6.00
180 Mattias Ekholm RC 5.00 12.00
181 Brendan Smith RC 2.50 6.00
182 Eddie Lack RC 2.50 6.00
183 Frederic St. Denis RC 2.50 6.00
184 Anders Nilsson RC 2.50 6.00
185 Kris Fredheim RC 2.50 6.00
186 Dmitry Orlov RC 6.00 15.00
187 Kevin Marshall RC 2.50 6.00
188 David Ullstrom RC 2.50 6.00
189 Louis Leblanc RC 2.50 6.00
190 Zack Kassian RC 3.00 8.00
191 Erik Gudbranson/99 RC 12.00 30.00
192 Adam Larsson/99 RC 25.00 50.00
193 Mika Zibanejad/99 RC 20.00 50.00
194 Mark Scheifele/99 RC 25.00 60.00
195 Brett Connolly/99 RC 20.00 40.00
196 Ryan Johansen/99 RC 30.00 60.00
197 Cody Hodgson/99 RC 15.00 40.00
198 Sean Couturier/99 RC 12.00 30.00
199 Gabriel Landeskog/99 RC 20.00 50.00
200 R.Nugent-Hopkins/99 RC 75.00 150.00

2011-12 SP Game Used Gold

*1-100 VETS/100: 1.2X TO 3X BASIC CARDS
*101-190 ROOK/50: .6X TO 1.5X BASIC RC
97 Nicklas Backstrom 3.00 8.00
191 Erik Gudbranson AU 12.00 30.00
192 Adam Larsson AU 12.00 30.00
193 Mika Zibanejad AU 12.00 30.00
194 Mark Scheifele AU 15.00 40.00
195 Brett Connolly AU 10.00 25.00
196 Ryan Johansen AU 30.00 80.00
197 Cody Hodgson AU 40.00 100.00
198 Sean Couturier AU 15.00 40.00
199 Gabriel Landeskog AU 40.00 100.00
200 Ryan Nugent-Hopkins AU 125.00 250.00

2011-12 SP Game Used 500 Goal Club Marks

500GCBH Brett Hull EXCH 60.00 120.00
500GCDH Dale Hawerchuk EXCH 50.00 100.00
500GCHU Bobby Hull 60.00 120.00
500GCJB Johnny Bucyk EXCH 30.00 60.00
500GCJK Jari Kurri EXCH 50.00 100.00
500GCMB Mike Bossy 40.00 80.00
500GCMG Mike Gartner 30.00 60.00
500GCML Mario Lemieux EXCH 100.00 200.00
500GCMM Mike Modano EXCH 30.00 60.00
500GCRF Ron Francis 15.00 40.00
500GCWG Wayne Gretzky EXCH 250.00 600.00

2011-12 SP Game Used Authentic Fabrics

*PATCH/25-35: .8X TO 2X BASIC JSY/100
AFAB Alexandre Burrows 2.50 6.00
AFAH Ales Hemsky 3.00 8.00
AFAK Anze Kopitar 6.00 15.00
AFAN Antti Niemi 3.00 8.00
AFAO Alexander Ovechkin 15.00 40.00
AFAS Alexander Semin 4.00 10.00
AFAT Alex Tanguay 2.50 6.00
AFAV Antoine Vermette 2.50 6.00
AFBH Brett Hull 8.00 20.00
AFBK David Backes 2.50 6.00
AFBP Brad Park 3.00 8.00
AFBR Daniel Briere 4.00 10.00
AFBY Dustin Byfuglien 4.00 10.00
AFCG Claude Giroux 4.00 10.00
AFCH Cody Hodgson 8.00 20.00
AFCK Matt Carkner 3.00 8.00
AFCN Cam Neely 4.00 10.00
AFCP Carey Price 8.00 20.00
AFDA Daniel Alfredsson 4.00 10.00
AFDB Dan Boyle 2.50 6.00
AFDC Dan Cleary 4.00 10.00
AFDD Drew Doughty 5.00 12.00
AFDE Derick Brassard 2.50 6.00
AFDK Duncan Keith 3.00 8.00
AFDR Derek Roy 2.50 6.00
AFDS Daniel Sedin 5.00 12.00
AFDU Dustin Penner 3.00 8.00
AFDW Drew Stafford 2.50 6.00
AFEM Evgeni Malkin 8.00 20.00
AFES Eric Staal 5.00 12.00
AFGL Guillaume Latendresse 3.00 8.00
AFGR Mike Green 3.00 8.00
AFHE Milan Hejduk 3.00 8.00
AFHL Henrik Lundqvist 4.00 10.00
AFHS Henrik Sedin 5.00 12.00
AFHZ Henrik Zetterberg 6.00 15.00
AFIB Ilya Bryzgalov 4.00 10.00
AFIK Ilya Kovalchuk 4.00 10.00
AFJC Jeff Carter 3.00 8.00
AFJE Jordan Eberle 5.00 12.00
AFJF Johan Franzen 3.00 8.00
AFJH Jim Howard 8.00 20.00
AFJI Jarome Iginla 5.00 12.00
AFJS Jason Spezza 4.00 10.00
AFJT John Tavares 6.00 15.00
AFJV James van Riemsdyk 3.00 8.00
AFKE Phil Kessel 4.00 10.00
AFKO Mikko Koivu 3.00 8.00
AFLC Logan Couture 5.00 12.00
AFLE Loui Eriksson 2.50 6.00
AFLU Milan Lucic 4.00 10.00
AFMB Martin Brodeur 10.00 25.00
AFMC Michael Cammalleri 3.00 8.00
AFMD Matt Duchene 4.00 10.00
AFMG Marian Gaborik 4.00 10.00
AFMH Marian Hossa 4.00 10.00
AFMK Miikka Kiprusoff 4.00 10.00
AFML Mario Lemieux 15.00 40.00
AFMM Mark Messier 8.00 20.00
AFMP Magnus Paajarvi 3.00 8.00
AFMR Mike Richards 3.00 8.00
AFMS Martin St. Louis 4.00 10.00
AFNB Nicklas Backstrom 4.00 10.00
AFNH Nathan Horton 4.00 10.00
AFNK Nikolai Kulemin 2.50 6.00
AFPA Paul Stastny 3.00 8.00
AFPB Patrice Bergeron 5.00 12.00
AFPD Pavel Datsyuk 6.00 15.00
AFPE Corey Perry 6.00 15.00
AFPG Chris Pronger 4.00 10.00
AFPK Patrick Kane 8.00 20.00
AFPM Patrick Marleau 4.00 10.00
AFPR Patrick Roy 10.00 25.00
AFPS Patrick Sharp 4.00 10.00
AFRB Ray Bourque 8.00 20.00
AFRG Ryan Getzlaf 4.00 10.00
AFRI Brad Richards 4.00 10.00
AFRK Ryan Kesler 4.00 10.00
AFRL Roberto Luongo 6.00 15.00
AFRM Ryan Miller 4.00 10.00
AFRN Rick Nash 4.00 10.00
AFRS Ryan Smyth 3.00 8.00
AFRY Bobby Ryan 3.00 8.00
AFSB Sergei Bobrovsky 6.00 15.00
AFSC Sidney Crosby 15.00 40.00
AFSD Shane Doan 3.00 8.00
AFSH Scott Hartnell 2.50 6.00
AFSM Steve Mason 3.00 8.00
AFSN Scott Niedermayer 4.00 10.00
AFSS Steven Stamkos 8.00 20.00
AFST Jordan Staal 3.00 8.00
AFSW Shea Weber 3.00 8.00
AFTE Tyler Ennis 2.50 6.00
AFTH Taylor Hall 6.00 15.00
AFTO Jonathan Toews 6.00 15.00
AFTS Tyler Seguin 5.00 12.00
AFTV Thomas Vanek 3.00 8.00
AFWG Wayne Gretzky 25.00 60.00
AFZC Zdeno Chara 4.00 10.00
AFZP Zach Parise 4.00 10.00

2011-12 SP Game Used Authentic Fabrics Gold

COMMON GROUP B-D 2.00 5.00
GRP B-D SEMISTARS 2.50 6.00
GRP B-D UNL.STARS 3.00 8.00
AFAO1 Alexander Ovechkin 8 C 12.00 30.00
AFBH1 Brett Hull 1 C 5.00 12.00
AFBY1 Dustin Byfuglien B C 4.00 10.00
AFCG1 Claude Giroux 2 C 6.00 10.00
AFCH1 Cody Hodgson D C 2.50 6.00
AFCK1 Matt Carkner E C 5.00 12.00
AFCN1 Cam Neely B C 3.00 8.00
AFCP1 Carey Price B C 6.00 15.00
AFDC1 Dan Cleary 1 C 4.00 10.00
AFDK1 Duncan Keith D C 4.00 10.00
AFEM1 Evgeni Malkin E C 6.00 15.00
AFHL1 Henrik Lundqvist G C 8.00 20.00
AFHZ1 Henrik Zetterberg E C 4.00 10.00
AFIK1 Ilya Kovalchuk K C 3.00 8.00
AFJE1 Jordan Eberle 1 C 6.00 15.00
AFJF1 Johan Franzen G C 2.50 6.00
AFJH1 Jim Howard H C 4.00 10.00
AFJI1 Jarome Iginla G C 4.00 10.00
AFJT1 John Tavares 1 C 5.00 12.00
AFMB1 Martin Brodeur 0 C 8.00 10.00
AFML1 Mario Lemieux 6 C 8.00 20.00
AFMM1 Mark Messier B C 6.00 15.00
AFMP1 Magnus Paajarvi 1 C 2.50 6.00
AFNB1 Nicklas Backstrom A D 3.00 8.00
AFNB2 Nicklas Backstrom H C 3.00 8.00
AFNB3 Nicklas Backstrom S C 3.00 8.00
AFNB4 Nicklas Backstrom W D 3.00 8.00
AFPB1 Patrice Bergeron C D 4.00 10.00
AFPD1 Pavel Datsyuk # C 4.00 10.00
AFPK1 Patrick Kane A C 6.00 15.00
AFPR1 Patrick Roy 0 C 8.00 20.00
AFRB1 Ray Bourque # D 5.00 12.00
AFRL1 Roberto Luongo 1 C 5.00 12.00
AFSB1 Sergei Bobrovsky # D 5.00 12.00
AFSC1 Sidney Crosby I C 12.00 30.00
AFSS1 Steven Stamkos # C 6.00 15.00
AFTH1 Taylor Hall A C 3.00 8.00
AFTO1 Jonathan Toews 1 C 5.00 12.00
AFTS1 Tyler Seguin C C 4.00 10.00
AFWG1 Wayne Gretzky 1 A 25.00 60.00

2011-12 SP Game Used Authentic Fabrics Dual

*PATCH/25: .8X TO 2X BASIC DUAL/100
AF2BG J.Benn/E.Godard/100 5.00 12.00
AF2BH D.Backes/J.Halak/100 5.00 12.00
AF2BK D.Byfuglien/E.Kane/100 5.00 12.00
AF2BP Brodeur/Parise/100 8.00 20.00
AF2BQ J.Quick/J.Bernier/100 6.00 15.00
AF2CK N.Kronwall/D.Cleary/100 5.00 12.00
AF2CL S.Crosby/K.Letang/100 20.00 50.00
AF2CS S.Crosby/J.Staal/100 20.00 50.00
AF2CZ Zetterberg/Cleary/100 6.00 15.00
AF2DF Datsyuk/J.Franzen/100 8.00 20.00
AF2EH J.Eberle/T.Hall/100 15.00 40.00
AF2EK Ericsson/N.Kronwall/100 5.00 12.00
AF2FJ M.Fleury/B.Johnson/100 10.00 25.00
AF2FK R.Francis/A.Kovalev/100 6.00 15.00
AF2GB Backstrom/M.Green/100 5.00 12.00
AF2GH R.Getzlaf/J.Hiller/100 6.00 15.00
AF2GK M.Koivu/Latendresse/100 4.00 10.00
AF2GL Gaborik/Lundqvist/100 8.00 20.00
AF2HO Howard/Osgood/100 6.00 15.00
AF2HS A.Hemsky/R.Smyth/100 4.00 10.00
AF2IK Iginla/Kiprusoff/100 6.00 15.00
AF2JR Bouwmster/Bourque/100 3.00 8.00
AF2KD Doughty/Kopitar/100 6.00 15.00
AF2KZ I.Kovalchuk/T.Zajac/100 5.00 12.00
AF2LB Brodeur/Luongo/100 12.00 30.00
AF2LG Gretzky/Lemieux/25 30.00 60.00
AF2LH Howard/Lidstrom/100 6.00 15.00
AF2LK Luongo/Kesler/100 8.00 20.00
AF2MB M.Staal/B.Dubinsky/100 3.00 8.00
AF2ME T.Ennis/T.Myers/100 5.00 12.00
AF2MG M.Messier/M.Gartner/100 10.00 25.00
AF2MV R.Miller/T.Vanek/100 5.00 12.00
AF2ND N.Horton/D.Krejci/100 5.00 12.00
AF2NM R.Nash/S.Mason/100 5.00 12.00
AF2NV Vokoun/M.Neuvirth/100 4.00 10.00
AF2PE T.Plekanec/L.Eller/100 3.00 8.00
AF2PG Perry/Getzlaf/100 6.00 15.00
AF2PH Pronger/S.Hartnell/100 5.00 12.00
AF2PO M.Paajarvi/L.Omark/100 5.00 12.00
AF2RO M.Ribeiro/S.Ott/100 3.00 8.00
AF2RS Robinson/P.Subban/100 6.00 15.00
AF2SD Duchene/P.Stastny/100 5.00 12.00
AF2SO Semin/Ovechkin/100 20.00 50.00
AF2SS H.Sedin/D.Sedin/100 6.00 15.00
AF2SW R.Suter/S.Weber/100 4.00 10.00
AF2TK J.Toews/P.Kane/100 10.00 25.00
AF2TM Moulson/Tavares/100 8.00 20.00
AF2TR T.Thomas/T.Rask/100 6.00 15.00
AF2VG Giroux/vanRiemsdk/100 5.00 12.00
AF2WB S.Weiss/D.Booth/100 4.00 10.00

2011-12 SP Game Used Authentic Fabrics Triples

*PATCH/15: .8X TO 2X BASIC TRIPLE/25
AF3ANA Getzlaf/Ryan/Hiller 8.00 20.00
AF3ATL Byfuglien/Pavelec/Kane 8.00 20.00
AF3AVS Duchene/Stastny/Johnson 8.00 20.00
AF3BOS Rask/Chara/Bergeron 10.00 25.00
AF3BUF Miller/Myers/Vanek 8.00 20.00
AF3CBJ Brassard/Mason/Nash 8.00 20.00
AF3CGY Kiprusoff/Iginla/Bouwm 10.00 25.00
AF3COL Bourque/Roy/Sakic 20.00 50.00
AF3DET Lidstrm/Zettr/Frnzen 10.00 25.00
AF3EDM Eberle/Hall/Paajarvi 15.00 40.00
AF3LAK Doughty/Kopitar/Quick 12.00 30.00
AF3NYI Moulsn/Tavrs/Okpso 12.00 30.00
AF3NYR Gaborik/Stepan/Staal 8.00 20.00
AF3OIL Gretzky/Messier/Kurri 50.00 100.00
AF3OTT Alfreds/Spezza/Andrsn 8.00 20.00
AF3PHI Giroux/Van Rms/Prngr 8.00 20.00
AF3SJS Marleau/Thrntn/Havlat 12.00 30.00
AF3STL Halak/Pietra/Backes 8.00 20.00
AF3TBL Stamkos/St. Ls/Lecav 10.00 25.00
AF3TGH Orr/Parros/Carkner 12.00 30.00
AF3VAN Sedin/Sedin/Kesler 10.00 25.00
AF3WAS Back/Ovechkin/Semin 30.00 80.00
AF3FLYR Hartnell/Briere/van Rm 10.00 25.00
AF3PENS Crosby/Staal/Malkin 15.00 40.00

2011-12 SP Game Used Career Legacy Dual

*PATCH/15: .8X TO 2X DUAL JSY/75
CL2BB Jay Bouwmeester 5.00 12.00
CL2EE Jordan Eberle 15.00 40.00
CL2GG Jean-Sebastien Giguere 6.00 15.00
CL2HH Brett Hull 12.00 30.00
CL2KK Phil Kessel 6.00 15.00

2011-12 SP Game Used Career Legacy Triple

CL3MH Marian Hossa 12.00 30.00

2011-12 SP Game Used Championship Marks

CMBM Brad Marchand EXCH 40.00 80.00
CMMR Michael Ryder EXCH 30.00 60.00
CMNH Nathan Horton EXCH 25.00 50.00
CMPB Patrice Bergeron EXCH 60.00 150.00
CMTS Tyler Seguin 30.00 80.00

2011-12 SP Game Used Extra SIGnificance

XSIGAA Larsson/Henrique 25.00 50.00
XSIGBK D.Byfuglien/A.Kulda 25.00 50.00
XSIGBM R.Miller/M.Brodeur 25.00 60.00
XSIGBR B.Orr/R.Bourque 150.00 300.00
XSIGBS D.Backes/C.Stewart 10.00 25.00
XSIGBT M.Bossy/J.Tavares 30.00 60.00
XSIGBV Carter/Brassard EXCH 10.00 25.00
XSIGCB D.Boyle/L.Couture 15.00 40.00
XSIGCR S.Couturier/M.Read 20.00 50.00
XSIGDB B.Barber/D.Schultz 15.00 40.00
XSIGDD Heatley/Setoguchi 10.00 25.00
XSIGDF P.Datsyuk/J.Franzen 25.00 50.00
XSIGEH J.Eberle/T.Hall 75.00 150.00
XSIGEP J.Eberle/M.Paajarvi 30.00 60.00
XSIGGC W.Gretzky/P.Coffey 200.00 500.00
XSIGHR Horton/Marchand EXCH 10.00 25.00
XSIGIB J.Iginla/J.Bouwmeester 15.00 40.00
XSIGJJ J.Skinner/J.McBain 15.00 40.00
XSIGKD A.Kopitar/D.Doughty 25.00 50.00
XSIGKH R.Kesler/C.Hodgson 20.00 50.00
XSIGLF N.Lidstrom/J.Franzen 15.00 40.00
XSIGLT Twist/Lafleur 15.00 40.00
XSIGMK Kulemin/MacArthur 8.00 20.00
XSIGMS Marleau/Thornton 25.00 50.00
XSIGNL RNH/Landeskog 75.00 200.00
XSIGNS A.Niemi/A.Stalock 10.00 25.00
XSIGOB Ovechkin/Backstrom 30.00 80.00
XSIGOC Coffey/Orr EXCH 75.00 150.00
XSIGOL Ovechkin/Larionov 50.00 100.00
XSIGPC J.Pavelski/L.Couture 20.00 40.00
XSIGRG S.Gagne/M.Richards 12.00 30.00
XSIGRM RNH/Scheifele 125.00 250.00
XSIGRS P.Roy/J.Sakic 60.00 120.00
XSIGSB P.Bergeron/T.Seguin 60.00 150.00
XSIGSD D.Doughty/B.Seabrook 25.00 50.00
XSIGSL Seabrook/Leddy EXCH 15.00 40.00
XSIGSM Marchand/Seguin EXCH 30.00 60.00
XSIGST J.Toews/B.Seabrook 40.00 80.00
XSIGTK J.Toews/P.Kane 40.00 80.00
XSIGTM T.Tatar/T.McCollum 10.00 25.00
XSIGTS S.Stamkos/J.Tavares 40.00 80.00
XSIGVE T.Vanek/T.Ennis 10.00 25.00
XSIGWB S.Weber/J.Blum 10.00 25.00
XSIGZM Zuccarello-Aasen/McDonagh 12.0030.00
XSIGZS Zuccarello-Aasen/D.Stepan 12.00 30.00

2011-12 SP Game Used Inked Sweaters

ISAO Alexander Ovechkin/15 50.00 100.00
ISAP Alex Pietrangelo/50 12.00 30.00
ISBR Brad Richards/50 10.00 25.00
ISBS Brayden Schenn/50 20.00 40.00
ISCH Cody Hodgson/50 20.00 50.00
ISCP Carey Price/50 30.00 60.00
ISCU Sean Couturier/50 20.00 50.00
ISDR Stefan Della Rovere/50 6.00 15.00
ISEK Evander Kane/50 12.00 30.00
ISEM Evgeni Malkin/50 25.00 50.00
ISGL Gabriel Landeskog/50 25.00 60.00
ISHL Henrik Lundqvist/50 15.00 40.00
ISJB Jamie Benn/50 10.00 25.00
ISJC Jared Cowen/50 10.00 25.00
ISJE Jordan Eberle/50 30.00 60.00
ISJF Jeff Carter/50 8.00 20.00
ISJH Jaroslav Halak/50 10.00 25.00
ISJT Jonathan Toews/15 40.00 80.00
ISKA Keith Aulie/50 8.00 20.00
ISKV Kris Versteeg/50 6.00 15.00
ISMB Martin Brodeur/15 40.00 80.00
ISMF Marc-Andre Fleury/50 12.00 30.00
ISMG Marian Gaborik/50 12.00 30.00
ISML Mario Lemieux/15 60.00 120.00
ISMM Mark Messier/15 40.00 80.00
ISNB Nicklas Backstrom/50 10.00 25.00
ISNL Nicklas Lidstrom/50 15.00 40.00
ISPC Patrice Cormier/50 6.00 15.00
ISPR Patrick Roy/15 50.00 100.00
ISPS P.K. Subban/50 20.00 50.00
ISRK Ryan Kesler/50 10.00 25.00
ISRM Ryan Miller/50 15.00 30.00
ISRY Ryan Nugent-Hopkins/50 30.00 80.00
ISSC Sidney Crosby/15 75.00 150.00
ISSS Steven Stamkos/50 20.00 50.00
ISTE Tyler Ennis/50 6.00 15.00
ISTH Taylor Hall/50 30.00 60.00
ISTV Thomas Vanek/50 8.00 20.00
ISWG Wayne Gretzky/15 200.00 500.00

2011-12 SP Game Used Inked Sweaters Dual

DISBP J.Bucyk/B.Park/15 20.00 50.00
DISCN J.Carter/R.Nash/15 15.00 40.00
DISDK Doughty/Kopitr/15 30.00 60.00
DISFR Fuhr/Ranford/15 40.00 80.00
DISGR R.Getzlaf/B.Ryan/15 25.00 50.00
DISIT Iginla/Thornton/15 40.00 80.00
DISLG Lundqvst/Gabork/15 30.00 60.00
DISMR R.Miller/D.Roy/15 12.00 30.00
DISRG Richards/Gagne/15 20.00 50.00
DISTK J.Toews/P.Kane/15 50.00 100.00

2011-12 SP Game Used Letter Marks

LMAS Alex Stalock 10.00 25.00
LMBB Bill Barber 15.00 40.00
LMCH Cody Hodgson 20.00 50.00
LMDB Dustin Byfuglien 15.00 40.00
LMEM Evgeni Malkin 30.00 60.00
LMJF Johan Franzen 12.00 30.00
LMJP Joe Pavelski 20.00 50.00
LMJS Jeff Skinner 25.00 60.00
LMJT Jonathan Toews 40.00 80.00
LMLR Larry Robinson 15.00 40.00
LMMH Milan Hejduk 15.00 40.00
LMMO John Moore 8.00 20.00
LMMT Maxime Talbot 15.00 40.00
LMNB Nicklas Backstrom 15.00 40.00
LMPB Patrice Bergeron EXCH 100.00 250.00
LMRL Reggie Leach 15.00 40.00
LMRV Rogie Vachon 20.00 50.00
LMSM Steve Mason 12.00 30.00
LMTL Ted Lindsay 15.00 40.00
LMTV Tomas Vokoun 20.00 50.00
LMVA Thomas Vanek 12.00 30.00
LMVL Ville Leino 15.00 40.00
LMWC Wendel Clark 30.00 60.00

2011-12 SP Game Used Number Marks

NMAO Ovechkin EXCH 60.00 120.00
NMAS Alex Stalock 12.00 30.00
NMBC Bobby Clarke 40.00 80.00
NMBY Dustin Byfuglien 15.00 40.00
NMCH Cody Hodgson 30.00 60.00
NMJE Jordan Eberle EXCH 100.00 175.00
NMJM Markstrom EXCH 30.00 60.00
NMJS Jeff Skinner EXCH 25.00 50.00
NMJV Jakub Voracek EXCH 30.00 60.00
NMMZ Zuccarello-Aasen EXCH 20.00 50.00
NMPS P.K. Subban EXCH 40.00 80.00
NMSC Sidney Crosby EXCH 150.00 250.00
NMSS Steven Stamkos 60.00 120.00
NMTS Tyler Seguin 40.00 100.00

2011-12 SP Game Used Rookie Exclusives Autographs

REAH Adam Henrique 12.00 30.00
REAL Anton Lander 5.00 12.00
REAM Andy Miele 6.00 15.00
REAP Aaron Palushaj 5.00 12.00
REAS Alex Stalock 4.00 10.00
REBC Brett Connolly 8.00 20.00
REBE Ben Scrivens 5.00 12.00
REBG Blake Geoffrion 5.00 12.00
REBH Ben Holmstrom 6.00 15.00
REBN Brendon Nash 5.00 12.00
REBS Brandon Saad 10.00 25.00
RECA Cam Atkinson 12.00 30.00
RECG Cameron Gaunce 4.00 10.00
RECH Cody Hodgson 8.00 20.00
RECK Carl Klingberg 5.00 12.00
RECS Craig Smith EXCH 10.00 25.00
RECT Colten Teubert 8.00 20.00
REDS Devante Smith-Pelly EXCH 6.00 15.00
REEG Erik Gudbranson 6.00 15.00
REGL Gabriel Landeskog 20.00 50.00
REGN Greg Nemisz 5.00 12.00
REGR Colin Greening 10.00 25.00
REGU Erik Gustafsson EXCH 6.00 15.00
REGV Gustav Nyquist EXCH 15.00 40.00
REHS Harri Sateri 10.00 25.00
REJB Jonathon Blum 5.00 12.00
REJC Joe Colborne 5.00 12.00
REJF Justin Faulk 8.00 20.00
REJG Jake Gardiner 12.00 30.00
REJM John Moore 5.00 12.00
REJV Joe Vitale 5.00 12.00
RELA Adam Larsson 10.00 25.00
RELL Louis Leblanc 15.00 40.00
RELP Lennart Petrell 6.00 15.00
REMF Matt Frattin 10.00 25.00
REMK Marcus Kruger 12.00 25.00
REMR Matt Read 15.00 40.00
REMS Mark Scheifele 15.00 40.00
REMZ Mika Zibanejad 12.00 30.00
REPP Paul Postma 5.00 12.00
REPW Patrick Wiercioch 5.00 12.00
RERD Raphael Diaz EXCH 5.00 12.00
RERH Roman Horak 5.00 12.00
RERJ Ryan Johansen 10.00 25.00
RERN Ryan Nugent-Hopkins 30.00 80.00
RESA David Savard 5.00 12.00
RESC Sean Couturier 15.00 40.00
REST Brian Strait 6.00 15.00
RETE Tim Erixon 5.00 12.00
RETH Teemu Hartikainen 5.00 12.00
RETV Tomas Vincour 6.00 15.00
REVV Viatcheslav Voynov 5.00 12.00
REYS Yann Sauve 5.00 12.00
REZK Zack Kassian 15.00 40.00

2011-12 SP Game Used SIGnificance

SIGAB Alexander Burmistrov/50 8.00 20.00
SIGAK Anze Kopitar/50 15.00 40.00
SIGAL Adam Larsson/50 8.00 20.00
SIGAN Antti Niemi/50 10.00 25.00
SIGAS Alex Stalock/50 5.00 12.00
SIGBA David Backes/50 5.00 12.00
SIGBB Bill Barber/50 8.00 20.00
SIGBC Brett Connolly/50 6.00 15.00
SIGBH Brett Hull/15 40.00 80.00
SIGBM Brad Marchand/50 EXCH 15.00 40.00
SIGBO Bobby Orr/15 150.00 250.00
SIGBR Bobby Ryan/50 6.00 15.00
SIGBS Brayden Schenn/50 10.00 25.00
SIGBY Dan Boyle/50 15.00 30.00
SIGCA Jeff Carter/50 EXCH 10.00 25.00
SIGCF Cam Fowler/50 8.00 20.00
SIGCG Claude Giroux/50 20.00 40.00
SIGCH Cody Hodgson/50 15.00 40.00
SIGCM Clarke MacArthur/50 6.00 15.00
SIGCP Carey Price/50 20.00 40.00
SIGCS Chris Stewart/50 6.00 15.00
SIGCU Sean Couturier/50 12.00 30.00
SIGCW Cam Ward/50 8.00 20.00
SIGDB Dustin Byfuglien/15 60.00 120.00
SIGDD Drew Doughty/50 10.00 25.00
SIGDP Dion Phaneuf/50 10.00 25.00
SIGDS Derek Stepan/50 5.00 12.00
SIGEC Jonathan Ericsson/50 5.00 12.00
SIGEG Evgeny Grachev/50 EX 6.00 15.00
SIGEK Evander Kane/50 10.00 25.00
SIGEM Evgeni Malkin/50 20.00 40.00
SIGFR Matt Frattin/50 8.00 20.00
SIGHA Jaroslav Halak/50 8.00 20.00
SIGHO Cody Hodgson/50 15.00 40.00
SIGHP Nugent-Hopkins/15 250.00 400.00
SIGJB Jonathon Blum/50 6.00 15.00
SIGJC Joe Colborne/50 6.00 15.00
SIGJE Jordan Eberle/50 25.00 50.00
SIGJH Jonas Hiller/50 6.00 15.00
SIGJK Jari Kurri/50 10.00 25.00
SIGJM Jacob Markstrom/50 8.00 20.00
SIGJS Jeff Skinner/50 10.00 25.00
SIGJT John Tavares/50 12.00 30.00
SIGJV James van Riemsdyk/50 6.00 15.00
SIGKE Phil Kessel/50 8.00 20.00
SIGKG Marcus Kruger/50 10.00 25.00
SIGKS Kevin Shattenkirk/50 5.00 12.00
SIGKV Kris Versteeg/50 5.00 12.00
SIGLC Logan Couture/50 10.00 25.00
SIGLD Gabriel Landeskog/50 25.00 50.00
SIGMA Rick MacLeish/50 8.00 20.00
SIGMB Martin Brodeur/15 60.00 120.00
SIGMC Thomas McCollum/50 6.00 15.00
SIGMD Matt Duchene/50 10.00 25.00
SIGMF Marc-Andre Fleury/50 12.00 30.00
SIGML Mario Lemieux/15 100.00 200.00
SIGMM Mark Messier/15 40.00 80.00
SIGMP Magnus Paajarvi/50 8.00 20.00
SIGMR Mike Richards/50 EXCH 10.00 25.00
SIGMS Martin St. Louis/50 10.00 25.00
SIGMZ Zuccarello-Aasen/50 8.00 20.00
SIGNB Nicklas Backstrom/50 8.00 20.00
SIGNH Nathan Horton/50 8.00 20.00
SIGNK Nazem Kadri/50 10.00 25.00
SIGOR Bobby Orr/50 75.00 150.00
SIGOV Alexander Ovechkin/15 60.00 150.00
SIGPA Patrice Bergeron/50 80.00 200.00
SIGPB Patrik Berglund/50 5.00 12.00
SIGPC Patrice Cormier/50 EXCH 6.00 15.00
SIGPM Patrick Marleau/50 8.00 20.00
SIGPR Patrick Roy/15 60.00 120.00
SIGPS Paul Stastny/50 6.00 15.00
SIGRF Bill Ranford/50 8.00 20.00
SIGRJ Ryan Johansen/50 20.00 50.00
SIGRK Ryan Kesler/50 10.00 25.00
SIGRM Ryan Miller/50 10.00 25.00
SIGRN Pekka Rinne/50 8.00 20.00
SIGRS Ryan Smyth/50 10.00 25.00
SIGRY Nugent-Hopkins/50 50.00 120.00
SIGSB Brent Seabrook/50 5.00 12.00
SIGSC Sidney Crosby/15 75.00 150.00
SIGSE Devin Setoguchi/50 6.00 15.00
SIGSF Mark Scheifele/50 20.00 50.00
SIGSG Simon Gagne/50 15.00 30.00
SIGSID Sidney Crosby/50 60.00 120.00
SIGSS Steven Stamkos/50 25.00 40.00
SIGST Jordan Staal/50 6.00 15.00
SIGSU P.K. Subban/50 20.00 50.00
SIGTB Tyler Bozak/50 6.00 15.00
SIGTH Taylor Hall/50 25.00 50.00
SIGTM Tyler Myers/50 5.00 12.00
SIGTO T.J. Oshie/50 8.00 20.00
SIGTR Tuukka Rask/50 10.00 25.00
SIGTS Tyler Seguin/15 30.00 60.00
SIGTT Tomas Tatar/50 5.00 12.00
SIGTV Thomas Vanek/50 6.00 15.00
SIGVL Ville Leino/50 6.00 15.00
SIGVO Tomas Vokoun/50 6.00 15.00
SIGWG Wayne Gretzky/15 250.00 600.00

2011-12 SP Game Used SIGnificant Numbers Autographs

SNAH Ales Hemsky/83 12.00 30.00
SNAN Antti Niemi/31 15.00 40.00
SNBH Brett Hull/16 125.00 200.00
SNBP Brad Park/22 15.00 40.00
SNBR Brad Richards/19 20.00 40.00
SNBY Dustin Byfuglien/33 20.00 40.00
SNCG Claude Giroux/28 30.00 60.00
SNCM Clarke MacArthur/16 25.00 50.00
SNCP Carey Price/31 30.00 60.00
SNDB David Backes/25 15.00 40.00
SNEG Erik Gudbranson/44 12.00 30.00
SNEM Evgeni Malkin/71 30.00 60.00
SNGL Gabriel Landeskog/92 25.00 60.00
SNHE Milan Hejduk/23 12.00 30.00
SNHL Henrik Lundqvist/30 30.00 60.00
SNIK Ilya Kovalchuk/17 25.00 50.00
SNJH Jaroslav Halak/41 15.00 40.00
SNJK Jari Kurri/17 20.00 50.00
SNJO Jonathan Toews/19 40.00 80.00
SNJT Joe Thornton/19 30.00 60.00
SNJV James van Riemsdyk/21 12.00 30.00
SNKE Phil Kessel/81 12.00 30.00
SNLR Luc Robitaille/20 20.00 40.00
SNMB Martin Brodeur/30 40.00 80.00
SNMF Marc-Andre Fleury/29 30.00 80.00
SNMH Marian Hossa/81 15.00 40.00
SNMP Magnus Paajarvi/91 8.00 20.00
SNMR Mike Richards/18 30.00 60.00
SNMS Martin St. Louis/26 12.00 30.00
SNMZ Mika Zibanejad/93 25.00 60.00
SNNB Nicklas Backstrom/19 25.00 50.00
SNNH Nathan Horton/18 30.00 60.00
SNNK Nikolai Kulemin/41 10.00 25.00
SNPA Paul Stastny/26 12.00 30.00
SNPB Patrice Bergeron/37 125.00 300.00
SNPE Patrik Elias/26 10.00 25.00
SNPS P.K. Subban/76 25.00 60.00
SNRG Ryan Getzlaf/15 25.00 50.00
SNRK Ryan Kesler/17 20.00 50.00
SNRM Ryan Miller/30 20.00 40.00
SNRN Ryan Nugent-Hopkins/93 40.00 100.00
SNSC Sidney Crosby/87 75.00 150.00
SNSS Steven Stamkos/91 40.00 80.00
SNTA John Tavares/91 25.00 50.00
SNTE Tyler Ennis/63 12.00 30.00
SNTO Tony Esposito/35 20.00 40.00
SNTR Tuukka Rask/40 15.00 40.00
SNTS Tyler Seguin/19 60.00 120.00
SNTV Thomas Vanek/26 12.00 30.00
SNVH Victor Hedman/77 12.00 30.00

2011-12 SP Game Used Team Marks Flyers

TMBS Brayden Schenn EXCH 20.00 50.00
TMCG Claude Giroux EXCH 30.00 60.00
TMEW Eric Wellwood EXCH 20.00 40.00
TMMT Maxime Talbot 10.00 25.00
TMVK Jakub Voracek EXCH 15.00 40.00

2011-12 SP Game Used Team Marks Oilers

TMCF Paul Coffey/25 40.00 80.00
TMDD Devan Dubnyk/50 25.00 50.00
TMGA G.Anderson/25 EXCH 25.00 50.00
TMGF Grant Fuhr/25 30.00 60.00
TMJE Jordan Eberle/50 60.00 150.00
TMJK Jari Kurri/25 EXCH 40.00 80.00
TMMM Mark Messier/25 30.00 60.00
TMMP M.Paajarvi/50 EXCH 20.00 50.00
TMSG Sam Gagner/50 EXCH 20.00 50.00
TMTH Taylor Hall/50 EXCH 60.00 120.00
TMWG W.Gretzky/25 EXCH 250.00 600.00

2011-12 SP Game Used Team Marks Team Canada

TMAP Alex Pietrangelo 30.00 60.00
TMCH Cody Hodgson 40.00 80.00
TMDT Dustin Tokarski 20.00 50.00
TMEB Jordan Eberle 50.00 120.00
TMEK Evander Kane 25.00 50.00
TMJT John Tavares 50.00 100.00
TMPC Patrice Cormier EXCH 12.00 30.00
TMPS P.K. Subban 40.00 80.00
TMTE Tyler Ennis 20.00 50.00
TMTM Tyler Myers 15.00 40.00

2011-12 SP Game Used Trophy Marks Calder

CALDERAO Alex Ovechkin EXCH 50.00 100.00
CALDEREM Evgeni Malkin EXCH 40.00 80.00
CALDERJS Jeff Skinner EXCH 30.00 60.00
CALDERPK Patrick Kane EXCH 30.00 60.00
CALDERSM Steve Mason 20.00 40.00
CALDERTM Tyler Myers EXCH 20.00 40.00

2011-12 SP Game Used Trophy Marks Hart

HARTBH Bobby Hull 60.00 120.00
HARTBO Bobby Orr 125.00 250.00
HARTJB Jean Beliveau 50.00 100.00

2012-13 SP Game Used

COMP.SET w/o RC's (100) 15.00 40.00
1 Dale Hawerchuk .75 2.00
2 Evander Kane .60 1.50
3 Alexander Ovechkin 2.50 6.00
4 Braden Holtby .75 2.00
5 Pavel Bure .60 1.50
6 Ryan Kesler .60 1.50
7 Alexandre Burrows .40 1.00
8 Richard Brodeur .60 1.50
9 Curtis Joseph .75 2.00
10 Dion Phaneuf .50 1.25
11 Phil Kessel .60 1.50
12 Steven Stamkos 1.25 3.00
13 Vincent Lecavalier .60 1.50
14 Alex Pietrangelo .50 1.25
15 Brett Hull 1.25 3.00
16 David Backes .40 1.00
17 Jaroslav Halak .60 1.50
18 Patrick Marleau .60 1.50
19 Joe Pavelski .75 2.00
20 Antti Niemi .50 1.25
21 Logan Couture .75 2.00
22 James Neal .40 1.00
23 Evgeni Malkin 1.25 3.00
24 Marc-Andre Fleury 1.25 3.00
25 Mario Lemieux 2.50 6.00
26 Sidney Crosby 2.50 6.00
27 Claude Giroux .60 1.50
28 Eric Lindros 1.00 2.50
29 Bernie Parent .75 2.00
30 Brayden Schenn .60 1.50
31 Dave Schultz .60 1.50
32 Ron Hextall .60 1.50
33 Erik Karlsson .75 2.00
34 Rick Nash .60 1.50
35 Brad Richards .60 1.50
36 Marian Gaborik .60 1.50
37 Mark Messier 1.25 3.00
38 Henrik Lundqvist 1.50 4.00
39 Mike Bossy .60 1.50
40 John Tavares 1.00 2.50
41 Bryan Trottier .60 1.50
42 Ilya Kovalchuk .60 1.50
43 Martin Brodeur 1.50 4.00
44 Adam Henrique .50 1.25
45 Pekka Rinne .60 1.50
46 Guy Lafleur .75 2.00
47 Jean Beliveau .60 1.50
48 Larry Robinson .60 1.50
49 P.K. Subban .75 2.00
50 Carey Price 1.25 3.00
51 Dany Heatley .50 1.25
52 Jari Kurri .60 1.50
53 Wayne Gretzky 2.50 6.00
54 Anze Kopitar 1.00 2.50
55 Drew Doughty .75 2.00
56 Simon Gagne .60 1.50
57 Luc Robitaille .60 1.50
58 Jonathan Quick .75 2.00
59 Ron Francis .75 2.00
60 Kris Versteeg .40 1.00
61 Stephen Weiss .50 1.25
62 Grant Fuhr 1.00 2.50
63 Bill Ranford .60 1.50
64 Jordan Eberle .60 1.50
65 Paul Coffey .60 1.50
66 Ryan Nugent-Hopkins .75 2.00
67 Taylor Hall .60 1.50
68 Johan Franzen .50 1.25
69 Nicklas Lidstrom .60 1.50
70 Pavel Datsyuk 1.00 2.50
71 Jamie Benn .60 1.50
72 Jaromir Jagr 2.00 5.00
73 Joe Sakic 1.25 3.00
74 Matt Duchene .60 1.50
75 Gabriel Landeskog .75 2.00
76 Denis Savard .60 1.50
77 Doug Wilson .50 1.25
78 Ed Belfour .60 1.50
79 Jonathan Toews 1.00 2.50
80 Patrick Kane 1.25 3.00
81 Jeff Skinner .75 2.00
82 Eric Staal .75 2.00
83 Jordan Staal .50 1.25
84 Doug Gilmour .75 2.00
85 Jarome Iginla .75 2.00
86 Thomas Vanek .50 1.25
87 Derek Roy .40 1.00
88 Ryan Miller .60 1.50
89 Dominik Hasek 1.00 2.50
90 Cody Hodgson .40 1.00
91 Bobby Orr 2.50 6.00
92 Cam Neely .60 1.50
93 Brad Marchand 1.25 3.00
94 Tuukka Rask .75 2.00
95 Patrice Bergeron .75 2.00
96 Ray Bourque 1.00 2.50
97 Terry O'Reilly .50 1.25
98 Tyler Seguin .75 2.00
99 Bobby Ryan .50 1.25
100 Jonas Hiller .50 1.25
101 Mat Clark/73 RC 8.00 20.00
102 Carter Camper/58 RC 6.00 15.00
103 Maxime Sauve/75 RC 6.00 15.00
104 L. MacDermid/64 RC 8.00 20.00
105 Torey Krug/47 RC 20.00 50.00
106 M. Hutchinson/70 RC 10.00 25.00
107 Travis Turnbull/65 RC 6.00 15.00
108 Sven Baertschi/47 RC 12.00 30.00
109 Akim Aliu/29 RC 12.00 30.00
110 Jeremy Welsh/23 RC 12.00 30.00
111 Brandon Bollig/52 RC 6.00 15.00
112 Tyson Barrie/41 RC 25.00 60.00
113 Mike Connolly/18 RC 15.00 40.00
114 Dalton Prout/47 RC 8.00 20.00
115 Cody Goloubef/48 RC 8.00 20.00
116 Shawn Hunwick/31 RC 8.00 20.00
117 Andrew Joudrey/23 RC 12.00 30.00
118 Ryan Garbutt/40 RC 8.00 20.00
119 Reilly Smith/18 RC 20.00 50.00
122 Riley Sheahan/15 RC 25.00 50.00
123 Philippe Cornet/51 RC 8.00 20.00
124 Colby Robak/47 RC 8.00 20.00
125 Jordan Nolan/71 RC 6.00 15.00
126 Kris Foucault/72 RC 6.00 15.00
127 Jason Zucker/16 RC 30.00 60.00
128 Tyler Cuma/65 RC 6.00 15.00
129 Chay Genoway/47 RC 8.00 20.00
130 Gabriel Dumont/37 RC 15.00 40.00
131 Robert Mayer/65 RC 10.00 25.00
132 Chet Pickard/37 RC 10.00 25.00
133 Aaron Ness/55 RC 6.00 15.00
134 Casey Cizikas/53 RC 8.00 20.00
135 Matt Donovan/46 RC 10.00 25.00
136 Chris Kreider/20 RC 60.00 120.00
137 Jakob Silfverberg/33 RC 50.00 100.00
138 Mark Stone/60 RC 25.00 50.00
139 Brandon Manning/23 RC 12.00 30.00
140 Michael Stone/26 RC 12.00 30.00
141 Matt Watkins/50 RC 6.00 15.00
142 Tyson Sexsmith/37 RC 30.00 60.00
143 Jake Allen/34 RC 25.00 60.00
145 J.T. Brown/19 RC 15.00 40.00
146 Carter Ashton/37 RC 15.00 40.00
147 Ryan Hamilton/48 RC 8.00 20.00
148 Jussi Rynnas/40 RC 8.00 20.00

2012-13 SP Game Used Authentic Fabrics

*GOLD/16-88: .6X TO 1.5X BASIC INSERTS
*PATCH/35: .75X TO 2X BASIC INSERTS
AFAK Anze Kopitar D 5.00 12.00
AFAO Alexander Ovechkin A 12.00 30.00
AFBH Brett Hull A 6.00 15.00
AFBR Bobby Ryan D 2.50 6.00
AFBS Brendan Shanahan D 3.00 8.00
AFCG Claude Giroux D 3.00 8.00
AFCJ Curtis Joseph A 4.00 10.00
AFCK Chris Kreider D 8.00 20.00
AFCP Carey Price D 6.00 15.00
AFDA Daniel Alfredsson D 3.00 8.00
AFDU Dustin Brown D 3.00 8.00
AFEL Eric Lindros D 5.00 12.00
AFGR Mike Green C 2.50 6.00
AFHE Milan Hejduk C 2.50 6.00
AFJC Jeff Carter D 2.50 6.00
AFJI Jarome Iginla B 4.00 10.00
AFJJ Jaromir Jagr B 10.00 25.00
AFJK Jake Allen D 6.00 15.00
AFJS Jason Spezza D 3.00 8.00
AFKA Evander Kane C 3.00 8.00
AFMB Martin Brodeur A 8.00 20.00
AFMF Marc-Andre Fleury D 6.00 15.00
AFMG Michael Grabner C 2.50 6.00
AFMK Miikka Kiprusoff D 3.00 8.00
AFMO Mike Modano B 5.00 12.00
AFRB Ray Bourque D 5.00 12.00
AFRF Ron Francis C 4.00 10.00
AFRG Ryan Getzlaf C 3.00 8.00
AFRI Pekka Rinne D 3.00 8.00
AFSG Scott Glennie C 2.50 6.00
AFSH Scott Hartnell D 2.00 5.00
AFSV Sven Baertschi D 3.00 8.00

AFTS Tyler Seguin D 4.00 10.00
AFZC Zdeno Chara D 3.00 8.00

2012-13 SP Game Used Authentic Fabrics Gold

AFBH Brett Hull/16 10.00 25.00
AFCG Claude Giroux/28 5.00 12.00
AFCJ Curtis Joseph/31 6.00 15.00
AFCK Chris Kreider/20 12.00 30.00
AFCP Carey Price/31 10.00 25.00
AFDU Dustin Brown/23 5.00 12.00
AFEL Eric Lindros/88 8.00 20.00
AFGR Mike Green/52 4.00 10.00
AFHE Milan Hejduk/23 4.00 10.00
AFJJ Jaromir Jagr/68 15.00 40.00
AFJK Jake Allen/34 10.00 25.00
AFJS Jason Spezza/19 5.00 12.00
AFMB Martin Brodeur/30 12.00 30.00
AFMF Marc-Andre Fleury/29 10.00 25.00
AFMG Michael Grabner/40 4.00 10.00
AFMK Miikka Kiprusoff/34 5.00 12.00
AFRB Ray Bourque/77 8.00 20.00
AFRI Pekka Rinne/35 5.00 12.00
AFSH Scott Hartnell/19 3.00 8.00
AFSV Sven Baertschi/47 5.00 12.00
AFTS Tyler Seguin/19 6.00 15.00
AFZC Zdeno Chara/33 5.00 12.00

2012-13 SP Game Used Authentic Fabrics Dual

*PATCH/25: .6X TO 1.5X BASIC DUAL
AF2CR S.Couturier/M.Read D 3.00 8.00
AF2CZ H.Zetterberg/D.Cleary D 5.00 12.00
AF2DD D.Brown/D.Penner D 4.00 10.00
AF2DF P.Datsyuk/J.Franzen D 6.00 15.00
AF2EA J.Ericsson/J.Abdelkader D 3.00 8.00
AF2EH J.Eberle/T.Hall C 4.00 10.00
AF2GB M.Green/N.Backstrom C 4.00 10.00
AF2GR R.Getzlaf/B.Ryan D 4.00 10.00
AF2GS P.Subban/J.Gorges D 5.00 12.00
AF2GV S.Varlamov/J.Giguere D 4.00 10.00
AF2HB S.Hartnell/D.Briere D 4.00 10.00
AF2IK J.Iginla/M.Kiprusoff 5.00 12.00
AF2KD A.Kopitar/D.Doughty D 6.00 15.00
AF2KE N.Kronwall/J.Ericsson D 3.00 8.00
AF2KH C.Kreider/C.Hagelin D 10.00 25.00
AF2LK R.Kesler/R.Luongo D 6.00 15.00
AF2MI M.Brodeur/I.Kovalchuk D 10.00 25.00
AF2MK D.Krejci/B.Marchand D 8.00 20.00
AF2MM T.Myers/R.Miller D 4.00 10.00
AF2PK O.Pavelec/E.Kane A 4.00 10.00
AF2RC M.Richards/J.Carter D 3.00 8.00
AF2TR T.Thomas/T.Rask D 5.00 12.00
AF2WV S.Weiss/K.Versteeg D 3.00 8.00

2012-13 SP Game Used Authentic Fabrics Eights

AF8USA USA Stars 10.00 25.00
AF8ALLSTAR All-Stars 50.00 125.00
AF8GOALIE Goalie Stars 20.00 50.00
AF8SWEDEN Swedish Stars 10.00 25.00

2012-13 SP Game Used Authentic Fabrics Fives

AF5BOS Boston 5 12.00 30.00
AF5BUF Buffalo 5 10.00 25.00
AF5CGY Calgary 5 12.00 30.00
AF5COL Colorado 5 12.00 30.00
AF5DET Detroit 5 15.00 40.00
AF5GR8 8 All-Time Greats 60.00 150.00
AF5LAK L.A. Kings 5 15.00 40.00
AF5STL St. Louis 5 10.00 25.00
AF5VAN Vancouver 5 12.00 30.00
AF5BEES Boston 5 15.00 40.00
AF5BLUE N.Y. Rangers 5 25.00 60.00
AF5LBBR Montreal 5 20.00 50.00
AF5PENS Pittsburgh 5 40.00 100.00

2012-13 SP Game Used Authentic Fabrics Quads

AF4BUF Miller/Vanek/Stafford/Myers 8.00 20.00
AF4LAK Gagne/Brown/Carter/Penner 8.00 20.00
AF4A3AK Spezza/Alfredsson Karlsson/Anderson 10.00 25.00
AF4RBJB Brod/Roy/Belfr/Josph 20.00 50.00
AF4KINGS Rich/Quick/Dghty/Kop 12.00 30.00

2012-13 SP Game Used Authentic Fabrics Sevens

AF7GR8 All-Time Greats 60.00 150.00
AF7LAK L.A. Kings Stars 12.00 30.00
AF7NYR N.Y. Rangers Stars 25.00 60.00
AF7PHI Philadelphia Flyers Stars 10.00 25.00
AF7GOALIE Goalie Greats 25.00 60.00
AF7ROOKIE Rookie Stars 25.00 60.00

2012-13 SP Game Used Authentic Fabrics Sixes

NYNY New York Stars 25.00 60.00
ANALA Anaheim/L.A. Stars 12.00 30.00
CGYVAN Calgary/Vancvr Stars 15.00 40.00
CHIDET Chicago/Detroit Stars 20.00 50.00
MTLBOS Montreal/Boston Stars 20.00 50.00
NYBOS NY/Boston Stars 25.00 60.00
PITPHI Pittsburgh/Philly Stars 20.00 50.00
PITWAS Pttsbrgh/Wshng Stars 40.00 100.00
STLDET St.Louis/Detroit Stars 15.00 40.00
WASTBY Wash/Tampa Stars 40.00 100.00

2012-13 SP Game Used Authentic Fabrics Team Canada

*PATCH/35: .8X TO 2X BASIC TC JSY
*FIGHT STRAP/15: 1.2X TO 3X TC GRP B-D
*FIGHT STRAP/15: .8X TO 2X TC GRP A
TC1 Carter Ashton D 2.50 6.00
TC2 Brett Connolly D 2.50 6.00
TC3 Dan Boyle C 2.50 6.00
TC4 Jared Cowen C 4.00 10.00
TC5 Casey Cizikas D 3.00 8.00
TC6 Colten Teubert C 2.50 6.00
TC7 Simon Despres D 3.00 8.00
TC8 Dany Heatley D 3.00 8.00
TC9 Calvin de Haan C 2.50 6.00
TC10 Erik Gudbranson C 2.50 6.00
TC11 Eric Staal D 5.00 12.00
TC12 Jamie Benn B 4.00 10.00
TC13 Ryan Ellis C 2.50 6.00
TC14 Patrice Bergeron D 5.00 12.00
TC15 Patrice Cormier C 4.00 10.00
TC16 Corey Perry D 6.00 15.00
TC17 Chris Pronger D 4.00 10.00
TC18 Chet Pickard D 3.00 8.00
TC19 Mark Scheifele D 6.00 15.00
TC20 Scott Niedermayer C 4.00 10.00
TC21 Devante Smith-Pelly C 3.00 8.00
TC22 Jaden Schwartz D 6.00 15.00
TC23 Tyson Barrie C 8.00 20.00
TC24 Wayne Gretzky A 40.00 80.00
TC25 Zach Boychuk C 2.50 6.00

2012-13 SP Game Used Authentic Fabrics Team Canada Gold

TC8 Dany Heatley/15 8.00 20.00
TC14 Patrice Bergeron/39 8.00 20.00
TC19 Mark Scheifele/19 8.00 20.00
TC24 Wayne Gretzky/99 40.00 80.00

2012-13 SP Game Used Authentic Fabrics Team Canada Dual

*PATCH/25: .8X TO 2X BASIC DUAL
TC26 R.Nash/M.Richards 5.00 12.00
TC27 B.Connolly/D.Smith-Pelly 4.00 10.00
TC28 C.Goloubef/C.Teubert 3.00 8.00
TC29 K.Aulie/R.Ellis 3.00 8.00
TC30 C.Ashton/C.Cizikas 4.00 10.00
TC31 J.Iginla/R.Getzlaf 8.00 20.00

2012-13 SP Game Used Authentic Fabrics Team Canada Fives

TC42 Eak/Sch/Leb/Fol/Ciz 10.00 25.00

2012-13 SP Game Used Authentic Fabrics Team Canada Quads

TC37 Schw/Schf/Cnlly/Smt-Ply 12.00 30.00
TC38 Igin/Thrntn/Htley/Getzlf 15.00 40.00
TC39 Ellis/Gudbn/Olsn/de Hn 6.00 15.00
TC40 Cowen/Dsprs/Brrie/Ellis 15.00 40.00
TC41 Dghty/Keith/Byle/Wber 12.00 30.00

2012-13 SP Game Used Authentic Fabrics Team Canada Triples

TC32 Schwrtz/Cnnlly/Smith-Ply 8.00 20.00
TC33 Despres/Olsen/Barrie 6.00 15.00
TC34 Leblanc/Johansen/Foligno 8.00 20.00
TC35 Schwartz/Cizikas/Ashton 8.00 20.00
TC36 Boyle/Thornton/Heatley 6.00 15.00

2012-13 SP Game Used Authentic Fabrics Triples

*PATCH/15: 1.2X TO 3X BASIC TRIPLE
AF3ASK Alfredsson/Spezza/Karlsson 6.00 15.00
AF3CBS Chara/Bergeron/Seguin 6.00 15.00
AF3DSS Staal/Stepan/Kreider 8.00 20.00
AF3DVE Doan/Vermette Ekman-Larsson 6.00 15.00
AF3GBC Brown/Carter/Gagne 5.00 12.00
AF3GRH Getzlaf/Ryan/Hiller 5.00 12.00
AF3IKC Iginla/Kiprusoff/Cammalleri 6.00 15.00
AF3MVM Miller/Vanek/Myers 5.00 12.00
AF3PHG Giroux/Hartnell/Schenn 5.00 12.00
AF3RQD Richards/Quick/Dghty 6.00 15.00
AF3SDL Stastny/Duchene/Land 6.00 15.00
AF3SHB Sakic/Hejduk/Bourque 10.00 25.00
AF3SSB Sedin/Burrows/Sedin 6.00 15.00

2012-13 SP Game Used Draft Day Marks

DDMCA1 Carter Ashton A/35 5.00 12.00
DDMCG1 Cody Goloubef B/35 5.00 12.00
DDMCI1 Casey Cizikas A/35 12.00 30.00
DDMCK1 Chris Kreider D/35 25.00 60.00
DDMCP1 Chet Pickard A/35 6.00 15.00
DDMEK1 Erik Karlsson A/10 60.00 120.00
DDMJA1 Jake Allen A/35 15.00 40.00
DDMJS1 Jeff Skinner E/10 40.00 80.00
DDMJT1 John Tavares A/20* 50.00 100.00
DDMJZ1 Jason Zucker C/35 12.00 30.00
DDMLC1 Logan Couture C/10 30.00 60.00
DDMRN1 Nugent-Hopkins E/10 100.00 200.00
DDMSB1 Sven Baertschi A/35 8.00 20.00
DDMSC1 Jaden Schwartz A/35 12.00 30.00
DDMSG1 Scott Glennie E/70* 12.00 30.00
DDMSH1 Riley Sheahan A/70* 15.00 40.00
DDMSI1 Jakob Silfverberg B/35 15.00 40.00
DDMTB1 Tyson Barrie A/35 15.00 40.00

2012-13 SP Game Used Gold Autographs

1 Dale Hawerchuk B 10.00 25.00
2 Evander Kane C 8.00 20.00
3 Alexander Ovechkin B 25.00 60.00
5 Pavel Bure B 25.00 60.00
6 Ryan Kesler C 8.00 20.00
8 Richard Brodeur B 8.00 20.00
9 Curtis Joseph B 10.00 25.00
10 Dion Phaneuf C 6.00 15.00
11 Phil Kessel B 8.00 20.00
12 Steven Stamkos A 15.00 40.00
13 Vincent Lecavalier B 8.00 20.00
14 Alex Pietrangelo B 6.00 15.00
15 Brett Hull B 15.00 40.00
16 David Backes C 5.00 12.00
17 Jaroslav Halak C 8.00 20.00
18 Patrick Marleau B 8.00 20.00
19 Joe Pavelski C 10.00 25.00
20 Antti Niemi B 6.00 15.00
21 Logan Couture B 10.00 25.00
22 James Neal C 5.00 12.00
23 Evgeni Malkin A 15.00 40.00
24 Marc-Andre Fleury B 15.00 40.00
25 Mario Lemieux A 30.00 80.00
26 Sidney Crosby A 60.00 150.00
27 Claude Giroux B 8.00 20.00
28 Eric Lindros A 12.00 30.00
30 Brayden Schenn C 8.00 20.00
31 Dave Schultz C 8.00 20.00
32 Ron Hextall B 8.00 20.00
34 Rick Nash B 8.00 20.00
35 Brad Richards C 8.00 20.00
36 Marian Gaborik B 8.00 20.00
37 Mark Messier A 15.00 40.00
38 Henrik Lundqvist B 20.00 50.00
39 Mike Bossy B 8.00 20.00
40 John Tavares C 12.00 30.00
41 Bryan Trottier B 8.00 20.00
43 Martin Brodeur B 20.00 50.00
44 Adam Henrique C 6.00 15.00
45 Pekka Rinne C 8.00 20.00
46 Guy Lafleur B 10.00 25.00
47 Jean Beliveau B 8.00 20.00
48 Larry Robinson B 8.00 20.00
49 P.K. Subban B 10.00 25.00
50 Carey Price B 15.00 40.00
51 Dany Heatley B 6.00 15.00
52 Jari Kurri C 8.00 20.00
53 Wayne Gretzky A 100.00 250.00
54 Anze Kopitar B 12.00 30.00
55 Drew Doughty B 10.00 25.00
56 Simon Gagne B 8.00 20.00
57 Luc Robitaille B 8.00 20.00
59 Ron Francis B 10.00 25.00
60 Kris Versteeg A 5.00 12.00
61 Stephen Weiss C 6.00 15.00
62 Grant Fuhr B 12.00 30.00
63 Bill Ranford C 8.00 20.00
64 Jordan Eberle C 8.00 20.00
65 Paul Coffey B 8.00 20.00
66 Ryan Nugent-Hopkins B 10.00 25.00
67 Taylor Hall B 8.00 20.00
68 Johan Franzen B 6.00 15.00
69 Nicklas Lidstrom B 8.00 20.00
70 Pavel Datsyuk B 12.00 30.00
71 Jamie Benn C 8.00 20.00
72 Jaromir Jagr A 25.00 60.00
73 Joe Sakic A 15.00 40.00
74 Matt Duchene B 8.00 20.00
75 Gabriel Landeskog B 10.00 25.00
76 Denis Savard B 8.00 20.00
77 Doug Wilson C 6.00 15.00
78 Ed Belfour B 8.00 20.00
79 Jonathan Toews A 12.00 30.00
80 Patrick Kane B 15.00 40.00
81 Jeff Skinner B 10.00 25.00
82 Eric Staal C 10.00 25.00
83 Jordan Staal C 6.00 15.00
84 Doug Gilmour B 10.00 25.00
85 Jarome Iginla B 10.00 25.00
86 Thomas Vanek C 6.00 15.00
87 Derek Roy B 5.00 12.00
88 Ryan Miller B 8.00 20.00
89 Dominik Hasek B 12.00 30.00
90 Cody Hodgson C 5.00 12.00
91 Bobby Orr A 60.00 150.00
92 Cam Neely B 8.00 20.00
93 Brad Marchand B 15.00 40.00
94 Tuukka Rask C 10.00 25.00
95 Patrice Bergeron B 10.00 25.00
96 Ray Bourque B 12.00 30.00
98 Tyler Seguin B 10.00 25.00
99 Bobby Ryan C 6.00 15.00
100 Jonas Hiller C 6.00 15.00
103 Maxime Sauve 5.00 12.00
108 Sven Baertschi 8.00 20.00
109 Akim Aliu 6.00 15.00
111 Brandon Bollig 5.00 12.00
112 Tyson Barrie 15.00 40.00
115 Cody Goloubef 5.00 12.00
119 Reilly Smith 15.00 40.00
120 Brenden Dillon 6.00 15.00
122 Riley Sheahan 8.00 20.00
125 Jordan Nolan 5.00 12.00
127 Jason Zucker 12.00 30.00
128 Tyler Cuma 5.00 12.00
130 Gabriel Dumont 6.00 15.00
132 Chet Pickard 6.00 15.00
136 Chris Kreider 20.00 50.00
137 Jakob Silfverberg 10.00 25.00
138 Mark Stone 15.00 40.00
140 Michael Stone 6.00 15.00
143 Jake Allen 6.00 15.00
144 Jaden Schwartz 15.00 40.00
145 J.T. Brown 6.00 15.00
146 Carter Ashton 5.00 12.00
148 Jussi Rynnas 5.00 12.00

2012-13 SP Game Used Inked Rookie Sweaters

IRSCA Carter Ashton 6.00 15.00
IRSCK Chris Kreider 25.00 60.00
IRSCP Chet Pickard 8.00 20.00
IRSJA Jake Allen 20.00 50.00
IRSRS Riley Sheahan 12.00 30.00
IRSSB Sven Baertschi 10.00 25.00
IRSSC Jaden Schwartz 15.00 40.00
IRSTB Tyson Barrie 20.00 50.00

2012-13 SP Game Used Inked Sweaters

ISAO Alexander Ovechkin/25 40.00 80.00
ISBP Brad Park/50 8.00 20.00
ISBS Brayden Schenn/99 8.00 20.00
ISCH Carl Hagelin/50 12.00 30.00
ISCP Carey Price/25 20.00 50.00
ISCS Cory Schneider/99 10.00 25.00
ISDB Dustin Brown/99 8.00 20.00
ISEK Evander Kane/99 8.00 20.00
ISEM Evgeni Malkin/25 25.00 60.00
ISGA Mike Gartner/50 12.00 30.00
ISGL Gabriel Landeskog/99 10.00 25.00
ISHL Henrik Lundqvist/25 15.00 40.00
ISHO Cody Hodgson/99 5.00 12.00
ISJE Jordan Eberle/50 20.00 50.00
ISJH Jaroslav Halak/50 10.00 25.00
ISKS Kevin Shattenkirk/99 5.00 12.00
ISKV Kris Versteeg/25 6.00 15.00
ISLA Luke Adam/99 6.00 15.00
ISMF Marc-Andre Fleury/50 15.00 30.00
ISMH Milan Hejduk/50 8.00 20.00
ISMR Matt Read/99 6.00 15.00
ISNB Nicklas Backstrom/50 10.00 25.00
ISNL Nicklas Lidstrom/25 20.00 40.00
ISPS P.K. Subban/50 12.00 30.00
ISRE Ryan Ellis/99 5.00 12.00
ISRK Ryan Kesler/50 10.00 25.00
ISRM Ryan Miller/50 10.00 25.00
ISSM Craig Smith/99 5.00 12.00
ISSS Steven Stamkos/25 20.00 50.00
ISTH Taylor Hall/50 25.00 50.00

2012-13 SP Game Used SIGnificant Numbers Autographs

COMMON CARD/20-92 8.00 20.00
SEMISTARS/20-92 10.00 25.00
UNL.STARS/20-92 12.00 30.00
SNBH Brett Hull/16 50.00 100.00
SNCG Claude Giroux/28 12.00 30.00
SNCK Chris Kreider/20 30.00 80.00
SNCP Carey Price/31 25.00 60.00
SNEM Evgeni Malkin/71 30.00 60.00
SNGL Gabriel Landeskog/92 15.00 40.00
SNHE Milan Hejduk/23 10.00 25.00
SNHG Carl Hagelin/62 8.00 20.00
SNHL Henrik Lundqvist/30 25.00 50.00
SNJA Jake Allen/34 25.00 60.00
SNJG Josh Gorges/26 10.00 25.00
SNMB Martin Brodeur/30 35.00 75.00
SNMF Marc-Andre Fleury/29 25.00 60.00
SNPS P.K. Subban/76 15.00 40.00
SNRG Ryan Getzlaf/15 15.00 30.00
SNRK Ryan Kesler/17 15.00 40.00
SNTS Tyler Seguin/19 20.00 50.00
SNTT Bryan Trottier/19 15.00 30.00

2012-13 SP Game Used Stanley Cup Finals Materials Net Cord

G1AK Anze Kopitar 50.00 100.00
G1AV Anton Volchenkov 15.00 40.00
G1CF Colin Fraser 15.00 40.00
G1JQ Jonathan Quick 75.00 150.00
G2DD Drew Doughty 40.00 80.00
G2DP Dustin Penner 15.00 40.00
G2JC Jeff Carter 25.00 50.00
G2JQ Jonathan Quick 50.00 100.00
G3AK Anze Kopitar 50.00 100.00
G3AM Alec Martinez 25.00 50.00
G3DB Dustin Brown 30.00 60.00
G3JQ Jonathan Quick 75.00 150.00
G3JW Justin Williams 30.00 80.00
G3MG Matt Greene 25.00 50.00
G3SV Viatcheslav Voynov 15.00 40.00
G3WG Wayne Gretzky 100.00 200.00
G3WM Willie Mitchell 25.00 60.00
G4AH Adam Henrique 40.00 80.00
G4AP Alexei Ponikarovsky 25.00 50.00
G4DC David Clarkson 15.00 40.00
G4DZ Dainius Zubrus 15.00 40.00
G4IK Ilya Kovalchuk 40.00 80.00
G4MB Martin Brodeur 50.00 100.00
G4MF Mark Fayne 15.00 40.00
G4PE Patrik Elias 20.00 50.00
G5BS Bryce Salvador 25.00 50.00
G5MB Martin Brodeur 50.00 100.00
G5TZ Travis Zajac 15.00 40.00
G5ZP Zach Parise 25.00 60.00
G6DB Dustin Brown 30.00 60.00
G6DD Drew Doughty 40.00 80.00
G6DK Dwight King 25.00 50.00
G6JC Jeff Carter 40.00 80.00
G6JQ Jonathan Quick 60.00 120.00
G6JS Jarret Stoll 30.00 60.00
G6LR Luc Robitaille 30.00 80.00
G6MR Mike Richards 30.00 60.00
G6RS Rob Scuderi 25.00 50.00
G6SG Simon Gagne 40.00 80.00
G6TL Trevor Lewis 30.00 60.00

2012-13 SP Game Used Stanley Cup Finals Materials Net Skirt Autographs

SCUPAH Adam Henrique C 15.00 40.00
SCUPAK Anze Kopitar B 40.00 100.00
SCUPDB Dustin Brown C 30.00 80.00
SCUPDD Drew Doughty B 75.00 150.00
SCUPLR Luc Robitaille B 40.00 100.00
SCUPMB Martin Brodeur A 175.00 350.00
SCUPWG Wayne Gretzky A 500.00 1200.00

2012-13 SP Game Used Tandem Twigs

TTLA W.Gretzky/M.Dionne 25.00 50.00
TTNY W.Gretzky/M.Moccior 20.00 60.00
TTBEES P.Esposito/J.Bucyk 10.00 25.00
TTBOS P.Esposito/R.Bourque 10.00 25.00
TTEDM W.Gretzky/M.Messier 40.00 80.00
TTMTL J.Beliveau/G.Lafleur 15.00 40.00
TTOTT D.Alfredsson/D.Hasek 15.00 40.00

2013-14 SP Game Used

COMP.SET w/o RC's (100) 15.00 40.00
1 Dale Hawerchuk .60 1.50
2 Evander Kane .50 1.25
3 Alexander Ovechkin 2.00 5.00
4 Braden Holtby .60 1.50
5 Nicklas Backstrom .50 1.25
6 Alexandre Burrows .30 .75
7 Markus Naslund .50 1.25
8 Ryan Kesler .50 1.25
9 Trevor Linden .50 1.25
10 Doug Gilmour .60 1.50
11 Nazem Kadri .60 1.50
12 Dion Phaneuf .40 1.00
13 Phil Kessel .50 1.25
14 Steven Stamkos 1.00 2.50
15 Chris Stewart .40 1.00
16 Curtis Joseph .60 1.50
17 Brett Hull 1.00 2.50
18 David Backes .30 .75
19 Jaroslav Halak .50 1.25
20 Patrick Marleau .50 1.25
21 Joe Pavelski .60 1.50
22 Antti Niemi .40 1.00
23 Chris Kunitz .50 1.25
24 Kris Letang .60 1.50
25 Paul Coffey .50 1.25
26 Evgeni Malkin 1.00 2.50
27 James Neal .30 .75
28 Mario Lemieux 2.00 5.00
29 Sidney Crosby 2.00 5.00
30 Mike Smith .50 1.25
31 Shane Doan .40 1.00
32 Claude Giroux .50 1.25
33 Eric Lindros .75 2.00
34 Scott Hartnell .30 .75
35 Dave Schultz .50 1.25
36 Erik Karlsson .60 1.50
37 Jason Spezza .50 1.25
38 Rick Nash .50 1.25
39 Theoren Fleury .60 1.50
40 Mark Messier 1.00 2.50
41 Henrik Lundqvist 1.25 3.00
42 Mike Bossy .50 1.25
43 John Tavares .75 2.00
44 Cory Schneider .50 1.25
45 Adam Henrique .40 1.00
46 Martin Brodeur 1.25 3.00
47 Pekka Rinne .50 1.25
48 Jean Beliveau .50 1.25
49 Larry Robinson .50 1.25
50 P.K. Subban .60 1.50
51 Carey Price 1.00 2.50
52 Zach Parise .50 1.25
53 Mikko Koivu .40 1.00
54 Niklas Backstrom .40 1.00
55 Jari Kurri .50 1.25
56 Wayne Gretzky 3.00 8.00
57 Anze Kopitar .75 2.00
58 Drew Doughty .60 1.50
59 Mike Richards .40 1.00
60 Jeff Carter .40 1.00
61 Jonathan Quick .60 1.50
62 Ron Francis .60 1.50
63 Pavel Bure .50 1.25
64 Grant Fuhr .75 2.00
65 Bill Ranford .50 1.25
66 Jordan Eberle .50 1.25
67 Ryan Nugent-Hopkins .60 1.50
68 Taylor Hall .50 1.25
69 Chris Osgood .50 1.25
70 Nicklas Lidstrom .50 1.25
71 Pavel Datsyuk .75 2.00
72 Jamie Benn .50 1.25
73 Marian Gaborik .50 1.25
74 Joe Sakic 1.00 2.50
75 Matt Duchene .50 1.25
76 Gabriel Landeskog .60 1.50
77 Corey Crawford .60 1.50
78 Tony Esposito .50 1.25
79 Jonathan Toews .75 2.00
80 Marian Hossa .50 1.25
81 Patrick Kane 1.00 2.50
82 Jeff Skinner .60 1.50
83 Eric Staal .60 1.50
84 Jordan Staal .40 1.00
85 Jiri Tlusty .30 .75
86 Thomas Vanek .40 1.00
87 Gilbert Perreault .50 1.25
88 Cody Hodgson .30 .75
89 Cam Neely .50 1.25
90 Brad Marchand 1.00 2.50
91 Tuukka Rask .60 1.50
92 Patrice Bergeron .60 1.50
93 Ray Bourque .75 2.00
94 Terry O'Reilly .40 1.00
95 Bobby Orr 2.00 5.00
96 Zdeno Chara .50 1.25
97 Jonas Hiller .40 1.00
98 Corey Perry .75 2.00
99 Ryan Getzlaf .50 1.25
100 Teemu Selanne 1.00 2.50
101 Alex Galchenyuk/27 RC 200.00 350.00
102 Zemgus Girgensons/28 RC 60.00 120.00
103 Richard Panik/71 RC 10.00 25.00
104 Ryan Murray/27 RC 40.00 80.00
105 Michael Latta/46 RC 15.00 40.00
106 Hampus Lindholm/47 RC 20.00 50.00
107 Mikael Granlund/64 RC 15.00 40.00
108 Boone Jenner/38 RC 15.00 40.00
109 Anton Belov/77 RC 10.00 25.00
110 Matt Tennyson/80 RC 6.00 15.00
112 Ondrej Palat/18 RC 30.00 60.00
113 Justin Schultz/19 RC 60.00 120.00
114 Drew Shore/15 RC 25.00 60.00
115 Ryan Spooner/51 RC 12.00 30.00
116 Austin Watson/52 RC 10.00 25.00
117 Tom Wilson/43 RC 20.00 50.00
121 Eric Gryba/62 RC 8.00 20.00
122 Stefan Matteau/15 RC 12.00 30.00
123 Tanner Pearson/70 RC 15.00 40.00
125 Cristopher Nilstorp/41 RC 10.00 25.00
126 Mark Arcobello/26 RC 15.00 40.00
127 Jordan Schroeder/45 RC 12.00 30.00
128 Joakim Nordstrom/42 RC 10.00 25.00
129 Sami Vatanen/45 RC 12.00 30.00
130 Matthew Irwin/52 RC 10.00 25.00
131 Quinton Howden/42 RC 10.00 25.00
132 Emerson Etem/65 RC 10.00 25.00
133 Rasmus Ristolainen/55 RC 40.00 80.00
134 Josh Leivo/32 RC 10.00 25.00
135 Tomas Hertl/48 RC 30.00 80.00
136 Dougie Hamilton/27 RC 50.00 100.00
138 Elias Lindholm/16 RC 30.00 60.00
139 Calvin Pickard/31 RC 15.00 40.00
140 Brian Flynn/65 RC 8.00 20.00
142 Jonas Brodin/25 RC 20.00 50.00
144 Cameron Schilling/45 RC 8.00 20.00
146 Michael Bournival/49 RC 12.00 30.00
147 Lucas Lessio/22 RC 15.00 40.00
148 Nick Petrecki/54 RC 8.00 20.00
149 Mathew Dumba/55 RC 8.00 20.00
151 Carl Soderberg/34 RC 12.00 30.00
152 Nathan MacKinnon/29 RC 700.00 1000.00
153 Cory Conacher/89 RC 6.00 15.00
155 Jarred Tinordi/24 RC 15.00 40.00
156 Nicklas Jensen/46 RC 10.00 25.00
158 Andrej Sustr/62 RC 6.00 15.00
159 Jamie Devane/59 RC 10.00 25.00
160 Aleksander Barkov/16 RC 125.00 200.00
163 Eric Gelinas/32 RC 12.00 30.00
165 Viktor Fasth/30 RC 12.00 30.00
167 Connor Carrick/58 RC 10.00 25.00
168 Vladimir Tarasenko/91 RC 60.00 120.00
169 Spencer Abbott/56 RC 10.00 25.00
171 Petr Mrazek/34 RC 25.00 60.00
172 Scott Laughton/21 RC 20.00 50.00
173 Matt Nieto/83 RC 8.00 20.00
174 Frank Corrado/26 RC 12.00 30.00
175 Chris Brown/44 RC 8.00 20.00
177 Christian Thomas/60 RC 8.00 20.00
179 Jean-Gabriel Pageau/44 RC 12.00 30.00
180 Rickard Rakell/67 RC 10.00 25.00
182 Edward Pasquale/32 RC 15.00 40.00
183 Sean Monahan/23 RC 100.00 200.00
184 Mikhail Grigorenko/25 RC 40.00 80.00
185 Nail Yakupov/64 RC 60.00 120.00
187 Valeri Nichushkin/43 RC 60.00 120.00
188 Max Reinhart/59 RC 12.00 30.00
189 Morgan Rielly/44 RC 50.00 100.00
190 Will Acton/41 RC 10.00 25.00
191 Brock Nelson/29 RC 30.00 80.00
192 Brian Lashoff/23 RC 12.00 30.00
193 Tye McGinn/15 RC 30.00 60.00
194 Tyler Toffoli/73 RC 30.00 60.00
196 Beau Bennett/19 RC 40.00 80.00
198 Nick Bjugstad/27 RC 25.00 50.00
199 Nathan Beaulieu/40 RC 15.00 40.00
200 Danny DeKeyser/65 RC 12.00 30.00

2013-14 SP Game Used Authentic Fabrics

*GOLD/52-99: .6X TO 1.5X BASIC JSY C-D
*GOLD/52-99: .5X TO 1.2X BASIC JSY A-B
*GOLD/31-46: .8X TO 2X BASIC JSY C-D
*GOLD/31-46: .6X TO 1.5X BASIC JSY A-B
*GOLD/15-26: 1X TO 2.5X BASIC JSY C-D
*GOLD/15-26: .8X TO 2X BASIC JSY A-B
*FIGHT STRAP/15: 1X TO 2.5X BASIC JSY C-D
*FIGHT STRAP/15: .8X TO 2X BASIC JSY A-B
*PATCH/35: 1X TO 2.5X BASIC JSY C-D
*PATCH/35: .8X TO 2X BASIC JSY A-B
AFAL Andrew Ladd D 2.00 5.00
AFAO Alexander Ovechkin C 12.00 30.00
AFBC Brian Campbell C 2.00 5.00
AFBE Brian Elliott D 2.50 6.00
AFBR Dustin Brown D 3.00 8.00
AFCP Carey Price D 4.00 10.00
AFCS Chris Stewart C 2.50 6.00
AFDB David Backes D 2.00 5.00
AFDK David Krejci D 3.00 8.00
AFDP Dion Phaneuf D 2.50 6.00
AFEL Eric Lindros A 6.00 15.00
AFES Eric Staal A 5.00 12.00
AFGF Grant Fuhr C 5.00 12.00
AFGL Gabriel Landeskog D 4.00 10.00
AFGR Mike Green D 2.50 6.00
AFHZ Henrik Zetterberg C 4.00 10.00
AFJA Jake Allen B 4.00 10.00
AFJB Jamie Benn D 3.00 8.00
AFJC Jeff Carter D 2.50 6.00
AFJE Jordan Eberle D 6.00 15.00
AFJH Jonas Hiller D 2.50 6.00
AFJQ Jonathan Quick D 4.00 10.00
AFJS Joe Sakic B 5.00 12.00
AFKL Kari Lehtonen D 2.50 6.00
AFKY Keith Yandle D 2.00 5.00
AFLE Lars Eller A 2.50 6.00
AFLS Luke Schenn D 3.00 8.00
AFLU Milan Lucic D 3.00 8.00
AFMC Michael Cammalleri D 2.50 6.00
AFMG Michel Goulet D 2.50 6.00
AFMK Mikko Koivu D 3.00 8.00
AFML Mario Lemieux A 15.00 40.00
AFMR Mike Richards D 2.50 6.00
AFMS Mats Sundin D 3.00 8.00
AFMT Maxime Talbot D 3.00 8.00
AFNB Nicklas Backstrom D 3.00 8.00
AFPA P.A. Parenteau D 2.00 5.00
AFPE Corey Perry D 5.00 12.00
AFPR Pekka Rinne D 3.00 8.00
AFPS P.K. Subban D 4.00 10.00
AFRC Ryan Callahan C 2.00 5.00
AFRG Ryan Getzlaf D 3.00 8.00
AFRN Ryan Nugent-Hopkins D 4.00 10.00
AFSC Sidney Crosby B 15.00 40.00
AFSD Shane Doan D 2.50 6.00
AFSG Simon Gagne D 3.00 8.00
AFST Paul Stastny C 2.50 6.00
AFSW Shea Weber D 2.50 6.00
AFTE Tyler Ennis D 3.00 8.00
AFTH Taylor Hall C 3.00 8.00
AFTM Tyler Myers A 2.50 6.00
AFTP Tomas Plekanec C 2.00 5.00
AFTV Thomas Vanek D 2.50 6.00
AFVV Slava Voynov D 2.50 6.00
AFWG Wayne Gretzky A 15.00 40.00
AFWS Wayne Simmonds A 5.00 12.00
AFZB Zach Bogocian A 3.00 8.00
AFZC Zdeno Chara C 3.00 8.00

2013-14 SP Game Used Authentic Fabrics Dual

*PATCH/25: .8X TO 2X BASIC DUAL
AF2BM E.Belfour/M.Modano C 6.00 15.00
AF2BS D.Backes/C.Stewart D 3.00 8.00
AF2CB Z.Chara/R.Bourque D 6.00 15.00
AF2CR T.Rask/Z.Chara D 5.00 12.00
AF2DV D.Doughty/S.Voynov D 6.00 15.00
AF2DY Datsyuk/S.Yzerman D 10.00 25.00
AF2EH J.Eberle/T.Hall D 4.00 10.00
AF2EK I.Kovalchuk/P.Elias B 5.00 12.00
AF2FH P.Forsberg/R.Hextall D 5.00 12.00
AF2FL M.Fleury/K.Letang C 6.00 15.00
AF2GB Backstrom/M.Green D 4.00 10.00
AF2GP R.Getzlaf/C.Perry D 6.00 15.00
AF2HG A.Hemsky/S.Gagner D 2.50 6.00
AF2HH J.Howard/D.Hasek D 6.00 15.00
AF2KC D.Keith/C.Crawford D 5.00 12.00
AF2LB K.Lehtonen/J.Benn D 4.00 10.00
AF2LM M.Lucic/B.Marchand D 8.00 20.00
AF2LS R.Luongo/H.Sedin D 6.00 15.00
AF2MT Marleau/J.Thornton D 6.00 15.00
AF2NH M.Neuvirth/B.Holtby D 5.00 12.00
AF2NQ A.Niemi/J.Quick D 5.00 12.00
AF2OH B.Holtby/A.Ovechkin D 5.00 12.00
AF2PD Parenteau/M.Duchene D 4.00 10.00
AF2PE T.Plekanec/L.Eller D 2.50 6.00
AF2PK O.Pavelec/E.Kane D 4.00 10.00
AF2PS Plekanec/P.Subban A 8.00 20.00
AF2RC M.Richards/J.Carter D 3.00 8.00
AF2RW S.Weber/P.Rinne D 4.00 10.00
AF2SA J.Spezza/C.Anderson C 4.00 10.00
AF2SG M.Sundin/D.Gilmour D 6.00 15.00
AF2SH J.Sakic/M.Hejduk D 8.00 20.00
AF2VS T.Vanek/D.Stafford D 3.00 8.00
AF2YJ K.Yandle/C.Joseph D 5.00 12.00

2013-14 SP Game Used Authentic Fabrics Dual Patches

AF2BL P.Bergeron/M.Lucic 10.00 25.00
AF2BM E.Belfour/M.Modano 12.00 30.00
AF2BS D.Backes/C.Stewart 6.00 15.00
AF2CB Z.Chara/R.Bourque 12.00 30.00
AF2CR T.Rask/Z.Chara 10.00 25.00
AF2CS R.Callahan/D.Stepan 5.00 12.00
AF2DV D.Doughty/S.Voynov 12.00 30.00
AF2EH J.Eberle/T.Hall 8.00 20.00
AF2EK I.Kovalchuk/P.Elias 8.00 20.00
AF2FL M.Fleury/K.Letang 12.00 30.00
AF2GB N.Backstrom/M.Green 8.00 20.00
AF2GL C.Giroux/S.Laughton 10.00 25.00
AF2GP R.Getzlaf/C.Perry 12.00 30.00
AF2GS C.Giroux/W.Simmonds 10.00 25.00
AF2HG A.Hemsky/S.Gagner 5.00 12.00
AF2HH J.Howard/D.Hasek 12.00 30.00
AF2KC D.Keith/C.Crawford 10.00 25.00
AF2KE N.Kronwall/J.Ericsson 6.00 15.00
AF2KY I.Kovalchuk/N.Yakupov 10.00 25.00
AF2LB K.Lehtonen/J.Benn 8.00 20.00
AF2LM M.Lucic/B.Marchand 15.00 40.00
AF2NH M.Neuvirth/B.Holtby 12.00 30.00
AF2NQ A.Niemi/J.Quick 10.00 25.00
AF2OH B.Holtby/A.Ovechkin 15.00 40.00
AF2PD P.Parenteau/M.Duchene 8.00 20.00
AF2PE T.Plekanec/L.Eller 5.00 12.00
AF2PS T.Plekanec/P.Subban 10.00 25.00
AF2RC M.Richards/J.Carter 6.00 15.00
AF2RW S.Weber/P.Rinne 8.00 20.00
AF2SA J.Spezza/C.Anderson 8.00 20.00
AF2SD P.Stastny/M.Duchene 8.00 20.00
AF2SH J.Sakic/M.Hejduk 15.00 40.00
AF2VS T.Vanek/D.Stafford 6.00 15.00
AF2YJ K.Yandle/C.Joseph 10.00 25.00

2013-14 SP Game Used Authentic Fabrics Eights

AF8CAN Canadian Stars 20.00 50.00
AF8NET Goalie Stars 20.00 50.00
AF8RUS Russian Stars 20.00 50.00
AF8SWE Swedish Stars 20.00 50.00
AF8STAR All-Stars 20.00 50.00

2013-14 SP Game Used Authentic Fabrics Fives

AF5CAP Ovc/Grn/Hlt/Bks/Nv 50.00 125.00
AF5COL Dch/Lnd/Sts/McK/Prn 25.00 50.00
AF5DAL Lht/Bn/Nls/Dly/Cmp 12.00 30.00
AF5DET Dts/Hwd/Lds/Mrz/DKy 15.00 40.00
AF5GR8 Grt/Ry/Yzr/Hwrk/Hll 60.00 120.00
AF5LAK Qck/Kpt/Crtr/Vyn/Tfli 25.00 60.00
AF5NJD Els/Kvlk/Hnr/Brdr/Zjc 30.00 80.00
AF5NYR Cln/Stp/Nsh/Lnd/Rch 12.00 30.00
AF5SJS Hrt/Ctr/Mrl/Ptrcki/Nmi 25.00 60.00
AF5STL Stw/Ptn/Elt/Bck/Brgl 10.00 25.00
AF5TOR Blf/Glm/Jsp/Lnd/Snd 20.00 50.00

2013-14 SP Game Used Authentic Fabrics Quads

AF4COL Dch/Lnds/Hjdk/Stst B 10.00 25.00
AF4DAL Mdn/Lhtn/Bnn/Dley B 12.00 30.00
AF4DET Yzm/Dts/Mrzk/DKy B 12.00 30.00
AF4EDM RNH/Ykv/Hll/Ebr B 12.00 30.00
AF4HOF Hll/Lmx/Skc/Sndn B 30.00 80.00
AF4KINGS Kptr/Qck/Dgh/Vyn B 12.00 30.00
AF4LAK Kptr/Rchr/Crtr/Wlms B 12.00 30.00
AF4NYR Stp/Nsh/Clhn/Hgln A 8.00 20.00
AF4OTT Spz/Andr/Krls/Cnch B 8.00 20.00
AF4PIT Mlkn/Ltng/Flry/Nl B 15.00 40.00
AF4STL Stwt/Aln/Ellt/Bcks B 8.00 20.00

2013-14 SP Game Used Authentic Fabrics Sevens

AF7G Goalie Stars 25.00 60.00
AF7CHI Chicago Stars 20.00 50.00
AF7EDM Edmonton Stars 20.00 50.00
AF7LAK L.A. Kings Stars 15.00 40.00
AF7MON Montreal Stars 25.00 60.00

2013-14 SP Game Used Authentic Fabrics Sixes

AF6CARNAS Carolina/Nashville 15.00 40.00
AF6CHISTL Chicago/St.Louis 15.00 40.00
AF6COLDET Colorado/Detroit 15.00 40.00
AF6LAKANA LA/Anaheim Stars 15.00 40.00
AF6LAKSJS LA/San Jose Stars 15.00 40.00

2013-14 SP Game Used Authentic Fabrics Triples

*PATCH/15: 1.2X TO 3X BASIC TRIPLE
AF3ANA Gtzlf/Prry/Hller B 8.00 20.00
AF3AVS Brque/Roy/Skic B 12.00 30.00
AF3BUF Myrs/Adam/Vnek B 4.00 10.00
AF3CAPS Ovchkn/Bkstrm/Hltby B 6.00 15.00
AF3CHI Toews/Kne/Kth B 10.00 25.00
AF3DAL Lhtnen/Benn/Dley B 5.00 12.00
AF3DRW Yzrmn/Dtsyk/DKysr B 8.00 20.00
AF3EDM Hpkns/Ebrle/Hall B 6.00 15.00
AF3GR8 Roy/Grtzky/Lmeux B 25.00 50.00
AF3HOF Skic/Sndin/Lmeux B 20.00 50.00
AF3JETS Byfgln/Pvlec/Kane B 5.00 12.00
AF3KINGS Rchrds/Crtr/Kptr B 8.00 20.00
AF3LAK Quick/Dghty/Kptar B 5.00 12.00
AF3LBBR Sbbn/Prce/Glchnyk B 6.00 15.00
AF3NJD Brdeur/Kvlchk/Hnrqe B 12.00 30.00
AF3OIL Ykpv/Hpkns/Hall B 8.00 20.00
AF3OTT Spzza/Krlssn/Lhnr B 6.00 15.00
AF3USA Brwn/Ststny/Quick A 6.00 15.00
AF3WIN Bgsian/Kne/Byfgln B 5.00 12.00

2013-14 SP Game Used Draft Day Marks

DDMAB1 A.Barkov A/35 25.00 60.00
DDMAG1 Alex Galchenyuk A/35 20.00 50.00
DDMAO1 A.Ovechkin C/10 60.00 120.00
DDMBH1 Brett Hull H/10 40.00 80.00
DDMBJ1 Nick Bjugstad A/35 15.00 40.00
DDMBN1 Brock Nelson E/35 12.00 30.00
DDMCC1 Charlie Coyle C/35 12.00 30.00
DDMCT1 Christian Thomas A/35 6.00 15.00
DDMDH1 Dougie Hamilton A/35 20.00 50.00
DDMDM1 Dylan McIlrath A/35 8.00 20.00
DDMEE1 Emerson Etem E/70* 8.00 20.00
DDMEL1 Eric Lindros D/10 40.00 80.00
DDMGR1 Mikael Granlund A/35 12.00 30.00
DDMJB1 Jonas Brodin B/35 10.00 25.00
DDMJC1 Jack Campbell A/35 12.00 30.00
DDMJH1 J.Huberdeau A/35 20.00 50.00
DDMJO1 Jamie Oleksiak A/35 6.00 15.00
DDMJU1 Justin Schultz C/35 8.00 20.00
DDMMA1 Stefan Matteau A/70* 6.00 15.00
DDMMD1 Mathew Dumba A/35 5.00 12.00
DDMMG1 M.Grigorenko E/35 5.00 12.00
DDMMJ1 Jon Merrill E/35 8.00 20.00
DDMMR1 Morgan Rielly E/35 40.00 80.00
DDMNB1 Nathan Beaulieu A/35 5.00 12.00
DDMNJ1 Nicklas Jensen E/70* 10.00 25.00
DDMNM1 N.MacKinnon A/35 125.00 300.00
DDMNY1 Nail Yakupov A/35 15.00 40.00
DDMPF1 Peter Forsberg B/10 100.00 175.00

DDMPK1 P.Kane A/10 EXCH 40.00 80.00
DDMPM1 Petr Mrazek A/35 15.00 40.00
DDMPR1 Patrick Roy O/10 150.00 225.00
DDMQH1 Quinton Howden D/35 8.00 20.00
DDMRM1 Ryan Murray A/35 12.00 30.00
DDMSJ1 Seth Jones E/35 15.00 40.00
DDMSM1 Sean Monahan A/70* 30.00 60.00
DDMTI1 Jarred Tinordi D/35 8.00 20.00
DDMTJ1 Jacob Trouba A/35 25.00 50.00
DDMTT1 Tyler Toffoli F/70* 30.00 60.00
DDMTW1 Tom Wilson I/35 15.00 40.00
DDMVN1 Valeri Nichushkin C/35 20.00 50.00
DDMZG1 Z.Girgensons E/35 25.00 50.00

2013-14 SP Game Used Gold Autographs

1 Dale Hawerchuk C 10.00 25.00
3 Alexander Ovechkin B 30.00 80.00
6 Alexandre Burrows D 5.00 12.00
7 Markus Naslund C 8.00 20.00
8 Ryan Kesler C 8.00 20.00
9 Trevor Linden D 8.00 20.00
10 Doug Gilmour A 10.00 25.00
12 Dion Phaneuf C 6.00 15.00
13 Phil Kessel C 8.00 20.00
14 Steven Stamkos B 15.00 40.00
15 Chris Stewart B 6.00 15.00
16 Curtis Joseph C 10.00 25.00
17 Brett Hull A 15.00 40.00
18 David Backes D 5.00 12.00
19 Jaroslav Halak D 8.00 20.00
21 Joe Pavelski B 10.00 25.00
22 Antti Niemi D 6.00 15.00
23 Chris Kunitz D 8.00 20.00
25 Paul Coffey C 8.00 20.00
26 Evgeni Malkin B 15.00 40.00
28 Mario Lemieux B 40.00 100.00
29 Sidney Crosby B 30.00 80.00
31 Shane Doan D 6.00 15.00
34 Scott Hartnell D 5.00 12.00
35 Dave Schultz C 8.00 20.00
37 Jason Spezza B 8.00 20.00
38 Rick Nash B 8.00 20.00
40 Mark Messier A 15.00 40.00
42 Mike Bossy B 8.00 20.00
43 John Tavares D 12.00 30.00
44 Cory Schneider D 8.00 20.00
45 Adam Henrique C 6.00 15.00
46 Martin Brodeur A 20.00 50.00
48 Jean Beliveau B 8.00 20.00
49 Larry Robinson C 8.00 20.00
52 Zach Parise C 8.00 20.00
55 Jari Kurri C 8.00 20.00
56 Wayne Gretzky C 150.00 400.00
57 Anze Kopitar C 12.00 30.00
59 Mike Richards C 6.00 15.00
60 Jeff Carter C 6.00 15.00
62 Ron Francis B 10.00 25.00
63 Pavel Bure A 8.00 20.00
64 Grant Fuhr B 12.00 30.00
65 Bill Ranford D 8.00 20.00
67 Ryan Nugent-Hopkins C 10.00 25.00
68 Taylor Hall C 8.00 20.00
69 Chris Osgood D 8.00 20.00
70 Nicklas Lidstrom C 8.00 20.00
71 Pavel Datsyuk B 12.00 30.00
72 Jamie Benn D 8.00 20.00
73 Marian Gaborik B 8.00 20.00
74 Joe Sakic A 15.00 40.00
78 Tony Esposito B 8.00 20.00
79 Jonathan Toews A 12.00 30.00
81 Patrick Kane A 15.00 40.00
82 Jeff Skinner B 10.00 25.00
83 Eric Staal B 10.00 25.00
84 Jordan Staal D 6.00 15.00
85 Jiri Tlusty D 5.00 12.00
87 Gilbert Perreault C 8.00 20.00
89 Cam Neely C 8.00 20.00
90 Brad Marchand B 15.00 40.00
91 Tuukka Rask D 10.00 25.00
92 Patrice Bergeron B 10.00 25.00
93 Ray Bourque B 12.00 30.00
94 Terry O'Reilly C 6.00 15.00
95 Bobby Orr C 30.00 80.00
101 Alex Galchenyuk D 20.00 50.00
103 Richard Panik B 8.00 20.00
104 Ryan Murray A 12.00 30.00
107 Mikael Granlund A 12.00 30.00
108 Boone Jenner D 15.00 40.00
113 Justin Schultz A 8.00 20.00
114 Drew Shore B 6.00 15.00
115 Ryan Spooner C 8.00 20.00
116 Austin Watson D 6.00 15.00
117 Tom Wilson D 15.00 40.00
122 Stefan Matteau D 6.00 15.00
123 Tanner Pearson D 8.00 20.00
125 Cristopher Nilstorp A 6.00 15.00
127 Jordan Schroeder B 8.00 20.00
131 Quinton Howden D 6.00 15.00
132 Emerson Etem B 8.00 20.00
133 Rasmus Ristolainen B 12.00 30.00
135 Tomas Hertl D 15.00 40.00
136 Dougie Hamilton B 12.00 30.00
137 Thomas Hickey D 6.00 15.00
138 Elias Lindholm A 20.00 50.00
141 Radko Gudas A 8.00 20.00
145 Alex Chiasson D 8.00 20.00
148 Nick Petrecki D 5.00 12.00
149 Mathew Dumba A 5.00 12.00
150 Mark Pysyk D 8.00 20.00
152 Nathan MacKinnon A 125.00 300.00
153 Cory Conacher C 5.00 12.00
155 Jarred Tinordi D 8.00 20.00
156 Nicklas Jensen C 6.00 15.00
160 Aleksander Barkov C 25.00 60.00
162 Seth Jones B 15.00 40.00
164 Jack Campbell D 20.00 50.00
165 Viktor Fasth D 8.00 20.00
170 Jamie Oleksiak D 6.00 15.00
171 Petr Mrazek B 15.00 40.00
172 Scott Laughton C 10.00 25.00
175 Chris Brown D 5.00 12.00
176 Jonathan Huberdeau A 20.00 50.00
177 Christian Thomas C 6.00 15.00
179 Jean-Gabriel Pageau D 8.00 20.00
181 Brendan Gallagher A 20.00 50.00
183 Sean Monahan B 12.00 30.00
184 Mikhail Grigorenko D 5.00 12.00
185 Nail Yakupov A 15.00 40.00
187 Valeri Nichushkin A 15.00 40.00
188 Max Reinhart D 8.00 20.00
189 Morgan Rielly B 20.00 50.00
191 Brock Nelson C 15.00 40.00
192 Brian Lashoff D 6.00 15.00
193 Tye McGinn D 8.00 20.00
194 Tyler Toffoli C 15.00 40.00
195 Jesper Fast D 8.00 20.00
196 Beau Bennett D 10.00 25.00
197 Jacob Trouba A 12.00 30.00
198 Nick Bjugstad C 10.00 25.00
199 Nathan Beaulieu D 5.00 12.00
200 Danny DeKeyser C 10.00 25.00

2013-14 SP Game Used Inked Rookie Sweaters

*PATCH/25: .6X TO 1.5X BASIC JSY AU
IRSAG Alex Galchenyuk 12.00 30.00
IRSBB Beau Bennett 6.00 15.00
IRSBG Brendan Gallagher 12.00 30.00
IRSCC Cory Conacher 3.00 8.00
IRSDH Dougie Hamilton 12.00 30.00
IRSEE Emerson Etem 6.00 15.00
IRSGR Mikhail Grigorenko 8.00 20.00
IRSJC Jack Campbell 5.00 12.00
IRSJH Jonathan Huberdeau 10.00 25.00
IRSJS Justin Schultz 5.00 12.00
IRSJT Jarred Tinordi 5.00 12.00
IRSMG Mikael Granlund 8.00 20.00
IRSNB Nathan Beaulieu 3.00 8.00
IRSNY Nail Yakupov 10.00 25.00
IRSPM Petr Mrazek 8.00 20.00
IRSQH Quinton Howden 4.00 10.00
IRSRS Ryan Spooner 8.00 20.00
IRSSC Jordan Schroeder 5.00 12.00
IRSSL Scott Laughton 8.00 20.00
IRSSM Stefan Matteau 6.00 15.00
IRSTT Tyler Toffoli 10.00 25.00
IRSVF Viktor Fasth 5.00 12.00

2013-14 SP Game Used Inked Sweaters

ISAH Adam Henrique/99 6.00 15.00
ISAK Anze Kopitar/99 12.00 30.00
ISAN Antti Niemi/99 6.00 15.00
ISAO Alexander Ovechkin/25 30.00 80.00
ISCP Carey Price/25 15.00 40.00
ISDB David Backes/99 5.00 12.00
ISDH Dale Hawerchuk/50 10.00 25.00
ISDP Dion Phaneuf/50 6.00 15.00
ISEM Evgeni Malkin/50 15.00 40.00
ISJS Jeff Skinner/50 10.00 25.00
ISJT Jonathan Toews/50 12.00 30.00
ISMB Martin Brodeur/25 20.00 50.00
ISMK Mikko Koivu/99 6.00 15.00
ISMR Matt Read/99 5.00 12.00
ISMS Marc Staal/99 5.00 12.00
ISPB Patrice Bergeron/50 10.00 25.00
ISPK Patrick Kane/25 15.00 40.00
ISRI Pekka Rinne/99 8.00 20.00
ISRN Ryan Nugent-Hopkins/50 10.00 25.00
ISSC Sidney Crosby/25 30.00 80.00
ISSG Sam Gagner/99 5.00 12.00
ISSW Shea Weber/50 6.00 15.00
ISTE Tony Esposito/25 8.00 20.00
ISTH Taylor Hall/50 8.00 20.00
ISVD Vincent Damphousse/99 6.00 15.00
ISWG Wayne Gretzky/25 100.00 250.00

2013-14 SP Game Used Rookie Fabrics

*FIGHT STRAP/15: 1.2X TO 3X BASIC JSY
*GOLD/40-91: .6X TO 1.5X BASIC JSY
*GOLD/25-34: .8X TO 2X BASIC JSY
*GOLD/19-24: 1X TO 2.5X BASIC JSY
*PATCH/35: .8X TO 2X BASIC JSY
RFAG Alex Galchenyuk B 6.00 15.00
RFBB Beau Bennett A 4.00 10.00
RFBG Brendan Gallagher B 5.00 12.00
RFCC Charlie Coyle B 4.00 10.00
RFCO Cory Conacher B 1.50 4.00
RFDB Damien Brunner B 2.00 5.00
RFDH Dougie Hamilton A 5.00 12.00
RFEE Emerson Etem A 2.50 6.00
RFGR Mikael Granlund B 4.00 10.00
RFJB Jonas Brodin B 3.00 8.00
RFJC Jack Campbell A 6.00 15.00
RFJH Jonathan Huberdeau B 4.00 10.00
RFJS Justin Schultz A 2.50 6.00
RFJT Jarred Tinordi B 2.50 6.00
RFMG Mikhail Grigorenko B 1.50 4.00
RFMO Sean Monahan B 8.00 20.00
RFMR Morgan Rielly B 6.00 15.00
RFMU Ryan Murray B 4.00 10.00
RFNB Nathan Beaulieu B 4.00 10.00
RFNM Nathan MacKinnon B 20.00 50.00
RFNY Nail Yakupov B 5.00 12.00
RFPM Petr Mrazek B 4.00 10.00
RFQH Quinton Howden B 2.00 5.00
RFRM Ryan Murphy B 2.50 6.00
RFSC Jordan Schroeder B 2.50 6.00
RFSL Scott Laughton B 3.00 8.00
RFTT Tyler Toffoli A 4.00 10.00
RFVF Viktor Fasth A 2.50 6.00
RFVN Valeri Nichushkin B 5.00 12.00
RFVT Vladimir Tarasenko B 4.00 10.00

2013-14 SP Game Used Rookie Fabrics Dual

*PATCH/25: .8X TO 2X BASIC DUAL
RF2BL B.Bennett/S.Laughton 3.00 8.00
RF2CG C.Coyle/M.Granlund 4.00 10.00
RF2CO J.Campbell/J.Oleksiak 6.00 15.00
RF2CP C.Conacher/J.Pageau 2.50 6.00
RF2DM D.DeKeyser/P.Mrazek 5.00 12.00
RF2GB A.Galchenyuk/N.Beaulieu 6.00 15.00
RF2GG A.Galchenyuk/B.Gallagher 6.00 15.00
RF2HH J.Huberdeau/Q.Howden 4.00 10.00
RF2HS D.Hamilton/R.Spooner 4.00 10.00
RF2MJ R.Murray/B.Jenner 5.00 12.00
RF2SY J.Schultz/N.Yakupov 5.00 12.00
RF2TG J.Tinordi/B.Gallagher 6.00 15.00
RF2TH T.Toffoli/T.Hertl 5.00 12.00
RF2YM N.Yakupov/N.MacKinnon 12.00 30.00

2013-14 SP Game Used Rookie Fabrics Fives

RF5DEF Hmln/Sch/Mph/Beli/Bdin 6.00 15.00
RF5FWD Yv/Gch/Hbr/Glghr/Cnc 10.00 25.00
RF5USA Etm/Cmbl/Cyl/Bnt/Schr 10.00 25.00
RF5EAST Hmt/Cnch/Glch/Ggr/Hbr 10.00 25.00
RF5WEST Ykv/Sch/MKn/Trsn/My 20.00 50.00
RF5CANADA Hbrd/Hw/Bel/Olk/Tfl 12.00 30.00

2013-14 SP Game Used Rookie Fabrics Quads

RF4MON Glch/Glghr/Tnrdi/Blieu 10.00 25.00
RF4RUS Grgn/Ykpv/Trsnko/Nch 6.00 15.00
RF4USA Etm/Bntt/Glchn/Tnrdi 8.00 20.00
RF4CAND Schltz/Hmltn/Mrph/Beli 4.00 10.00

2013-14 SP Game Used Rookie Fabrics Sevens

RF7DEF Hm/Olk/Sc/Br/Tn/Bl/Mp 10.00 25.00
RF7FWD Cn/Gr/MK/Yk/Hb/Gl/Ts 30.00 80.00
RF7USA Et/Cy/Gc/Tn/Mu/Bn/Sc 15.00 40.00
RF7CANADA Sp/Olk/Sc/Hw/Bl/Lg/Py 8.00 20.00

2013-14 SP Game Used Rookie Fabrics Triples

RF3G Mrzk/Pckrd/Cmpbll 6.00 15.00
RF3ANA Fasth/Etem/Rakell 3.00 8.00
RF3FWD Trsnko/Ykpv/Glchnyk 8.00 20.00
RF3MIN Grnlnd/Brdn/Cyle 5.00 12.00
RF3MON Blieu/Gllghr/Glchnyk 10.00 25.00

2013-14 SP Game Used SIGnificant Numbers Autographs

SNAG Alex Galchenyuk/27 100.00 175.00
SNCC Cory Conacher/89 5.00 12.00
SNCH Carl Hagelin/62 5.00 12.00
SNCO Charlie Coyle/63 12.00 30.00
SNJS Joe Sakic/19 20.00 40.00
SNJT Jonathan Toews/19 30.00 60.00
SNNY Nail Yakupov/64 30.00 60.00
SNRN Ryan Nugent-Hopkins/93 15.00 40.00

2013-14 SP Game Used Stanley Cup Finals Materials Game Used Puck

SCGUPAS Andrew Shaw 20.00 50.00
SCGUPBB Bryan Bickell 20.00 50.00
SCGUPBS Brent Seabrook 20.00 50.00
SCGUPCC Corey Crawford 40.00 100.00
SCGUPDB Dave Bolland 20.00 50.00
SCGUPDP Daniel Paille 20.00 50.00
SCGUPKA Patrick Kane 60.00 150.00
SCGUPML Milan Lucic 30.00 80.00
SCGUPPB Patrice Bergeron 40.00 100.00
SCGUPPK Patrick Kane 60.00 150.00
SCGUPRA Tuukka Rask 40.00 100.00
SCGUPTR Tuukka Rask 40.00 100.00

2013-14 SP Game Used Stanley Cup Finals Materials Net Cord

G1AF Andrew Ference 20.00 50.00
G1AS Andrew Shaw 20.00 50.00
G1CC Corey Crawford 40.00 100.00
G1DB Dave Bolland 20.00 50.00
G1DK Duncan Keith 50.00 125.00
G1ML Milan Lucic 30.00 80.00
G2CK Chris Kelly 20.00 50.00
G2DP Daniel Paille 20.00 50.00
G2MH Marian Hossa 50.00 125.00
G2PS Patrick Sharp 30.00 80.00
G2TR Tuukka Rask 40.00 100.00
G2TS Tyler Seguin 40.00 100.00
G3AS Andrew Shaw 20.00 50.00
G3JT Jonathan Toews 50.00 125.00
G3PB Patrice Bergeron 40.00 100.00
G3TR Tuukka Rask 40.00 100.00
G3TS Tyler Seguin 40.00 100.00
G3ZC Zdeno Chara 30.00 80.00
G4BS Brent Seabrook 20.00 50.00
G4CC Corey Crawford 40.00 100.00
G4DK Duncan Keith 25.00 60.00
G4JB Johnny Boychuk 25.00 60.00
G4JJ Jaromir Jagr 100.00 250.00
G4MH Michal Handzus 20.00 50.00
G4PB Patrice Bergeron 40.00 100.00
G4PK Patrick Kane 60.00 150.00
G4PS Patrick Sharp 30.00 80.00
G5BB Bryan Bickell 20.00 50.00
G5CC Corey Crawford 40.00 100.00
G5JO Johnny Oduya 25.00 60.00
G5JT Jonathan Toews 50.00 125.00
G5MH Michal Handzus 20.00 50.00
G5PK Patrick Kane 60.00 150.00
G5ZC Zdeno Chara 30.00 80.00
G6BB Bryan Bickell 20.00 50.00
G6CC Corey Crawford 40.00 100.00
G6DB Dave Bolland 20.00 50.00
G6JT Jonathan Toews 50.00 125.00
G6ML Milan Lucic 30.00 80.00
G6PK Patrick Kane 60.00 150.00
G6PS Patrick Sharp 30.00 80.00

2013-14 SP Game Used Stanley Cup Finals Materials Net Skirt Autographs

SCNSAAS Andrew Shaw B 60.00 150.00
SCNSABM Brad Marchand 40.00 100.00
SCNSABS Brandon Saad 40.00 100.00
SCNSAJT Jonathan Toews A 150.00 250.00
SCNSAPB Patrice Bergeron 60.00 150.00
SCNSAPK Patrick Kane A 80.00 200.00
SCNSASE Brent Seabrook 50.00 125.00

2013-14 SP Game Used Tandem Twigs

TTPP M.Lemieux/R.Francis A 25.00 60.00
TTANA T.Selanne/R.Getzlaf C 12.00 30.00
TTAVA P.Roy/J.Sakic A 15.00 40.00
TTBOS R.Bourque/C.Neely B 10.00 25.00
TTCOL P.Roy/P.Forsberg A 15.00 40.00
TTDET P.Datsyuk/H.Zetterberg B 10.00 25.00
TTDRW S.Yzerman/N.Lidstrom A 15.00 40.00
TTEDM P.Coffey/J.Kurri B 6.00 15.00
TTLAK D.Doughty/A.Kopitar C 10.00 25.00
TTLOS J.Quick/D.Doughty C 8.00 20.00
TTMNS D.Ciccarelli/M.Modano B 10.00 25.00
TTNYR R.Nash/H.Lundqvist B 15.00 40.00
TTOIL M.Messier/G.Anderson A 12.00 30.00
TTPEN M.Lemieux/E.Malkin A 25.00 60.00
TTPHI E.Lindros/C.Giroux B 10.00 25.00
TTRAN H.Lundqvist/M.Staal C 15.00 40.00
TTSAB T.Vanek/R.Miller C 6.00 15.00
TTTOR D.Gilmour/P.Kessel B 8.00 20.00
TTDUCKS T.Selanne/S.Koivu C 12.00 30.00
TTKINGS W.Gretzky/L.Robitaille A 40.00 100.00
TTSTAAL E.Staal/M.Staal C 8.00 20.00
TTGOALIE D.Hasek/R.Miller C 10.00 25.00
TTOILERS M.Messier/P.Coffey A 12.00 30.00
TTRWINGS S.Yzerman/H.Zetterberg B 15.0040.00

2013-14 SP Game Used Team Canada Fabrics

*FIGHT STRAP/15: 1.2X TO 3X JSY B-C
*FIGHT STRAP/15: 1X TO 2.5X JSY A
*GOLD/97: .5X TO 1.2X JSY B
*GOLD/17-28: 1X TO 2.5X JSY C
*PATCH/35: 1X TO 2.5X JSY B-C
*PATCH/35: .8X TO 2X JSY A
TCBG Brendan Gallagher C 6.00 15.00
TCDH Dougie Hamilton C 4.00 10.00
TCJH Jonathan Huberdeau C 5.00 12.00
TCJO Jamie Oleksiak A 4.00 10.00
TCJT Joe Thornton B 6.00 15.00
TCMF Marcus Foligno C 3.00 8.00
TCMP Mark Pysyk A 5.00 12.00
TCNB Nathan Beaulieu C 1.50 4.00
TCQH Quinton Howden C 3.00 8.00

2013-14 SP Game Used Team Canada Fabrics Dual

*PATCH/25: 1X TO 2.5X BASIC INSERTS
TC2HG Huberdeau/Gallagher 4.00 10.00
TC2HP D.Hamilton/M.Pysyk 4.00 10.00

2013-14 SP Game Used Team Canada Fabrics Quads

TC4DEF Hmltn/Pyk/Olksk/Blieu 4.00 10.00
TC42012F Hbrd/Gllgr/Hwdn/Stne 8.00 20.00

2013-14 SP Game Used Team Canada Fabrics Triples

*PATCH/15: 1X TO 2.5X BASIC TRIPLE
TC3HBO Hmltn/Blieu/Olksk 5.00 12.00
TC3HHG Hbrdau/Hwdn/Gllghr 5.00 12.00

2013-14 SP Game Used Winter Classic Materials Net Cord

WCNCAM Andrej Meszaros 10.00 25.00
WCNCAS Anton Stralman 10.00 25.00
WCNCBB Bill Barber 15.00 40.00
WCNCBC Bobby Clarke 25.00 60.00
WCNCBD Brandon Dubinsky 10.00 25.00
WCNCBI Stu Bickel 12.00 30.00
WCNCBL Brian Leetch 12.00 30.00
WCNCBO Brian Boyle 10.00 25.00
WCNCBP Brandon Prust 10.00 25.00
WCNCBR Brad Richards 15.00 40.00
WCNCBS Brayden Schenn 15.00 40.00
WCNCCG Claude Giroux 15.00 40.00
WCNCCH Carl Hagelin 10.00 25.00
WCNCCO Braydon Coburn 10.00 25.00
WCNCDB Daniel Briere 15.00 40.00
WCNCDG Daniel Girardi 10.00 25.00
WCNCDS Derek Stepan 10.00 25.00
WCNCEL Eric Lindros 25.00 60.00
WCNCGA Glenn Anderson 12.00 30.00
WCNCHL Henrik Lundqvist 40.00 100.00
WCNCJJ Jaromir Jagr 50.00 125.00
WCNCJM John Mitchell 10.00 25.00
WCNCJV James van Riemsdyk 12.00 30.00
WCNCMB Martin Biron 12.00 30.00
WCNCMC Matt Carle 12.00 30.00
WCNCMD Michael Del Zotto 12.00 30.00
WCNCMG Marian Gaborik 15.00 40.00
WCNCMI Mike Gartner 20.00 50.00
WCNCMM Mark Messier 30.00 80.00
WCNCMR Matt Read 10.00 25.00
WCNCMS Marc Staal 10.00 25.00
WCNCMT Maxime Talbot 10.00 25.00
WCNCPA Bernie Parent 20.00 50.00
WCNCRC Ryan Callahan 10.00 25.00
WCNCRM Ryan McDonagh 10.00 25.00
WCNCRU Michael Rupp 10.00 25.00
WCNCSB Sergei Bobrovsky 25.00 60.00
WCNCSC Sean Couturier 12.00 30.00
WCNCSH Scott Hartnell 10.00 25.00
WCNCVO Jakub Voracek 12.00 30.00
WCNCWS Wayne Simmonds 20.00 50.00

2013-14 SP Game Used Winter Classic Materials Net Skirt Autographs

WCNSABS Brayden Schenn B 30.00 80.00
WCNSAMM Mark Messier A 40.00 100.00

2014-15 SP Game Used

1 Wayne Gretzky/99 25.00 60.00
2 Jakub Voracek/93 3.00 8.00
3 Ryan Nugent-Hopkins/93 5.00 12.00
4 Gabriel Landeskog/92 5.00 12.00
5 John Tavares/91 6.00 15.00
6 Steven Stamkos/91 8.00 20.00
7 Tyler Seguin/91 5.00 12.00
8 Sidney Crosby/87 15.00 40.00
9 Phil Kessel/81 4.00 10.00
10 Jeff Carter/77 3.00 8.00
11 P.K. Subban/76 5.00 12.00
12 T.J. Oshie/74 4.00 10.00
13 Sergei Bobrovsky/72 6.00 15.00
14 Evgeni Malkin/71 8.00 20.00
15 Jaromir Jagr/68 12.00 30.00
16 Max Pacioretty/67 4.00 10.00
17 Mario Lemieux/66 15.00 40.00
18 Erik Karlsson/65 5.00 12.00
19 Mikael Granlund/64 3.00 8.00
20 Tyler Ennis/63 2.50 6.00
21 Rick Nash/61 4.00 10.00
22 Roberto Luongo/58 6.00 15.00
23 Jeff Skinner/53 5.00 12.00
24 Tyler Johnson/50 2.50 6.00
25 Tomas Hertl/48 4.00 10.00
26 Jonathan Bernier/45 3.00 8.00
27 David Backes/42 2.50 6.00
28 Tuukka Rask/40 5.00 12.00
29 Henrik Zetterberg/40 5.00 12.00
30 Dominik Hasek/39 6.00 15.00
31 Doug Gilmour/39 5.00 12.00
32 Logan Couture/39 5.00 12.00
33 Patrice Bergeron/37 5.00 12.00
34 Steve Mason/35 3.00 8.00
35 Cory Schneider/35 4.00 10.00
36 Jim Howard/35 5.00 12.00
37 Pekka Rinne/35 4.00 10.00
38 Mike Richter/35 4.00 10.00
39 Dustin Byfuglien/33 4.00 10.00
40 Kari Lehtonen/32 3.00 8.00
41 Jonathan Quick/32 5.00 12.00
42 Carey Price/31 8.00 20.00
43 Antti Niemi/31 3.00 8.00
44 Eddie Lack/31 3.00 8.00
45 Philipp Grubauer/31 4.00 10.00
46 Henrik Lundqvist/30 10.00 25.00
47 Martin Brodeur/30 10.00 25.00
48 Nathan MacKinnon/29 15.00 40.00
49 Jason Pominville/29 2.50 6.00
50 Claude Giroux/28 4.00 10.00
51 Martin St. Louis/26 4.00 10.00
52 Matt Moulson/26 2.50 6.00
53 Blake Wheeler/26 4.00 10.00
54 Jiri Hudler/24 3.00 8.00
55 Dustin Brown/23 4.00 10.00
56 Mike Bossy/22 4.00 10.00
57 Peter Forsberg/21 8.00 20.00
58 James van Riemsdyk/21 3.00 8.00
59 Brandon Saad/20 3.00 8.00
60 Ryan Suter/20 3.00 8.00
61 Alexander Steen/20 2.50 6.00
62 Chris Kreider/20 5.00 12.00
63 Jonathan Toews/19 6.00 15.00
64 Shane Doan/19 3.00 8.00
65 Jason Spezza/19 4.00 10.00
66 Nicklas Backstrom/19 4.00 10.00
67 Steve Yzerman/19 10.00 25.00
68 James Neal/18 2.50 6.00
69 Bryan Little/18 4.00 10.00
70 Radim Vrbata/17 2.50 6.00
71 Brandon Dubinsky/17 2.50 6.00
72 Ryan Kesler/17 4.00 10.00
73 Andrew Ladd/16 2.50 6.00
100 Ryan Johansen/19 3.00 8.00
101 Bo Horvat/53 RC 40.00 100.00
103 Cody Kunyk/28 RC 5.00 12.00
104 Landon Ferraro/29 RC 5.00 12.00
105 Oscar Klefbom/84 RC 25.00 60.00
107 Patrik Nemeth/37 RC 8.00 20.00
108 Joni Ortio/37 RC 10.00 25.00
109 Jiri Sekac/26 RC 6.00 15.00
110 Andrey Makarov/35 RC 8.00 20.00
111 A.Wennberg/41 RC 12.00 30.00
112 Johan Sundstrom/28 RC 8.00 20.00
114 Sam Reinhart/23 RC 100.00 200.00
115 Mike Halmo/43 RC 5.00 12.00
116 Vincent Trocheck/67 RC 15.00 40.00
117 John Persson/56 RC 6.00 15.00
118 Barclay Goodrow/89 RC 8.00 20.00
119 Jake McCabe/29 RC 8.00 20.00
121 Paul Carey/28 RC 5.00 12.00
122 Simon Moser/21 RC 5.00 12.00
123 Ty Rattie/18 RC 8.00 20.00
125 Colton Sissons/84 RC 8.00 20.00
126 Seth Griffith/53 RC 10.00 25.00
128 Josh Manson/42 RC 6.00 15.00
129 Chris Wagner/62 RC 8.00 20.00
130 Victor Rask/49 RC 8.00 20.00
131 Petteri Lindbohm/48 RC 6.00 15.00
132 A.Khokhlachev/76 RC 8.00 20.00
133 Marko Dano/56 RC 8.00 20.00
134 Patrick Brown/36 RC 8.00 20.00
135 Cedric Paquette/54 RC 8.00 20.00
136 Mirco Mueller/41 RC 8.00 20.00
137 V.Namestnikov/65 RC 12.00 30.00
138 Joe Morrow/45 RC 10.00 25.00
139 Jonathan Drouin/27 RC 150.00 250.00
140 Josh Jooris/86 RC 8.00 20.00
141 Adam Lowry/17 RC 12.00 30.00
142 Andrew Hammond/30 RC 12.00 30.00
143 Nicolas Deschamps/94 RC 8.00 20.00
144 Kristers Gudlevskis/37 RC 8.00 20.00
146 Ryan Sproul/48 RC 8.00 20.00
147 Leon Draisaitl/29 RC 150.00 400.00
148 Calle Jarnkrok/19 RC 8.00 20.00
149 Matt Carey/25 RC 6.00 15.00
151 Bogdan Yakimov/39 RC 8.00 20.00
154 Curtis Lazar/27 RC 8.00 20.00
155 Kevin Czuczman/24 RC 6.00 15.00
156 Teuvo Teravainen/86 RC 12.00 30.00
157 Rocco Grimaldi/23 RC 8.00 20.00
158 Joonas Nattinen/28 RC 8.00 20.00
159 Peter LeBlanc/64 RC 5.00 12.00
160 Stuart Percy/50 RC 8.00 20.00
161 Tyler Wotherspoon/56 RC 8.00 20.00
162 Teemu Pulkkinen/56 RC 10.00 25.00
163 William Karlsson/38 RC 25.00 60.00
164 Damon Severson/28 RC 8.00 20.00
166 Joey Hishon/38 RC 10.00 25.00
167 Greg McKegg/39 RC 6.00 15.00
168 Michael Zalewski/40 RC 6.00 15.00
169 Justin Johnson/49 RC 6.00 15.00
170 Matt Lindblad/52 RC 6.00 15.00
171 Johnny Gaudreau/53 RC 25.00 60.00
173 Evgeny Kuznetsov/92 RC 20.00 50.00
174 Nicolas Deslauriers/44 RC 8.00 20.00
175 Phil Varone/84 RC 6.00 15.00
176 Andrej Nestrasil/49 RC 8.00 20.00
177 Scott Mayfield/42 RC 6.00 15.00
178 Brett Gallant/59 RC 6.00 15.00
179 Brandon Kozun/67 RC 6.00 15.00
180 Mark Visentin/40 RC 8.00 20.00
181 Mark Van Guilder/29 RC 8.00 20.00
182 Garrett Wilson/28 RC 6.00 15.00
183 Dennis Everberg/45 RC 8.00 20.00
184 Chris Tierney/50 RC 8.00 20.00
185 Nathan Lieuwen/50 RC 6.00 15.00
186 Jonathan Racine/58 RC 8.00 20.00
188 Andre Burakovsky/65 RC 12.00 30.00
189 Brandon Gormley/33 RC 8.00 20.00
190 Anthony Duclair/63 RC 12.00 30.00
191 S.Gostisbehere/53 RC 15.00 40.00
192 Markus Granlund/60 RC 12.00 30.00
193 Bryce Van Brabant/48 RC 10.00 25.00
194 Bill Arnold/46 RC 6.00 15.00
196 T.van Riemsdyk/57 RC 12.00 30.00
197 Bobby Robins/64 RC 6.00 15.00
198 Adam Payerl/45 RC 6.00 15.00
199 P-E Bellemare/78 RC 8.00 20.00
200 Darnell Nurse/25 RC 60.00 150.00

2014-15 SP Game Used Authentic Fabrics

AFAN Antti Niemi E 3.00 8.00
AFBR Rod Brind'Amour E 3.00 8.00
AFBS Brandon Sutter B 2.50 6.00
AFCC Corey Crawford D 5.00 12.00
AFCE Cody Eakin E 2.50 6.00
AFEB Ed Belfour E 4.00 10.00
AFEK Evander Kane E 4.00 10.00
AFGR Michael Grabner A 3.00 8.00
AFJM Jake Muzzin C 4.00 10.00
AFJR Jeremy Roenick E 6.00 15.00
AFJZ Jeff Zatkoff A 3.00 8.00
AFMG Mike Gartner E 5.00 12.00
AFNH Nathan Horton E 4.00 10.00
AFPP Pete Peeters E 3.00 8.00
AFRB Ray Bourque E 6.00 15.00
AFRF Ron Francis C 5.00 12.00
AFVL Vincent Lecavalier E 4.00 10.00

2014-15 SP Game Used Authentic Fabrics Dual

AF2AL C.Anderson/Lehner C 5.00 12.00
AF2BS M.Sundin/E.Belfour B 5.00 12.00
AF2CH D.Hasek/C.Chelios C 8.00 20.00
AF2GK R.Getzlaf/A.Kopitar C 8.00 20.00
AF2HH M.Hackett/Hodgson A 3.00 8.00
AF2HT B.Hull/M.Turco C 10.00 25.00
AF2HY T.Hall/N.Yakupov C 5.00 12.00
AF2KB P.Kessel/J.Bernier A 5.00 12.00
AF2KD D.Keith/D.Doughty B 6.00 15.00
AF2LB Lehtonen/E.Belfour C 5.00 12.00
AF2PM P.Bure/M.Lemieux C 20.00 50.00
AF2PS C.Price/P.Subban C 10.00 25.00
AF2RR P.Rinne/T.Rask C 6.00 15.00
AF2ZH Zetterberg/J.Howard B 6.00 15.00

2014-15 SP Game Used Authentic Fabrics Quads

AF4CAN Keith/Doughty Price/Luongo C 6.00 15.00
AF4CHI Kruger/Leddy/Saad/Bickell A 2.50 6.00
AF4FIN Maatta/Niemi Lehtonen/Rask B 4.00 10.00
AF4SJLA Niemi/Thornton Quick/Brown C 5.00 12.00
AF4WINS Varlamov/Niemi Fleury/Bishop C 6.00 15.00

2014-15 SP Game Used Authentic Fabrics Sixes

AF6BOSMON Bq/Mry/Ot/Blw/Trg/Ry 15.00 40.00
AF6CENTRAL Cr/Vrl/Lh/Rn/Pv/Kmp 8.00 20.00
AF6CHINYR Sd/Kth/Ld/Zc/Stp/Mc 6.00 15.00
AF6NYRMON Hg/Mre/Zc/Pc/Elr/Mrk 12.00 30.00
AF6PACIFIC St/Qk/Nm/Lk/Sc/Rm 8.00 20.00
AF6PHINYR Ct/Gx/Ms/Stp/Ln/McD 15.00 40.00

2014-15 SP Game Used Authentic Fabrics Triples

AF3G Ramo/Smith/Scrivens A 5.00 12.00
AF3GK Smith/Lack/Ramo C 5.00 12.00
AF3QN Goulet/Nolan/Tardif C 5.00 12.00
AF3CBJ Bbrvsky/Hortn/Schltz C 8.00 20.00
AF3FIN Rask/Niemi/Lehtonen C 6.00 15.00
AF3FLY Coutr/Coburn/Giroux A 5.00 12.00
AF3LAK Brown/Toffoli/Quick C 6.00 15.00
AF3NET Lehtn/Kmper/Pavelec C 5.00 12.00
AF3NYR Moore/Zuccrl/Hagelin B 6.00 15.00
AF3BEES Brque/Murray/Oates C 8.00 20.00
AF3CAPS Kuzn/Green/Carlson A 20.00 50.00
AF3JETS Ladd/Kane/Pavelec C 5.00 12.00

2014-15 SP Game Used Autographs Blue

1 Wayne Gretzky C 150.00 400.00
3 Ryan Nugent-Hopkins D 8.00 20.00
4 Gabriel Landeskog D 8.00 20.00
5 John Tavares E 10.00 25.00
6 Steven Stamkos C 12.00 30.00
7 Tyler Seguin C 8.00 20.00
8 Sidney Crosby A 100.00 200.00
9 Phil Kessel D 6.00 15.00
13 Sergei Bobrovsky E 10.00 25.00
14 Evgeni Malkin D 12.00 30.00
15 Jaromir Jagr A 20.00 50.00
16 Max Pacioretty D 6.00 15.00
17 Mario Lemieux A 40.00 100.00
19 Mikael Granlund E 5.00 12.00
21 Rick Nash C 6.00 15.00
23 Jeff Skinner D 8.00 20.00
24 Tyler Johnson E 4.00 10.00
25 Tomas Hertl E 6.00 15.00
26 Jonathan Bernier E 5.00 12.00
27 David Backes E 4.00 10.00
28 Tuukka Rask E 8.00 20.00
30 Dominik Hasek B 10.00 25.00
31 Doug Gilmour C 8.00 20.00
32 Logan Couture C 8.00 20.00
33 Patrice Bergeron D 8.00 20.00
34 Steve Mason E 5.00 12.00
35 Cory Schneider D 6.00 15.00
36 Jim Howard E 8.00 20.00
37 Pekka Rinne E 6.00 15.00
38 Mike Richter D 6.00 15.00
43 Antti Niemi D 5.00 12.00
45 Philipp Grubauer E 6.00 15.00
47 Martin Brodeur B 15.00 40.00
48 Nathan MacKinnon D 25.00 60.00
49 Jason Pominville E 4.00 10.00
50 Claude Giroux C 6.00 15.00
51 Martin St. Louis C 6.00 15.00
55 Dustin Brown D 6.00 15.00
56 Mike Bossy C 6.00 15.00
57 Peter Forsberg B 12.00 30.00
58 James van Riemsdyk C 5.00 12.00
59 Brandon Saad E 5.00 12.00
62 Chris Kreider A 8.00 20.00
63 Jonathan Toews C 10.00 25.00
64 Shane Doan E 5.00 12.00
65 Jason Spezza D 6.00 15.00
67 Steve Yzerman B 15.00 40.00
68 James Neal E 4.00 10.00
72 Ryan Kesler D 6.00 15.00
77 Theoren Fleury C 8.00 20.00
78 Pavel Datsyuk C 10.00 25.00
79 Mats Sundin B 6.00 15.00
80 Eric Staal D 8.00 20.00
81 Anze Kopitar D 10.00 25.00
82 Brendan Gallagher B 6.00 15.00
83 Zach Parise C 6.00 15.00
84 Mark Messier B 12.00 30.00
87 Guy Lafleur C 8.00 20.00
89 Matt Duchene D 6.00 15.00
90 Teemu Selanne B 12.00 30.00
92 Alexander Ovechkin B 25.00 60.00
93 Joe Pavelski E 8.00 20.00
94 Kyle Turris E 6.00 15.00
95 Phil Esposito B 10.00 25.00
97 Shea Weber C 5.00 12.00
98 Taylor Hall B 6.00 15.00
99 Bobby Orr D 40.00 100.00
100 Ryan Johansen E 5.00 12.00
101 Bo Horvat D 15.00 40.00
102 Laurent Brossoit D 6.00 15.00
105 Oscar Klefbom D 12.00 30.00
108 Joni Ortio C 8.00 20.00
109 Jiri Sekac D 5.00 12.00
111 Alexander Wennberg D 10.00 25.00
113 Griffin Reinhart D 6.00 15.00
114 Sam Reinhart D 25.00 60.00
116 Vincent Trocheck D 12.00 30.00
119 Jake McCabe D 6.00 15.00
120 Kevin Hayes C EXCH 15.00 40.00
123 Ty Rattie D 6.00 15.00
125 Colton Sissons D 6.00 15.00
132 Alexander Khokhlachev D 6.00 15.00
133 Marko Dano D 6.00 15.00
134 Patrick Brown D 6.00 15.00
136 Mirco Mueller D 6.00 15.00
137 Vladislav Namestnikov D 10.00 25.00
138 Joe Morrow D 8.00 20.00
139 Jonathan Drouin D 12.00 30.00
141 Adam Lowry D 10.00 25.00
145 Tobias Rieder D 6.00 15.00
146 Ryan Sproul D 6.00 15.00
147 Leon Draisaitl D 100.00 250.00
150 Corban Knight D 6.00 15.00
153 Aaron Ekblad D 15.00 40.00
154 Curtis Lazar D 6.00 15.00
156 Teuvo Teravainen D 10.00 25.00
157 Rocco Grimaldi D 6.00 15.00
158 Joonas Nattinen D 6.00 15.00
160 Stuart Percy D 6.00 15.00
161 Tyler Wotherspoon D 6.00 15.00
162 Teemu Pulkkinen D 8.00 20.00
164 Damon Severson D 6.00 15.00
166 Joey Hishon D 8.00 20.00
167 Greg McKegg D 5.00 12.00
171 Johnny Gaudreau D 30.00 80.00
172 Jori Lehtera A 8.00 20.00
173 Evgeny Kuznetsov D 15.00 40.00
176 Andrej Nestrasil D 6.00 15.00
179 Brandon Kozun D 5.00 12.00
180 Mark Visentin D 6.00 15.00
183 Dennis Everberg D 6.00 15.00
184 Chris Tierney D 6.00 15.00
188 Andre Burakovsky D 10.00 25.00
189 Brandon Gormley D 6.00 15.00
190 Anthony Duclair C 10.00 25.00
192 Markus Granlund B 10.00 25.00
196 Trevor van Riemsdyk D 10.00 25.00
200 Darnell Nurse D 12.00 30.00

2014-15 SP Game Used Buyback Autographs

31 Nicklas Lidstrom/20 25.00 60.00

2014-15 SP Game Used Career Legacy Jerseys

CLDK Dominik Hasek D 12.00 30.00
CLEK Evander Kane C 4.00 10.00
CLJB Jonathan Bernier D 2.50 6.00
CLJJ Jaromir Jagr A 20.00 50.00
CLML Mario Lemieux B 10.00 25.00
CLSM Steve Mason D 2.50 6.00
CLSV Semyon Varlamov D 3.00 8.00

2014-15 SP Game Used Career Legacy Patches

CLAL Andrew Ladd/99 2.50 6.00
CLAT Alex Tanguay/99 8.00 20.00
CLBG Bill Guerin/99 6.00 15.00
CLCA Craig Anderson/50 5.00 12.00
CLDB Daniel Briere/99 10.00 25.00
CLDK Dominik Hasek/25 20.00 40.00
CLDP David Perron/99 3.00 8.00
CLJB Jonathan Bernier/99 15.00 40.00
CLJC Jeff Carter/99 3.00 8.00
CLJJ Jaromir Jagr/25 30.00 60.00
CLML Mario Lemieux/25 25.00 50.00
CLMR Mike Richards/99 3.00 8.00
CLSM Steve Mason/99 10.00 25.00
CLSV Semyon Varlamov/25 6.00 15.00
CLZC Zdeno Chara/99 4.00 10.00

2014-15 SP Game Used Draft Day Marks

DDMAC1 Adam Clendening C 12.00 30.00
DDMAE1 Aaron Ekblad E 30.00 80.00
DDMBH1 Bo Horvat EXCH 30.00 60.00
DDMBR1 Bobby Ryan R 15.00 40.00
DDMCJ1 Calle Jarnkrok EXCH 10.00 25.00
DDMCL1 Curtis Lazar L 25.00 50.00
DDMDN1 Darnell Nurse N 15.00 40.00
DDMEK1 Evander Kane K 25.00 60.00
DDMFF1 Filip Forsberg F 50.00 100.00
DDMGO1 Brandon Gormley G 12.00 30.00
DDMJB1 Jonathan Bernier B 12.00 30.00
DDMJD1 Jonathan Drouin D 30.00 60.00
DDMJE1 Jordan Eberle E/30* 30.00 80.00
DDMJG1 Johnny Gaudreau G 125.00 300.00
DDMJH1 Joey Hishon H/70* 15.00 40.00
DDMJM1 Joe Morrow M 15.00 40.00
DDMJT1 Jonathan Toews T 50.00 100.00
DDMKR1 Kerby Rychel R 10.00 25.00
DDMKZ1 Evgeny Kuznetsov K 20.00 50.00
DDMLD1 Leon Draisaitl D 40.00 100.00
DDMMF1 Marc-Andre Fleury F 30.00 60.00
DDMMV1 Mark Visentin V 12.00 30.00
DDMNA1 V.Namestnikov N/70* 15.00 40.00
DDMPK1 Phil Kessel K 20.00 50.00
DDMRG1 Griffin Reinhart R/70* 15.00 40.00
DDMRS1 Ryan Strome S 15.00 40.00
DDMSR1 Sam Reinhart R/70* 25.00 60.00
DDMTR1 Ty Rattie R 12.00 30.00
DDMTV1 Teuvo Teravainen T 30.00 60.00
DDMZP1 Zach Parise P 25.00 50.00

2014-15 SP Game Used Gold Jerseys

1 Wayne Gretzky B 15.00 40.00

5 John Tavares D 4.00 10.00
6 Steven Stamkos E 5.00 12.00
8 Sidney Crosby E 10.00 25.00
11 P.K. Subban E 3.00 8.00
13 Sergei Bobrovsky E 4.00 10.00
14 Evgeni Malkin E 5.00 12.00
16 Max Pacioretty E 2.50 6.00
17 Mario Lemieux E 10.00 25.00
21 Rick Nash E 2.50 6.00
22 Roberto Luongo B 4.00 10.00
27 David Backes E 1.50 4.00
28 Tuukka Rask E 3.00 8.00
29 Henrik Zetterberg E 3.00 8.00
30 Dominik Hasek A 4.00 10.00
31 Doug Gilmour E 3.00 8.00
32 Logan Couture E 3.00 8.00
33 Patrice Bergeron C 3.00 8.00
35 Cory Schneider C 2.50 6.00
36 Jim Howard E 3.00 8.00
37 Pekka Rinne E 2.50 6.00
38 Mike Richter B 2.50 6.00
40 Kari Lehtonen E 2.00 5.00
41 Jonathan Quick E 3.00 8.00
42 Carey Price E 5.00 12.00
43 Antti Niemi E 2.00 5.00
44 Eddie Lack E 2.00 5.00
46 Henrik Lundqvist E 6.00 15.00
47 Martin Brodeur E 6.00 15.00
52 Matt Moulson E 1.50 4.00
55 Dustin Brown C 2.50 6.00
62 Chris Kreider E 3.00 8.00
66 Nicklas Backstrom E 2.50 6.00
67 Steve Yzerman E 6.00 15.00
73 Andrew Ladd E 1.50 4.00
75 Jordan Eberle E 2.50 6.00
76 Jamie Benn E 2.50 6.00
77 Theoren Fleury E 3.00 8.00
81 Anze Kopitar E 4.00 10.00
84 Mark Messier E 5.00 12.00
85 Corey Perry D 4.00 10.00
88 Patrick Sharp E 2.50 6.00
91 Drew Doughty E 3.00 8.00
92 Alexander Ovechkin E 10.00 25.00
95 Phil Esposito B 4.00 10.00
96 Brent Seabrook D 1.50 4.00
98 Taylor Hall E 2.50 6.00
101 Bo Horvat 6.00 15.00
102 Laurent Brossoit 2.50 6.00
105 Oscar Klefbom 5.00 12.00
107 Patrik Nemeth 2.50 6.00
108 Joni Ortio 3.00 8.00
111 Alexander Wennberg 4.00 10.00
113 Griffin Reinhart 2.50 6.00
114 Sam Reinhart 10.00 25.00
116 Vincent Trocheck 5.00 12.00
119 Jake McCabe 2.50 6.00
123 Ty Rattie 2.50 6.00
125 Colton Sissons 2.50 6.00
130 Victor Rask 2.50 6.00
132 Alexander Khokhlachev 2.50 6.00
133 Marko Dano 2.50 6.00
136 Mirco Mueller 2.50 6.00
137 Vladislav Namestnikov 4.00 10.00
139 Jonathan Drouin 5.00 12.00
146 Ryan Sproul 2.50 6.00
147 Leon Draisaitl 12.00 30.00
150 Corban Knight 2.50 6.00
151 Bogdan Yakimov 2.50 6.00
153 Aaron Ekblad 6.00 15.00
154 Curtis Lazar 2.50 6.00
156 Teuvo Teravainen 4.00 10.00
157 Rocco Grimaldi 2.50 6.00
160 Stuart Percy 2.50 6.00
161 Tyler Wotherspoon 2.50 6.00
162 Teemu Pulkkinen 3.00 8.00
164 Damon Severson 2.50 6.00
166 Joey Hishon 2.50 6.00
167 Greg McKegg 2.00 5.00
171 Johnny Gaudreau 8.00 20.00
173 Evgeny Kuznetsov 6.00 15.00
177 Scott Mayfield 2.00 5.00
180 Mark Visentin 2.50 6.00
184 Chris Tierney 2.50 6.00
188 Andre Burakovsky 4.00 10.00
189 Brandon Gormley 2.50 6.00
192 Markus Granlund 4.00 10.00
200 Darnell Nurse 5.00 12.00

2014-15 SP Game Used Gold Spectrum Materials

1 Wayne Gretzky/25 30.00 80.00
2 Jakub Voracek/25 3.00 8.00
4 Gabriel Landeskog/99 2.50 6.00
5 John Tavares/50 6.00 15.00
8 Sidney Crosby/25 15.00 40.00
9 Phil Kessel/50 4.00 10.00
10 Jeff Carter/50 3.00 8.00
11 P.K. Subban/50 5.00 12.00
13 Sergei Bobrovsky/25 6.00 15.00
15 Jaromir Jagr/50 12.00 30.00
16 Max Pacioretty/50 4.00 10.00
17 Mario Lemieux/50 15.00 40.00
18 Erik Karlsson/50 5.00 12.00
20 Tyler Ennis/99 2.50 6.00
22 Roberto Luongo/25 6.00 15.00
26 Jonathan Bernier/25 3.00 8.00
27 David Backes/99 2.50 6.00
28 Tuukka Rask/50 5.00 12.00
29 Henrik Zetterberg/50 5.00 12.00
31 Doug Gilmour/99 5.00 12.00
32 Logan Couture/50 2.50 6.00
33 Patrice Bergeron/45 5.00 12.00
34 Steve Mason/50 3.00 8.00
35 Cory Schneider/99 4.00 10.00
36 Jim Howard/99 5.00 12.00
37 Pekka Rinne/50 4.00 10.00
38 Mike Richter/25 4.00 10.00
40 Kari Lehtonen/25 3.00 8.00
41 Jonathan Quick/50 5.00 12.00
42 Carey Price/99 8.00 20.00
43 Antti Niemi/50 2.50 6.00
44 Eddie Lack/99 3.00 8.00
45 Philipp Grubauer/50 4.00 10.00
46 Henrik Lundqvist/99 10.00 25.00
47 Martin Brodeur/50 10.00 25.00
50 Claude Giroux/99 4.00 10.00
51 Martin St. Louis/99 4.00 10.00
52 Matt Moulson/50 2.50 6.00
53 Blake Wheeler/90 4.00 10.00
55 Dustin Brown/99 4.00 10.00
57 Peter Forsberg/75 8.00 20.00
58 James van Riemsdyk/99 3.00 8.00
59 Brandon Saad/50 3.00 8.00
60 Ryan Suter/99 3.00 8.00
61 Alexander Steen/50 2.50 6.00
62 Chris Kreider/25 5.00 12.00
63 Jonathan Toews/25 6.00 15.00
64 Shane Doan/99 3.00 8.00
65 Jason Spezza/50 4.00 10.00
66 Nicklas Backstrom/25 4.00 10.00
67 Steve Yzerman/84 10.00 25.00
68 James Neal/90 2.50 6.00
69 Bryan Little/99 4.00 10.00
71 Brandon Dubinsky/90 2.50 6.00
73 Andrew Ladd/99 2.50 6.00
74 Ryan Getzlaf/25 4.00 10.00
75 Jordan Eberle/25 4.00 10.00
76 Jamie Benn/50 4.00 10.00
77 Theoren Fleury/25 5.00 12.00
78 Pavel Datsyuk/25 6.00 15.00
79 Mats Sundin/75 4.00 10.00
80 Eric Staal/75 5.00 12.00
81 Anze Kopitar/75 6.00 15.00
82 Brendan Gallagher/50 4.00 10.00
83 Zach Parise/50 4.00 10.00
84 Mark Messier/25 8.00 20.00
86 Pavel Bure/50 4.00 10.00
87 Guy Lafleur/99 5.00 12.00
88 Patrick Sharp/99 4.00 10.00
89 Matt Duchene/50 4.00 10.00
90 Teemu Selanne/50 8.00 20.00
91 Drew Doughty/99 5.00 12.00
92 Alexander Ovechkin/50 15.00 40.00
96 Brent Seabrook/25 2.50 6.00
97 Shea Weber/50 3.00 8.00
98 Taylor Hall/50 4.00 10.00
100 Ryan Johansen/50 3.00 8.00
101 Bo Horvat/99 10.00 25.00
102 Laurent Brossoit/99 4.00 10.00
105 Oscar Klefbom/99 8.00 20.00
107 Patrik Nemeth/99 4.00 10.00
108 Joni Ortio/99 5.00 12.00
111 Alexander Wennberg/99 6.00 15.00
113 Griffin Reinhart/99 4.00 10.00
114 Sam Reinhart/99 15.00 40.00
116 Vincent Trocheck/99 8.00 20.00
119 Jake McCabe/99 4.00 10.00
123 Ty Rattie/99 6.00 15.00
125 Colton Sissons/99 4.00 10.00
130 Victor Rask/99 4.00 10.00
132 Alexander Khokhlachev/99 4.00 10.00
133 Marko Dano/99 6.00 15.00
136 Mirco Mueller/99 4.00 10.00
137 Vladislav Namestnikov/99 6.00 15.00
139 Jonathan Drouin/99 8.00 20.00
146 Ryan Sproul/99 4.00 10.00
147 Leon Draisaitl/99 20.00 50.00
150 Corban Knight/99 4.00 10.00
151 Bogdan Yakimov/99 4.00 10.00
153 Aaron Ekblad/99 10.00 25.00
154 Curtis Lazar/99 4.00 10.00
156 Teuvo Teravainen/99 6.00 15.00
157 Rocco Grimaldi/99 4.00 10.00
160 Stuart Percy/99 4.00 10.00
161 Tyler Wotherspoon/99 4.00 10.00
164 Damon Severson/99 4.00 10.00
166 Joey Hishon/99 5.00 12.00
167 Greg McKegg/99 3.00 8.00
171 Johnny Gaudreau/99 12.00 30.00
173 Evgeny Kuznetsov/99 10.00 25.00
177 Scott Mayfield/99 3.00 8.00
180 Mark Visentin/99 4.00 10.00
184 Chris Tierney/99 4.00 10.00
188 Andre Burakovsky/99 6.00 15.00
189 Brandon Gormley/99 4.00 10.00
192 Markus Granlund/99 6.00 15.00
200 Darnell Nurse/99 8.00 20.00

2014-15 SP Game Used Heritage Classic Materials Net Cord

HCNCAB Alexandre Burrows 10.00 25.00
HCNCAE Alexander Edler 10.00 25.00
HCNCCC Cody Ceci 10.00 25.00
HCNCCG Colin Greening 10.00 25.00
HCNCCM Clarke MacArthur 10.00 25.00
HCNCCN Chris Neil 10.00 25.00
HCNCDH Dan Hamhuis 10.00 25.00
HCNCDS Daniel Sedin 20.00 50.00
HCNCEC Erik Condra 15.00 40.00
HCNCEG Eric Gryba 15.00 40.00
HCNCEK Erik Karlsson 20.00 50.00
HCNCEL Eddie Lack 12.00 30.00
HCNCHS Henrik Sedin 20.00 50.00
HCNCJG Jason Garrison 10.00 25.00
HCNCJH Jannik Hansen 12.00 30.00
HCNCJS Jason Spezza 15.00 40.00
HCNCMM Milan Michalek 10.00 25.00
HCNCRK Ryan Kesler 15.00 40.00
HCNCZK Zack Kassian 10.00 25.00
HCNCZS Zack Smith 10.00 25.00

2014-15 SP Game Used Inked Rookie Sweaters

IRSAB Andre Burakovsky 12.00 30.00
IRSAE Aaron Ekblad 15.00 40.00
IRSAK Alexander Khokhlachev 6.00 15.00
IRSAW Alexander Wennberg 8.00 20.00
IRSBG Brandon Gormley 5.00 12.00
IRSCK Corban Knight 6.00 15.00
IRSCL Curtis Lazar 12.00 30.00
IRSCT Chris Tierney 6.00 15.00
IRSDS Damon Severson 10.00 25.00
IRSEK Evgeny Kuznetsov 12.00 30.00
IRSGM Greg McKegg 5.00 12.00
IRSGR Griffin Reinhart 10.00 25.00
IRSJD Jonathan Drouin 15.00 40.00
IRSJG Johnny Gaudreau 60.00 150.00
IRSJH Joey Hishon 6.00 15.00
IRSJM Jake McCabe 8.00 20.00
IRSLB Laurent Brossoit 6.00 15.00
IRSLD Leon Draisaitl 25.00 60.00
IRSMD Marko Dano 10.00 25.00
IRSMM Mirco Mueller 15.00 40.00
IRSMV Mark Visentin 5.00 12.00
IRSRS Ryan Sproul 6.00 15.00
IRSSP Stuart Percy 6.00 15.00
IRSSR Sam Reinhart 15.00 40.00
IRSTR Ty Rattie 6.00 15.00
IRSTT Teuvo Teravainen 40.00 80.00
IRSVN Vladislav Namestnikov 8.00 20.00
IRSVT Vincent Trocheck 10.00 25.00

2014-15 SP Game Used Inked Rookie Sweaters Patches

*PATCH/49: .6X TO 1.5X BASIC JERSEY/149
IRSJG Johnny Gaudreau 125.00 300.00

2014-15 SP Game Used Inked Sweaters

ISAK Anze Kopitar/50 12.00 30.00
ISAO Adam Oates/50 8.00 20.00
ISBA David Backes/99 5.00 12.00
ISBH Brett Hull/25 15.00 40.00
ISCG Claude Giroux/99 8.00 20.00
ISCK Chris Kreider/99 10.00 25.00
ISDB Dustin Brown/99 8.00 20.00
ISDG Doug Gilmour/99 10.00 25.00
ISJB Jamie Benn/50 8.00 20.00
ISKL Kari Lehtonen/99 6.00 15.00
ISPE Phil Esposito/25 12.00 30.00
ISPF Peter Forsberg/50 15.00 40.00
ISPR Patrick Roy/25 50.00 125.00
ISPS Patrick Sharp/99 8.00 20.00
ISRB Ray Bourque/50 12.00 30.00
ISSC Sidney Crosby/25 80.00 200.00
ISSM Steve Mason/99 6.00 15.00
ISSY Steve Yzerman/25 30.00 80.00

2014-15 SP Game Used Stadium Series Materials Game Used Pucks

SSGUPBN Brock Nelson 20.00 50.00
SSGUPCP Corey Perry 30.00 80.00
SSGUPDC Daniel Carcillo 12.00 30.00
SSGUPDS Derek Stepan 12.00 30.00
SSGUPHL Henrik Lundqvist 50.00 125.00
SSGUPJQ Jonathan Quick 25.00 60.00
SSGUPMZ Mats Zuccarello 20.00 50.00
SSGUPPE Patrik Elias 20.00 50.00
SSGUPRG Ryan Getzlaf 20.00 50.00

2014-15 SP Game Used Stadium Series Materials Jerseys

SSAG Andy Greene E 2.50 6.00
SSAH Adam Henrique C 3.00 8.00
SSBB Bryan Bickell C 2.50 6.00
SSBG Brian Gibbons C 2.50 6.00
SSBL Ben Lovejoy E 2.50 6.00
SSBS Brent Seabrook B 2.50 6.00
SSCK Chris Kunitz D 4.00 10.00
SSCS Cory Schneider E 4.00 10.00
SSDB Damien Brunner A 2.50 6.00
SSDK Duncan Keith E 3.00 8.00
SSDM Dominic Moore E 2.50 6.00
SSDS Derek Stepan E 2.50 6.00
SSFN Frans Nielsen C 2.50 6.00
SSFO Cam Fowler C 4.00 10.00
SSFR Colin Fraser E 2.50 6.00
SSHL Hampus Lindholm C 2.50 6.00
SSJM Jake Muzzin E 2.50 6.00
SSJN Jordan Nolan D 2.50 6.00
SSJT John Tavares E 6.00 15.00
SSJZ Jeff Zatkoff E 3.00 8.00
SSKC Kyle Clifford D 2.50 6.00
SSKK Kevin Klein E 2.50 6.00
SSMD Matt Donovan E 2.50 6.00
SSMF Matt Frattin E 3.00 8.00
SSMG Michael Grabner A 3.00 8.00
SSMK Marcus Kruger D 2.50 6.00
SSMN Matt Niskanen D 3.00 8.00
SSMZ Mats Zuccarello D 4.00 10.00
SSNB Nick Bonino D 2.50 6.00
SSOM Olli Maatta C 2.50 6.00
SSSA Brandon Saad B 3.00 8.00
SSSG Stephen Gionta E 2.50 6.00
SSTH Thomas Hickey E 2.50 6.00

2014-15 SP Game Used Stadium Series Materials Net Cord Dodger Stadium

LANCAC Andrew Cogliano 8.00 20.00
LANCAK Anze Kopitar 20.00 50.00
LANCCF Cam Fowler 12.00 30.00
LANCCP Corey Perry 20.00 50.00
LANCDB Dustin Brown 12.00 30.00
LANCDD Drew Doughty 15.00 40.00
LANCFB Francois Beauchemin 8.00 20.00
LANCJC Jeff Carter 10.00 25.00
LANCJH Jonas Hiller 10.00 25.00
LANCJM Jake Muzzin 10.00 25.00
LANCJQ Jonathan Quick 15.00 40.00
LANCJS Jarret Stoll 10.00 25.00
LANCJW Justin Williams 10.00 25.00
LANCKP Kyle Palmieri 10.00 25.00
LANCMB Matt Beleskey 8.00 20.00
LANCMR Mike Richards 10.00 25.00
LANCNB Nick Bonino 8.00 20.00
LANCRG Ryan Getzlaf 15.00 40.00
LANCSK Saku Koivu 12.00 30.00
LANCSV Slava Voynov 12.00 30.00
LANCTS Teemu Selanne 25.00 60.00

2014-15 SP Game Used Stadium Series Materials Net Cord Soldier Field

SSCHBB Bryan Bickell 8.00 20.00
SSCHBO Brooks Orpik 8.00 20.00
SSCHBS Brandon Sutter 8.00 20.00
SSCHCC Corey Crawford 15.00 40.00
SSCHCK Chris Kunitz 12.00 30.00
SSCHDK Duncan Keith 10.00 25.00
SSCHEM Evgeni Malkin 25.00 60.00
SSCHJJ Jussi Jokinen 8.00 20.00
SSCHJN James Neal 8.00 20.00
SSCHJT Jonathan Toews 20.00 50.00
SSCHKV Kris Versteeg 8.00 20.00
SSCHMF Marc-Andre Fleury 25.00 60.00
SSCHMH Marian Hossa 8.00 20.00
SSCHMR Michal Rozsival 8.00 20.00
SSCHNL Nick Leddy 8.00 20.00
SSCHOM Olli Maatta 8.00 20.00
SSCHPK Patrick Kane 25.00 60.00
SSCHPS Patrick Sharp 12.00 30.00
SSCHSA Brandon Saad 10.00 25.00
SSCHSC Sidney Crosby 50.00 125.00
SSCHSD Simon Despres 12.00 30.00

2014-15 SP Game Used Stanley Cup Finals Materials Game Used Pucks

SCFGUPAK Anze Kopitar G3 80.00 200.00
SCFGUPAM Alec Martinez G5 30.00 80.00
SCFGUPBB Bryan Boyle G5 30.00 80.00
SCFGUPCH Carl Hagelin G1 30.00 80.00
SCFGUPDD Drew Doughty G1 60.00 150.00
SCFGUPHL Henrik Lundqvist G4 125.00 300.00
SCFGUPJC Jeff Carter G3 40.00 100.00
SCFGUPJQ Jonathan Quick G1 60.00 150.00
SCFGUPJW Justin Williams G1 40.00 100.00
SCFGUPLU Henrik Lundqvist G5 125.00 300.00
SCFGUPMG Marian Gaborik G5 50.00 125.00
SCFGUPMS Martin St. Louis G4 50.00 125.00
SCFGUPQU Jonathan Quick G3 60.00 150.00
SCFGUPTT Tyler Toffoli G5 50.00 125.00
SCFGUPWI Justin Williams G5 40.00 100.00

2014-15 SP Game Used Stanley Cup Finals Materials Net Cord

SCNCAK Anze Kopitar 30.00 80.00
SCNCAM Alec Martinez 12.00 30.00
SCNCAS Anton Stralman 12.00 30.00
SCNCBB Brian Boyle 12.00 30.00
SCNCBP Benoit Pouliot 12.00 30.00
SCNCBR Brad Richards 20.00 50.00
SCNCCH Carl Hagelin 12.00 30.00
SCNCCK Chris Kreider 25.00 60.00
SCNCDB Dustin Brown 20.00 50.00
SCNCDD Drew Doughty 25.00 60.00
SCNCDE Derick Brassard 12.00 30.00
SCNCDG Daniel Girardi 12.00 30.00
SCNCDK Dwight King 12.00 30.00
SCNCDM Dominic Moore 12.00 30.00
SCNCDO Derek Dorsett 12.00 30.00
SCNCDS Derek Stepan 12.00 30.00
SCNCGA Marian Gaborik 20.00 50.00
SCNCHL Henrik Lundqvist 50.00 120.00
SCNCJC Jeff Carter 15.00 40.00
SCNCJM Jake Muzzin 20.00 50.00
SCNCJN Jordan Nolan 20.00 50.00
SCNCJQ Jonathan Quick 25.00 60.00
SCNCJS Jarret Stoll 15.00 40.00
SCNCJW Justin Williams 12.00 30.00
SCNCKC Kyle Clifford 12.00 30.00
SCNCKK Kevin Klein 12.00 30.00
SCNCMG Matt Greene 12.00 30.00
SCNCMO John Moore 12.00 30.00
SCNCMR Mike Richards 15.00 40.00
SCNCMS Martin St. Louis 20.00 50.00
SCNCMZ Mats Zuccarello 20.00 50.00
SCNCRD Raphael Diaz 12.00 30.00
SCNCRM Ryan McDonagh 12.00 30.00
SCNCRN Rick Nash 20.00 50.00
SCNCRR Robyn Regehr 12.00 30.00
SCNCST Marc Staal 12.00 30.00
SCNCSV Slava Voynov 12.00 30.00
SCNCTL Trevor Lewis 12.00 30.00
SCNCTP Tanner Pearson 12.00 30.00
SCNCTT Tyler Toffoli 20.00 50.00
SCNCWM Willie Mitchell 12.00 30.00

2014-15 SP Game Used Winter Classic Materials Game Used Pucks

WCGUPDA Daniel Alfredsson 15.00 40.00
WCGUPJB Jonathan Bernier 12.00 30.00
WCGUPJR James van Riemsdyk 12.00 30.00

2014-15 SP Game Used Winter Classic Materials Jerseys

*PATCH/99: .6X TO 1.5X BASIC INSERTS
WCCF Cody Franson A 5.00 12.00
WCDC David Clarkson A 5.00 12.00
WCJB Jonathan Bernier B 6.00 15.00
WCNK Nazem Kadri B 10.00 25.00

2014-15 SP Game Used Winter Classic Materials Net Cord

WCBS Brendan Smith 6.00 15.00
WCCF Cody Franson 6.00 15.00
WCDA Daniel Alfredsson 10.00 25.00
WCDC David Clarkson 6.00 15.00
WCDD Danny DeKeyser 6.00 15.00
WCDP Dion Phaneuf 8.00 20.00
WCGN Gustav Nyquist 6.00 15.00
WCHZ Henrik Zetterberg 12.00 30.00
WCJA Justin Abdelkader 8.00 20.00
WCJH Jim Howard 12.00 30.00
WCJL Joffrey Lupul 6.00 15.00
WCJV James van Riemsdyk 8.00 20.00
WCNK Niklas Kronwall 8.00 20.00
WCKU Nikolai Kulemin 6.00 15.00
WCMR Morgan Rielly 10.00 25.00
WCNK Nazem Kadri 12.00 30.00
WCPD Pavel Datsyuk 15.00 40.00
WCPK Phil Kessel 10.00 25.00
WCTB Tyler Bozak 6.00 15.00
WCTT Tomas Tatar 6.00 15.00

2015-16 SP Game Used

1 Wayne Gretzky/99 15.00 30.00
2 Keith Yandle/93 3.00 8.00
3 Jakub Voracek/93 4.00 10.00
4 Steven Stamkos/91 10.00 25.00
5 John Tavares/91 8.00 20.00
6 Vladimir Tarasenko/91 6.00 15.00
7 Tyler Seguin/91 8.00 20.00
8 Jason Spezza/90 5.00 12.00
9 Brent Burns/88 4.00 10.00
10 Patrick Kane/88 10.00 25.00
11 David Pastrnak/88 12.00 30.00
12 Sidney Crosby/87 15.00 30.00
13 Nikita Kucherov/86 10.00 25.00
14 Marian Hossa/81 5.00 12.00
15 Phil Kessel/81 5.00 12.00
16 Phil Esposito/77 8.00 20.00
17 Victor Hedman/77 6.00 15.00
18 P.K. Subban/76 8.00 20.00
19 John Carlson/74 5.00 12.00
20 Tyler Toffoli/73 5.00 12.00
21 Sergei Bobrovsky/72 8.00 20.00
22 Evgeni Malkin/71 8.00 20.00
23 Nick Foligno/71 4.00 10.00
24 Jaromir Jagr/68 15.00 40.00
25 Max Pacioretty/67 5.00 12.00
26 Erik Karlsson/65 6.00 15.00
27 Mikael Granlund/64 4.00 10.00
28 Mark Stone/61 6.00 15.00
29 Roman Josi/59 5.00 12.00
30 Mark Scheifele/55 8.00 20.00
31 Jeff Skinner/53 6.00 15.00
32 Bo Horvat/53 6.00 15.00
33 David Krejci/46 6.00 15.00
34 Jonathan Bernier/45 5.00 12.00
35 Morgan Rielly/44 6.00 15.00
36 Henrik Zetterberg/40 8.00 20.00
37 Tuukka Rask/40 8.00 20.00
38 Logan Couture/39 8.00 20.00
39 Steve Mason/35 5.00 12.00
40 Cory Schneider/35 6.00 15.00
41 Pekka Rinne/35 6.00 15.00
42 Patrick Roy/33 25.00 50.00
43 Henrik Sedin/33 8.00 20.00
44 Zdeno Chara/33 10.00 25.00
45 Jonathan Quick/32 10.00 25.00
46 Carey Price/31 20.00 40.00
47 Frederik Andersen/31 10.00 25.00
48 Ryan Miller/30 15.00 30.00
49 Ben Bishop/30 6.00 15.00
50 Andrew Hammond/30 10.00 25.00
51 Henrik Lundqvist/30 20.00 50.00
52 Marc-Andre Fleury/29 15.00 40.00
53 Nathan MacKinnon/29 30.00 80.00
54 Claude Giroux/28 8.00 20.00
55 Ryan McDonagh/27 8.00 20.00
56 Anders Lee/27 8.00 20.00
57 Alex Galchenyuk/27 12.00 30.00
58 Nick Bjugstad/27 5.00 12.00
59 Blake Wheeler/26 8.00 20.00
60 Jiri Hudler/24 6.00 15.00
61 Sam Reinhart/23 15.00 40.00
62 Sean Monahan/23 5.00 12.00
63 Oliver Ekman-Larsson/23 8.00 20.00
64 Daniel Sedin/22 8.00 20.00
65 Peter Forsberg/21 15.00 40.00
66 James van Riemsdyk/21 6.00 15.00
67 Tomas Tatar/21 5.00 12.00
68 Derek Stepan/21 5.00 12.00
69 Ryan Johansen/19 8.00 20.00
70 Nicklas Backstrom/19 12.00 30.00
71 Jonathan Toews/19 30.00 60.00
72 Ondrej Palat/18 8.00 20.00
73 Ryan Strome/18 10.00 25.00
74 Jaden Schwartz/17 12.00 30.00
75 Ryan Kesler/17 10.00 25.00
76 Jason Zucker/16 10.00 25.00
77 Elias Lindholm/16 10.00 25.00
101 Rasmus Rissanen/62 RC 6.00 15.00
102 Anton Slepyshev/42 RC 8.00 20.00
103 Curtis Hamilton/70 RC 10.00 25.00
104 Antoine Bibeau/30 RC 15.00 40.00
105 Artemi Panarin/72 RC 150.00 300.00
106 Andreas Athanasiou/72 RC 20.00 40.00
107 Ben Hutton/27 RC 15.00 40.00
108 Keegan Lowe/45 RC 12.00 30.00
109 Stefan Noesen/64 RC 6.00 15.00
110 Brian O'Neill/18 RC 15.00 40.00
111 Stanislav Galiev/49 RC 12.00 30.00
112 Viktor Svedberg/27 RC 12.00 30.00
113 Colin Miller/48 RC 10.00 25.00
114 Oscar Dansk/35 RC 20.00 50.00
115 Colton Parayko/55 RC 25.00 60.00
116 Henrik Samuelsson/55 RC 8.00 20.00
117 Connor Brickley/86 RC 8.00 20.00
118 Josh Anderson/53 RC 25.00 60.00
119 Jordan Oesterle/82 RC 6.00 15.00
120 Oscar Lindberg/24 RC 20.00 50.00
121 Daniel Sprong/41 RC 75.00 125.00
122 Dylan DeMelo/74 RC 8.00 20.00
123 Viktor Arvidsson/38 RC 15.00 40.00
124 Dylan Larkin/71 RC 150.00 300.00
125 Malcolm Subban/70 RC 35.00 60.00
126 Evgeny Medvedev/82 RC 20.00 40.00
127 Jack Eichel/15 RC 1200.00 1800.00
128 Jared McCann/91 RC 12.00 30.00
129 Brendan Ranford/64 RC 8.00 20.00
130 Mike Lee/30 RC 10.00 25.00
131 Logan Shaw/48 RC 20.00 40.00
133 Joonas Donskoi/27 RC 40.00 80.00
134 Mackenzie Skapski/70 RC 12.00 30.00
135 Jordan Weal/19 RC 20.00 40.00
136 Jean-Francois Berube/30 RC 12.00 30.00
137 Casey Bailey/37 RC 15.00 40.00
138 Devin Shore/17 RC 40.00 80.00
139 Tyler Bunz/34 RC 15.00 40.00
141 Nick Shore/21 RC 8.00 20.00
142 David Musil/87 RC 8.00 20.00
143 Slater Koekkoek/29 RC 10.00 25.00
144 Max Domi/16 RC 500.00 800.00
145 Tanner Kero/36 RC 15.00 40.00
146 Matt Puempel/26 RC 12.00 30.00
147 Mike Condon/39 RC 75.00 125.00
148 Louis Domingue/35 RC 30.00 60.00
149 Mikko Rantanen/96 RC 40.00 80.00
150 Nicolas Petan/19 RC 60.00 150.00
151 Luke Witkowski/53 RC 8.00 20.00
152 Brett Kulak/61 RC 8.00 20.00
153 Ronalds Kenins/41 RC 8.00 20.00
154 Mark Alt/39 RC 10.00 25.00
155 Robby Fabbri/15 RC 75.00 150.00
156 Sergei Plotnikov/61 RC 6.00 15.00
157 Nikolaj Ehlers/27 RC 175.00 300.00
158 Erik Gustafsson/52 RC 40.00 80.00
159 Sergey Kalinin/51 RC 8.00 20.00
160 Petr Straka/51 RC 40.00 80.00
161 Tyler Randell/64 RC 10.00 25.00
162 Danny Biega/41 RC 8.00 20.00
163 Connor Hellebuyck/37 RC 50.00 100.00
164 Brian Ferlin/68 RC 8.00 20.00
165 Joonas Kemppainen/41 RC 8.00 20.00
166 Alex Biega/55 RC 8.00 20.00
167 Sam Brittain/31 RC 15.00 40.00
168 Jake Virtanen/18 RC 500.00 750.00
171 Ryan Hartman/38 RC 20.00 50.00
172 Brock McGinn/23 RC 40.00 80.00
173 Sam Bennett/93 RC 30.00 80.00
174 Ryan Sproul/25 RC 12.00 30.00
175 David Wolf/45 RC 8.00 20.00
178 Tommy Cross/56 RC 10.00 25.00
179 Nick Cousins/52 RC 12.00 30.00
180 Jacob de la Rose/25 RC 15.00 40.00
181 Kyle Baun/39 RC 15.00 40.00
182 Daniil Tarasov/71 RC 12.00 30.00
184 Vincent Hinostroza/48 RC 8.00 20.00
185 Emile Poirier/57 RC 10.00 25.00
187 Chris Wideman/45 RC 12.00 30.00
188 Chris Driedger/32 RC 12.00 30.00
189 Nikolay Goldobin/82 RC 10.00 25.00
190 Chandler Stephenson/18 RC 30.00 60.00
191 Andrew Miller/58 RC 10.00 25.00
192 Ryan Bourque/25 RC 12.00 30.00
193 Brett Pesce/54 RC 10.00 25.00
194 Raman Hrabarenka/34 RC 15.00 40.00
195 Brendan Gaunce/50 RC 15.00 40.00
196 Max McCormick/89 RC 8.00 20.00
197 Connor McDavid/97 RC 1000.00 2500.00
198 Kevin Fiala/56 RC 15.00 40.00
199 Linus Ullmark/35 RC 30.00 80.00
200 Matt O'Connor/29 RC 25.00 60.00
201 Brett Kulak/61 RC 10.00 25.00
202 Michael Mersch/49 RC 20.00 50.00
203 Dennis Rasmussen/70 RC 25.00 60.00
205 Taylor Leier/58 RC 20.00 50.00
206 Marek Langhamer/30 RC 25.00 60.00
207 Conor Sheary/43 RC 50.00 125.00
208 Phil Di Giuseppe/34 RC 20.00 50.00
209 Garret Sparks/31 RC 300.00 400.00
210 Adam Pelech/50 RC 15.00 40.00
211 Joseph Blandisi/64 RC 20.00 50.00
212 Anthony Stolarz/65 RC 50.00 125.00
213 Brady Skjei/76 RC 40.00 100.00
214 Charles Hudon/54 RC 20.00 50.00
215 Michael Keranen/36 RC 15.00 40.00
216 Shea Theodore/53 RC 60.00 150.00
217 Mike McCarron/34 RC 60.00 150.00
218 Gustav Olofsson/23 RC 40.00 100.00
219 Fredrik Claesson/49 RC 30.00 80.00
220 Frank Vatrano/72 RC 60.00 150.00
221 Markus Hannikainen/33 RC 60.00 150.00
222 Jujhar Khaira/54 RC 15.00 40.00
223 Ryan Carpenter/40 RC 80.00 150.00
224 Zachary Fucale/30 RC 80.00 150.00
225 Jaccob Slavin/74 RC 30.00 80.00
226 Alexandre Grenier/65 RC 30.00 80.00
227 Andreas Martinsen/27 RC 25.00 60.00
228 Andrey Pedan/29 RC 30.00 80.00
229 Nick Ritchie/37 RC 300.00 400.00
230 Christoph Bertschy/47 RC 80.00 150.00
231 Daniel Carr/43 RC 40.00 100.00
232 Byron Froese/56 RC 15.00 40.00
233 Laurent Dauphin/76 RC 20.00 50.00
234 Joonas Korpisalo/70 RC 30.00 80.00
235 Matt Murray/30 RC 500.00 700.00
236 Ryan Dzingel/43 RC 100.00 200.00

2015-16 SP Game Used '14 Stadium Series Materials Net Cord Soldier Field

SSNCBB Bryan Bickell 8.00 20.00
SSNCEM Evgeni Malkin 25.00 60.00
SSNCJN James Neal 8.00 20.00
SSNCJT Jonathan Toews 30.00 60.00
SSNCKV Kris Versteeg 8.00 20.00
SSNCPK Patrick Kane 30.00 60.00
SSNCPS Patrick Sharp 15.00 40.00
SSNCSC Sidney Crosby 30.00 60.00

2015-16 SP Game Used '14 Stadium Series Materials Net Cord Yankee Stadium

SSNCBN Brock Nelson Jan.29 12.00 30.00
SSNCBP Benoit Pouliot Jan.29 8.00 20.00
SSNCCH Carl Hagelin Jan.25 15.00 40.00
SSNCDC Daniel Carcillo Jan.29 8.00 20.00
SSNCDM Dominic Moore Jan.25 15.00 40.00
SSNCDS Derek Stepan Jan.25 25.00 50.00
SSNCEN Evgeni Nabokov Jan.29 12.00 30.00
SSNCJJ Jaromir Jagr Jan.25 40.00 80.00
SSNCMS Marc Staal Jan.25 8.00 20.00
SSNCMZ Mats Zuccarello Jan.25 25.00 50.00
SSNCPE Patrik Elias Jan.25 8.00 20.00
SSNCRN Rick Nash Jan.25 8.00 20.00
SSNCTZ Travis Zajac Jan.25 8.00 20.00
SSNCHL1 Henrik Lundqvist Jan.25 30.00 80.00
SSNCHL2 Henrik Lundqvist Jan.29 40.00 80.00

2015-16 SP Game Used '14 Winter Classic Materials Net Cord

WCNCDA Daniel Alfredsson 12.00 30.00
WCNCJA Justin Abdelkader 15.00 40.00
WCNCJB Jonathan Bernier 12.00 30.00
WCNCJL Joffrey Lupul 8.00 20.00
WCNCJV James van Riemsdyk 10.00 25.00
WCNCPD Pavel Datsyuk 15.00 40.00
WCNCTB Tyler Bozak 8.00 20.00

2015-16 SP Game Used All-Star Skills Fabrics

AS1 Bobby Ryan E 2.50 6.00
AS2 Jakub Voracek C 2.50 6.00
AS3 Zemgus Girgensons E 2.50 6.00
AS4 Roberto Luongo E 5.00 12.00
AS5 Justin Faulk E 2.50 6.00
AS6 Steven Stamkos B 5.00 12.00
AS7 Phil Kessel E 3.00 8.00
AS8 Filip Forsberg D 5.00 12.00
AS9 Jonathan Drouin D 2.50 6.00
AS10 Vladimir Tarasenko D 4.00 10.00
AS11 Drew Doughty E 2.50 6.00
AS12 Jaroslav Halak E 3.00 8.00
AS13 Anze Kopitar E 3.00 8.00
AS14 Patrice Bergeron E 4.00 10.00
AS15 Tyler Seguin E 4.00 10.00
AS16 Kevin Shattenkirk E 2.00 5.00
AS17 Radim Vrbata E 2.00 5.00
AS18 Dustin Byfuglien E 3.00 8.00
AS19 Carey Price E 6.00 15.00
AS20 Corey Crawford E 4.00 10.00
AS21 Patrik Elias E 3.00 8.00
AS22 Jiri Sekac E 2.00 5.00
AS23 Ryan Nugent-Hopkins E 4.00 10.00
AS24 Marc-Andre Fleury E 6.00 15.00
AS25 Shea Weber E 2.50 6.00
AS26 Brian Elliott E 2.50 6.00
AS27 Claude Giroux E 3.00 8.00
AS28 Rick Nash D 3.00 8.00
AS29 Alexander Ovechkin E 5.00 12.00
AS31 Mike Hoffman E 2.00 5.00
AS32 Duncan Keith E 3.00 8.00
AS33 Oliver Ekman-Larsson E 3.00 8.00
AS34 Mark Giordano E 3.00 8.00
AS36 Brent Seabrook E 2.00 5.00
AS37 Brent Burns E 3.00 8.00
AS38 Nick Foligno D 2.50 6.00
AS39 Aaron Ekblad E 4.00 10.00
AS41 Ryan Getzlaf A 5.00 12.00
AS43 Ryan Suter D 2.50 6.00
AS44 Ryan Johansen E 2.50 6.00

2015-16 SP Game Used All-Star Skills Fabrics Patch

*PATCH/35: 1X TO 2.5X BASIC JSY
AS9 Jonathan Drouin 5.00 12.00
AS20 Corey Crawford 8.00 20.00
AS30 John Tavares 10.00 25.00
AS35 Jonathan Toews 10.00 25.00
AS40 Patrick Kane 15.00 40.00
AS42 Johnny Gaudreau 10.00 25.00

2015-16 SP Game Used All-Star Skills Dual Fabrics

*PATCH/35: .6X TO 1.5X BASIC DUAL
AS21 N.Foligno/J.Toews 5.00 12.00
AS22 N.Foligno/R.Johansen 3.00 8.00
AS23 S.Stamkos/J.Drouin 8.00 20.00
AS24 J.Tavares/J.Halak 6.00 15.00
AS25 R.Luongo/A.Ekblad 6.00 15.00
AS26 Gaudreau/M.Giordano 6.00 15.00
AS27 Tarasenko/Shattenkirk 5.00 12.00
AS28 D.Keith/B.Seabrook 3.00 8.00
AS29 D.Doughty/A.Kopitar 6.00 15.00
AS210 S.Weber/F.Forsberg 6.00 15.00
AS211 J.Voracek/C.Giroux 4.00 10.00
AS212 B.Ryan/M.Hoffman 3.00 8.00
AS213 J.Toews/P.Kane 8.00 20.00
AS214 J.Tavares/J.Voracek 6.00 15.00
AS215 P.Bergeron/P.Elias 5.00 12.00
AS216 R.Getzlaf/A.Kopitar 6.00 15.00
AS217 J.Tavares/R.Nash 6.00 15.00
AS218 R.Suter/K.Shattenkirk 3.00 8.00
AS219 D.Byfuglien/J.Faulk 4.00 10.00
AS220 B.Elliott/C.Crawford 5.00 12.00
AS221 M.Fleury/R.Luongo 8.00 20.00

2015-16 SP Game Used All-Star Skills Quad Fabrics

*PATCH/15: 1.2X TO 3X BASIC QUAD
AS41 Toews/Gtzlf/Tvres/Nash 8.00 20.00
AS42 Kane/Stmkos/Ovch/Kptr 20.00 50.00
AS43 Webr/Sbrk/Ekblad/Suter 6.00 15.00
AS44 Dghty/Keith/Burns/Byfgln 6.00 15.00
AS45 Crwfrd/Halk/Prce/M.Flry 10.00 25.00
AS46 Tvres/Trsnk/Frsbrg/Gdru 8.00 20.00
AS47 Ovch/Stmks/Tws/Tvres 20.00 50.00
AS48 Gtzal/Segn/Kane/Kpitr 10.00 25.00
AS49 Frsbrg/Gdru/Grgns/RNH 8.00 20.00
AS410 Trsnko/Tvrs/Grx/RNH 8.00 20.00

2015-16 SP Game Used All-Star Skills Relics

*GOLD/49: .5X TO 1.2X BASIC JSY/125
ASAE Aaron Ekblad 5.00 12.00
ASAK Anze Kopitar 6.00 15.00
ASAO Alexander Ovechkin 6.00 15.00
ASBB Brent Burns 4.00 10.00
ASBE Brian Elliott 3.00 8.00
ASBR Bobby Ryan 3.00 8.00
ASBS Brent Seabrook 2.50 6.00
ASCC Corey Crawford 5.00 12.00
ASCG Claude Giroux 4.00 10.00
ASCP Carey Price 10.00 25.00
ASDB Dustin Byfuglien 4.00 10.00
ASDD Drew Doughty 5.00 12.00
ASDK Duncan Keith 5.00 12.00
ASFF Filip Forsberg 6.00 15.00
ASJD Jonathan Drouin 3.00 8.00
ASJF Justin Faulk 3.00 8.00
ASJG Johnny Gaudreau 6.00 15.00
ASJH Jaroslav Halak 4.00 10.00
ASJS Jiri Sekac 2.50 6.00
ASJV Jakub Voracek 3.00 8.00
ASKE Phil Kessel 4.00 10.00
ASKS Kevin Shattenkirk 2.50 6.00
ASMF Marc-Andre Fleury 8.00 20.00
ASMG Mark Giordano 3.00 8.00
ASMH Mike Hoffman 2.50 6.00
ASNA Rick Nash 4.00 10.00
ASNF Nick Foligno 3.00 8.00
ASOE Oliver Ekman-Larsson 3.00 8.00
ASPB Patrice Bergeron 5.00 12.00
ASPE Patrik Elias 3.00 8.00
ASRG Ryan Getzlaf 4.00 10.00
ASRJ Ryan Johansen 3.00 8.00
ASRL Roberto Luongo 6.00 15.00
ASRN Ryan Nugent-Hopkins 5.00 12.00
ASRS Ryan Suter 3.00 8.00
ASRV Radim Vrbata 2.50 6.00
ASSS Steven Stamkos 8.00 20.00
ASSW Shea Weber 3.00 8.00
ASTS Tyler Seguin 5.00 12.00
ASVT Vladimir Tarasenko 5.00 12.00
ASZG Zemgus Girgensons 3.00 8.00

2015-16 SP Game Used All-Star Skills Relics Platinum Blue Patch

*BLUE/25: .8X TO 2X BASIC JSY/125
ASCC Corey Crawford 10.00 25.00
ASJD Jonathan Drouin 6.00 15.00
ASJT Jonathan Toews 12.00 30.00
ASPK Patrick Kane 15.00 40.00
ASTA John Tavares 12.00 30.00

2015-16 SP Game Used All-Star Skills Six Fabrics

AS61 Wbr/Sbk/Ekb/Str/Grd/Flk 8.00 20.00
AS62 Dty/Kth/Byf/Brn/Shk/E-L 8.00 20.00
AS63 Crw/Lng/Hlk/Prc/Flry/Ell 12.00 30.00
AS65 Flg/Ovc/Kpt/Stm/Grx/Kne 30.00 80.00
AS66 Tws/Vrk/Trsk/Els/Fsg/Gdr 10.00 25.00
AS67 Jhn/Ksl/Ryn/Vrb/Gns/RNH 10.00 25.00
AS69 Tvr/Vrk/Nsh/Sgn/Frg/Ekb 15.00 40.00

2015-16 SP Game Used All-Star Skills Triple Fabrics Patch

*BASE TRIPLE: .15X TO .4X PATCH/25
AS31 Hoffman/Drouin/Sekac 8.00 20.00
AS32 Seguin/Tavares/Tarasenko 15.00 40.00
AS33 Kessel/Kane/Gaudreau 20.00 50.00
AS34 Faulk/Giordano/Ekman-Larsson 10.00 25.00
AS35 Shattenkirk/Burns/Suter 10.00 25.00
AS36 Nugent-Hopkins

Vrbata/Gaudreau 15.00 40.00
AS37 Girgensons/Elias/Ryan 10.00 25.00
AS38 Forsberg/Bergeron/Stamkos 20.00 50.00
AS39 Tarasenko/Ryan/Vrbata 12.00 30.00
AS310 Kessel/Voracek/Kane 20.00 50.00
AS311 Foligno/Nash/Ovechkin 40.00 100.00
AS312 Nugent-Hopkins
Getzlaf/Johansen 12.00 30.00
AS313 Kopitar/Seguin/Tavares 15.00 40.00
AS314 Price/Fleury/Halak 20.00 50.00
AS315 Drouin/Gaudreau/Hoffman 15.00 40.00

2015-16 SP Game Used Autographs Blue

1 Wayne Gretzky B 200.00 500.00
5 John Tavares C 10.00 25.00
7 Tyler Seguin B 8.00 20.00
8 Jason Spezza C 6.00 15.00
9 Brent Burns C 6.00 15.00
10 Patrick Kane B 12.00 30.00
12 Sidney Crosby B 60.00 150.00
15 Phil Kessel A 6.00 15.00
16 Phil Esposito B 10.00 25.00
17 Victor Hedman A 8.00 20.00
18 P.K. Subban A 8.00 20.00
19 John Carlson E 6.00 15.00
20 Tyler Toffoli E 6.00 15.00
22 Evgeni Malkin B 12.00 30.00
24 Jaromir Jagr B 30.00 80.00
25 Max Pacioretty C 6.00 15.00
27 Mikael Granlund E 5.00 12.00
30 Mark Scheifele E 10.00 25.00
31 Jeff Skinner C 8.00 20.00
32 Bo Horvat E 8.00 20.00
34 Jonathan Bernier C 5.00 12.00
38 Logan Couture B 8.00 20.00
39 Steve Mason D 5.00 12.00
40 Cory Schneider B 6.00 15.00
42 Patrick Roy B 30.00 80.00
45 Jonathan Quick B 8.00 20.00
46 Carey Price B 12.00 30.00
47 Frederik Andersen B 8.00 20.00
48 Ryan Miller B 6.00 15.00
49 Ben Bishop D 5.00 12.00
50 Andrew Hammond E 8.00 20.00
53 Nathan MacKinnon C 25.00 60.00
55 Ryan McDonagh D 4.00 10.00
56 Anders Lee E 6.00 15.00
57 Alex Galchenyuk C 4.00 10.00
59 Blake Wheeler B 6.00 15.00
61 Sam Reinhart C 12.00 30.00
65 Peter Forsberg B 12.00 30.00
66 James van Riemsdyk C 5.00 12.00
67 Tomas Tatar E 4.00 10.00
71 Jonathan Toews B 10.00 25.00
72 Ondrej Palat E 5.00 12.00
73 Ryan Strome E 6.00 15.00
75 Ryan Kesler D 6.00 15.00
76 Jason Zucker E 6.00 15.00
80 Jamie Benn B 6.00 15.00
81 Johnny Gaudreau D 10.00 25.00
82 Pavel Datsyuk B 10.00 25.00
83 Mark Messier B 12.00 30.00
84 Zach Parise B 6.00 15.00
85 Brendan Gallagher D 6.00 15.00
86 Jonathan Huberdeau B 8.00 20.00
87 Guy Lafleur B 8.00 20.00
88 Corey Perry B 10.00 25.00
89 Matt Duchene C 6.00 15.00
91 Bobby Hull B 12.00 30.00
92 Tyler Johnson D 4.00 10.00
93 Alexander Ovechkin B 25.00 60.00
95 Teemu Selanne B 12.00 30.00
96 Joe Pavelski B 8.00 20.00
97 Nicklas Lidstrom B 6.00 15.00
99 Taylor Hall B 6.00 15.00
100 Glenn Hall B 6.00 15.00
102 Anton Slepyshev D 4.00 10.00
104 Antoine Bibeau E 6.00 15.00
105 Artemi Panarin D 25.00 60.00
106 Andreas Athanasiou C 15.00 40.00
107 Ben Hutton C 6.00 15.00
109 Stefan Noesen E 4.00 10.00
113 Colin Miller E 5.00 12.00
115 Colton Parayko E 10.00 25.00
116 Henrik Samuelsson E 4.00 10.00
118 Josh Anderson E 12.00 30.00
120 Oscar Lindberg E 6.00 15.00
121 Daniel Sprong C 8.00 20.00
122 Dylan DeMelo D 5.00 12.00
124 Dylan Larkin C 20.00 50.00
125 Malcolm Subban D 10.00 25.00
128 Jared McCann E 8.00 20.00
129 Brendan Ranford E 5.00 12.00
133 Joonas Donskoi C 6.00 15.00
134 Mackenzie Skapski C 6.00 15.00
135 Jordan Weal D 4.00 10.00
136 Jean-Francois Berube E 5.00 12.00
140 Mattias Janmark C 6.00 15.00
141 Nick Shore B 4.00 10.00
143 Slater Koekkoek D 4.00 10.00
144 Max Domi C 12.00 30.00
146 Matt Puempel D 5.00 12.00
147 Mike Condon E 6.00 15.00
149 Mikko Rantanen C 30.00 80.00
150 Nicolas Petan D 6.00 15.00
153 Ronalds Kenins C 4.00 10.00
155 Robby Fabbri C 8.00 20.00
156 Sergei Plotnikov C 4.00 10.00
157 Nikolaj Ehlers D 12.00 30.00
163 Connor Hellebuyck C 25.00 60.00
167 Sam Brittain E 6.00 15.00
168 Jake Virtanen D 8.00 20.00
169 Andrew Copp E 6.00 15.00
170 Noah Hanifin C 10.00 25.00
172 Brock McGinn C 6.00 15.00
174 Derek Forbort B 5.00 12.00
175 Sam Bennett C 20.00 50.00
179 Nick Cousins D 6.00 15.00
180 Jacob de la Rose B 6.00 15.00
181 Kyle Baun E 6.00 15.00
183 Radek Faksa E 6.00 15.00
184 Vincent Hinostroza D 4.00 10.00
185 Emile Poirier C 5.00 12.00
186 Shane Prince D 4.00 10.00
189 Nikolay Goldobin C 6.00 15.00
190 Chandler Stephenson C 8.00 20.00
197 Connor McDavid A 300.00 800.00
198 Kevin Fiala C 8.00 20.00
201 Brett Kulak C 5.00 12.00
205 Taylor Leier C 6.00 15.00
208 Phil Di Giuseppe B 6.00 15.00
209 Garret Sparks A 6.00 15.00
210 Adam Pelech C 5.00 12.00
212 Anthony Stolarz C 15.00 40.00
213 Brady Skjei C 5.00 12.00
214 Charles Hudon A 6.00 15.00
216 Shea Theodore C 10.00 25.00
217 Mike McCarron A 8.00 20.00
218 Gustav Olofsson B 6.00 15.00
220 Frank Vatrano B 8.00 20.00
221 Markus Hannikainen B 5.00 12.00
222 Jujhar Khaira B 5.00 12.00
223 Ryan Carpenter C 6.00 15.00
224 Zachary Fucale A 5.00 12.00
225 Jaccob Slavin B 10.00 25.00
226 Alexandre Grenier C 5.00 12.00
229 Nick Ritchie A 6.00 15.00
230 Christoph Bertschy B 5.00 12.00
231 Daniel Carr C 5.00 12.00
232 Byron Froese B 5.00 12.00
234 Joonas Korpisalo C 12.00 30.00
235 Matt Murray A 25.00 60.00
236 Ryan Dzingel C 4.00 10.00

2015-16 SP Game Used Career Legacy Jerseys

*GOLD/49: .5X TO 1.2X BASIC JSY/125
*BLUE/25: .8X TO 2X BASIC JSY/125
CLDS Denis Savard 4.00 10.00
CLJS Jason Spezza 4.00 10.00
CLJT Joe Thornton 6.00 15.00
CLJV Jakub Voracek 3.00 8.00
CLKL Kari Lehtonen 3.00 8.00
CLMG Marian Gaborik 4.00 10.00
CLML Martin St. Louis 4.00 10.00
CLTS Tyler Seguin 5.00 12.00

2015-16 SP Game Used Copper Jerseys

1 Wayne Gretzky A 20.00 50.00
3 Jakub Voracek E 2.50 6.00
4 Steven Stamkos C 6.00 15.00
5 John Tavares C 5.00 12.00
6 Vladimir Tarasenko D 4.00 10.00
7 Tyler Seguin D 4.00 10.00
8 Jason Spezza E 3.00 8.00
9 Brent Burns D 3.00 8.00
10 Patrick Kane C 6.00 15.00
12 Sidney Crosby A 8.00 20.00
13 Nikita Kucherov E 6.00 15.00
14 Marian Hossa D 3.00 8.00
15 Phil Kessel D 3.00 8.00
17 Victor Hedman E 4.00 10.00
18 P.K. Subban E 4.00 10.00
19 John Carlson E 3.00 8.00
20 Tyler Toffoli E 3.00 8.00
21 Sergei Bobrovsky E 5.00 12.00
22 Evgeni Malkin D 6.00 15.00
25 Max Pacioretty D 3.00 8.00
26 Erik Karlsson E 4.00 10.00
27 Mikael Granlund E 2.50 6.00
28 Mark Stone E 4.00 10.00
29 Roman Josi E 3.00 8.00
30 Mark Scheifele E 5.00 12.00
31 Jeff Skinner D 4.00 10.00
33 David Krejci E 3.00 8.00
34 Jonathan Bernier E 2.50 6.00
35 Morgan Rielly E 3.00 8.00
36 Henrik Zetterberg B 5.00 12.00
37 Tuukka Rask C 4.00 10.00
38 Logan Couture D 4.00 10.00
39 Steve Mason E 2.50 6.00
40 Cory Schneider E 3.00 8.00
41 Pekka Rinne D 3.00 8.00
42 Patrick Roy A 10.00 25.00
43 Henrik Sedin D 4.00 10.00
44 Zdeno Chara D 3.00 8.00
45 Jonathan Quick D 4.00 10.00
46 Carey Price D 8.00 20.00
47 Frederik Andersen E 4.00 10.00
48 Ryan Miller E 3.00 8.00
50 Andrew Hammond E 4.00 10.00
51 Henrik Lundqvist C 8.00 20.00
52 Marc-Andre Fleury D 6.00 15.00
53 Nathan MacKinnon D 12.00 30.00
55 Ryan McDonagh E 2.00 5.00
56 Anders Lee E 3.00 8.00
57 Alex Galchenyuk C 2.00 5.00
58 Nick Bjugstad E 2.00 5.00
59 Blake Wheeler E 3.00 8.00
60 Jiri Hudler C 2.50 6.00
62 Sean Monahan D 2.00 5.00
63 Oliver Ekman-Larsson D 3.00 8.00
64 Daniel Sedin D 4.00 10.00
66 James van Riemsdyk C 2.50 6.00
67 Tomas Tatar E 2.00 5.00
68 Derek Stepan E 2.00 5.00
69 Ryan Johansen E 2.50 6.00
70 Nicklas Backstrom C 3.00 8.00
71 Jonathan Toews B 5.00 12.00
72 Ondrej Palat E 2.50 6.00
73 Ryan Strome E 3.00 8.00
74 Jaden Schwartz E 4.00 10.00
75 Ryan Kesler E 3.00 8.00
77 Elias Lindholm E 3.00 8.00
78 Ryan Getzlaf C 3.00 8.00
79 Jordan Eberle E 3.00 8.00
80 Jamie Benn C 3.00 8.00
81 Johnny Gaudreau D 5.00 12.00
82 Pavel Datsyuk B 6.00 15.00
83 Mark Messier A 6.00 15.00
84 Zach Parise D 3.00 8.00
85 Brendan Gallagher E 3.00 8.00
86 Jonathan Huberdeau E 4.00 10.00
87 Guy Lafleur A 5.00 12.00
88 Corey Perry E 5.00 12.00
90 Filip Forsberg C 5.00 12.00
92 Tyler Johnson B 2.50 6.00
93 Alexander Ovechkin C 5.00 12.00
94 Drew Doughty E 4.00 10.00
96 Joe Pavelski E 4.00 10.00
97 Nicklas Lidstrom C 3.00 8.00
98 Aaron Ekblad E 4.00 10.00
99 Taylor Hall D 3.00 8.00
100 Glenn Hall A 5.00 12.00
104 Antoine Bibeau 5.00 12.00
105 Artemi Panarin 15.00 30.00
106 Andreas Athanasiou 5.00 12.00
109 Stefan Noesen 3.00 8.00
111 Stanislav Galiev 5.00 12.00
114 Oscar Dansk 6.00 15.00
116 Henrik Samuelsson 3.00 8.00
118 Josh Anderson 10.00 25.00
121 Daniel Sprong 6.00 15.00
124 Dylan Larkin 15.00 40.00
125 Malcolm Subban 4.00 10.00
127 Jack Eichel 12.00 30.00
129 Brendan Ranford 4.00 10.00
134 Mackenzie Skapski 5.00 12.00
135 Jordan Weal 3.00 8.00
138 Devin Shore 5.00 12.00
141 Nick Shore 3.00 8.00
143 Slater Koekkoek 3.00 8.00
144 Max Domi 10.00 25.00
146 Matt Puempel 4.00 10.00
149 Mikko Rantanen 25.00 60.00
150 Nicolas Petan 5.00 12.00
153 Ronalds Kenins 3.00 8.00
155 Robby Fabbri 6.00 15.00
157 Nikolaj Ehlers 10.00 25.00
163 Connor Hellebuyck 20.00 50.00
168 Jake Virtanen 6.00 15.00
170 Noah Hanifin 8.00 20.00
171 Ryan Hartman 6.00 15.00
172 Brock McGinn 5.00 12.00
175 Sam Bennett 15.00 40.00
179 Nick Cousins 5.00 12.00
180 Jacob de la Rose 5.00 12.00
181 Kyle Baun 5.00 12.00
185 Emile Poirier 4.00 10.00
186 Shane Prince 3.00 8.00
189 Nikolay Goldobin 5.00 12.00
197 Connor McDavid 150.00 400.00
198 Kevin Fiala 6.00 15.00

2015-16 SP Game Used Draft Day Marks

DDMAB Antoine Bibeau/35 8.00 20.00
DDMBG Brendan Gaunce/35 10.00 25.00
DDMCH Connor Hellebuyck/35 25.00 50.00
DDMCM Connor McDavid/35 600.00 1500.00
DDMDF Derek Forbort/35 6.00 15.00
DDMDL Dylan Larkin/35 60.00 150.00
DDMEP Emile Poirier/35 6.00 15.00
DDMHS Henrik Samuelsson/35 5.00 12.00
DDMHS Hunter Shinkaruk/35 8.00 20.00
DDMHU Charles Hudon/35 12.00 30.00
DDMJV Jake Virtanen/35 10.00 25.00
DDMKF Kevin Fiala/35 10.00 25.00
DDMMD Max Domi/35 50.00 100.00
DDMMP Matt Puempel/35 6.00 15.00
DDMMS Mackenzie Skapski/35 8.00 20.00
DDMNC Nick Cousins/35 12.00 30.00
DDMNE Nikolaj Ehlers/35 15.00 40.00
DDMNH Noah Hanifin/35 12.00 30.00
DDMNP Nicolas Petan/35 12.00 30.00
DDMNR Nick Ritchie/35 8.00 20.00
DDMOK Oscar Klefbom/35 12.00 30.00
DDMRF Robby Fabbri/35 20.00 40.00
DDMRF Radek Faksa/35 8.00 20.00
DDMRH Ryan Hartman/35 10.00 25.00
DDMSB Sam Bennett/35 25.00 60.00
DDMSI Duncan Siemens/35 8.00 20.00
DDMSK Slater Koekkoek/35 5.00 12.00
DDMSN Stefan Noesen/35 5.00 12.00
DDMSP Shane Prince/35 5.00 12.00
DDMST Shea Theodore/35 12.00 30.00
DDMSU Malcolm Subban/35 20.00 40.00
DDMZF Zachary Fucale/35 30.00 60.00

2015-16 SP Game Used Gold Spectrum Materials

*ROOKIE/99: 1X TO 2.5X COPPER/399
3 Jakub Voracek/49 5.00 12.00
4 Steven Stamkos/25 15.00 40.00
5 John Tavares/15 12.00 30.00
6 Vladimir Tarasenko/49 8.00 20.00
7 Tyler Seguin/25 10.00 25.00
8 Jason Spezza/25 8.00 20.00
10 Patrick Kane/25 15.00 40.00
13 Nikita Kucherov/99 10.00 25.00
14 Marian Hossa/25 8.00 20.00
15 Phil Kessel/25 8.00 20.00
17 Victor Hedman/99 6.00 15.00
18 P.K. Subban/25 10.00 25.00
19 John Carlson/49 6.00 15.00
20 Tyler Toffoli/49 6.00 15.00
21 Sergei Bobrovsky/49 10.00 25.00
22 Evgeni Malkin/25 15.00 40.00
25 Max Pacioretty/25 8.00 20.00
26 Erik Karlsson/49 8.00 20.00
27 Mikael Granlund/49 5.00 12.00
28 Mark Stone/99 6.00 15.00
29 Roman Josi/49 6.00 15.00
30 Mark Scheifele/99 8.00 20.00
31 Jeff Skinner/49 8.00 20.00
33 David Krejci/49 6.00 15.00
34 Jonathan Bernier/49 5.00 12.00
35 Morgan Rielly/49 6.00 15.00
36 Henrik Zetterberg/25 10.00 25.00
37 Tuukka Rask/25 10.00 25.00
38 Logan Couture/49 8.00 20.00
39 Steve Mason/49 5.00 12.00
40 Cory Schneider/49 6.00 15.00
41 Pekka Rinne/49 6.00 15.00
43 Henrik Sedin/25 10.00 25.00
44 Zdeno Chara/25 8.00 20.00
45 Jonathan Quick/49 8.00 20.00
46 Carey Price/25 15.00 40.00
47 Frederik Andersen/99 6.00 15.00
48 Ryan Miller/49 6.00 15.00
49 Ben Bishop/49 5.00 12.00
50 Andrew Hammond/99 6.00 15.00
51 Henrik Lundqvist/15 12.00 30.00
52 Marc-Andre Fleury/49 12.00 30.00
53 Nathan MacKinnon/25 30.00 80.00
54 Claude Giroux/25 8.00 20.00
55 Ryan McDonagh/49 4.00 10.00
56 Anders Lee/99 5.00 12.00
57 Alex Galchenyuk/25 5.00 12.00
58 Nick Bjugstad/99 3.00 8.00
59 Blake Wheeler/99 5.00 12.00
60 Jiri Hudler/49 5.00 12.00
61 Sam Reinhart/49 12.00 30.00
62 Sean Monahan/25 5.00 12.00
63 Oliver Ekman-Larsson/49 6.00 15.00
64 Daniel Sedin/25 10.00 25.00
66 James van Riemsdyk/49 5.00 12.00
67 Tomas Tatar/99 3.00 8.00
70 Nicklas Backstrom/25 8.00 20.00
71 Jonathan Toews/25 12.00 30.00
72 Ondrej Palat/49 5.00 12.00
73 Ryan Strome/49 6.00 15.00
74 Jaden Schwartz/99 6.00 15.00
77 Elias Lindholm/49 6.00 15.00
78 Ryan Getzlaf/25 8.00 20.00
79 Jordan Eberle/49 6.00 15.00
80 Jamie Benn/49 6.00 15.00
81 Johnny Gaudreau/49 10.00 25.00
82 Pavel Datsyuk/25 12.00 30.00
84 Zach Parise/49 6.00 15.00
85 Brendan Gallagher/49 6.00 15.00
86 Jonathan Huberdeau/49 8.00 20.00
88 Corey Perry/49 10.00 25.00
89 Matt Duchene/49 6.00 15.00
90 Filip Forsberg/25 12.00 30.00
92 Tyler Johnson/25 5.00 12.00
94 Drew Doughty/49 8.00 20.00
95 Teemu Selanne/25 15.00 40.00
96 Joe Pavelski/49 8.00 20.00
97 Nicklas Lidstrom/15 8.00 20.00
98 Aaron Ekblad/49 8.00 20.00
99 Taylor Hall/25 8.00 20.00
171 Ryan Hartman/99 6.00 15.00
197 Connor McDavid/99 300.00 800.00

2015-16 SP Game Used Inked Rookie Sweaters

*PATCH/49: .6X TO 1.5X BASIC AU/149
IRSAB Antoine Bibeau 5.00 12.00
IRSAP Artemi Panarin EXCH 60.00 120.00
IRSBM Brock McGinn 5.00 12.00
IRSCM Connor McDavid 600.00 1500.00
IRSDF Derek Forbort 4.00 10.00
IRSDL Dylan Larkin 75.00 150.00
IRSDS Daniel Sprong EXCH 6.00 15.00
IRSEP Emile Poirier EXCH 4.00 10.00
IRSHS Henrik Samuelsson 3.00 8.00
IRSJA Josh Anderson 10.00 25.00
IRSJR Jacob de la Rose 5.00 12.00
IRSJV Jake Virtanen EXCH 6.00 15.00
IRSKB Kyle Baun 5.00 12.00
IRSKF Kevin Fiala 6.00 15.00
IRSMD Max Domi EXCH 10.00 25.00
IRSMP Matt Puempel 4.00 10.00
IRSMR Mikko Rantanen EXCH 25.00 60.00
IRSNC Nick Cousins 6.00 15.00
IRSNE Nikolaj Ehlers 10.00 25.00
IRSNG Nikolay Goldobin 5.00 12.00
IRSNH Noah Hanifin 8.00 20.00
IRSNP Nicolas Petan 5.00 12.00
IRSRF Robby Fabbri 12.00 30.00
IRSRH Ryan Hartman 6.00 15.00
IRSRK Ronalds Kenins 3.00 8.00
IRSSB Sam Bennett EXCH 15.00 40.00
IRSSK Slater Koekkoek 3.00 8.00
IRSSN Stefan Noesen 3.00 8.00
IRSSP Shane Prince 3.00 8.00
IRSSU Malcolm Subban 10.00 25.00

2015-16 SP Game Used Inked Sweaters

ISCP Carey Price/25 40.00 80.00
ISDK David Krejci/99 8.00 20.00
ISJB Jonathan Bernier/50 6.00 15.00
ISJS Jeff Skinner/99 10.00 25.00
ISJT Jonathan Toews/25 30.00 60.00
ISJV Jakub Voracek/99 6.00 15.00
ISLR Luc Robitaille/25 12.00 30.00
ISMF Marc-Andre Fleury/99 15.00 40.00
ISMG Mikael Granlund/99 6.00 15.00
ISMK Mike Keane/99 6.00 15.00
ISMS Martin St. Louis/50 8.00 20.00
ISNM Nathan MacKinnon/50 30.00 80.00
ISPM Patrick Marleau/50 8.00 20.00
ISPS Paul Stastny/50 6.00 15.00
ISRK Ryan Kesler/99 8.00 20.00
ISSH Scott Hartnell/99 5.00 12.00
ISTA John Tavares/25 20.00 50.00
ISTH Tomas Hertl/99 8.00 20.00
ISTS Tyler Seguin/25 15.00 40.00
ISTT Tyler Toffoli/99 8.00 20.00

2015-16 SP Game Used Media Guide Booklets

*PATCH/15: .8X TO 2X BASIC INSERTS/65
MGBV D.Backes/V.Tarasenko 10.00 25.00
MGCB P.Bergeron/Z.Chara 10.00 25.00
MGDJ R.Johansen/B.Dubinsky 6.00 15.00
MGDO M.Domi/O.Ekman-Larsson 8.00 20.00
MGEN R.Nugent-Hopkins/J.Eberle 10.00 25.00
MGFK M.Fleury/C.Kunitz 15.00 40.00
MGGB W.Gretzky/R.Blake 50.00 125.00
MGGC C.Coyle/M.Granlund 8.00 20.00
MGHE A.Ekblad/J.Huberdeau 10.00 25.00
MGIL J.Iginla/G.Landeskog 10.00 25.00
MGJJ J.Spezza/J.Benn 8.00 20.00
MGME C.McDavid/T.Hall 40.00 80.00
MGMG S.Monahan/J.Gaudreau 12.00 30.00
MGNK R.Nash/C.Kreider 10.00 25.00
MGOH A.Ovechkin/B.Holtby 15.00 40.00
MGOS R.Strome/K.Okposo 8.00 20.00
MGPC L.Couture/J.Pavelski 10.00 25.00
MGPG R.Getzlaf/C.Perry 12.00 30.00
MGQD J.Quick/D.Doughty 10.00 25.00
MGRK M.Rielly/N.Kadri 12.00 30.00
MGSK M.Keane/D.Savard 8.00 20.00
MGSP S.Stamkos/O.Palat 15.00 40.00
MGSS H.Sedin/D.Sedin 10.00 25.00
MGST J.Trouba/M.Scheifele 12.00 30.00
MGTK J.Toews/P.Kane 20.00 40.00
MGTZ K.Turris/M.Zibanejad 10.00 25.00
MGVG J.Voracek/C.Giroux 8.00 20.00
MGWJ S.Weber/S.Jones 8.00 20.00

2015-16 SP Game Used Rookie Phenoms Relics

*BLUE/25: .8X TO 2X BASIC INSERTS
*GOLD/49: .6X TO 1.5X BASIC INSERTS
RPAB Antoine Bibeau 2.00 5.00
RPAP Artemi Panarin 15.00 40.00
RPCH Connor Hellebuyck 8.00 20.00
RPCM Connor McDavid 125.00 300.00
RPDL Dylan Larkin 25.00 50.00
RPDS Daniel Sprong 4.00 10.00
RPEP Emile Poirier 1.50 4.00
RPHS Henrik Samuelsson 1.25 3.00
RPJA Josh Anderson 4.00 10.00
RPJD Jacob de la Rose 2.00 5.00
RPJE Jack Eichel 25.00 50.00
RPJV Jake Virtanen 2.50 6.00
RPKF Kevin Fiala 2.50 6.00
RPMD Max Domi 4.00 10.00
RPMP Matt Puempel 1.50 4.00
RPMR Mikko Rantanen 10.00 25.00
RPNE Nikolaj Ehlers 5.00 12.00
RPNH Noah Hanifin 3.00 8.00
RPNP Nicolas Petan 2.00 5.00
RPRF Robby Fabbri 4.00 10.00
RPRH Ryan Hartman 2.50 6.00
RPRK Ronalds Kenins 3.00 8.00
RPSB Sam Bennett 6.00 15.00
RPSM Mackenzie Skapski 2.00 5.00
RPSP Shane Prince 1.25 3.00

2015-16 SP Game Used Stadium Series Relics

*BLUE/25: .8X TO 2X BASIC JSY/125
*GOLD/49: .5X TO 1.2X BASIC JSY/125
LADB Dustin Brown 4.00 10.00
LADD Drew Doughty 5.00 12.00
LADK Dwight King 2.50 6.00
LAGR Matt Greene 2.50 6.00
LAJM Jamie McBain 2.50 6.00
LAJN Jordan Nolan 2.50 6.00
LAJW Justin Williams 3.00 8.00
LAMG Marian Gaborik 4.00 10.00
LAMJ Martin Jones 3.00 8.00
LANS Nick Shore 2.50 6.00
LATT Tyler Toffoli 4.00 10.00
SJAS Alex Stalock 2.50 6.00
SJBD Brenden Dillon 2.50 6.00
SJJS James Sheppard 2.50 6.00
SJLC Logan Couture 5.00 12.00
SJMI Matt Irwin 2.50 6.00
SJMK Melker Karlsson 2.50 6.00
SJMN Matt Nieto 2.50 6.00
SJPM Patrick Marleau 4.00 10.00

2015-16 SP Game Used Stanley Cup Finals Materials Net Cord

SCNCAK Alex Killorn 20.00 50.00
SCNCAN Andrew Shaw 20.00 50.00
SCNCAS Anton Stralman 20.00 50.00
SCNCAV Antoine Vermette 20.00 50.00
SCNCBB Ben Bishop 25.00 60.00
SCNCBR Brad Richards 30.00 80.00
SCNCBS Brent Seabrook 20.00 50.00
SCNCCC Corey Crawford 40.00 100.00
SCNCCP Cedric Paquette 20.00 50.00
SCNCDK Duncan Keith 25.00 60.00
SCNCJB J.T. Brown 20.00 50.00
SCNCJD Jonathan Drouin 25.00 60.00
SCNCJG Jason Garrison 20.00 50.00
SCNCJO Johnny Oduya 25.00 60.00
SCNCJT Jonathan Toews 75.00 125.00
SCNCKT Kimmo Timonen 20.00 50.00
SCNCMH Marian Hossa 30.00 80.00
SCNCNH Niklas Hjalmarsson 20.00 50.00
SCNCNK Nikita Kucherov 60.00 150.00
SCNCOP Ondrej Palat 25.00 60.00
SCNCPK Patrick Kane 90.00 150.00
SCNCPS Patrick Sharp 30.00 80.00
SCNCRC Ryan Callahan 20.00 50.00
SCNCSA Brandon Saad 25.00 60.00
SCNCSS Steven Stamkos 60.00 150.00
SCNCTJ Tyler Johnson 20.00 50.00
SCNCTT Teuvo Teravainen 30.00 80.00
SCNCVA Andrei Vasilevskiy 50.00 125.00
SCNCVF Valtteri Filppula 20.00 50.00
SCNCVH Victor Hedman 40.00 100.00

2015-16 SP Game Used Supreme Gloves

PAAK Anze Kopitar 30.00 80.00
PADB Dustin Brown 20.00 50.00
PADD Drew Doughty 25.00 60.00
PAJC Jeff Carter 15.00 40.00
PAMB Martin Brodeur 50.00 125.00
PAML Mario Lemieux 80.00 200.00
PAPA Pascal Dupuis 15.00 40.00
PARL Roberto Luongo 30.00 80.00
PASH Scott Hartnell 12.00 30.00
PASV Semyon Varlamov 20.00 50.00
PATT Tyler Toffoli 20.00 50.00

2015-16 SP Game Used Supreme Pads

PACO Chris Osgood 12.00 30.00
PACP Carey Price 40.00 100.00
PAGF Grant Fuhr 50.00 100.00
PAJQ Jonathan Quick 30.00 80.00
PAMA Marc-Andre Fleury 25.00 60.00
PAPD Pavel Datsyuk 30.00 80.00

2015-16 SP Game Used Supreme Patches

PAAE Alexander Edler 12.00 30.00
PAAG Alex Galchenyuk 12.00 30.00
PAAK Anze Kopitar 30.00 80.00
PAAM Alec Martinez 12.00 30.00
PAAP Alex Pietrangelo 15.00 40.00
PAAT Alex Tanguay 12.00 30.00
PABB Bob Bourne 12.00 30.00
PABE Patrik Berglund 12.00 30.00
PABH Braden Holtby 25.00 60.00
PABR Bill Ranford 20.00 50.00
PABW Blake Wheeler 20.00 50.00
PACA Craig Anderson 20.00 50.00
PACC Corey Crawford 25.00 60.00
PACG Claude Giroux 20.00 50.00
PACO Chris Osgood 20.00 50.00
PADB Dustin Brown 20.00 50.00
PADD Drew Doughty 25.00 60.00
PADG Doug Gilmour 25.00 60.00
PADK David Krejci 20.00 50.00
PADS Derek Stepan 12.00 30.00
PAEK Erik Karlsson 25.00 60.00
PAEM Evgeni Malkin 40.00 100.00
PAES Eric Staal 25.00 60.00
PAGF Grant Fuhr 30.00 80.00
PAGM Glen Murray 15.00 40.00
PAHZ Henrik Zetterberg 25.00 60.00
PAJB Jonathan Bernier 15.00 40.00
PAJC Jeff Carter 15.00 40.00
PAJH Jiri Hudler 15.00 40.00
PAJI Jarome Iginla 25.00 60.00
PAJJ Jack Johnson 12.00 30.00
PAJQ Jonathan Quick 25.00 60.00
PAJR Jeremy Roenick 30.00 80.00
PAJS Jason Spezza 20.00 50.00
PAJT John Tavares 30.00 80.00
PAKR Niklas Kronwall 15.00 40.00
PALA Gabriel Landeskog 25.00 60.00
PAMA Marc-Andre Fleury 40.00 100.00
PAMB Martin Brodeur 50.00 125.00
PAMG Mike Gartner 25.00 60.00
PAMI Mikael Granlund 15.00 40.00
PAMT Marty Turco 20.00 50.00
PANB Nicklas Backstrom 20.00 50.00
PAOV Alexander Ovechkin 80.00 200.00
PAPB Patrice Bergeron 25.00 60.00
PAPD Pavel Datsyuk 30.00 80.00
PAPE Corey Perry 30.00 80.00
PAPF Peter Forsberg 40.00 100.00
PAPK Patrick Kane 40.00 100.00
PAPM Patrick Marleau 20.00 50.00
PAPR Patrick Roy 50.00 125.00
PARB Rod Brind'Amour 15.00 40.00
PARG Ryan Getzlaf 20.00 50.00
PARI Morgan Rielly 20.00 50.00
PARJ Ryan Johansen 15.00 40.00
PARL Roberto Luongo 30.00 80.00
PARM Ryan McDonagh 12.00 30.00
PARY Bobby Ryan 15.00 40.00
PASA Denis Savard 20.00 50.00
PASB Brayden Schenn 20.00 50.00
PASC Sidney Crosby 80.00 200.00
PASD Shane Doan 15.00 40.00
PASE Daniel Sedin 25.00 60.00
PASH Scott Hartnell 12.00 30.00
PASJ Seth Jones 20.00 50.00
PAST Jordan Staal 15.00 40.00
PASU P.K. Subban 25.00 60.00
PASV Semyon Varlamov 20.00 50.00
PATH Joe Thornton 30.00 80.00
PATP Tanner Pearson 12.00 30.00
PATR Tuukka Rask 25.00 60.00
PATS Tyler Seguin 25.00 60.00
PAVD Vincent Damphousse 15.00 40.00
PAVH Victor Hedman 25.00 60.00
PAVO Jakub Voracek 15.00 40.00
PAWS Wayne Simmonds 25.00 60.00
PAZC Zdeno Chara 20.00 50.00
PATT Tyler Toffoli 20.00 50.00

2015-16 SP Game Used Supreme Skates

PAEM Evgeni Malkin 30.00 80.00
PALU Milan Lucic 12.00 30.00
PAMD Marcel Dionne 20.00 50.00
PASB Brayden Schenn 15.00 40.00

2015-16 SP Game Used Supreme Sticks

PAAG Alex Galchenyuk 12.00 30.00
PAAM Alec Martinez 12.00 30.00
PAAT Alex Tanguay 12.00 30.00
PABB Bob Bourne 12.00 30.00
PABC Bobby Clarke 30.00 80.00
PABE Patrik Berglund 12.00 30.00
PABL Rob Blake 20.00 50.00
PABR Bill Ranford 20.00 50.00
PABS Borje Salming 20.00 50.00
PABW Blake Wheeler 20.00 50.00
PACG Claude Giroux 20.00 50.00
PADE Devan Dubnyk 15.00 40.00
PADG Doug Gilmour 25.00 60.00
PADK David Krejci 20.00 50.00
PADS Derek Stepan 12.00 30.00
PAGC Guy Carbonneau 15.00 40.00
PAHZ Henrik Zetterberg 25.00 60.00
PAJB Jonathan Bernier 15.00 40.00
PAJH Jiri Hudler 15.00 40.00
PAJI Jarome Iginla 25.00 60.00
PAJJ Jack Johnson 12.00 30.00
PAJK Jari Kurri 20.00 50.00
PAJR Jeremy Roenick 30.00 80.00
PAJS Jason Spezza 20.00 50.00
PAJT John Tavares 30.00 80.00
PAKR Niklas Kronwall 15.00 40.00
PALR Larry Robinson 20.00 50.00
PAMG Mike Gartner 25.00 60.00
PAMM Mark Messier 40.00 100.00
PAMR Mike Richter 20.00 50.00
PAMT Marty Turco 20.00 50.00
PANB Nicklas Backstrom 20.00 50.00
PAOV Alexander Ovechkin 80.00 200.00
PAPB Patrice Bergeron 25.00 60.00
PAPF Peter Forsberg 40.00 100.00
PAPK Patrick Kane 40.00 100.00
PAPR Patrick Roy 50.00 125.00
PARM Ryan McDonagh 12.00 30.00
PASA Denis Savard 20.00 50.00
PASC Sidney Crosby 80.00 200.00
PASD Shane Doan 15.00 40.00
PASE Daniel Sedin 25.00 60.00
PASG Sam Gagner 12.00 30.00
PAST Jordan Staal 15.00 40.00
PASU P.K. Subban 25.00 60.00
PATE Teemu Selanne 40.00 100.00
PATH Joe Thornton 30.00 80.00
PATP Tanner Pearson 12.00 30.00
PAVA John Vanbiesbrouck 20.00 50.00
PAVD Vincent Damphousse 15.00 40.00
PAWC Wendel Clark 30.00 80.00
PAZC Zdeno Chara 20.00 50.00

2015-16 SP Game Used Winter Classic Materials Net Cord

WCNCAO Alexander Ovechkin 40.00 80.00
WCNCBO Brooks Orpik 20.00 50.00
WCNCBR Brad Richards 15.00 40.00
WCNCBS Brandon Saad 12.00 30.00
WCNCCC Corey Crawford 20.00 50.00
WCNCDK Duncan Keith 12.00 30.00
WCNCEF Eric Fehr 10.00 25.00
WCNCEK Evgeny Kuznetsov 25.00 60.00
WCNCJC John Carlson 15.00 40.00
WCNCJH Jack Hillen 10.00 25.00
WCNCJO Johnny Oduya 12.00 30.00
WCNCJT Jonathan Toews 30.00 60.00
WCNCKA Karl Alzner 15.00 40.00
WCNCMG Mike Green 15.00 40.00
WCNCMH Marian Hossa 30.00 60.00
WCNCMK Marcus Kruger 10.00 25.00
WCNCMN Matt Niskanen 12.00 30.00
WCNCNB Nicklas Backstrom 30.00 60.00
WCNCNH Niklas Hjalmarsson 10.00 25.00
WCNCPK Patrick Kane 30.00 60.00
WCNCPS Patrick Sharp 15.00 40.00
WCNCSE Brent Seabrook 10.00 25.00
WCNCTB Troy Brouwer 15.00 40.00
WCNCTW Tom Wilson 15.00 40.00

2016-17 SP Game Used

1 Sidney Crosby/87 20.00 50.00
2 Robby Fabbri/15 6.00 15.00
3 Joe Thornton/19 15.00 40.00
5 Mark Stone/61 6.00 15.00
6 Max Pacioretty/67 5.00 12.00
7 David Pastrnak/88 12.00 30.00
10 Jason Spezza/90 5.00 12.00
11 Andrew Ladd/16 6.00 15.00
12 Nathan MacKinnon/29 30.00 80.00
13 Sam Bennett/93 8.00 20.00
14 Rasmus Ristolainen/55 3.00 8.00
17 Jakob Silfverberg/33 5.00 12.00
18 Jonathan Toews/19 15.00 40.00
19 Petr Mrazek/34 8.00 20.00
20 David Backes/42 4.00 10.00
22 Nino Niederreiter/22 5.00 12.00
23 Nick Foligno/71 4.00 10.00
24 Rick Nash/61 5.00 12.00
26 Nikita Kucherov/86 10.00 25.00
27 Morgan Rielly/44 6.00 15.00
28 Henrik Sedin/33 10.00 25.00
29 Blake Wheeler/26 8.00 20.00
30 Victor Rask/49 4.00 10.00
31 Ryan Kesler/17 10.00 25.00
32 Ryan Spooner/51 4.00 10.00
33 Carey Price/31 15.00 40.00
35 Max Domi/16 10.00 25.00
36 John Tavares/91 8.00 20.00
37 Corey Crawford/50 8.00 20.00
38 Mikael Granlund/64 4.00 10.00
39 Chris Kreider/20 12.00 30.00
41 Jake Allen/34 8.00 20.00
42 Phil Kessel/81 5.00 12.00
43 Nikolaj Ehlers/27 8.00 20.00
45 Mike Hoffman/68 3.00 8.00
47 Ryan Miller/30 8.00 20.00
48 Ryan Getzlaf/15 10.00 25.00
49 Nazem Kadri/43 8.00 20.00
50 Connor McDavid/97 25.00 60.00
51 T.J. Oshie/77 5.00 12.00
52 Jaden Schwartz/17 12.00 30.00
54 Jakub Voracek/93 4.00 10.00
55 Victor Hedman/77 6.00 15.00
56 Alex Galchenyuk/27 5.00 12.00
57 Jaroslav Halak/41 6.00 15.00
58 Jeff Carter/77 4.00 10.00
59 Aleksander Barkov/16 15.00 40.00
60 Henrik Lundqvist/30 20.00 50.00
61 Boone Jenner/38 6.00 15.00
62 Gabriel Landeskog/92 6.00 15.00
63 Ryan Johansen/92 4.00 10.00
64 Jack Eichel/15 15.00 40.00
65 David Krejci/46 6.00 15.00
66 Derek Stepan/21 6.00 15.00
67 Bo Horvat/53 6.00 15.00
68 Cam Ward/30 8.00 20.00
69 Kyle Palmieri/21 8.00 20.00
70 Henrik Zetterberg/40 8.00 20.00
72 Sean Monahan/23 5.00 12.00
74 Tyler Toffoli/73 5.00 12.00
78 Frederik Andersen/31 10.00 25.00
80 Oliver Ekman-Larsson/23 8.00 20.00
81 Tom Wilson /43 6.00 15.00
82 Sam Reinhart/23 15.00 40.00
84 Mark Scheifele/55 8.00 20.00
85 Wayne Simmonds/17 12.00 30.00
86 Patrick Kane/88 10.00 25.00
87 Tomas Tatar/21 6.00 15.00
88 Anders Lee/27 8.00 20.00
90 Teuvo Teravainen/86 5.00 12.00
91 Matt Murray/30 12.00 30.00
92 Carl Hagelin/62 3.00 8.00
94 Patrick Roy/33 20.00 50.00
95 Larry Murphy/55 4.00 10.00
96 Pat LaFontaine/16 10.00 25.00
97 Mario Lemieux/66 20.00 50.00
98 Felix Potvin/29 12.00 30.00
100 Wayne Gretzky/99 30.00 80.00
101 Auston Matthews/34 RC 1250.00 1500.00
102 Pavel Zacha/37 RC 30.00 80.00
103 Christian Dvorak/18 RC 30.00 80.00
105 Justin Bailey/56 RC 15.00 40.00
108 Matthew Tkachuk/19 RC 100.00 250.00
109 Kyle Connor/81 RC 50.00 120.00
110 William Nylander/29 RC 100.00 250.00
111 Mikhail Sergachev/22 RC 40.00 100.00
112 Brandon Carlo/25 RC 40.00 100.00
113 Dylan Strome/20 RC 60.00 150.00
114 Jacob Larsson/51 RC 25.00 60.00
115 Miles Wood/44 RC 15.00 40.00
116 Lawson Crouse/67 RC 12.00 30.00
117 Zach Sanford/82 RC 30.00 80.00
118 Daniel Altshuller/40 RC 15.00 40.00
119 Anthony Beauvillier/72 RC 15.00 40.00
120 Anthony Mantha/39 RC 40.00 100.00
121 Casey Nelson/34 RC 20.00 50.00
122 Ondrej Kase/86 RC 15.00 40.00
123 Dominik Simon/49 RC 15.00 40.00
124 Nikita Zaitsev/22 RC 25.00 60.00
125 Nikita Soshnikov/26 RC 15.00 40.00
126 Gustav Forsling/42 RC 40.00 100.00
128 Esa Lindell/23 RC 25.00 60.00
129 Josh Archibald/45 RC 12.00 30.00
130 Mitch Marner/16 RC 700.00 900.00
131 Hudson Fasching/52 RC 15.00 40.00
132 Shane Harper/38 RC 30.00 80.00
133 Markus Nutivaara/65 RC 15.00 40.00
134 Nick Baptiste/73 RC 15.00 40.00
135 Oliver Bjorkstrand/28 RC 30.00 80.00
136 Sebastian Aho/20 RC 80.00 200.00
137 Ross Johnston/52 RC 15.00 40.00

138 Jared Coreau/31 RC 25.00 60.00
139 Jesse Puljujarvi/98 RC 30.00 80.00
140 Kasperi Kapanen/37 RC 30.00 80.00
141 Nick Sorensen /59 RC 15.00 40.00
142 Aaron Dell/30 RC 25.00 60.00
143 J.C. Lipon/46 RC 20.00 50.00
145 Pontus Aberg/46 RC 25.00 60.00
146 Kevin Labanc/62 RC 15.00 40.00
147 Artturi Lehkonen/62 RC 20.00 50.00
148 Michael Matheson/19 RC 25.00 60.00
149 Troy Stecher/51 RC 30.00 80.00
150 Sonny Milano/22 RC 30.00 80.00
151 Jimmy Vesey/26 RC 40.00 100.00
152 Denis Malgin/62 RC 12.00 30.00
154 Noel Acciari/55 RC 40.00 100.00
155 Oliver Kylington/58 RC 12.00 30.00
156 Lukas Sedlak/45 RC 20.00 50.00
159 Blake Speers/74 RC 15.00 40.00
160 Brendan Leipsic/49 RC 15.00 40.00
161 Tyler Motte/64 RC 15.00 40.00
162 Frederik Gauthier/54 RC 12.00 30.00
165 Sergey Tolchinsky/61 RC 12.00 30.00
166 Rob O'Gara/44 RC 20.00 50.00
168 Ben Harpur/67 RC 15.00 40.00
169 Thomas Chabot/72 RC 40.00 100.00
170 Charlie Lindgren/40 RC 30.00 80.00
171 Nikita Tryamkin/88 RC 12.00 30.00
172 Danton Heinen/43 RC 15.00 40.00
173 Oskar Sundqvist/40 RC 20.00 50.00
175 Steven Santini/34 RC 15.00 40.00
176 Brayden Point/21 RC 60.00 150.00
177 Nic Dowd/26 RC 20.00 50.00
181 Scott Kosmachuk/72 RC 15.00 40.00
182 Tristan Jarry/35 RC 40.00 100.00
183 Tobias Lindberg/46 RC 30.00 80.00
184 Blake Pietila/56 RC 15.00 40.00
185 Patrik Laine/29 RC 700.00 1000.00
187 Pavel Buchnevich/89 RC 8.00 20.00
188 Rinat Valiev/29 RC 30.00 80.00
189 Anthony DeAngelo/77 RC 12.00 30.00
190 Jason Dickinson/16 RC 20.00 50.00
191 Brett Lernout/36 RC 20.00 50.00
192 Josh Morrissey/44 RC 50.00 125.00
193 Tom Kuhnhackl/34 RC 15.00 40.00
195 Chase De Leo/77 RC 15.00 40.00
196 Mark McNeill/41 RC 20.00 50.00
197 Austin Czarnik/27 RC 40.00 100.00
198 Trevor Carrick/46 RC 20.00 50.00
199 Joseph Cramarossa/74 RC 15.00 40.00

2016-17 SP Game Used Gold

1 Sidney Crosby JSY B 25.00 60.00
2 Robby Fabbri JSY D 2.50 6.00
3 Joe Thornton JSY C 8.00 20.00
4 Brayden Schenn JSY D 4.00 10.00
5 Mark Stone JSY C 6.00 15.00
6 Max Pacioretty JSY C 5.00 12.00
8 Anze Kopitar JSY C 8.00 20.00
9 Jonathan Huberdeau JSY B 8.00 20.00
10 Jason Spezza JSY C 5.00 12.00
13 Sam Bennett JSY D 6.00 15.00
14 Rasmus Ristolainen JSY D 2.50 6.00
17 Jakob Silfverberg JSY D 2.50 6.00
18 Jonathan Toews JSY B 10.00 25.00
19 Petr Mrazek JSY C 5.00 12.00
20 David Backes JSY D 2.50 6.00
21 Filip Forsberg JSY D 6.00 15.00
22 Nino Niederreiter JSY D 2.50 6.00
23 Nick Foligno JSY D 3.00 8.00
24 Rick Nash JSY C 5.00 12.00
25 Alexander Ovechkin JSY B 25.00 60.00
27 Morgan Rielly JSY D 4.00 10.00
28 Henrik Sedin JSY C 6.00 15.00
29 Blake Wheeler JSY D 4.00 10.00
31 Ryan Kesler JSY C 5.00 12.00
33 Carey Price JSY B 12.00 30.00
34 Jarome Iginla JSY C 6.00 15.00
35 Max Domi JSY D 4.00 10.00
36 John Tavares JSY B 10.00 25.00
38 Mikael Granlund JSY D 3.00 8.00
39 Chris Kreider JSY C 6.00 15.00
40 John Klingberg JSY C 5.00 12.00
41 Jake Allen JSY D 4.00 10.00
42 Phil Kessel JSY C 5.00 12.00
43 Nikolaj Ehlers JSY D 4.00 10.00
45 Mike Hoffman JSY D 2.50 6.00
46 Duncan Keith JSY D 3.00 8.00
47 Ryan Miller JSY D 4.00 10.00
48 Ryan Getzlaf JSY C 5.00 12.00
49 Nazem Kadri JSY D 5.00 12.00
50 Connor McDavid JSY B 30.00 80.00
51 T.J. Oshie JSY D 4.00 10.00
52 Jaden Schwartz JSY D 5.00 12.00
53 Patrick Marleau JSY C 5.00 12.00
54 Jakub Voracek JSY D 3.00 8.00
55 Victor Hedman JSY C 6.00 15.00
56 Alex Galchenyuk JSY C 3.00 8.00
58 Jeff Carter JSY D 3.00 8.00
59 Aleksander Barkov JSY C 8.00 20.00
60 Henrik Lundqvist JSY C 12.00 30.00
62 Gabriel Landeskog JSY C 6.00 15.00
64 Jack Eichel JSY D 6.00 15.00
66 Derek Stepan JSY C 3.00 8.00
67 Bo Horvat JSY D 5.00 12.00
68 Cam Ward JSY D 4.00 10.00
70 Henrik Zetterberg JSY C 6.00 15.00
71 Jordan Eberle JSY D 4.00 10.00
72 Sean Monahan JSY D 2.50 6.00
73 Patrick Sharp JSY D 3.00 8.00
74 Tyler Toffoli JSY D 4.00 10.00
75 Zach Parise JSY D 4.00 10.00
76 Brendan Gallagher JSY C 5.00 12.00
78 Frederik Andersen JSY D 5.00 12.00
79 Michael Cammalleri JSY D 3.00 8.00
80 Oliver Ekman-Larsson JSY C 5.00 12.00
82 Sam Reinhart JSY D 8.00 20.00
83 Jake Muzzin JSY D 4.00 10.00
84 Mark Scheifele JSY A 12.00 30.00
85 Wayne Simmonds JSY D 5.00 12.00
86 Patrick Kane JSY B 12.00 30.00
87 Tomas Tatar JSY D 2.50 6.00
88 Anders Lee JSY D 4.00 10.00
89 Roberto Luongo JSY C 8.00 20.00
91 Matt Murray JSY C 8.00 20.00
93 Igor Larionov JSY B 6.00 15.00
94 Patrick Roy JSY A 20.00 50.00
95 Larry Murphy JSY B 5.00 12.00
97 Mario Lemieux JSY A 30.00 80.00
98 Felix Potvin JSY B 10.00 25.00
99 Pavel Bure JSY B 6.00 15.00
100 Wayne Gretzky JSY A 50.00 125.00
101 Auston Matthews JSY 25.00 60.00
102 Pavel Zacha JSY 6.00 15.00
103 Christian Dvorak JSY 5.00 12.00
104 Nick Schmaltz JSY 5.00 12.00
105 Justin Bailey JSY 4.00 10.00
106 Ivan Provorov JSY 6.00 15.00
107 Chris Bigras JSY 3.00 8.00
108 Matthew Tkachuk JSY 15.00 40.00
109 Kyle Connor JSY 12.00 30.00
111 Mikhail Sergachev JSY 6.00 15.00
112 Brandon Carlo JSY 6.00 15.00
113 Dylan Strome JSY 10.00 25.00
114 Jacob Larsson JSY 6.00 15.00
115 Miles Wood JSY 3.00 8.00
116 Lawson Crouse JSY 3.00 8.00
118 Daniel Altshuller JSY 3.00 8.00
119 Anthony Beauvillier JSY 4.00 10.00
120 Anthony Mantha JSY 8.00 20.00
123 Dominik Simon JSY 3.00 8.00
125 Nikita Soshnikov JSY 2.50 6.00
128 Esa Lindell JSY 4.00 10.00
130 Mitch Marner JSY 12.00 30.00
131 Hudson Fasching JSY 4.00 10.00
135 Oliver Bjorkstrand JSY 5.00 12.00
136 Sebastian Aho JSY 12.00 30.00
139 Jesse Puljujarvi JSY 8.00 20.00
140 Kasperi Kapanen JSY 6.00 15.00
143 J.C. Lipon JSY 4.00 10.00
145 Pontus Aberg JSY 5.00 12.00
146 Kevin Labanc JSY 4.00 10.00
148 Michael Matheson JSY 4.00 10.00
150 Sonny Milano JSY 5.00 12.00
151 Jimmy Vesey JSY 6.00 15.00
153 Mike Reilly JSY 3.00 8.00
155 Oliver Kylington JSY 3.00 8.00
160 Brendan Leipsic JSY 3.00 8.00
162 Frederik Gauthier JSY 3.00 8.00
170 Charlie Lindgren JSY 6.00 15.00
173 Oskar Sundqvist JSY 4.00 10.00
175 Steven Santini JSY 3.00 8.00
176 Brayden Point JSY 10.00 25.00
178 Ryan Pulock JSY 4.00 10.00
179 Jakob Chychrun JSY 8.00 20.00
180 Connor Brown JSY 6.00 15.00
185 Patrik Laine JSY 10.00 25.00
186 Zach Werenski JSY 12.00 30.00
187 Pavel Buchnevich JSY 6.00 15.00
189 Anthony DeAngelo JSY 3.00 8.00
190 Jason Dickinson JSY 3.00 8.00
193 Tom Kuhnhackl JSY 3.00 8.00
196 Mark McNeill JSY 4.00 10.00
198 Trevor Carrick JSY 4.00 10.00

2016-17 SP Game Used Red

2 Robby Fabbri JSY AU C 4.00 10.00
3 Joe Thornton JSY AU B 12.00 30.00
4 Brayden Schenn JSY AU C 6.00 15.00
5 Mark Stone JSY AU C 8.00 20.00
6 Max Pacioretty JSY AU B 8.00 20.00
8 Anze Kopitar JSY AU B 12.00 30.00
9 Jonathan Huberdeau JSY AU C 8.00 20.00
10 Jason Spezza JSY AU B 8.00 20.00
13 Sam Bennett JSY AU C 10.00 25.00
20 David Backes JSY AU B 5.00 12.00
22 Nino Niederreiter JSY AU C 4.00 10.00
24 Rick Nash JSY AU C 6.00 15.00
27 Morgan Rielly JSY AU C 6.00 15.00
34 Jarome Iginla JSY AU B 10.00 25.00
36 John Tavares JSY AU B 12.00 30.00
41 Jake Allen JSY AU C 6.00 15.00
43 Nikolaj Ehlers JSY AU C 6.00 15.00
45 Mike Hoffman JSY AU C 4.00 10.00
47 Ryan Miller JSY AU C 6.00 15.00
50 Connor McDavid JSY AU B 125.00 250.00
52 Jaden Schwartz JSY AU C 8.00 20.00
53 Patrick Marleau JSY AU C 6.00 15.00
54 Jakub Voracek JSY AU C 5.00 12.00
56 Alex Galchenyuk JSY AU B 5.00 12.00
59 Aleksander Barkov JSY AU C 10.00 25.00
60 Henrik Lundqvist JSY AU B 20.00 50.00
62 Gabriel Landeskog JSY AU B 10.00 25.00
66 Derek Stepan JSY AU C 4.00 10.00
67 Bo Horvat JSY AU C 8.00 20.00
68 Cam Ward JSY AU C 6.00 15.00
70 Henrik Zetterberg JSY AU B 10.00 25.00
72 Sean Monahan JSY AU C 4.00 10.00
74 Tyler Toffoli JSY AU C 6.00 15.00
75 Zach Parise JSY AU B 8.00 20.00
76 Brendan Gallagher JSY AU B 8.00 20.00
77 Bobby Ryan JSY AU B 6.00 15.00
83 Jake Muzzin JSY AU C 6.00 15.00
84 Mark Scheifele JSY AU C 10.00 25.00
87 Tomas Tatar JSY AU C 4.00 10.00
88 Anders Lee JSY AU C 6.00 15.00
89 Roberto Luongo JSY AU B 12.00 30.00
91 Matt Murray JSY AU C 25.00 60.00
93 Igor Larionov JSY AU B 8.00 20.00
94 Patrick Roy JSY AU B 20.00 50.00
95 Larry Murphy JSY AU B 6.00 15.00
97 Mario Lemieux JSY AU B 30.00 80.00
98 Felix Potvin JSY AU B 12.00 30.00
99 Pavel Bure JSY AU B 8.00 20.00
102 Pavel Zacha JSY AU C 10.00 25.00
103 Christian Dvorak JSY AU C 8.00 20.00
104 Nick Schmaltz JSY AU D 6.00 15.00
105 Justin Bailey JSY AU D 5.00 12.00
106 Ivan Provorov JSY AU B 12.00 30.00
107 Chris Bigras JSY AU D 4.00 10.00
108 Matthew Tkachuk JSY AU B 30.00 80.00
109 Kyle Connor JSY AU B 25.00 60.00
110 William Nylander JSY AU B 30.00 80.00
111 Mikhail Sergachev JSY AU B 12.00 30.00
113 Dylan Strome JSY AU C 15.00 40.00
115 Miles Wood JSY AU E 4.00 10.00
116 Lawson Crouse JSY AU D 4.00 10.00
118 Daniel Altshuller JSY AU E 4.00 10.00
119 Anthony Beauvillier JSY AU D 5.00 12.00
120 Anthony Mantha JSY AU C 12.00 30.00
123 Dominik Simon JSY AU C 5.00 12.00
125 Nikita Soshnikov JSY AU B 5.00 12.00
128 Esa Lindell JSY AU E 5.00 12.00
131 Hudson Fasching JSY AU D 5.00 12.00
135 Oliver Bjorkstrand JSY AU D 6.00 15.00
139 Jesse Puljujarvi JSY AU B 15.00 40.00
140 Kasperi Kapanen JSY AU C 10.00 25.00
143 J.C. Lipon JSY AU C 6.00 15.00
145 Pontus Aberg JSY AU C 8.00 20.00
146 Kevin Labanc JSY AU E 5.00 12.00
148 Michael Matheson JSY AU D 5.00 12.00
150 Sonny Milano JSY AU C 8.00 20.00
153 Mike Reilly JSY AU E 4.00 10.00
157 Travis Konecny JSY AU C 12.00 30.00
160 Brendan Leipsic JSY AU C 5.00 12.00
161 Tyler Motte JSY AU E 5.00 12.00
167 Mathew Barzal JSY AU B 25.00 60.00
169 Thomas Chabot JSY AU D 10.00 25.00
170 Charlie Lindgren JSY AU C 10.00 25.00
173 Oskar Sundqvist JSY AU D 5.00 12.00
175 Steven Santini JSY AU E 4.00 10.00
176 Brayden Point JSY AU C 15.00 40.00
178 Ryan Pulock JSY AU C 6.00 15.00
179 Jakob Chychrun JSY AU C 12.00 30.00
180 Connor Brown JSY AU C 10.00 25.00
185 Patrik Laine JSY AU B 20.00 50.00
186 Zach Werenski JSY AU B 25.00 60.00
187 Pavel Buchnevich JSY AU C 10.00 25.00
189 Anthony DeAngelo JSY AU E 4.00 10.00
190 Jason Dickinson JSY AU D 4.00 10.00
192 Josh Morrissey JSY AU D 12.00 30.00
193 Tom Kuhnhackl JSY AU D 4.00 10.00
196 Mark McNeill JSY AU E 5.00 12.00
198 Trevor Carrick JSY AU C 6.00 15.00

2016-17 SP Game Used All Star Skills Dual Fabrics

AS2BS J.Benn/T.Seguin 5.00 12.00
AS2HT T.Hall/V.Tarasenko 5.00 12.00
AS2KT P.Kane/J.Tavares 8.00 20.00
AS2LG D.Larkin/J.Gaudreau 6.00 15.00
AS2ML E.Malkin/K.Letang 8.00 20.00
AS2PB J.Pavelski/B.Burns 5.00 12.00
AS2PG C.Perry/J.Gibson 6.00 15.00
AS2QD J.Quick/D.Doughty 5.00 12.00
AS2SB S.Stamkos/B.Bishop 8.00 20.00
AS2SC C.Schneider/D.Dubnyk 4.00 10.00
AS2SK P.Subban/E.Karlsson 5.00 12.00

2016-17 SP Game Used All Star Skills Fabrics

ASAE Aaron Ekblad B 5.00 12
ASBB Ben Bishop C 2.50 6.00
ASBH Braden Holtby B 5.00 12.00
ASBS Brandon Saad C 2.50 6.00
ASBU Brent Burns B 4.00 10.00
ASCG Claude Giroux C 3.00 8.00
ASCP Corey Perry B 6.00 15.00
ASCS Cory Schneider C 3.00 8.00
ASDB Dustin Byfuglien C 3.00 8.00
ASDD Devan Dubnyk C 2.50 6.00
ASDL Dylan Larkin B 5.00 12.00
ASDO Drew Doughty C 4.00 10.00
ASDS Daniel Sedin B 5.00 12.00
ASEK Erik Karlsson B 5.00 12.00
ASEM Evgeni Malkin A 10.00 25.00
ASGI John Gibson C 3.00 8.00
ASJB Jamie Benn A 5.00 12.00
ASJF Justin Faulk C 2.50 6.00
ASJG Johnny Gaudreau B 6.00 15.00
ASJJ Jaromir Jagr A 15.00 40.00
ASJN James Neal C 2.00 5.00
ASJP Joe Pavelski B 5.00 12.00
ASJQ Jonathan Quick C 4.00 10.00
ASJS John Scott C 3.00 8.00
ASJT John Tavares A 8.00 20.00
ASKL Kris Letang B 5.00 12.00
ASKU Evgeny Kuznetsov B 5.00 12.00
ASLK Leo Komarov C 2.00 5.00
ASMD Matt Duchene C 3.00 8.00
ASMG Mark Giordano C 3.00 8.00
ASNB Nicklas Backstrom C 3.00 8.00
ASPB Patrice Bergeron C 4.00 10.00
ASPK Patrick Kane A 10.00 25.00
ASPR Pekka Rinne C 3.00 8.00
ASPS P.K. Subban A 6.00 15.00
ASRJ Roman Josi C 3.00 8.00
ASRL Roberto Luongo A 8.00 20.00
ASRM Ryan McDonagh C 2.00 5.00
ASRO Ryan O'Reilly C 3.00 8.00
ASSS Steven Stamkos A 10.00 25.00
ASSW Shea Weber C 2.50 6.00
ASTH Taylor Hall A 5.00 12.00
ASTS Tyler Seguin A 6.00 15.00
ASVT Vladimir Tarasenko A 6.00 15.00

2016-17 SP Game Used All Star Skills Quad Fabrics

AS4NSH Neal/Josi/Weber/Rinne B 5.00 12.00
AS4CAPT Kane/Tavares/Scott/Jagr A 15.00 40.00
AS4DMEN Faulk/McDonagh Giordano/Byfuglien B 5.00 12.00
AS4SCUP Malkin/Letang Pavelski/Burns A 10.00 25.00
AS4SOCAL Doughty/Quick Perry/Gibson B 8.00 20.00

2016-17 SP Game Used All Star Skills Relic Blends

ASBAE Aaron Ekblad 6.00 15.00
ASBBB Ben Bishop 4.00 10.00
ASBBH Braden Holtby 6.00 15.00
ASBBS Brandon Saad 4.00 10.00
ASBBU Brent Burns 5.00 12.00
ASBCG Claude Giroux 5.00 12.00
ASBCP Corey Perry 8.00 20.00
ASBCS Cory Schneider 5.00 12.00
ASBDB Dustin Byfuglien 5.00 12.00
ASBDD Devan Dubnyk 4.00 10.00
ASBDL Dylan Larkin 6.00 15.00
ASBDO Drew Doughty 6.00 15.00
ASBDS Daniel Sedin 6.00 15.00
ASBEK Erik Karlsson 6.00 15.00
ASBEM Evgeni Malkin 10.00 25.00
ASBGI John Gibson 5.00 12.00
ASBJB Jamie Benn 5.00 12.00
ASBJF Justin Faulk 4.00 10.00
ASBJG Johnny Gaudreau 8.00 20.00
ASBJJ Jaromir Jagr 15.00 40.00
ASBJN James Neal 3.00 8.00
ASBJP Joe Pavelski 6.00 15.00
ASBJQ Jonathan Quick 6.00 15.00
ASBJS John Scott 5.00 12.00
ASBJT John Tavares 8.00 20.00
ASBKL Kris Letang 6.00 15.00
ASBKU Evgeny Kuznetsov 6.00 15.00
ASBLK Leo Komarov 3.00 8.00
ASBMD Matt Duchene 5.00 12.00
ASBMG Mark Giordano 5.00 12.00
ASBNB Nicklas Backstrom 5.00 12.00
ASBPB Patrice Bergeron 6.00 15.00
ASBPK Patrick Kane 10.00 25.00
ASBPR Pekka Rinne 5.00 12.00
ASBPS P.K. Subban 6.00 15.00
ASBRJ Roman Josi 5.00 12.00
ASBRL Roberto Luongo 8.00 20.00
ASBRM Ryan McDonagh 3.00 8.00
ASBRO Ryan O'Reilly 5.00 12.00
ASBSS Steven Stamkos 10.00 25.00
ASBSW Shea Weber 4.00 10.00
ASBTH Taylor Hall 5.00 12.00
ASBTS Tyler Seguin 6.00 15.00
ASBVT Vladimir Tarasenko 6.00 15.00

2016-17 SP Game Used All Star Skills Six Fabrics

AS6-DEF Karlsson/Doughty/Letang Subban/Burns/Josi B 8.00 20.00
AS6AFWD Larkin/Bergeron/Jagr/Komarov O'Reilly/Stamkos B 20.00 50.00
AS6CFWD Kane/Benn/Tarasenko Duchene/Seguin/Neal A 15.00 40.00
AS6FPNP Neal/Weber/Rinne Jagr/Ekblad/Luongo B 20.00 50.00
AS6MFWD Kuznetsov/Malkin/Tavares/Giroux Saad/Backstrom A 15.00 40.00
AS6PFWD Gaudreau/Hall/Perry/Pavelski Scott/Sedin B 10.00 25.00
AS6ASTARS Kane/Benn/Gaudreau/Malkin Kuznetsov/Tavares A 15.00 40.00

2016-17 SP Game Used All Star Skills Triple Fabrics

AS3BHQ Bishop/Holtby/Quick 5.00 12.00
AS3BKH Backstrom/Kuznetsov/Holtby 5.00 12.00
AS3EJL Ekblad/Jagr/Luongo 12.00 30.00
AS3GBB Giordano/Burns/Byfuglien 4.00 10.00
AS3KSE Karlsson/Subban/Ekblad 5.00 12.00
AS3SBS Saad/Bergeron/Scott 5.00 12.00
AS3SGP Stamkos/Giroux/Pavelski 8.00 20.00
AS3SHD Seguin/Hall/Duchene 5.00 12.00
AS3-SOK Sedin/O'Reilly/Komarov 5.00 12.00

2016-17 SP Game Used Autographs Blue

2 Robby Fabbri D 2.00 5.00
4 Brayden Schenn D 3.00 8.00
6 Max Pacioretty C 5.00 12.00
8 Anze Kopitar C 8.00 20.00
9 Jonathan Huberdeau C 6.00 15.00
10 Jason Spezza C 5.00 12.00
11 Andrew Ladd C 3.00 8.00
13 Sam Bennett C 8.00 20.00
16 Taylor Hall C 5.00 12.00
22 Nino Niederreiter D 2.00 5.00
24 Rick Nash B 8.00 20.00
26 Nikita Kucherov D 6.00 15.00
27 Morgan Rielly C 5.00 12.00
32 Ryan Spooner D 2.50 6.00
33 Carey Price B 50.00 120.00
34 Jarome Iginla B 10.00 25.00
36 John Tavares B 12.00 30.00
41 Jake Allen D 3.00 8.00
43 Nikolaj Ehlers D 3.00 8.00
44 Tyler Johnson D 2.00 5.00
47 Ryan Miller C 5.00 12.00
50 Connor McDavid C 90.00 150.00
52 Jaden Schwartz D 4.00 10.00
53 Patrick Marleau C 5.00 12.00
54 Jakub Voracek C 4.00 10.00
56 Alex Galchenyuk B 5.00 12.00
57 Jaroslav Halak C 5.00 12.00
59 Aleksander Barkov C 8.00 20.00
60 Henrik Lundqvist B 25.00 60.00
61 Boone Jenner D 3.00 8.00
62 Gabriel Landeskog C 6.00 15.00
65 David Krejci C 5.00 12.00
66 Derek Stepan D 2.00 5.00
67 Bo Horvat D 4.00 10.00
68 Cam Ward C 5.00 12.00
69 Kyle Palmieri D 2.50 6.00
70 Henrik Zetterberg B 10.00 25.00
72 Sean Monahan C 3.00 8.00
74 Tyler Toffoli D 3.00 8.00
75 Zach Parise B 8.00 20.00
76 Brendan Gallagher C 5.00 12.00
77 Bobby Ryan C 4.00 10.00
81 Tom Wilson D 3.00 8.00
83 Jake Muzzin C 5.00 12.00
84 Mark Scheifele D 5.00 12.00
87 Tomas Tatar D 2.00 5.00
88 Anders Lee D 3.00 8.00
89 Roberto Luongo C 8.00 20.00
91 Matt Murray C 20.00 50.00
92 Carl Hagelin D 2.00 5.00
93 Igor Larionov B 8.00 20.00
94 Patrick Roy D 40.00 100.00
95 Larry Murphy C 4.00 10.00
97 Mario Lemieux B 50.00 120.00
98 Felix Potvin C 8.00 20.00
100 Wayne Gretzky C 250.00 600.00
101 Auston Matthews A 200.00 400.00
102 Pavel Zacha F 5.00 12.00
103 Christian Dvorak B 8.00 20.00
104 Nick Schmaltz D 5.00 12.00
105 Justin Bailey F 3.00 8.00
106 Ivan Provorov B 10.00 25.00
107 Chris Bigras F 2.50 6.00
108 Matthew Tkachuk C 20.00 50.00
109 Kyle Connor C 15.00 40.00
110 William Nylander C 20.00 50.00
111 Mikhail Sergachev B 10.00 25.00
113 Dylan Strome B 30.00 80.00
115 Miles Wood D 3.00 8.00
116 Lawson Crouse D 3.00 8.00
118 Daniel Altshuller E 3.00 8.00
119 Anthony Beauvillier B 6.00 15.00
120 Anthony Mantha D 8.00 20.00
123 Dominik Simon F 2.50 6.00
125 Nikita Soshnikov D 2.50 6.00
128 Esa Lindell F 3.00 8.00
131 Hudson Fasching B 6.00 15.00
135 Oliver Bjorkstrand F 4.00 10.00
139 Jesse Puljujarvi B 12.00 30.00
140 Kasperi Kapanen D 6.00 15.00
143 J.C. Lipon B 6.00 15.00
145 Pontus Aberg E 5.00 12.00
146 Kevin Labanc E 4.00 10.00
148 Michael Matheson F 3.00 8.00
150 Sonny Milano B 8.00 20.00
153 Mike Reilly F 2.50 6.00
160 Brendan Leipsic E 3.00 8.00
161 Tyler Motte D 4.00 10.00
165 Sergey Tolchinsky F 2.50 6.00
167 Mathew Barzal C 15.00 40.00
169 Thomas Chabot D 8.00 20.00
170 Charlie Lindgren F 5.00 12.00
172 Danton Heinen D 3.00 8.00
173 Oskar Sundqvist E 4.00 10.00
175 Steven Santini E 3.00 8.00
176 Brayden Point B 15.00 40.00
178 Ryan Pulock F 3.00 8.00
179 Jakob Chychrun F 6.00 15.00
180 Connor Brown F 5.00 12.00
186 Zach Werenski C 15.00 40.00
187 Pavel Buchnevich F 5.00 12.00
189 Anthony DeAngelo E 3.00 8.00
190 Jason Dickinson F 2.50 6.00
192 Josh Morrissey E 10.00 25.00
193 Tom Kuhnhackl D 3.00 8.00
195 Chase De Leo F 3.00 8.00
196 Mark McNeill F 3.00 8.00
198 Trevor Carrick F 3.00 8.00

2016-17 SP Game Used Banner Year All Star '16

BASAE Aaron Ekblad 6.00 15.00
BASBB Ben Bishop 4.00 10.00
BASBH Braden Holtby 6.00 15.00
BASBS Brandon Saad 4.00 10.00
BASBU Brent Burns 5.00 12.00
BASCG Claude Giroux 5.00 12.00
BASCP Corey Perry 8.00 20.00
BASCS Cory Schneider 5.00 12.00
BASDB Dustin Byfuglien 5.00 12.00
BASDD Devan Dubnyk 4.00 10.00
BASDL Dylan Larkin 6.00 15.00
BASDO Drew Doughty 6.00 15.00
BASDS Daniel Sedin 6.00 15.00
BASEK Evgeny Kuznetsov 6.00 15.00
BASEM Evgeni Malkin 10.00 25.00
BASGI John Gibson 5.00 12.00
BASJB Jamie Benn 5.00 12.00
BASJF Justin Faulk 4.00 10.00
BASJG Johnny Gaudreau 8.00 20.00
BASJJ Jaromir Jagr 15.00 40.00
BASJN James Neal 3.00 8.00
BASJP Joe Pavelski 6.00 15.00
BASJQ Jonathan Quick 6.00 15.00
BASJS John Scott SP 20.00 50.00
BASJT John Tavares 8.00 20.00
BASKA Erik Karlsson 6.00 15.00
BASKL Kris Letang 6.00 15.00
BASLK Leo Komarov 3.00 8.00
BASMD Matt Duchene 5.00 12.00
BASMG Mark Giordano 5.00 12.00
BASNB Nicklas Backstrom 5.00 12.00
BASPB Patrice Bergeron 6.00 15.00
BASPK Patrick Kane 10.00 25.00
BASPR Pekka Rinne 5.00 12.00
BASPS P.K. Subban 6.00 15.00
BASRJ Roman Josi 5.00 12.00
BASRL Roberto Luongo 8.00 20.00
BASRM Ryan McDonagh 3.00 8.00
BASRO Ryan O'Reilly 5.00 12.00
BASSS Steven Stamkos 10.00 25.00
BASSW Shea Weber 4.00 10.00
BASTH Taylor Hall 5.00 12.00
BASTS Tyler Seguin 6.00 15.00
BASVT Vladimir Tarasenko 6.00 15.00

2016-17 SP Game Used Banner Year All Star '16 Autographs

BASBU Brent Burns B 25.00 60.00
BASCS Cory Schneider B 25.00 60.00
BASGI John Gibson B 25.00 60.00
BASJB Jamie Benn B 25.00 60.00
BASJP Joe Pavelski B 30.00 80.00
BASJT John Tavares A 60.00 150.00
BASRJ Roman Josi B 25.00 60.00
BASRL Roberto Luongo A 60.00 150.00

2016-17 SP Game Used Banner Year Draft '12

BD12AA Andreas Athanasiou 6.00 15.00
BD12AG Alex Galchenyuk SP 4.00 10.00
BD12AV Andrei Vasilevskiy 10.00 25.00
BD12CB Connor Brown 10.00 25.00
BD12FA Frederik Andersen 8.00 20.00
BD12FF Filip Forsberg 10.00 25.00
BD12MM Matt Murray 10.00 25.00
BD12MR Morgan Rielly 6.00 15.00
BD12NY Nail Yakupov 4.00 10.00
BD12RM Ryan Murray 4.00 10.00
BD12SG Shayne Gostisbehere 6.00 15.00
BD12TH Tomas Hertl 6.00 15.00
BD12TT Teuvo Teravainen 6.00 15.00
BD12ZG Zemgus Girgensons 5.00 12.00

2016-17 SP Game Used Banner Year Draft '12 Autographs

BD12AA Andreas Athanasiou C 20.00 50.00
BD12AG Alex Galchenyuk B 20.00 50.00
BD12-MM Matt Murray C 20.00 50.00

2016-17 SP Game Used Banner Year Draft '14

BD14AE Aaron Ekblad SP 8.00 20.00
BD14DL Dylan Larkin 8.00 20.00
BD14DP David Pastrnak 15.00 40.00
BD14JV Jake Virtanen 8.00 20.00
BD14LD Leon Draisaitl 20.00 50.00
BD14NE Nikolaj Ehlers 6.00 15.00
BD14RF Robby Fabbri 4.00 10.00
BD14SB Sam Bennett 10.00 25.00
BD14SR Sam Reinhart 12.00 30.00
BD14WN William Nylander 25.00 60.00

2016-17 SP Game Used Banner Year Draft '14 Autographs

BD14AE Aaron Ekblad C 8.00 20.00
BD14LD Leon Draisaitl C 20.00 50.00
BD14SB Sam Bennett C 15.00 40.00
BD14-WN William Nylander B 30.00 80.00

2016-17 SP Game Used Banner Year Draft '15

BD15CM Connor McDavid 30.00 80.00
BD15DS Daniel Sprong 4.00 10.00
BD15JE Jack Eichel SP 10.00 25.00
BD15MA Mitch Marner 20.00 50.00
BD15NH Noah Hanifin 6.00 15.00
BD15PZ Pavel Zacha 10.00 25.00
BD15ST Dylan Strome 15.00 40.00

2016-17 SP Game Used Banner Year Draft '15 Autographs

BD15PZ Pavel Zacha C 10.00 25.00
BD15-ST Dylan Strome C 15.00 40.00

2016-17 SP Game Used Banner Year Draft '16

BD16AM Auston Matthews 40.00 100.00
BD16JP Jesse Puljujarvi SP 12.00 30.00
BD16MT Matthew Tkachuk 25.00 60.00
BD16-PL Patrik Laine 15.00 40.00

2016-17 SP Game Used Banner Year Draft '16 Autographs

BD16AM Auston Matthews B 200.00 300.00
BD16JP Jesse Puljujarvi B 25.00 60.00
BD16PL Patrik Laine B 150.00 300.00

2016-17 SP Game Used Banner Year Stadium Series '16

BSSAP Artemi Panarin 12.00 30.00
BSSCC Corey Crawford 8.00 20.00
BSSDL Dylan Larkin 8.00 20.00
BSSGL Gabriel Landeskog 8.00 20.00
BSSHZ Henrik Zetterberg 8.00 20.00
BSSJI Jarome Iginla 8.00 20.00
BSSJT Jonathan Toews 10.00 25.00
BSSMD Matt Duchene 6.00 15.00
BSSMK Mikko Koivu 5.00 12.00
BSSNM Nathan MacKinnon 25.00 60.00
BSSNN Nino Niederreiter 4.00 10.00
BSSPK Patrick Kane SP 12.00 30.00
BSSPM Petr Mrazek SP 6.00 15.00
BSSTT Tomas Tatar 4.00 10.00
BSSZP Zach Parise 6.00 15.00

2016-17 SP Game Used Banner Year Stadium Series '16 Autographs

BSSGL Gabriel Landeskog B 25.00 60.00
BSSHZ Henrik Zetterberg A 25.00 60.00
BSSJI Jarome Iginla B 25.00 60.00
BSSMD Matt Duchene B 20.00 50.00
BSSNN Nino Niederreiter B 12.00 30.00
BSSTT Tomas Tatar B 12.00 30.00
BSSZP Zach Parise B 20.00 50.00
BSS-JT Jonathan Toews A 30.00 80.00

2016-17 SP Game Used Banner Year Stanley Cup Finals

BSCAK Anze Kopitar 8.00 20.00
BSCBB Brent Burns 5.00 12.00
BSCBS Brandon Saad 4.00 10.00
BSCCC Corey Crawford SP 6.00 15.00
BSCDB Derick Brassard 3.00 8.00
BSCDD Drew Doughty SP 6.00 15.00
BSCDK Duncan Keith 4.00 10.00
BSCDS Derek Stepan 3.00 8.00
BSCEM Evgeni Malkin 10.00 25.00
BSCHL Henrik Lundqvist 12.00 30.00
BSCJC Jeff Carter 4.00 10.00
BSCJP Joe Pavelski 6.00 15.00
BSCJT Jonathan Toews 8.00 20.00
BSCJW Justin Williams 4.00 10.00
BSCKE Phil Kessel 5.00 12.00
BSCKL Kris Letang 6.00 15.00
BSCKR David Krejci 5.00 12.00
BSCMH Marian Hossa 5.00 12.00
BSCMJ Martin Jones 4.00 10.00
BSCMM Matt Murray SP 8.00 20.00
BSCMR Mike Richards 4.00 10.00
BSCMZ Mats Zuccarello 5.00 12.00
BSCPB Patrice Bergeron 6.00 15.00
BSCPK Patrick Kane 10.00 25.00
BSCSC Sidney Crosby 20.00 50.00
BSCTH Joe Thornton 8.00 20.00
BSCTR Tuukka Rask 6.00 15.00
BSCTT Tyler Toffoli 5.00 12.00
BSCZC Zdeno Chara 5.00 12.00
BSC-BM Brad Marchand 10.00 25.00

2016-17 SP Game Used Banner Year Stanley Cup Finals Autographs

BSCAK Anze Kopitar B 50.00 120.00
BSCDK David Krejci B 30.00 80.00
BSCHL Henrik Lundqvist A 80.00 200.00
BSCJT Jonathan Toews A 50.00 120.00
BSCMM Matt Murray B 50.00 125.00
BSCTH Joe Thornton B 50.00 125.00
BSCTT Tyler Toffoli B 30.00 80.00

2016-17 SP Game Used Banner Year Winter Classic

BWCAG Alex Galchenyuk 3.00 8.00
BWCAM Andrei Markov 3.00 8.00
BWCBG Brendan Gallagher SP 5.00 12.00
BWCBH Braden Holtby 6.00 15.00
BWCBS Brent Seabrook 3.00 8.00
BWCCC Corey Crawford 6.00 15.00
BWCEK Evgeny Kuznetsov 6.00 15.00
BWCJC John Carlson 5.00 12.00
BWCJT Jonathan Toews 8.00 20.00
BWCKE Duncan Keith 4.00 10.00
BWCLE Loui Eriksson 3.00 8.00
BWCMC Mike Condon 5.00 12.00
BWCMH Marian Hossa 5.00 12.00
BWCMJ Marcus Johansson 5.00 12.00
BWCMP Max Pacioretty 5.00 12.00
BWCMQ Adam McQuaid 3.00 8.00
BWCNB Nicklas Backstrom 5.00 12.00
BWCNH Niklas Hjalmarsson 3.00 8.00
BWCPB Patrice Bergeron 6.00 15.00
BWCPK Patrick Kane 10.00 25.00
BWCPS P.K. Subban 6.00 15.00
BWCRS Ryan Spooner 4.00 10.00
BWCTP Tomas Plekanec 3.00 8.00
BWCTR Tuukka Rask 6.00 15.00
BWCZC Zdeno Chara 5.00 12.00
BWC-AO Alexander Ovechkin SP 20.00 50.00

2016-17 SP Game Used Banner Year Winter Classic Autographs

BWCAG Alex Galchenyuk B 20.00 50.00
BWCAO Alexander Ovechkin A 125.00 300.00
BWCBG Brendan Gallagher B 30.00 80.00
BWCJT Jonathan Toews A 50.00 120.00
BWC-RS Ryan Spooner B 25.00 60.00

2016-17 SP Game Used Draft Day Marks

DDMAD Anthony DeAngelo/35 10.00 25.00
DDMAM Anthony Mantha/35 40.00 100.00
DDMBM Brandon Montour/35 30.00 80.00
DDMBP Brendan Perlini/35 12.00 30.00
DDMBP Brayden Point/35 30.00 80.00
DDMCB Chris Bigras/35 10.00 25.00
DDMCD Christian Dvorak/35 15.00 40.00
DDMDS Dylan Strome/35 30.00 80.00
DDMFA Hudson Fasching/35 12.00 30.00
DDMIP Ivan Provorov/35 30.00 80.00
DDMJC Jakob Chychrun/35 25.00 60.00
DDMJD Jason Dickinson/35 10.00 25.00
DDMJH Julius Honka/35 12.00 30.00
DDMJP Jesse Puljujarvi/35 30.00 80.00
DDMJV Jakub Vrana/35 15.00 40.00
DDMKC Kyle Connor/35 15.00 40.00
DDMKK Kasperi Kapanen/35 20.00 50.00
DDMLC Lawson Crouse/35 10.00 25.00
DDMMB Mathew Barzal/35 30.00 80.00
DDMMM Michael Matheson/35 12.00 30.00
DDMMM Mitch Marner/35 100.00 200.00
DDMMT Matthew Tkachuk/35 50.00 125.00
DDMNS Nick Schmaltz/35 15.00 40.00
DDMOB Oliver Bjorkstrand/35 15.00 40.00
DDMPB Pavel Buchnevich/35 20.00 50.00
DDMPL Patrik Laine/35 125.00 250.00
DDMPZ Pavel Zacha/35 20.00 50.00
DDMRP Ryan Pulock/35 12.00 30.00
DDMSM Sonny Milano/35 15.00 40.00
DDMTD Thatcher Demko/35 30.00 80.00
DDMTK Travis Konecny/35 25.00 60.00
DDMTM Timo Meier/35 25.00 60.00
DDMWN William Nylander/35 80.00 150.00
DDMZW Zach Werenski/35 40.00 100.00

2016-17 SP Game Used Frameworks Materials

FWAE Aaron Ekblad D 8.00 20.00
FWAH Adam Henrique D 5.00 12.00
FWAK Anze Kopitar C 12.00 30.00
FWAO Alexander Ovechkin C 30.00 80.00
FWBH Brett Hull B 20.00 50.00
FWBS Brandon Saad D 5.00 12.00
FWBW Blake Wheeler D 6.00 15.00
FWCA Carey Price B 20.00 50.00
FWCM Connor McDavid B 50.00 125.00
FWDS Daniel Sedin C 10.00 25.00
FWEM Evgeni Malkin B 20.00 50.00
FWHB Braden Holtby C 10.00 25.00
FWHL Henrik Lundqvist B 25.00 60.00
FWHZ Henrik Zetterberg A 20.00 50.00
FWJB Jamie Benn C 8.00 20.00
FWJG Johnny Gaudreau C 12.00 30.00
FWJJ Jaromir Jagr C 25.00 60.00
FWJS Jordan Staal D 5.00 12.00
FWJT Jonathan Toews B 15.00 40.00
FWKM Kirk McLean B 10.00 25.00
FWLR Larry Robinson A 15.00 40.00
FWMD Max Domi D 6.00 15.00
FWMJ Martin Jones D 5.00 12.00
FWML Mario Lemieux B 40.00 100.00
FWNK Nazem Kadri D 8.00 20.00
FWPB Patrice Bergeron D 8.00 20.00
FWPK Patrick Kane A 30.00 80.00
FWPR Patrick Roy B 25.00 60.00
FWRI Pekka Rinne C 8.00 20.00
FWSC Sidney Crosby B 40.00 100.00
FWSS Steven Stamkos C 15.00 40.00
FWSZ Steve Yzerman B 25.00 60.00
FWTA John Tavares B 15.00 40.00
FWTS Tyler Seguin C 10.00 25.00
FWVT Vladimir Tarasenko C 10.00 25.00
FWZP Zach Parise C 8.00 20.00

2016-17 SP Game Used Inked Sweaters

ISAE Aaron Ekblad/99 15.00 40.00
ISAH Adam Henrique/99 10.00 25.00
ISBB Brent Burns/50 15.00 40.00
ISHL Henrik Lundqvist/50 40.00 100.00
ISHZ Henrik Zetterberg/50 20.00 50.00
ISKM Kirk McLean/50 15.00 40.00
ISLD Leon Draisaitl/99 40.00 100.00
ISMB Matt Beleskey/99 10.00 25.00
ISMH Mike Hoffman/99 8.00 20.00
ISMP Max Pacioretty/50 15.00 40.00
ISMZ Mats Zuccarello/99 12.00 30.00
ISRJ Roman Josi/99 12.00 30.00

2016-17 SP Game Used Orange Rainbow Draft Year

1 Sidney Crosby/105 15.00 40.00
2 Robby Fabbri/114 2.50 6.00
3 Joe Thornton/197 5.00 12.00
4 Brayden Schenn/109 4.00 10.00
5 Mark Stone/110 5.00 12.00
6 Max Pacioretty/107 4.00 10.00
7 David Pastrnak/114 10.00 25.00
8 Anze Kopitar/105 6.00 15.00
9 Jonathan Huberdeau/111 5.00 12.00
10 Jason Spezza/101 4.00 10.00
11 Andrew Ladd/104 2.50 6.00
12 Nathan MacKinnon/113 15.00 40.00
13 Sam Bennett/114 6.00 15.00
14 Rasmus Ristolainen/113 2.50 6.00
15 Anthony Duclair/113 3.00 8.00
16 Taylor Hall/110 4.00 10.00
17 Jakob Silfverberg/109 2.50 6.00
18 Jonathan Toews/106 6.00 15.00
19 Petr Mrazek/110 4.00 10.00
20 David Backes/103 2.50 6.00
21 Filip Forsberg/112 6.00 15.00
22 Nino Niederreiter/110 2.50 6.00
23 Nick Foligno/106 3.00 8.00
24 Rick Nash/102 4.00 10.00
25 Alexander Ovechkin/104 15.00 40.00
26 Nikita Kucherov/111 8.00 20.00
27 Morgan Rielly/112 4.00 10.00

Card	Low	High
28 Henrik Sedin/199	4.00	10.00
29 Blake Wheeler/104	4.00	10.00
30 Victor Rask/111	2.50	6.00
31 Ryan Kesler/103	4.00	10.00
32 Ryan Spooner/110	3.00	8.00
33 Carey Price/105	8.00	20.00
34 Jarome Iginla/195	4.00	10.00
35 Max Domi/113	4.00	10.00
36 John Tavares/109	6.00	15.00
37 Corey Crawford/103	5.00	12.00
38 Mikael Granlund/110	3.00	8.00
39 Chris Kreider/109	5.00	12.00
40 John Klingberg/110	4.00	10.00
41 Jake Allen/108	4.00	10.00
42 Phil Kessel/106	4.00	10.00
43 Nikolaj Ehlers/114	4.00	10.00
44 Tyler Johnson /100	2.50	6.00
45 Mike Hoffman/109	2.50	6.00
46 Duncan Keith/102	3.00	8.00
47 Ryan Miller/199	3.00	8.00
48 Ryan Getzlaf/103	4.00	10.00
49 Nazem Kadri/109	5.00	12.00
50 Connor McDavid/115	20.00	50.00
51 T.J. Oshie/105	4.00	10.00
52 Jaden Schwartz/110	5.00	12.00
53 Patrick Marleau/197	3.00	8.00
54 Jakub Voracek/107	3.00	8.00
55 Victor Hedman/109	5.00	12.00
56 Alex Galchenyuk/112	2.50	6.00
57 Jaroslav Halak/103	4.00	10.00
58 Jeff Carter/103	3.00	8.00
59 Aleksander Barkov/113	6.00	15.00
60 Henrik Lundqvist/100	10.00	25.00
61 Boone Jenner/111	4.00	10.00
62 Gabriel Landeskog/111	5.00	12.00
63 Ryan Johansen/110	3.00	8.00
64 Jack Eichel/115	6.00	15.00
65 David Krejci/104	4.00	10.00
66 Derek Stepan/108	2.50	6.00
67 Bo Horvat/113	5.00	12.00
68 Cam Ward/102	4.00	10.00
69 Kyle Palmieri/109	3.00	8.00
70 Henrik Zetterberg/199	4.00	10.00
71 Jordan Eberle/108	4.00	10.00
72 Sean Monahan/113	2.50	6.00
73 Patrick Sharp/101	3.00	8.00
74 Tyler Toffoli/110	4.00	10.00
75 Zach Parise/103	4.00	10.00
76 Brendan Gallagher/110	4.00	10.00
77 Bobby Ryan/105	3.00	8.00
78 Frederik Andersen/110	5.00	12.00
79 Michael Cammalleri/101	3.00	8.00
80 Oliver Ekman-Larsson/109	4.00	10.00
81 Tom Wilson /112	4.00	10.00
82 Sam Reinhart/114	8.00	20.00
83 Jake Muzzin/107	4.00	10.00
84 Mark Scheifele/111	6.00	15.00
85 Wayne Simmonds/107	5.00	12.00
86 Patrick Kane/107	8.00	20.00
87 Tomas Tatar/109	2.50	6.00
88 Anders Lee/109	4.00	10.00
89 Roberto Luongo/197	5.00	12.00
90 Teuvo Teravainen/112	4.00	10.00
91 Matt Murray/112	6.00	15.00
92 Carl Hagelin/107	2.50	6.00
93 Igor Larionov/185	3.00	8.00
94 Patrick Roy/184	8.00	20.00
95 Larry Murphy/180	2.50	6.00
96 Pat LaFontaine/183	3.00	8.00
97 Mario Lemieux/184	12.00	30.00
98 Felix Potvin/190	5.00	12.00
99 Pavel Bure/189	3.00	8.00
100 Wayne Gretzky/100	25.00	60.00
101 Auston Matthews/116	80.00	150.00
102 Pavel Zacha/115	6.00	15.00
103 Christian Dvorak/114	5.00	12.00
104 Nick Schmaltz/114	5.00	12.00
105 Justin Bailey/113	4.00	10.00
106 Ivan Provorov/115	6.00	15.00
107 Chris Bigras/113	3.00	8.00
108 Matthew Tkachuk/116	15.00	40.00
109 Kyle Connor/115	12.00	30.00
110 William Nylander/114	15.00	40.00
111 Mikhail Sergachev/116	6.00	15.00
112 Brandon Carlo/115	6.00	15.00
113 Dylan Strome/115	10.00	25.00
114 Jacob Larsson/115	6.00	15.00
115 Miles Wood/113	3.00	8.00
116 Lawson Crouse/115	3.00	8.00
117 Zach Sanford/113	4.00	10.00
118 Daniel Altshuller/112	3.00	8.00
119 Anthony Beauvillier/115	4.00	10.00
120 Anthony Mantha/113	8.00	20.00
121 Casey Nelson/100	4.00	10.00
122 Ondrej Kase/114	4.00	10.00
123 Dominik Simon/115	3.00	8.00
124 Nikita Zaitsev/100	4.00	10.00
125 Nikita Soshnikov/100	2.50	6.00
126 Gustav Forsling/114	8.00	20.00
127 Brandon Tanev/100	5.00	12.00
128 Esa Lindell/112	4.00	10.00
129 Josh Archibald/111	2.50	6.00
130 Mitch Marner/115	25.00	60.00
131 Hudson Fasching/113	4.00	10.00
132 Shane Harper/100	6.00	15.00
133 Markus Nutivaara/100	4.00	10.00
134 Nick Baptiste/113	4.00	10.00
135 Oliver Bjorkstrand/113	5.00	12.00
136 Sebastian Aho/115	12.00	30.00
137 Ross Johnston/100	4.00	10.00
138 Jared Coreau/100	5.00	12.00
139 Jesse Puljujarvi/116	8.00	20.00
140 Kasperi Kapanen/114	6.00	15.00
141 Nick Sorensen /113	4.00	10.00
142 Aaron Dell/100	4.00	10.00
143 J.C. Lipon/113	4.00	10.00
144 Roman Lyubimov/100	4.00	10.00
145 Pontus Aberg/112	5.00	12.00
146 Kevin Labanc/114	4.00	10.00
147 Artturi Lehkonen/113	5.00	12.00
148 Michael Matheson/112	4.00	10.00
149 Troy Stecher/100	4.00	10.00
150 Sonny Milano/114	5.00	12.00
151 Jimmy Vesey/112	6.00	15.00
152 Denis Malgin/115	3.00	8.00
153 Mike Reilly/111	3.00	8.00
154 Noel Acciari/100	5.00	12.00
155 Oliver Kylington/115	3.00	8.00
156 Lukas Sedlak/111	4.00	10.00
157 Travis Konecny/115	8.00	20.00
158 Michal Kempny/100	4.00	10.00
159 Blake Speers/115	4.00	10.00
160 Brendan Leipsic/112	3.00	8.00
161 Tyler Motte/113	4.00	10.00
162 Frederik Gauthier/113	3.00	8.00
163 Nick Paul/113	5.00	12.00
164 Alan Quine/113	4.00	10.00
165 Sergey Tolchinsky/100	3.00	8.00
166 Rob O'Gara/111	4.00	10.00
167 Mathew Barzal/115	12.00	30.00
168 Ben Harpur/113	4.00	10.00
169 Thomas Chabot/115	8.00	20.00
170 Charlie Lindgren/100	6.00	15.00
171 Nikita Tryamkin/114	3.00	8.00
172 Danton Heinen/114	3.00	8.00
173 Oskar Sundqvist/112	4.00	10.00
174 Joel Eriksson Ek/115	6.00	15.00
175 Steven Santini/113	3.00	8.00
176 Brayden Point/114	10.00	25.00
177 Nic Dowd/109	3.00	8.00
178 Ryan Pulock/113	4.00	10.00
179 Jakob Chychrun/116	8.00	20.00
180 Connor Brown/112	6.00	15.00
181 Scott Kosmachuk/112	4.00	10.00
182 Tristan Jarry/113	8.00	20.00
183 Tobias Lindberg/113	6.00	15.00
184 Blake Pietila/111	4.00	10.00
185 Patrik Laine/116	30.00	80.00
186 Zach Werenski/115	12.00	30.00
187 Pavel Buchnevich/113	6.00	15.00
188 Rinat Valiev/114	5.00	12.00
189 Anthony DeAngelo/114	3.00	8.00
190 Jason Dickinson/113	3.00	8.00
191 Brett Lernout/114	4.00	10.00
192 Josh Morrissey/113	10.00	25.00
193 Tom Kuhnhackl/110	3.00	8.00
194 Zach Hyman/110	12.00	30.00
195 Chase De Leo/114	4.00	10.00
196 Mark McNeill/111	4.00	10.00
197 Austin Czarnik/100	6.00	15.00
198 Trevor Carrick/112	4.00	10.00
199 Joseph Cramarossa/111	4.00	10.00

2016-17 SP Game Used Red Spectrum

Card	Low	High
101 Auston Matthews PATCH AU	400.00	700.00
185 Patrik Laine PATCH AU	150.00	300.00

2016-17 SP Game Used Rookie Relic Blends

Card	Low	High
RRBAB Anthony Beauvillier	4.00	10.00
RRBAM Anthony Mantha	8.00	20.00
RRBAU Auston Matthews	25.00	60.00
RRBBL Brendan Leipsic	3.00	8.00
RRBCB Connor Brown	6.00	15.00
RRBCD Christian Dvorak	5.00	12.00
RRBDS Dylan Strome	10.00	25.00
RRBHF Hudson Fasching	4.00	10.00
RRBIP Ivan Provorov	6.00	15.00
RRBJM Josh Morrissey	10.00	25.00
RRBJP Jesse Puljujarvi	8.00	20.00
RRBJV Jimmy Vesey	6.00	15.00
RRBKC Kyle Connor	12.00	30.00
RRBKK Kasperi Kapanen	6.00	15.00
RRBMM Mitch Marner	12.00	30.00
RRBMT Matthew Tkachuk	15.00	40.00
RRBNS Nick Schmaltz	5.00	12.00
RRBPB Pavel Buchnevich	6.00	15.00
RRBPL Patrik Laine	20.00	50.00
RRBPZ Pavel Zacha	6.00	15.00
RRBSA Sebastian Aho	12.00	30.00
RRBSM Sonny Milano	5.00	12.00
RRBTK Travis Konecny	8.00	20.00
RRBTM Tyler Motte	4.00	10.00
RRBWN William Nylander	15.00	40.00
RRBZW Zach Werenski	12.00	30.00

2016-17 SP Game Used Rookie Sweaters

Card	Low	High
RSAM Auston Matthews	12.00	30.00
RSCB Connor Brown	3.00	8.00
RSCD Christian Dvorak	2.50	6.00
RSCL Charlie Lindgren	3.00	8.00
RSDS Dylan Strome	5.00	12.00
RSEL Esa Lindell	2.00	5.00
RSHF Hudson Fasching	2.00	5.00
RSIP Ivan Provorov	3.00	8.00
RSJD Brayden Point	5.00	12.00
RSJM Travis Konecny	4.00	10.00
RSJP Jesse Puljujarvi	4.00	10.00
RSJV Jimmy Vesey	3.00	8.00
RSKC Kyle Connor	6.00	15.00
RSKK Kasperi Kapanen	3.00	8.00
RSMA Anthony Mantha	4.00	10.00
RSMB Mathew Barzal	6.00	15.00
RSMI Michael Matheson	2.00	5.00
RSMM Mitch Marner	6.00	15.00
RSMR Mike Reilly	1.50	4.00
RSMT Matthew Tkachuk	8.00	20.00
RSNS Nick Schmaltz	2.50	6.00
RSOB Oliver Bjorkstrand	2.50	6.00
RSPB Pavel Buchnevich	3.00	8.00
RSPL Patrik Laine	5.00	12.00
RSPZ Pavel Zacha	3.00	8.00
RSSA Sebastian Aho	6.00	15.00
RSSM Sonny Milano	2.50	6.00
RSWN William Nylander	8.00	20.00
RSZW Zach Werenski	6.00	15.00

2016-17 SP Game Used Rookie Sweaters Inked Patch

*SINGLES: 1.25X TO 3X BASIC INSERTS

Card	Low	High
RSAM Auston Matthews/35	300.00	500.00
RSIP Ivan Provorov/99	40.00	100.00
RSMI Mitch Marner/35	125.00	300.00
RSPL Patrik Laine/99	150.00	300.00
RSWN William Nylander/99	50.00	120.00

2016-17 SP Game Used Stadium Series Materials Puck

Card	Low	High
SSGUPAP Artemi Panarin	40.00	100.00
SSGUPDL Dylan Larkin	25.00	60.00
SSGUPGL Gabriel Landeskog	25.00	60.00
SSGUPHZ Henrik Zetterberg	25.00	60.00
SSGUPJP Jason Pominville	12.00	30.00
SSGUPJT Jonathan Toews	30.00	80.00
SSGUPMD Matt Dumba	12.00	30.00
SSGUPNM Nathan MacKinnon	80.00	200.00
SSGUPNN Nino Niederreiter	12.00	30.00
SSGUPPK Patrick Kane	40.00	100.00
SSGUPTB Tyson Barrie	12.00	30.00
SSGUPTT Tomas Tatar	12.00	30.00

2016-17 SP Game Used Stadium Series Quad Fabrics

Card	Low	High
SS4CHI Toews/Keith Shaw/Hjalmarsson	8.00	20.00
SS4COL MacKinnon/Iginla Beauchemin/Holden	20.00	50.00
SS4DET Larkin/Abdelkader Green/Glendening	6.00	15.00
SS4-MIN Parise/Niederreiter Vanek/Carter	5.00	12.00

2016-17 SP Game Used Stadium Series Relic Blends

Card	Low	High
SSBAS Andrew Shaw	4.00	10.00
SSBDK Duncan Keith	5.00	12.00
SSBDL Dylan Larkin	8.00	20.00
SSBEJ Erik Johnson	4.00	10.00
SSBFB Francois Beauchemin	5.00	12.00
SSBHJ Niklas Hjalmarsson	4.00	10.00
SSBJA Justin Abdelkader	5.00	12.00
SSBJI Jarome Iginla	8.00	20.00
SSBJS Jared Spurgeon	6.00	15.00
SSBJT Jonathan Toews	10.00	25.00
SSBLG Luke Glendening	4.00	10.00
SSBMG Mike Green	5.00	12.00
SSBNH Nick Holden	4.00	10.00
SSBNM Nathan MacKinnon	25.00	60.00
SSBNN Nino Niederreiter	4.00	10.00
SSBRC Ryan Carter	6.00	15.00
SSBRS Riley Sheahan	4.00	10.00
SSBTV Trevor van Riemsdyk	5.00	12.00
SSBVA Thomas Vanek	5.00	12.00
SSBZP Zach Parise	6.00	15.00

2016-17 SP Game Used Stanley Cup Finals Materials Net Cord

Card	Low	High
SCNCBB Brent Burns	25.00	60.00
SCNCBR Bryan Rust	25.00	60.00
SCNCCH Carl Hagelin	15.00	40.00
SCNCCK Chris Kunitz	25.00	60.00
SCNCCS Conor Sheary	25.00	60.00
SCNCCT Chris Tierney Game 3	15.00	40.00
SCNCEM Evgeni Malkin	50.00	125.00
SCNCEV Evgeni Malkin	50.00	125.00
SCNCJB Justin Braun	15.00	40.00
SCNCJD Joonas Donskoi	15.00	40.00
SCNCJP Joe Pavelski	30.00	80.00
SCNCJT Joe Thornton	40.00	100.00
SCNCJW Joel Ward	20.00	50.00
SCNCKL Kris Letang	30.00	80.00
SCNCLC Logan Couture	30.00	80.00
SCNCMA Matt Murray	40.00	100.00
SCNCMC Matt Cullen	25.00	60.00
SCNCMJ Martin Jones	20.00	50.00
SCNCMK Melker Karlsson Game 5	15.00	40.00
SCNCMM Matt Murray	40.00	100.00
SCNCMV Marc-Edouard Vlasic	15.00	40.00
SCNCNB Nick Bonino	15.00	40.00
SCNCOM Olli Maatta	15.00	40.00
SCNCPH Patric Hornqvist	15.00	40.00
SCNCPK Phil Kessel	25.00	60.00
SCNCPM Patrick Marleau	25.00	60.00
SCNCSC Sidney Crosby	125.00	200.00
SCNCSI Sidney Crosby	125.00	200.00
SCNCTH Tomas Hertl	25.00	60.00
SCNCTJ Joe Thornton	40.00	100.00

2016-17 SP Game Used Winter Classic Materials Net Cord

Card	Low	High
WCNCAD Adam McQuaid	15.00	40.00
WCNCAG Alex Galchenyuk	15.00	40.00
WCNCAM Andrei Markov	15.00	40.00
WCNCBC Brett Connolly	15.00	40.00
WCNCBE Patrice Bergeron	30.00	80.00
WCNCBG Brendan Gallagher	25.00	60.00
WCNCDD David Desharnais	15.00	40.00
WCNCER Loui Eriksson	15.00	40.00
WCNCJH Jimmy Hayes	15.00	40.00
WCNCJM Joe Morrow	20.00	50.00
WCNCLE Lars Eller	15.00	40.00
WCNCMB Matt Beleskey	20.00	50.00
WCNCMC Mike Condon	25.00	60.00
WCNCMP Max Pacioretty	25.00	60.00
WCNCNB Nathan Beaulieu	15.00	40.00
WCNCPB Paul Byron	20.00	50.00
WCNCPS P.K. Subban	30.00	80.00
WCNCRS Ryan Spooner	20.00	50.00
WCNCTK Torey Krug	20.00	50.00
WCNCTP Tomas Plekanec	15.00	40.00
WCNCTR Tuukka Rask	30.00	80.00
WCNCZC Zdeno Chara	25.00	60.00

2017-18 SP Game Used

Card	Low	High
1 Auston Matthews/34	25.00	60.00
2 Victor Hedman/77	6.00	15.00
3 Tyler Seguin/91	8.00	20.00
4 Jake Guentzel/59	10.00	25.00
5 Henrik Zetterberg/40	6.00	15.00
8 Oliver Ekman-Larsson/23	10.00	25.00
10 Carey Price/31	12.00	30.00
11 Ryan O'Reilly/90	5.00	12.00
14 Sean Monahan/23	6.00	15.00
15 Vladimir Tarasenko/91	4.00	10.00
17 Patrik Laine/29	12.00	30.00
18 Ryan Spooner/51	4.00	10.00
19 Milan Lucic/27	5.00	12.00
20 Jonathan Toews/19	10.00	25.00
21 Aleksander Barkov/16	12.00	30.00
22 Roman Josi/59	5.00	12.00
23 Marc-Andre Fleury/29	12.00	30.00
24 Pavel Zacha/37	5.00	12.00
25 Erik Karlsson/65	6.00	15.00
26 Brock Nelson/29	5.00	12.00
27 Mats Zuccarello/36	6.00	15.00
28 Shayne Gostisbehere/53	8.00	20.00
29 Evgeny Kuznetsov/92	5.00	12.00
30 Loui Eriksson/21	6.00	15.00
31 Jason Spezza/90	5.00	12.00
32 Dylan Larkin/71	25.00	60.00
34 Sebastian Aho/20	10.00	25.00
35 Matt Murray/30	10.00	25.00
36 Logan Couture/39	6.00	15.00
37 John Gibson/36	6.00	15.00
38 Nikolaj Ehlers/27	10.00	25.00
41 Evgeni Malkin/71	6.00	15.00
42 Max Pacioretty/67	5.00	12.00
43 Patrice Bergeron/37	8.00	20.00
45 Steven Stamkos/91	6.00	15.00
46 Jonathan Quick/32	6.00	15.00
50 Sidney Crosby/87	15.00	40.00
51 Colton Parayko/55	15.00	40.00
52 William Karlsson/71	10.00	25.00
53 Leon Draisaitl/29	15.00	40.00
54 Pekka Rinne/35	6.00	15.00
55 Patrick Kane/88	5.00	12.00
56 Claude Giroux/28	15.00	40.00
59 Jonathan Drouin/92	10.00	25.00
60 Henrik Lundqvist/30	8.00	20.00
61 David Pastrnak/88	5.00	12.00
64 Henrik Sedin/33	8.00	20.00
65 Brent Burns/88	40.00	100.00
66 Nathan MacKinnon/29	8.00	20.00
68 Nikita Kucherov/86	6.00	15.00
69 Mark Stone/61	4.00	10.00
15 John Tavares/91	6.00	15.00
72 Ryan Johansen/92	6.00	15.00
73 Mark Scheifele/55	6.00	15.00
74 Mitch Marner/16	40.00	100.00
75 Derek Stepan/21	5.00	12.00
76 Nino Niederreiter/22	5.00	12.00
77 Connor McDavid/97	20.00	50.00
80 Steve Yzerman/19	15.00	40.00
83 Brett Hull/16	20.00	50.00
84 Ed Belfour/30	12.00	40.00
85 Wayne Gretzky/99	20.00	50.00
87 Charlie McAvoy/73 RC	300.00	400.00
88 Victor Mete/53 RC	50.00	120.00
89 Gabriel Carlsson/53 RC	12.00	30.00
90 Kailer Yamamoto/56 RC	30.00	80.00
92 Janne Kuokkanen/59 RC	15.00	40.00
93 Jan Rutta/44 RC	20.00	50.00
94 Evgeny Svechnikov/37 RC	25.00	60.00
95 Vadim Shipachyov/87 RC	40.00	100.00
96 Nathan Walker/78 RC	12.00	30.00
97 Tage Thompson/32 RC	60.00	150.00
98 Vladislav Kamenev/91 RC	12.00	30.00
99 Filip Chytil/72 RC	150.00	200.00
101 Valentin Zykov/73 RC	30.00	80.00
102 Alex Iafallo/19 RC	40.00	100.00
103 Marcus Sorensen/20 RC	40.00	100.00
104 Ville Husso/35 RC	40.00	100.00
105 Owen Tippett/74 RC	40.00	100.00
106 Jean-Sebastien Dea/39 RC	10.00	25.00
107 Ivan Barbashev/49 RC	30.00	80.00
108 Alex Formenton/59 RC	30.00	80.00
109 Brendan Lemieux/48 RC	15.00	40.00
111 Mike Vecchione/74 RC	20.00	50.00
112 Nelson Nogier/62 RC	15.00	40.00
113 Kevin Rooney/58 RC	25.00	60.00
117 John Hayden/40 RC	6.00	15.00
118 Andreas Borgman/55 RC	30.00	80.00
119 Christian Djoos/29 RC	40.00	100.00
120 Colin White/36 RC	50.00	120.00
121 Paul LaDue/38 RC	20.00	50.00
122 Evan McEneny/61 RC	6.00	15.00
123 Michael Kapla/32 RC	12.00	30.00
124 Alexandre Carrier/73 RC	15.00	40.00
127 Vince Dunn/29 RC	80.00	150.00
129 Filip Chlapik/78 RC	15.00	40.00
131 Riley Barber/24 RC	25.00	60.00
132 MacKenzie Weegar/52 RC	12.00	30.00
133 Michael Amadio/52 RC	20.00	50.00
135 Nikita Scherbak/38 RC	50.00	125.00
136 Peter Cehlarik/22 RC	40.00	100.00
137 Kalle Kossila/83 RC	10.00	25.00
138 Sean Malone/37 RC	40.00	100.00
139 Andrei Mironov/94 RC	15.00	40.00
140 Josh Ho-Sang/66 RC	25.00	60.00
141 Blake Coleman/40 RC	60.00	150.00
142 Viktor Antipin/93 RC	15.00	40.00
143 Rasmus Andersson/54 RC	12.00	30.00
145 Calle Rosen/48 RC	15.00	40.00
147 T.J. Tynan/68 RC	15.00	40.00
148 Remi Elie/40 RC	12.00	30.00
149 Andrew Poturalski/29 RC	15.00	40.00
150 Pierre-Luc Dubois/18 RC	150.00	250.00
151 Martin Necas/88 RC	40.00	100.00
152 Jonny Brodzinski/17 RC	30.00	80.00
153 Madison Bowey/22 RC	30.00	80.00
154 Anton Lindholm/54 RC	15.00	40.00
155 Jack Roslovic/52 RC	30.00	80.00
156 Samuel Girard/49 RC	25.00	60.00
157 Lucas Wallmark/72 RC	12.00	30.00
159 Dan Renouf/20 RC	80.00	150.00
160 Jakob Forsbacka-Karlsson/23 RC	50.00	120.00
161 Jordan Schmaltz/43 RC	12.00	30.00
162 Denis Gurianov/34 RC	15.00	40.00
163 Christian Jaros/83 RC	25.00	60.00
164 Luke Kunin/19 RC	50.00	120.00
165 Tyson Jost/17 RC	60.00	150.00
166 Matt Lorito/22 RC	20.00	50.00
167 Garrett Mitchell/76 RC	30.00	80.00
168 Jake Dotchin/59 RC	25.00	60.00
170 Jake DeBrusk/74 RC	50.00	120.00
171 Jon Gillies/32 RC	20.00	50.00
173 Tim Heed/72 RC	20.00	50.00
174 Carter Rowney/37 RC	15.00	40.00
175 Jesper Bratt/63 RC	30.00	80.00
176 Samuel Blais/64 RC	20.00	50.00
177 Alex Tuch/89 RC	30.00	80.00
178 Robbie Russo/18 RC	25.00	60.00
179 J.T. Compher/37 RC	30.00	80.00
180 Christian Fischer/36 RC	25.00	60.00
181 Logan Brown/21 RC	60.00	150.00
182 Alexander Nylander/92 RC	25.00	60.00
183 Jaycob Megna/75 RC	15.00	40.00
184 Kurtis MacDermid/56 RC	8.00	20.00
185 Nolan Patrick/19 RC	600.00	700.00

2017-18 SP Game Used Gold

Card	Low	High
COMMON CARD	2.00	5.00
SEMISTARS	2.50	6.00
UNLISTED STARS	3.00	8.00
COMMON CARD/399	2.00	5.00
SEMISTARS	2.50	6.00
UNLISTED STARS	3.00	8.00
50 Sidney Crosby JSY A	15.00	40.00

2017-18 SP Game Used Orange Rainbow

Card	Low	High
1 Auston Matthews/140	8.00	20.00
2 Victor Hedman/116	2.50	6.00
3 Tyler Seguin/137	2.50	6.00
4 Jake Guentzel/116	3.00	8.00
5 Henrik Zetterberg/143	2.50	6.00
6 Corey Perry/150	3.00	8.00
7 Anze Kopitar/134	3.00	8.00
8 Oliver Ekman-Larsson/123	2.00	5.00
9 Artemi Panarin/134	4.00	10.00
10 Carey Price/144	4.00	10.00
11 Ryan O'Reilly/128	2.00	5.00
12 Joe Pavelski/141	2.50	6.00
13 Brayden Schenn/126	2.00	5.00
14 Sean Monahan/131	1.25	3.00
15 Vladimir Tarasenko/140	2.50	6.00
16 Matt Duchene/130	2.00	5.00
17 Patrik Laine/136	2.50	6.00
18 Ryan Spooner/113	1.50	4.00
19 Milan Lucic/130	2.00	5.00
20 Jonathan Toews/134	3.00	8.00
21 Aleksander Barkov/128	3.00	8.00
22 Roman Josi/115	2.00	5.00
23 Marc-Andre Fleury/142	4.00	10.00
24 Pavel Zacha/108	1.50	4.00
25 Erik Karlsson/121	2.50	6.00
26 Brock Nelson/126	2.00	5.00
27 Mats Zuccarello/126	2.00	5.00
28 Shayne Gostisbehere/117	2.00	5.00
29 Evgeny Kuznetsov/120	2.50	6.00
30 Loui Eriksson/136	1.25	3.00
31 Jason Spezza/134	2.00	5.00
32 Dylan Larkin/123	2.50	6.00
33 Patrick Marleau/144	2.00	5.00
34 Sebastian Aho/124	3.00	8.00
35 Matt Murray/132	3.00	8.00
36 Logan Couture/132	2.50	6.00
37 John Gibson/125	2.00	5.00
38 Nikolaj Ehlers/125	2.00	5.00
39 Tyson Barrie/113	1.25	3.00
40 Alexander Ovechkin/165	8.00	20.00
41 Evgeni Malkin/150	4.00	10.00
42 Max Pacioretty/139	2.00	5.00
43 Patrice Bergeron/132	2.50	6.00
44 Eric Staal/145	2.50	6.00
45 Steven Stamkos/160	4.00	10.00
46 Jonathan Quick/140	2.50	6.00
47 Cam Atkinson/135	2.00	5.00
48 Johnny Gaudreau/130	3.00	8.00
49 Jack Eichel/124	3.00	8.00
50 Sidney Crosby/151	8.00	20.00
51 Colton Parayko/109	1.50	4.00
52 William Karlsson/109	2.50	6.00
53 Leon Draisaitl/129	6.00	15.00
54 Pekka Rinne/143	2.00	5.00
55 Patrick Kane/146	4.00	10.00
56 Claude Giroux/128	2.00	5.00
57 Noah Hanifin/104	2.00	5.00
58 Adam Henrique/130	1.50	4.00
59 Jonathan Drouin/121	1.50	4.00
60 Henrik Lundqvist/139	5.00	12.00
61 David Pastrnak/134	5.00	12.00
62 Justin Abdelkader/123	1.50	4.00
63 Mark Giordano/121	2.00	5.00
64 Henrik Sedin/129	2.50	6.00
65 Brent Burns/129	2.00	5.00
66 Nathan MacKinnon/124	8.00	20.00
67 Roberto Luongo/147	3.00	8.00
68 Nikita Kucherov/140	4.00	10.00
69 Mark Stone/126	2.50	6.00
70 John Tavares/138	3.00	8.00
71 Jamie Benn/141	2.00	5.00
72 Ryan Johansen/133	1.50	4.00
73 Mark Scheifele/132	3.00	8.00
74 Mitch Marner/119	3.00	8.00
75 Derek Stepan/122	1.25	3.00
76 Nino Niederreiter/125	1.25	3.00
77 Connor McDavid/130	10.00	25.00
78 Mark Messier/150	4.00	10.00
79 Rod Langway/111	2.00	5.00
80 Steve Yzerman/165	5.00	12.00
81 Mark Recchi/153	2.50	6.00
82 Teemu Selanne/176	4.00	10.00
83 Brett Hull/186	4.00	10.00
84 Ed Belfour/143	2.50	6.00
85 Wayne Gretzky/192	12.00	30.00
86 Nico Hischier/117	20.00	50.00
87 Charlie McAvoy/116	15.00	40.00
88 Victor Mete/116	6.00	15.00
89 Gabriel Carlsson/115	5.00	12.00
90 Kailer Yamamoto/117	15.00	40.00
91 Adrian Kempe/114	12.00	30.00
92 Janne Kuokkanen/116	6.00	15.00
93 Jan Rutta/100	6.00	15.00
94 Evgeny Svechnikov/115	12.00	30.00
95 Vadim Shipachyov/100	8.00	20.00
96 Nathan Walker/114	6.00	15.00
97 Tage Thompson/116	15.00	40.00
98 Vladislav Kamenev/114	6.00	15.00
99 Filip Chytil/117	6.00	15.00
100 Clayton Keller/116	15.00	40.00
101 Valentin Zykov/113	6.00	15.00
102 Alex Iafallo/100	6.00	15.00
103 Marcus Sorensen/110	5.00	12.00
104 Ville Husso/114	8.00	20.00
105 Owen Tippett/117	12.00	30.00
106 Jean-Sebastien Dea/100	6.00	15.00
107 Ivan Barbashev/114	8.00	20.00
108 Alex Formenton/117	6.00	15.00
109 Brendan Lemieux/114	6.00	15.00
110 Anders Bjork/114	8.00	20.00
111 Mike Vecchione/100	5.00	12.00
112 Nelson Nogier/114	6.00	15.00
113 Kevin Rooney/100	6.00	15.00
114 Alex Kerfoot/112	12.00	30.00
115 Brock Boeser/115	25.00	60.00
116 Travis Sanheim/114	6.00	15.00
117 John Hayden/113	5.00	12.00
118 Andreas Borgman/100	6.00	15.00
119 Christian Djoos/112	6.00	15.00
120 Colin White/115	8.00	20.00
121 Paul LaDue/112	5.00	12.00
122 Evan McEneny/100	6.00	15.00
123 Michael Kapla/100	6.00	15.00
124 Alexandre Carrier/115	5.00	12.00
125 Haydn Fleury/114	6.00	15.00
126 Robert Hagg/113	6.00	15.00
127 Vince Dunn/115	8.00	20.00
128 Eric Comrie/113	5.00	12.00
129 Filip Chlapik/115	5.00	12.00
130 Alex DeBrincat/116	15.00	40.00
131 Riley Barber/112	6.00	15.00
132 MacKenzie Weegar/113	8.00	20.00
133 Michael Amadio/114	6.00	15.00
134 Griffen Molino/100	5.00	12.00
135 Nikita Scherbak/114	8.00	20.00
136 Peter Cehlarik/113	6.00	15.00
137 Kalle Kossila/100	5.00	12.00
138 Sean Malone/113	6.00	15.00
139 Andrei Mironov/115	6.00	15.00
140 Josh Ho-Sang/114	8.00	20.00
141 Blake Coleman/111	6.00	15.00
142 Viktor Antipin/100	6.00	15.00
143 Rasmus Andersson/115	6.00	15.00
144 Oscar Fantenberg/100	6.00	15.00
145 Calle Rosen/100	6.00	15.00
146 Tucker Poolman/113	5.00	12.00
147 T.J. Tynan/111	5.00	12.00
148 Remi Elie/113	5.00	12.00
149 Andrew Poturalski/100	6.00	15.00
150 Pierre-Luc Dubois/116	10.00	25.00
151 Martin Necas/117	20.00	50.00
152 Jonny Brodzinski/113	6.00	15.00
153 Madison Bowey/113	4.00	10.00
154 Anton Lindholm/114	6.00	15.00
155 Jack Roslovic/115	8.00	20.00
156 Samuel Girard/116	6.00	15.00
157 Lucas Wallmark/114	6.00	15.00
158 Ian McCoshen/113	6.00	15.00
159 Dan Renouf/100	5.00	12.00
160 Jakob Forsbacka-Karlsson/115	6.00	15.00
161 Jordan Schmaltz/112	8.00	20.00
162 Denis Gurianov/115	15.00	40.00
163 Christian Jaros/115	5.00	12.00
164 Luke Kunin/116	6.00	15.00
165 Tyson Jost/116	12.00	30.00
166 Matt Lorito/100	6.00	15.00
167 Garrett Mitchell/109	6.00	15.00
168 Jake Dotchin/112	5.00	12.00
169 Samuel Morin/113	4.00	10.00
170 Jake DeBrusk/115	15.00	40.00
171 Jon Gillies/112	6.00	15.00
172 Will Butcher/113	8.00	20.00
173 Tim Heed/110	6.00	15.00
174 Carter Rowney/100	5.00	12.00
175 Jesper Bratt/116	12.00	30.00
176 Samuel Blais/114	6.00	15.00
177 Alex Tuch/114	15.00	40.00
178 Robbie Russo/111	6.00	15.00
179 J.T. Compher/113	6.00	15.00
180 Christian Fischer/115	8.00	20.00
181 Logan Brown/116	6.00	15.00
182 Alexander Nylander/116	10.00	25.00
183 Jaycob Megna/112	6.00	15.00
184 Kurtis MacDermid/100	6.00	15.00
185 Nolan Patrick/117	12.00	30.00

2017-18 SP Game Used Rainbow

Card	Low	High
86 Nico Hischier/218	5.00	12.00
87 Charlie McAvoy/219	4.00	10.00
88 Victor Mete/219	1.50	4.00
89 Gabriel Carlsson/220	1.25	3.00
90 Kailer Yamamoto/219	4.00	10.00
91 Adrian Kempe/221	3.00	8.00
92 Janne Kuokkanen/219	1.50	4.00
93 Jan Rutta/227	1.50	4.00
94 Evgeny Svechnikov/221	3.00	8.00
95 Vadim Shipachyov/230	2.00	5.00
96 Nathan Walker/223	1.50	4.00
97 Tage Thompson/220	4.00	10.00
98 Vladislav Kamenev/221	1.50	4.00
99 Filip Chytil/218	1.50	4.00
100 Clayton Keller/219	4.00	10.00
101 Valentin Zykov/222	1.50	4.00
102 Alex Iafallo/223	1.50	4.00
103 Marcus Sorensen/225	1.25	3.00
104 Ville Husso/222	2.00	5.00
105 Owen Tippett/218	3.00	8.00
106 Jean-Sebastien Dea/223	1.50	4.00
107 Ivan Barbashev/221	2.00	5.00
108 Alex Formenton/218	1.50	4.00
109 Brendan Lemieux/221	1.50	4.00
110 Anders Bjork/221	2.00	5.00
111 Mike Vecchione/224	1.25	3.00
112 Nelson Nogier/221	1.50	4.00
113 Kevin Rooney/224	1.50	4.00
114 Alex Kerfoot/223	3.00	8.00
115 Brock Boeser/220	4.00	10.00
116 Travis Sanheim/221	1.50	4.00
117 John Hayden/222	1.25	3.00
118 Andreas Borgman/222	1.50	4.00
119 Christian Djoos/223	1.50	4.00
120 Colin White/220	2.00	5.00
121 Paul LaDue/225	1.25	3.00
122 Evan McEneny/223	1.50	4.00
123 Michael Kapla/223	1.50	4.00
124 Alexandre Carrier/221	1.25	3.00
125 Haydn Fleury/221	1.50	4.00
126 Robert Hagg/222	1.50	4.00
127 Vince Dunn/221	2.00	5.00
128 Eric Comrie/222	1.25	3.00
129 Filip Chlapik/220	1.25	3.00
130 Alex DeBrincat/219	4.00	10.00
131 Riley Barber/223	1.50	4.00
132 MacKenzie Weegar/223	2.00	5.00
133 Michael Amadio/221	1.50	4.00
134 Griffen Molino/223	1.25	3.00
135 Nikita Scherbak/221	2.00	5.00
136 Peter Cehlarik/222	1.50	4.00
137 Kalle Kossila/224	1.25	3.00
138 Sean Malone/222	1.50	4.00
139 Andrei Mironov/223	1.50	4.00
140 Josh Ho-Sang/221	2.00	5.00
141 Blake Coleman/225	1.50	4.00
142 Viktor Antipin/224	1.50	4.00
143 Rasmus Andersson/221	1.50	4.00
144 Oscar Fantenberg/226	1.50	4.00
145 Calle Rosen/223	1.50	4.00
146 Tucker Poolman/224	1.25	3.00
147 T.J. Tynan/225	1.25	3.00
148 Remi Elie/222	1.25	3.00
149 Andrew Poturalski/223	1.50	4.00
150 Pierre-Luc Dubois/219	2.50	6.00
151 Martin Necas/218	5.00	12.00
152 Jonny Brodzinski/224	1.50	4.00
153 Madison Bowey/222	1.00	2.50
154 Anton Lindholm/222	1.50	4.00
155 Jack Roslovic/220	2.00	5.00
156 Samuel Girard/219	1.50	4.00
157 Lucas Wallmark/222	1.50	4.00
158 Ian McCoshen/222	1.50	4.00
159 Dan Renouf/223	1.25	3.00
160 Jakob Forsbacka-Karlsson/221	1.50	4.00
161 Jordan Schmaltz/224	2.00	5.00
162 Denis Gurianov/220	4.00	10.00
163 Christian Jaros/221	1.25	3.00
164 Luke Kunin/219	1.50	4.00
165 Tyson Jost/219	3.00	8.00
166 Matt Lorito/227	1.50	4.00
167 Garrett Mitchell/226	1.50	4.00
168 Jake Dotchin/223	1.25	3.00
169 Samuel Morin/222	1.00	2.50
170 Jake DeBrusk/221	4.00	10.00
171 Jon Gillies/223	1.50	4.00
172 Will Butcher/222	2.00	5.00
173 Tim Heed/226	1.50	4.00
174 Carter Rowney/228	1.25	3.00
175 Jesper Bratt/219	3.00	8.00
176 Samuel Blais/221	1.50	4.00
177 Alex Tuch/221	4.00	10.00
178 Robbie Russo/224	1.50	4.00
179 J.T. Compher/222	1.50	4.00
180 Christian Fischer/220	2.00	5.00
181 Logan Brown/219	1.50	4.00
182 Alexander Nylander/219	2.50	6.00
183 Jaycob Megna/224	1.50	4.00
184 Kurtis MacDermid/223	1.50	4.00
185 Nolan Patrick/219	3.00	8.00

2017-18 SP Game Used Red

Card	Low	High
1 Auston Matthews JSY AU A	100.00	200.00
10 Carey Price JSY AU A	25.00	60.00
77 Connor McDavid JSY AU A	150.00	250.00
85 Wayne Gretzky JSY AU A	200.00	500.00
115 Brock Boeser JSY AU A	80.00	200.00

2017-18 SP Game Used '16 Heritage Classic Game Used Pucks

Card	Low	High
HCGUPCT Cam Talbot	50.00	125.00
HCGUPMS Mark Scheifele	30.00	80.00
HCGUPPL Patrik Laine	30.00	80.00

2017-18 SP Game Used '16 Heritage Classic Materials Net Cord

Card	Low	High
HCNCAL Adam Larsson	10.00	25.00
HCNCBW Blake Wheeler	10.00	25.00
HCNCCM Connor McDavid	40.00	100.00
HCNCCT Cam Talbot	10.00	25.00
HCNCDB Dustin Byfuglien	10.00	25.00
HCNCLD Leon Draisaitl	30.00	80.00
HCNCML Milan Lucic	10.00	25.00
HCNCMS Mark Scheifele	25.00	60.00
HCNCNE Nikolaj Ehlers	10.00	25.00
HCNCOK Oscar Klefbom	8.00	20.00
HCNCPL Patrik Laine	30.00	80.00
HCNCRN Ryan Nugent-Hopkins	15.00	40.00

2017-18 SP Game Used '17 All Star Game Materials Net Cord

Card	Low	High
ASNCAM Auston Matthews	30.00	80.00
ASNCAO Alexander Ovechkin	30.00	80.00
ASNCBB Brent Burns	8.00	20.00
ASNCCM Connor McDavid	40.00	100.00
ASNCCP Carey Price	15.00	40.00
ASNCEK Erik Karlsson	10.00	25.00
ASNCJG Johnny Gaudreau	12.00	30.00
ASNCJT John Tavares	12.00	30.00
ASNCNM Nathan MacKinnon	30.00	80.00
ASNCPK Patrick Kane	15.00	40.00
ASNCPL Patrik Laine	10.00	25.00
ASNCPS P.K. Subban	10.00	25.00
ASNCRK Ryan Kesler	8.00	20.00
ASNCSB Sergei Bobrovsky	12.00	30.00
ASNCSC Sidney Crosby	30.00	80.00
ASNCTH Taylor Hall	8.00	20.00
ASNCTO Jonathan Toews	12.00	30.00
ASNCTS Tyler Seguin	10.00	25.00
ASNCVT Vladimir Tarasenko	10.00	25.00
ASNCWS Wayne Simmonds	10.00	25.00

2017-18 SP Game Used '17 All Star Game Used Pucks

Card	Low	High
ASGUPAM Auston Matthews	100.00	200.00
ASGUPAO Alexander Ovechkin	50.00	125.00
ASGUPCP Carey Price	60.00	150.00
ASGUPJG Johnny Gaudreau	25.00	60.00
ASGUPJT John Tavares	25.00	60.00

2017-18 SP Game Used '17 All Star Skills Dual Fabrics

Card	Low	High
AS2BP B.Burns/J.Pavelski	5.00	12.00
AS2CD J.Carter/D.Doughty	5.00	12.00
AS2KH N.Kucherov/V.Hedman	8.00	20.00
AS2MO C.McDavid/A.Ovechkin	20.00	50.00
AS2MR B.Marchand/T.Rask	8.00	20.00
AS2OH A.Ovechkin/B.Holtby	15.00	40.00
AS2TK J.Toews/P.Kane	8.00	20.00
AS2WP S.Weber/C.Price	8.00	20.00

2017-18 SP Game Used '17 All Star Skills Dual Fabrics Patch

*PATCH/25: 1X TO 2.5X BASIC INSERTS

Card	Low	High
AS2MO Connor McDavid Alexander Ovechkin	80.00	150.00

2017-18 SP Game Used '17 All Star Skills Fabrics

Card	Low	High
ASAM Auston Matthews	12.00	30.00
ASAO Alexander Ovechkin	12.00	30.00
ASBB Brent Burns	3.00	8.00
ASBH Braden Holtby	4.00	10.00
ASBM Brad Marchand	6.00	15.00
ASCA Cam Atkinson	3.00	8.00
ASCC Corey Crawford	4.00	10.00
ASCM Connor McDavid	15.00	40.00
ASCP Carey Price	6.00	15.00
ASDK Duncan Keith	2.50	6.00
ASDO Drew Doughty	4.00	10.00
ASEK Erik Karlsson	4.00	10.00
ASJG Johnny Gaudreau	5.00	12.00
ASJP Joe Pavelski	4.00	10.00
ASJT John Tavares	5.00	12.00

ASNK Nikita Kucherov 6.00 15.00
ASNM Nathan MacKinnon 12.00 30.00
ASPK Patrick Kane 6.00 15.00
ASPL Patrik Laine 4.00 10.00
ASPS P.K. Subban 4.00 10.00
ASRK Ryan Kesler 3.00 8.00
ASSC Sidney Crosby 12.00 30.00
ASSW Shea Weber 2.50 6.00
ASTA Vladimir Tarasenko 4.00 10.00
ASTH Taylor Hall 3.00 8.00
ASTO Jonathan Toews 5.00 12.00
ASTR Tuukka Rask 4.00 10.00
ASTS Tyler Seguin 4.00 10.00
ASVH Victor Hedman 4.00 10.00
ASWS Wayne Simmonds 4.00 10.00

2017-18 SP Game Used '17 All Star Skills Fabrics Patch

*PATCH/35: .75X TO 2X BASIC INSERTS
ASAM Auston Matthews 40.00 100.00

2017-18 SP Game Used '17 All Star Skills Quad Fabrics

AS4NET Price/Rask/Bobrovsky/Holtby 8.00 20.00
AS4DMEN Karlsson/Subban Doughty/Burns 5.00 12.00
AS4HAWKS Toews/Kane Keith/Crawford 8.00 20.00
AS4STARS Toews/Ovechkin McDavid/MacKinnon 20.00 50.00

2017-18 SP Game Used '17 Centennial Classic Fabrics

CCAA Andreas Athanasiou 3.00 8.00
CCAM Anthony Mantha 2.50 6.00
CCCB Connor Brown 2.50 6.00
CCDL Dylan Larkin 4.00 10.00
CCFA Frederik Andersen 4.00 10.00
CCFN Frans Nielsen 2.00 5.00
CCMM Mitch Marner 5.00 12.00
CCNK Nazem Kadri 4.00 10.00
CCNZ Nikita Zaitsev 2.50 6.00
CCWN William Nylander 6.00 15.00

2017-18 SP Game Used '17 Centennial Classic Materials Net Cord

CCNCAA Andreas Athanasiou 20.00 50.00
CCNCAM Anthony Mantha 15.00 40.00
CCNCDL Dylan Larkin 30.00 80.00
CCNCFA Frederik Andersen 25.00 60.00
CCNCFN Frans Nielsen 12.00 30.00
CCNCGN Gustav Nyquist 12.00 30.00
CCNCHZ Henrik Zetterberg 25.00 60.00
CCNCJV James van Riemsdyk 15.00 40.00
CCNCMA Auston Matthews 80.00 200.00
CCNCMM Mitch Marner 30.00 80.00
CCNCMR Morgan Rielly 20.00 50.00
CCNCNK Nazem Kadri 25.00 60.00
CCNCNZ Nikita Zaitsev 15.00 40.00
CCNCTT Tomas Tatar 12.00 30.00
CCNCWN William Nylander 40.00 100.00
CCNCZH Zach Hyman 30.00 80.00

2017-18 SP Game Used '17 Centennial Classic Quad Fabrics

CC4DRW Mantha/Athanasiou Nielsen/Helm 8.00 20.00
CC4TML Marner/Nylander Kadri/Andersen 15.00 40.00

2017-18 SP Game Used '17 Stadium Series Fabrics

PFBM Brandon Manning 2.50 6.00
PFIP Ivan Provorov 2.50 6.00
PFMR Matt Read 2.50 6.00
PFWS Wayne Simmonds 4.00 10.00
PPEM Evgeni Malkin 6.00 15.00
PPJG Jake Guentzel 5.00 12.00
PPJS Justin Schultz 3.00 8.00
PPMA Marc-Andre Fleury 6.00 15.00
PPPH Patric Hornqvist 2.00 5.00
PPSC Sidney Crosby 12.00 30.00

2017-18 SP Game Used '17 Stadium Series Materials Net Cord

SSNCCG Claude Giroux 20.00 50.00
SSNCCH Carl Hagelin 12.00 30.00
SSNCCO Sean Couturier 15.00 40.00
SSNCEM Evgeni Malkin 40.00 100.00
SSNCJG Jake Guentzel 30.00 80.00
SSNCJS Justin Schultz 20.00 50.00
SSNCJV Jakub Voracek 15.00 40.00
SSNCMM Matt Murray 30.00 80.00
SSNCPK Phil Kessel 20.00 50.00
SSNCSC Sidney Crosby 80.00 200.00
SSNCSG Shayne Gostisbehere 20.00 50.00
SSNCWS Wayne Simmonds 25.00 60.00

2017-18 SP Game Used '17 Stadium Series Quad Fabrics

SS4FLY Simmonds Manning/Provorov/Read 10.00 25.00
SS4PEN Malkin/Guentzel Hornqvist/Fleury 15.00 40.00

2017-18 SP Game Used '17 Stanley Cup Finals Materials Net Cord

SCNCBD Brian Dumoulin 15.00 40.00
SCNCBR Bryan Rust 20.00 50.00
SCNCCH Carl Hagelin 12.00 30.00
SCNCCJ Calle Jarnkrok 15.00 40.00
SCNCCS Conor Sheary 20.00 50.00
SCNCEM Evgeni Malkin 40.00 100.00
SCNCFF Filip Forsberg 30.00 80.00
SCNCFI Mike Fisher 12.00 30.00
SCNCJG Jake Guentzel 30.00 80.00
SCNCJN James Neal 12.00 30.00
SCNCJS Justin Schultz 20.00 50.00
SCNCMF Marc-Andre Fleury 40.00 100.00
SCNCMM Matt Murray 30.00 80.00
SCNCPH Patric Hornqvist 12.00 30.00
SCNCPK Phil Kessel 20.00 50.00
SCNCPR Pekka Rinne 20.00 50.00
SCNCPS P.K. Subban 25.00 60.00
SCNCRE Ryan Ellis 15.00 40.00
SCNCRJ Roman Josi 20.00 50.00
SCNCSC Sidney Crosby 80.00 200.00
SCNCSI Colton Sissons 12.00 30.00
SCNCVA Viktor Arvidsson 12.00 30.00

2017-18 SP Game Used '17 Winter Classic Materials Net Cord

WCNCAA Artem Anisimov 12.00 30.00
WCNCAP Artemi Panarin 40.00 100.00
WCNCAS Alexander Steen 12.00 30.00
WCNCBS Brent Seabrook 12.00 30.00
WCNCCC Corey Crawford 25.00 60.00
WCNCDK Duncan Keith 15.00 40.00
WCNCJA Jake Allen 20.00 50.00
WCNCJS Jaden Schwartz 25.00 60.00
WCNCJT Jonathan Toews 30.00 80.00
WCNCPI Alex Pietrangelo 15.00 40.00
WCNCPK Patrick Kane 40.00 100.00
WCNCVT Vladimir Tarasenko 25.00 60.00

2017-18 SP Game Used Autographs Blue

1 Auston Matthews A 150.00 250.00
2 Victor Hedman B 8.00 20.00
3 Tyler Seguin A 8.00 20.00
4 Jake Guentzel E 10.00 25.00
9 Artemi Panarin C 12.00 30.00
10 Carey Price A 30.00 80.00
12 Joe Pavelski B 8.00 20.00
13 Brayden Schenn E 10.00 25.00
14 Sean Monahan D 4.00 10.00
15 Vladimir Tarasenko A 15.00 40.00
16 Matt Duchene D 6.00 15.00
17 Patrik Laine B 25.00 60.00
18 Ryan Spooner E 5.00 12.00
20 Jonathan Toews A 25.00 60.00
21 Aleksander Barkov C 10.00 25.00
23 Marc-Andre Fleury E 30.00 80.00
24 Pavel Zacha E 5.00 12.00
27 Mats Zuccarello B 6.00 15.00
31 Jason Spezza B 6.00 15.00
34 Sebastian Aho E 10.00 25.00
35 Matt Murray D 10.00 25.00
36 Logan Couture B 8.00 20.00
37 John Gibson E 6.00 15.00
38 Nikolaj Ehlers D 6.00 15.00
40 Alexander Ovechkin A 30.00 80.00
42 Max Pacioretty B 6.00 15.00
45 Steven Stamkos A 12.00 30.00
47 Cam Atkinson D 6.00 15.00
50 Sidney Crosby A 100.00 200.00
51 Colton Parayko E 5.00 12.00
52 William Karlsson B 25.00 60.00
53 Leon Draisaitl D 20.00 50.00
55 Patrick Kane A 20.00 50.00
57 Noah Hanifin E 6.00 15.00
58 Adam Henrique E 5.00 12.00
60 Henrik Lundqvist A 40.00 100.00
63 Mark Giordano E 6.00 15.00
67 Roberto Luongo B 12.00 30.00
68 Nikita Kucherov E 12.00 30.00
69 Mark Stone E 8.00 20.00
70 John Tavares A 12.00 30.00
73 Mark Scheifele C 10.00 25.00
74 Mitch Marner C 25.00 60.00
76 Nino Niederreiter D 4.00 10.00
77 Connor McDavid A 150.00 250.00
78 Mark Messier A 20.00 50.00
79 Rod Langway B 6.00 15.00
80 Steve Yzerman A 25.00 60.00
82 Teemu Selanne A 20.00 50.00
83 Brett Hull A 12.00 30.00
84 Ed Belfour A 20.00 50.00
85 Wayne Gretzky A 200.00 500.00
87 Charlie McAvoy B 40.00 100.00
88 Victor Mete C 25.00 60.00
89 Gabriel Carlsson A 4.00 10.00
91 Adrian Kempe D 10.00 25.00
94 Evgeny Svechnikov C 10.00 25.00
95 Vadim Shipachyov E 6.00 15.00
97 Tage Thompson E 8.00 20.00
98 Vladislav Kamenev E 5.00 12.00
100 Clayton Keller D 12.00 30.00
101 Valentin Zykov E 5.00 12.00
105 Owen Tippett C 8.00 20.00
107 Ivan Barbashev A 6.00 15.00
110 Anders Bjork D 8.00 20.00
111 Mike Vecchione E 8.00 20.00
115 Brock Boeser A 100.00 200.00
116 Travis Sanheim E 5.00 12.00
119 Christian Djoos C 15.00 40.00
125 Haydn Fleury E 5.00 12.00
126 Robert Hagg A 5.00 12.00
127 Vince Dunn B 12.00 30.00
129 Filip Chlapik D 4.00 10.00
130 Alex DeBrincat D 12.00 30.00
131 Riley Barber E 5.00 12.00
133 Michael Amadio C 8.00 20.00
135 Nikita Scherbak B 6.00 15.00
136 Peter Cehlarik D 8.00 20.00
140 Josh Ho-Sang A 6.00 15.00
146 Tucker Poolman C 8.00 20.00
149 Andrew Poturalski C 5.00 12.00
150 Pierre-Luc Dubois C 8.00 20.00
153 Madison Bowey E 3.00 8.00
155 Jack Roslovic E 6.00 15.00
161 Jordan Schmaltz C 6.00 15.00
162 Denis Gurianov E 12.00 30.00
164 Luke Kunin D 8.00 20.00
165 Tyson Jost D 10.00 25.00
169 Samuel Morin C 3.00 8.00
171 Jon Gillies C 5.00 12.00
172 Will Butcher C 8.00 20.00
175 Jesper Bratt C 15.00 40.00
177 Alex Tuch D 15.00 40.00
179 J.T. Compher C 5.00 12.00
180 Christian Fischer A 8.00 20.00
182 Alexander Nylander E 8.00 20.00

2017-18 SP Game Used Banner Year All Star '17

BASAM Auston Matthews 12.00 30.00
BASAO Alexander Ovechkin 12.00 30.00
BASBB Brent Burns 3.00 8.00
BASCA Cam Atkinson 3.00 8.00
BASCM Connor McDavid 15.00 40.00
BASJG Johnny Gaudreau 5.00 12.00
BASJT John Tavares 5.00 12.00
BASNM Nathan MacKinnon 12.00 30.00
BASPK P.K. Subban 4.00 10.00
BASPL Patrik Laine 4.00 10.00
BASSC Sidney Crosby 12.00 30.00
BASTO Jonathan Toews 5.00 12.00
BASVH Victor Hedman 4.00 10.00
BASWS Wayne Simmonds 4.00 10.00

2017-18 SP Game Used Banner Year Centennial Classic '17

BCCAM Auston Matthews 15.00 40.00
BCCDL Dylan Larkin 6.00 15.00
BCCFA Frederik Andersen 6.00 15.00
BCCGN Gustav Nyquist 3.00 8.00
BCCHZ Henrik Zetterberg 6.00 15.00
BCCJV James van Riemsdyk 4.00 10.00
BCCMA Anthony Mantha 4.00 10.00
BCCMM Mitch Marner 12.00 30.00
BCCMR Morgan Rielly 5.00 12.00
BCCTT Tomas Tatar 3.00 8.00

2017-18 SP Game Used Banner Year Draft '03

BD03BB Brent Burns 8.00 20.00
BD03CC Corey Crawford 10.00 25.00
BD03MF Marc-Andre Fleury 15.00 40.00
BD03PB Patrice Bergeron 12.00 30.00
BD03RK Ryan Kesler 8.00 20.00

2017-18 SP Game Used Banner Year Draft '14

BD14IB Ivan Barbashev 3.00 8.00
BD14JH Josh Ho-Sang 3.00 8.00

2017-18 SP Game Used Banner Year Draft '15

BD15ES Evgeny Svechnikov 5.00 12.00
BD15JR Jack Roslovic 3.00 8.00

2017-18 SP Game Used Banner Year Draft '15 Autographs

BD15JR Jack Roslovic 12.00 30.00

2017-18 SP Game Used Banner Year Draft '16

BD16CK Clayton Keller 4.00 10.00
BD16CM Charlie McAvoy 4.00 10.00
BD16PD Pierre-Luc Dubois 2.50 6.00
BD16TJ Tyson Jost 3.00 8.00

2017-18 SP Game Used Banner Year Draft '17

BD17NH Nico Hischier 12.00 30.00
BD17NP Nolan Patrick 12.00 30.00

2017-18 SP Game Used Banner Year Stadium Series '17

BSSCG Claude Giroux 6.00 15.00
BSSEM Evgeni Malkin 12.00 30.00
BSSJG Jake Guentzel 10.00 25.00
BSSJV Jakub Voracek 5.00 12.00
BSSPH Patric Hornqvist 4.00 10.00
BSSPK Phil Kessel 6.00 15.00
BSSSG Shayne Gostisbehere 6.00 15.00
BSSWS Wayne Simmonds 8.00 20.00

2017-18 SP Game Used Banner Year Winter Classic '17

BWCAA Artem Anisimov 3.00 8.00
BWCCC Corey Crawford 6.00 15.00
BWCDK Duncan Keith 4.00 10.00
BWCJA Jake Allen 5.00 12.00
BWCJS Jaden Schwartz 6.00 15.00
BWCPK Patrick Kane 10.00 25.00
BWCRF Robby Fabbri 3.00 8.00
BWCVT Vladimir Tarasenko 6.00 15.00

2017-18 SP Game Used Draft Day Marks

DDMAD Alex DeBrincat 50.00 125.00
DDMAK Adrian Kempe 40.00 100.00
DDMAT Alex Tuch 50.00 125.00
DDMBB Brock Boeser 150.00 300.00
DDMCF Christian Fischer 25.00 60.00
DDMCK Clayton Keller 50.00 125.00
DDMCM Charlie McAvoy 50.00 125.00
DDMDG Denis Gurianov 50.00 125.00
DDMES Evgeny Svechnikov 40.00 100.00
DDMGC Gabriel Carlsson 15.00 40.00
DDMHF Haydn Fleury 20.00 50.00
DDMIB Ivan Barbashev 25.00 60.00
DDMJE Joel Eriksson Ek 15.00 40.00
DDMJG Jake Guentzel 40.00 100.00
DDMJG Jon Gillies 20.00 50.00
DDMJR Jack Roslovic 25.00 60.00
DDMLK Luke Kunin 20.00 50.00
DDMOT Owen Tippett 40.00 100.00
DDMPD Pierre-Luc Dubois 30.00 80.00
DDMSM Samuel Morin 12.00 30.00
DDMTJ Tyson Jost 40.00 100.00
DDMTT Tage Thompson 40.00 100.00
DDMVK Vladislav Kamenev 20.00 50.00
DDMVT Vladimir Tarasenko 40.00 100.00
DDMVZ Valentin Zykov 20.00 50.00

2017-18 SP Game Used Frameworks Materials

FWAG Alex Galchenyuk C 5.00 12.00
FWAL Andrew Ladd C 5.00 12.00
FWAM Anthony Mantha B 15.00 40.00
FWAW Alexander Wennberg A 5.00 12.00
FWBB Brent Burns B 8.00 20.00
FWBM Brad Marchand B 15.00 40.00
FWCC Corey Crawford C 10.00 25.00
FWCM Connor McDavid A 40.00 100.00
FWDG Doug Gilmour A 10.00 25.00
FWEB Ed Belfour B 10.00 25.00
FWEK Evgeny Kuznetsov A 10.00 25.00
FWHS Henrik Sedin B 10.00 25.00
FWJA Justin Abdelkader C 6.00 15.00
FWJH Jonathan Huberdeau C 10.00 25.00
FWJK John Klingberg C 8.00 20.00
FWJQ Jonathan Quick C 10.00 25.00
FWJS Joe Sakic A 15.00 40.00
FWKE Phil Kessel B 8.00 20.00
FWLD Leon Draisaitl B 25.00 60.00
FWMA Auston Matthews A 30.00 80.00
FWMK Mikko Koivu C 6.00 15.00
FWMM Mitch Marner B 12.00 30.00
FWMU Matt Murray B 12.00 30.00
FWMZ Mats Zuccarello B 8.00 20.00
FWNK Nikita Kucherov B 15.00 40.00
FWNM Nathan MacKinnon A 30.00 80.00
FWOE Oliver Ekman-Larsson B 8.00 20.00
FWPC Paul Coffey A 8.00 20.00
FWPF Peter Forsberg A 15.00 40.00
FWPL Patrik Laine B 10.00 25.00
FWPS P.K. Subban B 10.00 25.00
FWRB Ray Bourque A 12.00 30.00
FWRG Ryan Getzlaf B 8.00 20.00
FWRO Ryan O'Reilly B 8.00 20.00
FWSC Jaden Schwartz B 10.00 25.00
FWSG Shayne Gostisbehere C 8.00 20.00
FWSM Sean Monahan C 5.00 12.00
FWSW Shea Weber C 6.00 15.00
FWTH Taylor Hall B 8.00 20.00
FWVR Victor Rask C 5.00 12.00

2017-18 SP Game Used Goal Pucks

GPCA Cam Atkinson 15.00 40.00
GPDS Daniel Sedin 20.00 50.00
GPJP Joe Pavelski 20.00 50.00
GPJT Jonathan Toews 25.00 60.00
GPMG Mikael Granlund 12.00 30.00
GPMS Mark Stone 20.00 50.00
GPOE Oliver Ekman-Larsson 15.00 40.00
GPOP Ondrej Palat 12.00 30.00
GPRJ Roman Josi 15.00 40.00

2017-18 SP Game Used Inked Sweaters

ISAG Alex Galchenyuk/50 8.00 20.00
ISCC Chris Chelios/25 12.00 30.00
ISJO Joe Thornton/25 15.00 40.00
ISJT Jonathan Toews/25 30.00 80.00
ISMM Matt Murray/50 20.00 50.00
ISPL Patrik Laine/50 25.00 60.00
ISTA John Tavares/25 15.00 40.00
ISTS Tyler Seguin/50 8.00 20.00

2017-18 SP Game Used Inked Sweaters Patch

COMMON CARD 12.00 30.00
SEMISTARS 15.00 40.00
UNLISTED STARS 20.00 50.00
IPMM Matt Murray/25 40.00 100.00
IPPL Patrik Laine/25 40.00 100.00

2017-18 SP Game Used Rookie Sweaters

RSAB Anders Bjork/199 3.00 8.00
RSAD Alex DeBrincat/199 6.00 15.00
RSAK Adrian Kempe/199 5.00 12.00
RSAN Alexander Nylander/199 4.00 10.00
RSAT Alex Tuch/199 6.00 15.00
RSBB Brock Boeser/199 15.00 40.00
RSCF Christian Fischer/199 3.00 8.00
RSCK Clayton Keller/199 6.00 15.00
RSCM Charlie McAvoy/199 6.00 15.00
RSCW Colin White/199 3.00 8.00
RSES Evgeny Svechnikov/199 5.00 12.00
RSHF Haydn Fleury/199 2.50 6.00
RSIB Ivan Barbashev/199 3.00 8.00
RSJD Jake DeBrusk/199 6.00 15.00
RSJG Jon Gillies/199 2.50 6.00
RSJH Josh Ho-Sang/199 3.00 8.00
RSJK Janne Kuokkanen/199 2.50 6.00
RSJR Jack Roslovic/199 3.00 8.00
RSKY Kailer Yamamoto/199 6.00 15.00
RSLB Logan Brown/199 2.50 6.00
RSNH Nico Hischier/99 8.00 20.00
RSNP Nolan Patrick/99 5.00 12.00
RSNS Nikita Scherbak/199 3.00 8.00
RSOT Owen Tippett/199 5.00 12.00
RSPD Pierre-Luc Dubois/199 4.00 10.00
RSRB Riley Barber/199 2.50 6.00
RSSM Samuel Morin/199 1.50 4.00
RSTJ Tyson Jost/199 5.00 12.00
RSTT Tage Thompson/199 6.00 15.00
RSVS Vadim Shipachyov/199 3.00 8.00

2017-18 SP Game Used Rookie Sweaters Inked Patch

RSAB Anders Bjork 20.00 50.00
RSAD Alex DeBrincat 40.00 100.00
RSAK Adrian Kempe 30.00 80.00
RSAN Alexander Nylander 25.00 60.00
RSAT Alex Tuch 40.00 100.00
RSBB Brock Boeser 150.00 300.00
RSCF Christian Fischer 20.00 50.00
RSCK Clayton Keller 40.00 100.00
RSCM Charlie McAvoy 40.00 100.00
RSES Evgeny Svechnikov 30.00 80.00
RSHF Haydn Fleury 15.00 40.00
RSIB Ivan Barbashev 20.00 50.00
RSJG Jon Gillies 15.00 40.00
RSJH Josh Ho-Sang 20.00 50.00
RSJR Jack Roslovic 20.00 50.00
RSNS Nikita Scherbak 20.00 50.00
RSOT Owen Tippett 30.00 80.00
RSPD Pierre-Luc Dubois 25.00 60.00
RSRB Riley Barber 15.00 40.00
RSSM Samuel Morin 10.00 25.00
RSTJ Tyson Jost 30.00 80.00
RSTT Tage Thompson 40.00 100.00
RSVS Vadim Shipachyov 20.00 50.00

2017-18 SP Game Used Signing Day Marks

SDMMV Mike Vecchione 15.00 40.00
SDMVS Vadim Shipachyov 15.00 40.00

2018-19 SP Game Used

1 Connor McDavid/97 15.00 40.00
2 Nikita Kucherov/86 4.00 10.00
4 Max Pacioretty/67 8.00 20.00
5 Auston Matthews/34 20.00 50.00
6 Jake DeBrusk/74 5.00 12.00
7 Mikko Rantanen/96 5.00 12.00
9 Evgeni Malkin/71 12.00 30.00
10 Jonathan Quick/32 4.00 10.00
15 Vladimir Tarasenko/91 4.00 10.00
17 Dylan Larkin/71 6.00 15.00
18 Mark Scheifele/55 5.00 12.00
21 Teuvo Teravainen/86 2.50 6.00
24 Kyle Palmieri/21 2.50 6.00
25 Henrik Lundqvist/30 6.00 15.00
26 Vincent Trocheck/21 8.00 20.00
27 Anders Lee/27 3.00 8.00
31 Bo Horvat/53 3.00 8.00
32 Brayden Point/21 12.00 30.00
33 James van Riemsdyk/25 10.00 25.00
34 Danton Heinen/43 3.00 8.00
35 Jake Guentzel/59 4.00 10.00
36 Tomas Hertl/48 6.00 15.00
40 Marc-Andre Fleury/29 15.00 40.00
41 Stefan Noesen/23 3.00 8.00
42 Jaden Schwartz/17 6.00 15.00
43 Patrik Laine/29 6.00 15.00
44 Thomas Chabot/72 6.00 15.00
46 Matthew Tkachuk/19 8.00 20.00
47 Mike Hoffman/68 3.00 8.00
48 Derek Stepan/21 3.00 8.00
49 Viktor Arvidsson/33 6.00 15.00
50 Jonathan Toews/19 8.00 20.00
51 Kyle Okposo/21 6.00 15.00
52 Anthony Mantha/39 8.00 20.00
53 Tom Wilson/43 6.00 15.00
55 Nathan MacKinnon/29 10.00 25.00
56 Pierre-Luc Dubois/18 6.00 15.00
57 Mitch Marner/16 20.00 50.00
58 Brady Skjei/76 5.00 12.00
60 Carey Price/31 12.00 30.00
61 Mikael Granlund/64 6.00 15.00
62 Jonathan Marchessault/81 2.50 6.00
63 Leon Draisaitl/29 6.00 15.00
64 Jimmy Vesey/26 5.00 12.00
66 Alexander Radulov/47 4.00 10.00
67 Noah Hanifin/55 4.00 10.00
69 Kyle Connor/81 2.50 6.00
70 Evgeny Kuznetsov/92 2.50 6.00
73 Craig Anderson/41 3.00 8.00
74 Alex Galchenyuk/17 5.00 12.00
75 Andrei Vasilevskiy/88 3.00 8.00
76 David Krejci/46 5.00 12.00
78 Ryan O'Reilly/90 4.00 10.00
80 John Tavares/91 6.00 15.00
81 Sebastian Aho/20 6.00 15.00
82 Erik Karlsson/65 8.00 20.00
83 Ryan Nugent-Hopkins/93 5.00 12.00
84 Kevin Fiala/22 4.00 10.00
85 Sidney Crosby/87 10.00 25.00
90 Mario Lemieux/66 12.00 30.00
91 Curtis Joseph/31 4.00 10.00
92 Mike Bossy/22 4.00 10.00
93 Larry Robinson/19 10.00 25.00
97 Rod Brind'Amour/17 5.00 12.00
98 Markus Naslund/91 5.00 12.00
99 Luc Robitaille/20 6.00 15.00
100 Wayne Gretzky/99 15.00 40.00
101 Rasmus Dahlin/26 RC 300.00 400.00
102 Lias Andersson/50 RC 20.00 50.00
103 Michael Rasmussen/27 RC 30.00 80.00
104 Daniel Brickley/78 RC 15.00 40.00
105 Robert Thomas/18 RC 80.00 150.00
106 Ethan Bear/74 RC 40.00 100.00
107 Dillon Dube/29 RC 30.00 80.00
110 Ryan Donato/17 RC 100.00 200.00
111 Juuso Riikola/50 RC 25.00 60.00
115 Juho Lammikko/91 RC 6.00 15.00
117 Sam Steel/34 RC 30.00 80.00
121 Carl Dahlstrom/63 RC 12.00 30.00
123 Landon Bow/41 RC 12.00 30.00
125 Henrik Borgstrom/95 RC 12.00 30.00
126 Par Lindholm/26 RC 12.00 30.00
128 Dominik Kahun/24 RC 30.00 80.00
129 Ryan Lomberg/56 RC 6.00 15.00
130 Joey Anderson/49 RC 20.00 50.00
131 Ashton Sautner/59 RC 6.00 15.00
132 Christoffer Ehn/70 RC 8.00 20.00
134 Matthew Highmore/36 RC 5.00 12.00
135 Brett Howden/21 RC 25.00 60.00
136 Trevor Murphy/46 RC 3.00 8.00
138 Roope Hintz/24 RC 20.00 50.00
139 John Gilmour/58 RC 12.00 30.00
141 Dennis Cholowski/21 RC 100.00 200.00
142 Alex Broadhurst/25 RC 15.00 40.00
143 Kristian Vesalainen/93 RC 15.00 40.00
144 Samuel Montembeault/33 RC 20.00 50.00
145 Jaret Anderson-Dolan/28 RC 25.00 60.00
148 Ben Sexton/26 RC 100.00 200.00
152 Carson Soucy/60 RC 4.00 10.00
154 Libor Sulak/47 RC 10.00 25.00
155 Zach Aston-Reese/46 RC 20.00 50.00
158 Rourke Chartier/60 RC 8.00 20.00
159 Shane Gersich/63 RC 8.00 20.00
160 Casey Mittelstadt/37 RC 30.00 80.00
161 Victor Ejdsell/17 RC 20.00 50.00
162 Tomas Hyka/38 RC 12.00 30.00
163 Jacob MacDonald/23 RC 25.00 60.00
164 Austin Wagner/51 RC 20.00 50.00
166 Igor Ozhiganov/92 RC 4.00 10.00
167 Collin Delia/60 RC 15.00 40.00
168 Morgan Klimchuk/52 RC 4.00 10.00
169 Troy Terry/61 RC 25.00 60.00
170 Evan Bouchard/75 RC 30.00 80.00
171 Cooper Marody/65 RC 15.00 40.00
172 Mitch Reinke/39 RC 6.00 15.00
173 Kiefer Sherwood/64 RC 10.00 25.00
174 Mikhail Vorobyev/24 RC 15.00 40.00
175 Filip Hronek/17 RC 40.00 100.00
176 Urho Vaakanainen/58 RC 20.00 50.00
177 Sami Niku/83 RC 20.00 50.00
178 Jeremy Lauzon/79 RC 12.00 30.00
179 Neal Pionk/44 RC 20.00 50.00
180 Maxime Comtois/53 RC 25.00 60.00
181 Anthony Cirelli/71 RC 15.00 40.00
182 Louie Belpedio/47 RC 4.00 10.00
184 Maxim Mamin/78 RC 8.00 20.00
185 Travis Dermott/23 RC 80.00 150.00
186 Dylan Sikura/95 RC 12.00 30.00
189 Tyrell Goulbourne/39 RC 25.00 60.00
195 Adam Gaudette/88 RC 30.00 88.00
199 Christian Wolanin/86 RC 15.00 40.00
200 Elias Pettersson/40 RC 900.00 1500.00

2018-19 SP Game Used Gold

1 Connor McDavid JSY B 15.00 40.00
2 Nikita Kucherov JSY D 6.00 15.00
3 Nolan Patrick JSY E 3.00 8.00
4 Max Pacioretty JSY B 3.00 8.00
5 Auston Matthews JSY B 12.00 30.00
7 Mikko Rantanen JSY E 8.00 20.00
8 Adam Henrique JSY D 2.50 6.00
9 Evgeni Malkin JSY D 6.00 15.00
10 Jonathan Quick JSY D 4.00 10.00
11 Bobby Ryan JSY E 2.50 6.00
12 Max Domi JSY B 3.00 8.00
13 Duncan Keith JSY D 2.50 6.00
14 Filip Forsberg JSY D 5.00 12.00
15 Vladimir Tarasenko JSY B 4.00 10.00
16 Evander Kane JSY D 3.00 8.00
17 Dylan Larkin JSY D 4.00 10.00
18 Mark Scheifele JSY E 5.00 12.00
19 Jack Eichel JSY D 5.00 12.00
20 Johnny Gaudreau JSY D 5.00 12.00
21 Teuvo Teravainen JSY E 3.00 8.00
22 Alexander Wennberg JSY E 2.00 5.00
23 Zach Parise JSY E 3.00 8.00
24 Kyle Palmieri JSY E 2.50 6.00
25 Henrik Lundqvist JSY B 8.00 20.00
26 Vincent Trocheck JSY D 3.00 8.00
27 Anders Lee JSY D 2.50 6.00
28 Jamie Benn JSY D 3.00 8.00
29 Clayton Keller JSY D 4.00 10.00
30 Alexander Ovechkin JSY B 12.00 30.00
31 Bo Horvat JSY E 4.00 10.00
35 Jake Guentzel JSY D 5.00 12.00
36 Tomas Hertl JSY E 3.00 8.00
37 Ryan Getzlaf JSY D 3.00 8.00
38 Radek Faksa JSY D 2.50 6.00
39 Brendan Gallagher JSY D 3.00 8.00
40 Marc-Andre Fleury JSY B 6.00 15.00
42 Jaden Schwartz JSY D 4.00 10.00
43 Patrik Laine JSY D 4.00 10.00
45 Anze Kopitar JSY B 5.00 12.00
46 Matthew Tkachuk JSY D 6.00 15.00
48 Derek Stepan JSY E 2.00 5.00
49 Viktor Arvidsson JSY E 2.00 5.00
50 Jonathan Toews JSY B 5.00 12.00
52 Anthony Mantha JSY D 2.50 6.00
54 Mathew Barzal JSY D 4.00 10.00
55 Nathan MacKinnon JSY B 12.00 30.00
56 Pierre-Luc Dubois JSY D 2.50 6.00
57 Mitch Marner JSY D 5.00 12.00
59 Jake Muzzin JSY E 3.00 8.00
60 Carey Price JSY B 6.00 15.00
61 Mikael Granlund JSY E 2.50 6.00
62 Jonathan Marchessault JSY D 4.00 10.00
63 Leon Draisaitl JSY D 10.00 25.00
64 Jimmy Vesey JSY D 2.50 6.00
65 Taylor Hall JSY D 3.00 8.00
66 Alexander Radulov JSY E 3.00 8.00
67 Noah Hanifin JSY D 3.00 8.00
68 Brock Boeser JSY B 4.00 10.00
69 Kyle Connor JSY D 5.00 12.00
70 Evgeny Kuznetsov JSY D 4.00 10.00
71 Sean Couturier JSY D 2.50 6.00
73 Craig Anderson JSY E 2.50 6.00
74 Alex Galchenyuk JSY B 2.00 5.00
75 Andrei Vasilevskiy JSY D 5.00 12.00
76 David Krejci JSY E 3.00 8.00
77 Zach Werenski JSY E 5.00 12.00
79 Jonathan Huberdeau JSY D 4.00 10.00
80 John Tavares JSY B 5.00 12.00
81 Sebastian Aho JSY D 5.00 12.00
82 Erik Karlsson JSY B 4.00 10.00
83 Ryan Nugent-Hopkins JSY E 4.00 10.00
85 Sidney Crosby JSY B 12.00 30.00
86 Nico Hischier JSY B 5.00 12.00
88 Pavel Datsyuk JSY C 5.00 12.00
89 Owen Nolan JSY C 3.00 8.00
90 Mario Lemieux JSY B 12.00 30.00
93 Larry Robinson JSY C 3.00 8.00
95 Theoren Fleury JSY C 3.00 8.00
99 Luc Robitaille JSY C 3.00 8.00
100 Wayne Gretzky JSY A 20.00 50.00
101 Rasmus Dahlin JSY 8.00 20.00
102 Lias Andersson JSY 5.00 12.00
103 Michael Rasmussen JSY 4.00 10.00
104 Daniel Brickley JSY 3.00 8.00
105 Robert Thomas JSY 6.00 15.00
106 Ethan Bear JSY 5.00 12.00
107 Dillon Dube JSY 4.00 10.00
108 Marcus Pettersson JSY 3.00 8.00
109 Zach Whitecloud JSY 2.50 6.00
110 Ryan Donato JSY 5.00 12.00
112 Noah Juulsen JSY 3.00 8.00
113 Max Lajoie JSY 5.00 12.00
114 Dominic Turgeon JSY 3.00 8.00
117 Sam Steel JSY 3.00 8.00
118 Dylan Gambrell JSY 3.00 8.00
119 Spencer Foo JSY 2.50 6.00
120 Andrei Svechnikov JSY 8.00 20.00
122 Juuso Valimaki JSY 3.00 8.00
123 Landon Bow JSY 2.50 6.00
124 Isac Lundestrom JSY 2.50 6.00
125 Henrik Borgstrom JSY 5.00 12.00
127 Nicolas Roy JSY 2.00 5.00
130 Joey Anderson JSY 3.00 8.00
135 Brett Howden JSY 4.00 10.00
137 Jordan Greenway JSY 3.00 8.00
139 John Gilmour JSY 2.00 5.00
140 Jesperi Kotkaniemi JSY 6.00 15.00
141 Dennis Cholowski JSY 3.00 8.00
143 Kristian Vesalainen JSY 4.00 10.00
144 Samuel Montembeault JSY 6.00 15.00
145 Jaret Anderson-Dolan JSY 2.50 6.00
146 Blake Hillman JSY 3.00 8.00
150 Brady Tkachuk JSY 10.00 25.00
151 Oskar Lindblom JSY 5.00 12.00
155 Zach Aston-Reese JSY 5.00 12.00
157 Warren Foegele JSY 3.00 8.00
160 Casey Mittelstadt JSY 6.00 15.00
161 Victor Ejdsell JSY 2.50 6.00
162 Tomas Hyka JSY 3.00 8.00
165 Eeli Tolvanen JSY 6.00 15.00
168 Morgan Klimchuk JSY 3.00 8.00
169 Troy Terry JSY 5.00 12.00
170 Evan Bouchard JSY 8.00 20.00
175 Filip Hronek JSY 3.00 8.00
177 Sami Niku JSY 2.50 6.00
178 Jeremy Lauzon JSY 4.00 10.00
179 Neal Pionk JSY 3.00 8.00
180 Maxime Comtois JSY 3.00 8.00
181 Anthony Cirelli JSY 5.00 12.00
182 Louie Belpedio JSY 2.50 6.00
185 Travis Dermott JSY 5.00 12.00
186 Dylan Sikura JSY 4.00 10.00
187 Jordan Kyrou JSY 6.00 15.00
188 Michael Dal Colle JSY 3.00 8.00
190 Miro Heiskanen JSY 8.00 20.00
192 Antti Suomela JSY 2.50 6.00
193 Mackenzie Blackwood JSY 6.00 15.00
195 Adam Gaudette JSY 5.00 12.00
197 Henri Jokiharju JSY 2.50 6.00
200 Elias Pettersson JSY 20.00 50.00

2018-19 SP Game Used Rainbow

140 Jesperi Kotkaniemi/200 10.00 25.00
200 Elias Pettersson/298 20.00 50.00

2018-19 SP Game Used Red

1 Connor McDavid JSY AU A 150.00 250.00
2 Nikita Kucherov JSY AU A 15.00 40.00
5 Auston Matthews JSY AU A 30.00 80.00
7 Mikko Rantanen JSY AU B 20.00 50.00
9 Evgeni Malkin JSY AU A 15.00 40.00
11 Bobby Ryan JSY AU B 6.00 15.00
12 Max Domi JSY AU B 8.00 20.00
14 Filip Forsberg JSY AU A 12.00 30.00
15 Vladimir Tarasenko JSY AU A 10.00 25.00
16 Evander Kane JSY AU B 8.00 20.00
18 Mark Scheifele JSY AU A 12.00 30.00
20 Johnny Gaudreau JSY AU A 12.00 30.00
21 Teuvo Teravainen JSY AU B 8.00 20.00
22 Alexander Wennberg JSY AU B 5.00 12.00
23 Zach Parise JSY AU A 8.00 20.00
24 Kyle Palmieri JSY AU B 6.00 15.00
25 Henrik Lundqvist JSY AU A 20.00 50.00
26 Vincent Trocheck JSY AU B 8.00 20.00
27 Anders Lee JSY AU B 6.00 15.00
28 Jamie Benn JSY AU A 8.00 20.00
29 Clayton Keller JSY AU A 10.00 25.00
31 Bo Horvat JSY AU B 10.00 25.00
35 Jake Guentzel JSY AU A 12.00 30.00
36 Tomas Hertl JSY AU B 8.00 20.00
38 Radek Faksa JSY AU B 6.00 15.00
39 Brendan Gallagher JSY AU A 8.00 20.00
40 Marc-Andre Fleury JSY AU A 15.00 40.00
43 Patrik Laine JSY AU A 10.00 25.00
45 Anze Kopitar JSY AU A 12.00 30.00
46 Matthew Tkachuk JSY AU B 15.00 40.00
48 Derek Stepan JSY AU B 5.00 12.00
50 Jonathan Toews JSY AU A 12.00 30.00
52 Anthony Mantha JSY AU A 6.00 15.00
54 Mathew Barzal JSY AU A 10.00 25.00
56 Pierre-Luc Dubois JSY AU B 6.00 15.00
57 Mitch Marner JSY AU A 12.00 30.00
59 Jake Muzzin JSY AU B 8.00 20.00
60 Carey Price JSY AU A 15.00 40.00
61 Mikael Granlund JSY AU B 6.00 15.00
62 Jonathan Marchessault JSY AU B 10.00 25.00
63 Leon Draisaitl JSY AU A 25.00 60.00
64 Jimmy Vesey JSY AU B 6.00 15.00
65 Taylor Hall JSY AU A 8.00 20.00
66 Alexander Radulov JSY AU B 8.00 20.00
67 Noah Hanifin JSY AU B 8.00 20.00
68 Brock Boeser JSY AU A 10.00 25.00
69 Kyle Connor JSY AU B 12.00 30.00
70 Evgeny Kuznetsov JSY AU A 10.00 25.00
73 Craig Anderson JSY AU B 6.00 15.00
74 Alex Galchenyuk JSY AU B 5.00 12.00
75 Andrei Vasilevskiy JSY AU B 12.00 30.00
76 David Krejci JSY AU B 8.00 20.00
77 Zach Werenski JSY AU B 12.00 30.00
79 Jonathan Huberdeau JSY AU B 10.00 25.00
80 John Tavares JSY AU A 12.00 30.00
81 Sebastian Aho JSY AU B 12.00 30.00
82 Erik Karlsson JSY AU A 10.00 25.00
83 Ryan Nugent-Hopkins JSY AU A 10.00 25.00
88 Pavel Datsyuk JSY AU A 12.00 30.00
89 Owen Nolan JSY AU A 8.00 20.00
90 Mario Lemieux JSY AU A 30.00 80.00
91 Curtis Joseph JSY AU A 10.00 25.00
92 Mike Bossy JSY AU A 8.00 20.00
93 Larry Robinson JSY AU A 8.00 20.00
95 Theoren Fleury JSY AU A 8.00 20.00
97 Rod Brind'Amour JSY AU B 8.00 20.00
99 Luc Robitaille JSY AU A 8.00 20.00
100 Wayne Gretzky JSY AU A 200.00 500.00
102 Lias Andersson JSY AU C 12.00 30.00
103 Michael Rasmussen JSY AU C 10.00 25.00
104 Daniel Brickley JSY AU C 8.00 20.00
105 Robert Thomas JSY AU C 15.00 40.00
106 Ethan Bear JSY AU D 12.00 30.00
107 Dillon Dube JSY AU C 10.00 25.00
109 Zach Whitecloud JSY AU B 6.00 15.00
112 Noah Juulsen JSY AU C 8.00 20.00
113 Max Lajoie JSY AU B 12.00 30.00
114 Dominic Turgeon JSY AU D 8.00 20.00
117 Sam Steel JSY AU C 8.00 20.00
118 Dylan Gambrell JSY AU D 8.00 20.00
119 Spencer Foo JSY AU D 6.00 15.00
120 Andrei Svechnikov JSY AU B 20.00 50.00
122 Juuso Valimaki JSY AU C 8.00 20.00
123 Landon Bow JSY AU D 6.00 15.00
124 Isac Lundestrom JSY AU D 6.00 15.00
125 Henrik Borgstrom JSY AU C 12.00 30.00
127 Nicolas Roy JSY AU B 5.00 12.00
130 Joey Anderson JSY AU D 8.00 20.00
135 Brett Howden JSY AU C 10.00 25.00
137 Jordan Greenway JSY AU A 8.00 20.00
139 John Gilmour JSY AU C 5.00 12.00
140 Jesperi Kotkaniemi JSY AU B 15.00 40.00
141 Dennis Cholowski JSY AU B 8.00 20.00
143 Kristian Vesalainen JSY AU C 10.00 25.00
144 Samuel Montembeault JSY AU D 15.00 40.00
145 Jaret Anderson-Dolan JSY AU D 6.00 15.00
146 Blake Hillman JSY AU D 8.00 20.00
150 Brady Tkachuk JSY AU B 25.00 60.00
151 Oskar Lindblom JSY AU C 12.00 30.00
155 Zach Aston-Reese JSY AU D 12.00 30.00
156 Mathieu Joseph JSY AU D 10.00 25.00
157 Warren Foegele JSY AU C 8.00 20.00
160 Casey Mittelstadt JSY AU B 15.00 40.00
161 Victor Ejdsell JSY AU C 6.00 15.00
162 Tomas Hyka JSY AU C 8.00 20.00
165 Eeli Tolvanen JSY AU C 15.00 40.00
168 Morgan Klimchuk JSY AU C 8.00 20.00
169 Troy Terry JSY AU C 20.00 50.00
170 Evan Bouchard JSY AU C 20.00 50.00
175 Filip Hronek JSY AU C 8.00 20.00
177 Sami Niku JSY AU D 6.00 15.00
178 Jeremy Lauzon JSY AU D 10.00 25.00
179 Neal Pionk JSY AU C 8.00 20.00
180 Maxime Comtois JSY AU D 8.00 20.00
181 Anthony Cirelli JSY AU B 12.00 30.00
182 Louie Belpedio JSY AU B 6.00 15.00
185 Travis Dermott JSY AU C 12.00 30.00
186 Dylan Sikura JSY AU C 10.00 25.00
187 Jordan Kyrou JSY AU C 20.00 50.00
188 Michael Dal Colle JSY AU C 8.00 20.00
190 Miro Heiskanen JSY AU B 20.00 50.00
192 Antti Suomela JSY AU D 6.00 15.00
193 Mackenzie Blackwood JSY AU D 15.00 40.00

197 Henri Jokiharju JSY AU B 6.00 15.00
200 Elias Pettersson JSY AU B 200.00 300.00

2018-19 SP Game Used '16 All Star Game Materials Net Cord Dual

ASNCDBK N.Backstrom/E.Kuznetsov 20.00 50.00
ASNCDBS J.Benn/T.Seguin 20.00 50.00
ASNCDDQ D.Doughty/J.Quick 20.00 50.00
ASNCDGG J.Gaudreau/M.Giordano 25.00 60.00
ASNCDJL J.Jagr/R.Luongo 50.00 120.00
ASNCDJR R.Josi/P.Rinne 15.00 40.00
ASNCDLE D.Larkin/P.Bergeron 20.00 50.00
ASNCDML E.Malkin/K.Letang 30.00 80.00
ASNCDPB J.Pavelski/B.Burns 20.00 50.00
ASNCDST S.Stamkos/V.Tarasenko 30.00 80.00

2018-19 SP Game Used '17 100th Classic Game Used Pucks

NHL100AS Andrew Shaw 15.00 40.00
NHL100BG Brendan Gallagher 25.00 60.00
NHL100BR Bobby Ryan 20.00 50.00
NHL100CP Carey Price 50.00 125.00
NHL100EK Erik Karlsson 30.00 80.00
NHL100JD Jonathan Drouin 20.00 50.00

2018-19 SP Game Used '17 100th Classic Materials Net Cord

NNCAS Andrew Shaw 8.00 20.00
NNCBG Brendan Gallagher 12.00 30.00
NNCBR Bobby Ryan 10.00 25.00
NNCCA Craig Anderson 10.00 25.00
NNCCP Carey Price 25.00 60.00
NNCEK Erik Karlsson 15.00 40.00
NNCJD Jonathan Drouin 10.00 25.00
NNCKA Erik Karlsson 15.00 40.00
NNCMD Matt Duchene 12.00 30.00
NNCMP Max Pacioretty 12.00 30.00
NNCMS Mark Stone 15.00 40.00
NNCPR Carey Price 25.00 60.00
NNCSW Shea Weber 12.00 30.00

2018-19 SP Game Used '17 All Star Game Materials Net Cord Dual

ASNCDBD B.Burns/D.Doughty 15.00 40.00
ASNCDGL J.Gaudreau/P.Laine 20.00 50.00
ASNCDHS T.Hall/W.Simmonds 12.00 30.00
ASNCDKH N.Kucherov/V.Hedman 25.00 60.00
ASNCDKS D.Keith/P.Subban 15.00 40.00
ASNCDMM C.McDavid/A.Matthews 60.00 150.00
ASNCDMR B.Marchand/T.Rask 25.00 60.00
ASNCDMT N.MacKinnon
V.Tarasenko 50.00 120.00
ASNCDOH A.Ovechkin/B.Holtby 50.00 125.00
ASNCDTK J.Toews/P.Kane 25.00 60.00

2018-19 SP Game Used '18 All Star Game Used Pucks

ASGUPAM Auston Matthews 100.00 250.00
ASGUPAO Alexander Ovechkin 100.00 250.00
ASGUPBB Brock Boeser 30.00 80.00
ASGUPCM Connor McDavid 125.00 300.00
ASGUPMF Marc-Andre Fleury 50.00 125.00
ASGUPPK Patrick Kane 50.00 125.00
ASGUPSC Sidney Crosby 100.00 250.00

2018-19 SP Game Used '18 All Star Skills Fabrics

*PATCH/35: 1X TO 2.5X BASIC INSERTS
ASAB Aleksander Barkov 4.00 10.00
ASAK Anze Kopitar 4.00 10.00
ASAM Auston Matthews 10.00 25.00
ASAO Alexander Ovechkin 10.00 25.00
ASAP Alex Pietrangelo 2.00 5.00
ASAV Andrei Vasilevskiy 4.00 10.00
ASBB Brock Boeser 3.00 8.00
ASBH Braden Holtby 3.00 8.00
ASBM Brad Marchand 5.00 12.00
ASBO Brian Boyle 2.00 5.00
ASBP Brayden Point 3.00 8.00
ASBS Brayden Schenn 2.50 6.00
ASBU Brent Burns 2.50 6.00
ASBW Blake Wheeler 2.50 6.00
ASCC Claude Giroux 2.50 6.00
ASCH Connor Hellebuyck 5.00 12.00
ASCM Connor McDavid 12.00 30.00
ASCP Carey Price 5.00 12.00
ASDD Drew Doughty 3.00 8.00
ASEK Erik Karlsson 3.00 8.00
ASES Eric Staal 2.50 6.00
ASHL Henrik Lundqvist 6.00 15.00
ASJB Josh Bailey 2.00 5.00
ASJE Jack Eichel 4.00 10.00
ASJG Johnny Gaudreau 4.00 10.00
ASJK John Klingberg 2.50 6.00
ASJN James Neal 1.50 4.00
ASJT John Tavares 4.00 10.00
ASKL Kris Letang 3.00 8.00
ASMA Marc-Andre Fleury 5.00 12.00
ASMG Mike Green 2.00 5.00
ASMS Mike Smith 2.00 5.00
ASNH Noah Hanifin 2.50 6.00
ASNK Nikita Kucherov 5.00 12.00
ASNM Nathan MacKinnon 10.00 25.00
ASOK Oliver Ekman-Larsson 2.50 6.00
ASPK Patrick Kane 5.00 12.00
ASPR Pekka Rinne 2.50 6.00
ASPS P.K. Subban 3.00 8.00
ASRR Rickard Rakell 2.00 5.00
ASSC Sidney Crosby 10.00 25.00
ASSS Steven Stamkos 5.00 12.00
ASTS Tyler Seguin 3.00 8.00
ASZW Zach Werenski 4.00 10.00

2018-19 SP Game Used '18 All Star Skills Fabrics Dual

AS2BE B.Boeser/J.Eichel 5.00 12.00
AS2GS J.Gaudreau/M.Smith 5.00 12.00
AS2KD A.Kopitar/D.Doughty 5.00 12.00
AS2MM C.McDavid/A.Matthews 20.00 50.00
AS2OH A.Ovechkin/B.Holtby 12.00 30.00
AS2PA C.Price/M.Fleury 6.00 15.00
AS2SK T.Seguin/J.Klingberg 4.00 10.00
AS2SP B.Schenn/A.Pietrangelo 3.00 8.00
AS2SR P.Subban/P.Rinne 4.00 10.00
AS2WH B.Wheeler/C.Hellebuyck 6.00 15.00

2018-19 SP Game Used '18 All Star Skills Fabrics Quad

AS4NET Price/Lundqvist/Fleury/Rinne 10.00 25.00
AS4TBL Stamkos/Kucherov
Point/Vasilevskiy 8.00 20.00
AS4VETS MacKinnon
Marchand/Burns/Letang 15.00 40.00
AS4STARS McDavid/Boeser
Ovechkin/Kane 20.00 50.00

2018-19 SP Game Used '18 All Star Skills Relic Blends

ASRBAB Aleksander Barkov 4.00 10.00
ASRBAK Anze Kopitar 4.00 10.00
ASRBAM Auston Matthews 10.00 25.00
ASRBAO Alexander Ovechkin 10.00 25.00
ASRBAP Alex Pietrangelo 2.00 5.00
ASRBAV Andrei Vasilevskiy 4.00 10.00
ASRBBB Brock Boeser 3.00 8.00
ASRBBH Braden Holtby 3.00 8.00
ASRBBM Brad Marchand 5.00 12.00
ASRBBO Brian Boyle 2.00 5.00
ASRBBP Brayden Point 3.00 8.00
ASRBBS Brayden Schenn 2.50 6.00
ASRBBU Brent Burns 2.50 6.00
ASRBBW Blake Wheeler 2.50 6.00
ASRBCC Claude Giroux 2.50 6.00
ASRBCH Connor Hellebuyck 5.00 12.00
ASRBCM Connor McDavid 12.00 30.00
ASRBCP Carey Price 5.00 12.00
ASRBDD Drew Doughty 3.00 8.00
ASRBEK Erik Karlsson 3.00 8.00
ASRBES Eric Staal 2.50 6.00
ASRBHL Henrik Lundqvist 6.00 15.00
ASRBJB Josh Bailey 2.00 5.00
ASRBJE Jack Eichel 4.00 10.00
ASRBJG Johnny Gaudreau 4.00 10.00
ASRBJK John Klingberg 2.50 6.00
ASRBJN James Neal 1.50 4.00
ASRBJT John Tavares 4.00 10.00
ASRBKL Kris Letang 3.00 8.00
ASRBMF Marc-Andre Fleury 5.00 12.00
ASRBMG Mike Green 2.00 5.00
ASRBMS Mike Smith 2.00 5.00
ASRBNH Noah Hanifin 2.50 6.00
ASRBNK Nikita Kucherov 5.00 12.00
ASRBNM Nathan MacKinnon 10.00 25.00
ASRBOL Oliver Ekman-Larsson 2.50 6.00
ASRBPK Patrick Kane 5.00 12.00
ASRBPR Pekka Rinne 2.50 6.00
ASRBPS P.K. Subban 3.00 8.00
ASRBRR Rickard Rakell 2.00 5.00
ASRBSC Sidney Crosby 10.00 25.00
ASRBSS Steven Stamkos 5.00 12.00
ASRBTS Tyler Seguin 3.00 8.00
ASRBZW Zach Werenski 4.00 10.00

2018-19 SP Game Used '18 Rookie Relic Blends

RRBAC Anthony Cirelli 5.00 12.00
RRBAG Adam Gaudette 5.00 12.00
RRBAS Andrei Svechnikov 8.00 20.00
RRBBH Brett Howden 4.00 10.00
RRBBT Brady Tkachuk 10.00 25.00
RRBCM Casey Mittelstadt 6.00 15.00
RRBDC Dennis Cholowski 3.00 8.00
RRBDD Dillon Dube 4.00 10.00
RRBDO Ryan Donato 5.00 12.00
RRBDS Dylan Sikura 4.00 10.00
RRBEP Elias Pettersson 15.00 40.00
RRBET Eeli Tolvanen 6.00 15.00
RRBHB Henrik Borgstrom 5.00 12.00
RRBJG Jordan Greenway 3.00 8.00
RRBJK Jesperi Kotkaniemi 6.00 15.00
RRBLA Lias Andersson 5.00 12.00
RRBMC Maxime Comtois 3.00 8.00
RRBMH Miro Heiskanen 8.00 20.00
RRBML Max Lajoie 5.00 12.00
RRBNJ Noah Juulsen 3.00 8.00
RRBRD Rasmus Dahlin 12.00 30.00
RRBTT Troy Terry 5.00 12.00
RRBZR Zach Aston-Reese 5.00 12.00

2018-19 SP Game Used '18 Stadium Series Fabrics

SSAB Andre Burakovsky 2.00 5.00
SSAO Alexander Ovechkin 12.00 30.00
SSCD Christian Djoos 2.50 6.00
SSJC John Carlson 3.00 8.00
SSNB Nicklas Backstrom 3.00 8.00
SSNK Nazem Kadri 4.00 10.00
SSNZ Nikita Zaitsev 2.50 6.00
SSPM Patrick Marleau 3.00 8.00
SSWN William Nylander 6.00 15.00
SSZH Zach Hyman 5.00 12.00

2018-19 SP Game Used '18 Stadium Series Fabrics Quad

SS4CAPS Ovechkin/Carlson
Backstrom/Burakovsky 15.00 40.00
SS4LEAFS Marleau/Nylander
Kadri/Hyman 8.00 20.00

2018-19 SP Game Used '18 Stadium Series Game Used Pucks

SSGUPAO Alexander Ovechkin 100.00 250.00
SSGUPEK Evgeny Kuznetsov 30.00 80.00
SSGUPJC John Carlson 25.00 60.00
SSGUPMM Mitch Marner 40.00 100.00
SSGUPPM Patrick Marleau 25.00 60.00
SSGUPWN William Nylander 50.00 125.00

2018-19 SP Game Used '18 Stanley Cup Finals Game Used Pucks

SCGUPAO Alexander Ovechkin 100.00 250.00
SCGUPEK Evgeny Kuznetsov 30.00 80.00
SCGUPJM Jonathan Marchessault 30.00 80.00
SCGUPMF Marc-Andre Fleury 50.00 125.00
SCGUPNB Nicklas Backstrom 25.00 60.00
SCGUPWK William Karlsson 30.00 80.00

2018-19 SP Game Used '18 Stanley Cup Finals Materials Net Cord

SCNCAB Andre Burakovsky 8.00 20.00
SCNCAO Alexander Ovechkin 50.00 120.00
SCNCAT Alex Tuch 12.00 30.00
SCNCBH Braden Holtby 15.00 40.00
SCNCCM Colin Miller 8.00 20.00
SCNCEK Evgeny Kuznetsov 15.00 40.00
SCNCJC John Carlson 12.00 30.00
SCNCJM Jonathan Marchessault 15.00 40.00
SCNCJN James Neal 8.00 20.00
SCNCLE Lars Eller 8.00 20.00
SCNCMF Marc-Andre Fleury 25.00 60.00
SCNCNB Nicklas Backstrom 12.00 30.00
SCNCRS Reilly Smith 12.00 30.00
SCNCTO T.J. Oshie 12.00 30.00
SCNCTW Tom Wilson 12.00 30.00
SCNCWK William Karlsson 15.00 40.00

2018-19 SP Game Used '18 Winter Classic Game Used Pucks

WCGUPHL Henrik Lundqvist 60.00 150.00
WCGUPJE Jack Eichel 40.00 100.00
WCGUPKO Kyle Okposo 15.00 40.00
WCGUPKS Kevin Shattenkirk 15.00 40.00
WCGUPMZ Mats Zuccarello 25.00 60.00
WCGUPRR Rasmus Ristolainen 15.00 40.00

2018-19 SP Game Used A Piece of History 100 Point Season Club

100CG Claude Giroux 10.00 25.00
100CM Connor McDavid 50.00 125.00
100EM Evgeni Malkin 20.00 50.00
100JJ Jaromir Jagr 30.00 80.00
100JK Jari Kurri 10.00 25.00
100SC Sidney Crosby 40.00 100.00
100WG Wayne Gretzky 60.00 150.00

2018-19 SP Game Used A Piece of History 40 Win Season Club

40CH Connor Hellebuyck 20.00 50.00
40PR Patrick Roy 25.00 60.00
40RL Roberto Luongo 15.00 40.00

2018-19 SP Game Used A Piece of History 50 Goal Season Club

50AO Alexander Ovechkin 40.00 100.00
50JI Jarome Iginla 12.00 30.00
50PB Pavel Bure 10.00 25.00
50SS Steven Stamkos 20.00 50.00
50SY Steve Yzerman 25.00 60.00

2018-19 SP Game Used Autographs Blue

1 Connor McDavid C 150.00 250.00
2 Nikita Kucherov B 12.00 30.00
5 Auston Matthews C 25.00 60.00
6 Jake DeBrusk F 6.00 15.00
7 Mikko Rantanen D 15.00 40.00
9 Evgeni Malkin C 12.00 30.00
11 Bobby Ryan F 5.00 12.00
12 Max Domi C 6.00 15.00
15 Vladimir Tarasenko C 8.00 20.00
16 Evander Kane C 6.00 15.00
20 Johnny Gaudreau C 10.00 25.00
21 Teuvo Teravainen C 6.00 15.00
22 Alexander Wennberg D 4.00 10.00
24 Kyle Palmieri D 5.00 12.00
25 Henrik Lundqvist C 15.00 40.00
26 Vincent Trocheck E 6.00 15.00
27 Anders Lee E 5.00 12.00
29 Clayton Keller A 8.00 20.00
31 Bo Horvat C 8.00 20.00
32 Brayden Point D 8.00 20.00
34 Danton Heinen F 5.00 12.00
35 Jake Guentzel C 10.00 25.00
36 Tomas Hertl F 6.00 15.00
38 Radek Faksa F 5.00 12.00
40 Marc-Andre Fleury C 12.00 30.00
41 Stefan Noesen F 4.00 10.00
43 Patrik Laine A 8.00 20.00
44 Thomas Chabot D 6.00 15.00
46 Matthew Tkachuk D 12.00 30.00
48 Derek Stepan E 4.00 10.00
50 Jonathan Toews B 10.00 25.00
52 Anthony Mantha D 5.00 12.00
53 Tom Wilson C 6.00 15.00
56 Pierre-Luc Dubois C 5.00 12.00
57 Mitch Marner E 10.00 25.00
58 Brady Skjei F 5.00 12.00
59 Jake Muzzin E 6.00 15.00
60 Carey Price C 12.00 30.00
61 Mikael Granlund E 5.00 12.00
62 Jonathan Marchessault C 8.00 20.00
63 Leon Draisaitl C 20.00 50.00
64 Jimmy Vesey F 5.00 12.00
65 Taylor Hall A 6.00 15.00
66 Alexander Radulov C 6.00 15.00
67 Noah Hanifin E 6.00 15.00
68 Brock Boeser A 8.00 20.00
70 Evgeny Kuznetsov C 8.00 20.00
73 Craig Anderson E 5.00 12.00
74 Alex Galchenyuk C 4.00 10.00
75 Andrei Vasilevskiy D 10.00 25.00
76 David Krejci B 6.00 15.00
77 Zach Werenski E 10.00 25.00
79 Jonathan Huberdeau D 8.00 20.00
80 John Tavares C 10.00 25.00
81 Sebastian Aho D 10.00 25.00
84 Kevin Fiala F 5.00 12.00
87 Bobby Orr E 25.00 60.00
88 Pavel Datsyuk C 10.00 25.00
89 Owen Nolan E 6.00 15.00
90 Mario Lemieux C 25.00 60.00
91 Curtis Joseph D 8.00 20.00
92 Mike Bossy C 6.00 15.00
93 Larry Robinson A 6.00 15.00
96 Ted Lindsay B 6.00 15.00
97 Rod Brind'Amour E 6.00 15.00
99 Luc Robitaille C 6.00 15.00
100 Wayne Gretzky C 200.00 500.00
102 Lias Andersson B 10.00 25.00
103 Michael Rasmussen C 8.00 20.00
104 Daniel Brickley D 6.00 15.00
105 Robert Thomas B 12.00 30.00
106 Ethan Bear D 10.00 25.00
107 Dillon Dube C 8.00 20.00
109 Zach Whitecloud C 5.00 12.00
112 Noah Juulsen C 6.00 15.00
113 Max Lajoie D 10.00 25.00
114 Dominic Turgeon B 6.00 15.00
116 Andreas Johnsson C 8.00 20.00
117 Sam Steel C 6.00 15.00
118 Dylan Gambrell B 6.00 15.00
119 Spencer Foo B 5.00 12.00
120 Andrei Svechnikov B 15.00 40.00
122 Juuso Valimaki B 6.00 15.00
123 Landon Bow D 5.00 12.00
124 Isac Lundestrom B 5.00 12.00
125 Henrik Borgstrom C 10.00 25.00
127 Nicolas Roy B 4.00 10.00
130 Joey Anderson D 6.00 15.00
135 Brett Howden B 8.00 20.00
137 Jordan Greenway A 6.00 15.00
138 Roope Hintz C 15.00 40.00
139 John Gilmour A 4.00 10.00
140 Jesperi Kotkaniemi B 12.00 30.00
141 Dennis Cholowski B 6.00 15.00
143 Kristian Vesalainen B 8.00 20.00
144 Samuel Montembeault D 12.00 30.00
145 Jaret Anderson-Dolan D 5.00 12.00
146 Blake Hillman D 6.00 15.00
150 Brady Tkachuk B 20.00 50.00
151 Oskar Lindblom B 10.00 25.00
155 Zach Aston-Reese C 10.00 25.00
156 Mathieu Joseph B 8.00 20.00
157 Warren Foegele C 6.00 15.00
160 Casey Mittelstadt B 12.00 30.00
161 Victor Ejdsell C 5.00 12.00
162 Tomas Hyka B 6.00 15.00
164 Austin Wagner B 5.00 12.00
165 Eeli Tolvanen B 12.00 30.00
168 Morgan Klimchuk B 6.00 15.00
169 Troy Terry C 10.00 25.00
170 Evan Bouchard C 15.00 40.00
171 Cooper Marody B 6.00 15.00
173 Kiefer Sherwood B 5.00 12.00
174 Mikhail Vorobyev B 5.00 12.00
175 Filip Hronek B 6.00 15.00
177 Sami Niku C 5.00 12.00
178 Jeremy Lauzon C 8.00 20.00
179 Neal Pionk A 6.00 15.00
180 Maxime Comtois D 6.00 15.00
181 Anthony Cirelli C 10.00 25.00
182 Louie Belpedio B 5.00 12.00
185 Travis Dermott B 10.00 25.00
186 Dylan Sikura B 8.00 20.00
187 Jordan Kyrou C 20.00 50.00
188 Michael Dal Colle D 6.00 15.00
190 Miro Heiskanen B 15.00 40.00
192 Antti Suomela D 5.00 12.00
193 Mackenzie Blackwood C 12.00 30.00
197 Henri Jokiharju D 5.00 12.00
198 Joe Hicketts B 6.00 15.00
200 Elias Pettersson B 100.00 200.00

2018-19 SP Game Used Banner Year '18 All Star Game

BASAB Aleksander Barkov 5.00 12.00
BASAM Auston Matthews 12.00 30.00
BASAO Alexander Ovechkin 12.00 30.00
BASBB Brock Boeser 4.00 10.00
BASCH Connor Hellebuyck 6.00 15.00
BASCM Connor McDavid 15.00 40.00
BASCP Carey Price 6.00 15.00
BASDD Drew Doughty 4.00 10.00
BASMF Marc-Andre Fleury 6.00 15.00
BASNM Nathan MacKinnon 12.00 30.00
BASPK Patrick Kane 6.00 15.00
BASSC Sidney Crosby 12.00 30.00
BASSS Steven Stamkos 6.00 15.00
BASZW Zach Werenski 5.00 12.00

2018-19 SP Game Used Banner Year '18 Awards

BAWAK Anze Kopitar 8.00 20.00
BAWCM Connor McDavid 25.00 60.00
BAWMB Mathew Barzal 6.00 15.00
BAWPR Pekka Rinne 5.00 12.00
BAWTH Taylor Hall 5.00 12.00
BAWVH Victor Hedman 6.00 15.00

2018-19 SP Game Used Banner Year '18 Stanley Cup Finals

BSCAO Alexander Ovechkin 12.00 30.00
BSCAT Alex Tuch 3.00 8.00
BSCBH Braden Holtby 4.00 10.00
BSCEK Evgeny Kuznetsov 4.00 10.00
BSCJC John Carlson 3.00 8.00
BSCJM Jonathan Marchessault 4.00 10.00
BSCMF Marc-Andre Fleury 6.00 15.00
BSCNB Nicklas Backstrom 3.00 8.00
BSCRS Reilly Smith 3.00 8.00
BSCST Shea Theodore 4.00 10.00
BSCTO T.J. Oshie 3.00 8.00
BSCWK William Karlsson 4.00 10.00

2018-19 SP Game Used Banner Year '18 Winter Classic

BWCBS Brady Skjei 2.50 6.00
BWCHL Henrik Lundqvist 8.00 20.00
BWCJE Jack Eichel 5.00 12.00
BWCKO Kyle Okposo 2.00 5.00
BWCKS Kevin Shattenkirk 2.00 5.00
BWCMS Marc Staal 2.00 5.00
BWCMZ Mats Zuccarello 3.00 8.00
BWCRR Rasmus Ristolainen 2.00 5.00
BWCSR Sam Reinhart 6.00 15.00
BWCZI Mika Zibanejad 4.00 10.00

2018-19 SP Game Used Banner Year Draft '12

BD12CH Connor Hellebuyck 6.00 15.00
BD12TW Tom Wilson 3.00 8.00

2018-19 SP Game Used Banner Year Draft '12 Autographs

BD12CH Connor Hellebuyck 15.00 40.00

2018-19 SP Game Used Banner Year Draft '14

BD14AT Alex Tuch 3.00 8.00
BD14RD Ryan Donato 5.00 12.00

2018-19 SP Game Used Banner Year Draft '15

BD15BB Brock Boeser 4.00 10.00
BD15MB Mathew Barzal 4.00 10.00

2018-19 SP Game Used Banner Year Draft '17

BD17CM Casey Mittelstadt 6.00 15.00
BD17EP Elias Pettersson 10.00 25.00
BD17ET Eeli Tolvanen 6.00 15.00
BD17KV Kristian Vesalainen 4.00 10.00

2018-19 SP Game Used Battle Lines

BLBB Boston Bruins 12.00 30.00
BLBS Buffalo Sabres 12.00 30.00
BLCB Chicago Blackhawks 12.00 30.00
BLDR Detroit Red Wings 12.00 30.00
BLEO Edmonton Oilers 12.00 30.00
BLLA Los Angeles Kings 12.00 30.00
BLMC Montreal Canadiens 12.00 30.00
BLNY New York Rangers 12.00 30.00
BLPP Pittsburgh Penguins 12.00 30.00
BLSJ San Jose Sharks 12.00 30.00
BLTB Tampa Bay Lightning 12.00 30.00
BLTM Toronto Maples Leafs 12.00 30.00
BLWC Washington Capitals 12.00 30.00
BLWJ Winnipeg Jets 12.00 30.00

2018-19 SP Game Used Day with the Cup Materials Net Cord

DCNCAO Alexander Ovechkin 50.00 125.00
DCNCCC Corey Crawford 10.00 25.00
DCNCEK Evgeny Kuznetsov 15.00 40.00
DCNCEM Evgeni Malkin 25.00 60.00
DCNCJT Jonathan Toews 20.00 50.00
DCNCKE Phil Kessel 12.00 30.00
DCNCMM Matt Murray 12.00 30.00
DCNCNB Nicklas Backstrom 12.00 30.00
DCNCPK Patrick Kane 25.00 60.00
DCNCSC Sidney Crosby 50.00 125.00

2018-19 SP Game Used Draft Day Marks Rookies

DDMAC Anthony Cirelli 20.00 50.00
DDMAG Adam Gaudette 20.00 50.00
DDMAN Alexander Nylander 10.00 25.00
DDMAS Andrei Svechnikov 30.00 80.00
DDMCH Carter Hart 80.00 200.00
DDMCM Casey Mittelstadt 25.00 60.00
DDMCW Colin White 8.00 20.00
DDMDD Dillon Dube 15.00 40.00
DDMDG Dylan Gambrell 12.00 30.00
DDMDO Ryan Donato 20.00 50.00
DDMDS Dylan Sikura 15.00 40.00
DDMEP Elias Pettersson 100.00 250.00
DDMET Eeli Tolvanen 25.00 60.00
DDMHB Henrik Borgstrom 20.00 50.00
DDMIS Ilya Samsonov 25.00 60.00
DDMJD Jake DeBrusk 12.00 30.00
DDMJG Jordan Greenway 12.00 30.00
DDMJK Jordan Kyrou 50.00 125.00
DDMJS Josh Ho-Sang 10.00 25.00
DDMJZ Jakub Zboril 20.00 50.00
DDMLA Lias Andersson 20.00 50.00
DDMLB Logan Brown 12.00 30.00
DDMMC Michael Dal Colle 12.00 30.00
DDMMH Miro Heiskanen 30.00 80.00
DDMMM Michael McLeod 10.00 25.00
DDMMR Michael Rasmussen 15.00 40.00
DDMNJ Noah Juulsen 12.00 30.00
DDMRT Robert Thomas 25.00 60.00
DDMSN Sami Niku 10.00 25.00
DDMSS Sam Steel 12.00 30.00
DDMTD Travis Dermott 20.00 50.00
DDMTT Troy Terry 20.00 50.00
DDMVE Jimmy Vesey 10.00 25.00
DDMWF Warren Foegele 12.00 30.00

2018-19 SP Game Used Frameworks

FWAP Artemi Panarin C 12.00 30.00
FWAV Andrei Vasilevskiy C 10.00 25.00
FWBB Brock Boeser B 8.00 20.00
FWBO Bob Probert B 6.00 15.00
FWBP Bernie Parent B 8.00 20.00
FWBR Bobby Ryan C 5.00 12.00
FWBS Brayden Schenn D 6.00 15.00
FWCH Connor Hellebuyck C 12.00 30.00
FWCK Clayton Keller C 8.00 20.00
FWCO Shayne Corson B 5.00 12.00
FWCS Charlie Simmer B 4.00 10.00
FWDB Dustin Brown D 6.00 15.00
FWDL Dylan Larkin B 8.00 20.00
FWDP David Pastrnak D 15.00 40.00
FWGL Gabriel Landeskog D 8.00 20.00
FWIL Igor Larionov B 6.00 15.00
FWJB Jamie Benn A 6.00 15.00
FWJD Jonathan Drouin B 5.00 12.00
FWJG Johnny Gaudreau B 10.00 25.00
FWJI Jarome Iginla B 8.00 20.00
FWJJ Jaromir Jagr B 20.00 50.00
FWJT John Tavares B 10.00 25.00
FWKR Chris Kreider D 8.00 20.00
FWMA Marc-Andre Fleury B 12.00 30.00
FWMB Mathew Barzal B 8.00 20.00
FWMG Mikael Granlund D 5.00 12.00
FWML Milan Lucic D 5.00 12.00
FWMS Mark Scheifele A 10.00 25.00
FWNB Nicklas Backstrom B 6.00 15.00
FWNH Nico Hischier C 10.00 25.00
FWPK Patrick Kane B 12.00 30.00
FWPR Pekka Rinne C 6.00 15.00
FWPT Paul Stastny C 5.00 12.00
FWRR Rickard Rakell D 5.00 12.00
FWRS Reilly Smith D 6.00 15.00
FWSC Sidney Crosby B 25.00 60.00
FWTB Tom Barrasso B 6.00 15.00
FWTT Teuvo Teravainen D 6.00 15.00
FWWS Wayne Simmonds C 6.00 15.00

2018-19 SP Game Used Inked Rookie Sweaters Patch

RSAC Anthony Cirelli 20.00 50.00
RSAS Andrei Svechnikov 30.00 80.00
RSBH Brett Howden 15.00 40.00
RSBT Brady Tkachuk 40.00 100.00
RSCM Casey Mittelstadt 25.00 60.00
RSDC Michael Dal Colle 12.00 30.00
RSDD Dillon Dube 15.00 40.00
RSDS Dylan Sikura 15.00 40.00
RSDT Dominic Turgeon 12.00 30.00
RSEB Evan Bouchard 30.00 80.00
RSEP Elias Pettersson 200.00 300.00
RSET Eeli Tolvanen 25.00 60.00
RSHB Henrik Borgstrom 20.00 50.00
RSJG Jordan Greenway 12.00 30.00
RSJK Jesperi Kotkaniemi 25.00 60.00
RSKV Kristian Vesalainen 15.00 40.00
RSLA Lias Andersson 20.00 50.00
RSMC Maxime Comtois 12.00 30.00
RSMH Miro Heiskanen 30.00 80.00
RSML Max Lajoie 20.00 50.00
RSMR Michael Rasmussen 15.00 40.00
RSNJ Noah Juulsen 12.00 30.00
RSTD Travis Dermott 20.00 50.00
RSTT Troy Terry 50.00 125.00
RSWF Warren Foegele 12.00 30.00
RSZE Zach Aston-Reese 20.00 50.00

2018-19 SP Game Used Inked Sweaters

ISAL Anders Lee 6.00 15.00
ISBR Bobby Ryan 6.00 15.00
ISBS Brayden Schenn 8.00 20.00
ISDS Derek Stepan 5.00 12.00
ISJD Jonathan Drouin 6.00 15.00
ISJG John Gibson 8.00 20.00
ISJP Jesse Puljujarvi 8.00 20.00
ISKC Kyle Connor 12.00 30.00
ISKP Kyle Palmieri 6.00 15.00
ISMD Max Domi 8.00 20.00
ISMM Mitch Marner 12.00 30.00
ISMR Mikko Rantanen 20.00 50.00
ISMS Mark Scheifele 12.00 30.00
ISVT Vincent Trocheck 8.00 20.00

2018-19 SP Game Used Rookie Sweaters

RSAC Anthony Cirelli 4.00 10.00
RSAG Adam Gaudette 4.00 10.00
RSAS Andrei Svechnikov 6.00 15.00
RSBH Brett Howden 3.00 8.00
RSBT Brady Tkachuk 8.00 20.00
RSCM Casey Mittelstadt 5.00 12.00
RSDC Michael Dal Colle 2.50 6.00
RSDD Dillon Dube 3.00 8.00
RSDO Ryan Donato 4.00 10.00
RSDS Dylan Sikura 3.00 8.00
RSDT Dominic Turgeon 2.50 6.00
RSEB Evan Bouchard 6.00 15.00
RSEP Elias Pettersson 8.00 20.00
RSET Eeli Tolvanen 5.00 12.00
RSHB Henrik Borgstrom 4.00 10.00
RSJG Jordan Greenway 2.50 6.00
RSJK Jesperi Kotkaniemi 5.00 12.00
RSKV Kristian Vesalainen 3.00 8.00
RSLA Lias Andersson 4.00 10.00
RSMC Maxime Comtois 2.50 6.00
RSMH Miro Heiskanen 6.00 15.00
RSML Max Lajoie 4.00 10.00
RSMR Michael Rasmussen 3.00 8.00
RSNJ Noah Juulsen 2.50 6.00
RSRD Rasmus Dahlin 6.00 15.00
RSTD Travis Dermott 4.00 10.00
RSTT Troy Terry 4.00 10.00
RSWF Warren Foegele 2.50 6.00
RSZE Zach Aston-Reese 4.00 10.00

2018-19 SP Game Used Signing Day Marks

SDMDB Daniel Brickley 8.00 20.00
SDMZA Zach Aston-Reese 15.00 40.00

2018-19 SP Game Used Tools of The Game

TGAE Aaron Ekblad/75 8.00 20.00
TGAP Artemi Panarin/75 12.00 30.00
TGCJ Curtis Joseph/25 8.00 20.00
TGDG Doug Gilmour/25 8.00 20.00
TGIK Ilya Kovalchuk/25 5.00 12.00
TGJC Jeff Carter/75 5.00 12.00
TGJO Joe Thornton/75 10.00 25.00
TGMA Al MacInnis/75 8.00 20.00
TGMB Mathew Barzal/25 8.00 20.00
TGPK P.K. Subban/75 8.00 20.00
TGTB Tom Barrasso/75 6.00 15.00
TGTD Tie Domi/25 5.00 12.00
TGZC Zdeno Chara/75 6.00 15.00

2019-20 SP Game Used Blue

1 Wayne Gretzky AU B 200.00 500.00
2 Jesperi Kotkaniemi AU D 6.00 15.00
4 Jonathan Toews AU B 10.00 25.00
6 Ben Bishop AU D 5.00 12.00
7 Jake Guentzel AU E 10.00 25.00
8 Brady Tkachuk AU E 10.00 25.00
10 Jarome Iginla AU B 8.00 20.00
11 Connor Hellebuyck AU E 12.00 30.00
12 Steven Stamkos AU B 12.00 30.00
13 Joe Pavelski AU D 8.00 20.00
15 Pierre Turgeon AU D 5.00 12.00
16 Mitch Marner AU C 10.00 25.00
17 Seth Jones AU E 6.00 15.00
21 Bo Horvat AU C 8.00 20.00
24 Henrik Lundqvist AU B 15.00 40.00
28 Leon Draisaitl AU D 20.00 50.00
29 Brett Hull AU B 12.00 30.00
30 Jacob Trouba AU E 5.00 12.00
32 John Tavares AU C 10.00 25.00
35 Dylan Strome AU D 8.00 20.00
36 Anders Lee AU E 5.00 12.00
37 Alex DeBrincat AU E 8.00 20.00
39 Aaron Ekblad AU D 8.00 20.00
40 Ryan O'Reilly AU E 6.00 15.00
41 Sidney Crosby AU A 60.00 150.00
44 Brad Marchand AU D 12.00 30.00
45 Patrick Kane AU B 12.00 30.00
46 Patrick Roy AU B 50.00 125.00
48 Martin Brodeur AU A 15.00 40.00
50 Steve Yzerman AU B 15.00 40.00
52 Ron Hextall AU D 6.00 15.00
57 John Gibson AU E 6.00 15.00
58 Joe Sakic AU A 12.00 30.00
60 Carey Price AU B 12.00 30.00
61 Devan Dubnyk AU C 5.00 12.00
62 Nico Hischier AU D 10.00 25.00
63 Aleksander Barkov AU E 10.00 25.00
65 Joe Thornton AU C 10.00 25.00
67 Auston Matthews AU B 25.00 60.00
68 Evgenii Dadonov AU E 4.00 10.00
69 Mark Scheifele AU E 10.00 25.00
70 Mario Lemieux AU B 25.00 60.00
73 Chris Chelios AU B 6.00 15.00
76 Artemi Panarin AU D 12.00 30.00
78 Sergei Bobrovsky AU D 10.00 25.00
84 Marc-Andre Fleury AU C 12.00 30.00
85 Cam Atkinson AU E 6.00 15.00
91 Dylan Larkin AU D 8.00 20.00
92 Jack Eichel AU C 10.00 25.00
93 Brock Boeser AU D 8.00 20.00
97 Thomas Chabot AU E 6.00 15.00
98 Bobby Orr AU B 80.00 200.00
99 Doug Gilmour AU C 8.00 20.00
100 Connor McDavid AU B 150.00 250.00
102 Guillaume Brisebois AU C 6.00 15.00
104 Max Veronneau AU E 5.00 12.00
105 Cody Glass AU B 10.00 25.00
107 Blake Lizotte AU E 6.00 15.00
108 Mackenzie MacEachern AU E 6.00 15.00
109 Teddy Blueger AU C 6.00 15.00
110 Mario Ferraro AU D 5.00 12.00
112 Brandon Gignac AU E 5.00 12.00
113 Danil Yurtaykin AU E 5.00 12.00
115 Max Jones AU E 6.00 15.00
116 Vitaly Abramov AU C 6.00 15.00
117 Erik Brannstrom AU E 6.00 15.00
119 Philippe Myers AU D 5.00 12.00
120 Ilya Mikheyev AU C 10.00 25.00
122 Rasmus Sandin AU D 10.00 25.00
123 Martin Fehervary AU E 5.00 12.00
125 Connor Clifton AU E 6.00 15.00
126 Joel L'Esperance AU D 6.00 15.00
130 Matt Roy AU D 6.00 15.00
131 Libor Hajek AU E 5.00 12.00
133 Riley Stillman AU E 6.00 15.00
135 Carter Verhaeghe AU E 10.00 25.00
137 Ryan Poehling AU B 10.00 25.00
138 Filip Zadina AU B 60.00 150.00
140 Ryan Kuffner AU E 5.00 12.00
141 Nick Suzuki AU D 25.00 60.00
142 Trevor Moore AU E 5.00 12.00
144 Alexandre Texier AU E 6.00 15.00
147 Julien Gauthier AU E 6.00 15.00
149 Zach Senyshyn AU E 6.00 15.00
150 Zack MacEwen AU D 5.00 12.00
151 Dante Fabbro AU B 6.00 15.00
152 Nicolas Hague AU E 6.00 15.00
153 Nathan Bastian AU C 6.00 15.00
156 Oliver Wahlstrom AU C 10.00 25.00
157 Lean Bergmann AU C 5.00 12.00
158 Carl Grundstrom AU E 6.00 15.00
159 Jesper Boqvist AU C 5.00 12.00
160 Victor Olofsson AU E 12.00 30.00
163 Kole Sherwood AU E 6.00 15.00
165 Kaden Fulcher AU E 6.00 15.00
168 Tobias Bjornfot AU C 6.00 15.00
170 Joel Persson AU E 5.00 12.00
172 Jimmy Schuldt AU E 5.00 12.00
175 Noah Dobson AU E 15.00 40.00
176 Taro Hirose AU D 6.00 15.00
177 Brady Keeper AU E 6.00 15.00
181 Elvis Merzlikins AU D 12.00 30.00
183 Quinn Hughes AU A 60.00 150.00
184 Cale Makar AU B 60.00 150.00
185 Sam Lafferty AU E 5.00 12.00
186 Joey Daccord AU E 12.00 30.00
188 Rudolfs Balcers AU B 6.00 15.00
189 Nico Sturm AU E 5.00 12.00
190 Karson Kuhlman AU E 6.00 15.00
191 Dominik Kubalik AU D 12.00 30.00
192 Joel Farabee AU C 10.00 25.00
193 Kirby Dach AU B 12.00 30.00
195 Trent Frederic AU E 6.00 15.00
196 Emil Bemstrom AU E 6.00 15.00
199 Rem Pitlick AU E 6.00 15.00
200 Jack Hughes AU A 150.00 350.00

2019-20 SP Game Used Gold

*PATCH/25-65: 1.25X TO 3X BASIC INSERTS
3 Zach Werenski JSY B 5.00 12.00
4 Jonathan Toews JSY B 5.00 12.00
5 Matt Dumba JSY B 2.00 5.00
6 Ben Bishop JSY B 2.50 6.00
7 Jake Guentzel JSY B 5.00 12.00
8 Brady Tkachuk JSY B 5.00 12.00
9 Drew Doughty JSY B 4.00 10.00
11 Connor Hellebuyck JSY B 6.00 15.00
12 Steven Stamkos JSY B 6.00 15.00
13 Joe Pavelski JSY B 4.00 10.00
14 Nikita Kucherov JSY B 6.00 15.00
16 Mitch Marner JSY B 5.00 12.00
17 Seth Jones JSY B 3.00 8.00
18 Andrei Svechnikov JSY B 4.00 10.00
19 Miro Heiskanen JSY B 4.00 10.00
20 Tuukka Rask JSY B 4.00 10.00
21 Bo Horvat JSY B 4.00 10.00
22 Alexander Ovechkin JSY B 12.00 30.00
23 Anze Kopitar JSY B 5.00 12.00
24 Henrik Lundqvist JSY B 8.00 20.00
25 Mathew Barzal JSY B 4.00 10.00
26 Tyler Seguin JSY B 4.00 10.00
27 Brayden Point JSY B 4.00 10.00
28 Leon Draisaitl JSY B 10.00 25.00
29 Brett Hull JSY A 6.00 15.00
31 Ryan Johansen JSY B 2.50 6.00
32 John Tavares JSY B 5.00 12.00
33 Brent Burns JSY B 3.00 8.00
34 P.K. Subban JSY B 4.00 10.00
35 Dylan Strome JSY B 4.00 10.00
36 Anders Lee JSY B 2.50 6.00
37 Alex DeBrincat JSY B 4.00 10.00
38 Brendan Gallagher JSY B 3.00 8.00
39 Aaron Ekblad JSY B 4.00 10.00
40 Ryan O'Reilly JSY B 3.00 8.00
41 Sidney Crosby JSY A 12.00 30.00
42 Victor Hedman JSY B 4.00 10.00
43 Blake Wheeler JSY B 3.00 8.00
44 Brad Marchand JSY B 6.00 15.00
45 Patrick Kane JSY A 6.00 15.00
46 Patrick Roy JSY A 8.00 20.00
47 William Karlsson JSY B 4.00 10.00
48 Martin Brodeur JSY A 8.00 20.00
50 Steve Yzerman JSY A 8.00 20.00
51 Kris Letang JSY B 4.00 10.00
53 Clayton Keller JSY B 4.00 10.00
54 Matthew Tkachuk JSY B 6.00 15.00
55 Andreas Athanasiou JSY B 2.50 6.00
56 Phil Kessel JSY B 3.00 8.00
57 John Gibson JSY B 3.00 8.00
58 Joe Sakic JSY A 6.00 15.00
60 Carey Price JSY B 6.00 15.00
61 Devan Dubnyk JSY B 2.50 6.00
62 Nico Hischier JSY B 5.00 12.00
63 Aleksander Barkov JSY B 5.00 12.00
64 Patrik Laine JSY B 4.00 10.00
65 Joe Thornton JSY B 5.00 12.00

66 Sebastian Aho JSY B 5.00 12.00
67 Auston Matthews JSY A 12.00 30.00
68 Evgenii Dadonov JSY B 2.00 5.00
69 Mark Scheifele JSY B 5.00 12.00
70 Mario Lemieux JSY A 12.00 30.00
71 Alex Tuch JSY B 3.00 8.00
72 Nicklas Backstrom JSY B 3.00 8.00
73 Chris Chelios JSY A 3.00 8.00
74 Pierre-Luc Dubois JSY B 2.50 6.00
75 Viktor Arvidsson JSY B 2.00 5.00
77 John Carlson JSY B 3.00 8.00
78 Sergei Bobrovsky JSY B 5.00 12.00
79 Jordan Binnington JSY B 5.00 12.00
80 Teuvo Teravainen JSY B 3.00 8.00
81 Nazem Kadri JSY B 4.00 10.00
82 Johnny Gaudreau JSY B 5.00 12.00
83 Elias Pettersson JSY B 5.00 12.00
84 Marc-Andre Fleury JSY B 6.00 15.00
85 Cam Atkinson JSY B 3.00 8.00
86 Mikko Rantanen JSY B 8.00 20.00
87 Braden Holtby JSY B 4.00 10.00
88 Ryan Getzlaf JSY B 3.00 8.00
89 Claude Giroux JSY B 3.00 8.00
90 Roman Josi JSY B 3.00 8.00
91 Dylan Larkin JSY B 4.00 10.00
92 Jack Eichel JSY B 5.00 12.00
93 Brock Boeser JSY B 4.00 10.00
94 Nathan MacKinnon JSY B 12.00 30.00
96 Mats Zuccarello JSY B 3.00 8.00
99 Doug Gilmour JSY A 4.00 10.00
100 Connor McDavid JSY A 15.00 40.00
101 Kaapo Kakko JSY 5.00 12.00
102 Guillaume Brisebois JSY 3.00 8.00
104 Max Veronneau JSY 2.50 6.00
105 Cody Glass JSY 5.00 12.00
107 Blake Lizotte JSY 3.00 8.00
108 Mackenzie MacEachern JSY 3.00 8.00
109 Teddy Blueger JSY 3.00 8.00
110 Mario Ferraro JSY 2.50 6.00
112 Brandon Gignac JSY 2.50 6.00
115 Max Jones JSY 3.00 8.00
116 Vitaly Abramov JSY 3.00 8.00
117 Erik Brannstrom JSY 3.00 8.00
119 Philippe Myers JSY 2.50 6.00
120 Ilya Mikheyev JSY 5.00 12.00
122 Rasmus Sandin JSY 5.00 12.00
126 Joel L'Esperance JSY 3.00 8.00
127 Adam Fox JSY 8.00 20.00
130 Matt Roy JSY 3.00 8.00
131 Libor Hajek JSY 2.50 6.00
133 Riley Stillman JSY 3.00 8.00
135 Carter Verhaeghe JSY 5.00 12.00
137 Ryan Poehling JSY 5.00 12.00
138 Filip Zadina JSY 5.00 12.00
140 Ryan Kuffner JSY 2.50 6.00
141 Nick Suzuki JSY 12.00 30.00
142 Trevor Moore JSY 2.50 6.00
144 Alexandre Texier JSY 3.00 8.00
146 Nikita Gusev JSY 5.00 12.00
147 Julien Gauthier JSY 3.00 8.00
149 Zach Senyshyn JSY 3.00 8.00
150 Zack MacEwen JSY 2.50 6.00
151 Dante Fabbro JSY 3.00 8.00
154 Ryan Lindgren JSY 3.00 8.00
156 Oliver Wahlstrom JSY 5.00 12.00
158 Carl Grundstrom JSY 3.00 8.00
159 Jesper Boqvist JSY 2.50 6.00
160 Victor Olofsson JSY 6.00 15.00
162 Nikolay Prokhorkin JSY 2.50 6.00
163 Kole Sherwood JSY 3.00 8.00
164 Barrett Hayton JSY 6.00 15.00
165 Kaden Fulcher JSY 3.00 8.00
168 Tobias Bjornfot JSY 3.00 8.00
170 Joel Persson JSY 2.50 6.00
172 Jimmy Schuldt JSY 2.50 6.00
175 Noah Dobson JSY 8.00 20.00
176 Taro Hirose JSY 3.00 8.00
177 Brady Keeper JSY 3.00 8.00
181 Elvis Merzlikins JSY 6.00 15.00
183 Quinn Hughes JSY 15.00 40.00
184 Cale Makar JSY 30.00 80.00
186 Joey Daccord JSY 6.00 15.00
188 Rudolfs Balcers JSY 3.00 8.00
189 Nico Sturm JSY 2.50 6.00
190 Karson Kuhlman JSY 3.00 8.00
192 Joel Farabee JSY 5.00 12.00
193 Kirby Dach JSY 6.00 15.00
195 Trent Frederic JSY 3.00 8.00
196 Emil Bemstrom JSY 3.00 8.00
199 Rem Pitlick JSY 3.00 8.00
200 Jack Hughes JSY 15.00 40.00

2019-20 SP Game Used Rainbow

*ORANGE: .4X TO 1X BASIC CARDS
1 Wayne Gretzky/275 10.00 25.00
2 Jesperi Kotkaniemi/275 1.50 4.00
3 Zach Werenski/275 2.50 6.00
4 Jonathan Toews/275 2.50 6.00
5 Matt Dumba/275 1.00 2.50
6 Ben Bishop/275 1.25 3.00
7 Jake Guentzel/275 2.50 6.00
8 Brady Tkachuk/275 2.50 6.00
9 Drew Doughty/275 2.00 5.00
10 Jarome Iginla/275 2.00 5.00
11 Connor Hellebuyck/275 3.00 8.00
12 Steven Stamkos/275 3.00 8.00
13 Joe Pavelski/275 2.00 5.00
14 Nikita Kucherov/275 3.00 8.00
15 Pierre Turgeon/275 1.25 3.00
16 Mitch Marner/275 2.50 6.00
17 Seth Jones/275 1.50 4.00
18 Andrei Svechnikov/275 2.00 5.00
19 Miro Heiskanen/275 2.00 5.00
20 Tuukka Rask/275 2.00 5.00
21 Bo Horvat/275 2.00 5.00
22 Alexander Ovechkin/275 6.00 15.00
23 Anze Kopitar/275 2.50 6.00
24 Henrik Lundqvist/275 4.00 10.00
25 Mathew Barzal/275 2.00 5.00
26 Tyler Seguin/275 2.00 5.00
27 Brayden Point/275 2.00 5.00
28 Leon Draisaitl/275 5.00 12.00
29 Brett Hull/275 3.00 8.00
30 Jacob Trouba/275 1.25 3.00
31 Ryan Johansen/275 1.25 3.00
32 John Tavares/275 2.50 6.00
33 Brent Burns/275 1.50 4.00
34 P.K. Subban/275 2.00 5.00
35 Dylan Strome/275 2.00 5.00
36 Anders Lee/275 1.25 3.00
37 Alex DeBrincat/275 2.00 5.00
38 Brendan Gallagher/275 1.50 4.00
39 Aaron Ekblad/275 2.00 5.00
40 Ryan O'Reilly/275 1.50 4.00
41 Sidney Crosby/275 6.00 15.00
42 Victor Hedman/275 2.00 5.00
43 Blake Wheeler/275 1.50 4.00
44 Brad Marchand/275 3.00 8.00
45 Patrick Kane/275 3.00 8.00
46 Patrick Roy/275 4.00 10.00
47 William Karlsson/275 2.00 5.00
48 Martin Brodeur/275 4.00 10.00
49 Erik Karlsson/275 2.00 5.00
50 Steve Yzerman/275 4.00 10.00
51 Kris Letang/275 2.00 5.00
52 Ron Hextall/275 1.50 4.00
53 Clayton Keller/275 2.00 5.00
54 Matthew Tkachuk/275 3.00 8.00
55 Andreas Athanasiou/275 1.25 3.00
56 Phil Kessel/275 1.50 4.00
57 John Gibson/275 1.50 4.00
58 Joe Sakic/275 3.00 8.00
59 Jeff Skinner/275 1.50 4.00
60 Carey Price/275 3.00 8.00
61 Devan Dubnyk/275 1.25 3.00
62 Nico Hischier/275 2.50 6.00
63 Aleksander Barkov/275 2.50 6.00
64 Patrik Laine/275 2.00 5.00
65 Joe Thornton/275 2.50 6.00
66 Sebastian Aho/275 2.50 6.00
67 Auston Matthews/275 6.00 15.00
68 Evgenii Dadonov/275 1.00 2.50
69 Mark Scheifele/275 2.50 6.00
70 Mario Lemieux/275 6.00 15.00
71 Alex Tuch/275 1.50 4.00
72 Nicklas Backstrom/275 1.50 4.00
73 Chris Chelios/275 1.50 4.00
74 Pierre-Luc Dubois/275 1.25 3.00
75 Viktor Arvidsson/275 1.00 2.50
76 Artemi Panarin/275 3.00 8.00
77 John Carlson/275 1.50 4.00
78 Sergei Bobrovsky/275 2.50 6.00
79 Jordan Binnington/275 2.50 6.00
80 Teuvo Teravainen/275 1.50 4.00
81 Nazem Kadri/275 2.00 5.00
82 Johnny Gaudreau/275 2.50 6.00
83 Elias Pettersson/275 2.50 6.00
84 Marc-Andre Fleury/275 3.00 8.00
85 Cam Atkinson/275 1.50 4.00
86 Mikko Rantanen/275 4.00 10.00
87 Braden Holtby/275 2.00 5.00
88 Ryan Getzlaf/275 1.50 4.00
89 Claude Giroux/275 1.50 4.00
90 Roman Josi/275 1.50 4.00
91 Dylan Larkin/275 2.00 5.00
92 Jack Eichel/275 2.50 6.00
93 Brock Boeser/275 2.00 5.00
94 Nathan MacKinnon/275 6.00 15.00
95 Carter Hart/275 1.50 4.00
96 Mats Zuccarello/275 1.50 4.00
97 Thomas Chabot/275 1.50 4.00
98 Bobby Orr/275 6.00 15.00
99 Doug Gilmour/275 2.00 5.00
100 Connor McDavid/275 8.00 20.00
101 Kaapo Kakko/201 2.50 6.00
102 Guillaume Brisebois/297 1.50 4.00
103 Kevin Stenlund/296 1.25 3.00
104 Max Veronneau/295 1.25 3.00
105 Cody Glass/299 2.50 6.00
106 Joakim Nygard/293 1.25 3.00
107 Blake Lizotte/297 1.50 4.00
108 Mackenzie MacEachern/294 1.50 4.00
109 Teddy Blueger/294 1.50 4.00
110 Mario Ferraro/298 1.25 3.00
111 Scott Sabourin/292 1.25 3.00
112 Brandon Gignac/297 1.25 3.00
113 Danil Yurtaykin/297 1.25 3.00
114 Dmytro Timashov/296 1.50 4.00
115 Max Jones/298 1.50 4.00
116 Vitaly Abramov/298 1.50 4.00
117 Erik Brannstrom/299 1.50 4.00
118 Gaetan Haas/292 1.25 3.00
119 Philippe Myers/297 1.25 3.00
120 Ilya Mikheyev/294 2.50 6.00
121 Dennis Gilbert/296 1.25 3.00
122 Rasmus Sandin/200 2.50 6.00
123 Martin Fehervary/299 1.25 3.00
124 Kevin Boyle/292 1.50 4.00
125 Connor Clifton/295 1.50 4.00
126 Joel L'Esperance/295 1.50 4.00
127 Adam Fox/298 4.00 10.00
128 Conor Timmins/298 1.50 4.00
129 Ville Heinola/201 2.00 5.00
130 Matt Roy/295 1.50 4.00
131 Libor Hajek/298 1.25 3.00
132 Vladislav Gavrikov/295 1.25 3.00
133 Riley Stillman/298 1.50 4.00
134 Cale Fleury/298 2.00 5.00
135 Carter Verhaeghe/295 2.50 6.00
136 William Borgen/296 1.25 3.00
137 Ryan Poehling/299 2.50 6.00
138 Filip Zadina/219 2.50 6.00
139 Jacob Middleton/296 1.25 3.00
140 Ryan Kuffner/296 1.25 3.00
141 Nick Suzuki/299 6.00 15.00
142 Trevor Moore/295 1.25 3.00
143 Aleksi Saarela/297 1.50 4.00
144 Alexandre Texier/299 1.50 4.00
145 John Marino/297 2.50 6.00
146 Nikita Gusev/292 2.50 6.00
147 Julien Gauthier/297 1.50 4.00
148 Colton White/297 1.50 4.00
149 Zach Senyshyn/297 1.50 4.00
150 Zack MacEwen/296 1.25 3.00
151 Dante Fabbro/298 1.50 4.00
152 Nicolas Hague/298 1.50 4.00
153 Nathan Bastian/297 1.50 4.00
154 Ryan Lindgren/298 1.50 4.00
155 Adam Johnson/294 1.25 3.00
156 Oliver Wahlstrom/200 2.50 6.00
157 Lean Bergmann/298 1.25 3.00
158 Carl Grundstrom/297 1.50 4.00
159 Jesper Boqvist/298 1.25 3.00
160 Victor Olofsson/295 3.00 8.00
161 Colin Blackwell/293 1.50 4.00
162 Nikolay Prokhorkin/293 1.25 3.00
163 Kole Sherwood/297 1.50 4.00
164 Barrett Hayton/200 3.00 8.00
165 Kaden Fulcher/298 1.50 4.00
166 Nick Caamano/298 1.25 3.00
167 Josh Jacobs/296 1.25 3.00
168 Tobias Bjornfot/201 1.50 4.00
169 Josh Teves/295 1.25 3.00
170 Joel Persson/294 1.25 3.00
171 Givani Smith/298 1.25 3.00
172 Jimmy Schuldt/295 1.25 3.00
173 Josh Currie/292 1.25 3.00
174 David Gustafsson/200 1.25 3.00
175 Noah Dobson/200 4.00 10.00
176 Taro Hirose/296 1.50 4.00
177 Brady Keeper/296 1.50 4.00
178 Brogan Rafferty/295 1.50 4.00
179 Rhett Gardner/296 1.25 3.00
180 Carsen Twarynski/297 1.25 3.00
181 Elvis Merzlikins/294 3.00 8.00
182 Josh Brown/294 1.25 3.00
183 Quinn Hughes/299 8.00 20.00
184 Cale Makar/298 8.00 20.00
185 Sam Lafferty/295 1.25 3.00
186 Joey Daccord/296 3.00 8.00
187 Mark Friedman/295 1.25 3.00
188 Rudolfs Balcers/297 1.50 4.00
189 Nico Sturm/295 1.25 3.00
190 Karson Kuhlman/295 1.50 4.00
191 Dominik Kubalik/295 3.00 8.00
192 Joel Farabee/200 2.50 6.00
193 Kirby Dach/201 3.00 8.00
194 Connor Bunnaman/298 1.25 3.00
195 Trent Frederic/298 1.50 4.00
196 Emil Bemstrom/299 1.50 4.00
197 J.C. Beaudin/297 1.50 4.00
198 Jakob Lilja/293 1.25 3.00
199 Rem Pitlick/297 1.50 4.00
200 Jack Hughes/201 8.00 20.00

2019-20 SP Game Used Red

3 Zach Werenski JSY AU A 12.00 30.00
4 Jonathan Toews JSY AU B 12.00 30.00
6 Ben Bishop JSY AU C 6.00 15.00
7 Jake Guentzel JSY AU C 12.00 30.00
8 Brady Tkachuk JSY AU C 12.00 30.00
10 Jarome Iginla JSY AU A 10.00 25.00
11 Connor Hellebuyck JSY AU C 15.00 40.00
12 Steven Stamkos JSY AU A 15.00 40.00
13 Joe Pavelski JSY AU B 10.00 25.00
16 Mitch Marner JSY AU A 12.00 30.00
17 Seth Jones JSY AU C 8.00 20.00
21 Bo Horvat JSY AU C 10.00 25.00
24 Henrik Lundqvist JSY AU A 20.00 50.00
28 Leon Draisaitl JSY AU B 25.00 60.00
29 Brett Hull JSY AU A 15.00 40.00
32 John Tavares JSY AU A 12.00 30.00
33 Brent Burns JSY AU B 8.00 20.00
35 Dylan Strome JSY AU C 10.00 25.00
36 Anders Lee JSY AU C 6.00 15.00
37 Alex DeBrincat JSY AU C 10.00 25.00
39 Aaron Ekblad JSY AU B 10.00 25.00
40 Ryan O'Reilly JSY AU C 8.00 20.00
41 Sidney Crosby JSY AU A 30.00 80.00
44 Brad Marchand JSY AU B 15.00 40.00
45 Patrick Kane JSY AU A 15.00 40.00
46 Patrick Roy JSY AU A 20.00 50.00
47 William Karlsson JSY AU C 10.00 25.00
48 Martin Brodeur JSY AU A 20.00 50.00
50 Steve Yzerman JSY AU A 20.00 50.00
57 John Gibson JSY AU C 8.00 20.00
58 Joe Sakic JSY AU A 15.00 40.00
60 Carey Price JSY AU A 15.00 40.00
61 Devan Dubnyk JSY AU C 6.00 15.00
62 Nico Hischier JSY AU B 12.00 30.00
63 Aleksander Barkov JSY AU C 12.00 30.00
65 Joe Thornton JSY AU A 12.00 30.00
67 Auston Matthews JSY AU A 30.00 80.00
68 Evgenii Dadonov JSY AU C 5.00 12.00
69 Mark Scheifele JSY AU C 12.00 30.00
70 Mario Lemieux JSY AU A 30.00 80.00
73 Chris Chelios JSY AU B 8.00 20.00
78 Sergei Bobrovsky JSY AU B 12.00 30.00
83 Elias Pettersson JSY AU A 12.00 30.00
84 Marc-Andre Fleury JSY AU A 15.00 40.00
85 Cam Atkinson JSY AU C 8.00 20.00
91 Dylan Larkin JSY AU B 10.00 25.00
92 Jack Eichel JSY AU B 12.00 30.00
93 Brock Boeser JSY AU B 10.00 25.00
99 Doug Gilmour JSY AU A 10.00 25.00
100 Connor McDavid JSY AU A 150.00 250.00
102 Guillaume Brisebois JSY AU B 8.00 20.00
104 Max Veronneau JSY AU B 6.00 15.00
105 Cody Glass JSY AU A 12.00 30.00
107 Blake Lizotte JSY AU B 8.00 20.00
108 Mackenzie MacEachern JSY AU B 8.00 20.00
109 Teddy Blueger JSY AU B 8.00 20.00
110 Mario Ferraro JSY AU B 6.00 15.00
112 Brandon Gignac JSY AU B 6.00 15.00
115 Max Jones JSY AU A 8.00 20.00
116 Vitaly Abramov JSY AU B 8.00 20.00
117 Erik Brannstrom JSY AU A 8.00 20.00
119 Philippe Myers JSY AU B 6.00 15.00
120 Ilya Mikheyev JSY AU A 12.00 30.00
122 Rasmus Sandin JSY AU B 12.00 30.00
126 Joel L'Esperance JSY AU B 8.00 20.00
130 Matt Roy JSY AU B 8.00 20.00
131 Libor Hajek JSY AU B 6.00 15.00
133 Riley Stillman JSY AU B 8.00 20.00
135 Carter Verhaeghe JSY AU B 12.00 30.00
137 Ryan Poehling JSY AU A 12.00 30.00
138 Filip Zadina JSY AU A 12.00 30.00
140 Ryan Kuffner JSY AU B 6.00 15.00
141 Nick Suzuki JSY AU B 30.00 80.00
142 Trevor Moore JSY AU A 6.00 15.00
144 Alexandre Texier JSY AU A 8.00 20.00
147 Julien Gauthier JSY AU B 8.00 20.00
149 Zach Senyshyn JSY AU A 8.00 20.00
150 Zack MacEwen JSY AU B 6.00 15.00
151 Dante Fabbro JSY AU A 8.00 20.00
154 Ryan Lindgren JSY AU B 8.00 20.00
156 Oliver Wahlstrom JSY AU B 12.00 30.00
158 Carl Grundstrom JSY AU A 8.00 20.00
159 Jesper Boqvist JSY AU B 6.00 15.00
160 Victor Olofsson JSY AU B 15.00 40.00
163 Kole Sherwood JSY AU B 8.00 20.00
165 Kaden Fulcher JSY AU B 8.00 20.00
168 Tobias Bjornfot JSY AU B 8.00 20.00
170 Joel Persson JSY AU B 6.00 15.00
172 Jimmy Schuldt JSY AU B 6.00 15.00
175 Noah Dobson JSY AU B 20.00 50.00
176 Taro Hirose JSY AU B 8.00 20.00
177 Brady Keeper JSY AU B 8.00 20.00
181 Elvis Merzlikins JSY AU B 15.00 40.00
183 Quinn Hughes JSY AU A 40.00 100.00
184 Cale Makar JSY AU A 40.00 100.00
186 Joey Daccord JSY AU B 15.00 40.00
188 Rudolfs Balcers JSY AU B 8.00 20.00
189 Nico Sturm JSY AU A 6.00 15.00
190 Karson Kuhlman JSY AU B 8.00 20.00
192 Joel Farabee JSY AU B 12.00 30.00
193 Kirby Dach JSY AU B 15.00 40.00
195 Trent Frederic JSY AU A 8.00 20.00
196 Emil Bemstrom JSY AU A 8.00 20.00
199 Rem Pitlick JSY AU B 8.00 20.00
200 Jack Hughes JSY AU A 40.00 100.00

2019-20 SP Game Used '18 Global Series Game Used Pucks

GSGUPCM Connor McDavid 125.00 300.00
GSGUPKP Kyle Palmieri 20.00 50.00

2019-20 SP Game Used '19 All Star Game Materials Net Cord

ASNCAM Auston Matthews 50.00 125.00
ASNCAV Andrei Vasilevskiy 20.00 50.00
ASNCBH Braden Holtby 15.00 40.00
ASNCBW Blake Wheeler 12.00 30.00
ASNCCA Cam Atkinson 12.00 30.00
ASNCCG Claude Giroux 12.00 30.00
ASNCCM Connor McDavid 60.00 150.00
ASNCDP David Pastrnak 30.00 80.00
ASNCEK Erik Karlsson 15.00 40.00
ASNCGL Gabriel Landeskog 15.00 40.00
ASNCHL Henrik Lundqvist 30.00 80.00
ASNCJE Jack Eichel 20.00 50.00
ASNCJG Johnny Gaudreau 20.00 50.00
ASNCJP Joe Pavelski 15.00 40.00
ASNCJT John Tavares 20.00 50.00
ASNCKL Kris Letang 15.00 40.00
ASNCKP Kyle Palmieri 10.00 25.00
ASNCMB Mathew Barzal 15.00 40.00
ASNCMF Marc-Andre Fleury 25.00 60.00
ASNCMR Mikko Rantanen 30.00 80.00
ASNCMS Mark Scheifele 20.00 50.00
ASNCNM Nathan MacKinnon 50.00 120.00
ASNCPK Patrick Kane 25.00 60.00
ASNCPR Pekka Rinne 12.00 30.00
ASNCRJ Roman Josi 12.00 30.00
ASNCRO Ryan O'Reilly 12.00 30.00
ASNCSA Sebastian Aho 20.00 50.00
ASNCSC Sidney Crosby 50.00 125.00
ASNCSJ Seth Jones 12.00 30.00
ASNCSS Steven Stamkos 25.00 60.00

2019-20 SP Game Used '19 All Star Game Materials Net Cord Dual

ASDNCAJ C.Atkinson/S.Jones 12.00 30.00
ASDNCES J.Eichel/J.Skinner 20.00 50.00
ASDNCGR M.Rantanen/G.Landeskog 30.00 80.00
ASDNCHC B.Holtby/J.Carlson 15.00 40.00
ASDNCJR R.Josi/P.Rinne 12.00 30.00
ASDNCKB E.Karlsson/B.Burns 15.00 40.00
ASDNCMD C.McDavid/L.Draisaitl 60.00 150.00
ASDNCMT A.Matthews/J.Tavares 50.00 125.00
ASDNCSN S.Stamkos/N.Kucherov 25.00 60.00
ASDNCWS B.Wheeler/M.Scheifele 20.00 50.00

2019-20 SP Game Used '19 All Star Skills Fabrics

*PATCH/35: 1X TO 2.5X BASIC INSERTS
ASAM Auston Matthews 10.00 25.00
ASAV Andrei Vasilevskiy 4.00 10.00
ASBB Brent Burns 2.50 6.00
ASBH Braden Holtby 3.00 8.00
ASBW Blake Wheeler 2.50 6.00
ASCA Cam Atkinson 2.50 6.00
ASCG Claude Giroux 2.50 6.00
ASCK Clayton Keller 3.00 8.00
ASCM Connor McDavid 12.00 30.00
ASDD Drew Doughty 3.00 8.00
ASDP David Pastrnak 6.00 15.00
ASDU Devan Dubnyk 2.00 5.00
ASEK Erik Karlsson 3.00 8.00
ASEP Elias Pettersson 4.00 10.00
ASGI John Gibson 2.50 6.00
ASGL Gabriel Landeskog 3.00 8.00
ASHL Henrik Lundqvist 6.00 15.00
ASJC John Carlson 2.50 6.00
ASJE Jack Eichel 4.00 10.00
ASJG Johnny Gaudreau 4.00 10.00
ASJH Jim Howard 3.00 8.00
ASJP Joe Pavelski 3.00 8.00
ASJS Jeff Skinner 2.50 6.00
ASJT John Tavares 4.00 10.00
ASKL Kris Letang 3.00 8.00
ASKP Kyle Palmieri 2.00 5.00
ASKY Keith Yandle 1.50 4.00
ASLD Leon Draisaitl 8.00 20.00
ASMB Mathew Barzal 3.00 8.00
ASMF Marc-Andre Fleury 5.00 12.00
ASMH Miro Heiskanen 3.00 8.00
ASMR Mikko Rantanen 6.00 15.00
ASMS Mark Scheifele 4.00 10.00
ASNK Nikita Kucherov 5.00 12.00
ASNM Nathan MacKinnon 10.00 25.00
ASPK Patrick Kane 5.00 12.00
ASPR Pekka Rinne 2.50 6.00
ASRJ Roman Josi 2.50 6.00
ASRO Ryan O'Reilly 2.50 6.00
ASSA Sebastian Aho 4.00 10.00
ASSC Sidney Crosby 10.00 25.00
ASSJ Seth Jones 2.50 6.00
ASSS Steven Stamkos 5.00 12.00
ASTC Thomas Chabot 2.50 6.00

2019-20 SP Game Used '19 All Star Skills Fabrics Dual

*PATCH/25: 1X TO 2.5X BASIC INSERTS
AS2AJ C.Atkinson/S.Jones 3.00 8.00
AS2BK B.Burns/E.Karlsson 4.00 10.00
AS2ES J.Eichel/J.Skinner 5.00 12.00
AS2HC B.Holtby/J.Carlson 4.00 10.00
AS2JR R.Josi/P.Rinne 3.00 8.00
AS2MD C.McDavid/L.Draisaitl 15.00 40.00
AS2MR N.MacKinnon/M.Rantanen 12.00 30.00
AS2SD S.Stamkos/D.Doughty 6.00 15.00
AS2VK A.Vasilevskiy/N.Kucherov 6.00 15.00
AS2WS B.Wheeler/M.Scheifele 5.00 12.00

2019-20 SP Game Used '19 All Star Skills Relic Blends

ASRBAM Auston Matthews 10.00 25.00
ASRBAV Andrei Vasilevskiy 4.00 10.00
ASRBBB Brent Burns 2.50 6.00
ASRBBH Braden Holtby 3.00 8.00
ASRBBW Blake Wheeler 2.50 6.00
ASRBCA Cam Atkinson 2.50 6.00
ASRBCG Claude Giroux 2.50 6.00
ASRBCK Clayton Keller 3.00 8.00
ASRBCM Connor McDavid 12.00 30.00
ASRBDD Drew Doughty 3.00 8.00
ASRBDP David Pastrnak 6.00 15.00
ASRBDU Devan Dubnyk 2.00 5.00
ASRBEK Erik Karlsson 3.00 8.00
ASRBEP Elias Pettersson 4.00 10.00
ASRBGI John Gibson 2.50 6.00
ASRBGL Gabriel Landeskog 3.00 8.00
ASRBHL Henrik Lundqvist 6.00 15.00
ASRBJC John Carlson 2.50 6.00
ASRBJE Jack Eichel 4.00 10.00
ASRBJG Johnny Gaudreau 4.00 10.00
ASRBJH Jim Howard 3.00 8.00
ASRBJP Joe Pavelski 3.00 8.00
ASRBJS Jeff Skinner 2.50 6.00
ASRBJT John Tavares 4.00 10.00
ASRBKL Kris Letang 3.00 8.00
ASRBKP Kyle Palmieri 2.00 5.00
ASRBKY Keith Yandle 1.50 4.00
ASRBLD Leon Draisaitl 8.00 20.00
ASRBMB Mathew Barzal 3.00 8.00
ASRBMF Marc-Andre Fleury 5.00 12.00
ASRBMH Miro Heiskanen 3.00 8.00
ASRBMR Mikko Rantanen 6.00 15.00
ASRBMS Mark Scheifele 4.00 10.00
ASRBNK Nikita Kucherov 5.00 12.00
ASRBNM Nathan MacKinnon 10.00 25.00
ASRBPK Patrick Kane 5.00 12.00
ASRBPR Pekka Rinne 2.50 6.00
ASRBRJ Roman Josi 2.50 6.00
ASRBRO Ryan O'Reilly 2.50 6.00
ASRBSA Sebastian Aho 4.00 10.00
ASRBSC Sidney Crosby 10.00 25.00
ASRBSJ Seth Jones 2.50 6.00
ASRBSS Steven Stamkos 5.00 12.00
ASRBTC Thomas Chabot 2.50 6.00

2019-20 SP Game Used '19 All Star Weekend Banner Jersey

AWAM Auston Matthews 12.00 30.00
AWCA Cam Atkinson 3.00 8.00
AWCK Clayton Keller 4.00 10.00
AWCM Connor McDavid 15.00 40.00
AWDD Devan Dubnyk 2.50 6.00
AWJH Jim Howard 4.00 10.00
AWJP Joe Pavelski 4.00 10.00
AWJS Jeff Skinner 3.00 8.00
AWKL Kris Letang 4.00 10.00
AWKP Kyle Palmieri 2.50 6.00
AWKY Keith Yandle 2.00 5.00
AWNM Nathan MacKinnon 12.00 30.00
AWPK Patrick Kane 6.00 15.00
AWPR Pekka Rinne 3.00 8.00
AWSC Sidney Crosby 12.00 30.00

2019-20 SP Game Used '19 Rookie Relic Blends

RRBAF Adam Fox 8.00 20.00
RRBAT Alexandre Texier 3.00 8.00
RRBBH Barrett Hayton 6.00 15.00
RRBCG Carl Grundstrom 3.00 8.00
RRBCM Cale Makar 15.00 40.00
RRBDF Dante Fabbro 3.00 8.00
RRBEB Erik Brannstrom 3.00 8.00
RRBFZ Filip Zadina 5.00 12.00
RRBGL Cody Glass 5.00 12.00
RRBJB Jesper Boqvist 2.50 6.00
RRBJH Jack Hughes 15.00 40.00
RRBKD Kirby Dach 6.00 15.00
RRBKK Kaapo Kakko 5.00 12.00
RRBMJ Max Jones 3.00 8.00
RRBND Noah Dobson 8.00 20.00
RRBNG Nikita Gusev 5.00 12.00
RRBNS Nico Sturm 2.50 6.00
RRBPM Philippe Myers 2.50 6.00
RRBQH Quinn Hughes 15.00 40.00
RRBRP Ryan Poehling 5.00 12.00
RRBRS Rasmus Sandin 5.00 12.00
RRBSU Nick Suzuki 12.00 30.00
RRBTH Taro Hirose 3.00 8.00
RRBVA Vitaly Abramov 3.00 8.00

2019-20 SP Game Used '19 Stadium Series Fabrics

*PATCH/35: .75X TO 2X BASIC INSERTS
SSBE Brian Elliott 2.50 6.00
SSJM Jared McCann 2.50 6.00
SSMR Michael Raffl 2.00 5.00
SSNB Nick Bjugstad 2.00 5.00
SSNP Nolan Patrick 3.00 8.00
SSPK Phil Kessel 3.00 8.00
SSSC Sean Couturier 2.50 6.00
SSSL Scott Laughton 2.00 5.00
SSTK Travis Konecny 3.00 8.00
SSZA Zach Aston-Reese 3.00 8.00

2019-20 SP Game Used '19 Stadium Series Game Used Pucks

SSGUPCG Claude Giroux 25.00 60.00
SSGUPCO Sean Couturier 20.00 50.00
SSGUPEM Evgeni Malkin 50.00 125.00
SSGUPJS Justin Schultz 25.00 60.00
SSGUPJV Jakub Voracek 20.00 50.00
SSGUPSC Sidney Crosby 100.00 250.00

2019-20 SP Game Used '19 Stadium Series Materials Net Cord

SSNCBE Brian Elliott 10.00 25.00
SSNCCG Claude Giroux 12.00 30.00
SSNCCO Sean Couturier 10.00 25.00
SSNCEM Evgeni Malkin 25.00 60.00
SSNCJG Jake Guentzel 20.00 50.00
SSNCJS Justin Schultz 12.00 30.00
SSNCJV Jakub Voracek 10.00 25.00
SSNCKL Kris Letang 15.00 40.00
SSNCMM Matt Murray 12.00 30.00
SSNCNB Nick Bjugstad 8.00 20.00
SSNCNP Nolan Patrick 12.00 30.00
SSNCOL Oskar Lindblom 10.00 25.00
SSNCPK Phil Kessel 12.00 30.00
SSNCSC Sidney Crosby 50.00 125.00
SSNCTK Travis Konecny 12.00 30.00
SSNCTS Travis Sanheim 8.00 20.00
SSNCVR James van Riemsdyk 10.00 25.00
SSNCZA Zach Aston-Reese 12.00 30.00

2019-20 SP Game Used '19 Stanley Cup Final Game Used Pucks

SCGUPAP Alex Pietrangelo 20.00 50.00
SCGUPBM Brad Marchand 50.00 125.00
SCGUPBS Brayden Schenn 25.00 60.00
SCGUPCM Charlie McAvoy 30.00 80.00
SCGUPCP Colton Parayko 20.00 50.00
SCGUPDP David Pastrnak 60.00 150.00
SCGUPJB Jordan Binnington 40.00 100.00
SCGUPPB Patrice Bergeron 30.00 80.00
SCGUPRO Ryan O'Reilly 25.00 60.00
SCGUPRT Robert Thomas 25.00 60.00
SCGUPTR Tuukka Rask 30.00 80.00
SCGUPVT Vladimir Tarasenko 30.00 80.00
SCGUPZC Zdeno Chara 25.00 60.00

2019-20 SP Game Used '19 Stanley Cup Final Materials Net Cord

SCNCAP Alex Pietrangelo 10.00 25.00
SCNCBC Brandon Carlo 10.00 25.00
SCNCBM Brad Marchand 25.00 60.00
SCNCBS Brayden Schenn 12.00 30.00
SCNCCC Charlie Coyle 12.00 30.00
SCNCCG Carl Gunnarsson 8.00 20.00
SCNCCM Charlie McAvoy 15.00 40.00
SCNCCP Colton Parayko 10.00 25.00
SCNCDK David Krejci 12.00 30.00
SCNCDP David Pastrnak 30.00 80.00
SCNCIB Ivan Barbashev 10.00 25.00
SCNCJB Jordan Binnington 20.00 50.00
SCNCJD Jake DeBrusk 12.00 30.00
SCNCJS Jaden Schwartz 15.00 40.00
SCNCPB Patrice Bergeron 15.00 40.00
SCNCPE David Perron 10.00 25.00
SCNCRB Robert Bortuzzo 10.00 25.00
SCNCRO Ryan O'Reilly 12.00 30.00
SCNCSK Sean Kuraly 8.00 20.00
SCNCTK Torey Krug 10.00 25.00
SCNCTR Tuukka Rask 15.00 40.00
SCNCVT Vladimir Tarasenko 15.00 40.00
SCNCZC Zdeno Chara 12.00 30.00
SCNCZS Zach Sanford 8.00 20.00

2019-20 SP Game Used '19 Winter Classic Game Used Pucks

WCGUP1 Patrice Bergeron 30.00 80.00
WCGUP2 Erik Gustafsson 15.00 40.00
WCGUP3 David Pastrnak 60.00 150.00
WCGUP4 Jonathan Toews 40.00 100.00
WCGUP5 Brad Marchand 50.00 125.00
WCGUP6 Patrick Kane 50.00 125.00

2019-20 SP Game Used '19 Winter Classic Materials Net Cord

WCNCAD Alex DeBrincat 15.00 40.00
WCNCBM Brad Marchand 25.00 60.00
WCNCDA David Kampf 8.00 20.00
WCNCDK Duncan Keith 10.00 25.00
WCNCDP David Pastrnak 30.00 80.00
WCNCDS Dylan Strome 15.00 40.00
WCNCEG Erik Gustafsson 8.00 20.00
WCNCJT Jonathan Toews 20.00 50.00
WCNCKA Dominik Kahun 8.00 20.00
WCNCKR David Krejci 12.00 30.00
WCNCMG Matt Grzelcyk 10.00 25.00
WCNCMS Brent Seabrook 8.00 20.00
WCNCPB Patrice Bergeron 15.00 40.00
WCNCPK Patrick Kane 25.00 60.00
WCNCSK Sean Kuraly 8.00 20.00
WCNCTK Torey Krug 10.00 25.00
WCNCTR Tuukka Rask 15.00 40.00
WCNCZC Zdeno Chara 12.00 30.00

2019-20 SP Game Used A Piece of History 100 Point Season Club

100AO Alexander Ovechkin 30.00 80.00
100DG Doug Gilmour 10.00 25.00
100JT Joe Thornton 12.00 30.00
100NK Nikita Kucherov 15.00 40.00
100PK Patrick Kane 15.00 40.00
100PL Pat LaFontaine 8.00 20.00

2019-20 SP Game Used A Piece of History 40 Win Season Club

40AV Andrei Vasilevskiy 12.00 30.00
40CP Carey Price 15.00 40.00
40MB Martin Brodeur 20.00 50.00
40PR Pekka Rinne 8.00 20.00

2019-20 SP Game Used A Piece of History 50 Goal Season Club

50BH Brett Hull 15.00 40.00
50JJ Jaromir Jagr 25.00 60.00
50JS Joe Sakic 15.00 40.00
50ML Mario Lemieux 30.00 80.00

2019-20 SP Game Used Banner Year '19 All Star Game

BAS1 Connor McDavid 15.00 40.00
BAS2 Sidney Crosby 12.00 30.00
BAS3 Seth Jones 3.00 8.00
BAS4 Mark Scheifele 5.00 12.00
BAS5 Auston Matthews 12.00 30.00
BAS6 Thomas Chabot 3.00 8.00
BAS7 Jack Eichel 5.00 12.00
BAS8 Patrick Kane 6.00 15.00
BAS9 John Gibson 3.00 8.00
BAS10 John Tavares 5.00 12.00
BAS11 Leon Draisaitl 10.00 25.00
BAS12 Cam Atkinson 3.00 8.00
BAS13 Marc-Andre Fleury 6.00 15.00
BAS14 Ryan O'Reilly 3.00 8.00

2019-20 SP Game Used Banner Year '19 Winter Classic Autographs

BWC3 Dylan Strome/25 10.00 25.00
BWC6 Brad Marchand/25 15.00 40.00
BWC9 Alex DeBrincat/25 10.00 25.00

2019-20 SP Game Used Banner Year Draft '12

BD12BS Brady Skjei 2.50 6.00
BD12JT Jacob Trouba 2.50 6.00
BD12MD Matt Dumba 2.00 5.00

2019-20 SP Game Used Banner Year Draft '15

BD15IP Ivan Provorov 2.50 6.00
BD15MR Mikko Rantanen 8.00 20.00
BD15TC Thomas Chabot 3.00 8.00
BD15ZW Zach Werenski 5.00 12.00

2019-20 SP Game Used Banner Year Draft '17

BD17CG Cody Glass 5.00 12.00
BD17MH Miro Heiskanen 4.00 10.00
BD17RP Ryan Poehling 5.00 12.00

2019-20 SP Game Used Banner Year Draft '18

BD18QH Quinn Hughes 15.00 40.00

2019-20 SP Game Used Draft Day Marks Rookies

DDMAB Adam Boqvist/245* 12.00 30.00
DDMAF Adam Fox/105* 125.00 300.00
DDMBH Barrett Hayton/210* 30.00 80.00
DDMBT Brady Tkachuk/245* 25.00 60.00
DDMCG Carl Grundstrom/350* 15.00 40.00
DDMCM Cale Makar/175* 150.00 400.00
DDMDB Drake Batherson/315* 15.00 40.00
DDMDF Dante Fabbro/210* 15.00 40.00
DDMEB Erik Brannstrom/350* 15.00 40.00
DDMFZ Filip Zadina/210* 25.00 60.00
DDMGL Cody Glass/175* 25.00 60.00
DDMGR German Rubtsov/245* 12.00 30.00
DDMIS Igor Shesterkin/350* 60.00 150.00
DDMJB Jesper Boqvist/245* 12.00 30.00
DDMJF Joel Farabee/245* 25.00 60.00
DDMJG Julien Gauthier/280* 15.00 40.00
DDMJH Jack Hughes/210* 100.00 250.00
DDMJK Jesperi Kotkaniemi/350* 15.00 40.00
DDMKC Kale Clague/210* 12.00 30.00
DDMKD Kirby Dach/140* 30.00 80.00
DDMKO Klim Kostin/210* 15.00 40.00
DDMMF Morgan Frost/175* 25.00 60.00
DDMMJ Max Jones/175* 15.00 40.00
DDMND Noah Dobson/210* 40.00 100.00
DDMNE Martin Necas/175* 25.00 60.00
DDMNH Nico Hischier/280* 25.00 60.00
DDMOW Oliver Wahlstrom/315* 25.00 60.00
DDMQH Quinn Hughes/210* 80.00 200.00
DDMRA Rasmus Asplund/245* 12.00 30.00
DDMRS Rasmus Sandin/210* 25.00 60.00
DDMSU Nick Suzuki/210* 60.00 150.00
DDMTF Trent Frederic/280* 15.00 40.00
DDMVA Vitaly Abramov/245* 15.00 40.00

2019-20 SP Game Used Frameworks

FWAB Aleksander Barkov E 10.00 25.00
FWAD Alex DeBrincat E 8.00 20.00
FWAP Alex Pietrangelo D 5.00 12.00
FWAS Andrei Svechnikov E 8.00 20.00
FWBB Ben Bishop C 5.00 12.00
FWBP Brayden Point E 8.00 20.00
FWBT Brady Tkachuk E 10.00 25.00
FWCM Connor McDavid E 30.00 80.00
FWDD Drew Doughty E 8.00 20.00
FWEP Elias Pettersson E 10.00 25.00
FWES Eric Staal E 6.00 15.00
FWFF Filip Forsberg E 10.00 25.00
FWGU Jake Guentzel E 10.00 25.00
FWJA Jason Arnott A 5.00 12.00
FWJG John Gibson E 6.00 15.00
FWJR Jeremy Roenick C 10.00 25.00
FWMG Michel Goulet E 6.00 15.00
FWMR Mikko Rantanen E 15.00 40.00
FWNL Nicklas Lidstrom E 6.00 15.00
FWPL Pat LaFontaine E 6.00 15.00
FWRI Morgan Rielly D 6.00 15.00
FWRO Ryan O'Reilly E 6.00 15.00
FWSJ Seth Jones E 6.00 15.00
FWSN Scott Niedermayer B 6.00 15.00
FWVH Victor Hedman E 8.00 20.00
FWWG Wayne Gretzky E 40.00 100.00
FWWK William Karlsson E 8.00 20.00

2019-20 SP Game Used Inked Rookie Sweaters Patch

RSAT Alexandre Texier 12.00 30.00
RSCG Carl Grundstrom 12.00 30.00
RSCM Cale Makar 60.00 150.00
RSDF Dante Fabbro 12.00 30.00
RSEB Erik Brannstrom 12.00 30.00
RSFZ Filip Zadina 20.00 50.00
RSGL Cody Glass 20.00 50.00
RSIM Ilya Mikheyev 20.00 50.00
RSJB Jesper Boqvist 10.00 25.00
RSJG Jack Hughes 60.00 150.00
RSKD Kirby Dach 25.00 60.00
RSLH Libor Hajek 10.00 25.00
RSMJ Max Jones 12.00 30.00
RSND Noah Dobson 30.00 80.00
RSNS Nico Sturm 10.00 25.00
RSOW Oliver Wahlstrom 20.00 50.00
RSPM Philippe Myers 10.00 25.00
RSQH Quinn Hughes 80.00 200.00
RSRP Ryan Poehling 20.00 50.00
RSSU Nick Suzuki 50.00 125.00
RSTF Trent Frederic 12.00 30.00
RSTH Taro Hirose 12.00 30.00
RSVA Vitaly Abramov 12.00 30.00
RSVO Victor Olofsson 25.00 60.00
RSZS Zach Senyshyn 12.00 30.00

2019-20 SP Game Used Inked Sweaters

ISAB Aleksander Barkov 12.00 30.00
ISAT Alex Tuch 8.00 20.00
ISBB Ben Bishop 6.00 15.00
ISBO Brock Boeser 10.00 25.00

ISDL Dylan Larkin 10.00 25.00
ISDS Derek Stepan 5.00 12.00
ISJG John Gibson 8.00 20.00
ISJV Jakub Vrana 8.00 20.00
ISMM Matt Murray 8.00 20.00
ISSJ Seth Jones 8.00 20.00

2019-20 SP Game Used Rookie Sweaters

RSAF Adam Fox 6.00 15.00
RSAT Alexandre Texier 2.50 6.00
RSBH Barrett Hayton 5.00 12.00
RSCG Carl Grundstrom 2.50 6.00
RSCM Cale Makar 12.00 30.00
RSDF Dante Fabbro 2.50 6.00
RSEB Erik Brannstrom 2.50 6.00
RSFZ Filip Zadina 4.00 10.00
RSGL Cody Glass 4.00 10.00
RSIM Ilya Mikheyev 4.00 10.00
RSJB Jesper Boqvist 2.00 5.00
RSJG Jack Hughes 12.00 30.00
RSKD Kirby Dach 5.00 12.00
RSKK Kaapo Kakko 4.00 10.00
RSLH Libor Hajek 2.00 5.00
RSMJ Max Jones 2.50 6.00
RSND Noah Dobson 6.00 15.00
RSNG Nikita Gusev 4.00 10.00
RSNS Nico Sturm 2.00 5.00
RSOW Oliver Wahlstrom 4.00 10.00
RSPM Philippe Myers 2.00 5.00
RSQH Quinn Hughes 12.00 30.00
RSRP Ryan Poehling 4.00 10.00
RSSU Nick Suzuki 10.00 25.00
RSTF Trent Frederic 2.50 6.00
RSTH Taro Hirose 2.50 6.00
RSVA Vitaly Abramov 2.50 6.00
RSVO Victor Olofsson 5.00 12.00
RSZS Zach Senyshyn 2.50 6.00

2019-20 SP Game Used Showcase Standouts Jersey Autographs

SSAD Alex DeBrincat/50 15.00 40.00
SSBB Brock Boeser/50 15.00 40.00
SSBT Brady Tkachuk/50 20.00 50.00
SSCM Connor McDavid/25 60.00 150.00
SSDL Dylan Larkin/50 15.00 40.00
SSFZ Filip Zadina/50 20.00 50.00
SSJE Jack Eichel/25 20.00 50.00
SSJV Jakub Vrana/50 12.00 30.00
SSKL Kevin Labanc/50 8.00 20.00
SSMH Miro Heiskanen/50 15.00 40.00
SSMJ Max Jones/50 12.00 30.00
SSMM Mitch Marner/25 20.00 50.00
SSPM Philippe Myers/50 10.00 25.00

2019-20 SP Game Used Showcase Standouts Jerseys

*PATCH/25: 1X TO 2.5X BASIC INSERTS
SSAD Alex DeBrincat 3.00 8.00
SSBB Brock Boeser 3.00 8.00
SSBS Brady Skjei 2.00 5.00
SSBT Brady Tkachuk 4.00 10.00
SSCM Connor McDavid 12.00 30.00
SSDL Dylan Larkin 3.00 8.00
SSFZ Filip Zadina 4.00 10.00
SSJE Jack Eichel 4.00 10.00
SSJV Jakub Vrana 2.50 6.00
SSKL Kevin Labanc 1.50 4.00
SSMD Matt Dumba 1.50 4.00
SSMH Miro Heiskanen 3.00 8.00
SSMJ Max Jones 2.50 6.00
SSMM Mitch Marner 4.00 10.00
SSMT Matthew Tkachuk 5.00 12.00
SSNM Nathan MacKinnon 10.00 25.00
SSPD Pierre-Luc Dubois 2.00 5.00
SSPM Philippe Myers 2.00 5.00
SSTW Tom Wilson 2.50 6.00

2019-20 SP Game Used Signing Day Marks

SDMNG Nikita Gusev/175* 25.00 60.00
SDMPM Philippe Myers/175* 12.00 30.00
SDMTH Taro Hirose/210* 15.00 40.00

2019-20 SP Game Used Tools of the Game

TGAB Aleksander Barkov 5.00 12.00
TGAV Andrei Vasilevskiy 5.00 12.00
TGBG Brendan Gallagher 3.00 8.00
TGBW Blake Wheeler 3.00 8.00
TGCG Claude Giroux 3.00 8.00
TGCP Carey Price 6.00 15.00
TGDP David Pastrnak 8.00 20.00
TGFA Frederik Andersen 4.00 10.00
TGJG Johnny Gaudreau 5.00 12.00
TGMJ Martin Jones 2.50 6.00
TGMM Mitch Marner 5.00 12.00
TGNB Nicklas Backstrom 3.00 8.00
TGNM Nathan MacKinnon 12.00 30.00
TGRL Roberto Luongo 5.00 12.00
TGSC Sean Couturier 2.50 6.00
TGTS Tyler Seguin 4.00 10.00

2020-21 SP Game Used Golden Burst

1 Connor McDavid 8.00 20.00
2 Mark Stone 2.00 5.00
3 Ryan O'Reilly 1.50 4.00
4 Matthew Tkachuk 3.00 8.00
5 Andrei Vasilevskiy 2.50 6.00
6 Eric Staal 1.50 4.00
7 Quinn Hughes 4.00 10.00
8 Tomas Hertl 1.50 4.00
9 Niklas Hjalmarsson 1.00 2.50
10 Elias Pettersson 2.50 6.00
11 John Klingberg 1.50 4.00
12 Dylan Larkin 2.00 5.00
13 Sean Monahan 1.00 2.50
14 Teuvo Teravainen 1.50 4.00
15 Mark Scheifele 2.50 6.00
16 Colton Parayko 1.25 3.00
17 Elvis Merzlikins 1.50 4.00
18 Tom Wilson 1.50 4.00
19 Josh Morrissey 2.00 5.00
20 Leon Draisaitl 5.00 12.00
21 Anze Kopitar 2.50 6.00
22 Brock Boeser 2.00 5.00
23 Brent Burns 1.50 4.00
24 Steven Stamkos 3.00 8.00
25 Nathan MacKinnon 6.00 15.00
26 Anthony Mantha 1.25 3.00
27 Mika Zibanejad 2.00 5.00
28 Brendan Gallagher 1.50 4.00
29 Cale Makar 4.00 10.00
30 Nikita Kucherov 3.00 8.00
31 Pekka Rinne 1.50 4.00
32 Sebastian Aho 2.50 6.00
33 Johnny Gaudreau 2.50 6.00
34 Drew Doughty 2.00 5.00
35 Roman Josi 1.50 4.00
36 Zach Parise 1.50 4.00
37 Jake Guentzel 2.50 6.00
38 Matt Dumba 1.50 4.00
39 John Gibson 1.50 4.00
40 Jack Eichel 2.50 6.00
41 Seth Jones 1.50 4.00
42 Mathew Barzal 2.00 5.00
43 Shea Theodore 2.00 5.00
44 Igor Shesterkin 3.00 8.00
45 Jonathan Huberdeau 2.00 5.00
46 Mitch Marner 2.50 6.00
47 Josh Bailey 1.25 3.00
48 Pierre-Luc Dubois 1.25 3.00
49 Ryan Getzlaf 1.50 4.00
50 Auston Matthews 6.00 15.00
51 Brady Tkachuk 2.50 6.00
52 Nico Hischier 2.50 6.00
53 Carter Hart 1.50 4.00
54 John Tavares 2.50 6.00
55 Brayden Point 2.00 5.00
56 Thomas Chabot 1.50 4.00
57 Ryan Nugent-Hopkins 2.00 5.00
58 Sergei Bobrovsky 2.50 6.00
59 Jack Hughes 4.00 10.00
60 Brad Marchand 3.00 8.00
61 Claude Giroux 1.50 4.00
62 Andrei Svechnikov 2.00 5.00
63 Evgeni Malkin 3.00 8.00
64 Miro Heiskanen 2.00 5.00
65 Aleksander Barkov 2.50 6.00
66 Cam Atkinson 1.50 4.00
67 Mark Giordano 1.50 4.00
68 John Carlson 1.50 4.00
69 Philipp Grubauer 1.50 4.00
70 Artemi Panarin 3.00 8.00
71 David Perron 1.25 3.00
72 Alex DeBrincat 2.00 5.00
73 Jonathan Toews 2.50 6.00
74 Patrik Laine 2.00 5.00
75 David Pastrnak 4.00 10.00
76 Clayton Keller 2.00 5.00
77 Connor Hellebuyck 3.00 8.00
78 William Nylander 3.00 8.00
79 J.T. Miller 2.00 5.00
80 Patrick Kane 3.00 8.00
81 Oliver Ekman-Larsson 1.50 4.00
82 Patrice Bergeron 2.00 5.00
83 Elias Lindholm 1.50 4.00
84 Keith Yandle 1.00 2.50
85 Tyler Seguin 2.00 5.00
86 Victor Hedman 2.00 5.00
87 Nicklas Backstrom 1.50 4.00
88 Jamie Benn 1.50 4.00
89 Jonathan Drouin 1.25 3.00
90 Alex Ovechkin 6.00 15.00
91 Rasmus Dahlin 2.00 5.00
92 Alex Tuch 1.50 4.00
93 Jeff Carter 1.25 3.00
94 Filip Forsberg 2.50 6.00
95 Carey Price 3.00 8.00
96 Ben Bishop 1.25 3.00
97 Vladimir Tarasenko 2.00 5.00
98 William Karlsson 2.00 5.00
99 Kevin Hayes 1.25 3.00
100 Sidney Crosby 6.00 15.00
101 Billy Smith 1.50 4.00
102 Nicklas Lidstrom 1.50 4.00
103 Bill Ranford 1.25 3.00
104 Bernie Nicholls 1.25 3.00
105 Dominik Hasek 2.50 6.00
106 Olaf Kolzig 1.50 4.00
107 Pat LaFontaine 1.50 4.00
108 Ken Morrow 1.00 2.50
109 Patrick Roy 4.00 10.00
110 Henrik Zetterberg 2.00 5.00
111 Bob Bourne 1.00 2.50
112 Henrik Sedin 2.00 5.00
113 Jarome Iginla 2.00 5.00
114 Joe Sakic 3.00 8.00
115 John LeClair 1.50 4.00
116 Daniel Sedin 2.00 5.00
117 Saku Koivu 1.50 4.00
118 Steve Yzerman 4.00 10.00
119 Ty Smith TC 2.00 5.00
120 Dylan Cozens TC 3.00 8.00
121 Bowen Byram TC 4.00 10.00
122 Ty Dellandrea TC 2.00 5.00
123 Connor McMichael TC 3.00 8.00
124 Liam Foudy TC 2.00 5.00
125 Alexis Lafreniere TC 20.00 50.00
126 Ilya Sorokin 6.00 15.00
127 Vitek Vanecek 4.00 10.00
128 Nikolai Knyzhov 2.00 5.00
129 Brandon Hagel 3.00 8.00
130 Alexander Romanov 3.00 8.00
131 Matiss Kivlenieks 3.00 8.00
132 Logan Stanley 2.50 6.00
133 Egor Zamula 2.00 5.00
134 Pius Suter 3.00 8.00
135 Connor McMichael 4.00 10.00
136 Vitali Kravtsov 5.00 12.00
137 Philip Broberg 2.50 6.00
138 Martin Kaut 2.50 6.00
139 Gage Quinney 1.50 4.00
140 Bowen Byram 5.00 12.00
141 Nicolas Beaudin 2.50 6.00
142 Timothy Liljegren 2.50 6.00
143 Gustav Lindstrom 2.00 5.00
144 Shane Bowers 2.00 5.00
145 Joel Kiviranta 2.50 6.00
146 Jason Robertson 6.00 15.00
147 Alexander Barabanov 2.50 6.00
148 Alexander True 2.00 5.00
149 Thomas Harley 4.00 10.00
150 Alexis Lafreniere 30.00 80.00
151 Liam Foudy 2.50 6.00
152 Pierre-Olivier Joseph 2.50 6.00
153 Egor Korshkov 1.50 4.00
154 Morgan Geekie 2.50 6.00
155 Nick Robertson 4.00 10.00
156 Connor Ingram 2.00 5.00
157 Ian Mitchell 2.00 5.00
158 Mathias Brome 2.00 5.00
159 Ryan McLeod 2.50 6.00
160 Tim Stutzle 15.00 40.00
161 Gabe Vilardi 4.00 10.00
162 Tyler Benson 2.50 6.00
163 Mikey Anderson 2.50 6.00
164 Olli Juolevi 2.50 6.00
165 Nils Hoglander 2.50 6.00
166 Jani Hakanpaa 1.50 4.00
167 Keegan Kolesar 2.00 5.00
168 Calvin Thurkauf 2.00 5.00
169 Josh Norris 4.00 10.00
170 Ty Smith 4.00 10.00
171 Anthony Angello 2.00 5.00
172 Kieffer Bellows 2.00 5.00
173 Jonas Johansson 2.50 6.00
174 Alexander Alexeyev 2.00 5.00
175 K'Andre Miller 5.00 12.00
176 Jake Oettinger 6.00 15.00
177 Lucas Carlsson 2.00 5.00
178 Victor Soderstrom 2.00 5.00
179 Steven Lorentz 2.00 5.00
180 Kirill Kaprizov 60.00 150.00
181 Reid Duke 2.50 6.00
182 Alex Belzile 2.00 5.00
183 Ty Dellandrea 2.50 6.00
184 Kevin Lankinen 4.00 10.00
185 Dylan Cozens 10.00 25.00
186 Maxim Letunov 2.00 5.00
187 Philippe Maillet 2.00 5.00
188 Alexander Yelesin 2.00 5.00
189 Alec Regula 1.50 4.00
190 Peyton Krebs 4.00 10.00
191 Yegor Sharangovich 4.00 10.00
192 Jake Evans 2.50 6.00
193 Joseph Woll 5.00 12.00
194 Lukas Jasek 1.50 4.00
195 Cal Foote 3.00 8.00
196 Philipp Kurashev 3.00 8.00
197 Pavel Francouz 3.00 8.00
198 Chase Priskie 2.00 5.00

2020-21 SP Game Used Blue

*BLUE: 1.5X TO 4X GOLD.BURST
*BLUE.RC: 1.25X TO 3X GOLD.BURST
146 Jason Robertson AU D 40.00 100.00
160 Tim Stutzle AU C 100.00 250.00
180 Kirill Kaprizov AU D 250.00 600.00

2020-21 SP Game Used Blue Burst

*BLUE.BURST: .5X TO 1.25X GOLD.BURST
120 Dylan Cozens TC 10.00 25.00
126 Ilya Sorokin 15.00 40.00
150 Alexis Lafreniere 50.00 125.00

2020-21 SP Game Used Gold

*GOLD: 2X TO 5X GOLD.BURST
*GOLD.RC: 1.5X TO 4X GOLD.BURST

2020-21 SP Game Used Purple

*PURPLE: 1.5X TO 4X GOLD.BURST
126 Ilya Sorokin JSY AU/65 80.00 200.00
127 Vitek Vanecek JSY AU/65 10.00 25.00
146 Jason Robertson JSY AU/65 40.00 100.00
180 Kirill Kaprizov JSY AU/65 300.00 800.00

2020-21 SP Game Used Silver

*SILVER: .75X TO 2X GOLD.BURST
*SILVER.RC: .6X TO 1.5X GOLD.BURST

2020-21 SP Game Used '19 NHL Heritage Classic Banner Year Relics

HC20BL Bryan Little 2.50 6.00
HC20CH Connor Hellebuyck 6.00 15.00
HC20DR David Rittich 6.00 15.00
HC20JG Johnny Gaudreau 5.00 12.00
HC20JM Josh Morrissey 4.00 10.00
HC20KC Kyle Connor 5.00 12.00
HC20SM Sean Monahan 2.00 5.00

2020-21 SP Game Used '19 NHL Heritage Classic Game Used Pucks

HCPBL Bryan Little 25.00 60.00
HCPDR David Rittich 25.00 60.00
HCPEL Elias Lindholm 30.00 80.00
HCPJG Johnny Gaudreau 50.00 125.00
HCPJM Josh Morrissey 40.00 100.00
HCPKC Kyle Connor 50.00 120.00

2020-21 SP Game Used '20 NHL All Star Game Banner Jersey

BYJAD Anthony Duclair 2.50 6.00
BYJAK Anze Kopitar 5.00 12.00
BYJAP Alex Pietrangelo 2.50 6.00
BYJAV Andrei Vasilevskiy 5.00 12.00
BYJBH Braden Holtby 4.00 10.00
BYJBT Brady Tkachuk 5.00 12.00
BYJCA John Carlson 3.00 8.00
BYJCH Connor Hellebuyck 6.00 15.00
BYJCK Chris Kreider 4.00 10.00
BYJCM Connor McDavid 15.00 40.00
BYJDP David Pastrnak 8.00 20.00
BYJDR David Rittich 2.50 6.00
BYJEP Elias Pettersson 5.00 12.00
BYJES Eric Staal 3.00 8.00
BYJFA Frederik Andersen 4.00 10.00
BYJJB Jordan Binnington 5.00 12.00
BYJJE Jack Eichel 5.00 12.00
BYJJH Jonathan Huberdeau 4.00 10.00
BYJJM Jacob Markstrom 3.00 8.00
BYJJS Jaccob Slavin 2.50 6.00
BYJKL Kris Letang 4.00 10.00
BYJLD Leon Draisaitl 10.00 25.00
BYJMB Mathew Barzal 4.00 10.00
BYJMG Mark Giordano 2.00 5.00
BYJMM Mitch Marner 5.00 12.00
BYJMP Max Pacioretty 3.00 8.00
BYJMS Mark Scheifele 4.00 10.00
BYJMT Matthew Tkachuk 6.00 15.00
BYJNH Nico Hischier 5.00 12.00
BYJNM Nathan MacKinnon 12.00 30.00
BYJPE David Perron 2.50 6.00
BYJPK Patrick Kane 6.00 15.00
BYJQH Quinn Hughes 8.00 20.00
BYJRJ Roman Josi 3.00 8.00
BYJRO Ryan O'Reilly 3.00 8.00
BYJSJ Seth Jones 3.00 8.00
BYJSW Shea Weber 3.00 8.00
BYJTB Tyler Bertuzzi 2.50 6.00
BYJTH Tomas Hertl 3.00 8.00
BYJTJ Tristan Jarry 3.00 8.00
BYJTK Travis Konecny 3.00 8.00
BYJTO T.J. Oshie 3.00 8.00
BYJTS Tyler Seguin 4.00 10.00
BYJVH Victor Hedman 4.00 10.00

2020-21 SP Game Used '20 NHL All Star Game Banner Year Relics

AS20BT Brady Tkachuk 5.00 12.00
AS20CH Connor Hellebuyck 6.00 15.00
AS20CM Connor McDavid 15.00 40.00
AS20DP David Pastrnak 8.00 20.00
AS20EP Elias Pettersson 5.00 12.00
AS20JE Jack Eichel 5.00 12.00
AS20KL Kris Letang 4.00 10.00
AS20LD Leon Draisaitl 10.00 25.00
AS20MB Mathew Barzal 4.00 10.00
AS20MM Mitch Marner 5.00 12.00
AS20MS Mark Scheifele 5.00 12.00
AS20MT Matthew Tkachuk 6.00 15.00
AS20NM Nathan MacKinnon 12.00 30.00
AS20PK Patrick Kane 6.00 15.00
AS20QH Quinn Hughes 8.00 20.00
AS20RJ Roman Josi 3.00 8.00
AS20RO Ryan O'Reilly 3.00 8.00
AS20SJ Seth Jones 3.00 8.00
AS20SW Shea Weber 3.00 8.00
AS20TS Tyler Seguin 4.00 10.00
AS20VH Victor Hedman 4.00 10.00

2020-21 SP Game Used '20 NHL All Star Skills Fabrics

*PATCH/35: 1X TO 2.5X BASIC
ASVAK Anze Kopitar 4.00 10.00
ASVAP Alex Pietrangelo 2.00 5.00
ASVAV Andrei Vasilevskiy 4.00 10.00
ASVBH Braden Holtby 3.00 8.00
ASVCH Connor Hellebuyck 5.00 12.00
ASVEP Elias Pettersson 4.00 10.00
ASVES Eric Staal 2.50 6.00
ASVJC John Carlson 2.50 6.00
ASVJE Jack Eichel 4.00 10.00
ASVLD Leon Draisaitl 8.00 20.00
ASVMB Mathew Barzal 3.00 8.00
ASVMG Mark Giordano 2.50 6.00
ASVMS Mark Scheifele 4.00 10.00
ASVPK Patrick Kane 5.00 12.00
ASVRJ Roman Josi 2.50 6.00
ASVRO Ryan O'Reilly 2.50 6.00
ASVSJ Seth Jones 2.50 6.00
ASVSW Shea Weber 2.50 6.00
ASVTS Tyler Seguin 3.00 8.00
ASVVH Victor Hedman 3.00 8.00

2020-21 SP Game Used '20 NHL All Star Skills Fabrics 1st Year

*PATCH/35: 1X TO 2.5X BASIC
AS1AD Anthony Duclair 2.50 6.00
AS1BT Brady Tkachuk 5.00 12.00
AS1CK Chris Kreider 4.00 10.00
AS1DP David Perron 2.50 6.00
AS1DR David Rittich 2.50 6.00
AS1FA Frederik Andersen 4.00 10.00
AS1JB Jordan Binnington 5.00 12.00
AS1JH Jonathan Huberdeau 4.00 10.00
AS1JM Jacob Markstrom 3.00 8.00
AS1JS Jaccob Slavin 2.50 6.00
AS1MM Mitch Marner 5.00 12.00
AS1MP Max Pacioretty 3.00 8.00
AS1MT Matthew Tkachuk 6.00 15.00
AS1NH Nico Hischier 5.00 12.00
AS1QH Quinn Hughes 8.00 20.00
AS1TB Tyler Bertuzzi 2.50 6.00
AS1TH Tomas Hertl 3.00 8.00
AS1TJ Tristan Jarry 3.00 8.00
AS1TK Travis Konecny 3.00 8.00
AS1TO T.J. Oshie 3.00 8.00

2020-21 SP Game Used '20 NHL All Star Skills Fabrics Captains

*PATCH/35: 1X TO 2.5X BASIC
ASCCM Connor McDavid 20.00 50.00
ASCDP David Pastrnak 10.00 25.00
ASCKL Kris Letang 5.00 12.00
ASCNM Nathan MacKinnon 15.00 40.00

2020-21 SP Game Used '20 NHL All Star Skills Fabrics Quad

ASQHAVJ Holtby/Jarry
Vasilevskiy/Andersen 6.00 15.00
ASQKKSD Kane/Seguin
Draisaitl/Kopitar 12.00 30.00
ASQLMMP Pastrnak/Letang
MacKinnon/McDavid 20.00 50.00
ASQMBHR Binnington/Hellebuyck
Markstrom/Rittich 8.00 20.00
ASQMTPT Tkachuk/Tkachuk
Marner/Pettersson 8.00 20.00
ASQOBSH Oshie/Hischier
Barzal/Slavin 6.00 15.00
ASQPOSH O'Reilly/Scheifele
Pacioretty/Hertl 6.00 15.00
ASQSPHE Eichel/Huberdeau
Perron/Staal 6.00 15.00
ASQWCHJ Hedman/Weber
Carlson/Jones 5.00 12.00

2020-21 SP Game Used '20 NHL All Star Skills Materials Net Cord

ASNCAD Anthony Duclair 10.00 25.00
ASNCAK Anze Kopitar 20.00 50.00
ASNCAP Alex Pietrangelo 10.00 25.00
ASNCAV Andrei Vasilevskiy 20.00 50.00
ASNCBH Braden Holtby 15.00 40.00
ASNCBT Brady Tkachuk 20.00 50.00
ASNCCK Chris Kreider 15.00 40.00
ASNCCM Connor McDavid 60.00 150.00
ASNCDP David Pastrnak 30.00 80.00
ASNCDR David Rittich 10.00 25.00
ASNCEP Elias Pettersson 20.00 50.00
ASNCES Eric Staal 12.00 30.00
ASNCFA Frederik Andersen 15.00 40.00
ASNCHE Connor Hellebuyck 25.00 60.00
ASNCJB Jordan Binnington 20.00 50.00
ASNCJC John Carlson 12.00 30.00
ASNCJE Jack Eichel 20.00 50.00
ASNCJH Jonathan Huberdeau 15.00 40.00
ASNCJM Jacob Markstrom 12.00 30.00
ASNCJS Jaccob Slavin 10.00 25.00
ASNCKL Kris Letang 15.00 40.00
ASNCLD Leon Draisaitl 40.00 100.00
ASNCMB Mathew Barzal 15.00 40.00
ASNCMG Mark Giordano 12.00 30.00
ASNCMM Mitch Marner 20.00 50.00
ASNCMP Max Pacioretty 12.00 30.00
ASNCMS Mark Scheifele 20.00 50.00
ASNCMT Matthew Tkachuk 25.00 60.00
ASNCNH Nico Hischier 20.00 50.00
ASNCNM Nathan MacKinnon 50.00 120.00
ASNCPE David Perron 10.00 25.00
ASNCPK Patrick Kane 25.00 60.00
ASNCQH Quinn Hughes 30.00 80.00
ASNCRJ Roman Josi 12.00 30.00
ASNCRO Ryan O'Reilly 12.00 30.00
ASNCSJ Seth Jones 12.00 30.00
ASNCSW Shea Weber 12.00 30.00
ASNCTB Tyler Bertuzzi 10.00 25.00
ASNCTH Tomas Hertl 12.00 30.00
ASNCTJ Tristan Jarry 12.00 30.00
ASNCTK Travis Konecny 12.00 30.00
ASNCTO T.J. Oshie 12.00 30.00
ASNCTS Tyler Seguin 15.00 40.00
ASNCVH Victor Hedman 15.00 40.00

2020-21 SP Game Used '20 NHL All Star Skills Relic Blends

ASBAD Anthony Duclair 2.00 5.00
ASBAK Anze Kopitar 4.00 10.00
ASBAP Alex Pietrangelo 2.00 5.00
ASBAV Andrei Vasilevskiy 4.00 10.00
ASBBH Braden Holtby 3.00 8.00
ASBBT Brady Tkachuk 4.00 10.00
ASBCH Connor Hellebuyck 5.00 12.00
ASBCK Chris Kreider 3.00 8.00
ASBCM Connor McDavid 12.00 30.00
ASBDP David Perron 2.00 5.00
ASBDR David Rittich 2.00 5.00
ASBEP Elias Pettersson 4.00 10.00
ASBES Eric Staal 2.50 6.00
ASBFA Frederik Andersen 3.00 8.00
ASBJB Jordan Binnington 4.00 10.00
ASBJC John Carlson 2.50 6.00
ASBJE Jack Eichel 4.00 10.00
ASBJH Jonathan Huberdeau 3.00 8.00
ASBJM Jacob Markstrom 2.50 6.00
ASBJS Jaccob Slavin 2.00 5.00
ASBKL Kris Letang 3.00 8.00
ASBLD Leon Draisaitl 8.00 20.00
ASBMB Mathew Barzal 3.00 8.00
ASBMG Mark Giordano 2.50 6.00
ASBMM Mitch Marner 4.00 10.00
ASBMP Max Pacioretty 2.50 6.00
ASBMS Mark Scheifele 4.00 10.00
ASBMT Matthew Tkachuk 5.00 12.00
ASBNH Nico Hischier 4.00 10.00
ASBNM Nathan MacKinnon 10.00 25.00
ASBPA David Pastrnak 6.00 15.00
ASBPK Patrick Kane 5.00 12.00
ASBQH Quinn Hughes 6.00 15.00
ASBRO Ryan O'Reilly 2.50 6.00
ASBSJ Seth Jones 2.50 6.00
ASBSW Shea Weber 2.50 6.00
ASBTB Tyler Bertuzzi 2.00 5.00
ASBTH Tomas Hertl 2.50 6.00
ASBTJ Tristan Jarry 2.50 6.00
ASBTO T.J. Oshie 2.50 6.00
ASBTS Tyler Seguin 3.00 8.00
ASBVH Victor Hedman 3.00 8.00

2020-21 SP Game Used '20 NHL Stadium Series Banner Jersey

BYJBL Blake Lizotte 2.00 5.00
BYJDD Drew Doughty 4.00 10.00
BYJGL Gabriel Landeskog 4.00 10.00
BYJIC Ian Cole 2.00 5.00
BYJJC Jeff Carter 2.50 6.00
BYJJD Joonas Donskoi 2.00 5.00
BYJJQ Jonathan Quick 4.00 10.00
BYJKM Kurtis MacDermid 2.00 5.00
BYJKO Adrian Kempe 3.00 8.00
BYJMA Cale Makar 8.00 20.00
BYJMC Matt Calvert 2.00 5.00
BYJMN Matt Nieto 2.00 5.00
BYJPB Pierre-Edouard Bellemare 2.00 5.00
BYJTT Tyler Toffoli 3.00 8.00

2020-21 SP Game Used '20 NHL Stadium Series Banner Year Relics

SS20AI Alex Iafallo 2.50 6.00
SS20AK Anze Kopitar 6.00 15.00
SS20JQ Jonathan Quick 5.00 12.00
SS20MR Mikko Rantanen 10.00 25.00
SS20NM Nathan MacKinnon 15.00 40.00
SS20SG Samuel Girard 2.50 6.00
SS20TT Tyler Toffoli 4.00 10.00

2020-21 SP Game Used '20 NHL Stadium Series Fabrics

*PATCH: .75X TO 2X BASIC
SSFAK Adrian Kempe 3.00 8.00
SSFBL Blake Lizotte 2.00 5.00
SSFCM Cale Makar 8.00 20.00
SSFDD Drew Doughty 4.00 10.00
SSFGL Gabriel Landeskog 4.00 10.00
SSFIC Ian Cole 2.00 5.00
SSFJC Jeff Carter 2.50 6.00
SSFJD Joonas Donskoi 2.00 5.00
SSFJQ Jonathan Quick 4.00 10.00
SSFTT Tyler Toffoli 3.00 8.00

2020-21 SP Game Used '20 NHL Stadium Series Fabrics Dual

STATED ODDS 1:24 H/E 3.00 8.00
*PATCH/25: 1X TO 2.5X BASIC
SSDFCD J.Carter/D.Doughty 4.00 10.00
SSDFCN I.Cole/M.Nieto 2.00 5.00
SSDFDQ D.Doughty/J.Quick 4.00 10.00
SSDFKC A.Kempe/J.Carter 3.00 8.00
SSDFML C.Makar/G.Landeskog 8.00 20.00
SSDFTL T.Toffoli/B.Lizotte 3.00 8.00

2020-21 SP Game Used '20 NHL Stadium Series Game Used Pucks

SSPAI Alex Iafallo 15.00 40.00
SSPAK Anze Kopitar 40.00 100.00
SSPCM Cale Makar 60.00 150.00
SSPDD Drew Doughty 30.00 80.00
SSPJQ Jonathan Quick 30.00 80.00
SSPMR Mikko Rantanen 60.00 150.00
SSPNM Nathan MacKinnon 100.00 250.00
SSPSG Samuel Girard 15.00 40.00
SSPTT Tyler Toffoli 25.00 60.00

2020-21 SP Game Used '20 NHL Stadium Series Materials Net Cord

SSNCAI Alex Iafallo 8.00 20.00
SSNCAK Anze Kopitar 20.00 50.00
SSNCAM Alec Martinez 8.00 20.00
SSNCCM Cale Makar 30.00 80.00
SSNCDD Drew Doughty 15.00 40.00
SSNCGL Gabriel Landeskog 15.00 40.00
SSNCJC Jeff Carter 10.00 25.00
SSNCJD Joonas Donskoi 12.00 30.00
SSNCJQ Jonathan Quick 15.00 40.00
SSNCKE Adrian Kempe 12.00 30.00
SSNCMR Mikko Rantanen 30.00 80.00
SSNCNM Nathan MacKinnon 50.00 125.00
SSNCPG Philipp Grubauer 12.00 30.00
SSNCSG Samuel Girard 8.00 20.00
SSNCTT Tyler Toffoli 12.00 30.00

2020-21 SP Game Used '20 NHL Winter Classic Banner Year Relics

WC20BB Ben Bishop 5.00 12.00
WC20BC Blake Comeau 4.00 10.00
WC20FF Filip Forsberg 10.00 25.00
WC20JB Jamie Benn 6.00 15.00
WC20JK John Klingberg 6.00 15.00
WC20MD Matt Duchene 6.00 15.00
WC20RJ Roman Josi 6.00 15.00

2020-21 SP Game Used '20 NHL Winter Classic Game Used Pucks

WCPAR Alexander Radulov 25.00 60.00
WCPBB Ben Bishop 20.00 50.00
WCPBC Blake Comeau 15.00 40.00
WCPDF Dante Fabbro 25.00 60.00
WCPJK John Klingberg 25.00 60.00
WCPMD Matt Duchene 25.00 60.00
WCPPR Pekka Rinne 25.00 60.00
WCPRJ Roman Josi 25.00 60.00
WCPTS Tyler Seguin 30.00 80.00

2020-21 SP Game Used '20 NHL Winter Classic Materials Net Cord

WCNDAR Alexander Radulov 30.00 80.00
WCNDBB Ben Bishop 60.00 150.00
WCNDCP Corey Perry 50.00 120.00
WCNDDF Dante Fabbro 30.00 80.00
WCNDFF Filip Forsberg 25.00 60.00
WCNDJB Jamie Benn 40.00 100.00
WCNDJK John Klingberg 30.00 80.00
WCNDJO Ryan Johansen 25.00 60.00
WCNDJP Joe Pavelski 60.00 150.00
WCNDMD Matt Duchene 30.00 80.00
WCNDMH Miro Heiskanen 40.00 100.00
WCNDPR Pekka Rinne 30.00 80.00
WCNDRE Ryan Ellis 25.00 60.00
WCNDRJ Roman Josi 30.00 80.00
WCNDTS Tyler Seguin 40.00 100.00

2020-21 SP Game Used Distinctions Materials

*PATCH/25: 1X TO 2.5X BASIC
DMAL Alexis Lafreniere 12.00 30.00
DMAM Auston Matthews 12.00 30.00
DMAO Alex Ovechkin 12.00 30.00
DMAS Andrei Svechnikov 4.00 10.00
DMBM Brad Marchand 6.00 15.00
DMCG Claude Giroux 3.00 8.00
DMCM Connor McDavid 15.00 40.00
DMCP Carey Price 6.00 15.00
DMDL Dylan Larkin 4.00 10.00
DMDP David Pastrnak 8.00 20.00
DMEM Evgeni Malkin 6.00 15.00
DMEP Elias Pettersson 5.00 12.00
DMFK Erik Karlsson 4.00 10.00
DMJE Jack Eichel 5.00 12.00
DMJG Johnny Gaudreau 5.00 12.00
DMKC Kyle Connor 5.00 12.00
DMLD Leon Draisaitl 10.00 25.00
DMMB Mathew Barzal 4.00 10.00
DMMS Mark Stone 4.00 10.00
DMNH Nico Hischier 5.00 12.00
DMNK Nikita Kucherov 6.00 15.00
DMNM Nathan MacKinnon 12.00 30.00
DMPL Patrik Laine 4.00 10.00
DMRO Ryan O'Reilly 3.00 8.00
DMSC Sidney Crosby 12.00 30.00
DMSE Tyler Seguin 4.00 10.00
DMTS Tim Stutzle 8.00 20.00

2020-21 SP Game Used Draft Day Marks Rookies

DDMAL Alexis Lafreniere/350* 250.00 600.00
DDMBB Bowen Byram/175* 60.00 150.00
DDMBE Ethan Bear/140* 15.00 40.00
DDMCF Cal Foote/175* 40.00 100.00
DDMCM Connor McMichael/315* 50.00 125.00
DDMCP Cayden Primeau/245* 30.00 80.00
DDMDC Dylan Cozens/210* 50.00 150.00
DDMEM Elvis Merzlikins/350* 60.00 150.00
DDMGV Gabe Vilardi/245* 30.00 80.00
DDMHO Nils Hoglander/315* 30.00 80.00
DDMIM Ian Mitchell/280* 25.00 60.00
DDMJE Jake Evans/175* 30.00 80.00
DDMJM John Marino/210* 30.00 80.00
DDMJN Josh Norris/210* 50.00 125.00
DDMJR Jason Robertson/315* 125.00 300.00
DDMKB Kieffer Bellows/245* 25.00 60.00
DDMKK Kirill Kaprizov/280* 300.00 800.00
DDMLF Liam Foudy/175* 80.00 200.00
DDMMA Mikey Anderson/280* 30.00 80.00
DDMMK Martin Kaut/140* 30.00 80.00
DDMOJ Olli Juolevi/245* 30.00 80.00
DDMPJ Pierre-Olivier Joseph/210* 20.00 50.00
DDMPK Peyton Krebs/175* 50.00 125.00
DDMSB Shane Bowers/210* 25.00 60.00
DDMTB Tyler Benson/210* 30.00 80.00
DDMTD Ty Dellandrea/350* 30.00 80.00
DDMTH Thomas Harley/210* 25.00 60.00
DDMTL Timothy Liljegren/315* 25.00 60.00
DDMTS Tim Stutzle/245* 60.00 150.00
DDMTS Ty Smith/175* 50.00 125.00

2020-21 SP Game Used Draft Day Marks Veterans

DDMDH Dany Heatley/70* 60.00 150.00
DDMNH Niklas Hjalmarsson/110* 50.00 125.00

2020-21 SP Game Used Frameworks Materials

FAL Alexis Lafreniere 30.00 80.00
FAM Auston Matthews 30.00 80.00
FAO Alex Ovechkin 30.00 80.00
FBH Brett Hull 15.00 40.00
FCH Carter Hart 25.00 60.00
FCM Connor McDavid 40.00 100.00
FCP Carey Price 50.00 125.00
FDP David Pastrnak 20.00 50.00
FJE Jack Eichel 12.00 30.00
FJH Jonathan Huberdeau 10.00 25.00
FJS Joe Sakic 15.00 40.00
FLD Leon Draisaitl 25.00 60.00
FMA Mark Scheifele 12.00 30.00
FMB Mathew Barzal 10.00 25.00
FML Mario Lemieux 30.00 80.00
FMR Mike Richter 20.00 50.00
FMS Mark Stone 20.00 50.00
FNK Nikita Kucherov 12.00 30.00
FNM Nathan MacKinnon 30.00 80.00
FPK Patrick Kane 15.00 40.00
FQH Quinn Hughes 30.00 80.00
FRJ Roman Josi 8.00 20.00
FSA Sebastian Aho 12.00 30.00
FSC Sidney Crosby 30.00 80.00
FST Tim Stutzle 20.00 50.00
FSY Steve Yzerman 60.00 150.00
FTS Tyler Seguin 10.00 25.00

2020-21 SP Game Used Inked Rookie Sweaters Patch

RSBB Bowen Byram 40.00 100.00
RSGL Gustav Lindstrom 15.00 40.00
RSGV Gabe Vilardi 30.00 80.00
RSJN Josh Norris 60.00 150.00
RSJR Jason Robertson 80.00 200.00
RSKB Kieffer Bellows 15.00 40.00
RSKU Philipp Kurashev 25.00 60.00
RSLF Liam Foudy 20.00 50.00
RSMG Morgan Geekie 20.00 50.00
RSNB Nicolas Beaudin 25.00 60.00
RSNR Nick Robertson 30.00 80.00
RSOJ Olli Juolevi 20.00 50.00
RSPF Pavel Francouz 25.00 60.00
RSPK Peyton Krebs 60.00 150.00
RSSB Shane Bowers 15.00 40.00
RSTB Tyler Benson 20.00 50.00
RSTD Ty Dellandrea 20.00 50.00
RSTH Thomas Harley 30.00 80.00
RSTL Timothy Liljegren 20.00 50.00
RSTS Tim Stutzle 80.00 200.00
RSVS Victor Soderstrom 25.00 60.00

2020-21 SP Game Used Piece of History

400K Olaf Kolzig 8.00 20.00
50JC John LeClair 15.00 40.00
50JJ Jaromir Jagr 25.00 60.00
50SC Sidney Crosby 30.00 80.00
100BM Brad Marchand 15.00 40.00
100DH Dany Heatley 20.00 50.00
100EM Evgeni Malkin 15.00 40.00
100HS Henrik Sedin 15.00 40.00
100LD Leon Draisaitl 25.00 60.00
100NB Nicklas Backstrom 8.00 20.00

2020-21 SP Game Used Rookie Relic Blends

RBAA Alexander Alexeyev 2.50 6.00
RBAL Alexis Lafreniere 30.00 80.00
RBBB Bowen Byram 6.00 15.00
RBGL Gustav Lindstrom 2.50 6.00
RBGV Gabe Vilardi 5.00 12.00
RBJN Josh Norris 5.00 12.00
RBJR Jason Robertson 8.00 20.00
RBKB Kieffer Bellows 2.50 6.00
RBKU Philipp Kurashev 4.00 10.00
RBLF Liam Foudy 3.00 8.00
RBMG Morgan Geekie 3.00 8.00
RBNB Nicolas Beaudin 3.00 8.00
RBNR Nick Robertson 5.00 12.00
RBOJ Olli Juolevi 3.00 8.00
RBPF Pavel Francouz 4.00 10.00
RBPK Peyton Krebs 5.00 12.00
RBSB Shane Bowers 2.50 6.00
RBTB Tyler Benson 3.00 8.00
RBTD Ty Dellandrea 3.00 8.00
RBTH Thomas Harley 5.00 12.00
RBTL Timothy Liljegren 3.00 8.00
RBTS Tim Stutzle 30.00 80.00
RBVS Victor Soderstrom 2.50 6.00

2020-21 SP Game Used Rookie Sweaters

RSAA Alexander Alexeyev 2.50 6.00
RSAF Alexis Lafreniere 20.00 50.00
RSBB Bowen Byram 6.00 15.00
RSGL Gustav Lindstrom 2.50 6.00
RSGV Gabe Vilardi 5.00 12.00
RSJN Josh Norris 5.00 12.00
RSJR Jason Robertson 8.00 20.00
RSKB Kieffer Bellows 2.50 6.00
RSKU Philipp Kurashev 4.00 10.00
RSLF Liam Foudy 3.00 8.00
RSMG Morgan Geekie 3.00 8.00
RSNB Nicolas Beaudin 3.00 8.00
RSNR Nick Robertson 5.00 12.00
RSOJ Olli Juolevi 3.00 8.00
RSPF Pavel Francouz 4.00 10.00
RSPK Peyton Krebs 5.00 12.00

RSSB Shane Bowers 2.50 6.00
RSTB Tyler Benson 3.00 8.00
RSTD Ty Dellandrea 3.00 8.00
RSTH Thomas Harley 5.00 12.00
RSTL Timothy Liljegren 3.00 8.00
RSTS Tim Stutzle 15.00 40.00
RSVS Victor Soderstrom 3.00 8.00

2020-21 SP Game Used Signing Day Marks Rookies

SDMIM Ilya Mikheyev/280* 40.00 100.00

2020-21 SP Game Used Signing Day Marks Veterans

SDMMS Martin St. Louis/70* 40.00 100.00

2021-22 SP Game Used Blue Autographs

*VETS: 1.5X TO 4X RED.FRAG
*ROOKIES: 1.25X TO 2X RED.FRAG
145 Trevor Zegras B 80.00 200.00
150 Cole Caufield A 80.00 200.00

2021-22 SP Game Used Gold Fragment

*GOLD.FRAG: 1.5X TO 4X RED.FRAG

2021-22 SP Game Used Gold Jersey Autographs

*VETS: 3X TO 8X RED.FRAG
*ROOKIES: 2X TO 5X RED.FRAG
1 Connor McDavid/35 200.00 500.00
2 Sidney Crosby/35 150.00 400.00
3 Auston Matthews/35 200.00 500.00
19 Tim Stutzle/99 50.00 125.00
150 Cole Caufield/49 300.00 800.00

2021-22 SP Game Used Gold Premium Memorabilia

*VETS: 2X TO 5X RED.FRAG
*ROOKIES: 1.5X TO 4X RED.FRAG

2021-22 SP Game Used Red Fragment

1 Connor McDavid 8.00 20.00
2 Sidney Crosby 6.00 15.00
3 Auston Matthews 6.00 15.00
4 Patrick Kane 3.00 8.00
5 Kyle Connor 2.50 6.00
6 Patrice Bergeron 2.00 5.00
7 David Pastrnak 4.00 10.00
8 Cale Makar 4.00 10.00
9 Leon Draisaitl 5.00 12.00
10 Kirill Kaprizov 5.00 12.00
11 Jack Hughes 4.00 10.00
12 Artemi Panarin 3.00 8.00
13 Mitch Marner 2.50 6.00
14 Brayden Point 2.00 5.00
15 Quinn Hughes 4.00 10.00
16 Johnny Gaudreau 2.50 6.00
17 Sebastian Aho 2.50 6.00
18 Alexis Lafreniere 2.50 6.00
19 Tim Stutzle 2.00 5.00
20 Kris Letang 2.00 5.00
21 Ryan O'Reilly 1.50 4.00
22 Nick Suzuki 3.00 8.00
23 Miro Heiskanen 2.00 5.00
24 Anze Kopitar 2.50 6.00
25 Brady Tkachuk 2.50 6.00
26 Andrei Vasilevskiy 2.50 6.00
27 Elias Pettersson 2.50 6.00
28 Brent Burns 1.50 4.00
29 Mark Stone 2.00 5.00
30 Nathan MacKinnon 6.00 15.00
31 Jared Spurgeon 1.50 4.00
32 Maxime Comtois 1.25 3.00
33 Thatcher Demko 2.00 5.00
34 Oliver Bjorkstrand 1.25 3.00
35 Dylan Larkin 2.00 5.00
36 Jonathan Drouin 1.25 3.00
37 Martin Necas 2.50 6.00
38 Nikita Kucherov 3.00 8.00
39 Brock Nelson 1.50 4.00
40 Connor Hellebuyck 3.00 8.00
41 Juuse Saros 2.00 5.00
42 Jonathan Toews 2.50 6.00
43 Igor Shesterkin 3.00 8.00
44 Tom Wilson 1.50 4.00
45 David Perron 1.25 3.00
46 Matthew Tkachuk 3.00 8.00
47 Evgeni Malkin 3.00 8.00
48 Thomas Chabot 1.50 4.00
49 Charlie McAvoy 2.00 5.00
50 Jordan Binnington 2.50 6.00
51 Darnell Nurse 1.25 3.00
52 Roman Josi 1.50 4.00
53 John Klingberg 1.50 4.00
54 Jake Guentzel 2.50 6.00
55 Colton Parayko 1.25 3.00
56 Jonathan Marchessault 2.00 5.00
57 Brendan Gallagher 1.50 4.00
58 Sean Couturier 1.25 3.00
59 Sean Monahan 1.00 2.50
60 Carey Price 3.00 8.00
61 Shea Theodore 2.00 5.00
62 John Gibson 1.50 4.00
63 T.J. Oshie 1.50 4.00
64 Anders Lee 1.25 3.00
65 Matt Dumba 1.25 3.00
66 Ilya Samsonov 1.50 4.00
67 Tomas Hertl 1.50 4.00
68 Patrik Laine 2.00 5.00
69 Brock Boeser 2.00 5.00
70 Josh Bailey 1.25 3.00
71 Steven Stamkos 3.00 8.00
72 Andrei Svechnikov 2.00 5.00
73 Clayton Keller 2.00 5.00
74 Victor Hedman 2.00 5.00
75 Mark Scheifele 2.50 6.00
76 Jonathan Huberdeau 2.00 5.00
77 Yanni Gourde 1.25 3.00
78 Aleksander Barkov 2.50 6.00
79 Adam Fox 2.00 5.00
80 Mathew Barzal 2.00 5.00
81 Nico Hischier 2.50 6.00
82 John Tavares 2.50 6.00
83 Josh Morrissey 2.00 5.00
84 James van Riemsdyk 1.25 3.00
85 Alex DeBrincat 2.00 5.00
86 Tyler Bertuzzi 1.25 3.00
87 Jack Roslovic 1.00 2.50
88 Max Pacioretty 1.50 4.00
89 Carter Hart 1.50 4.00
90 Joe Pavelski 2.00 5.00
91 Brad Marchand 3.00 8.00
92 Jakob Chychrun 1.50 4.00
93 Jordan Eberle 1.50 4.00
94 Dylan Cozens 1.50 4.00
95 Mark Giordano 1.50 4.00
96 Ryan Nugent-Hopkins 2.00 5.00
97 Philipp Grubauer 1.50 4.00
98 Dustin Brown 1.50 4.00
99 Jean-Gabriel Pageau 1.00 2.50
100 Alex Ovechkin 6.00 15.00
101 Wayne Gretzky 10.00 25.00
102 Steve Yzerman 4.00 10.00
103 Jaromir Jagr 5.00 12.00
104 Teemu Selanne 3.00 8.00
105 Dominik Hasek 2.50 6.00
106 Saku Koivu 1.50 4.00
107 Joe Sakic 3.00 8.00
108 Guy Lafleur 2.00 5.00
109 Martin Brodeur 4.00 10.00
110 Brett Hull 2.50 6.00
111 Phil Esposito 2.50 6.00
112 Cam Neely 1.25 3.00
113 Pekka Rinne 1.50 4.00
114 Bernie Nicholls 1.25 3.00
115 Mike Modano 2.50 6.00
116 Eric Lindros 2.50 6.00
117 Grant Fuhr 2.50 6.00
118 Marcel Dionne 2.00 5.00
119 Ray Bourque 2.50 6.00
120 Vincent Lecavalier 1.50 4.00
121 Cole Sillinger 3.00 8.00
122 Tanner Jeannot 2.00 5.00
123 Justin Richards 2.00 5.00
124 Alexander Holtz 3.00 8.00
125 Jeremy Swayman 6.00 15.00
126 Cam York 2.00 5.00
127 Keaton Middleton 2.00 5.00
128 Aliaksei Protas 2.00 5.00
129 John-Jason Peterka 4.00 10.00
130 Vasily Podkolzin 2.50 6.00
131 Adam Beckman 2.00 5.00
132 Wade Allison 2.00 5.00
133 Seth Jarvis 5.00 12.00
134 Kyle Burroughs 2.00 5.00
135 Alex Newhook 3.00 8.00
136 Brandon Duhaime 2.00 5.00
137 Zac Jones 2.50 6.00
138 Alex Barre-Boulet 2.00 5.00
139 Scott Perunovich 2.00 5.00
140 Spencer Knight 4.00 10.00
141 Oskar Steen 2.50 6.00
142 David Farrance 2.00 5.00
143 Dawson Mercer 5.00 12.00
144 Kole Lind 2.50 6.00
145 Trevor Zegras 4.00 10.00
146 Mike Hardman 2.00 5.00
147 Rasmus Kupari 2.00 5.00
148 Jan Jenik 2.50 6.00
149 Jonas Rondbjerg 2.00 5.00
150 Cole Caufield 8.00 20.00
151 Tanner Laczynski 2.00 5.00
152 Morgan Barron 1.50 4.00
153 Joe Veleno 2.50 6.00
154 Jake Neighbours 4.00 10.00
155 Jamie Drysdale 3.00 8.00
156 Arttu Ruotsalainen 2.00 5.00
157 Riley Damiani 2.00 5.00
158 Ross Colton 2.50 6.00
159 Max Willman 1.25 3.00
160 Cole Perfetti 4.00 10.00
161 Jack Ahcan 2.00 5.00
162 Wyatt Kalynuk 2.00 5.00
163 Joey Keane 1.50 4.00
164 Ivan Prosvetov 2.00 5.00
165 Grigori Denisenko 2.50 6.00
166 Jake Leschyshyn 2.00 5.00
167 Sampo Ranta 2.00 5.00
168 Radim Zohorna 2.00 5.00
169 Mattias Samuelsson 2.00 5.00
170 Quinton Byfield 5.00 12.00
171 Jesse Ylonen 2.00 5.00
172 Ukko-Pekka Luukkonen 3.00 8.00
173 Garrett Pilon 2.50 6.00
174 Pavel Dorofeyev 2.50 6.00
175 Calen Addison 2.00 5.00
176 Jonah Gadjovich 2.00 5.00
177 Jacob Bryson 2.00 5.00
178 Hendrix Lapierre 2.00 5.00
179 Karel Vejmelka 2.50 6.00
180 Mason McTavish 4.00 10.00
181 Tyce Thompson 2.00 5.00
182 Jacob Bernard-Docker 2.00 5.00
183 Parker Kelly 2.00 5.00
184 Philip Tomasino 2.50 6.00
185 Shane Pinto 3.00 8.00
186 Brett Murray 2.00 5.00
187 Jasper Weatherby 2.00 5.00
188 Anton Lundell 4.00 10.00
189 Filip Gustavsson 4.00 10.00
190 William Eklund 5.00 12.00
191 Benoit-Olivier Groulx 2.00 5.00
192 Lane Pederson 2.00 5.00
193 Alex Turcotte 2.50 6.00
194 Nils Lundkvist 2.00 5.00
195 Moritz Seider 5.00 12.00
196 Logan Thompson 5.00 12.00
197 Tarmo Reunanen 2.00 5.00
198 Taylor Raddysh 3.00 8.00
199 Matthew Phillips 2.00 5.00
200 Lucas Raymond 6.00 15.00

2021-22 SP Game Used Red Jerseys

*VETS: .75X TO 2X RED.FRAG
*ROOKIES: .6X TO 1.5X RED.FRAG

2022-23 SP Game Used Red

1 Moritz Seider/221 2.00 5.00
2 Connor McDavid/225 8.00 20.00
3 Peyton Krebs/222 1.25 3.00
4 Brady Tkachuk/223 2.50 6.00
5 Ryan O'Reilly/232 1.50 4.00
6 Brad Marchand/234 3.00 8.00
7 Mathew Barzal/225 2.00 5.00
8 Trevor Zegras/221 1.50 4.00
9 Steven Stamkos/233 3.00 8.00
10 Jonathan Marchessault/232 2.00 5.00
11 Kirill Kaprizov/225 5.00 12.00
12 Mitch Marner/225 2.50 6.00
13 Elias Lindholm/228 1.50 4.00
14 Artemi Panarin/231 3.00 8.00
15 James van Riemsdyk/233 1.25 3.00
16 Brandon Saad/230 1.25 3.00
17 Elias Pettersson/224 2.50 6.00
18 Jason Robertson/222 2.50 6.00
19 Quinn Hughes/223 4.00 10.00
20 Lucas Raymond/220 2.50 6.00
21 Mikko Rantanen/226 4.00 10.00
22 Nico Hischier/224 2.50 6.00
23 Spencer Knight/221 1.50 4.00
24 Joe Pavelski/238 2.00 5.00
25 Alexis Lafreniere/221 2.50 6.00
26 Anze Kopitar/235 2.50 6.00
27 Miro Heiskanen/223 2.00 5.00
28 Cam Atkinson/233 1.50 4.00
29 Roope Hintz/226 2.00 5.00
30 Brock Boeser/225 2.00 5.00
31 Sidney Crosby/235 6.00 15.00
32 Philip Tomasino/220 1.00 2.50
33 Robert Thomas/223 1.50 4.00
34 Drake Batherson/224 1.50 4.00
35 Carey Price/235 3.00 8.00
36 Dawson Mercer/221 2.00 5.00
37 Seth Jarvis/221 2.00 5.00
38 Matthew Tkachuk/225 3.00 8.00
39 Sebastian Aho/225 2.50 6.00
40 Jake Guentzel/228 2.50 6.00
41 Blake Coleman/231 1.25 3.00
42 Adam Fox/225 2.00 5.00
43 Evgeny Kuznetsov/230 2.00 5.00
44 Filip Forsberg/228 2.50 6.00
45 Patrick Kane/234 3.00 8.00
46 Igor Shesterkin/227 3.00 8.00
47 Cale Makar/224 4.00 10.00
48 Tom Wilson/228 1.50 4.00
49 Anthony Beauvillier/225 1.00 2.50
50 Rasmus Dahlin/222 2.00 5.00
51 Jordan Eberle/232 1.50 4.00
52 Jaden Schwartz/231 1.25 3.00
53 Clayton Keller/223 2.00 5.00
54 Nick Suzuki/223 3.00 8.00
55 Nick Robertson/221 1.50 4.00
56 John Gibson/229 1.50 4.00
57 John Tavares/232 2.50 6.00
58 Victor Hedman/232 2.00 5.00
59 David Pastrnak/226 4.00 10.00
60 Nick Schmaltz/227 1.25 3.00
61 Tim Stutzle/221 2.00 5.00
62 Quinton Byfield/220 2.00 5.00
63 Kris Letang/235 2.00 5.00
64 Jack Roslovic/226 1.00 2.50
65 Mark Scheifele/229 2.50 6.00
66 Sean Couturier/230 1.25 3.00
67 Gabriel Landeskog/230 2.00 5.00
68 Cole Sillinger/219 1.25 3.00
69 Andrei Vasilevskiy/227 2.50 6.00
70 Ukko-Pekka Luukkonen/223 1.25 3.00
71 Logan Couture/233 2.00 5.00
72 Alex Pietrangelo/233 1.25 3.00
73 Brock Nelson/231 1.50 4.00
74 Mats Zuccarello/235 1.50 4.00
75 Jared McCann/226 1.25 3.00
76 Jonathan Toews/234 2.50 6.00
77 Nathan MacKinnon/227 6.00 15.00
78 Nikolaj Ehlers/226 1.50 4.00
79 Erik Karlsson/232 2.00 5.00
80 Alex Ovechkin/237 6.00 15.00
81 Jonathan Huberdeau/229 2.00 5.00
82 Jeremy Swayman/224 2.50 6.00
83 Jake Oettinger/224 2.50 6.00
84 Kyle Connor/220 2.50 6.00
85 Zach Werenski/225 2.50 6.00
86 Ryan Nugent-Hopkins/225 2.00 5.00
87 Roman Josi/232 1.50 4.00
88 Leon Draisaitl/227 5.00 12.00
89 Josh Norris/223 1.50 4.00
90 Joel Eriksson Ek/227 1.25 3.00
91 Evgeni Malkin/235 3.00 8.00
92 Cole Caufield/222 3.00 8.00
93 Tomas Hertl/229 1.50 4.00
94 Patrice Bergeron/236 2.00 5.00
95 Aleksander Barkov/227 2.50 6.00
96 Jack Hughes/221 4.00 10.00
97 Seth Jones/228 1.50 4.00
98 Auston Matthews/225 6.00 15.00
99 Darcy Kuemper/232 1.50 4.00
100 Andrei Svechnikov/223 2.00 5.00
101 Tage Thompson/225 2.00 5.00
102 Alex DeBrincat/225 2.00 5.00
103 Brent Burns/237 1.50 4.00
104 Ryan Strome/229 1.50 4.00
105 Johnny Gaudreau/229 2.50 6.00
106 Travis Konecny/225 1.50 4.00
107 Kirby Dach/222 1.50 4.00
108 Alex Iafallo/229 1.00 2.50
109 Dylan Larkin/225 2.00 5.00
110 Elvis Merzlikins/228 1.50 4.00
111 Jordan Kyrou/224 1.50 4.00
112 Marcus Foligno/231 1.25 3.00
113 Jonathan Quick/236 2.00 5.00
114 Anthony Cirelli/225 1.25 3.00
115 Vitek Vanecek/227 1.50 4.00
116 Jaccob Slavin/228 1.25 3.00
117 Sam Bennett/226 2.50 6.00
118 Jack Eichel/226 2.50 6.00
119 Robby Fabbri/227 1.00 2.50
120 Marc-Andre Fleury/238 3.00 8.00
121 Bobby Orr/274 6.00 15.00
122 Mario Lemieux/257 6.00 15.00
123 Wayne Gretzky/262 10.00 25.00
124 Teemu Selanne/252 3.00 8.00
125 Steve Yzerman/257 4.00 10.00
126 Patrick Roy/257 4.00 10.00
127 Ray Bourque/262 2.50 6.00
128 Dominik Hasek/257 2.50 6.00
129 Brett Hull/258 3.00 8.00
130 Martin Brodeur/250 4.00 10.00
131 Nicklas Lidstrom/252 1.50 4.00
132 Marcel Dionne/271 2.00 5.00
133 Jarome Iginla/245 2.00 5.00
134 Luc Robitaille/257 1.50 4.00
135 Ryan Getzlaf/237 1.50 4.00
136 Billy Smith/272 1.50 4.00
137 Keith Tkachuk/250 1.50 4.00
138 Pekka Rinne/240 1.50 4.00
139 Henrik Lundqvist/240 4.00 10.00
140 Grant Fuhr/260 2.50 6.00
141 Joe Sakic/253 3.00 8.00
142 Sergei Zubov/252 1.25 3.00
143 Jaromir Jagr/250 5.00 12.00
144 Vincent Lecavalier/242 1.50 4.00
145 John Vanbiesbrouck/259 1.50 4.00
146 Larry Robinson/271 1.50 4.00
147 Phil Esposito/281 2.50 6.00
148 Mark Messier/262 3.00 8.00
149 Eric Lindros/250 2.50 6.00
150 Paul Coffey/261 1.50 4.00
151 Michael Eyssimont/226 2.00 5.00
152 Erik Kallgren/226 2.00 5.00
153 Filip Hallander/222 2.00 5.00
154 Isaac Ratcliffe/223 2.00 5.00
155 Hunter Drew/224 2.00 5.00
156 Zack Hayes/223 1.50 4.00
157 Trey Fix-Wolansky/223 2.00 5.00
158 Samuel Fagemo/222 1.50 4.00
159 Kaedan Korczak/222 1.50 4.00
160 Jordan Spence/222 2.00 5.00
161 Mark Kastelic/223 1.50 4.00
162 Lukas Dostal/222 4.00 10.00
163 Pyotr Kochetkov/223 4.00 10.00
164 Jordan Harris/222 2.50 6.00
165 Nick Abruzzese/223 2.00 5.00
166 Matias Maccelli/222 3.00 8.00
167 Chase Pearson/225 1.50 4.00
168 Matt Boldy/221 6.00 15.00
169 Marc McLaughlin/223 2.00 5.00
170 Ronnie Attard/223 2.00 5.00
171 Brayden Tracey/221 1.50 4.00
172 Matty Beniers/220 5.00 12.00
173 Wyatt Johnston/219 8.00 20.00
174 Owen Power/220 4.00 10.00
175 Alex Vlasic/221 1.50 4.00
176 Thomas Bordeleau/221 2.00 5.00
177 Jacob Perreault/220 2.00 5.00
178 Jack Quinn/221 3.00 8.00
179 Lukas Reichel/220 4.00 10.00
180 Kent Johnson/220 4.00 10.00
181 Dylan Holloway/223 4.00 10.00
182 Marco Rossi/221 5.00 12.00
183 Reilly Walsh/223 2.00 5.00
184 Braden Schneider/221 3.00 8.00
185 Mads Sogaard/222 2.50 6.00
186 Noah Cates/224 2.00 5.00
187 Bobby Brink/221 2.00 5.00
188 Dylan Samberg/224 2.00 5.00
189 Jack McBain/223 2.00 5.00
190 Nathan Smith/224 1.50 4.00
191 Fredrik Karlstrom/225 1.50 4.00
192 Valtteri Puustinen/223 1.50 4.00
193 Kaiden Guhle/221 4.00 10.00
194 Jakub Lauko/222 2.50 6.00
195 Elmer Soderblom/218 4.00 10.00
196 Brandt Clarke/220 4.00 10.00
197 Vladislav Kolyachonok/221 1.50 4.00
198 Nikita Okhotiuk/222 1.50 4.00
199 Jacob Moverare/224 1.50 4.00
200 Filip Roos/224 1.50 4.00
201 Hayden Hodgson/227 1.50 4.00
202 Andrei Kuzmenko/227 4.00 10.00
203 Pontus Holmberg/224 2.00 5.00
204 Olle Lycksell/223 2.00 5.00
205 Johnathan Kovacevic/225 2.00 5.00
206 Ben Meyers/224 2.00 5.00
207 Cole Koepke/224 2.00 5.00
208 Nils Aman/223 2.00 5.00
209 Jake Christiansen/223 2.00 5.00
210 Nick Blankenburg/224 1.50 4.00
211 Arber Xhekaj/222 4.00 10.00
212 Nick Perbix/224 1.50 4.00
213 Pavol Regenda/223 2.00 5.00
214 Nick DeSimone/228 2.00 5.00
215 Jonatan Berggren/222 3.00 8.00
216 Nikita Alexandrov/222 2.00 5.00
217 Matej Blumel/222 2.50 6.00
218 Juuso Parssinen/222 2.00 5.00
219 Semyon Der-Arguchintsev/223 2.00 5.00
220 Aatu Raty/220 2.00 5.00
221 Oskar Olausson/220 2.00 5.00
222 Jake Sanderson/220 5.00 12.00
223 Jean-Luc Foudy/220 2.00 5.00
224 Lucas Johansen/226 1.50 4.00
225 Kirill Marchenko/222 5.00 12.00
226 Dylan Guenther/220 5.00 12.00
227 David Jiricek/219 4.00 10.00
228 Samuel Poulin/222 2.50 6.00
229 Juraj Slafkovsky/218 10.00 25.00
230 Shane Wright/219 5.00 12.00

2022-23 SP Game Used Crystal

*CRYSTAL: 1.5X TO 4X BASIC RED

2022-23 SP Game Used Gold

*GOLD: .5X TO 1.2X BASIC RED

2022-23 SP Game Used '01 Retro Rookies Crossover

*GOLD/25: 1.2X TO 3X BASIC
RC1 Owen Power 1.00 2.50
RC2 Matty Beniers 1.25 3.00
RC3 Matt Boldy 1.50 4.00
RC4 Juraj Slafkovsky 2.50 6.00
RC5 Shane Wright 1.25 3.00
RC6 Jack Quinn .75 2.00
RC7 Dylan Holloway 1.00 2.50
RC8 Lukas Dostal 1.00 2.50
RC9 Lukas Reichel 1.00 2.50
RC10 Kent Johnson 1.00 2.50
RC11 Jake Sanderson 1.25 3.00
RC12 Dylan Guenther 1.25 3.00
RC13 Brandt Clarke 1.00 2.50
RC14 Andrei Kuzmenko 1.00 2.50
RC15 Kaiden Guhle 1.00 2.50

2022-23 SP Game Used '01-02 Retro Rookies

*GOLD/25: 1.2X TO 3X BASIC
R1 Matt Boldy 1.50 4.00
R2 Chase Pearson .40 1.00
R3 Alex Vlasic .40 1.00
R4 Marc McLaughlin .50 1.25
R5 Bobby Brink .50 1.25
R6 Lukas Reichel 1.00 2.50
R7 Nathan Smith .40 1.00
R8 Trey Fix-Wolansky .50 1.25
R9 Valtteri Puustinen .40 1.00
R10 Lukas Dostal 1.00 2.50
R11 Matty Beniers 1.25 3.00
R12 Mark Kastelic .40 1.00
R13 Nick Abruzzese .50 1.25
R14 Jordan Harris .60 1.50
R15 Kent Johnson 1.00 2.50
R16 Kaedan Korczak .40 1.00
R17 Dylan Samberg .50 1.25
R18 Marco Rossi 1.25 3.00
R19 Dylan Holloway 1.00 2.50
R20 Jacob Perreault .50 1.25
R21 Mads Sogaard .60 1.50
R22 Owen Power 1.00 2.50
R23 Jack Quinn .75 2.00
R24 Fredrik Karlstrom .40 1.00
R25 Matias Maccelli .75 2.00
R26 Michael Eyssimont .50 1.25
R27 Isaac Ratcliffe .50 1.25
R28 Reilly Walsh .50 1.25
R29 Ronnie Attard .50 1.25
R30 Jordan Spence .50 1.25
R31 Samuel Fagemo .40 1.00
R32 Brayden Tracey .40 1.00
R33 Ben Meyers .50 1.25
R34 Hunter Drew .50 1.25
R35 Braden Schneider .75 2.00
R36 Jack McBain .50 1.25
R37 Noah Cates .50 1.25
R38 Filip Hallander .50 1.25
R39 Pyotr Kochetkov 1.00 2.50
R40 Erik Kallgren .50 1.25
R41 Thomas Bordeleau .50 1.25
R42 Shane Wright 1.25 3.00
R43 Juraj Slafkovsky 2.50 6.00
R44 Jake Sanderson 1.25 3.00
R45 Brandt Clarke 1.00 2.50
R46 Dylan Guenther 1.25 3.00
R47 Andrei Kuzmenko 1.00 2.50
R48 Elmer Soderblom 1.00 2.50
R49 Cole Koepke .50 1.25
R50 Arber Xhekaj 1.00 2.50
R51 Samuel Poulin .60 1.50
R52 Kaiden Guhle 1.00 2.50
R53 Jakub Lauko .60 1.50
R54 Wyatt Johnston 2.00 5.00
R55 Nils Aman .50 1.25
R56 Pontus Holmberg .50 1.25
R57 David Jiricek 1.00 2.50
R58 Pavol Regenda .50 1.25
R59 Filip Roos .40 1.00
R60 Jake Christiansen .50 1.25
R61 Nick DeSimone .50 1.25
R62 Marcus Bjork .50 1.25
R63 Kirill Marchenko 1.25 3.00
R64 Tyler Tucker .50 1.25
R65 Semyon Der-Arguchintsev .50 1.25
R66 Oskar Olausson .50 1.25
R67 Simon Holmstrom .50 1.25
R68 James Hamblin .50 1.25
R69 Lucas Johansen .40 1.00
R70 Jean-Luc Foudy .50 1.25

2022-23 SP Game Used '22 All Star Game Accuracy Target Relics

ASA1 Steven Stamkos 40.00 100.00
ASA2 Auston Matthews 40.00 100.00
ASA3 Nazem Kadri 12.00 30.00
ASA4 Joe Pavelski 12.00 30.00
ASA5 Brady Tkachuk 15.00 40.00

2022-23 SP Game Used '22 All Star Game Banner Year Relic Autographs

BYASCH Chance/25 100.00 250.00
BYASGR Gritty/25 125.00 300.00

2022-23 SP Game Used '22 All Star Game Banner Year Relics

BYASAD Alex DeBrincat 2.00 5.00
BYASAK Adrian Kempe 1.50 4.00
BYASAM Auston Matthews 6.00 15.00
BYASAP Adam Pelech 1.00 2.50
BYASAV Andrei Vasilevskiy 2.50 6.00
BYASBT Brady Tkachuk 2.50 6.00
BYASCG Claude Giroux 1.50 4.00
BYASCH Chance 6.00 15.00
BYASCK Chris Kreider 2.00 5.00
BYASCM Cale Makar 4.00 10.00
BYASCT Cam Talbot 1.50 4.00
BYASDL Dylan Larkin 2.00 5.00
BYASEK Evgeny Kuznetsov 2.00 5.00
BYASFA Frederik Andersen 2.00 5.00
BYASGA Johnny Gaudreau 2.50 6.00
BYASGI John Gibson 1.50 4.00
BYASGR Gritty 6.00 15.00
BYASHU Jack Hughes 4.00 10.00
BYASJC Jack Campbell 1.50 4.00
BYASJE Jordan Eberle 1.50 4.00
BYASJG Jake Guentzel 2.50 6.00
BYASJH Jonathan Huberdeau 2.00 5.00
BYASJK Jordan Kyrou 1.50 4.00
BYASJM Jonathan Marchessault 2.00 5.00
BYASJP Joe Pavelski 2.00 5.00
BYASJS Juuse Saros 2.00 5.00
BYASKC Kyle Connor 2.50 6.00
BYASKE Clayton Keller 2.00 5.00
BYASKK Kirill Kaprizov 5.00 12.00
BYASLD Leon Draisaitl 5.00 12.00
BYASMC Connor McDavid 8.00 20.00
BYASMS Mark Stone 2.00 5.00
BYASNK Nazem Kadri 2.00 5.00
BYASNS Nick Suzuki 3.00 8.00
BYASPB Patrice Bergeron 2.00 5.00
BYASPI Alex Pietrangelo 1.25 3.00
BYASRD Rasmus Dahlin 2.00 5.00
BYASRJ Roman Josi 1.50 4.00
BYASSA Sebastian Aho 2.50 6.00
BYASSS Steven Stamkos 3.00 8.00
BYASTD Thatcher Demko 2.00 5.00
BYASTJ Tristan Jarry 1.50 4.00
BYASTM Timo Meier 1.50 4.00
BYASTT Troy Terry 1.25 3.00
BYASTZ Trevor Zegras 1.50 4.00
BYASVH Victor Hedman 2.00 5.00
BYASWW Wild Wing 6.00 15.00
BYASZW Zach Werenski 2.50 6.00

2022-23 SP Game Used '22 All Star Game Dual Jerseys

*PATCH/35: .75X TO 2X BASIC
AS21 T.Terry/J.Gibson 3.00 8.00
AS22 T.Terry/T.Zegras 3.00 8.00
AS23 P.Bergeron/N.Suzuki 6.00 15.00
AS25 A.DeBrincat/B.Tkachuk 5.00 12.00
AS26 C.Makar/N.Kadri 8.00 20.00
AS27 C.McDavid/L.Draisaitl 15.00 40.00
AS28 C.Talbot/K.Kaprizov 10.00 25.00
AS29 R.Josi/Z.Werenski 5.00 12.00
AS210 R.Josi/J.Saros 4.00 10.00
AS211 A.Pelech/C.Kreider 4.00 10.00
AS212 T.Jarry/J.Guentzel 5.00 12.00
AS213 J.Kyrou/A.Kempe 3.00 8.00
AS214 S.Stamkos/V.Hedman 6.00 15.00
AS215 J.Campbell/A.Vasilevskiy 5.00 12.00
AS216 A.Matthews/J.Campbell 12.00 30.00
AS217 A.Pietrangelo/J.Hughes 8.00 20.00
AS218 M.Stone/A.Pietrangelo 4.00 10.00
AS219 J.Marchessault/M.Stone 4.00 10.00

2022-23 SP Game Used '22 All Star Game Jersey Banner Relic Autographs

ASJBGI John Gibson/25 10.00 25.00
ASJBJM Jonathan Marchessault/25 12.00 30.00
ASJBTD Thatcher Demko/25 12.00 30.00
ASJBTT Troy Terry/25 8.00 20.00

2022-23 SP Game Used '22 All Star Game Jersey Banner Relics

ASJBAD Alex DeBrincat 2.50 6.00
ASJBAK Adrian Kempe 2.00 5.00
ASJBAM Auston Matthews 8.00 20.00
ASJBAP Adam Pelech 1.25 3.00
ASJBAV Andrei Vasilevskiy 3.00 8.00
ASJBBT Brady Tkachuk 3.00 8.00
ASJBCG Claude Giroux 2.00 5.00
ASJBCK Chris Kreider 2.50 6.00
ASJBCM Cale Makar 5.00 12.00
ASJBCT Cam Talbot 2.00 5.00
ASJBDL Dylan Larkin 2.50 6.00
ASJBEK Evgeny Kuznetsov 2.50 6.00
ASJBFA Frederik Andersen 2.50 6.00
ASJBGA Johnny Gaudreau 3.00 8.00
ASJBGI John Gibson 2.00 5.00
ASJBHU Jack Hughes 5.00 12.00
ASJBJC Jack Campbell 2.00 5.00
ASJBJE Jordan Eberle 2.00 5.00
ASJBJG Jake Guentzel 3.00 8.00
ASJBJK Jordan Kyrou 2.00 5.00
ASJBJM Jonathan Marchessault 2.50 6.00
ASJBJP Joe Pavelski 2.50 6.00
ASJBJS Juuse Saros 2.50 6.00
ASJBKC Kyle Connor 3.00 8.00
ASJBKE Clayton Keller 2.50 6.00
ASJBKK Kirill Kaprizov 6.00 15.00
ASJBLD Leon Draisaitl 6.00 15.00
ASJBMC Connor McDavid 15.00 40.00
ASJBMS Mark Stone 2.50 6.00
ASJBNK Nazem Kadri 2.50 6.00
ASJBNS Nick Suzuki 4.00 10.00
ASJBPB Patrice Bergeron 2.50 6.00
ASJBPI Alex Pietrangelo 1.50 4.00
ASJBRD Rasmus Dahlin 2.50 6.00
ASJBRJ Roman Josi 2.00 5.00
ASJBSA Sebastian Aho 3.00 8.00
ASJBSS Steven Stamkos 4.00 10.00
ASJBTD Thatcher Demko 2.50 6.00
ASJBTJ Tristan Jarry 2.00 5.00
ASJBTM Timo Meier 2.00 5.00
ASJBTT Troy Terry 1.50 4.00
ASJBTZ Trevor Zegras 2.00 5.00
ASJBVH Victor Hedman 2.50 6.00
ASJBZW Zach Werenski 3.00 8.00

2022-23 SP Game Used '22 All Star Game Jerseys

*PATCH/49: 1.2X TO 3X BASIC
AS1 Auston Matthews 6.00 15.00
AS2 Brady Tkachuk 2.50 6.00
AS3 Patrice Bergeron 2.00 5.00
AS4 Jonathan Huberdeau 2.00 5.00
AS5 Dylan Larkin 2.00 5.00
AS6 Nick Suzuki 3.00 8.00
AS7 Steven Stamkos 3.00 8.00
AS8 Rasmus Dahlin 2.00 5.00
AS9 Victor Hedman 2.00 5.00
AS10 Jack Campbell 1.50 4.00
AS11 Andrei Vasilevskiy 2.50 6.00
AS12 Claude Giroux 1.50 4.00
AS13 Sebastian Aho 2.50 6.00
AS14 Trevor Zegras 1.50 4.00
AS15 Jake Guentzel 2.50 6.00
AS16 Jack Hughes 4.00 10.00
AS17 Chris Kreider 2.00 5.00
AS18 Evgeny Kuznetsov 2.00 5.00
AS19 Adam Pelech 1.00 2.50
AS20 Zach Werenski 2.50 6.00
AS21 Frederik Andersen 2.00 5.00
AS22 Tristan Jarry 1.50 4.00
AS23 Joe Pavelski 2.00 5.00
AS24 Kyle Connor 2.50 6.00
AS25 Alex DeBrincat 2.00 5.00
AS26 Kirill Kaprizov 5.00 12.00
AS27 Clayton Keller 2.00 5.00
AS28 Nazem Kadri 2.00 5.00
AS29 Jordan Kyrou 1.50 4.00
AS30 Cale Makar 4.00 10.00
AS31 Roman Josi 1.50 4.00
AS32 Juuse Saros 2.00 5.00
AS33 Cam Talbot 1.50 4.00
AS34 Connor McDavid 8.00 20.00
AS35 Leon Draisaitl 5.00 12.00
AS36 Jordan Eberle 1.50 4.00
AS37 Johnny Gaudreau 2.50 6.00
AS38 Adrian Kempe 1.50 4.00
AS39 Timo Meier 1.50 4.00
AS40 Mark Stone 2.00 5.00
AS41 Jonathan Marchessault 2.00 5.00
AS42 Troy Terry 1.25 3.00
AS43 Alex Pietrangelo 1.25 3.00
AS44 Thatcher Demko 2.00 5.00
AS45 John Gibson 1.50 4.00

2022-23 SP Game Used '22 All Star Game Net Cord

ASNAD Alex DeBrincat 20.00 50.00
ASNAM Auston Matthews 60.00 150.00
ASNAP Adam Pelech 10.00 25.00
ASNAV Andrei Vasilevskiy 25.00 60.00
ASNBT Brady Tkachuk 25.00 60.00
ASNCG Claude Giroux 15.00 40.00
ASNCK Chris Kreider 20.00 50.00
ASNCM Connor McDavid 80.00 200.00
ASNDL Dylan Larkin 20.00 50.00
ASNHU Jack Hughes 40.00 100.00
ASNJE Jordan Eberle 15.00 40.00
ASNJG Jake Guentzel 25.00 60.00
ASNJH Jonathan Huberdeau 20.00 50.00
ASNJP Joe Pavelski 20.00 50.00
ASNKC Kyle Connor 25.00 60.00
ASNKK Kirill Kaprizov 50.00 125.00
ASNLD Leon Draisaitl 50.00 125.00
ASNMA Cale Makar 40.00 100.00
ASNMS Mark Stone 20.00 50.00
ASNNK Nazem Kadri 20.00 50.00
ASNNS Nick Suzuki 30.00 80.00
ASNRD Rasmus Dahlin 20.00 50.00
ASNRJ Roman Josi 15.00 40.00
ASNSA Sebastian Aho 25.00 60.00
ASNSS Steven Stamkos 30.00 80.00
ASNTD Thatcher Demko 20.00 50.00
ASNTJ Tristan Jarry 15.00 40.00
ASNTT Troy Terry 12.00 30.00
ASNTW Tom Wilson 15.00 40.00
ASNVH Victor Hedman 20.00 50.00

2022-23 SP Game Used '22 All Star Game Pucks

ASPAM Auston Matthews 40.00 100.00
ASPAV Andrei Vasilevskiy 15.00 40.00
ASPCG Claude Giroux 10.00 25.00
ASPCM Connor McDavid 50.00 125.00
ASPHU Jack Hughes 25.00 60.00
ASPJH Jonathan Huberdeau 12.00 30.00
ASPLD Leon Draisaitl 30.00 80.00
ASPMA Cale Makar 25.00 60.00
ASPRJ Roman Josi 10.00 25.00
ASPSA Sebastian Aho 15.00 40.00

2022-23 SP Game Used '22 All Star Game Quad Jerseys

AS41 Makar/Dahlin/Hedman/Josi 8.00 20.00
AS42 Vasilevskiy/Jarry/Talbot/Demko 5.00 12.00
AS43 Giroux/Hughes/Aho/Kreider 8.00 20.00
AS44 Makar/Kaprizov Matthews/Huberdeau 12.00 30.00
AS45 Kadri/Stamkos/Pavelski/Tkachuk 6.00 15.00
AS46 Aho/Guentzel/Terry/Gaudreau 5.00 12.00
AS47 Pietrangelo/Hughes DeBrincat/Zegras 8.00 20.00
AS48 Makar/Kadri Stamkos/Vasilevskiy 8.00 20.00

2022-23 SP Game Used '22 All Star Game Rink Glass Relics

ASGAD Alex DeBrincat 20.00 50.00
ASGAK Adrian Kempe 15.00 40.00
ASGAM Auston Matthews 60.00 150.00
ASGAP Adam Pelech 10.00 25.00
ASGAU Auston Matthews 60.00 150.00
ASGAV Andrei Vasilevskiy 25.00 60.00
ASGBT Brady Tkachuk 25.00 60.00
ASGCG Claude Giroux 15.00 40.00
ASGCK Chris Kreider 20.00 50.00
ASGCM Cale Makar 40.00 100.00
ASGCO Connor McDavid 80.00 200.00
ASGCT Cam Talbot 15.00 40.00
ASGDL Dylan Larkin 20.00 50.00
ASGDR Leon Draisaitl 50.00 125.00
ASGEK Evgeny Kuznetsov 20.00 50.00
ASGFA Frederik Andersen 20.00 50.00
ASGGA Johnny Gaudreau 25.00 60.00
ASGGI John Gibson 15.00 40.00
ASGHU Jack Hughes 40.00 100.00
ASGJA Jack Hughes 40.00 100.00
ASGJC Jack Campbell 15.00 40.00
ASGJE Jordan Eberle 15.00 40.00
ASGJG Jake Guentzel 25.00 60.00
ASGJH Jonathan Huberdeau 20.00 50.00
ASGJK Jordan Kyrou 15.00 40.00
ASGJM Jonathan Marchessault 20.00 50.00
ASGJP Joe Pavelski 20.00 50.00
ASGJS Juuse Saros 20.00 50.00
ASGKA Kirill Kaprizov 50.00 125.00
ASGKC Kyle Connor 25.00 60.00
ASGKE Clayton Keller 20.00 50.00
ASGKK Kirill Kaprizov 50.00 125.00
ASGLD Leon Draisaitl 50.00 125.00
ASGMA Cale Makar 40.00 100.00
ASGMC Connor McDavid 80.00 200.00
ASGMS Mark Stone 20.00 50.00
ASGNK Nazem Kadri 20.00 50.00
ASGNS Nick Suzuki 30.00 80.00
ASGPB Patrice Bergeron 20.00 50.00
ASGPI Alex Pietrangelo 12.00 30.00
ASGRD Rasmus Dahlin 20.00 50.00
ASGRJ Roman Josi 15.00 40.00
ASGSA Sebastian Aho 25.00 60.00
ASGSS Steven Stamkos 30.00 80.00
ASGTD Thatcher Demko 20.00 50.00
ASGTJ Tristan Jarry 15.00 40.00
ASGTM Timo Meier 15.00 40.00
ASGTT Troy Terry 12.00 30.00
ASGTW Tom Wilson 15.00 40.00
ASGVH Victor Hedman 20.00 50.00

2022-23 SP Game Used '22 All Star Game Trio Jerseys

*PATCH/25: .75X TO 2X BASIC
AS31 Kuznetsov/Vasilevskiy/Kaprizov 10.00 25.00
AS32 Kyrou/Pavelski/DeBrincat 4.00 10.00
AS33 Terry/Gibson/Zegras 3.00 8.00
AS34 Gaudreau/Larkin/Keller 5.00 12.00
AS35 Kempe/Eberle/Meier 3.00 8.00
AS36 Kaprizov/Matthews/Makar 12.00 30.00
AS37 Giroux/Hughes/Guentzel 8.00 20.00
AS38 Giroux/Matthews/Pavelski 12.00 30.00
AS39 Hedman/Stamkos/Vasilevskiy 6.00 15.00
AS310 Stone/Pietrangelo Marchessault 4.00 10.00

2022-23 SP Game Used '22 Heritage Classic Banner Year Relic Autographs
BYHCDC Dylan Cozens/25 15.00 40.00
BYHCPK Peyton Krebs/25 12.00 30.00
BYHCRS Rasmus Sandin/25 12.00 30.00
BYHCTL Timothy Liljegren/25 10.00 25.00
BYHCTT Tage Thompson/25 20.00 50.00

2022-23 SP Game Used '22 Heritage Classic Banner Year Relics
BYHCAM Auston Matthews 8.00 20.00
BYHCDC Dylan Cozens 3.00 8.00
BYHCMM Mitch Marner 5.00 12.00
BYHCPK Peyton Krebs 2.50 6.00
BYHCRS Rasmus Sandin 2.50 6.00
BYHCTL Timothy Liljegren 2.00 5.00
BYHCTT Tage Thompson 4.00 10.00
BYHCVH Vincent Hinostroza 2.00 5.00
BYHCVO Victor Olofsson 3.00 8.00
BYHCWN William Nylander 6.00 15.00

2022-23 SP Game Used '22 Heritage Classic Net Cord
HCNAK Alex Kerfoot 25.00 60.00
HCNAM Auston Matthews 125.00 300.00
HCNAT Alex Tuch 30.00 80.00
HCNCM Casey Mittelstadt 30.00 80.00
HCNDC Dylan Cozens 30.00 80.00
HCNHJ Henri Jokiharju 20.00 50.00
HCNIM Ilya Mikheyev 25.00 60.00
HCNJH Justin Holl 20.00 50.00
HCNJT John Tavares 50.00 125.00
HCNKO Kyle Okposo 20.00 50.00
HCNMB Michael Bunting 30.00 80.00
HCNMM Mitch Marner 50.00 125.00
HCNMR Morgan Rielly 30.00 80.00
HCNPK Peyton Krebs 25.00 60.00
HCNRD Rasmus Dahlin 40.00 100.00
HCNTB T.J. Brodie 20.00 50.00
HCNTT Tage Thompson 40.00 100.00
HCNVH Vincent Hinostroza 20.00 50.00
HCNVO Victor Olofsson 30.00 80.00
HCNWN William Nylander 60.00 150.00

2022-23 SP Game Used '22 Heritage Classic Pucks
HCPAM Auston Matthews 125.00 300.00
HCPMB Michael Bunting 30.00 80.00
HCPMM Mitch Marner 50.00 125.00
HCPPK Tage Thompson 40.00 100.00
HCPRD Rasmus Dahlin 40.00 100.00

2022-23 SP Game Used '22 Stadium Series Banner Year Relics
BYSSAV Andrei Vasilevskiy 2.50 6.00
BYSSCF Cal Foote 1.25 3.00
BYSSCP Corey Perry 2.50 6.00
BYSSFF Filip Forsberg 2.50 6.00
BYSSPT Philip Tomasino 1.00 2.50
BYSSRJ Roman Josi 1.50 4.00
BYSSSS Steven Stamkos 3.00 8.00
BYSSTJ Tanner Jeannot 1.00 2.50
BYSSVH Victor Hedman 2.00 5.00

2022-23 SP Game Used '22 Stadium Series Jerseys
*PATCH/35: 2X TO 5X BASIC
STS1 Steven Stamkos 3.00 8.00
STS2 Ryan McDonagh 1.00 2.50
STS3 Mathieu Joseph 1.00 2.50
STS4 Brayden Point 2.00 5.00
STS5 Ondrej Palat 1.25 3.00
STS6 Corey Perry 2.50 6.00
STS7 Nikita Kucherov 3.00 8.00
STS8 Matt Luff 1.00 2.50
STS9 Eeli Tolvanen 1.50 4.00
STS10 Mark Borowiecki 1.00 2.50
STS11 David Rittich 1.00 2.50
STS12 Colton Sissons 1.00 2.50
STS13 Matt Duchene 1.50 4.00
STS14 Dante Fabbro 1.00 2.50
STS15 Filip Forsberg 2.50 6.00

2022-23 SP Game Used '22 Stadium Series Net Cord
SSNAK Alex Killorn 20.00 50.00
SSNAV Andrei Vasilevskiy 50.00 125.00
SSNBP Brayden Point 40.00 100.00
SSNCF Cal Foote 25.00 60.00
SSNET Eeli Tolvanen 30.00 80.00
SSNFF Filip Forsberg 50.00 125.00
SSNJS Juuse Saros 40.00 100.00
SSNMD Matt Duchene 30.00 80.00
SSNNK Nikita Kucherov 60.00 150.00
SSNPT Philip Tomasino 20.00 50.00
SSNRC Ross Colton 25.00 60.00
SSNRJ Roman Josi 30.00 80.00
SSNSS Steven Stamkos 60.00 150.00
SSNTJ Tanner Jeannot 20.00 50.00
SSNVH Victor Hedman 40.00 100.00

2022-23 SP Game Used '22 Stadium Series Pucks
SSPAV Andrei Vasilevskiy 50.00 125.00
SSPBP Brayden Point 40.00 100.00
SSPFF Filip Forsberg 50.00 125.00
SSPMD Matt Duchene 30.00 80.00
SSPNK Nikita Kucherov 60.00 150.00
SSPPT Philip Tomasino 20.00 50.00
SSPRJ Roman Josi 30.00 80.00
SSPSS Steven Stamkos 60.00 150.00
SSPTJ Tanner Jeannot 20.00 50.00
SSPVH Victor Hedman 40.00 100.00

2022-23 SP Game Used '22 Stanley Cup Final Banner Year Relic Autographs
BYSCCF Cal Foote/25 25.00 60.00
BYSCDT Devon Toews/25 25.00 60.00
BYSCNS Nico Sturm/25 20.00 50.00

2022-23 SP Game Used '22 Stanley Cup Final Banner Year Relics
BYSCAC Anthony Cirelli B 2.50 6.00
BYSCAK Alex Killorn B 2.00 5.00
BYSCAN Alex Newhook A 2.50 6.00
BYSCAV Andrei Vasilevskiy B 5.00 12.00
BYSCBB Bowen Byram B 4.00 10.00
BYSCCF Cal Foote B 2.50 6.00
BYSCCM Cale Makar B 8.00 20.00
BYSCCP Corey Perry B 5.00 12.00
BYSCDT Devon Toews A 2.50 6.00
BYSCEJ Erik Johnson A 2.00 5.00
BYSCGL Gabriel Landeskog A 4.00 10.00
BYSCJC J.T. Compher B 2.00 5.00
BYSCMR Mikko Rantanen B 8.00 20.00
BYSCNM Nathan MacKinnon B 12.00 30.00
BYSCNS Nico Sturm A 2.00 5.00
BYSCSS Steven Stamkos B 6.00 15.00
BYSCVH Victor Hedman B 4.00 10.00
BYSCVN Valeri Nichushkin B 3.00 8.00

2022-23 SP Game Used '22 Stanley Cup Final Net Cord
SCNAK Alex Killorn 25.00 60.00
SCNAN Alex Newhook 30.00 80.00
SCNAV Andrei Vasilevskiy 60.00 150.00
SCNBB Bowen Byram 50.00 125.00
SCNBH Brandon Hagel 30.00 80.00
SCNBP Brayden Point 50.00 125.00
SCNCM Cale Makar 150.00 400.00
SCNDK Darcy Kuemper 40.00 100.00
SCNDT Devon Toews 30.00 80.00
SCNGL Gabriel Landeskog 50.00 120.00
SCNKA Nazem Kadri 50.00 125.00
SCNMR Mikko Rantanen 100.00 250.00
SCNMS Mikhail Sergachev 30.00 80.00
SCNNK Nikita Kucherov 80.00 200.00
SCNNM Nathan MacKinnon 150.00 400.00
SCNOP Ondrej Palat 30.00 80.00
SCNRC Ross Colton 30.00 80.00
SCNSS Steven Stamkos 80.00 200.00
SCNVH Victor Hedman 50.00 125.00
SCNVN Valeri Nichushkin 40.00 100.00

2022-23 SP Game Used '22 Stanley Cup Final Pucks
SCPAC Anthony Cirelli 25.00 60.00
SCPAK Alex Killorn 20.00 50.00
SCPAN Alex Newhook 25.00 60.00
SCPAV Andrei Vasilevskiy 50.00 125.00
SCPBB Bowen Byram 40.00 100.00
SCPBH Brandon Hagel 25.00 60.00
SCPBP Brayden Point 40.00 100.00
SCPCM Cale Makar 80.00 200.00
SCPDK Darcy Kuemper 30.00 80.00
SCPDT Devon Toews 25.00 60.00
SCPGL Gabriel Landeskog 40.00 100.00
SCPKA Nazem Kadri 40.00 100.00
SCPMR Mikko Rantanen 80.00 200.00
SCPNK Nikita Kucherov 60.00 150.00
SCPNM Nathan MacKinnon 125.00 300.00
SCPOP Ondrej Palat 25.00 60.00
SCPRC Ross Colton 25.00 60.00
SCPSS Steven Stamkos 60.00 150.00
SCPVH Victor Hedman 40.00 100.00
SCPVN Valeri Nichushkin 30.00 80.00

2022-23 SP Game Used '22 Winter Classic Banner Year Relic Autographs
BYWCBD Brandon Duhaime/25 20.00 50.00
BYWCDP David Perron/25 25.00 60.00
BYWCMZ Mats Zuccarello/25 30.00 80.00
BYWCRP Kevin Fiala/25 25.00 60.00
BYWCSP Scott Perunovich/25 20.00 50.00
BYWCTK Torey Krug/25 25.00 60.00

2022-23 SP Game Used '22 Winter Classic Banner Year Relics
BYWCBD Brandon Duhaime 3.00 8.00
BYWCCA Calen Addison 3.00 8.00
BYWCDP David Perron 4.00 10.00
BYWCJB Jordan Binnington 8.00 20.00
BYWCKK Kirill Kaprizov 15.00 40.00
BYWCMZ Mats Zuccarello 5.00 12.00
BYWCRH Ryan Hartman 3.00 8.00
BYWCRP Kevin Fiala 4.00 10.00
BYWCSP Scott Perunovich 3.00 8.00
BYWCTK Torey Krug 4.00 10.00

2022-23 SP Game Used '22 Winter Classic Net Cord
WCNCA Calen Addison 25.00 60.00
WCNCT Cam Talbot 40.00 100.00
WCNDP David Perron 30.00 80.00
WCNJB Jordan Binnington 60.00 150.00
WCNJK Jordan Kyrou 40.00 100.00
WCNKF Kevin Fiala 30.00 80.00
WCNKK Kirill Kaprizov 125.00 300.00
WCNMD Matt Dumba 25.00 60.00
WCNMZ Mats Zuccarello 40.00 100.00
WCNPB Pavel Buchnevich 30.00 80.00
WCNRH Ryan Hartman 25.00 60.00
WCNRO Ryan O'Reilly 40.00 100.00
WCNRT Robert Thomas 40.00 100.00
WCNTK Torey Krug 30.00 80.00
WCNVT Vladimir Tarasenko 50.00 120.00

2022-23 SP Game Used A Piece of History
*PATCH/25: .5X TO 1.2X BASIC
AAK Anze Kopitar 20.00 50.00
ADP Denis Potvin 12.00 30.00
AEM Evgeni Malkin 25.00 60.00
AJQ Jonathan Quick 15.00 40.00
AJS Joe Sakic 25.00 60.00
AKK Kirill Kaprizov 40.00 100.00
AKT Keith Tkachuk 12.00 30.00
ALR Luc Robitaille 12.00 30.00
AMB Martin Brodeur 30.00 80.00
AMF Marc-Andre Fleury 25.00 60.00
AMT Matthew Tkachuk 25.00 60.00
ANB Nicklas Backstrom 12.00 30.00
APF Peter Forsberg 25.00 60.00
APK Patrick Kane 25.00 60.00
ARG Ryan Getzlaf 12.00 30.00
ASB Sergei Bobrovsky 20.00 50.00
ASC Sidney Crosby 50.00 125.00
ASS Steven Stamkos 25.00 60.00
ATE Tony Esposito 12.00 30.00

2022-23 SP Game Used Authentic Fabrics
AFAD Alex DeBrincat 2.00 5.00
AFAL Alexis Lafreniere 2.50 6.00
AFAM Auston Matthews 6.00 15.00
AFAO Alex Ovechkin 6.00 15.00
AFAP Artemi Panarin 3.00 8.00
AFBM Brad Marchand 3.00 8.00
AFBS Brayden Schenn 1.50 4.00
AFCC Cole Caufield 3.00 8.00
AFCM Connor McDavid 8.00 20.00
AFDP David Pastrnak 4.00 10.00
AFEK Erik Karlsson 2.00 5.00
AFEM Evgeni Malkin 3.00 8.00
AFEP Elias Pettersson 2.50 6.00
AFFF Filip Forsberg 2.50 6.00
AFGV Gabe Vilardi 1.50 4.00
AFHU Jonathan Huberdeau 2.00 5.00
AFJB Jamie Benn 1.50 4.00
AFJC Jakob Chychrun 1.50 4.00
AFJE Jack Eichel 2.50 6.00
AFJG Johnny Gaudreau 2.50 6.00
AFJH Jack Hughes 4.00 10.00
AFJR Jason Robertson 2.50 6.00
AFJT Jonathan Toews 2.50 6.00
AFKK Kirill Kaprizov 5.00 12.00
AFLD Leon Draisaitl 5.00 12.00
AFLR Lucas Raymond 2.50 6.00
AFMA Cale Makar 4.00 10.00
AFMB Mathew Barzal 2.00 5.00
AFMC Mason McTavish 1.50 4.00
AFMM Mitch Marner 2.50 6.00
AFMT Matthew Tkachuk 3.00 8.00
AFNK Nikita Kucherov 3.00 8.00
AFNM Nathan MacKinnon 6.00 15.00
AFPK Patrick Kane 3.00 8.00
AFRD Rasmus Dahlin 2.00 5.00
AFSC Sidney Crosby 6.00 15.00
AFSS Steven Stamkos 3.00 8.00
AFTK Travis Konecny 1.50 4.00
AFTT Tage Thompson 2.00 5.00
AFTZ Trevor Zegras 1.50 4.00

2022-23 SP Game Used Authentic Fabrics Patch
*PATCH/35: 1.5X TO 4X BASIC
AFCM Connor McDavid 40.00 100.00

2022-23 SP Game Used Autographs Blue
3 Peyton Krebs D 5.00 12.00
4 Brady Tkachuk C 10.00 25.00
5 Ryan O'Reilly D 6.00 15.00
6 Brad Marchand C 12.00 30.00
8 Trevor Zegras C 6.00 15.00
10 Jonathan Marchessault C 8.00 20.00
16 Brandon Saad E 5.00 12.00
17 Elias Pettersson B 10.00 25.00
23 Spencer Knight C 6.00 15.00
24 Joe Pavelski C 8.00 20.00
25 Alexis Lafreniere C 10.00 25.00
26 Anze Kopitar B 10.00 25.00
27 Miro Heiskanen D 8.00 20.00
28 Cam Atkinson E 6.00 15.00
29 Roope Hintz D 8.00 20.00
30 Brock Boeser D 8.00 20.00
33 Robert Thomas D 6.00 15.00
34 Drake Batherson E 6.00 15.00
35 Carey Price A 12.00 30.00
37 Seth Jarvis D 8.00 20.00
38 Matthew Tkachuk C 12.00 30.00
41 Blake Coleman D 5.00 12.00
42 Adam Fox C 8.00 20.00
47 Cale Makar A 15.00 40.00
49 Anthony Beauvillier D 4.00 10.00
51 Jordan Eberle D 6.00 15.00
53 Clayton Keller D 8.00 20.00
54 Nick Suzuki C 12.00 30.00
56 John Gibson E 6.00 15.00
58 Victor Hedman B 8.00 20.00
60 Nick Schmaltz E 5.00 12.00
61 Tim Stutzle D 8.00 20.00
64 Jack Roslovic E 4.00 10.00
70 Ukko-Pekka Luukkonen D 5.00 12.00
74 Mats Zuccarello D 6.00 15.00
75 Jared McCann E 5.00 12.00
80 Alex Ovechkin A 125.00 300.00
81 Jonathan Huberdeau C 8.00 20.00
82 Jeremy Swayman D 10.00 25.00
83 Jake Oettinger C 10.00 25.00
85 Zach Werenski D 10.00 25.00
89 Josh Norris D 6.00 15.00
93 Tomas Hertl D 6.00 15.00
95 Aleksander Barkov C 10.00 25.00
96 Jack Hughes B 15.00 40.00
99 Darcy Kuemper E 6.00 15.00
100 Andrei Svechnikov C 8.00 20.00
101 Tage Thompson D 8.00 20.00
102 Alex DeBrincat C 8.00 20.00
103 Brent Burns C 6.00 15.00
104 Ryan Strome E 6.00 15.00
107 Kirby Dach E 6.00 15.00
110 Elvis Merzlikins E 6.00 15.00
111 Jordan Kyrou C 6.00 15.00
112 Marcus Foligno E 5.00 12.00
113 Jonathan Quick B 8.00 20.00
114 Anthony Cirelli E 5.00 12.00
115 Vitek Vanecek E 6.00 15.00
116 Jaccob Slavin E 5.00 12.00
118 Jack Eichel C 10.00 25.00
119 Robby Fabbri E 4.00 10.00
120 Marc-Andre Fleury C 12.00 30.00
121 Bobby Orr A 80.00 200.00
124 Teemu Selanne A 12.00 30.00
125 Steve Yzerman A 15.00 40.00
126 Patrick Roy A 15.00 40.00
127 Ray Bourque B 10.00 25.00
128 Dominik Hasek B 10.00 25.00
129 Brett Hull B 12.00 30.00
130 Martin Brodeur B 15.00 40.00
131 Nicklas Lidstrom B 6.00 15.00
132 Marcel Dionne B 8.00 20.00
133 Jarome Iginla B 8.00 20.00
134 Luc Robitaille B 6.00 15.00
135 Ryan Getzlaf B 6.00 15.00
136 Billy Smith B 6.00 15.00
137 Keith Tkachuk C 6.00 15.00
139 Henrik Lundqvist B 15.00 40.00
140 Grant Fuhr C 10.00 25.00
141 Joe Sakic A 12.00 30.00
142 Sergei Zubov C 5.00 12.00
144 Vincent Lecavalier B 6.00 15.00
145 John Vanbiesbrouck B 6.00 15.00
146 Larry Robinson B 6.00 15.00
148 Mark Messier A 12.00 30.00
149 Eric Lindros A 10.00 25.00
150 Paul Coffey B 6.00 15.00
151 Michael Eyssimont F 6.00 15.00
152 Erik Kallgren F 6.00 15.00
154 Isaac Ratcliffe F 6.00 15.00
155 Hunter Drew F 6.00 15.00
156 Zack Hayes E 5.00 12.00
157 Trey Fix-Wolansky F 6.00 15.00
158 Samuel Fagemo D 5.00 12.00
159 Kaedan Korczak E 5.00 12.00
160 Jordan Spence D 6.00 15.00
161 Mark Kastelic F 5.00 12.00
162 Lukas Dostal D 12.00 30.00
163 Pyotr Kochetkov F 12.00 30.00
164 Jordan Harris F 8.00 20.00
165 Nick Abruzzese E 6.00 15.00
167 Chase Pearson F 5.00 12.00
168 Matt Boldy B 20.00 50.00
169 Marc McLaughlin F 6.00 15.00
170 Ronnie Attard E 6.00 15.00
171 Brayden Tracey D 5.00 12.00
172 Matty Beniers B 40.00 100.00
173 Wyatt Johnston C 25.00 60.00
174 Owen Power B 12.00 30.00
175 Alex Vlasic D 5.00 12.00
176 Thomas Bordeleau D 6.00 15.00
177 Jacob Perreault D 6.00 15.00
178 Jack Quinn C 10.00 25.00
179 Lukas Reichel B 12.00 30.00
180 Kent Johnson B 12.00 30.00
181 Dylan Holloway D 12.00 30.00
182 Marco Rossi B 15.00 40.00
183 Reilly Walsh F 6.00 15.00
184 Braden Schneider D 10.00 25.00
185 Mads Sogaard F 8.00 20.00
186 Noah Cates E 6.00 15.00
187 Bobby Brink D 6.00 15.00
188 Dylan Samberg F 6.00 15.00
189 Jack McBain F 6.00 15.00
190 Nathan Smith F 5.00 12.00
191 Fredrik Karlstrom F 5.00 12.00
192 Valtteri Puustinen F 5.00 12.00
193 Kaiden Guhle C 12.00 30.00
195 Elmer Soderblom D 12.00 30.00
196 Brandt Clarke C 12.00 30.00
199 Jacob Moverare E 5.00 12.00
200 Filip Roos E 5.00 12.00
201 Hayden Hodgson E 5.00 12.00
202 Andrei Kuzmenko C 12.00 30.00
203 Pontus Holmberg E 6.00 15.00
204 Olle Lycksell E 6.00 15.00
205 Johnathan Kovacevic E 6.00 15.00
206 Ben Meyers E 6.00 15.00
207 Cole Koepke E 6.00 15.00
208 Nils Aman F 6.00 15.00
209 Jake Christiansen E 6.00 15.00
210 Nick Blankenburg E 5.00 12.00
211 Arber Xhekaj E 12.00 30.00
212 Nick Perbix E 5.00 12.00
213 Pavol Regenda E 6.00 15.00
214 Nick DeSimone F 6.00 15.00
215 Jonatan Berggren D 10.00 25.00
216 Nikita Alexandrov F 6.00 15.00
218 Juuso Parssinen D 6.00 15.00
219 Semyon Der-Arguchintsev E 6.00 15.00
220 Aatu Raty C 6.00 15.00
221 Oskar Olausson D 6.00 15.00
222 Jake Sanderson C 15.00 40.00
223 Jean-Luc Foudy E 6.00 15.00
224 Lucas Johansen F 5.00 12.00
225 Kirill Marchenko E 15.00 40.00
226 Dylan Guenther C 15.00 40.00
227 David Jiricek A 12.00 30.00
228 Samuel Poulin C 8.00 20.00
230 Shane Wright B 15.00 40.00

2022-23 SP Game Used Back to Back All Stars Jersey Banner Relics
BBASAV Andrei Vasilevskiy 5.00 12.00
BBASBT Brady Tkachuk 5.00 12.00
BBASCM Connor McDavid 15.00 40.00
BBASJH Jonathan Huberdeau 4.00 10.00
BBASLD Leon Draisaitl 10.00 25.00
BBASRJ Roman Josi 3.00 8.00
BBASVH Victor Hedman 4.00 10.00

2022-23 SP Game Used Draft Day Marks Rookies
DDMAN Alex Newhook/245* 20.00 50.00
DDMAV Alex Vlasic/210* 20.00 50.00
DDMBB Bobby Brink/175* 25.00 60.00
DDMBS Braden Schneider/315* 40.00 100.00
DDMBU Michael Bunting/245* 25.00 60.00
DDMDH Dylan Holloway/280* 50.00 125.00
DDMHL Hendrix Lapierre/280* 15.00 40.00
DDMJB Justin Barron/210* 20.00 50.00
DDMJN Jake Neighbours/350* 25.00 60.00
DDMJP JJ Peterka/245* 25.00 60.00
DDMJP Jacob Perreault/315* 25.00 60.00
DDMJQ Jack Quinn/175* 40.00 100.00
DDMJS Jake Sanderson/315* 60.00 150.00
DDMKG Kaiden Guhle/175* 50.00 125.00
DDMKJ Kent Johnson/245* 50.00 125.00
DDMLD Lukas Dostal/210* 50.00 125.00
DDMLT Lassi Thomson/245* 15.00 40.00
DDMMB Matty Beniers/245* 60.00 150.00
DDMMB Matt Boldy/175* 80.00 200.00
DDMMM Mason McTavish/280* 25.00 60.00
DDMOP Owen Power/175* 50.00 125.00
DDMRE Lukas Reichel/245* 50.00 125.00
DDMSD Sean Durzi/175* 15.00 40.00
DDMSF Samuel Fagemo/210* 20.00 50.00
DDMSL Juraj Slafkovsky/350* 125.00 300.00
DDMSO Mads Sogaard/245* 30.00 80.00
DDMSP Jordan Spence/210* 25.00 60.00
DDMSP Samuel Poulin/210* 30.00 80.00
DDMSW Shane Wright/210* 60.00 150.00
DDMTB Thomas Bordeleau/315* 25.00 60.00
DDMVP Vasily Podkolzin/315* 15.00 40.00
DDMWA Wade Allison/245* 15.00 40.00
DDMWE William Eklund/210* 30.00 80.00
DDMWJ Wyatt Johnston/280* 100.00 250.00

2022-23 SP Game Used Draft Day Marks Veterans
DDMMP Max Pacioretty/100* 10.00 25.00
DDMTC Thomas Chabot/60* 15.00 40.00

2022-23 SP Game Used Inked Rookie Sweaters Patch
RSAK Andrei Kuzmenko 25.00 60.00
RSAX Arber Xhekaj 25.00 60.00
RSBC Brandt Clarke 25.00 60.00
RSBO Matt Boldy 80.00 200.00
RSBS Braden Schneider 20.00 50.00
RSCK Cole Koepke 12.00 30.00
RSDG Dylan Guenther 30.00 80.00
RSDH Dylan Holloway 25.00 60.00
RSDJ David Jiricek 25.00 60.00
RSES Elmer Soderblom 25.00 60.00
RSJH Jordan Harris 15.00 40.00
RSJM Jack McBain 12.00 30.00
RSJO Jordan Spence 12.00 30.00
RSJP Jacob Perreault 12.00 30.00
RSJQ Jack Quinn 20.00 50.00
RSJS Juraj Slafkovsky 125.00 300.00
RSKG Kaiden Guhle 25.00 60.00
RSKJ Kent Johnson 25.00 60.00
RSLD Lukas Dostal 25.00 60.00
RSLR Lukas Reichel 25.00 60.00
RSMB Matty Beniers 80.00 200.00
RSMK Mark Kastelic 10.00 25.00
RSMR Marco Rossi 30.00 80.00
RSMS Mads Sogaard 15.00 40.00
RSNA Nick Abruzzese 12.00 30.00
RSOP Owen Power 25.00 60.00
RSPK Pyotr Kochetkov 25.00 60.00
RSSA Jake Sanderson 30.00 80.00
RSSF Samuel Fagemo 10.00 25.00
RSSP Samuel Poulin 15.00 40.00
RSSW Shane Wright 30.00 80.00
RSTB Thomas Bordeleau 12.00 30.00
RSZH Zack Hayes 10.00 25.00

2022-23 SP Game Used Inked Sweaters
ISAH Alexander Holtz/35 10.00 25.00
ISBC Blake Coleman/35 8.00 20.00
ISBM Brad Marchand/25 20.00 50.00
ISCK Clayton Keller/35 12.00 30.00
ISDC Dylan Cozens/35 10.00 25.00
ISHL Hendrix Lapierre/35 6.00 15.00
ISJG John Gibson/35 10.00 25.00
ISJP Joe Pavelski/35 12.00 30.00
ISKD Kirby Dach/35 10.00 25.00
ISMH Miro Heiskanen/35 12.00 30.00
ISMT Matthew Tkachuk/35 20.00 50.00
ISTD Thatcher Demko/35 12.00 30.00
ISTK Torey Krug/35 8.00 20.00
ISTT Troy Terry/35 8.00 20.00
ISTZ Trevor Zegras/25 10.00 25.00
ISZW Zach Werenski/35 15.00 40.00

2022-23 SP Game Used Jersey Autographs Red
*GOLD: .5X TO 1.2X RED
3 Peyton Krebs/149 8.00 20.00
4 Brady Tkachuk/65 15.00 40.00
5 Ryan O'Reilly/65 10.00 25.00
6 Brad Marchand/35 20.00 50.00
8 Trevor Zegras/35 10.00 25.00
10 Jonathan Marchessault/65 12.00 30.00
15 James van Riemsdyk/99 8.00 20.00
16 Brandon Saad/99 8.00 20.00
23 Spencer Knight/99 10.00 25.00
24 Joe Pavelski/35 12.00 30.00
26 Anze Kopitar/35 15.00 40.00
27 Miro Heiskanen/99 12.00 30.00
28 Cam Atkinson/99 10.00 25.00
29 Roope Hintz/99 12.00 30.00
30 Brock Boeser/65 12.00 30.00
33 Robert Thomas/65 10.00 25.00
34 Drake Batherson/149 10.00 25.00
37 Seth Jarvis/99 12.00 30.00
38 Matthew Tkachuk/65 20.00 50.00
40 Jake Guentzel/65 15.00 40.00
41 Blake Coleman/149 8.00 20.00
48 Tom Wilson/35 10.00 25.00
49 Anthony Beauvillier/149 6.00 15.00
51 Jordan Eberle/65 10.00 25.00
53 Clayton Keller/99 12.00 30.00
54 Nick Suzuki/35 20.00 50.00
56 John Gibson/99 10.00 25.00
60 Nick Schmaltz/149 8.00 20.00
61 Tim Stutzle/35 12.00 30.00
64 Jack Roslovic/99 6.00 15.00
70 Ukko-Pekka Luukkonen/149 8.00 20.00
74 Mats Zuccarello/65 10.00 25.00
75 Jared McCann/149 8.00 20.00
81 Jonathan Huberdeau/35 12.00 30.00
82 Jeremy Swayman/99 15.00 40.00
85 Zach Werenski/99 15.00 40.00
89 Josh Norris/65 10.00 25.00
93 Tomas Hertl/99 10.00 25.00
95 Aleksander Barkov/35 15.00 40.00
99 Darcy Kuemper/99 10.00 25.00
100 Andrei Svechnikov/35 12.00 30.00
101 Tage Thompson/49 12.00 30.00
102 Alex DeBrincat/35 12.00 30.00
103 Brent Burns/65 10.00 25.00
104 Ryan Strome/149 10.00 25.00
107 Kirby Dach/99 10.00 25.00
111 Jordan Kyrou/65 10.00 25.00
112 Marcus Foligno/149 8.00 20.00
113 Jonathan Quick/35 12.00 30.00
115 Vitek Vanecek/35 10.00 25.00
118 Jack Eichel/99 15.00 40.00
119 Robby Fabbri/99 6.00 15.00
151 Michael Eyssimont/149 10.00 25.00
152 Erik Kallgren/149 10.00 25.00
154 Isaac Ratcliffe/99 10.00 25.00
156 Zack Hayes/149 8.00 20.00
157 Trey Fix-Wolansky/149 10.00 25.00
158 Samuel Fagemo/49 8.00 20.00
159 Kaedan Korczak/149 8.00 20.00
160 Jordan Spence/149 10.00 25.00
161 Mark Kastelic/149 8.00 20.00
162 Lukas Dostal/99 20.00 50.00
163 Pyotr Kochetkov/99 20.00 50.00
164 Jordan Harris/149 12.00 30.00
165 Nick Abruzzese/149 10.00 25.00
167 Chase Pearson/149 8.00 20.00
168 Matt Boldy/49 60.00 150.00
169 Marc McLaughlin/149 10.00 25.00
170 Ronnie Attard/149 10.00 25.00
171 Brayden Tracey/99 8.00 20.00
172 Matty Beniers/49 25.00 60.00
173 Wyatt Johnston/49 40.00 100.00
174 Owen Power/49 20.00 50.00
175 Alex Vlasic/149 8.00 20.00
176 Thomas Bordeleau/99 10.00 25.00
177 Jacob Perreault/49 10.00 25.00
178 Jack Quinn/49 15.00 40.00
179 Lukas Reichel/49 20.00 50.00
180 Kent Johnson/49 20.00 50.00
181 Dylan Holloway/49 20.00 50.00
182 Marco Rossi/49 25.00 60.00
183 Reilly Walsh/149 10.00 25.00
184 Braden Schneider/49 15.00 40.00
185 Mads Sogaard/99 12.00 30.00
186 Noah Cates/149 10.00 25.00
187 Bobby Brink/99 10.00 25.00
188 Dylan Samberg/149 10.00 25.00
189 Jack McBain/149 10.00 25.00
190 Nathan Smith/149 8.00 20.00
191 Fredrik Karlstrom/149 8.00 20.00
192 Valtteri Puustinen/149 8.00 20.00
193 Kaiden Guhle/149 20.00 50.00
195 Elmer Soderblom/99 20.00 50.00
196 Brandt Clarke/49 20.00 50.00
199 Jacob Moverare/149 8.00 20.00
200 Filip Roos/149 8.00 20.00
201 Hayden Hodgson/149 8.00 20.00
202 Andrei Kuzmenko/49 20.00 50.00
203 Pontus Holmberg/149 10.00 25.00
204 Olle Lycksell/149 10.00 25.00
205 Johnathan Kovacevic/149 10.00 25.00
206 Ben Meyers/149 10.00 25.00
207 Cole Koepke/149 10.00 25.00
208 Nils Aman/149 10.00 25.00
209 Jake Christiansen/149 10.00 25.00
210 Nick Blankenburg/149 8.00 20.00
211 Arber Xhekaj/149 20.00 50.00
212 Nick Perbix/149 8.00 20.00
213 Pavol Regenda/149 10.00 25.00
214 Nick DeSimone/149 10.00 25.00
215 Jonatan Berggren/99 15.00 40.00
216 Nikita Alexandrov/149 10.00 25.00
218 Juuso Parssinen/149 10.00 25.00
219 Semyon Der-Arguchintsev/149 10.00 25.00
221 Oskar Olausson/149 10.00 25.00
222 Jake Sanderson/149 25.00 60.00
224 Lucas Johansen/149 8.00 20.00
225 Kirill Marchenko/149 25.00 60.00
226 Dylan Guenther/49 25.00 60.00
227 David Jiricek/49 20.00 50.00
228 Samuel Poulin/99 12.00 30.00
229 Juraj Slafkovsky/49 80.00 200.00
230 Shane Wright/49 25.00 60.00

2022-23 SP Game Used Jerseys Red
1 Moritz Seider 4.00 10.00
2 Connor McDavid 15.00 40.00
3 Peyton Krebs 2.50 6.00
4 Brady Tkachuk 5.00 12.00
5 Ryan O'Reilly 3.00 8.00
6 Brad Marchand 6.00 15.00
7 Mathew Barzal 4.00 10.00
8 Trevor Zegras 3.00 8.00
9 Steven Stamkos 6.00 15.00
10 Jonathan Marchessault 4.00 10.00
11 Kirill Kaprizov 10.00 25.00
12 Mitch Marner 5.00 12.00
13 Elias Lindholm 3.00 8.00
14 Artemi Panarin 6.00 15.00
15 James van Riemsdyk 2.50 6.00
16 Brandon Saad 2.50 6.00
17 Elias Pettersson 5.00 12.00
18 Jason Robertson 5.00 12.00
19 Quinn Hughes 8.00 20.00
20 Lucas Raymond 5.00 12.00
21 Mikko Rantanen 8.00 20.00
22 Nico Hischier 5.00 12.00
23 Spencer Knight 3.00 8.00
24 Joe Pavelski 4.00 10.00
25 Alexis Lafreniere 5.00 12.00
26 Anze Kopitar 5.00 12.00
27 Miro Heiskanen 4.00 10.00
28 Cam Atkinson 3.00 8.00
29 Roope Hintz 4.00 10.00
30 Brock Boeser 4.00 10.00
31 Sidney Crosby 12.00 30.00
32 Philip Tomasino 2.00 5.00
33 Robert Thomas 3.00 8.00
34 Drake Batherson 3.00 8.00
35 Carey Price 6.00 15.00
36 Dawson Mercer 4.00 10.00
37 Seth Jarvis 4.00 10.00
38 Matthew Tkachuk 6.00 15.00
39 Sebastian Aho 5.00 12.00
40 Jake Guentzel 5.00 12.00
41 Blake Coleman 2.50 6.00
42 Adam Fox 4.00 10.00
43 Evgeny Kuznetsov 4.00 10.00
44 Filip Forsberg 5.00 12.00
45 Patrick Kane 6.00 15.00
46 Igor Shesterkin 6.00 15.00
47 Cale Makar 8.00 20.00
48 Tom Wilson 3.00 8.00
49 Anthony Beauvillier 2.00 5.00
50 Rasmus Dahlin 4.00 10.00
51 Jordan Eberle 3.00 8.00
52 Jaden Schwartz 2.50 6.00
53 Clayton Keller 4.00 10.00
54 Nick Suzuki 6.00 15.00
55 Nick Robertson 3.00 8.00
56 John Gibson 3.00 8.00
57 John Tavares 5.00 12.00
58 Victor Hedman 4.00 10.00
59 David Pastrnak 8.00 20.00
60 Nick Schmaltz 2.50 6.00
61 Tim Stutzle 4.00 10.00
62 Quinton Byfield 4.00 10.00
63 Kris Letang 4.00 10.00
64 Jack Roslovic 2.00 5.00
65 Mark Scheifele 5.00 12.00
66 Sean Couturier 2.50 6.00
67 Gabriel Landeskog 4.00 10.00
68 Cole Sillinger 2.50 6.00
69 Andrei Vasilevskiy 5.00 12.00
70 Ukko-Pekka Luukkonen 2.50 6.00
71 Logan Couture 4.00 10.00
72 Alex Pietrangelo 2.50 6.00
73 Brock Nelson 3.00 8.00
74 Mats Zuccarello 3.00 8.00
75 Jared McCann 2.50 6.00
76 Jonathan Toews 5.00 12.00
77 Nathan MacKinnon 12.00 30.00
78 Nikolaj Ehlers 3.00 8.00
79 Erik Karlsson 4.00 10.00
80 Alex Ovechkin 12.00 30.00
81 Jonathan Huberdeau 4.00 10.00
82 Jeremy Swayman 5.00 12.00
83 Jake Oettinger 5.00 12.00
84 Kyle Connor 5.00 12.00
85 Zach Werenski 5.00 12.00
86 Ryan Nugent-Hopkins 4.00 10.00
87 Roman Josi 3.00 8.00
88 Leon Draisaitl 10.00 25.00
89 Josh Norris 3.00 8.00
90 Joel Eriksson Ek 2.50 6.00
91 Evgeni Malkin 6.00 15.00
92 Cole Caufield 6.00 15.00
93 Tomas Hertl 3.00 8.00
94 Patrice Bergeron 4.00 10.00
95 Aleksander Barkov 5.00 12.00
96 Jack Hughes 8.00 20.00
97 Seth Jones 3.00 8.00
98 Auston Matthews 12.00 30.00
99 Darcy Kuemper 3.00 8.00
100 Andrei Svechnikov 4.00 10.00
101 Tage Thompson 4.00 10.00
102 Alex DeBrincat 4.00 10.00
103 Brent Burns 3.00 8.00
104 Ryan Strome 3.00 8.00
105 Johnny Gaudreau 5.00 12.00
106 Travis Konecny 3.00 8.00
107 Kirby Dach 3.00 8.00
109 Dylan Larkin 4.00 10.00
110 Elvis Merzlikins 3.00 8.00
111 Jordan Kyrou 3.00 8.00
112 Marcus Foligno 2.50 6.00
113 Jonathan Quick 4.00 10.00
115 Vitek Vanecek 3.00 8.00
116 Jaccob Slavin 2.50 6.00
117 Sam Bennett 5.00 12.00
118 Jack Eichel 5.00 12.00
119 Robby Fabbri 2.00 5.00
120 Marc-Andre Fleury 6.00 15.00
122 Mario Lemieux 12.00 30.00
124 Teemu Selanne 6.00 15.00
125 Steve Yzerman 8.00 20.00
126 Patrick Roy 8.00 20.00
127 Ray Bourque 5.00 12.00
128 Dominik Hasek 5.00 12.00
129 Brett Hull 6.00 15.00
130 Martin Brodeur 8.00 20.00
131 Nicklas Lidstrom 3.00 8.00
132 Marcel Dionne 4.00 10.00
133 Jarome Iginla 4.00 10.00
134 Luc Robitaille 3.00 8.00
135 Ryan Getzlaf 3.00 8.00
137 Keith Tkachuk 3.00 8.00
138 Pekka Rinne 3.00 8.00
139 Henrik Lundqvist 8.00 20.00
140 Grant Fuhr 5.00 12.00
141 Joe Sakic 6.00 15.00
142 Sergei Zubov 2.50 6.00
143 Jaromir Jagr 10.00 25.00
144 Vincent Lecavalier 3.00 8.00
146 Larry Robinson 3.00 8.00
147 Phil Esposito 5.00 12.00
148 Mark Messier 6.00 15.00
149 Eric Lindros 5.00 12.00
150 Paul Coffey 3.00 8.00
151 Michael Eyssimont 3.00 8.00
152 Erik Kallgren 3.00 8.00
153 Filip Hallander 3.00 8.00
154 Isaac Ratcliffe 3.00 8.00
156 Zack Hayes 2.50 6.00
157 Trey Fix-Wolansky 3.00 8.00
158 Samuel Fagemo 2.50 6.00
159 Kaedan Korczak 2.50 6.00
160 Jordan Spence 3.00 8.00
161 Mark Kastelic 2.50 6.00
162 Lukas Dostal 6.00 15.00
163 Pyotr Kochetkov 6.00 15.00
164 Jordan Harris 4.00 10.00
165 Nick Abruzzese 3.00 8.00
166 Matias Maccelli 5.00 12.00
167 Chase Pearson 2.50 6.00
168 Matt Boldy 10.00 25.00
169 Marc McLaughlin 3.00 8.00
170 Ronnie Attard 3.00 8.00
171 Brayden Tracey 2.50 6.00
172 Matty Beniers 8.00 20.00
173 Wyatt Johnston 12.00 30.00
174 Owen Power 6.00 15.00
175 Alex Vlasic 2.50 6.00
176 Thomas Bordeleau 3.00 8.00
177 Jacob Perreault 3.00 8.00
178 Jack Quinn 5.00 12.00
179 Lukas Reichel 6.00 15.00
180 Kent Johnson 6.00 15.00
181 Dylan Holloway 6.00 15.00
182 Marco Rossi 8.00 20.00
183 Reilly Walsh 3.00 8.00
184 Braden Schneider 5.00 12.00
185 Mads Sogaard 4.00 10.00
186 Noah Cates 3.00 8.00
187 Bobby Brink 3.00 8.00
188 Dylan Samberg 3.00 8.00
189 Jack McBain 3.00 8.00
190 Nathan Smith 2.50 6.00
191 Fredrik Karlstrom 2.50 6.00
192 Valtteri Puustinen 2.50 6.00
193 Kaiden Guhle 6.00 15.00
194 Jakub Lauko 4.00 10.00
195 Elmer Soderblom 6.00 15.00
196 Brandt Clarke 6.00 15.00
197 Vladislav Kolyachonok 2.50 6.00
198 Nikita Okhotiuk 2.50 6.00
199 Jacob Moverare 2.50 6.00
200 Filip Roos 2.50 6.00
201 Hayden Hodgson 2.50 6.00

202 Andrei Kuzmenko 6.00 15.00
203 Pontus Holmberg 3.00 8.00
204 Olle Lycksell 3.00 8.00
205 Johnathan Kovacevic 3.00 8.00
206 Ben Meyers 3.00 8.00
207 Cole Koepke 3.00 8.00
208 Nils Aman 3.00 8.00
209 Jake Christiansen 3.00 8.00
210 Nick Blankenburg 2.50 6.00
211 Arber Xhekaj 6.00 15.00
212 Nick Perbix 2.50 6.00
213 Pavol Regenda 3.00 8.00
214 Nick DeSimone 3.00 8.00
215 Jonatan Berggren 5.00 12.00
216 Nikita Alexandrov 3.00 8.00
217 Matej Blumel 4.00 10.00
218 Juuso Parssinen 3.00 8.00
219 Semyon Der-Arguchintsev 3.00 8.00
221 Oskar Olausson 3.00 8.00
222 Jake Sanderson 8.00 20.00
224 Lucas Johansen 2.50 6.00
225 Kirill Marchenko 8.00 20.00
226 Dylan Guenther 8.00 20.00
227 David Jiricek 6.00 15.00
228 Samuel Poulin 4.00 10.00
229 Juraj Slafkovsky 15.00 40.00
230 Shane Wright 8.00 20.00

2022-23 SP Game Used Jerseys Gold Premium Memorabilia

*GOLD: .6X TO 1.5X RED

2022-23 SP Game Used Mascot Marks

MMANA Wild Wing/280* 25.00 60.00
MMARI Howler the Coyote/495* 25.00 60.00
MMBOS Blades The Bruin/490* 25.00 60.00
MMBUF Sabretooth/330* 25.00 60.00
MMCAR Stormy/198* 25.00 60.00
MMCBJ Stinger/231* 25.00 60.00
MMCGY Harvey The Hound/490* 25.00 60.00
MMCHI Tommy Hawk/297* 25.00 60.00
MMCOL Bernie the St. Bernard/630* 25.00 60.00
MMDAL Victor E. Green/396* 25.00 60.00
MMDET Al The Octopus/420* 25.00 60.00
MMEDM Hunter/210* 30.00 80.00
MMFLA Stanley C. Panther/525* 25.00 60.00
MMLAK Bailey/210* 25.00 60.00
MMMIN Nordy/175* 25.00 60.00
MMMON Youppi!/231* 30.00 80.00
MMNJD N.J. Devil/231* 25.00 60.00
MMNSH Gnash/165* 30.00 80.00
MMNYI Sparky The Dragon/495* 20.00 50.00
MMOTT Spartacat/297* 25.00 60.00
MMPHI Gritty/198* 30.00 80.00
MMPIT Iceburgh/280* 25.00 60.00
MMSJS S.J. Sharkie/297* 25.00 60.00
MMSTL Louie/165* 25.00 60.00
MMTBL Thunderbug/330* 25.00 60.00
MMTOR Carlton the Bear/462* 25.00 60.00
MMVAN Fin/99* 40.00 100.00
MMVGK Chance/198* 40.00 100.00
MMWIN Moose/175* 25.00 60.00
MMWSH Slapshot/264* 15.00 40.00

2022-23 SP Game Used New Grooves Gold

*RED/99: .5X TO 1.2X GOLD
NG1 Matt Boldy 3.00 8.00
NG2 Owen Power 2.00 5.00
NG3 Matty Beniers 2.50 6.00
NG4 Kent Johnson 2.00 5.00
NG5 Jack Quinn 1.50 4.00
NG6 Marco Rossi 2.50 6.00
NG7 Lukas Dostal 2.00 5.00
NG8 Dylan Holloway 2.00 5.00
NG9 Lukas Reichel 2.00 5.00
NG10 Jonatan Berggren 1.50 4.00
NG11 Jacob Perreault 1.00 2.50
NG12 Juraj Slafkovsky 5.00 12.00
NG13 Shane Wright 2.50 6.00
NG14 Braden Schneider 1.50 4.00
NG15 Brandt Clarke 2.00 5.00
NG16 Andrei Kuzmenko 2.00 5.00
NG17 Samuel Poulin 1.25 3.00
NG18 David Jiricek 2.00 5.00
NG19 Jake Sanderson 2.50 6.00
NG20 Wyatt Johnston 4.00 10.00

2022-23 SP Game Used New Grooves Autographs

NG1 Matt Boldy C 20.00 50.00
NG2 Owen Power C 12.00 30.00
NG3 Matty Beniers C 15.00 40.00
NG4 Kent Johnson D 12.00 30.00
NG5 Jack Quinn E 10.00 25.00
NG6 Marco Rossi D 15.00 40.00
NG7 Lukas Dostal E 12.00 30.00
NG8 Dylan Holloway E 12.00 30.00
NG9 Lukas Reichel E 12.00 30.00
NG10 Jonatan Berggren E 10.00 25.00
NG11 Jacob Perreault E 6.00 15.00
NG12 Juraj Slafkovsky A 30.00 80.00
NG13 Shane Wright B 15.00 40.00
NG14 Braden Schneider E 10.00 25.00
NG15 Brandt Clarke D 12.00 30.00
NG16 Andrei Kuzmenko D 12.00 30.00
NG19 Jake Sanderson E 15.00 40.00
NG20 Wyatt Johnston D 25.00 60.00

2022-23 SP Game Used New Grooves Jersey Autographs

NG1 Matt Boldy 30.00 80.00
NG2 Owen Power 20.00 50.00
NG3 Matty Beniers 25.00 60.00
NG4 Kent Johnson 20.00 50.00
NG5 Jack Quinn 15.00 40.00
NG6 Marco Rossi 25.00 60.00
NG7 Lukas Dostal 20.00 50.00
NG8 Dylan Holloway 20.00 50.00
NG9 Lukas Reichel 20.00 50.00
NG10 Jonatan Berggren 15.00 40.00
NG11 Jacob Perreault 10.00 25.00
NG12 Juraj Slafkovsky 50.00 125.00
NG13 Shane Wright 25.00 60.00
NG14 Braden Schneider 15.00 40.00
NG15 Brandt Clarke 20.00 50.00
NG16 Andrei Kuzmenko 20.00 50.00
NG19 Jake Sanderson 25.00 60.00
NG20 Wyatt Johnston 40.00 100.00

2022-23 SP Game Used New Grooves Jerseys

*PATCH/25: .75X TO 2X BASIC
NG1 Matt Boldy 6.00 15.00
NG2 Owen Power 4.00 10.00
NG3 Matty Beniers 5.00 12.00
NG4 Kent Johnson 4.00 10.00
NG5 Jack Quinn 3.00 8.00
NG6 Marco Rossi 5.00 12.00
NG7 Lukas Dostal 4.00 10.00
NG8 Dylan Holloway 4.00 10.00
NG9 Lukas Reichel 4.00 10.00
NG10 Jonatan Berggren 3.00 8.00
NG11 Jacob Perreault 2.00 5.00
NG12 Juraj Slafkovsky 10.00 25.00
NG13 Shane Wright 5.00 12.00
NG14 Braden Schneider 3.00 8.00
NG15 Brandt Clarke 4.00 10.00
NG16 Andrei Kuzmenko 4.00 10.00
NG17 Samuel Poulin 2.50 6.00
NG18 David Jiricek 4.00 10.00
NG19 Jake Sanderson 5.00 12.00
NG20 Wyatt Johnston 8.00 20.00

2022-23 SP Game Used Purity

*PLATINUM/150: 1.5X TO 4X BASIC
*GOLD/35: 2.5X TO 6X BASIC
P1 Kirill Kaprizov 1.50 4.00
P2 Nathan MacKinnon 2.00 5.00
P3 Evgeni Malkin 1.00 2.50
P4 Brad Marchand 1.00 2.50
P5 Jack Hughes 1.25 3.00
P6 Artemi Panarin 1.00 2.50
P7 Andrei Vasilevskiy .75 2.00
P8 Alexis Lafreniere .75 2.00
P9 Jonathan Toews .75 2.00
P10 David Pastrnak 1.25 3.00
P11 Jonathan Huberdeau .60 1.50
P12 Matthew Tkachuk 1.00 2.50
P13 John Tavares .75 2.00
P14 Moritz Seider .60 1.50
P15 Trevor Zegras .50 1.25
P16 Tim Stutzle .60 1.50
P17 Jason Robertson .75 2.00
P18 Mitch Marner .75 2.00
P19 Ryan O'Reilly .50 1.25
P20 Quinn Hughes 1.25 3.00
P21 Andrei Svechnikov .60 1.50
P22 Cole Caufield 1.00 2.50
P23 Brady Tkachuk .75 2.00
P24 Alex Nedeljkovic .40 1.00
P25 Arthur Kaliyev .50 1.25
P26 Alex Iafallo .30 .75
P27 Zach Werenski .75 2.00
P28 Joe Pavelski .60 1.50
P29 Vitek Vanecek .50 1.25
P30 John Gibson .50 1.25
P31 Blake Coleman .40 1.00
P32 Brandon Saad .40 1.00
P33 Mason McTavish .50 1.25
P34 William Eklund .60 1.50
P35 Gabriel Landeskog .60 1.50
P36 Torey Krug .40 1.00
P37 Marcus Foligno .40 1.00
P38 Robby Fabbri .30 .75
P39 Ryan Strome .50 1.25
P40 Josh Bailey .40 1.00
P41 Mats Zuccarello .50 1.25
P42 Carey Price 1.00 2.50
P43 Patrick Kane 1.00 2.50
P44 Cale Makar 1.25 3.00
P45 Marc-Andre Fleury 1.00 2.50
P46 Alex Ovechkin 2.00 5.00
P47 Leon Draisaitl 1.50 4.00
P48 Sidney Crosby 2.00 5.00
P49 Auston Matthews 2.00 5.00
P50 Connor McDavid 2.50 6.00
P51 Ryan Getzlaf .50 1.25
P52 Grant Fuhr .75 2.00
P53 Jaromir Jagr 1.50 4.00
P54 Teemu Selanne 1.00 2.50
P55 Brett Hull 1.00 2.50
P56 Jarome Iginla .60 1.50
P57 Paul Coffey .60 1.50
P58 Larry Robinson .50 1.25
P59 Martin Brodeur 1.25 3.00
P60 Mike Liut .30 .75
P61 Martin St. Louis .50 1.25
P62 Vincent Lecavalier .50 1.25
P63 Bernie Nicholls .40 1.00
P64 Wendel Clark .75 2.00
P65 Lanny McDonald .50 1.25
P66 Dany Heatley .40 1.00
P67 Ron Hextall .50 1.25
P68 Trevor Linden .50 1.25
P69 Dave Taylor .40 1.00
P70 Billy Smith .50 1.25
P71 Bobby Orr 2.00 5.00
P72 Patrick Roy 1.25 3.00
P73 Dominik Hasek 1.00 2.50
P74 Mario Lemieux 2.00 5.00
P75 Wayne Gretzky 3.00 8.00
P76 Mads Sogaard .60 1.50
P77 Matias Maccelli .75 2.00
P78 Trey Fix-Wolansky .50 1.25
P79 Alex Vlasic .40 1.00
P80 Jordan Spence .50 1.25
P81 Nick Abruzzese .50 1.25
P82 Dylan Samberg .50 1.25
P83 Jordan Harris .50 1.25
P84 Samuel Fagemo .40 1.00
P85 Braden Schneider .75 2.00
P86 Elmer Soderblom 1.00 2.50
P87 Thomas Bordeleau .50 1.25
P88 Jacob Perreault .50 1.25
P89 Mark Kastelic .40 1.00
P90 Chase Pearson .40 1.00
P91 Owen Power 1.00 2.50
P92 Matty Beniers 1.25 3.00
P93 Matt Boldy 1.50 4.00
P94 Dylan Holloway .60 1.50
P95 Jack Quinn .75 2.00
P96 Lukas Reichel 1.00 2.50
P97 Kent Johnson 1.00 2.50
P98 Shane Wright 1.25 3.00
P99 Andrei Kuzmenko 1.00 2.50
P100 Juraj Slafkovsky 2.50 6.00

2022-23 SP Game Used Purity Autographs

P24 Alex Nedeljkovic/49 8.00 20.00
P25 Arthur Kaliyev/49 10.00 25.00
P27 Zach Werenski/49 15.00 40.00
P28 Joe Pavelski/49 12.00 30.00
P29 Vitek Vanecek/49 10.00 25.00
P30 John Gibson/49 10.00 25.00
P31 Blake Coleman/49 8.00 20.00
P32 Brandon Saad/49 8.00 20.00
P33 Mason McTavish/49 10.00 25.00
P34 William Eklund/49 12.00 30.00
P36 Torey Krug/49 8.00 20.00
P37 Marcus Foligno/49 8.00 20.00
P38 Robby Fabbri/49 6.00 15.00
P39 Ryan Strome/49 10.00 25.00
P40 Josh Bailey/49 8.00 20.00
P41 Mats Zuccarello/49 10.00 25.00
P51 Ryan Getzlaf/49 10.00 25.00
P52 Grant Fuhr/49 15.00 40.00
P56 Jarome Iginla/49 12.00 30.00
P58 Larry Robinson/49 12.00 30.00
P61 Martin St. Louis/49 10.00 25.00
P62 Vincent Lecavalier/49 10.00 25.00
P63 Bernie Nicholls/49 8.00 20.00
P64 Wendel Clark/49 15.00 40.00
P65 Lanny McDonald/49 10.00 25.00
P67 Ron Hextall/49 10.00 25.00
P69 Dave Taylor/49 8.00 20.00
P70 Billy Smith/49 10.00 25.00
P76 Mads Sogaard/25 12.00 30.00
P78 Trey Fix-Wolansky/25 10.00 25.00
P79 Alex Vlasic/25 8.00 20.00
P80 Jordan Spence/25 10.00 25.00
P81 Nick Abruzzese/25 10.00 25.00
P82 Dylan Samberg/25 10.00 25.00
P83 Jordan Harris/25 12.00 30.00
P84 Samuel Fagemo/25 8.00 20.00
P85 Braden Schneider/25 15.00 40.00
P86 Elmer Soderblom/25 20.00 50.00
P87 Thomas Bordeleau/25 10.00 25.00
P88 Jacob Perreault/25 10.00 25.00
P89 Mark Kastelic/25 8.00 20.00
P90 Chase Pearson/25 8.00 20.00
P91 Owen Power/25 20.00 50.00

2022-23 SP Game Used Rally Time Towels

RT1 Teemu Selanne 12.00 30.00
RT2 Mark Messier 12.00 30.00
RT3 Adam Graves 5.00 12.00
RT4 Mario Lemieux 25.00 60.00
RT5 Paul Coffey 6.00 15.00
RT6 Nicklas Lidstrom 6.00 15.00
RT7 Brett Hull 12.00 30.00
RT8 Mike Modano 10.00 25.00
RT9 Henrik Zetterberg 8.00 20.00
RT10 Artemi Panarin 12.00 30.00
RT11 Alexis Lafreniere 10.00 25.00
RT12 Nathan MacKinnon 25.00 60.00
RT13 Cale Makar 15.00 40.00
RT14 Gabriel Landeskog 8.00 20.00
RT15 Mikko Rantanen 15.00 40.00
RT16 Pavel Buchnevich 5.00 12.00
RT17 Brandon Saad 5.00 12.00
RT18 Jordan Kyrou 6.00 15.00
RT19 Kirill Kaprizov 20.00 50.00
RT20 Mats Zuccarello 6.00 15.00
RT21 Jared Spurgeon 6.00 15.00
RT22 Max Pacioretty 6.00 15.00
RT23 Jonathan Marchessault 8.00 20.00
RT24 William Karlsson 8.00 20.00
RT25 Carey Price 12.00 30.00
RT26 Cole Caufield 12.00 30.00
RT27 Jonathan Huberdeau 8.00 20.00
RT28 Aleksander Barkov 10.00 25.00
RT29 Sebastian Aho 8.00 20.00
RT30 Andrei Svechnikov 8.00 20.00
RT31 Erik Karlsson 8.00 20.00
RT32 Tomas Hertl 6.00 15.00
RT33 Jason Robertson 10.00 25.00
RT34 Joe Pavelski 8.00 20.00
RT35 Roope Hintz 8.00 20.00

2022-23 SP Game Used Retro Renovations Jerseys

RRAK Arthur Kaliyev 1.50 4.00
RRAS Andrei Svechnikov 2.00 5.00
RRBC Blake Coleman 1.25 3.00
RRBS Brandon Saad 1.25 3.00
RRBT Brady Tkachuk 2.50 6.00
RRCC Charlie Coyle 1.50 4.00
RRCK Clayton Keller 2.00 5.00
RRCM Connor McDavid 8.00 20.00
RRCP Carey Price 3.00 8.00
RRGL Gabriel Landeskog 2.00 5.00
RRJG John Gibson 1.50 4.00
RRJP Joe Pavelski 2.00 5.00
RRMB Mathew Barzal 2.00 5.00
RRMH Miro Heiskanen 2.00 5.00
RRNS Nick Schmaltz 1.25 3.00
RRPA Colton Parayko 1.25 3.00
RRRH Roope Hintz 2.00 5.00
RRSA Sebastian Aho 2.50 6.00
RRTK Torey Krug 1.25 3.00
RRZW Zach Werenski 2.50 6.00

2022-23 SP Game Used Retro Renovations Rookie Jerseys

*PATCH/35: .75X TO 2X BASIC
RRAX Arber Xhekaj 3.00 8.00
RRBE Matty Beniers 4.00 10.00
RRBO Matt Boldy 5.00 12.00
RRCL Brandt Clarke 3.00 8.00
RRDG Dylan Guenther 4.00 10.00
RRDH Dylan Holloway 3.00 8.00
RRDJ David Jiricek 3.00 8.00
RRDS Dylan Samberg 1.50 4.00
RRJA Jake Sanderson 4.00 10.00
RRJL Jakub Lauko 2.00 5.00
RRJQ Jack Quinn 2.50 6.00
RRJS Juraj Slafkovsky 8.00 20.00
RRKG Kaiden Guhle 3.00 8.00
RRKJ Kent Johnson 3.00 8.00
RRKU Andrei Kuzmenko 3.00 8.00
RRLD Lukas Dostal 3.00 8.00
RRLR Lukas Reichel 3.00 8.00
RRMM Matias Maccelli 2.50 6.00
RRMR Marco Rossi 4.00 10.00
RRMS Mads Sogaard 2.00 5.00
RROP Owen Power 3.00 8.00
RRPE Jacob Perreault 1.50 4.00
RRPK Pyotr Kochetkov 3.00 8.00
RRPO Samuel Poulin 2.00 5.00
RRSP Jordan Spence 1.50 4.00
RRSW Shane Wright 4.00 10.00
RRTB Thomas Bordeleau 1.50 4.00
RRTF Trey Fix-Wolansky 1.50 4.00
RRWJ Wyatt Johnston 6.00 15.00

2022-23 SP Game Used Rookie Blends Jerseys

RBAK Andrei Kuzmenko 3.00 8.00
RBAV Alex Vlasic 1.25 3.00
RBAX Arber Xhekaj 3.00 8.00
RBBC Brandt Clarke 3.00 8.00
RBBM Ben Meyers 1.50 4.00
RBBS Braden Schneider 2.50 6.00
RBBT Brayden Tracey 1.25 3.00
RBCK Cole Koepke 1.50 4.00
RBCP Chase Pearson 1.25 3.00
RBDG Dylan Guenther 4.00 10.00
RBDH Dylan Holloway 3.00 8.00
RBDJ David Jiricek 3.00 8.00
RBDS Dylan Samberg 1.50 4.00
RBES Elmer Soderblom 3.00 8.00
RBFH Filip Hallander 1.50 4.00
RBFK Fredrik Karlstrom 1.25 3.00
RBHD Hunter Drew 1.50 4.00
RBIR Isaac Ratcliffe 1.50 4.00
RBJB Jonatan Berggren 2.50 6.00
RBJH Jordan Harris 2.00 5.00
RBJL Jakub Lauko 2.00 5.00
RBJM Jack McBain 1.50 4.00
RBJP Jacob Perreault 1.50 4.00
RBJQ Jack Quinn 2.50 6.00
RBJS Jake Sanderson 4.00 10.00
RBKG Kaiden Guhle 3.00 8.00
RBKJ Kent Johnson 3.00 8.00
RBKK Kaeden Korczak 1.25 3.00
RBLD Lukas Dostal 3.00 8.00
RBLR Lukas Reichel 3.00 8.00
RBMB Matt Boldy 5.00 12.00
RBME Michael Eyssimont 1.50 4.00
RBMK Mark Kastelic 1.25 3.00
RBMM Matias Maccelli 2.50 6.00
RBMO Jacob Moverare 1.25 3.00
RBMR Marco Rossi 4.00 10.00
RBMS Mads Sogaard 2.00 5.00
RBNA Nick Abruzzese 1.50 4.00
RBNB Nick Blankenburg 1.25 3.00
RBOP Owen Power 3.00 8.00
RBPK Pyotr Kochetkov 3.00 8.00
RBPR Pavol Regenda 1.50 4.00
RBSF Samuel Fagemo 1.25 3.00
RBSL Juraj Slafkovsky 8.00 20.00
RBSP Samuel Poulin 2.00 5.00
RBSW Shane Wright 4.00 10.00
RBTB Thomas Bordeleau 1.50 4.00
RBTF Trey Fix-Wolansky 1.50 4.00
RBVP Valtteri Puustinen 1.25 3.00
RBZH Zack Hayes 1.25 3.00

2022-23 SP Game Used Rookie Outbursts Jersey Autographs

ROAK Andrei Kuzmenko B 10.00 25.00
ROAV Alex Vlasic C 4.00 10.00
ROAX Arber Xhekaj D 10.00 25.00
ROBB Bobby Brink C 5.00 12.00
ROBC Brandt Clarke C 10.00 25.00
ROBE Matty Beniers A 12.00 30.00
RODG Dylan Guenther B 12.00 30.00
RODH Dylan Holloway C 10.00 25.00
RODS Dylan Samberg D 5.00 12.00
ROEK Erik Kallgren D 5.00 12.00
ROES Elmer Soderblom C 10.00 25.00
ROIR Isaac Ratcliffe D 5.00 12.00
ROJB Jonatan Berggren C 8.00 20.00
ROJH Jordan Harris D 6.00 15.00
ROJP Jacob Perreault C 5.00 12.00
ROJQ Jack Quinn B 8.00 20.00
ROJS Jordan Spence C 5.00 12.00
ROKG Kaiden Guhle C 10.00 25.00
ROKJ Kent Johnson B 10.00 25.00
ROLD Lukas Dostal C 10.00 25.00
ROLR Lukas Reichel B 10.00 25.00
ROMB Matt Boldy A 15.00 40.00
ROMR Marco Rossi B 12.00 30.00
ROMS Mads Sogaard C 6.00 15.00
RONA Nick Abruzzese D 5.00 12.00
ROOP Owen Power A 10.00 25.00
ROPK Pyotr Kochetkov C 10.00 25.00
RORA Ronnie Attard D 5.00 12.00
RORW Reilly Walsh D 5.00 12.00
ROSA Jake Sanderson B 12.00 30.00
ROSF Samuel Fagemo B 4.00 10.00
ROSW Shane Wright A 12.00 30.00
ROTB Thomas Bordeleau C 5.00 12.00
ROTF Trey Fix-Wolansky D 5.00 12.00

2022-23 SP Game Used Rookie Outbursts Jerseys

ROAK Andrei Kuzmenko 3.00 8.00
ROAV Alex Vlasic 1.25 3.00
ROAX Arber Xhekaj 3.00 8.00
ROBB Bobby Brink 1.50 4.00
ROBC Brandt Clarke 3.00 8.00
ROBE Matty Beniers 4.00 10.00
RODG Dylan Guenther 4.00 10.00
RODH Dylan Holloway 3.00 8.00
RODJ David Jiricek 3.00 8.00
RODS Dylan Samberg 1.50 4.00
ROEK Erik Kallgren 1.50 4.00
ROES Elmer Soderblom 3.00 8.00
ROFH Filip Hallander 1.50 4.00
ROIR Isaac Ratcliffe 1.00 2.50
ROJB Jonatan Berggren 2.50 6.00
ROJH Jordan Harris 2.00 5.00
ROJP Jacob Perreault 1.50 4.00
ROJQ Jack Quinn 2.50 6.00
ROJS Jordan Spence 1.50 4.00
ROKG Kaiden Guhle 3.00 8.00
ROKJ Kent Johnson 3.00 8.00
ROLD Lukas Dostal 3.00 8.00
ROLR Lukas Reichel 3.00 8.00
ROMB Matt Boldy 5.00 12.00
ROMM Matias Maccelli 2.50 6.00
ROMR Marco Rossi 4.00 10.00
ROMS Mads Sogaard 2.00 5.00
RONA Nick Abruzzese 1.50 4.00
ROOP Owen Power 3.00 8.00
ROPK Pyotr Kochetkov 3.00 8.00
RORA Ronnie Attard 1.50 4.00
RORW Reilly Walsh 1.50 4.00
ROSA Jake Sanderson 4.00 10.00
ROSF Samuel Fagemo 1.25 3.00
ROSL Juraj Slafkovsky 8.00 20.00
ROSW Shane Wright 4.00 10.00
ROTB Thomas Bordeleau 1.50 4.00
ROTF Trey Fix-Wolansky 1.50 4.00

2022-23 SP Game Used Rookie Sweaters

RSAK Andrei Kuzmenko 3.00 8.00
RSAX Arber Xhekaj 3.00 8.00
RSBC Brandt Clarke 3.00 8.00
RSBO Matt Boldy 5.00 12.00
RSBS Braden Schneider 2.50 6.00
RSCK Cole Koepke 1.50 4.00
RSDG Dylan Guenther 4.00 10.00
RSDH Dylan Holloway 3.00 8.00
RSDJ David Jiricek 3.00 8.00
RSES Elmer Soderblom 3.00 8.00
RSJH Jordan Harris 2.00 5.00
RSJL Jakub Lauko 2.00 5.00
RSJM Jack McBain 1.50 4.00
RSJO Jordan Spence 1.50 4.00
RSJP Jacob Perreault 1.50 4.00
RSJQ Jack Quinn 2.50 6.00
RSJS Juraj Slafkovsky 8.00 20.00
RSKG Kaiden Guhle 3.00 8.00
RSKJ Kent Johnson 3.00 8.00
RSLD Lukas Dostal 3.00 8.00
RSLR Lukas Reichel 3.00 8.00
RSMB Matty Beniers 4.00 10.00
RSMK Mark Kastelic 1.25 3.00
RSMM Matias Maccelli 2.50 6.00
RSMR Marco Rossi 4.00 10.00
RSMS Mads Sogaard 2.00 5.00
RSNA Nick Abruzzese 1.50 4.00
RSOP Owen Power 3.00 8.00
RSPK Pyotr Kochetkov 3.00 8.00
RSSA Jake Sanderson 4.00 10.00
RSSF Samuel Fagemo 1.25 3.00
RSSP Samuel Poulin 2.00 5.00
RSSW Shane Wright 4.00 10.00
RSTB Thomas Bordeleau 1.50 4.00
RSZH Zack Hayes 1.25 3.00

2022-23 SP Game Used Signing Day Marks

SDMTJ Tanner Jeannot/245* 25.00 60.00
SDMWG Wayne Gretzky/70* 800.00 2000.00

2022-23 SP Game Used STI-XL Sticks

XLAM Auston Matthews 40.00 100.00
XLAO Alex Ovechkin 40.00 100.00
XLAV Andrei Vasilevskiy 15.00 40.00
XLBH Brett Hull 40.00 100.00
XLCC Chris Chelios 10.00 25.00
XLCM Connor McDavid 60.00 150.00
XLDH Dominik Hasek 15.00 40.00
XLEM Evgeni Malkin 20.00 50.00
XLJH Jack Hughes 25.00 60.00
XLJM Jonathan Marchessault 50.00 125.00
XLLM Lanny McDonald 30.00 80.00
XLML Mario Lemieux 40.00 100.00
XLMP Max Pacioretty 10.00 25.00
XLMR Mikko Rantanen 25.00 60.00
XLPC Paul Coffey 10.00 25.00
XLPR Patrick Roy 25.00 60.00
XLRB Ray Bourque 15.00 40.00
XLSC Sidney Crosby 60.00 150.00
XLTA John Tavares 15.00 40.00
XLWN William Nylander 20.00 50.00

2023-24 SP Game Used Crystal

*CRYSTAL/25: 1.5X TO 4X RED
202 Billy Sweezey 20.00 50.00
223 Luke Evangelista 20.00 50.00
226 Simon Edvinsson 20.00 50.00
227 Adam Fantilli 80.00 200.00
229 Logan Cooley 40.00 100.00
230 Connor Bedard 600.00 1500.00
232 Devon Levi 80.00 200.00
236 Matthew Coronato 15.00 40.00
238 Brock Faber 80.00 200.00
239 Tyson Foerster 30.00 80.00
252 Cole Guttman 12.00 30.00
273 John Beecher 30.00 80.00
280 Alex Laferriere 20.00 50.00

2023-24 SP Game Used Gold

*GOLD: .5X TO 1.2X RED

2023-24 SP Game Used Red

1 Viktor Arvidsson/230 1.00 2.50
2 Anthony Beauvillier/226 1.00 2.50
3 Timo Meier/227 1.50 4.00
4 Evgeni Malkin/231 3.00 8.00
5 William Karlsson/237 2.00 5.00
6 Sergei Bobrovsky/235 2.50 6.00
7 Mika Zibanejad/230 2.00 5.00
8 Dougie Hamilton/230 1.25 3.00
9 Filip Forsberg/229 2.50 6.00
10 Travis Konecny/226 1.50 4.00
11 Logan Couture/236 2.00 5.00
12 Morgan Rielly/229 1.50 4.00
13 Kris Letang/236 2.00 5.00
14 Jeff Skinner/233 1.50 4.00
15 John Tavares/231 2.50 6.00
16 Moritz Seider/222 2.00 5.00
17 Alexis Lafreniere/222 2.50 6.00
18 Jake Guentzel/229 2.50 6.00
19 Karel Vejmelka/227 1.00 2.50
20 Shane Wright/220 2.00 5.00
21 Matias Maccelli/223 1.25 3.00
22 Carter Hart/225 1.50 4.00
23 Jonathan Marchessault/233 2.00 5.00
24 Teuvo Teravainen/221 1.50 4.00
25 Kent Johnson/222 1.50 4.00
26 Cole Perfetti/229 1.50 4.00
27 Evgeny Kuznetsov/231 2.00 5.00
28 Jeremy Swayman/225 2.50 6.00
29 Ukko-Pekka Luukkonen/224 1.25 3.00
30 Bowen Byram/222 2.00 5.00
31 Miro Heiskanen/224 2.00 5.00
32 Aaron Ekblad/228 2.00 5.00
33 Jordan Eberle/233 1.50 4.00
34 Jamie Drysdale/228 1.25 3.00
35 Nick Schmaltz/230 1.25 3.00
36 J.T. Miller/221 2.00 5.00
37 Taylor Raddysh/226 1.25 3.00
38 Anze Kopitar/236 2.50 6.00
39 Sam Reinhart/228 3.00 8.00
40 Anton Lundell/219 1.50 4.00
41 Ryan Strome/231 1.50 4.00
42 Milan Lucic/231 1.25 3.00
43 Marcus Foligno/230 1.25 3.00
44 Brandon Hagel/223 1.25 3.00
45 Zach Hyman/228 2.50 6.00
46 Robert Thomas/222 1.50 4.00
47 Drake Batherson/227 1.50 4.00
48 Jared McCann/236 1.25 3.00
49 Blake Coleman/233 1.25 3.00
50 Juraj Slafkovsky/222 3.00 8.00
51 Brandon Saad/228 1.25 3.00
52 Brendan Gallagher/228 1.50 4.00
53 John Gibson/230 1.50 4.00
54 Robby Fabbri/225 1.00 2.50
55 Dylan Cozens/235 1.50 4.00
56 Seth Jarvis/232 2.00 5.00
57 Roope Hintz/232 2.00 5.00
58 Jacob Markstrom/228 1.50 4.00
59 Anders Lee/231 1.25 3.00
60 Shea Theodore/222 2.00 5.00
61 Nikolaj Ehlers/225 1.50 4.00
62 Jake Oettinger/233 2.50 6.00
63 Philipp Grubauer/224 1.50 4.00
64 Arthur Kaliyev/225 1.50 4.00
65 Tristan Jarry/232 1.50 4.00
66 Darcy Kuemper/227 1.50 4.00
67 Jack Campbell/236 1.50 4.00
68 Mats Zuccarello/232 1.50 4.00
69 Dylan Guenther/220 2.00 5.00
70 Boone Jenner/230 1.50 4.00
71 Mario Ferraro/225 1.00 2.50
72 Vitek Vanecek/228 1.25 3.00
73 Tom Wilson/229 1.50 4.00
74 Filip Hronek/230 1.00 2.50
75 Tomas Hertl/226 1.50 4.00
76 Mark Stone/231 2.00 5.00
77 Jaccob Slavin/263 1.25 3.00
78 Alexander Romanov/226 1.25 3.00
79 Owen Power/221 1.50 4.00
80 Kirby Dach/223 1.50 4.00
81 K'Andre Miller/226 1.25 3.00
82 Thomas Chabot/227 1.50 4.00
83 Jake Sanderson/221 2.00 5.00
84 Gabriel Landeskog/230 2.00 5.00
85 Ryan Nugent-Hopkins/226 2.00 5.00
86 Evan Bouchard/231 2.00 5.00
87 Neal Pionk/228 1.00 2.50
88 Noah Dobson/224 2.00 5.00
89 Shane Pinto/223 1.25 3.00
90 Boris Katchouk/225 1.00 2.50
91 Yegor Sharangovich/225 1.50 4.00
92 Noah Cates/225 1.00 2.50
93 Filip Gustavsson/225 1.50 4.00
94 David Jiricek/235 1.50 4.00
95 David Perron/220 1.25 3.00
96 Evgenii Dadonov/235 1.25 3.00
97 Arber Xhekaj/223 2.00 5.00
98 Andreas Athanasiou/229 1.25 3.00
99 Joe Veleno/226 1.25 3.00
100 Ryan O'Reilly/233 1.50 4.00
101 Trevor Zegras/222 2.00 5.00
102 Mathew Barzal/226 2.00 5.00
103 Nicklas Backstrom/236 1.50 4.00
104 Cole Caufield/223 3.00 8.00
105 Quinn Hughes/224 2.00 5.00
106 William Nylander/227 4.00 10.00
107 Steven Stamkos/234 3.00 8.00
108 Jordan Kyrou/225 1.50 4.00
109 Tage Thompson/226 2.00 5.00
110 Jack Eichel/227 2.50 6.00
111 Matty Beniers/221 2.00 5.00
112 Jonathan Huberdeau/230 2.00 5.00
113 Nico Hischier/225 2.50 6.00
114 Joe Pavelski/239 2.00 5.00
115 Brayden Point/227 2.00 5.00
116 Auston Matthews/226 6.00 15.00
117 Marc-Andre Fleury/239 3.00 8.00
118 Roman Josi/233 2.00 5.00
119 Brad Marchand/235 3.00 8.00
120 Victor Hedman/233 2.00 5.00
121 Seth Jones/229 1.50 4.00
122 Brady Tkachuk/224 2.50 6.00
123 Alex Ovechkin/238 6.00 15.00
124 Cale Makar/225 4.00 10.00
125 Clayton Keller/225 2.00 5.00
126 Bo Horvat/225 2.00 5.00
127 Nick Suzuki/224 2.00 5.00
128 Aleksander Barkov/228 2.50 6.00
129 Matthew Tkachuk/226 3.00 8.00
130 Chandler Stephenson/229 1.25 3.00
131 Kevin Fiala/227 1.50 4.00
132 Leon Draisaitl/228 5.00 12.00
133 Ilya Sorokin/228 2.50 6.00
134 Igor Shesterkin/227 3.00 8.00
135 Logan Thompson/223 2.00 5.00
136 Andrei Svechnikov/223 2.00 5.00
137 Connor Hellebuyck/230 3.00 8.00
138 Josh Morrissey/228 2.00 5.00
139 Juuse Saros/228 2.00 5.00
140 Jack Hughes/222 4.00 10.00
141 Sidney Crosby/236 6.00 15.00
142 Andrei Vasilevskiy/229 2.50 6.00
143 Mikko Rantanen/227 4.00 10.00
144 Connor McDavid/227 8.00 20.00
145 Troy Terry/226 1.50 4.00
146 Jason Robertson/224 2.50 6.00
147 Brock Nelson/232 1.50 4.00
148 Adam Fox/230 2.00 5.00
149 Rasmus Dahlin/225 2.00 5.00
150 Nathan MacKinnon/227 6.00 15.00
151 Linus Ullmark/230 1.50 4.00
152 Erik Karlsson/233 2.50 6.00
153 Vladimir Tarasenko/230 2.00 5.00
154 Artemi Panarin/232 3.00 8.00
155 Johnny Gaudreau/229 2.50 6.00
156 Kevin Hayes/227 1.25 3.00
157 Mitch Marner/227 2.50 6.00
158 Elias Pettersson/225 2.50 6.00
159 Dylan Larkin/227 2.00 5.00
160 Stuart Skinner/225 2.00 5.00
161 Nikita Kucherov/227 3.00 8.00
162 David Pastrnak/227 4.00 10.00
163 Nazem Kadri/233 2.00 5.00
164 Kirill Kaprizov/226 5.00 12.00
165 Jari Kurri/253 1.50 4.00
166 Doug Gilmour/260 2.00 5.00
167 Rod Brind'Amour/253 1.50 4.00
168 Chris Chelios/262 1.50 4.00
169 Sergei Zubov/253 1.25 3.00
170 Ron Hextall/259 1.50 4.00
171 Keith Tkachuk/251 1.50 4.00
172 Vincent Lecavalier/243 1.50 4.00
173 Rob Blake/254 1.50 4.00
174 Denis Potvin/270 1.50 4.00
175 Teemu Selanne/253 3.00 8.00
176 Mike Modano/253 2.50 6.00
177 John LeClair/254 1.50 4.00
178 Ron Francis/260 2.00 5.00
179 Jarome Iginla/246 2.00 5.00
180 Dany Heatley/243 1.25 3.00
181 Ryan Getzlaf/238 1.50 4.00
182 Joe Sakic/254 3.00 8.00
183 Joe Thornton/244 2.50 6.00
184 Larry Robinson/257 1.50 4.00
185 Shane Doan/247 1.25 3.00
186 Steve Yzerman/258 4.00 10.00
187 Luc Robitaille/258 1.50 4.00
188 Henrik Lundqvist/241 4.00 10.00
189 Martin Brodeur/251 4.00 10.00
190 Tim Thomas/249 1.50 4.00
191 Grant Fuhr/261 2.50 6.00
192 Patrick Roy/258 4.00 10.00
193 Pekka Rinne/241 1.50 4.00
194 Dominik Hasek/259 2.50 6.00
195 Henrik Zetterberg/243 2.00 5.00
196 Rick Nash/239 1.50 4.00
197 Mario Lemieux/258 6.00 15.00
198 Jaromir Jagr/252 5.00 12.00
199 Wayne Gretzky/263 10.00 25.00
200 Ray Bourque/263 2.50 6.00
201 Samuel Bolduc/223 2.00 5.00
202 Billy Sweezey/227 2.00 5.00
203 Arnaud Durandeau/225 2.00 5.00
204 Jake Livingstone/224 2.00 5.00
205 Matt Murray/225 2.00 5.00
206 Hunter McKown/221 2.00 5.00
207 Wyatt Kaiser/221 2.00 5.00
208 Joona Koppanen/225 1.50 4.00
209 Jonathan Gruden/223 2.00 5.00
210 Cole McWard/223 2.00 5.00
211 Adam Ginning/224 2.00 5.00
212 Hugh McGing/225 2.00 5.00
213 Owen Beck/219 3.00 8.00
214 Egor Afanasyev/223 2.00 5.00
215 Nick Swaney/226 2.00 5.00
216 Vincent Desharnais/227 2.50 6.00
217 Bobby McMann/227 3.00 8.00
218 Aidan McDonough/224 1.50 4.00
219 Jaxson Stauber/224 2.00 5.00
220 Akito Hirose/224 1.50 4.00
221 Jakob Pelletier/222 2.50 6.00
222 Ridly Greig/221 3.00 8.00
223 Luke Evangelista/221 3.00 8.00
224 Yaroslav Askarov/221 5.00 12.00
225 Marco Kasper/219 5.00 12.00
226 Simon Edvinsson/220 4.00 10.00
227 Adam Fantilli/219 6.00 15.00
228 Leo Carlsson/219 6.00 15.00
229 Logan Cooley/222 6.00 15.00
230 Connor Bedard/218 125.00 300.00
231 Luke Hughes/220 6.00 15.00
232 Devon Levi/222 5.00 12.00
233 Stanislav Svozil/221 1.50 4.00
234 Dustin Wolf/222 6.00 15.00
235 Matthew Knies/221 8.00 20.00
236 Matthew Coronato/221 3.00 8.00
237 Tye Kartye/222 2.00 5.00
238 Brock Faber/221 5.00 12.00
239 Tyson Foerster/222 4.00 10.00
240 Sean Farrell/222 2.00 5.00
241 Will Cuylle/222 3.00 8.00
242 Samuel Knazko/221 2.00 5.00
243 Elliot Desnoyers/222 2.00 5.00
244 Zach Benson/218 3.00 8.00
245 Henry Thrun/222 2.00 5.00
246 Lukas Rousek/224 1.50 4.00
247 Luke Philp/228 2.00 5.00
248 Nikita Nesterenko/222 2.00 5.00
249 Michael Kesselring/224 2.00 5.00
250 Jiri Patera/225 3.00 8.00
251 Olle Eriksson Ek/224 2.00 5.00
252 Cole Guttman/224 2.00 5.00
253 Milos Kelemen/224 2.00 5.00
254 Walker Duehr/226 1.50 4.00
255 Jet Greaves/222 3.00 8.00
256 William Dufour/222 1.50 4.00
257 Levi Merilainen/221 2.00 5.00
258 David Gust/229 2.00 5.00
259 Matthew Kessel/223 1.50 4.00
260 Jackson LaCombe/223 2.00 5.00
261 Drew Helleson/222 2.00 5.00
262 Lucas Condotta/226 2.00 5.00
263 Mikael Pyyhtia/222 2.00 5.00
264 Tyler Kleven/222 2.00 5.00
265 Tyler Angle/223 2.00 5.00
266 Maxence Guenette/222 2.00 5.00
267 Vincent Iorio/221 2.00 5.00
268 Damien Giroux/223 2.00 5.00
269 Joel Teasdale/224 2.00 5.00
270 Spencer Stastney/226 2.00 5.00
271 Emil Andrae/221 2.00 5.00
272 Fraser Minten/219 4.00 10.00
273 John Beecher/222 4.00 10.00
274 Pavel Mintyukov/220 3.00 8.00
275 Matt Savoie/219 4.00 10.00
276 Mackie Samoskevich/221 3.00 8.00
277 Kevin Korchinski/219 3.00 8.00
278 Tristan Luneau/220 2.00 5.00
279 Matthew Poitras/219 4.00 10.00
280 Alex Laferriere/222 3.00 8.00

2023-24 SP Game Used '01 Retro Rookie Crossover

RC1 Marco Kasper 2.50 6.00
RC2 Luke Hughes 3.00 8.00
RC3 Brock Faber 2.50 6.00
RC4 Luke Evangelista 1.50 4.00
RC6 Tyson Foerster 2.00 5.00
RC7 Connor Bedard 100.00 250.00
RC8 Adam Fantilli 3.00 8.00
RC9 Matthew Coronato 1.50 4.00
RC10 Matthew Knies 4.00 10.00
RC11 Simon Edvinsson 2.00 5.00
RC12 Owen Beck 1.50 4.00
RC13 Yaroslav Askarov 2.50 6.00
RC14 Logan Cooley 3.00 8.00
RC15 Zach Benson 1.50 4.00

2023-24 SP Game Used '03-04 Retro Rookie Debut

R1 Adam Fantilli 3.00 8.00
R2 Aidan McDonough .75 2.00
R3 Logan Cooley 3.00 8.00
R4 Dustin Wolf 3.00 8.00
R5 Brock Faber 2.50 6.00
R6 Connor Bedard 60.00 150.00
R7 Devon Levi 2.50 6.00
R8 Luke Hughes 3.00 8.00
R9 Ridly Greig 1.50 4.00
R10 Owen Beck 1.50 4.00
R11 Tyson Foerster 2.00 5.00
R12 Will Cuylle 1.50 4.00
R13 Yaroslav Askarov 2.50 6.00
R14 Matt Savoie 2.00 5.00
R15 Marco Kasper 2.50 6.00
R16 Matthew Knies 4.00 10.00
R17 Sean Farrell 1.00 2.50
R18 Simon Edvinsson 2.00 5.00
R19 Matthew Coronato 1.50 4.00
R20 Stanislav Svozil .75 2.00

2023-24 SP Game Used '03-04 Retro Rookie Debut Platinum Blue

*BLUE/25: 1.5X TO 4X BASIC
R1 Adam Fantilli 30.00 80.00
R3 Logan Cooley 20.00 50.00
R5 Brock Faber 30.00 80.00
R6 Connor Bedard 200.00 500.00
R8 Luke Hughes 40.00 100.00
R11 Tyson Foerster 15.00 40.00
R12 Will Cuylle 20.00 50.00

2023-24 SP Game Used '22 Global Series Fabrics

*PATCH/35: 1.2X TO 3X BASIC
GS1 Roman Josi 1.50 4.00
GS2 Filip Forsberg 2.50 6.00
GS3 Juuse Saros 2.00 5.00
GS4 Matt Duchene 1.50 4.00
GS5 Nino Niederreiter 1.00 2.50
GS6 Colton Sissons 1.00 2.50
GS7 Erik Karlsson 2.00 5.00
GS8 Timo Meier 1.50 4.00
GS9 Tomas Hertl 1.50 4.00
GS10 Nick Bonino 1.00 2.50
GS11 Logan Couture 2.00 5.00
GS12 Mario Ferraro 1.00 2.50
GS13 Devon Toews 1.25 3.00
GS15 Alexandar Georgiev 1.50 4.00
GS16 Cale Makar 4.00 10.00
GS17 Mikko Rantanen 4.00 10.00
GS19 Josh Manson 1.00 2.50
GS20 Boone Jenner 1.50 4.00
GS21 Patrik Laine 2.00 5.00
GS22 Cole Sillinger 1.25 3.00
GS23 Elvis Merzlikins 1.50 4.00
GS24 Johnny Gaudreau 2.50 6.00
GS25 Kent Johnson 1.50 4.00

2023-24 SP Game Used '22 Global Series Puck Relics

GSPCM Cale Makar 80.00 200.00
GSPEK Erik Karlsson 40.00 100.00
GSPFF Filip Forsberg 50.00 125.00
GSPJG Johnny Gaudreau 50.00 125.00
GSPJS Juuse Saros 40.00 100.00
GSPKJ Kent Johnson 30.00 80.00
GSPMR Mikko Rantanen 80.00 200.00
GSPNM Nathan MacKinnon 125.00 300.00
GSPRJ Roman Josi 30.00 80.00
GSPTM Timo Meier 30.00 80.00

2023-24 SP Game Used '23 All Star Game Net Cord Relics

ASNAF Adam Fox 20.00 50.00
ASNAO Alex Ovechkin 60.00 150.00
ASNAP Artemi Panarin 30.00 80.00
ASNAV Andrei Vasilevskiy 25.00 60.00
ASNBH Bo Horvat 20.00 50.00
ASNBT Brady Tkachuk 25.00 60.00
ASNCH Connor Hellebuyck 30.00 80.00
ASNCK Clayton Keller 20.00 50.00
ASNCM Connor McDavid 80.00 200.00
ASNCS Chandler Stephenson 12.00 30.00
ASNDL Dylan Larkin 20.00 50.00
ASNEK Erik Karlsson 20.00 50.00
ASNEP Elias Pettersson 25.00 60.00
ASNIS Igor Shesterkin 30.00 80.00
ASNJG Johnny Gaudreau 25.00 60.00
ASNJH Jack Hughes 40.00 100.00
ASNJM Josh Morrissey 20.00 50.00
ASNJR Jason Robertson 25.00 60.00
ASNJS Juuse Saros 20.00 50.00
ASNKF Kevin Fiala 12.00 30.00
ASNKK Kirill Kaprizov 50.00 125.00
ASNLD Leon Draisaitl 50.00 125.00
ASNLU Linus Ullmark 15.00 40.00
ASNMA Cale Makar 40.00 100.00
ASNMM Mitch Marner 25.00 60.00
ASNMR Mikko Rantanen 40.00 100.00
ASNMT Matthew Tkachuk 30.00 80.00
ASNNK Nikita Kucherov 30.00 80.00
ASNNM Nathan MacKinnon 60.00 150.00
ASNRD Rasmus Dahlin 20.00 50.00
ASNSC Sidney Crosby 60.00 150.00
ASNSO Ilya Sorokin 25.00 60.00
ASNTT Troy Terry 12.00 30.00

2023-24 SP Game Used '23 All Star Game Puck Relics

ASPAO Alex Ovechkin 50.00 120.00
ASPCM Connor McDavid 60.00 150.00
ASPDP David Pastrnak 30.00 80.00
ASPJH Jack Hughes 30.00 80.00
ASPJR Jason Robertson 20.00 50.00
ASPKK Kirill Kaprizov 40.00 100.00
ASPLD Leon Draisaitl 40.00 100.00
ASPNK Nikita Kucherov 25.00 60.00
ASPNM Nathan MacKinnon 50.00 125.00
ASPSC Sidney Crosby 50.00 125.00

2023-24 SP Game Used '23 All Star Mascot Fabrics

ASMBE Bernie the St. Bernard 6.00 15.00
ASMBL Bailey 6.00 15.00
ASMBT Blades The Bruin 6.00 15.00
ASMBY Buoy 6.00 15.00
ASMCH Chance 12.00 30.00
ASMCT Carlton the Bear 6.00 15.00
ASMFT Fin The Whale 6.00 15.00
ASMGN Gnash 6.00 15.00
ASMGR Gritty 25.00 60.00
ASMHO Howler 6.00 15.00
ASMHU Hunter 6.00 15.00
ASMIC Iceburgh 6.00 15.00
ASMLU Louie 6.00 15.00
ASMMO Moose 6.00 15.00
ASMND N.J. Devil 6.00 15.00
ASMNR Nordy 6.00 15.00
ASMPA Stanley C. Panther 6.00 15.00
ASMSB Sabretooth 6.00 15.00
ASMSC Spartacat 6.00 15.00
ASMSL Slapshot 6.00 15.00
ASMSP Sparky The Dragon 6.00 15.00
ASMSS S.J. Sharkie 6.00 15.00
ASMST Stormy 6.00 15.00
ASMTB Thunderbug 6.00 15.00
ASMTH Tommy Hawk 6.00 15.00
ASMVG Victor E. Green 6.00 15.00
ASMWW Wild Wing 6.00 15.00
ASMYP Youppi 12.00 30.00

2023-24 SP Game Used '23 All Star Mascot Fabrics Patch

*PATCH/35: .6X TO 1.5X BASIC
ASMBE Bernie the St. Bernard 25.00 60.00
ASMBY Buoy 30.00 80.00
ASMCH Chance 30.00 80.00
ASMCT Carlton the Bear 20.00 50.00
ASMGR Gritty 80.00 200.00
ASMSB Sabretooth 20.00 50.00
ASMSS S.J. Sharkie 20.00 50.00
ASMST Stormy 15.00 40.00
ASMVG Victor E. Green 15.00 40.00
ASMYP Youppi 25.00 60.00

2023-24 SP Game Used '23 All Star Skills Accuracy Jersey Relics

ASA1 Aleksander Barkov 15.00 40.00
ASA2 Leon Draisaitl 12.00 30.00
ASA3 Kevin Hayes 8.00 20.00
ASA4 Jack Hughes 12.00 30.00
ASA5 Nazem Kadri 12.00 30.00
ASA6 Nikita Kucherov 25.00 30.00
ASA7 Connor McDavid 20.00 50.00
ASA8 Brock Nelson 10.00 25.00
ASA9 Artemi Panarin 12.00 30.00
ASA10 Vladimir Tarasenko 12.00 30.00

2023-24 SP Game Used '23 All Star Skills Dual Jerseys

ASDAB Aleksander Barkov 5.00 12.00
ASDAO Alex Ovechkin 12.00 30.00
ASDAP Artemi Panarin 6.00 15.00
ASDBN Brock Nelson 3.00 8.00
ASDCK Clayton Keller 4.00 10.00
ASDCM Connor McDavid 15.00 40.00
ASDDL Dylan Larkin 4.00 10.00
ASDDP David Pastrnak 8.00 20.00
ASDEP Elias Pettersson 5.00 12.00
ASDIS Igor Shesterkin 6.00 15.00
ASDJH Jack Hughes 8.00 20.00
ASDJR Jason Robertson 5.00 12.00
ASDJS Juuse Saros 4.00 10.00
ASDKF Kevin Fiala 2.50 6.00
ASDLD Leon Draisaitl 10.00 25.00
ASDMA Cale Makar 8.00 20.00
ASDMM Mitch Marner 5.00 12.00
ASDMT Matthew Tkachuk 6.00 15.00
ASDNK Nikita Kucherov 6.00 15.00
ASDNM Nathan MacKinnon 12.00 30.00
ASDNS Nick Suzuki 6.00 15.00
ASDRD Rasmus Dahlin 4.00 10.00
ASDSC Sidney Crosby 12.00 30.00
ASDSJ Seth Jones 3.00 8.00

2023-24 SP Game Used '23 All Star Skills Dual Jerseys Patch

*PATCH/35: .75X TO 2X BASIC
ASDCM Connor McDavid 60.00 150.00
ASDKF Kevin Fiala 20.00 50.00
ASDMT Matthew Tkachuk 30.00 80.00
ASDSC Sidney Crosby 60.00 150.00

2023-24 SP Game Used '23 All Star Skills Net Cord Relics

SKNAB Aleksander Barkov 25.00 60.00
SKNAF Adam Fox 20.00 50.00
SKNAO Alex Ovechkin 60.00 150.00
SKNAS Andrei Svechnikov 20.00 50.00
SKNAV Andrei Vasilevskiy 25.00 60.00
SKNBN Brock Nelson 15.00 40.00
SKNBT Brady Tkachuk 25.00 60.00
SKNCH Connor Hellebuyck 30.00 80.00
SKNCM Connor McDavid 80.00 200.00
SKNCS Chandler Stephenson 12.00 30.00
SKNDP David Pastrnak 40.00 100.00
SKNEP Elias Pettersson 25.00 60.00
SKNJH Jack Hughes 40.00 100.00
SKNJM Josh Morrissey 20.00 50.00
SKNJR Jason Robertson 25.00 60.00
SKNJS Juuse Saros 20.00 50.00
SKNKF Kevin Fiala 12.00 30.00
SKNKH Kevin Hayes 12.00 30.00
SKNKU Nikita Kucherov 30.00 80.00
SKNLD Leon Draisaitl 50.00 125.00
SKNLT Logan Thompson 20.00 50.00
SKNLU Linus Ullmark 15.00 40.00
SKNMA Cale Makar 40.00 100.00
SKNMM Mitch Marner 25.00 60.00
SKNMR Mikko Rantanen 40.00 100.00
SKNMT Matthew Tkachuk 30.00 80.00
SKNNK Nazem Kadri 20.00 50.00
SKNNM Nathan MacKinnon 60.00 150.00
SKNNS Nick Suzuki 30.00 80.00
SKNRD Rasmus Dahlin 20.00 50.00
SKNSC Sidney Crosby 60.00 150.00
SKNSJ Seth Jones 15.00 40.00
SKNSS Stuart Skinner 20.00 50.00
SKNVT Vladimir Tarasenko 20.00 50.00

2023-24 SP Game Used '23 Debut Net Cord Relics

DEBCB Connor Bedard 1000.00 2500.00

2023-24 SP Game Used '23 Stadium Series Fabrics

*PATCH/35: 3X TO 8X BASIC
STS1 Sebastian Aho 3.00 8.00
STS2 Brent Burns 2.00 5.00
STS3 Andrei Svechnikov 2.50 6.00
STS4 Teuvo Teravainen 2.00 5.00
STS5 Martin Necas 3.00 8.00
STS6 Frederik Andersen 2.50 6.00
STS7 Seth Jarvis 2.50 6.00
STS8 Jesperi Kotkaniemi 2.00 5.00
STS9 Brady Skjei 1.25 3.00
STS10 Jaccob Slavin 1.50 4.00
STS11 T.J. Oshie 2.00 5.00
STS12 Nicklas Backstrom 2.00 5.00
STS13 Dylan Strome 2.50 6.00
STS14 Tom Wilson 2.00 5.00
STS15 Darcy Kuemper 2.00 5.00
STS16 Sonny Milano 1.50 4.00
STS17 Evgeny Kuznetsov 2.50 6.00
STS18 Dmitry Orlov 2.00 5.00
STS19 Erik Gustafsson 1.25 3.00
STS20 Garnet Hathaway 1.25 3.00

2023-24 SP Game Used '23 Stadium Series Puck Relics

SSPAS Andrei Svechnikov 30.00 80.00
SSPBB Brent Burns 25.00 60.00
SSPDK Darcy Kuemper 25.00 60.00
SSPDS Dylan Strome 30.00 80.00
SSPMN Martin Necas 40.00 100.00
SSPNB Nicklas Backstrom 25.00 60.00
SSPSA Sebastian Aho 40.00 100.00
SSPTO T.J. Oshie 25.00 60.00
SSPTT Teuvo Teravainen 25.00 60.00
SSPTW Tom Wilson 25.00 60.00

2023-24 SP Game Used '23 Stanley Cup Finals Net Cord Relics

SCNAB Aleksander Barkov 120.00 300.00
SCNAE Aaron Ekblad 100.00 250.00
SCNAH Adin Hill 80.00 200.00
SCNAL Anton Lundell 80.00 200.00
SCNAP Alex Pietrangelo 60.00 150.00
SCNBM Brandon Montour 100.00 250.00
SCNCS Chandler Stephenson 60.00 150.00
SCNCV Carter Verhaeghe 80.00 200.00
SCNJE Jack Eichel 150.00 400.00
SCNJM Jonathan Marchessault 100.00 250.00
SCNMS Mark Stone 100.00 250.00
SCNMT Matthew Tkachuk 150.00 400.00
SCNSB Sergei Bobrovsky 125.00 300.00
SCNSR Sam Reinhart 150.00 400.00
SCNST Shea Theodore 100.00 250.00
SCNWK William Karlsson 100.00 250.00

2023-24 SP Game Used '23 Stanley Cup Finals Puck Relics

SCPAB Aleksander Barkov 120.00 300.00
SCPAE Aaron Ekblad 100.00 250.00
SCPAH Adin Hill 80.00 200.00
SCPAP Alex Pietrangelo 60.00 150.00
SCPBM Brandon Montour 100.00 250.00
SCPCS Chandler Stephenson 60.00 150.00
SCPCV Carter Verhaeghe 80.00 200.00
SCPJE Jack Eichel 120.00 300.00
SCPJM Jonathan Marchessault 100.00 250.00
SCPMS Mark Stone 100.00 250.00
SCPMT Matthew Tkachuk 150.00 400.00
SCPSB Sergei Bobrovsky 125.00 300.00
SCPSR Sam Reinhart 150.00 400.00
SCPST Shea Theodore 100.00 250.00

2023-24 SP Game Used '23 Winter Classic Fabrics

WC1 David Pastrnak 8.00 20.00
WC2 Linus Ullmark 3.00 8.00
WC3 Brad Marchand 6.00 15.00
WC4 Patrice Bergeron 4.00 10.00
WC5 Charlie McAvoy 4.00 10.00
WC6 Hampus Lindholm 2.00 5.00
WC7 David Krejci 3.00 8.00
WC8 Pavel Zacha 2.50 6.00
WC9 Charlie Coyle 3.00 8.00
WC10 Brandon Carlo 2.50 6.00
WC11 Derek Forbort 2.00 5.00
WC12 Nick Foligno 2.00 5.00
WC13 Connor Clifton 2.00 5.00
WC14 Sidney Crosby 12.00 30.00
WC15 Evgeni Malkin 6.00 15.00
WC16 Jake Guentzel 5.00 12.00
WC17 Rickard Rakell 2.50 6.00
WC18 Tristan Jarry 3.00 8.00
WC19 Jeff Carter 2.50 6.00
WC20 Kasperi Kapanen 2.50 6.00
WC21 Pierre-Olivier Joseph 2.00 5.00
WC22 Bryan Rust 3.00 8.00
WC23 Jan Rutta 2.00 5.00
WC24 Danton Heinen 2.00 5.00
WC25 Jason Zucker 3.00 8.00

2023-24 SP Game Used '23 Winter Classic Fabrics Patch

*PATCH/35: 3X TO 8X BASIC
WC4 Patrice Bergeron 80.00 200.00
WC12 Nick Foligno 30.00 80.00
WC16 Jake Guentzel 15.00 40.00

2023-24 SP Game Used '23 Winter Classic Net Cord Relics

WCNBM Brad Marchand 60.00 150.00
WCNCM Charlie McAvoy 40.00 100.00
WCNDP David Pastrnak 80.00 200.00
WCNEM Evgeni Malkin 80.00 200.00
WCNHL Hampus Lindholm 20.00 50.00
WCNJC Jeff Carter 25.00 60.00
WCNJD Jake DeBrusk 30.00 80.00
WCNJG Jake Guentzel 50.00 120.00
WCNLU Linus Ullmark 30.00 80.00
WCNPB Patrice Bergeron 80.00 200.00
WCNPJ Pierre-Olivier Joseph 20.00 50.00
WCNPZ Pavel Zacha 25.00 60.00
WCNRR Rickard Rakell 25.00 60.00
WCNSC Sidney Crosby 100.00 250.00
WCNTJ Tristan Jarry 30.00 80.00

2023-24 SP Game Used '23 Winter Classic Puck Relics

WCPBM Brad Marchand 60.00 150.00
WCPCM Charlie McAvoy 40.00 100.00
WCPDP David Pastrnak 80.00 200.00
WCPEM Evgeni Malkin 60.00 150.00
WCPJG Jake Guentzel 50.00 120.00
WCPLU Linus Ullmark 30.00 80.00
WCPPB Patrice Bergeron 40.00 100.00
WCPRR Rickard Rakell 25.00 60.00
WCPSC Sidney Crosby 125.00 300.00
WCPTJ Tristan Jarry 30.00 80.00

2023-24 SP Game Used A Piece of History Jerseys

*PATCH/25: 2X TO 5X BASIC
AAG Alexandar Georgiev 15.00 40.00
ADP David Pastrnak 20.00 50.00
AEK Erik Karlsson 10.00 25.00
AHA Dale Hawerchuk 10.00 25.00
AHL Henrik Lundqvist 20.00 50.00
AJP Joe Pavelski 10.00 25.00
AJR Jason Robertson 12.00 30.00
ALU Linus Ullmark 12.00 30.00
AMH Marian Hossa 8.00 20.00
ANM Nathan MacKinnon 20.00 50.00
APC Paul Coffey 8.00 20.00
APK Patrick Kane 15.00 40.00
APR Patrick Roy 20.00 50.00
ASS Steven Stamkos 30.00 80.00

2023-24 SP Game Used Autographs

3 Timo Meier 8.00 20.00
5 William Karlsson SP 10.00 25.00
13 Kris Letang SP 10.00 25.00
15 John Tavares SP 12.00 30.00
17 Alexis Lafreniere SP 12.00 30.00
18 Jake Guentzel 12.00 30.00
19 Karel Vejmelka 5.00 12.00
20 Shane Wright SP 10.00 25.00
22 Carter Hart SP 8.00 20.00
23 Jonathan Marchessault 10.00 25.00
24 Teuvo Teravainen SP 8.00 20.00
25 Kent Johnson 8.00 20.00
26 Cole Perfetti 8.00 20.00
27 Evgeny Kuznetsov 10.00 25.00
29 Ukko-Pekka Luukkonen 6.00 15.00
31 Miro Heiskanen SP 10.00 25.00
33 Jordan Eberle 8.00 20.00
34 Jamie Drysdale SP 6.00 15.00
35 Nick Schmaltz 6.00 15.00
37 Taylor Raddysh 6.00 15.00
39 Sam Reinhart 15.00 40.00
40 Anton Lundell 8.00 20.00
41 Ryan Strome 8.00 20.00
44 Brandon Hagel SP 6.00 15.00
45 Zach Hyman SP 12.00 30.00
46 Robert Thomas SP 8.00 20.00
47 Drake Batherson 8.00 20.00
48 Jared McCann SP 6.00 15.00
49 Blake Coleman 6.00 15.00
51 Brandon Saad 6.00 15.00
52 Brendan Gallagher 8.00 20.00
53 John Gibson SP 8.00 20.00
55 Dylan Cozens SP 8.00 20.00
56 Seth Jarvis 10.00 25.00
57 Roope Hintz 10.00 25.00
58 Jacob Markstrom SP 8.00 20.00
59 Anders Lee 6.00 15.00
60 Shea Theodore 10.00 25.00
62 Jake Oettinger SP 12.00 30.00
66 Darcy Kuemper SP 8.00 20.00
67 Jack Campbell SP 8.00 20.00
69 Dylan Guenther 10.00 25.00
70 Boone Jenner 8.00 20.00
71 Mario Ferraro 5.00 12.00
73 Tom Wilson SP 8.00 20.00
75 Tomas Hertl SP 8.00 20.00
76 Mark Stone SP 10.00 25.00
77 Jaccob Slavin SP 6.00 15.00
78 Alexander Romanov 6.00 15.00
79 Owen Power SP 8.00 20.00
80 Kirby Dach 8.00 20.00
81 K'Andre Miller SP 6.00 15.00
82 Thomas Chabot 8.00 20.00
83 Jake Sanderson SP 10.00 25.00
84 Gabriel Landeskog SP 10.00 25.00
86 Evan Bouchard SP 10.00 25.00
87 Neal Pionk 5.00 12.00
89 Shane Pinto 6.00 15.00
90 Boris Katchouk 5.00 12.00
91 Yegor Sharangovich 8.00 20.00
92 Noah Cates 5.00 12.00
93 Filip Gustavsson 8.00 20.00
94 David Jiricek 8.00 20.00
96 Evgenii Dadonov 5.00 12.00
97 Arber Xhekaj SP 8.00 20.00
99 Joe Veleno 6.00 15.00
100 Ryan O'Reilly SP 8.00 20.00
110 Jack Eichel SP 12.00 30.00
111 Matty Beniers SP 10.00 25.00
112 Jonathan Huberdeau 10.00 25.00
113 Nico Hischier SP 12.00 30.00
114 Joe Pavelski 10.00 25.00
115 Brayden Point SP 10.00 25.00
117 Marc-Andre Fleury SP 15.00 40.00
118 Roman Josi 8.00 20.00
119 Brad Marchand SP 15.00 40.00
120 Victor Hedman SP 10.00 25.00
122 Brady Tkachuk 12.00 30.00
123 Alex Ovechkin SP 80.00 200.00
124 Cale Makar SP 30.00 80.00
125 Clayton Keller SP 10.00 25.00
127 Nick Suzuki SP 15.00 40.00
128 Aleksander Barkov 12.00 30.00
129 Matthew Tkachuk SP 15.00 40.00
130 Chandler Stephenson 6.00 15.00
131 Kevin Fiala 6.00 15.00
133 Ilya Sorokin SP 12.00 30.00
135 Logan Thompson 10.00 25.00
136 Andrei Svechnikov 10.00 25.00
137 Connor Hellebuyck 15.00 40.00
138 Josh Morrissey 10.00 25.00
139 Juuse Saros 10.00 25.00
140 Jack Hughes SP 50.00 125.00
141 Sidney Crosby SP 60.00 150.00
142 Andrei Vasilevskiy SP 12.00 30.00
143 Mikko Rantanen SP 20.00 50.00
144 Connor McDavid SP 250.00 600.00
145 Troy Terry 6.00 15.00
147 Brock Nelson 8.00 20.00
155 Johnny Gaudreau SP 12.00 30.00
156 Kevin Hayes 6.00 15.00
157 Mitch Marner SP 12.00 30.00
158 Elias Pettersson SP 12.00 30.00
159 Dylan Larkin SP 10.00 25.00
165 Jari Kurri SP 8.00 20.00
166 Doug Gilmour SP 10.00 25.00
167 Rod Brind'Amour SP 8.00 20.00
168 Chris Chelios SP 8.00 20.00
169 Sergei Zubov SP 6.00 15.00
170 Ron Hextall SP 8.00 20.00
171 Keith Tkachuk SP 8.00 20.00
172 Vincent Lecavalier SP 8.00 20.00
173 Rob Blake SP 8.00 20.00
174 Denis Potvin SP 8.00 20.00
175 Teemu Selanne SP 15.00 40.00
176 Mike Modano SP 12.00 30.00
177 John LeClair SP 8.00 20.00
178 Ron Francis SP 10.00 25.00
179 Jarome Iginla SP 10.00 25.00
180 Dany Heatley SP 6.00 15.00
182 Joe Sakic SP 15.00 40.00
183 Joe Thornton SP 12.00 30.00
184 Larry Robinson SP 8.00 20.00
186 Steve Yzerman SP 20.00 50.00
187 Luc Robitaille SP 8.00 20.00
188 Henrik Lundqvist SP 20.00 50.00
189 Martin Brodeur SP 20.00 50.00
190 Tim Thomas SP 8.00 20.00
191 Grant Fuhr SP 12.00 30.00
192 Patrick Roy SP 60.00 150.00
194 Dominik Hasek SP 12.00 30.00
195 Henrik Zetterberg SP 10.00 25.00
197 Mario Lemieux SP 80.00 200.00
200 Ray Bourque SP 12.00 30.00
201 Samuel Bolduc 8.00 20.00
202 Billy Sweezey 8.00 20.00
203 Arnaud Durandeau 8.00 20.00
205 Matt Murray 8.00 20.00
206 Hunter McKown SP 8.00 20.00
207 Wyatt Kaiser 8.00 20.00
208 Joona Koppanen 6.00 15.00
209 Jonathan Gruden 8.00 20.00
210 Cole McWard 8.00 20.00
211 Adam Ginning 8.00 20.00
212 Hugh McGing 8.00 20.00
213 Owen Beck 12.00 30.00
214 Egor Afanasyev 8.00 20.00
215 Nick Swaney 8.00 20.00
216 Vincent Desharnais 10.00 25.00
217 Bobby McMann 12.00 30.00
218 Aidan McDonough 6.00 15.00
219 Jaxson Stauber 8.00 20.00
220 Akito Hirose 6.00 15.00
221 Jakob Pelletier 10.00 25.00
222 Ridly Greig 12.00 30.00
224 Yaroslav Askarov SP 20.00 50.00
225 Marco Kasper 20.00 50.00
226 Simon Edvinsson 15.00 40.00
228 Leo Carlsson SP 80.00 200.00
230 Connor Bedard SP 800.00 2000.00
231 Luke Hughes SP 30.00 80.00
232 Devon Levi SP 30.00 80.00
233 Stanislav Svozil 6.00 15.00
234 Dustin Wolf SP 25.00 60.00
235 Matthew Knies 40.00 100.00
236 Matthew Coronato 12.00 30.00
237 Tye Kartye 12.00 30.00
238 Brock Faber 60.00 150.00
239 Tyson Foerster 15.00 40.00
240 Sean Farrell 8.00 20.00
241 Will Cuylle 12.00 30.00
242 Samuel Knazko 8.00 20.00
243 Elliot Desnoyers 8.00 20.00
244 Zach Benson 12.00 30.00
245 Henry Thrun 8.00 20.00
246 Lukas Rousek 6.00 15.00
247 Luke Philp 8.00 20.00
248 Nikita Nesterenko 8.00 20.00
249 Michael Kesselring 8.00 20.00
250 Jiri Patera 12.00 30.00
251 Olle Eriksson Ek 8.00 20.00
252 Cole Guttman 8.00 20.00
253 Milos Kelemen 8.00 20.00
254 Walker Duehr 6.00 15.00
255 Jet Greaves 12.00 30.00
256 William Dufour 6.00 15.00
257 Leevi Merilainen 8.00 20.00
258 David Gust 8.00 20.00
259 Matthew Kessel 6.00 15.00
264 Tyler Kleven 8.00 20.00
267 Vincent Iorio 8.00 20.00
273 John Beecher 15.00 40.00
274 Pavel Mintyukov 12.00 30.00
275 Matt Savoie SP 15.00 40.00
276 Mackie Samoskevich 12.00 30.00
277 Kevin Korchinski SP 12.00 30.00
278 Tristan Luneau 8.00 20.00
279 Matthew Poitras 15.00 40.00
280 Alex Laferriere 12.00 30.00

2023-24 SP Game Used Banner Year '21 Seattle Kraken Expansion Draft

BYKRBT Brandon Tanev 4.00 10.00
BYKRGE Morgan Geekie 3.00 8.00
BYKRJD Joonas Donskoi 3.00 8.00
BYKRJE Jordan Eberle 5.00 12.00
BYKRJM Jared McCann 4.00 10.00
BYKRJO Jamie Oleksiak 4.00 10.00
BYKRMG Mark Giordano 5.00 12.00
BYKRRF Ron Francis 6.00 15.00
BYKRVD Vince Dunn 4.00 10.00
BYKRYG Yanni Gourde 4.00 10.00

2023-24 SP Game Used Banner Year '22 Global Series

BYGSBB Bowen Byram 4.00 10.00
BYGSBJ Boone Jenner 3.00 8.00
BYGSCM Cale Makar 8.00 20.00
BYGSCS Cole Sillinger 2.50 6.00
BYGSFF Filip Forsberg 5.00 12.00
BYGSJG Johnny Gaudreau 5.00 12.00
BYGSJS Juuse Saros 4.00 10.00
BYGSKJ Kent Johnson 3.00 8.00
BYGSLC Logan Couture 4.00 10.00
BYGSMD Matt Duchene 3.00 8.00
BYGSMF Mario Ferraro 2.00 5.00
BYGSMR Mikko Rantanen 8.00 20.00
BYGSNM Nathan MacKinnon 8.00 20.00
BYGSTH Tomas Hertl 3.00 8.00
BYGSTM Timo Meier 3.00 8.00

2023-24 SP Game Used Banner Year '22 Global Series Autographs

BYGSBB Bowen Byram/25 25.00 60.00
BYGSBJ Boone Jenner/25 20.00 50.00
BYGSCS Cole Sillinger/25 15.00 40.00
BYGSKJ Kent Johnson/25 20.00 50.00
BYGSMD Matt Duchene/25 20.00 50.00
BYGSMF Mario Ferraro/25 12.00 30.00
BYGSTH Tomas Hertl/25 20.00 50.00

2023-24 SP Game Used Banner Year '23 Stadium Series

BYSSAS Andrei Svechnikov 4.00 10.00
BYSSBB Brent Burns 3.00 8.00
BYSSDK Darcy Kuemper 3.00 8.00
BYSSDO Dmitry Orlov 3.00 8.00
BYSSEG Erik Gustafsson 2.00 5.00
BYSSEK Evgeny Kuznetsov 4.00 10.00
BYSSJS Jaccob Slavin 2.50 6.00
BYSSMN Martin Necas 5.00 12.00
BYSSSA Sebastian Aho 5.00 12.00
BYSSSM Sonny Milano 2.50 6.00
BYSSTT Teuvo Teravainen 3.00 8.00
BYSSTW Tom Wilson 3.00 8.00

2023-24 SP Game Used Banner Year '23 Stadium Series Autographs

BYSSDK Darcy Kuemper/25 40.00 100.00
BYSSEG Erik Gustafsson/25 25.00 60.00
BYSSJS Jaccob Slavin/25 30.00 80.00
BYSSMN Martin Necas/25 60.00 150.00
BYSSTT Teuvo Teravainen/25 40.00 100.00

2023-24 SP Game Used Banner Year '23 Winter Classic

BYWCBM Brad Marchand 6.00 15.00
BYWCBR Bryan Rust 3.00 8.00
BYWCCC Charlie Coyle 3.00 8.00
BYWCCM Charlie McAvoy 4.00 10.00
BYWCDP David Pastrnak 8.00 20.00
BYWCEM Evgeni Malkin 6.00 15.00
BYWCHL Hampus Lindholm 2.00 5.00
BYWCJC Jeff Carter 2.50 6.00
BYWCJS Jeremy Swayman 5.00 12.00
BYWCKK Kasperi Kapanen 2.50 6.00
BYWCLU Linus Ullmark 3.00 8.00
BYWCPB Patrice Bergeron 4.00 10.00
BYWCPJ Pierre-Olivier Joseph 2.00 5.00
BYWCRR Rickard Rakell 2.50 6.00
BYWCSC Sidney Crosby 12.00 30.00
BYWCTJ Tristan Jarry 3.00 8.00

2023-24 SP Game Used Banner Year '23 Winter Classic Autographs

BYWCBR Bryan Rust/25 25.00 60.00
BYWCCC Charlie Coyle/25 25.00 60.00
BYWCKK Kasperi Kapanen/25 20.00 50.00
BYWCTJ Tristan Jarry/25 25.00 60.00

2023-24 SP Game Used Banner Year NHL Draft

BYDRAF Adam Fantilli 6.00 15.00
BYDRAM Auston Matthews 8.00 20.00
BYDRAS Andrei Svechnikov 2.50 6.00
BYDRAV Andrei Vasilevskiy 3.00 8.00
BYDRCB Connor Bedard 40.00 100.00
BYDRCH Carter Hart 2.00 5.00
BYDRCK Clayton Keller 2.50 6.00
BYDRCM Connor McDavid 10.00 25.00
BYDRDJ David Jiricek 2.00 5.00
BYDRJE Jack Eichel 3.00 8.00
BYDRJO Jake Oettinger 3.00 8.00
BYDRLC Logan Cooley 6.00 15.00
BYDRMA Cale Makar 5.00 12.00
BYDRMK Marco Kasper 5.00 12.00
BYDRMR Mikko Rantanen 5.00 12.00
BYDRMT Matthew Tkachuk 4.00 10.00
BYDRNH Nico Hischier 3.00 8.00
BYDROB Owen Beck 3.00 8.00
BYDRTH Tomas Hertl 2.00 5.00
BYDRTT Tage Thompson 2.50 6.00

2023-24 SP Game Used Deep Cuts

DC1 Matty Beniers 3.00 8.00
DC2 David Pastrnak 6.00 15.00
DC3 Connor McDavid 12.00 30.00
DC4 Mason McTavish 2.50 6.00
DC5 Nick Schmaltz 2.00 5.00
DC6 Arnaud Durandeau 2.50 6.00
DC7 Adam Fantilli 8.00 20.00
DC8 Connor Bedard 80.00 200.00
DC9 Mike Modano 4.00 10.00
DC10 Keith Primeau 2.00 5.00
DC11 Jack Hughes 6.00 15.00
DC12 Cale Makar 6.00 15.00
DC13 Dustin Wolf 8.00 20.00
DC14 Dylan Guenther 3.00 8.00
DC15 Brad Marchand 5.00 12.00
DC16 Owen Beck 4.00 10.00
DC17 Matthew Knies 10.00 25.00
DC18 Nico Hischier 4.00 10.00
DC19 Jeremy Swayman 4.00 10.00
DC20 Jakob Pelletier 3.00 8.00
DC21 Alex Tuch 2.50 6.00
DC22 Eric Lindros 4.00 10.00
DC23 Jonathan Huberdeau 3.00 8.00
DC24 Wyatt Kaiser 2.50 6.00
DC25 Matt Murray 2.50 6.00
DC26 Sean Farrell 2.50 6.00
DC27 Yaroslav Askarov 6.00 15.00
DC28 Seth Jarvis 3.00 8.00
DC29 Luke Hughes 8.00 20.00
DC30 Bowen Byram 3.00 8.00
DC31 Hunter McKown 2.50 6.00
DC32 Wyatt Johnston 5.00 12.00
DC33 Henrik Lundqvist 6.00 15.00
DC34 Jarome Iginla 3.00 8.00
DC35 Simon Edvinsson 5.00 12.00
DC36 Ridly Greig 4.00 10.00
DC37 Jake Oettinger 4.00 10.00
DC38 Will Cuylle 4.00 10.00
DC39 Matthew Tkachuk 5.00 12.00
DC40 Brandt Clarke 2.50 6.00
DC41 Matthew Coronato 4.00 10.00
DC42 Marco Kasper 6.00 15.00
DC43 Anton Lundell 2.50 6.00
DC44 Tim Thomas 2.50 6.00
DC45 Mats Zuccarello 2.50 6.00
DC46 Kirill Kaprizov 8.00 20.00
DC47 Nick Suzuki 5.00 12.00
DC48 Logan Cooley 8.00 20.00
DC49 Zach Benson 4.00 10.00
DC50 Juuse Saros 3.00 8.00
DC51 Ryan Getzlaf 2.50 6.00
DC52 Aidan McDonough 2.00 5.00
DC53 Luke Evangelista 4.00 10.00
DC54 Brock Faber 6.00 15.00
DC55 Teemu Selanne 5.00 12.00
DC56 Shane Doan 2.00 5.00
DC57 Drake Batherson 2.50 6.00
DC58 Jared McCann 2.00 5.00
DC59 Wayne Gretzky 15.00 40.00
DC60 Patrick Roy 6.00 15.00
DC61 Philipp Grubauer 2.50 6.00
DC62 Jake Sanderson 3.00 8.00
DC63 Noah Dobson 3.00 8.00
DC64 Tye Kartye 4.00 10.00
DC65 Mark Messier 5.00 12.00
DC66 Steve Yzerman 6.00 15.00
DC67 Jonathan Gruden 2.50 6.00
DC68 Tristan Jarry 2.50 6.00
DC69 Carter Hart 2.50 6.00
DC70 Chris Chelios 2.50 6.00
DC71 Devon Levi 6.00 15.00
DC72 Stanislav Svozil 2.00 5.00
DC73 Joona Koppanen 2.00 5.00
DC74 Connor Hellebuyck 5.00 12.00
DC75 Anze Kopitar 4.00 10.00
DC76 Jonathan Marchessault 3.00 8.00
DC77 Andrei Vasilevskiy 4.00 10.00
DC78 Rick Nash 2.50 6.00
DC79 Nikita Nesterenko 2.50 6.00
DC80 Danil Gushchin 2.50 6.00
DC81 Grant Fuhr 4.00 10.00
DC82 Pekka Rinne 2.50 6.00
DC83 Nathan MacKinnon 10.00 25.00
DC84 Jaccob Slavin 2.00 5.00
DC85 Martin Brodeur 6.00 15.00
DC86 Joe Pavelski 3.00 8.00
DC87 Jaromir Jagr 8.00 20.00
DC88 Adam Oates 2.50 6.00
DC89 Tage Thompson 3.00 8.00
DC90 Rasmus Dahlin 3.00 8.00
DC91 Luc Robitaille 2.50 6.00
DC92 Ryan Nugent-Hopkins 3.00 8.00
DC93 Dave Taylor 2.00 5.00
DC94 Rod Brind'Amour 2.50 6.00
DC95 Jari Kurri 2.50 6.00
DC96 Mark Stone 3.00 8.00
DC97 Jordan Kyrou 2.50 6.00
DC98 Joe Thornton 4.00 10.00
DC99 Auston Matthews 10.00 25.00
DC100 John Vanbiesbrouck 2.50 6.00

2023-24 SP Game Used Draft Day Marks

DDMAF Adam Fantilli/280* 125.00 300.00
DDMCA Leo Carlsson/280* 150.00 400.00
DDMCB Connor Bedard/210* 1500.00 4000.00
DDMCZ Connor Zary/140* 125.00 300.00
DDMDL Devon Levi/140* 60.00 150.00
DDMDW Dustin Wolf/140* 150.00 400.00
DDMJN Yaroslav Askarov/245* 80.00 200.00
DDMJP Jakob Pelletier/315* 30.00 80.00
DDMKK Kevin Korchinski/350* 40.00 100.00
DDMKN Matthew Knies/175* 200.00 500.00
DDMLC Logan Cooley/210* 80.00 200.00
DDMLE Luke Evangelista/385* 40.00 100.00
DDMLH Luke Hughes/210* 150.00 400.00
DDMMC Matthew Coronato/280* 40.00 100.00
DDMMK Marco Kasper/210* 60.00 150.00
DDMMS Matt Savoie/210* 50.00 125.00
DDMOB Owen Beck/140* 80.00 200.00
DDMRE Ryker Evans/175* 30.00 80.00
DDMRG Ridly Greig/175* 60.00 150.00
DDMSB Samuel Bolduc/210* 25.00 60.00
DDMSE Simon Edvinsson/315* 50.00 125.00
DDMSF Sean Farrell/245* 25.00 60.00
DDMSN Simon Nemec/175* 80.00 200.00
DDMSS Stanislav Svozil/210* 20.00 50.00
DDMTF Tyson Foerster/280* 60.00 150.00
DDMWC Will Cuylle/210* 80.00 200.00
DDMWD William Dufour/210* 20.00 50.00

2023-24 SP Game Used HOF Marks

HOFMAM Al MacInnis/280* 20.00 50.00
HOFMAO Adam Oates/175* 15.00 40.00
HOFMBH Bobby Hull/140* 30.00 80.00
HOFMBO Bobby Orr/105* 30.00 80.00
HOFMBP Bernie Parent/210* 20.00 50.00
HOFMBS Brendan Shanahan/280* 15.00 40.00
HOFMDA Dave Andreychuk/350* 15.00 40.00
HOFMEB Ed Belfour/245* 15.00 40.00
HOFMEG Ed Giacomin/280* 15.00 40.00
HOFMEL Eric Lindros/245* 40.00 100.00

HOFMFM Frank Mahovlich/315* 15.00 40.00
HOFMGA Glenn Anderson/280* 12.00 30.00
HOFMGF Grant Fuhr/140* 25.00 60.00
HOFMGH Gordie Howe/140* 50.00 125.00
HOFMGL Guy Lafleur/245* 20.00 50.00
HOFMHR Henri Richard/245* 15.00 40.00
HOFMJK Jari Kurri/175* 15.00 40.00
HOFMJN Joe Nieuwendyk/350* 12.00 30.00
HOFMMG Michel Goulet/210* 15.00 40.00
HOFMMR Maurice Richard/245* 40.00 100.00
HOFMPL Pat LaFontaine/350* 15.00 40.00
HOFMRG Rod Gilbert/245* 15.00 40.00
HOFMRV Rogie Vachon/210* 15.00 40.00
HOFMSA Syl Apps/140* 15.00 40.00
HOFMSB Borje Salming/245* 15.00 40.00
HOFMSM Billy Smith/175* 15.00 40.00
HOFMSY Steve Yzerman/245* 80.00 200.00
HOFMSZ Sergei Zubov/175* 12.00 30.00
HOFMTS Teemu Selanne/245* 50.00 125.00
HOFMYC Yvan Cournoyer/315* 15.00 40.00

2023-24 SP Game Used Inked Rookie Sweaters Patch

RSAD Arnaud Durandeau/49 10.00 25.00
RSAG Adam Ginning/49 10.00 25.00
RSAH Akito Hirose/49 8.00 20.00
RSAM Aidan McDonough/49 8.00 20.00
RSBF Brock Faber/35 100.00 250.00
RSBM Bobby McMann/49 10.00 25.00
RSDL Devon Levi/35 80.00 200.00
RSDW Dustin Wolf/35 30.00 80.00
RSHM Hunter McKown/49 10.00 25.00
RSJG Jonathan Gruden/49 10.00 25.00
RSJK Joona Koppanen/49 8.00 20.00
RSJP Jakob Pelletier/49 12.00 30.00
RSKA Marco Kasper/35 25.00 60.00
RSLC Logan Cooley/49 100.00 250.00
RSLE Luke Evangelista/49 15.00 40.00
RSMC Matthew Coronato/49 15.00 40.00
RSMK Matthew Knies/35 150.00 400.00
RSMM Matt Murray/49 10.00 25.00
RSNS Nick Swaney/49 10.00 25.00
RSOB Owen Beck/49 15.00 40.00
RSRG Ridly Greig/49 15.00 40.00
RSSE Simon Edvinsson/25 20.00 50.00
RSSF Sean Farrell/49 10.00 25.00
RSSS Stanislav Svozil/35 8.00 20.00
RSWC Will Cuylle/49 15.00 40.00
RSWK Wyatt Kaiser/49 10.00 25.00
RSYA Yaroslav Askarov/25 80.00 200.00

2023-24 SP Game Used Inked Sweaters

ISBB Brent Burns/25 12.00 30.00
ISCH Connor Hellebuyck/25 25.00 60.00
ISCK Clayton Keller/25 15.00 40.00
ISDC Dylan Cozens/25 12.00 30.00
ISIS Ilya Sorokin/25 20.00 50.00
ISJG John Gibson/25 15.00 40.00
ISJM Jared McCann/25 10.00 25.00
ISJO Jake Oettinger/25 20.00 50.00
ISMB Matty Beniers/25 15.00 40.00
ISMR Mikko Rantanen/25 30.00 80.00
ISVH Victor Hedman/25 15.00 40.00

2023-24 SP Game Used Jersey Autographs

2 Anthony Beauvillier/35 6.00 15.00
3 Timo Meier/35 10.00 25.00
20 Shane Wright/35 12.00 30.00
22 Carter Hart/99 10.00 25.00
23 Jonathan Marchessault/35 12.00 30.00
24 Teuvo Teravainen/99 10.00 25.00
25 Kent Johnson/99 10.00 25.00
26 Cole Perfetti/99 10.00 25.00
27 Evgeny Kuznetsov/99 12.00 30.00
29 Ukko-Pekka Luukkonen/149 10.00 25.00
31 Miro Heiskanen/99 12.00 30.00
32 Aaron Ekblad/149 12.00 30.00
33 Jordan Eberle/99 10.00 25.00
34 Jamie Drysdale/149 8.00 20.00
35 Nick Schmaltz/99 8.00 20.00
37 Taylor Raddysh/149 8.00 20.00
39 Sam Reinhart/99 20.00 50.00
40 Anton Lundell/149 10.00 25.00
41 Ryan Strome/99 10.00 25.00
44 Brandon Hagel/99 8.00 20.00
45 Zach Hyman/99 15.00 40.00
46 Robert Thomas/149 10.00 25.00
47 Drake Batherson/65 10.00 25.00
48 Jared McCann/65 8.00 20.00
49 Blake Coleman/65 8.00 20.00
51 Brandon Saad/99 8.00 20.00
52 Brendan Gallagher/99 10.00 25.00
53 John Gibson/35 10.00 25.00
55 Dylan Cozens/99 10.00 25.00
56 Seth Jarvis/65 12.00 30.00
57 Roope Hintz/65 12.00 30.00
58 Jacob Markstrom/65 10.00 25.00
59 Anders Lee/65 8.00 20.00
60 Shea Theodore/65 12.00 30.00
62 Jake Oettinger/65 15.00 40.00
63 Philipp Grubauer/65 10.00 25.00
66 Darcy Kuemper/99 10.00 25.00
69 Dylan Guenther/99 12.00 30.00
70 Boone Jenner/35 10.00 25.00
71 Mario Ferraro/149 6.00 15.00
73 Tom Wilson/35 10.00 25.00
75 Tomas Hertl/65 10.00 25.00
76 Mark Stone/35 12.00 30.00
77 Jaccob Slavin/35 8.00 20.00
78 Alexander Romanov/149 8.00 20.00
79 Owen Power/65 10.00 25.00
80 Kirby Dach/99 10.00 25.00
81 K'Andre Miller/99 8.00 20.00
82 Thomas Chabot/99 10.00 25.00
83 Jake Sanderson/99 12.00 30.00
84 Gabriel Landeskog/35 12.00 30.00
91 Yegor Sharangovich/149 10.00 25.00
110 Jack Eichel/35 15.00 40.00
111 Matty Beniers/99 12.00 30.00
112 Jonathan Huberdeau/65 12.00 30.00
113 Nico Hischier/35 15.00 40.00
114 Joe Pavelski/35 12.00 30.00
115 Brayden Point/35 12.00 30.00
118 Roman Josi/35 10.00 25.00
120 Victor Hedman/35 12.00 30.00
122 Brady Tkachuk/35 15.00 40.00
125 Clayton Keller/35 12.00 30.00
127 Nick Suzuki/35 20.00 50.00
128 Aleksander Barkov/35 15.00 40.00
129 Matthew Tkachuk/35 20.00 50.00
130 Chandler Stephenson/35 8.00 20.00
131 Kevin Fiala/35 8.00 20.00
133 Ilya Sorokin/35 8.00 20.00
136 Andrei Svechnikov/35 12.00 30.00
137 Connor Hellebuyck/35 20.00 50.00
138 Josh Morrissey/35 12.00 30.00
139 Juuse Saros/35 12.00 30.00
140 Jack Hughes/35 50.00 125.00
142 Andrei Vasilevskiy/35 15.00 40.00
143 Mikko Rantanen/35 25.00 60.00
201 Samuel Bolduc/149 10.00 25.00
202 Billy Sweezey/149 10.00 25.00
203 Arnaud Durandeau/149 10.00 25.00
205 Matt Murray/149 10.00 25.00
206 Hunter McKown/149 10.00 25.00
207 Wyatt Kaiser/149 10.00 25.00
208 Joona Koppanen/149 8.00 20.00
209 Jonathan Gruden/149 10.00 25.00
210 Cole McWard/149 10.00 25.00
211 Adam Ginning/149 10.00 25.00
212 Hugh McGing/149 10.00 25.00
213 Owen Beck/149 15.00 40.00
214 Egor Afanasyev/149 10.00 25.00
215 Nick Swaney/149 10.00 25.00
216 Vincent Desharnais/149 12.00 30.00
217 Bobby McMann/149 15.00 40.00
218 Aidan McDonough/149 8.00 20.00
219 Jaxson Stauber/149 10.00 25.00
220 Akito Hirose/149 8.00 20.00
221 Jakob Pelletier/149 10.00 25.00
222 Ridly Greig/149 15.00 40.00
223 Luke Evangelista/149 15.00 40.00
224 Yaroslav Askarov/99 25.00 60.00
225 Marco Kasper/99 25.00 60.00
226 Simon Edvinsson/99 20.00 50.00
228 Leo Carlsson/99 100.00 250.00
229 Logan Cooley/99 30.00 80.00
230 Connor Bedard/49 1500.00 4000.00
231 Luke Hughes/49 80.00 200.00
232 Devon Levi/49 25.00 60.00
233 Stanislav Svozil/149 8.00 20.00
234 Dustin Wolf/149 30.00 80.00
235 Matthew Knies/149 60.00 150.00
236 Matthew Coronato/149 15.00 40.00
237 Tye Kartye/149 12.00 30.00
238 Brock Faber/149 60.00 150.00
239 Tyson Foerster/149 20.00 50.00
240 Sean Farrell/149 8.00 20.00
241 Will Cuylle/149 15.00 40.00
242 Samuel Knazko/149 10.00 25.00
243 Elliot Desnoyers/149 10.00 25.00
244 Zach Benson/149 15.00 40.00
245 Henry Thrun/149 10.00 25.00
246 Lukas Rousek/149 8.00 20.00
247 Luke Philp/149 10.00 25.00
248 Nikita Nesterenko/149 10.00 25.00
249 Michael Kesselring/149 10.00 25.00
250 Jiri Patera/149 15.00 40.00
251 Olle Eriksson Ek/149 10.00 25.00
252 Cole Guttman/149 10.00 25.00
254 Walker Duehr/149 8.00 20.00
255 Jet Greaves/149 15.00 40.00
256 William Dufour/149 8.00 20.00
257 Leevi Merilainen/149 10.00 25.00
258 David Gust/149 10.00 25.00
259 Matthew Kessel/149 8.00 20.00
264 Tyler Kleven/149 10.00 25.00
267 Vincent Iorio/149 10.00 25.00
273 John Beecher/149 20.00 50.00
274 Pavel Mintyukov/149 15.00 40.00
275 Matt Savoie/149 20.00 50.00
276 Mackie Samoskevich/149 15.00 40.00
277 Kevin Korchinski/149 20.00 50.00
279 Matthew Poitras/149 20.00 50.00

2023-24 SP Game Used Jersey Autographs Premium Material

*PREMIUM: .6X TO 1.5X BASIC
202 Billy Sweezey/49 30.00 80.00
217 Bobby McMann/49 40.00 100.00
223 Luke Evangelista/49 40.00 100.00
226 Simon Edvinsson/25 60.00 150.00
228 Leo Carlsson/25 125.00 300.00
234 Dustin Wolf/35 50.00 125.00
235 Matthew Knies/35 200.00 500.00
238 Brock Faber/49 100.00 250.00
239 Tyson Foerster/49 30.00 80.00
241 Will Cuylle/49 30.00 80.00
244 Zach Benson/49 30.00 80.00
273 John Beecher/49 60.00 150.00
279 Matthew Poitras/49 60.00 150.00

2023-24 SP Game Used Jerseys

1 Viktor Arvidsson 2.00 5.00
2 Anthony Beauvillier 2.00 5.00
3 Timo Meier 3.00 8.00
4 Evgeni Malkin 6.00 15.00
5 William Karlsson 4.00 10.00
6 Sergei Bobrovsky 5.00 12.00
7 Mika Zibanejad 4.00 10.00
8 Dougie Hamilton 2.50 6.00
9 Filip Forsberg 5.00 12.00
10 Travis Konecny 3.00 8.00
11 Logan Couture 4.00 10.00
12 Morgan Rielly 3.00 8.00
13 Kris Letang 4.00 10.00
14 Jeff Skinner 3.00 8.00
15 John Tavares 5.00 12.00
16 Moritz Seider 4.00 10.00
17 Alexis Lafreniere 5.00 12.00
18 Jake Guentzel 5.00 12.00
19 Karel Vejmelka 2.00 5.00
20 Shane Wright 3.00 8.00
21 Matias Maccelli 2.50 6.00
22 Carter Hart 3.00 8.00
23 Jonathan Marchessault 4.00 10.00
24 Teuvo Teravainen 3.00 8.00
25 Kent Johnson 3.00 8.00
26 Cole Perfetti 3.00 8.00
27 Evgeny Kuznetsov 4.00 10.00
28 Jeremy Swayman 5.00 12.00
29 Ukko-Pekka Luukkonen 2.50 6.00
31 Miro Heiskanen 5.00 12.00
32 Aaron Ekblad 4.00 10.00
33 Jordan Eberle 3.00 8.00
34 Jamie Drysdale 2.50 6.00
35 Nick Schmaltz 2.50 6.00
36 J.T. Miller 4.00 10.00
37 Taylor Raddysh 2.50 6.00
38 Anze Kopitar 5.00 12.00
39 Sam Reinhart 6.00 15.00
40 Anton Lundell 3.00 8.00
41 Ryan Strome 3.00 8.00
42 Milan Lucic 2.50 6.00
43 Marcus Foligno 2.50 6.00
44 Brandon Hagel 2.50 6.00
45 Zach Hyman 5.00 12.00
46 Robert Thomas 3.00 8.00
47 Drake Batherson 3.00 8.00
48 Jared McCann 2.50 6.00
49 Blake Coleman 2.50 6.00
50 Juraj Slafkovsky 6.00 15.00
51 Brandon Saad 2.50 6.00
52 Brendan Gallagher 3.00 8.00
53 John Gibson 3.00 8.00
54 Robby Fabbri 2.00 5.00
55 Dylan Cozens 3.00 8.00
56 Seth Jarvis 4.00 10.00
57 Roope Hintz 4.00 10.00
58 Jacob Markstrom 3.00 8.00
59 Anders Lee 2.50 6.00
60 Shea Theodore 4.00 10.00
61 Nikolaj Ehlers 3.00 8.00
62 Jake Oettinger 5.00 12.00
63 Philipp Grubauer 3.00 8.00
64 Arthur Kaliyev 3.00 8.00
65 Tristan Jarry 3.00 8.00
66 Darcy Kuemper 3.00 8.00
67 Jack Campbell 3.00 8.00
68 Mats Zuccarello 3.00 8.00
69 Dylan Guenther 4.00 10.00
70 Boone Jenner 3.00 8.00
71 Mario Ferraro 2.00 5.00
73 Tom Wilson 3.00 8.00
75 Tomas Hertl 3.00 8.00
76 Mark Stone 4.00 10.00
77 Jaccob Slavin 2.50 6.00
78 Alexander Romanov 2.50 6.00
79 Owen Power 3.00 8.00
80 Kirby Dach 3.00 8.00
81 K'Andre Miller 2.50 6.00
82 Thomas Chabot 3.00 8.00
83 Jake Sanderson 4.00 10.00
84 Gabriel Landeskog 4.00 10.00
85 Ryan Nugent-Hopkins 4.00 10.00
91 Yegor Sharangovich 3.00 8.00
95 David Perron 2.50 6.00
96 Evgenii Dadonov 2.00 5.00
100 Ryan O'Reilly 3.00 8.00
101 Trevor Zegras 3.00 8.00
102 Mathew Barzal 4.00 10.00
103 Nicklas Backstrom 3.00 8.00
104 Cole Caufield 6.00 15.00
105 Quinn Hughes 8.00 20.00
106 William Nylander 6.00 15.00
107 Steven Stamkos 6.00 15.00
108 Jordan Kyrou 3.00 8.00
109 Tage Thompson 4.00 10.00
110 Jack Eichel 5.00 12.00
111 Matty Beniers 4.00 10.00
112 Jonathan Huberdeau 4.00 10.00
113 Nico Hischier 5.00 12.00
114 Joe Pavelski 4.00 10.00
115 Brayden Point 4.00 10.00
116 Auston Matthews 12.00 30.00
117 Marc-Andre Fleury 6.00 15.00
118 Roman Josi 3.00 8.00
119 Brad Marchand 6.00 15.00
120 Victor Hedman 3.00 8.00
121 Seth Jones 3.00 8.00
122 Brady Tkachuk 5.00 12.00
123 Alex Ovechkin 12.00 30.00
124 Cale Makar 8.00 20.00
125 Clayton Keller 4.00 10.00
126 Bo Horvat 3.00 8.00
127 Nick Suzuki 6.00 15.00
128 Aleksander Barkov 6.00 15.00
129 Matthew Tkachuk 6.00 15.00
130 Chandler Stephenson 2.50 6.00
131 Kevin Fiala 2.50 6.00
132 Leon Draisaitl 10.00 25.00
133 Ilya Sorokin 5.00 12.00
134 Igor Shesterkin 6.00 15.00
136 Andrei Svechnikov 4.00 10.00
137 Connor Hellebuyck 6.00 15.00
138 Josh Morrissey 4.00 10.00
139 Juuse Saros 4.00 10.00
140 Jack Hughes 8.00 20.00
141 Sidney Crosby 12.00 30.00
142 Andrei Vasilevskiy 5.00 12.00
143 Mikko Rantanen 8.00 20.00
144 Connor McDavid 15.00 40.00
145 Troy Terry 2.50 6.00
146 Jason Robertson 5.00 12.00
147 Brock Nelson 3.00 8.00
148 Adam Fox 4.00 10.00
149 Rasmus Dahlin 4.00 10.00
150 Nathan MacKinnon 12.00 30.00
151 Linus Ullmark 3.00 8.00
152 Erik Karlsson 4.00 10.00
153 Vladimir Tarasenko 4.00 10.00
154 Artemi Panarin 6.00 15.00
155 Johnny Gaudreau 5.00 12.00
156 Kevin Hayes 2.50 6.00
157 Mitch Marner 5.00 12.00
158 Elias Pettersson 5.00 12.00
159 Dylan Larkin 4.00 10.00
161 Nikita Kucherov 6.00 15.00
162 David Pastrnak 8.00 20.00
163 Nazem Kadri 4.00 10.00
164 Kirill Kaprizov 10.00 25.00
167 Rod Brind'Amour 3.00 8.00
168 Chris Chelios SP 3.00 8.00
169 Sergei Zubov 2.50 6.00
171 Keith Tkachuk 3.00 8.00
172 Vincent Lecavalier 3.00 8.00
173 Rob Blake SP 3.00 8.00
174 Denis Potvin SP 3.00 8.00
175 Teemu Selanne SP 6.00 15.00
177 John LeClair SP 3.00 8.00
178 Ron Francis SP 4.00 10.00
179 Jarome Iginla SP 4.00 10.00
180 Dany Heatley 2.50 6.00
181 Ryan Getzlaf 3.00 8.00
182 Joe Sakic SP 6.00 15.00
183 Joe Thornton SP 5.00 12.00
184 Larry Robinson SP 3.00 8.00
185 Shane Doan 3.00 8.00
186 Steve Yzerman 8.00 20.00
187 Luc Robitaille SP 3.00 8.00
188 Henrik Lundqvist SP 8.00 20.00
189 Martin Brodeur SP 8.00 20.00
190 Tim Thomas 3.00 8.00
191 Grant Fuhr SP 5.00 12.00
192 Patrick Roy SP 8.00 20.00
193 Pekka Rinne 3.00 8.00
194 Dominik Hasek SP 5.00 12.00
195 Henrik Zetterberg SP 4.00 10.00
196 Rick Nash 3.00 8.00
197 Mario Lemieux SP 12.00 30.00
198 Jaromir Jagr SP 10.00 25.00
200 Ray Bourque SP 5.00 12.00
201 Samuel Bolduc 3.00 8.00
202 Billy Sweezey 3.00 8.00
203 Arnaud Durandeau 3.00 8.00
204 Jake Livingstone 3.00 8.00
205 Matt Murray 3.00 8.00
206 Hunter McKown 3.00 8.00
207 Wyatt Kaiser 3.00 8.00
208 Joona Koppanen 2.50 6.00
209 Jonathan Gruden 3.00 8.00
210 Cole McWard 3.00 8.00
211 Adam Ginning 3.00 8.00
212 Hugh McGing 3.00 8.00
213 Owen Beck 5.00 12.00
214 Egor Afanasyev 3.00 8.00
215 Nick Swaney 3.00 8.00
216 Vincent Desharnais 4.00 10.00
217 Bobby McMann 5.00 12.00
218 Aidan McDonough 2.50 6.00
219 Jaxson Stauber 3.00 8.00
220 Akito Hirose 2.50 6.00
221 Jakob Pelletier 4.00 10.00
222 Ridly Greig 5.00 12.00
223 Luke Evangelista 5.00 12.00
224 Yaroslav Askarov 8.00 20.00
225 Marco Kasper 8.00 20.00
226 Simon Edvinsson 6.00 15.00
227 Adam Fantilli 10.00 25.00
228 Leo Carlsson 10.00 25.00
229 Logan Cooley 10.00 25.00
230 Connor Bedard 60.00 150.00
231 Luke Hughes 10.00 25.00
232 Devon Levi 8.00 20.00
233 Stanislav Svozil 2.50 6.00
234 Dustin Wolf 10.00 25.00
235 Matthew Knies 12.00 30.00
236 Matthew Coronato 5.00 12.00
237 Tye Kartye 5.00 12.00
238 Brock Faber 8.00 20.00
239 Tyson Foerster 6.00 15.00
240 Sean Farrell 3.00 8.00
241 Will Cuylle 5.00 12.00
242 Samuel Knazko 3.00 8.00
243 Elliot Desnoyers 3.00 8.00
244 Zach Benson 5.00 12.00
245 Henry Thrun 3.00 8.00
246 Lukas Rousek 2.50 6.00
247 Luke Philp 3.00 8.00
248 Nikita Nesterenko 3.00 8.00
249 Michael Kesselring 3.00 8.00
250 Jiri Patera 5.00 12.00
251 Olle Eriksson Ek 3.00 8.00
252 Cole Guttman 3.00 8.00
254 Walker Duehr 2.50 6.00
255 Jet Greaves 5.00 12.00
256 William Dufour 2.50 6.00
257 Leevi Merilainen 3.00 8.00
258 David Gust 3.00 8.00
259 Matthew Kessel 2.50 6.00
264 Tyler Kleven 3.00 8.00
267 Vincent Iorio 3.00 8.00
272 Fraser Minten 6.00 15.00
273 John Beecher 6.00 15.00
274 Pavel Mintyukov 5.00 12.00
275 Matt Savoie 6.00 15.00
276 Mackie Samoskevich 5.00 12.00
277 Kevin Korchinski 5.00 12.00
279 Matthew Poitras 6.00 15.00

2023-24 SP Game Used Jerseys Premium Materials

*PREMIUM: .75X TO 2X BASIC
*PREMIUM RC: 1X TO 2.5X BASIC
238 Brock Faber/25 50.00 125.00
239 Tyson Foerster/25 30.00 80.00

2023-24 SP Game Used New Grooves Red

*GOLD/99: .75X TO 2X RED
NG1 Dustin Wolf 3.00 8.00
NG2 Luke Evangelista 1.50 4.00
NG3 Marco Kasper 2.50 6.00
NG4 Simon Edvinsson 2.00 5.00
NG5 Leo Carlsson 3.00 8.00
NG6 Adam Fantilli 4.00 10.00
NG7 Tyson Foerster 2.00 5.00
NG8 Matthew Knies 4.00 10.00
NG9 Devon Levi 2.50 6.00
NG10 Brock Faber 2.50 6.00
NG11 Stanislav Svozil .75 2.00
NG12 Matthew Coronato 1.50 4.00
NG13 Owen Beck 1.50 4.00
NG14 Ridly Greig 1.50 4.00
NG15 Yaroslav Askarov 2.50 6.00
NG16 Connor Bedard 100.00 250.00
NG17 Luke Hughes 3.00 8.00
NG18 Tye Kartye 1.50 4.00
NG19 Logan Cooley 3.00 8.00
NG20 Aidan McDonough .75 2.00

2023-24 SP Game Used New Grooves Autographs

NG1 Dustin Wolf 20.00 50.00
NG2 Luke Evangelista SP 10.00 25.00
NG3 Marco Kasper 15.00 40.00
NG4 Simon Edvinsson 12.00 30.00
NG5 Leo Carlsson SP 60.00 150.00
NG7 Tyson Foerster 12.00 30.00
NG8 Matthew Knies 40.00 100.00
NG9 Devon Levi 25.00 60.00
NG10 Brock Faber 40.00 100.00
NG11 Stanislav Svozil 5.00 12.00
NG12 Matthew Coronato 10.00 25.00
NG13 Owen Beck 10.00 25.00
NG14 Ridly Greig 10.00 25.00
NG15 Yaroslav Askarov SP 15.00 40.00
NG18 Tye Kartye 10.00 25.00
NG19 Logan Cooley SP 20.00 50.00
NG20 Aidan McDonough 5.00 12.00

2023-24 SP Game Used New Grooves Jersey Autographs

NG1 Dustin Wolf 30.00 80.00
NG2 Luke Evangelista 15.00 40.00
NG3 Marco Kasper 25.00 60.00
NG4 Simon Edvinsson 25.00 60.00
NG5 Leo Carlsson 125.00 300.00
NG6 Adam Fantilli 80.00 200.00
NG7 Tyson Foerster 20.00 50.00
NG8 Matthew Knies 60.00 150.00
NG9 Devon Levi 50.00 125.00
NG10 Brock Faber 80.00 200.00
NG11 Stanislav Svozil 8.00 20.00
NG12 Matthew Coronato 15.00 40.00
NG13 Owen Beck 15.00 40.00
NG14 Ridly Greig 15.00 40.00
NG15 Yaroslav Askarov 25.00 60.00
NG16 Connor Bedard 1200.00 3000.00
NG17 Luke Hughes 80.00 200.00
NG18 Tye Kartye 15.00 40.00
NG19 Logan Cooley 30.00 80.00
NG20 Aidan McDonough 8.00 20.00

2023-24 SP Game Used New Grooves Jerseys

NG1 Dustin Wolf 5.00 12.00
NG2 Luke Evangelista 2.50 6.00
NG3 Marco Kasper 4.00 10.00
NG4 Simon Edvinsson 3.00 8.00
NG5 Leo Carlsson 5.00 12.00
NG6 Adam Fantilli 5.00 12.00
NG7 Tyson Foerster 3.00 8.00
NG8 Matthew Knies 6.00 15.00
NG9 Devon Levi 4.00 10.00
NG10 Brock Faber 4.00 10.00
NG11 Stanislav Svozil 1.25 3.00
NG12 Matthew Coronato 2.50 6.00
NG13 Owen Beck 2.50 6.00
NG14 Ridly Greig 2.50 6.00
NG15 Yaroslav Askarov 4.00 10.00
NG16 Connor Bedard 80.00 200.00
NG17 Luke Hughes 5.00 12.00
NG18 Tye Kartye 2.50 6.00
NG19 Logan Cooley 5.00 12.00
NG20 Aidan McDonough 1.25 3.00

2023-24 SP Game Used New Grooves Jerseys Patch

*PATCH: 2X TO 5X BASIC
NG8 Matthew Knies/25 30.00 80.00
NG9 Devon Levi/25 60.00 150.00

2023-24 SP Game Used Rally Time Towel Relics

RT1 Adin Hill 6.00 15.00
RT2 Sergei Bobrovsky 10.00 25.00
RT3 Sebastian Aho 10.00 25.00
RT4 Jonathan Marchessault 8.00 20.00
RT5 Jack Eichel 10.00 25.00
RT6 Matthew Tkachuk 12.00 30.00
RT8 Brandon Montour 8.00 20.00
RT9 Adrian Kempe 6.00 15.00
RT10 Patrick Kane 12.00 30.00
RT11 Jean-Sebastien Giguere 6.00 15.00
RT12 Patrice Bergeron 8.00 20.00
RT13 Brad Marchand 12.00 30.00
RT14 Sidney Crosby 25.00 60.00
RT15 Scott Niedermayer 6.00 15.00
RT16 Jason Robertson 10.00 25.00
RT17 Pekka Rinne 6.00 15.00
RT18 Joe Pavelski 6.00 15.00
RT19 Bo Horvat 8.00 20.00
RT20 Alex Ovechkin 25.00 60.00
RT21 Ryan O'Reilly 6.00 15.00
RT22 Nicklas Backstrom 6.00 15.00
RT25 Auston Matthews 25.00 60.00
RT26 Joe Nieuwendyk 5.00 12.00
RT27 Ed Belfour 6.00 15.00
RT28 Bryan Trottier 6.00 15.00
RT29 Mark Recchi 6.00 15.00
RT30 Matty Beniers 8.00 20.00

2023-24 SP Game Used Retro Renovations Jerseys

RRBH Brett Hull 12.00 30.00
RRCC Chris Chelios 6.00 15.00
RRDH Dominik Hasek 10.00 25.00
RRJJ Jaromir Jagr 20.00 50.00
RRJR Jeremy Roenick 10.00 25.00
RRJS Joe Sakic 12.00 30.00
RRJT Joe Thornton 10.00 25.00
RRMB Martin Brodeur 15.00 40.00
RRML Mario Lemieux 25.00 60.00
RRMM Mark Messier 12.00 30.00

2023-24 SP Game Used Rookie Sweaters

RSAD Arnaud Durandeau 2.00 5.00
RSAF Adam Fantilli 6.00 15.00
RSAG Adam Ginning 2.00 5.00
RSAH Akito Hirose 1.50 4.00
RSAM Aidan McDonough 1.50 4.00
RSBF Brock Faber 5.00 12.00
RSBM Bobby McMann 2.50 6.00
RSCB Connor Bedard 80.00 200.00
RSDL Devon Levi 5.00 12.00
RSDW Dustin Wolf 6.00 15.00
RSHM Hunter McKown 2.00 5.00
RSJG Jonathan Gruden 2.00 5.00
RSJK Joona Koppanen 1.50 4.00
RSJP Jakob Pelletier 2.50 6.00
RSKA Marco Kasper 5.00 12.00
RSLC Logan Cooley 6.00 15.00
RSLE Luke Evangelista 3.00 8.00
RSLH Luke Hughes 6.00 15.00
RSMC Matthew Coronato 3.00 8.00
RSMK Matthew Knies 8.00 20.00
RSMM Matt Murray 2.00 5.00
RSNS Nick Swaney 2.00 5.00
RSOB Owen Beck 3.00 8.00
RSRG Ridly Greig 3.00 8.00
RSSE Simon Edvinsson 4.00 10.00
RSSF Sean Farrell 2.00 5.00
RSSS Stanislav Svozil 1.50 4.00
RSWC Will Cuylle 3.00 8.00
RSWK Wyatt Kaiser 2.00 5.00
RSYA Yaroslav Askarov 5.00 12.00

2023-24 SP Game Used SIGNED

SNAD Alex DeBrincat 20.00 50.00
SNAO Alex Ovechkin SP 100.00 250.00

2023-24 SP Game Used Signing Day Marks

SDMTK Tye Kartye/210* 50.00 125.00

2024-25 SP Game Used

1 Jonathan Huberdeau .60 1.50
2 Zach Hyman .75 2.00
3 Timo Meier .50 1.25
4 Yanni Gourde .40 1.00
5 Jaccob Slavin .40 1.00
6 Darnell Nurse .40 1.00
7 Jean-Gabriel Pageau .30 .75
8 Vince Dunn .40 1.00
9 Brent Burns .50 1.25
10 Carter Verhaeghe .50 1.25
11 Noah Dobson .60 1.50
12 Jordan Kyrou .50 1.25
13 Nazem Kadri .60 1.50
14 Lucas Raymond .75 2.00
15 Jack Hughes 1.25 3.00
16 Fabian Zetterlund .30 .75
17 Sean Durzi .30 .75
18 Kirill Marchenko .60 1.50
19 Joel Eriksson Ek .40 1.00
20 Cam Atkinson .50 1.25
21 Noah Hanifin .50 1.25
22 Jordan Greenway .30 .75
23 Alex DeBrincat .60 1.50
24 Thomas Novak .30 .75
25 Thomas Bordeleau .30 .75
26 Cole Perfetti .50 1.25
27 Rasmus Dahlin .60 1.50
28 Dylan Larkin .60 1.50
29 Roman Josi .50 1.25
30 Mikael Granlund .40 1.00
31 Rasmus Kupari .30 .75
32 Alex Tuch .50 1.25
33 Miro Heiskanen .60 1.50
34 Luke Evangelista .40 1.00
35 Michael Bunting .40 1.00
36 Adam Lowry .40 1.00
37 Mason McTavish .50 1.25
38 Mikko Rantanen 1.25 3.00
39 Drew Doughty .50 1.25
40 Josh Norris .50 1.25
41 Victor Hedman .60 1.50
42 Tage Thompson .60 1.50
43 Jason Robertson .75 2.00
44 Ryan O'Reilly .50 1.25
45 Erik Karlsson .60 1.50
46 Mark Scheifele .75 2.00
47 Charlie Coyle .50 1.25
48 Roope Hintz .60 1.50
49 Josh Anderson .40 1.00
50 Kris Letang .60 1.50
51 John Carlson .50 1.25
52 Charlie McAvoy .60 1.50
53 Wyatt Johnston 1.00 2.50
54 Kaiden Guhle .50 1.25
55 Evgeni Malkin 1.00 2.50
56 T.J. Oshie .50 1.25
57 Yegor Sharangovich .50 1.25
58 Evan Bouchard .60 1.50
59 Dawson Mercer .60 1.50
60 Matty Beniers .60 1.50
61 Sebastian Aho .75 2.00
62 Ryan Nugent-Hopkins .60 1.50
63 Bo Horvat .60 1.50
64 Jared McCann .40 1.00
65 Ryan Strome .40 1.00
66 Kevin Korchinski .40 1.00
67 Kevin Fiala .40 1.00
68 Alexis Lafreniere .75 2.00
69 Anthony Cirelli .40 1.00
70 Troy Terry .40 1.00
71 Nick Foligno .30 .75
72 Anze Kopitar .75 2.00
73 Chris Kreider .60 1.50
74 Brayden Point .60 1.50
75 David Pastrnak 1.25 3.00
76 Zach Werenski .75 2.00
77 Juraj Slafkovsky 1.00 2.50
78 Jamie Drysdale .40 1.00
79 Dylan Strome .60 1.50
80 Matias Maccelli .40 1.00
81 Adam Fantilli .75 2.00
82 Brock Faber .60 1.50
83 Morgan Frost .40 1.00
84 William Karlsson .60 1.50
85 Mikael Backlund .40 1.00
86 J.T. Compher .40 1.00
87 Nico Hischier .75 2.00
88 Nico Sturm .30 .75
89 Jack McBain .30 .75
90 Samuel Girard .30 .75
91 Matt Boldy .75 2.00
92 Thomas Chabot .50 1.25
93 Jack Eichel .75 2.00
94 Isac Lundestrom .30 .75
95 Ross Colton .40 1.00
96 Quinton Byfield .50 1.25
97 Claude Giroux .50 1.25
98 Chandler Stephenson .40 1.00
99 Seth Jarvis .60 1.50
100 Aleksander Barkov .75 2.00
101 Anders Lee .40 1.00
102 Kevin Hayes .40 1.00
103 Brad Marchand 1.00 2.50
104 Kent Johnson .50 1.25
105 Cole Caufield 1.00 2.50
106 Travis Sanheim .30 .75
107 Alex Ovechkin 2.00 5.00
108 Connor Bedard 1.50 4.00
109 Matthew Tkachuk 1.00 2.50
110 Mika Zibanejad .60 1.50
111 Pavel Buchnevich .50 1.25
112 Logan Cooley .75 2.00
113 Devon Toews .40 1.00
114 Mats Zuccarello .50 1.25
115 Tim Stutzle .60 1.50
116 Tomas Hertl .50 1.25
117 Jason Dickinson .30 .75
118 Aaron Ekblad .60 1.50
119 Vincent Trocheck .50 1.25
120 Colton Parayko .40 1.00
121 Quinn Hughes 1.25 3.00
122 Elias Pettersson .75 2.00
123 Nikita Kucherov 1.00 2.50
124 Thatcher Demko .60 1.50
125 Kyle Connor .75 2.00
126 Brady Tkachuk .75 2.00
127 Jesper Bratt .50 1.25
128 Cam Talbot .50 1.25
129 Brock Boeser .60 1.50
130 J.T. Miller .60 1.50
131 Frank Vatrano .40 1.00
132 Auston Matthews 2.00 5.00
133 Morgan Rielly .50 1.25
134 William Nylander 1.00 2.50
135 Mitch Marner .75 2.00
136 Jake Oettinger .75 2.00
137 Clayton Keller .60 1.50
138 Mathew Barzal .60 1.50
139 Igor Shesterkin 1.00 2.50
140 Filip Forsberg .75 2.00
141 Alex DeBrincat .60 1.50
142 Vincent Trocheck .50 1.25
143 Nathan MacKinnon 2.00 5.00
144 Cale Makar 1.25 3.00
145 Sidney Crosby 2.00 5.00
146 Alexandar Georgiev .50 1.25
147 Kirill Kaprizov 1.50 4.00
148 Sebastian Aho .75 2.00
149 Tom Wilson .50 1.25
150 Jeremy Swayman .75 2.00
151 Travis Konecny .50 1.25
152 Elias Lindholm .50 1.25
153 Oliver Bjorkstrand .40 1.00
154 Connor McDavid 2.50 6.00
155 Leon Draisaitl 1.50 4.00
156 Connor Hellebuyck 1.00 2.50
157 David Pastrnak 1.25 3.00
158 Rasmus Dahlin .60 1.50
159 Robert Thomas .60 1.50
160 Sam Reinhart 1.00 2.50
161 Sergei Bobrovsky .75 2.00
162 Boone Jenner .50 1.25
163 Nick Suzuki 1.00 2.50
164 Tomas Hertl .50 1.25
165 Bill Guerin .50 1.25
166 Bryan Trottier .50 1.25
167 Brian Leetch .40 1.00
168 Rob Blake .50 1.25
169 Mike Modano .75 2.00
170 Doug Gilmour .60 1.50
171 Michel Goulet .50 1.25
172 Corey Crawford .50 1.25
173 Wayne Gretzky 3.00 8.00
174 Patrice Bergeron .60 1.50
175 Joe Thornton .75 2.00
176 Jari Kurri .50 1.25
177 Paul Coffey .50 1.25
178 Keith Primeau .40 1.00
179 Peter Bondra .50 1.25
180 Larry Robinson .50 1.25
181 Scott Niedermayer .50 1.25
182 Ron Francis .60 1.50
183 Eric Lindros .75 2.00
184 Teemu Selanne 1.00 2.50
185 Joe Pavelski .60 1.50
186 Alex Delvecchio .50 1.25
187 Rick Nash .50 1.25
188 Martin St. Louis .50 1.25
189 Charlie Simmer .30 .75
190 Joe Sakic 1.00 2.50
191 Keith Tkachuk .50 1.25
192 Al MacInnis .60 1.50
193 Peter Stastny .40 1.00
194 Pat LaFontaine .50 1.25
195 Henrik Zetterberg .60 1.50
196 Trevor Linden .50 1.25
197 Adam Graves .40 1.00
198 Jeremy Roenick .75 2.00
199 David Backes .30 .75
200 Dany Heatley .40 1.00
201 Jackson Blake RC 2.00 5.00
202 Brennan Othmann RC 1.50 4.00
203 Arshdeep Bains RC 1.25 3.00
204 Adam Klapka RC 1.00 2.50
205 Kyle MacLean RC 1.00 2.50
206 Cameron Crotty RC 1.00 2.50
207 Olen Zellweger RC 2.00 5.00
208 Brian Halonen RC 1.00 2.50
209 Josh Doan RC 1.50 4.00
210 Frank Nazar RC 3.00 8.00
211 Zack Ostapchuk RC 1.00 2.50
212 Mason Morelli RC 1.00 2.50
213 Logan Stankoven RC 2.50 6.00
214 Logan Morrison RC 1.00 2.50
215 Macklin Celebrini RC 10.00 25.00
216 Landon Slaggert RC 1.00 2.50
217 Ivan Fedotov RC 2.00 5.00
218 Lukas Cormier RC 1.00 2.50
219 Ethan Del Mastro RC 1.00 2.50
220 Vasily Ponomarev RC 1.00 2.50
221 Pierrick Dube RC 1.00 2.50
222 Jason Polin RC 1.00 2.50
223 Jack St. Ivany RC 1.00 2.50
224 Brad Lambert RC 1.25 3.00
225 Rutger McGroarty RC 2.00 5.00
226 Liam Ohgren RC 2.00 5.00
227 Declan Carlile RC 1.00 2.50
228 Seamus Casey RC 1.25 3.00
229 Nikolai Kovalenko RC .75 2.00
230 Collin Graf RC 1.00 2.50
231 Nikita Chibrikov RC 1.00 2.50
232 Samuel Honzek RC 1.00 2.50
233 Gavin Brindley RC 1.00 2.50
234 Shakir Mukhamadullin RC 1.25 3.00
235 Calum Ritchie RC 1.25 3.00
236 Luca Del Bel Belluz RC 1.00 2.50
237 Jack Thompson RC 1.00 2.50
238 Maxim Tsyplakov RC 1.50 4.00

239 Bradly Nadeau RC 1.50 4.00
240 Matt Rempe RC 2.00 5.00
241 Matt Villalta RC 1.00 2.50
242 Yan Kuznetsov RC 1.00 2.50
243 Ruslan Iskhakov RC 1.00 2.50
244 Maksymilian Szuber RC 1.00 2.50
245 Jesper Wallstedt RC 2.50 6.00
246 Emil Lilleberg RC 1.00 2.50
247 Will Smith RC 3.00 8.00
248 Joshua Roy RC 1.50 4.00
249 Maxwell Crozier RC 1.00 2.50
250 Matvei Michkov RC 4.00 10.00
251 James Malatesta RC 1.00 2.50
252 Devin Cooley RC 1.00 2.50
253 Oliver Kapanen RC 1.00 2.50
254 Mavrik Bourque RC 2.00 5.00
255 Zachary Bolduc RC 2.00 5.00
256 Conor Geekie RC 2.00 5.00
257 Scott Morrow RC 1.25 3.00
258 Brandon Scanlin RC 1.00 2.50
259 Brendan Brisson RC 1.25 3.00
260 Phil Kemp RC 1.00 2.50
261 Zach Dean RC 1.00 2.50
262 Jett Luchanko RC 2.00 5.00
263 Marat Khusnutdinov RC 1.00 2.50
264 Gage Goncalves RC 1.25 3.00
265 Albert Johansson RC 1.00 2.50
266 Justin Brazeau RC 1.00 2.50
267 Graeme Clarke RC 1.00 2.50
268 Patrik Koch RC 1.00 2.50
269 Cameron Butler RC 1.00 2.50
270 Georgi Romanov RC 1.25 3.00
271 Nolan Allan RC 1.00 2.50
272 Sam Colangelo RC 1.00 2.50
273 Logan Mailloux RC 1.50 4.00
274 Aku Raty RC 1.00 2.50
275 Akil Thomas RC 1.00 2.50
276 Victor Mancini RC 1.00 2.50
277 Andre Lee RC 1.00 2.50
278 Cutter Gauthier RC 2.50 6.00
279 Lane Hutson RC 5.00 12.00
280 Marshall Rifai RC 1.00 2.50

2024-25 SP Game Used Crystal
*CRYSTAL: 2X TO 5X BASIC
250 Matvei Michkov 125.00 300.00

2024-25 SP Game Used Gold
*GOLD/149: 1X TO 2.5X BASIC
215 Macklin Celebrini 40.00 100.00
250 Matvei Michkov 15.00 40.00
279 Lane Hutson 15.00 40.00

2024-25 SP Game Used Red
*RED: .5X TO 1.2X BASIC

2024-25 SP Game Used '22 Stanley Cup Carpet Relics
SCC1 Bowen Byram 25.00 60.00
SCC2 Nicolas Aube-Kubel 12.00 30.00
SCC3 J.T. Compher 12.00 30.00
SCC4 Pavel Francouz 15.00 40.00
SCC5 Erik Johnson 12.00 30.00
SCC6 Jack Johnson 12.00 30.00
SCC7 Nazem Kadri 25.00 60.00
SCC8 Gabriel Landeskog 25.00 60.00
SCC9 Artturi Lehkonen 15.00 40.00
SCC10 Nathan MacKinnon 40.00 100.00
SCC11 Cale Makar 40.00 100.00
SCC12 Josh Manson 15.00 40.00
SCC13 Alex Newhook 15.00 40.00
SCC14 Valeri Nichushkin 20.00 50.00
SCC15 Logan O'Connor 20.00 50.00
SCC16 Mikko Rantanen 40.00 100.00
SCC17 Nico Sturm 12.00 30.00
SCC18 Devon Toews 15.00 40.00
SCC19 Darcy Kuemper 20.00 50.00
SCC20 Andre Burakovsky 12.00 30.00

2024-25 SP Game Used '23 Global Series Melbourne Banner Year Relics
BYGSAK Anze Kopitar 6.00 15.00
BYGSCK Clayton Keller 5.00 12.00
BYGSDD Drew Doughty 4.00 10.00
BYGSKE Alex Kerfoot 3.00 8.00
BYGSKP Adrian Kempe 4.00 10.00
BYGSLC Logan Cooley 6.00 15.00
BYGSMI Matias Maccelli 3.00 8.00
BYGSQB Quinton Byfield 5.00 12.00
BYGSSD Sean Durzi 2.50 6.00
BYGSTM Trevor Moore 2.50 6.00

2024-25 SP Game Used '23 Global Series Melbourne Net Cord Relics
GSNAK Alex Kerfoot 12.00 30.00
GSNBH Barrett Hayton 15.00 40.00
GSNCI Connor Ingram 10.00 25.00
GSNCK Clayton Keller 20.00 50.00
GSNDA Phillip Danault 15.00 40.00
GSNDD Drew Doughty 15.00 40.00
GSNJZ Jason Zucker 15.00 40.00
GSNKE Adrian Kempe 15.00 40.00
GSNKF Kevin Fiala 12.00 30.00
GSNKO Anze Kopitar 25.00 60.00
GSNLC Logan Cooley 25.00 60.00
GSNMA Mikey Anderson 12.00 30.00
GSNMM Matias Maccelli 12.00 30.00
GSNNB Nick Bjugstad 10.00 25.00
GSNNS Nick Schmaltz 12.00 30.00
GSNPD Pierre-Luc Dubois 12.00 30.00
GSNQB Quinton Byfield 20.00 50.00
GSNSD Sean Durzi 10.00 25.00
GSNTL Trevor Lewis 10.00 25.00
GSNTM Trevor Moore 10.00 25.00

2024-25 SP Game Used '23 Global Series Melbourne Puck Relics
GSPAK Anze Kopitar 15.00 40.00
GSPCK Clayton Keller 12.00 30.00
GSPLC Logan Cooley 15.00 40.00
GSPTM Trevor Moore 6.00 15.00

2024-25 SP Game Used '23 Global Series Sweden Banner Year Relics
BYGSAD Alex DeBrincat 5.00 12.00
BYGSAM Auston Matthews 15.00 40.00
BYGSBF Brock Faber 5.00 12.00
BYGSBT Brady Tkachuk 6.00 15.00
BYGSCG Claude Giroux 4.00 10.00
BYGSDL Dylan Larkin 5.00 12.00
BYGSJN Josh Norris 4.00 10.00
BYGSJT John Tavares 6.00 15.00
BYGSKK Kirill Kaprizov 12.00 30.00
BYGSLR Lucas Raymond 6.00 15.00
BYGSMB Matt Boldy 6.00 15.00
BYGSMM Mitch Marner 6.00 15.00
BYGSMS Moritz Seider 5.00 12.00
BYGSMZ Mats Zuccarello 4.00 10.00
BYGSTS Tim Stutzle 5.00 12.00
BYGSWN William Nylander 8.00 20.00

2024-25 SP Game Used '23 Global Series Sweden Fabrics
*PATCH/35: 2X TO 5X BASIC
GSFAD Alex DeBrincat 2.00 5.00
GSFAM Auston Matthews 6.00 15.00
GSFAZ Artem Zub 1.00 2.50
GSFBF Brock Faber 2.00 5.00
GSFBT Brady Tkachuk 2.50 6.00
GSFCG Claude Giroux 1.50 4.00
GSFDB Drake Batherson 1.50 4.00
GSFDL Dylan Larkin 2.00 5.00
GSFDS Daniel Sprong 1.00 2.50
GSFJC J.T. Compher 1.00 2.50
GSFJN Josh Norris 1.50 4.00
GSFJS Jake Sanderson 2.00 5.00
GSFJT John Tavares 2.50 6.00
GSFKK Kirill Kaprizov 5.00 12.00
GSFLR Lucas Raymond 2.50 6.00
GSFMB Matt Boldy 2.50 6.00
GSFMJ Marcus Johansson 1.00 2.50
GSFMK Matthew Knies 3.00 8.00
GSFMM Mitch Marner 2.50 6.00
GSFMR Marco Rossi 2.00 5.00
GSFMS Moritz Seider 2.00 5.00
GSFMZ Mats Zuccarello 1.50 4.00
GSFRI Morgan Rielly 1.50 4.00
GSFTS Tim Stutzle 2.00 5.00
GSFWN William Nylander 3.00 8.00

2024-25 SP Game Used '23 Global Series Sweden Puck Relics
GSPAC Andrew Copp 10.00 25.00
GSPAD Alex DeBrincat 20.00 50.00
GSPAM Auston Matthews 40.00 100.00
GSPAZ Artem Zub 10.00 25.00
GSPBF Brock Faber 20.00 50.00
GSPBT Brady Tkachuk 25.00 60.00
GSPCG Claude Giroux 15.00 40.00
GSPDB Drake Batherson 15.00 40.00
GSPDL Dylan Larkin 20.00 50.00
GSPJB Jonas Brodin 10.00 25.00
GSPJC J.T. Compher 10.00 25.00
GSPJN Josh Norris 15.00 40.00
GSPJT John Tavares 25.00 60.00
GSPKK Kirill Kaprizov 25.00 60.00
GSPLR Lucas Raymond 25.00 60.00
GSPMB Matt Boldy 25.00 60.00
GSPMD Max Domi 15.00 40.00
GSPMJ Marcus Johansson 10.00 25.00
GSPMM Mitch Marner 25.00 60.00
GSPMR Morgan Rielly 15.00 40.00
GSPMS Moritz Seider 20.00 50.00
GSPMZ Mats Zuccarello 15.00 40.00
GSPTS Tim Stutzle 20.00 50.00
GSPWN William Nylander 30.00 80.00

2024-25 SP Game Used '23 Heritage Classic Banner Year Relics
BYHCCM Connor McDavid 20.00 50.00
BYHCEB Evan Bouchard 5.00 12.00
BYHCJH Jonathan Huberdeau 5.00 12.00
BYHCLD Leon Draisaitl 12.00 30.00
BYHCMC Matt Coronato 3.00 8.00
BYHCMW MacKenzie Weegar 3.00 8.00
BYHCNK Nazem Kadri 5.00 12.00
BYHCRN Ryan Nugent-Hopkins 5.00 12.00
BYHCYS Yegor Sharangovich 4.00 10.00
BYHCZH Zach Hyman 6.00 15.00

2024-25 SP Game Used '23 Heritage Classic Fabrics
*PATCH/35: 1X TO 2.5X BASIC
HCF1 Connor McDavid 20.00 50.00
HCF2 Evan Bouchard 5.00 12.00
HCF3 Leon Draisaitl 12.00 30.00
HCF4 Ryan Nugent-Hopkins 5.00 12.00
HCF5 Zach Hyman 6.00 15.00
HCF6 Jonathan Huberdeau 5.00 12.00
HCF7 MacKenzie Weegar 3.00 8.00
HCF8 Nazem Kadri 5.00 12.00
HCF9 Yegor Sharangovich 4.00 10.00
HCF10 Matt Coronato 3.00 8.00

2024-25 SP Game Used '23 Heritage Classic Net Cord Relics
HCNAM Andrew Mangiapane 30.00 80.00
HCNBC Blake Coleman 25.00 60.00
HCNCB Connor Brown 25.00 60.00
HCNCC Cody Ceci 20.00 50.00
HCNCM Connor McDavid 150.00 400.00
HCNDN Darnell Nurse 25.00 60.00
HCNEB Evan Bouchard 40.00 100.00
HCNEL Elias Lindholm 30.00 80.00
HCNJH Jonathan Huberdeau 40.00 100.00
HCNLD Leon Draisaitl 100.00 250.00
HCNMB Mikael Backlund 25.00 60.00
HCNMC Matt Coronato 25.00 60.00
HCNME Mattias Ekholm 25.00 60.00
HCNMW MacKenzie Weegar 25.00 60.00
HCNNK Nazem Kadri 40.00 100.00
HCNNZ Nikita Zadorov 20.00 50.00
HCNPB Phillip Broberg 20.00 50.00
HCNRN Ryan Nugent-Hopkins 40.00 100.00
HCNYS Yegor Sharangovich 30.00 80.00
HCNZH Zach Hyman 50.00 125.00

2024-25 SP Game Used '23 Heritage Classic Puck Relics
HCPCM Connor McDavid 80.00 200.00
HCPEB Evan Bouchard 20.00 50.00
HCPJH Jonathan Huberdeau 20.00 50.00
HCPLD Leon Draisaitl 50.00 125.00
HCPMW MacKenzie Weegar 12.00 30.00
HCPNK Nazem Kadri 20.00 50.00

2024-25 SP Game Used '24 All Star Skills Net Cord Relics
ASNAG Alexandar Georgiev 20.00 50.00
ASNAM Auston Matthews 80.00 200.00
ASNCH Connor Hellebuyck 40.00 100.00
ASNCM Connor McDavid 100.00 250.00
ASNCT Cam Talbot 20.00 50.00
ASNDP David Pastrnak 50.00 125.00
ASNEP Elias Pettersson 30.00 80.00
ASNIS Igor Shesterkin 40.00 100.00
ASNJM J.T. Miller 25.00 60.00
ASNJO Jake Oettinger 30.00 80.00
ASNJS Jeremy Swayman 30.00 80.00
ASNLD Leon Draisaitl 60.00 150.00
ASNMA Cale Makar 50.00 125.00
ASNMB Mathew Barzal 25.00 60.00
ASNNK Nikita Kucherov 40.00 100.00
ASNNM Nathan MacKinnon 80.00 200.00
ASNQH Quinn Hughes 50.00 125.00
ASNSB Sergei Bobrovsky 30.00 80.00
ASNTD Thatcher Demko 25.00 60.00
ASNWN William Nylander 40.00 100.00

2024-25 SP Game Used '24 All-Star Game Banner Year Relics
BYASAD Alex DeBrincat 2.50 6.00
BYASAM Auston Matthews 8.00 20.00
BYASBT Brady Tkachuk 3.00 8.00
BYASCM Cale Makar 5.00 12.00
BYASDP David Pastrnak 5.00 12.00
BYASEP Elias Pettersson 3.00 8.00
BYASFF Filip Forsberg 3.00 8.00
BYASKC Kyle Connor 3.00 8.00
BYASKK Kirill Kaprizov 6.00 15.00
BYASLD Leon Draisaitl 6.00 15.00
BYASMB Mathew Barzal 2.50 6.00
BYASMC Connor McDavid 10.00 25.00
BYASNK Nikita Kucherov 4.00 10.00
BYASNM Nathan MacKinnon 8.00 20.00
BYASNS Nick Suzuki 4.00 10.00
BYASQH Quinn Hughes 5.00 12.00
BYASRD Rasmus Dahlin 2.50 6.00
BYASSA Sebastian Aho 3.00 8.00
BYASSC Sidney Crosby 8.00 20.00
BYASWN William Nylander 4.00 10.00

2024-25 SP Game Used '24 All-Star Game Net Cord Relics
ASNAD Alex DeBrincat 25.00 60.00
ASNAG Alexandar Georgiev 20.00 50.00
ASNAM Auston Matthews 80.00 200.00
ASNBB Brock Boeser 25.00 60.00
ASNBJ Boone Jenner 20.00 50.00
ASNBT Brady Tkachuk 30.00 80.00
ASNCH Connor Hellebuyck 40.00 100.00
ASNCK Clayton Keller 25.00 60.00
ASNCM Connor McDavid 100.00 250.00
ASNCT Cam Talbot 20.00 50.00
ASNDP David Pastrnak 50.00 125.00
ASNEL Elias Lindholm 25.00 60.00
ASNEP Elias Pettersson 30.00 80.00
ASNFF Filip Forsberg 30.00 80.00
ASNFV Frank Vatrano 15.00 40.00
ASNIS Igor Shesterkin 40.00 100.00
ASNJB Jesper Bratt 20.00 50.00
ASNJM J.T. Miller 25.00 60.00
ASNJO Jake Oettinger 30.00 80.00
ASNJS Jeremy Swayman 30.00 80.00
ASNKC Kyle Connor 30.00 80.00
ASNKK Kirill Kaprizov 60.00 150.00
ASNLD Leon Draisaitl 60.00 150.00
ASNMA Cale Makar 50.00 125.00
ASNMB Mathew Barzal 25.00 60.00
ASNMM Mitch Marner 30.00 80.00
ASNMR Morgan Rielly 20.00 50.00
ASNNK Nikita Kucherov 40.00 100.00
ASNNM Nathan MacKinnon 80.00 200.00
ASNNS Nick Suzuki 40.00 100.00
ASNOB Oliver Bjorkstrand 15.00 40.00
ASNQH Quinn Hughes 50.00 125.00
ASNRD Rasmus Dahlin 25.00 60.00
ASNRT Robert Thomas 30.00 80.00
ASNSA Sebastian Aho 30.00 80.00
ASNSB Sergei Bobrovsky 30.00 80.00
ASNSC Sidney Crosby 80.00 200.00
ASNSR Sam Reinhart 40.00 100.00
ASNTD Thatcher Demko 25.00 60.00
ASNTH Tomas Hertl 20.00 50.00
ASNTK Travis Konecny 20.00 50.00
ASNTW Tom Wilson 20.00 50.00
ASNVT Vincent Trocheck 20.00 50.00
ASNWN William Nylander 40.00 100.00

2024-25 SP Game Used '24 All-Star Game Puck Relics
ASPAM Auston Matthews 50.00 125.00
ASPBB Brock Boeser 15.00 40.00
ASPCK Clayton Keller 15.00 40.00
ASPCM Cale Makar 30.00 80.00
ASPDP David Pastrnak 30.00 80.00
ASPFV Frank Vatrano 10.00 25.00
ASPJB Jesper Bratt 12.00 30.00
ASPLD Leon Draisaitl 40.00 100.00
ASPMC Connor McDavid 60.00 150.00
ASPMM Mitch Marner 20.00 50.00
ASPNK Nikita Kucherov 25.00 60.00
ASPNM Nathan MacKinnon 50.00 125.00
ASPOB Oliver Bjorkstrand 10.00 25.00
ASPQH Quinn Hughes 30.00 80.00
ASPRT Robert Thomas 12.00 30.00
ASPSC Sidney Crosby 50.00 125.00
ASPSR Sam Reinhart 25.00 60.00
ASPTK Travis Konecny 10.00 25.00
ASPVT Vincent Trocheck 12.00 30.00
ASPWN William Nylander 25.00 60.00

2024-25 SP Game Used '24 All-Star Mascot Fabrics
*PATCH/35: 1.5X TO 4X BASIC
ASMF1 Blades The Bruin 6.00 15.00
ASMF2 Sabretooth 6.00 15.00
ASMF3 Stormy 6.00 15.00
ASMF4 Tommy Hawk 6.00 15.00
ASMF5 Bernie the St. Bernard 6.00 15.00
ASMF6 Stinger 6.00 15.00
ASMF7 Victor E. Green 6.00 15.00
ASMF8 Hunter 6.00 15.00
ASMF9 Stanley C. Panther 6.00 15.00
ASMF10 Bailey 6.00 15.00
ASMF11 Youppi 10.00 25.00
ASMF12 Gnash 6.00 15.00
ASMF13 New Jersey Devils 6.00 15.00
ASMF14 Sparky The Dragon 6.00 15.00
ASMF15 Spartacat 6.00 15.00
ASMF16 Gritty 12.00 30.00
ASMF17 Iceburgh 6.00 15.00
ASMF18 SJ Sharkie 6.00 15.00
ASMF19 Buoy 6.00 15.00
ASMF20 Louie 6.00 15.00
ASMF21 Thunderbug 6.00 15.00
ASMF22 Chance 6.00 15.00
ASMF23 Slapshot 6.00 15.00
ASMF24 Mick E Moose 6.00 15.00
ASMF25 Howler 6.00 15.00

2024-25 SP Game Used '24 All-Star Skills Souvenirs Jersey Relics
SVAG Alexandar Georgiev 4.00 10.00
SVAM Auston Matthews 15.00 40.00
SVCH Connor Hellebuyck 8.00 20.00
SVCM Connor McDavid 20.00 50.00
SVCT Cam Talbot 4.00 10.00
SVDP David Pastrnak 10.00 25.00
SVEP Elias Pettersson 6.00 15.00
SVIS Igor Shesterkin 8.00 20.00
SVJM J.T. Miller 5.00 12.00
SVJO Jake Oettinger 6.00 15.00
SVJS Jeremy Swayman 6.00 15.00
SVLD Leon Draisaitl 12.00 30.00
SVMA Cale Makar 10.00 25.00
SVMB Mathew Barzal 5.00 12.00
SVNK Nikita Kucherov 8.00 20.00
SVNM Nathan MacKinnon 15.00 40.00
SVQH Quinn Hughes 10.00 25.00
SVSB Sergei Bobrovsky 6.00 15.00
SVTD Thatcher Demko 5.00 12.00
SVWN William Nylander 8.00 20.00

2024-25 SP Game Used '24 Stadium Series Banner Year Relics
BYSSAF Adam Fox 4.00 10.00
BYSSAL Alexis Lafreniere 5.00 12.00
BYSSAP Artemi Panarin 6.00 15.00
BYSSBH Bo Horvat 4.00 10.00
BYSSBN Brock Nelson 3.00 8.00
BYSSJB Jesper Bratt 3.00 8.00
BYSSJF Joel Farabee 3.00 8.00
BYSSJH Jack Hughes 8.00 20.00
BYSSJT Jacob Trouba 2.50 6.00
BYSSKM K'Andre Miller 2.50 6.00
BYSSLE Anders Lee 2.50 6.00
BYSSLH Luke Hughes 5.00 12.00
BYSSMB Mathew Barzal 4.00 10.00
BYSSMF Morgan Frost 2.50 6.00
BYSSND Noah Dobson 4.00 10.00
BYSSNH Nico Hischier 5.00 12.00
BYSSOT Owen Tippett 2.00 5.00
BYSSSC Sean Couturier 2.50 6.00
BYSSTK Travis Konecny 3.00 8.00
BYSSTM Timo Meier 3.00 8.00

2024-25 SP Game Used '24 Stadium Series Devils Flyers Net Cord Relics
SSNCL Curtis Lazar 20.00 50.00
SSNCY Cam York 20.00 50.00
SSNDM Dawson Mercer 40.00 100.00
SSNEH Erik Haula 20.00 50.00
SSNGH Garnet Hathaway 20.00 50.00
SSNJB Jesper Bratt 30.00 80.00
SSNJD Jamie Drysdale 25.00 60.00
SSNJF Joel Farabee 30.00 80.00
SSNJH Jack Hughes 80.00 200.00
SSNLH Luke Hughes 50.00 125.00
SSNMF Morgan Frost 25.00 60.00
SSNNC Noah Cates 20.00 50.00
SSNNH Nico Hischier 50.00 120.00
SSNOP Ondrej Palat 25.00 60.00
SSNOT Owen Tippett 20.00 50.00
SSNSC Sean Couturier 25.00 60.00
SSNSL Scott Laughton 20.00 50.00
SSNSN Simon Nemec 40.00 100.00
SSNTM Timo Meier 30.00 80.00
SSNTS Travis Sanheim 20.00 50.00

2024-25 SP Game Used '24 Stadium Series Devils Flyers Puck Relics
SSPJB Jesper Bratt 25.00 60.00
SSPJD Jamie Drysdale 20.00 50.00
SSPJF Joel Farabee 25.00 60.00
SSPJH Jack Hughes 60.00 150.00
SSPLH Luke Hughes 40.00 100.00
SSPMF Morgan Frost 20.00 50.00
SSPNC Noah Cates 15.00 40.00
SSPNH Nico Hischier 40.00 100.00
SSPSC Sean Couturier 20.00 50.00
SSPSN Simon Nemec 30.00 80.00

2024-25 SP Game Used '24 Stadium Series Fabrics
*PATCH/35: 1.2X TO 3X BASIC
GSF1 Adam Fox 5.00 12.00
GSF2 Noah Dobson 5.00 12.00
GSF3 Alexis Lafreniere 6.00 15.00
GSF4 Brock Nelson 4.00 10.00
GSF5 Artemi Panarin 8.00 20.00
GSF6 Mathew Barzal 5.00 12.00
GSF7 K'Andre Miller 3.00 8.00
GSF8 Kyle Palmieri 3.00 8.00
GSF9 Vincent Trocheck 4.00 10.00
GSF10 Anders Lee 3.00 8.00
GSF11 Jamie Drysdale 3.00 8.00
GSF12 Ondrej Palat 3.00 8.00
GSF13 Cam Atkinson 4.00 10.00
GSF14 Tyler Toffoli 4.00 10.00
GSF15 Travis Sanheim 2.50 6.00
GSF16 Luke Hughes 6.00 15.00
GSF17 Sean Couturier 3.00 8.00
GSF18 Nico Hischier 6.00 15.00
GSF19 Travis Konecny 4.00 10.00
GSF20 Jack Hughes 10.00 25.00

2024-25 SP Game Used '24 Stadium Series Islanders Rangers Net Cord Relics
SSNAF Adam Fox 40.00 100.00
SSNAL Alexis Lafreniere 50.00 125.00
SSNAP Artemi Panarin 60.00 150.00
SSNBH Bo Horvat 40.00 100.00
SSNBN Brock Nelson 30.00 80.00
SSNBS Braden Schneider 25.00 60.00
SSNCC Cal Clutterbuck 20.00 50.00
SSNEN Pierre Engvall 20.00 50.00
SSNJT Jacob Trouba 25.00 60.00
SSNKM K'Andre Miller 25.00 60.00
SSNKP Kyle Palmieri 25.00 60.00
SSNLE Anders Lee 25.00 60.00
SSNMB Mathew Barzal 40.00 100.00
SSNMZ Mika Zibanejad 40.00 100.00
SSNND Noah Dobson 40.00 100.00
SSNPE Adam Pelech 20.00 50.00
SSNRL Ryan Lindgren 20.00 50.00
SSNVT Vincent Trocheck 30.00 80.00

2024-25 SP Game Used '24 Stadium Series Islanders Rangers Puck Relics
SSPAF Adam Fox 30.00 80.00
SSPAL Alexis Lafreniere 40.00 100.00
SSPAP Artemi Panarin 50.00 125.00
SSPBH Bo Horvat 30.00 80.00
SSPCC Cal Clutterbuck 15.00 40.00
SSPKM K'Andre Miller 20.00 50.00
SSPLE Anders Lee 20.00 50.00
SSPMB Mathew Barzal 30.00 80.00
SSPMZ Mika Zibanejad 30.00 80.00
SSPND Noah Dobson 30.00 80.00

2024-25 SP Game Used '24 Stanley Cup Finals Banner Year Relics
BYSCAB Aleksander Barkov 6.00 15.00
BYSCCM Connor McDavid 20.00 50.00
BYSCCV Carter Verhaeghe 4.00 10.00
BYSCEB Evan Bouchard 5.00 12.00
BYSCLD Leon Draisaitl 12.00 30.00
BYSCMT Matthew Tkachuk 8.00 20.00
BYSCRN Ryan Nugent-Hopkins 5.00 12.00
BYSCSB Sergei Bobrovsky 6.00 15.00
BYSCSR Sam Reinhart 8.00 20.00
BYSCZH Zach Hyman 6.00 15.00

2024-25 SP Game Used '24 Stanley Cup Finals Net Cord Relics
SCNAB Aleksander Barkov 150.00 400.00
SCNCM Connor McDavid 500.00 1200.00
SCNEB Evan Bouchard 125.00 300.00
SCNLD Leon Draisaitl 300.00 800.00
SCNMT Matthew Tkachuk 200.00 500.00
SCNRN Ryan Nugent-Hopkins 125.00 300.00
SCNSB Sergei Bobrovsky 250.00 600.00
SCNSM Sam Bennett 150.00 400.00
SCNSR Sam Reinhart 200.00 500.00
SCNZH Zach Hyman 150.00 400.00

2024-25 SP Game Used '24 Stanley Cup Finals Puck Relics
SCPAB Aleksander Barkov 125.00 300.00
SCPAE Aaron Ekblad 100.00 250.00
SCPAL Anton Lundell 80.00 200.00
SCPBM Brandon Montour 100.00 250.00
SCPBO Sergei Bobrovsky 125.00 300.00
SCPCM Connor McDavid 400.00 1000.00
SCPCV Carter Verhaeghe 80.00 200.00
SCPEB Evan Bouchard 100.00 250.00
SCPER Evan Rodrigues 60.00 150.00
SCPGF Gustav Forsling 80.00 200.00
SCPLD Leon Draisaitl 250.00 600.00
SCPMT Matthew Tkachuk 150.00 400.00
SCPRN Ryan Nugent-Hopkins 100.00 250.00
SCPSB Sam Bennett 125.00 300.00
SCPSR Sam Reinhart 150.00 400.00
SCPZH Zach Hyman 125.00 300.00

2024-25 SP Game Used '24 Stanley Cup Playoffs Net Cord Relics
SCNAH Adam Henrique 80.00 200.00
SCNAL Anton Lundell 100.00 250.00
SCNBM Brandon Montour 125.00 300.00
SCNCV Carter Verhaeghe 100.00 250.00
SCNER Evan Rodrigues 80.00 200.00
SCNME Mattias Ekholm 80.00 200.00
SCNMJ Mattias Janmark 60.00 150.00
SCNOE Oliver Ekman-Larsson 125.00 300.00
SCNPB Philip Broberg 60.00 150.00
SCNSB Sergei Bobrovsky 250.00 600.00
SCNSS Stuart Skinner 120.00 300.00
SCNZH Zach Hyman 150.00 400.00

2024-25 SP Game Used '24 Winter Classic Banner Year Relics
BYWCAP Alex Pietrangelo 3.00 8.00
BYWCCS Chandler Stephenson 3.00 8.00
BYWCET Eeli Tolvanen 4.00 10.00
BYWCJD Joey Daccord 4.00 10.00
BYWCJE Jack Eichel 6.00 15.00
BYWCJM Jared McCann 4.00 10.00
BYWCMA Jonathan Marchessault 5.00 12.00
BYWCMB Matty Beniers 5.00 12.00
BYWCMS Mark Stone 5.00 12.00
BYWCVD Vince Dunn 3.00 8.00

2024-25 SP Game Used '24 Winter Classic Fabrics
*PATCH/35: 1.2X TO 3X BASIC
WCF1 Matty Beniers 6.00 15.00
WCF2 Vince Dunn 4.00 10.00
WCF3 Joey Daccord 5.00 12.00
WCF4 Jared McCann 4.00 10.00
WCF5 Eeli Tolvanen 5.00 12.00
WCF6 Alex Pietrangelo 4.00 10.00
WCF7 Chandler Stephenson 4.00 10.00
WCF8 Jack Eichel 8.00 20.00
WCF9 Jonathan Marchessault 6.00 15.00
WCF10 Mark Stone 6.00 15.00

2024-25 SP Game Used '24 Winter Classic Net Cord Relics
WCNAB Andre Burakovsky 25.00 60.00
WCNAL Adam Larsson 40.00 100.00
WCNAP Alex Pietrangelo 30.00 80.00
WCNBH Brett Howden 25.00 60.00
WCNBT Brandon Tanev 30.00 80.00
WCNCS Chandler Stephenson 30.00 80.00
WCNEJ Jack Eichel 60.00 150.00
WCNET Eeli Tolvanen 40.00 100.00
WCNIB Ivan Barbashev 30.00 80.00
WCNJD Joey Daccord 80.00 200.00
WCNJE Jordan Eberle 40.00 100.00
WCNJM Jonathan Marchessault 50.00 125.00
WCNMB Matty Beniers 50.00 125.00
WCNMC Jared McCann 30.00 80.00
WCNMS Mark Stone 50.00 125.00
WCNNH Nicolas Hague 25.00 60.00
WCNTK Tye Kartye 30.00 80.00
WCNVD Vince Dunn 30.00 80.00
WCNWK William Karlsson 50.00 125.00
WCNZW Zach Whitecloud 25.00 60.00

2024-25 SP Game Used Autographs Blue
1 Jonathan Huberdeau 10.00 25.00
5 Jacob Slavin 6.00 15.00
8 Vince Dunn 6.00 15.00
16 Fabian Zetterlund 5.00 12.00
17 Sean Durzi 5.00 12.00
18 Kirill Marchenko 10.00 25.00
24 Thomas Novak 5.00 12.00
25 Thomas Bordeleau 5.00 12.00
26 Cole Perfetti 8.00 20.00
29 Roman Josi SP 8.00 20.00
30 Mikael Granlund 6.00 15.00
33 Miro Heiskanen 10.00 25.00
34 Luke Evangelista 6.00 15.00
35 Michael Bunting 8.00 20.00
38 Mikko Rantanen SP 20.00 50.00
42 Tage Thompson 10.00 25.00
44 Ryan O'Reilly 8.00 20.00
49 Josh Anderson 6.00 15.00
50 Kris Letang 10.00 25.00
51 John Carlson 8.00 20.00
53 Wyatt Johnston 15.00 40.00
59 Dawson Mercer 10.00 25.00
60 Matty Beniers 10.00 25.00
62 Ryan Nugent-Hopkins SP 10.00 25.00
65 Ryan Strome 8.00 20.00
66 Kevin Korchinski 6.00 15.00
68 Alexis Lafreniere SP 12.00 30.00
70 Troy Terry 6.00 15.00
71 Nick Foligno 5.00 12.00
72 Anze Kopitar 12.00 30.00
77 Juraj Slafkovsky 15.00 40.00
80 Matias Maccelli 6.00 15.00
83 Morgan Frost SP 6.00 15.00
86 J.T. Compher 5.00 12.00
87 Nico Hischier SP 12.00 30.00
89 Jack McBain 5.00 12.00
90 Samuel Girard 5.00 12.00
91 Matt Boldy 12.00 30.00
93 Jack Eichel SP 12.00 30.00
95 Ross Colton 6.00 15.00
98 Chandler Stephenson 6.00 15.00
99 Seth Jarvis 10.00 25.00
100 Aleksander Barkov SP 12.00 30.00
101 Anders Lee 6.00 15.00
102 Kevin Hayes 6.00 15.00
104 Kent Johnson 8.00 20.00
107 Alex Ovechkin SP 100.00 250.00
109 Matthew Tkachuk SP 15.00 40.00
112 Logan Cooley 12.00 30.00
113 Devon Toews 6.00 15.00
117 Jason Dickinson 5.00 12.00
122 Elias Pettersson SP 12.00 30.00
123 Nikita Kucherov SP 15.00 40.00
124 Thatcher Demko SP 10.00 25.00
126 Brady Tkachuk SP 12.00 30.00
129 Brock Boeser SP 10.00 25.00
131 Frank Vatrano 6.00 15.00
139 Igor Shesterkin SP 15.00 40.00
144 Cale Makar SP 30.00 80.00
147 Kirill Kaprizov SP 25.00 60.00
150 Jeremy Swayman 12.00 30.00
153 Oliver Bjorkstrand 6.00 15.00
155 Leon Draisaitl SP 25.00 60.00
156 Connor Hellebuyck SP 15.00 40.00
159 Robert Thomas SP 8.00 20.00
160 Sam Reinhart SP 15.00 40.00
162 Boone Jenner SP 8.00 20.00
163 Nick Suzuki 15.00 40.00
164 Tomas Hertl SP 8.00 20.00
165 Bill Guerin SP 8.00 20.00
166 Bryan Trottier 8.00 20.00
167 Brian Leetch SP 6.00 15.00
168 Rob Blake 8.00 20.00
169 Mike Modano SP 12.00 30.00
170 Doug Gilmour SP 10.00 25.00
171 Michel Goulet SP 8.00 20.00
172 Corey Crawford SP 8.00 20.00
174 Patrice Bergeron 10.00 25.00
175 Joe Thornton SP 12.00 30.00
176 Jari Kurri SP 8.00 20.00
177 Paul Coffey 8.00 20.00
178 Keith Primeau SP 6.00 15.00
179 Peter Bondra SP 8.00 20.00
180 Larry Robinson 8.00 20.00
182 Ron Francis SP 10.00 25.00
183 Eric Lindros SP 12.00 30.00
185 Joe Pavelski SP 10.00 25.00
186 Alex Delvecchio 8.00 20.00
187 Rick Nash 8.00 20.00
188 Martin St. Louis 8.00 20.00
189 Charlie Simmer SP 5.00 12.00
190 Joe Sakic SP 15.00 40.00
191 Keith Tkachuk 8.00 20.00
192 Al MacInnis 10.00 25.00
195 Henrik Zetterberg 10.00 25.00
196 Trevor Linden SP 8.00 20.00
197 Adam Graves 6.00 15.00
198 Jeremy Roenick SP 12.00 30.00
199 David Backes SP 5.00 12.00
200 Dany Heatley 6.00 15.00
201 Jackson Blake 15.00 40.00
202 Brennan Othmann 12.00 30.00
203 Arshdeep Bains 10.00 25.00
204 Adam Klapka 8.00 20.00
205 Kyle MacLean 8.00 20.00
207 Olen Zellweger 15.00 40.00
208 Brian Halonen 8.00 20.00
209 Josh Doan 12.00 30.00
210 Frank Nazar 25.00 60.00
211 Zack Ostapchuk 8.00 20.00
212 Mason Morelli 8.00 20.00
213 Logan Stankoven 20.00 50.00
214 Logan Morrison 8.00 20.00
215 Macklin Celebrini 150.00 400.00
217 Ivan Fedotov 15.00 40.00
218 Lukas Cormier 8.00 20.00
219 Ethan Del Mastro 8.00 20.00
220 Vasily Ponomarev 8.00 20.00
221 Pierrick Dube 8.00 20.00
222 Jason Polin 8.00 20.00
225 Rutger McGroarty 15.00 40.00
226 Liam Ohgren 15.00 40.00
227 Declan Carlile 8.00 20.00
228 Seamus Casey 10.00 25.00
229 Nikolai Kovalenko 6.00 15.00
230 Collin Graf 8.00 20.00
231 Nikita Chibrikov 8.00 20.00
232 Samuel Honzek 8.00 20.00
234 Shakir Mukhamadullin 10.00 25.00
235 Calum Ritchie 10.00 25.00
237 Jack Thompson 8.00 20.00
239 Bradly Nadeau 12.00 30.00
240 Matt Rempe 15.00 40.00
241 Matt Villalta 8.00 20.00
242 Yan Kuznetsov 8.00 20.00
245 Jesper Wallstedt 20.00 50.00
246 Emil Lilleberg 8.00 20.00
247 Will Smith 40.00 100.00
248 Joshua Roy 12.00 30.00
249 Maxwell Crozier 8.00 20.00
250 Matvei Michkov 150.00 400.00
252 Devin Cooley 8.00 20.00
254 Mavrik Bourque 15.00 40.00
255 Zachary Bolduc 15.00 40.00
256 Conor Geekie 15.00 40.00
257 Scott Morrow 10.00 25.00
259 Brendan Brisson 10.00 25.00
260 Phil Kemp 8.00 20.00
261 Zach Dean 8.00 20.00
262 Jett Luchanko SP 15.00 40.00
263 Marat Khusnutdinov 8.00 20.00
264 Gage Goncalves 10.00 25.00
266 Justin Brazeau 8.00 20.00
267 Graeme Clarke 8.00 20.00
271 Nolan Allan 8.00 20.00
272 Sam Colangelo 8.00 20.00
273 Logan Mailloux 12.00 30.00
274 Aku Raty 8.00 20.00
275 Akil Thomas 8.00 20.00
276 Victor Mancini 8.00 20.00
278 Cutter Gauthier 20.00 50.00
279 Lane Hutson 150.00 400.00
280 Marshall Rifai 8.00 20.00

2024-25 SP Game Used Draft Day Marks
DDMBN Bradly Nadeau/210* 40.00 100.00
DDMBO Brennan Othmann/245* 40.00 100.00
DDMBO Mavrik Bourque/245* 50.00 125.00
DDMBR Brendan Brisson/245* 30.00 80.00
DDMCG Cutter Gauthier/280* 60.00 150.00
DDMFL Fabian Lysell/210* 60.00 150.00
DDMFN Frank Nazar/175* 125.00 300.00
DDMGB Gavin Brindley/280* 25.00 60.00
DDMGC Graeme Clarke/210* 25.00 60.00
DDMGE Conor Geekie/210* 50.00 125.00
DDMJD Josh Doan/140* 40.00 100.00
DDMJW Jesper Wallstedt/315* 60.00 150.00
DDMLC Lukas Cormier/245* 25.00 60.00
DDMLH Lane Hutson/210* 400.00 1000.00
DDMLO Liam Ohgren/210* 50.00 125.00
DDMLS Logan Stankoven/280* 60.00 150.00
DDMMC Macklin Celebrini/315* 500.00 1200.00
DDMMM Matvei Michkov/245* 250.00 600.00
DDMMR Matt Rempe/175* 50.00 125.00
DDMNC Nikita Chibrikov/315* 25.00 60.00
DDMOZ Olen Zellweger/315* 25.00 60.00
DDMSC Sam Colangelo/315* 25.00 60.00
DDMSC Sebastian Cossa/175* 60.00 150.00
DDMVP Vasily Ponomarev/315* 25.00 60.00
DDMWS Will Smith/175* 150.00 400.00
DDMZD Zach Dean/140* 25.00 60.00
DDMZO Zack Ostapchuk/315* 25.00 60.00

2024-25 SP Game Used Draft Swag Relics Jersey
DS1 Liam Ohgren 5.00 12.00
DS2 Bradly Nadeau 4.00 10.00
DS3 Lane Hutson 40.00 100.00
DS5 Matthew Poitras 2.50 6.00
DS6 Frank Nazar 8.00 20.00
DS7 Kevin Korchinski 2.00 5.00
DS8 Adam Fantilli 4.00 10.00
DS9 Connor Bedard 30.00 80.00
DS10 Gavin Brindley 2.50 6.00

2024-25 SP Game Used Draft Swag Relics Hat
*HAT/25: 1.5X TO 4X BASIC
DS2 Bradly Nadeau 25.00 60.00

2024-25 SP Game Used Frameworks Jerseys
FAF Adam Fox SP 10.00 25.00
FAK Anze Kopitar 12.00 30.00
FAO Alex Ovechkin SP 30.00 80.00
FCB Connor Bedard SP 25.00 60.00
FHU Jack Hughes 20.00 50.00
FJE Jack Eichel 12.00 30.00
FJK Jordan Kyrou 8.00 20.00
FKC Kyle Connor 12.00 30.00
FKK Kirill Kaprizov 20.00 50.00
FLS Logan Stankoven 20.00 50.00
FMB Matty Beniers 10.00 25.00
FMS Moritz Seider 10.00 25.00
FMT Matthew Tkachuk 15.00 40.00
FNK Nikita Kucherov 15.00 40.00
FRD Rasmus Dahlin 10.00 25.00
FRJ Roman Josi 8.00 20.00
FRN Ryan Nugent-Hopkins 10.00 25.00
FSA Sebastian Aho 12.00 30.00

FSC Sidney Crosby SP 30.00 80.00
FTK Travis Konecny 8.00 20.00

2024-25 SP Game Used Game Gear Rookies

GGBO Brennan Othmann 10.00 25.00
GGCG Cutter Gauthier 15.00 40.00
GGFN Frank Nazar 20.00 50.00
GGJR Joshua Roy 10.00 25.00
GGLH Lane Hutson 80.00 200.00
GGLO Liam Ohgren 12.00 30.00
GGLS Logan Stankoven 15.00 40.00
GGMC Macklin Celebrini 200.00 500.00
GGMM Matvei Michkov 80.00 200.00
GGOZ Olen Zellweger 12.00 30.00

2024-25 SP Game Used HOF Marks

HOFAB Andy Bathgate/280* 12.00 30.00
HOFBC Bobby Clarke/210* 25.00 60.00
HOFBF Bernie Federko/245* 12.00 30.00
HOFCC Chris Chelios/245* 15.00 40.00
HOFCP Chris Pronger/245* 15.00 40.00
HOFDP Denis Potvin/210* 15.00 40.00
HOFHM Howie Morenz/210* 15.00 40.00
HOFJI Jarome Iginla/210* 20.00 50.00
HOFJR Jean Ratelle/245* 12.00 30.00
HOFJS Joe Sakic/175* 60.00 150.00
HOFKC King Clancy/210* 15.00 40.00
HOFKL Kevin Lowe/140* 15.00 40.00
HOFLR Larry Robinson/280* 15.00 40.00
HOFMB Mike Bossy/175* 15.00 40.00
HOFMG Mike Gartner/245* 20.00 50.00
HOFML Mario Lemieux/245* 60.00 150.00
HOFMM Mike Modano/210* 25.00 60.00
HOFMR Mark Recchi/210* 15.00 40.00
HOFMS Mats Sundin/210* 30.00 80.00
HOFNL Nicklas Lidstrom/280* 15.00 40.00
HOFNU Norm Ullman/210* 15.00 40.00
HOFPF Peter Forsberg/280* 30.00 80.00
HOFRB Ray Bourque/245* 25.00 60.00
HOFRF Ron Francis/245* 20.00 50.00
HOFSA Sid Abel/140* 15.00 40.00
HOFSN Scott Niedermayer/385* 15.00 40.00
HOFTB Turk Broda/175* 15.00 40.00
HOFTE Tony Esposito/280* 15.00 40.00
HOFTH Tim Horton/210* 25.00 60.00
HOFWG Wayne Gretzky/245* 100.00 250.00

2024-25 SP Game Used Inked Rookie Sweaters

*PATCH/35: 1.5X TO 4X BASIC
IRSAT Akil Thomas 5.00 12.00
IRSBB Brendan Brisson 6.00 15.00
IRSBO Brennan Othmann 8.00 20.00
IRSCG Cutter Gauthier 20.00 50.00
IRSEL Emil Lilleberg 5.00 12.00
IRSFN Frank Nazar 25.00 60.00
IRSGC Graeme Clarke 5.00 12.00
IRSGG Gage Goncalves 6.00 15.00
IRSJB Justin Brazeau 5.00 12.00
IRSJD Josh Doan 8.00 20.00
IRSJR Joshua Roy 8.00 20.00
IRSJW Jesper Wallstedt 12.00 30.00
IRSLC Lukas Cormier 5.00 12.00
IRSLH Lane Hutson 200.00 500.00
IRSLO Liam Ohgren 10.00 25.00
IRSLS Logan Stankoven 15.00 40.00
IRSMB Mavrik Bourque 10.00 25.00
IRSMR Matt Rempe 15.00 40.00
IRSOZ Olen Zellweger 10.00 25.00
IRSSC Sam Colangelo 5.00 12.00
IRSSM Scott Morrow 6.00 15.00
IRSZB Zachary Bolduc 10.00 25.00
IRSZO Zack Ostapchuk 5.00 12.00

2024-25 SP Game Used Inked Sweaters

ISAB Aleksander Barkov 20.00 50.00
ISAL Anders Lee 10.00 25.00
ISAM Auston Matthews 80.00 200.00
ISAO Alex Ovechkin 150.00 400.00
ISBB Brock Boeser 15.00 40.00
ISBS Brandon Saad 10.00 25.00
ISBT Brady Tkachuk 20.00 50.00
ISCB Connor Bedard 125.00 300.00
ISCH Connor Hellebuyck 25.00 60.00
ISCV Carter Verhaeghe 12.00 30.00
ISKK Kirill Kaprizov 80.00 200.00
ISKM K'Andre Miller 10.00 25.00
ISMA Cale Makar 30.00 80.00
ISMH Miro Heiskanen 15.00 40.00
ISNS Nick Suzuki 25.00 60.00
ISQH Quinn Hughes 30.00 80.00
ISRJ Roman Josi 12.00 30.00
ISTD Thatcher Demko 15.00 40.00
ISTT Troy Terry 10.00 25.00

2024-25 SP Game Used Jersey Autographs Red

1 Jonathan Huberdeau/65 12.00 30.00
5 Jaccob Slavin/149 8.00 20.00
11 Noah Dobson/99 12.00 30.00
16 Fabian Zetterlund/149 6.00 15.00
18 Kirill Marchenko/149 12.00 30.00
24 Thomas Novak/149 6.00 15.00
26 Cole Perfetti/99 10.00 25.00
29 Roman Josi/35 10.00 25.00
30 Mikael Granlund/99 8.00 20.00
33 Miro Heiskanen/65 12.00 30.00
34 Luke Evangelista/149 8.00 20.00
35 Michael Bunting/149 10.00 25.00
38 Mikko Rantanen/65 25.00 60.00
42 Tage Thompson/65 12.00 30.00
44 Ryan O'Reilly/65 10.00 25.00
49 Josh Anderson/99 8.00 20.00
50 Kris Letang/35 12.00 30.00
51 John Carlson/65 10.00 25.00
53 Wyatt Johnston/65 20.00 50.00
59 Dawson Mercer/149 12.00 30.00
60 Matty Beniers/65 12.00 30.00
64 Jared McCann/65 8.00 20.00
65 Ryan Strome/99 10.00 25.00
66 Kevin Korchinski/149 8.00 20.00
68 Alexis Lafreniere/35 15.00 40.00
70 Troy Terry/99 8.00 20.00
77 Juraj Slafkovsky/35 20.00 50.00
80 Matias Maccelli/149 8.00 20.00
83 Morgan Frost/149 8.00 20.00
85 Mikael Backlund/65 8.00 20.00
86 J.T. Compher/149 6.00 15.00
87 Nico Hischier/35 15.00 40.00
90 Samuel Girard/99 6.00 15.00
91 Matt Boldy/65 15.00 40.00
93 Jack Eichel/35 15.00 40.00
94 Isac Lundestrom/149 6.00 15.00
98 Chandler Stephenson/99 8.00 20.00
99 Seth Jarvis/99 12.00 30.00
100 Aleksander Barkov/35 15.00 40.00
101 Anders Lee/99 8.00 20.00
104 Kent Johnson/149 10.00 25.00
106 Travis Sanheim/149 6.00 15.00
112 Logan Cooley/149 15.00 40.00
113 Devon Toews/99 8.00 20.00
115 Tim Stutzle/35 12.00 30.00
116 Tomas Hertl/149 10.00 25.00
121 Quinn Hughes/35 40.00 100.00
124 Thatcher Demko/65 12.00 30.00
126 Brady Tkachuk/35 15.00 40.00
129 Brock Boeser/35 12.00 30.00
131 Frank Vatrano/99 8.00 20.00
136 Jake Oettinger/65 15.00 40.00
144 Cale Makar/35 25.00 60.00
147 Kirill Kaprizov/35 30.00 80.00
150 Jeremy Swayman/65 15.00 40.00
153 Oliver Bjorkstrand/99 8.00 20.00
156 Connor Hellebuyck/35 20.00 50.00
159 Robert Thomas/65 10.00 25.00
160 Sam Reinhart/35 20.00 50.00
163 Nick Suzuki/35 20.00 50.00
164 Tomas Hertl/65 10.00 25.00
165 Bill Guerin/35 10.00 25.00
166 Bryan Trottier/65 10.00 25.00
167 Brian Leetch/65 8.00 20.00
172 Corey Crawford/99 10.00 25.00
174 Patrice Bergeron/65 12.00 30.00
175 Joe Thornton/35 15.00 40.00
176 Jari Kurri/65 10.00 25.00
177 Paul Coffey/35 10.00 25.00
178 Keith Primeau/99 8.00 20.00
182 Ron Francis/35 12.00 30.00
185 Joe Pavelski/99 12.00 30.00
190 Rick Nash/65 10.00 25.00
191 Keith Tkachuk/35 10.00 25.00
197 Adam Graves/35 8.00 20.00
201 Jackson Blake/99 20.00 50.00
202 Brennan Othmann/49 15.00 40.00
203 Arshdeep Bains/149 12.00 30.00
204 Adam Klapka/99 10.00 25.00
205 Kyle MacLean/149 10.00 25.00
207 Olen Zellweger/99 20.00 50.00
208 Brian Halonen/99 10.00 25.00
209 Josh Doan/49 15.00 40.00
210 Frank Nazar/99 30.00 80.00
211 Zack Ostapchuk/99 10.00 25.00
212 Mason Morelli/149 10.00 25.00
213 Logan Stankoven/49 25.00 60.00
214 Logan Morrison/149 10.00 25.00
215 Macklin Celebrini/49 250.00 600.00
217 Ivan Fedotov/99 20.00 50.00
218 Lukas Cormier/99 10.00 25.00
219 Ethan Del Mastro/99 10.00 25.00
220 Vasily Ponomarev/99 10.00 25.00
221 Pierrick Dube/99 10.00 25.00
222 Jason Polin/99 10.00 25.00
225 Rutger McGroarty/149 20.00 50.00
226 Liam Ohgren/49 15.00 40.00
227 Declan Carlile/149 10.00 25.00
228 Seamus Casey/149 12.00 30.00
229 Nikolai Kovalenko/99 8.00 20.00
230 Collin Graf/99 10.00 25.00
231 Nikita Chibrikov/49 10.00 25.00
234 Shakir Mukhamadullin/99 12.00 30.00
237 Jack Thompson/149 10.00 25.00
239 Bradly Nadeau/99 15.00 40.00
240 Matt Rempe/99 20.00 50.00
241 Matt Villalta/149 10.00 25.00
242 Yan Kuznetsov/99 10.00 25.00
245 Jesper Wallstedt/99 25.00 60.00
246 Emil Lilleberg/99 10.00 25.00
247 Will Smith/99 80.00 200.00
248 Joshua Roy/99 15.00 40.00
249 Maxwell Crozier/99 10.00 25.00
250 Matvei Michkov/99 125.00 300.00
252 Devin Cooley/149 10.00 25.00
254 Mavrik Bourque/49 20.00 50.00
255 Zachary Bolduc/99 20.00 50.00
256 Conor Geekie/149 20.00 50.00
257 Scott Morrow/99 12.00 30.00
259 Brendan Brisson/99 12.00 30.00
260 Phil Kemp/149 10.00 25.00
261 Zach Dean/99 10.00 25.00
264 Gage Goncalves/99 12.00 30.00
266 Justin Brazeau/99 10.00 25.00
267 Graeme Clarke/149 10.00 25.00
272 Sam Colangelo/49 10.00 25.00
274 Aku Raty/149 10.00 25.00
275 Akil Thomas/149 10.00 25.00
278 Cutter Gauthier/49 40.00 100.00
279 Lane Hutson/49 150.00 400.00
280 Marshall Rifai/99 10.00 25.00

2024-25 SP Game Used Jersey Autographs Premium Memorabilia Gold

*PREMIUM GOLD: .6X TO 1.5X BASIC
215 Macklin Celebrini/35 500.00 1200.00
247 Will Smith/35 125.00 300.00
250 Matvei Michkov/35 200.00 500.00

2024-25 SP Game Used Jerseys Red

*GOLD/25: .8X TO 2X BASIC
1 Jonathan Huberdeau 4.00 10.00
2 Zach Hyman 5.00 12.00
3 Timo Meier 3.00 8.00
4 Yanni Gourde 2.50 6.00
5 Jaccob Slavin 2.50 6.00
6 Darnell Nurse 2.50 6.00
7 Jean-Gabriel Pageau 2.00 5.00
8 Vince Dunn 2.50 6.00
9 Brent Burns 3.00 8.00
10 Carter Verhaeghe 3.00 8.00
11 Noah Dobson 4.00 10.00
12 Jordan Kyrou 3.00 8.00
13 Nazem Kadri 4.00 10.00
14 Lucas Raymond 5.00 12.00
15 Jack Hughes 8.00 20.00
16 Fabian Zetterlund 2.00 5.00
18 Kirill Marchenko 4.00 10.00
19 Joel Eriksson Ek 2.50 6.00
21 Noah Hanifin 3.00 8.00
23 Alex DeBrincat 4.00 10.00
24 Thomas Novak 2.00 5.00
26 Cole Perfetti 3.00 8.00
27 Rasmus Dahlin 4.00 10.00
28 Dylan Larkin 4.00 10.00
29 Roman Josi 3.00 8.00
30 Mikael Granlund 2.50 6.00
32 Alex Tuch 3.00 8.00
33 Miro Heiskanen 4.00 10.00
34 Luke Evangelista 2.50 6.00
35 Michael Bunting 3.00 8.00
37 Mason McTavish 3.00 8.00
38 Mikko Rantanen 8.00 20.00
39 Drew Doughty 3.00 8.00
40 Josh Norris 3.00 8.00
41 Victor Hedman 4.00 10.00
42 Tage Thompson 4.00 10.00
43 Jason Robertson 5.00 12.00
44 Ryan O'Reilly 3.00 8.00
45 Erik Karlsson 4.00 10.00
46 Mark Scheifele 5.00 12.00
47 Charlie Coyle 3.00 8.00
48 Roope Hintz 4.00 10.00
49 Josh Anderson 2.50 6.00
50 Kris Letang 4.00 10.00
51 John Carlson 3.00 8.00
52 Charlie McAvoy 4.00 10.00
53 Wyatt Johnston 6.00 15.00
54 Kaiden Guhle 3.00 8.00
55 Evgeni Malkin 6.00 15.00
56 T.J. Oshie 3.00 8.00
57 Yegor Sharangovich 3.00 8.00
58 Evan Bouchard 4.00 10.00
59 Dawson Mercer 4.00 10.00
60 Matty Beniers 4.00 10.00
61 Sebastian Aho 5.00 12.00
62 Ryan Nugent-Hopkins 4.00 10.00
63 Bo Horvat 4.00 10.00
64 Jared McCann 2.50 6.00
65 Ryan Strome 3.00 8.00
66 Kevin Korchinski 2.50 6.00
67 Kevin Fiala 2.50 6.00
68 Alexis Lafreniere 5.00 12.00
70 Troy Terry 2.50 6.00
72 Anze Kopitar 5.00 12.00
73 Chris Kreider 4.00 10.00
74 Brayden Point 4.00 10.00
75 David Pastrnak 8.00 20.00
76 Zach Werenski 3.00 8.00
77 Juraj Slafkovsky 6.00 15.00
78 Jamie Drysdale 2.50 6.00
79 Dylan Strome 4.00 10.00
80 Matias Maccelli 2.50 6.00
81 Adam Fantilli 5.00 12.00
82 Brock Faber 4.00 10.00
83 Morgan Frost 2.50 6.00
84 William Karlsson 4.00 10.00
85 Mikael Backlund 2.50 6.00
86 J.T. Compher 2.00 5.00
87 Nico Hischier 5.00 12.00
88 Nico Sturm 2.00 5.00
90 Samuel Girard 2.00 5.00
91 Matt Boldy 5.00 12.00
92 Thomas Chabot 3.00 8.00
93 Jack Eichel 5.00 12.00
94 Isac Lundestrom 2.00 5.00
96 Quinton Byfield 4.00 10.00
97 Claude Giroux 3.00 8.00
98 Chandler Stephenson 2.50 6.00
99 Seth Jarvis 4.00 10.00
100 Aleksander Barkov 5.00 12.00
101 Anders Lee 2.50 6.00
103 Brad Marchand 6.00 15.00
104 Kent Johnson 3.00 8.00
105 Cole Caufield 6.00 15.00
106 Travis Sanheim 2.00 5.00
107 Alex Ovechkin 12.00 30.00
108 Connor Bedard 10.00 25.00
109 Matthew Tkachuk 6.00 15.00
110 Mika Zibanejad 4.00 10.00
111 Pavel Buchnevich 2.50 6.00
112 Logan Cooley 5.00 12.00
113 Devon Toews 2.50 6.00
114 Mats Zuccarello 3.00 8.00
115 Tim Stutzle 4.00 10.00
116 Tomas Hertl 3.00 8.00
118 Aaron Ekblad 4.00 10.00
119 Vincent Trocheck 3.00 8.00
120 Colton Parayko 2.50 6.00
121 Quinn Hughes 8.00 20.00
122 Elias Pettersson 5.00 12.00
123 Nikita Kucherov 6.00 15.00
124 Thatcher Demko 4.00 10.00
125 Kyle Connor 5.00 12.00
126 Brady Tkachuk 5.00 12.00
127 Jesper Bratt 3.00 8.00
128 Brock Boeser 3.00 8.00
130 J.T. Miller 4.00 10.00
131 Frank Vatrano 2.50 6.00
132 Auston Matthews 12.00 30.00
133 Morgan Rielly 3.00 8.00
134 William Nylander 6.00 15.00
135 Mitch Marner 5.00 12.00
136 Jake Oettinger 5.00 12.00
137 Clayton Keller 4.00 10.00
138 Mathew Barzal 4.00 10.00
139 Igor Shesterkin 6.00 15.00
140 Filip Forsberg 5.00 12.00
141 Alex DeBrincat 4.00 10.00
142 Vincent Trocheck 3.00 8.00
143 Nathan MacKinnon 12.00 30.00
144 Cale Makar 8.00 20.00
145 Sidney Crosby 12.00 30.00
146 Alexandar Georgiev 3.00 8.00
147 Kirill Kaprizov 10.00 25.00
148 Sebastian Aho 5.00 12.00
149 Tom Wilson 3.00 8.00
150 Jeremy Swayman 5.00 12.00
151 Travis Konecny 3.00 8.00
152 Elias Lindholm 3.00 8.00
153 Oliver Bjorkstrand 2.50 6.00
154 Connor McDavid 15.00 40.00
155 Leon Draisaitl 10.00 25.00
156 Connor Hellebuyck 6.00 15.00
157 David Pastrnak 8.00 20.00
158 Rasmus Dahlin 4.00 10.00
159 Robert Thomas 3.00 8.00
160 Sam Reinhart 6.00 15.00
161 Sergei Bobrovsky 5.00 12.00
162 Boone Jenner 3.00 8.00
163 Nick Suzuki 6.00 15.00
164 Tomas Hertl 3.00 8.00
166 Bryan Trottier SP 3.00 8.00
167 Brian Leetch 2.50 6.00
174 Patrice Bergeron 4.00 10.00
175 Joe Thornton 5.00 12.00
176 Jari Kurri SP 3.00 8.00
180 Larry Robinson SP 3.00 8.00
182 Ron Francis 4.00 10.00
184 Teemu Selanne SP 6.00 15.00
185 Joe Pavelski SP 4.00 10.00
187 Rick Nash SP 3.00 8.00
189 Charlie Simmer SP 2.00 5.00
190 Joe Sakic SP 6.00 15.00
191 Keith Tkachuk SP 3.00 8.00
194 Pat LaFontaine SP 3.00 8.00
195 Henrik Zetterberg SP 4.00 10.00
197 Adam Graves SP 2.50 6.00
198 Jeremy Roenick SP 5.00 12.00
201 Jackson Blake 5.00 12.00
202 Brennan Othmann 5.00 12.00
203 Arshdeep Bains 4.00 10.00
204 Adam Klapka 3.00 8.00
205 Kyle MacLean 3.00 8.00
207 Olen Zellweger 6.00 15.00
208 Brian Halonen 3.00 8.00
209 Josh Doan 5.00 12.00
210 Frank Nazar 10.00 25.00
211 Zack Ostapchuk 3.00 8.00
212 Mason Morelli 3.00 8.00
213 Logan Stankoven 8.00 20.00
214 Logan Morrison 3.00 8.00
215 Macklin Celebrini 15.00 40.00
217 Ivan Fedotov 6.00 15.00
218 Lukas Cormier 3.00 8.00
219 Ethan Del Mastro 3.00 8.00
220 Vasily Ponomarev 3.00 8.00
221 Pierrick Dube 3.00 8.00
222 Jason Polin 3.00 8.00
225 Rutger McGroarty 6.00 15.00
226 Liam Ohgren 6.00 15.00
227 Declan Carlile 3.00 8.00
228 Seamus Casey 4.00 10.00
229 Nikolai Kovalenko 2.50 6.00
230 Collin Graf 3.00 8.00
231 Nikita Chibrikov 3.00 8.00
233 Gavin Brindley 3.00 8.00
234 Shakir Mukhamadullin 4.00 10.00
235 Calum Ritchie 4.00 10.00
236 Luca Del Bel Belluz 3.00 8.00
237 Jack Thompson 3.00 8.00
239 Bradly Nadeau 5.00 12.00
240 Matt Rempe 6.00 15.00
241 Matt Villalta 3.00 8.00
242 Yan Kuznetsov 3.00 8.00
245 Jesper Wallstedt 8.00 20.00
246 Emil Lilleberg 3.00 8.00
247 Will Smith 10.00 25.00
248 Joshua Roy 5.00 12.00
249 Maxwell Crozier 3.00 8.00
250 Matvei Michkov 12.00 30.00
252 Devin Cooley 3.00 8.00
254 Mavrik Bourque 6.00 15.00
255 Zachary Bolduc 6.00 15.00
256 Conor Geekie 6.00 15.00
257 Scott Morrow 4.00 10.00
259 Brendan Brisson 4.00 10.00
260 Phil Kemp 3.00 8.00
261 Zach Dean 3.00 8.00
264 Gage Goncalves 4.00 10.00
266 Justin Brazeau 3.00 8.00
267 Graeme Clarke 3.00 8.00
271 Nolan Allan 3.00 8.00
272 Sam Colangelo 3.00 8.00
274 Aku Raty 3.00 8.00
275 Akil Thomas 3.00 8.00
276 Victor Mancini 3.00 8.00
277 Andre Lee 3.00 8.00
278 Cutter Gauthier 8.00 20.00
279 Lane Hutson 15.00 40.00
280 Marshall Rifai 3.00 8.00

2024-25 SP Game Used New Grooves

*RED: .5X TO 1.2X BASIC
NG1 Cutter Gauthier 2.00 5.00
NG2 Frank Nazar 2.50 6.00
NG3 Logan Stankoven 2.00 5.00
NG4 Olen Zellweger 1.50 4.00
NG5 Bradly Nadeau 1.25 3.00
NG6 Gavin Brindley .75 2.00
NG7 Liam Ohgren 1.50 4.00
NG8 Jesper Wallstedt 2.00 5.00
NG9 Lane Hutson 4.00 10.00
NG10 Brennan Othmann 1.25 3.00
NG11 Luca Del Bel Belluz .75 2.00
NG12 Joshua Roy 1.25 3.00
NG13 Josh Doan 1.25 3.00
NG14 Brendan Brisson 1.00 2.50
NG15 Lukas Cormier .75 2.00
NG16 Scott Morrow 1.00 2.50
NG17 Mavrik Bourque 1.50 4.00
NG18 Marat Khusnutdinov .75 2.00
NG19 Shakir Mukhamadullin 1.00 2.50
NG20 Zachary Bolduc 1.50 4.00

2024-25 SP Game Used New Grooves Gold

*GOLD/99: .8X TO 2X BASIC
NG9 Lane Hutson 20.00 50.00

2024-25 SP Game Used New Grooves Autographs

NG1 Cutter Gauthier 10.00 25.00
NG2 Frank Nazar 12.00 30.00
NG3 Logan Stankoven 10.00 25.00
NG4 Olen Zellweger 8.00 20.00
NG5 Bradly Nadeau 6.00 15.00
NG7 Liam Ohgren 8.00 20.00
NG8 Jesper Wallstedt 10.00 25.00
NG9 Lane Hutson 125.00 300.00
NG10 Brennan Othmann 6.00 15.00
NG12 Joshua Roy 6.00 15.00
NG13 Josh Doan 6.00 15.00
NG14 Brendan Brisson 5.00 12.00
NG15 Lukas Cormier 4.00 10.00
NG16 Scott Morrow 5.00 12.00
NG17 Mavrik Bourque 8.00 20.00
NG18 Marat Khusnutdinov 4.00 10.00
NG19 Shakir Mukhamadullin 5.00 12.00
NG20 Zachary Bolduc 8.00 20.00

2024-25 SP Game Used New Grooves Jersey Autographs

NG1 Cutter Gauthier 20.00 50.00
NG2 Frank Nazar 25.00 60.00
NG3 Logan Stankoven 20.00 50.00
NG4 Olen Zellweger 15.00 40.00
NG5 Bradly Nadeau 12.00 30.00
NG7 Liam Ohgren 15.00 40.00
NG8 Jesper Wallstedt 20.00 50.00
NG10 Brennan Othmann 12.00 30.00
NG12 Joshua Roy 12.00 30.00
NG13 Josh Doan 12.00 30.00
NG14 Brendan Brisson 10.00 25.00
NG15 Lukas Cormier 8.00 20.00
NG16 Scott Morrow 10.00 25.00
NG17 Mavrik Bourque 15.00 40.00
NG19 Shakir Mukhamadullin 10.00 25.00
NG20 Zachary Bolduc 15.00 40.00

2024-25 SP Game Used New Grooves Jerseys

*PATCH/25: 2.5X TO 6X BASIC
NG1 Cutter Gauthier 3.00 8.00
NG2 Frank Nazar 4.00 10.00
NG3 Logan Stankoven 3.00 8.00
NG4 Olen Zellweger 2.50 6.00
NG5 Bradly Nadeau 2.00 5.00
NG6 Gavin Brindley 1.25 3.00
NG7 Liam Ohgren 2.50 6.00
NG8 Jesper Wallstedt 3.00 8.00
NG9 Lane Hutson 12.00 30.00
NG10 Brennan Othmann 2.00 5.00
NG11 Luca Del Bel Belluz 1.25 3.00
NG12 Joshua Roy 2.00 5.00
NG13 Josh Doan 2.00 5.00
NG14 Brendan Brisson 1.50 4.00
NG15 Lukas Cormier 1.25 3.00
NG16 Scott Morrow 1.50 4.00
NG17 Mavrik Bourque 2.50 6.00
NG19 Shakir Mukhamadullin 1.50 4.00
NG20 Zachary Bolduc 2.50 6.00

2024-25 SP Game Used Rookie Jumbo Patch

JRPAB Arshdeep Bains 15.00 40.00
JRPAT Akil Thomas 12.00 30.00
JRPBB Brendan Brisson 15.00 40.00
JRPBH Brian Halonen 12.00 30.00
JRPBL Jackson Blake 25.00 60.00
JRPBO Brennan Othmann 20.00 50.00
JRPCG Cutter Gauthier 30.00 80.00
JRPEL Emil Lilleberg 12.00 30.00
JRPFN Frank Nazar 40.00 100.00
JRPGB Gavin Brindley 12.00 30.00
JRPGC Graeme Clarke 12.00 30.00
JRPGG Gage Goncalves 15.00 40.00
JRPGR Collin Graf 12.00 30.00
JRPJB Justin Brazeau 12.00 30.00
JRPJD Josh Doan 20.00 50.00
JRPJP Jason Polin 12.00 30.00
JRPJR Joshua Roy 20.00 50.00
JRPJT Jack Thompson 12.00 30.00
JRPJW Jesper Wallstedt 30.00 80.00
JRPKM Kyle MacLean 12.00 30.00
JRPLC Lukas Cormier 12.00 30.00
JRPLD Luca Del Bel Belluz 12.00 30.00
JRPLM Logan Morrison 12.00 30.00
JRPLO Liam Ohgren 25.00 60.00
JRPLS Logan Stankoven 30.00 80.00
JRPMB Mavrik Bourque 25.00 60.00
JRPMC Maxwell Crozier 12.00 30.00
JRPMM Mason Morelli 12.00 30.00
JRPMR Matt Rempe 25.00 60.00
JRPOZ Olen Zellweger 25.00 60.00
JRPRI Marshall Rifai 12.00 30.00
JRPSC Sam Colangelo 12.00 30.00
JRPSM Scott Morrow 15.00 40.00
JRPVP Vasily Ponomarev 12.00 30.00
JRPZB Zachary Bolduc 25.00 60.00
JRPZD Zach Dean 12.00 30.00
JRPZO Zack Ostapchuk 12.00 30.00

2024-25 SP Game Used Rookie Sweaters

RSAT Akil Thomas 2.00 5.00
RSBB Brendan Brisson 2.50 6.00
RSBO Brennan Othmann 3.00 8.00
RSCG Cutter Gauthier 5.00 12.00
RSEL Emil Lilleberg 2.00 5.00
RSFN Frank Nazar 6.00 15.00
RSGB Gavin Brindley 2.00 5.00
RSGG Gage Goncalves 2.50 6.00
RSJD Josh Doan 3.00 8.00
RSJR Joshua Roy 3.00 8.00
RSLC Lukas Cormier 2.00 5.00
RSLH Lane Hutson 20.00 50.00
RSLO Liam Ohgren 4.00 10.00
RSLS Logan Stankoven 5.00 12.00
RSMB Mavrik Bourque 4.00 10.00
RSMC Macklin Celebrini 20.00 50.00
RSMM Matvei Michkov 15.00 40.00
RSMR Matt Rempe 4.00 10.00
RSOZ Olen Zellweger 4.00 10.00
RSSC Sam Colangelo 2.00 5.00
RSSM Scott Morrow 2.50 6.00
RSWS Will Smith 8.00 20.00
RSZB Zachary Bolduc 4.00 10.00
RSZO Zack Ostapchuk 2.00 5.00

2024-25 SP Game Used Rookie Sweaters Patch

*PATCH/49: 1X TO 2.5X BASIC
RSLH Lane Hutson 125.00 300.00
RSMC Macklin Celebrini 80.00 200.00
RSMM Matvei Michkov 80.00 200.00
RSWS Will Smith 25.00 60.00

2024-25 SP Game Used Signing Day Marks

SDMAB Arshdeep Bains/175* 15.00 40.00
SDMCY Devin Cooley/210* 20.00 50.00

2024-25 SP Game Used Stick to It

STIAD Alex DeBrincat 25.00 60.00
STIAM Al MacInnis 25.00 60.00
STIAO Alex Ovechkin 50.00 125.00
STIBB Brock Boeser 25.00 60.00
STIBC Bobby Clarke 30.00 80.00
STIBH Bobby Hull 40.00 100.00
STIBT Bryan Trottier 20.00 50.00
STICB Connor Bedard 125.00 300.00
STICC Chris Chelios 20.00 50.00
STIEL Eric Lindros 30.00 80.00
STIFM Frank Mahovlich 20.00 50.00
STIGL Guy Lafleur 25.00 60.00
STILR Luc Robitaille 20.00 50.00
STIMB Martin Brodeur 50.00 125.00
STIML Mario Lemieux 80.00 200.00
STINL Nicklas Lidstrom 20.00 50.00
STIPC Paul Coffey 20.00 50.00
STIPF Peter Forsberg 40.00 100.00
STISY Steve Yzerman 50.00 125.00

2024-25 SP Game Used Visible Spectrum

VS1 Sidney Crosby 10.00 25.00
VS2 Robert Thomas 1.25 3.00
VS3 Cale Makar 3.00 8.00
VS4 Mathew Barzal 1.50 4.00
VS5 Nathan MacKinnon 5.00 12.00
VS6 Bradly Nadeau 2.00 5.00
VS7 Aleksander Barkov 2.00 5.00
VS8 Zach Hyman 2.00 5.00
VS9 Nick Suzuki 2.50 6.00
VS10 William Nylander 2.50 6.00
VS11 Olen Zellweger 2.50 6.00
VS12 Roman Josi 1.25 3.00
VS13 Sebastian Aho 2.00 5.00
VS14 Mikko Rantanen 3.00 8.00
VS15 Cutter Gauthier 3.00 8.00
VS16 Steven Stamkos 2.50 6.00
VS17 Kirill Kaprizov 4.00 10.00
VS18 Joshua Roy 2.00 5.00
VS19 Filip Forsberg 2.00 5.00
VS20 Nikita Kucherov 2.50 6.00
VS21 Logan Stankoven 3.00 8.00
VS22 Connor McDavid 6.00 15.00
VS23 Brennan Othmann 2.00 5.00
VS24 Elias Pettersson 2.00 5.00
VS25 Artemi Panarin 2.50 6.00
VS26 Gavin Brindley 1.25 3.00
VS27 Leon Draisaitl 4.00 10.00
VS28 Liam Ohgren 2.50 6.00
VS29 David Pastrnak 3.00 8.00
VS30 Connor Bedard 4.00 10.00
VS31 Frank Nazar 4.00 10.00
VS32 Connor Hellebuyck 2.50 6.00
VS33 Auston Matthews 5.00 12.00
VS34 Lane Hutson 15.00 40.00
VS35 Quinn Hughes 3.00 8.00

2020-21 SP Signature Legends

1 Brad Richards .50 1.25
2 Daniel Sedin .60 1.50
3 Henrik Sedin .60 1.50
4 Scott Mellanby .40 1.00
5 Chris Phillips .40 1.00
6 Randy Carlyle .40 1.00
7 Greg Adams .40 1.00
8 Felix Potvin .75 2.00
9 Jean Pronovost .30 .75
10 Olaf Kolzig .50 1.25
11 Jacques Plante .50 1.25
12 Esa Tikkanen .40 1.00
13 Stan Mikita .50 1.25
14 Gerry Cheevers .50 1.25
15 Henrik Zetterberg .60 1.50
16 Jean Ratelle .40 1.00
17 Borje Salming .50 1.25
18 Jeremy Roenick .75 2.00
19 Clark Gillies .50 1.25
20 Lanny McDonald .40 1.00
21 Tim Horton .75 2.00
22 Wayne Cashman .30 .75
23 Terry Sawchuk .50 1.25
24 Steve Vickers .30 .75
25 Curtis Joseph .60 1.50
26 Mike Richter .50 1.25
27 Glenn Anderson .40 1.00
28 Michel Goulet .50 1.25
29 Guy Carbonneau .50 1.25
30 Janne Niinimaa .30 .75
31 Igor Larionov .50 1.25
32 Murray Craven .30 .75
33 Bob Probert .50 1.25
34 Mark Osborne .40 1.00
35 Bernie Geoffrion .40 1.00
36 Trevor Linden .50 1.25
37 Guy Lapointe .40 1.00
38 Harold Snepsts .30 .75
39 Michal Handzus .30 .75
40 Denis Savard .50 1.25
41 Keith Tkachuk .50 1.25
42 Kelly Hrudey .40 1.00
43 Turk Broda .50 1.25
44 Norm Ullman .50 1.25
45 Slava Kozlov .30 .75
46 Mario Marois .40 1.00
47 Bryan McCabe .30 .75
48 Bernie Federko .40 1.00
49 Joe Nieuwendyk .40 1.00
50 Bernie Nicholls .40 1.00
51 Howie Morenz .50 1.25
52 Darren Turcotte .30 .75
53 Murray Baron .30 .75
54 Bobby Smith .50 1.25
55 Martin St. Louis .50 1.25
56 Marc-Andre Bergeron .30 .75
57 Rick Kehoe .40 1.00
58 Charlie Simmer .30 .75
59 Mike Gartner .60 1.50
60 Pat Hickey .40 1.00
61 Randy McKay .30 .75
62 Doug Wilson .40 1.00
63 Bill Ranford .40 1.00
64 Shawn Chambers .30 .75
65 Filip Kuba .30 .75
66 John LeClair .50 1.25
67 Wendel Clark .75 2.00
68 Fredrik Olausson .30 .75
69 Bryan Trottier .50 1.25
70 Saku Koivu .50 1.25
71 Terry Crisp .30 .75
72 Bryce Salvador .30 .75
73 Craig Muni .30 .75
74 Peter Bondra .50 1.25
75 Bob Nystrom .40 1.00
76 Christian Ruuttu .40 1.00
77 Mikael Samuelsson .30 .75
78 Pat Hughes .30 .75
79 Bryan Berard .50 1.25
80 Rick Vaive .40 1.00
81 Chris Pronger .50 1.25
82 Steve Larmer .40 1.00
83 Dave Taylor .40 1.00
84 Terry O'Reilly .40 1.00
85 Joey Kocur .30 .75
86 Steven Reinprecht .30 .75
87 Owen Nolan .50 1.25
88 Ray Sheppard .30 .75
89 Keith Primeau .40 1.00
90 Ken Daneyko .40 1.00
91 Shayne Corson .40 1.00
92 Sergio Momesso .30 .75
93 Terry Carkner .30 .75
94 Michal Grosek .30 .75
95 Mikael Andersson .30 .75
96 Glenn Hall .50 1.25
97 Paul Reinhart .40 1.00
98 P.J. Axelsson .30 .75
99 Dick Duff .40 1.00
100 Niklas Hagman .30 .75
101 Brooks Orpik .30 .75
102 Kjell Samuelsson .30 .75
103 Bob Nevin .30 .75
104 Barret Jackman .30 .75
105 Brian MacLellan .40 1.00
106 Adam Graves .40 1.00
107 Rod Brind'Amour .50 1.25
108 Brian Holzinger .30 .75
109 Daniel Girardi .30 .75
110 Ryan Whitney .30 .75
111 Gord Murphy .30 .75
112 Ray Ferraro .40 1.00
113 Dave Barr .30 .75
114 Wayne Gretzky 3.00 8.00
115 Lucien DeBlois .30 .75
116 Darryl Shannon .30 .75
117 John Chabot .30 .75
118 Gilles Meloche .50 1.25
119 Brent Ashton .30 .75
120 Jean-Sebastien Giguere .50 1.25
121 Brian Engblom .30 .75
122 Harry Howell .40 1.00
123 Carey Wilson .40 1.00
124 Nick Schultz .30 .75
125 Nelson Emerson .40 1.00
126 Randy Wood .30 .75
127 Robert Picard .30 .75
128 Joe Cirella .30 .75
129 Terry Ruskowski .40 1.00
130 Brent Gilchrist .30 .75
131 Don Edwards .30 .75
132 Henri Richard .50 1.25
133 Chris Clark .30 .75
134 Johan Garpenlov .30 .75
135 Steve Thomas .40 1.00
136 R.J. Umberger .30 .75
137 Chris Mason .40 1.00
138 Scott Arniel .30 .75
139 Vernon Fiddler .30 .75
140 Chris Joseph .30 .75
141 Sami Salo .30 .75
142 Willie O'Ree .60 1.50
143 Mike Donnelly .30 .75
144 J.P. Dumont .30 .75
145 Dan McGillis .30 .75
146 Cory Cross .40 1.00
147 David Lumley .30 .75
148 Mathieu Dandenault .30 .75
149 Yvan Cournoyer .50 1.25
150 David Shaw .30 .75
151 Dave Brown .30 .75
152 Guy Chouinard .40 1.00
153 Jim Peplinski .30 .75
154 Alex Tanguay .40 1.00
155 Bill Berg .30 .75
156 Dany Heatley .40 1.00
157 Andreas Lilja .30 .75
158 John Grahame .30 .75
159 Andre St. Laurent .30 .75
160 Anders Hedberg .30 .75
161 Brian Propp .40 1.00
162 Paul Bissonnette .30 .75
163 Rod Langway .40 1.00
164 Dean Kennedy .30 .75
165 Steve Shutt .40 1.00
166 Patrick Roy 1.25 3.00
167 John Vanbiesbrouck .50 1.25
168 Hakan Loob .30 .75
169 Billy Smith .50 1.25
170 Patrice Brisebois .30 .75
171 Bill Hogaboam .30 .75
172 Dallas Smith .60 1.50
173 Reggie Leach .50 1.25
174 Murray Wilson .50 1.25
175 John Davidson .40 1.00
176 Hal Gill .30 .75
177 Dave Schultz .40 1.00
178 Darren Langdon .30 .75
179 Dan Bouchard .50 1.25
180 Al Iafrate .40 1.00
181 Rick Chartraw .30 .75
182 Gerry Meehan .30 .75
183 Daniel Briere .40 1.00
184 Randy Cunneyworth .30 .75
185 Daniel Marois .40 1.00
186 Jack Valiquette .40 1.00
187 Rich Preston .30 .75
188 Mark Recchi .60 1.50
189 Brian Campbell .40 1.00

190 John Druce .30 .75
191 Jim Vandermeer .30 .75
192 Nik Antropov .40 1.00
193 Andy Bathgate .40 1.00
194 Bob Carpenter .40 1.00
195 Bill Barber .50 1.25
196 Jarkko Ruutu .30 .75
197 Red Berenson .40 1.00
198 Greg Gilbert .40 1.00
199 Dirk Graham .40 1.00
200 Dave Andreychuk .50 1.25
201 Byron Dafoe .40 1.00
202 Mike Komisarek .40 1.00
203 Adam Creighton .30 .75
204 Ben Lovejoy .30 .75
205 Mark Bell .30 .75
206 Kip Miller .30 .75
207 Kevin Miller .30 .75
208 Shjon Podein .30 .75
209 Steve Kasper .30 .75
210 Robert Kron .30 .75
211 Peter Budaj .30 .75
212 Colin Patterson .40 1.00
213 Orest Kindrachuk .30 .75
214 Trevor Letowski .30 .75
215 John-Michael Liles .40 1.00
216 Bruce MacGregor .30 .75
217 Steve Rucchin .30 .75
218 Mike Weaver .30 .75
219 Eddy Beers .30 .75
220 Clint Malarchuk .30 .75
221 Dennis Ververgaert .30 .75
222 Eric Belanger .30 .75
223 Tim Hunter .30 .75
224 Jocelyn Lemieux .30 .75
225 Ossi Vaananen .30 .75
226 Mike Kitchen .30 .75
227 Larry Patey .30 .75
228 Matt Hendricks .30 .75
229 Andrew Raycroft .40 1.00
230 Jody Hull .30 .75
231 Mike Palmateer .50 1.25
232 Darrin Shannon .30 .75
233 Stephane Matteau .30 .75
234 Lorne Henning .30 .75
235 Guillaume Latendresse .30 .75
236 Randy Burridge .30 .75
237 Patrick O'Sullivan .30 .75
238 Jan Hlavac .30 .75
239 Chris Thorburn .30 .75
240 Rick Lanz .30 .75
241 Kyle Wellwood .40 1.00
242 Josh Gorges .30 .75
243 Greg de Vries .30 .75
244 Tom Chorske .30 .75
245 Donald Audette .40 1.00
246 Pierre Bouchard .30 .75
247 Claude Loiselle .40 1.00
248 Scott Hannan .30 .75
249 Jim Cummins .30 .75
250 Jason Marshall .30 .75
251 Willie Mitchell .40 1.00
252 Simon Gagne .40 1.00
253 Jorgen Pettersson .30 .75
254 Dennis Hextall .30 .75
255 Paul Ysebaert .30 .75
256 Mike Lalor .30 .75
257 Mike Sillinger .30 .75
258 Brian Mullen .30 .75
259 Stu Barnes .30 .75
260 Mike Hudson .30 .75
261 Jocelyn Thibault .40 1.00
262 Jeff Daniels .30 .75
263 Greg Fox .30 .75
264 Brad Lukowich .30 .75
265 Mike Zuke .30 .75
266 Stewart Gavin .30 .75
267 Mason Raymond .30 .75
268 Gino Odjick .30 .75
269 Rich Pilon .30 .75
270 Larry Melnyk .30 .75
271 Keith Acton .30 .75
272 Jiri Slegr .30 .75
273 Tuomo Ruutu .40 1.00
274 Paul Kruse .30 .75
275 Brian Lawton .40 1.00
276 Reijo Ruotsalainen .30 .75
277 Mike Commodore .30 .75
278 Sean McKenna .30 .75
279 Dainius Zubrus .30 .75
280 Chris Tamer .30 .75
281 Vesa Toskala .50 1.25
282 Kent Manderville .30 .75
283 Ed Olczyk .40 1.00
284 Jason Woolley .30 .75
285 Laurie Boschman .40 1.00
286 Yvon Lambert .50 1.25
287 Alexandre Burrows .30 .75
288 Dana Murzyn .30 .75
289 Kerry Huffman .30 .75
290 Chris Terreri .30 .75
291 Ed Van Impe .30 .75
292 Daniel Paille .30 .75
293 Blaine Stoughton .40 1.00
294 Fedor Tyutin .30 .75
295 Magnus Arvedson .30 .75
296 Dale McCourt .40 1.00
297 Dmitri Mironov .30 .75
298 Lars Lindgren .30 .75
299 Ray Whitney .30 .75
300 Jonas Hoglund .40 1.00
301 Gordie Howe SP 2.50 6.00
302 Bobby Clarke SP 1.25 3.00
303 Mark Messier SP 1.50 4.00
304 Johnny Bucyk SP .75 2.00
305 Luc Robitaille SP .75 2.00
306 Jarome Iginla SP 1.00 2.50
307 Al MacInnis SP 1.00 2.50
308 Bernie Parent SP 1.00 2.50
309 Doug Gilmour SP 1.00 2.50
310 Peter Forsberg SP 1.50 4.00
311 Frank Mahovlich SP .75 2.00
312 Paul Coffey SP .75 2.00
313 Nicklas Lidstrom SP .75 2.00
314 Jaromir Jagr SP 2.50 6.00
315 Denis Potvin SP .75 2.00
316 Grant Fuhr SP 1.25 3.00
317 Ed Belfour SP .75 2.00
318 Eric Lindros SP 1.25 3.00
319 Darryl Sittler SP 1.00 2.50
320 Dominik Hasek SP 1.25 3.00
321 Brett Hull SP 1.50 4.00
322 Mike Modano SP 1.25 3.00
323 Marcel Dionne SP 1.00 2.50
324 Joe Sakic SP 1.50 4.00
325 Mario Lemieux SP 3.00 8.00
326 Johnny Bower SP .75 2.00
327 Pat LaFontaine SP .75 2.00
328 Jean Beliveau SP .75 2.00
329 Chris Chelios SP .75 2.00
330 Phil Esposito SP 1.25 3.00
331 Patrick Roy SP 2.00 5.00
332 Brian Leetch SP .60 1.50
333 Bobby Hull SP 2.00 5.00
334 Mike Bossy SP .75 2.00
335 Guy Lafleur SP 1.00 2.50
336 Ron Hextall SP .75 2.00
337 Maurice Richard SP 1.50 4.00
338 Dale Hawerchuk SP 1.00 2.50
339 Steve Yzerman SP 2.00 5.00
340 Ted Lindsay SP .75 2.00
341 Brendan Shanahan SP .75 2.00
342 Martin Brodeur SP 2.00 5.00
343 Theoren Fleury SP .75 2.00
344 Teemu Selanne SP 1.50 4.00
345 Scott Niedermayer SP .75 2.00
346 Cam Neely SP .75 2.00
347 Jari Kurri SP .75 2.00
348 Mats Sundin SP .75 2.00
349 Ray Bourque SP 1.25 3.00
350 Wayne Gretzky SP 5.00 12.00
351 Bernie Nicholls ATFW AU/199 30.00 80.00
352 Rod Brind'Amour ATFW AU/199 40.00 100.00
353 Dave Taylor ATFW AU/199 30.00 80.00
354 Ed Olczyk ATFW/199 8.00 20.00
355 Trevor Linden ATFW AU/199 40.00 100.00
356 Doug Wilson ATFW AU/199 30.00 80.00
357 Brad Richards ATFW AU/199 40.00 100.00
358 Brian Propp ATFW AU/199 30.00 80.00
359 Ray Ferraro ATFW AU/199 30.00 80.00
360 Rod Langway ATFW AU/199 30.00 80.00
361 Lanny McDonald ATFW/199 8.00 20.00
362 Daniel Briere ATFW AU/199 30.00 80.00
363 Dave Andreychuk ATFW/199 10.00 25.00
364 Curtis Joseph ATFW AU/199 50.00 125.00
365 Bernie Parent ATFW AU/199 50.00 125.00
366 Owen Nolan ATFW AU/199 40.00 100.00
367 Denis Savard ATFW AU/199 40.00 100.00
368 Guy Carbonneau ATFW AU/199 40.00 100.00
369 Felix Potvin ATFW AU/199 60.00 150.00
370 Clark Gillies ATFW/199 10.00 25.00
371 Steve Shutt ATFW AU/199 30.00 80.00
372 Wendel Clark ATFW AU/199 60.00 150.00
373 Mark Recchi ATFW AU/199 50.00 125.00
374 Igor Larionov ATFW AU/199 40.00 100.00
375 Hakan Loob ATFW/199 6.00 15.00
376 John LeClair ATFW AU/199 40.00 100.00
377 Adam Graves ATFW AU/199 30.00 80.00
378 Steve Larmer ATFW AU/199 30.00 80.00
379 Peter Bondra ATFW AU/199 40.00 100.00
380 Steve Thomas ATFW AU/199 30.00 80.00
381 Rick Vaive ATFW AU/199 30.00 80.00
382 Dave Schultz ATFW AU/199 30.00 80.00
383 Chris Pronger ATFW AU/199 40.00 100.00
384 Randy Carlyle ATFW AU/199 30.00 80.00
385 Ron Hextall ATFW AU/199 40.00 100.00
386 Saku Koivu ATFW AU/199 40.00 100.00
387 Keith Tkachuk ATFW AU/199 40.00 100.00
388 Bob Carpenter ATFW AU/199 30.00 80.00
389 Slava Kozlov ATFW/199 6.00 15.00
390 Tim Kerr ATFW AU/199 25.00 60.00
391 Denis Potvin ATFW/99 10.00 25.00
392 Guy Lapointe ATFW/99 8.00 20.00
393 Jari Kurri ATFW AU/99 80.00 200.00
394 Brian Leetch ATFW AU/99 60.00 150.00
395 Henrik Sedin ATFW AU/99 100.00 250.00
396 Mike Gartner ATFW AU/99 100.00 250.00
397 Martin St. Louis ATFW AU/99 80.00 200.00
398 Daniel Sedin ATFW AU/99 100.00 250.00
399 Mike Richter ATFW AU/99 80.00 200.00
400 Scott Niedermayer ATFW/99 10.00 25.00
401 Jeremy Roenick ATFW AU/99 125.00 300.00
402 Mike Modano ATFW AU/99 125.00 300.00
403 Henrik Zetterberg ATFW AU/99 100.00 250.00
404 Paul Coffey ATFW AU/99 80.00 200.00
405 Bryan Trottier ATFW AU/99 80.00 200.00
406 Yvan Cournoyer ATFW AU/99 80.00 200.00
407 Chris Chelios ATFW AU/99 80.00 200.00
408 Bernie Federko ATFW AU/99 60.00 150.00
409 Frank Mahovlich ATFW AU/99 80.00 200.00
410 Luc Robitaille ATFW AU/99 80.00 200.00
411 Mike Bossy ATFW AU/99 80.00 200.00
412 Bobby Clarke ATFW AU/99 125.00 300.00
413 Theoren Fleury ATFW AU/99 80.00 200.00
414 Bill Barber ATFW AU/99 80.00 200.00
415 Dale Hawerchuk ATFW AU/99 100.00 250.00
416 Grant Fuhr ATFW AU/99 125.00 300.00
417 Borje Salming ATFW AU/99 80.00 200.00
418 Jarome Iginla ATFW AU/99 100.00 250.00
419 Pat LaFontaine ATFW AU/99 80.00 200.00
420 Doug Gilmour ATFW AU/99 100.00 250.00
421 Brendan Shanahan ATFW/99 10.00 25.00
422 Michel Goulet ATFW AU/99 80.00 200.00
423 Ed Belfour ATFW/99 10.00 25.00
424 Al MacInnis ATFW AU/99 100.00 250.00
425 Cam Neely ATFW AU/99 80.00 200.00
426 Ray Bourque ATFW AU/99 125.00 300.00
427 Darryl Sittler ATFW AU/99 100.00 250.00
428 Ted Lindsay ATFW AU/99 80.00 200.00
429 Phil Esposito ATFW AU/99 125.00 300.00
430 Marcel Dionne ATFW AU/99 100.00 250.00
431 Brett Hull ATFW AU/99 150.00 400.00
432 Peter Forsberg ATFW AU/99 150.00 400.00
433 Bobby Hull ATFW AU/99 200.00 500.00
434 Guy Lafleur ATFW AU/99 100.00 250.00
435 Terry Sawchuk ATFW/99 10.00 25.00
436 Dominik Hasek ATFW AU/49 500.00 1200.00
437 Joe Sakic ATFW AU/49 600.00 1500.00
438 Jacques Plante ATFW/49 10.00 25.00
439 Mark Messier ATFW AU/49 600.00 1500.00
440 Eric Lindros ATFW AU/49 500.00 1200.00
441 Teemu Selanne ATFW AU/49 600.00 1500.00
442 Jean Beliveau ATFW/49 10.00 25.00
443 Jaromir Jagr ATFW AU/49 1000.00 2500.00
444 Martin Brodeur ATFW AU/49 800.00 2000.00
445 Maurice Richard ATFW/49 20.00 50.00
446 Steve Yzerman ATFW AU/49 800.00 2000.00
447 Patrick Roy ATFW AU/49 800.00 2000.00
448 Mario Lemieux ATFW AU/49 1200.00 3000.00
449 Nicklas Lidstrom ATFW AU/49 300.00 800.00
450 Wayne Gretzky ATFW AU/49 2000.00 5000.00
451 Gordie Howe ATFW/199 30.00 80.00

2020-21 SP Signature Legends Gold

*GOLD: 1.2X TO 3X BASIC
314 Jaromir Jagr SP 8.00 20.00
325 Mario Lemieux SP 12.00 30.00
331 Patrick Roy SP 8.00 20.00
350 Wayne Gretzky SP 20.00 50.00

2020-21 SP Signature Legends Gold Spectrum

*GOLD.SPCTRM: 10X TO 25X BASIC
451 Gordie Howe ATFW AU/25 1000.00 2500.00

2020-21 SP Signature Legends '97 Legends Signatures

AL161 Patrice Brisebois E 12.00 30.00
AL162 Brian Campbell E 15.00 40.00
AL165 Bob Carpenter E 15.00 40.00
AL166 Scott Gomez D 15.00 40.00
AL167 Dick Duff E 15.00 40.00
AL168 Murray Craven D 12.00 30.00
AL169 Wayne Cashman D 12.00 30.00
AL170 Tim Hunter D 12.00 30.00
AL171 Simon Gagne C 15.00 40.00
AL172 Dirk Graham E 15.00 40.00
AL173 Steve Smith E 12.00 30.00
AL174 Bernie Parent A 25.00 60.00
AL175 Scott Mellanby B 15.00 40.00
AL176 Mario Marois D 15.00 40.00
AL178 Al Iafrate C 15.00 40.00
AL179 Curtis Joseph B 25.00 60.00
AL180 John LeClair C 20.00 50.00
AL181 John Davidson D 15.00 40.00
AL182 Ron Hextall D 20.00 50.00
AL183 John Vanbiesbrouck E 20.00 50.00
AL184 Jonathan Cheechoo D 15.00 40.00
AL185 Igor Larionov A 20.00 50.00
AL186 Daniel Briere A 15.00 40.00
AL187 Keith Primeau D 15.00 40.00
AL188 Adam Graves A 15.00 40.00
AL189 Owen Nolan A 20.00 50.00
AL190 Guy Chouinard C 15.00 40.00
AL191 Saku Koivu B 20.00 50.00
AL192 Mark Messier B 40.00 100.00
AL193 Bryan Trottier A 20.00 50.00
AL194 Lucien DeBlois E 12.00 30.00
AL195 Doug Weight E 15.00 40.00
AL197 Martin St. Louis C 20.00 50.00
AL198 Laurie Boschman E 15.00 40.00
AL199 Robert Picard D 12.00 30.00
AL200 Wendel Clark A 30.00 80.00
AL201 Bernie Federko B 15.00 40.00
AL202 Glenn Hall C 20.00 50.00
AL203 Steve Larmer A 15.00 40.00
AL204 Guy Carbonneau A 20.00 50.00
AL205 Gilles Meloche D 20.00 50.00
AL207 Dave Schultz B 15.00 40.00
AL208 Kelly Hrudey D 15.00 40.00
AL209 Terry O'Reilly C 15.00 40.00
AL211 Steve Rucchin E 12.00 30.00
AL212 Mike Liut D 12.00 30.00
AL213 Peter Bondra A 20.00 50.00
AL214 Reggie Leach D 20.00 50.00
AL216 Dominik Hasek B 30.00 80.00
AL217 Rod Brind'Amour A 20.00 50.00
AL218 Stephane Matteau C 12.00 30.00
AL219 Mike Gartner B 25.00 60.00
AL220 Guy Lafleur A 25.00 60.00
AL221 Stewart Gavin D 12.00 30.00
AL222 Harold Snepsts D 12.00 30.00
AL223 Luc Robitaille B 20.00 50.00
AL224 Paul Reinhart D 15.00 40.00
AL225 Al Secord C 15.00 40.00
AL227 Red Berenson C 15.00 40.00
AL228 Mike Modano B 30.00 80.00
AL229 Yvan Cournoyer B 20.00 50.00
AL230 Bernie Nicholls C 15.00 40.00
AL231 Blaine Stoughton D 15.00 40.00
AL232 P.J. Axelsson E 12.00 30.00
AL233 Rick Kehoe E 15.00 40.00
AL234 Doug Wilson A 15.00 40.00
AL235 Barret Jackman E 12.00 30.00
AL236 Paul Coffey B 20.00 50.00
AL237 Billy Smith C 20.00 50.00
AL239 Bob Nystrom E 15.00 40.00
AL240 Bryan Berard D 20.00 50.00
AL241 Brian Mullen D 12.00 30.00
AL242 Bryce Salvador D 12.00 30.00
AL244 Dallas Smith E 25.00 60.00
AL245 Larry Patey D 12.00 30.00
AL246 Denis Savard A 20.00 50.00
AL248 Martin Brodeur A 50.00 125.00
AL249 Orest Kindrachuk C 12.00 30.00
AL250 Jean Pronovost D 12.00 30.00
AL251 Steve Vickers E 12.00 30.00
AL252 Steve Shutt B 15.00 40.00
AL253 Tuomo Ruutu D 15.00 40.00
AL255 Bobby Smith D 20.00 50.00
AL256 Dave Taylor B 15.00 40.00
AL257 Al MacInnis A 25.00 60.00
AL258 Esa Tikkanen D 15.00 40.00
AL259 Dennis Ververgaert E 12.00 30.00
AL260 Fredrik Olausson D 12.00 30.00

2020-21 SP Signature Legends Behind the Boards

*GOLD/99: .75X TO 2X BASIC
BB1 Wayne Gretzky 4.00 10.00
BB2 Bill Ranford .50 1.25
BB3 Randy Carlyle .50 1.25
BB4 Scott Arniel .40 1.00
BB5 Terry O'Reilly .50 1.25
BB6 Steve Smith .40 1.00
BB7 Paul MacLean .40 1.00
BB8 Alexandre Burrows .40 1.00
BB9 Rod Brind'Amour .60 1.50
BB10 Patrick Roy 1.50 4.00

2020-21 SP Signature Legends Behind the Boards Autographs Silver

BB2 Bill Ranford 15.00 40.00
BB3 Randy Carlyle 15.00 40.00
BB5 Terry O'Reilly 40.00 100.00
BB6 Steve Smith 12.00 30.00
BB8 Alexandre Burrows 12.00 30.00
BB9 Rod Brind'Amour 20.00 50.00

2020-21 SP Signature Legends Century Legends Dual Signatures

CL2CG D.Gilmour/W.Clark 80.00 200.00
CL2KB P.Bondra/O.Kolzig 50.00 125.00
CL2MF L.McDonald/T.Fleury 40.00 100.00
CL2NB R.Bourque/C.Neely 80.00 200.00
CL2SF J.Sakic/P.Forsberg 100.00 250.00
CL2SK J.Kurri/T.Selanne 100.00 250.00
CL2YL S.Yzerman/N.Lidstrom 125.00 300.00

2020-21 SP Signature Legends Century Legends Signatures

CLAB Alexandre Burrows D 12.00 30.00
CLAM Al MacInnis B 25.00 60.00
CLBB Bill Barber C 20.00 50.00
CLBC Bobby Clarke B 30.00 80.00
CLBH Brett Hull B 40.00 100.00
CLBM Brian Mullen D 12.00 30.00
CLBN Bernie Nicholls D 15.00 40.00
CLBT Bryan Trottier B 20.00 50.00
CLCA Guy Carbonneau A 20.00 50.00
CLCN Cam Neely D 20.00 50.00
CLCP Chris Pronger B 20.00 50.00
CLCS Charlie Simmer C 12.00 30.00
CLDG Doug Gilmour C 25.00 60.00
CLDH Dominik Hasek C 60.00 150.00
CLDS Denis Savard B 20.00 50.00
CLDW Doug Wilson B 15.00 40.00
CLGC Gerry Cheevers D 20.00 50.00
CLGF Grant Fuhr C 30.00 80.00
CLGH Glenn Hall C 20.00 50.00
CLGO Michel Goulet C 20.00 50.00
CLJS Joe Sakic C 40.00 100.00
CLKL Ken Linseman D 20.00 50.00
CLLB Laurie Boschman D 15.00 40.00
CLMA Mario Marois C 15.00 40.00
CLMB Martin Brodeur B 80.00 200.00
CLMC Murray Craven E 12.00 30.00
CLMD Marcel Dionne D 25.00 60.00
CLMG Mike Gartner C 25.00 60.00
CLML Mario Lemieux B 125.00 300.00
CLMM Mark Messier C 80.00 200.00
CLMO Mike Modano B 40.00 100.00
CLNL Nicklas Lidstrom D 20.00 50.00
CLNU Norm Ullman E 20.00 50.00
CLPA Bernie Parent B 25.00 60.00
CLPC Paul Coffey C 20.00 50.00
CLPE Phil Esposito B 30.00 80.00
CLPR Patrick Roy B 80.00 200.00
CLRB Red Berenson D 15.00 40.00
CLRC Randy Carlyle B 15.00 40.00
CLSK Saku Koivu C 20.00 50.00
CLSM Scott Mellanby C 15.00 40.00
CLST Steve Thomas C 15.00 40.00
CLSY Steve Yzerman C 80.00 200.00
CLTF Theoren Fleury B 20.00 50.00
CLWC Wayne Cashman D 12.00 30.00
CLWG Wayne Gretzky B 300.00 800.00
CLYL Yvon Lambert E 20.00 50.00

2020-21 SP Signature Legends Century Legends Triple Signatures

CL3TDS Dave Taylor
Marcel Dionne
Charlie Simmer/25 60.00 150.00

2020-21 SP Signature Legends Decagons

DC1 Maurice Richard 5.00 12.00
DC2 Terry Sawchuk 2.50 6.00
DC3 Jacques Plante 2.50 6.00
DC4 Jean Beliveau 2.50 6.00
DC5 Gordie Howe 8.00 20.00
DC6 Johnny Bower 2.50 6.00
DC7 Stan Mikita 2.50 6.00
DC8 Frank Mahovlich 2.50 6.00
DC9 Glenn Hall 2.50 6.00
DC10 Bobby Hull 6.00 15.00
DC11 Dave Schultz 2.00 5.00
DC12 Denis Potvin 2.50 6.00
DC13 Darryl Sittler 3.00 8.00
DC14 Dennis Hextall 1.50 4.00
DC15 Guy Lapointe 2.00 5.00
DC16 Rick Kehoe 2.00 5.00
DC17 Orest Kindrachuk 1.50 4.00
DC18 Bernie Parent 3.00 8.00
DC19 Gerry Cheevers 2.50 6.00
DC20 Johnny Bucyk 2.50 6.00
DC21 Bobby Clarke 4.00 10.00
DC22 Guy Lafleur 3.00 8.00
DC23 Phil Esposito 4.00 10.00
DC24 Nick Libett 2.00 5.00
DC25 Joe Watson 1.50 4.00
DC26 Ian Turnbull 1.50 4.00
DC27 Chris Nilan 1.50 4.00
DC28 Dana Murzyn 1.50 4.00
DC29 Randy Carlyle 2.00 5.00
DC30 Ken Linseman 2.50 6.00
DC31 Bobby Smith 2.50 6.00
DC32 Dave Taylor 2.00 5.00
DC33 Charlie Simmer 1.50 4.00
DC34 Tim Hunter 1.50 4.00
DC35 Bernie Nicholls 2.00 5.00
DC36 John Ogrodnick 1.50 4.00
DC37 Mike Gartner 3.00 8.00
DC38 Laurie Boschman 2.00 5.00
DC39 Rick Vaive 2.00 5.00
DC40 Mike Bossy 2.50 6.00
DC41 Greg Gilbert 2.00 5.00
DC42 Mike Liut 1.50 4.00
DC43 Grant Fuhr 4.00 10.00
DC44 Billy Smith 2.50 6.00
DC45 Wayne Gretzky 15.00 40.00
DC46 Ray Bourque 4.00 10.00
DC47 Bryan Trottier 2.50 6.00
DC48 Hakan Loob 1.50 4.00
DC49 Dale Hawerchuk 3.00 8.00
DC50 Jari Kurri 2.50 6.00
DC51 Denis Savard 2.50 6.00
DC52 Jim Peplinski 1.50 4.00
DC53 Marcel Dionne 3.00 8.00
DC54 Tim Kerr 1.50 4.00
DC55 Ken Morrow 1.50 4.00
DC56 Gino Odjick 1.50 4.00
DC57 Michal Pivonka 1.50 4.00
DC58 Teemu Selanne 5.00 12.00
DC59 Peter Bondra 2.50 6.00
DC60 Shayne Corson 2.00 5.00
DC61 Randy McKay 1.50 4.00
DC62 Bill Ranford 2.00 5.00
DC63 Greg Adams 2.00 5.00
DC64 Trevor Linden 2.50 6.00
DC65 Ray Sheppard 1.50 4.00
DC66 Mike Modano 4.00 10.00
DC67 Ron Hextall 2.50 6.00
DC68 Dominik Hasek 4.00 10.00
DC69 Gord Murphy 1.50 4.00
DC70 Martin Brodeur 6.00 15.00
DC71 Ed Belfour 2.50 6.00
DC72 Fredrik Olausson 1.50 4.00
DC73 Mike Richter 2.50 6.00
DC74 Brian Leetch 2.00 5.00
DC75 Mario Lemieux 10.00 25.00
DC76 Patrick Roy 6.00 15.00
DC77 Jaromir Jagr 8.00 20.00
DC78 Joe Sakic 5.00 12.00
DC79 Steve Yzerman 6.00 15.00
DC80 Brett Hull 5.00 12.00
DC81 Theoren Fleury 2.50 6.00
DC82 Donald Audette 2.00 5.00
DC83 Mark Messier 5.00 12.00
DC84 Jeremy Roenick 4.00 10.00
DC85 Simon Gagne 2.00 5.00
DC86 Jonathan Cheechoo 2.00 5.00
DC87 Chris Neil 1.50 4.00
DC88 Dainius Zubrus 1.50 4.00
DC89 Filip Kuba 1.50 4.00
DC90 Brad Richards 2.50 6.00
DC91 Jean-Sebastien Giguere 2.50 6.00
DC92 Michal Handzus 1.50 4.00
DC93 Ray Whitney 1.50 4.00
DC94 Olaf Kolzig 2.50 6.00
DC95 Scott Hannan 1.50 4.00
DC96 Martin St. Louis 2.50 6.00
DC97 Alexandre Burrows 1.50 4.00
DC98 Tomas Plekanec 1.50 4.00
DC99 Daniel Sedin 3.00 8.00
DC100 Henrik Sedin 3.00 8.00

2020-21 SP Signature Legends Decagons Autographs Gold

DC5 Gordie Howe B 150.00 400.00
DC6 Johnny Bower B 20.00 50.00
DC9 Glenn Hall D 20.00 50.00
DC10 Bobby Hull D 50.00 125.00
DC11 Dave Schultz B 15.00 40.00
DC13 Darryl Sittler D 25.00 60.00
DC16 Rick Kehoe F 15.00 40.00
DC17 Orest Kindrachuk E 12.00 30.00
DC18 Bernie Parent A 25.00 60.00
DC19 Gerry Cheevers D 20.00 50.00
DC20 Johnny Bucyk B 20.00 50.00
DC21 Bobby Clarke B 30.00 80.00
DC23 Phil Esposito C 30.00 80.00
DC24 Nick Libett F 15.00 40.00
DC26 Ian Turnbull F 12.00 30.00
DC27 Chris Nilan D 12.00 30.00
DC28 Dana Murzyn F 12.00 30.00
DC30 Ken Linseman D 20.00 50.00
DC31 Bobby Smith D 20.00 50.00
DC32 Dave Taylor C 15.00 40.00
DC34 Tim Hunter C 12.00 30.00
DC35 Bernie Nicholls E 15.00 40.00
DC36 John Ogrodnick E 12.00 30.00
DC37 Mike Gartner C 25.00 60.00
DC38 Laurie Boschman D 15.00 40.00
DC39 Rick Vaive D 15.00 40.00
DC42 Mike Liut E 12.00 30.00
DC43 Grant Fuhr B 30.00 80.00
DC44 Billy Smith D 20.00 50.00
DC45 Wayne Gretzky B 300.00 800.00
DC46 Ray Bourque B 30.00 80.00
DC47 Bryan Trottier A 20.00 50.00
DC50 Jari Kurri B 20.00 50.00
DC51 Denis Savard A 20.00 50.00
DC52 Jim Peplinski E 12.00 30.00
DC53 Marcel Dionne D 25.00 60.00
DC54 Tim Kerr D 12.00 30.00
DC55 Ken Morrow F 12.00 30.00
DC56 Gino Odjick E 12.00 30.00
DC57 Michal Pivonka F 12.00 30.00
DC58 Teemu Selanne C 80.00 200.00
DC59 Peter Bondra E 20.00 50.00
DC60 Shayne Corson D 15.00 40.00
DC61 Randy McKay D 12.00 30.00
DC62 Bill Ranford D 15.00 40.00
DC64 Trevor Linden E 20.00 50.00
DC65 Ray Sheppard D 12.00 30.00
DC66 Mike Modano C 30.00 80.00
DC67 Ron Hextall D 20.00 50.00
DC68 Dominik Hasek A 100.00 250.00
DC69 Gord Murphy E 12.00 30.00
DC70 Martin Brodeur B 50.00 125.00
DC72 Fredrik Olausson D 12.00 30.00
DC73 Mike Richter A 20.00 50.00
DC74 Brian Leetch C 15.00 40.00
DC75 Mario Lemieux B 200.00 500.00
DC76 Patrick Roy B 100.00 250.00
DC77 Jaromir Jagr C 200.00 500.00
DC78 Joe Sakic C 60.00 150.00
DC79 Steve Yzerman A 125.00 300.00
DC80 Brett Hull A 40.00 100.00
DC81 Theoren Fleury C 20.00 50.00
DC82 Donald Audette E 15.00 40.00
DC83 Mark Messier B 40.00 100.00
DC84 Jeremy Roenick C 30.00 80.00
DC85 Simon Gagne D 15.00 40.00
DC86 Jonathan Cheechoo E 15.00 40.00
DC87 Chris Neil F 12.00 30.00
DC89 Filip Kuba E 12.00 30.00
DC93 Ray Whitney D 12.00 30.00
DC94 Olaf Kolzig E 20.00 50.00
DC95 Scott Hannan E 12.00 30.00
DC96 Martin St. Louis A 20.00 50.00
DC97 Alexandre Burrows C 12.00 30.00
DC98 Tomas Plekanec F 12.00 30.00
DC99 Daniel Sedin D 25.00 60.00
DC100 Henrik Sedin D 25.00 60.00

2020-21 SP Signature Legends Dominant Digits

*GOLD: 5X TO 12X BASIC
DD1 Ken Daneyko .50 1.25
DD2 Denis Savard .60 1.50
DD3 Bernie Parent .75 2.00
DD4 Teemu Selanne 1.25 3.00
DD5 Red Berenson .50 1.25
DD6 Scott Niedermayer .60 1.50
DD7 Dave Andreychuk .60 1.50
DD8 Dale Hawerchuk .75 2.00
DD9 Mike Bossy .60 1.50
DD10 Rod Brind'Amour .60 1.50
DD11 Mario Lemieux 2.50 6.00
DD12 Gordie Howe 2.00 5.00
DD13 Rod Langway .50 1.25
DD14 Doug Gilmour .75 2.00
DD15 Grant Fuhr 1.00 2.50
DD16 Joe Sakic 1.25 3.00
DD17 Jari Kurri .60 1.50
DD18 Yvan Cournoyer .60 1.50
DD19 Brett Hull 1.25 3.00
DD20 Ed Belfour .60 1.50
DD21 Curtis Joseph .75 2.00
DD22 Dave Taylor .50 1.25
DD23 Marcel Dionne .75 2.00
DD24 Mark Messier 1.25 3.00
DD25 Peter Forsberg 1.25 3.00
DD27 Bernie Federko .50 1.25
DD28 Terry O'Reilly .50 1.25
DD29 Keith Tkachuk .60 1.50
DD30 Steve Yzerman 1.50 4.00
DD31 Darryl Sittler .75 2.00
DD32 Guy Lafleur .75 2.00
DD33 Bryan Trottier .60 1.50
DD34 Patrick Roy 1.50 4.00
DD35 Bob Nystrom .50 1.25
DD36 Ray Bourque 1.00 2.50
DD37 Mike Modano 1.00 2.50
DD38 Pat LaFontaine .60 1.50
DD39 Chris Pronger .60 1.50
DD40 Chris Chelios .60 1.50
DD41 Luc Robitaille .60 1.50
DD42 Paul Coffey .60 1.50
DD43 Maurice Richard 1.25 3.00
DD44 Nicklas Lidstrom .60 1.50
DD45 Wayne Gretzky 4.00 10.00
DD46 Mike Gartner .75 2.00
DD47 Martin Brodeur 1.50 4.00
DD48 Martin St. Louis .60 1.50
DD49 Jean Beliveau .60 1.50
DD50 Jaromir Jagr 2.00 5.00

2020-21 SP Signature Legends Dominant Digits Autographs Gold

DD2 Denis Savard B 20.00 50.00
DD3 Bernie Parent B 25.00 60.00
DD4 Teemu Selanne C 40.00 100.00
DD5 Red Berenson C 15.00 40.00
DD10 Rod Brind'Amour B 20.00 50.00
DD13 Rod Langway C 15.00 40.00
DD14 Doug Gilmour B 25.00 60.00
DD15 Grant Fuhr C 30.00 80.00
DD16 Joe Sakic C 40.00 100.00
DD17 Jari Kurri C 20.00 50.00
DD18 Yvan Cournoyer C 20.00 50.00
DD19 Brett Hull A 40.00 100.00
DD21 Curtis Joseph B 25.00 60.00
DD22 Dave Taylor B 15.00 40.00
DD23 Marcel Dionne D 25.00 60.00
DD24 Mark Messier B 40.00 100.00
DD25 Peter Forsberg C 40.00 100.00
DD26 Dominik Hasek A 30.00 80.00
DD27 Bernie Federko C 15.00 40.00
DD28 Terry O'Reilly D 15.00 40.00
DD29 Keith Tkachuk B 20.00 50.00
DD31 Darryl Sittler C 25.00 60.00
DD33 Bryan Trottier B 20.00 50.00
DD35 Bob Nystrom C 15.00 40.00
DD36 Ray Bourque B 30.00 80.00
DD37 Mike Modano B 30.00 80.00
DD38 Pat LaFontaine D 20.00 50.00
DD39 Chris Pronger B 20.00 50.00
DD40 Chris Chelios C 20.00 50.00
DD41 Luc Robitaille C 20.00 50.00
DD42 Paul Coffey C 20.00 50.00
DD44 Nicklas Lidstrom A 20.00 50.00
DD45 Wayne Gretzky A 300.00 800.00
DD46 Mike Gartner C 25.00 60.00
DD48 Martin St. Louis A 20.00 50.00
DD50 Jaromir Jagr C 150.00 400.00

2020-21 SP Signature Legends Evolve

*GOLD/99: 1X TO 2.5X BASIC
E1 Wayne Gretzky 6.00 15.00
E2 Brett Hull 2.00 5.00
E3 Keith Tkachuk 1.00 2.50
E4 Cam Neely 1.00 2.50
E5 Josh Gorges .60 1.50
E6 Steve Yzerman 2.50 6.00
E7 Randy Carlyle .75 2.00
E8 John Tonelli .75 2.00
E9 Pat Hickey .75 2.00
E10 Sami Salo .60 1.50
E11 Dana Murzyn .60 1.50
E12 Joe Sakic 2.00 5.00
E13 Marcel Dionne 1.25 3.00
E14 Phil Esposito 1.50 4.00
E15 Bryan McCabe .60 1.50
E16 Teemu Selanne 2.00 5.00
E17 Mario Lemieux 4.00 10.00
E18 Mike Modano 1.50 4.00
E19 Luc Robitaille 1.00 2.50
E20 Ray Bourque 1.50 4.00
E21 Pat LaFontaine 1.00 2.50
E22 Chris Chelios 1.00 2.50
E23 Mike Richter 1.00 2.50
E24 Denis Savard 1.00 2.50
E25 Mike Liut .60 1.50
E26 Grant Fuhr 1.50 4.00
E27 Kelly Hrudey .75 2.00
E28 Dale Hawerchuk 1.25 3.00
E29 Martin St. Louis 1.00 2.50
E30 Frank Mahovlich 1.00 2.50
E31 Keith Primeau .75 2.00
E32 Brad Richards 1.00 2.50
E33 Dominik Hasek 1.50 4.00
E34 Alexandre Burrows .60 1.50
E35 Nicklas Lidstrom 1.00 2.50

2020-21 SP Signature Legends Evolve Autographs Silver Spectrum

E1 Wayne Gretzky 500.00 1200.00
E2 Brett Hull 80.00 200.00
E3 Keith Tkachuk 40.00 100.00
E4 Cam Neely 40.00 100.00
E5 Josh Gorges 25.00 60.00
E6 Steve Yzerman 100.00 250.00
E7 Randy Carlyle 30.00 80.00
E8 John Tonelli 30.00 80.00
E9 Pat Hickey 30.00 80.00
E11 Dana Murzyn 25.00 60.00
E12 Joe Sakic 80.00 200.00
E13 Marcel Dionne 50.00 125.00
E14 Phil Esposito 60.00 150.00
E15 Bryan McCabe 25.00 60.00
E16 Teemu Selanne 80.00 200.00
E17 Mario Lemieux 150.00 400.00
E18 Mike Modano 60.00 150.00
E19 Luc Robitaille 80.00 200.00
E20 Ray Bourque 60.00 150.00
E21 Pat LaFontaine 40.00 100.00
E22 Chris Chelios 40.00 100.00
E23 Mike Richter 40.00 100.00
E24 Denis Savard 40.00 100.00
E25 Mike Liut 25.00 60.00
E26 Grant Fuhr 60.00 150.00
E27 Kelly Hrudey 30.00 80.00
E29 Martin St. Louis 40.00 100.00
E31 Keith Primeau 30.00 80.00
E32 Brad Richards 40.00 100.00
E33 Dominik Hasek 150.00 400.00
E35 Nicklas Lidstrom 40.00 100.00

2020-21 SP Signature Legends Life After Hockey

*GOLD: 1.2X TO 3X BASIC
LA1 Jamal Mayers .75 2.00
LA2 Randy Gregg .60 1.50
LA3 Theoren Fleury 1.00 2.50
LA4 Ray Ferraro .75 2.00
LA5 Chris Nilan .60 1.50
LA6 Ryan Whitney .60 1.50
LA7 Paul Bissonnette .60 1.50
LA8 Al Secord .75 2.00
LA9 Clint Malarchuk .60 1.50
LA10 Sheldon Kennedy .60 1.50
LA11 Mike Richter 1.00 2.50
LA12 Wayne Gretzky 6.00 15.00
LA13 Lanny McDonald .75 2.00
LA14 Mike Richter 1.00 2.50
LA15 Stu Grimson 1.00 2.50
LA16 Ed Olczyk .75 2.00
LA17 Steve Yzerman 2.50 6.00
LA18 Doug Wilson .75 2.00
LA19 T.J. Galiardi .75 2.00
LA20 Stewart Gavin .60 1.50

2020-21 SP Signature Legends Life After Hockey Autographs Silver Spectrum

LA1 Jamal Mayers/99 15.00 40.00
LA3 Theoren Fleury/50 20.00 50.00
LA5 Chris Nilan/99 12.00 30.00
LA7 Paul Bissonnette/99 12.00 30.00
LA8 Al Secord/99 15.00 40.00
LA9 Clint Malarchuk/99 12.00 30.00
LA10 Sheldon Kennedy/99 12.00 30.00
LA13 Lanny McDonald/25 15.00 40.00
LA14 Mike Richter/50 20.00 50.00
LA15 Stu Grimson/99 20.00 50.00
LA17 Steve Yzerman/25 80.00 200.00
LA19 T.J. Galiardi/99 15.00 40.00

2020-21 SP Signature Legends Profiles

P1 Mark Messier 4.00 10.00
P2 Mark Messier 4.00 10.00
P3 Mark Messier 4.00 10.00
P4 Mark Messier 4.00 10.00
P5 Mark Messier 4.00 10.00
P6 Mark Messier 4.00 10.00
P7 Martin Brodeur 5.00 12.00
P8 Martin Brodeur 5.00 12.00
P9 Martin Brodeur 5.00 12.00
P10 Martin Brodeur 5.00 12.00
P11 Martin Brodeur 5.00 12.00
P12 Martin Brodeur 5.00 12.00
P13 Jaromir Jagr 6.00 15.00
P14 Jaromir Jagr 6.00 15.00
P15 Jaromir Jagr 6.00 15.00
P16 Jaromir Jagr 6.00 15.00
P17 Jaromir Jagr 6.00 15.00
P18 Jaromir Jagr 6.00 15.00
P19 Steve Yzerman 5.00 12.00
P20 Steve Yzerman 5.00 12.00
P21 Steve Yzerman 5.00 12.00
P22 Steve Yzerman 5.00 12.00
P23 Steve Yzerman 5.00 12.00
P24 Steve Yzerman 5.00 12.00
P25 Mario Lemieux 8.00 20.00
P26 Mario Lemieux 8.00 20.00
P27 Mario Lemieux 8.00 20.00
P28 Mario Lemieux 8.00 20.00
P29 Mario Lemieux 8.00 20.00
P30 Mario Lemieux 8.00 20.00
P31 Patrick Roy 5.00 12.00
P32 Patrick Roy 5.00 12.00
P33 Patrick Roy 5.00 12.00
P34 Patrick Roy 5.00 12.00
P35 Patrick Roy 5.00 12.00
P36 Patrick Roy 5.00 12.00
P37 Nicklas Lidstrom 2.00 5.00
P38 Nicklas Lidstrom 2.00 5.00
P39 Nicklas Lidstrom 2.00 5.00
P40 Nicklas Lidstrom 2.00 5.00
P41 Nicklas Lidstrom 2.00 5.00
P42 Nicklas Lidstrom 2.00 5.00

P43 Wayne Gretzky 12.00 30.00
P44 Wayne Gretzky 12.00 30.00
P45 Wayne Gretzky 12.00 30.00
P46 Wayne Gretzky 12.00 30.00
P47 Wayne Gretzky 12.00 30.00
P48 Wayne Gretzky 12.00 30.00

2020-21 SP Signature Legends UD Canvas Legends

C1 Mario Lemieux 4.00 10.00
C2 Ray Whitney .60 1.50
C3 Steve Shutt .75 2.00
C4 Brad Richards 1.00 2.50
C5 Joey Kocur .60 1.50
C6 Bernie Federko .75 2.00
C7 Michal Handzus .60 1.50
C8 Randy Carlyle .75 2.00
C9 Alexandre Burrows .60 1.50
C10 Bryan McCabe .60 1.50
C11 Doug Gilmour 1.25 3.00
C12 Scott Niedermayer 1.00 2.50
C13 Denis Potvin 1.00 2.50
C14 Paul Coffey 1.00 2.50
C15 Jeremy Roenick 1.50 4.00
C16 Chris Terreri .60 1.50
C17 Guy Lafleur 1.25 3.00
C18 Steve Yzerman 2.50 6.00
C19 Tim Hunter .60 1.50
C20 John Davidson .75 2.00
C21 Yvan Cournoyer 1.00 2.50
C22 Scott Mellanby .75 2.00
C23 Scott Gomez .75 2.00
C24 Ed Belfour 1.00 2.50
C25 Wayne Gretzky 6.00 15.00
C26 Steve Rucchin .60 1.50
C27 Kelly Hrudey .75 2.00
C28 Ken Daneyko .75 2.00
C29 Mike Modano 1.50 4.00
C30 Guy Chouinard .75 2.00
C31 Byron Dafoe .75 2.00
C32 Mike Sillinger .60 1.50
C33 Randy McKay .60 1.50
C34 Bob Kelly .60 1.50
C35 Mark Messier 2.00 5.00
C36 Brent Gilchrist .60 1.50
C37 Bill Ranford .75 2.00
C38 Wendel Clark 1.50 4.00
C39 Lanny McDonald .75 2.00
C40 Keith Tkachuk 1.00 2.50
C41 Grant Fuhr 1.50 4.00
C42 Ray Sheppard .60 1.50
C43 Bob Carpenter .75 2.00
C44 Jari Kurri 1.00 2.50
C45 Scott Hannan .60 1.50
C46 Alex Tanguay .75 2.00
C47 Willie Mitchell .75 2.00
C48 Olaf Kolzig 1.00 2.50
C49 Jaromir Jagr 3.00 8.00
C50 Mike Gartner 1.25 3.00
C51 Chris Chelios 1.00 2.50
C52 Kevin Weekes .75 2.00
C53 Joe Sakic 2.00 5.00
C54 Fedor Tyutin .60 1.50
C55 Ed Olczyk .75 2.00
C56 Bob Nystrom .75 2.00
C57 Steven Reinprecht .60 1.50
C58 Billy Smith 1.00 2.50
C59 Martin Brodeur 2.50 6.00
C60 Gilles Meloche 1.00 2.50
C61 Michal Grosek .60 1.50
C62 Ray Ferraro .75 2.00
C63 Bryan Berard 1.00 2.50
C64 Ron Hextall 1.00 2.50
C65 Al Secord .75 2.00
C66 Ed Westfall .75 2.00
C67 Michel Goulet 1.00 2.50
C68 Al Iafrate .75 2.00
C69 Stephane Matteau .60 1.50
C70 Ray Bourque 1.50 4.00
C71 Guillaume Latendresse .60 1.50
C72 Chris Phillips .75 2.00
C73 Mike Komisarek .75 2.00
C74 Clark Gillies 1.00 2.50
C75 Tiger Williams .60 1.50
C76 Murray Craven .60 1.50
C77 Randy Wood .60 1.50
C78 Pierre Bouchard .60 1.50
C79 Dale Hawerchuk 1.25 3.00
C80 Esa Tikkanen .75 2.00
C81 John LeClair 1.00 2.50
C82 Patrick Roy 2.50 6.00
C83 Murray Baron .60 1.50
C84 Borje Salming 1.00 2.50
C85 Rich Preston .60 1.50
C86 Denis Herron .75 2.00
C87 Brett Hull 2.00 5.00
C88 Rick Vaive .75 2.00
C89 John Tonelli .75 2.00
C90 Ed Johnston 1.00 2.50
C91 Robert Picard .60 1.50
C92 Wade Redden .75 2.00
C93 Stu Grimson 1.00 2.50
C94 Reijo Ruotsalainen .60 1.50
C95 Teemu Selanne 2.00 5.00
C96 Al MacInnis 1.25 3.00
C97 Rod Brind'Amour 1.00 2.50
C98 Jamal Mayers .75 2.00
C99 Sandy McCarthy .75 2.00
C100 Stu Barnes .60 1.50

2020-21 SP Signature Legends UD Canvas Legends Autographs

C2 Ray Whitney D 12.00 30.00
C3 Steve Shutt A 15.00 40.00
C4 Brad Richards B 20.00 50.00
C5 Joey Kocur E 12.00 30.00
C6 Bernie Federko C 15.00 40.00
C8 Randy Carlyle B 15.00 40.00
C9 Alexandre Burrows E 12.00 30.00
C10 Bryan McCabe E 12.00 30.00
C11 Doug Gilmour B 25.00 60.00
C14 Paul Coffey B 20.00 50.00
C15 Jeremy Roenick C 30.00 80.00
C16 Chris Terreri E 12.00 30.00
C18 Steve Yzerman B 150.00 400.00
C19 Tim Hunter D 12.00 30.00
C20 John Davidson D 15.00 40.00
C21 Yvan Cournoyer C 20.00 50.00
C22 Scott Mellanby C 15.00 40.00
C23 Scott Gomez E 15.00 40.00
C25 Wayne Gretzky B 300.00 800.00
C26 Steve Rucchin E 12.00 30.00
C27 Kelly Hrudey C 15.00 40.00
C29 Mike Modano B 30.00 80.00
C30 Guy Chouinard D 15.00 40.00
C31 Byron Dafoe E 15.00 40.00
C32 Mike Sillinger E 12.00 30.00
C33 Randy McKay D 12.00 30.00
C34 Bob Kelly E 12.00 30.00
C35 Mark Messier B 40.00 100.00
C36 Brent Gilchrist E 12.00 30.00
C37 Bill Ranford D 15.00 40.00
C38 Wendel Clark B 30.00 80.00
C39 Lanny McDonald B 15.00 40.00
C40 Keith Tkachuk B 20.00 50.00
C41 Grant Fuhr B 30.00 80.00
C42 Ray Sheppard D 12.00 30.00
C43 Bob Carpenter C 15.00 40.00
C44 Jari Kurri B 20.00 50.00
C45 Scott Hannan D 12.00 30.00
C46 Alex Tanguay E 15.00 40.00
C47 Willie Mitchell E 15.00 40.00
C48 Olaf Kolzig E 20.00 50.00
C49 Jaromir Jagr C 250.00 600.00
C51 Chris Chelios C 20.00 50.00
C52 Kevin Weekes E 15.00 40.00
C53 Joe Sakic B 80.00 200.00
C54 Fedor Tyutin E 12.00 30.00
C56 Bob Nystrom C 15.00 40.00
C57 Steven Reinprecht E 12.00 30.00
C58 Billy Smith D 20.00 50.00
C59 Martin Brodeur B 80.00 200.00
C60 Gilles Meloche D 20.00 50.00
C61 Michal Grosek E 12.00 30.00
C62 Ray Ferraro B 15.00 40.00
C63 Bryan Berard C 20.00 50.00
C64 Ron Hextall B 20.00 50.00
C65 Al Secord C 15.00 40.00
C66 Ed Westfall E 15.00 40.00
C67 Michel Goulet C 20.00 50.00
C68 Al Iafrate C 15.00 40.00
C69 Stephane Matteau D 12.00 30.00
C70 Ray Bourque B 30.00 80.00
C71 Guillaume Latendresse E 12.00 30.00
C73 Mike Komisarek E 15.00 40.00
C76 Murray Craven D 12.00 30.00
C77 Randy Wood E 12.00 30.00
C78 Pierre Bouchard D 12.00 30.00
C80 Esa Tikkanen D 15.00 40.00
C81 John LeClair A 20.00 50.00
C82 Patrick Roy B 80.00 200.00
C83 Murray Baron E 12.00 30.00
C85 Rich Preston E 12.00 30.00
C86 Denis Herron E 15.00 40.00
C87 Brett Hull B 80.00 200.00
C88 Rick Vaive C 15.00 40.00
C89 John Tonelli E 15.00 40.00
C90 Ed Johnston E 20.00 50.00
C92 Wade Redden E 15.00 40.00
C93 Stu Grimson E 20.00 50.00
C94 Reijo Ruotsalainen E 12.00 30.00
C95 Teemu Selanne B 40.00 100.00
C96 Al MacInnis B 25.00 60.00
C97 Rod Brind'Amour A 20.00 50.00
C98 Jamal Mayers D 15.00 40.00
C99 Sandy McCarthy E 15.00 40.00
C100 Stu Barnes E 12.00 30.00

1935 Sporting Events and Stars

31 Ice Hockey 20.00 40.00

2007 Sportkings Lumber Silver

L1 Martin Brodeur Stick 20.00 40.00
L2 Mario Lemieux Stick 25.00 50.00
L3 Patrick Roy Stick 30.00 60.00
L4 Terry Sawchuk Stick 25.00 50.00
L5 Maurice Richard Stick 30.00 60.00

2007 Sportkings Lumber Gold

*GOLD: .75X TO 1.5 BASIC

2012 Sportkings Double Memorabilia Silver

DM7 G.Lafleur/P.Roy 20.00 40.00
DM9 G.Lafleur/G.Lafleur 15.00 30.00

2012 Sportkings Greatest Moments Silver

GM2 Guy Lafleur 10.00 20.00

2013 Sportkings Cityscapes Double Silver

CSD1 S.Pippen/B.Hull 10.00 25.00
CSD5 G.Howe/C.Drexler 8.00 20.00

2013 Sportkings Cityscapes Triple Silver

CST2 Thomas/Pippen/Hull 10.00 25.00

2013 Sportkings National Convention VIP

COMPLETE SET (9) 6.00 15.00
VIP01 Bill Mosienko .60 1.50
VIP02 Bobby Hull 1.25 3.00
VIP03 Charlie Gardiner .60 1.50
VIP04 Glenn Hall .75 2.00
VIP05 Max Bentley .60 1.50
VIP06 Pierre Pilote .60 1.50
VIP07 Roy Conacher .60 1.50
VIP08 Stan Mikita .75 2.00
VIP09 Tony Esposito 1.00 2.50

1995 Sports Illustrated for Kids II

333 Jeremy Roenick HK .25 .60
338 John Vanbiesbrouck HK .20 .50
347 Mark Messier HK
kid photo) .25 .60
356 Felix Potvin HK .20 .50
366 Scott Stevens HK .20 .50
377 Paul Kariya HK 1.50 4.00
382 Jim Carey HK .20 .50
399 Eric Lindros HK .30 .75
413 Martin Brodeur HK 1.50 4.00
420 Paul Coffey HK
comic .20 .50
425 Peter Forsberg HK 1.50 4.00
432 Karyn Bye HK .20 .50

1977-79 Sportscaster Series 14

COMPLETE SET (24) 17.50 35.00
1423 Ken Dryden 2.00 4.00

1977-79 Sportscaster Series 15

COMPLETE SET (24) 12.50 25.00
1513 Yvan Cournoyer 1.25 2.50

1977-79 Sportscaster Series 18

COMPLETE SET (24) 12.50 25.00
1823 Garry Unger .50 1.00

1977-79 Sportscaster Series 19

COMPLETE SET (24) 25.00 50.00
1915 World Championship 1.00 2.00

1977-79 Sportscaster Series 51

COMPLETE SET (24) 20.00 40.00
5101 Czechoslovakia 1977 .75 1.50
5118 Guy Lafleur 1.50 3.00

1977-79 Sportscaster Series 74

COMPLETE SET (24) 200.00 400.00
7417 The 1978 WCH 2.00 4.00
7424 Vaclav Nedomansky 2.50 5.00

1977-79 Sportscaster Series 77

COMPLETE SET (24) 150.00 300.00
7710 Wayne Gretzky 125.00 250.00
7724 Expansion 2.00 4.00

1996-97 SPx

COMPLETE SET (50) 20.00 50.00
1 Paul Kariya .60 1.50
2 Teemu Selanne .60 1.50
3 Ray Bourque 1.00 2.50
4 Cam Neely .60 1.50
5 Theo Fleury .40 1.00
6 Chris Chelios .60 1.50
7 Jeremy Roenick .75 2.00
8 Peter Forsberg 1.00 2.50
9 Joe Sakic 1.25 3.00
10 Patrick Roy 2.50 6.00
11 Mike Modano .75 2.00
12 Joe Nieuwendyk .50 1.25
13 Sergei Fedorov .75 2.00
14 Steve Yzerman 2.50 6.00
15 Paul Coffey .60 1.50
16 Chris Osgood .50 1.25
17 Doug Weight .50 1.25
18 Pat LaFontaine .60 1.50
19 Brendan Shanahan .60 1.50
20 Vitali Yachmenev .40 1.00
21 Saku Koivu .60 1.50
22 Pierre Turgeon .50 1.25
23 Petr Sykora .40 1.00
24 Scott Stevens .50 1.25
25 Martin Brodeur 1.50 4.00
26 Brian Leetch .60 1.50
27 Mark Messier .60 1.50
28 Mike Richter .60 1.50
29 Zigmund Palffy .50 1.25
30 Todd Bertuzzi .60 1.50
31 Alexei Yashin .40 1.00
32 Daniel Alfredsson .50 1.25
33 Eric Lindros .60 1.50
34 John LeClair .60 1.50
35 Keith Tkachuk .60 1.50
36 Alexei Zhamnov .50 1.25
37 Mario Lemieux 2.50 6.00
38 Jaromir Jagr 1.00 2.50
39 Wayne Gretzky 3.00 8.00
40 Brett Hull .75 2.00
41 Owen Nolan .50 1.25
42 Roman Hamrlik .50 1.25
43 Mats Sundin .60 1.50
44 Felix Potvin .60 1.50
45 Doug Gilmour .50 1.25
46 Pavel Bure .60 1.50
47 Alexander Mogilny .50 1.25
48 Jim Carey .60 1.50
49 Peter Bondra .50 1.25
50 Eric Daze .50 1.25
P39 W.Gretzky PROMO .40 1.00
GF1 Great Futures 5.00 12.00
GS1 W.Gretzky Tribute AU 150.00 400.00
GT1 W.Gretzky Tribute 8.00 20.00

1996-97 SPx Gold

*GOLD: 1.2X TO 3X BASIC CARDS

1996-97 SPx Holoview Heroes

COMPLETE SET (10) 15.00 40.00
HH1 Ray Bourque 1.50 4.00
HH2 Patrick Roy 2.50 6.00
HH3 Steve Yzerman 2.50 6.00
HH4 Paul Coffey 1.00 2.50
HH5 Mark Messier 2.00 5.00
HH6 Mario Lemieux 4.00 10.00
HH7 Wayne Gretzky 6.00 15.00
HH8 Brett Hull 2.00 5.00
HH9 Doug Gilmour 1.25 3.00
HH10 Grant Fuhr 1.50 4.00

1997-98 SPx

COMPLETE SET (50) 15.00 40.00
1 Paul Kariya .50 1.25
2 Teemu Selanne 1.00 2.50
3 Ray Bourque .75 2.00
4 Dominik Hasek .75 2.00
5 Pat LaFontaine .50 1.25
6 Theo Fleury .60 1.50
7 Jarome Iginla .60 1.50
8 Tony Amonte .40 1.00
9 Chris Chelios .50 1.25
10 Patrick Roy 1.25 3.00
11 Peter Forsberg 1.00 2.50
12 Joe Sakic 1.00 2.50
13 Mike Modano .75 2.00
14 Steve Yzerman 1.25 3.00
15 Sergei Fedorov .75 2.00
16 Brendan Shanahan .50 1.25
17 Doug Weight .50 1.25
18 Jason Arnott .40 1.00
19 Curtis Joseph .60 1.50
20 John Vanbiesbrouck .50 1.25
21 Ed Jovanovski .30 .75
22 Geoff Sanderson .40 1.00
23 Rob Blake .50 1.25
24 Saku Koivu .50 1.25
25 Doug Gilmour .60 1.50
26 Scott Stevens .50 1.25
27 Martin Brodeur 1.25 3.00
28 Zigmund Palffy .50 1.25
29 Bryan Berard .30 .75
30 Wayne Gretzky 3.00 8.00
30S Wayne Gretzky SAMPLE 3.00 8.00
31 Mike Richter .50 1.25
32 Mark Messier 1.00 2.50
33 Brian Leetch .40 1.00
34 Daniel Alfredsson .50 1.25
35 Alexei Yashin .40 1.00
36 Eric Lindros .75 2.00
37 Janne Niinimaa .40 1.00
38 John LeClair .50 1.25
39 Jeremy Roenick .75 2.00
40 Keith Tkachuk .50 1.25
41 Ron Francis .60 1.50
42 Jaromir Jagr 1.50 4.00
43 Brett Hull 1.00 2.50
44 Owen Nolan .50 1.25
45 Chris Gratton .30 .75
46 Mats Sundin .50 1.25
47 Pavel Bure .50 1.25
48 Adam Oates .50 1.25
49 Joe Juneau .30 .75
50 Peter Bondra .50 1.25

1997-98 SPx Bronze

*BRONZE: 1X TO 2X BASIC CARDS

1997-98 SPx Gold

*GOLD: 4X TO 10X BASIC CARDS

1997-98 SPx Silver

*SILVER: 1.5X TO 4X BASIC CARDS

1997-98 SPx Steel

*STEEL: .8X TO 2X BASIC CARDS

1997-98 SPx Dimension

SPX1 Wayne Gretzky 20.00 50.00
SPX2 Jeremy Roenick 3.00 8.00
SPX3 Mark Messier 3.00 8.00
SPX4 Eric Lindros 2.50 6.00
SPX5 Doug Gilmour 2.00 5.00
SPX6 Pavel Bure 1.50 4.00
SPX7 Brendan Shanahan 1.50 4.00
SPX8 Bryan Berard 1.00 2.50
SPX9 Curtis Joseph 2.00 5.00
SPX10 Chris Chelios 1.50 4.00
SPX11 Sergei Fedorov 2.50 6.00
SPX12 Adam Oates 1.50 4.00
SPX13 Zigmund Palffy 1.50 4.00
SPX14 Theo Fleury 2.00 5.00
SPX15 Keith Tkachuk 1.50 4.00
SPX16 Peter Forsberg 3.00 8.00
SPX17 Mats Sundin 1.50 4.00
SPX18 Teemu Selanne 3.00 8.00
SPX19 Paul Kariya 1.50 4.00
SPX20 Brett Hull 3.00 8.00

1997-98 SPx DuoView

COMPLETE SET (10) 125.00 250.00
1 Wayne Gretzky 30.00 80.00
2 Jaromir Jagr 8.00 20.00
3 Martin Brodeur 20.00 50.00
4 Jarome Iginla 6.00 15.00
5 Steve Yzerman 25.00 60.00
6 Patrick Roy 25.00 60.00
7 Doug Weight 4.00 10.00
8 John Vanbiesbrouck 4.00 10.00
9 Dominik Hasek 10.00 25.00
10 Joe Sakic 10.00 25.00

1997-98 SPx DuoView Autographs

1 Wayne Gretzky 200.00 500.00
2 Jaromir Jagr 25.00 60.00
3 Martin Brodeur 50.00 120.00
4 Jarome Iginla 20.00 50.00
5 Patrick Roy 40.00 100.00
6 Doug Weight 12.50 30.00

1997-98 SPx Grand Finale

*GRAND FINALE: 20X TO 50X BASIC CARDS

1999-00 SPx

COMPLETE SET (180) 125.00 250.00
COMP.SET w/o SP's (162) 40.00 80.00
1 Damian Rhodes .25 .60
2 Nelson Emerson .10 .30
3 Ray Ferraro .10 .30
4 Paul Kariya .30 .75
5 Steve Rucchin .15 .40
6 Guy Hebert .25 .60
7 Oleg Tverdovsky .10 .30
8 Ted Donato .10 .30
9 Ray Bourque .50 1.25
10 Sergei Samsonov .25 .60
11 Joe Thornton .50 1.25
12 Jason Allison .10 .30
13 Byron Dafoe .25 .60
14 Jonathan Girard .10 .30
15 Dominik Hasek .60 1.50
16 Alexei Zhitnik .10 .30
17 Michael Peca .25 .60
18 Cory Sarich .25 .60
19 Martin Biron .25 .60
20 Miroslav Satan .25 .60
21 Valeri Bure .10 .30
22 Derek Morris .10 .30
23 Phil Housley .25 .60
24 Jarome Iginla .40 1.00
25 Rico Fata .10 .30
26 Jean-Sebastien Giguere .25 .60
27 Marc Savard .10 .30
28 Arturs Irbe .25 .60
29 Keith Primeau .10 .30
30 Sami Kapanen .10 .30
31 Ron Francis .10 .30
32 Wendel Clark .25 .60
33 J-P Dumont .25 .60
34 Ty Jones .10 .30
35 Tony Amonte .25 .60
36 Jocelyn Thibault .25 .60
37 Doug Gilmour .25 .60
38 Bryan McCabe .10 .30
39 Joe Sakic .60 1.50
40 Peter Forsberg .75 2.00
41 Alex Tanguay .25 .60
42 Chris Drury .25 .60
43 Patrick Roy 1.50 4.00
44 Sandis Ozolinsh .10 .30
45 Adam Deadmarsh .10 .30
46 Milan Hejduk .30 .75
47 Mike Modano .50 1.25
48 Brett Hull .40 1.00
49 Darryl Sydor .25 .60
50 Ed Belfour .30 .75
51 Jere Lehtinen .25 .60
52 Jamie Langenbrunner .10 .30
53 Joe Nieuwendyk .25 .60
54 Sergei Fedorov .50 1.25
55 Steve Yzerman 1.50 4.00
56 Brendan Shanahan .30 .75
57 Chris Osgood .25 .60
58 Nicklas Lidstrom .30 .75
59 Igor Larionov .10 .30
60 Chris Chelios .30 .75
61 Bill Guerin .10 .30
62 Doug Weight .15 .40
63 Mike Grier .10 .30
64 Tommy Salo .25 .60
65 Bill Ranford .25 .60
66 Tom Poti .10 .30
67 Daniel Cleary .10 .30
68 Mark Parrish .10 .30
69 Pavel Bure .30 .75
70 Oleg Kvasha .10 .30
71 Viktor Kozlov .25 .60
72 Trevor Kidd .25 .60
73 Rob Blake .25 .60
74 Pavel Rosa .10 .30
75 Luc Robitaille .25 .60
76 Zigmund Palffy .25 .60
77 Aki Berg .10 .30
78 Saku Koivu .30 .75
79 Jeff Hackett .25 .60
80 Trevor Linden .25 .60
81 Cliff Ronning .25 .60
82 David Legwand .25 .60
83 Mike Dunham .25 .60
84 Scott Stevens .25 .60
85 Martin Brodeur .75 2.00
86 Patrik Elias .25 .60
87 Brendan Morrison .25 .60
88 Scott Niedermayer .10 .30
89 Vadim Sharifijanov .10 .30
90 Mike Watt .10 .30
91 Felix Potvin .30 .75
92 Eric Brewer .10 .30
93 Jorgen Jonsson RC .25 .60
94 Kenny Jonsson .10 .30
95 Olli Jokinen .25 .60
96 Theo Fleury .10 .30
97 Brian Leetch .25 .60
98 Mike Richter .30 .75
99 Petr Nedved .25 .60
100 Adam Graves .10 .30
101 Manny Malhotra .25 .60
102 Alexei Yashin .10 .30
103 Daniel Alfredsson .15 .40
104 Ron Tugnutt .25 .60
105 Magnus Arvedson .10 .30
106 Sami Salo .10 .30
107 Marian Hossa .30 .75
108 Eric Lindros .30 .75
109 John Vanbiesbrouck .25 .60
110 John LeClair .30 .75
111 Rod Brind'Amour .25 .60
112 Mark Recchi .20 .50
113 Eric Desjardins .25 .60
114 Jeremy Roenick .40 1.00
115 Keith Tkachuk .30 .75
116 Rick Tocchet .25 .60
117 Robert Esche RC 1.00 2.50
118 Nikolai Khabibulin .25 .60
119 Teppo Numminen .10 .30
120 Jaromir Jagr .50 1.25
121 Martin Straka .10 .30
122 Jan Hrdina .10 .30
123 German Titov .10 .30
124 Alexei Kovalev .25 .60
125 Matthew Barnaby .25 .60
126 Vincent Damphousse .10 .30
127 Owen Nolan .25 .60
128 Jeff Friesen .10 .30
129 Patrick Marleau .25 .60
130 Marco Sturm .25 .60
131 Mike Vernon .25 .60
132 Pavol Demitra .25 .60
133 Al MacInnis .25 .60
134 Pierre Turgeon .25 .60
135 Chris Pronger .25 .60
136 Jochen Hecht RC 1.00 2.50
137 Vincent Lecavalier .30 .75
138 Paul Mara .25 .60
139 Dan Cloutier .25 .60
140 Andrei Zyuzin .10 .30
141 Pavel Kubina .10 .30
142 Kevin Hodson .25 .60
143 Mats Sundin .30 .75
144 Curtis Joseph .30 .75
145 Sergei Berezin .25 .60
146 Bryan Berard .10 .30
147 Tomas Kaberle .10 .30
148 Daniil Markov .10 .30
149 Mark Messier .30 .75
150 Bill Muckalt .25 .60
151 Markus Naslund .30 .75
152 Mattias Ohlund .25 .60
153 Ed Jovanovski .10 .30
154 Steve Kariya RC 1.00 2.50
155 Josh Holden .10 .30
156 Richard Zednik .10 .30
157 Jaroslav Svejkovsky .10 .30
158 Adam Oates .25 .60
159 Peter Bondra .25 .60
160 Sergei Gonchar .10 .30
161 Olaf Kolzig .25 .60
162 Jan Bulis .10 .30
163 Patrik Stefan AU RC 8.00 20.00
164 Daniel Sedin AU 6.00 15.00
165 Henrik Sedin AU 8.00 20.00
166 Pavel Brendl AU RC 8.00 20.00
167 Brian Finley AU 5.00 12.00
168 Taylor Pyatt AU 8.00 20.00
169 Jamie Lundmark AU 6.00 15.00
170 Denis Shvidki 2.50 6.00
171 Jani Rita 2.50 6.00
172 Oleg Saprykin AU RC 6.00 15.00
173 Nick Boynton 2.50 6.00
174 Tim Connolly AU 6.00 15.00
175 Kris Beech AU 5.00 12.00
176 Roberto Luongo 4.00 10.00
177 David Legwand 3.00 8.00
178 Dave Tanabe 2.50 6.00
179 Barret Jackman 2.50 6.00
180 Maxime Ouellet 4.00 10.00

1999-00 SPx Radiance

*RADIANCE 1-162: 20X TO 40X BASIC CARDS
*RADIANCE 163-180: 1X TO 3X BASIC SP
*RADIANCE 163-180: .5X TO 1.2X BASIC SP AU
164 Daniel Sedin 20.00 50.00
165 Henrik Sedin 25.00 60.00
166 Pavel Brendl 12.50 30.00
168 Taylor Pyatt 10.00 25.00

1999-00 SPx 99 Cheers

COMPLETE SET (15) 30.00 60.00
COMMON GRETZKY (CH1-15) 2.50 6.00

1999-00 SPx Highlight Heroes

COMPLETE SET (10) 15.00 30.00
HH1 Wayne Gretzky 4.00 10.00
HH2 Sergei Samsonov .60 1.50
HH3 Dominik Hasek 1.25 3.00
HH4 Jaromir Jagr 1.00 2.50
HH5 Patrick Roy 3.00 8.00
HH6 Paul Kariya 1.00 2.50
HH7 Pavel Bure .75 2.00
HH8 Peter Forsberg 1.50 4.00
HH9 Eric Lindros 1.50 4.00
HH10 Teemu Selanne 1.00 2.50

1999-00 SPx Prolifics

COMPLETE SET (15) 25.00 50.00
P1 Paul Kariya 1.00 2.50
P2 Jaromir Jagr 1.50 4.00
P3 Brett Hull 1.25 3.00
P4 Joe Sakic 2.00 5.00
P5 Sergei Samsonov 1.00 2.50
P6 Keith Tkachuk 1.00 2.50
P7 Brendan Shanahan 1.50 4.00
P8 Vincent Lecavalier 1.00 2.50
P9 Steve Yzerman 5.00 12.00
P10 Jeremy Roenick 1.25 3.00
P11 Mike Modano 1.50 4.00
P12 John LeClair 1.25 3.00
P13 Peter Forsberg 2.50 6.00
P14 Ray Bourque 1.50 4.00
P15 David Legwand 1.00 2.50

1999-00 SPx SPXcitement

COMPLETE SET (20) 20.00 40.00
X1 Wayne Gretzky 3.00 8.00
X2 Patrick Roy 2.50 6.00
X3 Pavel Bure .60 1.50
X4 Steve Yzerman 2.50 6.00
X5 David Legwand .50 1.25
X6 Dominik Hasek 1.00 2.50
X7 Sergei Samsonov .50 1.25
X8 Patrik Stefan 1.00 2.50
X9 Eric Lindros .75 2.00
X10 Brett Hull .60 1.50
X11 Steve Kariya .50 1.25
X12 Keith Tkachuk .50 1.25
X13 Alex Tanguay .50 1.25
X14 Peter Forsberg 1.25 3.00
X15 Jaromir Jagr .75 2.00
X16 Paul Kariya .50 1.25
X17 Brendan Shanahan .75 2.00
X18 Mike Modano .75 2.00
X19 John LeClair .60 1.50
X20 Teemu Selanne .50 1.25

1999-00 SPx SPXtreme

COMPLETE SET (20) 20.00 40.00
XT1 Al MacInnis .50 1.25
XT2 Keith Tkachuk .60 1.50
XT3 Peter Forsberg 1.50 4.00
XT4 Teemu Selanne .60 1.50
XT5 Patrick Roy 3.00 8.00
XT6 Sergei Samsonov .60 1.25
XT7 Brendan Shanahan 1.00 2.50
XT8 Mike Modano 1.00 2.50
XT9 Eric Lindros 1.00 2.50
XT10 Paul Kariya .60 1.50
XT11 Jaromir Jagr 1.00 2.50
XT12 Brett Hull .75 2.00
XT13 Mats Sundin .60 1.50
XT14 Dominik Hasek 1.25 3.00
XT15 Ray Bourque 1.00 2.50
XT16 Curtis Joseph .60 1.50
XT17 John LeClair .75 2.00
XT18 Ed Belfour .60 1.50
XT19 David Legwand .50 1.25
XT20 Wayne Gretzky 4.00 10.00

1999-00 SPx Starscape

COMPLETE SET (10) 12.00 25.00
S1 Brett Hull .75 2.00
S2 Jaromir Jagr 1.00 2.50
S3 Pavel Bure .75 2.00
S4 Dominik Hasek 1.25 3.00
S5 Eric Lindros 1.00 2.50
S6 Paul Kariya .60 1.50
S7 Peter Forsberg 1.50 4.00
S8 Teemu Selanne .60 1.50
S9 Patrick Roy 3.00 8.00
S10 Keith Tkachuk .60 1.50

1999-00 SPx Winning Materials

WM1 Mike Modano 12.00 30.00
WM2 Martin Brodeur 15.00 40.00
WM3 Steve Yzerman 25.00 60.00
WM4 Jaromir Jagr 15.00 40.00
WM5 Dominik Hasek 15.00 40.00
WM6 Brett Hull 12.00 30.00
WM7 Patrick Roy 20.00 50.00
WM8 Ray Bourque 15.00 40.00
WM9 Eric Lindros 12.00 30.00
WM10 Wayne Gretzky 50.00 100.00
WMA1 W.Gretzky AU/25 600.00 1500.00
WMA2 B.Hull AU/25 125.00 300.00

2000-01 SPx

COMPLETE SET (130) 250.00 500.00
COMP.SET w/o SP's (90) 20.00 40.00
1 Paul Kariya .30 .75
2 Teemu Selanne .60 1.50
3 Patrik Stefan .25 .60
4 Jason Allison .25 .60
5 Sergei Samsonov .25 .60
6 Dominik Hasek .50 1.25
7 Miroslav Satan .20 .50
8 Fred Brathwaite .25 .60
9 Valeri Bure .25 .60
10 Ron Francis .40 1.00
11 Arturs Irbe .25 .60
12 Tony Amonte .25 .60
13 Joe Sakic .60 1.50
14 Milan Hejduk .25 .60
15 Patrick Roy .75 2.00
16 Peter Forsberg .60 1.50
17 Ray Bourque .50 1.25
18 Ron Tugnutt .25 .60
19 Brett Hull .60 1.50
20 Ed Belfour .30 .75
21 Mike Modano .50 1.25
22 Sergei Fedorov .50 1.25
23 Brendan Shanahan .30 .75
24 Chris Osgood .30 .75
25 Steve Yzerman .75 2.00
26 Doug Weight .30 .75
27 Tommy Salo .25 .60
28 Pavel Bure .30 .75
29 Trevor Kidd .20 .50
30 Viktor Kozlov .25 .60
31 Rob Blake .30 .75
32 Zigmund Palffy .30 .75
33 Luc Robitaille .30 .75
34 Manny Fernandez .20 .50
35 Saku Koivu .30 .75
36 David Legwand .30 .75
37 Martin Brodeur .75 2.00
38 Patrik Elias .30 .75
39 Scott Gomez .25 .60
40 Scott Stevens .30 .75
41 Mariusz Czerkawski .20 .50
42 Tim Connolly .20 .50
43 Mark Messier .60 1.50
44 Mike York .20 .50
45 Theo Fleury .40 1.00
46 Marian Hossa .30 .75
47 Radek Bonk .25 .60
48 Simon Gagne .30 .75
49 Brian Boucher .25 .60
50 Rick Tocchet .25 .60
51 John LeClair .30 .75
52 Jeremy Roenick .50 1.25
53 Keith Tkachuk .30 .75
54 Jaromir Jagr 1.00 2.50
55 Jean-Sebastien Aubin .25 .60
56 Jeff Friesen .20 .50
57 Steve Shields .20 .50
58 Brad Stuart .25 .60
59 Chris Pronger .30 .75
60 Pavol Demitra .40 1.00
61 Roman Turek .25 .60
62 Dan Cloutier .25 .60
63 Vincent Lecavalier .30 .75
64 Nikolai Antropov .25 .60
65 Curtis Joseph .40 1.00
66 Mats Sundin .30 .75
67 Felix Potvin .50 1.25
68 Markus Naslund .30 .75
69 Adam Oates .30 .75
70 Olaf Kolzig .30 .75
71 Peter Forsberg XE .60 1.50
72 Brendan Shanahan XE .30 .75
73 Scott Stevens XE .30 .75
74 Mark Messier XE .60 1.50
75 John LeClair XE .30 .75
76 Keith Primeau XE .25 .60
77 Keith Tkachuk XE .30 .75
78 Jeremy Roenick XE .50 1.25
79 Owen Nolan XE .30 .75
80 Chris Pronger XE .30 .75
81 Paul Kariya PRO .30 .75
82 Dominik Hasek PRO .50 1.25
83 Patrick Roy PRO .75 2.00
84 Ray Bourque PRO .50 1.25
85 Mike Modano PRO .50 1.25
86 Steve Yzerman PRO .75 2.00
87 Pavel Bure PRO .30 .75
88 Martin Brodeur PRO .75 2.00
89 John LeClair PRO .30 .75
90 Jaromir Jagr PRO 1.00 2.50
91 Herbert Vasilijevs RC 1.50 4.00
92 Eric Nickulas RC 1.50 4.00
93 Brandon Smith RC 1.50 4.00
94 Jeff Cowan RC 1.50 4.00
95 Serge Aubin RC 2.00 5.00
96 Mike Minard RC 2.50 6.00
97 Steven Reinprecht RC 2.50 6.00
98 David Gosselin RC 2.00 5.00
99 Colin White RC 1.50 4.00
100 Willie Mitchell RC 2.50 6.00
101 Steve Brule RC 1.50 4.00
102 Steve Valiquette RC 2.00 5.00
103 Petr Mika RC 1.50 4.00
104 Chris Kenady RC 1.50 4.00
105 Johan Witehall RC 1.50 4.00
106 Jani Hurme RC 1.50 4.00
107 Jean-Guy Trudel RC 1.50 4.00
108 Dale Rominski RC 1.50 4.00
109 Greg Andrusak RC 2.00 5.00
110 Martin Havlat RC 5.00 12.00
111 Jeremy Stevenson RC 1.50 4.00
112 Sergei Vyshedkevich RC 1.50 4.00
113 Johnathan Aitken RC 1.50 4.00
114 Keith Aldridge RC 1.50 4.00
115 Rich Parent RC 2.00 5.00
116 Kaspars Astashenko RC 1.50 4.00
117 Matt Elich RC 2.00 5.00
118 Dieter Kochan RC 1.50 4.00
119 Kyle Freadrich RC 1.50 4.00
120 Justin Williams RC 4.00 10.00
121 Andrew Raycroft JSY RC 6.00 15.00
122 Zdenek Blatny JSY RC 2.50 6.00
123 Pavel Brendl JSY 2.50 6.00
124 Jason Jaspers JSY RC 2.50 6.00
125 Fedor Fedorov JSY RC 3.00 8.00
126 Jordan Krestanovich JSY RC 2.50 6.00
127 Marc-Andre Thinel JSY RC 2.50 6.00
128 Damian Surma JSY RC 2.50 6.00
129 Jeff Bateman JSY RC 2.50 6.00

130 Sheldon Keefe JSY 2.50 6.00
131 Ray Ferraro .20 .50
132 Bill Guerin .30 .75
133 Ronald Petrovicky RC 1.00 2.50
134 Shane Willis .20 .50
135 Chris Nielsen RC 1.00 2.50
136 Petteri Nummelin RC 1.00 2.50
137 Igor Larionov .30 .75
138 Shawn Horcoff RC 2.00 5.00
139 Lance Ward RC 1.00 2.50
140 Manny Fernandez .20 .50
141 Scott Niedermayer .30 .75
142 Alexei Yashin .25 .60
143 Claude Lemieux .25 .60
144 Mario Lemieux 1.25 3.00
145 Milan Kraft .20 .50
146 Evgeni Nabokov .25 .60
147 Keith Tkachuk .30 .75
148 Gary Roberts .20 .50
149 Daniel Sedin .40 1.00
150 Henrik Sedin .40 1.00
151 Kris Beech .20 .50
152 Lee Goren RC 1.50 4.00
153 Pavel Kolarik RC 1.50 4.00
154 Greg Kuznik RC 1.50 4.00
155 Josef Vasicek RC 4.00 10.00
156 Rick Berry RC 1.50 4.00
157 David Aebischer RC 3.00 8.00
158 Rostislav Klesla RC 4.00 10.00
159 Marty Turco RC 3.00 8.00
160 Tyler Bouck RC 1.50 4.00
161 Mike Comrie RC 4.00 10.00
162 Eric Belanger RC 2.00 5.00
163 Marian Gaborik RC 10.00 25.00
164 Scott Hartnell RC 4.00 10.00
165 Jason Labarbera RC 2.00 5.00
166 Rick DiPietro RC 3.00 8.00
167 Ruslan Fedotenko RC 1.50 4.00
168 Petr Hubacek RC 1.50 4.00
169 Roman Cechmanek RC 2.00 5.00
170 Roman Simicek RC 1.50 4.00
171 Mark Smith RC 1.50 4.00
172 Jakub Cutta RC 1.50 4.00
173 Marc Chouinard RC 1.50 4.00
174 Darcy Hordichuk RC 1.50 4.00
175 Bryan Adams RC 1.50 4.00
176 Jarno Kultanen RC 1.50 4.00
177 Eric Boulton RC 1.50 4.00
178 Brian Swanson RC 1.50 4.00
179 Lubomir Sekeras RC 1.50 4.00
180 Eric Landry RC 1.50 4.00
181 Mike Commodore RC 1.50 4.00
182 Johan Holmqvist RC 1.50 4.00
183 Jeff Ulmer RC 1.50 4.00
184 Ossi Vaananen RC 2.00 5.00
185 Alexander Khavanov RC 1.50 4.00
186 Bryce Salvador RC 2.00 5.00
187 Reed Low RC 1.50 4.00

2000-01 SPx Spectrum

*1-90 VETS/50: 10X TO 25X BASIC CARDS
*91-120 ROOKIES/50: 1.2X TO 3X RC/1500
*121-130 JSY/50: .8X TO 2X BASIC JSY

2000-01 SPx Highlight Heroes

COMPLETE SET (14) 10.00 20.00
HH1 Paul Kariya .60 1.50
HH2 Patrik Stefan .50 1.25
HH3 Joe Thornton 1.00 2.50
HH4 Valeri Bure .50 1.25
HH5 Milan Hejduk .60 1.50
HH6 Brett Hull .75 2.00
HH7 Brendan Shanahan 1.00 2.50
HH8 Pavel Bure .75 2.00
HH9 Marian Hossa .60 1.50
HH10 Brian Boucher .60 1.50
HH11 Jeremy Roenick .75 2.00
HH12 Jaromir Jagr 1.00 2.50
HH13 Chris Pronger .50 1.25
HH14 Curtis Joseph .60 1.50

2000-01 SPx Prolifics

COMPLETE SET (7) 8.00 15.00
P1 Dominik Hasek 1.25 3.00
P2 Ray Bourque 1.25 3.00
P3 Brett Hull .75 2.00
P4 Steve Yzerman 3.00 8.00
P5 Mark Messier .75 2.00
P6 John LeClair .75 2.00
P7 Jaromir Jagr 1.00 2.50

2000-01 SPx Rookie Redemption

RR1 Ilja Bryzgalov 4.00 10.00
RR2 Ilya Kovalchuk 10.00 25.00
RR3 Ivan Huml 2.00 5.00
RR4 Ales Kotalik 2.50 6.00
RR5 Scott Nichol 2.00 5.00
RR6 Erik Cole 3.00 8.00
RR7 Casey Hankinson 2.00 5.00
RR8 Vaclav Nedorost 2.00 5.00
RR9 Martin Spanhel 2.00 5.00
RR10 Niko Kapanen 2.00 5.00
RR11 Pavel Datsyuk 12.00 30.00
RR12 Ty Conklin 4.00 10.00
RR13 Kristian Huselius 3.00 8.00
RR14 Jaroslav Bednar 2.00 5.00
RR15 Nick Schultz 2.00 5.00
RR16 Martti Jarventie 2.00 5.00
RR17 Martin Erat 4.00 10.00
RR18 Andreas Salomonsson 2.00 5.00
RR19 Raffi Torres 3.00 8.00
RR20 Dan Blackburn 2.50 6.00
RR21 Ivan Ciernik 2.00 5.00
RR22 Jiri Dopita 2.00 5.00
RR23 Krys Kolanos 2.00 5.00
RR24 Billy Tibbetts 2.00 5.00
RR25 Jeff Jillson 2.00 5.00
RR26 Mark Rycroft 2.00 5.00
RR27 Nikita Alexeev 2.00 5.00
RR28 Bob Wren 2.00 5.00
RR29 Pat Kavanagh 2.00 5.00
RR30 Brian Sutherby 2.00 5.00

2000-01 SPx SPXcitement

COMPLETE SET (14) 10.00 20.00
X1 Teemu Selanne .60 1.50
X2 Sergei Samsonov .50 1.25
X3 Tony Amonte .50 1.25
X4 Joe Sakic 1.25 3.00
X5 Mike Modano 1.00 2.50
X6 Sergei Fedorov 1.25 3.00
X7 Pavel Bure .75 2.00
X8 Martin Brodeur 1.50 4.00
X9 Simon Gagne .50 1.25
X10 Jaromir Jagr 1.00 2.50
X11 Jeff Friesen .50 1.25
X12 Roman Turek .50 1.25
X13 Vincent Lecavalier .60 1.50
X14 Mats Sundin .60 1.50

2000-01 SPx SPXtreme

COMPLETE SET (7) 8.00 15.00
S1 Paul Kariya .75 2.00
S2 Peter Forsberg 1.50 4.00
S3 Mike Modano 1.00 2.50
S4 Martin Brodeur 1.50 4.00
S5 Mark Messier .75 2.00
S6 John LeClair .75 2.00
S7 Jaromir Jagr 1.00 2.50

2000-01 SPx Winning Materials

AC Anson Carter SP 4.00 10.00
BH Brett Hull SP 10.00 25.00
BS Brendan Shanahan 5.00 12.00
CJ Curtis Joseph 6.00 15.00
CO Chris Osgood 5.00 12.00
DH Dominik Hasek 8.00 20.00
FP Felix Potvin 8.00 20.00
JJ Jaromir Jagr 15.00 40.00
JL John LeClair 5.00 12.00
JR Jeremy Roenick 8.00 20.00
JS Joe Sakic 10.00 25.00
KJ Kenny Jonsson 3.00 8.00
KT Keith Tkachuk 5.00 12.00
MB Martin Brodeur SP 12.00 30.00
ML Mario Lemieux 20.00 50.00
MM Mike Modano SP 8.00 20.00
NL Nicklas Lidstrom 5.00 12.00
PD Pavol Demitra SP 6.00 15.00
PF Peter Forsberg 10.00 25.00
PK Paul Kariya SP 5.00 12.00
PR Patrick Roy 12.00 30.00
RB Ray Bourque 8.00 20.00
SF Sergei Fedorov 8.00 20.00
SY Steve Yzerman 12.00 30.00
TO Tony Amonte 4.00 10.00
TS Teemu Selanne 10.00 25.00
WG Wayne Gretzky 30.00 80.00
PBO Peter Bondra SP 5.00 12.00
WBC Brian Boucher Upd 4.00 10.00
WBE Ed Belfour Upd 5.00 12.00
WBI Martin Biron Upd 4.00 10.00
WBO Ray Bourque Upd 8.00 20.00
WBU Valeri Bure Upd 4.00 10.00
WFE Sergei Fedorov Upd 8.00 20.00
WGR Wayne Gretzky Upd 30.00 80.00
WJJ Jaromir Jagr Upd 15.00 40.00
WKA Paul Kariya Upd 5.00 12.00
WLE John LeClair Upd 5.00 12.00
WLU Roberto Luongo Upd 8.00 20.00
WRE Jeremy Roenick Upd 8.00 20.00
WRO Patrick Roy Upd 12.00 30.00
WSA Miroslav Satan Upd 3.00 8.00
WSE Teemu Selanne Upd 10.00 25.00
WSU Mats Sundin Upd 5.00 12.00
WTB Jocelyn Thibault Upd 4.00 10.00
WTH Joe Thornton Upd 8.00 20.00
WTK Keith Tkachuk Upd 5.00 12.00
WYZ Steve Yzerman Upd 12.00 30.00

2000-01 SPx Winning Materials Autographs

SBH Brett Hull 75.00 150.00
SCJ Curtis Joseph 40.00 100.00
SFP Felix Potvin 60.00 120.00
SJL John LeClair 40.00 100.00
SKT Keith Tkachuk 60.00 120.00
SMB Martin Brodeur 60.00 125.00
SML Mario Lemieux 150.00 300.00
SRB Ray Bourque 75.00 150.00
SSY Steve Yzerman 125.00 225.00
SWG Wayne Gretzky 250.00 600.00

2001-02 SPx

COMP.SET w/o SP's (155) 40.00 80.00
1 Paul Kariya .30 .75
2 Patrik Stefan .25 .60
3 Sergei Samsonov .25 .60
4 Joe Thornton .50 1.25
5 Bill Guerin .30 .75
6 Martin Biron .25 .60
7 Miroslav Satan .25 .60
8 Jarome Iginla .40 1.00
9 Marc Savard .20 .50
10 Arturs Irbe .25 .60
11 Tony Amonte .25 .60
12 Steve Sullivan .20 .50
13 Joe Sakic .60 1.50
14 Peter Forsberg .60 1.50
15 Ray Bourque .50 1.25
16 Milan Hejduk .25 .60
17 Patrick Roy .75 2.00
18 Ron Tugnutt .25 .60
19 Mike Modano .50 1.25
20 Ed Belfour .30 .75
21 Pierre Turgeon .25 .60
22 Steve Yzerman .75 2.00
23 Brendan Shanahan .30 .75
24 Sergei Fedorov .50 1.25
25 Luc Robitaille .30 .75
26 Dominik Hasek .50 1.25
27 Tommy Salo .25 .60
28 Mike Comrie .25 .60
29 Pavel Bure .30 .75
30 Zigmund Palffy .30 .75
31 Felix Potvin .50 1.25
32 Adam Deadmarsh .20 .50
33 Marian Gaborik .30 .75
34 Saku Koivu .30 .75
35 David Legwand .25 .60
36 Mike Dunham .25 .60
37 Martin Brodeur .75 2.00
38 Patrik Elias .30 .75
39 Jason Arnott .25 .60
40 Michael Peca .25 .60
41 Rick DiPietro .25 .60
42 Mark Messier .60 1.50
43 Theo Fleury .40 1.00
44 Marian Hossa .30 .75
45 Radek Bonk .20 .50
46 Jeremy Roenick .50 1.25
47 Roman Cechmanek .25 .60
48 Keith Primeau .25 .60
49 John LeClair .30 .75
50 Sean Burke .20 .50
51 Alexei Kovalev .25 .60
52 Mario Lemieux 1.25 3.00
53 Johan Hedberg .25 .60
54 Robert Lang .20 .50
55 Evgeni Nabokov .25 .60
56 Teemu Selanne .60 1.50
57 Owen Nolan .30 .75
58 Chris Pronger .30 .75
59 Keith Tkachuk .30 .75
60 Doug Weight .30 .75
61 Pavol Demitra .40 1.00
62 Brad Richards .30 .75
63 Vincent Lecavalier .30 .75
64 Curtis Joseph .40 1.00
65 Mats Sundin .30 .75
66 Markus Naslund .30 .75
67 Daniel Sedin .40 1.00
68 Jaromir Jagr 1.00 2.50
69 Peter Bondra .30 .75
70 Olaf Kolzig .30 .75
71 Paul Kariya XCT .30 .75
72 Peter Forsberg XCT .60 1.50
73 Mike Modano XCT .50 1.25
74 Sergei Fedorov XCT .50 1.25
75 Steve Yzerman XCT .75 2.00
76 Pavel Bure XCT .30 .75
77 Zigmund Palffy XCT .30 .75
78 Mario Lemieux XCT 1.25 3.00
79 Vincent Lecavalier XCT .30 .75
80 Markus Naslund XCT .30 .75
81 Joe Sakic XT .60 1.50
82 Chris Drury XT .25 .60
83 Patrick Roy XT .75 2.00
84 Mike Modano XT .50 1.25
85 Steve Yzerman XT .75 2.00
86 Pavel Bure XT .30 .75
87 Martin Brodeur XT .75 2.00
88 John LeClair XT .30 .75
89 Mario Lemieux XT 1.25 3.00
90 Chris Pronger XT .30 .75
91 Timo Parssinen RC 1.50 4.00
92 Ilja Bryzgalov RC 3.00 8.00
93 Kevin Sawyer RC 1.25 3.00
94 Dany Heatley SP 1.50 4.00
95 Zdenek Kutlak RC 1.25 3.00
96 Greg Crozier RC 1.25 3.00
97 Mika Noronen SP 1.25 3.00
98 Scott Nichol RC 1.25 3.00
99 Erik Cole RC 2.50 6.00
100 Casey Hankinson RC 1.25 3.00
101 Vaclav Nedorost RC 1.25 3.00
102 Jaroslav Obsut RC 1.25 3.00
103 Niko Kapanen RC 2.00 5.00
104 Pavel Datsyuk RC 30.00 80.00
105 Niklas Hagman RC 1.50 4.00
106 Kristian Huselius RC 2.00 5.00
107 Andrej Podkonicky RC 1.25 3.00
108 Francis Belanger RC 1.50 4.00
109 Martin Erat RC 1.50 4.00
110 Bill Bowler RC 1.25 3.00
111 Scott Clemmensen RC 1.25 3.00
112 Josef Boumedienne RC 1.25 3.00
113 Andreas Salomonsson RC 1.25 3.00
114 Mike Jefferson RC 1.25 3.00
115 Stanislav Gron RC 1.25 3.00
116 Radek Martinek RC 1.25 3.00
117 Dan Blackburn RC 1.50 4.00
118 Chris Neil RC 1.50 4.00
119 Ivan Ciernik RC 1.25 3.00
120 Pavel Brendl SP 1.25 3.00
121 David Cullen RC 1.25 3.00
122 Billy Tibbetts RC 1.25 3.00
123 Miikka Kiprusoff SP 2.00 5.00
124 Jeff Jillson RC 1.25 3.00
125 Michel Larocque RC 1.25 3.00
126 Mark Rycroft RC 1.50 4.00
127 Thomas Ziegler RC 1.50 4.00
128 Nikita Alexeev RC 1.25 3.00
129 Bob Wren RC 1.25 3.00
130 Mike Brown SP 1.50 4.00
131 Pat Kavanagh RC 1.50 4.00
132 Brian Sutherby RC 1.25 3.00
133A Brian Pothier AW/800 RC 1.25 3.00
133H Brian Pothier HM/800 RC 1.25 3.00
134A Dan Snyder AW/1500 RC 1.50 4.00
134H Dan Snyder HM/1500 RC 1.50 4.00
135A Jody Shelley AW/1500 RC 1.50 4.00
135H Jody Shelley HM/1500 RC 1.50 4.00
136A M.Spanhel AW/1500 RC 1.25 3.00
136H M.Spanhel HM/1500 RC 1.25 3.00
137A M.Darche AW/1500 RC 2.00 5.00
137H M.Darche HM/1500 RC 2.00 5.00
138A M.Davidson AW/1500 RC 1.25 3.00
138H M.Davidson HM/1500 RC 1.25 3.00
139A S.Selmser AW/1500 RC 1.25 3.00
139H S.Selmser HM/1500 RC 1.25 3.00
140A Jason Chimera AW/800 RC 1.25 3.00
140H Jason Chimera HM/800 RC 1.25 3.00
141A M.Matteucci AW/1500 RC 1.25 3.00
141H M.Matteucci HM/1500 RC 1.25 3.00
142A Pascal Dupuis AW/800 RC 2.00 5.00
142H Pascal Dupuis HM/800 RC 2.00 5.00
143A Peter Smrek AW/800 RC 1.25 3.00
143H Peter Smrek HM/800 RC 1.25 3.00
144A M.Samuelsson AW/1500 RC 1.50 4.00
144H M.Samuelsson HM/1500 RC 1.50 4.00
145A J.Kwiatkowski AW/1500 RC 1.25 3.00
145H J.Kwiatkowski HM/1500 RC 1.25 3.00
146A Kirby Law AW/1500 RC 1.25 3.00
146H Kirby Law HM/1500 RC 1.25 3.00
147A T.Divisek AW/1500 RC 1.50 4.00
147H T.Divisek HM/1500 RC 1.50 4.00
148A I.Kovalchuk AW/800 RC 10.00 25.00
148H I.Kovalchuk HM/800 RC 10.00 25.00
149A J.Bednar AW/800 RC 1.25 3.00
149H J.Bednar HM/800 RC 1.25 3.00
150A Jiri Dopita AW/800 RC 1.25 3.00
150H Jiri Dopita HM/800 RC 1.25 3.00
151A Krys Kolanos AW/800 RC 1.25 3.00
151H Krys Kolanos HM/800 RC 1.25 3.00
152 Jeff Friesen .20 .50
153 Jean-Sebastien Giguere .30 .75
154 Dany Heatley .25 .60
155 Pascal Rheaume .20 .50
156 Andy Hilbert .20 .50
157 Jozef Stumpel .20 .50
158 Glen Murray .25 .60
159 Maxim Afinogenov .20 .50
160 Roman Turek .25 .60
161 Craig Conroy .20 .50
162 Jeff O'Neill .25 .60
163 Sami Kapanen .20 .50
164 Jocelyn Thibault .25 .60
165 Mark Bell .20 .50
166 Kyle Calder .20 .50
167 Alex Tanguay .25 .60
168 Darius Kasparaitis .20 .50
169 Chris Drury .25 .60
170 Radim Vrbata .20 .50
171 Rostislav Klesla .20 .50
172 Brett Hull .60 1.50
173 Jani Rita .20 .50
174 Mike York .20 .50
175 Roberto Luongo .50 1.25
176 Jason Allison .25 .60
177 Andrew Brunette .20 .50
178 Sergei Berezin .20 .50
179 Donald Audette .20 .50
180 Brian Gionta .25 .60
181 Alexei Yashin .25 .60
182 Chris Osgood .30 .75
183 Pavel Bure .30 .75
184 Tom Poti .20 .50
185 Eric Lindros .50 1.25
186 Patrick Lalime .25 .60
187 Martin Havlat .25 .60
188 Brian Boucher .25 .60
189 Simon Gagne .30 .75
190 Brian Savage .20 .50
191 Brent Johnson .25 .60
192 Gordie Dwyer .20 .50
193 Nikolai Khabibulin .30 .75
194 Alexander Mogilny .25 .60
195 Brendan Morrison .25 .60
196 Trevor Linden .30 .75
197 Pasi Nurminen RC 1.25 3.00
198 Ivan Huml RC 1.25 3.00
199 Ales Kotalik RC 2.50 6.00
200 Mike Peluso RC 1.25 3.00
201 Riku Hahl RC 1.25 3.00
202 Kelly Fairchild RC 1.25 3.00
203 Blake Bellefeuille RC 1.25 3.00
204 Sean Avery RC 1.25 3.00
205 Brad Norton RC 1.25 3.00
206 Marcel Hossa RC 2.00 5.00
207 Olivier Michaud RC 2.00 5.00
208 Robert Schnabel RC 1.25 3.00
209 Christian Berglund RC 1.50 4.00
210 Raffi Torres RC 2.00 5.00
211 Toni Dahlman RC 1.25 3.00
212 Branko Radivojevic RC 1.25 3.00
213 Shane Endicott RC 1.25 3.00
214 Tom Kostopoulos RC 1.25 3.00
215 Sebastien Centomo RC 1.25 3.00
216 Karel Pilar RC 1.25 3.00
19 Steve Yzerman SAMPLE 2.00 5.00

2001-02 SPx Hidden Treasures

DTAD M.Afinogenov/J.Dumont 8.00 20.00
DTBJ P.Bondra/J.Jagr 10.00 25.00
DTBN R.Blake/V.Nieminen 8.00 20.00
DTFC R.Fedotenko/T.Connolly 8.00 20.00
DTGW S.Gagne/J.Williams 8.00 20.00
DTHB M.Hejduk/R.Blake 8.00 20.00
DTJD J.Allison/A.Deadmarsh 8.00 20.00
DTPS Z.Palffy/M.Satan 8.00 20.00
DTSF M.Sundin/P.Forsberg 10.00 25.00
DTSG S.Sullivan/S.Gagne 8.00 20.00
DTTD T.Amonte/C.Drury 8.00 20.00
DTTP J.Thibault/F.Potvin 10.00 25.00
DTTT J.Thibault/J.Theodore 8.00 20.00
DTYL M.York/B.Leetch 8.00 20.00
TTBSS Bondra/Selanne/Sundin 12.50 30.00
TTBTT Brodeur/Thibault/Theodore 15.00 40.00
TTDBA Dumont/Biron/Afinogenov 12.50 30.00
TTDSA Daze/Sullivan/Amonte 12.50 30.00
TTFSD Forsbrg/Shan./Deadmrsh 15.00 40.00
TTKBL Klesla/Blake/Lidstrom 12.50 30.00
TTTHN Tanguay/Hinote/Nieminen 12.50 30.00
TTYLS Yzerman/Lemieux/Sakic 100.00 200.00

2001-02 SPx Hockey Treasures

HTBH Brett Hull 6.00 15.00
HTCJ Curtis Joseph 5.00 12.00
HTDH Dominik Hasek 8.00 20.00
HTHU Brett Hull 6.00 15.00
HTJI Jarome Iginla 6.00 15.00
HTJL John LeClair 5.00 12.00
HTJN Joe Nieuwendyk 6.00 15.00
HTKP Keith Primeau 5.00 12.00
HTLE John LeClair 5.00 12.00
HTMB Martin Brodeur 10.00 25.00
HTML Mario Lemieux 15.00 40.00
HTMM Mike Modano 8.00 20.00
HTMO Mike Modano 6.00 15.00
HTPR Patrick Roy 12.50 30.00
HTRC Roman Cechmanek 5.00 12.00
HTSF Sergei Fedorov 6.00 15.00
HTSS Sergei Samsonov 5.00 12.00
HTSY Steve Yzerman 12.50 30.00
HTTS Teemu Selanne 5.00 12.00

2001-02 SPx Hockey Treasures Autographs

STBO Ray Bourque 75.00 200.00
STCJ Curtis Joseph 25.00 60.00
STJI Jarome Iginla 30.00 80.00
STJL John LeClair 15.00 40.00
STKE Keith Primeau 25.00 60.00
STKP Keith Primeau 25.00 60.00
STLE John LeClair 15.00 40.00
STRB Ray Bourque 75.00 150.00
STSY Steve Yzerman 75.00 200.00
STTU Marty Turco 30.00 80.00

2001-02 SPx Rookie Redemption

R1 Stanislav Chistov 2.00 5.00
R2 Mark Hartigan 2.00 5.00
R3 Tim Thomas 8.00 20.00
R4 Henrik Tallinder 2.00 5.00
R5 Chuck Kobasew 4.00 10.00
R6 Jaroslav Svoboda 2.00 5.00
R7 Shawn Thornton 4.00 10.00
R8 Jeff Paul 2.00 5.00
R9 Rick Nash 10.00 25.00
R10 John Erskine 2.00 5.00
R11 Henrik Zetterberg 12.50 30.00
R12 Ales Hemsky 6.00 15.00
R13 Jay Bouwmeester 4.00 10.00
R14 Alexander Frolov 5.00 12.00
R15 Pierre-Marc Bouchard 4.00 10.00
R16 Ron Hainsey 2.00 5.00
R17 Scottie Upshall 5.00 12.00
R18 Steve Ott 4.00 10.00
R19 Eric Godard 2.00 5.00
R20 Jamie Lundmark 2.00 5.00
R21 Jason Spezza 8.00 20.00
R22 Radovan Somik 2.00 5.00
R23 Jeff Taffe 2.00 5.00
R24 Shane Endicott 2.00 5.00
R25 Lynn Loyns 2.00 5.00
R26 Curtis Sanford 2.00 5.00
R27 Alexander Svitov 2.00 5.00
R28 Carlo Colaiacovo 2.00 5.00
R29 Fedor Fedorov 2.00 5.00
R30 Steve Eminger 2.00 5.00

2001-02 SPx Rookie Treasures

RTBP Brian Pothier 3.00 8.00
RTDA Mathieu Darche 3.00 8.00
RTDS Dan Snyder 6.00 15.00
RTIK Ilya Kovalchuk 12.00 30.00
RTJB Jaroslav Bednar 3.00 8.00
RTJC Jason Chimera 3.00 8.00
RTJD Jiri Dopita 3.00 8.00
RTJK Joel Kwiatkowski 3.00 8.00
RTJS Jody Shelley 6.00 15.00
RTKK Krys Kolanos 3.00 8.00
RTKL Kirby Law 3.00 8.00
RTMD Matt Davidson 3.00 8.00
RTMM Mike Matteucci 3.00 8.00
RTMS Martin Spanhel 3.00 8.00
RTMS Mikael Samuelsson 3.00 8.00
RTPD Pascal Dupuis 4.00 10.00
RTPS Peter Smrek 3.00 8.00
RTRT Raffi Torres 4.00 10.00
RTSS Sean Selmser 3.00 8.00
RTTD Tomas Divisek 3.00 8.00

2001-02 SPx Signs of Xcellence

BO Bobby Orr 150.00 250.00
DW Doug Weight 10.00 25.00
GH Gordie Howe 100.00 200.00
JL John LeClair 10.00 25.00
MC Mike Comrie 5.00 12.00
MM Mark Messier 40.00 100.00
SG Simon Gagne 10.00 25.00
TL Trevor Letowski 5.00 12.00
WG Wayne Gretzky 200.00 500.00

2001-02 SPx Yzerman Tribute

COMMON AUTO/19 175.00 300.00
COMMON DBL.MEM. (20-24) 15.00 40.00
COMMON SINGLE MEM. (25-26) 10.00 25.00

2002-03 SPx

COMP.SET w/o SP's (100) 20.00 50.00
1 Paul Kariya .30 .75
2 Jean-Sebastien Giguere .30 .75
3 Ilya Kovalchuk .40 1.00
4 Dany Heatley .25 .60
5 Joe Thornton .50 1.25
6 Sergei Samsonov .25 .60
7 Miroslav Satan .30 .75
8 Martin Biron .25 .60
9 Roman Turek .30 .75
10 Jarome Iginla .40 1.00
11 Jeff O'Neill .20 .50
12 Ron Francis .40 1.00
13 Arturs Irbe .25 .60
14 Eric Daze .20 .50
15 Jocelyn Thibault .25 .60
16 Patrick Roy .75 2.00
17 Chris Drury .30 .75
18 Joe Sakic .60 1.50
19 Peter Forsberg .60 1.50
20 Rob Blake .30 .75
21 Rostislav Klesla .20 .50
22 Marc Denis .25 .60
23 Mike Modano .50 1.25
24 Marty Turco .30 .75
25 Bill Guerin .30 .75
26 Steve Yzerman .75 2.00
27 Sergei Fedorov .50 1.25
28 Nicklas Lidstrom .30 .75
29 Brett Hull .60 1.50
30 Curtis Joseph .40 1.00
31 Brendan Shanahan .30 .75
32 Mike Comrie .30 .75
33 Tommy Salo .25 .60
34 Roberto Luongo .50 1.25
35 Kristian Huselius .20 .50
36 Felix Potvin .50 1.25
37 Zigmund Palffy .30 .75
38 Marian Gaborik .30 .75
39 Manny Fernandez .20 .50
40 Jose Theodore .30 .75
41 Saku Koivu .30 .75
42 Patrik Elias .30 .75
43 Martin Brodeur .75 2.00
44 Scott Hartnell .20 .50
45 Mike Dunham .25 .60
46 Alexei Yashin .25 .60
47 Chris Osgood .30 .75
48 Michael Peca .25 .60
49 Eric Lindros .50 1.25
50 Mike Richter .30 .75
51 Pavel Bure .30 .75
52 Patrick Lalime .25 .60
53 Marian Hossa .30 .75
54 Daniel Alfredsson .30 .75
55 Jeremy Roenick .50 1.25
56 Simon Gagne .30 .75
57 Roman Cechmanek .25 .60
58 Sean Burke .20 .50
59 Tony Amonte .25 .60
60 Alexei Kovalev .25 .60
61 Mario Lemieux 1.25 3.00
62 Owen Nolan .30 .75
63 Evgeni Nabokov .25 .60
64 Keith Tkachuk .30 .75
65 Chris Pronger .30 .75
66 Brent Johnson .25 .60
67 Nikolai Khabibulin .30 .75
68 Vincent Lecavalier .30 .75
69 Alexander Mogilny .25 .60
70 Mats Sundin .30 .75
71 Ed Belfour .30 .75
72 Todd Bertuzzi .30 .75
73 Markus Naslund .30 .75
74 Olaf Kolzig .30 .75
75 Jaromir Jagr 1.00 2.50
76 Paul Kariya .30 .75
77 Adam Oates .30 .75
78 Sergei Samsonov .25 .60
79 Bobby Orr 1.25 3.00
80 Joe Thornton .50 1.25
81 Jeff O'Neill .20 .50
82 Ron Francis .40 1.00
83 Joe Sakic .60 1.50
84 Patrick Roy .75 2.00
85 Peter Forsberg .60 1.50
86 Bill Guerin .30 .75
87 Mike Modano .50 1.25
88 Curtis Joseph .40 1.00
89 Gordie Howe 1.00 2.50
90 Steve Yzerman .75 2.00
91 Mike Comrie .30 .75
92 Jose Theodore .30 .75
93 Martin Brodeur .75 2.00
94 Pavel Bure .30 .75
95 Wayne Gretzky 2.00 5.00
96 John LeClair .30 .75
97 Mario Lemieux 1.25 3.00
98 Evgeni Nabokov .25 .60
99 Mats Sundin .30 .75
100 Jaromir Jagr 1.00 2.50
101 Pasi Nurminen SPR 1.50 4.00
102 Mark Hartigan SPR 1.50 4.00
103 Andy Hilbert SPR 1.50 4.00
104 Henrik Tallinder SPR 1.50 4.00
105 Jaroslav Svoboda SPR 1.50 4.00
106 Riku Hahl SPR 1.50 4.00
107 Jordan Krestanovich SPR 1.50 4.00
108 Andrej Nedorost SPR 1.50 4.00
109 Sean Avery SPR 2.00 5.00
110 Jani Rita SPR 1.50 4.00
111 Stephen Weiss SPR 2.50 6.00
112 Lukas Krajicek SPR 2.00 5.00
113 Tony Virta SPR 1.50 4.00
114 Marcel Hossa SPR 1.50 4.00
115 Jan Lasak SPR 2.00 5.00
116 Jonas Andersson SPR 2.00 5.00
117 Trent Hunter SPR 1.50 4.00
118 Martin Prusek SPR 1.50 4.00
119 Bruno St. Jacques SPR 1.50 4.00
120 Branko Radivojevic SPR 1.50 4.00
121 Shane Endicott SPR 1.50 4.00
122 Justin Papineau SPR 1.50 4.00
123 Sebastien Centomo SPR 1.50 4.00
124 Karel Pilar SPR 1.50 4.00
125 Sebastien Charpentier SPR 1.50 4.00
126 Mark Messier CA/1804 3.00 8.00
127 Ron Francis CA/1701 2.00 5.00
128 Steve Yzerman CA/1662 4.00 10.00
129 Mario Lemieux CA/1601 6.00 15.00
130 Luc Robitaille CA/1288 1.50 4.00
131 Joe Sakic CA/1257 3.00 8.00
132 Brett Hull CA/1246 3.00 8.00
133 Al MacInnis CA/1204 2.00 5.00
134 Pierre Turgeon CA/1192 1.25 3.00
135 Jaromir Jagr CA/1158 5.00 12.00
136 Mark Recchi CA/1074 2.00 5.00
137 Brendan Shanahan CA/1030 1.50 4.00
138 Jeremy Roenick CA/1014 2.50 6.00
139 Mike Modano CA/977 2.50 6.00
140 Mats Sundin CA/942 1.50 4.00
141 Sergei Fedorov CA/871 2.50 6.00
142 Teemu Selanne CA/855 3.00 8.00
143 Pavel Bure CA/749 1.50 4.00
144 Peter Bondra CA/734 1.50 4.00
145 Eric Lindros CA/732 2.50 6.00
146 A.Smirnov JSY AU/1250 RC 6.00 15.00
147 K.Sauer JSY AU/1250 RC 5.00 12.00
148 C.Kobasew JSY AU/1250 RC 6.00 15.00
149 R.Nash JSY AU/500 RC 20.00 50.00
150 J.Bouwmster JSY AU/500 RC 5.00 12.00
151 H.Zetterberg JSY AU/1250 RC 20.00 50.00
152 P.Bouchard JSY AU/1250 RC 8.00 20.00
153 R.Hainsey JSY AU/1250 RC 5.00 12.00
154 A.Hall JSY AU/1250 RC 5.00 12.00
155 S.Upshall JSY AU/1250 RC 6.00 15.00
156 S.Chistov JSY AU/500 RC 5.00 12.00
157 J.Taffe JSY AU/1250 RC 5.00 12.00
158 M.Tellqvist JSY AU/1250 RC 5.00 12.00
159 A.Svitov JSY AU/1250 RC 5.00 12.00
160 Ales Hemsky JSY RC 8.00 20.00
161 Alexander Frolov JSY RC 8.00 20.00
162 Steve Eminger JSY RC 3.00 8.00
163 Anton Volchenkov JSY RC 3.00 8.00
164 Sylvain Blouin JSY RC 3.00 8.00
165 Greg Koehler JSY RC 3.00 8.00
166 Martin Gerber JSY RC 5.00 12.00
167 Micki Dupont JSY RC 3.00 8.00
168 Jordan Leopold JSY RC 5.00 12.00
169 Tomi Pettinen JSY RC 3.00 8.00
170 Lynn Loyns JSY RC 3.00 8.00
171 Matt Henderson JSY RC 3.00 8.00
172 Radovan Somik JSY RC 3.00 8.00
173 Patrick Sharp JSY RC 10.00 25.00
174 Jeff Paul JSY RC 3.00 8.00
175 J.Spezza JSY AU/500 RC 25.00 60.00
176 Pascal LeClaire RC 1.50 4.00
177 Steve Ott RC 1.25 3.00
178 Brooks Orpik RC 1.25 3.00
179 Jared Aulin RC 1.25 3.00
180 Brandon Reid RC 1.25 3.00
181 Ray Emery RC 4.00 10.00
182 Ari Ahonen RC 1.25 3.00
183 Niko Dimitrakos RC 1.25 3.00
184 Jarret Stoll RC 5.00 12.00
185 Cristobal Huet RC 2.50 6.00
186 Mike Komisarek RC 2.00 5.00
187 Ryan Miller RC 8.00 20.00
188 Jason Bacashihua RC 1.50 4.00
189 Carlo Colaiacovo RC 2.00 5.00
190 Mike Cammalleri RC 4.00 10.00
191 Fernando Pisani RC 1.25 3.00
192 Alexei Semenov RC 1.25 3.00
193 Konstantin Koltsov RC 1.50 4.00

2002-03 SPx Spectrum Silver

*1-100 VETS/199: 2X TO 5X BASIC CARDS

2002-03 SPx Milestones

MBL Brian Leetch 5.00 12.00
MBO Peter Bondra 5.00 12.00
MBS Brendan Shanahan 5.00 12.00
MJR Jeremy Roenick 8.00 20.00
MJS Joe Sakic 10.00 25.00
MMB Martin Brodeur 12.50 30.00
MML Mario Lemieux 12.50 30.00
MMM Mike Modano 8.00 20.00
MMR Mark Recchi 5.00 12.00
MPB Pavel Bure 5.00 12.00
MPR Patrick Roy 12.50 30.00
MSF Sergei Fedorov 8.00 20.00
MSH Brendan Shanahan 5.00 12.00
MSY Steve Yzerman 12.50 30.00
MTS Teemu Selanne 6.00 15.00

2002-03 SPx Milestones Silver

*STARS: .75X TO 2X BASIC CARDS

2002-03 SPx Rookie Redemption

R194 Matthew Lombardi 3.00 8.00
R195 Pavel Vorobiev 3.00 8.00
R196 Marek Svatos 4.00 10.00
R197 Cody McCormick 3.00 8.00
R198 John-Michael Liles 3.00 8.00
R199 Antti Miettinen 3.00 8.00
R200 Brent Burns 3.00 8.00
R201 Christoph Brandner 3.00 8.00
R202 Chris Higgins 4.00 10.00
R203 Dan Hamhuis 3.00 8.00
R204 Marek Zidlicky 3.00 8.00
R205 Paul Martin 3.00 8.00
R206 Sean Bergenheim 3.00 8.00
R207 Antoine Vermette 4.00 10.00
R208 Matthew Spiller 3.00 8.00
R209 Christian Ehrhoff 3.00 8.00
R210 Peter Sejna 3.00 8.00
R211 Maxim Kondratiev 3.00 8.00
R212 Matt Stajan 4.00 10.00
R213 Boyd Gordon 3.00 8.00
R214 Joffrey Lupul 5.00 12.00
R215 Patrice Bergeron 10.00 25.00
R216 Eric Staal 12.00 30.00
R217 Tuomo Ruutu 5.00 12.00
R218 Nathan Horton 6.00 15.00
R219 Dustin Brown 10.00 20.00
R220 Jordin Tootoo 5.00 12.00
R221 Joni Pitkanen 4.00 10.00
R222 Marc-Andre Fleury 20.00 50.00
R223 Milan Michalek 6.00 15.00

2002-03 SPx Smooth Skaters

ED Eric Daze 5.00 12.00
JI Jarome Iginla 8.00 20.00
JJ Jaromir Jagr 8.00 20.00
JS Joe Sakic 10.00 25.00
JT Joe Thornton 10.00 25.00
ML Mario Lemieux 15.00 40.00
MM Mike Modano 8.00 20.00
MN Markus Naslund 5.00 12.00
MS Mats Sundin 5.00 12.00
PB Peter Bondra 5.00 12.00
PK Paul Kariya 5.00 12.00
SA Miroslav Satan 5.00 12.00
SG Simon Gagne 6.00 15.00
SS Sergei Samsonov 5.00 12.00
SU Steve Sullivan 5.00 12.00
SY Steve Yzerman 12.50 30.00
WG Wayne Gretzky 20.00 50.00

2002-03 SPx Smooth Skaters Silver

*STARS: .75X TO 2 X BASIC CARDS

2002-03 SPx Winning Materials

WMAY Alexei Yashin 5.00 12.00
WMBI Martin Biron 6.00 15.00
WMBL Brian Leetch 6.00 15.00
WMBO Ray Bourque COL 15.00 40.00
WMCJ Curtis Joseph 6.00 15.00
WMDH Dominik Hasek 20.00 50.00
WMDL David Legwand 6.00 15.00
WMDU J-P Dumont 5.00 12.00
WMEL Eric Lindros 6.00 15.00
WMFP Felix Potvin 8.00 20.00
WMIK Ilya Kovalchuk 15.00 40.00
WMJA Jaromir Jagr JSY/JSY 10.00 25.00
WMJG Jean-Sebastien Giguere 5.00 12.00
WMJJ Jaromir Jagr JSY/STK 10.00 25.00
WMJR Jeremy Roenick 12.50 30.00
WMJT Joe Thornton 10.00 25.00
WMKA Paul Kariya JSY/JSY 6.00 15.00
WMKO Olaf Kolzig 6.00 15.00
WMLE John LeClair 6.00 15.00
WMMB Martin Brodeur 20.00 50.00
WMML Mario Lemieux 25.00 60.00
WMMM Mike Modano 10.00 25.00
WMMN Markus Naslund 6.00 15.00
WMPA Zigmund Palffy 6.00 15.00
WMPB Pavel Bure 6.00 15.00
WMPF Peter Forsberg 15.00 40.00
WMPK Paul Kariya JSY/STK 6.00 15.00
WMPR Keith Primeau 5.00 12.00
WMRB Ray Bourque BOS 15.00 40.00
WMRO Patrick Roy 20.00 50.00
WMSG Simon Gagne 8.00 20.00
WMSS Sergei Samsonov 6.00 15.00
WMSY Steve Yzerman 20.00 50.00
WMTH Jose Theodore 8.00 20.00
WMZP Zigmund Palffy 6.00 15.00

2002-03 SPx Winning Materials Silver

*STARS: .75X TO 2X BASIC CARDS

2002-03 SPx Xtreme Talents Silver

*STARS: .75X TO 2X BASIC CARDS

2003-04 SPx

COMP.SET w/o SP's (100) 25.00 50.00
1 Jean-Sebastien Giguere .30 .75
2 Stanislav Chistov .20 .50

3 Sergei Fedorov .50 1.25
4 Dany Heatley .25 .60
5 Ilya Kovalchuk .30 .75
6 Joe Thornton .50 1.25
7 Sergei Samsonov .25 .60
8 Glen Murray .25 .60
9 Felix Potvin .50 1.25
10 Miroslav Satan .25 .60
11 Maxim Afinogenov .20 .50
12 Chris Drury .25 .60
13 Jarome Iginla .40 1.00
14 Roman Turek .25 .60
15 Steve Reinprecht .20 .50
16 Ron Francis .40 1.00
17 Jeff O'Neill .20 .50
18 Alexei Zhamnov .25 .60
19 Jocelyn Thibault .25 .60
20 Kyle Calder .20 .50
21 Joe Sakic .60 1.50
22 Teemu Selanne .60 1.50
23 Peter Forsberg .60 1.50
24 David Aebischer .25 .60
25 Paul Kariya .30 .75
26 Marc Denis .25 .60
27 Rick Nash .30 .75
28 Todd Marchant .20 .50
29 Bill Guerin .30 .75
30 Marty Turco .30 .75
31 Mike Modano .50 1.25
32 Henrik Zetterberg .40 1.00
33 Brendan Shanahan .30 .75
34 Steve Yzerman .75 2.00
35 Dominik Hasek .50 1.25
36 Ryan Smyth .25 .60
37 Ales Hemsky .30 .75
38 Tommy Salo .25 .60
39 Mike Comrie .25 .60
40 Stephen Weiss .20 .50
41 Roberto Luongo .50 1.25
42 Jay Bouwmeester .20 .50
43 Olli Jokinen .30 .75
44 Zigmund Palffy .30 .75
45 Alexander Frolov .25 .60
46 Roman Cechmanek .25 .60
47 Marian Gaborik .30 .75
48 Manny Fernandez .20 .50
49 Pierre-Marc Bouchard .30 .75
50 Jose Theodore .30 .75
51 Saku Koivu .30 .75
52 Mike Komisarek .20 .50
53 Marcel Hossa .20 .50
54 Tomas Vokoun .20 .50
55 David Legwand .25 .60
56 Scott Stevens .30 .75
57 Martin Brodeur .75 2.00
58 Patrik Elias .30 .75
59 Jamie Langenbrunner .25 .60
60 Alexei Yashin .25 .60
61 Rick DiPietro .25 .60
62 Michael Peca .25 .60
63 Mike Dunham .25 .60
64 Eric Lindros .50 1.25
65 Alex Kovalev .25 .60
66 Patrick Lalime .25 .60
67 Marian Hossa .30 .75
68 Daniel Alfredsson .30 .75
69 Jason Spezza .30 .75
70 John LeClair .30 .75
71 Tony Amonte .25 .60
72 Simon Gagne .30 .75
73 Jeremy Roenick .50 1.25
74 Chris Gratton .20 .50
75 Sean Burke .20 .50
76 Mike Johnson .20 .50
77 Martin Straka .20 .50
78 Mario Lemieux 1.25 3.00
79 Sebastien Caron .25 .60
80 Niko Dimitrakos .20 .50
81 Evgeni Nabokov .25 .60
82 Mike Ricci .20 .50
83 Chris Osgood .30 .75
84 Al MacInnis .40 1.00
85 Keith Tkachuk .30 .75
86 Chris Pronger .30 .75
87 Nikolai Khabibulin .30 .75
88 Martin St. Louis .30 .75
89 Vincent Lecavalier .30 .75
90 Owen Nolan .30 .75
91 Alexander Mogilny .25 .60
92 Ed Belfour .30 .75
93 Mats Sundin .30 .75
94 Markus Naslund .30 .75
95 Johan Hedberg .25 .60
96 Todd Bertuzzi .30 .75
97 Ed Jovanovski .25 .60
98 Jaromir Jagr 1.00 2.50
99 Olaf Kolzig .30 .75
100 Peter Bondra .30 .75
101 Wayne Gretzky LI 15.00 40.00
102 Gordie Howe LI 8.00 20.00
103 Bobby Orr LI 10.00 25.00
104 Bobby Clarke LI 4.00 10.00
105 Scotty Bowman LI 2.50 6.00
106 Lanny McDonald LI 2.00 5.00
107 Stan Mikita LI 3.00 8.00
108 Ted Lindsay LI 2.50 6.00
109 Marcel Dionne LI 3.00 8.00
110 Johnny Bucyk LI 2.50 6.00
111 Jean Beliveau LI 3.00 8.00
112 Mike Bossy LI 2.50 6.00
113 Guy Lafleur LI 3.00 8.00
114 Mario Lemieux LI 10.00 25.00
115 Mark Messier LI 5.00 12.00
116 Patrick Roy LI 6.00 15.00
117 Martin Brodeur LI 6.00 15.00
118 Jarome Iginla LI 3.00 8.00
119 Mike Modano LI 4.00 10.00
120 Steve Yzerman LI 6.00 15.00
121 Peter Forsberg LI 4.00 10.00
122 Marian Gaborik LI 2.50 6.00
123 Scott Stevens LI 2.50 6.00
124 Paul Kariya LI 2.50 6.00
125 Tie Domi LI 2.00 5.00
126 Joe Sakic LI 5.00 12.00
127 Brendan Shanahan LI 2.50 6.00
128 Jeremy Roenick LI 4.00 10.00
129 Joe Thornton LI 4.00 10.00
130 Mats Sundin LI 2.50 6.00
131 Jean-Sebastien Giguere Xcite 2.50 6.00
132 Marian Gaborik Xcite 2.50 6.00
133 Joe Thornton Xcite 4.00 10.00
134 Saku Koivu Xcite 2.50 6.00
135 Dany Heatley Xcite 2.00 5.00
136 Vincent Lecavalier Xcite 2.50 6.00
137 Todd Bertuzzi Xcite 2.50 6.00
138 Sergei Fedorov Xcite 4.00 10.00
139 Marty Turco Xcite 2.50 6.00
140 Paul Kariya Xcite 2.50 6.00
141 Marian Hossa Xcite 2.50 6.00
142 Alexei Yashin Xcite 2.00 5.00
143 Zigmund Palffy Xcite 2.50 6.00
144 Mario Lemieux Xcite 10.00 25.00
145 Ilya Kovalchuk Xcite 2.50 6.00
146 Henrik Zetterberg Xcite 3.00 8.00
147 Mike Modano Xcite 4.00 10.00
148 Tony Amonte Xcite 2.00 5.00
149 Jason Spezza Xcite 2.50 6.00
150 Owen Nolan Xcite 2.50 6.00
151 Ales Hemsky Xcite 2.50 6.00
152 Markus Naslund Xcite 2.50 6.00
153 Teemu Selanne Xcite 5.00 12.00
154 Sergei Samsonov Xcite 2.00 5.00
155 Martin Brodeur Xcite 6.00 15.00
156 Dany Heatley NG 2.50 6.00
157 Marian Hossa NG 3.00 8.00
158 Jean-Sebastien Giguere NG 3.00 8.00
159 Joe Thornton NG 5.00 12.00
160 Henrik Zetterberg NG 4.00 10.00
161 Rick Nash NG 3.00 8.00
162 Jay Bouwmeester NG 2.00 5.00
163 Jason Spezza NG 3.00 8.00
164 Pavel Datsyuk NG 5.00 12.00
165 Mike Komisarek NG 2.00 5.00
166 Ales Hemsky NG 3.00 8.00
167 Marian Gaborik NG 3.00 8.00
168 Alexander Frolov NG 2.50 6.00
169 Steve Ott NG 2.00 5.00
170 Justin Williams NG 2.50 6.00
171 Pierre-Marc Bouchard NG 3.00 8.00
172 Ryan Miller NG 3.00 8.00
173 Ilya Kovalchuk NG 3.00 8.00
174 Kyle Calder NG 2.00 5.00
175 David Aebischer NG 2.50 6.00
176 Mario Lemieux PRO 20.00 50.00
177 Joe Thornton PRO 8.00 20.00
178 Martin Brodeur PRO 12.00 30.00
179 Steve Yzerman PRO 12.00 30.00
180 Joe Sakic PRO 10.00 25.00
181 Mats Sundin PRO 5.00 12.00
182 Saku Koivu PRO 5.00 12.00
183 Sergei Fedorov PRO 8.00 20.00
184 Jeremy Roenick PRO 8.00 20.00
185 Roberto Luongo PRO 8.00 20.00
186 Mike Modano PRO 8.00 20.00
187 Todd Bertuzzi PRO 5.00 12.00
188 Zigmund Palffy PRO 5.00 12.00
189 Jean-Sebastien Giguere PRO 5.00 12.00
190 Markus Naslund PRO 5.00 12.00
191 Dan Fritsche JSY RC 3.00 8.00
192 Tim Gleason JSY RC 4.00 10.00
193 Lasse Kukkonen JSY RC 2.50 6.00
194 John-Michael Liles JSY RC 4.00 10.00
195 Paul Martin JSY RC 4.00 10.00
196 Esa Pirnes JSY RC 3.00 8.00
197 Tom Preissing JSY RC 3.00 8.00
198 David Hale JSY RC 3.00 8.00
199 Marek Svatos JSY RC 6.00 15.00
200 Boyd Kane JSY RC 3.00 8.00
201 Matthew Lombardi JSY RC 4.00 10.00
202 Marek Zidlicky JSY RC 3.00 8.00
203 Matthew Spiller JSY RC 4.00 10.00
204 Andrew Peters JSY RC 4.00 10.00
205 Greg Campbell JSY RC 3.00 8.00
206 Sean Bergenheim JSY RC 4.00 10.00
207 Boyd Gordon JSY RC 4.00 10.00
208 P.Sejna JSY AU/925 RC 3.00 8.00
209 M.Stajan JSY AU/925 RC 6.00 15.00
210 M.Michalek JSY AU/925 RC 8.00 20.00
211 P.Vorobiev JSY AU/925 RC 6.00 15.00
212 D.Hamhuis JSY AU/925 RC 5.00 12.00
213 C.Higgins JSY AU/925 RC 8.00 20.00
214 A.Miettinen JSY AU/925 RC 6.00 15.00
215 C.Ehrhoff JSY AU/925 RC 5.00 12.00
216 A.Semin JSY AU/925 RC 10.00 25.00
217 A.Vermette JSY AU/925 RC 8.00 20.00
218 T.Moen JSY AU/925 RC 6.00 15.00
219 J.Pitkanen JSY AU/925 RC 6.00 15.00
220 P.Bergeron JSY AU/925 RC 150.00 400.00
221 J.Hudler JSY AU/925 RC 12.00 30.00
222 M.Fleury JSY AU/500 RC 80.00 200.00
223 D.Brown JSY AU/500 RC 12.00 30.00
224 J.Lupul JSY AU/925 RC 10.00 25.00
225 T.Ruutu JSY AU/500 RC 8.00 20.00
226 J.Tootoo JSY AU/500 RC 10.00 25.00
227 E.Staal JSY AU/500 RC 15.00 40.00
228 N.Horton JSY AU/500 RC 12.00 30.00
229 T.Salmalainen JSY AU/925 RC 4.00 10.00
230 John Pohl JSY RC 3.00 8.00
231 Sergei Zinovjev JSY RC 3.00 8.00
232 Ryan Kesler JSY RC 8.00 20.00
233 Dominic Moore JSY RC 3.00 8.00
234 Peter Sarno JSY RC 3.00 8.00
235 Ryan Malone JSY RC 6.00 15.00
236 Nikolai Zherdev JSY RC 6.00 15.00
237 Fredrik Sjostrom JSY RC 4.00 10.00
238 Derek Roy JSY RC 5.00 12.00
239 Mikko Luoma JSY RC 3.00 8.00
240 Trevor Daley JSY RC 5.00 12.00

2003-04 SPx Radiance

*1-100 VETS/50: 8X TO 20X BASIC CARDS
*101-155 LI/XCI/50: 1X TO 2.5X LI/XCI/750
*156-175 NG/50.: 8X TO 2X NG/500
*176-190 PRO/50: .5X TO 1.2X PO/250
*191-207 ROOK.JSY/50: .5X TO 1.2X JSY/999
*ROOK.JSY/AU/50: .6X TO 1.5X JSY AU/925
*ROOK.JSY/AU/50: .5X TO 1.2X JSY AU/500
115 Mark Messier LI 12.00 30.00
220 Patrice Bergeron 250.00 600.00
222 Marc-Andre Fleury 100.00 250.00
227 Eric Staal 40.00 80.00
228 Nathan Horton 30.00 60.00

2003-04 SPx Big Futures

*LIMITED: .75X TO 2X
BFAA Ari Ahonen 6.00 15.00
BFAF Alexander Frolov 6.00 15.00
BFAH Ales Hemsky 10.00 25.00
BFAK Ales Kotalik 6.00 15.00
BFAS Alexander Svitov 6.00 15.00
BFBJ Barret Jackman 6.00 15.00
BFBO Brooks Orpik 6.00 15.00
BFCN Sebastien Caron 6.00 15.00
BFDB Dan Blackburn 6.00 15.00
BFDH Dany Heatley 10.00 25.00
BFHZ Henrik Zetterberg 12.50 30.00
BFIK Ilya Kovalchuk 12.50 30.00
BFIR Igor Radulov 6.00 15.00
BFJB Jay Bouwmeester 6.00 15.00
BFJB Jason Bacashihua 6.00 15.00
BFJL Jordan Leopold 6.00 15.00
BFJS Jason Spezza 12.50 30.00
BFJT Joe Thornton 15.00 40.00
BFMC Mike Cammalleri 8.00 20.00
BFMD Marc Denis 6.00 15.00
BFMG Mathieu Garon 6.00 15.00
BFMH Marcel Hossa 6.00 15.00
BFMP Mark Parrish 6.00 15.00
BFMT Marty Turco 8.00 20.00
BFOJ Olli Jokinen 6.00 15.00
BFPD Pavel Datsyuk 10.00 25.00
BFPL Pascal Leclaire 6.00 15.00
BFPMB Pierre-Marc Bouchard 6.00 15.00
BFRE Robert Esche 8.00 20.00
BFRN Rick Nash 12.50 30.00
BFSC Stanislav Chistov 6.00 15.00
BFSG Simon Gagne 10.00 25.00
BFSO Steve Ott 8.00 20.00
BFSW Stephen Weiss 8.00 20.00

2003-04 SPx Fantasy Franchise

*LIMITED/25: .5X TO 1.2X BASIC INSERTS
FFBLK Bure/Lindrs/Kova 10.00 25.00
FFDSA Drury/Satan/Afing 12.00 30.00
FFEHJ Elias/Hossa/Jagr 12.00 30.00
FFGC Fedrv/Gigre/Chstv 10.00 25.00
FFGRB Giguere/Roy/Brodr 30.00 80.00
FFHSL Hossa/Spez/Lalime 12.00 30.00
FFHYS Hull/Yzerman/Shan 25.00 60.00
FFHYZ Howe/Yzerman/Zett 40.00 100.00
FFKFB Koval/Fedorov/Bure 8.00 20.00
FFKSF Kariya/Selanne/Fors 25.00 60.00
FFKTH Kariya/Thorn/Heatley 15.00 40.00
FFLGH Lemieux/Gretz/Howe 50.00 120.00
FFLRA LeClair/JR/Amonte 15.00 40.00
FFMGT Modn/Guerin/Turco 15.00 40.00
FFNBM Naslund/Bert/Mrrison 15.00 40.00
FFNSM Nolan/Sundin/Mogilny 10.00 25.00
FFNSZ Nash/Spezza/Zetter 25.00 60.00
FFSBJ Steve/Brodeur/Jovo 15.00 40.00
FFTMS Thornt/Murry/Samsnv 15.00 40.00
FFTWM Tkchk/Wght/McInn 10.00 25.00

2003-04 SPx Hall Pass

*LIMITED: .75X TO 2X
HPBH Brett Hull 15.00 40.00
HPCC Chris Chelios 10.00 25.00
HPDG Doug Gilmour 10.00 25.00
HPDH Dominik Hasek 12.50 30.00
HPMB Martin Brodeur 25.00 60.00
HPML Mario Lemieux 20.00 50.00
HPMM Mark Messier 12.50 30.00
HPPR Patrick Roy 20.00 50.00
HPRB Ray Bourque 12.50 30.00
HPRF Ron Francis 8.00 20.00

2003-04 SPx Origins

OAY Alexei Yashin 8.00 20.00
OBL Brian Leetch 8.00 20.00
OBS Brendan Shanahan 8.00 20.00
ODH Dany Heatley 15.00 40.00
ODW Doug Weight 8.00 20.00
OEB Ed Belfour 12.50 30.00
OHZ Henrik Zetterberg 15.00 40.00
OJI Jarome Iginla 12.50 30.00
OJJ Jaromir Jagr 15.00 40.00
OJR Jeremy Roenick 15.00 40.00
OJS Jason Spezza 10.00 25.00
OJSG Jean-Sebastien Giguere 8.00 20.00
OJT Joe Thornton 12.50 30.00
OMB Martin Brodeur 20.00 50.00
OMH Marian Hossa 10.00 25.00
OML Mario Lemieux 25.00 60.00
OMN Markus Naslund 8.00 20.00
OMS Mats Sundin 10.00 25.00
OON Owen Nolan 8.00 20.00
OPB Pavel Bure 8.00 20.00
OPE Patrik Elias 8.00 20.00
OPF Peter Forsberg 15.00 40.00
OPR Patrick Roy 20.00 50.00
OSF Sergei Fedorov 15.00 40.00
OSS Sergei Samsonov 8.00 20.00
OTS Teemu Selanne 10.00 25.00
OZP Zigmund Palffy 8.00 20.00

2003-04 SPx Signature Threads

STAF Alexander Frolov 20.00 50.00
STAH Ales Hemsky 15.00 40.00
STEL Eric Lindros 20.00 50.00
STHZ Henrik Zetterberg 25.00 60.00
STIK Ilya Kovalchuk 40.00 100.00
STJI Jarome Iginla 25.00 60.00
STJL John LeClair 15.00 40.00
STJR Jeremy Roenick 30.00 80.00
STJS Jason Spezza 30.00 80.00
STJT Joe Thornton 40.00 100.00
STJT Jose Theodore 25.00 60.00
STJSG Jean-Sebastien Giguere 15.00 40.00
STMC Mike Comrie 15.00 40.00
STMH Marian Hossa 20.00 50.00
STMN Markus Naslund 20.00 50.00
STMT Marty Turco 15.00 40.00
STPB Pavel Bure 15.00 40.00
STRN Rick Nash 40.00 100.00
STSF Sergei Fedorov 25.00 60.00
STSK Saku Koivu 20.00 50.00
STSS Sergei Samsonov 15.00 40.00
STSY Steve Yzerman 75.00 150.00
STTB Todd Bertuzzi 20.00 50.00
STWG Wayne Gretzky 250.00 600.00
STZP Zigmund Palffy 15.00 40.00

2003-04 SPx Style

*LIMITED: .5X TO 1.25X
SPXBG Brodeur/Giguere/Luongo 15.00 40.00
SPXBS Bertuzzi/Shanahan/Tkachuk 12.50 30.00
SPXBT Belfour/Turco/Esche 12.50 30.00
SPXDS Domi/Stock/Shelley 12.50 30.00
SPXGS Gretzky/Spezza/Thornton 75.00 200.00
SPXHH Hejduk/Hossa/Jagr 20.00 50.00
SPXHN Howe/Nash/Bertuzzi 25.00 60.00
SPXHT Howe/Thornton/Bertuzzi 20.00 50.00
SPXJB Jovanovksi/Blake/Chara 12.50 30.00
SPXLH Lemieux/Heatley/Fedorov 20.00 50.00
SPXNZ Naslund/Zetterberg/Sundin 20.00 50.00
SPXRB Roy/Brodeur/Giguere 25.00 60.00

2003-04 SPx VIP

*LIMITED: .6X TO 1.5X
VIPDA C.Drury/M.Afinogenov 12.50 30.00
VIPFG S.Fedorov/J.Giguere 15.00 40.00
VIPFS P.Forsberg/J.Sakic 20.00 50.00
VIPKH S.Koivu/Marcel Hossa 12.50 30.00
VIPLS V.Lecavalier/M.St. Louis 15.00 40.00
VIPMG M.Modano/B.Guerin 12.50 30.00
VIPNB M.Naslund
T.Bertuzzi 12.50 30.00
VIPPF Z.Palffy/A.Frolov 12.50 30.00
VIPSB S.Stevens/M.Brodeur 25.00 60.00
VIPSK T.Selanne/P.Kariya 12.50 30.00
VIPTM J.Thornton/G.Murray 12.50 30.00
VIPYS S.Yzerman/B.Shanahan 25.00 60.00

2003-04 SPx Winning Materials

*LIMITED: .6X TO 1.5X
WMAD Adam Deadmarsh 6.00 15.00
WMBE Ed Belfour 8.00 20.00
WMBL Rob Blake 6.00 15.00
WMBO Peter Bondra 8.00 20.00
WMCD Chris Drury 6.00 15.00
WMDB Dan Blackburn 6.00 15.00
WMDH Dominik Hasek 12.50 30.00
WMEB Ed Belfour 8.00 20.00
WMFO Peter Forsberg 12.50 30.00
WMGR Wayne Gretzky 40.00 100.00
WMGY Wayne Gretzky 40.00 100.00
WMJB Jay Bouwmeester 6.00 15.00
WMJF Jeff Friesen 6.00 15.00
WMJG Jaromir Jagr 10.00 25.00
WMJI Jarome Iginla 10.00 25.00
WMJJ Jaromir Jagr 10.00 25.00
WMJR Jeremy Roenick 12.50 30.00
WMJS Joe Sakic 15.00 40.00
WMJZ Jason Spezza 12.50 30.00
WMMD Mike Dunham 6.00 15.00
WMMH Marian Hossa 8.00 20.00
WMMM Mark Messier 15.00 40.00
WMMN Markus Naslund 8.00 20.00
WMMO Mike Modano 12.50 30.00
WMMS Mats Sundin 8.00 20.00
WMMT Marty Turco 6.00 15.00
WMPB Pavel Bure 8.00 20.00
WMPF Peter Forsberg 12.50 30.00
WMPK Paul Kariya 8.00 20.00
WMPR Patrick Roy 20.00 50.00
WMRB Ray Bourque 10.00 25.00
WMRN Rick Nash 15.00 40.00
WMRY Patrick Roy 20.00 50.00
WMSA Jason Spezza 12.50 30.00
WMSB Sean Burke 6.00 15.00
WMSF Sergei Fedorov 10.00 25.00
WMSW Stephen Weiss 6.00 15.00
WMTA Tony Amonte 6.00 15.00
WMTB Todd Bertuzzi 8.00 20.00
WMTH Jose Theodore 12.50 30.00
WMTS Teemu Selanne 8.00 20.00
WMWG Wayne Gretzky 30.00 80.00

2005-06 SPx

COMP.SET w/o SP's (90) 12.50 25.00
*MULTICOLOR JSY: 1X TO 2.5X HI
1 Jean-Sebastien Giguere .40 1.00
2 Sergei Fedorov .60 1.50
3 Ilya Kovalchuk .60 1.50
4 Kari Lehtonen .30 .75
5 Marian Hossa .40 1.00
6 Patrice Bergeron .50 1.25
7 Joe Thornton .60 1.50
8 Andrew Raycroft .30 .75
9 Glen Murray .30 .75
10 Maxim Afinogenov .25 .60
11 Chris Drury .30 .75
12 Jarome Iginla .50 1.25
13 Miikka Kiprusoff .40 1.00
14 Tony Amonte .30 .75
15 Erik Cole .25 .60
16 Eric Staal .50 1.25
17 Tuomo Ruutu .40 1.00
18 Nikolai Khabibulin .40 1.00
19 Joe Sakic .75 2.00
20 David Aebischer .30 .75
21 Milan Hejduk .30 .75
22 Alex Tanguay .40 1.00
23 Rick Nash .40 1.00
24 Nikolai Zherdev .25 .60
25 Mike Modano .60 1.50
26 Bill Guerin .30 .75
27 Marty Turco .40 1.00
28 Steve Yzerman 1.00 2.50
29 Brendan Shanahan .40 1.00
30 Henrik Zetterberg .50 1.25
31 Nicklas Lidstrom .40 1.00
32 Ty Conklin .30 .75
33 Chris Pronger .40 1.00
34 Ryan Smyth .30 .75
35 Roberto Luongo .60 1.50
36 Stephen Weiss .25 .60
37 Joe Nieuwendyk .30 .75
38 Jeremy Roenick .60 1.50
39 Luc Robitaille .40 1.00
40 Alexander Frolov .25 .60
41 Marian Gaborik .40 1.00
42 Manny Fernandez .25 .60
43 Saku Koivu .40 1.00
44 Jose Theodore .40 1.00
45 Michael Ryder .30 .75
46 Mike Ribeiro .25 .60
47 Paul Kariya .40 1.00
48 Tomas Vokoun .30 .75
49 David Legwand .30 .75
50 Martin Brodeur 1.00 2.50
51 Patrik Elias .40 1.00
52 Alexander Mogilny .30 .75
53 Scott Gomez .30 .75
54 Alexei Yashin .30 .75
55 Rick DiPietro .30 .75
56 Miroslav Satan .30 .75
57 Jaromir Jagr 1.25 3.00
58 Tom Poti .25 .60
59 Kevin Weekes .30 .75
60 Dany Heatley .30 .75
61 Daniel Alfredsson .40 1.00
62 Martin Havlat .40 1.00
63 Dominik Hasek .60 1.50
64 Jason Spezza .30 .75
65 Peter Forsberg .75 2.00
66 Keith Primeau .30 .75
67 Simon Gagne .40 1.00
68 Robert Esche .30 .75
69 Shane Doan .30 .75
70 Brett Hull .75 2.00
71 Curtis Joseph .50 1.25
72 Mario Lemieux 1.50 4.00
73 Zigmund Palffy .40 1.00
74 Mark Recchi .50 1.25
75 Evgeni Nabokov .30 .75
76 Patrick Marleau .40 1.00
77 Jonathan Cheechoo .30 .75
78 Keith Tkachuk .40 1.00
79 Doug Weight .40 1.00
80 Vincent Lecavalier .40 1.00
81 Sean Burke .25 .60
82 Brad Richards .40 1.00
83 Martin St. Louis .40 1.00
84 Mats Sundin .40 1.00
85 Ed Belfour .40 1.00
86 Jason Allison .30 .75
87 Eric Lindros .60 1.50
88 Markus Naslund .40 1.00
89 Brendan Morrison .25 .60
90 Olaf Kolzig .40 1.00
91 Bernie Geoffrion JSY AU 50.00 100.00
92 Bobby Hull JSY AU 25.00 60.00
93 Bobby Clarke JSY AU 25.00 60.00
94 Borje Salming JSY AU 15.00 40.00
95 Brian Leetch JSY AU 100.00 200.00
96 Bryan Trottier JSY AU 250.00 500.00
97 Cam Neely JSY AU 60.00 120.00
98 Dominik Hasek JSY AU 100.00 200.00
99 Doug Weight JSY AU 60.00 150.00
100 Ed Jovanovski JSY AU 25.00 60.00
101 Gerry Cheevers JSY AU 60.00 120.00
102 Gilbert Perreault JSY AU 60.00 120.00
103 Gordie Howe JSY AU 400.00 600.00
104 Grant Fuhr JSY AU 50.00 100.00
105 Guy Lafleur JSY AU 30.00 80.00
106 Jari Kurri JSY AU 15.00 40.00
107 Jeremy Roenick JSY AU 80.00 200.00
108 Johnny Bucyk JSY AU 50.00 100.00
109 Luc Robitaille JSY AU 40.00 100.00
110 Marcel Dionne JSY AU 25.00 60.00
111 Martin Brodeur JSY AU SP 500.00 800.00
112 Mats Sundin JSY AU SP 500.00 800.00
113 Mike Bossy JSY AU 25.00 60.00
114 Mike Modano JSY AU SP 300.00 500.00
115 Michael Peca JSY AU 20.00 50.00
116 Miroslav Satan JSY AU SP 150.00 300.00
118 Peter Stastny JSY AU 25.00 60.00
119 Phil Esposito JSY AU SP 175.00 300.00
120 Ray Bourque JSY AU SP 500.00 1000.00
121 Roberto Luongo JSY AU 50.00 100.00
122 Rogie Vachon JSY AU 20.00 40.00
123 Ron Hextall JSY AU 60.00 150.00
125 Wayne Gretzky JSY AU/25 750.00 2000.00
126 Clark Gillies JSY AU SP 200.00 400.00
127 Lanny McDonald JSY AU 15.00 40.00
128 Tiger Williams JSY AU 15.00 40.00
129 Jean Beliveau JSY AU/25 250.00 400.00
131 Butch Goring JSY AU 12.00 30.00
132 Guy Lapointe JSY AU 60.00 120.00
133 Duncan Keith JSY RC 5.00 12.00
134 Jaroslav Balastik JSY RC 3.00 8.00
135 Jay McClement JSY RC 3.00 8.00
136 Jeff Hoggan JSY RC 3.00 8.00
137 Andrew Alberts JSY RC 3.00 8.00
138 Kevin Dallman JSY RC 4.00 10.00
139 Maxime Talbot JSY RC 5.00 12.00
140 Raitis Ivanans JSY RC 2.00 5.00
141 Niklas Nordgren JSY RC 5.00 12.00
142 Kevin Nastiuk JSY RC 3.00 8.00
143 Jim Slater JSY RC 3.00 8.00
144 George Parros JSY RC 3.00 8.00
145 David Leneveu JSY RC 4.00 10.00
146 Andrew Wozniewski JSY RC 4.00 10.00
147 Ryan Hollweg JSY RC 3.00 8.00
148 Brett Lebda JSY RC 3.00 8.00
149 Patrick Eaves JSY RC 5.00 12.00
150 Ryane Clowe JSY RC 6.00 15.00
151 Josh Gorges JSY RC 4.00 10.00
152 Brad Winchester JSY RC 5.00 12.00
153 Matt Foy JSY RC 3.00 8.00
154 Wojtek Wolski JSY AU RC 4.00 10.00
155 Rene Bourque JSY AU RC 5.00 12.00
156 Gilbert Brule JSY AU RC 6.00 15.00
157 Jeff Woywitka JSY AU RC 3.00 8.00
158 Hannu Toivonen JSY AU RC 5.00 12.00
159 Al Montoya JSY AU RC 5.00 12.00
160 Yann Danis JSY AU RC 4.00 10.00
161 Alexander Perezhogin JSY AU RC 4.00 10.00
162 Cam Barker JSY AU RC 4.00 10.00
163 Zach Parise JSY AU RC 12.00 30.00
164 Dion Phaneuf JSY AU RC 8.00 20.00
165 Mike Richards JSY AU RC 10.00 25.00
166 Cam Ward JSY AU RC 8.00 20.00
167 Robert Nilsson JSY AU RC 5.00 12.00
168 Petteri Nokelainen JSY AU RC 3.00 8.00
169 Alexander Steen JSY AU RC 15.00 40.00
170 Ryan Getzlaf JSY AU RC 15.00 40.00
171 Corey Perry JSY AU RC 12.00 30.00
172 Rostislav Olesz JSY AU RC 4.00 10.00
173 Henrik Lundqvist JSY AU RC 60.00 150.00
174 Petr Prucha JSY AU RC 5.00 12.00
175 Jim Howard JSY AU RC 12.00 30.00
176 Johan Franzen JSY AU RC 8.00 20.00
177 Thomas Vanek JSY AU RC 10.00 25.00
178 Andrej Meszaros JSY AU RC 4.00 10.00
179 Brandon Bochenski JSY AU RC 5.00 12.00
180 Jussi Jokinen JSY AU RC 5.00 12.00
181 Braydon Coburn JSY AU RC 5.00 12.00
182 Ryan Suter JSY AU RC 6.00 15.00
183 Peter Budaj JSY AU RC 6.00 15.00
184 Brent Seabrook JSY AU RC 10.00 25.00
185 Keith Ballard JSY AU RC 4.00 10.00
186 Milan Jurcina JSY AU RC 4.00 10.00
187 Anthony Stewart JSY AU RC 4.00 10.00
188 Eric Nystrom JSY AU RC 4.00 10.00
189 Jeff Carter JSY AU/499 RC 15.00 40.00
190 Alex Ovechkin
JSY AU/499 RC 1200.00 3000.00
191 Sidney Crosby JSY AU/499 RC 300.00800.00
192 Lee Stempniak RC 2.50 6.00
193 Andy Roach RC 1.50 4.00
194 Colin Hemingway RC 1.50 4.00
195 Mark Streit RC 1.50 4.00
196 Wade Skolney RC 1.50 4.00
197 Chris Campoli RC 1.50 4.00
198 Paul Ranger RC 1.50 4.00
199 Kyle Brodziak RC 1.50 4.00
200 Chris Holt RC 1.50 4.00
201 Brian McGrattan RC 1.50 4.00
202 Adam Berkhoel RC 2.00 5.00
203 Nick Tarnasky RC 1.50 4.00
204 Evgeny Artyukhin RC 2.00 5.00
205 Timo Helbling RC 1.50 4.00
206 Derek Boogaard RC 4.00 10.00
207 Michael Wall RC 2.00 5.00
208 Steve Goertzen RC 1.50 4.00
209 Junior Lessard RC 1.50 4.00
210 Vojtech Polak RC 1.50 4.00
211 Andrew Penner RC 2.00 5.00
212 Jordan Sigalet RC 1.50 4.00
213 Kevin Colley RC 2.00 5.00
214 Dimitri Patzold RC 1.50 4.00
215 Christoph Schubert RC 1.50 4.00
216 Zenon Konopka RC 1.50 4.00
217 Staffan Kronwall RC 1.50 4.00
218 Erik Christensen RC 1.50 4.00
219 Brian Eklund RC 2.00 5.00
220 Rob McVicar RC 2.00 5.00
221 Tomas Fleischmann RC 2.50 6.00
222 Chris Thorburn JSY AU RC 4.00 10.00
223 Daniel Paille JSY AU RC 5.00 12.00
224 Andrew Ladd JSY AU RC 6.00 15.00
225 Danny Richmond JSY AU RC 3.00 8.00
226 Brad Richardson JSY AU RC 5.00 12.00
227 Ole-Kristian Tollefsen JSY AU RC 4.00 10.00
228 Alexandre Picard JSY AU RC 3.00 8.00
229 Kyle Quincey JSY AU RC 4.00 10.00
230 Valtteri Filppula JSY AU RC 6.00 15.00
231 Jeff Tambellini JSY AU RC 3.00 8.00
232 Mikko Koivu JSY AU RC 6.00 15.00
233 Maxim Lapierre JSY AU RC 5.00 12.00
234 Andrei Kostitsyn JSY AU RC 6.00 15.00
235 Barry Tallackson JSY AU RC 4.00 10.00
236 Jeremy Colliton JSY AU RC 3.00 8.00
237 R.J. Umberger JSY AU RC 5.00 12.00
238 Ben Eager JSY AU RC 4.00 10.00
239 Ryan Whitney JSY AU RC 5.00 12.00
240 Steve Bernier JSY AU RC 5.00 12.00
241 Ryan Craig JSY AU RC 3.00 8.00
242 Kevin Bieksa JSY AU RC 8.00 20.00
243 Jakub Klepis JSY AU RC 3.00 8.00
244 Dustin Penner RC 2.50 6.00
245 Ben Walter RC 1.50 4.00
246 Eric Healey RC 2.00 5.00
247 Nathan Paetsch RC 2.00 5.00
248 Jiri Novotny RC 2.00 5.00
249 Richie Regehr RC 1.50 4.00
250 Chad Larose RC 2.00 5.00
251 Martin St. Pierre RC 2.00 5.00
252 Corey Crawford RC 12.00 25.00
253 James Wisniewski RC 2.00 5.00
254 Vitaly Kolesnik RC 2.00 5.00
255 Geoff Platt RC 2.00 5.00
256 Joakim Lindstrom RC 1.50 4.00
257 Danny Syvret RC 1.50 4.00
258 Kyle Brodziak RC 1.50 4.00
259 J-F Jacques RC 1.50 4.00
260 Mall Greene RC 1.50 4.00
261 Greg Jacina RC 1.50 4.00
262 Rob Globke RC 1.50 4.00
263 Yanick Lehoux RC 2.50 6.00
264 Connor James RC 2.00 5.00
265 Richard Petiot RC 2.00 5.00
266 Petr Kanko RC 2.00 5.00
267 Matt Ryan RC 2.00 5.00
268 J-P Cote RC 2.00 5.00
269 Jonathan Ferland RC 2.00 5.00
270 Greg Zanon RC 2.00 5.00
271 Kevin Klein RC 2.00 5.00
272 Pekka Rinne RC 4.00 10.00
273 Cam Janssen RC 2.00 5.00
274 Jason Ryznar RC 1.50 4.00
275 Bruno Gervais RC 1.50 4.00
276 Stefan Ruzicka RC 1.50 4.00
277 Alexandre Picard RC 1.50 4.00
278 Matt Jones RC 1.50 4.00
279 Colby Armstrong RC 2.50 6.00
280 Doug Murray RC 1.50 4.00
281 Grant Stevenson RC 1.50 4.00
282 Dennis Wideman RC 2.50 6.00
283 Chris Beckford-Tseu RC 2.00 5.00
284 Gerald Coleman RC 1.50 4.00
285 Darren Reid RC 1.50 4.00
286 Doug O'Brien RC 1.50 4.00
287 Jay Harrison RC 1.50 4.00
288 Rick Rypien RC 4.00 10.00
289 Alexandre Burrows RC 3.00 8.00
290 Tomas Mojzis RC 1.50 4.00
291 David Steckel RC 2.00 5.00
292 Mike Green RC 6.00 15.00
293 Joey Tenute RC 2.00 5.00

2005-06 SPx Spectrum

*STARS: 15X TO 40X BASE HI
*ROOKIE JSY: .75X TO 2X
*ROOKIE JSY/AU: 1X TO 2.5X
*ROOKIE: .6X TO 1.5X
28 Steve Yzerman 25.00 60.00
50 Martin Brodeur 25.00 60.00
72 Mario Lemieux 25.00 60.00
156 Gilbert Brule JSY AU 30.00 80.00
164 Dion Phaneuf JSY AU 60.00 150.00
166 Cam Ward JSY AU 60.00 120.00
170 Ryan Getzlaf JSY AU 60.00 120.00
173 Henrik Lundqvist JSY AU 125.00 300.00
189 Jeff Carter JSY AU 25.00 60.00
190 A.Ovechkin JSY AU 6000.00 15000.00
191 Sidney Crosby JSY AU 800.00 1200.00
224 Andrew Ladd 10.00 25.00
238 Ben Eager 6.00 15.00
242 Kevin Bieksa 12.00 30.00

2005-06 SPx Winning Combos

*GOLD/99: .6X TO 1.5X BASIC JSY/350
WCAB D.Aebischer
R.Blake 5.00 12.00
WCAN S.Fedorov/T.Selanne 10.00 25.00
WCBA M.Biron/M.Afinogenov 4.00 10.00
WCBB R.Bourque/R.Blake 8.00 20.00
WCBE M.Brodeur/P.Elias 12.00 30.00
WCBF D.Brown/A.Frolov 5.00 12.00
WCBH J.Bouwmeester/N.Horton 5.00 12.00
WCBK M.Bossy/J.Kurri 5.00 12.00
WCBL R.Bourque/B.Leetch 8.00 20.00
WCBM T.Bertuzzi/B.Morrison 5.00 12.00
WCBN M.Biron/M.Noronen 4.00 10.00
WCBO G.Murray/J.Thornton 8.00 20.00
WCBP R.Blake/C.Pronger 5.00 12.00
WCBT M.Brodeur/J.Theodore 12.00 30.00
WCCH Z.Chara/M.Havlat 5.00 12.00
WCCN D.Cloutier/M.Naslund 5.00 12.00
WCCP T.Conklin/C.Pronger 5.00 12.00
WCDA B.Guerin/M.Modano 8.00 20.00
WCDB C.Drury/D.Briere 5.00 12.00
WCDN M.Denis/R.Nash 5.00 12.00
WCDR M.Dionne/L.Robitaille 6.00 15.00
WCED R.Smyth/A.Hemsky 4.00 10.00
WCEJ E.Staal/J.Williams 6.00 15.00
WCEM E.Belfour/M.Turco 5.00 12.00
WCFG S.Fedorov/J.Giguere 8.00 20.00
WCFL J.Bouwmeester/R.Luongo 8.00 20.00
WCFP P.Forsberg/K.Primeau 10.00 25.00
WCFR S.Fedorov/J.Roenick 8.00 20.00
WCFS P.Forsberg/J.Sakic 10.00 25.00
WCGC W.Gretzky/S.Crosby 30.00 80.00
WCGF M.Gaborik/M.Fernandez 5.00 12.00
WCGM W.Gretzky/M.Messier 20.00 50.00
WCGR S.Gagne/B.Richards 5.00 12.00
WCHA D.Heatley/D.Alfredsson 5.00 12.00
WCHD B.Hull/S.Doan 10.00 25.00
WCHJ B.Hull/C.Joseph 10.00 25.00
WCHK M.Hossa/S.Koivu 5.00 12.00
WCJM J.Jagr/M.Messier 15.00 40.00
WCJP J.Thornton/P.Bergeron 8.00 20.00
WCJY J.Jagr/A.Yashin 15.00 40.00
WCKI M.Kiprusoff/J.Iginla 6.00 15.00
WCKN M.Kiprusoff/E.Nabokov 5.00 12.00
WCKR N.Khabibulin/T.Ruutu 5.00 12.00
WCLA L.Robitaille/J.Roenick 8.00 20.00
WCLF M.Lemieux/J.LeClair 10.00 25.00
WCLJ M.Lemieux/J.Jagr 12.00 30.00
WCLK G.Lafleur/S.Koivu 6.00 15.00
WCMI M.Hossa/I.Kovalchuk 5.00 12.00
WCMM M.Modano/B.Morrow 8.00 20.00
WCMN B.Morrison/M.Naslund 5.00 12.00
WCMP M.Ribeiro/P.Bergeron 6.00 15.00
WCMT M.Messier/B.Trottier 10.00 25.00
WCNA O.Nolan/N.Antropov 5.00 12.00
WCND L.Nagy/S.Doan 4.00 10.00
WCNY M.Bossy/B.Trottier 5.00 12.00
WCNZ R.Nash/N.Zherdev 5.00 12.00
WCOT D.Heatley/M.Havlat 5.00 12.00
WCPE K.Primeau/R.Esche 4.00 10.00
WCPG K.Primeau/S.Gagne 5.00 12.00
WCPH M.Peca/A.Hemsky 4.00 10.00
WCPR Z.Palffy/M.Recchi 6.00 15.00
WCPS M.Parrish/M.Satan 4.00 10.00
WCRB A.Raycroft/P.Bergeron 6.00 15.00
WCRC W.Redden/Z.Chara 5.00 12.00
WCRK M.Ryder/S.Koivu 5.00 12.00
WCRL A.Raycroft/K.Lehtonen 4.00 10.00
WCRR M.Ryder/M.Ribeiro 4.00 10.00
WCRT M.Ribeiro/J.Theodore 5.00 12.00
WCRW H.Zetterberg/N.Lidstrom 6.00 15.00
WCSA J.Spezza/D.Alfredsson 5.00 12.00
WCSB J.Spezza/P.Bergeron 6.00 15.00
WCSC R.Smyth/T.Conklin 4.00 10.00
WCSF M.St. Louis/R.Fedotenko 5.00 12.00
WCSH J.Sakic/M.Hejduk 10.00 25.00
WCSL M.St.Louis/V.Lecavalier 5.00 12.00
WCSN M.Sundin/O.Nolan 5.00 12.00
WCSR S.Stevens/B.Rafalski 5.00 12.00
WCST M.Turco/B.Morrow 5.00 12.00
WCSW M.Stajan/J.Williams 4.00 10.00
WCSY B.Shanahan/S.Yzerman 10.00 25.00
WCTB B.Richards/V.Lecavalier 5.00 12.00
WCTH A.Tanguay/M.Hejduk 5.00 12.00
WCTM M.Turco/M.Modano 8.00 20.00
WCTO M.Sundin/E.Belfour 5.00 12.00
WCVA E.Jovanovski/B.Morrison 4.00 10.00
WCVH T.Vokoun/D.Hasek 8.00 20.00
WCWH S.Weiss/N.Horton 5.00 12.00
WCWL P.Worrell/G.Laraque 4.00 10.00
WCWM D.Weight/A.MacInnis 6.00 15.00
WCWT D.Weight/K.Tkachuk 5.00 12.00
WCZD H.Zetterberg/K.Draper 6.00 15.00
WCZL H.Zetterberg/M.Legace 6.00 15.00

2005-06 SPx Winning Combos Autographs

AWCAB David Aebischer
Rob Blake 20.00 50.00
AWCAK A.Raycroft/K.Lehtonen 50.00 100.00
AWCBA Martin Biron
Maxim Afinogenov 30.00 80.00
AWCBB R.Bourque/R.Blake 30.00 80.00
AWCBF Dustin Brown
Alexander Frolov 20.00 50.00
AWCBL Jay Bouwmeester
Roberto Luongo 25.00 60.00
AWCBN Martin Biron
Mikka Noronen 20.00 50.00
AWCBO Andrew Raycroft
Patrice Bergeron 25.00 60.00
AWCBP R.Blake/C.Pronger 30.00 80.00
AWCBT M.Brodeur/J.Theodore 75.00 150.00
AWCCH Zdeno Chara
Martin Havlat 25.00 60.00
AWCCP Ty Conklin
Chris Pronger 20.00 50.00
AWCDB Chris Drury
Daniel Briere 20.00 50.00
AWCDR M.Dionne/Robitaille 30.00 80.00
AWCGC W.Gretzky/S.Crosby 2000.00 5000.00
AWCGR Simon Gagne

Brad Richards 20.00 50.00
AWCHA Dany Heatley
Daniel Alfredsson 30.00 80.00
AWCHH Dany Heatley
Martin Havlat 30.00 80.00
AWCHK M. Hossa/I. Kovalchuk 50.00 100.00
AWCJM Ed Jovanovski
Brendan Morrison 30.00 80.00
AWCLA Robitaille/Roenick 30.00 80.00
AWCLK Guy Lafleur
Saku Koivu 30.00 80.00
AWCMM Mike Modano
Brenden Morrow 30.00 80.00
AWCMN Brendan Morrison
Markus Naslund 20.00 50.00
AWCMS Marcel Hossa
Saku Koivu 20.00 50.00
AWCNA Owen Nolan
Nik Antropov 20.00 50.00
AWCND Ladislav Nagy
Shane Doan 25.00 60.00
AWCNY M.Bossy/B.Trottier 30.00 80.00
AWCNZ Rick Nash
Nikolai Zherdev 25.00 60.00
AWCOT J.Spezza/D.Alfredsson 25.00 60.00
AWCPE Keith Primeau
Robert Esche 20.00 50.00
AWCPH Michael Peca
Ales Hemsky 20.00 50.00
AWCPS Mark Parrish
Miroslav Satan 30.00 80.00
AWCRB Mike Ribeiro
Patrice Bergeron 20.00 50.00
AWCRL B.Richards/Lecavalier 30.00 60.00
AWCRR Michael Ryder
Mike Ribeiro 30.00 80.00
AWCSA Matt Stajan
Nik Antropov 30.00 80.00
AWCSC Ryan Smyth
Ty Conklin 30.00 80.00
AWCSF Martin St. Louis
Ruslan Fedotenko 30.00 80.00
AWCSH Ryan Smyth
Ales Hemsky 30.00 80.00
AWCSL Martin St. Louis
Vincent Lecavalier 30.00 80.00
AWCSW Eric Staal
Justin Williams 20.00 50.00
AWCTB Joe Thornton
Patrice Bergeron 30.00 80.00
AWCTH Alex Tanguay
Milan Hejduk 20.00 50.00
AWCTM Marty Turco
Brenden Morrow 20.00 50.00
AWCWH Stephen Weiss
Nathan Horton 30.00 80.00
AWCWL Peter Worrell
Georges Laraque 30.00 80.00
AWCZD Zetterberg/K.Draper 30.00 80.00
AWCZL Henrik Zetterberg
Manny Legace 30.00 80.00

2005-06 SPx Winning Materials

WMAE David Aebischer 3.00 8.00
WMAF Alexander Frolov 2.50 6.00
WMAH Ales Hemsky 3.00 8.00
WMAR Andrew Raycroft 3.00 8.00
WMAT Alex Tanguay 4.00 10.00
WMBG Bill Guerin 4.00 10.00
WMBH Brett Hull 8.00 20.00
WMBL Brian Leetch 3.00 8.00
WMBM Brendan Morrison 2.50 6.00
WMBR Brad Richards 4.00 10.00
WMBS Brendan Shanahan 4.00 10.00
WMBT Bryan Trottier 4.00 10.00
WMBY Mike Bossy 4.00 10.00
WMCD Chris Drury 3.00 8.00
WMCJ Curtis Joseph 5.00 12.00
WMCP Chris Pronger 4.00 10.00
WMDA Daniel Alfredsson 4.00 10.00
WMDB Daniel Briere 4.00 10.00
WMDH Dany Heatley 6.00 15.00
WMDW Doug Weight 4.00 10.00
WMEB Ed Belfour 4.00 10.00
WMED Eric Daze 3.00 8.00
WMEJ Ed Jovanovski 3.00 8.00
WMGL Guy Lafleur 5.00 12.00
WMHA Dominik Hasek 10.00 25.00
WMHO Marian Hossa 4.00 10.00
WMHV Martin Havlat 4.00 10.00
WMHZ Henrik Zetterberg 5.00 12.00
WMIK Ilya Kovalchuk 6.00 15.00
WMJG Jean-Sebastien Giguere 4.00 10.00
WMJI Jarome Iginla 6.00 15.00
WMJJ Jaromir Jagr 6.00 15.00
WMJL John LeClair 4.00 10.00
WMJO Jose Theodore 4.00 10.00
WMJR Jeremy Roenick 6.00 15.00
WMJS Joe Sakic 10.00 25.00
WMJT Joe Thornton 8.00 20.00
WMJW Justin Williams 3.00 8.00
WMKD Kris Draper 5.00 12.00
WMKF Miikka Kiprusoff 4.00 10.00
WMKL Kari Lehtonen 3.00 8.00
WMKP Keith Primeau 3.00 8.00
WMKT Keith Tkachuk 4.00 10.00
WMLN Ladislav Nagy 2.50 6.00
WMLR Luc Robitaille 4.00 10.00
WMLX Mario Lemieux 15.00 40.00
WMMB Martin Brodeur 12.00 30.00
WMMC Bryan McCabe 2.50 6.00
WMMD Marcel Dionne 5.00 12.00
WMMG Marian Gaborik 8.00 20.00
WMMH Milan Hejduk 3.00 8.00
WMML Manny Legace 4.00 10.00
WMMM Mike Modano 6.00 15.00
WMMN Markus Naslund 4.00 10.00
WMMP Mark Parrish 2.50 6.00
WMMR Mike Ribeiro 2.50 6.00
WMMS Mark Messier 8.00 20.00
WMMW Brenden Morrow 3.00 8.00
WMNA Nik Antropov 3.00 8.00
WMNH Nathan Horton 4.00 10.00
WMNK Nikolai Khabibulin 4.00 10.00
WMNZ Nikolai Zherdev 2.50 6.00
WMOK Olaf Kolzig 4.00 10.00
WMON Owen Nolan 4.00 10.00
WMPB Patrice Bergeron 5.00 12.00
WMPE Michael Peca 3.00 8.00
WMPF Peter Forsberg 6.00 15.00
WMPM Patrick Marleau 4.00 10.00
WMRE Robert Esche 3.00 8.00
WMRF Ruslan Fedotenko 2.50 6.00
WMRL Roberto Luongo 6.00 15.00
WMRN Rick Nash 4.00 10.00
WMRS Ryan Smyth 3.00 8.00
WMRY Michael Ryder 3.00 8.00
WMRZ Richard Zednik 2.50 6.00
WMSA Miroslav Satan 3.00 8.00
WMSC Sidney Crosby 40.00 80.00
WMSD Shane Doan 3.00 8.00
WMSF Sergei Fedorov 6.00 15.00
WMSG Simon Gagne 4.00 10.00
WMSK Saku Koivu 4.00 10.00
WMSL Martin St. Louis 4.00 10.00
WMSP Jason Spezza 4.00 10.00
WMST Matt Stajan 2.50 6.00
WMSU Mats Sundin 4.00 10.00
WMSW Stephen Weiss 2.50 6.00
WMSY Steve Yzerman 12.00 30.00
WMTC Ty Conklin 3.00 8.00
WMTR Tuomo Ruutu 4.00 10.00
WMTS Teemu Selanne 6.00 15.00
WMTU Marty Turco 4.00 10.00
WMVL Vincent Lecavalier 4.00 10.00
WMWG Wayne Gretzky 25.00 50.00
WMZC Zdeno Chara 4.00 10.00
WMZP Zigmund Palffy 4.00 10.00

2005-06 SPx Winning Materials Autographs

AWMAF Alexander Frolov 15.00 40.00
AWMAR Andrew Raycroft 15.00 40.00
AWMAT Alex Tanguay 15.00 40.00
AWMBL Brian Leetch 15.00 40.00
AWMBM Brenden Morrow 15.00 40.00
AWMBR Brad Richards 15.00 40.00
AWMCD Chris Drury 15.00 40.00
AWMCP Chris Pronger 15.00 40.00
AWMDA David Aebischer 15.00 40.00
AWMDH Dany Heatley 15.00 40.00
AWMDW Doug Weight 15.00 40.00
AWMED Eric Daze 15.00 40.00
AWMHA Dominik Hasek 40.00 80.00
AWMHO Marian Hossa 15.00 40.00
AWMHV Martin Havlat 15.00 40.00
AWMHZ Henrik Zetterberg 20.00 50.00
AWMIK Ilya Kovalchuk 30.00 80.00
AWMJI Jarome Iginla 25.00 60.00
AWMJO Joe Thornton 25.00 60.00
AWMJR Jeremy Roenick 20.00 50.00
AWMJS Jason Spezza 25.00 60.00
AWMJT Jose Theodore 20.00 50.00
AWMJW Justin Williams 15.00 40.00
AWMKD Kris Draper 15.00 40.00
AWMKP Keith Primeau 15.00 40.00
AWMMB Martin Brodeur 40.00 100.00
AWMMC Bryan McCabe 15.00 40.00
AWMMH Milan Hejduk 15.00 40.00
AWMMN Markus Naslund 20.00 50.00
AWMMO Mike Modano 30.00 60.00
AWMMR Mike Ribeiro 15.00 40.00
AWMMT Marty Turco 12.50 30.00
AWMNH Nathan Horton 15.00 40.00
AWMNZ Nikolai Zherdev 15.00 40.00
AWMOK Olaf Kolzig 12.50 30.00
AWMPE Michael Peca 15.00 40.00
AWMPR Patrick Roy 60.00 120.00
AWMRE Robert Esche 15.00 40.00
AWMRL Roberto Luongo 20.00 50.00
AWMRN Rick Nash 20.00 50.00
AWMRS Ryan Smyth 15.00 40.00
AWMRY Michael Ryder 15.00 40.00
AWMRZ Richard Zednik 15.00 40.00
AWMSD Shane Doan 15.00 40.00
AWMSG Simon Gagne 20.00 50.00
AWMSL Martin St. Louis 15.00 40.00
AWMTC Ty Conklin 15.00 40.00
AWMVL Vincent Lecavalier 25.00 60.00
AWMWG Wayne Gretzky 250.00 600.00
AWMZC Zdeno Chara 15.00 40.00

2005-06 SPx Winning Materials Gold

*GOLD: .6X TO 1.5X BASIC WM
WMES Eric Staal 12.00 30.00
WMMB Martin Brodeur 15.00 40.00
WMPK Paul Kariya 6.00 15.00
WMSC Sidney Crosby 50.00 120.00

2005-06 SPx Xcitement Legends

XLBB Bill Barber 2.00 5.00
XLBC Bobby Clarke 4.00 10.00
XLBG Bernie Geoffrion 2.00 5.00
XLBH Bobby Hull 5.00 12.00
XLBN Bob Nystrom 1.50 4.00
XLBO Johnny Bower 2.50 6.00
XLBP Brad Park 2.00 5.00
XLBT Bryan Trottier 2.50 6.00
XLBU Johnny Bucyk 2.50 6.00
XLCG Clark Gillies 2.50 6.00
XLCN Cam Neely 2.50 6.00
XLDC Don Cherry 2.50 6.00
XLDM Dickie Moore 1.50 4.00
XLDS Denis Savard 2.50 6.00
XLDT Dave Taylor 2.00 5.00
XLFM Frank Mahovlich 2.50 6.00
XLGA Glenn Anderson 2.00 5.00
XLGC Gerry Cheevers 2.50 6.00
XLGF Grant Fuhr 4.00 10.00
XLGH Gordie Howe 8.00 20.00
XLGL Guy Lafleur 3.00 8.00
XLGO Butch Goring 1.50 4.00
XLGP Gilbert Perreault 2.50 6.00
XLHL Hakan Loob 1.50 4.00
XLJB Jean Beliveau 2.50 6.00
XLJK Jari Kurri 2.50 6.00
XLKH Ken Hodge 2.00 5.00
XLKM Ken Morrow 1.50 4.00
XLLA Guy Lapointe 2.00 5.00
XLLM Lanny McDonald 2.50 6.00
XLMB Mike Bossy 2.50 6.00
XLMD Marcel Dionne 3.00 8.00
XLMN Mats Naslund 1.50 4.00
XLPE Phil Esposito 4.00 10.00
XLPR Patrick Roy 6.00 15.00
XLPS Peter Stastny 2.00 5.00
XLRH Ron Hextall 2.50 6.00
XLRK Red Kelly 2.50 6.00
XLRL Reggie Leach 1.50 4.00
XLRM Rick Martin 1.50 4.00
XLRR Rene Robert 1.50 4.00
XLRV Rogie Vachon 3.00 8.00
XLSA Derek Sanderson 2.50 6.00
XLSB Scotty Bowman 2.50 6.00
XLSM Stan Mikita 3.00 8.00
XLTE Tony Esposito 2.50 6.00
XLTO Terry O'Reilly 2.00 5.00
XLTW Tiger Williams 1.50 4.00
XLWC Wayne Cashman 1.50 4.00
XLWG Wayne Gretzky 15.00 40.00

2005-06 SPx Xcitement Legends Gold

*GOLD: .75X TO 2X

2005-06 SPx Xcitement Rookies

*GOLD/99: .8X TO 2X BASIC INSERTS
XRAA Andrew Alberts 1.25 3.00
XRAM Andrej Meszaros 1.50 4.00
XRAO Alexander Ovechkin 150.00 400.00
XRAP Alexander Perezhogin 1.50 4.00
XRAS Alexander Steen 3.00 8.00
XRAW Andrew Wozniewski 1.50 4.00
XRBB Brandon Bochenski 2.00 5.00
XRBC Braydon Coburn 2.00 5.00
XRBS Brent Seabrook 4.00 10.00
XRCB Cam Barker 1.50 4.00
XRCC Chris Campoli 1.25 3.00
XRCP Corey Perry 6.00 15.00
XRCW Cam Ward 3.00 8.00
XRDK Duncan Keith 4.00 10.00
XRDL David Leneveu 1.50 4.00
XRDP Dion Phaneuf 3.00 8.00
XREN Eric Nystrom 1.50 4.00
XRGB Gilbert Brule 2.00 5.00
XRHL Henrik Lundqvist 10.00 25.00
XRHT Hannu Toivonen 2.00 5.00
XRJC Jeff Carter 3.00 8.00
XRJF Johan Franzen 3.00 8.00
XRJH Jim Howard 4.00 10.00
XRJJ Jussi Jokinen 2.00 5.00
XRJM Jay McClement 1.25 3.00
XRJS Jim Slater 1.50 4.00
XRJW Jeff Woywitka 1.25 3.00
XRKB Keith Ballard 1.50 4.00
XRKD Kevin Dallman 1.50 4.00
XRKN Kevin Nastiuk 1.25 3.00
XRMF Matt Foy 1.25 3.00
XRMJ Milan Jurcina 1.50 4.00
XRMO Alvaro Montoya 2.00 5.00
XRMR Mike Richards 4.00 10.00
XRMT Maxime Talbot 2.00 5.00
XRPB Peter Budaj 2.50 6.00
XRPN Petteri Nokelainen 1.25 3.00
XRPP Petr Prucha 2.00 5.00
XRRB Rene Bourque 2.00 5.00
XRRC Ryane Clowe 2.50 6.00
XRRG Ryan Getzlaf 5.00 12.00
XRRN Robert Nilsson 2.00 5.00
XRRO Rostislav Olesz 1.50 4.00
XRRS Ryan Suter 2.50 6.00
XRSC Sidney Crosby 80.00 200.00
XRST Anthony Stewart 1.50 4.00
XRTV Thomas Vanek 4.00 10.00
XRWW Wojtek Wolski 1.50 4.00
XRYD Yann Danis 1.50 4.00
XRZP Zach Parise 5.00 12.00

2005-06 SPx Xcitement Superstars

XSAT Alex Tanguay 2.00 5.00
XSBG Bill Guerin 2.00 5.00
XSBH Brett Hull 4.00 10.00
XSBL Brian Leetch 1.50 4.00
XSBR Brad Richards 2.00 5.00
XSBS Brendan Shanahan 2.00 5.00
XSCP Chris Pronger 2.00 5.00
XSDA Daniel Alfredsson 2.00 5.00
XSDH Dany Heatley 1.50 4.00
XSEB Ed Belfour 2.00 5.00
XSED Eric Daze 1.50 4.00
XSEJ Ed Jovanovski 1.50 4.00
XSEN Evgeni Nabokov 1.50 4.00
XSHA Dominik Hasek 3.00 8.00
XSHK Milan Hejduk 1.50 4.00
XSHV Martin Havlat 2.00 5.00
XSHZ Henrik Zetterberg 2.50 6.00
XSIK Ilya Kovalchuk 2.00 5.00
XSJI Jarome Iginla 2.50 6.00
XSJJ Jaromir Jagr 6.00 15.00
XSJO Joe Thornton 3.00 8.00
XSJR Jeremy Roenick 3.00 8.00
XSJS Joe Sakic 4.00 10.00
XSJT Jose Theodore 2.00 5.00
XSKD Kris Draper 2.50 6.00
XSKP Keith Primeau 1.50 4.00
XSKT Keith Tkachuk 2.00 5.00
XSLR Luc Robitaille 2.00 5.00
XSMB Martin Brodeur 5.00 12.00
XSMG Marian Gaborik 2.00 5.00
XSMH Marian Hossa 2.00 5.00
XSML Mario Lemieux 8.00 20.00
XSMM Mark Messier 4.00 10.00
XSMN Markus Naslund 2.00 5.00
XSMO Mike Modano 3.00 8.00
XSMP Mark Parrish 1.25 3.00
XSMS Mats Sundin 2.00 5.00
XSMT Marty Turco 2.00 5.00
XSOK Olaf Kolzig 2.00 5.00
XSON Owen Nolan 2.00 5.00
XSRB Rob Blake 2.00 5.00
XSRL Roberto Luongo 3.00 8.00
XSRN Rick Nash 2.00 5.00
XSSD Shane Doan 1.50 4.00
XSSF Sergei Fedorov 3.00 8.00
XSSG Simon Gagne 2.00 5.00
XSSK Saku Koivu 2.00 5.00
XSSL Martin St. Louis 2.00 5.00
XSSY Steve Yzerman 5.00 12.00
XSVL Vincent Lecavalier 2.00 5.00

2005-06 SPx Xcitement Superstars Gold

*GOLD: .5X TO 1.25X
XSMM Mark Messier 5.00 12.00

2006-07 SPx

1 Chris Pronger .40 1.00
2 Teemu Selanne .75 2.00
3 Jean-Sebastien Giguere .40 1.00
4 Kari Lehtonen .30 .75
5 Marian Hossa .40 1.00
6 Ilya Kovalchuk .40 1.00
7 Patrice Bergeron .50 1.25
8 Zdeno Chara .40 1.00
9 Brad Boyes .25 .60
10 Ryan Miller .40 1.00
11 Chris Drury .30 .75
12 Alex Tanguay .25 .60
13 Dion Phaneuf .30 .75
14 Jarome Iginla .50 1.25
15 Miikka Kiprusoff .40 1.00
16 Eric Staal .50 1.25
17 Cam Ward .40 1.00
18 Rod Brind'Amour .40 1.00
19 Nikolai Khabibulin .40 1.00
20 Martin Havlat .25 .60
21 Tuomo Ruutu .40 1.00
22 Joe Sakic .75 2.00
23 Marek Svatos .25 .60
24 Jose Theodore .40 1.00
25 Milan Hejduk .30 .75
26 Rick Nash .40 1.00
27 Sergei Fedorov .60 1.50
28 Fredrik Modin .25 .60
29 Eric Lindros .60 1.50
30 Mike Modano .60 1.50
31 Brenden Morrow .30 .75
32 Marty Turco .40 1.00
33 Pavel Datsyuk .60 1.50
34 Gordie Howe 1.25 3.00
35 Nicklas Lidstrom .40 1.00
36 Henrik Zetterberg .50 1.25
37 Dominik Hasek .60 1.50
38 Ryan Smyth .30 .75
39 Ales Hemsky .30 .75
40 Joffrey Lupul .25 .60
41 Wayne Gretzky 2.50 6.00
42 Olli Jokinen .40 1.00
43 Todd Bertuzzi .40 1.00
44 Ed Belfour .40 1.00
45 Jay Bouwmeester .25 .60
46 Alexander Frolov .25 .60
47 Rob Blake .40 1.00
48 Marian Gaborik .40 1.00
49 Manny Fernandez .25 .60
50 Pavol Demitra .50 1.25
51 Alexei Kovalev .30 .75
52 Cristobal Huet .30 .75
53 Saku Koivu .40 1.00
54 Michael Ryder .25 .60
55 Mike Ribeiro .25 .60
56 Paul Kariya .40 1.00
57 Tomas Vokoun .30 .75
58 Jason Arnott .30 .75
59 Martin Brodeur 1.00 2.50
60 Brian Gionta .25 .60
61 Patrik Elias .40 1.00
62 Scott Gomez .30 .75
63 Rick DiPietro .30 .75
64 Miroslav Satan .30 .75
65 Alexei Yashin .30 .75
66 Brendan Shanahan .40 1.00
67 Henrik Lundqvist 1.00 2.50
68 Jaromir Jagr 1.25 3.00
69 Petr Prucha .30 .75
70 Daniel Alfredsson .40 1.00
71 Jason Spezza .40 1.00
72 Dany Heatley .30 .75
73 Martin Gerber .30 .75
74 Jeff Carter .30 .75
75 Peter Forsberg .75 2.00
76 Simon Gagne .40 1.00
77 Shane Doan .30 .75
78 Jeremy Roenick .60 1.50
79 Curtis Joseph .50 1.25
80 Mark Recchi .50 1.25
81 Sidney Crosby 1.50 4.00
82 Marc-Andre Fleury .75 2.00
83 Mario Lemieux 1.50 4.00
84 Patrick Marleau .40 1.00
85 Joe Thornton .60 1.50
86 Jonathan Cheechoo .30 .75
87 Keith Tkachuk .40 1.00
88 Doug Weight .40 1.00
89 Brad Richards .40 1.00
90 Vincent Lecavalier .40 1.00
91 Martin St. Louis .40 1.00
92 Mats Sundin .40 1.00
93 Andrew Raycroft .30 .75
94 Darcy Tucker .30 .75
95 Alexander Steen .25 .60
96 Roberto Luongo .60 1.50
97 Markus Naslund .40 1.00
98 Brendan Morrison .25 .60
99 Olaf Kolzig .40 1.00
100 Alexander Ovechkin 1.50 4.00
101 Teemu Selanne JSY 12.00 30.00
102 Ilya Kovalchuk JSY 6.00 15.00
103 Jarome Iginla JSY 8.00 20.00
104 Mark Recchi JSY 8.00 20.00
105 Eric Staal JSY 8.00 20.00
106 Joe Sakic JSY 12.00 30.00
107 Sergei Fedorov JSY 10.00 25.00
108 Mike Modano JSY 10.00 25.00
109 Brendan Shanahan JSY 6.00 15.00
110 Mats Sundin JSY 6.00 15.00
111 Bill Ranford JSY 6.00 15.00
112 Roberto Luongo JSY 10.00 25.00
113 Alexei Kovalev JSY 5.00 12.00
114 Paul Kariya JSY 6.00 15.00
115 Jaromir Jagr JSY 20.00 50.00
116 Peter Forsberg JSY 12.00 30.00
117 Richard Brodeur JSY 5.00 12.00
118 Peter Stastny JSY 5.00 12.00
119 Ron Hextall JSY 6.00 15.00
120 Eric Lindros JSY 10.00 25.00
121 Dave Williams JSY 4.00 10.00
122 Cam Neely JSY AU 12.00 30.00
123 Ray Bourque JSY AU 40.00 100.00
124 Gilbert Perreault JSY AU 12.00 30.00
125 Lanny McDonald JSY AU 12.00 30.00
126 Gordie Howe JSY AU 100.00 200.00
127 Grant Fuhr JSY AU 15.00 40.00
128 Wayne Gretzky JSY AU 250.00 600.00
129 Guy Lafleur JSY AU 40.00 100.00
130 Patrick Roy JSY AU 40.00 100.00
131 Martin Brodeur JSY AU 30.00 80.00
132 Mike Bossy JSY AU 12.00 30.00
133 D. Hasek JSY AU 20.00 50.00
134 Sidney Crosby JSY AU 75.00 150.00
135 Mario Lemieux SP JSY AU 125.00 250.00
136 Al MacInnis JSY AU 15.00 40.00
137 Borje Salming JSY AU 12.00 30.00
138 Darryl Sittler SP JSY AU 100.00 200.00
139 Steve Shutt JSY AU 12.00 30.00
140 Ed Belfour JSY AU 12.00 30.00
141 Bobby Clarke JSY AU 20.00 50.00
142 Billy Smith JSY AU 12.00 30.00
143 Dustin Byfuglien JSY RC 6.00 15.00
144 D. Stafford JSY AU RC EXCH 5.00 12.00
145 Frank Doyle JSY RC 3.00 8.00
146 Carsen Germyn JSY RC 2.50 6.00
147 David Printz JSY RC 2.50 6.00
148 Masi Marjamaki JSY RC 2.50 6.00
149 K.Pushkarev JSY RC 3.00 8.00
150 Michel Ouellet JSY RC 3.00 8.00
151 Billy Thompson JSY RC 2.50 6.00
152 Filip Novak JSY RC 2.50 6.00
153 M. Kopriva JSY RC 2.50 6.00
154 J. Johansson JSY RC 2.50 6.00
155 Shane O'Brien JSY RC 2.50 6.00
156 John Oduya JSY RC 4.00 10.00
157 Fredrik Norrena JSY RC 2.50 6.00
158 N. Backstrom JSY RC 5.00 12.00
159 D.J. King JSY RC 2.50 6.00
160 P. Thoresen JSY RC 2.50 6.00
161 D. Boyd JSY AU RC EXCH 3.00 8.00
162 Mikko Lehtonen JSY RC 3.00 8.00
163 Roman Polak JSY RC 3.00 8.00
164 Yan Stastny JSY AU RC 3.00 8.00
165 Mark Stuart JSY AU RC 3.00 8.00
166 Eric Fehr JSY AU RC 5.00 12.00
167 R. Potulny JSY AU RC 3.00 8.00
168 Ben Ondrus JSY AU RC 3.00 8.00
169 B. Bell JSY AU RC 3.00 8.00
170 Ian White JSY AU RC 4.00 10.00
171 J. Williams JSY AU RC 3.00 8.00
172 M-A Pouliot JSY AU RC 3.00 8.00
173 Noah Welch JSY AU RC 3.00 8.00
174 Shea Weber JSY AU RC 10.00 25.00
175 Jarkko Immonen JSY AU RC 4.00 10.00
176 Tomas Kopecky JSY AU RC 4.00 10.00
177 Matt Carle JSY AU RC 3.00 8.00
178 Ryan Shannon JSY AU RC 3.00 8.00
179 Anze Kopitar JSY AU RC 25.00 60.00
180 Travis Zajac JSY AU RC 6.00 15.00
181 Nigel Dawes JSY AU RC 3.00 8.00
182 K. Letang JSY AU RC 12.00 30.00
183 M-E Vlasic JSY AU RC 5.00 12.00
184 L. Smid JSY AU RC 3.00 8.00
185 L. Eriksson JSY AU RC 6.00 15.00
186 Paul Stastny JSY AU RC 8.00 20.00
187 A. Kaigorodov RC 1.25 3.00
188 P. O'Sullivan JSY AU RC 6.00 15.00
189 Phil Kessel JSY AU RC 12.00 30.00
190 G. Latendresse JSY AU RC 6.00 15.00
191 Jordan Staal JSY AU RC 8.00 20.00
192 L Bourdon JSY AU RC EXCH 8.00 20.00
193 Evgeni Malkin JSY AU RC 50.00 100.00
194 Keith Yandle JSY AU RC 8.00 20.00
195 A. Radulov JSY AU RC 6.00 15.00
196 Rob Collins RC 1.25 3.00
197 Steve Regier RC 1.25 3.00
198 Matt Koalska RC 1.25 3.00
199 Ryan Caldwell RC 1.25 3.00
200 David Liffiton RC 1.25 3.00
201 Erik Reitz RC 1.25 3.00
202 Adam Burish RC 2.00 5.00
203 Alex Brooks RC 1.25 3.00
204 Joel Perrault RC 1.25 3.00
205 Nate Thompson RC 1.25 3.00
206 Janis Sprukts RC 1.25 3.00
207 Alexei Mikhnov RC 1.25 3.00
208 Dave Bolland RC 2.00 5.00
209 Michael Blunden RC 1.25 3.00
210 Lars Jonsson RC 1.25 3.00
211 Triston Grant RC 1.25 3.00
212 Matt Lashoff RC 1.25 3.00
213 Bill Thomas RC 1.25 3.00

2006-07 SPx Spectrum

*VETS: 12X TO 30X BASIC CARDS
*FLASHBACK FABRIC: 1X TO 2.5X
*ROOKIES: 1.2X TO 3X
*ROOKIE JSY: .8X TO 2X
81 Sidney Crosby 100.00 250.00
123 Ray Bourque JSY AU 25.00 60.00
125 Lanny McDonald JSY AU 20.00 50.00
126 Gordie Howe JSY AU 75.00 150.00
127 Grant Fuhr JSY AU 20.00 50.00
128 Wayne Gretzky JSY AU 400.00 1000.00
130 Patrick Roy JSY AU 60.00 120.00
131 Martin Brodeur JSY AU 30.00 80.00
134 Sidney Crosby JSY AU 150.00 300.00
140 Ed Belfour JSY AU 30.00 80.00
193 Evgeni Malkin JSY AU 175.00 350.00

2006-07 SPx SPxcitement

*SPECTRUM/99: .8X TO 2X BASIC INSERTS
X1 Chris Pronger 2.00 5.00
X2 Teemu Selanne 4.00 10.00
X3 Ilya Kovalchuk 2.00 5.00
X4 Kari Lehtonen 1.50 4.00
X5 Marian Hossa 2.00 5.00
X6 Ray Bourque 3.00 8.00
X7 Cam Neely 2.00 5.00
X8 Patrice Bergeron 2.50 6.00
X9 Brad Boyes 1.25 3.00
X10 Phil Esposito 3.00 8.00
X11 Gilbert Perreault 2.00 5.00
X12 Ryan Miller 2.00 5.00
X13 Chris Drury 1.50 4.00
X14 Lanny McDonald 2.00 5.00
X15 Jarome Iginla 2.50 6.00
X16 Miikka Kiprusoff 2.00 5.00
X17 Alex Tanguay 1.25 3.00
X18 Dion Phaneuf 1.50 4.00
X19 Nikolai Khabibulin 2.00 5.00
X20 Martin Havlat 1.25 3.00
X21 Tuomo Ruutu 2.00 5.00
X22 Joe Sakic 4.00 10.00
X23 Jose Theodore 2.00 5.00
X24 Milan Hejduk 1.50 4.00
X25 Marek Svatos 1.25 3.00
X26 Rick Nash 2.00 5.00
X27 Sergei Fedorov 3.00 8.00
X28 Gilbert Brule 1.50 4.00
X29 Mike Modano 3.00 8.00
X30 Marty Turco 2.00 5.00
X31 Eric Lindros 3.00 8.00
X32 Brenden Morrow 1.50 4.00
X33 Gordie Howe 6.00 15.00
X34 Henrik Zetterberg 2.50 6.00
X35 Pavel Datsyuk 3.00 8.00
X36 Nicklas Lidstrom 2.00 5.00
X37 Ted Lindsay 2.00 5.00
X38 Grant Fuhr 3.00 8.00
X39 Wayne Gretzky 12.00 30.00
X40 Ales Hemsky 1.50 4.00
X41 Ryan Smyth 1.50 4.00
X42 Jay Bouwmeester 1.25 3.00
X43 Nathan Horton 2.00 5.00
X44 Olli Jokinen 2.00 5.00
X45 Todd Bertuzzi 2.00 5.00
X46 Ed Belfour 2.00 5.00
X47 Alexander Frolov 1.25 3.00
X48 Rob Blake 2.00 5.00
X49 Rogie Vachon 2.50 6.00
X50 Marian Gaborik 2.00 5.00
X51 Manny Fernandez 1.25 3.00
X52 Pavol Demitra 2.50 6.00
X53 Patrick Roy 5.00 12.00
X54 Guy Lafleur 2.50 6.00
X55 Saku Koivu 2.00 5.00
X56 Cristobal Huet 1.50 4.00
X57 Michael Ryder 1.25 3.00
X58 Paul Kariya 2.00 5.00
X59 Tomas Vokoun 1.50 4.00
X60 Martin Brodeur 5.00 12.00
X61 Patrik Elias 2.00 5.00
X62 Brian Gionta 1.25 3.00
X63 Mike Bossy 2.00 5.00
X64 Miroslav Satan 1.50 4.00
X65 Alexei Yashin 1.50 4.00
X66 Jaromir Jagr 6.00 15.00
X67 Henrik Lundqvist 5.00 12.00
X68 Brendan Shanahan 2.00 5.00
X69 Dany Heatley 1.50 4.00
X70 Jason Spezza 2.00 5.00
X71 Daniel Alfredsson 2.00 5.00
X72 Martin Gerber 1.50 4.00
X73 Peter Forsberg 4.00 10.00
X74 Simon Gagne 2.00 5.00
X75 Jeff Carter 1.50 4.00
X76 Shane Doan 1.50 4.00
X77 Jeremy Roenick 3.00 8.00
X78 Owen Nolan 2.00 5.00
X79 Mario Lemieux 8.00 20.00
X80 Sidney Crosby 8.00 20.00
X81 Marc-Andre Fleury 4.00 10.00
X82 Joe Thornton 3.00 8.00
X83 Jonathan Cheechoo 1.50 4.00
X84 Patrick Marleau 2.00 5.00
X85 Doug Weight 2.00 5.00
X86 Keith Tkachuk 2.00 5.00
X87 Joe Mullen 1.50 4.00
X88 Vincent Lecavalier 2.00 5.00
X89 Martin St. Louis 2.00 5.00
X90 Brad Richards 2.00 5.00
X91 Borje Salming 2.00 5.00
X92 Darryl Sittler 2.50 6.00
X93 Mats Sundin 2.00 5.00
X94 Andrew Raycroft 1.50 4.00
X95 Alexander Steen 1.25 3.00
X96 Markus Naslund 2.00 5.00
X97 Roberto Luongo 3.00 8.00
X98 Richard Brodeur 1.50 4.00
X99 Alexander Ovechkin 8.00 20.00
X100 Olaf Kolzig 2.00 5.00

2006-07 SPx Winning Materials

*SPECTRUM/99: .6X TO 1.5X BASIC JSY
WMAF Alexander Frolov 1.50 4.00
WMAH Ales Hemsky 2.00 5.00
WMAM Al MacInnis 3.00 8.00
WMAN Glenn Anderson 2.00 5.00
WMAO Alexander Ovechkin 10.00 25.00
WMAS Alexander Steen 1.50 4.00
WMAT Alex Tanguay 1.50 4.00
WMAY Alexei Yashin 2.00 5.00
WMBB Brad Boyes 1.50 4.00
WMBC Bobby Clarke 4.00 10.00
WMBG Bill Guerin 2.50 6.00
WMBL Brian Leetch 2.00 5.00
WMBM Bryan McCabe 1.50 4.00
WMBO Pierre-Marc Bouchard 2.50 6.00
WMBR Brad Richards 2.50 6.00
WMBS Billy Smith 2.50 6.00
WMBT Bryan Trottier 2.50 6.00
WMCA Jeff Carter 2.00 5.00
WMCC Chris Chelios 2.50 6.00
WMCD Chris Drury 2.00 5.00
WMCH Cristobal Huet 2.00 5.00
WMCJ Curtis Joseph 3.00 8.00
WMCN Cam Neely 2.50 6.00
WMCP Chris Pronger 2.50 6.00
WMCW Cam Ward 2.50 6.00
WMDA Daniel Alfredsson 2.50 6.00
WMDH Dany Heatley 2.00 5.00
WMDP Dion Phaneuf 2.00 5.00
WMDW Doug Weight 2.50 6.00
WMEB Ed Belfour 2.50 6.00
WMES Eric Staal 3.00 8.00
WMGA Simon Gagne 2.50 6.00
WMGF Grant Fuhr 4.00 10.00
WMGI Brian Gionta 1.50 4.00
WMHA Martin Havlat 1.50 4.00
WMHE Milan Hejduk 2.00 5.00
WMHK Dominik Hasek 4.00 10.00
WMHL Henrik Lundqvist 6.00 15.00
WMHO Tomas Holmstrom 2.00 5.00
WMHZ Henrik Zetterberg 3.00 8.00
WMIK Ilya Kovalchuk 2.50 6.00
WMJB Jay Bouwmeester 1.50 4.00
WMJC Jonathan Cheechoo 2.00 5.00
WMJG Jean-Sebastien Giguere 2.50 6.00
WMJI Jarome Iginla 3.00 8.00
WMJJ Jaromir Jagr 8.00 20.00
WMJL Joffrey Lupul 1.50 4.00
WMJS Joe Sakic 5.00 12.00
WMJT Jose Theodore 2.50 6.00
WMJW Justin Williams 2.00 5.00
WMKC Kyle Calder 1.50 4.00
WMKD Kris Draper 1.50 4.00
WMKL Kari Lehtonen 2.00 5.00
WMKT Keith Tkachuk 2.50 6.00
WMLM Lanny McDonald 2.50 6.00
WMMA Maxim Afinogenov 1.50 4.00
WMMB Martin Brodeur 6.00 15.00
WMMC Mike Cammalleri 1.50 4.00
WMMF Manny Fernandez 1.50 4.00
WMMG Marian Gaborik 2.50 6.00
WMMH Marian Hossa 2.50 6.00
WMMM Mike Modano 4.00 10.00
WMMN Markus Naslund 2.50 6.00
WMMO Brendan Morrison 1.50 4.00
WMMR Michael Ryder 1.50 4.00
WMMS Miroslav Satan 2.00 5.00
WMMT Marty Turco 2.50 6.00
WMMW Brenden Morrow 2.00 5.00
WMNL Nicklas Lidstrom 2.50 6.00
WMOJ Olli Jokinen 2.50 6.00
WMOK Olaf Kolzig 2.50 6.00
WMPB Patrice Bergeron 3.00 8.00
WMPD Pavel Datsyuk 4.00 10.00
WMPE Patrik Elias 2.50 6.00
WMPF Peter Forsberg 5.00 12.00
WMPK Paul Kariya 2.50 6.00
WMPM Patrick Marleau 2.50 6.00
WMPP Petr Prucha 2.00 5.00
WMPT Pierre Turgeon 2.00 5.00
WMRD Rick DiPietro 2.00 5.00
WMRE Robert Esche 2.00 5.00
WMRE Mark Recchi 3.00 8.00
WMRL Roberto Luongo 4.00 10.00
WMRN Rick Nash 2.50 6.00
WMRO Rob Blake 2.50 6.00
WMRS Ryan Smyth 2.00 5.00
WMSA Borje Salming 2.50 6.00
WMSC Sidney Crosby 10.00 25.00
WMSD Shane Doan 2.00 5.00
WMSF Sergei Federov 4.00 10.00
WMSG Scott Gomez 2.00 5.00
WMSK Saku Koivu 2.50 6.00
WMSP Jason Spezza 2.50 6.00
WMSS Sergei Samsonov 2.00 5.00
WMST Martin St. Louis 2.50 6.00
WMTH Joe Thornton 4.00 10.00
WMTR Tuomo Ruutu 2.50 6.00
WMTS Teemu Selanne 5.00 12.00
WMTV Tomas Vokoun 2.00 5.00
WMVL Vincent Lecavalier 2.50 6.00

2007-08 SPx

COMP.SET w/o SPs (100) 12.00 30.00
1 Jean-Sebastien Giguere .40 1.00
2 Ryan Getzlaf .40 1.00
3 Scott Niedermayer .40 1.00
4 Chris Pronger .40 1.00
5 Mike Modano .60 1.50
6 Mike Ribeiro .25 .60
7 Marty Turco .40 1.00
8 Anze Kopitar .60 1.50
9 Alexander Frolov .25 .60
10 Rob Blake .40 1.00
11 Shane Doan .30 .75
12 Ed Jovanovski .30 .75
13 David Aebischer .30 .75
14 Joe Thornton .60 1.50
15 Evgeni Nabokov .30 .75
16 Jonathan Cheechoo .30 .75
17 Patrick Marleau .40 1.00
18 Jarome Iginla .50 1.25
19 Miikka Kiprusoff .40 1.00
20 Alex Tanguay .30 .75
21 Dion Phaneuf .30 .75
22 Joe Sakic .75 2.00
23 Paul Stastny .30 .75
24 Milan Hejduk .30 .75
25 Ales Hemsky .30 .75
26 Dwayne Roloson .30 .75
27 Wayne Gretzky 2.50 6.00
28 Shawn Horcoff .25 .60
29 Marian Gaborik .40 1.00
30 Niklas Backstrom .40 1.00
31 Pierre-Marc Bouchard .40 1.00
32 Markus Naslund .40 1.00
33 Roberto Luongo .60 1.50
34 Henrik Sedin .50 1.25
35 Daniel Sedin .50 1.25
36 Martin Havlat .40 1.00
37 Nikolai Khabibulin .40 1.00
38 Duncan Keith .30 .75
39 Rick Nash .40 1.00
40 Fredrik Norrena .25 .60
41 Sergei Fedorov .60 1.50
42 Henrik Zetterberg .50 1.25
43 Gordie Howe 1.25 3.00
44 Pavel Datsyuk .60 1.50
45 Nicklas Lidstrom .40 1.00
46 Chris Mason .30 .75
47 Steve Sullivan .25 .60
48 Alexander Radulov .40 1.00
49 Doug Weight .40 1.00
50 Manny Legace .30 .75
51 Paul Kariya .40 1.00
52 Ilya Kovalchuk .40 1.00
53 Kari Lehtonen .30 .75
54 Marian Hossa .40 1.00
55 Eric Staal .50 1.25
56 Cam Ward .40 1.00
57 Justin Williams .30 .75
58 Nathan Horton .40 1.00
59 Tomas Vokoun .30 .75
60 Olli Jokinen .30 .75
61 Martin St. Louis .40 1.00
62 Vincent Lecavalier .40 1.00
63 Brad Richards .40 1.00
64 Alexander Ovechkin 1.50 4.00
65 Olaf Kolzig .40 1.00
66 Alexander Semin .40 1.00

67 Patrice Bergeron .50 1.25
68 Bobby Orr 1.50 4.00
69 Phil Kessel .40 1.00
70 Jason Pominville .25 .60
71 Ryan Miller .40 1.00
72 Thomas Vanek .30 .75
73 Saku Koivu .40 1.00
74 Cristobal Huet .30 .75
75 Michael Ryder .25 .60
76 Guillaume Latendresse .30 .75
77 Daniel Alfredsson .40 1.00
78 Jason Spezza .40 1.00
79 Ray Emery .30 .75
80 Dany Heatley .30 .75
81 Mats Sundin .40 1.00
82 Vesa Toskala .30 .75
83 Alexander Steen .25 .60
84 Darcy Tucker .30 .75
85 Martin Brodeur 1.00 2.50
86 Patrik Elias .40 1.00
87 Zach Parise .40 1.00
88 Rick DiPietro .30 .75
89 Miroslav Satan .30 .75
90 Bill Guerin .40 1.00
91 Henrik Lundqvist 1.00 2.50
92 Jaromir Jagr 1.25 3.00
93 Mark Messier .75 2.00
94 Simon Gagne .40 1.00
95 Daniel Briere .40 1.00
96 Jeff Carter .30 .75
97 Marc-Andre Fleury .75 2.00
98 Evgeni Malkin .75 2.00
99 Sidney Crosby 1.50 4.00
100 Mario Lemieux 1.50 4.00
101 Billy Smith JSY 8.00 20.00
102 Bob Nystrom JSY 5.00 12.00
103 Bobby Clarke JSY 12.00 30.00
104 Brendan Shanahan JSY 8.00 20.00
105 Brian Leetch JSY 6.00 15.00
106 Denis Savard JSY 8.00 20.00
107 Dino Ciccarelli JSY 8.00 20.00
108 Doug Gilmour JSY 10.00 25.00
109 Ed Belfour JSY 8.00 20.00
110 Frank Mahovlich JSY 8.00 20.00
111 Guy Lafleur JSY 10.00 25.00
112 Joe Sakic JSY 15.00 40.00
113 Keith Tkachuk JSY 8.00 20.00
114 Lanny McDonald JSY 8.00 20.00
115 Mark Recchi JSY 10.00 25.00
116 Mats Sundin JSY 8.00 20.00
117 Mike Modano JSY 12.00 30.00
118 Nicklas Lidstrom JSY 8.00 20.00
119 Paul Kariya JSY 8.00 20.00
120 Peter Forsberg JSY 15.00 40.00
121 Roberto Luongo JSY 12.00 30.00
122 Saku Koivu JSY 8.00 20.00
123 Sergei Fedorov JSY 12.00 30.00
124 Steve Shutt JSY 6.00 15.00
125 Teemu Selanne JSY 15.00 40.00
126 Al MacInnis JSY AU 25.00 60.00
127 Alexander Ovechkin JSY AU 75.00 150.00
128 Borje Salming JSY AU 20.00 50.00
129 Cam Neely JSY AU 20.00 50.00
130 D.Hawerchuk SP JSY AU 40.00 100.00
131 Dany Heatley JSY AU 15.00 40.00
132 Darryl Sittler JSY AU 25.00 60.00
133 Dominik Hasek JSY AU 30.00 80.00
134 Doug Wilson JSY AU 10.00 25.00
135 Evgeni Malkin JSY AU 25.00 60.00
136 Gordie Howe SP JSY AU 250.00 400.00
137 Grant Fuhr JSY AU 40.00 80.00
138 Jarome Iginla JSY AU 15.00 40.00
139 J.Beliveau SP JSY AU 150.00 250.00
140 Joe Thornton JSY AU 20.00 50.00
141 Larry Robinson JSY AU 20.00 50.00
142 M.Lemieux SP JSY AU 125.00 250.00
143 M.Messier SP JSY AU 60.00 120.00
144 Martin Brodeur JSY AU 40.00 100.00
145 Ray Bourque JSY AU 30.00 80.00
146 P.Roy SP JSY AU 100.00 200.00
147 Peter Stastny JSY AU 15.00 40.00
149 Sidney Crosby JSY AU 100.00 200.00
150 W.Gretzky SP JSY AU 500.00 1200.00
151 Ryan Carter RC 1.50 4.00
152 Mark Mancari RC 1.50 4.00
153 Patrick Kaleta RC 1.50 4.00
154 David Moss RC 2.50 6.00
155 Colin Fraser RC 1.50 4.00
156 Bryan Bickell RC 3.00 8.00
157 Magnus Johansson RC 1.50 4.00
158 Jonas Nordqvist RC 1.50 4.00
159 Jeff Finger RC 1.50 4.00
160 Tomas Popperle RC 1.50 4.00
161 Chris Conner RC 1.50 4.00
162 Bryan Young RC 1.50 4.00
163 Sebastien Bisaillon RC 1.50 4.00
164 Zach Stortini RC 1.50 4.00
165 Martin Lojek RC 1.50 4.00
166 Joe Piskula RC 1.50 4.00
167 John Zeiler RC 1.50 4.00
168 Brady Murray RC 1.50 4.00
169 Rich Peverley RC 1.50 4.00
170 Mark Fraser RC 1.50 4.00
171 David Clarkson RC 1.50 4.00
172 Denis Tolpeko RC 1.50 4.00
173 Daniel Carcillo RC 2.00 5.00
174 Craig Weller RC 1.50 4.00
175 Daniel Winnik RC 2.00 5.00
176 Thomas Plihal RC 1.50 4.00
177 Steve Wagner RC 1.50 4.00
178 Mike Lundin RC 1.50 4.00
179 Jannik Hansen RC 2.00 5.00
180 Mason Raymond RC 2.50 6.00
181 Jonas Hiller JSY RC 6.00 15.00
182 Tobias Enstrom JSY RC 5.00 12.00
183 Jonathan Sigalet JSY RC 3.00 8.00
184 Jaroslav Hlinka JSY RC 4.00 10.00
185 Tyler Weiman JSY RC 4.00 10.00
186 Jared Boll JSY RC 4.00 10.00
187 Marc Methot JSY RC 3.00 8.00
188 Tobias Stephan JSY RC 4.00 10.00
189 Matt Niskanen JSY RC 5.00 12.00
190 Devin Setoguchi JSY RC 5.00 12.00
191 Matt Ellis JSY RC 4.00 10.00
192 Tom Gilbert JSY RC 4.00 10.00
193 Tuukka Rask JSY AU RC 30.00 80.00
194 Ville Koistinen JSY RC 3.00 8.00
195 Rod Pelley JSY RC 3.00 8.00
196 Brandon Dubinsky JSY RC 6.00 15.00
197 Daniel Girardi JSY RC 4.00 10.00
198 Ryan Parent JSY RC 3.00 8.00
199 Torrey Mitchell JSY RC 4.00 10.00
200 Matt Smaby JSY RC 3.00 8.00
201 Bobby Ryan JSY AU RC 6.00 15.00
202 Drew Miller JSY AU RC 6.00 15.00
203 Bryan Little JSY AU RC 8.00 20.00
204 Brett Sterling JSY AU RC 5.00 12.00
205 David Krejci JSY AU RC 20.00 50.00
206 Milan Lucic JSY AU RC 20.00 40.00
207 Curtis McElhinney JSY AU RC 8.00 20.00
208 Kris Russell JSY AU RC 8.00 20.00
209 Sam Gagner JSY AU RC 10.00 25.00
210 Andrew Cogliano JSY AU RC 6.00 15.00
211 Rob Schremp JSY AU RC 6.00 15.00
212 Steve Downie JSY AU RC 6.00 15.00
213 Jack Johnson JSY AU RC 6.00 15.00
214 Jonathan Bernier JSY AU RC 10.00 25.00
215 Lauri Tukonen JSY AU RC 5.00 12.00
216 Petr Kalus JSY AU RC 5.00 12.00
217 James Sheppard JSY AU RC 5.00 12.00
218 Kyle Chipchura JSY AU RC 8.00 20.00
219 Jaroslav Halak JSY AU RC 10.00 25.00
220 Nicklas Bergfors JSY AU RC 5.00 12.00
221 Andy Greene JSY AU RC 6.00 15.00
222 Frans Nielsen JSY AU RC 8.00 20.00
223 Ryan Callahan JSY AU RC 12.50 30.00
224 Marc Staal JSY AU RC 8.00 20.00
225 Nick Foligno JSY AU RC 10.00 25.00
226 Brian Elliott JSY AU RC 10.00 25.00
227 Martin Hanzal JSY AU RC 6.00 15.00
228 David Perron JSY AU RC 10.00 25.00
229 Erik Johnson JSY AU RC 8.00 20.00
230 Anton Stralman JSY AU RC 5.00 12.00
231 Jonathan Toews JSY AU RC 75.00 135.00
232 Patrick Kane JSY AU RC 100.00 200.00
233 Carey Price JSY AU RC 100.00 250.00
234 Jiri Tlusty JSY AU RC 12.00 30.00
235 Peter Mueller JSY AU RC 10.00 25.00
236 Nicklas Backstrom JSY AU RC 25.00 60.00

2007-08 SPx Spectrum

*SPEC JSY (1-100): 6X TO 15X
*SPEC JSY (101-125): .5X TO 1.2X
*SPEC JSY AU (126-150): .4X TO 1X
*SPEC (151-180): .8X TO 2X
*SPEC JSY (181-200): .5X TO 1.2X
*SPEC JSY AU (201-230): .5X TO 1.2X
*SPEC JSY AU (231-236): .4X TO 1X
143 Mark Messier JSY AU 100.00 200.00
146 Patrick Roy JSY AU 100.00 200.00
149 Sidney Crosby JSY AU 200.00 400.00
231 Jonathan Toews JSY AU 300.00 600.00
232 Patrick Kane JSY AU 350.00 600.00
233 Carey Price JSY AU 200.00 500.00
236 Nicklas Backstrom JSY AU 50.00 100.00

2007-08 SPx Force Quad Holograms

F1 Lem/Sid/Gretz/Mess 15.00 40.00
F2 Roy/Brod/Luon/Gig 10.00 25.00
F3 Sakic/Lecav/Joe/Spez 8.00 20.00
F4 Iggy/St. L/Heat/Howe 12.00 30.00
F5 Lids/Nied/Orr/Dion 15.00 40.00

2007-08 SPx SPXtreme

COMPLETE SET (70) 75.00 150.00
X1 Wayne Gretzky 6.00 15.00
X2 Mario Lemieux 4.00 10.00
X3 Bobby Orr 4.00 10.00
X4 Mark Messier 2.00 5.00
X5 Gordie Howe 3.00 8.00
X6 Patrick Roy 2.50 6.00
X7 Phil Esposito 1.50 4.00
X8 Tony Esposito 1.00 2.50
X9 Stan Mikita 1.25 3.00
X10 Grant Fuhr 1.50 4.00
X11 Luc Robitaille 1.00 2.50
X12 Guy Lafleur 1.25 3.00
X13 Mike Bossy 1.00 2.50
X14 Denis Potvin 1.00 2.50
X15 Bobby Clarke 1.50 4.00
X16 Bernie Parent 1.25 3.00
X17 Darryl Sittler 1.25 3.00
X18 Lanny McDonald 1.00 2.50
X19 Peter Stastny .75 2.00
X20 Dale Hawerchuk 1.25 3.00
X21 Jean-Sebastien Giguere 1.00 2.50
X22 Ilya Kovalchuk 1.00 2.50
X23 Patrice Bergeron 1.25 3.00
X24 Ryan Miller 1.00 2.50
X25 Jarome Iginla 1.25 3.00
X26 Eric Staal 1.25 3.00
X27 Joe Sakic 2.00 5.00
X28 Rick Nash 1.00 2.50
X29 Mike Modano 1.50 4.00
X30 Henrik Zetterberg 1.25 3.00
X31 Marian Gaborik 1.00 2.50
X32 Saku Koivu 1.00 2.50
X33 Tomas Vokoun .75 2.00
X34 Martin Brodeur 2.50 6.00
X35 Jaromir Jagr 3.00 8.00
X36 Dany Heatley .75 2.00
X37 Simon Gagne 1.00 2.50
X38 Sidney Crosby 4.00 10.00
X39 Evgeni Malkin 2.00 5.00
X40 Joe Thornton 1.50 4.00
X41 Vincent Lecavalier 1.00 2.50
X42 Mats Sundin 1.00 2.50
X43 Roberto Luongo 1.50 4.00
X44 Alexander Ovechkin 4.00 10.00
X45 Miikka Kiprusoff 1.00 2.50
X46 Thomas Vanek .75 2.00
X47 Teemu Selanne 2.00 5.00
X48 Anze Kopitar 1.50 4.00
X49 Miroslav Satan .75 2.00
X50 Daniel Alfredsson 1.00 2.50
X51 Rob Schremp .75 2.00
X52 Jack Johnson .75 2.00
X53 Petr Kalus .60 1.50
X54 Carey Price 10.00 25.00
X55 Patrick Kane 15.00 40.00
X56 Nicklas Backstrom 2.00 5.00
X57 Marc Staal 1.00 2.50
X58 Peter Mueller .75 2.00
X59 Jonathan Toews 15.00 40.00
X60 Bobby Ryan 1.50 4.00
X61 Nicklas Bergfors .60 1.50
X62 Erik Johnson 1.00 2.50
X63 Sam Gagner 1.25 3.00
X64 Kyle Chipchura 1.00 2.50
X65 Bryan Little .75 2.00
X66 Jonathan Bernier 1.25 3.00
X67 Andrew Cogliano .75 2.00
X68 Nick Foligno 1.25 3.00
X69 Brett Sterling .60 1.50
X70 James Sheppard .60 1.50

2007-08 SPx SPXtreme Spectrum

*SPECTRUM/25: 2.5X TO 6X BASIC INSERTS
X4 Mark Messier 12.00 30.00
X54 Carey Price 40.00 100.00
X55 Patrick Kane 50.00 100.00
X59 Jonathan Toews 60.00 120.00

2007-08 SPx Winning Combos

WCAR J.Arnott/A.Radulov 5.00 12.00
WCBE M.Brodeur/P.Elias 12.00 30.00
WCBH E.Belfour/D.Hasek 8.00 20.00
WCBK P.Bergeron/P.Kessel 6.00 15.00
WCBL M.Brodeur/R.Luongo 8.00 20.00
WCBM M.Sundin/B.Salming 5.00 12.00
WCCM S.Crosby/E.Malkin 20.00 50.00
WCCO S.Crosby/A.Ovechkin 12.00 30.00
WCDA D.Sittler/A.Steen 6.00 15.00
WCDB Datsyuk/Brind'Amour 8.00 20.00
WCDG P.Demitra/M.Gaborik 6.00 15.00
WCDM D.Ciccarelli/M.Gaborik 5.00 12.00
WCDS R.DiPietro/B.Smith 5.00 12.00
WCDZ Datsyuk/Zetterberg 8.00 20.00
WCFK A.Frolov/A.Kopitar 8.00 20.00
WCFR G.Fuhr/D.Roloson 8.00 20.00
WCGB S.Gagne/M.Biron 5.00 12.00
WCHE D.Heatley/R.Emery 4.00 10.00
WCHK Havlat/Khabibulin 5.00 12.00
WCIM M.Hossa/I.Kovalchuk 5.00 12.00
WCIT J.Iginla/A.Tanguay 6.00 15.00
WCJD E.Jovanovski/S.Doan 4.00 10.00
WCJL J.Jagr/H.Lundqvist 15.00 40.00
WCJM J.Sakic/M.Hejduk 10.00 25.00
WCJS J.Jagr/P.Stastny 6.00 15.00
WCKO O.Kolzig/A.Ovechkin 8.00 20.00
WCKR S.Koivu/M.Ryder 5.00 12.00
WCLB N.Lidstrom/R.Bourque 8.00 20.00
WCLC M.Lemieux/S.Crosby 20.00 50.00
WCLH G.Lafleur/C.Higgins 6.00 15.00
WCLS Lecavalier/St. Louis 5.00 12.00
WCMM M.Modano/M.Turco 8.00 20.00
WCMT McDonald/Tanguay 5.00 12.00
WCMV R.Miller/T.Vanek 5.00 12.00
WCNF R.Nash/S.Fedorov 8.00 20.00
WCNG Niedermayer/Giguere 5.00 12.00
WCNK C.Neely/P.Kessel 5.00 12.00
WCNL M.Naslund/R.Luongo 8.00 20.00
WCOM A.Ovechkin/E.Malkin 15.00 40.00
WCPM D.Phaneuf/A.MacInnis 6.00 15.00
WCRB P.Roy/M.Brodeur 12.00 30.00
WCRH D.Roloson/A.Hemsky 4.00 10.00
WCSD M.Satan/R.DiPietro 4.00 10.00
WCSH D.Savard/M.Havlat 5.00 12.00
WCSS J.Sakic/B.Shanahan 6.00 15.00
WCST M.Sundin/D.Tucker 5.00 12.00
WCSW E.Staal/C.Ward 6.00 15.00
WCTN Thornton/Nabokov 8.00 20.00
WCVJ T.Vokoun/O.Jokinen 4.00 10.00
WCWK P.Kariya/D.Weight 5.00 12.00

2007-08 SPx Winning Combos Spectrum

*SPEC: .5X TO 1.2X

2007-08 SPx Winning Materials

*SPECTRUM/99: .5X TO 1.2X BASIC INSERTS
WMAH Ales Hemsky 3.00 8.00
WMAM Al MacInnis 5.00 12.00
WMAO Alexander Ovechkin 15.00 40.00
WMAT Alex Tanguay 3.00 8.00
WMBR Brad Richards 4.00 10.00
WMCN Cam Neely 4.00 10.00
WMCW Cam Ward 4.00 10.00
WMDA Daniel Alfredsson 4.00 10.00
WMDB Daniel Briere 4.00 10.00
WMDH Dany Heatley 3.00 8.00
WMDP Dion Phaneuf 3.00 8.00
WMDR Dwayne Roloson 3.00 8.00
WMES Eric Staal 5.00 12.00
WMHA Dominik Hasek 6.00 15.00
WMHL Henrik Lundqvist 10.00 25.00
WMHZ Henrik Zetterberg 5.00 12.00
WMIK Ilya Kovalchuk 4.00 10.00
WMJC Jonathan Cheechoo 3.00 8.00
WMJG Jean-Sebastien Giguere 4.00 10.00
WMJI Jarome Iginla 5.00 12.00
WMJJ Jaromir Jagr 12.00 30.00
WMJS Joe Sakic 8.00 20.00
WMJT Joe Thornton 6.00 15.00
WMKL Kari Lehtonen 3.00 8.00
WMMB Martin Brodeur 10.00 25.00
WMMG Marian Gaborik 4.00 10.00
WMMH Marian Hossa 4.00 10.00
WMMM Mike Modano 6.00 15.00
WMMN Markus Naslund 4.00 10.00
WMMR Michael Ryder 2.50 6.00
WMMS Mats Sundin 4.00 10.00
WMMT Marty Turco 4.00 10.00
WMNL Nicklas Lidstrom 4.00 10.00
WMPB Patrice Bergeron 5.00 12.00
WMPD Pavel Datsyuk 6.00 15.00
WMPF Peter Forsberg 8.00 20.00
WMPK Paul Kariya 4.00 10.00
WMPO Denis Potvin 4.00 10.00
WMRL Roberto Luongo 6.00 15.00
WMRN Rick Nash 4.00 10.00
WMSA Borje Salming 4.00 10.00
WMSC Sidney Crosby 15.00 40.00
WMSG Simon Gagne 4.00 10.00
WMSK Saku Koivu 4.00 10.00
WMTS Teemu Selanne 8.00 20.00
WMTV Tomas Vokoun 3.00 8.00
WMVA Thomas Vanek 3.00 8.00
WMVL Vincent Lecavalier 4.00 10.00
WMVT Vesa Toskala 3.00 8.00
WMZP Zach Parise 4.00 10.00

2007-08 SPx Winning Materials Radiance Autographs

WMAO Alexander Ovechkin 150.00 250.00
WMCN Cam Neely 12.00 30.00
WMDP Dion Phaneuf 40.00 80.00
WMHA Dominik Hasek 40.00 80.00
WMMG Marian Gaborik 40.00 80.00
WMNL Nicklas Lidstrom 30.00 60.00
WMSC Sidney Crosby 150.00 300.00

2008-09 SPx

COMP.SET w/o SPs (100) 15.00 40.00
1 Nicklas Backstrom .50 1.25
2 Alexander Ovechkin 2.00 5.00
3 Pavol Demitra .60 1.50
4 Roberto Luongo .75 2.00
5 Steve Bernier .30 .75
6 Mats Sundin .50 1.25
7 Vesa Toskala .60 1.50
8 Ryan Malone .30 .75
9 Vincent Lecavalier .50 1.25
10 Olaf Kolzig .50 1.25
11 David Perron .40 1.00
12 Paul Kariya .50 1.25
13 Joe Thornton .75 2.00
14 Jonathan Cheechoo .40 1.00
15 Patrick Marleau .50 1.25
16 Rob Blake .50 1.25
17 Jordan Staal .40 1.00
18 Sidney Crosby 2.00 5.00
19 Marc-Andre Fleury 1.00 2.50
20 Evgeni Malkin 1.00 2.50
21 Miroslav Satan .50 1.25
22 Shane Doan .40 1.00
23 Peter Mueller .40 1.00
24 Olli Jokinen .40 1.00
25 Mike Richards .40 1.00
26 Martin Biron .40 1.00
27 Simon Gagne .50 1.25
28 Daniel Briere .50 1.25
29 Jason Spezza .50 1.25
30 Martin Gerber .40 1.00
31 Chris Phillips .30 .75
32 Markus Naslund .50 1.25
33 Scott Gomez .40 1.00
34 Wade Redden .30 .75
35 Henrik Lundqvist 1.25 3.00
36 Chris Drury .40 1.00
37 Nikolai Zherdev .30 .75
38 Doug Weight .50 1.25
39 Rick DiPietro .40 1.00
40 Martin Brodeur 1.25 3.00
41 Patrik Elias .50 1.25
42 Zach Parise .50 1.25
43 Brian Gionta .30 .75
44 Shea Weber .40 1.00
45 Jason Arnott .40 1.00
46 Carey Price 1.00 2.50
47 Saku Koivu .50 1.25
48 Alex Kovalev .40 1.00
49 Alex Tanguay .30 .75
50 Marian Gaborik .50 1.25
51 Pierre-Marc Bouchard .50 1.25
52 Anze Kopitar .75 2.00
53 Tomas Vokoun .40 1.00
54 Stephen Weiss .30 .75
55 Shawn Horcoff .30 .75
56 Dwayne Roloson .40 1.00
57 Sam Gagner .30 .75
58 Marian Hossa .50 1.25
59 Tomas Holmstrom .40 1.00
60 Brian Rafalski .40 1.00
61 Henrik Zetterberg .60 1.50
62 Nicklas Lidstrom .50 1.25
63 Brad Richards .50 1.25
64 Mike Modano .75 2.00
65 Marty Turco .50 1.25
66 Mike Ribeiro .30 .75
67 Jere Lehtinen .30 .75
68 Pascal Leclaire .40 1.00
69 Rick Nash .50 1.25
70 Joe Sakic 1.00 2.50
71 Milan Hejduk .40 1.00
72 Paul Stastny .40 1.00
73 Peter Forsberg 1.00 2.50
74 Marek Svatos .30 .75
75 Darcy Tucker .40 1.00
76 Patrick Sharp .50 1.25
77 Jonathan Toews .75 2.00
78 Patrick Kane 1.00 2.50
79 Eric Staal .60 1.50
80 Cam Ward .50 1.25
81 Justin Williams .40 1.00
82 Mike Cammalleri .40 1.00
83 Jarome Iginla .60 1.50
84 Todd Bertuzzi .50 1.25
85 Dion Phaneuf .40 1.00
86 Tuukka Rask .60 1.50
87 Ryan Miller .50 1.25
88 Maxim Afinogenov .30 .75
89 Marc Savard .30 .75
90 Patrice Bergeron .60 1.50
91 Phil Kessel .50 1.25
92 Tim Thomas .50 1.25
93 Zdeno Chara .50 1.25
94 Michael Ryder .30 .75
95 Ilya Kovalchuk .50 1.25
96 Kari Lehtonen .60 1.50
97 Tobias Enstrom .30 .75
98 Corey Perry .75 2.00
99 Ryan Getzlaf .50 1.25
100 Teemu Selanne 1.00 2.50
101 Adam Pardy RC 2.50 6.00
102 Wayne Simmonds RC 5.00 12.00
103 Nathan Oystrick RC 3.00 8.00
104 Anssi Salmela RC 3.00 8.00
105 Jared Ross RC 3.00 8.00
106 Chris Porter RC 3.00 8.00
107 Janne Niskala RC 3.00 8.00
108 John Mitchell RC 2.50 6.00
109 Mike Brown RC 3.00 8.00
110 Kyle Greentree RC 3.00 8.00
111 Sami Lepisto RC 2.50 6.00
112 Zach Fitzgerald RC 3.00 8.00
113 Darryl Boyce RC 2.50 6.00
114 Jesse Winchester RC 2.00 5.00
115 Corey Locke RC 2.50 6.00
116 Brandon Nolan RC 2.50 6.00
117 Jordan Hendry RC 2.50 6.00
118 Pascal Pelletier RC 2.00 5.00
119 Tom Cavanagh RC 2.50 6.00
120 Theo Peckham RC 2.50 6.00
121 B.J. Crombeen RC 2.00 5.00
122 Joe Jensen RC 3.00 8.00
123 Josh Bailey RC 4.00 10.00
124 Garrett Stafford RC 3.00 8.00
125 Jonas Frogren RC 2.00 5.00
126 Alex Foster RC 2.50 6.00
127 David Brine RC 2.00 5.00
128 Colin Stuart RC 2.50 6.00
129 Andrew Murray RC 2.50 6.00
130 Niklas Hjalmarsson RC 3.00 8.00
131 Jonathan Ericsson JSY RC 4.00 10.00
132 Darren Helm JSY RC 4.00 10.00
133 Erik Ersberg JSY RC 3.00 8.00
134 Matthew Halischuk JSY RC 2.50 6.00
135 Mark Fistric JSY RC 3.00 8.00
136 Adam Pineault JSY RC 3.00 8.00
137 Oscar Moller JSY RC 3.00 8.00
138 Matt D'Agostini JSY RC 3.00 8.00
139 Mattias Ritola JSY RC 3.00 8.00
140 Ryan Stone JSY RC 2.50 6.00
141 Mike Iggulden JSY RC 3.00 8.00
142 Andrew Ebbett JSY RC 2.50 6.00
143 Dan LaCosta JSY RC 4.00 10.00
144 Teddy Purcell JSY RC 3.00 8.00
145 Jamie McGinn JSY RC 4.00 10.00
146 Tim Ramholt JSY RC 3.00 8.00
147 Jon Filewich JSY RC 3.00 8.00
148 Boris Valabik JSY RC 4.00 10.00
149 Cory Schneider JSY AU RC 10.00 25.00
150 Tyler Plante JSY RC 3.00 8.00
151 Petr Vrana JSY RC 2.50 6.00
152 Brian Boyle JSY RC 3.00 8.00
153 Tom Sestito JSY RC 4.00 10.00
154 Ryan Jones JSY RC 4.00 10.00
155 Andreas Nodl JSY RC 2.50 6.00
156 James Neal JSY AU RC 10.00 25.00
157 Jakub Voracek JSY AU RC 10.00 25.00
158 T.J. Oshie JSY AU RC 10.00 25.00
159 Nikita Filatov JSY AU RC 5.00 12.00
160 Brandon Sutter JSY AU RC 5.00 12.00
161 Steve Mason JSY AU RC 8.00 20.00
162 Derick Brassard JSY AU RC 5.00 12.00
163 Kevin Porter JSY AU RC 4.00 10.00
164 Viktor Tikhonov JSY AU RC 4.00 10.00
165 J.Abdelkader JSY AU RC 8.00 20.00
166 Michael Frolik JSY AU RC 5.00 12.00
167 Zach Boychuk JSY AU RC 5.00 12.00
168 Shawn Matthias JSY AU RC 5.00 12.00
169 F.Brunnstrom JSY AU RC 4.00 10.00
170 Patric Hornqvist JSY AU RC 5.00 12.00
171 Nikolai Kulemin JSY AU RC 5.00 12.00
172 Colton Gillies JSY AU RC 4.00 10.00
173 Kyle Okposo JSY AU RC 6.00 15.00
174 Patrik Berglund JSY AU RC 4.00 10.00
175 Lauri Korpikoski JSY AU RC 3.00 8.00
176 Brian Lee JSY AU RC 4.00 10.00
177 Ilya Zubov JSY AU RC 4.00 10.00
178 Robbie Earl JSY AU RC 3.00 8.00
179 Claude Giroux JSY AU RC 20.00 50.00
180 A.Pietrangelo JSY AU RC 8.00 20.00
181 Alex Goligoski JSY AU RC 6.00 15.00
182 Vladimir Mihalik JSY AU RC 3.00 8.00
183 Luca Sbisa JSY AU RC 3.00 8.00
184 Mikkel Boedker JSY AU RC 6.00 15.00
185 Kyle Turris JSY AU RC 10.00 25.00
186 Blake Wheeler JSY AU RC 15.00 40.00
187 Luke Schenn JSY AU RC 8.00 20.00
188 Zach Bogosian JSY AU RC 8.00 20.00
189 Drew Doughty JSY AU RC 15.00 40.00
190 S.Stamkos JSY AU RC 80.00 200.00
191 Theoren Fleury FF JSY 10.00 25.00
192 Adam Oates FF JSY 8.00 20.00
193 Grant Fuhr FF JSY 12.00 30.00
194 Zach Parise FF JSY 8.00 20.00
195 Lanny McDonald FF JSY 8.00 20.00
196 Nicklas Lidstrom FF JSY 8.00 20.00
197 Martin Brodeur FF JSY 20.00 50.00
198 Paul Kariya FF JSY 8.00 20.00
199 Teemu Selanne FF JSY 15.00 40.00
200 Peter Forsberg FF JSY 15.00 40.00
201 Mike Bossy FF JSY 8.00 20.00
202 Jeremy Roenick FF JSY 12.00 30.00
203 Joe Sakic FF JSY 15.00 40.00
204 Brendan Shanahan FF JSY 8.00 20.00
205 Chris Chelios FF JSY 8.00 20.00
206 Dominik Hasek FF JSY 12.00 30.00
207 Borje Salming FF JSY 8.00 20.00
208 Frank Mahovlich FF JSY 8.00 20.00
209 Gerry Cheevers FF JSY 8.00 20.00
210 Olli Jokinen FF JSY 6.00 15.00
211 Mats Sundin FF JSY 8.00 20.00
212 Marian Hossa FF JSY 8.00 20.00
213 Guy Carbonneau FF JSY 8.00 20.00
214 Marian Gaborik FF JSY 8.00 20.00
215 Marcel Dionne FF JSY 10.00 25.00
217 Al MacInnis FF JSY 10.00 25.00
218 Rod Langway FF JSY 6.00 15.00
219 Chris Drury FF JSY 6.00 15.00
220 Dale Hawerchuk FF JSY 10.00 25.00
221 Sidney Crosby FF JSY AU 80.00 200.00
222 Brian Leetch FF JSY AU 10.00 25.00
223 Bryan Trottier FF JSY AU 12.00 30.00
224 Borje Salming FF JSY AU 12.00 30.00
225 Ryan Smyth FF JSY AU 10.00 25.00
226 Mario Lemieux FF JSY AU 60.00 120.00
227 Bob Bourne FF JSY AU 8.00 20.00
228 Ron Hextall FF JSY AU 12.00 30.00
229 Steve Shutt FF JSY AU 12.00 30.00
230 Lanny McDonald FF JSY AU 12.00 30.00
231 Mike Modano FF JSY AU 20.00 50.00
232 Simon Gagne FF JSY AU 12.00 30.00
233 Bernie Nicholls FF JSY AU 10.00 25.00
234 Johnny Bucyk FF JSY AU 12.00 30.00
235 Joe Thornton FF JSY AU 20.00 50.00
236 Dominik Hasek FF JSY AU 20.00 50.00
237 Rick Vaive FF JSY AU 8.00 20.00
238 Bobby Hull FF JSY AU 25.00 60.00
239 Alex Ovechkin FF JSY AU 50.00 125.00
240 Mark Messier FF JSY AU 25.00 60.00
241 Rod Langway FF JSY AU 10.00 25.00
242 Dino Ciccarelli FF JSY AU 12.00 30.00
243 Jari Kurri FF JSY AU 12.00 30.00
244 Luc Robitaille FF JSY AU 12.00 30.00
245 Ray Bourque FF JSY AU 20.00 50.00
246 V.Lecavalier FF JSY AU 12.00 30.00
247 Tony Esposito FF JSY AU 12.00 30.00
248 H.Zetterberg FF JSY AU 15.00 40.00
249 Patrick Roy FF JSY AU 75.00 150.00
250 Wayne Gretzky FF JSY AU 150.00 400.00

2008-09 SPx Spectrum

*1-100 VET JSY: 4X TO 10X BASE JSY
*101-130 ROOKIE: .8X TO 2X BASE
*131-155 ROOK.JSY: .8X TO 2X BASE
*156-184 ROOK.JSY AU: 1.5X TO 4X JSY AU/999
*185-190 ROOK.JSY AU: 1.2X TO 3X JSY AU/499
*191-220 FF JSY: .6X TO 1.5X BASE
*221-250 FF JSY AU: .6X TO 1.5X BASE
1 Nicklas Backstrom JSY 5.00 12.00
179 Claude Giroux JSY AU 125.00 250.00
190 Steven Stamkos JSY AU 150.00 400.00

2008-09 SPx Memorable Moments

MMAM Al MacInnis 10.00 25.00
MMBH Bobby Hull 15.00 40.00
MMBO Bobby Orr 30.00 80.00
MMBS Billy Smith 8.00 20.00
MMBT Bryan Trottier 8.00 20.00
MMCJ Curtis Joseph 10.00 25.00
MMCP Chris Pronger 8.00 20.00
MMDA Dave Andreychuk 8.00 20.00
MMDC Dino Ciccarelli 8.00 20.00
MMDS Dave Schultz 8.00 20.00
MMGF Grant Fuhr 12.00 30.00
MMGH Gordie Howe 15.00 40.00
MMGL Guy Lafleur 10.00 25.00
MMGR Wayne Gretzky 20.00 50.00
MMHO Gordie Howe 25.00 60.00
MMHZ Henrik Zetterberg 10.00 25.00
MMJK Jari Kurri 8.00 20.00
MMJS Joe Sakic 10.00 25.00
MMJT Joe Thornton 12.00 30.00
MMLE Mario Lemieux 30.00 80.00
MMLR Larry Robinson 8.00 20.00
MMMB Martin Brodeur 20.00 50.00
MMMD Marcel Dionne 10.00 25.00
MMMI Mike Bossy 8.00 20.00
MMML Mario Lemieux 15.00 40.00
MMMM Mark Messier 15.00 40.00
MMMS Martin St. Louis 8.00 20.00
MMPE Phil Esposito 12.00 30.00
MMPF Peter Forsberg 15.00 40.00
MMPR Patrick Roy 20.00 50.00
MMRH Ron Hextall 8.00 20.00
MMRO Luc Robitaille 10.00 25.00
MMRV Rogie Vachon 10.00 25.00
MMSB Scotty Bowman 8.00 20.00
MMSC Sidney Crosby 20.00 50.00
MMSF Sergei Fedorov 12.00 30.00
MMSM Stan Mikita 10.00 25.00
MMTH Jose Theodore 8.00 20.00
MMTS Teemu Selanne 15.00 40.00
MMTW Tiger Williams 5.00 12.00
MMWA Wayne Gretzky 20.00 50.00
MMWG Wayne Gretzky 20.00 50.00

2008-09 SPx SPxcitement

COMPLETE SET (70) 150.00 300.00
X1 Alexander Ovechkin 6.00 15.00
X2 Andrew Cogliano 1.00 2.50
X3 Anze Kopitar 2.50 6.00
X4 Bobby Clarke 2.50 6.00
X5 Bobby Hull 3.00 8.00
X6 Bobby Orr 6.00 15.00
X7 Cam Neely 1.50 4.00
X8 Carey Price 3.00 8.00
X9 Dale Hawerchuk 2.00 5.00
X10 Daniel Alfredsson 1.50 4.00
X11 Dany Heatley 1.25 3.00
X12 Darryl Sittler 2.00 5.00
X13 Denis Potvin 1.50 4.00
X14 Dino Ciccarelli 1.50 4.00
X15 Eric Staal 2.00 5.00
X16 Evgeni Malkin 3.00 8.00
X17 Frank Mahovlich 1.50 4.00
X18 Guy Lafleur 2.00 5.00
X19 Gordie Howe 5.00 12.00
X20 Grant Fuhr 2.50 6.00
X21 Gilbert Perreault 1.50 4.00
X22 Henrik Lundqvist 4.00 10.00
X23 Henrik Zetterberg 2.00 5.00
X24 Ilya Kovalchuk 1.50 4.00
X25 Jari Kurri 1.50 4.00
X26 Jarome Iginla 2.00 5.00
X27 Dion Phaneuf 1.25 3.00
X28 Jean-Sebastien Giguere 1.50 4.00
X29 Joe Sakic 3.00 8.00
X30 Joe Thornton 2.50 6.00
X31 Jonathan Toews 2.50 6.00
X32 Jordan Staal 1.25 3.00
X33 Kyle Okposo 2.00 5.00
X34 Kyle Turris 2.50 6.00
X35 Lanny McDonald 1.50 4.00
X36 Luc Robitaille 1.50 4.00
X37 Marian Gaborik 1.50 4.00
X38 Mario Lemieux 6.00 15.00
X39 Mark Messier 3.00 8.00
X40 Martin Brodeur 4.00 10.00
X41 Martin St. Louis 1.50 4.00
X42 Mats Sundin 1.50 4.00
X43 Miikka Kiprusoff 1.50 4.00
X44 Mike Bossy 1.50 4.00
X45 Mike Modano 2.50 6.00
X46 Nicklas Backstrom 1.50 4.00
X47 Patrick Kane 3.00 8.00
X48 Patrick Roy 4.00 10.00
X49 Paul Stastny 1.25 3.00
X50 Peter Mueller 1.25 3.00
X51 Peter Stastny 1.25 3.00
X52 Phil Esposito 2.50 6.00
X53 Rick Nash 1.50 4.00
X54 Roberto Luongo 2.50 6.00
X55 Ron Hextall 1.50 4.00
X56 Ryan Getzlaf 1.50 4.00
X57 Ryan Miller 1.50 4.00
X58 Saku Koivu 1.50 4.00
X59 Sam Gagner 1.00 2.50
X60 Sidney Crosby 6.00 15.00
X61 Stan Mikita 2.00 5.00
X62 Steve Mason 2.50 6.00
X63 Teemu Selanne 3.00 8.00
X64 Nikita Filatov 1.50 4.00
X65 Tony Esposito 1.50 4.00
X66 Vincent Lecavalier 1.50 4.00
X67 Wayne Gretzky 10.00 25.00
X68 Blake Wheeler 4.00 10.00
X69 Fabian Brunnstrom 1.25 3.00
X70 Steven Stamkos 6.00 15.00

2008-09 SPx Spxcitement Spectrum

*SPECTRUM: 1X TO 2.5X BASE
X46 Nicklas Backstrom 4.00 10.00

2008-09 SPx Winning Combos

*SPECTRUM: .5X TO 1.2X BASE
WCBG M.Gaborik/P.Bouchard 5.00 12.00
WCBM N.Backstrom/P.Mueller 5.00 12.00
WCBO R.Bourque/A.Oates 8.00 20.00
WCBP M.Brodeur/C.Price 12.00 30.00
WCCB E.Cole/G.Brule 3.00 8.00
WCCH R.Hextall/B.Clarke 8.00 20.00
WCCP J.Cheechoo/C.Perry 8.00 20.00
WCDL D.Sittler/L.McDonald 6.00 15.00
WCEE T.Esposito/P.Esposito 8.00 20.00
WCEI E.Malkin/I.Kovalchuk 10.00 25.00
WCEM E.Staal/M.Staal 6.00 15.00
WCFA G.Fuhr/G.Anderson 8.00 20.00
WCFB P.Forsberg/N.Backstrom 10.00 25.00
WCGB S.Gagner/N.Backstrom 5.00 12.00
WCGR S.Gagner/D.Roloson 4.00 10.00
WCGZ S.Gomez/N.Zherdev 4.00 10.00
WCHB M.Hejduk/P.Budaj 4.00 10.00
WCHE M.Hossa/P.Elias 5.00 12.00
WCHH B.Hull/D.Hawerchuk 10.00 25.00
WCHL D.Hasek/N.Lidstrom 8.00 20.00
WCHM D.Hasek/R.Miller 8.00 20.00
WCKC P.Kane/E.Cole 10.00 25.00
WCKH S.Koivu/C.Higgins 5.00 12.00
WCKK J.Kurri/S.Koivu 5.00 12.00
WCKS S.Koivu/S.Shutt 5.00 12.00
WCLC V.Lecavalier/J.Cheechoo 5.00 12.00
WCLH N.Lidstrom/T.Holmstrom 5.00 12.00
WCMG E.Malkin/S.Gagne 10.00 25.00
WCMK M.Modano/P.Kane 10.00 25.00
WCML M.Lemieux/M.Messier 10.00 25.00
WCMM L.McDonald/A.MacInnis 6.00 15.00
WCMV L.McDonald/R.Vaive 5.00 12.00
WCNE M.Naslund/P.Elias 5.00 12.00
WCNG M.Naslund/S.Gomez 5.00 12.00
WCNL R.Nash/V.Lecavalier 5.00 12.00
WCOK A.Ovechkin/I.Kovalchuk 10.00 25.00
WCOM A.Ovechkin/E.Malkin 20.00 50.00
WCPS R.Malone/S.Weiss 3.00 8.00
WCPZ R.Nash/M.Peca 5.00 12.00
WCRK M.Ryder/P.Kessel 5.00 12.00
WCRL L.Robinson/R.Langway 5.00 12.00
WCRM M.Ribeiro/M.Turco 5.00 12.00
WCSD S.Doan/R.Smyth 4.00 10.00
WCSH S.Shutt/C.Higgins 5.00 12.00
WCSM E.Staal/R.Malone 6.00 15.00
WCSS E.Staal/J.Staal 6.00 15.00
WCTK P.Kane/J.Toews 10.00 25.00
WCVH D.Hasek/T.Vokoun 12.00 30.00
WCZH H.Zetterberg/T.Holmstrom 6.00 15.00

2008-09 SPx Winning Combos Radiance Autographs

WCBM N.Backstrom/P.Mueller 15.00 40.00
WCBO R.Bourque/A.Oates 25.00 60.00
WCBP M.Brodeur/C.Price 40.00 100.00
WCCH B.Clarke/R.Hextall 25.00 60.00
WCDL L.McDonald/D.Sittler 20.00 50.00
WCEE P.Esposito/T.Esposito 25.00 60.00
WCEI I.Kovalchuk/E.Malkin 30.00 80.00
WCEM E.Staal/M.Staal 20.00 50.00
WCFA G.Fuhr/G.Anderson 25.00 60.00
WCGB Gagner/Backstrom 15.00 40.00
WCGR D.Roloson/S.Gagner 12.00 30.00
WCGZ S.Gomez/N.Zherdev 12.00 30.00
WCHB M.Hejduk/P.Budaj 12.00 30.00
WCHE P.Elias/M.Hossa 15.00 40.00
WCHH D.Hull/D.Hawerchuk 30.00 80.00
WCHL N.Lidstrom/D.Hasek 25.00 60.00
WCHM R.Miller/D.Hasek 25.00 60.00
WCKC E.Cole/P.Kane 30.00 80.00
WCKK S.Koivu/J.Kurri 15.00 40.00
WCKS S.Koivu/S.Shutt 15.00 40.00
WCLC Lecavalier/Cheechoo 15.00 40.00
WCLH Holmstrom/Lidstrom 15.00 40.00
WCMG S.Gagne/E.Malkin 30.00 80.00
WCMK M.Modano/P.Kane 30.00 80.00
WCML M.Lemieux/M.Messier 60.00 150.00
WCMM McDonald/MacInnis 20.00 50.00
WCMV L.McDonald/R.Vaive 15.00 40.00
WCNE M.Naslund/P.Elias 15.00 40.00
WCNG S.Gomez/M.Naslund 15.00 40.00
WCNL R.Nash/V.Lecavalier 15.00 40.00
WCOK Kovalchuk/Ovechkin 60.00 150.00
WCOM A.Ovechkin/E.Malkin 60.00 150.00
WCPS S.Weiss/R.Malone 10.00 25.00
WCPZ M.Peca/R.Nash 15.00 40.00
WCRK P.Kessel/M.Ryder 15.00 40.00
WCRL Langway/Robinson 15.00 40.00
WCRM M.Ribeiro/M.Turco 15.00 40.00
WCSH S.Shutt/C.Higgins 15.00 40.00
WCSM R.Malone/E.Staal 20.00 50.00
WCSS J.Staal/E.Staal 20.00 50.00
WCTK J.Toews/P.Kane 30.00 80.00
WCVH T.Vokoun/D.Hasek 25.00 60.00
WCZH Zetterberg/Holmstrom 20.00 50.00

2008-09 SPx Winning Materials

*SPECTRUM/99: .5X TO 1.2X BASIC JSY
WMAM Andrei Markov 4.00 10.00
WMAO Adam Oates 4.00 10.00
WMBH Bobby Hull 8.00 20.00
WMCC Bobby Clarke 6.00 15.00
WMCH Jonathan Cheechoo 3.00 8.00
WMCN Cam Neely 4.00 10.00
WMCP Carey Price 8.00 20.00
WMDG Doug Gilmour 5.00 12.00
WMDH Dominik Hasek 6.00 15.00
WMES Eric Staal 5.00 12.00
WMGF Grant Fuhr 6.00 15.00
WMGG Sam Gagner 2.50 6.00
WMGZ Scott Gomez 3.00 8.00
WMHD Milan Hejduk 3.00 8.00
WMHG Chris Higgins 2.50 6.00

WMHZ Henrik Zetterberg 5.00 12.00
WMIK Ilya Kovalchuk 4.00 10.00
WMJM Joe Mullen 3.00 8.00
WMJS Jordan Staal 3.00 8.00
WMJT Jonathan Toews 6.00 15.00
WMKN Patrick Kane 8.00 20.00
WMLM Lanny McDonald 4.00 10.00
WMMB Martin Brodeur 10.00 25.00
WMMG Marian Gaborik 4.00 10.00
WMMH Marian Hossa 4.00 10.00
WMMM Mark Messier 8.00 20.00
WMMO Mike Modano 6.00 15.00
WMMP Michael Peca 3.00 8.00
WMMR Mike Ribeiro 2.50 6.00
WMNL Nicklas Lidstrom 4.00 10.00
WMOV Alexander Ovechkin 8.00 20.00
WMPE Patrik Elias 4.00 10.00
WMPK Phil Kessel 4.00 10.00
WMPM Peter Mueller 3.00 8.00
WMPS Peter Stastny 3.00 8.00
WMRL Rod Langway 3.00 8.00
WMRM Ryan Malone 2.50 6.00
WMRN Rick Nash 4.00 10.00
WMRV Rick Vaive 2.50 6.00
WMRY Michael Ryder 2.50 6.00
WMSB Steve Bernier 2.50 6.00
WMSC Sidney Crosby 10.00 25.00
WMSG Simon Gagne 4.00 10.00
WMSK Saku Koivu 4.00 10.00
WMSS Steve Shutt 4.00 10.00
WMST Matt Stajan 2.50 6.00
WMSW Shea Weber 3.00 8.00
WMTH Tomas Holmstrom 3.00 8.00
WMVL Vincent Lecavalier 4.00 10.00
WMWC Wendel Clark 6.00 15.00

2008-09 SPx Winning Materials Radiance Autographs

WMAO Adam Oates 15.00 40.00
WMBH Bobby Hull 30.00 80.00
WMCC Bobby Clarke 25.00 60.00
WMCN Cam Neely 15.00 40.00
WMCP Carey Price 30.00 80.00
WMDG Doug Gilmour 20.00 50.00
WMDH Dominik Hasek 25.00 60.00
WMES Eric Staal 20.00 50.00
WMGF Grant Fuhr 25.00 60.00
WMGG Sam Gagner 10.00 25.00
WMGZ Scott Gomez 12.00 30.00
WMHD Milan Hejduk 12.00 30.00
WMHG Chris Higgins 10.00 25.00
WMHZ Henrik Zetterberg 20.00 50.00
WMIK Ilya Kovalchuk 15.00 40.00
WMJM Joe Mullen 12.00 30.00
WMJS Jordan Staal 12.00 30.00
WMJT Jonathan Toews 25.00 60.00
WMKN Patrick Kane 30.00 80.00
WMLM Lanny McDonald 15.00 40.00
WMMB Martin Brodeur 40.00 100.00
WMMH Marian Hossa 15.00 40.00
WMMM Mark Messier 30.00 80.00
WMMO Mike Modano 25.00 60.00
WMMP Michael Peca 12.00 30.00
WMMR Mike Ribeiro 10.00 25.00
WMNL Nicklas Lidstrom 15.00 40.00
WMOV Alexander Ovechkin 60.00 150.00
WMPE Patrik Elias 15.00 40.00
WMPK Phil Kessel 15.00 40.00
WMPM Peter Mueller 12.00 30.00
WMPS Peter Stastny 12.00 30.00
WMRL Rod Langway 12.00 30.00
WMRM Ryan Malone 10.00 25.00
WMRN Rick Nash 15.00 40.00
WMRV Rick Vaive 10.00 25.00
WMRY Michael Ryder 10.00 25.00
WMSB Steve Bernier 10.00 25.00
WMSC Sidney Crosby 60.00 150.00
WMSG Simon Gagne 15.00 40.00
WMSK Saku Koivu 15.00 40.00
WMSS Steve Shutt 15.00 40.00
WMST Matt Stajan 10.00 25.00
WMTH Tomas Holmstrom 12.00 30.00
WMVL Vincent Lecavalier 15.00 40.00
WMWC Wendel Clark 25.00 60.00

2008-09 SPx Winning Trios

AKF Kovalv/Afinog/Fedor 12.00 30.00
AWL Arnott/Weber/Legwand 8.00 20.00
BMG Backstrm/Gagnr/Muell 10.00 25.00
BTK Backstrom/Toews/Kane 20.00 50.00
BTS Trottier/Bossy/Smith 10.00 25.00
CGY McDon/MacIns/Fleury 12.00 30.00
COM Crosby/Ovechkin/Malkin 25.00 60.00
DMJ Doan/Mueller/Jokinen 8.00 20.00
FCM Crosby/Malkin/Fleury 20.00 50.00
FSH Sakic/Forsberg/Hejduk 20.00 50.00
GBN Gaborik/Bouchrd/Nolan 10.00 25.00
GLM Gretz/Lemieux/Mess 40.00 100.00
GRC Richards/Carter/Gagne 10.00 25.00
HGA Howe/Gretzky/Beliveau 60.00 120.00
HLH Hasek/Lidstrm/Holmstrm 15.00 40.00
HPN Hextall/Parent/Niittymaki 12.00 30.00
HSF Forsberg/Smyth/Hejduk 20.00 50.00
KKS Kurri/Koivu/Selanne 20.00 50.00
KLS Kovalchk/Lecavalr/Staal 12.00 30.00
KTP Kariya/Tkachuk/Perron 10.00 25.00
LCN Lecavalr/Cheech/Nash 10.00 25.00
MLT Turco/Modano/Lehtinen 15.00 40.00
MSS Salming/McDonald/Sittler 12.00 30.00
NBO Neely/Bourque/Oates 15.00 40.00
NLP Nash/Leclaire/Peca 10.00 25.00
NLS Luongo/Demitra/Bernier 12.00 30.00
NPR Brodeur/Parise/Elias 15.00 40.00
OKK Ovech/Kovalck/Kovalev 20.00 50.00
OMK Ovech/Malkin/Kovalck 15.00 40.00
PKK Price/Kovalev/Koivu 30.00 80.00
PLG Phaneuf/Lidstrm/Gonchr 10.00 25.00
RBP Roy/Brodeur/Price 15.00 40.00
RDV Robitaille/Dionne/Vachon 12.00 30.00
RSB Roy/Sakic/Bourque 15.00 40.00
SBT Bergeron/Savard/Thomas 12.00 30.00
SFB Sund/Forsbrg/Backstrm 10.00 25.00
SKK Selanne/Koivu/Koivu 20.00 50.00
SNL Sund/Naslnd/Lndqvst 25.00 60.00
SSS Staal/Staal/Staal 12.00 30.00
STS Sundin/Toskala/Stajan 12.00 30.00
VHG Gaborik/Hossa/Vokoun 10.00 25.00

2009-10 SPx

COMP.SET w/o SPS (100) 12.00 30.00
1 Sidney Crosby 2.00 5.00
2 Phil Kessel .50 1.25
3 Mike Green .40 1.00
4 Henrik Lundqvist 1.25 3.00
5 Mark Messier 1.00 2.50
6 Devin Setoguchi .40 1.00
7 Jeff Carter .40 1.00
8 Henrik Zetterberg .60 1.50
9 Martin Brodeur 1.25 3.00
10 Jonathan Toews .75 2.00
11 Ryan Kesler .50 1.25
12 Bobby Orr 2.00 5.00
13 Eric Staal .60 1.50
14 David Perron .40 1.00
15 Steven Stamkos 1.00 2.50
16 Steve Mason .40 1.00
17 Marc-Andre Fleury 1.00 2.50
18 Ilya Kovalchuk .50 1.25
19 Marian Gaborik .50 1.25
20 Miikka Kiprusoff .50 1.25
21 Ryan Getzlaf .50 1.25
22 Alexander Ovechkin 2.00 5.00
23 Tim Thomas .50 1.25
24 Dany Heatley .40 1.00
25 Andrew Cogliano .30 .75
26 David Booth .30 .75
27 Pekka Rinne .50 1.25
28 Mike Ribeiro .30 .75
29 Carey Price 1.00 2.50
30 Shane Doan .40 1.00
31 Brian Campbell .40 1.00
32 Ryan Miller .50 1.25
33 Mike Richards .40 1.00
34 Patrick Marleau .50 1.25
35 Nicklas Lidstrom .30 .75
36 Luke Schenn .50 1.25
37 Anze Kopitar .75 2.00
38 Chris Drury .40 1.00
39 Tomas Vokoun .40 1.00
40 Rick DiPietro .40 1.00
41 Paul Stastny .40 1.00
42 Mario Lemieux 2.00 5.00
43 Sam Gagner .30 .75
44 Jason Spezza .50 1.25
45 Martin St. Louis .50 1.25
46 Alexander Semin .50 1.25
47 Rick Nash .50 1.25
48 Cam Ward .50 1.25
49 Bobby Ryan .40 1.00
50 Tomas Kaberle .30 .75
51 Patrik Berglund .30 .75
52 Thomas Vanek .40 1.00
53 Andrei Markov .50 1.25
54 Pavel Datsyuk .75 2.00
55 Patrick Roy 1.25 3.00
56 Dion Phaneuf .40 1.00
57 Shea Weber .40 1.00
58 Patrik Elias .50 1.25
59 Bryan Little .50 1.25
60 Marty Turco .50 1.25
61 Jussi Jokinen .30 .75
62 Patrick Kane 1.00 2.50
63 Niklas Backstrom .50 1.25
64 Simon Gagne .50 1.25
65 Joe Thornton .75 2.00
66 Scottie Upshall .30 .75
67 Marian Hossa .50 1.25
68 Milan Hejduk .40 1.00
69 Marc Savard .30 .75
70 Kyle Okposo .30 .75
71 Jason Blake .30 .75
72 Mike Modano .75 2.00
73 Jordan Staal .40 1.00
74 Ales Hemsky .40 1.00
75 Chris Osgood .50 1.25
76 Derek Roy .30 .75
77 Daniel Alfredsson .50 1.25
78 Drew Doughty .60 1.50
79 Steve Yzerman 1.25 3.00
80 Roberto Luongo .75 2.00
81 Michael Frolik .40 1.00
82 Teemu Selanne 1.00 2.50
83 Ryan Smyth .40 1.00
84 Nicklas Backstrom .50 1.25
85 Mike Cammalleri .40 1.00
86 Peter Mueller .40 1.00
87 Kari Lehtonen .40 1.00
88 Gordie Howe 1.50 4.00
89 Scott Gomez .40 1.00
90 Jarome Iginla .60 1.50
91 David Backes .30 .75
92 Zdeno Chara .50 1.25
93 Vincent Lecavalier .50 1.25
94 Mikko Koivu .50 1.25
95 Daniel Briere .50 1.25
96 Jason Arnott .40 1.00
97 Henrik Sedin .60 1.50
98 Derick Brassard .30 .75
99 Wayne Gretzky 3.00 8.00
100 Zach Parise .50 1.25
101 Guillaume Desbiens RC 4.00 10.00
102 Davis Drewiske RC 4.00 10.00
103 Ryan Vesce RC 3.00 8.00
104 Alec Martinez RC 5.00 12.00
105 David Schlemko RC 3.00 8.00
106 Jay Beagle RC 5.00 12.00
107 Steven Zalewski RC 3.00 8.00
108 Tim Wallace RC 2.50 6.00
109 Geoff Kinrade RC 4.00 10.00
110 Teemu Laakso RC 2.50 6.00
111 Jakub Petruzalek RC 4.00 10.00
112 Matt Gilroy RC 4.00 10.00
113 Tyson Strachan RC 2.50 6.00
114 James Reimer RC 10.00 25.00
115 Sean Collins RC 3.00 8.00
116 Frazer McLaren RC 3.00 8.00
117 Johan Backlund RC 4.00 10.00
118 Mathieu Perreault RC 5.00 12.00
119 Kevin Quick RC 2.50 6.00
120 Mika Pyorala RC 3.00 8.00
121 Tim Stapleton RC 4.00 10.00
122 Chris Durno RC 3.00 8.00
123 Jaime Sifers RC 3.00 8.00
124 Troy Bodie RC 3.00 8.00
125 Braden Holtby RC 10.00 25.00
126 Sean Bentivoglio RC 3.00 8.00
127 Phil Oreskovic RC 4.00 10.00
128 James Wright RC 4.00 10.00
129 Bryan Rodney RC 3.00 8.00
130 Alexander Sulzer RC 2.50 6.00
131 Matt Beleskey JSY RC 4.00 10.00
132 Jason Demers JSY RC 8.00 20.00
133 Dmitry Kulikov JSY RC 5.00 12.00
134 Cal O'Reilly JSY RC 4.00 10.00
135 Jay Rosehill JSY RC 5.00 12.00
136 T.J. Galiardi JSY RC 5.00 12.00
137 Michael Sauer JSY RC 4.00 10.00
138 Ryan O'Marra JSY RC 3.00 8.00
139 Benn Ferriero JSY RC 5.00 12.00
140 Chris Butler JSY RC 5.00 12.00
141 Mike Santorelli JSY RC 5.00 12.00
142 Andrew MacDonald JSY RC 3.00 8.00
143 John Scott JSY RC 5.00 12.00
144 Matt Pelech JSY RC 5.00 12.00
145 Ray Macias JSY RC 4.00 10.00
146 Cody Franson JSY RC 5.00 12.00
147 Kris Chucko JSY RC 3.00 8.00
148 Joel Rechlicz JSY RC 3.00 8.00
149 Perttu Lindgren JSY RC 4.00 10.00
150 Sergei Shirokov JSY RC 3.00 8.00
151 Spencer Machacek JSY RC 5.00 12.00
152 Yannick Weber JSY RC 5.00 12.00
153 Artem Anisimov JSY AU RC 4.00 10.00
154 Brian Salcido JSY AU RC 4.00 10.00
155 C.Hanson JSY AU RC 6.00 15.00
156 I.Vishnevskiy JSY AU RC 4.00 10.00
157 Jhonas Enroth JSY AU RC 8.00 20.00
158 M.Grabner JSY AU RC 6.00 15.00
159 Luca Caputi JSY AU RC 6.00 15.00
160 Brad Marchand JSY AU RC 60.00 150.00
161 Mikael Backlund JSY AU RC 10.00 25.00
162 Riku Helenius JSY AU RC 6.00 15.00
163 Ville Leino JSY AU RC 5.00 12.00
164 Lars Eller JSY AU RC 6.00 15.00
165 Erik Karlsson JSY AU RC 15.00 40.00
166 Tyler Myers JSY AU RC 6.00 15.00
167 Ryan O'Reilly JSY AU RC 12.00 30.00
168 Jamie Benn JSY AU RC 15.00 40.00
169 Logan Couture JSY AU RC 12.00 30.00
170 Michael Del Zotto JSY AU RC 6.00 15.00
171 Viktor Stalberg JSY AU RC 6.00 15.00
172 Antti Niemi JSY AU RC 10.00 25.00
173 Tyler Bozak JSY AU RC 10.00 25.00
174 Colin Wilson JSY AU RC 6.00 15.00
175 M.Duchene JSY AU RC/499 15.00 40.00
176 Gustavsson JSY AU RC/499 8.00 20.00
177 V.Hedman JSY AU RC/499 20.00 50.00
178 E.Kane JSY AU RC/499 12.00 30.00
179 van Riems JSY AU RC/499 12.00 30.00
180 J.Tavares JSY AU RC/499 60.00 150.00
189 Doug Gilmour FF JSY 8.00 20.00
190 Alexander Ovechkin FF JSY 25.00 60.00
191 Tony Esposito FF JSY 10.00 25.00
192 Steve Shutt FF JSY 6.00 15.00
193 Jay Bouwmeester FF JSY 4.00 10.00
194 Adam Oates FF JSY 6.00 15.00
195 Joe Mullen FF JSY 5.00 12.00
196 Jari Kurri FF JSY 6.00 15.00
197 Patrick Kane FF JSY 12.00 30.00
198 Scott Gomez FF JSY 5.00 12.00
199 Paul Kariya FF JSY 6.00 15.00
200 Mike Modano FF JSY 10.00 25.00
201 Larry Murphy FF JSY 5.00 12.00
202 Luc Robitaille FF JSY 6.00 15.00
203 Nicklas Lidstrom FF JSY 4.00 10.00
204 Vincent Lecavalier FF JSY 6.00 15.00
205 Zach Parise FF JSY 6.00 15.00
206 Ray Bourque FF JSY 10.00 25.00
207 Bernie Federko FF JSY 5.00 12.00
208 Cam Neely FF JSY 6.00 15.00
209 Wade Redden FF JSY 4.00 10.00
210 Bob Bourne FF JSY 4.00 10.00
211 Larry Robinson FF JSY 6.00 15.00
212 Dale Hawerchuk FF JSY 8.00 20.00
213 Teemu Selanne FF JSY 12.00 30.00
214 Johnny Bucyk FF JSY 6.00 15.00
215 Brent Sutter FF JSY 4.00 10.00
216 Grant Fuhr FF JSY 10.00 25.00
217 Alex Tanguay FF JSY 4.00 10.00
218 Gilbert Perreault FF JSY 6.00 15.00
219 Steve Yzerman FF JSY AU 150.00 250.00
220 Martin Brodeur FF JSY AU 50.00 100.00
221 Evgeni Malkin FF JSY AU 30.00 60.00
222 Denis Savard FF JSY AU 15.00 40.00
223 Scotty Bowman FF JSY AU 30.00 60.00
224 Darryl Sittler FF JSY AU 12.00 30.00
225 Patrick Roy FF JSY AU 50.00 100.00
226 Wendel Clark FF JSY AU 15.00 40.00
227 Phil Esposito FF JSY AU 25.00 60.00
228 Patrick Marleau FF JSY AU 15.00 40.00
229 S.Niedermayer FF JSY AU 20.00 50.00
230 Marian Hossa FF JSY AU 12.00 30.00
231 Mark Messier FF JSY AU 40.00 100.00
232 Marcel Dionne FF JSY AU 20.00 50.00
233 Peter Stastny FF JSY AU 12.00 30.00
234 Mario Lemieux FF JSY AU 60.00 120.00
235 Carey Price FF JSY AU 30.00 80.00
236 Pavel Datsyuk FF JSY AU 20.00 50.00
237 Saku Koivu FF JSY AU 15.00 40.00
238 N.Khabibulin FF JSY AU 15.00 40.00
239 Gordie Howe FF JSY AU 75.00 150.00
240 Frank Mahovlich FF JSY AU 15.00 40.00
241 Guy Lafleur FF JSY AU 20.00 50.00
242 D.Ciccarelli FF JSY AU EXCH 15.00 40.00
243 G.Carbonneau FF JSY AU 25.00 60.00
244 Dany Heatley FF JSY AU 12.00 30.00
245 Sidney Crosby FF JSY AU 100.00 200.00
246 Glenn Anderson FF JSY AU 12.00 30.00
247 Dave Taylor FF JSY AU 15.00 40.00
248 Wayne Gretzky FF JSY AU 200.00 500.00

2009-10 SPx Spectrum

1 Sidney Crosby JSY 25.00 60.00
2 Phil Kessel JSY 8.00 20.00
4 Henrik Lundqvist JSY 20.00 50.00
5 Mark Messier JSY 15.00 40.00
7 Jeff Carter JSY 6.00 15.00
8 Henrik Zetterberg JSY 10.00 25.00
9 Martin Brodeur JSY 20.00 50.00
10 Jonathan Toews JSY 12.00 30.00
11 Ryan Kesler JSY 8.00 20.00
13 Eric Staal JSY 10.00 25.00
17 Marc-Andre Fleury JSY 15.00 40.00
18 Ilya Kovalchuk JSY 8.00 20.00
19 Marian Gaborik JSY 8.00 20.00
20 Miikka Kiprusoff JSY 8.00 20.00
21 Ryan Getzlaf JSY 8.00 20.00
22 Alexander Ovechkin JSY 25.00 60.00
23 Tim Thomas JSY 8.00 20.00
25 Andrew Cogliano JSY 5.00 12.00
26 David Booth JSY 8.00 20.00
27 Pekka Rinne JSY 8.00 20.00
28 Mike Ribeiro JSY 5.00 12.00
29 Carey Price JSY 15.00 40.00
30 Shane Doan JSY 6.00 15.00
32 Ryan Miller JSY 8.00 20.00
33 Mike Richards JSY 6.00 15.00
34 Patrick Marleau JSY 8.00 20.00
35 Nicklas Lidstrom JSY 5.00 12.00
36 Luke Schenn JSY 8.00 20.00
37 Anze Kopitar JSY 12.00 30.00
38 Chris Drury JSY 6.00 15.00
39 Tomas Vokoun JSY 6.00 15.00
40 Rick DiPietro JSY 6.00 15.00
41 Paul Stastny JSY 6.00 15.00
42 Mario Lemieux JSY 30.00 80.00
43 Sam Gagner JSY 5.00 12.00
44 Jason Spezza JSY 8.00 20.00
45 Martin St. Louis JSY 8.00 20.00
46 Alexander Semin JSY 8.00 20.00
47 Rick Nash JSY 8.00 20.00
48 Cam Ward JSY 8.00 20.00
50 Tomas Kaberle JSY 5.00 12.00
51 Patrik Berglund JSY 5.00 12.00
52 Thomas Vanek JSY 6.00 15.00
53 Andrei Markov JSY 8.00 20.00
54 Pavel Datsyuk JSY 12.00 30.00
55 Patrick Roy JSY 20.00 50.00
56 Dion Phaneuf JSY 6.00 15.00
57 Shea Weber JSY 6.00 15.00
58 Patrik Elias JSY 8.00 20.00
60 Marty Turco JSY 8.00 20.00
61 Jussi Jokinen JSY 5.00 12.00
62 Patrick Kane JSY 15.00 40.00
64 Simon Gagne JSY 8.00 20.00
65 Joe Thornton JSY 12.00 30.00
67 Marian Hossa JSY 12.00 30.00
68 Milan Hejduk JSY 6.00 15.00
69 Marc Savard JSY 5.00 12.00
70 Kyle Okposo JSY 5.00 12.00
72 Mike Modano JSY 12.00 30.00
73 Jordan Staal JSY 6.00 15.00
74 Ales Hemsky JSY 6.00 15.00
75 Chris Osgood JSY 8.00 20.00
76 Derek Roy JSY 5.00 12.00
77 Daniel Alfredsson JSY 8.00 20.00
78 Drew Doughty JSY 10.00 25.00
79 Steve Yzerman JSY 20.00 50.00
80 Roberto Luongo JSY 12.00 30.00
82 Teemu Selanne JSY 15.00 40.00
83 Ryan Smyth JSY 6.00 15.00
84 Nicklas Backstrom JSY 8.00 20.00
85 Mike Cammalleri JSY 15.00 40.00
86 Peter Mueller JSY 6.00 15.00
87 Kari Lehtonen JSY 6.00 15.00
88 Gordie Howe JSY 25.00 60.00
89 Scott Gomez JSY 6.00 15.00
90 Jarome Iginla JSY 10.00 25.00
93 Vincent Lecavalier JSY 8.00 20.00
94 Mikko Koivu JSY 8.00 20.00
96 Jason Arnott JSY 6.00 15.00
98 Derick Brassard JSY 10.00 25.00
99 Wayne Gretzky JSY 25.00 60.00
100 Zach Parise JSY 8.00 20.00
101 Guillaume Desbiens 5.00 12.00
102 Davis Drewiske 5.00 12.00
103 Ryan Vesce 4.00 10.00
104 Alec Martinez 6.00 15.00
105 David Schlemko 4.00 10.00
106 Jay Beagle 6.00 15.00
107 Steven Zalewski 4.00 10.00
108 Tim Wallace 3.00 8.00
109 Geoff Kinrade 5.00 12.00
110 Teemu Laakso 3.00 8.00
111 Jakub Petruzalek 5.00 12.00
112 Matt Gilroy 5.00 12.00
113 Tyson Strachan 3.00 8.00
114 James Reimer 15.00 40.00
115 Sean Collins 4.00 10.00
116 Frazer McLaren 4.00 10.00
117 Johan Backlund 5.00 12.00
118 Mathieu Perreault 6.00 15.00
119 Kevin Quick 3.00 8.00
120 Mika Pyorala 4.00 10.00
121 Tim Stapleton 5.00 12.00
122 Chris Durno 4.00 10.00
123 Jaime Sifers 4.00 10.00
124 Troy Bodie 4.00 10.00
125 Braden Holtby 12.00 30.00
126 Sean Bentivoglio 4.00 10.00
127 Phil Oreskovic 5.00 12.00
128 James Wright 5.00 12.00
130 Alexander Sulzer 3.00 8.00
131 Matt Beleskey PATCH 10.00 25.00
132 Jason Demers PATCH 20.00 50.00
133 Dmitry Kulikov PATCH 12.00 30.00
134 Cal O'Reilly PATCH 10.00 25.00
135 Jay Rosehill PATCH 12.00 30.00
136 T.J. Galiardi PATCH 12.00 30.00
137 Michael Sauer PATCH 10.00 25.00
138 Ryan O'Marra PATCH 8.00 20.00
139 Benn Ferriero PATCH 15.00 40.00
140 Chris Butler PATCH 12.00 30.00
141 Mike Santorelli PATCH 12.00 30.00
142 Andrew MacDonald PATCH 8.00 20.00
143 John Scott PATCH 12.50 30.00
144 Matt Pelech PATCH 12.00 30.00
145 Ray Macias PATCH 10.00 25.00
146 Cody Franson PATCH 12.00 30.00
147 Kris Chucko PATCH 8.00 20.00
149 Perttu Lindgren PATCH 10.00 25.00
150 Sergei Shirokov PATCH 8.00 20.00
151 Spencer Machacek PATCH 12.00 30.00
152 Yannick Weber PATCH 12.00 30.00
153 Artem Anisimov PATCH AU 10.00 25.00
154 Brian Salcido PATCH AU 10.00 25.00
155 Christian Hanson PATCH AU 15.00 40.00
156 Vishnevskiy PATCH AU ERR 10.00 25.00
157 Jhonas Enroth PATCH AU 20.00 50.00
158 M.Grabner PATCH AU 15.00 40.00
159 Luca Caputi PATCH AU 15.00 40.00
160 Brad Marchand PATCH AU 125.00 300.00
161 M.Backlund PATCH AU 25.00 60.00
162 Riku Helenius PATCH AU 15.00 40.00
163 Ville Leino PATCH AU 12.00 30.00
164 Lars Eller PATCH AU 40.00 100.00
165 Erik Karlsson PATCH AU 125.00 300.00
166 Tyler Myers PATCH AU 250.00 400.00
168 Jamie Benn PATCH AU 40.00 100.00
169 Logan Couture PATCH AU 75.00 150.00
170 M.Del Zotto PATCH AU 15.00 40.00
171 Viktor Stalberg PATCH AU 15.00 40.00
172 Antti Niemi PATCH AU 25.00 60.00
173 Tyler Bozak PATCH AU 60.00 120.00
174 Colin Wilson PATCH AU 15.00 40.00
183 Matt Duchene PATCH AU 200.00 350.00
184 J.Gustavsson PATCH AU 100.00 200.00
185 Victor Hedman PATCH AU 60.00 150.00
186 Evander Kane PATCH AU 60.00 120.00
187 van Riemsdyk PATCH AU 100.00 200.00
188 John Tavares PATCH AU 250.00 500.00

2009-10 SPx Shadowbox

SH1 Wayne Gretzky 125.00 200.00
SH2 Evgeni Malkin 25.00 60.00
SH3 Henrik Zetterberg 60.00 120.00
SH4 Jeff Carter 30.00 60.00
SH5 Rick Nash 12.00 30.00
SH6 Zach Parise 15.00 40.00
SH7 Joe Thornton 40.00 80.00
SH8 Patrick Kane 60.00 120.00
SH9 Bobby Orr 60.00 120.00
SH10 Jarome Iginla 30.00 60.00
SH11 Martin St. Louis 25.00 50.00
SH12 Dany Heatley 15.00 40.00
SH13 Ryan Getzlaf 15.00 40.00
SH14 Jason Spezza 25.00 50.00
SH15 Steve Yzerman 60.00 120.00
SH16 Alexander Ovechkin 60.00 120.00
SH17 Mario Lemieux 50.00 100.00
SH18 Dion Phaneuf 12.00 30.00
SH19 Cam Neely 15.00 40.00
SH20 Ilya Kovalchuk 15.00 40.00
SH22 Jonathan Toews 60.00 120.00
SH23 Nicklas Backstrom 15.00 40.00
SH24 Mark Messier 40.00 80.00
SH25 Pavel Datsyuk 30.00 60.00
SH26 Eric Staal 25.00 50.00
SH27 Mike Green 15.00 40.00
SH28 Vincent Lecavalier 30.00 60.00
SH29 Gordie Howe 40.00 100.00
SH30 Sidney Crosby 40.00 100.00

2009-10 SPx Shadowbox Stoppers

ST1 Martin Brodeur 15.00 40.00
ST2 Patrick Roy 40.00 100.00
ST3 Marc-Andre Fleury 30.00 60.00
ST5 Tony Esposito 20.00 50.00
ST6 Miikka Kiprusoff 30.00 60.00
ST7 Carey Price 40.00 80.00
ST9 Grant Fuhr 25.00 50.00
ST10 Steve Mason 30.00 60.00
ST11 Ron Hextall 25.00 50.00
ST12 Ryan Miller 15.00 40.00

2009-10 SPx SPXcitement

COMPLETE SET (70) 200.00 400.00
X1 Wayne Gretzky 10.00 25.00
X2 Luke Schenn 1.50 4.00
X3 Carey Price 3.00 8.00
X4 Bobby Orr 6.00 15.00
X5 Henrik Zetterberg 2.00 5.00
X6 Marc-Andre Fleury 3.00 8.00
X7 Thomas Vanek 1.25 3.00
X8 Cam Neely 1.50 4.00
X9 Gordie Howe 5.00 12.00
X10 Patrick Marleau 1.50 4.00
X11 Mark Messier 3.00 8.00
X12 Miikka Kiprusoff 1.50 4.00
X14 Jonathan Toews 2.50 6.00
X15 Dany Heatley 1.25 3.00
X16 Bobby Clarke 2.50 6.00
X17 Steven Stamkos 3.00 8.00
X18 Alexander Ovechkin 6.00 15.00
X19 Steve Yzerman 4.00 10.00
X20 Phil Kessel 1.50 4.00
X21 Steve Mason 1.25 3.00
X22 Mike Bossy 1.50 4.00
X23 Sam Gagner 1.00 2.50
X24 Eric Staal 2.00 5.00
X25 Matt Duchene 3.00 8.00
X26 Ryan Getzlaf 1.50 4.00
X27 Evgeni Malkin 3.00 8.00
X28 Scott Gomez 1.25 3.00
X29 Joe Thornton 2.50 6.00
X30 Martin Brodeur 4.00 10.00
X31 Mike Ribeiro 1.00 2.50
X32 Pavel Datsyuk 2.50 6.00
X33 Patrick Roy 4.00 10.00
X34 Drew Doughty 2.00 5.00
X35 Vincent Lecavalier 1.50 4.00
X36 Mikko Koivu 1.50 4.00
X37 Zach Parise 1.50 4.00
X38 Marian Hossa 1.50 4.00
X39 Tomas Vokoun 1.25 3.00
X40 Jarome Iginla 2.00 5.00
X41 Ville Leino 1.25 3.00
X42 Henrik Lundqvist 4.00 10.00
X43 Jordan Staal 1.25 3.00
X44 Bobby Ryan 1.25 3.00
X45 Mike Green 1.25 3.00
X46 Ilya Kovalchuk 1.50 4.00
X47 Cam Ward 1.50 4.00
X48 Jonas Gustavsson 8.00 20.00
X49 Ryan Kesler 1.50 4.00
X50 Mikael Backlund 2.50 6.00
X51 Patrick Kane 3.00 8.00
X52 Jason Spezza 1.50 4.00
X53 Jeff Carter 1.25 3.00
X54 David Perron 1.25 3.00
X55 Shea Weber 1.25 3.00
X56 James van Riemsdyk 3.00 8.00
X57 Devin Setoguchi 1.25 3.00
X58 Tim Thomas 1.50 4.00
X59 Rick DiPietro 1.25 3.00
X60 Nicklas Lidstrom 1.00 2.50
X61 Rick Nash 1.50 4.00
X62 Artem Anisimov 1.00 2.50
X63 James Neal 1.00 2.50
X64 Ryan Miller 1.50 4.00
X65 Brian Campbell 1.25 3.00
X66 Mario Lemieux 6.00 15.00
X67 Paul Stastny 1.25 3.00
X68 Peter Mueller 1.25 3.00
X69 Roberto Luongo 2.50 6.00
X70 Sidney Crosby 6.00 15.00

2009-10 SPx SPXcitement Spectrum

*SINGLES: 1.5X TO 4X BASIC INSERTS
X13 John Tavares 60.00 120.00
X37 Zach Parise 6.00 15.00
X48 Jonas Gustavsson 25.00 60.00

2009-10 SPx Winning Combos

WCBK Koivu/Bouchard 5.00 12.00
WCCB Chara/Bergeron 6.00 15.00
WCCG Gilmour/Clark 8.00 20.00
WCCM Crosby/Malkin 12.00 30.00
WCCO Crosby/Ovechkin 20.00 50.00
WCCT Campbell/Toews 8.00 20.00
WCCW Campbell/Wilson 4.00 10.00
WCDL Doan/Lombardi 4.00 10.00
WCEH Esposito/Huet 8.00 20.00
WCER Brind`Amour/Staal 6.00 15.00
WCFK Frolov/Kopitar 8.00 20.00
WCGD Gaborik/Drury 5.00 12.00
WCGF Fleury/Gilmour 8.00 20.00
WCGG Giguere/Getzlaf 5.00 12.00
WCGL Letang/Gonchar 6.00 15.00
WCHB Booth/Horton 5.00 12.00
WCHD Datsyuk/Holmstrom 8.00 20.00
WCHS Sharp/Hossa 5.00 12.00
WCHW Redden/Lundqvist 12.00 30.00
WCKF Kurri/Fuhr 8.00 20.00
WCKK Koivu/Koivu 5.00 12.00
WCKS Kurri/Selanne 10.00 25.00
WCLD Datsyuk/Lidstrom 8.00 20.00
WCLR Raymond/Luongo 8.00 20.00
WCLS Salming/Lidstrom 5.00 12.00
WCMC Ciccarelli/Modano 8.00 20.00
WCMR Richards/Modano 8.00 20.00
WCNB Bourque/Neely 8.00 20.00
WCNV Voracek/Nash 5.00 12.00
WCOB Ovechkin/Backstrom 15.00 40.00
WCOM Ovechkin/Malkin 15.00 40.00
WCPP Plekanec/Price 10.00 25.00
WCPR Pominville/Roy 3.00 8.00
WCRD Stafford/Miller 5.00 12.00
WCRL Roy/Luongo 12.00 30.00
WCRT Taylor/Robitaille 6.00 15.00
WCSB Stoll/Brown 5.00 12.00
WCSH Hawerchuk/Selanne 10.00 25.00
WCSK Sharp/Kane 10.00 25.00
WCSM Sittler/McDonald 6.00 15.00
WCSR Shutt/Robinson 5.00 12.00
WCSS Staal/Staal 6.00 15.00
WCSW Svatos/Wolski 3.00 8.00
WCYB Bowman/Yzerman 12.00 30.00

2009-10 SPx Winning Combos Spectrum

WCBP Z.Parise/M.Brodeur 20.00 50.00
WCFC M.Fleury/S.Crosby 30.00 80.00
WCHS P.Sharp.M.Hossa 8.00 20.00
WCIK J.Iginla/M.Hossa 10.00 25.00
WCOB Ovechkin/Backstrom 20.00 50.00

2009-10 SPx Winning Materials

*PATCH/50: 1X TO 2.5X BASIC JSY
WMAC Andrew Cogliano 3.00 8.00
WMAF Alexander Frolov 4.00 10.00
WMBC Brian Campbell 4.00 10.00
WMBS Brent Seabrook 3.00 8.00
WMCH Cristobal Huet 5.00 12.00
WMCO Chris Osgood 5.00 12.00
WMCW Cam Ward 5.00 12.00
WMDB Dustin Brown 5.00 12.00
WMDC Dino Ciccarelli 5.00 12.00
WMDG Doug Gilmour 6.00 15.00
WMDH Dale Hawerchuk 6.00 15.00
WMDR Derek Roy 3.00 8.00
WMDS Darryl Sittler 6.00 15.00
WMDT Dave Taylor 6.00 15.00
WMFM Frank Mahovlich 5.00 12.00
WMGA Glenn Anderson 4.00 10.00
WMGP Gilbert Perreault 5.00 12.00
WMJB Josh Bailey 4.00 10.00
WMJC Jonathan Cheechoo 4.00 10.00
WMJG Jean-Sebastien Giguere 5.00 12.00
WMJI Jarome Iginla 6.00 15.00
WMJK Jari Kurri 5.00 12.00
WMJS Jason Spezza 5.00 12.00
WMJT Jonathan Toews 8.00 20.00
WMKL Kari Lehtonen 4.00 10.00
WMLM Lanny McDonald 5.00 12.00
WMLR Larry Robinson 5.00 12.00
WMLU Luc Robitaille 5.00 12.00
WMMD Marcel Dionne 6.00 15.00
WMMG Marian Gaborik 5.00 12.00
WMMI Milan Lucic 4.00 10.00
WMMK Mikko Koivu 5.00 12.00
WMMM Mark Messier 10.00 25.00
WMMT Marty Turco 5.00 12.00
WMNL Nicklas Lidstrom 3.00 8.00
WMPB Patrice Bergeron 6.00 15.00
WMPM Peter Mueller 4.00 10.00
WMPR Patrick Roy 12.00 30.00
WMPS Patrick Sharp 5.00 12.00
WMRD Rick DiPietro 4.00 10.00
WMRG Ryan Getzlaf 4.00 10.00
WMRL Roberto Luongo 8.00 20.00
WMSD Shane Doan 4.00 10.00
WMSG Simon Gagne 5.00 12.00
WMSK Saku Koivu 5.00 12.00
WMST Drew Stafford 3.00 8.00
WMWG Wayne Gretzky 30.00 80.00

2009-10 SPx Winning Materials Autographs

AWMAK Anze Kopitar 20.00 50.00
AWMAO Adam Oates 12.00 30.00
AWMBC Bobby Clarke 15.00 40.00
AWMBH Bobby Hull 25.00 60.00
AWMBS Brent Sutter 8.00 20.00
AWMCN Cam Neely 12.00 30.00
AWMCP Carey Price 30.00 80.00
AWMDD Drew Doughty 15.00 40.00
AWMEM Evgeni Malkin 25.00 60.00
AWMES Eric Staal 15.00 40.00
AWMFR Michael Frolik 10.00 25.00
AWMHL Henrik Lundqvist 30.00 80.00
AWMIK Ilya Kovalchuk 12.00 30.00
AWMJK Jari Kurri 10.00 25.00
AWMJP Jason Pominville 8.00 20.00
AWMJT Joe Thornton 20.00 50.00
AWMJV Jakub Voracek 10.00 25.00
AWMLS Luke Schenn 12.00 30.00
AWMMB Martin Brodeur 40.00 100.00
AWMMF Marc-Andre Fleury 15.00 40.00
AWMMR Mason Raymond 20.00 50.00
AWMNB Nicklas Backstrom 12.00 30.00
AWMNH Nathan Horton 12.00 30.00
AWMPB Patrik Berglund 12.00 30.00
AWMPD Pavel Datsyuk 15.00 40.00
AWMPE Patrik Elias 12.00 30.00
AWMPH Dion Phaneuf 10.00 25.00
AWMPK Patrick Kane 25.00 60.00
AWMPL Pascal Leclaire 12.00 30.00
AWMPM Peter Mueller 10.00 25.00
AWMPR Pekka Rinne 12.00 30.00
AWMRH Ron Hextall 12.00 30.00
AWMRI Mike Richards 15.00 40.00
AWMRM Ryan Miller 20.00 50.00
AWMRN Rick Nash 12.00 30.00
AWMRY Michael Ryder 12.50 30.00
AWMSC Sidney Crosby 75.00 150.00
AWMSH Steve Shutt 12.00 30.00
AWMSW Shea Weber 10.00 25.00
AWMTE Tony Esposito 20.00 50.00
AWMTO Jonathan Toews 20.00 50.00
AWMTV Tomas Vokoun 10.00 25.00
AWMVA Thomas Vanek 10.00 25.00

2009-10 SPx Winning Trios

WTAVS Hejduk/Wolski/Svatos 6.00 15.00
WTBBR Price/Gomez/Plekanc 15.00 40.00
WTBCO Price/Lucic/Kariya 15.00 40.00
WTBOS Thomas/Bergern/Rydr 12.00 30.00
WTBRU Oates/Bourque/Neely 12.00 30.00
WTBUF Roy/Vanek/Stafford 6.00 15.00
WTBWK Hextall/Osgood/Redden 8.00 20.00
WTCBH Kane/Toews/Campbell 15.00 40.00
WTCBJ Voracek/Brassard/Nash 8.00 20.00
WTCGY McDonald/MacIns/Gilmr 10.00 25.00
WTCHF Mikita/Hull/Esposito 15.00 40.00
WTCHI Campbell/Sharp/Huet 10.00 25.00
WTCOL Stastny/Hejduk/Tucker 6.00 15.00
WTCON Zetter/Malkn/Nieder 15.00 40.00
WTCPT Mario/Messier/Gretzky 50.00 125.00
WTCZE Elias/Hejduk/Plekanec 8.00 20.00
WTDEF Bouwmstr/Phanf/Weber 6.00 15.00
WTDET Draper/Holmstrm/Lidstrm 6.00 15.00
WTDRW Osgood/Zetter/Datsyk 12.00 30.00
WTEDM Khabib/O'Sullvn/Cogli 8.00 20.00
WTEHF Messier/Fuhr/Kurri 15.00 40.00
WTFIN Selanne/Kurri/Koivu 12.00 30.00
WTFLD Lehtn/Rinne/Kiprusff 8.00 20.00
WTFLM Kiprusff/Iginla/Jokin 10.00 25.00
WTFND Kiprusff/Koivu/Selan 12.00 30.00
WTHAB Mahov/Shutt/Robnsn 8.00 20.00
WTHAR Ovechkin/Iginla/Crosby 15.00 40.00
WTHOF Mario/Yzermn/Messier 40.00 100.00
WTHRT Datsyk/Ovech/Malkn 20.00 50.00
WTHUR Staal/Brind`Amour/Ward 10.00 25.00
WTKAM Iginla/Doan/Nieder 10.00 25.00
WTKIN Dionne/Taylor/Murphy 15.00 40.00
WTKIT Roy/Richards/Robinsn 8.00 20.00
WTLAK Williams/Stoll/Brown 8.00 20.00
WTLAV Luongo/Bossy/Mario 30.00 80.00
WTLND Thorntn/Gagner/Carter 12.00 30.00
WTLON Ciccarelli/Gagner/Nash 8.00 20.00
WTLOS Kopitar/Doughty/Frolov 10.00 25.00
WTMHF Robinsn/Beliveau/Roy 30.00 60.00
WTMTL Shutt/Carbon/Robinsn 12.00 30.00
WTNYI Weight/Bailey/DiPietro 8.00 20.00
WTNYR Messi/Andersn/Leetch 6.00 15.00
WTOTT Spezza/Leclaire/Foligno 8.00 20.00
WTPEN Crosby/Staal/Malkin 25.00 60.00
WTPET Staal/Staal/Yzerman 20.00 50.00
WTPHI Carter/Richards/Gagne 15.00 40.00
WTPHX Mueller/Boedker/Doan 6.00 15.00
WTPIT Fleury/Letang/Gonchar 15.00 40.00
WTPOR Neely/Hossa/Messier 15.00 40.00
WTQMJ Luongo/Ribeiro/St.L 12.00 30.00
WTQUE Gagne/Lafleur/Ribeiro 12.00 30.00
WTRIM Lecav/Richrds/Crsby 15.00 40.00
WTRNG Staal/Gaborik/Drury 8.00 20.00
WTRRT Lecav/Ovech/Cheech 30.00 80.00
WTRUS Ovech/Koval/Malkn 20.00 50.00
WTSAB Vanek/Pominvill/Millr 12.00 30.00
WTSAS Ward/Schenn/Getzlf 8.00 20.00
WTSCC Getzlaf/Crsby/Datsyk 25.00 60.00
WTSEA Osgd/Andersn/Marleau 8.00 20.00
WTSHF Hawer/MacIns/Fedrk 12.00 30.00
WTSHO Brodr/Luongo/Kiprsff 20.00 50.00
WTSSM Espo/Gretz/Thorntn 50.00 100.00
WTSTR Richrds/Ribeo/Modno 12.00 30.00
WTSWE Lundqst/Lidstrm/Zetter 20.00 50.00
WTTHF Mahov/Sittler/McDnald 10.00 25.00
WTTOR Salmng/Mahov/McDnld 8.00 20.00
WTUDC Gretzky/Yzer/Crosby 100.00 200.00
WTUSA Modano/Parise/Miller 15.00 40.00
WTUSP Mullen/Parise/Modano 12.00 30.00
WTVIC Hextall/Fuhr/Roy 20.00 50.00
WTWNG Yzermn/Zettr/Howe 25.00 60.00

2010-11 SPx

COMP.SET w/o SPs (100) 10.00 25.00
1 Corey Perry .60 1.50
2 Ryan Getzlaf .40 1.00
3 Bobby Ryan .30 .75
4 Dustin Byfuglien .40 1.00
5 Evander Kane .40 1.00
6 Nik Antropov .30 .75
7 Blake Wheeler .40 1.00
8 Tuukka Rask .50 1.25
9 Patrice Bergeron .50 1.25
10 Milan Lucic .40 1.00
11 Tyler Myers .25 .60
12 Ryan Miller .40 1.00
13 Thomas Vanek .30 .75
14 Jay Bouwmeester .25 .60
15 Jarome Iginla .50 1.25
16 Miikka Kiprusoff .40 1.00

17 Tuomo Ruutu .30 .75
18 Eric Staal .50 1.25
19 Cam Ward .40 1.00
20 Duncan Keith .30 .75
21 Patrick Kane .75 2.00
22 Marian Hossa .40 1.00
23 Patrick Sharp .40 1.00
24 Jonathan Toews .60 1.50
25 Peter Mueller .30 .75
26 Matt Duchene .40 1.00
27 Paul Stastny .30 .75
28 Derick Brassard .25 .60
29 Rick Nash .40 1.00
30 Steve Mason .30 .75
31 Kari Lehtonen .30 .75
32 Brad Richards .40 1.00
33 Loui Eriksson .25 .60
34 Johan Franzen .30 .75
35 Jim Howard .50 1.25
36 Henrik Zetterberg .50 1.25
37 Nicklas Lidstrom .40 1.00
38 Pavel Datsyuk .60 1.50
39 Ales Hemsky .30 .75
40 Sam Gagner .25 .60
41 Dustin Penner .25 .60
42 Michael Frolik .25 .60
43 Stephen Weiss .30 .75
44 Tomas Vokoun .30 .75
45 Anze Kopitar .60 1.50
46 Drew Doughty .50 1.25
47 Dustin Brown .40 1.00
48 Guillaume Latendresse .30 .75
49 Mikko Koivu .40 1.00
50 Niklas Backstrom .40 1.00
51 Tomas Plekanec .25 .60
52 Carey Price .75 2.00
53 Mike Cammalleri .40 1.00
54 Pekka Rinne .40 1.00
55 J.P. Dumont .25 .60
56 Shea Weber .30 .75
57 Ilya Kovalchuk .40 1.00
58 Jamie Langenbrunner .25 .60
59 Martin Brodeur 1.00 2.50
60 Zach Parise .40 1.00
61 Matt Moulson .30 .75
62 Kyle Okposo .25 .60
63 John Tavares .60 1.50
64 Marian Gaborik .40 1.00
65 Henrik Lundqvist 1.00 2.50
66 Chris Drury .30 .75
67 Daniel Alfredsson .40 1.00
68 Jason Spezza .40 1.00
69 Alex Kovalev .30 .75
70 Claude Giroux .40 1.00
71 Jeff Carter .30 .75
72 James van Riemsdyk .30 .75
73 Chris Pronger .40 1.00
74 Mike Richards .30 .75
75 Ilya Bryzgalov .30 .75
76 Shane Doan .30 .75
77 Wojtek Wolski .25 .60
78 Marc-Andre Fleury .75 2.00
79 Evgeni Malkin .75 2.00
80 Jordan Staal .30 .75
81 Sidney Crosby 1.50 4.00
82 Dany Heatley .30 .75
83 Joe Pavelski .50 1.25
84 Joe Thornton .60 1.50
85 Patrick Marleau .40 1.00
86 T.J. Oshie .40 1.00
87 David Backes .25 .60
88 Victor Hedman .50 1.25
89 Steven Stamkos .75 2.00
90 Martin St. Louis .40 1.00
91 Phil Kessel .40 1.00
92 Dion Phaneuf .30 .75
93 Jean-Sebastien Giguere .40 1.00
94 Henrik Sedin .50 1.25
95 Ryan Kesler .40 1.00
96 Roberto Luongo .60 1.50
97 Daniel Sedin .50 1.25
98 Alexander Ovechkin 1.50 4.00
99 Nicklas Backstrom .40 1.00
100 Mike Green .30 .75
101 Bobby Orr 6.00 15.00
102 Lanny McDonald 1.50 4.00
103 Phil Esposito 2.50 6.00
104 Patrick Roy 4.00 10.00
105 Steve Yzerman 4.00 10.00
106 Jari Kurri 1.50 4.00
107 Gordie Howe 5.00 12.00
108 Wayne Gretzky 10.00 25.00
109 Guy Lafleur 2.00 5.00
110 Mike Bossy 1.50 4.00
111 Mark Messier 3.00 8.00
112 Bobby Clarke 2.50 6.00
113 Mario Lemieux 6.00 15.00
114 Peter Stastny 1.25 3.00
115 Red Kelly 1.50 4.00
116 Jonas Holos/499 RC 3.00 8.00
117 Brandon Pirri/499 RC 3.00 8.00
118 Alexander Urbom/499 RC 3.00 8.00
119 Matt Taormina/499 RC 3.00 8.00
120 Jake Muzzin/499 RC 8.00 20.00
121 Ryan Reaves/499 RC 4.00 10.00
122 Justin Mercier/499 RC 3.00 8.00
123 Robin Lehner/499 RC 6.00 15.00
124 Evan Brophey/499 RC 3.00 8.00
125 Nikita Nikitin/499 RC 3.00 8.00
126 Mattias Tedenby/499 RC 3.00 8.00
127 Kyle Wilson/499 RC 4.00 10.00
128 Adam McQuaid/499 RC 4.00 10.00
129 Mark Dekanich/499 RC 3.00 8.00
130 Guillaume Desbiens/499 4.00 10.00
131 Evan Oberg/499 RC 4.00 10.00
132 Jerome Samson/499 RC 3.00 8.00
133 Dustin Kohn/499 RC 3.00 8.00
134 Michael Haley/499 RC 3.00 8.00
135 Ian Cole/499 RC 3.00 8.00
136 Dylan Reese/499 RC 3.00 8.00
137 Corey Elkins/499 RC 2.50 6.00
138 Eric Wellwood/499 RC 4.00 10.00
139 Richard Clune/499 RC 4.00 10.00
140 Matt Kassian/499 RC 3.00 8.00
141 Colby Cohen/499 RC 3.00 8.00
142 Johan Motin/499 RC 2.50 6.00
143 Marco Scandella/499 RC 3.00 8.00
144 Jeremy Morin/499 RC 3.00 8.00
145 Brad Mills/499 RC 3.00 8.00
146 Mike Duco/499 RC 3.00 8.00
147 Alexander Pechurski/499 RC 4.00 10.00
148 Justin Falk/499 RC 2.50 6.00
149 Raymond Sawada/499 RC 2.50 6.00
150 Linus Klasen/499 RC 3.00 8.00
151 Clayton Stoner/499 RC 3.00 8.00
152 Dean Arsene/499 RC 3.00 8.00
153 Casey Wellman/499 RC 3.00 8.00
154 Maxime Fortunus/499 RC 2.50 6.00
155 Ben Smith/499 RC 4.00 10.00
156 Kaspars Daugavins JSY RC 5.00 12.00
157 Arturs Kulda JSY RC 4.00 10.00
158 Mark Olver JSY RC 4.00 10.00
159 Kyle Clifford JSY RC 5.00 12.00
160 Maxim Noreau JSY RC 3.00 8.00
161 Cody Almond JSY RC 4.00 10.00
162 Matt Martin JSY RC 6.00 15.00
163 Nick Palmieri JSY RC 4.00 10.00
164 Nick Johnson JSY RC 3.00 8.00
165 Justin Falk JSY RC 3.00 8.00
166 Luke Adam JSY AU RC 5.00 12.00
167 Dustin Tokarski JSY AU RC 5.00 12.00
168 Nick Leddy JSY AU RC 8.00 20.00
169 Jacob Josefson JSY AU RC 6.00 15.00
170 Alex Plante JSY AU RC 5.00 12.00
171 Evgeny Grachev JSY AU RC 5.00 12.00
172 Dana Tyrell JSY AU RC 5.00 12.00
173 K.Shattenkirk JSY AU RC 10.00 25.00
174 Anders Lindback JSY AU RC 5.00 12.00
175 Jordan Caron JSY AU RC 6.00 15.00
176 Brandon Yip JSY AU RC 5.00 12.00
177 Zach Hamill JSY AU RC 5.00 12.00
178 Jared Cowen JSY AU RC 5.00 12.00
179 Jamie McBain JSY AU RC 5.00 12.00
180 Cam Fowler JSY AU RC 8.00 20.00
181 Zac Dalpe JSY AU RC 6.00 15.00
182 Ekman-Larsson JSY AU RC 8.00 20.00
183 N.Niederreiter JSY AU RC 8.00 20.00
184 Eric Tangradi JSY AU RC 5.00 12.00
185 Henrik Karlsson JSY AU RC 5.00 12.00
186 S.Bobrovsky JSY AU RC 20.00 50.00
187 A.Burmistrov JSY AU RC 5.00 12.00
188 M.Johansson JSY AU RC 8.00 20.00
189 Jeff Skinner JSY AU RC 12.00 30.00
190 M.Paajarvi JSY AU RC 6.00 15.00
191 B.Schenn JSY AU RC 6.00 15.00
192 D.Stepan JSY AU/499 RC 12.00 30.00
193 N.Kadri JSY AU/499 RC 8.00 20.00
194 P.Subban JSY AU/499 RC 30.00 80.00
195 J.Eberle JSY AU/499 RC 15.00 40.00
196 T.Seguin JSY AU/499 RC 40.00 80.00
197 Taylor Hall JSY AU/499 RC 30.00 80.00
198 Adam Foote FF JSY 5.00 12.00
199 Alex Kovalev FF JSY 6.00 15.00
200 Alex Tanguay FF JSY 5.00 12.00
201 Alexander Frolov FF JSY 5.00 12.00
202 Bernie Nicholls FF JSY 6.00 15.00
203 Bob Probert FF JSY 8.00 20.00
204 Brendan Morrison FF JSY 6.00 15.00
206 Chris Pronger FF JSY 8.00 20.00
207 Darcy Tucker FF JSY 6.00 15.00
208 Dino Ciccarelli FF JSY 8.00 20.00
209 Donald Brashear FF JSY 12.00 30.00
210 Doug Weight FF JSY 8.00 20.00
212 Gump Worsley FF JSY 8.00 20.00
213 Ilya Kovalchuk FF JSY 8.00 20.00
214 Jarret Stoll FF JSY 6.00 15.00
215 Jason Arnott FF JSY 6.00 15.00
216 Jason Blake FF JSY 10.00 25.00
217 Joe Sakic FF JSY 15.00 40.00
218 Jose Theodore FF JSY 8.00 20.00
219 Kari Lehtonen FF JSY 6.00 15.00
220 Marc Savard FF JSY 8.00 20.00
221 Marian Hossa FF JSY 8.00 20.00
222 Olli Jokinen FF JSY 6.00 15.00
223 Paul Kariya FF JSY 8.00 20.00
224 Roberto Luongo FF JSY 12.00 30.00
225 Scott Gomez FF JSY 6.00 15.00
226 Teemu Selanne FF JSY 12.00 30.00
227 Wendel Clark FF JSY 12.00 30.00
228 Adam Oates FF JSY AU 15.00 40.00
229 Alex Ovechkin FF JSY AU 100.00 200.00
230 B.Bourne FF JSY AU EXCH 12.00 30.00
231 Borje Salming FF JSY AU 15.00 40.00
232 Brian Leetch FF JSY AU 15.00 40.00
233 Chris Drury FF JSY AU 20.00 50.00
234 Dale Hawerchuk FF JSY AU 12.00 30.00
235 Dany Heatley FF JSY AU 12.00 30.00
236 Darryl Sittler FF JSY AU 15.00 40.00
237 Doug Gilmour FF JSY AU 20.00 50.00
238 Gilbert Perreault FF JSY AU 20.00 50.00
240 Grant Fuhr FF JSY AU 25.00 60.00
241 J.P. Dumont FF JSY AU 10.00 25.00
242 Jari Kurri FF JSY AU EXCH 15.00 40.00
243 Jay Bouwmeester FF JSY AU 10.00 25.00
244 Larry Robinson FF JSY AU 15.00 40.00
245 Luc Robitaille FF JSY AU 15.00 40.00
246 Marcel Dionne FF JSY AU 20.00 50.00
247 M.Gaborik FF JSY AU EXCH 15.00 40.00
248 Mario Lemieux FF JSY AU 60.00 120.00
249 Mark Messier FF JSY AU 40.00 80.00
250 Markus Naslund FF JSY AU 20.00 50.00
251 Martin Brodeur FF JSY AU 50.00 100.00
252 Mike Modano FF JSY AU 25.00 60.00
253 Patrick Roy FF JSY AU 150.00 250.00
254 Sidney Crosby FF JSY AU 100.00 200.00
255 Simon Gagne FF JSY AU 15.00 40.00
256 Steve Yzerman FF JSY AU 100.00 200.00
257 Wayne Gretzky FF JSY AU 300.00 800.00

2010-11 SPx Spectrum

COMMON VET JSY (2-100) 4.00 10.00
VET JSY SEMISTARS 5.00 12.00
VET JSY UNL.STARS 6.00 15.00
*101-115: .5X TO 1.2X BASE
*116-155: 1X TO 2.5X BASE
*156-165: .8X TO 2X BASE
*166-197: .6X TO 1.5X BASE
2 Ryan Getzlaf JSY 6.00 15.00
5 Evander Kane JSY 6.00 15.00
11 Tyler Myers JSY 4.00 10.00
15 Jarome Iginla JSY 8.00 20.00
19 Cam Ward JSY 8.00 20.00
21 Patrick Kane JSY 12.00 30.00
26 Matt Duchene JSY 6.00 15.00
29 Rick Nash JSY 10.00 25.00
35 Jim Howard JSY 8.00 20.00
36 Henrik Zetterberg JSY 8.00 20.00
38 Pavel Datsyuk JSY 8.00 20.00
46 Drew Doughty JSY 8.00 20.00
52 Carey Price JSY 12.00 30.00
59 Martin Brodeur JSY 15.00 40.00
63 John Tavares JSY 10.00 25.00
64 Marian Gaborik JSY 6.00 15.00
65 Henrik Lundqvist JSY 15.00 40.00
67 Daniel Alfredsson JSY 8.00 20.00
70 Claude Giroux JSY 6.00 15.00
72 James van Riemsdyk JSY 5.00 12.00
79 Evgeni Malkin JSY 12.00 30.00
81 Sidney Crosby JSY 25.00 60.00
84 Joe Thornton JSY 10.00 25.00
89 Steven Stamkos JSY 12.00 30.00
93 Jean-Sebastien Giguere JSY 10.00 25.00
94 Henrik Sedin JSY 8.00 20.00
95 Ryan Kesler JSY 10.00 25.00
96 Roberto Luongo JSY 10.00 25.00
98 Alexander Ovechkin JSY 15.00 40.00
99 Nicklas Backstrom JSY 6.00 15.00
162 Matt Martin PATCH 15.00 40.00
175 Jordan Caron PATCH AU 40.00 80.00
176 Brandon Yip PATCH AU 25.00 60.00
180 Cam Fowler PATCH AU 75.00 150.00
181 Zac Dalpe PATCH AU 20.00 50.00
185 Henrik Karlsson PATCH AU 25.00 60.00
187 A.Burmistrov PATCH AU 50.00 100.00
188 M.Johansson PATCH AU 60.00 120.00
189 Jeff Skinner PATCH AU 30.00 80.00
191 Brayden Schenn PATCH AU 25.00 60.00
192 Derek Stepan PATCH AU 50.00 120.00
193 Nazem Kadri PATCH AU 25.00 60.00
194 P.K. Subban PATCH AU 150.00 300.00
195 Jordan Eberle PATCH AU 100.00 200.00
196 Tyler Seguin PATCH AU 100.00 200.00
197 Taylor Hall PATCH AU 100.00 200.00

2010-11 SPx Finite Rookies

COMP.SET w/o SPs (18) 100.00 175.00
F1 Luke Adam 2.50 6.00
F2 Jacob Josefson 2.50 6.00
F3 Dustin Tokarski 2.50 6.00
F4 Evgeny Grachev 2.50 6.00
F5 Kevin Shattenkirk 6.00 15.00
F6 Dana Tyrell 2.50 6.00
F7 Anders Lindback 2.50 6.00
F8 Jordan Caron 3.00 8.00
F9 Brandon Yip 2.50 6.00
F10 Zach Hamill 2.50 6.00
F11 Jared Cowen 2.50 6.00
F12 Jamie McBain 2.50 6.00
F13 Cam Fowler 6.00 15.00
F14 Zac Dalpe 3.00 8.00
F15 Oliver Ekman-Larsson 4.00 10.00
F16 Nino Niederreiter 4.00 10.00
F17 Henrik Karlsson 2.50 6.00
F18 Sergei Bobrovsky 10.00 25.00
F19 Eric Tangradi/249 3.00 8.00
F20 Alexander Burmistrov/249 3.00 8.00
F21 Marcus Johansson/249 5.00 12.00
F22 Jeff Skinner/249 8.00 20.00
F23 Magnus Paajarvi/249 4.00 10.00
F24 Brayden Schenn/249 8.00 20.00
F25 Derek Stepan/99 6.00 15.00
F26 Nazem Kadri/99 10.00 25.00
F27 P.K. Subban/99 15.00 40.00
F28 Jordan Eberle/99 20.00 50.00
F29 Tyler Seguin/99 15.00 40.00
F30 Taylor Hall/99 40.00 80.00

2010-11 SPx Rookie Materials

RMAB Alexander Burmistrov L1 4.00 10.00
RMBS Brayden Schenn L1 5.00 12.00
RMDS Derek Stepan L2 3.00 8.00
RMJE Jordan Eberle L2 6.00 15.00
RMJJ Jacob Josefson L1 2.00 5.00
RMJS Jeff Skinner L1 5.00 12.00
RMMJ Marcus Johansson L1 3.00 8.00
RMMP Magnus Paajarvi L1 2.50 6.00
RMNK Nazem Kadri L2 8.00 20.00
RMNN Nino Niederreiter L1 3.00 8.00
RMOE Oliver Ekman-Larsson L1 4.00 10.00
RMPS P.K. Subban L2 8.00 20.00
RMSB Sergei Bobrovsky L1 8.00 20.00
RMTH Taylor Hall L2 6.00 15.00
RMTS Tyler Seguin L2 8.00 20.00
RMZD Zac Dalpe L1 4.00 10.00

2010-11 SPx Shadowbox

SB1 Wayne Gretzky 100.00 250.00
SB2 Mario Lemieux 60.00 150.00
SB3 Mark Messier 30.00 60.00
SB4 Brandon Yip 12.00 30.00
SB5 Evgeni Malkin 30.00 80.00
SB6 Jonathan Toews 25.00 60.00
SB7 John Tavares 25.00 60.00
SB8 Alexander Ovechkin 50.00 100.00
SB9 Matt Duchene 12.00 30.00
SB10 Tyler Myers 10.00 25.00
SB11 Steven Stamkos 20.00 50.00
SB12 Phil Esposito 25.00 60.00
SB13 Jari Kurri 15.00 40.00
SB14 Jarome Iginla 20.00 50.00
SB15 Bobby Hull 30.00 80.00
SB16 Henrik Zetterberg 20.00 50.00
SB17 Ray Bourque 25.00 60.00
SB18 Jamie McBain 12.00 30.00
SB19 Steve Yzerman 40.00 100.00
SB20 P.K. Subban 40.00 100.00
SB21 James van Riemsdyk 12.00 30.00
SB22 Nazem Kadri 40.00 100.00

2010-11 SPx Shadowbox Autographs

SBSBO Bobby Orr L1 300.00 600.00
SBSGH Gordie Howe L2 400.00 800.00
SBSSC Sidney Crosby L1 EXCH 250.00 500.00
SBSWG Wayne Gretzky L2 1250.00 3000.00

2010-11 SPx Shadowbox Stoppers

ST1 Roberto Luongo 30.00 80.00
ST2 Henrik Lundqvist 50.00 125.00
ST3 Patrick Roy 60.00 120.00
ST4 Ilya Bryzgalov 15.00 40.00
ST5 Jim Howard 25.00 60.00
ST6 Ryan Miller 20.00 50.00
ST7 Martin Brodeur 40.00 100.00
ST8 Carey Price 40.00 100.00
ST9 Jean-Sebastien Giguere 20.00 50.00
ST10 Jonas Gustavsson 20.00 50.00
ST11 Jaroslav Halak 20.00 50.00
ST12 Miikka Kiprusoff 20.00 50.00

2010-11 SPx Winning Combos

WCAE P.Elias/J.Arnott 5.00 12.00
WCBB D.Backes/P.Berglund 3.00 8.00
WCBK D.Byfuglien/E.Kane 5.00 12.00
WCBL R.Luongo/M.Brodeur 12.00 30.00
WCBR P.Bergeron/T.Rask 6.00 15.00
WCCG D.Carcillo/C.Giroux 5.00 12.00
WCFM E.Malkin/M.Fleury 10.00 25.00
WCGF M.Fleury/J.Giguere 10.00 25.00
WCGM M.Messier/W.Gretzky 20.00 50.00
WCGS L.Schenn/J.Giguere 5.00 12.00
WCGV J.van Riemsdyk/C.Giroux 5.00 12.00
WCHG M.Gaborik/M.Hossa 5.00 12.00
WCHK M.Hossa/P.Kane 10.00 25.00
WCHS M.Hejduk/P.Stastny 4.00 10.00
WCJS S.Sullivan/J.Dumont 3.00 8.00
WCKB A.Burrows/R.Kesler 8.00 20.00
WCKD A.Kopitar/D.Doughty 8.00 20.00
WCKK P.Kessel/N.Kulemin 5.00 12.00
WCLB M.Brodeur/H.Lundqvist 12.00 30.00
WCLM R.Luongo/R.Miller 8.00 20.00
WCLS S.Stamkos/V.Lecavalier 10.00 25.00
WCMH P.Marleau/D.Heatley 5.00 12.00
WCMP P.Roy/M.Brodeur 12.00 30.00
WCNP C.Neely/B.Park 5.00 12.00
WCNV J.Voracek/R.Nash 5.00 12.00
WCOG M.Green/A.Ovechkin 12.00 30.00
WCOM A.Ovechkin/E.Malkin 12.00 30.00
WCPM C.Price/S.Mason 10.00 25.00
WCRB R.Bourque/P.Roy 10.00 25.00
WCRG W.Gretzky/L.Robitaille 15.00 40.00
WCSD M.Duchene/P.Stastny 5.00 12.00
WCSG S.Gagne/M.St. Louis 5.00 12.00
WCSH S.Stamkos/V.Hedman 10.00 25.00
WCSW C.Ward/E.Staal 6.00 15.00
WCTD J.Tavares/M.Duchene 8.00 20.00
WCVW T.Vokoun/S.Weiss 4.00 10.00
WCYL S.Yzerman/N.Lidstrom 12.00 30.00
WCZF J.Franzen/H.Zetterberg 6.00 15.00

2010-11 SPx Winning Combos Patches

WCAE P.Elias/J.Arnott 12.00 30.00
WCAS J.Spezza/D.Alfredsson 12.00 30.00
WCBB D.Backes/P.Berglund 8.00 20.00
WCBK D.Byfuglien/E.Kane 12.00 30.00
WCBL R.Luongo/M.Brodeur 30.00 80.00
WCBR P.Bergeron/T.Rask 15.00 40.00
WCCG D.Carcillo/C.Giroux 12.00 30.00
WCFM E.Malkin/M.Fleury 25.00 60.00
WCGF M.Fleury/J.Giguere 25.00 60.00
WCGR M.Richards/C.Giroux 12.00 30.00
WCGS L.Schenn/J.Giguere 12.00 30.00
WCGV J.van Riemsdyk/C.Giroux 12.00 30.00
WCHG M.Gaborik/M.Hossa 12.00 30.00
WCHK M.Hossa/P.Kane 25.00 60.00
WCHS M.Hejduk/P.Stastny 10.00 25.00
WCIB R.Bourque/J.Iginla 15.00 40.00
WCJS S.Sullivan/J.Dumont 8.00 20.00
WCKB A.Burrows/R.Kesler 12.00 30.00
WCKD A.Kopitar/D.Doughty 20.00 50.00
WCKK P.Kessel/N.Kulemin 12.00 30.00
WCKR P.Kessel/B.Ryan 12.00 30.00
WCLB M.Brodeur/H.Lundqvist 30.00 80.00
WCLM R.Luongo/R.Miller 20.00 50.00
WCMH P.Marleau/D.Heatley 12.00 30.00
WCMS E.Malkin/J.Staal 25.00 60.00
WCNP C.Neely/B.Park 12.00 30.00
WCNT N.Backstrom/T.Rask 15.00 40.00
WCNV J.Voracek/R.Nash 12.00 30.00
WCOG M.Green/A.Ovechkin 25.00 60.00
WCOM A.Ovechkin/E.Malkin 50.00 120.00
WCPR M.Richards/C.Pronger 12.00 30.00
WCRK P.Kane/B.Ryan 20.00 50.00
WCRV D.Roy/T.Vanek 10.00 25.00
WCSD M.Duchene/P.Stastny 12.00 30.00
WCSG S.Gagne/M.St. Louis 12.00 30.00
WCSH S.Stamkos/V.Hedman 25.00 60.00
WCSS D.Sedin/H.Sedin 15.00 40.00
WCSW C.Ward/E.Staal 15.00 40.00
WCTD J.Tavares/M.Duchene 20.00 50.00
WCTP J.Thornton/J.Pavelski 20.00 50.00
WCVW T.Vokoun/S.Weiss 10.00 25.00
WCYL S.Yzerman/N.Lidstrom 30.00 80.00
WCZF J.Franzen/H.Zetterberg 15.00 40.00

2010-11 SPx Winning Materials

WMAK Anze Kopitar 6.00 15.00
WMAN Antti Niemi 3.00 8.00
WMAO Alexander Ovechkin 8.00 20.00
WMCG Claude Giroux 4.00 10.00
WMCN Cam Neely 4.00 10.00
WMCP Carey Price 8.00 20.00
WMCR Sidney Crosby 15.00 40.00
WMCW Cam Ward 4.00 10.00
WMDC Daniel Carcillo 2.50 6.00
WMDH Dany Heatley 3.00 8.00
WMDK Duncan Keith 6.00 15.00
WMDS Daniel Sedin 5.00 12.00
WMEK Evander Kane 4.00 10.00
WMEM Evgeni Malkin 8.00 20.00
WMES Eric Staal 5.00 12.00
WMGR Mike Green 3.00 8.00
WMHE Milan Hejduk 3.00 8.00
WMHZ Henrik Zetterberg 5.00 12.00
WMJC Jeff Carter 3.00 8.00
WMJG Jean-Sebastien Giguere 4.00 10.00
WMJS Jordan Staal 3.00 8.00
WMLR Luc Robitaille 4.00 10.00
WMMB Martin Brodeur 6.00 15.00
WMMD Matt Duchene 4.00 10.00
WMMG Marian Gaborik 4.00 10.00
WMMH Marian Hossa 4.00 10.00
WMMK Mikko Koivu 4.00 10.00
WMML Mario Lemieux 15.00 40.00
WMMM Mark Messier 8.00 20.00
WMPD Pavel Datsyuk 6.00 15.00
WMPE Patrik Elias 4.00 10.00
WMPK Patrick Kane 6.00 15.00
WMPS Patrick Sharp 4.00 10.00
WMRI Brad Richards 4.00 10.00
WMRK Ryan Kesler 6.00 15.00
WMSC Sidney Crosby 15.00 40.00
WMSD Shane Doan 3.00 8.00
WMSM Steve Mason 3.00 8.00
WMSY Steve Yzerman 10.00 25.00
WMTA John Tavares 6.00 15.00
WMVL Vincent Lecavalier 4.00 10.00
WMWG Wayne Gretzky 25.00 60.00

2010-11 SPx Winning Materials Autographs

WMAO Alexander Ovechkin 75.00 125.00
WMCP Carey Price 30.00 60.00
WMCR Sidney Crosby 90.00 150.00
WMCW Cam Ward 12.00 30.00
WMDH Dany Heatley 10.00 25.00
WMEK Evander Kane 12.00 30.00
WMEM Evgeni Malkin 30.00 60.00
WMES Eric Staal 12.00 30.00
WMHZ Henrik Zetterberg 30.00 60.00
WMJS Jordan Staal 20.00 50.00
WMMB Martin Brodeur 40.00 80.00
WMMD Matt Duchene 12.00 30.00
WMMH Marian Hossa 15.00 40.00
WMML Mario Lemieux 75.00 150.00
WMMM Mark Messier 30.00 60.00
WMRK Ryan Kesler 12.00 30.00
WMSC Sidney Crosby 90.00 150.00
WMSD Shane Doan 10.00 25.00
WMSS Steven Stamkos 40.00 80.00
WMSY Steve Yzerman 50.00 100.00
WMVL Vincent Lecavalier 20.00 50.00
WMWG Wayne Gretzky 250.00 600.00

2010-11 SPx Winning Materials Patches

*PATCH/35: 1X TO 2.5X BASIC WM
WMAK Anze Kopitar 15.00 40.00
WMDC Daniel Carcillo 12.00 30.00
WMDS Daniel Sedin 15.00 40.00
WMJG Jean-Sebastien Giguere 10.00 25.00
WMML Mario Lemieux 40.00 100.00
WMRI Brad Richards 12.00 30.00
WMRK Ryan Kesler 15.00 40.00

2010-11 SPx Winning Trios

WM31ST Stamkos/Kane/Tvares 15.00 40.00
WM3BOS Bergern/Lucic/Savard 10.00 25.00
WM3CGY McDnld/Mullen/Gilmour 10.00 25.00
WM3CPT Howe/Lidstrm/Yzermn 25.00 60.00
WM3DAL Ribeo/Eriksson/Richrds 8.00 20.00
WM3DEF Doughty/Myers/Weber 10.00 25.00
WM3DET Datsyuk/Zetter/Franzen 12.00 30.00
WM3GR8 Messier/Lemx/Gretzky 50.00 125.00
WM3HOF Yzermn/Lmieux/Mssier 30.00 80.00
WM3ISL Tavres/Okpso/Weight 12.00 30.00
WM3LAK Dghty/Brown/Kopitar 12.00 30.00
WM3MON Price/Gionta/Cammllri 15.00 40.00
WM3NYR Gabrik/Drury/Lndqvist 20.00 50.00
WM3RKP Tavares/Dchne/Myers 15.00 40.00
WM3RUS Datsyuk/Malkin/Ovech 15.00 40.00
WM3SLO Chara/Hossa/Gaborik 8.00 20.00
WM3TML Kulemin/Kess/Phaneuf 8.00 20.00
WM3VAN Burrows/Sedin/Kesler 15.00 40.00
WM3BEES Bourque/Chara/Park 12.00 30.00
WM3CAPS Ovech/Bckstrm/Grn 15.00 40.00
WM3ECAN Cammll/Kessel/Spezza 8.00 20.00
WM3NJD1 Langen/Elias/Brodr 12.00 30.00
WM3NJD2 Parise/Koval/Clarksn 8.00 20.00
WM3PITT Malkin/Crosby/Fleury 15.00 40.00
WM3SCF2 van R/Giroux/Carcillo 8.00 20.00
WM3SCW2 Keith/Hossa/Kane 15.00 40.00
WM3WCAN Penner/Sedin/Iginla 10.00 25.00
WM3WILD Bckstrm/Koivu/Bchrd 8.00 20.00
WM3FGHT2 Carkner/Carcillo/Orr 12.00 30.00
WM3GLDRS Ovech/Crsby/Stmkos 30.00 80.00

2011-12 SPx

COMP.SET w/o SP's (100) 12.00 30.00
1 Dustin Byfuglien .40 1.00
2 Ondrej Pavelec .40 1.00
3 Alexander Ovechkin 1.50 4.00
4 Nicklas Backstrom .40 1.00
5 Mike Green .30 .75
6 Alexander Semin .40 1.00
7 Henrik Sedin .50 1.25
8 Ryan Kesler .40 1.00
9 Roberto Luongo .60 1.50
10 Daniel Sedin .50 1.25
11 Phil Kessel .40 1.00
12 Dion Phaneuf .30 .75
13 Nikolai Kulemin .25 .60
14 Steven Stamkos .75 2.00
15 Martin St. Louis .40 1.00
16 Vincent Lecavalier .40 1.00
17 Patrik Berglund .25 .60
18 David Backes .25 .60
19 Chris Stewart .30 .75
20 Jaroslav Halak .40 1.00
21 Joe Thornton .60 1.50
22 Patrick Marleau .40 1.00
23 Marc-Andre Fleury .75 2.00
24 Evgeni Malkin .75 2.00
25 Jordan Staal .30 .75
26 Sidney Crosby 1.50 4.00
27 Oliver Ekman-Larsson .40 1.00
28 Ilya Bryzgalov .40 1.00
29 Claude Giroux .40 1.00
30 James van Riemsdyk .30 .75
31 Chris Pronger .40 1.00
32 Daniel Briere .40 1.00
33 Daniel Alfredsson .40 1.00
34 Jason Spezza .40 1.00
35 Marian Gaborik .40 1.00
36 Henrik Lundqvist 1.00 2.50
37 Derek Stepan .25 .60
38 Brad Richards .40 1.00
39 Matt Moulson .25 .60
40 John Tavares .60 1.50
41 Ilya Kovalchuk .40 1.00
42 Martin Brodeur 1.00 2.50
43 Zach Parise .40 1.00
44 Pekka Rinne .40 1.00
45 Shea Weber .30 .75
46 Tomas Plekanec .25 .60
47 Carey Price .75 2.00
48 Michael Cammalleri .30 .75
49 P.K. Subban .50 1.25
50 Dany Heatley .30 .75
51 Guillaume Latendresse .30 .75
52 Mikko Koivu .30 .75
53 Mike Richards .30 .75
54 Anze Kopitar .60 1.50
55 Drew Doughty .50 1.25
56 Dustin Brown .40 1.00
57 Stephen Weiss .30 .75
58 David Booth .25 .60
59 Ales Hemsky .30 .75
60 Sam Gagner .25 .60
61 Magnus Paajarvi .30 .75
62 Jordan Eberle .40 1.00
63 Taylor Hall .40 1.00
64 Johan Franzen .30 .75
65 Jim Howard .50 1.25
66 Henrik Zetterberg .50 1.25
67 Nicklas Lidstrom .25 .60
68 Pavel Datsyuk .60 1.50
69 Kari Lehtonen .30 .75
70 Loui Eriksson .25 .60
71 Jeff Carter .30 .75
72 Derick Brassard .25 .60
73 Rick Nash .40 1.00
74 Steve Mason .30 .75
75 Peter Mueller .30 .75
76 Matt Duchene .40 1.00
77 Paul Stastny .30 .75
78 Patrick Kane .75 2.00
79 Marian Hossa .40 1.00
80 Patrick Sharp .40 1.00
81 Jonathan Toews .60 1.50
82 Tomas Kaberle .25 .60
83 Eric Staal .50 1.25
84 Jussi Jokinen .25 .60
85 Olli Jokinen .30 .75
86 Jay Bouwmeester .25 .60
87 Jarome Iginla .50 1.25
88 Miikka Kiprusoff .40 1.00
89 Ryan Miller .40 1.00
90 Thomas Vanek .30 .75
91 Drew Stafford .25 .60
92 Derek Roy .25 .60
93 Patrice Bergeron .50 1.25
94 Milan Lucic .40 1.00
95 Tim Thomas .40 1.00
96 Zdeno Chara .40 1.00
97 Nathan Horton .40 1.00
98 Tyler Seguin .50 1.25
99 Bobby Ryan .30 .75
100 Ryan Getzlaf .40 1.00
101 Bobby Orr LEG 8.00 20.00
102 Phil Esposito LEG 3.00 8.00
103 Cam Neely LEG 2.00 5.00
104 Bobby Hull LEG 4.00 10.00
105 Joe Sakic LEG 4.00 10.00
106 Alex Delvecchio LEG 2.00 5.00
107 Ted Lindsay LEG 2.00 5.00
108 Wayne Gretzky LEG 6.00 15.00
109 Paul Coffey LEG 2.00 5.00
110 Jari Kurri LEG 2.00 5.00
111 Ron Francis LEG 2.50 6.00
112 Guy Lafleur LEG 2.50 6.00
113 Jean Beliveau LEG 2.00 5.00
114 Patrick Roy LEG 6.00 15.00
115 Mike Bossy LEG 2.00 5.00
116 Mark Messier LEG 4.00 10.00
117 Pelle Lindbergh LEG 4.00 10.00
118 Bobby Clarke LEG 3.00 8.00
119 Mario Lemieux LEG 8.00 20.00
120 Richard Brodeur LEG 2.00 5.00
121 Dale Hawerchuk LEG 2.50 6.00
122 Allen York RC 3.00 8.00
123 David Ullstrom RC 2.50 6.00
124 Carl Klingberg RC 2.50 6.00
125 Andy Miele RC 2.50 6.00
126 Ben Holmstrom RC 2.50 6.00
127 Ben Scrivens RC 5.00 12.00
128 Bracken Kearns RC 2.50 6.00
129 Brendon Nash RC 2.50 6.00
130 Brian Strait RC 3.00 8.00
131 Cam Talbot RC 6.00 15.00
132 Cameron Gaunce RC 2.00 5.00
133 Carson McMillan RC 3.00 8.00
134 Chris Vande Velde RC 4.00 10.00
135 Cody Eakin RC 5.00 12.00
136 Stefan Elliott RC 2.50 6.00
137 Colton Sceviour RC 2.50 6.00
138 Corey Tropp RC 2.50 6.00
139 Drew Bagnall RC 2.50 6.00
140 Erik Gudbranson 3.00 8.00
141 Gustav Nyquist RC 10.00 25.00
142 Harry Zolnierczyk RC 2.50 6.00
143 Hugh Jessiman RC 2.50 6.00
144 Leland Irving RC 2.50 6.00
145 Joe Vitale RC 2.50 6.00
146 Keith Kinkaid RC 2.50 6.00
147 Lance Bouma RC 2.50 6.00
148 Mattias Ekholm RC 5.00 12.00
149 Maxime Macenauer RC 2.50 6.00
150 Pat Maroon RC 2.50 6.00
151 Patrick Wiercioch RC 2.50 6.00
152 Paul Postma RC 2.50 6.00
153 Peter Holland RC 2.50 6.00
154 Robert Bortuzzo RC 2.50 6.00
155 Roman Wick RC 3.00 8.00
156 Ryan Thang RC 2.00 5.00
157 Scott Timmins RC 2.50 6.00
158 Stephane Da Costa RC 2.50 6.00
159 Cade Fairchild RC 2.00 5.00
160 Tomas Kubalik RC 2.50 6.00
161 Viatcheslav Voynov RC 2.50 6.00
162 Brayden McNabb RC 2.50 6.00
163 Zac Rinaldo RC 2.50 6.00
164 David Rundblad JSY RC 3.00 8.00
165 Yann Sauve JSY RC 3.00 8.00
166 Teemu Hartikainen JSY RC 3.00 8.00
167 Cam Atkinson JSY RC 8.00 20.00
168 Brett Bulmer JSY RC 4.00 10.00
169 Alexei Emelin JSY RC 3.00 8.00
170 Raphael Diaz JSY RC 3.00 8.00
171 Colin Greening JSY RC 3.00 8.00
172 Colten Teubert JSY RC 3.00 8.00
173 Roman Horak JSY RC 3.00 8.00
174 Justin Faulk JSY AU RC 8.00 20.00
175 John Moore JSY AU RC 5.00 12.00
176 Tomas Vincour JSY AU RC 5.00 12.00
177 Zack Kassian JSY AU RC 8.00 20.00
178 Craig Smith JSY AU RC 6.00 15.00
179 Tim Erixon JSY AU RC 5.00 12.00
180 D.Smith-Pelly JSY AU RC 6.00 15.00
181 Greg Nemisz JSY AU RC 5.00 12.00
182 Marcus Kruger JSY AU RC 8.00 20.00
183 Brandon Saad JSY AU RC 15.00 30.00
184 Anton Lander JSY AU RC 5.00 12.00
185 E.Gudbranson JSY AU RC 6.00 15.00
186 Aaron Palushaj JSY AU RC 5.00 12.00
187 Jonathon Blum JSY AU RC 5.00 12.00
188 Blake Geoffrion JSY AU RC 5.00 12.00
189 Adam Henrique JSY AU RC 12.00 30.00
190 Adam Larsson JSY AU RC 6.00 15.00
191 M.Zibanejad JSY AU RC 15.00 40.00
192 Matt Read JSY AU RC 6.00 15.00
193 Louis Leblanc JSY AU RC 6.00 15.00
194 Jake Gardiner JSY AU RC 5.00 12.00
195 Joe Colborne JSY AU RC 5.00 12.00
196 Matt Frattin JSY AU RC 5.00 12.00
197 Brendan Smith JSY AU RC 6.00 15.00
198 R.Johansen JSY AU RC 15.00 40.00
199 Lennart Petrell JSY AU RC 6.00 15.00
200 Cody Hodgson JSY AU RC 12.00 30.00
201 Brett Connolly JSY AU RC 8.00 20.00
202 Mark Scheifele JSY AU RC 30.00 80.00
203 Sean Couturier JSY AU RC 8.00 20.00
204 G.Landeskog JSY AU RC 25.00 60.00
205 Nugent-Hopk JSY AU RC 30.00 80.00
206 Jaromir Jagr FF JSY E 15.00 40.00
207 Jaromir Jagr FF JSY D 25.00 60.00
208 Bernie Nicholls FF JSY E 4.00 10.00
209 Bill Ranford FF JSY D 8.00 20.00
210 Chris Higgins FF JSY C 8.00 20.00
211 Chris Pronger FF JSY B 8.00 20.00
212 Craig Anderson FF JSY E 5.00 12.00
213 Daniel Paille FF JSY E 3.00 8.00
214 Dave Taylor FF JSY E 4.00 10.00
215 Doug Weight FF JSY D 8.00 20.00
216 Dustin Penner FF JSY E 4.00 10.00
217 Ed Jovanovski FF JSY E 3.00 8.00
218 Erik Johnson FF JSY E 3.00 8.00
219 Jaromir Jagr FF JSY D 25.00 60.00
220 Ilya Kovalchuk FF JSY E 5.00 12.00
221 Langenbrunner FF JSY E 3.00 8.00
222 Jason Arnott FF JSY E 4.00 10.00
223 Joe Mullen FF JSY E 4.00 10.00
224 Jordan Leopold FF JSY E 3.00 8.00
225 Jose Theodore FF JSY E 5.00 12.00
227 Kari Lehtonen FF JSY E 4.00 10.00
228 Matt Stajan FF JSY E 3.00 8.00
229 Michael Frolik FF JSY E 3.00 8.00
230 Nik Antropov FF JSY D 6.00 15.00
231 Raffi Torres FF JSY E 3.00 8.00
232 Roberto Luongo FF JSY C 10.00 25.00
233 Saku Koivu FF JSY E 5.00 12.00
234 Scott Gomez FF JSY E 5.00 12.00
235 Sergei Gonchar FF JSY E 3.00 8.00
236 A.Ovechkin FF JSY AU B 50.00 100.00
237 Cam Neely FF JSY AU D 20.00 50.00
238 Chris Drury FF JSY AU C 10.00 25.00
239 Guy Lafleur FF JSY AU A 60.00 100.00
240 Jari Kurri FF JSY AU D 25.00 50.00
241 Jarome Iginla FF JSY AU C 15.00 40.00
242 Alex Tanguay FF JSY AU D 8.00 20.00
243 Kris Versteeg FF JSY AU E 10.00 25.00
244 L.Robinson FF JSY AU E 12.00 30.00
245 Luc Robitaille FF JSY AU E 12.00 30.00
246 Marcel Dionne FF JSY AU D 20.00 50.00
247 M.Lemieux FF JSY AU B 60.00 120.00
248 Mark Messier FF JSY AU B 30.00 60.00
249 M.Brodeur FF JSY AU B 40.00 80.00
250 Marty Turco FF JSY AU E 12.00 30.00
251 Mike Bossy FF JSY AU C 15.00 40.00
252 Mike Modano FF JSY AU B 20.00 50.00
253 Joe Thornton FF JSY AU B 20.00 40.00
254 Patrick Roy FF JSY AU B 40.00 80.00
255 Peter Mueller FF JSY AU E 10.00 25.00
256 Peter Stastny FF JSY AU D 10.00 25.00
257 Phil Esposito FF JSY AU B 20.00 40.00
258 Phil Kessel FF JSY AU C 12.00 30.00
259 Ray Bourque FF JSY AU B 30.00 60.00
260 Ray Emery FF JSY AU D 10.00 25.00
261 Ron Francis FF JSY AU B 15.00 30.00
262 Ron Hextall FF JSY AU B 25.00 50.00
263 Sidney Crosby FF JSY AU B 60.00 120.00
264 Tony Esposito FF JSY AU B 25.00 50.00
265 W.Gretzky FF JSY AU C 300.00 800.00

2011-12 SPx Spectrum

*101-121 LEG/25: 1X TO 2.5X BASIC LEG/499
*122-163 ROOK/25: .6X TO 1.5X BASIC RC/499
*164-173 PATCH/35: 1X TO 2.5X JSY RC/799
*174-199 PTCH AU/25: 1X TO 2.5X JSY AU RC
*201-205 PTCH AU/25: 1X TO 2.5X JSY AU RC
1 Dustin Byfuglien PATCH 10.00 25.00
2 Ondrej Pavelec PATCH 10.00 25.00
3 Alexander Ovechkin PATCH 40.00 100.00
4 Nicklas Backstrom PATCH 10.00 25.00
5 Mike Green PATCH 8.00 20.00
6 Alexander Semin PATCH 10.00 25.00
7 Henrik Sedin PATCH 12.00 30.00
8 Ryan Kesler PATCH 10.00 25.00
9 Roberto Luongo PATCH 15.00 40.00
10 Daniel Sedin PATCH 12.00 30.00
11 Phil Kessel PATCH 10.00 25.00
12 Dion Phaneuf PATCH 8.00 20.00
13 Nikolai Kulemin PATCH 6.00 15.00
14 Steven Stamkos PATCH 20.00 50.00
15 Martin St. Louis PATCH 10.00 25.00
16 Vincent Lecavalier PATCH 10.00 25.00
17 Patrik Berglund PATCH 6.00 15.00
18 David Backes PATCH 6.00 15.00
19 Chris Stewart PATCH 8.00 20.00
20 Jaroslav Halak PATCH 10.00 25.00
21 Joe Thornton PATCH 15.00 40.00
22 Patrick Marleau PATCH 10.00 25.00
23 Marc-Andre Fleury PATCH 20.00 50.00
24 Evgeni Malkin PATCH 20.00 50.00
25 Jordan Staal PATCH 8.00 20.00
26 Sidney Crosby PATCH 30.00 80.00
27 Oliver Ekman-Larsson PATCH 10.00 25.00
28 Ilya Bryzgalov PATCH 10.00 25.00
29 Claude Giroux PATCH 10.00 25.00
30 James van Riemsdyk PATCH 8.00 20.00
31 Chris Pronger PATCH 10.00 25.00
32 Daniel Briere PATCH 10.00 25.00
33 Daniel Alfredsson PATCH 10.00 25.00
34 Jason Spezza PATCH 10.00 25.00
35 Marian Gaborik PATCH 10.00 25.00
36 Henrik Lundqvist PATCH 25.00 60.00

37 Derek Stepan PATCH 6.00 15.00
38 Brad Richards PATCH 10.00 25.00
39 Matt Moulson PATCH 6.00 15.00
40 John Tavares PATCH 15.00 40.00
41 Ilya Kovalchuk PATCH 10.00 25.00
42 Martin Brodeur PATCH 25.00 60.00
43 Zach Parise PATCH 10.00 25.00
44 Pekka Rinne PATCH 10.00 25.00
45 Shea Weber PATCH 8.00 20.00
46 Tomas Plekanec PATCH 6.00 15.00
47 Carey Price PATCH 20.00 50.00
48 Michael Cammalleri PATCH 8.00 20.00
49 P.K. Subban PATCH 12.00 30.00
50 Dany Heatley PATCH 8.00 20.00
51 Guillaume Latendresse PATCH 8.00 20.00
52 Mikko Koivu PATCH 8.00 20.00
53 Mike Richards PATCH 8.00 20.00
54 Anze Kopitar PATCH 15.00 40.00
55 Drew Doughty PATCH 12.00 30.00
56 Dustin Brown PATCH 10.00 25.00
57 Stephen Weiss PATCH 8.00 20.00
58 David Booth PATCH 6.00 15.00
59 Ales Hemsky PATCH 8.00 20.00
60 Sam Gagner PATCH 10.00 25.00
61 Magnus Paajarvi PATCH 8.00 20.00
62 Jordan Eberle PATCH 10.00 25.00
64 Johan Franzen PATCH 8.00 20.00
65 Jim Howard PATCH 12.00 30.00
66 Henrik Zetterberg PATCH 12.00 30.00
67 Nicklas Lidstrom PATCH 6.00 15.00
68 Pavel Datsyuk PATCH 15.00 40.00
69 Kari Lehtonen PATCH 12.00 30.00
70 Loui Eriksson PATCH 6.00 15.00
71 Jeff Carter PATCH 8.00 20.00
72 Derick Brassard PATCH 6.00 15.00
73 Rick Nash PATCH 10.00 25.00
74 Steve Mason PATCH 8.00 20.00
75 Peter Mueller PATCH 8.00 20.00
76 Matt Duchene PATCH 10.00 25.00
77 Paul Stastny PATCH 8.00 20.00
78 Patrick Kane PATCH 20.00 50.00
79 Marian Hossa PATCH 10.00 25.00
80 Patrick Sharp PATCH 10.00 25.00
81 Jonathan Toews PATCH 15.00 40.00
82 Tomas Kaberle PATCH 6.00 15.00
83 Eric Staal PATCH 12.00 30.00
84 Jussi Jokinen PATCH 6.00 15.00
85 Olli Jokinen PATCH 8.00 20.00
86 Jay Bouwmeester PATCH 6.00 15.00
87 Jarome Iginla PATCH 12.00 30.00
88 Miikka Kiprusoff PATCH 10.00 25.00
89 Ryan Miller PATCH 10.00 25.00
90 Thomas Vanek PATCH 8.00 20.00
91 Drew Stafford PATCH 6.00 15.00
92 Derek Roy PATCH 6.00 15.00
93 Patrice Bergeron PATCH 12.00 30.00
94 Milan Lucic PATCH 10.00 25.00
95 Tim Thomas PATCH 10.00 25.00
96 Zdeno Chara PATCH 10.00 25.00
97 Nathan Horton PATCH 10.00 25.00
98 Tyler Seguin PATCH 12.00 30.00
99 Bobby Ryan PATCH 8.00 20.00
100 Ryan Getzlaf PATCH 10.00 25.00
183 Brandon Saad PATCH AU 90.00 150.00
201 Brett Connolly PATCH AU 25.00 60.00
203 Sean Couturier PATCH AU 50.00 120.00
204 Gabriel Landeskog PATCH AU 80.00 200.00
205 Ryan Nugent-Hopkins PATCH AU 200.00 400.00

2011-12 SPx Finite Rookies

F1 Alexei Emelin/499 2.00 5.00
F2 Andy Miele/499 2.00 5.00
F3 Anton Lander/499 2.00 5.00
F4 Blake Geoffrion/499 2.00 5.00
F5 Mika Zibanejad/499 5.00 12.00
F6 Carl Klingberg/499 2.00 5.00
F7 Colin Greening/499 2.00 5.00
F8 Colten Teubert/499 2.00 5.00
F9 Erik Gudbranson/499 2.50 6.00
F10 Joe Colborne/499 2.00 5.00
F11 Gustav Nyquist/499 6.00 15.00
F12 Jonathon Blum/499 2.00 5.00
F13 Peter Holland/499 2.00 5.00
F14 Raphael Diaz/499 2.00 5.00
F15 Tim Erixon/499 2.00 5.00
F16 Brandon Saad/249 5.00 12.00
F17 Teemu Hartikainen/249 2.50 6.00
F18 Marcus Kruger/249 4.00 10.00
F19 Devante Smith-Pelly/249 3.00 8.00
F20 Adam Henrique/249 6.00 15.00
F21 Craig Smith/249 3.00 8.00
F22 Matt Frattin/249 2.50 6.00
F23 Lennart Petrell/249 3.00 8.00
F24 Cody Eakin/249 4.00 10.00
F25 David Rundblad/249 2.50 6.00
F26 Jake Gardiner/249 4.00 10.00
F27 Matt Read/249 8.00 20.00
F28 Louis Leblanc/99 25.00 50.00
F29 Zack Kassian/99 8.00 20.00
F30 Ryan Johansen/99 12.00 30.00
F31 Adam Larsson/99 5.00 12.00
F32 Brett Connolly/99 4.00 10.00
F33 Cody Hodgson/99 12.00 30.00
F34 Sean Couturier/99 20.00 40.00
F35 Mark Scheifele/99 12.00 30.00
F36 Gabriel Landeskog/99 12.00 30.00
F37 Ryan Nugent-Hopkins/99 15.00 40.00

2011-12 SPx Rookie Materials

*PATCH/25: 1X TO 2.5X BASIC GRP A
*PATCH/15: 1X TO 2.5X BASIC GRP B
RMAL Adam Larsson 3.00 8.00
RMBC Brett Connolly 3.00 8.00
RMCE Cody Eakin 4.00 10.00
RMCH Cody Hodgson 8.00 20.00
RMCS Craig Smith 3.00 8.00
RMEG Erik Gudbranson 3.00 8.00
RMGL Gabriel Landeskog 10.00 25.00
RMJG Jake Gardiner 4.00 10.00
RMLL Louis Leblanc 12.00 30.00
RMMF Matt Frattin 2.50 6.00
RMMR Matt Read 3.00 8.00
RMMS Mark Scheifele 10.00 25.00
RMMZ Mika Zibanejad 8.00 20.00
RMRJ Ryan Johansen 10.00 25.00
RMRN Ryan Nugent-Hopkins 15.00 40.00
RMSC Sean Couturier 6.00 15.00
RMTH Teemu Hartikainen 2.50 6.00
RMZK Zack Kassian 3.00 8.00

2011-12 SPx Shadowbox

SB1 Wayne Gretzky 60.00 120.00
SB2 Mario Lemieux 40.00 80.00
SB3 Mark Messier 30.00 80.00
SB4 Ron Francis 25.00 50.00
SB5 Joe Sakic 30.00 60.00
SB6 Mike Gartner 20.00 50.00
SB7 Guy Lafleur 20.00 50.00
SB8 Brett Hull 30.00 60.00
SB9 Jaromir Jagr 50.00 120.00
SB10 Evgeni Malkin 30.00 80.00
SB12 Alexander Semin 10.00 25.00
SB13 Rick Nash 20.00 50.00
SB14 Ryan Getzlaf 15.00 40.00
SB15 Drew Doughty 15.00 40.00
SB16 Patrick Kane 20.00 50.00
SB17 Zach Parise 15.00 40.00
SB18 Ilya Kovalchuk 15.00 40.00
SB19 Nicklas Lidstrom 30.00 60.00
SB20 Steven Stamkos AU 60.00 150.00

2011-12 SPx Shadowbox Programme of Excellence

PE1 John Tavares 25.00 60.00
PE2 P.K. Subban 25.00 60.00
PE3 Taylor Hall 15.00 40.00
PE4 Jordan Eberle 60.00 120.00
PE5 Tyler Ennis 10.00 25.00
PE6 Sidney Crosby 75.00 135.00
PE7 Jonathan Toews 40.00 80.00
PE8 Carey Price 40.00 80.00
PE9 Mike Richards 25.00 60.00
PE10 Roberto Luongo 50.00 100.00
PE11 Cody Hodgson AU 75.00 150.00

2011-12 SPx Shadowbox Stoppers

SBS1 Martin Brodeur 25.00 60.00
SBS2 Tim Thomas 30.00 60.00
SBS3 Bernie Parent 30.00 60.00
SBS4 Ryan Miller 15.00 40.00
SBS5 Corey Crawford 15.00 40.00
SBS6 Ondrej Pavelec 20.00 50.00
SBS7 Bill Ranford 15.00 40.00
SBS8 Terry Sawchuk 40.00 80.00
SBS9 Georges Vezina 50.00 100.00
SBS10 Patrick Roy AU EXCH 250.00 500.00

2011-12 SPx Winning Combos

*PATCH/15: .8X TO 2X BASIC GRP A
*PATCH/15: 1X TO 2.5X BASIC GRP B-C
WCAP A.Markov/P.Subban D 8.00 20.00
WCBH Bergeron/N.Horton E 6.00 15.00
WCBJ B.Schenn/J.Cowen E 5.00 12.00
WCBK D.Byfuglien/E.Kane E 5.00 12.00
WCBS P.Bergeron/E.Staal D 6.00 15.00
WCCF M.Fleury/S.Crosby C 10.00 25.00
WCCL M.Lemieux/S.Crosby C 20.00 50.00
WCDC Backes/C.Stewart E 4.00 10.00
WCDJ Cleary/Abdelkader E 5.00 12.00
WCEH T.Hall/J.Eberle E 8.00 20.00
WCFS M.Fleury/J.Staal E 10.00 25.00
WCGM Messier/W.Gretzky A 40.00 100.00
WCGR R.Getzlaf/B.Ryan E 5.00 12.00
WCGS M.Gaborik/D.Stepan E 5.00 12.00
WCGV Giroux/Van Riemsdyk E 6.00 15.00
WCHK V.Hedman/Karlsson E 6.00 15.00
WCHP Hemsky/M.Paajarvi E 5.00 12.00
WCHS H.Lundqvist/M.Staal E 12.00 30.00
WCIK J.Iginla/M.Kiprusoff E 6.00 15.00
WCKD Kopitar/D.Doughty D 8.00 20.00
WCKG J.Kurri/W.Gretzky B 12.00 30.00
WCKH R.Kesler/C.Hodgson C 3.00 8.00
WCKP Kovalchuk/Z.Parise E 6.00 15.00
WCLA Gagne/M.Richards E 5.00 12.00
WCLD Lidstrom/P.Datsyuk E 8.00 20.00
WCLK Luongo/M.Kiprusoff E 8.00 20.00
WCLM M.Lemieux/E.Malkin B 20.00 50.00
WCLS Lecavalier/St. Louis E 5.00 12.00
WCMK Kulemin/C.MacArthur E 3.00 8.00
WCMS R.Miller/D.Stafford E 5.00 12.00
WCNC M.Neuvirth/J.Carlson E 2.50 6.00
WCOB Ovechkin/Backstrom D 8.00 20.00
WCOG Ovechkin/M.Green C 5.00 12.00
WCPR P.Roy/R.Bourque D 8.00 20.00
WCRB P.Roy/M.Brodeur E 12.00 30.00
WCRG Robitaille/W.Gretzky A 25.00 50.00
WCRH Rinne/P.Hornqvist E 5.00 12.00
WCRL P.Roy/R.Luongo B 12.00 30.00
WCRV D.Roy/T.Vanek E 4.00 10.00
WCSD Duchene/P.Stastny E 4.00 10.00
WCSE D.Stafford/T.Ennis E 3.00 8.00
WCSS H.Sedin/D.Sedin E 6.00 15.00
WCTB Thornton/Bergeron D 5.00 12.00
WCTK J.Toews/P.Kane C 10.00 25.00
WCTM Moulson/J.Tavares E 5.00 12.00
WCTR T.Rask/T.Thomas E 6.00 15.00
WCTS J.Thornton/E.Staal D 5.00 12.00
WCVG J.Voracek/C.Giroux E 5.00 12.00
WCZF Zetterberg/Franzen E 5.00 12.00

2011-12 SPx Winning Materials

*PATCH/35: .6X TO 1.5X BASIC GRP B
*PATCH/35: .8X TO 2X BASIC GRP C-E
WMAH Ales Hemsky E 3.00 8.00
WMAK Anze Kopitar E 6.00 15.00
WMAO Alexander Ovechkin C 15.00 40.00
WMBA David Backes C 2.50 6.00
WMCN Cam Neely E 4.00 10.00
WMCS Chris Stewart E 3.00 8.00
WMDB Dustin Byfuglien C 4.00 10.00
WMDD Drew Doughty C 5.00 12.00
WMDR Derek Roy C 2.50 6.00
WMDS Daniel Sedin B 6.00 15.00
WMEL Eric Lindros E 6.00 15.00
WMEM Evgeni Malkin C 5.00 12.00
WMGL Guillaume Latendresse C 3.00 8.00
WMHL Henrik Lundqvist D 10.00 25.00
WMHW Jim Howard C 5.00 12.00
WMJC Jeff Carter E 3.00 8.00
WMJE Jordan Eberle D 5.00 12.00
WMJI Jarome Iginla E 5.00 12.00
WMJT Jonathan Toews D 6.00 15.00
WMKE Phil Kessel D 4.00 10.00
WMMB Martin Brodeur B 12.00 30.00
WMMD Matt Duchene E 4.00 10.00
WMMF Marc-Andre Fleury E 8.00 20.00
WMMG Marian Gaborik D 4.00 10.00
WMML Mario Lemieux B 8.00 20.00
WMMM Mark Messier B 6.00 15.00
WMMR Mike Richards E 3.00 8.00
WMMS Martin St. Louis D 4.00 10.00
WMNB Nicklas Backstrom E 4.00 10.00
WMNG Nathan Gerbe E 2.50 6.00
WMNL Nicklas Lidstrom C 5.00 12.00
WMPK Patrick Kane D 8.00 20.00
WMPM Patrick Marleau E 4.00 10.00
WMPR Pekka Rinne E 4.00 10.00
WMRB Ray Bourque E 6.00 15.00
WMRK Ryan Kesler C 4.00 10.00
WMRL Roberto Luongo E 6.00 15.00
WMRM Ryan Miller E 4.00 10.00
WMRN Rick Nash E 4.00 10.00
WMSC Sidney Crosby B 20.00 50.00
WMSF Drew Stafford E 2.50 6.00
WMSS Steven Stamkos B 10.00 25.00
WMST Jordan Staal D 3.00 8.00
WMTA John Tavares D 5.00 12.00
WMTH Taylor Hall B 5.00 12.00
WMTM Tyler Myers D 2.50 6.00
WMTS Tyler Seguin D 5.00 12.00
WMTV Thomas Vanek E 3.00 8.00
WMVL Vincent Lecavalier E 5.00 12.00
WMWG Wayne Gretzky A 50.00 100.00

2011-12 SPx Winning Materials Autographs

WMAH Ales Hemsky 10.00 25.00
WMAO Alexander Ovechkin 30.00 80.00
WMBA David Backes EXCH 8.00 20.00
WMCN Cam Neely 12.00 30.00
WMCS Chris Stewart 10.00 25.00
WMDD Drew Doughty 12.00 30.00
WMDR Derek Roy 10.00 25.00
WMEL Eric Lindros 60.00 120.00
WMEM Evgeni Malkin 25.00 50.00
WMHL Henrik Lundqvist 25.00 50.00
WMJC Jeff Carter EXCH 10.00 25.00
WMJE Jordan Eberle 50.00 100.00
WMJI Jarome Iginla 15.00 40.00
WMJT Jonathan Toews 25.00 50.00
WMKE Phil Kessel 12.00 30.00
WMMB Martin Brodeur 25.00 60.00
WMMD Matt Duchene 12.00 30.00
WMMF Marc-Andre Fleury 20.00 40.00
WMML Mario Lemieux 50.00 100.00
WMMR Mike Richards EXCH 20.00 40.00
WMMS Martin St. Louis 20.00 40.00
WMNB Nicklas Backstrom 12.00 30.00
WMNL Nicklas Lidstrom EXCH 8.00 20.00
WMPK Patrick Kane 15.00 40.00
WMPM Patrick Marleau 15.00 40.00
WMPR Pekka Rinne 12.00 30.00
WMRB Ray Bourque 20.00 50.00
WMRK Ryan Kesler 12.00 30.00
WMRN Rick Nash 12.00 30.00
WMSC Sidney Crosby 60.00 120.00
WMSS Steven Stamkos 30.00 60.00
WMST Jordan Staal 10.00 25.00
WMTA John Tavares 25.00 50.00
WMTM Tyler Myers 8.00 20.00
WMTS Tyler Seguin EXCH 30.00 60.00
WMTV Thomas Vanek 10.00 25.00
WMWG Wayne Gretzky 250.00 600.00

2011-12 SPx Winning Trios

WTBCK Boychk/Cormier/Kane 6.00 15.00
WTBKD Kopitar/Doughty/Brown 10.00 25.00
WTBKP Brodeur/Kovlchk/Parse 15.00 40.00
WTCBP Bourque/Park/Chara 10.00 25.00
WTCOS Crosby/Ovech/Stamks 15.00 40.00
WTCPP Price/Pleknc/Cammall 12.00 30.00
WTCTL Lucic/Chara/Thomas 6.00 15.00
WTDRW Kronwll/Howrd/Ericssn 8.00 20.00
WTEHP Eberle/Hall/Paajarvi 8.00 20.00
WTFCM Crosby/Malkn/Fleury 15.00 40.00
WTGLS Lundqvst/Gabrk/Staal 15.00 40.00
WTGVP Giroux/vanRiems/Prngr 6.00 15.00
WTHTK Toews/Kane/Hossa 12.00 30.00
WTIBK Iginla/Bouwm/Kiprsff 8.00 20.00
WTIKB Iginla/Kiprsff/Bourque 8.00 20.00
WTKOM Ovech/Malkn/Koval 25.00 60.00
WTLDZ Lidstrm/Zetter/Datsyk 12.00 30.00
WTLGM Messier/Gretzky/Mario 30.00 60.00
WTLKB Keslr/Burrws/Luong 12.00 30.00
WTLSM Messier/Mario/Sakic 15.00 40.00
WTMPK Miller/Kessel/Parise 8.00 20.00
WTNHT RNH/Hall/Tavares 25.00 60.00
WTOCC Orr/Carcillo/Carkner 5.00 12.00
WTOPC Orr/Parros/Carkner 5.00 12.00
WTPGR Getzlaf/Ryan/Hiller 6.00 15.00
WTPMS Myers/Subbn/Pietrng 8.00 20.00
WTPRM Pominville/Roy/Miller 6.00 15.00
WTRFB Roy/Forsbrg/Bourq 15.00 40.00
WTRLE Ribiero/Lehtn/Erikssn 5.00 12.00
WTRMM Roy/Miller/Myers 6.00 15.00
WTSCK Spezza/Kessl/Camlri 6.00 15.00
WTSFA Spezza/Flgno/Alfrdssn 6.00 15.00
WTSIH Iginla/Hemsky/Sedin 8.00 20.00
WTSKK Kessel/Kulemin/Schenn 6.00 15.00
WTSOB Backstrm/Semn/Ovech 25.00 60.00
WTSTK Toews/Kane/Sharp 12.00 30.00
WTTAB Tokarski/Aulie/Benn 6.00 15.00
WTTBS Thorntn/Bergrn/Staal 10.00 25.00
WTTCG Luongo/Brodr/Fleury 15.00 40.00
WTTSH Stamkos/Hall/Tavares 12.00 30.00

2013-14 SPx

COMP.SET w/o RC's (100) 12.00 30.00
1 Bobby Ryan .30 .75
2 Jonathan Toews .60 1.50
3 Shea Weber .30 .75
4 Ryan Suter .30 .75
5 Jamie Benn .40 1.00
6 Henrik Sedin .50 1.25
7 Eric Staal .50 1.25
8 Slava Voynov .40 1.00
9 Craig Anderson .40 1.00
10 Adam Henrique .30 .75
11 Patrik Elias .40 1.00
12 Max Pacioretty .40 1.00
13 Ryan Johansen .30 .75
14 Mike Ribeiro .25 .60
15 Cory Schneider .40 1.00
16 Milan Lucic .40 1.00
17 James van Riemsdyk .30 .75
18 Chris Stewart .30 .75
19 Tomas Fleischmann .25 .60
20 Jeff Skinner .50 1.25
21 Ales Hemsky .25 .60
22 Derek Roy .25 .60
23 Oliver Ekman-Larsson .40 1.00
24 Lee Stempniak .25 .60
25 David Krejci .40 1.00
26 Pascal Dupuis .25 .60
27 Claude Giroux .40 1.00
28 Matt Moulson .25 .60
29 Patrick Sharp .40 1.00
30 Kyle Okposo .25 .60
31 Steven Stamkos .75 2.00
32 Tyler Ennis .25 .60
33 James Neal .25 .60
34 Marian Gaborik .40 1.00
35 Carey Price .75 2.00
36 Ryan Callahan .25 .60
37 Paul Stastny .30 .75
38 Corey Perry .60 1.50
39 Jakub Voracek .30 .75
40 Jordan Eberle .40 1.00
41 Sergei Bobrovsky .60 1.50
42 Tuukka Rask .50 1.25
43 Nicklas Backstrom .40 1.00
44 Jonathan Quick .50 1.25
45 Alex Pietrangelo .30 .75
46 Cam Ward .40 1.00
47 Joe Thornton .60 1.50
48 Henrik Lundqvist 1.00 2.50
49 Pavel Datsyuk .60 1.50
50 Anze Kopitar .60 1.50
51 Derek Stepan .25 .60
52 Matt Duchene .40 1.00
53 Steve Mason .30 .75
54 Brent Seabrook .25 .60
55 Erik Karlsson .50 1.25
56 Jim Howard .50 1.25
57 Evgeni Nabokov .40 1.00
58 Phil Kessel .40 1.00
59 Evgeni Malkin .75 2.00
60 Jacob Markstrom .40 1.00
61 David Legwand .30 .75
62 Chris Kunitz .40 1.00
63 Alexandre Burrows .25 .60
64 Shane Doan .30 .75
65 Dan Boyle .25 .60
66 Zdeno Chara .40 1.00
67 David Clarkson .25 .60
68 Jakob Silfverberg .25 .60
69 Alexander Ovechkin 1.50 4.00
70 Andrew Ladd .25 .60
71 Taylor Hall .40 1.00
72 P.A. Parenteau .25 .60
73 David Backes .25 .60
74 Blake Wheeler .40 1.00
75 Mike Fisher .25 .60
76 Jonathan Bernier .30 .75
77 Zach Parise .40 1.00
78 Jiri Tlusty .25 .60
79 Tyler Seguin .50 1.25
80 Nazem Kadri .50 1.25
81 Patrick Marleau .40 1.00
82 Martin Brodeur 1.00 2.50
83 Joe Pavelski .50 1.25
84 Niklas Kronwall .30 .75
85 Cody Hodgson .25 .60
86 Mikael Backlund .30 .75
87 Logan Couture .50 1.25
88 Michael Cammalleri .30 .75
89 Evander Kane .40 1.00
90 Kari Lehtonen .30 .75
91 Ondrej Pavelec .40 1.00
92 Brian Elliott .30 .75
93 Sidney Crosby 1.50 4.00
94 Teddy Purcell .25 .60
95 Patrick Kane .75 2.00
96 Henrik Zetterberg .50 1.25
97 Martin St. Louis .40 1.00
98 Gabriel Landeskog .50 1.25
99 Ryan Getzlaf .40 1.00
100 Lars Eller .25 .60
101 Scott Laughton RC 1.50 4.00
102 Jack Campbell RC 3.00 8.00
103 Frank Corrado RC .75 2.00
104 Jacob Trouba RC 2.00 5.00
105 Tyler Toffoli RC 2.50 6.00
106 Marek Mazanec RC 1.25 3.00
107 Brett Bellemore RC 1.00 2.50
108 Eric Gryba RC 1.00 2.50
109 Calvin Pickard RC 1.50 4.00
110 Martin Jones RC 2.00 5.00
111 Jonas Brodin RC 1.50 4.00
112 Nathan Beaulieu RC .75 2.00
113 Jarred Tinordi RC 1.25 3.00
114 Max Reinhart RC 1.25 3.00
115 Nicklas Jensen RC 1.00 2.50
116 Tanner Pearson RC 1.25 3.00
117 Nikita Zadorov RC .75 2.00
118 Morgan Rielly RC 3.00 8.00
119 Michael Bournival RC 1.25 3.00
120 Cory Conacher RC .75 2.00
121 Frederik Andersen RC 3.00 8.00
122 Danny DeKeyser RC 1.50 4.00
123 Tomas Jurco RC 1.50 4.00
124 Radko Gudas RC 1.25 3.00
125 Alex Chiasson RC 1.25 3.00
126 Olli Maatta RC 2.00 5.00
127 Freddie Hamilton RC 1.25 3.00
128 Joakim Nordstrom RC 1.00 2.50
129 Justin Fontaine RC 1.25 3.00
130 Mark Arcobello RC 1.25 3.00
131 Jon Merrill RC 1.25 3.00
132 Zemgus Girgensons RC 2.00 5.00
133 Ryan Murphy RC 1.25 3.00
134 Damien Brunner RC 1.00 2.50
135 Ryan Strome RC 2.00 5.00
136 Sami Vatanen RC 1.25 3.00
137 Hampus Lindholm RC 2.00 5.00
138 Michael Latta RC 1.00 2.50
139 Mathew Dumba RC .75 2.00
140 Antti Raanta RC 2.50 6.00
141 Boone Jenner RC 2.50 6.00
142 Brendan Gallagher RC 3.00 8.00
143 Sean Monahan RC 2.00 5.00
144 Dougie Hamilton RC 2.00 5.00
145 Jonathan Huberdeau RC 15.00 40.00
146 Valeri Nichushkin RC 2.50 6.00
147 Alex Galchenyuk RC 8.00 20.00
148 Nail Yakupov RC 2.50 6.00
149 Seth Jones RC 2.50 6.00
150 Charlie Coyle RC 2.00 5.00
151 Nathan MacKinnon RC 6.00 15.00
152 Elias Lindholm RC 3.00 8.00
153 Vladimir Tarasenko RC 3.00 8.00
154 Mikhail Grigorenko RC .75 2.00
155 Aleksander Barkov RC 4.00 10.00
156 Ryan Murray RC 2.00 5.00
157 Justin Schultz RC 1.25 3.00
158 Rasmus Ristolainen RC 2.00 5.00
159 Tomas Hertl RC 2.50 6.00
160 Petr Mrazek RC 2.50 6.00
161 Tomas Jurco JSY AU/499 6.00 15.00
162 Ryan Murray JSY AU/499 8.00 20.00
163 Q.Howden AU/499 RC 4.00 10.00
164 A.Watson AU/499 RC 4.00 10.00
165 J.Schroeder AU/499 RC 5.00 12.00
166 A.Chiasson AU/499 5.00 12.00
167 F.Forsberg AU/499 RC 20.00 40.00
168 Nicklas Jensen JSY AU/499 6.00 15.00
169 D.Brunner AU/499 6.00 15.00
170 R.Spooner AU/499 RC 5.00 12.00
171 R.Ristolainen AU/499 8.00 20.00
172 B.Bennett AU/249 RC 8.00 20.00
173 C.Coyle AU/499 8.00 20.00
174 C.Conacher AU/499 3.00 8.00
175 Tarasenko JSY AU/249 EXCH 50.00 100.00
176 Mathew Dumba JSY AU/499 3.00 8.00
177 C.Thomas AU/499 RC 4.00 10.00
178 M.Granlund AU/499 RC 8.00 20.00
179 Morgan Rielly JSY AU/499 12.00 30.00
180 N.Bjugstad AU/499 RC 6.00 15.00
181 Jonas Brodin JSY AU/499 8.00 20.00
182 Jarred Tinordi JSY AU/499 5.00 12.00
183 Jack Campbell JSY AU/499 20.00 50.00
184 Petr Mrazek JSY AU/499 10.00 25.00
185 N.Beaulieu AU/499 3.00 8.00
186 M.Grigorenko AU/499 3.00 8.00
187 B.Nelson AU/499 RC 10.00 25.00
188 T.Pearson AU/499 8.00 20.00
189 E.Etem AU/499 RC 5.00 12.00
190 Elias Lindholm JSY AU/499 12.00 30.00
191 Ryan Murphy JSY AU/499 5.00 12.00
192 Jacob Trouba JSY AU/499 12.00 30.00
193 H.Lindholm AU/499 8.00 20.00
194 Tyler Toffoli JSY AU/499 12.00 30.00
195 S.Laughton AU/499 6.00 15.00
196 T.Wilson AU/499 RC 10.00 25.00
197 B.Jenner AU/499 10.00 25.00
198 V.Fasth AU/499 RC 5.00 12.00
199 V.Nichushkin AU/249 40.00 100.00
200 S.Monahan AU/249 10.00 25.00
201 A.Barkov AU/249 20.00 50.00
202 J.Huberdeau AU/249 15.00 40.00
203 Tomas Hertl JSY AU/249 15.00 40.00
204 Justin Schultz JSY AU/249 6.00 15.00
205 D.Hamilton AU/249 12.00 30.00
206 A.Galchenyuk AU/249 25.00 60.00
207 Seth Jones JSY AU/249 15.00 30.00
208 Nail Yakupov JSY AU/249 15.00 40.00
209 N.MacKinnon AU/249 125.00 300.00
210 B.Gallagher AU/249 25.00 50.00

2013-14 SPx Spectrum

*161-210 JSY AU/30: .8X TO 2X JSY AU/499
*161-210 JSY AU/30: 1X TO 2.5X JSY AU/249
101 Scott Laughton AU 20.00 50.00
102 Jack Campbell AU 40.00 100.00
104 Jacob Trouba AU 40.00 100.00
105 Tyler Toffoli AU 20.00 50.00
112 Nathan Beaulieu AU 10.00 25.00
113 Jarred Tinordi AU 15.00 40.00
114 Max Reinhart AU 15.00 40.00
115 Nicklas Jensen AU 12.00 30.00
116 Tanner Pearson AU 15.00 40.00
118 Morgan Rielly AU 60.00 125.00
120 Cory Conacher AU 10.00 25.00
121 Frederik Andersen AU 40.00 80.00
122 Danny DeKeyser AU 20.00 50.00
124 Radko Gudas AU 15.00 40.00
125 Alex Chiasson AU 15.00 40.00
128 Joakim Nordstrom AU 12.00 30.00
129 Justin Fontaine AU 15.00 40.00
130 Mark Arcobello AU 15.00 40.00
131 Jon Merrill AU 15.00 40.00
134 Damien Brunner AU 12.00 30.00
135 Ryan Strome AU 25.00 60.00
137 Hampus Lindholm AU 25.00 60.00
139 Mathew Dumba AU 10.00 25.00
141 Boone Jenner AU 30.00 80.00
143 Sean Monahan AU 50.00 100.00
144 Dougie Hamilton AU 50.00 100.00
145 Jonathan Huberdeau AU 40.00 80.00
146 Valeri Nichushkin AU 90.00 150.00
147 Alex Galchenyuk AU 75.00 150.00
148 Nail Yakupov AU 50.00 100.00
149 Seth Jones AU 40.00 80.00
150 Charlie Coyle AU 25.00 60.00
151 Nathan MacKinnon AU 150.00 400.00
152 Elias Lindholm AU 40.00 100.00
154 Mikhail Grigorenko AU 10.00 25.00
155 Aleksander Barkov AU 50.00 120.00
156 Ryan Murray AU 25.00 60.00
157 Justin Schultz AU 15.00 40.00
158 Rasmus Ristolainen AU 25.00 60.00
159 Tomas Hertl AU 30.00 80.00
160 Petr Mrazek AU 60.00 120.00
175 Vladimir Tarasenko PATCH AU 125.00200.00
199 Valeri Nichushkin PATCH AU 80.00 200.00
203 Tomas Hertl PATCH AU 30.00 80.00
206 Alex Galchenyuk PATCH AU 125.00 250.00
208 Nail Yakupov PATCH AU 100.00 200.00
209 Nathan MacKinnon PATCH AU 400.00600.00

2013-14 SPx 96-97 SPx Retro

1 Taylor Hall 1.50 4.00
2 Chris Osgood 1.50 4.00
3 Ryan Getzlaf 1.50 4.00
4 Jarome Iginla 2.00 5.00
5 P.K. Subban 2.00 5.00
6 Bobby Clarke 3.00 8.00
7 Guy Lafleur 2.50 6.00
8 Jonathan Quick 2.00 5.00
9 Eric Lindros 3.00 8.00
10 Martin St. Louis 1.50 4.00
11 Grant Fuhr 3.00 8.00
12 Pavel Bure 1.50 4.00
13 Tony Esposito 2.00 5.00
14 Joe Thornton 2.50 6.00
15 Bobby Hull 4.00 10.00
16 Mats Sundin 2.00 5.00
17 Zdeno Chara 1.50 4.00
18 Mario Lemieux 8.00 20.00
19 Carey Price 3.00 8.00
20 Sidney Crosby 6.00 15.00
21 Bobby Orr 8.00 20.00
22 Henrik Zetterberg 2.00 5.00
23 Theoren Fleury 2.00 5.00
24 Steve Yzerman 5.00 12.00
25 Patrick Kane 3.00 8.00
26 Tyler Seguin 2.00 5.00
27 Patrick Roy 5.00 12.00
28 Mike Bossy 2.00 5.00
29 Scott Hartnell 1.00 2.50
30 Jonathan Toews 2.50 6.00
31 Luc Robitaille 1.50 4.00
32 Alexander Ovechkin 6.00 15.00
33 Claude Giroux 1.50 4.00
34 Brad Marchand 3.00 8.00
35 John Tavares 2.50 6.00
36 Wayne Gretzky 5.00 12.00
37 Martin Brodeur 4.00 10.00
38 Henrik Lundqvist 4.00 10.00
39 Zach Parise 1.50 4.00
40 Steven Stamkos 3.00 8.00
41 Nathan MacKinnon 8.00 20.00
42 Aleksander Barkov 5.00 12.00
43 Seth Jones 3.00 8.00
44 Elias Lindholm 4.00 10.00
45 Sean Monahan 2.50 6.00
46 Tomas Hertl 3.00 8.00
47 Ryan Murray 2.50 6.00
48 Jacob Trouba 2.50 6.00
49 Boone Jenner 3.00 8.00
50 Valeri Nichushkin 3.00 8.00

2013-14 SPx 96-97 SPx Retro Autographs

ARAG Alex Galchenyuk B 20.00 50.00
ARBB Beau Bennett A 25.00 50.00
ARBG Brendan Gallagher A 15.00 40.00
ARCC Charlie Coyle C 8.00 20.00
ARCO Cory Conacher C 6.00 15.00
ARDB Damien Brunner A 15.00 30.00
ARDH Dougie Hamilton B 20.00 40.00
ARFF Filip Forsberg B 15.00 40.00
ARGR Mikael Granlund B 10.00 25.00
ARJB Jonas Brodin C 6.00 15.00
ARJH Jonathan Huberdeau B 15.00 30.00
ARJS Justin Schultz B 6.00 15.00
ARMG Mikhail Grigorenko C 3.00 8.00
ARNB Nathan Beaulieu C 3.00 8.00
ARNY Nail Yakupov B 20.00 50.00
ARPM Petr Mrazek C 20.00 40.00
ARTT Tyler Toffoli C 10.00 25.00
ARVF Viktor Fasth C 5.00 12.00
ARVT Vladimir Tarasenko C 12.00 30.00

2013-14 SPx Buyback Autographs

39 W.Gretzky '96-97 SPx/24 200.00 500.00
63 J.Tavares '10-11 SPx/91 20.00 40.00

2013-14 SPx Rookie Materials

RMAG Alex Galchenyuk 6.00 15.00
RMBB Beau Bennett 3.00 8.00
RMBE Nathan Beaulieu 1.50 4.00
RMBG Brendan Gallagher 5.00 12.00
RMCC Cory Conacher 1.50 4.00
RMCO Charlie Coyle 4.00 10.00
RMDH Dougie Hamilton 5.00 12.00
RMEL Elias Lindholm 6.00 15.00
RMJB Jonas Brodin 3.00 8.00
RMJC Jack Campbell 6.00 15.00
RMJH Jonathan Huberdeau 5.00 12.00
RMJM J.T. Miller 6.00 15.00
RMJS Jordan Schroeder 2.50 6.00
RMJT Jarred Tinordi 2.50 6.00
RMMG Mikhail Grigorenko 1.50 4.00
RMMR Morgan Rielly 6.00 15.00
RMMU Ryan Murphy 2.50 6.00
RMNB Nick Bjugstad 3.00 8.00
RMNM Nathan MacKinnon 10.00 25.00
RMNY Nail Yakupov 5.00 12.00
RMPM Petr Mrazek 5.00 12.00
RMRM Ryan Murray 4.00 10.00
RMRR Rasmus Ristolainen 4.00 10.00
RMSC Justin Schultz 2.50 6.00
RMSJ Seth Jones 5.00 12.00
RMSM Sean Monahan 5.00 12.00
RMTH Tomas Hertl 6.00 15.00
RMTT Tyler Toffoli 5.00 12.00
RMVN Valeri Nichushkin 5.00 12.00
RMVT Vladimir Tarasenko 5.00 12.00

2013-14 SPx Rookie Materials Combos

*PATCH/25: 1.2X TO 3X BASIC COMBO
RM2D M.Dumba/R.Ristolainen C 5.00 12.00
RM21ST MacKinnon/Yakupov A 8.00 20.00
RM22ND R.Murray/A.Barkov A 5.00 12.00
RM2BUF Grigorenko/Girgensons C 5.00 12.00
RM2CAN Galchenyuk/Gallagher A 10.00 25.00
RM2CBJ B.Jenner/R.Murray B 5.00 12.00
RM2DAL Chiasson/Nichushkin B 6.00 15.00
RM2LAK T.Toffoli/T.Pearson C 5.00 12.00
RM2NET V.Fasth/P.Mrazek B 6.00 15.00
RM2NASH F.Forsberg/S.Jones B 8.00 20.00
RM2WILD C.Coyle/M.Dumba C 5.00 12.00
RM2SCORER S.Monahan/T.Hertl A 6.00 15.00

2013-14 SPx Rookie Materials Trios

RM3C Monhn/Galchn/Hubrd B 10.00 25.00
RM3D Jones/Rielly/Dumba A 10.00 25.00
RM3RW Taras/Bennett/Chiasn B 6.00 15.00
RM3CCE Conacher/Coyle/Etem C 6.00 15.00
RM3DEF Murray/Trouba/Ristol C 6.00 15.00
RM3NET Mrazek/Fasth/Cmpbl B 20.00 40.00
RM3FWDS MacKin/Taras/Yakpv A 20.00 40.00
RM3CENTER MacKin/Hertl/Jenner B 25.00 50.00

2013-14 SPx Shadowbox

SH1 Henrik Lundqvist 20.00 50.00
SH2 Dominik Hasek 12.00 30.00
SH3 Dany Heatley 6.00 15.00
SH4 Steven Stamkos 15.00 40.00
SH5 Sidney Crosby 25.00 60.00
SH6 Corey Crawford 10.00 25.00
SH7 Martin St. Louis 8.00 20.00
SH8 Bobby Orr 30.00 80.00
SH9 Alexander Ovechkin 30.00 80.00
SH10 Claude Giroux 8.00 20.00
SH11 Roberto Luongo 12.00 30.00
SH12 Nazem Kadri 10.00 25.00
SH13 Cory Conacher 6.00 15.00
SH14 Jakub Voracek 6.00 15.00
SH15 Eric Lindros 12.00 30.00
SH16 Brendan Gallagher 10.00 25.00
SH17 Evgeni Malkin 15.00 40.00
SH18 Shea Weber 6.00 15.00
SH19 Logan Couture 10.00 25.00
SH20 Marian Hossa 10.00 25.00
SH21 Milan Lucic 8.00 20.00
SH22 James van Riemsdyk 6.00 15.00
SH23 Henrik Zetterberg 10.00 25.00
SH24 Patrick Sharp 8.00 20.00
SH25 Chris Osgood 8.00 20.00
SH26 Drew Doughty 10.00 25.00
SH27 Grant Fuhr 12.00 30.00
SH28 Oliver Ekman-Larsson 8.00 20.00
SH29 Brent Seabrook 5.00 12.00
SH30 Claude Lemieux 6.00 15.00
SH31 P.K. Subban 10.00 25.00
SH32 Jonathan Quick 10.00 25.00
SH33 Thomas Vanek 6.00 15.00
SH34 Ryan Callahan 5.00 12.00
SH35 Corey Perry 12.00 30.00
SH36 Guy Lafleur 10.00 25.00

2013-14 SPx Winning Combos

*PATCH/15: .6X TO 1.5X COMBO GRP A
*PATCH/15: .8X TO 2X COMBO GRP B
*PATCH/15: 1X TO 2.5X COMBO GRP C-D
WCAQ A.Kopitar/J.Quick B 8.00 20.00
WCBB D.Backes/P.Berglund A 4.00 10.00
WCBG M.Grabner/J.Bailey D 3.00 8.00
WCBH E.Belfour/B.Hull A 12.00 30.00
WCBN P.Bure/M.Naslund B 5.00 12.00
WCBV D.Brown/S.Voynov D 4.00 10.00
WCCB R.Bourque/Z.Chara C 8.00 20.00
WCCS R.Callahan/D.Stepan B 2.50 6.00
WCEH J.Eberle/T.Hall C 5.00 12.00
WCGB M.Green/Backstrom D 4.00 10.00
WCGH R.Getzlaf/J.Hiller C 5.00 12.00
WCGP C.Price/J.Gorges C 5.00 12.00
WCHH D.Hasek/J.Howard B 8.00 20.00
WCHM R.Hextall/S.Mason D 6.00 15.00
WCHN T.Hall/Nugent-Hopkins C 5.00 12.00
WCKD A.Kopitar/D.Doughty D 6.00 15.00
WCLD N.Lidstrom/P.Datsyuk C 6.00 15.00
WCLF R.Francis/M.Lemieux B 8.00 20.00
WCLK R.Luongo/R.Kesler C 4.00 10.00
WCLS J.Spezza/R.Lehner C 4.00 10.00
WCMD D.Krejci/M.Lucic C 4.00 10.00
WCME R.Miller/T.Ennis D 4.00 10.00
WCMG M.Messier/M.Gartner A 15.00 40.00
WCML E.Lindros/M.Messier B 12.00 30.00
WCNF M.Naslund/R.Francis C 5.00 12.00
WCPF C.Perry/C.Fowler D 6.00 15.00
WCRC J.Carter/M.Richards D 3.00 8.00
WCRO Ovechkin/Robitaille B 20.00 50.00
WCRS L.Robinson/P.Subban B 6.00 15.00
WCRW P.Rinne/S.Weber D 4.00 10.00
WCSD Duchene/P.Stastny C 4.00 10.00
WCSK P.Sharp/D.Keith B 5.00 12.00
WCSW D.Savard/D.Wilson C 4.00 10.00

2013-14 SPx Winning Materials

*PATCH/15: 1.2X TO 3X BASIC GRP C
*PATCH/15: .8X TO 2X BASIC GRP A-B
WMAO Alexander Ovechkin C 12.00 30.00
WMCF Cam Fowler C 3.00 8.00
WMCP Carey Price B 10.00 25.00
WMDG Doug Gilmour B 6.00 15.00
WMDU Matt Duchene C 3.00 8.00
WMEK Erik Karlsson C 4.00 10.00
WMEL Eric Lindros B 8.00 20.00
WMGA Glenn Anderson B 4.00 10.00
WMHA Dominik Hasek B 8.00 20.00
WMJB Johnny Bucyk B 5.00 12.00
WMJC Jeff Carter C 2.50 6.00
WMJE Jordan Eberle C 3.00 8.00
WMJK Jari Kurri B 5.00 12.00
WMJS Jason Spezza C 3.00 8.00
WMLU Milan Lucic C 3.00 8.00
WMMD Marcel Dionne B 6.00 15.00
WMMF Marc-Andre Fleury C 5.00 12.00
WMMG Michel Goulet B 5.00 12.00
WMML Mario Lemieux B 20.00 50.00
WMMM Mark Messier A 6.00 15.00
WMMR Mike Richards C 2.50 6.00
WMPD Pavel Datsyuk C 5.00 12.00
WMPE Phil Esposito B 8.00 20.00
WMPR Patrick Roy A 12.00 30.00
WMPS P.K. Subban C 4.00 10.00
WMRB Ray Bourque B 8.00 20.00
WMRF Ron Francis B 6.00 15.00
WMRG Ryan Getzlaf C 3.00 8.00
WMRH Ron Hextall C 3.00 8.00
WMRL Roberto Luongo C 5.00 12.00
WMRM Ryan Miller B 4.00 10.00
WMRN Rick Nash C 3.00 8.00
WMSC Sidney Crosby C 15.00 40.00
WMSS Steven Stamkos C 6.00 15.00
WMTE Tony Esposito B 6.00 15.00
WMTH Taylor Hall C 3.00 8.00
WMTT Tony Twist C 3.00 8.00

2013-14 SPx Winning Trios

W3LA Richards/Cartr/Vynv B 6.00 15.00
W3AVS Ststny/Varlmv/Dchne B 6.00 15.00
W3BOS Lucic/Rask/Chara B 8.00 20.00
W3COL Roy/Sakic/Bourque B 15.00 40.00
W3DET Datsyuk/Zetter/Lidstrm B 10.00 25.00
W3DRW Howard/Mrazek/Hasek B 12.00 30.00
W3EDM Yakupov/RNH/Hall B 6.00 15.00
W3GR8 Gretzky/Lemx/Messier A 25.00 60.00
W3LAK Quick/Brown/Kopitar B 6.00 15.00
W3OIL Hall/Gagner/Eberle B 6.00 15.00
W3OTT Spezza/Karlsn/Lehner B 8.00 20.00

W3AMZG Lmux/Skic/Lndrs A 25.00 50.00
W3CAPS Ovech/Bckstrm/Holtby B 25.00 60.00
W3JETS Pavelec/Kane/Bytgln B 6.00 15.00
W3LBBR Gorges/Price/Subban B 12.00 30.00
W3PITT Fleury/Malkin/Letang A 12.00 30.00
W3KINGS Kopitr/Quick/Doughty B 10.00 25.00

2014-15 SPx

*RC AU/50: .6X TO 1.5X BASIC INSERTS
1 Andrew Cogliano .25 .60
2 Ryan Getzlaf .40 1.00
3 Corey Perry .60 1.50
4 Zdeno Chara .40 1.00
5 Tuukka Rask .50 1.25
6 Patrice Bergeron .50 1.25
7 Tyler Ennis .25 .60
8 Cody Hodgson .25 .60
9 Jiri Hudler .30 .75
10 Sean Monahan .25 .60
11 Eric Staal .50 1.25
12 Cam Ward .40 1.00
13 Jeff Skinner .50 1.25
14 Corey Crawford .50 1.25
15 Jonathan Toews .60 1.50
16 Patrick Kane .75 2.00
17 Duncan Keith .30 .75
18 Matt Duchene .40 1.00
19 Nathan MacKinnon 1.50 4.00
20 Ryan O'Reilly .40 1.00
21 Ryan Johansen .30 .75
22 Sergei Bobrovsky .60 1.50
23 Scott Hartnell .25 .60
24 Tyler Seguin .50 1.25
25 Jamie Benn .40 1.00
26 Kari Lehtonen .30 .75
27 Henrik Zetterberg .50 1.25
28 Pavel Datsyuk .60 1.50
29 Gustav Nyquist .25 .60
30 Taylor Hall .40 1.00
31 Jordan Eberle .40 1.00
32 Ryan Nugent-Hopkins .40 1.00
33 Roberto Luongo .60 1.50
34 Scottie Upshall .25 .60
35 Anze Kopitar .60 1.50
36 Drew Doughty .50 1.25
37 Jonathan Quick .50 1.25
38 Marian Gaborik .40 1.00
39 Jason Pominville .25 .60
40 Zach Parise .40 1.00
41 Mikko Koivu .30 .75
42 P.K. Subban .50 1.25
43 Max Pacioretty .40 1.00
44 Carey Price .75 2.00
45 Pekka Rinne .40 1.00
46 Shea Weber .30 .75
47 James Neal .25 .60
48 Jaromir Jagr 1.25 3.00
49 Adam Henrique .30 .75
50 Cory Schneider .40 1.00
51 Kyle Okposo .25 .60
52 John Tavares .60 1.50
53 Jaroslav Halak .40 1.00
54 Martin St. Louis .40 1.00
55 Henrik Lundqvist 1.00 2.50
56 Rick Nash .40 1.00
57 Erik Karlsson .50 1.25
58 Craig Anderson .40 1.00
59 Kyle Turris .40 1.00
60 Claude Giroux .40 1.00
61 Wayne Simmonds .50 1.25
62 Steve Mason .30 .75
63 Keith Yandle .25 .60
64 Shane Doan .30 .75
65 Mike Smith .40 1.00
66 Sidney Crosby 1.50 4.00
67 Evgeni Malkin .75 2.00
68 Chris Kunitz .40 1.00
69 Marc-Andre Fleury .75 2.00
70 Joe Pavelski .40 1.00
71 Patrick Marleau .40 1.00
72 Logan Couture .50 1.25
73 Martin Brodeur 1.00 2.50
74 T.J. Oshie .40 1.00
75 David Backes .25 .60
76 Steven Stamkos .75 2.00
77 Ben Bishop .30 .75
78 Valtteri Filppula .25 .60
79 Phil Kessel .40 1.00
80 James van Riemsdyk .30 .75
81 James Reimer .40 1.00
82 Henrik Sedin .50 1.25
83 Daniel Sedin .50 1.25
84 Eddie Lack .30 .75
85 Alexander Ovechkin 1.50 4.00
86 Nicklas Backstrom .40 1.00
87 Joel Ward .25 .60
88 Blake Wheeler .40 1.00
89 Dustin Byfuglien .40 1.00
90 Evander Kane .40 1.00
91 Teemu Selanne .75 2.00
92 Mats Sundin .40 1.00
93 Bobby Clarke .60 1.50
94 Mark Messier .75 2.00
95 Joe Sakic .75 2.00
96 Guy Lafleur .50 1.25
97 Dominik Hasek .60 1.50
98 Steve Yzerman 1.00 2.50
99 Wayne Gretzky 2.50 6.00
100 Bobby Orr 1.50 4.00
101 Jordan Binnington RC 8.00 20.00
102 Landon Ferraro RC 1.00 2.50
103 Sven Andrighetto RC 2.00 5.00
104 Anton Forsberg RC 1.25 3.00
105 Shayne Gostisbehere RC 3.00 8.00
106 Troy Grosenick RC 1.25 3.00
107 William Karlsson RC 5.00 12.00
108 Petter Granberg RC 1.25 3.00
109 Markus Granlund RC 2.50 6.00
110 Josh Jooris RC 1.50 4.00
111 Sam Carrick RC 1.50 4.00
112 Mike Halmo RC 1.00 2.50
113 Scott Mayfield RC 1.25 3.00
114 Seth Helgeson RC 1.25 3.00
115 Kevin Czuczman RC 1.25 3.00
116 Borna Rendulic RC 1.50 4.00
117 Phillip Danault RC 3.00 8.00
118 Scott Darling RC 3.00 8.00
119 Colin Smith RC 1.50 4.00
120 Kevin Hayes RC 4.00 10.00
121 Johan Sundstrom RC 1.50 4.00
122 Mike Zalewski RC 1.25 3.00
123 Victor Rask RC 1.50 4.00
124 Andrew Agozzino RC 1.25 3.00
125 Andrey Makarov RC 1.50 4.00
126 Brody Sutter RC 1.00 2.50
127 Kristers Gudlevskis RC 1.50 4.00
128 Chris Wagner RC 1.50 4.00
129 Christian Folin RC 1.50 4.00
130 Oscar Klefbom RC 3.00 8.00
131 Curtis McKenzie AU RC EXCH 5.00 12.00
132 Joe Morrow AU RC 8.00 20.00
133 David Pastrnak AU RC 125.00 300.00
134 Brandon Kozun AU RC 5.00 12.00
135 Cedric Paquette AU RC 6.00 15.00
136 Joonas Nattinen AU RC 6.00 15.00
137 Tyler Wotherspoon AU RC 6.00 15.00
138 Stuart Percy AU RC 6.00 15.00
139 A.Clendening JSY AU RC 6.00 15.00
140 T.Pulkkinen JSY AU RC 8.00 20.00
141 Joni Ortio JSY AU RC 8.00 20.00
142 Patrik Nemeth JSY AU RC 6.00 15.00
143 Ryan Sproul JSY AU RC 6.00 15.00
144 A.Duclair JSY AU RC EXCH 10.00 25.00
145 Mark Visentin JSY AU RC 6.00 15.00
146 V.Namestnikov JSY AU RC 10.00 25.00
147 Calle Jarnkrok JSY AU RC 6.00 15.00
148 Kerby Rychel JSY AU RC 5.00 12.00
149 A.Wennberg JSY AU RC 10.00 25.00
150 A.Khokhlachev JSY AU RC 6.00 15.00
151 Joey Hishon JSY AU RC 8.00 20.00
152 Greg McKegg JSY AU RC 5.00 12.00
153 Ty Rattie JSY AU RC 6.00 15.00
154 Vincent Trocheck JSY AU RC 12.00 30.00
155 Chris Tierney JSY AU RC 6.00 15.00
156 Mirco Mueller JSY AU RC 6.00 15.00
157 Corban Knight JSY AU RC 6.00 15.00
158 Jake McCabe JSY AU RC 6.00 15.00
159 Tobias Rieder JSY AU RC 6.00 15.00
160 Griffin Reinhart JSY AU RC 6.00 15.00
161 Darnell Nurse JSY AU RC 12.00 30.00
162 Seth Griffith JSY AU RC 6.00 15.00
163 Marko Dano JSY AU RC 6.00 15.00
164 Colton Sissons JSY AU RC 6.00 15.00
165 Damon Severson JSY AU RC 6.00 15.00
166 Brandon Gormley JSY AU RC 6.00 15.00
167 Laurent Brossoit JSY AU RC 6.00 15.00
168 Adam Lowry JSY AU RC 10.00 25.00
169 J.Drouin JSY AU/249 RC 12.00 30.00
170 Jiri Sekac JSY AU/249 RC 5.00 12.00
171 T.Teravainen JSY AU/249 RC 10.00 25.00
172 Bo Horvat JSY AU/249 RC 15.00 40.00
173 E.Kuznetsov JSY AU/249 RC 15.00 40.00
174 Aaron Ekblad JSY AU/249 RC 15.00 40.00
175 Sam Reinhart JSY AU/249 RC 25.00 60.00
176 Leon Draisaitl JSY AU/249 RC 100.00 250.00
177 A.Burakovsky JSY AU/249 RC 10.00 25.00
178 Curtis Lazar JSY AU/249 RC 6.00 15.00
179 J.Gaudreau JSY AU/249 RC 80.00 200.00
180 Jori Lehtera JSY
AU/249 RC EXCH 8.00 20.00
203 Marian Hossa FF JSY A 3.00 8.00
204 Marian Gaborik FF JSY A 3.00 8.00
205 Peter Forsberg FF JSY A 6.00 15.00
206 Nikolai Khabibulin FF JSY C 3.00 8.00
207 Zach Parise FF JSY C 3.00 8.00
208 Jonathan Bernier FF JSY C 2.50 6.00
209 Wayne Simmonds FF JSY C 4.00 10.00
210 Tyler Seguin FF JSY A 5.00 12.00
211 Rick Nash FF JSY C 3.00 8.00
212 Jeff Carter FF JSY C 2.50 6.00
213 Phil Kessel FF JSY C 3.00 8.00
214 Jaromir Jagr FF JSY B 10.00 25.00
215 Matt Moulson FF JSY C 2.00 5.00
216 Brad Richards FF JSY C 3.00 8.00
217 D.Alfredsson FF JSY 3.00 8.00
218 Joe Thornton FF JSY C 5.00 12.00
219 Brett Hull FF JSY A 6.00 15.00
220 Dale Hawerchuk FF JSY B 4.00 10.00
223 Doug Gilmour FF JSY B 4.00 10.00
224 Grant Fuhr FF JSY B 5.00 12.00
225 Dominik Hasek FF JSY B 5.00 12.00
226 Rob Blake FF JSY B 3.00 8.00
227 Ron Francis FF JSY B 4.00 10.00
228 Ed Belfour FF JSY B 3.00 8.00
229 Mario Lemieux FF JSY A 12.00 30.00
230 Patrick Roy FF JSY A 8.00 20.00
231 Mats Sundin FF JSY B 3.00 8.00
232 Steve Yzerman FF JSY A 8.00 20.00

2014-15 SPx Spectrum Blue

179 Johnny Gaudreau JSY AU 150.00 400.00

2014-15 SPx 97-98 SPx Retro

*ACTIVE/50: 1X TO 2.5X BASIC INSERTS
*RETIRED/50: .8X TO 2X BASIC INSERTS
1 Sidney Crosby 6.00 15.00
2 Ryan Getzlaf 1.50 4.00
3 Claude Giroux 1.50 4.00
4 Tyler Seguin 2.00 5.00
5 Corey Perry 2.50 6.00
6 Phil Kessel 1.50 4.00
7 Taylor Hall 1.50 4.00
8 Alexander Ovechkin 6.00 15.00
9 Joe Pavelski 1.50 4.00
10 Jamie Benn 1.50 4.00
11 Nicklas Backstrom 1.50 4.00
12 Evgeni Malkin 3.00 8.00
13 Anze Kopitar 2.50 6.00
14 Patrick Kane 3.00 8.00
15 Jonathan Toews 2.50 6.00
16 Matt Duchene 1.50 4.00
17 Martin St. Louis 1.50 4.00
18 Blake Wheeler 1.50 4.00
19 Kyle Okposo 1.00 2.50
20 Jaromir Jagr 5.00 12.00
21 John Tavares 2.50 6.00
22 Jordan Eberle 1.50 4.00
23 Erik Karlsson 2.00 5.00
24 Drew Doughty 2.00 5.00
25 Duncan Keith 1.25 3.00
26 P.K. Subban 2.00 5.00
27 Carey Price 3.00 8.00
28 Henrik Lundqvist 4.00 10.00
29 Jonathan Quick 2.00 5.00
30 Tuukka Rask 2.00 5.00
31 Roberto Luongo 2.50 6.00
32 Steven Stamkos 3.00 8.00
33 Patrice Bergeron 2.00 5.00
34 Zach Parise 1.50 4.00
35 Nathan MacKinnon 6.00 15.00
36 Shea Weber 1.25 3.00
37 Joe Thornton 2.50 6.00
38 Eric Staal 2.00 5.00
39 Martin Brodeur 6.00 15.00
40 Max Pacioretty 1.50 4.00
41 T.J. Oshie 1.50 4.00
42 Henrik Zetterberg 2.00 5.00
43 Pavel Datsyuk 2.50 6.00
44 Jonathan Bernier 1.25 3.00
45 Patrick Sharp 1.50 4.00
46 Mats Sundin 1.50 4.00
47 Jean Beliveau 3.00 8.00
48 Dominik Hasek 3.00 8.00
49 Teemu Selanne 3.00 8.00
50 Jeremy Roenick 3.00 8.00
51 Nicklas Lidstrom 2.00 5.00
52 Mike Bossy 2.00 5.00
53 Joe Sakic 4.00 10.00
54 Patrick Roy 5.00 12.00
55 Mario Lemieux 8.00 20.00
56 Guy Lafleur 2.50 6.00
57 Doug Harvey 2.00 5.00
58 Terry Sawchuk 2.00 5.00
59 Steve Yzerman 5.00 12.00
60 Wayne Gretzky 8.00 20.00
61 Teuvo Teravainen 2.50 6.00
62 Ty Rattie 1.25 3.00
63 Evgeny Kuznetsov 4.00 10.00
64 Brandon Gormley 1.50 4.00
65 Johnny Gaudreau 5.00 12.00
66 Marko Dano 1.50 4.00
67 Anthony Duclair 2.50 6.00
68 Chris Tierney 1.50 4.00
69 David Pastrnak 20.00 50.00
70 Stuart Percy 1.50 4.00
71 Alexander Khokhlachev 1.50 4.00
72 Sam Reinhart 6.00 15.00
73 Kerby Rychel 1.25 3.00
74 Adam Clendening 1.25 3.00
75 Jiri Sekac 1.25 3.00
76 Seth Griffith 2.00 5.00
77 Calle Jarnkrok 2.00 5.00
78 Damon Severson 2.00 5.00
79 Leon Draisaitl 12.00 30.00
80 Sven Andrighetto 2.00 5.00
81 Bo Horvat 4.00 10.00
82 Griffin Reinhart 1.50 4.00
83 Alexander Wennberg 2.50 6.00
84 Curtis Lazar 2.00 5.00
85 Kevin Hayes 4.00 10.00
86 Jori Lehtera 1.50 4.00
87 Andre Burakovsky 2.50 6.00
88 Darnell Nurse 5.00 12.00
89 Aaron Ekblad 4.00 10.00
90 Jonathan Drouin 3.00 8.00

2014-15 SPx Finite Rookies

1 Adam Clendening/299 2.00 5.00
2 Damon Severson/299 2.00 5.00
3 Alexander Khokhlachev/299 2.00 5.00
4 Brandon Kozun/299 1.50 4.00
5 Teuvo Teravainen/299 5.00 12.00
6 Evgeny Kuznetsov/299 6.00 15.00
7 Darnell Nurse/299 4.00 10.00
8 Vladislav Namestnikov/299 3.00 8.00
9 Seth Griffith/299 2.50 6.00
10 Jiri Sekac/299 1.50 4.00
11 Griffin Reinhart/299 2.00 5.00
12 Kevin Hayes/299 5.00 12.00
13 Brandon Gormley/299 2.00 5.00
14 Marko Dano/299 2.00 5.00
15 Ty Rattie/299 4.00 10.00
16 Alexander Wennberg/299 3.00 8.00
17 Stuart Percy/299 2.00 5.00
18 Victor Rask/299 3.00 8.00
19 Teemu Pulkkinen/299 2.50 6.00
20 Adam Lowry/299 3.00 8.00
21 Curtis Lazar/299 2.00 5.00
22 Andre Burakovsky/199 4.00 10.00
23 Johnny Gaudreau/199 8.00 20.00
24 Anthony Duclair/199 4.00 10.00
25 Sam Reinhart/199 10.00 25.00
26 Bo Horvat/199 6.00 15.00
27 Leon Draisaitl/199 12.00 30.00
28 Jonathan Drouin/149 5.00 12.00
29 Aaron Ekblad/149 12.00 30.00
30 Jori Lehtera/149 2.00 5.00

2014-15 SPx Finite Rookies Autographs

1 Adam Clendening/125 5.00 12.00
2 Damon Severson/125 5.00 12.00
3 Alexander Khokhlachev/125 5.00 12.00
4 Brandon Kozun/125 5.00 12.00
5 Teuvo Teravainen/125 20.00 40.00
6 Evgeny Kuznetsov/125 12.00 30.00
7 Darnell Nurse/125 15.00 30.00
8 Vladislav Namestnikov/125 8.00 20.00
9 Seth Griffith/125 6.00 15.00
10 Jiri Sekac/125 4.00 10.00
11 Griffin Reinhart/125 5.00 12.00
12 Kevin Hayes/125 EXCH 25.00 50.00
13 Brandon Gormley/125 5.00 12.00
14 Marko Dano/125 5.00 12.00
15 Ty Rattie/125 5.00 12.00
16 Alexander Wennberg/125 8.00 20.00
17 Stuart Percy/125 5.00 12.00
18 Victor Rask/125 5.00 12.00
19 Teemu Pulkkinen/125 8.00 20.00
20 Adam Lowry/125 8.00 20.00
21 Curtis Lazar/125 8.00 20.00
22 Andre Burakovsky/49 12.00 30.00
23 Johnny Gaudreau/49 80.00 200.00
24 Anthony Duclair/49 EXCH 25.00 60.00
25 Sam Reinhart/49 40.00 80.00
26 Bo Horvat/49 20.00 50.00
27 Leon Draisaitl/49 100.00 250.00
28 Jonathan Drouin/25 30.00 80.00
29 Aaron Ekblad/25 25.00 60.00
30 Jori Lehtera/25 12.00 30.00

2014-15 SPx Flashback Fabrics Patch

*203-232 PATCH/15: .8X TO 2X GRP A FF
*203-232 PATCH/15: 1X TO 2.5X GRP B FF
*203-232 PATCH/15: 1.2X TO 3X GRP C FF

2014-15 SPx Rookie Inaugural Jerseys

*PATCH/99: .6X TO 1.5X BASIC JSY
RPMAB Andre Burakovsky 4.00 10.00
RPMAE Aaron Ekblad 5.00 12.00
RPMAL Adam Lowry 4.00 10.00
RPMAW Alexander Wennberg 4.00 10.00
RPMBH Bo Horvat 6.00 15.00
RPMCJ Calle Jarnkrok 2.50 6.00
RPMCK Corban Knight 2.50 6.00
RPMCL Curtis Lazar 2.50 6.00
RPMCT Chris Tierney 2.50 6.00
RPMDN Darnell Nurse 5.00 12.00
RPMEK Evgeny Kuznetsov 6.00 15.00
RPMGR Griffin Reinhart 2.50 6.00
RPMJD Jonathan Drouin 5.00 12.00
RPMJG Johnny Gaudreau 8.00 20.00
RPMJH Joey Hishon 3.00 8.00
RPMLD Leon Draisaitl 12.00 30.00
RPMMD Marko Dano 2.50 6.00
RPMMV Alexander Khokhlachev 2.50 6.00
RPMSG Seth Griffith 3.00 8.00
RPMSR Sam Reinhart 10.00 25.00
RPMTR Ty Rattie 2.50 6.00
RPMTT Teuvo Teravainen 5.00 12.00
RPMWK Adam Clendening 2.50 6.00

2014-15 SPx Rookie Inaugural Jerseys Combos

*PATCH/49: .8X TO 2X BASIC JSY
RPM2EN A.Ekblad/D.Nurse 6.00 15.00
RPM2ER A.Ekblad/S.Reinhart 6.00 15.00
RPM2GK J.Gaudreau/C.Knight 10.00 25.00
RPM2GM B.Gormley/M.Visentin 3.00 8.00
RPM2KB Kuznetsov/Burakovsky 6.00 15.00
RPM2KG Khokhlachev/S.Griffith 4.00 10.00
RPM2ND D.Nurse/L.Draisaitl 5.00 12.00
RPM2RM S.Reinhart/J.McCabe 5.00 12.00
RPM2WD A.Wennberg/M.Dano 5.00 12.00

2014-15 SPx Rookie Inaugural Jerseys Trios

*PATCH/25: .8X TO 2X BASIC JSY
RPM3DNW Drouin/Nurse/Wenn 8.00 20.00
RPM3ENG Ekblad/Nurse/Gorm 10.00 25.00
RPM3ERD Ekblad/S.Rein/Drais 20.00 50.00
RPM3GOK Gaudr/Ortio/Knight 12.00 30.00
RPM3LRW Lazar/S.Rein/Wenn 6.00 15.00
RPM3NDB Nurse/Drais/Brossoit 20.00 50.00

2014-15 SPx Shadow Box

SH1 Sidney Crosby 30.00 80.00
SH2 Ryan Getzlaf 8.00 20.00
SH3 Claude Giroux 8.00 20.00
SH4 Tyler Seguin 10.00 25.00
SH5 Corey Perry 12.00 30.00
SH6 Taylor Hall 8.00 20.00
SH7 Alexander Ovechkin 30.00 80.00
SH8 Joe Pavelski 10.00 25.00
SH9 Jamie Benn 8.00 20.00
SH10 Anze Kopitar 12.00 30.00
SH11 Patrick Kane 15.00 40.00
SH12 Jonathan Toews 25.00 60.00
SH13 Martin St. Louis 8.00 20.00
SH14 Henrik Lundqvist 20.00 50.00
SH15 Jaromir Jagr 40.00 100.00
SH16 Nathan MacKinnon 30.00 80.00
SH17 P.K. Subban 10.00 25.00
SH18 Drew Doughty 10.00 25.00
SH19 Patrice Bergeron 12.00 30.00
SH20 Pavel Datsyuk 12.00 30.00
SH21 Zach Parise 8.00 20.00
SH22 Erik Karlsson 10.00 25.00
SH23 T.J. Oshie 8.00 20.00
SH24 Steven Stamkos 15.00 40.00
SH25 Jordan Eberle 8.00 20.00
SH26 Duncan Keith 6.00 15.00
SH27 Peter Forsberg 25.00 60.00
SH28 Joe Sakic 25.00 60.00
SH29 Doug Gilmour 15.00 40.00
SH30 Nicklas Lidstrom 20.00 50.00
SH31 Bobby Clarke 20.00 50.00
SH32 Bobby Orr 50.00 120.00
SH33 Dominik Hasek 20.00 50.00
SH34 Jean Beliveau 12.00 30.00
SH35 Doug Harvey 8.00 20.00
SH36 Mats Sundin 8.00 20.00
SH38 Teemu Selanne AU 40.00 80.00
SH39 Wayne Gretzky AU 200.00 500.00
SH40 Teuvo Teravainen AU 60.00 150.00
SH42 Evgeny Kuznetsov AU 50.00 100.00

2014-15 SPx Winning Combos

WCBF G.Fuhr/E.Belfour 8.00 20.00
WCBH M.Brodeur/A.Henrique 12.00 30.00
WCBK N.Kadri/J.Bernier 8.00 20.00
WCBV S.Bobrovsky/S.Varlamov 6.00 15.00
WCCN C.Crawford/A.Niemi 5.00 12.00
WCDK D.Doughty/D.Keith 5.00 12.00
WCDM E.Malkin/P.Datsyuk 12.00 30.00
WCDZ H.Zetterberg/P.Datsyuk 6.00 15.00
WCEH T.Hall/J.Eberle 4.00 10.00
WCEP E.Karlsson/P.Subban 5.00 12.00
WCGS C.Giroux/W.Simmonds 5.00 12.00
WCHB D.Harvey/J.Beliveau 10.00 25.00
WCHS T.Seguin/T.Hall 6.00 15.00
WCKD A.Kopitar/D.Doughty 6.00 15.00
WCKM E.Malkin/C.Kunitz 10.00 25.00
WCLF M.Lemieux/R.Francis 8.00 20.00
WCLH D.Harvey/G.Lafleur 15.00 30.00
WCLQ H.Lundqvist/J.Quick 15.00 40.00
WCLR K.Lehtonen/P.Rinne 5.00 12.00
WCPP M.Pacioretty/C.Price 8.00 20.00
WCRB P.Roy/M.Brodeur 12.00 30.00
WCRL R.Nash/H.Lundqvist 20.00 50.00
WCRS J.Sakic/P.Roy 12.00 30.00
WCRW P.Rinne/S.Weber 5.00 12.00
WCSF P.Forsberg/J.Sakic 10.00 25.00
WCSK J.Kurri/T.Selanne 8.00 20.00
WCTK J.Toews/P.Kane 10.00 25.00
WCVB V.Hedman/B.Bishop 6.00 15.00
WCVD M.Duchene/S.Varlamov 4.00 10.00

2014-15 SPx Winning Materials

WMAK Anze Kopitar B 8.00 20.00
WMBP Brad Park C 3.00 8.00
WMCG Claude Giroux C 4.00 10.00
WMCP Carey Price E 6.00 15.00
WMDB David Backes D 2.50 6.00
WMDD Drew Doughty E 4.00 10.00
WMDG Doug Gilmour C 5.00 12.00
WMDO Doug Harvey C 8.00 20.00
WMEM Evgeni Malkin C 8.00 20.00
WMES Eric Staal E 4.00 10.00
WMGF Grant Fuhr D 6.00 15.00
WMHA Dominik Hasek D 6.00 15.00
WMHL Henrik Lundqvist A 15.00 40.00
WMJB Jean Beliveau A 12.00 30.00
WMJQ Jonathan Quick C 5.00 12.00
WMLR Luc Robitaille E 3.00 8.00
WMMB Martin Brodeur E 6.00 15.00
WMMD Matt Duchene E 3.00 8.00
WMML Mario Lemieux C 10.00 25.00
WMOV Alexander Ovechkin D 15.00 40.00
WMSC Sidney Crosby B 12.00 30.00
WMTH Taylor Hall E 3.00 8.00
WMTO Jonathan Toews D 4.00 10.00
WMTR Tuukka Rask E 4.00 10.00
WMTS Tyler Seguin B 6.00 15.00

2015-16 SPx

1 Alexander Ovechkin 1.50 4.00
2 Carey Price .75 2.00
3 Cory Schneider .40 1.00
4 David Backes .25 .60
5 Erik Karlsson .50 1.25
6 Ryan Strome .40 1.00
7 Sidney Crosby 1.50 4.00
8 Jarome Iginla .50 1.25
9 Corey Perry .60 1.50
10 James van Riemsdyk .30 .75
11 Henrik Lundqvist 1.00 2.50
12 Oliver Ekman-Larsson .40 1.00
13 Claude Giroux .40 1.00
14 Adam Henrique .30 .75
15 Jamie Benn .40 1.00
16 Dustin Brown .40 1.00
17 Brayden Schenn .40 1.00
18 Jonathan Toews .60 1.50
19 Jordan Eberle .40 1.00
20 Gabriel Landeskog .50 1.25
21 Zach Parise .40 1.00
22 Ryan O'Reilly .40 1.00
23 Steven Stamkos .75 2.00
24 Daniel Sedin .50 1.25
25 Logan Couture .50 1.25
26 Andrew Ladd .25 .60
27 Johnny Gaudreau .60 1.50
28 Eric Staal .50 1.25
29 Brendan Gallagher .40 1.00
30 Aaron Ekblad .50 1.25
31 Filip Forsberg .60 1.50
32 P.K. Subban .50 1.25
33 Henrik Zetterberg .50 1.25
34 Evgeni Malkin .75 2.00
35 Tyler Johnson .25 .60
36 Anze Kopitar .60 1.50
37 Rick Nash .40 1.00
38 Nicklas Backstrom .40 1.00
39 Jiri Hudler .30 .75
40 Vladimir Tarasenko .50 1.25
41 Ben Bishop .30 .75
42 Jonathan Bernier .30 .75
43 Tyler Seguin .50 1.25
44 Radim Vrbata .25 .60
45 John Tavares .60 1.50
46 Joe Pavelski .50 1.25
47 Ryan Getzlaf .40 1.00
48 Max Pacioretty .40 1.00
49 Blake Wheeler .40 1.00
50 Brent Seabrook .25 .60
51 Ryan Nugent-Hopkins .50 1.25
52 Jason Pominville .25 .60
53 Patrice Bergeron .50 1.25
54 Jordan Staal .30 .75
55 Ryan Johansen .30 .75
56 Bobby Hull .75 2.00
57 Martin St. Louis .40 1.00
58 Wayne Gretzky 2.50 6.00
59 Mark Messier .75 2.00
60 Grant Fuhr .60 1.50
61 Aaron Ekblad SC .50 1.25
62 Alex Galchenyuk SC .25 .60
63 Viktor Arvidsson SC .40 1.00
64 Nathan MacKinnon SC 1.50 4.00
65 Max Domi SC .75 2.00
66 Tyler Johnson SC .25 .60
67 Sean Monahan SC .25 .60
68 Aleksander Barkov SC .60 1.50
69 Mark Stone SC .60 1.50
70 Nikolay Goldobin SC .40 1.00
71 Nikolaj Ehlers SC .75 2.00
72 Sam Bennett SC 1.25 3.00
73 Artemi Panarin SC 1.50 4.00
74 Dylan Larkin SC 1.25 3.00
75 Connor McDavid SC 15.00 40.00
76 Alexander Ovechkin SW 1.50 4.00
77 Bobby Ryan SW .30 .75
78 Ryan Johansen SW .30 .75
79 Evgeni Malkin SW .75 2.00
80 Patrick Kane SW .75 2.00
81 Matt Duchene SW .40 1.00
82 Pavel Datsyuk SW .60 1.50
83 Johnny Gaudreau SW .60 1.50
84 Jason Spezza SW .40 1.00
85 Jaromir Jagr SW 1.25 3.00
86 Aleksander Barkov SW .60 1.50
87 Sidney Crosby SW 1.50 4.00
88 Logan Couture SW .50 1.25
89 Connor McDavid SW 25.00 60.00
90 Matt Moulson SW .25 .60
91 Claude Giroux NOF .40 1.00
92 David Krejci NOF .40 1.00
93 Alexander Ovechkin NOF 1.50 4.00
94 Joe Sakic NOF .75 2.00
95 Mario Lemieux NOF 1.50 4.00
96 Mike Bossy NOF .40 1.00
97 Jonathan Toews NOF .60 1.50
98 Nicklas Lidstrom NOF .40 1.00
99 Steve Yzerman NOF 1.00 2.50
100 Bobby Clarke NOF .60 1.50
101 Brian Ferlin RC 1.00 2.50
102 Luke Witkowski RC 1.00 2.50
103 Linus Ullmark RC 3.00 8.00
104 Byron Froese RC 1.25 3.00
105 Connor Brickley RC 1.25 3.00
106 Erik Gustafsson RC 2.00 5.00
107 Logan Shaw RC 1.50 4.00
108 Vincent Hinostroza RC 1.00 2.50
109 Chandler Stephenson RC 2.00 5.00
110 Zachary Fucale RC 1.25 3.00
111 Tommy Cross RC 1.25 3.00
112 Nick Shore RC 1.00 2.50
113 Chris Wideman RC 1.50 4.00
114 Joel Edmundson RC 1.25 3.00
115 Andrew Copp RC 1.50 4.00
116 Max McCormick RC 1.25 3.00
117 Brendan Ranford RC 1.25 3.00
118 Sergey Kalinin RC 1.00 2.50
119 Brett Pesce RC 1.25 3.00
120 Mike Condon RC 1.50 4.00
121 Chris Driedger RC 1.25 3.00
122 Tyler Randell RC 1.50 4.00
123 Tanner Kero RC 1.50 4.00
124 Viktor Svedberg RC 1.25 3.00
125 Brendan Gaunce RC 2.00 5.00
126 Dylan DeMelo RC 1.25 3.00
127 Joonas Kemppainen RC 1.00 2.50
128 Brian O'Neill RC 1.25 3.00
129 Anton Slepyshev RC 1.00 2.50
130 Evgeny Medvedev RC 1.25 3.00
131 Mike Condon AU 6.00 15.00
132 Sergei Plotnikov AU RC 4.00 10.00
133 Mattias Janmark AU RC 6.00 15.00
134 Ben Hutton AU RC 6.00 15.00
135 Andreas Athanasiou AU RC 20.00 50.00
136 Colton Parayko AU RC 10.00 25.00
137 Joonas Donskoi AU RC 6.00 15.00
138 Oscar Lindberg AU RC 6.00 15.00
139 Antoine Bibeau JSY AU/499 RC 5.00 12.00
140 Malcolm Subban JSY AU/499 RC 8.00 20.00
141 Matt Puempel JSY AU/499 RC 4.00 10.00
142 Nikolay Goldobin JSY AU/499 RC 5.00 12.00
143 Nick Cousins JSY AU/499 RC 5.00 12.00
144 Connor Hellebuyck
JSY AU/499 RC 20.00 50.00
145 Shane Prince JSY AU/499 RC 3.00 8.00
146 Jordan Weal JSY AU/499 RC 3.00 8.00
147 Mikko Rantanen JSY AU/499 RC 30.00 80.00
148 Brendan Gaunce JSY AU/499 RC 6.00 15.00
149 Slater Koekkoek JSY AU/499 RC 3.00 8.00
150 Daniel Sprong JSY AU/499 RC 6.00 15.00
151 Ryan Hartman JSY AU/499 RC 6.00 15.00
152 Jared McCann JSY AU/499 RC 6.00 15.00
153 Jake Virtanen JSY AU/499 RC 6.00 15.00
154 Hunter Shinkaruk JSY AU/499 RC 5.00 12.00
155 Nick Ritchie JSY AU/499 RC 5.00 12.00
156 Derek Forbort JSY AU/499 RC 4.00 10.00
157 Zachary Fucale JSY AU/499 4.00 10.00
158 Kevin Fiala JSY AU/499 RC 6.00 15.00
159 Robby Fabbri JSY AU/499 RC 6.00 15.00
160 Henrik Samuelsson
JSY AU/499 RC 3.00 8.00
161 Mackenzie Skapski
JSY AU/499 RC 5.00 12.00
162 Noah Hanifin JSY AU/499 RC 8.00 20.00
163 Emile Poirier JSY AU/499 RC 4.00 10.00
164 Nicolas Petan JSY AU/499 RC 5.00 12.00
165 Brock McGinn JSY AU/499 RC 5.00 12.00
166 Sam Bennett JSY AU/399 RC 20.00 50.00
167 Nikolaj Ehlers JSY AU/399 RC 12.00 30.00
168 Dylan Larkin JSY AU/399 RC 60.00 120.00
169 Connor McDavid
JSY AU/399 RC 1000.00 2500.00
170 Artemi Panarin JSY AU/399 RC 50.00 100.00
171 Max Domi JSY AU/199 RC 15.00 40.00
172 Jack Eichel JSY/399 RC 25.00 60.00

2015-16 SPx Red

*RED: .6X TO 1.5X AU/499 RC
*RED: .5X TO 1.2X AU/399 RC
*RED: .5X TO 1.2X AU/299 RC
151 Ryan Hartman JSY AU 10.00 25.00
168 Dylan Larkin JSY AU 100.00 200.00
169 Connor McDavid JSY AU 1200.00 3000.00
170 Artemi Panarin JSY AU 100.00 200.00

2015-16 SPx '05-06 Retro Rookie Autograph Jerseys

SPXRAB Antoine Bibeau/399 5.00 12.00
SPXRCH Connor Hellebuyck/399 20.00 50.00
SPXRCM Connor McDavid/299 600.00 1500.00
SPXRDF Derek Forbort/399 4.00 10.00
SPXRDL Dylan Larkin/299 60.00 120.00
SPXRDS Daniel Sprong/399 6.00 15.00
SPXREP Emile Poirier/399 4.00 10.00
SPXRJA Josh Anderson/399 10.00 25.00
SPXRJM Jared McCann/399 6.00 15.00
SPXRJV Jake Virtanen/299 6.00 15.00
SPXRKB Kyle Baun/399 5.00 12.00
SPXRKF Kevin Fiala/399 6.00 15.00
SPXRMR Mikko Rantanen/399 30.00 80.00
SPXRNC Nick Cousins/399 5.00 12.00
SPXRNE Nikolaj Ehlers/399 8.00 20.00
SPXRNG Nikolay Goldobin/399 5.00 12.00
SPXRNH Noah Hanifin/399 8.00 20.00
SPXRNP Nicolas Petan/399 5.00 12.00
SPXRNR Nick Ritchie/399 5.00 12.00
SPXRRB Robby Fabbri/399 6.00 15.00
SPXRSH Hunter Shinkaruk/399 5.00 12.00
SPXRSP Shane Prince/399 3.00 8.00
SPXRZF Zachary Fucale/399 10.00 25.00

2015-16 SPx '05-06 Retro Rookie Jerseys

SPXR-AB Antoine Bibeau D 2.50 6.00
SPXR-AP Artemi Panarin B 10.00 25.00
SPXR-BM Brock McGinn D 2.50 6.00
SPXR-CH Connor Hellebuyck D 10.00 25.00
SPXR-CM Connor McDavid B 100.00 250.00
SPXR-DF Derek Forbort D 2.00 5.00
SPXR-DL Dylan Larkin B 8.00 20.00
SPXR-DS Daniel Sprong C 3.00 8.00
SPXR-EP Emile Poirier A 6.00 15.00
SPXR-JA Josh Anderson D 5.00 12.00
SPXR-JE Jack Eichel B 10.00 25.00
SPXR-JM Jared McCann C 3.00 8.00
SPXR-JV Jake Virtanen B 3.00 8.00
SPXR-KB Kyle Baun D 2.50 6.00
SPXR-KF Kevin Fiala D 3.00 8.00
SPXR-MD Max Domi B 5.00 12.00
SPXR-MR Mikko Rantanen C 12.00 30.00
SPXR-NC Nick Cousins D 2.50 6.00
SPXR-NE Nikolaj Ehlers B 5.00 12.00
SPXR-NG Nikolay Goldobin B 2.50 6.00
SPXR-NH Noah Hanifin B 4.00 10.00
SPXR-NP Nicolas Petan C 2.50 6.00
SPXR-NR Nick Ritchie C 2.50 6.00
SPXR-RB Robby Fabbri B 3.00 8.00
SPXR-RH Ryan Hartman D 3.00 8.00
SPXR-SH Hunter Shinkaruk C 2.50 6.00
SPXR-SP Shane Prince C 1.50 4.00
SPXR-ZF Zachary Fucale C 2.00 5.00

2015-16 SPx Monochromatics

MAE Aaron Ekblad C 5.00 12.00
MAH Adam Henrique D 3.00 8.00
MAO Alexander Ovechkin B 15.00 40.00
MBB Ben Bishop D 3.00 8.00
MBE Jamie Benn C 4.00 10.00
MBG Brendan Gallagher C 4.00 10.00
MBS Brayden Schenn D 4.00 10.00
MCG Claude Giroux C 4.00 10.00
MCP Carey Price B 8.00 20.00
MCS Cory Schneider D 4.00 10.00
MDB David Backes D 2.50 6.00
MDS Daniel Sedin D 5.00 12.00
MEM Evgeni Malkin B 8.00 20.00
MGF Grant Fuhr B 6.00 15.00
MGL Gabriel Landeskog D 5.00 12.00
MJE Jordan Eberle D 4.00 10.00
MJG Johnny Gaudreau C 6.00 15.00
MJH Jiri Hudler D 3.00 8.00
MJI Jarome Iginla C 5.00 12.00
MJS Jordan Staal D 3.00 8.00
MLC Logan Couture D 5.00 12.00
MMS Martin St. Louis B 4.00 10.00
MNB Nicklas Backstrom C 4.00 10.00
MNK Nazem Kadri A 5.00 12.00
MOE Oliver Ekman-Larsson C 4.00 10.00
MRJ Ryan Johansen C 3.00 8.00
MRN Ryan Nugent-Hopkins C 5.00 12.00
MRS Ryan Strome D 4.00 10.00
MSE Brent Seabrook D 2.50 6.00
MSS Steven Stamkos B 8.00 20.00
MTS Tyler Seguin B 5.00 12.00
MVT Vladimir Tarasenko B 5.00 12.00
MZP Zach Parise C 4.00 10.00

2015-16 SPx Sweet Shot Stick Signings

SSS-CM Connor McDavid 250.00 400.00
SSS-DL Dylan Larkin 25.00 60.00
SSS-DS Daniel Sprong 10.00 25.00
SSS-EP Emile Poirier 6.00 15.00
SSS-JD Jacob de la Rose 8.00 20.00
SSS-JM Jared McCann 10.00 25.00
SSS-KF Kevin Fiala 10.00 25.00
SSS-MR Mikko Rantanen 40.00 100.00
SSS-MS Malcolm Subban 12.00 30.00
SSS-NE Nikolaj Ehlers 15.00 40.00
SSS-NP Nicolas Petan 8.00 20.00
SSS-OL Oscar Lindberg 8.00 20.00
SSS-SP Shane Prince 8.00 20.00

2015-16 SPx X Jersey Dual

XDBL S.Bennett/D.Larkin C 12.00 30.00
XDBT T.Seguin/J.Benn C 5.00 12.00
XDDL P.Datsyuk/N.Lidstrom A 6.00 15.00
XDDP M.Domi/A.Panarin B 15.00 40.00
XDHE N.Hanifin/J.Eichel B 15.00 40.00
XDKQ A.Kopitar/J.Quick C 6.00 15.00
XDKS R.Getzlaf/R.Kesler D 4.00 10.00
XDMG W.Gretzky/C.McDavid B 60.00 120.00
XDMP E.Malkin/C.Perry D 8.00 20.00
XDOB A.Ovechkin/N.Backstrom C 15.00 40.00
XDRB P.Roy/M.Brodeur B 10.00 25.00
XDSG P.Subban/A.Galchenyuk D 5.00 12.00
XDSL D.Stepan/H.Lundqvist D 10.00 25.00
XDTK J.Toews/P.Kane B 8.00 20.00

2015-16 SPx X Jersey Quad

XQBPPH Benn/Parise/Pavelski/Hall C 6.00 15.00
XQDPRE Domi/Panarin
Rantanen/Ehlers B 25.00 60.00
XQFCRR Fleury/Coffey
Robitaille/Robinson A 5.00 12.00
XQMHNE McDavid/Hall
Nugent-Hopkins/Eberle A 80.00 200.00
XQOTSS Ovechkin
Tavares/Seguin/Stamkos B 20.00 50.00
XQPKTV Perry/Kane
Tarasenko/Voracek C 10.00 25.00
XQPRLR Price/Rinne
Lundqvist/Rask C 12.00 30.00
XQPSGP Pacioretty/Subban
Galchenyuk/Price C 10.00 25.00
XQTKKC Toews/Kane
Keith/Crawford B 10.00 25.00

2016-17 SPx

1 John Gibson 3.00 8.00
2 Oliver Ekman-Larsson 3.00 8.00
3 David Krejci 3.00 8.00
4 Ray Bourque 5.00 12.00
5 Ryan O'Reilly 3.00 8.00
6 Dale Hawerchuk 4.00 10.00
7 Sean Monahan 2.00 5.00
8 Jonathan Toews 5.00 12.00
9 Patrick Kane 6.00 15.00
10 Nathan MacKinnon 12.00 30.00
11 Boone Jenner 3.00 8.00
12 Jamie Benn 3.00 8.00
13 Steve Yzerman 8.00 20.00
14 Dylan Larkin 4.00 10.00
15 Wayne Gretzky 20.00 50.00
16 Connor McDavid 15.00 40.00
17 Aleksander Barkov 5.00 12.00
18 Pavel Bure 3.00 8.00
19 Jaromir Jagr 10.00 25.00
20 Rob Blake 3.00 8.00
21 Drew Doughty 4.00 10.00
22 Zach Parise 3.00 8.00
23 Patrick Roy 8.00 20.00
24 Carey Price 6.00 15.00
25 Pekka Rinne 3.00 8.00
26 Cory Schneider 3.00 8.00
27 Jaroslav Halak 3.00 8.00
28 John Tavares 5.00 12.00
29 Derek Stepan 2.00 5.00
30 Rick Nash 3.00 8.00
31 Henrik Lundqvist 8.00 20.00
32 Mark Stone 3.00 8.00
33 Jakub Voracek 2.50 6.00
34 Sidney Crosby 12.00 30.00
35 Mario Lemieux 12.00 30.00

Card	Low	High
36 Joe Pavelski	4.00	10.00
37 Brent Burns	3.00	8.00
38 Jake Allen	3.00	8.00
39 Brett Hull	6.00	15.00
40 Steven Stamkos	6.00	15.00
41 Tyler Johnson	2.00	5.00
42 Nikita Kucherov	6.00	15.00
43 James van Riemsdyk	2.50	6.00
44 Morgan Rielly	3.00	8.00
45 Ryan Miller	3.00	8.00
46 Kirk McLean	3.00	8.00
47 Alexander Ovechkin	12.00	30.00
48 Braden Holtby	4.00	10.00
49 Mark Scheifele	5.00	12.00
50 Nikolaj Ehlers	3.00	8.00
51 William Nylander RC	12.00	30.00
52 Pavel Zacha RC	5.00	12.00
53 Anthony Mantha RC	6.00	15.00
54 Hudson Fasching RC	3.00	8.00
55 Kasperi Kapanen RC	5.00	12.00
56 Sonny Milano RC	4.00	10.00
57 Josh Morrissey RC	8.00	20.00
58 Justin Bailey RC	3.00	8.00
59 Connor Brown RC	5.00	12.00
60 Steven Santini RC	2.50	6.00
61 Oliver Bjorkstrand RC	4.00	10.00
62 Jason Dickinson RC	2.50	6.00
63 Nick Schmaltz RC	4.00	10.00
64 Dylan Strome RC	8.00	20.00
65 Kyle Connor RC	10.00	25.00
66 Mathew Barzal RC	10.00	25.00
67 Matthew Tkachuk RC	12.00	30.00
68 Mikhail Sergachev RC	5.00	12.00
69 Jimmy Vesey RC	5.00	12.00
70 Travis Konecny RC	6.00	15.00
71 Mitch Marner RC	20.00	50.00
72 Ivan Provorov RC	5.00	12.00
73 Jesse Puljujarvi RC	6.00	15.00
74 Patrik Laine RC	20.00	50.00
75 Auston Matthews RC	40.00	100.00

2016-17 SPx Blue

Card	Low	High
1 John Gibson AU/99	6.00	15.00
3 David Krejci AU/99	6.00	15.00
7 Sean Monahan AU/99	4.00	10.00
10 Nathan MacKinnon AU/49	40.00	100.00
11 Boone Jenner AU/99	6.00	15.00
12 Jamie Benn AU/49	10.00	25.00
17 Aleksander Barkov AU/99	10.00	25.00
22 Zach Parise AU/99	6.00	15.00
24 Carey Price AU/49	40.00	80.00
26 Cory Schneider AU/49	10.00	25.00
27 Jaroslav Halak AU/99	6.00	15.00
28 John Tavares AU/49	15.00	40.00
29 Derek Stepan AU/99	4.00	10.00
30 Rick Nash AU/99	6.00	15.00
31 Henrik Lundqvist AU/49	25.00	60.00
33 Jakub Voracek AU/99	5.00	12.00
36 Joe Pavelski AU/99	8.00	20.00
37 Brent Burns AU/99	6.00	15.00
38 Jake Allen AU/99	6.00	15.00
41 Tyler Johnson AU/99	4.00	10.00
42 Nikita Kucherov AU/99	12.00	30.00
43 James van Riemsdyk AU/99	5.00	12.00
44 Morgan Rielly AU/99	6.00	15.00
49 Mark Scheifele AU/99	10.00	25.00
50 Nikolaj Ehlers AU/99	6.00	15.00
51 William Nylander AU/199	30.00	80.00
52 Pavel Zacha AU/199	10.00	25.00
54 Hudson Fasching AU/199	6.00	15.00
56 Sonny Milano AU/199	8.00	20.00
57 Josh Morrissey AU/199	15.00	40.00
58 Justin Bailey AU/199	6.00	15.00
59 Connor Brown AU/199	10.00	25.00
60 Steven Santini AU/199	5.00	12.00
61 Oliver Bjorkstrand AU/199	8.00	20.00
62 Jason Dickinson AU/199	5.00	12.00
63 Nick Schmaltz AU/199	8.00	20.00
64 Dylan Strome AU/199	15.00	40.00
66 Mathew Barzal AU/199	20.00	50.00
67 Matthew Tkachuk AU/199	25.00	60.00
68 Mikhail Sergachev AU/199	10.00	25.00
71 Mitch Marner AU/199	80.00	200.00
72 Ivan Provorov AU/199	10.00	25.00
73 Jesse Puljujarvi AU/199	15.00	40.00
74 Patrik Laine AU/199	75.00	150.00

2016-17 SPx Gold

Card	Low	High
7 Sean Monahan PATCH AU/49	10.00	25.00
10 Nathan MacKinnon PATCH AU/25	80.00	200.00
17 Aleksander Barkov PATCH AU/49	25.00	60.00
22 Zach Parise PATCH AU/49	15.00	40.00
24 Carey Price BLKR AU/25	50.00	120.00
26 Cory Schneider PATCH AU/25	20.00	50.00
27 Jaroslav Halak PATCH AU/49	15.00	40.00
28 John Tavares PATCH AU/25	30.00	80.00
29 Derek Stepan PATCH AU/49	10.00	25.00
31 Henrik Lundqvist PATCH AU/25	50.00	120.00
32 Mark Stone PATCH AU/49	20.00	50.00
33 Jakub Voracek PATCH AU/49	12.00	30.00
37 Brent Burns PATCH AU/49	15.00	40.00
38 Jake Allen PATCH AU/49	15.00	40.00
41 Tyler Johnson PATCH AU/49	10.00	25.00
42 Nikita Kucherov PATCH AU/49	30.00	80.00
43 James van Riemsdyk PATCH AU/49	12.00	30.00
44 Morgan Rielly PATCH AU/49	15.00	40.00
45 Ryan Miller STK AU/49	15.00	40.00
49 Mark Scheifele PATCH AU/49	25.00	60.00
50 Nikolaj Ehlers PATCH AU/49	15.00	40.00
51 William Nylander PATCH AU	40.00	80.00
52 Pavel Zacha PATCH AU	20.00	50.00
53 Anthony Mantha PATCH AU	25.00	60.00
54 Hudson Fasching PATCH AU	12.00	30.00
55 Kasperi Kapanen PATCH AU	20.00	50.00
56 Sonny Milano PATCH AU	15.00	40.00
57 Josh Morrissey PATCH AU	30.00	80.00
58 Justin Bailey PATCH AU	12.00	30.00
59 Connor Brown PATCH AU	20.00	50.00
60 Steven Santini PATCH AU	10.00	25.00
61 Oliver Bjorkstrand PATCH AU	15.00	40.00
62 Jason Dickinson PATCH AU	10.00	25.00
63 Nick Schmaltz PATCH AU	15.00	40.00
64 Dylan Strome PATCH AU	30.00	80.00
65 Kyle Connor PATCH AU	40.00	100.00
66 Mathew Barzal PATCH AU	30.00	80.00
67 Matthew Tkachuk PATCH AU	30.00	80.00
68 Mikhail Sergachev PATCH AU	20.00	50.00
70 Travis Konecny PATCH AU	15.00	40.00
71 Mitch Marner PATCH AU	150.00	400.00
72 Ivan Provorov PATCH AU	30.00	80.00
73 Jesse Puljujarvi PATCH AU	25.00	60.00
74 Patrik Laine PATCH AU	250.00	400.00
75 Auston Matthews PATCH AU	400.00	600.00

2016-17 SPx Red

Card	Low	High
1 John Gibson JSY C	4.00	10.00
2 Oliver Ekman-Larsson JSY B	4.00	10.00
5 Ryan O'Reilly JSY B	4.00	10.00
7 Sean Monahan JSY B	2.50	6.00
8 Jonathan Toews JSY B	6.00	15.00
10 Nathan MacKinnon JSY B	15.00	40.00
12 Jamie Benn JSY B	4.00	10.00
13 Steve Yzerman JSY	10.00	25.00
14 Dylan Larkin JSY C	5.00	12.00
15 Wayne Gretzky JSY	25.00	60.00
16 Connor McDavid JSY A	20.00	50.00
17 Aleksander Barkov JSY C	6.00	15.00
19 Jaromir Jagr JSY B	12.00	30.00
20 Rob Blake JSY	4.00	10.00
21 Drew Doughty JSY A	5.00	12.00
22 Zach Parise JSY C	4.00	10.00
23 Patrick Roy JSY	10.00	25.00
24 Carey Price JSY A	8.00	20.00
25 Pekka Rinne JSY C	4.00	10.00
26 Cory Schneider JSY C	4.00	10.00
28 John Tavares JSY B	6.00	15.00
29 Derek Stepan JSY C	2.50	6.00
31 Henrik Lundqvist JSY B	10.00	25.00
32 Mark Stone JSY C	5.00	12.00
33 Jakub Voracek JSY C	3.00	8.00
34 Sidney Crosby JSY A	15.00	40.00
35 Mario Lemieux JSY	15.00	40.00
37 Brent Burns JSY B	4.00	10.00
38 Jake Allen JSY C	4.00	10.00
39 Brett Hull JSY	8.00	20.00
40 Steven Stamkos JSY A	8.00	20.00
41 Tyler Johnson JSY B	2.50	6.00
42 Nikita Kucherov JSY B	8.00	20.00
43 James van Riemsdyk JSY C	3.00	8.00
44 Morgan Rielly JSY C	4.00	10.00
45 Ryan Miller JSY C	4.00	10.00
46 Kirk McLean JSY	4.00	10.00
47 Alexander Ovechkin JSY A	15.00	40.00
48 Braden Holtby JSY A	5.00	12.00
49 Mark Scheifele JSY B	6.00	15.00
51 William Nylander JSY	20.00	50.00
52 Pavel Zacha JSY	8.00	20.00
53 Anthony Mantha JSY	10.00	25.00
54 Hudson Fasching JSY	5.00	12.00
55 Kasperi Kapanen JSY	8.00	20.00
56 Sonny Milano JSY	6.00	15.00
57 Josh Morrissey JSY	12.00	30.00
58 Justin Bailey JSY	5.00	12.00
59 Connor Brown JSY	8.00	20.00
60 Steven Santini JSY	4.00	10.00
61 Oliver Bjorkstrand JSY	6.00	15.00
62 Jason Dickinson JSY	4.00	10.00
63 Nick Schmaltz JSY	6.00	15.00
64 Dylan Strome JSY	12.00	30.00
65 Kyle Connor JSY	15.00	40.00
66 Mathew Barzal JSY	15.00	40.00
67 Matthew Tkachuk JSY	20.00	50.00
68 Mikhail Sergachev JSY	8.00	20.00
69 Jimmy Vesey JSY	8.00	20.00
70 Travis Konecny JSY	10.00	25.00
71 Mitch Marner JSY	15.00	40.00
72 Ivan Provorov JSY	8.00	20.00
73 Jesse Puljujarvi JSY	10.00	25.00
74 Patrik Laine JSY	12.00	30.00
75 Auston Matthews JSY	30.00	80.00

2016-17 SPx Double XL Duos Materials

Card	Low	High
XDBM S.Bennett/S.Monahan/99	8.00	20.00
XDJL J.Jagr/R.Luongo/99	15.00	40.00
XDKH E.Kuznetsov/B.Holtby/99	6.00	15.00
XDLC P.Laine/K.Connor/99	15.00	40.00
XDLG M.Lemieux/W.Gretzky/49	30.00	80.00
XDMM A.Matthews/M.Marner/99	50.00	120.00
XDNB W.Nylander/C.Brown/99	20.00	50.00
XDRE S.Reinhart/J.Eichel/99	10.00	25.00
XDZS P.Zacha/S.Santini/99	8.00	20.00

2016-17 SPx Double XL Materials

Card	Low	High
XXLAH Adam Henrique/99	3.00	8.00
XXLAO Alexander Ovechkin/99	15.00	40.00
XXLBD Brandon Dubinsky/199	2.00	5.00
XXLBR Bill Ranford/99	4.00	10.00
XXLBS Brayden Schenn/199	3.00	8.00
XXLCG Claude Giroux/199	3.00	8.00
XXLDB Dustin Byfuglien/199	3.00	8.00
XXLEK Erik Karlsson/99	5.00	12.00
XXLFF Filip Forsberg/199	5.00	12.00
XXLGL Gabriel Landeskog/199	4.00	10.00
XXLHS Henrik Sedin/199	4.00	10.00
XXLJG Johnny Gaudreau/199	5.00	12.00
XXLJV Jimmy Vesey/199	5.00	12.00
XXLKC Kyle Connor/199	10.00	25.00
XXLMD Max Domi/199	3.00	8.00
XXLMM Mitch Marner/199	10.00	25.00
XXLNH Noah Hanifin/199	3.00	8.00
XXLNN Nino Niederreiter/199	2.00	5.00
XXLON Owen Nolan/99	4.00	10.00
XXLPZ Pavel Zacha/199	5.00	12.00
XXLSB Sam Bennett/199	5.00	12.00
XXLSC Sidney Crosby/199	12.00	30.00
XXLWN William Nylander/199	12.00	30.00

2016-17 SPx Extraordinary Material Autographs Black

Card	Low	High
EMAM Auston Matthews/25	250.00	400.00
EMBB Brent Burns/49	15.00	40.00
EMCM Connor McDavid/25	250.00	400.00
EMCS Cory Schneider/49	5.00	12.00
EMDT Dave Taylor/25	15.00	40.00
EMHL Henrik Lundqvist/25	20.00	50.00
EMHZ Henrik Zetterberg/25	20.00	50.00
EMIP Ivan Provorov/49	15.00	40.00
EMJS Jason Spezza/49	5.00	12.00
EMJT John Tavares/25	30.00	80.00
EMNK Nikita Kucherov/49	20.00	50.00
EMPL Patrik Laine/25	200.00	350.00
EMSB Sam Bennett/49	8.00	20.00
EMZP Zach Parise/49	12.00	30.00

2016-17 SPx Extraordinary Materials

Card	Low	High
EMAE Aaron Ekblad/25	12.00	30.00
EMAM Auston Matthews/25	60.00	150.00
EMBB Brent Burns/25	10.00	25.00
EMCS Cory Schneider/25	10.00	25.00
EMDT Dave Taylor/25	10.00	25.00
EMFF Filip Forsberg/25	15.00	40.00
EMGF Grant Fuhr/25	15.00	40.00
EMHL Henrik Lundqvist/25	25.00	60.00
EMIP Ivan Provorov/25	15.00	40.00
EMJS Jason Spezza/25	10.00	25.00
EMJT John Tavares/25	15.00	40.00
EMMM Mitch Marner/25	30.00	80.00
EMMS Mark Stone/25	12.00	30.00
EMNK Nikita Kucherov/25	20.00	50.00

2016-17 SPx Extravagant Materials

Card	Low	High
EXAB Aleksander Barkov D	5.00	12.00
EXAM Anthony Mantha D	6.00	15.00
EXDD Drew Doughty C	4.00	10.00
EXDK Duncan Keith C	2.50	6.00
EXDS Dylan Strome D	8.00	20.00
EXEK Evgeny Kuznetsov D	4.00	10.00
EXEM Evgeni Malkin A	6.00	15.00
EXJC Jeff Carter A	2.50	6.00
EXJE Jack Eichel C	5.00	12.00
EXMJ Martin Jones D	2.50	6.00
EXML Mario Lemieux A	12.00	30.00
EXMR Morgan Rielly C	3.00	8.00
EXPB Patrice Bergeron C	4.00	10.00
EXPK Patrick Kane B	6.00	15.00
EXRG Ryan Getzlaf C	3.00	8.00
EXSS Steven Stamkos B	6.00	15.00
EXVH Victor Hedman D	4.00	10.00
EXVT Vladimir Tarasenko B	4.00	10.00

2016-17 SPx Extreme Black Holo Shield

Card	Low	High
EBAB Aleksander Barkov	8.00	20.00
EBAM Auston Matthews	50.00	120.00
EBAO Alexander Ovechkin	20.00	50.00
EBBB Brent Burns	5.00	12.00
EBBL Rob Blake	5.00	12.00
EBCD Christian Dvorak	6.00	15.00
EBCM Connor McDavid	25.00	60.00
EBCP Carey Price	10.00	25.00
EBDH Dale Hawerchuk	6.00	15.00
EBDK David Krejci	5.00	12.00
EBDL Dylan Larkin	6.00	15.00
EBDS Derek Stepan	3.00	8.00
EBHF Hudson Fasching	5.00	12.00
EBHL Henrik Lundqvist	12.00	30.00
EBIP Ivan Provorov	8.00	20.00
EBJA Jake Allen	5.00	12.00
EBJB Jamie Benn	5.00	12.00
EBJE Joel Eriksson Ek	8.00	20.00
EBJG John Gibson	5.00	12.00
EBJP Joe Pavelski	6.00	15.00
EBJT Jonathan Toews	8.00	20.00
EBJV Jakub Voracek	4.00	10.00
EBKC Kyle Connor	15.00	40.00
EBKM Kirk McLean	5.00	12.00
EBLA Patrik Laine	12.00	30.00
EBLE Loui Eriksson	3.00	8.00
EBMA Anthony Mantha	10.00	25.00
EBMB Mathew Barzal	15.00	40.00
EBMI Sonny Milano	6.00	15.00
EBMM Mitch Marner	15.00	40.00
EBMR Morgan Rielly	5.00	12.00
EBMS Mark Scheifele	8.00	20.00
EBMT Matthew Tkachuk	20.00	50.00
EBNK Nikita Kucherov	10.00	25.00
EBNM Nathan MacKinnon	20.00	50.00
EBPB Pavel Buchnevich	8.00	20.00
EBPK Patrick Kane	10.00	25.00
EBPU Jesse Puljujarvi	10.00	25.00
EBPZ Pavel Zacha	8.00	20.00
EBRB Ray Bourque	8.00	20.00
EBSA Sebastian Aho	15.00	40.00
EBSC Sidney Crosby	20.00	50.00
EBSE Mikhail Sergachev	8.00	20.00
EBSM Sean Monahan	3.00	8.00
EBTA John Tavares	8.00	20.00
EBTK Travis Konecny	10.00	25.00
EBVE Jimmy Vesey	8.00	20.00
EBWG Wayne Gretzky	25.00	60.00
EBWN William Nylander	20.00	50.00
EBZP Zach Parise	5.00	12.00

2016-17 SPx Ice Shredders Materials

Card	Low	High
ISAM Auston Matthews A	25.00	60.00
ISAO Alexander Ovechkin B	15.00	40.00
ISBW Blake Wheeler D	4.00	10.00
ISCM Connor McDavid B	20.00	50.00
ISDL Dylan Larkin C	5.00	12.00
ISEK Erik Karlsson C	5.00	12.00
ISGA Marian Gaborik D	4.00	10.00
ISGL Guy Lafleur A	5.00	12.00
ISJD Jonathan Drouin D	3.00	8.00
ISJT John Tavares B	6.00	15.00
ISJV Jimmy Vesey C	6.00	15.00
ISMG Mike Gartner B	5.00	12.00
ISNM Nathan MacKinnon C	15.00	40.00
ISPB Pavel Bure A	12.00	30.00
ISPK Phil Kessel D	4.00	10.00
ISPL Patrik Laine B	10.00	25.00
ISPZ Pavel Zacha C	6.00	15.00
ISSC Sidney Crosby A	15.00	40.00
ISWN William Nylander C	15.00	40.00

2016-17 SPx Ice Shredders Materials Premium Black

Card	Low	High
ISAM Auston Matthews/25	125.00	200.00
ISPL Patrik Laine/25	50.00	120.00

2016-17 SPx Impressions Autographs

Card	Low	High
IABB Brent Burns/199	10.00	25.00
IACC Chris Chelios/99	10.00	25.00
IADK David Krejci/199	10.00	25.00
IADT Dave Taylor/99	10.00	25.00
IAHL Henrik Lundqvist/25	50.00	120.00
IAHZ Henrik Zetterberg/25	25.00	60.00
IAIL Igor Larionov/25	20.00	50.00
IAJG John Gibson/199	10.00	25.00
IAJM Jake Muzzin/99	10.00	25.00
IALD Leon Draisaitl/199	30.00	80.00
IAMM Mike Modano/25	30.00	80.00
IAMS Mark Scheifele/199	15.00	40.00
IANB Nick Bjugstad/199	6.00	15.00
IANK Nikita Kucherov/99	20.00	50.00
IANN Nino Niederreiter/199	6.00	15.00
IARB Ray Bourque/25	30.00	80.00
IARJ Roman Josi/199	10.00	25.00
IAZP Zach Parise/99	10.00	25.00

2016-17 SPx Rookies

Card	Low	High
RAB Anthony Beauvillier	1.50	4.00
RAD Anthony DeAngelo	1.25	3.00
RAL Artturi Lehkonen	2.00	5.00
RAM Auston Matthews	25.00	60.00
RBI Chris Bigras	1.25	3.00
RBL Brendan Leipsic	1.25	3.00
RBP Brayden Point	4.00	10.00
RCB Connor Brown	2.50	6.00
RCD Christian Dvorak	2.00	5.00
RCL Charlie Lindgren	2.50	6.00
RDH Danton Heinen	1.25	3.00
RDL Chase De Leo	1.50	4.00
RDS Dylan Strome	4.00	10.00
REL Esa Lindell	1.50	4.00
RHF Hudson Fasching	1.50	4.00
RIP Ivan Provorov	2.50	6.00
RJB Justin Bailey	1.50	4.00
RJC Jakob Chychrun	25.00	60.00
RJE Joel Eriksson Ek	2.50	6.00
RJM Josh Morrissey	4.00	10.00
RJP Jesse Puljujarvi	4.00	10.00
RJV Jimmy Vesey	2.50	6.00
RKC Kyle Connor	5.00	12.00
RKK Kasperi Kapanen	2.50	6.00
RKL Kevin Labanc	1.50	4.00
RKU Tom Kuhnhackl	1.25	3.00
RLC Lawson Crouse	1.25	3.00
RMA Anthony Mantha	5.00	12.00
RMB Mathew Barzal	5.00	12.00
RMI Michael Matheson	1.50	4.00
RMM Mitch Marner	12.00	30.00
RMR Mike Reilly	1.25	3.00
RMS Mikhail Sergachev	2.50	6.00
RMT Matthew Tkachuk	6.00	15.00
RMW Miles Wood	1.25	3.00
RNS Nick Schmaltz	2.00	5.00
ROB Oliver Bjorkstrand	2.00	5.00
ROK Oliver Kylington	1.25	3.00
RPB Pavel Buchnevich	2.50	6.00
RPL Patrik Laine	10.00	25.00
RPZ Pavel Zacha	2.50	6.00
RRP Ryan Pulock	1.50	4.00
RSA Sebastian Aho	5.00	12.00
RSM Sonny Milano	2.00	5.00
RSO Nikita Soshnikov	1.00	2.50
RSS Steven Santini	1.25	3.00
RTK Travis Konecny	3.00	8.00
RTM Tyler Motte	1.50	4.00
RWN William Nylander	6.00	15.00
RZW Zach Werenski	5.00	12.00

2017-18 SPx

Card	Low	High
1 Sidney Crosby	6.00	15.00
2 Auston Matthews	6.00	15.00
3 Taylor Hall	1.50	4.00
4 Aleksander Barkov	2.50	6.00
5 Jonathan Toews	2.50	6.00
6 Marc-Andre Fleury	3.00	8.00
7 Carey Price	3.00	8.00
8 Erik Karlsson	2.00	5.00
9 Kevin Shattenkirk	1.00	2.50
10 Nikita Kucherov	3.00	8.00
11 Vladimir Tarasenko	2.00	5.00
12 Anze Kopitar	2.50	6.00
13 Patrik Laine	2.00	5.00
14 Alexander Wennberg	1.00	2.50
15 Henrik Zetterberg	2.00	5.00
16 John Tavares	2.50	6.00
17 Joe Pavelski	2.00	5.00
18 Devan Dubnyk	1.25	3.00
19 Alexander Ovechkin	6.00	15.00
20 Connor McDavid	8.00	20.00
21 Mario Lemieux	6.00	15.00
22 Patrick Roy	4.00	10.00
23 Pavel Bure	1.50	4.00
24 Steve Yzerman	4.00	10.00
25 Wayne Gretzky	10.00	25.00
26 Logan Brown RC	5.00	12.00
27 Will Butcher RC	6.00	15.00
28 Haydn Fleury RC	5.00	12.00
29 Adrian Kempe RC	10.00	25.00
30 Anders Bjork RC	6.00	15.00
31 Kailer Yamamoto RC	12.00	30.00
32 Jake DeBrusk RC	12.00	30.00
33 Luke Kunin RC	5.00	12.00
34 Owen Tippett RC	10.00	25.00
35 Alex Tuch RC	12.00	30.00
36 Jack Roslovic RC	6.00	15.00
37 Evgeny Svechnikov RC	10.00	25.00
38 Ivan Barbashev RC	6.00	15.00
39 Colin White RC	6.00	15.00
40 Josh Ho-Sang RC	6.00	15.00
41 Tyson Jost RC	10.00	25.00
42 Christian Fischer RC	6.00	15.00
43 Alexander Nylander RC	8.00	20.00
44 Charlie McAvoy RC	12.00	30.00
45 Brock Boeser RC	30.00	80.00
46 Clayton Keller RC	12.00	30.00
47 Pierre-Luc Dubois RC	8.00	20.00
48 Alex DeBrincat RC	20.00	50.00
49 Nolan Patrick RC	10.00	25.00
50 Nico Hischier RC	15.00	40.00

2017-18 SPx Double XL Duos Materials

Card	Low	High
XDBM A.Bjork/C.McAvoy/199	10.00	25.00
XDBT I.Barbashev/T.Thompson/199	10.00	25.00
XDFH J.Faulk/N.Hanifin/199	4.00	10.00
XDGB W.Gretzky/R.Blake/99	25.00	60.00
XDGN M.Granlund/N.Niederreiter/199	3.00	8.00
XDHB B.Hull/E.Belfour/99	12.00	30.00
XDMD C.McDavid/L.Draisaitl/199	20.00	50.00
XDML E.Malkin/K.Letang/199	8.00	20.00
XDSS H.Sedin/D.Sedin/199	5.00	12.00
XDTS J.Toews/B.Saad/199	6.00	15.00
XDWB C.White/L.Brown/199	5.00	12.00
XDYL S.Yzerman/I.Larionov/99	12.00	30.00

2017-18 SPx Extravagant Materials

Card	Low	High
EXBB Brent Burns C	2.50	6.00
EXBH Brett Hull B	5.00	12.00
EXBM Brad Marchand D	5.00	12.00
EXBW Blake Wheeler C	2.50	6.00
EXCC Corey Crawford E	3.00	8.00
EXCM Connor McDavid B	12.00	30.00
EXCP Corey Perry E	4.00	10.00
EXCT Cam Talbot E	2.50	6.00
EXDP David Pastrnak C	6.00	15.00
EXEK Erik Karlsson C	3.00	8.00
EXJB Jamie Benn D	2.50	6.00
EXJG Johnny Gaudreau D	4.00	10.00
EXJQ Jonathan Quick E	3.00	8.00
EXMM Mitch Marner D	4.00	10.00
EXNM Nathan MacKinnon C	10.00	25.00
EXPA Colton Parayko E	2.00	5.00
EXSC Sidney Crosby B	10.00	25.00
EXWN William Nylander D	5.00	12.00

2017-18 SPx Impressions Autographs

Card	Low	High
IAAB Aleksander Barkov/249	12.00	30.00
IABE Brian Elliott/249	8.00	20.00
IACA Cam Atkinson/249	8.00	20.00
IACS Conor Sheary/249	8.00	20.00
IAJK Jari Kurri/249	8.00	20.00
IAJP Jason Pominville/249	5.00	12.00
IAJV John Vanbiesbrouck/249	8.00	20.00
IALC Logan Couture/125	10.00	25.00
IALD Leon Draisaitl/125	20.00	50.00
IALR Larry Robinson/125	10.00	25.00
IAMG Mark Giordano/249	8.00	20.00
IANE Nikolaj Ehlers/249	8.00	20.00
IAPL Patrik Laine/125	20.00	50.00
IARB Rod Brind'Amour/249	8.00	20.00
IARL Roberto Luongo/125	12.00	30.00
IAWS Wayne Simmonds/125	10.00	25.00

2017-18 SPx Lasting Marks

Card	Low	High
LMBB Brock Boeser	100.00	200.00
LMBO Bobby Orr	100.00	200.00
LMCK Clayton Keller	30.00	80.00
LMDG Doug Gilmour	60.00	150.00
LMEM Evgeni Malkin	25.00	60.00
LMFK Jakob Forsbacka-Karlsson	10.00	25.00
LMGL Guy Lafleur	15.00	40.00
LMHS Josh Ho-Sang	8.00	20.00
LMJJ Joe Thornton	8.00	20.00
LMJT Jonathan Toews	15.00	40.00
LMMB Martin Brodeur	30.00	80.00
LMMP Max Pacioretty	6.00	15.00
LMPF Peter Forsberg	50.00	125.00
LMSS Steven Stamkos	15.00	40.00
LMVS Vadim Shipachyov	20.00	50.00

2017-18 SPx Materials

Card	Low	High
1 Sidney Crosby A	8.00	20.00
2 Auston Matthews A	8.00	20.00
3 Taylor Hall B	2.00	5.00
4 Aleksander Barkov C	3.00	8.00
5 Jonathan Toews A	3.00	8.00
6 Marc-Andre Fleury C	4.00	10.00
7 Carey Price B	4.00	10.00
8 Erik Karlsson A	2.50	6.00
9 Kevin Shattenkirk C	1.25	3.00
10 Nikita Kucherov B	4.00	10.00
11 Vladimir Tarasenko C	2.50	6.00
12 Anze Kopitar C	3.00	8.00
13 Patrik Laine C	2.50	6.00
14 Alexander Wennberg C	1.25	3.00
15 Henrik Zetterberg C	2.50	6.00
16 John Tavares A	3.00	8.00
17 Joe Pavelski C	2.50	6.00
18 Devan Dubnyk C	1.50	4.00
19 Alexander Ovechkin B	8.00	20.00
20 Connor McDavid A	10.00	25.00
21 Mario Lemieux B	12.00	30.00
22 Patrick Roy C	10.00	25.00
23 Pavel Bure C	6.00	15.00
24 Steve Yzerman B	10.00	25.00
25 Wayne Gretzky A	20.00	50.00

2017-18 SPx Rookies

Card	Low	High
RAD Alex DeBrincat	6.00	15.00
RAK Adrian Kempe	5.00	12.00
RAN Alexander Nylander	4.00	10.00
RBB Brock Boeser	20.00	50.00
RCF Christian Fischer	3.00	8.00
RCK Clayton Keller	6.00	15.00
RCM Charlie McAvoy	6.00	15.00
RCW Colin White	3.00	8.00
RES Evgeny Svechnikov	5.00	12.00
RFC Filip Chytil	2.50	6.00
RIB Ivan Barbashev	3.00	8.00
RJH Josh Ho-Sang	3.00	8.00
RJR Jack Roslovic	3.00	8.00
RJT J.T. Compher	2.50	6.00
RKY Kailer Yamamoto	6.00	15.00
RLB Logan Brown	2.50	6.00
RLK Luke Kunin	2.50	6.00
RNH Nico Hischier	8.00	20.00
RNP Nolan Patrick	5.00	12.00
RNS Nikita Scherbak	3.00	8.00
ROT Owen Tippett	5.00	12.00
RPD Pierre-Luc Dubois	4.00	10.00
RTJ Tyson Jost	5.00	12.00
RVM Victor Mete	2.50	6.00
RWB Will Butcher	3.00	8.00

2017-18 SPx Rookies Gold

*PATCH/49: X TO X BASIC INSERTS

Card	Low	High
RAK Adrian Kempe PATCH AU/49	25.00	60.00

2017-18 SPx Rookie Variations

Card	Low	High
26 Logan Brown AU/148	10.00	25.00
27 Will Butcher AU/148	12.00	30.00
28 Haydn Fleury AU/148	10.00	25.00
29 Adrian Kempe AU/148	20.00	50.00
30 Anders Bjork AU/148	12.00	30.00
31 Kailer Yamamoto AU/148	25.00	60.00
32 Jake DeBrusk AU/148	25.00	60.00
33 Luke Kunin AU/148	10.00	25.00
34 Owen Tippett AU/148	20.00	50.00
35 Alex Tuch AU/148	25.00	60.00
36 Jack Roslovic AU/148	12.00	30.00
37 Evgeny Svechnikov AU/148	20.00	50.00
38 Ivan Barbashev AU/148	12.00	30.00
39 Colin White AU/148	12.00	30.00
40 Josh Ho-Sang AU/148	12.00	30.00
41 Tyson Jost AU/148	20.00	50.00
42 Christian Fischer AU/148	12.00	30.00
43 Alexander Nylander AU/148	15.00	40.00
44 Charlie McAvoy AU/98	60.00	150.00
45 Brock Boeser AU/98	250.00	350.00
46 Clayton Keller AU/98	30.00	80.00
47 Pierre-Luc Dubois AU/98	20.00	50.00
48 Alex DeBrincat AU/98	25.00	60.00
49 Nolan Patrick/98	20.00	50.00
50 Nico Hischier/98	20.00	50.00

2017-18 SPx Rookies Autographs

Card	Low	High
RAD Alex DeBrincat/199	20.00	50.00
RAK Adrian Kempe/199	15.00	40.00
RAN Alexander Nylander/199	12.00	30.00
RBB Brock Boeser/99	100.00	200.00
RCF Christian Fischer/199	10.00	25.00
RCK Clayton Keller/99	15.00	40.00
RCM Charlie McAvoy/99	60.00	150.00
RCW Colin White/199	10.00	25.00
RES Evgeny Svechnikov/199	15.00	40.00
RFC Filip Chytil/199	8.00	20.00
RIB Ivan Barbashev/199	10.00	25.00
RJH Josh Ho-Sang/199	10.00	25.00
RJR Jack Roslovic/199	10.00	25.00
RJT J.T. Compher/199	8.00	20.00
RKY Kailer Yamamoto/199	20.00	50.00
RLB Logan Brown/199	8.00	20.00
RLK Luke Kunin/199	8.00	20.00
RNS Nikita Scherbak/199	10.00	25.00
ROT Owen Tippett/199	12.00	30.00
RPD Pierre-Luc Dubois/199	12.00	30.00
RTJ Tyson Jost/199	15.00	40.00
RVM Victor Mete/199	8.00	20.00
RWB Will Butcher/199	10.00	25.00

2017-18 SPx Rookies Materials

Card	Low	High
RAD Alex DeBrincat	8.00	20.00
RAK Adrian Kempe	6.00	15.00
RAN Alexander Nylander	5.00	12.00
RBB Brock Boeser	8.00	20.00
RCF Christian Fischer	4.00	10.00
RCK Clayton Keller	8.00	20.00
RCM Charlie McAvoy	8.00	20.00
RCW Colin White	4.00	10.00
RES Evgeny Svechnikov	6.00	15.00
RFC Filip Chytil	3.00	8.00
RIB Ivan Barbashev	4.00	10.00
RJH Josh Ho-Sang	4.00	10.00
RJR Jack Roslovic	4.00	10.00
RJT J.T. Compher	3.00	8.00
RKY Kailer Yamamoto	8.00	20.00
RLB Logan Brown	3.00	8.00
RLK Luke Kunin	3.00	8.00
RNH Nico Hischier	10.00	25.00
RNP Nolan Patrick	6.00	15.00
RNS Nikita Scherbak	4.00	10.00
ROT Owen Tippett	6.00	15.00
RPD Pierre-Luc Dubois	5.00	12.00
RTJ Tyson Jost	6.00	15.00

2018-19 SPx

Card	Low	High
1 Connor McDavid	4.00	10.00
2 Jack Eichel	1.25	3.00
3 Erik Karlsson	1.00	2.50
4 Marc-Andre Fleury	1.50	4.00
5 John Tavares	1.25	3.00
6 Patrick Kane	1.50	4.00
7 Steven Stamkos	1.50	4.00
8 Brock Boeser	1.00	2.50
9 Claude Giroux	.75	2.00
10 Connor Hellebuyck	1.50	4.00
11 Taylor Hall	.75	2.00
12 Nikita Kucherov	1.50	4.00
13 Aaron Ekblad	1.00	2.50
14 Charlie McAvoy	1.00	2.50
15 Nathan MacKinnon	3.00	8.00
16 Alexander Ovechkin	3.00	8.00
17 Mathew Barzal	1.00	2.50
18 Mark Scheifele	1.25	3.00
19 Auston Matthews	3.00	8.00
20 Sidney Crosby	3.00	8.00
21 Ray Bourque	1.25	3.00
22 Pat LaFontaine	.75	2.00
23 Martin Brodeur	2.00	5.00
24 Patrick Roy	2.00	5.00
25 Wayne Gretzky	5.00	12.00
26 Rasmus Dahlin RC	15.00	40.00
27 Brett Howden RC	3.00	8.00
28 Jordan Kyrou RC	5.00	12.00
29 Michael Rasmussen RC	3.00	8.00
30 Jordan Greenway RC	2.50	6.00
31 Miro Heiskanen RC	6.00	15.00
32 Brady Tkachuk RC	8.00	20.00
33 Troy Terry RC	4.00	10.00
34 Ryan Donato RC	4.00	10.00
35 Sam Steel RC	2.50	6.00
36 Andreas Johnsson RC	3.00	8.00
37 Robert Thomas RC	5.00	12.00
38 Henri Jokiharju RC	2.00	5.00
39 Kristian Vesalainen RC	3.00	8.00
40 Evan Bouchard RC	6.00	15.00
41 Henrik Borgstrom RC	4.00	10.00
42 Jesperi Kotkaniemi RC	5.00	12.00
43 Andrei Svechnikov RC	6.00	15.00
44 Dylan Sikura RC	3.00	8.00
45 Juuso Valimaki RC	2.50	6.00
46 Eeli Tolvanen RC	5.00	12.00
47 Adam Gaudette RC	4.00	10.00
48 Casey Mittelstadt RC	5.00	12.00
49 Lias Andersson RC	4.00	10.00
50 Elias Pettersson RC	30.00	80.00

2018-19 SPx Gold

*GOLD: X TO X BASIC CARDS

Card	Low	High
4 Marc-Andre Fleury PATCH AU/25	100.00	200.00

2018-19 SPx '08-09 Retro Rookies

Card	Low	High
08AS Andrei Svechnikov	8.00	20.00
08BH Brett Howden	4.00	10.00
08BT Brady Tkachuk	10.00	25.00
08CM Casey Mittelstadt	6.00	15.00
08DO Ryan Donato	5.00	12.00
08EP Elias Pettersson	10.00	25.00
08ET Eeli Tolvanen	6.00	15.00
08HJ Henri Jokiharju	2.50	6.00
08JB Jake Bean	3.00	8.00
08JK Jesperi Kotkaniemi	6.00	15.00
08KY Jordan Kyrou	6.00	15.00
08MH Miro Heiskanen	8.00	20.00
08MM Michael McLeod	2.50	6.00
08MR Michael Rasmussen	4.00	10.00
08RD Rasmus Dahlin	8.00	20.00

2018-19 SPx Autographs

Card	Low	High
5 John Tavares/49	20.00	50.00
10 Connor Hellebuyck/149	12.00	30.00
11 Taylor Hall/149	6.00	15.00
12 Nikita Kucherov/149	12.00	30.00
13 Aaron Ekblad/149	8.00	20.00

2018-19 SPx Double XL Duos Materials

Card	Low	High
XDDM R.Dahlin/C.Mittelstadt	6.00	15.00
XDGM W.Gretzky/C.McDavid	15.00	40.00
XDGP C.Giroux/N.Patrick	2.50	6.00
XDHH T.Hall/N.Hischier	4.00	10.00
XDKJ J.Kotkaniemi/N.Juulsen	5.00	12.00
XDKT P.Kane/J.Toews	5.00	12.00
XDLC M.Lemieux/S.Crosby	10.00	25.00
XDMM A.Matthews/M.Marner	12.00	30.00
XDPB D.Pastrnak/P.Bergeron	6.00	15.00
XDPG E.Pettersson/A.Gaudette	8.00	20.00
XDRP P.Roy/C.Price	6.00	15.00
XDSJ P.Subban/R.Josi	3.00	8.00

2018-19 SPx Extravagant Materials

Card	Low	High
EXAM Auston Matthews A	8.00	20.00
EXAO Alexander Ovechkin A	8.00	20.00
EXBB Brock Boeser B	2.50	6.00
EXBH Braden Holtby C	2.50	6.00
EXBM Brad Marchand B	4.00	10.00
EXBW Blake Wheeler C	2.00	5.00
EXCG Claude Giroux B	2.00	5.00
EXDD Drew Doughty A	2.50	6.00
EXEM Evgeni Malkin A	4.00	10.00
EXFF Filip Forsberg D	3.00	8.00
EXGL Gabriel Landeskog D	2.50	6.00
EXHL Henrik Lundqvist B	5.00	12.00
EXJG Johnny Gaudreau B	3.00	8.00
EXJQ Jonathan Quick D	2.50	6.00
EXJT Jonathan Toews A	3.00	8.00
EXNB Nicklas Backstrom C	2.00	5.00
EXNM Nathan MacKinnon A	8.00	20.00
EXPS P.K. Subban C	2.50	6.00
EXVH Victor Hedman C	2.50	6.00
EXVT Vladimir Tarasenko C	2.50	6.00

2018-19 SPx Extravagant Materials Premium

*PATCH: .75X TO 2X BASIC INSERTS

Card	Low	High
EXHL Henrik Lundqvist/25	12.00	30.00

2018-19 SPx Impressions Autographs

Card	Low	High
IAAR Alexander Radulov/125	10.00	25.00
IABM Brandon Montour/249	12.00	30.00
IACA Craig Anderson/249	8.00	20.00
IACH Connor Hellebuyck/125	20.00	50.00
IADN Darnell Nurse/249	8.00	20.00
IAGL Guy Lafleur/25	15.00	40.00
IAJP Jesse Puljujarvi/249	10.00	25.00
IAJT John Tavares/25	25.00	60.00
IAKT Kyle Turris/249	8.00	20.00
IAMP Max Pacioretty/125	10.00	25.00
IAMR Mikko Rantanen/249	25.00	60.00
IAPD Pavel Datsyuk/25	20.00	50.00
IARE Ryan Ellis/249	8.00	20.00
IASM Sean Monahan/125	6.00	15.00
IATA Tony Amonte/249	8.00	20.00
IATS Travis Sanheim/249	6.00	15.00
IAWG Wayne Gretzky/25	200.00	500.00
IAWK William Karlsson/125	12.00	30.00

2018-19 SPx Lasting Marks

Card	Low	High
LMBO Bobby Orr	60.00	150.00
LMCM Connor McDavid	150.00	250.00
LMCP Carey Price	30.00	80.00
LMML Mario Lemieux	60.00	150.00
LMPR Patrick Roy	40.00	100.00
LMSY Steve Yzerman	40.00	100.00
LMWG Wayne Gretzky	200.00	500.00

2018-19 SPx Materials

Card	Low	High
1 Connor McDavid A	10.00	25.00
2 Jack Eichel C	3.00	8.00
4 Marc-Andre Fleury C	4.00	10.00
5 John Tavares A	3.00	8.00
6 Patrick Kane B	4.00	10.00
7 Steven Stamkos B	4.00	10.00
8 Brock Boeser D	2.50	6.00
9 Claude Giroux C	2.00	5.00
10 Connor Hellebuyck D	4.00	10.00
11 Taylor Hall B	2.00	5.00
12 Nikita Kucherov C	4.00	10.00
13 Aaron Ekblad D	2.50	6.00
14 Charlie McAvoy D	2.50	6.00
15 Nathan MacKinnon B	8.00	20.00
16 Alexander Ovechkin B	8.00	20.00
17 Mathew Barzal D	2.50	6.00
18 Mark Scheifele C	3.00	8.00
19 Auston Matthews A	8.00	20.00
20 Sidney Crosby A	8.00	20.00
21 Ray Bourque C	10.00	25.00
22 Pat LaFontaine C	10.00	25.00
23 Martin Brodeur B	12.00	30.00
24 Patrick Roy A	12.00	30.00
25 Wayne Gretzky A	15.00	40.00

2018-19 SPx Rookies

Card	Low	High
RAJ Andreas Johnsson	2.00	5.00
RAS Andrei Svechnikov	4.00	10.00
RBT Brady Tkachuk	5.00	12.00
RCM Casey Mittelstadt	3.00	8.00
RDB Drake Batherson	3.00	8.00
RDC Dennis Cholowski	1.50	4.00
RDO Ryan Donato	2.50	6.00
REP Elias Pettersson	15.00	40.00
RET Eeli Tolvanen	3.00	8.00
RHB Henrik Borgstrom	2.50	6.00
RHJ Henri Jokiharju	1.25	3.00
RIS Ilya Samsonov	3.00	8.00
RJG Jordan Greenway	1.50	4.00
RJK Jesperi Kotkaniemi	3.00	8.00
RJV Juuso Valimaki	1.50	4.00
RKY Jordan Kyrou	3.00	8.00
RLA Lias Andersson	2.50	6.00

RMH Miro Heiskanen 4.00 10.00
RML Maxime Lajoie 2.50 6.00
RMR Michael Rasmussen 2.00 5.00
ROL Oskar Lindblom 2.50 6.00
RRD Rasmus Dahlin 4.00 10.00
RRT Robert Thomas 3.00 8.00
RSS Sam Steel 1.50 4.00
RTD Travis Dermott 2.50 6.00

2018-19 SPx Rookies Materials

RAJ Andreas Johnsson 4.00 10.00
RAS Andrei Svechnikov 8.00 20.00
RBT Brady Tkachuk 10.00 25.00
RCM Casey Mittelstadt 6.00 15.00
RDB Drake Batherson 6.00 15.00
RDC Dennis Cholowski 3.00 8.00
RDO Ryan Donato 5.00 12.00
REP Elias Pettersson 10.00 25.00
RET Eeli Tolvanen 6.00 15.00
RHB Henrik Borgstrom 5.00 12.00
RHJ Henri Jokiharju 2.50 6.00
RIS Ilya Samsonov 6.00 15.00
RJG Jordan Greenway 3.00 8.00
RJK Jesperi Kotkaniemi 6.00 15.00
RJV Juuso Valimaki 3.00 8.00
RKY Jordan Kyrou 6.00 15.00
RLA Lias Andersson 5.00 12.00
RMH Miro Heiskanen 8.00 20.00
RML Maxime Lajoie 5.00 12.00
RMR Michael Rasmussen 4.00 10.00
ROL Oskar Lindblom 5.00 12.00
RRD Rasmus Dahlin 8.00 20.00
RRT Robert Thomas 6.00 15.00
RSS Sam Steel 3.00 8.00
RTD Travis Dermott 5.00 12.00

2018-19 SPx SPxcitement Swatches

XSAE Aaron Ekblad C 5.00 12.00
XSCH Connor Hellebuyck B 8.00 20.00
XSCP Carey Price A 8.00 20.00
XSDK Duncan Keith B 3.00 8.00
XSDL Dylan Larkin C 5.00 12.00
XSDP David Pastrnak A 10.00 25.00
XSES Eric Staal B 4.00 10.00
XSJG Jake Guentzel C 6.00 15.00
XSJK John Klingberg A 4.00 10.00
XSMZ Mats Zuccarello C 4.00 10.00
XSPM Patrick Marleau A 4.00 10.00
XSRJ Roman Josi B 4.00 10.00
XSRR Rickard Rakell C 3.00 8.00
XSTJ Tyler Johnson B 2.50 6.00
XSVT Vladimir Tarasenko A 5.00 12.00

2018-19 SPx Superscripts

SSAG Alex Galchenyuk B 6.00 15.00
SSAI Arturs Irbe F 8.00 20.00
SSAL Andrew Ladd E 6.00 15.00
SSBO Bobby Orr A 60.00 150.00
SSBR Bobby Ryan D 8.00 20.00
SSCC Chris Chelios B 10.00 25.00
SSCM Connor McDavid A 150.00 250.00
SSCO Charlie Coyle C 10.00 25.00
SSCS Charlie Simmer F 6.00 15.00
SSCW Colin White E 6.00 15.00
SSDH Danton Heinen F 8.00 20.00
SSDS Daniel Sprong F 6.00 15.00
SSEG Erik Gudbranson F 6.00 15.00
SSEK Evander Kane C 10.00 25.00
SSJD Jonathan Drouin E 8.00 20.00
SSJK John Klingberg F 10.00 25.00
SSJM Jake Muzzin E 10.00 25.00
SSJV Jake Virtanen F 8.00 20.00
SSMA Mitch Marner D 15.00 40.00
SSMD Max Domi D 10.00 25.00
SSMG Mark Giordano C 10.00 25.00
SSMZ Mats Zuccarello F 10.00 25.00
SSNB Nick Bjugstad F 6.00 15.00
SSOK Oscar Klefbom F 8.00 20.00
SSPD Pierre-Luc Dubois E 8.00 20.00
SSPM Patrick Marleau B 10.00 25.00
SSPR Patrick Roy A 25.00 60.00
SSRF Radek Faksa F 8.00 20.00
SSRM Ryan Murray F 8.00 20.00
SSSB Sam Bennett F 15.00 40.00
SSTM Timo Meier F 10.00 25.00
SSVA Viktor Arvidsson E 6.00 15.00
SSVE Jimmy Vesey F 8.00 20.00
SSVR Jakub Vrana F 10.00 25.00
SSWG Wayne Gretzky A 200.00 500.00

2019-20 SPx

1 Patrice Bergeron/149 1.00 2.50
2 Viktor Arvidsson/149 .50 1.25
3 Johnny Gaudreau/149 1.25 3.00
4 Ryan Getzlaf/149 .75 2.00
5 Blake Wheeler/149 .75 2.00
6 Elias Pettersson/149 1.25 3.00
7 Matthew Tkachuk/149 1.50 4.00
8 Ryan O'Reilly/149 .75 2.00
9 Connor McDavid/99 12.00 30.00
10 Brent Burns/149 .75 2.00
11 Jonathan Drouin/149 .60 1.50
12 Nikita Kucherov/99 1.50 4.00
13 Claude Giroux/149 .75 2.00
14 Thomas Chabot/149 .75 2.00
15 Seth Jones/149 .75 2.00
16 Clayton Keller/149 1.00 2.50
17 Alex DeBrincat/149 1.00 2.50
18 Mitch Marner/99 1.25 3.00
19 Sean Couturier/149 .60 1.50
20 Mathew Barzal/149 1.00 2.50
21 Matt Murray/149 .75 2.00
22 Roman Josi/149 .75 2.00
23 Cam Atkinson/149 .75 2.00
24 Logan Couture/149 1.00 2.50
25 Henrik Lundqvist/99 2.00 5.00
26 Sebastian Aho/149 1.25 3.00
27 Ben Bishop/149 .60 1.50
28 Auston Matthews/99 3.00 8.00
29 Aleksander Barkov/149 1.25 3.00
30 Carey Price/99 6.00 15.00
31 Nico Hischier/149 1.25 3.00
32 Sidney Crosby/99 12.00 30.00
33 Steven Stamkos/99 1.50 4.00
34 Brad Marchand/99 1.50 4.00
35 Nathan MacKinnon/99 3.00 8.00
36 Marc-Andre Fleury/99 1.50 4.00
37 Tyler Seguin/99 1.00 2.50
38 Alexander Ovechkin/99 3.00 8.00
39 Jack Eichel/149 1.25 3.00
40 Brady Tkachuk/149 1.25 3.00
41 Leon Draisaitl/99 2.50 6.00
42 Vladimir Tarasenko/149 1.00 2.50
43 Mikko Rantanen/149 2.00 5.00
44 Brock Boeser/149 1.00 2.50
45 Dylan Larkin/149 1.00 2.50
46 Eric Staal/149 .75 2.00
47 Patrick Kane/99 1.50 4.00
48 Drew Doughty/149 1.00 2.50
49 Andrei Svechnikov/149 1.00 2.50
50 Connor Hellebuyck/149 1.50 4.00
51 Quinn Hughes/199 RC 12.00 30.00
52 Oliver Wahlstrom/349 RC 4.00 10.00
53 Barrett Hayton/199 RC 5.00 12.00
54 Morgan Frost/199 RC 4.00 10.00
55 Klim Kostin/349 RC 2.50 6.00
56 Noah Dobson/199 RC 6.00 15.00
57 Trevor Moore/349 RC 2.00 5.00
58 Nick Suzuki/199 RC 10.00 25.00
59 Kirby Dach/199 RC 5.00 12.00
60 Emil Bemstrom/349 RC 2.50 6.00
61 Philippe Myers/199 RC 2.00 5.00
62 Libor Hajek/349 RC 2.00 5.00
63 Conor Timmins/349 RC 2.50 6.00
64 Connor Clifton/349 RC 2.50 6.00
65 Adam Fox/199 RC 6.00 15.00
66 Jesper Boqvist/349 RC 2.00 5.00
67 Kaapo Kakko/199 RC 4.00 10.00
68 Ryan Poehling/199 RC 4.00 10.00
69 Martin Fehervary/349 RC 2.00 5.00
70 Max Jones/349 RC 2.50 6.00
71 Nicolas Hague/199 RC 2.50 6.00
72 Mario Ferraro/349 RC 2.00 5.00
73 Joel Farabee/199 RC 4.00 10.00
74 Blake Lizotte/349 RC 2.50 6.00
75 Carl Grundstrom/349 RC 2.50 6.00
76 Rasmus Sandin/199 RC 4.00 10.00
77 Carter Verhaeghe/349 RC 4.00 10.00
78 Trent Frederic/349 RC 2.50 6.00
79 Filip Zadina/199 RC 10.00 25.00
80 Teddy Blueger/349 RC 2.50 6.00
81 Taro Hirose/199 RC 2.50 6.00
82 Adam Boqvist/199 RC 2.50 6.00
83 Cale Makar/199 RC 12.00 30.00
84 German Rubtsov/349 RC 2.00 5.00
85 Alexandre Texier/349 RC 2.50 6.00
86 Dante Fabbro/199 RC 2.50 6.00
87 Cale Fleury/349 RC 3.00 8.00
88 Tobias Bjornfot/349 RC 2.50 6.00
89 Karson Kuhlman/349 RC 2.50 6.00
90 Nikita Gusev/199 RC 4.00 10.00
91 Ilya Mikheyev/199 RC 4.00 10.00
92 Ville Heinola/349 RC 3.00 8.00
93 Joel L'Esperance/349 RC 2.50 6.00
94 Victor Olofsson/199 RC 5.00 12.00
95 Erik Brannstrom/199 RC 2.50 6.00
96 Cody Glass/199 RC 4.00 10.00
97 Vitaly Abramov/349 RC 2.50 6.00
98 Dominik Kubalik/199 RC 5.00 12.00
99 Sam Lafferty/349 RC 2.00 5.00
100 Jack Hughes/199 RC 12.00 30.00

2019-20 SPx '09-10 Retro Rookie Jersey Autographs

*PATCH/25: .5X TO 1.25X BASIC INSERTS
09AF Adam Fox/99 60.00 150.00
09BH Barrett Hayton/99 15.00 40.00
09CG Cody Glass/35 12.00 30.00
09CM Cale Makar/35 60.00 150.00
09FZ Filip Zadina/99 12.00 30.00
09JH Jack Hughes/35 80.00 200.00
09KD Kirby Dach/35 15.00 40.00
09MF Morgan Frost/99 12.00 30.00
09ND Noah Dobson/99 20.00 50.00
09NS Nick Suzuki/99 30.00 80.00
09OW Oliver Wahlstrom/99 25.00 60.00
09QH Quinn Hughes/35 60.00 150.00
09RP Ryan Poehling/35 12.00 30.00
09TH Taro Hirose/99 8.00 20.00
09VO Victor Olofsson/99 15.00 40.00

2019-20 SPx Autographs

2 Viktor Arvidsson E 4.00 10.00
8 Ryan O'Reilly E 6.00 15.00
10 Brent Burns C 6.00 15.00
11 Jonathan Drouin E 5.00 12.00
14 Thomas Chabot E 6.00 15.00
15 Seth Jones E 6.00 15.00
17 Alex DeBrincat E 8.00 20.00
18 Mitch Marner B 10.00 25.00
21 Matt Murray E 6.00 15.00
23 Cam Atkinson D 6.00 15.00
26 Sebastian Aho E 10.00 25.00
27 Ben Bishop E 5.00 12.00
28 Auston Matthews A 25.00 60.00
29 Aleksander Barkov D 10.00 25.00
30 Carey Price A 12.00 30.00
31 Nico Hischier C 15.00 40.00
34 Brad Marchand D 12.00 30.00
36 Marc-Andre Fleury B 12.00 30.00
37 Tyler Seguin C 8.00 20.00
39 Jack Eichel B 10.00 25.00
41 Leon Draisaitl E 12.00 30.00
44 Brock Boeser D 8.00 20.00
45 Dylan Larkin C 8.00 20.00
46 Eric Staal E 6.00 15.00
51 Quinn Hughes/49 40.00 100.00
52 Oliver Wahlstrom/149 12.00 30.00
53 Barrett Hayton/149 15.00 40.00
54 Morgan Frost/149 12.00 30.00
55 Klim Kostin/299 8.00 20.00
56 Noah Dobson/149 20.00 50.00
57 Trevor Moore/299 6.00 15.00
58 Nick Suzuki/49 30.00 80.00
59 Kirby Dach/49 15.00 40.00
60 Emil Bemstrom/299 8.00 20.00
61 Philippe Myers/299 6.00 15.00
62 Libor Hajek/299 6.00 15.00
64 Connor Clifton/299 8.00 20.00
65 Adam Fox/299 40.00 100.00
66 Jesper Boqvist/299 6.00 15.00
68 Ryan Poehling/149 12.00 30.00
69 Martin Fehervary/299 6.00 15.00
70 Max Jones/299 8.00 20.00
71 Nicolas Hague/299 8.00 20.00
72 Mario Ferraro/299 6.00 15.00
73 Joel Farabee/149 12.00 30.00
74 Blake Lizotte/299 8.00 20.00
75 Carl Grundstrom/299 8.00 20.00
76 Rasmus Sandin/299 12.00 30.00
77 Carter Verhaeghe/299 12.00 30.00
78 Trent Frederic/299 8.00 20.00
79 Filip Zadina/149 12.00 30.00
80 Teddy Blueger/299 8.00 20.00
81 Taro Hirose/299 8.00 20.00
82 Adam Boqvist/149 8.00 20.00
83 Cale Makar/49 60.00 150.00
84 German Rubtsov/299 6.00 15.00
85 Alexandre Texier/299 8.00 20.00
86 Dante Fabbro/299 8.00 20.00
88 Tobias Bjornfot/299 8.00 20.00
89 Karson Kuhlman/299 8.00 20.00
90 Nikita Gusev/149 12.00 30.00
91 Ilya Mikheyev/299 12.00 30.00
92 Ville Heinola/299 10.00 25.00
93 Joel L'Esperance/299 8.00 20.00
94 Victor Olofsson/149 15.00 40.00
95 Erik Brannstrom/149 8.00 20.00
96 Cody Glass/149 12.00 30.00
97 Vitaly Abramov/299 8.00 20.00
98 Dominik Kubalik/299 10.00 25.00
99 Sam Lafferty/299 8.00 20.00
100 Jack Hughes/49 50.00 125.00

2019-20 SPx Double XL Duos Materials

XDAS S.Aho/A.Svechnikov 10.00 25.00
XDBN M.Barzal/B.Nelson 5.00 12.00
XDDD M.Domi/J.Drouin 4.00 10.00
XDGM J.Guentzel/E.Malkin 8.00 20.00
XDHH Q.Hughes/J.Hughes 50.00 125.00
XDJD S.Jones/P.Dubois 4.00 10.00
XDKS N.Kucherov/S.Stamkos 8.00 20.00
XDLA D.Larkin/A.Athanasiou 5.00 12.00
XDMD C.McDavid/L.Draisaitl 30.00 80.00
XDMM A.Matthews/M.Marner 15.00 40.00
XDMR N.MacKinnon/M.Rantanen 15.00 40.00
XDOK A.Ovechkin/E.Kuznetsov 15.00 40.00
XDPM D.Pastrnak/C.McAvoy 12.00 30.00
XDSW M.Scheifele/B.Wheeler 6.00 15.00
XDTT M.Tkachuk/B.Tkachuk 8.00 20.00

2019-20 SPx Extravagant Materials

*PATCH/25: .75X TO 2X BASIC INSERTS
EXAD Alex DeBrincat B 2.50 6.00
EXCM Connor McDavid A 10.00 25.00
EXEP Elias Pettersson A 3.00 8.00
EXHU Jonathan Huberdeau B 2.50 6.00
EXJB Jamie Benn B 2.00 5.00
EXJC John Carlson B 2.00 5.00
EXJG John Gibson B 2.00 5.00
EXJH Jack Hughes A 10.00 25.00
EXJT John Tavares A 3.00 8.00
EXJV Jakub Voracek B 1.50 4.00
EXKC Kyle Connor B 3.00 8.00
EXKK Kaapo Kakko A 3.00 8.00
EXMA Cale Makar A 10.00 25.00
EXMF Marc-Andre Fleury B 4.00 10.00
EXPB Patrice Bergeron A 2.50 6.00
EXQH Quinn Hughes A 10.00 25.00
EXRJ Ryan Johansen B 1.50 4.00
EXSC Sidney Crosby A 8.00 20.00
EXTH Taylor Hall A 2.00 5.00
EXTT Teuvo Teravainen B 2.00 5.00

2019-20 SPx Material Autographs Premium

2 Viktor Arvidsson/49 4.00 10.00
10 Brent Burns/25 6.00 15.00
11 Jonathan Drouin/25 5.00 12.00
14 Thomas Chabot/49 6.00 15.00
15 Seth Jones/25 6.00 15.00
16 Clayton Keller/25 8.00 20.00
17 Alex DeBrincat/25 8.00 20.00
21 Matt Murray/49 6.00 15.00
23 Cam Atkinson/25 6.00 15.00
26 Sebastian Aho/49 10.00 25.00
27 Ben Bishop/25 5.00 12.00
29 Aleksander Barkov/25 10.00 25.00
31 Nico Hischier/49 15.00 40.00
37 Tyler Seguin/25 8.00 20.00
39 Jack Eichel/25 10.00 25.00
44 Brock Boeser/49 8.00 20.00
45 Dylan Larkin/25 8.00 20.00
46 Eric Staal/49 6.00 15.00
49 Andrei Svechnikov/49 8.00 20.00
50 Connor Hellebuyck/49 12.00 30.00
51 Quinn Hughes/35 60.00 150.00
52 Oliver Wahlstrom/35 12.00 30.00
53 Barrett Hayton/35 15.00 40.00
54 Morgan Frost/35 12.00 30.00
55 Klim Kostin/35 8.00 20.00
56 Noah Dobson/35 20.00 50.00
57 Trevor Moore/35 6.00 15.00
58 Nick Suzuki/35 60.00 150.00
59 Kirby Dach/35 40.00 100.00
60 Emil Bemstrom/35 8.00 20.00
61 Philippe Myers/35 6.00 15.00
62 Libor Hajek/35 6.00 15.00
65 Adam Fox/35 125.00 300.00
66 Jesper Boqvist/35 10.00 25.00
68 Ryan Poehling/35 12.00 30.00
69 Martin Fehervary/35 6.00 15.00
70 Max Jones/35 8.00 20.00
72 Mario Ferraro/35 6.00 15.00
73 Joel Farabee/35 30.00 80.00
74 Blake Lizotte/35 8.00 20.00
75 Carl Grundstrom/35 8.00 20.00
76 Rasmus Sandin/35 12.00 30.00
77 Carter Verhaeghe/35 12.00 30.00
78 Trent Frederic/35 8.00 20.00
79 Filip Zadina/35 12.00 30.00
80 Teddy Blueger/35 8.00 20.00
81 Taro Hirose/35 8.00 20.00
82 Adam Boqvist/35 25.00 60.00
83 Cale Makar/35 40.00 100.00
84 German Rubtsov/35 6.00 15.00
85 Alexandre Texier/35 8.00 20.00
86 Dante Fabbro/35 8.00 20.00
88 Tobias Bjornfot/35 8.00 20.00
89 Karson Kuhlman/35 8.00 20.00
90 Nikita Gusev/35 12.00 30.00
91 Ilya Mikheyev/35 12.00 30.00
93 Joel L'Esperance/35 8.00 20.00
94 Victor Olofsson/35 15.00 40.00
95 Erik Brannstrom/35 8.00 20.00
96 Cody Glass/35 12.00 30.00
97 Vitaly Abramov/35 8.00 20.00
98 Dominik Kubalik/35 30.00 80.00
99 Sam Lafferty/35 6.00 15.00
100 Jack Hughes/35 125.00 300.00

2019-20 SPx Materials

1 Patrice Bergeron/199 2.50 6.00
2 Viktor Arvidsson/199 1.25 3.00
3 Johnny Gaudreau/199 3.00 8.00
4 Ryan Getzlaf/199 2.00 5.00
5 Blake Wheeler/199 2.00 5.00
6 Elias Pettersson/199 3.00 8.00
7 Matthew Tkachuk/199 4.00 10.00
8 Ryan O'Reilly/199 2.00 5.00
9 Connor McDavid/199 12.00 30.00
10 Brent Burns/199 2.00 5.00
11 Jonathan Drouin/199 1.50 4.00
12 Nikita Kucherov/199 4.00 10.00
13 Claude Giroux/199 2.00 5.00
14 Thomas Chabot/199 2.00 5.00
15 Seth Jones/199 2.00 5.00
16 Clayton Keller/199 2.50 6.00
17 Alex DeBrincat/199 2.50 6.00
18 Mitch Marner/199 3.00 8.00
19 Sean Couturier/199 1.50 4.00
20 Mathew Barzal/199 2.50 6.00
21 Matt Murray/199 2.00 5.00
22 Roman Josi/199 2.00 5.00
23 Cam Atkinson/199 2.00 5.00
24 Logan Couture/199 2.50 6.00
25 Henrik Lundqvist/199 5.00 12.00
26 Sebastian Aho/199 3.00 8.00
27 Ben Bishop/199 1.50 4.00
28 Auston Matthews/199 8.00 20.00
29 Aleksander Barkov/199 3.00 8.00
30 Carey Price/199 4.00 10.00
31 Nico Hischier/199 3.00 8.00
32 Sidney Crosby/199 12.00 30.00
33 Steven Stamkos/199 4.00 10.00
34 Brad Marchand/199 4.00 10.00
35 Nathan MacKinnon/199 8.00 20.00
36 Marc-Andre Fleury/199 4.00 10.00
37 Tyler Seguin/199 2.50 6.00
38 Alexander Ovechkin/199 8.00 20.00
39 Jack Eichel/199 3.00 8.00
40 Brady Tkachuk/199 3.00 8.00
41 Leon Draisaitl/199 6.00 15.00
42 Vladimir Tarasenko/199 2.50 6.00
43 Mikko Rantanen/199 5.00 12.00
44 Brock Boeser/199 2.50 6.00
45 Dylan Larkin/199 2.50 6.00
46 Eric Staal/199 2.00 5.00
47 Patrick Kane/199 4.00 10.00
48 Drew Doughty/199 2.50 6.00
49 Andrei Svechnikov/199 2.50 6.00
50 Connor Hellebuyck/199 4.00 10.00
51 Quinn Hughes/199 10.00 25.00
52 Oliver Wahlstrom/199 3.00 8.00
53 Barrett Hayton/199 4.00 10.00
54 Morgan Frost/199 3.00 8.00
55 Klim Kostin/199 2.00 5.00
56 Noah Dobson/199 5.00 12.00
57 Trevor Moore/399 1.50 4.00
58 Nick Suzuki/199 8.00 20.00
59 Kirby Dach/199 4.00 10.00
60 Emil Bemstrom/399 2.00 5.00
61 Philippe Myers/399 1.50 4.00
62 Libor Hajek/399 1.50 4.00
65 Adam Fox/199 15.00 40.00
66 Jesper Boqvist/199 1.50 4.00
67 Kaapo Kakko/199 3.00 8.00
68 Ryan Poehling/199 3.00 8.00
69 Martin Fehervary/399 1.50 4.00
70 Max Jones/399 2.00 5.00
72 Mario Ferraro/399 1.50 4.00
73 Joel Farabee/199 3.00 8.00
74 Blake Lizotte/199 2.00 5.00
75 Carl Grundstrom/399 2.00 5.00
76 Rasmus Sandin/199 3.00 8.00
77 Carter Verhaeghe/399 3.00 8.00
78 Trent Frederic/399 2.00 5.00
79 Filip Zadina/199 3.00 8.00
80 Teddy Blueger/399 2.00 5.00
81 Taro Hirose/199 2.00 5.00
82 Adam Boqvist/199 2.00 5.00
83 Cale Makar/199 10.00 25.00
84 German Rubtsov/399 1.50 4.00
85 Alexandre Texier/399 2.00 5.00
86 Dante Fabbro/399 2.00 5.00
88 Tobias Bjornfot/399 2.00 5.00
89 Karson Kuhlman/399 2.00 5.00
90 Nikita Gusev/199 3.00 8.00
91 Ilya Mikheyev/199 3.00 8.00
93 Joel L'Esperance/399 2.00 5.00
94 Victor Olofsson/199 4.00 10.00
95 Erik Brannstrom/199 2.00 5.00
96 Cody Glass/199 3.00 8.00
97 Vitaly Abramov/399 2.00 5.00
98 Dominik Kubalik/399 4.00 10.00
99 Sam Lafferty/399 1.50 4.00
100 Jack Hughes/199 10.00 25.00

2019-20 SPx Rookie Superscripts

RSSBH Barrett Hayton C 12.00 30.00
RSSCG Cody Glass B 10.00 25.00
RSSFZ Filip Zadina C 15.00 40.00
RSSJH Jack Hughes B 50.00 125.00
RSSKD Kirby Dach B 12.00 30.00
RSSNS Nick Suzuki B 25.00 60.00
RSSRS Rasmus Sandin C 10.00 25.00

2019-20 SPx Shadow Box

SAV Andrei Vasilevskiy 5.00 12.00
SBB Brent Burns 3.00 8.00
SBM Brad Marchand 6.00 15.00
SCM Connor McDavid 15.00 40.00
SJE Jack Eichel 5.00 12.00
SJT John Tavares 5.00 12.00
SMS Mark Scheifele 5.00 12.00
SRO Ryan O'Reilly 3.00 8.00
SSC Sidney Crosby 20.00 50.00

2019-20 SPx Shadow Box Autographs

SBB Brent Burns/49 10.00 25.00
SBM Brad Marchand/49 20.00 50.00
SRO Ryan O'Reilly/99 25.00 60.00

2019-20 SPx Shadow Box Rookie Autographs

SAF Adam Fox/150 40.00 100.00
SAT Alexandre Texier/150 10.00 25.00
SBH Barrett Hayton/150 20.00 50.00
SCG Cody Glass/150 15.00 40.00
SDF Dante Fabbro/150 10.00 25.00
SDK Dominik Kubalik/150 40.00 100.00
SEB Erik Brannstrom/150 10.00 25.00
SJB Jesper Boqvist/150 8.00 20.00
SJH Jack Hughes/75 60.00 150.00
SKD Kirby Dach/150 20.00 50.00
SMA Cale Makar/75 50.00 125.00
SMJ Max Jones/150 10.00 25.00
SNG Nikita Gusev/150 15.00 40.00
SNS Nick Suzuki/150 40.00 100.00
SOW Oliver Wahlstrom/150 15.00 40.00
SPM Philippe Myers/150 8.00 20.00
SQH Quinn Hughes/75 80.00 200.00
SRP Ryan Poehling/75 15.00 40.00
SRS Rasmus Sandin/150 15.00 40.00
STB Tobias Bjornfot/150 10.00 25.00
STH Taro Hirose/150 10.00 25.00
SVO Victor Olofsson/150 15.00 40.00

2019-20 SPx Shadow Box Rookies

SAF Adam Fox 10.00 25.00
SAT Alexandre Texier 4.00 10.00
SBH Barrett Hayton 8.00 20.00
SCG Cody Glass 6.00 15.00
SDF Dante Fabbro 4.00 10.00
SDK Dominik Kubalik 8.00 20.00
SEB Erik Brannstrom 4.00 10.00
SFZ Filip Zadina 6.00 15.00
SJB Jesper Boqvist 3.00 8.00
SJH Jack Hughes 20.00 50.00
SKD Kirby Dach 8.00 20.00
SKK Kaapo Kakko 6.00 15.00
SMA Cale Makar 20.00 50.00
SMJ Max Jones 4.00 10.00
SNG Nikita Gusev 6.00 15.00
SNS Nick Suzuki 15.00 40.00
SOW Oliver Wahlstrom 6.00 15.00
SPM Philippe Myers 3.00 8.00
SQH Quinn Hughes 20.00 50.00
SRP Ryan Poehling 6.00 15.00
SRS Rasmus Sandin 6.00 15.00
STB Tobias Bjornfot 4.00 10.00
STH Taro Hirose 4.00 10.00
SVO Victor Olofsson 8.00 20.00

2019-20 SPx Superscripts

*GOLD: .50X TO 1.25X BASIC INSERTS
SSAI Arturs Irbe E 8.00 20.00
SSAT Alex Tuch E 10.00 25.00
SSBB Brent Burns B 10.00 25.00
SSBN Bernie Nicholls D 8.00 20.00
SSBP Brayden Point D 12.00 30.00
SSBR Brock Boeser B 12.00 30.00
SSCA Cam Atkinson C 10.00 25.00
SSCM Connor McDavid A 100.00 250.00
SSDG Dirk Graham D 8.00 20.00
SSDH Danton Heinen D 8.00 20.00
SSDN Darnell Nurse D 8.00 20.00
SSDS Dylan Strome C 12.00 30.00
SSHL Henrik Lundqvist A 25.00 60.00
SSJG Jake Guentzel E 15.00 40.00
SSJK John Klingberg C 10.00 25.00
SSKF Kevin Fiala D 8.00 20.00
SSKM Kirk McLean D 8.00 20.00
SSKP Kyle Palmieri E 8.00 20.00
SSMD Matt Dumba C 6.00 15.00
SSMG Mikael Granlund D 8.00 20.00
SSMH Miro Heiskanen D 12.00 30.00
SSML Mike Liut E 6.00 15.00
SSMU Matt Murray D 10.00 25.00
SSPR Patrick Roy A 40.00 100.00
SSRA Bill Ranford E 8.00 20.00
SSSA Sebastian Aho C 8.00 20.00
SSSC Shayne Corson E 8.00 20.00
SSST Shea Theodore E 12.00 30.00
SSTB Tyler Bertuzzi E 8.00 20.00
SSTJ Tyson Jost B 8.00 20.00
SSTT Teuvo Teravainen D 10.00 25.00
SSYG Yanni Gourde E 8.00 20.00

2020-21 SPx

1 Connor McDavid 10.00 25.00
2 Alex Ovechkin 3.00 8.00
3 Travis Konecny .75 2.00
4 Brayden Point 1.00 2.50
5 John Tavares 1.25 3.00
6 Brock Boeser 1.00 2.50
7 Brady Tkachuk 1.25 3.00
8 Ryan Nugent-Hopkins 1.00 2.50
9 J.T. Miller 1.00 2.50
10 Artemi Panarin 1.50 4.00
11 Anze Kopitar 1.25 3.00
12 Alex DeBrincat 1.00 2.50
13 Johnny Gaudreau 1.25 3.00
14 Sean Couturier .60 1.50
15 Ryan Getzlaf .75 2.00
16 Aleksander Barkov 1.25 3.00
17 Clayton Keller 1.00 2.50
18 Pierre-Luc Dubois .60 1.50
19 Jonathan Toews 1.25 3.00
20 Sebastian Aho 1.25 3.00
21 Niklas Hjalmarsson .50 1.25
22 Kevin Fiala .60 1.50
23 Sam Reinhart 1.50 4.00
24 Kaapo Kakko .60 1.50
25 David Pastrnak 2.00 5.00
26 Blake Wheeler .75 2.00
27 Anders Lee .60 1.50
28 Claude Giroux .75 2.00
29 Leon Draisaitl 2.50 6.00
30 Robert Thomas .75 2.00
31 Carey Price 1.50 4.00
32 Jack Eichel 1.25 3.00
33 David Rittich .60 1.50
34 Auston Matthews 3.00 8.00
35 Pekka Rinne .75 2.00
36 John Gibson .75 2.00
37 Andrei Svechnikov 1.00 2.50
38 Nico Hischier 1.25 3.00
39 Mathew Barzal 1.00 2.50
40 Elias Pettersson 1.25 3.00
41 Joe Pavelski 1.00 2.50
42 Nikita Kucherov 1.50 4.00
43 Quinn Hughes 2.00 5.00
44 Miro Heiskanen 1.00 2.50
45 Logan Couture 1.00 2.50
46 Brent Burns .75 2.00
47 Frederik Andersen 1.00 2.50
48 Thomas Chabot .75 2.00
49 Adam Fox 1.00 2.50
50 Jordan Binnington 1.25 3.00
51 Matthew Tkachuk 1.50 4.00
52 Teuvo Teravainen .75 2.00
53 Bo Horvat 1.00 2.50
54 Shea Theodore 1.00 2.50
55 Mark Scheifele 1.25 3.00
56 Mark Giordano .75 2.00
57 Dustin Brown .75 2.00
58 Zach Hyman 1.25 3.00
59 Tyler Bertuzzi .60 1.50
60 Drew Doughty 1.00 2.50
61 Mark Stone 1.00 2.50
62 Dominik Kubalik .75 2.00
63 Brad Marchand 1.50 4.00
64 Nick Schmaltz .60 1.50
65 Jake Guentzel 1.25 3.00
66 William Karlsson 1.00 2.50
67 Tomas Hertl .75 2.00
68 Andrei Vasilevskiy 1.25 3.00
69 Jakub Vrana .75 2.00
70 Nikita Gusev .60 1.50
71 Evgeni Malkin 1.50 4.00
72 Sergei Bobrovsky 1.25 3.00
73 Nick Suzuki 1.50 4.00
74 James van Riemsdyk .60 1.50
75 Eric Staal .75 2.00
76 Seth Jones .75 2.00
77 Dylan Larkin 1.00 2.50
78 Cam Atkinson .75 2.00
79 Carter Hart .75 2.00
80 Cale Makar 2.00 5.00
81 Brendan Gallagher .75 2.00
82 Roman Josi .75 2.00
83 Kyle Connor 1.25 3.00
84 John Carlson .75 2.00
85 Patrice Bergeron 1.00 2.50
86 Jack Hughes 2.00 5.00
87 Sidney Crosby 10.00 25.00
88 Patrick Kane 1.50 4.00
89 Elvis Merzlikins .75 2.00
90 Ryan O'Reilly .75 2.00
91 Steven Stamkos 1.50 4.00
92 Nathan MacKinnon 3.00 8.00
93 Tyler Seguin 1.00 2.50
94 Dougie Hamilton .60 1.50
95 Phillip Danault .75 2.00
96 Mackenzie Blackwood .75 2.00
97 Max Pacioretty .75 2.00
98 Mitch Marner 1.25 3.00
99 Zach Parise .75 2.00
100 Vladimir Tarasenko 1.00 2.50

2020-21 SPx Autographs

1 Connor McDavid A 150.00 400.00
5 John Tavares A 12.00 30.00
8 Ryan Nugent-Hopkins D 10.00 25.00
9 J.T. Miller D 10.00 25.00
11 Anze Kopitar C 12.00 30.00
16 Aleksander Barkov B 12.00 30.00
19 Jonathan Toews A 12.00 30.00
21 Niklas Hjalmarsson D 5.00 12.00
23 Sam Reinhart D 15.00 40.00
27 Anders Lee B 6.00 15.00
29 Leon Draisaitl A 25.00 60.00
31 Carey Price A 30.00 80.00
35 Pekka Rinne D 8.00 20.00
36 John Gibson C 8.00 20.00
37 Andrei Svechnikov E 10.00 25.00
38 Nico Hischier C 12.00 30.00
41 Joe Pavelski D 10.00 25.00
44 Miro Heiskanen E 10.00 25.00
46 Brent Burns B 8.00 20.00
49 Adam Fox C 20.00 50.00
52 Teuvo Teravainen E 8.00 20.00
54 Shea Theodore D 10.00 25.00
55 Mark Scheifele B 12.00 30.00
56 Mark Giordano D 8.00 20.00
57 Dustin Brown D 8.00 20.00
58 Zach Hyman E 12.00 30.00
62 Dominik Kubalik E 8.00 20.00
63 Brad Marchand C 15.00 40.00
65 Jake Guentzel D 12.00 30.00
66 William Karlsson B 10.00 25.00
68 Andrei Vasilevskiy C 12.00 30.00
69 Jakub Vrana D 8.00 20.00
70 Nikita Gusev C 6.00 15.00
72 Sergei Bobrovsky C 12.00 30.00
73 Nick Suzuki C 20.00 50.00
74 James van Riemsdyk C 6.00 15.00
75 Eric Staal E 8.00 20.00
78 Cam Atkinson D 8.00 20.00
81 Brendan Gallagher A 8.00 20.00
82 Roman Josi A 8.00 20.00
89 Elvis Merzlikins E 8.00 20.00
93 Tyler Seguin B 10.00 25.00
94 Dougie Hamilton E 6.00 15.00
95 Phillip Danault D 8.00 20.00

2020-21 SPx Double XL Duos Materials

XDBO A.Ovechkin/N.Backstrom/49 10.00 25.00
XDBP P.Bergeron/D.Pastrnak/49 10.00 25.00
XDCT B.Tkachuk/T.Chabot/99 6.00 15.00
XDHH K.Hayes/C.Hart/99 4.00 10.00
XDMM N.MacKinnon/C.Makar/49 15.00 40.00
XDNT T.Teravainen/N.Niederreiter/99 4.00 10.00
XDPW C.Price/S.Weber/99 8.00 20.00
XDTM A.Matthews/J.Tavares/49 15.00 40.00
XDZP A.Panarin/M.Zibanejad/49 8.00 20.00

2020-21 SPx Extravagant Materials

EXAL Alexis Lafreniere 20.00 50.00
EXAM Auston Matthews 8.00 20.00
EXAO Alex Ovechkin 8.00 20.00
EXCM Connor McDavid 10.00 25.00
EXDP David Pastrnak 5.00 12.00
EXJE Jack Eichel 3.00 8.00
EXJG Johnny Gaudreau 3.00 8.00
EXKK Kirill Kaprizov 30.00 80.00
EXMZ Mika Zibanejad 2.50 6.00
EXNM Nathan MacKinnon 8.00 20.00
EXPK Patrick Kane 4.00 10.00
EXSS Steven Stamkos 4.00 10.00
EXTR Tuukka Rask 2.50 6.00
EXTS Tim Stutzle 5.00 12.00

2020-21 SPx Finite Rookies

*SPECTRUM/35: .6X TO 1.5X BASIC
F1 Kirill Kaprizov 12.00 30.00
F2 Alexander Alexeyev 2.50 6.00
F3 Mikhail Berdin 3.00 8.00
F4 Martin Kaut 3.00 8.00
F5 Connor McMichael 5.00 12.00
F6 Morgan Geekie 3.00 8.00
F7 Bowen Byram 6.00 15.00
F8 Philipp Kurashev 4.00 10.00
F9 Pavel Francouz 4.00 10.00
F10 Jason Robertson 8.00 20.00
F11 Mikey Anderson 3.00 8.00
F12 Thomas Harley 5.00 12.00
F13 Timothy Liljegren 3.00 8.00
F14 Tyler Benson 3.00 8.00
F15 Shane Bowers 2.50 6.00
F16 Vitali Kravtsov 6.00 15.00
F17 Nick Robertson 5.00 12.00
F18 Ty Dellandrea 3.00 8.00
F19 Egor Zamula 2.50 6.00
F20 Josh Norris 5.00 12.00
F21 Gabe Vilardi 5.00 12.00
F22 Dylan Cozens 5.00 12.00
F23 Ilya Sorokin 8.00 20.00
F24 Michael DiPietro 4.00 10.00
F25 Philip Broberg 12.00 30.00
F26 Kieffer Bellows 2.50 6.00
F27 Peyton Krebs 8.00 20.00
F28 Liam Foudy 3.00 8.00
F29 Victor Soderstrom 2.50 6.00
F30 Alexis Lafreniere 10.00 25.00

2020-21 SPx Jerseys

1 Connor McDavid 10.00 25.00
2 Alex Ovechkin 8.00 20.00
3 Travis Konecny 2.00 5.00
4 Brayden Point 2.50 6.00
5 John Tavares 3.00 8.00
6 Brock Boeser 2.50 6.00
7 Brady Tkachuk 3.00 8.00
8 Ryan Nugent-Hopkins 2.50 6.00
9 J.T. Miller 2.50 6.00
10 Artemi Panarin 4.00 10.00
11 Anze Kopitar 3.00 8.00
12 Alex DeBrincat 2.50 6.00
13 Johnny Gaudreau 3.00 8.00
14 Sean Couturier 1.50 4.00
15 Ryan Getzlaf 2.00 5.00
16 Aleksander Barkov 3.00 8.00
17 Clayton Keller 2.50 6.00
19 Jonathan Toews 3.00 8.00
20 Sebastian Aho 3.00 8.00
21 Niklas Hjalmarsson 1.25 3.00
23 Sam Reinhart 4.00 10.00
24 Kaapo Kakko 1.50 4.00
25 David Pastrnak 5.00 12.00
26 Blake Wheeler 2.00 5.00
27 Anders Lee 1.50 4.00
28 Claude Giroux 2.00 5.00
29 Leon Draisaitl 6.00 15.00
30 Robert Thomas 2.00 5.00
31 Carey Price 4.00 10.00
32 Jack Eichel 3.00 8.00
34 Auston Matthews 8.00 20.00
35 Pekka Rinne 2.00 5.00
36 John Gibson 2.00 5.00
37 Andrei Svechnikov 2.50 6.00
38 Nico Hischier 3.00 8.00
39 Mathew Barzal 2.50 6.00
40 Elias Pettersson 3.00 8.00
41 Joe Pavelski 2.50 6.00
42 Nikita Kucherov 4.00 10.00
43 Quinn Hughes 5.00 12.00
44 Miro Heiskanen 2.50 6.00
45 Logan Couture 2.50 6.00
46 Brent Burns 2.00 5.00
47 Frederik Andersen 2.50 6.00
48 Thomas Chabot 2.00 5.00
49 Adam Fox 2.50 6.00
50 Jordan Binnington 3.00 8.00
51 Matthew Tkachuk 4.00 10.00
52 Teuvo Teravainen 2.00 5.00
53 Bo Horvat 2.50 6.00
54 Shea Theodore 2.50 6.00
55 Mark Scheifele 3.00 8.00
56 Mark Giordano 2.00 5.00
57 Dustin Brown 2.00 5.00
58 Zach Hyman 3.00 8.00
59 Tyler Bertuzzi 1.50 4.00
60 Drew Doughty 2.50 6.00
61 Mark Stone 2.50 6.00
63 Brad Marchand 4.00 10.00
64 Nick Schmaltz 1.50 4.00
65 Jake Guentzel 3.00 8.00
66 William Karlsson 2.50 6.00
67 Tomas Hertl 2.00 5.00
68 Andrei Vasilevskiy 3.00 8.00
69 Jakub Vrana 2.00 5.00
70 Nikita Gusev 1.50 4.00
71 Evgeni Malkin 4.00 10.00
72 Sergei Bobrovsky 3.00 8.00
74 James van Riemsdyk 1.50 4.00
76 Seth Jones 2.00 5.00
77 Dylan Larkin 2.50 6.00
78 Cam Atkinson 2.00 5.00
79 Carter Hart 2.00 5.00
80 Cale Makar 5.00 12.00
81 Brendan Gallagher 2.00 5.00
82 Roman Josi 2.00 5.00
83 Kyle Connor 3.00 8.00
84 John Carlson 2.00 5.00
85 Patrice Bergeron 2.50 6.00
86 Jack Hughes 5.00 12.00
87 Sidney Crosby 8.00 20.00
88 Patrick Kane 4.00 10.00

90 Ryan O'Reilly 2.00 5.00
91 Steven Stamkos 4.00 10.00
92 Nathan MacKinnon 8.00 20.00
93 Tyler Seguin 2.50 6.00
94 Dougie Hamilton 1.50 4.00
98 Mitch Marner 3.00 8.00
99 Zach Parise 2.00 5.00
100 Vladimir Tarasenko 2.50 6.00

2020-21 SPx Rookie Jersey Autographs

*GOLD: .5X TO 1.25X BASIC
AB Alex Belzile/375 8.00 20.00
AL Alexis Lafreniere/75 150.00 400.00
AN Anthony Angello/375 8.00 20.00
AR Alexander Romanov/165 40.00 100.00
AT Alexander True/375 8.00 20.00
AY Alexander Yelesin/375 8.00 20.00
BB Bowen Byram/165 30.00 80.00
BH Brandon Hagel/375 12.00 30.00
CI Connor Ingram/375 8.00 20.00
CM Connor McMichael/165 30.00 80.00
CT Calvin Thurkauf/375 8.00 20.00
DC Dylan Cozens/165 60.00 150.00
GL Gustav Lindstrom/375 8.00 20.00
GQ Gage Quinney/375 6.00 15.00
GV Gabe Vilardi/375 15.00 40.00
IS Ilya Sorokin/165 60.00 150.00
JE Jake Evans/375 10.00 25.00
JH Jani Hakanpaa/375 6.00 15.00
JJ Jonas Johansson/375 10.00 25.00
JN Josh Norris/165 40.00 100.00
JR Jason Robertson/375 25.00 60.00
KA Martin Kaut/375 10.00 25.00
KB Kieffer Bellows/375 8.00 20.00
KK Kirill Kaprizov/165 150.00 400.00
KO Keegan Kolesar/375 8.00 20.00
KR Peyton Krebs/165 15.00 40.00
LC Lucas Carlsson/375 8.00 20.00
LF Liam Foudy/375 10.00 25.00
MA Mikey Anderson/375 10.00 25.00
MG Morgan Geekie/375 10.00 25.00
MK Matiss Kivlenieks/375 40.00 100.00
ML Maxim Letunov/375 8.00 20.00
NB Nicolas Beaudin/375 10.00 25.00
NH Nils Hoglander/165 40.00 100.00
NK Nikolai Knyzhov/375 8.00 20.00
NR Nick Robertson/165 15.00 40.00
OJ Olli Juolevi/375 10.00 25.00
PJ Pierre-Olivier Joseph/375 10.00 25.00
RM Ryan McLeod/375 8.00 20.00
SB Shane Bowers/375 8.00 20.00
TB Tyler Benson/375 10.00 25.00
TD Ty Dellandrea/165 10.00 25.00
TH Thomas Harley/375 15.00 40.00
TL Timothy Liljegren/375 10.00 25.00
TS Tim Stutzle/165 60.00 150.00
VS Victor Soderstrom/375 8.00 20.00

2020-21 SPx Rookie Jerseys

RJAA Alexander Alexeyev 2.50 6.00
RJAB Alex Belzile 2.50 6.00
RJAK Arthur Kaliyev 5.00 12.00
RJAL Alexis Lafreniere 25.00 60.00
RJAN Anthony Angello 2.50 6.00
RJAR Alexander Romanov 4.00 10.00
RJAY Alexander Yelesin 2.50 6.00
RJBB Bowen Byram 6.00 15.00
RJBH Brandon Hagel 4.00 10.00
RJCI Connor Ingram 2.50 6.00
RJCM Connor McMichael 5.00 12.00
RJCT Calvin Thurkauf 2.50 6.00
RJDC Dylan Cozens 5.00 12.00
RJEK Egor Korshkov 2.00 5.00
RJGL Gustav Lindstrom 2.50 6.00
RJGQ Gage Quinney 2.00 5.00
RJGV Gabe Vilardi 5.00 12.00
RJIS Ilya Sorokin 8.00 20.00
RJJE Jake Evans 3.00 8.00
RJJH Jani Hakanpaa 2.00 5.00
RJJJ Jonas Johansson 3.00 8.00
RJJN Josh Norris 5.00 12.00
RJJR Jason Robertson 8.00 20.00
RJKA Kirill Kaprizov 30.00 80.00
RJKB Kieffer Bellows 2.50 6.00
RJKI Matiss Kivlenieks 8.00 20.00
RJKK Keegan Kolesar 2.50 6.00
RJKM K'Andre Miller 6.00 15.00
RJKR Peyton Krebs 5.00 12.00
RJLC Lucas Carlsson 2.50 6.00
RJLF Liam Foudy 3.00 8.00
RJMA Mikey Anderson 3.00 8.00
RJMG Morgan Geekie 3.00 8.00
RJMK Martin Kaut 3.00 8.00
RJML Maxim Letunov 2.50 6.00
RJNB Nicolas Beaudin 3.00 8.00
RJNH Nils Hoglander 3.00 8.00
RJNK Nikolai Knyzhov 2.50 6.00
RJNR Nick Robertson 5.00 12.00
RJOJ Olli Juolevi 3.00 8.00
RJPJ Pierre-Olivier Joseph 3.00 8.00
RJPK Philipp Kurashev 4.00 10.00
RJRM Ryan McLeod 2.50 6.00
RJSB Shane Bowers 2.50 6.00
RJTB Tyler Benson 3.00 8.00
RJTD Ty Dellandrea 3.00 8.00
RJTH Thomas Harley 5.00 12.00
RJTL Timothy Liljegren 3.00 8.00
RJTR Alexander True 2.50 6.00
RJVS Victor Soderstrom 2.50 6.00

2020-21 SPx Rookie Jerseys Gold Spectrum

*GOLD/99: .5X TO 1.25X BASIC
RJAL Alexis Lafreniere 40.00 100.00
RJJR Jason Robertson 10.00 25.00
RJKA Kirill Kaprizov 60.00 150.00

2020-21 SPx Rookie Superscript

RSAR Alexander Romanov B 12.00 30.00
RSBB Bowen Byram C 20.00 50.00
RSDC Dylan Cozens B 15.00 40.00
RSKK Kirill Kaprizov A 400.00 1000.00
RSLF Liam Foudy D 10.00 25.00
RSNR Nick Robertson C 15.00 40.00
RSPK Peyton Krebs C 15.00 40.00
RSTD Ty Dellandrea D 12.00 30.00

2020-21 SPx Shadow Box

SB1 Alexis Lafreniere 60.00 150.00
SB2 Alexander Romanov 6.00 15.00
SB3 Bowen Byram 20.00 50.00
SB4 Dylan Cozens 15.00 40.00
SB5 Kirill Kaprizov 60.00 150.00
SB6 Ilya Sorokin 12.00 30.00
SB7 Ty Smith 8.00 20.00
SB8 K'Andre Miller 20.00 50.00
SB9 Connor McMichael 8.00 20.00
SB10 Josh Norris 8.00 20.00
SB11 Gabe Vilardi 8.00 20.00
SB12 Philipp Kurashev 6.00 15.00
SB13 Nick Robertson 8.00 20.00
SB14 Peyton Krebs 8.00 20.00
SB15 Victor Soderstrom 4.00 10.00
SB16 Ty Dellandrea 5.00 12.00
SB17 Timothy Liljegren 5.00 12.00
SB18 Alexander Alexeyev 4.00 10.00
SB19 Jason Robertson 12.00 30.00
SB20 Liam Foudy 5.00 12.00
SB21 Kieffer Bellows 4.00 10.00
SB22 Morgan Geekie 5.00 12.00
SB23 Martin Kaut 5.00 12.00
SB24 Tyler Benson 5.00 12.00
SB25 Cale Makar 10.00 25.00
SB26 Roman Josi 4.00 10.00
SB27 Aleksander Barkov 6.00 15.00
SB28 Andrei Svechnikov 5.00 12.00
SB29 Carey Price 8.00 20.00
SB30 Tomas Hertl 4.00 10.00
SB31 Elias Pettersson 6.00 15.00
SB32 Auston Matthews 15.00 40.00
SB33 Connor McDavid 20.00 50.00

2020-21 SPx Superscript

*GOLD/25: .75X TO 2X BASIC
SAB Aleksander Barkov B 15.00 40.00
SAF Adam Fox E 12.00 30.00
SAS Andrei Svechnikov D 12.00 30.00
SAV Andrei Vasilevskiy E 15.00 40.00
SBB Brock Boeser A 12.00 30.00
SBG Brendan Gallagher A 10.00 25.00
SBO Adam Boqvist D 8.00 20.00
SCH Connor Hellebuyck B 20.00 50.00
SDH Dany Heatley D 8.00 20.00
SDK Dominik Kubalik E 10.00 25.00
SDW Doug Wilson E 8.00 20.00
SES Eric Staal E 10.00 25.00
SFP Felix Potvin D 15.00 40.00
SJL John LeClair C 10.00 25.00
SJS Jaccob Slavin D 8.00 20.00
SJV James van Riemsdyk B 8.00 20.00
SMF Mike Fisher C 6.00 15.00
SMG Mark Giordano E 10.00 25.00
SMR Mike Richter D 10.00 25.00
SMS Mark Scheifele E 15.00 40.00
SPB Peter Bondra B 10.00 25.00
SPD Phillip Danault D 10.00 25.00
SRI Pekka Rinne D 10.00 25.00
SRJ Roman Josi A 10.00 25.00
SSE Mikhail Sergachev C 8.00 20.00
SWC Wendel Clark A 15.00 40.00
SZH Zach Hyman D 15.00 40.00

2021-22 SPx

1 Kirill Kaprizov 2.50 6.00
2 Dylan Larkin 1.00 2.50
3 Jonathan Toews 1.25 3.00
4 Miro Heiskanen 1.00 2.50
5 Cam Atkinson .75 2.00
6 Jakob Chychrun .75 2.00
7 Jordan Eberle .75 2.00
8 Alex Ovechkin 3.00 8.00
9 Jack Roslovic .50 1.25
10 Artemi Panarin 1.50 4.00
11 Jonathan Huberdeau 1.00 2.50
12 Alex DeBrincat 1.00 2.50
13 Alexis Lafreniere 1.25 3.00
14 Johnny Gaudreau 1.25 3.00
15 Dylan Strome 1.00 2.50
16 Joe Pavelski 1.00 2.50
17 Josh Anderson .60 1.50
18 Matthew Tkachuk 1.50 4.00
19 Nicklas Backstrom .75 2.00
20 Sebastian Aho 1.25 3.00
21 Jason Robertson 1.25 3.00
22 Keith Yandle .50 1.25
23 Pius Suter .60 1.50
24 Dylan Cozens .75 2.00
25 Nils Hoglander .60 1.50
26 Kyle Palmieri .60 1.50
27 Brayden Point 1.00 2.50
28 Aleksander Barkov 1.25 3.00
29 Nathan MacKinnon 3.00 8.00
30 Marc-Andre Fleury 1.50 4.00
31 Philipp Grubauer .75 2.00
32 Casey Mittelstadt .75 2.00
33 Cam Talbot .75 2.00
34 Auston Matthews 3.00 8.00
35 Tristan Jarry .75 2.00
36 John Gibson .75 2.00
37 Patrice Bergeron 1.00 2.50
38 Yanni Gourde .60 1.50
39 Alex Nedeljkovic .60 1.50
40 Elias Pettersson 1.25 3.00
41 Anze Kopitar 1.25 3.00
42 Gabe Vilardi .75 2.00
43 Quinn Hughes 2.00 5.00
44 Maxime Comtois .60 1.50
45 Josh Morrissey 1.00 2.50
46 Bowen Byram 1.00 2.50
47 Nick Suzuki 1.50 4.00
48 Yegor Sharangovich .75 2.00
49 Drake Batherson .75 2.00
50 Jordan Binnington 1.25 3.00
51 Brock Boeser 1.00 2.50
52 Eeli Tolvanen .75 2.00
53 Jared Spurgeon .75 2.00
54 Mathew Barzal 1.00 2.50
55 Mark Scheifele 1.25 3.00
56 Jordan Kyrou .75 2.00
57 Teuvo Teravainen .75 2.00
58 Devon Toews .60 1.50
59 Tyler Bertuzzi .60 1.50
60 Erik Karlsson 1.00 2.50
61 Max Pacioretty .75 2.00
62 Joel Farabee .75 2.00
63 Brad Marchand 1.50 4.00
64 Aaron Ekblad 1.00 2.50
65 Oliver Wahlstrom .50 1.25
66 Tim Stutzle 1.00 2.50
67 Brent Burns .75 2.00
68 Carter Hart .75 2.00
69 Anthony Cirelli .60 1.50
70 Adam Fox 1.00 2.50
71 Taylor Hall .75 2.00
72 Joonas Donskoi .50 1.25
73 Mitch Marner 1.25 3.00
74 Brady Tkachuk 1.25 3.00
75 K'Andre Miller .60 1.50
76 Kris Letang 1.00 2.50
77 David Pastrnak 2.00 5.00
78 Cale Makar 2.00 5.00
79 Evgeni Malkin 1.50 4.00
80 Robin Lehner .60 1.50
81 Jonathan Marchessault 1.00 2.50
82 Phil Kessel .75 2.00
83 Anthony Beauvillier .50 1.25
84 William Karlsson 1.00 2.50
85 Ryan Nugent-Hopkins 1.00 2.50
86 Jack Hughes 2.00 5.00
87 Sidney Crosby 3.00 8.00
88 Patrick Kane 1.50 4.00
89 Connor Hellebuyck 1.50 4.00
90 Ryan O'Reilly .75 2.00
91 John Tavares 1.25 3.00
92 Roman Josi .75 2.00
93 Andrei Svechnikov 1.00 2.50
94 Mark Stone 1.00 2.50
95 Carey Price 1.50 4.00
96 Mikko Rantanen 2.00 5.00
97 Connor McDavid 4.00 10.00
98 Nikita Kucherov 1.50 4.00
99 Andrei Vasilevskiy 1.25 3.00
100 Leon Draisaitl 2.50 6.00

2021-22 SPx Autographs

4 Miro Heiskanen C 10.00 25.00
5 Cam Atkinson F 8.00 20.00
7 Jordan Eberle F 8.00 20.00
9 Jack Roslovic G 5.00 12.00
11 Jonathan Huberdeau E 10.00 25.00
13 Alexis Lafreniere C 12.00 30.00
15 Dylan Strome G 10.00 25.00
16 Joe Pavelski E 10.00 25.00
18 Matthew Tkachuk E 15.00 40.00
21 Jason Robertson E 12.00 30.00
23 Pius Suter G 6.00 15.00
24 Dylan Cozens E 8.00 20.00
25 Nils Hoglander G 6.00 15.00
26 Kyle Palmieri G 6.00 15.00
28 Aleksander Barkov D 12.00 30.00
30 Marc-Andre Fleury B 15.00 40.00
31 Philipp Grubauer E 8.00 20.00
33 Cam Talbot E 8.00 20.00
34 Auston Matthews A 80.00 200.00
38 Yanni Gourde F 6.00 15.00
39 Alex Nedeljkovic F 6.00 15.00
41 Anze Kopitar B 12.00 30.00
42 Gabe Vilardi G 8.00 20.00
43 Quinn Hughes D 20.00 50.00
44 Maxime Comtois F 6.00 15.00
45 Josh Morrissey G 10.00 25.00
46 Bowen Byram F 10.00 25.00
48 Yegor Sharangovich G 8.00 20.00
49 Drake Batherson F 8.00 20.00
51 Brock Boeser E 10.00 25.00
58 Devon Toews F 6.00 15.00
59 Tyler Bertuzzi F 6.00 15.00
61 Max Pacioretty C 8.00 20.00
63 Brad Marchand E 15.00 40.00
66 Tim Stutzle D 20.00 50.00
67 Brent Burns E 8.00 20.00
68 Carter Hart D 8.00 20.00
74 Brady Tkachuk E 12.00 30.00
75 K'Andre Miller G 6.00 15.00
76 Kris Letang D 10.00 25.00
78 Cale Makar A 20.00 50.00
83 Anthony Beauvillier F 5.00 12.00
85 Ryan Nugent-Hopkins C 10.00 25.00
89 Connor Hellebuyck F 15.00 40.00
91 John Tavares A 12.00 30.00
92 Roman Josi B 8.00 20.00
93 Andrei Svechnikov E 10.00 25.00
94 Mark Stone C 10.00 25.00
95 Carey Price B 30.00 80.00
97 Connor McDavid A 150.00 400.00
99 Andrei Vasilevskiy B 12.00 30.00
100 Leon Draisaitl A 25.00 60.00

2021-22 SPx Base Jerseys

1 Kirill Kaprizov 8.00 20.00
2 Dylan Larkin 3.00 8.00
3 Jonathan Toews 4.00 10.00
4 Miro Heiskanen 3.00 8.00
5 Cam Atkinson 2.50 6.00
6 Jakob Chychrun 2.50 6.00
7 Jordan Eberle 2.50 6.00
8 Alex Ovechkin 10.00 25.00
9 Jack Roslovic 1.50 4.00
10 Artemi Panarin 5.00 12.00
11 Jonathan Huberdeau 3.00 8.00
12 Alex DeBrincat 3.00 8.00
13 Alexis Lafreniere 4.00 10.00
14 Johnny Gaudreau 4.00 10.00
15 Dylan Strome 3.00 8.00
16 Joe Pavelski 3.00 8.00
17 Josh Anderson 2.00 5.00
18 Matthew Tkachuk 5.00 12.00
19 Nicklas Backstrom 2.50 6.00
20 Sebastian Aho 4.00 10.00
21 Jason Robertson 4.00 10.00
24 Dylan Cozens 2.50 6.00
27 Brayden Point 3.00 8.00
28 Aleksander Barkov 4.00 10.00
29 Nathan MacKinnon 10.00 25.00
30 Marc-Andre Fleury 5.00 12.00
31 Philipp Grubauer 2.50 6.00
32 Casey Mittelstadt 2.50 6.00
33 Cam Talbot 2.50 6.00
34 Auston Matthews 10.00 25.00
35 Tristan Jarry 2.50 6.00
36 John Gibson 2.50 6.00
37 Patrice Bergeron 3.00 8.00
38 Yanni Gourde 2.00 5.00
39 Alex Nedeljkovic 2.00 5.00
40 Elias Pettersson 4.00 10.00
41 Anze Kopitar 4.00 10.00
43 Quinn Hughes 6.00 15.00
44 Maxime Comtois 2.00 5.00
45 Josh Morrissey 3.00 8.00
46 Bowen Byram 3.00 8.00
47 Nick Suzuki 5.00 12.00
48 Yegor Sharangovich 2.50 6.00
49 Drake Batherson 2.50 6.00
50 Jordan Binnington 4.00 10.00
51 Brock Boeser 3.00 8.00
52 Eeli Tolvanen 2.50 6.00
53 Jared Spurgeon 2.50 6.00
54 Mathew Barzal 3.00 8.00
55 Mark Scheifele 4.00 10.00
57 Teuvo Teravainen 2.50 6.00
59 Tyler Bertuzzi 2.00 5.00
60 Erik Karlsson 3.00 8.00
61 Max Pacioretty 2.50 6.00
62 Joel Farabee 2.50 6.00
63 Brad Marchand 5.00 12.00
64 Aaron Ekblad 3.00 8.00
66 Tim Stutzle 3.00 8.00
67 Brent Burns 2.50 6.00
68 Carter Hart 2.50 6.00
70 Adam Fox 3.00 8.00
71 Taylor Hall 2.50 6.00
73 Mitch Marner 4.00 10.00
74 Brady Tkachuk 4.00 10.00
77 David Pastrnak 6.00 15.00
78 Cale Makar 6.00 15.00
79 Evgeni Malkin 5.00 12.00
80 Robin Lehner 2.00 5.00
81 Jonathan Marchessault 3.00 8.00
82 Phil Kessel 2.50 6.00
83 Anthony Beauvillier 1.50 4.00
84 William Karlsson 3.00 8.00
85 Ryan Nugent-Hopkins 3.00 8.00
86 Jack Hughes 6.00 15.00
87 Sidney Crosby 10.00 25.00
89 Connor Hellebuyck 5.00 12.00
90 Ryan O'Reilly 2.50 6.00
91 John Tavares 4.00 10.00
92 Roman Josi 2.50 6.00
93 Andrei Svechnikov 3.00 8.00
94 Mark Stone 3.00 8.00
95 Carey Price 5.00 12.00
96 Mikko Rantanen 6.00 15.00
97 Connor McDavid 12.00 30.00
98 Nikita Kucherov 5.00 12.00
99 Andrei Vasilevskiy 4.00 10.00
100 Leon Draisaitl 8.00 20.00

2021-22 SPx Double XL Duos Materials

XLAM A.Matthews/M.Marner/49 15.00 40.00
XLAS A.Svechnikov/S.Aho/99 6.00 15.00
XLBL P.Laine/O.Bjorkstrand/99 5.00 12.00
XLCM S.Crosby/E.Malkin/49 15.00 40.00
XLEM J.McCann/J.Eberle/99 4.00 10.00
XLHR J.Robertson/M.Heiskanen/99 6.00 15.00
XLMD C.McDavid/L.Draisaitl/49 20.00 50.00
XLMM N.MacKinnon/C.Makar/49 15.00 40.00
XLNS J.Norris/T.Stutzle/99 5.00 12.00
XLPL A.Panarin/A.Lafreniere/49 8.00 20.00

2021-22 SPx Extravagant Material Autographs

*PREMIUM/25: .6X TO 1.5X BASIC
EMAB Aleksander Barkov/50 15.00 40.00
EMAL Alexis Lafreniere/25 15.00 40.00
EMAV Andrei Vasilevskiy/25 15.00 40.00
EMBB Brent Burns/25 10.00 25.00
EMBM Brad Marchand/25 20.00 50.00
EMCH Carter Hart/50 10.00 25.00
EMCM Connor McDavid/25 200.00 500.00
EMCP Carey Price/25 20.00 50.00
EMJB Josh Bailey/50 8.00 20.00
EMJT John Tavares/25 15.00 40.00
EMLD Leon Draisaitl/25 30.00 80.00
EMMA Cale Makar/25 25.00 60.00
EMQH Quinn Hughes/25 25.00 60.00
EMRJ Roman Josi/50 10.00 25.00
EMSA Sebastian Aho/50 15.00 40.00
EMST Mark Stone/50 12.00 30.00

2021-22 SPx Extravagant Materials

*PREMIUM/25: .75X TO 2X BASIC
EMAL Alexis Lafreniere 4.00 10.00
EMAM Auston Matthews 10.00 25.00
EMAV Andrei Vasilevskiy 4.00 10.00
EMBB Brent Burns 2.50 6.00
EMBM Brad Marchand 5.00 12.00
EMCH Carter Hart 2.50 6.00
EMCM Connor McDavid 12.00 30.00
EMCP Carey Price 5.00 12.00
EMJB Josh Bailey 2.00 5.00
EMJT John Tavares 4.00 10.00
EMKK Kirill Kaprizov 8.00 20.00
EMLD Leon Draisaitl 8.00 20.00
EMMA Cale Makar 6.00 15.00
EMMH Miro Heiskanen 3.00 8.00
EMMP Max Pacioretty 2.50 6.00
EMNS Nick Suzuki 5.00 12.00
EMQH Quinn Hughes 6.00 15.00
EMRJ Roman Josi 2.50 6.00
EMSA Sebastian Aho 4.00 10.00
EMSS Steven Stamkos 5.00 12.00

2021-22 SPx Finite Rookies

*GOLD/299: .5X TO 1.2X BASIC
*GREEN/199: .6X TO 1.5X BASIC
*PLATINUM/99: .75X TO 2X BASIC
*SILVER/75: 1X TO 2.5X BASIC
*GOLD.SPCTRM/35: 1.2X TO 3X BASIC
F1 Trevor Zegras 5.00 12.00
F2 Cole Caufield 10.00 25.00
F3 Quinton Byfield 6.00 15.00
F4 Spencer Knight 5.00 12.00
F5 Jeremy Swayman 8.00 20.00
F6 Jamie Drysdale 4.00 10.00
F7 Calen Addison 2.50 6.00
F8 Grigori Denisenko 3.00 8.00
F9 Shane Pinto 4.00 10.00
F10 Alex Newhook 4.00 10.00
F11 David Farrance 2.50 6.00
F12 Zac Jones 3.00 8.00
F13 Ross Colton 3.00 8.00
F14 Arttu Ruotsalainen 2.50 6.00
F15 Ivan Prosvetov 2.50 6.00
F16 Matthew Phillips 2.50 6.00
F17 Jan Jenik 3.00 8.00
F18 Ukko-Pekka Luukkonen 4.00 10.00
F19 Wyatt Kalynuk 2.50 6.00
F20 Joe Veleno 3.00 8.00
F21 Rasmus Kupari 2.50 6.00
F22 Jacob Bernard-Docker 2.50 6.00
F23 Wade Allison 2.50 6.00
F24 Kole Lind 3.00 8.00
F25 Joey Keane 2.00 5.00
F26 Jesse Ylonen 2.50 6.00
F27 Tanner Laczynski 2.50 6.00
F28 Sampo Ranta 2.50 6.00
F29 Morgan Barron 2.00 5.00
F30 Tyce Thompson 2.50 6.00
F31 Logan Thompson 6.00 15.00
F32 Mattias Samuelsson 2.50 6.00
F33 Radim Zohorna 2.50 6.00
F34 Alex Barre-Boulet 2.50 6.00
F35 Cam York 2.50 6.00
F36 Filip Gustavsson 5.00 12.00
F37 Jack Ahcan 2.50 6.00
F38 Mike Hardman 2.50 6.00
F39 Jacob Bryson 2.50 6.00
F40 Parker Kelly 2.50 6.00
F41 Dawson Mercer 6.00 15.00
F42 Nils Lundkvist 2.50 6.00
F43 Vasily Podkolzin 3.00 8.00
F44 Moritz Seider 6.00 15.00
F45 Lucas Raymond 8.00 20.00
F46 Mason McTavish 5.00 12.00
F47 Cole Perfetti 5.00 12.00
F48 William Eklund 6.00 15.00
F49 Cole Sillinger 4.00 10.00
F50 Anton Lundell 5.00 12.00

2021-22 SPx Jerseys

*GOLD/65: 1X TO 2.5X BASIC
*PATCH/25: 1.5X TO 4X BASIC
JAF Adam Fox 2.50 6.00
JAK Anze Kopitar 3.00 8.00
JAM Auston Matthews 8.00 20.00
JAO Alex Ovechkin 8.00 20.00
JAP Artemi Panarin 4.00 10.00
JAS Andrei Svechnikov 2.50 6.00
JBB Brent Burns 2.00 5.00
JBM Brad Marchand 4.00 10.00
JBO Brock Boeser 2.50 6.00
JBT Brady Tkachuk 3.00 8.00
JCA Cale Makar 5.00 12.00
JCK Clayton Keller 2.50 6.00
JCM Connor McDavid 10.00 25.00
JDL Dylan Larkin 2.50 6.00
JDN Darnell Nurse 1.50 4.00
JDP David Pastrnak 5.00 12.00
JJC John Carlson 2.00 5.00
JJE Jordan Eberle 2.00 5.00
JJH Jack Hughes 5.00 12.00
JKE Phil Kessel 2.00 5.00
JKF Kevin Fiala 1.50 4.00
JMA Mark Scheifele 3.00 8.00
JMB Mathew Barzal 2.50 6.00
JMC Maxime Comtois 1.50 4.00
JMH Miro Heiskanen 2.50 6.00
JMM Mitch Marner 3.00 8.00
JMS Mark Stone 2.50 6.00
JMT Matthew Tkachuk 4.00 10.00
JNM Nathan MacKinnon 8.00 20.00
JNS Nick Suzuki 4.00 10.00
JRO Ryan O'Reilly 2.00 5.00
JSA Sebastian Aho 3.00 8.00
JSC Sidney Crosby 8.00 20.00
JSS Steven Stamkos 4.00 10.00

2021-22 SPx Patch Autographs

2 Dylan Larkin/25 20.00 50.00
5 Cam Atkinson/49 15.00 40.00
7 Jordan Eberle/49 15.00 40.00
9 Jack Roslovic/49 10.00 25.00
11 Jonathan Huberdeau/25 20.00 50.00
13 Alexis Lafreniere/25 40.00 100.00
15 Dylan Strome/49 20.00 50.00
16 Joe Pavelski/49 20.00 50.00
18 Matthew Tkachuk/49 30.00 80.00
21 Jason Robertson/25 8.00 200.00
24 Dylan Cozens/49 15.00 40.00
28 Aleksander Barkov/49 25.00 60.00
31 Philipp Grubauer/49 15.00 40.00
32 Casey Mittelstadt/49 15.00 40.00
33 Cam Talbot/49 15.00 40.00
35 Tristan Jarry/49 15.00 40.00
36 John Gibson/49 15.00 40.00
38 Yanni Gourde/49 12.00 30.00
39 Alex Nedeljkovic/49 12.00 30.00
44 Maxime Comtois/49 12.00 30.00
46 Bowen Byram/49 20.00 50.00
48 Yegor Sharangovich/49 15.00 40.00
49 Drake Batherson/49 15.00 40.00
57 Teuvo Teravainen/25 15.00 40.00
59 Tyler Bertuzzi/49 12.00 30.00
61 Max Pacioretty/25 15.00 40.00
63 Brad Marchand/25 40.00 100.00
66 Tim Stutzle/25 20.00 50.00
67 Brent Burns/25 15.00 40.00
74 Brady Tkachuk/25 25.00 60.00
81 Jonathan Marchessault/25 20.00 50.00
83 Anthony Beauvillier/49 10.00 25.00
84 William Karlsson/49 20.00 50.00
85 Ryan Nugent-Hopkins/25 20.00 50.00
89 Connor Hellebuyck/25 30.00 80.00
90 Ryan O'Reilly/25 15.00 40.00
92 Roman Josi/25 15.00 40.00
93 Andrei Svechnikov/25 20.00 50.00
94 Mark Stone/25 20.00 50.00

2021-22 SPx Radiance F/X

*RED/150: .5X TO 1.2X BASIC
*GOLD/50: 1X TO 2.5X BASIC
*GREEN/25: 1.5X TO 4X BASIC
RFX1 Connor McDavid 10.00 25.00
RFX2 Auston Matthews 8.00 20.00
RFX3 Nathan MacKinnon 8.00 20.00
RFX4 Leon Draisaitl 6.00 15.00
RFX5 Alex Ovechkin 8.00 20.00
RFX6 Brad Marchand 4.00 10.00
RFX7 Ryan O'Reilly 2.00 5.00
RFX8 Patrick Kane 4.00 10.00
RFX9 Marc-Andre Fleury 4.00 10.00
RFX10 Patrice Bergeron 2.50 6.00
RFX11 Kris Letang 2.50 6.00
RFX12 Evgeni Malkin 4.00 10.00
RFX13 David Pastrnak 5.00 12.00
RFX14 Cale Makar 5.00 12.00
RFX15 Kirill Kaprizov 6.00 15.00
RFX16 Jack Hughes 5.00 12.00
RFX17 Artemi Panarin 4.00 10.00
RFX18 Steven Stamkos 4.00 10.00
RFX19 Alexis Lafreniere 3.00 8.00
RFX20 Nikita Kucherov 4.00 10.00
RFX21 Andrei Svechnikov 2.50 6.00
RFX22 Maxime Comtois 1.50 4.00
RFX23 Miro Heiskanen 2.50 6.00
RFX24 Tristan Jarry 2.00 5.00
RFX25 Gabe Vilardi 2.00 5.00
RFX26 Anthony Cirelli 1.50 4.00
RFX27 Cam Atkinson 2.00 5.00
RFX28 Dylan Cozens 2.00 5.00
RFX29 Nils Hoglander 1.50 4.00
RFX30 K'Andre Miller 1.50 4.00
RFX31 Philipp Grubauer 2.00 5.00
RFX32 Victor Hedman 2.50 6.00
RFX33 Carey Price 4.00 10.00
RFX34 Johnny Gaudreau 3.00 8.00
RFX35 Matthew Tkachuk 4.00 10.00
RFX36 Aleksander Barkov 3.00 8.00
RFX37 Brock Boeser 2.50 6.00
RFX38 Nikita Kucherov 4.00 10.00
RFX39 Max Pacioretty 2.00 5.00
RFX40 Robin Lehner 1.50 4.00
RFX41 Mark Scheifele 3.00 8.00
RFX42 Nick Suzuki 4.00 10.00
RFX43 Mikko Rantanen 5.00 12.00
RFX44 John Gibson 2.00 5.00
RFX45 Devon Toews 1.50 4.00
RFX46 Jason Robertson 3.00 8.00
RFX47 Tim Stutzle 2.50 6.00
RFX48 Brent Burns 2.00 5.00
RFX49 Jake Guentzel 3.00 8.00
RFX50 Jordan Binnington 3.00 8.00
RFX51 Cole Caufield 8.00 20.00
RFX52 Trevor Zegras 4.00 10.00
RFX53 Alex Newhook 3.00 8.00
RFX54 Jeremy Swayman 6.00 15.00
RFX55 Spencer Knight 4.00 10.00
RFX56 Jamie Drysdale 3.00 8.00
RFX57 Quinton Byfield 5.00 12.00
RFX58 Calen Addison 2.00 5.00
RFX59 Zac Jones 2.50 6.00
RFX60 Grigori Denisenko 2.50 6.00
RFX61 Cam York 2.00 5.00
RFX62 Ross Colton 2.50 6.00
RFX63 Ukko-Pekka Luukkonen 3.00 8.00
RFX64 Wyatt Kalynuk 2.00 5.00
RFX65 Arttu Ruotsalainen 2.00 5.00
RFX66 Joe Veleno 2.50 6.00
RFX67 Rasmus Kupari 2.00 5.00
RFX68 Mattias Samuelsson 2.00 5.00
RFX69 Parker Kelly 2.00 5.00
RFX70 Jesse Ylonen 2.00 5.00
RFX71 Jacob Bernard-Docker 2.00 5.00
RFX72 Filip Gustavsson 4.00 10.00
RFX73 Tanner Laczynski 2.00 5.00
RFX74 Wade Allison 2.00 5.00
RFX75 Shane Pinto 3.00 8.00
RFX76 Logan Thompson 5.00 12.00
RFX77 Kole Lind 2.50 6.00
RFX78 Joey Keane 1.50 4.00
RFX79 Jacob Bryson 2.00 5.00
RFX80 Jan Jenik 2.50 6.00
RFX81 Jack Ahcan 2.00 5.00
RFX82 Morgan Barron 1.50 4.00
RFX83 Ivan Prosvetov 2.00 5.00
RFX84 Mike Hardman 2.00 5.00
RFX85 Sampo Ranta 2.00 5.00
RFX86 Matthew Phillips 2.00 5.00
RFX87 Tyce Thompson 2.00 5.00
RFX88 Alex Barre-Boulet 2.00 5.00
RFX89 Garrett Pilon 2.50 6.00
RFX90 Lucas Raymond 6.00 15.00
RFX91 Vasily Podkolzin 2.50 6.00
RFX92 Mason McTavish 4.00 10.00
RFX93 Anton Lundell 4.00 10.00
RFX94 Philip Tomasino 2.50 6.00
RFX95 William Eklund 5.00 12.00
RFX96 Nils Lundkvist 2.00 5.00
RFX97 Jonathan Dahlen 2.00 5.00
RFX98 Cole Perfetti 4.00 10.00
RFX99 Benoit-Olivier Groulx 2.00 5.00
RFX100 Moritz Seider 5.00 12.00

2021-22 SPx Rookie Jersey Autographs

AB Alex Barre-Boulet/375 8.00 20.00
AD Adam Beckman/375 8.00 20.00
AH Alexander Holtz/175 12.00 30.00
AL Anton Lundell/175 15.00 40.00
AN Alex Newhook/175 12.00 30.00
AR Arttu Ruotsalainen/375 8.00 20.00
AT Alex Turcotte/175 10.00 25.00
BE Jacob Bernard-Docker/375 8.00 20.00
BG Benoit-Olivier Groulx/375 8.00 20.00
BK Boris Katchouk/375 6.00 15.00
CA Calen Addison/375 8.00 20.00
CP Cole Perfetti/175 15.00 40.00
CS Cole Sillinger/375 12.00 30.00
CY Cam York/375 8.00 20.00
DA Jonathan Dahlen/375 8.00 20.00
DM Dawson Mercer/375 25.00 60.00
FG Filip Gustavsson/375 15.00 40.00
GD Grigori Denisenko/175 10.00 25.00
HL Hendrix Lapierre/375 8.00 20.00
IP Ivan Prosvetov/375 8.00 20.00
JA Jack Ahcan/375 8.00 20.00
JB Jacob Bryson/375 8.00 20.00
JD Jamie Drysdale/175 12.00 30.00
JJ Jan Jenik/375 10.00 25.00
JK Joey Keane/375 6.00 15.00
JL Jake Leschyshyn/375 8.00 20.00
JN Jake Neighbours/375 15.00 40.00
JP John-Jason Peterka/175 15.00 40.00
JS Jeremy Swayman/175 60.00 150.00
JV Joe Veleno/375 10.00 25.00
JY Jesse Ylonen/375 8.00 20.00
LP Lane Pederson/375 8.00 20.00
LT Logan Thompson/375 25.00 60.00
MB Morgan Barron/375 6.00 15.00
MH Mike Hardman/375 8.00 20.00
MM Mason McTavish/175 25.00 60.00
MS Moritz Seider/75 100.00 250.00
NL Nils Lundkvist/375 8.00 20.00
OS Oskar Steen/375 10.00 25.00
PE Scott Perunovich/375 8.00 20.00
PK Parker Kelly/375 8.00 20.00
PT Philip Tomasino/175 10.00 25.00
QB Quinton Byfield/75 20.00 50.00
RC Ross Colton/375 10.00 25.00
RD Riley Damiani/375 8.00 20.00
RK Rasmus Kupari/375 8.00 20.00
SA Mattias Samuelsson/375 8.00 20.00
SK Spencer Knight/175 15.00 40.00
SP Shane Pinto/375 12.00 30.00
SR Sampo Ranta/375 8.00 20.00
TR Taylor Raddysh/375 12.00 30.00
TT Tyce Thompson/375 8.00 20.00
TZ Trevor Zegras/75 80.00 200.00
UL Ukko-Pekka Luukkonen/375 12.00 30.00
WA Wade Allison/375 8.00 20.00
WE William Eklund/175 20.00 50.00
WK Wyatt Kalynuk/375 8.00 20.00
ZJ Zac Jones/375 10.00 25.00

2021-22 SPx Rookie Jersey Autographs Spectrum

*SPECTRUM: .5X TO 1.2X BASIC
DM Dawson Mercer/65 40.00 100.00
MM Mason McTavish/35 40.00 100.00

2021-22 SPx Rookie Jerseys

*GOLD/99: .5X TO 1.2X BASIC
*PATCH/35: 1.2X TO 3X BASIC
RJAB Alex Barre-Boulet 2.50 6.00
RJAD Adam Beckman 2.50 6.00
RJAH Alexander Holtz 4.00 10.00
RJAL Anton Lundell 5.00 12.00
RJAN Alex Newhook 4.00 10.00
RJAR Arttu Ruotsalainen 2.50 6.00
RJBE Jacob Bernard-Docker 2.50 6.00
RJBG Benoit-Olivier Groulx 2.50 6.00
RJBK Boris Katchouk 2.00 5.00
RJCA Calen Addison 2.50 6.00
RJCC Cole Caufield 10.00 25.00
RJCP Cole Perfetti 5.00 12.00
RJCS Cole Sillinger 4.00 10.00
RJCY Cam York 2.50 6.00
RJDA Jonathan Dahlen 2.50 6.00
RJDF David Farrance 2.50 6.00
RJDM Dawson Mercer 6.00 15.00
RJGD Grigori Denisenko 3.00 8.00
RJHL Hendrix Lapierre 2.50 6.00
RJIP Ivan Prosvetov 2.50 6.00
RJJA Jack Ahcan 2.50 6.00
RJJB Jacob Bryson 2.50 6.00
RJJD Jamie Drysdale 4.00 10.00
RJJJ Jan Jenik 3.00 8.00
RJJK Joey Keane 2.00 5.00
RJJL Jake Leschyshyn 2.50 6.00
RJJN Jake Neighbours 5.00 12.00
RJJS Jeremy Swayman 8.00 20.00
RJJV Joe Veleno 3.00 8.00
RJJY Jesse Ylonen 2.50 6.00
RJKB Kasper Bjorkqvist 2.50 6.00
RJLP Lane Pederson 2.50 6.00
RJLR Lucas Raymond 8.00 20.00
RJLT Logan Thompson 6.00 15.00
RJMB Morgan Barron 2.00 5.00
RJMH Mike Hardman 2.50 6.00
RJMM Mason McTavish 5.00 12.00
RJMS Mattias Samuelsson 2.50 6.00
RJNL Nils Lundkvist 2.50 6.00
RJOS Oskar Steen 3.00 8.00
RJPE Scott Perunovich 2.50 6.00
RJPK Parker Kelly 2.50 6.00
RJPT Philip Tomasino 3.00 8.00
RJQB Quinton Byfield 6.00 15.00
RJRC Ross Colton 3.00 8.00
RJRD Riley Damiani 2.50 6.00
RJRK Rasmus Kupari 2.50 6.00
RJRZ Radim Zohorna 2.50 6.00
RJSE Moritz Seider 6.00 15.00
RJSK Spencer Knight 5.00 12.00
RJSP Shane Pinto 4.00 10.00
RJSR Sampo Ranta 2.50 6.00
RJTL Tanner Laczynski 2.50 6.00
RJTR Taylor Raddysh 4.00 10.00
RJTT Tyce Thompson 2.50 6.00
RJTZ Trevor Zegras 5.00 12.00
RJUL Ukko-Pekka Luukkonen 4.00 10.00
RJVP Vasily Podkolzin 3.00 8.00
RJWA Wade Allison 2.50 6.00
RJWE William Eklund 6.00 15.00
RJWK Wyatt Kalynuk 2.50 6.00
RJZJ Zac Jones 3.00 8.00

2021-22 SPx Rookie Superscripts

*GOLD: .6X TO 1.5X BASIC
RSSAB Adam Beckman E 8.00 20.00
RSSAL Anton Lundell B 15.00 40.00
RSSAN Alex Newhook C 12.00 30.00
RSSAR Arttu Ruotsalainen E 8.00 20.00
RSSAT Alex Turcotte B 10.00 25.00
RSSBG Benoit-Olivier Groulx D 8.00 20.00
RSSBM Brett Murray E 8.00 20.00
RSSBR Jacob Bryson E 8.00 20.00
RSSCA Calen Addison D 8.00 20.00
RSSCP Cole Perfetti B 15.00 40.00
RSSCS Cole Sillinger D 12.00 30.00
RSSCY Cam York E 8.00 20.00
RSSDA Jonathan Dahlen D 8.00 20.00
RSSDF David Farrance E 8.00 20.00
RSSDM Dawson Mercer C 20.00 50.00
RSSFG Filip Gustavsson E 15.00 40.00
RSSGD Grigori Denisenko B 10.00 25.00
RSSGP Garrett Pilon E 10.00 25.00
RSSHL Hendrix Lapierre E 8.00 20.00
RSSIP Ivan Prosvetov E 8.00 20.00
RSSJA Jack Ahcan E 8.00 20.00
RSSJB Jacob Bernard-Docker D 8.00 20.00
RSSJD Jamie Drysdale B 12.00 30.00
RSSJJ Jan Jenik E 10.00 25.00
RSSJK Joey Keane E 6.00 15.00
RSSJL Jake Leschyshyn E 8.00 20.00
RSSJN Jake Neighbours D 15.00 40.00

RSSJS Jeremy Swayman B 25.00 60.00
RSSJV Joe Veleno D 10.00 25.00
RSSJY Jesse Ylonen E 8.00 20.00
RSSKL Kole Lind E 10.00 25.00
RSSLR Lucas Raymond B 25.00 60.00
RSSLT Logan Thompson E 20.00 50.00
RSSMB Morgan Barron E 6.00 15.00
RSSMH Mike Hardman E 8.00 20.00
RSSMP Matthew Phillips E 8.00 20.00
RSSMS Mattias Samuelsson E 8.00 20.00
RSSMT Mason McTavish D 15.00 40.00
RSSNL Nils Lundkvist D 8.00 20.00
RSSOS Oskar Steen E 10.00 25.00
RSSPD Pavel Dorofeyev E 10.00 25.00
RSSPE John-Jason Peterka C 15.00 40.00
RSSPK Parker Kelly E 8.00 20.00
RSSPT Philip Tomasino D 10.00 25.00
RSSQB Quinton Byfield B 20.00 50.00
RSSRC Ross Colton C 10.00 25.00
RSSRD Riley Damiani E 8.00 20.00
RSSRK Rasmus Kupari C 8.00 20.00
RSSRS Robin Salo E 8.00 20.00
RSSSE Moritz Seider B 20.00 50.00
RSSSK Spencer Knight B 15.00 40.00
RSSSP Shane Pinto E 12.00 30.00
RSSSR Sampo Ranta E 8.00 20.00
RSSTL Tanner Laczynski E 8.00 20.00
RSSTT Tyce Thompson E 8.00 20.00
RSSTZ Trevor Zegras B 15.00 40.00
RSSUL Ukko-Pekka Luukkonen E 12.00 30.00
RSSVP Vasily Podkolzin B 10.00 25.00
RSSWA Wade Allison E 8.00 20.00
RSSWE William Eklund B 20.00 50.00
RSSWK Wyatt Kalynuk E 8.00 20.00
RSSZJ Zac Jones E 10.00 25.00

2021-22 SPx Shadow Box

SB1 Cole Caufield 30.00 80.00
SB2 Trevor Zegras 8.00 20.00
SB3 Quinton Byfield 10.00 25.00
SB4 Spencer Knight 8.00 20.00
SB5 Jeremy Swayman 15.00 40.00
SB6 Alex Newhook 6.00 15.00
SB7 Jamie Drysdale 6.00 15.00
SB8 Grigori Denisenko 5.00 12.00
SB9 Zac Jones 5.00 12.00
SB10 Cam York 4.00 10.00
SB11 Joe Veleno 5.00 12.00
SB12 Ross Colton 5.00 12.00
SB13 Alex Barre-Boulet 4.00 10.00
SB14 Shane Pinto 6.00 15.00
SB15 David Farrance 4.00 10.00
SB16 Calen Addison 4.00 10.00
SB17 Filip Gustavsson 8.00 20.00
SB18 Rasmus Kupari 4.00 10.00
SB19 Kole Lind 5.00 12.00
SB20 Moritz Seider 20.00 50.00
SB21 Lucas Raymond 12.00 30.00
SB22 Vasily Podkolzin 5.00 12.00
SB23 Cole Perfetti 8.00 20.00
SB24 William Eklund 10.00 25.00
SB25 Andrei Vasilevskiy 6.00 15.00
SB26 Patrick Kane 8.00 20.00
SB27 Cale Makar 10.00 25.00
SB28 Quinn Hughes 10.00 25.00
SB29 Jordan Binnington 6.00 15.00
SB30 Teuvo Teravainen 4.00 10.00
SB31 Philipp Grubauer 4.00 10.00
SB32 Nick Suzuki 8.00 20.00
SB33 Dylan Cozens 4.00 10.00

2021-22 SPx Shadow Box Autographs

SBAAB Alex Barre-Boulet/175 10.00 25.00
SBAAN Alex Newhook/75 15.00 40.00
SBAAV Andrei Vasilevskiy/25 15.00 40.00
SBACA Calen Addison/175 10.00 25.00
SBACM Cale Makar/25 50.00 125.00
SBACP Cole Perfetti/75 20.00 50.00
SBADC Dylan Cozens/99 10.00 25.00
SBADF David Farrance/175 10.00 25.00
SBAFG Filip Gustavsson/175 20.00 50.00
SBAGD Grigori Denisenko/75 12.00 30.00
SBAJD Jamie Drysdale/75 15.00 40.00
SBAJS Jeremy Swayman/75 80.00 200.00
SBAJV Joe Veleno/175 12.00 30.00
SBAKL Kole Lind/175 12.00 30.00
SBAMS Moritz Seider/35 125.00 300.00
SBANL Nils Lundkvist/175 10.00 25.00
SBANS Nick Suzuki/99 20.00 50.00
SBAPK Patrick Kane/25 30.00 80.00
SBAQB Quinton Byfield/75 25.00 60.00
SBAQH Quinn Hughes/25 25.00 60.00
SBARC Ross Colton/175 12.00 30.00
SBARK Rasmus Kupari/175 10.00 25.00
SBASK Spencer Knight/75 20.00 50.00
SBASP Shane Pinto/175 15.00 40.00
SBATZ Trevor Zegras/35 100.00 250.00
SBAVP Vasily Podkolzin/35 12.00 30.00
SBAWE William Eklund/75 40.00 100.00
SBAZJ Zac Jones/175 12.00 30.00

2021-22 SPx Signature Fabrics

SFAT Alex Tuch/49 10.00 25.00
SFBB Brock Boeser/25 12.00 30.00
SFBH Brandon Hagel/49 8.00 20.00
SFCO Connor McMichael/49 10.00 25.00
SFDC Dylan Cozens/49 10.00 25.00
SFGV Gabe Vilardi/49 10.00 25.00
SFHE Tomas Hertl/49 10.00 25.00
SFJM J.T. Miller/49 12.00 30.00
SFMA Maxime Comtois/49 8.00 20.00
SFMH Miro Heiskanen/49 12.00 30.00
SFMO Josh Morrissey/49 12.00 30.00
SFPG Philipp Grubauer/25 10.00 25.00
SFRT Robert Thomas/49 10.00 25.00
SFTB Tyler Bertuzzi/49 8.00 20.00
SFTJ Tristan Jarry/49 10.00 25.00

2021-22 SPx Signature Fabrics Spectrum

*SPECTRUM: .5X TO 1.2X BASIC
SFAT Alex Tuch/25 20.00 50.00

2021-22 SPx SPx Rookie Signatures

*GOLD/25: .5X TO 1.2X BASIC
SPXRAN Alex Newhook C 10.00 25.00
SPXRAR Arttu Ruotsalainen E 6.00 15.00
SPXRCP Cole Perfetti B 12.00 30.00
SPXRCY Cam York E 6.00 15.00
SPXRDM Dawson Mercer C 15.00 40.00
SPXRFG Filip Gustavsson E 12.00 30.00
SPXRGD Grigori Denisenko D 8.00 20.00
SPXRGP Garrett Pilon E 8.00 20.00
SPXRIP Ivan Prosvetov E 6.00 15.00
SPXRJA Jack Ahcan E 6.00 15.00
SPXRJB Jacob Bryson E 6.00 15.00
SPXRJD Jamie Drysdale B 10.00 25.00
SPXRJJ Jan Jenik E 8.00 20.00
SPXRJK Joey Keane E 5.00 12.00
SPXRJP John-Jason Peterka C 12.00 30.00
SPXRJV Joe Veleno D 8.00 20.00
SPXRMB Morgan Barron E 5.00 12.00
SPXRMH Mike Hardman E 6.00 15.00
SPXRMP Matthew Phillips E 6.00 15.00
SPXRMS Mattias Samuelsson E 6.00 15.00
SPXRPK Parker Kelly E 6.00 15.00
SPXRPT Philip Tomasino C 8.00 20.00
SPXRRC Ross Colton D 8.00 20.00
SPXRRK Rasmus Kupari C 6.00 15.00
SPXRSE Moritz Seider B 100.00 250.00
SPXRSK Spencer Knight B 12.00 30.00
SPXRSP Shane Pinto E 10.00 25.00
SPXRSR Sampo Ranta E 6.00 15.00
SPXRTT Tyce Thompson E 6.00 15.00
SPXRZJ Zac Jones E 8.00 20.00

2021-22 SPx SPx Signatures

SPXBB Brent Burns C 8.00 20.00
SPXBM Brad Marchand C 15.00 40.00
SPXBO Brock Boeser D 10.00 25.00
SPXCH Connor Hellebuyck D 15.00 40.00
SPXCT Cam Talbot C 8.00 20.00
SPXDC Dylan Cozens C 8.00 20.00
SPXDH Dougie Hamilton D 6.00 15.00
SPXDS Dylan Strome E 10.00 25.00
SPXFH Filip Hronek E 5.00 12.00
SPXGV Gabe Vilardi E 8.00 20.00
SPXHZ Henrik Zetterberg B 10.00 25.00
SPXIM Ilya Mikheyev E 6.00 15.00
SPXJM Jacob Markstrom C 8.00 20.00
SPXJP Jean-Gabriel Pageau E 5.00 12.00
SPXJR Jack Roslovic E 5.00 12.00
SPXJT John Tavares A 12.00 30.00
SPXMN Martin Necas E 12.00 30.00
SPXMO Josh Morrissey E 10.00 25.00
SPXMS Mark Stone D 10.00 25.00
SPXNE Nikolaj Ehlers D 8.00 20.00
SPXPA Joe Pavelski D 10.00 25.00
SPXPD Pierre-Luc Dubois B 6.00 15.00
SPXSB Sergei Bobrovsky D 12.00 30.00
SPXZH Zach Hyman B 12.00 30.00

2021-22 SPx Superscripts

*GOLD/25: .6X TO 1.5X BASIC
SSAB Aleksander Barkov B 15.00 40.00
SSAK Anze Kopitar B 15.00 40.00
SSAL Anders Lee D 8.00 20.00
SSAR Alexander Romanov D 8.00 20.00
SSAS Andrei Svechnikov D 12.00 30.00
SSBB Brock Boeser B 12.00 30.00
SSBU Brent Burns B 10.00 25.00
SSBY Bowen Byram D 12.00 30.00
SSCH Connor Hellebuyck C 20.00 50.00
SSCT Cam Talbot C 10.00 25.00
SSCV Carter Verhaeghe A 10.00 25.00
SSDB Drake Batherson D 10.00 25.00
SSDC Dylan Cozens D 10.00 25.00
SSDS Dylan Strome D 12.00 30.00
SSDV Dan Vladar D 8.00 20.00
SSFH Filip Hronek D 6.00 15.00
SSGC Gerry Cheevers B 10.00 25.00
SSHE Tomas Hertl D 10.00 25.00
SSJE Jake Evans D 6.00 15.00
SSJM Jonathan Marchessault C 12.00 30.00
SSJR Jason Robertson C 25.00 60.00
SSJZ Jason Zucker D 10.00 25.00
SSKF Kevin Fiala D 8.00 20.00
SSKM K'Andre Miller D 8.00 20.00
SSLF Liam Foudy D 8.00 20.00
SSMC Maxime Comtois D 8.00 20.00
SSMJ Jared McCann D 8.00 20.00
SSMO Josh Morrissey D 12.00 30.00
SSMP Max Pacioretty B 10.00 25.00
SSMZ Mats Zuccarello C 10.00 25.00
SSNE Nikolaj Ehlers D 10.00 25.00
SSNH Nils Hoglander D 8.00 20.00
SSNR Nick Robertson D 10.00 25.00
SSPS Pius Suter D 8.00 20.00
SSRH Roope Hintz D 12.00 30.00
SSRO Jack Roslovic D 6.00 15.00
SSRR Ryan Reaves D 8.00 20.00
SSSA Sebastian Aho C 15.00 40.00
SSSL Steven Lorentz D 6.00 15.00
SSTS Travis Sanheim D 6.00 15.00
SSVN Vladislav Namestnikov D 6.00 15.00
SSVV Vitek Vanecek D 10.00 25.00
SSYG Yanni Gourde D 8.00 20.00
SSYS Yegor Sharangovich D 10.00 25.00
SSZH Zach Hyman A 15.00 40.00

2021-22 SPx Winning Combos Materials

*PREMIUM/25: .75X TO 2X BASIC
WCADSJ A.DeBrincat/S.Jones 4.00 10.00
WCALAF A.Lafreniere/A.Fox 5.00 12.00
WCAMJT A.Matthews/J.Tavares 12.00 30.00
WCBBQH B.Boeser/Q.Hughes 8.00 20.00
WCBMTH B.Marchand/T.Hall 6.00 15.00
WCCMRN C.McDavid
R.Nugent-Hopkins 15.00 40.00
WCDCCM D.Cozens/C.Mittelstadt 3.00 8.00
WCJPJA J.Petry/J.Anderson 3.00 8.00
WCKCCH K.Connor/C.Hellebuyck 6.00 15.00
WCMHRH M.Heiskanen/R.Hintz 4.00 10.00
WCOBJR O.Bjorkstrand/J.Roslovic 2.50 6.00
WCPGYG P.Grubauer/Y.Gourde 3.00 8.00
WCROCP R.O'Reilly/C.Parayko 3.00 8.00
WCSATT S.Aho/T.Teravainen 5.00 12.00

2021-22 SPx Winning Combos Materials Autographs

WCBBQH B.Boeser/Q.Hughes/25 50.00 125.00
WCDCCM D.Cozens/C.Mittelstadt/50 20.0050.00
WCJPJA J.Petry/J.Anderson/25 20.00 50.00
WCMHRH M.Heiskanen/R.Hintz/50 25.00 60.00
WCPGYG P.Grubauer/Y.Gourde/50 20.00 50.00
WCROCP R.O'Reilly/C.Parayko/50 20.00 50.00

2021-22 SPx Winning Combos Materials Autographs Premium

*PREMIUM: .75X TO 2X BASIC
WCPGYG Philipp Grubauer
Yanni Gourde/25 80.00 200.00

2021-22 SPx Winning Materials

*PREMIUM: 1X TO 2.5X BASIC
WMAB Aleksander Barkov 6.00 15.00
WMAD Alex DeBrincat 5.00 12.00
WMAF Adam Fox 5.00 12.00
WMAK Anze Kopitar 6.00 15.00
WMAL Alexis Lafreniere 6.00 15.00
WMAM Auston Matthews 15.00 40.00
WMAV Andrei Vasilevskiy 6.00 15.00
WMBB Brent Burns 4.00 10.00
WMBM Brad Marchand 8.00 20.00
WMBN Bernie Nicholls 3.00 8.00
WMBP Brayden Point 5.00 12.00
WMBR Bill Ranford 3.00 8.00
WMCC Cole Caufield 15.00 40.00
WMCH Carter Hart 4.00 10.00
WMCM Connor McDavid 20.00 50.00
WMCP Colton Parayko 3.00 8.00
WMDM Dawson Mercer 10.00 25.00
WMDS Daniel Sedin 5.00 12.00
WMGU Jake Guentzel 6.00 15.00
WMHE Connor Hellebuyck 8.00 20.00
WMHZ Henrik Zetterberg 5.00 12.00
WMJB Josh Bailey 3.00 8.00
WMJG John Gibson 4.00 10.00
WMKK Kirill Kaprizov 12.00 30.00
WMLD Leon Draisaitl 12.00 30.00
WMMA Cale Makar 10.00 25.00
WMMD Matt Dumba 3.00 8.00
WMMH Miro Heiskanen 5.00 12.00
WMMN Martin Necas 6.00 15.00
WMMP Max Pacioretty 4.00 10.00
WMMS Mats Sundin 4.00 10.00
WMNS Nick Suzuki 8.00 20.00
WMPK Patrick Kane 8.00 20.00
WMPL Pat LaFontaine 4.00 10.00
WMQB Quinton Byfield 10.00 25.00
WMQH Quinn Hughes 10.00 25.00
WMRJ Roman Josi 4.00 10.00
WMRO Ryan O'Reilly 4.00 10.00
WMSA Sebastian Aho 6.00 15.00
WMSC Mark Scheifele 6.00 15.00
WMSK Saku Koivu 4.00 10.00
WMSM Sean Monahan 2.50 6.00
WMSP Scott Perunovich 4.00 10.00
WMST Mark Stone 5.00 12.00
WMTD Thatcher Demko 5.00 12.00
WMTT Tyler Toffoli 4.00 10.00
WMTZ Trevor Zegras 8.00 20.00

2021-22 SPx Winning Materials Autographs

WMAB Aleksander Barkov/50 20.00 50.00
WMAF Adam Fox/50 15.00 40.00
WMAK Anze Kopitar/25 20.00 50.00
WMAL Alexis Lafreniere/25 20.00 50.00
WMAV Andrei Vasilevskiy/25 20.00 50.00
WMBB Brent Burns/25 12.00 30.00
WMBM Brad Marchand/25 25.00 60.00
WMBN Bernie Nicholls/25 10.00 25.00
WMBR Bill Ranford/50 10.00 25.00
WMCP Colton Parayko/99 10.00 25.00
WMDM Dawson Mercer/25 30.00 80.00
WMDS Daniel Sedin/99 15.00 40.00
WMGU Jake Guentzel/99 20.00 50.00
WMHE Connor Hellebuyck/99 25.00 60.00
WMHZ Henrik Zetterberg/50 15.00 40.00
WMJB Josh Bailey/99 10.00 25.00
WMJG John Gibson/99 12.00 30.00
WMLD Leon Draisaitl/25 40.00 100.00
WMMA Cale Makar/25 30.00 80.00
WMMN Martin Necas/99 20.00 50.00
WMNS Nick Suzuki/25 25.00 60.00
WMPL Pat LaFontaine/50 12.00 30.00
WMQB Quinton Byfield/25 25.00 60.00
WMQH Quinn Hughes/50 30.00 80.00
WMRJ Roman Josi/50 12.00 30.00
WMRO Ryan O'Reilly/50 12.00 30.00
WMSA Sebastian Aho/99 20.00 50.00
WMSK Saku Koivu/50 12.00 30.00
WMSM Sean Monahan/99 8.00 20.00
WMSP Scott Perunovich/99 12.00 30.00
WMST Mark Stone/50 15.00 40.00
WMTS Tim Stutzle/99 30.00 80.00
WMTZ Trevor Zegras/25 80.00 200.00

2022-23 SPx

1 Aleksander Barkov 1.25 3.00
2 Adam Fox 1.00 2.50
3 Anze Kopitar 1.25 3.00
4 Anton Lundell .75 2.00
5 Auston Matthews 3.00 8.00
6 Alex Ovechkin 3.00 8.00
7 Artemi Panarin 1.50 4.00
8 Andrei Vasilevskiy 1.25 3.00
9 Bowen Byram 1.00 2.50
10 Brandon Hagel .60 1.50
11 Brad Marchand 1.50 4.00
12 Brandon Saad .60 1.50
13 Brady Tkachuk 1.25 3.00
14 Michael Bunting .75 2.00
15 Cam Atkinson .75 2.00
16 Josh Anderson .60 1.50
17 Clayton Keller 1.00 2.50
18 Cale Makar 2.00 5.00
19 Cole Caufield 1.50 4.00
20 Drake Batherson .75 2.00
21 Connor McMichael .75 2.00
22 David Pastrnak 2.00 5.00
23 Devon Toews .60 1.50
24 Evgenii Dadonov .50 1.25
25 Mason McTavish .75 2.00
26 Elias Lindholm .75 2.00
27 Elvis Merzlikins .75 2.00
28 Evgeni Malkin 1.50 4.00
29 Jake Guentzel 1.25 3.00
30 Mattias Ekholm .60 1.50
31 Jack Hughes 2.00 5.00
32 Igor Shesterkin 1.50 4.00
33 Josh Bailey .60 1.50
34 Jordan Eberle .75 2.00
35 Johnny Gaudreau 1.25 3.00
36 Jonathan Huberdeau 1.00 2.50
37 Jacob Markstrom .75 2.00
38 Josh Norris .75 2.00
39 Cole Perfetti .75 2.00
40 Joe Pavelski 1.00 2.50
41 Jason Robertson 1.25 3.00
42 Jeremy Swayman 1.25 3.00
43 Jonathan Toews 1.25 3.00
44 James van Riemsdyk .60 1.50
45 Arthur Kaliyev .75 2.00
46 Kyle Connor 1.25 3.00
47 Kevin Fiala .60 1.50
48 Kirill Kaprizov 2.50 6.00
49 Karel Vejmelka .50 1.25
50 Leon Draisaitl 2.50 6.00
51 Anders Lee .60 1.50
52 Lucas Raymond 1.25 3.00
53 John Marino .75 2.00
54 Mathew Barzal 1.00 2.50
55 Connor McDavid 4.00 10.00
56 Marc-Andre Fleury 1.50 4.00
57 Mikael Granlund .60 1.50
58 Miro Heiskanen 1.00 2.50
59 Mitch Marner 1.25 3.00
60 Moritz Seider 1.00 2.50
61 Matthew Tkachuk 1.50 4.00
62 Mats Zuccarello .75 2.00
63 Dawson Mercer 1.00 2.50
64 Nikolaj Ehlers .75 2.00
65 Bo Horvat 1.00 2.50
66 Nathan MacKinnon 3.00 8.00
67 Nick Suzuki 1.50 4.00
68 Oliver Bjorkstrand .60 1.50
69 Oskar Lindblom .60 1.50
70 Patrice Bergeron 1.00 2.50
71 Pierre-Luc Dubois .60 1.50
72 Martin Necas 1.25 3.00
73 Philipp Grubauer .75 2.00
74 Patrick Kane 1.50 4.00
75 Patrik Laine 1.00 2.50
76 Quinn Hughes 2.00 5.00
77 Rasmus Dahlin 1.00 2.50
78 Robby Fabbri .50 1.25
79 Roman Josi .75 2.00
80 Ryan Nugent-Hopkins 1.00 2.50
81 Ryan O'Reilly .75 2.00
82 Ryan Strome .75 2.00
83 Robert Thomas .75 2.00
84 Sebastian Aho 1.25 3.00
85 Sidney Crosby 3.00 8.00
86 Jonathan Marchessault 1.00 2.50
87 Jaccob Slavin .60 1.50
88 Steven Stamkos 1.50 4.00
89 Mark Stone 1.00 2.50
90 John Tavares 1.25 3.00
91 Teuvo Teravainen .75 2.00
92 Tomas Hertl .75 2.00
93 Timo Meier .75 2.00
94 Tim Stutzle 1.00 2.50
95 Tage Thompson 1.00 2.50
96 Cole Sillinger .60 1.50
97 Trevor Zegras .75 2.00
98 Ville Husso .50 1.25
99 Vasily Podkolzin .50 1.25
100 Yanni Gourde .60 1.50
101 Shane Wright RC 5.00 12.00
102 Matt Boldy RC 6.00 15.00
103 Marco Rossi RC 5.00 12.00
104 Jacob Perreault RC 2.00 5.00
105 Jordan Spence RC 2.00 5.00
106 Reilly Walsh RC 2.00 5.00
107 Jack Quinn RC 3.00 8.00
108 Owen Power RC 4.00 10.00
109 Pyotr Kochetkov RC 4.00 10.00
110 Braden Schneider RC 3.00 8.00
111 Lukas Reichel RC 4.00 10.00
112 Nick Abruzzese RC 2.00 5.00
113 Kent Johnson RC 4.00 10.00
114 Bobby Brink RC 2.00 5.00
115 Matias Maccelli RC 3.00 8.00
116 Matty Beniers RC 5.00 12.00
117 Lukas Dostal RC 4.00 10.00
118 Thomas Bordeleau RC 2.00 5.00
119 Kaedan Korczak RC 1.50 4.00
120 Dylan Holloway RC 4.00 10.00
121 Brayden Tracey RC 1.50 4.00
122 Samuel Fagemo RC 1.50 4.00
123 Erik Kallgren RC 2.00 5.00
124 Trey Fix-Wolansky RC 2.00 5.00
125 Isaac Ratcliffe RC 2.00 5.00
126 Ronnie Attard RC 2.00 5.00
127 Noah Cates RC 2.00 5.00
128 Jordan Harris RC 2.50 6.00
129 Jack McBain RC 2.00 5.00
130 Dylan Samberg RC 2.00 5.00
131 Mads Sogaard RC 2.50 6.00
132 Alex Vlasic RC 1.50 4.00
133 Marc McLaughlin RC 2.00 5.00
134 Zack Hayes RC 1.50 4.00
135 Filip Hallander RC 2.00 5.00
136 Fredrik Karlstrom RC 1.50 4.00
137 Hunter Drew RC 2.00 5.00
138 Mark Kastelic RC 1.50 4.00
139 Michael Eyssimont RC 2.00 5.00
140 Valtteri Puustinen RC 1.50 4.00
141 Andrei Kuzmenko RC 4.00 10.00
142 Kaiden Guhle RC 4.00 10.00
143 Juraj Slafkovsky RC 10.00 25.00
144 Marcus Bjork RC 2.00 5.00
145 Brandt Clarke RC 4.00 10.00
146 Jeff Malott RC 2.00 5.00
147 Jake Sanderson RC 5.00 12.00
148 Bokondji Imama RC 1.50 4.00
149 Samuel Poulin RC 2.50 6.00
150 Dylan Guenther RC 5.00 12.00
151 Nick Perbix RC 1.50 4.00
152 Brayden Pachal RC 1.50 4.00
153 Declan Chisholm RC 2.00 5.00
154 Matej Blumel RC 2.50 6.00
155 Oskar Olausson RC 2.00 5.00
156 Arber Xhekaj RC 4.00 10.00
157 Pontus Holmberg RC 2.00 5.00
158 Pavol Regenda RC 2.00 5.00
159 Olle Lycksell RC 2.00 5.00
160 Aatu Raty RC 2.00 5.00
161 Mitchell Chaffee RC 1.50 4.00
162 Johnathan Kovacevic RC 2.00 5.00
163 Brandon Biro RC 3.00 8.00
164 Adam Raska RC 2.00 5.00
165 Linus Hogberg RC 1.50 4.00
166 Nick Blankenburg RC 1.50 4.00
167 Elmer Soderblom RC 4.00 10.00
168 Samuel Ersson RC 4.00 10.00
169 Filip Kral RC 2.50 6.00
170 Ben Meyers RC 2.00 5.00
171 Nils Aman RC 2.00 5.00
172 Viktor Lodin RC 2.00 5.00
173 Simon Holmstrom RC 2.00 5.00
174 Vladislav Kolyachonok RC 1.50 4.00
175 Carson Meyer RC 1.50 4.00
176 Kirill Marchenko RC 5.00 12.00
177 Filip Roos RC 1.50 4.00
178 William Bitten RC 2.00 5.00
179 Jack LaFontaine RC 2.00 5.00
180 Jakub Galvas RC 2.00 5.00
181 Jakub Lauko RC 2.50 6.00
182 James Hamblin RC 2.00 5.00
183 Chase Pearson RC 1.50 4.00
184 Cole Koepke RC 2.00 5.00
185 Wyatt Johnston RC 8.00 20.00
186 Jean-Luc Foudy RC 2.00 5.00
187 Jonatan Berggren RC 3.00 8.00
188 Lucas Johansen RC 1.50 4.00
189 Mac Hollowell RC 2.00 5.00
190 David Jiricek RC 4.00 10.00
191 Hayden Hodgson RC 1.50 4.00
192 Juuso Parssinen RC 2.00 5.00
193 Nathan Smith RC 1.50 4.00
194 Jacob Moverare RC 1.50 4.00
195 Cole Reinhardt RC 2.00 5.00
196 Nick DeSimone RC 2.00 5.00
197 Linus Sandin RC 1.50 4.00
198 Jake Christiansen RC 2.00 5.00
199 Nikita Okhotiuk RC 1.50 4.00
200 Nikita Alexandrov RC 2.00 5.00

2022-23 SPx Colored HoloFoil

*HOLOFOIL/149: .5X TO 1.2X BASIC

2022-23 SPx Grand Finale

*FINALE/50: 1X TO 2.5X BASIC
*FINALE RC/50: .75X TO 2X BASIC
55 Connor McDavid 25.00 60.00

2022-23 SPx Radiance

*RADIANCE/100: .6X TO 1.5X BASIC
*RADIANCE RC/100: .5X TO 1.2X BASIC

2022-23 SPx NHL Shield Die Cut Hologram

*SHIELD/25: 1.5X TO 4X
*SHIELD RC/25: 1X TO 2.5X
55 Connor McDavid 30.00 80.00

2022-23 SPx '02-03 SPx Retro

R1 Patrice Bergeron 1.50 4.00
R2 Mitch Marner 2.00 5.00
R3 Patrik Laine 1.50 4.00
R4 Connor McDavid 6.00 15.00
R5 Kirill Kaprizov 4.00 10.00
R6 Adam Fox 1.50 4.00
R7 Jonathan Toews 2.00 5.00
R8 Rasmus Dahlin 1.50 4.00
R9 Kole Lind .75 2.00
R10 Vladimir Tarasenko 1.50 4.00
R11 Pius Suter 1.00 2.50
R12 Claude Giroux 1.25 3.00
R13 Nick Suzuki 2.50 6.00
R14 Maxime Comtois 1.00 2.50
R15 Steven Stamkos 2.50 6.00
R16 Chris Wideman .75 2.00
R17 Brent Burns 1.25 3.00
R18 Anze Kopitar 2.00 5.00
R19 Brock Boeser 1.50 4.00
R20 Aleksander Barkov 2.00 5.00
R21 Thomas Chabot 1.25 3.00
R22 Elias Lindholm 1.25 3.00
R23 John Gibson 1.25 3.00
R24 Miro Heiskanen 1.50 4.00
R25 Jonathan Huberdeau 1.50 4.00
R26 Sonny Milano 1.00 2.50
R27 Ryan O'Reilly 1.25 3.00
R28 Mark Stone 1.50 4.00
R29 Jack Campbell 1.25 3.00
R30 Sam Bennett 2.00 5.00
R31 Timo Meier 1.25 3.00
R32 Ryan Strome 1.25 3.00
R33 Tyler Bertuzzi 1.00 2.50
R34 Brock Nelson 1.25 3.00
R35 Joel Eriksson Ek 1.00 2.50
R36 Robin Lehner 1.00 2.50
R37 Tristan Jarry 1.25 3.00
R38 Alex Nedeljkovic 1.00 2.50
R39 Tage Thompson 1.50 4.00
R40 Vitek Vanecek 1.25 3.00
R41 Jared McCann 1.00 2.50
R42 John Marino 1.25 3.00
R43 Torey Krug 1.00 2.50
R44 Pavel Francouz 1.00 2.50
R45 Jeff Petry 1.25 3.00
R46 Mattias Ekholm 1.00 2.50
R47 Jaccob Slavin 1.00 2.50
R48 Nick Schmaltz 1.00 2.50
R49 Kirby Dach 1.25 3.00
R50 Blake Coleman 1.00 2.50
R51 Shane Wright 3.00 8.00
R52 Owen Power 2.50 6.00
R53 Kent Johnson 2.50 6.00
R54 Jakub Lauko 1.50 4.00
R55 Mads Sogaard 1.50 4.00
R56 Elmer Soderblom 2.50 6.00
R57 Mark Kastelic 1.00 2.50
R58 Juraj Slafkovsky 6.00 15.00
R59 Kaedan Korczak 1.00 2.50
R60 Filip Hallander 1.25 3.00
R61 Matty Beniers 3.00 8.00
R62 Jake Sanderson 3.00 8.00
R63 Noah Cates 1.25 3.00
R64 Alex Vlasic 1.00 2.50
R65 David Jiricek 2.50 6.00
R66 Wyatt Johnston 5.00 12.00
R67 Trey Fix-Wolansky 1.25 3.00
R68 Brandt Clarke 2.50 6.00
R69 Andrei Kuzmenko 2.50 6.00
R70 Matt Boldy 4.00 10.00
R71 Michael Eyssimont 1.25 3.00
R72 Dylan Holloway 2.50 6.00
R73 Lukas Dostal 2.50 6.00
R74 Matias Maccelli 2.00 5.00
R75 Ben Meyers 1.25 3.00
R76 Jacob Perreault 1.25 3.00
R77 Jacob Moverare 1.00 2.50
R78 Jonatan Berggren 2.00 5.00
R79 Erik Kallgren 1.25 3.00
R80 Nikita Okhotiuk 1.00 2.50
R81 Nick Abruzzese 1.25 3.00
R82 Arber Xhekaj 2.50 6.00
R83 Jordan Harris 1.50 4.00
R84 Fredrik Karlstrom 1.00 2.50
R85 Ronnie Attard 1.25 3.00
R86 Braden Schneider 2.00 5.00
R87 Kirill Marchenko 3.00 8.00
R88 Dylan Guenther 3.00 8.00
R89 Lukas Reichel 2.50 6.00
R90 Thomas Bordeleau 1.25 3.00
R91 Bobby Brink 1.25 3.00
R92 Samuel Poulin 1.50 4.00
R93 Kaiden Guhle 2.50 6.00
R94 Cole Koepke 1.25 3.00
R95 Pyotr Kochetkov 2.50 6.00
R96 Isaac Ratcliffe 1.25 3.00
R97 Brayden Tracey 1.00 2.50
R98 Marco Rossi 3.00 8.00
R99 Jack McBain 1.25 3.00
R100 Jack Quinn 2.00 5.00

2022-23 SPx '02-03 SPx Retro Autographs Lunar Waves

R6 Adam Fox 10.00 25.00
R9 Kole Lind 5.00 12.00
R11 Pius Suter 6.00 15.00
R13 Nick Suzuki 30.00 80.00
R14 Maxime Comtois 6.00 15.00
R16 Chris Wideman 5.00 12.00
R17 Brent Burns 8.00 20.00
R18 Anze Kopitar 12.00 30.00
R19 Brock Boeser 10.00 25.00
R20 Aleksander Barkov 12.00 30.00
R21 Thomas Chabot 8.00 20.00
R23 John Gibson 8.00 20.00
R24 Miro Heiskanen 10.00 25.00
R25 Jonathan Huberdeau 10.00 25.00
R26 Sonny Milano 6.00 15.00
R28 Mark Stone 10.00 25.00
R29 Jack Campbell 8.00 20.00
R35 Joel Eriksson Ek 6.00 15.00
R36 Robin Lehner 6.00 15.00
R37 Tristan Jarry 8.00 20.00
R38 Alex Nedeljkovic 6.00 15.00
R39 Tage Thompson 25.00 60.00
R40 Vitek Vanecek 8.00 20.00
R41 Jared McCann 6.00 15.00
R43 Torey Krug 6.00 15.00
R44 Pavel Francouz 6.00 15.00
R47 Jaccob Slavin 6.00 15.00
R48 Nick Schmaltz 6.00 15.00
R49 Kirby Dach 8.00 20.00
R50 Blake Coleman 6.00 15.00
R53 Kent Johnson B 15.00 40.00
R54 Jakub Lauko C 10.00 25.00
R55 Mads Sogaard C 10.00 25.00
R56 Elmer Soderblom C 15.00 40.00
R57 Mark Kastelic C 6.00 15.00
R59 Kaedan Korczak C 6.00 15.00
R60 Filip Hallander C 8.00 20.00
R62 Jake Sanderson C 20.00 50.00
R63 Noah Cates C 8.00 20.00
R64 Alex Vlasic C 6.00 15.00
R65 David Jiricek B 15.00 40.00
R66 Wyatt Johnston B 30.00 80.00
R68 Brandt Clarke B 15.00 40.00
R69 Andrei Kuzmenko B 15.00 40.00
R70 Matt Boldy B 25.00 60.00
R71 Michael Eyssimont C 8.00 20.00
R72 Dylan Holloway B 15.00 40.00
R73 Lukas Dostal C 15.00 40.00
R74 Matias Maccelli C 12.00 30.00
R75 Ben Meyers C 8.00 20.00
R76 Jacob Perreault C 8.00 20.00
R77 Jacob Moverare A 6.00 15.00
R78 Jonatan Berggren B 12.00 30.00
R79 Erik Kallgren C 8.00 20.00
R81 Nick Abruzzese C 8.00 20.00
R82 Arber Xhekaj C 15.00 40.00
R83 Jordan Harris C 10.00 25.00
R84 Fredrik Karlstrom C 6.00 15.00
R85 Ronnie Attard C 8.00 20.00
R86 Braden Schneider C 12.00 30.00
R87 Kirill Marchenko B 20.00 50.00
R88 Dylan Guenther B 20.00 50.00
R89 Lukas Reichel C 15.00 40.00
R90 Thomas Bordeleau C 8.00 20.00
R91 Bobby Brink C 8.00 20.00
R92 Samuel Poulin C 10.00 25.00
R93 Kaiden Guhle B 15.00 40.00
R94 Cole Koepke C 8.00 20.00
R95 Pyotr Kochetkov C 15.00 40.00
R97 Brayden Tracey C 6.00 15.00
R98 Marco Rossi B 20.00 50.00
R99 Jack McBain C 8.00 20.00
R100 Jack Quinn B 12.00 30.00

2022-23 SPx Autographs

1 Aleksander Barkov C 12.00 30.00
2 Adam Fox A 10.00 25.00
3 Anze Kopitar A 12.00 30.00
4 Anton Lundell C 8.00 20.00
5 Auston Matthews A 80.00 200.00
6 Alex Ovechkin A 125.00 300.00
8 Andrei Vasilevskiy A 12.00 30.00
10 Brandon Hagel C 6.00 15.00
11 Brad Marchand A 15.00 40.00
12 Brandon Saad C 6.00 15.00
13 Brady Tkachuk A 12.00 30.00
14 Michael Bunting C 8.00 20.00
15 Cam Atkinson C 8.00 20.00
17 Clayton Keller B 10.00 25.00
18 Cale Makar A 20.00 50.00
20 Drake Batherson C 8.00 20.00
23 Devon Toews C 6.00 15.00
24 Evgenii Dadonov C 5.00 12.00
25 Mason McTavish C 8.00 20.00
27 Elvis Merzlikins C 8.00 20.00
29 Jake Guentzel A 12.00 30.00
32 Igor Shesterkin A 15.00 40.00
33 Josh Bailey C 6.00 15.00
34 Jordan Eberle B 8.00 20.00
36 Jonathan Huberdeau A 10.00 25.00
37 Jacob Markstrom B 8.00 20.00
38 Josh Norris C 8.00 20.00
39 Cole Perfetti B 8.00 20.00
40 Joe Pavelski B 10.00 25.00
42 Jeremy Swayman B 12.00 30.00
44 James van Riemsdyk C 6.00 15.00
45 Arthur Kaliyev C 8.00 20.00
47 Kevin Fiala B 6.00 15.00
49 Karel Vejmelka C 5.00 12.00
50 Leon Draisaitl A 25.00 60.00
51 Anders Lee C 6.00 15.00
55 Connor McDavid A 150.00 400.00
56 Marc-Andre Fleury A 15.00 40.00
57 Mikael Granlund C 6.00 15.00
58 Miro Heiskanen B 10.00 25.00
61 Matthew Tkachuk A 15.00 40.00
62 Mats Zuccarello C 8.00 20.00
63 Dawson Mercer B 10.00 25.00
64 Nikolaj Ehlers C 8.00 20.00
67 Nick Suzuki A 15.00 40.00
72 Martin Necas C 12.00 30.00
73 Philipp Grubauer B 8.00 20.00
78 Robby Fabbri C 5.00 12.00
80 Ryan Nugent-Hopkins A 10.00 25.00
83 Robert Thomas C 8.00 20.00
86 Jonathan Marchessault A 10.00 25.00
87 Jaccob Slavin C 6.00 15.00
89 Mark Stone C 10.00 25.00
91 Teuvo Teravainen C 8.00 20.00
92 Tomas Hertl B 8.00 20.00
94 Tim Stutzle A 10.00 25.00
95 Tage Thompson C 10.00 25.00
98 Ville Husso C 5.00 12.00
99 Vasily Podkolzin B 5.00 12.00
101 Shane Wright D 25.00 60.00
102 Matt Boldy D 30.00 80.00
103 Marco Rossi C 25.00 60.00
104 Jacob Perreault B 10.00 25.00
107 Jack Quinn C 15.00 40.00
108 Owen Power D 20.00 50.00
109 Pyotr Kochetkov D 20.00 50.00
110 Braden Schneider D 15.00 40.00
111 Lukas Reichel D 20.00 50.00
112 Nick Abruzzese D 10.00 25.00
113 Kent Johnson C 20.00 50.00
114 Bobby Brink D 10.00 25.00
115 Matias Maccelli D 15.00 40.00
117 Lukas Dostal D 20.00 50.00
118 Thomas Bordeleau D 10.00 25.00
119 Kaedan Korczak D 8.00 20.00
120 Dylan Holloway C 20.00 50.00
121 Brayden Tracey D 8.00 20.00
122 Samuel Fagemo D 8.00 20.00
123 Erik Kallgren D 10.00 25.00
125 Isaac Ratcliffe B 10.00 25.00
126 Ronnie Attard D 10.00 25.00
127 Noah Cates D 10.00 25.00
128 Jordan Harris D 12.00 30.00
129 Jack McBain D 10.00 25.00
130 Dylan Samberg D 10.00 25.00
131 Mads Sogaard D 12.00 30.00
132 Alex Vlasic D 8.00 20.00
133 Marc McLaughlin B 10.00 25.00
134 Zack Hayes D 8.00 20.00
135 Filip Hallander D 10.00 25.00
136 Fredrik Karlstrom D 8.00 20.00
138 Mark Kastelic D 8.00 20.00
139 Michael Eyssimont D 10.00 25.00
140 Valtteri Puustinen D 8.00 20.00
141 Andrei Kuzmenko C 20.00 50.00
142 Kaiden Guhle C 20.00 50.00
143 Juraj Slafkovsky C 60.00 150.00
145 Brandt Clarke C 20.00 50.00
147 Jake Sanderson D 25.00 60.00
149 Samuel Poulin D 12.00 30.00
150 Dylan Guenther C 25.00 60.00
151 Nick Perbix D 8.00 20.00
154 Matej Blumel D 12.00 30.00
155 Oskar Olausson D 10.00 25.00
156 Arber Xhekaj D 20.00 50.00
157 Pontus Holmberg D 10.00 25.00
159 Olle Lycksell D 10.00 25.00
160 Aatu Raty D 10.00 25.00
162 Johnathan Kovacevic D 10.00 25.00
166 Nick Blankenburg D 8.00 20.00
167 Elmer Soderblom D 20.00 50.00
170 Ben Meyers D 10.00 25.00
174 Vladislav Kolyachonok D 8.00 20.00
176 Kirill Marchenko C 25.00 60.00
177 Filip Roos D 8.00 20.00
178 William Bitten C 10.00 25.00
181 Jakub Lauko D 12.00 30.00
183 Chase Pearson D 8.00 20.00
184 Cole Koepke D 10.00 25.00
185 Wyatt Johnston C 40.00 100.00
186 Jean-Luc Foudy D 10.00 25.00
187 Jonatan Berggren D 15.00 40.00
188 Lucas Johansen D 8.00 20.00
190 David Jiricek C 20.00 50.00
192 Juuso Parssinen D 10.00 25.00
193 Nathan Smith D 8.00 20.00
194 Jacob Moverare A 8.00 20.00
196 Nick DeSimone D 10.00 25.00
198 Jake Christiansen D 10.00 25.00
200 Nikita Alexandrov D 10.00 25.00

2022-23 SPx Finite Rookies

*GOLD/299: .5X TO 1.2X BASIC
*GREEN/199: .6X TO 1.5X BASIC
*PLATINUM/99: .75X TO 2X BASIC
*SLVR SPEC/49: 1.2X TO 3X BASIC
*GOLD SPEC/25: 2X TO 5X BASIC
F1 Juraj Slafkovsky 5.00 12.00
F2 Marco Rossi 2.50 6.00
F3 Matty Beniers 2.50 6.00
F4 Jordan Spence 1.00 2.50
F5 Lukas Dostal 2.00 5.00
F6 Jack Quinn 1.50 4.00
F7 Matt Boldy 3.00 8.00
F8 David Jiricek 2.00 5.00
F9 Arber Xhekaj 2.00 5.00
F10 Jake Sanderson 2.50 6.00
F11 Elmer Soderblom 2.00 5.00
F12 Shane Wright 2.50 6.00
F13 Mads Sogaard 1.25 3.00

F14 Lukas Reichel 2.00 5.00
F15 Bobby Brink 1.00 2.50
F16 Nick Blankenburg .75 2.00
F17 Dylan Samberg 1.00 2.50
F18 Ronnie Attard 1.00 2.50
F19 Samuel Fagemo .75 2.00
F20 Dylan Guenther 2.50 6.00
F21 Brayden Tracey .75 2.00
F22 Kent Johnson 2.00 5.00
F23 Alex Vlasic .75 2.00
F24 Trey Fix-Wolansky 1.00 2.50
F25 Kaedan Korczak .75 2.00
F26 Chase Pearson .75 2.00
F27 Filip Hallander 1.00 2.50
F28 Jacob Perreault 1.00 2.50
F29 Noah Cates 1.00 2.50
F30 Kaiden Guhle 2.00 5.00
F31 Isaac Ratcliffe 1.00 2.50
F32 Michael Eyssimont 1.00 2.50
F33 Jack McBain 1.00 2.50
F34 Ben Meyers 1.00 2.50
F35 Matias Maccelli 1.50 4.00
F36 Andrei Kuzmenko 2.00 5.00
F37 Samuel Poulin 1.25 3.00
F38 Fredrik Karlstrom .75 2.00
F39 Nick Abruzzese 1.00 2.50
F40 Jordan Harris 1.25 3.00
F41 Erik Kallgren 1.00 2.50
F42 Braden Schneider 1.50 4.00
F43 Mark Kastelic .75 2.00
F44 Nathan Smith .75 2.00
F45 Cole Koepke 1.00 2.50
F46 Dylan Holloway 2.00 5.00
F47 Thomas Bordeleau 1.00 2.50
F48 Wyatt Johnston 4.00 10.00
F49 Brandt Clarke 2.00 5.00
F50 Owen Power 2.00 5.00

2022-23 SPx HoloChampions

*RED/65: .6X TO 1.5X BASIC
HCAK Anze Kopitar 4.00 10.00
HCAO Alex Ovechkin 10.00 25.00
HCBH Brett Hull 5.00 12.00
HCBM Brad Marchand 5.00 12.00
HCBP Brayden Point 3.00 8.00
HCCM Cale Makar 6.00 15.00
HCCO Chris Osgood 2.50 6.00
HCDK Darcy Kuemper 2.50 6.00
HCDP David Perron 2.00 5.00
HCEM Evgeni Malkin 5.00 12.00
HCJQ Jonathan Quick 3.00 8.00
HCJT Jonathan Toews 4.00 10.00
HCML Mario Lemieux 10.00 25.00
HCPK Patrick Kane 5.00 12.00
HCPR Patrick Roy 6.00 15.00
HCRO Ryan O'Reilly 2.50 6.00
HCSC Sidney Crosby 10.00 25.00
HCVH Victor Hedman 3.00 8.00
HCWG Wayne Gretzky 15.00 40.00

2022-23 SPx HoloChampions Gold

*GOLD/35: 1X TO 2.5X BASIC
HCPR Patrick Roy 30.00 80.00
HCWG Wayne Gretzky 80.00 200.00

2022-23 SPx HoloGraphs

*RED/25: .6X TO 1.5X BASIC
*GOLD/25: .6X TO 1.5X BASIC
HGAD Alex DeBrincat/49 10.00 25.00
HGAE Aaron Ekblad/49 10.00 25.00
HGAM Auston Matthews/25 80.00 200.00
HGAO Alex Ovechkin/25 80.00 200.00
HGAV Andrei Vasilevskiy/25 12.00 30.00
HGBM Brad Marchand/49 20.00 50.00
HGCM Connor McDavid/25 125.00 300.00
HGDC Dylan Cozens/49 8.00 20.00
HGIS Igor Shesterkin/25 40.00 100.00
HGJK Jordan Kyrou/49 8.00 20.00
HGJS Jeremy Swayman/99 25.00 60.00
HGKF Kevin Fiala/99 6.00 15.00
HGNS Nick Suzuki/25 25.00 60.00
HGPF Pavel Francouz/99 6.00 15.00
HGSM Sonny Milano/99 6.00 15.00

2022-23 SPx HoloGraphs Rookies

*RED: .5X TO 1.2X BASIC
*GOLD/25: .6X TO 1.5X BASIC
HGRAK Andrei Kuzmenko/49 15.00 40.00
HGRBC Brandt Clarke/49 30.00 80.00
HGRBS Braden Schneider/99 12.00 30.00
HGRDG Dylan Guenther/49 20.00 50.00
HGRDH Dylan Holloway/49 15.00 40.00
HGRDJ David Jiricek/49 15.00 40.00
HGREK Erik Kallgren/99 8.00 20.00
HGRES Elmer Soderblom/99 15.00 40.00
HGRJQ Jack Quinn/49 12.00 30.00
HGRKG Kaiden Guhle/99 15.00 40.00
HGRKJ Kent Johnson/49 15.00 40.00
HGRKK Kaedan Korczak/99 6.00 15.00
HGRLR Lukas Reichel/49 15.00 40.00
HGRMK Mark Kastelic/99 6.00 15.00
HGRMR Marco Rossi/49 20.00 50.00
HGRMS Mads Sogaard/99 10.00 25.00
HGRNA Nick Abruzzese/49 8.00 20.00
HGRSA Jake Sanderson/49 20.00 50.00
HGRSP Samuel Poulin/99 10.00 25.00
HGRTB Thomas Bordeleau/49 8.00 20.00
HGRWJ Wyatt Johnston/49 30.00 80.00

2022-23 SPx Patch Autographs

1 Aleksander Barkov/25 25.00 60.00
2 Adam Fox/25 20.00 50.00
3 Anze Kopitar/25 25.00 60.00
4 Anton Lundell/25 15.00 40.00
8 Andrei Vasilevskiy/25 25.00 60.00
11 Brad Marchand/25 30.00 80.00
12 Brandon Saad/25 12.00 30.00
13 Brady Tkachuk/25 25.00 60.00
14 Michael Bunting/25 15.00 40.00
15 Cam Atkinson/25 15.00 40.00
17 Clayton Keller/25 20.00 50.00
20 Drake Batherson/25 15.00 40.00
21 Connor McMichael/25 15.00 40.00
25 Mason McTavish/25 15.00 40.00
27 Elvis Merzlikins/25 15.00 40.00
29 Jake Guentzel/25 25.00 60.00
33 Josh Bailey/25 12.00 30.00
34 Jordan Eberle/25 15.00 40.00
36 Jonathan Huberdeau/25 20.00 50.00
37 Jacob Markstrom/25 15.00 40.00
38 Josh Norris/25 15.00 40.00
39 Cole Perfetti/25 15.00 40.00
40 Joe Pavelski/25 20.00 50.00
41 Jason Robertson/25 25.00 60.00
42 Jeremy Swayman/25 25.00 60.00
44 James van Riemsdyk/49 12.00 30.00
45 Arthur Kaliyev/25 15.00 40.00
47 Kevin Fiala/25 12.00 30.00
51 Anders Lee/25 12.00 30.00
57 Mikael Granlund/25 12.00 30.00
58 Miro Heiskanen/25 20.00 50.00
62 Mats Zuccarello/49 15.00 40.00
64 Nikolaj Ehlers/25 15.00 40.00
78 Robby Fabbri/25 10.00 25.00
80 Ryan Nugent-Hopkins/25 20.00 50.00
81 Ryan O'Reilly/25 15.00 40.00
83 Robert Thomas/25 15.00 40.00
86 Jonathan Marchessault/25 20.00 50.00
87 Jaccob Slavin/25 12.00 30.00
89 Mark Stone/25 20.00 50.00
91 Teuvo Teravainen/25 15.00 40.00
92 Tomas Hertl/25 15.00 40.00
96 Cole Sillinger/25 12.00 30.00
103 Marco Rossi/25 40.00 100.00
104 Jacob Perreault/25 15.00 40.00
106 Reilly Walsh/49 15.00 40.00
110 Braden Schneider/25 25.00 60.00
111 Lukas Reichel/25 40.00 100.00
112 Nick Abruzzese/49 15.00 40.00
114 Bobby Brink/49 15.00 40.00
115 Matias Maccelli/25 25.00 60.00
117 Lukas Dostal/25 30.00 80.00
118 Thomas Bordeleau/25 15.00 40.00
119 Kaedan Korczak/49 12.00 30.00
120 Dylan Holloway/25 30.00 80.00
121 Brayden Tracey/49 12.00 30.00
122 Samuel Fagemo/49 12.00 30.00
123 Erik Kallgren/49 15.00 40.00
125 Isaac Ratcliffe/49 15.00 40.00
126 Ronnie Attard/49 15.00 40.00
127 Noah Cates/25 15.00 40.00
128 Jordan Harris/25 20.00 50.00
129 Jack McBain/49 15.00 40.00
130 Dylan Samberg/49 15.00 40.00
131 Mads Sogaard/49 20.00 50.00
132 Alex Vlasic/49 12.00 30.00
133 Marc McLaughlin/49 15.00 40.00
134 Zack Hayes/49 12.00 30.00
135 Filip Hallander/49 15.00 40.00
136 Fredrik Karlstrom/49 12.00 30.00
138 Mark Kastelic/49 12.00 30.00
139 Michael Eyssimont/49 15.00 40.00
140 Valtteri Puustinen/49 12.00 30.00
142 Kaiden Guhle/25 30.00 80.00
145 Brandt Clarke/25 60.00 150.00
147 Jake Sanderson/25 40.00 100.00
149 Samuel Poulin/25 20.00 50.00
150 Dylan Guenther/25 40.00 100.00
151 Nick Perbix/49 12.00 30.00
154 Matej Blumel/49 20.00 50.00
156 Arber Xhekaj/25 30.00 80.00
157 Pontus Holmberg/49 15.00 40.00
159 Olle Lycksell/49 15.00 40.00
166 Nick Blankenburg/49 12.00 30.00
167 Elmer Soderblom/25 30.00 80.00
170 Ben Meyers/49 15.00 40.00
171 Nils Aman/49 15.00 40.00
174 Vladislav Kolyachonok/49 12.00 30.00
176 Kirill Marchenko/25 40.00 100.00
177 Filip Roos/49 12.00 30.00
178 William Bitten/49 15.00 40.00
181 Jakub Lauko/49 20.00 50.00
183 Chase Pearson/49 12.00 30.00
184 Cole Koepke/49 15.00 40.00
185 Wyatt Johnston/25 80.00 200.00
187 Jonatan Berggren/25 25.00 60.00
188 Lucas Johansen/49 12.00 30.00
190 David Jiricek/25 30.00 80.00
192 Juuso Parssinen/49 15.00 40.00
193 Nathan Smith/49 12.00 30.00
194 Jacob Moverare/49 12.00 30.00
196 Nick DeSimone/49 15.00 40.00
198 Jake Christiansen/49 15.00 40.00

2022-23 SPx Radiance FX

*BLUE/399: .5X TO 1.2X BASIC
*RED/249: .6X TO 1.5X BASIC
*GOLD/99: .75X TO 2X BASIC
RFX1 Wayne Gretzky 8.00 20.00
RFX2 Patrick Roy 3.00 8.00
RFX3 Mario Lemieux 5.00 12.00
RFX4 Mark Messier 2.50 6.00
RFX5 Jean Beliveau 1.25 3.00
RFX6 Gordie Howe 4.00 10.00
RFX7 Trevor Linden 1.25 3.00
RFX8 Brett Hull 2.50 6.00
RFX9 Dale Hawerchuk 1.50 4.00
RFX10 Bobby Orr 5.00 12.00
RFX11 Steve Yzerman 3.00 8.00
RFX12 Mike Modano 2.00 5.00
RFX13 Jarome Iginla 1.50 4.00
RFX14 Martin Brodeur 3.00 8.00
RFX15 Mike Bossy 1.25 3.00
RFX16 Dominik Hasek 2.00 5.00
RFX17 Teemu Selanne 2.50 6.00
RFX18 Mats Sundin 1.25 3.00
RFX19 Eric Lindros 2.00 5.00
RFX20 Ryan Getzlaf 1.25 3.00
RFX21 Trevor Zegras 1.25 3.00
RFX22 Clayton Keller 1.50 4.00
RFX23 Taylor Hall 1.25 3.00
RFX24 David Pastrnak 3.00 8.00
RFX25 Matthew Tkachuk 2.50 6.00
RFX26 Sebastian Aho 2.00 5.00
RFX27 Patrick Kane 2.50 6.00
RFX28 Jonathan Toews 2.00 5.00
RFX29 Cale Makar 3.00 8.00
RFX30 Nathan MacKinnon 5.00 12.00
RFX31 Johnny Gaudreau 2.00 5.00
RFX32 Jason Robertson 2.00 5.00
RFX33 Moritz Seider 1.50 4.00
RFX34 Connor McDavid 6.00 15.00
RFX35 Leon Draisaitl 4.00 10.00
RFX36 Spencer Knight 1.25 3.00
RFX37 Quinton Byfield 1.50 4.00
RFX38 Jonathan Huberdeau 1.50 4.00
RFX39 Marc-Andre Fleury 2.50 6.00
RFX40 Kirill Kaprizov 4.00 10.00
RFX41 Cole Caufield 2.50 6.00
RFX42 Roman Josi 1.25 3.00
RFX43 Jack Hughes 3.00 8.00
RFX44 Mathew Barzal 1.50 4.00
RFX45 Alexis Lafreniere 2.00 5.00
RFX46 Igor Shesterkin 2.50 6.00
RFX47 Alex DeBrincat 1.50 4.00
RFX48 Tim Stutzle 1.50 4.00
RFX49 Sidney Crosby 5.00 12.00
RFX50 Erik Karlsson 1.50 4.00
RFX51 Yanni Gourde 1.00 2.50
RFX52 Ryan O'Reilly 1.25 3.00
RFX53 Andrei Vasilevskiy 2.00 5.00
RFX54 Auston Matthews 5.00 12.00
RFX55 Mitch Marner 2.00 5.00
RFX56 Quinn Hughes 3.00 8.00
RFX57 Elias Pettersson 2.00 5.00
RFX58 Jack Eichel 2.00 5.00
RFX59 Alex Ovechkin 5.00 12.00
RFX60 Kyle Connor 2.00 5.00
RFX61 Shane Wright 3.00 8.00
RFX62 Andrei Kuzmenko 2.50 6.00
RFX63 Dylan Holloway 2.50 6.00
RFX64 Jonatan Berggren 2.00 5.00
RFX65 Jack Quinn 2.00 5.00
RFX66 Jordan Harris 1.50 4.00
RFX67 Bobby Brink 1.25 3.00
RFX68 Jack McBain 1.25 3.00
RFX69 Kaiden Guhle 2.50 6.00
RFX70 Brayden Tracey 1.00 2.50
RFX71 Kent Johnson 2.50 6.00
RFX72 Lukas Dostal 2.50 6.00
RFX73 Matt Boldy 4.00 10.00
RFX74 Arber Xhekaj 2.50 6.00
RFX75 Owen Power 2.50 6.00
RFX76 Wyatt Johnston 5.00 12.00
RFX77 Nick Abruzzese 1.25 3.00
RFX78 David Jiricek 2.50 6.00
RFX79 Pyotr Kochetkov 2.50 6.00
RFX80 Thomas Bordeleau 1.25 3.00
RFX81 Elmer Soderblom 2.50 6.00
RFX82 Marco Rossi 3.00 8.00
RFX83 Lukas Reichel 2.50 6.00
RFX84 Matty Beniers 3.00 8.00
RFX85 Ben Meyers 1.25 3.00
RFX86 Dylan Guenther 3.00 8.00
RFX87 Filip Hallander 1.25 3.00
RFX88 Isaac Ratcliffe 1.25 3.00
RFX89 Jake Sanderson 3.00 8.00
RFX90 Mads Sogaard 1.50 4.00
RFX91 Brandt Clarke 2.50 6.00
RFX92 Jordan Spence 1.25 3.00
RFX93 Fredrik Karlstrom 1.00 2.50
RFX94 Samuel Poulin 1.50 4.00
RFX95 Kaedan Korczak 1.00 2.50
RFX96 Mark Kastelic 1.00 2.50
RFX97 Braden Schneider 2.00 5.00
RFX98 Erik Kallgren 1.25 3.00
RFX99 Jacob Perreault 1.25 3.00
RFX100 Juraj Slafkovsky 6.00 15.00

2022-23 SPx Radiance FX Autographs Purple

RFX32 Jason Robertson/35 20.00 50.00
RFX36 Spencer Knight/35 12.00 30.00
RFX38 Jonathan Huberdeau/35 15.00 40.00
RFX45 Alexis Lafreniere/35 20.00 50.00
RFX47 Alex DeBrincat/35 15.00 40.00
RFX52 Ryan O'Reilly/35 12.00 30.00
RFX62 Andrei Kuzmenko/35 25.00 60.00
RFX63 Dylan Holloway/35 25.00 60.00
RFX64 Jonatan Berggren/35 20.00 50.00
RFX65 Jack Quinn/35 20.00 50.00
RFX66 Jordan Harris/35 15.00 40.00
RFX67 Bobby Brink/35 12.00 30.00
RFX68 Jack McBain/35 12.00 30.00
RFX69 Kaiden Guhle/35 25.00 60.00
RFX70 Brayden Tracey/35 10.00 25.00
RFX71 Kent Johnson/35 25.00 60.00
RFX72 Lukas Dostal/35 25.00 60.00
RFX73 Matt Boldy/35 40.00 100.00
RFX74 Arber Xhekaj/35 25.00 60.00
RFX76 Wyatt Johnston/35 50.00 125.00
RFX77 Nick Abruzzese/35 12.00 30.00
RFX78 David Jiricek/35 25.00 60.00
RFX79 Pyotr Kochetkov/35 25.00 60.00
RFX80 Thomas Bordeleau/35 12.00 30.00
RFX81 Elmer Soderblom/35 25.00 60.00
RFX83 Lukas Reichel/35 25.00 60.00
RFX85 Ben Meyers/35 12.00 30.00
RFX86 Dylan Guenther/35 30.00 80.00
RFX87 Filip Hallander/35 12.00 30.00
RFX89 Jake Sanderson/35 30.00 80.00
RFX90 Mads Sogaard/35 15.00 40.00
RFX91 Brandt Clarke/35 25.00 60.00
RFX93 Fredrik Karlstrom/35 10.00 25.00
RFX94 Samuel Poulin/35 15.00 40.00
RFX95 Kaedan Korczak/35 10.00 25.00
RFX96 Mark Kastelic/35 10.00 25.00
RFX97 Braden Schneider/35 20.00 50.00
RFX99 Jacob Perreault/35 12.00 30.00

2022-23 SPx Rookie Jersey Autographs

AB Nick Abruzzese/375 10.00 25.00
AK Andrei Kuzmenko/175 20.00 50.00
AV Alex Vlasic/375 8.00 20.00
AX Arber Xhekaj/375 20.00 50.00
BB Bobby Brink/375 10.00 25.00
BC Brandt Clarke/175 20.00 50.00
BE Jonatan Berggren/175 15.00 40.00
BH Braden Schneider/375 15.00 40.00
BO Matt Boldy/75 30.00 80.00
BT Brayden Tracey/375 8.00 20.00
CE Chase Pearson/375 8.00 20.00
CK Cole Koepke/375 10.00 25.00
DG Dylan Guenther/175 25.00 60.00
DH Dylan Holloway/175 20.00 50.00
DJ David Jiricek/375 20.00 50.00
DS Dylan Samberg/375 10.00 25.00
EK Erik Kallgren/375 10.00 25.00
ES Elmer Soderblom/175 20.00 50.00
JB Jack McBain/375 10.00 25.00
JC Jake Christiansen/375 10.00 25.00
JH Jordan Harris/375 12.00 30.00
JL Jakub Lauko/375 12.00 30.00
JQ Jack Quinn/175 15.00 40.00
KG Kaiden Guhle/375 20.00 50.00
KJ Kent Johnson/175 20.00 50.00
KM Kirill Marchenko/175 25.00 60.00
LD Lukas Dostal/375 20.00 50.00
MB Matty Beniers/75 100.00 250.00
MC Matias Maccelli/375 15.00 40.00
MK Mark Kastelic/375 8.00 20.00
MM Marc McLaughlin/375 10.00 25.00
MO Jacob Moverare/375 8.00 20.00
MR Marco Rossi/175 25.00 60.00
MY Michael Eyssimont/375 10.00 25.00
NA Nils Aman/375 10.00 25.00
NB Nick Blankenburg/375 8.00 20.00
NC Noah Cates/375 10.00 25.00
NP Nick Perbix/375 8.00 20.00
NS Nathan Smith/375 8.00 20.00
OL Olle Lycksell/375 10.00 25.00
OP Owen Power/75 50.00 125.00
PE Jacob Perreault/375 10.00 25.00
PK Pyotr Kochetkov/375 20.00 50.00
PR Pavol Regenda/375 10.00 25.00
RA Ronnie Attard/375 10.00 25.00
RE Lukas Reichel/175 20.00 50.00
RW Reilly Walsh/375 10.00 25.00
SA Jake Sanderson/175 25.00 60.00
SE Jordan Spence/375 10.00 25.00
SF Samuel Fagemo/175 8.00 20.00
SO Mads Sogaard/375 12.00 30.00
SP Samuel Poulin/175 12.00 30.00
SW Shane Wright/75 25.00 60.00
TB Thomas Bordeleau/375 10.00 25.00
WJ Wyatt Johnston/175 30.00 80.00
ZH Zack Hayes/375 8.00 20.00

2022-23 SPx Rookie Jersey Autographs Spectrum

*SPECTRUM: .6X TO 1.5X BASIC
MR Marco Rossi/35 50.00 125.00

2022-23 SPx Rookie Superscripts

SSRAM Nils Aman D 8.00 20.00
SSRAV Alex Vlasic D 6.00 15.00
SSRAX Arber Xhekaj D 25.00 60.00
SSRBB Bobby Brink D 8.00 20.00
SSRBC Brandt Clarke D 15.00 40.00
SSRBM Ben Meyers D 8.00 20.00
SSRBO Matt Boldy C 30.00 80.00
SSRBS Braden Schneider D 12.00 30.00
SSRBT Brayden Tracey B 6.00 15.00
SSRCK Cole Koepke D 8.00 20.00
SSRCP Chase Pearson D 6.00 15.00
SSRDG Dylan Guenther D 20.00 50.00
SSRDH Dylan Holloway C 15.00 40.00
SSRDJ David Jiricek A 15.00 40.00
SSRDS Dylan Samberg D 8.00 20.00
SSREK Erik Kallgren C 8.00 20.00
SSRES Elmer Soderblom D 15.00 40.00
SSRFH Filip Hallander D 8.00 20.00
SSRFK Fredrik Karlstrom D 6.00 15.00
SSRJC Jake Christiansen D 8.00 20.00
SSRJH Jordan Harris D 10.00 25.00
SSRJL Jakub Lauko A 10.00 25.00
SSRJM Jack McBain D 8.00 20.00
SSRJP Jacob Perreault C 8.00 20.00
SSRJQ Jack Quinn C 12.00 30.00
SSRJS Juraj Slafkovsky B 50.00 125.00
SSRKG Kaiden Guhle D 15.00 40.00
SSRKJ Kent Johnson C 15.00 40.00
SSRKK Kaedan Korczak D 6.00 15.00
SSRKM Kirill Marchenko A 20.00 50.00
SSRKU Andrei Kuzmenko B 15.00 40.00
SSRLD Lukas Dostal D 15.00 40.00
SSRLR Lukas Reichel D 15.00 40.00
SSRMC Marc McLaughlin A 8.00 20.00
SSRME Michael Eyssimont D 8.00 20.00
SSRMK Mark Kastelic A 6.00 15.00
SSRMM Matias Maccelli D 12.00 30.00
SSRMR Marco Rossi B 20.00 50.00
SSRMS Mads Sogaard D 10.00 25.00
SSRNA Nick Abruzzese D 8.00 20.00
SSRNC Noah Cates D 8.00 20.00
SSRNP Nick Perbix D 6.00 15.00
SSRNS Nathan Smith D 6.00 15.00
SSROP Owen Power C 15.00 40.00
SSRPK Pyotr Kochetkov D 25.00 60.00
SSRRA Ronnie Attard D 8.00 20.00
SSRRW Reilly Walsh D 8.00 20.00
SSRSA Jake Sanderson D 20.00 50.00
SSRSF Samuel Fagemo D 6.00 15.00
SSRSP Samuel Poulin D 10.00 25.00
SSRSW Shane Wright C 20.00 50.00
SSRTB Thomas Bordeleau D 8.00 20.00
SSRVK Vladislav Kolyachonok D 6.00 15.00
SSRVP Valtteri Puustinen D 6.00 15.00
SSRWJ Wyatt Johnston C 30.00 80.00
SSRZH Zack Hayes D 6.00 15.00

2022-23 SPx Rookie Superscripts Gold

*GOLD: .6X TO 1.5X BASIC
SSRDJ David Jiricek/25 50.00 125.00
SSRJS Juraj Slafkovsky/25 125.00 300.00

2022-23 SPx Shadow Box

*GOLD/99: 1X TO 2.5X BASIC
SB1 Connor McDavid 15.00 40.00
SB2 Patrice Bergeron 4.00 10.00
SB3 Matthew Tkachuk 6.00 15.00
SB4 Mikko Rantanen 8.00 20.00
SB5 Jonathan Huberdeau 4.00 10.00
SB6 Kirill Kaprizov 10.00 25.00
SB7 Anze Kopitar 5.00 12.00
SB8 Alex Ovechkin 12.00 30.00
SB9 Igor Shesterkin 6.00 15.00
SB10 Sidney Crosby 12.00 30.00
SB11 Brayden Point 4.00 10.00
SB12 William Nylander 6.00 15.00
SB13 Elias Pettersson 5.00 12.00
SB14 Claude Giroux 3.00 8.00
SB15 Jack Hughes 8.00 20.00
SB16 Matt Boldy 10.00 25.00
SB17 Kent Johnson 6.00 15.00
SB18 Lukas Reichel 6.00 15.00
SB19 Thomas Bordeleau 3.00 8.00
SB20 Wyatt Johnston 12.00 30.00
SB21 Owen Power 6.00 15.00
SB22 Nick Abruzzese 3.00 8.00
SB23 Dylan Samberg 3.00 8.00
SB24 Andrei Kuzmenko 6.00 15.00
SB25 Samuel Poulin 4.00 10.00
SB26 Trey Fix-Wolansky 3.00 8.00
SB27 Elmer Soderblom 6.00 15.00
SB28 Marco Rossi 8.00 20.00
SB29 Noah Cates 3.00 8.00
SB30 Jacob Perreault 3.00 8.00
SB31 Dylan Guenther 8.00 20.00
SB32 Matty Beniers 8.00 20.00
SB33 Shane Wright 8.00 20.00
SB34 Matias Maccelli 5.00 12.00
SB35 Lukas Dostal 6.00 15.00
SB36 Jordan Spence 3.00 8.00
SB37 Jack Quinn 5.00 12.00
SB38 Kaiden Guhle 6.00 15.00
SB39 Brandt Clarke 6.00 15.00
SB40 Juraj Slafkovsky 15.00 40.00
SB41 Filip Hallander 3.00 8.00
SB42 David Jiricek 6.00 15.00
SB43 Mads Sogaard 4.00 10.00
SB44 Cole Koepke 3.00 8.00
SB45 Jordan Harris 4.00 10.00
SB46 Braden Schneider 5.00 12.00
SB47 Bobby Brink 3.00 8.00
SB48 Mark Kastelic 2.50 6.00
SB49 Arber Xhekaj 6.00 15.00
SB50 Jake Sanderson 8.00 20.00

2022-23 SPx Signature Fabrics

*SPECTRUM/25: .5X TO 1.2X BASIC
SFAS Andrei Svechnikov/25 12.00 30.00
SFBG Brendan Gallagher/49 10.00 25.00
SFBS Brandon Saad/49 8.00 20.00
SFCO Blake Coleman/49 8.00 20.00
SFJE Joel Eriksson Ek/49 8.00 20.00
SFLE Anders Lee/49 8.00 20.00
SFNS Nick Schmaltz/49 8.00 20.00
SFRL Robin Lehner/49 8.00 20.00
SFTH Taylor Hall/25 10.00 25.00
SFTT Teuvo Teravainen/49 10.00 25.00

2022-23 SPx Superscripts

*GOLD/25: .6X TO 1.5X BASIC
SSAC Andrew Copp C 6.00 15.00
SSAK Arthur Kaliyev C 10.00 25.00
SSAL Anders Lee C 8.00 20.00
SSAN Alex Nedeljkovic C 8.00 20.00
SSBA Josh Bailey C 8.00 20.00
SSBC Blake Coleman C 8.00 20.00
SSBH Brandon Hagel C 8.00 20.00
SSBJ Boone Jenner C 10.00 25.00
SSBS Brandon Saad C 8.00 20.00
SSCC Charlie Coyle C 10.00 25.00
SSCI Anthony Cirelli C 8.00 20.00
SSCK Clayton Keller B 12.00 30.00
SSCM Casey Mittelstadt C 10.00 25.00
SSCW Chris Wideman C 6.00 15.00
SSDB Drake Batherson C 10.00 25.00
SSDK Darcy Kuemper C 10.00 25.00
SSDT Devon Toews C 8.00 20.00
SSED Evgenii Dadonov C 6.00 15.00
SSEM Elvis Merzlikins C 10.00 25.00
SSJA Jake Allen C 10.00 25.00
SSJE Joel Eriksson Ek C 8.00 20.00
SSJG John Gibson C 10.00 25.00
SSJK John Klingberg A 10.00 25.00
SSJM Jacob Markstrom C 10.00 25.00
SSJS Jeremy Swayman C 15.00 40.00
SSJZ Jason Zucker C 10.00 25.00
SSKL Kole Lind C 6.00 15.00
SSMC Maxime Comtois C 8.00 20.00
SSMF Marcus Foligno C 8.00 20.00
SSMG Mikael Granlund C 8.00 20.00
SSNE Nikolaj Ehlers C 10.00 25.00
SSNS Nick Schmaltz C 8.00 20.00
SSPE Cal Petersen C 6.00 15.00
SSPS Pius Suter C 8.00 20.00
SSRF Robby Fabbri C 6.00 15.00
SSRL Robin Lehner C 8.00 20.00
SSRU Bryan Rust C 10.00 25.00
SSSJ Seth Jarvis C 12.00 30.00
SSSL Jaccob Slavin C 8.00 20.00
SSSM Sonny Milano C 8.00 20.00
SSSR Sam Reinhart C 20.00 50.00
SSTJ Tristan Jarry C 10.00 25.00
SSTK Torey Krug C 8.00 20.00
SSTS Ty Smith B 10.00 25.00
SSTT Tyler Toffoli B 10.00 25.00
SSVH Ville Husso B 6.00 15.00
SSVV Vitek Vanecek C 10.00 25.00
SSYS Yegor Sharangovich C 10.00 25.00

2022-23 SPx White Out Autographs

WOAB Aleksander Barkov A 12.00 30.00
WOAE Aaron Ekblad B 10.00 25.00
WOAK Arthur Kaliyev C 8.00 20.00
WOAS Andrei Svechnikov B 10.00 25.00
WOBB Brock Boeser B 10.00 25.00
WOCA Cam Atkinson C 8.00 20.00
WODC Dylan Cozens B 8.00 20.00
WODP David Perron C 6.00 15.00
WOJA Jake Allen C 8.00 20.00
WOJC Jack Campbell C 8.00 20.00
WOJD Jamie Drysdale C 6.00 15.00
WOJG Jake Guentzel B 12.00 30.00
WOJM Jared McCann B 6.00 15.00
WOJP Jeff Petry C 8.00 20.00
WOKD Kirby Dach C 8.00 20.00
WOKM K'Andre Miller A 6.00 15.00
WOMT Matthew Tkachuk A 15.00 40.00
WONR Nick Robertson C 8.00 20.00
WOPG Philipp Grubauer C 8.00 20.00
WORH Roope Hintz C 10.00 25.00
WOTC Thomas Chabot C 8.00 20.00
WOTD Thatcher Demko C 10.00 25.00
WOTK Torey Krug C 6.00 15.00
WOYS Yegor Sharangovich C 8.00 20.00
WOZP Zach Parise B 8.00 20.00
WOZW Zach Werenski C 12.00 30.00

2022-23 SPx White Out Rookie Autographs

WORAK Andrei Kuzmenko B 15.00 40.00
WORAV Alex Vlasic C 6.00 15.00
WORBC Brandt Clarke D 15.00 40.00
WORDG Dylan Guenther D 20.00 50.00
WORDH Dylan Holloway C 15.00 40.00
WORDJ David Jiricek A 15.00 40.00
WORDS Dylan Samberg D 8.00 20.00
WORES Elmer Soderblom C 15.00 40.00
WORJH Jordan Harris D 10.00 25.00
WORJM Jack McBain D 8.00 20.00
WORJP Jacob Perreault C 8.00 20.00
WORJQ Jack Quinn B 12.00 30.00
WORKG Kaiden Guhle D 15.00 40.00
WORKJ Kent Johnson C 15.00 40.00
WORKK Kaedan Korczak D 6.00 15.00
WORLD Lukas Dostal D 15.00 40.00
WORLR Lukas Reichel D 15.00 40.00
WORMB Matt Boldy C 25.00 60.00
WORMK Mark Kastelic D 6.00 15.00
WORMM Matias Maccelli D 12.00 30.00
WORMR Marco Rossi B 20.00 50.00
WORMS Mads Sogaard D 10.00 25.00
WORNA Nick Abruzzese D 8.00 20.00
WORNB Nick Blankenburg D 6.00 15.00
WOROP Owen Power C 30.00 80.00
WORSA Jake Sanderson D 20.00 50.00
WORSF Samuel Fagemo D 6.00 15.00
WORSP Samuel Poulin D 10.00 25.00
WORSW Shane Wright C 20.00 50.00
WORTB Thomas Bordeleau D 8.00 20.00
WORWJ Wyatt Johnston D 30.00 80.00

2023-24 SPx

1 Connor McDavid 4.00 10.00
2 Anze Kopitar 1.25 3.00
3 John Tavares 1.25 3.00
4 Alex DeBrincat 1.00 2.50
5 Dylan Larkin 1.00 2.50
6 Nick Suzuki 1.50 4.00
7 Erik Karlsson 1.00 2.50
8 Jordan Eberle .75 2.00
9 Jake Oettinger 1.25 3.00
10 Joel Eriksson Ek .60 1.50
11 Alex Ovechkin 3.00 8.00
12 William Nylander 1.50 4.00
13 Jack Eichel 1.25 3.00
14 Dylan Guenther 1.00 2.50
15 Seth Jones .75 2.00
16 Johnny Gaudreau 1.25 3.00
17 Seth Jarvis 1.00 2.50
18 Juuse Saros 1.00 2.50
19 Bo Horvat 1.00 2.50
20 Aleksander Barkov 1.25 3.00
21 Sebastian Aho 1.25 3.00
22 Ryan Nugent-Hopkins 1.00 2.50
23 Charlie McAvoy 1.00 2.50
24 Jack Hughes 2.00 5.00
25 Matt Duchene .75 2.00
26 Jared McCann .60 1.50
27 K'Andre Miller .60 1.50
28 Elias Pettersson 1.25 3.00
29 Roman Josi .75 2.00
30 Mitch Marner 1.25 3.00
31 Nathan MacKinnon 3.00 8.00
32 Karel Vejmelka .50 1.25
33 Lucas Raymond 1.25 3.00
34 Darcy Kuemper .75 2.00
35 Mikko Rantanen 2.00 5.00
36 Juraj Slafkovsky 1.50 4.00
37 Kyle Connor 1.25 3.00
38 Andrei Kuzmenko .75 2.00
39 Carter Hart .75 2.00
40 Jordan Kyrou .75 2.00
41 Matty Beniers 1.00 2.50
42 Timo Meier .75 2.00
43 Tomas Hertl .75 2.00
44 Cale Makar 2.00 5.00
45 Kirby Dach .75 2.00
46 Mathew Barzal 1.00 2.50
47 Moritz Seider 1.00 2.50
48 Matthew Tkachuk 1.50 4.00
49 Leon Draisaitl 2.50 6.00
50 Mason McTavish .75 2.00
51 Nikolaj Ehlers .75 2.00
52 Kirill Kaprizov 2.50 6.00
53 John Gibson .75 2.00
54 Brent Burns .75 2.00
55 Jeremy Swayman 1.25 3.00
56 Carter Verhaeghe .75 2.00
57 Brayden Point 1.00 2.50
58 Brady Tkachuk 1.25 3.00
59 J.T. Miller 1.00 2.50
60 Jacob Markstrom .75 2.00
61 Brad Marchand 1.50 4.00
62 Roope Hintz 1.00 2.50
63 Tage Thompson 1.00 2.50
64 Connor Hellebuyck 1.50 4.00
65 Jonathan Marchessault 1.00 2.50
66 Alex Iafallo .50 1.25
67 Mattias Ekholm .60 1.50
68 Tim Stutzle 1.00 2.50
69 Clayton Keller 1.00 2.50
70 Sidney Crosby 3.00 8.00
71 Marcus Foligno .60 1.50
72 Trevor Zegras .75 2.00
73 Lukas Reichel .75 2.00
74 Oskar Lindblom .60 1.50
75 Josh Norris .75 2.00
76 Cole Caufield 1.50 4.00
77 Jake Neighbours .75 2.00
78 Adam Fox 1.00 2.50
79 Ilya Sorokin 1.25 3.00
80 Samuel Girard .50 1.25
81 Bryan Rust .75 2.00
82 Igor Shesterkin 1.50 4.00
83 Travis Konecny .75 2.00
84 Patrik Laine 1.00 2.50
85 Jonathan Huberdeau 1.00 2.50
86 David Pastrnak 2.00 5.00
87 Aaron Ekblad 1.00 2.50
88 Rasmus Dahlin 1.00 2.50
89 Quinton Byfield 1.00 2.50
90 Dylan Cozens .75 2.00
91 Vitek Vanecek .75 2.00
92 Andrei Vasilevskiy 1.25 3.00
93 Quinn Hughes 2.00 5.00
94 Alexis Lafreniere 1.25 3.00
95 Nikita Kucherov 1.50 4.00
96 Evgeni Malkin 1.50 4.00
97 Tyler Toffoli .75 2.00
98 Mark Stone 1.00 2.50
99 Jason Robertson 1.25 3.00
100 Auston Matthews 3.00 8.00
101 Connor Bedard RC 100.00 250.00
102 Luke Hughes RC 6.00 15.00
103 Ridly Greig RC 3.00 8.00
104 Logan Cooley RC 6.00 15.00
105 Marco Kasper RC 5.00 12.00
106 Adam Fantilli RC 6.00 15.00
107 Brock Faber RC 5.00 12.00
108 Will Cuylle RC 3.00 8.00
109 Leo Carlsson RC 6.00 15.00
110 Devon Levi RC 5.00 12.00
111 Ilya Solovyov RC 2.00 5.00
112 Stanislav Svozil RC 1.50 4.00
113 Cole McWard RC 2.00 5.00
114 William Dufour RC 1.50 4.00
115 Tyson Foerster RC 4.00 10.00
116 Connor Zary RC 4.00 10.00
117 Elliot Desnoyers RC 2.00 5.00
118 Jakob Pelletier RC 2.50 6.00
119 Jiri Kulich RC 4.00 10.00
120 Joel Teasdale RC 2.00 5.00
121 Matt Savoie RC 4.00 10.00
122 Simon Edvinsson RC 4.00 10.00
123 Adam Edstrom RC 2.00 5.00
124 Vincent Desharnais RC 2.50 6.00
125 Vincent Iorio RC 2.00 5.00
126 Nikita Nesterenko RC 2.00 5.00
127 Samuel Bolduc RC 2.00 5.00
128 Martin Pospisil RC 2.50 6.00
129 Samuel Knazko RC 2.00 5.00
130 Raphael Lavoie RC 2.00 5.00
131 Matt Murray RC 2.00 5.00
132 Aidan McDonough RC 1.50 4.00
133 Alex Laferriere RC 3.00 8.00
134 Matthew Knies RC 8.00 20.00
135 Dmitri Voronkov RC 2.50 6.00
136 Lucas Condotta RC 2.00 5.00
137 Tristen Robins RC 2.00 5.00
138 Fraser Minten RC 4.00 10.00
139 Jackson LaCombe RC 2.00 5.00
140 Danil Gushchin RC 2.00 5.00
141 Justin Sourdif RC 2.00 5.00
142 Wyatt Kaiser RC 2.00 5.00
143 Mackie Samoskevich RC 3.00 8.00
144 Jet Greaves RC 3.00 8.00
145 Ryker Evans RC 2.50 6.00
146 Matthew Coronato RC 3.00 8.00
147 Ryan Shea RC 2.00 5.00
148 Billy Sweezey RC 2.00 5.00
149 Mason Lohrei RC 3.00 8.00
150 Bobby McMann RC 3.00 8.00
151 Drew Helleson RC 2.00 5.00
152 Simon Nemec RC 4.00 10.00
153 Akito Hirose RC 1.50 4.00
154 Dustin Wolf RC 6.00 15.00
155 Adam Ginning RC 2.00 5.00
156 Kevin Korchinski RC 3.00 8.00
157 Luke Philp RC 2.00 5.00
158 John Beecher RC 4.00 10.00
159 Damien Giroux RC 2.00 5.00
160 Matthew Kessel RC 1.50 4.00
161 Olle Eriksson Ek RC 2.00 5.00
162 Jayden Struble RC 2.50 6.00
163 Egor Afanasyev RC 2.00 5.00
164 Maxence Guenette RC 2.00 5.00
165 Milos Kelemen RC 2.00 5.00
166 Isak Rosen RC 2.00 5.00
167 Hunter McKown RC 2.00 5.00
168 Jonathan Gruden RC 2.00 5.00
169 Matthew Poitras RC 4.00 10.00
170 Sean Farrell RC 2.00 5.00
171 Pavel Mintyukov RC 3.00 8.00
172 Nick Swaney RC 2.00 5.00
173 Spencer Stastney RC 2.00 5.00
174 Joona Koppanen RC 1.50 4.00
175 Emil Andrae RC 2.00 5.00
176 Cole Guttman RC 2.00 5.00
177 Hardy Haman Aktell RC 2.00 5.00
178 David Gust RC 2.00 5.00
179 Tye Kartye RC 3.00 8.00
180 Michael Kesselring RC 2.00 5.00
181 Arturs Silovs RC 4.00 10.00
182 Jaxson Stauber RC 2.00 5.00
183 Tyler Kleven RC 2.00 5.00
184 Hugh McGing RC 2.00 5.00
185 Owen Beck RC 3.00 8.00
186 Ryan Johnson RC 2.50 6.00
187 Tyler Angle RC 2.00 5.00
188 Ty Emberson RC 2.00 5.00
189 Lukas Rousek RC 1.50 4.00
190 Leevi Merilainen RC 2.00 5.00
191 Jiri Patera RC 3.00 8.00
192 Walker Duehr RC 1.50 4.00
193 Jake Livingstone RC 2.00 5.00

194 Ondrej Pavel RC 2.00 5.00
195 Luke Evangelista RC 3.00 8.00
196 Henry Thrun RC 2.00 5.00
197 Mikael Pyyhtia RC 2.00 5.00
198 Arnaud Durandeau RC 2.00 5.00
199 Zach Benson RC 3.00 8.00
200 Yaroslav Askarov RC 5.00 12.00

2023-24 SPx Grand Finale
*FINALE/50: 1X TO 2.5X BASIC
*FINALE RC/50: .75X TO 2X BASIC
1 Connor McDavid 30.00 80.00
100 Auston Matthews 15.00 40.00
101 Connor Bedard 300.00 800.00

2023-24 SPx NHL Shield Die Cut Hologram
*SHIELD/25: 1.5X TO 4X
*SHIELD RC/25: 1X TO 2.5X
1 Connor McDavid 40.00 100.00
100 Auston Matthews 30.00 80.00
101 Connor Bedard 400.00 1000.00
102 Luke Hughes 30.00 80.00
104 Logan Cooley 30.00 80.00
106 Adam Fantilli 30.00 80.00
107 Brock Faber 30.00 80.00
109 Leo Carlsson 25.00 60.00
110 Devon Levi 25.00 60.00

2023-24 SPx Parallax Purple
*PURPLE/149: .5X TO 1.2X BASIC

2023-24 SPx Radiance
*RADIANCE/100: .6X TO 1.5X BASIC
101 Connor Bedard 150.00 400.00

2023-24 SPx '03-04 Retro Rookie Jersey Autographs
20BF Brock Faber 50.00 125.00
20DG Danil Gushchin 8.00 20.00
20JP Jakob Pelletier 10.00 25.00
20KN Matthew Knies 30.00 80.00
20LC Logan Cooley 50.00 125.00
20MK Marco Kasper 25.00 60.00
20OB Owen Beck 12.00 30.00
20SB Samuel Bolduc 8.00 20.00
20SE Simon Edvinsson 15.00 40.00
20TF Tyson Foerster 25.00 60.00
20WC Will Cuylle 12.00 30.00

2023-24 SPx '03-04 Retro Rookie Jersey Autographs Spectrum
*SPCTRM/25: .6X TO 1.5X BASIC
20CA Leo Carlsson 60.00 150.00

2023-24 SPx Autographs
1 Connor McDavid SP 150.00 400.00
3 John Tavares SP 12.00 30.00
8 Jordan Eberle 8.00 20.00
9 Jake Oettinger 12.00 30.00
10 Joel Eriksson Ek 6.00 15.00
13 Jack Eichel SP 12.00 30.00
17 Seth Jarvis 10.00 25.00
18 Juuse Saros SP 10.00 25.00
20 Aleksander Barkov 12.00 30.00
26 Jared McCann 6.00 15.00
27 K'Andre Miller 6.00 15.00
28 Elias Pettersson SP 12.00 30.00
29 Roman Josi 8.00 20.00
32 Karel Vejmelka 5.00 12.00
34 Darcy Kuemper 8.00 20.00
36 Juraj Slafkovsky 15.00 40.00
38 Andrei Kuzmenko 8.00 20.00
42 Timo Meier 8.00 20.00
43 Tomas Hertl 8.00 20.00
49 Leon Draisaitl SP 25.00 60.00
53 John Gibson 8.00 20.00
54 Brent Burns SP 8.00 20.00
56 Carter Verhaeghe 8.00 20.00
60 Jacob Markstrom 8.00 20.00
63 Tage Thompson 10.00 25.00
64 Connor Hellebuyck 15.00 40.00
65 Jonathan Marchessault SP 10.00 25.00
66 Alex Iafallo 5.00 12.00
68 Tim Stutzle 10.00 25.00
73 Lukas Reichel 8.00 20.00
74 Oskar Lindblom 6.00 15.00
77 Jake Neighbours 8.00 20.00
80 Samuel Girard 5.00 12.00
81 Bryan Rust 8.00 20.00
82 Igor Shesterkin SP 15.00 40.00
83 Travis Konecny 8.00 20.00
85 Jonathan Huberdeau 10.00 25.00
90 Dylan Cozens 8.00 20.00
92 Andrei Vasilevskiy SP 12.00 30.00
93 Quinn Hughes SP 20.00 50.00
98 Mark Stone 10.00 25.00
100 Auston Matthews SP 80.00 200.00
102 Luke Hughes SP 50.00 125.00
103 Ridly Greig 12.00 30.00
104 Logan Cooley SP 60.00 150.00
105 Marco Kasper 20.00 50.00
106 Adam Fantilli SP 50.00 125.00
107 Brock Faber 80.00 200.00
108 Will Cuylle 12.00 30.00
109 Leo Carlsson 60.00 150.00
110 Devon Levi SP 20.00 50.00
111 Ilya Solovyov SP 8.00 20.00
112 Stanislav Svozil 6.00 15.00
113 Cole McWard 8.00 20.00
114 William Dufour 6.00 15.00
115 Tyson Foerster 15.00 40.00
116 Connor Zary 15.00 40.00
117 Elliot Desnoyers 8.00 20.00
119 Jiri Kulich 15.00 40.00
121 Matt Savoie 15.00 40.00
122 Simon Edvinsson SP 15.00 40.00
124 Vincent Desharnais 10.00 25.00
125 Vincent Iorio 8.00 20.00
126 Nikita Nesterenko 8.00 20.00
127 Samuel Bolduc 8.00 20.00
128 Martin Pospisil 10.00 25.00
129 Samuel Knazko 8.00 20.00
130 Raphael Lavoie 8.00 20.00
131 Matt Murray 8.00 20.00
132 Aidan McDonough 6.00 15.00
133 Alex Laferriere 12.00 30.00
134 Matthew Knies 40.00 100.00
137 Tristen Robins 8.00 20.00
138 Fraser Minten 15.00 40.00
140 Danil Gushchin 8.00 20.00
142 Wyatt Kaiser 8.00 20.00
143 Mackie Samoskevich SP 12.00 30.00
144 Jet Greaves 12.00 30.00
145 Ryker Evans 10.00 25.00
146 Matthew Coronato 12.00 30.00
148 Billy Sweezey 8.00 20.00
153 Akito Hirose 6.00 15.00
154 Dustin Wolf SP 25.00 60.00
155 Adam Ginning 8.00 20.00
156 Kevin Korchinski 12.00 30.00
157 Luke Philp 8.00 20.00
158 John Beecher 15.00 40.00
159 Damien Giroux 6.00 15.00
160 Matthew Kessel 6.00 15.00
161 Olle Eriksson Ek 8.00 20.00
163 Egor Afanasyev 8.00 20.00
164 Maxence Guenette 8.00 20.00
165 Milos Kelemen 8.00 20.00
166 Isak Rosen 8.00 20.00
169 Matthew Poitras 30.00 80.00
170 Sean Farrell SP 8.00 20.00
172 Nick Swaney 8.00 20.00
174 Joona Koppanen 6.00 15.00
179 Tye Kartye 12.00 30.00
182 Jaxson Stauber 8.00 20.00
185 Owen Beck SP 12.00 30.00
187 Tyler Angle 8.00 20.00
189 Lukas Rousek 6.00 15.00
190 Leevi Merilainen 8.00 20.00
191 Jiri Patera 12.00 30.00
192 Walker Duehr 6.00 15.00
193 Jake Livingstone 8.00 20.00
195 Luke Evangelista SP 12.00 30.00
196 Henry Thrun 8.00 20.00
198 Arnaud Durandeau 8.00 20.00
199 Zach Benson 12.00 30.00
200 Yaroslav Askarov SP 25.00 60.00

2023-24 SPx Finite Rookies
*GOLD/399: .5X TO 1.2X BASIC
*GREEN/199: .6X TO 1.5X BASIC
*PLATINUM/99: .8X TO 2X BASIC
F1 Leo Carlsson 3.00 8.00
F2 Luke Hughes 3.00 8.00
F3 Matthew Knies 4.00 10.00
F4 Ridly Greig 1.50 4.00
F5 Zach Benson 1.50 4.00
F6 Stanislav Svozil .75 2.00
F7 Marco Kasper 2.50 6.00
F8 Akito Hirose .75 2.00
F9 Wyatt Kaiser 1.00 2.50
F10 Connor Zary 2.00 5.00
F11 William Dufour .75 2.00
F12 Yaroslav Askarov 2.50 6.00
F13 Jackson LaCombe 1.00 2.50
F14 Arnaud Durandeau 1.00 2.50
F15 Connor Bedard 40.00 100.00
F16 Tye Kartye 1.50 4.00
F17 Luke Evangelista 1.50 4.00
F18 Devon Levi 2.50 6.00
F19 Bobby McMann 1.50 4.00
F20 Adam Fantilli 3.00 8.00
F21 Jonathan Gruden 1.00 2.50
F22 Owen Beck 1.50 4.00
F23 Samuel Bolduc 1.00 2.50
F24 Elliot Desnoyers 1.00 2.50
F25 Simon Nemec 2.00 5.00
F26 Jiri Patera 1.00 2.50
F27 Sean Farrell 1.00 2.50
F28 Lukas Rousek .75 2.00
F29 Egor Afanasyev 1.00 2.50
F30 Tyson Foerster 2.00 5.00
F31 Nikita Nesterenko 1.00 2.50
F32 Brock Faber 2.50 6.00
F33 Luke Philp 1.00 2.50
F34 Hunter McKown 1.00 2.50
F35 Matt Savoie 2.00 5.00
F36 Hugh McGing 1.00 2.50
F37 Matthew Coronato 1.50 4.00
F38 Olle Eriksson Ek 1.00 2.50
F39 Vincent Desharnais 1.25 3.00
F40 Kevin Korchinski 1.50 4.00
F41 Michael Kesselring 1.00 2.50
F42 Dustin Wolf 3.00 8.00
F43 Will Cuylle 1.50 4.00
F44 Leevi Merilainen 1.00 2.50
F45 Pavel Mintyukov 1.50 4.00
F46 Joona Koppanen .75 2.00
F47 Jakob Pelletier 1.25 3.00
F48 Vincent Iorio 1.00 2.50
F49 Matt Murray 1.00 2.50
F50 Henry Thrun 1.00 2.50

2023-24 SPx Finite Rookies Gold Spectrum
*GOLD SPEC/25: 2X TO 5X BASIC
F15 Connor Bedard 400.00 1000.00

2023-24 SPx Finite Rookies Silver Spectrum
*SLVR SPEC/49: 1.2X TO 3X BASIC
F15 Connor Bedard 150.00 400.00

2023-24 SPx Force
*RED/30: .8X TO 2X BASIC
SFASBN Aho/Svechnikov/Burns/Necas 6.00 15.00
SFBCCH Bedard/Cooley/Carlsson/Hughes 100.00 250.00
SFCSHS Connor/Scheifele/Hawerchuk/Selanne 8.00 20.00
SFESMS Eichel/Stone/Marchessault/Stephenson 6.00 15.00
SFKDRB Kopitar/Doughty/Robitaille/Blake 6.00 15.00
SFKHIN Kadri/Huberdeau/Iginla/Nieuwendyk 5.00 12.00
SFPDTC Power/Dahlin/Thompson/Cozens 5.00 12.00
SFRHMH Robertson/Heiskanen/Modano/Hull 8.00 20.00
SFSNGT Stutzle/Norris/Giroux/Tkachuk 6.00 15.00
SFUVSS Ullmark/Vasilevskiy/Shesterkin/Sorokin 8.00 20.00

2023-24 SPx Hardwired for Success
*RED/65: .5X TO 1.2X BASIC
*GOLD/35: 1.2X TO 3X BASIC
HWAM Auston Matthews 8.00 20.00
HWCC Cole Caufield 4.00 10.00
HWCM Connor McDavid 10.00 25.00
HWEP Elias Pettersson 3.00 8.00
HWJE Jack Eichel 3.00 8.00
HWJR Jason Robertson 3.00 8.00
HWMA Cale Makar 5.00 12.00
HWMB Matty Beniers 2.50 6.00
HWMB Matt Boldy 3.00 8.00
HWMS Moritz Seider 2.50 6.00
HWMT Matthew Tkachuk 4.00 10.00
HWPL Patrik Laine 2.50 6.00
HWTM Timo Meier 2.00 5.00
HWTS Tim Stutzle 2.50 6.00
HWTZ Trevor Zegras 2.00 5.00

2023-24 SPx Holograph Autographs
*RED: .6X TO 1.5X BASIC
*GOLD/49: .6X TO 1.5X BASIC
HGAS Andrei Svechnikov/49 10.00 25.00
HGBH Bo Horvat/49 10.00 25.00
HGDC Dylan Cozens/25 8.00 20.00
HGJE Jack Eichel/25 12.00 30.00
HGJN Jake Neighbours/99 8.00 20.00
HGKF Kevin Fiala/49 6.00 15.00
HGLT Logan Thompson/99 10.00 25.00
HGMB Matt Boldy/49 12.00 30.00
HGOP Owen Power/49 8.00 20.00
HGRK Rasmus Kupari/99 5.00 12.00
HGRO Ryan O'Reilly/49 8.00 20.00
HGSP Shane Pinto/99 6.00 15.00

2023-24 SPx Holograph Rookie Autographs
HGRAH Akito Hirose/99 6.00 15.00
HGRCM Cole McWard/99 8.00 20.00
HGRKA Marco Kasper/49 20.00 50.00
HGRLC Logan Cooley/49 40.00 100.00
HGRLM Leevi Merilainen/99 8.00 20.00
HGRLP Luke Philp/99 8.00 20.00
HGRLR Lukas Rousek/49 8.00 20.00
HGRMK Matthew Knies/49 40.00 100.00
HGROB Owen Beck/49 12.00 30.00
HGROE Olle Eriksson Ek/99 8.00 20.00
HGRPA Jiri Patera/99 12.00 30.00
HGRRG Ridly Greig/49 12.00 30.00
HGRSE Simon Edvinsson/49 15.00 40.00
HGRSN Simon Nemec/49 15.00 40.00
HGRSS Stanislav Svozil/99 6.00 15.00
HGRTF Tyson Foerster/49 25.00 60.00
HGRTK Tye Kartye/49 12.00 30.00
HGRVD Vincent Desharnais/99 10.00 25.00
HGRWK Wyatt Kaiser/99 8.00 20.00
HGRZB Zach Benson/49 12.00 30.00

2023-24 SPx Holograph Rookie Autographs Gold
*GOLD/25: .6X TO 1.5X BASIC
HGRBM Bobby McMann/25 20.00 50.00

2023-24 SPx Holograph Rookie Autographs Red
*RED: .5X TO 1.2X BASIC
HGRLC Logan Cooley/25 60.00 150.00
HGRTF Tyson Foerster/25 40.00 100.00

2023-24 SPx Patch Autographs
4 Alex DeBrincat/25 20.00 50.00
8 Jordan Eberle/25 15.00 40.00
9 Jake Oettinger/25 25.00 60.00
10 Joel Eriksson Ek/40 12.00 30.00
17 Seth Jarvis/49 12.00 30.00
18 Juuse Saros/25 20.00 50.00
19 Bo Horvat/25 20.00 50.00
20 Aleksander Barkov/25 25.00 60.00
26 Jared McCann/25 12.00 30.00
27 K'Andre Miller/25 12.00 30.00
29 Roman Josi/25 15.00 40.00
32 Karel Vejmelka/49 10.00 25.00
34 Darcy Kuemper/49 15.00 40.00
36 Juraj Slafkovsky/25 30.00 80.00
37 Kyle Connor/25 20.00 50.00
38 Andrei Kuzmenko/25 15.00 40.00
41 Matty Beniers/25 20.00 50.00
42 Timo Meier/25 15.00 40.00
43 Tomas Hertl/49 15.00 40.00
50 Mason McTavish/25 20.00 50.00
55 Jeremy Swayman/25 25.00 60.00
56 Carter Verhaeghe/25 15.00 40.00
58 Brady Tkachuk/25 25.00 60.00
60 Jacob Markstrom/25 15.00 40.00
64 Connor Hellebuyck/25 30.00 80.00
74 Oskar Lindblom/49 12.00 30.00
77 Jake Neighbours/49 15.00 40.00
80 Samuel Girard/49 10.00 25.00
81 Bryan Rust/49 15.00 40.00
83 Travis Konecny/49 15.00 40.00
90 Dylan Cozens/25 15.00 40.00
91 Vitek Vanecek/49 15.00 40.00
98 Mark Stone/25 20.00 50.00
102 Luke Hughes/25 125.00 300.00
103 Ridly Greig/25 30.00 80.00
105 Marco Kasper/25 50.00 125.00
108 Will Cuylle/25 30.00 80.00
110 Devon Levi/25 50.00 125.00
112 Stanislav Svozil/49 15.00 40.00
113 Cole McWard/49 20.00 50.00
114 William Dufour/25 15.00 40.00
115 Tyson Foerster/25 40.00 100.00
116 Connor Zary/25 40.00 100.00
117 Elliot Desnoyers/49 15.00 40.00
119 Jiri Kulich/49 40.00 100.00
121 Matt Savoie/25 40.00 100.00
122 Simon Edvinsson/25 40.00 100.00
124 Vincent Desharnais/49 25.00 60.00
125 Vincent Iorio/49 20.00 50.00
126 Nikita Nesterenko/49 20.00 50.00
127 Samuel Bolduc/49 20.00 50.00
128 Martin Pospisil/25 25.00 60.00
129 Samuel Knazko/49 20.00 50.00
130 Raphael Lavoie/49 20.00 50.00
131 Matt Murray/49 20.00 50.00
132 Aidan McDonough/49 15.00 40.00
133 Alex Laferriere/25 30.00 80.00
134 Matthew Knies/25 80.00 200.00
137 Tristen Robins/49 20.00 50.00
138 Fraser Minten/49 40.00 100.00
140 Danil Gushchin/25 30.00 80.00
141 Justin Sourdif/49 20.00 50.00
142 Wyatt Kaiser/49 20.00 50.00
143 Mackie Samoskevich/49 30.00 80.00
144 Jet Greaves/49 30.00 80.00
145 Ryker Evans/49 25.00 60.00
146 Matthew Coronato/25 30.00 80.00
148 Billy Sweezey/49 20.00 50.00
152 Simon Nemec/25 80.00 200.00
153 Akito Hirose/49 15.00 40.00
154 Dustin Wolf/25 60.00 150.00
155 Adam Ginning/49 20.00 50.00
156 Kevin Korchinski/25 30.00 80.00
157 Luke Philp/49 20.00 50.00
158 John Beecher/49 40.00 100.00
160 Matthew Kessel/49 15.00 40.00
161 Olle Eriksson Ek/49 20.00 50.00
163 Egor Afanasyev/25 20.00 50.00
165 Milos Kelemen/25 20.00 50.00
166 Isak Rosen/49 20.00 50.00
169 Matthew Poitras/25 40.00 100.00
170 Sean Farrell/25 20.00 50.00
171 Pavel Mintyukov/25 30.00 80.00
172 Nick Swaney/49 20.00 50.00
174 Joona Koppanen/49 15.00 40.00
179 Tye Kartye/49 30.00 80.00
182 Jaxson Stauber/49 20.00 50.00
185 Owen Beck/25 20.00 50.00
189 Lukas Rousek/49 15.00 40.00
190 Leevi Merilainen/49 20.00 50.00
191 Jiri Patera/49 30.00 80.00
192 Walker Duehr/49 15.00 40.00
193 Jake Livingstone/49 20.00 50.00
195 Luke Evangelista/25 30.00 80.00
196 Henry Thrun/49 20.00 50.00
198 Arnaud Durandeau/49 20.00 50.00
199 Zach Benson/25 30.00 80.00
200 Yaroslav Askarov/25 80.00 200.00

2023-24 SPx Radiance FX
RFX1 Mario Lemieux 4.00 10.00
RFX2 Eric Lindros 1.50 4.00
RFX3 Henrik Zetterberg 1.25 3.00
RFX4 Luc Robitaille 1.00 2.50
RFX5 Brad Park .75 2.00
RFX6 Ron Francis 1.25 3.00
RFX7 Peter Forsberg 2.00 5.00
RFX8 Denis Potvin 1.00 2.50
RFX9 Guy Lapointe .75 2.00
RFX10 Frank Mahovlich 1.00 2.50
RFX11 Ed Belfour 1.00 2.50
RFX12 Sid Abel 1.00 2.50
RFX13 Marcel Dionne 1.25 3.00
RFX14 Joe Sakic 2.00 5.00
RFX15 Scott Niedermayer 1.00 2.50
RFX16 Brendan Shanahan 1.00 2.50
RFX17 Todd Bertuzzi .75 2.00
RFX18 Marty Turco .75 2.00
RFX19 Maurice Richard 2.00 5.00
RFX20 Wayne Gretzky 8.00 20.00
RFX21 Jack Hughes 2.50 6.00
RFX22 Miro Heiskanen 1.25 3.00
RFX23 Auston Matthews 4.00 10.00
RFX24 Matthew Tkachuk 2.00 5.00
RFX25 Bo Horvat 1.25 3.00
RFX26 Jack Eichel 1.50 4.00
RFX27 Moritz Seider 1.25 3.00
RFX28 Patrik Laine 1.25 3.00
RFX29 Brady Tkachuk 1.50 4.00
RFX30 Dylan Larkin 1.25 3.00
RFX31 Mathew Barzal 1.25 3.00
RFX32 John Tavares 1.50 4.00
RFX33 Tim Stutzle 1.25 3.00
RFX34 Cole Caufield 2.00 5.00
RFX35 Clayton Keller 1.25 3.00
RFX36 Connor McDavid 5.00 12.00
RFX37 Leon Draisaitl 3.00 8.00
RFX38 Jordan Kyrou 1.00 2.50
RFX39 Jacob Markstrom 1.00 2.50
RFX40 Trevor Zegras 1.25 3.00
RFX41 Sidney Crosby 4.00 10.00
RFX42 Adam Fox 1.25 3.00
RFX43 Mika Zibanejad 1.25 3.00
RFX44 Matty Beniers 1.25 3.00
RFX45 David Pastrnak 2.50 6.00
RFX46 Anze Kopitar 1.50 4.00
RFX47 Juuse Saros 1.25 3.00
RFX48 Tage Thompson 1.25 3.00
RFX49 Elias Pettersson 1.50 4.00
RFX50 Kirill Kaprizov 3.00 8.00
RFX51 Alex Ovechkin 4.00 10.00
RFX52 Connor Hellebuyck 1.50 4.00
RFX53 Travis Konecny 1.25 3.00
RFX54 Nathan MacKinnon 4.00 10.00
RFX55 Brent Burns 1.00 2.50
RFX56 Erik Karlsson 1.25 3.00
RFX57 Rasmus Dahlin 1.25 3.00
RFX58 Cale Makar 2.50 6.00
RFX59 Seth Jones 1.00 2.50
RFX60 Steven Stamkos 2.00 5.00
RFX61 Simon Nemec 2.00 5.00
RFX62 Luke Hughes 3.00 8.00
RFX63 Ridly Greig 1.50 4.00
RFX64 William Dufour .75 2.00
RFX65 Simon Edvinsson 1.50 4.00
RFX66 Ryker Evans 1.25 3.00
RFX67 Marco Kasper 2.50 6.00
RFX68 Tyson Foerster 2.00 5.00
RFX69 Owen Beck 1.50 4.00
RFX70 Dustin Wolf 3.00 8.00
RFX71 Matt Savoie 2.00 5.00
RFX72 Will Cuylle 1.50 4.00
RFX73 Adam Fantilli 3.00 8.00
RFX74 Akito Hirose .75 2.00
RFX75 Devon Levi 2.50 6.00
RFX76 Ivan Miroshnichenko 1.50 4.00
RFX77 Zach Benson 1.50 4.00
RFX78 Lukas Rousek .75 2.00
RFX79 Yaroslav Askarov 2.50 6.00
RFX80 Jackson LaCombe 1.00 2.50
RFX81 Jiri Patera 1.50 4.00
RFX82 Jakob Pelletier 1.25 3.00
RFX83 Leo Carlsson 3.00 8.00
RFX84 Vincent Iorio 1.00 2.50
RFX85 Brock Faber 2.50 6.00
RFX86 Samuel Bolduc 1.00 2.50
RFX87 Vincent Desharnais 1.25 3.00
RFX88 Connor Zary 2.00 5.00
RFX89 Drew Helleson 1.00 2.50
RFX90 Luke Evangelista 1.50 4.00
RFX91 Sean Farrell 1.00 2.50
RFX92 Tye Kartye 1.50 4.00
RFX93 Logan Cooley 3.00 8.00
RFX94 Bobby McMann 1.50 4.00
RFX95 Nikita Nesterenko 1.00 2.50
RFX96 Pavel Mintyukov 1.50 4.00
RFX97 Matthew Coronato 1.50 4.00
RFX98 Luke Philp 1.00 2.50
RFX99 Matthew Knies 4.00 10.00
RFX100 Connor Bedard 30.00 80.00

2023-24 SPx Radiance FX Blue
*BLUE/299: .6X TO 1.5X BASIC
RFX20 Wayne Gretzky 20.00 50.00

2023-24 SPx Radiance FX Gold
*GOLD/99: 1X TO 2.5X BASIC
RFX20 Wayne Gretzky 60.00 150.00
RFX36 Connor McDavid 20.00 50.00
RFX100 Connor Bedard 125.00 300.00

2023-24 SPx Rookie Jersey Autographs
AD Arnaud Durandeau/375 10.00 25.00
AG Adam Ginning/375 10.00 25.00
AH Akito Hirose/375 8.00 20.00
AM Aidan McDonough/375 8.00 20.00
BF Brock Faber/75 60.00 150.00
BM Bobby McMann/375 15.00 40.00
CB Connor Bedard/75 600.00 1500.00
CM Cole McWard/375 10.00 25.00
CO Logan Cooley/75 50.00 125.00
DG Danil Gushchin/375 10.00 25.00
DW Dustin Wolf/175 30.00 80.00
EA Egor Afanasyev/375 10.00 25.00
ED Elliot Desnoyers/375 10.00 25.00
EV Luke Evangelista/175 15.00 40.00
GU Danil Gust/375 10.00 25.00
HM Hugh McGing/375 10.00 25.00
HT Henry Thrun/375 10.00 25.00
JK Joona Koppanen/375 8.00 20.00
JS Jaxson Stauber/375 10.00 25.00
KA Marco Kasper/175 25.00 60.00
KK Kevin Korchinski/375 15.00 40.00
KN Matthew Knies/175 30.00 80.00
LC Leo Carlsson/75 60.00 150.00
LH Luke Hughes/75 60.00 150.00
LI Jake Livingstone/375 10.00 25.00
LM Leevi Merilainen/375 10.00 25.00
LP Luke Philp/375 10.00 25.00
LR Lukas Rousek/375 8.00 20.00
MC Matthew Coronato/375 15.00 40.00
MK Milos Kelemen/375 10.00 25.00
MM Matt Murray/375 10.00 25.00
MS Matt Savoie/175 20.00 50.00
NN Nikita Nesterenko/375 10.00 25.00
OB Owen Beck/175 15.00 40.00
OE Olle Eriksson Ek/375 10.00 25.00
PA Jiri Patera/375 15.00 40.00
PM Pavel Mintyukov/175 15.00 40.00
RG Ridly Greig/175 15.00 40.00
SB Samuel Bolduc/375 10.00 25.00
SE Simon Edvinsson/75 20.00 50.00
SF Sean Farrell/375 10.00 25.00
SN Simon Nemec/175 20.00 50.00
SS Stanislav Svozil/375 8.00 20.00
TF Tyson Foerster/175 20.00 50.00
TK Tye Kartye/375 15.00 40.00
TR Tristen Robins/375 10.00 25.00
VI Vincent Iorio/375 10.00 25.00
WC Will Cuylle/375 15.00 40.00
WD William Dufour/375 8.00 20.00
YA Yaroslav Askarov/175 25.00 60.00

2023-24 SPx Rookie Jersey Autographs Patch Spectrum
*PATCH SPEC: .6X TO 1.5X BASIC
BF Brock Faber/35 125.00 300.00
KN Matthew Knies/25 60.00 150.00
YA Yaroslav Askarov/25 60.00 150.00

2023-24 SPx Rookie Jersey Autographs Spectrum
*SPCTRM: .5X TO 1.2X BASIC
CO Logan Cooley/25 80.00 200.00
LC Leo Carlsson/25 80.00 200.00
LH Luke Hughes/25 100.00 250.00
YA Yaroslav Askarov/35 40.00 100.00

2023-24 SPx Rookie Superscripts
SSRAD Arnaud Durandeau 8.00 20.00
SSRAF Adam Fantilli SP 40.00 100.00
SSRAG Adam Ginning 8.00 20.00
SSRAM Aidan McDonough 6.00 15.00
SSRBF Brock Faber SP 40.00 100.00
SSRBS Billy Sweezey 8.00 20.00
SSRCA Leo Carlsson SP 40.00 100.00
SSRCM Cole McWard 8.00 20.00
SSRCZ Connor Zary SP 15.00 40.00
SSRDG Danil Gushchin 8.00 20.00
SSRDU Walker Duehr 6.00 15.00
SSRDW Dustin Wolf SP 25.00 60.00
SSREA Egor Afanasyev 8.00 20.00
SSRED Elliot Desnoyers 8.00 20.00
SSRHT Henry Thrun 8.00 20.00
SSRIM Ivan Miroshnichenko SP 12.00 30.00
SSRJG Jet Greaves 12.00 30.00
SSRJK Joona Koppanen 6.00 15.00
SSRJL Jake Livingstone 8.00 20.00
SSRJS Jaxson Stauber 8.00 20.00
SSRKA Marco Kasper SP 20.00 50.00
SSRKE Matthew Kessel 6.00 15.00
SSRKK Kevin Korchinski 12.00 30.00
SSRLC Logan Cooley SP 25.00 60.00
SSRLE Luke Evangelista SP 12.00 30.00
SSRLH Luke Hughes SP 40.00 100.00
SSRLM Leevi Merilainen 8.00 20.00
SSRLP Luke Philp 8.00 20.00
SSRLR Lukas Rousek 6.00 15.00
SSRMC Matthew Coronato SP 12.00 30.00
SSRMK Matthew Knies SP 40.00 100.00
SSRMM Matt Murray 8.00 20.00
SSRMP Matthew Poitras 15.00 40.00
SSRMS Matt Savoie SP 15.00 40.00
SSRNS Nick Swaney 8.00 20.00
SSROB Owen Beck SP 12.00 30.00
SSROE Olle Eriksson Ek 8.00 20.00
SSRPA Jiri Patera 12.00 30.00
SSRPM Pavel Mintyukov 12.00 30.00
SSRRG Ridly Greig SP 12.00 30.00
SSRSB Samuel Bolduc 8.00 20.00
SSRSE Simon Edvinsson SP 15.00 40.00
SSRSF Sean Farrell SP 8.00 20.00
SSRSK Samuel Knazko 8.00 20.00
SSRSN Simon Nemec SP 15.00 40.00
SSRSS Stanislav Svozil 6.00 15.00
SSRTF Tyson Foerster SP 15.00 40.00
SSRTK Tye Kartye 12.00 30.00
SSRTR Tristen Robins 8.00 20.00
SSRVD Vincent Desharnais 10.00 25.00
SSRVI Vincent Iorio 8.00 20.00
SSRWC Will Cuylle SP 12.00 30.00
SSRWD William Dufour 6.00 15.00
SSRWK Wyatt Kaiser 8.00 20.00
SSRYA Yaroslav Askarov SP 20.00 50.00
SSRZB Zach Benson SP 12.00 30.00

2023-24 SPx Rookie Superscripts Gold
*GOLD: .5X TO 1.2X BASIC
SSRAF Adam Fantilli/25 60.00 150.00
SSRBF Brock Faber/25 60.00 150.00
SSRCA Leo Carlsson/25 60.00 150.00
SSRLH Luke Hughes/25 60.00 150.00
SSRMK Matthew Knies/25 60.00 150.00

2023-24 SPx Signature Fabrics
*SPECTRUM: .5X TO 1.2X BASIC
SFBS Brandon Saad/99 6.00 15.00
SFJN Jake Neighbours/99 8.00 20.00
SFJS Jaccob Slavin/99 6.00 15.00
SFJT John Tavares/35 20.00 50.00
SFMB Michael Bunting/99 8.00 20.00
SFMF Mario Ferraro/99 5.00 12.00
SFNO Josh Norris/99 8.00 20.00
SFPG Philipp Grubauer/99 8.00 20.00
SFRH Roope Hintz/99 10.00 25.00
SFST Shea Theodore/99 10.00 25.00
SFTR Taylor Raddysh/99 6.00 15.00
SFZH Zach Hyman/35 20.00 50.00

2023-24 SPx Starscape Shadow Box
*SILVER/99: 1X TO 2.5X BASIC
SS1 Nathan MacKinnon 12.00 30.00
SS2 Kirill Kaprizov 10.00 25.00
SS3 David Pastrnak 8.00 20.00
SS4 Leon Draisaitl 10.00 25.00
SS5 Nikita Kucherov 6.00 15.00
SS6 Ilya Sorokin 5.00 12.00
SS7 Auston Matthews 12.00 30.00
SS8 Alex Ovechkin 12.00 30.00
SS9 Tage Thompson 4.00 10.00
SS10 Artemi Panarin 6.00 15.00
SS11 Timo Meier 3.00 8.00
SS12 Connor McDavid 15.00 40.00
SS13 Sidney Crosby 12.00 30.00
SS14 Dylan Larkin 4.00 10.00
SS15 Connor Hellebuyck 6.00 15.00
SS16 Luke Hughes 10.00 25.00
SS17 Jackson LaCombe 3.00 8.00
SS18 Adam Fantilli 10.00 25.00
SS19 Yaroslav Askarov 8.00 20.00
SS20 Arnaud Durandeau 3.00 8.00
SS21 Akito Hirose 2.50 6.00
SS22 Owen Beck 5.00 12.00
SS23 Dustin Wolf 10.00 25.00
SS24 Simon Nemec 6.00 15.00
SS25 Luke Evangelista 5.00 12.00
SS26 Elliot Desnoyers 3.00 8.00
SS27 Tyson Foerster 6.00 15.00
SS28 Pavel Mintyukov 5.00 12.00
SS29 Ridly Greig 5.00 12.00
SS30 Connor Zary 6.00 15.00
SS31 Matthew Knies 12.00 30.00
SS32 Danil Gushchin 3.00 8.00
SS33 Matthew Poitras 6.00 15.00
SS34 Connor Bedard 100.00 250.00
SS35 Will Cuylle 5.00 12.00
SS36 Lukas Rousek 2.50 6.00
SS37 Marco Kasper 8.00 20.00
SS38 Sean Farrell 3.00 8.00
SS39 Vincent Iorio 3.00 8.00
SS40 Leo Carlsson 10.00 25.00
SS41 Jakob Pelletier 4.00 10.00
SS42 Vincent Desharnais 4.00 10.00
SS43 William Dufour 2.50 6.00
SS44 Samuel Bolduc 3.00 8.00
SS45 Devon Levi 8.00 20.00
SS46 Wyatt Kaiser 3.00 8.00
SS47 Brock Faber 8.00 20.00
SS48 Tye Kartye 5.00 12.00
SS49 Simon Edvinsson 6.00 15.00
SS50 Logan Cooley 10.00 25.00

2023-24 SPx Superscripts
*GOLD/25: .5X TO 1.2X BASIC
SSAM Mikey Anderson 6.00 15.00
SSAS Andrei Svechnikov SP 10.00 25.00
SSBJ Boone Jenner 8.00 20.00
SSBK Boris Katchouk 5.00 12.00
SSBR Bryan Rust 8.00 20.00
SSCC Charlie Coyle 8.00 20.00
SSDC Dylan Cozens SP 8.00 20.00
SSDJ Dakota Joshua 5.00 12.00
SSED Evgenii Dadonov 5.00 12.00
SSFL Marc-Andre Fleury SP 60.00 150.00
SSGV Gabe Vilardi SP 8.00 20.00
SSJB Josh Bailey 6.00 15.00
SSJE Jordan Eberle SP 8.00 20.00
SSJH Jordan Harris SP 5.00 12.00
SSJL Jake Leschyshyn 5.00 12.00
SSJP Joe Pavelski 10.00 25.00
SSJV Joe Veleno 6.00 15.00
SSJY Jesse Ylonen 5.00 12.00
SSLD Lukas Dostal 8.00 20.00
SSLE Anders Lee 6.00 15.00
SSMA Matias Maccelli 6.00 15.00
SSME Michael Eyssimont SP 5.00 12.00
SSMF Mario Ferraro 5.00 12.00
SSMG Matt Grzelcyk 6.00 15.00
SSMI Jacob Middleton 5.00 12.00
SSMM Mason Marchment 6.00 15.00
SSNL Nils Lundkvist 5.00 12.00
SSNP Neal Pionk 5.00 12.00
SSOL Oskar Lindblom 6.00 15.00
SSPE Jeff Petry SP 8.00 20.00
SSPK Peyton Krebs 6.00 15.00
SSRC Ross Colton 6.00 15.00
SSRE Sam Reinhart 15.00 40.00
SSSC Braden Schneider 6.00 15.00
SSST Shea Theodore SP 10.00 25.00
SSTK Torey Krug SP 6.00 15.00
SSTR Taylor Raddysh 6.00 15.00
SSTT Tyce Thompson 5.00 12.00
SSTW Tom Wilson SP 8.00 20.00
SSVP Vasily Podkolzin 5.00 12.00
SSYS Yegor Sharangovich 8.00 20.00
SSZW Zach Werenski SP 12.00 30.00

2023-24 SPx X Marks the Spot Autographs
XMAB Aleksander Barkov SP 10.00 25.00
XMBB Brent Burns SP 6.00 15.00
XMEM Elvis Merzlikins 6.00 15.00
XMFG Filip Gustavsson 6.00 15.00
XMJB Jonatan Berggren 5.00 12.00
XMJC Jalen Chatfield 4.00 10.00
XMJE Joel Eriksson Ek SP 5.00 12.00
XMJH Jonathan Huberdeau 8.00 20.00
XMJM Jacob Markstrom 6.00 15.00
XMKM K'Andre Miller 5.00 12.00
XMLR Lukas Reichel 6.00 15.00
XMLT Logan Thompson 8.00 20.00
XMMA Kirill Marchenko 8.00 20.00
XMMB Michael Bunting 6.00 15.00
XMMC Jared McCann 5.00 12.00
XMMS Mark Stone SP 20.00 50.00
XMNS Nick Schmaltz SP 5.00 12.00
XMPK Pyotr Kochetkov 6.00 15.00
XMSP Shane Pinto 5.00 12.00
XMTT Tyler Toffoli 6.00 15.00
XMZH Zach Hyman 10.00 25.00

2023-24 SPx X Marks the Spot Rookie Autographs
*GOLD/35: .5X TO 1.2X BASIC
XMRAD Arnaud Durandeau 8.00 20.00
XMRAG Adam Ginning 8.00 20.00
XMRBF Brock Faber SP 50.00 125.00
XMRBS Billy Sweezey 8.00 20.00
XMRDG Danil Gushchin 8.00 20.00
XMRDL Devon Levi SP 20.00 50.00
XMRDW Dustin Wolf SP 25.00 60.00
XMRKA Marco Kasper SP 20.00 50.00
XMRKN Matthew Knies SP 50.00 125.00
XMRLC Leo Carlsson SP 25.00 60.00
XMRLE Luke Evangelista SP 12.00 30.00
XMRLH Luke Hughes SP 60.00 150.00
XMRLM Leevi Merilainen 8.00 20.00
XMRMC Matthew Coronato SP 12.00 30.00
XMRMK Matthew Kessel 6.00 15.00
XMRNS Nick Swaney 8.00 20.00
XMROB Owen Beck SP 12.00 30.00
XMROE Olle Eriksson Ek 8.00 20.00
XMRPA Jiri Patera 12.00 30.00
XMRRG Ridly Greig SP 12.00 30.00
XMRSB Samuel Bolduc 8.00 20.00
XMRSE Simon Edvinsson SP 15.00 40.00
XMRSK Samuel Knazko 8.00 20.00
XMRSS Stanislav Svozil 6.00 15.00
XMRTF Tyson Foerster SP 15.00 40.00
XMRTR Tristen Robins 8.00 20.00
XMRWC Will Cuylle SP 12.00 30.00
XMRWD William Dufour 6.00 15.00
XMRWK Wyatt Kaiser 8.00 20.00
XMRYA Yaroslav Askarov SP 25.00 60.00

2024-25 SPx
1 Jeremy Swayman 1.25 3.00
2 Fabian Zetterlund .50 1.25
3 Brayden Point 1.00 2.50
4 Miro Heiskanen 1.00 2.50
5 Tim Stutzle 1.00 2.50
6 Brock Boeser 1.00 2.50
7 Brock Faber 1.00 2.50
8 Alex Ovechkin 3.00 8.00
9 Filip Forsberg 1.25 3.00
10 Artemi Panarin 1.50 4.00
11 Trevor Zegras .75 2.00
12 Matt Boldy 1.25 3.00
13 Kent Johnson .75 2.00
14 Nick Suzuki 1.50 4.00
15 Mitch Marner 1.25 3.00
16 Aleksander Barkov 1.25 3.00
17 Kyle Connor 1.25 3.00
18 Zach Hyman 1.25 3.00
19 Matthew Tkachuk 1.50 4.00
20 Sebastian Aho 1.25 3.00
21 Jason Robertson 1.25 3.00
22 Cole Caufield 1.50 4.00
23 Mason McTavish .75 2.00
24 Jack Eichel 1.25 3.00
25 Jordan Kyrou .75 2.00
26 Rasmus Dahlin 1.00 2.50
27 J.T. Miller 1.00 2.50
28 Sergei Bobrovsky 1.25 3.00
29 Nathan MacKinnon 3.00 8.00
30 Ilya Sorokin 1.00 2.50

31 Igor Shesterkin 1.50 4.00
32 Mark Scheifele 1.25 3.00
33 Adam Fantilli 1.25 3.00
34 Auston Matthews 3.00 8.00
35 Alexis Lafreniere 1.25 3.00
36 Tom Wilson .75 2.00
37 Andrei Svechnikov 1.00 2.50
38 Cale Makar 2.00 5.00
39 Noah Dobson 1.00 2.50
40 Elias Pettersson 1.25 3.00
41 Matty Beniers 1.00 2.50
42 Jake Oettinger 1.25 3.00
43 Quinn Hughes 2.00 5.00
44 Kevin Fiala .60 1.50
45 Nico Hischier 1.25 3.00
46 John Tavares 1.25 3.00
47 Brent Burns .75 2.00
48 Tomas Hertl .75 2.00
49 Leon Draisaitl 2.50 6.00
50 Thatcher Demko 1.00 2.50
51 Juraj Slafkovsky 1.50 4.00
52 MacKenzie Weegar .60 1.50
53 Wyatt Johnston 1.50 4.00
54 Travis Sanheim .50 1.25
55 Mikko Rantanen 2.00 5.00
56 Brock Nelson .75 2.00
57 Morgan Rielly .75 2.00
58 Kris Letang 1.00 2.50
59 Roman Josi .75 2.00
60 Moritz Seider 1.00 2.50
61 Mark Stone 1.00 2.50
62 Bo Horvat 1.00 2.50
63 Brad Marchand 1.50 4.00
64 Adam Fox 1.00 2.50
65 Erik Karlsson 1.00 2.50
66 Thomas Harley .75 2.00
67 Jake Neighbours .75 2.00
68 Luke Hughes 1.25 3.00
69 Travis Konecny .75 2.00
70 Jared McCann .60 1.50
71 Dylan Larkin 1.00 2.50
72 Tage Thompson 1.00 2.50
73 Charlie McAvoy 1.00 2.50
74 Juuse Saros 1.00 2.50
75 Kirill Kaprizov 2.50 6.00
76 William Eklund 1.00 2.50
77 Victor Hedman 1.00 2.50
78 Carter Verhaeghe .75 2.00
79 Mathew Barzal 1.00 2.50
80 Evgeni Malkin 1.50 4.00
81 William Karlsson 1.00 2.50
82 Anze Kopitar 1.25 3.00
83 Nikita Kucherov 1.50 4.00
84 Lucas Raymond 1.25 3.00
85 Marc-Andre Fleury 1.50 4.00
86 Jack Hughes 2.00 5.00
87 Sidney Crosby 3.00 8.00
88 David Pastrnak 2.00 5.00
89 Owen Tippett .50 1.25
90 Andrei Vasilevskiy 1.25 3.00
91 Nazem Kadri 1.00 2.50
92 John Carlson .75 2.00
93 Mika Zibanejad 1.00 2.50
94 Brady Tkachuk 1.25 3.00
95 Robert Thomas .75 2.00
96 William Nylander 1.50 4.00
97 Connor McDavid 4.00 10.00
98 Connor Bedard 2.50 6.00
99 Connor Hellebuyck 1.50 4.00
100 Quinton Byfield 1.00 2.50
101 Mavrik Bourque RC 3.00 8.00
102 Collin Graf RC 1.50 4.00
103 Ivan Fedotov RC 2.50 6.00
104 Akil Thomas RC 1.50 4.00
105 Josh Doan RC 2.50 6.00
106 James Malatesta RC 1.50 4.00
107 Logan Morrison RC 1.50 4.00
108 Devin Cooley RC 1.50 4.00
109 Cameron Crotty RC 1.50 4.00
110 Jack St. Ivany RC 1.50 4.00
111 Zach Dean RC 1.50 4.00
112 Landon Slaggert RC 1.50 4.00
113 Marat Khusnutdinov RC 1.50 4.00
114 Zack Ostapchuk RC 1.50 4.00
115 Logan Stankoven RC 4.00 10.00
116 Arshdeep Bains RC 2.00 5.00
117 Mason Morelli RC 1.50 4.00
118 Matt Rempe RC 3.00 8.00
119 Matt Villalta RC 1.50 4.00
120 Shakir Mukhamadullin RC 2.00 5.00
121 Olen Zellweger RC 3.00 8.00
122 Kyle MacLean RC 1.50 4.00
123 Brendan Brisson RC 2.00 5.00
124 Joshua Roy RC 2.50 6.00
125 Phil Kemp RC 1.50 4.00
126 Maxwell Crozier RC 1.50 4.00
127 Gage Goncalves RC 2.00 5.00
128 Jesper Wallstedt RC 4.00 10.00
129 Yan Kuznetsov RC 1.50 4.00
130 Graeme Clarke RC 1.50 4.00
131 Emil Lilleberg RC 1.50 4.00
132 Jack Thompson RC 1.50 4.00
133 Vasily Ponomarev RC 1.50 4.00
134 Brennan Othmann RC 2.50 6.00
135 Lukas Cormier RC 1.50 4.00
136 Pierrick Dube RC 1.50 4.00
137 Zachary Bolduc RC 2.50 6.00
138 Liam Ohgren RC 3.00 8.00
139 Lane Hutson RC 8.00 20.00
140 Frank Nazar RC 5.00 12.00
141 Ruslan Iskhakov RC 1.50 4.00
142 Sam Colangelo RC 1.50 4.00
143 Brad Lambert RC 2.00 5.00
144 Gavin Brindley RC 1.50 4.00
145 Bradly Nadeau RC 2.50 6.00
146 Ethan Del Mastro RC 1.50 4.00
147 Marshall Rifai RC 1.50 4.00
148 Scott Morrow RC 2.00 5.00
149 Cutter Gauthier RC 4.00 10.00
150 Logan Mailloux RC 2.50 6.00
151 Jakub Dobes EXT RC 6.00 15.00
152 Lian Bichsel EXT RC 3.00 8.00
153 Jett Luchanko EXT RC 3.00 8.00
154 Conor Geekie EXT RC 3.00 8.00
155 Jonathan Lekkerimaki EXT RC 4.00 10.00
156 Sebastian Cossa EXT RC 4.00 10.00
157 Denton Mateychuk EXT RC 3.00 8.00
158 Will Smith EXT RC 5.00 12.00
159 Matvei Michkov EXT RC 6.00 15.00
160 Macklin Celebrini EXT RC 8.00 20.00
161 Cutter Gauthier HOLO 12.00 30.00
162 Lane Hutson HOLO 40.00 100.00
163 Mavrik Bourque HOLO 10.00 25.00
164 Frank Nazar HOLO 15.00 40.00
165 Olen Zellweger HOLO 10.00 25.00
166 Macklin Celebrini HOLO 125.00 300.00
167 Brennan Othmann HOLO 12.00 30.00
168 Brad Lambert HOLO 6.00 15.00
169 Matvei Michkov HOLO 60.00 150.00
170 Liam Ohgren HOLO 10.00 25.00
171 Conor Geekie HOLO 10.00 25.00
172 Josh Doan HOLO 8.00 20.00
173 Logan Stankoven HOLO 12.00 30.00
174 Will Smith HOLO 15.00 40.00
175 Seamus Casey HOLO 6.00 15.00

2024-25 SPx Gold

*GOLD: .6X TO 1.5X BASIC
151 Jakub Dobes EXT 20.00 50.00
155 Jonathan Lekkerimaki EXT 8.00 20.00
156 Sebastian Cossa EXT 15.00 40.00
159 Matvei Michkov EXT 30.00 80.00
160 Macklin Celebrini EXT 40.00 100.00

2024-25 SPx Grand Finale

*GRAND FINALE/50: 1X TO 2.5X BASIC
139 Lane Hutson 80.00 200.00
151 Jakub Dobes EXT 40.00 100.00
152 Lian Bichsel EXT 30.00 80.00
153 Jett Luchanko EXT 12.00 30.00
157 Denton Mateychuk EXT 8.00 20.00
158 Will Smith EXT 20.00 50.00
159 Matvei Michkov EXT 80.00 200.00
160 Macklin Celebrini EXT 150.00 400.00

2024-25 SPx Radiance

*RADIANCE/100: .6X TO 1.5X BASIC
*RADIANCE RC/100: .8X TO 2X BASIC
139 Lane Hutson 50.00 125.00
151 Jakub Dobes EXT 30.00 80.00
152 Lian Bichsel EXT 12.00 30.00
155 Jonathan Lekkerimaki EXT 8.00 20.00
156 Sebastian Cossa EXT 15.00 40.00
159 Matvei Michkov EXT 40.00 100.00
160 Macklin Celebrini EXT 50.00 125.00

2024-25 SPx Rookie Holograms Blue

*HOLO BLUE/25: .8X TO 2X BASIC
162 Lane Hutson 50.00 125.00
166 Macklin Celebrini 150.00 400.00

2024-25 SPx Silver

*SILVER: .5X TO 1.2X BASIC
151 Jakub Dobes EXT 10.00 25.00

2024-25 SPx Silver Spectrum

*SILVER SPEC/25: 1.2X TO 3X BASIC
151 Jakub Dobes EXT 50.00 125.00
153 Jett Luchanko EXT 15.00 40.00

2024-25 SPx All-Time Holoview

ATGAM Al MacInnis 3.00 8.00
ATGAO Adam Oates 2.50 6.00
ATGBE Jean Beliveau 2.50 6.00
ATGBL Brian Leetch 2.50 6.00
ATGBO Bobby Orr 10.00 25.00
ATGBR Martin Brodeur 6.00 15.00
ATGCC Chris Chelios 2.50 6.00
ATGCN Cam Neely 2.50 6.00
ATGDH Dominik Hasek 4.00 10.00
ATGDP Denis Potvin 2.50 6.00
ATGEB Ed Belfour 2.50 6.00
ATGEL Eric Lindros 4.00 10.00
ATGGF Grant Fuhr 4.00 10.00
ATGHE Dany Heatley 2.00 5.00
ATGHZ Henrik Zetterberg 3.00 8.00
ATGJB Johnny Bucyk 2.50 6.00
ATGJJ Jaromir Jagr 8.00 20.00
ATGJK Jari Kurri 2.50 6.00
ATGJP Jacques Plante 2.50 6.00
ATGJS Joe Sakic 5.00 12.00
ATGJT Joe Thornton 4.00 10.00
ATGLI Trevor Linden 2.50 6.00
ATGLR Luc Robitaille 2.50 6.00
ATGMB Mike Bossy 2.50 6.00
ATGME Mark Messier 5.00 12.00
ATGMG Mike Gartner 3.00 8.00
ATGML Mario Lemieux 15.00 40.00
ATGMM Mike Modano 4.00 10.00
ATGMR Maurice Richard 5.00 12.00
ATGMS Martin St. Louis 2.50 6.00
ATGNL Nicklas Lidstrom 2.50 6.00
ATGPC Paul Coffey 2.50 6.00
ATGPR Patrick Roy 12.00 30.00
ATGRB Rod Brind'Amour 2.50 6.00
ATGRF Ron Francis 3.00 8.00
ATGRG Ryan Getzlaf 2.50 6.00
ATGRI Mike Ricci 1.50 4.00
ATGRN Rick Nash 2.50 6.00
ATGRO Larry Robinson 2.50 6.00
ATGRV Rogie Vachon 2.50 6.00
ATGSD Shane Doan 2.00 5.00
ATGSE Teemu Selanne 5.00 12.00
ATGSM Stan Mikita 2.50 6.00
ATGSY Steve Yzerman 12.00 30.00
ATGSZ Sergei Zubov 2.00 5.00
ATGTA Tony Amonte 2.00 5.00
ATGTL Ted Lindsay 2.50 6.00
ATGTS Terry Sawchuk 2.50 6.00
ATGTW Tiger Williams 1.50 4.00
ATGWG Wayne Gretzky 15.00 40.00

2024-25 SPx Autographs Blue

101 Mavrik Bourque/99 15.00 40.00
102 Collin Graf/199 8.00 20.00
104 Akil Thomas/199 8.00 20.00
107 Logan Morrison/199 8.00 20.00
108 Devin Cooley/199 8.00 20.00
111 Zach Dean/99 8.00 20.00
113 Marat Khusnutdinov/199 8.00 20.00
114 Zack Ostapchuk/199 8.00 20.00
115 Logan Stankoven/99 20.00 50.00
116 Arshdeep Bains/199 10.00 25.00
117 Mason Morelli/199 8.00 20.00
120 Shakir Mukhamadullin/99 10.00 25.00
121 Olen Zellweger/99 15.00 40.00
124 Joshua Roy/199 12.00 30.00
125 Phil Kemp/199 8.00 20.00
127 Gage Goncalves/199 10.00 25.00
128 Jesper Wallstedt/99 20.00 50.00
129 Yan Kuznetsov/199 8.00 20.00
130 Graeme Clarke/199 8.00 20.00
131 Emil Lilleberg/199 8.00 20.00
132 Jack Thompson/199 8.00 20.00
133 Vasily Ponomarev/199 8.00 20.00
134 Brennan Othmann/99 12.00 30.00
135 Lukas Cormier/199 8.00 20.00
136 Pierrick Dube/199 8.00 20.00
137 Zachary Bolduc/99 15.00 40.00
138 Liam Ohgren/199 15.00 40.00
139 Lane Hutson/199 150.00 400.00
140 Frank Nazar/199 25.00 60.00
142 Sam Colangelo/199 8.00 20.00
145 Bradly Nadeau/199 12.00 30.00
147 Marshall Rifai/199 8.00 20.00
148 Scott Morrow/199 10.00 25.00
150 Logan Mailloux/199 12.00 30.00
151 Jakub Dobes/99 EXT 60.00 150.00
152 Lian Bichsel/99 EXT 50.00 125.00
154 Conor Geekie/99 EXT 15.00 40.00
157 Denton Mateychuk/99 EXT 15.00 40.00
158 Will Smith/99 EXT 60.00 150.00
159 Matvei Michkov/99 EXT 150.00 400.00
160 Macklin Celebrini/99 EXT 250.00 600.00

2024-25 SPx Bound For Glory

BFG1 Adam Fantilli 2.00 5.00
BFG2 Macklin Celebrini 6.00 15.00
BFG3 Cole Caufield 2.50 6.00
BFG4 Cale Makar 3.00 8.00
BFG5 Brock Faber 1.50 4.00
BFG6 Thomas Harley 1.25 3.00
BFG7 Lane Hutson 6.00 15.00
BFG8 Alexis Lafreniere 2.00 5.00
BFG9 Wyatt Johnston 2.50 6.00
BFG10 Matvei Michkov 5.00 12.00
BFG11 Brady Tkachuk 2.00 5.00
BFG12 Lucas Raymond 2.00 5.00
BFG13 Luke Hughes 2.00 5.00
BFG14 Connor Bedard 4.00 10.00
BFG15 Logan Stankoven 3.00 8.00
BFG16 Noah Dobson 1.50 4.00
BFG17 Jason Robertson 2.00 5.00
BFG18 Cole Perfetti 1.25 3.00
BFG19 Jack Hughes 3.00 8.00
BFG20 Quinton Byfield 1.50 4.00
BFG21 Moritz Seider 1.50 4.00
BFG22 Evan Bouchard 1.50 4.00
BFG23 Owen Power 1.25 3.00
BFG24 Matt Boldy 2.00 5.00
BFG25 Will Smith 4.00 10.00

2024-25 SPx Bound For Glory Blue

*BLUE/199: .6X TO 1.5X BASIC
BFG2 Macklin Celebrini 25.00 60.00
BFG7 Lane Hutson 25.00 60.00
BFG10 Matvei Michkov 20.00 50.00
BFG14 Connor Bedard 10.00 25.00
BFG25 Will Smith 12.00 30.00

2024-25 SPx Excellence Redefined

*BLUE/199: .6X TO 1.5X BASIC
EX1 A.Ovechkin/A.Panarin 5.00 12.00
EX2 A.Vasilevskiy/I.Shesterkin 2.50 6.00
EX3 V.Hedman/R.Dahlin 1.50 4.00
EX4 D.Doughty/C.Makar 3.00 8.00
EX5 A.Barkov/J.Hughes 3.00 8.00
EX6 C.McDavid/S.Crosby 6.00 15.00
EX7 P.Kane/K.Kaprizov 4.00 10.00
EX8 A.Matthews/A.Fantilli 5.00 12.00
EX9 C.Bedard/N.MacKinnon 5.00 12.00
EX10 W.Johnston/J.Eichel 2.50 6.00

2024-25 SPx Finite

*BRONZE/599: .5X TO 1.2X BASIC
*SILVER/399: .5X TO 1.2X BASIC
*GOLD/199: .6X TO 1.5X BASIC
*PURPLE/99: .8X TO 2X BASIC
*TUXEDO/50: 2X TO 5X BASIC
F1 Leo Carlsson 1.50 4.00
F2 Matthew Tkachuk 2.00 5.00
F3 Jordan Kyrou 1.00 2.50
F4 Nathan MacKinnon 4.00 10.00
F5 Cole Caufield 2.00 5.00
F6 Sidney Crosby 4.00 10.00
F7 Connor Bedard 3.00 8.00
F8 Tomas Hertl 1.00 2.50
F9 Adam Fantilli 1.50 4.00
F10 Travis Konecny 1.00 2.50
F11 Kirill Kaprizov 3.00 8.00
F12 Jeremy Swayman 1.50 4.00
F13 Auston Matthews 4.00 10.00
F14 Dylan Larkin 1.25 3.00
F15 Matty Beniers 1.25 3.00
F16 Leon Draisaitl 3.00 8.00
F17 Ilya Sorokin 1.50 4.00
F18 Jason Robertson 1.50 4.00
F19 Jack Hughes 2.50 6.00
F20 David Pastrnak 2.50 6.00
F21 Nick Suzuki 1.50 4.00
F22 Anze Kopitar 1.50 4.00
F23 Alex Ovechkin 4.00 10.00
F24 Connor McDavid 5.00 12.00
F25 Filip Forsberg 1.50 4.00
F26 Zachary Bolduc 2.00 5.00
F27 Joshua Roy 1.50 4.00
F28 Collin Graf 1.50 4.00
F29 Arshdeep Bains 1.25 3.00
F30 Olen Zellweger 2.00 5.00
F31 Logan Morrison 1.00 2.50
F32 Yan Kuznetsov 1.00 2.50
F33 Landon Slaggert 1.00 2.50
F34 Mavrik Bourque 2.00 5.00
F35 Kyle MacLean 1.00 2.50
F36 Matt Rempe 2.00 5.00
F37 Jack St. Ivany 1.00 2.50
F38 Graeme Clarke 1.00 2.50
F39 Zack Ostapchuk 1.00 2.50
F40 Ivan Fedotov 2.00 5.00
F41 Brendan Brisson 1.50 4.00
F42 Zach Dean 1.00 2.50
F43 Gage Goncalves 1.25 3.00
F44 Josh Doan 1.50 4.00
F45 Jesper Wallstedt 2.50 6.00
F46 Logan Stankoven 2.50 6.00
F47 Brennan Othmann 1.50 4.00
F48 Akil Thomas 1.00 2.50
F49 James Malatesta 1.00 2.50
F50 Shakir Mukhamadullin 1.25 3.00

2024-25 SPx Finite Autographs Silver Spectrum

F1 Leo Carlsson/49 10.00 25.00
F8 Tomas Hertl/49 6.00 15.00
F9 Adam Fantilli/49 10.00 25.00
F17 Ilya Sorokin/49 15.00 40.00
F28 Collin Graf/99 6.00 15.00
F29 Arshdeep Bains/99 8.00 20.00
F31 Logan Morrison/99 6.00 15.00
F32 Yan Kuznetsov/99 6.00 15.00
F34 Mavrik Bourque/99 12.00 30.00
F38 Graeme Clarke/99 6.00 15.00
F39 Zack Ostapchuk/99 6.00 15.00
F42 Zach Dean/99 6.00 15.00
F43 Gage Goncalves/99 8.00 20.00
F45 Jesper Wallstedt/99 15.00 40.00
F46 Logan Stankoven/99 15.00 40.00
F48 Akil Thomas/99 6.00 15.00
F50 Shakir Mukhamadullin/99 8.00 20.00

2024-25 SPx Force

SFASNJ Aho/Svechnikov/Necas/Jarvis 6.00 15.00
SFBDNH Barzal/Dobson/ Nelson/Horvat 5.00 12.00
SFBERK Boldy/Eriksson Ek/Rossi/Kaprizov 12.00 30.00
SFBMBD Beniers/McCann Bjorkstrand/Dunn 5.00 12.00
SFCSMH Connor/Scheifele Morrissey/Hellebuyck 8.00 20.00
SFDHHB Draisaitl/Hyman/Nugent-Hopkins/Bouchard 12.00 30.00
SFDPTS Draisaitl/Pastrnak Thomas/Suzuki 12.00 30.00
SFEBCO Esposito/Bucyk Cheevers/Orr 15.00 40.00
SFFKTS Foerster/Konecny Tippett/Sanheim 4.00 10.00
SFFOJS Forsberg/O'Reilly/Josi/Saros 6.00 15.00
SFGMFJ Gaudreau/Marchenko Fantilli/Jenner 6.00 15.00
SFHHBM Hischier/Hughes Bratt/Mercer 10.00 25.00
SFJRBH Johnston/Robertson Benn/Hintz 8.00 20.00
SFKBHP Kucherov/Bratt Hughes/Pettersson 10.00 25.00
SFKDJB Kurashev/Dickinson Jones/Bedard 12.00 30.00
SFKFBM Kopitar/Fiala/Byfield/Moore 6.00 15.00
SFKLMB Kopitar/Larkin/Letang Malkin/Bunting 8.00 20.00
SFKMCS Keller/Maccelli Cooley/Schmaltz 6.00 15.00
SFKPZL Kreider/Panarin Zibanejad/Lafreniere 8.00 20.00
SFLRSD Larkin/Raymond Seider/DeBrincat 6.00 15.00
SFMCZT McTavish/Carlsson Zegras/Terry 6.00 15.00
SFMKCG Messier/Kurri Coffey/Gretzky 25.00 60.00
SFMMKA MacKinnon/Makar Kaprizov/Aho 15.00 40.00
SFMMRT MacKinnon/Makar Rantanen/Toews 15.00 40.00
SFMNRM Matthews/Nylander Rielly/Marner 15.00 40.00
SFOBMM Oettinger/Barzal Marner/Matthews 15.00 40.00
SFOWOC Ovechkin/Wilson Oshie/Carlson 15.00 40.00
SFPHHK Point/Hagel Hedman/Kucherov 8.00 20.00
SFPMBH Pettersson/Miller Boeser/Hughes 10.00 25.00
SFPMLM Pastrnak/McAvoy Lindholm/Marchand 10.00 25.00
SFSCMS Suzuki/Caufield Matheson/Slafkovsky 8.00 20.00
SFSHKE Stone/Hertl/Karlsson/Eichel 6.00 15.00
SFTBSN Tkachuk/Batherson Stutzle/Norris 6.00 15.00
SFTKNP Thomas/Kyrou Neighbours/Parayko 4.00 10.00
SFTRPP Thompson/Dahlin Power/Peterka 5.00 12.00
SFTVEB Tkachuk/Verhaeghe Ekblad/Barkov 8.00 20.00
SFVSBS Vasilevskiy/Shesterkin Bobrovsky/Sorokin 8.00 20.00

2024-25 SPx Force Autographs

SFBMBD Matty Beniers
Jared McCann
Oliver Bjorkstrand
Vince Dunn/49 6.00 15.00
SFCSMH Kyle Connor
Mark Scheifele
Josh Morrissey
Connor Hellebuyck/49 10.00 25.00
SFDHHB Leon Draisaitl
Zach Hyman
Ryan Nugent-Hopkins
Evan Bouchard/25 15.00 40.00
SFFKTS Tyson Foerster
Travis Konecny
Owen Tippett
Travis Sanheim/49 5.00 12.00
SFFOJS Filip Forsberg
Ryan O'Reilly
Roman Josi
Juuse Saros/49 8.00 20.00
SFGMFJ Johnny Gaudreau
Kirill Marchenko
Adam Fantilli
Boone Jenner/49 8.00 20.00
SFJRBH Wyatt Johnston
Jason Robertson
Jamie Benn
Roope Hintz/49 10.00 25.00
SFKLMB Erik Karlsson
Kris Letang
Evgeni Malkin
Michael Bunting/49 10.00 25.00
SFKMCS Clayton Keller
Matias Maccelli
Logan Cooley
Nick Schmaltz/49 8.00 20.00
SFMMRT Nathan MacKinnon
Cale Makar
Mikko Rantanen
Devon Toews/49 20.00 50.00
SFOWOC Alex Ovechkin
Tom Wilson
T.J. Oshie
John Carlson/49 20.00 50.00
SFTKNP Robert Thomas
Jordan Kyrou
Jake Neighbours
Colton Parayko/49 5.00 12.00
SFTRPP Tage Thompson
Rasmus Dahlin
Owen Power
JJ Peterka/49 6.00 15.00
SFTVEB Matthew Tkachuk
Carter Verhaeghe
Aaron Ekblad
Aleksander Barkov/49 10.00 25.00
SFVSBS Andrei Vasilevskiy
Igor Shesterkin
Sergei Bobrovsky
Ilya Sorokin/25 10.00 25.00

2024-25 SPx Force Rookie Autographs

SFRDBSB Dean/Bolduc Stankoven/Bourque 12.00 30.00
SFRZMDT Zellweger/Mukhamadullin Doan/Thomas 10.00 25.00

2024-25 SPx Force Rookies

SFRBWCO Brisson/Wallstedt Clarke/Othmann 8.00 20.00
SFRDBSB Dean/Bolduc Stankoven/Bourque 8.00 20.00
SFRZMDT Zellweger/Mukhamadullin Doan/Thomas 6.00 15.00

2024-25 SPx Game Film

*BLUE/199: .6X TO 1.5X BASIC
GF1 Matt Boldy 1.50 4.00
GF2 Anze Kopitar 1.50 4.00
GF3 Connor Bedard 3.00 8.00
GF4 Mark Stone 1.25 3.00
GF5 Brock Boeser 1.25 3.00
GF6 Connor McDavid 5.00 12.00
GF7 Patrick Kane 2.00 5.00
GF8 Alex Ovechkin 4.00 10.00
GF9 Sidney Crosby 4.00 10.00
GF10 Nick Suzuki 1.50 4.00
GF11 Nathan MacKinnon 4.00 10.00
GF12 Auston Matthews 4.00 10.00
GF13 Brady Tkachuk 1.50 4.00
GF14 Aleksander Barkov 1.50 4.00
GF15 Quinn Hughes 2.50 6.00

2024-25 SPx Holo'd Hardware

HHAM Auston Matthews 15.00 40.00
HHAO Alex Ovechkin 15.00 40.00
HHBC Bobby Clarke 6.00 15.00
HHCM Connor McDavid 40.00 100.00
HHCP Corey Perry 6.00 15.00
HHEM Evgeni Malkin 8.00 20.00
HHGH Gordie Howe 12.00 30.00
HHLD Leon Draisaitl 12.00 30.00
HHML Mario Lemieux 30.00 80.00
HHMM Mark Messier 8.00 20.00
HHNK Nikita Kucherov 8.00 20.00
HHPK Patrick Kane 8.00 20.00
HHSC Sidney Crosby 15.00 40.00
HHTH Taylor Hall 4.00 10.00
HHWG Wayne Gretzky 25.00 60.00

2024-25 SPx Holographs

*GOLD/25: .6X TO 1.5X BASIC
HOLOAD Alex DeBrincat 10.00 25.00
HOLOAL Alexis Lafreniere 12.00 30.00
HOLOBN Brock Nelson 8.00 20.00
HOLOBO Mavrik Bourque 15.00 40.00
HOLOCH Connor Hellebuyck 15.00 40.00
HOLOIS Ilya Sorokin 12.00 30.00
HOLOJB Jordan Binnington 12.00 30.00
HOLOJD Josh Doan 12.00 30.00
HOLOJS Juraj Slafkovsky 15.00 40.00
HOLOJW Jesper Wallstedt 20.00 50.00
HOLOKL Kris Letang 10.00 25.00
HOLOLD Leon Draisaitl 25.00 60.00
HOLOLS Logan Stankoven 20.00 50.00
HOLOMB Matt Boldy 12.00 30.00
HOLOMR Mikko Rantanen 20.00 50.00
HOLONK Nikita Kucherov 15.00 40.00
HOLONS Nick Suzuki 15.00 40.00
HOLOQH Quinn Hughes 20.00 50.00
HOLOSW Shane Wright 10.00 25.00

2024-25 SPx Holoview F/X

HV1 Nathan MacKinnon 4.00 10.00
HV2 Jason Robertson 1.50 4.00
HV3 Sidney Crosby 4.00 10.00
HV4 Connor Bedard 3.00 8.00
HV5 Filip Forsberg 1.50 4.00
HV6 Kyle Connor 1.50 4.00
HV7 Alex Ovechkin 4.00 10.00
HV8 Connor McDavid 5.00 12.00
HV9 William Nylander 2.00 5.00
HV10 Cole Caufield 2.00 5.00
HV11 Auston Matthews 4.00 10.00
HV12 Dylan Larkin 1.25 3.00
HV13 Jack Eichel 1.50 4.00
HV14 Tage Thompson 1.25 3.00
HV15 Leon Draisaitl 3.00 8.00
HV16 Elias Pettersson 1.50 4.00
HV17 Jack Hughes 2.50 6.00
HV18 Sebastian Aho 1.50 4.00
HV19 David Pastrnak 2.50 6.00
HV20 Kirill Kaprizov 3.00 8.00
HV21 Brad Marchand 2.00 5.00
HV22 Matthew Tkachuk 2.00 5.00
HV23 Wyatt Johnston 2.00 5.00
HV24 Artemi Panarin 2.00 5.00
HV25 Cale Makar 2.50 6.00
HV26 Quinn Hughes 2.50 6.00
HV27 Nick Suzuki 2.00 5.00
HV28 Nikita Kucherov 2.00 5.00
HV29 Mathew Barzal 1.25 3.00
HV30 Mitch Marner 1.50 4.00
HV31 Brad Lambert 1.25 3.00
HV32 Lane Hutson 5.00 12.00
HV33 Brennan Othmann 1.50 4.00
HV34 Josh Doan 1.50 4.00
HV35 Matvei Michkov 4.00 10.00
HV36 Rutger McGroarty 2.00 5.00
HV37 Will Smith 3.00 8.00
HV38 Logan Stankoven 2.50 6.00
HV39 Brendan Brisson 1.25 3.00
HV40 Jesper Wallstedt 2.50 6.00
HV41 Zachary Bolduc 2.00 5.00
HV42 Frank Nazar 3.00 8.00
HV43 Conor Geekie 2.00 5.00
HV44 Mavrik Bourque 2.00 5.00
HV45 Cutter Gauthier 2.50 6.00
HV46 Jett Luchanko 2.00 5.00
HV47 Olen Zellweger 2.00 5.00
HV48 Macklin Celebrini 5.00 12.00
HV49 Seamus Casey 1.25 3.00
HV50 Liam Ohgren 2.00 5.00

2024-25 SPx Holoview F/X Blue

*BLUE/399: .6X TO 1.5X BASIC
HV32 Lane Hutson 30.00 80.00
HV35 Matvei Michkov 25.00 60.00
HV48 Macklin Celebrini 30.00 80.00

2024-25 SPx Holoview F/X Red

*RED/25: 2X TO 5X BASIC
HV3 Sidney Crosby 30.00 80.00
HV8 Connor McDavid 40.00 100.00
HV19 David Pastrnak 25.00 60.00
HV35 Matvei Michkov 125.00 300.00
HV36 Rutger McGroarty 40.00 100.00
HV41 Zachary Bolduc 15.00 40.00
HV45 Cutter Gauthier 40.00 100.00
HV46 Jett Luchanko 30.00 80.00
HV49 Seamus Casey 15.00 40.00

2024-25 SPx Salute

SAO Alex Ovechkin 30.00 80.00
SBO Bobby Orr 30.00 80.00
SCM Connor McDavid 40.00 100.00
SSC Sidney Crosby 30.00 80.00
SWG Wayne Gretzky 50.00 125.00

2024-25 SPx Salute Autographs

SAO Alex Ovechkin 250.00 600.00

2024-25 SPx SPxCellence

XCAB Aleksander Barkov 3.00 8.00
XCAM Auston Matthews 8.00 20.00
XCAO Alex Ovechkin 8.00 20.00
XCAP Artemi Panarin 4.00 10.00
XCBB Brock Boeser 2.50 6.00
XCBH Bo Horvat 2.50 6.00
XCCB Connor Bedard 6.00 15.00
XCCH Connor Hellebuyck 4.00 10.00
XCCK Clayton Keller 2.50 6.00
XCCM Cale Makar 5.00 12.00
XCDL Dylan Larkin 2.50 6.00
XCDP David Pastrnak 5.00 12.00
XCEP Elias Pettersson 3.00 8.00
XCJD Josh Doan 3.00 8.00
XCJE Jack Eichel 3.00 8.00
XCJH Jack Hughes 5.00 12.00
XCJM Vince Dunn 1.50 4.00
XCJN Jake Neighbours 2.50 6.00
XCJS Juraj Slafkovsky 4.00 10.00
XCJT John Tavares 3.00 8.00
XCKC Kyle Connor 3.00 8.00
XCKK Kirill Kaprizov 6.00 15.00
XCLC Logan Cooley 3.00 8.00
XCLD Leon Draisaitl 6.00 15.00
XCLS Logan Stankoven 5.00 12.00
XCMA Mitch Marner 3.00 8.00
XCMC Connor McDavid 10.00 25.00
XCMM Mason McTavish 2.00 5.00
XCNK Nikita Kucherov 4.00 10.00
XCNM Nathan MacKinnon 8.00 20.00
XCNS Nick Suzuki 4.00 10.00
XCRD Rasmus Dahlin 2.50 6.00
XCSA Sebastian Aho 3.00 8.00
XCSC Sidney Crosby 8.00 20.00
XCTH Tomas Hertl 2.00 5.00
XCTM Trevor Moore 1.25 3.00
XCWJ Wyatt Johnston 4.00 10.00
XCWN William Nylander 4.00 10.00
XCYS Yegor Sharangovich 2.00 5.00
XCZH Zach Hyman 3.00 8.00

2024-25 SPx SPxCellence Autographs

XCAB Aleksander Barkov/49 15.00 40.00
XCCH Connor Hellebuyck/99 20.00 50.00
XCJM Vince Dunn/99 8.00 20.00
XCLC Logan Cooley/99 25.00 60.00
XCLS Logan Stankoven/99 15.00 40.00
XCMM Mason McTavish/99 10.00 25.00
XCTH Tomas Hertl/99 10.00 25.00
XCWJ Wyatt Johnston/49 25.00 60.00
XCYS Yegor Sharangovich/99 10.00 25.00

2024-25 SPx Star Focus Signatures

SFAT Alex Tuch 6.00 15.00
SFBB Brock Boeser 8.00 20.00
SFEP Elias Pettersson 10.00 25.00
SFJE Jack Eichel 10.00 25.00
SFMA Cale Makar 40.00 100.00
SFMH Miro Heiskanen 8.00 20.00
SFMS Mark Stone 8.00 20.00

2024-25 SPx SuperScripts

SSAR Alexander Romanov 6.00 15.00
SSAT Alex Turcotte 5.00 12.00
SSCL Charlie Lindgren 6.00 15.00
SSCS Cole Sillinger 6.00 15.00
SSET Eeli Tolvanen 8.00 20.00
SSFV Frank Vatrano 6.00 15.00
SSJC J.T. Compher 5.00 12.00
SSJD Jamie Drysdale 6.00 15.00
SSJQ Jack Quinn 6.00 15.00
SSJS Jared Spurgeon 8.00 20.00
SSJW Joseph Woll 12.00 30.00
SSMA Mikey Anderson 6.00 15.00
SSMG Morgan Geekie 5.00 12.00
SSQU Jonathan Quick 25.00 60.00
SSRR Ryan Reaves 6.00 15.00
SSSP Shane Pinto 6.00 15.00
SSTN Thomas Novak 5.00 12.00
SSTT Teuvo Teravainen 8.00 20.00

2024-25 SPx SuperScripts Gold

*GOLD: .5X TO 1.2X BASIC
SSQU Jonathan Quick/25 40.00 100.00

2024-25 SPx SuperScripts Rookies

*GOLD/99: .5X TO 1.2X BASIC
SSRAB Arshdeep Bains 8.00 20.00
SSRAT Akil Thomas 6.00 15.00
SSRBB Brendan Brisson 8.00 20.00
SSRBO Brennan Othmann 10.00 25.00
SSRCG Collin Graf 6.00 15.00
SSRDC Devin Cooley 6.00 15.00
SSRFN Frank Nazar 20.00 50.00
SSRGA Cutter Gauthier 15.00 40.00
SSRGC Graeme Clarke 6.00 15.00
SSRIF Ivan Fedotov 12.00 30.00
SSRJD Josh Doan 10.00 25.00
SSRJR Joshua Roy 10.00 25.00
SSRJW Jesper Wallstedt 15.00 40.00
SSRLM Logan Morrison 6.00 15.00
SSRLS Logan Stankoven 15.00 40.00
SSRMB Mavrik Bourque 12.00 30.00
SSRMK Marat Khusnutdinov 6.00 15.00
SSRMM Mason Morelli 6.00 15.00
SSRMR Matt Rempe 12.00 30.00
SSROZ Olen Zellweger 12.00 30.00
SSRRI Marshall Rifai 6.00 15.00
SSRSM Shakir Mukhamadullin 8.00 20.00
SSRZB Zachary Bolduc 12.00 30.00
SSRZD Zach Dean 6.00 15.00

1998-99 SPx Finite

COMP BASE SET (90) 30.00 80.00
1 Teemu Selanne .60 1.50
2 Guy Hebert .50 1.25
3 Josef Marha .20 .50
4 Travis Green .20 .50
5 Sergei Samsonov .50 1.25
6 Jason Allison .20 .50
7 Byron Dafoe .50 1.25
8 Dominik Hasek 1.25 3.00
9 Michael Peca .20 .50
10 Erik Rasmussen .20 .50
11 Matthew Barnaby .20 .50
12 Theo Fleury .20 .50
13 Derek Morris .20 .50
14 Valeri Bure .20 .50
15 Trevor Kidd .50 1.25
16 Sami Kapanen .20 .50
17 Bates Battaglia .20 .50
18 Tony Amonte .50 1.25
19 Dmitri Nabokov .20 .50
20 Daniel Cleary .20 .50
21 Jeff Hackett .50 1.25
22 Joe Sakic 1.25 3.00
23 Valeri Kamensky .50 1.25
24 Patrick Roy 2.00 5.00
25 Wade Belak .20 .50
26 Joe Nieuwendyk .50 1.25
27 Mike Keane .20 .50
28 Jere Lehtinen .20 .50
29 Ed Belfour .50 1.25
30 Steve Yzerman 3.00 8.00
31 Dmitri Mironov .20 .50
32 Brendan Shanahan .60 1.50
33 Nicklas Lidstrom .60 1.50
34 Doug Weight .50 1.25
35 Janne Niinimaa .20 .50
36 Bill Guerin .50 1.25
37 Ray Whitney .20 .50
38 Robert Svehla .20 .50
39 Ed Jovanovski .50 1.25
40 Vladimir Tsyplakov .20 .50
41 Jozef Stumpel .50 1.25
42 Rob Blake .50 1.25
43 Mark Recchi .50 1.25
44 Andy Moog .50 1.25
45 Matt Higgins RC .20 .50
46 Martin Brodeur 1.50 4.00
47 Doug Gilmour .50 1.25
48 Brendan Morrison .50 1.25
49 Patrik Elias .50 1.25
50 Trevor Linden .50 1.25
51 Bryan Berard .20 .50
52 Zdeno Chara 3.00 8.00
53 Wayne Gretzky 3.00 8.00
54 Marc Savard .20 .50
55 Daniel Goneau .20 .50
56 Pat Lafontaine .60 1.50
57 Alexei Yashin .20 .50
58 Marian Hossa .60 1.50
59 Wade Redden .20 .50
60 John LeClair .60 1.50
61 Alexandre Daigle .20 .50
62 Rod Brind'Amour .50 1.25
63 Chris Therien .20 .50
64 Keith Tkachuk .60 1.50
65 Brad Isbister .20 .50
66 Nikolai Khabibulin .50 1.25
67 Robert Dome .20 .50
68 Alexei Morozov .20 .50
69 Stu Barnes .20 .50
70 Tom Barrasso .50 1.25
71 Owen Nolan .50 1.25
72 Marco Sturm .50 1.25
73 Patrick Marleau .20 .50
74 Pierre Turgeon .50 1.25
75 Chris Pronger .50 1.25
76 Pavol Demitra .20 .50
77 Grant Fuhr .50 1.25
78 Stephane Richer .50 1.25
79 Zac Bierk RC .50 1.25
80 Alexander Selivanov .20 .50
81 Mike Johnson .50 1.25
82 Mats Sundin .60 1.50
83 Alyn McAuley .50 1.25
84 Pavel Bure .60 1.50
85 Todd Bertuzzi .60 1.50
86 Garth Snow .50 1.25
87 Peter Bondra .50 1.25
88 Olaf Kolzig .50 1.25
89 Jan Bulis .20 .50

90 Sergei Gonchar .20 .50
91 Pavel Bure GI .75 2.00
92 Joe Sakic GI 2.00 5.00
93 Steve Yzerman GI 5.00 12.00
94 Jaromir Jagr GI 1.50 4.00
95 Peter Forsberg GI 2.50 6.00
96 Brendan Shanahan GI 1.00 2.50
97 Brett Hull GI 1.25 3.00
98 Alexei Yashin GI .75 2.00
99 Wayne Gretzky GI 6.00 15.00
100 Eric Lindros GI 1.00 2.50
101 Sergei Samsonov GI .75 2.00
102 John LeClair GI 1.00 2.50
103 Dominik Hasek GI 2.00 5.00
104 Teemu Selanne GI 1.00 2.50
105 Martin Brodeur GI 2.50 6.00
106 Tony Amonte GI .75 2.00
107 Theo Fleury GI .75 2.00
108 Rob Blake GI .75 2.00
109 Mike Modano GI 1.50 4.00
110 Peter Bondra GI .75 2.00
111 Brian Leetch GI 1.00 2.50
112 Nicklas Lidstrom GI 1.00 2.50
113 Doug Weight GI .75 2.00
114 Zigmund Palffy GI .60 1.50
115 Saku Koivu GI 1.00 2.50
116 Paul Kariya GI 1.00 2.50
117 Ray Bourque GI 1.50 4.00
118 Mats Sundin GI 1.00 2.50
119 Patrick Roy GI 1.50 4.00
120 Chris Chelios GI 1.00 2.50
121 Sergei Samsonov SS 1.50 4.00
122 Mike Johnson SS .60 1.50
123 Patrik Elias SS 1.50 4.00
124 Josef Marha SS .60 1.50
125 Dan Cloutier SS .60 1.50
126 Cameron Mann SS .60 1.50
127 Mattias Ohlund SS .60 1.50
128 Daniel Cleary SS .60 1.50
129 Anders Eriksson SS .60 1.50
130 Patrick Marleau SS .60 1.50
131 Jan Bulis SS .60 1.50
132 Alyn McCauley SS .60 1.50
133 Joe Thornton SS 3.00 8.00
134 Andrei Zyuzin SS .60 1.50
135 Richard Zednik SS .60 1.50
136 Derek Morris SS .60 1.50
137 Bates Battaglia SS .60 1.50
138 Mike Watt SS .60 1.50
139 Olli Jokinen SS 1.50 4.00
140 Marian Hossa SS 2.00 5.00
141 Daniel Goneau SS .60 1.50
142 Erik Rasmussen SS .60 1.50
143 Daniel Briere SS .60 1.50
144 Norm Maracle SS RC 2.50 6.00
145 Brendan Morrison SS 1.50 4.00
146 Brad Isbister SS .60 1.50
147 Robert Dome SS .60 1.50
148 Zac Bierk SS .60 1.50
149 Alexei Morozov SS .60 1.50
150 Marco Sturm SS .60 1.50
151 Wayne Gretzky MP 12.50 30.00
152 Eric Lindros MP 2.00 5.00
153 Paul Kariya MP 2.00 5.00
154 Patrick Roy MP 6.00 15.00
155 Sergei Samsonov MP 2.00 5.00
156 Steve Yzerman MP 8.00 20.00
157 Teemu Selanne MP 2.00 5.00
158 Brendan Shanahan MP 2.00 5.00
159 Dominik Hasek MP 4.00 10.00
160 Mark Messier MP 2.00 5.00
161 Martin Brodeur MP 6.00 15.00
162 Mats Sundin MP 2.00 5.00
163 Joe Sakic MP 4.00 10.00
164 John LeClair MP 2.00 5.00
165 Jaromir Jagr MP 4.00 10.00
166 Peter Forsberg MP 4.00 10.00
167 Theo Fleury MP 1.50 4.00
168 Peter Bondra MP 1.50 4.00
169 Mike Modano MP 3.00 8.00
170 Pavel Bure MP 2.00 5.00
171 Patrick Roy LL 12.50 30.00
172 Eric Lindros LL 6.00 15.00
173 Dominik Hasek LL 10.00 20.00
174 Jaromir Jagr LL 6.00 15.00
175 Steve Yzerman LL 12.50 30.00
176 Martin Brodeur LL 12.50 30.00
177 Ray Bourque LL 6.00 15.00
178 Peter Forsberg LL 10.00 25.00
179 Paul Kariya LL 6.00 15.00
180 Wayne Gretzky LL 8.00 20.00
S99 Wayne Gretzky SAMPLE .75 2.00

1998-99 SPx Finite Radiance

*RADIANCE 1-90: .8X TO 2X BASIC
*RADIANCE GI 91-120: .8X TO 2X BASIC
*RADIANCE SS 121-150: .8X TO 2X BASIC
*RADIANCE MP 151-170: 1X TO 2.5X BASIC
*RADIANCE LL 171-180: .8X TO 2X BASIC

1998-99 SPx Finite Spectrum

*SPECTRUM 1-90: 5X TO 15X BASIC
*SPECTRUM GI 91-120: 8X TO 18X BASIC
*SPECTRUM SS 121-150: 6X TO 15X BASIC
*SPECTRUM MP 151-170: 10X TO 20X BASIC

1998-99 SPx Top Prospects

COMPLETE SET (90) 60.00 150.00
COMP.SET w/o SP's (60) 15.00 40.00
1 Paul Kariya .60 1.50
2 Teemu Selanne .60 1.50
3 Ray Bourque 1.00 2.50
4 Sergei Samsonov .40 1.00
5 Joe Thornton 1.00 2.50
6 Dominik Hasek 1.25 3.00
7 Theo Fleury .40 1.00
8 Keith Primeau .20 .50
9 Tony Amonte .40 1.00
10 Doug Gilmour .40 1.00
11 J-P Dumont .20 .50
12 Chris Chelios .60 1.50
13 Peter Forsberg 1.50 4.00
14 Patrick Roy 3.00 8.00
15 Joe Sakic 1.25 3.00
16 Milan Hejduk RC 3.00 8.00
17 Chris Drury .40 1.00
18 Mike Modano 1.00 2.50
19 Brett Hull .75 2.00
20 Ed Belfour .60 1.50
21 Steve Yzerman 2.00 5.00
22 Brendan Shanahan .60 1.50
23 Sergei Fedorov 1.00 2.50
24 Chris Osgood .40 1.00
25 Nicklas Lidstrom .60 1.50
26 Bill Guerin .20 .50
27 Doug Weight .40 1.00
28 Tom Poti .20 .50
29 Mark Parrish RC 1.00 2.50
30 Rob Blake .40 1.00
31 Pavel Rosa RC .40 1.00
32 Vincent Damphousse .20 .50
33 Saku Koivu .60 1.50
34 Mike Dunham .20 .50
35 Martin Brodeur 1.50 4.00
36 Zigmund Palffy .40 1.00
37 Eric Brewer .20 .50
38 Wayne Gretzky 4.00 10.00
39 Brian Leetch .60 1.50
40 Manny Malhotra .20 .50
41 Petr Nedved .20 .50
42 Alexei Yashin .20 .50
43 Eric Lindros .60 1.50
44 John LeClair .40 1.00
45 John Vanbiesbrouck .40 1.00
46 Keith Tkachuk .40 1.00
47 Jeremy Roenick .75 2.00
48 Daniel Briere .20 .50
49 Jaromir Jagr 1.00 2.50
50 Patrick Marleau .40 1.00
51 Al MacInnis .20 .50
52 Chris Pronger .40 1.00
53 Vincent Lecavalier .60 1.50
54 Curtis Joseph .60 1.50
55 Mats Sundin .60 1.50
56 Tomas Kaberle RC 1.00 2.50
57 Mark Messier .60 1.50
58 Pavel Bure .60 1.50
59 Bill Muckalt RC .40 1.00
60 Peter Bondra .40 1.00
61 Brian Finley RC 1.50 4.00
62 Roberto Luongo 2.00 5.00
63 Mike Van Ryn 1.50 4.00
64 Harold Druken 1.50 4.00
65 Daniel Tkaczuk 1.50 4.00
66 Brenden Morrow RC 5.00 12.00
67 Jani Rita RC 1.50 4.00
68 Tommi Santala RC 1.50 4.00
69 Teemu Virkkunen RC 1.50 4.00
70 Arto Laaktikainen RC 1.50 4.00
71 Ilkka Mikkola RC 1.50 4.00
72 Miko Jokela RC 1.50 4.00
73 Kirill Safronov RC 1.50 4.00
74 Denis Shvidki 1.50 4.00
75 Denis Arkhipov RC 1.50 4.00
76 Maxim Afinogenov 2.00 5.00
77 Alexander Zevakhin RC 1.50 4.00
78 Alexei Volkov RC 1.50 4.00
79 Daniel Sedin AU 8.00 20.00
80 Henrik Sedin AU 8.00 20.00
81 Jimmie Olvestad RC 1.50 4.00
82 Mattias Weinhandl RC 1.50 4.00
83 Mathias Tjarnqvist RC 1.50 4.00
84 Jakob Johansson RC 1.50 4.00
85 Barrett Heisten RC 1.50 4.00
86 Tim Connolly RC 2.00 5.00
87 Andy Hilbert RC 1.50 4.00
88 David Legwand 1.50 4.00
89 Joe Blackburn RC 1.50 4.00
90 Dave Tanabe RC 1.50 4.00

1998-99 SPx Top Prospects Radiance

*RADIANCE 1-60: 10X TO 25X BASIC CARDS
*RADIANCE 61-90: 1.2X TO 3X BASIC CARDS
*ROOKIES: 2X TO 5X BASIC CARDS

1998-99 SPx Top Prospects Highlight Heroes

COMPLETE SET (30) 75.00 150.00
H1 Paul Kariya 1.50 4.00
H2 Teemu Selanne 1.50 4.00
H3 Ray Bourque 2.50 6.00
H4 Sergei Samsonov 1.25 3.00
H5 Dominik Hasek 3.00 8.00
H6 Theo Fleury 1.25 3.00
H7 Doug Gilmour 1.25 3.00
H8 Joe Sakic 3.00 8.00
H9 Patrick Roy 8.00 20.00
H10 Peter Forsberg 4.00 10.00
H11 Mike Modano 2.50 6.00
H12 Brett Hull 2.00 5.00
H13 Brendan Shanahan 1.50 4.00
H14 Steve Yzerman 8.00 20.00
H15 Sergei Fedorov 2.50 6.00
H16 Saku Koivu 1.50 4.00
H17 Martin Brodeur 4.00 10.00
H18 Wayne Gretzky 10.00 25.00
H19 Zigmund Palffy 1.25 3.00
H20 John Vanbiesbrouck 1.25 3.00
H21 Eric Lindros 1.50 4.00
H22 John LeClair 1.50 4.00
H23 Keith Tkachuk 1.50 4.00
H24 Jeremy Roenick 2.00 5.00
H25 Jaromir Jagr 2.50 6.00
H26 Vincent Lecavalier 1.50 4.00
H27 Mats Sundin 1.50 4.00
H28 Curtis Joseph 1.50 4.00
H29 Pavel Bure 1.50 4.00
H30 Peter Bondra 1.25 3.00

1998-99 SPx Top Prospects Lasting Impressions

COMPLETE SET (30) 40.00 80.00
L1 Vincent Lecavalier .75 2.00
L2 John Vanbiesbrouck .60 1.50
L3 Paul Kariya .75 2.00
L4 Keith Tkachuk .75 2.00
L5 Mike Modano 1.25 3.00
L6 Dominik Hasek 1.25 3.00
L7 Teemu Selanne .75 2.00
L8 Mats Sundin .75 2.00
L9 Brendan Shanahan .75 2.00
L10 Pavel Bure .75 2.00
L11 Theo Fleury .75 2.00
L12 Curtis Joseph .75 2.00
L13 Joe Sakic 1.50 4.00
L14 Eric Lindros .75 2.00
L15 Peter Bondra .60 1.50
L16 Brett Hull 1.00 2.50
L17 Ray Bourque 1.25 3.00
L18 Jaromir Jagr 1.25 3.00
L19 Steve Yzerman 4.00 10.00
L20 Jeremy Roenick 1.00 2.50
L21 Martin Brodeur 2.00 5.00
L22 Saku Koivu .75 2.00
L23 Patrick Roy 4.00 10.00
L24 John LeClair .75 2.00
L25 Doug Gilmour .60 1.50
L26 Sergei Fedorov 1.25 3.00
L27 Wayne Gretzky 5.00 12.00
L28 Peter Forsberg 2.00 5.00
L29 Zigmund Palffy .60 1.50
L30 Sergei Samsonov .60 1.50

1998-99 SPx Top Prospects Premier Stars

COMPLETE SET (30) 100.00 200.00
PS1 Wayne Gretzky 15.00 40.00
PS2 Sergei Samsonov 2.00 5.00
PS3 Ray Bourque 4.00 10.00
PS4 Dominik Hasek 5.00 12.00
PS5 Martin Brodeur 6.00 15.00
PS6 Brian Leetch 2.50 6.00
PS7 Mike Richter 2.50 6.00
PS8 Eric Lindros 3.00 8.00
PS9 John LeClair 2.50 6.00
PS10 John Vanbiesbrouck 2.00 5.00
PS11 Jaromir Jagr 4.00 10.00
PS12 Vincent Lecavalier 2.50 6.00
PS13 Mats Sundin 2.50 6.00
PS14 Curtis Joseph 2.50 6.00
PS15 Peter Bondra 2.00 5.00
PS16 Wayne Gretzky 15.00 40.00
PS17 Teemu Selanne 2.50 6.00
PS18 Paul Kariya 2.50 6.00
PS19 Theo Fleury 2.50 6.00
PS20 Tony Amonte 2.00 5.00
PS21 Patrick Roy 12.50 30.00
PS22 Joe Sakic 5.00 12.00
PS23 Peter Forsberg 6.00 15.00
PS24 Mike Modano 4.00 10.00
PS25 Brett Hull 3.00 8.00
PS26 Steve Yzerman 12.50 30.00
PS27 Brendan Shanahan 2.50 6.00
PS28 Doug Weight 2.00 5.00
PS29 Keith Tkachuk 2.50 6.00
PS30 Mark Messier 2.50 6.00

1998-99 SPx Top Prospects Winning Materials

CJ Curtis Joseph 8.00 20.00
CO Chris Osgood 8.00 20.00
EL Eric Lindros 10.00 25.00
FP Felix Potvin 10.00 25.00
JJ Jaromir Jagr 12.50 30.00
JL John LeClair 8.00 20.00
JS Joe Sakic 15.00 40.00
JV John Vanbiesbrouck 8.00 20.00
MR Mike Richter 8.00 20.00
MS Mats Sundin 8.00 20.00
PR Patrick Roy 30.00 80.00
RB Ray Bourque 15.00 40.00

1998-99 SPx Top Prospects Year of the Great One

COMPLETE SET (30) 150.00 300.00
COMMON GRETZKY (WG1-WG30) 5.00 12.00

1992 Sport-Flash

COMPLETE SET (15) 4.00 10.00
1 Jacques Laperriere .25 .60
2 Larry Carriere .20 .50
3 Chuck Rayner .30 .75
4 Jean Beliveau .75 2.00
5 BoomBoom Geoffrion .60 1.50
6 Gilles Gilbert .30 .75
7 Marcel Bonin .20 .50
8 Leon Rochefort .20 .50
9 Maurice Richard 2.00 5.00
10 Rejean Houle .20 .50
11 Pierre Mondou .20 .50
12 Yvan Cournoyer .30 .75
13 Henri Richard .40 1.00
14 Checklist Card .02 .10
15 Certification of Limited Edition .02 .10

1992 Sport-Flash Autographs

COMPLETE SET (15) 80.00 200.00
1 Jacques Laperriere 4.00 10.00
2 Larry Carriere 4.00 10.00
3 Chuck Rayner 4.00 10.00
4 Jean Beliveau 25.00 50.00
5 BoomBoom Geoffrion 12.00 30.00
6 Gilles Gilbert 4.00 10.00
7 Marcel Bonin 4.00 10.00
8 Leon Rochefort 4.00 10.00
9 Maurice Richard 20.00 50.00
10 Rejean Houle 4.00 10.00
11 Pierre Mondou 4.00 10.00
12 Yvan Cournoyer 6.00 15.00
13 Henri Richard 8.00 20.00

1991-92 Stadium Club

1 Wayne Gretzky 1.00 2.50
2 Randy Moller .12 .30
3 Ray Ferraro .12 .30
4 Craig Wolanin .12 .30
5 Shayne Corson .12 .30
6 Chris Chelios .15 .40
7 Joe Mullen .12 .30
8 Ken Wregget .12 .30
9 Rob Cimetta .12 .30
10 Mike Liut .10 .25
11 Martin Gelinas .12 .30
12 Mario Marois .12 .30
13 Rick Vaive .10 .25
14 Brad McCrimmon .12 .30
15 Mark Hunter .12 .30
16 Jim Wiemer .12 .30
17 Sergio Momesso .12 .30
18 Claude Lemieux .12 .30
19 Brian Hayward .12 .30
20 Pat Flatley .12 .30
21 Mark Osborne .12 .30
22 Mike Hudson .12 .30
23 Rejean Lemelin .10 .25
24 Slava Fetisov .12 .30
25 Bobby Smith .12 .30
26 Kris King .12 .30
27 Randy Velischek .12 .30
28 Steve Bozek .12 .30
29 Mike Foligno .15 .40
30 Scott Arniel .10 .25
31 Sergei Makarov .12 .30
32 Rick Zombo .12 .30
33 Christian Ruuttu .12 .30
34 Gino Cavallini .12 .30
35 Rick Tocchet .12 .30
36 Jiri Hrdina .12 .30
37 Peter Bondra .15 .40
38 Craig Ludwig .12 .30
39 Mikael Andersson .12 .30
40 Bob Kudelski .10 .25
41 Guy Carbonneau .12 .30
42 Geoff Smith .12 .30
43 Russ Courtnall .12 .30
44 Michal Pivonka .12 .30
45 Todd Krygier .12 .30
46 Jeremy Roenick .25 .60
47 Doug Brown .12 .30
48 Paul Cavallini .12 .30
49 Ron Sutter .12 .30
50 Paul Ranheim .15 .40
51 Mike Gartner .20 .50
52 Greg Adams .12 .30
53 Dave Capuano .12 .30
54 Mike Krushelnyski .12 .30
55 Ulf Dahlen .12 .30
56 Steven Finn .10 .25
57 Ed Olczyk .12 .30
58 Steve Duchesne .10 .25
59 Bob Probert .15 .40
60 Joe Nieuwendyk .12 .30
61 Petr Klima .12 .30
62 Uwe Krupp .12 .30
63 Jay Miller .12 .30
64 Cam Neely .15 .40
65 Phil Housley .12 .30
66 Michel Goulet .12 .30
67 Brett Hull .30 .75
68 Mike Ridley .12 .30
69 Esa Tikkanen .12 .30
70 Kjell Samuelsson .12 .30
71 Corey Millen RC .15 .40
72 Doug Lidster .12 .30
73 Ron Francis .20 .50
74 Scott Young .12 .30
75 Bob Sweeney .10 .25
76 Sean Burke .15 .40
77 Pierre Turgeon .12 .30
78 David Reid .10 .25
79 Al MacInnis .20 .50
80 Mike Hough .12 .30
81 Steve Yzerman .50 1.25
82 Derek King .10 .25
83 Brad Shaw .10 .25
84 Trevor Linden .15 .40
85 Rick Meagher .12 .30
86 Stephane Richer .12 .30
87 Brian Bellows .12 .30
88 Pete Peeters .10 .25
89 Adam Creighton .12 .30
90 Brent Ashton .12 .30
91 Bryan Trottier .15 .40
92 Mike Richter .15 .40
93 Dave Andreychuk .15 .40
94 Randy Carlyle .12 .30
95 Dave Christian .10 .25
96 Doug Gilmour .20 .50
97 Tony Granato .10 .25
98 Jeff Norton .12 .30
99 Neal Broten .12 .30
100 Jody Hull .10 .25
101 Shawn Burr .12 .30
102 Pat Verbeek .12 .30
103 Ken Daneyko .12 .30
104 Peter Zezel .10 .25
105 Kirk McLean .12 .30
106 Kelly Miller .12 .30
107 Patrick Roy .40 1.00
108 Adam Oates .15 .40
109 Steve Thomas .12 .30
110 Scott Mellanby .12 .30
111 Mark Messier .30 .75
112 Larry Murphy .12 .30
113 Mark Janssens .12 .30
114 Doug Bodger .12 .30
115 Ron Tugnutt .12 .30
116 Glenn Anderson .12 .30
117 Dave Gagner .12 .30
118 Dino Ciccarelli .12 .30
119 Randy Burridge .12 .30
120 Kelly Hrudey .12 .30
121 Jimmy Carson .12 .30
122 Bruce Driver .12 .30
123 Pat LaFontaine .15 .40
124 Wendel Clark .25 .60
125 Peter Sidorkiewicz .12 .30
126 Gary Roberts .12 .30
127 Petr Svoboda .12 .30
128 Vincent Riendeau .12 .30
129 Brian Skrudland .12 .30
130 Tim Kerr .10 .25
131 Doug Wilson .12 .30
132 Pat Elynuik .12 .30
133 Craig MacTavish .12 .30
134 Troy Mallette .12 .30
135 Mike Ramsey .12 .30
136 Tony Hrkac .12 .30
137 Craig Simpson .10 .25
138 Jon Casey .12 .30
139 Steve Kasper .10 .25
140 Kevin Hatcher .12 .30
141 Dave Barr .12 .30
142 Brad Lauer .12 .30
143 Gary Suter .10 .25
144 John MacLean .12 .30
145 Dean Evason .12 .30
146 Vincent Damphousse .12 .30
147 Craig Janney .12 .30
148 Jeff Brown .12 .30
149 Geoff Courtnall .12 .30
150 Igor Larionov .12 .30
151 Jan Erixon .12 .30
152 Bob Essensa .12 .30
153 Gaetan Duchesne .10 .25
154 Jyrki Lumme .12 .30
155 Tom Barrasso .12 .30
156 Curtis Leschyshyn .12 .30
157 Benoit Hogue .12 .30
158 Gary Leeman .12 .30
159 Luc Robitaille .15 .40
160 Jamie Macoun .12 .30
161 Bob Carpenter .12 .30
162 Kevin Dineen .12 .30
163 Gary Nylund .12 .30
164 Dale Hunter .12 .30
165 Gerard Gallant .10 .25
166 Jacques Cloutier .12 .30
167 Troy Murray .12 .30
168 Phil Bourque .12 .30
169 Grant Ledyard .12 .30
170 Joel Otto .12 .30
171 Paul Ysebaert UER
Photo actually Mike Sillinger .12 .30
172 Luke Richardson .12 .30
173 Ron Hextall .15 .40
174 Mario Lemieux .60 1.50
175 Garry Galley .12 .30
176 Murray Craven .12 .30
177 Walt Poddubny .10 .25
178 Scott Pearson .12 .30
179 Kevin Lowe .12 .30
180 Brent Sutter .12 .30
181 Dirk Graham .12 .30
182 Pelle Eklund .12 .30
183 Sylvain Cote .12 .30
184 Rod Brind'Amour .12 .30
185 Fredrik Olausson .12 .30
186 Kelly Kisio .12 .30
187 Mike Modano .30 .75
188 Calle Johansson .12 .30
189 John Tonelli .12 .30
190 Glen Wesley .12 .30
191 Bob Errey .12 .30
192 Rich Sutter .12 .30
193 Kirk Muller .10 .25
194 Rob Zettler .12 .30
195 Alexander Mogilny .12 .30
196 Adrien Plavsic .12 .30
197 Daniel Marois .12 .30
198 Yves Racine .12 .30
199 Brendan Shanahan .15 .40
200 Rob Brown .12 .30
201 Brian Leetch .12 .30
202 Dave McLlwain .12 .30
203 Charlie Huddy .12 .30
204 David Volek .12 .30
205 Trent Yawney .12 .30
206 Brian MacLellan .12 .30
207 Thomas Steen .12 .30
208 Sylvain Lefebvre .12 .30
209 Tomas Sandstrom .12 .30
210 Mike McPhee .12 .30
211 Andy Moog .15 .40
212 Paul Coffey .15 .40
213 Denis Savard .15 .40
214 Eric Desjardins .15 .40
215 Wayne Presley .12 .30
216 Stephane Morin UER .12 .30
217 Ric Nattress .12 .30
218 Troy Gamble .10 .25
219 Terry Carkner .12 .30
220 Dave Hannan .12 .30
221 Randy Wood .12 .30
222 Brian Mullen .12 .30
223 Garth Butcher .12 .30
224 Tim Cheveldae .12 .30
225 Rod Langway .12 .30
226 Stephen Leach .12 .30
227 Perry Berezan .12 .30
228 Zarley Zalapski .12 .30
229 Patrik Sundstrom .12 .30
230 Steve Smith .15 .40
231 Daren Puppa .12 .30
232 Dave Taylor .12 .30
233 Ray Bourque .25 .60
234 Kevin Stevens .12 .30
235 Frank Musil .12 .30
236 Mike Keane .10 .25
237 Brian Propp .12 .30
238 Brent Fedyk .12 .30
239 Rob Ramage .12 .30
240 Robert Kron .12 .30
241 Mike McNeil .12 .30
242 Greg Gilbert .12 .30
243 Dan Quinn .12 .30
244 Chris Nilan .10 .25
245 Bernie Nicholls .12 .30
246 Don Beaupre .12 .30
247 Keith Acton .12 .30
248 Gord Murphy .12 .30
249 Bill Ranford .12 .30
250 Dave Chyzowski .10 .25
251 Clint Malarchuk .12 .30
252 Larry Robinson .15 .40
253 Dave Poulin .12 .30
254 Paul MacDermid .12 .30
255 Doug Smail .12 .30
256 Mark Recchi .20 .50
257 Brian Bradley .12 .30
258 Grant Fuhr .25 .60
259 Owen Nolan .15 .40
260 Hubie McDonough .12 .30
261 Mikko Makela .12 .30
262 Mathieu Schneider .12 .30
263 Peter Stastny .12 .30
264 Jim Hrivnak .12 .30
265 Scott Stevens .15 .40
266 Mike Tomlak .12 .30
267 Marty McSorley .12 .30
268 Johan Garpenlov .12 .30
269 Mike Vernon .12 .30
270 Steve Larmer .12 .30
271 Phil Sykes .12 .30
272 Jay Mazur .10 .25
273 John Ogrodnick .12 .30
274 Dave Ellett .12 .30
275 Randy Gilhen .12 .30
276 Tom Chorske .12 .30
277 James Patrick .12 .30
278 Darin Kimble .12 .30
279 Paul Cyr .12 .30
280 Petr Nedved .12 .30
281 Tony McKegney .12 .30
282 Alexei Kasatonov .10 .25
283 Stephen Lebeau .12 .30
284 Everett Sanipass .12 .30
285 Tony Tanti .12 .30
286 Kevin Miller .12 .30
287 Moe Mantha .12 .30
288 Alan May .12 .30
289 John Cullen .12 .30
290 Daniel Berthiaume .12 .30
291 Mark Pederson .12 .30
292 Laurie Boschman .12 .30
293 Neil Wilkinson .12 .30
294 Rick Wamsley .10 .25
295 Ken Linseman .12 .30
296 Jamie Leach .12 .30
297 Chris Terreri .12 .30
298 Cliff Ronning .10 .25
299 Bobby Holik .15 .40
300 Mats Sundin .15 .40
301 Carey Wilson .12 .30
302 Teppo Numminen .12 .30
303 Dave Lowry .12 .30
304 Joe Reekie .12 .30
305 Keith Primeau .12 .30
306 David Shaw .12 .30
307 Nick Kypreos .12 .30
308 Dave Manson .12 .30
309 Mick Vukota .12 .30
310 Todd Elik .12 .30
311 Michel Petit .12 .30
312 Dale Hawerchuk .20 .50
313 Joe Murphy .12 .30
314 Chris Dahlquist .12 .30
315 Petri Skriko .10 .25
316 Sergei Fedorov .25 .60
317 Lee Norwood .10 .25
318 Garry Valk .12 .30
319 Glen Featherstone .10 .25
320 Dave Snuggerud .10 .25
321 Doug Evans .10 .25
322 Marc Bureau .12 .30
323 John Vanbiesbrouck .15 .40
324 John McIntyre .12 .30
325 Wes Walz .12 .30
326 Daryl Reaugh .12 .30
327 Paul Fenton .12 .30
328 Ulf Samuelsson .12 .30
329 Andrew Cassels .12 .30
330 Alexei Gusarov RC .12 .30
331 John Druce .12 .30
332 Adam Graves .12 .30
333 Ed Belfour .40 1.00
334 Murray Baron .12 .30
335 John Tucker .10 .25
336 Todd Gill .12 .30
337 Martin Hostak .10 .25
338 Gino Odjick .10 .25
339 Eric Weinrich .15 .40
340 Todd Ewen .12 .30
341 Mike Hartman .12 .30
342 Danton Cole .05 .15
343 Jaromir Jagr .50 1.25
344 Mike Craig .12 .30
345 Mark Fitzpatrick .12 .30
346 Darren Turcotte .12 .30
347 Ron Wilson .12 .30
348 Rob Blake .15 .40
349 Dale Kushner .12 .30
350 Jeff Beukeboom .12 .30
351 Tim Bergland .12 .30
352 Peter Ing .12 .30
353 Wayne McBean .10 .25
354 Jim McKenzie RC .15 .40
355 Theo Fleury .12 .30
356 Jocelyn Lemieux .12 .30
357 Ken Hodge Jr. .12 .30
358 Shawn Anderson .12 .30
359 Dimitri Khristich .12 .30
360 Jon Morris .12 .30
361 Darrin Shannon .12 .30
362 Chris Joseph .12 .30
363 Normand Lacombe .12 .30
364 Frank Pietrangelo .12 .30
365 Joey Kocur .10 .25
366 Anatoli Semenov .12 .30
367 Bob Bassen .12 .30
368 Brad Jones .12 .30
369 Glenn Healy .15 .40
370 Don Sweeney .10 .25
371 Brad Dalgarno .10 .25
372 Al Iafrate .12 .30
373 Patrick Lebeau UER RC .12 .30
374 Terry Yake .12 .30
375 Roger Johansson .12 .30
376 Paul Broten .10 .25
377 Andre Racicot RC .12 .30
378 Scott Thornton .12 .30
379 Zdeno Ciger .12 .30
380 Paul Stanton .12 .30
381 Ray Sheppard .12 .30
382 Kevin Haller RC .15 .40
383 Vladimir Ruzicka .12 .30
384 Bryan Marchment RC .12 .30
385 Bill Berg .12 .30
386 Mike Ricci .10 .25
387 Pat Conacher .12 .30
388 Brian Glynn .12 .30
389 Joe Sakic .50 1.25
390 Mikhail Tatarinov .12 .30
391 Stephane Matteau .12 .30
392 Mark Tinordi .12 .30
393 Robert Reichel .30 .75
394 Tim Sweeney .12 .30
395 Rick Tabaracci .12 .30
396 Ken Sabourin .12 .30
397 Jeff Lazaro .12 .30
398 Checklist 1-133 .05 .15
399 Checklist 134-266 .05 .15
400 Checklist 267-400 .05 .15

1992-93 Stadium Club

1 Brett Hull .20 .50
2 Theo Fleury .15 .40
3 Joe Sakic .20 .50
4 Mike Modano .25 .60
5 Dmitri Mironov .05 .15
6 Yves Racine .05 .15
7 Igor Kravchuk .05 .15
8 Philippe Bozon .05 .15
9 Stephane Richer .07 .20
10 Dave Lowry .07 .20
11 Dean Evason .05 .15
12 Mark Fitzpatrick .07 .20
13 Dave Poulin .05 .15
14 Phil Housley .07 .20
15 Adrien Plavsic .05 .15
16 Claude Boivin .05 .15
17 Bill Guerin RC .20 .50
18 Wayne Gretzky .60 1.50
19 Steve Yzerman .25 .60
20 Joe Mullen .07 .20
21 Brad McCrimmon .05 .15
22 Dan Quinn .07 .20
23 Rob Blake .07 .20
24 Wayne Presley .05 .15
25 Zarley Zalapski .05 .15
26 Bryan Trottier .10 .25
27 Peter Sidorkiewicz .05 .15
28 John MacLean .07 .20
29 Brad Schlegel .05 .15
30 Marc Bureau .07 .20
31 Troy Murray .05 .15
32 Tony Amonte .07 .20
33 Rob DiMaio .05 .15
34 Joe Murphy .05 .15
35 Jim Waite .07 .20
36 Ron Sutter .05 .15
37 Joe Nieuwendyk .07 .20
38 Kevin Haller .05 .15
39 Andrew Cassels .05 .15
40 Dale Hunter .07 .20
41 Craig Janney .07 .20
42 Sergio Momesso .05 .15
43 Nicklas Lidstrom .07 .20
44 Luc Robitaille .10 .25
45 Adam Creighton .05 .15
46 Norm Maciver .05 .15
47 Mikhail Tatarinov .05 .15
48 Gary Roberts .05 .15
49 Gord Hynes .05 .15
50 Claude Lemieux .05 .15
51 Brad May .05 .15
52 Paul Stanton .05 .15
53 Rick Wamsley .05 .15
54 Steve Larmer .05 .15
55 Darrin Shannon .05 .15
56 Pat Falloon .05 .15
57 Chris Dahlquist .07 .20
58 John Vanbiesbrouck .10 .25
59 Sylvain Turgeon .05 .15
60 Jay More .05 .15
61 Randy Burridge .05 .15
62 Slava Kozlov .07 .20
63 Daniel Marois .05 .15
64 Curt Giles .05 .15
65 Brad Shaw .05 .15
66 Bill Ranford .07 .20
67 Frank Musil .07 .20
68 Steve Leach .05 .15
69 Michel Goulet .07 .20
70 Mathieu Schneider .05 .15
71 Steve Kasper .05 .15
72 Darryl Sydor .05 .15
73 Brian Leetch .07 .20
74 Chris Terreri .07 .20
75 Jim Johnson .07 .20
76 Rick Tocchet .07 .20
77 Teppo Numminen .05 .15
78 Owen Nolan .10 .25
79 Grant Ledyard .05 .15
80 Trevor Linden .10 .25
81 Luciano Borsato .05 .15
82 Derek King .05 .15
83 Robert Cimetta .07 .20
84 Geoff Smith .05 .15
85 Ray Sheppard .05 .15
86 Dimitri Khristich .05 .15
87 Chris Chelios .10 .25
88 Alexander Godynyuk .05 .15
89 Perry Anderson .05 .15
90 Neal Broten .07 .20
91 Brian Benning .05 .15
92 Brent Thompson .07 .20
93 Claude LaPointe .05 .15
94 Mario Lemieux .40 1.00
95 Pat LaFontaine .10 .25
96 Frank Pietrangelo .07 .20
97 Gerald Diduck .07 .20
98 Paul DiPietro .05 .15
99 Valeri Zelepukin .05 .15
100 Rick Zombo .05 .15
101 Daniel Berthiaume .07 .20
102 Tom Fitzgerald .05 .15
103 Ken Baumgartner .05 .15
104 Esa Tikkanen .05 .15
105 Steve Chiasson .05 .15
106 Bobby Holik .07 .20
107 Dominik Hasek .15 .40
108 Jeff Hackett .07 .20
109 Paul Broten .05 .15
110 Kevin Stevens .07 .20

111 Geoff Sanderson .07 .20
112 Donald Audette .07 .20
113 Jarmo Myllys .05 .15
114 Brian Skrudland .07 .20
115 Andrei Lomakin .05 .15
116 Keith Tkachuk .10 .25
117 John McIntyre .05 .15
118 Jacques Cloutier .07 .20
119 Michel Picard .07 .20
120 Dave Babych .07 .20
121 Dave Gagner .07 .20
122 Bob Carpenter .07 .20
123 Ray Ferraro .05 .15
124 Glenn Anderson .07 .20
125 Craig MacTavish .05 .15
126 Shawn Burr .05 .15
127 Tim Bergland .05 .15
128 Al MacInnis .12 .30
129 Jeff Beukeboom .05 .15
130 Ken Wregget .07 .20
131 Arturs Irbe .07 .20
132 Dave Andreychuk .10 .25
133 Patrick Roy .25 .60
134 Benoit Brunet .05 .15
135 Rick Tabaracci .05 .15
136 Jamie Baker .05 .15
137 Yanic Dupre .05 .15
138 Jari Kurri .10 .25
139 Adam Burt .05 .15
140 Peter Stastny .07 .20
141 Brad Jones .05 .15
142 Jeff Odgers .05 .15
143 Anatoli Semenov UER .05 .15
144 Paul Ranheim .05 .15
145 Sylvain Cote .07 .20
146 Brent Ashton .05 .15
147 Doug Bodger .05 .15
148 Bryan Marchment .07 .20
149 Bob Kudelski .07 .20
150 Adam Graves .05 .15
151 Scott Stevens .10 .25
152 Russ Courtnall .05 .15
153 Darcy Wakaluk .07 .20
154 Pelle Eklund .07 .20
155 Robert Kron .05 .15
156 Randy Ladouceur .05 .15
157 Ed Olczyk .05 .15
158 Jiri Hrdina .05 .15
159 John Tonelli .07 .20
160 John Cullen .05 .15
161 Jan Erixon .07 .20
162 David Shaw .07 .20
163 Brian Bradley .05 .15
164 Russ Romaniuk .05 .15
165 Eric Weinrich .05 .15
166 Steve Heinze .05 .15
167 Jeremy Roenick .15 .40
168 Mark Pederson .05 .15
169 Paul Coffey .10 .25
170 Bob Errey .07 .20
171 Brian Lawton .07 .20
172 Vincent Riendeau .07 .20
173 Marc Fortier .05 .15
174 Marc Bergevin .07 .20
175 Jim Sandlak .05 .15
176 Bob Bassen .05 .15
177 Uwe Krupp .05 .15
178 Paul MacDermid .07 .20
179 Bob Corkum .07 .20
180 Robert Reichel .05 .15
181 John LeClair .10 .25
182 Mike Hudson .05 .15
183 Mark Recchi .12 .30
184 Rollie Melanson .05 .15
185 Gordie Roberts .07 .20
186 Clint Malarchuk .05 .15
187 Kris King .05 .15
188 Adam Oates .10 .25
189 Jarrod Skalde .05 .15
190 Mike Lalor .07 .20
191 Vincent Damphousse .07 .20
192 Peter Ahola .05 .15
193 Kirk McLean .05 .15
194 Murray Baron .05 .15
195 Michel Petit .05 .15
196 Stephane Fiset .05 .15
197 Pat Verbeek .05 .15
198 Jon Casey .05 .15
199 Tim Cheveldae .05 .15
200 Mike Ridley .05 .15
201 Scott Lachance .05 .15
202 Rod Brind'Amour .05 .15
203 Bret Hedican RC .07 .20
204 Wendel Clark .15 .40
205 Shawn McEachern .05 .15
206 Randy Wood .05 .15
207 Ulf Dahlen .05 .15
208 Andy Brickley .05 .15
209 Scott Niedermayer .10 .25
210 Bob Essensa .07 .20
211 Patrick Poulin .05 .15
212 Johan Garpenlov .05 .15
213 Marty McInnis .05 .15
214 Josef Beranek .05 .15
215 Rod Langway .07 .20
216 Dave Christian .05 .15
217 Sergei Makarov .05 .15
218 Gerard Gallant .05 .15
219 Neil Wilkinson UER .05 .15
220 Tomas Sandstrom .07 .20
221 Shayne Corson .07 .20
222 John Ogrodnick .05 .15
223 Keith Acton .07 .20
224 Paul Fenton .07 .20
225 Rob Zettler .05 .15
226 Todd Elik .05 .15
227 Petr Svoboda .07 .20
228 Zdeno Ciger .05 .15
229 Kevin Miller .05 .15
230 Rich Pilon .05 .15
231 Pat Jablonski .07 .20
232 Greg Adams .05 .15
233 Martin Brodeur .25 .60
234 Dave Taylor .07 .20
235 Kelly Buchberger .05 .15
236 Steve Konroyd .07 .20
237 Guy Larose .05 .15
238 Patrice Brisebois .05 .15
239 Checklist 1-125 .05 .15
240 Checklist 126-250 .05 .15
241 Mark Messier MC .20 .50
242 Mike Richter MC .10 .25
243 Ed Belfour MC .10 .25
244 Sergei Fedorov MC .15 .40
245 Adam Oates MC .10 .25
246 Pavel Bure MC .10 .25
247 Luc Robitaille MC .10 .25
248 Brian Leetch MC .07 .20
249 Ray Bourque MC .15 .40
250 Tony Amonte MC .07 .20
251 Mario Lemieux MC .40 1.00
252 Patrick Roy MC .25 .60
253 Nicklas Lidstrom MC .07 .20
254 Steve Yzerman MC .25 .60
255 Jeremy Roenick MC .15 .40
256 Wayne Gretzky MC .60 1.50
257 Kevin Stevens MC .07 .20
258 Brett Hull MC .20 .50
259 Pat Falloon MC .05 .15
260 Guy Carbonneau MC .07 .20
261 Todd Gill .05 .15
262 Mike Sullivan .05 .15
263 Jeff Brown .07 .20
264 Joe Reekie .05 .15
265 Geoff Courtnall .05 .15
266 Mike Richter .10 .25
267 Ray Bourque .15 .40
268 Mike Craig .05 .15
269 Scott King .05 .15
270 Don Beaupre .07 .20
271 Ted Donato .05 .15
272 Gary Leeman .05 .15
273 Steve Weeks .05 .15
274 Keith Brown .07 .20
275 Greg Paslawski .05 .15
276 Pierre Turgeon .07 .20
277 Jimmy Carson .05 .15
278 Tom Fergus .05 .15
279 Glen Wesley .05 .15
280 Tomas Forslund .05 .15
281 Tony Granato .05 .15
282 Phil Bourque .05 .15
283 Dave Ellett .05 .15
284 David Bruce .05 .15
285 Stu Barnes .05 .15
286 Peter Bondra .10 .25
287 Garth Butcher .07 .20
288 Ron Hextall .10 .25
289 Guy Carbonneau .07 .20
290 Louie DeBrusk .05 .15
291 Dave Barr .05 .15
292 Ken Sutton .05 .15
293 Brian Bellows .07 .20
294 Mike McNeill .07 .20
295 Rob Brown .05 .15
296 Corey Millen .05 .15
297 Joe Juneau .05 .15
298 Jeff Chychrun UER .05 .15
299 Igor Larionov .05 .15
300 Sergei Fedorov .15 .40
301 Kevin Hatcher .05 .15
302 Al Iafrate .07 .20
303 James Black .05 .15
304 Steph Beauregard .07 .20
305 Joel Otto .05 .15
306 Nelson Emerson .05 .15
307 Gaetan Duchesne .05 .15
308 J.J. Daigneault .05 .15
309 Jamie Macoun .07 .20
310 Laurie Boschman .05 .15
311 Mike Gartner .12 .30
312 Tony Tanti .05 .15
313 Steve Duchesne .05 .15
314 Martin Gelinas .05 .15
315 Dominic Roussel .07 .20
316 Cam Neely .10 .25
317 Craig Wolanin .05 .15
318 Randy Gilhen .05 .15
319 David Volek .05 .15
320 Alexander Mogilny .07 .20
321 Jyrki Lumme .05 .15
322 Jeff Reese .05 .15
323 Greg Gilbert .07 .20
324 Jeff Norton .07 .20
325 Jim Hrivnak .07 .20
326 Eric Desjardins .07 .20
327 Curtis Joseph .12 .30
328 Ric Nattress .07 .20
329 Jamie Leach .05 .15
330 Christian Ruuttu .05 .15
331 Doug Brown .07 .20
332 Randy Carlyle .07 .20
333 Ed Belfour .10 .25
334 Doug Smail .05 .15
335 Hubie McDonough .05 .15
336 Pat MacLeod .05 .15
337 Don Sweeney .05 .15
338 Felix Potvin .20 .50
339 Kent Manderville .05 .15
340 Sergei Nemchinov .05 .15
341 Calle Johansson .05 .15
342 Dirk Graham .05 .15
343 Craig Billington .07 .20
344 Valeri Kamensky .05 .15
345 Mike Vernon .07 .20
346 Fredrik Olausson .05 .15
347 Peter Ing .05 .15
348 Mikael Andersson .05 .15
349 Mike Keane .05 .15
350 Stephane Quintal .05 .15
351 Tom Chorske .07 .20
352 Ron Francis .12 .30
353 Dana Murzyn .05 .15
354 Craig Ludwig .07 .20
355 Bob Probert .10 .25
356 Glenn Healy .07 .20
357 Troy Loney .05 .15
358 Vladimir Ruzicka .05 .15
359 Doug Gilmour .12 .30
360 Darren Turcotte .05 .15
361 Kelly Miller .05 .15
362 Dennis Vaske .05 .15
363 Stephane Matteau .05 .15
364 Brian Hayward .05 .15
365 Kevin Dineen .05 .15
366 Igor Ulanov .05 .15
367 Sylvain Lefebvre .05 .15
368 Petr Klima .05 .15
369 Steve Thomas .07 .20
370 Daren Puppa .07 .20
371 Brendan Shanahan .10 .25
372 Charlie Huddy .07 .20
373 Cliff Ronning .05 .15
374 Brian Propp .05 .15
375 Larry Murphy .07 .20
376 Bruce Driver .05 .15
377 Rob Pearson .05 .15
378 Paul Ysebaert .05 .15
379 Mark Osborne .05 .15
380 Doug Weight .20 .50
381 Kerry Huffman UER .05 .15
382 Michal Pivonka .05 .15
383 Steve Smith .05 .15
384 Steven Finn .05 .15
385 Kevin Lowe .07 .20
386 Mike Ramsey .05 .15
387 Kirk Muller .05 .15
388 John LeBlanc RC .07 .20
389 Rich Sutter .05 .15
390 Brent Fedyk .05 .15
391 Kelly Hrudey .07 .20
392 Slava Fetisov .05 .15
393 Glen Murray .07 .20
394 James Patrick .05 .15
395 Tom Draper .05 .15
396 Mark Hunter .07 .20
397 Wayne McBean .05 .15
398 Joe Sacco .05 .15
399 Dino Ciccarelli .07 .20
400 Brian Noonan .05 .15
401 Guy Hebert RC .15 .40
402 Peter Douris .05 .15
403 Gilbert Dionne .05 .15
404 Doug Lidster .07 .20
405 John Druce .05 .15
406 Alexei Kasatonov .05 .15
407 Chris Lindberg .05 .15
408 Mike Ricci .05 .15
409 Tom Kurvers .05 .15
410 Pat Elynuik .05 .15
411 Mike Donnelly .05 .15
412 Grant Fuhr .15 .40
413 Curtis Leschyshyn .07 .20
414 Derian Hatcher .05 .15
415 Michel Mongeau .07 .20
416 Tom Barrasso .07 .20
417 Joey Kocur .05 .15
418 Vladimir Konstantinov .10 .25
419 Dale Hawerchuk .12 .30
420 Brian Mullen .05 .15
421 Mark Greig .07 .20
422 Claude Vilgrain .07 .20
423 Gary Suter .05 .15
424 Garry Galley .05 .15
425 Benoit Hogue .05 .15
426 Jeff Finley RC .05 .15
427 Bobby Smith .07 .20
428 Brent Sutter .05 .15
429 Ron Wilson .07 .20
430 Andy Moog .10 .25
431 Stephan Lebeau .05 .15
432 Troy Mallette .05 .15
433 Peter Zezel .05 .15
434 Mike Hough .07 .20
435 Mark Tinordi .05 .15
436 Dave Manson .05 .15
437 Jim Paek .07 .20
438 Frantisek Kucera .07 .20
439 Rob Zamuner RC .07 .20
440 Ulf Samuelsson .05 .15
441 Perry Berezan .05 .15
442 Murray Craven .05 .15
443 Mark Messier .20 .50
444 Alexander Semak .05 .15
445 Gord Murphy .07 .20
446 Jocelyn Lemieux .05 .15
447 Paul Cavallini .05 .15
448 Bernie Nicholls .07 .20
449 Brent Gilchrist .05 .15
450 Randy McKay .07 .20
451 Alexei Gusarov .05 .15
452 Mike McPhee .05 .15
453 Kimbi Daniels .05 .15
454 Kelly Kisio .07 .20
455 Bob Sweeney .05 .15
456 Luke Richardson .07 .20
457 Petr Nedved .07 .20
458 Craig Berube .05 .15
459 Kay Whitmore .07 .20
460 Randy Velischek .05 .15
461 David Williams RC .05 .15
462 Scott Mellanby .05 .15
463 Terry Carkner .07 .20
464 Dale Craigwell .05 .15
465 Kevin Todd .05 .15
466 Kjell Samuelsson .07 .20
467 Denis Savard .10 .25
468 Adam Foote .07 .20
469 Stephane Morin .05 .15
470 Doug Wilson .07 .20
471 Shawn Cronin .05 .15
472 Brian Glynn UER .05 .15
473 Craig Simpson .05 .15
474 Todd Krygier .07 .20
475 Brad Miller .05 .15
476 Yvon Corriveau .05 .15
477 Patrick Flatley .07 .20
478 Mats Sundin .10 .25
479 Joe Cirella .07 .20
480 Gino Cavallini .05 .15
481 Marty McSorley .07 .20
482 Brad Marsh .07 .20
483 Bob McGill .05 .15
484 Randy Moller .05 .15
485 Keith Primeau .07 .20
486 Darin Kimble .05 .15
487 Mike Krushelnyski .05 .15
488 Sutter Brothers .05 .15
489 Pavel Bure .10 .25
490 Ray Whitney RC .15 .40
491 Dave McLlwain .05 .15
492 Per Djoos .07 .20
493 Garry Valk .05 .15
494 Mike Bullard .07 .20
495 Greg Hawgood .05 .15
496 Terry Yake .05 .15
497 Mike Hartman .05 .15
498 Jaromir Jagr .20 .50
499 Checklist 251-384 .05 .15
500 Checklist 385-500 .05 .15
501 Eric Lindros .15 .40

1993-94 Stadium Club

1 Guy Carbonneau .07 .20
2 Joe Cirella .07 .20
3 Laurie Boschman .07 .20
4 Arturs Irbe .10 .25
5 Adam Creighton .07 .20
6 Mike McPhee .07 .20
7 Jeff Beukeboom .07 .20
8 Kevin Todd .07 .20
9 Yvon Corriveau .07 .20
10 Eric Lindros .20 .50
11 Martin Rucinsky .07 .20
12 Michel Goulet .07 .20
13 Scott Pellerin RC .12 .30
14 Mike Eagles .07 .20
15 Steve Heinze .07 .20
16 Gerard Gallant .07 .20
17 Kelly Miller .07 .20
18 Petr Nedved .07 .20
19 Joe Mullen .10 .25
20 Pat LaFontaine .12 .30
21 Garth Butcher .07 .20
22 Jeff Reese .07 .20
23 Dave Andreychuk .12 .30
24 Patrick Flatley .07 .20
25 Tomas Sandstrom .07 .20
26 Andre Racicot .07 .20
27 Patrice Brisebois .07 .20
28 Neal Broten .10 .25
29 Mark Freer .07 .20
30 Kelly Kisio .07 .20
31 Scott Mellanby .10 .25
32 Joe Sakic .25 .60
33 Kerry Huffman .07 .20
34 Evgeny Davydov .07 .20
35 Mark Messier .25 .60
36 Pat Verbeek .07 .20
37 Greg Gilbert .07 .20
38 John Tucker .07 .20
39 Claude Lemieux .07 .20
40 Shayne Corson .10 .25
41 Gordie Roberts .07 .20
42 Jiri Slegr .07 .20
43 Kevin Dineen .07 .20
44 Johan Garpenlov .07 .20
45 Sergei Fedorov .20 .50
46 Rich Sutter .07 .20
47 Dave Hannan .07 .20
48 Sylvain Lefebvre .07 .20
49 Pat Elynuik .07 .20
50 Ray Ferraro .07 .20
51 Brent Ashton .07 .20
52 Paul Stanton .07 .20
53 Kevin Haller .07 .20
54 Kelly Hrudey .10 .25
55 Russ Courtnall .07 .20
56 Alexei Zhamnov .10 .25
57 Andrei Lomakin .07 .20
58 Keith Brown .07 .20
59 Glen Murray .10 .25
60 Kay Whitmore .07 .20
61 Stephane Richer .10 .25
62 Todd Gill .07 .20
63 Bob Sweeney .07 .20
64 Mike Richter .12 .30
65 Brett Hull .25 .60
66 Sylvain Cote .07 .20
67 Kirk Muller .07 .20
68 Ronnie Stern .07 .20
69 Josef Beranek .07 .20
70 Steve Yzerman .30 .75
71 Don Beaupre .10 .25
72 Ed Courtenay .07 .20
73 Zdeno Ciger .07 .20
74 Andrew Cassels .07 .20
75 Roman Hamrlik .07 .20
76 Benoit Hogue .07 .20
77 Andrei Kovalenko .07 .20
78 Rod Brind'Amour .10 .25
79 Tom Barrasso .10 .25
80 Al Iafrate .07 .20
81 Brett Hedican .07 .20
82 Peter Bondra .12 .30
83 Ted Donato .07 .20
84 Chris Lindberg .07 .20
85 John Vanbiesbrouck .12 .30
86 Ron Sutter .07 .20
87 Luc Robitaille .12 .30
88 Brian Leetch .10 .25
89 Randy Wood .07 .20
90 Dirk Graham .07 .20
91 Alexander Mogilny .10 .25
92 Mike Keane .07 .20
93 Adam Oates .12 .30
94 Viacheslav Butsayev .07 .20
95 John LeClair .12 .30
96 Joe Nieuwendyk .10 .25
97 Mikael Andersson .07 .20
98 Jaromir Jagr .40 1.00
99 Ed Belfour .12 .30
100 David Reid .07 .20
101 Darius Kasparaitis .07 .20
102 Zarley Zalapski .07 .20
103 Christian Ruuttu .07 .20
104 Phil Housley .10 .25
105 Al MacInnis .15 .40
106 Tommy Sjodin .07 .20
107 Richard Smehlik .07 .20
108 Jyrki Lumme .07 .20
109 Dominic Roussel .10 .25
110 Mike Gartner .15 .40
111 Bernie Nicholls .10 .25
112 Mark Howe .12 .30
113 Rich Pilon .07 .20
114 Jeff Odgers .07 .20
115 Gilbert Dionne .07 .20
116 Peter Zezel .07 .20
117 Don Sweeney .07 .20
118 Jimmy Carson .07 .20
119 Igor Korolev .07 .20
120 Bob Kudelski .07 .20
121 Dave Lowry .07 .20
122 Steve Kasper .07 .20
123 Mike Ridley .07 .20
124 Dave Tippett .07 .20
125 Cliff Ronning .07 .20
126 Bruce Driver .07 .20
127 Stephane Matteau .07 .20
128 Joel Otto .07 .20
129 Alexei Kovalev .10 .25
130 Mike Modano .20 .50
131 Bill Ranford .10 .25
132 Petr Svoboda .07 .20
133 Roger Johansson .07 .20
134 Marc Bureau .07 .20
135 Keith Tkachuk .12 .30
136 Mark Recchi .15 .40
137 Bob Probert .12 .30
138 Uwe Krupp .07 .20
139 Mike Sullivan .07 .20
140 Doug Gilmour .15 .40
141 Teemu Selanne TW .25 .60
142 Dave Poulin TW .07 .20
143 Mario Lemieux TW .50 1.25
144 Ed Belfour TW .12 .30
145 Pierre Turgeon TW .10 .25
146 Mario Lemieux TW .50 1.25
147 Chris Chelios TW .12 .30
148 Mario Lemieux TW .50 1.25
149 Doug Gilmour TW .15 .40
150 Ed Belfour TW .12 .30
151 Paul Ranheim .07 .20
152 Gino Cavallini .07 .20
153 Kevin Hatcher .07 .20
154 Marc Bergevin .07 .20
155 Marty McSorley .10 .25
156 Brian Bellows .10 .25
157 Patrick Poulin .07 .20
158 Kevin Stevens .10 .25
159 Bobby Holik .07 .20
160 Ray Bourque .20 .50
161 Bryan Marchment .07 .20
162 Curtis Joseph .15 .40
163 Kirk McLean .10 .25
164 Teppo Numminen .07 .20
165 Kevin Lowe .07 .20
166 Tim Cheveldae .10 .25
167 Brad Dalgarno .07 .20
168 Glenn Anderson .10 .25
169 Frank Musil .07 .20
170 Eric Desjardins .10 .25
171 Doug Zmolek .07 .20
172 Mark Lamb .07 .20
173 Craig Ludwig .07 .20
174 Rob Gaudreau RC .12 .30
175 Bob Carpenter .10 .25
176 Mike Ricci .07 .20
177 Brian Skrudland .07 .20
178 Dominik Hasek .20 .50
179 Pat Conacher .07 .20
180 Mark Janssens .07 .20
181 Brent Fedyk .07 .20
182 Rob DiMaio .07 .20
183 Dave Manson .07 .20
184 Janne Ojanen .07 .20
185 Ryan Walter .07 .20
186 Michael Nylander .07 .20
187 Steve Leach .07 .20
188 Jeff Brown .07 .20
189 Shawn McEachern .07 .20
190 Jeremy Roenick .20 .50
191 Darrin Shannon .07 .20
192 Wendel Clark .20 .50
193 Kevin Miller .07 .20
194 Paul DiPietro .07 .20
195 Steve Thomas .07 .20
196 Nicklas Lidstrom .12 .30
197 Ed Olczyk .07 .20
198 Robert Reichel .07 .20
199 Neil Brady .07 .20
200 Wayne Gretzky .75 2.00
201 Adrien Plavsic .07 .20
202 Joe Juneau .07 .20
203 Brad May .10 .25
204 Igor Kravchuk .07 .20
205 Keith Acton .07 .20
206 Ken Daneyko .07 .20
207 Sean Burke .07 .20
208 Jay More .07 .20
209 John Cullen .07 .20
210 Teemu Selanne .25 .60
211 Brent Sutter .07 .20
212 Brian Bradley .07 .20
213 Donald Audette .07 .20
214 Philippe Bozon .07 .20
215 Derek King .07 .20
216 Cam Neely .12 .30
217 Keith Primeau .10 .25
218 Steve Smith .07 .20
219 Ken Sutton .07 .20
220 Dale Hawerchuk .15 .40
221 Alexei Zhitnik .07 .20
222 Glen Wesley .07 .20
223 Nelson Emerson .07 .20
224 Pat Falloon .07 .20
225 Darryl Sydor .07 .20
226 Tony Amonte .10 .25
227 Brian Mullen .07 .20
228 Gary Suter .07 .20
229 David Shaw .07 .20
230 Troy Murray .07 .20
231 Patrick Roy .30 .75
232 Mitchel Petit .07 .20
233 Wayne Presley .07 .20
234 Keith Jones .07 .20
235 Gary Roberts .07 .20
236 Steve Larmer .10 .25
237 Valeri Kamensky .10 .25
238 Ulf Dahlen .07 .20
239 Danton Cole .07 .20
240 Vincent Damphousse .10 .25
241 Yuri Khmylev .07 .20
242 Stephane Quintal .07 .20
243 Peter Taglianetti .07 .20
244 Gary Leeman .07 .20
245 Sergei Nemchinov .07 .20
246 Rob Blake .10 .25
247 Steve Chiasson .07 .20
248 Vladimir Malakhov .07 .20
249 Checklist 1-125 .05 .15
250 Checklist 126-250 .05 .15
251 Kjell Samuelsson .07 .20
252 Terry Carkner .07 .20
253 Bill Lindsay .07 .20
254 Bob Essensa .10 .25
255 Jocelyn Lemieux .07 .20
256 Joe Sacco .07 .20
257 Marty McInnis .07 .20
258 Warren Rychel .07 .20
259 David Maley .07 .20
260 Grant Fuhr .20 .50
261 Scott Young .07 .20
262 Ed Ronan .07 .20
263 Micah Aivazoff RC .12 .30
264 Murray Craven .07 .20
265 Slava Fetisov .07 .20
266 Chris Dahlquist .07 .20
267 Norm Maciver .07 .20
268 Alexander Godynyuk .07 .20
269 Mikael Renberg .12 .30
270 Adam Graves .07 .20
271 Randy Ladouceur .07 .20
272 Frank Pietrangelo .10 .25
273 Basil McRae .07 .20
274 Bryan Smolinski .07 .20
275 Daren Puppa .07 .20
276 Darcy Wakaluk .07 .20
277 Dimitri Khristich .07 .20
278 Vladimir Vujtek .07 .20
279 Tom Kurvers .07 .20
280 Felix Potvin .25 .60
281 Keith Brown .07 .20
282 Thomas Steen .07 .20
283 Larry Murphy .10 .25
284 Bob Corkum .07 .20
285 Tony Granato .07 .20
286 Cam Russell .07 .20
287 John MacLean .10 .25
288 Shawn Antoski .07 .20
289 Pelle Eklund .07 .20
290 Chris Pronger .12 .30
291 Alexander Karpovtsev .07 .20
292 Paul Laus RC .07 .20
293 Jaroslav Otevrel .07 .20
294 Dino Ciccarelli .10 .25
295 Guy Hebert .10 .25
296 Dave Karpa .07 .20
297 Denis Savard .12 .30
298 Jim Johnson .07 .20
299 Kirk Maltby RC .12 .30
300 Alexandre Daigle .07 .20
301 Dave Poulin .07 .20
302 James Patrick .07 .20
303 Jon Casey .10 .25
304 Yves Racine .07 .20
305 Craig Simpson .07 .20
306 Mike Krushelnyski .07 .20
307 Mark Fitzpatrick .07 .20
308 Charlie Huddy .07 .20
309 Todd Ewen .07 .20
310 Mario Lemieux .50 1.25
311 Mark Astley RC .12 .30
312 Sergei Zubov .10 .25
313 Shawn Burr .07 .20
314 Valeri Zelepukin .07 .20
315 Stephane Fiset .10 .25
316 C.J. Young .07 .20
317 Luciano Borsato .07 .20
318 Darcy Loewen .07 .20
319 Mike Vernon .10 .25
320 Chris Gratton .10 .25
321 Matthew Barnaby .10 .25
322 Mike Rathje .07 .20
323 Sergio Momesso .07 .20
324 David Volek .07 .20
325 Ron Tugnutt .10 .25
326 Jeff Hackett .07 .20
327 Robb Stauber .07 .20
328 Chris Terreri .10 .25
329 Rick Tocchet .10 .25
330 John Vanbiesbrouck .12 .30
331 Drake Berehowsky .07 .20
332 Alexei Kasatonov .07 .20
333 Vladimir Konstantinov .10 .25
334 John Blue .10 .25
335 Craig Janney .10 .25
336 Curtis Leschyshyn .07 .20
337 Todd Krygier .07 .20
338 Boris Mironov .07 .20
339 Joby Messier RC .12 .30
340 Tommy Soderstrom .10 .25
341 Randy Cunneyworth .07 .20
342 Mark Ferner RC .07 .20
343 Stephan Lebeau .07 .20
344 Jody Hull .07 .20
345 Jason Arnott RC .25 .60
346 Gerard Gallant .07 .20
347 Stephane Richer .10 .25
348 Jeff Shantz RC .07 .20
349 Brian Skrudland .07 .20
350 Chris Osgood RC .75 2.00
351 Gary Shuchuk .07 .20
352 Martin Brodeur .30 .75
353 Bob Rouse .07 .20
354 Doug Bodger .07 .20
355 Mike Craig .07 .20
356 Ulf Samuelsson .07 .20
357 Trevor Linden .12 .30
358 Dennis Vaske .07 .20
359 Alexei Yashin .10 .25
360 Paul Ysebaert .07 .20
361 Shaun Van Allen .07 .20
362 Sandis Ozolinsh .07 .20
363 Todd Elik .07 .20
364 German Titov RC .12 .30
365 Alexander Semak .07 .20
366 Allen Pedersen .07 .20
367 Greg Johnson .07 .20
368 Anatoli Semenov .07 .20
369 Scott Mellanby .10 .25
370 Mats Sundin .12 .30
371 Mattias Norstrom RC .12 .30
372 Glen Featherstone .07 .20
373 Sergei Petrenko .07 .20
374 Mike Donnelly .07 .20
375 Nikolai Borschevsky .07 .20
376 Rob Zamuner .07 .20
377 Steven King .07 .20
378 Rick Tabaracci .07 .20
379 Dave Lowry .07 .20
380 Pierre Turgeon .10 .25
381 Garry Galley .07 .20
382 Doug Weight .10 .25
383 Scott Stevens .12 .30
384 Mark Tinordi .07 .20
385 Ron Francis .15 .40
386 Mark Greig .07 .20
387 Sean Hill .07 .20
388 Slava Kozlov .10 .25
389 Brendan Shanahan .12 .30
390 Theo Fleury .07 .20
391 Mathieu Schneider .07 .20
392 Tom Fitzgerald .07 .20
393 Markus Naslund .12 .30
394 Travis Green .10 .25
395 Troy Loney .07 .20
396 Gord Donnelly .07 .20
397 Owen Nolan .12 .30
398 Steve Larmer .10 .25
399 Dave Archibald .07 .20
400 Jari Kurri .12 .30
401 Jim Paek .07 .20
402 Andrei Lomakin .07 .20
403 Scott Niedermayer .12 .30
404 Bob Errey .07 .20
405 Michal Pivonka .07 .20
406 Doug Lidster .07 .20
407 Garry Valk .07 .20
408 Geoff Sanderson .10 .25
409 Stewart Malgunas RC .12 .30
410 Craig MacTavish .07 .20
411 Jaroslav Modry RC .12 .30
412 Shawn Chambers .07 .20
413 Geoff Courtnall .07 .20
414 Mark Hardy .07 .20
415 Martin Straka .07 .20
416 Randy Burridge .07 .20
417 Kent Manderville .07 .20
418 Darren Rumble .07 .20
419 Bill Houlder .07 .20
420 Chris Chelios .12 .30
421 Jim Hrivnak .07 .20
422 Benoit Brunet .07 .20
423 Aaron Ward RC .12 .30
424 Alexei Gusarov .07 .20
425 Mats Sundin SWE .12 .30
426 Kjell Samuelsson .07 .20
427 Mikael Andersson .07 .20
428 Ulf Dahlen .07 .20
429 Nicklas Lidstrom .12 .30
430 Tommy Soderstrom SWE .10 .25
431 Darrin Madeley RC .12 .30
432 Kevin Dahl .07 .20
433 Ron Hextall .12 .30
434 Patrick Carnback RC .12 .30
435 Randy Moller .07 .20
436 Dave Gagner .10 .25
437 Corey Millen .07 .20
438 Olaf Kolzig .12 .30
439 Gord Murphy .07 .20
440 Cam Stewart RC .12 .30
441 Darren McCarty RC .20 .50
442 Frantisek Kucera .07 .20
443 Ted Drury .07 .20
444 Troy Mallette .07 .20
445 Robin Bawa RC .07 .20
446 Steven Rice .07 .20
447 Pat Elynuik .07 .20
448 Jim Cummins RC .07 .20
449 Rob Niedermayer .10 .25
450 Paul Coffey .12 .30
451 Calle Johansson .07 .20
452 Mike Needham .07 .20
453 Glenn Healy .10 .25
454 Dixon Ward .07 .20
455 Al Iafrate .07 .20
456 Jon Casey .10 .25
457 Kevin Stevens USA .10 .25
458 Tony Amonte .10 .25
459 Chris Chelios .12 .30
460 Pat LaFontaine USA .12 .30
461 Jamie Baker .07 .20
462 Andre Faust .07 .20
463 Bobby Dollas .07 .20
464 Steven Finn .07 .20
465 Scott Lachance .07 .20
466 Mike Hough .07 .20
467 Bill Guerin .12 .30
468 Dimitri Filimonov .07 .20
469 Dave Ellett .07 .20
470 Andy Moog .12 .30
471 Scott Thomas RC .12 .30
472 Trent Yawney .07 .20
473 Tim Sweeney .07 .20
474 Shjon Podein RC .12 .30
475 J.J. Daigneault .07 .20
476 Darren Turcotte .07 .20
477 Esa Tikkanen .07 .20
478 Vitali Karamnov .07 .20
479 Jocelyn Thibault RC .12 .30
480 Pavel Bure .12 .30
481 Steve Konowalchuk .07 .20
482 Sylvain Turgeon .07 .20
483 Jeff Daniels .07 .20
484 Dallas Drake RC .12 .30
485 Iain Fraser RC .12 .30
486 Joe Reekie .07 .20
487 Evgeny Davydov .07 .20
488 Jozef Stumpel .07 .20
489 Brent Thompson .07 .20
490 Terry Yake .07 .20
491 Derek Plante RC .12 .30
492 Dimitri Yushkevich .07 .20
493 Wayne McBean .07 .20
494 Derian Hatcher .07 .20
495 Jeff Norton .07 .20
496 Adam Foote .07 .20
497 Mike Peluso .07 .20

498 Rob Pearson .07 .20
499 Checklist 251-375 .05 .15
500 Checklist 376-500 .05 .15

1993-94 Stadium Club Members Only Parallel

COMPLETE SET (500) 150.00 300.00
*MEMBERS ONLY: 3X TO 8X BASIC CARDS

1993-94 Stadium Club OPC

COMPLETE SET (250) 12.00 30.00
COMP.SERIES 1 (250) 6.00 15.00
COMP.SERIES 2 (250) 6.00 15.00
*O-PEE-CHEE: .4X TO 1X BASIC CARDS

1993-94 Stadium Club First Day Issue

*VETS: 12X TO 30X BASIC CARDS
*ROOKIE STARS: 5X TO 12X BASIC RC
*SER.1 OPC: .5X TO 1.2X BASIC FIRST DAY

1993-94 Stadium Club All-Stars

COMPLETE SET (23) 30.00 60.00
*O-PEE-CHEE: .4X TO 1X BASIC INSERTS
1 P.Roy/E.Belfour 6.00 15.00
2 R.Bourque/P.Coffey 2.00 5.00
3 A.Iafrate/C.Chelios 1.50 4.00
4 J.Jagr/B.Hull 2.00 5.00
5 P.LaFontaine/S.Yzerman 5.00 12.00
6 K.Stevens/P.Bure 2.00 5.00
7 C.Billington/J.Casey .75 2.00
8 S.Duchesne/S.Chiasson .75 2.00
9 S.Stevens/P.Housley .75 2.00
10 P.Bondra/K.Kisio 1.50 4.00
11 A.Oates/B.Bradley 1.50 4.00
12 A.Mogilny/J.Kurri 1.50 4.00
13 P.Sidorkiewicz/M.Vernon .75 2.00
14 Z.Zalapski/D.Manson .75 2.00
15 B.Marsh/R.Carlyle .75 2.00
16 K.Muller/G.Roberts .75 2.00
17 J.Sakic/D.Gilmour 3.00 8.00
18 M.Recchi/L.Robitaille 1.50 4.00
19 K.Lowe/G.Butcher .75 2.00
20 R.Tocchet/J.Roenick 2.00 5.00
21 P.Turgeon/M.Modano 2.00 5.00
22 M.Gartner/T.Selanne 2.00 5.00
23 M.Lemieux/W.Gretzky 10.00 25.00

1993-94 Stadium Club All-Stars Members Only Parallel

COMPLETE SET (23)
*MEMBERS ONLY: .6X TO 1.5X BASIC CARD

1993-94 Stadium Club Finest Inserts

COMPLETE SET (12) 15.00 40.00
1 Wayne Gretzky 5.00 12.00
2 Jeff Brown .20 .50
3 Brett Hull 1.25 3.00
4 Paul Coffey .75 2.00
5 Felix Potvin .75 2.00
6 Mike Gartner .40 1.00
7 Luc Robitaille .40 1.00
8 Marty McSorley .20 .50
9 Gary Roberts .20 .50
10 Mario Lemieux 4.00 10.00
11 Patrick Roy 4.00 10.00
12 Ray Bourque 1.50 4.00

1993-94 Stadium Club Finest Members Only Parallel

COMPLETE SET (12)
*MEMBERS ONLY: .6X TO 1.5X BASIC CARD

1993-94 Stadium Club Master Photos

COMPLETE SET (24) 12.00 30.00
COMP.SERIES 1 (12) 8.00 20.00
COMP.SERIES 2 (12) 4.00 10.00
*WINNER EXCH: .5X TO 1.2X JUMBOS
*WINNER MEM.ONLY: .6X TO 1.5X JUMBOS
1 Pat LaFontaine .30 .75
2 Doug Gilmour .30 .75
3 Ray Bourque .60 1.50
4 Teemu Selanne .30 .75
5 Eric Lindros .50 1.25
6 Ray Ferraro .07 .20
7 Patrick Roy 2.50 6.00
8 Wayne Gretzky 4.00 10.00
9 Brett Hull .50 1.25
10 John Vanbiesbrouck .30 .75
11 Adam Oates .15 .40
12 Tom Barrasso .20 .50
13 Esa Tikkanen .10 .25
14 Jari Kurri .30 .75
15 Grant Fuhr .40 1.00
16 Scott Lachance .07 .20
17 Theo Fleury .25 .75
18 Adam Graves .07 .20
19 Rick Tabaracci .15 .40
20 Pierre Turgeon .15 .40
21 Steven Finn .07 .20
22 Craig Janney .15 .40
23 Mathieu Schneider .07 .20
24 Felix Potvin .75 2.00

1993-94 Stadium Club Team USA

COMPLETE SET (23) 8.00 20.00
1 Mark Beaufait .40 1.00
2 Jim Campbell .60 1.50
3 Ted Crowley .40 1.00
4 Mike Dunham .60 1.50
5 Chris Ferraro .40 1.00
6 Peter Ferraro .40 1.00
7 Brett Hauer .40 1.00
8 Darby Hendrickson .40 1.00
9 Jon Hillebrandt .40 1.00
10 Chris Imes .40 1.00
11 Craig Johnson .40 1.00
12 Peter Laviolette .40 1.00
13 Jeff Lazaro .40 1.00
14 John Lilley .40 1.00
15 Todd Marchant .60 1.50
16 Matt Martin .40 1.00
17 Ian Moran .40 1.00
18 Travis Richards .40 1.00
19 Barry Richter .40 1.00
20 David Roberts .40 1.00
21 Brian Rolston .60 1.50
22 David Sacco .40 1.00
23 Jim Storm .40 1.00

1993-94 Stadium Club Team USA Members Only Parallel

COMPLETE SET (23)
*MEMBERS ONLY: .8X TO 2X BASIC CARD

1994 Stadium Club Members Only 50

COMP.FACT SET (50) 8.00 20.00
1 Felix Potvin .30 .75
2 Chris Chelios .20 .50
3 Paul Coffey .20 .50
4 Pavel Bure .60 1.50
5 Wayne Gretzky 1.50 4.00
6 Brett Hull .30 .75
7 Al MacInnis .08 .25
8 Rob Blake .08 .25
9 Alexei Kasatonov .02 .10
10 Teemu Selanne .50 1.25
11 Sandis Ozolinsh .08 .25
12 Shayne Corson .02 .10
13 Dave Andreychuk .05 .15
14 Dave Taylor .02 .10
15 Sergei Fedorov .50 1.25
16 Brendan Shanahan .40 1.00
17 Arturs Irbe .20 .50
18 Joe Nieuwendyk .08 .25
19 Russ Courtnall .02 .10
20 Jeremy Roenick .30 .75
21 Doug Gilmour .20 .50
22 Curtis Joseph .30 .75
23 Patrick Roy 1.25 3.00
24 Brian Leetch .20 .50
25 Ray Bourque .40 1.00
26 Alexander Mogilny .20 .50
27 Mark Messier .30 .75
28 Eric Lindros .60 1.50
29 Garry Galley .02 .10
30 Scott Stevens .05 .15
31 Al Iafrate .02 .10
32 Larry Murphy .02 .10
33 Joe Mullen .02 .10
34 Mark Recchi .20 .50
35 Adam Graves .05 .15
36 Geoff Sanderson .02 .10
37 Adam Oates .20 .50
38 Pierre Turgeon .20 .50
39 Joe Sakic .50 1.25
40 John Vanbiesbrouck .20 .50
41 Brian Bradley .02 .10
42 Alexei Yashin .08 .25
43 Bob Kudelski .02 .10
44 Jaromir Jagr .75 2.00
45 Mike Richter .30 .75
46 Martin Brodeur .60 1.50
47 Mikael Renberg .08 .25
48 Derek Plante .02 .10
49 Jason Arnott .08 .25
50 Alexandre Daigle .02 .10

1994-95 Stadium Club

1 Mark Messier .20 .50
2 Brad May .05 .15
3 Mike Ricci .05 .15
4 Scott Stevens .10 .25
5 Keith Tkachuk .10 .25
6 Guy Hebert .07 .20
7 Jason Arnott .07 .20
8 Cam Neely .10 .25
9 Adam Graves .05 .15
10 Pavel Bure .10 .25
11 Jeff Odgers .05 .15
12 Dimitri Khristich .05 .15
13 Patrick Poulin .05 .15
14 Mike Donnelly .05 .15
15 Felix Potvin .15 .40
16 Keith Primeau .07 .20
17 Fred Knipscheer .05 .15
18 Mike Keane .05 .15
19 Vitali Prokhorov .05 .15
20 Ray Ferraro .05 .15
21 Shane Churla .05 .15
22 Rob Niedermayer .07 .20
23 Adam Creighton .05 .15
24 Tommy Soderstrom .07 .20
25 Theo Fleury .10 .25
26 Jim Storm .07 .20
27 Bret Hedican .05 .15
28 Sean Hill .05 .15
29 Bill Ranford .07 .20
30 Derek Plante .05 .15
31 Dave McLlwain .05 .15
32 Iain Fraser .05 .15
33 Patrick Roy .25 .60
34 Martin Straka .05 .15
35 Bruce Driver .05 .15
36 Brian Skrudland .05 .15
37 Bob Errey .05 .15
38 Randy Cunneyworth .05 .15
39 John Slaney .05 .15
40 Ray Sheppard .07 .20
41 Sergei Nemchinov .05 .15
42 Dave Ellett .05 .15
43 Vincent Riendeau .05 .15
44 Trent Yawney .05 .15
45 Dave Gagner .07 .20
46 Igor Korolev .05 .15
47 Gary Shuchuk .07 .20
48 Rob Zamuner .05 .15
49 Frantisek Kucera .05 .15
50 Joe Mullen .07 .20
51 Ron Hextall .10 .25
52 J.J. Daigneault .05 .15
53 Patrik Carnback .05 .15
54 Steven Rice .05 .15
55 Brian Leetch PP .07 .20
56 Al MacInnis PP .12 .30
57 Luc Robitaille PP .10 .25
58 Dave Andreychuk PP .10 .25
59 Jeremy Roenick PP .15 .40
60 Mario Lemieux PP .40 1.00
61 Dave Manson .05 .15
62 Pat Falloon .05 .15
63 Jesse Belanger .05 .15
64 Philippe Boucher .05 .15
65 Sergio Momesso .10 .25
66 Evgeny Davydov .05 .15
67 Alexei Gusarov .07 .20
68 Jaromir Jagr .30 .75
69 Randy Ladouceur .07 .20
70 Chris Chelios .10 .25
71 John Druce .07 .20
72 Kris Draper .05 .15
73 Joey Kocur .05 .15
74 Rick Tabaracci .07 .20
75 Mikael Andersson .05 .15
76 Mark Osborne .05 .15
77 Ray Bourque .15 .40
78 Dimitri Yushkevich .05 .15
79 Mike Vernon .07 .20
80 Steve Thomas .05 .15
81 Steve Duchesne .05 .15
82 Dean Evason .05 .15
83 Jason Smith .07 .20
84 Bryan Marchment .07 .20
85 Boris Mironov .05 .15
86 Jeff Norton .05 .15
87 Donald Audette .05 .15
88 Eric Lindros .15 .40
89 Garry Valk .05 .15
90 Mats Sundin .10 .25
91 Gerald Diduck .05 .15
92 Jeff Shantz .05 .15
93 Scott Niedermayer .10 .25
94 Troy Mallette .05 .15
95 John Vanbiesbrouck .10 .25
96 Ron Francis .12 .30
97 Slava Kozlov .07 .20
98 Ken Baumgartner .05 .15
99 Wayne Gretzky .60 1.50
100 Brett Hull .20 .50
101 Marc Bergevin .05 .15
102 Owen Nolan .10 .25
103 Bryan Smolinski .05 .15
104 Lyle Odelein .07 .20
105 Mike Ridley .05 .15
106 Trevor Kidd .07 .20
107 Derian Hatcher .05 .15
108 Derek King .05 .15
109 Rob Zettler .05 .15
110 Alexandre Daigle GE .05 .15
111 Chris Pronger GE .10 .25
112 Chris Gratton GE .05 .15
113 John Slaney GE .05 .15
114 Jocelyn Thibault GE .07 .20
115 Jason Arnott GE .07 .20
116 Alexei Yashin GE .10 .25
117 Rob Niedermayer GE .07 .20
118 Jason Allison GE .07 .20
119 Martin Brodeur GE .25 .60
120 Pat Verbeek .07 .20
121 Kelly Buchberger .05 .15
122 Doug Lidster .05 .15
123 Sergei Makarov .05 .15
124 Kris King .05 .15
125 Dominik Hasek .15 .40
126 Martin Rucinsky .05 .15
127 Kerry Huffman .05 .15
128 Gord Murphy .05 .15
129 Bobby Holik .05 .15
130 Kirk Muller .05 .15
131 Christian Ruuttu .05 .15
132 Jyrki Lumme .05 .15
133 Ken Wregget .07 .20
134 Dale Hunter .05 .15
135 Rob Blake .10 .25
136 Petr Klima .05 .15
137 Steve Heinze .05 .15
138 Chris Osgood .15 .40
139 John Lilley .05 .15
140 Dave Andreychuk .10 .25
141 Zarley Zalapski .05 .15
142 Curtis Joseph .12 .30
143 Brent Gilchrist .05 .15
144 Vladimir Malakhov .05 .15
145 Mikael Renberg .07 .20
146 Robert Kron .05 .15
147 Dean McAmmond .05 .15
148 Doug Bodger .05 .15
149 Ray Whitney .05 .15
150 Brian Leetch .07 .20
151 Martin Lapointe .05 .15
152 Teppo Numminen .05 .15
153 Scott Young .05 .15
154 Nick Kypreos .05 .15
155 Ed Belfour .10 .25
156 Greg Adams .05 .15
157 Brian Benning .05 .15
158 Bob Carpenter .07 .20
159 Vladimir Konstantinov .07 .20
160 Rick Tocchet .07 .20
161 Joe Sacco .05 .15
162 Daren Puppa .07 .20
163 Randy Burridge .05 .15
164 Darryl Sydor .05 .15
165 Jay More .05 .15
166 Joe Nieuwendyk .07 .20
167 Mike Eastwood .05 .15
168 Murray Baron .05 .15
169 Brent Fedyk .05 .15
170 Russ Courtnall .05 .15
171 Sean Burke .07 .20
172 Uwe Krupp .05 .15
173 Kevin Lowe .05 .15
174 Guy Carbonneau .05 .15
175 Alexei Yashin .10 .25
176 Thomas Steen .05 .15
177 Sandis Ozolinsh .05 .15
178 Patrick Roy SO .25 .60
179 Dominik Hasek SO .15 .40
180 Ed Belfour SO .10 .25
181 Mike Richter SO .10 .25
182 Ron Hextall SO .10 .25
183 Daren Puppa SO .07 .20
184 Jon Casey SO .07 .20
185 Felix Potvin SO .15 .40
186 Martin Brodeur SO .25 .60
187 Darcy Wakaluk SO .07 .20
188 Kirk McLean SO .07 .20
189 Mike Vernon SO .07 .20
190 Arturs Irbe SO .07 .20
191 Dino Ciccarelli .07 .20
192 Steven Finn .05 .15
193 Pierre Sevigny .05 .15
194 Jim Dowd .05 .15
195 Chris Gratton .05 .15
196 Wayne Presley .05 .15
197 Joel Otto .05 .15
198 Fredrik Olausson .05 .15
199 Jody Hull .05 .15
200 Cliff Ronning .05 .15
201 Darren Turcotte RR .05 .15
202 Al Iafrate RR .05 .15
203 Eric Lindros RR .15 .40
204 Sandis Ozolinsh RR .05 .15
205 Petr Nedved .07 .20
206 Mark Lamb .05 .15
207 Shaun Van Allen .05 .15
208 Kelly Hrudey .07 .20
209 Nikolai Borschevsky .05 .15
210 Glen Wesley .05 .15
211 Shawn McEachern .05 .15
212 Mark Janssens .05 .15
213 Brian Mullen .05 .15
214 Craig Ludwig .05 .15
215 Mike Rathje .05 .15
216 Stephane Matteau .05 .15
217 Tim Cheveldae .07 .20
218 Brent Sutter .07 .20
219 Gord Dineen UER
Ottawa Senators
(Listed as born .05 .15
220 Kevin Hatcher .05 .15
221 Todd Simon RC .05 .15
222 Bill Lindsay .05 .15
223 Kirk McLean .07 .20
224 Chris Joseph .05 .15
225 Valeri Zelepukin .05 .15
226 Terry Yake .05 .15
227 Benoit Brunet .05 .15
228 Nicklas Lidstrom .10 .25
229 Zdeno Ciger .05 .15
230 Gary Roberts .05 .15
231 Andy Moog .10 .25
232 Ed Patterson .05 .15
233 Philippe Bozon .07 .20
234 Brent Hughes .05 .15
235 Chris Pronger .10 .25
236 Travis Green .07 .20
237 Pat Conacher .05 .15
238 Bob Rouse .05 .15
239 Yves Racine .05 .15
240 Nelson Emerson .05 .15
241 Oleg Petrov .05 .15
242 Steve Larmer .07 .20
243 Dan Laperriere .05 .15
244 John McIntyre .05 .15
245 Alexander Semak .05 .15
246 Stephane Fiset UER .07 .20
247 Peter Bondra .10 .25
248 Dale Hawerchuk .12 .30
249 Jamie Baker .05 .15
250 Sergei Fedorov .15 .40
251 Derek Mayer .05 .15
252 Ivan Droppa .05 .15
253 Kent Manderville .05 .15
254 Sergei Zholtok .05 .15
255 Murray Craven .05 .15
256 Todd Krygier .05 .15
257 Brent Grieve RC .05 .15
258 Esa Tikkanen .05 .15
259 Brad Dalgarno .05 .15
260 Russ Romaniuk .05 .15
261 Stu Barnes .05 .15
262 Dan Keczmer .05 .15
263 Eric Desjardins .07 .20
264 Martin Brodeur TW .25 .60
265 Adam Graves TW .05 .15
266 Cam Neely TW .10 .25
267 Ray Bourque TW .15 .40
268 Sergei Fedorov TW .15 .40
269 Dominik Hasek TW .15 .40
270 Wayne Gretzky TW .60 1.50

1994-95 Stadium Club Members Only Parallel

COMPLETE SET (270) 150.00 300.00
*MEMBERS ONLY: 3X TO 8X BASIC CARDS

1994-95 Stadium Club First Day Issue

*VETS: 15X TO 40X BASIC CARDS

1994-95 Stadium Club Dynasty and Destiny

COMPLETE SET (5) 5.00 12.00
1 T.Barrasso/A.Irbe 1.25 3.00
2 M.Messier/E.Lindros 1.50 4.00
3 B.Hull/P.Bure 2.00 5.00
4 Robitaille/Renberg 1.25 3.00
5 C.Chelios/C.Pronger 1.50 4.00

1994-95 Stadium Club Dynasty and Destiny Members Only Parallel

*MEMBERS ONLY: .6X TO 1.5X BASIC CARD

1994-95 Stadium Club Finest Inserts

COMPLETE SET (9) 15.00 40.00
1 Mario Lemieux 5.00 12.00
2 Brett Hull 1.25 3.00
3 Mark Messier 1.00 2.50
4 Wayne Gretzky 6.00 15.00
5 Pavel Bure 1.00 2.50
6 Sergei Fedorov 1.50 4.00
7 Brian Leetch 1.00 2.50
8 Ray Bourque 1.50 4.00
9 Patrick Roy 5.00 12.00

1994-95 Stadium Club Finest Inserts Members Only Parallel

*MEMBERS ONLY: .6X TO 1.5X BASIC CARD

1994-95 Stadium Club Super Teams

COMPLETE SET (26) 25.00 60.00
1 Anaheim Mighty Ducks 1.00 2.50
2 Bruins/Oates/Bourque 1.00 2.50
3 Sabres/D.Hasek 1.00 2.50
4 Flames/Trefilov/Fleury 1.00 2.50
5 Blackhawks/E.Belfour 1.00 2.50
6 Stars/M.Modano 1.00 2.50
7 Detroit Red Wings 2.00 5.00
8 Edmonton Oilers 1.00 2.50
9 Florida Panthers 1.00 2.50
10 Hartford Whalers 1.00 2.50
11 Los Angeles Kings 1.00 2.50
12 Canadiens/P.Roy 2.50 6.00
13 Devils/M.Brodeur WIN 4.00 10.00
14 New York Islanders 1.00 2.50
15 Rangers/M.Messier 2.00 5.00
16 Ottawa Senators 1.00 2.50
17 Flyers/Lindros/Recchi/Bowen 1.00 2.50
18 Pittsburgh Penguins 2.00 5.00
19 Nordiques/J.Sakic 2.00 5.00
20 Blues/C.Joseph 1.00 2.50
21 San Jose Sharks 1.00 2.50
22 Tampa Bay Lightning 1.00 2.50
23 Toronto Maple Leafs 1.00 2.50
24 Canucks/P.Bure 2.00 5.00
25 Washington Capitals 1.00 2.50
26 Jets/Selanne/Zhamnov 2.00 5.00

1994-95 Stadium Club Super Teams Members Only Parallel

*MEMBERS ONLY: .6X TO 1.5X BASIC CARD

1994-95 Stadium Club Super Team Winner

COMPLETE SET (270) 50.00 100.00
*ST WINNERS: 2X TO 5X BASIC CARDS

1995 Stadium Club Members Only 50

COMP. FACT SET (50) 10.00 25.00
1 Patrick Roy 1.00 2.50
2 Ray Bourque .20 .50
3 Brian Leetch .20 .50
4 Cam Neely .15 .40
5 Jaromir Jagr .60 1.50
6 Alexander Mogilny .15 .40
7 John Vanbiesbrouck .40 1.00
8 Geoff Sanderson .05 .15
9 Mark Recchi .08 .25
10 Scott Stevens .02 .10
11 Roman Hamrlik .05 .15
12 Dominik Hasek .40 1.00
13 Joe Sakic .40 1.00
14 Alexei Yashin .20 .50
15 Eric Lindros .60 1.50
16 Adam Oates .08 .25
17 Ulf Samuelsson .02 .10
18 Wendel Clark .05 .15
19 Mark Messier .30 .75
20 Pierre Turgeon .08 .25
21 Mark Tinordi .02 .10
22 Ron Francis .08 .25
23 Jeff Brown .02 .10
24 Tom Kurvers .02 .10
25 Mike Modano .30 .75
26 Mats Sundin .20 .50
27 Jeremy Roenick .20 .50
28 Kevin Hatcher .02 .10
29 Curtis Joseph .20 .50
30 Paul Coffey .20 .50
31 Jason Arnott .08 .25
32 Wayne Gretzky 1.25 3.00
33 Theo Fleury .20 .50
34 Al MacInnis .07 .20
35 Ed Belfour .20 .50
36 Sergei Fedorov .40 1.00
37 Brett Hull .30 .75
38 Chris Chelios .20 .50
39 Keith Tkachuk .30 .75
40 Felix Potvin .20 .50
41 Pavel Bure .40 1.00
42 Ulf Dahlen .02 .10
43 Teemu Selanne .40 1.00
44 Doug Gilmour .20 .50
45 Phil Housley .05 .15
46 Paul Kariya FIN 2.50 6.00
47 Peter Forsberg FIN 2.00 5.00
48 Jim Carey FIN .60 1.50
49 Todd Marchant FIN .20 .50
50 Blaine Lacher FIN .30 .75

1995-96 Stadium Club

1 Alexander Mogilny .07 .20
2A Ray Bourque .15 .40
2B Bill Ranford UER .07 .20
3 Garry Galley .05 .15
4 Glen Wesley .05 .15
5 Dave Andreychuk .10 .25
6 Daren Puppa .07 .20
7 Shayne Corson .07 .20
8 Kelly Hrudey .07 .20
9 Russ Courtnall .05 .15
10 Chris Chelios .10 .25
11 Ulf Samuelsson .05 .15
12 Mike Vernon .07 .20
13 Al MacInnis .12 .30
14 Joel Otto .05 .15
15 Patrick Roy .25 .60
16 Steve Thomas .07 .20
17 Pat Verbeek .07 .20
18 Joe Nieuwendyk .07 .20
19 Todd Krygier .05 .15
20 Steve Yzerman .25 .60
22 Ron Francis .12 .30
23 Sylvain Cote .05 .15
24 Grant Fuhr .15 .40
25 Brendan Shanahan .10 .25
26 John MacLean .07 .20
27 Darren Turcotte .05 .15
28 Bernie Nicholls .07 .20
29 Sean Burke .05 .15
30 Brian Leetch .07 .20
31 Dave Gagner .05 .15
32 Rick Tocchet .07 .20
33 Ron Hextall .10 .25
34 Paul Coffey .10 .25
35 John Vanbiesbrouck .10 .25
36 Rod Brind'Amour .10 .25
37 Brian Savage .05 .15
38 Nelson Emerson .05 .15
39 Brian Bradley .07 .20
40 Adam Oates .10 .25
41 Kirk McLean. .07 .20
42 Kevin Hatcher .07 .20
43 Mike Keane .05 .15
44 Don Beaupre .07 .20
45 Scott Stevens .10 .25
46 Dale Hawerchuk .12 .30
47 Scott Young .05 .15
48 Mark Recchi .12 .30
49 Mike Richter .10 .25
50 Kevin Stevens .07 .20
51 Mike Ridley .05 .15
52 Joe Murphy .05 .15
53 Stephane Fiset .07 .20
54 Donald Audette .07 .20
55 Ed Belfour .07 .20
56 Rob Blake .07 .20
57 Adam Graves .07 .20
58 Arturs Irbe .07 .20
59 Mathieu Schneider .05 .15
60 Dominik Hasek .15 .40
61 Andrew Cassels .05 .15
62 Johan Garpenlov .05 .15
63 Kyle McLaren RC .05 .15
64 Petr Nedved .07 .20
65 Owen Nolan .10 .25
66 Keith Primeau .07 .20
67 Mark Tinordi .05 .15
68 Dimitri Khristich .05 .15
69 Chris Pronger .10 .25
70 Jaromir Jagr .30 .75
71 Mike Ricci .05 .15
72 Trevor Kidd .07 .20
73 Stu Barnes .05 .15
74 Doug Weight .10 .25
75 Mats Sundin .10 .25
76 Scott Niedermayer .10 .25
77 John LeClair .10 .25
78 Derian Hatcher .07 .20
79 Brad May .05 .15
80 Felix Potvin .15 .40
81 Derek King .07 .20
82 Guy Hebert .07 .20
83 Shawn McEachern .05 .15
84 Slava Kozlov .07 .20
85 Martin Brodeur .25 .60
86 Ray Whitney .07 .20
87 Martin Straka .05 .15
88 Keith Jones .07 .20
89 Roman Hamrlik .05 .15
90 Keith Tkachuk .10 .25
91 Jim Dowd .05 .15
92 Sergei Zubov .07 .20
93 Bryan McCabe .10 .25
94 Rob Niedermayer .07 .20
95 Alexei Zhamnov .10 .25
96 Zarley Zalapski .05 .15
97 Alexandre Daigle .05 .15
98 Jocelyn Thibault .07 .20
99 Zigmund Palffy .10 .25
100 Luc Robitaille .10 .25
101 Radek Bonk .05 .15
102 Todd Marchant .05 .15
103 Todd Harvey .05 .15
104 Blaine Lacher .07 .20
105 Peter Forsberg .20 .50
106 Jeff Friesen .05 .15
107 Kenny Jonsson .10 .25
108 Brett Lindros .05 .15
109 David Oliver .05 .15
110 Mikael Renberg .07 .20
111 Alexander Selivanov .07 .20
112 Stanislav Neckar .05 .15
113 Oleg Tverdovsky .10 .25
114 Shean Donovan .05 .15
115 Jim Carey .07 .20
116 Tony Granato .05 .15
117 Tony Amonte .07 .20
118 Tomas Sandstrom .07 .20
119 Rick Tabaracci .07 .20
120 Ray Ferraro .05 .15
121 Brian Noonan .05 .15
122 Miroslav Satan RC .12 .30
123 Sergio Momesso .05 .15
124 Gary Suter .05 .15
125 Eric Desjardins .07 .20
126 Steve Duchesne .05 .15
127 Zdeno Ciger .07 .20
128 Cliff Ronning .05 .15
129 Nicklas Lidstrom .10 .25
130 Bill Guerin .10 .25
131 Igor Korolev .05 .15
132 Roman Oksiuta .05 .15
133 Jesse Belanger .05 .15
134 Chris Gratton .05 .15
135 Chris Osgood .10 .25
136 Pat Peake .05 .15
137 Viktor Kozlov .07 .20
138 Aaron Gavey .05 .15
139 Zdenek Nedved .05 .15
140 Rhett Warrener .05 .15
141 Marko Kiprusoff .07 .20
142 Dan Quinn .07 .20
143 Alexei Zhitnik .05 .15
144 Larry Murphy .07 .20
145 Phil Housley .07 .20
146 Don Sweeney .05 .15
147 Jason Dawe .05 .15
148 Marcus Ragnarsson RC .12 .30
149 Andrei Nikolishin .05 .15
150 Dino Ciccarelli .07 .20
151 Jari Kurri .10 .25
152 Bob Probert .10 .25
153 Randy McKay .05 .15
154 Michael Nylander .05 .15
155 Wendel Clark .15 .40
156 Antti Tormanen RC .05 .15
157 Nikolai Khabibulin .07 .20
158 Tom Barrasso .07 .20
159 Vincent Damphousse .07 .20
160 Trevor Linden .10 .25
161 Valeri Kamensky .07 .20
162 Mike Gartner .12 .30
163 Cam Neely EC .25 .60
164 Pat LaFontaine EC .25 .60
165 Theo Fleury EC .30 .75
166 Jeremy Roenick EC .40 1.00
167 Joe Sakic EC .50 1.25
168 Mike Modano EC .40 1.00
169 Sergei Fedorov EC .40 1.00
170 Scott Mellanby EC .20 .50
171 Jason Arnott EC .20 .50
172 Geoff Sanderson EC .15 .40
173 Wayne Gretzky EC 1.50 4.00
174 Paul Kariya EC .25 .60
175 Pierre Turgeon EC .20 .50
176 Stephane Richer EC .20 .50
177 Kirk Muller EC .20 .50
178 Mark Messier EC .50 1.25
179 Craig Janney EC .15 .40
180 Mario Lemieux EC 1.00 2.50
181 Eric Lindros EC .40 1.00
182 Alexei Yashin EC .20 .50
183 Brett Hull EC .50 1.25
184 Doug Gilmour EC .30 .75
185 Petr Klima EC .15 .40
186 Pavel Bure EC .25 .60
187 Joe Juneau EC .15 .40
188 Teemu Selanne EC .50 1.25
189 Claude Lemieux EC .25 .60
190 Vitali Yachmenev ER .25 .60
191 Jason Bonsignore ER .15 .40
192 Jeff O'Neill ER .25 .60
193 Brendan Witt ER .25 .60
194 Brian Holzinger ER RC .50 1.25
195 Eric Daze ER .50 1.25
196 Ed Jovanovski ER .25 .60
197 Deron Quint ER .20 .50
198 Marty Murray ER .25 .60
199 Jere Lehtinen ER .20 .50
200 Radek Dvorak ER RC .30 .75
201 Aki Berg ER RC .25 .60
202 Chad Kilger ER RC .25 .60
203 Saku Koivu ER .25 .60
204 Todd Bertuzzi ER RC .30 .75
205 Niklas Sundstrom ER .25 .60
206 Daniel Alfredsson ER RC 1.25 3.00
207 Shane Doan ER RC .75 2.00
208 Richard Park .25 .60
209 Peter Bondra .25 .60
210 Bryan Smolinski .15 .40
211 Tommy Salo .40 1.00
212 Patrick Poulin .15 .40
213 Mathieu Dandenault RC .50 1.25
214 Steve Rucchin .20 .50
215 Ray Sheppard .20 .50
216 Robert Svehla RC .15 .40
217 Olaf Kolzig .25 .60
218 Alexei Kovalev .20 .50
219 Ian Moran .15 .40
220 Valeri Bure .15 .40
221 Dean Malkoc .15 .40
222 Jason Doig .25 .60
223 David Nemirovsky RC .20 .50
224 Jamie Pushor .20 .50
225 Ricard Persson .20 .50

1995-96 Stadium Club Members Only Parallel

COMPLETE SET (225) 150.00 300.00
*MEMBERS ONLY: 3X TO 8X BASIC CARDS

1995-96 Stadium Club Extreme North

COMPLETE SET (9) 20.00 40.00
EN1 Pavel Bure 2.00 5.00
EN2 Teemu Selanne 2.00 5.00
EN3 Felix Potvin 2.00 5.00
EN4 Patrick Roy 8.00 20.00
EN5 Theo Fleury 1.25 3.00
EN6 Bill Ranford 1.25 3.00
EN7 Pierre Turgeon 1.25 3.00
EN8 Doug Gilmour 1.25 3.00
EN9 Alexander Mogilny 1.25 3.00

1995-96 Stadium Club Extreme North Members Only Parallel

*MEMBERS ONLY: .6X TO 1.5X BASIC INSERTS

1995-96 Stadium Club Fearless

COMPLETE SET (9) 8.00 15.00
F1 Brendan Shanahan 1.50 4.00
F2 Chris Chelios 1.50 4.00
F3 Keith Primeau .75 2.00
F4 Scott Stevens 1.25 3.00
F5 Rick Tocchet 1.25 3.00
F6 Kevin Stevens .75 2.00
F7 Ulf Samuelsson .75 2.00
F8 Wendel Clark 1.25 3.00
F9 Keith Tkachuk 1.50 4.00

1995-96 Stadium Club Fearless Members Only Parallel

*MEMBERS ONLY: .6X TO 1.5X BASIC INSERTS

1995-96 Stadium Club Generation TSC

COMPLETE SET (9) 15.00 30.00
GT1 Paul Kariya 1.50 4.00
GT2 Teemu Selanne 1.50 4.00
GT3 Jaromir Jagr 2.00 5.00
GT4 Peter Forsberg 3.00 8.00
GT5 Martin Brodeur 4.00 10.00
GT6 Jim Carey .75 2.00
GT7 Mikael Renberg .75 2.00
GT8 Scott Niedermayer .75 2.00
GT9 Ed Jovanovski .75 2.00

1995-96 Stadium Club Generation TSC Members Only Parallel

*MEMBERS ONLY: .6X TO 1.5X BASIC INSERTS

1995-96 Stadium Club Metalists

COMPLETE SET (12) 25.00 60.00
M1 Wayne Gretzky 10.00 25.00
M2 Mario Lemieux 6.00 15.00
M3 Patrick Roy 6.00 15.00
M4 Ray Bourque 1.50 4.00
M5 Ed Belfour 1.50 4.00
M6 Tom Barrasso 1.00 2.50
M7 Joe Mullen 1.00 2.50
M8 Brian Leetch 1.00 2.50
M9 Mark Messier 1.50 4.00
M10 Dominik Hasek 3.00 8.00
M11 Paul Coffey 1.00 2.50
M12 Guy Carbonneau 1.00 2.50

1995-96 Stadium Club Metalists Members Only Parallel

*MEMBERS ONLY: .6X TO 1.5X BASIC INSERTS

1995-96 Stadium Club Nemeses

COMPLETE SET (9) 25.00 60.00
N1 E.Lindros/S.Stevens 1.50 4.00
N2 W.Gretzky/M.Lemieux 10.00 25.00

N3 C.Lemieux/C.Neely 1.50 4.00
N4 P.Bure/M.Richter 1.50 4.00
N5 B.Leetch/R.Bourque 2.50 6.00
N6 M.Brodeur/D.Hasek 4.00 10.00
N7 D.Gilmour/S.Fedorov 2.50 6.00
N8 M.Messier/J.Otto 1.50 4.00
N9 P.Kariya/P.Forsberg 4.00 10.00

1995-96 Stadium Club Nemeses Members Only Parallel

*MEMBERS ONLY: .6X TO 1.5X BASIC INSERTS

1995-96 Stadium Club Power Streak

COMPLETE SET (10) 5.00 12.00
PS1 Pierre Turgeon .40 1.00
PS2 Eric Lindros 1.25 3.00
PS3 Ron Francis .75 2.00
PS4 Paul Coffey .75 2.00
PS5 Mikael Renberg .40 1.00
PS6 John LeClair .40 1.00
PS7 Dino Ciccarelli .40 1.00
PS8 Wendel Clark .75 2.00
PS9 Brett Hull 1.25 3.00
PS10 Stephane Richer .40 1.00

1995-96 Stadium Club Power Streak Members Only Parallel

*MEMBERS ONLY: .6X TO 1.5X BASIC INSERTS

1995-96 Stadium Club Master Photo Test

COMPLETE SET (9) 25.00 60.00
1 Jason Arnott 2.00 5.00
2 Theo Fleury 4.00 10.00
3 Doug Gilmour 4.00 10.00
4 Trevor Linden 4.00 10.00
5 Kirk McLean 2.00 5.00
6 Alexander Mogilny 2.00 5.00
7 Felix Potvin 4.00 10.00
8 Mats Sundin 6.00 15.00
9 Alexei Yashin 2.00 5.00

1996 Stadium Club Members Only 50

COMPLETE SET (50) 8.00 20.00
1 Wayne Gretzky 1.50 4.00
2 Paul Kariya 1.00 2.50
3 Brett Hull .30 .75
4 Chris Chelios .25 .60
5 Paul Coffey .25 .60
6 Ed Belfour .25 .60
7 Theo Fleury .25 .60
8 Owen Nolan .08 .25
9 Al MacInnis .08 .25
10 Alexander Mogilny .20 .50
11 Kevin Hatcher .02 .10
12 Doug Weight .15 .40
13 Felix Potvin .20 .50
14 Teemu Selanne .50 1.25
15 Sergei Fedorov .50 1.25
16 Larry Murphy .02 .10
17 Joe Sakic .50 1.25
18 Mats Sundin .25 .60
19 Nicklas Lidstrom .08 .25
20 Peter Forsberg .60 1.50
21 Chris Osgood .25 .60
22 Mike Gartner .05 .15
23 D.Savard
C.MacTavish .05 .15
24 Mario Lemieux 1.25 3.00
25 Jaromir Jagr .75 2.00
26 Brendan Shanahan .50 1.25
27 Scott Stevens .05 .15
28 Ray Bourque .30 .75
29 Martin Brodeur .60 1.50
30 Eric Lindros .75 2.00
31 Peter Bondra .25 .60
32 Scott Mellanby .02 .10
33 Brian Leetch .25 .60
34 John Vanbiesbrouck .25 .60
35 Pat Verbeek .07 .20
36 Cam Neely .20 .50
37 Roman Hamrlik .15 .40
38 Daniel Alfredsson .20 .50
39 Pierre Turgeon .20 .50
40 Mark Messier .30 .75
41 Eric Desjardins .02 .10
42 Dominik Hasek .50 1.25
43 John LeClair .40 1.00
44 Mathieu Schneider .02 .10
45 Ron Francis .20 .50
46 Saku Koivu 1.25 3.00
47 Ed Jovanovski .75 2.00
48 Vitali Yachmenev .40 1.00
49 Petr Sykora .75 2.00
50 Eric Daze .75 2.00

1999-00 Stadium Club Promos

COMPLETE SET (6) .75 2.00
PP1 Chris Osgood .20 .50
PP2 Steve Konowalchuk .08 .25
PP3 Jeremy Roenick .40 1.00
PP4 Rod Brind'Amour .20 .50
PP5 Mattias Norstrom .08 .25
PP6 Clarke Wilm .08 .25

1999-00 Stadium Club

COMPLETE SET (200) 30.00 60.00
1 Jaromir Jagr .30 .75
2 Mats Sundin .20 .50
3 Mark Messier .20 .50
4 Paul Kariya .20 .50
5 Ray Bourque .30 .75
6 Tony Amonte .15 .40
7 Dominik Hasek .40 1.00
8 Peter Forsberg .50 1.25
9 Pavel Bure .20 .50
10 Nicklas Lidstrom .20 .50
11 Kenny Jonsson .05 .15
12 Brian Leetch .20 .50
13 Eric Lindros .20 .50
14 Al MacInnis .15 .40
15 Keith Tkachuk .20 .50
16 Martin Brodeur .60 1.50
17 Saku Koivu .20 .50
18 Jeff Friesen .05 .15
19 Olaf Kolzig .15 .40
20 Mike Modano .30 .75
21 Jarome Iginla .25 .60
22 Alexei Kovalev .05 .15
23 Vincent Lecavalier .20 .50
24 Greg Johnson .05 .15
25 Ron Francis .15 .40
26 Steve Konowalchuk .05 .15
27 Luc Robitaille .15 .40
28 Alexei Yashin .05 .15
29 Mark Parrish .05 .15
30 Todd Warriner .05 .15
31 Brett Hull .25 .60
32 Steve Dubinsky .05 .15
33 Rod Brind'Amour .15 .40
34 Bill Muckalt .05 .15
35 Bryan Berard .05 .15
36 Manny Malhotra .15 .40
37 Jozef Stumpel .15 .40
38 Sergei Fedorov .30 .75
39 Roman Vopat .15 .40
40 Teemu Selanne .20 .50
41 Teppo Numminen .05 .15
42 Mats Lindgren .05 .15
43 Chris Gratton .05 .15
44 Owen Nolan .15 .40
45 Scott Niedermayer .05 .15
46 Sergei Krivokrasov .05 .15
47 Joe Sakic .40 1.00
48 Bill Guerin .05 .15
49 Shayne Corson .05 .15
50 Eric Daze .15 .40
51 Clarke Wilm .05 .15
52 Magnus Arvedson .05 .15
53 Sergei Berezin .05 .15
54 Derian Hatcher .05 .15
55 Jeremy Roenick .25 .60
56 Adam Oates .15 .40
57 Dixon Ward .05 .15
58 Petr Nedved .15 .40
59 Joe Reekie .05 .15
60 Milan Hejduk .20 .50
61 Mike Grier .05 .15
62 Martin Straka .05 .15
63 Petr Sykora .05 .15
64 Harry York .05 .15
65 John LeClair .20 .50
66 Patrick Roy .60 1.50
67 Arturs Irbe .15 .40
68 Murray Baron .05 .15
69 Felix Potvin .30 .75
70 Pavol Demitra .15 .40
71 Ray Whitney .15 .40
72 Patrick Marleau .20 .50
73 Tom Fitzgerald .05 .15
74 Jamal Mayers .05 .15
75 Joe Thornton .30 .75
76 Craig Rivet .05 .15
77 Ed Belfour .20 .50
78 Stephane Fiset .15 .40
79 Alexander Karpovtsev .05 .15
80 Miroslav Satan .05 .15
81 Doug Weight .15 .40
82 Marian Hossa .20 .50
83 Markus Naslund .20 .50
84 Derek Morris .05 .15
85 Mike Richter .20 .50
86 Scott Young .05 .15
87 Darcy Tucker .05 .15
88 Jason Allison .05 .15
89 Chris Osgood .15 .40
90 Doug Gilmour .15 .40
91 Ron Tugnutt .15 .40
92 Adam Deadmarsh .05 .15
93 Byron Dafoe .15 .40
94 Rick Tocchet .15 .40
95 Mike Johnson .05 .15
96 Guy Hebert .15 .40
97 Cory Stillman .15 .40
98 Daniel Alfredsson .15 .40
99 Tom Barrasso .15 .40
100 Peter Bondra .15 .40
101 Rob Blake .15 .40
102 Gary Roberts .05 .15
103 Cliff Ronning .15 .40
104 Jason Woolley .05 .15
105 Keith Primeau .05 .15
106 Brendan Shanahan .20 .50
107 Alexei Zhamnov .15 .40
108 Bobby Holik .05 .15
109 Mark Recchi .15 .40
110 Eric Brewer .05 .15
111 Mike Ricci .15 .40
112 Pierre Turgeon .15 .40
113 Martin Rucinsky .05 .15
114 Chris McAllister RC .05 .15
115 Patrik Elias .15 .40
116 Alexander Selivanov .05 .15
117 Fredrik Olausson .05 .15
118 Curtis Joseph .20 .50
119 Wade Redden .05 .15
120 Nikolai Khabibulin .15 .40
121 Chris Drury .15 .40
122 Chris Chelios .20 .50
123 Vincent Damphousse .05 .15
124 Mattias Ohlund .15 .40
125 Mike Dunham .15 .40
126 John Vanbiesbrouck .15 .40
127 John MacLean .15 .40
128 Jocelyn Thibault .15 .40
129 Jan Hrdina .05 .15
130 Mariusz Czerkawski .05 .15
131 Pavel Kubina .05 .15
132 Scott Stevens .15 .40
133 Mattias Norstrom .05 .15
134 Sami Kapanen .05 .15
135 Sergei Samsonov .15 .40
136 Tom Poti .05 .15
137 Steve Shields .15 .40
138 Anson Carter .15 .40
139 Chris McAlpine .05 .15
140 Rob Niedermayer .05 .15
141 Michael Peca .05 .15
142 Valeri Bure .05 .15
143 Joe Nieuwendyk .15 .40
144 Jose Theodore .25 .60
145 Steve Yzerman 1.00 2.50
146 Chris Pronger .15 .40
147 Marty McInnis .05 .15
148 Jere Lehtinen .15 .40
149 Adam Graves .05 .15
150 Deron Quint .05 .15
151 Ray Ferraro .05 .15
152 Niklas Sundstrom .05 .15
153 Damian Rhodes .15 .40
154 Zigmund Palffy .15 .40
155 Valeri Kamensky .15 .40
156 Oleg Tverdovsky .15 .40
157 Bill Ranford .15 .40
158 Kelly Buchberger .05 .15
159 Trevor Linden .05 .15
160 Bryan McCabe .05 .15
161 Dan Cloutier .05 .15
162 Olli Jokinen .15 .40
163 Theo Fleury .05 .15
164 Dave Andreychuk .15 .40
165 Gord Murphy .05 .15
166 Steve Duchesne .15 .40
167 Marc Savard .05 .15
168 Maxim Afinogenov .05 .15
169 Mark Eaton RC .15 .40
170 Pavel Patera RC .05 .15
171 Nikolai Antropov RC .60 1.50
172 Ivan Novoseltsev RC .40 1.00
173 Jochen Hecht RC 1.00 2.50
174 Mike Ribeiro .05 .15
175 Yuri Butsayev RC .05 .15
176 Jorgen Jonsson RC .05 .15
177 Dan Hinote RC .20 .50
178 Dave Tanabe .05 .15
179 John Grahame RC .50 1.25
180 Mika Alatalo RC .15 .40
181 Patrik Stefan RC .40 1.00
182 Mike Fisher RC .40 1.00
183 Niclas Havelid RC .15 .40
184 Paul Comrie RC .05 .15
185 Michal Rozsival RC .05 .15
186 Oleg Saprykin RC .40 1.00
187 Martin Skoula RC .20 .50
188 Simon Gagne .20 .50
189 Brian Rafalski RC .50 1.25
190 J-P Dumont .15 .40
191 Martin Biron .15 .40
192 Rico Fata .05 .15
193 Jan Hlavac .05 .15
194 Alex Tanguay .15 .40
195 Brad Stuart .15 .40
196 Brian Boucher .20 .50
197 Steve Kariya RC .20 .50
198 Scott Gomez .05 .15
199 Tim Connolly .25 .60
200 David Legwand .15 .40

1999-00 Stadium Club First Day Issue

*VETS: 12.5X TO 30X BASIC CARDS
*ROOKIES: 3X TO 8X BASIC CARDS

1999-00 Stadium Club One of a Kind

*VETS: 12.5X TO 25X BASIC CARDS
*ROOKIES: 3X TO 8X BASIC CARDS

1999-00 Stadium Club Capture the Action

COMPLETE SET (30) 40.00 80.00
*GAME VIEW/100: 3X TO 8X BASIC INSERTS
CA1 Bill Muckalt .60 1.50
CA2 Chris Drury .75 2.00
CA3 Milan Hejduk 1.00 2.50
CA4 Mark Parrish .60 1.50
CA5 Marian Hossa 1.00 2.50
CA6 Manny Malhotra .75 2.00
CA7 J-P Dumont .75 2.00
CA8 Eric Brewer .60 1.50
CA9 Vincent Lecavalier 1.00 2.50
CA10 Jan Hrdina .60 1.50
CA11 Paul Kariya 1.00 2.50
CA12 Peter Forsberg 2.50 6.00
CA13 Eric Lindros 1.25 3.00
CA14 Martin Brodeur 2.50 6.00
CA15 Teemu Selanne 1.00 2.50
CA16 Keith Tkachuk 1.00 2.50
CA17 Mats Sundin 1.00 2.50
CA18 Pavel Bure 1.25 3.00
CA19 Mike Modano 1.50 4.00
CA20 Nicklas Lidstrom 1.25 3.00
CA21 Ray Bourque 1.50 4.00
CA22 Dominik Hasek 2.00 5.00
CA23 Patrick Roy 5.00 12.00
CA24 Mark Messier 1.00 2.50
CA25 Steve Yzerman 5.00 12.00
CA26 Jaromir Jagr 1.50 4.00
CA27 Paul Coffey 1.00 2.50
CA28 Brett Hull 1.25 3.00
CA29 Al MacInnis .75 2.00
CA30 Larry Murphy .75 2.00

1999-00 Stadium Club Chrome

COMPLETE SET (50) 30.00 60.00
*REFRACTORS: .8X TO 2X BASIC INSERTS
1 Jaromir Jagr 1.00 2.50
2 Mats Sundin .60 1.50
3 Mark Messier .60 1.50
4 Paul Kariya .60 1.50
5 Ray Bourque 1.00 2.50
6 Tony Amonte .50 1.25
7 Dominik Hasek 1.25 3.00
8 Peter Forsberg 1.50 4.00
9 Pavel Bure .60 1.50
10 Nicklas Lidstrom .60 1.50
11 Brian Leetch .50 1.25
12 Eric Lindros .60 1.50
13 Al MacInnis .50 1.25
14 Keith Tkachuk .60 1.50
15 Martin Brodeur 1.50 4.00
16 Saku Koivu .60 1.50
17 Jeff Friesen .50 1.25
18 Mike Modano 1.00 2.50
19 Vincent Lecavalier .60 1.50
20 Luc Robitaille .50 1.25
21 Brett Hull .75 2.00
22 Teemu Selanne .60 1.50
23 Joe Sakic 1.25 3.00
24 Jeremy Roenick .75 2.00
25 John LeClair .60 1.50
26 Patrick Roy 3.00 8.00
27 Joe Thornton 1.00 2.50
28 Ed Belfour .60 1.50
29 Doug Weight .50 1.25
30 Marian Hossa .60 1.50
31 Chris Osgood .50 1.25
32 Daniel Alfredsson .50 1.25
33 Peter Bondra .50 1.25
34 Brendan Shanahan .60 1.50
35 Curtis Joseph .60 1.50
36 Chris Drury .50 1.25
37 Sergei Samsonov .50 1.25
38 Anson Carter .50 1.25
39 Joe Nieuwendyk .50 1.25
40 Steve Yzerman 3.00 8.00
41 Zigmund Palffy .50 1.25
42 Theo Fleury .50 1.25
43 Patrik Stefan 1.00 2.50
44 Simon Gagne .60 1.50
45 J-P Dumont .50 1.25
46 Alex Tanguay .50 1.25
47 Steve Kariya .50 1.25
48 Scott Gomez .50 1.25
49 Tim Connolly .75 2.00
50 David Legwand .50 1.25

1999-00 Stadium Club Chrome Oversized

COMPLETE SET (20) 50.00 100.00
*REFRACTORS: .8X TO 2X BASIC INSERTS
1 Jaromir Jagr 1.50 4.00
2 Mats Sundin 1.00 2.50
3 Paul Kariya 1.00 2.50
4 Ray Bourque 1.50 4.00
5 Dominik Hasek 2.00 5.00
6 Peter Forsberg 2.50 6.00
7 Pavel Bure 1.00 2.50
8 Eric Lindros 1.00 2.50
9 Martin Brodeur 2.50 6.00
10 Mike Modano 1.50 4.00
11 Teemu Selanne 1.00 2.50
12 Joe Sakic 2.00 5.00
13 Patrick Roy 5.00 12.00
14 Marian Hossa 1.00 2.50
15 Curtis Joseph 1.00 2.50
16 Steve Yzerman 5.00 12.00
17 Theo Fleury .75 2.00
18 Patrik Stefan 1.50 4.00
19 Steve Kariya .75 2.00
20 David Legwand .75 2.00

1999-00 Stadium Club Co-Signers

CS1 C.Drury/B.Morrison 10.00 25.00
CS2 B.Morrison/M.Hossa 10.00 25.00
CS3 M.Hossa/C.Drury 10.00 25.00
CS4 J.Jagr/M.Sundin 30.00 80.00
CS5 J.Jagr/A.Yashin 25.00 60.00
CS6 J.LeClair/J.Jagr 40.00 100.00
CS7 A.Yashin/M.Sundin 12.00 30.00
CS8 M.Sundin/J.LeClair 12.00 30.00
CS9 A.Yashin/J.LeClair 10.00 25.00
CS10 C.Osgood/E.Belfour 30.00 80.00
CS11 C.Osgd/C.Joseph 25.00 60.00
CS12 E.Belfr/C.Joseph 30.00 80.00
CS13 R.Bourque/A.MacInnis 40.00 100.00
CS14 A.MacInnis/W.Redden 10.00 25.00
CS15 W.Redden/R.Bourque 25.00 60.00

1999-00 Stadium Club Eyes of the Game

COMPLETE SET (10) 8.00 15.00
*REFRACTORS: 1.5X TO 4X BASIC INSERTS
EG1 Jaromir Jagr 1.00 2.50
EG2 Peter Forsberg 1.50 4.00
EG3 Paul Kariya .60 1.50
EG4 Teemu Selanne .60 1.50
EG5 Joe Sakic 1.25 3.00
EG6 Eric Lindros .60 1.50
EG7 Jason Allison .50 1.25
EG8 Mats Sundin .60 1.50
EG9 Pavol Demitra .50 1.25
EG10 Rod Brind'Amour .50 1.25

1999-00 Stadium Club Goalie Cam

COMPLETE SET (7) 8.00 15.00
GC1 Dominik Hasek 2.00 5.00
GC2 Martin Brodeur 2.50 6.00
GC3 Byron Dafoe .75 2.00
GC4 Olaf Kolzig .75 2.00
GC5 Mike Richter 1.00 2.50
GC6 Ron Tugnutt .75 2.00
GC7 Tom Barrasso .75 2.00

1999-00 Stadium Club Lone Star Signatures

LS1 Jaromir Jagr 40.00 100.00
LS2 Alexei Yashin 5.00 12.00
LS3 Mats Sundin 25.00 60.00
LS4 Ray Bourque 25.00 60.00
LS5 Al MacInnis 6.00 15.00
LS6 Wade Redden 5.00 12.00
LS7 Chris Osgood 6.00 15.00
LS8 Ed Belfour 8.00 20.00
LS9 Curtis Joseph 20.00 50.00
LS10 John LeClair 8.00 20.00
LS11 Chris Drury 6.00 15.00
LS12 Brendan Morrison 6.00 15.00
LS13 Marian Hossa 8.00 20.00

1999-00 Stadium Club Onyx Extreme

COMPLETE SET (10) 8.00 15.00
*DIE-CUT: 1.5X TO 4X BASIC INSERTS
OE1 Jaromir Jagr 1.00 2.50
OE2 Peter Forsberg 1.50 4.00
OE3 Dominik Hasek 1.25 3.00
OE4 Eric Lindros .50 1.25
OE5 Paul Kariya .50 1.25
OE6 Joe Sakic 1.25 3.00
OE7 Nicklas Lidstrom .50 1.25
OE8 Teemu Selanne .50 1.25
OE9 John LeClair .50 1.25
OE10 Pavel Bure .50 1.25

1999-00 Stadium Club Souvenirs

SAM Al MacInnis S 5.00 12.00
SCO Chris Osgood J 5.00 12.00
SEB Ed Belfour S 6.00 15.00
SJL John LeClair S 10.00 25.00
SMH Marian Hossa J 5.00 12.00
SMS Mats Sundin J 5.00 12.00

2000-01 Stadium Club

1 Pavel Bure .15 .40
2 Brendan Shanahan .15 .40
3 Chris Pronger .15 .40
4 Doug Weight .15 .40
5 Peter Forsberg .30 .75
6 Jaromir Jagr .50 1.25
7 Ed Belfour .15 .40
8 Rod Brind'Amour .15 .40
9 Mike Richter .15 .40
10 Mike Ricci .10 .25
11 Dimitri Yushkevich .10 .25
12 Dominik Hasek .25 .60
13 Teemu Selanne .30 .75
14 Ed Jovanovski .12 .30
15 Damian Rhodes .10 .25
16 Martin Brodeur .40 1.00
17 Keith Primeau .12 .30
18 Byron Dafoe .12 .30
19 Jeff Hackett .10 .25
20 Brad Isbister .10 .25
21 Jeremy Roenick .25 .60
22 Jocelyn Thibault .12 .30
23 Ray Bourque .25 .60
24 Steve Yzerman .40 1.00
25 Mike Dunham .10 .25
26 Bill Guerin .15 .40
27 Dan Cloutier .12 .30
28 Pavol Demitra .20 .50
29 Richard Smehlik .10 .25
30 Ron Francis .20 .50
31 Zigmund Palffy .15 .40
32 David Legwand .15 .40
33 Scott Stevens .15 .40
34 Daniel Alfredsson .15 .40
35 Michal Rozsival .10 .25
36 John LeClair .15 .40
37 Vincent Lecavalier .15 .40
38 Jason Allison .12 .30
39 Kenny Jonsson .10 .25
40 Patrick Roy .40 1.00
41 Derian Hatcher .12 .30
42 Chris Osgood .15 .40
43 Owen Nolan .15 .40
44 Mike York .10 .25
45 Ryan Smyth .12 .30
46 Alexei Kovalev .12 .30
47 Roman Turek .12 .30
48 Mark Recchi .20 .50
49 Ray Ferraro .10 .25
50 Sergei Samsonov .12 .30
51 Paul Kariya .15 .40
52 Jarome Iginla .20 .50
53 Martin Biron .12 .30
54 Tom Poti .10 .25
55 Trevor Linden .15 .40
56 Pierre Turgeon .12 .30
57 Scott Gomez .12 .30
58 Mattias Ohlund .10 .25
59 Tony Amonte .12 .30
60 Yannick Tremblay .10 .25
61 Cliff Ronning .10 .25
62 Marc Savard .10 .25
63 Viktor Kozlov .12 .30
64 Pavel Kubina .10 .25
65 Arturs Irbe .12 .30
66 Stephane Fiset .10 .25
67 John Madden .12 .30
68 Steve Shields .10 .25
69 Theo Fleury .20 .50
70 Chris Simon .10 .25
71 Andy Delmore .10 .25
72 Radek Bonk .12 .30
73 Michal Handzus .10 .25
74 Tommy Salo .12 .30
75 Felix Potvin .25 .60
76 Teppo Numminen .10 .25
77 Bobby Holik .10 .25
78 Phil Housley .12 .30
79 Sergei Gonchar .10 .25
80 Shawn McEachern .10 .25
81 Simon Gagne .15 .40
82 Mike Sillinger .10 .25
83 Tim Connolly .10 .25
84 Eric Daze .12 .30
85 Andrew Brunette .10 .25
86 Mike Modano .25 .60
87 Chris Drury .12 .30
88 Nicklas Lidstrom .15 .40
89 Joe Thornton .25 .60
90 Michael Peca .12 .30
91 Matt Cullen .10 .25
92 Robyn Regehr .10 .25
93 Todd Marchant .10 .25
94 Brett Hull .30 .75
95 Rob Blake .15 .40
96 Sergei Zholtok .10 .25
97 Eric Lindros .25 .60
98 Jean-Sebastien Aubin .12 .30
99 Jason Arnott .12 .30
100 Keith Tkachuk .15 .40
101 Wade Redden .10 .25
102 Sean Burke .10 .25
103 Marian Hossa .15 .40
104 Robert Lang .10 .25
105 Curtis Joseph .20 .50
106 Jeff Friesen .10 .25
107 Dennis Bonvie .10 .25
108 Alexander Korolyuk .10 .25
109 Eric Lacroix .10 .25
110 Todd Bertuzzi .12 .30
111 Bates Battaglia .10 .25
112 Jozef Stumpel .10 .25
113 Alexei Zhamnov .12 .30
114 Milan Hejduk .12 .30
115 Chris Chelios .15 .40
116 Adam Graves .12 .30
117 Patrik Stefan .12 .30
118 Guy Hebert .12 .30
119 Anson Carter .12 .30
120 Fred Brathwaite .12 .30
121 Maxim Afinogenov .10 .25
122 Eric Messier .10 .25
123 Ray Whitney .12 .30
124 Bob Bassen .10 .25
125 Patrick Lalime .12 .30
126 Jonas Hoglund .10 .25
127 Mike Johnson .10 .25
128 Peter Schaefer .10 .25
129 Olaf Kolzig .15 .40
130 Jamie Langenbrunner .12 .30
131 Scott Niedermayer .15 .40
132 Mariusz Czerkawski .10 .25
133 Petr Buzek .10 .25
134 Michal Grosek .10 .25
135 Valeri Bure .12 .30
136 Igor Korolev .10 .25
137 Oleg Tverdovsky .10 .25
138 Fredrik Modin .10 .25
139 Kyle McLaren .10 .25
140 Todd Gill .10 .25
141 Miroslav Satan .10 .25
142 Jeff O'Neill .12 .30
143 Steve Sullivan .10 .25
144 Jon Klemm .10 .25
145 Joe Nieuwendyk .12 .30
146 Luc Robitaille .15 .40
147 Patrice Brisebois .10 .25
148 Travis Green .10 .25
149 Patric Kjellberg .10 .25
150 Mats Sundin .15 .40
151 Brian Rolston .12 .30
152 Patrik Elias .15 .40
153 Markus Naslund .15 .40
154 Trevor Letowski .10 .25
155 Brad Stuart .12 .30
156 Doug Gilmour .20 .50
157 Alexander Mogilny .12 .30
158 Glen Wesley .10 .25
159 Petr Nedved .12 .30
160 Peter Bondra .15 .40
161 Alex Tanguay .12 .30
162 Steve Rucchin .10 .25
163 Nikolai Antropov .12 .30
164 Anders Eriksson .10 .25
165 Martin Rucinsky .10 .25
166 Trevor Kidd .10 .25
167 Zdeno Chara .15 .40
168 Adam Oates .15 .40
169 Eric Desjardins .12 .30
170 Petr Sykora .12 .30
171 Brenden Morrow .12 .30
172 AL MacInnis .20 .50
173 Ethan Moreau .10 .25
174 Chris Tamer .10 .25
175 Jaroslav Spacek .10 .25
176 Paul Mara .10 .25
177 Bryan Smolinski .12 .30
178 Yanic Perreault .10 .25
179 Vaclav Prospal .10 .25
180 Vitali Yachmenev .10 .25
181 Pavel Trnka .10 .25
182 Joe Sakic .30 .75
183 Vincent Damphousse .12 .30
184 Sergei Fedorov .25 .60
185 Brian Rafalski .10 .25
186 Jochen Hecht .10 .25
187 Shane Doan .12 .30
188 Saku Koivu .15 .40
189 Richard Zednik .10 .25
190 Brian Boucher .12 .30
191 Jeff Halpern .10 .25
192 Matt Cooke .10 .25
193 Darcy Tucker .10 .25
194 Brian Leetch .12 .30
195 Glen Murray .12 .30
196 Robert Svehla .10 .25
197 Kimmo Timonen .10 .25
198 Claude Lapointe .10 .25
199 Brian Savage .10 .25
200 Sami Kapanen .10 .25
201 Scott Pellerin .10 .25
202 Cam Stewart .10 .25
203 Sergei Krivokrasov .10 .25
204 Manny Fernandez .10 .25
205 Darby Hendrickson .10 .25
206 Jamie McLennan .10 .25
207 Kevyn Adams .10 .25
208 Lyle Odelein .10 .25
209 Marc Denis .12 .30
210 Ron Tugnutt .12 .30
211 Tyler Wright .10 .25
212 Geoff Sanderson .12 .30
213 Mark Messier .30 .75
214 Mike Vernon .12 .30
215 Dave Andreychuk .15 .40
216 Chris Murray .10 .25
217 Joe Juneau .10 .25
218 Vladimir Malakhov .10 .25
219 Paul Coffey .15 .40
220 Roberto Luongo .25 .60
221 Roman Hamrlik .10 .25
222 Sandis Ozolinsh .10 .25
223 Gary Roberts .10 .25
224 Boyd Devereaux .10 .25
225 Scott Thornton .12 .30
226 Igor Larionov .15 .40
227 John Vanbiesbrouck .15 .40
228 Milan Kraft SP .40 1.00
229 Steven McCarthy SP .40 1.00
230 Kris Beech SP .40 1.00
231 Henrik Sedin SP .75 2.00
232 Daniel Sedin SP .75 2.00
233 Oleg Saprykin SP .40 1.00
234 Maxime Ouellet SP .60 1.50
235 Taylor Pyatt SP .40 1.00
236 Brent Johnson SP .50 1.25
237 Shawn Heins SP .40 1.00
238 Mika Noronen SP .40 1.00
239 Samuel Pahlsson SP .40 1.00
240 Dimitri Kalinin SP .40 1.00
241 Marian Gaborik RC 3.00 8.00
242 Petr Svoboda RC .50 1.25
243 Niclas Wallin RC .50 1.25
244 Dale Purinton RC .40 1.00
245 Justin Williams RC 1.00 2.50
246 Roman Simicek RC .40 1.00
247 Brad Tapper RC .40 1.00
248 Rostislav Klesla RC 1.00 2.50
249 Martin Havlat RC 1.25 3.00
250 Scott Hartnell RC 1.00 2.50
251 Andrew Raycroft RC 1.00 2.50
252 Ossi Vaananen RC .50 1.25
253 Steven Reinprecht RC .60 1.50
254 Josef Vasicek RC 1.00 2.50
255 Petr Hubacek RC .40 1.00
256 Lubomir Sekeras RC .40 1.00
257 David Aebischer RC .75 2.00
258 Jani Hurme RC .40 1.00
259 Marty Turco RC 1.50 4.00
260 Jarno Kultanen RC .40 1.00

2000-01 Stadium Club Beam Team

COMPLETE SET (30) 150.00 300.00
BT1 Paul Kariya 4.00 10.00
BT2 Peter Forsberg 10.00 25.00
BT3 Mike Modano 6.00 15.00
BT4 Steve Yzerman 12.00 30.00
BT5 Pavel Bure 5.00 12.00
BT6 Jaromir Jagr 6.00 15.00
BT7 Brett Hull 5.00 12.00
BT8 Joe Sakic 8.00 20.00
BT9 Scott Gomez 3.00 8.00
BT10 Teemu Selanne 8.00 20.00
BT11 Vincent Lecavalier 4.00 10.00
BT12 Patrick Roy 15.00 40.00
BT13 Martin Brodeur 10.00 25.00
BT14 Dominik Hasek 8.00 20.00
BT15 Joe Thornton 6.00 15.00
BT16 Valeri Bure 3.00 8.00
BT17 Ed Belfour 4.00 10.00
BT18 Ray Bourque 8.00 20.00
BT19 Mark Messier 5.00 12.00
BT20 Curtis Joseph 4.00 10.00
BT21 Jason Arnott 3.00 8.00
BT22 Brian Boucher 4.00 10.00
BT23 Tony Amonte 3.00 8.00
BT24 Milan Hejduk 4.00 10.00
BT25 Mark Recchi 3.00 8.00
BT26 Patrik Elias 3.00 8.00
BT27 Zigmund Palffy 3.00 8.00
BT28 Jeremy Roenick 5.00 12.00
BT29 Eric Lindros 6.00 15.00
BT30 Chris Pronger 3.00 8.00

2000-01 Stadium Club Capture the Action

COMPLETE SET (15) 10.00 20.00
*GAME VIEW/100: 4X TO 10X
CA1 Jaromir Jagr 1.00 2.50
CA2 Martin Brodeur 1.50 4.00
CA3 Scott Gomez .50 1.25
CA4 Ed Belfour .60 1.50
CA5 Dominik Hasek 1.25 3.00
CA6 Olaf Kolzig .50 1.25
CA7 Pavel Bure .60 1.50
CA8 John LeClair .60 1.50
CA9 Curtis Joseph .60 1.50
CA10 Chris Pronger .50 1.25
CA11 Peter Forsberg 1.50 4.00
CA12 Teemu Selanne .60 1.50
CA13 Patrik Stefan .50 1.25
CA14 Vincent Lecavalier .60 1.50
CA15 Tim Connolly .50 1.25

2000-01 Stadium Club Co-Signers

CO1 P.Bure/P.Demitra 15.00 40.00
CO2 S.Gomez/M.Brodeur 60.00 150.00
CO3 N.Antropov/D.Alfredsson 12.00 30.00
CO4 A.Carter/M.York 15.00 40.00

2000-01 Stadium Club Glove Save

COMPLETE SET (10) 20.00 40.00
GS1 Martin Brodeur 3.00 8.00
GS2 Ed Belfour 1.25 3.00
GS3 Patrick Roy 6.00 15.00
GS4 Curtis Joseph 1.25 3.00
GS5 Brian Boucher 1.00 2.50
GS6 Roman Turek 1.00 2.50
GS7 Olaf Kolzig 1.00 2.50
GS8 Dominik Hasek 2.50 6.00
GS9 Chris Osgood 1.00 2.50
GS10 Fred Brathwaite 1.00 2.50

2000-01 Stadium Club Lone Star Signatures

LS1 Pavel Bure 10.00 25.00
LS2 Martin Brodeur 30.00 80.00
LS3 Scott Gomez 8.00 20.00
LS4 Daniel Alfredsson 8.00 20.00
LS5 Nikolai Antropov 8.00 20.00
LS6 Jose Theodore 10.00 25.00
LS7 Anson Carter 8.00 20.00
LS8 Pavol Demitra 8.00 20.00
LS9 Mike York 8.00 20.00
LS10 Brad Stuart 8.00 20.00

2000-01 Stadium Club Promos

COMPLETE SET (6) 2.00 4.00
PP1 Bill Guerin .30 .75
PP2 Alexei Kovalev .30 .75
PP3 Keith Primeau .30 .75
PP4 Jocelyn Thibault .30 .75
PP5 Brad Isbister .30 .75
PP6 Adam Graves .30 .75

2000-01 Stadium Club Souvenirs

SCS1 Wade Redden 2.50 6.00
SCS2 Joe Sakic 8.00 20.00
SCS3 Derian Hatcher 3.00 8.00
SCS4 Jeff Hackett 2.50 6.00
SCS5 Kenny Jonsson 2.50 6.00
SCS6 Sergei Samsonov 3.00 8.00
SCS7 Darren McCarty 6.00 15.00
SCS8 Tie Domi 4.00 10.00

2000-01 Stadium Club Special Forces

COMPLETE SET (20) 15.00 30.00
SF1 Scott Stevens .60 1.50
SF2 Chris Pronger .60 1.50
SF3 Paul Kariya .60 1.50
SF4 Peter Forsberg 1.25 3.00
SF5 Mike Modano 1.00 2.50
SF6 Steve Yzerman 1.50 4.00
SF7 Pavel Bure .60 1.50
SF8 Jaromir Jagr 2.00 5.00
SF9 John LeClair .60 1.50
SF10 Mats Sundin .60 1.50
SF11 Owen Nolan .60 1.50
SF12 Brendan Shanahan .60 1.50
SF13 Pavol Demitra .75 2.00

SF14 Nicklas Lidstrom .60 1.50
SF15 Ron Francis .75 2.00
SF16 Patrick Roy 1.50 4.00
SF17 Martin Brodeur 1.50 4.00
SF18 Dominik Hasek 1.00 2.50
SF19 Keith Tkachuk .60 1.50
SF20 Curtis Joseph .75 2.00

2001-02 Stadium Club

COMPLETE SET (140) 60.00 120.00
1 Martin Brodeur .50 1.25
2 Peter Forsberg .40 1.00
3 Chris Pronger .20 .50
4 Paul Kariya .20 .50
5 Mike Modano .30 .75
6 Curtis Joseph .25 .60
7 Jason Allison .15 .40
8 Brendan Shanahan .20 .50
9 Peter Bondra .20 .50
10 Mark Messier .40 1.00
11 Owen Nolan .20 .50
12 Saku Koivu .20 .50
13 Tony Amonte .15 .40
14 Vincent Lecavalier .20 .50
15 Marian Hossa .20 .50
16 Pavel Bure .20 .50
17 Daniel Sedin .25 .60
18 Mario Lemieux 1.25 3.00
19 Rick DiPietro .15 .40
20 Zigmund Palffy .20 .50
21 Ron Tugnutt .15 .40
22 Ron Francis .25 .60
23 Maxim Afinogenov .12 .30
24 Steve Yzerman .50 1.25
25 Ray Ferraro .12 .30
26 Tommy Salo .15 .40
27 Marian Gaborik .20 .50
28 Claude Lemieux .15 .40
29 David Legwand .15 .40
30 Roman Cechmanek .15 .40
31 Jarome Iginla .25 .60
32 Sergei Fedorov .30 .75
33 Bill Guerin .20 .50
34 Brian Leetch .15 .40
35 Alexei Kovalev .15 .40
36 Pavol Demitra .25 .60
37 Olaf Kolzig .20 .50
38 Jose Theodore .20 .50
39 Johan Hedberg .15 .40
40 Teemu Selanne .40 1.00
41 Adam Deadmarsh .12 .30
42 Miroslav Satan .15 .40
43 Henrik Sedin .25 .60
44 Ed Belfour .20 .50
45 Sean Burke .12 .30
46 Patrik Elias .20 .50
47 Daniel Alfredsson .20 .50
48 Evgeni Nabokov .15 .40
49 Markus Naslund .20 .50
50 Mats Sundin .20 .50
51 Milan Hejduk .15 .40
52 Eric Belanger .12 .30
53 Darren McCarty .12 .30
54 Keith Tkachuk .20 .50
55 Steve Sullivan .12 .30
56 Mark Recchi .25 .60
57 Rob Blake .20 .50
58 Manny Fernandez .12 .30
59 Patrick Lalime .15 .40
60 Adam Oates .20 .50
61 Joe Sakic .40 1.00
62 Lubomir Visnovsky .12 .30
63 Jeff Halpern .12 .30
64 Shane Willis .12 .30
65 Todd Bertuzzi .20 .50
66 Jeff Friesen .12 .30
67 Mike Dunham .15 .40
68 Alex Tanguay .15 .40
60 J P Dumont .12 .30
70 Patrick Marleau .20 .50
71 Martin Straka .12 .30
72 Petr Sykora .12 .30
73 Arturs Irbe .15 .40
74 Patrik Stefan .15 .40
75 Brad Richards .20 .50
76 Mike Comrie .15 .40
77 Jason Arnott .15 .40
78 Tie Domi .15 .40
79 Martin Havlat .15 .40
80 Roberto Luongo .30 .75
81 Nicklas Lidstrom .20 .50
82 Simon Gagne .20 .50
83 Marc Savard .12 .30
84 John LeClair .20 .50
85 Gary Roberts .12 .30
86 Ryan Smyth .15 .40
87 Patrick Roy .50 1.25
88 Petr Nedved .15 .40
89 Brent Johnson .15 .40
90 Scott Gomez .15 .40
91 Joe Thornton .30 .75
92 Felix Potvin .30 .75
93 Chris Drury .15 .40
94 Keith Primeau .15 .40
95 Rod Brind'Amour .20 .50
96 Joe Nieuwendyk .15 .40
97 Espen Knutsen .12 .30
98 Adam Foote .15 .40
99 Brad Isbister .12 .30
100 Marc Denis .15 .40
101 Eric Lindros TR .60 1.50
102 Alexei Yashin TR .30 .75
103 Dominik Hasek TR .60 1.50
104 Michael Peca TR .30 .75
105 Brett Hull TR .75 2.00
106 Pierre Turgeon TR .30 .75
107 Doug Weight TR .40 1.00
108 Alexander Mogilny TR .30 .75
109 Jaromir Jagr TR 1.25 3.00
110 Jeremy Roenick TR .60 1.50
111 Dany Heatley PP 1.00 2.50
112 Rostislav Klesla PP .75 2.00
113 Pavel Brendl PP .75 2.00
114 Barrett Heisten PP .75 2.00
115 Miikka Kiprusoff PP 1.25 3.00
116 Kris Beech PP .75 2.00
117 Pierre Dagenais PP .75 2.00
118 Bryan Allen PP .75 2.00
119 Jason Williams PP .75 2.00
120 Milan Kraft PP .75 2.00
121 Ilya Kovalchuk RC 5.00 12.00
122 Peter Smrek RC 1.00 2.50
123 Jiri Dopita RC 1.00 2.50
124 Jeff Jillson RC 1.00 2.50
125 Jukka Hentunen RC 1.00 2.50
126 Vaclav Nedorost RC 1.00 2.50
127 Timo Parssinen RC 1.25 3.00
128 Niklas Hagman RC 1.25 3.00
129 Andreas Salomonsson RC 1.00 2.50
130 Scott Nichol RC 1.00 2.50
131 Dan Blackburn RC 1.25 3.00
132 Kristian Huselius RC 1.50 4.00
133 Ivan Ciernik RC 1.00 2.50
134 Scott Clemmensen RC 1.00 2.50
135 Pascal Dupuis RC 1.50 4.00
136 Jason Chimera RC 1.00 2.50
137 Erik Cole RC 2.00 5.00
138 Brian Sutherby RC 1.00 2.50
139 Pavel Datsyuk RC 6.00 15.00
140 Niko Kapanen RC 1.50 4.00

2001-02 Stadium Club Award Winners

*VETS: 4X TO 10X BASIC CARDS
*ROOKIES: .5X TO 1.5X BASIC CARDS
31 Jarome Iginla 10.00 25.00
38 Jose Theodore 20.00 50.00
81 Nicklas Lidstrom 10.00 25.00
111 Dany Heatley 8.00 20.00

2001-02 Stadium Club Master Photos

*1-100 VETS/100: 8X TO 20X BASIC CARDS
*101-110 TR/100: 4X TO 10X BASIC TR
*111-120 PP/100: 1.2X TO 3X BASIC PP
*121-140 ROOKIE/100: 1X TO 2.5X BASIC RC

2001-02 Stadium Club Gallery

COMPLETE SET (40) 30.00 60.00
*GOLD/50: 5X TO 12X BASIC INSERT
G1 Curtis Joseph .60 1.50
G2 Brendan Shanahan .60 1.50
G3 Mats Sundin .60 1.50
G4 Patrik Elias .50 1.25
G5 Martin Havlat .50 1.25
G6 Joe Sakic 1.25 3.00
G7 Mike Modano 1.00 2.50
G8 Chris Drury .50 1.25
G9 Scott Stevens .50 1.25
G10 Olaf Kolzig .50 1.25
G11 Roberto Luongo .75 2.00
G12 Roman Cechmanek .50 1.25
G13 Ed Belfour .60 1.50
G14 Teemu Selanne .60 1.50
G15 Henrik Sedin .60 1.50
G16 Jaromir Jagr 1.00 2.50
G17 Marian Gaborik 1.25 3.00
G18 John LeClair .60 1.50
G19 Keith Tkachuk .60 1.50
G20 Paul Kariya .60 1.50
G21 Mario Lemieux 4.00 10.00
G22 Sergei Fedorov 1.00 2.50
G23 Martin Brodeur 1.50 4.00
G24 Pavel Bure .60 1.50
G25 Mike Comrie .50 1.25
G26 Zigmund Palffy .50 1.25
G27 Milan Hejduk .60 1.50
G28 Nicklas Lidstrom .60 1.50
G29 Patrick Roy 3.00 8.00
G30 Bill Guerin .50 1.25
G31 Evgeni Nabokov .50 1.25
G32 Tony Amonte .50 1.25
G33 Peter Forsberg 1.50 4.00
G34 Rick DiPietro .50 1.25
G35 Saku Koivu .60 1.50
G36 Chris Pronger .50 1.25
G37 Steve Yzerman 3.00 8.00
G38 Daniel Sedin .60 1.50
G39 Vincent Lecavalier .60 1.50
G40 Mark Messier .60 1.50

2001-02 Stadium Club Heart and Soul

COMPLETE SET (10) 15.00 30.00
HS1 Mark Messier 1.00 2.50
HS2 Patrick Roy 4.00 10.00
HS3 Steve Yzerman 4.00 10.00
HS4 Mario Lemieux 5.00 12.00
HS5 Chris Pronger .60 1.50
HS6 Scott Stevens .60 1.50
HS7 Peter Forsberg 2.00 5.00
HS8 Curtis Joseph .60 1.50
HS9 Mike Modano 1.25 3.00
HS10 Brendan Shanahan 1.25 3.00

2001-02 Stadium Club Lone Star Signatures

LS1 Milan Hejduk 8.00 20.00
LS2 Olaf Kolzig 8.00 20.00
LS3 Marian Gaborik 12.50 30.00
LS4 Martin Havlat 8.00 20.00
LS5 Patrik Elias 8.00 20.00
LS6 Adam Oates 8.00 20.00
LS7 Ilya Kovalchuk 12.50 30.00

2001-02 Stadium Club New Regime

NR1 Marty Turco 2.00 5.00
NR2 David Aebischer 2.00 5.00
NR3 Brent Johnson 2.00 5.00
NR4 Evgeni Nabokov 2.00 5.00
NR5 Marc Denis 2.00 5.00
NR6 Roberto Luongo 2.50 6.00
NR7 Manny Fernandez 2.00 5.00
NR8 Roman Cechmanek 2.00 5.00
NR9 Jani Hurme 2.00 5.00
NR10 Johan Hedberg 2.00 5.00
NR11 Rick DiPietro 2.00 5.00
NRABJ Brent Johnson AU 8.00 20.00
NRADA David Aebischer AU 10.00 25.00
NRAEN Evgeni Nabokov AU 8.00 20.00
NRAJHE Johan Hedberg AU 8.00 20.00
NRAMD Marc Denis AU 8.00 20.00
NRAMF Manny Fernandez AU 8.00 20.00
NRAMT Marty Turco AU 10.00 25.00
NRARC Roman Cechmanek AU 8.00 20.00
NRARL Roberto Luongo AU 10.00 25.00

2001-02 Stadium Club NHL Passport

COMPLETE SET (20) 20.00 40.00
NHLP1 Peter Forsberg 1.50 4.00
NHLP2 Nicklas Lidstrom .60 1.50
NHLP3 Mats Sundin .60 1.50
NHLP4 Pavel Bure .75 2.00
NHLP5 Sergei Fedorov 1.25 3.00
NHLP6 Alexei Kovalev .50 1.25
NHLP7 Saku Koivu .75 2.00
NHLP8 Teemu Selanne .60 1.50
NHLP9 Roman Cechmanek .50 1.25
NHLP10 Patrik Elias .50 1.25
NHLP11 Milan Hejduk .60 1.50
NHLP12 Petr Sykora .50 1.25
NHLP13 Chris Drury .50 1.25
NHLP14 Bill Guerin .50 1.25
NHLP15 John LeClair .75 2.00
NHLP16 Mike Modano 1.00 2.50
NHLP17 Paul Kariya .60 1.50
NHLP18 Mario Lemieux 4.00 10.00
NHLP19 Joe Sakic 1.25 3.00
NHLP20 Steve Yzerman 3.00 8.00

2001-02 Stadium Club Perennials

COMPLETE SET (15) 20.00 40.00
P1 Pavel Bure .75 2.00
P2 Joe Sakic 1.25 3.00
P3 Martin Brodeur 1.50 4.00
P4 Peter Forsberg 1.50 4.00
P5 Patrick Roy 3.00 8.00
P6 John LeClair .75 2.00
P7 Paul Kariya .60 1.50
P8 Steve Yzerman 3.00 8.00
P9 Mario Lemieux 4.00 10.00
P10 Ed Belfour .60 1.50
P11 Keith Tkachuk .60 1.50
P12 Sergei Fedorov 1.25 3.00
P13 Curtis Joseph .60 1.50
P14 Zigmund Palffy .60 1.50
P15 Tony Amonte .60 1.50

2001-02 Stadium Club Souvenirs

AZ Alexei Zhamnov 4.00 10.00
CO Chris Osgood 6.00 15.00
JI Jarome Iginla 15.00 40.00
JT Joe Thornton 8.00 20.00
MB Martin Brodeur 15.00 40.00
MP Matt Pettinger 4.00 10.00
MR Mark Recchi 6.00 15.00
MT Marty Turco 6.00 15.00
PB Pavel Bure 4.00 10.00
PF Peter Forsberg 15.00 40.00
PK Paul Kariya 8.00 20.00
PM Patrick Marleau 6.00 15.00
SB Sean Burke 6.00 15.00
SF Sergei Fedorov 10.00 25.00
SK Saku Koivu 4.00 10.00
TD Tie Domi 6.00 15.00
TK Tomas Kloucek 4.00 10.00
JHA Jeff Hackett 4.00 10.00
JHL Jan Hlavac 4.00 10.00
MAS Marc Savard 4.00 10.00
MIS Miroslav Satan 6.00 15.00
EBMB E.Belfour/M.Brodeur 60.00 120.00
JHSK J.Hackett/S.Koivu 20.00 50.00
JSCD J.Sakic/C.Drury 30.00 80.00
MTEB M.Turco/E.Belfour 20.00 50.00
PFCD P.Forsberg/C.Drury 30.00 80.00
PFJS P.Forsberg/J.Sakic 50.00 100.00
PRMB P.Roy/M.Brodeur 60.00 120.00
SFPB S.Fedorov/P.Bure 30.00 80.00
SSPB S.Samsonov/P.Bure 20.00 50.00
TDDM T.Domi/D.McCarty 20.00 50.00
TKMM T.Kloucek/M.Mottau 20.00 50.00
EBMBPR Belfour/Brodeur/Roy 100.00 250.00
JSCDPF Sakic/Drury/Forsberg 100.00 200.00
JTJA33 Thorn/Allison/Samsonov 75.00 150.00

2001-02 Stadium Club Toronto Fall Expo

COMPLETE SET (6) 1.50 4.00
1 Marian Hossa .40 1.00
2 Peter Forsberg .75 2.00
3 Daniel Alfredsson .20 .50
4 Nicklas Lidstrom .20 .50
5 Brendan Shanahan .30 .75
6 Pavel Bure .40 1.00

2002-03 Stadium Club

COMPLETE SET (140) 75.00 150.00
COMP.SET w/o SP's (120) 25.00 50.00
1 Jose Theodore .30 .75
2 Jarome Iginla .40 1.00
3 Nicklas Lidstrom .30 .75
4 Ron Francis .40 1.00
5 Jaromir Jagr 1.00 2.50
6 Mario Lemieux 1.25 3.00
7 Owen Nolan .30 .75
8 Martin Brodeur .75 2.00
9 Joe Sakic .60 1.50
10 Ilya Kovalchuk .40 1.00
11 Mike Modano .50 1.25
12 Jason Allison .25 .60
13 Sean Burke .20 .50
14 Mats Sundin .30 .75
15 Markus Naslund .30 .75
16 Jeremy Roenick .50 1.25
17 Eric Lindros .50 1.25
18 Brent Johnson .25 .60
19 Sergei Fedorov .50 1.25
20 Sergei Samsonov .25 .60
21 Chris Drury .30 .75
22 Ryan Smyth .25 .60
23 Scott Hartnell .20 .50
24 Simon Gagne .30 .75
25 Dan Cloutier .25 .60
26 Vincent Lecavalier .30 .75
27 Martin Havlat .25 .60
28 Patrik Elias .30 .75
29 Roberto Luongo .50 1.25
30 Rob Blake .30 .75
31 J-P Dumont .20 .50
32 Jeff O'Neill .20 .50
33 Pavel Datsyuk .50 1.25
34 Dan Blackburn .25 .60
35 Alexei Kovalev .25 .60
36 Olaf Kolzig .30 .75
37 Milan Hejduk .25 .60
38 Steve Yzerman .75 2.00
39 Marc Denis .25 .60
40 Michael Peca .25 .60
41 Saku Koivu .30 .75
42 Marian Gaborik .30 .75
43 Brad Richards .30 .75
44 Alexander Mogilny .25 .60
45 Mike Comrie .30 .75
46 Peter Forsberg .60 1.50
47 Dany Heatley .25 .60
48 Steve Sullivan .20 .50
49 Keith Tkachuk .30 .75
50 Todd Bertuzzi .30 .75
51 Evgeni Nabokov .25 .60
52 David Legwand .25 .60
53 Scott Stevens .30 .75
54 Eric Daze .20 .50
55 Martin Biron .25 .60
56 Zigmund Palffy .30 .75
57 Paul Kariya .30 .75
58 Krys Kolanos .20 .50
59 Pavel Bure .30 .75
60 Darcy Tucker .20 .50
61 Marian Hossa .30 .75
62 Roman Cechmanek .25 .60
63 Mark Parrish .20 .50
64 Arturs Irbe .25 .60
65 Brian Rolston .25 .60
66 Marty Turco .30 .75
67 Peter Bondra .30 .75
68 Johan Hedberg .30 .75
69 Chris Pronger .30 .75
70 Patrick Lalime .25 .60
71 Mike Dunham .25 .60
72 Kristian Huselius .20 .50
73 Patrick Roy .75 2.00
74 Joe Thornton .50 1.25
75 Andrew Brunette .20 .50
76 Alexei Yashin .25 .60
77 John LeClair .30 .75
78 Miroslav Satan .30 .75
79 Doug Weight .30 .75
80 Gary Roberts .20 .50
81 Tommy Salo .25 .60
82 Daniel Alfredsson .30 .75
83 Marco Sturm .20 .50
84 Rostislav Klesla .20 .50
85 Richard Zednik .20 .50
86 Roman Turek .30 .75
87 Brian Leetch .25 .60
88 Chris Osgood .30 .75
89 Brendan Morrison .25 .60
90 Jocelyn Thibault .25 .60
91 Teemu Selanne .60 1.50
92 Jean-Sebastien Giguere .30 .75
93 Nikolai Khabibulin .30 .75
94 Pavol Demitra .40 1.00
95 Brendan Shanahan .30 .75
96 Mark Recchi .40 1.00
97 Felix Potvin .50 1.25
98 Shane Doan .25 .60
99 Erik Cole .20 .50
100 Brett Hull .60 1.50
101 Curtis Joseph .40 1.00
102 Bobby Holik .20 .50
103 Ed Belfour .30 .75
104 Bill Guerin .30 .75
105 Petr Sykora .25 .60
106 Scott Young .20 .50
107 Adam Oates .30 .75
108 Jeff Friesen .20 .50
109 Darius Kasparaitis .20 .50
110 Tony Amonte .25 .60
111 Marcel Hossa .20 .50
112 Jamie Lundmark .25 .60
113 Pavel Brendl .20 .50
114 Jaroslav Svoboda .20 .50
115 Stephen Weiss .30 .75
116 Martin Prusek .20 .50
117 Jani Rita .20 .50
118 Petr Cajanek .20 .50
119 Trent Hunter .20 .50
120 Jonathan Cheechoo .25 .60
121 Stanislav Chistov RC 1.00 2.50
122 Alexander Svitov RC 1.00 2.50
123 Alexander Frolov RC 2.50 6.00
124 Alexei Smirnov RC 1.25 3.00
125 Chuck Kobasew RC 1.25 3.00
126 Rick Nash RC 6.00 15.00
127 Henrik Zetterberg RC 8.00 20.00
128 Jay Bouwmeester RC 3.00 8.00
129 Ales Hemsky RC 4.00 10.00
130 Martin Gerber RC 1.50 4.00
131 Ron Hainsey RC 1.00 2.50
132 P-M Bouchard RC 1.50 4.00
133 Jason Spezza RC 5.00 12.00
134 Kurt Sauer RC 1.00 2.50
135 Lasse Pirjeta RC 1.00 2.50
136 Adam Hall RC 1.00 2.50
137 Dennis Seidenberg RC 1.50 4.00
138 Patrick Sharp RC 3.00 8.00
139 Steve Eminger RC 1.00 2.50
140 Dmitri Bykov RC 1.00 2.50

2002-03 Stadium Club Silver Decoy Cards

*DECOYS: .5X TO 1.2X BASIC CARDS

2002-03 Stadium Club Proofs

*1-120 VETS/250: 2X TO 5X BASIC CARDS
*121-140 ROOKIES/100: .8X TO 2X BASIC RC

2002-03 Stadium Club Beam Team

COMPLETE SET (15) 20.00 40.00
BT1 Steve Yzerman 3.00 8.00
BT2 Mario Lemieux 4.00 10.00
BT3 Patrick Roy 3.00 8.00
BT4 Jarome Iginla 1.00 2.50
BT5 Jose Theodore .75 2.00
BT6 Brendan Shanahan 1.00 2.50
BT7 Chris Pronger .50 1.25
BT8 Dany Heatley .75 2.00
BT9 Joe Thornton 1.00 2.50
BT10 Peter Forsberg 1.50 4.00
BT11 Ron Francis .50 1.25
BT12 Owen Nolan .50 1.25
BT13 Todd Bertuzzi .60 1.50
BT14 Rob Blake .50 1.25
BT15 Paul Kariya .60 1.50

2002-03 Stadium Club Champions Fabric

FC1 Rob Blake 4.00 10.00
FC2 Derian Hatcher 4.00 10.00
FC3 Alex Tanguay 4.00 10.00
FC4 Martin Brodeur 10.00 25.00
FC5 Milan Hejduk 4.00 10.00
FC6 Mike Modano 6.00 15.00
FC7 Scott Niedermayer 4.00 10.00
FC8 Brian Leetch 4.00 10.00
FC9 Sergei Zubov 4.00 10.00
FC10 Chris Drury 4.00 10.00

2002-03 Stadium Club Champions Patches

*PATCHES: 2X TO 5X BASIC JERSEY

2002-03 Stadium Club Lone Star Signatures Blue

LSBG Brian Gionta 8.00 20.00
LSBR Brad Richards 8.00 20.00
LSCP Chris Pronger SP 12.50 30.00
LSDB Daniel Briere 8.00 20.00
LSEC Erik Cole 6.00 15.00
LSED Eric Daze 6.00 15.00
LSIL Ilya Kovalchuk 10.00 25.00
LSJI Jarome Iginla 12.50 30.00
LSJT Jose Theodore 12.50 30.00
LSPL Patrick Lalime 8.00 20.00
LSRK Rostislav Klesla 6.00 15.00
LSSG Simon Gagne 10.00 30.00
LSSW Stephen Weiss 8.00 20.00
LSTB Todd Bertuzzi 10.00 25.00

2002-03 Stadium Club Lone Star Signatures Red

*RED SIGS: .5X TO 1.25X BLUE

2002-03 Stadium Club Passport Jerseys

1 Saku Koivu 5.00 12.00
2 Daniel Alfredsson 4.00 10.00
3 Eric Lindros 5.00 15.00
4 Mats Sundin 6.00 15.00
5 Todd Bertuzzi 5.00 12.00
6 Simon Gagne 6.00 15.00
7 Marian Hossa 5.00 12.00
8 Paul Kariya 5.00 12.00
9 Vincent Lecavalier 6.00 15.00
10 Miroslav Satan 4.00 10.00
11 Markus Naslund 6.00 15.00
12 Zigmund Palffy 4.00 10.00
13 Tony Amonte 4.00 10.00
14 Brian Rolston 4.00 10.00
15 Maxim Afinogenov 4.00 10.00
16 Sergei Samsonov 4.00 10.00
17 Marco Sturm 4.00 10.00

2002-03 Stadium Club Puck Stops Here

COMPLETE SET (15) 10.00 20.00
PSH1 Brent Johnson .50 1.25
PSH2 Roman Cechmanek .50 1.25
PSH3 Evgeni Nabokov .50 1.25
PSH4 Jose Theodore .75 2.00
PSH5 Martin Biron .50 1.25
PSH6 Chris Osgood .50 1.25
PSH7 Marty Turco .50 1.25
PSH8 Nikolai Khabibulin .60 1.50
PSH9 Roberto Luongo 1.00 2.50
PSH10 Martin Brodeur 1.25 3.00
PSH11 Sean Burke .50 1.25
PSH12 Tommy Salo .50 1.25
PSH13 Mike Richter .60 1.50
PSH14 Patrick Roy 1.50 4.00
PSH15 Jean-Sebastien Giguere .50 1.25

2002-03 Stadium Club St. Patrick Relics

SAS P.Roy STK AU/50 100.00 250.00
CAJ P.Roy JSY 12.50 30.00
MCJ P.Roy JSY 12.50 30.00
CAJA P.Roy JSY AU/250 60.00 150.00
MCJA P.Roy JSY AU/250 60.00 150.00
SPS P.Roy STK 12.50 30.00
CAJP P.Roy PATCH/100 30.00 80.00
MCJP P.Roy PATCH/100 30.00 80.00
CAMCJ P.Roy 2 JSY/500 30.00 80.00
CAMCJA P.Roy 2 JSY AU/50 200.00 500.00
CAMCJS P.Roy JSY/STK/50 60.00 120.00
CAMCJSA P.Roy JSY/STK AU/25 200.00 500.00
CAJPA P.Roy PATCH AU/10
MCJPA P.Roy PATCH AU/10
CAMCJP P.Roy DUAL PATCH/25
CAMCJPA P.Roy DUAL PATCH AU/5

2002-03 Stadium Club World Stage

COMPLETE SET (20) 15.00 30.00
WS1 Sergei Fedorov 1.25 3.00
WS2 Chris Drury .50 1.25
WS3 Martin Brodeur 1.50 4.00
WS4 Joe Sakic 1.25 3.00
WS5 Mike Modano 1.00 2.50
WS6 Jeremy Roenick .75 2.00
WS7 Brett Hull .75 2.00
WS8 Ilya Kovalchuk 1.00 2.50
WS9 Nicklas Lidstrom .60 1.50
WS10 Jaromir Jagr 1.00 2.50
WS11 Alexei Yashin .50 1.25
WS12 Zigmund Palffy .50 1.25
WS13 Marian Gaborik .75 2.00
WS14 Teemu Selanne .60 1.50
WS15 Alexei Kovalev .50 1.25
WS16 Patrik Elias .50 1.25
WS17 Peter Bondra .50 1.25
WS18 Pavel Bure .75 2.00
WS19 Mats Sundin .60 1.50
WS20 Daniel Alfredsson .50 1.25

2002-03 Stadium Club YoungStars Relics

YSS1 Ilya Kovalchuk 12.50 30.00
YSS2 Pavel Datsyuk 8.00 20.00
YSS3 Mike Comrie 4.00 10.00
YSS4 Dan Blackburn 4.00 10.00
YSS5 Dany Heatley 6.00 15.00
YSS6 Marian Gaborik 8.00 20.00
YSS7 Kristian Huselius 5.00 12.00
YSS8 David Legwand 5.00 12.00
YSS9 Roberto Luongo 8.00 20.00
YSS10 Brad Richards 5.00 12.00
YSS11 Justin Williams 5.00 12.00
YSS12 Kyle Calder 4.00 10.00
YSS13 Dave Tanabe 4.00 10.00
YSS14 Brenden Morrow 5.00 12.00
YSS15 Scott Hartnell 4.00 10.00
YSS16 Mike Fisher 5.00 12.00
YSS17 Tim Connolly 5.00 12.00
YSS18 Nick Boynton 4.00 10.00
YSS19 Paul Mara 4.00 10.00
YSS20 Mike Ribeiro 5.00 12.00
YSS21 Robyn Regehr 4.00 10.00
YSS22 Andrew Ference 4.00 10.00
YSS23 Karel Rachunek 4.00 10.00
YSDS1 D.Heatley/I.Kovalchuk 25.00 60.00
YSDS2 D.Legwand/S.Hartnell 10.00 25.00
YSDS3 K.Huselius/R.Luongo 20.00 50.00
YSDS4 M.Gaborik/P.Datsyuk 25.00 60.00
YSDS5 J.Williams/M.Comrie 8.00 20.00
YSDS6 B.Richards/D.Blackburn 10.00 25.00
APIK Kovalchuk Puck AU/200 20.00 50.00

1994-95 Stars HockeyKaps

COMPLETE SET (25) 3.00 8.00
1 Dave Barr .08 .25
2 Brad Berry .08 .25
3 Neal Broten .20 .50
4 Paul Broten .08 .25
5 Paul Cavallini .08 .25
6 Shane Churla .20 .50
7 Russ Courtnall .15 .40
8 Mike Craig .08 .25
9 Ulf Dahlen .15 .40
10 Dean Evason .08 .25
11 Dave Gagner .15 .40
12 Bob Gainey CO .15 .40
13 Brent Gilchrist .08 .25
14 Derian Hatcher .15 .40
15 Doug Jarvis ACO .02 .10
16 Jim Johnson .08 .25
17 Trent Klatt .08 .25
18 Grant Ledyard .08 .25
19 Craig Ludwig .08 .25
20 Mike McPhee .08 .25
21 Mike Modano .60 1.50
22 Andy Moog .40 1.00
23 Mark Tinordi .08 .25
24 Darcy Wakaluk .15 .40
25 Rick Wilson ACO .02 .10

1994-95 Stars Pinnacle Sheet

COMPLETE SHEET (9) 2.00 5.00
3 Mike Modano .60 1.50
55 Derian Hatcher .20 .50
133 Russ Courtnall .20 .50
157 Darcy Wakaluk .20 .50
185 Brent Gilchrist .08 .25
262 Todd Harvey .20 .50
315 Andy Moog .40 1.00
334 Dave Gagner .20 .50
433 Paul Broten .08 .25

1994-95 Stars Postcards

COMPLETE SET (23) 6.00 15.00
1 Paul Broten .20 .50
2 Paul Cavallini .20 .50
3 Shane Churla .30 .75
4 Gord Donnelly .20 .50
5 Mike Donnelly .20 .50
6 Dean Evason .20 .50
7 Dave Gagner .30 .75
8 Brent Gilchrist .20 .50
9 Todd Harvey .30 .75
10 Derian Hatcher .30 .75
11 Kevin Hatcher .20 .50
12 Mike Kennedy .20 .50
13 Trent Klatt .20 .50
14 Mike Lalor .20 .50
15 Grant Ledyard .20 .50
16 Craig Ludwig .20 .50
17 Richard Matvichuk .30 .75
18 Corey Millen .20 .50
19 Mike Modano 1.25 3.00
20 Andy Moog .75 2.00
21 Darcy Wakaluk .30 .75
22 Peter Zezel .20 .50
23 Doug Zmolek .20 .50

1994-95 Stars Score Sheet

COMPLETE SHEET (9) 2.00 5.00
17 Mike McPhee .08 .25
43 Russ Courtnall .08 .25
68 Mark Tinordi .08 .25
94 Paul Cavallini .08 .25
113 Neal Broten .20 .50
148 Derian Hatcher .20 .50
173 Andy Moog .40 1.00
188 Mike Modano .60 1.50
NNO Shane Churla .40 1.00

1995-96 Stars Score Sheet

COMPLETE SHEET (1) 2.00 5.00
12 Kevin Hatcher .08 .25
38 Todd Harvey .20 .50
64 Andy Moog .40 1.00
89 Greg Adams .20 .50
120 Mike Modano .75 2.00
197 Darcy Wakaluk .20 .50
225 Derian Hatcher .20 .50
229 Joe Nieuwendyk .40 1.00
261 Brent Gilchrist .08 .25

1996-97 Stars Postcards

COMPLETE SET 6.00 15.00
1 Greg Adams .20 .50
2 Bob Bassen .20 .50
3 Neal Broten .30 .75
4 Guy Carbonneau .20 .50
5 Bob Gainey .20 .50
6 Brent Gilchrist .20 .50
7 Todd Harvey .30 .75
8 Derian Hatcher .30 .75
9 Ken Hitchcock CO .20 .50
10 Benoit Hogue .20 .50
11 Bill Huard .20 .50
12 Arturs Irbe .30 .75
13 Mike Kennedy .20 .50
14 Mike Lalor .20 .50
15 Jamie Langenbrunner .30 .75
16 Grant Ledyard .20 .50
17 Jere Lehtinen .30 .75
18 Craig Ludwig .20 .50
19 Grant Marshall .20 .50
20 Richard Matvichuk .20 .50
21 Mike Modano 1.00 2.50
22 Joe Nieuwendyk .30 .75
23 Andy Moog .60 1.50
24 Dave Reid .20 .50
25 Darryl Sydor .20 .50
26 Pat Verbeek .30 .75
27 Sergei Zubov .20 .50

1996-97 Stars Score Sheet

COMPLETE SHEET 2.00 5.00
39 Greg Adams .20 .50
72 Mike Modano .75 2.00
86 Todd Harvey .20 .50
94 Pat Verbeek .20 .50
104 Andy Moog .40 1.00
152 Joe Nieuwendyk .30 .75
171 Sergei Zubov .20 .50
246 Jere Lehtinen .20 .50
NNO Derian Hatcher .20 .50

1997-98 Stars Postcards

COMPLETE SET (17) 4.00 10.00
1 Greg Adams .20 .50
2 Ed Belfour 1.00 2.50
3 Guy Carbonneau .20 .50
4 Bob Errey .20 .50
5 Derian Hatcher .20 .50
6 Benoit Hogue .20 .50
7 Jere Lehtinen .20 .50
8 Juha Lind .20 .50
9 Craig Ludwig .20 .50
10 Grant Marshall .20 .50
11 Mike Modano 1.00 2.50
12 Joe Nieuwendyk .60 1.50
13 Dave Reid .20 .50
14 Darryl Sydor .20 .50
15 Roman Turek .20 .50
16 Pat Verbeek .20 .50
17 Sergei Zubov .20 .50

1999-00 Stars Postcards

COMPLETE SET (27) 8.00 20.00
1 Keith Aldridge .20 .50
2 Ed Belfour .75 2.00
3 Guy Carbonneau .30 .75
4 Shawn Chambers .20 .50
5 Manny Fernandez .40 1.00
6 Aaron Gavey .20 .50
7 Derian Hatcher .30 .75
8 Brett Hull .75 2.00
9 Mike Keane .20 .50
10 Jamie Langenbrunner .30 .75
11 Jere Lehtinen .40 1.00
12 Alan Letang .20 .50
13 Juha Lind .20 .50
14 Warren Luhning .20 .50
15 Brad Lukowich .20 .50
16 Grant Marshall .20 .50
17 Richard Matvichuk .20 .50
18 Mike Modano 1.25 3.00
19 Chris Murray .20 .50
20 Joe Nieuwendyk .40 1.00
21 Pavel Patera .20 .50
22 Derek Plante .20 .50
23 Jamie Pushor .20 .50
24 Brian Skrudland .20 .50
25 Blake Sloan .20 .50
26 Darryl Sydor .20 .50
27 Sergei Zubov .20 .50

2000-01 Stars Postcards

COMPLETE SET (26) 8.00 20.00
1 Ed Belfour .80 2.00
2 Tyler Bouck .30 .75
3 Gerald Diduck .20 .50
4 Ted Donato .20 .50
5 Derian Hatcher .30 .75
6 Sami Helenius .20 .50
7 Ken Hitchcock HCO .20 .50
8 Brett Hull .80 2.00
9 Richard Jackman .20 .50
10 Mike Keane .20 .50
11 Jamie Langenbrunner .20 .50
12 Jere Lehtinen .60 1.50
13 Brad Lukowich .20 .50
14 Roman Lyashenko .30 .75
15 Grant Marshall .20 .50
16 Richard Matvichuk .20 .50
17 Mike Modano .80 2.00
18 Brenden Morrow .60 1.50
19 Kirk Muller .20 .50
20 Joe Nieuwendyk .30 .75
21 Jon Sim .20 .50
22 Blake Sloan .20 .50
23 Darryl Sydor .20 .50
24 Marty Turco .80 2.00
25 Shaun Van Allen .20 .50
26 Sergei Zubov .20 .50

2001-02 Stars Postcards

COMPLETE SET (26) 8.00 20.00
COMMON CARD (1-26)
1 Ed Belfour .75 2.00
2 Benoit Brunet .20 .50
3 Rob DiMaio .20 .50
4 John Erskine .20 .50
5 Derian Hatcher .30 .75
6 Sami Helenius .30 .75
7 Ken Hitchcock CO .20 .50
8 Benoit Hogue .20 .50
9 Valeri Kamensky .20 .50
10 Niko Kapanen .40 1.00
11 Jamie Langenbrunner .40 1.00
12 Jere Lehtinen .40 1.00
13 Brad Lukowich .20 .50
14 Roman Lyashenko .20 .50
15 Dave Manson .20 .50
16 Richard Matvichuk .20 .50
17 Mike Modano 1.25 3.00
18 Brenden Morrow .40 1.00
19 Kirk Muller .20 .50
20 Joe Nieuwendyk .40 1.00
21 Martin Rucinsky .20 .50

22 Darryl Sydor .20 .50
23 Marty Turco .60 1.50
24 Pierre Turgeon .30 .75
25 Pat Verbeek .20 .50
26 Sergei Zubov .20 .50

2001-02 Stars Team Issue

1 Brenden Morrow .75 2.00
2 Derian Hatcher .75 2.00
3 John Erskine .40 1.00
4 Niko Kapanen .40 1.00

2002-03 Stars Postcards

COMPLETE SET (24) 10.00 20.00
1 Scott Pellerin .20 .50
2 Sami Helenius .20 .50
3 John Erskine .40 1.00
4 Stephane Robidas .20 .50
5 Jere Lehtinen .60 1.50
6 Sergei Zubov .20 .50
7 Kirk Muller .20 .50
8 Brenden Morrow .40 1.00
9 Mike Modano 1.25 3.00
10 Richard Matvichuk .20 .50
11 Manny Malhotra .20 .50
12 Derian Hatcher .20 .50
13 Scott Young .20 .50
14 Niko Kapanen .40 1.00
15 Bill Guerin .60 1.50
16 Aaron Downey .75 2.00
17 Rob Dimaio .20 .50
18 Pierre Turgeon .30 .75
19 Marty Turco 1.25 3.00
20 Ron Tugnutt .40 1.00
21 Darryl Sydor .20 .50
22 Ulf Dahlen .20 .50
23 Philippe Boucher .20 .50
24 Jason Arnott .30 .75

2003-04 Stars Postcards

COMPLETE SET (31) 10.00 20.00
1 Jason Arnott .20 .50
2 Stu Barnes .20 .50
3 Philippe Boucher .20 .50
4 Trevor Daley .20 .50
5 Rob DiMaio .20 .50
6 Aaron Downey .40 1.00
7 John Erskine .20 .50
8 Steve Gainey .20 .50
9 Bill Guerin .40 1.00
10 Niko Kapanen .30 .75
11 Jon Klemm .20 .50
12 Jere Lehtinen .40 1.00
13 Jeff MacMillan .20 .50
14 Richard Matvichuk .20 .50
15 Antti Miettinen .20 .50
16 Mike Modano .75 2.00
17 Gavin Morgan .20 .50
18 Brenden Morrow .60 1.50
19 Teppo Numminen .20 .50
20 David Oliver .20 .50
21 Steve Ott .75 2.00
22 Blake Sloan .20 .50
23 Mike Smith 1.25 3.00
24 Don Sweeney .20 .50
25 Mathias Tjarnqvist .20 .50
26 Ron Tugnutt .30 .75
27 Marty Turco .75 2.00
28 Pierre Turgeon .20 .50
29 Rob Valicevic .20 .50
30 Scott Young .20 .50
31 Sergei Zubov .20 .50

2006-07 Stars Team Postcards

COMPLETE SET (28) 15.00 30.00
1 Krys Barch .75 2.00
2 Matthew Barnaby .75 2.00
3 Stu Barnes .40 1.00
4 Philippe Boucher .40 1.00
5 Trevor Daley .40 1.00
6 Loui Eriksson .75 2.00
7 Niklas Hagman .40 1.00
8 Jeff Halpern .40 1.00
9 Jussi Jokinen .40 1.00
10 Jon Klemm .40 1.00
11 Jere Lehtinen .75 2.00
12 Eric Lindros .75 2.00
13 Joel Lundqvist .75 2.00
14 Antti Miettinen .40 1.00
15 Mike Modano 1.25 3.00
16 Brenden Morrow .75 2.00
17 Steve Ott .75 2.00
18 Mike Ribeiro .40 1.00
19 Stephane Robidas .40 1.00
20 Mike Smith .75 2.00
21 Patrik Stefan .40 1.00
22 Darryl Sydor .40 1.00
23 Marty Turco .75 2.00
24 Sergei Zubov .40 1.00
25 Dave Tippett CO .10 .25
26 Celena Rae .40 1.00
27 Brett Hull 1.25 3.00
28 Craig Ludwig .40 1.00

2007-08 Stars Team Issue

COMPLETE SET (25) 15.00 30.00
1 Krys Barch .75 2.00
2 Stu Barnes .40 1.00
3 Philippe Boucher .40 1.00
4 Trevor Daley .40 1.00
5 Loui Eriksson .75 2.00
6 Todd Fedoruk .75 2.00
7 Niklas Grossman .40 1.00
8 Niklas Hagman .40 1.00
9 Jeff Halpern .40 1.00
10 Jussi Jokinen .40 1.00
11 Jere Lehtinen .75 2.00
12 Joel Lundqvist .40 1.00
13 Antti Miettinen .40 1.00
14 Mike Modano 1.25 3.00
15 Brenden Morrow 1.25 3.00
16 Matt Niskanen .75 2.00
17 Mattias Norstrom .40 1.00
18 Steve Ott .75 2.00
19 Mike Ribeiro .40 1.00
20 Stephane Robidas .40 1.00
21 Mike Smith .75 2.00
22 Marty Turco .75 2.00
23 Brad Winchester .40 1.00
24 Sergei Zubov .40 1.00
25 Dave Tippett HC .40 1.00

1975-76 Stingers Kahn's

COMPLETE SET (14) 62.50 125.00
1 Serge Aubry 5.00 10.00
2 Bryan Campbell 5.00 10.00
3 Rick Dudley 7.50 15.00
4 Pierre Guite 5.00 10.00
5 John Hughes 5.00 10.00
6 Claude Larose 6.00 12.00
7 Jacques Locas UER 5.00 10.00
8 Bernie MacNeil 5.00 10.00
9 Mike Pelyk 5.00 10.00
10 Ron Plumb 5.00 10.00
11 Dave Smedsmo 5.00 10.00
12 Dennis Sobchuk 5.00 10.00
13 Gene Sobchuk 5.00 10.00
14 Gary Veneruzzo 5.00 10.00

1976-77 Stingers Kahn's

COMPLETE SET (6) 62.50 125.00
1 Rick Dudley 15.00 30.00
2 Dave Inkpen 12.50 25.00
3 John Hughes 10.00 20.00
4 Claude Larose 12.50 25.00
5 Jacques Locas 10.00 20.00
6 Ron Plumb 10.00 20.00
7 Dennis Sobchuk 10.00 20.00

1997-98 Studio

1 Wayne Gretzky 1.00 2.50
2 Dominik Hasek .25 .60
3 Eric Lindros .25 .60
4 Paul Kariya .15 .40
5 Jaromir Jagr .50 1.25
6 Brendan Shanahan .15 .40
7 Patrick Roy .40 1.00
8 Keith Tkachuk .15 .40
9 Mark Messier .30 .75
10 Steve Yzerman .40 1.00
11 Brett Hull .30 .75
12 Jarome Iginla .20 .50
13 Mike Modano .25 .60
14 Pavel Bure .15 .40
15 Peter Forsberg .30 .75
16 Ryan Smyth .12 .30
17 John Vanbiesbrouck .15 .40
18 Teemu Selanne .30 .75
19 Saku Koivu .15 .40
20 Martin Brodeur .40 1.00
21 Sergei Fedorov .25 .60
22 John LeClair .15 .40
23 Joe Sakic .30 .75
24 Jose Theodore .15 .40
25 Marc Denis .15 .40
26 Dainius Zubrus .12 .30
27 Bryan Berard .10 .25
28 Ray Bourque .25 .60
29 Curtis Joseph .20 .50
30 Chris Chelios .15 .40
31 Alexei Yashin .12 .30
32 Adam Oates .15 .40
33 Anson Carter .10 .25
34 Jim Campbell .10 .25
35 Jason Arnott .12 .30
36 Derek Plante .12 .30
37 Guy Hebert .12 .30
38 Oleg Tverdovsky .12 .30
39 Ed Jovanovski .10 .25
40 Jeremy Roenick .25 .60
41 Scott Mellanby .12 .30
42 Keith Primeau .12 .30
43 Ron Hextall .15 .40
44 Daren Puppa .12 .30
45 Jim Carey .10 .25
46 Zigmund Palffy .15 .40
47 Jaroslav Svejkovsky .12 .30
48 Daymond Langkow .10 .25
49 Mikael Renberg .12 .30
50 Pat LaFontaine .15 .40
51 Mike Grier .12 .30
52 Stephane Fiset .12 .30
53 Luc Robitaille .15 .40
54 Joe Thornton .25 .60
55 Joe Nieuwendyk .12 .30
56 Mike Dunham .12 .30
57 Mark Recchi .20 .50
58 Ed Belfour .15 .40
59 Mike Richter .15 .40
60 Peter Bondra .15 .40
61 Trevor Kidd .10 .25
62 Sean Burke .10 .25
63 Nikolai Khabibulin .15 .40
64 Pierre Turgeon .12 .30
65 Dino Ciccarelli .15 .40
66 Felix Potvin .25 .60
67 Mats Sundin .15 .40
68 Joe Juneau .10 .25
69 Mike Vernon .12 .30
70 Adam Deadmarsh .10 .25
71 Damian Rhodes .12 .30
72 Mike Peca .12 .30
73 Jean-Sebastien Giguere .15 .40
74 Ron Francis .20 .50
75 Roman Hamrlik .10 .25
76 Vincent Damphousse .12 .30
77 Jocelyn Thibault .12 .30
78 Claude Lemieux .12 .30
79 Steve Shields RC .15 .40
80 Dimitri Khristich .12 .30
81 Theo Fleury .20 .50
82 Sandis Ozolinsh .10 .25
83 Ethan Moreau .10 .25
84 Geoff Sanderson .12 .30
85 Paul Coffey .15 .40
86 Brian Leetch .12 .30
87 Chris Osgood .15 .40
88 Kirk McLean .12 .30
89 Mike Gartner .20 .50
90 Chris Gratton .10 .25
91 Eric Fichaud .12 .30
92 Alexandre Daigle .10 .25
93 Doug Gilmour .20 .50
94 Daniel Alfredsson .15 .40
95 Doug Weight .15 .40
96 Derian Hatcher .12 .30
97 Wade Redden .10 .25
98 Jeff Friesen .12 .30
99 Tony Amonte .12 .30
100 Janne Niinimaa .12 .30
101 Trevor Linden .15 .40
102 Grant Fuhr .25 .60
103 Chris Phillips .12 .30
104 Sergei Berezin .12 .30
105 Brendan Shanahan CL .15 .40
106 Steve Yzerman CL .40 1.00
107 Teemu Selanne CL .30 .75
108 Eric Lindros CL .25 .60
109 Wayne Gretzky CL 1.00 2.50
110 Patrick Roy CL .40 1.00
P3 Eric Lindros PROMO .25 .60

1997-98 Studio Press Proofs Silver

*PP SILVER: 10X TO 25X BASIC CARDS

1997-98 Studio Press Proofs Gold

*PP GOLD: 15X TO 40X BASIC CARDS

1997-98 Studio Hard Hats

COMPLETE SET (24) 75.00 150.00
1 Wayne Gretzky 12.00 30.00
2 Eric Lindros 3.00 8.00
3 Paul Kariya 3.00 8.00
4 Bryan Berard .75 2.00
5 Dainius Zubrus .75 2.00
6 Daymond Langkow .75 2.00
7 Keith Tkachuk 1.50 4.00
8 Ryan Smyth 1.50 4.00
9 Brendan Shanahan 3.00 8.00
10 Steve Yzerman 12.00 30.00
11 Teemu Selanne 3.00 8.00
12 Jarome Iginla 4.00 10.00
13 Zigmund Palffy 1.50 4.00
14 Sergei Berezin .75 2.00
15 Saku Koivu 3.00 8.00
16 Peter Forsberg 8.00 20.00
17 Joe Sakic 6.00 15.00
18 Pavel Bure 3.00 8.00
19 Jaromir Jagr 5.00 12.00
20 Brett Hull 4.00 10.00
21 Sergei Fedorov 4.00 10.00
22 Mike Grier .75 2.00
23 Ethan Moreau .75 2.00
24 Mats Sundin 3.00 8.00

1997-98 Studio Portraits 8x10

COMPLETE SET (36) 30.00 60.00
1 Wayne Gretzky 2.00 5.00
2 Dominik Hasek .75 2.00
3 Eric Lindros .50 1.25
4 Paul Kariya .30 .75
5 Jaromir Jagr .50 1.25
6 Brendan Shanahan .30 .75
7 Patrick Roy 1.50 4.00
8 Keith Tkachuk .30 .75
9 Mark Messier .40 1.00
10 Steve Yzerman 1.25 3.00
11 Brett Hull .50 1.25
12 Jarome Iginla .50 1.25
13 Mike Modano .50 1.25
14 Pavel Bure .40 1.00
15 Peter Forsberg .50 1.25
16 Ryan Smyth .25 .60
17 John Vanbiesbrouck .30 .75
18 Teemu Selanne .40 1.00
19 Saku Koivu .30 .75
20 Martin Brodeur .50 1.25
21 Sergei Fedorov .50 1.25
22 Joe Thornton .75 2.00
23 Joe Sakic .75 2.00
24 Bryan Berard .30 .75
25 John LeClair .40 1.00
26 Marc Denis .25 .60
27 Dainius Zubrus .30 .75
28 Chris Chelios .40 1.00
29 Jason Arnott .30 .75
30 Jeremy Roenick .50 1.25
31 Zigmund Palffy .25 .60
32 Jaroslav Svejkovsky .25 .60
33 Mike Richter .40 1.00
34 Felix Potvin .50 1.25
35 Brian Leetch .40 1.00
36 Chris Osgood .40 1.00
NNOA Martin Brodeur AU/700 40.00 100.00
NNOB Jarome Iginla AU/1000 15.00 40.00
NNOC Ryan Smyth AU/1000 6.00 15.00

1997-98 Studio Silhouettes

COMPLETE SET (24) 100.00 200.00
*8X10 JUMBO/3000: .3X TO .8X INSERT/1500
1 Wayne Gretzky 10.00 25.00
2 Eric Lindros 3.00 8.00
3 Patrick Roy 8.00 20.00
4 Martin Brodeur 6.00 15.00
5 Paul Kariya 2.50 6.00
6 Mark Messier 3.00 8.00
7 Dominik Hasek 5.00 12.00
8 Brett Hull 4.00 10.00
9 Pavel Bure 3.00 8.00
10 Steve Yzerman 6.00 15.00
11 Brendan Shanahan 3.00 8.00
12 Joe Sakic 6.00 15.00
13 Peter Forsberg 3.00 8.00
14 Sergei Fedorov 4.00 10.00
15 John LeClair 2.50 6.00
16 John Vanbiesbrouck 2.50 6.00
17 Teemu Selanne 3.00 8.00
18 Keith Tkachuk 2.50 6.00
19 Mike Modano 4.00 10.00
20 Felix Potvin 5.00 12.00
21 Ryan Smyth 2.00 5.00
22 Jaromir Jagr 5.00 12.00
23 Brian Leetch 2.50 6.00
24 Jarome Iginla 5.00 12.00

1995-96 Summit

1 Mark Messier .20 .50
2 Paul Kariya .10 .25
3 Alexei Zhamnov .10 .25
4 Adam Oates .10 .25
5 Dale Hunter .07 .20
6 Valeri Kamensky .07 .20
7 Pavel Bure .10 .25
8 Theo Fleury .12 .30
9 Mats Sundin .10 .25
10 Joe Murphy .05 .15
11 Brian Bellows .07 .20
12 Owen Nolan .10 .25
13 Brett Hull .20 .50
14 Mike Modano .15 .40
15 Ulf Dahlen .05 .15
16 Paul Coffey .10 .25
17 Jaromir Jagr .30 .75
18 Jason Arnott .07 .20
19 Eric Lindros .15 .40
20 Jesse Belanger .05 .15
21 Alexandre Daigle .05 .15
22 Darren Turcotte .05 .15
23 Brian Leetch .07 .20
24 Wayne Gretzky .60 1.50
25 Mathieu Schneider .05 .15
26 Mark Recchi .12 .30
27 Martin Brodeur .25 .60
28 Igor Korolev .05 .15
29 Jocelyn Thibault .07 .20
30 Chris Pronger .10 .25
31 Sergei Fedorov .15 .40
32 Jari Kurri .10 .25
33 Ray Bourque .15 .40
34 Pat LaFontaine .10 .25
35 Don Beaupre .07 .20
36 Dave Andreychuk .10 .25
37 Oleg Tverdovsky .10 .25
38 Geoff Sanderson .05 .15
39 Chris Chelios .10 .25
40 Phil Housley .07 .20
41 Kevin Hatcher .07 .20
42 Ron Francis .12 .30
43 Pierre Turgeon .07 .20
44 Mikael Renberg .07 .20
45 Chris Gratton .05 .15
46 Tommy Soderstrom .07 .20
47 Stu Barnes .05 .15
48 Alexander Mogilny .07 .20
49 Craig Janney .05 .15
50 Scott Niedermayer .10 .25
51 Jim Carey .07 .20
52 Stephane Richer .07 .20
53 Dave Gagner .05 .15
54 Teemu Selanne .20 .50
55 Kelly Hrudey .07 .20
56 Roman Hamrlik .05 .15
57 Scott Mellanby .07 .20
58 Guy Hebert .07 .20
59 Gary Suter .05 .15
60 Travis Green .07 .20
61 Joe Sakic .20 .50
62 Doug Gilmour .12 .30
63 Peter Bondra .10 .25
64 Vincent Damphousse .07 .20
65 Dino Ciccarelli .07 .20
66 Adam Graves .07 .20
67 Kevin Stevens .07 .20
68 Jeff Friesen .05 .15
69 Kirk McLean .07 .20
70 Brad May .05 .15
71 Bill Ranford .07 .20
72 Derian Hatcher .07 .20
73 Glen Wesley .05 .15
74 Sergei Zubov .07 .20
75 John LeClair .10 .25
76 Igor Larionov .05 .15
77 Ray Sheppard .07 .20
78 Ulf Samuelsson .05 .15
79 Rod Brind'Amour .10 .25
80 Felix Potvin .15 .40
81 Cam Neely .10 .25
82 Jeremy Roenick .15 .40
83 Slava Kozlov .07 .20
84 Arturs Irbe .07 .20
85 Daren Puppa .07 .20
86 Rob Blake .07 .20
87 Steve Heinze .05 .15
88 Tom Barrasso .07 .20
89 Luc Robitaille .10 .25
90 Al MacInnis .12 .30
91 Petr Nedved .07 .20
92 Joe Mullen .07 .20
93 Mark Tinordi .05 .15
94 Tomas Sandstrom .07 .20
95 Dale Hawerchuk .12 .30
96 Andy Moog .10 .25
97 Alexei Kovalev .07 .20
98 David Oliver .05 .15
99 Patrick Poulin .05 .15
100 Tony Granato .05 .15
101 Alexei Yashin .07 .20
102 Trevor Linden .10 .25
103 Rick Tocchet .07 .20
104 Brett Lindros .05 .15
105 Rob Niedermayer .07 .20
106 John MacLean .07 .20
107 Pat Verbeek .07 .20
108 Ray Ferraro .05 .15
109 Mike Ricci .05 .15
110 Doug Weight .10 .25
111 Bill Guerin .10 .25
112 Ken Wregget .07 .20
113 Teppo Numminen .05 .15
114 Mike Vernon .07 .20
115 Mike Richter .10 .25
116 Dan Quinn .07 .20
117 Peter Forsberg .20 .50
118 Mario Lemieux .40 1.00
119 Geoff Courtnall .05 .15
120 Ed Belfour .07 .20
121 Kirk Muller .07 .20
122 Chris Osgood .10 .25
123 Radek Bonk .05 .15
124 Brendan Shanahan .10 .25
125 Sean Burke .05 .15
126 Larry Murphy .07 .20
127 Blaine Lacher .07 .20
128 Russ Courtnall .05 .15
129 Claude Lemieux .10 .25
130 John Vanbiesbrouck .10 .25
131 Wendel Clark .15 .40
132 Nelson Emerson .05 .15
133 Ron Hextall .10 .25
134 Scott Stevens .10 .25
135 Bernie Nicholls .07 .20
136 Brian Skrudland .05 .15
137 Sandis Ozolinsh .05 .15
138 Trevor Kidd .07 .20
139 Joe Juneau .05 .15
140 Keith Primeau .07 .20
141 Petr Klima .05 .15
142 Viktor Kozlov .07 .20
143 Mike Gartner .12 .30
144 Zigmund Palffy .10 .25
145 Steve Duchesne .05 .15
146 Brian Bradley .07 .20
147 Michal Pivonka .05 .15
148 Todd Harvey .05 .15
149 Patrick Roy .25 .60
150 Gary Roberts .05 .15
151 Shayne Corson .07 .20
152 Keith Tkachuk .10 .25
153 Dimitri Khristich .05 .15
154 Steve Yzerman .25 .60
155 Shawn McEachern .05 .15
156 Bryan Smolinski .05 .15
157 Vladimir Malakhov .05 .15
158 Andrew Cassels .05 .15
159 Dominik Hasek .15 .40
160 Stephane Fiset .07 .20
161 Steve Thomas .07 .20
162 Joe Nieuwendyk .07 .20
163 Sergio Momesso .05 .15
164 Jyrki Lumme .05 .15
165 Tony Amonte .07 .20
166 Yanic Perreault .05 .15
167 Brian Savage .05 .15
168 Brian Holzinger RC .20 .50
169 Radek Dvorak RC .12 .30
170 Jamie Langenbrunner .05 .15
171 Ed Jovanovski .10 .25
172 Bryan McCabe .10 .25
173 Jere Lehtinen .07 .20
174 Antti Tormanen .05 .15
175 Aki Berg RC .10 .25
176 Ryan Smyth .07 .20
177 Shean Donovan .05 .15
178 Darby Hendrickson .05 .15
179 Chad Kilger RC .10 .25
180 Vitali Yachmenev .10 .25
181 Deron Quint .07 .20
182 Daniel Alfredsson RC .50 1.25
183 Jeff O'Neill .10 .25
184 Corey Hirsch .07 .20
185 Sandy Moger RC .05 .15
186 Saku Koivu .10 .25
187 Niklas Sundstrom .10 .25
188 Shane Doan RC .30 .75
189 Brendan Witt .10 .25
190 Eric Daze .20 .50
191 Marty Murray .10 .25
192 Byron Dafoe .07 .20
193 Todd Bertuzzi RC .12 .30
194 Kyle McLaren RC .05 .15
195 Marcus Ragnarsson RC .12 .30
196 Robert Svehla RC .05 .15
197 Valeri Bure .05 .15
198 Paul Coffey .10 .25
199 Checklist (1-198) .05 .15
200 Checklist (inserts) .05 .15

1995-96 Summit Artist's Proofs

*VETS: 20X TO 50X BASIC CARDS
*ROOKIES: 12X TO 30X

1995-96 Summit Ice

*VETS: 5X TO 12X BASIC CARDS
*ROOKIES: 3X TO 8X

1995-96 Summit GM's Choice

1 Patrick Roy 5.00 12.00
2 Martin Brodeur 5.00 12.00
3 Chris Chelios 2.00 5.00
4 Brian Leetch 1.50 4.00
5 Eric Lindros 3.00 8.00
6 Keith Tkachuk 2.00 5.00
7 Pavel Bure 2.00 5.00
8 Scott Stevens 2.00 5.00
9 Paul Coffey 2.00 5.00
10 Mario Lemieux 8.00 20.00
11 Jaromir Jagr 6.00 15.00
12 Cam Neely 2.00 5.00
13 Ray Bourque 3.00 8.00
14 Al MacInnis 2.50 6.00
15 Sergei Fedorov 3.00 8.00
16 Mark Messier 4.00 10.00
17 Brett Hull 4.00 10.00
18 Wayne Gretzky 12.00 30.00
19 Paul Kariya 2.00 5.00
20 Brendan Shanahan 2.00 5.00
21 Mike McPhee 2.00 5.00

1995-96 Summit In The Crease

COMPLETE SET (15) 25.00 60.00
1 Martin Brodeur 6.00 15.00
2 Dominik Hasek 4.00 10.00
3 Patrick Roy 10.00 25.00
4 Ed Belfour 2.00 5.00
5 Felix Potvin 2.00 5.00
6 Jim Carey 1.25 3.00
7 Jocelyn Thibault 1.25 3.00
8 Stephane Fiset 1.25 3.00
9 Chris Osgood 2.00 5.00
10 Ron Hextall 2.00 5.00
11 Mike Richter 2.00 5.00
12 Andy Moog 1.25 3.00
13 Sean Burke 1.25 3.00
14 Kirk McLean 1.25 3.00
15 John Vanbiesbrouck 2.00 5.00

1995-96 Summit Mad Hatters

COMPLETE SET (15) 15.00 30.00
1 Lindros
Nolan
Nicholls 1.50 4.00
2 Brett Hull 2.00 5.00
3 John LeClair .75 2.00
4 Cam Neely 1.50 4.00
5 Alexei Zhamnov .60 1.50
6 Jason Arnott .60 1.50
7 Pavel Bure 1.50 4.00
8 Wendel Clark .75 2.00
9 Sergei Fedorov 2.00 5.00
10 Jaromir Jagr 2.50 6.00
11 Peter Bondra .75 2.00
12 Alexei Yashin .60 1.50
13 Joe Nieuwendyk .75 2.00
14 Luc Robitaille .75 2.00
15 Todd Harvey .60 1.50

1995-96 Summit Promos

8 Wendel Clark .75 2.00
16 Paul Coffey .75 2.00
17 Jaromir Jagr 1.00 2.50
33 Ray Bourque 1.00 2.50
43 Pierre Turgeon .75 2.00
61 Joe Sakic .75 2.00
75 John LeClair .75 2.00
100 Brendan Shanahan .75 2.00

1996-97 Summit

*AP: 6X TO 15X BASIC CARDS
1 Joe Sakic .20 .50
2 Dominik Hasek .15 .40
3 Paul Coffey .10 .25
4 Todd Gill .07 .20
5 Pat Verbeek .05 .15
6 John LeClair .10 .25
7 Joe Juneau .05 .15
8 Scott Mellanby .07 .20
9 Scott Stevens .10 .25
10 Ron Francis .12 .30
11 Larry Murphy .07 .20
12 Sandis Ozolinsh .05 .15
13 Luc Robitaille .10 .25
14 Grant Fuhr .15 .40
15 Adam Oates .10 .25
16 Keith Primeau .07 .20
17 Mark Recchi .12 .30
18 Brian Bradley .05 .15
19 Zdeno Ciger .05 .15
20 Zigmund Palffy .10 .25
21 Damian Rhodes .07 .20
22 Russ Courtnall .05 .15
23 Mike Modano .15 .40
24 Geoff Sanderson .07 .20
25 Michal Pivonka .05 .15
26 Randy Burridge .05 .15
27 Dimitri Khristich .05 .15
28 Mike Gartner .12 .30
29 Cam Neely .10 .25
30 Mathieu Schneider .05 .15
31 Steve Thomas .05 .15
32 Mario Lemieux .40 1.00
33 Darryl Sydor .05 .15
34 Alexei Yashin .07 .20
35 Brett Hull .20 .50
36 Trevor Kidd .05 .15
37 Alexei Zhamnov .07 .20
38 Uwe Krupp .05 .15
39 Brian Skrudland .05 .15
40 Igor Larionov .10 .25
41 Nikolai Khabibulin .07 .20
42 Pavel Bure .10 .25
43 Chris Chelios .10 .25
44 Andrew Cassels .05 .15
45 Owen Nolan .10 .25
46 Todd Harvey .05 .15
47 Jari Kurri .10 .25
48 Olaf Kolzig .10 .25
49 Greg Johnson .05 .15
50 Dominic Roussel .05 .15
51 Mats Sundin .10 .25
52 Robert Svehla .05 .15
53 Sandy Moger .05 .15
54 Darren Turcotte .05 .15
55 Teppo Numminen .05 .15
56 Benoit Hogue .05 .15
57 Scott Niedermayer .10 .25
58 Alexander Selivanov .05 .15
59 Valeri Kamensky .07 .20
60 Ken Wregget .07 .20
61 Travis Green .07 .20
62 Peter Bondra .10 .25
63 Vladimir Konstantinov .07 .20
64 Craig Janney .07 .20
65 Joe Nieuwendyk .07 .20
66 John Vanbiesbrouck .10 .25
67 Wayne Gretzky .60 1.50
68 Kirk McLean .07 .20
69 Alexei Zhitnik .05 .15
70 Mike Ricci .05 .15
71 Jeff Beukeboom .05 .15
72 Felix Potvin .15 .40
73 Mikael Renberg .07 .20
74 Jamie Baker .05 .15
75 Guy Hebert .07 .20
76 Steve Yzerman .25 .60
77 Daren Puppa .07 .20
78 Scott Young .05 .15
79 Martin Gelinas .05 .15
80 Dave Gagner .10 .25
81 Tomas Sandstrom .05 .15
82 Alexei Kovalev .07 .20
83 Ray Whitney .05 .15
84 Vyacheslav Kozlov .05 .15
85 Jaromir Jagr .30 .75
86 Joe Murphy .05 .15
87 Patrick Roy .25 .60
88 Ray Sheppard .07 .20
89 Chris Terreri .07 .20
90 Pierre Turgeon .07 .20
91 Theo Fleury .20 .50
92 Doug Weight .10 .25
93 Tom Barrasso .07 .20
94 Jim Carey .10 .25
95 Greg Adams .05 .15
96 Brian Leetch .07 .20
97 Ed Belfour .10 .25
98 Stephane Fiset .07 .20
99 Stephane Richer .07 .20
100 Ron Hextall .10 .25
101 Mike Vernon .07 .20
102 Jocelyn Thibault .07 .20
103 Jason Arnott .07 .20
104 Keith Tkachuk .10 .25
105 Sergei Fedorov .15 .40
106 Alexandre Daigle .05 .15
107 Alexander Mogilny .07 .20
108 German Titov .05 .15
109 Sean Burke .05 .15
110 Arturs Irbe .07 .20
111 Mark Messier .20 .50
112 Nicklas Lidstrom .12 .30
113 Claude Lemieux .05 .15
114 Martin Brodeur .25 .60
115 Bernie Nicholls .07 .20
116 Paul Kariya .10 .25
117 Eric Lindros .15 .40
118 Doug Gilmour .12 .30
119 Sergei Zubov .07 .20
120 Adam Graves .05 .15
121 Phil Housley .07 .20
122 Bob Bassen .05 .15
123 Rod Brind'Amour .10 .25
124 Dave Andreychuk .10 .25
125 Corey Hirsch .07 .20
126 Kelly Hrudey .07 .20
127 Pat LaFontaine .10 .25
128 Slava Fetisov .05 .15
129 Oleg Tverdovsky .07 .20
130 Andy Moog .10 .25
131 Stu Barnes .05 .15
132 Roman Hamrlik .05 .15
133 Teemu Selanne .20 .50
134 Trevor Linden .10 .25
135 Chris Osgood .10 .25
136 Vincent Damphousse .07 .20
137 Shayne Corson .07 .20
138 Jeremy Roenick .15 .40
139 Brendan Shanahan .10 .25
140 Wendel Clark .15 .40
141 Ray Bourque .15 .40
142 Peter Forsberg .20 .50
143 John MacLean .07 .20
144 Jeff Friesen .05 .15
145 Mike Richter .10 .25
146 Dave Reid .05 .15
147 Rob Niedermayer .07 .20
148 Petr Nedved .07 .20
149 Sylvain Lefebvre .05 .15
150 Curtis Joseph .12 .30
151 Eric Daze .07 .20
152 Saku Koivu .10 .25
153 Jere Lehtinen .05 .15
154 Todd Bertuzzi .10 .25
155 Chad Kilger .05 .15
156 Stephane Yelle .05 .15
157 Bryan McCabe .05 .15
158 Aaron Gavey .05 .15
159 Kyle McLaren .05 .15
160 Valeri Bure .05 .15
161 Antti Tormanen .05 .15
162 Brendan Witt .05 .15
163 Ed Jovanovski .07 .20
164 Aki Berg .05 .15
165 Marcus Ragnarsson .05 .15
166 Miroslav Satan .05 .15
167 Daniel Alfredsson .10 .25
168 Jeff O'Neill .05 .15
169 Radek Dvorak .07 .20
170 Petr Sykora .05 .15
171 Vitali Yachmenev .05 .15
172 Niklas Andersson .05 .15
173 Nolan Baumgartner .05 .15
174 Brandon Convery .05 .15
175 Ralph Intranuovo .05 .15
176 Niklas Sundblad .05 .15
177 Patrick Labrecque .05 .15
178 Eric Fichaud .07 .20
179 Martin Biron RC .12 .30
180 Steve Sullivan RC .07 .20
181 Peter Ferraro .05 .15
182 Jose Theodore .12 .30
183 Kevin Hodson RC .10 .25
184 Ethan Moreau RC .10 .25
185 Curtis Brown .05 .15
186 Daymond Langkow .07 .20
187 Jan Caloun RC .10 .25
188 Landon Wilson .05 .15
189 Tommy Salo .07 .20
190 Anders Eriksson .05 .15
191 David Nemirovsky .05 .15
192 Jamie Langenbrunner .05 .15
193 Zdenek Nedved .05 .15
194 Todd Hlushko .05 .15
195 Alexei Yegorov RC .10 .25
196 Jamie Pushor .05 .15
197 Anders Myrvold .05 .15
198 Mark Messier CL .20 .50
199 Brett Hull CL .20 .50
200 Pavel Bure CL .10 .25

1996-97 Summit Ice

*VETS: 6X TO 15X BASIC CARDS
*ROOKIES: 2.5X TO 6X

1996-97 Summit Metal

COMPLETE SET (200) 20.00 50.00
*METAL: 1.5X TO 4X BASIC CARDS

1996-97 Summit Premium Stock

COMPLETE SET (200) 20.00 50.00
*VETS: 1.5X TO 4X BASIC CARDS
*ROOKIES: .6X TO 1.5X BASIC CARDS

1996-97 Summit High Voltage

COMPLETE SET (16) 60.00 150.00
*MIRAGE: .8X TO 2X BASIC INSERTS
1 Mark Messier 4.00 10.00
2 Joe Sakic 8.00 20.00
3 Paul Kariya 4.00 10.00
4 Daniel Alfredsson 2.00 5.00
5 Wayne Gretzky 12.00 30.00
6 Peter Forsberg 6.00 15.00
7 Eric Daze 2.00 5.00
8 Mario Lemieux 8.00 20.00
9 Eric Lindros 4.00 10.00
10 Jeremy Roenick 4.00 10.00
11 Alexander Mogilny 2.00 5.00
12 Teemu Selanne 4.00 10.00
13 Sergei Fedorov 4.00 10.00
14 Saku Koivu 4.00 10.00
15 Jaromir Jagr 6.00 15.00
16 Brett Hull 4.00 10.00
P16 Eric Lindros PROMO 2.00 5.00

1996-97 Summit In The Crease

COMPLETE SET (16) 30.00 80.00
*PREM.STOCK: .8X TO 2X BASIC INSERTS
1 Patrick Roy 6.00 15.00
2 Mike Richter 2.50 6.00
3 Ed Belfour 2.50 6.00
4 Daren Puppa 1.50 4.00
5 Curtis Joseph 2.50 6.00

6 Jim Carey 1.50 4.00
7 Damian Rhodes 1.50 4.00
8 Martin Brodeur 6.00 15.00
9 Felix Potvin 3.00 8.00
10 John Vanbiesbrouck 2.00 5.00
11 Jocelyn Thibault 1.50 4.00
12 Nikolai Khabibulin 1.50 4.00
13 Chris Osgood 1.50 4.00
14 Dominik Hasek 4.00 10.00
15 Corey Hirsch 1.50 4.00
16 Ron Hextall 1.50 4.00

1996-97 Summit Untouchables

COMPLETE SET (18) 75.00 150.00
1 Mario Lemieux 10.00 25.00
2 Jaromir Jagr 4.00 10.00
3 Joe Sakic 8.00 20.00
4 Ron Francis 2.00 5.00
5 Peter Forsberg 4.00 10.00
6 Eric Lindros 5.00 12.00
7 Paul Kariya 3.00 8.00
8 Teemu Selanne 6.00 15.00
9 Alexander Mogilny 2.00 5.00
10 Sergei Fedorov 4.00 10.00
11 Doug Weight 2.00 5.00
12 Wayne Gretzky 25.00 60.00
13 Chris Osgood 2.00 5.00
14 Jim Carey 2.00 5.00
15 Patrick Roy 10.00 25.00
16 Martin Brodeur 8.00 20.00
17 Felix Potvin 6.00 15.00
18 Ron Hextall 3.00 8.00

1980 Superstar Matchbook

COMPLETE SET 30.00 60.00
3 Ray Bourque 4.00 8.00
5 Gordie Howe 3.00 6.00
7 Guy LaFleur 2.00 4.00
9 Bobby Orr 5.00 10.00

1910-11 Sweet Caporal Postcards

COMPLETE SET (45) 9000.00 18000.00
1 Paddy Moran 250.00 500.00
2 Joe Hall 175.00 350.00
3 Barney Holden 100.00 200.00
4 Joe Malone 500.00 1000.00
5 Ed Oatman 100.00 200.00
6 Tom Dunderdale 175.00 350.00
7 Ken Mallen 100.00 200.00
8 Jack MacDonald 100.00 200.00
9 Fred Lake 100.00 200.00
10 Albert Kerr 100.00 200.00
11 Marty Walsh 175.00 350.00
12 Hamby Shore 100.00 200.00
13 Alex Currie 100.00 200.00
14 Bruce Ridpath 100.00 200.00
15 Bruce Stuart 175.00 350.00
16 Percy Lesueur 175.00 350.00
17 Jack Darragh 175.00 350.00
18 Steve Vair 100.00 200.00
19 Don Smith 100.00 200.00
20 Cyclone Taylor 600.00 1200.00
21 Bert Lindsay 125.00 250.00
22 H.L. Gilmour 175.00 350.00
23 Bobby Rowe 100.00 200.00
24 Sprague Cleghorn 300.00 600.00
25 Odie Cleghorn 125.00 250.00
26 Skein Ronan 100.00 200.00
27 Walter Smaill 125.00 250.00
28 Ernest Johnson 200.00 400.00
29 Jack Marshall 175.00 350.00
30 Harry Hyland 175.00 350.00
31 Art Ross 600.00 1200.00
32 Riley Hern 175.00 350.00
33 Gordon Roberts 175.00 350.00
34 Frank Glass 100.00 200.00
35 Ernest Russell 200.00 400.00
36 James Gardner 175.00 350.00
37 Art Bernier 100.00 200.00
38 Georges Vezina 2000.00 4000.00
39 Henri Dallaire 100.00 200.00
40 R.(Rocket) Power 100.00 200.00
41 Didier Pitre 175.00 350.00
42 Newsy Lalonde 600.00 1200.00
43 Eugene Payan 100.00 200.00
44 George Poulin 100.00 200.00
45 Jack Laviolette 200.00 400.00

1934-35 Sweet Caporal

COMPLETE SET (48) 2500.00 5000.00
1 Gerald Carson MC 25.00 50.00
2 Nels Crutchfield MC 25.00 50.00
3 Wilfrid Cude MC 30.00 60.00
4 Roger Jenkins MC 25.00 50.00
5 Aurel Joliat MC 175.00 350.00
6 Joe Lamb MC 25.00 50.00
7 Wildor Larochelle MC 25.00 50.00
8 Pete Lepine MC 25.00 50.00
9 Georges Mantha MC 25.00 50.00
10 Sylvio Mantha MC 50.00 100.00
11 Jack McGill MC 25.00 50.00
12 Armand Mondou MC 25.00 50.00
13 Paul Marcel Raymond MC 25.00 50.00
14 Jack Riley MC 25.00 50.00
15 Russ Blinco MM 25.00 50.00
16 Herb Cain MM 40.00 80.00
17 Lionel Conacher MM 125.00 250.00
18 Alex Connell MM 62.50 125.00
19 Stewart Evans MM 25.00 50.00
20 Norman Gainor MM 25.00 50.00
21 Paul Haynes MM 25.00 50.00
22 Gus Marker MM 25.00 50.00
23 Baldy Northcott MM 30.00 60.00
24 Earl Robinson MM 25.00 50.00
25 Hooley Smith MM 50.00 100.00
26 Dave Trottier MM 25.00 50.00
27 Jimmy Ward MM 25.00 50.00
28 Cy Wentworth MM 30.00 60.00
29 Eddie Shore BB 250.00 500.00
30 Babe Siebert BB 62.50 125.00
31 Nels Stewart BB 75.00 150.00
32 Tiny Thompson BB 75.00 150.00
33 Lorne Chabot CBH 50.00 100.00
34 Mush March CBH 25.00 50.00
35 Howie Morenz CBH 400.00 800.00
36 Larry Aurie DRW 25.00 50.00
37 Ebbie Goodfellow DRW 50.00 100.00
38 Herbie Lewis DRW 25.00 50.00
39 Ralph Weiland DRW 50.00 100.00
40 Bill Cook NYR 50.00 100.00
41 Bun Cook NYR 50.00 100.00
42 Ivan(Ching) Johnson NYR 67.50 135.00
43 Dave Kerr NYR 40.00 80.00
44 King Clancy 200.00 400.00
45 Charlie Conacher TML 200.00 400.00
46 Red Horner TML 62.50 125.00
47 Busher Jackson TML 75.00 150.00
48 Joe Primeau TML 100.00 200.00

2006-07 Sweet Shot

1 Teemu Selanne 2.00 5.00
2 Chris Pronger 1.00 2.50
3 Jean-Sebastien Giguere 1.00 2.50
4 Ilya Kovalchuk 1.00 2.50
5 Marian Hossa 1.00 2.50
6 Kari Lehtonen .75 2.00
7 Patrice Bergeron 1.25 3.00
8 Zdeno Chara 1.00 2.50
9 Cam Neely 1.00 2.50
10 Bobby Orr 8.00 20.00
11 Phil Esposito 1.50 4.00
12 Ray Bourque 1.50 4.00
13 Ryan Miller 1.00 2.50
14 Maxim Afinogenov .60 1.50
15 Chris Drury .75 2.00
16 Gilbert Perreault 1.00 2.50
17 Alex Tanguay .60 1.50
18 Dion Phaneuf .75 2.00
19 Jarome Iginla 1.25 3.00
20 Miikka Kiprusoff 1.00 2.50
21 Cam Ward 1.00 2.50
22 Eric Staal 1.25 3.00
23 Nikolai Khabibulin 1.00 2.50
24 Martin Havlat .60 1.50
25 Bobby Hull 2.00 5.00
26 Tony Esposito 1.00 2.50
27 Joe Sakic 2.00 5.00
28 Jose Theodore 1.00 2.50
29 Milan Hejduk .75 2.00
30 Patrick Roy 2.50 6.00
31 Rick Nash 1.00 2.50
32 Sergei Fedorov 1.50 4.00
33 Pascal LeClaire .75 2.00
34 Mike Modano 1.50 4.00
35 Eric Lindros 1.50 4.00
36 Marty Turco 1.00 2.50
37 Henrik Zetterberg 1.25 3.00
38 Nicklas Lidstrom 1.00 2.50
39 Pavel Datsyuk 1.50 4.00
40 Dominik Hasek 1.50 4.00
41 Gordie Howe 3.00 8.00
42 Ted Lindsay 1.00 2.50
43 Ales Hemsky .75 2.00
44 Dwayne Roloson .75 2.00
45 Wayne Gretzky 8.00 20.00
46 Jari Kurri 1.00 2.50
47 Grant Fuhr 1.50 4.00
48 Ed Belfour 1.00 2.50
49 Olli Jokinen 1.00 2.50
50 Rob Blake 1.00 2.50
51 Alexander Frolov .60 1.50
52 Manny Fernandez .60 1.50
53 Pavol Demitra 1.25 3.00
54 Marian Gaborik 1.00 2.50
55 Saku Koivu 1.00 2.50
56 Cristobal Huet .75 2.00
57 Michael Ryder .60 1.50
58 Guy Lafleur 1.25 3.00
59 Larry Robinson 1.00 2.50
60 Paul Kariya 1.00 2.50
61 Tomas Vokoun .75 2.00
62 Brian Gionta .60 1.50
63 Martin Brodeur 2.50 6.00
64 Patrik Elias 1.00 2.50
65 Rick DiPietro .75 2.00
66 Alexei Yashin .75 2.00
67 Mike Bossy 1.00 2.50
68 Billy Smith 1.00 2.50
69 Denis Potvin 1.00 2.50
70 Jaromir Jagr 3.00 8.00
71 Henrik Lundqvist 2.50 6.00
72 Brendan Shanahan 1.00 2.50
73 Dany Heatley .75 2.00
74 Jason Spezza 1.00 2.50
75 Daniel Alfredsson 1.00 2.50
76 Peter Forsberg 2.00 5.00
77 Simon Gagne 1.00 2.50
78 Bobby Clarke 1.50 4.00
79 Jeremy Roenick 1.50 4.00
80 Shane Doan .75 2.00
81 Curtis Joseph 1.25 3.00
82 Sidney Crosby 6.00 15.00
83 Marc-Andre Fleury 2.00 5.00
84 Mario Lemieux 4.00 10.00
85 Peter Stastny .75 2.00
86 Joe Thornton 1.50 4.00
87 Patrick Marleau 1.00 2.50
88 Jonathan Cheechoo .75 2.00
89 Doug Weight 1.00 2.50
90 Brad Richards 1.00 2.50
91 Vincent Lecavalier 1.00 2.50
92 Martin St. Louis 1.00 2.50
93 Mats Sundin 1.00 2.50
94 Andrew Raycroft .75 2.00
95 Darcy Tucker .75 2.00
96 Johnny Bower 1.00 2.50
97 Darryl Sittler 1.25 3.00
98 Roberto Luongo 1.50 4.00
99 Markus Naslund 1.00 2.50
100 Alexander Ovechkin 4.00 10.00
101 Shane O'Brien JSY RC 2.50 6.00
102 Ryan Shannon JSY RC 2.50 6.00
103 David McKee JSY RC 2.50 6.00
104 Phil Kessel JSY RC 8.00 20.00
105 Yan Stastny JSY RC 2.50 6.00
106 Mark Stuart JSY RC 2.50 6.00
107 Matt Lashoff JSY RC 2.50 6.00
108 Clarke MacArthur JSY RC 3.00 8.00
109 Drew Stafford JSY RC 4.00 10.00
110 Masi Marjamaki JSY RC 2.50 6.00
111 Michael Funk JSY RC 2.50 6.00
112 Brandon Prust JSY RC 2.50 6.00
113 Dustin Boyd JSY RC 2.50 6.00
114 Dustin Byfuglien JSY RC 6.00 15.00
115 Dave Bolland JSY RC 4.00 10.00
116 Michael Blunden JSY RC 2.50 6.00
117 Paul Stastny JSY RC 6.00 15.00
118 Fredrik Norrena JSY RC 2.50 6.00
119 Niklas Grossman JSY RC 4.00 10.00
120 Loui Eriksson JSY RC 5.00 12.00
121 Tomas Kopecky JSY RC 3.00 8.00
122 Stefan Liv JSY RC 2.50 6.00
123 Patrick Thoresen JSY RC 2.50 6.00
124 Marc-Antoine Pouliot JSY RC 2.50 6.00
125 Ladislav Smid JSY RC 2.50 6.00
126 Janis Sprukts JSY RC 2.50 6.00
127 Jeff Deslauriers JSY RC 2.50 6.00
128 David Booth JSY RC 3.00 8.00
129 Konstantin Pushkarev JSY RC 3.00 8.00
130 Anze Kopitar JSY RC 12.00 30.00
131 Patrick O'Sullivan JSY RC 4.00 10.00
132 Benoit Pouliot JSY RC 3.00 8.00
133 Niklas Backstrom JSY RC 5.00 12.00
134 Guillaume Latendresse JSY RC 4.00 10.00
135 Shea Weber JSY RC 6.00 15.00
136 Alexander Radulov JSY RC 5.00 12.00
137 Travis Zajac JSY RC 5.00 12.00
138 Nigel Dawes JSY RC 2.50 6.00
139 Jarkko Immonen JSY RC 3.00 8.00
140 Josh Hennessy JSY RC 2.50 6.00
141 Jussi Timonen JSY RC 3.00 8.00
142 Ryan Potulny JSY RC 2.50 6.00
143 Keith Yandle JSY RC 6.00 15.00
144 Michel Ouellet JSY RC 3.00 8.00
145 Jordan Staal JSY RC 6.00 15.00
146 Evgeni Malkin JSY RC 20.00 40.00
147 Noah Welch JSY RC 2.50 6.00
148 Kristopher Letang JSY RC 10.00 25.00
149 Matt Carle JSY RC 2.50 6.00
150 M-E Vlasic JSY RC 4.00 10.00
151 Joe Pavelski JSY RC 12.00 30.00
152 Marek Schwarz JSY RC 4.00 10.00
153 Karri Ramo JSY RC 2.50 6.00
154 Blair Jones JSY RC 2.50 6.00
155 Ian White JSY RC 3.00 8.00
156 Jeremy Williams JSY RC 2.50 6.00
157 Luc Bourdon JSY RC 4.00 10.00
158 Jesse Schultz JSY RC 2.50 6.00
159 Alexander Edler JSY RC 4.00 10.00
160 Eric Fehr JSY RC 4.00 10.00

2006-07 Sweet Shot Endorsed Equipment

EEAR Andrew Raycroft 50.00 100.00
EEBR Bill Ranford 50.00 100.00
EEEB Ed Belfour 50.00 100.00
EEGC Gerry Cheevers 60.00 125.00
EEGF Grant Fuhr 50.00 100.00
EEJT Jose Theodore EXCH 30.00 80.00
EEMF Marc-Andre Fleury 100.00 150.00
EEMT Marty Turco 50.00 100.00
EEPR Patrick Roy 150.00 300.00
EETE Tony Esposito 60.00 125.00

2006-07 Sweet Shot Rookie Jerseys Autographs

101 Shane O'Brien 12.00 30.00
102 Ryan Shannon 12.00 30.00
103 David McKee 12.00 30.00
104 Phil Kessel 30.00 80.00
105 Yan Stastny 12.00 30.00
106 Mark Stuart 12.00 30.00
107 Matt Lashoff 12.00 30.00
108 Clarke MacArthur 15.00 40.00
109 Drew Stafford 40.00 100.00
110 Masi Marjamaki 12.00 30.00
111 Michael Funk 12.00 30.00
112 Brandon Prust 12.00 30.00
113 Dustin Boyd 12.00 30.00
114 Dustin Byfuglien 30.00 80.00
115 Dave Bolland 20.00 50.00
116 Michael Blunden 12.00 30.00
117 Paul Stastny 40.00 100.00
118 Fredrik Norrena 12.00 30.00
119 Niklas Grossman 20.00 50.00
120 Loui Eriksson 25.00 60.00
121 Tomas Kopecky 15.00 40.00
122 Stefan Liv 12.00 30.00
123 Patrick Thoresen 12.00 30.00
124 Marc-Antoine Pouliot 12.00 30.00
125 Ladislav Smid 12.00 30.00
126 Janis Sprukts 12.00 30.00
127 Jeff Deslauriers 12.00 30.00
128 David Booth 15.00 40.00
129 Konstantin Pushkarev 15.00 40.00
130 Anze Kopitar 50.00 120.00
131 Patrick O'Sullivan 20.00 50.00
132 Benoit Pouliot 15.00 40.00
133 Niklas Backstrom 25.00 60.00
134 Guillaume Latendresse 20.00 50.00
135 Shea Weber 30.00 80.00
136 Alexander Radulov 25.00 60.00
137 Travis Zajac 25.00 60.00
138 Nigel Dawes 12.00 30.00
139 Jarkko Immonen 15.00 40.00
140 Josh Hennessy 12.00 30.00
141 Jussi Timonen 15.00 40.00
142 Ryan Potulny 12.00 30.00
143 Keith Yandle 30.00 80.00
144 Michel Ouellet 15.00 40.00
145 Jordan Staal 40.00 100.00
146 Evgeni Malkin 75.00 200.00
147 Noah Welch 12.00 30.00
148 Kristopher Letang 50.00 125.00
149 Matt Carle 12.00 30.00
150 Marc-Edouard Vlasic 20.00 50.00
151 Joe Pavelski 60.00 150.00
152 Marek Schwarz 20.00 50.00
153 Karri Ramo 12.00 30.00
154 Blair Jones 12.00 30.00
155 Ian White 15.00 40.00
156 Jeremy Williams 12.00 30.00
157 Luc Bourdon 20.00 50.00
158 Jesse Schultz 12.00 30.00
159 Alexander Edler 20.00 50.00
160 Eric Fehr 20.00 50.00

2006-07 Sweet Shot Signature Shots/Saves

SSAF Alexander Frolov 5.00 12.00
SSAH Ales Hemsky 6.00 15.00
SSAK Anze Kopitar 25.00 60.00
SSAO Adam Oates 8.00 20.00
SSAR Andrew Raycroft 6.00 15.00
SSAT Alex Tanguay SP 5.00 12.00
SSBB Brad Boyes 5.00 12.00
SSBE Jean Beliveau SP 8.00 20.00
SSBF Bernie Federko 6.00 15.00
SSBG Brian Gionta 5.00 12.00
SSBH Bobby Hull SP 15.00 40.00
SSBI Martin Biron 6.00 15.00
SSBM Brenden Morrow 6.00 15.00
SSBO Pierre-Marc Bouchard 8.00 20.00
SSBR Martin Brodeur SP 20.00 50.00
SSCA Colby Armstrong 6.00 15.00
SSCH Jonathan Cheechoo 6.00 15.00
SSCI Dino Ciccarelli 8.00 20.00
SSCN Cam Neely SP 8.00 20.00
SSCP Corey Perry 12.00 30.00
SSCW Cam Ward 8.00 20.00
SSDC Don Cherry SP 12.00 30.00
SSDH Dominik Hasek 12.00 30.00
SSDI Dick Irvin 5.00 12.00
SSDP Denis Potvin SP 8.00 20.00
SSDR Dwayne Roloson 6.00 15.00
SSDS Drew Stafford 8.00 20.00
SSEM Evgeni Malkin 30.00 80.00
SSES Eric Staal 10.00 25.00
SSGB Gilbert Brule 6.00 15.00
SSGE Martin Gerber 6.00 15.00
SSGF Grant Fuhr SP 12.00 30.00
SSGH Gordie Howe 25.00 60.00
SSGL Guillaume Latendresse 8.00 20.00
SSGO Scott Gomez 6.00 15.00
SSHA Dale Hawerchuk 10.00 25.00
SSHE Dany Heatley SP 6.00 15.00
SSHI Chris Higgins 5.00 12.00
SSHU Cristobal Huet 6.00 15.00
SSHZ H. Zetterberg SP EXCH 10.00 25.00
SSIK Ilya Kovalchuk 8.00 20.00
SSJB Johnny Bucyk SP 8.00 20.00
SSJC Jeff Carter 6.00 15.00
SSJG Jean-Sebastien Giguere 8.00 20.00
SSJI Jarome Iginla 10.00 25.00
SSJP Joni Pitkanen 5.00 12.00
SSJS Jarret Stoll 6.00 15.00
SSJT Joe Thornton SP 12.00 30.00
SSKD Kris Draper 5.00 12.00
SSKL Kari Lehtonen 6.00 15.00
SSMA Matt Carle SP 5.00 12.00
SSMB Mike Bossy SP 8.00 20.00
SSMC Mike Cammalleri 5.00 12.00
SSME Barry Melrose 6.00 15.00
SSMF Marc-Andre Fleury 15.00 40.00
SSMG Marian Gaborik 8.00 20.00
SSMH Martin Havlat 5.00 12.00
SSMI Milan Hejduk 6.00 15.00
SSMK Miikka Kiprusoff 8.00 20.00
SSML Mario Lemieux SP 80.00 150.00
SSMM Marty McSorley 6.00 15.00
SSMO Mike Modano SP 15.00 40.00
SSMP Michael Peca 6.00 15.00
SSMR Michael Ryder 5.00 12.00
SSMS Marc Savard 5.00 12.00
SSMT Marty Turco 8.00 20.00
SSND Nigel Dawes 5.00 12.00
SSNL Nicklas Lidstrom SP 20.00 50.00
SSNZ Nikolai Zherdev 5.00 12.00
SSOR Bobby Orr 80.00 150.00
SSPB Patrice Bergeron 40.00 100.00
SSPE Patrik Elias 8.00 20.00
SSPK Phil Kessel 15.00 40.00
SSPM Patrick Marleau SP 8.00 20.00
SSPO Patrick O'Sullivan 8.00 20.00
SSPP Petr Prucha 6.00 15.00
SSPS Paul Stastny 12.00 30.00
SSRA Alexander Radulov 10.00 25.00
SSRB Ray Bourque SP 20.00 50.00
SSRH Ron Hextall 8.00 20.00
SSRM Ryan Miller 8.00 20.00
SSRN Rick Nash 8.00 20.00
SSRS Ryan Smyth 6.00 15.00
SSSC Sidney Crosby 60.00 150.00
SSSG Simon Gagne 8.00 20.00
SSST Jordan Staal 12.00 30.00
SSSV Marek Svatos 5.00 12.00
SSTH Jose Theodore SP 8.00 20.00
SSTO Terry O'Reilly 5.00 12.00
SSTV Tomas Vokoun 6.00 15.00
SSVL Vincent Lecavalier SP 12.00 30.00
SSVT Vesa Toskala 6.00 15.00
SSWG Wayne Gretzky SP 250.00 600.00
SSWO Willie O'Ree 12.00 30.00
SSZC Zdeno Chara 12.00 30.00

2006-07 Sweet Shot Signature Shots/Saves Ice Signings

SSIAH Ales Hemsky 6.00 15.00
SSIAR Alex Radulov EXCH 15.00 40.00
SSIBB Brad Boyes 6.00 15.00
SSIBO Bobby Orr 100.00 200.00
SSICA Colby Armstrong 12.00 30.00
SSICW Cam Ward 10.00 25.00
SSIDH Dominik Hasek 25.00 60.00
SSIEM Evgeni Malkin 50.00 120.00
SSIES Eric Staal 10.00 25.00
SSIGH Gordie Howe 40.00 100.00
SSIHE Dany Heatley 15.00 40.00
SSIHZ Henrik Zetterberg 15.00 40.00
SSIIK Ilya Kovalchuk 12.00 30.00
SSIJG Jean-Sebastien Giguere 15.00 40.00
SSIJI Jarome Iginla 20.00 50.00
SSIJK Jari Kurri 20.00 50.00
SSIJS Jarret Stoll 6.00 15.00
SSIJT Joe Thornton 30.00 80.00
SSIKL Kari Lehtonen 12.00 30.00
SSILR Larry Robinson 10.00 25.00
SSIMB Martin Brodeur 25.00 60.00
SSIMD Marcel Dionne 10.00 25.00
SSIMG Marian Gaborik 20.00 50.00
SSIMH Martin Havlat 12.00 30.00
SSIMK Miikka Kiprusoff 15.00 40.00
SSIMM Mike Modano 12.00 30.00
SSIMR Michael Ryder 10.00 25.00
SSIMS Marek Svatos 6.00 15.00
SSIMT Marty Turco 12.00 30.00
SSINL Nicklas Lidstrom 20.00 50.00
SSIPE Patrik Elias 6.00 15.00
SSIPK Phil Kessel 20.00 50.00
SSIRB Ray Bourque 30.00 80.00
SSIRK Red Kelly 12.00 30.00
SSIRM Ryan Miller 20.00 50.00
SSIRN Rick Nash 15.00 40.00
SSISC Sidney Crosby 100.00 200.00
SSISG Simon Gagne 10.00 25.00
SSIST Jordan Staal 25.00 60.00
SSITV Tomas Vokoun 10.00 25.00
SSIWG Wayne Gretzky 250.00 600.00

2006-07 Sweet Shot Signature Shots/Saves Sticks

SSSAB Andy Bathgate 15.00 40.00
SSSAF Alexander Frolov 15.00 40.00
SSSAH Ales Hemsky 25.00 60.00
SSSAK Anze Kopitar 75.00 150.00
SSSAR Andrew Raycroft 20.00 50.00
SSSBB Brad Boyes 40.00
SSSBC Bobby Clarke 25.00 60.00
SSSBG Brian Gionta 20.00 50.00
SSSBH Bobby Hull 40.00 100.00
SSSBM Brenden Morrow 25.00 60.00
SSSBO Mike Bossy 30.00 80.00
SSSBP Bernie Parent 50.00 125.00
SSSBR Brent Sutter 15.00 40.00
SSSBS Borje Salming 15.00 40.00
SSSBU Johnny Bucyk 20.00 50.00
SSSCA Colby Armstrong
SSSCD Chris Drury 25.00 60.00
SSSCH Cristobal Huet 20.00 50.00
SSSCN Cam Neely 30.00 80.00
SSSDC Don Cherry 75.00 150.00
SSSDE Denis Potvin 20.00 50.00
SSSDH Dominik Hasek 30.00 80.00
SSSDP Dion Phaneuf 30.00 60.00
SSSDR Dwayne Roloson 25.00 60.00
SSSDS Denis Savard 20.00 50.00
SSSDT Dave Taylor 20.00 50.00
SSSDW Doug Wilson 15.00 40.00
SSSEM Evgeni Malkin 50.00 120.00
SSSES Eric Staal 25.00 60.00
SSSGB Gilbert Brule 25.00 60.00
SSSGE Martin Gerber 15.00 30.00
SSSGF Grant Fuhr 30.00 80.00
SSSGH Gordie Howe 75.00 150.00
SSSGL Guillaume Latendresse 40.00 100.00
SSSGP Gilbert Perreault
SSSHE Dany Heatley 20.00 50.00
SSSHZ Henrik Zetterberg 40.00 100.00
SSSIK Ilya Kovalchuk 30.00 80.00
SSSJA Jason Arnott
SSSJB Jean Beliveau 50.00 125.00
SSSJC Jonathan Cheechoo 20.00 50.00
SSSJE Jeff Carter 20.00 50.00
SSSJI Jarome Iginla 30.00 80.00
SSSJK Jari Kurri 30.00 80.00
SSSJO Johnny Bower
SSSJR Jeremy Roenick 30.00 80.00
SSSJS Jordan Staal 100.00 200.00
SSSJT Jose Theodore
SSSKL Kari Lehtonen
SSSLA Guy Lafleur 40.00 100.00
SSSLR Luc Robitaille
SSSMA Matt Carle 15.00 40.00
SSSMB Martin Brodeur 100.00 200.00
SSSMC Mike Cammalleri 25.00 60.00
SSSMD Marcel Dionne 30.00 60.00
SSSMF Marc-Andre Fleury 25.00 60.00
SSSMG Marian Gaborik 20.00 50.00
SSSMH Martin Havlat 25.00 60.00
SSSMI Milan Hejduk
SSSMK Miikka Kiprusoff 25.00 60.00
SSSML Mario Lemieux 100.00 200.00
SSSMM Mike Modano 30.00 80.00
SSSMP Michael Peca
SSSMR Michael Ryder 25.00 60.00
SSSMS Marek Svatos 20.00 50.00
SSSMT Marty Turco 20.00 50.00
SSSNL Nicklas Lidstrom 25.00 60.00
SSSNZ Nikolai Zherdev 20.00 50.00
SSSOR Bobby Orr 200.00 400.00
SSSPA Patrice Bergeron 25.00 60.00
SSSPB Pierre-Marc Bouchard
SSSPE Patrik Elias 20.00 50.00
SSSPH Phil Esposito 50.00 125.00
SSSPK Phil Kessel 30.00 80.00
SSSPM Patrick Marleau 30.00 60.00
SSSPO Patrick O'Sullivan 15.00 40.00
SSSPS Paul Stastny 50.00 125.00
SSSRA Alexander Radulov 40.00 100.00
SSSRB Ray Bourque 40.00 100.00
SSSRH Ron Hextall 40.00 100.00
SSSRM Ryan Miller 25.00 60.00
SSSRN Rick Nash 25.00 60.00
SSSRO Larry Robinson 20.00 50.00
SSSRS Ryan Smyth 30.00 60.00
SSSRV Rick Vaive 25.00 60.00
SSSSC Sidney Crosby 150.00 300.00
SSSSG Scott Gomez 20.00 50.00
SSSSI Darryl Sittler 25.00 60.00
SSSSJ Jarret Stoll 15.00 40.00
SSSSK Saku Koivu 25.00 60.00
SSSST Peter Stastny 30.00 80.00
SSSSU Brian Sutter 15.00 40.00
SSSTE Tony Esposito 25.00 60.00
SSSTH Joe Thornton 40.00 100.00
SSSTL Ted Lindsay
SSSTV Tomas Vokoun 30.00 60.00
SSSVL Vincent Lecavalier 25.00 60.00
SSSWG Wayne Gretzky 400.00 1000.00

2006-07 Sweet Shot Signature Sticks

STAM Al MacInnis 30.00 80.00
STAO Adam Oates 20.00 50.00
STAR Andrew Raycroft 25.00 60.00
STBB Bob Bourne 25.00 60.00
STBC Bobby Clarke 60.00 125.00
STBH Bobby Hull 75.00 150.00
STBL Rob Blake 15.00 40.00
STBO Bobby Orr 400.00 600.00
STBP Bernie Parent 75.00 150.00
STBS Billy Smith 30.00 80.00
STCD Chris Drury 30.00 80.00
STCG Clark Gillies
STCH Cristobal Huet 30.00 80.00
STCW Cam Ward 30.00 80.00
STDA David Aebischer 30.00 80.00
STDB Daniel Briere 30.00 80.00
STDG Doug Gilmour 100.00 175.00
STDH Dominik Hasek 60.00 125.00
STDP Dion Phaneuf 30.00 80.00
STDR Dwayne Roloson 30.00 80.00
STEM Evgeni Malkin 100.00 200.00
STES Eric Staal 30.00 80.00
STFM Frank Mahovlich 60.00 150.00
STGH Gordie Howe 175.00 300.00
STGL Guy Lafleur 60.00 125.00
STGP Gilbert Perreault 40.00 100.00
STHA Dale Hawerchuk 30.00 80.00
STHE Dany Heatley 60.00 125.00
STHZ Henrik Zetterberg 75.00 150.00
STIK Ilya Kovalchuk 60.00 125.00
STJB Jean Beliveau 75.00 150.00
STJC Jonathan Cheechoo 60.00 125.00
STJG Jean-Sebastien Giguere 25.00 60.00
STJI Jarome Iginla 100.00 200.00
STJK Jari Kurri 60.00 125.00
STJL Joffrey Lupul 25.00 60.00
STJM Joe Mullen 25.00 60.00
STJP Joni Pitkanen 25.00 60.00
STJR Jeremy Roenick 75.00 150.00
STJT Joe Thornton 75.00 175.00
STKL Kari Lehtonen 30.00 80.00
STLE Manny Legace 25.00 60.00
STLM Larry Murphy 25.00 60.00
STLR Luc Robitaille 40.00 100.00
STMB Martin Brodeur 75.00 150.00
STMG Marian Gaborik 75.00 150.00
STMH Milan Hejduk 25.00 60.00
STMI Mike Bossy 75.00 125.00
STMK Miikka Kiprusoff 60.00 125.00
STML Mario Lemieux 175.00 300.00
STMM Mike Modano 60.00 125.00
STMN Markus Naslund 30.00 80.00
STMP Michael Peca 30.00 80.00
STMR Michael Ryder 30.00 80.00
STMS Martin St. Louis 40.00 100.00
STMT Marty Turco 30.00 80.00
STNL Nicklas Lidstrom 40.00 100.00
STNZ Nikolai Zherdev 30.00 80.00
STPB Patrice Bergeron 30.00 80.00
STPE Patrik Elias 25.00 60.00
STPI Pierre-Marc Bouchard 30.00 60.00
STPK Phil Kessel 60.00 125.00
STPM Patrick Marleau 30.00 80.00
STPO Denis Potvin 30.00 80.00
STPR Patrick Roy 150.00 300.00
STRB Ray Bourque 75.00 150.00
STRH Ron Hextall 30.00 80.00
STRM Ryan Malone 25.00 60.00
STRN Rick Nash 60.00 125.00
STRO Larry Robinson 25.00 60.00
STRY Ryan Miller 40.00 100.00
STSA Denis Savard 25.00 60.00
STSK Saku Koivu 40.00 100.00
STST Jordan Staal 100.00 200.00
STSV Marek Svatos 25.00 60.00
STTE Tony Esposito 30.00 80.00
STTR Tuomo Ruutu 25.00 60.00
STTV Tomas Vokoun 40.00 100.00
STWG Wayne Gretzky 600.00 1500.00

2006-07 Sweet Shot Sweet Stitches

*DUAL/50: .8X TO 2X SINGLE SWATCH
*TRIPLE/25: 1X TO 2.5X SINGLE SWATCH
SSAF Alexander Frolov 2.50 6.00
SSAH Ales Hemsky 3.00 8.00
SSAL Daniel Alfredsson 4.00 10.00
SSAN Antero Niittymaki 3.00 8.00
SSAO Alexander Ovechkin 15.00 40.00
SSAR Andrew Raycroft 3.00 8.00
SSAS Alexander Steen 2.50 6.00
SSAT Alex Tanguay 2.50 6.00
SSBG Brian Gionta 2.50 6.00
SSBL Rob Blake 4.00 10.00
SSBO Pierre-Marc Bouchard 4.00 10.00
SSBR Brendan Shanahan 4.00 10.00
SSBS Billy Smith 4.00 10.00
SSBT Bryan Trottier 4.00 10.00
SSCD Chris Drury 3.00 8.00
SSCH Cristobal Huet 3.00 8.00
SSCN Cam Neely 4.00 10.00
SSCP Chris Pronger 4.00 10.00
SSCW Cam Ward 4.00 10.00
SSDA Dany Heatley 3.00 8.00
SSDH Dominik Hasek 6.00 15.00
SSDP Dion Phaneuf 3.00 8.00
SSDS Darryl Sittler 5.00 12.00
SSDW Doug Weight 4.00 10.00
SSEL Eric Lindros 6.00 15.00
SSES Eric Staal 5.00 12.00
SSFM Frank Mahovlich 4.00 10.00
SSGF Grant Fuhr 6.00 15.00
SSGL Guy Lafleur 5.00 12.00
SSGP Gilbert Perreault 4.00 10.00
SSHA Dale Hawerchuk 5.00 12.00
SSHE Milan Hejduk 3.00 8.00
SSHL Henrik Lundqvist 10.00 25.00
SSHO Marian Hossa 4.00 10.00
SSHZ Henrik Zetterberg 5.00 12.00
SSIK Ilya Kovalchuk 4.00 10.00
SSJC Jonathan Cheechoo 3.00 8.00
SSJG Jean-Sebastien Giguere 4.00 10.00
SSJI Jarome Iginla 5.00 12.00
SSJJ Jaromir Jagr 12.00 30.00
SSJL Joffrey Lupul 2.50 6.00
SSJM Joe Mullen 3.00 8.00
SSJS Joe Sakic 8.00 20.00
SSJT Jose Theodore 4.00 10.00
SSKL Kari Lehtonen 3.00 8.00
SSLR Luc Robitaille 4.00 10.00
SSMA Maxim Afinogenov 2.50 6.00
SSMB Martin Brodeur 10.00 25.00
SSMF Manny Fernandez 2.50 6.00
SSMG Marian Gaborik 4.00 10.00
SSMH Martin Havlat 2.50 6.00
SSMI Mike Bossy 4.00 10.00
SSMK Miikka Kiprusoff 4.00 10.00
SSML Mario Lemieux 15.00 40.00
SSMM Mike Modano 6.00 15.00
SSMN Markus Naslund 4.00 10.00
SSMR Michael Ryder 2.50 6.00
SSMS Marek Svatos 2.50 6.00
SSMT Marty Turco 4.00 10.00
SSNL Nicklas Lidstrom 4.00 10.00
SSOJ Olli Jokinen 4.00 10.00
SSOK Olaf Kolzig 4.00 10.00
SSPB Patrice Bergeron 5.00 12.00
SSPD Pavel Datsyuk 6.00 15.00
SSPE Patrik Elias 4.00 10.00
SSPF Peter Forsberg 8.00 20.00
SSPK Paul Kariya 4.00 10.00
SSPL Pascal LeClaire 3.00 8.00
SSPM Patrick Marleau 4.00 10.00
SSPO Denis Potvin 4.00 10.00
SSPR Patrick Roy 10.00 25.00
SSPS Peter Stastny 3.00 8.00
SSRB Ray Bourque 6.00 15.00
SSRE Mark Recchi 5.00 12.00
SSRH Ron Hextall 4.00 10.00
SSRI Brad Richards 4.00 10.00
SSRL Roberto Luongo 6.00 15.00
SSRM Ryan Miller 4.00 10.00
SSRN Rick Nash 4.00 10.00
SSRO Larry Robinson 4.00 10.00
SSRS Ryan Smyth 3.00 8.00
SSRV Rogie Vachon 5.00 12.00
SSSA Miroslav Satan 3.00 8.00
SSSB Borje Salming 4.00 10.00
SSSC Sidney Crosby 12.00 30.00
SSSD Shane Doan 3.00 8.00
SSSF Sergei Fedorov 6.00 15.00
SSSH Steve Shutt 4.00 10.00
SSSK Saku Koivu 4.00 10.00
SSSP Jason Spezza 4.00 10.00
SSSS Sergei Samsonov 3.00 8.00
SSST Martin St. Louis 4.00 10.00
SSSU Mats Sundin 4.00 10.00
SSSZ Sergei Zubov 3.00 8.00
SSTH Joe Thornton 6.00 15.00
SSTS Teemu Selanne 8.00 20.00
SSTV Tomas Vokoun 3.00 8.00
SSVL Vincent Lecavalier 4.00 10.00
SSWG Wayne Gretzky 25.00 60.00
SSZC Zdeno Chara 4.00 10.00

2007-08 Sweet Shot

1 Ales Hemsky .50 1.25
2 Al MacInnis .75 2.00
3 Alexander Ovechkin 2.50 6.00
4 Bobby Orr 2.50 6.00
5 Alexander Semin .60 1.50
6 Anze Kopitar 1.00 2.50
7 Bernie Federko .50 1.25
8 Cam Neely .60 1.50
9 Gordie Howe 2.00 5.00
10 Alexander Radulov .60 1.50
11 Mark Messier 1.25 3.00
12 Borje Salming .60 1.50
13 Brad Richards .60 1.50
14 Brendan Morrison .40 1.00
15 Brendan Shanahan .60 1.50
16 Brian Leetch .50 1.25
17 Billy Smith .60 1.50
18 Cam Ward .60 1.50
19 Daniel Alfredsson .60 1.50
20 Daniel Briere .60 1.50
21 Dany Heatley .50 1.25
22 Darryl Sittler .75 2.00
23 Denis Potvin .60 1.50
24 Dino Ciccarelli .60 1.50
25 Dion Phaneuf .50 1.25
26 Dominik Hasek 1.00 2.50
27 Manny Legace .50 1.25
28 Drew Stafford .40 1.00
29 Eric Staal .75 2.00
30 Patrice Bergeron .75 2.00
31 Frank Mahovlich .60 1.50
32 Gilbert Perreault .60 1.50
33 Patrick Roy 1.50 4.00
34 Grant Fuhr 1.00 2.50
35 Guy Lafleur .75 2.00
36 Henrik Lundqvist 1.50 4.00
37 Henrik Zetterberg .75 2.00
38 Ilya Kovalchuk .60 1.50
39 Jari Kurri .60 1.50
40 Jarome Iginla .75 2.00
41 Jaromir Jagr 2.00 5.00
42 Jason Spezza .60 1.50
43 Jean Beliveau .75 2.00
44 Jean-Sebastien Giguere .60 1.50
45 Joe Mullen .50 1.25
46 Joe Sakic 1.25 3.00
47 Joe Thornton 1.00 2.50
48 Johnny Bucyk .60 1.50
49 Jonathan Cheechoo .50 1.25
50 Jordan Staal .50 1.25
51 Kari Lehtonen .50 1.25
52 Larry Robinson .60 1.50
53 Luc Robitaille .60 1.50
54 Marc-Andre Fleury 1.25 3.00
55 Marian Gaborik .60 1.50
56 Marian Hossa .60 1.50
57 Miikka Kiprusoff .60 1.50
58 Bobby Hull 1.25 3.00
59 Mark Recchi .75 2.00
60 Markus Naslund .60 1.50
61 Martin Brodeur 1.50 4.00
62 Martin St. Louis .60 1.50
63 Marty Turco .60 1.50
64 Mats Sundin .60 1.50
65 Michael Ryder .40 1.00
66 Mario Lemieux 2.50 6.00
67 Mike Bossy .60 1.50
68 Mike Modano 1.00 2.50
69 Nathan Horton .60 1.50
70 Nicklas Lidstrom .60 1.50
71 Evgeni Malkin 1.25 3.00
72 Patrick Marleau .60 1.50
73 Bobby Clarke 1.00 2.50
74 Paul Kariya .60 1.50
75 Pavel Datsyuk 1.00 2.50
76 Peter Stastny .50 1.25
77 Ray Bourque 1.00 2.50
78 Phil Esposito 1.00 2.50
79 Phil Kessel .60 1.50
80 Paul Stastny .50 1.25
81 Rick DiPietro .50 1.25
82 Rick Nash .60 1.50
83 Roberto Luongo 1.00 2.50
84 Ron Hextall .60 1.50
85 Ryan Miller .60 1.50
86 Ryan Smyth .50 1.25
87 Sidney Crosby 2.50 6.00
88 Scott Niedermayer .60 1.50

89 Patrik Elias .60 1.50
90 Shane Doan .50 1.25
91 Saku Koivu .60 1.50
92 Simon Gagne .60 1.50
93 Stan Mikita .75 2.00
94 Teemu Selanne 1.25 3.00
95 Thomas Vanek .50 1.25
96 Tomas Vokoun .50 1.25
97 Tony Esposito .60 1.50
98 Vincent Lecavalier .60 1.50
99 Wayne Gretzky 4.00 10.00
100 Zach Parise .60 1.50
101 Bobby Ryan JSY RC 3.00 8.00
102 Jonathan Toews JSY RC 8.00 20.00
103 Sam Gagner JSY RC 2.50 6.00
104 Carey Price JSY RC 8.00 20.00
105 Nicklas Bergfors JSY RC 1.25 3.00
106 Erik Johnson JSY RC 2.00 5.00
107 Nicklas Backstrom JSY RC 4.00 10.00
108 Jack Johnson JSY RC 1.50 4.00
109 Jonathan Bernier JSY RC 2.50 6.00
110 Bryan Little JSY RC 2.00 5.00
111 Patrick Kane JSY RC 15.00 40.00
112 Kris Russell JSY RC 2.00 5.00
113 Matt Niskanen JSY RC 2.00 5.00
114 Andrew Cogliano JSY RC 1.50 4.00
115 Marc Staal JSY RC 2.00 5.00
116 Nick Foligno JSY RC 2.50 6.00
117 Peter Mueller JSY RC 1.50 4.00
118 Ondrej Pavelec JSY RC 2.50 6.00
119 Martin Hanzal JSY RC 1.50 4.00
120 Matt Smaby JSY RC 1.25 3.00
121 Petr Kalus JSY RC 1.25 3.00
122 Andy Greene JSY RC 1.50 4.00
123 Frans Nielsen JSY RC 2.00 5.00
124 Rob Schremp JSY RC 1.50 4.00
125 James Sheppard JSY RC 1.25 3.00
126 Kyle Chipchura JSY RC 2.00 5.00
127 Ryan Parent JSY RC 1.25 3.00
128 David Krejci JSY RC 4.00 10.00
129 Lauri Tukonen JSY RC 1.25 3.00
130 Tobias Enstrom JSY RC 2.00 5.00
131 Mason Raymond JSY RC 2.00 5.00
132 Brandon Dubinsky JSY RC 2.50 6.00
133 Curtis McElhinney JSY RC 2.00 5.00
134 Brian Elliott JSY RC 2.50 6.00
135 Drew Miller JSY RC 1.50 4.00
136 Ryan Callahan JSY RC 2.50 6.00
137 Ville Koistinen JSY RC 1.25 3.00
138 Torrey Mitchell JSY RC 1.50 4.00
139 David Perron JSY RC 2.50 6.00
140 Jannik Hansen JSY RC 1.50 4.00
141 Jaroslav Halak JSY RC 4.00 10.00
142 Sergei Kostitsyn JSY RC 1.50 4.00
143 Milan Lucic JSY RC 5.00 12.00
144 Tyler Weiman JSY RC 1.50 4.00
145 Jaroslav Hlinka JSY RC 1.50 4.00
146 Tobias Stephan JSY RC 1.50 4.00
147 Tuukka Rask JSY RC 5.00 12.00
148 Ryan Carter JSY RC 1.25 3.00
149 Jared Boll JSY RC 1.50 4.00
150 Casey Borer JSY RC 1.25 3.00
151 Steve Downie JSY RC 1.50 4.00
152 Lukas Kaspar JSY RC 1.25 3.00
153 Matt Ellis JSY RC 1.50 4.00
154 Jiri Tlusty JSY RC 2.00 5.00
155 Daniel Carcillo JSY RC 1.50 4.00
156 Devin Setoguchi JSY RC 2.00 5.00
157 T.J. Hensick JSY RC 1.50 4.00
158 Anton Stralman JSY RC 1.25 3.00
159 David Jones JSY RC 1.25 3.00
160 Jack Skille JSY RC 1.50 4.00

2007-08 Sweet Shot Rookie Jerseys Autographs

COMMON CARD/100 8.00 20.00
SEMISTARS/100 10.00 25.00
UNLISTED STARS/100 12.00 30.00
101 Bobby Ryan 20.00 50.00
102 Jonathan Toews 60.00 120.00
103 Sam Gagner 12.00 30.00
104 Carey Price 60.00 150.00
106 Erik Johnson 12.00 30.00
107 Nicklas Backstrom 25.00 60.00
109 Jonathan Bernier 15.00 40.00
111 Patrick Kane 50.00 100.00
114 Andrew Cogliano 10.00 25.00
118 Ondrej Pavelec 15.00 40.00
128 David Krejci 25.00 60.00
136 Ryan Callahan 15.00 40.00
141 Jaroslav Halak 15.00 40.00
143 Milan Lucic 25.00 50.00
147 Tuukka Rask 40.00 80.00

2007-08 Sweet Shot Signature Saves Ice Signings

SSRBP Bernie Parent 15.00 40.00
SSRBR Bill Ranford 12.00 30.00
SSRGF Grant Fuhr 20.00 50.00
SSRJG Jean-Sebastien Giguere 12.00 30.00
SSRMB Martin Brodeur 30.00 80.00
SSRMF Marc-Andre Fleury 25.00 60.00
SSRMT Marty Turco 12.00 30.00
SSRPR Patrick Roy/50 50.00 125.00
SSRRM Ryan Miller 12.00 30.00
SSRTE Tony Esposito 25.00 50.00

2007-08 Sweet Shot Signature Saves Puck Signings

SSPBI Bill Ranford 10.00 25.00
SSPBP Bernie Parent 12.00 30.00
SSPCP Carey Price 30.00 80.00
SSPGF Grant Fuhr 15.00 40.00
SSPHA Dominik Hasek 25.00 60.00
SSPJG Jean-Sebastien Giguere 10.00 25.00
SSPMT Marty Turco 10.00 25.00
SSPRA Andrew Raycroft 8.00 20.00
SSPRB Richard Brodeur 8.00 20.00
SSPRM Ryan Miller 10.00 25.00
SSPTE Tony Esposito 20.00 40.00

2007-08 Sweet Shot Signature Saves Stick Signings

SSSBP Bernie Parent 30.00 80.00
SSSBR Bill Ranford 25.00 60.00
SSSCP Carey Price 100.00 200.00
SSSDH Dominik Hasek 40.00 100.00
SSSDR Dwayne Roloson 20.00 50.00
SSSGF Grant Fuhr 40.00 100.00
SSSJG Jean-Sebastien Giguere 20.00 50.00
SSSMB Martin Brodeur 60.00 150.00
SSSMT Marty Turco
SSSRH Ron Hextall 25.00 60.00
SSSRI Richard Brodeur 20.00 50.00
SSSRM Ryan Miller 25.00 60.00
SSSTE Tony Esposito 50.00 100.00
SSSVO Tomas Vokoun 20.00 50.00

2007-08 Sweet Shot Signature Shots Ice Signings

SSRAK Anze Kopitar 20.00 50.00
SSRAT Alex Tanguay 10.00 25.00
SSRBO Mike Bossy 12.00 30.00
SSRDH Dany Heatley 10.00 25.00
SSRDP Denis Potvin 12.00 30.00
SSREM Evgeni Malkin 40.00 100.00
SSRGH Gordie Howe/50 50.00 100.00
SSRGL Guy Lafleur 30.00 60.00
SSRGP Gilbert Perreault 12.00 30.00
SSRHZ Henrik Zetterberg 15.00 40.00
SSRIK Ilya Kovalchuk 12.00 30.00
SSRJI Jarome Iginla 15.00 40.00
SSRJK Jari Kurri 12.00 30.00
SSRJT Joe Thornton 20.00 50.00
SSRLR Larry Robinson 12.00 30.00
SSRMG Marian Gaborik 12.00 30.00
SSRMM Mike Modano 20.00 50.00
SSRMN Markus Naslund 12.00 30.00
SSRMR Michael Ryder 8.00 20.00
SSRMS Martin St. Louis 12.00 30.00
SSRNL Nicklas Lidstrom 20.00 40.00
SSRPB Patrice Bergeron 15.00 40.00
SSRRB Ray Bourque 25.00 50.00
SSRRN Rick Nash 12.00 30.00
SSRSC Sidney Crosby 75.00 150.00
SSRSG Simon Gagne 12.00 30.00
SSRVL Vincent Lecavalier 12.00 30.00

2007-08 Sweet Shot Signature Shots Puck Signings

SSPAK Anze Kopitar 10.00 25.00
SSPAM Andy McDonald 5.00 12.00
SSPAR Alexander Radulov 6.00 15.00
SSPAT Alex Tanguay 5.00 12.00
SSPBB Brad Boyes 4.00 10.00
SSPBC Bobby Clarke 10.00 25.00
SSPBE1 Jean Beliveau
SSPBG Brian Gionta 4.00 10.00
SSPBH Bobby Hull
SSPBL Bryan Little 5.00 12.00
SSPBM Brendan Morrison 4.00 10.00
SSPBO Bobby Orr 75.00 150.00
SSPBR Bobby Ryan 10.00 25.00
SSPCA Mike Cammalleri 5.00 12.00
SSPDB Dan Boyle 4.00 10.00
SSPDM Dickie Moore
SSPDP David Perron 8.00 20.00
SSPDS Darryl Sutter 5.00 12.00
SSPDT Darcy Tucker 5.00 12.00
SSPDU Duane Sutter 4.00 10.00
SSPEJ Erik Johnson 6.00 15.00
SSPEM Evgeni Malkin 40.00 80.00
SSPGA Simon Gagne 6.00 15.00
SSPGH Gordie Howe 40.00 100.00
SSPGL Guy Lafleur 25.00 50.00
SSPGO Scott Gomez 5.00 12.00
SSPGP Gilbert Perreault 6.00 15.00
SSPIK Ilya Kovalchuk 15.00 30.00
SSPJC Jonathan Cheechoo 5.00 12.00
SSPJI Jarome Iginla 8.00 20.00
SSPJJ Jack Johnson 5.00 12.00
SSPJK Jari Kurri 6.00 15.00
SSPJP Joni Pitkanen 4.00 10.00
SSPJT Jonathan Toews 30.00 60.00
SSPKD Kris Draper 4.00 10.00
SSPKE Phil Kessel 6.00 15.00
SSPLR Larry Robinson 6.00 15.00
SSPMC Matt Carle 4.00 10.00
SSPMG Marian Gaborik 10.00 25.00
SSPMH Milan Hejduk 5.00 12.00
SSPMN Markus Naslund 6.00 15.00
SSPMO Brenden Morrow 5.00 12.00
SSPMP Michael Peca 5.00 12.00
SSPMR Michael Ryder 4.00 10.00
SSPMS Marc Staal 6.00 15.00
SSPMU Peter Mueller 5.00 12.00
SSPNB Nicklas Backstrom 12.00 30.00
SSPNF Nick Foligno 8.00 20.00
SSPNL Nicklas Lidstrom 10.00 25.00
SSPOS Patrick O'Sullivan 5.00 12.00
SSPPB Patrice Bergeron 8.00 20.00
SSPPE Corey Perry 10.00 25.00
SSPPK Patrick Kane 40.00 80.00
SSPPO Denis Potvin 6.00 15.00
SSPPS Paul Stastny 5.00 12.00
SSPRG Ryan Getzlaf 12.00 30.00
SSPRI Mike Richards 5.00 12.00
SSPRN Rick Nash 6.00 15.00
SSPRP Ryan Potulny 4.00 10.00
SSPRS Rob Schremp 5.00 12.00
SSPRV Rick Vaive 5.00 12.00
SSPSB Scotty Bowman 6.00 15.00
SSPSC Sidney Crosby 60.00 120.00
SSPSG Sam Gagner 8.00 20.00
SSPSH Steve Shutt 5.00 12.00
SSPSM Ryan Smyth 5.00 12.00
SSPST Martin St. Louis 6.00 15.00
SSPSU Brent Sutter 4.00 10.00
SSPSV Marek Svatos 4.00 10.00
SSPSW Stephen Weiss 4.00 10.00
SSPTH Tomas Holmstrom 6.00 15.00
SSPTS Tomas Steen 4.00 10.00
SSPTV Thomas Vanek 5.00 12.00
SSPVL Vincent Lecavalier 6.00 15.00
SSPWG Wayne Gretzky 250.00 600.00

2007-08 Sweet Shot Signature Shots Stick Signings

SSSAK Anze Kopitar 25.00 60.00
SSSAM Al MacInnis 20.00 50.00
SSSAO Alexander Ovechkin 60.00 150.00
SSSAR Alexander Radulov 15.00 40.00
SSSAT Alex Tanguay 12.00 30.00
SSSBC Bobby Clarke 25.00 60.00
SSSBE Jean Beliveau 20.00 50.00
SSSBH Bobby Hull 30.00 80.00
SSSBL Brian Leetch 12.00 30.00
SSSBM Brendan Morrison 10.00 25.00
SSSBO Bobby Orr 60.00 150.00
SSSCH Jonathan Cheechoo 12.00 30.00
SSSCN Cam Neely 15.00 40.00
SSSCR Sidney Crosby 60.00 150.00
SSSDA Dany Heatley EXCH 12.00 30.00
SSSDC Dino Ciccarelli 15.00 40.00
SSSDS Darryl Sittler 20.00 50.00
SSSDT Darcy Tucker 12.00 30.00
SSSEM Evgeni Malkin 30.00 80.00
SSSGH Gordie Howe 80.00 200.00
SSSGL Guillaume Latendresse 12.00 30.00
SSSGP Gilbert Perreault 15.00 40.00
SSSHA Dale Hawerchuk 20.00 50.00
SSSHE Milan Hejduk 12.00 30.00
SSSHZ Henrik Zetterberg 20.00 50.00
SSSIK Ilya Kovalchuk 15.00 40.00
SSSJB Johnny Bucyk 15.00 40.00
SSSJC Jeff Carter 12.00 30.00
SSSJI Jarome Iginla 20.00 50.00
SSSJJ Jack Johnson 12.00 30.00
SSSJK Jari Kurri 15.00 40.00
SSSJM Joe Mullen 12.00 30.00
SSSJS Jordan Staal 12.00 30.00
SSSJT Jonathan Toews 60.00 150.00
SSSKA Patrick Kane 300.00 500.00
SSSLA Guy Lafleur 20.00 50.00
SSSLM Lanny McDonald 15.00 40.00
SSSLR Luc Robitaille 15.00 40.00
SSSMD Marcel Dionne 20.00 50.00
SSSME Mark Messier/10
SSSMG Marian Gaborik 15.00 40.00
SSSMH Marian Hossa 15.00 40.00
SSSMI Mike Bossy 15.00 40.00
SSSML Mario Lemieux/10
SSSMM Mike Modano 25.00 60.00
SSSMN Markus Naslund 15.00 40.00
SSSMR Michael Ryder 10.00 25.00
SSSMS Martin St. Louis 15.00 40.00
SSSNH Nathan Horton 15.00 40.00
SSSNL Nicklas Lidstrom 15.00 40.00
SSSPB Patrice Bergeron 20.00 50.00
SSSPK Phil Kessel 15.00 40.00
SSSPM Peter Mueller 12.00 30.00
SSSPO Denis Potvin 15.00 40.00
SSSPS Paul Stastny 12.00 30.00
SSSRB Ray Bourque 25.00 60.00
SSSRE Ron Ellis 10.00 25.00
SSSRN Rick Nash 15.00 40.00
SSSRO Larry Robinson 15.00 40.00
SSSRS Ryan Smyth 12.00 30.00
SSSSA Borje Salming 15.00 40.00
SSSSG Sam Gagner 20.00 50.00
SSSSI Simon Gagne 15.00 40.00
SSSSK Saku Koivu 15.00 40.00
SSSSM Stan Mikita 20.00 50.00
SSSSP Peter Stastny 12.00 30.00
SSSSS Steve Shutt 12.00 30.00
SSSSV Marek Svatos 10.00 25.00
SSSTH Joe Thornton 25.00 60.00
SSSTV Thomas Vanek 12.00 30.00
SSSVL Vincent Lecavalier 15.00 40.00
SSSWG Wayne Gretzky/10

2007-08 Sweet Shot Sweet Spot Signatures Baseball Skins

SBSAO Alexander Ovechkin 80.00 200.00
SBSBC Bobby Clarke 30.00 80.00
SBSBH Bobby Hull 40.00 100.00
SBSBO Bobby Orr 80.00 200.00
SBSBP Bernie Parent 25.00 60.00
SBSBU Johnny Bucyk 20.00 50.00
SBSDH Dany Heatley 15.00 40.00
SBSDP Denis Potvin 20.00 50.00
SBSDS Darryl Sittler 25.00 60.00
SBSEM Evgeni Malkin 40.00 100.00
SBSGH Gordie Howe 60.00 150.00
SBSGL Guy Lafleur 25.00 60.00
SBSHA Dominik Hasek 30.00 80.00
SBSHL Henrik Lundqvist 50.00 120.00
SBSJI Jarome Iginla 25.00 60.00
SBSJK Jari Kurri 20.00 50.00
SBSJM Joe Mullen 15.00 40.00
SBSJT Joe Thornton 30.00 80.00
SBSLM Lanny McDonald 20.00 50.00
SBSMB Martin Brodeur 50.00 125.00
SBSMD Marcel Dionne 25.00 60.00
SBSMF Marc-Andre Fleury 40.00 100.00
SBSMH Milan Hejduk 15.00 40.00
SBSML Mario Lemieux 80.00 200.00
SBSMM Mark Messier 40.00 100.00
SBSMN Markus Naslund 20.00 50.00
SBSMR Michael Ryder 12.00 30.00
SBSMS Martin St. Louis 20.00 50.00
SBSMT Marty Turco 20.00 50.00
SBSPB Patrice Bergeron 25.00 60.00
SBSPR Patrick Roy 50.00 125.00
SBSRB Ray Bourque 30.00 80.00
SBSRH Ron Hextall 20.00 50.00
SBSRN Rick Nash 20.00 50.00
SBSRO Larry Robinson 20.00 50.00
SBSSC Sidney Crosby 80.00 200.00
SBSSG Simon Gagne 20.00 50.00
SBSTE Tony Esposito 20.00 50.00
SBSTL Ted Lindsay 20.00 50.00
SBSVL Vincent Lecavalier 20.00 50.00
SBSWG Wayne Gretzky 250.00 600.00

2007-08 Sweet Shot Sweet Stitches Triples

SSTAH Ales Hemsky 4.00 10.00
SSTAK Alex Kovalev 4.00 10.00
SSTAM Al MacInnis 6.00 15.00
SSTAO Alexander Ovechkin 20.00 50.00
SSTAR Alexander Radulov 5.00 12.00
SSTAS Alexander Steen 3.00 8.00
SSTAT Alex Tanguay 4.00 10.00
SSTBC Bobby Clarke 8.00 20.00
SSTBL Brian Leetch 4.00 10.00
SSTBN Bernie Nicholls 4.00 10.00
SSTBO Mike Bossy 5.00 12.00
SSTBS Brendan Shanahan 5.00 12.00
SSTCN Cam Neely 5.00 12.00
SSTCP Chris Pronger 5.00 12.00
SSTDA Daniel Alfredsson 5.00 12.00
SSTDE Denis Savard 5.00 12.00
SSTDG Doug Gilmour 6.00 15.00
SSTDH Dale Hawerchuk 6.00 15.00
SSTDP Denis Potvin 5.00 12.00
SSTDR Dwayne Roloson 4.00 10.00
SSTDS Daniel Sedin 6.00 15.00
SSTDW Doug Weight 5.00 12.00
SSTEM Evgeni Malkin 12.00 30.00
SSTEN Evgeni Nabokov 4.00 10.00
SSTES Eric Staal 6.00 15.00
SSTFM Frank Mahovlich 5.00 12.00
SSTGF Grant Fuhr 8.00 20.00
SSTGL Guy Lafleur 10.00 25.00
SSTGP Gilbert Perreault 5.00 12.00
SSTHA Dominik Hasek 8.00 20.00
SSTHE Dany Heatley 4.00 10.00
SSTHL Henrik Lundqvist 12.00 30.00
SSTHM Milan Hejduk 4.00 10.00
SSTHS Henrik Sedin 6.00 15.00
SSTHZ Henrik Zetterberg 6.00 15.00
SSTIK Ilya Kovalchuk 5.00 12.00
SSTJI Jarome Iginla 6.00 15.00
SSTJJ Jaromir Jagr 15.00 40.00
SSTJO Joe Sakic 12.00 30.00
SSTJS Jason Spezza 5.00 12.00
SSTJT Joe Thornton 8.00 20.00
SSTKL Kari Lehtonen 4.00 10.00
SSTKO Anze Kopitar 8.00 20.00
SSTKP Miikka Kiprusoff 5.00 12.00
SSTLM Lanny McDonald 5.00 12.00
SSTLR Larry Robinson 5.00 12.00
SSTMA Martin Havlat 5.00 12.00
SSTMB Martin Brodeur 12.00 30.00
SSTMF Marc-Andre Fleury 10.00 25.00
SSTMG Marian Gaborik 5.00 12.00
SSTMH Marian Hossa 5.00 12.00
SSTMI Stan Mikita 6.00 15.00
SSTMK Mikko Koivu 4.00 10.00
SSTML Mario Lemieux 12.00 30.00
SSTMM Mark Messier 10.00 25.00
SSTMN Markus Naslund 5.00 12.00
SSTMO Mike Modano 8.00 20.00
SSTMR Mark Recchi 6.00 15.00
SSTMS Martin St. Louis 5.00 12.00
SSTMT Marty Turco 5.00 12.00
SSTMV Miroslav Satan 4.00 10.00
SSTNL Nicklas Lidstrom 5.00 12.00
SSTPB Patrice Bergeron 6.00 15.00
SSTPD Pavel Datsyuk 8.00 20.00
SSTPF Peter Forsberg 10.00 25.00
SSTPH Dion Phaneuf 4.00 10.00
SSTPK Paul Kariya 5.00 12.00
SSTPM Patrick Marleau 5.00 12.00
SSTPR Patrick Roy 12.00 30.00
SSTPS Peter Stastny 4.00 10.00
SSTRB Ray Bourque 8.00 20.00
SSTRE Ray Emery 4.00 10.00
SSTRG Ryan Getzlaf 5.00 12.00
SSTRH Ron Hextall 5.00 12.00
SSTRL Roberto Luongo 8.00 20.00
SSTRM Ryan Miller 5.00 12.00
SSTRN Rick Nash 5.00 12.00
SSTRO Luc Robitaille 5.00 12.00
SSTRS Ryan Smyth 4.00 10.00
SSTRV Rogie Vachon 6.00 15.00
SSTRY Michael Ryder 3.00 8.00
SSTSA Borje Salming 5.00 12.00
SSTSC Sidney Crosby 12.00 30.00
SSTSD Shane Doan 4.00 10.00
SSTSF Sergei Fedorov 8.00 20.00
SSTSG Simon Gagne 5.00 12.00
SSTSH Steve Shutt 4.00 10.00
SSTSI Darryl Sittler 6.00 15.00
SSTSK Saku Koivu 5.00 12.00
SSTSM Billy Smith 5.00 12.00
SSTSN Scott Niedermayer 5.00 12.00
SSTSS Scott Stevens 5.00 12.00
SSTST Jordan Staal 4.00 10.00
SSTSU Mats Sundin 5.00 12.00
SSTTS Teemu Selanne 10.00 25.00
SSTTV Tomas Vokoun 4.00 10.00
SSTTW Tiger Williams 3.00 8.00
SSTVL Vincent Lecavalier 5.00 12.00
SSTWG Wayne Gretzky 20.00 50.00
SSTZP Zach Parise 5.00 12.00

2017-18 Synergy Blue

*VETS: .5X TO 1.25X RED
*ROOKIES: .5X TO 1.25X RED
30 Auston Matthews 4.00 10.00

2017-18 Synergy Green

*VETS: 1X TO 2.5X RED
*ROOKIES: 1.25X TO 3X RED
50 Wayne Gretzky 12.00 30.00

2017-18 Synergy Purple

*VETS: 1.5X TO 4X RED
*ROOKIES: 2.5X TO 5X RED
89 Alex Tuch 40.00 100.00
92 Brock Boeser 80.00 150.00
93 Owen Tippett 15.00 40.00
94 Alex DeBrincat 20.00 50.00
95 Clayton Keller 25.00 60.00
96 Josh Ho-Sang 15.00 40.00
97 Pierre-Luc Dubois 25.00 60.00
98 Charlie McAvoy 25.00 60.00

2017-18 Synergy Red

COMMON CARD .40 1.00
SEMISTARS .50 1.25
UNLISTED STARS .60 1.50
COMMON RC 1.00 2.50
RC.SEMISTARS 1.25 3.00
RC.UNL.STAR 1.50 4.00
*BOUNTY: .6X TO 1.5X BASIC CARDS
1 Connor McDavid 3.00 8.00
2 Johnny Gaudreau 1.00 2.50
3 Henrik Zetterberg .75 2.00
4 Jamie Benn .60 1.50
5 P.K. Subban .75 2.00
6 Brad Marchand 1.25 3.00
7 John Tavares 1.00 2.50
8 Jack Eichel 1.00 2.50
9 Taylor Hall .60 1.50
10 Sidney Crosby 2.50 6.00
11 Claude Giroux .60 1.50
12 Vladimir Tarasenko .75 2.00
13 Aaron Ekblad .75 2.00
14 Leon Draisaitl 2.00 5.00
15 Carey Price 1.25 3.00
16 Ryan Getzlaf .60 1.50
17 Devan Dubnyk .50 1.25
18 Nathan MacKinnon 2.50 6.00
19 Max Domi .60 1.50
20 Alexander Ovechkin 2.50 6.00
21 Jonathan Toews 1.00 2.50
22 Drew Doughty .75 2.00
23 Nikita Kucherov 1.25 3.00
24 Mark Scheifele 1.00 2.50
25 Erik Karlsson .75 2.00
26 Daniel Sedin .75 2.00
27 Evgeni Malkin 1.25 3.00
28 Artemi Panarin 1.25 3.00
29 Nicklas Backstrom .60 1.50
30 Auston Matthews 3.00 8.00
31 Marc-Andre Fleury 1.25 3.00
32 David Pastrnak 1.50 4.00
33 Steven Stamkos 1.25 3.00
34 Brent Burns .60 1.50
35 Henrik Lundqvist 1.50 4.00
36 Jeff Skinner .75 2.00
37 Patrik Laine .75 2.00
38 Ryan Johansen .50 1.25
39 Jeff Carter .50 1.25
40 Patrick Kane 1.25 3.00
41 Mario Lemieux 2.50 6.00
42 Martin Brodeur 1.50 4.00
43 Pat LaFontaine .60 1.50
44 Pavel Bure .60 1.50
45 Patrick Roy 1.50 4.00
46 Joe Sakic 1.25 3.00
47 Mike Bossy .60 1.50
48 Ray Bourque 1.00 2.50
49 Mark Messier 1.25 3.00
50 Wayne Gretzky 4.00 10.00
51 Carter Rowney 1.25 3.00
52 Nicolas Kerdiles 1.50 4.00
53 Vince Dunn 2.00 5.00
54 Calle Rosen 1.50 4.00
55 Haydn Fleury 1.50 4.00
56 Tim Heed 1.50 4.00
57 Alex Kerfoot 3.00 8.00
58 Nikita Scherbak 2.00 5.00
59 J.T. Compher 1.50 4.00
60 Jack Roslovic 2.00 5.00
61 Denis Gurianov 4.00 10.00
62 Ivan Barbashev 2.00 5.00
63 Jakob Forsbacka-Karlsson 1.50 4.00
64 Samuel Girard 1.50 4.00
65 Madison Bowey 1.00 2.50
66 Lucas Wallmark 1.50 4.00
67 Janne Kuokkanen 1.50 4.00
68 Jon Gillies 1.50 4.00
69 Christian Fischer 2.00 5.00
70 Christian Djoos 1.50 4.00
71 Logan Brown 1.50 4.00
72 Alexander Nylander 2.50 6.00
73 Anders Bjork 2.00 5.00
74 Adrian Kempe 3.00 8.00
75 Colin White 2.00 5.00
76 Victor Mete 1.50 4.00
77 Luke Kunin 1.50 4.00
78 Tyson Jost 3.00 8.00
79 Jake DeBrusk 4.00 10.00
80 Kailer Yamamoto 4.00 10.00
81 Travis Sanheim 1.50 4.00
82 Jesper Bratt 3.00 8.00
83 Filip Chytil 1.50 4.00
84 Filip Chlapik 1.25 3.00
85 Evgeny Svechnikov 3.00 8.00
86 Tage Thompson 4.00 10.00
87 Samuel Blais 1.50 4.00
88 Martin Necas 5.00 12.00
89 Alex Tuch 4.00 10.00
90 Alex Formenton 1.50 4.00
91 Will Butcher 2.00 5.00
92 Brock Boeser 20.00 50.00
93 Owen Tippett 6.00 15.00
94 Alex DeBrincat 8.00 20.00
95 Clayton Keller 12.00 30.00
96 Josh Ho-Sang 8.00 20.00
97 Pierre-Luc Dubois 12.00 30.00
98 Charlie McAvoy 20.00 50.00
99 Nolan Patrick 3.00 8.00
100 Nico Hischier 8.00 20.00

2017-18 Synergy Autographs

AAA Artem Anisimov B 6.00 15.00
AAB Aleksander Barkov B 15.00 40.00
AAD Alex DeBrincat D 25.00 60.00
AAG Alex Galchenyuk B 6.00 15.00
AAL Anders Lee C 10.00 25.00
AAM Anthony Mantha C 8.00 20.00
AAN Alexander Nylander C 15.00 40.00
AAO Alexander Ovechkin A 40.00 100.00
AAT Alex Tuch D 25.00 60.00
AAV Andrei Vasilevskiy C 15.00 40.00
AAW Alexander Wennberg C 6.00 15.00
ABB Brock Boeser C 100.00 200.00
ABJ Anders Bjork C 12.00 30.00
ABO Bobby Orr C 80.00 150.00
ABS Brayden Schenn B 10.00 25.00
ACA Cam Atkinson C 10.00 25.00
ACF Christian Fischer D 12.00 30.00
ACK Clayton Keller C 25.00 60.00
ACM Connor McDavid A 50.00 125.00
ACP Carey Price A 20.00 50.00
ACS Conor Sheary C 10.00 25.00
ADG Denis Gurianov D 25.00 60.00
ADH Dominik Hasek A 15.00 40.00
ADS Darryl Sittler A 12.00 30.00
AEK Erik Karlsson A 12.00 30.00
AEM Evgeni Malkin A 20.00 50.00
AES Evgeny Svechnikov D 20.00 50.00
AFA Frederik Andersen C 12.00 30.00
AGI Jon Gillies D 10.00 25.00
AGL Guy Lafleur A 12.00 30.00
AGR Mikael Granlund C 8.00 20.00
AHL Henrik Lundqvist A 25.00 60.00
AJA Jake Allen B 10.00 25.00
AJB Jesper Bratt D 20.00 50.00
AJC John Carlson B 10.00 25.00
AJE Jeff Carter B 8.00 20.00
AJO Joe Sakic A 20.00 50.00
AJP Joe Pavelski B 12.00 30.00
AJR Jack Roslovic D 12.00 30.00
AJS Jason Spezza C 10.00 25.00
AJT Jonathan Toews A 15.00 40.00
AKA Evander Kane C 10.00 25.00
AKE Adrian Kempe D 20.00 50.00
AKP Kyle Palmieri C 8.00 20.00
ALD Leon Draisaitl B 30.00 80.00
ALK Luke Kunin C 10.00 25.00
AMA Auston Matthews A 40.00 100.00
AMB Madison Bowey D 6.00 15.00
AMC Charlie McAvoy B 25.00 60.00
AME Mark Messier A 20.00 50.00
AMF Marc-Andre Fleury B 20.00 50.00
AMG Mark Giordano C 10.00 25.00
AMI Mitch Marner B 15.00 40.00
AMM Matt Murray B 15.00 40.00
ANE Nikolaj Ehlers C 10.00 25.00
ANK Nikita Kucherov B 20.00 50.00
ANS Nikita Scherbak C 12.00 30.00
APB Pavel Buchnevich D 8.00 20.00
APD Pierre-Luc Dubois D 15.00 40.00
APK Patrick Kane B 20.00 50.00
APL Patrik Laine B 12.00 30.00
APO Jason Pominville C 6.00 15.00
APR Patrick Roy A 25.00 60.00
ARA Radek Faksa D 8.00 20.00
ARK Ryan Kesler B 10.00 25.00
ARL Roberto Luongo B 15.00 40.00
ARS Ryan Spooner C 8.00 20.00
ASA Sebastian Aho C 15.00 40.00
ASC Sidney Crosby A 40.00 100.00
ASK Brady Skjei C 8.00 20.00
ASM Samuel Morin D 6.00 15.00
ASS Steven Stamkos A 20.00 50.00
ASY Steve Yzerman A 25.00 60.00
ATA Tage Thompson D 25.00 60.00
ATJ Tyler Johnson B 6.00 15.00
ATS Tyler Seguin A 12.00 30.00
ATT Teuvo Teravainen C 10.00 25.00
ATV John Tavares A 15.00 40.00
ATY Tyson Jost D 20.00 50.00
AVH Victor Hedman B 12.00 30.00
AVK Vladislav Kamenev D 10.00 25.00
AVT Vladimir Tarasenko B 12.00 30.00
AVZ Valentin Zykov D 10.00 25.00
AWG Wayne Gretzky C 200.00 500.00
AWN William Nylander B 20.00 50.00
AWS Wayne Simmonds B 12.00 30.00

2017-18 Synergy Career Spanning

CS1 Wayne Gretzky 6.00 15.00
CS2 Steve Yzerman 2.50 6.00
CS3 Martin Brodeur 2.50 6.00
CS4 Ray Bourque 1.50 4.00
CS5 Lanny McDonald 1.00 2.50
CS6 Mark Messier 2.00 5.00
CS7 Mark Recchi 1.25 3.00
CS8 Dominik Hasek 1.50 4.00
CS9 Joe Sakic 2.00 5.00
CS10 Mario Lemieux 4.00 10.00

2017-18 Synergy Career Spanning Red

*RED/35: 1.5X TO 4X BASIC INSERTS
CS1 Wayne Gretzky 25.00 60.00

2017-18 Synergy Cast For Greatness

CG1 Sidney Crosby 40.00 100.00
CG2 Henrik Lundqvist 25.00 60.00
CG3 Mark Scheifele 15.00 40.00
CG4 Brad Marchand 20.00 50.00
CG5 Claude Giroux 10.00 25.00
CG6 Anze Kopitar 15.00 40.00
CG7 Henrik Zetterberg 12.00 30.00
CG8 Auston Matthews 40.00 100.00
CG9 Jamie Benn 10.00 25.00
CG10 Jonathan Toews 15.00 40.00
CG11 Marc-Andre Fleury 20.00 50.00
CG12 Ryan Getzlaf 10.00 25.00
CG13 Johnny Gaudreau 15.00 40.00
CG14 John Tavares 15.00 40.00
CG15 Patrik Laine 12.00 30.00
CG16 Mario Lemieux 40.00 100.00
CG17 Evgeni Malkin 20.00 50.00
CG18 Mark Messier 20.00 50.00
CG19 Nikita Kucherov 20.00 50.00
CG20 Erik Karlsson 12.00 30.00
CG21 Nolan Patrick 20.00 50.00
CG22 Brent Burns 10.00 25.00
CG23 Josh Ho-Sang 12.00 30.00
CG24 Steven Stamkos 20.00 50.00
CG25 Wayne Gretzky 60.00 150.00
CG26 Clayton Keller 25.00 60.00
CG27 Vladimir Tarasenko 12.00 30.00
CG28 Nicklas Backstrom 10.00 25.00
CG29 Bobby Orr 50.00 125.00
CG30 Patrick Kane 20.00 50.00
CG31 P.K. Subban 12.00 30.00
CG32 Pierre-Luc Dubois 15.00 40.00
CG33 Brock Boeser 25.00 60.00
CG34 Joe Sakic 20.00 50.00
CG35 Nico Hischier 30.00 80.00
CG36 Connor McDavid 50.00 125.00

2017-18 Synergy Color Shift

C1 Connor McDavid 40.00 100.00
C2 P.K. Subban 10.00 25.00
C3 John Tavares 12.00 30.00
C4 Nico Hischier 25.00 60.00
C5 Alex Ovechkin 30.00 80.00
C6 Jonathan Toews 12.00 30.00
C7 Patrik Laine 10.00 25.00
C8 Carey Price 15.00 40.00
C9 Johnny Gaudreau 12.00 30.00
C10 Sidney Crosby 30.00 80.00
C11 Mario Lemieux 30.00 80.00
C12 Steve Yzerman 20.00 50.00
C13 Ryan Getzlaf 8.00 20.00
C14 Brock Boeser 50.00 125.00
C15 Patrick Kane 15.00 40.00
C16 Brad Marchand 15.00 40.00
C17 Steven Stamkos 15.00 40.00
C18 Vladimir Tarasenko 10.00 25.00
C19 Nolan Patrick 15.00 40.00
C20 Auston Matthews 30.00 80.00
C21 Peter Forsberg 15.00 40.00
C22 Brent Burns 8.00 20.00
C23 Patrick Roy 20.00 50.00
C24 Henrik Lundqvist 20.00 50.00
C25 Erik Karlsson 10.00 25.00
C26 Pierre-Luc Dubois 12.00 30.00
C27 Evgeni Malkin 15.00 40.00
C28 Clayton Keller 20.00 50.00
C29 Nikita Kucherov 15.00 40.00
C30 Wayne Gretzky 50.00 125.00

2017-18 Synergy Exceptional Talent

ET1 Mark Scheifele 1.50 4.00
ET2 Henrik Lundqvist 2.50 6.00
ET3 Tyson Jost 2.00 5.00
ET4 Evgeny Svechnikov 2.00 5.00
ET5 Alexander Nylander 1.50 4.00
ET6 Owen Tippett 2.00 5.00
ET7 Filip Chytil 1.00 2.50
ET8 Brent Burns 1.00 2.50
ET9 Nikita Kucherov 2.00 5.00
ET10 Nicklas Backstrom 1.00 2.50
ET11 Jeff Carter .75 2.00
ET12 P.K. Subban 1.25 3.00
ET13 Artemi Panarin 2.00 5.00
ET14 Ryan Getzlaf 1.00 2.50
ET15 John Tavares 1.50 4.00
ET16 Steven Stamkos 2.00 5.00
ET17 Jack Eichel 1.50 4.00
ET18 Jamie Benn 1.00 2.50
ET19 Jonathan Toews 1.50 4.00
ET20 Patrik Laine 1.25 3.00
ET21 Johnny Gaudreau 1.50 4.00
ET22 Carey Price 2.00 5.00
ET23 Brad Marchand 2.00 5.00
ET24 Vladimir Tarasenko 1.25 3.00
ET25 Pierre-Luc Dubois 1.50 4.00
ET26 Will Butcher 1.25 3.00
ET27 Alex DeBrincat 2.50 6.00
ET28 Kailer Yamamoto 2.50 6.00
ET29 Alexander Ovechkin 4.00 10.00
ET30 Patrick Kane 2.00 5.00
ET31 Brock Boeser 2.50 6.00
ET32 Clayton Keller 2.50 6.00
ET33 Charlie McAvoy 2.50 6.00
ET34 Josh Ho-Sang 1.25 3.00
ET35 Erik Karlsson 1.25 3.00
ET36 Evgeni Malkin 2.00 5.00
ET37 Nico Hischier 3.00 8.00
ET38 Nolan Patrick 2.00 5.00
ET39 Auston Matthews 4.00 10.00
ET40 Connor McDavid 5.00 12.00
ET41 Sidney Crosby 4.00 10.00
ET42 Wayne Gretzky 6.00 15.00

2017-18 Synergy Impact Players

IP1 Wayne Gretzky 5.00 12.00
IP2 Henrik Zetterberg 1.00 2.50
IP3 Mitch Marner 1.25 3.00
IP4 Patrick Marleau .75 2.00
IP5 Nico Hischier 2.50 6.00
IP6 Corey Perry 1.25 3.00
IP7 Daniel Sedin 1.00 2.50
IP8 Drew Doughty 1.00 2.50
IP9 Brock Boeser 2.00 5.00
IP10 Steven Stamkos 1.50 4.00
IP11 Pavel Bure .75 2.00
IP12 Ryan McDonagh .50 1.25
IP13 Patrice Bergeron 1.00 2.50
IP14 Tyler Seguin 1.00 2.50
IP15 Patrik Laine 1.00 2.50
IP16 Filip Forsberg 1.25 3.00
IP17 Mike Bossy .75 2.00
IP18 Nolan Patrick 1.50 4.00
IP19 Ryan Johansen .60 1.50
IP20 Patrick Kane 1.50 4.00
IP21 Clayton Keller 2.00 5.00
IP22 Cam Atkinson .75 2.00
IP23 Evgeni Malkin 1.50 4.00
IP24 Marc-Andre Fleury 1.50 4.00
IP25 Connor McDavid 4.00 10.00
IP26 Nathan MacKinnon 3.00 8.00
IP27 Alex DeBrincat 2.00 5.00
IP28 Peter Forsberg 1.50 4.00
IP29 Taylor Hall .75 2.00
IP30 Erik Karlsson 1.00 2.50
IP31 Anders Bjork 1.00 2.50
IP32 Bobby Orr 3.00 8.00
IP33 Blake Wheeler .75 2.00
IP34 Duncan Keith .60 1.50
IP35 Dominik Hasek 1.25 3.00
IP36 Nikita Kucherov 1.50 4.00
IP37 Mario Lemieux 3.00 8.00
IP38 Nicklas Lidstrom .75 2.00
IP39 Claude Giroux .75 2.00
IP40 Auston Matthews 3.00 8.00
IP41 Pat LaFontaine .75 2.00
IP42 Will Butcher 1.00 2.50
IP43 Max Pacioretty .75 2.00
IP44 Kailer Yamamoto 2.00 5.00
IP45 Josh Ho-Sang 1.00 2.50
IP46 Shea Weber .60 1.50
IP47 Pierre-Luc Dubois 1.25 3.00
IP48 Jean Beliveau .75 2.00
IP49 Joe Pavelski 1.00 2.50
IP50 Sidney Crosby 3.00 8.00

2017-18 Synergy Impact Players Blue

*BLUE/26: 2X TO 5X BASIC INSERTS
IP15 Patrik Laine 15.00 40.00
IP32 Bobby Orr 25.00 60.00

2017-18 Synergy Noteworthy Newcomers

NN1 Nico Hischier 2.50 6.00
NN2 Evgeny Svechnikov 1.50 4.00
NN3 Haydn Fleury .75 2.00
NN4 Adrian Kempe 1.50 4.00
NN5 Pierre-Luc Dubois 1.25 3.00
NN6 Jack Roslovic 1.00 2.50
NN7 Owen Tippett 1.50 4.00
NN8 Tyson Jost 1.50 4.00
NN9 Anders Bjork 1.00 2.50
NN10 Clayton Keller 2.00 5.00
NN11 Colin White 1.00 2.50
NN12 Martin Necas 2.50 6.00
NN13 Jesper Bratt 1.50 4.00
NN14 Alex DeBrincat 2.00 5.00
NN15 Josh Ho-Sang 1.00 2.50
NN16 Filip Chytil .75 2.00
NN17 Alex Kerfoot 1.50 4.00
NN18 Logan Brown .75 2.00
NN19 Alexander Nylander 1.25 3.00

NN20 Charlie McAvoy 2.00 5.00
NN21 Ian McCoshen .75 2.00
NN22 Victor Mete .75 2.00
NN23 Christian Fischer 1.00 2.50
NN24 Will Butcher 1.00 2.50
NN25 Brock Boeser 2.00 5.00
NN26 Alex Tuch 2.00 5.00
NN27 Robert Hagg .75 2.00
NN28 Brendan Lemieux .75 2.00
NN29 Kailer Yamamoto 2.00 5.00
NN30 Nolan Patrick 1.50 4.00

2017-18 Synergy Noteworthy Newcomers Red

NN5 Pierre-Luc Dubois 12.00 30.00
NN12 Martin Necas 12.00 30.00

2018-19 Synergy Blue

*VETS: .5X TO 1.25X BASIC CARDS
*ROOKIES: .5X TO 1.25X BASIC CARDS
96 Jesperi Kotkaniemi 4.00 10.00
100 Elias Pettersson 25.00 60.00

2018-19 Synergy Purple

93 Carter Hart/79 50.00 120.00
100 Elias Pettersson/40 50.00 120.00

2018-19 Synergy Red

1 Connor McDavid 3.00 8.00
2 Jack Eichel 1.00 2.50
3 Johnny Gaudreau 1.00 2.50
4 Sebastian Aho 1.00 2.50
5 P.K. Subban .75 2.00
6 Brad Marchand 1.25 3.00
7 Patrik Laine .75 2.00
8 Patrick Kane 1.25 3.00
9 Nathan MacKinnon 2.50 6.00
10 John Tavares 1.00 2.50
11 Artemi Panarin 1.25 3.00
12 Jamie Benn .60 1.50
13 Matt Duchene .60 1.50
14 Claude Giroux .60 1.50
15 Erik Karlsson .75 2.00
16 Aaron Ekblad .75 2.00
17 Dylan Larkin .75 2.00
18 Drew Doughty .75 2.00
19 Zach Parise .60 1.50
20 Marc-Andre Fleury 1.25 3.00
21 Henrik Lundqvist 1.50 4.00
22 Taylor Hall .60 1.50
23 Ryan Getzlaf .60 1.50
24 Clayton Keller .75 2.00
25 Sidney Crosby 2.50 6.00
26 Steven Stamkos 1.25 3.00
27 Mathew Barzal .75 2.00
28 Vladimir Tarasenko .75 2.00
29 Brock Boeser .75 2.00
30 Alexander Ovechkin 2.50 6.00
31 Carey Price 1.25 3.00
32 Steve Yzerman 1.50 4.00
33 Brett Hull 1.25 3.00
34 Mark Messier 1.25 3.00
35 Dominik Hasek 1.00 2.50
36 Lanny McDonald .60 1.50
37 Chris Chelios .60 1.50
38 Peter Forsberg 1.25 3.00
39 Larry Robinson .60 1.50
40 Wayne Gretzky 4.00 10.00
41 Jakub Zboril 2.50 6.00
42 Cal Petersen 1.25 3.00
43 Josh Mahura 1.25 3.00
44 Sami Niku 1.25 3.00
45 Kristian Vesalainen 2.00 5.00
46 Rourke Chartier 1.25 3.00
47 Par Lindholm 1.50 4.00
48 Ethan Bear 2.50 6.00
49 Mathieu Joseph 2.00 5.00
50 Maxime Lajoie 2.50 6.00
51 Adam Gaudette 1.50 4.00
52 Filip Hronek 1.50 4.00
53 Antti Suomela 1.25 3.00
54 Zach Aston-Reese 2.50 6.00
55 Spencer Foo 1.25 3.00
56 Mikhail Vorobyev 1.25 3.00
57 Christoffer Ehn 1.25 3.00
58 Travis Dermott 2.50 6.00
59 Kiefer Sherwood 1.25 3.00
60 Jaret Anderson-Dolan 1.25 3.00
61 Isac Lundestrom 1.25 3.00
62 Maxim Mamin 1.50 4.00
63 Andreas Johnsson 2.00 5.00
64 Joe Hicketts 1.50 4.00
65 Dylan Gambrell 1.50 4.00
66 Dillon Dube 2.00 5.00
67 Dominik Kahun 1.50 4.00
68 Roope Hintz 4.00 10.00
69 Dylan Sikura 2.00 5.00
70 Anthony Cirelli 2.50 6.00
71 Warren Foegele 1.50 4.00
72 Oskar Lindblom 2.50 6.00
73 Austin Wagner 1.25 3.00
74 Noah Juulsen 1.50 4.00
75 Maxime Comtois 1.50 4.00
76 Robert Thomas 3.00 8.00
77 Ilya Samsonov 3.00 8.00
78 Brett Howden 2.00 5.00
79 Jordan Kyrou 3.00 8.00
80 Henri Jokiharju 1.25 3.00
81 Jordan Greenway 1.50 4.00
82 Henrik Borgstrom 2.50 6.00
83 Evan Bouchard 4.00 10.00
84 Troy Terry 2.50 6.00
85 Ryan Donato 2.50 6.00
86 Lias Andersson 2.50 6.00
87 Juuso Valimaki 1.50 4.00
88 Dennis Cholowski 1.50 4.00
89 Michael Rasmussen 2.00 5.00
90 Sam Steel 1.50 4.00
91 Drake Batherson 3.00 8.00
92 Miro Heiskanen 4.00 10.00
93 Carter Hart 30.00 80.00
94 Brady Tkachuk 5.00 12.00
95 Eeli Tolvanen 3.00 8.00
96 Jesperi Kotkaniemi 3.00 8.00
97 Andrei Svechnikov 4.00 10.00
98 Casey Mittelstadt 3.00 8.00
99 Rasmus Dahlin 4.00 10.00
100 Elias Pettersson 12.00 30.00

2018-19 Synergy Autographs

AAD Alex Delvecchio A 8.00 20.00
AAK Anze Kopitar A 12.00 30.00
AAL Anders Lee E 6.00 15.00
AAM Auston Matthews A 100.00 200.00
AAN Anthony Mantha B 6.00 15.00
AAP Artemi Panarin B 15.00 40.00
AAR Alexander Radulov C 8.00 20.00
AAS Andrei Svechnikov D 20.00 50.00
AAV Andrei Vasilevskiy C 12.00 30.00
ABB Brock Boeser B 10.00 25.00
ABE Jake Bean E 8.00 20.00
ABO Johnny Bower B 8.00 20.00
ABS Brady Skjei D 6.00 15.00
ABT Brady Tkachuk D 25.00 60.00
ACA Craig Anderson C 6.00 15.00
ACC Chris Chelios B 8.00 20.00
ACH Connor Hellebuyck C 15.00 40.00
ACK Clayton Keller B 10.00 25.00
ACM Connor McDavid B 40.00 100.00
ACO Colton Parayko C 6.00 15.00
ACP Carey Price A 15.00 40.00
ADB Drake Batherson C 15.00 40.00
ADH Dominik Hasek B 12.00 30.00
AEB Evan Bouchard E 20.00 50.00
AED Evgenii Dadonov C 5.00 12.00
AEK Evgeny Kuznetsov C 10.00 25.00
AEM Evgeni Malkin B 15.00 40.00
AEP Elias Pettersson D 40.00 100.00
AET Eeli Tolvanen E 15.00 40.00
AGI John Gibson B 8.00 20.00
AGU Jake Guentzel A 12.00 30.00
AHJ Henri Jokiharju E 6.00 15.00
AHL Henrik Lundqvist A 20.00 50.00
AHO Brett Howden E 10.00 25.00
AHU Brett Hull A 15.00 40.00
AIS Ilya Samsonov E 15.00 40.00
AJB Jamie Benn B 8.00 20.00
AJD Jonathan Drouin B 6.00 15.00
AJG Johnny Gaudreau A 12.00 30.00
AJJ Jaromir Jagr B 25.00 60.00
AJK Jari Kurri B 8.00 20.00
AJM Jonathan Marchessault C 10.00 25.00
AJT John Tavares B 25.00 60.00
AJV Jakub Voracek B 6.00 15.00
AKA Evander Kane C 15.00 40.00
AKL John Klingberg C 8.00 20.00
AKO Jesperi Kotkaniemi D 15.00 40.00
AKV Kristian Vesalainen E 10.00 25.00
AKY Jordan Kyrou E 15.00 40.00
ALA Maxime Lajoie D 12.00 30.00
ALD Leon Draisaitl B 25.00 60.00
AMA Mitch Marner C 12.00 30.00
AMB Mike Bossy B 8.00 20.00
AMC Michael McLeod E 8.00 20.00
AMD Max Domi B 8.00 20.00
AMF Marc-Andre Fleury B 15.00 40.00
AMH Miro Heiskanen D 20.00 50.00
AMI Casey Mittelstadt C 15.00 40.00
AMJ Martin Jones B 15.00 40.00
AML Mario Lemieux A 30.00 80.00
AMM Mark Messier A 15.00 40.00
AMP Max Pacioretty B 30.00 80.00
AMR Michael Rasmussen E 10.00 25.00
AMS Mark Scheifele B 12.00 30.00
ANE Nikolaj Ehlers A 8.00 20.00
ANH Noah Hanifin C 8.00 20.00
ANK Nikita Kucherov B 15.00 40.00
AOR Bobby Orr C 40.00 100.00
APD Pavel Datsyuk B 12.00 30.00
APF Peter Forsberg B 15.00 40.00
APK Patrick Kane A 20.00 50.00
APL Patrik Laine B 10.00 25.00
APR Patrick Roy B 20.00 50.00
ARE Ryan Ellis C 6.00 15.00
ART Robert Thomas D 15.00 40.00
ASA Sebastian Aho C 12.00 30.00
ASB Sergei Bobrovsky B 12.00 30.00
ASM Sean Monahan C 5.00 12.00
AST Mark Stone B 10.00 25.00
ASY Steve Yzerman A 20.00 50.00
ATH Taylor Hall A 8.00 20.00
ATO Jonathan Toews B 12.00 30.00
AVL Vladimir Tarasenko B 10.00 25.00
AVT Vincent Trocheck B 8.00 20.00
AWG Wayne Gretzky B 200.00 500.00
AWK William Karlsson C 10.00 25.00

2018-19 Synergy Cast for Greatness

CG1 Connor McDavid 30.00 80.00
CG2 Patrick Kane 12.00 30.00
CG3 Casey Mittelstadt 12.00 30.00
CG4 Taylor Hall 6.00 15.00
CG5 Patrick Roy 15.00 40.00
CG6 Drew Doughty 8.00 20.00
CG7 Steve Yzerman 15.00 40.00
CG8 Brock Boeser 8.00 20.00
CG9 David Pastrnak 15.00 40.00
CG10 Wayne Gretzky 40.00 100.00
CG11 Patrice Bergeron 8.00 20.00
CG12 Artemi Panarin 8.00 20.00
CG13 Jakub Voracek 5.00 12.00
CG14 Sidney Crosby 25.00 60.00
CG15 Brady Tkachuk 20.00 50.00
CG16 Carey Price 12.00 30.00
CG17 Andrei Svechnikov 15.00 40.00
CG18 Filip Forsberg 10.00 25.00
CG19 Patrik Laine 8.00 20.00
CG20 John Tavares 10.00 25.00
CG21 Henrik Lundqvist 15.00 40.00
CG22 Nathan MacKinnon 25.00 60.00
CG23 Marc-Andre Fleury 12.00 30.00
CG24 Erik Karlsson 8.00 20.00
CG25 Alexander Ovechkin 25.00 60.00
CG26 Jesperi Kotkaniemi 12.00 30.00
CG27 Dylan Larkin 8.00 20.00
CG28 Mathew Barzal 8.00 20.00
CG29 Lanny McDonald 6.00 15.00
CG30 Auston Matthews 25.00 60.00
CG31 Tyler Seguin 8.00 20.00
CG32 Pavel Bure 6.00 15.00
CG33 Steven Stamkos 12.00 30.00
CG34 Jack Eichel 10.00 25.00
CG35 Rasmus Dahlin 15.00 40.00
CG36 Elias Pettersson 20.00 50.00

2018-19 Synergy Exceptional Talent

ET1 Rasmus Dahlin 1.50 4.00
ET2 Maxime Comtois .60 1.50
ET3 Eeli Tolvanen 1.25 3.00
ET4 Evan Bouchard 1.50 4.00
ET5 Ryan Donato 1.00 2.50
ET6 Jakub Zboril 1.00 2.50
ET7 Dennis Cholowski .60 1.50
ET8 Travis Dermott 1.00 2.50
ET9 Warren Foegele .60 1.50
ET10 Maxime Lajoie 1.00 2.50
ET11 Juuso Valimaki .60 1.50
ET12 Jake Bean .60 1.50
ET13 Mikhail Vorobyev .50 1.25
ET14 Dylan Sikura .75 2.00
ET15 Dillon Dube .75 2.00
ET16 Lias Andersson 1.00 2.50
ET17 Sam Steel .60 1.50
ET18 Josh Mahura .50 1.25
ET19 Miro Heiskanen 1.50 4.00
ET20 Jesperi Kotkaniemi 1.25 3.00
ET21 Jordan Kyrou 1.25 3.00
ET22 Ilya Samsonov 1.25 3.00
ET23 Henri Jokiharju .50 1.25
ET24 Robert Thomas 1.25 3.00
ET25 Brady Tkachuk 2.00 5.00
ET26 Troy Terry 1.00 2.50
ET27 Jordan Greenway .60 1.50
ET28 Brett Howden .75 2.00
ET29 Jaret Anderson-Dolan .50 1.25
ET30 Andrei Svechnikov 1.50 4.00
ET31 Adam Gaudette 1.00 2.50
ET32 Zach Aston-Reese 1.00 2.50
ET33 Rourke Chartier .50 1.25
ET34 Anthony Cirelli 1.00 2.50
ET35 Noah Juulsen .60 1.50
ET36 Andreas Johnsson .75 2.00
ET37 Michael Rasmussen .75 2.00
ET38 Drake Batherson 1.25 3.00
ET39 Henrik Borgstrom 1.00 2.50
ET40 Casey Mittelstadt 1.25 3.00
ET41 Kristian Vesalainen .75 2.00
ET42 Elias Pettersson 5.00 12.00

2018-19 Synergy Glow Shift

G1 Connor McDavid 40.00 100.00
G2 Auston Matthews 30.00 80.00
G3 John Tavares 12.00 30.00
G4 Patrick Kane 15.00 40.00
G5 Dylan Larkin 10.00 25.00
G6 Henrik Lundqvist 20.00 50.00
G8 Sidney Crosby 30.00 80.00
G9 Steven Stamkos 15.00 40.00
G10 P.K. Subban 10.00 25.00
G11 Drew Doughty 10.00 25.00
G13 Brock Boeser 10.00 25.00
G14 Patrik Laine 10.00 25.00
G15 David Pastrnak 20.00 50.00
G17 Patrick Roy 20.00 50.00
G18 Pavel Bure 8.00 20.00
G19 Pavel Datsyuk 12.00 30.00
G20 Chris Chelios 8.00 20.00
G21 Rasmus Dahlin 20.00 50.00
G22 Andrei Svechnikov 20.00 50.00
G23 Elias Pettersson 25.00 60.00
G24 Casey Mittelstadt 15.00 40.00
G25 Jesperi Kotkaniemi 15.00 40.00

2018-19 Synergy Last Line Of Defense

LD1 Carey Price .75 2.00
LD2 Corey Crawford .30 .75
LD3 Connor Hellebuyck .75 2.00
LD4 Frederik Andersen .50 1.25
LD5 Henrik Lundqvist 1.00 2.50
LD6 Martin Jones .30 .75
LD7 Pekka Rinne .40 1.00
LD8 Jonathan Quick .50 1.25
LD9 Sergei Bobrovsky .60 1.50
LD10 Andrei Vasilevskiy .60 1.50
LD11 Devan Dubnyk .30 .75
LD12 Braden Holtby .50 1.25
LD13 Tuukka Rask .50 1.25
LD14 Matt Murray .60 1.50
LD15 Marc-Andre Fleury .75 2.00

2018-19 Synergy Post Season Perfection

PS1 Wayne Gretzky 2.50 6.00
PS2 Mario Lemieux 1.50 4.00
PS3 Patrick Roy 1.00 2.50
PS4 Maurice Richard .75 2.00
PS5 Bobby Orr 1.50 4.00
PS6 Joe Sakic .75 2.00
PS7 Mark Messier .75 2.00
PS8 Mike Bossy .40 1.00
PS9 Paul Coffey .40 1.00
PS10 Jonathan Quick .50 1.25
PS11 Patrick Kane .75 2.00
PS12 Cam Ward .40 1.00
PS13 Evgeni Malkin .75 2.00
PS14 Bob Baun .40 1.00
PS15 Sidney Crosby 1.50 4.00
PS16 Jake Guentzel .60 1.50
PS17 Steve Yzerman 1.00 2.50
PS18 Ray Bourque .60 1.50
PS19 Martin Brodeur 1.00 2.50
PS20 Alexander Ovechkin 1.50 4.00

2018-19 Synergy Significant Selections

SS1 Connor McDavid 4.00 10.00
SS2 Jack Eichel 1.25 3.00
SS3 Mitch Marner 1.25 3.00
SS4 Brock Boeser 1.00 2.50
SS5 Casey Mittelstadt 1.50 4.00
SS6 Jesperi Kotkaniemi 1.50 4.00
SS7 Andrei Svechnikov 2.00 5.00
SS8 Drake Batherson 1.50 4.00
SS9 Ryan Donato 1.25 3.00
SS10 Auston Matthews 3.00 8.00
SS11 Eeli Tolvanen 1.50 4.00
SS12 Patrik Laine 1.00 2.50
SS13 Brady Tkachuk 2.50 6.00
SS14 Rasmus Dahlin 2.00 5.00
SS15 Elias Pettersson 2.50 6.00

2018-19 Synergy Significant Selections Green

*GREEN: .5X TO 1.25X BASIC INSERTS
SS15 Elias Pettersson 15.00 40.00

2018-19 Synergy Significant Selections Purple

*PURPLE: 2.5X TO 6X BASIC INSERTS
SS7 Andrei Svechnikov 12.00 30.00
SS15 Elias Pettersson 25.00 60.00

2019-20 Synergy Green

*GREEN.VETS: .75X TO 2X BASIC CARDS
*GREEN.RC: 1.25X TO 3X BASIC CARDS
91 Cale Makar AU/99 40.00 100.00
92 Quinn Hughes AU/99 40.00 100.00
93 Filip Zadina AU/99 12.00 30.00
94 Ryan Poehling AU/99 12.00 30.00
95 Nikita Gusev AU/99 12.00 30.00
96 Cody Glass AU/99 12.00 30.00
97 Nick Suzuki AU/99 30.00 80.00
98 Kirby Dach AU/99 15.00 40.00
99 Kaapo Kakko/99 12.00 30.00
100 Jack Hughes AU/99 40.00 100.00

2019-20 Synergy Red

*BLUE.VETS: .5X TO 1.25X BASIC CARDS
*BLUE.RC/199-399: .5X TO 1.25X BASIC CARDS
1 Connor McDavid 3.00 8.00
2 Tuukka Rask .75 2.00
3 Sebastian Aho 1.00 2.50
4 Pierre-Luc Dubois .50 1.25
5 John Tavares 1.00 2.50
6 Mathew Barzal .75 2.00
7 Mika Zibanejad .75 2.00
8 Carter Hart .60 1.50
9 Jack Eichel 1.00 2.50
10 Steven Stamkos 1.25 3.00
11 Dylan Larkin .75 2.00
12 Aleksander Barkov 1.00 2.50
13 Carey Price 1.25 3.00
14 Brady Tkachuk 1.00 2.50
15 Nathan MacKinnon 2.50 6.00
16 Ben Bishop .50 1.25
17 Devan Dubnyk .50 1.25
18 Roman Josi .60 1.50
19 Ryan O'Reilly .60 1.50
20 Patrick Kane 1.25 3.00
21 Blake Wheeler .60 1.50
22 John Gibson .60 1.50
23 Oliver Ekman-Larsson .60 1.50
24 Matthew Tkachuk 1.25 3.00
25 Alexander Ovechkin 2.50 6.00
26 Drew Doughty .75 2.00
27 Brent Burns .60 1.50
28 Elias Pettersson 1.00 2.50
29 Marc-Andre Fleury 1.25 3.00
30 Sidney Crosby 2.50 6.00
31 Taylor Hall .60 1.50
32 Mikko Rantanen AS 1.50 4.00
33 Sidney Crosby AS 2.50 6.00
34 P.K. Subban AS .75 2.00
35 Henrik Lundqvist AS 1.50 4.00
36 Connor McDavid AS 3.00 8.00
37 Nikita Kucherov AS 1.25 3.00
38 Elias Pettersson AS 1.00 2.50
39 Erik Karlsson AS .75 2.00
40 Auston Matthews AS 2.50 6.00
41 Max Jones 1.50 4.00
42 Teddy Blueger 1.50 4.00
43 Nico Sturm 1.25 3.00
44 Taro Hirose 1.50 4.00
45 Rem Pitlick 1.50 4.00
46 Libor Hajek 1.25 3.00
47 Max Veronneau 1.25 3.00
48 Matt Roy 1.50 4.00
49 Karson Kuhlman 1.50 4.00
50 Trent Frederic 1.25 3.00
51 Aleksi Saarela 1.50 4.00
52 Kevin Stenlund 1.25 3.00
53 Vladislav Gavrikov 1.25 3.00
54 Joel L'Esperance 1.50 4.00
55 Zack MacEwen 1.25 3.00
56 Zach Senyshyn 1.50 4.00
57 Guillaume Brisebois 1.50 4.00
58 Jacob Middleton 1.25 3.00
59 Ryan Kuffner 1.25 3.00
60 Rudolfs Balcers 1.50 4.00
61 Nathan Bastian 1.50 4.00
62 Joey Daccord 3.00 8.00
63 Jimmy Schuldt 1.25 3.00
64 Brandon Gignac 1.25 3.00
65 Blake Lizotte 1.50 4.00
66 Kaden Fulcher 1.50 4.00
67 Vitaly Abramov 1.50 4.00
68 Josh Jacobs 1.25 3.00
69 Julien Gauthier 1.50 4.00
70 Adam Johnson 1.50 4.00
71 Brady Keeper 1.50 4.00
72 Brogan Rafferty 1.50 4.00
73 Colin Blackwell 1.50 4.00
74 Mackenzie MacEachern 1.50 4.00
75 Dennis Gilbert 1.25 3.00
76 Philippe Myers 1.25 3.00
77 Erik Brannstrom 1.50 4.00
78 Dante Fabbro 1.50 4.00
79 Alexandre Texier 1.50 4.00
80 Victor Olofsson 3.00 8.00
81 Carl Grundstrom 1.50 4.00
82 Oliver Wahlstrom 2.50 6.00
83 Rasmus Sandin 2.50 6.00
84 Adam Fox 4.00 10.00
85 Connor Clifton 1.50 4.00
86 Barrett Hayton 3.00 8.00
87 Ilya Mikheyev 2.50 6.00
88 Jesper Boqvist 2.50 6.00
89 Tobias Bjornfot 1.50 4.00
90 Noah Dobson 4.00 10.00
91 Cale Makar 8.00 20.00
92 Quinn Hughes 8.00 20.00
93 Filip Zadina 2.50 6.00
94 Ryan Poehling 2.50 6.00
95 Nikita Gusev 2.50 6.00
96 Cody Glass 2.50 6.00
97 Nick Suzuki 6.00 15.00
98 Kirby Dach 3.00 8.00
99 Kaapo Kakko 2.50 6.00
100 Jack Hughes 8.00 20.00

2019-20 Synergy All Star Journey First Appearance

AP1 Sidney Crosby 1.50 4.00
AP2 John Tavares .60 1.50
AP3 Henrik Lundqvist 1.00 2.50
AP4 Johnny Gaudreau .60 1.50
AP5 Connor McDavid 2.00 5.00
AP6 Erik Karlsson .50 1.25

2019-20 Synergy Autographs

AAV Andrei Vasilevskiy C 12.00 30.00
ABB Ben Bishop C 6.00 15.00
ABT Brady Tkachuk C 12.00 30.00
ABU Brent Burns C 8.00 20.00
ADD Dillon Dube D 5.00 12.00
ADF Dante Fabbro D 8.00 20.00
ADS Dylan Strome B 10.00 25.00
AEP Elias Pettersson A 12.00 30.00
AHL Henrik Lundqvist A 20.00 50.00
AJB Jamie Benn A 8.00 20.00
AJE Jack Eichel B 12.00 30.00
AJG Jake Guentzel C 12.00 30.00
AJH Joe Thornton A 12.00 30.00
AJM Jonathan Marchessault D 10.00 25.00
AJO Jonathan Toews A 12.00 30.00
AJT John Tavares A 12.00 30.00
AJV Jakub Voracek B 6.00 15.00
AJW Jordan Weal D 5.00 12.00
ALD Leon Draisaitl C 25.00 60.00
AMA Marc-Andre Fleury A 15.00 40.00
AMC Connor McDavid B 150.00 250.00
AME Mark Scheifele C 12.00 30.00
AMM Mitch Marner D 12.00 30.00
AMS Mark Stone C 10.00 25.00
ANY Shea Theodore D 10.00 25.00
APZ Petr Mrazek D 8.00 20.00
ARM Ryan Murray C 6.00 15.00
ASA Sebastian Aho D 12.00 30.00
ASE Sam Steel D 6.00 15.00
ASJ Seth Jones C 8.00 20.00
ASM Sean Monahan C 5.00 12.00
ASS Steven Stamkos A 15.00 40.00
AWK William Karlsson C 10.00 25.00

2019-20 Synergy Cast For Greatness

CG1 Ryan Poehling 10.00 25.00
CG2 Filip Zadina 10.00 25.00
CG3 Quinn Hughes 30.00 80.00
CG4 Cale Makar 30.00 80.00
CG5 Erik Brannstrom 6.00 15.00
CG6 Alexandre Texier 6.00 15.00
CG7 Carter Hart 6.00 15.00
CG8 Nikita Kucherov 12.00 30.00
CG9 Alexander Ovechkin 25.00 60.00
CG10 Connor McDavid 30.00 80.00
CG11 Brad Marchand 12.00 30.00
CG12 Nathan MacKinnon 25.00 60.00
CG13 Patrick Kane 12.00 30.00
CG14 Leon Draisaitl 20.00 50.00
CG15 David Pastrnak 15.00 40.00
CG16 Auston Matthews 25.00 60.00
CG17 Sidney Crosby 25.00 60.00
CG18 Patrice Bergeron 8.00 20.00
CG19 Ben Bishop 5.00 12.00
CG20 Andrei Vasilevskiy 10.00 25.00
CG21 Brent Burns 6.00 15.00
CG22 Mikko Rantanen 15.00 40.00
CG23 Steven Stamkos 12.00 30.00
CG24 Jakub Voracek 5.00 12.00
CG25 Jonathan Toews 10.00 25.00
CG26 Max Pacioretty 6.00 15.00
CG27 Carey Price 12.00 30.00
CG28 Johnny Gaudreau 10.00 25.00
CG29 John Tavares 10.00 25.00
CG30 Blake Wheeler 6.00 15.00
CG31 Mark Scheifele 10.00 25.00
CG32 Matthew Tkachuk 12.00 30.00
CG33 John Gibson 6.00 15.00
CG34 Taylor Hall 6.00 15.00
CG35 Claude Giroux 6.00 15.00

2019-20 Synergy Impactful Performers

GC1 Nikita Kucherov .75 2.00
GC2 Alexander Ovechkin 1.50 4.00
GC3 Connor McDavid 2.00 5.00
GC4 Brad Marchand .75 2.00
GC5 Nathan MacKinnon 1.50 4.00
GC6 Patrick Kane .75 2.00
GC7 Leon Draisaitl 1.25 3.00
GC8 David Pastrnak 1.00 2.50
GC9 Auston Matthews 1.50 4.00
GC10 Sidney Crosby 1.50 4.00
GC11 Steven Stamkos .75 2.00
GC12 Ben Bishop .30 .75
GC13 Claude Giroux .40 1.00
GC14 Brent Burns .40 1.00
GC15 Johnny Gaudreau .60 1.50
GC16 Elias Pettersson .60 1.50
GC17 Aleksander Barkov .60 1.50
GC18 John Tavares .60 1.50
GC19 Blake Wheeler .40 1.00
GC20 Marc-Andre Fleury .75 2.00

2019-20 Synergy NHL Journey '18-19 Season

NP1 Steven Stamkos .75 2.00
NP2 Sidney Crosby 1.50 4.00
NP3 Patrick Kane .75 2.00
NP4 Nathan MacKinnon 1.50 4.00
NP5 Matthew Tkachuk .75 2.00
NP6 Connor McDavid 2.00 5.00
NP7 Carey Price .75 2.00
NP8 David Pastrnak 1.00 2.50
NP9 Auston Matthews 1.50 4.00
NP10 Alexander Ovechkin 1.50 4.00

2019-20 Synergy NHL Journey Draft Day

NP1 Steven Stamkos .75 2.00
NP2 Sidney Crosby 1.50 4.00
NP3 Patrick Kane .75 2.00
NP4 Nathan MacKinnon 1.50 4.00
NP5 Matthew Tkachuk .75 2.00
NP6 Connor McDavid 2.00 5.00
NP7 Carey Price .75 2.00
NP8 David Pastrnak 1.00 2.50
NP9 Auston Matthews 1.50 4.00
NP10 Alexander Ovechkin 1.50 4.00

2019-20 Synergy NHL Journey Rookie Season

NP1 Steven Stamkos .75 2.00
NP2 Sidney Crosby 1.50 4.00
NP3 Patrick Kane .75 2.00
NP4 Nathan MacKinnon 1.50 4.00
NP5 Matthew Tkachuk .75 2.00
NP6 Connor McDavid 2.00 5.00
NP7 Carey Price .75 2.00
NP8 David Pastrnak 1.00 2.50
NP9 Auston Matthews 1.50 4.00
NP10 Alexander Ovechkin 1.50 4.00

2019-20 Synergy Rookie Autographs

AAT Alexandre Texier D 8.00 20.00
ABH Barrett Hayton C 15.00 40.00
ACG Carl Grundstrom C 8.00 20.00
ACM Cale Makar D 40.00 100.00
AEB Erik Brannstrom D 8.00 20.00
AFZ Filip Zadina D 12.00 30.00
AJA Jack Hughes A 40.00 100.00
AKK Karson Kuhlman C 8.00 20.00
AMJ Max Jones D 8.00 20.00
APM Philippe Myers D 6.00 15.00
AQH Quinn Hughes C 40.00 100.00
ARP Ryan Poehling D 12.00 30.00
ATH Taro Hirose D 8.00 20.00
AVO Victor Olofsson C 15.00 40.00

2019-20 Synergy Rookie Journey Away Jersey

RP1 Cale Makar 2.00 5.00
RP2 Quinn Hughes 2.00 5.00
RP3 Filip Zadina .60 1.50
RP4 Ryan Poehling UER .60 1.50
RP5 Max Jones .40 1.00
RP6 Carl Grundstrom .40 1.00
RP7 Erik Brannstrom .40 1.00
RP8 Vitaly Abramov .40 1.00
RP9 Dante Fabbro .40 1.00
RP10 Alexandre Texier .40 1.00
RP11 Kaapo Kakko .60 1.50
RP12 Nick Suzuki 1.50 4.00
RP13 Cody Glass .60 1.50
RP14 Rasmus Sandin .60 1.50
RP16A Jack Hughes 2.00 5.00
RP16B Jack Hughes VAR 2.00 5.00

2019-20 Synergy Rookie Journey Draft Day

RP1 Cale Makar 2.00 5.00
RP2 Quinn Hughes 2.00 5.00
RP3 Filip Zadina .60 1.50
RP4 Ryan Poehling .60 1.50
RP5 Max Jones .40 1.00
RP6 Carl Grundstrom .40 1.00
RP7 Erik Brannstrom .40 1.00
RP8 Vitaly Abramov .40 1.00
RP9 Dante Fabbro .40 1.00
RP10 Alexandre Texier .40 1.00
RP11 Kaapo Kakko .60 1.50
RP12 Nick Suzuki 1.50 4.00
RP13 Cody Glass .60 1.50
RP14 Rasmus Sandin .60 1.50
RP15 Noah Dobson 1.00 2.50
RP16 Jack Hughes 2.00 5.00

2019-20 Synergy Rookie Journey Home Jersey

RP1 Cale Makar 2.00 5.00
RP2 Quinn Hughes 2.00 5.00
RP3 Filip Zadina .60 1.50
RP4 Ryan Poehling .60 1.50
RP5 Max Jones .40 1.00
RP6 Carl Grundstrom .40 1.00
RP7 Erik Brannstrom .40 1.00
RP8 Vitaly Abramov .40 1.00
RP9 Dante Fabbro .40 1.00
RP10 Alexandre Texier .40 1.00
RP11 Kaapo Kakko .60 1.50
RP12 Nick Suzuki 1.50 4.00
RP13 Cody Glass .60 1.50
RP14 Rasmus Sandin .60 1.50
RP15 Noah Dobson 1.00 2.50
RP16 Jack Hughes 2.00 5.00

2020-21 Synergy Red

1 Alex Ovechkin 2.50 6.00
2 Mark Stone .75 2.00
3 Artemi Panarin 1.25 3.00
4 David Pastrnak 1.50 4.00
5 John Tavares 1.00 2.50
6 Andrei Vasilevskiy 1.00 2.50
7 Ryan O'Reilly .60 1.50
8 Patrick Kane 1.25 3.00
9 Connor Hellebuyck 1.00 2.50
10 Dylan Larkin .75 2.00
11 Brady Tkachuk 1.00 2.50
12 Jean-Gabriel Pageau .40 1.00
13 Mitch Marner 1.00 2.50
14 Jack Eichel 1.00 2.50
15 Sebastian Aho 1.00 2.50
16 John Carlson .60 1.50
17 Aleksander Barkov 1.00 2.50
18 Roman Josi .60 1.50
19 Tomas Hertl .60 1.50
20 Ryan Suter .50 1.25
21 Connor McDavid 3.00 8.00
22 Elias Pettersson 1.00 2.50
23 Brad Marchand 1.25 3.00
24 Oliver Ekman-Larsson .60 1.50
25 Carey Price 1.25 3.00
26 Tyler Seguin .75 2.00
27 Nathan MacKinnon 2.50 6.00
28 Mark Scheifele .60 1.50
29 Anze Kopitar 1.00 2.50
30 Nikita Kucherov 1.25 3.00
31 Zach Werenski 1.00 2.50
32 Sidney Crosby 2.50 6.00
33 John Gibson .60 1.50
34 Nico Hischier 1.00 2.50
35 Matthew Tkachuk 1.25 3.00
36 Cale Makar 1.50 4.00
37 Carter Hart .60 1.50
38 Leon Draisaitl 2.00 5.00
39 Auston Matthews 2.50 6.00
40 Quinn Hughes 1.50 4.00
41 John Klingberg .60 1.50
42 Patrice Bergeron .75 2.00
43 Sean Monahan .40 1.00
44 Teuvo Teravainen .60 1.50
45 Seth Jones .60 1.50
46 Max Pacioretty .60 1.50
47 Pekka Rinne .60 1.50
48 Tyler Bertuzzi .50 1.25
49 Victor Hedman .75 2.00
50 Igor Shesterkin 1.25 3.00
51 Sean Couturier .50 1.25
52 Jonathan Huberdeau .75 2.00
53 Evgeni Malkin 1.25 3.00
54 Brock Boeser .75 2.00
55 Mathew Barzal .75 2.00
56 Steven Stamkos 1.25 3.00
57 Ryan Getzlaf .60 1.50
58 Jack Hughes 1.50 4.00
59 Miro Heiskanen .75 2.00
60 Rasmus Dahlin .75 2.00
61 Wendel Clark 1.00 2.50
62 Mark Recchi .75 2.00
63 Darryl Sittler .75 2.00
64 Martin St. Louis .60 1.50
65 Guy Lafleur .75 2.00
66 Bobby Orr 2.50 6.00
67 Trevor Linden .60 1.50
68 Billy Smith .60 1.50
69 John LeClair .60 1.50
70 Mario Lemieux 2.50 6.00
71 Mike Richter .60 1.50
72 Brett Hull 1.25 3.00
73 Gerry Cheevers .60 1.50
74 Peter Bondra .60 1.50
75 Wayne Gretzky 4.00 10.00
76 Joel Kiviranta 2.00 5.00
77 Joseph Woll 4.00 10.00
78 Reid Duke 2.00 5.00
79 Alexander True 1.50 4.00
80 Jani Hakanpaa 1.25 3.00
81 Calvin Thurkauf 1.50 4.00
82 Matiss Kivlenieks 2.50 6.00
83 Alec Regula 1.25 3.00
84 Gustav Lindstrom 1.50 4.00
85 Lucas Carlsson 1.50 4.00
86 Gage Quinney 1.25 3.00
87 Dylan Coghlan 2.00 5.00
88 Steven Lorentz 1.50 4.00
89 Artem Zagidulin 2.00 5.00
90 Brandon Hagel 2.50 6.00
91 Maxim Letunov 1.50 4.00
92 Vitek Vanecek 3.00 8.00
93 Jonas Johansson 2.00 5.00
94 Egor Korshkov 1.25 3.00
95 Anthony Angello 1.50 4.00
96 Stuart Skinner 4.00 10.00
97 MacKenzie Entwistle 1.50 4.00
98 Alexander Yelesin 1.50 4.00
99 Jansen Harkins 1.50 4.00
100 Brayden Burke 1.50 4.00
101 Thomas Harley 3.00 8.00
102 Kieffer Bellows 1.50 4.00
103 Connor Ingram 1.50 4.00
104 Philip Broberg 2.00 5.00
105 Michael DiPietro 2.50 6.00
106 Timothy Liljegren 2.00 5.00
107 Jake Oettinger 5.00 12.00
108 Shane Bowers 1.50 4.00
109 Ty Dellandrea 2.00 5.00
110 Olli Juolevi 2.00 5.00
111 Mikey Anderson 2.00 5.00
112 Alexander Alexeyev 1.50 4.00
113 Morgan Geekie 2.00 5.00
114 Pierre-Olivier Joseph 2.00 5.00
115 Philipp Kurashev 2.50 6.00
116 Jake Evans 2.00 5.00
117 Nicolas Beaudin 2.00 5.00
118 Egor Zamula 1.50 4.00
119 Victor Soderstrom 1.50 4.00
120 Martin Kaut 2.00 5.00
121 Ryan McLeod 1.50 4.00
122 Mikhail Berdin 2.00 5.00
123 Tyler Benson 2.00 5.00
124 Pavel Francouz 2.50 6.00
125 Alex Belzile 1.50 4.00
126 Gabe Vilardi SP 10.00 25.00
127 Liam Foudy SP 6.00 15.00
128 Jason Robertson SP 8.00 20.00
129 Josh Norris SP 15.00 40.00
130 Alexis Lafreniere SP 80.00 200.00
131 Vitali Kravtsov SP 30.00 80.00
132 Connor McMichael SP 10.00 25.00
133 Nick Robertson SP 10.00 25.00
134 Peyton Krebs SP 25.00 60.00
135 Bowen Byram SP 12.00 30.00

2020-21 Synergy Purple

*PURP.NON.AU: 2X TO 5X RED
6 Andrei Vasilevskiy AU/35 15.00 40.00
10 Dylan Larkin AU/65 12.00 30.00
13 Mitch Marner AU/35 15.00 40.00
19 Tomas Hertl AU/35 10.00 25.00
22 Elias Pettersson AU/35 30.00 80.00
23 Brad Marchand AU/35 20.00 50.00
26 Tyler Seguin AU/35 12.00 30.00
28 Mark Scheifele AU/65 15.00 40.00
36 Cale Makar AU/35 30.00 80.00
37 Carter Hart AU/35 40.00 100.00
40 Quinn Hughes AU/35 40.00 100.00
54 Brock Boeser AU/35 12.00 30.00
58 Jack Hughes AU/35 40.00 100.00
61 Wendel Clark AU/35 15.00 40.00
62 Mark Recchi AU/35 10.00 25.00
63 Darryl Sittler AU/35 12.00 30.00
69 John LeClair AU/35 25.00 60.00
73 Gerry Cheevers AU/35 15.00 40.00
74 Peter Bondra AU/35 30.00 80.00
76 Joel Kiviranta AU/35 12.00 30.00
78 Reid Duke AU/35 12.00 30.00
82 Matiss Kivlenieks AU/35 25.00 60.00
101 Thomas Harley AU/35 20.00 50.00
102 Kieffer Bellows AU/35 10.00 25.00
103 Connor Ingram AU/35 10.00 25.00
105 Michael DiPietro/35 40.00 100.00
106 Timothy Liljegren AU/35 12.00 30.00
107 Jake Oettinger AU/35 25.00 60.00
109 Ty Dellandrea AU/35 12.00 30.00

110 Olli Juolevi AU/35 12.00 30.00
113 Morgan Geekie AU/35 20.00 50.00
116 Jake Evans AU/35 12.00 30.00
117 Nicolas Beaudin AU/35 12.00 30.00
120 Martin Kaut AU/35 12.00 30.00
123 Tyler Benson AU/35 12.00 30.00

2020-21 Synergy Red Codes
*CODES: .6X TO 1.5X RED
*CODES.SP: 3X TO 8X RED
127 Liam Foudy SP 120.00 300.00
128 Jason Robertson SP 40.00 100.00
130 Alexis Lafreniere SP 125.00 300.00
131 Vitali Kravtsov SP 80.00 200.00
134 Peyton Krebs SP 250.00 600.00

2020-21 Synergy Autographs
AAB Aleksander Barkov B 15.00 40.00
AAM Auston Matthews A 80.00 200.00
AAP Artemi Panarin B 20.00 50.00
AAS Andrei Svechnikov C 12.00 30.00
AAV Andrei Vasilevskiy C 15.00 40.00
ABB Brock Boeser B 12.00 30.00
ABG Brendan Gallagher C 10.00 25.00
ABH Brett Hull B 20.00 50.00
ABM Brad Marchand B 10.00 25.00
ABO Adam Boqvist D 8.00 20.00
ABU Brent Burns B 10.00 25.00
ACH Carter Hart C 30.00 80.00
ACM Cale Makar B 25.00 60.00
ACP Colton Parayko D 8.00 20.00
ADK Dominik Kubalik D 25.00 60.00
AEM Elvis Merzlikins D 10.00 25.00
AEP Elias Pettersson B 30.00 80.00
AGC Gerry Cheevers B 10.00 25.00
AHA Noah Hanifin D 10.00 25.00
AHE Connor Hellebuyck C 20.00 50.00
AHJ Niklas Hjalmarsson D 6.00 15.00
AJB Jamie Benn B 10.00 25.00
AJM John Marino D 10.00 25.00
AJP Jean-Gabriel Pageau D 6.00 15.00
AJT John Tavares B 15.00 40.00
AJV Jakub Vrana C 10.00 25.00
AKY Kailer Yamamoto D 10.00 25.00
AMC Connor McDavid C 125.00 300.00
AMG Mark Giordano D 10.00 25.00
AML Mario Lemieux A 40.00 100.00
AMM Mitch Marner B 15.00 40.00
AMS Mark Scheifele C 15.00 40.00
AMT Matthew Tkachuk C 20.00 50.00
ANH Nico Hischier C 15.00 40.00
ANS Nick Suzuki C 20.00 50.00
APB Peter Bondra B 10.00 25.00
APD Phillip Danault D 10.00 25.00
APK Patrick Kane B 20.00 50.00
APR Cayden Primeau D 15.00 40.00
ARN Ryan Nugent-Hopkins C 12.00 30.00
AST Shea Theodore D 20.00 50.00
ATL Trevor Linden B 10.00 25.00
ATS Tyler Seguin B 12.00 30.00
ATT Teuvo Teravainen D 10.00 25.00
AVA James van Riemsdyk C 8.00 20.00
AVO Victor Olofsson D 6.00 15.00
AWC Wendel Clark B 15.00 40.00

2020-21 Synergy Autographs Red
*RED: .6X TO 1.5X BASIC
ABO Adam Boqvist/49 15.00 40.00
ACP Colton Parayko/25 15.00 40.00
AJM John Marino/49 20.00 50.00

2020-21 Synergy Cast for Greatness
*PURPLE: .6X TO 1.5X BASIC
*GREEN/50: .75X TO 2X BASIC
CG1 Auston Matthews 12.00 30.00
CG2 Nikita Kucherov 6.00 15.00
CG3 Elias Pettersson 5.00 12.00
CG4 Patrick Kane 6.00 15.00
CG5 Nathan MacKinnon 12.00 30.00
CG6 Matthew Tkachuk 6.00 15.00
CG7 Alex Ovechkin 12.00 30.00
CG8 Leon Draisaitl 10.00 25.00
CG9 John Carlson 3.00 8.00
CG10 Mark Stone 4.00 10.00
CG11 Nick Suzuki 6.00 15.00
CG12 Jack Eichel 5.00 12.00
CG13 Quinn Hughes 8.00 20.00
CG14 Sebastian Aho 5.00 12.00
CG15 Ryan O'Reilly 3.00 8.00
CG16 Connor Hellebuyck 6.00 15.00
CG17 Aleksander Barkov 5.00 12.00
CG18 Brady Tkachuk 5.00 12.00
CG19 David Pastrnak 8.00 20.00
CG20 Evgeni Malkin 6.00 15.00
CG21 Nico Hischier 5.00 12.00
CG22 Cale Makar 8.00 20.00
CG23 Tuukka Rask 4.00 10.00
CG24 Mitch Marner 5.00 12.00
CG25 Artemi Panarin 6.00 15.00
CG26 Dylan Larkin 4.00 10.00
CG27 Sidney Crosby 12.00 30.00
CG28 Igor Shesterkin 6.00 15.00
CG29 Connor McDavid 15.00 40.00
CG30 Gabe Vilardi 6.00 15.00
CG31 Josh Norris 6.00 15.00
CG32 Jason Robertson 10.00 25.00
CG33 Kieffer Bellows 3.00 8.00
CG34 Timothy Liljegren 4.00 10.00
CG35 Liam Foudy 4.00 10.00
CG36 Alexis Lafreniere Bounty 12.00 30.00

2020-21 Synergy Cast for Greatness Signatures
CGSAB Aleksander Barkov 30.00 80.00
CGSAV Andrei Vasilevskiy 30.00 80.00
CGSBG Brendan Gallagher 30.00 80.00
CGSBM Brad Marchand 40.00 100.00
CGSCM Connor McDavid 400.00 1000.00
CGSEP Elias Pettersson 30.00 80.00
CGSJT John Tavares 30.00 80.00
CGSMS Mark Scheifele 30.00 80.00
CGSSM Sean Monahan 40.00 100.00
CGSTS Tyler Seguin 25.00 60.00

2020-21 Synergy Constant Threats
CT1 Alex Ovechkin 2.00 5.00
CT2 Nikita Kucherov 1.00 2.50
CT3 Connor McDavid 2.50 6.00
CT4 Sebastian Aho .75 2.00
CT5 John Tavares .75 2.00
CT6 Mika Zibanejad .60 1.50
CT7 Brad Marchand 1.00 2.50
CT8 Nathan MacKinnon 2.00 5.00
CT9 Mark Stone .60 1.50
CT10 Leon Draisaitl 1.50 4.00
CT11 Steven Stamkos 1.00 2.50
CT12 Patrick Kane 1.00 2.50
CT13 Elias Pettersson .75 2.00
CT14 Auston Matthews 2.00 5.00
CT15 Sidney Crosby 2.00 5.00
CT16 Artemi Panarin 1.00 2.50
CT17 Jack Eichel .75 2.00
CT18 Mark Scheifele .75 2.00
CT19 Tomas Hertl .50 1.25
CT20 David Pastrnak 1.25 3.00

2020-21 Synergy Exceptional Futures
*GOLD/449: .6X TO 1.5X BASIC
*BLACK/99: 1.25X TO 3X BASIC
EFSAF Alexis Lafreniere 4.00 10.00
EFSBB Bowen Byram 2.50 6.00
EFSCM Connor McMichael 2.00 5.00
EFSDK Dylan Coghlan 1.25 3.00
EFSEZ Egor Zamula 1.00 2.50
EFSGV Gabe Vilardi 2.00 5.00
EFSJE Jake Evans 1.25 3.00
EFSJN Josh Norris 2.00 5.00
EFSJR Jason Robertson 3.00 8.00
EFSKB Kieffer Bellows 1.00 2.50
EFSLF Liam Foudy 1.25 3.00
EFSMA Mikey Anderson 1.25 3.00
EFSMD Michael DiPietro 1.50 4.00
EFSMG Morgan Geekie 1.25 3.00
EFSMK Martin Kaut 1.25 3.00
EFSNB Nicolas Beaudin 1.25 3.00
EFSNR Nick Robertson 2.00 5.00
EFSPJ Pierre-Olivier Joseph 1.25 3.00
EFSPK Peyton Krebs 2.00 5.00
EFSRM Ryan McLeod 1.00 2.50
EFSSB Shane Bowers 1.00 2.50
EFSTB Tyler Benson 1.25 3.00
EFSTD Ty Dellandrea 1.25 3.00
EFSTH Thomas Harley 2.00 5.00
EFSTL Timothy Liljegren 1.25 3.00
EFSVK Vitali Kravtsov 2.50 6.00
EFSVS Victor Soderstrom 1.00 2.50

2020-21 Synergy Exceptional Stars
*GOLD: .5X TO 1.25X BASIC
*BLACK: .6X TO 1.5X BASIC
ES1 Patrick Kane 2.00 5.00
ES2 Victor Hedman 1.25 3.00
ES3 John Klingberg 1.00 2.50
ES4 Tuukka Rask 1.25 3.00
ES5 Anze Kopitar 1.50 4.00
ES6 Steven Stamkos 2.00 5.00
ES7 Ryan O'Reilly 1.00 2.50
ES8 Johnny Gaudreau 1.50 4.00
ES9 Artemi Panarin 2.00 5.00
ES10 Mark Stone 1.25 3.00
ES11 Connor Hellebuyck 2.00 5.00
ES12 Tomas Hertl 1.00 2.50
ES13 Blake Wheeler .75 2.00
ES14 John Tavares 1.50 4.00
ES15 Alex Ovechkin 4.00 10.00
ES16 Patrice Bergeron 1.25 3.00
ES17 Evgeni Malkin 2.00 5.00
ES18 Roman Josi 1.00 2.50
ES19 Nikita Kucherov 2.00 5.00
ES20 Seth Jones 1.00 2.50
ES21 Jordan Binnington 1.50 4.00
ES22 Zach Parise 1.00 2.50
ES23 John Gibson 1.00 2.50
ES24 Sean Monahan .60 1.50
ES25 Sean Couturier .75 2.00
ES26 Brad Marchand 2.00 5.00
ES27 Tomas Tatar .60 1.50
ES28 Mika Zibanejad 1.25 3.00
ES29 Teuvo Teravainen 1.00 2.50
ES30 Andrei Vasilevskiy 1.50 4.00
ES31 John Carlson 1.00 2.50
ES32 Sidney Crosby 4.00 10.00
ES33 Morgan Rielly 1.00 2.50
ES34 Darcy Kuemper 1.00 2.50
ES35 Drew Doughty 1.25 3.00
ES36 Nathan MacKinnon 4.00 10.00
ES37 Brayden Schenn 1.00 2.50
ES38 Max Pacioretty 1.00 2.50
ES39 Kris Letang 1.25 3.00
ES40 Leon Draisaitl 3.00 8.00

2020-21 Synergy Exceptional Young Stars
*GOLD: .5X TO 1.25X BASIC
*BLACK: .75X TO 2X BASIC
EY1 Cale Makar 3.00 8.00
EY2 Andrei Svechnikov 1.50 4.00
EY3 Dylan Larkin 1.50 4.00
EY4 Mathew Barzal 1.50 4.00
EY5 Carter Hart 1.25 3.00
EY6 Brady Tkachuk 2.00 5.00
EY7 Kyle Connor 2.00 5.00
EY8 William Nylander 2.50 6.00
EY9 Nico Hischier 2.00 5.00
EY10 Pierre-Luc Dubois 1.00 2.50
EY11 Igor Shesterkin 2.50 6.00
EY12 Mikko Rantanen 3.00 8.00
EY13 Rasmus Dahlin 1.50 4.00
EY14 Connor McDavid 6.00 15.00
EY15 Aleksander Barkov 2.00 5.00
EY16 Zach Werenski 2.00 5.00
EY17 Quinn Hughes 3.00 8.00
EY18 Miro Heiskanen 1.50 4.00
EY19 Matthew Tkachuk 2.50 6.00
EY20 Nick Schmaltz 1.00 2.50
EY21 Mitch Marner 2.00 5.00
EY22 Jack Eichel 2.00 5.00
EY23 Brayden Point 1.50 4.00
EY24 Elias Pettersson 2.00 5.00
EY25 Dominik Kubalik 1.25 3.00
EY26 Sebastian Aho 2.00 5.00
EY27 Auston Matthews 5.00 12.00
EY28 Nick Suzuki 2.50 6.00
EY29 David Pastrnak 3.00 8.00
EY30 Thomas Chabot 1.25 3.00

2020-21 Synergy Perennial All Stars
PA1 Andrei Vasilevskiy .50 1.25
PA2 Patrick Kane .60 1.50
PA3 Johnny Gaudreau .50 1.25
PA4 Marc-Andre Fleury .60 1.50
PA5 Connor McDavid 1.50 4.00
PA6 Shea Weber .30 .75
PA7 Tyler Seguin .40 1.00
PA8 Sidney Crosby 1.25 3.00
PA9 Claude Giroux .30 .75
PA10 Eric Staal .30 .75
PA11 Alex Ovechkin 1.25 3.00
PA12 Erik Karlsson .40 1.00

2020-21 Synergy Roaring 20s
R1 Quinn Hughes 1.00 2.50
R2 Auston Matthews 1.50 4.00
R3 Josh Norris .75 2.00
R4 Matthew Tkachuk .75 2.00
R5 Aleksander Barkov .60 1.50
R6 Jason Robertson 1.25 3.00
R7 David Pastrnak 1.00 2.50
R8 Andrei Svechnikov .50 1.25
R9 Gabe Vilardi .75 2.00
R10 Cale Makar 1.00 2.50
R11 Vitali Kravtsov 1.00 2.50
R12 Mitch Marner .60 1.50
R13 Kieffer Bellows .40 1.00
R14 Brady Tkachuk .60 1.50
R15 Tyler Benson .50 1.25
R16 Timothy Liljegren .50 1.25
R17 Liam Foudy .50 1.25
R18 Connor McDavid 2.00 5.00

2020-21 Synergy Rookie Autographs
*RED: .5X TO 1.25X BASIC
ARAB Alex Belzile D 5.00 12.00
ARAL Alexis Lafreniere A 150.00 400.00
ARAR Alec Regula B 4.00 10.00
ARBH Brandon Hagel D 8.00 20.00
ARCT Calvin Thurkauf D 5.00 12.00
AREK Egor Korshkov C 4.00 10.00
ARGQ Gage Quinney D 4.00 10.00
ARJH Jani Hakanpaa D 4.00 10.00
ARJK Joel Kiviranta C 12.00 30.00
ARJO Jake Oettinger A 15.00 40.00
ARJR Jason Robertson B 20.00 50.00
ARKK Keegan Kolesar D 5.00 12.00
ARLC Lucas Carlsson C 5.00 12.00
ARLF Liam Foudy A 6.00 15.00
ARMG Morgan Geekie B 6.00 15.00
ARMK Matiss Kivlenieks C 20.00 50.00
ARML Maxim Letunov D 5.00 12.00
ARNB Nicolas Beaudin C 6.00 15.00
ARNK Nikolai Knyzhov C 5.00 12.00
AROJ Olli Juolevi B 6.00 15.00
ARPK Peyton Krebs A 10.00 25.00
ARRD Reid Duke D 6.00 15.00
ARSL Steven Lorentz D 5.00 12.00
ARTB Tyler Benson B 6.00 15.00
ARTD Ty Dellandrea B 6.00 15.00
ARTL Timothy Liljegren B 6.00 15.00
ARTR Alexander True D 5.00 12.00
ARVS Victor Soderstrom B 5.00 12.00
ARVV Vitek Vanecek C 10.00 25.00

2020-21 Synergy Rookie Journey Draft
*AWAY: .5X TO 1.25X BASIC
*HOME: .6X TO 1.5X BASIC
RJAL Alexis Lafreniere 50.00 125.00
RJBB Bowen Byram 2.00 5.00
RJCM Connor McMichael 1.50 4.00
RJGV Gabe Vilardi 1.50 4.00
RJJN Josh Norris 1.50 4.00
RJKB Kieffer Bellows .75 2.00
RJLF Liam Foudy 1.00 2.50
RJMA Mikey Anderson 1.00 2.50
RJMD Michael DiPietro 1.25 3.00
RJMK Martin Kaut 1.00 2.50
RJNB Nicolas Beaudin 1.00 2.50
RJNR Nick Robertson 1.50 4.00
RJPK Peyton Krebs 1.50 4.00
RJTB Tyler Benson 1.00 2.50
RJTL Timothy Liljegren 1.00 2.50

2020-21 Synergy Rookie Portrait Autographs Purple
*PURPLE: .5X TO 1.25X RED
A128 Jason Robertson 80.00 200.00
A130 Alexis Lafreniere 1000.00 2500.00
A134 Peyton Krebs 25.00 60.00

2020-21 Synergy Rookie Portrait Autographs Red
A126 Gabe Vilardi 15.00 40.00
A127 Liam Foudy 10.00 25.00
A128 Jason Robertson 25.00 60.00
A129 Josh Norris 15.00 40.00
A130 Alexis Lafreniere 500.00 1200.00
A133 Nick Robertson 40.00 100.00
A134 Peyton Krebs 15.00 40.00
A135 Bowen Byram 20.00 50.00

2020-21 Synergy Stanley Cup Journey Regular Season
*POSTSEASON: .5X TO 1.25X BASIC
*WINNING: .6X TO 1.5X BASIC
CJAK Anze Kopitar 1.25 3.00
CJAO Alex Ovechkin 3.00 8.00
CJDD Drew Doughty 1.00 2.50
CJDK Duncan Keith .60 1.50
CJEM Evgeni Malkin 1.50 4.00
CJES Eric Staal .75 2.00
CJJB Jordan Binnington 1.25 3.00
CJJT Jonathan Toews 1.25 3.00
CJMB Martin Brodeur 2.00 5.00
CJML Mario Lemieux 3.00 8.00
CJNL Nicklas Lidstrom .75 2.00
CJPB Patrice Bergeron 1.00 2.50
CJPK Patrick Kane 1.50 4.00
CJPR Patrick Roy 2.00 5.00
CJRO Ryan O'Reilly .75 2.00
CJSC Sidney Crosby 3.00 8.00
CJSY Steve Yzerman 2.00 5.00
CJWG Wayne Gretzky 5.00 12.00

2020-21 Synergy Star Quest
SQ1 Sidney Crosby 12.00 30.00
SQ2 Nathan MacKinnon 15.00 40.00
SQ3 Carter Hart 25.00 40.00
SQ4 Auston Matthews 15.00 40.00
SQ5 Sean Monahan 2.50 6.00
SQ6 Kyle Connor 6.00 15.00
SQ7 Henrik Lundqvist 10.00 25.00
SQ8 Brent Burns 4.00 10.00
SQ9 Mark Stone 5.00 12.00
SQ10 Cam Atkinson 4.00 10.00
SQ11 Andrei Vasilevskiy 6.00 15.00
SQ12 Sergei Bobrovsky 6.00 15.00
SQ13 Roman Josi 4.00 10.00
SQ14 Aleksander Barkov 6.00 15.00
SQ15 Miro Heiskanen 15.00 40.00
SQ16 Jake Guentzel 6.00 15.00
SQ17 Mark Scheifele 6.00 15.00
SQ18 Kirby Dach 4.00 10.00
SQ19 Teuvo Teravainen 4.00 10.00
SQ20 Connor McDavid 10.00 25.00
SQ21 Bowen Byram 10.00 25.00
SQ22 Nick Robertson 12.00 30.00
SQ23 Jason Robertson 12.00 30.00
SQ24 Gabe Vilardi 4.00 10.00
SQ25 Alexis Lafreniere 150.00 350.00

2020-21 Synergy Synergy FX
*PURPLE: .5X TO 1.25X BASIC
FX1 Auston Matthews 4.00 10.00
FX2 Patrick Kane 2.00 5.00
FX3 Nathan MacKinnon 4.00 10.00
FX4 Carey Price 2.00 5.00
FX5 Sidney Crosby 4.00 10.00
FX6 Artemi Panarin 2.00 5.00
FX7 Mitch Marner 1.50 4.00
FX8 David Pastrnak 2.50 6.00
FX9 Matthew Tkachuk 2.00 5.00
FX10 Roman Josi 1.00 2.50
FX11 Andrei Vasilevskiy 1.50 4.00
FX12 Miro Heiskanen 1.25 3.00
FX13 Jack Eichel 1.50 4.00
FX14 Nikita Kucherov 2.00 5.00
FX15 Mark Stone 1.25 3.00
FX16 Leon Draisaitl 3.00 8.00
FX17 Ryan O'Reilly 1.00 2.50
FX18 Mark Scheifele 1.50 4.00
FX19 Brad Marchand 2.00 5.00
FX20 Sebastian Aho 1.50 4.00
FX21 Sean Monahan .60 1.50
FX22 Brock Boeser 1.25 3.00
FX23 Tomas Hertl 1.00 2.50
FX24 Elias Pettersson 1.50 4.00
FX25 Evgeni Malkin 2.00 5.00
FX26 Seth Jones 1.00 2.50
FX27 Alex Ovechkin 4.00 10.00
FX28 Carter Hart 1.00 2.50
FX29 Teuvo Teravainen 1.00 2.50
FX30 Dylan Larkin 1.25 3.00
FX31 Anze Kopitar 1.50 4.00
FX32 John Klingberg 1.00 2.50
FX33 Brady Tkachuk 1.50 4.00
FX34 Nico Hischier 1.50 4.00
FX35 Quinn Hughes 2.50 6.00
FX36 John Tavares 1.50 4.00
FX37 Igor Shesterkin 2.00 5.00
FX38 Connor Hellebuyck 2.00 5.00
FX39 Patrice Bergeron 1.25 3.00
FX40 Cale Makar 2.50 6.00
FX41 Oliver Ekman-Larsson 1.00 2.50
FX42 Max Pacioretty 1.00 2.50
FX43 John Carlson 1.00 2.50
FX44 Aleksander Barkov 1.50 4.00
FX45 Mathew Barzal 1.25 3.00
FX46 John Gibson 1.00 2.50
FX47 Rasmus Dahlin 1.25 3.00
FX48 Victor Hedman 1.25 3.00
FX49 Jonathan Huberdeau 1.25 3.00
FX50 Connor McDavid 5.00 12.00

2020-21 Synergy Synergy FX Green
*GREEN.NON.AU: .6X TO 1.5X BASIC
FX1 Auston Matthews AU/25 60.00 150.00
FX24 Elias Pettersson AU/25 30.00 80.00
FX28 Carter Hart AU/25 30.00 80.00
FX50 Connor McDavid AU/25 150.00 400.00

2020-21 Synergy Synergy FX Rookies
*PURPLE: .6X TO 1.5X BASIC
FXRAA Alexander Alexeyev 1.00 2.50
FXRAB Alex Belzile 1.00 2.50
FXRAL Alexis Lafreniere 50.00 125.00
FXRAT Alexander True 1.00 2.50
FXRBB Bowen Byram 2.50 6.00
FXRCI Connor Ingram 1.00 2.50
FXRCM Connor McMichael 5.00 12.00
FXRDC Dylan Coghlan 1.25 3.00
FXREK Egor Korshkov .75 2.00
FXREZ Egor Zamula 1.00 2.50
FXRGV Gabe Vilardi 2.00 5.00
FXRJE Jake Evans 1.25 3.00
FXRJK Joel Kiviranta 1.25 3.00
FXRJN Josh Norris 2.00 5.00
FXRJO Jake Oettinger 3.00 8.00
FXRJR Jason Robertson 3.00 8.00
FXRJW Joseph Woll 2.50 6.00
FXRKB Kieffer Bellows 1.00 2.50
FXRKU Philipp Kurashev 1.50 4.00
FXRLF Liam Foudy 1.25 3.00
FXRMA Mikey Anderson 1.25 3.00
FXRMB Mikhail Berdin 1.25 3.00
FXRMD Michael DiPietro 1.50 4.00
FXRMG Morgan Geekie 1.25 3.00
FXRMK Martin Kaut 1.25 3.00
FXRNB Nicolas Beaudin 1.25 3.00
FXRNR Nick Robertson 2.00 5.00
FXROJ Olli Juolevi 1.25 3.00
FXRPB Philip Broberg 1.25 3.00
FXRPF Pavel Francouz 4.00 10.00
FXRPJ Pierre-Olivier Joseph 1.25 3.00
FXRPK Peyton Krebs 4.00 10.00
FXRRM Ryan McLeod 1.00 2.50
FXRSB Shane Bowers 1.00 2.50
FXRTB Tyler Benson 1.25 3.00
FXRTD Ty Dellandrea 1.25 3.00
FXRTH Thomas Harley 2.00 5.00
FXRTL Timothy Liljegren 1.25 3.00
FXRVK Vitali Kravtsov 4.00 10.00
FXRVS Victor Soderstrom 1.00 2.50

2020-21 Synergy Synergy FX Rookies Green
*GREEN.NON.AU: .6X TO 1.5X BASIC
FXRAL Alexis Lafreniere AU/49 800.00 2000.00
FXRBB Bowen Byram AU/49 80.00 200.00
FXRCI Connor Ingram AU/99 8.00 20.00
FXRCM Connor McMichael/99 10.00 25.00
FXRGV Gabe Vilardi AU/49 15.00 40.00
FXRJE Jake Evans AU/99 10.00 25.00
FXRJK Joel Kiviranta AU/99 10.00 25.00
FXRJN Josh Norris AU/49 15.00 40.00
FXRJO Jake Oettinger AU/49 25.00 60.00
FXRJR Jason Robertson AU/99 40.00 100.00
FXRKB Kieffer Bellows AU/99 8.00 20.00
FXRLF Liam Foudy AU/99 10.00 25.00
FXRMB Mikhail Berdin/99 8.00 20.00
FXRMD Michael DiPietro/99 10.00 25.00
FXRMG Morgan Geekie AU/99 10.00 25.00
FXRMK Martin Kaut AU/99 10.00 25.00
FXRNB Nicolas Beaudin AU/99 10.00 25.00
FXRNR Nick Robertson AU/49 15.00 40.00
FXROJ Olli Juolevi AU/99 10.00 25.00
FXRPB Philip Broberg/99 10.00 25.00
FXRPF Pavel Francouz/99 15.00 40.00
FXRPJ Pierre-Olivier Joseph AU/99 10.00 25.00
FXRPK Peyton Krebs AU/49 15.00 40.00
FXRTB Tyler Benson AU/99 10.00 25.00
FXRTD Ty Dellandrea AU/99 10.00 25.00
FXRTL Timothy Liljegren AU/49 10.00 25.00
FXRVK Vitali Kravtsov/99 8.00 20.00

2021-22 Synergy Red
1 Igor Shesterkin 1.25 3.00
2 Jared McCann .50 1.25
3 Troy Terry .50 1.25
4 Jason Robertson 1.00 2.50
5 Elias Lindholm .60 1.50
6 Taylor Hall .60 1.50
7 Marc-Andre Fleury 1.25 3.00
8 Alex Ovechkin 2.50 6.00
9 Clayton Keller .75 2.00
10 Brady Tkachuk 1.00 2.50
11 Jonathan Huberdeau .75 2.00
12 Kyle Connor 1.00 2.50
13 Brad Marchand 1.25 3.00
14 Anze Kopitar 1.00 2.50
15 Jordan Eberle .60 1.50
16 Matthew Tkachuk 1.25 3.00
17 Connor Hellebuyck 1.25 3.00
18 Kevin Fiala .50 1.25
19 Andrei Svechnikov .75 2.00
20 Tyler Bertuzzi .50 1.25
21 Aleksander Barkov 1.00 2.50
22 Connor McDavid 3.00 8.00
23 John Carlson .60 1.50
24 Juuse Saros .75 2.00
25 Steven Stamkos 1.25 3.00
26 Dylan Cozens .60 1.50
27 Tyler Toffoli .60 1.50
28 Kirill Kaprizov 2.00 5.00
29 Nathan MacKinnon 2.50 6.00
30 Jack Hughes 1.50 4.00
31 Auston Matthews 2.50 6.00
32 Anders Lee .50 1.25
33 Boone Jenner .60 1.50
34 Mark Stone .75 2.00
35 Andrei Vasilevskiy 1.00 2.50
36 Jesper Bratt .60 1.50
37 Teuvo Teravainen .60 1.50
38 Mathew Barzal .75 2.00
39 Cale Makar 1.50 4.00
40 Leon Draisaitl 2.00 5.00
41 Nick Suzuki 1.25 3.00
42 Joe Pavelski .75 2.00
43 Alex Nedeljkovic .50 1.25
44 Brock Boeser .75 2.00
45 Jake Guentzel 1.00 2.50
46 Jordan Kyrou .60 1.50
47 Patrick Kane 1.25 3.00
48 Artemi Panarin 1.25 3.00
49 Carter Hart .60 1.50
50 Mitch Marner 1.00 2.50
51 Brent Burns .60 1.50
52 Roman Josi .60 1.50
53 Alex DeBrincat .75 2.00
54 Jonathan Marchessault .75 2.00
55 Drake Batherson .60 1.50
56 Sidney Crosby 2.50 6.00
57 Claude Giroux .60 1.50
58 Quinn Hughes 1.50 4.00
59 Ryan O'Reilly .60 1.50
60 John Tavares 1.00 2.50
61 Paul Coffey .75 2.00
62 Ray Bourque 1.00 2.50
63 Dave Taylor .50 1.25
64 Peter Forsberg 1.25 3.00
65 Teemu Selanne 1.25 3.00
66 Doug Gilmour .75 2.00
67 Vincent Lecavalier .60 1.50
68 Lanny McDonald .60 1.50
69 Jaromir Jagr 2.00 5.00
70 Wayne Gretzky 4.00 10.00
71 Jarome Iginla .75 2.00
72 Pat LaFontaine .60 1.50
73 Mike Modano 1.00 2.50
74 Steve Yzerman 1.50 4.00
75 Theoren Fleury .60 1.50
76 Zac Jones 2.00 5.00
77 Quinton Byfield 4.00 10.00
78 Ukko-Pekka Luukkonen 2.50 6.00
79 Alex Barre-Boulet 1.50 4.00
80 Grigori Denisenko 2.00 5.00
81 Ross Colton 2.00 5.00
82 Alex Newhook 2.50 6.00
83 Jamie Drysdale 2.50 6.00
84 Shane Pinto 2.50 6.00
85 Jeremy Swayman 5.00 12.00
86 Kole Lind 2.00 5.00
87 Cam York 1.50 4.00
88 Jacob Bernard-Docker 1.50 4.00
89 Trevor Zegras 3.00 8.00
90 Joe Veleno 2.00 5.00
91 Jan Jenik 2.00 5.00
92 Filip Gustavsson 3.00 8.00
93 Mike Hardman 1.50 4.00
94 Jonah Gadjovich 1.50 4.00
95 Sampo Ranta 1.50 4.00
96 Arttu Ruotsalainen 1.50 4.00
97 Calen Addison 1.50 4.00
98 Spencer Knight 3.00 8.00
99 Cole Caufield 6.00 15.00
100 Rasmus Kupari 1.50 4.00
101 Jake Leschyshyn 1.50 4.00
102 Hendrix Lapierre 1.50 4.00
103 Tanner Jeannot 1.50 4.00
104 Justin Barron 2.50 6.00
105 John-Jason Peterka 3.00 8.00
106 Scott Perunovich 1.50 4.00
107 Cole Perfetti 3.00 8.00
108 Vasily Podkolzin 2.00 5.00
109 Mattias Samuelsson 1.50 4.00
110 Adam Beckman 1.50 4.00
111 Philip Tomasino 2.00 5.00
112 Moritz Seider 4.00 10.00
113 Michael Pezzetta 1.50 4.00
114 Anton Lundell 3.00 8.00
115 William Eklund 4.00 10.00
116 Jacob Peterson 1.50 4.00
117 Nils Lundkvist 1.50 4.00
118 Cole Sillinger 2.50 6.00
119 Lucas Raymond 5.00 12.00
120 Jack Drury 2.50 6.00
121 Jake Neighbours 3.00 8.00
122 Alex Turcotte 2.00 5.00
123 Yegor Chinakhov 2.50 6.00
124 Robin Salo 1.50 4.00
125 Dawson Mercer 4.00 10.00
126 Seth Jarvis 4.00 10.00
127 Brandon Duhaime 1.50 4.00
128 Karel Vejmelka 2.00 5.00
129 Mason McTavish 3.00 8.00
130 Riley Damiani 1.50 4.00
131 Adam Ruzicka 1.50 4.00
132 Aliaksei Protas 1.50 4.00
133 Alexander Holtz 2.50 6.00
134 Jonathan Dahlen 1.50 4.00
135 Benoit-Olivier Groulx 1.50 4.00

2021-22 Synergy Purple
*PURP.NON.AU: 2X TO 5X RED

2021-22 Synergy Red Codes
*CODES: .5X TO 1.2X RED

2021-22 Synergy Autographs
AAB Aleksander Barkov D 15.00 40.00
AAK Anze Kopitar C 15.00 40.00
AAL Alexis Lafreniere C 15.00 40.00
AAM Auston Matthews A 80.00 200.00
AAN Alex Nedeljkovic D 8.00 20.00
AAS Andrei Svechnikov D 12.00 30.00
ABB Brent Burns B 10.00 25.00
ABJ Boone Jenner E 10.00 25.00
ABM Brad Marchand C 20.00 50.00
ABN Brock Nelson F 10.00 25.00
ABT Brady Tkachuk D 15.00 40.00
ACT Cam Talbot E 10.00 25.00
ADH Dougie Hamilton E 8.00 20.00
AGI John Gibson F 10.00 25.00
AJE Jordan Eberle E 10.00 25.00
AJG Jake Guentzel D 15.00 40.00
AJI Jarome Iginla A 12.00 30.00
AJN Josh Norris E 10.00 25.00
AJR Jason Robertson D 15.00 40.00
AJS Joe Sakic A 20.00 50.00
AJT John Tavares A 15.00 40.00
AKC Kyle Connor D 15.00 40.00
AMC Connor McDavid A 125.00 300.00
AMH Miro Heiskanen D 12.00 30.00
AMM Mitch Marner B 15.00 40.00
AMT Matthew Tkachuk D 20.00 50.00
ANS Nick Suzuki C 20.00 50.00
APK Patrick Kane A 20.00 50.00
ASB Sam Bennett E 15.00 40.00
ASC Sidney Crosby A 125.00 300.00
ASS Steven Stamkos B 20.00 50.00
ATB Tyler Bertuzzi B 8.00 20.00
ATE Teuvo Teravainen C 10.00 25.00
ATT Troy Terry E 8.00 20.00
AWG Wayne Gretzky A 125.00 300.00
AWO Willie O'Ree C 12.00 30.00
AYG Yanni Gourde E 8.00 20.00

2021-22 Synergy Autographs Red
*RED: .6X TO 1.5X BASIC
AAM Auston Matthews 150.00 400.00
AMC Connor McDavid 200.00 500.00
ASC Sidney Crosby 250.00 600.00
AWG Wayne Gretzky 200.00 500.00

2021-22 Synergy Cast for Greatness
CG1 Connor McDavid 30.00 80.00
CG2 Jason Robertson 10.00 25.00
CG3 Auston Matthews 25.00 60.00
CG4 Mikko Rantanen 15.00 40.00
CG5 David Pastrnak 15.00 40.00
CG6 Quinn Hughes 15.00 40.00
CG7 Jake Guentzel 10.00 25.00
CG8 Joe Pavelski 8.00 20.00
CG9 Nick Suzuki 12.00 30.00
CG10 Artemi Panarin 12.00 30.00
CG11 Jonathan Huberdeau 8.00 20.00
CG12 Brayden Point 8.00 20.00
CG13 Max Pacioretty 6.00 15.00
CG14 Alex DeBrincat 8.00 20.00
CG15 Sebastian Aho 10.00 25.00
CG16 Roman Josi 6.00 15.00
CG17 Sidney Crosby 25.00 60.00
CG18 Jack Hughes 15.00 40.00
CG19 John Tavares 10.00 25.00
CG20 Kirill Kaprizov 20.00 50.00
CG21 Nathan MacKinnon 25.00 60.00
CG22 Mathew Barzal 8.00 20.00
CG23 Brady Tkachuk 10.00 25.00
CG24 Marc-Andre Fleury 12.00 30.00
CG25 Tyler Bertuzzi 5.00 12.00
CG26 Clayton Keller 8.00 20.00
CG27 Alex Ovechkin 25.00 60.00
CG28 Kyle Connor 10.00 25.00
CG29 John Gibson 6.00 15.00
CG30 Jesper Bratt 6.00 15.00
CG31 Spencer Knight 12.00 30.00
CG32 Trevor Zegras 12.00 30.00
CG33 Cole Caufield 25.00 60.00
CG34 Moritz Seider 15.00 40.00
CG35 Quinton Byfield 15.00 40.00
GS36 Lucas Raymond Bounty 20.00 50.00

2021-22 Synergy Cast For Greatness Signatures
CGSAS Andrei Svechnikov 25.00 60.00
CGSEP Elias Pettersson 30.00 80.00
CGSMM Mitch Marner 30.00 80.00
CGSMT Matthew Tkachuk 40.00 100.00
CGSPR Patrick Roy 80.00 200.00

2021-22 Synergy Exceptional Futures
*RED/499: .6X TO 1.5X BASIC
*BLUE/299: .75X TO 2X BASIC
*PURPLE/199: 1X TO 2.5X BASIC
*GREEN/99: 1.2X TO 3X BASIC
*PINK/25: 2.5X TO 6X BASIC
EFAH Alexander Holtz 1.50 4.00
EFAL Anton Lundell 2.00 5.00
EFAN Alex Newhook 1.50 4.00
EFAT Alex Turcotte 1.25 3.00
EFCC Cole Caufield 4.00 10.00
EFCP Cole Perfetti 2.00 5.00
EFCS Cole Sillinger 1.50 4.00
EFCY Cam York 1.00 2.50
EFDM Dawson Mercer 2.50 6.00
EFHL Hendrix Lapierre 1.00 2.50
EFJD Jonathan Dahlen 1.00 2.50
EFJP John-Jason Peterka 2.00 5.00
EFJS Jeremy Swayman 3.00 8.00
EFKL Kole Lind 1.25 3.00
EFKV Karel Vejmelka 1.25 3.00
EFLR Lucas Raymond
EFMM Mason McTavish 2.00 5.00
EFMS Moritz Seider 2.50 6.00
EFNL Nils Lundkvist 1.00 2.50
EFPT Philip Tomasino 1.25 3.00
EFQB Quinton Byfield 2.50 6.00
EFRC Ross Colton 1.25 3.00
EFRD Riley Damiani 1.00 2.50
EFSJ Seth Jarvis 2.50 6.00
EFSK Spencer Knight 2.00 5.00
EFSP Shane Pinto 1.50 4.00
EFTJ Tanner Jeannot 1.00 2.50
EFTZ Trevor Zegras 2.00 5.00
EFVP Vasily Podkolzin 1.25 3.00
EFWE William Eklund 2.50 6.00

2021-22 Synergy Exceptional Phenoms
*RED/499: .6X TO 1.5X BASIC
*BLUE/299: .75X TO 2X BASIC
*PURPLE/199: 1X TO 2.5X BASIC
*GREEN/99: 1.2X TO 3X BASIC
*PINK/25: 2.5X TO 6X BASIC
EPAD Alex DeBrincat 1.25 3.00
EPAE Aaron Ekblad 1.25 3.00
EPAF Adam Fox 1.25 3.00
EPAM Auston Matthews 4.00 10.00
EPBP Brayden Point 1.25 3.00
EPBT Brady Tkachuk 1.50 4.00
EPCH Carter Hart 1.00 2.50
EPCM Cale Makar 2.50 6.00
EPDC Dylan Cozens 1.00 2.50
EPDL Dylan Larkin 1.25 3.00
EPDP David Pastrnak 2.50 6.00
EPEP Elias Pettersson 1.50 4.00
EPJH Jack Hughes 2.50 6.00
EPJK Jordan Kyrou 1.00 2.50
EPJM Jared McCann .75 2.00
EPJP Jesse Puljujarvi 1.00 2.50
EPJR Jason Robertson 1.50 4.00
EPKC Kyle Connor 1.50 4.00
EPKK Kirill Kaprizov 3.00 8.00
EPMB Mathew Barzal 1.25 3.00
EPMC Charlie McAvoy 1.25 3.00
EPMH Miro Heiskanen 1.25 3.00
EPMM Mitch Marner 1.50 4.00
EPMT Matthew Tkachuk 2.00 5.00
EPNS Nick Suzuki 2.00 5.00
EPQH Quinn Hughes 2.50 6.00
EPSA Sebastian Aho 1.50 4.00
EPSB Sam Bennett 1.50 4.00
EPTM Timo Meier 1.00 2.50
EPTT Troy Terry .75 2.00

2021-22 Synergy Exceptional Stars
*RED/499: .6X TO 1.5X BASIC
*BLUE/299: .75X TO 2X BASIC
*PURPLE/199: 1X TO 2.5X BASIC
*GREEN/99: 1.2X TO 3X BASIC
*PINK/25: 2.5X TO 6X BASIC
ESAB Aleksander Barkov 1.50 4.00
ESAK Anze Kopitar 1.50 4.00
ESAN Alex Nedeljkovic .75 2.00
ESAO Alex Ovechkin 4.00 10.00
ESAP Artemi Panarin 2.00 5.00
ESAV Andrei Vasilevskiy 1.50 4.00
ESBH Bo Horvat 1.25 3.00
ESBJ Boone Jenner 1.00 2.50
ESBM Brad Marchand 2.00 5.00
ESCH Connor Hellebuyck 2.00 5.00
ESCM Connor McDavid 5.00 12.00
ESEL Elias Lindholm 1.00 2.50
ESFA Frederik Andersen 1.25 3.00
ESGA Johnny Gaudreau 1.50 4.00
ESGU Jake Guentzel 1.50 4.00
ESIS Igor Shesterkin 2.00 5.00
ESJG John Gibson 1.00 2.50
ESJH Jonathan Huberdeau 1.25 3.00
ESJM J.T. Miller 1.25 3.00
ESJP Joe Pavelski 1.25 3.00
ESJS Jeff Skinner 1.00 2.50
ESJT Jonathan Toews 1.50 4.00
ESKA Patrick Kane 2.00 5.00
ESKU Nikita Kucherov 2.00 5.00
ESLD Leon Draisaitl 3.00 8.00
ESMA Mark Scheifele 1.50 4.00
ESMD Matt Duchene 1.00 2.50
ESMS Mark Stone 1.25 3.00
ESMZ Mats Zuccarello 1.00 2.50

ESNB Nicklas Backstrom 1.00 2.50
ESNK Nazem Kadri 1.25 3.00
ESNM Nathan MacKinnon 4.00 10.00
ESPB Patrice Bergeron 1.25 3.00
ESPG Philipp Grubauer 1.00 2.50
ESPK Phil Kessel 1.00 2.50
ESSC Sidney Crosby 4.00 10.00
ESTA John Tavares 1.50 4.00
ESTB Tyler Bertuzzi .75 2.00
ESTT Tyler Toffoli 1.00 2.50
ESVT Vladimir Tarasenko 1.25 3.00

2021-22 Synergy FX

*ORANGE/449: .5X TO 1.2X BASIC
*PURPLE/275: .6X TO 1.5X BASIC
FXAB Aleksander Barkov 1.50 4.00
FXAD Alex DeBrincat 1.25 3.00
FXAF Adam Fox 1.25 3.00
FXAK Anze Kopitar 1.50 4.00
FXAO Alex Ovechkin 4.00 10.00
FXBT Brady Tkachuk 1.50 4.00
FXCA Cam Atkinson 1.00 2.50
FXCG Claude Giroux 1.00 2.50
FXCK Clayton Keller 1.25 3.00
FXCM Cale Makar 2.50 6.00
FXDL Dylan Larkin 1.25 3.00
FXDP David Pastrnak
FXEL Elias Lindholm 1.00 2.50
FXHA Ryan Hartman .60 1.50
FXJB Jesper Bratt 1.00 2.50
FXJE Jordan Eberle 1.00 2.50
FXJG Jake Guentzel 1.50 4.00
FXJH Jonathan Huberdeau 1.25 3.00
FXJK Jordan Kyrou 1.00 2.50
FXJM J.T. Miller 1.25 3.00
FXJT John Tavares 1.50 4.00
FXKC Kyle Connor 1.50 4.00
FXKK Kirill Kaprizov 3.00 8.00
FXLD Leon Draisaitl 3.00 8.00
FXMB Mathew Barzal 1.25 3.00
FXMC Connor McDavid 5.00 12.00
FXMP Max Pacioretty 1.00 2.50
FXMS Mark Scheifele 1.50 4.00
FXMT Matthew Tkachuk 2.00 5.00
FXMZ Mika Zibanejad 1.25 3.00
FXNM Nathan MacKinnon 4.00 10.00
FXNS Nick Suzuki 2.00 5.00
FXPB Patrice Bergeron 1.25 3.00
FXPK Patrick Kane 2.00 5.00
FXRD Rasmus Dahlin 1.25 3.00
FXRH Roope Hintz 1.25 3.00
FXRJ Roman Josi 1.00 2.50
FXSA Sebastian Aho 1.50 4.00
FXSC Sidney Crosby 4.00 10.00
FXSS Steven Stamkos 2.00 5.00
FXTB Tyler Bertuzzi .75 2.00
FXTM Timo Meier 1.00 2.50
FXTT Troy Terry .75 2.00
FXVH Victor Hedman 1.25 3.00
FXZW Zach Werenski 1.50 4.00

2021-22 Synergy FX Rookies

*ORANGE/449: .5X TO 1.2X BASIC
*PURPLE/275: .6X TO 1.5X BASIC
FXRAB Alex Barre-Boulet 1.00 2.50
FXRAH Alexander Holtz 1.50 4.00
FXRAL Anton Lundell 2.00 5.00
FXRAN Alex Newhook 1.50 4.00
FXRAP Aliaksei Protas 1.00 2.50
FXRAT Alex Turcotte 1.25 3.00
FXRBD Brandon Duhaime 1.00 2.50
FXRBG Benoit-Olivier Groulx 1.00 2.50
FXRBK Boris Katchouk .75 2.00
FXRBL Brett Leason 1.00 2.50
FXRCA Calen Addison 1.00 2.50
FXRCC Cole Caufield 4.00 10.00
FXRCS Cole Sillinger 1.50 4.00
FXRCY Cam York 1.00 2.50
FXRDA Jonathan Dahlen 1.00 2.50
FXRDM Dysin Mayo 1.00 2.50
FXRFG Filip Gustavsson 2.00 5.00
FXRGD Grigori Denisenko 1.25 3.00
FXRHL Hendrix Lapierre 1.00 2.50
FXRJA Jack Ahcan 1.00 2.50
FXRJD Jamie Drysdale 1.50 4.00
FXRJJ Jan Jenik 1.25 3.00
FXRJL Jake Leschyshyn 1.00 2.50
FXRJN Jake Neighbours 2.00 5.00
FXRJP John-Jason Peterka 2.00 5.00
FXRJS Jeremy Swayman 3.00 8.00
FXRJV Joe Veleno 1.25 3.00
FXRJW Jasper Weatherby 1.00 2.50
FXRKL Kole Lind 1.25 3.00
FXRKV Karel Vejmelka 1.25 3.00
FXRLR Lucas Raymond 3.00 8.00
FXRLT Lassi Thomson 1.00 2.50
FXRME Dawson Mercer 2.50 6.00
FXRMH Mike Hardman 1.00 2.50
FXRMM Mason McTavish 2.00 5.00
FXRMP Michael Pezzetta 1.00 2.50
FXRMS Moritz Seider 2.50 6.00
FXRNL Nils Lundkvist 1.00 2.50
FXRPE Jacob Peterson 1.00 2.50
FXRPT Philip Tomasino 1.25 3.00
FXRQB Quinton Byfield 2.50 6.00
FXRRC Ross Colton 1.25 3.00
FXRRD Riley Damiani 1.00 2.50
FXRRS Robin Salo 1.00 2.50
FXRSC Scott Perunovich 1.00 2.50
FXRSJ Seth Jarvis 2.50 6.00
FXRSK Spencer Knight 2.00 5.00
FXRSL Josiah Slavin 1.00 2.50
FXRSP Shane Pinto 1.50 4.00
FXRTJ Tanner Jeannot 1.00 2.50
FXRTZ Trevor Zegras 2.00 5.00
FXRUL Ukko-Pekka Luukkonen 1.50 4.00
FXRWE William Eklund 2.50 6.00
FXRYC Yegor Chinakhov 1.50 4.00
FXRZJ Zac Jones 1.25 3.00

2021-22 Synergy Postseason Brilliance

PB1 Mathew Barzal .75 2.00
PB2 Brayden Point .75 2.00
PB3 Nathan MacKinnon 2.50 6.00
PB4 Andrei Vasilevskiy 1.00 2.50
PB5 Cole Caufield 2.50 6.00
PB6 Nick Suzuki 1.25 3.00
PB7 David Pastrnak 1.50 4.00
PB8 Josh Bailey .50 1.25
PB9 William Karlsson .75 2.00
PB10 Jonathan Huberdeau .75 2.00
PB11 Carey Price 1.25 3.00
PB12 Nikita Kucherov 1.25 3.00

2021-22 Synergy Roaring 20s

R201 Quinn Hughes 1.00 2.50
R202 Brady Tkachuk .60 1.50
R203 Cole Caufield 1.50 4.00
R204 Trevor Zegras .75 2.00
R205 Rasmus Dahlin .50 1.25
R206 Kirby Dach .40 1.00
R207 Jack Hughes 1.00 2.50
R208 Andrei Svechnikov .50 1.25
R209 Dylan Cozens .40 1.00
R2010 Alexis Lafreniere .60 1.50
R2011 Grigori Denisenko .50 1.25
R2012 Tim Stutzle .50 1.25
R2013 Clayton Keller .50 1.25
R2014 Kirill Kaprizov 1.25 3.00
R2015 Jason Robertson .60 1.50
R2016 Spencer Knight .75 2.00
R2017 Alex Turcotte .50 1.25
R2018 Lucas Raymond 1.25 3.00

2021-22 Synergy Rookie Autographs

ARAH Alexander Holtz C 8.00 20.00
ARAL Anton Lundell B 10.00 25.00
ARAN Alex Newhook C 8.00 20.00
ARAT Alex Turcotte C 6.00 15.00
ARBG Benoit-Olivier Groulx E 5.00 12.00
ARCA Calen Addison E 5.00 12.00
ARCC Cole Caufield A 80.00 200.00
ARCP Cole Perfetti B 10.00 25.00
ARCS Cole Sillinger C 8.00 20.00
ARDM Dawson Mercer C
ARFG Filip Gustavsson E 10.00 25.00
ARHL Hendrix Lapierre D 5.00 12.00
ARJB Jacob Bryson E 5.00 12.00
ARJD Jonathan Dahlen E 5.00 12.00
ARJJ Jan Jenik E 6.00 15.00
ARJL Jake Leschyshyn E 5.00 12.00
ARJN Jake Neighbours E 10.00 25.00
ARJP John-Jason Peterka C 10.00 25.00
ARJS Jeremy Swayman C 30.00 80.00
ARJV Joe Veleno D 6.00 15.00
ARJY Jesse Ylonen E 5.00 12.00
ARKL Kole Lind D 6.00 15.00
ARMM Mason McTavish B 10.00 25.00
ARMS Moritz Seider B 12.00 30.00
ARNL Nils Lundkvist C 5.00 12.00
ARPK Parker Kelly E 5.00 12.00
ARQB Quinton Byfield B 25.00 60.00
ARRC Ross Colton D 6.00 15.00
ARRD Riley Damiani D 5.00 12.00
ARSK Spencer Knight C 10.00 25.00
ARSP Shane Pinto E 8.00 20.00
ARTJ Tanner Jeannot D 5.00 12.00
ARTZ Trevor Zegras B 80.00 200.00
ARVP Vasily Podkolzin C 6.00 15.00
ARWE William Eklund C 12.00 30.00

2021-22 Synergy Rookie Autographs Red

*RED: .6X TO 1.5X BASIC
ARCC Cole Caufield 100.00 250.00
ARJS Jeremy Swayman 40.00 100.00
ARMS Moritz Seider 30.00 80.00
ARQB Quinton Byfield 30.00 80.00
ARSK Spencer Knight 25.00 60.00
ARTZ Trevor Zegras 100.00 250.00

2021-22 Synergy Rookie Journey Away

*RED/399: .75X TO 2X BASIC
*GOLD/149: 1.2X TO 3X BASIC
RJ1 Lucas Raymond 1.50 4.00
RJ2 Quinton Byfield 1.25 3.00
RJ3 William Eklund 1.25 3.00
RJ4 Mason McTavish 1.00 2.50
RJ5 Cole Caufield 2.00 5.00
RJ6 Jeremy Swayman 1.50 4.00
RJ7 Alex Newhook .75 2.00
RJ8 Dawson Mercer 1.25 3.00
RJ9 Cole Sillinger .75 2.00
RJ10 Trevor Zegras 1.00 2.50
RJ11 Moritz Seider 1.25 3.00
RJ12 Vasily Podkolzin .60 1.50
RJ13 Alex Turcotte .60 1.50
RJ14 Alexander Holtz .75 2.00
RJ15 Anton Lundell 1.00 2.50

2021-22 Synergy Rookie Journey Draft

*RED/499: .75X TO 2X BASIC
*GOLD/249: 1.2X TO 3X BASIC
RJ1 Lucas Raymond 1.50 4.00
RJ2 Quinton Byfield 1.25 3.00
RJ3 William Eklund 1.25 3.00
RJ4 Mason McTavish 1.00 2.50
RJ5 Cole Caufield 2.00 5.00
RJ6 Jeremy Swayman 1.50 4.00
RJ7 Alex Newhook .75 2.00
RJ8 Dawson Mercer 1.25 3.00
RJ9 Cole Sillinger .75 2.00
RJ10 Trevor Zegras 1.00 2.50
RJ11 Moritz Seider 1.25 3.00
RJ12 Vasily Podkolzin .60 1.50
RJ13 Alex Turcotte .60 1.50
RJ14 Alexander Holtz .75 2.00
RJ15 Anton Lundell 1.00 2.50

2021-22 Synergy Rookie Journey Home

*RED/299: .75X TO 2X BASIC
*GOLD/99: 1.2X TO 3X BASIC
RJ1 Lucas Raymond 1.50 4.00
RJ2 Quinton Byfield 1.25 3.00
RJ3 William Eklund 1.25 3.00
RJ4 Mason McTavish 1.00 2.50
RJ5 Cole Caufield 2.00 5.00
RJ6 Jeremy Swayman 1.50 4.00
RJ7 Alex Newhook .75 2.00
RJ8 Dawson Mercer 1.25 3.00
RJ9 Cole Sillinger .75 2.00
RJ10 Trevor Zegras 1.00 2.50
RJ11 Moritz Seider 1.25 3.00
RJ12 Vasily Podkolzin .60 1.50
RJ13 Alex Turcotte .60 1.50
RJ14 Alexander Holtz .75 2.00
RJ15 Anton Lundell 1.00 2.50

2021-22 Synergy Rookie Portraits Autographs Red

RPAL Anton Lundell 40.00 100.00
RPAN Alex Newhook 30.00 80.00
RPAT Alex Turcotte 25.00 60.00
RPCC Cole Caufield 80.00 200.00
RPCP Cole Perfetti 40.00 100.00
RPCS Cole Sillinger 30.00 80.00
RPDM Dawson Mercer 50.00 125.00
RPJS Jeremy Swayman 60.00 150.00
RPLR Lucas Raymond 60.00 150.00
RPMM Mason McTavish 40.00 100.00
RPMS Moritz Seider 50.00 125.00
RPQB Quinton Byfield 50.00 125.00
RPTZ Trevor Zegras 40.00 100.00
RPWE William Eklund 50.00 125.00

2021-22 Synergy Star of the Show

SOS1 Auston Matthews 1.50 4.00
SOS2 Kirill Kaprizov 1.25 3.00
SOS3 David Pastrnak 1.00 2.50
SOS4 Leon Draisaitl 1.25 3.00
SOS5 Nathan MacKinnon 1.50 4.00
SOS6 Nikita Kucherov .75 2.00
SOS7 Cale Makar 1.00 2.50
SOS8 Sebastian Aho .60 1.50
SOS9 Aleksander Barkov .60 1.50
SOS10 Mathew Barzal .50 1.25
SOS11 Elias Pettersson .60 1.50
SOS12 Mark Stone .50 1.25
SOS13 Mark Scheifele .60 1.50
SOS14 Alex Ovechkin 1.50 4.00
SOS15 Andrei Vasilevskiy .60 1.50
SOS16 Artemi Panarin .75 2.00
SOS17 Sidney Crosby 1.50 4.00
SOS18 Philipp Grubauer .40 1.00
SOS19 Connor McDavid 2.00 5.00
SOS20 Patrick Kane

2021-22 Synergy Star Quest

SQ1 Alex Ovechkin 15.00 40.00
SQ2 Leon Draisaitl 12.00 30.00
SQ3 Cole Caufield 15.00 40.00
SQ4 Auston Matthews 15.00 40.00
SQ5 Kirill Kaprizov 12.00 30.00
SQ6 Jonathan Huberdeau 5.00 12.00
SQ7 David Pastrnak 10.00 25.00
SQ8 Quinton Byfield 10.00 25.00
SQ9 Sidney Crosby 15.00 40.00
SQ10 Mika Zibanejad 5.00 12.00
SQ11 Roman Josi 4.00 10.00
SQ12 Chandler Stephenson 3.00 8.00
SQ13 Trevor Zegras 8.00 20.00
SQ14 Tanner Jeannot 4.00 10.00
SQ15 Kyle Connor 6.00 15.00
SQ16 Josh Norris 4.00 10.00
SQ17 Nick Suzuki 8.00 20.00
SQ18 Jake Guentzel 6.00 15.00
SQ19 Cam Atkinson 4.00 10.00
SQ20 Johnny Gaudreau 6.00 15.00
SQ21 Steven Stamkos 8.00 20.00
SQ22 Lucas Raymond 12.00 30.00
SQ23 Anze Kopitar 6.00 15.00
SQ24 Patrick Kane 8.00 20.00
SQ25 Jordan Kyrou 4.00 10.00

2021-22 Synergy Synergistic Duos Stars

*RED/499: .6X TO 1.5X BASIC
*GOLD/249: .75X TO 2X BASIC
SD1 A.Ovechkin/N.Backstrom 4.00 10.00
SD2 A.Kopitar/A.Kempe 1.50 4.00
SD3 N.MacKinnon/C.Makar 4.00 10.00
SD4 S.Stamkos/N.Kucherov 2.00 5.00
SD5 E.Pettersson/J.iller 1.50 4.00
SD6 D.Larkin/T.Bertuzzi 1.25 3.00
SD7 M.Scheifele/K.Connor 1.50 4.00
SD8 C.Price/N.Suzuki
SD9 J.Pavelski/M.Heiskanen 1.25 3.00
SD10 R.O'Reilly/J.Kyrou 1.00 2.50
SD11 R.Dahlin/V.Olofsson 1.25 3.00
SD12 S.Aho/A.Svechnikov 1.50 4.00
SD13 B.Burns/T.Hertl 1.00 2.50
SD14 D.Pastrnak/B.Marchand 2.50 6.00
SD15 J.Huberdeau/A.Barkov 1.50 4.00
SD16 T.Terry/J.Gibson 1.00 2.50
SD17 J.Hughes/N.Hischier 2.50 6.00
SD18 C.Atkinson/C.Hart 1.00 2.50

2021-22 Synergy Synergistic Duos Stars and Legends

*RED/399: .6X TO 1.5X BASIC
*GOLD/149: .75X TO 2X BASIC
SD1 A.Ovechkin/P.Bondra 4.00 10.00
SD2 A.Kopitar/W.Gretzky 6.00 15.00
SD3 N.MacKinnon/J.Sakic 4.00 10.00
SD4 S.Stamkos/V.Lecavalier 2.00 5.00
SD5 E.Pettersson/H.Sedin 1.50 4.00
SD6 D.Larkin/S.Yzerman 2.50 6.00
SD7 M.Scheifele/K.Tkachuk 1.50 4.00
SD8 C.Price/P.Roy 2.50 6.00
SD9 J.Pavelski/M.Modano 1.50 4.00
SD10 R.O'Reilly/B.Hull 1.50 4.00
SD11 R.Dahlin/P.LaFontaine 1.25 3.00
SD12 S.Aho/R.Brind'Amour 1.50 4.00
SD13 Brent Burns/Doug Wilson 1.00 2.50
SD14 D.Pastrnak/B.Orr 4.00 10.00
SD15 J.Huberdeau/J.Vanbiesbrouck 1.25 3.00
SD16 T.Terry/T.Selanne 2.00 5.00
SD17 J.Hughes/M.Brodeur 2.50 6.00
SD18 C.Atkinson/E.Lindros 1.50 4.00

2021-22 Synergy Synergistic Duos Stars and Rookies

*RED/299: .6X TO 1.5X BASIC
*GOLD/99: .75X TO 2X BASIC
SD1 A.Ovechkin/H.Lapierre 4.00 10.00
SD2 A.Kopitar/Q.Byfield 2.50 6.00
SD3 N.MacKinnon/A.Newhook 4.00 10.00
SD4 S.Stamkos/R.Colton 2.00 5.00
SD5 E.Pettersson/V.Podkolzin 1.50 4.00
SD6 D.Larkin/L.Raymond 3.00 8.00
SD7 M.Scheifele/C.Perfetti 2.00 5.00
SD8 C.Price/C.Caufield 4.00 10.00
SD9 J.Pavelski/R.Damiani 1.25 3.00
SD10 R.O'Reilly/J.Neighbours 2.00 5.00
SD11 R.Dahlin/J.Peterka 2.00 5.00
SD12 S.Aho/S.Jarvis 2.50 6.00
SD13 B.Burns/W.Eklund 2.50 6.00
SD14 D.Pastrnak/J.Swayman 3.00 8.00
SD15 J.Huberdeau/A.Lundell 2.00 5.00
SD16 T.Terry/T.Zegras 2.00 5.00
SD17 J.Hughes/D.Mercer 2.50 6.00
SD18 C.Atkinson/C.York 1.00 2.50

2022-23 Synergy Red

1 Moritz Seider .75 2.00
2 Kyle Connor 1.00 2.50
3 Josh Bailey .50 1.25
4 Jack Eichel 1.00 2.50
5 Trevor Zegras .60 1.50
6 Victor Hedman .75 2.00
7 Taylor Hall .60 1.50
8 Kirill Kaprizov 2.00 5.00
9 Carey Price 1.25 3.00
10 Brandon Saad .50 1.25
11 Mathew Barzal .75 2.00
12 Alexis Lafreniere 1.00 2.50
13 Jack Hughes 1.50 4.00
14 Gabriel Landeskog .75 2.00
15 Leon Draisaitl 2.00 5.00
16 Evgeni Malkin 1.25 3.00
17 Cale Makar 1.50 4.00
18 Ryan O'Reilly .60 1.50
19 Auston Matthews 2.50 6.00
20 James van Riemsdyk .50 1.25
21 Marc-Andre Fleury 1.25 3.00
22 Blake Coleman .50 1.25
23 Miro Heiskanen .75 2.00
24 Andrei Vasilevskiy 1.00 2.50
25 Tom Wilson .60 1.50
26 Elias Pettersson 1.00 2.50
27 Zach Werenski 1.00 2.50
28 Jordan Eberle .60 1.50
29 Jordan Kyrou .60 1.50
30 Brady Tkachuk 1.00 2.50
31 John Gibson .60 1.50
32 Clayton Keller .75 2.00
33 Dylan Cozens .60 1.50
34 Tomas Hertl .60 1.50
35 Quinn Hughes 1.50 4.00
36 Sidney Crosby 2.50 6.00
37 Jonathan Toews 1.00 2.50
38 Brad Marchand 1.25 3.00
39 Rasmus Dahlin .75 2.00
40 Tyler Toffoli .60 1.50
41 Aaron Ekblad .75 2.00
42 Roman Josi .60 1.50
43 Patrick Kane 1.25 3.00
44 Igor Shesterkin 1.25 3.00
45 Jared McCann .50 1.25
46 Kirby Dach .60 1.50
47 Mitch Marner 1.00 2.50
48 Anze Kopitar 1.00 2.50
49 Jaccob Slavin .50 1.25
50 Connor McDavid 3.00 8.00
51 Carter Hart .60 1.50
52 Lucas Raymond 1.00 2.50
53 Josh Norris .60 1.50
54 Jason Robertson 1.00 2.50
55 Tanner Jeannot .40 1.00
56 Dawson Mercer .75 2.00
57 Sebastian Aho 1.00 2.50
58 Nathan MacKinnon 2.50 6.00
59 Alex Ovechkin 2.50 6.00
60 Nikolaj Ehlers .60 1.50
61 Glenn Hall .60 1.50
62 Joe Sakic 1.25 3.00
63 Bobby Orr 2.50 6.00
64 Bernie Nicholls .50 1.25
65 John Vanbiesbrouck .60 1.50
66 Mario Lemieux 2.50 6.00
67 Patrick Roy 1.50 4.00
68 Nicklas Lidstrom .60 1.50
69 Mike Gartner .75 2.00
70 Wendel Clark 1.00 2.50
71 Dominik Hasek 1.00 2.50
72 Ryan Getzlaf .60 1.50
73 Phil Esposito 1.00 2.50
74 Larry Robinson .60 1.50
75 Wayne Gretzky 4.00 10.00
76 Braden Schneider 2.50 6.00
77 Samuel Fagemo 1.25 3.00
78 Fredrik Karlstrom 1.25 3.00
79 Bobby Brink 1.50 4.00
80 Erik Kallgren 1.50 4.00
81 Filip Hallander 1.50 4.00
82 Valtteri Puustinen 1.25 3.00
83 Hunter Drew 1.50 4.00
84 Jack LaFontaine 1.50 4.00
85 Michael Eyssimont 1.50 4.00
86 Chase Pearson 1.25 3.00
87 Isaac Ratcliffe 1.50 4.00
88 Mads Sogaard 2.00 5.00
89 Nick Abruzzese 1.50 4.00
90 Matias Maccelli 2.50 6.00
91 Jordan Harris 2.00 5.00
92 Mark Kastelic 1.25 3.00
93 Pyotr Kochetkov 3.00 8.00
94 Ronnie Attard 1.50 4.00
95 Thomas Bordeleau 1.50 4.00
96 Linus Hogberg 1.25 3.00
97 Jakub Galvas 1.50 4.00
98 Jordan Spence 1.50 4.00
99 Carson Meyer 1.25 3.00
100 Bokondji Imama 1.25 3.00
101 Jack McBain 1.50 4.00
102 Kaedan Korczak 1.25 3.00
103 Marc McLaughlin 1.50 4.00
104 Reilly Walsh 1.50 4.00
105 Zack Hayes 1.25 3.00
106 Dylan Samberg 1.50 4.00
107 Brayden Tracey 1.25 3.00
108 Trey Fix-Wolansky 1.50 4.00
109 Jordan Spence 1.50 4.00
110 Alex Vlasic 1.25 3.00
111 Nathan Smith 1.25 3.00
112 Noah Cates 1.50 4.00
113 Johnathan Kovacevic 1.50 4.00
114 Vladislav Kolyachonok 1.25 3.00
115 Nikita Okhotiuk 1.25 3.00
116 Matt Boldy 5.00 12.00
117 Owen Power 3.00 8.00
118 Kent Johnson 3.00 8.00
119 Matty Beniers 4.00 10.00
120 Marco Rossi 4.00 10.00
121 Jack Quinn 2.50 6.00
122 Jacob Perreault 1.50 4.00
123 Lukas Reichel 3.00 8.00
124 Dylan Holloway 3.00 8.00
125 Braden Schneider 2.50 6.00
RDG Dylan Guenther 4.00 10.00
RJA Jake Sanderson 4.00 10.00
RJS Juraj Slafkovsky 8.00 20.00
RSW Shane Wright 4.00 10.00

2022-23 Synergy Purple

*PURP.NON.AU: 2X TO 5X RED
119 Matty Beniers AU/49 150.00 400.00
RSI Juraj Slafkovsky AU/99 80.00 200.00
RSW Shane Wright AU/99 50.00 125.00

2022-23 Synergy Red Codes

*CODES: .5X TO 1.2X RED

2022-23 Synergy 2030

1 Elias Pettersson 1.00 2.50
2 Cale Makar 1.50 4.00
3 Cole Caufield 1.25 3.00
4 Andrei Svechnikov .75 2.00
5 Trevor Zegras .60 1.50
6 Lucas Raymond 1.00 2.50
7 Matt Boldy
8 Tim Stutzle .75 2.00
9 Alexis Lafreniere 1.00 2.50
10 Spencer Knight .60 1.50
11 Jason Robertson 1.00 2.50
12 Quinn Hughes 1.50 4.00
13 Kirill Kaprizov 2.00 5.00
14 Alex Newhook .50 1.25
15 Shane Wright 1.50 4.00
16 Moritz Seider .75 2.00
17 Cole Perfetti .60 1.50
18 Anton Lundell .60 1.50

2022-23 Synergy Cast For Greatness

CG1 Patrick Roy 15.00 40.00
CG2 Connor McDavid 30.00 80.00
CG3 Andrei Vasilevskiy 10.00 25.00
CG4 Kirill Kaprizov 20.00 50.00
CG5 Kent Johnson 12.00 30.00
CG6 Alex Ovechkin 25.00 60.00
CG7 Gordie Howe 20.00 50.00
CG8 Cale Makar 15.00 40.00
CG9 Sidney Crosby 25.00 60.00
CG10 Matty Beniers 15.00 40.00
CG11 Jonathan Huberdeau 8.00 20.00
CG12 Artemi Panarin 12.00 30.00
CG13 Nathan MacKinnon 25.00 60.00
CG14 Mario Lemieux 25.00 60.00
CG15 Owen Power 12.00 30.00
CG16 Aleksander Barkov 10.00 25.00
CG17 Mitch Marner 10.00 25.00
CG18 Roman Josi 6.00 15.00
CG19 Matthew Tkachuk 12.00 30.00
CG20 Marco Rossi 15.00 40.00
CG21 Wayne Gretzky 40.00 100.00
CG22 Mark Scheifele 10.00 25.00
CG23 David Pastrnak 15.00 40.00
CG24 Steven Stamkos 12.00 30.00
CG25 Matt Boldy 20.00 50.00
CG26 Andrei Svechnikov 8.00 20.00
CG27 Carey Price 12.00 30.00
CG28 Bobby Hull 12.00 30.00
CG29 Leon Draisaitl 20.00 50.00
CG30 Anze Kopitar 10.00 25.00
CG31 Igor Shesterkin 12.00 30.00
CG32 Patrick Kane 12.00 30.00
CG33 Trevor Zegras 6.00 15.00
CG34 Auston Matthews 25.00 60.00
CG35 Nikita Kucherov 12.00 30.00
CG36 Dylan Holloway 12.00 30.00

2022-23 Synergy Cast For Greatness Signatures

CGSBO Bobby Orr/25 80.00 200.00
CGSET Eeli Tolvanen/25 20.00 50.00
CGSIS Igor Shesterkin/25 40.00 100.00
CGSJJ Jaromir Jagr/25 60.00 150.00
CGSJR Jason Robertson/25 30.00 80.00
CGSKC Kyle Connor/25 30.00 80.00
CGSSB Sam Bennett/25 30.00 80.00
CGSTS Tim Stutzle/25 25.00 60.00

2022-23 Synergy Cranked Up

*RED/399: .5X TO 1.2X BASIC
*BLUE/249: .6X TO 1.5X BASIC
*PURPLE/99: .75X TO 2X BASIC
*GREEN/65: 1X TO 2.5X BASIC
*PINK/25: 2X TO 5X BASIC
CUAB Aleksander Barkov 1.50 4.00
CUAF Adam Fox 1.25 3.00
CUAK Anze Kopitar 1.50 4.00
CUAM Andrew Mangiapane 1.00 2.50
CUAO Alex Ovechkin 4.00 10.00
CUAP Artemi Panarin 2.00 5.00
CUAU Auston Matthews 4.00 10.00
CUAV Alex Vlasic .75 2.00
CUBC Bobby Clarke 1.50 4.00
CUBE Matty Beniers 2.50 6.00
CUBH Brendan Shanahan 1.00 2.50
CUBM Ben Meyers 1.00 2.50
CUBO Matt Boldy 3.00 8.00
CUBP Brayden Point 1.25 3.00
CUBS Braden Schneider 1.50 4.00
CUBT Brayden Tracey .75 2.00
CUBU Johnny Bucyk 1.00 2.50
CUCA Cole Caufield 2.00 5.00
CUCE Chris Chelios 1.00 2.50
CUCM Connor McDavid 5.00 12.00
CUDH Dominik Hasek 1.50 4.00
CUDL Dylan Larkin 1.25 3.00
CUDO Lukas Dostal 2.00 5.00
CUDP David Pastrnak 2.50 6.00
CUDS Dylan Samberg 1.00 2.50
CUEB Jordan Eberle 1.00 2.50
CUEK Evgeny Kuznetsov 1.25 3.00
CUEL Eric Lindros 1.50 4.00
CUFH Filip Hallander 1.00 2.50
CUFK Fredrik Karlstrom .75 2.00
CUGH Gordie Howe 3.00 8.00
CUHS Jordan Harris 1.25 3.00
CUHU Jack Hughes 2.50 6.00
CUHY Dylan Holloway 2.00 5.00
CUIR Isaac Ratcliffe 1.00 2.50
CUJB Jordan Binnington 1.50 4.00
CUJC John Carlson 1.00 2.50
CUJD Jamie Drysdale .75 2.00
CUJE Jack Eichel 1.50 4.00
CUJF Joel Farabee 1.00 2.50
CUJG Johnny Gaudreau 1.50 4.00
CUJH Jonathan Huberdeau 1.25 3.00
CUJK Johnathan Kovacevic 1.00 2.50
CUJM Jacob Markstrom 1.00 2.50
CUJN Josh Norris 1.00 2.50
CUJO Joel Eriksson Ek .75 2.00
CUJP Joe Pavelski 1.25 3.00
CUJQ Jack Quinn 1.50 4.00
CUJT John Tavares 1.50 4.00
CUKA Kirill Kaprizov 3.00 8.00
CUKJ Kent Johnson 2.00 5.00
CUKO Kaedan Korczak .75 2.00
CUKR Erik Kallgren 1.00 2.50
CUKV Pyotr Kochetkov 2.00 5.00
CULA Jack LaFontaine 1.00 2.50
CULC Logan Couture 1.25 3.00
CULD Leon Draisaitl 3.00 8.00
CULE Luc Robitaille 1.00 2.50
CULR Lucas Raymond 1.50 4.00
CUMA Matias Maccelli 1.50 4.00
CUMB Mathew Barzal 1.25 3.00
CUMC Jack McBain 1.00 2.50
CUMD Matt Duchene 1.00 2.50
CUME Mark Messier 2.00 5.00
CUMH Miro Heiskanen 1.25 3.00
CUMI J.T. Miller 1.25 3.00
CUMK Mark Kastelic .75 2.00
CUML Mario Lemieux 4.00 10.00
CUNC Noah Cates 1.00 2.50
CUNH Nico Hischier 1.50 4.00
CUNM Nathan MacKinnon 4.00 10.00
CUNO Nikita Okhotiuk .75 2.00
CUOP Owen Power 2.00 5.00
CUPB Patrice Bergeron
CUPD Pierre-Luc Dubois .75 2.00
CUPE Jacob Perreault 1.00 2.50
CUPF Peter Forsberg 2.00 5.00
CUPK Phil Kessel 1.00 2.50
CUPR Patrick Roy 2.50 6.00
CUQH Quinn Hughes 2.50 6.00
CURE Lukas Reichel 2.00 5.00
CURO Marco Rossi 2.50 6.00
CURT Robert Thomas 1.00 2.50
CURW Reilly Walsh 1.00 2.50
CUSC Sidney Crosby 4.00 10.00
CUSF Samuel Fagemo .75 2.00
CUSJ Seth Jones 1.00 2.50
CUSK Jeff Skinner 1.00 2.50
CUSO Mads Sogaard 1.25 3.00
CUSP Jordan Spence 1.00 2.50
CUST Tim Stutzle 1.25 3.00
CUSY Steve Yzerman 2.50 6.00
CUTB Thomas Bordeleau 1.00 2.50
CUTE Teuvo Teravainen 1.00 2.50
CUTF Trey Fix-Wolansky 1.00 2.50
CUTS Teemu Selanne 2.00 5.00
CUTT Tage Thompson 1.25 3.00
CUVH Victor Hedman 1.25 3.00
CUWG Wayne Gretzky 6.00 15.00
CUWN William Nylander 2.00 5.00

2022-23 Synergy Greater Than Signatures

*ORANGE: .5X TO 1.2X BASIC
GTAL Anton Lundell 10.00 25.00
GTAS Andrei Svechnikov 12.00 30.00
GTBB Brent Burns 10.00 25.00
GTBE Matty Beniers 25.00 60.00
GTBM Brad Marchand 20.00 50.00
GTCP Carey Price 20.00 50.00
GTDB Drake Batherson 10.00 25.00
GTDC Dylan Cozens 10.00 25.00
GTDM Dawson Mercer 12.00 30.00
GTJM Jarod McCann 8.00 20.00
GTJP Joe Pavelski 12.00 30.00
GTKC Kyle Connor 15.00 40.00
GTKJ Kent Johnson 20.00 50.00
GTKL Kris Letang 12.00 30.00
GTMB Matt Boldy 30.00 80.00
GTMR Marco Rossi 25.00 60.00
GTMT Matthew Tkachuk 20.00 50.00
GTRH Roope Hintz 12.00 30.00
GTRJ Roman Josi 10.00 25.00
GTST Mark Stone 12.00 30.00
GTTS Tim Stutzle 25.00 60.00

2022-23 Synergy Light Up The Night

*NEON YLW/699: .5X TO 1.2X BASIC
*BLUE/399: .6X TO 1.5X BASIC
*GREEN/99: .75X TO 2X BASIC
*PINK/75: 1X TO 2.5X BASIC
LNAK Arthur Kaliyev 1.00 2.50
LNAL Anders Lee .75 2.00
LNAM Auston Matthews 4.00 10.00
LNAO Alex Ovechkin 4.00 10.00
LNAP Artemi Panarin 2.00 5.00
LNAS Andrei Svechnikov 1.25 3.00
LNAV Andrei Vasilevskiy 1.50 4.00
LNBH Brandon Hagel .75 2.00
LNBM Brad Marchand 2.00 5.00
LNBS Brandon Saad .75 2.00
LNCK Clayton Keller 1.25 3.00
LNCM Connor McDavid 5.00 12.00
LNCP Carey Price 2.00 5.00
LNDP David Pastrnak 2.50 6.00
LNEM Evgeni Malkin 2.00 5.00
LNEP Elias Pettersson 1.50 4.00
LNHA Taylor Hall 1.00 2.50
LNIS Igor Shesterkin 2.00 5.00
LNJE Jack Eichel 1.50 4.00
LNJG John Gibson 1.00 2.50
LNJH Jack Hughes 2.50 6.00
LNJK Jordan Kyrou 1.00 2.50
LNJP Joe Pavelski 1.25 3.00
LNJR Jason Robertson 1.50 4.00
LNJS Jaccob Slavin .75 2.00
LNJT John Tavares 1.50 4.00
LNKK Kirill Kaprizov 3.00 8.00
LNKM K'Andre Miller .75 2.00
LNLA Alexis Lafreniere 1.50 4.00
LNLD Leon Draisaitl 3.00 8.00
LNLR Lucas Raymond 1.50 4.00
LNMA Cale Makar 2.50 6.00
LNME Elvis Merzlikins 1.00 2.50
LNMF Marc-Andre Fleury 2.00 5.00
LNMH Miro Heiskanen 1.25 3.00
LNMN Martin Necas 1.50 4.00
LNMS Mattias Samuelsson .60 1.50
LNNE Nikolaj Ehlers 1.00 2.50
LNNK Nikita Kucherov 2.00 5.00
LNPB Patrice Bergeron 1.25 3.00
LNPK Patrick Kane 2.00 5.00
LNPO Colton Parayko .75 2.00
LNRF Robby Fabbri .60 1.50
LNRK Rasmus Kupari .60 1.50
LNSA Sebastian Aho 1.50 4.00
LNSC Sidney Crosby 4.00 10.00
LNSM Sean Monahan .60 1.50
LNSR Sam Reinhart 2.00 5.00
LNSS Steven Stamkos 2.00 5.00
LNTH Tomas Hertl 1.00 2.50
LNTS Tim Stutzle 1.25 3.00
LNTT Tage Thompson 1.25 3.00
LNTW Tom Wilson 1.00 2.50
LNTZ Trevor Zegras 1.00 2.50
LNWE William Eklund 1.25 3.00

2022-23 Synergy Light Up the Night Green Autographs

LNAK Arthur Kaliyev/99 10.00 25.00
LNAL Anders Lee/99 8.00 20.00
LNAS Andrei Svechnikov/25 12.00 30.00
LNAV Andrei Vasilevskiy/25 15.00 40.00
LNBH Brandon Hagel/49 8.00 20.00
LNBM Brad Marchand/25 20.00 50.00
LNJP Joe Pavelski/25 12.00 30.00
LNJR Jason Robertson/25 15.00 40.00
LNJS Jaccob Slavin/99 8.00 20.00
LNJT John Tavares/25 15.00 40.00
LNKM K'Andre Miller/25 8.00 20.00
LNLA Alexis Lafreniere/25 15.00 40.00
LNMH Miro Heiskanen/49 12.00 30.00
LNMN Martin Necas/25 15.00 40.00
LNMS Mattias Samuelsson/25 6.00 15.00
LNNE Nikolaj Ehlers/25 10.00 25.00
LNRF Robby Fabbri/99 6.00 15.00
LNRK Rasmus Kupari/25 6.00 15.00
LNSM Sean Monahan/25 6.00 15.00
LNSR Sam Reinhart/25 20.00 50.00
LNTH Tomas Hertl/49 10.00 25.00
LNTS Tim Stutzle/25 12.00 30.00
LNTT Tage Thompson/49 60.00 150.00
LNTW Tom Wilson/25 10.00 25.00
LNWE William Eklund/25 12.00 30.00

2022-23 Synergy Light Up the Night Green Rookie Autographs

LNRBB Bobby Brink/49 10.00 25.00
LNRBT Brayden Tracey/49 8.00 20.00
LNRDH Dylan Holloway/49 20.00 50.00
LNRDO Lukas Dostal/49 20.00 50.00
LNRDS Dylan Samberg/49 10.00 25.00
LNREK Erik Kallgren/99 10.00 25.00
LNRFH Filip Hallander/99 10.00 25.00
LNRFK Fredrik Karlstrom/99 8.00 20.00
LNRIR Isaac Ratcliffe/49 10.00 25.00
LNRJA Jacob Perreault/49 10.00 25.00
LNRJM Jack McBain/99 10.00 25.00
LNRJO Jordan Harris/49 12.00 30.00
LNRJQ Jack Quinn/49 15.00 40.00
LNRKA Kaedan Korczak/49 8.00 20.00
LNRKJ Kent Johnson/49 20.00 50.00
LNRKO Pyotr Kochetkov/99 20.00 50.00
LNRMB Matt Boldy/49 30.00 80.00
LNRMC Marc McLaughlin/49 10.00 25.00
LNRME Michael Eyssimont/99 10.00 25.00
LNRMK Mark Kastelic/49 8.00 20.00
LNRMR Marco Rossi/49 25.00 60.00
LNRMS Mads Sogaard/99 12.00 30.00
LNRNA Nick Abruzzese/49 10.00 25.00
LNRNC Noah Cates/99 10.00 25.00
LNRNS Nathan Smith/99 8.00 20.00
LNROP Owen Power/49 20.00 50.00
LNRPE Chase Pearson/99 8.00 20.00
LNRRA Ronnie Attard/49 10.00 25.00
LNRRE Lukas Reichel/49 25.00 60.00
LNRSF Samuel Fagemo/49 8.00 20.00
LNRTB Thomas Bordeleau/49 10.00 25.00
LNRTF Trey Fix-Wolansky/49 10.00 25.00
LNRVL Alex Vlasic/49 8.00 20.00
LNRVP Valtteri Puustinen/99 8.00 20.00
LNRZH Zack Hayes/99 8.00 20.00

2022-23 Synergy Light Up The Night Rookies

*NEON YLW/699: .5X TO 1.2X BASIC
*BLUE/399: .6X TO 1.5X BASIC
*PINK/75: 1X TO 2.5X BASIC
LNRAR Adam Raska 1.00 2.50
LNRBB Bobby Brink 1.00 2.50
LNRBE Matty Beniers 2.50 6.00
LNRBR Braden Schneider 1.50 4.00
LNRBT Brayden Tracey .75 2.00
LNRDH Dylan Holloway 2.00 5.00
LNRDO Lukas Dostal 2.00 5.00
LNRDS Dylan Samberg 1.00 2.50
LNREK Erik Kallgren 1.00 2.50
LNRFH Filip Hallander 1.00 2.50
LNRFK Fredrik Karlstrom .75 2.00
LNRHD Hunter Drew 1.00 2.50
LNRIR Isaac Ratcliffe 1.00 2.50
LNRJA Jacob Perreault 1.00 2.50
LNRJL Jack LaFontaine 1.00 2.50
LNRJM Jack McBain 1.00 2.50
LNRJO Jordan Harris 1.25 3.00
LNRJQ Jack Quinn 1.50 4.00
LNRKA Kaedan Korczak .75 2.00
LNRKJ Kent Johnson 2.00 5.00
LNRKO Pyotr Kochetkov 2.00 5.00
LNRMA Jeff Malott 1.00 2.50
LNRMB Matt Boldy 3.00 8.00
LNRMC Marc McLaughlin 1.00 2.50
LNRME Michael Eyssimont 1.00 2.50
LNRMK Mark Kastelic .75 2.00
LNRMM Matias Maccelli 1.50 4.00
LNRMR Marco Rossi 2.50 6.00
LNRMS Mads Sogaard 1.25 3.00

LNRNA Nick Abruzzese 1.00 2.50
LNRNC Noah Cates 1.00 2.50
LNRNS Nathan Smith .75 2.00
LNROP Owen Power 2.00 5.00
LNRPE Chase Pearson .75 2.00
LNRRA Ronnie Attard 1.00 2.50
LNRRE Lukas Reichel 2.00 5.00
LNRRW Reilly Walsh 1.00 2.50
LNRSF Samuel Fagemo .75 2.00
LNRSP Jordan Spence 1.00 2.50
LNRTB Thomas Bordeleau 1.00 2.50
LNRTF Trey Fix-Wolansky 1.00 2.50
LNRVK Vladislav Kolyachonok .75 2.00
LNRVL Alex Vlasic .75 2.00
LNRVP Valtteri Puustinen .75 2.00
LNRZH Zack Hayes .75 2.00

2022-23 Synergy Rink Ink

*ORANGE: .5X TO 1.2X BASIC
RIAL Alexis Lafreniere 20.00 50.00
RIBJ Boone Jenner 12.00 30.00
RIBT Brady Tkachuk 20.00 50.00
RICC Charlie Coyle 12.00 30.00
RICN Cam Neely 12.00 30.00
RIDM Dawson Mercer 15.00 40.00
RIHE Ron Hextall 12.00 30.00
RIJB Josh Bailey 10.00 25.00
RIJM Janis Moser 8.00 20.00
RIJR Jason Robertson 20.00 50.00
RIKD Kirby Dach 12.00 30.00
RIMA Maxime Comtois 10.00 25.00
RIMC Jared McCann 10.00 25.00
RIML Mike Liut 8.00 20.00
RIMM Mike Modano 20.00 50.00
RIPS Pius Suter 10.00 25.00
RIPT Philip Tomasino 8.00 20.00
RIRC Ross Colton 10.00 25.00
RIRH Roope Hintz 15.00 40.00
RISC Shayne Corson 10.00 25.00
RITF Theoren Fleury 12.00 30.00
RITN Tage Thompson 15.00 40.00
RITS Tim Stutzle 15.00 40.00
RITT Teuvo Teravainen 12.00 30.00

2022-23 Synergy Rink Ink Rookies

RIRAV Alex Vlasic C 6.00 15.00
RIRBB Bobby Brink C 8.00 20.00
RIRBE Matty Beniers 100.00 250.00
RIRBO Thomas Bordeleau D 8.00 20.00
RIRBT Brayden Tracey C 6.00 15.00
RIRCP Chase Pearson D 6.00 15.00
RIRDS Dylan Samberg C 8.00 20.00
RIRFH Filip Hallander C 8.00 20.00
RIRFK Fredrik Karlstrom C 6.00 15.00
RIRIR Isaac Ratcliffe C 8.00 20.00
RIRJH Jordan Harris D 10.00 25.00
RIRJP Jacob Perreault B 8.00 20.00
RIRJQ Jack Quinn A 12.00 30.00
RIRKJ Kent Johnson B 15.00 40.00
RIRKK Kaedan Korczak C 6.00 15.00
RIRLD Lukas Dostal C 15.00 40.00
RIRLR Lukas Reichel B 15.00 40.00
RIRMB Matt Boldy A 25.00 60.00
RIRME Michael Eyssimont D 8.00 20.00
RIRMK Mark Kastelic D 6.00 15.00
RIRMR Marco Rossi A 20.00 50.00
RIRMS Mads Sogaard D 10.00 25.00
RIRNA Nick Abruzzese D 8.00 20.00
RIROP Owen Power A 15.00 40.00
RIRPK Pyotr Kochetkov D 15.00 40.00
RIRTF Trey Fix-Wolansky D 8.00 20.00
RIRVP Valtteri Puustinen C 6.00 15.00

2022-23 Synergy Rink Ink Rookies Orange

*ORANGE: .5X TO 1.2X BASIC
RIRPK Pyotr Kochetkov/49 80.00 200.00

2022-23 Synergy Rookie Journey Away

*RED/499: .5X TO 1.2X BASIC
*GREEN/249: .6X TO 1.5X BASIC
*GOLD/99: .75X TO 2X BASIC
RJ1 Matt Boldy 4.00 10.00
RJ2 Kent Johnson 2.50 6.00
RJ3 Jacob Perreault 1.25 3.00
RJ4 Marco Rossi 3.00 8.00
RJ5 Matty Beniers 3.00 8.00
RJ6 Jack Quinn 2.00 5.00
RJ7 Braden Schneider 2.00 5.00
RJ8 Brayden Tracey 1.00 2.50
RJ9 Lukas Reichel 2.50 6.00
RJ10 Owen Power 2.50 6.00
RJ11 Dylan Holloway 2.50 6.00
RJ12 Pyotr Kochetkov 2.50 6.00
RJ13 Isaac Ratcliffe 1.25 3.00
RJ14 Mads Sogaard 1.50 4.00
RJ15 Jordan Spence 1.25 3.00

2022-23 Synergy Rookie Journey Draft

*RED/499: .5X TO 1.2X BASIC
*GREEN/249: .6X TO 1.5X BASIC
*GOLD/99: .75X TO 2X BASIC
RJ1 Matt Boldy 4.00 10.00
RJ2 Kent Johnson 2.50 6.00
RJ3 Jacob Perreault 1.25 3.00
RJ4 Marco Rossi 3.00 8.00
RJ5 Matty Beniers 3.00 8.00
RJ6 Jack Quinn 2.00 5.00
RJ7 Braden Schneider 2.00 5.00
RJ8 Brayden Tracey 1.00 2.50
RJ9 Lukas Reichel 2.50 6.00
RJ10 Owen Power 2.50 6.00
RJ11 Dylan Holloway 2.50 6.00
RJ12 Pyotr Kochetkov 2.50 6.00
RJ13 Isaac Ratcliffe 1.25 3.00
RJ14 Mads Sogaard 1.50 4.00
RJ15 Jordan Spence 1.25 3.00

2022-23 Synergy Rookie Journey Home

*RED/499: .5X TO 1.2X BASIC
*GREEN/249: .6X TO 1.5X BASIC
*GOLD/99: .75X TO 2X BASIC
RJ1 Matt Boldy 4.00 10.00
RJ2 Kent Johnson 2.50 6.00
RJ3 Jacob Perreault 1.25 3.00
RJ4 Marco Rossi 3.00 8.00
RJ5 Matty Beniers 3.00 8.00
RJ6 Jack Quinn 2.00 5.00
RJ7 Braden Schneider 2.00 5.00
RJ8 Brayden Tracey 1.00 2.50
RJ9 Lukas Reichel 2.50 6.00
RJ10 Owen Power 2.50 6.00
RJ11 Dylan Holloway 2.50 6.00
RJ12 Pyotr Kochetkov 2.50 6.00
RJ13 Isaac Ratcliffe 1.25 3.00
RJ14 Mads Sogaard 1.50 4.00
RJ15 Jordan Spence 1.25 3.00

2022-23 Synergy Rookie Portraits Red Autographs

RPDG Dylan Guenther 40.00 100.00
RPDH Dylan Holloway 30.00 80.00
RPJP Jacob Perreault 15.00 40.00
RPJQ Jack Quinn 25.00 60.00
RPJS Jake Sanderson 40.00 100.00
RPKJ Kent Johnson 30.00 80.00
RPLR Lukas Reichel 30.00 80.00
RPMB Matt Boldy 50.00 125.00
RPMR Marco Rossi 40.00 100.00
RPOP Owen Power 30.00 80.00
RPSW Shane Wright 40.00 100.00

2022-23 Synergy Star Of The Show

SOS1 Andrei Vasilevskiy .60 1.50
SOS2 Connor McDavid 2.00 5.00
SOS3 Alex Ovechkin 1.50 4.00
SOS4 Auston Matthews 1.50 4.00
SOS5 Kirill Kaprizov 1.25 3.00
SOS6 Sidney Crosby 1.50 4.00
SOS7 Artemi Panarin .75 2.00
SOS8 Carey Price .75 2.00
SOS9 Elias Pettersson .60 1.50
SOS10 Cale Makar 1.00 2.50
SOS11 Johnny Gaudreau .60 1.50
SOS12 Patrick Kane .75 2.00
SOS13 Kyle Connor .60 1.50
SOS14 David Pastrnak 1.00 2.50
SOS15 Roman Josi .40 1.00
SOS16 Jason Robertson .60 1.50
SOS17 Mitch Marner .60 1.50
SOS18 Sebastian Aho .60 1.50
SOS19 Leon Draisaitl 1.25 3.00
SOS20 Igor Shesterkin .75 2.00

2022-23 Synergy Star Quest

SQ1 Brad Marchand 8.00 20.00
SQ2 Patrick Kane 8.00 20.00
SQ3 Michael Bunting 4.00 10.00
SQ4 Steven Stamkos 8.00 20.00
SQ5 Connor McDavid 20.00 50.00
SQ6 Alex Ovechkin 15.00 40.00
SQ7 Andrei Vasilevskiy 6.00 15.00
SQ8 Taylor Hall 4.00 10.00
SQ9 Dylan Holloway 8.00 20.00
SQ10 Sidney Crosby 15.00 40.00
SQ11 Sebastian Aho 6.00 15.00
SQ12 Cale Makar 10.00 25.00
SQ13 Braden Schneider 6.00 15.00
SQ14 Alexis Lafreniere 6.00 15.00
SQ15 Jeremy Swayman 6.00 15.00
SQ16 Connor Hellebuyck 8.00 20.00
SQ17 Seth Jarvis 5.00 12.00
SQ18 Igor Shesterkin 8.00 20.00
SQ19 Jake Guentzel 6.00 15.00
SQ20 Thomas Bordeleau 4.00 10.00
SQ21 Joe Pavelski 5.00 12.00
SQ22 Anze Kopitar 6.00 15.00
SQ23 Leon Draisaitl 12.00 30.00
SQ24 Troy Terry 3.00 8.00
SQ25 Victor Hedman 5.00 12.00

2022-23 Synergy Synergistic Duos Stars

*RED/499: .5X TO 1.2X BASIC
*GREEN/249: .6X TO 1.5X BASIC
*GOLD/99: .75X TO 2X BASIC
SD1 Jason Robertson
Roope Hintz 2.00 5.00
SD2 Zach Werenski
Patrik Laine 2.00 5.00
SD3 Brady Tkachuk
Tim Stutzle 2.00 5.00
SD4 Patrick Kane
Jonathan Toews 2.50 6.00
SD5 Nick Suzuki
Cole Caufield 2.50 6.00
SD6 Moritz Seider
Lucas Raymond 2.00 5.00
SD7 Trevor Zegras
Jamie Drysdale 1.25 3.00
SD8 Aleksander Barkov
Aaron Ekblad 2.00 5.00
SD9 John Carlson
Tom Wilson 1.25 3.00
SD10 Gabriel Landeskog
Mikko Rantanen 3.00 8.00
SD11 Kirill Kaprizov
Marc-Andre Fleury 4.00 10.00
SD12 Rasmus Dahlin
Tage Thompson 1.50 4.00
SD13 Brad Marchand
Patrice Bergeron 2.50 6.00
SD14 Auston Matthews
Mitch Marner 5.00 12.00
SD15 Andrei Vasilevskiy
Steven Stamkos 2.50 6.00
SD16 Igor Shesterkin
Artemi Panarin 2.50 6.00
SD17 Sidney Crosby
Evgeni Malkin 5.00 12.00
SD18 Connor McDavid
Leon Draisaitl 6.00 15.00

2022-23 Synergy Synergistic Duos Stars Legends

*RED/499: .5X TO 1.2X BASIC
*GREEN/249: .6X TO 1.5X BASIC
*GOLD/99: .75X TO 2X BASIC
SD1 Jason Robertson
Mike Modano 2.00 5.00
SD2 Cole Caufield
Guy Lafleur 2.50 6.00
SD3 Brady Tkachuk
Dany Heatley 2.00 5.00
SD4 Patrick Kane
Bobby Hull 2.50 6.00
SD5 Nick Suzuki
Jean Beliveau 2.50 6.00
SD6 Moritz Seider
Nicklas Lidstrom 1.50 4.00
SD7 Trevor Zegras
Teemu Selanne 2.50 6.00
SD8 Anze Kopitar
Luc Robitaille 2.00 5.00
SD9 John Carlson
Mike Gartner 1.50 4.00
SD10 Gabriel Landeskog
Joe Sakic 2.50 6.00
SD11 Alexis Lafreniere
Rod Gilbert 2.00 5.00
SD12 Rasmus Dahlin
Dominik Hasek 2.00 5.00
SD13 Brad Marchand
Cam Neely 2.50 6.00
SD14 Auston Matthews
Darryl Sittler 5.00 12.00
SD15 Andrei Vasilevskiy
Martin St. Louis 2.00 5.00
SD16 Adam Fox
Brian Leetch 1.50 4.00
SD17 Sidney Crosby
Mario Lemieux 5.00 12.00
SD18 Connor McDavid
Wayne Gretzky 8.00 20.00

2022-23 Synergy Synergistic Duos Stars Rookies

*RED/499: .5X TO 1.2X BASIC
*GREEN/249: .6X TO 1.5X BASIC
*GOLD/99: .75X TO 2X BASIC
SD1 John Gibson
Lukas Dostal 2.50 6.00
SD2 Kirill Kaprizov
Matt Boldy 4.00 10.00
SD3 Rasmus Dahlin
Owen Power 2.50 6.00
SD4 Jordan Eberle
Matty Beniers 3.00 8.00
SD5 Tage Thompson
Jack Quinn 2.00 5.00
SD6 Leon Draisaitl
Dylan Holloway 4.00 10.00
SD7 Patrik Laine
Kent Johnson 2.50 6.00
SD8 Anze Kopitar
Samuel Fagemo 2.00 5.00
SD9 Adam Fox
Braden Schneider 2.00 5.00
SD10 Tomas Hertl
Thomas Bordeleau 1.25 3.00
SD11 Marc-Andre Fleury
Marco Rossi 3.00 8.00
SD12 Patrick Kane
Lukas Reichel 2.50 6.00
SD13 Brady Tkachuk
Mads Sogaard 2.00 5.00
SD14 Troy Terry
Jacob Perreault 1.25 3.00
SD15 Travis Konecny
Isaac Ratcliffe 1.25 3.00
SD16 Andrei Svechnikov
Pyotr Kochetkov 2.50 6.00
SD17 Nick Suzuki
Jordan Harris 2.50 6.00
SD18 Mitch Marner
Nick Abruzzese 2.00 5.00

2022-23 Synergy Thrill Rides

TR1 Trevor Zegras .60 1.50
TR2 Connor McDavid 3.00 8.00
TR3 Cale Makar 1.50 4.00
TR4 Nikita Kucherov 1.25 3.00
TR5 Auston Matthews 2.50 6.00
TR6 Andrei Svechnikov .75 2.00
TR7 Leon Draisaitl 2.00 5.00
TR8 Igor Shesterkin 1.25 3.00
TR9 Sidney Crosby 2.50 6.00
TR10 Nathan MacKinnon 2.50 6.00
TR11 Moritz Seider .75 2.00
TR12 Kirill Kaprizov 2.00 5.00

2023-24 Synergy Red

1 Connor McDavid 3.00 8.00
2 Auston Matthews 2.50 6.00
3 Sidney Crosby 2.50 6.00
4 Alex Ovechkin 2.50 6.00
5 Cale Makar 1.50 4.00
6 Brad Marchand 1.25 3.00
7 Leon Draisaitl 2.00 5.00
8 Jack Eichel 1.00 2.50
9 Andrei Vasilevskiy 1.00 2.50
10 Jason Robertson 1.00 2.50
11 Cole Caufield 1.25 3.00
12 Trevor Zegras .60 1.50
13 Tim Stutzle .75 2.00
14 Marc-Andre Fleury 1.25 3.00
15 Matthew Tkachuk 1.25 3.00
16 Nick Suzuki 1.25 3.00
17 Mark Stone .75 2.00
18 Roman Josi .60 1.50
19 Aleksander Barkov 1.00 2.50
20 Andrei Svechnikov .75 2.00
21 Jonathan Huberdeau .75 2.00
22 Ilya Sorokin 1.00 2.50
23 Ryan O'Reilly .60 1.50
24 Kyle Connor .60 1.50
25 Roope Hintz .75 2.00
26 Jordan Eberle .60 1.50
27 Jordan Kyrou .60 1.50
28 Tage Thompson .75 2.00
29 Matt Boldy 1.00 2.50
30 Lukas Reichel .60 1.50
31 Wyatt Johnston 1.25 3.00
32 Andrei Kuzmenko .60 1.50
33 Josh Norris .60 1.50
34 Zach Hyman 1.00 2.50
35 Juraj Slafkovsky 1.25 3.00
36 David Pastrnak 1.50 4.00
37 Jack Hughes 1.50 4.00
38 Nathan MacKinnon 2.50 6.00
39 Kirill Kaprizov 2.00 5.00
40 Patrick Kane 1.25 3.00
41 Evgeni Malkin 1.25 3.00
42 Steven Stamkos 1.25 3.00
43 Mitch Marner 1.00 2.50
44 Clayton Keller .75 2.00
45 Elias Pettersson 1.00 2.50
46 Moritz Seider .75 2.00
47 Matty Beniers .75 2.00
48 Johnny Gaudreau 1.00 2.50
49 Travis Konecny .60 1.50
50 Anze Kopitar 1.00 2.50
51 Erik Karlsson .75 2.00
52 Mason McTavish .60 1.50
53 Sebastian Aho 1.00 2.50
54 Dylan Larkin .75 2.00
55 Igor Shesterkin 1.25 3.00
56 Artemi Panarin 1.25 3.00
57 Nico Hischier 1.00 2.50
58 Rasmus Dahlin .75 2.00
59 Lucas Raymond 1.00 2.50
60 Brock Nelson .60 1.50
61 Wayne Gretzky 4.00 10.00
62 Bobby Orr 2.50 6.00
63 Mark Messier 1.25 3.00
64 Mario Lemieux 2.50 6.00
65 Gordie Howe 2.00 5.00
66 Dominik Hasek 1.00 2.50
67 Henrik Lundqvist 1.50 4.00
68 Patrick Roy 1.50 4.00
69 Maurice Richard 1.25 3.00
70 Joe Thornton 1.00 2.50
71 Peter Forsberg 1.25 3.00
72 Teemu Selanne 1.25 3.00
73 Eric Lindros 1.00 2.50
74 Rod Brind'Amour .60 1.50
75 Johnny Bucyk .60 1.50
76 Tye Kartye 3.00 8.00
77 Jackson LaCombe 2.00 5.00
78 Tyler Kleven 2.00 5.00
79 Henry Thrun 2.00 5.00
80 Drew Helleson 2.00 5.00
81 Matthew Coronato 3.00 8.00
82 Dustin Wolf 6.00 15.00
83 Sean Farrell 2.00 5.00
84 Owen Beck 3.00 8.00
85 Luke Evangelista 3.00 8.00
86 Yaroslav Askarov 5.00 12.00
87 Tyson Foerster 4.00 10.00
88 Nikita Nesterenko 2.00 5.00
89 Jakob Pelletier 2.50 6.00
90 Stanislav Svozil 2.00 5.00
91 Brock Faber 5.00 12.00
92 William Dufour 1.50 4.00
93 Will Cuylle 3.00 8.00
94 Ridly Greig 3.00 8.00
95 Adam Ginning 2.00 5.00
96 Vincent Iorio 2.00 5.00
97 Tristen Robins 2.00 5.00
98 Samuel Bolduc 2.00 5.00
99 Leevi Merilainen 2.00 5.00
100 Danil Gushchin 2.00 5.00
101 Samuel Knazko 2.00 5.00
102 Wyatt Kaiser 2.00 5.00
103 Jonathan Gruden 2.00 5.00
104 Jaxson Stauber 2.00 5.00
105 Joona Koppanen 1.50 4.00
106 Hugh McGing 2.00 5.00
107 Matthew Kessel 1.50 4.00
108 Olle Eriksson Ek 2.00 5.00
109 Matt Murray 2.00 5.00
110 Jake Livingstone 2.00 5.00
111 Bobby McMann 3.00 8.00
112 Cole McWard 2.00 5.00
113 Akito Hirose 1.50 4.00
114 Arnaud Durandeau 2.00 5.00
115 Vincent Desharnais 2.50 6.00
116 Aidan McDonough 1.50 4.00
117 Nick Swaney 2.00 5.00
118 Luke Philp 2.00 5.00
119 David Gust 2.00 5.00
120 Egor Afanasyev 2.00 5.00
121 Luke Hughes 6.00 15.00
122 Matthew Knies 8.00 20.00
123 Devon Levi 5.00 12.00
124 Marco Kasper 5.00 12.00
125 Simon Edvinsson 4.00 10.00
RAF Adam Fantilli 6.00 15.00
RCB Connor Bedard 80.00 200.00
RCZ Connor Zary 4.00 10.00
RLC Logan Cooley 6.00 15.00
RLE Leo Carlsson 6.00 15.00
RSN Simon Nemec 4.00 10.00

2023-24 Synergy Purple

*PURPLE AU: 8X TO 20X RED
*PURPLE NON-AU:1.5X TO 4X RED
*PURPLE AU RC: 2X TO 5X RED
*PURP NON-AU RC: .6X TO 1.5X RED
31 Wyatt Johnston/65 AU 30.00 80.00
35 Juraj Slafkovsky/65 AU 60.00 150.00
68 Patrick Roy/35 AU 150.00 400.00
71 Peter Forsberg/35 AU 80.00 200.00
RCB Connor Bedard/13 AU 800.00 2000.00

2023-24 Synergy Red Codes

*CODES: 1X TO 2.5X RED
*CODES RC: .5X TO 1.2X RED
121 Luke Hughes 60.00 150.00
122 Matthew Knies 60.00 150.00
123 Devon Levi 100.00 250.00
124 Marco Kasper 25.00 60.00
125 Simon Edvinsson 12.00 30.00

2023-24 Synergy 2030

10F18 Mason McTavish .60 1.50
20F18 Jake Sanderson .75 2.00
30F18 Owen Power .60 1.50
40F18 Wyatt Johnston 1.25 3.00
50F18 Jack Quinn .60 1.50
60F18 Adam Fox .75 2.00
70F18 Ilya Sorokin 1.00 2.50
80F18 Seth Jarvis .75 2.00
90F18 Juraj Slafkovsky 1.25 3.00
100F18 Jeremy Swayman 1.00 2.50
110F18 Nick Suzuki 1.25 3.00
120F18 Igor Shesterkin 1.25 3.00
130F18 Jack Hughes 1.50 4.00
140F18 Kent Johnson .60 1.50
150F18 Rasmus Dahlin .75 2.00
160F18 Matt Boldy 1.00 2.50
170F18 Matty Beniers .75 2.00
180F18 Jordan Kyrou .60 1.50

2023-24 Synergy Barnburners

BARN1 Simon Edvinsson 4.00 10.00
BARN2 Luke Hughes 6.00 15.00
BARN3 Devon Levi 5.00 12.00
BARN4 Mario Lemieux 8.00 20.00
BARN5 Mark Messier 4.00 10.00
BARN6 Alex Ovechkin 8.00 20.00
BARN7 Sidney Crosby 8.00 20.00
BARN8 Connor McDavid 10.00 25.00
BARN9 Auston Matthews 8.00 20.00
BARN10 Jason Robertson 3.00 8.00
BARN11 David Pastrnak 5.00 12.00
BARN12 Trevor Zegras 2.00 5.00
BARN13 Nick Suzuki 4.00 10.00
BARN14 Matty Beniers 2.50 6.00
BARN15 Artemi Panarin 4.00 10.00

2023-24 Synergy Cast for Greatness

*PURPLE: .6X TO 1.5X BASIC
CG1 Connor McDavid 15.00 40.00
CG2 Leon Draisaitl 10.00 25.00
CG3 Auston Matthews 12.00 30.00
CG4 Mitch Marner 5.00 12.00
CG5 Sidney Crosby 12.00 30.00
CG6 Evgeni Malkin 6.00 15.00
CG7 Brad Marchand 6.00 15.00
CG8 David Pastrnak 8.00 20.00
CG9 Kirill Kaprizov 10.00 25.00
CG10 Cole Caufield 6.00 15.00
CG11 Nick Suzuki 6.00 15.00
CG12 Cale Makar 8.00 20.00
CG13 Nathan MacKinnon 12.00 30.00
CG14 Matty Beniers 4.00 10.00
CG15 Lucas Raymond 5.00 12.00
CG16 Moritz Seider 4.00 10.00
CG17 Andrei Vasilevskiy 5.00 12.00
CG18 Artemi Panarin 6.00 15.00
CG19 Jack Hughes 8.00 20.00
CG20 Tage Thompson 4.00 10.00
CG21 Matthew Tkachuk 6.00 15.00
CG22 Jason Robertson 5.00 12.00
CG23 Mark Stone 4.00 10.00
CG24 Alex Tuch 3.00 8.00
CG25 Dylan Cozens 3.00 8.00
CG26 Wayne Gretzky 20.00 50.00
CG27 Mario Lemieux 12.00 30.00
CG28 Dominik Hasek 5.00 12.00
CG29 Steve Yzerman 8.00 20.00
CG30 Joe Sakic 6.00 15.00
CG31 Matthew Knies 12.00 30.00
CG32 Simon Edvinsson 6.00 15.00
CG33 Marco Kasper 8.00 20.00
CG34 Devon Levi 8.00 20.00
CG35 Luke Hughes 10.00 25.00
CG36 Connor Bedard 30.00 80.00

2023-24 Synergy Cast for Greatness Signatures

CGSBT Brady Tkachuk 30.00 80.00
CGSCM Connor McDavid 150.00 400.00
CGSCP Carey Price 40.00 100.00
CGSJE Jack Eichel 30.00 80.00
CGSJO Jake Oettinger 30.00 80.00
CGSMM Mark Messier 40.00 100.00
CGSMR Mikko Rantanen 20.00 50.00
CGSSY Steve Yzerman 50.00 125.00

2023-24 Synergy Cranked Up

*RED/599: .5X TO 1.2X BASIC
*BLUE/399: .6X TO 1.5X BASIC
*PURPLE/199: .8X TO 2X BASIC
CRAB Aleksander Barkov 1.50 4.00
CRAF Adam Fantilli 3.00 8.00
CRAG Adam Ginning 1.00 2.50
CRAK Anze Kopitar 1.50 4.00
CRAM Auston Matthews 4.00 10.00
CRAO Alex Ovechkin 4.00 10.00
CRAP Artemi Panarin 2.00 5.00
CRBA Mathew Barzal 1.25 3.00
CRBE Matty Beniers 1.25 3.00
CRBF Brock Faber 2.50 6.00
CRBH Brett Hull 2.00 5.00
CRBM Brad Marchand 2.00 5.00
CRBN Brock Nelson 1.00 2.50
CRBO Bobby Orr 4.00 10.00
CRBR Martin Brodeur 2.50 6.00
CRBT Brady Tkachuk 1.50 4.00
CRCB Connor Bedard 20.00 50.00
CRCC Cole Caufield 2.00 5.00
CRCK Clayton Keller 1.25 3.00
CRCM Connor McDavid 5.00 12.00
CRDC Dylan Cozens 1.00 2.50
CRDG Doug Gilmour 1.25 3.00
CRDH Dominik Hasek 1.50 4.00
CRDL Dylan Larkin 1.25 3.00
CRDP David Pastrnak 2.50 6.00
CRDW Dustin Wolf 3.00 8.00
CREK Erik Karlsson 1.25 3.00
CREM Evgeni Malkin 2.00 5.00
CREP Elias Pettersson 1.50 4.00
CREV Luke Evangelista 1.50 4.00
CRGU Danil Gushchin 1.00 2.50
CRHE Drew Helleson 1.00 2.50
CRHL Henrik Lundqvist 2.50 6.00
CRJE Jack Eichel 1.50 4.00
CRJG Johnny Gaudreau 1.50 4.00
CRJH Jack Hughes 2.50 6.00
CRJI Jarome Iginla 1.25 3.00
CRJK Jordan Kyrou 1.00 2.50
CRJL Jackson LaCombe 1.00 2.50
CRJP Joe Pavelski 1.25 3.00
CRJR Jason Robertson 1.50 4.00
CRKC Kyle Connor 1.50 4.00
CRKF Kevin Fiala .75 2.00
CRKK Kirill Kaprizov 3.00 8.00
CRKL Tyler Kleven 1.00 2.50
CRKN Matthew Knies 4.00 10.00
CRKO Joona Koppanen .75 2.00
CRLD Leon Draisaitl 3.00 8.00
CRLE Devon Levi 2.50 6.00
CRLH Luke Hughes 3.00 8.00
CRLM Leevi Merilainen 1.00 2.50
CRLR Lucas Raymond 1.50 4.00
CRMB Matt Boldy 1.50 4.00
CRMC Matthew Coronato 1.50 4.00
CRMD Matt Duchene 1.00 2.50
CRMK Marco Kasper 2.50 6.00
CRML Mario Lemieux 4.00 10.00
CRMM Mark Messier 2.00 5.00
CRMN Martin Necas 1.50 4.00
CRMO Mike Modano 1.50 4.00
CRMR Mikko Rantanen 2.50 6.00
CRMT Matthew Tkachuk 2.00 5.00
CRMZ Mika Zibanejad 1.25 3.00
CRNH Nico Hischier 1.50 4.00
CRNL Nicklas Lidstrom 1.00 2.50
CRNM Nathan MacKinnon 4.00 10.00
CRNN Nikita Nesterenko 1.00 2.50
CRNS Nick Suzuki 2.00 5.00
CROB Owen Beck 1.50 4.00
CRPE Jakob Pelletier 1.25 3.00
CRPF Peter Forsberg 2.00 5.00
CRPR Patrick Roy 2.50 6.00
CRRF Ron Francis 1.25 3.00
CRRG Ridly Greig 1.50 4.00
CRRJ Roman Josi 1.00 2.50
CRRO Tristen Robins 1.00 2.50
CRSA Sebastian Aho 1.50 4.00
CRSB Samuel Bolduc 1.00 2.50
CRSC Sidney Crosby 4.00 10.00
CRSE Simon Edvinsson 2.00 5.00
CRSF Sean Farrell 1.00 2.50
CRSS Steven Stamkos 2.00 5.00
CRSV Stanislav Svozil .75 2.00
CRTF Tyson Foerster 2.00 5.00
CRTH Tage Thompson 1.25 3.00
CRTK Travis Konecny 1.00 2.50
CRTO Tyler Toffoli 1.00 2.50
CRTR Tyler Raddysh .75 2.00
CRTS Tim Stutzle 1.25 3.00
CRTT Troy Terry .75 2.00
CRTZ Trevor Zegras 1.00 2.50
CRVI Vincent Iorio 1.00 2.50
CRWC Will Cuylle 1.50 4.00
CRWD William Dufour .75 2.00
CRWG Wayne Gretzky 6.00 15.00
CRWK Wyatt Kaiser 1.00 2.50
CRYA Yaroslav Askarov 2.50 6.00

2023-24 Synergy Cranked Up Green

*GREEN/49: 1.2X TO 3X BASIC
CRCB Connor Bedard 80.00 200.00
CRCM Connor McDavid 25.00 60.00
CRML Mario Lemieux 20.00 50.00

2023-24 Synergy Cranked Up Pink

*PNK/25: 2X TO 5X BASIC
CRCB Connor Bedard 100.00 250.00
CRCM Connor McDavid 60.00 150.00
CRML Mario Lemieux 40.00 100.00

2023-24 Synergy Fearless Leaders

*SPCTRM/25: 1X TO 2.5X BASIC
LD1 Wayne Gretzky 12.00 30.00
LD2 Mark Messier 4.00 10.00
LD3 Patrick Roy 12.00 30.00
LD4 Alex Ovechkin 8.00 20.00
LD5 Bobby Orr 8.00 20.00
LD6 Mario Lemieux 8.00 20.00
LD7 John Tavares 3.00 8.00
LD8 Evgeni Malkin 4.00 10.00
LD9 Paul Coffey 2.00 5.00
LD10 Ray Bourque 3.00 8.00
LD11 Keith Tkachuk 2.00 5.00
LD12 Nicklas Lidstrom 2.00 5.00
LD13 Phil Esposito 3.00 8.00
LD14 Guy Lafleur 2.50 6.00
LD15 Joe Sakic 4.00 10.00
LD16 Martin St. Louis 2.00 5.00
LD17 Gordie Howe 6.00 15.00
LD18 Eric Lindros 3.00 8.00
LD19 Jean Beliveau 2.00 5.00
LD20 Saku Koivu 2.00 5.00
LD21 Connor McDavid 10.00 25.00
LD22 Stan Mikita 2.00 5.00
LD23 Trevor Linden 2.00 5.00
LD24 Ted Lindsay 2.00 5.00
LD25 Sidney Crosby 8.00 20.00

2023-24 Synergy Flammable

*SPCTRM/25: 1X TO 2.5X BASIC
FL1 Marco Kasper 5.00 12.00
FL2 Luke Hughes 6.00 15.00
FL3 Matthew Knies 8.00 20.00
FL4 Devon Levi 5.00 12.00
FL5 Simon Edvinsson 4.00 10.00
FL6 Dominik Hasek 3.00 8.00
FL7 Henrik Lundqvist 5.00 12.00
FL8 Peter Forsberg 4.00 10.00
FL9 Mario Lemieux 8.00 20.00
FL10 Wayne Gretzky 12.00 30.00
FL11 Alex Ovechkin 8.00 20.00
FL12 Auston Matthews 8.00 20.00
FL13 Andrei Vasilevskiy 3.00 8.00
FL14 Evgeni Malkin 4.00 10.00
FL15 Tim Stutzle 2.50 6.00
FL16 Cole Caufield 4.00 10.00
FL17 Kirill Kaprizov 6.00 15.00
FL18 Connor McDavid 10.00 25.00
FL19 Trevor Zegras 2.00 5.00
FL20 Rasmus Dahlin 2.00 5.00
FL21 Cale Makar 5.00 12.00
FL22 Lucas Raymond 3.00 8.00
FL23 Jack Hughes 5.00 12.00
FL24 Artemi Panarin 4.00 10.00
FL25 Matty Beniers 2.50 6.00

2023-24 Synergy Greater Than Signatures

*GREEN: .5X TO 1.2X BASIC
GTAL Anders Lee 6.00 15.00
GTAN Alex Newhook 6.00 15.00
GTAS Andrei Svechnikov SP 10.00 25.00
GTBC Blake Coleman 6.00 15.00
GTBM Brad Marchand SP 15.00 40.00
GTBS Brandon Saad 6.00 15.00
GTEK Evgeny Kuznetsov 10.00 25.00
GTFG Filip Gustavsson 8.00 20.00
GTJN Josh Norris 8.00 20.00
GTJQ Jonathan Quick SP 25.00 60.00
GTKA Marco Kasper SP 20.00 50.00
GTLT Logan Thompson 10.00 25.00
GTMA Mikey Anderson 6.00 15.00
GTMD Matt Duchene 8.00 20.00
GTMK Matthew Knies SP 30.00 80.00
GTMM Mason Marchment 6.00 15.00
GTNH Nico Hischier 12.00 30.00
GTOB Owen Beck 12.00 30.00
GTRF Robby Fabbri 5.00 12.00
GTRH Roope Hintz 10.00 25.00
GTRS Ryan Strome 8.00 20.00
GTSE Simon Edvinsson SP 15.00 40.00
GTSM Sonny Milano 6.00 15.00
GTSP Shane Pinto 6.00 15.00
GTTF Tyson Foerster 15.00 40.00
GTTR Taylor Raddysh 6.00 15.00
GTZH Zach Hyman 12.00 30.00

2023-24 Synergy Let's Goooo

*SPCTRM/25: 1.2X TO 3X BASIC
LG1 Connor McDavid 6.00 15.00
LG2 Sidney Crosby 5.00 12.00
LG3 David Pastrnak 3.00 8.00
LG4 Kirill Kaprizov 4.00 10.00
LG5 Kyle Connor 2.00 5.00
LG6 Elias Pettersson 2.00 5.00
LG7 Cole Caufield 2.50 6.00
LG8 Auston Matthews 5.00 12.00
LG9 Mikko Rantanen 3.00 8.00
LG10 Jack Hughes 3.00 8.00
LG11 Artemi Panarin 2.50 6.00
LG12 Brock Nelson 1.25 3.00
LG13 Travis Konecny 1.25 3.00
LG14 Brayden Point 1.50 4.00
LG15 Matthew Tkachuk 2.50 6.00
LG16 Tage Thompson 1.50 4.00
LG17 Tim Stutzle 1.50 4.00
LG18 Lucas Raymond 2.00 5.00
LG19 Jordan Kyrou 1.25 3.00
LG20 Clayton Keller 1.50 4.00
LG21 Jonathan Marchessault 1.50 4.00
LG22 Adrian Kempe 1.25 3.00
LG23 Jared McCann 1.00 2.50
LG24 Erik Karlsson 1.50 4.00
LG25 Trevor Zegras 1.25 3.00

2023-24 Synergy Light Up the Night

*PINK/699: .5X TO 1.2X BASIC
*BLUE/499: .6X TO 1.5X BASIC
LNAB Aleksander Barkov 1.50 4.00
LNAK Andrei Kuzmenko 1.00 2.50
LNAM Auston Matthews 4.00 10.00
LNAO Alex Ovechkin 4.00 10.00
LNAP Artemi Panarin 2.00 5.00
LNAS Andrei Svechnikov 1.25 3.00
LNAT Alex Tuch 1.00 2.50
LNAV Andrei Vasilevskiy 1.50 4.00
LNBE Matty Beniers 1.25 3.00
LNBM Brad Marchand 2.00 5.00
LNBT Brady Tkachuk 1.50 4.00
LNCC Cole Caufield 2.00 5.00
LNCK Clayton Keller 1.25 3.00
LNCM Cale Makar 2.50 6.00
LNDP David Pastrnak 2.50 6.00
LNEK Erik Karlsson 1.25 3.00
LNEM Evgeni Malkin 2.00 5.00
LNEP Elias Pettersson 1.50 4.00
LNHU Jack Hughes 2.50 6.00
LNIS Ilya Sorokin 1.50 4.00
LNJE Jack Eichel 1.50 4.00
LNJG Johnny Gaudreau 1.50 4.00
LNJH Jonathan Huberdeau 1.25 3.00
LNJK Jordan Kyrou 1.00 2.50
LNJP Joe Pavelski 1.25 3.00
LNJR Jason Robertson 1.50 4.00
LNJS Jeremy Swayman 1.50 4.00
LNKK Kirill Kaprizov 3.00 8.00
LNKO Anze Kopitar 1.50 4.00
LNLD Leon Draisaitl 3.00 8.00
LNLR Lukas Reichel 1.00 2.50
LNMB Matt Boldy 1.50 4.00
LNMC Connor McDavid 5.00 12.00
LNMF Marc-Andre Fleury 2.00 5.00
LNMR Mikko Rantanen 2.50 6.00
LNMT Matthew Tkachuk 2.00 5.00
LNNH Nico Hischier 1.50 4.00
LNNS Nick Suzuki 2.00 5.00
LNRJ Roman Josi 1.00 2.50
LNRN Ryan Nugent-Hopkins 1.25 3.00
LNSC Sidney Crosby 4.00 10.00
LNTK Travis Konecny 1.00 2.50
LNTT Tage Thompson 1.25 3.00
LNTZ Trevor Zegras 1.25 3.00
LNWJ Wyatt Johnston 2.00 5.00

2023-24 Synergy Light Up the Night Green

*GREEN NON AU: .8X TO 2X BASIC
*GREEN AU: 5X TO 12X BASIC
LNWJ Wyatt Johnston/99 AU 30.00 80.00

2023-24 Synergy Light Up the Night Rookies

*PINK/699: .5X TO 1.2X BASIC
*GREEN NON AU: .8X TO 2X BASIC
*GREEN AU: 5X TO 12X BASIC
LNAD Arnaud Durandeau 1.00 2.50
LNAF Adam Fantilli 3.00 8.00
LNAG Adam Ginning 1.00 2.50
LNAH Akito Hirose .75 2.00
LNBF Brock Faber 2.50 6.00
LNBS Billy Sweezey 1.00 2.50
LNCA Leo Carlsson 3.00 8.00
LNCB Connor Bedard 15.00 40.00
LNCO Matthew Coronato 1.50 4.00
LNCZ Connor Zary 2.00 5.00
LNDG Danil Gushchin 1.00 2.50
LNDH Drew Helleson 1.00 2.50
LNDL Devon Levi 2.50 6.00
LNDW Dustin Wolf 3.00 8.00
LNEA Egor Afanasyev 1.00 2.50
LNGJ Jonathan Gruden 1.00 2.50
LNGR Jet Greaves 1.50 4.00
LNHM Hugh McGing 1.00 2.50
LNJL Jackson LaCombe 1.00 2.50
LNJO Joona Koppanen .75 2.00
LNKA Marco Kasper 2.50 6.00
LNKN Matthew Knies 4.00 10.00
LNLC Logan Cooley 3.00 8.00

LNLE Luke Evangelista 1.50 4.00
LNLH Luke Hughes 3.00 8.00
LNLI Jake Livingstone 1.00 2.50
LNLM Leevi Merilainen 1.00 2.50
LNMH Hunter McKown 1.00 2.50
LNMK Matthew Kessel .75 2.00
LNMM Matt Murray 1.00 2.50
LNNN Nikita Nesterenko 1.00 2.50
LNOB Owen Beck 1.50 4.00
LNOE Olle Eriksson Ek 1.00 2.50
LNPA Jiri Patera 1.50 4.00
LNPE Jakob Pelletier 1.25 3.00
LNRG Ridly Greig 1.50 4.00
LNRO Lukas Rousek .75 2.00
LNSB Samuel Bolduc 1.00 2.50
LNSE Simon Edvinsson 2.00 5.00
LNSF Sean Farrell 1.00 2.50
LNSK Samuel Knazko 1.00 2.50
LNSN Simon Nemec 2.00 5.00
LNSS Stanislav Svozil .75 2.00
LNST Jaxson Stauber 1.00 2.50
LNTF Tyson Foerster 2.00 5.00
LNTR Tristen Robins 1.00 2.50
LNVD Vincent Desharnais 1.25 3.00
LNWC Will Cuylle 1.50 4.00
LNWD William Dufour .75 2.00
LNWK Wyatt Kaiser 1.00 2.50
LNYA Yaroslav Askarov 2.50 6.00

2023-24 Synergy Light Up the Night Rookies Blue

*BLUE/499: .6X TO 1.5X BASIC
LNCB Connor Bedard 30.00 80.00

2023-24 Synergy Rookie Journey Away

*RED/599: .5X TO 1.2X BASIC
*GREEN/399: .6X TO 1.5X BASIC
RJ1 Devon Levi 3.00 8.00
RJ2 Luke Hughes 4.00 10.00
RJ3 Matthew Knies 5.00 12.00
RJ4 Egor Afanasyev 1.25 3.00
RJ5 Simon Edvinsson 2.50 6.00
RJ6 Yaroslav Askarov 3.00 8.00
RJ7 Matthew Coronato 2.00 5.00
RJ8 Marco Kasper 3.00 8.00
RJ9 Jakob Pelletier 1.50 4.00
RJ10 Owen Beck 2.00 5.00
RJ11 Adam Fantilli 4.00 10.00
RJ12 Connor Bedard 30.00 80.00
RJ13 Connor Zary 2.50 6.00
RJ14 Matt Savoie 2.50 6.00
RJ15 Leo Carlsson 4.00 10.00

2023-24 Synergy Rookie Journey Away Gold

*GOLD/149: .8X TO 2X BASIC
RJ12 Connor Bedard 80.00 200.00

2023-24 Synergy Rookie Journey Draft

*RED/599: .5X TO 1.2X BASIC
*GREEN/399: .6X TO 1.5X BASIC
RJ1 Devon Levi 3.00 8.00
RJ2 Luke Hughes 4.00 10.00
RJ3 Matthew Knies 5.00 12.00
RJ4 Egor Afanasyev 1.25 3.00
RJ5 Simon Edvinsson 2.50 6.00
RJ6 Yaroslav Askarov 3.00 8.00
RJ7 Matthew Coronato 2.00 5.00
RJ8 Marco Kasper 3.00 8.00
RJ9 Jakob Pelletier 1.50 4.00
RJ10 Owen Beck 2.00 5.00
RJ11 Adam Fantilli 4.00 10.00
RJ12 Connor Bedard 25.00 60.00
RJ13 Connor Zary 2.50 6.00
RJ14 Matt Savoie 2.50 6.00
RJ15 Leo Carlsson 4.00 10.00

2023-24 Synergy Rookie Journey Draft Gold

*GOLD/149: .8X TO 2X BASIC
RJ12 Connor Bedard 80.00 200.00

2023-24 Synergy Rookie Journey Home

*RED/599: .5X TO 1.2X BASIC
RJ1 Devon Levi 3.00 8.00
RJ2 Luke Hughes 4.00 10.00
RJ3 Matthew Knies 5.00 12.00
RJ4 Egor Afanasyev 1.25 3.00
RJ5 Simon Edvinsson 2.50 6.00
RJ6 Yaroslav Askarov 3.00 8.00
RJ7 Matthew Coronato 2.00 5.00
RJ8 Marco Kasper 3.00 8.00
RJ9 Jakob Pelletier 1.50 4.00
RJ10 Owen Beck 2.00 5.00
RJ11 Adam Fantilli 4.00 10.00
RJ12 Connor Bedard 25.00 60.00
RJ13 Connor Zary 2.50 6.00
RJ14 Matt Savoie 2.50 6.00
RJ15 Leo Carlsson 4.00 10.00

2023-24 Synergy Rookie Journey Home Gold

*GOLD/149: .8X TO 2X BASIC
RJ12 Connor Bedard 100.00 250.00

2023-24 Synergy Rookie Journey Home Green

*GREEN/399: .6X TO 1.5X BASIC
RJ12 Connor Bedard 50.00 125.00

2023-24 Synergy Rookie Portraits Autographs Red

RPAF Adam Fantilli 60.00 150.00
RPCB Connor Bedard 800.00 2000.00
RPKA Marco Kasper 50.00 125.00
RPLH Luke Hughes 60.00 150.00
RPMC Matthew Coronato 30.00 80.00
RPMK Matthew Knies 80.00 200.00
RPSE Simon Edvinsson 40.00 100.00
RPSN Simon Nemec 40.00 100.00

2023-24 Synergy Rookie Sygnatures

*GREEN: .6X TO 1.5X BASIC
SAD Arnaud Durandeau 6.00 15.00
SAF Adam Fantilli SP 50.00 125.00
SAG Adam Ginning 6.00 15.00
SAI Aidan McDonough 5.00 12.00
SBF Brock Faber 30.00 80.00
SCO Matthew Coronato SP 10.00 25.00
SDG Danil Gushchin 6.00 15.00
SDW Dustin Wolf SP 20.00 50.00
SEA Egor Afanasyev 6.00 15.00
SHM Hunter McKown 6.00 15.00
SJI Jiri Patera 10.00 25.00
SKA Marco Kasper SP 20.00 50.00
SKN Matthew Knies SP 30.00 80.00
SLM Leevi Merilainen 6.00 15.00
SLR Lukas Rousek 5.00 12.00
SMK Matthew Kessel 5.00 12.00
SOB Owen Beck 10.00 25.00
SOE Olle Eriksson Ek 6.00 15.00
SPE Jakob Pelletier 8.00 20.00
SRG Ridly Greig 10.00 25.00
SSB Samuel Bolduc 6.00 15.00
SSE Simon Edvinsson SP 12.00 30.00
SSS Stanislav Svozil 5.00 12.00
SST Jaxson Stauber 6.00 15.00
STF Tyson Foerster SP 12.00 30.00
STR Tristen Robins 6.00 15.00
SVD Vincent Desharnais 8.00 20.00

2023-24 Synergy Star Of The Show

SOS1 Nathan MacKinnon 1.50 4.00
SOS2 David Pastrnak 1.00 2.50
SOS3 Cole Caufield .75 2.00
SOS4 Alex Ovechkin 1.50 4.00
SOS5 Jack Hughes 1.00 2.50
SOS6 Matthew Tkachuk .75 2.00
SOS7 Steven Stamkos .75 2.00
SOS8 Auston Matthews 1.50 4.00
SOS9 Dylan Larkin .50 1.25
SOS10 Connor McDavid 2.00 5.00
SOS11 Sidney Crosby 1.50 4.00
SOS12 Tage Thompson .50 1.25
SOS13 Tim Stutzle .50 1.25
SOS14 Jason Robertson .60 1.50
SOS15 Kirill Kaprizov 1.25 3.00
SOS16 Artemi Panarin .75 2.00
SOS17 Trevor Zegras .40 1.00
SOS18 Jack Eichel .60 1.50
SOS19 Elias Pettersson .60 1.50
SOS20 Anze Kopitar .60 1.50

2023-24 Synergy Star Quest '98

*GREEN/99: .6X TO 1.5X BASIC
*RED/49: 1.2X TO 3X BASIC
SQ1 Wayne Gretzky 20.00 50.00
SQ2 Patrick Roy 8.00 20.00
SQ3 Dominik Hasek 5.00 12.00
SQ4 Teemu Selanne 6.00 15.00
SQ5 Jaromir Jagr 10.00 25.00
SQ6 Luke Hughes 10.00 25.00
SQ7 Devon Levi 8.00 20.00
SQ8 Simon Edvinsson 6.00 15.00
SQ9 Matthew Knies 12.00 30.00
SQ10 Marco Kasper 8.00 20.00
SQ11 Alex Ovechkin 12.00 30.00
SQ12 Auston Matthews 12.00 30.00
SQ13 Connor McDavid 15.00 40.00
SQ14 Sidney Crosby 12.00 30.00
SQ15 David Pastrnak 8.00 20.00
SQ16 Cole Caufield 6.00 15.00
SQ17 Trevor Zegras 3.00 8.00
SQ18 Kirill Kaprizov 10.00 25.00
SQ19 Jack Hughes 8.00 20.00
SQ20 Tim Stutzle 4.00 10.00
SQ21 Nikita Kucherov 6.00 15.00
SQ22 Matty Beniers 4.00 10.00
SQ23 Nathan MacKinnon 12.00 30.00
SQ24 Artemi Panarin 6.00 15.00
SQ25 Elias Pettersson 5.00 12.00

2023-24 Synergy Sygnatures

SAL Anton Lundell 6.00 15.00
SAV Andrei Vasilevskiy SP 10.00 25.00
SBG Brendan Gallagher 6.00 15.00
SCC Chris Chelios SP 6.00 15.00
SCP Cole Perfetti 6.00 15.00
SCS Chandler Stephenson 5.00 12.00
SEB Evan Bouchard 8.00 20.00
SJB Johnny Bucyk SP 6.00 15.00
SJH Jonathan Huberdeau 8.00 20.00
SJM John Marino 6.00 15.00
SJP Jeff Petry 6.00 15.00
SJQ Jonathan Quick SP 8.00 20.00
SJS Juuse Saros 8.00 20.00
SJV Joe Veleno 5.00 12.00
SKM K'Andre Miller 5.00 12.00
SMF Mario Ferraro 4.00 10.00
SMH Miro Heiskanen 8.00 20.00
SNE Nikolaj Ehlers 6.00 15.00
SPA Joe Pavelski SP 8.00 20.00
SPF Peter Forsberg SP 12.00 30.00
SRC Ross Colton 5.00 12.00
SRF Ron Francis SP 30.00 80.00
SRO Ryan O'Reilly 6.00 15.00
SRS Ryan Strome 6.00 15.00
SSP Shane Pinto 5.00 12.00
STO Tyler Toffoli 6.00 15.00
STT Teuvo Teravainen 6.00 15.00
SZH Zach Hyman 10.00 25.00

2023-24 Synergy Synergistic Duos Star Legend

*RED/599: .5X TO 1.2X BASIC
*GREEN/399: .6X TO 1.5X BASIC
*GOLD/149: .8X TO 2X BASIC
SD1 M.Seider/S.Yzerman 2.50 6.00
SD2 J.Hughes/M.Brodeur 2.50 6.00
SD3 M.Barzal/D.Potvin 1.25 3.00
SD4 T.Thompson/D.Hasek 1.50 4.00
SD5 T.Raddysh/S.Mikita 1.00 2.50
SD6 A.Ovechkin/M.Gartner 4.00 10.00
SD7 A.Panarin/M.Messier 2.00 5.00
SD8 A.Matthews/D.Gilmour 4.00 10.00
SD9 D.Pastrnak/B.Orr 4.00 10.00
SD10 T.Stutzle/M.Hossa 1.25 3.00
SD11 T.Konecny/B.Clarke 1.50 4.00
SD12 J.Saros/P.Rinne 1.25 3.00
SD13 E.Pettersson/T.Linden 1.50 4.00
SD14 N.Suzuki/M.Richard 2.00 5.00
SD15 L.Couture/E.Nabokov 1.25 3.00
SD16 J.Robertson/M.Modano 1.50 4.00
SD17 J.Kyrou/B.Hull 2.00 5.00
SD18 J.Huberdeau/A.MacInnis 1.25 3.00

2023-24 Synergy Synergistic Duos Star Rookie

*RED/599: .5X TO 1.2X BASIC
*GREEN/399: .6X TO 1.5X BASIC
*GOLD/149: .8X TO 2X BASIC
SD1 M.Seider/S.Edvinsson 2.50 6.00
SD2 J.Hughes/L.Hughes 4.00 10.00
SD3 M.Barzal/W.Dufour 1.50 4.00
SD4 T.Thompson/D.Levi 3.00 8.00
SD5 T.Raddysh/C.Bedard 10.00 25.00
SD6 A.Ovechkin/V.Iorio 5.00 12.00
SD7 A.Panarin/W.Cuylle 2.50 6.00
SD8 A.Matthews/M.Knies 5.00 12.00
SD9 D.Pastrnak/J.Koppanen 3.00 8.00
SD10 T.Stutzle/R.Greig 2.00 5.00
SD11 T.Konecny/T.Foerster 2.50 6.00
SD12 J.Saros/Y.Askarov 3.00 8.00
SD13 E.Pettersson/A.Hirose 2.00 5.00
SD14 C.Caufield/S.Farrell 2.50 6.00
SD15 L.Couture/D.Gushchin 1.50 4.00
SD16 J.Robertson/M.Murray 2.00 5.00
SD17 J.Kyrou/H.McGing 1.25 3.00
SD18 J.Huberdeau/M.Coronato 2.00 5.00

2023-24 Synergy Synergistic Duos Star Rookie Gold

*GOLD/149: .8X TO 2X BASIC
SD5 Taylor Raddysh
Connor Bedard 30.00 80.00

2023-24 Synergy Synergistic Duos Star Rookie Green

*GREEN/399: .6X TO 1.5X BASIC
SD5 Taylor Raddysh
Connor Bedard 25.00 60.00

2023-24 Synergy Synergistic Duos Star Rookie Red

*RED/599: .5X TO 1.2X BASIC
SD5 Taylor Raddysh
Connor Bedard 20.00 50.00

2023-24 Synergy Synergistic Duos Star Star

*RED/599: .5X TO 1.2X BASIC
*GREEN/399: .6X TO 1.5X BASIC
*GOLD/149: .8X TO 2X BASIC
SD1 M.Seider/L.Raymond 1.50 4.00
SD2 J.Hughes/N.Hischier 2.50 6.00
SD3 M.Barzal/B.Nelson 1.25 3.00
SD4 T.Thompson/D.Cozens 1.25 3.00
SD5 T.Raddysh/S.Jones 1.00 2.50
SD6 A.Ovechkin/E.Kuznetsov 4.00 10.00
SD7 A.Panarin/A.Fox 2.00 5.00
SD8 A.Matthews/M.Marner 4.00 10.00
SD9 D.Pastrnak/B.Marchand 2.50 6.00
SD10 T.Stutzle/B.Tkachuk 1.50 4.00
SD11 T.Konecny/C.Hart 1.00 2.50
SD12 J.Saros/R.Josi 1.25 3.00
SD13 E.Pettersson/Q.Hughes 2.50 6.00
SD14 N.Suzuki/C.Caufield 2.00 5.00
SD15 L.Couture/T.Hertl 1.25 3.00
SD16 J.Robertson/J.Pavelski 1.50 4.00
SD17 J.Kyrou/P.Buchnevich 1.00 2.50
SD18 J.Huberdeau/N.Kadri 1.25 3.00

2023-24 Synergy Thrill Rides

TR1 Alex Ovechkin 2.50 6.00
TR2 Connor McDavid 3.00 8.00
TR3 Auston Matthews 2.50 6.00
TR4 David Pastrnak 1.50 4.00
TR5 Kirill Kaprizov 2.00 5.00
TR6 Tage Thompson .75 2.00
TR7 Jack Hughes 1.50 4.00
TR8 Artemi Panarin 1.25 3.00
TR9 Cole Caufield 1.25 3.00
TR10 Kyle Connor 1.00 2.50
TR11 Jordan Kyrou .60 1.50
TR12 Sidney Crosby 2.50 6.00

2023-24 Synergy Waffleboarded

WF1 Dominik Hasek 4.00 10.00
WF2 Patrick Roy 6.00 15.00
WF3 Jeremy Swayman 4.00 10.00
WF4 Andrei Vasilevskiy 4.00 10.00
WF5 Igor Shesterkin 5.00 12.00
WF6 Jake Oettinger 4.00 10.00
WF7 Marc-Andre Fleury 5.00 12.00
WF8 Ilya Sorokin 4.00 10.00
WF9 Adin Hill 2.50 6.00
WF10 Juuse Saros 3.00 8.00

2024-25 Synergy Red

1 Kirill Kaprizov 2.00 5.00
2 Kris Letang .75 2.00
3 Brady Tkachuk 1.00 2.50
4 Charlie McAvoy .75 2.00
5 Roman Josi .60 1.50
6 Alex Ovechkin 2.50 6.00
7 Rasmus Dahlin .75 2.00
8 Cale Makar 1.50 4.00
9 Clayton Keller .75 2.00
10 Martin Necas 1.00 2.50
11 Quinn Hughes 1.50 4.00
12 Vince Dunn .50 1.25
13 Mathew Barzal .75 2.00
14 Nick Suzuki 1.25 3.00
15 Roope Hintz .75 2.00
16 Mitch Marner 1.00 2.50
17 Jack Hughes 1.50 4.00
18 Moritz Seider .75 2.00
19 Matthew Tkachuk 1.25 3.00
20 Sebastian Aho 1.00 2.50
21 Jason Robertson 1.00 2.50
22 Victor Hedman .75 2.00
23 Mason McTavish .60 1.50
24 Travis Sanheim .40 1.00
25 Brock Boeser .75 2.00
26 Artemi Panarin 1.25 3.00
27 Luke Hughes 1.00 2.50
28 Jared McCann .50 1.25
29 Nathan MacKinnon 2.50 6.00
30 Connor McDavid 3.00 8.00
31 Kyle Connor 1.00 2.50
32 Leo Carlsson 1.00 2.50
33 Trevor Moore .40 1.00
34 Auston Matthews 2.50 6.00
35 Carter Verhaeghe .60 1.50
36 Logan Cooley 1.25 3.00
37 Tage Thompson .75 2.00
38 Matt Boldy 1.00 2.50
39 Connor Hellebuyck 1.25 3.00
40 Sidney Crosby 2.50 6.00
41 Filip Forsberg 1.00 2.50
42 Elias Pettersson 1.00 2.50
43 Johnny Gaudreau 1.00 2.50
44 Jack Eichel 1.00 2.50
45 Travis Konecny .60 1.50
46 Nikita Kucherov 1.25 3.00
47 Brock Faber .75 2.00
48 Nazem Kadri .75 2.00
49 Leon Draisaitl 2.00 5.00
50 William Eklund .75 2.00
51 Pierre-Luc Dubois .50 1.25
52 John Carlson .60 1.50
53 Dylan Larkin .75 2.00
54 William Nylander 1.25 3.00
55 Robert Thomas .60 1.50
56 Igor Shesterkin 1.25 3.00
57 Connor Bedard 2.00 5.00
58 Cole Caufield 1.25 3.00
59 Brock Nelson .60 1.50
60 David Pastrnak 1.50 4.00
61 Rick Nash .60 1.50
62 Ron Francis .75 2.00
63 Rogie Vachon .60 1.50
64 Patrick Roy 1.50 4.00
65 Felix Potvin 1.00 2.50
66 Al MacInnis .75 2.00
67 Joe Thornton 1.00 2.50
68 Jari Kurri .60 1.50
69 Mark Messier 1.25 3.00
70 Tom Barrasso .50 1.25
71 Maurice Richard 1.25 3.00
72 Wayne Gretzky 4.00 10.00
73 Bryan Trottier .60 1.50
74 Mario Lemieux 2.50 6.00
75 Jarome Iginla .75 2.00
76 Maksymilian Szuber 2.00 5.00
77 Emil Lilleberg 2.00 5.00
78 Logan Morrison 2.00 5.00
79 Joshua Roy 3.00 8.00
80 Yan Kuznetsov 2.00 5.00
81 Kyle MacLean 2.00 5.00
82 Olen Zellweger 4.00 10.00
83 Jesper Wallstedt 5.00 12.00
84 Ethan Del Mastro 2.00 5.00
85 Shakir Mukhamadullin 2.50 6.00
86 Lukas Cormier 2.00 5.00
87 Devin Cooley 2.00 5.00
88 Gage Goncalves 2.50 6.00
89 Sam Colangelo 2.00 5.00
90 Arshdeep Bains 2.50 6.00
91 Phil Kemp 2.00 5.00
92 Pierrick Dube 2.00 5.00
93 Cameron Crotty 2.00 5.00
94 Maxwell Crozier 2.00 5.00
95 Mason Morelli 2.00 5.00
96 Collin Graf 2.00 5.00
97 Brennan Othmann 3.00 8.00
98 Graeme Clarke 2.00 5.00
99 Jack St. Ivany 2.00 5.00
100 Matt Villalta 2.00 5.00
101 Josh Doan 3.00 8.00
102 Mavrik Bourque 4.00 10.00
103 Akil Thomas 2.00 5.00
104 Landon Slaggert 2.00 5.00
105 Zack Ostapchuk 2.00 5.00
106 Zach Dean 2.00 5.00
107 Brad Lambert 2.50 6.00
108 Lane Hutson 20.00 50.00
109 Scott Morrow 2.50 6.00
110 Marat Khusnutdinov 2.00 5.00
111 Matt Rempe 4.00 10.00
112 Ivan Fedotov 4.00 10.00
113 Vasily Ponomarev 2.00 5.00
114 Zachary Bolduc 4.00 10.00
115 Gavin Brindley 2.00 5.00
116 Luca Del Bel Belluz 2.00 5.00
117 Jackson Blake 4.00 10.00
118 Logan Mailloux 3.00 8.00
119 Bradly Nadeau 3.00 8.00
120 James Malatesta 2.00 5.00
121 Cutter Gauthier 5.00 12.00
122 Logan Stankoven 5.00 12.00
123 Frank Nazar 6.00 15.00
124 Liam Ohgren 4.00 10.00
125 Brendan Brisson 2.50 6.00
RCG Conor Geekie EXT 4.00 10.00
RMC Macklin Celebrini EXT 40.00 100.00
RMM Matvei Michkov EXT 50.00 125.00

2024-25 Synergy Gold Bounty

*GOLD/25: 4X TO 10X RED
*GOLD RC/25: 2X TO 5X RED
108 Lane Hutson 125.00 300.00
121 Cutter Gauthier 40.00 100.00
122 Logan Stankoven 60.00 150.00
123 Frank Nazar 30.00 80.00
126 Logan Stankoven
Portrait 25.00 60.00
127 Josh Doan
Portrait 15.00 40.00
128 Frank Nazar
Portrait 30.00 80.00
129 Brennan Othmann
Portrait 15.00 40.00
130 Olen Zellweger
Portrait 20.00 50.00
131 Lane Hutson
Portrait 125.00 300.00
RMC Macklin Celebrini EXT 150.00 400.00
RWS Will Smith EXT 60.00 150.00
RPMC Macklin Celebrini EXT
Portrait 150.00 400.00
RPWS Will Smith EXT
Portrait 80.00 200.00

2024-25 Synergy Purple

108 Lane Hutson AU/99 200.00 500.00
111 Matt Rempe AU/99 30.00 80.00
117 Jackson Blake AU/99 30.00 80.00
122 Logan Stankoven AU/49 25.00 60.00
RMC Macklin Celebrini EXT AU/99 300.00 800.00
RMM Matvei Michkov EXT AU/99 300.00 800.00
RWS Will Smith EXT AU/99 80.00 200.00

2024-25 Synergy Red Codes

*RED CODES: 1X TO 2.5X RED
*RED CODES RC: .5X TO 1.2X RED
108 Lane Hutson 30.00 80.00
121 Cutter Gauthier 30.00 80.00
122 Logan Stankoven 30.00 80.00
123 Frank Nazar 30.00 80.00
124 Liam Ohgren 50.00 125.00

2024-25 Synergy #1 Hits

1H1 Sidney Crosby 2.50 6.00
1H2 Alex Ovechkin 2.50 6.00
1H3 Connor McDavid 3.00 8.00
1H4 Auston Matthews 2.50 6.00
1H5 Kirill Kaprizov 2.00 5.00
1H6 David Pastrnak 1.50 4.00
1H7 Nathan MacKinnon 2.50 6.00
1H8 Leon Draisaitl 2.00 5.00
1H9 Jack Hughes 1.50 4.00
1H10 Nikita Kucherov 1.25 3.00

2024-25 Synergy All-Star Assembly

AA1 David Pastrnak 2.50 6.00
AA2 Connor Hellebuyck 2.00 5.00
AA3 Igor Shesterkin 2.00 5.00
AA4 Mitch Marner 1.50 4.00
AA5 Nikita Kucherov 2.00 5.00
AA6 Connor McDavid 5.00 12.00
AA7 Mathew Barzal 1.25 3.00
AA8 Nathan MacKinnon 4.00 10.00
AA9 Auston Matthews 4.00 10.00
AA10 Kirill Kaprizov 3.00 8.00
AA11 Elias Pettersson 1.50 4.00
AA12 Nick Suzuki 2.00 5.00
AA13 Clayton Keller 1.25 3.00
AA14 Sidney Crosby 4.00 10.00
AA15 Morgan Rielly 1.00 2.50
AA16 Sebastian Aho 1.50 4.00
AA17 Leon Draisaitl 3.00 8.00
AA18 Tom Wilson 1.00 2.50
AA19 Quinn Hughes 2.50 6.00
AA20 William Nylander 2.00 5.00
AA21 Thatcher Demko 1.25 3.00
AA22 Rasmus Dahlin 1.25 3.00
AA23 Brady Tkachuk 1.50 4.00
AA24 Filip Forsberg 1.50 4.00
AA25 Cale Makar 2.50 6.00

2024-25 Synergy All-Synergy Team

*GOLD/25: .6X TO 1.5X BASIC
AS1 Andrei Vasilevskiy 3.00 8.00
AS2 Connor Hellebuyck 4.00 10.00
AS3 Rasmus Dahlin 2.50 6.00
AS4 Quinn Hughes 5.00 12.00
AS5 Erik Karlsson 2.50 6.00
AS6 Cale Makar 5.00 12.00
AS7 Artemi Panarin 4.00 10.00
AS8 Kirill Kaprizov 6.00 15.00
AS9 Auston Matthews 8.00 20.00
AS10 Connor McDavid 10.00 25.00
AS11 Nikita Kucherov 4.00 10.00
AS12 Mikko Rantanen 5.00 12.00

2024-25 Synergy Cast For Greatness

*PURPLE: .5X TO 1.2X BASIC
CG1 Pekka Rinne 3.00 8.00
CG2 Morgan Rielly 3.00 8.00
CG3 Brady Tkachuk 5.00 12.00
CG4 Cutter Gauthier 8.00 20.00
CG5 Sidney Crosby 12.00 30.00
CG6 Jason Robertson 5.00 12.00
CG7 Joe Thornton 5.00 12.00
CG8 Mitch Marner 5.00 12.00
CG9 Mikko Rantanen 8.00 20.00
CG10 Nathan MacKinnon 12.00 30.00
CG11 Frank Nazar 10.00 25.00
CG12 Brayden Point 4.00 10.00
CG13 Anze Kopitar 5.00 12.00
CG14 Mike Gartner 4.00 10.00
CG15 Patrick Kane 6.00 15.00
CG16 Brennan Othmann 5.00 12.00
CG17 Brock Boeser 4.00 10.00
CG18 Chris Kreider 4.00 10.00
CG19 Nikolaj Ehlers 3.00 8.00
CG20 David Pastrnak 8.00 20.00
CG21 Logan Stankoven 8.00 20.00
CG22 Leon Draisaitl 10.00 25.00
CG23 Alex Ovechkin 12.00 30.00
CG24 Adam Fox 4.00 10.00
CG25 Phil Esposito 5.00 12.00
CG26 Logan Cooley 6.00 15.00
CG27 Mark Stone 4.00 10.00
CG28 Artemi Panarin 6.00 15.00
CG29 Brad Lambert 4.00 10.00
CG30 Jordan Kyrou 3.00 8.00
CG31 Evgeni Malkin 6.00 15.00
CG32 Mike Modano 5.00 12.00
CG33 J.T. Miller 4.00 10.00
CG34 Zach Hyman 5.00 12.00
CG35 Mavrik Bourque 6.00 15.00
CG36 Jared McCann 2.50 6.00

2024-25 Synergy Colorways

*YELLOW: .5X TO 1.2X BASIC
*BLUE/99: 1.2X TO 3X BASIC
*PINK/49: 1.5X TO 4X BASIC
*GREEN/25: 2X TO 5X BASIC
L1 Ryan Nugent-Hopkins 1.25 3.00
L2 Joel Eriksson Ek .75 2.00
L3 Josh Doan 1.50 4.00
L4 Terry Sawchuk 1.00 2.50
L5 Liam Ohgren 2.00 5.00
L6 Anze Kopitar 1.50 4.00
L7 Brady Tkachuk 1.50 4.00
L8 Alex Ovechkin 4.00 10.00
L9 Jack Eichel 1.50 4.00
L10 Artemi Panarin 2.00 5.00
L11 Adam Fantilli 1.50 4.00
L12 Mavrik Bourque 2.00 5.00
L13 Mathew Barzal 1.25 3.00
L14 Jamie Benn 1.00 2.50
L15 Borje Salming 1.00 2.50
L16 Mitch Marner 1.50 4.00
L17 Fabian Zetterlund .60 1.50
L18 Tim Stutzle 1.25 3.00
L19 Matthew Tkachuk 2.00 5.00
L20 Sebastian Aho 1.50 4.00
L21 Jason Robertson 1.50 4.00
L22 Kevin Fiala .75 2.00
L23 Adam Fox 1.25 3.00
L24 Brendan Brisson 1.25 3.00
L25 Scott Niedermayer 1.00 2.50
L26 Rasmus Dahlin 1.25 3.00
L27 Robert Thomas 1.00 2.50
L28 Zachary Bolduc 1.50 4.00
L29 Nathan MacKinnon 4.00 10.00
L30 Gordie Howe 3.00 8.00
L31 Igor Shesterkin 2.00 5.00
L32 Paul Coffey 1.00 2.50
L33 MacKenzie Weegar .75 2.00
L34 Auston Matthews 4.00 10.00
L35 Clayton Keller 1.25 3.00
L36 Ray Bourque 1.50 4.00
L37 Quinton Byfield 1.25 3.00
L38 Owen Tippett .60 1.50
L39 Tim Horton 1.50 4.00
L40 Trevor Zegras 1.00 2.50
L41 Leon Draisaitl 3.00 8.00
L42 Dylan Strome 1.25 3.00
L43 Luke Hughes 1.50 4.00
L44 Josh Morrissey 1.25 3.00
L45 Kirill Kaprizov 3.00 8.00
L46 Teemu Selanne 2.00 5.00
L47 Brock Nelson 1.00 2.50
L48 Larry Robinson 1.00 2.50
L49 Travis Sanheim .60 1.50
L50 Matty Beniers 1.25 3.00
L51 Owen Power 1.00 2.50
L52 Nikita Kucherov 2.00 5.00
L53 Wyatt Johnston 2.00 5.00
L54 Pavel Buchnevich .75 2.00
L55 Mikko Rantanen 2.50 6.00
L56 Quinn Hughes 2.50 6.00
L57 Howie Morenz 1.00 2.50
L58 Logan Mailloux 2.00 5.00
L59 Roman Josi 1.00 2.50
L60 Mario Lemieux 4.00 10.00
L61 Oliver Bjorkstrand .75 2.00
L62 Olen Zellweger 2.00 5.00
L63 Brent Burns 1.00 2.50
L64 Moritz Seider 1.25 3.00
L65 Zach Dean 1.00 2.50
L66 Luc Robitaille 1.00 2.50
L67 Nick Suzuki 2.00 5.00
L68 Mark Scheifele 1.50 4.00
L69 Philipp Kurashev .75 2.00
L70 William Karlsson 1.25 3.00
L71 Dylan Larkin 1.25 3.00
L72 Sergei Bobrovsky 1.50 4.00
L73 Matias Maccelli .75 2.00
L74 Jesper Wallstedt 2.50 6.00
L75 Jonathan Huberdeau 1.25 3.00
L76 Logan Stankoven 2.50 6.00
L77 Victor Hedman 1.25 3.00
L78 Jean Ratelle .75 2.00
L79 Cole Caufield 2.00 5.00
L80 Gavin Brindley 1.00 2.50
L81 Cale Makar 2.50 6.00
L82 Elias Pettersson 1.50 4.00
L83 Evgeni Malkin 2.00 5.00
L84 Charlie McAvoy 1.25 3.00
L85 Shakir Mukhamadullin 1.25 3.00
L86 Jack Hughes 2.50 6.00
L87 Sidney Crosby 4.00 10.00
L88 Patrick Kane 2.00 5.00
L89 Johnny Gaudreau 1.50 4.00
L90 Ryan O'Reilly 1.00 2.50
L91 Leo Carlsson 1.50 4.00
L92 Cutter Gauthier 2.50 6.00
L93 William Eklund 1.25 3.00
L94 David Pastrnak 2.50 6.00
L95 Serge Savard 1.00 2.50
L96 Brennan Othmann 1.50 4.00
L97 Connor McDavid 5.00 12.00
L98 Connor Bedard 3.00 8.00
L99 Wayne Gretzky 6.00 15.00
L100 Frank Nazar 3.00 8.00

2024-25 Synergy D2D

*GOLD/25: 1.5X TO 4X BASIC
D2DLA D.Doughty/M.Anderson 2.50 6.00
D2DNJ L.Hughes/S.Nemec 4.00 10.00
D2DTB V.Hedman/R.McDonagh 3.00 8.00
D2DBOS H.Lindholm/C.McAvoy 3.00 8.00
D2DBUF O.Power/R.Dahlin 3.00 8.00
D2DCAR B.Burns/J.Slavin 2.50 6.00
D2DCGY M.Weegar/R.Andersson 2.00 5.00
D2DCOL D.Toews/C.Makar 6.00 15.00
D2DDAL M.Heiskanen/T.Harley 3.00 8.00
D2DDET S.Edvinsson/M.Seider 3.00 8.00
D2DMIN J.Middleton/B.Faber 3.00 8.00
D2DMTL M.Matheson/A.Xhekaj 2.50 6.00
D2DNSH R.Josi/A.Carrier 2.50 6.00
D2DNYI N.Dobson/A.Romanov 3.00 8.00
D2DNYR A.Fox/J.Trouba 3.00 8.00
D2DOTT J.Sanderson/T.Chabot 3.00 8.00
D2DPHI T.Sanheim/J.Drysdale 2.00 5.00
D2DPIT E.Karlsson/K.Letang 3.00 8.00
D2DSEA V.Dunn/R.Evans 2.00 5.00
D2DSTL C.Parayko/T.Krug 2.00 5.00
D2DUTA J.Valimaki/S.Durzi 1.50 4.00
D2DVAN Q.Hughes/F.Hronek 6.00 15.00
D2DVGK B.McNabb/S.Theodore 3.00 8.00
D2DWPG J.Morrissey/D.DeMelo 3.00 8.00
D2DWSH J.Carlson/R.Sandin 2.50 6.00

2024-25 Synergy Drop the Hammer

*GOLD/25: 1X TO 2.5X BASIC
DH1 Tom Wilson 3.00 8.00
DH2 Kris Letang 4.00 10.00
DH3 Moritz Seider 4.00 10.00
DH4 Ryan Reaves 2.50 6.00
DH5 Radko Gudas 2.00 5.00
DH6 Brady Tkachuk 5.00 12.00
DH7 Zdeno Chara 3.00 8.00
DH8 Matt Rempe 6.00 15.00
DH9 Jamie Benn 3.00 8.00
DH10 Evander Kane 3.00 8.00
DH11 Chris Chelios 3.00 8.00
DH12 Arber Xhekaj 3.00 8.00
DH13 Nick Foligno 2.00 5.00
DH14 Brad Marchand 6.00 15.00
DH15 Alex Ovechkin 12.00 30.00
DH16 Matthew Tkachuk 6.00 15.00
DH17 Drew Doughty 3.00 8.00
DH18 Mark Messier 6.00 15.00
DH19 Brendan Gallagher 3.00 8.00
DH20 Brent Burns 3.00 8.00

2024-25 Synergy Generators

G1 Clayton Keller 1.00 2.50
G2 Connor McDavid 4.00 10.00
G3 Sebastian Aho 1.25 3.00
G4 Connor Bedard 2.50 6.00
G5 Evgeni Malkin 1.50 4.00
G6 Tage Thompson 1.00 2.50
G7 Lucas Raymond 1.25 3.00
G8 Artemi Panarin 1.50 4.00
G9 Trevor Zegras .75 2.00
G10 Jason Robertson 1.25 3.00
G11 Mitch Marner 1.25 3.00
G12 Cole Caufield 1.50 4.00
G13 Roman Josi .75 2.00
G14 Zach Hyman 1.25 3.00
G15 Robert Thomas .75 2.00
G16 Cale Makar 2.00 5.00
G17 Matt Boldy 1.25 3.00
G18 Brady Tkachuk 1.25 3.00
G19 Quinn Hughes 2.00 5.00
G20 Kyle Connor 1.25 3.00

2024-25 Synergy Interdimensional

IBO Brennan Othmann 12.00 30.00
ICG Cutter Gauthier 10.00 25.00
IJD Josh Doan 6.00 15.00
ILH Lane Hutson 40.00 100.00
ILO Liam Ohgren 8.00 20.00
ILS Logan Stankoven 10.00 25.00
IMB Mavrik Bourque 8.00 20.00
IMC Macklin Celebrini 125.00 300.00
IOZ Olen Zellweger 8.00 20.00
IZB Zachary Bolduc 6.00 15.00

2024-25 Synergy Monuments

M1 Luc Robitaille 1.00 2.50
M2 Patrick Roy 2.50 6.00
M3 Willie O'Ree 1.25 3.00
M4 Sidney Crosby 4.00 10.00
M5 Dominik Hasek 1.50 4.00
M6 Gordie Howe 3.00 8.00
M7 Alex Ovechkin 4.00 10.00
M8 Pavel Datsyuk 1.50 4.00
M9 Mark Messier 2.00 5.00
M10 Teemu Selanne 2.00 5.00
M11 Wayne Gretzky 6.00 15.00
M12 Mario Lemieux 4.00 10.00
M13 Joe Sakic 2.00 5.00
M14 Stan Mikita 1.00 2.50
M15 Steve Yzerman 2.50 6.00
M16 Jacques Plante 1.00 2.50
M17 Mats Sundin 1.00 2.50
M18 Bobby Orr 4.00 10.00

2024-25 Synergy New Game

NG1 Matthew Knies 1.50 4.00
NG2 Simon Nemec 1.00 2.50
NG3 Leo Carlsson 1.25 3.00
NG4 Thomas Harley .75 2.00
NG5 Alexander Holtz .75 2.00
NG6 Samuel Ersson .75 2.00
NG7 Brock Faber 1.00 2.50
NG8 Jake Neighbours .75 2.00
NG9 JJ Peterka .75 2.00
NG10 Evan Bouchard 1.00 2.50
NG11 Adam Fantilli 1.25 3.00
NG12 Matt Boldy 1.25 3.00
NG13 Logan Cooley 1.50 4.00
NG14 Kevin Korchinski .60 1.50
NG15 Lucas Raymond 1.25 3.00
NG16 Juraj Slafkovsky 1.50 4.00
NG17 Thomas Bordeleau .50 1.25
NG18 Quinton Byfield 1.00 2.50
NG19 Wyatt Johnston 1.50 4.00
NG20 Jack Hughes 2.00 5.00
NG21 Kirill Marchenko 1.00 2.50
NG22 Cole Perfetti .75 2.00
NG23 Marco Rossi 1.00 2.50
NG24 Luke Hughes 1.25 3.00
NG25 Matty Beniers 1.00 2.50
NG26 Cole Caufield 1.50 4.00
NG27 Noah Dobson 1.00 2.50
NG28 Connor Bedard 2.50 6.00
NG29 Fabian Zetterlund .50 1.25
NG30 Mason McTavish .75 2.00

2024-25 Synergy New Game Signatures

*RED: .6X TO 1.5X BASIC
NGS1 Matthew Knies 15.00 40.00
NGS4 Thomas Harley SP 8.00 20.00
NGS5 Alexander Holtz 8.00 20.00
NGS6 Samuel Ersson 8.00 20.00
NGS8 Jake Neighbours 8.00 20.00
NGS12 Matt Boldy SP 12.00 30.00
NGS13 Logan Cooley 15.00 40.00
NGS14 Kevin Korchinski 6.00 15.00
NGS16 Juraj Slafkovsky 15.00 40.00
NGS17 Thomas Bordeleau 5.00 12.00
NGS18 Quinton Byfield SP 10.00 25.00
NGS19 Wyatt Johnston 15.00 40.00
NGS21 Kirill Marchenko 10.00 25.00
NGS22 Cole Perfetti 8.00 20.00
NGS23 Marco Rossi 10.00 25.00
NGS24 Luke Hughes SP 12.00 30.00
NGS25 Matty Beniers SP 10.00 25.00
NGS27 Noah Dobson 10.00 25.00
NGS28 Connor Bedard SP 150.00 400.00
NGS29 Fabian Zetterlund 5.00 12.00

2024-25 Synergy NHL Impressions

*MAGENTA: .5X TO 1.2X BASIC
IM1 Logan Cooley 2.50 6.00
IM2 Wyatt Johnston 2.50 6.00
IM3 Nathan MacKinnon 5.00 12.00
IM4 Dylan Larkin 1.50 4.00
IM5 Mark Stone 1.50 4.00
IM6 Connor McDavid 6.00 15.00
IM7 Auston Matthews 5.00 12.00
IM8 Filip Forsberg 2.00 5.00
IM9 Anze Kopitar 2.00 5.00
IM10 Jamie Drysdale 1.00 2.50

IM11 Brock Faber 1.50 4.00
IM12 Bo Horvat 1.50 4.00
IM13 Cole Caufield 2.50 6.00
IM14 Aleksander Barkov 2.00 5.00
IM15 Jack Hughes 3.00 8.00
IM16 Brad Marchand 2.50 6.00
IM17 Artemi Panarin 2.50 6.00
IM18 Elias Pettersson 2.00 5.00
IM19 Connor Bedard 4.00 10.00
IM20 Kirill Kaprizov 4.00 10.00
IM21 Travis Konecny 1.25 3.00
IM22 Sidney Crosby 5.00 12.00
IM23 David Pastrnak 3.00 8.00
IM24 Jared McCann 1.00 2.50
IM25 Alex Ovechkin 5.00 12.00
IM26 Andrei Svechnikov 1.50 4.00
IM27 William Nylander 2.50 6.00
IM28 Leon Draisaitl 4.00 10.00
IM29 J.T. Miller 1.50 4.00
IM30 Mika Zibanejad 1.50 4.00
IM31 Zach Hyman 2.00 5.00
IM32 Tomas Hertl 1.25 3.00
IM33 Jake Neighbours 1.25 3.00
IM34 Tage Thompson 1.50 4.00
IM35 Kyle Connor 2.00 5.00
IM36 Yegor Sharangovich 1.25 3.00
IM37 Brayden Point 1.50 4.00
IM38 Alexis Lafreniere 2.00 5.00
IM39 Lucas Raymond 2.00 5.00
IM40 Cale Makar 3.00 8.00
IM41 Andrei Vasilevskiy 2.00 5.00
IM42 Jordan Binnington 2.00 5.00
IM43 John Gibson 1.25 3.00
IM44 Igor Shesterkin 2.50 6.00
IM45 Juuse Saros 1.50 4.00
IM46 Jeremy Swayman 2.00 5.00
IM47 Ukko-Pekka Luukkonen 1.00 2.50
IM48 Jake Oettinger 2.00 5.00
IM49 Stuart Skinner 1.50 4.00
IM50 Sergei Bobrovsky 2.00 5.00
IM51 Darcy Kuemper 1.25 3.00
IM52 Frederik Andersen 1.50 4.00
IM53 Connor Hellebuyck 2.50 6.00
IM54 Logan Thompson 1.50 4.00
IM55 Alexandar Georgiev 1.25 3.00
IM56 Ilya Sorokin 2.00 5.00
IM57 Tristan Jarry 1.25 3.00
IM58 Thatcher Demko 1.50 4.00
IM59 Joey Daccord 1.25 3.00
IM60 Jonathan Quick 1.50 4.00
IM61 Akil Thomas 1.25 3.00
IM62 Frank Nazar 4.00 10.00
IM63 Zach Dean 1.25 3.00
IM64 Logan Stankoven 3.00 8.00
IM65 Collin Graf 1.25 3.00
IM66 Olen Zellweger 2.50 6.00
IM67 Logan Morrison 1.25 3.00
IM68 Zack Ostapchuk 1.25 3.00
IM69 Liam Ohgren 2.50 6.00
IM70 Brendan Brisson 1.50 4.00
IM71 Ivan Fedotov 2.00 5.00
IM72 Brennan Othmann 2.00 5.00
IM73 Lane Hutson 10.00 25.00
IM74 Josh Doan 2.00 5.00
IM75 Graeme Clarke 1.25 3.00
IM76 Scott Morrow 1.50 4.00
IM77 Matt Rempe 2.50 6.00
IM78 Landon Slaggert 1.25 3.00
IM79 Cutter Gauthier 3.00 8.00
IM80 Marat Khusnutdinov 1.25 3.00
IM81 Arshdeep Bains 1.50 4.00
IM82 Mavrik Bourque 2.50 6.00
IM83 Joshua Roy 2.00 5.00
IM84 Shakir Mukhamadullin 1.50 4.00
IM85 Sam Colangelo 1.25 3.00
IM86 Kyle MacLean 1.25 3.00
IM87 Jesper Wallstedt 3.00 8.00
IM88 Zachary Bolduc 2.00 5.00
IM89 Gage Goncalves 1.50 4.00
IM90 Ethan Del Mastro 1.25 3.00
IM91 Al MacInnis 1.50 4.00
IM92 Mike Modano 2.00 5.00
IM93 Steve Yzerman 3.00 8.00
IM94 Charlie Simmer .75 2.00
IM95 Guy Carbonneau 1.25 3.00
IM96 Brian Propp 1.00 2.50
IM97 Tiger Williams .75 2.00
IM98 Shane Doan 1.00 2.50
IM99 Alex Delvecchio 1.25 3.00
IM100 Johnny Bucyk 1.25 3.00

2024-25 Synergy NHL Impressions Green

*GREEN/149: .6X TO 1.5X BASIC
*GREEN AU/49-99: 2.5X TO 6X BASIC
*GREEN AU/25: 4X TO 10X BASIC
IM77 Matt Rempe AU/99 40.00 100.00

2024-25 Synergy Rookie Journey Away

*GOLD/25: 2.5X TO 6X BASIC
RJ1 Mavrik Bourque 2.50 6.00
RJ2 Brennan Othmann 2.00 5.00
RJ3 Liam Ohgren 2.50 6.00
RJ4 Brendan Brisson 1.50 4.00
RJ5 Cutter Gauthier 3.00 8.00
RJ6 Zachary Bolduc 2.00 5.00
RJ7 Josh Doan 2.00 5.00
RJ8 Shakir Mukhamadullin 1.50 4.00
RJ9 Logan Stankoven 3.00 8.00
RJ10 Frank Nazar 4.00 10.00
RJ11 Olen Zellweger 2.50 6.00
RJ12 Jesper Wallstedt 3.00 8.00
RJ13 Lane Hutson 12.00 30.00
RJ14 Bradly Nadeau 2.00 5.00
RJ15 Brad Lambert 1.50 4.00

2024-25 Synergy Rookie Journey Away Green

*GREEN/199: .6X TO 1.5X BASIC
RJ13 Lane Hutson 30.00 80.00

2024-25 Synergy Rookie Journey Away Red

*RED/499: .5X TO 1.2X BASIC
RJ13 Lane Hutson 25.00 60.00

2024-25 Synergy Rookie Journey Draft

*RED/499: .5X TO 1.2X BASIC
*GREEN/199: .6X TO 1.5X BASIC
*GOLD/25: 2.5X TO 6X BASIC
RJ1 Mavrik Bourque 2.50 6.00
RJ2 Brennan Othmann 2.00 5.00
RJ3 Liam Ohgren 2.50 6.00
RJ4 Brendan Brisson 1.50 4.00
RJ5 Cutter Gauthier 3.00 8.00
RJ6 Zachary Bolduc 2.00 5.00
RJ7 Josh Doan 2.00 5.00
RJ8 Shakir Mukhamadullin 1.50 4.00
RJ9 Logan Stankoven 3.00 8.00
RJ10 Frank Nazar 4.00 10.00
RJ11 Olen Zellweger 2.50 6.00
RJ12 Jesper Wallstedt 3.00 8.00
RJ13 Lane Hutson 12.00 30.00
RJ14 Bradly Nadeau 2.00 5.00
RJ15 Brad Lambert 1.50 4.00

2024-25 Synergy Rookie Journey Home

*RED/499: .5X TO 1.2X BASIC
*GOLD/25: 2.5X TO 6X BASIC
RJ1 Mavrik Bourque 2.50 6.00
RJ2 Brennan Othmann 2.00 5.00
RJ3 Liam Ohgren 2.50 6.00
RJ4 Brendan Brisson 1.50 4.00
RJ5 Cutter Gauthier 3.00 8.00
RJ6 Zachary Bolduc 2.00 5.00
RJ7 Josh Doan 2.00 5.00
RJ8 Shakir Mukhamadullin 1.50 4.00
RJ9 Logan Stankoven 3.00 8.00
RJ10 Frank Nazar 4.00 10.00
RJ11 Olen Zellweger 2.50 6.00
RJ12 Jesper Wallstedt 3.00 8.00
RJ13 Lane Hutson 12.00 30.00
RJ14 Bradly Nadeau 2.00 5.00
RJ15 Brad Lambert 1.50 4.00

2024-25 Synergy Rookie Journey Home Green

*GREEN/199: .6X TO 1.5X BASIC
RJ13 Lane Hutson 30.00 80.00

2024-25 Synergy Rookie Journey Photo Variant

*RED/49: 2X TO 5X BASIC
RJ9 Logan Stankoven 1.50 4.00

2024-25 Synergy Rookie Sygnatures

*RED: .6X TO 1.5X BASIC
SRAB Arshdeep Bains 8.00 20.00
SRAT Akil Thomas 6.00 15.00
SRBB Brendan Brisson 8.00 20.00
SRBN Bradly Nadeau 10.00 25.00
SRCG Collin Graf 6.00 15.00
SRDC Devin Cooley 6.00 15.00
SRFN Frank Nazar 20.00 50.00
SRGA Cutter Gauthier 15.00 40.00
SRGC Graeme Clarke 6.00 15.00
SRJD Josh Doan 10.00 25.00
SRJR Joshua Roy 10.00 25.00
SRJW Jesper Wallstedt 15.00 40.00
SRLH Lane Hutson 150.00 400.00
SRLM Logan Mailloux 12.00 30.00
SRLO Liam Ohgren 12.00 30.00
SRLS Logan Stankoven 15.00 40.00
SRMB Mavrik Bourque 12.00 30.00
SRMC Macklin Celebrini 150.00 400.00
SRMK Marat Khusnutdinov 6.00 15.00
SRML Logan Morrison 6.00 15.00
SRMM Mason Morelli 6.00 15.00
SRMO Scott Morrow 8.00 20.00
SROZ Olen Zellweger 12.00 30.00
SRSM Shakir Mukhamadullin 8.00 20.00
SRZB Zachary Bolduc 10.00 25.00
SRZD Zach Dean 6.00 15.00
SRZO Zack Ostapchuk 6.00 15.00

2024-25 Synergy StarQuest

*GREEN: .5X TO 1.2X BASIC
*PURPLE: .8X TO 2X BASIC
SQ1 Liam Ohgren 4.00 10.00
SQ2 Cale Makar 5.00 12.00
SQ3 Leon Draisaitl 6.00 15.00
SQ4 Filip Forsberg 3.00 8.00
SQ5 Frank Nazar 6.00 15.00
SQ6 Nikita Kucherov 4.00 10.00
SQ7 Connor Bedard 6.00 15.00
SQ8 Quinn Hughes 5.00 12.00
SQ9 Cutter Gauthier 5.00 12.00
SQ10 Kirill Kaprizov 6.00 15.00
SQ11 Artemi Panarin 4.00 10.00
SQ12 Jason Robertson 3.00 8.00
SQ13 Victor Hedman 2.50 6.00
SQ14 Logan Stankoven 5.00 12.00
SQ15 Matthew Tkachuk 4.00 10.00
SQ16 Jack Eichel 3.00 8.00
SQ17 Nathan MacKinnon 8.00 20.00
SQ18 Sidney Crosby 8.00 20.00
SQ19 David Pastrnak 5.00 12.00
SQ20 Jack Hughes 5.00 12.00
SQ21 Nick Suzuki 4.00 10.00
SQ22 Connor McDavid 10.00 25.00
SQ23 Alex Ovechkin 8.00 20.00
SQ24 Brad Lambert 2.50 6.00
SQ25 Tage Thompson 2.50 6.00

2024-25 Synergy Start your Engines

SYE1 Logan Mailloux 1.50 4.00
SYE2 Bradly Nadeau 1.25 3.00
SYE3 Zachary Bolduc 1.25 3.00
SYE4 Josh Doan 1.25 3.00
SYE5 Shakir Mukhamadullin 1.00 2.50
SYE6 Akil Thomas .75 2.00
SYE7 Gavin Brindley .75 2.00
SYE8 Frank Nazar 2.50 6.00
SYE9 Joshua Roy 1.25 3.00
SYE10 Logan Stankoven 2.00 5.00
SYE11 Graeme Clarke .75 2.00
SYE12 Olen Zellweger 1.50 4.00
SYE13 Jesper Wallstedt 2.00 5.00
SYE14 Matt Rempe 1.50 4.00
SYE15 Brendan Brisson 1.00 2.50
SYE16 Marat Khusnutdinov .75 2.00
SYE17 Zach Dean .75 2.00
SYE18 Cutter Gauthier 2.00 5.00
SYE19 Mavrik Bourque 1.50 4.00
SYE20 Lane Hutson 12.00 30.00
SYE21 Liam Ohgren 1.50 4.00
SYE22 Brennan Othmann 1.25 3.00

2024-25 Synergy Sygnatures

SAG Adam Graves SP 8.00 20.00
SAI Alex Iafallo 6.00 15.00
SAL Alexis Lafreniere SP 15.00 40.00
SAM Auston Matthews SP 40.00 100.00
SAT Alex Tuch 10.00 25.00
SBC Brady Tkachuk SP 15.00 40.00
SBS Brayden Schenn 10.00 25.00
SCO Chris Osgood 10.00 25.00
SCR Corey Crawford SP 12.00 30.00
SEP Elias Pettersson SP 15.00 40.00
SGV Gabe Vilardi 10.00 25.00
SJS Juraj Slafkovsky 20.00 50.00
SJV Joe Veleno 8.00 20.00
SJW Joseph Woll 15.00 40.00
SLD Leon Draisaitl SP 30.00 80.00
SMF Marc-Andre Fleury SP 20.00 50.00
SMR Marco Rossi 12.00 30.00
SND Noah Dobson 12.00 30.00
SPM Pavel Mintyukov 8.00 20.00
SRC Ross Colton 8.00 20.00
SRO Ryan O'Reilly 10.00 25.00
SSG Samuel Girard 6.00 15.00
SSW Shane Wright SP 12.00 30.00
STF Tyson Foerster 10.00 25.00
STL Trevor Linden SP 10.00 25.00
STM Timo Meier 10.00 25.00
STT Tony Twist 6.00 15.00
STW Tom Wilson 10.00 25.00

2024-25 Synergy Sygnatures Red Backcheck

SCR Corey Crawford/49 20.00 50.00

2024-25 Synergy Synergistic Duos Stars

*RED/499: .5X TO 1.2X BASIC
*GREEN/199: .6X TO 1.5X BASIC
*GOLD/25: 2X TO 5X BASIC
SD1 N.Suzuki/C.Caufield 2.50 6.00
SD2 S.Aho/A.Svechnikov 2.00 5.00
SD3 E.Malkin/S.Crosby 5.00 12.00
SD4 T.Konecny/O.Tippett 1.25 3.00
SD5 A.Kopitar/Q.Byfield 2.00 5.00
SD6 Q.Hughes/E.Pettersson 3.00 8.00
SD7 R.Thomas/J.Kyrou 1.25 3.00
SD8 W.Eklund/F.Zetterlund 1.50 4.00
SD9 M.McTavish/L.Carlsson 2.00 5.00
SD10 M.Stone/T.Hertl 1.50 4.00
SD11 A.Panarin/V.Trocheck 2.50 6.00
SD12 N.Kucherov/B.Point 2.50 6.00
SD13 J.Hughes/L.Hughes 3.00 8.00
SD14 L.Draisaitl/C.McDavid 6.00 15.00
SD15 B.Jenner/A.Fantilli 2.00 5.00
SD16 B.Horvat/B.Nelson 1.50 4.00
SD17 C.Bedard/P.Kurashev 4.00 10.00
SD18 R.Hintz/J.Robertson 2.00 5.00

2024-25 Synergy Synergistic Duos Stars and Legends

*RED/499: .5X TO 1.2X BASIC
*GREEN/199: .6X TO 1.5X BASIC
*GOLD/25: 2X TO 5X BASIC
SD1 N.Suzuki/M.Richard 2.50 6.00
SD2 S.Aho/R.Brind'Amour 2.00 5.00
SD3 E.Malkin/M.Lemieux 5.00 12.00
SD4 T.Konecny/E.Lindros 2.00 5.00
SD5 A.Kopitar/L.Robitaille 2.00 5.00
SD6 Q.Hughes/T.Linden 3.00 8.00
SD7 R.Thomas/A.MacInnis 1.50 4.00
SD8 W.Eklund/J.Thornton 2.00 5.00
SD9 M.McTavish/T.Selanne 2.50 6.00
SD10 M.Stone/M.Fleury 2.50 6.00
SD11 A.Panarin/A.Graves 2.50 6.00
SD12 N.Kucherov/M.St. Louis 2.50 6.00
SD13 J.Hughes/M.Brodeur 3.00 8.00
SD14 L.Draisaitl/W.Gretzky 8.00 20.00
SD15 B.Jenner/R.Nash 1.25 3.00
SD16 B.Horvat/B.Trottier 1.50 4.00
SD17 C.Bedard/T.Amonte 4.00 10.00
SD18 R.Hintz/M.Modano 2.00 5.00

2024-25 Synergy Synergistic Duos Stars and Rookies

*RED/499: .5X TO 1.2X BASIC
*GOLD/25: 2X TO 5X BASIC
SD1 N.Suzuki/L.Hutson 8.00 20.00
SD2 S.Aho/B.Nadeau 2.00 5.00
SD3 E.Malkin/J.St. Ivany 2.50 6.00
SD4 T.Konecny/I.Fedotov 2.00 5.00
SD5 A.Kopitar/A.Thomas 2.00 5.00
SD6 Q.Hughes/A.Bains 3.00 8.00
SD7 R.Thomas/Z.Bolduc 2.50 6.00
SD8 W.Eklund/S.Mukhamadullin 1.50 4.00
SD9 M.McTavish/C.Gauthier 3.00 8.00
SD10 M.Stone/B.Brisson 1.50 4.00
SD11 A.Panarin/B.Othmann 2.50 6.00
SD12 N.Kucherov/G.Goncalves 2.50 6.00
SD13 J.Hughes/B.Halonen 3.00 8.00
SD14 L.Draisaitl/P.Kemp 4.00 10.00
SD15 B.Jenner/G.Brindley 1.25 3.00
SD16 B.Horvat/R.Iskhakov 1.50 4.00
SD17 C.Bedard/F.Nazar 6.00 15.00
SD18 R.Hintz/L.Stankoven 3.00 8.00

2024-25 Synergy Synergistic Duos Stars and Rookies Green

*GREEN/199: .6X TO 1.5X BASIC
SD17 Connor Bedard
Frank Nazar 15.00 40.00

2024-25 Synergy Waffleboarded

*GOLD/25: .8X TO 2X BASIC
WB1 Thatcher Demko 4.00 10.00
WB2 Juuse Saros 4.00 10.00
WB3 Jake Oettinger 5.00 12.00
WB4 Andrei Vasilevskiy 5.00 12.00
WB5 Jonathan Quick 4.00 10.00
WB6 Jeremy Swayman 5.00 12.00
WB7 Marc-Andre Fleury 6.00 15.00
WB8 Sergei Bobrovsky 5.00 12.00
WB9 Martin Brodeur 25.00 60.00
WB10 Igor Shesterkin 6.00 15.00
WB11 Stuart Skinner 4.00 10.00
WB12 Connor Hellebuyck 6.00 15.00
WB13 Alexandar Georgiev 3.00 8.00
WB14 Dominik Hasek 5.00 12.00
WB15 John Gibson 3.00 8.00
WB16 Jordan Binnington 5.00 12.00
WB17 Henrik Lundqvist 8.00 20.00
WB18 Ilya Sorokin 5.00 12.00

1981-82 TCMA

COMPLETE SET (13) 24.00 60.00
1 Norm Ullman 1.25 3.00
2 Gump Worsley 2.00 5.00
3 J.C. Tremblay .60 1.50
4 Lou Fontinato .60 1.50
5 Johnny Bucyk 1.25 3.00
6 Harry Howell .75 2.00
7 Henri Richard 2.00 5.00
8 Andy Bathgate 1.25 3.00
9 Bobby Orr 10.00 25.00
10 Frank Mahovlich 2.00 5.00
11 Jean Beliveau 4.00 10.00
12 Jacques Plante 4.00 10.00
13 Stan Mikita 3.00 8.00

1935 TCTA

NNO Maple Leaf Arena 25.00 50.00

1974 Team Canada L'Equipe WHA

COMPLETE SET (24) 25.00 50.00
1 Ralph Backstrom 1.00 2.00
2 Serge Bernier .75 1.50
3 Gerry Cheevers 5.00 10.00
4 Al Hamilton 1.00 2.00
5 Billy Harris CO .50 1.00
6 Jim Harrison .75 1.50
7 Ben Hatskin OWN .75 1.50
8 Paul Henderson 2.00 4.00
9 Rejean Houle 1.00 2.00
10 Mark Howe 4.00 8.00
11 Marty Howe 1.00 2.00
12 Bill Hunter .50 1.00
13 Gordon W. Juckes .50 1.00
14 Rick Ley 1.00 2.00
15 Frank Mahovlich 4.00 8.00
16 John McKenzie 1.00 2.00
17 Don McLeod .75 1.50
18 Rick Noonan .75 1.50
19 Brad Selwood .75 1.50
20 Rick Smith .75 1.50
21 Pat Stapleton 1.00 2.00
22 Marc Tardif 1.00 2.00
23 Mike Walton 1.00 2.00
24 Tom Webster 1.00 2.00

2002 Team Canada Coca Cola Coins

1 Mario Lemieux 4.00 10.00
2 Steve Yzerman 4.00 10.00
3 Joe Sakic 1.50 4.00
4 Chris Pronger 1.00 2.50
5 Owen Nolan 1.00 2.50
6 Scott Niedermayer 1.00 2.50
7 Rob Blake 1.00 2.50
8 Paul Kariya 1.50 4.00

1996-97 Team Out

COMPLETE SET (89) 10.00 25.00
1 Paul Kariya .60 1.50
2 Luc Robitaille .08 .25
3 John LeClair .20 .50
4 Theo Fleury .20 .50
5 Scott Mellanby .08 .25
6 Adam Graves .08 .25
7 Esa Tikkanen .02 .10
8 Slava Kozlov .08 .25
9 Eric Daze .08 .25
10 Ryan Smyth .08 .25
11 Shayne Corson .08 .25
12 Kevin Stevens .08 .25
13 Murray Craven .02 .10
14 Keith Tkachuk .20 .50
15 Zigmund Palffy .20 .50
16 Eric Lindros .40 1.00
17 Mario Lemieux 1.00 2.50
18 Joe Sakic .40 1.00
19 Wayne Gretzky 1.25 3.00
20 Mark Messier .20 .50
21 Sergei Fedorov .40 1.00
22 Jason Arnott .08 .25
23 Chris Gratton .08 .25
24 Pierre Turgeon .08 .25
25 Mike Modano .20 .50
26 Saku Koivu .20 .50
27 Alexei Yashin .08 .25
28 Steve Yzerman .75 2.00
29 Peter Forsberg .40 1.00
30 Adam Oates .08 .25
31 Brett Hull .20 .50
32 Jaromir Jagr .40 1.00
33 Pavel Bure .40 1.00
34 Teemu Selanne .30 .75
35 Stephane Richer .02 .10
36 Mike Gartner .08 .25
37 Claude Lemieux .08 .25
38 Rick Tocchet .08 .25
39 Alexander Mogilny .08 .25
40 Peter Bondra .08 .25
41 Mats Sundin .08 .25
42 Daniel Alfredsson .08 .25
43 Owen Nolan .02 .10
44 Joe Juneau .08 .25
45 Mikael Renberg .08 .25
46 Chris Chelios .20 .50
47 Ray Bourque .30 .75
48 Scott Stevens .08 .25
49 Paul Coffey .20 .50
50 Glen Wesley .02 .10
51 Nicklas Lidstrom .20 .50
52 Scott Niedermayer .08 .25
53 Larry Murphy .02 .10
54 Sandis Ozolinsh .08 .25
55 Vladimir Malakhov .02 .10
56 Robert Svehla .02 .10
57 Steve Duchesne .02 .10
58 Sergei Gonchar .02 .10
59 Darius Kasparaitis .08 .25
60 Patrick Roy 1.00 2.50
61 Martin Brodeur .40 1.00
62 Mike Richter .20 .50
63 John Vanbiesbrouck .20 .50
64 Ron Hextall .08 .25
65 Nikolai Khabibulin .08 .25
66 Grant Fuhr .08 .25
67 Kirk McLean .08 .25
68 Jim Carey .20 .50
69 Dominik Hasek .30 .75
70 Ed Belfour .20 .50
71 Chris Osgood .20 .50
72 Guy Hebert .08 .25
73 Trevor Kidd .08 .25
74 Felix Potvin .20 .50
75 Roman Hamrlik .08 .25
76 Alexei Zhitnik .08 .25
77 Al MacInnis .02 .10
78 Brian Leetch .20 .50
79 Rob Blake .08 .25
80 Derian Hatcher .02 .10
81 Mathieu Schneider .02 .10
82 Gary Suter .02 .10
83 Jeff Brown .02 .10
84 Jyrki Lumme .02 .10
85 Ed Jovanovski .08 .25
86 Eric Desjardins .08 .25
87 Stephane Quintal .02 .10
88 Marcus Ragnarsson .02 .10
89 Zarley Zalapski .02 .10

2005-06 The Cup

1 Jean-Sebastien Giguere 6.00 15.00
2 Teemu Selanne 12.00 30.00
3 Ilya Kovalchuk 6.00 15.00
4 Marian Hossa 6.00 15.00
5 Kari Lehtonen 5.00 12.00
6 Cam Neely 6.00 15.00
7 Patrice Bergeron 8.00 20.00
8 Ray Bourque 10.00 25.00
9 Johnny Bucyk 6.00 15.00
10 Phil Esposito 10.00 25.00
11 Don Cherry 6.00 15.00
12 Brian Leetch 5.00 12.00
13 Gerry Cheevers 6.00 15.00
14 Gilbert Perreault 6.00 15.00
15 Chris Drury 5.00 12.00
16 Ryan Miller 6.00 15.00
17 Jarome Iginla 8.00 20.00
18 Lanny McDonald 6.00 15.00
19 Miikka Kiprusoff 6.00 15.00
20 Joe Mullen 5.00 12.00
21 Eric Staal 8.00 20.00
22 Doug Weight 6.00 15.00
23 Martin Gerber 5.00 12.00
24 Nikolai Khabibulin 6.00 15.00
25 Denis Savard 6.00 15.00
26 Bobby Hull 12.00 30.00
27 Tony Esposito 6.00 15.00
28 Joe Sakic 12.00 30.00
29 Alex Tanguay 6.00 15.00
30 Milan Hejduk 5.00 12.00
31 Jose Theodore 6.00 15.00
32 Marek Svatos 5.00 12.00
33 Rick Nash 6.00 15.00
34 Sergei Fedorov 10.00 25.00
35 Mike Modano 10.00 25.00
36 Marty Turco 6.00 15.00
37 Brenden Morrow 5.00 12.00
38 Steve Yzerman 15.00 40.00
39 Gordie Howe 20.00 50.00
40 Brendan Shanahan 6.00 15.00
41 Scotty Bowman 6.00 15.00
42 Pavel Datsyuk 10.00 25.00
43 Henrik Zetterberg 8.00 20.00
44 Chris Pronger 6.00 15.00
45 Wayne Gretzky 40.00 100.00
46 Grant Fuhr 10.00 25.00
47 Roberto Luongo 10.00 25.00
48 Olli Jokinen 6.00 15.00
49 Jeremy Roenick 10.00 25.00
50 Luc Robitaille 6.00 15.00
51 Rogie Vachon 8.00 20.00
52 Marian Gaborik 6.00 15.00
53 Saku Koivu 6.00 15.00
54 Jean Beliveau 6.00 15.00
55 Steve Shutt 6.00 15.00
56 Patrick Roy 15.00 40.00
57 Guy Lafleur 8.00 20.00
58 Guy Lapointe 5.00 12.00
59 Michael Ryder 5.00 12.00
60 Tomas Vokoun 5.00 12.00
61 Paul Kariya 6.00 15.00
62 Martin Brodeur 15.00 40.00
63 Patrik Elias 6.00 15.00
64 Alexei Yashin 5.00 12.00
65 Mike Bossy 6.00 15.00
66 Denis Potvin 6.00 15.00
67 Bryan Trottier 6.00 15.00
68 Clark Gillies 6.00 15.00
69 Jaromir Jagr 20.00 50.00
70 Dominik Hasek 10.00 25.00
71 Dany Heatley 5.00 12.00
72 Jason Spezza 6.00 15.00
73 Daniel Alfredsson 6.00 15.00
74 Peter Forsberg 12.00 30.00
75 Ron Hextall 6.00 15.00
76 Simon Gagne 6.00 15.00
77 Bobby Clarke 10.00 25.00
78 Keith Primeau 5.00 12.00
79 Bernie Parent 8.00 20.00
80 Shane Doan 5.00 12.00
81 Curtis Joseph 8.00 20.00
82 Mario Lemieux 25.00 60.00
83 Marc-Andre Fleury 12.00 30.00
84 Jonathan Cheechoo 5.00 12.00
85 Evgeni Nabokov 5.00 12.00
86 Joe Thornton 10.00 25.00
87 Patrick Marleau 6.00 15.00
88 Keith Tkachuk 6.00 15.00
89 Martin St. Louis 6.00 15.00
90 Vincent Lecavalier 6.00 15.00
91 Brad Richards 6.00 15.00
92 Ed Belfour 6.00 15.00
93 Darryl Sittler 8.00 20.00
94 Mats Sundin 6.00 15.00
95 Eric Lindros 10.00 25.00
96 Doug Gilmour 8.00 20.00
97 Markus Naslund 6.00 15.00
98 Todd Bertuzzi 6.00 15.00
99 Ed Jovanovski 5.00 12.00
100 Olaf Kolzig 6.00 15.00
101 R.Getzlaf JSY AU RC 150.00 300.00
102 R.Whitney JSY AU RC EX 20.00 50.00
103 R.J. Umberger JSY AU RC 40.00 100.00
104 Cam Ward JSY AU RC 40.00 100.00
105 B.Seabrook JSY AU RC 80.00 150.00
106 Eric Nystrom JSY AU RC 15.00 40.00
107 Gilbert Brule JSY AU RC 25.00 60.00
108 H.Toivonen JSY AU RC 20.00 50.00
109 R.Nilsson JSY AU RC 20.00 50.00
110 R.Olesz JSY AU RC 15.00 40.00
111 Ryan Suter JSY AU RC 40.00 100.00
112 J.Jokinen JSY AU RC EX 30.00 80.00
113 Zach Parise JSY AU RC 100.00 250.00
114 W.Wolski JSY AU RC 15.00 40.00
115 A.Meszaros JSY AU RC 15.00 40.00
116 J.Franzen JSY AU RC 30.00 80.00
117 P.Budaj JSY AU RC 25.00 60.00
118 D.Leneveu JSY AU RC 15.00 40.00
119 A.Alberts JSY AU RC 12.00 30.00
120 S.Bernier JSY AU RC 20.00 50.00
121 M.Koivu JSY AU RC 50.00 120.00
122 C.Campoli JSY AU RC 12.00 30.00
123 E.Artyukhin JSY AU RC 15.00 40.00
124 C.Schubert JSY AU RC 12.00 30.00
125 T.Fleischmann JSY AU RC 20.00 50.00
126 M.Talbot JSY AU RC 20.00 50.00
127 J.Sigalet JSY AU RC 12.00 30.00
128 D.Richmond JSY AU RC 12.00 30.00
129 M.Lapierre JSY AU RC 30.00 80.00
130 D.Patzold JSY AU RC 12.00 30.00
131 R.Bourque JSY AU RC 20.00 50.00
132 Y.Danis JSY AU RC 15.00 40.00
133 B.Winchester JSY AU RC 20.00 50.00
134 Jim Slater JSY AU RC 15.00 40.00
135 Petr Prucha JSY AU RC 20.00 50.00
136 Jim Howard JSY AU RC 80.00 200.00
137 P.Eaves JSY AU RC 20.00 50.00
138 R.Clowe JSY AU RC 25.00 60.00
139 B.Coburn JSY AU RC 20.00 50.00
140 B.Richardson JSY AU RC 20.00 50.00
141 M.Jurcina JSY AU RC 15.00 40.00
142 J.Woywitka JSY AU RC 12.00 30.00
143 A.Kostitsyn JSY AU RC 25.00 60.00
144 Derek Boogaard AU RC 25.00 60.00
145 B.Tallackson JSY AU RC 15.00 40.00
146 J.Klepis JSY AU RC EX 12.00 30.00
147 A.Montoya JSY AU RC 20.00 50.00
148 A.Ladd JSY AU RC 40.00 100.00
149 B.Bochenski JSY AU RC 20.00 50.00
150 J.Tambellini JSY AU RC 12.00 30.00
151 J.Balastik JSY AU RC 12.00 30.00
152 L.Stempniak JSY AU RC 20.00 50.00
153 K.Dallman JSY AU RC 15.00 40.00
154 N.Nordgren JSY AU RC 20.00 50.00
155 K.Nastiuk JSY AU RC 12.00 30.00
156 R.Craig JSY AU RC 12.00 30.00
157 E.Christensen JSY AU RC 12.00 30.00
158 C.Thorburn JSY AU RC 15.00 40.00
159 J.Gorges JSY AU RC 15.00 40.00
160 Matt Foy JSY AU RC 12.00 30.00
161 O.Tollefsen JSY AU RC 15.00 40.00
162 K.Bieksa JSY AU RC 30.00 80.00
163 K.Quincey JSY AU RC 15.00 40.00
164 A.Wozniewski JSY AU RC 15.00 40.00
165 Jeff Hoggan JSY AU RC 12.00 30.00
166 J.Colliton JSY AU RC 12.00 30.00
167 A.Picard JSY AU RC 12.00 30.00
168 Ben Eager JSY AU RC 15.00 40.00
169 D.Paille JSY AU RC 20.00 50.00
170 V.Filppula JSY AU RC 40.00 100.00
171 A. Perezhogin JSY AU RC 15.00 40.00
172 M.Richards JSY AU RC 60.00 120.00
173 Corey Perry JSY AU RC 150.00 300.00
174 A.Steen JSY AU RC 40.00 100.00
175 T.Vanek JSY AU RC 100.00 200.00
176 J.Carter JSY AU RC 30.00 80.00
177 H.Lundqvist JSY AU RC 400.00 1000.00
178 D.Phaneuf JSY AU/99 RC 250.00 600.00
179 A.Ovechkin
JSY AU/99 RC 25000.00 60000.00
180 S.Crosby JSY AU/99 RC 4000.00 10000.00
181 Brett Lebda AU RC 10.00 25.00
182 Jay McClement AU RC 10.00 25.00
183 Cam Barker JSY AU RC 15.00 40.00
184 P.Nokelainen AU RC 10.00 25.00
185 Keith Ballard AU RC 12.00 30.00
186 Duncan Keith AU RC 100.00 200.00
187 George Parros AU RC 10.00 25.00
188 Adam Berkhoel AU RC 12.00 30.00
189 Anthony Stewart AU RC 12.00 30.00
190 Ryan Hollweg AU RC 10.00 25.00
191 Ben Walter AU RC 10.00 25.00

2005-06 The Cup Gold

*1-100 GOLD: 1.2X TO 3X BASE HI
2 Teemu Selanne 30.00 80.00
3 Ilya Kovalchuk 25.00 60.00
8 Ray Bourque 25.00 60.00
11 Don Cherry 25.00 60.00
17 Jarome Iginla 25.00 60.00
21 Eric Staal 25.00 60.00
26 Bobby Hull 25.00 60.00
28 Joe Sakic 50.00 100.00
33 Rick Nash 40.00 80.00
35 Mike Modano 25.00 60.00
38 Steve Yzerman 60.00 125.00
39 Gordie Howe 30.00 80.00
42 Pavel Datsyuk 25.00 60.00
43 Henrik Zetterberg 25.00 60.00
45 Wayne Gretzky 250.00 400.00
47 Roberto Luongo 25.00 60.00
50 Luc Robitaille 25.00 60.00
52 Marian Gaborik 25.00 60.00
53 Saku Koivu 25.00 60.00
56 Patrick Roy 75.00 150.00
57 Guy Lafleur 25.00 60.00
62 Martin Brodeur 30.00 80.00
69 Jaromir Jagr 25.00 60.00
70 Dominik Hasek 25.00 60.00
71 Dany Heatley 25.00 60.00
72 Jason Spezza 25.00 60.00
74 Peter Forsberg 25.00 60.00
82 Mario Lemieux 60.00 150.00
83 Marc-Andre Fleury 25.00 60.00
86 Joe Thornton 25.00 60.00
90 Vincent Lecavalier 25.00 60.00

2005-06 The Cup Autographed Rookie Patches Gold Rainbow

101 Ryan Getzlaf/51 250.00 500.00
102 Ryan Whitney/19
103 R.J. Umberger/20 75.00 150.00
104 Cam Ward/30 200.00 300.00
106 Eric Nystrom/23 75.00 150.00
107 Gilbert Brule/17 75.00 150.00
108 Hannu Toivonen/33 25.00 60.00
109 Robert Nilsson/21 100.00 200.00
110 Rostislav Olesz/85 20.00 50.00
111 Ryan Suter/20 75.00 150.00
112 Jussi Jokinen/36 80.00 150.00
116 Johan Franzen/39 100.00 200.00
117 Peter Budaj/31 125.00 250.00
118 David Leneveu/30 50.00 120.00
119 Andrew Alberts/41 30.00 60.00
120 Steve Bernier/26 75.00 150.00
121 Mikko Koivu/21 60.00 120.00
123 Evgeny Artyukhin/76 20.00 50.00
125 Tomas Fleischmann/43 60.00 120.00
126 Maxime Talbot/25 60.00 120.00
127 Jordan Sigalet/57 40.00 100.00
128 Danny Richmond/51 15.00 40.00
129 Maxim Lapierre/40 25.00 50.00
130 Dimitri Patzold/30 40.00 80.00
132 Yann Danis/75 15.00 40.00
133 Brad Winchester/26 30.00 60.00
134 Jim Slater/23 25.00 50.00
135 Petr Prucha/25 30.00 60.00
136 Jim Howard/35 125.00 200.00
137 Patrick Eaves/44 50.00 120.00
138 Ryane Clowe/29 75.00 150.00
141 Milan Jurcina/68 25.00 60.00
142 Jeff Woywitka/29 20.00 50.00
143 Andrei Kostitsyn/46 40.00 100.00
145 Barry Tallackson/27 25.00 50.00
146 Jakub Klepis/38 25.00 60.00
147 Alvaro Montoya/29 30.00 80.00
148 Andrew Ladd/16 40.00 80.00
151 Jaroslav Balastik/40 15.00 40.00
153 Kevin Dallman/38 25.00 50.00
154 Niklas Nordgren/44 15.00 40.00
155 Kevin Nastiuk/35 15.00 50.00
156 Ryan Craig/34 25.00 50.00
157 Erik Christensen/16 30.00 60.00
160 Matt Foy/83 15.00 50.00
161 Ole-Kristian Tollefsen/55 25.00 50.00
162 Kevin Bieksa/25 50.00 125.00
164 Andrew Wozniewski/56 15.00 40.00
165 Jeff Hoggan/22 30.00 60.00
166 Jeremy Colliton/27 40.00 80.00
167 Alexandre Picard/19 25.00 50.00
168 Ben Eager/55 25.00 50.00
169 Daniel Paille/20 60.00 120.00
171 Alexander Perezhogin/42 25.00 60.00
172 Mike Richards/18 125.00 250.00
173 Corey Perry/61 125.00 250.00
175 Thomas Vanek/26 125.00 250.00
176 Jeff Carter/17 50.00 125.00
177 Henrik Lundqvist/30 300.00 800.00
180 Sidney Crosby/87 4000.00 10000.00
183 Cam Barker/25 50.00 120.00
187 George Parros/57 30.00 60.00
189 Anthony Stewart/57

2005-06 The Cup Honorable Numbers

HNAH Ales Hemsky/83 20.00 50.00
HNAT Alex Tanguay/18 25.00 60.00
HNAY Alexei Yashin/79 15.00 40.00
HNBI Martin Biron/43 12.00 30.00
HNBL Brian Leetch/22 40.00 100.00
HNBM Bryan McCabe/24 15.00 40.00
HNBT Bryan Trottier/19 100.00 200.00
HNBY Mike Bossy/22 30.00 80.00
HNCD Chris Drury/23 15.00 40.00
HNCP Chris Pronger/44 40.00 100.00
HNDG Doug Gilmour/93 30.00 80.00
HNDR Dwayne Roloson/30 15.00 40.00
HNDS Darryl Sittler/27 30.00 80.00
HNDW Doug Weight/39 20.00 50.00
HNED Eric Daze/55 12.00 30.00
HNGC Gerry Cheevers/30 25.00 60.00
HNGE Martin Gerber/29 25.00 60.00
HNGF Grant Fuhr/31 40.00 100.00
HNGM Glen Murray/27 25.00 60.00
HNHK Dominik Hasek/39 40.00 100.00
HNIK Ilya Kovalchuk/17 25.00 60.00
HNJO Joe Thornton/19 30.00 80.00
HNJS Jean-Sebastien Giguere/35 15.00 40.00
HNJT Jose Theodore/60 40.00 100.00
HNKL Kari Lehtonen/32 30.00 80.00
HNKP Keith Primeau/25 30.00 80.00
HNLR Luc Robitaille/20 30.00 80.00
HNMB Martin Brodeur/30 100.00 200.00
HNMH Milan Hejduk/23 20.00 50.00
HNMK Miikka Kiprusoff/34 30.00 80.00
HNMN Markus Naslund/19 30.00 80.00
HNMP Mark Parrish/37 20.00 50.00
HNMS Marek Svatos/40 20.00 50.00
HNMT Marty Turco/35 25.00 60.00
HNOK Olaf Kolzig/37 25.00 60.00
HNPB Patrice Bergeron/37 50.00 125.00
HNPE Michael Peca/37 12.00 30.00
HNPR Patrick Roy/33 200.00 300.00
HNRB Ray Bourque/77 30.00 80.00
HNRE Robert Esche/42 12.00 30.00
HNRH Ron Hextall/27 40.00 100.00
HNRN Rick Nash/61 30.00 80.00
HNSA Miroslav Satan/81 25.00 60.00
HNSC Sidney Crosby/87 2000.00 5000.00
HNSL Martin St. Louis/26 25.00 60.00
HNTB Todd Bertuzzi/44 15.00 40.00
HNTE Tony Esposito/35 30.00 80.00
HNTV Tomas Vokoun/29 25.00 60.00
HNZP Zigmund Palffy/33 25.00 60.00
HNDS2 Denis Savard/18 25.00 60.00

2005-06 The Cup Limited Logos Autographs

LLAO Alexander Ovechkin 6000.00 15000.00
LLAT Alex Tanguay 30.00 80.00
LLAY Alexei Yashin 25.00 60.00
LLBH Bobby Hull/25 60.00 150.00
LLBI Martin Biron 25.00 60.00
LLBL Rob Blake 30.00 80.00
LLBS Billy Smith 30.00 80.00

LLBY Mike Bossy 30.00 80.00
LLCD Chris Drury 25.00 60.00
LLCP Chris Pronger 30.00 80.00
LLDA David Aebischer 25.00 60.00
LLDP Denis Potvin 30.00 80.00
LLDW Doug Weight/35 30.00 80.00
LLED Eric Daze 25.00 60.00
LLEN Evgeni Nabokov/20 25.00 60.00
LLES Eric Staal 40.00 100.00
LLFM Frank Mahovlich/20 40.00 100.00
LLGE Martin Gerber 25.00 60.00
LLGF Grant Fuhr/45 50.00 125.00
LLGM Glen Murray 25.00 60.00
LLGP Gilbert Perreault 30.00 80.00
LLHA Dominik Hasek 50.00 125.00
LLHJ Milan Hejduk 25.00 60.00
LLHV Martin Havlat 30.00 80.00
LLIK Ilya Kovalchuk 30.00 80.00
LLJC Jonathan Cheechoo/25 25.00 60.00
LLJI Jarome Iginla 40.00 100.00
LLJO Joe Thornton 50.00 125.00
LLJS Jean-Sebastien Giguere 30.00 80.00
LLJT Jose Theodore 30.00 80.00
LLKD Kris Draper 40.00 100.00
LLKP Keith Primeau 25.00 60.00
LLLM Lanny McDonald/25 30.00 80.00
LLLU Luc Robitaille 30.00 80.00
LLMB Martin Brodeur 80.00 200.00
LLMC Bryan McCabe 20.00 50.00
LLMG Marian Gaborik 30.00 80.00
LLMH Marian Hossa 30.00 80.00
LLMK Miikka Kiprusoff 30.00 80.00
LLMM Mike Modano 50.00 125.00
LLMN Markus Naslund 30.00 80.00
LLMO Brendan Morrison 20.00 50.00
LLMP Michael Peca/30 25.00 60.00
LLMT Marty Turco 30.00 80.00
LLMW Brenden Morrow 25.00 60.00
LLOJ Olli Jokinen 30.00 80.00
LLOK Olaf Kolzig 30.00 80.00
LLPB Patrice Bergeron/25 40.00 100.00
LLPM Patrick Marleau/30 30.00 80.00
LLPR Patrick Roy/21 250.00 400.00
LLRB Ray Bourque/45 50.00 125.00
LLRE Robert Esche 25.00 60.00
LLRL Roberto Luongo/40 50.00 125.00
LLRM Ryan Miller 30.00 80.00
LLRN Rick Nash/20 30.00 80.00
LLRS Ryan Smyth 25.00 60.00
LLRV Rogie Vachon/20 40.00 100.00
LLRY Michael Ryder 25.00 60.00
LLSA Miroslav Satan 25.00 60.00
LLSC Sidney Crosby 2500.00 6000.00
LLSD Shane Doan 25.00 60.00
LLSG Simon Gagne 30.00 80.00
LLSK Saku Koivu 30.00 80.00
LLSL Martin St. Louis/25 30.00 80.00
LLSN Scott Niedermayer 30.00 80.00
LLSS Steve Shutt 30.00 80.00
LLSW Stephen Weiss 20.00 50.00
LLTB Todd Bertuzzi 30.00 80.00
LLTC Ty Conklin 25.00 60.00
LLTV Tomas Vokoun 25.00 60.00
LLVL Vincent Lecavalier 30.00 80.00
LLZP Zigmund Palffy 30.00 80.00

2005-06 The Cup Noble Numbers

NNBB Rob Blake
Jay Bouwmeester/4
NNBC Brodeur/Cheevers/30 80.00 200.00
NNBE Ray Bourque
Phil Esposito/7
NNBL Jean Beliveau
Vincent Lecavalier/4
NNBS Bossy/Shutt/22 30.00 80.00
NNDZ Pavel Datsyuk
Nikolai Zherdev/13
NNFJ Fuhr/Joseph/31 50.00 125.00
NNFS Forsberg/Salming/21 60.00 150.00
NNGM Simon Gagne
Patrick Marleau/12
NNGT Giguere/Turco/35 30.00 80.00
NNGV Gerber/Vokoun/29 25.00 60.00
NNHD Hejduk/Drury/23 25.00 60.00
NNHM Bobby Hull
Lanny McDonald/9
NNHR Dany Heatley
Tuomo Ruutu/15
NNIG Jarome Iginla
Simon Gagne/12
NNJJ Jagr/Jurcina/68 100.00 250.00
NNJS J.Spezza/Doan/19 30.00 80.00
NNKA Saku Koivu
Daniel Alfredsson/11
NNKC Kovalchuk/Carter/17 50.00 125.00
NNKL Kiprusoff/Legace/34 30.00 80.00
NNLA Roberto Luongo
David Aebischer/1
NNLM Lundqvist/Miller/30 150.00 400.00
NNLR Roberto Luongo
Andrew Raycroft/1
NNMJ Murphy/Jovanovski/55 25.00 60.00
NNMK Mike Modano
Paul Kariya/9
NNMM Lanny McDonald
Joe Mullen/7
NNMS Mahovlich/Sittler/27 40.00 100.00
NNMT Joe Mullen
Keith Tkachuk/7
NNNP Nash/Perry/61 100.00 250.00
NNPB Pronger/Bertuzzi/44 30.00 80.00
NNPK Gilbert Perreault
Saku Koivu/11
NNPM Denis Potvin
Larry Murphy/5
NNSC Brendan Shanahan
Jonathan Cheechoo/14
NNSD Mats Sundin
Pavel Datsyuk/13
NNSE Stastny/Elias/26 30.00 80.00
NNSI Eric Staal
Jarome Iginla/12
NNSL Stastny/St. Louis/26 30.00 80.00
NNSM Eric Staal
Patrick Marleau/12
NNSR Spezza/B.Richards/19 30.00 80.00
NNSS Mats Sundin
Teemu Selanne/13
NNST D.Savard/Tanguay/18 30.00 80.00
NNTN Thornton/Naslund/19 50.00 125.00
NNTS Thornton/Spezza/19 50.00 125.00
NNYS Yzerman/Sakic/19 80.00 200.00
NNYT Yzerman/Thornton/19 80.00 200.00
NNZS Zetterberg/Svatos/40 40.00 100.00

2005-06 The Cup Platinum Rookies

101 Ryan Getzlaf 60.00 120.00
102 Ryan Whitney 50.00 100.00
103 R.J. Umberger 25.00 60.00
104 Cam Ward 25.00 60.00
105 Brent Seabrook 40.00 100.00
106 Eric Nystrom 15.00 40.00
107 Gilbert Brule 12.00 30.00
108 Hannu Toivonen 20.00 50.00
109 Robert Nilsson 20.00 50.00
110 Rostislav Olesz 15.00 40.00
111 Ryan Suter 25.00 60.00
112 Jussi Jokinen 20.00 50.00
113 Zach Parise 75.00 135.00
114 Wojtek Wolski 15.00 40.00
115 Andrej Meszaros 15.00 40.00
116 Johan Franzen 30.00 80.00
117 Peter Budaj 25.00 60.00
118 David Leneveu 15.00 40.00
119 Andrew Alberts 12.00 30.00
120 Steve Bernier 20.00 50.00
121 Mikko Koivu 25.00 60.00
122 Chris Campoli 12.00 30.00
123 Evgeny Artyukhin 15.00 40.00
124 Christoph Schubert 12.00 30.00
125 Tomas Fleischmann 20.00 50.00
126 Maxime Talbot 20.00 50.00
127 Jordan Sigalet 12.00 30.00
128 Danny Richmond 12.00 30.00
129 Maxim Lapierre 20.00 50.00
130 Dimitri Patzold 12.00 30.00
131 Rene Bourque 20.00 50.00
132 Yann Danis 15.00 40.00
133 Brad Winchester 20.00 50.00
134 Jim Slater 15.00 40.00
135 Petr Prucha 30.00 80.00
136 Jim Howard 40.00 100.00
137 Patrick Eaves 20.00 50.00
138 Ryane Clowe 25.00 60.00
139 Braydon Coburn 20.00 50.00
140 Brad Richardson 20.00 50.00
141 Milan Jurcina 15.00 40.00
142 Jeff Woywitka 12.00 30.00
143 Andrei Kostitsyn 20.00 50.00
144 Derek Boogaard 30.00 80.00
145 Barry Tallackson 15.00 40.00
146 Jakub Klepis 12.00 30.00
147 Alvaro Montoya 20.00 50.00
148 Andrew Ladd 25.00 60.00
149 Brandon Bochenski 20.00 50.00
150 Jeff Tambellini 12.00 30.00
151 Jaroslav Balastik 12.00 30.00
152 Lee Stempniak 20.00 50.00
153 Kevin Dallman 15.00 40.00
154 Niklas Nordgren 20.00 50.00
155 Kevin Nastiuk 12.00 30.00
156 Ryan Craig 12.00 30.00
157 Erik Christensen 12.00 30.00
158 Chris Thorburn 15.00 40.00
159 Josh Gorges 15.00 40.00
160 Matt Foy 12.00 30.00
161 Ole-Kristian Tollefsen 30.00 80.00
162 Kevin Bieksa 30.00 80.00
163 Kyle Quincey 15.00 40.00
164 Andrew Wozniewski 15.00 40.00
165 Jeff Hoggan 12.00 30.00
166 Jeremy Colliton 12.00 30.00
167 Alexandre Picard 12.00 30.00
168 Ben Eager 15.00 40.00
169 Daniel Paille 20.00 50.00
170 Valtteri Filppula 25.00 60.00
171 Alexander Perezhogin 15.00 40.00
172 Mike Richards 50.00 125.00
173 Corey Perry 75.00 150.00
174 Alexander Steen 50.00 100.00
175 Thomas Vanek 50.00 100.00
176 Jeff Carter 60.00 120.00
177 Henrik Lundqvist 100.00 250.00
178 Dion Phaneuf 50.00 120.00
179 Alexander Ovechkin 2500.00 6000.00
180 Sidney Crosby 800.00 1200.00
181 Brett Lebda 12.00 30.00
182 Jay McClement 12.00 30.00
183 Cam Barker 15.00 40.00
184 Petteri Nokelainen 12.00 30.00
185 Keith Ballard 15.00 40.00
186 Duncan Keith 40.00 100.00
187 George Parros 12.00 30.00
188 Adam Berkhoel 15.00 40.00
189 Anthony Stewart 15.00 40.00
190 Ryan Hollweg 12.00 30.00
191 Ben Walter 12.00 30.00

2005-06 The Cup Scripted Numbers

SNBC Brodeur/Cheevers/30 80.00 200.00
SNBL Mike Bossy
Brian Leetch/22 30.00 80.00
SNBN Ed Belfour
Evgeni Nabokov/20 30.00 80.00
SNBP Bergeron/Peca/37 40.00 100.00
SNBR Ed Belfour
Luc Robitaille/20 30.00 80.00
SNBS Mike Bossy
Steve Shutt/22 30.00 80.00
SNET Turco/Tony O/35 30.00 80.00
SNGT Giguere/Turco/35 30.00 80.00
SNGV Gerber/Vokoun/29 25.00 60.00
SNHD Hejduk/Drury/23 25.00 60.00
SNKC Ilya Kovalchuk
Jeff Carter/17 50.00 125.00
SNKL Kiprusoff/Legace/34 30.00 80.00
SNLM Lundqvist/Miller/30 150.00 400.00
SNMN Murray/Nieder/27 30.00 80.00
SNMS Big M/Sittler/27 40.00 100.00
SNND Markus Naslund
Shane Doan/19 30.00 80.00
SNNP Nash/Perry/61 20.00 50.00
SNPB Pronger/Bertuzzi/44 30.00 80.00
SNST Denis Savard
Alex Tanguay
/18 30.00 80.00
SNTH Alex Tanguay
Marian Hossa/18 30.00 80.00
SNTN Joe Thornton
Markus Naslund/19 50.00 125.00
SNZS Zetterberg/Svatos/40 40.00 100.00

2005-06 The Cup Scripted Swatches

SSAF Alexander Frolov/25 20.00 50.00
SSAH Ales Hemsky/25 25.00 60.00
SSAR Andrew Raycroft/25 25.00 60.00
SSAS Alexander Steen/25 50.00 120.00
SSAT Alex Tanguay/25 30.00 80.00
SSAY Alexei Yashin/25 25.00 60.00
SSBL Rob Blake/25 25.00 60.00
SSBY Mike Bossy/25 30.00 80.00
SSCD Chris Drury/25 25.00 60.00
SSCN Cam Neely/18 30.00 80.00
SSDG Doug Gilmour/25 40.00 100.00
SSDH Dany Heatley/25 25.00 60.00
SSDP Dion Phaneuf/25 50.00 125.00
SSDT Dave Taylor/25 25.00 60.00
SSDW Doug Weight/25 30.00 80.00
SSEN Evgeni Nabokov/25 25.00 60.00
SSER Eric Staal/25 40.00 100.00
SSGC Gerry Cheevers/25 30.00 80.00
SSGE Martin Gerber/25 25.00 60.00
SSGF Grant Fuhr/25 50.00 125.00
SSGL Guy Lafleur/20 40.00 100.00
SSGM Glen Murray/25 25.00 60.00
SSHK Dominik Hasek/25 50.00 125.00
SSHL Henrik Lundqvist/25 150.00 400.00
SSHO Marian Hossa/25 30.00 80.00
SSHV Martin Havlat/25 30.00 80.00
SSIK Ilya Kovalchuk/25 30.00 80.00
SSJB Jean Beliveau/25 30.00 80.00
SSJC Jeff Carter/25 25.00 60.00
SSJI Jarome Iginla/25 40.00 100.00
SSJO Joe Thornton/25 50.00 125.00
SSJS Jean-Sebastien Giguere/25 30.00 80.00
SSJT Jose Theodore/25 30.00 80.00
SSKL Kari Lehtonen/25 25.00 60.00
SSKP Keith Primeau/25 25.00 60.00
SSLR Luc Robitaille/25 30.00 80.00
SSLU Joffrey Lupul/25 20.00 50.00
SSMB Martin Brodeur/25 80.00 200.00
SSMG Marian Gaborik/25 30.00 80.00
SSMH Milan Hejduk/25 25.00 60.00
SSMK Miikka Kiprusoff/25 30.00 80.00
SSMM Mike Modano/25 50.00 125.00
SSMN Markus Naslund/25 30.00 80.00
SSMO Brendan Morrison/25 20.00 50.00
SSMP Mark Parrish/25 20.00 50.00
SSMT Marty Turco/25 30.00 80.00
SSMW Brenden Morrow/25 25.00 60.00
SSOJ Olli Jokinen/25 30.00 80.00
SSOK Olaf Kolzig/25 30.00 80.00
SSPE Michael Peca/25 25.00 60.00
SSRE Robert Esche/25 25.00 60.00
SSRM Ryan Miller/25 30.00 80.00
SSRY Michael Ryder/25 25.00 60.00
SSSA Miroslav Satan/25 25.00 60.00
SSSD Shane Doan/25 25.00 60.00
SSSG Simon Gagne/25 30.00 80.00
SSSK Saku Koivu/25 30.00 80.00
SSST Matt Stajan/25 20.00 50.00
SSTB Todd Bertuzzi/25 30.00 80.00
SSTE Tony Esposito/25 30.00 80.00
SSTV Thomas Vanek/25 60.00 150.00
SSVL Vincent Lecavalier/25 30.00 80.00
SSZP Zigmund Palffy/25 30.00 80.00
SSPR1 Patrick Roy/25 80.00 200.00
SSPR2 Patrick Roy/25 80.00 200.00
SSRB1 Ray Bourque/25 50.00 125.00
SSRB2 Ray Bourque/25 50.00 125.00

2005-06 The Cup Signature Patches

SPAF Alexander Frolov 12.00 30.00
SPAH Ales Hemsky 15.00 40.00
SPAO Alexander Ovechkin 2500.00 6000.00
SPAR Andrew Raycroft 15.00 40.00
SPAT Alex Tanguay 20.00 50.00
SPAY Alexei Yashin 15.00 40.00
SPBK Rob Blake 20.00 50.00
SPBL Brian Leetch 15.00 40.00
SPBS Billy Smith 30.00 80.00
SPBY Mike Bossy 30.00 80.00
SPCD Chris Drury 15.00 40.00
SPCN Cam Neely/25 60.00 100.00
SPCP Chris Pronger 40.00 80.00
SPDA David Aebischer 15.00 40.00
SPDG Doug Gilmour 25.00 60.00
SPDH Dany Heatley 15.00 40.00
SPDO Dominik Hasek 50.00 80.00
SPDP Dion Phaneuf 50.00 120.00
SPDW Doug Weight 20.00 50.00
SPES Eric Staal 30.00 80.00
SPFM Frank Mahovlich 20.00 50.00
SPGA Glenn Anderson 15.00 40.00
SPGC Gerry Cheevers/65 30.00 80.00
SPGE Martin Gerber 15.00 40.00
SPGL Guy Lafleur 25.00 60.00
SPGM Glen Murray 15.00 40.00
SPGO Scott Gomez 15.00 40.00
SPGP Gilbert Perreault/40 50.00 125.00
SPHJ Milan Hejduk 15.00 40.00
SPHL Henrik Lundqvist 60.00 120.00
SPHV Martin Havlat 20.00 50.00
SPIK Ilya Kovalchuk 30.00 80.00
SPJC Jeff Carter 15.00 40.00
SPJI Jarome Iginla 25.00 60.00
SPJM Joe Mullen 15.00 40.00
SPJO Joe Thornton 40.00 100.00
SPJP Joni Pitkanen 12.00 30.00
SPJS Jean-Sebastien Giguere 20.00 50.00
SPJT Jose Theodore 20.00 50.00
SPKD Kris Draper 25.00 60.00
SPKP Keith Primeau 15.00 40.00
SPLM Lanny McDonald 20.00 50.00
SPLR Luc Robitaille 25.00 60.00
SPLU Joffrey Lupul 12.00 30.00
SPMB Martin Brodeur 60.00 120.00
SPMG Marian Gaborik 25.00 60.00
SPMH Marian Hossa 20.00 50.00
SPMK Miikka Kiprusoff 40.00 100.00
SPMM Mike Modano 25.00 60.00
SPMN Markus Naslund 20.00 50.00
SPMP Mark Parrish 12.00 30.00
SPMR Mike Richards 25.00 60.00
SPMS Miroslav Satan 15.00 40.00
SPMT Marty Turco 20.00 50.00
SPOJ Olli Jokinen 20.00 50.00
SPOK Olaf Kolzig 20.00 50.00
SPPB Patrice Bergeron 25.00 60.00
SPPE Corey Perry/60 30.00 80.00
SPPO Denis Potvin 20.00 50.00
SPPR Patrick Roy 75.00 150.00
SPRB Ray Bourque 50.00 100.00
SPRE Robert Esche 15.00 40.00
SPRH Ron Hextall/40 50.00 100.00
SPRL Roberto Luongo 50.00 100.00
SPRM Ryan Miller 30.00 80.00
SPRN Rick Nash/40 40.00 100.00
SPRY Michael Ryder 15.00 40.00
SPSC Sidney Crosby 350.00 600.00
SPSD Shane Doan/25 50.00 100.00
SPSG Simon Gagne 20.00 50.00
SPSH Steve Shutt 20.00 50.00
SPSK Saku Koivu 20.00 50.00
SPSL Martin St. Louis/65 20.00 50.00
SPSN Scott Niedermayer 20.00 50.00
SPSV Marek Svatos 15.00 40.00
SPTB Todd Bertuzzi 20.00 50.00
SPTI Tiger Williams 12.00 30.00
SPTV Thomas Vanek 30.00 80.00
SPVL Vincent Lecavalier 25.00 60.00
SPVO Tomas Vokoun 15.00 40.00
SPWG Wayne Gretzky/25 500.00 1200.00
SPWR Wade Redden 12.00 30.00
SPZC Zdeno Chara 20.00 50.00

2006-07 The Cup

1 Teemu Selanne 6.00 15.00
2 Jean-Sebastian Giguere 3.00 8.00
3 Kari Lehtonen 2.50 6.00
4 Ilya Kovalchuk 3.00 8.00
5 Phil Esposito 5.00 12.00
6 Don Cherry 5.00 12.00
7 Ray Bourque 5.00 12.00
8 Bobby Orr 12.00 30.00
9 Cam Neely 3.00 8.00
10 Patrice Bergeron 4.00 10.00
11 Johnny Bucyk 3.00 8.00
12 Ryan Miller 3.00 8.00
13 Gilbert Perreault 3.00 8.00
14 Jarome Iginla 4.00 10.00
15 Miikka Kiprusoff 3.00 8.00
16 Al MacInnis 4.00 10.00
17 Eric Staal 4.00 10.00
18 Cam Ward 3.00 8.00
19 Bobby Hull 6.00 15.00
20 Tony Esposito 3.00 8.00
21 Stan Mikita 4.00 10.00
22 Joe Sakic 6.00 15.00
23 Patrick Roy 8.00 20.00
24 Rick Nash 3.00 8.00
25 Sergei Fedorov 5.00 12.00
26 Mike Modano 5.00 12.00
27 Dominik Hasek 5.00 12.00
28 Henrik Zetterberg 4.00 10.00
29 Gordie Howe 10.00 25.00
30 Scotty Bowman 3.00 8.00
31 Ted Lindsay 3.00 8.00
32 Red Kelly 3.00 8.00
33 Ales Hemsky 2.50 6.00
34 Grant Fuhr 5.00 12.00
35 Jari Kurri 3.00 8.00
36 Ed Belfour 3.00 8.00
37 Wayne Gretzky 20.00 50.00
38 Rob Blake 3.00 8.00
39 Marcel Dionne 4.00 10.00
40 Luc Robitaille 3.00 8.00
41 Rogie Vachon 4.00 10.00
42 Dino Ciccarelli 3.00 8.00
43 Marian Gaborik 3.00 8.00
44 Saku Koivu 3.00 8.00
45 Michael Ryder 2.00 5.00
46 Guy Lafleur 4.00 10.00
47 Larry Robinson 3.00 8.00
48 Jean Beliveau 3.00 8.00
49 Jacques Lemaire 2.50 6.00
50 Paul Kariya 3.00 8.00
51 Tomas Vokoun 2.50 6.00
52 Martin Brodeur 8.00 20.00
53 Scott Stevens 3.00 8.00
54 Alexei Yashin 2.50 6.00
55 Al Arbour 2.50 6.00
56 Mike Bossy 3.00 8.00
57 Billy Smith 3.00 8.00
58 Denis Potvin 3.00 8.00
59 Jaromir Jagr 10.00 25.00
60 Brendan Shanahan 3.00 8.00
61 Henrik Lundqvist 8.00 20.00
62 Gump Worsley 3.00 8.00
63 Andy Bathgate 2.50 6.00
64 Jason Spezza 3.00 8.00
65 Dany Heatley 2.50 6.00
66 Peter Forsberg 6.00 15.00
67 Simon Gagne 3.00 8.00
68 Bernie Parent 4.00 10.00
69 Bobby Clarke 5.00 12.00
70 Ron Hextall 3.00 8.00
71 Jeremy Roenick 5.00 12.00
72 Shane Doan 2.50 6.00
73 Sidney Crosby 12.00 30.00
74 Marc-Andre Fleury 6.00 15.00
75 Mario Lemieux 12.00 30.00
76 Peter Stastny 2.50 6.00
77 Joe Thornton 5.00 12.00
78 Jonathan Cheechoo 2.50 6.00
79 Patrick Marleau 3.00 8.00
80 Bernie Federko 2.50 6.00
81 Vincent Lecavalier 3.00 8.00
82 Mats Sundin 3.00 8.00
83 Frank Mahovlich 3.00 8.00
84 Darryl Sittler 4.00 10.00
85 Johnny Bower 3.00 8.00
86 Borje Salming 3.00 8.00
87 Roberto Luongo 5.00 12.00
88 Markus Naslund 3.00 8.00
89 Alexander Ovechkin 12.00 30.00
90 Dale Hawerchuk 4.00 10.00
91 Nate Thompson AU RC 6.00 15.00
92 Mike Brown AU RC 6.00 15.00
93 Mike Card AU RC 6.00 15.00
94 Adam Dennis AU RC 6.00 15.00
95 Carsen Germyn AU RC 6.00 15.00
96 Adam Burish AU RC 10.00 25.00
97 Drew Larman AU RC 6.00 15.00
98 Jonas Johansson AU RC 6.00 15.00
99 Joel Perrault AU RC 6.00 15.00
100 Mikko Lehtonen AU RC 8.00 20.00
101 Alex Brooks AU RC 6.00 15.00
102 Frank Doyle AU RC 8.00 20.00
103 Billy Thompson AU RC 6.00 15.00
104 Kelly Guard AU RC 8.00 20.00
105 David Printz AU RC 6.00 15.00
106 D.J. King AU RC 6.00 15.00
107 J-F. Racine AU RC 8.00 20.00
108 Nathan McIver AU RC 6.00 15.00
109 S.O'Brien JSY AU/50 50.00 125.00
110 R.Shannon JSY AU/125 RC 15.00 40.00
111 David McKee JSY AU RC 12.00 30.00
112 Mark Stuart JSY AU RC 12.00 30.00
113 Matt Lashoff JSY AU RC 12.00 30.00
114 D.Stafford JSY AU RC 20.00 50.00
115 C.MacArthur JSY AU RC EX 15.00 40.00
116 Michael Funk JSY AU RC 12.00 30.00
117 Brandon Prust JSY AU RC 12.00 30.00
118 Dustin Boyd JSY AU RC 12.00 30.00
119 D.Byfuglien JSY AU RC 30.00 80.00
120 Dave Bolland JSY AU RC 20.00 50.00
121 M. Blunden JSY AU RC 12.00 30.00
122 Filip Novak JSY AU RC 12.00 30.00
123 F.Norrena JSY AU RC 12.00 30.00
124 N.Grossman JSY AU RC 20.00 50.00
125 Loui Eriksson JSY AU RC 25.00 60.00
126 T.Kopecky JSY AU RC 15.00 40.00
127 Stefan Liv JSY AU RC 25.00 60.00
128 P. Thoresen JSY AU RC EX 12.00 30.00
129 M-A.Pouliot JSY AU RC 12.00 30.00
130 Ladislav Smid JSY AU RC 12.00 30.00
131 Janis Sprukts JSY AU RC 12.00 30.00
132 J.Deslauriers JSY AU RC 12.00 30.00
133 David Booth JSY AU RC 15.00 40.00
134 K.Pushkarev JSY AU RC 15.00 40.00
135 P. O'Sullivan JSY AU RC 20.00 50.00
136 B.Pouliot JSY AU RC 15.00 40.00
137 N.Backstrom JSY AU RC 25.00 60.00
138 G.Latendresse JSY AU RC 20.00 50.00
139 Shea Weber JSY AU RC 80.00 200.00
140 J.Oduya JSY AU RC 20.00 50.00
141 Travis Zajac JSY AU RC 25.00 60.00
142 M.Marjamaki JSY AU RC 12.00 30.00
143 Nigel Dawes JSY AU RC 12.00 30.00
144 J.Immonen JSY AU RC 15.00 40.00
145 J.Hennessy JSY AU RC 12.00 30.00
146 Ryan Potulny JSY AU RC 12.00 30.00
147 J.Timonen JSY AU RC 15.00 40.00
148 Keith Yandle JSY AU RC 30.00 80.00
149 Michel Ouellet JSY AU RC 15.00 40.00
150 Noah Welch JSY AU RC 12.00 30.00
151 K. Letang JSY AU RC 100.00 250.00
152 Joe Pavelski JSY AU RC 150.00 400.00
153 Matt Carle JSY AU RC 12.00 30.00
154 M-E Vlasic JSY AU RC 20.00 50.00
155 Yan Stastny JSY AU RC 12.00 30.00
156 M. Schwarz JSY AU RC 20.00 50.00
157 R. Polak JSY AU RC 15.00 40.00
158 Karri Ramo JSY AU RC 12.00 30.00
159 Blair Jones JSY AU RC 12.00 30.00
160 Brendan Bell JSY AU RC 12.00 30.00
161 Ian White JSY AU RC 15.00 40.00
162 Ben Ondrus JSY AU RC 12.00 30.00
163 J. Williams JSY AU RC 12.00 30.00
164 M.Kopriva JSY AU RC 12.00 30.00
165 L. Bourdon JSY AU RC 25.00 60.00
166 J. Schultz JSY AU RC 12.00 30.00
167 A. Edler JSY AU RC 20.00 50.00
168 Eric Fehr JSY AU RC 20.00 50.00
169 J.Staal JSY AU/99 RC 150.00 300.00
170 P.Kessel JSY AU/99 RC 125.00 300.00
171 E.Malkin JSY AU/99 RC 700.00 1200.00
172 P.Stastny JSY AU/99 RC 150.00 300.00
173 A.Kopitar JSY AU/99 RC 800.00 2000.00
174 A.Radulov JSY AU/99 RC 50.00 125.00

2006-07 The Cup Foundations

CQAH Ales Hemsky 5.00 12.00
CQAK Anze Kopitar 20.00 50.00
CQAM Al MacInnis 8.00 20.00
CQAO Adam Oates 6.00 15.00
CQAR Andrew Raycroft 5.00 12.00
CQAY Alexei Yashin 5.00 12.00
CQBB Brad Boyes 4.00 10.00
CQBL Rob Blake 6.00 15.00
CQBS Billy Smith 6.00 15.00
CQCJ Curtis Joseph 8.00 20.00
CQCN Cam Neely 6.00 15.00
CQCP Chris Pronger 6.00 15.00
CQCW Cam Ward 6.00 15.00
CQDA Daniel Alfredsson 6.00 15.00
CQDC Dino Ciccarelli 6.00 15.00
CQDG Doug Gilmour 8.00 20.00
CQDH Dale Hawerchuk 6.00 15.00
CQDS Denis Savard 6.00 15.00
CQEB Ed Belfour 6.00 15.00
CQEL Eric Lindros 10.00 25.00
CQEM Evgeni Malkin 25.00 60.00
CQEN Evgeni Nabokov 5.00 12.00
CQES Eric Staal 8.00 20.00
CQFM Frank Mahovlich 6.00 15.00
CQGC Gerry Cheevers 6.00 15.00
CQGF Grant Fuhr 10.00 25.00
CQGH Gordie Howe 20.00 50.00
CQGL Guy Lafleur 8.00 20.00
CQGP Gilbert Perreault 6.00 15.00
CQHA Dominik Hasek 10.00 25.00
CQHE Dany Heatley 6.00 15.00
CQHL Henrik Lundqvist 15.00 40.00
CQHM Milan Hejduk 6.00 15.00
CQHZ Henrik Zetterberg 8.00 20.00
CQIK Ilya Kovalchuk 6.00 15.00
CQJB Jean Beliveau 6.00 15.00
CQJC Jonathan Cheechoo 5.00 12.00
CQJI Jarome Iginla 8.00 20.00
CQJJ Jaromir Jagr 20.00 50.00
CQJK Jari Kurri 6.00 15.00
CQJO Joe Sakic 12.00 30.00
CQJR Jeremy Roenick 10.00 25.00
CQJS Jordan Staal 10.00 25.00
CQJT Joe Thornton 10.00 25.00
CQKE Phil Kessel 12.00 30.00
CQKL Kari Lehtonen 5.00 12.00
CQLM Lanny McDonald 6.00 15.00
CQLR Larry Robinson 6.00 15.00
CQMA Stan Mikita 8.00 20.00
CQMB Martin Brodeur 15.00 40.00
CQMD Marcel Dionne 8.00 20.00
CQMG Marian Gaborik 6.00 15.00
CQMH Marian Hossa 6.00 15.00
CQMI Mike Bossy 6.00 15.00
CQML Mario Lemieux 25.00 60.00
CQMM Mike Modano 10.00 25.00
CQMN Markus Naslund 6.00 15.00
CQMR Michael Ryder 4.00 10.00
CQMS Martin St. Louis 6.00 15.00
CQMT Marty Turco 6.00 15.00
CQNL Nicklas Lidstrom 6.00 15.00
CQOK Olaf Kolzig 6.00 15.00
CQOV Alexander Ovechkin 25.00 60.00
CQPB Patrice Bergeron 8.00 20.00
CQPD Pavel Datsyuk 10.00 25.00
CQPE Patrik Elias 6.00 15.00
CQPF Peter Forsberg 12.00 30.00
CQPH Dion Phaneuf 5.00 12.00
CQPK Paul Kariya 6.00 15.00
CQPM Patrick Marleau 6.00 15.00
CQPR Patrick Roy 15.00 40.00
CQPS Peter Stastny 5.00 12.00
CQRB Ray Bourque 10.00 25.00
CQRD Rick DiPietro 5.00 12.00
CQRE Ron Ellis 4.00 10.00
CQRH Ron Hextall 6.00 15.00
CQRL Roberto Luongo 10.00 25.00
CQRM Ryan Miller 6.00 15.00
CQRN Rick Nash 6.00 15.00
CQRO Luc Robitaille 6.00 15.00
CQRS Ryan Smyth 5.00 12.00
CQRV Rogie Vachon 8.00 20.00
CQSA Borje Salming 6.00 15.00
CQSC Sidney Crosby 25.00 60.00
CQSF Sergei Fedorov 10.00 25.00
CQSG Simon Gagne 6.00 15.00
CQSH Brendan Shanahan 6.00 15.00
CQSK Saku Koivu 6.00 15.00
CQSM Miroslav Satan 5.00 12.00
CQSP Jason Spezza 6.00 15.00
CQSS Scott Stevens 6.00 15.00
CQST Steve Shutt 6.00 15.00
CQSU Mats Sundin 6.00 15.00
CQTE Tony Esposito 6.00 15.00
CQTH Jose Theodore 6.00 15.00
CQTS Teemu Selanne 12.00 30.00
CQTV Tomas Vokoun 5.00 12.00
CQVL Vincent Lecavalier 6.00 15.00
CQWG Wayne Gretzky 40.00 100.00

2006-07 The Cup Enshrinements

EAK Anze Kopitar 50.00 125.00
EAR Andrew Raycroft 12.00 30.00
EBO Bobby Orr 60.00 150.00
EBP Benoit Pouliot 12.00 30.00
ECD Chris Drury 12.00 30.00
ECN Cam Neely 15.00 40.00
ECW Cam Ward 15.00 40.00
EDB Dustin Boyd 10.00 25.00
EDH Dominik Hasek 25.00 60.00
EDP Dion Phaneuf 12.00 30.00
EDS Drew Stafford 15.00 40.00
EEM Evgeni Malkin 60.00 150.00
EES Eric Staal 20.00 50.00
EFM Frank Mahovlich 15.00 40.00
EGH Gordie Howe 50.00 125.00
EGL G. Latendresse 12.00 30.00
EGR Wayne Gretzky 200.00 500.00
EHE Dany Heatley 12.00 30.00
EHZ Henrik Zetterberg 20.00 50.00
EIK Ilya Kovalchuk 15.00 40.00
EJB Johnny Bucyk 15.00 40.00
EJC Jonathan Cheechoo 12.00 30.00
EJG J-S Giguere 15.00 40.00
EJI Jarome Iginla 20.00 50.00
EJK Jari Kurri 15.00 40.00
EJM Joe Mullen 12.00 30.00
EJS Jordan Staal 25.00 60.00
EJT Joe Thornton 25.00 60.00
EKL Kari Lehtonen 12.00 30.00
ELR Larry Robinson 15.00 40.00
EMB Martin Brodeur 40.00 100.00
EMD Marcel Dionne 20.00 50.00
EMF Marc-Andre Fleury 30.00 80.00
EMG Marian Gaborik 15.00 40.00
EML Mario Lemieux 60.00 150.00
EMR Michael Ryder 10.00 25.00
EMS Marek Svatos 10.00 25.00
EMT Marty Turco 15.00 40.00
ENL Nicklas Lidstrom 15.00 40.00
EPK Phil Kessel 30.00 80.00
EPL Pat LaFontaine 15.00 40.00
EPR Patrick Roy 40.00 100.00
EPS Paul Stastny 25.00 60.00
ERA Alexander Radulov 25.00 60.00
ERB Ray Bourque 25.00 60.00
ERH Ron Hextall 15.00 40.00
ERL Roberto Luongo 25.00 60.00
ERM Ryan Miller 15.00 40.00
ERN Rick Nash 15.00 40.00
ERS Ryan Smyth 15.00 40.00
ESC Sidney Crosby 100.00 200.00
ESS Steve Shutt 15.00 40.00
EST Scott Stevens 15.00 40.00
ETE Tony Esposito 15.00 40.00
ETV Tomas Vokoun 12.00 30.00
ETZ Travis Zajac 20.00 50.00
EVA Thomas Vanek 15.00 40.00
EVL Vincent Lecavalier 15.00 40.00
EVT Vesa Toskala 12.00 30.00
EWG Wayne Gretzky 200.00 500.00

2006-07 The Cup Gold

*GOLD: 1X TO 2.5X HI COLUMN
1 Teemu Selanne 15.00 40.00
2 Jean-Sebastien Giguere 12.00 30.00
3 Kari Lehtonen 15.00 40.00
4 Ilya Kovalchuk 20.00 50.00
5 Phil Esposito 20.00 50.00
6 Don Cherry 15.00 40.00
7 Ray Bourque 25.00 60.00
8 Bobby Orr 50.00 100.00
9 Cam Neely 20.00 50.00
10 Patrice Bergeron 15.00 40.00
11 Johnny Bucyk 10.00 25.00
12 Ryan Miller 15.00 40.00
13 Gilbert Perreault 15.00 40.00
14 Jarome Iginla 20.00 50.00
15 Miikka Kiprusoff 15.00 40.00
16 Al MacInnis 8.00 20.00
17 Eric Staal 15.00 40.00
18 Cam Ward 15.00 40.00
19 Bobby Hull 25.00 60.00
20 Tony Esposito 15.00 40.00
21 Stan Mikita 15.00 40.00
22 Joe Sakic 30.00 80.00
23 Patrick Roy 40.00 100.00
24 Rick Nash 15.00 40.00
25 Sergei Fedorov 12.00 30.00
26 Mike Modano 15.00 40.00
27 Dominik Hasek 25.00 60.00
28 Henrik Zetterberg 20.00 50.00
29 Gordie Howe 30.00 80.00
30 Scotty Bowman 10.00 25.00
31 Ted Lindsay 8.00 20.00
32 Red Kelly 8.00 20.00
33 Ales Hemsky 8.00 20.00
34 Grant Fuhr 20.00 50.00
35 Jari Kurri 20.00 50.00
36 Ed Belfour 15.00 40.00
37 Wayne Gretzky 50.00 150.00
38 Rob Blake 12.00 30.00
39 Marcel Dionne 15.00 40.00
40 Luc Robitaille 12.00 30.00
41 Rogie Vachon 12.00 30.00
42 Dino Ciccarelli 8.00 20.00
43 Marian Gaborik 20.00 50.00
44 Saku Koivu 12.00 30.00
45 Michael Ryder 12.00 30.00
46 Guy Lafleur 25.00 60.00
47 Larry Robinson 12.00 30.00
48 Jean Beliveau 20.00 50.00
49 Jacques Lemaire 12.00 30.00
50 Paul Kariya 15.00 40.00
51 Tomas Vokoun 15.00 40.00
52 Martin Brodeur 40.00 100.00
53 Scott Stevens 12.00 30.00
54 Alexei Yashin 8.00 20.00
55 Al Arbour 8.00 20.00
56 Mike Bossy 12.00 30.00
57 Billy Smith 12.00 30.00
58 Denis Potvin 12.00 30.00
59 Jaromir Jagr 25.00 60.00
60 Brendan Shanahan 15.00 40.00
61 Henrik Lundqvist 20.00 50.00
62 Gump Worsley 12.00 30.00
63 Andy Bathgate 8.00 20.00
64 Jason Spezza 12.00 30.00
65 Dany Heatley 20.00 50.00
66 Peter Forsberg 25.00 60.00
67 Simon Gagne 15.00 40.00
68 Bernie Parent 15.00 40.00
69 Bobby Clarke 15.00 40.00
70 Ron Hextall 12.00 30.00
71 Jeremy Roenick 12.00 30.00
72 Shane Doan 8.00 20.00
73 Sidney Crosby 100.00 200.00
74 Marc-Andre Fleury 20.00 50.00
75 Mario Lemieux 40.00 100.00
76 Peter Stastny 12.00 30.00
77 Joe Thornton 25.00 60.00
78 Jonathan Cheechoo 15.00 40.00
79 Patrick Marleau 12.00 30.00
80 Bernie Federko 8.00 20.00
81 Vincent Lecavalier 15.00 40.00
82 Mats Sundin 15.00 40.00
83 Frank Mahovlich 15.00 40.00
84 Darryl Sittler 15.00 40.00
85 Johnny Bower 12.00 30.00
86 Borje Salming 12.00 30.00
87 Roberto Luongo 20.00 50.00
88 Markus Naslund 15.00 40.00
89 Alexander Ovechkin 40.00 100.00
90 Dale Hawerchuk 8.00 20.00

2006-07 The Cup Gold Rainbow Autographed Rookie Patches

*WHITE SWATCHES: .5X to 1X LO
109 Shane O'Brien/37 30.00 80.00
110 Ryan Shannon/38 30.00 80.00
111 David McKee/41 30.00 80.00
112 Mark Stuart/45 25.00 60.00
113 Matt Lashoff/49 25.00 60.00
114 Drew Stafford/21 50.00 100.00
115 C. MacArthur/41 EXCH 50.00 100.00
117 Brandon Prust/37 20.00 50.00
118 Dustin Boyd/43 20.00 50.00
119 Dustin Byfuglien/52 40.00 100.00
120 Dave Bolland/36 50.00 100.00
121 Michael Blunden/28 20.00 50.00
122 Filip Novak/17 20.00 50.00
123 Fredrik Norrena/30 40.00 100.00
125 Loui Eriksson/21 60.00 120.00
126 Tomas Kopecky/32 20.00 50.00
127 Stefan Liv/32 25.00 60.00
128 Patrick Thoresen/28 20.00 50.00
129 M-A Pouliot/36 30.00 80.00
131 Janis Sprukts/38 25.00 60.00
132 Jeff Deslauriers/39 20.00 50.00
133 David Booth/46 25.00 60.00
136 Benoit Pouliot/67 25.00 60.00
137 Niklas Backstrom/32 60.00 150.00
138 G.Latendresse/84 50.00 100.00
140 Johnny Oduya/29 20.00 50.00
141 Travis Zajac/19 40.00 100.00
142 Masi Marjamaki/58 30.00 80.00
144 Jarkko Immonen/38 25.00 60.00
145 Josh Hennesy/36 30.00 80.00
147 J. Timonen/46 EXCH 25.00 60.00
151 Kris Letang/58 75.00 150.00
152 Joe Pavelski/53 125.00 300.00
153 Matt Carle/18
154 M-E Vlasic/43 30.00 80.00
155 Yan Stastny/43 25.00 60.00
156 M. Schwarz/40 EXCH
157 Roman Polak/46 15.00 40.00
158 Karri Ramo/31 25.00 60.00
159 Blair Jones/49 20.00 50.00
160 Brendan Bell/36 20.00 50.00

162 Ben Ondrus/46 20.00 50.00
163 Jeremy Williams/48 20.00 50.00
164 Miroslav Kopriva/31 25.00 60.00
166 Jesse Schultz/20 40.00 100.00
167 Alexander Edler/23 40.00 100.00
170 Phil Kessel/81 100.00 250.00
171 Evgeni Malkin/71 400.00 800.00
172 Paul Stastny/26 60.00 120.00
173 Anze Kopitar/11 500.00 700.00
174 A. Radulov/47 EXCH 100.00 250.00

2006-07 The Cup Gold Rainbow Autographed Rookies

91 Nate Thompson/52 10.00 25.00
92 Mike Brown/70 10.00 25.00
93 Mike Card/33 10.00 25.00
94 Adam Dennis/35
95 Carsen Germyn/39 10.00 25.00
96 Adam Burish/37 8.00 20.00
97 Drew Larman/50 10.00 25.00
98 Jonas Johansson/45 8.00 20.00
99 Joel Perrault/26 10.00 25.00
100 Mikko Lehtonen/42 8.00 20.00
101 Alex Brooks/8
102 Frank Doyle/1
103 Billy Thompson/31
104 Kelly Guard/32 12.00 30.00
105 David Printz/28 12.00 30.00
106 D.J. King/19 12.00 30.00
107 J-F Racine/35 12.00 30.00
108 Nathan McIver/45 10.00 25.00

2006-07 The Cup Honorable Numbers

HNAH A. Hemsky/83 EXCH 25.00 60.00
HNAO Adam Oates/12
HNBC Bobby Clarke/16
HNBS Billy Smith/31 50.00 100.00
HNCH Jonathan Cheechoo/14
HNCW Cam Ward/30 40.00 80.00
HNDC D. Ciccarelli/20 EXCH 40.00 80.00
HNDE Denis Savard/18 60.00 125.00
HNDS Darryl Sittler/27 40.00 80.00
HNDW Doug Wilson/24 50.00 100.00
HNEM Evgeni Malkin/71 150.00 300.00
HNEN Evgeni Nabokov/20 50.00 100.00
HNES Eric Staal/12 20.00 50.00
HNGF Grant Fuhr/31 50.00 100.00
HNGL G. Latendresse/84 15.00 40.00
HNGO S. Gomez/23 EXCH 50.00 100.00
HNHA Dominik Hasek/39 40.00 80.00
HNHE Dany Heatley/15 20.00 50.00
HNHL Henrik Lundqvist/30 100.00 200.00
HNHM Milan Hejduk/23 30.00 80.00
HNHZ Henrik Zetterberg/40 75.00 150.00
HNIK Ilya Kovalchuk/17 40.00 100.00
HNJC Jeff Carter/17 60.00 125.00
HNJG Jean-Sebastien Giguere/35 40.00 80.00
HNJI Jarome Iginla/12 30.00 80.00
HNJK Jari Kurri/17 125.00 250.00
HNJS Jason Spezza/19 80.00 140.00
HNJT Joe Thornton/19 75.00 150.00
HNKL K.Lehtonen/32 EXCH 50.00 100.00
HNLE Loui Eriksson/21 30.00 80.00
HNLR Larry Robinson/19 40.00 80.00
HNMA Stan Mikita/21 60.00 125.00
HNMB Martin Brodeur/30 125.00 250.00
HNMC Matt Carle/18 40.00 100.00
HNMD Marcel Dionne/16 60.00 125.00
HNMH Martin Havlat/24 20.00 50.00
HNMI Mike Bossy/22 50.00 100.00
HNML Mario Lemieux/66 100.00 200.00
HNMN Markus Naslund/19 75.00 150.00
HNMR Michael Ryder/73 15.00 40.00
HNMS Martin St. Louis/26 50.00 100.00
HNMT Marty Turco/35 25.00 60.00
HNMU Larry Murphy/55 15.00 40.00
HNNZ Nikolai Zherdev/13 20.00 50.00
HNPA Paul Henderson/19 50.00 100.00
HNPB Patrice Bergeron/37 40.00 80.00
HNPE Patrik Elias/26 25.00 60.00
HNPK Phil Kessel/81 40.00 80.00
HNPL Pat LaFontaine/16
HNPM Patrick Marleau/12 50.00 100.00
HNPO Patrick O'Sullivan/12 30.00 80.00
HNPR Patrick Roy/33 125.00 250.00
HNPS Paul Stastny/26 50.00 120.00
HNRA A. Radulov/47 EXCH 60.00 125.00
HNRH Ron Hextall/27 40.00 100.00
HNRM Ryan Miller/30 50.00 120.00
HNRN Rick Nash/61 30.00 80.00
HNRO Luc Robitaille/20 25.00 60.00
HNRS Ryan Smyth/94 EXCH 25.00 60.00
HNSA Borje Salming/21 40.00 80.00
HNSC Sidney Crosby/87 150.00 300.00
HNSG Simon Gagne/12 30.00 80.00
HNSH Steve Shutt/22 25.00 60.00
HNSM Miroslav Satan/81 25.00 60.00
HNST Peter Stastny/26 40.00 80.00
HNSV Marek Svatos/40 25.00 60.00
HNTE Tony Esposito/35 60.00 125.00
HNTH Jose Theodore/60 12.00 30.00
HNTV Tomas Vokoun/29 40.00 80.00
HNTW Tiger Williams/22 25.00 60.00
HNWG Wayne Gretzky/99 400.00 1000.00
HNZC Zdeno Chara/33 25.00 60.00

2006-07 The Cup Jerseys

1 Teemu Selanne 12.00 30.00
2 Jean-Sebastien Giguere 6.00 15.00
3 Kari Lehtonen 5.00 12.00
4 Ilya Kovalchuk 6.00 15.00
7 Ray Bourque 10.00 25.00
9 Cam Neely 6.00 15.00
10 Patrice Bergeron 8.00 20.00
12 Ryan Miller 6.00 15.00
13 Gilbert Perreault 6.00 15.00
14 Jarome Iginla 8.00 20.00
15 Miikka Kiprusoff 6.00 15.00
16 Al MacInnis 8.00 20.00
17 Eric Staal 8.00 20.00
18 Cam Ward 6.00 15.00
19 Bobby Hull 12.00 30.00
20 Tony Esposito 6.00 15.00
21 Stan Mikita 8.00 20.00
22 Joe Sakic 12.00 30.00
23 Patrick Roy 15.00 40.00
24 Rick Nash 6.00 15.00
25 Sergei Fedorov 10.00 25.00
26 Mike Modano 10.00 25.00
27 Dominik Hasek 10.00 25.00
28 Henrik Zetterberg 8.00 20.00
29 Gordie Howe 20.00 50.00
33 Ales Hemsky 5.00 12.00
34 Grant Fuhr 10.00 25.00
35 Jari Kurri 6.00 15.00
36 Ed Belfour 6.00 15.00
37 Wayne Gretzky 40.00 100.00
38 Rob Blake 6.00 15.00
39 Marcel Dionne 8.00 20.00
40 Luc Robitaille 6.00 15.00
41 Rogie Vachon 8.00 20.00
42 Dino Ciccarelli 6.00 15.00
43 Marian Gaborik 6.00 15.00
44 Saku Koivu 6.00 15.00
45 Michael Ryder 4.00 10.00
46 Guy Lafleur 8.00 20.00
47 Larry Robinson 6.00 15.00
48 Jean Beliveau 6.00 15.00
50 Paul Kariya 6.00 15.00
51 Tomas Vokoun 5.00 12.00
52 Martin Brodeur 15.00 40.00
53 Scott Stevens 6.00 15.00
54 Alexei Yashin 5.00 12.00
56 Mike Bossy 6.00 15.00
57 Billy Smith 6.00 15.00
59 Jaromir Jagr 20.00 50.00
60 Brendan Shanahan 6.00 15.00
61 Henrik Lundqvist 15.00 40.00
62 Gump Worsley 6.00 15.00
64 Jason Spezza 6.00 15.00
65 Dany Heatley 5.00 12.00
66 Peter Forsberg 12.00 30.00
67 Simon Gagne 6.00 15.00
69 Bobby Clarke 10.00 25.00
70 Ron Hextall 6.00 15.00
71 Jeremy Roenick 10.00 25.00
72 Shane Doan 5.00 12.00
73 Sidney Crosby 25.00 60.00
74 Marc-Andre Fleury 12.00 30.00
75 Mario Lemieux 25.00 60.00
76 Peter Stastny 5.00 12.00
77 Joe Thornton 10.00 25.00
78 Jonathan Cheechoo 5.00 12.00
79 Patrick Marleau 6.00 15.00
80 Bernie Federko 5.00 12.00
81 Vincent Lecavalier 6.00 15.00
82 Mats Sundin 6.00 15.00
83 Frank Mahovlich 6.00 15.00
84 Darryl Sittler 8.00 20.00
86 Borje Salming 6.00 15.00
87 Roberto Luongo 10.00 25.00
88 Markus Naslund 6.00 15.00
89 Alexander Ovechkin 25.00 60.00
90 Dale Hawerchuk 8.00 20.00

2006-07 The Cup Limited Logos Autographs

*SINGLE COLOR SWATCH: .5X TO 1X LO
LLAF Alexander Frolov/50 75.00 150.00
LLAH Ales Hemsky/50 30.00 80.00
LLAK Anze Kopitar/50 150.00 300.00
LLAM Al MacInnis/50 60.00 125.00
LLAO Adam Oates/50 30.00 80.00
LLAR Andrew Raycroft/50 30.00 80.00
LLAT Alex Tanguay/50 25.00 60.00
LLAY Alexei Yashin/50 30.00 80.00
LLBB Brad Boyes/50 20.00 50.00
LLBC Bobby Clarke/50 60.00 120.00
LLBF Bernie Federko/50 30.00 80.00
LLBG Brian Gionta/50 30.00 80.00
LLBL Bill Ranford/50 30.00 80.00
LLBO Mike Bossy/50 75.00 150.00
LLBS Billy Smith/50 30.00 80.00
LLCA Jeff Carter/50 50.00 120.00
LLCN Cam Neely/50 75.00 200.00
LLCW Cam Ward/50 30.00 80.00
LLDA David Aebischer/50 30.00 80.00
LLDB Daniel Briere/50 30.00 80.00
LLDC Dino Ciccarelli/50 30.00 80.00
LLDE Denis Savard/50 60.00 125.00
LLDG Doug Gilmour/50 75.00 150.00
LLDH Dale Hawerchuk/50 40.00 100.00
LLDO Dominik Hasek/50 60.00 125.00
LLDR Dwayne Roloson/50 30.00 80.00
LLDS Darryl Sittler/50 30.00 80.00
LLDW Doug Wilson/50 30.00 80.00
LLEM Evgeni Malkin/50 125.00 250.00
LLES Eric Staal/50 25.00 60.00
LLGA Glenn Anderson/50 25.00 60.00
LLGE Martin Gerber/50
LLGH Gordie Howe/10
LLGL Guy Lafleur/50 60.00 125.00
LLGP Gilbert Perreault/50 40.00 100.00
LLHE Dany Heatley/50 25.00 60.00
LLHL Henrik Lundqvist/50 100.00 200.00
LLHZ Henrik Zetterberg/50 75.00 150.00
LLIK Ilya Kovalchuk/50 40.00 100.00
LLJC Jonathan Cheechoo/50 30.00 80.00
LLJG Jean-Sebastien Giguere/50 50.00 100.00
LLJI Jarome Iginla/50 75.00 150.00
LLJK Jari Kurri/50 60.00 125.00
LLJM Joe Mullen/50 25.00 60.00
LLJR Jeremy Roenick/50 40.00 100.00
LLJS Jordan Staal/50 40.00 100.00
LLJT Joe Thornton/50 75.00 150.00
LLKL Kari Lehtonen/50 25.00 60.00
LLLM Lanny McDonald/50 20.00 50.00
LLLR Larry Robinson/50 30.00 80.00
LLMB Martin Brodeur/50 100.00 200.00
LLMG Marian Gaborik/50 30.00 80.00
LLMH Martin Havlat/50 25.00 60.00
LLMI Milan Hejduk/50 25.00 60.00
LLML Mario Lemieux/50 150.00 300.00
LLMM Mike Modano/50 40.00 100.00
LLMR Michael Ryder/50 25.00 60.00
LLMS Marek Svatos/50 20.00 50.00
LLMT Marty Turco/50 25.00 60.00
LLMU Larry Murphy/50
LLNK Nikolai Khabibulin/50 30.00 80.00
LLNL Nicklas Lidstrom/50 60.00 125.00
LLNZ Nikolai Zherdev/50 20.00 50.00
LLON Owen Nolan/50 25.00 60.00
LLOV Alexander Ovechkin/50 1200.00 3000.00
LLPA Paul Henderson/25 75.00 150.00
LLPB Patrice Bergeron/50 30.00 80.00
LLPE Patrik Elias/50 25.00 60.00
LLPH Dion Phaneuf/50 100.00 200.00
LLPK Phil Kessel/25 75.00 150.00
LLPL Pat LaFontaine/50 60.00 125.00
LLPM Patrick Marleau/50 30.00 80.00
LLPR Patrick Roy/50 150.00 300.00
LLPS Peter Stastny/50 30.00 80.00
LLRL Roberto Luongo/50 60.00 125.00
LLRM Ryan Miller/50 50.00 100.00
LLRN Rick Nash/50 60.00 150.00
LLRS Ryan Smyth/50 30.00 80.00
LLRV Rogie Vachon/50 30.00 80.00
LLSA Borje Salming/50 40.00 100.00
LLSC Sidney Crosby/50 300.00 600.00
LLSG Simon Gagne/50 30.00 80.00
LLSH Steve Shutt/50 30.00 80.00
LLSK Saku Koivu/50 30.00 80.00
LLSM Miroslav Satan/50 30.00 80.00
LLSS Scott Stevens/50 30.00 80.00
LLST Martin St. Louis/50 40.00 100.00
LLTB Todd Bertuzzi/50 30.00 80.00
LLTH Jose Theodore/50 25.00 60.00
LLTU Darcy Tucker/50 40.00 100.00
LLTV Tomas Vokoun/50 40.00 100.00
LLVL Vincent Lecavalier/50 100.00 200.00
LLVT Vesa Toskala/50 30.00 80.00
LLWC Wendel Clark/50 75.00 150.00
LLWG Wayne Gretzky/50 500.00 1200.00
LLZC Zdeno Chara/50 30.00 80.00

2006-07 The Cup Rookies Platinum

91 Nate Thompson 8.00 20.00
92 Mike Brown 8.00 20.00
93 Mike Card 8.00 20.00
94 Adam Dennis 8.00 20.00
95 Carsen Germyn 8.00 20.00
96 Adam Burish 12.00 30.00
97 Drew Larman 8.00 20.00
98 Jonas Johansson 8.00 20.00
99 Joel Perrault 8.00 20.00
100 Mikko Lehtonen 10.00 25.00
101 Alex Brooks 8.00 20.00
102 Frank Doyle 10.00 25.00
103 Billy Thompson 8.00 20.00
104 Kelly Guard 10.00 25.00
105 David Printz 8.00 20.00
106 D.J. King 8.00 20.00
107 Jean-Francois Racine 10.00 25.00
108 Nathan McIver 8.00 20.00
109 Shane O'Brien 8.00 20.00
110 Ryan Shannon 8.00 20.00
111 David McKee 8.00 20.00
112 Mark Stuart 8.00 20.00
113 Matt Lashoff 8.00 20.00
114 Drew Stafford 12.00 30.00
115 Clarke MacArthur 10.00 25.00
116 Michael Funk 8.00 20.00
117 Brandon Prust 8.00 20.00
118 Dustin Boyd 8.00 20.00
119 Dustin Byfuglien 20.00 50.00
120 Dave Bolland 12.00 30.00
121 Michael Blunden 8.00 20.00
122 Filip Novak 8.00 20.00
123 Fredrik Norrena 8.00 20.00
124 Niklas Grossman 12.00 30.00
125 Loui Eriksson 15.00 40.00
126 Tomas Kopecky 10.00 25.00
127 Stefan Liv 8.00 20.00
128 Patrick Thoresen 8.00 20.00
129 Marc-Antoine Pouliot 8.00 20.00
130 Ladislav Smid 8.00 20.00
131 Janis Sprukts 8.00 20.00
132 Jeff Drouin-Deslauriers 8.00 20.00
133 David Booth 10.00 25.00
134 Konstantin Pushkarev 10.00 25.00
135 Patrick O'Sullivan 12.00 30.00
136 Benoit Pouliot 10.00 25.00
137 Niklas Backstrom 15.00 40.00
138 Guillaume Latendresse 12.00 30.00
139 Shea Weber 20.00 50.00
140 Johnny Oduya 12.00 30.00
141 Travis Zajac 15.00 40.00
142 Masi Marjamaki 8.00 20.00
143 Nigel Dawes 8.00 20.00
144 Jarkko Immonen 10.00 25.00
145 Josh Hennessy 8.00 20.00
146 Ryan Potulny 8.00 20.00
147 Jussi Timonen 10.00 25.00
148 Keith Yandle 20.00 50.00
149 Michel Ouellet 10.00 25.00
150 Noah Welch 8.00 20.00
151 Kristopher Letang 50.00 125.00
152 Joe Pavelski 75.00 150.00
153 Matt Carle 8.00 20.00
154 Marc-Edouard Vlasic 12.00 30.00
155 Yan Stastny 8.00 20.00
156 Marek Schwarz 12.00 30.00
157 Roman Polak 10.00 25.00
158 Karri Ramo 8.00 20.00
159 Blair Jones 8.00 20.00
160 Brendan Bell 8.00 20.00
161 Ian White 10.00 25.00
162 Ben Ondrus 8.00 20.00
163 Jeremy Williams 8.00 20.00
164 Miroslav Kopriva 8.00 20.00
165 Luc Bourdon 12.00 30.00
166 Jesse Schultz 8.00 20.00
167 Alexander Edler 12.00 30.00
168 Eric Fehr 12.00 30.00
169 Jordan Staal 50.00 125.00
170 Phil Kessel 25.00 60.00
171 Evgeni Malkin 150.00 300.00
172 Paul Stastny 50.00 125.00
173 Anze Kopitar 60.00 125.00
174 Alexander Radulov 15.00 40.00

2006-07 The Cup Scripted Swatches

SSAO Alexander Ovechkin 1500.00 4000.00
SSAR Andrew Raycroft 25.00 60.00
SSAT Alex Tanguay 25.00 60.00
SSBO Mike Bossy 50.00 100.00
SSBR Bill Ranford 30.00 80.00
SSBS Borje Salming 30.00 80.00
SSCD Chris Drury 25.00 60.00
SSCN Cam Neely 50.00 100.00
SSCW Cam Ward 25.00 60.00
SSDB Daniel Briere 30.00 80.00
SSDC D. Ciccarelli EXCH 30.00 80.00
SSDH Dale Hawerchuk 30.00 80.00
SSDS Denis Savard 30.00 80.00
SSDT Dave Taylor/10 125.00 250.00
SSDW Dave Williams 20.00 50.00
SSEM Evgeni Malkin 100.00 200.00
SSES Eric Staal 25.00 60.00
SSGA Glenn Anderson 25.00 60.00
SSGC Gerry Cheevers 30.00 80.00
SSGF Grant Fuhr 30.00 80.00
SSGL Guy Lafleur 50.00 100.00
SSGP Gilbert Perreault 30.00 80.00
SSHA Dominik Hasek 40.00 100.00
SSHE Dany Heatley 20.00 50.00
SSHL Henrik Lundqvist 100.00 200.00
SSHZ H. Zetterberg EXCH 75.00 150.00
SSIK Ilya Kovalchuk 30.00 80.00
SSJC Jonathan Cheechoo 25.00 60.00
SSJG Jean-Sebastien Giguere 25.00 60.00
SSJI Jarome Iginla 50.00 100.00
SSJK Jari Kurri 50.00 100.00
SSJM Joe Mullen 20.00 50.00
SSJS Jason Spezza
SSJT Joe Thornton 50.00 100.00
SSLR Larry Robinson 30.00 80.00
SSMB Martin Brodeur 150.00 250.00
SSMD Marcel Dionne 30.00 80.00
SSMG Marian Gaborik 30.00 80.00
SSMH Martin Havlat 20.00 50.00
SSMI Milan Hejduk 30.00 80.00
SSML Mario Lemieux 100.00 250.00
SSMM Mike Modano 30.00 80.00
SSMN Markus Naslund 30.00 80.00
SSMR Michael Ryder 25.00 60.00
SSMS Martin St. Louis 25.00 60.00
SSMT Marty Turco 25.00 60.00
SSNL Nicklas Lidstrom 30.00 80.00
SSPB Patrice Bergeron 30.00 80.00
SSPH Dion Phaneuf 30.00 80.00
SSPK Phil Kessel 30.00 80.00
SSPL P. LaFontaine EXCH 30.00 80.00
SSPM Patrick Marleau 25.00 60.00
SSPR Patrick Roy 75.00 150.00
SSRA A. Radulov EXCH 50.00 100.00
SSRB Ray Bourque 60.00 120.00
SSRE Ron Ellis 25.00 60.00
SSRH Ron Hextall 30.00 80.00
SSRL Roberto Luongo
SSRM Ryan Miller 50.00 100.00
SSRN Rick Nash 30.00 80.00
SSRO Luc Robitaille 30.00 80.00
SSRS Ryan Smyth 15.00 40.00
SSSC Sidney Crosby 150.00 300.00
SSSG Simon Gagne 25.00 60.00
SSSH Steve Shutt 20.00 50.00
SSSK Saku Koivu 25.00 60.00
SSSS Scott Stevens 60.00 125.00
SSST Jordan Staal 60.00 150.00
SSTE Tony Esposito 50.00 100.00
SSTH Jose Theodore 25.00 60.00
SSTV Tomas Vokoun 25.00 60.00
SSVL Vincent Lecavalier 50.00 100.00

2006-07 The Cup Signature Patches

*WHITE SWATCHES: .5X TO 1X LO
SPAF Alexander Frolov 20.00 50.00
SPAH A. Hemsky EXCH 20.00 50.00
SPAK Anze Kopitar 40.00 100.00
SPAM Al MacInnis 25.00 60.00
SPAO Alexander Ovechkin 1200.00 3000.00
SPAR A. Radulov EXCH 25.00 60.00
SPAT Alex Tanguay 25.00 60.00
SPBC Bobby Clarke 40.00 80.00
SPBR Martin Brodeur 75.00 150.00
SPBS Billy Smith 25.00 60.00
SPCH Cristobal Huet 20.00 50.00
SPCN Cam Neely 25.00 60.00
SPCW Cam Ward 25.00 60.00
SPDA David Aebischer 15.00 40.00
SPDB Daniel Briere 15.00 40.00
SPDC D. Ciccarelli EXCH 25.00 60.00
SPDH Dale Hawerchuk 25.00 60.00
SPDI Dion Phaneuf 25.00 60.00
SPDS Denis Savard 25.00 60.00
SPDT Dave Taylor 25.00 60.00
SPDW Doug Wilson 15.00 40.00
SPEL Patrik Elias 15.00 40.00
SPEM Evgeni Malkin 75.00 150.00
SPES Eric Staal 20.00 50.00
SPGC Gerry Cheevers 30.00 60.00
SPGF Grant Fuhr 30.00 60.00
SPGH Gordie Howe/25 175.00 300.00
SPGL Guy Lafleur 25.00 60.00
SPGO Scott Gomez 20.00 50.00
SPGP Gilbert Perreault 25.00 60.00
SPHA Dominik Hasek 40.00 80.00
SPHE Dany Heatley 20.00 50.00
SPHZ H. Zetterberg EXCH 30.00 80.00
SPIK Ilya Kovalchuk 25.00 60.00
SPJC Jonathan Cheechoo 25.00 60.00
SPJG Jean-Sebastien Giguere 25.00 60.00
SPJI Jarome Iginla 30.00 80.00
SPJK Jari Kurri 20.00 50.00
SPJO Jordan Staal 30.00 60.00
SPJR Jeremy Roenick 25.00 60.00
SPJS J. Spezza EXCH 20.00 50.00
SPJT Joe Thornton 30.00 80.00
SPKL Kari Lehtonen 25.00 60.00
SPLA G. Latendresse 25.00 60.00
SPLB Luc Bourdon 30.00 60.00
SPLM Lanny McDonald 15.00 40.00
SPLR Larry Robinson 15.00 40.00
SPLX Mario Lemieux/25 250.00 400.00
SPMB Mike Bossy 40.00 80.00
SPMC Matt Carle 15.00 40.00
SPMD Marcel Dionne/25 50.00 120.00
SPMG Marian Gaborik 25.00 60.00
SPMI Milan Hejduk 25.00 60.00
SPMM Mike Modano 25.00 60.00
SPMR Michael Ryder 25.00 60.00
SPMS Martin St. Louis 20.00 50.00
SPMT Marty Turco 15.00 40.00
SPNL Nicklas Lidstrom 20.00 50.00
SPPA Brad Park 15.00 40.00
SPPB Patrice Bergeron 20.00 50.00
SPPH Paul Henderson 25.00 50.00
SPPK Phil Kessel 30.00 80.00
SPPM Patrick Marleau 20.00 50.00
SPPO Patrick O'Sullivan 20.00 50.00
SPPS Paul Stastny 40.00 100.00
SPRA Andrew Raycroft 12.00 30.00
SPRE Ron Ellis 15.00 40.00
SPRH Ron Hextall 25.00 60.00
SPRI Richard Brodeur 15.00 40.00
SPRL Roberto Luongo 30.00 60.00
SPRM Ryan Miller 25.00 60.00
SPRN Rick Nash 20.00 50.00
SPRO Luc Robitaille 40.00 80.00
SPRS Ryan Smyth 25.00 60.00
SPRV Rogie Vachon 25.00 60.00
SPSA Borje Salming 20.00 50.00
SPSC Sidney Crosby 175.00 350.00
SPSE Scott Stevens 50.00 100.00
SPSG Simon Gagne 12.00 30.00
SPSK Saku Koivu 20.00 50.00
SPSM Stan Mikita 30.00 80.00
SPSS Steve Shutt 20.00 50.00
SPST Peter Stastny 15.00 40.00
SPSU Brent Sutter 15.00 40.00
SPSV Marek Svatos 15.00 40.00
SPTB Todd Bertuzzi 20.00 50.00
SPTE Tony Esposito 25.00 60.00
SPTH Jose Theodore 15.00 40.00
SPTV Tomas Vokoun 15.00 40.00
SPVL Vincent Lecavalier 20.00 50.00
SPWG Wayne Gretzky/25 400.00 1000.00
SPBO1 Ray Bourque 40.00 80.00
SPBO2 Ray Bourque 40.00 80.00
SPPR1 Patrick Roy 60.00 150.00
SPPR2 Patrick Roy 60.00 150.00

2006-07 The Cup Stanley Cup Signatures

CSAA Al Arbour 30.00 60.00
CSAM Al MacInnis 40.00 80.00
CSAT Alex Tanguay 25.00 50.00
CSBA Bob Baun 30.00 60.00
CSBC Bobby Clarke 30.00 60.00
CSBD Butch Bouchard 40.00 80.00
CSBH Bobby Hull 50.00 100.00
CSBI Bill Ranford 40.00 100.00
CSBO Bobby Orr 150.00 300.00
CSBP Bernie Parent 40.00 80.00
CSBR Martin Brodeur 100.00 200.00
CSBS Billy Smith 40.00 80.00
CSBU Johnny Bucyk 40.00 80.00
CSCG Clark Gillies 25.00 50.00
CSCM Craig MacTavish 25.00 50.00
CSCS Clint Smith 60.00 125.00
CSCW Cam Ward 30.00 80.00
CSDG Doug Gilmour 30.00 60.00
CSDH Dominik Hasek 50.00 100.00
CSDP Denis Potvin 25.00 50.00
CSES Eric Staal 30.00 60.00
CSFM Frank Mahovlich 40.00 80.00
CSFR Frank Mahovlich 30.00 60.00
CSGA Glenn Anderson 40.00 80.00
CSGC Gerry Cheevers 30.00 60.00
CSGF Grant Fuhr 40.00 80.00
CSGH Gordie Howe 75.00 175.00
CSGL Guy Lafleur 60.00 125.00
CSHE Milan Hejduk 25.00 50.00
CSJB Jean Beliveau 50.00 100.00
CSJK Jari Kurri 40.00 100.00
CSJL Jacques Lemaire 30.00 60.00
CSJM Joe Mullen 30.00 60.00
CSJO Johnny Bower 25.00 60.00
CSKE Red Kelly 30.00 60.00
CSLA Larry Murphy
CSLE Elmer Lach 40.00 80.00
CSLR Larry Robinson 20.00 50.00
CSMB Mike Bossy 40.00 80.00
CSML Mario Lemieux 150.00 300.00
CSMM Mike Modano 50.00 100.00
CSMS Milt Schmidt 40.00 80.00
CSMU Joe Mullen 30.00 60.00
CSNL Nicklas Lidstrom 40.00 80.00
CSPE Phil Esposito 30.00 60.00
CSPR Patrick Roy 150.00 250.00
CSRB Ray Bourque 50.00 100.00
CSRK Red Kelly 20.00 50.00
CSRL Reggie Leach
CSRO Patrick Roy 75.00 150.00
CSRV Rogie Vachon 30.00 60.00
CSSB Scotty Bowman 40.00 80.00
CSSH Steve Shutt 25.00 50.00
CSSM Stan Mikita 30.00 60.00
CSSS Scott Stevens
CSST Martin St. Louis 25.00 50.00
CSTL Ted Lindsay 30.00 60.00
CSVL Vincent Lecavalier 30.00 60.00
CSWG W. Gretzky 400.00 1000.00

2007-08 The Cup

1 Dale Hawerchuk 4.00 10.00
2 Bobby Hull 6.00 15.00
3 Alexander Ovechkin 12.00 30.00
4 Dino Ciccarelli 3.00 8.00
5 Markus Naslund 3.00 8.00
6 Roberto Luongo 5.00 12.00
7 Richard Brodeur 2.50 6.00
8 Mats Sundin 3.00 8.00
9 Frank Mahovlich 3.00 8.00
10 Darryl Sittler 4.00 10.00
11 Borje Salming 3.00 8.00
12 Vincent Lecavalier 3.00 8.00
13 Martin St. Louis 3.00 8.00
14 Brad Richards 3.00 8.00
15 Paul Kariya 3.00 8.00
16 Bernie Federko 2.50 6.00
17 Joe Mullen 2.50 6.00
18 Joe Thornton 5.00 12.00
19 Jonathan Cheechoo 2.50 6.00
20 Patrick Marleau 3.00 8.00
21 Sidney Crosby 12.00 30.00
22 Evgeni Malkin 6.00 15.00
23 Mario Lemieux 12.00 30.00
24 Marc-Andre Fleury 6.00 15.00
25 Jordan Staal 2.50 6.00
26 Shane Doan 2.50 6.00
27 Simon Gagne 3.00 8.00
28 Bobby Clarke 5.00 12.00
29 Ron Hextall 3.00 8.00
30 Bernie Parent 4.00 10.00
31 Dany Heatley 2.50 6.00
32 Jason Spezza 3.00 8.00
33 Daniel Alfredsson 3.00 8.00
34 Mark Messier 6.00 15.00
35 Jaromir Jagr 10.00 25.00
36 Brendan Shanahan 3.00 8.00
37 Brian Leetch 2.50 6.00
38 Andy Bathgate 2.50 6.00
39 Mike Bossy 3.00 8.00
40 Clark Gillies 3.00 8.00
41 Denis Potvin 3.00 8.00
42 Billy Smith 3.00 8.00
43 Martin Brodeur 8.00 20.00
44 Zach Parise 3.00 8.00
45 Alexander Radulov 3.00 8.00
46 Peter Forsberg 6.00 15.00
47 Saku Koivu 3.00 8.00
48 Michael Ryder 2.00 5.00
49 Larry Robinson 3.00 8.00
50 Guy Lafleur 4.00 10.00
51 Patrick Roy 8.00 20.00
52 Jean Beliveau 4.00 10.00
53 Marian Gaborik 3.00 8.00
54 Mikko Koivu 2.50 6.00
55 Marcel Dionne 4.00 10.00
56 Anze Kopitar 5.00 12.00
57 Rob Blake 3.00 8.00
58 Gordie Howe 10.00 25.00
59 Tomas Vokoun 2.50 6.00
60 Jari Kurri 3.00 8.00
61 Grant Fuhr 5.00 12.00
62 Wayne Gretzky 20.00 50.00
63 Ales Hemsky 2.50 6.00
64 Dwayne Roloson 2.50 6.00
65 Dominik Hasek 5.00 12.00
66 Henrik Zetterberg 4.00 10.00
67 Nicklas Lidstrom 3.00 8.00
68 Pavel Datsyuk 5.00 12.00
69 Marty Turco 3.00 8.00
70 Mike Modano 5.00 12.00
71 Rick Nash 3.00 8.00
72 Sergei Fedorov 5.00 12.00
73 Joe Sakic 6.00 15.00
74 Paul Stastny 2.50 6.00
75 Milan Hejduk 2.50 6.00
76 Stan Mikita 4.00 10.00
77 Tony Esposito 3.00 8.00
78 Nikolai Khabibulin 3.00 8.00
79 Denis Savard 3.00 8.00
80 Eric Staal 4.00 10.00
81 Cam Ward 3.00 8.00
82 Jarome Iginla 4.00 10.00
83 Miikka Kiprusoff 3.00 8.00
84 Lanny McDonald 3.00 8.00
85 Al MacInnis 4.00 10.00
86 Ryan Miller 3.00 8.00
87 Gilbert Perreault 3.00 8.00
88 Thomas Vanek 2.50 6.00
89 Patrice Bergeron 4.00 10.00
90 Ray Bourque 5.00 12.00
91 Cam Neely 3.00 8.00
92 Bobby Orr 12.00 30.00
93 Johnny Bucyk 3.00 8.00
94 Phil Kessel 3.00 8.00
95 Ilya Kovalchuk 3.00 8.00
96 Marian Hossa 3.00 8.00
97 Kari Lehtonen 2.50 6.00
98 Jean-Sebastien Giguere 3.00 8.00
99 Ryan Getzlaf 3.00 8.00
100 Teemu Selanne 6.00 15.00
101 Matt Keetley AU RC 6.00 15.00
102 Tyler Kennedy AU RC 6.00 15.00
103 Petteri Wirtanen AU RC 6.00 15.00
104 Matt Hunwick AU RC 6.00 15.00
105 Tomas Popperle AU RC 6.00 15.00
106 Johnny Boychuk AU RC 10.00 25.00
107 Alexander Nikulin AU RC 6.00 15.00
108 Mark Mancari AU RC 6.00 15.00
109 Craig Weller AU RC 6.00 15.00
110 Jake Dowell AU RC 6.00 15.00
111 David Clarkson AU RC 6.00 15.00
112 Drew MacIntyre AU RC 6.00 15.00
113 Kris Versteeg AU RC 20.00 50.00
114 Greg Moore AU RC 6.00 15.00
115 Tomas Plihal AU RC 6.00 15.00
116 Mike Lundin AU RC 6.00 15.00
117 Rich Peverley AU RC 6.00 15.00
118 Cody Bass AU RC 6.00 15.00
119 Bobby Ryan JSY AU RC 15.00 40.00
120 Ondrej Pavelec JSY AU RC 25.00 60.00
121 Jack Johnson JSY AU RC 8.00 20.00
122 Nicklas Bergfors JSY AU RC 6.00 15.00
123 Erik Johnson JSY AU RC 10.00 25.00
124 Bryan Little JSY AU RC 10.00 25.00
125 Kris Russell JSY AU RC 10.00 25.00
126 Matt Niskanen JSY AU RC 10.00 25.00
127 A.Cogliano JSY AU RC 8.00 20.00
128 J.Bernier JSY AU RC 12.00 30.00
129 Marc Staal JSY AU RC 10.00 25.00
130 Nick Foligno JSY AU RC 12.00 30.00
131 Peter Mueller JSY AU RC 8.00 20.00
132 Brett Sterling JSY AU RC 6.00 15.00
133 Petr Kalus JSY AU RC 6.00 15.00
134 Rob Schremp JSY AU RC 8.00 20.00
135 Andy Greene JSY AU RC 8.00 20.00
136 Frans Nielsen JSY AU RC 25.00 60.00
137 Martin Hanzal JSY AU RC 8.00 20.00
138 Devin Setoguchi JSY AU RC 10.00 25.00
139 Matt Smaby JSY AU RC 6.00 15.00
140 James Sheppard JSY AU RC 6.00 15.00
141 Kyle Chipchura JSY AU RC 10.00 25.00
142 Ryan Parent JSY AU RC 6.00 15.00
143 David Krejci JSY AU RC 40.00 100.00
144 Lauri Tukonen JSY AU RC 6.00 15.00
145 Anton Stralman JSY AU RC 6.00 15.00
146 Tobias Enstrom JSY AU RC 10.00 25.00
147 B.Dubinsky JSY AU RC 12.00 30.00
148 M.Raymond JSY AU RC 10.00 25.00
149 Drew Miller JSY AU RC 8.00 20.00
150 Curtis McElhinney JSY AU RC 10.00 25.00
151 Ryan Callahan JSY AU RC 12.00 30.00
152 Brian Elliott JSY AU RC 12.00 30.00
153 J.Sigalet JSY AU RC 6.00 15.00
154 Ville Koistinen JSY AU RC 6.00 15.00
155 Torrey Mitchell JSY AU RC 8.00 20.00
156 David Perron JSY AU RC 20.00 50.00
157 Jannik Hansen JSY AU RC 8.00 20.00
158 Jaroslav Halak JSY AU RC 20.00 50.00
159 Milan Lucic JSY AU RC 25.00 60.00
160 Lukas Kaspar JSY AU RC 6.00 15.00
161 Marc Methot JSY AU RC 6.00 15.00
162 Tyler Weiman JSY AU RC 8.00 20.00
163 Ryan Carter JSY AU RC 6.00 15.00
164 Jared Boll JSY AU RC 8.00 20.00
165 Jonas Hiller JSY AU RC 12.00 30.00
166 J.Hlinka JSY AU RC 8.00 20.00
167 Matt Ellis JSY AU RC 8.00 20.00
168 Cory Murphy JSY AU RC 6.00 15.00
169 Steve Wagner JSY AU RC 6.00 15.00
170 Stefan Meyer JSY AU RC 8.00 20.00
171 Daniel Carcillo JSY AU RC 8.00 20.00
172 Tuukka Rask JSY AU RC 60.00 150.00
173 David Jones JSY AU RC 6.00 15.00
174 Tobias Stephan JSY AU RC 8.00 20.00
175 Tom Gilbert JSY AU RC 8.00 20.00
176 Cal Clutterbuck JSY AU RC 10.00 25.00
177 Rod Pelley JSY AU RC 6.00 15.00
178 Daniel Girardi JSY AU RC 8.00 20.00
179 Chris Bourque JSY AU RC 8.00 20.00
180 T.J. Hensick JSY AU RC 8.00 20.00
181 Steve Downie JSY AU RC 8.00 20.00
182 Jack Skille JSY AU RC 8.00 20.00
183 Casey Borer JSY AU RC 6.00 15.00
184 S.Kostitsyn JSY AU RC 8.00 20.00
185 P.Kane JSY AU/99 RC 800.00 1500.00
186 S.Gagner JSY AU/99 RC 30.00 80.00
187 N.Backstrom JSY AU/99 RC 200.00 500.00
188 Jiri Tlusty JSY AU/99 RC 25.00 60.00
189 C.Price JSY AU/99 RC 1500.00 4000.00
190 J.Toews JSY AU/99 RC 1500.00 3000.00

2007-08 The Cup Chirography

CCAM Al MacInnis 15.00 40.00
CCAO Alexander Ovechkin 50.00 120.00
CCBC Bobby Clarke 20.00 50.00
CCBF Bernie Federko 10.00 25.00
CCBH Bobby Hull 25.00 60.00
CCBL Brian Leetch 10.00 25.00
CCBO Bobby Orr 50.00 125.00
CCBP Bernie Parent 15.00 40.00
CCBR Martin Brodeur 30.00 80.00
CCCG Clark Gillies 12.00 30.00
CCCN Cam Neely 12.00 30.00
CCDC Dino Ciccarelli 12.00 30.00
CCDH Dany Heatley 10.00 25.00
CCDP Denis Potvin 12.00 30.00
CCDS Darryl Sittler 15.00 40.00
CCEM Evgeni Malkin 25.00 60.00
CCES Eric Staal 15.00 40.00
CCFM Frank Mahovlich 12.00 30.00
CCGF Grant Fuhr 20.00 50.00
CCGH Gordie Howe 60.00 150.00
CCGL Guy Lafleur 30.00 80.00
CCGP Gilbert Perreault 12.00 30.00
CCHA Dale Hawerchuk 15.00 40.00
CCIK Ilya Kovalchuk 12.00 30.00
CCJB Jean Beliveau 30.00 80.00
CCJC Jonathan Cheechoo 10.00 25.00
CCJI Jarome Iginla 15.00 40.00
CCJK Jari Kurri 12.00 30.00
CCJM Joe Mullen 10.00 25.00
CCJT Joe Thornton 20.00 50.00
CCLM Lanny McDonald 12.00 30.00
CCLR Luc Robitaille 12.00 30.00
CCMB Mike Bossy 12.00 30.00
CCMD Marcel Dionne 15.00 40.00
CCMG Marian Gaborik 12.00 30.00
CCML Mario Lemieux 50.00 125.00
CCMM Mark Messier 25.00 60.00
CCMN Markus Naslund 12.00 30.00
CCMO Mike Modano 20.00 50.00
CCMS Martin St. Louis 12.00 30.00
CCMT Marty Turco 12.00 30.00
CCPE Phil Esposito 20.00 50.00
CCPR Patrick Roy 50.00 125.00
CCRB Ray Bourque 20.00 50.00
CCRH Ron Hextall 12.00 30.00
CCRO Larry Robinson 12.00 30.00
CCSA Borje Salming 12.00 30.00
CCSC Sidney Crosby 50.00 125.00
CCSD Shane Doan 10.00 25.00
CCSG Simon Gagne 12.00 30.00
CCSK Saku Koivu 12.00 30.00
CCSM Stan Mikita 25.00 60.00
CCTE Tony Esposito 12.00 30.00
CCVL Vincent Lecavalier 12.00 30.00
CCWG Wayne Gretzky 250.00 600.00

2007-08 The Cup Enshrinements

EAM Al MacInnis 15.00 40.00
EAO Alexander Ovechkin 150.00 400.00
EBC Bobby Clarke 20.00 50.00
EBF Bernie Federko 10.00 25.00
EBH Bobby Hull 25.00 60.00
EBL Brian Leetch 10.00 25.00
EBO Bobby Orr 50.00 125.00
EBP Bernie Parent 15.00 40.00
ECG Clark Gillies 12.00 30.00
ECN Cam Neely 12.00 30.00
EDC Dino Ciccarelli 12.00 30.00
EDH Dany Heatley 10.00 25.00
EDP Denis Potvin 12.00 30.00
EDS Darryl Sittler 15.00 40.00
EEM Evgeni Malkin 25.00 60.00
EES Eric Staal 15.00 40.00
EFM Frank Mahovlich 12.00 30.00
EGF Grant Fuhr 20.00 50.00
EGH Gordie Howe 50.00 125.00
EGL Guy Lafleur 15.00 40.00
EGP Gilbert Perreault 12.00 30.00
EHA Dale Hawerchuk 15.00 40.00
EIK Ilya Kovalchuk 12.00 30.00
EJB Jean Beliveau 15.00 40.00
EJC Jonathan Cheechoo 10.00 25.00
EJI Jarome Iginla 15.00 40.00
EJK Jari Kurri 12.00 30.00
EJM Joe Mullen 10.00 25.00
EJT Joe Thornton 20.00 50.00
ELM Lanny McDonald 12.00 30.00
ELR Luc Robitaille 12.00 30.00
EMB Martin Brodeur 30.00 80.00
EMD Marcel Dionne 15.00 40.00
EMG Marian Gaborik 12.00 30.00
EMI Mike Bossy 12.00 30.00
EML Mario Lemieux 50.00 125.00
EMM Mark Messier 25.00 60.00

EMN Markus Naslund 12.00 30.00
EMO Mike Modano 20.00 50.00
EMS Martin St. Louis 12.00 30.00
EMT Marty Turco 12.00 30.00
EPE Phil Esposito 20.00 50.00
EPR Patrick Roy 30.00 80.00
ERB Ray Bourque 20.00 50.00
ERH Ron Hextall 12.00 30.00
ERO Larry Robinson 12.00 30.00
ESA Borje Salming 12.00 30.00
ESC Sidney Crosby 50.00 125.00
ESD Shane Doan 10.00 25.00
ESG Simon Gagne 12.00 30.00
ESK Saku Koivu 12.00 30.00
ESM Stan Mikita 15.00 40.00
ETE Tony Esposito 12.00 30.00
EVL Vincent Lecavalier 12.00 30.00
EWG Wayne Gretzky 250.00 600.00

2007-08 The Cup Enshrinements Duals

E2BG M.Bossy/C.Gillies 25.00 60.00
E2BR J.Beliveau/L.Robinson 30.00 80.00
E2CP B.Clarke/B.Parent 40.00 100.00
E2DH S.Doan/D.Heatley 20.00 50.00
E2EB P.Esposito/R.Bourque 40.00 100.00
E2EM T.Esposito/S.Mikita 30.00 80.00
E2EP T.Esposito/G.Perreault 25.00 60.00
E2FK G.Fuhr/J.Kurri 40.00 100.00
E2FM B.Federko/A.MacInnis 30.00 80.00
E2FS M.Fleury/J.Staal 50.00 125.00
E2GM W.Gretzky/M.Messier 300.00 800.00
E2GS S.Gagne/M.St. Louis 15.00 40.00
E2HM G.Howe/M.Messier 80.00 200.00
E2HP R.Hextall/B.Parent 30.00 80.00
E2IM J.Iginla/L.McDonald 30.00 80.00
E2KO Kovalchuk/Ovechkin 200.00 500.00
E2LC Lecavalier/Cheechoo 25.00 60.00
E2LM M.Lemieux/E.Malkin 100.00 250.00
E2LS Lidstrom/Salming 25.00 60.00
E2MM M.Modano/J.Mullen 40.00 100.00
E2MS F.Mahovlich/D.Sittler 30.00 80.00
E2OG B.Orr/W.Gretzky 200.00 500.00
E2OH B.Orr/G.Howe 100.00 250.00
E2PR D.Potvin/L.Robinson 25.00 60.00
E2RD L.Robitaille/M.Dionne 30.00 80.00
E2RH L.Robitaille/B.Hull 50.00 125.00
E2RL P.Roy/M.Lemieux 100.00 250.00
E2SH P.Stastny/D.Hawerchuk 30.00 80.00
E2TS J.Thornton/E.Staal 40.00 100.00

2007-08 The Cup Foundations

CFAK Anze Kopitar 10.00 25.00
CFAM Al MacInnis 8.00 20.00
CFAO Adam Oates 6.00 15.00
CFAR Alexander Radulov 6.00 15.00
CFAS Alexander Steen 4.00 10.00
CFAT Alex Tanguay 5.00 12.00
CFBC Bobby Clarke 10.00 25.00
CFBH Bobby Hull 12.00 30.00
CFBL Brian Leetch 5.00 12.00
CFBO Mike Bossy 6.00 15.00
CFBR Bill Ranford 6.00 15.00
CFBS Billy Smith 6.00 15.00
CFBU Johnny Bucyk 6.00 15.00
CFCN Cam Neely 6.00 15.00
CFCP Chris Pronger 6.00 15.00
CFDA Daniel Alfredsson 6.00 15.00
CFDC Dino Ciccarelli 6.00 15.00
CFDE Denis Savard 6.00 15.00
CFDH Dale Hawerchuk 8.00 20.00
CFDP Denis Potvin 6.00 15.00
CFDR Dwayne Roloson 5.00 12.00
CFDS Darryl Sittler 8.00 20.00
CFEM Evgeni Malkin 12.00 30.00
CFEN Evgeni Nabokov 5.00 12.00
CFEP Phil Esposito 10.00 25.00
CFES Eric Staal 8.00 20.00
CFFM Frank Mahovlich 6.00 15.00
CFGF Grant Fuhr 10.00 25.00
CFGH Gordie Howe 20.00 50.00
CFGL Guy Lafleur 8.00 20.00
CFGP Gilbert Perreault 6.00 15.00
CFHA Dominik Hasek 10.00 25.00
CFHE Dany Heatley 5.00 12.00
CFHL Henrik Lundqvist 15.00 40.00
CFHO Marian Hossa 6.00 15.00
CFHZ Henrik Zetterberg 8.00 20.00
CFIK Ilya Kovalchuk 6.00 15.00
CFJB Jean Beliveau 8.00 20.00
CFJI Jarome Iginla 8.00 20.00
CFJJ Jaromir Jagr 20.00 50.00
CFJK Jari Kurri 6.00 15.00
CFJO Joe Sakic 12.00 30.00
CFJS Jason Spezza 6.00 15.00
CFJT Joe Thornton 10.00 25.00
CFKI Miikka Kiprusoff 6.00 15.00
CFKL Kari Lehtonen 5.00 12.00
CFLM Lanny McDonald 6.00 15.00
CFLR Larry Robinson 6.00 15.00
CFMB Martin Brodeur 15.00 40.00
CFMF Marc-Andre Fleury 12.00 30.00
CFMG Marian Gaborik 6.00 15.00
CFMH Milan Hejduk 5.00 12.00
CFMK Mikko Koivu 5.00 12.00
CFML Mario Lemieux 25.00 60.00
CFMM Mark Messier 12.00 30.00
CFMN Markus Naslund 6.00 15.00
CFMO Mike Modano 10.00 25.00
CFMR Mark Recchi 8.00 20.00
CFMS Martin St. Louis 6.00 15.00
CFNL Nicklas Lidstrom 6.00 15.00
CFOV Alexander Ovechkin 25.00 60.00
CFPB Patrice Bergeron 8.00 20.00
CFPD Pavel Datsyuk 10.00 25.00
CFPE Corey Perry 10.00 25.00
CFPF Peter Forsberg 12.00 30.00
CFPH Dion Phaneuf 5.00 12.00
CFPK Paul Kariya 6.00 15.00
CFPM Patrick Marleau 6.00 15.00
CFPR Patrick Roy 15.00 40.00
CFPS Peter Stastny 5.00 12.00
CFRB Ray Bourque 10.00 25.00
CFRE Ron Ellis 4.00 10.00
CFRH Ron Hextall 6.00 15.00
CFRI Brad Richards 6.00 15.00
CFRL Roberto Luongo 10.00 25.00
CFRN Rick Nash 6.00 15.00
CFRO Luc Robitaille 6.00 15.00
CFRS Ryan Smyth 5.00 12.00
CFRV Rogie Vachon 8.00 20.00
CFRY Michael Ryder 4.00 10.00
CFSA Borje Salming 6.00 15.00
CFSC Sidney Crosby 25.00 60.00
CFSD Shane Doan 5.00 12.00
CFSF Sergei Fedorov 10.00 25.00
CFSG Simon Gagne 6.00 15.00
CFSH Brendan Shanahan 6.00 15.00
CFSK Saku Koivu 6.00 15.00
CFSL Steve Sullivan 4.00 10.00
CFSM Stan Mikita 8.00 20.00
CFSN Scott Niedermayer 6.00 15.00
CFSS Steve Shutt 5.00 12.00
CFST Scott Stevens 6.00 15.00
CFSU Mats Sundin 6.00 15.00
CFTS Teemu Selanne 12.00 30.00
CFTV Tomas Vokoun 5.00 12.00
CFTW Tiger Williams 4.00 10.00
CFVL Vincent Lecavalier 6.00 15.00
CFVT Vesa Toskala 5.00 12.00
CFWG Wayne Gretzky 40.00 100.00
CFZP Zach Parise 6.00 15.00

2007-08 The Cup Gold Jerseys

*GOLD JSY: 1X TO 2.5X
1 Dale Hawerchuk 15.00 40.00
2 Bobby Hull 25.00 60.00
3 Alexander Ovechkin 50.00 125.00
4 Dino Ciccarelli 12.00 30.00
5 Markus Naslund 12.00 30.00
6 Roberto Luongo 20.00 50.00
7 Richard Brodeur 10.00 25.00
8 Mats Sundin 12.00 30.00
9 Frank Mahovlich 12.00 30.00
10 Darryl Sittler 15.00 40.00
11 Borje Salming 12.00 30.00
12 Vincent Lecavalier 12.00 30.00
13 Martin St. Louis 12.00 30.00
14 Brad Richards 12.00 30.00
15 Paul Kariya 12.00 30.00
16 Bernie Federko 10.00 25.00
17 Joe Mullen 10.00 25.00
18 Joe Thornton 20.00 50.00
19 Jonathan Cheechoo 10.00 25.00
20 Patrick Marleau 12.00 30.00
21 Sidney Crosby 50.00 125.00
22 Evgeni Malkin 20.00 50.00
23 Mario Lemieux 50.00 125.00
24 Marc-Andre Fleury 25.00 60.00
25 Jordan Staal 10.00 25.00
26 Shane Doan 10.00 25.00
27 Simon Gagne 12.00 30.00
28 Bobby Clarke 20.00 50.00
29 Ron Hextall 12.00 30.00
30 Bernie Parent 15.00 40.00
31 Dany Heatley 10.00 25.00
32 Jason Spezza 15.00 40.00
33 Daniel Alfredsson 12.00 30.00
34 Mark Messier 25.00 60.00
35 Jaromir Jagr 40.00 100.00
36 Brendan Shanahan 12.00 30.00
37 Brian Leetch 10.00 25.00
39 Mike Bossy 12.00 30.00
40 Clark Gillies 12.00 30.00
41 Denis Potvin 12.00 30.00
42 Billy Smith 12.00 30.00
43 Martin Brodeur 30.00 80.00
44 Zach Parise 12.00 30.00
45 Alexander Radulov 12.00 30.00
46 Peter Forsberg 25.00 60.00
47 Saku Koivu 12.00 30.00
48 Michael Ryder 8.00 20.00
49 Larry Robinson 12.00 30.00
50 Guy Lafleur 15.00 40.00
51 Patrick Roy 30.00 80.00
52 Jean Beliveau 15.00 40.00
53 Marian Gaborik 12.00 30.00
54 Mikko Koivu 10.00 25.00
55 Marcel Dionne 15.00 40.00
56 Anze Kopitar 20.00 50.00
57 Rob Blake 12.00 30.00
58 Gordie Howe 40.00 100.00
59 Tomas Vokoun 10.00 25.00
60 Jari Kurri 12.00 30.00
61 Grant Fuhr 20.00 50.00
62 Wayne Gretzky 80.00 200.00
63 Ales Hemsky 10.00 25.00
64 Dwayne Roloson 10.00 25.00
65 Dominik Hasek 20.00 50.00
66 Henrik Zetterberg 15.00 40.00
67 Nicklas Lidstrom 12.00 30.00
68 Pavel Datsyuk 20.00 50.00
69 Marty Turco 12.00 30.00
70 Mike Modano 20.00 50.00
71 Rick Nash 12.00 30.00
72 Sergei Fedorov 12.00 30.00
73 Joe Sakic 25.00 60.00
74 Paul Stastny 10.00 25.00
75 Milan Hejduk 10.00 25.00
76 Stan Mikita 15.00 40.00
77 Tony Esposito 12.00 30.00
78 Nikolai Khabibulin 12.00 30.00
79 Denis Savard 12.00 30.00
80 Eric Staal 15.00 40.00
81 Cam Ward 12.00 30.00
82 Jarome Iginla 15.00 40.00
83 Miikka Kiprusoff 12.00 30.00
84 Lanny McDonald 12.00 30.00
85 Al MacInnis 15.00 40.00
86 Ryan Miller 12.00 30.00
87 Gilbert Perreault 12.00 30.00
88 Thomas Vanek 10.00 25.00
89 Patrice Bergeron 15.00 40.00
90 Ray Bourque 20.00 50.00
91 Cam Neely 12.00 30.00
93 Johnny Bucyk 12.00 30.00
94 Phil Kessel 12.00 30.00
95 Ilya Kovalchuk 12.00 30.00
96 Marian Hossa 12.00 30.00
97 Kari Lehtonen 10.00 25.00
98 Jean-Sebastien Giguere 12.00 30.00
99 Ryan Getzlaf 12.00 30.00
100 Teemu Selanne 25.00 60.00

2007-08 The Cup Gold Rainbow Autographed Rookies

101 Matt Keetley/36 12.00 30.00
102 Tyler Kennedy/34 25.00 60.00
103 Petteri Wirtanen/56 6.00 15.00
104 Matt Hunwick/48 8.00 20.00
105 Tomas Popperle/1
106 Johnny Boychuk/28 15.00 40.00
107 Alexander Nikulin/6
108 Mark Mancari/25 50.00 100.00
109 Craig Weller/12
110 Jake Dowell/49 8.00 20.00
111 David Clarkson/27 25.00 60.00
112 Drew MacIntyre/34 15.00 40.00
113 Kris Versteeg/32 125.00 250.00
114 Greg Moore/47 15.00 40.00
115 Tomas Plihal/59 10.00 25.00
116 Mike Lundin/39 10.00 25.00
117 Rich Peverley/37 8.00 20.00
118 Cody Bass/21 15.00 40.00

2007-08 The Cup Gold Rainbow Autographed Rookie Patches

119 Bobby Ryan/54 30.00 80.00
120 Ondrej Pavelec/33 30.00 60.00
121 Jack Johnson/33 40.00 100.00
128 Jonathan Bernier/45 60.00 120.00
129 Marc Staal/18
130 Nick Foligno/71 15.00 40.00
131 Peter Mueller/88 25.00 60.00
132 Brett Sterling/21 15.00 40.00
133 Petr Kalus/23 15.00 40.00
134 Rob Schremp/44 15.00 40.00
136 Frans Nielsen/51 20.00 50.00
138 Devin Setoguchi/16 30.00 80.00
139 Matt Smaby/32 25.00 60.00
140 James Sheppard/15 15.00 40.00
141 Kyle Chipchura/28 20.00 60.00
142 Ryan Parent/77 25.00 60.00
143 David Krejci/46 60.00 150.00
144 Lauri Tukonen/28 20.00 50.00
145 Anton Stralman/36 12.00 30.00
146 Tobias Enstrom/39 20.00 50.00
147 Brandon Dubinsky/54 40.00 100.00
148 Mason Raymond/21 30.00 80.00
149 Drew Miller/18 20.00 40.00
150 Curtis McElhinney/31 15.00 40.00
151 Ryan Callahan/43 25.00 60.00
152 Brian Elliott/30 25.00 60.00
153 Jonathan Sigalet/50 12.00 30.00
155 Torrey Mitchell/17 20.00 50.00
156 David Perron/57 40.00 100.00
157 Jannik Hansen/59 15.00 40.00
158 Jaroslav Halak/41 75.00 150.00
159 Milan Lucic/17 125.00 200.00
160 Lukas Kaspar/43 15.00 40.00
161 Marc Methot/48 12.00 30.00
162 Tyler Weiman/35 20.00 50.00
163 Ryan Carter/52 15.00 40.00
164 Jared Boll/40 20.00 50.00
166 Jaroslav Hlinka/17 20.00 50.00
168 Cory Murphy/21 25.00 60.00
169 Steve Wagner/49 12.00 30.00
170 Stefan Meyer/64 20.00 50.00
172 Tuukka Rask/40 150.00 400.00
173 David Jones/36 15.00 40.00
174 Tobias Stephan/31 15.00 40.00
175 Tom Gilbert/77 20.00 50.00
176 Cal Clutterbuck/22 25.00 60.00
177 Rod Pelley/22 15.00 40.00
178 Daniel Girardi/46 15.00 40.00
179 Chris Bourque/56 15.00 40.00
180 T.J. Hensick/34 15.00 40.00
181 Steve Downie/25 15.00 40.00
182 Jack Skille/48 25.00 60.00
183 Casey Borer/25 15.00 40.00
184 Sergei Kostitsyn/25 20.00 50.00
185 Patrick Kane/88 500.00 1000.00
186 Sam Gagner/89 40.00 100.00
187 Nicklas Backstrom/19 250.00 400.00
188 Jiri Tlusty/41 60.00 120.00
189 Carey Price/31 500.00 1200.00
190 Jonathan Toews/19 1000.00 1500.00

2007-08 The Cup Honorable Numbers

HNAC Andrew Cogliano/13
HNAM Al MacInnis/2
HNAO Alexander Ovechkin/8
HNBC Bobby Clarke/16 50.00 100.00
HNBL Brian Leetch/2
HNBN Bernie Nicholls/9
HNBR Martin Brodeur/30 150.00 300.00
HNBS Borje Salming/21
HNCN Cam Neely/8
HNCP Carey Price/31 300.00 600.00
HNDC Dino Ciccarelli/22 40.00 100.00
HNDH Dale Hawerchuk/10
HNDS Darryl Sittler/27 20.00 50.00
HNEM Evgeni Malkin/71 60.00 120.00
HNES Eric Staal/12
HNGA Sam Gagner/89 40.00 100.00
HNGF Grant Fuhr/31 40.00 80.00
HNGH Gordie Howe/9
HNGP Gilbert Perreault/11
HNHA Dominik Hasek/39 40.00 100.00
HNHE Dany Heatley/15 40.00 80.00
HNHZ Henrik Zetterberg/40 40.00 100.00
HNIK Ilya Kovalchuk/17 50.00 100.00
HNJB Jonathan Bernier/45 50.00 120.00
HNJC Jonathan Cheechoo/14
HNJG Jean-Sebastien Giguere/35 25.00 60.00
HNJI Jarome Iginla/12
HNJK Jari Kurri/17 50.00 100.00
HNJM Joe Mullen/7
HNJO Jonathan Toews/19 500.00 800.00
HNJS Jordan Staal/11
HNJT Joe Thornton/19 75.00 150.00
HNLM Lanny McDonald/9
HNLR Larry Robinson/19 40.00 80.00
HNMD Marcel Dionne/16 60.00 120.00
HNMF Marc-Andre Fleury/29 75.00 150.00
HNMG Marian Gaborik/10
HNML Mario Lemieux/66 175.00 350.00
HNMM Mark Messier/11
HNMN Markus Naslund/19 20.00 50.00
HNMO Mike Modano/9
HNMS Martin St. Louis/26 20.00 50.00
HNMT Marty Turco/35 20.00 50.00
HNNB Nicklas Backstrom/19 100.00 200.00
HNPE Phil Esposito/7
HNPK Patrick Kane/88 300.00 500.00
HNPM Peter Mueller/88 15.00 40.00
HNPR Patrick Roy/33 125.00 250.00
HNPS Paul Stastny/26 40.00 80.00
HNRB Ray Bourque/77 40.00 80.00
HNRG Ryan Getzlaf/15 50.00 100.00
HNRM Ryan Miller/30 40.00 100.00
HNRN Rick Nash/61 30.00 80.00
HNRO Luc Robitaille/20 25.00 60.00
HNRS Ryan Smyth/94 15.00 40.00
HNSC Sidney Crosby/87 150.00 300.00
HNSD Shane Doan/19 25.00 60.00
HNSG Simon Gagne/12
HNSH Steve Shutt/22 15.00 40.00
HNSK Saku Koivu/11
HNST Peter Stastny/26 50.00 100.00
HNTE Tony Esposito/35 40.00 80.00
HNTL Jiri Tlusty/41 25.00 60.00
HNTV Thomas Vanek/26 25.00 60.00
HNVL Vincent Lecavalier/4

2007-08 The Cup Honorable Numbers Dual

HN2BS M.Bossy/S.Shutt/22 50.00 100.00
HN2DC M.Dionne/B.Clarke/16 40.00 100.00
HN2GT J.Giguere/M.Turco/35 40.00 100.00
HN2RC L.Robitaille/D.Ciccarelli/20 40.00 80.00
HN2SK M.Satan/P.Kessel/81 25.00 60.00
HN2SS P.Stastny/P.Stastny/26 60.00 150.00
HN2TD J.Thornton/S.Doan/19 40.00 100.00

2007-08 The Cup Limited Logos Autographs

LLAC Andrew Cogliano/25 40.00 80.00
LLAH Ales Hemsky/50 20.00 50.00
LLAK Anze Kopitar/31 60.00 120.00
LLAM Al MacInnis/30 30.00 80.00
LLAO Adam Oates/50 25.00 60.00
LLAR Alexander Radulov/50 25.00 60.00
LLAT Alex Tanguay/50 20.00 50.00
LLBG Brian Gionta/50 15.00 40.00
LLBL Brian Leetch/50 20.00 50.00
LLBN Bernie Nicholls/50 25.00 60.00
LLBR Bill Ranford/50 25.00 60.00
LLCA Jeff Carter/50 40.00 80.00
LLCD Chris Drury/50 20.00 50.00
LLCN Cam Neely/25 60.00 120.00
LLCW Cam Ward/50 25.00 60.00
LLCY Carey Price/50 125.00 300.00
LLDC Dino Ciccarelli/50 25.00 60.00
LLDG Doug Gilmour/50 30.00 80.00
LLDH Dale Hawerchuk/50 30.00 80.00
LLDR Dwayne Roloson/50 20.00 50.00
LLEL Patrik Elias/50 25.00 60.00
LLEM Evgeni Malkin/25 125.00 250.00
LLEN Evgeni Nabokov/50 20.00 50.00
LLES Eric Staal/50 30.00 80.00
LLGA Sam Gagner/25 60.00 120.00
LLGF Grant Fuhr/25 30.00 80.00
LLGL Guy Lafleur/3
LLGP Gilbert Perreault/25 30.00 80.00
LLHA Dominik Hasek/50 40.00 100.00
LLHE Dany Heatley/50 25.00 60.00
LLHZ Henrik Zetterberg/50 50.00 120.00
LLIK Ilya Kovalchuk/50 40.00 120.00
LLJA Jason Arnott/50 20.00 50.00
LLJB Jonathan Bernier/50 60.00 120.00
LLJC Jonathan Cheechoo/50 20.00 50.00
LLJG Jean-Sebastien Giguere/50 30.00 80.00
LLJI Jarome Iginla/50 30.00 80.00
LLJK Jari Kurri/25 30.00 80.00
LLJM Joe Mullen/50 20.00 50.00
LLJO Jonathan Toews/50 175.00 350.00
LLJS Jordan Staal/50 20.00 50.00
LLJT Joe Thornton/50 40.00 100.00
LLJW Justin Williams/50 20.00 50.00
LLLM Lanny McDonald/50 40.00 80.00
LLLR Larry Robinson/28 25.00 60.00
LLMA Martin Brodeur/50 75.00 150.00
LLMD Marcel Dionne/22 60.00 120.00
LLMF Marc-Andre Fleury/50 30.00 80.00
LLMG Marian Gaborik/50 40.00 100.00
LLMH Marian Hossa/50 30.00 80.00
LLMI Milan Hejduk/50 20.00 50.00
LLML Mario Lemieux/50 100.00 200.00
LLMM Mark Messier/50 50.00 100.00
LLMN Markus Naslund/50 25.00 60.00
LLMO Mike Modano/50 30.00 75.00
LLMS Martin St. Louis/50 25.00 60.00
LLMT Marty Turco/50 25.00 60.00
LLNB Nicklas Backstrom/50 90.00 150.00
LLNL Nicklas Lidstrom/50 60.00 120.00
LLOV Alexander Ovechkin/50 125.00 250.00
LLPB Patrice Bergeron/50 30.00 80.00
LLPK Patrick Kane/50 600.00 1500.00
LLPM Peter Mueller/50 25.00 60.00
LLPR Patrick Roy/50 125.00 250.00
LLPS Paul Stastny/50 20.00 50.00
LLRB Ray Bourque/50 40.00 100.00
LLRG Ryan Getzlaf/50 25.00 60.00
LLRI Richard Brodeur/50 20.00 50.00
LLRM Ryan Miller/50 25.00 60.00
LLRN Rick Nash/50 25.00 60.00
LLRO Luc Robitaille/50 25.00 60.00
LLRS Ryan Smyth/50 20.00 50.00
LLSA Borje Salming/50 25.00 60.00
LLSC Sidney Crosby/50 300.00 500.00
LLSD Shane Doan/50 20.00 50.00
LLSG Simon Gagne/50 25.00 60.00
LLSH Steve Shutt/50 20.00 50.00
LLSK Saku Koivu/50 25.00 60.00
LLSM Stan Mikita/25 60.00 120.00
LLST Peter Stastny/32 60.00 120.00
LLSV Marek Svatos/50 15.00 40.00
LLTL Jiri Tlusty/50 25.00 60.00
LLTR Tuomo Ruutu/50 25.00 60.00
LLTV Thomas Vanek/50 25.00 60.00
LLVL Vincent Lecavalier/50 50.00 100.00
LLVO Tomas Vokoun/50 20.00 50.00
LLWG Wayne Gretzky/5

2007-08 The Cup Rookies Platinum

101 Matt Keetley 6.00 15.00
102 Tyler Kennedy 6.00 15.00
103 Petteri Wirtanen 6.00 15.00
104 Matt Hunwick 6.00 15.00
105 Tomas Popperle 6.00 15.00
106 Johnny Boychuk 10.00 25.00
107 Alexander Nikulin 6.00 15.00
108 Mark Mancari 6.00 15.00
109 Craig Weller 6.00 15.00
110 Jake Dowell 6.00 15.00
111 David Clarkson 6.00 15.00
112 Drew MacIntyre 6.00 15.00
113 Kris Versteeg 50.00 120.00
114 Greg Moore 6.00 15.00
115 Tomas Plihal 6.00 15.00
116 Mike Lundin 6.00 15.00
117 Rich Peverley 6.00 15.00
118 Cody Bass 6.00 15.00
119 Bobby Ryan 15.00 40.00
120 Ondrej Pavelec 12.00 30.00
121 Jack Johnson 8.00 20.00
122 Nicklas Bergfors 6.00 15.00
123 Erik Johnson 10.00 25.00
124 Bryan Little 8.00 20.00
125 Kris Russell 10.00 25.00
126 Matt Niskanen 10.00 25.00
127 Andrew Cogliano 40.00 80.00
128 Jonathan Bernier 12.00 30.00
129 Marc Staal 10.00 25.00
130 Nick Foligno 12.00 30.00
131 Peter Mueller 8.00 20.00
132 Brett Sterling 6.00 15.00
133 Petr Kalus 6.00 15.00
134 Rob Schremp 8.00 20.00
135 Andy Greene 8.00 20.00
136 Frans Nielsen 10.00 25.00
137 Martin Hanzal 8.00 20.00
138 Devin Setoguchi 10.00 25.00
139 Matt Smaby 6.00 15.00
140 James Sheppard 6.00 15.00
141 Kyle Chipchura 10.00 25.00
142 Ryan Parent 6.00 15.00
143 David Krejci 25.00 60.00
144 Lauri Tukonen 6.00 15.00
145 Anton Stralman 6.00 15.00
146 Tobias Enstrom 10.00 25.00
147 Brandon Dubinsky 12.00 30.00
148 Mason Raymond 10.00 25.00
149 Drew Miller 8.00 20.00
150 Curtis McElhinney 10.00 25.00
151 Ryan Callahan 12.00 30.00
152 Brian Elliott 12.00 30.00
153 Jonathan Sigalet 6.00 15.00
154 Ville Koistinen 6.00 15.00
155 Torrey Mitchell 8.00 20.00
156 David Perron 12.00 30.00
157 Jannik Hansen 8.00 20.00
158 Jaroslav Halak 60.00 120.00
159 Milan Lucic 25.00 60.00
160 Lukas Kaspar 6.00 15.00
161 Marc Methot 6.00 15.00
162 Tyler Weiman 8.00 20.00
163 Ryan Carter 6.00 15.00
164 Jared Boll 8.00 20.00
165 Jonas Hiller 12.00 30.00
166 Jaroslav Hlinka 8.00 20.00
167 Matt Ellis 8.00 20.00
168 Cory Murphy 6.00 15.00
169 Steve Wagner 6.00 15.00
170 Stefan Meyer 8.00 20.00
171 Daniel Carcillo 8.00 20.00
172 Tuukka Rask 25.00 60.00
173 David Jones 6.00 15.00
174 Tobias Stephan 8.00 20.00
175 Tom Gilbert 8.00 20.00
176 Cal Clutterbuck 10.00 25.00
177 Rod Pelley 6.00 15.00
178 Daniel Girardi 8.00 20.00
179 Chris Bourque 8.00 20.00
180 T.J. Hensick 8.00 20.00
181 Steve Downie 8.00 20.00
182 Jack Skille 8.00 20.00
183 Casey Borer 6.00 15.00
184 Sergei Kostitsyn 25.00 60.00
185 Patrick Kane 100.00 200.00
186 Sam Gagner 40.00 80.00
187 Nicklas Backstrom 80.00 200.00
188 Jiri Tlusty 10.00 25.00
189 Carey Price 200.00 350.00
190 Jonathan Toews 75.00 150.00

2007-08 The Cup Scripted Swatches

SSGH Gordie Howe/10
SSAC Andrew Cogliano 20.00 50.00
SSAO Alexander Ovechkin 75.00 150.00
SSAR Alexander Radulov 25.00 60.00
SSAT Alex Tanguay 25.00 60.00
SSBC Bobby Clarke 50.00 120.00
SSBL Brian Leetch 25.00 60.00
SSBR Martin Brodeur 100.00 200.00
SSCN Cam Neely/10
SSCP Carey Price 100.00 200.00
SSCW Cam Ward 30.00 80.00
SSDC Dino Ciccarelli 30.00 80.00
SSDG Doug Gilmour 40.00 100.00
SSDH Dale Hawerchuk 40.00 100.00
SSDS Darryl Sittler/10
SSEL Patrik Elias 30.00 80.00
SSEM Evgeni Malkin 75.00 150.00
SSES Eric Staal 40.00 100.00
SSGA Sam Gagner 25.00 60.00
SSGP Gilbert Perreault/10
SSHA Dominik Hasek 30.00 80.00
SSHE Dany Heatley 30.00 80.00
SSHZ Henrik Zetterberg 60.00 120.00
SSIK Ilya Kovalchuk 30.00 80.00
SSJB Jonathan Bernier 25.00 60.00
SSJG Jean-Sebastien Giguere 30.00 80.00
SSJI Jarome Iginla 40.00 100.00
SSJM Joe Mullen 25.00 60.00
SSJO Jonathan Toews 125.00 250.00
SSJS Jordan Staal 25.00 60.00
SSJT Joe Thornton 50.00 125.00
SSLM Lanny McDonald 30.00 80.00
SSLR Larry Robinson 30.00 80.00
SSMB Mike Bossy/10
SSMD Marcel Dionne 40.00 100.00
SSMF Marc-Andre Fleury 60.00 150.00
SSMG Marian Gaborik 30.00 80.00
SSMH Marian Hossa 30.00 80.00
SSMI Milan Hejduk 25.00 60.00
SSML Mario Lemieux 125.00 250.00
SSMM Mark Messier 125.00 250.00
SSMN Markus Naslund 30.00 80.00
SSMO Mike Modano 50.00 125.00
SSMS Martin St. Louis 25.00 60.00
SSMT Marty Turco 30.00 80.00
SSNB Nicklas Backstrom 100.00 200.00
SSNL Nicklas Lidstrom 30.00 80.00
SSPB Patrice Bergeron 40.00 100.00
SSPK Patrick Kane 75.00 150.00
SSPM Peter Mueller 25.00 60.00
SSPR Patrick Roy 100.00 200.00
SSPS Paul Stastny 25.00 60.00
SSRB Ray Bourque 60.00 120.00
SSRG Ryan Getzlaf 30.00 80.00
SSRM Ryan Miller 25.00 60.00
SSRN Rick Nash 30.00 80.00
SSRO Luc Robitaille 30.00 80.00
SSRS Ryan Smyth 25.00 60.00
SSSA Borje Salming 30.00 80.00
SSSC Sidney Crosby 200.00 300.00
SSSD Shane Doan 20.00 50.00
SSSG Simon Gagne 30.00 80.00
SSSH Steve Shutt 25.00 60.00
SSSK Saku Koivu 30.00 80.00
SSST Peter Stastny 25.00 60.00
SSTL Jiri Tlusty 20.00 50.00
SSVL Vincent Lecavalier 30.00 80.00
SSWG Wayne Gretzky 500.00 1200.00

2007-08 The Cup Signature Patches

SPAK Anze Kopitar/75 25.00 60.00
SPAO Alexander Ovechkin/75 75.00 150.00
SPAT Alex Tanguay/75 15.00 40.00
SPBL Brian Leetch/75 15.00 40.00
SPBR Martin Brodeur/25 75.00 150.00
SPBS Borje Salming/75 20.00 50.00
SPCD Chris Drury/75 15.00 40.00
SPCH Jonathan Cheechoo/75 15.00 40.00
SPCN Cam Neely/10
SPCP Carey Price/75 200.00 350.00
SPCW Cam Ward/75 20.00 50.00
SPDC Dino Ciccarelli/75 20.00 50.00
SPDH Dominik Hasek/25 75.00 150.00
SPEM Evgeni Malkin/75 15.00 40.00
SPES Eric Staal/75 25.00 60.00
SPGA Sam Gagner/75 25.00 60.00
SPGF Grant Fuhr/10
SPGP Gilbert Perreault/10
SPHA Dale Hawerchuk/75 25.00 60.00
SPHE Dany Heatley/75 15.00 40.00
SPIK Ilya Kovalchuk/75 20.00 50.00
SPJA Jason Arnott/75 15.00 40.00
SPJB Jonathan Bernier/75 20.00 50.00
SPJG Jean-Sebastien Giguere/75 20.00 50.00
SPJI Jarome Iginla/75 25.00 60.00
SPJM Joe Mullen/75 15.00 40.00
SPJS Jordan Staal/75 20.00 50.00
SPJT Joe Thornton/25 30.00 80.00
SPKE Patrick Kane/75 150.00 250.00
SPLM Lanny McDonald/75 20.00 50.00
SPLR Luc Robitaille/75 20.00 50.00
SPMB Mike Bossy/10
SPMG Marian Gaborik/75 30.00 80.00
SPMH Milan Hejduk/75 15.00 40.00
SPML Mario Lemieux/25 100.00 200.00
SPMM Mike Modano/75 25.00 60.00
SPMN Markus Naslund/75 20.00 50.00
SPMS Martin St. Louis/75 20.00 50.00
SPMT Marty Turco/75 20.00 50.00
SPNB Nicklas Backstrom/75 50.00 100.00
SPNL Nicklas Lidstrom/75 20.00 50.00
SPPB Patrice Bergeron/75 40.00 80.00
SPPE Patrik Elias/75 15.00 40.00
SPPK Phil Kessel/75 20.00 50.00
SPPM Peter Mueller/75 15.00 40.00
SPPR Patrick Roy/25 100.00 200.00
SPPS Peter Stastny/75 15.00 40.00
SPRB Ray Bourque/25 25.00 60.00
SPRM Ryan Miller/75 20.00 50.00
SPRN Rick Nash/75 20.00 50.00
SPSC Sidney Crosby/75 150.00 300.00
SPSD Shane Doan/75 15.00 40.00
SPSG Simon Gagne/75 15.00 40.00
SPSK Saku Koivu/75 25.00 60.00
SPST Paul Stastny/75 15.00 40.00
SPTL Jiri Tlusty/75 15.00 40.00
SPTO Jonathan Toews/75 150.00 250.00
SPTV Tomas Vokoun/75 15.00 40.00
SPVL Vincent Lecavalier/75 15.00 40.00

2007-08 The Cup Stanley Cup Signatures

SCAM Andy McDonald 25.00 60.00
SCBC Bobby Clarke 50.00 125.00
SCBD Bill Dineen 25.00 60.00
SCBG Brian Gionta 20.00 50.00
SCBH Bobby Hull 40.00 100.00
SCBL Brian Leetch 25.00 60.00
SCBN Bob Nystrom 20.00 50.00
SCBO Mike Bossy 30.00 80.00
SCBP Bernie Parent 40.00 100.00
SCBS Brent Sutter 20.00 50.00
SCCD Chris Drury 25.00 60.00
SCDB Dan Boyle 20.00 50.00
SCDP Denis Potvin 30.00 80.00
SCEL Patrik Elias 20.00 50.00
SCFM1 Frank Mahovlich 25.00 60.00
SCFM2 Frank Mahovlich 25.00 60.00
SCGF Grant Fuhr 25.00 60.00
SCGH Gordie Howe 100.00 200.00
SCGL Guy Lafleur 60.00 120.00
SCHL Hakan Loob 25.00 60.00
SCJA Jason Arnott 25.00 60.00
SCJB Johnny Bucyk 30.00 80.00
SCJG Jean-Sebastien Giguere 25.00 60.00
SCJK Jari Kurri 30.00 80.00
SCJW Justin Williams 15.00 40.00
SCKD Kris Draper 20.00 50.00
SCLM Lanny McDonald 30.00 80.00
SCLR Larry Robinson 25.00 60.00
SCLU Luc Robitaille 15.00 40.00
SCMB Martin Brodeur 125.00 250.00
SCME Mark Messier 100.00 200.00
SCML Mario Lemieux 100.00 200.00
SCMM Mark Messier 100.00 200.00
SCMO Mike Modano 50.00 125.00
SCNB Neal Broten 20.00 50.00
SCOR Bobby Orr 200.00 400.00
SCPE Phil Esposito 25.00 60.00
SCPR1 Patrick Roy 125.00 250.00
SCPR2 Patrick Roy 125.00 250.00
SCRE Ron Ellis 20.00 50.00
SCRG Ryan Getzlaf 25.00 60.00
SCSA Denis Savard 20.00 50.00
SCSB Scotty Bowman 30.00 80.00
SCSC Scotty Bowman 30.00 80.00
SCSG Scott Gomez
SCSM Stan Mikita 40.00 100.00
SCSU Duane Sutter 20.00 50.00
SCWG Wayne Gretzky 400.00 1000.00

2008-09 The Cup

*VETS/25: .6X TO 1.5X BASIC CARDS
*RC/25: .6X TO 1.5X BASIC CARDS
1 Wayne Gretzky 20.00 50.00
2 Vincent Lecavalier 3.00 8.00
3 Tony Esposito 3.00 8.00
4 Thomas Vanek 2.50 6.00
5 Teemu Selanne 6.00 15.00
6 Brian Leetch 2.50 6.00
7 Sidney Crosby 12.00 30.00
8 Saku Koivu 3.00 8.00
9 Ryan Miller 3.00 8.00
10 Ryan Getzlaf 3.00 8.00
11 Ron Hextall 3.00 8.00
12 Roberto Luongo 5.00 12.00
13 Rick Nash 3.00 8.00
14 Ray Bourque 5.00 12.00
15 Phil Esposito 5.00 12.00
16 Brendan Shanahan 3.00 8.00
17 Pavel Datsyuk 5.00 12.00
18 Paul Stastny 2.50 6.00
19 Paul Kariya 3.00 8.00
20 Mats Sundin 3.00 8.00
21 Patrick Roy 8.00 20.00
22 Patrick Kane 6.00 15.00
23 Nicklas Lidstrom 3.00 8.00
24 Mike Richards 2.50 6.00
25 Marty Turco 3.00 8.00
26 Martin St. Louis 3.00 8.00
27 Martin Brodeur 8.00 20.00
28 Markus Naslund 3.00 8.00
29 Mark Messier 6.00 15.00
30 Mario Lemieux 12.00 30.00
31 Marian Gaborik 3.00 8.00
32 Marc-Andre Fleury 6.00 15.00
33 Luc Robitaille 3.00 8.00
34 Lanny McDonald 3.00 8.00
35 Jonathan Toews 5.00 12.00
36 Joe Thornton 5.00 12.00
37 Joe Sakic 6.00 15.00
38 Joe Mullen 2.50 6.00
39 Jean Beliveau 3.00 8.00
40 Jason Spezza 3.00 8.00
41 Jarome Iginla 4.00 10.00
42 Jari Kurri 3.00 8.00
43 Ilya Kovalchuk 3.00 8.00
44 Henrik Zetterberg 4.00 10.00
45 Guy Lafleur 4.00 10.00
46 Grant Fuhr 5.00 12.00
47 Gordie Howe 10.00 25.00
48 Frank Mahovlich 3.00 8.00
49 Evgeni Malkin 6.00 15.00
50 Eric Staal 4.00 10.00
51 Dominik Hasek 5.00 12.00
52 Dino Ciccarelli 3.00 8.00
53 Dany Heatley 2.50 6.00
54 Dale Hawerchuk 4.00 10.00
55 Carey Price 6.00 15.00
56 Cam Neely 3.00 8.00
57 Bobby Orr 12.00 30.00
58 Bobby Hull 6.00 15.00
59 Alexander Ovechkin 12.00 30.00
60 Al MacInnis 4.00 10.00
61 Nathan Oystrick AU RC 10.00 25.00
62 Marc-Andre Gragnani AU RC 8.00 20.00
63 Derek Dorsett AU RC 12.00 30.00
64 Maxsim Mayorov AU RC 10.00 25.00
65 Wayne Simmonds AU RC 15.00 40.00
66 Danny Taylor AU RC 8.00 20.00
67 Tim Ramholt AU RC 8.00 20.00
68 Mike Iggulden AU RC 8.00 20.00
69 Trevor Smith AU RC 8.00 20.00
70 Dane Byers AU RC 8.00 20.00
71 Dustin Jeffrey AU RC 10.00 25.00
72 Tom Cavanagh AU RC 8.00 20.00
73 Derek Joslin AU RC 8.00 20.00
74 Paul Szczechura AU RC 10.00 25.00
75 Jonas Frogren AU RC 6.00 15.00
76 John Mitchell AU RC 8.00 20.00
77 Simeon Varlamov AU RC 20.00 50.00
78 Oskar Osala AU RC 10.00 25.00
79 Andrew Ebbett JSY AU RC 10.00 25.00
80 B.Mikkelson JSY AU RC 10.00 25.00
81 Zach Bogosian JSY AU RC 20.00 50.00
82 Boris Valabik JSY AU RC 15.00 40.00
83 Nathan Gerbe JSY AU RC 15.00 40.00
84 Tim Kennedy JSY AU RC 15.00 40.00
85 Zach Boychuk JSY AU RC 15.00 40.00
86 Brandon Sutter JSY AU RC 15.00 40.00
87 Chris Stewart JSY AU RC 15.00 40.00
88 Dan LaCosta JSY AU RC 15.00 40.00
89 Steve Mason JSY AU RC 25.00 60.00
90 Tom Sestito JSY AU RC 15.00 40.00
91 Nikita Filatov JSY AU RC 15.00 40.00
92 Jakub Voracek JSY AU RC 30.00 80.00
93 Adam Pineault JSY AU RC 12.00 30.00
94 Derick Brassard JSY AU RC 15.00 40.00
95 Mark Fistric JSY AU RC 12.00 30.00
96 Fabian Brunnstrom JSY AU RC 12.00 30.00
97 James Neal JSY AU RC 30.00 80.00
98 J.Abdelkader JSY AU RC 25.00 60.00
99 J.Ericsson JSY AU RC 15.00 40.00
100 Mattias Ritola JSY AU RC 12.00 30.00
101 Darren Helm JSY AU RC 15.00 40.00
102 Michael Frolik JSY AU RC 15.00 40.00
103 Shawn Matthias JSY AU RC 15.00 40.00
104 Tyler Plante JSY AU RC 12.00 30.00
105 Michal Repik JSY AU RC 15.00 40.00
106 K.McArdle JSY AU RC 12.00 30.00
107 Brian Boyle JSY AU RC 12.00 30.00
108 Oscar Moller JSY AU RC 12.00 30.00

109 Erik Ersberg JSY AU RC 12.00 30.00
110 Teddy Purcell JSY AU RC 12.00 30.00
111 Colton Gillies JSY AU RC 12.00 30.00
112 Max Pacioretty JSY AU RC 30.00 80.00
113 Matt D'Agostini JSY AU RC 12.00 30.00
114 Ben Maxwell JSY AU RC 15.00 40.00
115 Patric Hornqvist JSY AU RC 15.00 40.00
116 Ryan Jones JSY AU RC 15.00 40.00
117 M.Halischuk JSY AU RC 10.00 25.00
118 Petr Vrana JSY AU RC 10.00 25.00
119 Josh Bailey JSY AU RC 20.00 50.00
120 Kyle Okposo JSY AU RC 20.00 50.00
121 Trevor Lewis JSY AU RC 15.00 40.00
122 Lauri Korpikoski JSY AU RC 10.00 25.00
123 Brian Lee JSY AU RC 12.00 30.00
124 Ilya Zubov JSY AU RC 12.00 30.00
125 Claude Giroux JSY AU RC 150.00 250.00
126 Luca Sbisa JSY AU RC 10.00 25.00
127 Andreas Nodl JSY AU RC 10.00 25.00
128 Viktor Tikhonov JSY AU RC 12.00 30.00
129 Kevin Porter JSY AU RC 12.00 30.00
130 Mikkel Boedker JSY AU RC 20.00 50.00
131 Alex Goligoski JSY AU RC 20.00 50.00
132 Jonathan Filewich JSY AU RC 12.00 30.00
133 Ryan Stone JSY AU RC 10.00 25.00
134 Jamie McGinn JSY AU RC 15.00 40.00
135 Alex Pietrangelo JSY AU RC 25.00 60.00
136 Patrik Berglund JSY AU RC 12.00 30.00
137 Ben Bishop JSY AU RC 25.00 60.00
138 T.J. Oshie JSY AU RC 30.00 80.00
139 Vladimir Mihalik JSY AU RC 10.00 25.00
140 Ty Wishart JSY AU RC 12.00 30.00
141 Robbie Earl JSY AU RC 10.00 25.00
142 Nikolai Kulemin JSY AU RC 15.00 40.00
143 Cory Schneider JSY AU RC 40.00 100.00
144 Karl Alzner JSY AU RC 10.00 25.00
145 J.Pogge JSY AU RC/99 20.00 50.00
146 D.Doughty JSY AU RC/99 250.00 400.00
147 B.Wheeler JSY AU RC/99 100.00 200.00
148 L.Schenn JSY AU RC/99 50.00 125.00
149 Kyle Turris JSY AU RC/99 30.00 80.00
150 S.Stamkos JSY AU RC/99 1000.00 2500.00

2008-09 The Cup Gold Rainbow

*RC RAINBOW: .6X TO 1.5X BASIC CARDS
150 S.Stamkos PATCH AU/91 500.00 1200.00

2008-09 The Cup Platinum Jerseys

1 Wayne Gretzky 50.00 125.00
2 Vincent Lecavalier 8.00 20.00
3 Tony Esposito 8.00 20.00
4 Thomas Vanek 6.00 15.00
5 Teemu Selanne 15.00 40.00
6 Brian Leetch 6.00 15.00
7 Sidney Crosby 30.00 80.00
8 Saku Koivu 8.00 20.00
9 Ryan Miller 8.00 20.00
10 Ryan Getzlaf 8.00 20.00
11 Ron Hextall 8.00 20.00
12 Roberto Luongo 12.00 30.00
13 Rick Nash 8.00 20.00
14 Ray Bourque 12.00 30.00
15 Phil Esposito 12.00 30.00
16 Brendan Shanahan 8.00 20.00
17 Pavel Datsyuk 12.00 30.00
18 Paul Stastny 6.00 15.00
19 Paul Kariya 8.00 20.00
20 Mats Sundin 8.00 20.00
21 Patrick Roy 20.00 50.00
22 Patrick Kane 15.00 40.00
23 Nicklas Lidstrom 8.00 20.00
24 Mike Richards 6.00 15.00
25 Marty Turco 8.00 20.00
26 Martin St. Louis 8.00 20.00
27 Martin Brodeur 20.00 50.00
28 Markus Naslund 8.00 20.00
29 Mark Messier 15.00 40.00
30 Mario Lemieux 30.00 80.00
31 Marian Gaborik 8.00 20.00
32 Marc-Andre Fleury 15.00 40.00
33 Luc Robitaille 8.00 20.00
34 Lanny McDonald 8.00 20.00
35 Jonathan Toews 12.00 30.00
36 Joe Thornton 12.00 30.00
37 Joe Sakic 15.00 40.00
38 Joe Mullen 6.00 15.00
39 Jean Beliveau 8.00 20.00
40 Jason Spezza 8.00 20.00
41 Jarome Iginla 10.00 25.00
42 Jari Kurri 8.00 20.00
43 Ilya Kovalchuk 8.00 20.00
44 Henrik Zetterberg 10.00 25.00
45 Guy Lafleur 10.00 25.00
46 Grant Fuhr 12.00 30.00
47 Gordie Howe 25.00 60.00
48 Frank Mahovlich 8.00 20.00
49 Evgeni Malkin 15.00 40.00
50 Eric Staal 10.00 25.00
51 Dominik Hasek 12.00 30.00
52 Dino Ciccarelli 8.00 20.00
53 Dany Heatley 6.00 15.00
54 Dale Hawerchuk 10.00 25.00
55 Carey Price 15.00 40.00
56 Cam Neely 8.00 20.00
57 Brett Hull 12.00 30.00
58 Bobby Hull 15.00 40.00
59 Alexander Ovechkin 20.00 50.00
60 Al MacInnis 10.00 25.00

2008-09 The Cup Auto Draft Boards

DBAC Andrew Cogliano 12.00 30.00
DBAK Anze Kopitar 30.00 80.00
DBAP Alex Pietrangelo 30.00 80.00
DBBE Jonathan Bernier 15.00 40.00
DBBO Zach Boychuk 20.00 50.00
DBBR Bobby Ryan 15.00 40.00
DBBS Brandon Sutter 20.00 50.00
DBCG Colton Gillies 15.00 40.00
DBCP Carey Price 40.00 100.00
DBCS Chris Stewart 20.00 50.00
DBDB Derick Brassard 20.00 50.00
DBDD Drew Doughty 50.00 125.00
DBDS Devin Setoguchi 15.00 40.00
DBFO Nick Foligno 20.00 50.00
DBGI Claude Giroux 40.00 100.00
DBJB Josh Bailey 25.00 60.00
DBJS Jordan Staal 15.00 40.00
DBJT Jonathan Toews 30.00 80.00
DBJV Jakub Voracek 40.00 100.00
DBKA Karl Alzner 12.00 30.00
DBKE Phil Kessel 20.00 50.00
DBKM Kenndal McArdle 15.00 40.00
DBKO Kyle Okposo 25.00 60.00
DBKT Kyle Turris 30.00 80.00
DBLE Brian Lee 15.00 40.00
DBLS Luke Schenn 25.00 60.00
DBLW Trevor Lewis 20.00 50.00
DBMB Mikkel Boedker 25.00 60.00
DBMF Michael Frolik 20.00 50.00
DBMH Martin Hanzal 15.00 40.00
DBMN Matt Niskanen 15.00 40.00
DBMP Max Pacioretty 40.00 100.00
DBMS Marc Staal 12.00 30.00
DBNB Nicklas Backstrom 20.00 50.00
DBNF Nikita Filatov 20.00 50.00
DBNI Nicklas Bergfors 30.00 80.00
DBPB Patrik Berglund 15.00 40.00
DBPK Patrick Kane 40.00 100.00
DBPM Peter Mueller 15.00 40.00
DBSB Luca Sbisa 12.00 30.00
DBSC Sidney Crosby 350.00 500.00
DBSD Steve Downie 20.00 50.00
DBSG Sam Gagner 12.00 30.00
DBSH James Sheppard 12.00 30.00
DBSS Steven Stamkos 150.00 400.00
DBSV Simeon Varlamov 40.00 100.00
DBTO T.J. Oshie 30.00 80.00
DBTR Tuukka Rask 25.00 60.00
DBTW Ty Wishart 15.00 40.00
DBVT Viktor Tikhonov 15.00 40.00
DBZB Zach Bogosian 25.00 60.00

2008-09 The Cup Chirography

CCAO Alexander Ovechkin 50.00 120.00
CCBH Bobby Hull 25.00 60.00
CCBO Bobby Orr 60.00 150.00
CCBR Martin Brodeur 30.00 80.00
CCEM Evgeni Malkin 25.00 60.00
CCFM Frank Mahovlich 12.00 30.00
CCGH Gordie Howe 80.00 200.00
CCGP Gilbert Perreault 12.00 30.00
CCIK Ilya Kovalchuk 12.00 30.00
CCJB Jean Beliveau 12.00 30.00
CCJI Jarome Iginla 15.00 40.00
CCJT Joe Thornton 20.00 50.00
CCMB Mike Bossy 12.00 30.00
CCML Mario Lemieux 50.00 125.00
CCMM Mark Messier 25.00 60.00
CCPE Phil Esposito 20.00 50.00
CCPR Patrick Roy 30.00 80.00
CCRB Ray Bourque 20.00 50.00
CCRH Ron Hextall 12.00 30.00
CCRO Larry Robinson 12.00 30.00
CCSC Sidney Crosby 80.00 200.00
CCVL Vincent Lecavalier 12.00 30.00
CCWG Wayne Gretzky 200.00 500.00

2008-09 The Cup Enshrinements

CEAB Andy Bathgate 15.00 40.00
CEAO Alexander Ovechkin 60.00 150.00
CEBB Butch Bouchard 20.00 50.00
CEBC Bobby Clarke 25.00 60.00
CEBH Bobby Hull 30.00 80.00
CEBL Brian Leetch 12.00 30.00
CEBO Bobby Orr 60.00 150.00
CEBS Borje Salming 15.00 40.00
CEBU Johnny Bucyk 15.00 40.00
CECN Cam Neely 15.00 40.00
CEDH Dany Heatley 12.00 30.00
CEEM Evgeni Malkin 30.00 80.00
CEES Eric Staal 15.00 40.00
CEFM Frank Mahovlich 15.00 40.00
CEGF Grant Fuhr 25.00 60.00
CEGH Gordie Howe 50.00 125.00
CEGP Gilbert Perreault 15.00 40.00
CEHA Dominik Hasek 25.00 60.00
CEHZ Henrik Zetterberg 20.00 50.00
CEJB Jean Beliveau 15.00 40.00
CEJI Jarome Iginla 20.00 50.00
CEJK Jari Kurri 15.00 40.00
CEJO Johnny Bower 15.00 40.00
CEJT Joe Thornton 25.00 60.00
CELR Larry Robinson 15.00 40.00
CEMB Martin Brodeur 40.00 100.00
CEML Mario Lemieux 60.00 150.00
CEMM Mark Messier 30.00 80.00
CEMO Mike Modano 25.00 60.00
CENL Nicklas Lidstrom 30.00 80.00
CEPE Phil Esposito 25.00 60.00
CEPH Dion Phaneuf 12.00 30.00
CEPR Patrick Roy 40.00 100.00
CERB Ray Bourque 25.00 60.00
CERL Rod Langway 12.00 30.00
CERN Rick Nash 15.00 40.00
CESC Sidney Crosby 60.00 150.00
CETE Tony Esposito 15.00 40.00
CEWG Wayne Gretzky 200.00 500.00

2008-09 The Cup Enshrinements Dual

CE2BH Beliveau/Howe 150.00 250.00
CE2BL Lindsay/Bouchard 25.00 60.00
CE2BM Bucyk/Mahovlich 20.00 50.00
CE2BT Turco/Brodeur 50.00 125.00
CE2HM Hull/Mikita 40.00 100.00
CE2HN Nash/Heatley 20.00 50.00
CE2IS Iginla/E.Staal 25.00 60.00
CE2KH Kurri/Hawerchuk 25.00 60.00
CE2KM Kovalchuk/Malkin 40.00 100.00
CE2LB B.Leetch/A.Bathgate 20.00 50.00
CE2LG Langway/Gillies 20.00 50.00
CE2NB Lidstrom/Salming 20.00 50.00
CE2PB Bowman/Potvin 20.00 50.00
CE2RD Roy/Duff 50.00 125.00
CE2SM Savard/Mullen 20.00 50.00

2008-09 The Cup Foundations Jerseys

CFAK Anze Kopitar 12.00 30.00
CFAO Adam Oates 8.00 20.00
CFBC Bobby Clarke 12.00 30.00
CFBH Bobby Hull 15.00 40.00
CFBK Mikkel Boedker 10.00 25.00
CFBL Brian Leetch 6.00 15.00
CFBM Ben Maxwell 8.00 20.00
CFBS Brandon Sutter 8.00 20.00
CFBT Bryan Trottier 8.00 20.00
CFBU Johnny Bucyk 8.00 20.00
CFBW Blake Wheeler 20.00 50.00
CFCG Colton Gillies 6.00 15.00
CFCS Cory Schneider 25.00 60.00
CFDB Derick Brassard 8.00 20.00
CFDD Drew Doughty 20.00 50.00
CFDE Denis Savard 8.00 20.00
CFEM Evgeni Malkin 15.00 40.00
CFEP Phil Esposito 12.00 30.00
CFES Eric Staal 10.00 25.00
CFFB Fabian Brunnstrom 6.00 15.00
CFGF Grant Fuhr 12.00 30.00
CFGH Gordie Howe 25.00 60.00
CFHA Dominik Hasek 12.00 30.00
CFHE Dany Heatley 6.00 15.00
CFHL Henrik Lundqvist 20.00 50.00
CFHO Marian Hossa 8.00 20.00
CFHZ Henrik Zetterberg 10.00 25.00
CFIK Ilya Kovalchuk 8.00 20.00
CFJI Jarome Iginla 10.00 25.00
CFJK Carey Price 15.00 40.00
CFJN James Neal 15.00 40.00
CFJO Joe Sakic 15.00 40.00
CFJP Jean-Pierre Dumont 5.00 12.00
CFJS Jason Spezza 8.00 20.00
CFJT Joe Thornton 12.00 30.00
CFJV Jakub Voracek 15.00 40.00
CFKA Karl Alzner 5.00 12.00
CFKL Karl Lehtonen 10.00 25.00
CFKO Kyle Okposo 10.00 25.00
CFKT Kyle Turris 10.00 25.00
CFKV Alex Kovalev 6.00 15.00
CFLS Luke Schenn 10.00 25.00
CFMB Martin Brodeur 20.00 50.00
CFMF Marc-Andre Fleury 15.00 40.00
CFMG Sam Gagner 5.00 12.00
CFMH Milan Hejduk 6.00 15.00
CFMK Nicklas Backstrom 8.00 20.00
CFML Mario Lemieux 30.00 80.00
CFMM Mark Messier 15.00 40.00
CFMO Mike Modano 12.00 30.00
CFMR Mike Richards 6.00 15.00
CFMS Martin St. Louis 8.00 20.00
CFMT Marty Turco 8.00 20.00
CFNF Nikita Filatov 8.00 20.00
CFNL Nicklas Lidstrom 8.00 20.00
CFOV Alexander Ovechkin 30.00 80.00
CFPB Patrice Bergeron 10.00 25.00
CFPD Pavel Datsyuk 12.00 30.00
CFPH Dion Phaneuf 6.00 15.00
CFPK Paul Kariya 8.00 20.00
CFPR Patrick Roy 20.00 50.00
CFPS Paul Stastny 6.00 15.00
CFRB Ray Bourque 12.00 30.00
CFRL Roberto Luongo 12.00 30.00
CFRN Rick Nash 8.00 20.00
CFRS Ryan Smyth 6.00 15.00
CFRV Rogie Vachon 10.00 25.00
CFSC Sidney Crosby 30.00 80.00
CFSD Shane Doan 6.00 15.00
CFSF Sergei Fedorov 12.00 30.00
CFSG Simon Gagne 8.00 20.00
CFSK Saku Koivu 8.00 20.00
CFSL Jordan Staal 6.00 15.00
CFSS Steven Stamkos 30.00 80.00
CFST Chris Stewart 8.00 20.00
CFSU Mats Sundin 8.00 20.00
CFSV Simeon Varlamov 15.00 40.00
CFSY Peter Stastny 6.00 15.00
CFTH Tomas Holmstrom 6.00 15.00
CFTS Teemu Selanne 15.00 40.00
CFTV Thomas Vanek 6.00 15.00
CFTW Peter Mueller 6.00 15.00
CFVL Vincent Lecavalier 8.00 20.00
CFWG Wayne Gretzky 50.00 125.00
CFWR Wade Redden 5.00 12.00
CFZB Zach Bogosian 10.00 25.00
CFZP Zach Parise 8.00 20.00

2008-09 The Cup Honorable Numbers

HNAP Alex Pietrangelo/27 25.00 60.00
HNBK Mikkel Boedker/89 20.00 50.00
HNBS Brandon Sutter/16 15.00 40.00
HNBW Blake Wheeler/26 40.00 100.00
HNCG Colton Gillies/18 12.00 30.00
HNCP Carey Price/31 30.00 80.00
HNDB Derick Brassard/16 15.00 40.00
HNDC Dino Ciccarelli/22 15.00 40.00
HNEM Evgeni Malkin/71 30.00 80.00
HNFB Fabian Brunnstrom/96 12.00 30.00
HNGA Sam Gagner/89 10.00 25.00
HNGF Grant Fuhr/31 25.00 60.00
HNHL Henrik Lundqvist/30 40.00 100.00
HNIK Ilya Kovalchuk/17 15.00 40.00
HNJT Jonathan Toews/19 25.00 60.00
HNJV Jakub Voracek/93 30.00 80.00
HNKO Kyle Okposo/21 20.00 50.00
HNKT Kyle Turris/91 25.00 60.00
HNMB Martin Brodeur/30 40.00 100.00
HNMF Michael Frolik/67 15.00 40.00
HNML Mario Lemieux/66 60.00 150.00
HNMT Marty Turco/35 15.00 40.00
HNNB Nicklas Backstrom/19 15.00 40.00
HNNF Nikita Filatov/28 15.00 40.00
HNPK Patrick Kane/88 30.00 80.00
HNPM Peter Mueller/88 12.00 30.00
HNPR Patrick Roy/33 40.00 100.00
HNRB Ray Bourque/77 25.00 60.00
HNRM Ryan Miller/30 15.00 40.00
HNRN Rick Nash/61 15.00 40.00
HNSC Sidney Crosby/87 150.00 300.00
HNSS Steven Stamkos/91 125.00 300.00
HNTH Joe Thornton/19 25.00 60.00
HNTV Thomas Vanek/26 12.00 30.00

2008-09 The Cup Honorable Numbers Dual

HN2BM Brodeur/Miller/30 30.00 80.00
HN2BS Sutter/Brassard/16 12.00 30.00
HN2DB Doan/Backstrom/19 12.00 30.00
HN2FG Giroux/Filatov/28 25.00 60.00
HN2FP Price/Fuhr/31 25.00 60.00
HN2GS Stewart/Gerbe/42 12.00 30.00
HN2KK Kurri/Kovalchuk/17 12.00 30.00
HN2KM Kane/Mueller/88 25.00 60.00
HN2NG Gillies/Neal/18 25.00 60.00
HN2NR Richards/Neal/18 25.00 60.00
HN2SG Giguere/Schneider/35 30.00 80.00
HN2SS Stastny/Stastny/26 10.00 25.00
HN2SW Wheeler/Pa.Stastny/26 30.00 80.00
HN2TB Thornton/Backstrom/19 20.00 50.00
HN2TK Kulemin/Tikhonov/41 12.00 30.00
HN2TS Turris/Stamkos/91 50.00 125.00
HN2TT Toews/Thornton/19 20.00 50.00

2008-09 The Cup Limited Logos Autographs

LLAP Alex Pietrangelo 25.00 60.00
LLBL Brian Leetch 12.00 30.00
LLBO Mikkel Boedker 20.00 50.00
LLBS Brandon Sutter 15.00 40.00
LLBW Blake Wheeler 40.00 100.00
LLCD Chris Drury 12.00 30.00
LLCG Colton Gillies 12.00 30.00
LLCP Carey Price 30.00 80.00
LLCS Cory Schneider 40.00 100.00
LLCW Cam Ward 15.00 40.00
LLDB Derick Brassard 15.00 40.00
LLDD Drew Doughty 40.00 100.00
LLDG Doug Gilmour 20.00 50.00
LLDH Dany Heatley 12.00 30.00
LLDS Daniel Sedin 20.00 50.00
LLEM Evgeni Malkin 100.00 250.00
LLES Eric Staal 20.00 50.00
LLFR Michael Frolik 15.00 40.00
LLGA Glenn Anderson 12.00 30.00
LLHA Dominik Hasek 25.00 60.00
LLHE Milan Hejduk 12.00 30.00
LLHL Henrik Lundqvist 40.00 100.00
LLHS Henrik Sedin 20.00 50.00
LLHZ Henrik Zetterberg 20.00 50.00
LLIK Ilya Kovalchuk 15.00 40.00
LLJC Jeff Carter 12.00 30.00
LLJI Jarome Iginla 20.00 50.00
LLJN James Neal 30.00 80.00
LLJS Jordan Staal 12.00 30.00
LLJT Joe Thornton 25.00 60.00
LLJV Jakub Voracek 30.00 80.00
LLKA Karl Alzner 10.00 25.00
LLKE Phil Kessel 15.00 40.00
LLKO Anze Kopitar 25.00 60.00
LLKT Kyle Turris 25.00 60.00
LLLK Lauri Korpikoski 10.00 25.00
LLLR Luc Robitaille 15.00 40.00
LLLS Luke Schenn 20.00 50.00
LLMB Martin Brodeur 40.00 100.00
LLMC Mike Cammalleri 12.00 30.00
LLMF Marc-Andre Fleury 30.00 80.00
LLMG Marian Gaborik 15.00 40.00
LLMH Marian Hossa 15.00 40.00
LLML Mario Lemieux 60.00 150.00
LLMM Mark Messier 30.00 80.00
LLMN Markus Naslund 15.00 40.00
LLMO Mike Modano 25.00 60.00
LLMS Martin St. Louis 15.00 40.00
LLMT Marty Turco 15.00 40.00
LLNB Nicklas Backstrom 15.00 40.00
LLNF Nikita Filatov 15.00 40.00
LLNK Nikolai Kulemin 15.00 40.00
LLNL Nicklas Lidstrom 15.00 40.00
LLOS T.J. Oshie 30.00 80.00
LLPB Patrice Bergeron 12.00 30.00
LLPD Pavel Datsyuk 25.00 60.00
LLPH Patric Hornqvist 15.00 40.00
LLPK Patrick Kane 30.00 80.00
LLPM Peter Mueller 12.00 30.00
LLPR Patrick Roy 80.00 200.00
LLPV Petr Vrana 10.00 25.00
LLRB Ray Bourque 25.00 60.00
LLRI Mike Richards 12.00 30.00
LLRM Ryan Miller 15.00 40.00
LLRN Rick Nash 15.00 40.00
LLSC Sidney Crosby 250.00 350.00
LLSG Sam Gagner 10.00 25.00
LLSH Steve Shutt 15.00 40.00
LLSI Simon Gagne 15.00 40.00
LLSK Saku Koivu 15.00 40.00
LLSP Peter Stastny 12.00 30.00
LLSS Steven Stamkos 500.00 1200.00
LLTO Jonathan Toews 80.00 200.00
LLVL Vincent Lecavalier 15.00 40.00
LLVO Tomas Vokoun 15.00 40.00
LLZB Zach Bogosian 20.00 50.00

2008-09 The Cup Scripted Swatches

SSBO Mikkel Boedker 15.00 40.00
SSBS Brandon Sutter 12.00 30.00
SSBW Blake Wheeler 30.00 80.00
SSCG Claude Giroux 25.00 60.00
SSCP Carey Price 25.00 60.00
SSCW Cam Ward 15.00 40.00
SSDB Derick Brassard 12.00 30.00
SSDC Dino Ciccarelli 15.00 40.00
SSDD Drew Doughty 30.00 80.00
SSDG Doug Gilmour 15.00 40.00
SSDH Dany Heatley 10.00 25.00
SSEM Evgeni Malkin 25.00 60.00
SSES Eric Staal 15.00 40.00
SSFB Fabian Brunnstrom 10.00 25.00
SSFR Michael Frolik 15.00 40.00
SSGA Simon Gagne 12.00 30.00
SSGI Colton Gillies 10.00 25.00
SSHA Dominik Hasek 20.00 50.00
SSHL Henrik Lundqvist 30.00 80.00
SSHZ Henrik Zetterberg 15.00 40.00
SSIK Ilya Kovalchuk 15.00 40.00
SSJI Jarome Iginla 15.00 40.00
SSJN James Neal 25.00 60.00
SSJT Joe Thornton 25.00 60.00
SSJV Jakub Voracek 25.00 60.00
SSKO Kyle Okposo 15.00 40.00
SSKT Kyle Turris 20.00 50.00
SSLS Luke Schenn 12.00 30.00
SSMB Martin Brodeur 30.00 80.00
SSMC Mike Cammalleri 10.00 25.00
SSMF Marc-Andre Fleury 25.00 60.00
SSML Mario Lemieux 50.00 125.00
SSMM Mark Messier 25.00 60.00
SSMN Markus Naslund 12.00 30.00
SSMS Martin St. Louis 12.00 30.00
SSMT Marty Turco 12.00 30.00
SSNB Nicklas Backstrom 12.00 30.00
SSNF Nikita Filatov 12.00 30.00
SSNL Nicklas Lidstrom 12.00 30.00
SSOS T.J. Oshie 25.00 60.00
SSPB Patrik Berglund 10.00 25.00
SSPH Patric Hornqvist 12.00 30.00
SSPK Patrick Kane 25.00 60.00
SSPM Peter Mueller 10.00 25.00
SSPR Patrick Roy 30.00 80.00
SSRN Rick Nash 12.00 30.00
SSSC Sidney Crosby 150.00 250.00
SSSD Shane Doan 10.00 25.00
SSSG Sam Gagner 8.00 20.00
SSSS Steven Stamkos 50.00 125.00
SSST Peter Stastny 10.00 25.00
SSTO Jonathan Toews 20.00 50.00
SSTV Thomas Vanek 10.00 25.00
SSVL Vincent Lecavalier 12.00 30.00
SSZB Zach Bogosian 15.00 40.00

2008-09 The Cup Signature Patches

SPPS Paul Stastny 12.00 30.00
SPAK Anze Kopitar 25.00 60.00
SPBH Bobby Hull/25 30.00 80.00
SPBK Mikkel Boedker 20.00 50.00
SPBS Brandon Sutter 15.00 40.00
SPBW Blake Wheeler 40.00 100.00
SPCG Colton Gillies 12.00 30.00
SPCP Carey Price 30.00 80.00
SPDB Derick Brassard 15.00 40.00
SPDD Drew Doughty 40.00 100.00
SPDH Dany Heatley 12.00 30.00
SPEM Evgeni Malkin 30.00 80.00
SPES Eric Staal 20.00 50.00
SPFB Fabian Brunnstrom 12.00 30.00
SPFL Marc-Andre Fleury 30.00 80.00
SPGH Gordie Howe/25 50.00 125.00
SPHA Dale Hawerchuk 20.00 50.00
SPHK Dominik Hasek 25.00 60.00
SPIK Ilya Kovalchuk 15.00 40.00
SPJI Jarome Iginla 20.00 50.00
SPJN James Neal 30.00 80.00
SPJT Jonathan Toews 25.00 60.00
SPJV Jakub Voracek 30.00 80.00
SPKA Patrick Kane 30.00 80.00
SPKT Kyle Turris 25.00 60.00
SPLS Luke Schenn 20.00 50.00
SPMB Martin Brodeur/25 60.00 150.00
SPME Mark Messier/25 30.00 80.00
SPMF Michael Frolik 15.00 40.00
SPML Mario Lemieux/25 100.00 200.00
SPMM Mark Messier 30.00 80.00
SPMR Mike Richards 12.00 30.00
SPMS Martin St. Louis 15.00 40.00
SPMT Marty Turco 15.00 40.00
SPNB Nicklas Backstrom 15.00 40.00
SPNF Nikita Filatov 15.00 40.00
SPNL Nicklas Lidstrom 15.00 40.00
SPPK Phil Kessel 15.00 40.00
SPPM Peter Mueller 12.00 30.00
SPPR Patrick Roy/25 60.00 150.00
SPRB Ray Bourque 25.00 60.00
SPRN Rick Nash 15.00 40.00
SPSC Sidney Crosby/25 150.00 300.00
SPSG Simon Gagne 15.00 40.00
SPSS Steven Stamkos 200.00 500.00
SPTH Joe Thornton 25.00 60.00
SPVL Vincent Lecavalier 15.00 40.00
SPWG Wayne Gretzky/25 300.00 800.00
SPZB Zach Boychuk 15.00 40.00

2008-09 The Cup Stanley Cup Signatures

SCSBH Bobby Hull 30.00 80.00
SCSBO Bobby Orr 60.00 150.00
SCSES Eric Staal 20.00 50.00
SCSFM Frank Mahovlich 15.00 40.00
SCSGF Grant Fuhr 25.00 60.00
SCSGH Gordie Howe 50.00 125.00
SCSHZ Henrik Zetterberg 20.00 50.00
SCSJB Jean Beliveau 15.00 40.00
SCSJM Joe Mullen 12.00 30.00
SCSLM Lanny McDonald 12.00 30.00
SCSMB Martin Brodeur 40.00 100.00
SCSMI Mike Bossy 15.00 40.00
SCSML Mario Lemieux 60.00 150.00
SCSMM Mark Messier 30.00 80.00
SCSMS Martin St. Louis 15.00 40.00
SCSNL Nicklas Lidstrom 15.00 40.00
SCSPD Pavel Datsyuk 25.00 60.00
SCSPR Patrick Roy 60.00 150.00
SCSRB Ray Bourque 25.00 60.00
SCSVL Vincent Lecavalier 15.00 40.00
SCSWG Wayne Gretzky 250.00 600.00

2009-10 The Cup

1 Sidney Crosby 8.00 20.00
2 Ray Bourque 3.00 8.00
3 Jarome Iginla 2.50 6.00
4 Marian Gaborik 2.00 5.00
5 Anze Kopitar 3.00 8.00
6 Shane Doan 1.50 4.00
7 Sam Gagner 1.25 3.00
8 Alexander Ovechkin 8.00 20.00
9 Jonathan Toews 5.00 12.00
10 David Perron 1.50 4.00
11 Mark Messier 4.00 10.00
12 Pavel Datsyuk 3.00 8.00
13 Phil Kessel 2.00 5.00
14 Brad Richards 2.00 5.00
15 Bobby Hull 4.00 10.00
16 Teemu Selanne 4.00 10.00
17 Vincent Lecavalier 2.00 5.00
18 Cam Ward 2.00 5.00
19 Steve Yzerman 5.00 12.00
20 Carey Price 4.00 10.00
21 Saku Koivu 2.00 5.00
22 Patrick Marleau 2.00 5.00
23 Bobby Orr 8.00 20.00
24 Paul Kariya 2.00 5.00
25 Steve Mason 1.50 4.00
26 Mike Richards 1.50 4.00
27 Denis Potvin 2.00 5.00
28 Borje Salming 2.00 5.00
29 Jean Beliveau 2.00 5.00
30 Marty Turco 2.00 5.00
31 Derick Brassard 1.25 3.00
32 Martin Brodeur 5.00 12.00
33 Henrik Sedin 2.50 6.00
34 Jason Spezza 2.00 5.00
35 Gilbert Perreault 2.00 5.00
36 Phil Esposito 3.00 8.00
37 Paul Stastny 1.50 4.00
38 Brian Leetch 1.50 4.00
39 Simon Gagne 2.00 5.00
40 Miikka Kiprusoff 2.00 5.00
41 Scott Niedermayer 2.00 5.00
42 Guy Lafleur 2.50 6.00
43 Marc-Andre Fleury 4.00 10.00
44 Chris Drury 1.50 4.00
45 Joe Thornton 3.00 8.00
46 Ron Hextall 2.00 5.00
47 Ryan Miller 2.00 5.00
48 Mario Lemieux 8.00 20.00
49 Luke Schenn 2.00 5.00
50 Rick DiPietro 1.50 4.00
51 Ilya Kovalchuk 2.00 5.00
52 Mike Bossy 2.00 5.00
53 Shea Weber 1.50 4.00
54 Jari Kurri 2.00 5.00
55 Drew Doughty 2.50 6.00
56 Henrik Zetterberg 2.50 6.00
57 Dino Ciccarelli 2.00 5.00
58 Steven Stamkos 4.00 10.00
59 Grant Fuhr 3.00 8.00
60 Patrick Roy 5.00 12.00
61 Rick Nash 2.00 5.00
62 Tomas Vokoun 1.50 4.00
63 Eric Staal 2.50 6.00
64 Luc Robitaille 2.00 5.00
65 Mikko Koivu 2.00 5.00
66 Cam Neely 2.00 5.00
67 Dale Hawerchuk 2.50 6.00
68 Patrick Kane 4.00 10.00
69 Ryan Getzlaf 2.00 5.00
70 Daniel Sedin 2.50 6.00
71 Evgeni Malkin 4.00 10.00
72 Gordie Howe 6.00 15.00
73 Andrew Cogliano 1.25 3.00
74 Henrik Lundqvist 5.00 12.00
75 Mike Modano 3.00 8.00
76 Peter Mueller 1.50 4.00
77 Roberto Luongo 3.00 8.00
78 Bobby Clarke 3.00 8.00
79 Thomas Vanek 1.50 4.00
80 Marian Hossa 2.00 5.00
81 Larry Robinson 2.00 5.00
82 Tim Thomas 2.00 5.00
83 Dany Heatley 1.50 4.00
84 Peter Stastny 1.50 4.00
85 Jeff Carter 1.50 4.00
86 Nicklas Lidstrom 1.25 3.00
87 Martin St. Louis 2.00 5.00
88 Clark Gillies 2.00 5.00
89 Zach Parise 2.00 5.00
90 Wayne Gretzky 12.00 30.00
91 Taylor Chorney AU RC 8.00 20.00
92 Antti Khudobin AU RC 12.00 30.00
93 Alexander Salak AU RC 6.00 15.00
94 John Negrin AU RC 8.00 20.00
95 James Reimer AU RC 20.00 50.00
96 Steven Zalewski AU RC 6.00 15.00
97 Teemu Laakso AU RC 5.00 12.00
98 Braden Holtby AU RC 80.00 200.00
99 Aaron Gagnon AU RC 5.00 12.00
100 Tom Pyatt AU RC 8.00 20.00
101 Mathieu Carle AU RC 8.00 20.00
102 Mark Letestu AU RC 8.00 20.00
103 Carl Gunnarsson AU RC 5.00 12.00
104 Mathieu Perreault AU RC 10.00 25.00
105 Ryan Vesce AU RC 6.00 15.00
106 Tom Wandell AU RC 8.00 20.00
107 Mike Brodeur AU RC 6.00 15.00
108 Phil Oreskovic AU RC 8.00 20.00
109 Peter Regin AU RC 6.00 15.00
110 Tyler Eckford AU RC 6.00 15.00
111 David Laliberte AU RC 6.00 15.00
112 Oskars Bartulis JSY AU RC 8.00 20.00
113 Ryan O'Marra JSY AU RC 8.00 20.00
114 Lars Eller JSY AU RC 12.00 30.00
115 Brad Marchand JSY AU RC 200.00 500.00
116 Logan Couture JSY AU RC 40.00 100.00
117 Perttu Lindgren JSY AU RC 10.00 25.00
118 M.Grabner JSY AU RC 15.00 40.00
119 Cody Franson JSY AU RC 15.00 40.00
120 Tyler Bozak JSY AU RC 20.00 50.00
121 Sergei Shirokov JSY AU RC 8.00 20.00
122 J.Gustavsson JSY AU RC 15.00 40.00
123 Viktor Stalberg JSY AU RC 15.00 40.00
124 Victor Hedman JSY AU RC 150.00 400.00
125 Erik Karlsson JSY AU RC 200.00 400.00
126 M.Del Zotto JSY AU RC 12.00 30.00
127 Matt Gilroy JSY AU RC 12.00 30.00
128 Colin Wilson JSY AU RC 12.00 30.00
129 Dmitry Kulikov JSY AU RC 12.00 30.00
130 Jamie Benn JSY AU RC 80.00 200.00
131 Ryan O'Reilly JSY AU RC 60.00 150.00
132 Tyler Myers JSY AU RC 25.00 60.00
133 Evander Kane JSY AU RC 40.00 100.00
134 Antti Niemi JSY AU RC 20.00 50.00
135 Ville Leino JSY AU RC 10.00 25.00
136 M.Neuvirth JSY AU RC 15.00 40.00
137 Matt Pelech JSY AU RC 6.00 15.00
138 Kris Chucko JSY AU RC 8.00 20.00
139 Riku Helenius JSY AU RC 12.00 30.00
140 I.Vishnevskiy JSY AU RC 8.00 20.00
141 Jhonas Enroth JSY AU RC 15.00 40.00
142 Artem Anisimov JSY AU RC 20.00 50.00
143 M.Backlund JSY AU RC 20.00 50.00
144 C.Hanson JSY AU RC 12.00 30.00
145 Yannick Weber JSY AU RC 12.00 30.00
146 T.J. Galiardi JSY AU RC 12.00 30.00
147 S.Machacek JSY AU RC 12.00 30.00
148 Luca Caputi JSY AU RC 12.00 30.00
149 Brian Salcido JSY AU RC 8.00 20.00
150 Matt Beleskey JSY AU RC 20.00 50.00
151 Michael Sauer JSY AU RC 10.00 25.00
152 Jesse Joensuu JSY AU RC 10.00 25.00
153 Cal O'Reilly JSY AU RC 10.00 25.00
154 Ray Macias JSY AU RC 10.00 25.00
155 Keaton Ellerby JSY AU RC 10.00 25.00
156 Jakub Kindl JSY AU RC 12.00 30.00
157 Mike Santorelli JSY AU RC 10.00 25.00
158 Drayson Bowman JSY AU RC 12.00 30.00
159 A.MacDonald JSY AU RC 8.00 20.00
160 Ryan Stoa JSY AU RC 10.00 25.00
161 John Scott JSY AU RC 10.00 25.00
162 Matt Hendricks JSY AU RC 10.00 25.00
163 Byron Bitz JSY AU RC 10.00 25.00
164 Joel Rechlicz JSY AU RC 8.00 20.00
165 Alec Martinez JSY AU RC 15.00 40.00
166 Jason Demers JSY AU RC 15.00 40.00
167 Benn Ferriero JSY AU RC 12.00 30.00
168 Frazer McLaren JSY AU RC 10.00 25.00
169 Matthew Corrente JSY AU RC 10.00 25.00
170 Jay Rosehill JSY AU RC 10.00 25.00
171 Chris Butler JSY AU RC 8.00 20.00
172 Tyler Ennis JSY AU RC 15.00 40.00
173 Daniel Larsson JSY AU RC 10.00 25.00
174 Bobby Sanguinetti JSY AU RC 8.00 20.00
175 Colin McDonald JSY AU RC 10.00 25.00
176 Devan Dubnyk JSY AU RC 30.00 80.00
177 Danny Irmen JSY AU RC 8.00 20.00
178 M.Duchene JSY AU RC/99 300.00 700.00
179 van Riemsdyk JSY AU RC/99 150.00 400.00
180 J.Tavares JSY AU RC/99 1500.00 2000.00

2009-10 The Cup Gold

*GOLD 1-90: .8X TO 2X BASE
COMMON ROOKIE (91-177) 8.00 20.00
ROOKIE SEMISTARS 10.00 25.00
ROOKIE UNL.STARS 12.00 30.00
95 James Reimer 30.00 80.00
98 Braden Holtby 50.00 100.00
104 Mathieu Perreault 15.00 40.00
115 Brad Marchand 50.00 125.00
116 Logan Couture 25.00 60.00
120 Tyler Bozak 20.00 50.00
122 Jonas Gustavsson 15.00 40.00
123 Viktor Stalberg 12.00 30.00
124 Victor Hedman 30.00 80.00
125 Erik Karlsson 60.00 120.00
126 Michael Del Zotto 12.00 30.00
130 Jamie Benn 30.00 80.00
131 Ryan O'Reilly 25.00 60.00
132 Tyler Myers 20.00 50.00
134 Antti Niemi 25.00 60.00
136 Michal Neuvirth 15.00 40.00
141 Jhonas Enroth 15.00 40.00
148 Luca Caputi 12.00 30.00
150 Matt Beleskey 10.00 25.00
172 Tyler Ennis 15.00 40.00
176 Devan Dubnyk 15.00 40.00
178 Matt Duchene 40.00 100.00
179 James van Riemsdyk 60.00 120.00
180 John Tavares 125.00 250.00

2009-10 The Cup Gold Jerseys

1 Sidney Crosby 40.00 100.00
2 Ray Bourque 15.00 40.00
3 Jarome Iginla 8.00 20.00
4 Marian Gaborik 6.00 15.00
5 Anze Kopitar 10.00 25.00
6 Shane Doan 6.00 15.00
7 Sam Gagner 4.00 10.00
8 Alexander Ovechkin 20.00 50.00
9 Jonathan Toews 10.00 25.00
11 Mark Messier 12.00 30.00
12 Pavel Datsyuk 12.00 30.00
13 Phil Kessel 6.00 15.00
14 Brad Richards 6.00 15.00
15 Bobby Hull 12.00 30.00
16 Teemu Selanne 12.00 30.00
17 Vincent Lecavalier 6.00 15.00
18 Cam Ward 6.00 15.00
19 Steve Yzerman 15.00 40.00
20 Carey Price 12.00 30.00
21 Saku Koivu 6.00 15.00
22 Patrick Marleau 8.00 20.00
24 Paul Kariya 12.00 30.00
25 Steve Mason 5.00 12.00
26 Mike Richards 5.00 12.00
27 Denis Potvin 6.00 15.00
28 Borje Salming 12.00 30.00
29 Jean Beliveau 8.00 20.00
30 Marty Turco 6.00 15.00
31 Derick Brassard 5.00 12.00
32 Martin Brodeur 15.00 40.00
33 Henrik Sedin 8.00 20.00
34 Jason Spezza 6.00 15.00
35 Gilbert Perreault 6.00 15.00
36 Phil Esposito 10.00 25.00
37 Paul Stastny 5.00 12.00
38 Brian Leetch 10.00 25.00
39 Simon Gagne 6.00 15.00
40 Miikka Kiprusoff 8.00 20.00
41 Scott Niedermayer 8.00 20.00
42 Guy Lafleur 8.00 20.00
43 Marc-Andre Fleury 20.00 50.00
44 Chris Drury 5.00 12.00
45 Joe Thornton 10.00 25.00
46 Ron Hextall 8.00 20.00
47 Ryan Miller 12.00 30.00
48 Mario Lemieux 20.00 50.00
49 Luke Schenn 6.00 15.00
50 Rick DiPietro 8.00 20.00
51 Ilya Kovalchuk 10.00 25.00
52 Mike Bossy 15.00 40.00
53 Shea Weber 8.00 20.00
54 Jari Kurri 12.00 30.00
55 Drew Doughty 8.00 20.00
56 Henrik Zetterberg 8.00 20.00
57 Dino Ciccarelli 6.00 15.00
58 Steven Stamkos 10.00 25.00
59 Grant Fuhr 20.00 50.00
60 Patrick Roy 25.00 60.00
61 Rick Nash 10.00 25.00
62 Tomas Vokoun 6.00 15.00
63 Eric Staal 8.00 20.00
64 Luc Robitaille 6.00 15.00
65 Mikko Koivu 12.00 30.00
66 Cam Neely 6.00 15.00
67 Dale Hawerchuk 15.00 40.00
68 Patrick Kane 12.00 30.00
69 Ryan Getzlaf 6.00 15.00
70 Daniel Sedin 8.00 20.00
71 Evgeni Malkin 12.00 30.00
72 Gordie Howe 20.00 50.00
73 Andrew Cogliano 5.00 12.00
74 Henrik Lundqvist 15.00 40.00
75 Mike Modano 10.00 25.00
76 Peter Mueller 5.00 12.00
77 Roberto Luongo 20.00 50.00
79 Thomas Vanek 8.00 20.00
80 Marian Hossa 6.00 15.00
81 Larry Robinson 6.00 15.00
82 Tim Thomas 6.00 15.00

Card	Low	High
83 Dany Heatley	5.00	12.00
84 Peter Stastny	8.00	20.00
85 Jeff Carter	8.00	20.00
86 Nicklas Lidstrom	10.00	25.00
87 Martin St. Louis	8.00	20.00
88 Clark Gillies	6.00	15.00
89 Zach Parise	8.00	20.00
90 Wayne Gretzky	40.00	100.00

2009-10 The Cup Auto Draft Boards

Card	Low	High
DBBS Bobby Sanguinetti	15.00	40.00
DBCW Colin Wilson	25.00	60.00
DBDK Dmitry Kulikov	50.00	100.00
DBDU Matt Duchene	150.00	250.00
DBEK Erik Karlsson	175.00	300.00
DBIV Ivan Vishnevskiy	15.00	40.00
DBJK Jakub Kindl	50.00	100.00
DBJT John Tavares	250.00	500.00
DBJV James van Riemsdyk	60.00	120.00
DBKA Evander Kane	75.00	150.00
DBLC Logan Couture	100.00	200.00
DBLE Lars Eller	30.00	80.00
DBMB Mikael Backlund	60.00	120.00
DBMC Matthew Corrente	20.00	50.00
DBMD Michael Del Zotto	60.00	120.00
DBMG Michael Grabner	60.00	120.00
DBMP Matt Pelech	25.00	60.00
DBRH Riku Helenius	25.00	60.00
DBRO Ryan O'Marra	15.00	40.00
DBTE Tyler Ennis	40.00	100.00
DBTM Tyler Myers	100.00	200.00
DBVH Victor Hedman	60.00	150.00

2009-10 The Cup Emblems of Endorsement

Card	Low	High
EEAO Alexander Ovechkin		
EEBR Martin Brodeur	125.00	200.00
EEBS Bobby Sanguinetti	20.00	50.00
EECN Cam Neely	50.00	100.00
EECP Carey Price	175.00	300.00
EECW Colin Wilson	20.00	50.00
EEDB Drayson Bowman	20.00	50.00
EEDD Devan Dubnyk	30.00	80.00
EEDH Dany Heatley		
EEDP Dion Phaneuf	15.00	40.00
EEEK Evander Kane	50.00	100.00
EEEM Evgeni Malkin	90.00	150.00
EEES Eric Staal	25.00	60.00
EEHZ Henrik Zetterberg	75.00	135.00
EEIK Ilya Kovalchuk	25.00	60.00
EEJC Jeff Carter	30.00	80.00
EEJG Jonas Gustavsson	25.00	60.00
EEJI Jarome Iginla	90.00	150.00
EEJK Jari Kurri	25.00	60.00
EEJT Joe Thornton	30.00	80.00
EEJV James van Riemsdyk	100.00	175.00
EEKA Patrick Kane	40.00	100.00
EELC Logan Couture	60.00	120.00
EEMD Matt Duchene	100.00	175.00
EEMF Marc-Andre Fleury	75.00	135.00
EEMG Marian Gaborik	20.00	50.00
EEML Mario Lemieux	100.00	250.00
EEMM Mark Messier	75.00	125.00
EEMO Mike Modano	30.00	80.00
EEMR Mike Richards	75.00	125.00
EEMS Martin St. Louis	20.00	50.00
EEMT Marty Turco	25.00	60.00
EENB Nicklas Backstrom	50.00	100.00
EENL Nicklas Lidstrom	60.00	120.00
EEPD Pavel Datsyuk	40.00	80.00
EEPK Phil Kessel	25.00	60.00
EEPR Patrick Roy		
EERB Ray Bourque	50.00	100.00
EERM Ryan Miller	30.00	80.00
FFRN Rick Nash	75.00	125.00
EERO Luc Robitaille	25.00	60.00
EESC Sidney Crosby	300.00	500.00
EESD Shane Doan	25.00	60.00
EESM Steve Mason	25.00	60.00
EESS Sergei Shirokov	12.00	30.00
EEST Steven Stamkos	125.00	200.00
EESY Steve Yzerman	150.00	250.00
EETA John Tavares	150.00	250.00
EETM Tyler Myers	50.00	100.00
EETO Jonathan Toews	75.00	150.00
EETV Thomas Vanek	15.00	40.00
EEVH Victor Hedman	50.00	125.00
EEVL Vincent Lecavalier	25.00	60.00
EEVS Viktor Stalberg	20.00	50.00
EEWG Wayne Gretzky	600.00	1500.00

2009-10 The Cup Enshrinements

Card	Low	High
CEAO Alexander Ovechkin	30.00	80.00
CEBC Bobby Clarke	15.00	40.00
CEBH Bobby Hull	25.00	60.00
CEBO Bobby Orr	50.00	120.00
CECN Cam Neely	12.00	30.00
CECP Carey Price	25.00	60.00
CEDG Doug Gilmour	20.00	40.00
CEDH Dany Heatley		
CEEK Evander Kane	12.00	30.00
CEEM Evgeni Malkin	25.00	60.00
CEES Eric Staal	15.00	40.00
CEGF Grant Fuhr	20.00	50.00
CEGH Gordie Howe	50.00	100.00
CEGP Gilbert Perreault	12.00	30.00
CEHL Henrik Lundqvist	30.00	80.00
CEHZ Henrik Zetterberg	15.00	40.00
CEIK Ilya Kovalchuk	12.00	30.00
CEJB Jean Beliveau	30.00	60.00
CEJC Jeff Carter	10.00	25.00
CEJI Jarome Iginla	15.00	40.00
CEJK Jari Kurri	12.00	30.00
CEJT Jonathan Toews	20.00	50.00
CEJV James van Riemsdyk	20.00	50.00
CEKA Patrick Kane	25.00	60.00
CELR Luc Robitaille	15.00	40.00
CEMB Martin Brodeur	30.00	80.00
CEMD Matt Duchene	20.00	50.00
CEME Mark Messier	30.00	80.00
CEMG Marian Gaborik	12.00	30.00
CEMI Mike Bossy	12.00	30.00
CEML Mario Lemieux	50.00	100.00
CEMM Mike Modano	15.00	40.00
CEMR Mike Richards	10.00	25.00
CEMS Martin St. Louis	12.00	30.00
CEMT Marty Turco	8.00	20.00
CENL Nicklas Lidstrom	8.00	20.00
CEPE Phil Esposito	20.00	50.00
CEPK Phil Kessel	12.00	30.00
CEPR Patrick Roy	75.00	150.00
CERB Ray Bourque	20.00	50.00
CERN Rick Nash	15.00	40.00
CERO Larry Robinson	12.00	30.00
CESC Sidney Crosby	75.00	150.00
CESY Steve Yzerman	60.00	120.00
CETA John Tavares	50.00	100.00
CETH Joe Thornton	20.00	50.00
CEVH Victor Hedman	30.00	80.00
CEVL Vincent Lecavalier	12.00	30.00
CEWG Wayne Gretzky	200.00	500.00

2009-10 The Cup Enshrinements Dual

Card	Low	High
CE2BR Bourque/Orr	80.00	150.00
CE2BS Stalberg/Bozak	25.00	60.00
CE2CB Benn/Couture	30.00	80.00
CE2CR Richards/Clarke	25.00	60.00
CE2CV Carter/van Riemsdyk	12.00	30.00
CE2DM Datsyuk/Malkin	30.00	80.00
CE2DO O'Reilly/Duchene	30.00	80.00
CE2EN P.Esposito/Neely	25.00	60.00
CE2FW Wilson/Franson	15.00	40.00
CE2GB Bozak/Gustavsson	25.00	60.00
CE2GK Kessel/Gilmour	25.00	60.00
CE2GL Gaborik/Lundqvist	40.00	100.00
CE2GM Messier/Gretzky	250.00	600.00
CE2GS Shirokov/Grabner	15.00	40.00
CE2HT Toews/Hull	40.00	100.00
CE2IN Nash/Iginla	20.00	50.00
CE2KK Kovalchuk/Kane	10.00	25.00
CE2LD Leetch/Del Zotto	15.00	40.00
CE2LH Lidstrom/Hedman	80.00	200.00
CE2LY Yzerman/Lemieux	100.00	200.00
CE2ME Ennis/Myers	25.00	60.00
CE2MK Modano/Kane	30.00	80.00
CE2OB Ovech/Backstrm	60.00	150.00
CE2OM Ovechkin/Malkin	60.00	150.00
CE2PM Mason/Price	30.00	80.00
CE2RB Roy/Brodeur	80.00	150.00
CE2TD Tavares/Duchene	40.00	100.00
CE2TH Heatley/Thornton	25.00	60.00
CE2TS Tavares/Stamkos	50.00	120.00
CE2YH Yzerman/Howe	100.00	225.00

2009-10 The Cup Enshrinements Triples

Card	Low	High
CE3BGH Hedman/Gstvsn/Bcklnd	40.00	80.00
CE3DOM Malkin/Ovech/Datsyuk	125.00	200.00
CE3EBO P.Espo/Bucyk/Orr	125.00	200.00
CE3FKM Messier/Kurri/Fuhr	90.00	150.00
CE3KVW E.Kane/Wilson/Rmsdyk	40.00	100.00
CE3LAM Leetch/G.Andrsn/Messier	60.00	120.00
CE3LYG Yzermn/Gretzky/Lemieux	500.00	1200.00
CE3RBF M.Fleury/Brodeur/Roy	75.00	125.00
CE3RBL Roy/Beliveau/Lafleur	175.00	300.00
CE3TDH Hedmn/Tavares/Dchne	30.00	80.00

2009-10 The Cup Foundations Jerseys

Card	Low	High
CFAK Anze Kopitar	12.00	30.00
CFAM Al MacInnis	10.00	25.00
CFAN Antti Niemi	8.00	20.00
CFAO Alexander Ovechkin	15.00	40.00
CFBA Mikael Backlund	8.00	20.00
CFBL Brian Leetch	5.00	12.00
CFBM Brad Marchand	20.00	50.00
CFBR Bobby Ryan	6.00	15.00
CFBS Borje Salming	12.00	30.00
CFCG Claude Giroux	12.00	30.00
CFCN Cam Neely	6.00	15.00
CFCP Carey Price	15.00	40.00
CFCW Colin Wilson	5.00	12.00
CFDB Derick Brassard	5.00	12.00
CFDD Drew Doughty	10.00	25.00
CFDE Michael Del Zotto	5.00	12.00
CFDH Dany Heatley	10.00	25.00
CFDS Devin Setoguchi	6.00	15.00
CFDU Matt Duchene	12.00	30.00
CFDW Doug Wilson	6.00	15.00
CFEK Evander Kane	8.00	20.00
CFEM Evgeni Malkin	15.00	40.00
CFES Eric Staal	10.00	25.00
CFES Phil Esposito	12.00	30.00
CFGA Glenn Anderson	5.00	12.00
CFGH Gordie Howe	20.00	50.00
CFGP Gilbert Perreault	6.00	15.00
CFGR Michael Grabner	5.00	12.00
CFHA Dale Hawerchuk	8.00	20.00
CFHL Henrik Lundqvist	20.00	50.00
CFHZ Henrik Zetterberg	10.00	25.00
CFIK Ilya Kovalchuk	8.00	20.00
CFJB Jamie Benn	15.00	40.00
CFJC Jeff Carter	6.00	15.00
CFJG Jonas Gustavsson	6.00	15.00
CFJI Jarome Iginla	10.00	25.00
CFJO Jordan Staal	8.00	20.00
CFJS Jason Spezza	8.00	20.00
CFJT Joe Thornton	8.00	25.00
CFJV James van Riemsdyk	25.00	60.00
CFKA Paul Kariya	8.00	20.00
CFKE Phil Kessel	8.00	20.00
CFKO Mikko Koivu	8.00	20.00
CFLC Logan Couture	10.00	25.00
CFLE Lars Eller	5.00	12.00
CFLM Lanny McDonald	6.00	15.00
CFLR Larry Robinson	6.00	15.00
CFMA Martin Brodeur	20.00	50.00
CFMD Marcel Dionne	8.00	20.00
CFME Mark Messier	12.00	30.00
CFMF Marc-Andre Fleury	15.00	40.00
CFMG Marian Gaborik	12.00	30.00
CFMH Marian Hossa	8.00	20.00
CFMK Miikka Kiprusoff	8.00	20.00
CFML Mario Lemieux	20.00	50.00
CFMM Mike Modano	12.00	30.00
CFMR Mike Richards	6.00	15.00
CFMS Martin St. Louis	8.00	20.00
CFMT Marty Turco	8.00	20.00
CFNB Nicklas Backstrom	8.00	20.00
CFNL Nicklas Lidstrom	8.00	20.00
CFPD Pavel Datsyuk	12.00	30.00
CFPE Peter Stastny	8.00	20.00
CFPK Patrick Kane	15.00	40.00
CFPM Patrick Marleau	8.00	20.00
CFPR Patrick Roy	15.00	40.00
CFPS Paul Stastny	6.00	15.00
CFRB Ray Bourque	10.00	25.00
CFRG Ryan Getzlaf	8.00	20.00
CFRH Ron Hextall	15.00	40.00
CFRL Roberto Luongo	12.00	30.00
CFRM Ryan Miller	8.00	20.00
CFRN Rick Nash	8.00	20.00
CFRO Ryan O'Reilly	10.00	25.00
CFSC Sidney Crosby	50.00	120.00
CFSD Shane Doan	6.00	15.00
CFSK Saku Koivu	8.00	20.00
CFSM Steve Mason	6.00	15.00
CFSS Steve Shutt	6.00	15.00
CFST Steven Stamkos	12.00	30.00
CFSY Steve Yzerman	15.00	40.00
CFTA John Tavares	20.00	50.00
CFTB Tyler Bozak	10.00	25.00
CFTE Tony Esposito	10.00	25.00
CFTM Tyler Myers	8.00	20.00
CFTO Jonathan Toews	12.00	30.00
CFTT Tim Thomas	8.00	20.00
CFTV Tomas Vokoun	10.00	25.00
CFVH Victor Hedman	12.00	30.00
CFVI Ville Leino	4.00	10.00
CFVL Vincent Lecavalier	8.00	20.00
CFWA Cam Ward	10.00	25.00
CFWG Wayne Gretzky	50.00	100.00
CFZC Zdeno Chara	10.00	25.00
CFZP Zach Parise	8.00	20.00

2009-10 The Cup Honorable Numbers

Card	Low	High
HNCP Carey Price/31	50.00	120.00
HNCW Colin Wilson/33	20.00	50.00
HNEM Evgeni Malkin/71	40.00	100.00
HNGI Matt Gilroy/97	15.00	40.00
HNHL Henrik Lundqvist/30	40.00	100.00
HNHZ Henrik Zetterberg/40	75.00	150.00
HNIK Ilya Kovalchuk/17	30.00	80.00
HNJG Jonas Gustavsson/50	30.00	80.00
HNJK Jari Kurri/17	30.00	80.00
HNJT John Tavares/91	60.00	120.00
HNJV James van Riemsdyk/21	50.00	120.00
HNKA Erik Karlsson/65	75.00	150.00
HNKI Jakub Kindl/46	15.00	40.00
HNLC Logan Couture/39	30.00	80.00
HNLR Luc Robitaille/20	25.00	50.00
HNMA Martin Brodeur/30	60.00	120.00
HNMB Mikael Backlund/60	20.00	50.00
HNMF Marc-Andre Fleury/29	25.00	60.00
HNMG Mike Green/52	30.00	80.00
HNML Mario Lemieux/66	75.00	150.00
HNMR Mike Richards/18	25.00	60.00
HNMS Martin St. Louis/26	20.00	50.00
HNMT Marty Turco/35	20.00	50.00
HNNB Nicklas Backstrom/19	40.00	80.00
HNPA Patrick Kane/88	50.00	125.00
HNPE Patrik Elias/26	20.00	50.00
HNPK Phil Kessel/81	30.00	60.00
HNPS Paul Stastny/26	25.00	60.00
HNRB Ray Bourque/77	30.00	80.00
HNRM Ryan Miller/30	25.00	60.00
HNRN Rick Nash/61	30.00	60.00
HNRS Ryan Stoa/29	20.00	50.00
HNSD Shane Doan/19	30.00	60.00
HNSG Scott Gomez/91	15.00	40.00
HNSS Sergei Shirokov/25	15.00	40.00
HNSY Steve Yzerman/19	125.00	200.00
HNTH Joe Thornton/19	30.00	60.00
HNTM Tyler Myers/57	25.00	60.00
HNTO Jonathan Toews/19	50.00	100.00
HNVH Victor Hedman/77	80.00	200.00
HNVS Viktor Stalberg/45	15.00	40.00

2009-10 The Cup Honorable Numbers Dual

Card	Low	High
HN2BH Hedman/Bourque/77	80.00	200.00
HN2BL Lundqvist/Brodeur/30	125.00	250.00
HN2EB P.Esposito/Bourque/77	50.00	120.00
HN2EN Eller/Nash/61	40.00	80.00
HN2ES Stastny/Elias/26	30.00	60.00
HN2GH Gaborik/Hawerchuk/10		
HN2GT Gomez/Tavares/91	25.00	60.00
HN2HH Hull/Howe/9		
HN2IS Iginla/Staal/12		
HN2KC Kovalchuk/Carter/17	25.00	60.00
HN2KD Kane/Duchene/9		
HN2KK Kovalchuk/Kurri/17	30.00	80.00
HN2KM Kane/Mueller/88	30.00	60.00
HN2LS Schenn/Leetch/2		
HN2LV van Riemsdyk/Leino/21	25.00	60.00
HN2MD Modano/Duchene/9		
HN2NO Ovechkin/Neely/8		
HN2RC Ciccarelli/Robitaille/20		
HN2SS Stastny/Stastny/26	20.00	50.00
HN2SW Sedin/Wilson/33		
HN2TD Doan/Thornton/19		
HN2TY Thornton/Yzerman/19	75.00	150.00
HN2YT Yzerman/Toews/19	125.00	200.00

2009-10 The Cup Limited Logos Autographs

Card	Low	High
LLAO Alexander Ovechkin	75.00	150.00
LLBA Mikael Backlund	40.00	100.00
LLCN Cam Neely	30.00	80.00
LLCW Colin Wilson	30.00	80.00
LLDB Drayson Bowman	25.00	60.00
LLDK Dmitry Kulikov	25.00	60.00
LLDP Dion Phaneuf	20.00	50.00
LLDU Matt Duchene	40.00	100.00
LLEK Evander Kane	50.00	125.00
LLEM Evgeni Malkin	50.00	100.00
LLES Eric Staal	15.00	40.00
LLGI Matt Gilroy	15.00	40.00
LLGR Mike Green	30.00	80.00
LLHZ Henrik Zetterberg	40.00	100.00
LLIK Ilya Kovalchuk	25.00	60.00
LLJB Jamie Benn	40.00	100.00
LLJC Jeff Carter	20.00	50.00
LLJG Jonas Gustavsson	20.00	50.00
LLJI Jarome Iginla	25.00	60.00
LLJK Jakub Kindl	25.00	60.00
LLJT John Tavares	50.00	100.00
LLJV James van Riemsdyk	25.00	60.00
LLKA Erik Karlsson	60.00	150.00
LLKE Phil Kessel	25.00	60.00
LLLC Logan Couture	30.00	80.00
LLLE Ville Leino	25.00	60.00
LLMB Martin Brodeur	60.00	120.00
LLMD Michael Del Zotto	20.00	50.00
LLMG Marian Gaborik	25.00	60.00
LLML Mario Lemieux	75.00	150.00
LLMM Mike Modano	40.00	100.00
LLMR Mike Richards	20.00	50.00
LLMS Martin St. Louis	25.00	60.00
LLNB Nicklas Backstrom	30.00	80.00
LLOR Ryan O'Reilly	30.00	80.00
LLPD Pavel Datsyuk	20.00	50.00
LLPK Patrick Kane	60.00	120.00
LLPR Patrick Roy	100.00	200.00
LLRB Ray Bourque	40.00	100.00
LLRM Ryan Miller	25.00	60.00
LLRN Rick Nash	30.00	80.00
LLRO Luc Robitaille	40.00	100.00
LLSA Bobby Sanguinetti	15.00	40.00
LLSG Scott Gomez	20.00	50.00
LLSI Simon Gagne	15.00	40.00
LLSM Steve Mason	20.00	50.00
LLSS Sergei Shirokov	15.00	40.00
LLST Steven Stamkos	100.00	200.00
LLSY Steve Yzerman	75.00	150.00
LLTH Joe Thornton	40.00	100.00
LLTM Tyler Myers	30.00	80.00
LLTO Jonathan Toews	60.00	120.00
LLTV Thomas Vanek	20.00	50.00
LLVH Victor Hedman	40.00	80.00
LLVL Vincent Lecavalier	25.00	60.00
LLVS Viktor Stalberg	15.00	40.00

2009-10 The Cup Scripted Swatches

Card	Low	High
SSAC Andrew Cogliano	10.00	25.00
SSAO Alexander Ovechkin	75.00	150.00
SSBL Brian Leetch	40.00	80.00
SSCP Carey Price	30.00	80.00
SSCW Colin Wilson	15.00	40.00
SSDP Dion Phaneuf	12.00	30.00
SSEK Evander Kane	30.00	80.00
SSEM Evgeni Malkin	75.00	150.00
SSHL Henrik Lundqvist	50.00	100.00
SSJB Jamie Benn	50.00	125.00
SSJC Jeff Carter	40.00	100.00
SSJG Jonas Gustavsson	20.00	50.00
SSJK Jari Kurri	40.00	100.00
SSJS Jordan Staal	12.00	30.00
SSJT Joe Thornton	25.00	60.00
SSJV James van Riemsdyk	30.00	80.00
SSKA Patrick Kane	30.00	80.00
SSLC Logan Couture	40.00	100.00
SSMA Martin Brodeur	60.00	120.00
SSMB Mikael Backlund	25.00	60.00
SSMD Matt Duchene	100.00	200.00
SSMF Marc-Andre Fleury	25.00	60.00
SSMG Marian Gaborik	25.00	60.00
SSMM Mike Modano	30.00	80.00
SSMR Mike Richards	30.00	80.00
SSMS Martin St. Louis	15.00	40.00
SSMT Marty Turco	15.00	40.00
SSPD Pavel Datsyuk	25.00	60.00
SSPK Phil Kessel	20.00	50.00
SSPS Paul Stastny	12.00	30.00
SSSC Sidney Crosby	100.00	200.00
SSSM Steve Mason	12.00	30.00
SSSS Steven Stamkos	80.00	200.00
SSSY Steve Yzerman	75.00	150.00
SSTA John Tavares	100.00	200.00
SSTM Tyler Myers	50.00	100.00
SSVH Victor Hedman	80.00	200.00
SSVL Vincent Lecavalier	15.00	40.00

2009-10 The Cup Signature Patches

Card	Low	High
SPAA Artem Anisimov	8.00	20.00
SPAK Anze Kopitar	25.00	60.00
SPAO Alexander Ovechkin/25	100.00	200.00
SPBA Mikael Backlund	20.00	50.00
SPBE Jamie Benn	50.00	100.00
SPBH Bobby Hull/35	25.00	60.00
SPBL Brian Leetch	10.00	25.00
SPBO Tyler Bozak	20.00	50.00
SPBR Bobby Ryan/35	12.00	30.00
SPBS Brian Salcido	10.00	25.00
SPCD Chris Drury	12.00	30.00
SPCG Claude Giroux	30.00	80.00
SPCP Carey Price	75.00	150.00
SPCU Logan Couture	25.00	60.00
SPCW Colin Wilson	15.00	40.00
SPDB Derick Brassard	10.00	25.00
SPDG Doug Gilmour		
SPDK Dmitry Kulikov	15.00	40.00
SPDR Drayson Bowman	12.00	30.00
SPDU Matt Duchene	40.00	100.00
SPEK Evander Kane	25.00	60.00
SPEM Evgeni Malkin	30.00	80.00
SPES Eric Staal	20.00	50.00
SPGA Glenn Anderson	15.00	40.00
SPGI Matt Gilroy	12.00	30.00
SPGO Scott Gomez	12.00	30.00
SPHL Henrik Lundqvist	40.00	100.00
SPHZ Henrik Zetterberg	20.00	50.00
SPIK Ilya Kovalchuk	15.00	40.00
SPJC Jeff Carter	12.00	30.00
SPJG Jonas Gustavsson	15.00	40.00
SPJI Jarome Iginla/25	40.00	100.00
SPJK Jari Kurri	20.00	50.00
SPJS Jordan Staal	20.00	50.00
SPJT John Tavares	100.00	200.00
SPJV James van Riemsdyk	25.00	60.00
SPKA Erik Karlsson	50.00	100.00
SPKE Phil Kessel	15.00	40.00
SPKI Jakub Kindl	12.00	30.00
SPLC Luca Caputi	15.00	40.00
SPLE Ville Leino	10.00	25.00
SPMA Martin Brodeur/25	60.00	120.00
SPMD Michael Del Zotto	12.00	30.00
SPMF Marc-Andre Fleury	25.00	60.00
SPMG Marian Gaborik	15.00	40.00
SPML Mario Lemieux/25	100.00	200.00
SPMM Mark Messier/25	40.00	80.00
SPMO Mike Modano	20.00	50.00
SPMR Mike Richards	15.00	40.00
SPMS Martin St. Louis	15.00	40.00
SPMT Marty Turco	12.00	30.00
SPNB Nicklas Backstrom	25.00	60.00
SPNL Nicklas Lidstrom	10.00	25.00
SPOR Ryan O'Reilly	25.00	60.00
SPPD Pavel Datsyuk	40.00	100.00
SPPE Phil Esposito/25	30.00	80.00
SPPH Dion Phaneuf	12.00	30.00
SPPK Patrick Kane	50.00	100.00
SPPR Patrick Roy/25	75.00	150.00
SPPS Paul Stastny	12.00	30.00
SPRB Ray Bourque/25	30.00	80.00
SPRH Ron Hextall/35	12.00	30.00
SPRM Ryan Miller	20.00	50.00
SPRN Rick Nash	15.00	40.00
SPRO Luc Robitaille	20.00	50.00
SPRS Ryan Stoa	10.00	25.00
SPSC Sidney Crosby	175.00	300.00
SPSD Shane Doan		
SPSE Devin Setoguchi	12.00	30.00
SPSH Sergei Shirokov	8.00	20.00
SPSI Simon Gagne	15.00	40.00
SPSM Steve Mason	12.00	30.00
SPSS Steve Shutt	12.00	30.00
SPST Steven Stamkos	60.00	150.00
SPSW Shea Weber	20.00	50.00
SPSY Steve Yzerman/25	60.00	120.00
SPTH Joe Thornton	15.00	40.00
SPTM Tyler Myers	20.00	50.00
SPTO Jonathan Toews	40.00	80.00
SPTV Thomas Vanek	12.00	30.00
SPVH Victor Hedman	80.00	200.00
SPVL Vincent Lecavalier	10.00	25.00
SPVO Tomas Vokoun	12.00	30.00
SPVS Viktor Stalberg	12.00	30.00
SPWA Cam Ward	15.00	40.00
SPWG Wayne Gretzky/25	300.00	800.00

2009-10 The Cup Signature Patches Dual

Card	Low	High
SP2BG Grabner/Backlund		
SP2BN Bourque/Neely	60.00	120.00
SP2CG Gagner/Cogliano		
SP2CS Couture/Setoguchi	40.00	100.00
SP2CT Carter/Toews	30.00	80.00
SP2CV Carter/van Riemsdyk	40.00	100.00
SP2DK Kane/Duchene		
SP2DO Duchene/O'Reilly	40.00	100.00
SP2FM Malkin/Fleury	50.00	100.00
SP2FW Franson/Wilson	40.00	100.00
SP2GA Gaborik/Anisimov		
SP2GB Gustavsson/Bozak	20.00	50.00
SP2GL Gaborik/Lundqvist	50.00	125.00
SP2GM Messier/Gretzky	300.00	800.00
SP2GP Gomez/Price	25.00	60.00
SP2GS Grabner/Shirokov	20.00	50.00
SP2HB Hanson/Bozak	25.00	60.00
SP2HN Nash/Heatley		
SP2HT Hossa/Toews	75.00	150.00
SP2IB Backlund/Iginla	30.00	80.00
SP2ID Iginla/Doan		
SP2IS Iginla/St. Louis	25.00	60.00
SP2JS Stalberg/Gustavsson	25.00	60.00
SP2JV Hedman/Tavares	60.00	125.00
SP2KB Bozak/Kessel		
SP2KD Doughty/Kopitar	60.00	120.00
SP2KK Kane/Kovalchuk	40.00	100.00
SP2KM Kane/Modano		
SP2KV Kane/van Riemsdyk	40.00	100.00
SP2LD Leetch/Del Zotto		
SP2LG Gretzky/Lemieux	500.00	1200.00
SP2LM Leetch/Messier	40.00	100.00
SP2LN Niemi/Leino	50.00	100.00
SP2LS Lecavalier/Stamkos	40.00	100.00
SP2LY Yzerman/Lemieux	150.00	300.00
SP2LZ Lidstrom/Zetterberg	50.00	100.00
SP2MB Modano/Benn		
SP2ME Miller/Enroth	30.00	80.00
SP2MH Myers/Hedman	20.00	50.00
SP2MJ Kurri/Messier	40.00	100.00
SP2NB Nash/Brassard	30.00	80.00
SP2OB Ovechkin/Backstrom		
SP2OD Ovechkin/Datsyuk		
SP2OG Ovechkin/Green		
SP2OM Ovechkin/Malkin		
SP2PM Mason/Price	25.00	60.00
SP2PP Stastny/Stastny	15.00	40.00
SP2SD Stastny/Duchene	40.00	100.00
SP2SG Schenn/Gustavsson	40.00	80.00
SP2SS Sedin/Sedin		
SP2SW Ward/Staal	25.00	60.00
SP2TC Thornton/Couture	40.00	100.00
SP2TD Duchene/Tavares	125.00	250.00
SP2TH Heatley/Thornton		
SP2TK Kane/Toews	75.00	150.00
SP2TS Stamkos/Tavares	100.00	200.00
SP2TT Ennis/Myers	50.00	100.00
SP2VW Wilson/van Riemsdyk	30.00	80.00

2009-10 The Cup Stanley Cup Signatures

Card	Low	High
SCAD Alex Delvecchio		
SCAL Andrew Ladd	6.00	15.00
SCAM Al MacInnis	12.00	30.00
SCAN Glenn Anderson	8.00	20.00
SCAT Alex Tanguay	6.00	15.00
SCBB Bob Bourne		
SCBC Bobby Clarke	15.00	40.00
SCBH Bobby Hull	20.00	50.00
SCBL Brian Leetch	12.00	30.00
SCBO Bobby Orr	60.00	120.00
SCCD Chris Drury	8.00	20.00
SCCG Clark Gillies	10.00	25.00
SCCO Chris Osgood		
SCCW Cam Ward	10.00	25.00
SCDG Doug Gilmour	15.00	40.00
SCDP Denis Potvin	10.00	25.00
SCEM Evgeni Malkin	30.00	80.00
SCES Eric Staal	12.00	30.00
SCGA Glenn Anderson	8.00	20.00
SCGF Grant Fuhr	15.00	40.00
SCGH Gordie Howe	30.00	80.00
SCHZ Henrik Zetterberg	25.00	60.00
SCJA Jason Arnott	8.00	20.00
SCJB Johnny Bucyk	12.00	30.00
SCJG Jean-Sebastien Giguere	12.00	30.00
SCJK Jari Kurri	15.00	40.00
SCJS Jordan Staal	20.00	50.00
SCLR Larry Robinson	10.00	25.00
SCMB Martin Brodeur	30.00	80.00
SCME Mark Messier	30.00	80.00
SCMF Marc-Andre Fleury	20.00	50.00
SCMH Milan Hejduk	8.00	20.00
SCMI Mike Bossy	15.00	40.00
SCML Mario Lemieux	40.00	100.00
SCMM Mark Messier	30.00	80.00
SCMO Mike Modano	15.00	40.00
SCMS Martin St. Louis	10.00	25.00
SCMT Maxime Talbot	15.00	40.00
SCNL Nicklas Lidstrom	15.00	40.00
SCPA Patrick Roy	50.00	100.00
SCPD Pavel Datsyuk	15.00	40.00
SCPE Patrik Elias	10.00	25.00
SCPH Phil Esposito	15.00	40.00
SCPR Patrick Roy	50.00	100.00
SCRB Ray Bourque	12.00	30.00
SCRO Luc Robitaille	12.00	30.00
SCSB Scotty Bowman	12.00	30.00
SCSC Sidney Crosby	100.00	200.00
SCSG Scott Gomez	8.00	20.00
SCSY Steve Yzerman	60.00	120.00
SCTH Tomas Holmstrom		
SCTL Ted Lindsay	10.00	25.00
SCVF Valtteri Filppula	15.00	40.00
SCVL Vincent Lecavalier	15.00	40.00
SCWG Wayne Gretzky	200.00	500.00

2009-10 The Cup Stanley Cup Signatures Dual

Card	Low	High
SC2AE Elias/Arnott	15.00	40.00
SC2BG Bossy/Gillies	25.00	60.00
SC2BO Bucyk/Orr	75.00	150.00
SC2BP Bossy/Potvin	25.00	60.00
SC2DT Drury/Tanguay	20.00	50.00
SC2DZ Zetterberg/Datsyuk	30.00	60.00
SC2EO Orr/Esposito	75.00	150.00
SC2FA Anderson/Fuhr	25.00	50.00
SC2FT Fleury/Talbot		
SC2GA Delvecchio/Howe	40.00	100.00
SC2GB Gomez/Brodeur	30.00	80.00
SC2GM Gilmour/MacInnis	25.00	60.00
SC2HD Hejduk/Drury	10.00	25.00
SC2KG Kurri/Gretzky	250.00	600.00
SC2LD Delvecchio/Lindsay	20.00	50.00
SC2LM Leetch/Messier	40.00	100.00
SC2LS Lecavalier/St. Louis	15.00	40.00
SC2LZ Zetterberg/Lidstrom	30.00	80.00
SC2MC Modano/Carbonneau		
SC2MS Malkin/Staal		
SC2RB Roy/Bourque	40.00	80.00
SC2SB Boyle/St. Louis	12.00	30.00
SC2SL Staal/Ladd		
SC2SW Ward/Staal	15.00	40.00
SC2WM Messier/Gretzky	200.00	500.00
SC2YB Yzerman/Bowman	60.00	120.00
SC2YR Yzerman/Robitaille	60.00	120.00

2009-10 The Cup Trios Jerseys

Card	Low	High
CTASK Alfredssn/Kovalv/Spez	8.00	20.00
CTBGB Gillies/Bossy/Bourne		
CTBMR MacIns/Robinsn/Bourque	12.00	30.00
CTBPB Bourne/Bossy/Potvin		
CTBSW Ward/Staal/Brind`Amour	15.00	40.00
CTCBP Backlund/Chucko/Pelech	12.00	30.00
CTCDF Demers/Ferriero/Couture	10.00	25.00
CTCOM Malkin/Crosby/Ovechkin	30.00	80.00
CTCTS Stamkos/Crosby/Tavares	30.00	80.00
CTCWM Couture/Wilson/Mrchnd	15.00	40.00
CTDCP Clarke/Dionne/Perreault		
CTDGL Drury/Lundqvist/Gaborik	20.00	50.00
CTDMO McDnld/O'Marra/Dubnyk	15.00	40.00
CTEHH Hull/Esposito/Howe	50.00	100.00
CTEME Ennis/Enroth/Myers	12.00	30.00
CTENW Esposito/Wheeler/Neely		
CTFCM Crosby/Fleury/Malkin	30.00	80.00
CTFKM Fuhr/Messier/Kurri		
CTFOW Wilsn/Fransn/O'Reilly	8.00	20.00
CTGBS Stalberg/Bozak/Gustav	15.00	40.00
CTGDO Duchene/Galrdi/O'Rlly	20.00	50.00
CTGKH Karlsn/Gustav/Hedmn	25.00	60.00
CTHGV Hossa/Gaborik/Voracek	8.00	20.00
CTHTK Hossa/Kane/Toews	15.00	40.00
CTKBS Bozak/Kessel/Stalberg	12.00	30.00
CTKLK Kane/Lehtonen/Koval	12.00	30.00
CTKLN Lehton/Niemi/Kiprussf	12.00	30.00
CTKNG Koivu/Niedermyr/Getzlf	15.00	40.00
CTKOM Malkin/Koval/Ovech	30.00	80.00
CTKWM Marchand/Kane/Wilsn	30.00	80.00
CTLAM Messr/Andersn/Leetch	15.00	40.00
CTLCM Malkin/Mario/Crosby	30.00	80.00
CTLDZ Zetter/Lidstrm/Datsk	15.00	40.00
CTLEG Gustav/Lundqvst/Enroth	20.00	50.00
CTLIN Iginla/Nash/Lecavalier	10.00	25.00
CTLMM Modano/Leetch/Mullen		
CTLPM Mason/Price/Luongo	15.00	40.00
CTLSD Leetch/Sanguntt/Del Z	8.00	20.00
CTLSH Salming/Lidstrm/Hedmn	20.00	50.00
CTLSS Lecav/St. Louis/Stamks	15.00	40.00
CTLVB Vishnevsk/Benn/Lindgrn	25.00	60.00
CTLYM Yzrmn/Mssr/Lemieux	30.00	80.00
CTLYT Lemx/Tavares/Yzermn	30.00	80.00
CTMGK McDnld/Gilmour/Kessel		
CTMMG McDnld/Mullen/Gilmour		
CTMRB Benn/Richards/Modano	25.00	60.00
CTMTC Couture/Thrntn/Mrleau	15.00	40.00
CTMVM Miller/Myers/Vanek	20.00	50.00
CTNBM Nash/Mason/Brassrd	8.00	20.00
CTPKW Wilson/Kane/Parise	15.00	40.00
CTRBF Brodeur/Roy/Fleury	20.00	50.00
CTRBL Roy/Brodeur/Luongo	20.00	50.00
CTRCR Roy/Robinson/Carbon	20.00	50.00
CTRCV Richards/Carter/van R	20.00	50.00
CTRST Richards/Toews/Stastny	12.00	30.00
CTRTG Robitaille/Taylor/Gretzky	50.00	125.00
CTSDG Del Zotto/Sangntti/Gilry	8.00	20.00
CTSDH Hawrchk/Selann/Doan		
CTSDO Stastny/O'Reill/Duchen	12.00	30.00
CTSHN Heatly/Nash/St. Louis	8.00	20.00
CTSRL Lemaire/Robinson/Shutt	8.00	20.00
CTTDH Hedman/Tavars/Duchen	20.00	50.00
CTTKD Duchene/Tavares/Kane	30.00	80.00
CTVWG Wilson/vRmsdk/Gilry	20.00	50.00
CTYGM Messier/Yzermn/Gretz	50.00	125.00
CTYOD Yzermn/Osgood/Drapr	20.00	50.00
CTYZH Zetterbrg/Howe/Yzermn	40.00	100.00

2010-11 The Cup

Card	Low	High
1 Mike Green	2.50	6.00
2 Alexander Ovechkin	12.00	30.00
3 Alexander Semin	3.00	8.00
4 Nicklas Backstrom	3.00	8.00
5 Roberto Luongo	5.00	12.00
6 Daniel Sedin	4.00	10.00
7 Henrik Sedin	4.00	10.00
8 Jean-Sebastien Giguere	3.00	8.00
9 Phil Kessel	3.00	8.00
10 Dion Phaneuf	2.50	6.00
11 Tyler Bozak	2.00	5.00
12 Vincent Lecavalier	3.00	8.00
13 Martin St. Louis	3.00	8.00
14 Steven Stamkos	6.00	15.00
15 Jaroslav Halak	3.00	8.00
16 Antti Niemi	2.50	6.00
17 Patrick Marleau	3.00	8.00
18 Dany Heatley	2.50	6.00
19 Joe Thornton	5.00	12.00
20 Jordan Staal	2.50	6.00
21 Evgeni Malkin	6.00	15.00
22 Mario Lemieux	10.00	25.00
23 Marc-Andre Fleury	6.00	15.00
24 Sidney Crosby	12.00	30.00
25 Shane Doan	2.50	6.00
26 Mike Richards	2.50	6.00
27 Jeff Carter	2.50	6.00
28 Bobby Clarke	4.00	10.00
29 Eric Lindros	4.00	10.00
30 Jason Spezza	3.00	8.00
31 Mark Messier	5.00	12.00
32 Marian Gaborik	3.00	8.00
33 Henrik Lundqvist	8.00	20.00
34 Brian Leetch	2.00	5.00
35 Clark Gillies	2.50	6.00
36 Mike Bossy	2.50	6.00
37 John Tavares	5.00	12.00
38 Denis Potvin	2.50	6.00
39 Zach Parise	3.00	8.00
40 Ilya Kovalchuk	3.00	8.00
41 Martin Brodeur	8.00	20.00
42 Shea Weber	2.50	6.00
43 Carey Price	6.00	15.00
44 Larry Robinson	2.50	6.00
45 Guy Lafleur	3.00	8.00
46 Lars Eller	2.00	5.00
47 Mikko Koivu	3.00	8.00
48 Marcel Dionne	3.00	8.00
49 Anze Kopitar	5.00	12.00
50 Wayne Gretzky	15.00	40.00
51 Luc Robitaille	2.50	6.00
52 Drew Doughty	4.00	10.00
53 Ron Francis	3.00	8.00
54 Gordie Howe	8.00	20.00
55 Tomas Vokoun	2.50	6.00
56 Grant Fuhr	4.00	10.00
57 Jari Kurri	2.50	6.00
58 Steve Yzerman	6.00	15.00
59 Pavel Datsyuk	5.00	12.00
60 Nicklas Lidstrom	3.00	8.00
61 Johan Franzen	2.50	6.00
62 Henrik Zetterberg	4.00	10.00
63 Brad Richards	3.00	8.00
64 Steve Mason	2.50	6.00
65 Rick Nash	3.00	8.00
66 Chris Stewart	2.50	6.00
67 Patrick Roy	6.00	15.00
68 Matt Duchene	3.00	8.00
69 Paul Stastny	2.50	6.00
70 Milan Hejduk	2.50	6.00
71 Ray Bourque	4.00	10.00
72 Bobby Hull	5.00	12.00
73 Jonathan Toews	5.00	12.00
74 Patrick Kane	6.00	15.00
75 Phil Esposito	4.00	10.00
76 Marty Turco	3.00	8.00
77 Cam Ward	3.00	8.00
78 Eric Staal	4.00	10.00
79 Jarome Iginla	4.00	10.00
80 Miikka Kiprusoff	3.00	8.00
81 Tyler Myers	2.00	5.00
82 Thomas Vanek	2.50	6.00
83 Ryan Miller	3.00	8.00
84 Gilbert Perreault	2.50	6.00
85 Bobby Orr	10.00	25.00
86 Tuukka Rask	4.00	10.00
87 Cam Neely	2.50	6.00
88 Evander Kane	3.00	8.00
89 Teemu Selanne	6.00	15.00
90 Ryan Getzlaf	3.00	8.00
91 Philip McRae AU RC	6.00	15.00
92 Nick Bonino AU RC	8.00	20.00
93 Derek Smith AU RC	6.00	15.00
94 Nikita Nikitin AU RC	6.00	15.00
95 Matt Hackett AU RC	8.00	20.00
96 Johan Motin AU RC	5.00	12.00
97 Adam McQuaid AU RC	10.00	25.00
98 Robin Lehner AU RC	12.00	30.00
99 Cory Emmerton AU RC	8.00	20.00
100 Jeff Penner AU RC	10.00	25.00
101 Brayden Irwin AU RC	6.00	15.00
102 Matt Kassian AU RC	6.00	15.00
103 Brandon McMillan AU RC	6.00	15.00
104 Grant Clitsome AU RC	6.00	15.00
105 Nate Prosser AU RC	6.00	15.00
106 Maxime Fortunus AU RC	5.00	12.00
107 Chad Kolarik AU RC	6.00	15.00
108 Richard Bachman AU RC	8.00	20.00
109 J.T. Wyman JSY AU RC	10.00	25.00
110 Tommy Wingels JSY AU RC	10.00	25.00
111 Dustin Kohn JSY AU RC	10.00	25.00
112 A.Bodnarchuk JSY AU RC	10.00	25.00
113 R.McDonagh JSY AU RC	30.00	80.00
114 K.Daugavins JSY AU RC	12.00	30.00
115 T.J. Brodie JSY AU RC	10.00	25.00
116 Jim O'Brien JSY AU RC	12.00	30.00
117 Brett MacLean JSY AU RC	12.00	30.00
118 Tomas Tatar JSY AU RC	30.00	80.00
119 Zuccarello-Aasen JSY AU RC	30.00	80.00
120 Patrice Cormier JSY AU RC	12.00	30.00
121 Casey Wellman JSY AU RC	10.00	25.00
122 Matt Martin JSY AU RC	25.00	60.00
123 S.Della Rovere JSY AU RC	10.00	25.00
124 Nick Spaling JSY AU RC	10.00	25.00
125 Justin Mercier JSY AU RC	10.00	25.00
126 Keith Aulie JSY AU RC	10.00	25.00
127 Nick Palmieri JSY AU RC	10.00	25.00
128 Philip Larsen JSY AU RC	10.00	25.00
129 Pechurski JSY AU RC EX	12.00	30.00
130 Justin Falk JSY AU RC	8.00	20.00
131 Maxim Noreau JSY AU RC	8.00	20.00
132 Arturs Kulda JSY AU RC	10.00	25.00

133 Mark Olver JSY AU RC 10.00 25.00
134 Cody Almond JSY AU RC 10.00 25.00
135 Nick Johnson JSY AU RC 8.00 20.00
136 Evan Brophey JSY AU RC 10.00 25.00
137 Jeremy Morin JSY AU RC 10.00 25.00
138 Jamie Arniel JSY AU RC 10.00 25.00
139 J.Markstrom JSY AU RC 40.00 100.00
140 Henrik Karlsson JSY AU RC 10.00 25.00
141 Kyle Clifford JSY AU RC 12.00 30.00
142 Alex Plante JSY AU RC 10.00 25.00
143 Ian Cole JSY AU RC 10.00 25.00
144 Jared Cowen JSY AU RC 10.00 25.00
145 Dana Tyrell JSY AU RC 10.00 25.00
146 M.Scandella JSY AU RC 10.00 25.00
147 D.Tokarski JSY AU RC 10.00 25.00
148 Zach Hamill JSY AU RC 10.00 25.00
149 Jamie McBain JSY AU RC 10.00 25.00
150 Colby Cohen JSY AU RC 10.00 25.00
151 Nick Leddy JSY AU RC 12.00 30.00
152 A.Lindback JSY AU RC 10.00 25.00
153 Brandon Pirri JSY AU RC 10.00 25.00
154 Brandon Yip JSY AU RC 10.00 25.00
155 Eric Wellwood JSY AU RC 12.00 30.00
156 T.McCollum JSY AU RC 12.00 30.00
157 C.Fowler JSY AU RC EXCH 25.00 60.00
158 Kyle Palmieri JSY AU RC 20.00 50.00
159 Eric Tangradi JSY AU RC 10.00 25.00
160 E.Grachev JSY AU RC 10.00 25.00
161 Zac Dalpe JSY AU RC 12.00 30.00
162 Luke Adam JSY AU RC 10.00 25.00
163 Ekman-Larsson JSY AU RC 30.00 80.00
164 K.Shattenkirk JSY AU RC 25.00 60.00
165 Johansson JSY AU RC EX 60.00 150.00
166 Jacob Josefson JSY AU RC 10.00 25.00
167 Jordan Caron JSY AU RC 12.00 30.00
168 B.Schenn JSY AU RC 30.00 80.00
169 N.Niederreiter JSY AU RC 20.00 50.00
170 Mattias Tedenby JSY AU RC 10.00 25.00
171 A.Burmistrov JSY AU RC 15.00 40.00
172 M.Paajarvi JSY AU RC 12.00 30.00
173 Derek Stepan JSY AU RC 20.00 50.00
174 Nazem Kadri JSY AU RC 60.00 150.00
175 S.Bobrovsky JSY AU RC 200.00 500.00
176 P.K. Subban JSY AU RC 150.00 400.00
177 Jeff Skinner JSY AU RC 100.00 250.00
178 Jordan Eberle JSY AU RC 400.00 1000.00
179 Tyler Seguin JSY AU RC 300.00 800.00
180 Taylor Hall JSY AU RC 600.00 1200.00

2010-11 The Cup Gold

*GOLD 1-90: .8X TO 2X BASE
COMMON ROOKIE (91-180) 8.00 20.00
ROOKIE SEMISTARS 10.00 25.00
ROOKIE UNL.STARS 12.00 30.00
4 Nicklas Backstrom 6.00 15.00
22 Mario Lemieux 15.00 40.00
23 Marc-Andre Fleury 10.00 25.00
24 Sidney Crosby 25.00 60.00
27 Jeff Carter 12.00 30.00
29 Eric Lindros 12.00 30.00
50 Wayne Gretzky 50.00 100.00
98 Robin Lehner 20.00 50.00
99 Linus Omark 12.00 30.00
100 Jeff Penner 15.00 40.00
113 Ryan McDonagh 25.00 60.00
118 Tomas Tatar 30.00 60.00
119 Mats Zuccarello-Aasen 20.00 50.00
126 Keith Aulie 10.00 25.00
137 Jeremy Morin 10.00 25.00
139 Jacob Markstrom 25.00 60.00
156 Thomas McCollum 12.00 30.00
157 Cam Fowler 30.00 80.00
162 Luke Adam 10.00 25.00
163 Oliver Ekman-Larsson 15.00 40.00
164 Kevin Shattenkirk 20.00 50.00
165 Marcus Johansson 15.00 40.00
166 Jacob Josefson 10.00 25.00
167 Jordan Caron 12.00 30.00
168 Brayden Schenn 75.00 150.00
169 Nino Niederreiter 15.00 40.00
170 Mattias Tedenby 10.00 25.00
171 Alexander Burmistrov 10.00 25.00
172 Magnus Paajarvi 12.00 30.00
173 Derek Stepan 25.00 60.00
174 Nazem Kadri 30.00 80.00
175 Sergei Bobrovsky 40.00 100.00
176 P.K. Subban 100.00 200.00
177 Jeff Skinner 100.00 200.00
178 Jordan Eberle 100.00 200.00
179 Tyler Seguin 100.00 250.00
180 Taylor Hall 150.00 300.00

2010-11 The Cup Silver Jerseys

1 Mike Green 5.00 12.00
2 Alexander Ovechkin 25.00 60.00
3 Alexander Semin 6.00 15.00
4 Nicklas Backstrom 6.00 15.00
5 Roberto Luongo 10.00 25.00
6 Daniel Sedin 8.00 20.00
7 Henrik Sedin 8.00 20.00
8 Jean-Sebastien Giguere
9 Phil Kessel 6.00 15.00
10 Dion Phaneuf 5.00 12.00
11 Tyler Bozak 4.00 10.00
12 Vincent Lecavalier 6.00 15.00
13 Martin St. Louis 8.00 20.00
14 Steven Stamkos 12.00 30.00
15 Jaroslav Halak 6.00 15.00
17 Patrick Marleau 6.00 15.00
19 Joe Thornton 10.00 25.00
20 Jordan Staal 5.00 12.00
21 Evgeni Malkin 12.00 30.00
22 Mario Lemieux 25.00 60.00
23 Marc-Andre Fleury 8.00 20.00
24 Sidney Crosby 25.00 60.00
25 Shane Doan 8.00 20.00
26 Mike Richards 5.00 12.00
27 Jeff Carter 5.00 12.00
29 Eric Lindros 6.00 15.00
30 Jason Spezza 6.00 15.00
31 Mark Messier 12.00 30.00
32 Marian Gaborik 12.00 30.00
33 Henrik Lundqvist 15.00 40.00
34 Brian Leetch 5.00 12.00
35 Clark Gillies 6.00 15.00
36 Mike Bossy 6.00 15.00
37 John Tavares 12.00 30.00
39 Zach Parise 6.00 15.00
40 Ilya Kovalchuk 6.00 15.00
41 Martin Brodeur 15.00 40.00
42 Shea Weber 5.00 12.00
43 Carey Price 12.00 30.00
44 Larry Robinson 6.00 15.00
46 Lars Eller 4.00 10.00
47 Mikko Koivu 6.00 15.00
48 Marcel Dionne 8.00 20.00
49 Anze Kopitar 10.00 25.00
50 Wayne Gretzky 40.00 100.00
51 Luc Robitaille 8.00 20.00
52 Drew Doughty 8.00 20.00
54 Gordie Howe 20.00 50.00
55 Tomas Vokoun 5.00 12.00
57 Jari Kurri 6.00 15.00
58 Steve Yzerman 15.00 40.00
59 Pavel Datsyuk 10.00 25.00
60 Nicklas Lidstrom 6.00 15.00
61 Johan Franzen 8.00 20.00
62 Henrik Zetterberg 8.00 20.00
63 Brad Richards 6.00 15.00
64 Steve Mason 5.00 12.00
65 Rick Nash 6.00 15.00
66 Chris Stewart 5.00 12.00
67 Patrick Roy 15.00 40.00
68 Matt Duchene 6.00 15.00
69 Paul Stastny 5.00 12.00
70 Milan Hejduk 5.00 12.00
71 Ray Bourque 6.00 15.00
73 Jonathan Toews 10.00 25.00
74 Patrick Kane 12.00 30.00
75 Phil Esposito 10.00 25.00
76 Marty Turco 6.00 15.00
77 Cam Ward 6.00 15.00
78 Eric Staal 8.00 20.00
79 Jarome Iginla 8.00 20.00
80 Miikka Kiprusoff 6.00 15.00
81 Tyler Myers 4.00 10.00
82 Thomas Vanek 5.00 12.00
83 Ryan Miller 6.00 15.00
84 Gilbert Perreault 6.00 15.00
86 Tuukka Rask 8.00 20.00
87 Cam Neely 6.00 15.00
88 Evander Kane 6.00 15.00
90 Ryan Getzlaf 6.00 15.00

2010-11 The Cup Emblems of Endorsement

EEBR Martin Brodeur 100.00 200.00
EECP Carey Price 100.00 200.00
EEEL Eric Lindros 150.00 250.00
EEEM Evgeni Malkin 60.00 120.00
EEIL Igor Larionov 40.00 100.00
EEJE Jordan Eberle 200.00 400.00
EEJS Joe Sakic 150.00 250.00
EEJT John Tavares 40.00 100.00
EEMB Mike Bossy 60.00 120.00
EEMD Marcel Dionne 50.00 125.00
EEML Mario Lemieux 150.00 400.00
EEMM Mark Messier 80.00 200.00
EEMP Magnus Paajarvi 40.00 100.00
EENB Nicklas Backstrom 40.00 100.00
EEPD Pavel Datsyuk 60.00 150.00
EEPK Patrick Kane 80.00 200.00
EEPR Patrick Roy
EEPS P.K. Subban 200.00 400.00
EERF Ron Francis 40.00 100.00
EERM Ryan Miller 40.00 100.00
EESC Sidney Crosby EXCH 300.00 500.00
EESS Steven Stamkos 150.00 300.00
EESY Steve Yzerman 125.00 250.00
EETO Jonathan Toews 100.00 200.00
EETS Tyler Seguin 100.00 250.00
EEWG Wayne Gretzky 750.00 2000.00

2010-11 The Cup Enshrinements

CEAO Alexander Ovechkin 150.00 400.00
CEBC Bobby Clarke 20.00 50.00
CEBH Bobby Hull 15.00 40.00
CEBO Bobby Orr 75.00 150.00
CECN Cam Neely 12.00 30.00
CECP Carey Price 25.00 50.00
CECW Cam Ward 12.00 30.00
CEDI Marcel Dionne 15.00 40.00
CEDS Derek Stepan 8.00 20.00
CEEL Eric Lindros 30.00 60.00
CEEM Evgeni Malkin 25.00 60.00
CEES Eric Staal 15.00 40.00
CEGH Gordie Howe 60.00 120.00
CEGP Gilbert Perreault 12.00 30.00
CEHL Henrik Lundqvist 25.00 50.00
CEIL Igor Larionov 15.00 40.00
CEJB Johnny Bucyk 12.00 30.00
CEJE Jordan Eberle 50.00 100.00
CEJF Jeff Skinner 25.00 60.00
CEJG Jean-Sebastien Giguere 12.00 30.00
CEJH Jaroslav Halak 12.00 30.00
CEJI Jarome Iginla 15.00 40.00
CEJK Jari Kurri 12.00 30.00
CEJO Joe Thornton 20.00 50.00
CEJS Joe Sakic 25.00 60.00
CEJT Jonathan Toews 20.00 50.00
CEKE Phil Kessel 12.00 30.00
CELR Luc Robitaille 12.00 30.00
CEMB Martin Brodeur 30.00 80.00
CEMD Matt Duchene 12.00 30.00
CEME Mark Messier 25.00 60.00
CEMG Marian Gaborik 12.00 30.00
CEMH Milan Hejduk 10.00 25.00
CEMI Mike Bossy 12.00 30.00
CEML Mario Lemieux 50.00 100.00
CEMZ Mats Zuccarello-Aasen 12.00 30.00
CENB Nicklas Backstrom 15.00 40.00
CENK Nazem Kadri 20.00 50.00
CENL Nicklas Lidstrom 20.00 40.00
CEPE Phil Esposito 20.00 50.00
CEPK Patrick Kane 30.00 60.00
CEPR Patrick Roy 30.00 80.00
CEPS P.K. Subban 20.00 50.00
CERB Ray Bourque 20.00 50.00
CERF Ron Francis 20.00 50.00
CERG Ryan Getzlaf 12.00 30.00
CERK Red Kelly 10.00 25.00
CERM Ryan Miller 12.00 30.00
CERN Rick Nash 15.00 40.00
CESB Sergei Bobrovsky 30.00 80.00
CESC Sidney Crosby 75.00 150.00
CESY Steve Yzerman
CETA John Tavares 20.00 50.00
CETH Taylor Hall 15.00 40.00
CETS Tyler Seguin 25.00 60.00
CETV Thomas Vanek 10.00 25.00
CEWG Wayne Gretzky 150.00 400.00

2010-11 The Cup Enshrinements Dual

CE2CR B.Clarke/M.Richards EX 30.00 80.00
CE2FH G.Howe/R.Francis 60.00 150.00
CE2GB G.Howe/B.Orr 100.00 200.00
CE2GH W.Gretzky/T.Hall 400.00 1000.00
CE2GM W.Gretzky/M.Messier EX 250.00 600.00
CE2HC B.Hull/B.Clarke 40.00 100.00
CE2HD M.Duchene/M.Hejduk 20.00 50.00
CE2HE T.Hall/J.Eberle 75.00 150.00
CE2KK P.Kessel/N.Kadri 50.00 100.00
CE2KS J.Kurri/M.Paajarvi 30.00 80.00
CE2LB S.Bowman/I.Larionov 20.00 50.00
CE2ME M.Messier/J.Eberle 75.00 150.00
CE2MV R.Miller/T.Vanek 15.00 40.00
CE2NB C.Neely/R.Bourque 30.00 80.00
CE2OB Ovechkin/N.Bckstm EX 250.00 600.00
CE2OH B.Orr/B.Hull 100.00 200.00
CE2OM A.Ovechkin/E.Malkin EX 250.00 600.00
CE2PS C.Price/P.Subban 75.00 150.00
CE2RB P.Roy/M.Brodeur 100.00 200.00
CE2RS J.Sakic/P.Roy EX 75.00 150.00
CE2SC S.Crosby/S.Crosby EX 200.00 350.00
CE2SD J.Sakic/M.Duchene EX 50.00 100.00
CE2SZ Zuccarello-Asn/Stepan 25.00 60.00
CE2TD J.Tavares/M.Duchene 30.00 60.00
CE2TK P.Kane/J.Toews 40.00 100.00
CE2TS S.Stamkos/J.Tavares EX 60.00 120.00
CE2TT T.Seguin/T.Rask 30.00 80.00
CE2YH S.Yzerman/G.Howe 100.00 200.00

2010-11 The Cup Enshrinements Triple

CE3AVS Sakic/Roy/Bourque 125.00 250.00
CE3BOS Orr/Bucyk/Esposito 125.00 200.00
CE3CPT Gretzky/Mario/Yzerman 400.00 1000.00
CE3EDM Gretzky/Messier/Kurri
CE3NYR Z-Aasen/Grachv/Stepn 40.00 80.00
CE3OG6 Howe/Orr/Hull 175.00 300.00

2010-11 The Cup Foundations Jerseys

CFAK Anze Kopitar 12.00 30.00
CFAO Alexander Ovechkin 30.00 80.00
CFBO Mike Bossy 12.00 30.00
CFCP Carey Price 15.00 40.00
CFDP Dion Phaneuf 6.00 15.00
CFDU Matt Duchene 8.00 20.00
CFEK Evander Kane 8.00 20.00
CFEM Evgeni Malkin
CFES Eric Staal 10.00 25.00
CFHL Henrik Lundqvist 20.00 50.00
CFIK Ilya Kovalchuk 8.00 20.00
CFIL Igor Larionov 12.00 30.00
CFJC Jeff Carter 6.00 15.00
CFJE Jordan Eberle 25.00 60.00
CFJF Johan Franzen 8.00 20.00
CFJG Jean-Sebastien Giguere 10.00 25.00
CFJH Jaroslav Halak 8.00 20.00
CFJI Jarome Iginla 10.00 25.00
CFJS Joe Sakic 15.00 40.00
CFJT Joe Thornton 12.00 30.00
CFKE Phil Kessel 8.00 20.00
CFLR Luc Robitaille 10.00 25.00
CFMB Martin Brodeur 20.00 50.00
CFMD Marcel Dionne 8.00 20.00
CFMG Marian Gaborik 8.00 20.00
CFML Mario Lemieux 25.00 60.00
CFMM Mark Messier 20.00 50.00
CFMP Magnus Paajarvi 5.00 12.00
CFMR Mike Richards 6.00 15.00
CFNB Nicklas Backstrom 8.00 20.00
CFNL Nicklas Lidstrom 8.00 20.00
CFPD Pavel Datsyuk 12.00 30.00
CFPK Patrick Kane 15.00 40.00
CFPS P.K. Subban 25.00 60.00
CFRF Ron Francis 15.00 40.00
CFRH Ron Hextall 6.00 15.00
CFRL Roberto Luongo 12.00 30.00
CFRM Ryan Miller 8.00 20.00
CFRN Rick Nash 8.00 20.00
CFSC Sidney Crosby 30.00 80.00
CFSS Steven Stamkos 15.00 40.00
CFSY Steve Yzerman 15.00 40.00
CFTA John Tavares 12.00 30.00
CFTH Taylor Hall 10.00 25.00
CFTO Jonathan Toews 12.00 30.00
CFTS Tyler Seguin 12.00 30.00
CFWG Wayne Gretzky 50.00 100.00
CFZP Zach Parise 8.00 20.00

2010-11 The Cup Foundations Jerseys Autographs

CFAK Anze Kopitar 25.00 50.00
CFAO Alexander Ovechkin 60.00 120.00
CFBO Mike Bossy 25.00 50.00
CFCP Carey Price 50.00 100.00
CFDP Dion Phaneuf 12.00 30.00
CFDU Matt Duchene 15.00 40.00
CFEK Evander Kane 15.00 40.00
CFEM Evgeni Malkin 40.00 80.00
CFES Eric Staal 20.00 50.00
CFHL Henrik Lundqvist EXCH
CFIL Igor Larionov 25.00 50.00
CFJC Jeff Carter 12.00 30.00
CFJE Jordan Eberle 60.00 120.00
CFJF Johan Franzen 12.00 30.00
CFJG Jean-Sebastien Giguere 15.00 40.00
CFJH Jaroslav Halak 15.00 40.00
CFJI Jarome Iginla 20.00 50.00
CFJS Joe Sakic 40.00 80.00
CFJT Joe Thornton 25.00 60.00
CFKE Phil Kessel 15.00 40.00
CFLR Luc Robitaille 15.00 40.00
CFMB Martin Brodeur 40.00 80.00
CFMD Marcel Dionne 20.00 50.00
CFMG Marian Gaborik 15.00 40.00
CFML Mario Lemieux 60.00 120.00
CFMM Mark Messier 40.00 80.00
CFMP Magnus Paajarvi 25.00 50.00
CFNB Nicklas Backstrom 25.00 50.00
CFNL Nicklas Lidstrom 25.00 50.00
CFPD Pavel Datsyuk 30.00 60.00
CFPK Patrick Kane 40.00 80.00
CFPS P.K. Subban 40.00 100.00
CFRF Ron Francis 25.00 50.00
CFRH Ron Hextall 15.00 40.00
CFRM Ryan Miller 15.00 40.00
CFRN Rick Nash 15.00 40.00
CFSC Sidney Crosby 100.00 175.00
CFSS Steven Stamkos 50.00 100.00
CFSY Steve Yzerman 50.00 100.00
CFTA John Tavares 40.00 80.00
CFTO Jonathan Toews 75.00 150.00
CFWG Wayne Gretzky 250.00 600.00

2010-11 The Cup Honorable Numbers

HNAK Anze Kopitar/11
HNAO Alex Ovechkin/8
HNBB Sergei Bobrovsky/35 100.00 250.00
HNBL Brian Leetch/2
HNBR Bobby Ryan/9
HNCN Cam Neely/8
HNCP Carey Price/31 50.00 100.00
HNCS Chris Stewart/25 20.00 50.00
HNCW Cam Ward/30 20.00 50.00
HNDP Dion Phaneuf/3
HNEK Evander Kane/9
HNEM Evgeni Malkin/71 50.00 100.00
HNES Eric Staal/12
HNHL Henrik Lundqvist/30 60.00 120.00
HNIL Igor Larionov/8
HNJC Jeff Carter/17 25.00 50.00
HNJE Jordan Eberle/14
HNJF Johan Franzen/93 20.00 50.00
HNJG J-S Giguere/35 20.00 50.00
HNJI Jarome Iginla/12
HNJO Joe Thornton/19 40.00 80.00
HNJS Joe Sakic/19 100.00 200.00
HNJT Jonathan Toews/19 60.00 120.00
HNJV James van Riemsdyk/21 25.00 60.00
HNKE Phil Kessel/81 15.00 40.00
HNKS Kevin Shattenkirk/8
HNLR Luc Robitaille/20 50.00 100.00
HNMA Martin Brodeur/30 50.00 100.00
HNMD Matt Duchene/9
HNME Mark Messier/11
HNMF Marc-Andre Fleury/29 50.00 120.00
HNMG Marian Gaborik/10
HNMH Marian Hossa/81 30.00 60.00
HNML Mario Lemieux/6
HNMP Magnus Paajarvi/91 15.00 40.00
HNMS Martin St. Louis/26 25.00 60.00
HNMZ Mats Zuccarello-Aasen/36 25.00 60.00
HNNB Nicklas Backstrom/19 40.00 80.00
HNNK Nazem Kadri/43 30.00 80.00
HNPE Derek Stepan/21 30.00 60.00
HNPK Patrick Kane/88 50.00 100.00
HNPR Patrick Roy/33 125.00 225.00
HNPS P.K. Subban/76 75.00 150.00
HNRB Ray Bourque/77 100.00 175.00
HNRG Ryan Getzlaf/15 30.00 60.00
HNRI Brad Richards/91 15.00 40.00
HNRK Ryan Kesler/17 50.00 100.00
HNRM Ryan Miller/30 20.00 50.00
HNRN Rick Nash/61 30.00 80.00
HNSC Sidney Crosby/87 15.00 300.00
HNSD Shane Doan/19 25.00 50.00
HNSK Jeff Skinner/53 30.00 80.00
HNSM Steve Mason/1
HNSS Steven Stamkos/91 150.00 400.00
HNST Paul Stastny/26 20.00 50.00
HNSY Steve Yzerman/19 125.00 200.00
HNTA John Tavares/91 40.00 100.00
HNTM Tyler Myers/57 25.00 60.00
HNTR Tuukka Rask/40 40.00 80.00
HNTS Tyler Seguin/19 100.00 250.00
HNTT Tomas Tatar/12
HNTV Thomas Vanek/26 25.00 60.00
HNVL Vincent Lecavalier/4
HNWG Wayne Gretzky/9 EXCH

2010-11 The Cup Honorable Numbers Dual

BM Brodeur/Miller/30 EXCH 100.00 200.00
CC S.Crosby Dual/87 200.00 400.00
DJ D.Stepan/VanRmsdyk/21 30.00 60.00
ES T.Espo/S.Bobrvsky/35 100.00 250.00
HK M.Hossa/P.Kessel/81 25.00 60.00
KC R.Kesler/J.Carter/17 30.00 60.00
NB Naslund/Backstrom/19 50.00 100.00
SY J.Sakic/S.Yzerman/19 225.00 400.00
TS S.Stamkos/J.Tavares/91 100.00 250.00
TT Thornton/Toews/19
YS Yzerman/Seguin/19 EXCH 125.00 300.00

2010-11 The Cup Limited Logos Autographs

LLAK Anze Kopitar 60.00 150.00
LLAO Alexander Ovechkin 60.00 150.00
LLBB Sergei Bobrovsky 125.00 300.00
LLBD Brandon Dubinsky 15.00 40.00
LLBO Mike Bossy/25 60.00 150.00
LLBS Brayden Schenn 30.00 80.00
LLCF Cam Fowler 50.00 125.00
LLCG Claude Giroux 30.00 80.00
LLCN Cam Neely 25.00 60.00
LLCP Carey Price 60.00 150.00
LLCW Cam Ward 25.00 60.00
LLDD Drew Doughty 60.00 150.00
LLDS Derek Stepan 20.00 50.00
LLDU Matt Duchene 25.00 60.00
LLEL Eric Lindros 50.00 125.00
LLEM Evgeni Malkin 50.00 125.00
LLHL Henrik Lundqvist 40.00 100.00
LLIL Igor Larionov/25 50.00 125.00
LLJE Jordan Eberle 80.00 200.00
LLJF Johan Franzen 15.00 40.00
LLJG Jean-Sebastien Giguere 25.00 60.00
LLJH Jaroslav Halak 30.00 80.00
LLJI Jarome Iginla 25.00 60.00
LLJS Joe Sakic 50.00 125.00
LLKE Phil Kessel 25.00 60.00
LLKN Patrick Kane 50.00 125.00
LLKS Kevin Shattenkirk 20.00 50.00
LLLR Luc Robitaille 30.00 80.00
LLMB Martin Brodeur 60.00 150.00
LLMD Marcel Dionne/25 80.00 200.00
LLMF Marc-Andre Fleury 25.00 60.00
LLMG Marian Gaborik 25.00 60.00
LLML Mario Lemieux 80.00 200.00
LLMM Mark Messier 50.00 125.00
LLMP Magnus Paajarvi 25.00 60.00
LLMZ Mats Zuccarello-Aasen 40.00 100.00
LLNB Nicklas Backstrom 25.00 60.00
LLNK Nazem Kadri 25.00 60.00
LLNL Nicklas Lidstrom 60.00 150.00
LLNN Nino Niederreiter 30.00 80.00
LLPA Paul Stastny 20.00 50.00
LLPD Pavel Datsyuk 40.00 100.00
LLPK P.K. Subban 60.00 150.00
LLPR Patrick Roy 80.00 200.00
LLRF Ron Francis 20.00 50.00
LLRG Ryan Getzlaf 25.00 60.00
LLRK Ryan Kesler 30.00 80.00
LLRM Ryan Miller 30.00 80.00
LLRN Rick Nash 30.00 80.00
LLSC Sidney Crosby 120.00 300.00
LLSK Jeff Skinner 60.00 150.00
LLSM Steve Mason 30.00 80.00
LLSS Steven Stamkos 60.00 150.00
LLST Jordan Staal 20.00 50.00
LLSY Steve Yzerman 50.00 125.00
LLTA John Tavares 40.00 100.00
LLTH Taylor Hall 60.00 150.00
LLTM Tyler Myers 25.00 60.00
LLTO Jonathan Toews 60.00 150.00
LLTR Tuukka Rask 40.00 100.00
LLTS Tyler Seguin 80.00 200.00
LLTT Tomas Tatar 40.00 100.00
LLTV Thomas Vanek 25.00 60.00
LLWG Wayne Gretzky/10 EXCH

2010-11 The Cup Auto Draft Boards

DBAB Alexander Burmistrov 60.00 150.00
DBAP Alex Plante 30.00 80.00
DBBS Brayden Schenn 125.00 250.00
DBCA Jordan Caron 75.00 150.00
DBCF Cam Fowler EXCH 75.00 150.00
DBIC Ian Cole 20.00 50.00
DBJC Jared Cowen 20.00 50.00
DBJE Jordan Eberle 400.00 800.00
DBJJ Jacob Josefson 20.00 50.00
DBJN John Carlson 60.00 120.00
DBJS Jeff Skinner 225.00 400.00
DBKP Kyle Palmieri 40.00 100.00
DBKS Kevin Shattenkirk 40.00 80.00
DBMJ Marcus Johansson EXCH 100.00 200.00
DBMP Magnus Paajarvi 75.00 150.00
DBMT Mattias Tedenby 20.00 50.00
DBNK Nazem Kadri 100.00 200.00
DBNL Nick Leddy 40.00 80.00
DBNN Nino Niederreiter 60.00 120.00
DBOB Jim O'Brien 25.00 60.00
DBOE Oliver Ekman-Larsson 60.00 120.00
DBRM Ryan McDonagh 50.00 100.00
DBTH Taylor Hall 600.00 900.00
DBTS Tyler Seguin 250.00 500.00
DBZH Zach Hamill 30.00 80.00

2010-11 The Cup Rookie Bookmarks Dual Autographs

RBKANA C.Fowler/K.Palmieri 30.00 80.00
RBKATL Burmistrov/P.Cormier 40.00 100.00
RBKCAR J.Skinner/Z.Dalpe 125.00 250.00
RBKCHI N.Leddy/J.Morin 125.00 200.00
RBKEDM J.Eberle/M.Paajarvi 100.00 200.00
RBKLAK B.Schenn/K.Clifford 100.00 200.00
RBKNJD M.Tedenby/J.Josefson 75.00 150.00
RBKNYR Stepan/Zuccarello-Asn 125.00 250.00
RBKPHI Bobrovsky/E.Wellwood 75.00 150.00
RBKPHX Ekman-Larsson/MacLn 40.00 100.00
RBK12 T.Hall/T.Seguin 300.00 600.00
RBKPKNK P.Subban/N.Kadri 200.00 400.00
RBKTBAY D.Tyrell/D.Tokarski 30.00 80.00

2010-11 The Cup Rookie Gear Autographs

ARGAB Alexander Burmistrov 75.00 200.00
ARGBS Brayden Schenn 100.00 200.00
ARGDS Derek Stepan 100.00 200.00
ARGJC Jordan Caron 25.00 60.00
ARGJE Jordan Eberle 350.00 600.00
ARGJS Jeff Skinner 175.00 300.00
ARGKS Kevin Shattenkirk 60.00 120.00
ARGMJ Marcus Johansson EXCH 175.00 350.00
ARGMP Magnus Paajarvi 125.00 250.00
ARGMT Mattias Tedenby 30.00 80.00
ARGMZ Mats Zuccarello-Aasen 60.00 120.00
ARGNK Nazem Kadri 150.00 300.00
ARGNN Nino Niederreiter 50.00 120.00
ARGPS P.K. Subban 350.00 600.00
ARGSB Sergei Bobrovsky 100.00 250.00
ARGTH Taylor Hall 350.00 600.00
ARGTS Tyler Seguin 350.00 600.00
ARGTT Tomas Tatar 75.00 150.00

2010-11 The Cup Scripted Sticks

SAO Alexander Ovechkin 200.00 350.00
SGH Gordie Howe 175.00 300.00
SPR Patrick Roy 150.00 300.00
SSC Sidney Crosby 250.00 500.00
SWG Wayne Gretzky 500.00 1200.00

2010-11 The Cup Scripted Swatches

SSAO Alexander Ovechkin 50.00 100.00
SSEL Eric Lindros 50.00 120.00
SSEM Evgeni Malkin 30.00 80.00
SSJE Jordan Eberle 75.00 150.00
SSJT Jonathan Toews 50.00 100.00
SSMB Martin Brodeur 50.00 120.00
SSML Mario Lemieux 100.00 175.00
SSMM Mark Messier 50.00 100.00
SSNB Nicklas Backstrom 40.00 80.00
SSPD Pavel Datsyuk 30.00 80.00
SSPK Patrick Kane 40.00 100.00
SSPS P.K. Subban 75.00 150.00
SSRF Ron Francis 25.00 60.00
SSRG Ryan Getzlaf 25.00 60.00
SSRM Ryan Miller 25.00 60.00
SSSC Sidney Crosby 200.00 300.00
SSSS Steven Stamkos 75.00 150.00
SSSY Steve Yzerman 60.00 120.00
SSTH Taylor Hall 150.00 300.00
SSTS Tyler Seguin 40.00 100.00
SSWG Wayne Gretzky EXCH 400.00 1000.00

2010-11 The Cup Scripted Swatches Dual

SS2BM M.Brodeur/R.Miller 75.00 150.00
SS2DK D.Doughty/A.Kopitar
SS2EP J.Eberle/M.Paajarvi 60.00 150.00
SS2GR W.Gretzky/L.Robitaille 500.00 1200.00
SS2LC M.Lemieux/S.Crosby
SS2LF M.Lemieux/R.Francis 125.00 200.00
SS2NJ N.Lidstrom/J.Franzen 50.00 120.00
SS2OB A.Ovechkin/N.Backstrom
SS2OG E.Lindros/J.Tavares 75.00 150.00
SS2OM A.Ovechkin/E.Malkin 250.00 400.00
SS2RS P.Roy/J.Sakic 100.00 200.00
SS2TK J.Toews/P.Kane
SS2YL S.Yzerman/I.Larionov 100.00 175.00

2010-11 The Cup Signature Patches

SPAB Alexander Burmistrov 10.00 25.00
SPAK Anze Kopitar 25.00 60.00
SPAN Antti Niemi 12.00 30.00
SPAO Alex Ovechkin/35 75.00 150.00
SPBB Sergei Bobrovsky 50.00 125.00
SPBD Brad Richards 15.00 40.00
SPBL Brian Leetch 10.00 25.00
SPBN Jonathan Bernier 12.00 30.00
SPBO Mike Bossy/35 20.00 50.00
SPBR Bobby Ryan 12.00 30.00
SPBS Brayden Schenn 15.00 40.00
SPBW Jay Bouwmeester 10.00 25.00
SPCD Chris Drury 12.00 30.00
SPCG Claude Giroux 15.00 40.00
SPCN Cam Neely 20.00 50.00
SPCW Cam Ward 15.00 40.00
SPDD Drew Doughty 20.00 50.00
SPDI Marcel Dionne/35 50.00 100.00
SPDK Derek Stepan 15.00 40.00
SPEG Evgeny Grachev 12.00 30.00
SPEK Evander Kane 15.00 40.00
SPEL Eric Lindros 25.00 60.00
SPEM Evgeni Malkin 30.00 80.00
SPES Eric Staal 12.50 30.00
SPET Eric Tangradi 12.00 30.00
SPHL Henrik Lundqvist 40.00 100.00
SPIL Igor Larionov/35 20.00 50.00
SPJC Jeff Carter 12.00 30.00
SPJE Jordan Eberle 40.00 100.00
SPJF Johan Franzen
(inserted in 2011-12 Cup packs) 15.00 40.00
SPJH Jaroslav Halak 15.00 40.00
SPJI Jarome Iginla 20.00 50.00
SPJO Jordan Caron 15.00 40.00
SPJS Joe Sakic/35 50.00 100.00
SPJT John Tavares 25.00 60.00
SPJV James van Riemsdyk 12.00 30.00
SPKA Patrick Kane 30.00 80.00
SPKS Phil Kessel 15.00 40.00
SPKV Kevin Shattenkirk 15.00 40.00
SPLR Larry Robinson 12.00 30.00
SPMA Marian Gaborik 15.00 40.00
SPMC Ryan McDonagh 20.00 50.00
SPMD Matt Duchene 20.00 50.00
SPMF Marc-Andre Fleury 20.00 50.00
SPMH Marian Hossa 30.00 60.00
SPML Mario Lemieux/35 100.00 200.00
SPMM Mark Messier/35 40.00 100.00
SPMS Martin St. Louis 15.00 30.00
SPMT Marty Turco 12.00 30.00
SPMZ Mats Zuccarello-Aasen 20.00 50.00
SPNB Nicklas Backstrom 15.00 40.00
SPNH Nathan Horton EXCH 12.00 30.00
SPNK Nazem Kadri 50.00 100.00
SPNL Nicklas Lidstrom 15.00 40.00
SPNN Nino Niederreiter 15.00 40.00
SPOE Oliver Ekman-Larsson 15.00 40.00
SPPC Patrice Cormier 15.00 40.00
SPPH Dion Phaneuf 12.00 30.00
SPPJ Magnus Paajarvi 12.00 30.00
SPPK P.K. Subban 60.00 120.00
SPPM Patrick Marleau 15.00 40.00
SPPS Paul Stastny 12.00 30.00
SPRF Ron Francis/35 25.00 60.00
SPRG Ryan Getzlaf 15.00 40.00
SPRH Ron Hextall 15.00 40.00
SPRK Ryan Kesler 12.00 30.00
SPRM Ryan Miller 25.00 60.00
SPRN Rick Nash 15.00 40.00
SPRO Luc Robitaille 15.00 40.00
SPRS Ryan Smyth 15.00 40.00
SPSC Sidney Crosby 100.00 200.00
SPSD Shane Doan 12.00 30.00
SPSE Devin Setoguchi 12.00 30.00
SPSK Jeff Skinner 25.00 60.00
SPSM Steve Mason 12.00 30.00
SPSS Steven Stamkos 50.00 100.00
SPST Jordan Staal 15.00 40.00
SPSV Semyon Varlamov 15.00 40.00
SPTH Taylor Hall 60.00 120.00
SPTM Tyler Myers 12.00 30.00
SPTO Jonathan Toews 25.00 60.00
SPTS Tyler Seguin 30.00 80.00
SPTT Tomas Tatar 40.00 80.00
SPVO Tomas Vokoun 12.00 30.00

2010-11 The Cup Signature Patches Dual

SP2AT A.Pechurski/E.Tangradi 20.00 50.00
SP2BM M.Messier/B.Leetch 50.00 100.00
SP2CP C.Price/M.Cammalleri 75.00 150.00
SP2CS P.Subban/J.Cowen 50.00 120.00
SP2DS Dubinsky/Stepan 15.00 40.00
SP2EJ E.Staal/J.Staal 25.00 60.00
SP2GM W.Gretzky/M.Messier 600.00 1500.00
SP2GR R.Getzlaf/B.Ryan 20.00 50.00
SP2HB J.Halak/D.Backes 15.00 40.00
SP2HE T.Hall/J.Eberle 200.00 400.00
SP2HT J.Toews/M.Hossa 75.00 100.00
SP2IB J.Iginla/J.Bouwmeester 20.00 50.00
SP2IK J.Iginla/E.Kane 20.00 50.00
SP2JM J.Staal/M.Staal 20.00 50.00
SP2KD A.Kopitar/D.Doughty 50.00 100.00
SP2LC M.Lemieux/S.Crosby 400.00 800.00
SP2LF N.Lidstrom/J.Franzen 30.00 80.00
SP2LG W.Gretzky/M.Lemieux 1500.00 4000.00
SP2LS V.Lecavalier/M.St. Louis 20.00 50.00
SP2LY M.Lemieux/S.Yzerman 100.00 200.00
SP2ME T.Myers/T.Ennis 25.00 60.00
SP2MJ J.Sakic/M.Duchene 50.00 120.00
SP2ML M.Modano/N.Lidstrom 40.00 80.00
SP2MV T.Vanek/R.Miller 15.00 40.00
SP2NB R.Bourque/C.Neely 30.00 80.00
SP2NM R.Nash/S.Mason 20.00 50.00
SP2OB Ovechkin/Backstrom 100.00 200.00
SP2PP P.Stastny/P.Stastny 40.00 100.00
SP2RB M.Brodeur/P.Roy 100.00 200.00
SP2SD P.Stastny/M.Duchene 20.00 50.00
SP2SK P.Subban/N.Kadri 40.00 100.00
SP2SS M.St. Louis/S.Stamkos 40.00 100.00
SP2SW E.Staal/C.Ward 25.00 60.00
SP2TD J.Tavares/M.Duchene 50.00 100.00
SP2TJ T.Hall/J.Tavares 75.00 150.00
SP2TK J.Toews/P.Kane 100.00 200.00
SP2TN J.Thornton/A.Niemi 30.00 80.00
SP2YL S.Yzerman/I.Larionov 75.00 150.00
SP2ZS Zuccarello-Asn/Stepan 20.00 50.00

2010-11 The Cup Stanley Cup Signatures

SCAD Alex Delvecchio 10.00 25.00
SCAN Antti Niemi 8.00 20.00
SCAT Alex Tanguay 6.00 15.00
SCBC Bobby Clarke 15.00 40.00
SCBH Bobby Hull 12.00 30.00
SCBL Brian Leetch 15.00 40.00
SCBO Bobby Orr 60.00 120.00
SCBR Brad Richards 10.00 25.00
SCBS Brent Seabrook 15.00 40.00
SCCD Chris Drury 8.00 20.00
SCCG Clark Gillies 10.00 25.00
SCCW Cam Ward 10.00 25.00
SCDB Dustin Byfuglien 10.00 25.00
SCDG Doug Gilmour 12.00 30.00
SCDP Denis Potvin 10.00 25.00
SCEM Evgeni Malkin 20.00 50.00
SCES Eric Staal 12.00 30.00
SCFR Ron Francis 12.00 30.00
SCGA Glenn Anderson 8.00 20.00
SCGH Gordie Howe 60.00 120.00
SCHE Milan Hejduk 8.00 20.00
SCIL Igor Larionov 10.00 25.00
SCJB Johnny Bucyk 10.00 25.00
SCJF Johan Franzen 12.00 30.00
SCJG Jean-Sebastien Giguere 12.00 30.00
SCJK Jari Kurri 10.00 25.00
SCJS Joe Sakic 40.00 80.00
SCJT Jonathan Toews 40.00 80.00
SCKV Kris Versteeg 12.00 30.00
SCLF Guy Lafleur 25.00 60.00
SCLR Luc Robitaille 12.00 30.00
SCMA Mark Messier 20.00 50.00
SCMB Martin Brodeur 40.00 80.00
SCME Mark Messier 40.00 80.00
SCMF Marc-Andre Fleury 15.00 40.00
SCMH Marian Hossa 20.00 50.00
SCMI Mike Bossy 12.00 30.00
SCML Mario Lemieux 40.00 100.00
SCNL Nicklas Lidstrom 25.00 50.00
SCOS Chris Osgood 10.00 25.00
SCPA Patrick Roy 50.00 100.00
SCPE Phil Esposito 15.00 40.00
SCPK Patrick Kane 40.00 80.00
SCPR Patrick Roy 50.00 100.00
SCRB Ray Bourque 15.00 40.00
SCRK Red Kelly 10.00 25.00
SCRO Larry Robinson 10.00 25.00
SCSB Scotty Bowman 15.00 30.00
SCSC Sidney Crosby 100.00 175.00
SCST Jordan Staal 8.00 20.00
SCTL Ted Lindsay 10.00 25.00
SCVL Vincent Lecavalier 10.00 25.00
SCWG Wayne Gretzky 200.00 500.00

2010-11 The Cup Stanley Cup Signatures Dual

SC2AE J.Arnott/P.Elias 12.00 30.00
SC2BG M.Bossy/C.Gillies 20.00 50.00
SC2BK D.Byfuglien/P.Kane 25.00 60.00
SC2BO B.Orr/J.Bucyk 60.00 120.00
SC2BP M.Bossy/D.Potvin 20.00 50.00
SC2DT M.Hejduk/C.Drury 10.00 25.00
SC2EA E.Staal/A.Ladd 15.00 40.00
SC2EO B.Orr/P.Esposito 60.00 120.00
SC2FM M.Fleury/E.Malkin 40.00 80.00
SC2GM W.Gretzky/M.Messier 200.00 500.00
SC2HD G.Howe/Delvecchio 60.00 120.00
SC2HN M.Hossa/A.Niemi 40.00 80.00
SC2JP J.Sakic/P.Roy 100.00 200.00
SC2KG W.Gretzky/J.Kurri 250.00 600.00
SC2LD T.Lindsay/Delvecchio 15.00 40.00
SC2LF M.Lemieux/R.Francis 60.00 120.00
SC2LM M.Messier/B.Leetch 40.00 80.00
SC2LR Lecavalier/B.Richards 20.00 50.00
SC2NJ N.Lidstrom/J.Franzen 30.00 80.00
SC2RB P.Roy/R.Bourque 50.00 100.00
SC2RS B.Richards/St. Louis 12.00 30.00
SC2SB J.Sakic/R.Bourque 75.00 150.00
SC2SW E.Staal/C.Ward 20.00 50.00
SC2TK J.Toews/P.Kane 50.00 100.00
SC2YL S.Yzerman/I.Larionov 60.00 120.00
SC2YR S.Yzerman/Robitaille 50.00 120.00

2010-11 The Cup Trios Jerseys

C3BU Drury/DiPietro/Shatten 12.00 30.00
C3NY Stepan/Niederter/Adam 30.00 60.00
C3ANA Getzlaf/Perry/Fowler 15.00 40.00
C3ATL Cormier/Burmis/Kulda 8.00 20.00
C3AVS Duchn/Stastny/Muellr 8.00 20.00
C3BML Brodr/Miller/Lundqvist 20.00 50.00
C3BOS Rask/Bergeron/Horton 12.00 30.00
C3BUF Vanek/Myers/Miller 8.00 20.00
C3CAR Skinner/McBain/Dalpe 20.00 50.00
C3CHI Pirri/Leddy/Brophey 20.00 40.00
C3COL Sakic/Roy/Tanguay 20.00 50.00
C3CPT Sakic/Yzerman/Lemieux 15.00 40.00
C3DET Lidst/Zetter/Holmstrom 10.00 25.00
C3DRW Yzrmn/Larionv/Lidstrm 20.00 50.00
C3FLY Richrds/Cartr/Bobrvsky 25.00 60.00
C3GR8 Gretzky/Lemieux/Sakic 50.00 125.00
C3HSE Hall/Seguin/Eberle 30.00 80.00
C3LAK Doughty/Kopitar/Brown 15.00 40.00
C3MIN Scandella/Noreau/Almnd 6.00 15.00
C3NJD Tedenby/Josefsn/Palmri 6.00 15.00
C3NYI Tavrs/Niederrtr/Martn 12.00 30.00
C3NYR Lundqvst/Gabrik/Dbnsky 20.00 50.00
C3OIL Hall/Eberle/Paajarvi 40.00 100.00
C3OTT Spezza/Alfred/Kovalev 8.00 20.00
C3PEN Mario/Francs/Kovlv 15.00 40.00

C3PHI Clarke/Lindrs/Richrds 20.00 50.00
C3PHX Doan/Ekmn-Lars/MacLn 10.00 25.00
C3PIT Crosby/Malkin/Staal 20.00 50.00
C3SES Seguin/Eberle/Skinner 20.00 50.00
C3SJS Marleau/Htley/Thornton 12.00 30.00
C3STL Shatten/Cole/Dlla Rvere 12.00 30.00
C3SWE Pjarvi/Johnsn/Tedenby 10.00 25.00
C3TBL Stamkos/St.Lou/Lecav 15.00 40.00
C3TCG Luongo/Brodeur/Fleury 25.00 60.00
C3TOR Giguer/Phaneuf/Kessl 20.00 50.00
C3VAN Luongo/Sedin/Sedin 20.00 50.00
C3WJC Kadri/Subban/Cowen 20.00 50.00
C3BEES Seguin/Caron/Hamill 25.00 60.00
C3BLUE Zucc-A/Stpan/Grchv 12.00 30.00
C3CAPS Ovech/Backstr/Green 15.00 40.00
C3GMGG Crosby/Toews/Perry 20.00 50.00
C3HABD Subbn/Markv/Hamrlk 20.00 50.00
C3HAWK Espo/Wilsn/Probrt 15.00 40.00
C3LBBR Price/Cammallr/Markv 20.00 50.00
C3PITT Tangradi/Pchski/Jhnsn 12.00 30.00
C3SCUP Toews/Kane/Hossa 20.00 50.00
C3WASH Ovech/Backstrm/Semn 30.00 80.00
C3WILD Koivu/Latend/Bouchrd 8.00 20.00
C3WISC Stepn/McBan/McDngh 20.00 50.00
C3CANES Staal/Skinner/Ward 15.00 40.00
C3CWALL Gilmour/Brodr/Hawr 25.00 60.00
C3GOALS Sid/Ovie/Stamks 25.00 60.00
C3KMLPS Igin/Doan/Niedermyr 10.00 25.00
C3LAGR8 Gretz/Dionn/Robitlle 50.00 125.00
C3RMSKI Sid/Richrds/Lecav 20.00 50.00
C3ROOKD Subbn/Ekmn-Lrs/Shattn 25.00 60.00
C3WNDSR Hall/Fowler/Wellwd 30.00 80.00
C3PHILLY Richrds/Cartr/Giroux 8.00 20.00

2011-12 The Cup

1 Bobby Ryan 2.50 6.00
2 Ryan Getzlaf 3.00 8.00
3 Jonas Hiller 2.50 6.00
4 Ray Bourque 5.00 12.00
5 Bobby Orr 12.00 30.00
6 Phil Esposito 5.00 12.00
7 Cam Neely 3.00 8.00
8 Tim Thomas 3.00 8.00
9 Zdeno Chara 3.00 8.00
10 Nathan Horton 3.00 8.00
11 Tyler Seguin 4.00 10.00
12 Thomas Vanek 2.50 6.00
13 Ryan Miller 3.00 8.00
14 Derek Roy 2.00 5.00
15 Dominik Hasek 5.00 12.00
16 Miikka Kiprusoff 3.00 8.00
17 Jarome Iginla 4.00 10.00
18 Jeff Skinner 4.00 10.00
19 Patrick Kane 6.00 15.00
20 Tony Esposito 3.00 8.00
21 Bobby Hull 6.00 15.00
22 Jonathan Toews 5.00 12.00
23 Joe Sakic 6.00 15.00
24 Patrick Roy 8.00 20.00
25 Matt Duchene 3.00 8.00
26 Paul Stastny 2.50 6.00
27 Rick Nash 3.00 8.00
28 Jeff Carter 2.50 6.00
29 Steve Mason 2.50 6.00
30 Ed Belfour 3.00 8.00
31 Jim Howard 4.00 10.00
32 Pavel Datsyuk 5.00 12.00
33 Nicklas Lidstrom 2.00 5.00
34 Johan Franzen 2.50 6.00
35 Henrik Zetterberg 4.00 10.00
36 Ryan Smyth 2.50 6.00
37 Taylor Hall 3.00 8.00
38 Grant Fuhr 5.00 12.00
39 Jari Kurri 3.00 8.00
40 Jordan Eberle 3.00 8.00
41 Anze Kopitar 5.00 12.00
42 Mike Richards 2.50 6.00
43 Luc Robitaille 3.00 8.00
44 Drew Doughty 4.00 10.00
45 Mike Modano 5.00 12.00
46 Dino Ciccarelli 3.00 8.00
47 Carey Price 6.00 15.00
48 Larry Robinson 3.00 8.00
49 P.K. Subban 4.00 10.00
50 Pekka Rinne 3.00 8.00
51 Ilya Kovalchuk 3.00 8.00
52 Martin Brodeur 8.00 20.00
53 Zach Parise 3.00 8.00
54 John Tavares 5.00 12.00
55 Mike Bossy 3.00 8.00
56 Wayne Gretzky 20.00 50.00
57 Marian Gaborik 3.00 8.00
58 Henrik Lundqvist 8.00 20.00
59 Mark Messier 6.00 15.00
60 Jason Spezza 3.00 8.00
61 Eric Lindros 5.00 12.00
62 James van Riemsdyk 2.50 6.00
63 Jaromir Jagr 10.00 25.00
64 Claude Giroux 3.00 8.00
65 Jordan Staal 2.50 6.00
66 Evgeni Malkin 6.00 15.00
67 Mario Lemieux 12.00 30.00
68 Marc-Andre Fleury 6.00 15.00
69 Sidney Crosby 12.00 30.00
70 Ron Francis 4.00 10.00
71 Paul Coffey 3.00 8.00
72 Antti Niemi 2.50 6.00
73 Patrick Marleau 3.00 8.00
74 Joe Thornton 5.00 12.00
75 Logan Couture 4.00 10.00
76 Jaroslav Halak 3.00 8.00
77 Brett Hull 6.00 15.00
78 Vincent Lecavalier 3.00 8.00
79 Steven Stamkos 6.00 15.00
80 Phil Kessel 3.00 8.00
81 Dion Phaneuf 2.50 6.00
82 Roberto Luongo 5.00 12.00
83 Daniel Sedin 4.00 10.00
84 Henrik Sedin 4.00 10.00
85 Ryan Kesler 3.00 8.00
86 Trevor Linden 3.00 8.00
87 Alexander Ovechkin 12.00 30.00
88 Nicklas Backstrom 3.00 8.00
89 Dale Hawerchuk 4.00 10.00
90 Ondrej Pavelec 3.00 8.00
91 Zac Rinaldo RC 4.00 10.00
92 David Rundblad RC 4.00 10.00
93 Erik Condra RC 4.00 10.00
94 Robert Bortuzzo AU RC 6.00 15.00
95 Kevin Marshall AU RC 6.00 15.00
96 Ryan Thang AU RC 5.00 12.00
97 Pat Maroon AU RC 20.00 50.00
98 Eddie Lack AU RC 6.00 15.00
99 Jimmy Hayes AU RC 8.00 20.00
100 D.Ullstrom AU RC 6.00 15.00
101 Dylan Olsen AU RC 8.00 20.00
102 Frederic St. Denis AU RC 6.00 15.00
103 Brian Strait AU RC 8.00 20.00
104 Allen York AU RC 8.00 20.00
105 Stu Bickel AU RC 6.00 15.00
106 Paul Postma AU RC 6.00 15.00
107 Anders Nilsson AU RC 6.00 15.00
108 Mikko Koskinen AU RC 8.00 20.00
109 Ryan Ellis JSY AU RC 20.00 50.00
110 Marcus Foligno JSY AU RC 12.00 30.00
111 Zack Kassian JSY AU RC 10.00 25.00
112 B.McNabb JSY AU RC 8.00 20.00
113 Leland Irving JSY AU RC 8.00 20.00
114 Brendan Smith JSY AU RC 8.00 20.00
115 Peter Holland JSY AU RC 8.00 20.00
116 Gustav Nyquist JSY AU RC 20.00 50.00
117 Colten Teubert JSY AU RC 8.00 20.00
118 Andy Miele JSY AU RC 8.00 20.00
119 Jake Gardiner JSY AU RC 12.00 30.00
120 Carl Klingberg JSY AU RC 8.00 20.00
121 Mika Zibanejad JSY AU RC 80.00 200.00
122 Dmitry Orlov JSY AU RC EX 20.00 50.00
123 Aaron Palushaj JSY AU RC 8.00 20.00
124 Adam Larsson JSY AU RC 10.00 25.00
125 Matt Read JSY AU RC 10.00 25.00
126 Matt Frattin JSY AU RC 8.00 20.00
127 Blake Geoffrion JSY AU RC 8.00 20.00
128 D.Smith-Pelly JSY AU RC 10.00 25.00
129 E.Gudbranson JSY AU RC 10.00 25.00
130 Jonathon Blum JSY AU RC 8.00 20.00
131 Anton Lander JSY AU RC 8.00 20.00
132 Brandon Saad JSY AU RC 40.00 100.00
133 Adam Henrique JSY AU RC 20.00 50.00
134 Brett Connolly JSY AU RC 8.00 20.00
135 Harri Sateri JSY AU RC 8.00 20.00
136 Joe Colborne JSY AU RC 8.00 20.00
137 Marcus Kruger JSY AU RC 12.00 30.00
138 Greg Nemisz JSY AU RC 8.00 20.00
139 Ryan Johansen JSY AU RC 25.00 60.00
140 Simon Despres JSY AU RC 8.00 20.00
141 Keith Kinkaid JSY AU RC 8.00 20.00
142 Stefan Elliott JSY AU RC 8.00 20.00
143 Roman Horak JSY AU RC 8.00 20.00
144 John Moore JSY AU RC 8.00 20.00
145 Colin Greening JSY AU RC 8.00 20.00
146 Cam Atkinson JSY AU RC 20.00 50.00
147 Tomas Vincour JSY AU RC 8.00 20.00
148 Yann Sauve JSY AU RC 8.00 20.00
149 Alexei Emelin JSY AU RC 8.00 20.00
150 Cody Eakin JSY AU RC 12.00 30.00
151 Justin Faulk JSY AU RC 12.00 30.00
152 C.Gaunce JSY AU RC 6.00 15.00
153 Joe Vitale JSY AU RC 8.00 20.00
154 Brendon Nash JSY AU RC 8.00 20.00
155 Erik Gustafsson JSY AU RC 10.00 25.00
156 Raphael Diaz JSY AU RC 8.00 20.00
157 David Savard JSY AU RC 8.00 20.00
158 Tim Erixon JSY AU RC 8.00 20.00
159 T.Hartikainen JSY AU RC 8.00 20.00
160 Ben Scrivens JSY AU RC 8.00 20.00
161 Carl Hagelin JSY AU RC 12.00 30.00
162 Craig Smith JSY AU RC 10.00 25.00
163 P.Wiercioch JSY AU RC 8.00 20.00
164 Calvin de Haan JSY AU RC 8.00 20.00
165 Brett Bulmer JSY AU RC 8.00 20.00
166 Da Costa JSY AU RC 8.00 20.00
167 Voynov JSY AU RC EX 8.00 20.00
168 Roman Wick JSY AU RC 10.00 25.00
169 Mike Murphy JSY AU RC 8.00 20.00
170 Lance Bouma JSY AU RC 8.00 20.00
171 Andrew Shaw JSY AU RC 20.00 50.00
172 Ben Holmstrom JSY AU RC 8.00 20.00
173 Corey Tropp JSY AU RC 8.00 20.00
174 Lennart Petrell JSY AU RC 10.00 25.00
175 L.Leblanc JSY AU/99 RC 30.00 80.00
176 Scheifele JSY AU/99 RC 400.00 800.00
177 Hodgsn JSY AU/99 RC EX 50.00 120.00
178 S.Couturier JSY AU/99 RC 150.00 300.00
179 Landeskg JSY AU/99 RC 250.00 600.00
180 RNH JSY AU/99 RC 400.00 1000.00

2011-12 The Cup Gold

1 Bobby Ryan 5.00 12.00
2 Ryan Getzlaf 6.00 15.00
4 Ray Bourque 10.00 25.00
5 Bobby Orr 25.00 60.00
6 Phil Esposito 10.00 25.00
7 Cam Neely 6.00 15.00
8 Tim Thomas 6.00 15.00
10 Nathan Horton 6.00 15.00
11 Tyler Seguin 8.00 20.00
12 Thomas Vanek 5.00 12.00
13 Ryan Miller 6.00 15.00
15 Dominik Hasek 10.00 25.00
16 Miikka Kiprusoff 6.00 15.00
17 Jarome Iginla 8.00 20.00
18 Jeff Skinner 8.00 20.00
19 Patrick Kane 12.00 30.00
20 Tony Esposito 6.00 15.00
21 Bobby Hull 12.00 30.00
22 Jonathan Toews 10.00 25.00
23 Joe Sakic 12.00 30.00
24 Patrick Roy 15.00 40.00
25 Matt Duchene 6.00 15.00
26 Paul Stastny 5.00 12.00
27 Rick Nash 6.00 15.00
28 Jeff Carter 5.00 12.00
30 Ed Belfour 6.00 15.00
31 Jim Howard 8.00 20.00
32 Pavel Datsyuk 10.00 25.00
33 Nicklas Lidstrom 4.00 10.00
34 Johan Franzen 5.00 12.00
35 Henrik Zetterberg 8.00 20.00
37 Taylor Hall 6.00 15.00
38 Grant Fuhr 10.00 25.00
39 Jari Kurri 6.00 15.00
40 Jordan Eberle 6.00 15.00
41 Anze Kopitar 10.00 25.00
42 Mike Richards 5.00 12.00
43 Luc Robitaille 6.00 15.00
44 Drew Doughty 8.00 20.00
45 Mike Modano 10.00 25.00
46 Dino Ciccarelli 6.00 15.00
47 Carey Price 12.00 30.00
48 Larry Robinson 6.00 15.00
49 P.K. Subban 8.00 20.00
50 Pekka Rinne 6.00 15.00
51 Ilya Kovalchuk 6.00 15.00
52 Martin Brodeur 15.00 40.00
53 Zach Parise 6.00 15.00
54 John Tavares 10.00 25.00
55 Mike Bossy 6.00 15.00
56 Wayne Gretzky 40.00 100.00
57 Marian Gaborik 6.00 15.00
58 Henrik Lundqvist 15.00 40.00
59 Mark Messier 12.00 30.00
60 Jason Spezza 6.00 15.00
61 Eric Lindros 10.00 25.00
62 James van Riemsdyk 5.00 12.00
63 Jaromir Jagr 20.00 50.00
64 Claude Giroux 6.00 15.00
65 Jordan Staal 5.00 12.00
66 Evgeni Malkin 12.00 30.00
67 Mario Lemieux 25.00 60.00
68 Marc-Andre Fleury 12.00 30.00
69 Sidney Crosby 25.00 60.00
70 Ron Francis 8.00 20.00
71 Paul Coffey 6.00 15.00
73 Patrick Marleau 6.00 15.00
74 Joe Thornton 10.00 25.00
75 Logan Couture 8.00 20.00
76 Jaroslav Halak 6.00 15.00
77 Brett Hull 12.00 30.00
79 Steven Stamkos 12.00 30.00
80 Phil Kessel 6.00 15.00
81 Dion Phaneuf 5.00 12.00
82 Roberto Luongo 10.00 25.00
83 Daniel Sedin 8.00 20.00
84 Henrik Sedin 8.00 20.00
85 Ryan Kesler 6.00 15.00
86 Trevor Linden 6.00 15.00
87 Alexander Ovechkin 25.00 60.00
88 Nicklas Backstrom 6.00 15.00
89 Dale Hawerchuk 8.00 20.00
90 Ondrej Pavelec 6.00 15.00
91 Zac Rinaldo 5.00 12.00
92 David Rundblad 5.00 12.00
93 Erik Condra 5.00 12.00
94 Robert Bortuzzo 5.00 12.00
95 Kevin Marshall 5.00 12.00
97 Pat Maroon 15.00 40.00
98 Eddie Lack 5.00 12.00
99 Jimmy Hayes 6.00 15.00
100 David Ullstrom 5.00 12.00
101 Dylan Olsen 6.00 15.00
102 Frederic St. Denis 5.00 12.00
103 Brian Strait 6.00 15.00
104 Allen York 6.00 15.00
105 Stu Bickel 5.00 12.00
106 Paul Postma 5.00 12.00
107 Anders Nilsson 5.00 12.00
108 Mikko Koskinen 6.00 15.00
109 Ryan Ellis 5.00 12.00
110 Marcus Foligno 8.00 20.00
111 Zack Kassian 6.00 15.00
112 Brayden McNabb 5.00 12.00
113 Leland Irving 5.00 12.00
114 Brendan Smith 5.00 12.00
115 Peter Holland 5.00 12.00
116 Gustav Nyquist 12.00 30.00
117 Colten Teubert 5.00 12.00
118 Andy Miele 5.00 12.00
119 Jake Gardiner 8.00 20.00
120 Carl Klingberg 5.00 12.00
121 Mika Zibanejad 100.00 250.00
122 Dmitry Orlov 12.00 30.00
123 Aaron Palushaj 5.00 12.00
124 Adam Larsson 6.00 15.00
125 Matt Read 6.00 15.00
126 Matt Frattin 5.00 12.00
127 Blake Geoffrion 5.00 12.00
128 Devante Smith-Pelly 6.00 15.00
129 Erik Gudbranson 6.00 15.00
130 Jonathon Blum 5.00 12.00
131 Anton Lander 5.00 12.00
132 Brandon Saad 10.00 25.00
133 Adam Henrique 12.00 30.00
134 Brett Connolly 5.00 12.00
135 Harri Sateri 5.00 12.00
136 Joe Colborne 5.00 12.00
137 Marcus Kruger 8.00 20.00
138 Greg Nemisz 5.00 12.00
139 Ryan Johansen 15.00 40.00
140 Simon Despres 5.00 12.00
141 Keith Kinkaid 5.00 12.00
142 Stefan Elliott 5.00 12.00
143 Roman Horak 5.00 12.00
144 John Moore 5.00 12.00
145 Colin Greening 5.00 12.00
146 Cam Atkinson 12.00 30.00
147 Tomas Vincour 5.00 12.00
148 Yann Sauve 5.00 12.00
149 Alexei Emelin 5.00 12.00
150 Cody Eakin 8.00 20.00
151 Justin Faulk 8.00 20.00
153 Joe Vitale 5.00 12.00
154 Brendon Nash 5.00 12.00
155 Erik Gustafsson 6.00 15.00
156 Raphael Diaz 5.00 12.00
157 David Savard 5.00 12.00
158 Tim Erixon 5.00 12.00
159 Teemu Hartikainen 5.00 12.00
160 Ben Scrivens 5.00 12.00
161 Carl Hagelin 8.00 20.00
162 Craig Smith 6.00 15.00
163 Patrick Wiercioch 5.00 12.00
164 Calvin de Haan 5.00 12.00
165 Brett Bulmer 5.00 12.00
166 Stephane Da Costa 5.00 12.00
167 Viatcheslav Voynov 5.00 12.00
168 Roman Wick 6.00 15.00
169 Mike Murphy 5.00 12.00
170 Lance Bouma 5.00 12.00
171 Andrew Shaw 12.00 30.00
172 Ben Holmstrom 5.00 12.00
173 Corey Tropp 5.00 12.00
174 Lennart Petrell 6.00 15.00
175 Louis Leblanc 5.00 12.00
176 Mark Scheifele 20.00 50.00
177 Cody Hodgson 8.00 20.00
178 Sean Couturier 10.00 25.00
179 Gabriel Landeskog 15.00 40.00
180 Ryan Nugent-Hopkins 20.00 50.00

2011-12 The Cup Gold Rainbow

91 Zac Rinaldo/36 12.00 30.00
93 Erik Condra/22 12.00 30.00
94 Robert Bortuzzo AU/41 12.00 30.00
95 Kevin Marshall AU/46 12.00 30.00
96 Ryan Thang AU/65 8.00 20.00
97 Pat Maroon AU/62 25.00 60.00
98 Eddie Lack AU/31 12.00 30.00
99 Jimmy Hayes AU/39 15.00 40.00
100 David Ullstrom AU/41 EXCH 12.00 30.00
101 Dylan Olsen AU/34 15.00 40.00
102 Frederic St. Denis AU/62 10.00 25.00
103 Brian Strait AU/37 15.00 40.00
104 Allen York AU/41 15.00 40.00
105 Stu Bickel AU/41 12.00 30.00
106 Paul Postma AU/38 12.00 30.00
107 Anders Nilsson AU/45 12.00 30.00
109 Ryan Ellis JSY AU/49 12.00 30.00
110 Marcus Foligno JSY AU/82 20.00 50.00
111 Zack Kassian JSY AU/54 15.00 40.00
112 Brayden McNabb JSY AU/81 12.00 30.00
113 Leland Irving JSY AU/37 12.00 30.00
115 Peter Holland JSY AU/74 12.00 30.00
117 Colten Teubert JSY AU/33 12.00 30.00
118 Andy Miele JSY AU/21 12.00 30.00
119 Jake Gardiner JSY AU/51 20.00 50.00
120 Carl Klingberg JSY AU/48 EXCH 12.00 30.00
121 Mika Zibanejad JSY AU/93 80.00 200.00
122 Dmitry Orlov JSY AU/81 30.00 80.00
123 Aaron Palushaj JSY AU/60 12.00 30.00
125 Matt Read JSY AU/24 15.00 40.00
126 Matt Frattin JSY AU/39 12.00 30.00
128 Devante Smith-Pelly JSY AU/77 15.00 40.00
129 Erik Gudbranson JSY AU/44 15.00 40.00
131 Anton Lander JSY AU/57 12.00 30.00
132 Brandon Saad JSY AU/43 25.00 60.00
135 Harri Sateri JSY AU/35 12.00 30.00
136 Joe Colborne JSY AU/32 12.00 30.00
137 Marcus Kruger JSY AU/16 20.00 50.00
138 Greg Nemisz JSY AU/48 12.00 30.00
139 Ryan Johansen JSY AU/19 40.00 100.00
140 Simon Despres JSY AU/47 12.00 30.00
141 Keith Kinkaid JSY AU/35 12.00 30.00
142 Stefan Elliott JSY AU/46 12.00 30.00
143 Roman Horak JSY AU/51 12.00 30.00
147 Tomas Vincour JSY AU/81 12.00 30.00
148 Yann Sauve JSY AU/47 12.00 30.00
149 Alexei Emelin JSY AU/74 12.00 30.00
150 Cody Eakin JSY AU/50 20.00 50.00
151 Justin Faulk JSY AU/28 20.00 50.00
152 Cameron Gaunce JSY AU/43 10.00 25.00
153 Joe Vitale JSY AU/45 12.00 30.00
154 Brendon Nash JSY AU/47 12.00 30.00
155 Erik Gustafsson JSY AU/26 15.00 40.00
156 Raphael Diaz JSY AU/61 12.00 30.00
157 David Savard JSY AU/58 12.00 30.00
158 Tim Erixon JSY AU/53 12.00 30.00
159 Teemu Hartikainen JSY AU/56 12.00 30.00
160 Ben Scrivens JSY AU/30 12.00 30.00
161 Carl Hagelin JSY AU/62 20.00 50.00
163 Patrick Wiercioch JSY AU/46 12.00 30.00
164 Calvin de Haan JSY AU/44 12.00 30.00
165 Brett Bulmer JSY AU/19 12.00 30.00
166 Stephane Da Costa JSY AU/24 12.00 30.00
167 Viatcheslav Voynov JSY AU/26 12.00 30.00
168 Roman Wick JSY AU/43 15.00 40.00
169 Mike Murphy JSY AU/70 EXCH 12.00 30.00
170 Lance Bouma JSY AU/57 12.00 30.00
171 Andrew Shaw JSY AU/65 30.00 80.00
172 Ben Holmstrom JSY AU/22 12.00 30.00
173 Corey Tropp JSY AU/78 12.00 30.00
174 Lennart Petrell JSY AU/37 15.00 40.00
175 Louis Leblanc JSY AU/71 12.00 30.00
176 Mark Scheifele JSY AU/55 50.00 125.00
179 Landeskog JSY AU/92 125.00 300.00
180 Nugent-Hopkins JSY AU/93 100.00 250.00

2011-12 The Cup Auto Draft Boards

DBAL Adam Larsson 30.00 80.00
DBBC Brett Connolly 25.00 60.00
DBBS Brendan Smith 20.00 50.00
DBCH Cody Hodgson 30.00 80.00
DBCS Chris Summers 15.00 40.00
DBCT Colten Teubert 20.00 50.00
DBDH Calvin de Haan 30.00 80.00
DBDO Dylan Olsen 25.00 60.00
DBEG Erik Gudbranson 20.00 50.00
DBGL Gabriel Landeskog 75.00 150.00
DBGN Greg Nemisz 15.00 40.00
DBJB Jonathon Blum 20.00 50.00
DBJC Joe Colborne 15.00 40.00
DBJF Joe Finley 20.00 50.00
DBJG Jake Gardiner 30.00 80.00
DBJM John Moore 20.00 50.00
DBLI Leland Irving 20.00 50.00
DBLL Louis Leblanc 50.00 120.00
DBMS Mark Scheifele 80.00 200.00
DBMZ Mika Zibanejad 60.00 150.00
DBNH Riley Nash 20.00 50.00
DBPH Peter Holland 20.00 50.00
DBRE Ryan Ellis 20.00 50.00
DBRJ Ryan Johansen 60.00 150.00
DBRN Ryan Nugent-Hopkins 400.00 800.00
DBSC Sean Couturier 100.00 200.00
DBSD Simon Despres 25.00 60.00
DBTE Tim Erixon 20.00 50.00
DBTM Thomas McCollum 20.00 50.00
DBZK Zack Kassian 30.00 80.00

2011-12 The Cup Enshrinements

CEAH Adam Henrique 25.00 60.00
CEAL Adam Larsson 12.00 30.00
CEAO Alexander Ovechkin 150.00 400.00
CEBB Bill Barber 12.00 30.00
CEBC Bobby Clarke 20.00 50.00
CEBH Brett Hull 25.00 60.00
CEBO Bobby Orr 50.00 125.00
CEBR Martin Brodeur 30.00 80.00
CEBU Johnny Bucyk 12.00 30.00
CECH Cody Hodgson 15.00 40.00
CECN Cam Neely 12.00 30.00
CECO Brett Connolly 10.00 25.00
CECP Carey Price 25.00 60.00
CECU Sean Couturier 20.00 50.00
CEDH Dominik Hasek 20.00 50.00
CEDS Dave Schultz 12.00 30.00
CEEB Ed Belfour 12.00 30.00
CEEL Eric Lindros 20.00 50.00
CEEM Evgeni Malkin 25.00 60.00
CEGF Grant Fuhr 20.00 50.00
CEGL Gabriel Landeskog 30.00 80.00
CEHA Dale Hawerchuk 15.00 40.00
CEHL Henrik Lundqvist 30.00 80.00
CEHU Bobby Hull 25.00 60.00
CEJE Jordan Eberle 12.00 30.00
CEJK Jari Kurri 12.00 30.00
CEJS Joe Sakic 25.00 60.00
CEJT Jonathan Toews 20.00 50.00
CELL Louis Leblanc 10.00 25.00
CELR Luc Robitaille 12.00 30.00
CEMB Mike Bossy 12.00 30.00
CEMD Matt Duchene 12.00 30.00
CEMG Mike Gartner 15.00 40.00
CEML Mario Lemieux 50.00 125.00
CEMM Mark Messier 25.00 60.00
CEMN Markus Naslund 12.00 30.00
CEMS Mark Scheifele 40.00 100.00
CENB Nicklas Backstrom 12.00 30.00
CENL Nicklas Lidstrom 8.00 20.00
CEPC Paul Coffey 12.00 30.00
CEPK Patrick Kane 25.00 60.00
CEPS P.K. Subban 15.00 40.00
CERB Ray Bourque 20.00 50.00
CERF Ron Francis 15.00 40.00
CERJ Ryan Johansen 30.00 80.00
CERM Ryan Miller 12.00 30.00
CERN Rick Nash 12.00 30.00
CERNH Ryan Nugent-Hopkins 40.00 100.00
CESC Sidney Crosby 60.00 150.00
CESK Jeff Skinner 15.00 40.00
CETA John Tavares 20.00 50.00
CETH Taylor Hall 12.00 30.00
CETK Tim Kerr 8.00 20.00
CETL Trevor Linden 12.00 30.00
CETS Tyler Seguin 15.00 40.00
CEWG Wayne Gretzky 200.00 500.00

2011-12 The Cup Enshrinements Dual

CE2CM P.Coffey/M.Messier 30.00 80.00
CE2CR S.Couturier/M.Read 25.00 60.00
CE2EH T.Hall/J.Eberle 15.00 40.00
CE2EO P.Esposito/B.Orr 60.00 150.00
CE2FC R.Francis/P.Coffey 20.00 50.00
CE2FM E.Malkin/M.Fleury 30.00 80.00
CE2GM W.Gretzky/M.Messier 200.00 500.00
CE2GN Gretzky/Nugent-Hopkins 200.00 500.00
CE2HS T.Seguin/T.Hall 20.00 50.00
CE2HT B.Hull/J.Toews 30.00 80.00
CE2KH J.Kurri/T.Hartikainen 15.00 40.00
CE2KS Klingberg/M.Scheifele 50.00 125.00
CE2LC S.Crosby/Lemieux 200.00 300.00
CE2MK S.Mikita/P.Kane 30.00 80.00
CE2NB R.Bourque/C.Neely 25.00 60.00
CE2NL Nugent-Hopkins/Landes 25.00 60.00
CE2OB Ovechkin/Backstrom 200.00 500.00
CE2OH B.Orr/B.Hull 60.00 150.00
CE2PS C.Price/P.Subban 30.00 80.00
CE2RB P.Roy/M.Brodeur 40.00 100.00
CE2RG G.Fuhr/R.Miller 25.00 60.00
CE2RK M.Richards/Kopitar 25.00 60.00
CE2RL Lundqvist/B.Richards 40.00 100.00
CE2RS P.Roy/J.Sakic 40.00 100.00
CE2SB J.Sakic/R.Bourque 30.00 80.00
CE2SL P.Subban/L.Leblanc 20.00 50.00
CE2TD J.Tavares/M.Duchene 25.00 60.00
CE2TK P.Kane/J.Toews 30.00 80.00
CE2WM W.Gretzky/M.Messier 200.00 500.00

2011-12 The Cup Foundations Jerseys

CFAH Adam Henrique 12.00 30.00
CFAO Alexander Ovechkin 25.00 60.00
CFCG Claude Giroux 6.00 15.00
CFCH Cody Hodgson 8.00 20.00
CFCP Carey Price 12.00 30.00
CFCS Chris Stewart 5.00 12.00
CFCU Sean Couturier 10.00 25.00
CFDB David Backes 4.00 10.00
CFDD Drew Doughty 8.00 20.00
CFDH Dale Hawerchuk 8.00 20.00
CFDR Derek Roy 4.00 10.00
CFDS Denis Savard 6.00 15.00
CFEL Eric Lindros 10.00 25.00
CFEM Evgeni Malkin 12.00 30.00
CFGL Gabriel Landeskog 15.00 40.00
CFHL Henrik Lundqvist 15.00 40.00
CFJC Jeff Carter 5.00 12.00
CFJE Jordan Eberle 6.00 15.00
CFJH Jaroslav Halak 6.00 15.00
CFJI Jarome Iginla 8.00 20.00
CFJS Joe Sakic 12.00 30.00
CFJT John Tavares 10.00 25.00
CFLL Louis Leblanc 5.00 12.00
CFLR Larry Robinson 6.00 15.00
CFMB Martin Brodeur 15.00 40.00
CFMD Matt Duchene 6.00 15.00
CFMF Marc-Andre Fleury 12.00 30.00
CFML Mario Lemieux 25.00 60.00
CFMM Mark Messier 12.00 30.00
CFMR Mike Richards 5.00 12.00
CFNB Nicklas Backstrom 6.00 15.00
CFNH Ryan Nugent-Hopkins 20.00 50.00
CFNL Nicklas Lidstrom 4.00 10.00
CFPK Patrick Kane 12.00 30.00
CFPR Patrick Roy 15.00 40.00
CFPS P.K. Subban 8.00 20.00
CFRF Ron Francis 8.00 20.00
CFRK Ryan Kesler 6.00 15.00
CFRL Roberto Luongo 10.00 25.00
CFRM Ryan Miller 6.00 15.00
CFRN Rick Nash 6.00 15.00
CFSC Sidney Crosby 25.00 60.00
CFSS Steven Stamkos 12.00 30.00
CFST Jordan Staal 5.00 12.00
CFTH Taylor Hall 6.00 15.00
CFTL Trevor Linden 6.00 15.00
CFTO Jonathan Toews 10.00 25.00
CFTT Tim Thomas 6.00 15.00
CFWG Wayne Gretzky 40.00 100.00
CFZP Zach Parise 6.00 15.00

2011-12 The Cup Honorable Numbers

HNBM Brad Marchand/63 40.00 100.00
HNCG Claude Giroux/28 20.00 50.00
HNCO Chris Osgood/30 20.00 50.00
HNCP Carey Price/31 40.00 100.00
HNEM Evgeni Malkin/71 40.00 100.00
HNGL Gabriel Landeskog/92 50.00 125.00
HNHG Cody Hodgson/18 25.00 60.00
HNJF Johan Franzen/93 15.00 40.00
HNJG J-S Giguere/35 20.00 50.00
HNKE Evander Kane/29 20.00 50.00
HNLR Luc Robitaille/20 20.00 50.00
HNMB Martin Brodeur/30 50.00 125.00
HNMH Marian Hossa/81 20.00 50.00
HNNB Nicklas Backstrom/19 20.00 50.00
HNPA Paul Stastny/26 15.00 40.00
HNRH Nugent-Hopkins/93 60.00 150.00
HNRK Ryan Kesler/17 20.00 50.00
HNRM Ryan Miller/30 20.00 50.00
HNRN Rick Nash/61 20.00 50.00
HNSA Joe Sakic/19 40.00 100.00
HNSC Sidney Crosby/87 200.00 300.00
HNSF Mark Scheifele/55 60.00 150.00
HNSN Scott Niedermayer/27 20.00 50.00
HNTE Tony Esposito/35 20.00 50.00
HNTO Jonathan Toews/19 30.00 80.00
HNTS Tyler Seguin/19 25.00 60.00
HNTV John Tavares/19 30.00 80.00
HNVO Tomas Vokoun/29 15.00 40.00

2011-12 The Cup Honorable Numbers Dual

DHNBB M.Brodeur/E.Belfour/30 50.00 125.00
DHNHL B.Hull/T.Linden/16 40.00 100.00
DHNNB Backstrom/Naslnd/19 20.00 50.00
DHNNZ RNH/M.Zibanejad/93 25.00 60.00
DHNST J.Sakic/J.Toews/19 40.00 100.00

2011-12 The Cup Silver Jerseys

1 Bobby Ryan 6.00 15.00
2 Ryan Getzlaf 8.00 20.00
3 Jonas Hiller 6.00 15.00
4 Ray Bourque 12.00 30.00
6 Phil Esposito 12.00 30.00
7 Cam Neely 8.00 20.00
8 Tim Thomas 8.00 20.00
9 Zdeno Chara 8.00 20.00
10 Nathan Horton 8.00 20.00
11 Tyler Seguin 10.00 25.00
12 Thomas Vanek 6.00 15.00
13 Ryan Miller 8.00 20.00
14 Derek Roy 5.00 12.00
15 Dominik Hasek 12.00 30.00
16 Miikka Kiprusoff 8.00 20.00
17 Jarome Iginla 10.00 25.00
18 Jeff Skinner 10.00 25.00
19 Patrick Kane 15.00 40.00
20 Tony Esposito 8.00 20.00
22 Jonathan Toews 12.00 30.00
23 Joe Sakic 15.00 40.00
24 Patrick Roy 20.00 50.00
25 Matt Duchene 8.00 20.00
26 Paul Stastny 6.00 15.00
27 Rick Nash 8.00 20.00
28 Jeff Carter 6.00 15.00
29 Steve Mason 6.00 15.00
30 Ed Belfour 8.00 20.00
31 Jim Howard 10.00 25.00
32 Pavel Datsyuk 12.00 30.00
33 Nicklas Lidstrom 5.00 12.00
34 Johan Franzen 6.00 15.00
35 Henrik Zetterberg 10.00 25.00
36 Ryan Smyth 6.00 15.00
37 Taylor Hall 8.00 20.00
38 Grant Fuhr 12.00 30.00
39 Jari Kurri 8.00 20.00
40 Jordan Eberle 8.00 20.00
41 Anze Kopitar 12.00 30.00
42 Mike Richards 6.00 15.00
43 Luc Robitaille 8.00 20.00
44 Drew Doughty 10.00 25.00
45 Mike Modano 12.00 30.00
46 Dino Ciccarelli 8.00 20.00
47 Carey Price 15.00 40.00
48 Larry Robinson 8.00 20.00
49 P.K. Subban 10.00 25.00
50 Pekka Rinne 8.00 20.00
51 Ilya Kovalchuk 8.00 20.00
52 Martin Brodeur 20.00 50.00
53 Zach Parise 8.00 20.00
54 John Tavares 12.00 30.00
56 Wayne Gretzky 50.00 125.00
57 Marian Gaborik 8.00 20.00
58 Henrik Lundqvist 20.00 50.00
59 Mark Messier 15.00 40.00
60 Jason Spezza 8.00 20.00
61 Eric Lindros 12.00 30.00
62 James van Riemsdyk 6.00 15.00
63 Jaromir Jagr 25.00 60.00
64 Claude Giroux 8.00 20.00
65 Jordan Staal 6.00 15.00
66 Evgeni Malkin 15.00 40.00
67 Mario Lemieux 30.00 80.00
68 Marc-Andre Fleury 15.00 40.00
69 Sidney Crosby 30.00 80.00
70 Ron Francis 10.00 25.00
71 Paul Coffey 8.00 20.00
72 Antti Niemi 6.00 15.00
73 Patrick Marleau 10.00 25.00
74 Joe Thornton 12.00 30.00
75 Logan Couture 10.00 25.00
76 Jaroslav Halak 8.00 20.00
77 Brett Hull 15.00 40.00
78 Vincent Lecavalier 8.00 20.00
79 Steven Stamkos 15.00 40.00
80 Phil Kessel 8.00 20.00
81 Dion Phaneuf 6.00 15.00
82 Roberto Luongo 12.00 30.00
83 Daniel Sedin 10.00 25.00
84 Henrik Sedin 10.00 25.00
85 Ryan Kesler 8.00 20.00
86 Trevor Linden 8.00 20.00
87 Alexander Ovechkin 30.00 80.00
88 Nicklas Backstrom 8.00 20.00
89 Dale Hawerchuk 10.00 25.00
90 Ondrej Pavelec 8.00 20.00

2011-12 The Cup Limited Logos Autographs

LLAH Adam Henrique/50 40.00 100.00
LLAL Adam Larsson/50 20.00 50.00
LLBC Brett Connolly/50 15.00 40.00
LLBH Brett Hull/50 40.00 100.00
LLBM Brad Marchand/50 40.00 100.00
LLBR Bobby Ryan/50 15.00 40.00
LLBS Brayden Schenn/50 20.00 50.00
LLCG Claude Giroux/50 20.00 50.00
LLCH Cody Hodgson/50 25.00 60.00
LLCJ Curtis Joseph/50 25.00 60.00
LLCP Carey Price/50 40.00 100.00
LLCU Sean Couturier/50 30.00 80.00
LLDD Drew Doughty/50 25.00 60.00
LLDH Dany Heatley/50 15.00 40.00
LLDR Derek Roy/50 12.00 30.00
LLEB Ed Belfour/50 20.00 50.00
LLEK Evander Kane/50 20.00 50.00
LLEL Eric Lindros/50 30.00 80.00
LLEM Evgeni Malkin/50 40.00 100.00
LLES Eric Staal/50 25.00 60.00
LLGA Marian Gaborik/25 20.00 50.00
LLGC Guy Carbonneau/50 20.00 50.00
LLGL Gabriel Landeskog/50 50.00 125.00
LLHO Cody Hodgson/50 25.00 60.00
LLJE Jordan Eberle/50 20.00 50.00
LLJF Johan Franzen/50 15.00 40.00
LLJI Jarome Iginla/50 25.00 60.00
LLJS Jordan Staal/50 15.00 40.00
LLJT John Tavares/50 30.00 80.00
LLLL Louis Leblanc/50 15.00 40.00
LLMB Martin Brodeur/50 50.00 125.00
LLMD Matt Duchene/50 20.00 50.00
LLMF Marc-Andre Fleury/50 40.00 100.00
LLMG Mike Gartner/50 25.00 60.00
LLML Mario Lemieux/50 80.00 200.00
LLNB Nicklas Backstrom/50 20.00 50.00
LLNH Ryan Nugent-Hopkins/50 60.00 150.00
LLPB Patrice Bergeron/50 200.00 500.00
LLPD Pavel Datsyuk/50 30.00 80.00
LLPM Patrick Marleau/50 20.00 50.00
LLPS P.K. Subban/50 25.00 60.00
LLRB Ray Bourque/50 30.00 80.00
LLRE Pekka Rinne/50 20.00 50.00
LLRG Ryan Getzlaf/50 20.00 50.00
LLRJ Ryan Johansen/50 50.00 125.00
LLRK Ryan Kesler/50 20.00 50.00
LLRM Ryan Miller/50 20.00 50.00
LLRN Rick Nash/50 20.00 50.00
LLSA Joe Sakic/50 40.00 100.00
LLSC Sidney Crosby/50 80.00 200.00
LLSF Mark Scheifele/50 60.00 150.00
LLSU P.K. Subban/50 25.00 60.00
LLTH Taylor Hall/50 20.00 50.00
LLTL Trevor Linden/50 20.00 50.00
LLTO Jonathan Toews/50 30.00 80.00
LLTS Tyler Seguin/50 25.00 60.00
LLTT Tony Twist/50 12.00 30.00
LLZK Zack Kassian/50 20.00 50.00

2011-12 The Cup Rookie Bookmarks Dual Autographs

ARBCR S.Couturier/M.Read 75.00 150.00
ARBHS Hodgson/M.Scheifele 75.00 150.00
ARBLD L.Leblanc/R.Diaz 60.00 120.00
ARBLH A.Larsson/A.Henrique 50.00 100.00
ARBNL Nugent-Hpkins/Landskg 150.00 300.00
ARBSG J.Gardiner/B.Scrivens 75.00 150.00
ARBSN B.Smith/G.Nyquist 60.00 120.00
ARBZG Zibanejad/C.Greening 50.00 100.00

2011-12 The Cup Rookie Evolution Video Cards

REAH Adam Henrique 125.00 200.00
REBC Brett Connolly 25.00 60.00
REBG Blake Geoffrion 25.00 60.00
REBS Brendan Smith 30.00 80.00
RECE Cody Eakin 30.00 80.00
REGL Gabriel Landeskog 30.00 80.00
REJG Jake Gardiner 50.00 100.00
REMZ Mika Zibanejad 30.00 80.00
RERE Ryan Ellis 40.00 100.00
RERN Ryan Nugent-Hopkins 100.00 200.00
RESD Simon Despres 30.00 80.00
REZK Zack Kassian 30.00 80.00
NNO EXCH CARD 30.00 80.00

2011-12 The Cup Rookie Gear Autographs

ARGAH Adam Henrique 100.00 250.00
ARGAL Adam Larsson 50.00 120.00
ARGBC Brett Connolly 40.00 100.00
ARGCE Cody Eakin 60.00 150.00
ARGCH Cody Hodgson 60.00 150.00
ARGCS Craig Smith 50.00 125.00
ARGGL G.Landeskog 125.00 300.00
ARGLL Louis Leblanc 40.00 100.00
ARGMR Matt Read 50.00 125.00
ARGMS Mark Scheifele 150.00 400.00
ARGMZ Mika Zibanejad 125.00 300.00
ARGRE Ryan Ellis 40.00 100.00
ARGRJ Ryan Johansen 125.00 300.00
ARGRN Ryan Nugent-Hopkins 200.00 400.00
ARGSC Sean Couturier 80.00 200.00
ARGZK Zack Kassian 50.00 125.00

2011-12 The Cup Scripted Sticks

SAO Alexander Ovechkin 100.00 175.00
SBH Bobby Hull 30.00 60.00
SCP Carey Price 75.00 150.00
SDH Dale Hawerchuk 40.00 80.00
SEL Eric Lindros 60.00 120.00
SJS Joe Sakic 60.00 120.00
SLR Larry Robinson 25.00 50.00
SMB Martin Brodeur 100.00 200.00
SMM Mark Messier 50.00 120.00
SNL Nicklas Lidstrom 75.00 150.00
SPR Patrick Roy 75.00 150.00
SSC Sidney Crosby 200.00 350.00
SWG Wayne Gretzky 400.00 1000.00

2011-12 The Cup Scripted Sticks Dual

DSBL J.Beliveau/G.Lafleur 100.00 200.00
DSBP M.Bossy/D.Potvin 60.00 120.00
DSEB P.Esposito/J.Bucyk 60.00 120.00
DSGM W.Gretzky/M.Messier
DSKG W.Gretzky/J.Kurri
DSLC S.Crosby/Lemieux
DSMC D.Ciccarelli/M.Modano
DSOM A.Ovechkin/E.Malkin
DSRP P.Roy/C.Price 150.00 250.00
DSRS P.Roy/J.Sakic 175.00 300.00

2011-12 The Cup Scripted Swatches

SSAO Alexander Ovechkin/15 175.00 300.00
SSBC Brett Connolly/35 25.00 50.00
SSCU Sean Couturier/35 20.00 50.00
SSGL G.Landeskog/35 EXCH 50.00 120.00
SSJS Joe Sakic/35 75.00 150.00
SSMB Martin Brodeur/35
SSMF Marc-Andre Fleury/35 30.00 80.00
SSML Mario Lemieux/35 100.00 175.00
SSNH Nugent-Hopkins/35 75.00 150.00
SSRF Ron Francis/35 25.00 60.00
SSSC Sidney Crosby/35 150.00 250.00
SSWG Wayne Gretzky/35 300.00 800.00

2011-12 The Cup Scripted Swatches Dual

DSSCF Coffey/Francis/15 50.00 100.00
DSSCL S.Crosby/Lemieux/15
DSSCR Couturier/Read/15 40.00 100.00
DSSPS Price/Subban/15 100.00 200.00
DSSRG RNH/Landeskg/15 100.00 200.00
DSSRS Roy/Sakic/15 125.00 200.00

2011-12 The Cup Signature Patches

SPAH Adam Henrique 20.00 50.00
SPAK Anze Kopitar 25.00 60.00
SPAO Alexander Ovechkin/35 50.00 100.00
SPBC Brett Connolly 15.00 40.00
SPBH Brett Hull/35 50.00 120.00
SPBJ Jonathon Blum 10.00 25.00
SPBR Bill Ranford 15.00 40.00
SPBY Dustin Byfuglien 15.00 40.00
SPCF Cam Fowler 15.00 40.00
SPCG Claude Giroux 15.00 40.00
SPCH Cody Hodgson 15.00 40.00
SPCO Chris Osgood 12.00 30.00
SPCP Carey Price/35 60.00 120.00
SPCU Sean Couturier 15.00 40.00
SPDB Dan Boyle 10.00 25.00
SPDD Drew Doughty 30.00 60.00
SPDE Devin Setoguchi 10.00 25.00
SPDH Dany Heatley 15.00 40.00
SPDP Dion Phaneuf 12.00 30.00
SPDR Derek Roy 10.00 25.00
SPDS Derek Stepan 10.00 25.00
SPDW Doug Wilson 12.00 30.00
SPEK Evander Kane 25.00 50.00
SPEL Eric Lindros/35 30.00 80.00
SPES Eric Staal 12.00 30.00
SPGL Gabriel Landeskog 60.00 150.00
SPGT Mike Gartner 20.00 50.00
SPJB Jay Bouwmeester 10.00 25.00
SPJC Jeff Carter 8.00 20.00
SPJE Jordan Eberle 20.00 50.00
SPJF Johan Franzen 12.00 30.00
SPJI Jarome Iginla 25.00 50.00
SPJM John Moore 12.00 30.00
SPJS Joe Sakic/35 40.00 100.00
SPJT Joe Thornton/35 15.00 40.00
SPLL Louis Leblanc 15.00 40.00
SPLR Larry Robinson 15.00 40.00
SPLU Luc Robitaille 25.00 50.00
SPMB Martin Brodeur/35 60.00 125.00
SPMD Matt Duchene 15.00 40.00
SPMF Marc-Andre Fleury 12.00 30.00
SPMH Marian Hossa 15.00 40.00
SPMK Mike Modano/35 25.00 60.00
SPML Mario Lemieux/35 50.00 100.00
SPNB Nicklas Backstrom 20.00 40.00
SPPA Paul Stastny 12.00 30.00
SPPD Pavel Datsyuk 25.00 60.00
SPPR Patrick Roy/35 75.00 150.00
SPPS P.K. Subban 20.00 50.00
SPRF Ron Francis/35 25.00 60.00
SPRG Ryan Getzlaf 12.00 30.00
SPRH Ron Hextall 15.00 40.00
SPRJ Ryan Johansen 30.00 80.00
SPRK Ryan Kesler 10.00 25.00
SPRM Ryan Miller 15.00 40.00
SPRN Rick Nash 25.00 50.00
SPRNH Ryan Nugent-Hopkins 50.00 100.00
SPRY Bobby Ryan 12.00 30.00
SPSC Sidney Crosby/35 100.00 200.00
SPSE Brent Seabrook 10.00 25.00
SPST Jordan Staal 12.00 30.00
SPSV Denis Savard 12.00 30.00
SPSW Shea Weber
SPTE Tony Esposito/35 30.00 60.00
SPTH Taylor Hall 25.00 50.00
SPTM Tyler Myers
SPTS Tyler Seguin 25.00 60.00
SPTW Jonathan Toews 30.00 60.00
SPVA James van Riemsdyk 12.00 30.00
SPVO Tomas Vokoun 12.00 30.00
SPWG Wayne Gretzky/35 300.00 800.00
SPZK Zack Kassian 12.00 30.00

2011-12 The Cup Signature Patches Dual

SP2AA Henriq/Lrssn/35 20.00 50.00
SP2BM Richrds/Gabrk/35
SP2BS Boyle/Seabrook/35 15.00 40.00
SP2CL Crosby/Lemieux/25 300.00 600.00
SP2DD Heatley/Setogch/35 15.00 40.00
SP2DS Dubinsky/Stepan/35 12.00 30.00
SP2EP Eberle/Paajarvi/35 30.00 80.00
SP2FC Francis/Coffey/35 20.00 50.00
SP2FS Fleury/Staal/35 40.00 100.00
SP2GR Getzlaf/Ryan/35 20.00 50.00
SP2GV Giroux/vanRmsdk/35 25.00 60.00
SP2HC Hodgson/Benn/25 30.00 80.00
SP2HS Heatley/Staal/35 30.00 60.00
SP2IB Iginla/Bouwmstr/35 20.00 50.00
SP2LS Lecav/St.Louis/35 30.00 60.00
SP2MT Marleau/Thorntn/35 30.00 60.00
SP2MV Miller/Vanek/35
SP2NB Neely/Bourque/35 40.00 80.00
SP2NL RNH/Landeskog/35 EX 25.00 60.00
SP2NM Mason/Nash/35 12.00 30.00
SP2OB Ovechkn/Backstrm/35 40.00 80.00
SP2PS Price/Subban/35 75.00 135.00
SP2RA RNH/Lander/35 EX 75.00 150.00
SP2RG M.Richards/Gagne/35 15.00 40.00
SP2RM Roy/Miller/35 25.00 50.00
SP2RS Roy/Sakic/35 75.00 150.00
SP2RV Roy/Vanek/35
SP2SD Stastny/Duchene/35 20.00 50.00
SP2SG Sakic/Gretzky/35 300.00 800.00
SP2SK Scheifel/Klingbrg/35 30.00 80.00
SP2SL Lafleur/Stastny/35 25.00 60.00
SP2SM Couturier/Read/35 25.00 60.00
SP2TH Tavares/Hall/35 EXCH 50.00 100.00
SP2TT Hall/Seguin/35 40.00 80.00
SP2WB S.Weber/D.Boyle/35 15.00 40.00

2011-12 The Cup Stanley Cup Signatures

SCSAD Alex Delvecchio 12.00 30.00
SCSAT Alex Tanguay 8.00 20.00
SCSBB Bill Barber 10.00 25.00
SCSBC Bobby Clarke 12.00 30.00
SCSBH Bobby Hull 25.00 60.00
SCSBL Brian Leetch 10.00 25.00
SCSBM Brad Marchand 25.00 60.00
SCSBO Bobby Orr 60.00 120.00
SCSBW Johnny Bower 20.00 50.00
SCSCL Claude Lemieux 10.00 25.00
SCSCO Paul Coffey
SCSCR Sidney Crosby 90.00 150.00
SCSDP Denis Potvin 12.00 30.00
SCSDS Denis Savard 20.00 40.00
SCSEB Ed Belfour 20.00 40.00
SCSEM Evgeni Malkin 30.00 60.00
SCSGA Glenn Anderson 12.00 30.00
SCSGF Grant Fuhr 12.00 30.00
SCSGL Guy Lafleur 12.00 30.00
SCSHE Milan Hejduk 10.00 25.00
SCSHU Brett Hull 25.00 50.00
SCSIL Igor Larionov 12.00 30.00
SCSJB Johnny Bucyk 12.00 30.00
SCSJF Johan Franzen 10.00 25.00
SCSJG Jean-Sebastien Giguere 20.00 40.00
SCSJK Jari Kurri 15.00 40.00
SCSJS Joe Sakic 25.00 50.00
SCSJT Jonathan Toews 30.00 60.00
SCSLR Larry Robinson 12.00 30.00
SCSMA Mark Messier 30.00 60.00
SCSMB Martin Brodeur 30.00 60.00
SCSME Mark Messier 30.00 60.00
SCSMF Marc-Andre Fleury 20.00 40.00
SCSMH Marian Hossa 20.00 50.00
SCSMI Mike Bossy 15.00 40.00
SCSML Mario Lemieux 50.00 100.00
SCSMM Mike Modano 20.00 40.00
SCSMS Milt Schmidt 15.00 40.00
SCSNL Nicklas Lidstrom 25.00 50.00
SCSPC Paul Coffey 20.00 40.00
SCSPD Pavel Datsyuk 25.00 50.00
SCSPE Phil Esposito 20.00 50.00
SCSPK Patrick Kane 40.00 80.00
SCSRB Ray Bourque 25.00 50.00
SCSRF Ron Francis 25.00 50.00
SCSRG Ryan Getzlaf 12.00 30.00
SCSRK Red Kelly 12.00 30.00
SCSRM Rick MacLeish 12.00 30.00
SCSRO Patrick Roy 60.00 120.00
SCSSC Dave Schultz 12.00 30.00
SCSSN Scott Niedermayer 12.00 30.00
SCSST Jordan Staal 12.00 30.00
SCSTL Ted Lindsay 12.00 30.00
SCSTS Tyler Seguin 40.00 80.00
SCSWG Wayne Gretzky 250.00 600.00

2011-12 The Cup Stanley Cup Signatures Dual

SC2BG C.Gillies/M.Bossy EX 15.00 40.00
SC2BM P.Bergeron/Marchand 30.00 80.00
SC2BN M.Brodeur/S.Niedermayer
SC2BP D.Potvin/M.Bossy 25.00 50.00
SC2BT B.Marchand/T.Seguin 25.00 60.00
SC2CL M.Lemieux/P.Coffey 60.00 125.00
SC2CM M.Messier/P.Coffey 30.00 60.00
SC2DF J.Franzen/P.Datsyuk 25.00 50.00
SC2DL N.Lidstrom/P.Datsyuk 30.00 60.00
SC2EO B.Orr/P.Esposito 75.00 150.00
SC2FC P.Coffey/R.Francis EX 30.00 60.00
SC2FK G.Fuhr/J.Kurri EX 20.00 50.00
SC2GM W.Gretzky/M.Messier EX 250.00 600.00
SC2HM B.Hull/S.Mikita 50.00 100.00
SC2HT J.Toews/M.Hossa 40.00 100.00
SC2KG W.Gretzky/J.Kurri 250.00 600.00
SC2LC S.Crosby/Lemieux 150.00 300.00
SC2LD A.Delvecchio/T.Lindsay 25.00 60.00
SC2LF M.Lemieux/R.Francis 60.00 125.00
SC2LL I.Larionov/N.Lidstrom 25.00 60.00
SC2LM M.Messier/B.Leetch
SC2MS E.Malkin/J.Staal 30.00 80.00
SC2OS B.Orr/M.Schmidt 75.00 150.00
SC2PG P.Coffey/G.Fuhr 25.00 60.00
SC2RB P.Roy/R.Bourque 50.00 125.00
SC2RR Patrick Roy 125.00 250.00
SC2RS J.Sakic/P.Roy 75.00 125.00
SC2SB J.Sakic/R.Bourque 40.00 80.00
SC2TK J.Toews/P.Kane 75.00 150.00

2011-12 The Cup Trios Jerseys

C3ANA Perry/Getzlaf/Ryan 10.00 25.00
C3AVS Duchene/Ststny/Lndskg 15.00 40.00
C3BOS Bergeron/Horton/Seguin 8.00 20.00
C3BUF Miller/Vanek/Myers 6.00 15.00
C3CHI Crawford/Keith/Sharp 8.00 20.00
C3DRW Shanhn/Hasek/Lidstrm 10.00 25.00
C3LAK Kopitar/Richards/Brown 10.00 25.00
C3NJD Parise/Brodeur/Kovalchk 15.00 40.00
C3NYI Tavares/Moulson/Grabnr 10.00 25.00
C3NYR Callahan/Dubinsky/Stepn 4.00 10.00
C3OIL Hall/RNH/Eberle 20.00 50.00
C3PHI Giroux/Briere/vanRiems 6.00 15.00
C3QGF Brodeur/Luongo/Fleury 15.00 40.00
C3STL Halak/Pietrangelo/Stwrt 6.00 15.00
C3VAN Luongo/Sedin/Sedin 10.00 25.00
C3BEES Thomas/Krejci/Chara 6.00 15.00
C3BLUE Lundqvist/Staal/Gaborik 15.00 40.00
C3CAPS Ovech/Backstrom/Semin 25.00 60.00
C3JAGR Jagr/Jagr/Jagr 20.00 50.00
C3PENS Malkin/Staal/Fleury 12.00 30.00
C3PITT Fleury/Malkin/Letang 12.00 30.00
C3RAVS Landskg/Elliott/Gaunce 15.00 40.00
C3RCBJ Johnsn/Moore/Savard 15.00 40.00
C3RNJD Larsson/Henrq/Kinkaid 12.00 30.00
C3RPHI Coutier/Read/Gustafsn 10.00 25.00
C3WASH Green/Ovech/Vokoun 25.00 60.00
C3WJC1 Schenn/Coutier/Kassian 10.00 25.00
C3WJC2 Connolly/Leblanc/Johnsn 15.00 40.00
C3WJC3 Despres/Ellis/Gudbrnsn 6.00 15.00
C3BEESD Thomas/Rask/Chara 8.00 20.00
C3BLUES Hull/Joseph/Twist 12.00 30.00
C3DUCKS Hiller/Getzlaf/Fowler 6.00 15.00
C3GOLD1 Toews/Iginla/Staal 10.00 25.00
C3GOLD2 Perry/Bergrn/Morrow 10.00 25.00
C3GOLD3 Luongo/Brodr/Fleury 15.00 40.00
C3GOLD4 Seabrk/Dghty/Wbr 8.00 20.00
C3GOLD5 Thorntn/Marlu/Heatly 10.00 25.00
C3GOLD6 Nash/Richrds/Getzlf 6.00 15.00
C3GOLD7 Keith/Prongr/Niedrmyr 6.00 15.00
C3HAWKS Toews/Kane/Hossa 12.00 30.00
C3KINGS Quick/Dghty/Johnsn 8.00 20.00
C3NUCKS Hodgsn/Keslr/Burrws 8.00 20.00
C3RJETS Scheifl/Klingbrg/Pstm 20.00 50.00
C3RMTL1 Leblanc/Emelin/Diaz 5.00 12.00
C3RMTL2 Leblanc/Palshj/Nash 5.00 12.00
C3RNASH Ellis/Smith/Blum 6.00 15.00
C3ROIL1 RNH/Teubrt/Hartkn 20.00 50.00
C3ROIL2 RNH/Petrell/Lander 20.00 50.00
C3RPENS Despres/Vitale/Strait 6.00 15.00
C3RSENS Zibanjd/Grng/Wrcch 15.00 40.00
C3SABRE Roy/Staffrd/Pomnvll 4.00 10.00
C3WINGS Howrd/Frnzn/Krnwll 8.00 20.00
C390PENS Mario/Jagr/Murphy 25.00 60.00
C3ALLSTARG Brodeur/Belfr/Jsph 15.00 40.00
C3BHAWKS Savard/Wilsn/Espo 6.00 15.00
C3FLAMES Iginla/Cammllr/Kiprsff 8.00 20.00
C3RFLAMES Irving/Nemisz/Hork 5.00 12.00
C3RLEAFS Gardinr/Colbrn/Frttn 8.00 20.00
C3RSABRE Kassn/Flgno/McNb 8.00 20.00
C3STAR90S Mario/Sakic/Jagr 25.00 60.00

2012-13 The Cup

1 Ryan Getzlaf 2.50 6.00
2 Teemu Selanne 5.00 12.00
3 Ray Bourque 4.00 10.00
4 Bobby Orr 10.00 25.00
5 Tuukka Rask 3.00 8.00
6 Cam Neely 2.50 6.00
7 Zdeno Chara 2.50 6.00
8 Tyler Seguin 3.00 8.00
9 Brad Marchand 5.00 12.00
10 Thomas Vanek 2.00 5.00
11 Theoren Fleury 3.00 8.00
12 Miikka Kiprusoff 2.50 6.00
13 Jarome Iginla 3.00 8.00
14 Jeff Skinner 3.00 8.00
15 Phil Esposito 4.00 10.00
16 Patrick Kane 5.00 12.00
17 Tony Esposito 2.50 6.00
18 Bobby Hull 5.00 12.00
19 Jonathan Toews 4.00 10.00
20 Joe Sakic 5.00 12.00
21 Patrick Roy 6.00 15.00
22 Matt Duchene 2.50 6.00
23 Gabriel Landeskog 3.00 8.00
24 Jaromir Jagr 8.00 20.00
25 Dominik Hasek 4.00 10.00
26 Jim Howard 3.00 8.00
27 Pavel Datsyuk 4.00 10.00
28 Nicklas Lidstrom 2.50 6.00
29 Johan Franzen 2.00 5.00
30 Henrik Zetterberg 3.00 8.00
31 Ryan Smyth 2.00 5.00
32 Taylor Hall 2.50 6.00
33 Grant Fuhr 4.00 10.00
34 Jari Kurri 2.50 6.00
35 Jordan Eberle 2.50 6.00
36 Paul Coffey 2.50 6.00
37 Andy Moog 2.50 6.00
38 Ryan Nugent-Hopkins 3.00 8.00
39 Ed Belfour 2.50 6.00
40 Jeff Carter 2.00 5.00
41 Anze Kopitar 4.00 10.00
42 Mike Richards 2.00 5.00
43 Luc Robitaille 2.50 6.00
44 Drew Doughty 3.00 8.00
45 Wayne Gretzky 15.00 40.00
46 Jonathan Quick 3.00 8.00
47 Mike Modano 4.00 10.00
48 Zach Parise 2.50 6.00
49 Carey Price 5.00 12.00
50 Larry Robinson 2.50 6.00
51 P.K. Subban 3.00 8.00
52 Pekka Rinne 2.50 6.00
53 Ilya Kovalchuk 2.50 6.00
54 Martin Brodeur 6.00 15.00
55 Adam Henrique 2.00 5.00
56 John Tavares 4.00 10.00
57 Mike Bossy 2.50 6.00
58 Rick Nash 2.50 6.00
59 Marian Gaborik 2.50 6.00
60 Henrik Lundqvist 6.00 15.00
61 Mark Messier 5.00 12.00
62 Jason Spezza 2.50 6.00
63 Eric Lindros 4.00 10.00
64 Claude Giroux 2.50 6.00
65 Evgeni Malkin 5.00 12.00
66 Mario Lemieux 10.00 25.00
67 Marc-Andre Fleury 5.00 12.00
68 Sidney Crosby 10.00 25.00
69 Ron Francis 3.00 8.00
70 Kris Letang 3.00 8.00
71 Scott Hartnell 1.50 4.00
72 Antti Niemi 2.00 5.00
73 Patrick Marleau 2.50 6.00
74 Logan Couture 3.00 8.00
75 Jaroslav Halak 2.50 6.00
76 Brett Hull 5.00 12.00
77 Steven Stamkos 5.00 12.00
78 Phil Kessel 2.50 6.00
79 Dion Phaneuf 2.00 5.00
80 Mats Sundin 4.00 10.00
81 Alexandre Burrows 1.50 4.00
82 Daniel Sedin 3.00 8.00
83 Henrik Sedin 3.00 8.00
84 Ryan Kesler 2.50 6.00
85 Trevor Linden 2.50 6.00
86 Pavel Bure 2.50 6.00
87 Alexander Ovechkin 10.00 25.00
88 Nicklas Backstrom 2.50 6.00
89 Dale Hawerchuk 3.00 8.00
90 Ondrej Pavelec 2.50 6.00
91 M.Sauve JSY AU/249 RC 6.00 15.00
92 L.MacDermid JSY AU/249 RC 8.00 20.00
93 Torey Krug JSY AU/249 RC 30.00 80.00
94 M.Hutchinson JSY AU/249 RC 10.00 25.00
95 Akim Aliu JSY AU/249 RC 8.00 20.00
96 J.Welsh JSY AU/249 RC 8.00 20.00
97 Brandon Bollig JSY AU/249 RC 6.00 15.00
98 T.Barrie JSY AU/249 RC 30.00 80.00
99 M.Connolly JSY AU/249 RC 8.00 20.00
100 D.Prout JSY AU/249 RC 6.00 15.00
101 C.Goloubef JSY AU/249 RC 6.00 15.00
102 S.Hunwick JSY AU/249 RC 6.00 15.00
103 R.Garbutt JSY AU/249 RC 6.00 15.00
104 Reilly Smith JSY AU/249 RC 15.00 40.00
105 B.Dillon JSY AU/249 RC 8.00 20.00
106 S.Glennie JSY AU/249 RC 8.00 20.00
107 R.Sheahan JSY AU/249 RC 10.00 25.00
108 Philippe Cornet/199 RC 4.00 10.00
109 J.Nolan JSY AU/249 RC 6.00 15.00
110 J.Zucker JSY AU/249 RC 15.00 40.00
111 Tyler Cuma JSY AU/249 RC 6.00 15.00
112 C.Genoway JSY AU/249 RC 6.00 15.00
113 G.Dumont JSY AU/249 RC 8.00 20.00
114 Robert Mayer/199 RC 5.00 12.00
115 C.Pickard JSY AU/249 RC 12.00 30.00
116 Aaron Ness JSY AU/249 RC 6.00 15.00
117 C.Cizikas JSY AU/249 RC 12.00 30.00
118 M.Donovan JSY AU/249 RC 8.00 20.00
119 J.Silfverberg JSY AU/249 RC 25.00 60.00
120 Mark Stone JSY AU/249 RC 50.00 125.00
121 B.Manning JSY AU/249 RC 8.00 20.00
122 M.Stone JSY AU/249 RC 8.00 20.00
123 M.Watkins JSY AU/249 RC 6.00 15.00
124 Tyson Sexsmith/199 RC 3.00 8.00
125 Jake Allen JSY AU/249 RC 30.00 80.00
126 J.T. Brown JSY AU/249 RC 8.00 20.00
127 C.Ashton JSY AU/249 RC 6.00 15.00
128 R.Hamilton JSY AU/249 RC 6.00 15.00
129 J.Rynnas JSY AU/249 RC 6.00 15.00
130 S.Baertschi JSY AU/99 RC 80.00 200.00
131 Chris Kreider JSY AU/99 RC 100.00 250.00
132 J.Schwartz JSY AU/99 RC 150.00 400.00

2012-13 The Cup Gold

*1-90 VETS/25: 1X TO 2.5X BASIC CARDS
88 Nicklas Backstrom 8.00 20.00
91 Maxime Sauve 5.00 12.00
92 Lane MacDermid 6.00 15.00
93 Torey Krug 15.00 40.00
94 Michael Hutchinson 8.00 20.00
95 Akim Aliu 6.00 15.00
96 Jeremy Welsh 6.00 15.00
97 Brandon Bollig 5.00 12.00
98 Tyson Barrie 15.00 40.00
99 Mike Connolly 6.00 15.00
100 Dalton Prout 5.00 12.00
101 Cody Goloubef 5.00 12.00
102 Shawn Hunwick 5.00 12.00
103 Ryan Garbutt 8.00 20.00
104 Reilly Smith 12.00 30.00
105 Brenden Dillon 6.00 15.00
106 Scott Glennie 6.00 15.00
107 Riley Sheahan 10.00 25.00
108 Philippe Cornet 6.00 15.00
109 Jordan Nolan 5.00 12.00
110 Jason Zucker 12.00 30.00
111 Tyler Cuma 5.00 12.00
112 Chay Genoway 5.00 12.00
113 Gabriel Dumont 6.00 15.00
114 Robert Mayer 8.00 20.00
115 Chet Pickard 6.00 15.00
116 Aaron Ness 5.00 12.00
117 Casey Cizikas 6.00 15.00
118 Matt Donovan 6.00 15.00
119 Jakob Silfverberg 25.00 50.00
120 Mark Stone 100.00 250.00
121 Brandon Manning 6.00 15.00
122 Michael Stone 6.00 15.00
123 Matt Watkins 5.00 12.00
124 Tyson Sexsmith 5.00 12.00
125 Jake Allen 15.00 40.00
126 J.T. Brown 6.00 15.00
127 Carter Ashton 5.00 12.00
128 Ryan Hamilton 5.00 12.00
129 Jussi Rynnas 5.00 12.00
130 Sven Baertschi 8.00 20.00
131 Chris Kreider 20.00 50.00
132 Jaden Schwartz 20.00 50.00

2012-13 The Cup Gold Rainbow

*ROOKIE/55-74: .5X TO 1.2X JSY AU RC/249
*ROOKIE/31-49: .6X TO 1.5X JSY AU RC/249
*ROOKIE/20-29: .8X TO 2X JSY AU RC/249
*ROOKIE/15-18: 1X TO 2.5X JSY AU RC/249
93 Torey Krug JSY AU/47 60.00 120.00
119 Jakob Silfverberg JSY AU/33 30.00 80.00
130 Sven Baertschi JSY AU/47 30.00 80.00
131 Chris Kreider JSY AU/20 150.00 300.00

2012-13 The Cup Auto Draft Boards

DBCA Carter Ashton 8.00 20.00
DBCK Chris Kreider 40.00 100.00
DBCP Chet Pickard 10.00 25.00
DBJS Jaden Schwartz 25.00 60.00
DBRS Riley Sheahan 12.00 30.00
DBSB Sven Baertschi 12.00 30.00
DBTC Tyler Cuma 8.00 20.00

2012-13 The Cup Brilliance Autographs

BAM Andy Moog C 8.00 20.00
BAO Alexander Ovechkin A 30.00 80.00
BBH Brett Hull A 15.00 40.00
BBO Bobby Orr C 40.00 100.00
BCK Chris Kreider C 20.00 50.00
BCP Carey Price C 15.00 40.00
BEL Eric Lindros A 30.00 80.00
BEM Evgeni Malkin 15.00 40.00
BGL Gabriel Landeskog 10.00 25.00
BJA Jaden Schwartz C 15.00 40.00
BJE Jordan Eberle 8.00 20.00
BJI Jarome Iginla A 10.00 25.00
BJJ Jaromir Jagr A 50.00 125.00
BJQ Jonathan Quick 25.00 60.00
BJS Jeff Skinner C 10.00 25.00
BJT Jonathan Toews B 30.00 80.00
BMB Martin Brodeur 30.00 80.00
BMF Marc-Andre Fleury B 15.00 40.00
BML Mario Lemieux A 50.00 125.00
BMM Mark Messier A 25.00 60.00
BMS Mats Sundin A 25.00 60.00
BPB Pavel Bure A 30.00 80.00
BPF Peter Forsberg B 30.00 80.00
BPK Patrick Kane B 30.00 80.00
BPR Patrick Roy A 50.00 125.00
BPS P.K. Subban 10.00 25.00
BRI Pekka Rinne 8.00 20.00
BRN R.Nugent-Hopkins B EXCH 12.00 30.00
BSA Joe Sakic A 15.00 40.00
BSB Sven Baertschi C 8.00 20.00
BSC Sidney Crosby A 30.00 80.00
BSE Teemu Selanne 15.00 40.00
BTA John Tavares C 12.00 30.00
BTF Theoren Fleury B 10.00 25.00
BTH Taylor Hall B 8.00 20.00
BTL Trevor Linden B 8.00 20.00
BTS Tyler Seguin 10.00 25.00
BWG Wayne Gretzky A 100.00 250.00
BZP Zach Parise B 8.00 20.00

2012-13 The Cup Enshrinements

CEAM Andy Moog 10.00 25.00
CEAO Alexander Ovechkin 150.00 400.00
CEBC Bobby Clarke 15.00 40.00
CEBE Jean Beliveau 10.00 25.00
CEBH Brett Hull 20.00 50.00
CEBM Brad Marchand 20.00 50.00
CEBO Bobby Orr 40.00 100.00
CEBR Martin Brodeur 30.00 80.00
CECJ Curtis Joseph 12.00 30.00
CECK Chris Kreider 25.00 60.00
CECN Cam Neely 10.00 25.00
CECP Carey Price 20.00 50.00
CEDH Dominik Hasek 15.00 40.00
CEDS Dave Schultz 10.00 25.00
CEEB Ed Belfour 10.00 25.00
CEEL Eric Lindros 15.00 40.00
CEEM Evgeni Malkin 20.00 50.00
CEGF Grant Fuhr 15.00 40.00
CEGL Guy Lafleur 12.00 30.00
CEGP Gilbert Perreault 10.00 25.00
CEHA Dale Hawerchuk 12.00 30.00
CEHU Bobby Hull 40.00 100.00
CEJA Jaden Schwartz 20.00 50.00
CEJB Johnny Bucyk 10.00 25.00
CEJE Jordan Eberle 10.00 25.00
CEJK Jari Kurri 10.00 25.00
CEJR Jussi Rynnas 6.00 15.00
CEJS Jakob Silfverberg 12.00 30.00
CEJT Jonathan Toews 15.00 40.00
CEKV Mikko Koivu 8.00 20.00
CELA Gabriel Landeskog 12.00 30.00
CEMB Mike Bossy 10.00 25.00
CEML Mario Lemieux 40.00 100.00
CEMM Mark Messier 20.00 50.00
CEMS Mats Sundin 15.00 40.00
CEPB Pavel Bure 10.00 25.00
CEPC Paul Coffey 10.00 25.00
CEPE Phil Esposito 15.00 40.00
CEPF Peter Forsberg 20.00 50.00
CEPK Patrick Kane 20.00 50.00
CEPR Patrick Roy 40.00 100.00
CEPS P.K. Subban 12.00 30.00
CERB Ray Bourque 15.00 40.00
CERF Ron Francis 12.00 30.00
CESA Joe Sakic 20.00 50.00
CESB Sven Baertschi 10.00 25.00
CESC Sidney Crosby EXCH 100.00 200.00
CESE Teemu Selanne 20.00 50.00
CESK Jeff Skinner 12.00 30.00
CETA John Tavares 15.00 40.00
CETF Theoren Fleury 12.00 30.00
CETH Taylor Hall 10.00 25.00
CETS Tyler Seguin 12.00 30.00
CEVD Vincent Damphousse 8.00 20.00
CEWG Wayne Gretzky 200.00 500.00
CEZP Zach Parise 10.00 25.00

2012-13 The Cup Foundations Jerseys

CFAB Alexandre Burrows 3.00 8.00
CFAL Jake Allen 10.00 25.00
CFAO Alexander Ovechkin 20.00 50.00
CFBH Braden Holtby 6.00 15.00
CFBM Brad Marchand 10.00 25.00
CFBU Pavel Bure 5.00 12.00
CFCG Claude Giroux 5.00 12.00
CFCK Chris Kreider 12.00 30.00
CFCP Carey Price 10.00 25.00
CFDD Drew Doughty 6.00 15.00
CFDH Dale Hawerchuk 6.00 15.00
CFEL Eric Lindros 8.00 20.00
CFEM Evgeni Malkin 10.00 25.00
CFGL Gabriel Landeskog 6.00 15.00
CFJA Jaden Schwartz 10.00 25.00
CFJE Jordan Eberle 5.00 12.00
CFJI Jarome Iginla 6.00 15.00
CFJN James Neal 3.00 8.00
CFJQ Jonathan Quick 6.00 15.00
CFJS Jeff Skinner 6.00 15.00
CFJT Jonathan Toews 8.00 20.00
CFLX Claude Lemieux 4.00 10.00
CFMB Martin Brodeur 12.00 30.00
CFMD Matt Duchene 5.00 12.00
CFMF Marc-Andre Fleury 10.00 25.00
CFML Mario Lemieux 20.00 50.00
CFMR Mike Richards 4.00 10.00
CFPB Patrice Bergeron 6.00 15.00
CFPC Paul Coffey 5.00 12.00
CFPF Peter Forsberg 10.00 25.00
CFPM Patrick Marleau 5.00 12.00
CFPR Patrick Roy 12.00 30.00
CFPS P.K. Subban 6.00 15.00
CFRF Ron Francis 6.00 15.00
CFRK Ryan Kesler 5.00 12.00
CFRN Ryan Nugent-Hopkins 6.00 15.00
CFSA Joe Sakic 10.00 25.00
CFSB Sven Baertschi 5.00 12.00
CFSC Sidney Crosby 20.00 50.00
CFSS Steven Stamkos 10.00 25.00
CFSV Jakob Silfverberg 6.00 15.00
CFTF Theoren Fleury 6.00 15.00
CFTH Taylor Hall 5.00 12.00
CFTR Tuukka Rask 6.00 15.00
CFTS Tyler Seguin 6.00 15.00
CFWG Wayne Gretzky 30.00 80.00

2012-13 The Cup Honorable Numbers

HNCP Carey Price/31 50.00 125.00
HNMB Martin Brodeur/30 50.00 125.00
HNSA Joe Sakic/19 50.00 125.00
HNSB Sven Baertschi/47 40.00 100.00

2012-13 The Cup Honorable Numbers Dual

DHNJP C.Joseph/C.Price/31 90.00 150.00
DHNMI J.Iginla/P.Marleau/12 50.00 100.00
DHNSD M.Sundin/Datsyuk/13 100.00 200.00

2012-13 The Cup Limited Logos Autographs

LLAH Adam Henrique/50 20.00 50.00
LLAJ Jake Allen/50 30.00 60.00
LLBM Brad Marchand/25 40.00 100.00
LLCA Carter Ashton/50 15.00 40.00
LLCJ Curtis Joseph/25 30.00 80.00
LLCK Chris Kreider/50 25.00 60.00
LLCP Carey Price/50 60.00 120.00
LLCS Cory Schneider/50 25.00 60.00
LLDG Doug Gilmour/50 40.00 100.00
LLDO Dominik Hasek/50 25.00 60.00
LLEB Ed Belfour/50 25.00 60.00
LLEL Eric Lindros/50 30.00 80.00
LLGG Sam Gagner/50 20.00 50.00
LLGL Gabriel Landeskog/50 25.00 60.00
LLGO Michel Goulet/25 20.00 50.00
LLHT Scott Hartnell/50 20.00 50.00
LLJE Jordan Eberle/50 20.00 50.00
LLJI Jarome Iginla/50 30.00 80.00
LLJJ Jaromir Jagr/50 80.00 200.00
LLJS Joe Sakic/50 50.00 120.00
LLJZ Jason Zucker/25 15.00 40.00
LLLX Claude Lemieux/50 20.00 50.00
LLMA Mark Stone/50 40.00 100.00
LLMB Martin Brodeur/50 60.00 150.00
LLMD Matt Duchene/25 40.00 80.00
LLMF Marc-Andre Fleury/30 40.00 80.00
LLML Mario Lemieux/25 75.00 135.00
LLMR Mike Richards/50 20.00 50.00
LLNL Nicklas Lidstrom/50 30.00 80.00
LLPB Patrice Bergeron/50 30.00 80.00
LLPC Paul Coffey/50 25.00 60.00
LLPF Peter Forsberg/50 EXCH 60.00 120.00
LLPI Chet Pickard/40 12.00 30.00
LLPM Patrick Marleau/50 25.00 60.00
LLRF Ron Francis/25 40.00 100.00
LLRG Ryan Getzlaf/50 25.00 60.00
LLRI Pekka Rinne/50 25.00 60.00
LLRK Ryan Kesler/40 20.00 50.00
LLRY Reilly Smith/50 25.00 50.00
LLSB Sven Baertschi/50 20.00 50.00
LLSU Mats Sundin/50 30.00 80.00
LLSV Jakob Silfverberg/40 25.00 60.00
LLSY Paul Stastny/50 15.00 40.00
LLTL Theoren Fleury/40 40.00 80.00
LLTY Tyson Barrie/50 15.00 40.00

2012-13 The Cup Rookie Bookmarks Dual Autographs

DABAS J.Allen/J.Schwartz 75.00 135.00
DABBS S.Baertschi/J.Silfverberg 60.00 120.00
DABSK C.Kreider/J.Schwartz 75.00 150.00

2012-13 The Cup Rookie Evolution Video Cards

EVO Redemption Card 20.00 50.00

2012-13 The Cup Rookie Gear Autographs

ARGCA Carter Ashton 15.00 40.00
ARGCK Chris Kreider 60.00 150.00
ARGCP Chet Pickard 20.00 50.00
ARGJA Jake Allen 50.00 100.00
ARGJR Jussi Rynnas 30.00 80.00
ARGJS Jaden Schwartz 50.00 125.00
ARGJZ Jason Zucker 40.00 100.00
ARGRS Riley Sheahan 40.00 80.00
ARGSB Sven Baertschi 60.00 120.00
ARGSI Jakob Silfverberg 50.00 100.00
ARGTB Tyson Barrie 50.00 125.00

2012-13 The Cup Scripted Sticks

SSAO Alexander Ovechkin 75.00 150.00
SSEL Eric Lindros 50.00 100.00
SSJB Jean Beliveau 100.00 175.00
SSJS Joe Sakic 50.00 120.00
SSMB Martin Brodeur 50.00 120.00
SSML Mario Lemieux 125.00 250.00
SSMM Mark Messier 90.00 150.00
SSPB Pavel Bure 100.00 200.00
SSPC Paul Coffey
SSPR Patrick Roy 75.00 150.00
SSTS Teemu Selanne 40.00 100.00
SSWG Wayne Gretzky 500.00 1200.00

2012-13 The Cup Scripted Swatches

SWAO Alexander Ovechkin/35 60.00 120.00
SWBH Brett Hull/35 75.00 150.00
SWCK Chris Kreider/35 30.00 80.00
SWEL Eric Lindros/35 40.00 100.00
SWJJ Jaromir Jagr/35 50.00 100.00
SWJS Jaden Schwartz/35 40.00 100.00
SWMB Martin Brodeur 50.00 100.00
SWML Mario Lemieux/15 100.00 175.00
SWPB Pavel Bure/35 75.00 150.00
SWSA Joe Sakic/35 50.00 100.00
SWSN Mats Sundin/35 50.00 100.00
SWSV Sven Baertschi/35 25.00 60.00
SWTF Theoren Fleury/35 40.00 100.00

2012-13 The Cup Scripted Swatches Dual

DSWJL M.Lemieux/J.Jagr 150.00 250.00
DSWLG C.Giroux/E.Lindros 175.00 300.00
DSWOB P.Bure/A.Ovechkin 200.00 350.00
DSWSH D.Hawerchuk/T.Selanne 90.00 150.00

2012-13 The Cup Signature Patches

SPAB Alexandre Burrows/99 10.00 25.00
SPAO Alexander Ovechkin/35 60.00 120.00
SPBH Braden Holtby/99 15.00 40.00
SPBM Brad Marchand/99 30.00 80.00
SPBR Bobby Ryan/99 10.00 25.00
SPBS Brayden Schenn/99 10.00 25.00
SPCJ Curtis Joseph/75 15.00 40.00
SPCK Chris Kreider/99 30.00 60.00
SPCO Chris Osgood/99 15.00 40.00
SPCP Carey Price/35 40.00 80.00
SPCS Cory Schneider/99 12.00 30.00
SPDB Dustin Brown/99 15.00 40.00
SPDH Dominik Hasek/75 30.00 80.00
SPEB Ed Belfour/75 12.00 30.00
SPEL Eric Lindros/35 20.00 50.00
SPFZ Johan Franzen/75 12.00 30.00
SPGL Gabriel Landeskog/75 15.00 40.00
SPGU Michel Goulet/75 12.00 30.00
SPHE Adam Henrique/99 12.00 30.00
SPHU Brett Hull/35 30.00 60.00
SPJA Jake Allen/75 20.00 50.00
SPJE Jordan Eberle/75 15.00 40.00
SPJF Jeff Skinner/75 20.00 50.00
SPJI Jarome Iginla/75 20.00 50.00
SPJJ Jaromir Jagr/35 60.00 150.00
SPJN James Neal/75 6.00 15.00
SPJS Joe Sakic/35 30.00 80.00
SPLR Luc Robitaille/75 15.00 40.00
SPLX Mario Lemieux/15 75.00 150.00
SPMA Patrick Marleau/75 15.00 40.00
SPMB Martin Brodeur/35 60.00 120.00
SPMD Matt Duchene/99 10.00 25.00
SPMF Marc-Andre Fleury/75 30.00 80.00
SPMP Magnus Paajarvi/75 10.00 25.00
SPMS Marc Staal/99 10.00 25.00
SPNF Nick Foligno/75 12.00 30.00
SPPB Patrice Bergeron/75 20.00 50.00
SPPC Paul Coffey/35 15.00 40.00
SPPD Pavel Datsyuk/75 25.00 60.00
SPPR Patrick Roy/15 75.00 135.00
SPPS P.K. Subban/75 30.00 60.00
SPPV Pavel Bure/35 100.00 175.00
SPRB Ray Bourque/75 30.00 60.00
SPRE Pekka Rinne/75 15.00 40.00
SPRG Ryan Getzlaf/75 15.00 40.00
SPRH Ron Hextall/25 20.00 50.00
SPRK Ryan Kesler/35 12.00 30.00
SPRS Ryan Smyth/75 12.00 30.00
SPSB Sven Baertschi/99 12.00 30.00
SPSC Jaden Schwartz/99 15.00 40.00
SPSD Shane Doan/75 12.00 30.00
SPSI Jakob Silfverberg/99 15.00 40.00
SPSN Mats Sundin/35 40.00 80.00
SPSU Mats Sundin/75 20.00 50.00
SPSW Stephen Weiss/99 12.00 30.00
SPTF Theoren Fleury/35 25.00 60.00
SPTS Teemu Selanne/75 40.00 80.00
SPWG Wayne Gretzky/15 400.00 1000.00

2012-13 The Cup Signature Patches Dual

DSPCB B.Schenn/C.Giroux
DSPEH J.Eberle/T.Hall 25.00 60.00
DSPGB S.Gagne/D.Brown 15.00 40.00
DSPGR B.Ryan/R.Getzlaf 25.00 50.00
DSPGS R.Smith/S.Glennie 15.00 40.00
DSPIB J.Iginla/S.Baertschi 25.00 60.00
DSPLJ J.Jagr/M.Lemieux 150.00 250.00
DSPRP C.Pickard/P.Rinne 25.00 60.00
DSPSJ Baertschi/Silfverberg 30.00 80.00
DSPSK J.Schwartz/C.Kreider 40.00 80.00

2012-13 The Cup Silver Jerseys

1 Ryan Getzlaf 8.00 20.00
3 Ray Bourque 10.00 25.00
5 Tuukka Rask 8.00 20.00
6 Cam Neely 6.00 15.00
7 Zdeno Chara 6.00 15.00
8 Tyler Seguin 8.00 20.00
9 Brad Marchand 8.00 20.00
10 Thomas Vanek 5.00 12.00
12 Miikka Kiprusoff 6.00 15.00
14 Jeff Skinner 8.00 20.00
15 Phil Esposito 8.00 20.00
16 Patrick Kane 12.00 30.00
17 Tony Esposito 6.00 15.00
20 Joe Sakic 12.00 30.00
21 Patrick Roy 15.00 40.00
22 Matt Duchene 6.00 15.00
23 Gabriel Landeskog 8.00 20.00
24 Jaromir Jagr 12.00 30.00
26 Jim Howard 8.00 20.00
27 Pavel Datsyuk 10.00 25.00
30 Henrik Zetterberg 8.00 20.00
32 Taylor Hall 6.00 15.00
34 Jari Kurri 6.00 15.00
35 Jordan Eberle 6.00 15.00
36 Paul Coffey 6.00 15.00
38 Ryan Nugent-Hopkins 8.00 20.00
39 Ed Belfour 8.00 20.00
40 Jeff Carter 5.00 12.00
41 Anze Kopitar 10.00 25.00
42 Mike Richards 5.00 12.00
43 Luc Robitaille 6.00 15.00
44 Drew Doughty 8.00 20.00
45 Wayne Gretzky 40.00 100.00
46 Jonathan Quick 8.00 20.00
49 Carey Price 12.00 30.00
50 Larry Robinson 8.00 20.00
51 P.K. Subban 8.00 20.00
52 Pekka Rinne 6.00 15.00
53 Ilya Kovalchuk 6.00 15.00
54 Martin Brodeur 15.00 40.00
55 Adam Henrique 5.00 12.00
56 John Tavares 10.00 25.00
59 Marian Gaborik 6.00 15.00
62 Jason Spezza 6.00 15.00
63 Eric Lindros 10.00 25.00
64 Claude Giroux 6.00 15.00
65 Evgeni Malkin 12.00 30.00
66 Mario Lemieux 25.00 60.00
67 Marc-Andre Fleury 8.00 20.00
68 Sidney Crosby 25.00 60.00
69 Ron Francis 8.00 20.00
71 Scott Hartnell 4.00 10.00
73 Patrick Marleau 6.00 15.00

74 Logan Couture 8.00 20.00
75 Jaroslav Halak 6.00 15.00
76 Brett Hull 10.00 25.00
77 Steven Stamkos 12.00 30.00
78 Phil Kessel 6.00 15.00
79 Dion Phaneuf 5.00 12.00
80 Mats Sundin 10.00 25.00
81 Alexandre Burrows 4.00 10.00
83 Henrik Sedin 8.00 20.00
84 Ryan Kesler 10.00 25.00
86 Pavel Bure 15.00 40.00
87 Alexander Ovechkin 15.00 40.00
88 Nicklas Backstrom 6.00 15.00
89 Dale Hawerchuk 8.00 20.00
90 Ondrej Pavelec 10.00 25.00

2012-13 The Cup Trios Jerseys

C3TC Pickard/Benn/Kane 8.00 20.00
C3AVS Ststny/Dchne/Landskg 8.00 20.00
C3CGY Kiprusoff/Aliu/Baertschi 5.00 12.00
C3CHI Keith/Crawford/Bolland 10.00 25.00
C3DET Krnwall/Filppula/Ericsson 6.00 15.00
C3DRW Datsyuk/Zettrbrg/Franzn 12.00 30.00
C3LAK Brown/Kopitar/Doughty 12.00 30.00
C3LAK Kopitar/Quick/Doughty 12.00 30.00
C3MTL Markov/Subban/Diaz 8.00 20.00
C3NJD Brodr/Clrksn/Kovalchk 10.00 25.00
C3OIL Eberle/Hall/Nugent-Hop 10.00 25.00
C3PHX Doan/Bdkr/Ekman-Lars 8.00 20.00
C3TML Phaneuf/Kessel/Kulmn 8.00 20.00
C3BEES Chara/Horton/Rask 8.00 20.00
C3DALL Glennie/Garbutt/Smith 15.00 40.00
C3GOON Domi/Twist/Probert 20.00 50.00
C3HABS Gionta/Plekanec/Eller 5.00 12.00
C3LBBR Price/Subban/Eller 12.00 30.00
C3PITT Fleury/Letang/Malkin 15.00 40.00
C3SENS Alfreds/Spzza/Andersn 8.00 20.00
C3WASH Ovechkin/Green/Holtby 10.00 25.00
C3ASTAR Brodeur/Belfour/Joseph 12.00 30.00
C3BLUES Perron/Schwartz/Allen 10.00 25.00
C3DUCKS Perry/Getzlaf/Ryan 12.00 30.00
C3KINGS Penner/Richards/Carter 8.00 20.00
C3PFBRG Forsberg triple 10.00 25.00
C3ROOK2 Ashton/Glennie/Cizikas 6.00 15.00
C3ROOK4 Pickard/Allen/Rynnas 10.00 25.00
C3BOS Chara/Bergeron/Lucic 10.00 25.00
C3DEVILS Kovlchk/Henrq/Larsn 8.00 20.00
C3DSTARS Hull/Lindros/Modano 15.00 40.00
C3FLYERS Schenn/Couturier/Read 12.00 30.00

2013-14 The Cup

1 Corey Perry 5.00 12.00
2 Ryan Getzlaf 3.00 8.00
3 Jonas Hiller 2.50 6.00
4 Teemu Selanne 6.00 15.00
5 Bobby Orr 12.00 30.00
6 Milan Lucic 3.00 8.00
7 Brad Marchand 6.00 15.00
8 Ray Bourque 5.00 12.00
9 Tuukka Rask 4.00 10.00
10 Dominik Hasek 5.00 12.00
11 Theoren Fleury 4.00 10.00
12 Al MacInnis 4.00 10.00
13 Eric Staal 4.00 10.00
14 Corey Crawford 4.00 10.00
15 Tony Esposito 3.00 8.00
16 Patrick Kane 6.00 15.00
17 Jonathan Toews 5.00 12.00
18 Brent Seabrook 2.00 5.00
19 Matt Duchene 3.00 8.00
20 Joe Sakic 6.00 15.00
21 Peter Forsberg 6.00 15.00
22 Marian Gaborik 3.00 8.00
23 Sergei Bobrovsky 5.00 12.00
24 Ed Belfour 3.00 8.00
25 Pavel Datsyuk 5.00 12.00
26 Jim Howard 4.00 10.00
27 Steve Yzerman 8.00 20.00
28 Nicklas Lidstrom 3.00 8.00
29 Johan Franzen 2.50 6.00
30 Henrik Zetterberg 4.00 10.00
31 Chris Osgood 3.00 8.00
32 Glenn Anderson 2.50 6.00
33 Grant Fuhr 5.00 12.00
34 Wayne Gretzky 20.00 50.00
35 Jordan Eberle 3.00 8.00
36 Taylor Hall 3.00 8.00
37 Drew Doughty 4.00 10.00
38 Luc Robitaille 3.00 8.00
39 Jonathan Quick 4.00 10.00
40 Jari Kurri 3.00 8.00
41 Anze Kopitar 5.00 12.00
42 Zach Parise 3.00 8.00
43 Ryan Suter 2.50 6.00
44 Dany Heatley 2.50 6.00
45 Larry Robinson 3.00 8.00
46 P.K. Subban 4.00 10.00
47 Patrick Roy 8.00 20.00
48 Carey Price 6.00 15.00
49 Pekka Rinne 3.00 8.00
50 Shea Weber 2.50 6.00
51 Martin Brodeur 8.00 20.00
52 Jaromir Jagr 10.00 25.00
53 Thomas Vanek 2.50 6.00
54 John Tavares 5.00 12.00
55 Mike Bossy 3.00 8.00
56 Mark Messier 6.00 15.00
57 Eric Lindros 5.00 12.00
58 Rick Nash 3.00 8.00
59 Phil Esposito 5.00 12.00
60 Henrik Lundqvist 8.00 20.00
61 Craig Anderson 3.00 8.00
62 Jason Spezza 3.00 8.00
63 Bobby Clarke 5.00 12.00
64 Claude Giroux 3.00 8.00
65 Shane Doan 2.50 6.00
66 Mario Lemieux 12.00 30.00
67 Evgeni Malkin 6.00 15.00
68 Marc-Andre Fleury 6.00 15.00
69 Sidney Crosby 12.00 30.00
70 Paul Coffey 3.00 8.00
71 Kris Letang 4.00 10.00
72 Logan Couture 4.00 10.00
73 Antti Niemi 2.50 6.00
74 Curtis Joseph 4.00 10.00
75 Jaroslav Halak 3.00 8.00
76 Martin St. Louis 3.00 8.00
77 Steven Stamkos 6.00 15.00
78 Phil Kessel 3.00 8.00
79 Nazem Kadri 4.00 10.00
80 Mats Sundin 3.00 8.00
81 Pavel Bure 3.00 8.00
82 Roberto Luongo 5.00 12.00
83 Alexandre Burrows 2.00 5.00
84 Ryan Kesler 3.00 8.00
85 Nicklas Backstrom 3.00 8.00
86 Braden Holtby 4.00 10.00
87 Alexander Ovechkin 12.00 30.00
88 Bobby Hull 6.00 15.00
89 Dale Hawerchuk 4.00 10.00
90 Vincent Damphousse 2.50 6.00
91 Sami Vatanen RC 5.00 12.00
92 J.T. Miller RC 12.00 30.00
93 Connor Carrick AU RC 6.00 15.00
94 Reid Boucher AU RC 8.00 20.00
95 Eric Gelinas AU RC 8.00 20.00
96 Martin Marincin AU RC 6.00 15.00
97 Ondrej Palat AU RC 15.00 40.00
98 Jeff Zatkoff AU RC 8.00 20.00
99 Marek Mazanec AU RC 8.00 20.00
100 Darcy Kuemper AU RC 30.00 80.00
101 Antti Raanta JSY AU/249 RC 30.00 80.00
102 Chris Brown JSY AU/249 RC 10.00 25.00
103 Jesper Fast JSY AU/249 RC 15.00 40.00
104 A.Ciasson JSY AU/249 RC 15.00 40.00
105 Petr Mrazek JSY AU/249 RC 25.00 60.00
106 Laughton JSY AU/249 RC 20.00 50.00
107 T.Hickey JSY AU/249 RC 12.00 30.00
108 D.Brunner JSY AU/249 RC 12.00 30.00
109 John Gibson JSY AU/249 RC 60.00 150.00
110 M.Bournival JSY AU/249 RC 15.00 40.00
111 J.Fontaine JSY AU/249 RC 15.00 40.00
112 Ristolainen JSY AU/249 RC 30.00 80.00
113 S.Matteau JSY AU/249 RC 12.00 30.00
114 M.Granlund JSY AU/249 RC 30.00 80.00
115 Jonas Brodin JSY AU/249 RC 20.00 50.00
116 Viktor Fasth JSY AU/249 RC 15.00 40.00
117 Will Acton JSY AU/249 RC 12.00 30.00
118 D.DeKeyser JSY AU/249 RC 20.00 50.00
119 Seth Jones JSY AU/249 RC 30.00 80.00
120 Q.Howden JSY AU/249 RC 12.00 30.00
121 Morgan Rielly JSY AU/249 RC 60.00 150.00
122 R.Rakell JSY AU/249 RC 40.00 100.00
123 J.Nordstrom JSY AU/249 RC 12.00 30.00
124 P.Grubauer JSY AU/249 RC 60.00 150.00
125 Justin Schultz JSY AU/249 RC 25.00 60.00
126 M.Dumba JSY AU/249 RC 20.00 50.00
127 Dylan McIlrath JSY AU/249 RC 10.00 25.00
128 Brock Nelson JSY AU/249 RC 30.00 80.00
129 Dmitrij Jaskin JSY AU/249 RC 15.00 40.00
130 Tomas Jurco JSY AU/249 RC 20.00 50.00
131 E.Pasquale JSY AU/249 RC 10.00 25.00
132 Ryan Strome JSY AU/249 RC 40.00 100.00
133 Martin Jones JSY AU/249 RC 25.00 60.00
134 A.Watson JSY AU/249 RC 12.00 30.00
135 Filip Forsberg JSY AU/249 RC 80.00 200.00
136 Drew Shore JSY AU/249 RC 12.00 30.00
137 J.Schroeder JSY AU/249 RC 15.00 40.00
138 B.Gallagher JSY AU/249 RC 80.00 200.00
139 Charlie Coyle JSY AU/249 RC 30.00 80.00
140 N.Bjugstad JSY AU/249 RC 20.00 50.00
141 Max Reinhart JSY AU/249 RC 15.00 40.00
142 R.Sooner JSY AU/249 RC 15.00 40.00
143 Matt Irwin JSY AU/249 RC 12.00 30.00
144 N.Jensen JSY AU/249 RC 12.00 30.00
145 Gustafsson JSY AU/249 RC 20.00 50.00
146 N.Beaulieu JSY AU/249 RC 10.00 25.00
147 Brian Flynn JSY AU/249 RC 12.00 30.00
148 Carl Soderberg JSY AU/249 RC 15.00 40.00
149 C.Thomas JSY AU/249 RC 12.00 30.00
150 Ryan Murphy JSY AU/249 RC 15.00 40.00
151 Grigorenko JSY AU/249 RC 10.00 25.00
152 Tyler Toffoli JSY AU/249 RC 30.00 80.00
153 Ryan Murray JSY AU/249 RC 25.00 60.00
154 Cory Conacher JSY AU/249 RC 10.00 25.00
155 Tom Wilson JSY AU/249 RC 30.00 80.00
156 T.Pearson JSY AU/249 RC 25.00 60.00
157 Josh Leivo JSY AU/249 RC 12.00 30.00
158 Lucas Lessio JSY AU/249 RC 10.00 25.00
159 Linden Vey JSY AU/249 RC 10.00 25.00
160 Tarasenko JSY AU/249 RC EX 300.00 800.00
161 Xavier Ouellet JSY AU/249 RC 15.00 40.00
162 J.Campbell JSY AU/249 RC 50.00 125.00
163 D.Hamilton JSY AU/249 RC 25.00 60.00
164 F.Andersen JSY AU/249 RC 40.00 100.00
165 H.Lindholm JSY AU/249 RC 25.00 60.00
166 Mark Arcobello JSY AU/249 RC 15.00 40.00
167 Tyler Johnson JSY AU/249 RC 40.00 100.00
168 Alex Killorn JSY AU/249 RC 30.00 80.00
169 F.Hamilton JSY AU/249 RC 15.00 40.00
170 A.Barkov JSY AU/249 RC 150.00 400.00
171 Olli Maatta JSY AU/249 RC 25.00 60.00
172 Beau Bennett JSY AU/249 RC 20.00 50.00
173 N.Zadorov JSY AU/249 RC 10.00 25.00
174 Emerson Etem JSY AU/249 RC 15.00 40.00
175 Jon Merrill JSY AU/249 RC 15.00 40.00
176 Boone Jenner JSY AU/249 RC 25.00 60.00
177 Matt Nieto JSY AU/249 RC 12.00 30.00
178 Elias Lindholm JSY AU/249 RC 30.00 80.00
179 Jarred Tinordi JSY AU/249 RC 15.00 40.00
180 Michael Latta JSY AU/249 RC 12.00 30.00
181 Jacob Trouba JSY AU/249 RC 25.00 60.00
182 Girgensons JSY AU/249 RC 25.00 60.00
183 Cody Ceci JSY AU/249 RC 12.00 30.00
184 Huberdeau JSY AU/249 RC 150.00 400.00
185 Nichushkin JSY AU/99 RC EX 125.00 300.00
186 Yakupov JSY AU/99 RC EX 100.00 250.00
187 N.MacKinnon
JSY AU/99 RC 2500.00 5000.00
188 Galchenyuk JSY AU/99 RC 400.00 1000.00
189 Tomas Hertl JSY AU/99 RC 100.00 250.00
190 S.Monahan JSY AU/99 RC 400.00 1000.00

2013-14 The Cup Gold

*1-90 VETS/25: 1X TO 2.5X BASIC CARDS
*91-92 ROOK/25: .6X TO 1.5X BASIC ROOK
*93-99 ROOK AU/25: .6X TO 1.5X BASIC AU/99
14 Corey Crawford 10.00 25.00
85 Nicklas Backstrom 8.00 20.00
92 J.T. Miller 15.00 40.00
101 Antti Raanta AU 25.00 60.00
102 Chris Brown AU 8.00 20.00
103 Jesper Fast AU 10.00 25.00
104 Alex Chiasson AU 12.00 30.00
105 Petr Mrazek AU 25.00 60.00
106 Scott Laughton AU 15.00 40.00
107 Thomas Hickey AU 10.00 25.00
108 Damien Brunner AU 10.00 25.00
109 John Gibson AU 30.00 80.00
110 Michael Bournival AU 12.00 30.00
111 Justin Fontaine AU 12.00 30.00
112 Rasmus Ristolainen AU 20.00 50.00
113 Stefan Matteau AU 10.00 25.00
114 Mikael Granlund AU
115 Jonas Brodin AU 15.00 40.00
116 Viktor Fasth AU 12.00 30.00
117 Will Acton AU 10.00 25.00
118 Danny DeKeyser AU 15.00 40.00
119 Seth Jones AU 25.00 60.00
120 Quinton Howden AU 10.00 25.00
121 Morgan Rielly AU 30.00 80.00
122 Rickard Rakell AU 12.00 30.00
123 Joakim Nordstrom AU 10.00 25.00
124 Philipp Grubauer AU 80.00 200.00
125 Justin Schultz AU 10.00 25.00
126 Mathew Dumba AU 8.00 20.00
127 Dylan McIlrath AU 8.00 20.00
128 Brock Nelson AU 25.00 60.00
129 Dmitrij Jaskin AU 12.00 30.00
130 Tomas Jurco AU 15.00 40.00
131 Edward Pasquale AU 8.00 20.00
132 Ryan Strome AU 20.00 50.00
133 Martin Jones AU 20.00 50.00
134 Austin Watson AU 10.00 25.00
135 Filip Forsberg AU 50.00 100.00
136 Drew Shore AU 10.00 25.00
137 Jordan Schroeder AU 12.00 30.00
138 Brendan Gallagher AU 30.00 80.00
139 Charlie Coyle AU 20.00 50.00
140 Nick Bjugstad AU 15.00 40.00
141 Max Reinhart AU 10.00 25.00
142 Ryan Spooner AU 12.00 30.00
143 Matt Irwin AU 10.00 25.00
144 Nicklas Jensen AU 10.00 25.00
145 Johan Gustafsson AU 12.00 30.00
146 Nathan Beaulieu AU 8.00 20.00
147 Brian Flynn AU 10.00 25.00
148 Carl Soderberg AU 12.00 30.00
149 Christian Thomas AU 10.00 25.00
150 Ryan Murphy AU 12.00 30.00
151 Mikhail Grigorenko AU 8.00 20.00
152 Tyler Toffoli AU 40.00 80.00
154 Cory Conacher AU 8.00 20.00
155 Tom Wilson AU 15.00 40.00
156 Tanner Pearson AU 30.00 60.00
157 Josh Leivo AU 10.00 25.00
158 Lucas Lessio AU 8.00 20.00
159 Linden Vey AU 8.00 20.00
161 Xavier Ouellet AU 12.00 30.00
163 Dougie Hamilton AU 20.00 50.00
164 Frederik Andersen AU 30.00 80.00
165 Hampus Lindholm AU 20.00 50.00
166 Mark Arcobello AU 12.00 30.00
167 Tyler Johnson AU 125.00 200.00
168 Alex Killorn AU 20.00 50.00
169 Freddie Hamilton AU 10.00 25.00
170 Aleksander Barkov AU 40.00 100.00
171 Olli Maatta AU 20.00 50.00
172 Beau Bennett AU 20.00 50.00
173 Nikita Zadorov AU 8.00 20.00
174 Emerson Etem AU 12.00 30.00
175 Jon Merrill AU 12.00 30.00
176 Boone Jenner AU 25.00 60.00
177 Matt Nieto AU 10.00 25.00
178 Elias Lindholm AU 30.00 80.00
179 Jarred Tinordi AU 12.00 30.00
180 Michael Latta AU 10.00 25.00
181 Jacob Trouba AU 20.00 50.00
182 Zemgus Girgensons AU 20.00 50.00
183 Cody Ceci AU 10.00 25.00
184 Jonathan Huberdeau AU 30.00 80.00
185 Valeri Nichushkin AU 30.00 80.00
186 Nail Yakupov AU 25.00 60.00
187 Nathan MacKinnon AU 4000.00 8000.00
188 Alex Galchenyuk AU 100.00 200.00
189 Tomas Hertl AU 25.00 60.00
190 Sean Monahan AU 20.00 50.00

2013-14 The Cup Gold Rainbow

*ROOKIE/51-89: .5X TO 1.2X RC/249
*ROOKIE/30-49: .6X TO 1.5X RC/249
*ROOKIE/20-29: .8X TO 2X RC/249
*ROOKIE/15-19: 1X TO 2.5X RC/249
121 Morgan Rielly JSY AU/44 80.00 200.00
185 V.Nichushkin JSY AU/43 100.00 200.00
186 Nail Yakupov JSY AU/64 100.00 200.00
187 N.MacKinnon JSY AU/29 8000.00 15000.00
188 A.Galchenyuk JSY AU/27 200.00 400.00
189 Tomas Hertl JSY AU/48 100.00 200.00
190 S.Monahan JSY AU/23 150.00 250.00

2013-14 The Cup Auto Draft Boards

DBBN Brock Nelson 30.00 80.00
DBBR Jonas Brodin 20.00 50.00
DBCC Charlie Coyle 25.00 60.00
DBEE Emerson Etem 15.00 40.00
DBHA Dougie Hamilton 25.00 60.00
DBJH Jonathan Huberdeau 40.00 100.00
DBMG Mikael Granlund 25.00 60.00
DBNB Nathan Beaulieu 10.00 25.00
DBNJ Nicklas Jensen 12.00 30.00
DBPY Mark Pysyk 15.00 40.00
DBQH Quinton Howden 12.00 30.00
DBRR Rickard Rakell 15.00 40.00
DBRS Ryan Strome 25.00 60.00
DBSJ Jordan Schroeder 15.00 40.00
DBVT Vladimir Tarasenko 40.00 100.00

2013-14 The Cup Brilliance Autographs

BAK Anze Kopitar 20.00 50.00
BAN Antti Niemi 10.00 25.00
BAO Alexander Ovechkin 40.00 80.00
BBB Bill Barber 12.00 30.00
BBC Bobby Clarke 15.00 40.00
BBH Bobby Hull 25.00 60.00
BBO Bobby Orr 60.00 150.00
BBR Bill Ranford 12.00 30.00
BCL Claude Lemieux 12.00 30.00
BCN Cam Neely 12.00 30.00
BCP Corey Perry 20.00 50.00
BCS Cory Schneider 12.00 30.00
BDH Dominik Hasek 40.00 100.00
BDP Dion Phaneuf 10.00 25.00
BDS Darryl Sittler 15.00 40.00
BEB Ed Belfour 12.00 30.00
BEK Evander Kane 12.00 30.00
BEM Evgeni Malkin 25.00 60.00
BES Eric Staal 15.00 40.00
BFP Felix Potvin 12.00 30.00
BGA Glenn Anderson 10.00 25.00
BGF Grant Fuhr 20.00 50.00
BGI Clark Gillies 12.00 30.00
BGL Guy Lafleur 25.00 50.00
BGO Michel Goulet 10.00 25.00
BGP Gilbert Perreault 12.00 30.00
BHU Brett Hull 20.00 40.00
BJB Johnny Bucyk 12.00 30.00
BJI Jarome Iginla 15.00 40.00
BJJ Jaromir Jagr 50.00 100.00
BJK Jari Kurri 12.00 30.00
BJT Jonathan Toews 30.00 60.00
BKA Patrick Kane 30.00 60.00
BLR Larry Robinson 12.00 30.00
BMA Marian Gaborik 15.00 40.00
BMB Mike Bossy 12.00 30.00
BMD Marcel Dionne 15.00 40.00
BMF Marc-Andre Fleury 20.00 40.00
BMG Mike Gartner 15.00 40.00
BML Mario Lemieux 50.00 100.00
BMN Markus Naslund 12.00 30.00
BMS Mats Sundin 25.00 50.00
BMT Marty Turco 12.00 30.00
BPE Phil Esposito 20.00 50.00
BPF Peter Forsberg 25.00 50.00
BPK Phil Kessel 12.00 30.00
BPR Patrick Roy 60.00 120.00
BRB Ray Bourque 20.00 50.00
BRF Ron Francis 15.00 40.00
BRH Ron Hextall 15.00 40.00
BRI Mike Richter 12.00 30.00
BRV Rogie Vachon 15.00 40.00
BRY Bobby Ryan 10.00 25.00
BSC Sidney Crosby 100.00 200.00
BSM Stan Mikita 20.00 40.00
BSS Steve Shutt 10.00 25.00
BSW Shea Weber 10.00 25.00
BSY Steve Yzerman 60.00 150.00
BTA Taylor Hall 12.00 30.00
BTE Tony Esposito 20.00 40.00
BTF Theoren Fleury 15.00 40.00
BTS Tyler Seguin 15.00 40.00
BWG Wayne Gretzky 250.00 600.00
BZP Zach Parise 12.00 30.00

2013-14 The Cup Enshrinements

CEAB Aleksander Barkov 15.00 40.00
CEAG Alex Galchenyuk 12.00 30.00
CEAK Anze Kopitar 25.00 50.00
CEAM Al MacInnis 12.00 30.00
CEAN Antti Niemi 8.00 20.00
CEAO Adam Oates 10.00 25.00
CEBB Bill Barber 10.00 25.00
CEBC Bobby Clarke 12.00 30.00
CEBH Bobby Hull 15.00 40.00
CEBJ Boone Jenner 8.00 20.00
CEBO Bobby Orr 50.00 100.00
CEBR Bill Ranford 10.00 25.00
CECG Clark Gillies 10.00 25.00
CECL Claude Lemieux 10.00 25.00
CEDS Darryl Sittler 12.00 30.00
CEES Eric Staal 12.00 30.00
CEFF Filip Forsberg 15.00 40.00
CEFP Felix Potvin 20.00 50.00
CEGA Glenn Anderson 8.00 20.00
CEGF Grant Fuhr 15.00 40.00
CEGL Guy Lafleur 12.00 30.00
CEGM Glen Murray 8.00 20.00
CEGP Gilbert Perreault 10.00 25.00
CEGR Mikhail Grigorenko 3.00 8.00
CEJA Jacob Trouba 8.00 20.00
CEJB Johnny Bucyk 10.00 25.00
CEJH Jonathan Huberdeau 30.00 80.00
CEJI Jarome Iginla 12.00 30.00
CEJK Jari Kurri 10.00 25.00
CEJQ Jonathan Quick 15.00 40.00
CEJS Justin Schultz 10.00 25.00
CEJT Jonathan Toews 15.00 40.00
CELI Elias Lindholm 12.00 30.00
CELR Larry Robinson 10.00 25.00
CEMB Mike Bossy 10.00 25.00
CEMD Marcel Dionne 12.00 30.00
CEMG Mikael Granlund 8.00 20.00
CEMI Mike Gartner 12.00 30.00
CENL Nicklas Lidstrom 15.00 40.00
CENM Nathan MacKinnon 150.00 400.00
CENY Nail Yakupov 10.00 25.00
CEPB Pavel Bure 20.00 50.00
CEPC Paul Coffey 10.00 25.00
CEPE Phil Esposito 15.00 40.00
CEPK Phil Kessel 10.00 25.00
CERB Ray Bourque 15.00 40.00
CERH Ron Hextall 10.00 25.00
CERI Richard Brodeur 10.00 25.00
CERM Ryan Murray 8.00 20.00
CERR Rasmus Ristolainen 8.00 20.00
CERV Rogie Vachon 12.00 30.00
CERY Bobby Ryan 8.00 20.00
CESE Sean Monahan 8.00 20.00
CESJ Seth Jones 10.00 25.00
CESK Saku Koivu 10.00 25.00
CESM Stan Mikita 12.00 30.00
CESS Steve Shutt 8.00 20.00
CETE Tony Esposito 10.00 25.00
CETH Tomas Hertl 15.00 40.00
CEVN Valeri Nichushkin 10.00 25.00
CEVT Vladimir Tarasenko
CEWG Wayne Gretzky 200.00 500.00
CEZP Zach Parise 10.00 25.00

2013-14 The Cup Enshrinements Dual

CE2BG M.Bossy/C.Gillies 15.00 40.00
CE2CB B.Barber/B.Clarke 25.00 60.00
CE2DV M.Dionne/R.Vachon 20.00 50.00
CE2FE V.Fasth/E.Etem 15.00 40.00
CE2FI R.Francis/A.Irbe 20.00 50.00
CE2GG Galchenyuk/Gallagher 40.00 100.00
CE2HB A.Barkov/Huberdeau 50.00 125.00
CE2HM D.Hasek/R.Miller 25.00 60.00
CE2JF S.Jones/F.Forsberg 50.00 120.00
CE2JM B.Jenner/R.Murray 30.00 80.00
CE2KP P.Kessel/D.Phaneuf 15.00 40.00
CE2LS G.Lafleur/S.Shutt 20.00 50.00
CE2MC J.Campbell/P.Mrazek 30.00 80.00
CE2MY MacKinnon/Yakupov 80.00 200.00
CE2OB B.Orr/J.Bucyk 60.00 150.00
CE2WJ S.Weber/S.Jones 30.00 80.00
CE2YS Yakupov/J.Schultz 30.00 80.00
CE21983 B.Hull/S.Mikita 30.00 80.00
CE21988 G.Lafleur/T.Esposito 20.00 50.00
CE21989 D.Sittler/B.Park 20.00 50.00
CE21990 G.Perreault/B.Barber 15.00 40.00
CE22011 D.Gilmour/E.Belfour 20.00 50.00
CE22012A M.Sundin/J.Sakic 30.00 80.00

2013-14 The Cup Foundations Jerseys

CFAB Aleksander Barkov 12.00 30.00
CFAN Antti Niemi 3.00 8.00
CFAO Alexander Ovechkin 15.00 40.00
CFBB Bryan Bickell 2.50 6.00
CFCP Corey Perry 6.00 15.00
CFDH Dominik Hasek 6.00 15.00
CFEB Ed Belfour 4.00 10.00
CFEL Elias Lindholm 10.00 25.00
CFES Eric Lindros 6.00 15.00
CFJH Jim Howard 5.00 12.00
CFJQ Jonathan Quick 5.00 12.00
CFJR Jeremy Roenick 6.00 15.00
CFKL Phil Kessel 4.00 10.00
CFLR Luc Robitaille 4.00 10.00
CFMA Patrick Marleau 4.00 10.00
CFME Mark Messier 8.00 20.00
CFMG Mike Gartner 5.00 12.00
CFML Mario Lemieux 15.00 40.00
CFMS Mats Sundin 4.00 10.00
CFNM Nathan MacKinnon 20.00 50.00
CFPB Pavel Bure 4.00 10.00
CFPR Pekka Rinne 4.00 10.00
CFPS P.K. Subban 5.00 12.00
CFRB Ray Bourque 6.00 15.00
CFRF Ron Francis 5.00 12.00
CFRL Roberto Luongo 6.00 15.00
CFRO Patrick Roy 10.00 25.00
CFRS Ryan Strome 6.00 15.00
CFSC Sidney Crosby 15.00 40.00
CFSD Shane Doan 3.00 8.00
CFSJ Seth Jones 8.00 20.00
CFSM Sean Monahan 6.00 15.00
CFSW Shea Weber 3.00 8.00
CFTE Tony Esposito 4.00 10.00
CFTH Taylor Hall 4.00 10.00
CFTS Tyler Seguin 5.00 12.00
CFVT Vladimir Tarasenko 10.00 25.00
CFWG Wayne Gretzky 25.00 60.00

2013-14 The Cup Honorable Numbers

HNAB Aleksander Barkov/16 100.00 250.00
HNAG Alex Galchenyuk/27 40.00 100.00
HNBB Beau Bennett/19 20.00 50.00
HNBH Brett Hull/16 30.00 80.00
HNBI Bryan Bickell/29 10.00 25.00
HNBJ Boone Jenner/38 30.00 80.00
HNCC Cory Conacher/89 10.00 25.00
HNCH Cody Hodgson/19 10.00 25.00
HNCJ Curtis Joseph/31 20.00 50.00
HNCP Carey Price/31 30.00 80.00
HNDO Dominik Hasek/39 25.00 60.00
HNDW Doug Weight 15.00 40.00
HNEB Ed Belfour 15.00 40.00
HNEE Emerson Etem/65 15.00 40.00
HNEL Elias Lindholm/16 40.00 100.00
HNGC Guy Carbonneau/21 25.00 60.00
HNGF Grant Fuhr/31 25.00 60.00
HNGR Mikhail Grigorenko/25 10.00 25.00
HNHA Dougie Hamilton/27 25.00 60.00
HNHE Tomas Hertl/48 30.00 80.00
HNJQ Jonathan Quick 20.00 50.00
HNJS Justin Schultz/19 15.00 40.00
HNJT Jonathan Toews/19 100.00 250.00
HNLC Logan Couture/39 20.00 50.00
HNLO Martin St. Louis/26 25.00 60.00
HNLR Luc Robitaille/20 25.00 60.00
HNMB Martin Brodeur/30 40.00 100.00
HNMG Mike Gartner/22 25.00 60.00
HNMI Mikael Granlund/64 25.00 60.00
HNMJ Martin Jones/31 25.00 60.00
HNMO Sean Monahan/23 25.00 60.00
HNMR Morgan Rielly/44 50.00 125.00
HNNM Nathan MacKinnon/29 300.00 800.00
HNNY Nail Yakupov/64 30.00 80.00
HNPF Peter Forsberg/21 30.00 80.00
HNPM Petr Mrazek/34 30.00 80.00
HNPR Pekka Rinne 15.00 40.00
HNRH Ryan Nugent-Hopkins 20.00 50.00
HNRM Ryan Murray 25.00 60.00
HNRS Ryan Spooner/51 15.00 40.00
HNSA Joe Sakic/19 30.00 80.00
HNSL Scott Laughton/21 20.00 50.00
HNSM Stan Mikita/21 20.00 50.00
HNSY Steve Yzerman/19 40.00 100.00
HNTT Tyler Toffoli/73 20.00 50.00
HNTW Tom Wilson/43 30.00 80.00
HNVF Viktor Fasth/30 15.00 40.00
HNVT Vladimir Tarasenko/91 40.00 100.00

2013-14 The Cup Honorable Numbers Dual

HNBL A.Barkov/Lindholm/16 20.00 50.00
HNBR Belfour/L.Robitaille/20 30.00 80.00
HNGM Galchenyuk/Murray/27 75.00 150.00
HNGY Yakupov/Granlund/64 50.00 120.00
HNSN J.Sakic/M.Naslund/19 50.00 120.00
HNST J.Toews/J.Spezza/19 100.00 200.00
HNWN Nichushkin/T.Wilson/43 40.00 100.00
HNYT S.Yzerman/J.Toews/19 125.00 250.00

2013-14 The Cup Limited Logos Autographs

LLAB Aleksander Barkov/50 50.00 120.00
LLAG Alex Galchenyuk/50 40.00 100.00
LLAH Adam Henrique/50 12.00 30.00
LLAK Anze Kopitar 25.00 60.00
LLAL Alex Chiasson/50 15.00 40.00
LLAN Antti Niemi/50 12.00 30.00
LLAO Alexander Ovechkin/25 1500.00 4000.00
LLAT Alex Tanguay/50 10.00 25.00
LLBA David Backes/50 10.00 25.00
LLBG Brendan Gallagher/50 40.00 100.00
LLBJ Boone Jenner/50 30.00 80.00
LLCC Charlie Coyle/50 25.00 60.00
LLCF Cody Franson/50 10.00 25.00
LLCK Chris Kreider/50 20.00 50.00
LLCO Cory Conacher/50 10.00 25.00
LLCP Carey Price/25 30.00 80.00
LLCT Christian Thomas/50 12.00 30.00
LLDB Damien Brunner/50 12.00 30.00
LLDH Dominik Hasek/25 25.00 60.00
LLDL David Legwand/50 12.00 30.00
LLDM Dylan McIlrath/50 10.00 25.00
LLDW Doug Weight 15.00 40.00
LLEM Evgeni Malkin/25 30.00 80.00
LLFO Peter Forsberg/25 30.00 80.00
LLGF Grant Fuhr/50 25.00 60.00
LLGR Mikhail Grigorenko/50 10.00 25.00
LLGU Bill Guerin/50 15.00 40.00
LLHA Dale Hawerchuk/50 20.00 50.00
LLJA Jason Spezza/50 15.00 40.00
LLJF Justin Fontaine/50 15.00 40.00
LLJH Jonathan Huberdeau/50 40.00 100.00
LLJK Jari Kurri/50 15.00 40.00
LLJL John LeClair/50 15.00 40.00
LLJM Jon Merrill/50 15.00 40.00
LLJO John Tavares/25 25.00 60.00
LLJS Justin Schultz/50 15.00 40.00
LLJT Joe Thornton/50 25.00 60.00
LLKL Kari Lehtonen/50 12.00 30.00
LLKT Kyle Turris/50 10.00 25.00
LLLI Elias Lindholm/50 40.00 100.00
LLMC Ryan McDonagh/50 10.00 25.00
LLMD Matt Duchene/50 15.00 40.00
LLMG Mikael Granlund/50 25.00 60.00
LLMN Markus Naslund/50 15.00 40.00
LLMO Mike Modano/50 25.00 60.00
LLMP Max Pacioretty/50 15.00 40.00
LLMR Morgan Rielly/50 40.00 100.00
LLMS Mats Sundin/25 15.00 40.00
LLMU Ryan Murphy/50 15.00 40.00
LLNA Markus Naslund/25 15.00 40.00
LLNM Nathan MacKinnon/50 400.00 1000.00
LLNY Nail Yakupov/50 30.00 80.00
LLPE Patrik Elias/50 15.00 40.00
LLPM Petr Mrazek/50 30.00 80.00
LLPP P.A. Parenteau/25 10.00 25.00
LLRB Richard Brodeur/25 15.00 40.00
LLRI Mike Richter/25 15.00 40.00
LLRM Ryan Murray 25.00 60.00
LLRN Rick Nash/50 15.00 40.00
LLRO Jeremy Roenick/50 25.00 60.00
LLRR Rasmus Ristolainen/50 25.00 60.00
LLRS Ryan Smyth/50 12.00 30.00
LLRY Ryan Strome/50 25.00 60.00
LLSB Sergei Bobrovsky/50 25.00 60.00
LLSG Simon Gagne/50 15.00 40.00
LLSH Scott Hartnell/50 10.00 25.00
LLSJ Seth Jones/50 30.00 80.00
LLSK Saku Koivu/50 15.00 40.00
LLSM Sean Monahan/50 25.00 60.00
LLST Steve Mason/50 12.00 30.00
LLSW Shea Weber/50 12.00 30.00
LLTH Tomas Hertl/50 30.00 80.00
LLTJ Tomas Jurco/50 20.00 50.00
LLTP Tomas Plekanec/50 10.00 25.00
LLTR Jacob Trouba/50 25.00 60.00
LLVN Valeri Nichushkin/50 30.00 80.00
LLVT Vladimir Tarasenko/50 40.00 100.00
LLZG Zemgus Girgensons/50 25.00 60.00

2013-14 The Cup Rookie Bookmarks Dual Autographs

DABBT N.Beaulieu/J.Tinordi 60.00 120.00
DABFJ S.Jones/F.Forsberg 60.00 120.00
DABFM P.Mrazek/V.Fasth 40.00 100.00
DABGC M.Granlund/C.Coyle 60.00 120.00
DABGG A.Galchenyuk/B.Gallagher 150.00 250.00
DABHB J.Huberdeau/A.Barkov 100.00 200.00
DABMY N.MacKinnon/N.Yakupov 150.00 300.00
DABSH D.Hamilton/R.Spooner 40.00 80.00
DABSY N.Yakupov/J.Schultz 30.00 80.00
DABTP T.Toffoli/T.Pearson 90.00 150.00

2013-14 The Cup Rookie Brilliance Autographs

BAB Aleksander Barkov 15.00 40.00
BBJ Boone Jenner 15.00 40.00
BCC Cory Conacher 5.00 12.00
BFF Filip Forsberg 20.00 50.00
BGR Mikael Granlund 12.00 30.00
BHA Dougie Hamilton 12.00 30.00
BJH Jonathan Huberdeau 30.00 80.00
BJS Justin Schultz 8.00 20.00
BMR Morgan Rielly 20.00 50.00
BNM Nathan MacKinnon 150.00 400.00
BNY Nail Yakupov 15.00 40.00
BSJ Seth Jones 15.00 40.00
BTH Tomas Hertl 15.00 40.00
BVF Viktor Fasth 8.00 20.00
BVN Valeri Nichushkin 12.00 30.00
BVT Vladimir Tarasenko

2013-14 The Cup Rookie Evolution Video Cards

EVOAG Alex Galchenyuk 40.00 100.00
EVOCC Charlie Coyle 15.00 40.00
EVOJH Jonathan Huberdeau 25.00 60.00
EVONY Nail Yakupov 20.00 50.00
EVOSZ Justin Schultz 20.00 50.00
EVOTT Tyler Toffoli 40.00 80.00

2013-14 The Cup Rookie Gear Autographs

ARGAG Alex Galchenyuk 150.00 300.00
ARGBB Beau Bennett 40.00 100.00
ARGBG Brendan Gallagher 150.00 250.00
ARGCC Cory Conacher 15.00 40.00
ARGDB Damien Brunner 25.00 60.00
ARGDH Dougie Hamilton 75.00 150.00
ARGEE Emerson Etem 25.00 60.00
ARGEL Elias Lindholm 60.00 150.00
ARGFF Filip Forsberg 60.00 120.00
ARGGR Mikael Granlund 50.00 100.00
ARGJH Jonathan Huberdeau 75.00 150.00
ARGJS Justin Schultz 25.00 60.00
ARGMG Mikhail Grigorenko 30.00 80.00
ARGNM Nathan MacKinnon 300.00 600.00
ARGNY Nail Yakupov 60.00 120.00
ARGPM Petr Mrazek 75.00 150.00
ARGSJ Seth Jones 30.00 80.00
ARGSM Sean Monahan 60.00 120.00
ARGVF Viktor Fasth 25.00 60.00
ARGVT Vladimir Tarasenko

2013-14 The Cup Scripted Sticks

SSAK Anze Kopitar 25.00 60.00
SSAM Al MacInnis 20.00 50.00
SSBH Bobby Hull 30.00 80.00
SSCN Cam Neely 15.00 40.00
SSCP Carey Price 30.00 80.00
SSDG Doug Gilmour 20.00 50.00
SSDH Dale Hawerchuk 20.00 50.00
SSDP Dion Phaneuf 12.00 30.00
SSEM Evgeni Malkin 30.00 80.00
SSGA Marian Gaborik 15.00 40.00
SSGC Guy Carbonneau 15.00 40.00
SSGF Grant Fuhr 25.00 60.00
SSGL Guy Lafleur 20.00 50.00
SSHE Dany Heatley 12.00 30.00
SSHU Brett Hull 30.00 80.00
SSJK Jari Kurri 15.00 40.00
SSJL John LeClair 15.00 40.00
SSJS Joe Sakic 30.00 80.00
SSKE Phil Kessel 15.00 40.00
SSLC Logan Couture 20.00 50.00
SSLR Larry Robinson 15.00 40.00
SSMB Mike Bossy 15.00 40.00
SSMG Mike Gartner 20.00 50.00
SSMM Mark Messier 30.00 80.00
SSPC Paul Coffey 15.00 40.00
SSPE Phil Esposito 25.00 60.00
SSPF Peter Forsberg 30.00 80.00
SSPK Patrick Kane 50.00 125.00
SSPS P.K. Subban 20.00 50.00
SSRB Ray Bourque 25.00 60.00
SSRF Ron Francis 20.00 50.00
SSSC Sidney Crosby 150.00 250.00
SSTE Tony Esposito 15.00 40.00
SSTH Taylor Hall 15.00 40.00
SSWG Wayne Gretzky 300.00 800.00

2013-14 The Cup Scripted Swatches

SWAB Aleksander Barkov/35 30.00 80.00
SWAH Adam Henrique/35 8.00 20.00
SWAN Antti Niemi/35 8.00 20.00
SWAO Alexander Ovechkin/15
SWBB Brian Bellows/35 8.00 20.00
SWCC Charlie Coyle/35 15.00 40.00
SWCP Carey Price/35 40.00 100.00
SWDW Doug Weight/35 10.00 25.00
SWGF Grant Fuhr/35 25.00 60.00
SWGL Gabriel Landeskog/35 12.00 30.00
SWJF Justin Fontaine/35 10.00 25.00
SWJH Jonas Hiller/15
SWJJ Jaromir Jagr/35 30.00 80.00
SWJS Jason Spezza/35 10.00 25.00
SWMD Matt Duchene/15
SWMF Marc-Andre Fleury/35 20.00 50.00
SWMG Mikael Granlund/35 15.00 40.00
SWMN Markus Naslund/5
SWMR Morgan Rielly/35 25.00 60.00
SWMS Mats Sundin/35 10.00 25.00
SWNM Nathan MacKinnon/35 125.00 300.00
SWNY Nail Yakupov/35 20.00 50.00
SWPA Patrik Elias/35 10.00 25.00
SWPE Corey Perry/35 15.00 40.00
SWPF Peter Forsberg/35 20.00 50.00
SWPM Petr Mrazek/35 20.00 50.00
SWRB Richard Brodeur/35 10.00 25.00
SWRM Ryan Miller/35 10.00 25.00
SWRS Ryan Strome/35 15.00 40.00
SWSA Joe Sakic/35 20.00 50.00
SWSC Sidney Crosby/35 EXCH 100.00 200.00
SWSJ Seth Jones/35 20.00 50.00
SWST Martin St. Louis/35 10.00 25.00
SWSW Shea Weber/15
SWSY Steve Yzerman/35 25.00 60.00
SWTH Taylor Hall/35 10.00 25.00
SWTT Tyler Toffoli/35 20.00 50.00
SWVT Vladimir Tarasenko/35 60.00 150.00

2013-14 The Cup Signature Patches

SPAA Marc Staal/99 8.00 20.00
SPAG Alex Galchenyuk/99 30.00 80.00
SPAH Adam Henrique/99 10.00 25.00
SPAK Anze Kopitar/99 20.00 50.00
SPAO Alexander Ovechkin/25 50.00 125.00
SPBB Bill Barber/99 12.00 30.00
SPBG Brendan Gallagher/99 30.00 80.00
SPBJ Boone Jenner/99 25.00 60.00
SPCA Carey Price/99 25.00 60.00
SPCC Cory Conacher/99 8.00 20.00
SPCH Cody Hodgson/99 8.00 20.00
SPCP Corey Perry/99 20.00 50.00
SPCS Cory Schneider/25 12.00 30.00
SPDK David Krejci/99 12.00 30.00
SPDM Dylan McIlrath/99 8.00 20.00
SPDU Mathew Dumba/99 8.00 20.00
SPDW Doug Weight/99 12.00 30.00
SPES Eric Staal/25 15.00 40.00
SPGL Guy Lafleur/99 15.00 40.00
SPGM Glen Murray/99 10.00 25.00
SPHU Jonathan Huberdeau/99 80.00 200.00
SPJB Jonathan Bernier/25 10.00 25.00
SPJH Jonas Hiller/99 10.00 25.00
SPJO Jordan Schroeder/99 12.00 30.00
SPJS Jason Spezza/99 12.00 30.00
SPJT John Tavares/25 20.00 50.00
SPKL Kari Lehtonen/99 10.00 25.00
SPLC Logan Couture/25 15.00 40.00
SPLR Luc Robitaille/25 12.00 30.00
SPMB Martin Brodeur/25 30.00 80.00
SPMG Mikhail Grigorenko/99 8.00 20.00
SPMM Mike Modano/99 20.00 50.00
SPMN Markus Naslund/99 12.00 30.00
SPMS Mats Sundin/25 12.00 30.00
SPNM Nathan MacKinnon/99 300.00 800.00
SPNY Nail Yakupov/99 25.00 60.00
SPPB Pavel Bure/25 12.00 30.00
SPPE Patrik Elias/99 12.00 30.00
SPPP P.A. Parenteau/99 8.00 20.00
SPPR Pekka Rinne/99 12.00 30.00
SPRI Morgan Rielly/99 40.00 100.00
SPRK Ryan Kesler/99 12.00 30.00
SPRM Ryan Miller/25 12.00 30.00
SPRR Tyler Toffoli/99 25.00 60.00
SPRS Ryan Strome/99 20.00 50.00

Card	Low	High
SPSC Sidney Crosby/25	150.00	300.00
SPSE Tyler Seguin/99	15.00	40.00
SPSM Sean Monahan/99	20.00	50.00
SPSW Shea Weber/25	10.00	25.00
SPTH Tomas Hertl/99	25.00	60.00
SPVN Valeri Nichushkin/99	25.00	60.00
SPZG Zemgus Girgensons/99	20.00	50.00

2013-14 The Cup Signature Patches Dual

Card	Low	High
DSPBH M.Brodeur/Henrique/35	40.00	100.00
DSPBP D.Phaneuf/J.Bernier/35	10.00	25.00
DSPGG Gallagher/Galchnyk/35	30.00	80.00
DSPHM J.Howard/P.Mrazek/35	25.00	60.00
DSPJH C.Joseph/D.Hasek/15		
DSPJS M.Sundin/C.Joseph/15		
DSPKP D.Phaneuf/P.Kessel/35	12.00	30.00
DSPLG Gretzky/M.Lemieux/15		
DSPMB G.Murray/R.Bourque/35	20.00	50.00
DSPML Landeskog/MacKinn/35	200.00	500.00
DSPNM MacKinnon/Duchne/35	60.00	150.00
DSPNS M.Staal/R.Nash/35	12.00	30.00
DSPPE C.Perry/E.Etem/35	20.00	50.00
DSPPJ J.Bernier/P.Kessel/35	12.00	30.00
DSPRG J.Roenick/C.Giroux/35	20.00	50.00
DSPRR Robitaille/J.Roenick/35	20.00	50.00
DSPSF P.Forsberg/J.Sakic/15		
DSPSS J.Sakic/M.Sundin/15		
DSPTC C.Conacher/K.Turris/35	8.00	20.00
DSPTD Tavares/M.Duchene/35	20.00	50.00
DSPTV Seguin/V.Nichushkin/35	30.00	80.00
DSPWJ S.Jones/S.Weber/35	25.00	60.00
DSPYO S.Yzerman/C.Osgood/15		

2013-14 The Cup Signature Renditions

Card	Low	High
SRAB Aleksander Barkov	30.00	80.00
SRAG Alex Galchenyuk	25.00	60.00
SRBB Bill Barber	10.00	25.00
SRBC Bobby Clarke	15.00	40.00
SRBH Bobby Hull	20.00	50.00
SRBO Bobby Orr	40.00	100.00
SRCL Claude Lemieux	10.00	25.00
SRCN Cam Neely	10.00	25.00
SRDH Dominik Hasek	15.00	40.00
SREB Ed Belfour	10.00	25.00
SREM Evgeni Malkin	20.00	50.00
SRES Eric Staal	12.00	30.00
SRGF Grant Fuhr	15.00	40.00
SRGL Guy Lafleur	12.00	30.00
SRGP Gilbert Perreault	10.00	25.00
SRGR Mikhail Grigorenko	6.00	15.00
SRGW Wayne Gretzky	250.00	600.00
SRHE Tomas Hertl	20.00	50.00
SRHU Brett Hull	20.00	50.00
SRJH Jonathan Huberdeau	25.00	60.00
SRJJ Jaromir Jagr	30.00	80.00
SRJK Jari Kurri	10.00	25.00
SRJP Jean-Gabriel Pageau	10.00	25.00
SRJQ Jonathan Quick	12.00	30.00
SRJT John Tavares	15.00	40.00
SRKE Phil Kessel	10.00	25.00
SRLI Elias Lindholm	25.00	60.00
SRLR Larry Robinson	10.00	25.00
SRMB Martin Brodeur	25.00	60.00
SRMD Marcel Dionne	12.00	30.00
SRMG Mike Gartner	12.00	30.00
SRMI Mike Bossy	10.00	25.00
SRMM Mark Messier	20.00	50.00
SRMO Sean Monahan	15.00	40.00
SRMS Mats Sundin	10.00	25.00
SRMT Marty Turco	10.00	25.00
SRNL Nicklas Lidstrom	10.00	25.00
SRNM Nathan MacKinnon	50.00	125.00
SRNY Nail Yakupov	20.00	50.00
SROR Bobby Orr	60.00	150.00
SRPC Paul Coffey	10.00	25.00
SRPE Phil Esposito	15.00	40.00
SRPK Patrick Kane	20.00	50.00
SRRB Ray Bourque	15.00	40.00
SRRF Ron Francis	12.00	30.00
SRRH Ron Hextall	10.00	25.00
SRRM Ryan Murray	15.00	40.00
SRRV Rogie Vachon	12.00	30.00
SRSB Sergei Bobrovsky	15.00	40.00
SRSJ Seth Jones	20.00	50.00
SRSM Stan Mikita	12.00	30.00
SRSW Shea Weber	8.00	20.00
SRTE Tony Esposito	10.00	25.00
SRTF Theoren Fleury	12.00	30.00
SRTH Taylor Hall	10.00	25.00
SRTO Jonathan Toews	15.00	40.00
SRTS Tyler Seguin	12.00	30.00
SRVL Valeri Nichushkin	20.00	50.00
SRVT Vladimir Tarasenko	25.00	60.00
SRWA Wayne Gretzky	250.00	600.00
SRWG Wayne Gretzky	250.00	600.00

2013-14 The Cup Silver Jerseys

Card	Low	High
1 Corey Perry	10.00	25.00
2 Ryan Getzlaf	6.00	15.00
3 Jonas Hiller	5.00	12.00
4 Teemu Selanne	12.00	30.00
6 Milan Lucic	6.00	15.00
7 Brad Marchand	12.00	30.00
8 Ray Bourque	12.00	30.00
9 Tuukka Rask	8.00	20.00
13 Eric Staal	8.00	20.00
14 Corey Crawford	8.00	20.00
15 Tony Esposito	6.00	15.00
16 Patrick Kane	12.00	30.00
17 Jonathan Toews	10.00	25.00
18 Brent Seabrook	4.00	10.00
19 Matt Duchene	6.00	15.00
20 Joe Sakic	12.00	30.00
21 Peter Forsberg	12.00	30.00
23 Sergei Bobrovsky	10.00	25.00
25 Pavel Datsyuk	10.00	25.00
26 Jim Howard	8.00	20.00
27 Steve Yzerman	15.00	40.00
28 Nicklas Lidstrom	6.00	15.00
29 Johan Franzen	5.00	12.00
30 Henrik Zetterberg	8.00	20.00
31 Chris Osgood	6.00	15.00
33 Grant Fuhr	8.00	20.00
34 Wayne Gretzky	40.00	100.00
35 Jordan Eberle	6.00	15.00
36 Taylor Hall	6.00	15.00
37 Drew Doughty	8.00	20.00
38 Luc Robitaille	8.00	20.00
39 Jonathan Quick	8.00	20.00
41 Anze Kopitar	10.00	25.00
46 P.K. Subban	8.00	20.00
47 Patrick Roy	15.00	40.00
48 Carey Price	12.00	30.00
49 Pekka Rinne	6.00	15.00
50 Shea Weber	5.00	12.00
51 Martin Brodeur	15.00	40.00
53 Thomas Vanek	5.00	12.00
54 John Tavares	10.00	25.00
55 Mike Bossy	8.00	20.00
56 Mark Messier	8.00	20.00
57 Eric Lindros	10.00	25.00
60 Henrik Lundqvist	15.00	40.00
61 Craig Anderson	6.00	15.00
62 Jason Spezza	6.00	15.00
64 Claude Giroux	6.00	15.00
65 Shane Doan	5.00	12.00
66 Mario Lemieux	25.00	60.00
67 Evgeni Malkin	12.00	30.00
68 Marc-Andre Fleury	12.00	30.00
69 Sidney Crosby	25.00	60.00
71 Kris Letang	8.00	20.00
72 Logan Couture	8.00	20.00
73 Antti Niemi	5.00	12.00
75 Jaroslav Halak	6.00	15.00
76 Martin St. Louis	8.00	20.00
77 Steven Stamkos	12.00	30.00
78 Phil Kessel	6.00	15.00
80 Mats Sundin	6.00	15.00
82 Roberto Luongo	10.00	25.00
84 Ryan Kesler	6.00	15.00
85 Nicklas Backstrom	6.00	15.00
86 Braden Holtby	8.00	20.00
87 Alexander Ovechkin	25.00	60.00
89 Dale Hawerchuk	8.00	20.00

2013-14 The Cup Trios Jerseys

Card	Low	High
C3AD Slnne/Kvu/Gtzlf	10.00	25.00
C3BB Mrchnd/Lcc/Krjci	15.00	40.00
C3EO NgntHpkns/Ykpv/Hll	12.00	30.00
C3VC Kslr/Schrdr/Edlr	8.00	20.00
C3WC Crlsn/Grn/Bckstrm	8.00	20.00
C3ANA Fsth/Gbsn/Andrsn	12.00	30.00
C3AVS Ry/Skc/McKnn	25.00	50.00
C3BEES Prk/Mrry/Brque	12.00	30.00
C3BLUES Elltt/Trsnko/Brglnd	12.00	30.00
C3BOS Spner/Sdrbrg/Hmltn	15.00	40.00
C3BUF Grgnko/Rstln/Grgsns	8.00	20.00
C3CAN Blleu/Trnrdi/Brnvl	8.00	20.00
C3CAPS Ovchkn/Crrck/Hltby	30.00	80.00
C3CAR Wrd/Stl/Lndhlm	20.00	50.00
C3CHI Shrp/Sbrk/Bckll	8.00	20.00
C3COL Dchne/Ststny/Lndskg	10.00	25.00
C3DAL Nchshkn/Sgn/Chssn	10.00	25.00
C3DET Hsk/Hwrd/Mrzk	10.00	25.00
C3DEV Hnrque/Schder/Mrrll	8.00	20.00
C3DRW Hwrd/Dtsyk/Frnzn	12.00	30.00
C3DUCKS Gtzlt/Prry/Etm	12.00	30.00
C3EDM Ykpv/Schltz/Hll	10.00	25.00
C3FLO Hbrdeau/Brkv/Hwdn	15.00	40.00
C3FLY Lghtn/Grx/Hrtnll	10.00	25.00
C3GOAL Fhr/Jsph/Hxtll	12.00	30.00
C3GR8 Hll/Chls/Frsbrg	15.00	40.00
C3HABS Bnvl/Gllghr/Glchnyk	15.00	40.00
C3HAWKS Shrp/Kne/Tws	15.00	40.00
C3KINGS Prsn/Vy/Jnes	8.00	20.00
C3LAK Kptr/Tffli/Rchrds	15.00	40.00
C3LBBR Glchnyk/Pcrtty/Mrkv	15.00	40.00
C3LEAFS Blfr/Fhr/Brnr	12.00	30.00
C3LOS Kptr/Tffli/Qck	15.00	40.00
C3MINW Grnlnd/Cyle/Brdn	8.00	20.00
C3MON Prce/Ry/Thdre	25.00	50.00
C3MTL Prce/Gllghr/Glchnyk	15.00	40.00
C3NASH Jnes/Rnne/Wbr	10.00	25.00
C3NET Hsk/Espsto/Blfr	12.00	30.00
C3NJD Brdr/Zjc/Mrrll	20.00	50.00
C3NYI Tvrs/Nlsn/Hcky	15.00	40.00
C3NYR Grtnr/Lndrs/Flry	12.00	30.00
C3OIL Hll/Ebrle/NgntHpkns	10.00	25.00
C3OILRS Hmsky/Schltz/Hll	8.00	20.00
C3OTT Hsk/Spzza/Krlssn	20.00	40.00
C3PEN Lmx/Mlkn/Bnntt	15.00	40.00
C3PHI Rnck/Hxtll/LeClr	12.00	30.00
C3PIT Mlkn/Flry/Ltng	15.00	40.00
C3PREDS Frsbrg/Wtsn/Jnes	15.00	40.00
C3RWINGS Lshff/DKysr/Jrco	6.00	15.00
C3STAR Nsh/Kth/Sknnr	12.00	30.00
C3STARS Lhtnn/Bnn/Cmpbll	20.00	50.00
C3TBL Pnk/Kllrn/Gds	12.00	30.00
C3TOR Blfr/Sndn/Lndrs	12.00	30.00
C3VAN Kslr/Edlr/Jnsn	8.00	20.00
C3WAS Bckstrm/Grn/Wlsn	15.00	40.00
C3WINGS Hwrd/Mrzk/Jrco	10.00	25.00

2014-15 The Cup

Card	Low	High
1 Teemu Selanne	3.00	8.00
2 Ryan Getzlaf	1.50	4.00
3 Shane Doan	1.25	3.00
4 Bobby Orr	6.00	15.00
5 Patrice Bergeron	2.00	5.00
6 Phil Esposito	2.50	6.00
7 Ray Bourque	2.50	6.00
8 Tuukka Rask	2.00	5.00
9 Cam Neely	1.50	4.00
10 Zemgus Girgensons	1.25	3.00
11 Dominik Hasek	2.50	6.00
12 Sean Monahan	1.00	2.50
13 Theoren Fleury	2.00	5.00
14 Eric Staal	2.00	5.00
15 Jonathan Toews	2.50	6.00
16 Patrick Kane	3.00	8.00
17 Patrick Sharp	1.50	4.00
18 Steve Larmer	1.25	3.00
19 Nathan MacKinnon	6.00	15.00
20 Matt Duchene	1.50	4.00
21 Semyon Varlamov	1.50	4.00
22 Joe Sakic	3.00	8.00
23 Gabriel Landeskog	2.00	5.00
24 Rob Blake	1.50	4.00
25 Sergei Bobrovsky	2.50	6.00
26 Brandon Dubinsky	1.00	2.50
27 Tyler Seguin	2.00	5.00
28 Jason Spezza	1.50	4.00
29 Jamie Benn	1.50	4.00
30 Pavel Datsyuk	2.50	6.00
31 Chris Chelios	1.50	4.00
32 Steve Yzerman	4.00	10.00
33 Henrik Zetterberg	2.00	5.00
34 Wayne Gretzky	10.00	25.00
35 Taylor Hall	1.50	4.00
36 Ryan Nugent-Hopkins	2.00	5.00
37 Glenn Anderson	1.25	3.00
38 Roberto Luongo	2.50	6.00
39 Aleksander Barkov	2.50	6.00
40 Jonathan Quick	2.00	5.00
41 Marian Gaborik	1.50	4.00
42 Anze Kopitar	2.50	6.00
43 Zach Parise	1.50	4.00
44 Thomas Vanek	1.25	3.00
45 P.K. Subban	2.00	5.00
46 Max Pacioretty	1.50	4.00
47 Patrick Roy	4.00	10.00
48 Vincent Damphousse	1.25	3.00
49 Carey Price	3.00	8.00
50 Alex Galchenyuk	1.00	2.50
51 Filip Forsberg	2.50	6.00
52 Pekka Rinne	1.50	4.00
53 Shea Weber	1.25	3.00
54 Jaromir Jagr	5.00	12.00
55 Cory Schneider	1.50	4.00
56 Kyle Okposo	1.00	2.50
57 John Tavares	2.50	6.00
58 Mike Bossy	1.50	4.00
59 Henrik Lundqvist	4.00	10.00
60 Rick Nash	1.50	4.00
61 Martin St. Louis	1.50	4.00
62 John Vanbiesbrouck	1.50	4.00
63 Mark Messier	3.00	8.00
64 Erik Karlsson	2.00	5.00
65 Bobby Ryan	1.25	3.00
66 Claude Giroux	1.50	4.00
67 Sidney Crosby	10.00	25.00
68 Evgeni Malkin	3.00	8.00
69 Marc-Andre Fleury	3.00	8.00
70 Mario Lemieux	6.00	15.00
71 Mats Sundin	1.50	4.00
72 Logan Couture	2.00	5.00
73 Joe Pavelski	2.00	5.00
74 Arturs Irbe	3.00	8.00
75 Tomas Hertl	1.50	4.00
76 David Backes	1.00	2.50
77 Vladimir Tarasenko	2.00	5.00
78 Brett Hull	3.00	8.00
79 Steven Stamkos	3.00	8.00
80 Ben Bishop	1.25	3.00
81 Darryl Sittler	2.00	5.00
82 Phil Kessel	1.50	4.00
83 Jonathan Bernier	1.25	3.00
84 James van Riemsdyk	1.25	3.00
85 Ryan Miller	1.50	4.00
86 Trevor Linden	1.50	4.00
87 Nicklas Backstrom	1.50	4.00
88 Alexander Ovechkin	6.00	15.00
89 Mike Gartner	2.00	5.00
90 Evander Kane	1.50	4.00
91 Joel Armia RC	5.00	12.00
92 Klas Dahlbeck AU RC	6.00	15.00
93 Andrej Nestrasil AU RC	8.00	20.00
94 Scott Mayfield AU RC	6.00	15.00
95 Patrick Brown AU RC	8.00	20.00
96 Patrik Nemeth AU RC	8.00	20.00
97 Corban Knight AU RC	8.00	20.00
98 Joey Hishon AU RC	10.00	25.00
99 Mike Halmo AU RC	5.00	12.00
100 Laurent Brossoit AU RC EXCH	15.00	40.00
101 Joonas Nattinen JSY AU RC	10.00	25.00
102 Liam O'Brien JSY AU RC EXCH	10.00	25.00
103 Curtis McKenzie JSY AU RC	8.00	20.00
104 C.Paquette JSY AU RC EX	10.00	25.00
105 Tyler Graovac JSY AU RC	8.00	20.00
106 Jake McCabe JSY AU RC	10.00	25.00
107 N.Deslauriers JSY AU RC	10.00	25.00
108 Seth Helgeson JSY AU RC	8.00	20.00
109 Dennis Everberg JSY AU RC	10.00	25.00
110 Colin Smith JSY AU RC EXCH	10.00	25.00
111 Rocco Grimaldi JSY AU RC	10.00	25.00
112 Greg McKegg JSY AU RC	8.00	20.00
113 Bryan Rust JSY AU RC	250.00	600.00
114 J.Klingberg JSY AU RC EXCH	25.00	60.00
115 P-E Bellemare JSY AU RC	12.00	30.00
116 Rob Zepp JSY AU RC	15.00	40.00
117 Mark Visentin JSY AU RC	10.00	25.00
118 M.Karlsson JSY AU RC	10.00	25.00
119 Christian Folin JSY AU RC	10.00	25.00
120 Brandon Kozun JSY AU RC	8.00	20.00
121 Wotherspoon JSY AU/249 RC	10.00	25.00
122 Derrick Pouliot JSY AU RC	12.00	30.00
123 Barclay Goodrow JSY AU RC	20.00	50.00
124 A.Vasilevskiy JSY AU RC	400.00	1000.00
125 B.Gormley JSY AU RC	10.00	25.00
126 Ryan Sproul JSY AU RC	10.00	25.00
127 Joni Ortio JSY AU RC	12.00	30.00
128 Calle Jarnkrok JSY AU RC	10.00	25.00
129 Scott Harrington JSY AU RC	10.00	25.00
130 Griffin Reinhart JSY AU RC	10.00	25.00
131 Andy Andreoff JSY AU RC	10.00	25.00
132 Justin Hodgman JSY AU RC	8.00	20.00
133 Khokhlachev JSY AU RC EX	10.00	25.00
134 Josh Jooris JSY AU RC	10.00	25.00
135 P.Lindbohm JSY AU RC EX	15.00	40.00
136 Hammond JSY AU RC EXCH	15.00	40.00
137 M.Granlund JSY AU RC EX	15.00	40.00
138 Jordan Binnington JSY AU RC	100.00	250.00
139 Scott Darling JSY AU RC	20.00	50.00
140 Vincent Trocheck JSY AU RC	100.00	250.00
141 Colton Sissons JSY AU RC	10.00	25.00
142 Joe Morrow JSY AU RC	12.00	30.00
143 Teemu Pulkkinen JSY AU RC	15.00	40.00
144 Namestnikov JSY AU/249 RC EX	15.00	40.00
145 Brett Ritchie JSY AU RC	10.00	25.00
146 Mirco Mueller JSY AU RC	10.00	25.00
147 Marko Dano JSY AU RC	10.00	25.00
148 Ty Rattie JSY AU RC	10.00	25.00
149 A.Clendening JSY AU/249 RC	10.00	25.00
150 Tobias Rieder JSY AU RC	10.00	25.00
151 Victor Rask JSY AU RC	10.00	25.00
152 Karlsson JSY AU RC EXCH	30.00	80.00
153 B.Yakimov JSY AU/249 RC	10.00	25.00
154 K.Hayes JSY AU RC EXCH	25.00	60.00
155 T.van Riemsdyk JSY AU/249 RC	15.00	40.00
156 Pastrnak JSY AU/249 RC EXCH	800.00	2000.00
157 S.Andrighetto JSY AU/249 RC	12.00	30.00
158 Adam Lowry JSY AU RC	15.00	40.00
159 C.Tierney JSY AU RC EXCH	10.00	25.00
160 L.Draisaitl JSY AU RC EXCH	1000.00	2000.00
161 Kerby Rychel JSY AU RC	8.00	20.00
162 Darnell Nurse JSY AU RC	50.00	125.00
163 S.Gostisbehere JSY AU/249 RC	80.00	200.00
164 D.Severson JSY AU/249 RC	10.00	25.00
165 Phillip Danault JSY AU RC	20.00	50.00
166 Stuart Percy JSY AU RC	10.00	25.00
167 Jiri Sekac JSY AU RC	8.00	20.00
168 S.Griffith JSY AU RC EXCH	12.00	30.00
169 A.Wennberg JSY AU/249 RC	15.00	40.00
170 Curtis Lazar JSY AU RC	10.00	25.00
171 Duclair JSY AU/249 RC EXCH	15.00	40.00
172 Jori Lehtera JSY AU RC	12.00	30.00
173 E.Kuznetsov JSY AU/249 RC	30.00	80.00
174 A.Burakovsky JSY AU/249 RC	15.00	40.00
175 J.Gaudreau JSY AU/99 RC	400.00	1000.00
176 Bo Horvat JSY AU/99 RC	200.00	500.00
177 T.Teravainen JSY AU/99 RC	100.00	250.00
178 Sam Reinhart JSY AU/99 RC	200.00	400.00
179 Aaron Ekblad JSY AU/99 RC	60.00	150.00
180 Drouin JSY AU/99 RC EXCH	200.00	500.00

2014-15 The Cup Gold Spectrum

*ROOKIES/25: .6X TO 1.5X BASIC RC/249

Card	Low	High
91 Joel Armia	8.00	20.00
92 Klas Dahlbeck AU	10.00	25.00
93 Andrej Nestrasil AU	12.00	30.00
94 Scott Mayfield AU	10.00	25.00
95 Patrick Brown AU	12.00	30.00
96 Patrik Nemeth AU	12.00	30.00
97 Corban Knight AU	12.00	30.00
99 Mike Halmo AU	8.00	20.00
101 Joonas Nattinen AU	12.00	30.00
102 Liam O'Brien AU	12.00	30.00
103 Curtis McKenzie AU	10.00	25.00
104 Cedric Paquette AU	12.00	30.00
105 Tyler Graovac AU	10.00	25.00
106 Jake McCabe AU	12.00	30.00
107 Nicolas Deslauriers AU	12.00	30.00
108 Seth Helgeson AU	10.00	25.00
109 Dennis Everberg AU	12.00	30.00
110 Colin Smith AU	12.00	30.00
111 Rocco Grimaldi AU	12.00	30.00
112 Greg McKegg AU	10.00	25.00
113 Bryan Rust AU	150.00	400.00
114 John Klingberg AU	25.00	60.00
115 Pierre-Edouard Bellemare AU	15.00	40.00
116 Rob Zepp AU	20.00	50.00
117 Mark Visentin AU	12.00	30.00
118 Melker Karlsson AU	12.00	30.00
119 Christian Folin AU	12.00	30.00
120 Brandon Kozun AU	10.00	25.00
121 Tyler Wotherspoon AU	12.00	30.00
122 Derrick Pouliot AU	15.00	40.00
123 Barclay Goodrow AU	12.00	30.00
124 Andrei Vasilevskiy AU	200.00	500.00
125 Brandon Gormley AU	12.00	30.00
126 Ryan Sproul AU	12.00	30.00
127 Joni Ortio AU	15.00	40.00
129 Scott Harrington AU	12.00	30.00
130 Griffin Reinhart AU	12.00	30.00
131 Andy Andreoff AU	12.00	30.00
135 Petteri Lindbohm AU	10.00	25.00
137 Markus Granlund AU	20.00	50.00
138 Jordan Binnington AU	40.00	100.00
139 Scott Darling AU	50.00	100.00
140 Vincent Trocheck AU	25.00	50.00
141 Colton Sissons AU	12.00	30.00
142 Joe Morrow AU	15.00	40.00
143 Teemu Pulkkinen AU	60.00	100.00
147 Marko Dano AU	12.00	30.00
148 Ty Rattie AU	12.00	30.00
149 Adam Clendening AU	12.00	30.00
150 Tobias Rieder AU	12.00	30.00
151 Victor Rask AU	12.00	30.00
152 William Karlsson AU	40.00	100.00
153 Bogdan Yakimov AU	12.00	30.00
154 Kevin Hayes AU	50.00	120.00
155 Trevor van Riemsdyk AU	20.00	50.00
156 David Pastrnak AU	250.00	600.00
157 Sven Andrighetto AU	15.00	40.00
158 Adam Lowry AU	20.00	50.00
160 Leon Draisaitl AU	300.00	600.00
161 Kerby Rychel AU	10.00	25.00
162 Darnell Nurse AU	40.00	80.00
163 Shayne Gostisbehere AU	60.00	100.00
164 Damon Severson AU	12.00	30.00
165 Phillip Danault AU	25.00	60.00
166 Stuart Percy AU	12.00	30.00
167 Jiri Sekac AU	10.00	25.00
169 Alexander Wennberg AU	20.00	50.00
170 Curtis Lazar AU	12.00	30.00
172 Jori Lehtera AU	15.00	40.00
173 Evgeny Kuznetsov AU	20.00	50.00
174 Andre Burakovsky AU	40.00	80.00
175 Johnny Gaudreau AU	125.00	300.00
176 Bo Horvat AU	60.00	120.00
177 Teuvo Teravainen AU	75.00	150.00
178 Sam Reinhart AU	60.00	120.00
179 Aaron Ekblad AU	50.00	125.00
180 Jonathan Drouin AU	100.00	200.00

2014-15 The Cup Auto Draft Boards

Card	Low	High
ARDBBG Brandon Gormley	8.00	20.00
ARDBEK Evgeny Kuznetsov	60.00	150.00
ARDBJM Joe Morrow	10.00	25.00
ARDBKH Kevin Hayes	20.00	50.00
ARDBMV Mark Visentin	8.00	20.00
ARDBOK Oscar Klefbom	15.00	40.00
ARDBPD Phillip Danault	15.00	40.00
ARDBSP Stuart Percy	8.00	20.00

2014-15 The Cup Brilliance Autographs

Card	Low	High
BAO Adam Oates E	8.00	20.00
BBO Bobby Orr B	50.00	125.00
BCC Chris Chelios B	12.00	30.00
BCN Cam Neely C	8.00	20.00
BDA Dave Schultz E	8.00	20.00
BDH Dominik Hasek C	30.00	80.00
BDS Denis Savard D	8.00	20.00
BES Eric Staal D	10.00	25.00
BFP Felix Potvin D	15.00	40.00
BHU Brett Hull D	15.00	40.00
BJI Jarome Iginla D	10.00	25.00
BJL John LeClair E	8.00	20.00
BJP Joe Pavelski E	10.00	25.00
BJR Jeremy Roenick B	12.00	30.00
BJT John Tavares D	12.00	30.00
BMB Mike Bossy C	8.00	20.00
BMC Marty McSorley E	6.00	15.00
BML Mario Lemieux A	50.00	125.00
BMM Mark Messier A	20.00	50.00
BMN Markus Naslund D	8.00	20.00
BMP Max Pacioretty B	8.00	20.00
BNL Nicklas Lidstrom B	15.00	40.00
BPR Patrick Roy A	50.00	125.00
BPT Pierre Turgeon E	6.00	15.00
BSC Sidney Crosby A	100.00	200.00
BSW Shea Weber E	6.00	15.00
BSY Steve Yzerman B	40.00	100.00
BTB Tom Barrasso D	8.00	20.00
BTF Theoren Fleury D	10.00	25.00
BTH Taylor Hall C	8.00	20.00
BTS Teemu Selanne B	25.00	60.00
BWG Wayne Gretzky A	250.00	600.00

2014-15 The Cup Enshrinements

Card	Low	High
EAD Anthony Duclair/99	12.00	30.00
EAE Aaron Ekblad/99	20.00	50.00
EAI Arturs Irbe/99	6.00	15.00
EAO Alexander Ovechkin/25	200.00	500.00
EBE Jamie Benn/99	8.00	20.00
EBH Bobby Hull/25	20.00	50.00
EBO Bobby Orr/25	100.00	250.00
ECL Curtis Lazar/99	8.00	20.00
ECN Cam Neely/50	8.00	20.00
ECP Carey Price/50	15.00	40.00
EDA Dave Schultz/50	8.00	20.00
EDH Dominik Hasek/50	30.00	80.00
EDP David Pastrnak/99	150.00	400.00
EDS Damon Severson/99	8.00	20.00
EEK Evgeny Kuznetsov/99	20.00	50.00
EEM Evgeni Malkin/50	15.00	40.00
EES Eric Staal/99	10.00	25.00
EGF Grant Fuhr/50	20.00	50.00
EGM Glen Murray/99	6.00	15.00
EHU Brett Hull/25	15.00	40.00
EJB Jordan Binnington/99	40.00	100.00
EJG Johnny Gaudreau/99	125.00	300.00
EJI Jarome Iginla/99	10.00	25.00
EJJ Jaromir Jagr/50	25.00	60.00
EJL Jori Lehtera/99	10.00	25.00
EJP Joe Pavelski/99	10.00	25.00
EJR Jeremy Roenick/50	12.00	30.00
EJT John Tavares/50	12.00	30.00
EKR Kerby Rychel/99	6.00	15.00
ELS Leon Draisaitl/99	200.00	500.00
EMA Marty McSorley/99	6.00	15.00
EMB Martin Brodeur/25	60.00	150.00
EMI Mike Bossy/50	8.00	20.00
EML Mario Lemieux/25	30.00	80.00
EMM Mark Messier/25	15.00	40.00
EMP Max Pacioretty/99	8.00	20.00
EMS Mats Sundin/50	20.00	50.00
EPR Patrick Roy/25	60.00	150.00
ESA Sven Andrighetto/99	10.00	25.00
ESB Sergei Bobrovsky/99	12.00	30.00
ESC Sidney Crosby/50	100.00	250.00
ESE Jiri Sekac/99	6.00	15.00
ESL Steve Larmer/99	6.00	15.00
ESM Sean Monahan/99	5.00	12.00
ESP Stuart Percy/99	8.00	20.00
ESR Sam Reinhart/99	30.00	80.00
ESW Shea Weber/50	6.00	15.00
ESY Steve Yzerman/25	20.00	50.00
ETB Tom Barrasso/99	8.00	20.00
ETH Taylor Hall/50	8.00	20.00
ETO Jonathan Toews/50	12.00	30.00
ETS Teemu Selanne/99	25.00	60.00
ETT Teuvo Teravainen/99	12.00	30.00
EWG Wayne Gretzky/25	300.00	800.00

2014-15 The Cup Enshrinements Dual

Card	Low	High
E2BG W.Gretzky/R.Blake	200.00	500.00
E2BS J.Benn/J.Spezza	12.00	30.00
E2DE A.Ekblad/J.Drouin	30.00	80.00
E2DO A.Ovechkin/P.Datsyuk	250.00	600.00
E2EA Kuznetsov/Burakovsky	30.00	80.00
E2MK M.Messier/J.Kurri	25.00	60.00
E2PP C.Price/M.Pacioretty	25.00	60.00
E2RR S.Reinhart/G.Reinhart	50.00	125.00
E2VB Vasilevskiy/J.Binnington	60.00	150.00
E2YL S.Yzerman/N.Lidstrom	30.00	80.00

2014-15 The Cup Exquisite Collection Inserts

Card	Low	High
1 Wayne Gretzky AU/25	250.00	600.00
2 Mike Bossy AU/25	15.00	40.00
3 Grant Fuhr AU/25	25.00	60.00
4 Alexander Ovechkin AU/25	60.00	150.00
5 Bobby Orr AU/25	60.00	150.00
6 Mario Lemieux AU/25	60.00	150.00
7 Guy Lafleur AU/25	20.00	50.00
8 Carey Price AU/25	30.00	80.00
9 Jaromir Jagr AU/25	50.00	120.00
10 Ray Bourque AU/25	25.00	60.00
11 Mark Messier AU/25	30.00	80.00
12 Patrick Roy AU/25	40.00	100.00
13 Marcel Dionne AU/25	20.00	50.00
14 Jonathan Toews AU/25	25.00	60.00
15 Sidney Crosby AU/25	60.00	150.00
17 Kerby Rychel JSY AU/52	12.00	30.00
19 A.Duclair JSY AU/63 EX	25.00	60.00
21 N.Deslauriers JSY AU/44	15.00	40.00
22 A.Hammond JSY AU/30 EXCH	25.00	60.00
23 A.Burakovsky JSY AU/65	25.00	60.00
24 A.Vasilevskiy JSY AU/88	400.00	1000.00
25 Colton Sissons JSY AU/84	15.00	40.00
26 William Karlsson JSY AU/38	50.00	120.00
27 T.Teravainen JSY AU/86	25.00	60.00
28 Jake McCabe JSY AU/29	15.00	40.00
29 Curtis Lazar JSY AU/27	15.00	40.00
30 Josh Jooris JSY AU/86	15.00	40.00
31 B.Yakimov JSY AU/39	15.00	40.00
32 T.van Riemsdyk JSY AU/57	25.00	60.00
33 Adam Lowry JSY AU/17	30.00	80.00
34 Seth Helgeson JSY AU/25	12.00	30.00
36 V.Namestnikov JSY AU/65 EX	25.00	60.00
37 Darnell Nurse JSY AU/25	30.00	80.00
38 E.Kuznetsov JSY AU/92	40.00	100.00
39 Joni Ortio JSY AU/37	20.00	50.00
40 V.Trocheck JSY AU/67	30.00	80.00
41 Brandon Gormley JSY AU/33	15.00	40.00
42 Jiri Sekac JSY AU/26	12.00	30.00
44 S.Gostisbehere JSY AU/53	30.00	80.00
46 Mark Visentin JSY AU/29	15.00	40.00
47 C.Tierney JSY AU/50 EXCH	15.00	40.00
48 Teemu Pulkkinen JSY AU/56	20.00	50.00
49 Brandon Kozun JSY AU/67	12.00	30.00
50 Leon Draisaitl JSY AU/29	300.00	800.00
51 David Pastrnak JSY AU/88	200.00	500.00
52 P-E Bellemare JSY AU/78	15.00	40.00
53 Barclay Goodrow JSY AU/89	15.00	40.00
54 Joe Morrow JSY AU/45	20.00	50.00
56 Joey Hishon JSY AU/38	20.00	50.00
57 A.Wennberg JSY AU/41	25.00	60.00
58 Phillip Danault JSY AU/24	30.00	80.00
60 S.Andrighetto JSY AU/58	20.00	50.00
61 Ty Rattie JSY AU/18	15.00	40.00
62 Brett Ritchie JSY AU/25	15.00	40.00
63 Mirco Mueller JSY AU/41	15.00	40.00
64 Dennis Everberg JSY AU/45	15.00	40.00
65 J.Drouin JSY AU/27 EX	30.00	80.00
66 Victor Rask JSY AU/49	15.00	40.00
67 Liam O'Brien JSY AU/87	15.00	40.00
68 Sam Reinhart JSY AU/23	60.00	150.00
69 Joonas Nattinen JSY AU/28	15.00	40.00
70 Patrik Nemeth JSY AU/37	15.00	40.00
71 Jordan Binnington JSY AU/30	50.00	125.00
72 T.Wotherspoon JSY AU/56	15.00	40.00
73 Damon Severson JSY AU/28	15.00	40.00
75 Derrick Pouliot JSY AU/25	20.00	50.00
78 Stuart Percy JSY AU/50	15.00	40.00
79 Ryan Sproul JSY AU/48	15.00	40.00
80 Calle Jarnkrok JSY AU/19	15.00	40.00
81 Rocco Grimaldi JSY AU/23	15.00	40.00
82 Bo Horvat JSY AU/53	40.00	100.00
83 Patrick Brown JSY AU/36	15.00	40.00
85 J.Gaudreau JSY AU/53	200.00	500.00
86 Seth Griffith JSY AU/53	20.00	50.00
87 Greg McKegg JSY AU/39	12.00	30.00
88 Marko Dano JSY AU/56	15.00	40.00
89 M.Granlund JSY AU/60 EX	25.00	60.00

2014-15 The Cup Foundations Jerseys

Card	Low	High
CFAE Aaron Ekblad	10.00	25.00
CFAF Marc-Andre Fleury	8.00	20.00
CFAO Alexander Ovechkin	15.00	40.00
CFBH Brett Hull	8.00	20.00
CFCH Cody Hodgson	2.50	6.00
CFCK Chris Kunitz	4.00	10.00
CFDB David Backes	2.50	6.00
CFDE Derek Stepan	2.50	6.00
CFDK David Krejci	4.00	10.00
CFDO Dominik Hasek	6.00	15.00
CFDS Denis Savard	4.00	10.00
CFDU Dustin Brown	4.00	10.00
CFEB Ed Belfour	4.00	10.00
CFES Eric Staal	5.00	12.00
CFFA Frederik Andersen	5.00	12.00
CFGF Grant Fuhr	6.00	15.00
CFHA Dale Hawerchuk	5.00	12.00
CFHE Tomas Hertl	4.00	10.00
CFJJ Jaromir Jagr	12.00	30.00
CFJP Jason Pominville	2.50	6.00
CFJT John Tavares	6.00	15.00
CFKO Kyle Okposo	2.50	6.00
CFLC Logan Couture	5.00	12.00
CFMA Steve Mason	3.00	8.00
CFMG Marian Gaborik	4.00	10.00
CFML Mario Lemieux	15.00	40.00
CFMM Matt Moulson	2.50	6.00
CFNK Niklas Kronwall	3.00	8.00
CFNM Nathan MacKinnon	15.00	40.00
CFNU Ryan Nugent-Hopkins	5.00	12.00
CFPA Joe Pavelski	5.00	12.00
CFPF Peter Forsberg	8.00	20.00
CFPK Phil Kessel	4.00	10.00
CFPR Patrick Roy	10.00	25.00
CFPS Paul Stastny	3.00	8.00
CFRG Ryan Getzlaf	4.00	10.00
CFRM Ryan Miller	4.00	10.00
CFRN Rick Nash	4.00	10.00
CFSB Sergei Bobrovsky	6.00	15.00
CFSC Sidney Crosby	15.00	40.00
CFSH Patrick Sharp	4.00	10.00
CFSJ Seth Jones	4.00	10.00
CFSS Steven Stamkos	8.00	20.00
CFSW Shea Weber	3.00	8.00

2014-15 The Cup Honorable Numbers

Card	Low	High
HNAB Aleksander Barkov/16	25.00	60.00
HNCP Carey Price/31	80.00	200.00
HNDB Dustin Brown/23	15.00	40.00
HNDS Denis Savard/18	15.00	40.00
HNDW Doug Weight/39	25.00	60.00
HNJG John Gibson/36	15.00	40.00
HNJP Jason Pominville/29	10.00	25.00
HNJQ Jonathan Quick/32	20.00	50.00
HNKO Kyle Okposo/21	10.00	25.00
HNMB Martin Biron/43	12.00	30.00
HNNB Nick Bjugstad/27	10.00	25.00
HNPE Patrik Elias/26	15.00	40.00
HNRJ Ryan Johansen/19	12.00	30.00
HNRK Ryan Kesler/17	15.00	40.00
HNRM Ryan Miller/30	15.00	40.00
HNRS Ryan Strome/18	15.00	40.00
HNSH Scott Hartnell/43	10.00	25.00
HNSM Sean Monahan/23	10.00	25.00

2014-15 The Cup Honorable Numbers Dual

Card	Low	High
DHNHJ C.Hodgson/R.Johansen	40.00	100.00
DHNSY S.Yzerman/J.Sakic/19	100.00	200.00

2014-15 The Cup Limited Logos Autographs

Card	Low	High
LLAB Aleksander Barkov/50	30.00	80.00
LLAE Aaron Ekblad/50	50.00	120.00
LLAG Alex Galchenyuk/50	12.00	30.00
LLAN Antti Niemi/50	15.00	40.00
LLBG Bill Guerin/50	20.00	50.00
LLBH Brett Hull/25	40.00	100.00
LLBR Bobby Ryan/50	15.00	40.00
LLCC Charlie Coyle/50	20.00	50.00
LLCH Cody Hodgson/50	12.00	30.00
LLCK Chris Kunitz/50	20.00	50.00
LLCP Carey Price/25	40.00	100.00
LLDB David Backes/50	12.00	30.00
LLDU Dustin Brown/50	20.00	50.00
LLDW Doug Weight/50	20.00	50.00
LLGA Marian Gaborik/50	20.00	50.00
LLGF Grant Fuhr/25	30.00	80.00
LLGI John Gibson/50	20.00	50.00
LLGM Glen Murray/50	15.00	40.00
LLGN Gustav Nyquist/50	12.00	30.00
LLJB Jamie Benn/25	20.00	50.00
LLJD Jonathan Drouin/50	40.00	100.00
LLJG Johnny Gaudreau/50	150.00	400.00
LLJH Jonathan Huberdeau/50	25.00	60.00
LLJI Jarome Iginla/50	25.00	60.00
LLJJ Jaromir Jagr/25	60.00	150.00
LLJL John LeClair/50	20.00	50.00
LLJP Jason Pominville/50	12.00	30.00
LLJR James van Riemsdyk/50	15.00	40.00
LLJS Joe Sakic/25 EXCH	40.00	100.00
LLJT John Tavares/25	30.00	80.00
LLJU Tomas Jurco/50	12.00	30.00
LLKL Kari Lehtonen/50	15.00	40.00
LLKO Kyle Okposo/50	12.00	30.00
LLKU Evgeny Kuznetsov/50	50.00	125.00
LLLD Leon Draisaitl/50	1200.00	3000.00
LLMB Martin Biron/50	15.00	40.00
LLMG Mikael Granlund/50	15.00	40.00
LLMO Matt Moulson/50	12.00	30.00
LLMP Max Pacioretty/50	20.00	50.00
LLMR Morgan Rielly/50	20.00	50.00
LLMS Mats Sundin/25	20.00	50.00
LLMZ Mats Zuccarello/50	20.00	50.00
LLOK Olaf Kolzig/50	20.00	50.00
LLON Owen Nolan/50	20.00	50.00
LLPD Pavel Datsyuk/50	30.00	80.00
LLPK Patrick Kane/50	40.00	100.00
LLPM Patrick Marleau/50	20.00	50.00
LLRA Ray Bourque/25	30.00	80.00
LLRB Rod Brind'Amour/50	15.00	40.00
LLRI Rick Nash/50	20.00	50.00
LLRJ Ryan Johansen/50	15.00	40.00
LLRK Ryan Kesler/50	20.00	50.00
LLRM Ryan McDonagh/50	12.00	30.00
LLRY Ryan Miller/50	20.00	50.00
LLSJ Seth Jones/50	20.00	50.00
LLSK Jeff Skinner/50	25.00	60.00
LLSM Sean Monahan/50	12.00	30.00
LLSP Jason Spezza/50	20.00	50.00
LLSR Sam Reinhart/50	80.00	200.00
LLST Steve Mason/50	15.00	40.00
LLSV Semyon Varlamov/50	20.00	50.00
LLSW Shea Weber/50	15.00	40.00
LLTH Tomas Hertl/50	20.00	50.00
LLTJ Jonathan Toews/25	30.00	80.00
LLTR Jacob Trouba/50	15.00	40.00
LLTS Teemu Selanne/25	40.00	100.00
LLZP Zach Parise/50	20.00	50.00

2014-15 The Cup Rookie Bookmarks Dual Autographs

Card	Low	High
DARBBK Burakovsky/Kuznetsov	40.00	100.00
DARBPK S.Percy/B.Kozun	15.00	40.00
DARBWR A.Wennberg/K.Rychel	25.00	60.00

2014-15 The Cup Rookie Gear Autographs

Card	Low	High
ARGAE Aaron Ekblad	50.00	125.00
ARGAW Alexander Wennberg	30.00	80.00
ARGBH Bo Horvat	50.00	125.00
ARGCL Curtis Lazar	20.00	50.00
ARGDS Damon Severson	20.00	50.00
ARGGR Griffin Reinhart	20.00	50.00
ARGJD Jonathan Drouin EXCH	40.00	100.00
ARGLD Leon Draisaitl	300.00	800.00
ARGSA Sven Andrighetto	25.00	60.00
ARGSR Sam Reinhart	80.00	200.00

2014-15 The Cup Scripted Sticks

Card	Low	High
SSAM Andy Moog	20.00	50.00
SSAO Alexander Ovechkin	80.00	200.00
SSBH Brett Hull	40.00	100.00
SSBL Rob Blake	20.00	50.00
SSBP Brad Park	15.00	40.00
SSCC Chris Chelios	20.00	50.00
SSES Eric Staal	25.00	60.00
SSGL Glenn Anderson	15.00	40.00
SSJI Jarome Iginla	25.00	60.00
SSLA Guy Lafleur	25.00	60.00
SSMB Martin Brodeur	50.00	125.00
SSMD Marcel Dionne	25.00	60.00
SSMG Marian Gaborik	20.00	50.00
SSML Mario Lemieux	80.00	200.00
SSMM Marty McSorley	15.00	40.00
SSMR Mike Richter	20.00	50.00
SSPR Patrick Roy	50.00	125.00
SSRB Ray Bourque	30.00	80.00
SSRF Ron Francis	25.00	60.00
SSSC Sidney Crosby	150.00	250.00
SSSL Steve Larmer	15.00	40.00
SSSP Jason Spezza	20.00	50.00
SSSY Steve Yzerman	50.00	125.00
SSTS Teemu Selanne	40.00	100.00
SSWC Wendel Clark	30.00	80.00
SSWG Wayne Gretzky	250.00	600.00

2014-15 The Cup Scripted Swatches

Card	Low	High
SWAO Alexander Ovechkin	50.00	100.00
SWBH Brett Hull	30.00	60.00
SWBR Dustin Brown	15.00	40.00
SWCC Chris Chelios	15.00	40.00
SWCO Chris Osgood	15.00	40.00
SWCP Carey Price	30.00	60.00
SWCW Cam Ward	15.00	40.00
SWDB David Backes	10.00	25.00
SWDS Denis Savard	12.00	30.00
SWDW Doug Weight	15.00	40.00
SWGN Gustav Nyquist	15.00	40.00
SWJL John LeClair	15.00	40.00
SWJP Jason Pominville	10.00	25.00
SWJS Jeff Skinner	20.00	50.00
SWJT John Tavares	40.00	80.00
SWKO Kyle Okposo	10.00	25.00
SWKT Kyle Turris	15.00	40.00
SWMB Martin Biron	12.00	30.00
SWMG Marian Gaborik	25.00	50.00
SWMP Max Pacioretty	25.00	50.00
SWMZ Mats Zuccarello	25.00	50.00
SWPD Pavel Datsyuk	25.00	50.00
SWPM Patrick Marleau	15.00	40.00
SWRK Ryan Kesler	15.00	40.00
SWRN Rick Nash	15.00	40.00

SWSA Joe Sakic EXCH 40.00 80.00
SWSM Sean Monahan 10.00 25.00
SWSW Shea Weber 15.00 40.00
SWTH Taylor Hall 30.00 60.00

2014-15 The Cup Signature Patches

SPAB Aleksander Barkov/99 20.00 50.00
SPAE Aaron Ekblad/99 30.00 80.00
SPAV Andrei Vasilevskiy/99 125.00 300.00
SPBH Bo Horvat/99 60.00 150.00
SPBI Ben Bishop/99 10.00 25.00
SPBR Brett Ritchie/99 12.00 30.00
SPCK Chris Kunitz/99 12.00 30.00
SPCW Cam Ward/99 12.00 30.00
SPDB Dustin Brown/99 12.00 30.00
SPDK David Krejci/99 12.00 30.00
SPDP Derrick Pouliot/99 15.00 40.00
SPDW Doug Weight/99 12.00 30.00
SPGN Gustav Nyquist/99 8.00 20.00
SPGR Mikael Granlund/99 10.00 25.00
SPJA Jake Allen/99 12.00 30.00
SPJB Jonathan Bernier/25 10.00 25.00
SPJG John Gibson/99 12.00 30.00
SPJH Jonathan Huberdeau/99 15.00 40.00
SPJI Jarome Iginla/25 15.00 40.00
SPJL John LeClair/99 12.00 30.00
SPJP Jason Pominville/99 8.00 20.00
SPJS Joe Sakic/25 30.00 80.00
SPJV James van Riemsdyk/99 10.00 25.00
SPKA Patrick Kane/25 30.00 80.00
SPLD Leon Draisaitl/99 400.00 1000.00
SPMB Martin Biron/99 10.00 25.00
SPMN Markus Naslund/99 12.00 30.00
SPOK Olaf Kolzig/99 12.00 30.00
SPOV Alexander Ovechkin/25 50.00 125.00
SPRB Ray Bourque/25 30.00 80.00
SPRJ Ryan Johansen/99 10.00 25.00
SPRK Ryan Kesler/99 12.00 30.00
SPRM Rod Brind'Amour/99 10.00 25.00
SPSG Shayne Gostisbehere/99 25.00 60.00
SPSH Scott Hartnell/99 8.00 20.00
SPSK Jeff Skinner/99 15.00 40.00
SPSM Sean Monahan/99 8.00 20.00
SPSP Jason Spezza/99 12.00 30.00
SPSR Sam Reinhart/99 50.00 125.00
SPSV Semyon Varlamov/99 12.00 30.00
SPTJ Tomas Jurco/99 8.00 20.00
SPVD Vincent Damphousse/99 10.00 25.00
SPZP Zach Parise/99 12.00 30.00

2014-15 The Cup Signature Patches Dual

DSPDN L.Draisaitl/D.Nurse/35 40.00 100.00
DSPHB Huberdeau/A.Barkov/35 25.00 60.00
DSPJL J.Jagr/M.Lemieux/15
DSPJT J.Pavelski/T.Hertl/15
DSPKB Kuznetsov/Burakovsky/35 15.00 40.00
DSPPH J.Pavelski/T.Hertl/35 20.00 50.00
DSPRL J.LeClair/J.Roenick/35 12.00 30.00
DSPRR S.Reinhart/G.Reinhart/35 15.00 40.00
DSPWW Doug Weight/35 12.00 30.00
DSPYL S.Yzerman/N.Lidstrom/15

2014-15 The Cup Signature Renditions

SRBC Bobby Clarke D 25.00 60.00
SRBE Jamie Benn D 15.00 40.00
SRBO Bobby Orr D 60.00 150.00
SRCR Sidney Crosby A 60.00 150.00
SRDS Darryl Sittler C 20.00 50.00
SRES Eric Staal E 20.00 50.00
SRGA Marian Gaborik D 15.00 40.00
SRGL Guy Lafleur C 20.00 50.00
SRGR Wayne Gretzky B 250.00 600.00
SRHU Brett Hull C 30.00 80.00
SRJI Jarome Iginla C 20.00 50.00
SRJJ Jaromir Jagr B 50.00 125.00
SRJP Joe Pavelski E 20.00 50.00
SRJV James van Riemsdyk E 12.00 30.00
SRLE Mario Lemieux A 60.00 150.00
SRMB Mike Bossy C 15.00 40.00
SRMD Marcel Dionne D 20.00 50.00
SRML Mario Lemieux A 60.00 150.00
SRMM Mark Messier A 30.00 80.00
SRPD Pavel Datsyuk C 25.00 60.00
SRPE Phil Esposito A 25.00 60.00
SRPR Carey Price D 30.00 80.00
SRRB Ray Bourque B 25.00 60.00
SRSC Sidney Crosby B 60.00 150.00
SRSE Teemu Selanne B 30.00 80.00
SRSY Steve Yzerman A 40.00 100.00
SRTA John Tavares E 25.00 60.00
SRTH Taylor Hall D 15.00 40.00
SRTS Teemu Selanne C 30.00 80.00
SRWA Wayne Gretzky B 250.00 600.00
SRWC Wendel Clark E 25.00 60.00
SRWG Wayne Gretzky A 250.00 600.00
SRYZ Steve Yzerman B 40.00 100.00
SRZP Zach Parise C 15.00 40.00

2014-15 The Cup Signature Renditions Combos

SRCGM W.Gretzky/M.Messier 2000.00 5000.00
SRCHD P.Datsyuk/B.Hull 50.00 125.00
SRCJB M.Brodeur/J.Jagr 80.00 200.00
SRCOT J.Tavares/K.Okposo 40.00 100.00
SRCYH D.Hasek/S.Yzerman 60.00 150.00
SRCDRAFT Ekb/Rnht/Drstl EX 125.00 300.00

2014-15 The Cup Trios Jerseys

C3ANA Gtzlf/Kslr/Prry 6.00 15.00
C3AVS Skc/Ry/Blke 10.00 25.00
C3BEES Ots/Brge/Mrry 6.00 15.00
C3BOLTS Drn/Vslvsky/Nmstnkv 12.00 30.00
C3BRUINS Brgrn/Chra/Rsk 5.00 12.00
C3BUF Mlsn/Grgnsns/Hdgsn 3.00 8.00
C3CAN Mllr/Sdn/Sdn 5.00 12.00
C3CAPS Ovchkn/Bckstrm/Kzntsv 15.00 40.00
C3CAR Stl/Sknnr/Lndhlm 5.00 12.00
C3CB Sd/Hssa/Shrp 4.00 10.00
C3CBJ Wnnbrg/Dno/Rychl 6.00 15.00
C3CGY Mnhn/Gdru/Hllr 12.00 30.00
C3CHI Trvnn/Clndnng/Drllt 8.00 20.00
C3CHIC Crwfrd/Kth/Sbrk 5.00 12.00
C3COL Ignla/Dchne/Lndskg 5.00 12.00
C3D Ekbld/Nrse/Plt 10.00 25.00
C3DAL Sgn/Spzza/Bnn 8.00 20.00
C3DEF Wbr/Dghty/Sbbn 5.00 12.00
C3DET Zttrbrg/Krnwll/Dtsyk 6.00 15.00
C3EDM Hll/NgntHpkns/Ebrle 5.00 12.00
C3FIN Rsk/Rnne/Nmi 5.00 12.00
C3FLA Brkv/Hbrdu/Bjgstd 6.00 15.00
C3GOALS Sgn/Nsh/Pvlski 5.00 12.00
C3GR8 Stmks/Ovchkn/Prry 15.00 40.00
C3HAWKS Shrp/Tws/Kne 8.00 20.00
C3JAC Jhnsn/Hrtnll/Bbrvsky 6.00 15.00
C3JETS Whlr/Trba/Schfle 6.00 15.00
C3KINGS Qck/Kptr/Dghty 6.00 15.00
C3LAK Crtr/Tffli/Prsn 4.00 10.00
C3MET Nsh/Tvrs/Jgr 12.00 30.00
C3MTL Prce/Prtty/Sbbn 8.00 20.00
C3NET Vslvsky/Brngtn/Ortio 12.00 30.00
C3NJD Jgr/Hnrqe/Schndr 12.00 30.00
C3NYI Tvrs/Okpso/Strme 6.00 15.00
C3NYR Nsh/St.Ls/Zccrllo 4.00 10.00
C3OTT Ryn/Zbnjd/Trrs 5.00 12.00
C3PHI Schnn/Vrck/Grx 4.00 10.00
C3PIT Kntz/Flry/Mlkn 8.00 20.00
C3PRED Rnne/Wbr/Jns 4.00 10.00
C3ROOK1 Drn/Gdru/Rnhrt 15.00 40.00
C3ROOK2 Drn/Ekbld/Drstl 20.00 50.00
C3SHARKS Pvlski/Mrlu/Hrtl 5.00 12.00
C3SJS Thrntn/Ctre/Nmi 6.00 15.00
C3ST Bcks/Trsnko/Oshe 5.00 12.00
C3STARS Gtzlf/Tws/Grx 6.00 15.00
C3TBL Hdmn/Bshp/Stmks 8.00 20.00
C3TML Brnr/Kssl/vn Rmsdk 4.00 10.00
C3TOR Kssl/Kdri/vn Rmsdk 5.00 12.00
C3VAN Sdn/Kssn/Brrws 5.00 12.00
C3WAS Bckstrm/Crlsn/Hltby 5.00 12.00
C3WILD Prse/Pmnvlle/Grnlnd 4.00 10.00
C3WIN Pvlc/Kne/Schfle 6.00 15.00
C3ZONA Ggnr/Dn/EkmnLrssn 4.00 10.00

2015-16 The Cup

1 Wayne Gretzky 15.00 40.00
2 Corey Perry 5.00 12.00
3 Ryan Getzlaf 3.00 8.00
4 Teemu Selanne 6.00 15.00
5 Oliver Ekman-Larsson 3.00 8.00
6 Anthony Duclair 2.50 6.00
7 Tuukka Rask 4.00 10.00
8 David Krejci 3.00 8.00
9 Bobby Orr 12.00 30.00
10 Patrice Bergeron 4.00 10.00
11 Rasmus Ristolainen 2.00 5.00
12 Ryan O'Reilly 3.00 8.00
13 Jiri Hudler 2.50 6.00
14 Johnny Gaudreau 5.00 12.00
15 Sean Monahan 3.00 8.00
16 Cam Ward 3.00 8.00
17 Justin Faulk 2.50 6.00
18 Duncan Keith 2.50 6.00
19 Jonathan Toews 5.00 12.00
20 Patrick Kane 6.00 15.00
21 Jarome Iginla 4.00 10.00
22 Matt Duchene 3.00 8.00
23 Nathan MacKinnon 12.00 30.00
24 Joe Sakic 6.00 15.00
25 Patrick Roy 8.00 20.00
26 Sergei Bobrovsky 5.00 12.00
27 Scott Hartnell 2.00 5.00
28 Jason Spezza 3.00 8.00
29 Tyler Seguin 4.00 10.00
30 Jamie Benn 3.00 8.00
31 Tomas Tatar 2.00 5.00
32 Pavel Datsyuk 5.00 12.00
33 Henrik Zetterberg 4.00 10.00
34 Steve Yzerman 8.00 20.00
35 Dominik Hasek 5.00 12.00
36 Paul Coffey 3.00 8.00
37 Taylor Hall 3.00 8.00
38 Ryan Nugent-Hopkins 3.00 8.00
39 Roberto Luongo 5.00 12.00
40 Aaron Ekblad 4.00 10.00
41 Jaromir Jagr 10.00 25.00
42 Jonathan Quick 4.00 10.00
43 Tyler Toffoli 3.00 8.00
44 Anze Kopitar 5.00 12.00
45 Zach Parise 3.00 8.00
46 Jason Zucker 3.00 8.00
47 Alex Galchenyuk 2.00 5.00
48 Guy Lafleur 4.00 10.00
49 Carey Price 6.00 15.00
50 Max Pacioretty 4.00 10.00
51 Filip Forsberg 5.00 12.00
52 Shea Weber 2.50 6.00
53 Pekka Rinne 3.00 8.00
54 Martin Brodeur 8.00 20.00
55 Cory Schneider 3.00 8.00
56 Adam Henrique 2.50 6.00
57 Anders Lee 3.00 8.00
58 John Tavares 5.00 12.00
59 Jaroslav Halak 3.00 8.00
60 Ryan Strome 3.00 8.00
61 Henrik Lundqvist 8.00 20.00
62 Rick Nash 3.00 8.00
63 Mats Zuccarello 3.00 8.00
64 Mark Messier 6.00 15.00
65 Kyle Turris 2.50 6.00
66 Erik Karlsson 4.00 10.00
67 Mark Stone 4.00 10.00
68 Mike Hoffman 3.00 8.00
69 Claude Giroux 5.00 12.00
70 Jakub Voracek 2.50 6.00
71 Steve Mason 2.50 6.00
72 Sidney Crosby 12.00 30.00
73 Evgeni Malkin 6.00 15.00
74 Mario Lemieux 12.00 30.00
75 Marc-Andre Fleury 6.00 15.00
76 Peter Forsberg 4.00 10.00
77 Brent Burns 3.00 8.00
78 Joe Pavelski 4.00 10.00
79 Patrick Marleau 3.00 8.00
80 Jori Lehtera 2.00 5.00
81 Vladimir Tarasenko 4.00 10.00
82 Jake Allen 3.00 8.00
83 Victor Hedman 4.00 10.00
84 Steven Stamkos 6.00 15.00
85 Nikita Kucherov 6.00 15.00
86 Morgan Rielly 4.00 10.00
87 James van Riemsdyk 2.50 6.00
88 Doug Gilmour 5.00 12.00
89 Nazem Kadri 4.00 10.00
90 Ryan Miller 3.00 8.00
91 Henrik Sedin 4.00 10.00
92 Daniel Sedin 4.00 10.00
93 Pavel Bure 3.00 8.00
94 Evgeny Kuznetsov 4.00 10.00
95 Alexander Ovechkin 12.00 30.00
96 Nicklas Backstrom 3.00 8.00
97 Braden Holtby 4.00 10.00
98 Blake Wheeler 3.00 8.00
99 Mark Scheifele 5.00 12.00
100 Andrew Ladd 2.00 5.00
101 Joonas Kemppainen AU RC 6.00 15.00
102 Byron Froese AU RC 8.00 20.00
103 Frank Vatrano AU RC 12.00 30.00
104 Adam Pelech AU RC 8.00 20.00
105 Brett Kulak AU RC 8.00 20.00
106 Christoph Bertschy AU RC 8.00 20.00
107 Tanner Kero AU RC 12.00 30.00
108 Michael Keranen AU RC 8.00 20.00
109 Daniel Carr AU RC 8.00 20.00
110 Max McCormick AU RC 8.00 20.00
111 Petr Straka AU RC 6.00 15.00
112 Sergei Kalinin AU RC 15.00 40.00
113 Tyler Randell AU RC 10.00 25.00
114 Viktor Svedberg JSY AU RC 12.00 30.00
115 Matt Murray JSY AU RC 150.00 300.00
116 Jacob Slavin JSY AU RC 25.00 60.00
117 Linus Ullmark JSY AU RC 30.00 80.00
118 Juuse Saros JSY AU RC 80.00 200.00
119 Andrew Copp JSY AU RC 15.00 40.00
120 Chris Wideman JSY AU RC 15.00 40.00
121 Sergei Plotnikov JSY AU RC 15.00 40.00
122 Phil Di Giuseppe JSY AU RC 15.00 40.00
123 Joseph Blandisi JSY AU RC 15.00 40.00
124 Louis Domingue JSY AU RC 15.00 40.00
125 Keegan Lowe JSY AU RC 15.00 40.00
126 Mike Condon JSY AU RC 15.00 40.00
127 Chris Driedger JSY AU RC 25.00 60.00
128 Mike McCarron JSY AU RC 20.00 50.00
129 Joonas Korpisalo JSY AU RC 60.00 150.00
130 Robby Fabbri JSY AU RC 20.00 50.00
131 Anton Slepyshev JSY AU RC 10.00 25.00
132 Mark Alt JSY AU RC 10.00 25.00
133 Jean-Francois Berube JSY AU RC 12.00 30.00
134 Joonas Donskoi JSY AU RC 15.00 40.00
135 Charles Hudon JSY AU RC 15.00 40.00
136 Mattias Janmark JSY AU RC 15.00 40.00
137 Matt O'Connor JSY AU RC 12.00 30.00
138 Taylor Leier JSY AU RC 15.00 40.00
139 Viktor Arvidsson JSY AU RC 30.00 80.00
140 Garret Sparks JSY AU RC 15.00 40.00
141 Dylan DeMelo JSY AU RC 12.00 30.00
142 Colin Miller JSY AU RC 12.00 30.00
143 Sam Brittain JSY AU RC 15.00 40.00
144 Ben Hutton JSY AU RC 15.00 40.00
145 Antoine Bibeau JSY AU RC 15.00 40.00
146 Stefan Noesen JSY AU RC 10.00 25.00
147 David Musil JSY AU RC 12.00 30.00
148 Ronalds Kenins JSY AU RC 15.00 40.00
149 Radek Faksa JSY AU RC 15.00 40.00
150 Joel Edmundson JSY AU RC 12.00 30.00
151 Mackenzie Skapski JSY AU RC 15.00 40.00
152 Devin Shore JSY AU RC 15.00 40.00
153 Jujhar Khaira JSY AU RC 12.00 30.00
154 Andreas Athanasiou JSY AU RC 40.00 100.00
155 Jordan Weal JSY AU RC 10.00 25.00
156 Nick Cousins JSY AU RC 12.00 30.00
157 Jacob de la Rose JSY AU RC 15.00 40.00
158 Henrik Samuelsson JSY AU RC 10.00 25.00
159 Duncan Siemens JSY AU RC 15.00 40.00
160 Kyle Baun JSY AU RC 15.00 40.00
161 Derek Forbort JSY AU RC 12.00 30.00
162 Slater Koekkoek JSY AU RC 10.00 25.00
163 Laurent Dauphin JSY AU RC 15.00 40.00
164 Vincent Hinostroza JSY AU RC 10.00 25.00
165 Colton Parayko JSY AU RC 25.00 60.00
166 Mikko Rantanen JSY AU RC 250.00 600.00
167 Nicolas Petan JSY AU RC 15.00 40.00
168 Daniel Sprong JSY AU RC 20.00 50.00
169 Jared McCann JSY AU RC 20.00 50.00
170 Gustav Olofsson JSY AU RC 15.00 40.00
171 Josh Anderson JSY AU RC 25.00 60.00
172 Malcolm Subban JSY AU RC 25.00 60.00
173 Brendan Ranford JSY AU RC 12.00 30.00
174 Shea Theodore JSY AU RC 25.00 60.00
175 Zachary Fucale JSY AU RC 15.00 40.00
176 Emile Poirier JSY AU RC 12.00 30.00
177 Matt Puempel JSY AU RC 12.00 30.00
178 Nikolay Goldobin JSY AU RC 15.00 40.00
179 Kevin Fiala JSY AU RC 30.00 80.00
180 Brock McGinn JSY AU RC 15.00 40.00
181 Nick Ritchie JSY AU RC 15.00 40.00
182 Shane Prince JSY AU RC 10.00 25.00
183 Jake Virtanen JSY AU RC 25.00 60.00
184 Anthony Stolarz JSY AU RC 40.00 100.00
185 Brady Skjei JSY AU RC 12.00 30.00
186 Ryan Hartman JSY AU RC 20.00 50.00
187 Connor Hellebuyck JSY AU RC 200.00 500.00
188 Hunter Shinkaruk JSY AU RC 15.00 40.00
189 Brendan Gaunce JSY AU RC 20.00 50.00
190 Brett Pesce JSY AU RC 12.00 30.00
191 Chandler Stephenson JSY AU RC 20.00 50.00
192 Noah Hanifin JSY AU RC 25.00 60.00
193 Oscar Lindberg JSY AU RC 15.00 40.00
194 Sam Bennett JSY AU/99 RC 100.00 250.00
195 Artemi Panarin JSY AU/99 RC 350.00 600.00
196 Nikolaj Ehlers JSY AU/99 RC 350.00 600.00
197 Connor McDavid
JSY AU/99 RC 10000.00 20000.00
198 Max Domi JSY AU/99 RC 150.00 400.00
199 Dylan Larkin JSY AU/99 RC 350.00 700.00
200A Jack Eichel JSY/99 RC 400.00 1000.00
200B Jack Eichel JSY AU/99 XRC 600.00 1500.00

2015-16 The Cup Gold

*ROOKIES: .6X TO 1.50X BASIC CARDS
115 Matt Murray JSY AU 200.00 500.00
126 Mike Condon JSY AU 15.00 40.00
128 Mike McCarron JSY AU 12.00 30.00
129 Joonas Korpisalo JSY AU 120.00 300.00
130 Robby Fabbri JSY AU 40.00 100.00
135 Charles Hudon JSY AU 40.00 100.00
139 Viktor Arvidsson JSY AU 50.00 125.00
166 Mikko Rantanen JSY AU 200.00 500.00
168 Daniel Sprong JSY AU 30.00 80.00
171 Josh Anderson JSY AU 50.00 125.00
183 Jake Virtanen JSY AU 40.00 100.00
186 Ryan Hartman JSY AU 25.00 60.00
187 Connor Hellebuyck JSY AU 300.00 800.00

2015-16 The Cup Gold Spectrum

*ROOKIES: .5X TO 1.25X BASIC CARDS
115 Matt Murray AU 60.00 150.00
129 Joonas Korpisalo AU 80.00 200.00
130 Robby Fabbri AU 20.00 50.00
135 Charles Hudon AU 15.00 40.00
139 Viktor Arvidsson AU 25.00 60.00
166 Mikko Rantanen AU 80.00 200.00
168 Daniel Sprong AU 20.00 50.00
171 Josh Anderson AU 20.00 50.00
183 Jake Virtanen AU 20.00 50.00
187 Connor Hellebuyck AU 80.00 200.00

2015-16 The Cup 12-Way Relics

12WRC1 ROOKIES 200.00 500.00
12WCOLO AVS 50.00 125.00
12WVET1 VETS 50.00 120.00
12WFLYERS FLYERS 25.00 60.00
12WKINGS KINGS 20.00 50.00

2015-16 The Cup 6-Way Relics

6WCAN CANADA 25.00 60.00
6WNET NETMINDERS 25.00 60.00
6WRC1 ROOKIES 1 150.00 400.00
6WRC2 ROOKIES 2 50.00 125.00
6WVAN CANUCKS 12.00 30.00
6WVET VETS 40.00 100.00
6WARIZ COYOTES 20.00 50.00
6WHAWKS BLACK HAWKS 40.00 100.00
6WWINGS RED WINGS 30.00 80.00
6WFLAMES FLAMES 30.00 80.00
6WOILERS OILERS 150.00 400.00
6WSABRES SABRES 40.00 100.00

2015-16 The Cup Brilliance Autographs

BAI Artus Irbe 8.00 20.00
BAK Anze Kopitar 15.00 40.00
BAO Alexander Ovechkin 80.00 200.00
BBO Bobby Orr 60.00 150.00
BCM Connor McDavid 1200.00 3000.00
BJB Jamie Benn 10.00 25.00
BJT Jonathan Toews 15.00 40.00
BJV Jake Virtanen 12.00 30.00
BML Mario Lemieux 40.00 100.00
BMM Mark Messier 20.00 50.00
BMR Mikko Rantanen 100.00 250.00
BNE Nikolaj Ehlers 20.00 50.00
BPB Pavel Bure 10.00 25.00
BPR Patrick Roy 40.00 100.00
BRF Robby Fabbri 12.00 30.00
BSB Sam Bennett 30.00 80.00
BSC Sidney Crosby 100.00 250.00
BTH Taylor Hall 10.00 25.00
BWG Wayne Gretzky 200.00 500.00
BZF Zachary Fucale 8.00 20.00

2015-16 The Cup Enshrinements

EAE Aaron Ekblad/99 12.00 30.00
EAG Alex Galchenyuk/99 6.00 15.00
EAI Arturs Irbe 8.00 20.00
EAM Al MacInnis/99 12.00 30.00
EAO Alexander Ovechkin/25 150.00 400.00
EBO Bobby Orr/25 80.00 200.00
ECM Connor McDavid/99 2000.00 5000.00
EDH Dominik Hasek/99 25.00 60.00
EDL Dylan Larkin/99 30.00 80.00
EGA Glenn Anderson/99 8.00 20.00
EGC Guy Carbonneau/99 8.00 20.00
EJD Jonathan Drouin/99 8.00 20.00
EJG Johnny Gaudreau/99 15.00 40.00
EJK Jari Kurri/99 10.00 25.00
EJP Joe Pavelski/99 12.00 30.00
EJT Jonathan Toews/99 25.00 60.00
EML Mario Lemieux/25 80.00 200.00
ENE Nikolaj Ehlers/99 20.00 50.00
EPB Pavel Bure/99 25.00 60.00
EPR Patrick Roy/25 60.00 150.00
ERM Ryan Miller/99 10.00 25.00
ESB Sam Bennett/99 20.00 50.00
ESC Sidney Crosby/25 250.00 350.00
ESE Tyler Seguin/99 12.00 30.00
ETF Theoren Fleury/99 12.00 30.00
ETS Teemu Selanne/99 25.00 60.00
EWG Wayne Gretzky/25 300.00 800.00
EZF Zachary Fucale/99 8.00 20.00

2015-16 The Cup Enshrinements Dual

E2BS J.Benn/T.Seguin/25 20.00 50.00
E2JE J.Jagr/A.Ekblad/25 30.00 80.00
E2MB M.Messier/P.Bure/25 60.00 150.00
E2RH L.Robitaille/B.Hull/25 40.00 100.00

2015-16 The Cup Foundations Jerseys

CFAB Aleksander Barkov 8.00 20.00
CFAE Aaron Ekblad 6.00 15.00
CFAG Alex Galchenyuk 3.00 8.00
CFAL Andrew Ladd 3.00 8.00
CFAO Alexander Ovechkin 20.00 50.00
CFAP Artemi Panarin 20.00 50.00
CFCM Connor McDavid 400.00 1000.00
CFCP Carey Price 10.00 25.00
CFCW Cam Ward 5.00 12.00
CFDL Dylan Larkin 15.00 40.00
CFEM Evgeni Malkin 10.00 25.00
CFGF Grant Fuhr 6.00 15.00
CFGH Glenn Hall 5.00 12.00
CFJC John Carlson 5.00 12.00
CFJE Jack Eichel 20.00 50.00
CFJF Justin Faulk 4.00 10.00
CFJG Johnny Gaudreau 8.00 20.00
CFJH Jiri Hudler 4.00 10.00
CFJJ Jaromir Jagr 15.00 40.00
CFJS Joe Sakic 8.00 20.00
CFJT John Tavares 8.00 20.00
CFLE Anders Lee 5.00 12.00
CFMA Mark Scheifele 8.00 20.00
CFMD Max Domi 10.00 25.00
CFMH Mike Hoffman 3.00 8.00
CFML Mario Lemieux 20.00 50.00
CFMS Martin St. Louis 5.00 12.00
CFNE Nikolaj Ehlers 10.00 25.00
CFNR Nick Ritchie 5.00 12.00
CFPB Pavel Bure 6.00 15.00
CFPD Pavel Datsyuk 8.00 20.00
CFPR Patrick Roy 12.00 30.00
CFRF Robby Fabbri 6.00 15.00
CFRM Ryan Miller 5.00 12.00
CFRN Rick Nash 5.00 12.00
CFSB Sam Bennett 15.00 40.00
CFSC Sidney Crosby 20.00 50.00
CFSY Steve Yzerman 12.00 30.00
CFTH Taylor Hall 5.00 12.00
CFTO Jonathan Toews 8.00 20.00
CFTT Tyler Toffoli 5.00 12.00
CFWG Wayne Gretzky 30.00 80.00
CFZF Zachary Fucale 4.00 10.00

2015-16 The Cup Honorable Numbers

HNAG Alex Galchenyuk/27 15.00 40.00
HNAL Anders Lee/27 25.00 60.00
HNCW Cam Ward/30 25.00 60.00
HNDE Derek Stepan/21 15.00 40.00
HNEK Evgeny Kuznetsov/92 30.00 80.00
HNJH Jiri Hudler/24 20.00 50.00
HNJJ Jaromir Jagr/68 80.00 200.00
HNJT Jonathan Toews/19 40.00 100.00
HNMF Marc-Andre Fleury/29 50.00 125.00
HNMH Mike Hoffman/68 15.00 40.00
HNMP Max Pacioretty/67 25.00 60.00
HNMR Morgan Rielly/44 25.00 60.00
HNMS Mark Stone/61 30.00 80.00
HNNM Nathan MacKinnon/29 100.00 250.00
HNPF Peter Forsberg/21 50.00 125.00
HNPT Pierre Turgeon/87 20.00 50.00
HNRB Rod Brind'Amour/17 20.00 50.00
HNRO Ryan O'Reilly/90 25.00 60.00
HNSC Mark Scheifele/55 40.00 100.00
HNST Martin St. Louis/26 25.00 60.00
HNTT Tyler Toffoli/73 25.00 60.00
HNVT Vladimir Tarasenko/91 30.00 80.00
HNWP Willi Plett/25 25.00 60.00

2015-16 The Cup Honorable Numbers Dual

DHNGL A.Galchenyuk/A.Lee/27 25.00 60.00
DHNMW R.Miller/C.Ward/30 25.00 60.00
DHNVS D.Stepan/J.van Reimsdyk/21 25.00 60.00

2015-16 The Cup Honorable Numbers Rookies

HNRCM Connor McDavid/97 1500.00 4000.00
HNRDL Dylan Larkin/71 60.00 150.00
HNRJM Jared McCann/91 15.00 40.00
HNRMD Max Domi/16 30.00 80.00
HNRNE Nikolaj Ehlers/27 60.00 150.00
HNRNR Nick Ritchie/37 15.00 40.00
HNRSB Sam Bennett/93 15.00 40.00
HNRZF Zachary Fucale/30 20.00 50.00

2015-16 The Cup Limited Logos Autographs

LLAG Alex Galchenyuk/50 15.00 40.00
LLAK Anze Kopitar/50 40.00 100.00
LLBB Ben Bishop/50 20.00 50.00
LLBH Brett Hull/25 50.00 125.00
LLBL Rob Blake/50 25.00 60.00
LLCM Connor McDavid/50 3000.00 8000.00
LLCP Carey Price/25 50.00 125.00
LLDK David Krejci/50 25.00 60.00
LLDO Max Domi/50 25.00 60.00
LLDU Matt Duchene/50 25.00 60.00
LLEK Evgeny Kuznetsov/50 30.00 80.00
LLEM Evgeni Malkin/25 50.00 125.00
LLJB Jamie Benn/50 25.00 60.00
LLJC John Carlson/50 25.00 60.00
LLJE Jack Eichel/50 (No Auto) 100.00 250.00
LLJF Justin Faulk/50 20.00 50.00
LLJG Johnny Gaudreau/50 40.00 100.00
LLJJ Jaromir Jagr/50 80.00 200.00
LLJP Joe Pavelski/50 30.00 80.00
LLJR Jeremy Roenick/50 25.00 60.00
LLJS Joe Sakic/25 50.00 125.00
LLJT Jonathan Toews/25 40.00 100.00
LLMA Nathan MacKinnon/50 100.00 250.00
LLMD Marcel Dionne/50 30.00 80.00
LLMF Marc-Andre Fleury/50 50.00 125.00
LLMH Mike Hoffman/50 15.00 40.00
LLMM Mike Modano/50 40.00 100.00
LLMP Max Pacioretty/50 25.00 60.00
LLMS Martin St. Louis/50 25.00 60.00
LLNE Nikolaj Ehlers/50 50.00 125.00
LLNH Noah Hanifin/50 40.00 100.00
LLON Owen Nolan/50 25.00 60.00
LLOV Alexander Ovechkin/25 100.00 250.00
LLPC Paul Coffey/25 25.00 60.00
LLPT Pierre Turgeon/50 25.00 60.00
LLRB Ray Bourque/25 40.00 100.00
LLRM Ryan Miller/50 25.00 60.00
LLSB Sam Bennett/50 80.00 200.00
LLSE Tyler Seguin/50 25.00 60.00
LLTA John Tavares/50 40.00 100.00
LLTH Taylor Hall/50 25.00 60.00
LLTJ Tyler Johnson/50 15.00 40.00
LLTS Teemu Selanne/25 50.00 125.00

2015-16 The Cup Monumental Sticks

MSDD Drew Doughty/20 25.00 60.00
MSDS Daniel Sedin/20 20.00 50.00
MSHZ Henrik Zetterberg/20 25.00 60.00
MSJB Jean Beliveau/20 25.00 60.00
MSJQ Jonathan Quick/20 25.00 60.00
MSLR Luc Robitaille/20 20.00 50.00
MSMB Martin Brodeur/20 50.00 125.00
MSML Mario Lemieux/20 80.00 200.00
MSPB Patrice Bergeron/20 25.00 60.00
MSPF Peter Forsberg/20 40.00 100.00
MSPK Phil Kessel/20 20.00 50.00
MSPS P.K. Subban/20 25.00 60.00
MSRG Ryan Getzlaf/20 20.00 50.00

2015-16 The Cup Monumental Sticks Autographs

AMSFP Felix Potvin/20 80.00 200.00
AMSRB Rob Blake/20 50.00 125.00
AMSRM Ryan Miller/20 50.00 125.00

2015-16 The Cup Monumental Sticks Dual Autographs

DMSLG B.Guerin/J.LeClair/20 50.00 125.00

2015-16 The Cup Quads Jerseys

C4CAN Bure/Sedin/Sedin/Virtanen 6.00 15.00
C4CAP Ovechkin
Carlson/Backstrom/Holtby 20.00 50.00
C4EDM Gretzky/Hall
Eberle/McDavid 80.00 200.00
C4FLO Bure/Jagr/Huberdeau/Luongo 15.00 40.00
C4NYR Fleury/St. Louis
Nash/Lundqvist 12.00 30.00
C4TBL Kucherov/Hedman
Johnson/Stamkos 10.00 25.00
C4ARIZ Roenick/Hanzal
Ekman-Larsson/Domi 10.00 25.00
C4HABS Pacioretty/Galchenyuk
Price/Condon 10.00 25.00
C4JETS Wheeler/Scheifele
Ehlers/Hellebuyck 20.00 50.00
C4RET1 Messier/Yzerman
Lemieux/Sakic 20.00 50.00
C4RET2 Robinson/Bourque
Coffey/Blake 8.00 20.00
C4RET4 Forsberg/LeClair
Hextall/Roenick 10.00 25.00
C4RET5 Brodeur/Roy/Hall/Fuhr 12.00 30.00
C4RIV1 Zuccarello/Tavares/Nash/Lee 8.00 20.00
C4RIV2 Bergeron/Subban
Eriksson/Pacioretty 6.00 15.00
C4RIV3 Hall/Gaudreau
Eberle/Monahan 8.00 20.00
C4BLUES Tarasenko/Steen
Shattenkirk/Backes 6.00 15.00
C4DUCKS Perry/Getzlaf
Ritchie/Theodore 8.00 20.00
C4HAWKS Savard/Toews
Kane/Panarin 20.00 50.00
C4KINGS Toffoli/Kopitar/Carter/Brown 8.00 20.00
C4SABRE Hawerchuk
Ristolainen/O'Reilly/Eichel 20.00 50.00
C4STARS Spezza/Benn
Seguin/Lehtonen 6.00 15.00
C4BRUINS Bourque
Bergeron/Krejci/Rask 8.00 20.00
C4FLAMES Fleury/Monahan
Gaudreau/Bennett 15.00 40.00
C4FLYERS Simmonds/Giroux
Voracek/Schenn 6.00 15.00
C4POINT1 Jagr/Thornton
Iginla/Hossa 15.00 40.00
C4POINT2 Marleau/Elias
Sedin/Datsyuk 8.00 20.00
C4VEZINA Price/Rask/Bobrovsky
Lundqvist 12.00 30.00

2015-16 The Cup Rookie Bookmarks Dual Autographs

DARBFP R.Fabbri/C.Parayko 30.00 80.00
DARBFR K.Fiala/M.Rantanen 200.00 500.00
DARBHF Z.Fucale/C.Hudon 20.00 50.00
DARBLS O.Lindberg/D.Sprong 25.00 60.00
DARBME N.Ehlers/J.McCann 40.00 100.00
DARBML C.McDavid/D.Larkin 600.00 1000.00
DARBPP S.Prince/M.Puempel 15.00 40.00
DARBSC M.Subban/M.Condon 30.00 80.00
DARBVS J.Virtanen/H.Shinkaruk 25.00 60.00

2015-16 The Cup Rookie Gear Relic Autographs

ARGAP Artemi Panarin 60.00 150.00
ARGCH Charles Hudon 15.00 40.00
ARGCM Connor McDavid 600.00 1000.00
ARGDL Dylan Larkin 100.00 250.00
ARGHS Hunter Shinkaruk 15.00 40.00
ARGJM Jared McCann 20.00 50.00
ARGJV Jake Virtanen 20.00 50.00
ARGKF Kevin Fiala 20.00 50.00
ARGMC Mike Condon 15.00 40.00
ARGMR Mikko Rantanen 125.00 300.00
ARGMS Malcolm Subban 25.00 60.00
ARGNE Nikolaj Ehlers 30.00 80.00
ARGNG Nikolay Goldobin 15.00 40.00
ARGNH Noah Hanifin 25.00 60.00
ARGNR Nick Ritchie 15.00 40.00
ARGOL Oscar Lindberg 15.00 40.00
ARGSB Sam Bennett 50.00 125.00
ARGZF Zachary Fucale 12.00 30.00

2015-16 The Cup Scripted Sticks

SSAK Anze Kopitar 30.00 80.00
SSAO Alexander Ovechkin 600.00 1500.00
SSBC Bobby Clarke 30.00 80.00
SSBG Brendan Gallagher 20.00 50.00
SSBS Borje Salming 20.00 50.00
SSCJ Curtis Joseph 25.00 60.00
SSCP Carey Price 40.00 100.00
SSDG Doug Gilmour 25.00 60.00
SSDH Dominik Hasek 30.00 80.00
SSDS Denis Savard 20.00 50.00
SSFP Felix Potvin 30.00 80.00
SSJI Jarome Iginla 25.00 60.00
SSJJ Jaromir Jagr 60.00 150.00
SSJK Jari Kurri 20.00 50.00
SSJS Joe Sakic 40.00 100.00
SSLR Larry Robinson 20.00 50.00
SSMB Martin Brodeur 50.00 125.00
SSML Mario Lemieux 80.00 200.00
SSMM Mark Messier 40.00 100.00
SSMP Max Pacioretty 20.00 50.00
SSPR Patrick Roy 50.00 125.00
SSRB Rob Blake 20.00 50.00
SSRO Luc Robitaille 20.00 50.00
SSSC Sidney Crosby 80.00 200.00
SSSY Steve Yzerman 50.00 125.00
SSTS Teemu Selanne 40.00 100.00

2015-16 The Cup Scripted Swatches

SWAK Anze Kopitar 40.00 100.00
SWAO Alexander Ovechkin 600.00 1500.00
SWCM Connor McDavid 500.00 800.00
SWDL Dylan Larkin 50.00 125.00
SWEM Evgeni Malkin 50.00 125.00
SWJB Jamie Benn 25.00 60.00
SWJF Justin Faulk 20.00 50.00
SWJG Johnny Gaudreau 40.00 100.00
SWJI Jarome Iginla 30.00 80.00
SWJJ Jaromir Jagr 80.00 200.00
SWJT Jonathan Toews 40.00 100.00
SWJV Jake Virtanen 30.00 80.00
SWMD Max Domi 50.00 125.00
SWML Mario Lemieux 100.00 250.00
SWNM Nathan MacKinnon 100.00 250.00
SWON Owen Nolan 25.00 60.00
SWPC Paul Coffey 25.00 60.00
SWPR Carey Price 50.00 125.00
SWRF Robby Fabbri 30.00 80.00
SWRO Patrick Roy 60.00 150.00
SWSB Sam Bennett 80.00 200.00
SWSC Sidney Crosby 100.00 250.00
SWTH Taylor Hall 25.00 60.00
SWTS Teemu Selanne 50.00 125.00
SWWG Wayne Gretzky 300.00 800.00
SWZF Zachary Fucale 20.00 50.00

2015-16 The Cup Signature Patches

SPAE Aaron Ekblad/99 20.00 50.00
SPAK Anze Kopitar/99 25.00 60.00
SPAO Alexander Ovechkin/25 800.00 2000.00
SPBG Brendan Gallagher/99 15.00 40.00
SPCC Chris Chelios/99 15.00 40.00
SPCM Connor McDavid/99 250.00 600.00
SPDL Dylan Larkin/99 50.00 125.00
SPDS Daniel Sprong/99 20.00 50.00
SPHS Hunter Shinkaruk/99 15.00 40.00
SPJB Jamie Benn/99 15.00 40.00
SPJG Johnny Gaudreau/99 25.00 60.00
SPJH Jiri Hudler/99 12.00 30.00
SPJI Jarome Iginla/99 20.00 50.00
SPJJ Jaromir Jagr/25 50.00 125.00
SPJM Jared McCann/99 20.00 50.00
SPJP Joe Pavelski/99 20.00 50.00
SPJR Jeremy Roenick/25 25.00 60.00
SPJT John Tavares/99 25.00 60.00
SPKF Kevin Fiala/99 30.00 80.00
SPLR Luc Robitaille/99 15.00 40.00
SPMC Mike Condon/99 20.00 50.00
SPMF Marc-Andre Fleury/99 30.00 80.00
SPMG Marian Gaborik/25 15.00 40.00
SPMP Max Pacioretty/99 15.00 40.00
SPMR Mikko Rantanen/99 80.00 200.00
SPMS Mark Stone/99 20.00 50.00
SPNE Nikolaj Ehlers/99 30.00 80.00
SPNH Noah Hanifin/99 25.00 60.00
SPNR Nick Ritchie/99 15.00 40.00
SPOL Oscar Lindberg/99 15.00 40.00
SPPA Colton Parayko/99 25.00 60.00
SPPB Pavel Bure/99 15.00 40.00
SPPC Paul Coffey/25 25.00 60.00
SPPD Pavel Datsyuk/25 30.00 80.00
SPPR Carey Price/25 30.00 80.00
SPRF Robby Fabbri/99 20.00 50.00
SPRM Ryan Miller/99 15.00 40.00
SPRN Rick Nash/99 15.00 40.00
SPRO Ryan O'Reilly/99 15.00 40.00
SPSB Sam Bennett/99 50.00 125.00
SPSC Sidney Crosby/25 150.00 250.00
SPSE Teemu Selanne/25 40.00 100.00
SPSH Shea Theodore/99 25.00 60.00
SPST Martin St. Louis/25 15.00 40.00
SPSU Malcolm Subban/99 25.00 60.00
SPTH Taylor Hall/99 15.00 40.00
SPTO Jonathan Toews/25 40.00 100.00
SPTS Tyler Seguin/99 20.00 50.00
SPVI Jake Virtanen/99 20.00 50.00
SPZF Zachary Fucale/99 12.00 30.00

2015-16 The Cup Signature Patches Dual

DSPDL D.Larkin/M.Domi/35 50.00 125.00
DSPDM M.Duchene
N.MacKinnon/35 60.00 150.00
DSPFC Z.Fucale/M.Condon/35 15.00 40.00
DSPFM E.Malkin/M.Fleury/35 30.00 80.00
DSPHG B.Hull/B.Guerin/35 30.00 80.00
DSPHS M.Stone/M.Hoffman/35 20.00 50.00
DSPJH J.Huberdeau/J.Jagr/35 50.00 125.00
DSPJI J.Jagr/J.Iginla/35 30.00 80.00
DSPJT J.Benn/T.Seguin/35 20.00 50.00
DSPKT A.Kopitar/T.Toffoli/35 25.00 60.00
DSPMD C.McDavid/M.Domi/35 800.00 2000.00
DSPMP C.Price/R.Miller/35 30.00 80.00
DSPNH R.Nash/K.Hayes/35 15.00 40.00
DSPPG M.Pacioretty
A.Galchenyuk/35 15.00 40.00
DSPPP C.Price/M.Pacioretty/35 40.00 100.00
DSPRB L.Robitaille/R.Blake/35 15.00 40.00
DSPST V.Tarasenko/J.Schwartz/35 20.00 50.00
DSPTN G.Nyquist/T.Tatar/35 10.00 25.00
DSPVS J.Virtanen/H.Shinkaruk/35 20.00 50.00

2015-16 The Cup Signature Renditions

SRAO Alexander Ovechkin 40.00 100.00
SRBC Bobby Clarke 15.00 40.00
SRBO Bobby Orr 40.00 100.00
SRCM Connor McDavid 500.00 1200.00
SRCP Carey Price 40.00 100.00
SRDG Doug Gilmour 30.00 80.00
SRDL Dylan Larkin 30.00 80.00
SREM Evgeni Malkin 25.00 60.00
SRFP Felix Potvin 15.00 40.00
SRGC Guy Carbonneau 8.00 20.00
SRJJ Jaromir Jagr 30.00 80.00
SRJT Jonathan Toews 40.00 100.00
SRNM Nathan MacKinnon 50.00 125.00
SROL Oscar Lindberg 10.00 25.00
SRPB Pavel Bure 15.00 40.00
SRRB Rod Brind'Amour 8.00 20.00
SRRM Ryan Miller 10.00 25.00
SRRO Ryan O'Reilly 10.00 25.00
SRSM Sean Monahan 6.00 15.00
SRTF Theoren Fleury 12.00 30.00
SRTH Taylor Hall 10.00 25.00
SRWG Wayne Gretzky 300.00 800.00

2015-16 The Cup Signature Renditions Combos

SRCKT A.Kopitar/T.Toffoli 25.00 60.00
SRCMF C.McDavid/Z.Fucale 250.00 400.00
SRCMK J.Kurri/M.Messier 30.00 80.00
SRCPP C.Price/M.Pacioretty 30.00 80.00
SRCBSK Jamie Benn
John Klingberg
Tyler Seguin 20.00 50.00
SRCJEB Jagr/Barkov/Ekblad 80.00 200.00

2015-16 The Cup Trios Jerseys

C3LW Ovechkin/Benn/Hall 15.00 40.00
C3RW Kane/Tarasenko/Toffoli 8.00 20.00
C3CAL Gaudreau/Monahan/Hamilton 6.00 15.00
C3CAP Ovechkin/Holtby/Kuznetsov 15.00 40.00
C3CBJ Foligno/Saad/Hartnell 3.00 8.00
C3CEN Seguin/Toews/Malkin 8.00 20.00

2015-16 The Cup Trios Jerseys

C3FLO Barkov/Luongo/Jagr 12.00 30.00
C3NET Holtby/Price/Rask 8.00 20.00
C3NYI Tavares/Halak/Lee 6.00 15.00
C3NYR Zuccarello/Lundqvist/Nash 10.00 25.00
C3TBL Kucherov/Bishop/Stamkos 8.00 20.00
C3VAN Sedin/Miller/Sedin 5.00 12.00
C3COLO Landeskog
MacKinnon/Duchene 15.00 40.00
C3COYO Smith/Ekman
Larsson/Duclair 4.00 10.00
C3HABS Gallagher/Price/Pacioretty 8.00 20.00
C3JETS Scheifele/Wheeler/Byfuglien 6.00 15.00
C3NASH Josi/Rinne/Weber 4.00 10.00
C3RET1 Sakic/Yzerman/Lemieux 15.00 40.00
C3RET2 Coffey/Savard/Hawerchuk 5.00 12.00
C3RET5 Sakic/Bourque/Roy 10.00 25.00
C3ROTY Ekblad/MacKinnon/Panarin 15.00 40.00
C3WILD Koivu/Dubnyk/Parise 4.00 10.00
C3BLUES Tarasenko/Allen/Steen 5.00 12.00
C3CANES Lindholm/Faulk/Skinner 5.00 12.00
C3DUCKS Perry/Andersen/Getzlaf 6.00 15.00
C3LEAFS Rielly/van Riemsdyk/Kadri 5.00 12.00
C3PENGU Malkin/Fleury/Kessel 8.00 20.00
C3ROOK1 McDavid/Eichel/Larkin 60.00 150.00
C3ROOK2 McDavid/Panarin/Domi 60.00 150.00
C3ROOK3 Eichel/Bennett/Virtanen 15.00 40.00
C3ROOK4 Panarin
Hinostroza/Hartman 15.00 40.00
C3ROOK5 Theodore/Ritchie/Noesen 6.00 15.00
C3ROOK6 McCarron/Condon/Fucale 4.00 10.00
C3ROOK7 Lindberg/Skjei/Skapski 4.00 10.00
C3ROOK8 Hanifin/Pesce/McGinn 6.00 15.00
C3ROOK9 Virtanen/McCann/Hutton 5.00 12.00
C3STARS Seguin/Benn/Sharp 5.00 12.00
C3BRUINS Bergeron/Rask/Eriksson 5.00 12.00
C3DEVILS Henrique
Schneider/Cammalleri 4.00 10.00
C3GOALIE Crawford/Quick/Lundqvist 10.00 25.00
C3OILERS Nugent-
Hopkins/Hall/Eberle 5.00 12.00
C3ROOK10 Ehlers/Hellebuyck/Petan 15.00 40.00
C3SABRES O'Reilly
Reinhart/Ristolainen 8.00 20.00
C3SHARKS Pavelski/Jones/Marleau 5.00 12.00

2016-17 The Cup

1 Steve Yzerman 8.00 20.00
2 Ray Bourque 5.00 12.00
3 Corey Perry 5.00 12.00
4 John Gibson 3.00 8.00
5 Teemu Selanne 6.00 15.00
6 Oliver Ekman-Larsson 3.00 8.00
7 Max Domi 3.00 8.00
8 David Backes 2.00 5.00
9 Patrice Bergeron 4.00 10.00
10 Bobby Orr 12.00 30.00
11 Cam Neely 3.00 8.00
12 Ryan O'Reilly 3.00 8.00
13 Jack Eichel 5.00 12.00
14 Dale Hawerchuk 4.00 10.00
15 Mark Giordano 3.00 8.00
16 Sam Bennett 5.00 12.00
17 Sean Monahan 2.00 5.00
18 Jordan Staal 2.50 6.00
19 Teuvo Teravainen 3.00 8.00
20 Cam Ward 3.00 8.00
21 Artemi Panarin 6.00 15.00
22 Jonathan Toews 5.00 12.00
23 Chris Chelios 3.00 8.00
24 Patrick Kane 6.00 15.00
25 Nathan MacKinnon 12.00 30.00
26 Matt Duchene 3.00 8.00
27 Joe Sakic 6.00 15.00
28 Brandon Saad 2.50 6.00
29 Boone Jenner 3.00 8.00
30 Sergei Bobrovsky 5.00 12.00
31 Jamie Benn 3.00 8.00
32 Tyler Seguin 4.00 10.00
33 Mike Modano 5.00 12.00
34 Andreas Athanasiou 3.00 8.00
35 Dylan Larkin 4.00 10.00
36 Henrik Zetterberg 4.00 10.00
37 Igor Larionov 3.00 8.00
38 Leon Draisaitl 10.00 25.00
39 Connor McDavid 15.00 40.00
40 Wayne Gretzky 20.00 50.00
41 Jaromir Jagr 10.00 25.00
42 Aaron Ekblad 4.00 10.00
43 Roberto Luongo 5.00 12.00
44 Tyler Toffoli 3.00 8.00
45 Anze Kopitar 5.00 12.00
46 Drew Doughty 4.00 10.00
47 Jake Muzzin 3.00 8.00
48 Devan Dubnyk 2.50 6.00
49 Nino Niederreiter 2.00 5.00
50 Ryan Suter 2.50 6.00
51 Alex Galchenyuk 2.00 5.00
52 Patrick Roy 8.00 20.00
53 Shea Weber 2.50 6.00
54 Carey Price 6.00 15.00
55 P.K. Subban 4.00 10.00
56 Ryan Johansen 2.50 6.00
57 Roman Josi 3.00 8.00
58 Taylor Hall 3.00 8.00
59 Cory Schneider 3.00 8.00
60 Martin Brodeur 8.00 20.00
61 Adam Henrique 2.50 6.00
62 Pat LaFontaine 3.00 8.00
63 John Tavares 5.00 12.00
64 Andrew Ladd 2.00 5.00
65 Erik Karlsson 4.00 10.00
66 Mike Hoffman 2.00 5.00
67 Bobby Ryan 2.50 6.00
68 Craig Anderson 3.00 8.00
69 Claude Giroux 3.00 8.00
70 Bobby Clarke 5.00 12.00
71 Jakub Voracek 2.50 6.00
72 Jeremy Roenick 5.00 12.00
73 Matt Murray 5.00 12.00
74 Sidney Crosby 12.00 30.00
75 Mario Lemieux 12.00 30.00
76 Evgeni Malkin 6.00 15.00
77 Joe Pavelski 4.00 10.00
78 Brent Burns 3.00 8.00
79 Martin Jones 2.50 6.00
80 Joe Thornton 5.00 12.00
81 Alex Pietrangelo 2.50 6.00
82 Brett Hull 6.00 15.00
83 Vladimir Tarasenko 4.00 10.00
84 Jake Allen 3.00 8.00
85 Steven Stamkos 6.00 15.00
86 Dave Andreychuk 3.00 8.00
87 Nikita Kucherov 6.00 15.00
88 Nazem Kadri 4.00 10.00
89 Morgan Rielly 3.00 8.00
90 Felix Potvin 5.00 12.00
91 Frederik Andersen 4.00 10.00
92 Daniel Sedin 4.00 10.00
93 Loui Eriksson 2.00 5.00
94 Bo Horvat 4.00 10.00
95 Alexander Ovechkin 12.00 30.00
96 Braden Holtby 4.00 10.00
97 Nicklas Backstrom 3.00 8.00
98 Blake Wheeler 3.00 8.00
99 Nikolaj Ehlers 3.00 8.00
100 Mark Scheifele 5.00 12.00
101 Ivan Provorov JSY AU/249 RC 30.00 80.00
102 Matthew Tkachuk
JSY AU/249 RC 150.00 400.00
103 Pavel Zacha JSY AU/249 RC 30.00 80.00
104 Anthony Mantha
JSY AU/249 RC 250.00 400.00
105 Travis Konecny JSY AU/249 RC 60.00 150.00
106 Sebastian Aho JSY AU/249 RC 150.00 400.00
107 Mathew Barzal JSY AU/249 RC 300.00 700.00
108 Dylan Strome JSY AU/249 RC 50.00 125.00
109 Zach Werenski JSY AU/249 RC 40.00 100.00
110 Pavel Buchnevich
JSY AU/249 RC 40.00 100.00
111 Tyler Motte JSY AU/249 RC 12.00 30.00
112 Kyle Connor JSY AU/249 RC 100.00 250.00
113 Stephen Johns JSY AU/249 RC 15.00 40.00
114 Troy Stecher AU/249 RC 20.00 50.00
115 Tyler Bertuzzi JSY AU/249 RC 50.00 125.00
116 Zach Hyman JSY AU/249 RC 60.00 150.00
117 Nic Dowd JSY AU/249 RC 15.00 40.00
118 Nick Baptiste JSY AU/249 RC 20.00 50.00
119 Gustav Forsling JSY AU/249 RC 40.00 100.00
120 Brendan Guhle JSY AU/249 RC 20.00 50.00
121 Brandon Tanev JSY AU/249 RC 25.00 60.00
122 Mark Jankowski JSY AU/249 RC 15.00 40.00
123 Nikita Tryamkin JSY AU/249 RC 15.00 40.00
124 Tristan Jarry JSY AU/249 RC 60.00 150.00
125 A.J. Greer JSY AU/249 RC 20.00 50.00
126 Artturi Lehkonen JSY AU/249 RC 25.00 60.00
127 Austin Czarnik JSY AU/249 RC 30.00 80.00
128 Danton Heinen JSY AU/249 RC 15.00 40.00
129 Sergey Tolchinsky
JSY AU/249 RC 15.00 40.00
130 Brandon Montour
JSY AU/249 RC 50.00 125.00
131 Jakub Vrana JSY AU/249 RC 100.00 250.00
132 Timo Meier JSY AU/249 RC 40.00 100.00
133 Thatcher Demko
JSY AU/249 RC 80.00 200.00
134 Jake Guentzel JSY AU/249 RC 100.00 250.00
135 Julius Honka JSY AU/249 RC 20.00 50.00
136 Michael Matheson
JSY AU/249 RC 20.00 50.00
137 Jakob Chychrun
JSY AU/249 RC 40.00 100.00
138 Nikita Soshnikov JSY AU/249 RC 12.00 30.00
139 Brendan Perlini JSY AU/249 RC 30.00 80.00
140 Mikhail Sergachev
JSY AU/249 RC 40.00 100.00
141 Anthony Beauvillier
JSY AU/249 RC 25.00 60.00
142 Brayden Point JSY AU/249 RC 200.00 500.00
143 Christian Dvorak JSY AU/249 RC 25.00 60.00
144 Joel Eriksson Ek
JSY AU/249 RC 50.00 125.00
145 Kasperi Kapanen JSY AU/249 RC 30.00 80.00
146 Anthony DeAngelo
JSY AU/249 RC 15.00 40.00
147 Tom Kuhnhackl JSY AU/249 RC 15.00 40.00
148 Dominik Simon JSY AU/249 RC 15.00 40.00
149 Trevor Carrick JSY AU/249 RC 20.00 50.00
150 Brendan Leipsic JSY AU/249 RC 15.00 40.00
151 Nick Schmaltz JSY AU/249 RC 25.00 60.00
152 Esa Lindell JSY AU/249 RC 20.00 50.00
153 Hudson Fasching
JSY AU/249 RC 20.00 50.00
154 Justin Bailey JSY AU/249 RC 20.00 50.00
155 Connor Brown JSY AU/249 RC 20.00 50.00
156 Mike Reilly JSY AU/249 RC 15.00 40.00
157 Steven Santini JSY AU/249 RC 15.00 40.00
158 Chase De Leo JSY AU/249 RC 20.00 50.00
159 Oliver Bjorkstrand
JSY AU/249 RC 25.00 60.00
160 Daniel Altshuller JSY AU/249 RC 15.00 40.00
161 Lawson Crouse JSY AU/249 RC 15.00 40.00
162 Chris Bigras JSY AU/249 RC 15.00 40.00
163 Blake Speers JSY AU/249 RC 20.00 50.00
164 John Quenneville JSY AU/249 RC 20.00 50.00
165 Pontus Aberg JSY AU/249 RC 25.00 60.00
166 JC Lipon JSY AU/249 RC 20.00 50.00
167 Josh Morrissey JSY AU/249 RC 40.00 100.00
168 Jason Dickinson JSY AU/249 RC 15.00 40.00
169 Oskar Sundqvist JSY AU/249 RC 20.00 50.00
170 Mark McNeill JSY AU/249 RC 20.00 50.00
171 Kevin Labanc JSY AU/249 RC 20.00 50.00
172 Sonny Milano JSY AU/249 RC 25.00 60.00
173 Thomas Chabot JSY AU/249 RC 40.00 100.00
174 Ryan Pulock JSY AU/249 RC 20.00 50.00
175 Patrik Laine JSY AU/99 RC 400.00 1000.00
176 Mitch Marner JSY AU/99 RC 900.00 1500.00
177 Jesse Puljujarvi JSY AU/99 RC 125.00 300.00
178 William Nylander
JSY AU/99 RC 500.00 800.00
179 Jimmy Vesey JSY AU/99 RC 125.00 300.00
180 Auston Matthews
JSY AU/99 RC 7000.00 12000.00
181 Miles Wood JSY AU/249 RC 15.00 40.00
182 Oliver Kylington JSY AU/249 RC 15.00 40.00
183 Charlie Lindgren JSY AU/249 RC 30.00 80.00
184 Brandon Carlo JSY AU/249 RC 30.00 80.00
185 Jared Coreau RC 6.00 15.00
186 Markus Nutivaara RC 5.00 12.00
187 Adam Erne RC 6.00 15.00
188 Alan Quine RC 6.00 15.00
189 Joseph Cramarossa RC 5.00 12.00
190 Matt Puempel RC 5.00 12.00
191 Wade Megan RC 5.00 12.00
192 Matthew Benning RC 6.00 15.00
193 Nikita Zaitsev RC 6.00 15.00
194 Aaron Dell RC 5.00 12.00
195 Drake Caggiula RC 5.00 12.00
196 Denis Malgin RC 4.00 10.00
197 William Carrier RC 5.00 12.00
198 Jacob Larsson RC 8.00 20.00
199 Ondrej Kase RC 5.00 12.00
200 Kevin Gravel RC 8.00 20.00

2016-17 The Cup Brilliance Autographs

BAG Alex Galchenyuk B 4.00 10.00
BAM Auston Matthews A 250.00 600.00
BAV Andrei Vasilevskiy D 10.00 25.00
BDS Darryl Sittler A 20.00 50.00
BFA Frederik Andersen D 20.00 50.00
BJD Jonathan Drouin 5.00 12.00
BJG John Gibson D 6.00 15.00
BJH Julius Honka D 6.00 15.00
BJP Jesse Puljujarvi C 12.00 30.00
BLA Patrik Laine A 50.00 125.00
BLD Leon Draisaitl C 12.00 30.00
BMH Mike Hoffman C 4.00 10.00
BMM Matt Murray C 15.00 40.00
BMT Matthew Tkachuk C 80.00 200.00
BNE Nikolaj Ehlers D 8.00 20.00
BNK Nikita Kucherov C 20.00 50.00
BNN Nino Niederreiter D 4.00 10.00
BPB Peter Bondra C 8.00 20.00
BPL Pat LaFontaine C 8.00 20.00
BRJ Roman Josi B 8.00 20.00
BRK Ryan Kesler B 6.00 15.00
BRV Rogie Vachon B 12.00 30.00
BSA Derek Sanderson C 8.00 20.00
BTB Tyson Barrie C 4.00 10.00
BTD Thatcher Demko D 30.00 80.00
BTF Theoren Fleury B 12.00 30.00
BTK Travis Konecny D 25.00 60.00
BVD Vincent Damphousse B 6.00 15.00
BWC Wendel Clark A 15.00 40.00
BWG Wayne Gretzky A 300.00 800.00

2016-17 The Cup Enshrinements

EAB Anthony Beauvillier/99 8.00 20.00
EAG Alex Galchenyuk/99 5.00 12.00
EAO Alexander Ovechkin/25 150.00 400.00
EBC Bobby Clarke/99 12.00 30.00
ECN Cam Neely/99 8.00 20.00
EDP Denis Potvin/99 8.00 20.00
EDS Derek Sanderson/99 8.00 20.00
EEM Evgeni Malkin/99 15.00 40.00
EGL Guy Lafleur/25 25.00 60.00
EIP Ivan Provorov/99 8.00 20.00
EJB Jamie Benn/99 8.00 20.00
EJE Joel Eriksson Ek/99 12.00 30.00
EJM Jake Muzzin/99 5.00 12.00
EJT Joe Thornton/99 20.00 50.00
EJV Jimmy Vesey/99 12.00 30.00
EKM Kirk Muller/99 8.00 20.00
ELD Leon Draisaitl/99 15.00 40.00
ELE Loui Eriksson/99 5.00 12.00
EMB Martin Brodeur/25 40.00 100.00
EMG Mark Giordano/99 8.00 20.00
EMH Mike Hoffman/99 5.00 12.00
EMR Morgan Rielly/99 8.00 20.00
EMS Mark Scheifele/99 12.00 30.00
EPH Phil Housley/99 6.00 15.00
EPK Patrick Kane/99 25.00 60.00
ERL Roberto Luongo/99 12.00 30.00
ESC Sidney Crosby/25 150.00 250.00
EWG Wayne Gretzky/25 250.00 600.00
EZW Zach Werenski/99 25.00 60.00

2016-17 The Cup Enshrinements Dual

E2LC P.Laine/K.Connor/25 100.00 250.00
E2SL J.Sakic/G.Lafleur/25 60.00 150.00
E2SM D.Sittler/L.McDonald/25 30.00 80.00

2016-17 The Cup Foundations Jerseys

FAE Aaron Ekblad/25 8.00 20.00
FAG Alex Galchenyuk/25 4.00 10.00
FAK Anze Kopitar/25 10.00 25.00
FAM Auston Matthews/49 150.00 400.00
FAO Alexander Ovechkin/25 20.00 50.00
FAP Alex Pietrangelo/25 5.00 12.00
FAV Andrei Vasilevskiy/25 10.00 25.00
FAW Alexander Wennberg/25 4.00 10.00
FBB Brent Burns/25 6.00 15.00
FBE Brian Elliott/25 4.00 10.00
FCM Connor McDavid/25 30.00 80.00
FCP Carey Price/25 20.00 50.00
FDB David Backes/25 8.00 20.00
FDD Devan Dubnyk/25 5.00 12.00
FEK Erik Karlsson/25 8.00 20.00
FEM Evgeni Malkin/25 12.00 30.00
FES Eric Staal/25 8.00 20.00
FHL Henrik Lundqvist/25 15.00 40.00
FHZ Henrik Zetterberg/25 8.00 20.00
FJA Jake Allen/25 6.00 15.00
FJG John Gibson/25 6.00 15.00
FJJ Joe Thornton/25 8.00 20.00
FJM Jake Muzzin/25 6.00 15.00
FJP Jesse Puljujarvi/49 15.00 40.00
FJT Jonathan Toews/25 12.00 30.00
FJV Jimmy Vesey/49 8.00 20.00
FLE Loui Eriksson/25 4.00 10.00
FMA Anthony Mantha/49 12.00 30.00
FMG Mark Giordano/25 8.00 20.00
FMH Mike Hoffman/25 4.00 10.00
FMM Mitch Marner/49 20.00 50.00
FMR Morgan Rielly/25 8.00 20.00
FMS Mark Scheifele/25 8.00 20.00
FMT Matthew Tkachuk/49 25.00 60.00
FMZ Mats Zuccarello/25 6.00 15.00
FPB Pavel Buchnevich/49 10.00 25.00
FPK Patrick Kane/25 12.00 30.00
FPL Patrik Laine/49 15.00 40.00
FPS P.K. Subban/25 8.00 20.00
FRK Ryan Kesler/25 6.00 15.00
FRL Roberto Luongo/25 10.00 25.00
FSB Sergei Bobrovsky/25 10.00 25.00
FSC Sidney Crosby/25 25.00 60.00
FSS Steven Stamkos/25 12.00 30.00
FTA John Tavares/25 8.00 20.00
FTH Taylor Hall/25 8.00 20.00
FTK Travis Konecny/49 12.00 30.00
FTS Tyler Seguin/25 8.00 20.00
FWS Wayne Simmonds/25 8.00 20.00
FZW Zach Werenski/49 20.00 50.00

2016-17 The Cup Honorable Numbers

HNAM Auston Matthews/34 450.00 850.00
HNAV Andrei Vasilevskiy/88 20.00 50.00
HNCC Chris Chelios/24 20.00 50.00
HNCP Carey Price/31 80.00 200.00
HNDB David Backes/42 12.00 30.00
HNHL Henrik Lundqvist/30 30.00 80.00
HNJG Jake Guentzel/59 60.00 150.00
HNJP Jesse Puljujarvi/98 100.00 250.00
HNJS Joe Sakic/19 50.00 125.00
HNJT Joe Thornton/19 12.00 30.00
HNLD Leon Draisaitl/29 50.00 125.00
HNMA Michael Matheson/19 15.00 40.00
HNMM Matt Murray/30 30.00 80.00
HNMR Morgan Rielly/44 20.00 50.00
HNMS Mark Scheifele/55 20.00 50.00
HNNE Nikolaj Ehlers/27 20.00 50.00
HNNN Nino Niederreiter/22 8.00 20.00
HNPB Pavel Buchnevich/89 15.00 40.00
HNPL Patrik Laine/29 100.00 250.00
HNPR Patrick Roy/33 80.00 200.00
HNRK Ryan Kesler/17 20.00 50.00
HNTS Tyler Seguin/91 20.00 50.00
HNVE Jimmy Vesey/26 20.00 50.00
HNWS Wayne Simmonds/17 15.00 40.00

2016-17 The Cup Honorable Numbers Dual

HN2ST T.Seguin/J.Tavares/91 25.00 60.00

2016-17 The Cup Limited Logos Autographs

LLAE Aaron Ekblad/50 30.00 80.00
LLAG Alex Galchenyuk/50 15.00 40.00
LLAK Anze Kopitar/50 40.00 100.00
LLAM Auston Matthews/50 600.00 1000.00
LLBB Brent Burns 25.00 60.00
LLBE Brian Elliott/50 20.00 50.00
LLBO Bo Horvat/50 30.00 80.00
LLCP Carey Price/25 50.00 125.00
LLCS Cory Schneider/50 25.00 60.00
LLDB David Backes/50 15.00 40.00
LLGI Mark Giordano/50 25.00 60.00
LLGN Gustav Nyquist/50 15.00 40.00
LLHL Henrik Lundqvist/25 60.00 150.00
LLHZ Henrik Zetterberg/25 60.00 150.00
LLIP Ivan Provorov/50 15.00 40.00
LLJA Jaromir Jagr/50 80.00 200.00
LLJB Jamie Benn 25.00 60.00
LLJG John Gibson/50 25.00 60.00
LLJI Jarome Iginla/25 30.00 80.00
LLJJ Joe Thornton/25 40.00 100.00
LLJO Roman Josi/50 25.00 60.00
LLJP Jesse Puljujarvi/50 40.00 100.00
LLJR Jeremy Roenick 40.00 100.00
LLJS Jaden Schwartz/50 30.00 80.00
LLJT Jonathan Toews/25 60.00 150.00
LLLD Leon Draisaitl/50 80.00 200.00
LLLE Loui Eriksson/50 15.00 40.00
LLMA Mitch Marner/25 400.00 1000.00
LLMG Marian Gaborik/50 25.00 60.00
LLMH Mike Hoffman/50 15.00 40.00
LLMM Matt Murray/50 40.00 100.00
LLMS Mark Scheifele/50 40.00 100.00
LLNF Nick Foligno/50 20.00 50.00
LLNK Nikita Kucherov/50 50.00 125.00
LLNN Nino Niederreiter/50 15.00 40.00
LLPK Patrick Kane/25 50.00 125.00
LLPL Patrik Laine/50 200.00 500.00
LLRI Morgan Rielly/50 25.00 60.00
LLRK Ryan Kesler/50 25.00 60.00
LLRL Roberto Luongo/50 40.00 100.00
LLRN Rick Nash/50 25.00 60.00
LLTA John Tavares/50 40.00 100.00
LLTB Tyson Barrie/50 15.00 40.00
LLTH Taylor Hall/50 25.00 60.00
LLWS Wayne Simmonds/50 25.00 60.00
LLZW Zach Werenski/50 80.00 200.00

2016-17 The Cup Rookie Bookmarks Dual Autographs

DARBKP T.Konecny/I.Provorov 60.00 150.00
DARBLC P.Laine/K.Connor 80.00 200.00
DARBMB M.Marner/C.Brown 150.00 300.00
DARBMN Auston Matthews
William Nylander 1200.00 3000.00
DARBMS Tyler Motte
Nick Schmaltz 25.00 60.00
DARBSL M.Sergachev/A.Lehkonen 25.00 60.00
DARBVB J.Vesey/P.Buchnevich 60.00 150.00
DARBWB Z.Werenski/O.Bjorkstrand 25.00 60.00

2016-17 The Cup Rookie Gear Relic Autographs

ARGAM Auston Matthews 1000.00 2500.00
ARGBM Brandon Montour 50.00 125.00
ARGDS Dylan Strome 50.00 125.00
ARGIP Ivan Provorov 30.00 80.00
ARGJG Jake Guentzel 60.00 150.00
ARGJP Jesse Puljujarvi 40.00 100.00
ARGJV Jimmy Vesey 40.00 100.00
ARGKC Kyle Connor 60.00 150.00
ARGMA Anthony Mantha 40.00 100.00
ARGMM Mitch Marner 400.00 1000.00
ARGMS Mikhail Sergachev 30.00 80.00
ARGMT Matthew Tkachuk 80.00 200.00
ARGPL Patrik Laine 50.00 125.00
ARGPZ Pavel Zacha 30.00 80.00
ARGTK Travis Konecny 40.00 100.00
ARGTM Timo Meier 40.00 100.00
ARGZW Zach Werenski 60.00 150.00

2016-17 The Cup Scripted Materials

SMAB Aleksander Barkov 15.00 40.00
SMAE Aaron Ekblad 12.00 30.00
SMAG Alex Galchenyuk 6.00 15.00
SMAM Auston Matthews 300.00 800.00
SMAO Alexander Ovechkin 40.00 100.00
SMAV Andrei Vasilevskiy 15.00 40.00
SMAW Alexander Wennberg 6.00 15.00
SMBB Brent Burns 10.00 25.00
SMBE Brian Elliott 8.00 20.00
SMBH Brett Hull 20.00 50.00
SMBS Brayden Schenn 10.00 25.00
SMCM Connor McDavid 250.00 400.00
SMCP Carey Price 20.00 50.00
SMCS Cory Schneider 10.00 25.00
SMDB David Backes 6.00 15.00
SMEM Evgeni Malkin 20.00 50.00
SMFA Frederik Andersen 12.00 30.00
SMGL Guy Lafleur 12.00 30.00
SMHL Henrik Lundqvist 25.00 60.00
SMHZ Henrik Zetterberg 12.00 30.00
SMIL Igor Larionov 6.00 15.00
SMJD Jonathan Drouin 8.00 20.00
SMJE Joel Eriksson Ek 15.00 40.00
SMJG John Gibson 10.00 25.00
SMJI Jarome Iginla 12.00 30.00
SMJJ Joe Thornton 15.00 40.00
SMJM Jake Muzzin 10.00 25.00
SMJO Roman Josi 10.00 25.00
SMJP Jesse Puljujarvi 80.00 200.00
SMJT Jonathan Toews 15.00 40.00
SMJV Jimmy Vesey 15.00 40.00
SMLD Leon Draisaitl 30.00 80.00
SMLE Loui Eriksson 6.00 15.00
SMMG Mark Giordano 10.00 25.00
SMMH Mike Hoffman 6.00 15.00
SMMM Matt Murray 15.00 40.00
SMMR Morgan Rielly 10.00 25.00
SMMS Mark Scheifele 15.00 40.00
SMMT Mark Stone 12.00 30.00
SMNK Nikita Kucherov 20.00 50.00
SMNN Nino Niederreiter 6.00 15.00
SMPC Paul Coffey 10.00 25.00
SMPE Corey Perry 15.00 40.00
SMPK Patrick Kane 25.00 60.00
SMPL Patrik Laine 30.00 80.00
SMRK Ryan Kesler 10.00 25.00
SMSC Sidney Crosby 100.00 250.00
SMTA John Tavares 15.00 40.00
SMTH Taylor Hall 10.00 25.00
SMTK Travis Konecny 20.00 50.00
SMTS Tyler Seguin 12.00 30.00
SMWS Wayne Simmonds 12.00 30.00
SMZW Zach Werenski 30.00 80.00

2016-17 The Cup Signature Materials

SIAB Anthony Beauvillier/99 10.00 25.00
SIAG Alex Galchenyuk/99 6.00 15.00
SIAM Auston Matthews/99 500.00 1200.00
SIAO Alexander Ovechkin/25 80.00 150.00
SIAV Andrei Vasilevskiy/99 15.00 40.00
SIBE Brian Elliott/99 8.00 20.00
SIBH Bo Horvat/99 12.00 30.00
SIBM Brandon Montour/99 15.00 40.00
SICD Christian Dvorak/99 12.00 30.00
SICM Connor McDavid/25 250.00 450.00
SICP Carey Price/25 80.00 150.00
SIEM Evgeni Malkin/25 80.00 150.00
SIHL Henrik Lundqvist/25 60.00 150.00
SIHZ Henrik Zetterberg/99 12.00 30.00
SIJB Jamie Benn/99 8.00 20.00
SIJD Jonathan Drouin/99 8.00 20.00
SIJE Joel Eriksson Ek/99 12.00 30.00
SIJH Julius Honka/99 6.00 15.00
SIJJ Jaromir Jagr/25 150.00 250.00
SIJM Jake Muzzin/99 8.00 20.00
SIJP Jesse Puljujarvi/99 20.00 50.00
SIJS Jaden Schwartz/99 12.00 30.00
SIJV Jimmy Vesey/99 15.00 40.00
SIKC Kyle Connor/99 30.00 80.00
SIMA Anthony Mantha/99 80.00 150.00
SIMB Mathew Barzal/99 30.00 80.00
SIMG Mark Giordano/99 10.00 25.00
SIMH Mike Hoffman/99 8.00 20.00
SIMM Michael Matheson/99 10.00 25.00
SIMR Morgan Rielly/99 12.00 30.00
SIMS Mark Scheifele/99 15.00 40.00
SIMT Matthew Tkachuk/99 125.00 300.00
SINE Nikolaj Ehlers/99 12.00 30.00
SINN Nino Niederreiter/99 6.00 15.00
SINS Nick Schmaltz/99 12.00 30.00
SIPB Pavel Buchnevich/99 15.00 40.00
SIPE Corey Perry/99 15.00 40.00
SIPK Patrick Kane/25 80.00 150.00
SIPL Patrik Laine/99 100.00 250.00
SIRK Ryan Kesler/99 15.00 40.00
SIRL Roberto Luongo/99 15.00 40.00
SIRN Rick Nash/99 10.00 25.00
SIRS Ryan Spooner/99 8.00 20.00
SISC Sidney Crosby/25 300.00 400.00
SITA John Tavares/99 15.00 40.00
SITB Tyson Barrie/99 6.00 15.00
SITH Joe Thornton/99 15.00 40.00
SITM Timo Meier/99 20.00 50.00
SIWS Wayne Simmonds/99 12.00 30.00
SIZW Zach Werenski/99 30.00 80.00

2016-17 The Cup Signature Materials Dual

SI2BE A.Barkov/A.Ekblad/35 20.00 50.00
SI2BS J.Benn/T.Seguin/35 15.00 40.00
SI2CB Logan Couture
Brent Burns 15.00 40.00
SI2HE B.Horvat/L.Eriksson/35 15.00 40.00
SI2KD Nikita Kucherov
Jonathan Drouin 25.00 60.00
SI2PG C.Price/A.Galchenyuk/35 25.00 60.00
SI2RA Morgan Rielly
Frederik Andersen 15.00 40.00
SI2SM S.Monahan/M.Giordano/35 12.00 30.00
SI2SS W.Simmonds/B.Schenn/35 15.00 40.00
SI2WB Zach Werenski
Oliver Bjorkstrand 40.00 100.00

2016-17 The Cup Signature Renditions

SRAM Auston Matthews C 600.00 1500.00
SRAO Alexander Ovechkin C 60.00 150.00
SRBO Bobby Orr A 100.00 200.00
SRCM Connor McDavid B 200.00 400.00
SRCN Cam Neely E 15.00 40.00
SRCP Carey Price C 30.00 80.00
SRDA Dave Andreychuk E 15.00 40.00
SREM Evgeni Malkin D 30.00 80.00
SRHL Henrik Lundqvist C 30.00 80.00
SRJB Jamie Benn 15.00 40.00
SRJE Joel Eriksson Ek E 25.00 60.00
SRJJ Jaromir Jagr B 100.00 200.00
SRJT Joe Thornton D 25.00 60.00
SRJV Jimmy Vesey E 25.00 60.00
SRLM Lanny McDonald D 15.00 40.00
SRMD Marcel Dionne E 20.00 50.00
SRML Mario Lemieux A 80.00 200.00
SRMO Mike Modano D 25.00 60.00
SRPH Phil Housley E 12.00 30.00
SRPL Patrik Laine D 50.00 125.00
SRPR Patrick Roy B 40.00 100.00
SRRB Ray Bourque C 25.00 60.00
SRRL Roberto Luongo E 25.00 60.00
SRSC Sidney Crosby B 150.00 300.00
SRWG Wayne Gretzky A 250.00 600.00
SRZW Zach Werenski E 50.00 125.00

2016-17 The Cup Signature Renditions Combos

SR2CB P.Coffey/R.Bourque 50.00 125.00
SR2CL C.Chelios/N.Lidstrom 80.00 150.00
SR2MN Auston Matthews
William Nylander 500.00 1200.00

2016-17 The Cup The Show Autographs

TSAM Auston Matthews C 400.00 1000.00
TSEM Evgeni Malkin C 30.00 80.00
TSGL Guy Lafleur B 20.00 50.00
TSJS Joe Sakic B 30.00 80.00
TSJV Jimmy Vesey D 25.00 60.00
TSMM Mitch Marner D 50.00 125.00
TSMT Matthew Tkachuk D 60.00 150.00
TSPK Patrick Kane C 30.00 80.00
TSPL Patrik Laine C 60.00 150.00
TSRB Ray Bourque B 25.00 60.00
TSWG Wayne Gretzky A 400.00 1000.00
TSZW Zach Werenski D 50.00 125.00

2016-17 The Cup Ticket Inscriptions

TBAK Anze Kopitar/17 100.00 200.00
TBBS Brayden Schenn/14 40.00 100.00
TBGN Gustav Nyquist/12 30.00 80.00
TBJB Jamie Benn 40.00 100.00
TBPE Corey Perry/13 25.00 60.00
TBRN Rick Nash/15 60.00 150.00
TBTA John Tavares/27 150.00 250.00
TBWS Wayne Simmonds/23 40.00 100.00

2016-17 The Cup Trios Jerseys

C3ACR Chychrun/Strome/Dvorak 20.00 50.00
C3ANA Gibson/Getzlaf/Perry 10.00 25.00
C3ARI Domi/Ekman-Larsson/Smith 6.00 15.00
C3ASL Thornton/Jagr/Iginla 20.00 50.00
C3AVS Sakic/Roy/Blake 15.00 40.00
C3BB1 Marchand/Bergeron/Pastrnak 15.00 40.00
C3BB2 Spooner/Rask/Backes 8.00 20.00
C3BJR Bjorkstrand/Werenski/Milano 20.00 50.00
C3BUF O'Reilly/Eichel/Reinhart 12.00 30.00
C3CAL Monahan/Gaudreau/Bennett 10.00 25.00
C3CAR Hanifin/Teravainen/Lindholm 6.00 15.00
C3CDN Kane/Toews/Crawford 12.00 30.00
C3CBJ Wennberg/Bobrovsky/Jones 10.00 25.00
C3COL MacKinnon/Barrie/Duchene 25.00 60.00
C3DAL Seguin/Benn/Klingberg 8.00 20.00
C3DEF Hedman/Burns/Weber 8.00 20.00
C3DET Yzerman/Lidstrom/Larionov 15.00 40.00
C3DRW Larkin/Zetterberg/Athanasiou 15.00 40.00
C3EDM Lucic/McDavid/Draisaitl 40.00 100.00
C3FLO Trocheck/Ekblad/Barkov 10.00 25.00
C3GOA Dubnyk/Holtby/Bobrovsky 10.00 25.00
C3LA1 Toffoli/Kopitar/Carter 10.00 25.00
C3LA2 Doughty/Quick/Muzzin 8.00 20.00
C3MCR Lehkonen
Sergachev/Lindgren 10.00 25.00
C3MLR Nylander/Matthews/Marner 80.00 200.00
C3MON Pacioretty/Price/Weber 12.00 30.00
C3MW1 Suter/Dubnyk/Staal 8.00 20.00
C3MW2 Parise/Koivu/Niederreiter 6.00 15.00
C3NAS Forsberg/Subban/Johansen 10.00 25.00
C3NJD Henrique/Schneider/Hall 6.00 15.00
C3NOR Keith/Karlsson/Doughty 8.00 20.00
C3NYI Nelson/Tavares/Leddy 10.00 25.00
C3NYR Nash/McDonagh/Zibanejad 8.00 20.00
C3OIL Kurri/Gretzky/Messier 40.00 100.00
C3OTT Hoffman/Karlsson/Stone 8.00 20.00
C3PHI Schenn/Giroux/Simmonds 8.00 20.00
C3PIT Kessel/Malkin/Letang 12.00 30.00
C3RRT Perry/Stamkos/Ovechkin 25.00 60.00
C3SAS Marleau/Thornton/Couture 10.00 25.00
C3SCW Martinez/Letang/Keith 8.00 20.00
C3SEL Toews/Bergeron/Kopitar 10.00 25.00
C3SJS Burns/Pavelski/Jones 8.00 20.00
C3STL Pietrangelo/Tarasenko/Fabbri 8.00 20.00
C3TBL Hedman/Stamkos/Kucherov 12.00 30.00
C3TML Rielly/Andersen/Kadri 8.00 20.00
C3VAN Eriksson/Sedin/Sedin 8.00 20.00
C3WC1 Backstrom/Ovechkin/Holtby 25.00 60.00
C3WC2 Oshie/Kuznetsov/Burakovsky 8.00 20.00
C3WIN Scheifele/Wheeler/Byfuglien 8.00 20.00
C3WJR Connor/Laine/Morrissey 20.00 50.00

2017-18 The Cup

1 Guy Lafleur 4.00 10.00
2 Ryan Getzlaf 3.00 8.00
3 Adam Henrique 2.50 6.00
4 Derek Stepan 2.00 5.00
5 Oliver Ekman-Larsson 3.00 8.00
6 Bobby Orr 12.00 30.00
7 Brad Marchand 6.00 15.00
8 Jack Eichel 6.00 15.00
9 Jason Pominville 2.00 5.00
10 Dale Hawerchuk 4.00 10.00
11 Matthew Tkachuk 6.00 15.00
12 Jaromir Jagr 10.00 25.00
13 Johnny Gaudreau 5.00 12.00
14 Jeff Skinner 4.00 10.00
15 Sebastian Aho 5.00 12.00
16 Justin Williams 2.50 6.00
17 Tony Amonte 2.50 6.00
18 Patrick Kane 6.00 15.00
19 Duncan Keith 2.50 6.00
20 Jonathan Toews 5.00 12.00
21 Nathan MacKinnon 12.00 30.00
22 Mikko Rantanen 8.00 20.00
23 Patrick Roy 8.00 20.00
24 Artemi Panarin 6.00 15.00
25 Sergei Bobrovsky 5.00 12.00
26 Zach Werenski 5.00 12.00
27 Jamie Benn 3.00 8.00
28 Tyler Seguin 4.00 10.00
29 Alexander Radulov 3.00 8.00
30 Steve Yzerman 8.00 20.00
31 Anthony Mantha 2.50 6.00
32 Dylan Larkin 4.00 10.00
33 Connor McDavid 15.00 40.00
34 Leon Draisaitl 10.00 25.00
35 Aaron Ekblad 4.00 10.00
36 Aleksander Barkov 6.00 15.00
37 Vincent Trocheck 3.00 8.00
38 Jeff Carter 2.50 6.00
39 Anze Kopitar 5.00 12.00
40 Jonathan Quick 4.00 10.00
41 Devan Dubnyk 2.50 6.00
42 Mikael Granlund 2.50 6.00
43 Nino Niederreiter 2.00 5.00
44 Larry Robinson 3.00 8.00
45 Carey Price 6.00 15.00
46 Jonathan Drouin 2.50 6.00
47 Viktor Arvidsson 2.00 5.00
48 P.K. Subban 4.00 10.00
49 Filip Forsberg 5.00 12.00
50 Martin Brodeur 8.00 20.00
51 Taylor Hall 3.00 8.00
52 Jordan Eberle 3.00 8.00
53 John Tavares 5.00 12.00
54 Pat LaFontaine 3.00 8.00
55 Mark Messier 6.00 15.00
56 Henrik Lundqvist 8.00 20.00
57 Kevin Shattenkirk 2.00 5.00
58 Wayne Gretzky 20.00 50.00
59 Erik Karlsson 4.00 10.00
60 Mark Stone 4.00 10.00
61 Craig Anderson 3.00 8.00
62 Claude Giroux 3.00 8.00
63 Travis Konecny 3.00 8.00
64 Mark Recchi 4.00 10.00
65 Mario Lemieux 12.00 30.00
66 Sidney Crosby 12.00 30.00
67 Matt Murray 5.00 12.00
68 Brent Burns 3.00 8.00
69 Joe Thornton 5.00 12.00
70 Owen Nolan 3.00 8.00
71 Brayden Schenn 3.00 8.00
72 Vladimir Tarasenko 4.00 10.00
73 Brett Hull 6.00 15.00
74 Steven Stamkos 6.00 15.00
75 Nikita Kucherov 6.00 15.00
76 Victor Hedman 4.00 10.00
77 Auston Matthews 12.00 30.00
78 Patrick Marleau 3.00 8.00
79 Doug Gilmour 4.00 10.00
80 Pavel Bure 3.00 8.00
81 Henrik Sedin 4.00 10.00
82 Bo Horvat 4.00 10.00
83 Marc-Andre Fleury 6.00 15.00
84 Jonathan Marchessault 4.00 10.00
85 Alexander Ovechkin 12.00 30.00
86 John Carlson 3.00 8.00
87 Evgeny Kuznetsov 3.00 8.00
88 Mark Scheifele 5.00 12.00
89 Patrik Laine 4.00 10.00
90 Blake Wheeler 3.00 8.00
91 John Hayden JSY 249 RC 15.00 40.00
92 Eric Comrie JSY 249 RC 15.00 40.00
93 Vadim Shipachyov JSY 249 RC 25.00 60.00
94 Samuel Blais RC 10.00 25.00
95 C.J. Smith RC 8.00 20.00
96 Maxime Lagace RC 10.00 25.00
97 Adin Hill JSY AU 249 RC 80.00 200.00
98 Tim Heed JSY AU 249 RC 20.00 50.00
99 Brendan Lemieux JSY AU 249 RC 20.00 50.00
100 Andreas Borgman AU RC 40.00 100.00
101 Alex Kerfoot JSY AU 249 RC 40.00 100.00
102 Christian Jaros RC 8.00 20.00
103 Jan Rutta RC 10.00 25.00
104 Roland McKeown JSY AU 249 RC 20.00 50.00
105 Henrik Haapala RC 10.00 25.00
106 Kevin Roy RC 10.00 25.00
107 Sebastian Aho RC 8.00 20.00
108 Vinni Lettieri RC 8.00 20.00
109 Alex Iafallo JSY AU 249 RC 15.00 40.00
110 Filip Chytil JSY AU 249 RC 15.00 40.00
111 Remi Elie JSY AU 249 RC 12.00 30.00
112 Nathan Walker JSY AU 249 RC 15.00 40.00
113 Samuel Girard JSY AU 249 RC 15.00 40.00
114 Christian Djoos JSY AU 249 RC 15.00 40.00
116 Martin Necas AU RC 60.00 150.00
117 Alex Formenton JSY AU 249 RC 25.00 60.00
118 Jake DeBrusk JSY AU 249 RC 40.00 100.00
119 Mike Vecchione JSY AU 249 RC 12.00 30.00
120 Anders Bjork JSY AU 249 RC 20.00 50.00
121 Will Butcher JSY AU 249 RC 20.00 50.00
122 Owen Tippett JSY AU 249 RC 30.00 80.00
123 Josh Ho-Sang JSY AU 249 RC 20.00 50.00
124 Alexander Nylander
JSY AU 249 RC 25.00 60.00
125 Samuel Morin JSY AU 249 RC 10.00 25.00
126 Nicolas Kerdiles JSY AU 249 RC 15.00 40.00
127 Nick Merkley JSY AU 249 RC 15.00 40.00
128 Jordan Schmaltz JSY AU 249 RC 20.00 50.00
129 Peter Cehlarik JSY AU 249 RC 15.00 40.00
130 Riley Barber JSY AU 249 RC 15.00 40.00
131 Tucker Poolman JSY AU 249 RC 12.00 30.00
132 Valentin Zykov JSY AU 249 RC 15.00 40.00
133 Filip Chlapik JSY AU 249 RC 12.00 30.00
134 Ville Husso JSY AU 249 RC 20.00 50.00
135 Andrew Mangiapane
JSY AU 249 RC 125.00 300.00
136 Andrew Poturalski
JSY AU 249 RC 15.00 40.00
137 Alexandre Carrier JSY AU 249 RC 12.00 30.00
138 Michael Amadio JSY AU 249 RC 15.00 40.00
139 Kalle Kossila JSY AU 249 RC 12.00 30.00
140 Jonny Brodzinski JSY AU 249 RC 20.00 50.00
141 Ian McCoshen JSY AU 249 RC 15.00 40.00
143 Vladislav Kamenev
JSY AU 249 RC 15.00 40.00
144 Vince Dunn JSY AU 249 RC 20.00 50.00
145 Alex Nedeljkovic JSY AU 249 RC 25.00 60.00
146 Robert Hagg JSY AU 249 RC 15.00 40.00
147 Nikita Scherbak JSY AU 249 RC 20.00 50.00
148 Madison Bowey JSY AU 249 RC 10.00 25.00
149 Lucas Wallmark JSY AU 249 RC 15.00 40.00
150 Jon Gillies JSY AU 249 RC 15.00 40.00
151 Janne Kuokkanen JSY AU 249 RC 15.00 40.00
152 Jakob Forsbacka-Karlsson
JSY AU 249 RC 15.00 40.00

153 Jack Roslovic JSY AU 249 RC 20.00 50.00
154 J.T. Compher JSY AU 249 RC 15.00 40.00
155 Ivan Barbashev JSY AU 249 RC 20.00 50.00
156 Haydn Fleury JSY AU 249 RC 15.00 40.00
157 Evgeny Svechnikov JSY AU 249 RC 30.00 80.00
158 Denis Gurianov JSY AU 249 RC 40.00 100.00
159 Colin White JSY AU 249 RC 20.00 50.00
160 Christian Fischer JSY AU 249 RC 20.00 50.00
161 Kailer Yamamoto JSY AU 249 RC 80.00 200.00
162 Adrian Kempe JSY AU 249 RC 30.00 80.00
163 Victor Mete JSY AU 249 RC 15.00 40.00
164 Travis Sanheim JSY AU 249 RC 15.00 40.00
165 Tage Thompson JSY AU 249 RC 150.00 400.00
166 Luke Kunin JSY AU 249 RC 15.00 40.00
167 Logan Brown RC 10.00 25.00
168 Tyson Jost JSY AU 249 RC 30.00 80.00
169 Jesper Bratt JSY AU 249 RC 125.00 300.00
170 Alex Tuch JSY AU 99 RC 300.00 500.00
171 Pierre-Luc Dubois JSY AU 99 RC 200.00 500.00
172 Alex DeBrincat JSY AU/99 RC 300.00 800.00
173 Charlie McAvoy JSY AU 99 RC 200.00 500.00
174 Clayton Keller JSY AU 99 RC 600.00 800.00
175 Brock Boeser JSY AU 99 RC 200.00 500.00
176 Nolan Patrick JSY 99 RC 150.00 350.00
177A Nico Hischier JSY/99 RC 125.00 300.00

2017-18 The Cup Brilliance Autographs

BAB Anders Bjork C 12.00 30.00
BAD Alex Delvecchio B 10.00 25.00
BBB Bill Barber C 10.00 25.00
BBH Bo Horvat A 12.00 30.00
BBS Brady Skjei C 8.00 20.00
BCA Cam Atkinson B 10.00 25.00
BCS Conor Sheary B 10.00 25.00
BCW Colin White B 12.00 30.00
BDD Devan Dubnyk A 8.00 20.00
BFP Felix Potvin A 15.00 40.00
BHF Haydn Fleury B 10.00 25.00
BJC John Carlson B 10.00 25.00
BJG Jake Gardiner B 6.00 15.00
BJH Josh Ho-Sang A 12.00 30.00
BJT Jacob Trouba C 8.00 20.00
BLC Logan Couture A 12.00 30.00
BLK Luke Kunin C 10.00 25.00
BLR Larry Robinson A 12.00 30.00
BMG Mikael Granlund A 8.00 20.00
BMP Max Pacioretty C 10.00 25.00
BMS Mark Scheifele A 15.00 40.00
BPM Patrick Marleau A 10.00 25.00
BRE Ryan Ellis B 8.00 20.00
BRL Rod Langway B 10.00 25.00
BTJ Tyson Jost B 20.00 50.00
BTP Tanner Pearson B 8.00 20.00
BVH Ville Husso C 12.00 30.00
BVM Victor Mete C 15.00 40.00
BWB Will Butcher C 12.00 30.00
BWO Willie O'Ree A 12.00 30.00
BZW Zach Werenski C 15.00 40.00

2017-18 The Cup Color Coded Autographs

CCAD Alex DeBrincat/44 50.00 125.00
CCAM Anthony Mantha/33 15.00 40.00
CCBA Bill Barber/33 20.00 50.00
CCBB Brock Boeser/44 150.00 250.00
CCBH Bo Horvat/33 25.00 60.00
CCBO Bobby Orr/33 80.00 200.00
CCCA Craig Anderson/33 20.00 50.00
CCCK Clayton Keller/44 50.00 125.00
CCCM Connor McDavid/33 100.00 250.00
CCFP Felix Potvin/33 30.00 80.00
CCGL Guy Lafleur/33 25.00 60.00
CCGR Mikael Granlund/33 15.00 40.00
CCJC John Carlson/33 20.00 50.00
CCJG Jake Guentzel/33 30.00 80.00
CCJR Jack Roslovic/44 25.00 60.00
CCKM Kirk Muller/33 15.00 40.00
CCMC Charlie McAvoy/44 50.00 125.00
CCMD Marcel Dionne/33 25.00 60.00
CCMF Marc-Andre Fleury/33 40.00 100.00
CCMG Mike Gartner/33 25.00 60.00
CCOT Owen Tippett/44 40.00 100.00
CCPR Patrick Roy/33 50.00 125.00
CCPT Pierre Turgeon/33 15.00 40.00
CCRE Ryan Ellis/33 15.00 40.00
CCTA Tony Amonte/33 15.00 40.00

2017-18 The Cup Enshrinements

EAD Alex DeBrincat/99 40.00 100.00
EAT Alex Tuch/99 60.00 150.00
EBB Brock Boeser/99 150.00 250.00
EBH Bo Horvat/99 12.00 30.00
EBO Bobby Orr/25 150.00 250.00
ECA Cam Atkinson/99 10.00 25.00
ECK Clayton Keller/99 40.00 100.00
ECP Colton Parayko/99 8.00 20.00
EDS Dave Schultz/99 10.00 25.00
EEK Erik Karlsson/25 60.00 150.00
EGC Gerry Cheevers/99 10.00 25.00
EJC John Carlson/99 10.00 25.00
EJG Jake Guentzel/99 15.00 40.00
EJK Jari Kurri/99 10.00 25.00
EJN James Neal/99 6.00 15.00
EJP Joe Pavelski/99 12.00 30.00
EKY Kailer Yamamoto/99 25.00 60.00
ELM Lanny McDonald/25 10.00 25.00
EMF Marc-Andre Fleury/99 40.00 100.00
EMG Mikael Granlund/99 8.00 20.00
EMP Max Pacioretty/99 10.00 25.00
EMS Mark Scheifele/99 20.00 50.00
ENE Nikolaj Ehlers/99 10.00 25.00
EPT Pierre Turgeon/99 8.00 20.00
ETP Tanner Pearson/99 8.00 20.00
ETR Vincent Trocheck/99 10.00 25.00
EVH Victor Hedman/99 12.00 30.00
EWG Wayne Gretzky/25 250.00 600.00

2017-18 The Cup Foundations Jerseys

FAA Artem Anisimov/25 5.00 12.00
FAB Aleksander Barkov/25 12.00 30.00
FAD Alex DeBrincat/49 20.00 50.00
FAE Aaron Ekblad/25 10.00 25.00
FAM Auston Matthews/25 30.00 80.00
FAN Alexander Nylander/49 12.00 30.00
FAO Alexander Ovechkin/25 30.00 80.00
FAV Andrei Vasilevskiy/25 12.00 30.00
FBB Brock Boeser/49 20.00 50.00
FBH Bo Horvat/25 10.00 25.00
FBM Brandon Montour/25 8.00 20.00
FCA Cam Atkinson/25 8.00 20.00
FCK Clayton Keller/49 20.00 50.00
FCM Connor McDavid/25 40.00 100.00
FCP Colton Parayko/25 6.00 15.00
FDD Devan Dubnyk/25 6.00 15.00
FDK Duncan Keith/25 6.00 15.00
FEK Erik Karlsson/25 10.00 25.00
FGU Jake Guentzel/25 12.00 30.00
FHZ Henrik Zetterberg/25 10.00 25.00
FJB Jamie Benn/25 8.00 20.00
FJC Jeff Carter/25 6.00 15.00
FJD Jonathan Drouin/25 6.00 15.00
FJG Johnny Gaudreau/25 12.00 30.00
FJN James Neal/25 5.00 12.00
FJO Ryan Johansen/25 6.00 15.00
FJP Joe Pavelski/25 10.00 25.00
FJT John Tavares/25 12.00 30.00
FKS Kevin Shattenkirk/25 5.00 12.00
FLD Leon Draisaitl/25 25.00 60.00
FMC Charlie McAvoy/49 20.00 50.00
FMF Marc-Andre Fleury/25 15.00 40.00
FMG Mikael Granlund/25 6.00 15.00
FMM Matt Murray/25 12.00 30.00
FNB Nicklas Backstrom/25 8.00 20.00
FNE Nikolaj Ehlers/25 8.00 20.00
FNH Nico Hischier/49 25.00 60.00
FNK Nikita Kucherov/25 15.00 40.00
FNP Nolan Patrick/49 15.00 40.00
FPD Pierre-Luc Dubois/49 12.00 30.00
FPL Patrik Laine/25 10.00 25.00
FPM Patrick Marleau/25 8.00 20.00
FRJ Roman Josi/25 8.00 20.00
FSA Sebastian Aho/25 12.00 30.00
FTH Joe Thornton/25 12.00 30.00
FTJ Tyson Jost/49 15.00 40.00
FTP Tanner Pearson/25 6.00 15.00
FVH Victor Hedman/25 10.00 25.00
FVT Vladimir Tarasenko/25 10.00 25.00
FWB Will Butcher/49 12.00 30.00

2017-18 The Cup Honorable Numbers

HNAN Alexander Nylander/70 30.00 80.00
HNAT Alex Tuch/89 25.00 60.00
HNAV Andrei Vasilevskiy/88 20.00 50.00
HNDD Devan Dubnyk/40 15.00 40.00
HNJC Jeff Carter/77 12.00 30.00
HNJD Jonathan Drouin/92 30.00 80.00
HNJN James Neal/18 25.00 60.00
HNKY Kailer Yamamoto/56 30.00 80.00
HNMF Marc-Andre Fleury/29 80.00 200.00
HNMR Mikko Rantanen/96 40.00 100.00
HNMS Mark Scheifele/55 50.00 125.00
HNNK Nikita Kucherov/86 125.00 300.00
HNNP Nolan Patrick/19 80.00 200.00
HNPD Pierre-Luc Dubois/18 30.00 80.00
HNSB Sergei Bobrovsky/72 20.00 50.00
HNTJ Tyson Jost/17 30.00 80.00
HNTP Tanner Pearson/70 12.00 30.00

2017-18 The Cup Honorable Numbers Dual

HN2CH J.Carter/V.Hedman 20.00 50.00
HN2HB Patric Hornqvist
Sergei Bobrovsky/72 40.00 100.00
HN2LD P.Laine/L.Draisaitl 60.00 150.00
HNSLM H.Lundqvist/M.Murray 50.00 125.00

2017-18 The Cup Limited Logos Autographs

LLAA Artem Anisimov/50 15.00 40.00
LLAT Cam Atkinson/50 25.00 60.00
LLBA Mathew Barzal/50 30.00 80.00
LLBB Brock Boeser/50 60.00 150.00
LLBM Brandon Montour/50 12.00 30.00
LLCA Craig Anderson/50 25.00 60.00
LLCK Clayton Keller/50 60.00 150.00
LLCM Charlie McAvoy/50 60.00 150.00
LLCP Colton Parayko/50 20.00 50.00
LLDD Devan Dubnyk/25 20.00 50.00
LLDK Duncan Keith/50 20.00 50.00
LLEK Erik Karlsson/25 30.00 80.00
LLJC Jeff Carter/50 20.00 50.00
LLJD Jonathan Drouin/50 20.00 50.00
LLJN James Neal/50 15.00 40.00
LLJP Jason Pominville/50 15.00 40.00
LLJT Jacob Trouba/50 12.00 30.00
LLKS Kevin Shattenkirk/50 15.00 40.00
LLLC Logan Couture/50 30.00 80.00
LLMF Marc-Andre Fleury/25 50.00 125.00
LLMG Mikael Granlund/50 15.00 40.00
LLMR Mikko Rantanen/50 60.00 150.00
LLMZ Mats Zuccarello/50 25.00 60.00
LLNE Nikolaj Ehlers/50 25.00 60.00
LLNH Nico Hischier/25 (No Auto) 80.00 200.00
LLNP Nolan Patrick/25 (No Auto) 50.00 125.00
LLPH Patric Hornqvist/50 15.00 40.00
LLPL Pierre-Luc Dubois/50 40.00 100.00
LLPM Patrick Marleau/25 25.00 60.00
LLSA Sebastian Aho/50 40.00 100.00
LLSB Sergei Bobrovsky/25 40.00 100.00
LLSH Conor Sheary/50 25.00 60.00
LLSS Steven Stamkos/25 80.00 200.00
LLTJ Tyson Jost/50 50.00 125.00
LLTP Tanner Pearson/50 20.00 50.00
LLTR Vincent Trocheck/50 25.00 60.00
LLTS Tyler Seguin/25 30.00 80.00
LLVH Victor Hedman/25 30.00 80.00
LLVT Vladimir Tarasenko/25 30.00 80.00

2017-18 The Cup Rookie Gear Relic Autographs

ARGAD Alex DeBrincat 50.00 125.00
ARGAK Alex Kerfoot 40.00 100.00
ARGAT Alex Tuch 40.00 100.00
ARGBB Brock Boeser 50.00 120.00
ARGCK Clayton Keller 50.00 125.00
ARGCW Colin White 25.00 60.00
ARGHF Haydn Fleury 20.00 50.00
ARGJB Jesper Bratt 40.00 100.00
ARGJD Jake DeBrusk 50.00 120.00
ARGJR Jack Roslovic 25.00 60.00
ARGKY Kailer Yamamoto 50.00 125.00
ARGLK Luke Kunin 20.00 50.00
ARGNM Nick Merkley 20.00 50.00
ARGPD Pierre-Luc Dubois 30.00 80.00
ARGTJ Tyson Jost 40.00 100.00
ARGWB Will Butcher 25.00 60.00

2017-18 The Cup Scripted Sticks

SSAE Aaron Ekblad 25.00 60.00
SSAV Andrei Vasilevskiy 30.00 80.00
SSCC Chris Chelios 20.00 50.00
SSCM Connor McDavid 100.00 250.00
SSCN Cam Neely 20.00 50.00
SSCP Carey Price 40.00 100.00
SSDD Devan Dubnyk 15.00 40.00
SSDP Denis Potvin 20.00 50.00
SSDT Dave Taylor 15.00 40.00
SSMG Mike Gartner 25.00 60.00
SSTP Tanner Pearson 15.00 40.00

2017-18 The Cup Scripted Swatches

SWAD Alex DeBrincat/35 50.00 125.00
SWAN Craig Anderson/35 20.00 50.00
SWAT Alex Tuch/35 50.00 125.00
SWBB Brock Boeser/35 50.00 120.00
SWCA John Carlson/35 20.00 50.00
SWCK Clayton Keller/35 50.00 125.00
SWCM Connor McDavid/35 100.00 250.00
SWDD Devan Dubnyk/35 15.00 40.00
SWHL Henrik Lundqvist/35 50.00 125.00
SWJC Jeff Carter/35 15.00 40.00
SWKS Kevin Shattenkirk/35 12.00 30.00
SWMC Charlie McAvoy/35 50.00 125.00
SWMF Marc-Andre Fleury/35 40.00 100.00
SWMS Mark Scheifele/35 30.00 80.00
SWNK Nikita Kucherov/35 40.00 100.00
SWPD Pierre-Luc Dubois/35 30.00 80.00
SWPL Patrik Laine/35 25.00 60.00
SWPM Patrick Marleau/35 20.00 50.00
SWTJ Tyson Jost/35 40.00 100.00
SWTS Tyler Seguin/35 25.00 60.00
SWWB Will Butcher/35 25.00 60.00
SWZW Zach Werenski/35 30.00 80.00

2017-18 The Cup Signature Patches

SPAA Artem Anisimov/99 10.00 25.00
SPAD Alex DeBrincat/99 80.00 200.00
SPAO Alexander Ovechkin/25 60.00 150.00
SPAT Cam Atkinson/99 15.00 40.00
SPAV Andrei Vasilevskiy/99 25.00 60.00
SPBB Brock Boeser/99 40.00 100.00
SPBH Brett Hull/25 40.00 100.00
SPBO Bo Horvat/99 25.00 60.00
SPCA John Carlson/99 15.00 40.00
SPCK Clayton Keller/99 40.00 100.00
SPCM Connor McDavid/25 300.00 450.00
SPCP Colton Parayko/99 12.00 30.00
SPCW Colin White/99 20.00 50.00
SPDK Duncan Keith/99 20.00 50.00
SPEK Erik Karlsson/25 30.00 80.00
SPGU Jake Guentzel/99 25.00 60.00
SPHL Henrik Lundqvist/25 50.00 125.00
SPJB Jesper Bratt/99 30.00 80.00
SPJC Jeff Carter/99 12.00 30.00
SPJD Jake DeBrusk/99 40.00 100.00
SPJG Jake Gardiner/99 10.00 25.00
SPJH Josh Ho-Sang/99 20.00 50.00
SPJM Jonathan Marchessault/99 20.00 50.00
SPJN James Neal/99 10.00 25.00
SPJP Joe Pavelski/99 20.00 50.00
SPJR Jack Roslovic/99 20.00 50.00
SPJT Jonathan Toews/25 50.00 125.00
SPKS Kevin Shattenkirk/99 10.00 25.00
SPKY Kailer Yamamoto/99 40.00 100.00
SPLC Logan Couture/99 20.00 50.00
SPLD Leon Draisaitl/99 50.00 125.00
SPLK Luke Kunin/99 15.00 40.00
SPLR Larry Robinson/25 20.00 50.00
SPMC Charlie McAvoy/99 100.00 250.00
SPMG Mikael Granlund/99 12.00 30.00
SPMP Max Pacioretty/99 15.00 40.00
SPNE Nikolaj Ehlers/99 15.00 40.00
SPNM Nick Merkley/99 15.00 40.00
SPOT Owen Tippett/99 30.00 80.00
SPPL Patrik Laine/99 30.00 80.00
SPRA Mikko Rantanen/99 40.00 100.00
SPSS Steven Stamkos/25 30.00 80.00
SPTJ Tyson Jost/99 30.00 80.00
SPTP Tanner Pearson/99 12.00 30.00
SPTR Vincent Trocheck/99 15.00 40.00
SPVH Victor Hedman/99 15.00 40.00
SPZW Zach Werenski/99 25.00 60.00

2017-18 The Cup Signature Patches Dual

SP2DG D.Dubnyk/M.Granlund/35 12.00 30.00
SP2MN J.Marchessault/J.Neal/35 20.00 50.00
SP2PC J.Pavelski/L.Couture/35 20.00 50.00
SP2SL K.Shattenkirk/H.Lundqvist/35 40.00 100.00
SP2TJ T.Pearson/J.Carter/35 12.00 30.00
SP2VH A.Vasilevskiy/V.Hedman/35 25.00 60.00

2017-18 The Cup Signature Renditions

SRAB Alex DeBrincat E 40.00 100.00
SRAM Andy Moog E 15.00 40.00
SRAO Alexander Ovechkin B 60.00 150.00
SRAS Brock Boeser MVP E 40.00 100.00
SRAT Alex Tuch E 40.00 100.00
SRBB Brock Boeser Hat Trick D 40.00 100.00
SRBH Brett Hull B 30.00 80.00
SRBO Bobby Orr A 60.00 150.00
SRCK Clayton Keller D 40.00 100.00
SRCM Connor McDavid A 80.00 200.00
SRDD Devan Dubnyk E 12.00 30.00
SREK Erik Karlsson A 20.00 50.00
SRGC Gerry Cheevers E 15.00 40.00
SRJG Jake Guentzel E 25.00 60.00
SRJN James Neal E 10.00 25.00
SRKY Kailer Yamamoto E 40.00 100.00
SRMC Charlie McAvoy E 50.00 120.00
SRMF Marc-Andre Fleury C 30.00 80.00
SRMS Mark Scheifele E 25.00 60.00
SRPD Pierre-Luc Dubois E 25.00 60.00
SRPM Patrick Marleau C 15.00 40.00
SRPR Patrick Roy A 40.00 100.00
SRPT Pierre Turgeon E 12.00 30.00
SRSB Scotty Bowman B 20.00 50.00
SRTA Tony Amonte E 12.00 30.00
SRWB Will Butcher D 20.00 50.00
SRWG Wayne Gretzky A 200.00 500.00

2018-19 The Cup

1 Teemu Selanne 3.00 8.00
2 John Gibson 1.50 4.00
3 Clayton Keller 2.00 5.00
4 Bobby Orr 6.00 15.00
5 Brad Marchand 3.00 8.00
6 Dominik Hasek 2.50 6.00
7 Jack Eichel 2.50 6.00
8 Sean Monahan 1.00 2.50
9 Matthew Tkachuk 3.00 8.00
10 Teuvo Teravainen 1.50 4.00
11 Sebastian Aho 2.50 6.00
12 Alex DeBrincat 2.50 6.00
13 Patrick Kane 3.00 8.00
14 Nathan MacKinnon 6.00 15.00
15 Mikko Rantanen 4.00 10.00
16 Seth Jones 1.50 4.00
17 John Klingberg 1.50 4.00
18 Tyler Seguin 2.00 5.00
19 Steve Yzerman 4.00 10.00
20 Dylan Larkin 2.00 5.00
21 Connor McDavid 8.00 20.00
22 Leon Draisaitl 5.00 12.00
23 Aleksander Barkov 2.50 6.00
24 Vincent Trocheck 1.50 4.00
25 Wayne Gretzky 10.00 25.00
26 Drew Doughty 2.00 5.00
27 Eric Staal 1.50 4.00
28 Mikael Granlund 1.25 3.00
29 Carey Price 3.00 8.00
30 Patrick Roy 4.00 10.00
31 P.K. Subban 2.00 5.00
32 Filip Forsberg 2.50 6.00
33 Taylor Hall 1.50 4.00
34 Nico Hischier 2.50 6.00
35 Mathew Barzal 2.00 5.00
36 Anders Lee 1.25 3.00
37 Henrik Lundqvist 4.00 10.00
38 Jaromir Jagr 5.00 12.00
39 Mark Stone 2.00 5.00
40 Thomas Chabot 1.50 4.00
41 Sean Couturier 1.25 3.00
42 Claude Giroux 1.50 4.00
43 Sidney Crosby 6.00 15.00
44 Mario Lemieux 6.00 15.00
45 Brent Burns 1.50 4.00
46 Tomas Hertl 1.50 4.00
47 Ryan O'Reilly 1.50 4.00
48 Vladimir Tarasenko 2.00 5.00
49 Steven Stamkos 3.00 8.00
50 Andrei Vasilevskiy 2.50 6.00
51 Auston Matthews 6.00 15.00
52 John Tavares 2.50 6.00
53 Bo Horvat 2.00 5.00
54 Brock Boeser 2.00 5.00
55 Marc-Andre Fleury 3.00 8.00
56 William Karlsson 2.00 5.00
57 Alexander Ovechkin 6.00 15.00
58 Evgeny Kuznetsov 2.00 5.00
59 Mark Scheifele 2.50 6.00
60 Blake Wheeler 1.50 4.00
61 Elias Pettersson JSY AU/99 RC 1200.00 3000.00
62 Andrei Svechnikov JSY AU/99 RC 600.00 1500.00
63 Casey Mittelstadt JSY AU/99 RC 100.00 250.00
64 Eeli Tolvanen JSY AU/99 RC 100.00 250.00
65 Jesperi Kotkaniemi JSY AU/99 RC 80.00 200.00
66 Brady Tkachuk JSY AU/99 RC 400.00 1000.00
67 Rasmus Dahlin JSY/99 RC 150.00 400.00
68 Michael Rasmussen JSY AU/249 RC 20.00 50.00
69 Ilya Samsonov JSY AU/249 RC 100.00 200.00
70 Noah Juulsen JSY AU/249 RC 15.00 40.00
71 Nicolas Roy JSY AU/249 RC 10.00 25.00
72 Sami Niku JSY AU/249 RC 12.00 30.00
73 Troy Terry JSY AU/249 XRC 150.00 400.00
74 Victor Ejdsell JSY AU/249 RC 12.00 30.00
75 Ryan Donato JSY/249 RC 25.00 60.00
76 Jakub Zboril JSY AU/249 RC 25.00 60.00
77 Michael Dal Colle JSY AU/249 RC 15.00 40.00
78 Cooper Marody JSY AU/249 RC 25.00 60.00
79 Jaret Anderson-Dolan JSY AU/249 RC 12.00 30.00
80 Dominic Turgeon JSY AU/249 RC 15.00 40.00
81 Ethan Bear JSY AU/249 RC 25.00 60.00
82 John Gilmour JSY AU/249 RC 10.00 25.00
83 Warren Foegele JSY AU/249 RC 15.00 40.00
84 Henrik Borgstrom JSY AU/249 RC 25.00 60.00
85 Zach Aston-Reese JSY AU/249 RC 25.00 60.00
86 Brett Howden JSY AU/249 RC 20.00 50.00
87 Jordan Kyrou JSY AU/249 RC 100.00 250.00
88 Daniel Brickley JSY AU/249 RC 15.00 40.00
89 Anthony Cirelli JSY AU/249 RC 25.00 60.00
90 Oskar Lindblom JSY AU/249 RC 25.00 60.00
91 Henri Jokiharju JSY AU/249 RC 12.00 30.00
92 Spencer Foo JSY AU/249 RC 12.00 30.00
93 Tomas Hyka JSY AU/249 RC 15.00 40.00
94 Robert Thomas JSY AU/249 RC 30.00 80.00
95 Blake Hillman JSY AU/249 RC 15.00 40.00
96 Jordan Greenway JSY AU/249 RC 15.00 40.00
97 Miro Heiskanen JSY AU/249 RC 100.00 250.00
98 Lias Andersson JSY AU/249 RC 25.00 60.00
99 Dylan Gambrell JSY AU/249 RC 15.00 40.00
100 Louie Belpedio JSY AU/249 RC 12.00 30.00
101 Travis Dermott JSY AU/249 RC 25.00 60.00
102 Dylan Sikura JSY AU/249 RC 20.00 50.00
103 Adam Gaudette JSY AU/249 RC 25.00 60.00
104 Sam Steel JSY AU/249 RC 30.00 80.00
105 Dillon Dube JSY AU/249 RC 20.00 50.00
106 Antti Suomela JSY AU/249 RC 12.00 30.00
107 Jeremy Lauzon JSY AU/249 RC 20.00 50.00
108 Maxime Lajoie JSY AU/249 RC 25.00 60.00
109 Evan Bouchard JSY AU/249 RC 100.00 250.00
110 Juuso Valimaki JSY AU/249 RC 15.00 40.00
111 Isac Lundestrom JSY AU/249 RC 12.00 30.00
112 Maxime Comtois JSY AU/249 RC 40.00 100.00
113 Mackenzie Blackwood JSY AU/249 RC 30.00 80.00
114 Kristian Vesalainen JSY AU/249 RC 20.00 50.00
115 Mathieu Joseph JSY AU/249 RC 20.00 50.00
116 Mikhail Vorobyev JSY AU/249 RC 12.00 30.00
117 Kiefer Sherwood JSY AU/249 RC 12.00 30.00
118 Samuel Montembeault JSY AU/249 RC 30.00 80.00
119 Mitch Reinke JSY AU/249 RC 12.00 30.00
120 Neal Pionk JSY AU/249 RC 15.00 40.00
121 Maxim Mamin/249 RC 3.00 8.00
122 Andreas Johnsson JSY AU/249 RC 50.00 125.00
123 Joey Anderson JSY AU/249 RC 15.00 40.00
124 Landon Bow JSY AU/249 RC 12.00 30.00
125 Par Lindholm JSY AU/249 RC 12.00 30.00
126 Filip Hronek JSY AU/249 RC 15.00 40.00
127 Dan Vladar JSY AU/249 RC 20.00 50.00
128 Moritz Klimchuk JSY AU/249 RC 15.00 40.00
129 Zach Whitecloud JSY AU/249 RC 12.00 30.00
130 Carter Hart JSY AU/249 RC 200.00 450.00
131 Roope Hintz AU/249 RC 60.00 150.00
132 Austin Wagner AU/249 RC 12.00 30.00
133 Brett Seney JSY AU/249 RC 12.00 30.00
134 Jonas Siegenthaler JSY AU/249 RC 15.00 40.00
135 Urho Vaakanainen JSY AU/249 RC 30.00 80.00
136 Dennis Cholowski JSY AU/249 RC 15.00 40.00
137 Dominik Kahun JSY AU/249 RC 15.00 40.00
138 Josh Mahura JSY AU/249 RC 12.00 30.00
139 Jayce Hawryluk JSY AU/249 RC 12.00 30.00
140 Cal Petersen JSY AU/249 RC 12.00 30.00
141 Jake Bean JSY AU/249 RC 15.00 40.00
142 Ben Hicketts JSY AU/249 RC 15.00 40.00
143 Christoffer Ehn JSY AU/249 RC 12.00 30.00
144 Michael McLeod JSY AU/249 RC 12.00 30.00
145 Drake Batherson JSY AU/249 RC 80.00 200.00
146 Conor Garland JSY AU/249 RC 15.00 40.00
147 Marcus Pettersson JSY AU/249 RC 15.00 40.00
148 Matt Luff/249 RC 5.00 12.00
149 Collin Delia/249 RC 4.00 10.00
150 Mason Appleton/249 RC 2.50 6.00

2018-19 The Cup Brilliance Autographs

BAL Anders Lee 10.00 25.00
BAM Andy Moog 12.00 30.00
BAS Andrei Svechnikov 30.00 80.00
BBB Brock Boeser 15.00 40.00
BBO Bobby Orr 50.00 125.00
BCH Carter Hart 25.00 60.00
BCM Connor McDavid 200.00 300.00
BED Evgenii Dadonov 8.00 20.00
BEP Elias Pettersson 60.00 150.00
BHL Henrik Lundqvist 30.00 80.00
BJB Jake Bean 10.00 25.00
BJK Jesperi Kotkaniemi 25.00 60.00
BJT Joe Thornton 20.00 50.00
BKT Kyle Turris 10.00 25.00
BMA Anthony Mantha 15.00 40.00
BMG Mike Gartner 15.00 40.00
BMM Michael McLeod 12.00 30.00
BPR Patrick Roy 30.00 80.00
BTT Teuvo Teravainen 12.00 30.00
BTW Tom Wilson 12.00 30.00
BWG Wayne Gretzky 250.00 600.00

2018-19 The Cup Color Coded Autographs

CCAI Arturs Irbe/22 20.00 50.00
CCAS Andrei Svechnikov/33 60.00 150.00
CCBH Brett Howden/33 20.00 50.00
CCBM Brad Marchand/22 50.00 125.00
CCBO Bobby Orr/22 100.00 250.00
CCBT Brady Tkachuk/33 80.00 200.00
CCCA Cam Atkinson/22 25.00 60.00
CCCH Carter Hart/33 50.00 125.00
CCCJ Curtis Joseph/22 30.00 80.00
CCCM Connor McDavid/22 200.00 350.00
CCDB Drake Batherson/33 50.00 125.00
CCEP Elias Pettersson/33 150.00 400.00
CCGL Guy Lafleur/22 30.00 80.00
CCHJ Henri Jokiharju/33 20.00 50.00
CCJE Jack Eichel/22 80.00 200.00
CCJK Jesperi Kotkaniemi/33 50.00 125.00
CCJT John Tavares/22 50.00 125.00
CCMH Miro Heiskanen/33 80.00 200.00
CCMS Mark Scheifele/22 40.00 100.00
CCNH Nico Hischier/22 40.00 100.00
CCPR Patrick Roy/22 80.00 200.00
CCWG Wayne Gretzky/22 250.00 600.00

2018-19 The Cup Enshrinements

EAI Arturs Irbe/99 15.00 40.00
EAS Andrei Svechnikov/99 60.00 150.00
EAT Alex Tuch/99 20.00 50.00
EBM Brad Marchand/99 40.00 100.00
EBO Bobby Orr/25 80.00 200.00
EBS Brayden Schenn/99 20.00 50.00
EBT Brady Tkachuk/99 60.00 150.00
ECH Carter Hart/99 40.00 100.00
ECM Connor McDavid/25 250.00 350.00
EEP Elias Pettersson/99 60.00 150.00
EES Eric Staal/99 20.00 50.00
EFP Felix Potvin/99 30.00 80.00
EHB Henrik Borgstrom/99 30.00 80.00
EJB Jake Bean/99 20.00 50.00
EJK Jesperi Kotkaniemi/99 40.00 100.00
EMH Miro Heiskanen/99 50.00 125.00
EMS Mark Stone/99 25.00 60.00
ENU Norm Ullman/99 20.00 50.00
EPL Pat LaFontaine/25 50.00 125.00
EPR Patrick Roy/25 50.00 125.00
ERH Ron Hextall/99 20.00 50.00
ERL Rod Langway/99 15.00 40.00
ETH Tomas Hertl/99 20.00 50.00
ETW Tom Wilson/99 20.00 50.00
EWG Wayne Gretzky/25 250.00 600.00

2018-19 The Cup Foundations Jerseys

FAJ Andreas Johnsson 8.00 20.00
FAM Auston Matthews 25.00 60.00
FAS Andrei Svechnikov 15.00 40.00
FBB Brent Burns 6.00 15.00
FBM Brad Marchand 12.00 30.00
FBP Brayden Point 8.00 20.00
FBT Brady Tkachuk 20.00 50.00
FCH Carter Hart 12.00 30.00
FCM Connor McDavid 30.00 80.00
FCP Carey Price 12.00 30.00
FEK Evgeny Kuznetsov 8.00 20.00
FEP Elias Pettersson 20.00 50.00
FES Eric Staal 6.00 15.00
FET Eeli Tolvanen 12.00 30.00
FJE Jack Eichel 10.00 25.00
FJG Johnny Gaudreau 10.00 25.00
FJJ Joe Thornton 10.00 25.00
FJK Jesperi Kotkaniemi 12.00 30.00
FJQ Jonathan Quick 8.00 20.00
FJT John Tavares 10.00 25.00
FMH Miro Heiskanen 15.00 40.00
FMI Casey Mittelstadt 12.00 30.00
FMR Michael Rasmussen 8.00 20.00
FMS Mark Scheifele 10.00 25.00
FNH Nico Hischier 10.00 25.00
FPD Pierre-Luc Dubois 5.00 12.00
FSC Sidney Crosby 25.00 60.00
FSM Sean Monahan 4.00 10.00
FSS Steven Stamkos 12.00 30.00
FWK William Karlsson 6.00 15.00

2018-19 The Cup Hockey Hall of Fame Anniversary 75/25 Patch Autographs

HOFBB Bill Barber 12.00 30.00
HOFBC Bobby Clarke 20.00 50.00
HOFBO Bobby Orr 100.00 200.00
HOFBR Martin Brodeur 30.00 80.00
HOFCC Chris Chelios 12.00 30.00
HOFDG Doug Gilmour 15.00 40.00
HOFDH Dale Hawerchuk 15.00 40.00
HOFFM Frank Mahovlich 12.00 30.00
HOFGB Brett Hull 25.00 60.00
HOFGC Gerry Cheevers 12.00 30.00
HOFGJ Bobby Hull 25.00 60.00
HOFGL Guy Lafleur 15.00 40.00
HOFLM Lanny McDonald 12.00 30.00
HOFLR Larry Robinson 12.00 30.00
HOFMB Mike Bossy 12.00 30.00
HOFMG Mike Gartner 15.00 40.00
HOFML Mario Lemieux 50.00 125.00
HOFMM Mark Messier 25.00 60.00
HOFNL Nicklas Lidstrom 12.00 30.00
HOFNU Norm Ullman 12.00 30.00
HOFPC Paul Coffey 12.00 30.00
HOFPL Pat LaFontaine 12.00 30.00
HOFPR Patrick Roy 30.00 80.00
HOFRB Ray Bourque 20.00 50.00
HOFWG Wayne Gretzky 250.00 600.00
HOFWO Willie O'Ree 15.00 40.00

2018-19 The Cup Hockey Hall of Fame Anniversary 75/25 Patches

HOFAB Andy Bathgate 5.00 12.00
HOFBL Brian Leetch 5.00 12.00
HOFBP Brad Park 5.00 12.00
HOFBT Bryan Trottier 6.00 15.00
HOFDS Darryl Sittler 8.00 20.00
HOFES Eddie Shore 6.00 15.00
HOFGF Grant Fuhr 10.00 25.00
HOFHM Howie Morenz 6.00 15.00
HOFJB Jean Beliveau 6.00 15.00
HOFJK Jari Kurri 6.00 15.00
HOFJO Johnny Bower 6.00 15.00
HOFJP Jacques Plante 6.00 15.00
HOFMR Maurice Richard 12.00 30.00
HOFMS Mats Sundin 6.00 15.00
HOFPA Bernie Parent 8.00 20.00
HOFPF Peter Forsberg 12.00 30.00
HOFSM Stan Mikita 6.00 15.00
HOFSS Serge Savard 6.00 15.00
HOFTH Tim Horton 10.00 25.00
HOFTL Ted Lindsay 6.00 15.00
HOFTS Terry Sawchuk 6.00 15.00

2018-19 The Cup Honorable Numbers

HNCH Connor Hellebuyck/37 50.00 125.00
HNDB Drake Batherson/79 40.00 100.00
HNDS Daniel Sedin/22 40.00 100.00
HNED Evgenii Dadonov/63 20.00 50.00
HNEP Elias Pettersson/40 250.00 600.00
HNJM Jonathan Marchessault/81 40.00 100.00
HNRD Rasmus Dahlin/26 60.00 150.00
HNTH Tomas Hertl/48 30.00 80.00

2018-19 The Cup Limited Logos Autographs

LLAL Anders Lee/50 20.00 50.00
LLAM Anthony Mantha/50 20.00 50.00
LLAS Andrei Svechnikov/50 125.00 300.00
LLAT Alex Tuch/50 25.00 60.00
LLBS Brayden Schenn/50 25.00 60.00
LLBT Brady Tkachuk/50 80.00 200.00
LLCH Connor Hellebuyck/50 50.00 125.00
LLDS Daniel Sedin/25 30.00 80.00
LLED Evgenii Dadonov/50 15.00 40.00
LLEP Elias Pettersson/50 80.00 200.00
LLES Eric Staal/50 25.00 60.00
LLGR Jordan Greenway/50 20.00 50.00
LLHS Henrik Sedin/25 30.00 80.00
LLJE Jack Eichel/25 40.00 100.00
LLJG Jake Guentzel/50 30.00 80.00
LLJM Jonathan Marchessault/50 30.00 80.00
LLJT Joe Thornton/25 40.00 100.00
LLKT Kyle Turris/50 20.00 50.00
LLMH Miro Heiskanen/50 60.00 150.00
LLMS Mark Stone/50 30.00 80.00
LLRD Rasmus Dahlin/25 (No Auto) 60.00 150.00
LLRE Ryan Ellis/50 20.00 50.00
LLSA Sebastian Aho/50 40.00 100.00
LLSM Sean Monahan/50 15.00 40.00
LLTA John Tavares/25 40.00 100.00
LLTH Tomas Hertl/50 25.00 60.00
LLTT Teuvo Teravainen/50 25.00 60.00
LLTW Tom Wilson/50 25.00 60.00

2018-19 The Cup Rookie Class of 2019

2019AJ Andreas Johnsson 6.00 15.00
2019AS Andrei Svechnikov 12.00 30.00
2019BH Brett Howden 6.00 15.00
2019BT Brady Tkachuk 15.00 40.00
2019CH Carter Hart 10.00 25.00
2019CM Casey Mittelstadt 10.00 25.00
2019DB Drake Batherson 10.00 25.00
2019DC Dennis Cholowski 5.00 12.00
2019DD Dillon Dube 6.00 15.00
2019DO Ryan Donato 8.00 20.00
2019EB Evan Bouchard 12.00 30.00
2019EP Elias Pettersson 15.00 40.00
2019ET Eeli Tolvanen 10.00 25.00
2019HB Henrik Borgstrom 8.00 20.00
2019HJ Henri Jokiharju 4.00 10.00
2019IS Ilya Samsonov 10.00 25.00
2019JK Jesperi Kotkaniemi 10.00 25.00
2019JV Juuso Valimaki 5.00 12.00
2019KV Kristian Vesalainen 6.00 15.00
2019KY Jordan Kyrou 10.00 25.00
2019LA Lias Andersson 8.00 20.00
2019MB Mackenzie Blackwood 10.00 25.00
2019MC Maxime Comtois 5.00 12.00
2019MH Miro Heiskanen 12.00 30.00
2019ML Maxime Lajoie 8.00 20.00
2019MR Michael Rasmussen 6.00 15.00
2019RD Rasmus Dahlin 12.00 30.00
2019RT Robert Thomas 10.00 25.00
2019SS Sam Steel 5.00 12.00
2019TD Travis Dermott 8.00 20.00

2018-19 The Cup Rookie Class of 2019 Gold

2019AJ Andreas Johnsson AU 25.00 60.00
2019AS Andrei Svechnikov AU 50.00 125.00
2019BH Brett Howden AU 25.00 60.00
2019BT Brady Tkachuk AU 60.00 150.00
2019CH Carter Hart AU 40.00 100.00
2019DB Drake Batherson AU 40.00 100.00
2019DC Dennis Cholowski AU 20.00 50.00
2019DD Dillon Dube AU 25.00 60.00
2019EB Evan Bouchard AU 25.00 60.00
2019EP Elias Pettersson AU 60.00 150.00
2019HB Henrik Borgstrom AU 30.00 80.00
2019HJ Henri Jokiharju AU 15.00 40.00
2019JK Jesperi Kotkaniemi AU 40.00 100.00
2019JV Juuso Valimaki AU 20.00 50.00
2019KV Kristian Vesalainen AU 25.00 60.00
2019KY Jordan Kyrou AU 40.00 100.00
2019MC Maxime Comtois AU 20.00 50.00
2019MH Miro Heiskanen AU 50.00 120.00
2019ML Maxime Lajoie AU 30.00 80.00
2019MR Michael Rasmussen AU 25.00 60.00
2019RT Robert Thomas AU 40.00 100.00
2019SS Sam Steel AU 20.00 50.00
2019TD Travis Dermott AU 30.00 80.00

2018-19 The Cup Rookie Gear Relic Autographs

ARGAS Andrei Svechnikov 80.00 200.00
ARGBH Brett Howden 40.00 100.00
ARGBT Brady Tkachuk 100.00 250.00
ARGCH Carter Hart 250.00 400.00
ARGDB Drake Batherson 60.00 150.00
ARGDC Dennis Cholowski 30.00 80.00
ARGEP Elias Pettersson 300.00 800.00
ARGHJ Henri Jokiharju 25.00 60.00
ARGJG Jordan Greenway 25.00 60.00
ARGLA Lias Andersson 50.00 125.00
ARGMH Miro Heiskanen 80.00 200.00
ARGMR Michael Rasmussen 80.00 200.00
ARGTD Travis Dermott 50.00 125.00

2018-19 The Cup Scripted Swatches

SWAL Anders Lee 15.00 40.00
SWAV Andrei Vasilevskiy 30.00 80.00
SWBH Brett Howden 25.00 60.00
SWBO Brock Boeser 25.00 60.00
SWBT Brady Tkachuk 60.00 150.00
SWCH Carter Hart 40.00 100.00
SWCH Connor Hellebuyck 40.00 100.00
SWCM Connor McDavid 150.00 250.00
SWDC Dennis Cholowski 20.00 50.00
SWEP Elias Pettersson 60.00 150.00
SWES Eric Staal 20.00 50.00
SWEV Evgeny Kuznetsov 20.00 50.00
SWHL Henrik Lundqvist 50.00 125.00
SWJE Jack Eichel 30.00 80.00
SWJZ Jakub Zboril 30.00 80.00
SWKO Jesperi Kotkaniemi 40.00 100.00
SWNH Nico Hischier 30.00 80.00
SWRA Michael Rasmussen 25.00 60.00
SWRD Ryan Donato 30.00 80.00
SWTD Travis Dermott 30.00 80.00
SWTW Tom Wilson 25.00 60.00

2018-19 The Cup Signature Renditions

SRAI Arturs Irbe 12.00 30.00
SRAS Andrei Svechnikov 40.00 100.00
SRBH Brett Howden 20.00 50.00
SRBO Brock Boeser 20.00 50.00
SRCC Chris Chelios 15.00 40.00
SRCM Connor McDavid 150.00 250.00
SRCP Cal Petersen 12.00 30.00
SREP Elias Pettersson 100.00 250.00
SRHL Henrik Lundqvist 40.00 100.00
SRJE Jack Eichel 30.00 80.00
SRJJ Joe Thornton 25.00 60.00
SRJK Jesperi Kotkaniemi 30.00 80.00
SRJT John Tavares 25.00 60.00
SRMH Miro Heiskanen 40.00 100.00
SRNH Nico Hischier 25.00 60.00
SRPM Patrick Marleau 15.00 40.00
SRPR Patrick Roy 40.00 100.00
SRRH Ron Hextall 15.00 40.00
SRSC Sidney Crosby 350.00 450.00
SRTH Tomas Hertl 15.00 40.00
SRWG Wayne Gretzky 200.00 500.00
SRWO Willie O'Ree 20.00 50.00

2018-19 The Cup Team Canada Juniors Rookie Tribute

104 Anthony Mantha 3.00 8.00
107 Mathew Barzal 5.00 12.00
109 Ryan Ellis 3.00 8.00
138 Brendan Gallagher 4.00 10.00
142 Brayden Point 5.00 12.00
162 Darnell Nurse 3.00 8.00
176 Mark Scheifele 6.00 15.00
178 Sean Couturier 3.00 8.00
180 Jonathan Drouin 3.00 8.00
197 Connor McDavid 30.00 80.00

2018-19 The Cup The Show Autographs

TSAS Andrei Svechnikov 60.00 150.00
TSBO Bobby Orr 100.00 250.00
TSBT Brady Tkachuk 80.00 200.00
TSCH Carter Hart 50.00 125.00
TSCM Connor McDavid 125.00 300.00
TSEP Elias Pettersson 80.00 200.00
TSJK Jesperi Kotkaniemi 50.00 125.00
TSMH Miro Heiskanen 60.00 150.00
TSML Mario Lemieux 100.00 250.00
TSPR Patrick Roy 60.00 150.00
TSWG Wayne Gretzky 250.00 600.00

2018-19 The Cup Trilaterals Materials

TLAM Auston Matthews 40.00 100.00
TLAO Alexander Ovechkin 40.00 100.00
TLAS Andrei Svechnikov 25.00 60.00
TLBB Brent Burns 10.00 25.00
TLBL Mackenzie Blackwood 20.00 50.00
TLBT Brady Tkachuk 30.00 80.00
TLCH Carter Hart 20.00 50.00
TLCM Connor McDavid 50.00 125.00
TLCP Carey Price 20.00 50.00
TLDB Drake Batherson 20.00 50.00
TLEP Elias Pettersson 30.00 80.00
TLES Eric Staal 10.00 25.00
TLET Eeli Tolvanen 20.00 50.00
TLIS Ilya Samsonov 20.00 50.00
TLJE Jack Eichel 15.00 40.00
TLJK Jesperi Kotkaniemi 20.00 50.00
TLJQ Jonathan Quick 12.00 30.00
TLJT John Tavares 15.00 40.00
TLMB Martin Brodeur 25.00 60.00
TLMH Miro Heiskanen 25.00 60.00
TLMI Casey Mittelstadt 20.00 50.00
TLMR Mikko Rantanen 25.00 60.00
TLNH Nico Hischier 15.00 40.00
TLNM Nathan MacKinnon 40.00 100.00
TLPK Patrick Kane 20.00 50.00
TLRA Michael Rasmussen 12.00 30.00
TLRB Ray Bourque 15.00 40.00
TLRD Rasmus Dahlin 25.00 60.00
TLSC Sidney Crosby 40.00 100.00
TLSY Steve Yzerman 25.00 60.00
TLWK William Karlsson 12.00 30.00

2018-19 The Cup Trios Jerseys

C3AD1 Henrique/Kase/Rakell 8.00 20.00
C3AD2 Getzlaf/Perry/Gibson 15.00 40.00
C3ARI Stepan/Keller/Ekman-Larsson 12.00 30.00
C3AZC Dvorak/Galchenyuk
Hjalmarsson 8.00 20.00
C3BHR Kahun/Jokiharju/Sikura 12.00 30.00
C3BOS Pastrnak/Bergeron/Marchand 25.00 60.00
C3BUF Eichel/Okposo/Pominville 15.00 40.00
C3CAR Teravainen/Aho/Hamilton 15.00 40.00
C3CBH Toews/Kane/DeBrincat 20.00 50.00
C3CBJ Atkinson/Dubois/Werenski 15.00 40.00
C3CF1 Lindholm/Gaudreau/Tkachuk 20.00 50.00
C3CF2 Monahan/Giordano/Hanifin 10.00 25.00
C3COL Rantanen/MacKinnon
Landeskog 40.00 100.00
C3DAL Seguin/Benn/Klingberg 12.00 30.00
C3DRW Athanasiou/Larkin/Bertuzzi 12.00 30.00
C3EDM Nurse/Draisaitl
Nugent-Hopkins 30.00 80.00
C3FP1 Dadonov/Hoffman/Trocheck 10.00 25.00
C3FP2 Barkov/Huberdeau/Ekblad 15.00 40.00
C3LAK Kovalchuk/Kopitar/Carter 15.00 40.00
C3MC1 Gallagher/Shaw/Drouin 10.00 25.00
C3MC2 Weber/Price/Domi 20.00 50.00
C3MW1 Granlund/Parise/Staal 10.00 25.00
C3MW2 Dumba/Suter/Dubnyk 8.00 20.00
C3NJD Palmieri/Hall/Hischier 15.00 40.00
C3NP1 Johansen/Arvidsson/Forsberg 15.00 40.00
C3NP2 Subban/Josi/Rinne 12.00 30.00
C3NY1 Zibanejad/Kreider/Hayes 12.00 30.00
C3NY2 Lundqvist/Skjei/Shattenkirk 25.00 60.00
C3NYI Bailey/Barzal/Lee 12.00 30.00
C3OTT White/Ryan/Chabot 10.00 25.00
C3PF1 van Riemsdyk/Giroux/Patrick 10.00 25.00
C3PF2 Couturier/Provorov
Gostisbehere 10.00 25.00
C3PIT Letang/Malkin/Guentzel 20.00 50.00
C3RC1 Pettersson/Dahlin/Kotkaniemi 30.00 80.00
C3RC2 Tkachuk/Svechnikov
Heiskanen 30.00 80.00
C3RCG Hart/Vladar/Samsonov 20.00 50.00
C3RWR Rasmussen
Cholowski/Hronek 12.00 30.00
C3ST1 Perron/O'Reilly/Schenn 10.00 25.00
C3ST2 Tarasenko
Pietrangelo/Parayko 12.00 30.00
C3TB1 Point/Stamkos/Kucherov 20.00 50.00
C3TB2 Johnson/Hedman/Vasilevskiy 15.00 40.00
C3TML Tavares/Marner/Marleau 15.00 40.00
C3VAN Boeser/Baertschi/Horvat 12.00 30.00
C3VGK Fleury/Tuch/Karlsson 20.00 50.00
C3WC1 Ovechkin/Kuznetsov
Backstrom 40.00 100.00
C3WC2 Oshie/Wilson/Carlson 10.00 25.00
C3WJ1 Laine/Scheifele/Wheeler 15.00 40.00
C3WJ2 Byfuglien/Connor/Hellebuyck 20.00 50.00

2019-20 The Cup

1 John Gibson 2.00 5.00
2 Phil Kessel 2.00 5.00
3 Keith Tkachuk 2.00 5.00
4 David Pastrnak 5.00 12.00
5 Brad Marchand 4.00 10.00
6 Jack Eichel 3.00 8.00
7 Sam Reinhart 4.00 10.00
8 Matthew Tkachuk 4.00 10.00
9 Doug Gilmour 2.50 6.00
10 Sebastian Aho 3.00 8.00
11 Andrei Svechnikov 2.50 6.00
12 Patrick Kane 4.00 10.00
13 Alex DeBrincat 2.50 6.00
14 Nathan MacKinnon 8.00 20.00
15 Patrick Roy 5.00 12.00
16 Cam Atkinson 2.00 5.00
17 Miro Heiskanen 2.50 6.00
18 Ben Bishop 1.50 4.00
19 Dylan Larkin 2.50 6.00
20 Anthony Mantha 1.50 4.00
21 Connor McDavid 10.00 25.00
22 Leon Draisaitl 6.00 15.00
23 Wayne Gretzky 12.00 30.00
24 Aleksander Barkov 3.00 8.00
25 Jonathan Huberdeau 2.50 6.00
26 Anze Kopitar 3.00 8.00
27 Eric Staal 2.00 5.00
28 Carey Price 4.00 10.00
29 Jonathan Drouin 1.50 4.00
30 Roman Josi 2.00 5.00
31 Pekka Rinne 2.00 5.00
32 Nico Hischier 3.00 8.00
33 Anders Lee 1.50 4.00
34 Billy Smith 2.00 5.00
35 Artemi Panarin 4.00 10.00
36 Jacob Trouba 1.50 4.00
37 Thomas Chabot 2.00 5.00
38 Brady Tkachuk 3.00 8.00
39 Claude Giroux 2.00 5.00
40 Carter Hart 2.00 5.00
41 Sidney Crosby 8.00 20.00
42 Jake Guentzel 3.00 8.00
43 Brent Burns 2.00 5.00
44 Logan Couture 2.50 6.00
45 Ryan O'Reilly 2.00 5.00
46 Jordan Binnington 3.00 8.00
47 Steven Stamkos 4.00 10.00
48 Nikita Kucherov 4.00 10.00
49 Auston Matthews 8.00 20.00
50 John Tavares 3.00 8.00
51 Mitch Marner 3.00 8.00
52 Elias Pettersson 3.00 8.00
53 Brock Boeser 2.50 6.00
54 Bo Horvat 2.50 6.00
55 Marc-Andre Fleury 4.00 10.00
56 Mark Stone 2.50 6.00
57 Alex Ovechkin 8.00 20.00
58 John Carlson 2.00 5.00
59 Mark Scheifele 3.00 8.00
60 Connor Hellebuyck 4.00 10.00
61 Quinn Hughes JSY AU/99 RC 600.00 1500.00
62 Cale Makar JSY AU/99 RC 3000.00 8000.00
63 Cody Glass JSY AU/99 RC 30.00 80.00
65 Barrett Hayton JSY AU/249 RC 125.00 300.00
66 Jack Hughes JSY AU/99 RC 2500.00 6000.00
67 Vitaly Abramov JSY AU/249 RC 20.00 50.00
68 Zach Senyshyn JSY AU/249 RC 20.00 50.00
69 Joey Daccord JSY AU/249 RC 40.00 100.00
70 Victor Olofsson JSY AU/249 RC 125.00 300.00
71 Taro Hirose JSY AU/249 RC 20.00 50.00
72 Brady Keeper JSY AU/249 RC 20.00 50.00
73 Alexandre Texier JSY AU/249 RC 20.00 50.00
74 Mackenzie MacEachern
JSY AU/249 RC 20.00 50.00
75 Ryan Poehling JSY AU/249 RC 60.00 150.00
76 Zack MacEwen JSY AU/249 RC 15.00 40.00
77 Trent Frederic JSY AU/249 RC 20.00 50.00
78 Max Jones JSY AU/249 RC 20.00 50.00
79 Filip Zadina JSY AU/249 RC 125.00 300.00
80 Kole Sherwood JSY AU/249 RC 20.00 50.00
81 Joel Farabee JSY AU/249 RC 125.00 300.00
82 Jimmy Schuldt JSY AU/249 RC 15.00 40.00
83 Max Veronneau JSY AU/249 RC 15.00 40.00
84 Nico Sturm JSY AU/249 RC 15.00 40.00
85 Libor Hajek JSY AU/249 RC 15.00 40.00
86 Erik Brannstrom JSY AU/249 RC 20.00 50.00
87 Brandon Gignac JSY AU/249 RC 15.00 40.00
88 Kaden Fulcher JSY AU/249 RC 20.00 50.00
89 Rudolfs Balcers JSY AU/249 RC 20.00 50.00
91 Ryan Lindgren JSY AU/249 RC 20.00 50.00
92 Guillaume Brisebois
JSY AU/249 RC 20.00 50.00
93 Dante Fabbro JSY AU/249 RC 20.00 50.00
94 Blake Lizotte JSY AU/249 RC 20.00 50.00
95 Philippe Myers JSY AU/249 RC 15.00 40.00
96 Teddy Blueger JSY AU/249 RC 25.00 60.00
97 Ryan Kuffner JSY AU/249 RC 15.00 40.00
98 Rem Pitlick JSY AU/249 RC 20.00 50.00
99 Noah Dobson JSY AU/249 RC 80.00 200.00
100 Karson Kuhlman JSY AU/249 RC 20.00 50.00
101 Carl Grundstrom JSY AU/249 RC 20.00 50.00
102 Riley Stillman JSY AU/249 RC 20.00 50.00
103 Jesper Boqvist JSY AU/249 RC 15.00 40.00
104 Adam Fox JSY AU/249 RC 250.00 600.00
105 Nikita Gusev JSY AU/249 RC 30.00 80.00
106 Mario Ferraro JSY AU/249 RC 15.00 40.00
107 Oliver Wahlstrom
JSY AU/249 RC 125.00 300.00
108 Emil Bemstrom JSY AU/249 RC 20.00 50.00
109 Ilya Mikheyev JSY AU/249 RC 30.00 80.00
110 Morgan Frost JSY AU/249 RC 50.00 125.00
111 Igor Shesterkin
JSY AU/249 RC 400.00 1000.00
112 Jake Walman JSY AU/249 RC 25.00 60.00
113 Joachim Blichfeld
JSY AU/249 RC 20.00 50.00
114 Kale Clague JSY AU/249 RC 15.00 40.00
115 Julien Gauthier JSY AU/249 RC 20.00 50.00
116 Adam Boqvist JSY AU/249 RC 20.00 50.00
117 Klim Kostin JSY AU/249 RC 20.00 50.00
118 Dominik Kubalik
JSY AU/249 RC 80.00 200.00
119 Rhett Gardner JSY AU/249 RC 15.00 40.00
120 Otto Koivula AU/249 RC 12.00 30.00
121 Eetu Luostarinen JSY AU/249 RC 20.00 50.00
122 Jonathan Davidsson
JSY AU/249 RC 12.00 30.00
123 Rasmus Asplund JSY AU/249 RC 15.00 40.00
124 Mitchell Stephens
JSY AU/249 RC 12.00 30.00
125 John Marino JSY AU/249 RC 40.00 100.00
126 Andrew Peeke JSY AU/249 RC 12.00 30.00
127 Alexander Volkov JSY AU/249 RC 15.00 40.00
128 Cayden Primeau
JSY AU/249 RC 100.00 250.00
129 David Gustafsson
JSY AU/249 RC 15.00 40.00
130 Tobias Bjornfot JSY AU/249 RC 20.00 50.00
131 Ville Heinola JSY AU/249 RC 100.00 250.00
132 Sam Lafferty JSY AU/249 RC 15.00 40.00
133 Nicolas Hague JSY AU/249 RC 20.00 50.00
134 Nathan Bastian JSY AU/249 RC 20.00 50.00
135 Trevor Moore JSY AU/249 RC 15.00 40.00
136 Rasmus Sandin JSY AU/249 RC 50.00 125.00
137 Carter Verhaeghe
JSY AU/249 RC 60.00 150.00
138 Martin Fehervary JSY AU/249 RC 15.00 40.00
139 Matt Roy JSY AU/249 RC 20.00 50.00
140 Joel L'Esperance JSY AU/249 RC 20.00 50.00
141 Joel Persson JSY AU/249 RC 15.00 40.00
142 Connor Clifton JSY AU/249 RC 20.00 50.00
143 Elvis Merzlikins
JSY AU/249 RC 100.00 250.00
144 Lean Bergmann JSY AU/249 RC 15.00 40.00
145 German Rubtsov JSY AU/249 RC 15.00 40.00
146 Danil Yurtaykin JSY AU/249 RC 15.00 40.00
147 Adam Brooks JSY AU/249 RC 12.00 30.00
148 Ryan MacInnis JSY AU/249 RC 15.00 40.00
149 Givani Smith JSY AU/249 RC 15.00 40.00
150 Noah Gregor/249 RC 15.00 40.00
151 Kaapo Kakko JSY/99 RC 600.00 1500.00
152 Cale Fleury/249 RC 6.00 15.00
153 Conor Timmins JSY/249 RC 20.00 50.00
154 Nikolai Prokhorkin JSY/249 RC 15.00 40.00
155 Yakov Trenin JSY/249 RC 15.00 40.00
156 Jack Studnicka JSY/249 RC 20.00 50.00
157 Aleksi Saarela AU/249 RC 20.00 50.00
158 Dmytro Timashov/249 RC 20.00 50.00

2019-20 The Cup All Time Alum

ATABB Bill Barber 3.00 8.00
ATADS Daniel Sedin 4.00 10.00
ATAHS Henrik Sedin 4.00 10.00
ATALR Larry Robinson 3.00 8.00
ATAML Mario Lemieux 12.00 30.00
ATAMM Mike Modano 5.00 12.00
ATAPR Patrick Roy 8.00 20.00
ATARB Ray Bourque 5.00 12.00
ATASY Steve Yzerman 12.00 30.00
ATAWG Wayne Gretzky 20.00 50.00

2019-20 The Cup All Time Alum Alum Autographs

ATABB Bill Barber/50 20.00 50.00
ATADS Daniel Sedin/50 30.00 80.00
ATAHS Henrik Sedin/50 25.00 60.00
ATALR Larry Robinson/50 20.00 50.00
ATAMM Mike Modano/50 30.00 80.00
ATAPR Patrick Roy/25 100.00 250.00
ATASY Steve Yzerman/25 100.00 250.00

2019-20 The Cup Brilliance Autographs

BAP Artemi Panarin A 40.00 100.00
BBH Bobby Hull A 50.00 125.00
BCC Chris Chelios B 20.00 50.00
BCM Cale Makar C 150.00 400.00
BCN Cam Neely C 20.00 50.00
BDK Dominik Kubalik C 40.00 100.00
BDS Daniel Sedin A 40.00 100.00
BHS Henrik Sedin A 30.00 80.00
BIS Igor Shesterkin B 80.00 200.00
BJH Jack Hughes A 125.00 300.00
BJV James van Riemsdyk C 15.00 40.00
BKD Kirby Dach C 40.00 100.00
BKL Kevin Labanc C 12.00 30.00
BKY Keith Yandle C 12.00 30.00
BMB Martin Brodeur A 100.00 250.00
BMC Connor McDavid A 250.00 600.00
BMF Morgan Frost C 30.00 80.00
BMM Mike Modano B 30.00 80.00
BNL Nicklas Lidstrom A 20.00 50.00
BNS Nick Suzuki C 80.00 200.00
BPF Peter Forsberg A 40.00 100.00
BPL Pat LaFontaine C 20.00 50.00
BPR Patrick Roy A 125.00 300.00
BQH Quinn Hughes B 40.00 100.00
BRH Ron Hextall B 20.00 50.00
BSR Sam Reinhart C 40.00 100.00
BTK Tim Kerr C 12.00 30.00

2019-20 The Cup Color Coded Autographs

CCAB Aleksander Barkov 40.00 100.00
CCAP Artemi Panarin 80.00 200.00
CCBH Barrett Hayton 30.00 80.00
CCCM Cale Makar 600.00 1500.00
CCDB Dustin Brown 25.00 60.00
CCDF Dante Fabbro 25.00 60.00
CCDS Daniel Sedin 30.00 80.00
CCHS Henrik Sedin 30.00 80.00
CCIS Igor Shesterkin 150.00 400.00
CCJH Jack Hughes 400.00 1000.00
CCJT Joe Thornton 80.00 200.00
CCKD Kirby Dach 200.00 500.00
CCKY Keith Yandle 15.00 40.00
CCMG Mark Giordano 25.00 60.00
CCNL Nicklas Lidstrom 25.00 60.00
CCNS Nick Suzuki 100.00 250.00
CCPF Peter Forsberg 50.00 125.00
CCQH Quinn Hughes 150.00 400.00
CCRS Rasmus Sandin 40.00 100.00
CCSR Sam Reinhart 50.00 125.00

2019-20 The Cup Day With the Cup Signature Combos

DC2BK A.Kopitar/D.Brown B 60.00 150.00
DC2LJ J.Jagr/M.Lemieux A 800.00 2000.00

2019-20 The Cup Day With the Cup Signatures

DCBO Brooks Orpik B 15.00 40.00
DCJG Jake Guentzel B 30.00 80.00
DCPF Peter Forsberg A 150.00 400.00
DCPR Patrick Roy A 125.00 300.00
DCTT Teuvo Teravainen B 25.00 60.00
DCTW Tom Wilson B 30.00 80.00

2019-20 The Cup Enshrinements

EAB Aleksander Barkov/99 30.00 80.00
EAM Auston Matthews/25 150.00 400.00
EAS Anton Stastny/99 20.00 50.00
EBN Bernie Nicholls/99 15.00 40.00
EBS Bobby Smith/99 20.00 50.00
ECM Cale Makar/99 150.00 400.00
ECP Carey Price/25 40.00 100.00
EDW Doug Weight/99 20.00 50.00
EFR Morgan Frost/99 30.00 80.00
EGH Glenn Hall/99 20.00 50.00
EJF Joel Farabee/99 30.00 80.00
EJG John Gibson/99 20.00 50.00
EJH Jack Hughes/99 150.00 400.00
EJL Jacques Lemaire/99 15.00 40.00
EJS Jaccob Slavin/99 15.00 40.00
EKK Kasperi Kapanen/99 15.00 40.00
EKM Kirk McLean/99 40.00 100.00
ELD Leon Draisaitl 60.00 150.00
EMB Martin Brodeur/25 50.00 125.00
EMC Connor McDavid/25 300.00 800.00
EMF Marc-Andre Fleury/25 40.00 100.00
EMG Mark Giordano/99 20.00 50.00
ENH Nicolas Hague/99 20.00 50.00
ENL Nicklas Lidstrom/25 30.00 80.00
EOK Olaf Kolzig/99 30.00 80.00
EOW Oliver Wahlstrom/99 30.00 80.00
EPF Peter Forsberg/25 100.00 250.00
EQH Quinn Hughes/99 100.00 250.00
ESB Sergei Bobrovsky/99 30.00 80.00
ESC Sidney Crosby/25 300.00 800.00
ESR Sam Reinhart/99 40.00 100.00
EWC Wendel Clark/99 30.00 80.00
EWG Wayne Gretzky/25 300.00 800.00

2019-20 The Cup Foundations Jerseys

FAB Aleksander Barkov/49 10.00 25.00
FAB Adam Boqvist/49 6.00 15.00
FAD Alex DeBrincat/49 8.00 20.00
FAP Artemi Panarin/49 12.00 30.00
FBB Ben Bishop/49 5.00 12.00
FCG Cody Glass/99 10.00 25.00
FCH Connor Hellebuyck/49 12.00 30.00
FCM Connor McDavid/49 30.00 80.00
FCP Carey Price/49 12.00 30.00
FDL Dylan Larkin/49 8.00 20.00
FFR Morgan Frost/99 10.00 25.00
FFZ Filip Zadina/99 10.00 25.00
FGI John Gibson/49 6.00 15.00
FIS Igor Shesterkin/49 25.00 60.00
FJB Jesper Boqvist/49 5.00 12.00
FJD Jonathan Drouin/49 5.00 12.00
FJF Joel Farabee/49 20.00 50.00
FJG Jake Guentzel/49 10.00 25.00
FJH Jack Hughes/99 80.00 200.00
FJT Jonathan Toews/49 10.00 25.00
FJV James van Riemsdyk/49 5.00 12.00
FKD Kirby Dach/99 12.00 30.00
FKK Kaapo Kakko/99 10.00 25.00
FKO Klim Kostin/49 6.00 15.00
FLD Leon Draisaitl/49 20.00 50.00
FMA Cale Makar/99 60.00 150.00
FMF Marc-Andre Fleury/49 12.00 30.00
FMH Miro Heiskanen/49 8.00 20.00
FNG Nikita Gusev/49 10.00 25.00
FNS Nick Suzuki/99 25.00 60.00
FPM Philippe Myers/49 5.00 12.00
FPR Pekka Rinne/49 6.00 15.00
FQH Quinn Hughes/99 30.00 80.00
FRP Ryan Poehling/99 10.00 25.00
FRS Rasmus Sandin/49 10.00 25.00
FSB Sergei Bobrovsky/49 10.00 25.00
FTB Tobias Bjornfot/49 6.00 15.00
FTC Thomas Chabot/49 6.00 15.00
FTW Tom Wilson/49 6.00 15.00
FVO Victor Olofsson/49 12.00 30.00

2019-20 The Cup Honorable Numbers

HRCH Connor Hellebuyck/37 60.00 150.00
HREM Elvis Merzlikins/90 60.00 150.00
HRIM Ilya Mikheyev/65 25.00 60.00
HRJG John Gibson/36 30.00 80.00
HRJP Joe Pavelski/16 60.00 150.00
HRKD Kirby Dach/77 100.00 250.00
HRQH Quinn Hughes/43 125.00 300.00
HRSB Sergei Bobrovsky/72 25.00 60.00
HRTC Thomas Chabot/72 30.00 80.00
HRTW Tom Wilson/43 30.00 80.00

2019-20 The Cup Honorable Numbers Dual

HN2SH A.Svechnikov
C.Hellebuyck/37 60.00 150.00
HN2WG D.Weight/D.Gilmour/39 60.00 150.00

2019-20 The Cup Inked Insignias

IIAB Adam Brooks/75 20.00 50.00
IIAD Alex DeBrincat/25 40.00 100.00
IIAV Alexander Volkov/75 25.00 60.00
IIBH Barrett Hayton/75 30.00 80.00
IIBO Bobby Orr/25 400.00 1000.00
IIBR Erik Brannstrom/75 40.00 100.00
IICG Cody Glass/75 50.00 120.00
IICH Carter Hart/25 30.00 80.00
IICM Cale Makar/75 400.00 1000.00
IICP Carey Price/25 125.00 300.00
IIDF Dante Fabbro/75 50.00 125.00
IIEB Emil Bemstrom/75 30.00 80.00
IIFR Morgan Frost/75 30.00 80.00
IIGI John Gibson/25 30.00 80.00
IIHE Connor Hellebuyck/25 60.00 150.00
IIIM Ilya Mikheyev/75 50.00 125.00
IIIS Igor Shesterkin/75 150.00 400.00
IIJB Joachim Blichfeld/75 30.00 80.00
IIJF Joel Farabee/75 50.00 125.00
IIJG Jake Guentzel/25 50.00 120.00
IIJH Jack Hughes/75 200.00 500.00
IIJK John Klingberg/25 30.00 80.00
IIJT John Tavares/25 100.00 250.00
IIJW Jake Walman/75 40.00 100.00
IIKD Kirby Dach/75 60.00 150.00
IIKM Kirk McLean/25 25.00 60.00
IIKY Keith Yandle/25 20.00 50.00
IIMC Connor McDavid/25 400.00 1000.00
IIMF Marc-Andre Fleury/25 80.00 200.00
IIMG Mark Giordano/25 30.00 80.00
IIML Mario Lemieux/25 400.00 1000.00
IIMM Mike Modano/25 80.00 200.00
IINS Nick Suzuki/75 200.00 500.00
IIPR Patrick Roy/25 80.00 200.00
IIQH Quinn Hughes/75 80.00 200.00
IIRH Ron Hextall/25 60.00 150.00
IIRP Ryan Poehling/75 20.00 50.00
IISR Sam Reinhart/25 60.00 150.00
IIST Nico Sturm/75 25.00 60.00
IISV Andrei Svechnikov/25 40.00 100.00
IITB Tobias Bjornfot/75 20.00 50.00
IITS Teemu Selanne/25 60.00 150.00
IITT Teuvo Teravainen/25 30.00 80.00
IITW Tom Wilson/25 30.00 80.00
IIVO Victor Olofsson/75 60.00 150.00
IIWG Wayne Gretzky/25 1250.00 3000.00

2019-20 The Cup Limited Logos Autographs

LLAB Aleksander Barkov/25 60.00 150.00
LLAD Alex DeBrincat/50 60.00 150.00
LLAL Anders Lee/50 30.00 80.00
LLAP Artemi Panarin/25 150.00 400.00
LLAS Andrei Svechnikov/50 80.00 200.00
LLAT Alex Tuch/50 40.00 100.00
LLAV Andrei Vasilevskiy/50 60.00 150.00
LLBE Tyler Bertuzzi/50 30.00 80.00
LLBT Brady Tkachuk/50 60.00 150.00
LLCH Connor Hellebuyck/50 80.00 200.00
LLCM Cale Makar/50 1500.00 4000.00
LLCP Carey Price/25 125.00 300.00
LLDB Dustin Brown/50 50.00 125.00
LLES Eric Staal/50 40.00 100.00
LLGI John Gibson/50 40.00 100.00
LLHA Carter Hart/50 150.00 400.00
LLHL Henrik Lundqvist/25 100.00 250.00
LLJG Jake Guentzel/50 60.00 150.00
LLJH Jack Hughes/50 300.00 800.00
LLJK Jesperi Kotkaniemi/50 40.00 100.00
LLJP Joe Pavelski/50 50.00 125.00
LLJS Jaccob Slavin/50 30.00 80.00
LLJT Jacob Trouba/50 30.00 80.00
LLJV James van Riemsdyk/50 30.00 80.00
LLKD Kirby Dach/50 300.00 800.00
LLKL John Klingberg/50 40.00 100.00
LLKP Kyle Palmieri/50 20.00 50.00
LLMF Marc-Andre Fleury/25 125.00 300.00
LLMG Mark Giordano/50 40.00 100.00
LLMH Miro Heiskanen/50 50.00 125.00
LLMS Mark Scheifele/50 30.00 80.00
LLMT Matthew Tkachuk/50 125.00 300.00
LLNH Nico Hischier/50 60.00 150.00
LLPG Philipp Grubauer/50 60.00 150.00
LLSB Sergei Bobrovsky/50 60.00 150.00
LLSR Sam Reinhart/50 80.00 200.00
LLTC Thomas Chabot/50 60.00 150.00
LLTH Joe Thornton/25 60.00 150.00
LLTT Teuvo Teravainen/50 40.00 100.00
LLTW Tom Wilson/50 40.00 100.00

2019-20 The Cup Overshadow Patch Autographs

OSAP Artemi Panarin/25 60.00 150.00
OSAS Andrei Svechnikov/25 40.00 100.00
OSBM Brad Marchand/25 60.00 150.00
OSCH Connor Hellebuyck/25 60.00 150.00
OSCP Carey Price/25 80.00 200.00
OSGI John Gibson/25 30.00 80.00
OSJG Jake Guentzel/25 50.00 120.00
OSJP Joe Pavelski/25 40.00 100.00
OSMA Marc-Andre Fleury/25 60.00 150.00
OSMH Miro Heiskanen/25 40.00 100.00
OSSB Sergei Bobrovsky/25 50.00 125.00
OSTC Thomas Chabot/25 30.00 80.00
OSTW Tom Wilson/25 30.00 80.00

2019-20 The Cup Overshadow Rookie Patch Autographs

OSAB Adam Boqvist/55 30.00 80.00
OSAF Adam Fox/55 80.00 200.00
OSBH Barrett Hayton/55 60.00 150.00
OSCG Cody Glass/55 30.00 80.00
OSCM Cale Makar/25 300.00 800.00
OSDK Dominik Kubalik/55 50.00 125.00
OSEM Elvis Merzlikins/55 60.00 150.00
OSIM Ilya Mikheyev/55 25.00 60.00
OSJF Joel Farabee/55 50.00 120.00
OSJH Jack Hughes/25 250.00 600.00
OSKD Kirby Dach/25 80.00 200.00
OSMF Morgan Frost/55 30.00 80.00
OSNS Nick Suzuki/25 125.00 300.00
OSQH Quinn Hughes/25 125.00 300.00
OSRP Ryan Poehling/25 50.00 125.00
OSRS Rasmus Sandin/55 30.00 80.00
OSVO Victor Olofsson/25 60.00 150.00

2019-20 The Cup Quads Jerseys

C4AJDW Dub/Atk/Wer/Jon 20.00 50.00
C4BCKD Kop/Car/Bro/Dou 20.00 50.00
C4BCKO Ove/Kuz/Bac/Car 50.00 125.00
C4BCWT Tka/Whi/Bro/Cha 20.00 50.00
C4CBMP Mar/Ber/Pas/Cha 30.00 80.00
C4CKHM Cou/Her/Mei/Kar 15.00 40.00
C4ENLB Nel/Lee/Ebe/Bar 15.00 40.00
C4FSMK Sto/Mar/Kar/Fle 25.00 60.00
C4GFRG Get/Rak/Fow/Gib 12.00 30.00
C4KESK Kes/Sch/Kel/Ekm 15.00 40.00
C4KLMR Mac/Ran/Lan/Kad 50.00 125.00
C4LELP Pan/Lun/Lee/Ebe 30.00 80.00
C4LKFS Kak/Fox/Lin/She 50.00 125.00
C4LZTP Pan/Zib/Tro/Lun 30.00 80.00
C4MHBP Pet/Hor/Boe/Mil 20.00 50.00
C4MLGC Gir/Cou/Mal/Let 25.00 60.00
C4MLGT Gau/Tka/Mon/Lin 25.00 60.00
C4MLMG Mal/Gue/Let/Mur 25.00 60.00
C4MRFF Fro/Far/Rub/Mye 20.00 50.00
C4NGDT Gau/Tka/Dra/Nug 40.00 100.00
C4NKKD Dra/Nug/Kle/Kos 40.00 100.00
C4NTAS Sve/Aho/Ter/Nie 20.00 50.00
C4OTBP O'R/Tar/Par/Bin 20.00 50.00
C4PGDD Dro/Dom/Gal/Pri 25.00 60.00
C4RDJF For/Duc/Jos/Rin 20.00 50.00
C4RPBS Pav/Ben/Seg/Rad 15.00 40.00
C4SEMD Eic/Ski/Dah/Mil 20.00 50.00
C4SHBK Sta/Kuc/Bar/Hub 25.00 60.00
C4SHKP Sta/Kuc/Poi/Hed 25.00 60.00
C4SPDD Sta/Par/Dum/Dub 12.00 30.00
C4SSPM Suz/Poe/Mik/San 50.00 125.00
C4TKSD Kan/Toe/Str/DeB 25.00 60.00
C4TNMM Mat/Tav/Mar/Nyl 50.00 125.00
C4WSEL Sch/Whe/Lai/Ehl 20.00 50.00
C4YBHB Bar/Hub/Yan/Bob 20.00 50.00

2019-20 The Cup Rookie Class of 2020

2020AB Adam Boqvist 5.00 12.00
2020AF Adam Fox 12.00 30.00
2020AT Alexandre Texier 5.00 12.00
2020AV Alexander Volkov 4.00 10.00
2020BE Emil Bemstrom 5.00 12.00
2020BH Barrett Hayton 10.00 25.00
2020CG Cody Glass 8.00 20.00
2020CM Cale Makar 25.00 60.00
2020DF Dante Fabbro 5.00 12.00
2020DK Dominik Kubalik 10.00 25.00
2020EB Erik Brannstrom 5.00 12.00
2020FZ Filip Zadina 12.00 30.00
2020IM Ilya Mikheyev 8.00 20.00
2020IS Igor Shesterkin 25.00 60.00
2020JF Joel Farabee 8.00 20.00
2020JH Jack Hughes 25.00 60.00
2020KD Kirby Dach 10.00 25.00
2020KK Kaapo Kakko 15.00 40.00
2020MF Morgan Frost 8.00 20.00
2020ND Noah Dobson 12.00 30.00
2020NG Nikita Gusev 8.00 20.00
2020NS Nick Suzuki 25.00 60.00
2020OW Oliver Wahlstrom 8.00 20.00
2020QH Quinn Hughes 15.00 40.00
2020RP Ryan Poehling 8.00 20.00
2020RS Rasmus Sandin 12.00 30.00
2020TB Tobias Bjornfot 5.00 12.00
2020TH Taro Hirose 5.00 12.00
2020VH Ville Heinola 6.00 15.00
2020VO Victor Olofsson 10.00 25.00

2019-20 The Cup Rookie Class of 2020 Autographs

2020AB Adam Boqvist 15.00 40.00
2020AF Adam Fox 80.00 200.00
2020AT Alexandre Texier 25.00 60.00
2020AV Alexander Volkov 12.00 30.00
2020BE Emil Bemstrom 15.00 40.00
2020BH Barrett Hayton 15.00 40.00
2020CG Cody Glass 25.00 60.00
2020CM Cale Makar 250.00 600.00
2020DF Dante Fabbro 15.00 40.00
2020DK Dominik Kubalik 25.00 60.00
2020EB Erik Brannstrom 15.00 40.00
2020IM Ilya Mikheyev 15.00 40.00
2020IS Igor Shesterkin 80.00 200.00
2020JF Joel Farabee 40.00 100.00
2020JH Jack Hughes 200.00 500.00
2020KD Kirby Dach 30.00 80.00
2020MF Morgan Frost 25.00 60.00
2020NS Nick Suzuki 60.00 150.00
2020OW Oliver Wahlstrom 60.00 150.00
2020QH Quinn Hughes 125.00 300.00
2020RP Ryan Poehling 25.00 60.00
2020RS Rasmus Sandin 25.00 60.00
2020TB Tobias Bjornfot 15.00 40.00
2020TH Taro Hirose 15.00 40.00
2020VH Ville Heinola 20.00 50.00
2020VO Victor Olofsson 30.00 80.00

2019-20 The Cup Rookie Gear Relic Autographs

ARGAB Adam Boqvist 30.00 80.00
ARGAF Adam Fox 200.00 500.00
ARGCG Cody Glass 50.00 120.00
ARGIS Igor Shesterkin 250.00 600.00
ARGJF Joel Farabee 50.00 125.00
ARGJH Jack Hughes 250.00 600.00
ARGJW Jake Walman 40.00 100.00
ARGKC Kale Clague 25.00 60.00
ARGKD Kirby Dach 150.00 400.00
ARGMF Morgan Frost 50.00 125.00
ARGNS Nick Suzuki 250.00 600.00
ARGQH Quinn Hughes 125.00 300.00
ARGRP Ryan Poehling 50.00 125.00
ARGVO Victor Olofsson 60.00 150.00

2019-20 The Cup Rookie Marks Dual Autographs

DARBCB T.Bjornfot/K.Clague 40.00 100.00
DARBFS A.Fox/I.Shesterkin 600.00 1500.00
DARBHG C.Glass/N.Hague 50.00 125.00
DARBHH J.Hughes/Q.Hughes 300.00 800.00
DARBSM R.Sandin/I.Mikheyev 150.00 400.00

2019-20 The Cup Scripted Swatches

SMAB Aleksander Barkov 40.00 100.00
SMAP Artemi Panarin 50.00 125.00
SMBM Brad Marchand 30.00 80.00
SMCM Cale Makar 200.00 500.00
SMCP Carey Price 50.00 125.00
SMEM Elvis Merzlikins 50.00 125.00
SMFR Morgan Frost 40.00 100.00
SMJH Jack Hughes 250.00 600.00
SMJK Jesperi Kotkaniemi 25.00 60.00
SMJP Joe Pavelski 30.00 80.00
SMJV James van Riemsdyk 20.00 50.00
SMKD Kirby Dach 50.00 125.00
SMKL John Klingberg 25.00 60.00
SMKP Kyle Palmieri 20.00 50.00
SMMC Connor McDavid 200.00 500.00
SMMF Marc-Andre Fleury 80.00 200.00
SMMH Miro Heiskanen 30.00 80.00
SMNS Nick Suzuki 80.00 200.00
SMQH Quinn Hughes 125.00 300.00
SMRA Rasmus Asplund 20.00 50.00
SMRS Rasmus Sandin 40.00 100.00
SMSB Sergei Bobrovsky 40.00 100.00
SMTC Thomas Chabot 25.00 60.00

2019-20 The Cup Signature Materials

SPAB Adam Boqvist/99 20.00 50.00
SPAF Adam Fox/99 125.00 300.00
SPAL Anders Lee/99 15.00 40.00
SPAP Artemi Panarin/25 40.00 100.00
SPBA Aleksander Barkov/25 30.00 80.00
SPBE Tyler Bertuzzi/99 15.00 40.00
SPBH Barrett Hayton/99 40.00 100.00
SPBJ Tobias Bjornfot/99 20.00 50.00
SPBO Brock Boeser/99 25.00 60.00
SPBR Erik Brannstrom/99 20.00 50.00
SPCG Cody Glass/99 15.00 40.00
SPCH Connor Hellebuyck/99 40.00 100.00
SPCM Cale Makar/99 500.00 1200.00
SPCP Carey Price/25 100.00 250.00
SPCV Carter Verhaeghe/99 60.00 150.00
SPDK Dominik Kubalik/99 25.00 60.00
SPEB Emil Bemstrom/99 20.00 50.00
SPFR Morgan Frost/99 30.00 80.00
SPGA Julien Gauthier/99 20.00 50.00
SPGB Guillaume Brisebois/99 20.00 50.00
SPGI John Gibson/99 20.00 50.00
SPIM Ilya Mikheyev/99 30.00 80.00
SPIS Igor Shesterkin/99 150.00 400.00
SPJB Jesper Boqvist/99 15.00 40.00
SPJF Joel Farabee/99 60.00 150.00
SPJG Jake Guentzel/99 30.00 80.00
SPJH Jack Hughes/99 250.00 600.00
SPJK Jesperi Kotkaniemi/99 20.00 50.00
SPJQ Jonathan Quick/25 25.00 60.00
SPJS Jimmy Schuldt/99 15.00 40.00
SPJT Jacob Trouba/99 15.00 40.00
SPJV James van Riemsdyk/99 15.00 40.00
SPJW Jake Walman/99 25.00 60.00
SPKD Kirby Dach/99 100.00 250.00
SPKL John Klingberg/99 20.00 50.00
SPKP Kyle Palmieri/99 15.00 40.00
SPME Elvis Merzlikins/99 60.00 150.00
SPMF Marc-Andre Fleury/25 40.00 100.00
SPNS Nick Suzuki/99 125.00 300.00
SPOW Oliver Wahlstrom/99 60.00 150.00
SPPG Philipp Grubauer/99 20.00 50.00
SPQH Quinn Hughes/99 200.00 500.00
SPRA Rasmus Asplund/99 15.00 40.00
SPRP Ryan Poehling/99 30.00 80.00
SPRS Rasmus Sandin/99 80.00 200.00
SPST Nico Sturm/99 15.00 40.00
SPTC Thomas Chabot/99 20.00 50.00
SPTH Joe Thornton/25 30.00 80.00
SPTW Tom Wilson/99 20.00 50.00
SPVO Victor Olofsson/99 60.00 150.00

2019-20 The Cup Signature Renditions

SRAP Artemi Panarin A 40.00 100.00
SRBR Bill Ranford B 15.00 40.00
SRCH Connor Hellebuyck B 20.00 50.00
SRCJ Curtis Joseph B 30.00 80.00
SRCM Cale Makar B 250.00 600.00
SRJH Jack Hughes A 125.00 300.00
SRJS Joe Sakic A 100.00 250.00
SRKD Kirby Dach B 40.00 100.00
SRKM Kirk McLean B 40.00 100.00
SRMR Manon Rheaume B 125.00 300.00
SRRP Ryan Poehling B 30.00 80.00
SRVO Victor Olofsson B 40.00 100.00

2019-20 The Cup The NHL Collection Patch Autographs

NHLAB Aleksander Barkov/25 50.00 120.00
NHLBG Brendan Gallagher/25 30.00 80.00
NHLCH Connor Hellebuyck/25 60.00 150.00
NHLCM Cale Makar/35 1000.00 2500.00
NHLCV Carter Verhaeghe/35 50.00 120.00
NHLDK Dominik Kubalik/35 60.00 150.00
NHLEM Elvis Merzlikins/35 60.00 150.00
NHLGA Julien Gauthier/35 30.00 80.00
NHLGB Guillaume Brisebois/35 30.00 80.00
NHLIS Igor Shesterkin/35 250.00 600.00
NHLJF Joel Farabee/35 80.00 200.00
NHLJG John Gibson/25 30.00 80.00
NHLJH Jack Hughes/35 250.00 600.00
NHLJK Jesperi Kotkaniemi/25 30.00 80.00
NHLJS Jaccob Slavin/25 25.00 60.00
NHLJW Jake Walman/35 40.00 100.00
NHLKL John Klingberg/25 60.00 150.00
NHLKS Kole Sherwood/35 30.00 80.00
NHLKY Keith Yandle/25 20.00 50.00
NHLMF Mario Ferraro/35 25.00 60.00
NHLMH Miro Heiskanen/25 40.00 100.00
NHLNS Nico Sturm/35 25.00 60.00
NHLOW Oliver Wahlstrom/35 50.00 125.00
NHLPA Colton Parayko/25 25.00 60.00
NHLQH Quinn Hughes/35 250.00 600.00
NHLRA Rasmus Asplund/35 25.00 60.00
NHLRP Rem Pitlick/35 30.00 80.00
NHLSC Jimmy Schuldt/35 25.00 60.00
NHLSR Sam Reinhart/25 60.00 150.00
NHLYG Yanni Gourde/25 25.00 60.00

2019-20 The Cup Trilaterals Jerseys

TLAB Adam Boqvist 8.00 20.00
TLAD Alex DeBrincat 10.00 25.00
TLBB Brock Boeser 10.00 25.00
TLCG Cody Glass 12.00 30.00
TLCM Connor McDavid 40.00 100.00
TLCO Sean Couturier 6.00 15.00
TLDH Dougie Hamilton 6.00 15.00
TLDK Dominik Kubalik 15.00 40.00
TLDL Dylan Larkin 10.00 25.00
TLDP David Pastrnak 20.00 50.00
TLFF Filip Forsberg 12.00 30.00
TLFZ Filip Zadina 12.00 30.00
TLGU Jake Guentzel 12.00 30.00
TLIS Igor Shesterkin 30.00 80.00
TLJD Jonathan Drouin 6.00 15.00
TLJH Jack Hughes 40.00 100.00
TLJS Joe Sakic 15.00 40.00
TLJT Jonathan Toews 12.00 30.00
TLKD Kirby Dach 15.00 40.00
TLMA Cale Makar 80.00 200.00
TLMR Morgan Rielly 8.00 20.00
TLND Noah Dobson 20.00 50.00
TLNS Nick Suzuki 30.00 80.00
TLQH Quinn Hughes 40.00 100.00
TLRP Ryan Poehling 12.00 30.00
TLSC Sidney Crosby 30.00 80.00
TLTH Tomas Hertl 8.00 20.00
TLTS Teemu Selanne 15.00 40.00
TLVO Victor Olofsson 15.00 40.00
TLWG Wayne Gretzky 50.00 125.00

2019-20 The Cup Trios Jerseys

C3BAB Abramov/Balcers/Brannstrom 10.00 25.00
C3BKH Hertl/Karlsson/Burns 12.00 30.00
C3BWO Ovechkin/Backstrom/Wilson 40.00 100.00
C3CBR Bergeron/Chara/Rask 12.00 30.00
C3CHE Huberdeau/Connolly/Ekblad 12.00 30.00
C3CLB Lizotte/Bjornfot/Clague 10.00 25.00
C3CWT Tkachuk/White/Chabot 15.00 40.00
C3DBK Dach/Boqvist/Kubalik 20.00 50.00
C3DJF Duchene/Forsberg/Johansen 15.00 40.00
C3ELB Barzal/Eberle/Lee 12.00 30.00
C3GCH Giroux/Couturier/Hayes 10.00 25.00
C3GDD Domi/Gallagher/Drouin 10.00 25.00
C3GRG Getzlaf/Rakell/Gibson 10.00 25.00
C3HGS Glass/Hague/Schuldt 15.00 40.00
C3JDW Dubois/Jones/Werenski 15.00 40.00
C3JMB Klingberg/Heiskanen/Bishop 12.00 30.00
C3KDK Kopitar/Kempe/Doughty 15.00 40.00
C3KEK Kessel/Ekman-Larsson/Keller 12.00 30.00
C3KFS Kakko/Fox/Shesterkin 80.00 200.00
C3KKD Draisaitl/Klefbom/Koskinen 30.00 80.00
C3KMR MacKinnon/Kadri/Rantanen 40.00 100.00
C3LMG Guentzel/Letang/Murray 15.00 40.00
C3MBP Pettersson/Boeser/Miller 15.00 40.00
C3MFF Frost/Farabee/Myers 15.00 40.00
C3MGT Gaudreau/Monahan/Tkachuk 20.00 50.00
C3MHO Hughes/Makar/Olofsson 50.00 125.00
C3MLB Mantha/Larkin/Bertuzzi 12.00 30.00

C3MPM Pastrnak/Marchand/McAvoy 25.00 60.00
C3MTC Marleau/Thornton/Couture 15.00 40.00
C3OBP O'Reilly/Parayko/Binnington 15.00 40.00
C3OCK Kuznetsov/Oshie/Carlson 12.00 30.00
C3PBS Seguin/Pavelski/Benn 12.00 30.00
C3PST Schenn/Thomas/Pietrangelo 10.00 25.00
C3RAN Nylander/Rielly/Andersen 20.00 50.00
C3RED Eichel/Reinhart/Dahlin 20.00 50.00
C3RJA Arvidsson/Josi/Rinne 10.00 25.00
C3SEL Scheifele/Laine/Ehlers 15.00 40.00
C3SFK Frederic/Kuhlman/Senyshyn 10.00 25.00
C3SKP Point/Kucherov/Stamkos 20.00 50.00
C3SMK Stone/Karlsson/Marchessault 12.00 30.00
C3SPC Palmieri/Coleman/Subban 12.00 30.00
C3SPP Poehling/Suzuki/Primeau 40.00 100.00
C3SPZ Zuccarello/Parise/Staal 10.00 25.00
C3TAS Svechnikov/Teravainen/Aho 15.00 40.00
C3TKD Toews/Kane/DeBrincat 20.00 50.00
C3TMB Texier/Bemstrom/Merzlikins 20.00 50.00
C3TMM Tavares/Matthews/Marner 40.00 100.00
C3WKM Kostin/MacEachern/Walman 12.00 30.00
C3YBB Barkov/Yandle/Bobrovsky 15.00 40.00
C3ZTP Panarin/Zibanejad/Trouba 20.00 50.00

2020-21 The Cup

1 Connor McDavid 10.00 25.00
2 Eric Lindros 3.00 8.00
3 Anders Lee 1.50 4.00
4 Conor Garland 1.50 4.00
5 Mikko Rantanen 5.00 12.00
6 Jacob Markstrom 2.00 5.00
7 Brent Burns 2.00 5.00
8 Jordan Greenway 1.50 4.00
9 Artemi Panarin 4.00 10.00
10 Patrice Bergeron 2.50 6.00
11 Rickard Rakell 1.50 4.00
12 Sean Couturier 1.50 4.00
13 Ryan Suter 1.50 4.00
14 Ryan O'Reilly 2.00 5.00
15 Jack Eichel 3.00 8.00
16 Mathew Barzal 2.50 6.00
17 Carter Hart 2.00 5.00
18 Jaromir Jagr 6.00 15.00
19 Teemu Selanne 4.00 10.00
20 Bill Ranford 1.50 4.00
21 David Pastrnak 5.00 12.00
22 Robin Lehner 1.50 4.00
23 Mike Richter 2.00 5.00
24 Mark Scheifele 3.00 8.00
25 Mario Lemieux 8.00 20.00
26 Jonathan Marchessault 2.50 6.00
27 Auston Matthews 8.00 20.00
28 Dylan Larkin 2.50 6.00
29 Jonathan Huberdeau 2.50 6.00
30 Sebastian Aho 3.00 8.00
31 Roman Josi 2.00 5.00
32 Andrei Vasilevskiy 3.00 8.00
33 Seth Jones 2.00 5.00
34 Brock Boeser 2.50 6.00
35 Jason Zucker 2.00 5.00
36 Jakub Vrana 2.00 5.00
37 Tom Wilson 2.00 5.00
38 Alex DeBrincat 2.50 6.00
39 Rasmus Dahlin 2.50 6.00
40 Connor Hellebuyck 4.00 10.00
41 Thomas Chabot 2.00 5.00
42 Jordan Eberle 2.00 5.00
43 Clayton Keller 2.50 6.00
44 Pavel Buchnevich 1.50 4.00
45 J.T. Miller 2.50 6.00
46 Kevin Fiala 1.50 4.00
47 Miro Heiskanen 2.50 6.00
48 Cale Makar 5.00 12.00
49 Victor Hedman 2.50 6.00
50 Patrick Roy 5.00 12.00
51 Pierre-Luc Dubois 1.50 4.00
52 Kyle Connor 3.00 8.00
53 Jacob Trouba 1.50 4.00
54 Dominik Kubalik 2.00 5.00
55 Nick Suzuki 4.00 10.00
56 Alex Ovechkin 8.00 20.00
57 Eric Staal 2.00 5.00
58 John Tavares 3.00 8.00
59 Elias Lindholm 2.00 5.00
60 Josh Morrissey 2.50 6.00
61 John LeClair 2.00 5.00
62 Saku Koivu 2.00 5.00
63 Aleksander Barkov 3.00 8.00
64 Patrick Kane 4.00 10.00
65 Hampus Lindholm 1.25 3.00
66 Henrik Zetterberg 2.50 6.00
67 Leon Draisaitl 6.00 15.00
68 Jonathan Drouin 1.50 4.00
69 Matt Duchene 2.00 5.00
70 Matt Murray 2.00 5.00
71 Carey Price 4.00 10.00
72 David Perron 1.50 4.00
73 Joe Pavelski 2.50 6.00
74 Elias Pettersson 3.00 8.00
75 Wayne Gretzky 12.00 30.00
76 Brady Tkachuk 3.00 8.00
77 Mark Stone 2.50 6.00
78 Matthew Tkachuk 4.00 10.00
79 Evander Kane 2.00 5.00
80 Brad Marchand 4.00 10.00
81 William Nylander 4.00 10.00
82 Sidney Crosby 8.00 20.00
83 Jaccob Slavin 1.50 4.00
84 Mika Zibanejad 2.50 6.00
85 Nathan MacKinnon 8.00 20.00
86 Nick Schmaltz 1.50 4.00
87 Cam Atkinson 2.00 5.00
88 Anze Kopitar 3.00 8.00
89 Steven Stamkos 4.00 10.00
90 Timo Meier 2.00 5.00
91 Brayden Schenn 2.00 5.00
92 Sergei Bobrovsky 3.00 8.00
93 Teuvo Teravainen 2.00 5.00
94 Andrei Svechnikov 2.50 6.00
95 Brett Hull 4.00 10.00
96 Anthony Mantha 1.50 4.00
97 Andreas Johnsson 2.00 5.00
98 Matt Dumba 1.25 3.00
99 Jack Hughes 5.00 12.00
100 Bobby Orr 8.00 20.00
101 Alexis Lafreniere
JSY AU/99 RC 800.00 2000.00
102 Thomas Harley/249 RC 5.00 12.00
103 Jonas Johansson JSY AU/249 RC 25.00 60.00
104 Ryan McLeod JSY AU/249 RC 20.00 50.00
105 Connor Ingram/249 RC 2.50 6.00
106 Timothy Liljegren
JSY AU/49 RC 25.00 60.00
107 Liam Foudy JSY AU/249 RC 25.00 60.00
108 Reid Duke JSY AU/249 RC 25.00 60.00
109 Philipp Kurashev JSY AU/249 RC 30.00 80.00
110 Calvin Thurkauf JSY AU/249 RC 20.00 50.00
111 Alexander Yelesin/249 RC 2.50 6.00
112 Gage Quinney JSY AU/249 RC 15.00 40.00
113 Alexander Alexeyev
JSY AU/49 RC 20.00 50.00
114 Alex Belzile JSY AU/249 RC 20.00 50.00
115 Gustav Lindstrom
JSY AU/49 RC 20.00 50.00
116 Nicolas Beaudin JSY AU/249 RC 25.00 60.00
117 Mikey Anderson JSY AU/249 RC 25.00 60.00
118 Jason Robertson
JSY AU/99 RC 200.00 500.00
119 Dylan Coghlan/249 RC 3.00 8.00
120 Alec Regula JSY AU/249 RC 15.00 40.00
121 Gabe Vilardi JSY AU/249 RC 60.00 150.00
122 Pierre-Olivier Joseph
JSY AU/49 RC 25.00 60.00
123 Philippe Maillet/249 RC 2.50 6.00
124 Nick Robertson JSY AU/49 RC 60.00 150.00
125 Victor Soderstrom
JSY AU/49 RC 20.00 50.00
126 Egor Korshkov/249 RC 2.00 5.00
127 Jani Hakanpaa JSY AU/249 RC 15.00 40.00
128 Nikolai Knyzhov JSY AU/249 RC 20.00 50.00
129 Maxim Letunov JSY AU/249 RC 20.00 50.00
130 Peyton Krebs JSY AU/49 RC 40.00 100.00
131 Lucas Carlsson JSY AU/249 RC 20.00 50.00
132 Joel Kiviranta JSY AU/249 RC 25.00 60.00
133 Anthony Angello JSY AU/249 RC 20.00 50.00
134 Jake Evans JSY AU/249 RC 25.00 60.00
135 Ty Dellandrea JSY AU/249 RC 25.00 60.00
136 Olli Juolevi JSY AU/249 RC 25.00 60.00
137 Jake Oettinger JSY AU/249 RC 150.00 400.00
138 Keegan Kolesar JSY AU/249 RC 20.00 50.00
139 Josh Norris JSY AU/49 RC 80.00 200.00
140 Martin Kaut JSY AU/249 RC 25.00 60.00
141 Morgan Geekie JSY AU/249 RC 25.00 60.00
142 Tyler Benson JSY AU/249 RC 25.00 60.00
143 Vitek Vanecek JSY AU/249 RC 80.00 200.00
144 Bowen Byram JSY AU/99 RC 400.00 1000.00
145 Shane Bowers JSY AU/249 RC 20.00 50.00
146 Alexander True JSY AU/249 RC 20.00 50.00
147 Matiss Kivlenieks/249 RC 4.00 10.00
148 Brandon Hagel/249 RC 4.00 10.00
149 Kieffer Bellows JSY AU/249 RC 20.00 50.00
150 Steven Lorentz JSY AU/249 RC 20.00 50.00
151 Chase Priskie JSY AU/249 RC 20.00 50.00
152 Pavel Francouz JSY AU/249 RC 50.00 125.00
153 Dylan Cozens JSY AU/99 RC 300.00 800.00
154 Alexander Romanov
JSY AU/99 RC 80.00 200.00
155 Ian Mitchell/249 RC 2.50 6.00
156 Logan Stanley/249 RC 3.00 8.00
157 Kirill Kaprizov
JSY AU/99 RC 2500.00 6000.00
158 Pius Suter JSY AU/249 RC 30.00 80.00
159 Nils Hoglander JSY AU/249 RC 25.00 60.00
160 Ilya Sorokin JSY AU/49 RC 300.00 800.00
161 Tim Stutzle JSY AU/99 RC 600.00 1500.00
162 Cal Foote JSY AU/249 RC 30.00 80.00
163 Yegor Sharangovich
JSY AU/249 RC 40.00 100.00
164 Connor McMichael
JSY AU/249 RC 40.00 100.00
165 Arthur Kaliyev JSY AU/249 RC 40.00 100.00
166 Ty Smith JSY AU/49 RC 40.00 100.00
167 Alexander Barabanov
JSY AU/49 RC 25.00 60.00
168 Jack Rathbone JSY AU/249 RC 25.00 60.00
169 Drew O'Connor JSY AU/249 RC 25.00 60.00
170 Joel Hofer JSY AU/249 RC 25.00 60.00
171 Cameron Hillis/249 RC 2.50 6.00
172 Kevin Bahl/249 RC 2.50 6.00
173 Stuart Skinner JSY AU/249 RC 50.00 120.00
174 Gilles Senn/249 RC 2.50 6.00
175 John Leonard JSY AU/249 RC 20.00 50.00
176 Kevin Lankinen/249 RC 5.00 12.00
177 Mikko Lehtonen JSY AU/249 RC 20.00 50.00
178 Mathias Brome JSY AU/249 RC 20.00 50.00
179 Sasha Chmelevski
JSY AU/49 RC 20.00 50.00
180 Mikhail Berdin/249 RC 3.00 8.00
181 Mikhail Maltsev/249 RC 2.50 6.00
182 K'Andre Miller JSY AU/249 RC 125.00 300.00
183 Nolan Foote JSY AU/249 RC 25.00 60.00
184 Fredrik Handemark/249 RC 2.50 6.00
185 Michael DiPietro/249 RC 4.00 10.00
186 Aleksi Heponiemi/249 RC 4.00 10.00
187 Philip Broberg/249 RC 3.00 8.00
188 Joseph Woll/249 RC 6.00 15.00
189 Alexei Melnichuk/249 RC 2.00 5.00
190 Vitali Kravtsov/249 RC 6.00 15.00
191 Jansen Harkins/249 RC 2.50 6.00
192 Jalen Chatfield/249 RC 2.50 6.00
193 William Lagesson/249 RC 3.00 8.00
194 Artem Zub/249 RC 2.50 6.00
195 Nicolas Meloche/249 RC 2.50 6.00
196 Glenn Gawdin/249 RC 2.50 6.00
197 Reese Johnson/249 RC 2.50 6.00
198 Austin Strand/249 RC 2.50 6.00
199 Cam Johnson/249 RC 2.50 6.00
200 Michael McNiven/249 RC 2.50 6.00

2020-21 The Cup All Time Alum

ATABO Bobby Orr 12.00 30.00
ATAEL Eric Lindros 5.00 12.00
ATAGL Guy Lafleur 4.00 10.00
ATAJI Jarome Iginla 4.00 10.00
ATAJS Joe Sakic 6.00 15.00
ATAMR Mike Richter 3.00 8.00
ATAMS Martin St. Louis 3.00 8.00
ATANL Nicklas Lidstrom 3.00 8.00
ATAPB Peter Bondra 3.00 8.00
ATAWG Wayne Gretzky 20.00 50.00

2020-21 The Cup All Time Alum Autographs

ATABO Bobby Orr/25 150.00 400.00
ATAEL Eric Lindros/25 200.00 500.00
ATAJI Jarome Iginla/50 150.00 400.00
ATAJS Joe Sakic/25 150.00 400.00
ATAMR Mike Richter/50 80.00 200.00
ATAMS Martin St. Louis/50 40.00 100.00
ATAPB Peter Bondra/50 40.00 100.00
ATAWG Wayne Gretzky/25 400.00 1000.00

2020-21 The Cup Brilliance Autographs

BAK Arthur Kaliyev C 40.00 100.00
BAL Alexis Lafreniere B 80.00 200.00
BAT Alex Tuch C 20.00 50.00
BBO Bobby Orr A 80.00 200.00
BCM Connor McDavid A 300.00 800.00
BDC Dylan Cozens C 40.00 100.00
BDG Dirk Graham C 15.00 40.00
BFP Felix Potvin B 30.00 80.00
BHZ Henrik Zetterberg A 25.00 60.00
BLF Liam Foudy C 25.00 60.00
BMC Connor McMichael C 15.00 40.00
BNH Nils Hoglander C 25.00 60.00
BPR Patrick Roy A 100.00 250.00
BRS Ryan Suter C 15.00 40.00
BTP Tomas Plekanec C 12.00 30.00
BVA John Vanbiesbrouck C 20.00 50.00
BWG Wayne Gretzky A 500.00 1200.00

2020-21 The Cup Chemical Composition Autographs Mantle

CCAB Alexander Barabanov C 8.00 20.00
CCAK Arthur Kaliyev C 12.00 30.00
CCAL Alexis Lafreniere A 80.00 200.00
CCAR Alexander Romanov C 10.00 25.00
CCAT Alex Tuch C 6.00 15.00
CCAV Andrei Vasilevskiy A 20.00 50.00
CCBS Brayden Schenn A 6.00 15.00
CCCA Cam Atkinson B 6.00 15.00
CCCM Connor McDavid A 300.00 800.00
CCDC Dylan Cozens B 12.00 30.00
CCJH Jonathan Huberdeau A 8.00 20.00
CCJM J.T. Miller B 8.00 20.00
CCKM K'Andre Miller C 15.00 40.00
CCLE Anders Lee B 5.00 12.00
CCLF Liam Foudy C 8.00 20.00
CCMC Connor McMichael C 12.00 30.00
CCNE Nikolaj Ehlers B 6.00 15.00
CCNF Nolan Foote A 8.00 20.00
CCNH Nils Hoglander C 8.00 20.00
CCPK Peyton Krebs C 12.00 30.00
CCPS Pius Suter C 10.00 25.00
CCRO Ryan O'Reilly B 6.00 15.00
CCRS Ryan Suter B 5.00 12.00
CCTD Ty Dellandrea C 8.00 20.00
CCTH Tomas Hertl A 6.00 15.00

2020-21 The Cup Chemical Composition Jersey Autographs Outer Core

CCAB Alexander Barabanov 12.00 30.00
CCAK Arthur Kaliyev 20.00 50.00
CCAL Alexis Lafreniere 80.00 200.00
CCAR Alexander Romanov 15.00 40.00
CCAT Alex Tuch 10.00 25.00
CCAV Andrei Vasilevskiy 15.00 40.00
CCBS Brayden Schenn 10.00 25.00
CCCA Cam Atkinson 10.00 25.00
CCCM Connor McDavid 400.00 1000.00
CCDC Dylan Cozens 20.00 50.00
CCJH Jonathan Huberdeau 12.00 30.00
CCJM J.T. Miller 12.00 30.00
CCKM K'Andre Miller 25.00 60.00
CCLE Anders Lee 8.00 20.00
CCLF Liam Foudy 12.00 30.00
CCMC Connor McMichael 20.00 50.00
CCNE Nikolaj Ehlers 10.00 25.00
CCNF Nolan Foote 12.00 30.00
CCNH Nils Hoglander 12.00 30.00
CCPK Peyton Krebs 20.00 50.00
CCPS Pius Suter 15.00 40.00
CCRO Ryan O'Reilly 10.00 25.00
CCRS Ryan Suter 8.00 20.00
CCTD Ty Dellandrea 12.00 30.00
CCTH Tomas Hertl 10.00 25.00

2020-21 The Cup Day With the Cup Signatures

DCAV Andrei Vasilevskiy C 60.00 150.00
DCDP David Perron C 50.00 125.00
DCHZ Henrik Zetterberg B 100.00 250.00
DCLM Lanny McDonald B 50.00 125.00
DCMS Martin St. Louis C 40.00 100.00
DCRO Ryan O'Reilly C 40.00 100.00
DCSC Sidney Crosby A 400.00 1000.00
DCSS Steven Stamkos B 125.00 300.00
DCWG Wayne Gretzky A 400.00 1000.00

2020-21 The Cup Enshrinements

EAL Alexis Lafreniere/99 80.00 200.00
EAR Alexander Romanov/99 30.00 80.00
EAV Andrei Vasilevskiy/99 30.00 80.00
EBH Brett Hull/25 40.00 100.00
EBO Bobby Orr/25 80.00 200.00
ECA Cam Atkinson/99 20.00 50.00
ECM Connor McMichael/99 40.00 100.00
EDC Dylan Cozens/99 25.00 60.00
EDP David Perron/99 15.00 40.00
EDW Doug Wilson/99 15.00 40.00
EEL Eric Lindros/25 150.00 400.00
EES Eric Staal/99 20.00 50.00
EGS Gary Suter/99 12.00 30.00
EJM J.T. Miller/99 8.00 20.00
EKK Kirill Kaprizov/99 250.00 600.00
EKM K'Andre Miller/99 50.00 125.00
ELE Anders Lee/99 15.00 40.00
EMS Martin St. Louis/25 30.00 80.00
ENE Nikolaj Ehlers/99 20.00 50.00
ENS Nick Suzuki/99 40.00 100.00
EPB Peter Bondra/99 20.00 50.00
EPR Patrick Roy/25 125.00 300.00
ERH Ron Hextall/99 20.00 50.00
ESK Saku Koivu/99 20.00 50.00
ETS Tim Stutzle/99 150.00 400.00
EWG Wayne Gretzky/25 300.00 800.00

2020-21 The Cup Enshrinements Duos

E2HB Aleksander Barkov
Jonathan Huberdeau/25 40.00 100.00
E2LM Alexis Lafreniere
K'Andre Miller/25 100.00 250.00
E2SO Ryan O'Reilly
Brayden Schenn/25 25.00 60.00

2020-21 The Cup Foundations Jerseys

FAK Anze Kopitar/49 10.00 25.00
FAL Alexis Lafreniere/99 25.00 60.00
FAO Alex Ovechkin/49 30.00 80.00
FAP Artemi Panarin/49 12.00 30.00
FAR Alexander Romanov/99 10.00 25.00
FAV Andrei Vasilevskiy/49 10.00 25.00
FBB Bowen Byram/99 15.00 40.00
FBT Brady Tkachuk/49 10.00 25.00
FCF Cal Foote/99 10.00 25.00
FCG Claude Giroux/49 6.00 15.00
FCK Clayton Keller/49 8.00 20.00
FCM Connor McDavid/49 80.00 200.00
FDC Dylan Cozens/99 12.00 30.00
FDL Dylan Larkin/49 8.00 20.00
FDP David Pastrnak/49 15.00 40.00
FGV Gabe Vilardi/99 12.00 30.00
FIM Ian Mitchell/99 6.00 15.00
FIS Ilya Sorokin/99 20.00 50.00
FJE Jack Eichel/49 10.00 25.00
FJH Jonathan Huberdeau/49 8.00 20.00
FJK Jesperi Kotkaniemi/49 6.00 15.00
FJM J.T. Miller/49 8.00 20.00
FJO Jake Oettinger/99 20.00 50.00
FJR Jason Robertson/99 20.00 50.00
FJS Jordan Staal/49 5.00 12.00
FJT John Tavares/49 10.00 25.00
FKA Arthur Kaliyev/99 12.00 30.00
FKK Kirill Kaprizov/99 100.00 250.00
FKU Philipp Kurashev/99 10.00 25.00
FKY Keith Yandle/49 4.00 10.00
FLF Liam Foudy/99 8.00 20.00
FMA Mikey Anderson/99 8.00 20.00
FMB Mathew Barzal/49 8.00 20.00
FMC Connor McMichael/99 12.00 30.00
FMS Mark Stone/49 8.00 20.00
FNE Nikolaj Ehlers/49 6.00 15.00
FNH Nils Hoglander/99 8.00 20.00
FNM Nathan MacKinnon/49 25.00 60.00
FNR Nick Robertson/99 12.00 30.00
FPK Peyton Krebs/99 12.00 30.00
FPS Pius Suter/99 10.00 25.00
FRG Ryan Getzlaf/49 6.00 15.00
FRS Ryan Suter/49 5.00 12.00
FSC Sidney Crosby/49 30.00 80.00
FSJ Seth Jones/49 6.00 15.00
FSM Ty Smith/99 12.00 30.00
FTD Ty Dellandrea/99 8.00 20.00
FTS Tim Stutzle/99 30.00 80.00
FYS Yegor Sharangovich/99 12.00 30.00

2020-21 The Cup Honorable Numbers

HRAK Arthur Kaliyev/34 40.00 100.00
HRAR Alexander Romanov/27 30.00 80.00
HRDC Dylan Cozens/24 150.00 400.00
HRDW Doug Wilson/24 15.00 40.00
HRKK Kirill Kaprizov/97 800.00 2000.00
HRLF Liam Foudy/19 25.00 60.00
HRMR Mike Richter/35 150.00 400.00
HRMS Mark Stone/61 30.00 80.00
HRNH Nils Hoglander/36 25.00 60.00
HROK Olaf Kolzig/37 125.00 300.00
HRPS Pius Suter/24 30.00 80.00
HRRS Ryan Suter/20 15.00 40.00
HRST Shea Theodore/27 25.00 60.00

2020-21 The Cup Honorable Numbers Dual

HN2CS D.Cozens/P.Suter 40.00 100.00
HN2LE N.Ehlers/A.Lee 50.00 125.00
HN2TZ A.Tanguay/H.Zetterberg 60.00 150.00

2020-21 The Cup Inked Insignias

IIAK Arthur Kaliyev/75 60.00 150.00
IIAL Alexis Lafreniere/75 125.00 300.00
IIAR Alexander Romanov/75 50.00 125.00
IIAV Andrei Vasilevskiy/25 50.00 125.00
IIBB Bowen Byram/75 60.00 150.00
IIBM Brad Marchand/25 100.00 250.00
IICM Connor McDavid/25 600.00 1500.00
IIDC Dylan Cozens/75 40.00 100.00
IIDW Doug Wilson/25 25.00 60.00
IIJI Jarome Iginla/25 125.00 300.00
IIJL John LeClair/25 30.00 80.00
IIJM J.T. Miller/25 60.00 150.00
IIJV John Vanbiesbrouck/25 125.00 300.00
IIKK Kirill Kaprizov/75 400.00 1000.00
IIKM K'Andre Miller/75 80.00 200.00
IILF Liam Foudy/75 40.00 100.00
IIMB Martin Brodeur/25 150.00 400.00
IIMC Connor McMichael/75 60.00 150.00
IINH Nils Hoglander/75 60.00 150.00
IIPB Peter Bondra/25 125.00 300.00
IIPK Peyton Krebs/75 60.00 150.00
IIPR Patrick Roy/25 300.00 800.00
IIPS Pius Suter/75 50.00 125.00
IIRI Mike Richter/25 30.00 80.00
IIRO Ryan O'Reilly/25 30.00 80.00
IISC Brayden Schenn/25 60.00 150.00
IISM Martin St. Louis/25 50.00 125.00
IIST Mark Stone/25 30.00 80.00
IISY Steve Yzerman/25 250.00 600.00
IITD Ty Dellandrea/75 40.00 100.00
IITI Tim Stutzle/75 80.00 200.00
IITY Ty Smith/75 60.00 150.00
IIVS Victor Soderstrom/75 30.00 80.00

2020-21 The Cup Lamp Lighters Autographs

LLAB Alexander Barabanov B 25.00 60.00
LLAK Arthur Kaliyev B 40.00 100.00
LLAL Alexis Lafreniere A 125.00 300.00
LLAR Alexander Romanov B 30.00 80.00
LLAT Alex Tuch B 20.00 50.00
LLBB Brent Burns A 20.00 50.00
LLBH Brett Hull A 40.00 100.00
LLBS Bobby Smith B 20.00 50.00
LLBT Brady Tkachuk B 30.00 80.00
LLBY Bowen Byram B 50.00 125.00
LLCA Cam Atkinson B 20.00 50.00
LLCM Connor McMichael B 40.00 100.00
LLCO Maxime Comtois B 15.00 40.00
LLCT Calvin Thurkauf C 20.00 50.00
LLDC Dylan Cozens A 30.00 80.00
LLDP David Perron B 15.00 40.00
LLDS Daniel Sedin A 25.00 60.00
LLEL Eric Lindros A 200.00 500.00
LLES Eric Staal A 20.00 50.00
LLGE Morgan Geekie B 25.00 60.00
LLHE Tomas Hertl B 20.00 50.00
LLHS Henrik Sedin A 25.00 60.00
LLJC Jonathan Cheechoo A 15.00 40.00
LLJH Jonathan Huberdeau A 25.00 60.00
LLJI Jarome Iginla A 25.00 60.00
LLJM J.T. Miller B 25.00 60.00
LLJN Josh Norris B 40.00 100.00
LLKM K'Andre Miller B 50.00 125.00
LLKP Kyle Palmieri A 15.00 40.00
LLKR Peyton Krebs C 40.00 100.00
LLLD Leon Draisaitl A 60.00 150.00
LLLE Anders Lee B 15.00 40.00
LLLF Liam Foudy B 25.00 60.00
LLLV Maxim Letunov B 20.00 50.00
LLMG Marian Gaborik A 20.00 50.00
LLMM Mark Messier A 60.00 150.00
LLMO Mike Modano B 30.00 80.00
LLMS Martin St. Louis A 20.00 50.00
LLMT Matthew Tkachuk A 40.00 100.00
LLNE Nikolaj Ehlers B 20.00 50.00
LLNH Nils Hoglander A 25.00 60.00
LLPB Peter Bondra A 20.00 50.00
LLPS Pius Suter B 30.00 80.00
LLRO Ryan O'Reilly B 20.00 50.00
LLRT Robert Thomas B 20.00 50.00
LLSI Darryl Sittler A 25.00 60.00
LLSR Sam Reinhart B 40.00 100.00
LLSS Steven Stamkos A 60.00 150.00
LLST Mark Stone B 25.00 60.00
LLSY Steve Yzerman A 200.00 500.00
LLTA John Tavares A 30.00 80.00
LLTH Shea Theodore B 25.00 60.00
LLTM Tim Stutzle A 125.00 300.00
LLWG Wayne Gretzky A 400.00 1000.00
LLWK William Karlsson A 25.00 60.00
LLYS Yegor Sharangovich B 20.00 50.00

2020-21 The Cup Limited Logos Autographs

LLAL Anders Lee/50 30.00 80.00
LLAT Alex Tuch/50 40.00 100.00
LLAV Andrei Vasilevskiy/25 200.00 500.00
LLBB Brent Burns/25 40.00 100.00
LLBM Brad Marchand/25 80.00 200.00
LLBO Brock Boeser/25 50.00 125.00
LLBS Brayden Schenn/50 40.00 100.00
LLBT Brady Tkachuk/50 60.00 150.00
LLCA Cam Atkinson/50 40.00 100.00
LLCP Carey Price/25 80.00 200.00
LLDS Dylan Strome/50 50.00 125.00
LLHE Connor Hellebuyck/50 80.00 200.00
LLIS Ilya Sorokin/50 250.00 600.00
LLJH Jonathan Huberdeau/50 50.00 125.00
LLJM J.T. Miller/50 50.00 125.00
LLKK Kirill Kaprizov/50 500.00 1200.00
LLKP Kyle Palmieri/50 30.00 80.00
LLLA Alexis Lafreniere/25 250.00 600.00
LLMT Matthew Tkachuk/50 80.00 200.00
LLNE Nikolaj Ehlers/50 40.00 100.00
LLRO Ryan O'Reilly/50 40.00 100.00
LLRS Ryan Suter/50 30.00 80.00
LLSB Sergei Bobrovsky/50 60.00 150.00
LLSS Steven Stamkos/25 250.00 600.00
LLST Mark Stone/50 50.00 125.00
LLTH Shea Theodore/50 50.00 125.00
LLTS Tim Stutzle/50 300.00 800.00
LLWK William Karlsson/50 50.00 125.00

2020-21 The Cup Quads Jerseys

C4BBKF Byram/Bowers
Kaut/Francouz 30.00 80.00
C4BCKH Couture/Burns/Kane/Hertl 15.00 40.00
C4BCKO Backstrom/Ovechkin
Kuznetsov/Carlson 50.00 125.00
C4BDKK Doughty/Kopitar
Kempe/Brown 20.00 50.00
C4BENB Barzal/Eberle/Bailey/Nelson 15.00 40.00
C4BLMS Lafreniere/Miller
Sorokin/Bellows 50.00 125.00
C4BRMP Pastrnak/Bergeron
Marchand/Rask 30.00 80.00
C4BWPP Bergeron/Pastrnak
Weber/Price 30.00 80.00
C4BZWS Subban/Blackwood
Zacha/Wood 15.00 40.00
C4CLTK TRUE/Chmelevski
Knyzhov/Letunov 12.00 30.00
C4DJJF Forsberg/Johansen
Duchene/Josi 20.00 50.00
C4DRHO Robertson/Dellandrea
Harley/Oettinger 40.00 100.00
C4FSTT Stone/Tuch/Theodore/Fleury 25.00 60.00
C4GLBZ Bertuzzi/Greiss
Larkin/Zadina 15.00 40.00
C4GMGT Giordano/Tkachuk
Gaudreau/Monahan 25.00 60.00
C4GSRG Getzlaf/Silfverberg
Rakell/Gibson 12.00 30.00
C4HBPH Pettersson/Boeser
Horvat/Hughes 30.00 80.00
C4KDSK Kessel/Keller
Schmaltz/Dvorak 15.00 40.00
C4KKSD DeBrincat
Strome/Kane/Keith 25.00 60.00
C4LMRM MacKinnon/Landeskog
Rantanen/Makar 50.00 125.00
C4MGVG Giroux/van Riemsdyk
Malkin/Guentzel 25.00 60.00
C4MKRS Regula/Mitchell
Suter/Kurashev 20.00 50.00
C4NLGD Gaudreau/Lindholm
Draisaitl/Nugent-Hopkins 40.00 100.00
C4NNDP Nugent-
Hopkins/Draisaitl/Puljujarvi/Nurse 40.00 100.00
C4PSEG Greenway/Parise
Eriksson Ek/Suter 12.00 30.00
C4PSOS O'Reilly/Perron
Schenn/Schwartz 15.00 40.00
C4REDO Eichel/Olofsson
Reinhart/Dahlin 25.00 60.00
C4SHPV Stamkos/Point
Hedman/Vasilevskiy 25.00 60.00
C4STAS Staal/Aho
Teravainen/Svechnikov 20.00 50.00
C4TPBF Panarin/Buchnevich
Fox/Trouba 25.00 60.00
C4TRAM Matthews/Tavares
Rielly/Andersen 50.00 125.00
C4VGVH Giroux/Voracek/van
Riemsdyk/Hayes 12.00 30.00
C4WPGD Gallagher/Drouin
Weber/Price 25.00 60.00
C4WSEC Scheifele/Connor
Ehlers/Wheeler 20.00 50.00
C4YHEB Huberdeau/Barkov
Ekblad/Yandle 20.00 50.00

2020-21 The Cup Rookie Bookmarks Dual Autographs

DARBBB B.Byram/S.Bowers 80.00 200.00
DARBDO T.Dellandrea/J.Oettinger 100.00 250.00
DARBFT L.Foudy/C.Thurkauf 40.00 100.00
DARBLK A.Lafreniere/K.Kaprizov 500.00 1200.00
DARBSS Y.Sharangovich/T.Smith 60.00 150.00

2020-21 The Cup Rookie Class of '21

2020AA Alexander Alexeyev 3.00 8.00
2020AB Alexander Barabanov 4.00 10.00
2020BE Kieffer Bellows 3.00 8.00
2020DO Drew O'Connor 4.00 10.00
2020GL Gustav Lindstrom 3.00 8.00
2020GQ Gage Quinney 2.50 6.00
2020HA Jani Hakanpaa 2.50 6.00
2020JH Joel Hofer 4.00 10.00
2020JL John Leonard 3.00 8.00
2020JO Jake Oettinger 10.00 25.00
2020JR Jason Robertson 10.00 25.00
2020KB Kevin Bahl 3.00 8.00
2020KO Keegan Kolesar 3.00 8.00
2020LC Lucas Carlsson 3.00 8.00
2020MB Mathias Brome 3.00 8.00
2020MG Morgan Geekie 4.00 10.00
2020MK Martin Kaut 4.00 10.00
2020ML Maxim Letunov 3.00 8.00
2020NB Nicolas Beaudin 4.00 10.00
2020NF Nolan Foote 4.00 10.00
2020PJ Pierre-Olivier Joseph 4.00 10.00
2020RA Jack Rathbone 4.00 10.00
2020RE Alec Regula 2.50 6.00
2020RM Ryan McLeod 3.00 8.00
2020SB Shane Bowers 3.00 8.00
2020SC Sasha Chmelevski 3.00 8.00
2020SL Steven Lorentz 3.00 8.00
2020SS Stuart Skinner 8.00 20.00
2020TB Tyler Benson 4.00 10.00
2020TD Ty Dellandrea 4.00 10.00
2020TH Thomas Harley 6.00 15.00
2020TL Timothy Liljegren 4.00 10.00
2020VS Victor Soderstrom 3.00 8.00
2021AK Arthur Kaliyev 6.00 15.00
2021AL Alexis Lafreniere 12.00 30.00
2021AR Alexander Romanov 5.00 12.00
2021BB Bowen Byram 8.00 20.00
2021BH Brandon Hagel 5.00 12.00
2021CF Cal Foote 5.00 12.00
2021CM Connor McMichael 6.00 15.00
2021DC Dylan Cozens 6.00 15.00
2021GV Gabe Vilardi 6.00 15.00
2021IM Ian Mitchell 3.00 8.00
2021IS Ilya Sorokin 10.00 25.00
2021JE Jake Evans 4.00 10.00
2021JN Josh Norris 6.00 15.00
2021KK Kirill Kaprizov 30.00 80.00
2021KL Kevin Lankinen 6.00 15.00
2021KM K'Andre Miller 8.00 20.00
2021KU Philipp Kurashev 6.00 15.00
2021LF Liam Foudy 4.00 10.00
2021LS Logan Stanley 4.00 10.00
2021MA Mikey Anderson 3.00 8.00
2021NH Nils Hoglander 4.00 10.00
2021NK Nikolai Knyzhov 4.00 10.00
2021NR Nick Robertson 6.00 15.00
2021OJ Olli Juolevi 4.00 10.00
2021PK Peyton Krebs 6.00 15.00
2021PS Pius Suter 5.00 12.00
2021SM Ty Smith 6.00 15.00
2021TS Tim Stutzle 15.00 40.00
2021VV Vitek Vanecek 6.00 15.00
2021YS Yegor Sharangovich 6.00 15.00

2020-21 The Cup Rookie Class of '21 Autographs

2021AK Arthur Kaliyev 20.00 50.00
2021AL Alexis Lafreniere 40.00 100.00
2021AR Alexander Romanov 15.00 40.00
2021BB Bowen Byram 40.00 100.00
2021BH Brandon Hagel 15.00 40.00
2021CF Cal Foote 15.00 40.00
2021CM Connor McMichael 25.00 60.00
2021DC Dylan Cozens 25.00 60.00
2021JE Jake Evans 12.00 30.00
2021JN Josh Norris 20.00 50.00
2021KM K'Andre Miller 25.00 60.00
2021LF Liam Foudy 12.00 30.00
2021MA Mikey Anderson 12.00 30.00
2021NH Nils Hoglander 12.00 30.00
2021NK Nikolai Knyzhov 10.00 25.00
2021PK Peyton Krebs 20.00 50.00
2021PS Pius Suter 15.00 40.00
2021SM Ty Smith 20.00 50.00
2021TS Tim Stutzle 50.00 125.00
2021VV Vitek Vanecek 20.00 50.00
2021YS Yegor Sharangovich 20.00 50.00

2020-21 The Cup Rookie Class of '21 Patch Autographs

2020AA Alexander Alexeyev 12.00 30.00
2020AB Alexander Barabanov 15.00 40.00
2020BE Kieffer Bellows 12.00 30.00
2020DO Drew O'Connor 12.00 30.00
2020JH Joel Hofer 15.00 40.00
2020JL John Leonard 15.00 40.00
2020JO Jake Oettinger 80.00 200.00
2020JR Jason Robertson 200.00 500.00
2020KO Keegan Kolesar 12.00 30.00
2020MG Morgan Geekie 15.00 40.00
2020ML Maxim Letunov 12.00 30.00
2020NF Nolan Foote 15.00 40.00
2020PJ Pierre-Olivier Joseph 15.00 40.00
2020RA Jack Rathbone 15.00 40.00
2020RE Alec Regula 10.00 25.00
2020RM Ryan McLeod 12.00 30.00
2020SB Shane Bowers 12.00 30.00
2020SC Sasha Chmelevski 12.00 30.00
2020SL Steven Lorentz 12.00 30.00
2020SS Stuart Skinner 30.00 80.00
2020TD Ty Dellandrea 15.00 40.00
2020VS Victor Soderstrom 12.00 30.00
2021AK Arthur Kaliyev 25.00 60.00
2021AL Alexis Lafreniere 80.00 200.00
2021AR Alexander Romanov 20.00 50.00
2021BB Bowen Byram 60.00 150.00
2021BH Brandon Hagel 20.00 50.00
2021CF Cal Foote
2021CM Connor McMichael 25.00 60.00
2021DC Dylan Cozens 80.00 200.00
2021JN Josh Norris 100.00 250.00
2021KK Kirill Kaprizov 400.00 1000.00
2021KM K'Andre Miller 40.00 100.00
2021LF Liam Foudy 15.00 40.00
2021MA Mikey Anderson 25.00 60.00
2021NH Nils Hoglander 15.00 40.00
2021NK Nikolai Knyzhov 12.00 30.00
2021PK Peyton Krebs 25.00 60.00
2021PS Pius Suter 25.00 60.00
2021SM Ty Smith 25.00 60.00
2021TS Tim Stutzle 150.00 400.00
2021VV Vitek Vanecek 40.00 100.00
2021YS Yegor Sharangovich 25.00 60.00

2020-21 The Cup Rookie Class of '21 Patches

2021AK Arthur Kaliyev 10.00 25.00
2021AL Alexis Lafreniere 20.00 50.00
2021AR Alexander Romanov 8.00 20.00
2021BB Bowen Byram 12.00 30.00
2021BH Brandon Hagel 8.00 20.00
2021CF Cal Foote 8.00 20.00
2021CM Connor McMichael 10.00 25.00
2021DC Dylan Cozens 10.00 25.00
2021GV Gabe Vilardi 10.00 25.00
2021IM Ian Mitchell 5.00 12.00
2021IS Ilya Sorokin 40.00 100.00
2021JE Jake Evans 6.00 15.00
2021JN Josh Norris 10.00 25.00
2021KK Kirill Kaprizov 100.00 250.00
2021KM K'Andre Miller 12.00 30.00
2021KU Philipp Kurashev 8.00 20.00
2021LF Liam Foudy 6.00 15.00
2021LS Logan Stanley 6.00 15.00
2021MA Mikey Anderson 6.00 15.00
2021NH Nils Hoglander 6.00 15.00
2021NK Nikolai Knyzhov 5.00 12.00
2021NR Nick Robertson 10.00 25.00
2021OJ Olli Juolevi 6.00 15.00
2021PK Peyton Krebs 10.00 25.00
2021PS Pius Suter 8.00 20.00
2021SM Ty Smith 8.00 20.00
2021TS Tim Stutzle 40.00 100.00
2021VV Vitek Vanecek 10.00 25.00
2021YS Yegor Sharangovich 10.00 25.00

2020-21 The Cup Rookie Gear Relic Autographs

ARGAL Alexis Lafreniere 80.00 200.00
ARGAR Alexander Romanov 30.00 80.00
ARGBB Bowen Byram 50.00 125.00
ARGCM Connor McMichael 40.00 100.00
ARGDC Dylan Cozens 40.00 100.00
ARGJR Jason Robertson 80.00 200.00
ARGKM K'Andre Miller 50.00 125.00
ARGLF Liam Foudy 25.00 60.00
ARGPK Peyton Krebs 40.00 100.00
ARGPS Pius Suter 25.00 60.00
ARGYS Yegor Sharangovich 40.00 100.00

2020-21 The Cup Scripted Swatches

SCAK Arthur Kaliyev 50.00 125.00
SCAL Alexis Lafreniere 100.00 250.00
SCAT Alex Tuch 25.00 60.00
SCAV Andrei Vasilevskiy 40.00 100.00
SCBB Bowen Byram 60.00 150.00
SCBS Brayden Schenn 25.00 60.00
SCCM Connor McDavid 300.00 800.00
SCDC Dylan Cozens 80.00 200.00
SCKM K'Andre Miller 60.00 150.00
SCLE Anders Lee 20.00 50.00
SCLF Liam Foudy 30.00 80.00
SCNH Nils Hoglander 25.00 60.00
SCPS Pius Suter 40.00 100.00
SCRS Ryan Suter 20.00 50.00
SCWK William Karlsson 30.00 80.00
SCYS Yegor Sharangovich 50.00 125.00

2020-21 The Cup Signature Home Unis

*AWAY: .4X TO 1X BASIC
SHJAL Alexis Lafreniere/49 60.00 150.00
SHJAV Andrei Vasilevskiy/35 25.00 60.00
SHJBB Bowen Byram/49 80.00 200.00
SHJBS Brayden Schenn/35 15.00 40.00
SHJCH Connor Hellebuyck/35 30.00 80.00
SHJCM Connor McDavid/35 600.00 1500.00
SHJCP Carey Price/35 80.00 200.00
SHJDC Dylan Cozens/49 30.00 80.00
SHJDH Dominik Hasek/35 150.00 400.00
SHJHZ Henrik Zetterberg/35 25.00 60.00
SHJJH Jonathan Huberdeau/35 20.00 50.00
SHJJM J.T. Miller/35 20.00 50.00
SHJJR Jason Robertson/49 80.00 200.00
SHJLF Liam Foudy/49 20.00 50.00
SHJMG Marian Gaborik/35 15.00 40.00
SHJRO Ryan O'Reilly/49 15.00 40.00
SHJTD Ty Dellandrea/49 15.00 40.00
SHJTS Tim Stutzle/49 100.00 250.00
SHJTW Tom Wilson/35 15.00 40.00
SHJYS Yegor Sharangovich/49 30.00 80.00

2020-21 The Cup Signature Materials

SPAK Arthur Kaliyev/99 30.00 80.00
SPAL Alexis Lafreniere/99 150.00 400.00
SPAR Alexander Romanov/99 25.00 60.00
SPAT Alex Tuch/99 15.00 40.00
SPAV Andrei Vasilevskiy/25 60.00 150.00
SPBB Bowen Byram/99 125.00 300.00
SPBH Brandon Hagel/99 25.00 60.00
SPBS Brayden Schenn/99 15.00 40.00

SPCA Cam Atkinson/99 15.00 40.00
SPCO Connor McMichael/99 30.00 80.00
SPCR Sidney Crosby/10
SPDC Dylan Cozens/99 25.00 60.00
SPDP David Perron/99 12.00 30.00
SPDS Dylan Strome/99 20.00 50.00
SPHE Connor Hellebuyck/25 30.00 80.00
SPJH Jonathan Huberdeau/25 20.00 50.00
SPJM J.T. Miller/99 20.00 50.00
SPJP Joe Pavelski/99 20.00 50.00
SPKK Kirill Kaprizov/99 600.00 1500.00
SPKM K'Andre Miller/99 80.00 200.00
SPLD Leon Draisaitl/10
SPLE Anders Lee/99 12.00 30.00
SPLF Liam Foudy/99 20.00 50.00
SPMC Connor McDavid/10
SPMS Mark Stone/25 25.00 60.00
SPMT Matthew Tkachuk/25 30.00 80.00
SPNE Nikolaj Ehlers/99 15.00 40.00
SPNH Nils Hoglander/99 20.00 50.00
SPPJ Pierre-Olivier Joseph/99 20.00 50.00
SPPR Pekka Rinne/99 15.00 40.00
SPPS Pius Suter/99 25.00 60.00
SPRS Ryan Suter/99 12.00 30.00
SPSC Sasha Chmelevski/99 15.00 40.00
SPSL Steven Lorentz/99 15.00 40.00
SPSR Sam Reinhart/99 30.00 80.00
SPTH Tomas Hertl/99 15.00 40.00
SPTS Tim Stutzle/99 150.00 400.00
SPTW Tom Wilson/99 15.00 40.00
SPYS Yegor Sharangovich/99 30.00 80.00
SPZP Zach Parise/99 15.00 40.00

2020-21 The Cup Signature Renditions

SRAL Alexis Lafreniere A 60.00 150.00
SRBB Brent Burns B 15.00 40.00
SRCM Connor McDavid A 400.00 1000.00
SRCP Carey Price A 30.00 80.00
SRJV John Vanbiesbrouck C 15.00 40.00
SRKM Ken Morrow C 10.00 25.00
SRNH Nils Hoglander C 20.00 50.00
SRPS Pius Suter C 25.00 60.00
SRRS Ryan Suter C 12.00 30.00
SRTS Tim Stutzle C 50.00 125.00

2020-21 The Cup Signature Renditions Combos

SR2LM A.Lafreniere/K.Miller 150.00 400.00
SR2MD L.Draisaitl/C.McDavid 400.00 1000.00
SR2PS Z.Parise/R.Suter 20.00 50.00
SR2SS H.Sedin/D.Sedin 80.00 200.00

2020-21 The Cup Stick and Move

SMCC Chris Chelios/35 15.00 40.00
SMCP Carey Price/35 30.00 80.00
SMDP David Perron/50 12.00 30.00
SMGF Grant Fuhr/35 25.00 60.00
SMHZ Henrik Zetterberg/50 20.00 50.00
SMJV John Vanbiesbrouck/50 15.00 40.00
SMMG Marian Gaborik/35 15.00 40.00
SMMO Mike Modano/35 25.00 60.00
SMPC Paul Coffey/50 15.00 40.00
SMPD Pierre-Luc Dubois/35 12.00 30.00
SMRH Ron Hextall/35 15.00 40.00
SMSA Sebastian Aho/50 25.00 60.00
SMTT Tyler Toffoli/50 15.00 40.00
SMTU Alex Tuch/50 15.00 40.00

2020-21 The Cup The NHL Collection Patch Autographs

NHLAK Arthur Kaliyev/35 40.00 100.00
NHLAL Alexis Lafreniere/35 100.00 250.00
NHLAR Alec Regula/35 12.00 30.00
NHLAT Alex Tuch/25 30.00 80.00
NHLBB Bowen Byram/35 100.00 250.00
NHLCA Cam Atkinson/25 15.00 40.00
NHLDC Dylan Cozens/35 30.00 80.00
NHLDP David Perron/25 12.00 30.00
NHLJH Jonathan Huberdeau/25 20.00 50.00
NHLJM J.T. Miller/25 20.00 50.00
NHLJP Joe Pavelski/25 30.00 80.00
NHLKK Kirill Kaprizov/35 600.00 1500.00
NHLKM K'Andre Miller/35 40.00 100.00
NHLLF Liam Foudy/35 20.00 50.00
NHLNE Nikolaj Ehlers/25 15.00 40.00
NHLNF Nolan Foote/35 20.00 50.00
NHLNH Nils Hoglander/35 20.00 50.00
NHLNK Nikolai Knyzhov/35 15.00 40.00
NHLOR Ryan O'Reilly/25 15.00 40.00
NHLPK Peyton Krebs/35 30.00 80.00
NHLPS Pius Suter/35 25.00 60.00
NHLRO Alexander Romanov/35 25.00 60.00
NHLRT Robert Thomas/25 15.00 40.00
NHLSR Sam Reinhart/25 30.00 80.00
NHLST Dylan Strome/25 20.00 50.00
NHLTH Tomas Hertl/25 15.00 40.00
NHLTS Tim Stutzle/35 125.00 300.00
NHLYS Yegor Sharangovich/35 30.00 80.00

2020-21 The Cup Trios Jerseys

C3ABW Atkinson Bjorkstrand/Werenski 15.00 40.00
C3BBK Byram/Bowers/Kaut 25.00 60.00
C3BCT Tkachuk/Brown/Chabot 15.00 40.00
C3BKD Kopitar/Brown/Doughty 15.00 40.00
C3BKO Ovechkin Backstrom/Kuznetsov 40.00 100.00
C3BLB Barzal/Lee/Bailey 12.00 30.00
C3BMP Marchand/Bergeron/Pastrnak 25.00 60.00
C3BPH Pettersson/Boeser/Hughes 25.00 60.00
C3CKH Couture/Kane/Hertl 12.00 30.00
C3CLS Cozens/Sorokin/Lafreniere 15.00 40.00
C3CQK Kempe/Carter/Quick 12.00 30.00
C3DJF Forsberg/Duchene/Josi 15.00 40.00
C3DRO Robertson Dellandrea/Oettinger 30.00 80.00
C3DSK Dvorak/Schmaltz/Keller 12.00 30.00
C3FTK Fleury/Karlsson/Theodore 20.00 50.00
C3GBT Tkachuk/Backlund/Giordano 20.00 50.00
C3GHC Giroux/Hart/Couturier 10.00 25.00
C3GLM Gaudreau Lindholm/Monahan 15.00 40.00
C3GLZ Larkin/Greiss/Zadina 12.00 30.00
C3HEB Barkov/Huberdeau/Ekblad 15.00 40.00
C3HPV Point/Hedman/Vasilevskiy 15.00 40.00
C3KKD Kane/DeBrincat/Keith 20.00 50.00
C3KRM Krejci/McAvoy/Rask 12.00 30.00
C3KSS Kaprizov/Suter/Stutzle 50.00 125.00
C3LJJ Laine/Jenner/Jones 12.00 30.00
C3LRB Robertson Barabanov/Liljegren 20.00 50.00
C3MHD Horvat/Miller/Demko 12.00 30.00
C3MLG Malkin/Guentzel/Letang 20.00 50.00
C3MRM MacKinnon Rantanen/Makar 40.00 100.00
C3NHS Niederreiter/Slavin/Hamilton 8.00 20.00
C3NMM Matthews/Marner/Nylander 40.00 100.00
C3NND Draisaitl Nugent-Hopkins/Nurse 30.00 80.00
C3PBF Panarin/Buchnevich/Fox 20.00 50.00
C3PKH Pavelski/Klingberg/Heiskanen 12.00 30.00
C3POS Schwartz/Perron/O'Reilly 12.00 30.00
C3PST Stone/Pacioretty/Tuch 12.00 30.00
C3REO Eichel/Reinhart/Olofsson 20.00 50.00
C3SAS Svechnikov/Staal/Aho 15.00 40.00
C3SBP Schenn/Parayko/Binnington 15.00 40.00
C3SEG Greenway/Eriksson Ek/Jared 10.00 25.00
C3SFS Foote/Sharangovich/Smith 20.00 50.00
C3SJP Stamkos/Palat/Johnson 20.00 50.00
C3SRL Silfverberg/Rakell/Lindholm 8.00 20.00
C3TRA Tavares/Rielly/Andersen 15.00 40.00
C3VAM McMichael/Alexeyev/Vanecek 20.00 50.00
C3VVH van Riemsdyk/Kevin/Jakub 8.00 20.00
C3WPG Gallagher/Weber/Price 20.00 50.00
C3WSE Scheifele/Ehlers/Wheeler 15.00 40.00
C3ZWB Blackwood/Wood/Zacha 10.00 25.00

2021-22 The Cup

1 Marc-Andre Fleury 4.00 10.00
2 John Gibson 2.00 5.00
3 Brad Marchand 4.00 10.00
4 Jason Robertson 3.00 8.00
5 Patrick Kane 4.00 10.00
6 Brock Boeser 2.50 6.00
7 Eeli Tolvanen 2.00 5.00
8 Quinn Hughes 5.00 12.00
9 Yanni Gourde 1.50 4.00
10 Carey Price 4.00 10.00
11 Jarome Iginla 2.50 6.00
12 Max Pacioretty 2.00 5.00
13 Auston Matthews 8.00 20.00
14 Jordan Eberle 2.00 5.00
15 Victor Olofsson 2.00 5.00
16 Roman Josi 2.00 5.00
17 Sidney Crosby 8.00 20.00
18 Jeff Petry 2.00 5.00
19 Mark Stone 2.50 6.00
20 Drake Batherson 2.00 5.00
21 Andrei Vasilevskiy 3.00 8.00
22 Ryan O'Reilly 2.00 5.00
23 Miro Heiskanen 2.50 6.00
24 Philipp Grubauer 2.00 5.00
25 Alex Nedeljkovic 1.50 4.00
26 Brett Hull 3.00 8.00
27 Kyle Connor 3.00 8.00
28 John Tavares 3.00 8.00
29 Jonathan Huberdeau 2.50 6.00
30 Anders Lee 1.50 4.00
31 Cale Makar 5.00 12.00
32 Aleksander Barkov 3.00 8.00
33 Seth Jones 2.00 5.00
34 Dougie Hamilton 1.50 4.00
35 Joe Pavelski 2.50 6.00
36 Alex Ovechkin 8.00 20.00
37 Kevin Fiala 1.50 4.00
38 Cal Petersen 1.25 3.00
39 Tomas Hertl 2.00 5.00
40 Conor Garland 1.50 4.00
41 Tyler Bertuzzi 1.50 4.00
42 Sean Monahan 1.25 3.00
43 Martin Necas 3.00 8.00
44 Teemu Selanne 4.00 10.00
45 Taylor Hall 2.00 5.00
46 Casey Mittelstadt 2.00 5.00
47 Nikolaj Ehlers 2.00 5.00
48 Brady Tkachuk 3.00 8.00
49 Kris Letang 2.50 6.00
50 Connor McDavid 10.00 25.00
51 Mark Giordano 2.00 5.00
52 Sergei Bobrovsky 3.00 8.00
53 Cam Talbot 2.00 5.00
54 Teuvo Teravainen 2.00 5.00
55 Mathew Barzal 2.50 6.00
56 Matthew Tkachuk 4.00 10.00
57 Sam Reinhart 4.00 10.00
58 Jack Roslovic 1.25 3.00
59 Brent Burns 2.00 5.00
60 Robin Lehner 1.50 4.00
61 Tim Stutzle 2.50 6.00
62 Connor Hellebuyck 4.00 10.00
63 Anze Kopitar 3.00 8.00
64 Andrei Svechnikov 2.50 6.00
65 Patrick Roy 5.00 12.00
66 Leon Draisaitl 6.00 15.00
67 Clayton Keller 2.50 6.00
68 Victor Hedman 2.50 6.00
69 David Pastrnak 5.00 12.00
70 Mitch Marner 3.00 8.00
71 John Carlson 2.00 5.00
72 Sean Couturier 1.50 4.00
73 Evgeni Malkin 4.00 10.00
74 Nathan MacKinnon 8.00 20.00
75 Patrik Laine 2.50 6.00
76 Nicklas Backstrom 2.00 5.00
77 Nico Hischier 3.00 8.00
78 Mike Bossy 2.00 5.00
79 Sebastian Aho 3.00 8.00
80 Jordan Binnington 3.00 8.00
81 Steven Stamkos 4.00 10.00
82 Brayden Schenn 2.00 5.00
83 Mark Scheifele 3.00 8.00
84 Nick Suzuki 4.00 10.00
85 Dylan Larkin 2.50 6.00
86 Claude Giroux 2.00 5.00
87 Adam Fox 2.50 6.00
88 Jack Hughes 5.00 12.00
89 Elias Pettersson 3.00 8.00
90 Artemi Panarin 4.00 10.00
91 Jakob Chychrun 2.00 5.00
92 Igor Shesterkin 4.00 10.00
93 Ryan Nugent-Hopkins 2.50 6.00
94 Kirill Kaprizov 6.00 15.00
95 Jacob Markstrom 2.00 5.00
96 Doug Gilmour 2.50 6.00
97 Marcel Dionne 2.50 6.00
98 Paul Coffey 2.50 6.00
99 Wayne Gretzky 12.00 30.00
100 Cam Neely 1.50 4.00
101 Jeremy Swayman JSY AU/249 RC 200.00 500.00
102 Cam York/249 RC 2.50 6.00
103 Morgan Barron JSY AU/249 RC 15.00 40.00
104 Joe Veleno JSY AU/249 RC 25.00 60.00
105 Zac Jones JSY AU/249 RC 25.00 60.00
106 Ivan Prosvetov/249 RC 2.50 6.00
107 Lane Pederson JSY AU/249 RC 20.00 50.00
108 Wyatt Kalynuk JSY AU/249 RC 20.00 50.00
109 Mattias Samuelsson JSY AU/249 RC 20.00 50.00
110 Kole Lind JSY AU/249 RC 25.00 60.00
111 Oskar Steen JSY AU/249 RC 25.00 60.00
112 Calen Addison JSY AU/249 RC 20.00 50.00
113 Jacob Bryson JSY AU/249 RC 20.00 50.00
114 Matthew Phillips JSY AU/249 RC 20.00 50.00
115 Grigori Denisenko JSY AU/249 RC 25.00 60.00
116 Tanner Laczynski JSY AU/249 RC 20.00 50.00
117 Jacob Bernard-Docker JSY AU/249 RC 20.00 50.00
118 Brett Murray JSY AU/249 RC 20.00 50.00
119 Alex Newhook JSY AU/249 RC 30.00 80.00
120 Jacob Peterson/249 RC 2.50 6.00
121 Shane Pinto JSY AU/249 RC 30.00 80.00
122 David Farrance JSY AU/249 RC 20.00 50.00
123 Sampo Ranta JSY AU/249 RC 20.00 50.00
124 Tyce Thompson JSY AU/249 RC 20.00 50.00
125 Garrett Pilon JSY AU/249 RC 25.00 60.00
126 Parker Kelly JSY AU/249 RC 20.00 50.00
127 Adam Ruzicka/249 RC 2.50 6.00
128 Jamie Drysdale JSY AU/249 RC 80.00 200.00
129 Ross Colton JSY AU/249 RC 25.00 60.00
130 Wade Allison JSY AU/249 RC 20.00 50.00
131 J.J. Moser JSY AU/249 RC 20.00 50.00
132 Filip Gustavsson/249 RC 5.00 12.00
133 Jack Ahcan JSY AU/249 RC 20.00 50.00
134 Rasmus Kupari JSY AU/249 RC 20.00 50.00
135 Connor Dewar JSY AU/249 RC 20.00 50.00
136 Arttu Ruotsalainen JSY AU/249 RC 20.00 50.00
137 Jesse Ylonen JSY AU/249 RC 20.00 50.00
138 Gabriel Fortier JSY AU/249 RC 20.00 50.00
139 Michael Bunting JSY AU/249 RC 20.00 50.00
140 Jan Jenik/249 RC 3.00 8.00
141 Radim Zohorna/249 RC 2.50 6.00
142 Logan Thompson JSY AU/249 RC 40.00 100.00
143 Joey Keane/249 RC 2.00 5.00
144 Fabian Zetterlund JSY AU/249 RC 20.00 50.00
145 Mike Hardman JSY AU/249 RC 20.00 50.00
146 Ukko-Pekka Luukkonen JSY AU/249 RC 30.00 80.00
147 Cole Caufield JSY AU/99 RC 1200.00 3000.00
148 Spencer Knight JSY AU/99 RC 150.00 400.00
149 Trevor Zegras JSY AU/99 RC 250.00 600.00
150 Quinton Byfield JSY AU/99 RC 600.00 1500.00
151 Alex Barre-Boulet AU/249 RC 12.00 30.00
152 Sean Durzi/249 RC 2.50 6.00
153 Karel Vejmelka AU/249 RC 15.00 40.00
154 Egor Sokolov AU/249 RC 12.00 30.00
155 Nico Daws AU/249 RC 30.00 80.00
156 Mason McTavish AU/249 RC 60.00 150.00
157 Yegor Chinakhov/249 RC 4.00 10.00
158 Cole Sillinger AU/249 RC 30.00 80.00
159 Tanner Jeannot AU/249 RC 12.00 30.00
160 William Eklund AU/249 RC 40.00 100.00
161 Seth Jarvis JSY AU/249 RC 125.00 300.00
162 Aliaksei Protas JSY AU/249 RC 20.00 50.00
163 Daniil Miromanov/249 RC 2.50 6.00
164 Nils Lundkvist/249 RC 2.50 6.00
165 Riley Damiani JSY AU/249 RC 20.00 50.00
166 Brett Leason JSY AU/249 RC 20.00 50.00
167 Cole Schwindt JSY AU/249 RC 20.00 50.00
168 Jake Leschyshyn JSY AU/249 RC 20.00 50.00
169 Brandon Duhaime JSY AU/249 RC 20.00 50.00
170 Riley Tufte JSY AU/249 RC 20.00 50.00
171 Alex Turcotte JSY AU/249 RC 25.00 60.00
172 Boris Katchouk JSY AU/249 RC 15.00 40.00
173 Paul Cotter JSY AU/249 RC 20.00 50.00
174 Daniil Tarasov/249 RC 2.50 6.00
175 Jake Neighbours JSY AU/249 RC 40.00 100.00
176 Ryan Merkley/249 RC 3.00 8.00
177 Robin Salo/249 RC 2.50 6.00
178 Philip Tomasino JSY AU/249 RC 25.00 60.00
179 Alexander Holtz JSY AU/249 RC 30.00 80.00
180 Benoit-Olivier Groulx JSY AU/249 RC 20.00 50.00
181 Jonathan Dahlen/249 RC 2.50 6.00
182 J.J. Peterka JSY AU/249 RC 125.00 300.00
183 Cole Perfetti JSY AU/249 RC 60.00 150.00
184 Adam Beckman JSY AU/249 RC 20.00 50.00
185 Justin Barron JSY AU/249 RC 30.00 80.00
186 Kasper Bjorkqvist JSY AU/249 RC 20.00 50.00
187 Anton Lundell JSY AU/249 RC 60.00 150.00
188 Jack Drury JSY AU/249 RC 30.00 80.00
189 Dawson Mercer JSY AU/249 RC 150.00 400.00
190 Hendrix Lapierre JSY AU/249 RC 20.00 50.00
191 Scott Perunovich JSY AU/249 RC 20.00 50.00
192 Vasily Podkolzin JSY AU/249 RC 25.00 60.00
193 Jasper Weatherby JSY AU/249 RC 20.00 50.00
194 Taylor Raddysh JSY AU/249 RC 30.00 80.00
195 Justus Annunen JSY AU/249 RC 25.00 60.00
196 Lassi Thomson JSY AU/249 RC 20.00 50.00
197 Pavel Dorofeyev JSY AU/249 RC 25.00 60.00
198 Thomas Novak/249 RC 2.50 6.00
199 Moritz Seider JSY AU/99 RC 800.00 2000.00
200 Lucas Raymond JSY AU/99 RC 300.00 800.00

2021-22 The Cup All Time Alum

ATABS Billy Smith 3.00 8.00
ATADH Dominik Hasek 5.00 12.00
ATADS Darryl Sittler 3.00 8.00
ATAJJ Jaromir Jagr 10.00 25.00
ATAJV John Vanbiesbrouck 3.00 8.00
ATAMD Marcel Dionne 4.00 10.00
ATAMG Mike Gartner 4.00 10.00
ATAMM Mark Messier 6.00 15.00
ATAPE Phil Esposito 5.00 12.00
ATARH Ron Hextall 3.00 8.00

2021-22 The Cup All Time Alum Autographs

ATADH Dominik Hasek/25 150.00 400.00
ATADS Darryl Sittler/25 40.00 100.00
ATAJV John Vanbiesbrouck/50 40.00 100.00
ATAMD Marcel Dionne/50 50.00 125.00
ATAMG Mike Gartner/50 30.00 80.00
ATAMM Mark Messier/25 80.00 200.00
ATARH Ron Hextall/50 60.00 150.00

2021-22 The Cup Brilliance Autographs

BBT Brady Tkachuk C 30.00 80.00
BCM Connor McDavid A 300.00 800.00
BDS Darryl Sittler A 20.00 50.00
BGC Gerry Cheevers B 20.00 50.00
BGF Grant Fuhr B 40.00 100.00
BKC Kyle Connor B 30.00 80.00
BMS Martin St. Louis A 20.00 50.00
BNL Nils Lundkvist A 20.00 50.00
BTJ Tristan Jarry C 20.00 50.00
BWG Wayne Gretzky D 300.00 800.00

2021-22 The Cup Cup Quads Jerseys

C4ASSN Andersen/Slavin Svechnikov/Necas 20.00 50.00
C4BCKM Burns/Couture Karlsson/Meier 15.00 40.00
C4BCKO Backstrom/Carlson Kuznetsov/Ovechkin 50.00 120.00
C4BHEB Bobrovsky/Huberdeau Ekblad/Barkov 20.00 50.00
C4BKQD Brown/Kopitar Quick/Doughty 20.00 50.00
C4BNRA Barron/Newhook Ranta/Annunen 20.00 50.00
C4BRPM Bergeron/Rask Pastrnak/McAvoy 30.00 80.00
C4BSKH Benn/Seguin Klingberg/Heiskanen 15.00 40.00
C4CTNS Chabot/Tkachuk Norris/Stutzle 20.00 50.00
C4DBPH Demko/Boeser Pettersson/Hughes 30.00 80.00
C4DJFS Duchene/Josi Forsberg/Saros 20.00 50.00
C4DPEW Dahlen/Pederson Eklund/Weatherby 30.00 80.00
C4GCHP Giroux/Couturier Hayes/Provorov 12.00 30.00
C4GDZM Groulx/Drysdale Zegras/McTavish 25.00 60.00
C4GESG Giordano/Eberle Schwartz/Gourde 12.00 30.00
C4KGCK Kessel/Gostisbehere Chychrun/Keller 15.00 40.00
C4KLMR Kadri/Landeskog MacKinnon/Rantanen 50.00 125.00
C4LBNZ Larkin/Bertuzzi Nedeljkovic/Zadina 15.00 40.00
C4LPBS Luukkonen/Peterka Bryson/Samuelsson 20.00 50.00
C4MGHT Monahan Gaudreau/Hanifin/Tkachuk 25.00 60.00
C4MZJG Malkin/Zucker Jarry/Guentzel 25.00 60.00
C4NNDP Nugent-Hopkins/Nurse/Draisaitl Puljujarvi 40.00 100.00
C4OSCD Okposo/Skinner Cozens/Dahlin 15.00 40.00
C4PGPS Price/Gallagher/Petry/Suzuki 25.00 60.00
C4PLTK Pacioretty/Lehner Theodore/Karlsson 15.00 40.00
C4RMNM Rielly/Mrazek Nylander/Marner 25.00 60.00
C4SBBP Schenn/Binnington Buchnevich/Parayko 20.00 50.00
C4SEGK Spurgeon/Eriksson Ek/Greenway/Kaprizov 40.00 100.00
C4SHBH Subban/Hamilton Blackwood/Hughes 30.00 80.00
C4SHKP Stamkos/Hedman Kucherov/Point 25.00 60.00
C4TKDD Toews/Kane/DeBrincat/Dach 25.00 60.00
C4VBWL Voracek/Bjorkstrand Werenski/Laine 20.00 50.00
C4VNPB Varlamov/Nelson Pageau/Barzal 15.00 40.00
C4WSHC Wheeler/Scheifele Hellebuyck/Connor 25.00 60.00
C4ZKPS Zibanejad/Kreider Panarin/Shesterkin 25.00 60.00

2021-22 The Cup Cup Trios Jerseys

C3ABD Addison/Beckman/Duhaime 10.00 25.00
C3BCO Ovechkin Backstrom/Carlson 40.00 100.00
C3BHH Blackwood/Hischier/Hughes 25.00 60.00
C3BKH Burns/Karlsson/Hertl 12.00 30.00
C3BMP Bergeron/Marchand/Pastrnak 25.00 60.00
C3BPH Boeser/Pettersson/Hughes 25.00 60.00
C3BTN Batherson/Tkachuk/Norris 15.00 40.00
C3DEW Dahlen/Eklund/Weatherby 25.00 60.00
C3DKL Denisenko/Knight/Lundell 20.00 50.00
C3EBR Ekblad/Barkov/Reinhart 20.00 50.00
C3FTK Fleury/Toews/Kane 20.00 50.00
C3GCH Giroux/Couturier/Hart 10.00 25.00
C3GDZ Groulx/Drysdale/Zegras 20.00 50.00
C3GGG Giordano/Grubauer/Gourde 10.00 25.00
C3GGT Getzlaf/Gibson/Terry 10.00 25.00
C3GPB Gustavsson/Pinto Bernard-Docker 20.00 50.00
C3GTS Gallagher/Toffoli/Suzuki 20.00 50.00
C3HRO Heiskanen Robertson/Oettinger 15.00 40.00
C3JFS Josi/Forsberg/Saros 15.00 40.00
C3JKA Jarvis/Keane/Aho 25.00 60.00
C3KBT Kupari/Byfield/Turcotte 25.00 60.00
C3KCK Kessel/Chychrun/Keller 12.00 30.00
C3KDP Kopitar/Danault/Petersen 15.00 40.00
C3LBN Larkin/Bertuzzi/Nedeljkovic 12.00 30.00
C3LPS Luukkonen Peterka/Samuelsson 15.00 40.00
C3MDO Mittelstadt/Dahlin/Olofsson 12.00 30.00
C3MHT Mercer/Holtz/Thompson 25.00 60.00
C3MJG Malkin/Jarry/Guentzel 20.00 50.00
C3MLT Markstrom/Lindholm/Tkachuk 20.00 50.00
C3MRM MacKinnon Rantanen/Makar 40.00 100.00
C3NMM Nylander/Marner/Matthews 40.00 100.00
C3NND Nugent-Hopkins Nurse/Draisaitl 30.00 80.00
C3NPB Nelson/Pulock/Beauvillier 10.00 25.00
C3PBS Pavelski/Benn/Seguin 12.00 30.00
C3PFS Panarin/Fox/Shesterkin 20.00 50.00
C3PLT Pacioretty/Lehner/Theodore 12.00 30.00
C3PPV Palat/Point/Vasilevskiy 15.00 40.00
C3SAS Swayman/Ahcan/Steen 30.00 80.00
C3SBB Schenn/Binnington Buchnevich 15.00 40.00
C3SEH Scheifele/Ehlers/Hellebuyck 20.00 50.00
C3SHK Stamkos/Hedman/Kucherov 20.00 50.00
C3TAS Teravainen/Aho/Svechnikov 15.00 40.00
C3TFE Talbot/Fiala/Eriksson Ek 10.00 25.00
C3TJF Tomasino/Jeannot/Farrance 12.00 30.00
C3TLD Thompson/Leschyshyn Dorofeyev 25.00 60.00
C3VLB Varlamov/Lee/Barzal 12.00 30.00
C3VSR Veleno/Seider/Raymond 30.00 80.00
C3VWL Voracek/Werenski/Laine 15.00 40.00
C3YAL York/Allison/Laczynski 10.00 25.00
C3ZKK Zibanejad/Kreider/Kakko 12.00 30.00

2021-22 The Cup Day With The Cup Signatures

DCAO Alex Ovechkin A 40.00 1000.00
DCBK Bob Kelly D 40.00 100.00
DCBM Brad Marchand B 125.00 300.00
DCDH Dominik Hasek A 125.00 300.00
DCJL John LeClair C 60.00 150.00
DCMO Mike Modano B 100.00 250.00
DCTS Teemu Selanne A 100.00 250.00

2021-22 The Cup Effervescence Autographs

EFAH Alexander Holtz C 30.00 80.00
EFAL Alexis Lafreniere B 40.00 100.00
EFAN Alex Newhook C 25.00 60.00
EFAT Alex Turcotte C 12.00 30.00
EFAV Andrei Vasilevskiy A 50.00 125.00
EFBD Brandon Duhaime E 10.00 25.00
EFBU Michael Bunting D 10.00 25.00
EFCA Cam Atkinson D 10.00 25.00
EFCP Cole Perfetti B 20.00 50.00
EFDF David Farrance E 10.00 25.00
EFHL Hendrix Lapierre C 10.00 25.00
EFJD Jamie Drysdale C 15.00 40.00
EFJG John Gibson C 10.00 25.00
EFJP Joe Pavelski B 25.00 60.00
EFJY Jesse Ylonen E 10.00 25.00
EFLU Anton Lundell A 20.00 50.00
EFMD Marcel Dionne B 20.00 50.00
EFMM Mike Modano A 15.00 40.00
EFNE Nikolaj Ehlers C 10.00 25.00
EFNL Nils Lundkvist C 10.00 25.00
EFPB Peter Bondra C 25.00 60.00
EFPG Philipp Grubauer C 10.00 25.00
EFPI Shane Pinto D 15.00 40.00
EFQB Quinton Byfield C 50.00 125.00
EFSJ Seth Jones C 10.00 25.00
EFSP Scott Perunovich D 12.00 30.00
EFTJ Tanner Jeannot E 10.00 25.00
EFTS Tim Stutzle B 40.00 100.00
EFTT Tyler Toffoli C 10.00 25.00
EFVP Vasily Podkolzin D 12.00 30.00
EFWC Wendel Clark C 25.00 60.00
EFWK Wyatt Kalynuk E 10.00 25.00

2021-22 The Cup Enshrinements

EAL Alexis Lafreniere/25 80.00 200.00
EDH Dany Heatley/99 15.00 40.00
EMB Martin Brodeur/25 125.00 300.00
EMC Kirk McLean/99 15.00 40.00
EPF Peter Forsberg/25 100.00 250.00
ERC Ross Colton/99 25.00 60.00
ERR Rob Ray/99 20.00 50.00
ERS Ryan Suter/99 15.00 40.00

2021-22 The Cup Foundations Jerseys

FAH Alexander Holtz/99 10.00 25.00
FAK Anze Kopitar/49 10.00 25.00
FAN Alex Newhook/99 10.00 25.00
FAT Alex Turcotte/99 8.00 20.00
FAV Andrei Vasilevskiy/49 10.00 25.00
FBB Brock Boeser/49 8.00 20.00
FBU Brent Burns/49 6.00 15.00
FCC Cole Caufield/99 25.00 60.00
FCH Connor Hellebuyck/49 12.00 30.00
FCM Connor McDavid/49 30.00 80.00
FCP Cole Perfetti/99 12.00 30.00
FCY Cam York/99 6.00 15.00
FDM Dawson Mercer/99 15.00 40.00
FGI John Gibson/49 6.00 15.00
FHE Tomas Hertl/49 6.00 15.00
FHL Hendrix Lapierre/99 6.00 15.00
FJE Jordan Eberle/49 6.00 15.00
FJG Jake Guentzel/49 10.00 25.00
FJH Jonathan Huberdeau/49 8.00 20.00
FJL Jake Leschyshyn/99 6.00 15.00
FJN Jake Neighbours/99 12.00 30.00
FJP Joe Pavelski/49 8.00 20.00
FJT John Tavares/49 10.00 25.00
FKC Kyle Connor/49 10.00 25.00
FKL Kris Letang/49 8.00 20.00
FLR Lucas Raymond/99 20.00 50.00
FLU Anton Lundell/99 12.00 30.00
FMA Cale Makar/49 15.00 40.00
FMF Marc-Andre Fleury/49 12.00 30.00
FMM Mason McTavish/99 12.00 30.00
FMO Moritz Seider/99 15.00 40.00
FMS Mark Stone/49 8.00 20.00
FNL Nils Lundkvist/99 6.00 15.00
FPT Philip Tomasino/99 8.00 20.00
FQB Quinton Byfield/99 15.00 40.00
FQH Quinn Hughes/49 15.00 40.00
FRC Ross Colton/99 8.00 20.00
FRO Ryan O'Reilly/49 6.00 15.00
FSJ Seth Jarvis/99 15.00 40.00
FSK Spencer Knight/99 12.00 30.00
FSM Sean Monahan/49 4.00 10.00
FSW Jeremy Swayman/99 20.00 50.00
FTB Tyler Bertuzzi/49 5.00 12.00
FTH Taylor Hall/49 6.00 15.00
FTT Tyler Toffoli/49 6.00 15.00
FTZ Trevor Zegras/99 12.00 30.00
FUL Ukko-Pekka Luukkonen/99 10.00 25.00
FVO Victor Olofsson/49 6.00 15.00
FVP Vasily Podkolzin/99 8.00 20.00
FWE William Eklund/99 15.00 40.00

2021-22 The Cup Honorable Numbers

HRAT Alex Turcotte/39 30.00 80.00
HRBN Bernie Nicholls/19 30.00 80.00
HRJI Jarome Iginla/20 150.00 400.00
HRPT Philip Tomasino/26 60.00 150.00
HRQB Quinton Byfield/55 200.00 500.00
HRRL Robin Lehner/19 40.00 100.00
HRST Tim Stutzle/20 80.00 200.00
HRTZ Trevor Zegras/46 150.00 400.00

2021-22 The Cup Inked Insignias

IIAH Alexander Holtz/75 50.00 125.00
IIAL Anton Lundell/75 60.00 150.00
IIAN Alex Newhook/75 50.00 125.00
IIAP Aliaksei Protas/75 30.00 80.00
IIAV Andrei Vasilevskiy/25 50.00 125.00
IIBM Brad Marchand/25 80.00 200.00
IICC Cole Caufield/75 250.00 600.00
IICH Carter Hart/25 30.00 80.00
IICM Cale Makar/25 80.00 200.00
IICP Cole Perfetti/75 60.00 150.00
IICT Cam Talbot/25 30.00 80.00
IIHL Hendrix Lapierre/75 30.00 80.00
IIJD Jamie Drysdale/75 80.00 200.00
IIJG Jake Guentzel/25 50.00 125.00
IIJL Jake Leschyshyn/75 30.00 80.00
IIJM Jared McCann/25 30.00 80.00
IIJN Josh Norris/25 30.00 80.00
IIJR Jack Roslovic/25 20.00 50.00
IILE Anders Lee/25 25.00 60.00
IILR Lucas Raymond/75 125.00 300.00
IIMB Michael Bunting/75 30.00 80.00
IIMC Connor McDavid/25 400.00 1000.00
IIMT Matthew Tkachuk/25 60.00 150.00
IINE Jake Neighbours/75 60.00 150.00
IINL Nils Lundkvist/75 30.00 80.00
IIPT Philip Tomasino/75 40.00 100.00
IIQB Quinton Byfield/75 125.00 300.00
IIRL Robin Lehner/25 40.00 100.00
IISP Scott Perunovich/75 30.00 80.00
IITT Troy Terry/25 25.00 60.00
IIVP Vasily Podkolzin/75 40.00 100.00
IIWK Wyatt Kalynuk/75 30.00 80.00

2021-22 The Cup Limited Logos

LLAV Andrei Vasilevskiy AU/25 60.00 150.00
LLCC Cole Caufield AU/50 600.00 1500.00
LLCG Claude Giroux/50 25.00 60.00
LLDD Drew Doughty/25 30.00 80.00
LLEK Erik Karlsson/50 30.00 80.00
LLGL Gabriel Landeskog/50 30.00 80.00
LLGU Jake Guentzel AU/25 80.00 200.00
LLJG John Gibson AU/50 60.00 150.00
LLKC Kyle Connor AU/50 60.00 150.00
LLLR Lucas Raymond AU/50 250.00 600.00
LLMB Mathew Barzal/25 30.00 80.00
LLMS Moritz Seider AU/50 400.00 1000.00
LLNB Nicklas Backstrom/25 25.00 60.00
LLOK Olaf Kolzig AU/50 40.00 100.00
LLPK Phil Kessel/50 25.00 60.00
LLPL Patrik Laine/25 30.00 80.00
LLQB Quinton Byfield AU/50 200.00 500.00
LLRB Ray Bourque AU/25 60.00 150.00
LLSJ Seth Jones AU/25 100.00 250.00
LLSM Sean Monahan AU/50 25.00 60.00
LLTJ Tristan Jarry AU/50 60.00 150.00
LLTO Jonathan Toews/25 80.00 200.00
LLTZ Trevor Zegras AU/50 125.00 300.00

2021-22 The Cup National Colors Autographs

NCJL John LeClair/50 30.00 80.00
NCMD Marcel Dionne/25 40.00 100.00
NCMM Mike Modano/20 50.00 125.00
NCPB Peter Bondra/50 125.00 300.00
NCPG Philipp Grubauer/50 30.00 80.00
NCPR Pekka Rinne/50 30.00 80.00
NCTS Tim Stutzle/30 40.00 100.00

2021-22 The Cup Player Plaques Autographs

PPAL Anton Lundell/35 80.00 200.00
PPMT Matthew Tkachuk/25 40.00 100.00
PPRH Ron Hextall/25 80.00 200.00

2021-22 The Cup Rendition Relics

RRAK Anze Kopitar 10.00 25.00
RRAL Anton Lundell 12.00 30.00
RRAM Auston Matthews 25.00 60.00
RRAN Alex Newhook 10.00 25.00
RRAO Alex Ovechkin 25.00 60.00
RRAP Artemi Panarin 12.00 30.00
RRAT Alex Turcotte 8.00 20.00
RRCC Cole Caufield 25.00 60.00
RRCG Claude Giroux 6.00 15.00
RRCM Connor McDavid 30.00 80.00
RRDM Dawson Mercer 15.00 40.00
RRDP David Pastrnak 15.00 40.00
RRDS Daniel Sedin 8.00 20.00
RRHL Hendrix Lapierre 6.00 15.00
RRHS Henrik Sedin 8.00 20.00
RRJD Jamie Drysdale 10.00 25.00
RRJE Jordan Eberle 6.00 15.00
RRJH Jack Hughes 15.00 40.00
RRJS Jeremy Swayman 20.00 50.00
RRJV Jakub Voracek 5.00 12.00
RRLD Leon Draisaitl 20.00 50.00
RRLR Lucas Raymond 20.00 50.00
RRMA Cale Makar 15.00 40.00
RRMB Michael Bunting 6.00 15.00
RRML Mario Lemieux 25.00 60.00
RRMS Mark Scheifele 10.00 25.00
RRNB Nicklas Backstrom 6.00 15.00
RRNK Nikita Kucherov 12.00 30.00
RRNL Nils Lundkvist 6.00 15.00
RRNM Nathan MacKinnon 25.00 60.00
RRPB Patrice Bergeron 8.00 20.00
RRPT Philip Tomasino 8.00 20.00
RRQB Quinton Byfield 15.00 40.00
RRRC Ross Colton 8.00 20.00
RRRG Ryan Getzlaf 6.00 15.00
RRSC Sidney Crosby 25.00 60.00
RRSE Moritz Seider 15.00 40.00
RRSJ Seth Jarvis 15.00 40.00
RRSK Spencer Knight 12.00 30.00
RRSY Steve Yzerman 15.00 40.00
RRTJ Tanner Jeannot 6.00 15.00
RRTZ Trevor Zegras 12.00 30.00
RRVH Victor Hedman 8.00 20.00
RRVP Vasily Podkolzin 8.00 20.00
RRWG Wayne Gretzky 40.00 100.00

2021-22 The Cup Rookie Class of '22

2022AB Adam Beckman 3.00 8.00
2022AH Alexander Holtz 5.00 12.00
2022AL Anton Lundell 6.00 15.00
2022AN Alex Newhook 5.00 12.00
2022AP Aliaksei Protas 3.00 8.00
2022BD Brandon Duhaime 3.00 8.00
2022BG Benoit-Olivier Groulx 3.00 8.00
2022BU Michael Bunting 3.00 8.00
2022CC Cole Caufield 12.00 30.00
2022CP Cole Perfetti 6.00 15.00
2022CS Cole Sillinger 5.00 12.00
2022CY Cam York 3.00 8.00
2022DA Jonathan Dahlen 3.00 8.00
2022DF David Farrance 3.00 8.00
2022FG Filip Gustavsson 6.00 15.00
2022GD Grigori Denisenko 4.00 10.00
2022HL Hendrix Lapierre 3.00 8.00
2022IP Ivan Prosvetov 3.00 8.00
2022JB Jacob Bernard-Docker 3.00 8.00
2022JD Jamie Drysdale 5.00 12.00
2022JJ Jan Jenik 4.00 10.00
2022JN Jake Neighbours 6.00 15.00
2022JS Jeremy Swayman 10.00 25.00
2022JV Joe Veleno 4.00 10.00
2022JW Jasper Weatherby 3.00 8.00
2022JY Jesse Ylonen 3.00 8.00
2022LR Lucas Raymond 10.00 25.00
2022LT Logan Thompson 8.00 20.00
2022MB Morgan Barron 2.50 6.00
2022MM Mason McTavish 6.00 15.00
2022MS Moritz Seider 8.00 20.00
2022NL Nils Lundkvist 3.00 8.00
2022PD Pavel Dorofeyev 4.00 10.00
2022PE Scott Perunovich 3.00 8.00
2022PT Philip Tomasino 4.00 10.00
2022RC Ross Colton 4.00 10.00
2022SJ Seth Jarvis 8.00 20.00
2022SK Spencer Knight 6.00 15.00
2022SP Shane Pinto 5.00 12.00
2022SR Sampo Ranta 3.00 8.00
2022TJ Tanner Jeannot 3.00 8.00
2022TR Taylor Raddysh 5.00 12.00
2022VP Vasily Podkolzin 4.00 10.00
2022WE William Eklund 8.00 20.00
2022WK Wyatt Kalynuk 3.00 8.00

2021-22 The Cup Rookie Class of '22 Autographs

2022AB Adam Beckman 10.00 25.00
2022AH Alexander Holtz 15.00 40.00
2022AL Anton Lundell 20.00 50.00
2022AP Aliaksei Protas 10.00 25.00
2022BD Brandon Duhaime 10.00 25.00
2022BU Michael Bunting 10.00 25.00
2022CP Cole Perfetti 20.00 50.00
2022DF David Farrance 10.00 25.00
2022FG Filip Gustavsson 20.00 50.00
2022GD Grigori Denisenko 12.00 30.00
2022HL Hendrix Lapierre 10.00 25.00
2022JB Jacob Bernard-Docker 10.00 25.00
2022JD Jamie Drysdale 15.00 40.00
2022JN Jake Neighbours 20.00 50.00
2022JV Joe Veleno 12.00 30.00
2022JW Jasper Weatherby 10.00 25.00
2022JY Jesse Ylonen 10.00 25.00
2022LR Lucas Raymond 60.00 150.00
2022LT Logan Thompson 25.00 60.00
2022MB Morgan Barron 8.00 20.00
2022MM Mason McTavish 20.00 50.00
2022NL Nils Lundkvist 10.00 25.00
2022PD Pavel Dorofeyev 12.00 30.00
2022PE Scott Perunovich 10.00 25.00
2022PT Philip Tomasino 12.00 30.00
2022RC Ross Colton 12.00 30.00
2022SJ Seth Jarvis 30.00 80.00
2022SP Shane Pinto 15.00 40.00
2022SR Sampo Ranta 10.00 25.00
2022TJ Tanner Jeannot 10.00 25.00
2022TR Taylor Raddysh 15.00 40.00
2022VP Vasily Podkolzin 12.00 30.00
2022WE William Eklund 25.00 60.00
2022WK Wyatt Kalynuk 10.00 25.00

2021-22 The Cup Rookie Class of '22 Patches

2022AB Adam Beckman 6.00 15.00
2022AH Alexander Holtz 10.00 25.00
2022AL Anton Lundell 12.00 30.00
2022AN Alex Newhook 10.00 25.00
2022AP Aliaksei Protas 6.00 15.00
2022BD Brandon Duhaime 6.00 15.00
2022BG Benoit-Olivier Groulx 6.00 15.00
2022BU Michael Bunting 6.00 15.00
2022CP Cole Perfetti 12.00 30.00
2022CS Cole Sillinger 10.00 25.00
2022CY Cam York 6.00 15.00
2022DA Jonathan Dahlen 6.00 15.00
2022DF David Farrance 6.00 15.00
2022FG Filip Gustavsson 12.00 30.00
2022GD Grigori Denisenko 8.00 20.00
2022HL Hendrix Lapierre 6.00 15.00
2022IP Ivan Prosvetov 6.00 15.00
2022JB Jacob Bernard-Docker 6.00 15.00
2022JD Jamie Drysdale 10.00 25.00
2022JJ Jan Jenik 8.00 20.00
2022JN Jake Neighbours 12.00 30.00
2022JS Jeremy Swayman 30.00 80.00
2022JV Joe Veleno 8.00 20.00
2022JW Jasper Weatherby 6.00 15.00
2022JY Jesse Ylonen 6.00 15.00
2022LR Lucas Raymond 20.00 50.00
2022LT Logan Thompson 15.00 40.00
2022MB Morgan Barron 5.00 12.00
2022MM Mason McTavish 12.00 30.00
2022MS Moritz Seider 40.00 100.00
2022NL Nils Lundkvist 6.00 15.00

2022PD Pavel Dorofeyev 8.00 20.00
2022PE Scott Perunovich 6.00 15.00
2022PT Philip Tomasino 8.00 20.00
2022RC Ross Colton 8.00 20.00
2022SJ Seth Jarvis 15.00 40.00
2022SK Spencer Knight 12.00 30.00
2022SP Shane Pinto 10.00 25.00
2022SR Sampo Ranta 6.00 15.00
2022TJ Tanner Jeannot 6.00 15.00
2022TR Taylor Raddysh 10.00 25.00
2022VP Vasily Podkolzin 8.00 20.00
2022WE William Eklund 15.00 40.00
2022WK Wyatt Kalynuk 6.00 15.00

2021-22 The Cup Rookie Gear Relic Autographs

RGAH Alexander Holtz 30.00 80.00
RGAL Anton Lundell 40.00 100.00
RGAT Alex Turcotte 25.00 60.00
RGBG Benoit-Olivier Groulx 25.00 60.00
RGCC Cole Caufield 400.00 1000.00
RGCP Cole Perfetti 100.00 250.00
RGLR Lucas Raymond 100.00 250.00
RGMB Michael Bunting 20.00 50.00
RGNL Nils Lundkvist 20.00 50.00
RGPT Philip Tomasino 25.00 60.00
RGQB Quinton Byfield 150.00 400.00
RGVP Vasily Podkolzin 25.00 60.00

2021-22 The Cup Scripted Swatches

SSAT Alex Turcotte 30.00 80.00
SSCM Connor McDavid 200.00 500.00
SSCP Cole Perfetti 50.00 125.00
SSDB Drake Batherson 25.00 60.00
SSDS Dylan Strome 30.00 80.00
SSJG Jake Guentzel 40.00 100.00
SSJR Jack Roslovic 15.00 40.00
SSKF Kevin Fiala 20.00 50.00
SSPT Philip Tomasino 30.00 80.00
SSQB Quinton Byfield 80.00 200.00
SSSM Sean Monahan 15.00 40.00
SSTH Tomas Hertl 25.00 60.00
SSTS Tim Stutzle 80.00 200.00
SSTT Tyler Toffoli 25.00 60.00
SSVP Vasily Podkolzin 30.00 80.00

2021-22 The Cup Signature Materials

SPAB Anthony Beauvillier/99 12.00 30.00
SPAH Alexander Holtz/99 30.00 80.00
SPBA Aleksander Barkov/99 30.00 80.00
SPBO Benoit-Olivier Groulx/99 20.00 50.00
SPCA Cam Atkinson/99 20.00 50.00
SPCM Cale Makar/25 200.00 500.00
SPCP Cole Perfetti/99 40.00 100.00
SPDS Dylan Strome/99 25.00 60.00
SPGI John Gibson/99 20.00 50.00
SPHL Hendrix Lapierre/99 20.00 50.00
SPJE Jordan Eberle/99 20.00 50.00
SPJG Jake Guentzel/99 30.00 80.00
SPJH Jonathan Huberdeau/25 25.00 60.00
SPJM Jonathan Marchessault/99 25.00 60.00
SPJN Josh Norris/99 20.00 50.00
SPJR Jack Roslovic/99 12.00 30.00
SPJT John Tavares/25 30.00 80.00
SPKF Kevin Fiala/99 15.00 40.00
SPLR Lucas Raymond/99 80.00 200.00
SPLU Anton Lundell/99 40.00 100.00
SPMP Max Pacioretty/99 20.00 50.00
SPPA Joe Pavelski/99 25.00 60.00
SPPR Carey Price/99 50.00 125.00
SPQB Quinton Byfield/99 150.00 400.00
SPQH Quinn Hughes/25 50.00 125.00
SPRD Riley Damiani/99 20.00 50.00
SPSR Sam Reinhart/99 40.00 100.00
SPSV Andrei Svechnikov/99 25.00 60.00
SPTH Tomas Hertl/99 20.00 50.00
SPTJ Tristan Jarry/99 30.00 80.00
SPTZ Trevor Zegras/99 200.00 500.00
SPVP Vasily Podkolzin/99 25.00 60.00
SPWK William Karlsson/99 25.00 60.00

2021-22 The Cup Signature Renditions

SRAM Auston Matthews A 250.00 600.00
SRAN Alex Nedeljkovic C 12.00 30.00
SRAT Alex Turcotte A 20.00 50.00
SRBN Bernie Nicholls C 12.00 30.00
SRCM Connor McDavid A 400.00 1000.00
SRJE Jordan Eberle B 25.00 60.00
SRJP Joe Pavelski B 40.00 100.00
SRKT Keith Tkachuk B 15.00 40.00
SRMF Marc-Andre Fleury A 30.00 80.00
SRPB Paul Bissonnette C 80.00 200.00
SRPG Philipp Grubauer B 40.00 100.00
SRPI Shane Pinto C 25.00 60.00
SRPL Pat LaFontaine B 15.00 40.00
SRQH Quinn Hughes A 40.00 100.00
SRRC Ross Colton C 20.00 50.00
SRSP Scott Perunovich C 15.00 40.00
SRWK William Karlsson C 20.00 50.00

2021-22 The Cup Signature Renditions Combos

SR2DS M.Dionne/D.Sittler 40.00 100.00
SR2GP J.Petry/B.Gallagher 30.00 80.00
SR2YG W.Gretzky/S.Yzerman 2000.00 5000.00
SR2ZT M.Zuccarello/C.Talbot 20.00 50.00

2021-22 The Cup The Basics Autographs

TBBD Jacob Bernard-Docker E 10.00 25.00
TBBU Michael Bunting E 10.00 25.00
TBBY Quinton Byfield C 60.00 150.00
TBCL Cole Caufield B 200.00 500.00
TBCM Connor McDavid A 250.00 600.00
TBDV David Perron D 8.00 20.00
TBJC Jack Campbell D 10.00 25.00
TBJO Jake Oettinger D 15.00 40.00
TBLM Mario Lemieux C 125.00 300.00
TBLN Anton Lundell D 20.00 50.00
TBMC Mason McTavish D 20.00 50.00
TBMO Mike Modano B 15.00 40.00
TBPE Scott Perunovich D 10.00 25.00
TBPF Cole Perfetti E 20.00 50.00
TBRS Ryan Suter D 8.00 20.00
TBRY Lucas Raymond B 30.00 80.00
TBSP Shane Pinto E 15.00 40.00
TBTC Alex Tuch D 10.00 25.00
TBTL Trevor Linden C 10.00 25.00
TBTU Alex Turcotte C 12.00 30.00
TBVY Vasily Podkolzin E 12.00 30.00
TBWC Wendel Clark C 60.00 150.00
TBWE William Eklund C 25.00 60.00

2021-22 The Cup The Basics Patch Autographs

TBAH Alexander Holtz/25 30.00 80.00
TBAT Alex Turcotte/25 25.00 60.00
TBCC Cole Caufield/25 200.00 500.00
TBCP Cole Perfetti/25 40.00 100.00
TBHL Hendrix Lapierre/25 40.00 100.00
TBLU Anton Lundell/25 40.00 100.00
TBNL Nils Lundkvist/25 20.00 50.00
TBQB Quinton Byfield/25 80.00 200.00
TBRD Riley Damiani/25 20.00 50.00
TBTJ Tanner Jeannot/25 20.00 50.00
TBVP Vasily Podkolzin/25 25.00 60.00

2021-22 The Cup The Basics Patches

TBAS Andrei Svechnikov 10.00 25.00
TBBT Brady Tkachuk 12.00 30.00
TBDD Drew Doughty 10.00 25.00
TBDP David Pastrnak 40.00 100.00
TBEM Evgeni Malkin 30.00 80.00
TBJB Jordan Binnington 12.00 30.00
TBJH Jack Hughes 30.00 80.00
TBLD Leon Draisaitl 25.00 60.00
TBMM Mitch Marner 12.00 30.00
TBMR Mikko Rantanen 20.00 50.00
TBNK Nikita Kucherov 15.00 40.00
TBNM Nathan MacKinnon 30.00 80.00
TBNS Nick Suzuki 15.00 40.00
TBPB Patrice Bergeron 25.00 60.00
TBPK Phil Kessel 8.00 20.00
TBSA Sebastian Aho 12.00 30.00
TBSC Mark Scheifele 12.00 30.00
TBSS Steven Stamkos 15.00 40.00
TBZW Zach Werenski 12.00 30.00

2021-22 The Cup The NHL Collection Patch Autographs

NHLAH Alexander Holtz/35 30.00 80.00
NHLAN Alex Nedeljkovic/25 15.00 40.00
NHLCA Cam Atkinson/35 20.00 50.00
NHLCC Cole Caufield/35 200.00 500.00
NHLCP Cole Perfetti/35 50.00 125.00
NHLHL Hendrix Lapierre/35 20.00 50.00
NHLJA Seth Jarvis/35 50.00 125.00
NHLJD Jamie Drysdale/35 30.00 80.00
NHLJE Jordan Eberle/25 20.00 50.00
NHLKC Kyle Connor/25 30.00 80.00
NHLLR Lucas Raymond/35 80.00 200.00
NHLLU Nils Lundkvist/35 20.00 50.00
NHLMS Mark Stone/25 40.00 100.00
NHLNE Nikolaj Ehlers/25 20.00 50.00
NHLPL Pat LaFontaine/25 20.00 50.00
NHLPT Philip Tomasino/35 25.00 60.00
NHLQB Quinton Byfield/35 80.00 200.00
NHLSP Scott Perunovich/35 20.00 50.00
NHLTJ Tanner Jeannot/35 20.00 50.00
NHLTZ Trevor Zegras/35 125.00 300.00
NHLVP Vasily Podkolzin/35 25.00 60.00

2021-22 The Cup The Show

*BLACK: 4X TO 1X BASIC
SW1 Wayne Gretzky/49 60.00 150.00
SW2 Dominik Hasek/49 8.00 20.00
SW3 Bobby Hull/49 8.00 20.00
SW4 Gordie Howe/49 15.00 40.00
SW5 Marcel Dionne/49 6.00 15.00
SW6 Auston Matthews/49 20.00 50.00
SW7 Saku Koivu/49 5.00 12.00
SW8 Nathan MacKinnon/49 20.00 50.00
SW9 Alex Ovechkin/49 20.00 50.00
SW10 Connor McDavid/49 40.00 100.00
SW11 Steve Yzerman/49 12.00 30.00
SW12 Mario Lemieux/49 20.00 50.00
SW13 Kirill Kaprizov/49 15.00 40.00
SW14 Wendel Clark/49 8.00 20.00
SW15 Gerry Cheevers/49 12.00 30.00
SW16 Quinn Hughes/49 12.00 30.00
SW17 Marc-Andre Fleury/49 10.00 25.00
SW18 Mathew Barzal/49 6.00 15.00
SW19 Sidney Crosby/49 20.00 50.00
SW20 Mark Stone/49 6.00 15.00
SW21 Jaromir Jagr/49 15.00 40.00
SW22 Mike Liut/49 3.00 8.00
SW23 Patrick Roy/49 12.00 30.00
SW24 Ryan Suter/49 4.00 10.00
SW25 Lanny McDonald/49 5.00 12.00
SW26 David Pastrnak/49 12.00 30.00
SW27 Leon Draisaitl/49 15.00 40.00
SW28 Brendan Gallagher/49 5.00 12.00
SW29 Patrick Kane/49 10.00 25.00
SW30 Bobby Orr/49 20.00 50.00
SW31 Trevor Zegras/99 10.00 25.00
SW32 Vasily Podkolzin/99 6.00 15.00
SW33 Alex Newhook/99 8.00 20.00
SW34 Moritz Seider/99 12.00 30.00
SW35 Cole Sillinger/99 8.00 20.00
SW36 Alex Turcotte/99 6.00 15.00
SW37 Seth Jarvis/99 12.00 30.00
SW38 William Eklund/99 12.00 30.00
SW39 Dawson Mercer/99 12.00 30.00
SW40 J.J. Peterka/99 10.00 25.00
SW41 Cam York/99 5.00 12.00
SW42 Anton Lundell/99 10.00 25.00
SW43 Mason McTavish/99 10.00 25.00
SW44 Cole Perfetti/99 10.00 25.00
SW45 Lucas Raymond/99 15.00 40.00
SW46 Cole Caufield/99 20.00 50.00
SW47 Shane Pinto/99 8.00 20.00
SW48 Alexander Holtz/99 8.00 20.00
SW49 Spencer Knight/99 10.00 25.00
SW50 Quinton Byfield/99 12.00 30.00

2022-23 The Cup

1 Jack Hughes 5.00 12.00
2 Wendel Clark 3.00 8.00
3 Jared McCann 1.50 4.00
4 Matthew Tkachuk 4.00 10.00
5 Clayton Keller 2.50 6.00
6 Nathan MacKinnon 8.00 20.00
7 Trevor Zegras 2.00 5.00
8 Connor McDavid 10.00 25.00
9 Ryan Getzlaf 2.00 5.00
10 Bo Horvat 2.50 6.00
11 Zach Werenski 3.00 8.00
12 Auston Matthews 8.00 20.00
13 Bobby Hull 4.00 10.00
14 Mason McTavish 2.00 5.00
15 Kevin Fiala 1.50 4.00
16 Torey Krug 1.50 4.00
17 Johnny Gaudreau 3.00 8.00
18 Vitek Vanecek 2.00 5.00
19 Andrew Copp 1.25 3.00
20 Marc-Andre Fleury 4.00 10.00
21 Alex DeBrincat 2.50 6.00
22 Seth Jarvis 2.50 6.00
23 Josh Bailey 1.50 4.00
24 Glenn Hall 2.00 5.00
25 Brock Nelson 2.00 5.00
26 Kyle Connor 3.00 8.00
27 Ryan O'Reilly 2.00 5.00
28 Tim Stutzle 2.50 6.00
29 Tage Thompson 2.50 6.00
30 Yegor Sharangovich 2.00 5.00
31 Jacob Markstrom 2.00 5.00
32 Nick Robertson 2.00 5.00
33 Igor Shesterkin 4.00 10.00
34 Roope Hintz 2.50 6.00
35 Patrick Kane 4.00 10.00
36 Patrick Roy 5.00 12.00
37 Tomas Hertl 2.00 5.00
38 Jordan Kyrou 2.00 5.00
39 David Pastrnak 5.00 12.00
40 Cam Atkinson 2.00 5.00
41 Joe Sakic 4.00 10.00
42 Filip Forsberg 3.00 8.00
43 Miro Heiskanen 2.50 6.00
44 Alex Nedeljkovic 1.50 4.00
45 Sergei Zubov 1.50 4.00
46 Leon Draisaitl 6.00 15.00
47 Moritz Seider 2.50 6.00
48 Juuse Saros 2.50 6.00
49 Quinn Hughes 5.00 12.00
50 Cale Makar 5.00 12.00
51 Thatcher Demko 2.50 6.00
52 Jesse Puljujarvi 2.00 5.00
53 Quinton Byfield 2.50 6.00
54 James van Riemsdyk 1.50 4.00
55 Alex Newhook 1.50 4.00
56 Anders Lee 1.50 4.00
57 Andrei Vasilevskiy 3.00 8.00
58 Joe Pavelski 2.50 6.00
59 Brandon Saad 1.50 4.00
60 Tanner Jeannot 1.25 3.00
61 Wayne Gretzky 12.00 30.00
62 Teuvo Teravainen 2.00 5.00
63 Aaron Ekblad 2.50 6.00
64 Sebastian Aho 3.00 8.00
65 Chris Kreider 2.50 6.00
66 Brayden Point 2.50 6.00
67 Henrik Zetterberg 2.50 6.00
68 Mats Zuccarello 2.00 5.00
69 Bobby Orr 8.00 20.00
70 Josh Norris 2.00 5.00
71 Jake Oettinger 3.00 8.00
72 Sam Bennett 3.00 8.00
73 Darcy Kuemper 2.00 5.00
74 Taylor Hall 2.00 5.00
75 Sidney Crosby 8.00 20.00
76 Gabriel Landeskog 2.50 6.00
77 Elias Lindholm 2.00 5.00
78 Kirby Dach 2.00 5.00
79 Nick Schmaltz 1.50 4.00
80 Jeremy Swayman 3.00 8.00
81 Jonathan Huberdeau 2.50 6.00
82 Boone Jenner 2.00 5.00
83 Dawson Mercer 2.50 6.00
84 Kirill Kaprizov 6.00 15.00
85 Jeff Skinner 2.00 5.00
86 Mark Stone 2.50 6.00
87 Timo Meier 2.00 5.00
88 Jordan Eberle 3.00 8.00
89 Jack Eichel 3.00 8.00
90 Carey Price 4.00 10.00
91 Jonathan Toews 3.00 8.00
92 Steven Stamkos 3.00 8.00
93 Mitch Marner 3.00 8.00
94 Cole Caufield 4.00 10.00
95 Patrice Bergeron 2.50 6.00
96 Tristan Jarry 2.00 5.00
97 Alex Ovechkin 8.00 20.00
98 Brock Boeser 2.50 6.00
99 Oskar Lindblom 1.50 4.00
100 Mark Scheifele 3.00 8.00
101 Jack Quinn JSY AU/249 RC 100.00 250.00
102 Kaedan Korczak JSY AU/249 RC 15.00 40.00
103 Jake Christiansen
JSY AU/249 RC 20.00 50.00
104 Samuel Fagemo JSY AU/249 RC 15.00 40.00
105 Samuel Poulin/249 RC 3.00 8.00
106 Matias Maccelli JSY AU/249 RC 80.00 200.00
107 Brayden Tracey JSY AU/249 RC 15.00 40.00
108 Isaac Ratcliffe JSY AU/249 RC 20.00 50.00
109 Filip Hallander JSY AU/249 RC 20.00 50.00
110 Lukas Dostal JSY AU/249 RC 150.00 400.00
111 David Jiricek JSY AU/249 RC 100.00 250.00
112 Mads Sogaard JSY AU/249 RC 25.00 60.00
113 Jordan Harris JSY AU/249 RC 25.00 60.00
114 Elmer Soderblom
JSY AU/249 RC 40.00 100.00
115 Dylan Samberg JSY AU/249 RC 20.00 50.00
116 Cole Koepke JSY AU/249 RC 20.00 50.00
117 Marco Rossi JSY AU/249 RC 100.00 250.00
118 Alex Vlasic JSY AU/249 RC 15.00 40.00
119 Kaiden Guhle JSY AU/249 RC 80.00 200.00
120 Jack McBain JSY AU/249 RC 30.00 80.00
121 Jake Sanderson
JSY AU/249 RC 125.00 300.00
122 Brandt Clarke JSY AU/249 RC 60.00 150.00
123 Ben Meyers JSY AU/249 RC 20.00 50.00
124 Jakub Lauko JSY AU/249 RC 25.00 60.00
125 Nick Blankenburg
JSY AU/249 RC 15.00 40.00
126 Dylan Guenther
JSY AU/99 RC 150.00 400.00
127 Chase Pearson JSY AU/249 RC 15.00 40.00
128 Andrei Kuzmenko
JSY AU/99 RC 40.00 100.00
129 Michael Eyssimont
JSY AU/249 RC 20.00 50.00
130 Jacob Moverare JSY AU/249 RC 15.00 40.00
131 Dylan Holloway JSY AU/249 RC 60.00 150.00
132 Thomas Bordeleau
JSY AU/249 RC 20.00 50.00
133 Arber Xhekaj JSY AU/249 RC 80.00 200.00
134 Pavol Regenda JSY AU/249 RC 20.00 50.00
135 Mark Kastelic JSY AU/249 RC 15.00 40.00
136 Jordan Spence/249 RC 2.50 6.00
137 Valtteri Puustinen
JSY AU/249 RC 15.00 40.00
138 Lukas Reichel JSY AU/249 RC 40.00 100.00
139 Braden Schneider
JSY AU/249 RC 40.00 100.00
140 Jacob Perreault/249 RC 2.50 6.00
141 Pyotr Kochetkov
JSY AU/249 RC 60.00 150.00
142 Vladislav Kolyachonok
JSY AU/249 RC 15.00 40.00
143 Nick Perbix JSY AU/249 RC 15.00 40.00
144 Olle Lycksell JSY AU/249 RC 20.00 50.00
145 Matt Boldy JSY AU/99 RC 400.00 1000.00
146 Matty Beniers JSY AU/99 RC 500.00 1200.00
147 Kent Johnson JSY AU/99 RC 150.00 400.00
148 Owen Power JSY AU/99 RC 200.00 500.00
149 Shane Wright JSY AU/99 RC 400.00 1000.00
150 Juraj Slafkovsky
JSY AU/99 RC 1200.00 3000.00
151 Samuel Ersson/249 RC 5.00 12.00
152 Hunter Drew/249 RC 2.50 6.00
153 Filip Roos AU/249 RC 10.00 25.00
154 Trey Fix-Wolansky/249 RC 2.50 6.00
155 Aatu Raty AU/249 RC 12.00 30.00
156 Nick Abruzzese JSY/249 RC 5.00 12.00
157 Nikita Okhotiuk JSY/249 RC 4.00 10.00
158 Ronnie Attard JSY/249 RC 5.00 12.00
159 Zack Hayes JSY/249 RC 4.00 10.00
160 Ollie Lycksell JSY/249 RC 5.00 12.00
161 Marc McLaughlin
JSY AU/249 RC 20.00 50.00
162 James Hamblin/249 RC 2.50 6.00
163 Mac Hollowell/249 RC 2.50 6.00
164 Callahan Burke/249 RC 2.50 6.00
165 Cole Reinhardt/249 RC 2.50 6.00
166 Noah Cates JSY AU/249 RC 20.00 50.00
167 Fredrik Karlstrom JSY AU/249 RC 15.00 40.00
168 Brandon Biro/249 RC 4.00 10.00
169 Declan Chisholm/249 RC 2.50 6.00
170 Erik Kallgren/249 RC 2.50 6.00
171 Reilly Walsh JSY AU/249 RC 20.00 50.00
172 Nick Cicek/249 RC 2.50 6.00
173 Oskar Olausson/249 RC 2.50 6.00
174 Jake Lucchini/249 RC 2.50 6.00
175 Nikita Alexandrov
JSY AU/249 RC 20.00 50.00
176 Johnathan Kovacevic
JSY AU/249 RC 20.00 50.00
177 Matej Blumel/249 RC 3.00 8.00
178 Nick DeSimone JSY AU/249 RC 20.00 50.00
179 Jonatan Berggren
JSY AU/99 RC 30.00 80.00
180 Simon Holmstrom
JSY AU/249 RC 20.00 50.00
181 William Bitten JSY AU/249 RC 20.00 50.00
182 Nils Aman JSY AU/249 RC 20.00 50.00
183 Lucas Johansen/249 RC 2.00 5.00
184 Carson Meyer/249 RC 2.00 5.00
185 Brayden Pachal/249 RC 2.00 5.00
186 Jeff Malott/249 RC 2.50 6.00
187 Jean-Luc Foudy JSY AU/249 RC 20.00 50.00
188 Tyler Tucker/249 RC 2.50 6.00
189 Mitchell Chaffee/249 RC 2.00 5.00
190 Hayden Hodgson JSY AU/249 RC 15.00 40.00
191 Jakub Galvas/249 RC 2.50 6.00
192 Pontus Holmberg
JSY AU/249 RC 20.00 50.00
193 Samuel Walker/249 RC 2.50 6.00
194 Kirill Marchenko
JSY AU/249 RC 50.00 125.00
195 Semyon Der-Arguchintsev/249 RC 2.50 6.00
196 Nathan Smith JSY AU/249 RC 15.00 40.00
197 Marcus Bjork/249 RC 2.50 6.00
198 Bobby Brink JSY AU/249 RC 20.00 50.00
199 Juuso Parssinen/249 RC 2.50 6.00
200 Wyatt Johnston
JSY AU/99 RC 800.00 2000.00

2022-23 The Cup All Time Alum

ATACC Chris Chelios 3.00 8.00
ATACN Cam Neely 3.00 8.00
ATAEL Eric Lindros 5.00 12.00
ATAFP Felix Potvin 5.00 12.00
ATAGC Gerry Cheevers 3.00 8.00
ATAJK Jari Kurri 3.00 8.00
ATAMM Mike Modano 5.00 12.00

2022-23 The Cup All Time Alum Autographs Gold

ATAAG Adam Graves/50 30.00 80.00
ATACC Chris Chelios/25 60.00 150.00
ATACN Cam Neely/25 50.00 125.00
ATADT Dave Taylor/50 30.00 80.00
ATAEL Eric Lindros/25 100.00 250.00
ATAFP Felix Potvin/25 100.00 250.00
ATAGC Gerry Cheevers/50 40.00 100.00
ATAJK Jari Kurri/50 40.00 100.00
ATAMM Mike Modano/25 60.00 150.00

2022-23 The Cup Brilliance Autographs

BAG Adam Graves 30.00 80.00
BAL Anton Lundell 20.00 50.00
BBO Matt Boldy 60.00 150.00
BBS Brandon Saad 15.00 40.00
BCE Brandt Clarke 40.00 100.00
BDG Dylan Guenther 60.00 150.00
BJM Jacob Middleton 12.00 30.00
BJS Juraj Slafkovsky 125.00 300.00
BKM K'Andre Miller 15.00 40.00
BOP Owen Power 60.00 150.00
BOR Bobby Orr SP 150.00 400.00
BPR Patrick Roy SP 125.00 300.00
BSW Shane Wright 50.00 125.00
BWG Wayne Gretzky SP 250.00 600.00

2022-23 The Cup Championship Reflections

CRAG Adam Graves 15.00 40.00
CRBR Bill Ranford 20.00 50.00
CRBS Brandon Saad 15.00 40.00
CRCC Chris Chelios 20.00 50.00
CRGF Grant Fuhr 30.00 80.00
CRJL John LeClair 20.00 50.00
CRLR Larry Robinson 20.00 50.00
CRMB Martin Brodeur 100.00 250.00
CRMM Mark Messier 40.00 100.00
CRMR Mikko Rantanen 50.00 125.00
CRPR Patrick Roy 150.00 400.00
CRRB Rod Brind'Amour 50.00 125.00
CRRG Ryan Getzlaf 20.00 50.00
CRSZ Sergei Zubov 15.00 40.00
CRWG Wayne Gretzky 400.00 1000.00

2022-23 The Cup Cup Quads Jerseys

C4BASJ Aho/Svechnikov
Burns/Jarvis 20.00 50.00
C4BBTL Tkachuk/Barkov
Lundell/Bennett 25.00 60.00
C4BMPM Pastrnak/Marchand
McAvoy/Bergeron 30.00 80.00
C4BOWO Ovechkin/Oshie
Backstrom/Wilson 50.00 125.00
C4BPHG Hughes/Pettersson
Boeser/Garland 30.00 80.00
C4CKHM Meier/Hertl
Karlsson/Couture 15.00 40.00
C4CLSR Seider/Raymond
Larkin/Copp 20.00 50.00
C4CNDH Draisaitl/Nugent-Hopkins/Campbell/Hyman 40.00 100.00
C4CSPJ Power/Clarke
Sanderson/Jiricek 30.00 80.00
C4DJFS Josi/Forsberg
Duchene/Saros 20.00 50.00
C4EGMG McCann/Eberle
Grubauer/Gourde 12.00 30.00
C4FZEK Kaprizov/Fleury
Zuccarello/Eriksson Ek 40.00 100.00
C4GASC Caufield/Suzuki
Gallagher/Anderson 25.00 60.00
C4GDTS Tkachuk/DeBrincat
Stutzle/Giroux 20.00 50.00
C4GSKV Keller/Schmaltz
Gostisbehere/Vejmelka 15.00 40.00
C4GWLS Laine/Gaudreau
Werenski/Sillinger 20.00 50.00
C4JJSK Slafkovsky/Kuzmenko
Johnston/Johnson 60.00 150.00
C4KDDF Kopitar/Doughty
Fiala/Danault 20.00 50.00
C4KPLF Lafreniere/Kreider
Fox/Panarin 25.00 60.00
C4LBSR Barzal/Sorokin/Lee/Romanov 20.00 50.00
C4MHTL Huberdeau/Toffoli
Lindholm/Markstrom 15.00 40.00
C4MLJG Markstrom/Letang
Guentzel/Jarry 25.00 60.00
C4MRTM MacKinnon/Makar
Rantanen/Toews 50.00 125.00
C4OSKT Thomas/Kyrou/O'Reilly/Saad 12.00 30.00
C4PHHO Heiskanen/Oettinger
Pavelski/Hintz 20.00 50.00
C4RBWB Beniers/Boldy
Wright/Rossi 40.00 100.00
C4SDZM Strome/Zegras
McTavish/Drysdale 12.00 30.00
C4SHKP Stamkos/Hedman
Kucherov/Point 25.00 60.00
C4SMSE Eichel/Stone
Marchessault/Stephenson 20.00 50.00
C4TCDP Thompson/Dahlin
Cozens/Power 25.00 60.00
C4TKJK Kane/Jones/Toews/Kurashev 25.00 60.00
C4TMHH Hughes/Holtz/Tatar/Mercer 30.00 80.00
C4TNMM Matthews/Marner
Tavares/Nylander 50.00 125.00
C4WSEC Connor/Scheifele
Ehlers/Wheeler 20.00 50.00

2022-23 The Cup Cup Trios Jerseys

C3ASC Anderson/Caufield/Suzuki 20.00 50.00
C3BAS Aho/Svechnikov/Burns 15.00 40.00
C3BBB Boldy/Berggren/Beniers 30.00 80.00
C3BCP Pastrnak/Bergeron/Coyle 25.00 60.00
C3BPH Pettersson/Boeser/Hughes 25.00 60.00
C3BRJ Reichel/Boldy/Johnson 30.00 80.00
C3CAL Cates/Attard/Lycksell 10.00 25.00
C3CCK Cates/Kuzmenko/Clarke 20.00 50.00
C3CHB Hertl/Couture/Barabanov 12.00 30.00
C3CMO Crosby/McDavid/Ovechkin 50.00 120.00
C3CND Draisaitl/Nugent-Hopkins/Campbell 30.00 80.00
C3DFP Fiala/Danault/Petersen 10.00 25.00
C3DKK Kallgren/Kochetkov/Dostal 20.00 50.00
C3EGG Grubauer/Gourde/Eberle 10.00 25.00
C3FOM Foudy/Meyers/Olausson 10.00 25.00
C3FSR Seider/Raymond/Fabbri 15.00 40.00
C3GSK Keller/Schmaltz/Gostisbehere 12.00 30.00
C3GSX Slafkovsky/Guhle/Xhekaj 50.00 125.00
C3GTN Giroux/Norris/Tkachuk 15.00 40.00
C3GWM Gaudreau
Werenski/Merzlikins 15.00 40.00
C3HHH Harris/Holloway/Holmberg 20.00 50.00
C3HTL Lindholm/Toffoli/Huberdeau 12.00 30.00
C3JGF Josi/Forsberg/Granlund 15.00 40.00
C3JKB Johnston/Blumel/Karlstrom 40.00 100.00
C3JMJ Johnson/Marchenko/Jiricek 25.00 60.00
C3KPK Kyrou/Parayko/Krug 10.00 25.00
C3KPL Kreider/Panarin/Lafreniere 20.00 50.00
C3KSS Kastelic/Sanderson/Sogaard 25.00 60.00
C3LBR Romanov/Lee/Barzal 12.00 30.00
C3MGM Maccelli/Guenther/McBain 25.00 60.00
C3MLR Malkin/Letang/Rust 20.00 50.00
C3MMG MacKinnon/Makar/Girard 40.00 100.00
C3OCO Ovechkin/Carlson/Oshie 40.00 100.00
C3PBB Power/Beniers/Bordeleau 25.00 60.00
C3PSH Seguin/Pavelski/Hintz 12.00 30.00
C3RBL Bennett/Reinhart/Lundell 20.00 50.00
C3RPP Parssinen/Perbix/Rossi 25.00 60.00
C3SKP Stamkos/Point/Kucherov 20.00 50.00
C3SQH Quinn/Schneider/Holmstrom 15.00 40.00
C3SSS Shesterkin/Saros/Sorokin 20.00 50.00
C3TBH Hughes/Tatar/Bratt 25.00 60.00
C3TCD Thompson/Dahlin/Cozens 12.00 30.00
C3TKJ Kane/Jones/Toews 20.00 50.00
C3TKS Karlsson
Theodore/Stephenson 12.00 30.00
C3TRM Marner/Tavares/Rielly 15.00 40.00
C3TZM Zegras/McTavish/Terry 10.00 25.00
C3WJS Wright/Slafkovsky/Johnston 50.00 125.00
C3WSP Perfetti/Scheifele/Wheeler 15.00 40.00
C3ZEK Eriksson Ek
Zuccarello/Kaprizov 30.00 80.00

2022-23 The Cup Enshrinements

EAM Auston Matthews/25 200.00 500.00
EBC Brandt Clarke/99 40.00 100.00
EBO Matt Boldy/99 40.00 100.00
EDG Dylan Guenther/99 50.00 125.00
EJA Tristan Jarry/99 20.00 50.00
EJS Juraj Slafkovsky/99 150.00 400.00
EMB Martin Brodeur/25 80.00 200.00
EMH Miro Heiskanen/99 25.00 60.00
EML Mario Lemieux/25 250.00 600.00
EMM Mark Messier/25 80.00 200.00
EMS Mark Stone/99 25.00 60.00
END Noah Dobson/99 25.00 60.00
EOP Owen Power/99 40.00 100.00
EPR Patrick Roy/25 400.00 1000.00
ERB Rod Brind'Amour/99 20.00 50.00
ERG Ryan Getzlaf/99 20.00 50.00
ERH Ron Hextall/99 20.00 50.00
ERM Rick Middleton/99 20.00 50.00
ESW Shane Wright/99 50.00 125.00
ESY Steve Yzerman/25 100.00 250.00
ESZ Sergei Zubov/99 15.00 40.00
ETJ Tanner Jeannot/99 12.00 30.00
ETK Torey Krug/99 15.00 40.00
EWG Wayne Gretzky/25 600.00 1500.00

2022-23 The Cup Expanded Material Autographs

EMCS Chandler Stephenson 30.00 80.00
EMJE Jordan Eberle 25.00 60.00
EMTH Tage Thompson 30.00 80.00
EMTK Torey Krug 20.00 50.00
EMTS Tim Stutzle 50.00 125.00
EMVV Vitek Vanecek 25.00 60.00

2022-23 The Cup Expanded Rookie Material Autographs

ERBC Brandt Clarke 50.00 125.00
ERGR Dylan Guenther 100.00 250.00
ERJB Jonatan Berggren 30.00 60.00
ERJN Kent Johnson 50.00 125.00
ERJO Wyatt Johnston 125.00 300.00
ERKG Kaiden Guhle 80.00 200.00
ERLR Lukas Reichel 125.00 300.00
ERNC Noah Cates 25.00 60.00
ERPR Owen Power 50.00 125.00
ERRS Matty Beniers 60.00 150.00
ERSL Juraj Slafkovsky 300.00 800.00
ERSN Jake Sanderson 60.00 150.00
ERSR Braden Schneider 40.00 100.00
ERWT Shane Wright 80.00 200.00

2022-23 The Cup Foundations Jerseys

FAK Anze Kopitar/49 10.00 25.00
FAL Anders Lee/49 5.00 12.00
FAM Auston Matthews/49 25.00 60.00
FAO Alex Ovechkin/49 25.00 60.00
FAV Andrei Vasilevskiy/49 10.00 25.00
FAX Arber Xhekaj/99 12.00 30.00
FBC Brandt Clarke/99 12.00 30.00
FBE Matty Beniers/99 15.00 40.00
FBM Brad Marchand/49 12.00 30.00
FBS Braden Schneider/99 10.00 25.00
FCM Cale Makar/49 15.00 40.00
FCR Clayton Keller/49 8.00 20.00
FCS Chandler Stephenson/49 5.00 12.00
FDG Dylan Guenther/99 15.00 40.00
FDH Dylan Holloway/99 12.00 30.00
FDJ David Jiricek/99 12.00 30.00
FDM Dawson Mercer/49 8.00 20.00
FGV Gabe Vilardi/49 8.00 20.00
FIS Ilya Sorokin/49 10.00 25.00
FJB Jonatan Berggren/99 10.00 25.00
FJH Jordan Harris/99 8.00 20.00
FJM Jared McCann/49 5.00 12.00
FJQ Jack Quinn/99 10.00 25.00
FJS Juraj Slafkovsky/99 30.00 80.00
FKG Kaiden Guhle/99 12.00 30.00
FKJ Kent Johnson/99 12.00 30.00
FKM Kirill Marchenko/99 15.00 40.00
FKO Andrei Kuzmenko/99 12.00 30.00
FLR Lukas Reichel/99 12.00 30.00
FMB Matt Boldy/99 20.00 50.00
FMC Connor McDavid/49 50.00 125.00
FMJ J.T. Miller/49 8.00 20.00
FMM Matias Maccelli/99 10.00 25.00
FNP Nick Perbix/99 6.00 15.00
FOP Owen Power/99 12.00 30.00
FPH Pontus Holmberg/99 6.00 15.00
FPK Pyotr Kochetkov/99 12.00 30.00
FRJ Roman Josi/49 6.00 15.00
FRN Ryan Nugent-Hopkins/49 8.00 20.00
FRO Ryan O'Reilly/49 6.00 15.00
FSA Jake Sanderson/99 15.00 40.00
FSW Shane Wright/99 15.00 40.00
FTJ Tristan Jarry/49 6.00 15.00
FTM Timo Meier/49 6.00 15.00
FTO Tyler Toffoli/49 6.00 15.00
FTS Tim Stutzle/49 8.00 20.00
FTT Tage Thompson/49 8.00 20.00
FWJ Wyatt Johnston/99 25.00 60.00
FZH Zach Hyman/49 6.00 15.00
FZW Zach Werenski/49 10.00 25.00

2022-23 The Cup Honorable Numbers

HRBC Brandt Clarke/92 40.00 100.00
HRBT Brady Tkachuk/45 30.00 80.00
HRJM Jonathan Marchessault/30 25.00 60.00
HRJO Jake Oettinger/30 30.00 80.00
HRKJ Kent Johnson/91 60.00 150.00
HRMF Mario Ferraro/49 12.00 30.00
HRMS Mark Stone/33 50.00 125.00
HRPR Patrick Roy/33 150.00 400.00
HRRB Ray Bourque/19 200.00 500.00
HRRH Roope Hintz/72 25.00 60.00
HRRJ Roman Josi/96 20.00 50.00
HRSA Jake Sanderson/85 50.00 125.00
HRSW Shane Wright/51 100.00 250.00
HRSY Juraj Slafkovsky/20 600.00 1500.00
HRTH Tage Thompson/68 25.00 60.00
HRTJ Tanner Jeannot/41 30.00 80.00

2022-23 The Cup Inked Impressions

IIAD Alex DeBrincat 20.00 50.00
IIBB Brent Burns 25.00 60.00
IIEL Eric Lindros 125.00 300.00
IIFP Felix Potvin 60.00 150.00
IIGC Gerry Cheevers 25.00 60.00
IIGF Grant Fuhr 40.00 100.00
IIJH Jonathan Huberdeau 20.00 50.00
IIJS Juuse Saros 30.00 80.00
IIMD Marcel Dionne 30.00 80.00
IIMS Martin St. Louis 25.00 60.00
IIND Noah Dobson 50.00 125.00
IINS Nick Suzuki 60.00 150.00
IIRB Rob Blake 25.00 60.00
IIWO Willie O'Ree 30.00 80.00

2022-23 The Cup Limited Logos

LLBE Matty Beniers AU/50 200.00 500.00
LLCS Chandler Stephenson AU/50 30.00 80.00
LLDP David Pastrnak/25 125.00 300.00
LLEP Elias Pettersson/50 40.00 100.00
LLIS Ilya Sorokin AU/50 100.00 250.00
LLJG Johnny Gaudreau/50 100.00 250.00
LLJS Juraj Slafkovsky AU/50 600.00 1500.00
LLKJ Kent Johnson AU/50 80.00 200.00
LLMS Mark Scheifele/50 40.00 100.00
LLNS Nick Suzuki AU/50 125.00 300.00
LLOP Owen Power AU/50 150.00 400.00
LLPG Philipp Grubauer AU/50 40.00 100.00
LLPK Patrick Kane/25 50.00 125.00
LLQH Quinn Hughes/25 60.00 150.00
LLSA Juuse Saros AU/50 60.00 150.00
LLSS Steven Stamkos/25 80.00 200.00
LLSW Shane Wright AU/50 125.00 300.00
LLTN Tage Thompson AU/25 50.00 125.00
LLTZ Trevor Zegras/50 25.00 60.00
LLWN William Nylander/25 100.00 250.00

2022-23 The Cup LogoMarks

LMAG Adam Graves 8.00 20.00
LMAL Anders Lee 8.00 20.00
LMCM Connor McDavid SP 250.00 600.00
LMRO Ryan O'Reilly SP 10.00 25.00
LMRR Ryan Reaves 8.00 20.00
LMSD Shane Doan 8.00 20.00
LMST Shea Theodore 12.00 30.00
LMSZ Sergei Zubov 8.00 20.00
LMTK Torey Krug 8.00 20.00
LMTT Tage Thompson 12.00 30.00
LMVV Vitek Vanecek 10.00 25.00
LMWO Willie O'Ree 12.00 30.00
LMYC Yvan Cournoyer 15.00 40.00

2022-23 The Cup LogoMarks Rookies

LMBC Brandt Clarke 30.00 80.00
LMGR Dylan Guenther 40.00 100.00
LMJB Jonatan Berggren 15.00 40.00
LMJS Juraj Slafkovsky 125.00 300.00
LMKJ Kent Johnson 30.00 80.00
LMLR Lukas Reichel 20.00 50.00
LMMB Matt Boldy 50.00 125.00
LMOP Owen Power 30.00 80.00
LMSA Jake Sanderson SP 30.00 80.00
LMSW Shane Wright 40.00 100.00
LMWJ Wyatt Johnston 80.00 200.00

2022-23 The Cup MaterialiSticks

MSAM Auston Matthews 100.00 250.00
MSAO Alex Ovechkin 80.00 200.00
MSBP Bob Probert 80.00 200.00
MSBS Brendan Shanahan 40.00 100.00
MSHL Henrik Lundqvist 60.00 150.00
MSJH Jack Hughes 80.00 200.00
MSJJ Jaromir Jagr 150.00 400.00
MSJM Jonathan Marchessault 60.00 150.00
MSJQ Jonathan Quick 60.00 150.00
MSJT Jonathan Toews 60.00 150.00
MSMR Mark Recchi 50.00 125.00
MSMS Mark Stone 60.00 150.00
MSNM Nathan MacKinnon 80.00 200.00
MSRB Ray Bourque 80.00 200.00
MSSA Joe Sakic 100.00 250.00

2022-23 The Cup On Display Jersey Autographs

ODABE Matty Beniers/49 30.00 80.00
ODADG Dylan Guenther/49 50.00 125.00
ODAJE Jordan Eberle/25 12.00 30.00
ODAJS Juraj Slafkovsky/49 80.00 200.00
ODAKJ Kent Johnson/49 25.00 60.00
ODAMC Jared McCann/25 10.00 25.00
ODAOP Owen Power/49 25.00 60.00
ODARG Ryan Getzlaf/25 20.00 50.00
ODASA Jake Sanderson/49 20.00 50.00
ODASD Shane Doan/25 10.00 25.00
ODATS Tim Stutzle/25 15.00 40.00
ODATT Tage Thompson/25 30.00 80.00
ODAWJ Wyatt Johnston/49 50.00 125.00

2022-23 The Cup On Display Jerseys

ODAF Adam Fox/49 5.00 12.00
ODBC Brandt Clarke/75 8.00 20.00
ODBO Matt Boldy/75 12.00 30.00
ODBS Brendan Shanahan/49 4.00 10.00
ODBT Bryan Trottier/49 4.00 10.00
ODCC Cole Caufield/49 8.00 20.00
ODCP Chris Pronger/49 4.00 10.00
ODCW Cam Ward/49 4.00 10.00
ODDD Drew Doughty/49 5.00 12.00
ODDH Dale Hawerchuk/49 5.00 12.00
ODDP David Pastrnak/49 10.00 25.00
ODDS Denis Savard/49 4.00 10.00
ODEK Erik Karlsson/49 5.00 12.00
ODEL Elias Lindholm/49 4.00 10.00
ODEM Evgeni Malkin/49 8.00 20.00
ODFF Filip Forsberg/49 6.00 15.00
ODJB Jonatan Berggren/75 6.00 15.00
ODJH Jack Hughes/49 10.00 25.00
ODJP Juuso Parssinen/75 6.00 15.00
ODJR Jason Robertson/49 6.00 15.00
ODKK Kirill Kaprizov/49 12.00 30.00
ODKV Pyotr Kochetkov/75 8.00 20.00
ODLR Lukas Reichel/75 8.00 20.00

2022-23 The Cup On Display Jerseys

ODMB Matty Beniers/75 10.00 25.00
ODMM Mitch Marner/49 6.00 15.00
ODNC Noah Cates/75 4.00 10.00
ODNM Nathan MacKinnon/49 15.00 40.00
ODPF Peter Forsberg/49 8.00 20.00
ODPK Patrick Kane/49 8.00 20.00
ODQH Quinn Hughes/49 10.00 25.00
ODRB Ray Bourque/49 6.00 15.00
ODRM Ryan Miller/49 4.00 10.00
ODRN Rick Nash/49 4.00 10.00
ODSK Saku Koivu/49 4.00 10.00
ODSR Braden Schneider/75 6.00 15.00
ODSS Steven Stamkos/49 8.00 20.00
ODSW Shane Wright/75 10.00 25.00
ODTZ Trevor Zegras/49 4.00 10.00
ODVT Vladimir Tarasenko/49 5.00 12.00

2022-23 The Cup Renditions Relics

RRAD Alex DeBrincat 8.00 20.00
RRAK Andrei Kuzmenko 12.00 30.00
RRAO Alex Ovechkin SP 25.00 60.00
RRAP Artemi Panarin 12.00 30.00
RRBC Brandt Clarke 12.00 30.00
RRBE Matty Beniers 15.00 40.00
RRBP Brayden Point 8.00 20.00
RRCC Cole Caufield 12.00 30.00
RRCK Clayton Keller 8.00 20.00
RRCM Connor McDavid SP 30.00 80.00
RRCV Carter Verhaeghe 6.00 15.00
RRDG Dylan Guenther 15.00 40.00
RRDP David Pastrnak 15.00 40.00
RREK Erik Karlsson 8.00 20.00
RREM Evgeni Malkin 12.00 30.00
RREP Elias Pettersson 10.00 25.00
RRIS Igor Shesterkin 12.00 30.00
RRJB Jonatan Berggren 10.00 25.00
RRJG Johnny Gaudreau 10.00 25.00
RRJH Jack Hughes 15.00 40.00
RRJQ Jack Quinn 10.00 25.00
RRJR Jason Robertson SP 10.00 25.00
RRJS Juraj Slafkovsky 30.00 80.00
RRJT Jonathan Toews 10.00 25.00
RRKJ Kent Johnson 12.00 30.00
RRKK Kirill Kaprizov SP 20.00 50.00
RRKV Pyotr Kochetkov 12.00 30.00
RRLR Lucas Raymond 10.00 25.00
RRMB Matt Boldy 20.00 50.00
RRMM Mitch Marner 10.00 25.00
RRMS Moritz Seider 8.00 20.00
RRNM Nathan MacKinnon 25.00 60.00
RROP Owen Power 12.00 30.00
RRPB Patrice Bergeron 8.00 20.00
RRPK Patrick Kane 12.00 30.00
RRQH Quinn Hughes 15.00 40.00
RRRL Lukas Reichel 12.00 30.00
RRSA Jake Sanderson 15.00 40.00
RRSC Mark Scheifele 10.00 25.00
RRSW Shane Wright 15.00 40.00
RRTK Travis Konecny 6.00 15.00
RRTT Tage Thompson 8.00 20.00
RRTZ Trevor Zegras 6.00 15.00
RRWJ Wyatt Johnston 25.00 60.00
RRWN William Nylander 12.00 30.00

2022-23 The Cup Rookie Class of '23

2023AK Andrei Kuzmenko 5.00 12.00
2023AX Arber Xhekaj 5.00 12.00
2023BC Brandt Clarke 5.00 12.00
2023BE Matty Beniers 6.00 15.00
2023BO Matt Boldy 8.00 20.00
2023DG Dylan Guenther 6.00 15.00
2023DH Dylan Holloway 5.00 12.00
2023DJ David Jiricek 5.00 12.00
2023JQ Jack Quinn 4.00 10.00
2023KG Kaiden Guhle 5.00 12.00
2023KJ Kent Johnson 5.00 12.00
2023KM Kirill Marchenko 6.00 15.00
2023LD Lukas Dostal 5.00 12.00
2023LR Lukas Reichel 5.00 12.00
2023MM Matias Maccelli 4.00 10.00
2023MR Marco Rossi 6.00 15.00
2023OP Owen Power 5.00 12.00
2023PK Pyotr Kochetkov 5.00 12.00
2023SA Jake Sanderson 6.00 15.00
2023SL Juraj Slafkovsky 12.00 30.00
2023SW Shane Wright 6.00 15.00

2022-23 The Cup Rookie Class of '23 Autographs Gold

2023AX Arber Xhekaj 20.00 50.00
2023BC Brandt Clarke 20.00 50.00
2023BM Ben Meyers 10.00 25.00
2023BO Matt Boldy 50.00 125.00
2023CK Cole Koepke 10.00 25.00
2023DG Dylan Guenther 25.00 60.00
2023JB Jonatan Berggren 15.00 40.00
2023JP Juuso Parssinen 10.00 25.00
2023KG Kaiden Guhle 20.00 50.00
2023KJ Kent Johnson 20.00 50.00
2023KK Kaedan Korczak 8.00 20.00
2023LD Lukas Dostal 20.00 50.00
2023LJ Lucas Johansen 8.00 20.00
2023LR Lukas Reichel 20.00 50.00
2023MC Marc McLaughlin 10.00 25.00
2023MR Marco Rossi 25.00 60.00
2023NC Noah Cates 10.00 25.00
2023ND Nick DeSimone 10.00 25.00
2023NP Nick Perbix 8.00 20.00
2023OP Owen Power 40.00 100.00
2023PH Pontus Holmberg 10.00 25.00
2023RA Ronnie Attard 10.00 25.00
2023RW Reilly Walsh 10.00 25.00
2023SA Jake Sanderson 25.00 60.00
2023SL Juraj Slafkovsky 125.00 300.00
2023SW Shane Wright 50.00 125.00

2022-23 The Cup Rookie Class of '23 Patches

2023AK Andrei Kuzmenko 12.00 30.00
2023AX Arber Xhekaj 12.00 30.00
2023BC Brandt Clarke 12.00 30.00
2023BE Matty Beniers 15.00 40.00
2023BM Ben Meyers 6.00 15.00
2023BO Matt Boldy 20.00 50.00
2023BS Braden Schneider 10.00 25.00
2023CK Cole Koepke 6.00 15.00
2023DG Dylan Guenther 15.00 40.00
2023DH Dylan Holloway 12.00 30.00
2023DJ David Jiricek 12.00 30.00
2023EK Erik Kallgren 6.00 15.00
2023JB Jonatan Berggren 10.00 25.00
2023JL Jakub Lauko 8.00 20.00
2023JP Juuso Parssinen 6.00 15.00
2023JQ Jack Quinn 10.00 25.00
2023JS Jordan Spence 6.00 15.00
2023KG Kaiden Guhle 12.00 30.00
2023KJ Kent Johnson 12.00 30.00
2023KK Kaedan Korczak 5.00 12.00
2023KM Kirill Marchenko 15.00 40.00
2023LD Lukas Dostal 12.00 30.00
2023LJ Lucas Johansen 5.00 12.00
2023LR Lukas Reichel 12.00 30.00
2023MB Matej Blumel 8.00 20.00
2023MC Marc McLaughlin 6.00 15.00
2023ME Michael Eyssimont 6.00 15.00
2023MM Matias Maccelli 10.00 25.00
2023MR Marco Rossi 15.00 40.00
2023MS Mads Sogaard 8.00 20.00
2023NB Nick Blankenburg 5.00 12.00
2023NC Noah Cates 6.00 15.00
2023ND Nick DeSimone 6.00 15.00
2023NP Nick Perbix 5.00 12.00
2023OP Owen Power 12.00 30.00
2023PH Pontus Holmberg 6.00 15.00
2023PK Pyotr Kochetkov 12.00 30.00
2023RA Ronnie Attard 6.00 15.00
2023RW Reilly Walsh 6.00 15.00
2023SA Jake Sanderson 15.00 40.00
2023SL Juraj Slafkovsky 40.00 100.00
2023SP Samuel Poulin 8.00 20.00
2023SW Shane Wright 15.00 40.00
2023TB Thomas Bordeleau 6.00 15.00
2023WB William Bitten 6.00 15.00

2022-23 The Cup Rookie Gear Relic Autographs

RGBC Brandt Clarke 40.00 100.00
RGBE Matty Beniers 125.00 300.00
RGDG Dylan Guenther 50.00 125.00
RGJB Jonatan Berggren 30.00 80.00
RGJS Jake Sanderson 80.00 200.00
RGKJ Kent Johnson 60.00 150.00
RGLR Lukas Reichel 40.00 100.00
RGOP Owen Power 125.00 300.00
RGSW Shane Wright 125.00 300.00
RGWJ Wyatt Johnston 150.00 400.00

2022-23 The Cup Scripted Swatches

SMBC Brandt Clarke 50.00 125.00
SMBM Brad Marchand 50.00 125.00
SMCA Cam Atkinson 25.00 60.00
SMCM Connor McDavid 300.00 800.00
SMDG Dylan Guenther 80.00 200.00
SMFP Felix Potvin 125.00 300.00
SMIS Ilya Sorokin 40.00 100.00
SMJP Juuso Parssinen 25.00 60.00
SMJS Juraj Slafkovsky 200.00 500.00
SMMB Matty Beniers 100.00 250.00
SMMS Mark Stone 125.00 300.00
SMOP Owen Power 50.00 125.00
SMSW Shane Wright 80.00 200.00
SMTE Teuvo Teravainen 25.00 60.00
SMTM Timo Meier 25.00 60.00
SMTT Tage Thompson 30.00 80.00

2022-23 The Cup Sepia Signature Patches

SSPCM Connor McDavid 400.00 1000.00
SSPIS Ilya Sorokin 40.00 100.00
SSPJH Jonathan Huberdeau 30.00 80.00
SSPJS Juraj Slafkovsky 250.00 600.00
SSPKJ Kent Johnson 50.00 125.00
SSPMB Matty Beniers 60.00 150.00
SSPOP Owen Power 50.00 125.00
SSPRH Roope Hintz 30.00 80.00
SSPSA Juuse Saros 50.00 125.00
SSPSW Shane Wright 60.00 150.00
SSPTS Tim Stutzle 30.00 80.00
SSPTT Tage Thompson 30.00 80.00
SSPWJ Wyatt Johnston 100.00 250.00

2022-23 The Cup Signature Patches

SPAV Andrei Vasilevskiy/99 30.00 80.00
SPBC Brandt Clarke/99 40.00 100.00
SPBE Matty Beniers/99 200.00 500.00
SPBM Brad Marchand/25 60.00 150.00
SPCC Charlie Coyle/99 20.00 50.00
SPCS Chandler Stephenson/99 15.00 40.00
SPDG Dylan Guenther/99 50.00 125.00
SPGL Gabriel Landeskog/99 30.00 80.00
SPIS Ilya Sorokin/99 30.00 80.00
SPJA Tristan Jarry/99 20.00 50.00
SPJB Jonatan Berggren/99 30.00 80.00
SPKG Kaiden Guhle/99 40.00 100.00
SPKJ Kent Johnson/99 40.00 100.00
SPKV Arthur Kaliyev/99 20.00 50.00
SPLR Lukas Reichel/99 40.00 100.00
SPMH Miro Heiskanen/99 25.00 60.00
SPMR Mikko Rantanen/25 60.00 150.00
SPNS Nick Suzuki/25 60.00 150.00
SPOP Owen Power/99 80.00 200.00
SPPG Philipp Grubauer/99 20.00 50.00
SPRH Roope Hintz/25 30.00 80.00
SPRJ Roman Josi/25 40.00 100.00
SPSA Jake Sanderson/99 50.00 125.00
SPSR Sam Reinhart/25 30.00 80.00
SPSW Shane Wright/99 100.00 250.00
SPSY Juraj Slafkovsky/99 1200.00 3000.00
SPSZ Nick Schmaltz/99 15.00 40.00
SPTJ Tanner Jeannot/99 12.00 30.00
SPTK Torey Krug/99 6.00 15.00
SPTN Tage Thompson/25 40.00 100.00
SPTS Tim Stutzle/25 60.00 150.00
SPWJ Wyatt Johnston/99 150.00 400.00

2022-23 The Cup Signature Renditions

SRBB Brent Burns 15.00 40.00
SRBC Brandt Clarke 30.00 80.00
SRBO Matt Boldy 50.00 125.00
SRCM Connor McDavid SP 250.00 600.00
SRJS Juraj Slafkovsky 150.00 400.00
SROR Bobby Orr SP 100.00 250.00
SRRH Roope Hintz 20.00 50.00
SRSD Shane Doan 12.00 30.00
SRSW Shane Wright 40.00 100.00
SRTJ Tanner Jeannot 10.00 25.00
SRTT Tage Thompson 20.00 50.00
SRWE William Eklund 20.00 50.00
SRWG Wayne Gretzky SP 300.00 800.00

2022-23 The Cup Signature Renditions Combos

SR2GM Mark Messier Wayne Gretzky SP 800.00 2000.00

2022-23 The Cup The NHL Collection Patch Autographs

NHLAL Alexis Lafreniere/25 150.00 400.00
NHLBC Brandt Clarke/35 100.00 250.00
NHLBE Matty Beniers/35 150.00 400.00
NHLBR Bill Ranford/25 15.00 40.00
NHLDG Dylan Guenther/35 80.00 200.00
NHLIS Ilya Sorokin/25 60.00 150.00
NHLJB Jonatan Berggren/35 30.00 80.00
NHLJH Jonathan Huberdeau/25 25.00 60.00
NHLJS Juraj Slafkovsky/35 400.00 1000.00
NHLKJ Kent Johnson/35 60.00 150.00
NHLMB Matt Boldy/35 100.00 250.00
NHLMF Mario Ferraro/25 12.00 30.00
NHLMR Mikko Rantanen/25 80.00 200.00
NHLMS Mark Stone/25 100.00 250.00
NHLOP Owen Power/35 125.00 300.00
NHLPG Philipp Grubauer/25 20.00 50.00
NHLRL Lukas Reichel/35 80.00 200.00
NHLSA Jake Sanderson/35 80.00 200.00
NHLSR Sam Reinhart/25 40.00 100.00
NHLSW Shane Wright/35 80.00 200.00
NHLTT Tage Thompson/25 25.00 60.00
NHLWJ Wyatt Johnston/35 200.00 500.00

2022-23 The Cup The Show

SWAP Artemi Panarin 10.00 25.00
SWBH Bobby Hull 10.00 25.00
SWBO Bobby Orr 20.00 50.00
SWBP Brayden Point 6.00 15.00
SWBS Braden Schneider 8.00 20.00
SWBY Matt Boldy 15.00 40.00
SWCC Cole Caufield 10.00 25.00
SWCM Connor McDavid 25.00 60.00
SWDG Dylan Guenther 12.00 30.00
SWEM Evgeni Malkin 10.00 25.00
SWJB Jonatan Berggren 8.00 20.00
SWJH Jack Hughes 12.00 30.00
SWJR Jason Robertson 8.00 20.00
SWJS Juraj Slafkovsky 25.00 60.00
SWKJ Kent Johnson 10.00 25.00
SWKK Kirill Kaprizov 15.00 40.00
SWKM Kirill Marchenko 12.00 30.00
SWMB Matty Beniers 12.00 30.00
SWNM Nathan MacKinnon 20.00 50.00
SWOP Owen Power 10.00 25.00
SWPR Patrick Roy 12.00 30.00
SWSC Sidney Crosby 20.00 50.00
SWTZ Trevor Zegras 5.00 12.00
SWWG Wayne Gretzky 30.00 80.00
SWWJ Wyatt Johnston 20.00 50.00

2022-23 The Cup The Show Autographs

SWBO Bobby Orr SP 150.00 250.00
SWBY Matt Boldy 60.00 150.00
SWCM Connor McDavid SP 250.00 600.00
SWDG Dylan Guenther 50.00 125.00
SWJB Jonatan Berggren 30.00 80.00
SWJS Juraj Slafkovsky 150.00 400.00
SWKJ Kent Johnson 40.00 100.00
SWOP Owen Power 40.00 100.00
SWPR Patrick Roy SP 80.00 200.00
SWWG Wayne Gretzky SP 500.00 1200.00
SWWJ Wyatt Johnston 125.00 300.00

2022-23 The Cup The Show Autographs Black

SBBC Brandt Clarke 40.00 100.00
SBCM Connor McDavid SP 250.00 600.00
SBJM Jared McCann 15.00 40.00
SBJO Jake Oettinger 30.00 80.00
SBJS Juraj Slafkovsky 150.00 400.00
SBMD Marcel Dionne 25.00 60.00
SBMG Mike Gartner 25.00 60.00
SBMR Mikko Rantanen 50.00 125.00
SBRG Ryan Getzlaf 20.00 50.00
SBRO Ryan O'Reilly 20.00 50.00
SBSA Jake Sanderson SP 50.00 125.00
SBSW Shane Wright 50.00 125.00
SBSY Steve Yzerman SP 125.00 300.00
SBTT Tage Thompson 25.00 60.00
SBWG Wayne Gretzky SP 500.00 1200.00

2022-23 The Cup The Show Black

SBAK Andrei Kuzmenko 10.00 25.00
SBBC Brandt Clarke 10.00 25.00
SBBH Bo Horvat 6.00 15.00
SBBO Matt Boldy 15.00 40.00
SBCM Connor McDavid 25.00 60.00
SBDH Dylan Holloway 10.00 25.00
SBDJ David Jiricek 10.00 25.00
SBJM Jared McCann 4.00 10.00
SBJO Jake Oettinger 8.00 20.00
SBJS Juraj Slafkovsky 25.00 60.00
SBKM Kirill Marchenko 12.00 30.00
SBMA Jonathan Marchessault 6.00 15.00
SBMB Matty Beniers 12.00 30.00
SBMD Marcel Dionne 6.00 15.00
SBMG Mike Gartner 6.00 15.00
SBMR Mikko Rantanen 12.00 30.00
SBMZ Mats Zuccarello 5.00 12.00
SBPR Patrick Roy 12.00 30.00
SBRG Ryan Getzlaf 5.00 12.00
SBRO Ryan O'Reilly 5.00 12.00
SBSA Jake Sanderson 12.00 30.00
SBSW Shane Wright 12.00 30.00
SBSY Steve Yzerman 12.00 30.00
SBTT Tage Thompson 6.00 15.00
SBWG Wayne Gretzky 30.00 80.00

2023-24 The Cup

1 Jake Guentzel 3.00 8.00
2 Steven Stamkos 4.00 10.00
3 Matty Beniers 2.50 6.00
4 Bobby Orr 8.00 20.00
5 Martin Brodeur 5.00 12.00
6 Igor Shesterkin 4.00 10.00
7 Mark Stone 2.50 6.00
8 Kyle Connor 3.00 8.00
9 Mikko Rantanen 5.00 12.00
10 Troy Terry 1.50 4.00
11 Patrick Roy 5.00 12.00
12 Mitch Marner 3.00 8.00
13 Dylan Larkin 2.50 6.00
14 Carter Verhaeghe 2.00 5.00
15 Brent Burns 2.00 5.00
16 Andrei Vasilevskiy 3.00 8.00
17 Jeremy Swayman 3.00 8.00
18 Nico Hischier 3.00 8.00
19 Kevin Fiala 1.50 4.00
20 Petr Mrazek 1.50 4.00
21 Nazem Kadri 2.50 6.00
22 Sebastian Aho 3.00 8.00
23 Brad Marchand 4.00 10.00
24 Brock Nelson 2.00 5.00
25 Mason McTavish 2.00 5.00
26 Alexis Lafreniere 3.00 8.00
27 Travis Konecny 2.00 5.00
28 Logan Couture 2.50 6.00
29 Ilya Sorokin 3.00 8.00
30 Alex DeBrincat 2.50 6.00
31 Clayton Keller 2.50 6.00
32 Jacob Markstrom 2.00 5.00
33 Anze Kopitar 3.00 8.00
34 Mark Messier 4.00 10.00
35 Moritz Seider 2.50 6.00
36 William Nylander 4.00 10.00
37 Rasmus Dahlin 2.50 6.00
38 Brady Tkachuk 3.00 8.00
39 Wyatt Johnston 4.00 10.00
40 Brian Leetch 1.50 4.00
41 Marc-Andre Fleury 4.00 10.00
42 Jordan Kyrou 2.00 5.00
43 Roman Josi 2.00 5.00
44 Connor McDavid 10.00 25.00
45 Joel Farabee 2.00 5.00
46 Jason Robertson 3.00 8.00
47 Artemi Panarin 4.00 10.00
48 Andrei Kuzmenko 2.00 5.00
49 Corey Crawford 2.00 5.00
50 Nathan MacKinnon 8.00 20.00
51 Johnny Gaudreau 3.00 8.00
52 Trevor Zegras 2.00 5.00
53 Cole Perfetti 2.00 5.00
54 Elias Pettersson 3.00 8.00
55 John Carlson 2.00 5.00
56 Casey Mittelstadt 2.00 5.00
57 Jordan Binnington 3.00 8.00
58 Kirill Kaprizov 6.00 15.00
59 Cale Makar 5.00 12.00
60 Shane Wright 2.50 6.00
61 Juraj Slafkovsky 4.00 10.00
62 Tom Wilson 2.00 5.00
63 Brock Boeser 2.50 6.00
64 Nick Suzuki 4.00 10.00
65 Jack Eichel 3.00 8.00
66 Roope Hintz 2.50 6.00
67 Cole Sillinger 1.50 4.00
68 Evgeni Malkin 4.00 10.00
69 Tomas Hertl 2.00 5.00
70 Jack Hughes 5.00 12.00
71 Ryan Nugent-Hopkins 2.50 6.00
72 Tim Stutzle 2.50 6.00
73 Boone Jenner 2.00 5.00
74 Nikita Kucherov 4.00 10.00
75 Wayne Gretzky 12.00 30.00
76 Aleksander Barkov 3.00 8.00
77 Vladimir Tarasenko 3.00 8.00
78 Leon Draisaitl 6.00 15.00
79 Teuvo Teravainen 2.00 5.00
80 Robert Thomas 2.00 5.00
81 Travis Sanheim 1.25 3.00
82 Jonathan Huberdeau 2.50 6.00
83 Tage Thompson 2.50 6.00
84 Andrei Svechnikov 2.50 6.00
85 David Pastrnak 5.00 12.00
86 Kris Letang 2.50 6.00
87 Sidney Crosby 8.00 20.00
88 Philipp Grubauer 2.00 5.00
89 Matt Boldy 3.00 8.00
90 Mike Richter 2.00 5.00
91 Matthew Tkachuk 4.00 10.00
92 Juuse Saros 2.50 6.00
93 Auston Matthews 8.00 20.00
94 Cole Caufield 4.00 10.00
95 Mathew Barzal 2.50 6.00
96 Nick Schmaltz 1.50 4.00
97 Joe Pavelski 2.50 6.00
98 Chandler Stephenson 1.50 4.00
99 Patrick Kane 4.00 10.00
100 Ryan O'Reilly 2.00 5.00
101 Cole McWard JSY AU/249 RC 20.00 50.00
102 Bobby McMann JSY AU/249 RC 50.00125.00
103 Henry Thrun JSY AU/249 RC 20.00 50.00
104 Brock Faber JSY AU/249 RC 250.00 600.00
105 Tyler Kleven JSY AU/249 RC 20.00 50.00
106 Jake Livingstone JSY AU/249 RC 20.0050.00
107 Hunter McKown/249 RC 3.00 8.00
108 Nikita Nesterenko JSY AU/249 RC 20.00 50.00
109 Walker Duehr JSY AU/249 RC 15.00 40.00
110 Tyson Foerster JSY AU/249 RC 80.00 200.00
111 Danil Gushchin JSY AU/249 RC 20.00 50.00
112 Owen Beck JSY AU/249 RC 40.00 100.00
113 Devon Levi JSY AU/249 RC 150.00 400.00
114 Luke Philp JSY AU/249 RC 20.00 50.00
115 Arnaud Durandeau JSY AU/249 RC 20.00 50.00
116 Yaroslav Askarov JSY AU/249 RC 150.00 400.00
117 Ridly Greig JSY AU/249 RC 50.00 125.00
118 Tye Kartye JSY AU/249 RC 30.00 80.00
119 Matt Murray JSY AU/249 RC 20.00 50.00
120 David Gust JSY AU/249 RC 20.00 50.00
121 Samuel Bolduc JSY AU/249 RC 20.00 50.00
122 Lukas Rousek JSY AU/249 RC 15.00 40.00
123 Joona Koppanen JSY AU/249 RC 15.0040.00
124 Marco Kasper JSY AU/249 RC 125.00300.00
125 Jakob Pelletier JSY AU/249 RC 25.00 60.00
126 Jiri Patera JSY AU/249 RC 30.00 80.00
127 Luke Evangelista JSY AU/249 RC 40.00 100.00
128 Matthew Knies JSY AU/249 RC 500.00 1200.00
129 Vincent Desharnais JSY AU/249 RC 25.00 60.00
130 Wyatt Kaiser JSY AU/249 RC 20.00 50.00
131 Will Cuylle JSY AU/249 RC 125.00 300.00
132 Dustin Wolf JSY AU/249 RC 300.00 800.00
133 Stanislav Svozil JSY AU/249 RC 15.00 40.00
134 Aidan McDonough JSY AU/249 RC 15.00 40.00
135 Sean Farrell JSY AU/249 RC 20.00 50.00
136 Cole Guttman JSY AU/249 RC 20.00 50.00
137 William Dufour JSY AU/249 RC 15.00 40.00
138 Adam Ginning JSY AU/249 RC 20.00 50.00
139 Vincent Iorio JSY AU/249 RC 20.00 50.00
140 Leevi Merilainen JSY AU/249 RC 20.0050.00
141 Matt Coronato JSY AU/249 RC 100.00250.00
142 Elliot Desnoyers JSY AU/249 RC 20.0050.00
143 Simon Edvinsson JSY AU/249 RC 80.00 200.00
144 Egor Afanasyev/249 RC 3.00 8.00
145 Tristen Robins JSY AU/249 RC 20.00 50.00
146 Jaxson Stauber JSY AU/249 RC 20.00 50.00
147 Adam Fantilli JSY AU/99 RC 1200.003000.00
148 Luke Hughes JSY AU/99 RC 400.00 1000.00
149 Logan Cooley JSY AU/99 RC 600.001500.00
150 Connor Bedard JSY AU/99 RC 8000.00 20000.00
151 Ivan Miroshnichenko JSY AU/249 RC 50.00 125.00
152 Justin Sourdif JSY AU/249 RC 20.00 50.00
153 Jonathan Gruden JSY AU/249 RC 20.0050.00
154 Ryker Evans JSY AU/249 RC 30.00 80.00
155 Alex Laferriere JSY AU/249 RC 50.00 125.00
156 Nick Swaney/249 RC 3.00 8.00
157 Zach Benson JSY AU/249 RC 80.00 200.00
158 Hugh McGing JSY AU/249 RC 20.00 50.00
159 Jet Greaves/249 RC 5.00 12.00
160 Milos Kelemen JSY AU/249 RC 20.00 50.00
161 Kevin Korchinski JSY AU/249 RC 50.00 125.00
162 Jiri Kulich JSY AU/249 RC 80.00 200.00
163 Matthew Kessel JSY AU/249 RC 15.00 40.00
164 Akito Hirose JSY AU/249 RC 15.00 40.00
165 Samuel Knazko JSY AU/249 RC 20.00 50.00
166 Jayden Struble/249 RC 4.00 10.00
167 John Beecher JSY AU/249 RC 40.00 100.00
168 Drew Helleson/249 RC 3.00 8.00
169 Michael Kesselring JSY AU/249 RC 20.00 50.00
170 Tristan Luneau JSY AU/249 RC 20.00 50.00
171 Isak Rosen JSY AU/249 RC 20.00 50.00
172 Raphael Lavoie JSY AU/249 RC 20.00 50.00
173 Martin Pospisil JSY AU/249 RC 25.00 60.00
174 Billy Sweezey JSY AU/249 RC 20.00 50.00
175 Matthew Poitras JSY AU/249 RC 100.00 250.00
176 Pavel Mintyukov JSY AU/249 RC 50.00 125.00
177 Fraser Minten JSY AU/249 RC 40.00 100.00
178 Mackie Samoskevich JSY AU/249 RC 60.00 150.00
179 Connor Zary JSY AU/249 RC 60.00 150.00
180 Matt Savoie JSY AU/249 RC 100.00 250.00
181 Olle Eriksson Ek/249 RC 3.00 8.00
182 Angus Crookshank/249 RC 3.00 8.00
183 Arturs Silovs/249 RC 15.00 40.00
184 Emil Andrae/249 RC 3.00 8.00
185 Ryan Shea/249 RC 3.00 8.00
186 Ty Emberson/249 RC 3.00 8.00
187 Dmitri Voronkov/249 RC 4.00 10.00
188 Daemon Hunt/249 RC 3.00 8.00
189 Mason Lohrei/249 RC 15.00 40.00
190 Marc Del Gaizo/249 RC 3.00 8.00
191 Uvis Balinskis JSY AU/249 RC 20.00 50.00
192 Ryan Johnson/249 RC 4.00 10.00
193 Jackson LaCombe/249 RC 3.00 8.00
194 Roby Jarventie/249 RC 3.00 8.00
195 Ryan Winterton/249 RC 3.00 8.00
196 Sam Malinski/249 RC 3.00 8.00
197 John Ludvig/249 RC 3.00 8.00
198 Emil Heineman/249 RC 4.00 10.00
199 Leo Carlsson JSY AU/99 RC 800.00 2000.00
200 Simon Nemec JSY AU/99 RC 80.00 200.00

2023-24 The Cup Gold Spectrum Variation

101 Cole McWard AU/36 12.00 30.00
102 Bobby McMann AU/36 20.00 50.00
103 Henry Thrun AU/36 12.00 30.00
105 Tyler Kleven AU/36 20.00 50.00
106 Jake Livingstone AU/36 12.00 30.00
108 Nikita Nesterenko AU/36 12.00 30.00
109 Walker Duehr AU/36 10.00 25.00
110 Tyson Foerster AU/36 40.00 100.00
111 Danil Gushchin AU/36 20.00 50.00
112 Owen Beck AU/36 20.00 50.00
113 Devon Levi AU/36 40.00 100.00
114 Luke Philp AU/36 12.00 30.00
115 Arnaud Durandeau AU/36 12.00 30.00
116 Yaroslav Askarov AU/36 40.00 100.00
117 Ridly Greig AU/36 20.00 50.00
118 Tye Kartye AU/36 20.00 50.00
119 Matt Murray AU/36 12.00 30.00
120 David Gust AU/36 12.00 30.00
121 Samuel Bolduc AU/36 12.00 30.00
122 Lukas Rousek AU/36 10.00 25.00
123 Joona Koppanen AU/36 10.00 25.00
124 Marco Kasper AU/36 50.00 125.00
125 Jakob Pelletier AU/36 15.00 40.00
126 Jiri Patera AU/36 20.00 50.00
127 Luke Evangelista AU/36 20.00 50.00
129 Vincent Desharnais AU/36 15.00 40.00
130 Wyatt Kaiser AU/36 12.00 30.00
131 Will Cuylle AU/36 20.00 50.00
132 Dustin Wolf AU/36 150.00 400.00
133 Stanislav Svozil AU/36 10.00 25.00
134 Aidan McDonough AU/36 10.00 25.00
135 Sean Farrell AU/36 12.00 30.00
136 Cole Guttman AU/36 12.00 30.00
137 William Dufour AU/36 10.00 25.00
138 Adam Ginning AU/36 12.00 30.00
139 Vincent Iorio AU/36 12.00 30.00
140 Leevi Merilainen AU/36 15.00 40.00
141 Matt Coronato AU/36 20.00 50.00
142 Elliot Desnoyers AU/36 12.00 30.00
143 Simon Edvinsson AU/36 25.00 60.00
145 Tristen Robins AU/36 12.00 30.00
146 Jaxson Stauber AU/36 12.00 30.00
150 Connor Bedard AU/24 2000.00 5000.00
151 Ivan Miroshnichenko AU/36 20.00 50.00
152 Justin Sourdif AU/36 12.00 30.00
153 Jonathan Gruden AU/36 12.00 30.00
154 Ryker Evans AU/36 15.00 40.00
155 Alex Laferriere AU/36 20.00 50.00
156 Nick Swaney AU/36 12.00 30.00
157 Zach Benson AU/36 20.00 50.00
158 Hugh McGing AU/36 12.00 30.00
159 Jet Greaves AU/36 30.00 80.00
160 Milos Kelemen AU/36 12.00 30.00
161 Kevin Korchinski AU/36 20.00 50.00
162 Jiri Kulich AU/36 40.00 100.00
164 Akito Hirose AU/36 10.00 25.00
165 Samuel Knazko AU/36 15.00 40.00
167 John Beecher AU/36 25.00 60.00
169 Michael Kesselring AU/36 20.00 50.00
170 Tristan Luneau AU/36 12.00 30.00
171 Isak Rosen AU/36 12.00 30.00
172 Raphael Lavoie AU/36 12.00 30.00
173 Martin Pospisil AU/36 20.00 50.00
174 Billy Sweezey AU/36 12.00 30.00
175 Matthew Poitras AU/36 25.00 60.00
176 Pavel Mintyukov AU/36 20.00 50.00
177 Fraser Minten AU/36 25.00 60.00
179 Connor Zary AU/36 25.00 60.00
180 Matt Savoie AU/36 25.00 60.00
181 Olle Eriksson Ek AU/36 12.00 30.00
189 Mason Lohrei AU/36 20.00 50.00
191 Uvis Balinskis AU/36 12.00 30.00
195 Ryan Winterton AU/36 12.00 30.00
199 Leo Carlsson AU/24 125.00 400.00

2023-24 The Cup Baroque Autographs

BQAM Al MacInnis 30.00 80.00
BQDG Doug Gilmour 30.00 80.00
BQDP Denis Potvin 25.00 60.00
BQJK Jari Kurri 25.00 60.00
BQJS Joe Sakic SP 125.00 300.00
BQKP Keith Primeau 15.00 40.00
BQKS Kevin Stevens 20.00 50.00
BQNL Nicklas Lidstrom 60.00 150.00
BQPE Phil Esposito SP 40.00 100.00
BQRL Rejean Lemelin 15.00 40.00
BQRV Rogie Vachon 25.00 60.00
BQSB Scotty Bowman 25.00 60.00
BQTL Trevor Linden 25.00 60.00
BQWO Willie O'Ree 30.00 80.00
BQYC Yvan Cournoyer 25.00 60.00

2023-24 The Cup Color Coded Autographs

CCBB Brock Boeser 15.00 40.00
CCBP Brian Propp 10.00 25.00
CCCB Connor Bedard SP 600.00 1500.00
CCCO Logan Cooley SP 150.00 400.00
CCDL Devon Levi 30.00 80.00
CCDS Darryl Sittler 12.00 30.00
CCHZ Henrik Zetterberg SP 60.00 150.00
CCIM Ivan Miroshnichenko 20.00 50.00
CCLC Leo Carlsson 125.00 300.00
CCSN Simon Nemec 25.00 60.00
CCSW Shane Wright 15.00 40.00
CCTG Tony Granato 8.00 20.00
CCVT Vladimir Tarasenko SP 20.00 50.00
CCZB Zach Benson 20.00 50.00

2023-24 The Cup Cup Coronation

CRAD Alex Delvecchio AU 20.00 50.00
CREM Evgeni Malkin PATCH 20.00 50.00
CRLR Larry Robinson AU 80.00 200.00
CRMS Mark Stone PATCH 12.00 30.00
CRNM Nathan MacKinnon PATCH 40.00 100.00
CRRT Robert Thomas PATCH 60.00 150.00
CRSS Steven Stamkos PATCH 20.00 50.00
CRTB Tom Barrasso AU 50.00 125.00

2023-24 The Cup Cup Quads Jerseys

C4BASJ Aho/Svechnikov Burns/Jarvis 20.00 50.00
C4BFCF Bedard/Fantilli Faber/Cooley 80.00 200.00
C4BRTL Tkachuk/Barkov Reinhart/Lundell 25.00 60.00
C4BSHJ Benn/Seguin/Johnston/Hintz 25.0060.00
C4CGFE Couture/Ferraro/Eklund/Hertl 15.0040.00
C4CKSF Couturier/Konecny Sanheim/Foerster 25.00 60.00
C4CKWO Ovechkin/Carlson Wilson/Kuemper 50.00 125.00
C4DBPH Hughes/Pettersson Boeser/Demko 30.00 80.00
C4FHKC Hughes/Foerster Knies/Carlsson 50.00 125.00
C4GTSS Sanderson/Tkachuk Stutzle/Giroux 20.00 50.00
C4GZEB Greig/Evangelista Zary/Benson 25.00 60.00
C4JGFM Gaudreau/Jenner Fantilli/Marchenko 40.00 100.00
C4KDDF Kopitar/Doughty Danault/Fiala 25.00 60.00
C4KMHL Huberdeau/Kadri Lindholm/Markstrom 15.00 40.00
C4KNDS Draisaitl/Nugent-Hopkins Kane/Skinner 40.00 100.00
C4LCSR Seider/Raymond Larkin/Compher 20.00 50.00
C4MHHN Hughes/Hughes Nemec/Mercer 40.00 100.00
C4MLKG Malkin/Letang Karlsson/Guentzel 25.00 60.00
C4MMBG MacKinnon/Makar Georgiev/Byram 50.00 125.00
C4MRKB Bedard/Raddysh Kurashev/Mrazek 80.00 200.00
C4MSCS Caufield/Suzuki Slafkovsky/Montembeault 25.00 60.00
C4MUPM Pastrnak/Marchand Ullmark/McAvoy 30.00 80.00
C4NLBS Nelson/Barzal/Lee/Sorokin 20.00 50.00
C4NMMK Matthews/Marner Nylander/Knies 50.00 125.00
C4OJFS Josi/O'Reilly/Saros/Forsberg 20.0050.00
C4PLFS Panarin/Fox Lafreniere/Shesterkin 25.00 60.00
C4SBKT Kyrou/Binnington Thomas/Saad 20.00 50.00
C4SHVC Hellebuyck/Connor Scheifele/Vilardi 25.00 60.00
C4SKPV Kucherov/Point Stamkos/Vasilevskiy 30.00 80.00
C4SMGB McCann/Beniers Schwartz/Gourde 15.00 40.00
C4SSEH Eichel/Stone Hill/Stephenson 20.00 50.00
C4TCDP Dahlin/Thompson Cozens/Power 15.00 40.00
C4TZMC Zegras/McTavish Carlsson/Terry 40.00 100.00
C4ZBKF Kaprizov/Boldy Faber/Zuccarello 40.00 100.00
C4ZSKC Keller/Cooley Schmaltz/Zucker 40.00 100.00

2023-24 The Cup Cup Trios Jerseys

C3AEA Askarov/Evangelista Afanasyev 20.00 50.00
C3BDS Barzal/Sorokin/Dobson 12.00 30.00
C3BFC Bedard/Carlsson/Fantilli 50.00 125.00
C3BFS Struble/Beck/Farrell 12.00 30.00
C3BKG Bedard/Korchinski/Guttman 50.00 125.00
C3BRT Tkachuk/Barkov/Reinhart 15.00 40.00
C3CMO McDavid/Crosby/Ovechkin 40.00 100.00
C3CWO Ovechkin/Carlson/Wilson 30.00 80.00
C3DGS Georgiev/Demko/Swayman 12.00 30.00
C3DPH Pettersson/Hughes/Demko 20.00 50.00
C3DRF Doughty/Rielly/Fox 10.00 25.00
C3EKP Poitras/Evangelista/Knies 30.00 80.00
C3FBK Kaprizov/Boldy/Fleury 25.00 60.00
C3FHN Nemec/Faber/Hughes 25.00 60.00
C3GLM Gaudreau/Marchenko/Laine 12.00 30.00
C3GSF Savoie/Foerster/Greig 15.00 40.00
C3HFE Hertl/Eklund/Ferraro 10.00 25.00
C3HKT Thomas/Kyrou/Hayes 8.00 20.00
C3JMR Raddysh/Jones/Mrazek 8.00 20.00
C3KFD Kopitar/Fiala/Dubois 15.00 40.00
C3KFF Foerster/Konecny/Farabee 15.00 40.00
C3KHL Huberdeau/Lindholm/Kadri 10.00 25.00
C3KMM McMann/Knies/Minten 30.00 80.00
C3KPS Panarin/Shesterkin/Kreider 15.00 40.00
C3LDS Seider/DeBrincat/Larkin 10.00 25.00
C3MCL Carlsson/Mintyukov/Luneau 25.00 60.00
C3MHH Hughes/Hischier/Meier 20.00 50.00
C3MKG Malkin/Guentzel/Karlsson 15.00 40.00
C3MPM Pastrnak/Marchand/McAvoy 20.0050.00
C3MRM MacKinnon/Makar/Rantanen 30.0080.00
C3MWB McCann/Beniers/Wright 10.00 25.00
C3NDS Draisaitl/Nugent-Hopkins/Skinner 25.00 60.00
C3NMM Matthews/Marner/Nylander 30.00 80.00
C3OJF Josi/Forsberg/O'Reilly 12.00 30.00
C3PRJ Robertson/Johnston/Pavelski 15.00 40.00
C3RBK Kulich/Benson/Rosen 15.00 40.00
C3SCS Caufield/Suzuki/Slafkovsky 15.00 40.00
C3SFG Fantilli/Svozil/Greaves 25.00 60.00
C3SHC Connor/Scheifele/Hellebuyck 15.0040.00
C3SHV Vasilevskiy/Stamkos/Hedman 15.0040.00
C3SKM Keller/Schmaltz/Maccelli 10.00 25.00
C3SLR Savoie/Rousek/Levi 20.00 50.00
C3SME Eichel/Stone/Marchessault 12.00 30.00
C3TAS Aho/Svechnikov/Teravainen 12.00 30.00
C3TSS Tkachuk/Stutzle/Sanderson 12.00 30.00
C3TTD Dahlin/Thompson/Tuch 10.00 25.00
C3TZM Zegras/Terry/McTavish 8.00 20.00
C3WAL Wolf/Askarov/Levi 25.00 60.00
C3WZC Zary/Coronato/Wolf 25.00 60.00
C3ZBC Cooley/Benson/Zary 25.00 60.00

2023-24 The Cup Enshrinements

EKK Kirill Kaprizov/25 60.00 150.00
ENS Nick Suzuki/99 30.00 80.00
ESN Simon Nemec/99 30.00 80.00
ESW Shane Wright/99 20.00 50.00

2023-24 The Cup Expanded Material Autographs

EMCO Logan Cooley/25 100.00 250.00
EMDL Devon Levi/25 80.00 200.00
EMIM Ivan Miroshnichenko/25 50.00 125.00
EMLC Leo Carlsson/25 100.00 250.00
EMSA Mackie Samoskevich/25 50.00 125.00
EMSN Simon Nemec/25 60.00 150.00
EMTF Tyson Foerster/25 60.00 150.00

2023-24 The Cup Foundations Jerseys

FAF Adam Fantilli/99 20.00 50.00
FAV Andrei Vasilevskiy/49 10.00 25.00
FBB Brock Boeser/49 8.00 20.00
FBF Brock Faber/99 15.00 40.00
FBM Brad Marchand/49 12.00 30.00
FBN Brock Nelson/49 6.00 15.00
FCB Connor Bedard/99 125.00 300.00
FCM Cale Makar/49 15.00 40.00
FCO Logan Cooley/99 20.00 50.00
FCZ Connor Zary/99 12.00 30.00
FDL Devon Levi/99 15.00 40.00
FDW Dustin Wolf/99 20.00 50.00
FEP Elias Pettersson/49 10.00 25.00
FGU Jake Guentzel/49 10.00 25.00
FGV Gabe Vilardi/49 6.00 15.00
FHU Jack Hughes/49 15.00 40.00
FIR Isak Rosen/99 6.00 15.00
FJB John Beecher/99 12.00 30.00
FJG Johnny Gaudreau/49 10.00 25.00
FJH Jonathan Huberdeau/49 8.00 20.00
FJK Jiri Kulich/99 12.00 30.00
FJN Josh Norris/49 6.00 15.00
FKH Kevin Hayes/49 5.00 12.00
FKI Kevin Korchinski/99 10.00 25.00
FKK Kirill Kaprizov/49 20.00 50.00
FKN Matthew Knies/99 25.00 60.00
FLC Leo Carlsson/99 20.00 50.00
FLE Luke Evangelista/99 10.00 25.00
FMC Connor McDavid/49 30.00 80.00
FMH Miro Heiskanen/49 8.00 20.00
FMK Marco Kasper/99 15.00 40.00
FMP Matthew Poitras/99 12.00 30.00
FMS Matt Savoie/99 12.00 30.00
FNH Nico Hischier/49 10.00 25.00
FNS Nick Schmaltz/49 5.00 12.00
FPD Pierre-Luc Dubois/49 5.00 12.00
FPG Philipp Grubauer/49 6.00 15.00
FPM Pavel Mintyukov/99 10.00 25.00

FRG Ridly Greig/99 10.00 25.00
FSA Sebastian Aho/49 10.00 25.00
FSE Simon Edvinsson/99 12.00 30.00
FSN Simon Nemec/99 12.00 30.00
FTF Tyson Foerster/99 12.00 30.00
FTT Troy Terry/49 5.00 12.00
FTW Tom Wilson/49 6.00 15.00
FWC Will Cuylle/99 10.00 25.00
FYA Yaroslav Askarov/99 15.00 40.00
FZB Zach Benson/99 10.00 25.00

2023-24 The Cup Graduates Patch Autographs

GDCM Connor McDavid 1000.00 2500.00

2023-24 The Cup Honorable Numbers

HRAV Andrei Vasilevskiy/19 80.00 200.00
HRBR Martin Brodeur/30 150.00 400.00
HRCH Connor Hellebuyck/44 60.00 150.00
HRCO Logan Cooley/92 150.00 400.00
HRDL Devon Levi/27 150.00 400.00
HRHL Henrik Lundqvist/64 80.00 200.00
HRHZ Henrik Zetterberg/40 80.00 200.00
HRKC Kyle Connor/47 40.00 100.00
HRKK Kirill Kaprizov/21 150.00 400.00
HRKM Kirill Marchenko/86 40.00 100.00
HRLC Leo Carlsson/91 100.00 250.00
HRLH Luke Hughes/43 150.00 400.00
HRSA Sebastian Aho/38 80.00 200.00
HRSN Simon Nemec/17 125.00 300.00
HRSW Shane Wright/51 150.00 400.00

2023-24 The Cup Inked Impressions

IIGF Grant Fuhr/25 40.00 100.00
IIJT Joe Thornton/25 40.00 100.00
IIKM Kirill Marchenko/50 30.00 80.00
IIKS Kevin Stevens/50 20.00 50.00
IIMH Miro Heiskanen/50 30.00 80.00
IINE Nikolaj Ehlers/50 25.00 60.00
IINH Nico Hischier/50 40.00 100.00
IITH Tomas Hertl/50 25.00 60.00
IIVT Vladimir Tarasenko/25 40.00 100.00

2023-24 The Cup Limited Logos

LLAF Adam Fantilli AU/50 500.00 1200.00
LLBJ Boone Jenner AU/50 50.00 125.00
LLBT Bryan Trottier AU/25 250.00 600.00
LLCB Connor Bedard AU/50 2000.00 5000.00
LLCC Cole Caufield/50 50.00 125.00
LLCD Corey Crawford AU/25 125.00 300.00
LLCO Logan Cooley AU/50 300.00 800.00
LLDG Dylan Guenther AU/50 60.00 150.00
LLDM Dawson Mercer AU/50 60.00 150.00
LLDP David Pastrnak/25 100.00 250.00
LLDS Derek Sanderson AU/50 80.00 200.00
LLEM Evgeni Malkin/25 50.00 125.00
LLEP Elias Pettersson AU/25 80.00 200.00
LLFG Filip Gustavsson AU/50 50.00 125.00
LLFP Felix Potvin AU/25 200.00 500.00
LLHE Connor Hellebuyck AU/50 100.00 250.00
LLJA Josh Anderson AU/50 40.00 100.00
LLJL John LeClair AU/50 50.00 125.00
LLLC Leo Carlsson AU/50 250.00 600.00
LLMB Matty Beniers/50 30.00 80.00
LLMK Matthew Knies AU/50 800.00 2000.00
LLMS Moritz Seider/50 125.00 300.00
LLMT Matthew Tkachuk/25 125.00 300.00
LLSJ Seth Jarvis AU/50 100.00 250.00
LLSS Sergei Samsonov AU/50 40.00 100.00
LLTA Tony Amonte AU/50 40.00 100.00
LLTM Timo Meier AU/50 50.00 125.00
LLTS Tim Stutzle AU/50 125.00 300.00

2023-24 The Cup LogoMarks

LMAF Adam Fantilli SP 40.00 100.00
LMBN Brock Nelson 12.00 30.00
LMCB Connor Bedard SP 300.00 800.00
LMCC Chris Chelios SP 12.00 30.00
LMCN Cam Neely SP 12.00 30.00
LMCO Chris Osgood 30.00 80.00
LMCP Cole Perfetti 12.00 30.00
LMCY Logan Cooley SP 40.00 100.00
LMCZ Connor Zary 25.00 60.00
LMDL Devon Levi 30.00 80.00
LMJB Johnny Bucyk SP 12.00 30.00
LMJW Joseph Woll 25.00 60.00
LMKU Jari Kurri SP 12.00 30.00
LMLC Leo Carlsson SP 80.00 200.00
LMLH Luke Hughes SP 40.00 100.00
LMMK Matthew Knies 125.00 300.00
LMMP Matthew Poitras 25.00 60.00
LMMR Mike Ricci 30.00 80.00
LMMV Pavel Mintyukov 20.00 50.00
LMSN Simon Nemec 25.00 60.00
LMZB Zach Benson 20.00 50.00

2023-24 The Cup Materialisticks

MSAD Alex DeBrincat/25 20.00 50.00
MSAP Alex Pietrangelo/25 15.00 40.00
MSBT Brady Tkachuk/25 25.00 60.00
MSCG Claude Giroux/25 15.00 40.00
MSDB Drake Batherson/25 15.00 40.00
MSDG Doug Gilmour/25 20.00 50.00
MSDH Dominik Hasek/25 25.00 60.00
MSDL Dylan Larkin/25 20.00 50.00
MSDN Darnell Nurse/25 12.00 30.00
MSEB Ed Belfour/25 15.00 40.00
MSEL Eric Lindros/25 25.00 60.00
MSEM Evgeni Malkin/25 30.00 80.00
MSHZ Henrik Zetterberg/25 20.00 50.00
MSJL John LeClair/25 15.00 40.00
MSJN Joe Nieuwendyk/25 12.00 30.00
MSJS Joe Sakic/25 30.00 80.00
MSWN William Nylander/25 30.00 80.00

2023-24 The Cup Renditions Relics

RRAF Adam Fantilli 20.00 50.00
RRAK Anze Kopitar 10.00 25.00
RRAO Alex Ovechkin 25.00 60.00
RRAP Artemi Panarin 12.00 30.00
RRBF Brock Faber 15.00 40.00
RRBP Brayden Point 8.00 20.00
RRBS Borje Salming 6.00 15.00
RRCB Connor Bedard 40.00 100.00
RRCM Connor McDavid 30.00 80.00
RRCO Logan Cooley 20.00 50.00
RRCP Chris Pronger 6.00 15.00
RRDL Devon Levi 15.00 40.00
RRDP David Pastrnak 15.00 40.00
RREB Ed Belfour 6.00 15.00
RREK Erik Karlsson 8.00 20.00
RRIS Igor Shesterkin 12.00 30.00
RRJR Jeremy Roenick 10.00 25.00
RRJS Joe Sakic 12.00 30.00
RRJT Joe Thornton 10.00 25.00
RRKK Kirill Kaprizov 20.00 50.00
RRLC Leo Carlsson 20.00 50.00
RRLD Leon Draisaitl 20.00 50.00
RRLH Luke Hughes 20.00 50.00
RRMB Martin Brodeur 15.00 40.00
RRMK Matthew Knies 25.00 60.00
RRMS Mats Sundin 6.00 15.00
RRNL Nicklas Lidstrom 6.00 15.00
RRNM Nathan MacKinnon 25.00 60.00
RRPF Peter Forsberg 12.00 30.00
RRPT Pierre Turgeon 5.00 12.00
RRRG Ridly Greig 10.00 25.00
RRRO Jason Robertson 10.00 25.00
RRSC Sidney Crosby 25.00 60.00
RRSE Moritz Seider 8.00 20.00
RRSN Simon Nemec 12.00 30.00

2023-24 The Cup Rookie Gear Relic Autographs

RGBF Brock Faber 80.00 200.00
RGCB Connor Bedard 600.00 1500.00
RGCO Logan Cooley 100.00 250.00
RGDL Devon Levi 80.00 200.00
RGDW Dustin Wolf 100.00 250.00
RGLC Leo Carlsson 100.00 250.00
RGLH Luke Hughes 100.00 250.00
RGMP Matthew Poitras 60.00 150.00
RGSN Simon Nemec 60.00 150.00
RGTF Tyson Foerster 60.00 150.00
RGZB Zach Benson 50.00 125.00

2023-24 The Cup Rookie Rink Gallery

RGAFV1 Adam Fantilli 6.00 15.00
RGAFV2 Adam Fantilli 6.00 15.00
RGAFV3 Adam Fantilli 6.00 15.00
RGAFV4 Adam Fantilli 6.00 15.00
RGCAV1 Leo Carlsson 6.00 15.00
RGCAV2 Leo Carlsson 6.00 15.00
RGCAV3 Leo Carlsson 6.00 15.00
RGCAV4 Leo Carlsson 6.00 15.00
RGCBV1 Connor Bedard 12.00 30.00
RGCBV2 Connor Bedard 50.00 125.00
RGCBV3 Connor Bedard 50.00 125.00
RGCBV4 Connor Bedard 50.00 125.00
RGCZV1 Connor Zary 4.00 10.00
RGCZV2 Connor Zary 4.00 10.00
RGCZV3 Connor Zary 4.00 10.00
RGCZV4 Connor Zary 4.00 10.00
RGDLV1 Devon Levi 5.00 12.00
RGDLV2 Devon Levi 5.00 12.00
RGDLV3 Devon Levi 5.00 12.00
RGDLV4 Devon Levi 5.00 12.00
RGKKV1 Kevin Korchinski 3.00 8.00
RGKKV2 Kevin Korchinski 3.00 8.00
RGKKV3 Kevin Korchinski 3.00 8.00
RGKKV4 Kevin Korchinski 3.00 8.00
RGLCV1 Logan Cooley 6.00 15.00
RGLCV2 Logan Cooley 6.00 15.00
RGLCV3 Logan Cooley 6.00 15.00
RGLCV4 Logan Cooley 6.00 15.00
RGLEV1 Luke Evangelista 3.00 8.00
RGLEV2 Luke Evangelista 3.00 8.00
RGLEV3 Luke Evangelista 3.00 8.00
RGLEV4 Luke Evangelista 3.00 8.00
RGLHV1 Luke Hughes 6.00 15.00
RGLHV2 Luke Hughes 6.00 15.00
RGLHV3 Luke Hughes 6.00 15.00
RGLHV4 Luke Hughes 6.00 15.00
RGMKV1 Matthew Knies 8.00 20.00
RGMKV2 Matthew Knies 8.00 20.00
RGMKV3 Matthew Knies 8.00 20.00
RGMKV4 Matthew Knies 8.00 20.00
RGMPV1 Matthew Poitras 4.00 10.00
RGMPV2 Matthew Poitras 4.00 10.00
RGMPV3 Matthew Poitras 4.00 10.00
RGMPV4 Matthew Poitras 4.00 10.00
RGMSV1 Matt Savoie 4.00 10.00
RGMSV2 Matt Savoie 4.00 10.00
RGMSV3 Matt Savoie 4.00 10.00
RGMSV4 Matt Savoie 4.00 10.00
RGPMV1 Pavel Mintyukov 3.00 8.00
RGPMV2 Pavel Mintyukov 3.00 8.00
RGPMV3 Pavel Mintyukov 3.00 8.00
RGPMV4 Pavel Mintyukov 3.00 8.00
RGRGV1 Ridly Greig 3.00 8.00
RGRGV2 Ridly Greig 3.00 8.00
RGRGV3 Ridly Greig 3.00 8.00
RGRGV4 Ridly Greig 3.00 8.00
RGYAV1 Yaroslav Askarov 5.00 12.00
RGYAV2 Yaroslav Askarov 5.00 12.00
RGYAV3 Yaroslav Askarov 5.00 12.00
RGYAV4 Yaroslav Askarov 5.00 12.00

2023-24 The Cup Rookie Rink Gallery Autographs

RGCAV1 Leo Carlsson 40.00 100.00
RGCAV2 Leo Carlsson 40.00 100.00
RGCAV3 Leo Carlsson 40.00 100.00
RGCAV4 Leo Carlsson 40.00 100.00
RGCBV1 Connor Bedard 500.00 1200.00
RGCBV2 Connor Bedard 500.00 1200.00
RGCBV3 Connor Bedard 500.00 1200.00
RGCBV4 Connor Bedard 500.00 1200.00
RGDLV1 Devon Levi 30.00 80.00
RGDLV2 Devon Levi 30.00 80.00
RGDLV3 Devon Levi 30.00 80.00
RGDLV4 Devon Levi 30.00 80.00
RGKKV1 Kevin Korchinski 20.00 50.00
RGKKV2 Kevin Korchinski 20.00 50.00
RGKKV3 Kevin Korchinski 20.00 50.00
RGKKV4 Kevin Korchinski 20.00 50.00
RGLCV1 Logan Cooley 60.00 150.00
RGLCV2 Logan Cooley 60.00 150.00
RGLCV3 Logan Cooley 60.00 150.00
RGLCV4 Logan Cooley 60.00 150.00
RGLHV1 Luke Hughes 40.00 100.00
RGLHV2 Luke Hughes 40.00 100.00
RGLHV3 Luke Hughes 40.00 100.00
RGLHV4 Luke Hughes 40.00 100.00
RGMPV1 Matthew Poitras 25.00 60.00
RGMPV2 Matthew Poitras 25.00 60.00
RGMPV3 Matthew Poitras 25.00 60.00
RGMPV4 Matthew Poitras 25.00 60.00
RGMSV1 Matt Savoie 25.00 60.00
RGMSV2 Matt Savoie 25.00 60.00
RGMSV3 Matt Savoie 25.00 60.00
RGMSV4 Matt Savoie 25.00 60.00
RGRGV1 Ridly Greig 20.00 50.00
RGRGV2 Ridly Greig 20.00 50.00
RGRGV3 Ridly Greig 20.00 50.00
RGRGV4 Ridly Greig 20.00 50.00

2023-24 The Cup Rookie Rink Gallery Jerseys

*PATCH/35: 1X TO 2.5X BASIC
RGAFV1 Adam Fantilli 8.00 20.00
RGAFV2 Adam Fantilli 8.00 20.00
RGAFV3 Adam Fantilli 8.00 20.00
RGAFV4 Adam Fantilli 8.00 20.00
RGCAV1 Leo Carlsson 8.00 20.00
RGCAV2 Leo Carlsson 8.00 20.00
RGCAV3 Leo Carlsson 8.00 20.00
RGCAV4 Leo Carlsson 8.00 20.00
RGCBV1 Connor Bedard 60.00 150.00
RGCBV2 Connor Bedard 60.00 150.00
RGCBV3 Connor Bedard 60.00 150.00
RGCBV4 Connor Bedard 60.00 150.00
RGCZV1 Connor Zary 5.00 12.00
RGCZV2 Connor Zary 5.00 12.00
RGCZV3 Connor Zary 5.00 12.00
RGCZV4 Connor Zary 5.00 12.00
RGDLV1 Devon Levi 6.00 15.00
RGDLV2 Devon Levi 6.00 15.00
RGDLV3 Devon Levi 6.00 15.00
RGDLV4 Devon Levi 6.00 15.00
RGKKV1 Kevin Korchinski 4.00 10.00
RGKKV2 Kevin Korchinski 4.00 10.00
RGKKV3 Kevin Korchinski 4.00 10.00
RGKKV4 Kevin Korchinski 4.00 10.00
RGLCV1 Logan Cooley 8.00 20.00
RGLCV2 Logan Cooley 8.00 20.00
RGLCV3 Logan Cooley 8.00 20.00
RGLCV4 Logan Cooley 8.00 20.00
RGLEV1 Luke Evangelista 4.00 10.00
RGLEV2 Luke Evangelista 4.00 10.00
RGLEV3 Luke Evangelista 4.00 10.00
RGLEV4 Luke Evangelista 4.00 10.00
RGLHV1 Luke Hughes 8.00 20.00
RGLHV2 Luke Hughes 8.00 20.00
RGLHV3 Luke Hughes 8.00 20.00
RGLHV4 Luke Hughes 8.00 20.00
RGMKV1 Matthew Knies 10.00 25.00
RGMKV2 Matthew Knies 10.00 25.00
RGMKV3 Matthew Knies 10.00 25.00
RGMKV4 Matthew Knies 10.00 25.00
RGMPV1 Matthew Poitras 5.00 12.00
RGMPV2 Matthew Poitras 5.00 12.00
RGMPV3 Matthew Poitras 5.00 12.00
RGMPV4 Matthew Poitras 5.00 12.00
RGMSV1 Matt Savoie 5.00 12.00
RGMSV2 Matt Savoie 5.00 12.00
RGMSV3 Matt Savoie 5.00 12.00
RGMSV4 Matt Savoie 5.00 12.00
RGPMV1 Pavel Mintyukov 4.00 10.00
RGPMV2 Pavel Mintyukov 4.00 10.00
RGPMV3 Pavel Mintyukov 4.00 10.00
RGPMV4 Pavel Mintyukov 4.00 10.00
RGRGV1 Ridly Greig 4.00 10.00
RGRGV2 Ridly Greig 4.00 10.00
RGRGV3 Ridly Greig 4.00 10.00
RGRGV4 Ridly Greig 4.00 10.00
RGYAV1 Yaroslav Askarov 6.00 15.00
RGYAV2 Yaroslav Askarov 6.00 15.00
RGYAV3 Yaroslav Askarov 6.00 15.00
RGYAV4 Yaroslav Askarov 6.00 15.00

2023-24 The Cup Scripted Swatches

SSAV Andrei Vasilevskiy 30.00 80.00
SSCB Connor Bedard 600.00 1500.00
SSCM Connor McDavid 300.00 800.00
SSCO Logan Cooley 125.00 300.00
SSDL Devon Levi 50.00 125.00
SSEP Elias Pettersson 30.00 80.00
SSHL Henrik Lundqvist 125.00 300.00
SSJH Jonathan Huberdeau 25.00 60.00
SSKC Kyle Connor 30.00 80.00
SSKK Kirill Kaprizov 60.00 150.00
SSKL Kris Letang 25.00 60.00
SSLC Leo Carlsson 60.00 150.00
SSMF Marc-Andre Fleury 80.00 200.00
SSSN Simon Nemec 40.00 100.00
SSSW Shane Wright 25.00 60.00

2023-24 The Cup Signature Materials

SMBN Brock Nelson/99 20.00 50.00
SMBR Bryan Rust/99 20.00 50.00
SMCB Connor Bedard/99 1500.00 4000.00
SMCO Logan Cooley/99 125.00 300.00
SMCV Carter Verhaeghe/99 20.00 50.00
SMCZ Connor Zary/99 40.00 100.00
SMDW Dustin Wolf/99 80.00 200.00
SMJH Jonathan Huberdeau/99 25.00 60.00
SMJK Jiri Kulich/99 40.00 100.00
SMJP JJ Peterka/99 20.00 50.00
SMJS Jared Spurgeon/99 20.00 50.00
SMJT John Tavares/25 30.00 80.00
SMKC Kyle Connor/25 30.00 80.00
SMKL Kris Letang/99 25.00 60.00
SMLC Leo Carlsson/99 80.00 200.00
SMLI Devon Levi/99 50.00 125.00
SMMF Marc-Andre Fleury/25 200.00 500.00
SMMH Miro Heiskanen/25 25.00 60.00
SMMP Matthew Poitras/99 40.00 100.00
SMNE Nikolaj Ehlers/99 20.00 50.00
SMNH Nico Hischier/25 40.00 100.00
SMSA Sebastian Aho/99 30.00 80.00
SMSI Nick Suzuki/25 40.00 100.00
SMSW Shane Wright/99 25.00 60.00
SMTF Tyson Foerster/99 40.00 100.00
SMTH Tomas Hertl/99 20.00 50.00
SMTM Timo Meier/99 20.00 50.00
SMTW Tom Wilson/99 20.00 50.00
SMWC Will Cuylle/99 50.00 125.00
SMYA Yaroslav Askarov/99 50.00 125.00

2023-24 The Cup Signature Renditions

SRAD Alex Delvecchio SP 25.00 60.00
SRAF Adam Fantilli 60.00 150.00
SRAM Auston Matthews SP 150.00 400.00
SRBB Brock Boeser 25.00 60.00
SRBT Bryan Trottier 20.00 50.00
SRCA Leo Carlsson 60.00 150.00
SRCB Connor Bedard SP 600.00 1500.00
SRCC Corey Crawford 40.00 100.00
SRCM Connor McDavid SP 600.00 1500.00
SRDS Darryl Sittler SP 30.00 80.00
SRHL Henrik Lundqvist SP 125.00 300.00
SRJQ Jonathan Quick 60.00 150.00
SRJT John Tavares SP 30.00 80.00
SRLC Logan Cooley 60.00 150.00
SRMA Cale Makar SP 200.00 500.00
SRMF Marc-Andre Fleury SP 125.00 300.00
SRMT Mason Marchment 15.00 40.00
SRSN Simon Nemec 40.00 100.00
SRTB Tom Barrasso 25.00 60.00
SRWG Wayne Gretzky SP 800.00 2000.00

2023-24 The Cup Signature Renditions Combos

SR2DW V.Dunn/S.Wright 30.00 80.00
SR2TD K.Tkachuk/S.Doan SP 15.00 40.00

2023-24 The Cup Signature Renditions Retirement

SRRAM Al MacInnis 25.00 60.00
SRRBO Bobby Orr SP 250.00 600.00
SRRCN Cam Neely 40.00 100.00
SRREL Eric Lindros 125.00 300.00
SRRWG Wayne Gretzky SP 400.00 1000.00

2023-24 The Cup The Basics Autographs

BAL Alex Laferriere 15.00 40.00
BBK Owen Beck 15.00 40.00
BBL Brian Leetch SP 25.00 60.00
BCC Chris Chelios 15.00 40.00
BDS Darryl Sittler SP 10.00 25.00
BGS Jet Greaves 15.00 40.00
BIM Ivan Miroshnichenko 15.00 40.00
BJG John Gibson 10.00 25.00
BJT John Tavares SP 15.00 40.00
BKH Jiri Kulich 20.00 50.00
BKK Kevin Korchinski 15.00 40.00
BLC Logan Cooley 50.00 125.00
BMC Matt Coronato 15.00 40.00
BMK Marco Kasper 25.00 60.00
BMP Matthew Poitras 20.00 50.00
BRH Roope Hintz SP 12.00 30.00
BSE Simon Edvinsson 20.00 50.00
BSN Simon Nemec 20.00 50.00
BTL Trevor Linden SP 10.00 25.00
BWC Will Cuylle 15.00 40.00
BYA Yaroslav Askarov 40.00 100.00

2023-24 The Cup The Basics Patch Autographs

BAF Adam Fantilli/25 50.00 125.00
BAV Yaroslav Askarov/25 60.00 150.00
BCB Connor Bedard/25 1000.00 2500.00
BCN Leo Carlsson/25 50.00 125.00
BCO Logan Cooley/25 80.00 200.00
BCZ Connor Zary/25 30.00 80.00
BDL Devon Levi/25 40.00 100.00
BDW Dustin Wolf/25 125.00 300.00
BFR Brock Faber/25 40.00 100.00
BKI Kevin Korchinski/25 25.00 60.00
BNC Simon Nemec/25 30.00 80.00
BPM Pavel Mintyukov/25 25.00 60.00
BPS Matthew Poitras/25 30.00 80.00
BSV Matt Savoie/25 30.00 80.00
BTF Tyson Foerster/25 60.00 150.00
BZB Zach Benson/25 25.00 60.00

2023-24 The Cup The Basics Patches

BBE Matty Beniers 10.00 25.00
BCK Clayton Keller 10.00 25.00
BDP David Pastrnak 20.00 50.00
BLH Luke Hughes 25.00 60.00
BNM Nathan MacKinnon 30.00 80.00
BSC Mark Scheifele 12.00 30.00
BTS Tyler Seguin 10.00 25.00
BTZ Trevor Zegras 8.00 20.00
BVH Victor Hedman 10.00 25.00
BWN William Nylander 15.00 40.00

2023-24 The Cup The NHL Collection Patch Autographs

NHLCB Connor Bedard/35 1200.00 3000.00
NHLCM Cale Makar/25 150.00 400.00
NHLCO Logan Cooley/35 100.00 250.00
NHLDL Devon Levi/35 50.00 125.00
NHLDW Dustin Wolf/35 150.00 400.00
NHLJK Jiri Kulich/35 60.00 150.00
NHLKC Kyle Connor/25 30.00 80.00
NHLLC Leo Carlsson/35 100.00 250.00
NHLMP Matthew Poitras/35 40.00 100.00
NHLTF Tyson Foerster/35 40.00 100.00
NHLWC Will Cuylle/35 50.00 125.00

2023-24 The Cup The Show Black

SBAD Alex Delvecchio 5.00 12.00
SBAF Adam Fantilli 15.00 40.00
SBAO Alex Ovechkin 25.00 60.00
SBBF Brock Faber 12.00 30.00
SBBP Brian Propp 4.00 10.00
SBCA Guy Carbonneau 5.00 12.00
SBCB Connor Bedard 60.00 150.00
SBCC Corey Crawford 5.00 12.00
SBCM Connor McDavid 25.00 60.00
SBCO Logan Cooley 15.00 40.00
SBCS Gerry Cheevers 5.00 12.00
SBDL Devon Levi 12.00 30.00
SBDS Derek Sanderson 5.00 12.00
SBDW Dustin Wolf 15.00 40.00
SBFM Fraser Minten 10.00 25.00
SBGF Ryan Getzlaf 5.00 12.00
SBGU Jake Guentzel 8.00 20.00
SBIR Isak Rosen 5.00 12.00
SBJB John Beecher 10.00 25.00
SBJG Johnny Gaudreau 8.00 20.00
SBJH Jonathan Huberdeau 6.00 15.00
SBKB Kevin Bieksa 4.00 10.00
SBKC Kyle Connor 8.00 20.00
SBKK Kirill Kaprizov 15.00 40.00
SBKN Matthew Knies 25.00 60.00
SBKP Keith Primeau 3.00 8.00
SBLC Leo Carlsson 15.00 40.00
SBLD Leon Draisaitl 15.00 40.00
SBLH Luke Hughes 15.00 40.00
SBMA Cale Makar 12.00 30.00
SBMB Matt Boldy 8.00 20.00
SBMD Marcel Dionne 6.00 15.00
SBMH Miro Heiskanen 6.00 15.00
SBMK Marco Kasper 12.00 30.00
SBML Mike Liut 3.00 8.00
SBMM Mitch Marner 8.00 20.00
SBMR Mark Recchi 5.00 12.00
SBMY Matt Murray 5.00 12.00
SBQH Quinn Hughes 12.00 30.00
SBRG Ridly Greig 8.00 20.00
SBRN Rick Nash 5.00 12.00
SBSA Sebastian Aho 8.00 20.00
SBSC Shayne Corson 4.00 10.00
SBSF Sean Farrell 5.00 12.00
SBTK Tye Kartye 8.00 20.00
SBTL Trevor Linden 5.00 12.00
SBTS Tim Stutzle 6.00 15.00
SBWC Will Cuylle 8.00 20.00
SBYA Yaroslav Askarov 12.00 30.00
SBZB Zach Benson 8.00 20.00

2023-24 The Cup The Show Black Autographs

SBAD Alex Delvecchio SP 15.00 40.00
SBAF Adam Fantilli SP 50.00 125.00
SBAO Alex Ovechkin SP 80.00 200.00
SBBP Brian Propp SP 12.00 30.00
SBCA Guy Carbonneau 15.00 40.00
SBCB Connor Bedard SP 400.00 1000.00
SBCC Corey Crawford SP 40.00 100.00
SBCM Connor McDavid SP 300.00 800.00
SBCO Logan Cooley SP 50.00 125.00
SBCS Gerry Cheevers SP 15.00 40.00
SBDL Devon Levi 40.00 100.00
SBDS Derek Sanderson SP 15.00 40.00
SBDW Dustin Wolf 50.00 125.00
SBGF Ryan Getzlaf SP 15.00 40.00
SBJH Jonathan Huberdeau 20.00 50.00
SBKK Kirill Kaprizov SP 80.00 200.00
SBKN Matthew Knies 100.00 250.00
SBKP Keith Primeau SP 10.00 25.00
SBLC Leo Carlsson SP 50.00 125.00
SBLD Leon Draisaitl SP 100.00 250.00
SBLH Luke Hughes SP 60.00 150.00
SBMA Cale Makar SP 80.00 200.00
SBMB Matt Boldy 25.00 60.00
SBMD Marcel Dionne SP 20.00 50.00
SBMH Miro Heiskanen 20.00 50.00
SBMK Marco Kasper 40.00 100.00
SBMR Mark Recchi 15.00 40.00
SBSA Sebastian Aho 25.00 60.00
SBTL Trevor Linden SP 30.00 80.00
SBTS Tim Stutzle SP 30.00 80.00
SBWC Will Cuylle 25.00 60.00
SBYA Yaroslav Askarov 40.00 100.00
SBZB Zach Benson 25.00 60.00

2023-24 The Cup The Show White

SWAF Adam Fantilli 15.00 40.00
SWAL Alex Laferriere 8.00 20.00
SWAM Al MacInnis 6.00 15.00
SWBB Brent Burns 5.00 12.00
SWBG Bill Guerin 5.00 12.00
SWBM Brad Marchand 10.00 25.00
SWBO Brock Boeser 6.00 15.00
SWBP Brad Park 4.00 10.00
SWBR Brian Rolston 4.00 10.00
SWCB Connor Bedard 60.00 150.00
SWCJ Craig Janney 4.00 10.00
SWCM Connor McDavid 25.00 60.00
SWCO Logan Cooley 15.00 40.00
SWCS Charlie Simmer 3.00 8.00
SWCZ Connor Zary 10.00 25.00
SWDL Dylan Larkin 6.00 15.00
SWEP Elias Pettersson 8.00 20.00
SWIM Ivan Miroshnichenko 8.00 20.00
SWJG Jet Greaves 8.00 20.00
SWJH Jack Hughes 12.00 30.00
SWJK Jiri Kulich 10.00 25.00
SWJT John Tavares 8.00 20.00
SWKI Kevin Korchinski 8.00 20.00
SWKK Kirill Kaprizov 15.00 40.00
SWKS Kevin Stevens 4.00 10.00
SWKT Keith Tkachuk 5.00 12.00
SWLC Leo Carlsson 15.00 40.00
SWLE Luke Evangelista 8.00 20.00
SWMB Mathew Barzal 6.00 15.00
SWMC Matt Coronato 8.00 20.00
SWMF Marc-Andre Fleury 10.00 25.00
SWMM Mitch Marner 8.00 20.00
SWMP Matthew Poitras 10.00 25.00
SWMR Mike Ricci 3.00 8.00
SWMS Matt Savoie 10.00 25.00
SWPB Peter Bondra 5.00 12.00
SWPM Pavel Mintyukov 8.00 20.00
SWRN Ryan Nugent-Hopkins 6.00 15.00
SWRV Rogie Vachon 5.00 12.00
SWSA Mackie Samoskevich 8.00 20.00
SWSC Sidney Crosby 20.00 50.00
SWSD Shane Doan 4.00 10.00
SWSE Simon Edvinsson 10.00 25.00
SWSN Simon Nemec 10.00 25.00
SWTB Tom Barrasso 4.00 10.00
SWTF Tyson Foerster 10.00 25.00
SWTL Tristan Luneau 5.00 12.00
SWTN Joe Thornton 8.00 20.00
SWTT Troy Terry 4.00 10.00
SWTW Tiger Williams 3.00 8.00

2023-24 The Cup The Show White Autographs

SWAF Adam Fantilli SP 50.00 125.00
SWAL Alex Laferriere 25.00 60.00
SWAM Al MacInnis SP 20.00 50.00
SWBO Brock Boeser 20.00 50.00
SWCB Connor Bedard SP 400.00 1000.00
SWCJ Craig Janney SP 12.00 30.00
SWCM Connor McDavid SP 300.00 800.00
SWCO Logan Cooley SP 50.00 125.00
SWCS Charlie Simmer SP 10.00 25.00
SWCZ Connor Zary 30.00 80.00
SWEP Elias Pettersson SP 40.00 100.00
SWIM Ivan Miroshnichenko 25.00 60.00
SWJG Jet Greaves 25.00 60.00
SWJK Jiri Kulich 40.00 100.00
SWJT John Tavares 25.00 60.00
SWKI Kevin Korchinski 25.00 60.00
SWKK Kirill Kaprizov SP 80.00 200.00
SWKS Kevin Stevens SP 12.00 30.00
SWKT Keith Tkachuk SP 15.00 40.00
SWLC Leo Carlsson SP 50.00 125.00
SWMC Matt Coronato 25.00 60.00
SWMM Mitch Marner SP 25.00 60.00
SWMP Matthew Poitras 30.00 80.00
SWMR Mike Ricci 10.00 25.00
SWMS Matt Savoie 30.00 80.00
SWPB Peter Bondra SP 25.00 60.00
SWPM Pavel Mintyukov 25.00 60.00
SWRV Rogie Vachon SP 40.00 100.00
SWSA Mackie Samoskevich 25.00 60.00
SWSC Sidney Crosby SP 300.00 800.00
SWSD Shane Doan SP 12.00 30.00
SWSE Simon Edvinsson 30.00 80.00
SWSN Simon Nemec 30.00 80.00
SWTB Tom Barrasso SP 25.00 60.00
SWTF Tyson Foerster 30.00 80.00
SWTN Joe Thornton SP 40.00 100.00
SWTW Tiger Williams 10.00 25.00

2023-24 The Cup Trilaterals Jerseys

TLAF Adam Fantilli 12.00 30.00
TLBB Brock Boeser 5.00 12.00
TLBF Brock Faber 10.00 25.00
TLBO Matt Boldy 6.00 15.00
TLCB Connor Bedard 40.00 100.00
TLCC Charlie Coyle 4.00 10.00
TLCM Connor McDavid 20.00 50.00
TLCO Logan Cooley 12.00 30.00
TLCZ Connor Zary 8.00 20.00
TLDL Devon Levi 10.00 25.00
TLGN John Gibson 4.00 10.00
TLJE Jack Eichel 6.00 15.00
TLJG Jake Guentzel 6.00 15.00
TLJK Jordan Kyrou 4.00 10.00
TLJP JJ Peterka 4.00 10.00
TLJS Jeremy Swayman 6.00 15.00
TLLC Leo Carlsson 12.00 30.00
TLLE Luke Evangelista 6.00 15.00
TLMB Mathew Barzal 5.00 12.00
TLMH Miro Heiskanen 5.00 12.00
TLMK Matthew Knies 15.00 40.00
TLMP Matthew Poitras 8.00 20.00
TLNK Nikita Kucherov 10.00 25.00
TLRG Ridly Greig 6.00 15.00
TLRH Roope Hintz 5.00 12.00
TLSN Simon Nemec 8.00 20.00
TLTF Tyson Foerster 8.00 20.00
TLTK Travis Konecny 4.00 10.00
TLYA Yaroslav Askarov 10.00 25.00
TLZB Zach Benson 6.00 15.00

2002-03 Thrashers Postcards

COMPLETE SET (20) 10.00 25.00
1 Lubos Bartecko .40 1.00
2 Yuri Butsayev .40 1.00
3 Jeff Cowan .40 1.00
4 Dany Heatley 2.00 5.00
5 Milan Hnilicka .40 1.00
6 Tony Hrkac .40 1.00
7 Frantisek Kaberle .40 1.00
8 Ilya Kovalchuk 2.00 5.00
9 Slava Kozlov .40 1.00
10 Francis Lessard .40 1.00
11 Pasi Nurminen .60 1.50
12 Jeff Odgers .60 1.50
13 Kamil Piros .40 1.00
14 Dan Snyder .75 2.00
15 Patrik Stefan .40 1.00
16 Per Svartvadet .40 1.00
16 Andy Sutton .40 1.00
17 Chris Tamer .40 1.00
18 Brad Tapper .40 1.00
20 J.P. Vigier .40 1.00

2003-04 Thrashers Postcards

COMPLETE SET (23) 10.00 25.00
1 Serge Aubin .40 1.00
2 Jeff Cowan .40 1.00
3 Byron Dafoe .60 1.50
4 Garnet Exelby .60 1.50
5 Bob Hartley CO .20 .50
6 Frank Kaberle .40 1.00
7 Tomas Kloucek .40 1.00
8 Slava Kozlov .40 1.00
9 Ilya Kovalchuk 2.00 5.00
10 Brad Larsen .40 1.00
11 Francis Lessard .40 1.00
12 Ivan Majesky .40 1.00
13 Shawn McEachern .40 1.00
14 Pasi Nurminen .40 1.00
15 Ronald Petrovicky .40 1.00
16 Randy Robitaille .40 1.00
17 Marc Savard .60 1.50
18 Ben Simon .40 1.00
19 Patrik Stefan .40 1.00
20 Andy Sutton .40 1.00
21 Chris Tamer .40 1.00
22 Daniel Tjarnqvist .40 1.00
23 J.P. Vigier .40 1.00

2000-01 Titanium

COMPLETE SET w/o SP's (100) 25.00 50.00
1 Paul Kariya .30 .75
2 Teemu Selanne .60 1.50
3 Donald Audette .25 .60
4 Jason Allison .25 .60
5 Byron Dafoe .25 .60
6 Bill Guerin .30 .75
7 Joe Thornton .50 1.25
8 J-P Dumont .20 .50
9 Doug Gilmour .40 1.00
10 Dominik Hasek .50 1.25
11 Jarome Iginla .40 1.00
12 Marc Savard .20 .50
13 Mike Vernon .25 .60
14 Ron Francis .40 1.00
15 Arturs Irbe .25 .60
16 Tony Amonte .25 .60
17 Steve Sullivan .20 .50
18 Jocelyn Thibault .25 .60
19 Ray Bourque .50 1.25
20 Peter Forsberg .60 1.50
21 Milan Hejduk .25 .60
22 Patrick Roy .75 2.00
23 Joe Sakic .60 1.50
24 Alex Tanguay .25 .60
25 Geoff Sanderson .25 .60
26 Ron Tugnutt .25 .60
27 Ed Belfour .30 .75
28 Brett Hull .60 1.50
29 Mike Modano .50 1.25
30 Joe Nieuwendyk .25 .60
31 Sergei Fedorov .50 1.25
32 Manny Legace .20 .50
33 Nicklas Lidstrom .30 .75
34 Brendan Shanahan .30 .75
35 Steve Yzerman .75 2.00
36 Tommy Salo .25 .60
37 Ryan Smyth .25 .60
38 Doug Weight .30 .75
39 Pavel Bure .30 .75
40 Trevor Kidd .20 .50
41 Rob Blake .30 .75
42 Ziggy Palffy .30 .75
43 Luc Robitaille .30 .75
44 Jamie Storr .25 .60
45 Manny Fernandez .20 .50
46 Scott Pellerin .20 .50
47 Saku Koivu .30 .75
48 Trevor Linden .30 .75
49 Martin Rucinsky .20 .50
50 Jose Theodore .30 .75
51 David Legwand .30 .75
52 Cliff Ronning .20 .50
53 Jason Arnott .25 .60
54 Martin Brodeur .75 2.00
55 Patrik Elias .30 .75
56 Alexander Mogilny .25 .60
57 Tim Connolly .20 .50
58 Mariusz Czerkawski .20 .50
59 John Vanbiesbrouck .30 .75
60 Theo Fleury .40 1.00
61 Brian Leetch .25 .60
62 Mark Messier .60 1.50
63 Mike Richter .30 .75
64 Radek Bonk .25 .60
65 Marian Hossa .30 .75
66 Patrick Lalime .25 .60
67 Alexei Yashin .25 .60
68 Brian Boucher .25 .60
69 Simon Gagne .30 .75
70 John LeClair .30 .75
71 Eric Lindros .50 1.25
72 Sean Burke .20 .50
73 Jeremy Roenick .50 1.25
74 Keith Tkachuk .30 .75
75 Jaromir Jagr 1.00 2.50
76 Alexei Kovalev .25 .60
77 Mario Lemieux 1.25 3.00
78 Garth Snow .25 .60
79 Martin Straka .25 .60
80 Pavol Demitra .40 1.00
81 Chris Pronger .30 .75
82 Roman Turek .25 .60
83 Pierre Turgeon .25 .60
84 Vincent Damphousse .25 .60
85 Patrick Marleau .30 .75
86 Owen Nolan .30 .75
87 Steve Shields .20 .50
88 Mike Johnson .20 .50
89 Vincent Lecavalier .30 .75
90 Sergei Berezin .20 .50
91 Curtis Joseph .40 1.00
92 Gary Roberts .20 .50
93 Mats Sundin .30 .75
94 Andrew Cassels .20 .50
95 Brendan Morrison .30 .75
96 Markus Naslund .30 .75
97 Felix Potvin .50 1.25
98 Peter Bondra .30 .75
99 Olaf Kolzig .30 .75
100 Adam Oates .30 .75
101 Samuel Pahlsson SP 6.00 15.00
102 Scott Fankhouser SP 6.00 15.00
103 Tomi Kallio SP 6.00 15.00
104 Brad Tapper SP RC 6.00 15.00
105 Andrew Raycroft SP RC 10.00 25.00
106 Denis Hamel SP 6.00 15.00
107 Jeff Cowan SP RC 6.00 15.00
108 Oleg Saprykin SP 6.00 15.00
109 Josef Vasicek SP RC 15.00 40.00
110 Shane Willis SP 6.00 15.00
111 David Aebischer SP RC 12.00 30.00
112 Serge Aubin SP RC 8.00 20.00
113 Marc Denis SP 8.00 20.00
114 Chris Nielsen SP RC 6.00 15.00
115 David Vyborny SP 6.00 15.00
116 Marty Turco SP RC 15.00 40.00
117 Mike Comrie SP RC 15.00 40.00
118 Shawn Horcoff SP RC 12.00 30.00
119 Dominic Pittis SP 6.00 15.00
120 Roberto Luongo SP 15.00 40.00
121 Ivan Novoseltsev SP 6.00 15.00
122 Serge Payer SP 6.00 15.00
123 Denis Shvidki SP 6.00 15.00
124 Steven Reinprecht SP RC 10.00 25.00
125 Lubomir Visnovsky SP RC 12.00 30.00
126 Marian Gaborik SP RC 40.00 100.00
127 Filip Kuba SP 6.00 15.00
128 Mathieu Garon SP 6.00 15.00
129 Eric Landry SP RC 6.00 15.00
130 Andrei Markov SP 12.00 30.00
131 Marian Cisar SP 6.00 15.00
132 Scott Hartnell SP RC 15.00 40.00
133 Rick DiPietro SP RC 12.00 30.00
134 Martin Havlat SP RC 20.00 50.00
135 Jani Hurme SP RC 6.00 15.00
136 Petr Schastlivy SP 6.00 15.00
137 Ruslan Fedotenko SP RC 6.00 15.00
138 Justin Williams SP RC 15.00 40.00
139 Robert Esche SP 6.00 15.00
140 Milan Kraft SP 6.00 15.00
141 Brent Johnson SP 8.00 20.00
142 Reed Low SP RC 6.00 15.00

143 Evgeni Nabokov SP 8.00 20.00
144 Alexander Kharitonov SP RC 6.00 15.00
145 Dieter Kochan SP RC 6.00 15.00
146 Brad Richards SP 10.00 25.00
147 Adam Mair SP 6.00 15.00
148 Daniel Sedin SP 12.00 30.00
149 Henrik Sedin SP 12.00 30.00
150 Trent Whitfield SP 6.00 15.00

2000-01 Titanium Blue

*VETS/60-97: 5X TO 12X BASIC CARDS
*VETS/30-45: 8X TO 20X BASIC CARDS
*VETS/15-29: 10X TO 25X BASIC CARDS

2000-01 Titanium Gold

*GOLD/99: 5X TO 12X BASIC CARDS
62 Mark Messier 10.00 25.00

2000-01 Titanium Premiere Date

*PREM.DATE/185: 4X TO 10X BASIC CARDS

2000-01 Titanium Red

*RED/299: 3X TO 8X BASIC CARDS
62 Mark Messier 6.00 15.00

2000-01 Titanium Retail

*1-100 VETS: .4X TO 1X HOBBY
*101-150 ROOK/SP/199: .25X TO .6X SP/99
62 Mark Messier .75 2.00

2000-01 Titanium All-Stars

COMPLETE SET (20) 50.00 100.00
1W Dominik Hasek 2.50 6.00
1NA Paul Kariya 1.25 3.00
2W Peter Forsberg 3.00 8.00
2NA Bill Guerin 1.00 2.50
3W Sergei Fedorov 2.50 6.00
3NA Ray Bourque 2.50 6.00
4W Nicklas Lidstrom 1.25 3.00
4NA Patrick Roy 6.00 15.00
5W Pavel Bure 1.50 4.00
5NA Joe Sakic 2.50 6.00
6W Ziggy Palffy 1.00 2.50
6NA Brett Hull 1.50 4.00
7W Marian Hossa 1.25 3.00
7NA Martin Brodeur 4.00 10.00
8W Evgeni Nabokov 2.50 6.00
8NA Theo Fleury 1.00 2.50
9W Mats Sundin 1.25 3.00
9NA Mario Lemieux 6.00 15.00
10A North-American Team/100 8.00 20.00
10W World Team/100 8.00 20.00

2000-01 Titanium Game Gear

*PATCH/250-450: .8X TO 2X BASIC JSY
*PATCH/50-200: 1X TO 2.5X BASIC JSY
1 Phil Housley/212 6.00 15.00
2 Martin Gelinas/255 6.00 12.00
3 Sami Kapanen/246 6.00 15.00
4 Sandis Ozolinsh/244 6.00 15.00
5 Tony Amonte/251 6.00 15.00
6 Alexei Zhamnov/206 6.00 15.00
7 Peter Forsberg/235 8.00 20.00
8 Patrick Roy/255 15.00 40.00
9 Joe Sakic/224 12.00 30.00
10 Stephane Yelle/253 6.00 12.00
11 Marc Denis/253 6.00 12.00
12 Kevin Dineen/248 5.00 12.00
13 Ron Tugnutt/253 6.00 15.00
14 Ted Donato/247 6.00 12.00
15 Brett Hull/224 10.00 25.00
16 Chris Chelios/252 8.00 20.00
17 Steve Yzerman/212 20.00 50.00
18 Olli Jokinen/249 6.00 15.00
19 Rob Blake/253 6.00 15.00
20 Rob Blake/251 6.00 15.00
21 Nelson Emerson/193 6.00 12.00
22 Ziggy Palffy/252 6.00 15.00
23 Zigmund Palffy 6.00 15.00
24 Bryan Smolinski/213 5.00 12.00
25 Jozef Stumpel/252 6.00 12.00
26 Jeff Hackett/245 6.00 12.00
27 Trevor Linden/246 8.00 20.00
28 Trevor Linden/247 6.00 20.00
29 Eric Weinrich/252 5.00 12.00
30 Alexander Mogilny/251 6.00 15.00
31 Mariusz Czerkawski/251 6.00 12.00
32 Radek Dvorak/205 6.00 15.00
33 Theo Fleury/203 6.00 20.00
34 Adam Graves/242 6.00 15.00
35 Valeri Kamensky/237 6.00 15.00
36 Brian Leetch/206 6.00 15.00
37 Sandy McCarthy/214 6.00 15.00
38 Kirk McLean/254 6.00 15.00
39 Kirk McLean/251 8.00 20.00
40 Petr Nedved/253 6.00 15.00
41 Daniel Alfredsson/251 6.00 15.00
42 John LeClair/248 8.00 20.00
43 Teppo Numminen/254 6.00 12.00
44 Mario Lemieux/254 15.00 40.00
45 Roman Turek/255 6.00 15.00
46 Yanic Perreault/245 6.00 15.00
47 Gary Roberts/211 6.00 15.00
48 Andrew Cassels/254 6.00 12.00
49 Felix Potvin/254 10.00 25.00
50 Steve Konowalchuk/243 6.00 12.00
51 Guy Hebert 3.00 8.00
52 Guy Hebert 3.00 8.00
53 Mike Leclerc 2.50 6.00
54 Teemu Selanne 6.00 15.00
55 Per Johan Axelsson 2.50 6.00
56 Byron Dafoe 2.50 6.00
57 Andre Savage 2.50 6.00
58 Stu Barnes 2.50 6.00
59 Dominik Hasek 8.00 20.00
60 Erik Rasmussen 2.50 6.00
61 Rob Ray 2.50 6.00
62 Richard Smehlik 2.50 6.00
63 Alexei Zhitnik 3.00 8.00
64 Fred Brathwaite 2.50 6.00
65 Valeri Bure 2.50 6.00
66 Rico Fata 2.50 6.00
67 Phil Housley 3.00 8.00
68 Jarome Iginla 5.00 12.00
69 Marc Savard 3.00 8.00
70 Jeff Shantz 2.50 6.00
71 Cory Stillman 2.50 6.00
72 Boris Mironov 2.50 6.00
73 Alexei Zhamnov 3.00 8.00
74 Peter Forsberg 4.00 10.00
75 Jon Klemm 2.50 6.00
76 Aaron Miller 2.50 6.00
77 Dave Reid 2.50 6.00
78 Patrick Roy 12.00 30.00
79 Joe Sakic 8.00 20.00
80 Lyle Odelein 2.50 6.00
81 Ed Belfour 4.00 10.00
82 Derian Hatcher 2.50 6.00
83 Benoit Hogue 2.50 6.00
84 Brett Hull 5.00 12.00
85 Mike Keane 2.50 6.00
86 Jamie Langenbrunner 2.50 6.00
87 Jere Lehtinen 2.50 6.00
88 Grant Marshall 2.50 6.00
89 Mike Modano 5.00 12.00
90 Joe Nieuwendyk 3.00 8.00
91 Blake Sloan 2.50 6.00
92 Darryl Sydor 2.50 6.00
93 Sergei Zubov 2.50 6.00
94 Chris Chelios 4.00 10.00
95 Mathieu Dandenault 4.00 10.00
96 Chris Osgood 4.00 10.00
97 Brendan Shanahan 4.00 10.00
98 Steve Yzerman 10.00 25.00
99 Robert Svehla 2.50 6.00
100 Benoit Brunet 2.50 6.00
101 Eric Weinrich 2.50 6.00
102 Sergei Zholtok 4.00 10.00
103 Patric Kjellberg 2.50 6.00
104 David Legwand 3.00 8.00
105 Martin Brodeur 12.50 30.00
106 Scott Niedermayer 3.00 8.00
107 Chris Terreri 2.50 6.00
108 Mariusz Czerkawski 2.50 6.00
109 Wade Flaherty 2.50 6.00
110 Kenny Jonsson 2.50 6.00
111 Theo Fleury 4.00 10.00
112 Theo Fleury 4.00 10.00
113 Adam Graves 3.00 8.00
114 Brian Leetch 3.00 8.00
115 Sylvain Lefebvre 2.50 6.00
116 Manny Malhotra 2.50 6.00
117 Petr Nedved 2.50 6.00
118 Mike Richter 4.00 10.00
119 Daniel Alfredsson 3.00 8.00
120 Alexei Yashin 3.00 8.00
121 Eric Desjardins 2.50 6.00
122 John LeClair 4.00 10.00
123 Mika Alatalo 2.50 6.00
124 Sean Burke 2.50 6.00
125 Shane Doan 2.50 6.00
126 Nikolai Khabibulin 4.00 10.00
127 Jyrki Lumme 2.50 6.00
128 Teppo Numminen 2.50 6.00
129 Jeremy Roenick 5.00 12.00
130 Jean-Sebastien Aubin 4.00 10.00
131 Rene Corbet 2.50 6.00
132 Jan Hrdina 2.50 6.00
133 Jaromir Jagr 6.00 15.00
134 Darius Kasparaitis 2.50 6.00
135 Alexei Kovalev 3.00 8.00
136 Robert Lang 2.50 6.00
137 Alexei Morozov 2.50 6.00
138 Rich Parent 2.50 6.00
139 Wayne Primeau 2.50 6.00
140 Michal Rozsival 2.50 6.00
141 Kevin Stevens 2.50 6.00
142 Martin Straka 2.50 6.00
143 Matthew Barnaby 2.50 6.00
144 Tie Domi 2.50 6.00
145 Glenn Healy 2.50 6.00
146 Curtis Joseph 4.00 10.00
147 Dimitri Yushkevich 2.50 6.00
148 Dan Cloutier 2.50 6.00
149 Felix Potvin 5.00 12.00
150 Olaf Kolzig 3.00 8.00
151 Mario Lemieux/100 30.00 80.00
152 M.Lemieux/J.Jagr/100 100.00 200.00
153 P.Forsberg/J.Sakic/100 20.00 50.00
154 B.Hull/M.Modano/100 25.00 60.00
155 Kovalev/Straka/100 15.00 40.00

2000-01 Titanium Three-Star Selections

COMPLETE SET (30) 40.00 80.00
1 Dominik Hasek 1.25 3.00
2 Patrick Roy 3.00 8.00
3 Ed Belfour .75 2.00
4 Martin Brodeur 1.50 4.00
5 Mike Richter .75 2.00
6 Brian Boucher .60 1.50
7 Roman Turek .60 1.50
8 Curtis Joseph .75 2.00
9 Felix Potvin 1.50 4.00
10 Olaf Kolzig .60 1.50
11 Paul Kariya .75 2.00
12 Joe Sakic 1.50 4.00
13 Mike Modano 1.25 3.00
14 Sergei Fedorov 1.25 3.00
15 Ziggy Palffy .60 1.50
16 Theo Fleury .60 1.50
17 Jaromir Jagr 1.25 3.00
18 Mario Lemieux 5.00 12.00
19 Vincent Lecavalier .75 2.00
20 Mats Sundin .75 2.00
21 Shane Willis 1.50 4.00
22 Steven Reinprecht 2.00 5.00
23 Marian Gaborik 6.00 15.00
24 Rick DiPietro 5.00 12.00
25 Martin Havlat 6.00 15.00
26 Brent Johnson 1.25 3.00
27 Evgeni Nabokov 4.00 10.00
28 Brad Richards 2.00 5.00
29 Daniel Sedin 2.00 5.00
30 Henrik Sedin 2.00 5.00

2001-02 Titanium

1 Jeff Friesen .15 .40
2 Jean-Sebastien Giguere .25 .60
3 Paul Kariya .25 .60
4 Dany Heatley .20 .50
5 Milan Hnilicka .20 .50
6 Patrik Stefan .20 .50
7 Byron Dafoe .20 .50
8 Bill Guerin .25 .60
9 Brian Rolston .20 .50
10 Sergei Samsonov .20 .50
11 Joe Thornton .40 1.00
12 Stu Barnes .20 .50
13 Martin Biron .20 .50
14 Tim Connolly .15 .40
15 J-P Dumont .15 .40
16 Miroslav Satan .20 .50
17 Craig Conroy .15 .40
18 Jarome Iginla .30 .75
19 Dean McAmmond .15 .40
20 Derek Morris .15 .40
21 Marc Savard .15 .40
22 Roman Turek .20 .50
23 Tom Barrasso .20 .50
24 Ron Francis .30 .75
25 Arturs Irbe .20 .50
26 Sami Kapanen .15 .40
27 Jeff O'Neill .20 .50
28 Tony Amonte .20 .50
29 Mark Bell .20 .50
30 Kyle Calder .15 .40
31 Eric Daze .20 .50
32 Jocelyn Thibault .20 .50
33 Alexei Zhamnov .20 .50
34 Rob Blake .25 .60
35 Milan Hejduk .20 .50
36 Patrick Roy .60 1.50
37 Joe Sakic .50 1.25
38 Radim Vrbata .15 .40
39 Marc Denis .20 .50
40 Rostislav Klesla .15 .40
41 Ron Tugnutt .20 .50
42 Ray Whitney .15 .40
43 Ed Belfour .25 .60
44 Jere Lehtinen .15 .40
45 Mike Modano .40 1.00
46 Joe Nieuwendyk .20 .50
47 Pierre Turgeon .20 .50
48 Sergei Fedorov .40 1.00
49 Dominik Hasek .40 1.00
50 Brett Hull .50 1.25
51 Nicklas Lidstrom .25 .60
52 Luc Robitaille .25 .60
53 Brendan Shanahan .25 .60
54 Steve Yzerman .60 1.50
55 Anson Carter .20 .50
56 Mike Comrie .20 .50
57 Tommy Salo .20 .50
58 Ryan Smyth .20 .50
59 Pavel Bure .25 .60
60 Viktor Kozlov .15 .40
61 Roberto Luongo .40 1.00
62 Marcus Nilsson .15 .40
63 Jason Allison .20 .50
64 Adam Deadmarsh .15 .40
65 Steve Heinze .15 .40
66 Zigmund Palffy .25 .60
67 Felix Potvin .40 1.00
68 Andrew Brunette .15 .40
69 Jim Dowd .15 .40
70 Marian Gaborik .25 .60
71 Dwayne Roloson .20 .50
72 Doug Gilmour .30 .75
73 Yanic Perreault .15 .40
74 Mike Ribeiro .15 .40
75 Brian Savage .15 .40
76 Jose Theodore .25 .60
77 Mike Dunham .20 .50
78 Scott Hartnell .15 .40
79 David Legwand .20 .50
80 Cliff Ronning .15 .40
81 Jason Arnott .20 .50
82 Martin Brodeur .60 1.50
83 J-F Damphousse .15 .40
84 Patrik Elias .25 .60
85 Scott Stevens .25 .60
86 Mariusz Czerkawski .15 .40
87 Rick DiPietro .20 .50
88 Chris Osgood .20 .50
89 Mark Parrish .15 .40
90 Michael Peca .20 .50
91 Alexei Yashin .20 .50
92 Theo Fleury .30 .75
93 Brian Leetch .25 .60
94 Eric Lindros .40 1.00
95 Mark Messier .50 1.25
96 Mike Richter .25 .60
97 Mike York .15 .40
98 Daniel Alfredsson .25 .60
99 Martin Havlat .20 .50
100 Marian Hossa .25 .60
101 Patrick Lalime .20 .50
102 Todd White .15 .40
103 Roman Cechmanek .20 .50
104 Simon Gagne .25 .60
105 John LeClair .25 .60
106 Mark Recchi .30 .75
107 Jeremy Roenick .40 1.00
108 Sean Burke .25 .60
109 Daymond Langkow .20 .50
110 Claude Lemieux .15 .40
111 Johan Hedberg .20 .50
112 Alexei Kovalev .20 .50
113 Robert Lang .15 .40
114 Mario Lemieux 1.00 2.50
115 Pavol Demitra .30 .75
116 Brent Johnson .20 .50
117 Al MacInnis .25 .60
118 Chris Pronger .25 .60
119 Keith Tkachuk .25 .60
120 Doug Weight .25 .60
121 Vincent Damphousse .15 .40
122 Evgeni Nabokov .20 .50
123 Owen Nolan .20 .50
124 Teemu Selanne .50 1.25
125 Nikolai Khabibulin .25 .60
126 Vincent Lecavalier .25 .60
127 Brad Richards .20 .50
128 Martin St. Louis .25 .60
129 Curtis Joseph .30 .75
130 Alexander Mogilny .20 .50
131 Gary Roberts .15 .40
132 Mats Sundin .25 .60
133 Darcy Tucker .15 .40
134 Todd Bertuzzi .25 .60
135 Dan Cloutier .25 .60
136 Brendan Morrison .20 .50
137 Markus Naslund .25 .60
138 Daniel Sedin .30 .75
139 Henrik Sedin .30 .75
140 Peter Bondra .25 .60
141 Sergei Gonchar .15 .40
142 Jaromir Jagr .75 2.00
143 Olaf Kolzig .25 .60
144 Adam Oates .25 .60
145 Ilja Bryzgalov/30 RC 30.00 80.00
146 Timo Parssinen/29 RC 20.00 50.00
147 Ilya Kovalchuk/17 RC 150.00 250.00
148 Kamil Piros/25 RC 15.00 40.00
149 Brian Pothier/3 RC
150 Andy Hilbert/29 RC 15.00 40.00
151 Jukka Hentunen/24 RC 15.00 40.00
152 Erik Cole/26 RC 30.00 80.00
153 Vaclav Nedorost/22 RC 15.00 40.00
154 John Erskine/3 RC
155 Niko Kapanen/39 RC 20.00 50.00
156 Pavel Datsyuk/13 RC
157 Jason Chimera/28 RC 15.00 40.00
158 Ty Conklin/1 RC
159 Jussi Markkanen/30 RC 12.00 30.00
160 Niklas Hagman/14 RC
161 Kristian Huselius/22 RC 25.00 60.00
162 Jaroslav Bednar/7 RC
163 David Cullen/24 RC 15.00 40.00
164 Pascal Dupuis/11 RC
165 Nick Schultz/55 RC 10.00 25.00
166 Martin Erat/19 RC 20.00 50.00
167 Brian Gionta/14 RC
168 Andreas Salomonsson/15 RC 15.00 40.00
169 Radek Martinek/24 RC 15.00 40.00
170 Raffi Torres/16 RC 25.00 60.00
171 Dan Blackburn/31 RC 15.00 40.00
172 Mikael Samuelsson/37 RC 15.00 40.00
173 Chris Neil/25 RC 20.00 50.00
174 Jiri Dopita/20 RC 15.00 40.00
175 Bruno St. Jacques/42 RC 12.00 30.00
176 Krystofer Kolanos/36 RC 12.00 30.00
177 Josef Melichar/2 RC
178 Billy Tibbetts/12 RC
179 Mark Rycroft/42 RC 15.00 40.00
180 Jeff Jillson/5 RC
181 Nikita Alexeev/15 RC 15.00 40.00
182 Brad Leeb/38 RC 15.00 40.00
183 Chris Corrinet/48 RC 10.00 25.00
184 Brian Sutherby/41 RC 12.00 30.00

2001-02 Titanium Hobby Red

*RED/94: 5X TO 12X BASIC HOBBY

2001-02 Titanium Premiere Date

*VETS/94: 5X TO 12X BASIC HOBBY

2001-02 Titanium Retail

*1-144 VETS: .4X TO 1X HOBBY
145 Ilja Bryzgalov RC 6.00 15.00
146 Timo Parssinen RC 3.00 8.00
147 Ilya Kovalchuk RC 15.00 40.00
148 Kamil Piros RC 2.50 6.00
149 Brian Pothier RC 2.50 6.00
150 Andy Hilbert SP 2.50 6.00
151 Jukka Hentunen RC 2.50 6.00
152 Erik Cole RC 5.00 12.00
153 Vaclav Nedorost RC 2.50 6.00
154 John Erskine RC 2.50 6.00
155 Niko Kapanen RC 4.00 10.00
156 Pavel Datsyuk RC 20.00 50.00
157 Jason Chimera RC 2.50 6.00
158 Ty Conklin RC 4.00 10.00
159 Jussi Markkanen SP 2.50 6.00
160 Niklas Hagman RC 3.00 8.00
161 Kristian Huselius RC 4.00 10.00
162 Jaroslav Bednar RC 2.50 6.00
163 David Cullen RC 2.50 6.00
164 Pascal Dupuis RC 4.00 10.00
165 Nick Schultz RC 2.50 6.00
166 Martin Erat RC 3.00 8.00
167 Brian Gionta SP 3.00 8.00
168 Andreas Salomonsson RC 2.50 6.00
169 Radek Martinek RC 2.50 6.00
170 Raffi Torres RC 4.00 10.00
171 Dan Blackburn RC 3.00 8.00
172 Mikael Samuelsson RC 3.00 8.00
173 Chris Neil RC 2.50 6.00
174 Jiri Dopita RC 2.50 6.00
175 Bruno St. Jacques RC 2.50 6.00
176 Krystofer Kolanos RC 2.50 6.00
177 Josef Melichar SP 2.50 6.00
178 Billy Tibbetts RC 2.50 6.00
179 Mark Rycroft RC 3.00 8.00
180 Jeff Jillson RC 2.50 6.00
181 Nikita Alexeev RC 2.50 6.00
182 Brad Leeb SP 2.50 6.00
183 Chris Corrinet RC 2.50 6.00
184 Brian Sutherby RC 2.50 6.00

2001-02 Titanium All-Stars

1 Joe Thornton 1.00 2.50
2 Jarome Iginla .75 2.00
3 Sami Kapanen .40 1.00
4 Eric Daze .50 1.25
5 Rob Blake .60 1.50
6 Patrick Roy 1.50 4.00
7 Dominik Hasek 1.00 2.50
8 Sergei Fedorov 1.00 2.50
9 Nicklas Lidstrom .60 1.50
10 Brendan Shanahan .60 1.50
11 Zigmund Palffy .60 1.50
12 Jose Theodore .60 1.50
13 Patrik Elias .60 1.50
14 Alexei Yashin .50 1.25
15 Chris Pronger .60 1.50
16 Owen Nolan .60 1.50
17 Teemu Selanne 1.25 3.00
18 Nikolai Khabibulin .60 1.50
19 Mats Sundin .60 1.50
20 Jaromir Jagr 1.25 3.00

2001-02 Titanium Double-Sided Jerseys

1 S.Rucchin/P.Kariya 2.00 5.00
2 J.Friesen/O.Tverdovsky 1.25 3.00
3 S.Samsonov/B.Guerin 2.00 5.00
4 J.Dumont/A.Zhitnik 1.25 3.00
5 M.Savard/R.Turek 1.50 4.00
6 R.Turek/B.Boughner 1.50 4.00
7 J.Iginla/M.Savard 2.50 6.00
8 T.Amonte/B.Mironov 1.50 4.00
9 K.Calder/M.Nylander 1.25 3.00
10 A.Zhamnov/S.Sullivan 1.25 3.00
11 M.Hejduk/C.Drury 1.50 4.00
12 J.Sakic/A.Tanguay 4.00 10.00
13 P.Roy/R.Blake 5.00 12.00
14 A.Tanguay/V.Nedorost 1.50 4.00
15 L.Odelein/J.McLennan 1.25 3.00
16 M.Modano/J.Langenbrunner 3.00 8.00
17 F.Potvin/Z.Palffy 3.00 8.00
18 A.Deadmarsh/B.Smolinski 1.25 3.00
19 R.Blake/A.Miller 2.00 5.00
20 J.Theodore/F.Potvin 3.00 8.00
21 J.Dumont/S.Stevens 2.00 5.00
22 C.Ronning/T.Fitzgerald 1.25 3.00
23 I.Kovalchuk/D.Heatley 6.00 15.00
24 E.Daze/M.Bell 1.50 4.00
25 E.Lindros/T.Fleury 3.00 8.00
26 B.Leetch/R.Fata 1.50 4.00
27 E.Lindros/M.Messier 4.00 10.00
28 M.York/T.Fleury 2.50 6.00
29 M.Richter/B.Leetch 2.00 5.00
30 D.Alfredsson/M.Sundin 2.00 5.00
31 P.Brendl/J.Hrdina 1.25 3.00
32 M.Lemieux/A.Morozov 8.00 20.00
33 P.Brendl/J.Beranek 1.25 3.00
34 M.Straka/M.Rozsival 1.25 3.00
35 J.Hrdina/I.Moran 1.25 3.00
36 A.Kovalev/R.Parent 1.50 4.00
37 M.Eastwood/F.Brathwaite 1.50 4.00
38 S.Young/J.Hecht 1.50 4.00
39 T.Selanne/I.Kovalchuk STK 6.00 15.00
40 V.Lecavalier/P.Svoboda 2.00 5.00
41 C.Joseph/G.Healy 2.50 6.00
42 M.Sundin/J.Sakic 4.00 10.00
43 J.Jagr/D.Zubrus 6.00 15.00
44 T.Barrasso/A.Irbe 1.50 4.00
45 R.Francis/J.O'Neill 2.50 6.00
46 R.Brind'mour/E.Cole 2.50 6.00
47 M.Havlat/M.Hossa 2.00 5.00
48 D.Alfredsson/P.Lalime 2.00 5.00
49 J.Dopita/R.Cechmanek 1.50 4.00
50 J.Roenick/J.LeClair 3.00 8.00
51 S.Gagne/J.LeClair 2.00 5.00
52 M.Modano/P.Turgeon 3.00 8.00
53 M.Turco/E.Belfour 2.00 5.00
54 H.Sedin/D.Sedin 2.50 6.00
55 T.Bertuzzi/B.Morrison 2.00 5.00
56 M.Naslund/D.Cloutier 2.00 5.00
57 B.Morrison/M.Turco 2.00 5.00
58 M.Naslund/D.Alfredsson 2.00 5.00
59 J.Roenick/T.Barrasso 3.00 8.00
60 M.Havlat/R.Cechmanek 2.00 5.00
61 R.Francis/A.Irbe 2.50 6.00
62 J.O'Neill/E.Cole 2.50 6.00
63 M.Hossa/J.Dopita 2.00 5.00
64 P.Lalime/S.Gagne 2.00 5.00
65 E.Belfour/P.Turgeon 2.00 5.00
66 M.Biron/M.Satan 1.50 4.00
67 M.Gaborik/M.Fernandez 2.00 5.00
68 M.Brodeur/J.Arnott 5.00 12.00
69 P.Elias/S.Gomez 2.00 5.00
70 J.McLennan/F.Kuba 1.25 3.00
71 K.Kolanos/D.Langkow 1.50 4.00
72 M.Handzus/S.Berezin 1.25 3.00
73 S.Sullivan/M.Bell 1.25 3.00
74 J.Thornton/B.Guerin 3.00 8.00
75 J.Allison/Z.Palffy 2.00 5.00

2001-02 Titanium Rookie Team

1 Dany Heatley 10.00 25.00
2 Ilya Kovalchuk 10.00 25.00
3 Erik Cole 8.00 20.00
4 Mark Bell 4.00 10.00
5 Radim Vrbata 2.00 5.00
6 Kristian Huselius 2.00 5.00
7 Mike Ribeiro 2.00 5.00
8 Rick DiPietro 6.00 15.00
9 Raffi Torres 4.00 10.00
10 Krystofer Kolanos 2.00 5.00

2001-02 Titanium Saturday Knights

COMPLETE SET (20) 40.00 80.00
1 Paul Kariya 1.00 2.50
2 Joe Thornton 1.50 4.00
3 Jarome Iginla 1.25 3.00
4 Ed Belfour 1.00 2.50
5 Dominik Hasek 2.00 5.00
6 Brendan Shanahan 1.00 2.50
7 Steve Yzerman 5.00 12.00
8 Mike Comrie .75 2.00
9 Pavel Bure 1.00 2.50
10 Marian Gaborik 2.00 5.00
11 Jose Theodore 2.00 5.00
12 Martin Brodeur 2.50 6.00
13 Mike Peca .75 2.00
14 Eric Lindros 1.50 4.00
15 Daniel Alfredsson .75 2.00
16 Martin Havlat .75 2.00
17 Jeremy Roenick 1.25 3.00
18 Mario Lemieux 6.00 15.00
19 Curtis Joseph 1.00 2.50
20 Mats Sundin 1.00 2.50

2001-02 Titanium Three-Star Selections

COMPLETE SET (30) 15.00 40.00
1 Roman Turek .50 1.25
2 Tom Barrasso .50 1.25
3 Patrick Roy 3.00 8.00
4 Dominik Hasek 1.25 3.00
5 Martin Brodeur 1.50 4.00
6 Curtis Joseph .60 1.50
7 Chris Osgood .50 1.25
8 Evgeni Nabokov .50 1.25
9 Nikolai Khabibulin .60 1.50
10 Curtis Joseph .60 1.50
11 Paul Kariya .60 1.50
12 Jarome Iginla 1.00 2.50
13 Joe Sakic 1.50 4.00
14 Brendan Shanahan .60 1.50
15 Steve Yzerman 4.00 10.00
16 Eric Lindros .60 1.50
17 Mike York .50 1.25
18 Mario Lemieux 3.00 8.00
19 Mats Sundin .75 2.00
20 Jaromir Jagr 1.00 2.50
21 Dany Heatley .60 1.50
22 Ilya Kovalchuk 6.00 15.00
23 Erik Cole .60 1.50
24 Mark Bell 1.50 4.00
25 Radim Vrbata 1.50 4.00
26 Kristian Huselius 1.50 4.00
27 Mike Ribeiro 1.50 4.00
28 Rick DiPietro 1.50 4.00
29 Raffi Torres 1.50 4.00
30 Krystofer Kolanos 1.50 4.00

2002-03 Titanium

COMP.SET w/o SP's (100) 20.00 50.00
1 Jean-Sebastien Giguere .40 1.00
2 Paul Kariya .40 1.00
3 Petr Sykora .30 .75
4 Dany Heatley .30 .75
5 Ilya Kovalchuk .50 1.25
6 Pasi Nurminen .25 .60
7 Glen Murray .30 .75
8 Brian Rolston .30 .75
9 Steve Shields .30 .75
10 Joe Thornton .60 1.50
11 Martin Biron .30 .75
12 Chris Gratton .25 .60
13 Miroslav Satan .40 1.00
14 Chris Drury .40 1.00
15 Jarome Iginla .50 1.25
16 Roman Turek .40 1.00
17 Rod Brind'Amour .40 1.00
18 Ron Francis .50 1.25
19 Jeff O'Neill .25 .60
20 Kevin Weekes .30 .75
21 Tyler Arnason .30 .75
22 Theo Fleury .50 1.25
23 Jocelyn Thibault .30 .75
24 Peter Forsberg .75 2.00
25 Milan Hejduk .30 .75
26 Patrick Roy 1.00 2.50
27 Joe Sakic .75 2.00
28 Andrew Cassels .25 .60
29 Marc Denis .30 .75
30 Geoff Sanderson .30 .75
31 Bill Guerin .40 1.00
32 Mike Modano .60 1.50
33 Marty Turco .40 1.00
34 Pierre Turgeon .40 1.00
35 Sergei Fedorov .60 1.50
36 Brett Hull .75 2.00
37 Curtis Joseph .50 1.25
38 Nicklas Lidstrom .40 1.00
39 Brendan Shanahan .40 1.00
40 Steve Yzerman 1.00 2.50
41 Anson Carter .30 .75
42 Mike Comrie .40 1.00
43 Tommy Salo .30 .75
44 Ryan Smyth .30 .75
45 Kristian Huselius .25 .60
46 Olli Jokinen .40 1.00
47 Roberto Luongo .60 1.50
48 Jason Allison .30 .75
49 Eric Belanger .25 .60
50 Ziggy Palffy .30 .75
51 Felix Potvin .60 1.50
52 Manny Fernandez .25 .60
53 Marian Gaborik .40 1.00
54 Cliff Ronning .25 .60
55 Saku Koivu .40 1.00
56 Yanic Perreault .25 .60
57 Jose Theodore .40 1.00
58 Richard Zednik .25 .60
59 Andreas Johansson .25 .60
60 David Legwand .30 .75
61 Tomas Vokoun .30 .75
62 Martin Brodeur 1.00 2.50
63 Scott Gomez .30 .75
64 John Madden .25 .60
65 Rick DiPietro .30 .75
66 Michael Peca .30 .75
67 Alexei Yashin .30 .75
68 Pavel Bure .40 1.00
69 Eric Lindros .60 1.50
70 Tom Poti .25 .60
71 Daniel Alfredsson .40 1.00
72 Marian Hossa .40 1.00
73 Patrick Lalime .40 1.00
74 Roman Cechmanek .40 1.00
75 Simon Gagne .40 1.00
76 Jeremy Roenick .60 1.50
77 Tony Amonte .30 .75
78 Brian Boucher .30 .75
79 Shane Doan .30 .75
80 Johan Hedberg .40 1.00
81 Alex Kovalev .40 1.00
82 Mario Lemieux 1.50 4.00
83 Brent Johnson .30 .75
84 Cory Stillman .25 .60
85 Doug Weight .30 .75
86 Patrick Marleau .30 .75
87 Evgeni Nabokov .30 .75
88 Teemu Selanne .75 2.00
89 Nikolai Khabibulin .40 1.00
90 Vincent Lecavalier .40 1.00
91 Martin St. Louis .40 1.00
92 Ed Belfour .40 1.00
93 Alexander Mogilny .40 1.00
94 Mats Sundin .40 1.00
95 Todd Bertuzzi .40 1.00
96 Dan Cloutier .30 .75
97 Brendan Morrison .30 .75
98 Markus Naslund .40 1.00
99 Jaromir Jagr 1.25 3.00
100 Michael Nylander .25 .60
101 Stanislav Chistov RC 6.00 15.00
102 Martin Gerber RC 10.00 25.00
103 Kurt Sauer RC 6.00 15.00
104 Alexei Smirnov RC 8.00 20.00
105 Shaone Morrisonn RC 8.00 20.00
106 Tim Thomas RC 20.00 50.00
107 Ryan Miller RC 30.00 80.00
108 Chuck Kobasew RC 8.00 20.00
109 Jordan Leopold RC 10.00 25.00
110 Pascal Leclaire RC 8.00 20.00
111 Rick Nash RC 75.00 150.00
112 Steve Ott RC 6.00 15.00
113 Dmitri Bykov RC 6.00 15.00
114 Henrik Zetterberg RC 40.00 100.00
115 Ales Hemsky RC 25.00 60.00
116 Jay Bouwmeester RC 20.00 50.00
117 Michael Cammalleri RC 20.00 50.00
118 Alexander Frolov RC 15.00 40.00
119 P-M Bouchard RC 10.00 25.00
120 Stephane Veilleux RC 6.00 15.00
121 Kyle Wanvig 6.00 15.00
122 Ron Hainsey RC 6.00 15.00
123 Vernon Fiddler RC 8.00 20.00
124 Adam Hall RC 6.00 15.00
125 Scottie Upshall RC 8.00 20.00
126 Jason Spezza RC 100.00 175.00
127 Anton Volchenkov RC 6.00 15.00
128 Dennis Seidenberg RC 10.00 25.00
129 Radovan Somik RC 6.00 15.00
130 Jeff Taffe RC 6.00 15.00
131 Sebastien Caron 8.00 20.00
132 Brooks Orpik RC 6.00 15.00
133 Dick Tarnstrom RC 6.00 15.00
134 Tom Koivisto RC 6.00 15.00
135 Curtis Sanford RC 10.00 25.00
136 Lynn Loyns RC 6.00 15.00
137 Alexander Svitov RC 6.00 15.00
138 Carlo Colaiacovo RC 10.00 25.00
139 Mikael Tellqvist RC 6.00 15.00
140 Steve Eminger RC 6.00 15.00

2002-03 Titanium Blue

*1-100 VETS/450: 1X TO 2.5X BASIC CARDS
*101-140 SP/450: .1X TO .25X BASIC SP

2002-03 Titanium Red

*1-100 VETS/299: 1.2X TO 3X BASIC CARDS
*101-140 SP/299: .12X TO .3X BASIC SP

2002-03 Titanium Retail

COMP.SET w/o SP's (100) 20.00 50.00
*1-100 VETS: .4X TO 1X HOBBY
*101-40 SP/1475: .06X TO .15X HOB

2002-03 Titanium Jerseys

*PATCH/100-250: 1X TO 2.5X JSY/503-1403
*PATCH/100-250: .8X TO 2X JSY/253-439
*PATCH/110-225: .6X TO 1.5X JSY/253-439
*PATCH/40-85: 1.2X TO 3X JSY/561-1099
*PATCH/60-65: 1X TO 2.5X JSY/228-316
*PATCH/20-35: 1.5X TO 4X JSY/606-1307
*PATCH/15: 2X TO 5X JSY/1249
*PATCH/15: 1.5X TO 4X JSY/439
*RETAIL/99-160: .6X TO 1.5X HOB/503-1403
*RETAIL/99-160: .5X TO 1.2X HOB/253-439
1 Mike Leclerc/376 2.50 6.00
2 Dany Heatley/715 2.50 6.00
3 Ilya Kovalchuk/606 4.00 10.00
4 Patrik Stefan/1183 2.50 6.00
5 Joe Thornton/160 8.00 20.00
6 Martin Biron/1019 2.50 6.00
7 J-P Dumont/948 2.50 6.00
8 Rod Brind'Amour/1231 3.00 8.00
9 Arturs Irbe/829 2.50 6.00
10 Jeff O'Neill/283 2.50 6.00
11 Chris Drury/514 3.00 8.00
12 Roman Turek/1160 3.00 8.00
13 Mark Bell/957 2.50 6.00
14 Sergei Berezin/304 2.50 6.00
15 Steve Sullivan/641 2.00 5.00
16 Rob Blake/1020 3.00 8.00
17 Milan Hejduk/1160 2.50 6.00
18 Patrick Roy/150 15.00 40.00
19 Rostislav Klesla/1099 2.00 5.00
20 Geoff Sanderson/1307 2.50 6.00
21 Ron Tugnutt/1338 2.50 6.00
22 Marty Turco/552 3.00 8.00
23 Sergei Fedorov/561 5.00 12.00
24 Dominik Hasek/253 6.00 15.00
25 Brett Hull/899 6.00 15.00
26 Luc Robitaille/717 3.00 8.00
27 Jason Williams/1270 2.00 5.00
28 Mike Comrie/503 3.00 8.00
29 Tommy Salo/801 2.50 6.00
30 Ryan Smyth/1052 2.50 6.00
31 Valeri Bure/1352 2.50 6.00
32 Kristian Huselius/1305 2.00 5.00
33 Roberto Luongo/1403 5.00 12.00
34 Marian Gaborik/342 4.00 10.00
35 Yanic Perreault/1285 2.00 5.00
36 Jose Theodore/316 4.00 10.00
37 David Legwand/857 2.50 6.00
38 Scott Walker/1307 2.50 6.00
39 Scott Gomez/872 2.50 6.00
40 Scott Stevens/1273 3.00 8.00
41 Michael Peca/553 2.50 6.00
42 Alexei Yashin/743 2.50 6.00
43 Pavel Bure/908 3.00 8.00
44 Eric Lindros/583 5.00 12.00
45 Mark Messier/809 6.00 15.00
46 Daniel Alfredsson/532 3.00 8.00
47 Martin Havlat/545 2.50 6.00
48 Patrick Lalime/826 3.00 8.00
49 Simon Gagne/1028 3.00 8.00
50 Michal Handzus/636 2.50 6.00
51 Tomi Kallio/1301 2.00 5.00
52 John LeClair/942 3.00 8.00
53 Johan Hedberg/1004 3.00 8.00
54 Mario Lemieux/288 15.00 40.00
55 Toby Petersen/1320 2.00 5.00
56 Pavol Demitra/1256 4.00 10.00
57 Ray Ferraro/1288 2.50 6.00
58 Chris Pronger/1249 3.00 8.00
59 Keith Tkachuk/914 3.00 8.00
60 Sergei Varlamov/1152 2.50 6.00
61 Miikka Kiprusoff/1203 3.00 8.00
62 Patrick Marleau/730 3.00 8.00
63 Owen Nolan/439 4.00 10.00
64 Nikolai Khabibulin/1002 3.00 8.00
65 Fredrik Modin/1260 2.00 5.00
66 Alexander Mogilny/710 2.50 6.00
67 Gary Roberts/1260 2.00 5.00
68 Darcy Tucker/1260 2.00 5.00
69 Dan Cloutier/867 2.50 6.00
70 Brendan Morrison/638 2.50 6.00
71 Daniel Sedin/1105 4.00 10.00
72 Henrik Sedin/1100 4.00 10.00
73 Peter Bondra/1289 3.00 8.00
74 Jaromir Jagr/171 15.00 40.00
75 Olaf Kolzig/1303 3.00 8.00

2002-03 Titanium Saturday Knights

COMPLETE SET (10) 10.00 25.00
1 Jarome Iginla 1.00 2.50
2 Patrick Roy 3.00 8.00
3 Joe Sakic 1.50 4.00
4 Steve Yzerman 3.00 8.00
5 Jose Theodore 1.00 2.50
6 Marian Hossa .75 2.00

7 Mario Lemieux 4.00 10.00
8 Ed Belfour .75 2.00
9 Mats Sundin .75 2.00
10 Todd Bertuzzi .75 2.00

2002-03 Titanium Masked Marauders

COMPLETE SET (8) 10.00 25.00
1 Patrick Roy 3.00 8.00
2 Marty Turco 1.25 3.00
3 Curtis Joseph 1.25 3.00
4 Jose Theodore 1.50 4.00
5 Martin Brodeur 2.50 6.00
6 Nikolai Khabibulin 1.25 3.00
7 Ed Belfour 1.25 3.00
8 Dan Cloutier 1.25 3.00

2002-03 Titanium Right on Target

COMPLETE SET (20) 20.00 50.00
1 Stanislav Chistov 1.25 3.00
2 Ivan Huml .75 2.00
3 Chuck Kobasew 1.25 3.00
4 Jordan Leopold .75 2.00
5 Tyler Arnason .75 2.00
6 Rick Nash 2.50 6.00
7 Henrik Zetterberg 2.00 5.00
8 Ales Hemsky 1.50 4.00
9 Jay Bouwmeester 1.25 3.00
10 Stephen Weiss 1.25 3.00
11 Michael Cammalleri 1.25 3.00
12 Alexander Frolov 1.25 3.00
13 P-M Bouchard 1.25 3.00
14 Scottie Upshall 1.25 3.00
15 Rick DiPietro 1.50 4.00
16 Jamie Lundmark .75 2.00
17 Jason Spezza 2.00 5.00
18 Barret Jackman .75 2.00
19 Jonathan Cheechoo 1.25 3.00
20 Fedor Fedorov .75 2.00

2002-03 Titanium Shadows

COMPLETE SET (6) 30.00 60.00
1 Ilya Kovalchuk 1.50 4.00
2 Joe Thornton 1.50 4.00
3 Patrick Roy 6.00 15.00
4 Joe Sakic 2.50 6.00
5 Steve Yzerman 6.00 15.00
6 Marian Gaborik 2.00 6.00

2003-04 Titanium

COMP.SET w/o SP's (100) 15.00 30.00
1 Martin Gerber .15 .40
2 Steve Rucchin .15 .40
3 Petr Sykora .20 .50
4 Frantisek Kaberle .15 .40
5 Slava Kozlov .20 .50
6 Pasi Nurminen .20 .50
7 Marc Savard .15 .40
8 Mike Knuble .15 .40
9 Glen Murray .20 .50
10 Felix Potvin .40 1.00
11 Andrew Raycroft .20 .50
12 Martin Biron .20 .50
13 Daniel Briere .25 .60
14 J-P Dumont .15 .40
15 Miroslav Satan .20 .50
16 Shean Donovan .15 .40
17 Miikka Kiprusoff .25 .60
18 Jordan Leopold .15 .40
19 Erik Cole .15 .40
20 Ron Francis .30 .75
21 Jeff O'Neill .15 .40
22 Josef Vasicek .15 .40
23 Kevin Weekes .20 .50
24 Mark Bell .15 .40
25 Kyle Calder .15 .40
26 Jocelyn Thibault .20 .50
27 Alexei Zhamnov .20 .50
28 Rob Blake .25 .60
29 Alex Tanguay .20 .50
30 Marc Denis .20 .50
31 Rick Nash .25 .60
32 David Vyborny .15 .40
33 Jason Arnott .20 .50
34 Jere Lehtinen .20 .50
35 Pavel Datsyuk .40 1.00
36 Dominik Hasek .40 1.00
37 Curtis Joseph .30 .75
38 Henrik Zetterberg .30 .75
39 Tommy Salo .20 .50
40 Raffi Torres .15 .40
41 Mike York .15 .40
42 Valeri Bure .15 .40
43 Viktor Kozlov .15 .40
44 Stephen Weiss .15 .40
45 Roman Cechmanek .20 .50
46 Alexander Frolov .20 .50
47 Cristobal Huet .20 .50
48 Luc Robitaille .25 .60
49 Andrew Brunette .15 .40
50 Alexandre Daigle .20 .50
51 Manny Fernandez .15 .40
52 Marian Gaborik .25 .60
53 Dwayne Roloson .20 .50
54 Marcel Hossa .15 .40
55 Mike Ribeiro .15 .40
56 Michael Ryder .20 .50
57 Sheldon Souray .15 .40
58 David Legwand .20 .50
59 Tomas Vokoun .20 .50
60 Jeff Friesen .15 .40
61 Scott Gomez .20 .50
62 Scott Niedermayer .25 .60
63 Jason Blake .15 .40
64 Mariusz Czerkawski .15 .40
65 Trent Hunter .15 .40
66 Garth Snow .20 .50
67 Mike Dunham .20 .50
68 Brian Leetch .20 .50
69 Mark Messier .50 1.25
70 Radek Bonk .20 .50
71 Zdeno Chara .25 .60
72 Peter Schaefer .15 .40
73 Tony Amonte .20 .50
74 Robert Esche .15 .40
75 Michal Handzus .20 .50
76 Mark Recchi .30 .75
77 Sean Burke .15 .40
78 Shane Doan .20 .50
79 Ladislav Nagy .15 .40
80 Sebastien Caron .20 .50
81 Rico Fata .15 .40
82 Dick Tarnstrom .15 .40
83 Pavol Demitra .30 .75
84 Chris Pronger .25 .60
85 Keith Tkachuk .25 .60
86 Jonathan Cheechoo .20 .50
87 Vincent Damphousse .20 .50
88 Patrick Marleau .25 .60
89 Evgeni Nabokov .20 .50
90 Marco Sturm .15 .40
91 John Grahame .15 .40
92 Cory Stillman .15 .40
93 Joe Nieuwendyk .20 .50
94 Darcy Tucker .20 .50
95 Jason King .15 .40
96 Daniel Sedin .30 .75
97 Henrik Sedin .30 .75
98 Peter Bondra .25 .60
99 Sergei Gonchar .15 .40
100 Robert Lang .15 .40
101 Garrett Burnett RC 3.00 8.00
102 Tony Martensson RC 3.00 8.00
103 Sergei Zinovjev RC 3.00 8.00
104 Andrew Peters RC 4.00 10.00
105 Brent Krahn RC 3.00 8.00
106 Eric Staal RC 20.00 50.00
107 Travis Moen RC 4.00 10.00
108 Tuomo Ruutu RC 5.00 12.00
109 Pavel Vorobiev RC 4.00 10.00
110 Mikhail Yakubov RC 3.00 8.00
111 Cody McCormick RC 4.00 10.00
112 Dan Fritsche RC 3.00 8.00
113 Kent McDonell RC 4.00 10.00
114 Nikolai Zherdev RC 6.00 15.00
115 Trevor Daley RC 5.00 12.00
116 Antti Miettinen RC 5.00 12.00
117 Jiri Hudler RC 8.00 20.00
118 Niklas Kronwall RC 6.00 15.00
119 Nathan Robinson RC 3.00 8.00
120 Peter Sarno RC 3.00 8.00
121 Tim Gleason RC 4.00 10.00
122 Esa Pirnes RC 3.00 8.00
123 Brent Burns RC 20.00 50.00
124 Dan Hamhuis RC 4.00 10.00
125 Marek Zidlicky RC 3.00 8.00
126 David Hale RC 3.00 8.00
127 Paul Martin RC 4.00 10.00
128 Sean Bergenheim RC 4.00 10.00
129 Dominic Moore RC 3.00 8.00
130 Joni Pitkanen RC 5.00 12.00
131 Fredrik Sjostrom RC 5.00 12.00
132 Marc-Andre Fleury RC 40.00 100.00
133 Matt Murley RC 4.00 10.00
134 John Pohl RC 3.00 8.00
135 Peter Sejna RC 4.00 10.00
136 Milan Michalek RC 6.00 15.00
137 Maxim Kondratiev RC 3.00 8.00
138 Ryan Kesler RC 12.00 30.00
139 Alexander Semin RC 10.00 25.00
140 Rastislav Stana RC 5.00 12.00
141 Stanislav Chistov JSY 2.00 5.00
142 Sergei Fedorov JSY 5.00 12.00
143 J-S Giguere JSY 3.00 8.00
144 Sergei Samsonov JSY 2.50 6.00
145 Ryan Miller JSY/785 3.00 8.00
146 Jarome Iginla JSY 4.00 10.00
147 David Aebischer JSY 2.50 6.00
148 Milan Hejduk JSY 2.50 6.00
149 Joe Sakic JSY 6.00 15.00
150 Teemu Selanne JSY 6.00 15.00
151 Mike Modano JSY 5.00 12.00
152 Marty Turco JSY 3.00 8.00
153 Brendan Shanahan JSY 3.00 8.00
154 Ales Hemsky JSY 3.00 8.00
155 Ryan Smyth JSY 2.50 6.00
156 Jay Bouwmeester JSY 2.00 5.00
157 Olli Jokinen JSY 3.00 8.00
158 Roberto Luongo JSY 5.00 12.00
159 Jason Allison JSY 2.50 6.00
160 Ziggy Palffy JSY 3.00 8.00
161 Saku Koivu JSY 3.00 8.00
162 Jose Theodore JSY 3.00 8.00
163 Richard Zednik JSY 2.00 5.00
164 Martin Erat JSY 2.00 5.00
165 Scott Walker JSY 2.00 5.00
166 Patrik Elias JSY 3.00 8.00
167 Rick DiPietro JSY 2.50 6.00
168 Michael Peca JSY 2.50 6.00
169 Alexei Yashin JSY 2.50 6.00
170 Jaromir Jagr JSY 10.00 25.00
171 Eric Lindros JSY 5.00 12.00
172 Daniel Alfredsson JSY 3.00 8.00
173 Marian Hossa JSY 3.00 8.00
174 Patrick Lalime JSY 2.50 6.00
175 Jason Spezza JSY 3.00 8.00
176 Jeff Hackett JSY 2.50 6.00
177 Jeremy Roenick JSY 5.00 12.00
178 Barret Jackman JSY 2.00 5.00
179 Chris Osgood JSY 3.00 8.00
180 Doug Weight JSY 3.00 8.00
181 Nikolai Khabibulin JSY 3.00 8.00
182 Vincent Lecavalier JSY 3.00 8.00
183 Martin St. Louis JSY/640 3.00 8.00
184 Owen Nolan JSY 3.00 8.00
185 Gary Roberts JSY/835 2.00 5.00
186 Mats Sundin JSY 3.00 8.00
187 Dan Cloutier JSY 2.50 6.00
188 Brendan Morrison JSY 2.50 6.00
189 Markus Naslund JSY 3.00 8.00
190 Olaf Kolzig JSY 3.00 8.00
191 Ilya Kovalchuk JSY 4.00 10.00
192 Dany Heatley JSY/39 3.00 8.00
193 Joe Thornton JSY 6.00 15.00
194 Peter Forsberg JSY 8.00 20.00
195 Paul Kariya JSY 4.00 10.00
196 Bill Guerin JSY 4.00 10.00
197 Brett Hull JSY 8.00 20.00
198 Nicklas Lidstrom JSY 4.00 10.00
199 Steve Yzerman JSY 10.00 25.00
200 Martin Brodeur JSY 10.00 25.00
201 Pavel Bure JSY 4.00 10.00
202 John LeClair JSY 4.00 10.00
203 Mario Lemieux JSY 12.00 30.00
204 Ed Belfour JSY 4.00 10.00
205 Todd Bertuzzi JSY 4.00 10.00
206 Joffrey Lupul/15 30.00 60.00
207 Patrice Bergeron/37 60.00 150.00
208 Matthew Lombardi/18 15.00 30.00
209 Nathan Horton/16 60.00 120.00
210 Dustin Brown/23 40.00 80.00
211 Christopher Higgins/88 5.00 12.00
212 Jordin Tootoo/55 20.00 50.00
213 Antoine Vermette/20
214 Matt Stajan/14
215 Boyd Gordon/15 12.00 30.00

2003-04 Titanium Hobby Jersey Number Parallels

*1-100 VETS/150: 3X TO 8X BASIC CARDS
*101-140 ROOKIES/199: .15X TO .4X RC/99
*JERSEY/50: .8X TO 2X JSY/640-875
69 Mark Messier 5.00 12.00

2003-04 Titanium Patches

*PATCH/25-165: .8X TO 2X BASIC JSY

2003-04 Titanium Retail

*1-100 VETS: .4X TO 1X HOBBY
*101-140 ROOK/750: .1X TO .3X HOB/99
*141-190 JSY/170: .5X TO 1.2X JSY/640-875
69 Mark Messier .60 1.50

2003-04 Titanium Retail Jersey Number Parallels

*1-100 VETS/250: 2.5X TO 6X BASIC CARDS
*101-140 ROOKIES/225: .15X TO .4X RC/99
69 Mark Messier 4.00 10.00

2003-04 Titanium Highlight Reels

COMPLETE SET (8) 10.00 25.00
1 Ilya Kovalchuk 1.25 3.00
2 Joe Thornton 1.25 3.00
3 Peter Forsberg 1.50 4.00
4 Joe Sakic 1.50 4.00
5 Dominik Hasek 1.50 4.00
6 Steve Yzerman 3.00 8.00
7 Martin Brodeur 2.00 5.00
8 Mario Lemieux 3.00 8.00

2003-04 Titanium Masked Marauders

COMPLETE SET (10) 10.00 20.00
1 Jean-Sebastien Giguere .60 1.50
2 David Aebischer .60 1.50
3 Marty Turco .60 1.50
4 Dominik Hasek 1.50 4.00
5 Jose Theodore 1.00 2.50
6 Martin Brodeur 2.00 5.00
7 Rick DiPietro .60 1.50
8 Patrick Lalime .60 1.50
9 Nikolai Khabibulin .75 2.00
10 Ed Belfour .75 2.00

2003-04 Titanium Right on Target

COMPLETE SET (16) 10.00 20.00
1 Joffrey Lupul .30 .75
2 Patrice Bergeron 1.50 4.00
3 Eric Staal .75 2.00
4 Rick Nash .50 1.25
5 Henrik Zetterberg .60 1.50
6 Ales Hemsky .30 .75
7 Jay Bouwmeester .30 .75
8 Nathan Horton .75 2.00
9 Michael Ryder .30 .75
10 Jordin Tootoo .60 1.50
11 Jason Spezza .60 1.50
12 Joni Pitkanen .30 .75
13 Marc-Andre Fleury 2.00 5.00
14 Barret Jackman .30 .75
15 Matt Stajan .30 .75
16 Jason King .30 .75

2003-04 Titanium Stat Masters

COMPLETE SET (10) 8.00 15.00
1 Sergei Fedorov .75 2.00
2 Ilya Kovalchuk .75 2.00
3 Peter Forsberg 1.00 2.50
4 Rick Nash .75 2.00
5 Pavel Datsyuk .60 1.50
6 Brett Hull .75 2.00
7 Marian Hossa .60 1.50
8 Mario Lemieux 1.50 4.00
9 Todd Bertuzzi .60 1.50
10 Markus Naslund .60 1.50

2000-01 Titanium Draft Day Edition

COMP.SET w/o JSYs (76) 150.00 350.00
1 Jean-Sebastien Giguere/1010 3.00 8.00
2 Mike Leclerc/520 3.00 8.00
3 P.J. Axelsson/520 3.00 8.00
4 Byron Dafoe/520 3.00 8.00
5 Kyle McLaren/520 3.00 8.00
6 Sergei Samsonov/520 6.00 15.00
7 Don Sweeney/535 3.00 8.00
8 Joe Thornton/535 8.00 20.00
9 Eric Weinrich/1020 3.00 8.00
10 Stu Barnes/535 3.00 8.00
11 Dominik Hasek/535 8.00 20.00
12 Erik Rasmussen/1020 3.00 8.00
13 Fred Brathwaite/1010 3.00 8.00
14 Valeri Bure/1020 3.00 8.00
15 Marc Savard/1020 3.00 8.00
16 Tony Amonte/1020 3.00 8.00
17 Eric Daze/1020 3.00 8.00
18 Boris Mironov/1020 3.00 8.00
19 Michael Nylander/1020 3.00 8.00
20 Steve Sullivan/1020 3.00 8.00
21 Jocelyn Thibault/1020 3.00 8.00
22 Alexei Zhamnov/1020 3.00 8.00
23 Chris Dingman/520 3.00 8.00
24 Peter Forsberg/520 10.00 25.00
25 Patrick Roy/68 75.00 200.00
26 Joe Sakic/535 8.00 20.00
27 Lyle Odelein/535 3.00 8.00
28 Ed Belfour/110 10.00 25.00
29 Derian Hatcher/990 3.00 8.00
30 Brett Hull/115 12.00 30.00
31 Jamie Langenbrunner/985 3.00 8.00
32 Jere Lehtinen/520 3.00 8.00
33 Mike Modano/1015 6.00 15.00
34 Joe Nieuwendyk/1015 3.00 8.00
35 Darryl Sydor/835 3.00 8.00
36 Chris Chelios/520 4.00 10.00
37 Matthieu Dandenault/520 3.00 8.00
38 Nicklas Lidstrom/110 6.00 15.00
39 Darren McCarty/520 3.00 8.00
40 Chris Osgood/1020 3.00 8.00
41 Brendan Shanahan/520 6.00 15.00
42 Steve Yzerman/105 25.00 60.00
43 Anson Carter/55 12.50 30.00
44 Ryan Smyth/1015 3.00 8.00
45 Doug Weight/520 3.00 8.00
46 Pavel Bure/55 15.00 40.00
47 Robert Svehla/1015 3.00 8.00
48 Felix Potvin/100 10.00 25.00
49 Benoit Brunet/1015 3.00 8.00
50 Jeff Hackett/520 3.00 8.00
51 Sergei Zholtok/1010 3.00 8.00
52 Mike Dunham/1020 3.00 8.00
53 Tom Fitzgerald/520 3.00 8.00
54 Patric Kjellberg/520 3.00 8.00
55 David Legwand/520 3.00 8.00
56 Cliff Ronning/520 3.00 8.00
57 Kimmo Timonen/520 3.00 8.00
58 Scott Walker/520 3.00 8.00
59 Bobby Holik/520 3.00 8.00
60 Scott Niedermayer/995 3.00 8.00
61 Mariusz Czerkawski/1020 3.00 8.00
62 Kenny Jonsson/520 3.00 8.00
63 Claude Lapointe/1015 3.00 8.00
64 Chris Terreri/1020 3.00 8.00
65 Theo Fleury/870 3.00 8.00
66 Brian Leetch/520 3.00 8.00
67 Petr Nedved/1015 3.00 8.00
68 Mike Richter/1010 4.00 10.00
69 Mike York/1015 3.00 8.00
70 Daniel Alfredsson/520 3.00 8.00
71 Alexei Yashin/285 3.00 8.00
72 Eric Desjardins/520 3.00 8.00
73 John LeClair/520 4.00 10.00
74 Mika Alatalo/535 3.00 8.00
75 Sean Burke/1010 3.00 8.00
76 Shane Doan/535 3.00 8.00
77 Jyrki Lumme/520 3.00 8.00
78 Jeremy Roenick/520 6.00 15.00
79 Radoslav Suchy/1015 2.50 6.00
80 Jean-Sebastien Aubin/1015 3.00 8.00
81 Jan Hrdina/1020 3.00 8.00
82 Jaromir Jagr/520 8.00 20.00
83 Darius Kasparaitis/1010 3.00 8.00
84 Alexei Kovalev/1015 3.00 8.00
85 Milan Kraft/1015 3.00 8.00
86 Mario Lemieux/115 25.00 60.00
87 Kevin Stevens/1020 3.00 8.00
88 Martin Straka/1010 3.00 8.00
89 Dallas Drake/535 3.00 8.00
90 Cory Stillman/1010 3.00 8.00
91 Vincent Damphousse/1015 3.00 8.00
92 Teemu Selanne/1020 4.00 10.00
93 Vincent Lecavalier/535 6.00 15.00
94 Shayne Corson/1010 3.00 8.00
95 Tie Domi/535 3.00 8.00
96 Curtis Joseph/535 6.00 15.00
97 Mats Sundin/535 6.00 15.00
98 Peter Bondra/15 30.00 60.00
99 Ulf Dahlen/535 3.00 8.00
100 Dainius Zubrus/520 3.00 8.00
101 Samuel Pahlsson 1.50 4.00
102 Scott Fankhouser 1.50 4.00
103 Tomi Kallio 1.50 4.00
104 Brad Tapper RC 2.00 5.00
105 Andrew Raycroft RC 6.00 15.00
106 Denis Hamel 1.50 4.00
107 Jeff Cowan RC 2.00 5.00
108 Oleg Saprykin 1.50 4.00
109 Josef Vasicek RC 2.00 5.00
110 Shane Willis 1.50 4.00
111 David Aebischer RC 6.00 15.00
112 Serge Aubin RC 2.00 5.00
113 Marc Denis 1.50 4.00
114 Chris Nielsen RC 2.00 5.00
115 David Vyborny 1.50 4.00
116 Marty Turco RC 8.00 20.00
117 Mike Comrie RC 3.00 8.00
118 Shawn Horcoff RC 3.00 8.00
119 Dominic Pittis 1.50 4.00
120 Roberto Luongo 2.50 6.00
121 Ivan Novoseltsev 1.50 4.00
122 Serge Payer 1.50 4.00
123 Denis Shvidki 1.50 4.00
124 Steven Reinprecht RC 3.00 8.00
125 Lubomir Visnovsky RC 2.00 5.00
126 Marian Gaborik RC 8.00 20.00
127 Filip Kuba 1.50 4.00
128 Mathieu Garon 1.50 4.00
129 Eric Landry RC 2.00 5.00
130 Andrei Markov 4.00 10.00
131 Marian Cisar 1.50 4.00
132 Scott Hartnell RC 4.00 10.00
133 Rick DiPietro RC 6.00 15.00
134 Martin Havlat RC 6.00 15.00
135 Jani Hurme RC 3.00 8.00
136 Petr Schastlivy 1.50 4.00
137 Ruslan Fedotenko RC 2.00 5.00
138 Justin Williams RC 4.00 10.00
139 Robert Esche 1.50 4.00
140 Milan Kraft 1.50 4.00
141 Brent Johnson 1.50 4.00
142 Reed Low RC 2.00 5.00
143 Evgeni Nabokov 6.00 15.00
144 Alexander Kharitonov RC 2.00 5.00
145 Dieter Kochan RC 2.00 5.00
146 Brad Richards 1.50 4.00
147 Adam Mair 1.50 4.00
148 Daniel Sedin 2.00 5.00
149 Henrik Sedin 2.00 5.00
150 Trent Whitfield 1.50 4.00
151 Marc Chouinard RC 2.00 5.00
152 Jonas Ronnqvist RC 2.00 5.00
153 Petr Tenkrat RC 2.00 5.00
154 Ronald Petrovicky RC 2.00 5.00
155 Craig Adams RC 2.00 5.00
156 Niclas Wallin RC 2.00 5.00
157 Rostislav Klesla RC 3.00 8.00
158 Petteri Nummelin RC 2.00 5.00
159 Tyler Bouck RC 2.00 5.00
160 Michel Riesen RC 2.00 5.00
161 Eric Belanger RC 2.00 5.00
162 Roman Simicek RC 2.00 5.00
163 Xavier Delisle 1.50 4.00
164 Greg Classen RC 2.00 5.00
165 Mike Commodore RC 2.00 5.00
166 Sascha Goc RC 2.00 5.00
167 Jeff Ulmer RC 2.00 5.00
168 Shane Hnidy RC 2.00 5.00
169 Roman Cechmanek RC 2.00 5.00
170 Todd Fedoruk RC 2.00 5.00
171 Ossi Vaananen RC 2.00 5.00
172 Bryce Salvador RC 2.00 5.00
173 Mark Smith RC 2.00 5.00
174 Mike Brown RC 2.00 5.00
175 Jakub Cutta RC 2.00 5.00
176 Johan Hedberg RC 3.00 8.00

2000-01 Titanium Draft Day Edition Patches

*PATCHES: 1.2X TO 3X BASIC JSY
8 Joe Thornton/24 30.00 80.00
44 Ryan Smyth/24 15.00 40.00
46 Pavel Bure/116 15.00 40.00

2000-01 Titanium Draft Day Edition Promos

COMPLETE SET (76) 200.00 400.00
101 Samuel Pahlsson 2.00 5.00
102 Scott Fankhouser 2.00 5.00
103 Tomi Kallio 2.00 5.00
104 Brad Tapper 2.00 5.00
105 Andrew Raycroft 3.00 8.00
106 Denis Hamel 2.00 5.00
107 Jeff Cowan 2.00 5.00
108 Oleg Saprykin 2.00 5.00
109 Josef Vasicek 2.00 5.00
110 Shane Willis 2.00 5.00
111 David Aebischer 2.00 5.00
112 Serge Aubin 2.00 5.00
113 Marc Denis 3.00 8.00
114 Chris Nielsen 2.00 5.00
115 David Vyborny 2.00 5.00
116 Marty Turco 3.00 8.00
117 Mike Comrie 2.00 5.00
118 Shawn Horcoff 2.00 5.00
119 Dominic Pittis 2.00 5.00
120 Roberto Luongo 5.00 12.00
121 Ivan Novoseltsev 2.00 5.00
122 Serge Payer 2.00 5.00
123 Denis Shvidki 2.00 5.00
124 Steven Reinprecht 2.00 5.00
125 Lubomir Visnovsky 2.00 5.00
126 Marian Gaborik 8.00 20.00
127 Filip Kuba 2.00 5.00
128 Mathieu Garon 2.00 5.00
129 Eric Landry 2.00 5.00
130 Andrei Markov 5.00 12.00
131 Marian Cisar 2.00 5.00
132 Scott Hartnell 3.00 8.00
133 Rick DiPietro 3.00 8.00
134 Martin Havlat 3.00 8.00
135 Jani Hurme 2.00 5.00
136 Petr Schastlivy 2.00 5.00
137 Ruslan Fedotenko 2.00 5.00
138 Justin Williams 2.00 5.00
139 Robert Esche 2.00 5.00
140 Milan Kraft 2.00 5.00
141 Brent Johnson 2.00 5.00
142 Reed Low 2.00 5.00
143 Evgeni Nabokov 2.00 5.00
144 Alexander Kharitonov 3.00 8.00
145 Dieter Kochan 2.00 5.00
146 Brad Richards 3.00 8.00
147 Adam Mair 2.00 5.00
148 Daniel Sedin 8.00 20.00
149 Henrik Sedin 8.00 20.00
150 Trent Whitfield 2.00 5.00
151 Marc Chouinard 2.00 5.00
152 Jonas Ronnqvist 2.00 5.00
163 Potr Tonkrat 2.00 5.00
154 Ronald Petrovicky 2.00 5.00
155 Craig Adams 2.00 5.00
156 Niclas Wallin 2.00 5.00
157 Rostislav Klesla 2.00 5.00
158 Petteri Nummelin 2.00 5.00
159 Tyler Bouck 2.00 5.00
160 Michel Riesen 2.00 5.00
161 Eric Belanger 2.00 5.00
162 Roman Simicek 2.00 5.00
163 Xavier Delisle 2.00 5.00
164 Greg Classen 2.00 5.00
165 Mike Commodore 2.00 5.00
166 Sascha Goc 2.00 5.00
167 Jeff Ulmer 2.00 5.00
168 Shane Hnidy 2.00 5.00
169 Roman Cechmanek 2.00 5.00
170 Todd Fedoruk 2.00 5.00
171 Ossi Vaananen 2.00 5.00
172 Bryce Salvador 2.00 5.00
173 Mark Smith 2.00 5.00
174 Mike Brown 2.00 5.00
175 Jakub Cutta 2.00 5.00
176 Johan Hedberg 2.00 5.00

2001-02 Titanium Draft Day Edition

1 Jeff Friesen 2.50 6.00
1AU Ilya Kovalchuk AU/500* 12.00 30.00
2 Paul Kariya 4.00 10.00
3 Oleg Tverdovsky 2.50 6.00
4 Dany Heatley 3.00 8.00
5 Milan Hnilicka 3.00 8.00
6 Tomi Kallio 2.50 6.00
7 Ilya Kovalchuk 12.00 30.00
8 Patrik Stefan 3.00 8.00
9 Bill Guerin 4.00 10.00
10 Kyle McLaren 2.50 6.00
11 Joe Thornton 6.00 15.00
12 Martin Biron 3.00 8.00
13 J-P Dumont 2.50 6.00
14 Erik Rasmussen 2.50 6.00
15 Jarome Iginla 5.00 12.00
16 Marc Savard 2.50 6.00
17 Roman Turek 3.00 8.00
18 Erik Cole 5.00 12.00
19 Jeff O'Neill 3.00 8.00
20 Tony Amonte 3.00 8.00
21 Kyle Calder 2.50 6.00
22 Tom Fitzgerald 2.50 6.00
23 Phil Housley 3.00 8.00
24 Steve Sullivan 2.50 6.00
25 Rob Blake 4.00 10.00
26 Vaclav Nedorost 2.50 6.00
27 Joe Sakic 8.00 20.00
28 Alex Tanguay 3.00 8.00
29 Marc Denis 3.00 8.00
30 Rostislav Klesla 2.50 6.00
31 Ron Tugnutt 3.00 8.00
32 Jason Arnott 3.00 8.00
33 Derian Hatcher 2.50 6.00
34 Mike Modano 6.00 15.00
35 Pierre Turgeon 3.00 8.00
36 Sergei Zubov 3.00 8.00
37 Dominik Hasek 6.00 15.00
38 Brett Hull 8.00 20.00
39 Mike Comrie 3.00 8.00
40 Jochen Hecht 2.50 6.00
41 Jason Allison 3.00 8.00
42 Adam Deadmarsh 2.50 6.00
43 Felix Potvin 6.00 15.00
44 Manny Fernandez 2.50 6.00
45 Marian Gaborik 4.00 10.00
46 Filip Kuba 2.50 6.00
47 Jamie McLennan 2.50 6.00
48 Sergei Berezin 2.50 6.00
49 Jeff Hackett 3.00 8.00
50 Jukka Hentunen 2.50 6.00
51 Martin Brodeur 10.00 25.00
52 Scott Gomez 3.00 8.00
53 Bobby Holik 2.50 6.00
54 Jamie Langenbrunner 2.50 6.00
55 Scott Stevens 4.00 10.00
56 Mats Lindgren 2.50 6.00
57 Kip Miller 2.50 6.00
58 Chris Osgood 4.00 10.00
59 Theo Fleury 5.00 12.00
60 Brian Leetch 3.00 8.00
61 Eric Lindros 6.00 15.00
62 Mark Messier 8.00 20.00
63 Mike Richter 4.00 10.00
64 Daniel Alfredsson 4.00 10.00
65 Martin Havlat 3.00 8.00
66 Marian Hossa 4.00 10.00
67 Patrick Lalime 3.00 8.00
68 Roman Cechmanek 3.00 8.00
69 Jiri Dopita 2.50 6.00
70 Simon Gagne 4.00 10.00
71 John LeClair 4.00 10.00
72 Jeremy Roenick 6.00 15.00
73 Michal Handzus 2.50 6.00
74 Krystofer Kolanos 2.50 6.00
75 Daymond Langkow 3.00 8.00
76 Teppo Numminen 2.50 6.00
77 Kris Beech 2.50 6.00
78 Johan Hedberg 3.00 8.00
79 Robert Lang 2.50 6.00
80 Mario Lemieux 15.00 40.00
81 Rich Parent 2.50 6.00
82 Toby Petersen 2.50 6.00
83 Mike Eastwood 2.50 6.00
84 Ray Ferraro 2.50 6.00
85 Patrick Marleau 4.00 10.00
86 Evgeni Nabokov 3.00 8.00
87 Owen Nolan 4.00 10.00
88 Vincent Lecavalier 4.00 10.00
89 Tom Barrasso 3.00 8.00
90 Mats Sundin 4.00 10.00
91 Dimitri Yushkevich 2.50 6.00
92 Todd Bertuzzi 4.00 10.00
93 Andrew Cassels 2.50 6.00
94 Dan Cloutier 3.00 8.00
95 Brendan Morrison 3.00 8.00
96 Markus Naslund 4.00 10.00
97 Daniel Sedin 5.00 12.00
98 Henrik Sedin 5.00 12.00
99 Peter Bondra 4.00 10.00
100 Jaromir Jagr 12.00 30.00
101 Ilja Bryzgalov RC 6.00 15.00
102 Andy McDonald 2.50 6.00
103 Timo Parssinen RC 3.00 8.00
104 Dany Heatley 3.00 8.00
105 Ilya Kovalchuk RC 12.00 30.00
106 Pasi Nurminen RC 2.50 6.00
107 Kamil Piros RC 2.50 6.00
108 Brian Pothier RC 2.50 6.00
109 Daniel Tjarnqvist 2.50 6.00
110 Andy Hilbert 2.50 6.00
111 Ales Kotalik RC 5.00 12.00
112 Mika Noronen 2.50 6.00
113 Erik Cole RC 5.00 12.00
114 Tyler Arnason RC 3.00 8.00
115 Mark Bell 2.50 6.00
116 Vaclav Nedorost RC 2.50 6.00
117 Radim Vrbata 2.50 6.00
118 Brian Willsie 2.50 6.00
119 Mathieu Darche RC 4.00 10.00
120 Rostislav Klesla 2.50 6.00
121 Jody Shelley RC 3.00 8.00
122 Martin Spanhel RC 2.50 6.00
123 John Erskine RC 2.50 6.00
124 Niko Kapanen RC 4.00 10.00
125 Sean Avery RC 2.50 6.00
126 Pavel Datsyuk RC 15.00 40.00
127 Maxim Kuznetsov 2.50 6.00
128 Jason Chimera RC 2.50 6.00
129 Ty Conklin RC 4.00 10.00
130 Jussi Markkanen 2.50 6.00
131 Niklas Hagman RC 3.00 8.00
132 Kristian Huselius RC 4.00 10.00
133 Stephen Weiss RC 6.00 15.00
134 Jaroslav Bednar RC 2.50 6.00
135 David Cullen RC 2.50 6.00
136 Pascal Dupuis RC 4.00 10.00
137 Nick Schultz RC 2.50 6.00
138 Mathieu Garon 3.00 8.00
139 Marcel Hossa RC 4.00 10.00
140 Mike Ribeiro 2.50 6.00
141 Bubba Berenzweig 2.50 6.00
142 Martin Erat RC 3.00 8.00
143 Jukka Hentunen RC 2.50 6.00
144 Nathan Perrott RC 2.50 6.00
145 Christian Berglund RC 3.00 8.00
146 Scott Clemmensen RC 2.50 6.00
147 J-F Damphousse 2.50 6.00
148 Brian Gionta 3.00 8.00
149 Andreas Salomonsson RC 2.50 6.00
150 Radek Martinek RC 2.50 6.00
151 Raffi Torres RC 4.00 10.00
152 Dan Blackburn RC 3.00 8.00
153 Mikael Samuelsson RC 3.00 8.00
154 Chris Neil RC 3.00 8.00
155 Pavel Brendl 2.50 6.00
156 Jiri Dopita RC 2.50 6.00
157 Bruno St. Jacques RC 2.50 6.00
158 Billy Tibbetts RC 2.50 6.00
159 Darcy Hordichuk 2.50 6.00
160 Krystofer Kolanos RC 2.50 6.00
161 Josef Melichar 2.50 6.00
162 Mark Rycroft RC 3.00 8.00
163 Sergei Varlamov 2.50 6.00
164 Matt Bradley 2.50 6.00
165 Jeff Jillson RC 2.50 6.00
166 Vesa Toskala 2.50 6.00
167 Nikita Alexeev RC 2.50 6.00
168 Alexei Ponikarovsky 2.50 6.00
169 Chris Corrinet RC 2.50 6.00
170 Stephen Peat 2.50 6.00
171 Matt Pettinger 2.50 6.00
172 Brian Sutherby RC 2.50 6.00

1993 Titrex Guy Lafleur Insert

1 Guy Lafleur
(Wearing Titrex jersey) 1.25 3.00

1994 Titrex Guy Lafleur

COMPLETE SET (24) 12.00 30.00
COMMON LAFLEUR (1-24) .75 2.00

1954-55 Topps

1 Dick Gamble 200.00 500.00
2 Bob Chrystal RC 80.00 200.00
3 Harry Howell 80.00 200.00
4 Johnny Wilson 50.00 125.00
5 Red Kelly 80.00 200.00
6 Real Chevrefils 40.00 100.00
7 Bob Armstrong 50.00 125.00
8 Gordie Howe 1200.00 3000.00
9 Benny Woit 30.00 80.00
10 Gump Worsley 100.00 250.00
11 Andy Bathgate 80.00 200.00
12 Bucky Hollingworth RC 60.00 150.00
13 Ray Timgren 30.00 80.00
14 Jack Evans 30.00 80.00
15 Paul Ronty 25.00 60.00
16 Glen Skov 40.00 100.00
17 Gus Mortson 50.00 125.00
18 Doug Mohns RC 50.00 125.00
19 Leo Labine 50.00 125.00
20 Bill Gadsby 40.00 100.00
21 Jerry Toppazzini 30.00 80.00
22 Wally Hergesheimer 40.00 100.00
23 Danny Lewicki 30.00 80.00
24 Metro Prystai 30.00 80.00
25 Fern Flaman 40.00 100.00
26 Al Rollins 80.00 200.00
27 Marcel Pronovost 60.00 150.00
28 Lou Jankowski 40.00 100.00
29 Nick Mickoski 40.00 100.00
30 Frank Martin 40.00 100.00
31 Lorne Ferguson 40.00 100.00
32 Camille Henry RC 40.00 100.00
33 Pete Conacher 30.00 80.00
34 Marty Pavelich 40.00 100.00
35 Don McKenney RC 60.00 150.00
36 Fleming Mackell 30.00 80.00
37 Jim Henry 60.00 150.00
38 Hal Laycoe 40.00 100.00
39 Alex Delvecchio 125.00 300.00
40 Larry Wilson 20.00 50.00
41 Allan Stanley 40.00 100.00
42 George Sullivan 30.00 80.00
43 Jack McIntyre 40.00 100.00
44 Ivan Irwin RC 50.00 125.00
45 Tony Leswick 60.00 150.00
46 Bob Goldham 50.00 125.00
47 Cal Gardner 50.00 125.00
48 Ed Sandford 20.00 125.00
49 Bill Quackenbush 40.00 100.00
50 Warren Godfrey 30.00 80.00
51 Tod Lindsay 150.00 400.00
52 Earl Reibel 25.00 60.00
53 Don Raleigh 50.00 125.00
54 Bill Mosienko 100.00 250.00
55 Larry Popein RC 60.00 150.00
56 Edgar Laprade 30.00 80.00
57 Bill Dineen 50.00 125.00
58 Terry Sawchuk 300.00 800.00
59 Marcel Bonin RC 100.00 250.00
60 Milt Schmidt 150.00 400.00

1957-58 Topps

1 Real Chevrefils 25.00 60.00
2 Jack Bionda RC 12.00 30.00
3 Bob Armstrong 8.00 20.00
4 Fern Flaman 15.00 40.00
5 Jerry Toppazzini 20.00 50.00
6 Larry Regan RC 10.00 25.00
7 Bronco Horvath RC 15.00 40.00
8 Jack Caffery 12.00 30.00
9 Leo Labine 10.00 25.00
10 Johnny Bucyk RC 250.00 600.00
11 Vic Stasiuk 10.00 25.00
12 Doug Mohns 15.00 40.00
13 Don McKenney 15.00 40.00
14 Don Simmons RC 50.00 125.00
15 Allan Stanley 15.00 40.00
16 Fleming Mackell 12.00 30.00
17 Larry Hillman RC 20.00 50.00
18 Leo Boivin 10.00 25.00
19 Bob Bailey 10.00 25.00
20 Glenn Hall RC 300.00 800.00
21 Ted Lindsay 25.00 60.00
22 Pierre Pilote RC 100.00 250.00
23 Jim Thomson 10.00 25.00
24 Eric Nesterenko 10.00 25.00
25 Gus Mortson 40.00 100.00
26 Ed Litzenberger RC 25.00 60.00
27 Elmer Vasko RC 12.00 30.00
28 Jack McIntyre 8.00 20.00
29 Ron Murphy 10.00 25.00
30 Glen Skov 25.00 60.00
31 Hec Lalande RC 8.00 20.00
32 Nick Mickoski 8.00 20.00
33 Wally Hergesheimer 10.00 25.00
34 Alex Delvecchio 20.00 50.00
35 Terry Sawchuk UER 125.00 300.00

36 Guyle Fielder RC 10.00 25.00
37 Tom McCarthy 8.00 20.00
38 Al Arbour 25.00 60.00
39 Billy Dea RC 15.00 40.00
40 Lorne Ferguson 12.00 30.00
41 Warren Godfrey 12.00 30.00
42 Gordie Howe 300.00 800.00
43 Marcel Pronovost 12.00 30.00
44 Bill McNeil RC 10.00 25.00
45 Earl Reibel 10.00 25.00
46 Norm Ullman RC 100.00 250.00
47 Johnny Wilson 12.00 30.00
48 Red Kelly 20.00 50.00
49 Bill Dineen 20.00 50.00
50 Forbes Kennedy RC 15.00 40.00
51 Harry Howell 25.00 60.00
52 Jean-Guy Gendron RC 25.00 60.00
53 Gump Worsley 30.00 80.00
54 Larry Popein 20.00 50.00
55 Jack Evans 15.00 40.00
56 George Sullivan 10.00 25.00
57 Gerry Foley RC 15.00 40.00
58 Andy Hebenton RC 10.00 25.00
59 Larry Cahan 8.00 20.00
60 Andy Bathgate 20.00 50.00
61 Danny Lewicki 12.00 30.00
62 Dean Prentice 15.00 40.00
63 Camille Henry 10.00 25.00
64 Lou Fontinato RC 15.00 40.00
65 Bill Gadsby 12.00 30.00
66 Dave Creighton 50.00 125.00

1958-59 Topps

1 Bob Armstrong 40.00 100.00
2 Terry Sawchuk 100.00 250.00
3 Glen Skov 15.00 40.00
4 Leo Labine 10.00 25.00
5 Dollard St.Laurent 20.00 50.00
6 Danny Lewicki 20.00 50.00
7 John Hanna RC 8.00 20.00
8 Gordie Howe UER 250.00 600.00
9 Vic Stasiuk 20.00 50.00
10 Larry Regan 10.00 25.00
11 Forbes Kennedy 20.00 50.00
12 Elmer Vasko 10.00 25.00
13 Glenn Hall 40.00 100.00
14 Ken Wharram RC 20.00 50.00
15 Len Lunde RC 20.00 50.00
16 Ed Litzenberger 20.00 50.00
17 Norm Johnson RC 15.00 40.00
18 Earl Ingarfield RC 8.00 20.00
19 Les Colwill RC 8.00 20.00
20 Leo Boivin 12.00 30.00
21 Andy Bathgate 20.00 50.00
22 Johnny Wilson 8.00 20.00
23 Larry Cahan 25.00 60.00
24 Marcel Pronovost 25.00 60.00
25 Larry Hillman 10.00 25.00
26 Jim Bartlett RC 20.00 50.00
27 Nick Mickoski 20.00 50.00
28 Larry Popein 20.00 50.00
29 Fleming Mackell 10.00 25.00
30 Eddie Shack RC 125.00 300.00
31 Jack Evans 15.00 40.00
32 Dean Prentice 20.00 50.00
33 Claude Laforge RC 20.00 50.00
34 Bill Gadsby 20.00 50.00
35 Bronco Horvath 10.00 25.00
36 Pierre Pilote 40.00 100.00
37 Earl Balfour 15.00 40.00
38 Gus Mortson 15.00 40.00
39 Gump Worsley 50.00 125.00
40 Johnny Bucyk 50.00 125.00
41 Lou Fontinato 15.00 40.00
42 Tod Sloan 8.00 20.00
43 Charlie Burns RC 8.00 20.00
44 Don Simmons 20.00 50.00
45 Jerry Toppazzini 20.00 50.00
46 Andy Hebenton 10.00 25.00
47 Pete Goegan RC 20.00 50.00
48 George Sullivan 12.00 30.00
49 Hank Ciesla RC 20.00 50.00
50 Doug Mohns 15.00 40.00
51 Jean-Guy Gendron 8.00 20.00
52 Alex Delvecchio 40.00 100.00
53 Eric Nesterenko 15.00 40.00
54 Camille Henry 10.00 25.00
55 Lorne Ferguson 12.00 30.00
56 Fern Flaman 10.00 25.00
57 Earl Reibel 20.00 50.00
58 Warren Godfrey 20.00 50.00
59 Ron Murphy 12.00 30.00
60 Harry Howell 20.00 30.00
61 Red Kelly 30.00 80.00
62 Don McKenney 8.00 20.00
63 Ted Lindsay 30.00 80.00
64 Al Arbour 25.00 60.00
65 Norm Ullman 30.00 80.00
66 Bobby Hull RC 3000.00 8000.00

1959-60 Topps

1 Eric Nesterenko 60.00 150.00
2 Pierre Pilote 40.00 100.00
3 Elmer Vasko 80.00 200.00
4 Peter Goegan 15.00 40.00
5 Lou Fontinato 10.00 25.00
6 Ted Lindsay 20.00 50.00
7 Leo Labine 15.00 40.00
8 Alex Delvecchio 20.00 50.00
9 Don McKenney UER 8.00 20.00
10 Earl Ingarfield 8.00 20.00
11 Don Simmons 10.00 25.00
12 Glen Skov 8.00 20.00
13 Tod Sloan 10.00 25.00
14 Vic Stasiuk 8.00 20.00
15 Gump Worsley 25.00 60.00
16 Andy Hebenton 10.00 25.00
17 Dean Prentice 15.00 40.00
18 Pronovost/Bartlett IA 8.00 20.00
19 Fleming Mackell 10.00 25.00
20 Harry Howell 10.00 25.00
21 Larry Popein 8.00 20.00
22 Len Lunde 8.00 20.00
23 Johnny Bucyk 25.00 60.00
24 Jean-Guy Gendron 8.00 20.00
25 Barry Cullen 8.00 20.00
26 Leo Boivin 12.00 30.00
27 Warren Godfrey 15.00 40.00
28 G.Hall/C.Henry IA 15.00 40.00
29 Fern Flaman 10.00 25.00
30 Jack Evans 15.00 40.00
31 John Hanna 8.00 20.00
32 Glenn Hall 30.00 80.00
33 Murray Balfour RC 10.00 25.00
34 Andy Bathgate 15.00 40.00
35 Al Arbour 10.00 25.00
36 Jim Morrison 8.00 20.00
37 Nick Mickoski 8.00 20.00
38 Jerry Toppazzini 8.00 20.00
39 Bob Armstrong 10.00 25.00
40 Charlie Burns UER 20.00 50.00
41 Bill McNeil 8.00 20.00
42 Terry Sawchuk 80.00 200.00
43 Dollard St.Laurent 8.00 20.00
44 Marcel Pronovost 30.00 80.00
45 Norm Ullman 25.00 60.00
46 Camille Henry 12.00 30.00
47 Bobby Hull 250.00 600.00
48 G.Howe/J.Evans IA 60.00 150.00
49 Lou Marcon RC 8.00 20.00
50 Earl Balfour 12.00 30.00
51 Jim Bartlett 8.00 20.00
52 Forbes Kennedy 8.00 20.00
53 N.Mickoski/J.Hanna IA 8.00 20.00
54 G.Worsley/H.Howell IA 15.00 40.00
55 Brian Cullen 8.00 20.00
56 Bronco Horvath 10.00 25.00
57 Eddie Shack 30.00 80.00
58 Doug Mohns 10.00 25.00
59 George Sullivan 10.00 25.00
60 P.Pilote/F.Mackell IA 8.00 20.00
61 Ed Litzenberger 8.00 20.00
62 Bill Gadsby 12.00 30.00
63 Gordie Howe 200.00 500.00
64 Claude Laforge 8.00 20.00
65 Red Kelly 30.00 80.00
66 Ron Murphy 20.00 50.00

1960-61 Topps

1 Lester Patrick ATG 30.00 80.00
2 Paddy Moran ATG 15.00 40.00
3 Joe Malone ATG 12.00 30.00
4 Ernest Johnson 8.00 20.00
5 Nels Stewart ATG 12.00 30.00
6 Bill Hay RC 20.00 50.00
7 Eddie Shack 20.00 50.00
8 Cy Denneny ATG 40.00 100.00
9 Jim Morrison 6.00 15.00
10 Bill Cook ATG 12.00 30.00
11 Johnny Bucyk 25.00 60.00
12 Murray Balfour 6.00 15.00
13 Leo Labine 6.00 15.00
14 Stan Mikita RC 600.00 1500.00
15 George Hay ATG RC 10.00 25.00
16 Red Dutton ATG 20.00 50.00
17 Dickie Boon ATG RC 6.00 15.00
18 George Sullivan 6.00 15.00
19 Georges Vezina ATG 30.00 80.00
20 Eddie Shore ATG 50.00 125.00
21 Ed Litzenberger 6.00 15.00
22 Bill Gadsby 8.00 20.00
23 Elmer Vasko 12.00 30.00
24 Charlie Burns 12.00 30.00
25 Glenn Hall 40.00 100.00
26 Dit Clapper ATG 12.00 30.00
27 Art Ross ATG 15.00 40.00
28 Jerry Toppazzini 6.00 15.00
29 Frank Boucher ATG 25.00 60.00
30 Jack Evans 6.00 15.00
31 Jean-Guy Gendron 30.00 80.00
32 Chuck Gardiner ATG 10.00 25.00
33 Ab McDonald 20.00 50.00
34 Frank Fredrickson ATG RC 10.00 25.00
35 Frank Nighbor ATG 20.00 50.00
36 Gump Worsley 20.00 50.00
37 Dean Prentice 8.00 20.00
38 Hugh Lehman ATG RC 12.00 30.00
39 Jack McCartan RC 30.00 80.00
40 Don McKenney UER
(Misspelled McKenny
on card front 8.00 20.00
41 Ron Murphy 10.00 25.00
42 Andy Hebenton 10.00 25.00
43 Don Simmons 30.00 80.00
44 Herb Gardiner ATG 8.00 20.00
45 Andy Bathgate 15.00 40.00
46 Cyclone Taylor ATG 15.00 40.00
47 King Clancy ATG 15.00 40.00
48 Newsy Lalonde ATG 12.00 30.00
49 Harry Howell 10.00 25.00
50 Ken Schinkel RC 6.00 15.00
51 Tod Sloan 12.00 30.00
52 Doug Mohns 10.00 25.00
53 Camille Henry 10.00 25.00
54 Bronco Horvath 40.00 100.00
55 Tiny Thompson ATG 25.00 60.00
56 Bob Armstrong 20.00 50.00
57 Fern Flaman 8.00 20.00
58 Bobby Hull 200.00 500.00
59 Howie Morenz ATG 15.00 40.00
60 Dick Irvin ATG RC 25.00 60.00
61 Lou Fontinato 15.00 40.00
62 Leo Boivin 8.00 20.00
63 Moose Goheen ATG RC 25.00 60.00
64 Al Arbour 8.00 20.00
65 Pierre Pilote 15.00 40.00
66 Vic Stasiuk 12.00 30.00

1961-62 Topps Stamps

COMPLETE SET (52) 900.00 1500.00
*PANELS: .6X TO 1.5X SUM OF SINGLE STAMPS
1 Murray Balfour 15.00 30.00
2 Andy Bathgate 15.00 30.00
3 Leo Boivin 12.50 25.00
4 Dickie Boon 15.00 30.00
5 Frank Boucher 20.00 40.00
6 Johnny Bucyk 20.00 40.00
7 Charlie Burns 10.00 20.00
8 King Clancy 20.00 50.00
9 Dit Clapper 15.00 30.00
10 Sprague Cleghorn 20.00 40.00
11 Alex Connell 15.00 30.00
12 Bill Cook 15.00 30.00
13 Cy Denneny 15.00 30.00
14 Jack Evans 10.00 20.00
15 Frank Fredrickson 15.00 30.00
16 Chuck Gardiner 15.00 30.00
17 Herb Gardiner 15.00 30.00
18 Eddie Gerard 15.00 30.00
19 Moose Goheen 15.00 30.00
20 Glenn Hall 25.00 50.00
21 Doug Harvey 20.00 40.00
22 Bill Hay 15.00 30.00
23 George Hay 15.00 30.00
24 Andy Hebenton 10.00 20.00
25 Camille Henry 12.50 25.00
26 Bronco Horvath 10.00 20.00
27 Harry Howell 12.50 25.00
28 Bobby Hull 75.00 150.00
29 Dick Irvin 15.00 30.00
30 Ernest Johnson 15.00 30.00
31 Newsy Lalonde 20.00 40.00
32 Albert Langlois 15.00 30.00
33 Hugh Lehman 15.00 30.00
34 Joe Malone 20.00 40.00
35 Don McKenney 10.00 20.00
36 Stan Mikita 50.00 100.00
37 Doug Mohns 10.00 20.00
38 Paddy Moran 15.00 30.00
39 Howie Morenz 30.00 60.00
40 Ron Murphy 15.00 30.00
41 Frank Nighbor 25.00 50.00
42 Murray Oliver 10.00 20.00
43 Pierre Pilote 15.00 30.00
44 Dean Prentice 10.00 20.00
45 Andre Pronovost 10.00 20.00
46 Art Ross 25.00 50.00
47 Dallas Smith 10.00 20.00
48 Nels Stewart 15.00 30.00
49 Cyclone Taylor 15.00 30.00
50 Elmer Vasko 10.00 20.00
51 Georges Vezina 40.00 80.00
52 Gump Worsley 20.00 40.00

1961-62 Topps

COMMON CARD (1-66) 6.00 15.00
SEMISTARS 8.00 20.00
UNLISTED STARS 10.00 25.00
1 Phil Watson CO 25.00 60.00
2 Ted Green RC 15.00 40.00
3 Earl Balfour 80.00 200.00
4 Dallas Smith RC 20.00 50.00
5 Andre Pronovost UER
(Misspelled Provonost
on card back 10.00 25.00
6 Dick Meissner RC 5.00 12.00
7 Leo Boivin 15.00 40.00
8 Johnny Bucyk 40.00 100.00
9 Jerry Toppazzini 10.00 25.00
10 Doug Mohns 6.00 15.00
11 Charlie Burns 6.00 15.00
12 Don McKenney 8.00 20.00
13 Bob Armstrong 8.00 20.00
14 Murray Oliver 5.00 12.00
15 Orland Kurtenbach RC 30.00 80.00
16 Terry Gray RC 12.00 30.00
17 Don Head RC 6.00 15.00
18 Pat Stapleton RC 20.00 50.00
19 Cliff Pennington RC 5.00 12.00
20 Bruins Team Picture 15.00 40.00
21 E.Balfour/F.Flaman IA 10.00 25.00
22 A.Bathgate/G.Hall IA 10.00 25.00
23 Rudy Pilous CO RC 25.00 60.00
24 Pierre Pilote 25.00 60.00
25 Elmer Vasko 20.00 50.00
26 Reg Fleming RC 6.00 15.00
27 Ab McDonald 5.00 12.00
28 Eric Nesterenko 6.00 15.00
29 Bobby Hull 80.00 200.00
30 Ken Wharram 6.00 15.00
31 Dollard St.Laurent 5.00 12.00
32 Glenn Hall 25.00 60.00
33 Murray Balfour 20.00 50.00
34 Ron Murphy 5.00 12.00
35 Bill Hay 25.00 60.00
36 Stan Mikita 60.00 150.00
37 Denis DeJordy RC 15.00 40.00
38 Wayne Hillman RC 12.00 30.00
39 Rino Robazzo RC 20.00 50.00
40 Bronco Horvath 5.00 12.00
41 Bob Turner 8.00 20.00
42 Blackhawks Team Picture 15.00 40.00
43 Ken Wharram IA 15.00 40.00
44 St.Laurent/G.Hall IA 10.00 25.00
45 Doug Harvey CO 25.00 40.00
46 Junior Langlois 5.00 12.00
47 Irv Spencer RC 5.00 12.00
48 George Sullivan 5.00 12.00
49 Earl Ingarfield 5.00 12.00
50 Gump Worsley 15.00 40.00
51 Harry Howell 6.00 15.00
52 Larry Cahan 5.00 12.00
53 Andy Bathgate 8.00 20.00
54 Dean Prentice 6.00 15.00
55 Andy Hebenton 5.00 12.00
56 Camille Henry 6.00 15.00
57 Jean-Guy Gendron 5.00 12.00
58 Pat Hannigan RC 5.00 12.00
59 Ted Hampson 5.00 12.00
60 Jean Ratelle RC 125.00 300.00
61 Al Lebrun RC 30.00 80.00
62 Rod Gilbert RC 125.00 300.00
63 Rangers Team Picture 25.00 60.00
64 D.Meissner/G.Worsley IA 15.00 40.00
65 Gump Worsley IA 30.00 80.00
66 Checklist Card 60.00 150.00

1962-63 Topps

COMMON CARD (1-66) 6.00 15.00
SEMISTARS 8.00 20.00
UNLISTED STARS 10.00 25.00
1 Phil Watson CO 15.00 40.00
2 Bob Perreault RC 15.00 40.00
3 Bruce Gamble RC 15.00 40.00
4 Warren Godfrey 6.00 15.00
5 Leo Boivin 6.00 15.00
6 Doug Mohns 6.00 15.00
7 Ted Green 6.00 15.00
8 Pat Stapleton 6.00 15.00
9 Dallas Smith 15.00 40.00
10 Don McKenney 6.00 15.00
11 Johnny Bucyk 15.00 40.00
12 Murray Oliver 6.00 15.00
13 Jerry Toppazzini 15.00 40.00
14 Cliff Pennington 12.00 30.00
15 Charlie Burns 6.00 15.00
16 Jean-Guy Gendron 15.00 40.00
17 Irv Spencer 10.00 25.00
18 Wayne Connelly 6.00 15.00
19 Andre Pronovost 6.00 15.00
20 Terry Gray 6.00 15.00
21 Tom Williams RC 6.00 15.00
22 Bruins Team 15.00 40.00
23 Rudy Pilous CO 12.00 30.00
24 Glenn Hall 20.00 50.00
25 Denis DeJordy 6.00 15.00
26 Jack Evans 10.00 25.00
27 Elmer Vasko 6.00 15.00
28 Pierre Pilote 15.00 40.00
29 Bob Turner 6.00 15.00
30 Dollard St.Laurent 6.00 15.00
31 Wayne Hillman 8.00 20.00
32 Al McNeil 6.00 15.00
33 Bobby Hull 100.00 250.00
34 Stan Mikita 40.00 100.00
35 Bill Hay 8.00 20.00
36 Murray Balfour 8.00 20.00
37 Chico Maki RC 8.00 20.00
38 Ab McDonald 6.00 15.00
39 Ken Wharram 6.00 15.00
40 Ron Murphy 6.00 15.00
41 Eric Nesterenko 10.00 25.00
42 Reg Fleming 8.00 20.00
43 Murray Hall RC 6.00 15.00
44 Blackhawks Team 15.00 40.00
45 Gump Worsley 15.00 40.00
46 Harry Howell 6.00 15.00
47 Albert Langlois 6.00 15.00
48 Larry Cahan 6.00 15.00
49 Jim Neilson RC 12.00 30.00
50 Al Lebrun 8.00 20.00
51 Earl Ingarfield 6.00 15.00
52 Andy Bathgate 8.00 20.00
53 Dean Prentice 6.00 15.00
54 Andy Hebenton 6.00 15.00
55 Ted Hampson 6.00 15.00
56 Dave Balon RC 8.00 20.00
57 Bert Olmstead 6.00 15.00
58 Jean Ratelle 30.00 80.00
59 Rod Gilbert 30.00 80.00
60 Vic Hadfield RC 25.00 60.00
61 Frank Paice TR RC 6.00 15.00
62 Camille Henry 12.00 30.00
63 Bronco Horvath 8.00 20.00
64 Pat Hannigan 10.00 25.00
65 Rangers Team 12.00 30.00
66 Checklist Card 60.00 150.00

1962-63 Topps Hockey Bucks

COMPLETE SET (24) 600.00 1000.00
COMMON CARD (1-24) 20.00 40.00
1 Dave Balon 20.00 40.00
2 Andy Bathgate 20.00 40.00
3 Leo Boivin 20.00 40.00
4 Johnny Bucyk 25.00 50.00
5 Reg Fleming 20.00 40.00
6 Warren Godfrey 20.00 40.00
7 Ted Green 20.00 40.00
8 Glenn Hall 40.00 80.00
9 Bill Hay 25.00 50.00
10 Andy Hebenton 20.00 40.00
11 Harry Howell 20.00 40.00
12 Bobby Hull 100.00 200.00
13 Earl Ingarfield 20.00 40.00
14 Albert Langlois 20.00 40.00
15 Ab McDonald 20.00 40.00
16 Don McKenney 20.00 40.00
17 Stan Mikita 50.00 100.00
18 Doug Mohns 20.00 40.00
19 Murray Oliver 20.00 40.00
20 Pierre Pilote 25.00 50.00
21 Dean Prentice 20.00 40.00
22 Jerry Toppazzini 20.00 40.00
23 Elmer Vasko 20.00 40.00
24 Gump Worsley 40.00 80.00

1963-64 Topps

COMMON CARD (1-66) 6.00 15.00
SEMISTARS 8.00 20.00
UNLISTED STARS 10.00 25.00
1 Milt Schmidt CO 12.00 30.00
2 Ed Johnston RC 15.00 40.00
3 Doug Mohns 12.00 30.00
4 Tom Johnson 10.00 25.00
5 Leo Boivin 10.00 25.00
6 Bob McCord RC 5.00 12.00
7 Ted Green 8.00 20.00
8 Ed Westfall RC 12.00 30.00
9 Charlie Burns 6.00 15.00
10 Murray Oliver 8.00 15.00
11 Johnny Bucyk 40.00 100.00
12 Tom Williams 6.00 15.00
13 Dean Prentice 8.00 20.00
14 Bob Leiter RC 15.00 40.00
15 Andy Hebenton 5.00 12.00
16 Jean-Guy Gendron 12.00 30.00
17 Wayne Rivers RC 5.00 12.00
18 Jerry Toppazzini 10.00 25.00
19 Forbes Kennedy 5.00 12.00
20 Orland Kurtenbach 12.00 30.00
21 Bruins Team 15.00 40.00
22 Billy Reay CO 6.00 15.00
23 Glenn Hall 15.00 40.00
24 Denis DeJordy 20.00 50.00
25 Pierre Pilote 12.00 30.00
26 Elmer Vasko 5.00 12.00
27 Wayne Hillman 6.00 15.00
28 Al McNeil 5.00 12.00
29 Howie Young RC 10.00 25.00
30 Ed Van Impe RC 10.00 25.00
31 R.Fleming/G.Howe 8.00 20.00
32 Bob Turner 12.00 30.00
33 Bobby Hull 100.00 250.00
34 Bill Hay 5.00 12.00
35 Murray Balfour 5.00 12.00
36 Stan Mikita 20.00 50.00
37 Ab McDonald 5.00 12.00
38 Ken Wharram 6.00 15.00
39 Eric Nesterenko 6.00 15.00
40 Ron Murphy 4.00 10.00
41 Chico Maki 8.00 20.00
42 John McKenzie 6.00 15.00
43 Blackhawks Team 12.00 30.00
44 George Sullivan 8.00 20.00
45 Jacques Plante 30.00 80.00
46 Gilles Villemure RC 20.00 50.00
47 Doug Harvey 15.00 40.00
48 Harry Howell 8.00 20.00
49 Albert Langlois 5.00 12.00
50 Jim Neilson 6.00 15.00
51 Larry Cahan 5.00 12.00
52 Andy Bathgate 12.00 30.00
53 Don McKenney 5.00 12.00
54 Vic Hadfield 15.00 40.00
55 Earl Ingarfield 5.00 12.00
56 Camille Henry 8.00 20.00
57 Rod Gilbert 12.00 30.00
58 P.Goyette/G.Howe 6.00 15.00
59 Don Marshall 6.00 15.00
60 Dick Meissner 5.00 12.00
61 Val Fonteyne 6.00 15.00
62 Ken Schinkel 5.00 12.00
63 Jean Ratelle 12.00 30.00
64 Don Johns RC 5.00 12.00
65 Rangers Team 15.00 40.00
66 Checklist Card 80.00 200.00

1964-65 Topps

COMMON CARD 12.00 30.00
SEMISTARS 15.00 40.00
UNLISTED STARS 20.00 50.00
1 Pit Martin RC 60.00 150.00
2 Gilles Tremblay 60.00 150.00
3 Terry Harper 40.00 100.00
4 John Ferguson 30.00 80.00
5 Elmer Vasko 12.00 30.00
6 Terry Sawchuk UER 80.00 200.00
7 Bill Hay 40.00 100.00
8 Gary Bergman SP RC 60.00 150.00
9 Doug Barkley 30.00 80.00
10 Bob McCord 20.00 50.00
11 Parker MacDonald 15.00 40.00
12 Glenn Hall 60.00 150.00
13 Albert Langlois 15.00 40.00
14 Camille Henry SP 40.00 100.00
15 Norm Ullman 25.00 60.00
16 Ab McDonald 15.00 40.00
17 Charlie Hodge 30.00 80.00
18 Orland Kurtenbach 25.00 60.00
19 Dean Prentice 12.00 30.00
20 Bobby Hull SP 200.00 500.00
21 Ed Johnston 30.00 80.00
22 Denis DeJordy 25.00 60.00
23 Claude Provost 12.00 30.00
24 Rod Gilbert 25.00 60.00
25 Doug Mohns 20.00 50.00
26 Al McNeil 15.00 40.00
27 Billy Harris SP 60.00 150.00
28 Ken Wharram SP 20.00 50.00
29 George Sullivan 10.00 25.00
30 John McKenzie 30.00 80.00
31 Stan Mikita 40.00 100.00
32 Ted Green SP 30.00 80.00
33 Jean Beliveau SP 150.00 400.00
34 Arnie Brown RC 15.00 40.00
35 Reg Fleming 25.00 60.00
36 Jim Mikol RC 25.00 60.00
37 Dave Balon 25.00 60.00
38 Billy Reay CO 12.00 30.00
39 Marcel Pronovost SP 60.00 150.00
40 Johnny Bower 60.00 150.00
41 Wayne Hillman 20.00 50.00
42 Floyd Smith 15.00 40.00
43 Toe Blake CO 15.00 40.00
44 Red Kelly 30.00 80.00
45 Punch Imlach CO 30.00 80.00
46 Dick Duff 25.00 60.00
47 Roger Crozier RC 60.00 150.00
48 Henri Richard SP 125.00 300.00
49 Larry Jeffrey 12.00 30.00
50 Leo Boivin 12.00 30.00
51 Ed Westfall SP 50.00 125.00
52 Jean-Guy Talbot 50.00 125.00
53 Jacques Laperriere 30.00 80.00
54 1st Checklist 150.00 400.00
55 2nd Checklist SP 400.00 1000.00
56 Ron Murphy 30.00 80.00
57 Bob Baun 20.00 50.00
58 Tom Williams SP 400.00 1000.00
59 Pierre Pilote SP 400.00 1000.00
60 Bob Pulford 60.00 150.00
61 Red Berenson 20.00 50.00
62 Vic Hadfield 20.00 50.00
63 Bob Leiter 20.00 50.00
64 Jim Pappin RC 25.00 60.00
65 Earl Ingarfield 40.00 100.00
66 Lou Angotti RC 30.00 80.00
67 Rod Seiling RC 60.00 150.00
68 Jacques Plante 125.00 300.00
69 George Armstrong UER 40.00 100.00
70 Milt Schmidt CO 20.00 50.00
71 Eddie Shack 60.00 150.00
72 Gary Dornhoefer SP RC 500.00 1200.00
73 Chico Maki SP 200.00 500.00
74 Gilles Villemure SP 200.00 500.00
75 Carl Brewer 20.00 50.00
76 Bruce MacGregor 25.00 60.00
77 Bob Nevin 25.00 60.00
78 Ralph Backstrom 60.00 150.00
79 Murray Oliver 40.00 100.00
80 Bobby Rousseau SP 200.00 500.00
81 Don McKenney 25.00 60.00
82 Ted Lindsay 30.00 80.00
83 Harry Howell 30.00 80.00
84 Doug Robinson RC 25.00 60.00
85 Frank Mahovlich 60.00 150.00
86 Andy Bathgate 50.00 125.00
87 Phil Goyette 30.00 80.00
88 J.C. Tremblay 30.00 80.00
89 Gordie Howe 250.00 600.00
90 Murray Balfour 50.00 125.00
91 Eric Nesterenko SP 250.00 600.00
92 Marcel Paille SP RC 300.00 800.00
93 Sid Abel CO 30.00 80.00
94 Dave Keon 80.00 200.00
95 Alex Delvecchio 80.00 200.00
96 Bill Gadsby 40.00 100.00
97 Don Marshall 20.00 50.00
98 Bill Hicke SP 150.00 400.00
99 Ron Stewart 30.00 80.00
100 Johnny Bucyk 80.00 200.00
101 Tom Johnson 20.00 50.00
102 Tim Horton 60.00 150.00
103 Jim Neilson 25.00 60.00
104 Allan Stanley 40.00 100.00
105 Tim Horton AS SP 400.00 1000.00
106 Stan Mikita AS SP 100.00 250.00
107 Bobby Hull AS 80.00 200.00
108 Ken Wharram AS 25.00 60.00
109 Pierre Pilote AS 125.00 300.00
110 Glenn Hall AS 300.00 800.00

1965-66 Topps

COMMON CARD 5.00 12.00
SEMISTARS 6.00 15.00
UNLISTED STARS 8.00 20.00
1 Toe Blake CO 80.00 200.00
2 Gump Worsley 60.00 150.00
3 Jacques Laperriere 20.00 50.00
4 Jean-Guy Talbot 15.00 40.00
5 Ted Harris RC 25.00 60.00
6 Jean Beliveau 25.00 60.00
7 Dick Duff 15.00 40.00
8 Claude Provost DP 5.00 12.00
9 Red Berenson 5.00 12.00
10 John Ferguson 12.00 30.00
11 Punch Imlach CO 20.00 50.00
12 Terry Sawchuk 50.00 125.00
13 Bob Baun 5.00 12.00
14 Kent Douglas 12.00 30.00
15 Red Kelly 8.00 20.00
16 Jim Pappin 8.00 20.00
17 Dave Keon 25.00 60.00
18 Bob Pulford 5.00 12.00
19 George Armstrong 12.00 30.00
20 Orland Kurtenbach 12.00 30.00
21 Ed Giacomin RC 100.00 250.00
22 Harry Howell 5.00 12.00
23 Rod Seiling 12.00 30.00
24 Mike McMahon RC 5.00 12.00
25 Jean Ratelle 10.00 25.00
26 Doug Robinson 5.00 12.00
27 Vic Hadfield 12.00 30.00
28 Garry Peters UER RC 10.00 25.00
29 Don Marshall 5.00 12.00
30 Bill Hicke 5.00 12.00
31 Gerry Cheevers RC 150.00 400.00
32 Leo Boivin 8.00 20.00
33 Albert Langlois 8.00 20.00
34 Murray Oliver DP 5.00 12.00
35 Tom Williams 12.00 30.00
36 Ron Schock RC 5.00 12.00
37 Ed Westfall 6.00 15.00
38 Gary Dornhoefer 10.00 25.00
39 Bob Dillabough 20.00 50.00
40 Paul Popiel RC 12.00 30.00
41 Sid Abel CO 5.00 12.00
42 Roger Crozier 25.00 60.00
43 Doug Barkley 8.00 20.00
44 Bill Gadsby 6.00 15.00
45 Bryan Watson RC 6.00 15.00
46 Bob McCord 5.00 12.00
47 Alex Delvecchio 25.00 60.00
48 Andy Bathgate 12.00 30.00
49 Norm Ullman 6.00 15.00
50 Ab McDonald 5.00 12.00
51 Paul Henderson RC 80.00 200.00
52 Pit Martin 5.00 12.00
53 Billy Harris DP 12.00 30.00
54 Billy Reay CO 8.00 20.00
55 Glenn Hall 30.00 80.00
56 Pierre Pilote 12.00 30.00
57 Al McNeil 12.00 30.00
58 Camille Henry 5.00 12.00
59 Bobby Hull 50.00 125.00
60 Stan Mikita 30.00 80.00
61 Ken Wharram 12.00 30.00
62 Bill Hay 10.00 25.00
63 Fred Stanfield RC 20.00 50.00
64 Dennis Hull DP RC 40.00 100.00
65 Ken Hodge RC 50.00 125.00
66 Checklist Card 100.00 250.00
67 Charlie Hodge 12.00 30.00
68 Terry Harper 20.00 50.00
69 J.C. Tremblay 5.00 12.00
70 Bobby Rousseau DP 12.00 30.00
71 Henri Richard 40.00 100.00
72 Dave Balon 6.00 15.00
73 Ralph Backstrom 5.00 12.00
74 Jim Roberts RC 15.00 40.00
75 Claude Larose RC 8.00 20.00
76 Yvan Cournoyer DP RC 150.00 400.00
77 Johnny Bower DP 30.00 80.00
78 Carl Brewer 5.00 12.00
79 Tim Horton 20.00 50.00
80 Marcel Pronovost 8.00 20.00
81 Frank Mahovlich 25.00 60.00
82 Ron Ellis RC 20.00 50.00
83 Larry Jeffrey 5.00 12.00
84 Peter Stemkowski RC 10.00 25.00
85 Eddie Joyal RC 8.00 20.00
86 Mike Walton RC 5.00 12.00
87 George Sullivan 6.00 15.00
88 Don Simmons 8.00 20.00
89 Jim Neilson 5.00 12.00
90 Arnie Brown 8.00 20.00
91 Rod Gilbert 20.00 50.00
92 Phil Goyette 10.00 25.00
93 Bob Nevin 20.00 50.00
94 John McKenzie 10.00 25.00
95 Ted Taylor RC 6.00 15.00
96 Milt Schmidt CO DP 10.00 25.00
97 Ed Johnston 8.00 20.00
98 Ted Green 6.00 15.00
99 Don Awrey RC 8.00 20.00
100 Bob Woytowich DP RC 6.00 15.00
101 Johnny Bucyk 20.00 50.00
102 Dean Prentice 15.00 40.00
103 Ron Stewart 6.00 15.00
104 Reg Fleming 6.00 15.00
105 Parker MacDonald 6.00 15.00
106 Hank Bassen 5.00 12.00
107 Gary Bergman 6.00 15.00
108 Gordie Howe DP 100.00 250.00
109 Floyd Smith 50.00 125.00
110 Bruce MacGregor 12.00 30.00
111 Ron Murphy 5.00 12.00
112 Don McKenney 5.00 12.00
113 Denis DeJordy DP 5.00 12.00
114 Elmer Vasko 5.00 12.00
115 Matt Ravlich RC 10.00 25.00
116 Phil Esposito RC 600.00 1500.00
117 Chico Maki 12.00 30.00
118 Doug Mohns 8.00 20.00
119 Eric Nesterenko 6.00 15.00
120 Pat Stapleton 5.00 12.00
121 Checklist Card 125.00 300.00
122 Gordie Howe 600 SP 100.00 250.00
123 Toronto Maple Leafs SP 25.00 60.00
124 Chicago Blackhawks SP 40.00 100.00
125 Detroit Red Wings SP 40.00 100.00
126 Montreal Canadiens SP 25.00 60.00
127 New York Rangers SP 40.00 100.00
128 Boston Bruins SP 100.00 250.00

1966-67 Topps

COMMON CARD 6.00 15.00
SEMISTARS 8.00 20.00
UNLISTED STARS 10.00 25.00
1 Toe Blake CO 125.00 300.00
2 Gump Worsley 15.00 40.00
3 Jean-Guy Talbot 15.00 40.00
4 Gilles Tremblay 20.00 50.00
5 J.C. Tremblay 25.00 60.00
6 Jim Roberts 12.00 30.00
7 Bobby Rousseau 15.00 40.00
8 Henri Richard 40.00 100.00
9 Claude Provost 25.00 60.00
10 Claude Larose 15.00 40.00
11 Punch Imlach CO 40.00 100.00
12 Johnny Bower 30.00 80.00
13 Terry Sawchuk 40.00 100.00
14 Mike Walton 40.00 100.00
15 Pete Stemkowski 6.00 15.00
16 Allan Stanley 15.00 40.00
17 Eddie Shack 15.00 40.00
18 Brit Selby RC 20.00 50.00
19 Bob Pulford 6.00 15.00
20 Marcel Pronovost 6.00 15.00
21 Emile Francis CO RC 60.00 150.00
22 Rod Seiling 20.00 50.00
23 Ed Giacomin 50.00 125.00
24 Don Marshall 25.00 60.00
25 Orland Kurtenbach 10.00 25.00
26 Rod Gilbert 12.00 30.00
27 Bob Nevin 25.00 60.00
28 Phil Goyette 6.00 15.00
29 Jean Ratelle 20.00 50.00
30 Earl Ingarfield 6.00 15.00
31 Harry Sinden CO RC 60.00 150.00
32 Ed Westfall 20.00 50.00
33 Joe Watson RC 25.00 60.00
34 Bob Woytowich 20.00 50.00
35 Bobby Orr RC 6000.00 15000.00
36 Gilles Marotte RC 30.00 80.00
37 Ted Green 15.00 40.00
38 Tom Williams 25.00 60.00
39 Johnny Bucyk 40.00 100.00
40 Wayne Connelly 20.00 50.00
41 Pit Martin 8.00 20.00
42 Sid Abel CO 12.00 30.00
43 Roger Crozier 6.00 15.00
44 Andy Bathgate 25.00 60.00
45 Dean Prentice 6.00 15.00
46 Paul Henderson 10.00 25.00
47 Gary Bergman 30.00 80.00
48 Bryan Watson 8.00 20.00
49 Bob Wall RC 15.00 40.00
50 Leo Boivin 15.00 40.00
51 Bert Marshall RC 12.00 30.00
52 Norm Ullman 8.00 20.00
53 Billy Reay CO 6.00 15.00
54 Glenn Hall 12.00 30.00
55 Wally Boyer RC 20.00 50.00
56 Fred Stanfield 6.00 15.00
57 Pat Stapleton 6.00 15.00
58 Matt Ravlich 6.00 15.00
59 Pierre Pilote 6.00 15.00
60 Eric Nesterenko 20.00 50.00
61 Doug Mohns 6.00 15.00
62 Stan Mikita 20.00 50.00
63 Phil Esposito 80.00 200.00
64 Bobby Hull LL 100.00 250.00
65 C.Hodge/G.Worsley 30.00 80.00
66 Checklist Card 150.00 400.00
67 Jacques Laperriere 6.00 15.00
68 Terry Harper 20.00 50.00
69 Ted Harris 25.00 60.00
70 John Ferguson 10.00 25.00
71 Dick Duff 20.00 50.00
72 Yvan Cournoyer 25.00 60.00
73 Jean Beliveau 25.00 60.00
74 Dave Balon 20.00 50.00
75 Ralph Backstrom 20.00 50.00
76 Jim Pappin 10.00 25.00
77 Frank Mahovlich 15.00 40.00
78 Dave Keon 40.00 100.00
79 Red Kelly 25.00 60.00
80 Tim Horton 60.00 150.00
81 Ron Ellis 15.00 40.00
82 Kent Douglas 20.00 50.00
83 Bob Baun 25.00 60.00
84 George Armstrong 8.00 20.00
85 Bernie Geoffrion 30.00 80.00
86 Vic Hadfield 6.00 15.00
87 Wayne Hillman 20.00 50.00
88 Jim Neilson 12.00 30.00
89 Al McNeil 20.00 50.00
90 Arnie Brown 6.00 15.00
91 Harry Howell 25.00 60.00
92 Red Berenson 15.00 40.00
93 Reg Fleming 20.00 50.00
94 Ron Stewart 6.00 15.00
95 Murray Oliver 12.00 30.00
96 Ron Murphy 8.00 20.00
97 John McKenzie 6.00 15.00
98 Bob Dillabough 12.00 30.00
99 Ed Johnston 15.00 40.00
100 Ron Schock 25.00 60.00
101 Dallas Smith 10.00 25.00
102 Alex Delvecchio 20.00 50.00
103 Peter Mahovlich RC 15.00 40.00
104 Bruce MacGregor 20.00 50.00
105 Murray Hall 6.00 15.00
106 Floyd Smith 6.00 15.00
107 Hank Bassen 20.00 50.00

108 Val Fonteyne 15.00 40.00
109 Gordie Howe 150.00 400.00
110 Chico Maki 30.00 80.00
111 Doug Jarrett RC 20.00 50.00
112 Bobby Hull 50.00 125.00
113 Dennis Hull 6.00 15.00
114 Ken Hodge 25.00 60.00
115 Denis DeJordy 25.00 60.00
116 Lou Angotti 10.00 25.00
117 Ken Wharram 15.00 40.00
118 Montreal Canadiens 50.00 125.00
119 Detroit Red Wings 40.00 100.00
120 Checklist Card 300.00 800.00
121 Gordie Howe AS 30.00 80.00
122 Jacques Laperriere AS 12.00 30.00
123 Pierre Pilote AS 20.00 50.00
124 Stan Mikita AS 40.00 100.00
125 Bobby Hull AS 30.00 80.00
126 Glenn Hall AS 15.00 40.00
127 Jean Beliveau AS 30.00 80.00
128 Allan Stanley AS 10.00 25.00
129 Pat Stapleton AS 40.00 100.00
130 Gump Worsley AS 50.00 125.00
131 Frank Mahovlich AS 40.00 100.00
132 Bobby Rousseau AS 50.00 125.00

1966-67 Topps USA Test

COMPLETE SET (66) 8000.00 12000.00
COMMON CARD (1-66) 25.00 50.00
SEMISTARS/GOALIES 35.00 60.00
UNLISTED STARS 40.00 70.00
1 Dennis Hull 50.00 80.00
2 Gump Worsley 70.00 120.00
3 Dallas Smith 25.00 50.00
4 Gilles Tremblay 25.00 50.00
5 J.C. Tremblay 25.00 50.00
6 Ralph Backstrom 25.00 50.00
7 Bobby Rousseau 25.00 50.00
8 Henri Richard 125.00 200.00
9 Claude Provost 25.00 50.00
10 Red Berenson 25.00 50.00
11 Punch Imlach CO 25.00 50.00
12 Johnny Bower 70.00 120.00
13 Yvan Cournoyer 90.00 150.00
14 Mike Walton 25.00 50.00
15 Pete Stemkowski 25.00 50.00
16 Allan Stanley 40.00 70.00
17 George Armstrong 40.00 70.00
18 Harry Howell 35.00 60.00
19 Vic Hadfield 25.00 50.00
20 Marcel Pronovost 35.00 60.00
21 Pete Mahovlich 35.00 60.00
22 Rod Seiling 25.00 50.00
23 Gordie Howe 500.00 800.00
24 Don Marshall 25.00 50.00
25 Orland Kurtenbach 25.00 50.00
26 Rod Gilbert 50.00 80.00
27 Bob Nevin 25.00 50.00
28 Phil Goyette 25.00 50.00
29 Jean Ratelle 60.00 100.00
30 Dave Keon 90.00 150.00
31 Jean Beliveau 175.00 300.00
32 Ed Westfall 25.00 50.00
33 Ron Murphy 25.00 50.00
34 Wayne Hillman 25.00 50.00
35 Bobby Orr 5000.00 8000.00
36 Boom Boom Geoffrion 90.00 150.00
37 Ted Green 25.00 50.00
38 Tom Williams 25.00 50.00
39 Johnny Bucyk 50.00 80.00
40 Bobby Hull 350.00 600.00
41 Ted Harris 25.00 50.00
42 Red Kelly 50.00 80.00
43 Roger Crozier 35.00 60.00
44 Ken Wharram 25.00 50.00
45 Dean Prentice 25.00 50.00
46 Paul Henderson 50.00 80.00
47 Gary Bergman 25.00 50.00
48 Arnie Brown 25.00 50.00
49 Jim Pappin 25.00 50.00
50 Denis DeJordy 35.00 60.00
51 Frank Mahovlich 75.00 125.00
52 Norm Ullman 50.00 80.00
53 Chico Maki 25.00 50.00
54 Reg Fleming 25.00 50.00
55 Jim Neilson 25.00 50.00
56 Bruce MacGregor 25.00 50.00
57 Pat Stapleton 25.00 50.00
58 Matt Ravlich 25.00 50.00
59 Pierre Pilote 40.00 70.00
60 Eric Nesterenko 25.00 50.00
61 Doug Mohns 25.00 50.00
62 Stan Mikita 175.00 300.00
63 Alex Delvecchio 60.00 100.00
64 Ed Johnston 35.00 60.00
65 John Ferguson 35.00 60.00
66 John McKenzie 50.00 80.00

1967-68 Topps

COMMON CARD 5.00 12.00
SEMISTARS 6.00 15.00
UNLISTED STARS 8.00 20.00
1 Gump Worsley 80.00 200.00
2 Dick Duff 12.00 30.00
3 Jacques Lemaire RC 125.00 300.00
4 Claude Larose 6.00 15.00
5 Gilles Tremblay 12.00 30.00
6 Terry Harper 5.00 12.00
7 Jacques Laperriere 5.00 12.00
8 Garry Monahan RC 5.00 12.00
9 Carol Vadnais RC 5.00 12.00
10 Ted Harris 12.00 30.00
11 Dave Keon 25.00 60.00
12 Pete Stemkowski 5.00 12.00
13 Allan Stanley 12.00 30.00
14 Ron Ellis 5.00 12.00
15 Mike Walton 5.00 12.00
16 Tim Horton 20.00 50.00
17 Brian Conacher RC 20.00 50.00
18 Bruce Gamble 5.00 12.00
19 Bob Pulford 12.00 30.00
20 Duane Rupp RC 15.00 40.00
21 Larry Jeffrey 5.00 12.00
22 Wayne Hillman 5.00 12.00
23 Don Marshall 5.00 12.00
24 Red Berenson 6.00 15.00
25 Phil Goyette 5.00 12.00
26 Camille Henry 6.00 15.00
27 Rod Seiling 8.00 20.00
28 Bob Nevin 5.00 12.00
29 Bernie Geoffrion 12.00 30.00
30 Reg Fleming 5.00 12.00
31 Jean Ratelle 6.00 15.00
32 Phil Esposito 50.00 125.00
33 Derek Sanderson RC 80.00 200.00
34 Eddie Shack 10.00 25.00
35 Ross Lonsberry RC 5.00 12.00
36 Fred Stanfield 5.00 12.00
37 Don Awrey UER 5.00 12.00
38 Glen Sather RC 30.00 80.00
39 John McKenzie 6.00 15.00
40 Tom Williams 5.00 12.00
41 Dallas Smith 8.00 20.00
42 Johnny Bucyk 8.00 20.00
43 Gordie Howe 60.00 150.00
44 Gary Jarrett RC 5.00 12.00
45 Dean Prentice 5.00 12.00
46 Bert Marshall 5.00 12.00
47 Gary Bergman 8.00 20.00
48 Roger Crozier 5.00 12.00
49 Howie Young 5.00 12.00
50 Doug Roberts RC 5.00 12.00
51 Alex Delvecchio 12.00 30.00
52 Floyd Smith 5.00 12.00
53 Doug Shelton RC 5.00 12.00
54 Gerry Goyer RC 5.00 12.00
55 Wayne Maki RC 6.00 15.00
56 Dennis Hull 5.00 12.00
57 Dave Dryden RC 30.00 80.00
58 Paul Terbenche RC 15.00 40.00
59 Gilles Marotte 5.00 12.00
60 Eric Nesterenko 5.00 12.00
61 Pat Stapleton 5.00 12.00
62 Pierre Pilote 5.00 12.00
63 Doug Mohns 5.00 12.00
64 Stan Mikita Triple 12.00 30.00
65 G.Hall/D.DeJordy 8.00 20.00
66 Checklist Card 150.00 400.00
67 Ralph Backstrom 5.00 12.00
68 Bobby Rousseau 5.00 12.00
69 John Ferguson 6.00 15.00
70 Yvan Cournoyer 40.00 100.00
71 Claude Provost 12.00 30.00
72 Henri Richard 12.00 30.00
73 J.C. Tremblay 5.00 12.00
74 Jean Beliveau 60.00 150.00
75 Rogatien Vachon RC 125.00 300.00
76 Johnny Bower 40.00 100.00
77 Wayne Carleton RC 15.00 40.00
78 Jim Pappin 5.00 12.00
79 Frank Mahovlich 40.00 100.00
80 Larry Hillman 5.00 12.00
81 Marcel Pronovost 8.00 20.00
82 Murray Oliver 5.00 12.00
83 George Armstrong 20.00 50.00
84 Harry Howell 5.00 12.00
85 Ed Giacomin 12.00 30.00
86 Gilles Villemure 5.00 12.00
87 Orland Kurtenbach 8.00 20.00
88 Vic Hadfield 5.00 12.00
89 Arnie Brown 5.00 12.00
90 Rod Gilbert 40.00 100.00
91 Jim Neilson 5.00 12.00
92 Bobby Orr 600.00 1500.00
93 Skip Krake UER RC 5.00 12.00
94 Ted Green 15.00 40.00
95 Ed Westfall 12.00 30.00
96 Ed Johnston 12.00 30.00
97 Gary Doak RC 8.00 20.00
98 Ken Hodge 6.00 15.00
99 Gerry Cheevers 15.00 40.00
100 Ron Murphy 6.00 15.00
101 Norm Ullman 6.00 15.00
102 Bruce MacGregor 5.00 12.00
103 Paul Henderson 15.00 40.00
104 Jean-Guy Talbot 5.00 12.00
105 Bart Crashley RC 5.00 12.00
106 Roy Edwards RC 15.00 40.00
107 Jim Watson RC 5.00 12.00
108 Ted Hampson 5.00 12.00
109 Bill Orban RC 8.00 20.00
110 Geoffrey Powis RC 5.00 12.00
111 Chico Maki 5.00 12.00
112 Doug Jarrett 5.00 12.00
113 Bobby Hull 30.00 80.00
114 Stan Mikita 15.00 40.00
115 Denis DeJordy 5.00 12.00
116 Pit Martin 5.00 12.00
117 Ken Wharram 5.00 12.00
118 Bobby Orr Calder 250.00 600.00
119 Harry Howell Norris 5.00 12.00
120 Checklist Card 60.00 150.00
121 Harry Howell AS 5.00 12.00
122 Pierre Pilote AS 5.00 12.00
123 Ed Giacomin AS 6.00 15.00
124 Bobby Hull AS 25.00 60.00
125 Ken Wharram AS 5.00 12.00
126 Stan Mikita AS 20.00 50.00
127 Tim Horton AS 8.00 20.00
128 Bobby Orr AS 200.00 500.00
129 Glenn Hall AS 40.00 100.00
130 Don Marshall AS 5.00 12.00
131 Gordie Howe AS 50.00 125.00
132 Norm Ullman AS 8.00 20.00

1968-69 Topps

COMMON CARD 2.00 5.00
SEMISTARS 2.50 6.00
UNLISTED STARS 3.00 8.00
1 Gerry Cheevers 40.00 100.00
2 Bobby Orr 200.00 500.00
3 Don Awrey UER 5.00 12.00
4 Ted Green 6.00 15.00
5 Johnny Bucyk 30.00 80.00
6 Derek Sanderson 20.00 50.00
7 Phil Esposito 30.00 80.00
8 Ken Hodge 5.00 12.00
9 John McKenzie 5.00 12.00
10 Fred Stanfield 10.00 25.00
11 Tom Williams 6.00 15.00
12 Denis DeJordy 8.00 20.00
13 Doug Jarrett 8.00 20.00
14 Gilles Marotte 5.00 12.00
15 Pat Stapleton 10.00 25.00
16 Bobby Hull 30.00 80.00
17 Chico Maki 6.00 15.00
18 Pit Martin 10.00 25.00
19 Doug Mohns 5.00 12.00
20 Stan Mikita 30.00 80.00
21 Jim Pappin 6.00 15.00
22 Ken Wharram 5.00 12.00
23 Roger Crozier 8.00 20.00
24 Bob Baun 6.00 15.00
25 Gary Bergman 8.00 20.00
26 Kent Douglas 6.00 15.00
27 Ron Harris 5.00 12.00
28 Alex Delvecchio 5.00 12.00
29 Gordie Howe 80.00 200.00
30 Bruce MacGregor 5.00 12.00
31 Frank Mahovlich 15.00 40.00
32 Dean Prentice 5.00 12.00
33 Pete Stemkowski 5.00 12.00
34 Terry Sawchuk 30.00 80.00
35 Larry Cahan 5.00 12.00
36 Real Lemieux RC 10.00 25.00
37 Bill White RC 5.00 12.00
38 Gord Labossiere 8.00 20.00
39 Ted Irvine 8.00 20.00
40 Eddie Joyal 10.00 25.00
41 Dale Rolfe RC 5.00 12.00
42 Lowell MacDonald RC 6.00 15.00
43 Skip Krake UER 8.00 20.00
44 Terry Gray 8.00 20.00
45 Cesare Maniago 12.00 30.00
46 Mike McMahon 5.00 12.00
47 Wayne Hillman 5.00 12.00
48 Larry Hillman 5.00 12.00
49 Bob Woytowich 5.00 12.00
50 Wayne Connelly 10.00 25.00
51 Claude Larose 6.00 15.00
52 Danny Grant UER
John Vanderburg pictured 10.00 25.00
53 Andre Boudrias 5.00 12.00
54 Ray Cullen RC 5.00 12.00
55 Parker MacDonald 5.00 12.00
56 Gump Worsley 20.00 50.00
57 Terry Harper 8.00 20.00
58 Jacques Laperriere 5.00 12.00
59 J.C. Tremblay 12.00 30.00
60 Ralph Backstrom 8.00 20.00
61 Jean Beliveau 40.00 100.00
62 Yvan Cournoyer 20.00 50.00
63 Jacques Lemaire 20.00 50.00
64 Henri Richard 15.00 40.00
65 Bobby Rousseau 5.00 12.00
66 Gilles Tremblay 20.00 50.00
67 Ed Giacomin 20.00 50.00
68 Arnie Brown 8.00 20.00
69 Harry Howell 8.00 20.00
70 Jim Neilson 8.00 20.00
71 Rod Seiling 8.00 20.00
72 Rod Gilbert 20.00 50.00
73 Phil Goyette 5.00 12.00
74 Vic Hadfield 15.00 40.00
75 Don Marshall 8.00 20.00
76 Bob Nevin 6.00 15.00
77 Jean Ratelle 8.00 20.00
78 Charlie Hodge 10.00 25.00
79 Bert Marshall 5.00 12.00
80 Billy Harris 6.00 15.00
81 Carol Vadnais 5.00 12.00
82 Howie Young 8.00 20.00
83 John Brenneman RC 8.00 20.00
84 Gerry Ehman 5.00 12.00
85 Ted Hampson 5.00 12.00
86 Bill Hicke 5.00 12.00
87 Gary Jarrett 8.00 20.00
88 Doug Roberts 6.00 15.00
89 Bernie Parent RC 80.00 200.00
90 Joe Watson 12.00 30.00
91 Ed Van Impe 5.00 12.00
92 Larry Zeidel 8.00 20.00
93 John Miszuk RC 6.00 15.00
94 Gary Dornhoefer 8.00 20.00
95 Leon Rochefort RC 15.00 40.00
96 Brit Selby 5.00 12.00
97 Forbes Kennedy 12.00 30.00
98 Ed Hoekstra 5.00 12.00
99 Garry Peters 6.00 15.00
100 Les Binkley RC 12.00 30.00
101 Leo Boivin 12.00 30.00
102 Earl Ingarfield 8.00 20.00
103 Lou Angotti 5.00 12.00
104 Andy Bathgate 8.00 20.00
105 Wally Boyer 10.00 25.00
106 Ken Schinkel 8.00 20.00
107 Ab McDonald 8.00 20.00
108 Charlie Burns 8.00 20.00
109 Val Fonteyne 6.00 15.00
110 Noel Price 6.00 15.00
111 Glenn Hall 10.00 25.00
112 Bob Plager RC 10.00 25.00
113 Jim Roberts 15.00 40.00
114 Red Berenson 6.00 15.00
115 Larry Keenan 5.00 12.00
116 Camille Henry 6.00 15.00
117 Gary Sabourin RC 5.00 12.00
118 Ron Schock 8.00 20.00
119 Gary Veneruzzo RC 5.00 12.00
120 Gerry Melnyk 5.00 12.00
121 Checklist Card 40.00 100.00
122 Johnny Bower 25.00 60.00
123 Tim Horton 25.00 60.00
124 Pierre Pilote 6.00 15.00
125 Marcel Pronovost 8.00 20.00
126 Ron Ellis 8.00 20.00
127 Paul Henderson 15.00 40.00
128 Dave Keon 15.00 40.00
129 Bob Pulford 5.00 12.00
130 Floyd Smith 6.00 15.00
131 Norm Ullman 12.00 30.00
132 Mike Walton 20.00 50.00

1969-70 Topps

COMMON CARD 1.25 3.00
SEMISTARS 1.50 4.00
UNLISTED STARS 2.00 5.00
1 Gump Worsley 6.00 15.00
2 Ted Harris 4.00 10.00
3 Jacques Laperriere 4.00 10.00
4 Serge Savard RC 30.00 80.00
5 80 4.00 10.00
6 Yvan Cournoyer 4.00 10.00
7 John Ferguson 4.00 10.00
8 Jacques Lemaire 10.00 25.00
9 Bobby Rousseau 4.00 10.00
10 Jean Beliveau 40.00 100.00
11 Henri Richard 4.00 10.00
12 Glenn Hall 4.00 10.00
13 Bob Plager 4.00 10.00
14 Jim Roberts 4.00 10.00
15 Jean-Guy Talbot 4.00 10.00
16 Andre Boudrias 4.00 10.00
17 Camille Henry 4.00 10.00
18 Ab McDonald 4.00 10.00
19 Gary Sabourin 4.00 10.00
20 Red Berenson 4.00 10.00
21 Phil Goyette 4.00 10.00
22 Gerry Cheevers 15.00 40.00
23 Ted Green 4.00 10.00
24 Bobby Orr 200.00 500.00
25 Dallas Smith 4.00 10.00
26 Johnny Bucyk 4.00 10.00
27 Ken Hodge 4.00 10.00
28 John McKenzie 4.00 10.00
29 Ed Westfall 4.00 10.00
30 Phil Esposito 15.00 40.00
31 Derek Sanderson 8.00 20.00
32 Fred Stanfield 4.00 10.00
33 Ed Giacomin 12.00 30.00
34 Arnie Brown 4.00 10.00
35 Jim Neilson 4.00 10.00
36 Rod Seiling 4.00 10.00
37 Rod Gilbert 15.00 40.00
38 Vic Hadfield 4.00 10.00
39 Don Marshall 4.00 10.00
40 Bob Nevin 4.00 10.00
41 Ron Stewart 4.00 10.00
42 Jean Ratelle 4.00 10.00
43 Walt Tkaczuk RC 4.00 10.00
44 Bruce Gamble 4.00 10.00
45 Tim Horton 6.00 15.00
46 Ron Ellis 4.00 10.00
47 Paul Henderson 4.00 10.00
48 Brit Selby 4.00 10.00
49 Floyd Smith 4.00 10.00
50 Mike Walton 4.00 10.00
51 Dave Keon 12.00 30.00
52 Murray Oliver 4.00 10.00
53 Bob Pulford 4.00 10.00
54 Norm Ullman 4.00 10.00
55 Roger Crozier 4.00 10.00
56 Roy Edwards 4.00 10.00
57 Bob Baun 4.00 10.00
58 Gary Bergman 4.00 10.00
59 Carl Brewer 4.00 10.00
60 Wayne Connelly 4.00 10.00
61 Gordie Howe 30.00 80.00
62 Frank Mahovlich 12.00 30.00
63 Bruce MacGregor 4.00 10.00
64 Alex Delvecchio 20.00 50.00
65 Pete Stemkowski 4.00 10.00
66 Denis DeJordy 4.00 10.00
67 Doug Jarrett 4.00 10.00
68 Gilles Marotte 4.00 10.00
69 Pat Stapleton 4.00 10.00
70 Bobby Hull 25.00 60.00
71 Dennis Hull 12.00 30.00
72 Doug Mohns 4.00 10.00
73 Jim Pappin 4.00 10.00
74 Ken Wharram 4.00 10.00
75 Pit Martin 4.00 10.00
76 Stan Mikita 10.00 25.00
77 Charlie Hodge 4.00 10.00
78 Gary Smith 4.00 10.00
79 Harry Howell 4.00 10.00
80 Bert Marshall 4.00 10.00
81 Doug Roberts 4.00 10.00
82 Carol Vadnais 4.00 10.00
83 Gerry Ehman 4.00 10.00
84 Bill Hicke 4.00 10.00
85 Gary Jarrett 4.00 10.00
86 Ted Hampson 4.00 10.00
87 Earl Ingarfield 4.00 10.00
88 Doug Favell RC 5.00 12.00
89 Bernie Parent 10.00 25.00
90 Larry Hillman 4.00 10.00
91 Wayne Hillman 4.00 10.00
92 Ed Van Impe 4.00 10.00
93 Joe Watson 4.00 10.00
94 Gary Dornhoefer 4.00 10.00
95 Reg Fleming 4.00 10.00
96 Jean-Guy Gendron 4.00 10.00
97 Jim Johnson 4.00 10.00
98 Andre Lacroix 4.00 10.00
99 Gerry Desjardins RC 4.00 10.00
100 Dale Rolfe 4.00 10.00
101 Bill White 4.00 10.00
102 Bill Flett 4.00 10.00
103 Ted Irvine 4.00 10.00
104 Ross Lonsberry 4.00 10.00
105 Leon Rochefort 4.00 10.00
106 Eddie Shack 4.00 10.00
107 Dennis Hextall RC 4.00 10.00
108 Eddie Joyal 4.00 10.00
109 Gord Labossiere 4.00 10.00
110 Les Binkley 4.00 10.00
111 Tracy Pratt 4.00 10.00
112 Bryan Watson 4.00 10.00
113 Bob Woytowich 4.00 10.00
114 Keith McCreary 4.00 10.00
115 Dean Prentice 4.00 10.00
116 Glen Sather 4.00 10.00
117 Ken Schinkel 4.00 10.00
118 Wally Boyer 4.00 10.00
119 Val Fonteyne 4.00 10.00
120 Ron Schock 4.00 10.00
121 Cesare Maniago 4.00 10.00
122 Leo Boivin 4.00 10.00
123 Bob McCord 4.00 10.00
124 John Miszuk 4.00 10.00
125 Danny Grant UER
John Vanderburg pictured 4.00 10.00
126 Claude Larose 4.00 10.00
127 Jean-Paul Parise 4.00 10.00
128 Tom Williams 4.00 10.00
129 Charlie Burns 4.00 10.00
130 Ray Cullen 4.00 10.00
131 Danny O'Shea RC 4.00 10.00
132 Checklist Card 20.00 50.00

1970-71 Topps

1 Gerry Cheevers 12.00 30.00
2 Johnny Bucyk 25.00 60.00
3 Bobby Orr 100.00 250.00
4 Don Awrey 4.00 10.00
5 Fred Stanfield 4.00 10.00
6 John McKenzie 4.00 10.00
7 Wayne Cashman RC 5.00 12.00
8 Ken Hodge 4.00 10.00
9 Wayne Carleton 4.00 10.00
10 Garnet Bailey RC 4.00 10.00
11 Phil Esposito 20.00 50.00
12 Lou Angotti 4.00 10.00
13 Jim Pappin 4.00 10.00
14 Dennis Hull 4.00 10.00
15 Bobby Hull 20.00 50.00
16 Doug Mohns 4.00 10.00
17 Pat Stapleton 4.00 10.00
18 Pit Martin 4.00 10.00
19 Eric Nesterenko 4.00 10.00
20 Stan Mikita 10.00 25.00
21 Roy Edwards 4.00 10.00
22 Frank Mahovlich 4.00 10.00
23 Ron Harris 4.00 10.00
24 Bob Baun 4.00 10.00
25 Pete Stemkowski 4.00 10.00
26 Garry Unger 4.00 10.00
27 Bruce MacGregor 4.00 10.00
28 Larry Jeffrey 4.00 10.00
29 Gordie Howe 30.00 80.00
30 Billy Dea 4.00 10.00
31 Denis DeJordy 4.00 10.00
32 Matt Ravlich 4.00 10.00
33 Dave Amadio 4.00 10.00
34 Gilles Marotte 4.00 10.00
35 Eddie Shack 4.00 10.00
36 Bob Pulford 4.00 10.00
37 Ross Lonsberry 4.00 10.00
38 Gord Labossiere 4.00 10.00
39 Eddie Joyal 4.00 10.00
40 Gump Worsley 4.00 10.00
41 Bob McCord 4.00 10.00
42 Leo Boivin 4.00 10.00
43 Tom Reid RC 4.00 10.00
44 Charlie Burns 4.00 10.00
45 Bob Barlow 4.00 10.00
46 Bill Goldsworthy 4.00 10.00
47 Danny Grant 4.00 10.00
48 Norm Beaudin RC 4.00 10.00
49 Rogatien Vachon 12.00 30.00
50 Yvan Cournoyer 4.00 10.00
51 Serge Savard 4.00 10.00
52 Jacques Laperriere 4.00 10.00
53 Terry Harper 4.00 10.00
54 Ralph Backstrom 4.00 10.00
55 Jean Beliveau 10.00 25.00
56 Claude Larose UER 4.00 10.00
57 Jacques Lemaire 4.00 10.00
58 Peter Mahovlich 4.00 10.00
59 Tim Horton 10.00 25.00
60 Bob Nevin 4.00 10.00
61 Dave Balon 4.00 10.00
62 Vic Hadfield 4.00 10.00
63 Rod Gilbert 4.00 10.00
64 Ron Stewart 4.00 10.00
65 Ted Irvine 4.00 10.00
66 Arnie Brown 4.00 10.00
67 Brad Park RC 20.00 50.00
68 Ed Giacomin 4.00 10.00
69 Gary Smith 4.00 10.00
70 Carol Vadnais 4.00 10.00
71 Doug Roberts 4.00 10.00
72 Harry Howell 4.00 10.00
73 Joe Szura 4.00 10.00
74 Mike Laughton 4.00 10.00
75 Gary Jarrett 4.00 10.00
76 Bill Hicke 4.00 10.00
77 Paul Andrea RC 4.00 10.00
78 Bernie Parent 8.00 20.00
79 Joe Watson 4.00 10.00
80 Ed Van Impe 4.00 10.00
81 Larry Hillman 4.00 10.00
82 George Swarbrick 4.00 10.00
83 Bill Sutherland 4.00 10.00
84 Andre Lacroix 4.00 10.00
85 Gary Dornhoefer 4.00 10.00
86 Jean-Guy Gendron 4.00 10.00
87 Al Smith RC 4.00 10.00
88 Bob Woytowich 4.00 10.00
89 Duane Rupp 4.00 10.00
90 Jim Morrison 4.00 10.00
91 Ron Schock 4.00 10.00
92 Ken Schinkel 4.00 10.00
93 Keith McCreary 4.00 10.00
94 Bryan Hextall 4.00 10.00
95 Wayne Hicks RC 4.00 10.00
96 Gary Sabourin 4.00 10.00
97 Ernie Wakely RC 4.00 10.00
98 Bob Wall 4.00 10.00
99 Barclay Plager 4.00 10.00
100 Jean-Guy Talbot 4.00 10.00
101 Gary Veneruzzo 4.00 10.00
102 Tim Ecclestone 4.00 10.00
103 Red Berenson 4.00 10.00
104 Larry Keenan 4.00 10.00
105 Bruce Gamble 4.00 10.00
106 Jim Dorey 4.00 10.00
107 Mike Pelyk RC 4.00 10.00
108 Rick Ley 4.00 10.00
109 Mike Walton 4.00 10.00
110 Norm Ullman 4.00 10.00
111 Brit Selby 4.00 10.00
112 Garry Monahan 4.00 10.00
113 George Armstrong 4.00 10.00
114 Gary Doak 4.00 10.00
115 Darryl Sly RC 4.00 10.00
116 Wayne Maki 4.00 10.00
117 Orland Kurtenbach 4.00 10.00
118 Murray Hall 4.00 10.00
119 Marc Reaume 4.00 10.00
120 Pat Quinn 4.00 10.00
121 Andre Boudrias 4.00 10.00
122 Paul Popiel 4.00 10.00
123 Paul Terbenche 4.00 10.00
124 Howie Menard 4.00 10.00
125 Gerry Meehan RC 4.00 10.00
126 Skip Krake 4.00 10.00
127 Phil Goyette 4.00 10.00
128 Reg Fleming 4.00 10.00
129 Don Marshall 4.00 10.00
130 Bill Inglis RC 4.00 10.00
131 Gilbert Perreault RC 60.00 150.00
132 Checklist Card 30.00 80.00

1970-71 Topps/OPC Sticker Stamps

COMPLETE SET (33) 300.00 450.00
1 Jean Beliveau 15.00 30.00
2 Red Berenson 6.00 12.00
3 Wayne Carleton 6.00 12.00
4 Tim Ecclestone 6.00 12.00
5 Ron Ellis 6.00 12.00
6 Phil Esposito 15.00 30.00
7 Tony Esposito 15.00 40.00
8 Bill Flett 6.00 12.00
9 Ed Giacomin 10.00 20.00
10 Rod Gilbert 10.00 20.00
11 Danny Grant 6.00 12.00
12 Bill Hicke 6.00 12.00
13 Gordie Howe 20.00 50.00
14 Bobby Hull 15.00 40.00
15 Earl Ingarfield 6.00 12.00
16 Eddie Joyal 6.00 12.00
17 Dave Keon 15.00 30.00
18 Andre Lacroix 6.00 12.00
19 Jacques Laperriere 6.00 12.00
20 Jacques Lemaire 10.00 20.00
21 Frank Mahovlich 10.00 20.00
22 Keith McCreary 6.00 12.00
23 Stan Mikita 10.00 20.00
24 Bobby Orr 40.00 100.00
25 Jean-Paul Parise 6.00 12.00
26 Jean Ratelle 7.50 20.00
27 Derek Sanderson 12.50 25.00
28 Frank St.Marseille 6.00 12.00
29 Ron Schock 6.00 12.00
30 Garry Unger 6.00 12.00
31 Carol Vadnais 6.00 12.00
32 Ed Van Impe 6.00 12.00
33 Bob Woytowich 6.00 12.00

1971-72 Topps

COMPLETE SET (132) 200.00 350.00
1 Espo/Bucyk/B.Hull LL 20.00 50.00
2 Orr/Espo/Bucyk LL 12.00 30.00
3 Espo/Orr/Bucyk LL 20.00 50.00
4 Espo/EJ/Cheev/Giaco LL 12.00 30.00
5 Giaco/Espo/Maniago LL 8.00 20.00
6 Plante/Giaco/T.Espo LL 15.00 40.00
7 Fred Stanfield 3.00 8.00
8 Mike Robitaille RC 3.00 8.00
9 Vic Hadfield 3.00 8.00
10 Jacques Plante 15.00 40.00
11 Bill White 3.00 8.00
12 Andre Boudrias 3.00 8.00
13 Jim Lorentz 3.00 8.00
14 Arnie Brown 3.00 8.00
15 Yvan Cournoyer 3.00 8.00
16 Bryan Hextall 3.00 8.00
17 Gary Croteau 3.00 8.00
18 Gilles Villemure 3.00 8.00
19 Serge Bernier RC 3.00 8.00
20 Phil Esposito 5.00 12.00
21 Charlie Burns 3.00 8.00
22 Doug Barrie RC 3.00 8.00
23 Eddie Joyal 3.00 8.00
24 Rosaire Paiement 3.00 8.00
25 Pat Stapleton 3.00 8.00
26 Garry Unger 3.00 8.00
27 Al Smith 3.00 8.00
28 Bob Woytowich 3.00 8.00
29 Marc Tardif 3.00 8.00
30 Norm Ullman 3.00 8.00
31 Tom Williams 3.00 8.00
32 Ted Harris 3.00 8.00
33 Andre Lacroix 3.00 8.00
34 Mike Byers 3.00 8.00
35 Johnny Bucyk 3.00 8.00
36 Roger Crozier 3.00 8.00
37 Alex Delvecchio 3.00 8.00
38 Frank St.Marseille 3.00 8.00
39 Pit Martin 3.00 8.00
40 Brad Park 4.00 10.00
41 Greg Polis RC 3.00 8.00
42 Orland Kurtenbach 3.00 8.00
43 Jim McKenny RC 3.00 8.00
44 Bob Nevin 3.00 8.00
45 Ken Dryden RC 80.00 200.00
46 Carol Vadnais 3.00 8.00
47 Bill Flett 3.00 8.00
48 Jim Johnson 3.00 8.00
49 Al Hamilton 3.00 8.00
50 Bobby Hull 25.00 60.00
51 Chris Bordeleau RC 3.00 8.00
52 Tim Ecclestone 3.00 8.00
53 Rod Seiling 3.00 8.00
54 Gerry Cheevers 8.00 20.00
55 Bill Goldsworthy 3.00 8.00
56 Ron Schock 3.00 8.00
57 Jim Dorey 3.00 8.00
58 Wayne Maki 3.00 8.00
59 Terry Harper 3.00 8.00
60 Gilbert Perreault 12.00 30.00
61 Ernie Hicke RC 3.00 8.00
62 Wayne Hillman 3.00 8.00
63 Denis DeJordy 3.00 8.00
64 Ken Schinkel 3.00 8.00
65 Derek Sanderson 12.00 30.00
66 Barclay Plager 3.00 8.00
67 Paul Henderson 3.00 8.00
68 Jude Drouin 3.00 8.00
69 Keith Magnuson 3.00 8.00
70 Gordie Howe 25.00 60.00
71 Jacques Lemaire 3.00 8.00
72 Doug Favell 3.00 8.00
73 Bert Marshall 3.00 8.00
74 Gerry Meehan 3.00 8.00
75 Walt Tkaczuk 3.00 8.00
76 Bob Berry RC 3.00 8.00
77 Syl Apps RC 3.00 8.00
78 Tom Webster 3.00 8.00
79 Danny Grant 3.00 8.00
80 Dave Keon 3.00 8.00
81 Ernie Wakely 3.00 8.00
82 John McKenzie 3.00 8.00
83 Doug Roberts 3.00 8.00
84 Peter Mahovlich 3.00 8.00
85 Dennis Hull 3.00 8.00
86 Juha Widing RC 3.00 8.00
87 Gary Doak 3.00 8.00
88 Phil Goyette 3.00 8.00
89 Gary Dornhoefer 3.00 8.00
90 Ed Giacomin 3.00 8.00
91 Red Berenson 3.00 8.00
92 Mike Pelyk 3.00 8.00
93 Gary Jarrett 3.00 8.00
94 Bob Pulford 3.00 8.00
95 Dale Tallon 3.00 8.00
96 Eddie Shack 3.00 8.00
97 Jean Ratelle 3.00 8.00
98 Jim Pappin 3.00 8.00
99 Roy Edwards 3.00 8.00
100 Bobby Orr 60.00 150.00
101 Ted Hampson 3.00 8.00
102 Mickey Redmond 3.00 8.00
103 Bob Plager 3.00 8.00
104 Bruce Gamble 3.00 8.00
105 Frank Mahovlich 3.00 8.00
106 Tony Featherstone RC 3.00 8.00
107 Tracy Pratt 3.00 8.00
108 Ralph Backstrom 3.00 8.00
109 Murray Hall 3.00 8.00
110 Tony Esposito 10.00 25.00
111 Checklist Card 30.00 80.00
112 Jim Neilson 3.00 8.00
113 Ron Ellis 3.00 8.00
114 Bobby Clarke 20.00 50.00
115 Ken Hodge 3.00 8.00
116 Jim Roberts 3.00 8.00
117 Cesare Maniago 3.00 8.00
118 Jean Pronovost 3.00 8.00
119 Gary Bergman 3.00 8.00
120 Henri Richard 3.00 8.00
121 Ross Lonsberry 3.00 8.00
122 Pat Quinn 3.00 8.00
123 Rod Gilbert 3.00 8.00
124 Gary Smith 3.00 8.00
125 Stan Mikita 20.00 50.00
126 Ed Van Impe 3.00 8.00
127 Wayne Connelly 3.00 8.00
128 Dennis Hextall 3.00 8.00
129 Wayne Cashman 3.00 8.00
130 J.C. Tremblay 3.00 8.00
131 Bernie Parent 3.00 8.00
132 Dunc McCallum RC 8.00 20.00

1972-73 Topps

1 Bruins Team DP 10.00 25.00
2 Playoff Game 1 3.00 8.00
3 Playoff Game 2 3.00 8.00
4 Playoff Game 3 3.00 8.00
5 Playoff Game 4 DP 3.00 8.00
6 Playoff Game 5 DP 3.00 8.00
7 Playoff Game 6 DP 3.00 8.00
8 Stanley Cup Trophy 20.00 50.00
9 Ed Van Impe DP 3.00 8.00
10 Yvan Cournoyer DP 3.00 8.00
11 Syl Apps DP 3.00 8.00
12 Bill Plager RC 3.00 8.00
13 Ed Johnston DP 3.00 8.00
14 Walt Tkaczuk 3.00 8.00
15 Dale Tallon DP 3.00 8.00
16 Gerry Meehan 3.00 8.00
17 Reggie Leach 3.00 8.00
18 Marcel Dionne DP 8.00 20.00
19 Andre Dupont RC 8.00 8.00
20 Tony Esposito 8.00 20.00
21 Bob Berry DP 3.00 8.00
22 Craig Cameron 3.00 8.00
23 Ted Harris 3.00 8.00
24 Jacques Plante 8.00 20.00
25 Jacques Lemaire DP 3.00 8.00
26 Simon Nolet DP 3.00 8.00
27 Keith McCreary DP 3.00 8.00
28 Duane Rupp 3.00 8.00
29 Wayne Cashman 3.00 8.00
30 Brad Park 3.00 8.00
31 Roger Crozier 3.00 8.00
32 Wayne Maki 3.00 8.00
33 Tim Ecclestone 3.00 8.00
34 Rick Smith 3.00 8.00
35 Garry Unger DP 3.00 8.00
36 Serge Bernier DP 3.00 8.00
37 Brian Glennie 3.00 8.00
38 Gerry Desjardins DP 3.00 8.00
39 Danny Grant 3.00 8.00
40 Bill White DP 3.00 8.00
41 Gary Dornhoefer DP 3.00 8.00
42 Peter Mahovlich 3.00 8.00
43 Greg Polis DP 3.00 8.00
44 Larry Hale DP RC 3.00 8.00
45 Dallas Smith 3.00 8.00
46 Orland Kurtenbach DP 3.00 8.00
47 Steve Atkinson 3.00 8.00
48 Joey Johnston DP 3.00 8.00
49 Gary Bergman 3.00 8.00
50 Jean Ratelle 3.00 8.00
51 Rogatien Vachon DP 3.00 8.00
52 Phil Roberto DP 3.00 8.00
53 Brian Spencer DP 3.00 8.00
54 Jim McKenny DP 3.00 8.00
55 Gump Worsley 3.00 8.00
56 Stan Mikita DP 8.00 20.00
57 Guy Lapointe 3.00 8.00
58 Lew Morrison DP 3.00 8.00
59 Ron Schock DP 3.00 8.00
60 Johnny Bucyk 3.00 8.00
61 Espo/Hadf/B.Hull LL 5.00 12.00
62 Orr/Espo/Ratelle LL DP 6.00 15.00
63 Espo/Orr/Ratelle LL DP 4.00 10.00
64 Espo/Villem/Worsley LL 3.00 8.00
65 Wtsn/Magn/Dorn LL 3.00 8.00
66 Jim Neilson 3.00 8.00
67 Nick Libett DP 3.00 8.00
68 Jim Lorentz 3.00 8.00
69 Gilles Meloche RC 12.00 30.00
70 Pat Stapleton 3.00 8.00
71 Frank St.Marseille DP 3.00 8.00
72 Butch Goring 3.00 8.00
73 Paul Henderson DP 3.00 8.00
74 Doug Favell 3.00 8.00
75 Jocelyn Guevremont DP 3.00 8.00
76 Tom Miller RC 3.00 8.00

77 Bill MacMillan RC 3.00 8.00
78 Doug Mohns 3.00 8.00
79 Guy Lafleur DP 12.00 30.00
80 Rod Gilbert DP 3.00 8.00
81 Gary Doak 3.00 8.00
82 Dave Burrows DP RC 3.00 8.00
83 Gary Croteau 3.00 8.00
84 Tracy Pratt DP 3.00 8.00
85 Carol Vadnais DP 3.00 8.00
86 Jacques Caron DP RC 3.00 8.00
87 Keith Magnuson 3.00 8.00
88 Dave Keon 3.00 8.00
89 Mike Corrigan 3.00 8.00
90 Bobby Clarke 6.00 15.00
91 Dunc Wilson DP 3.00 8.00
92 Gerry Hart RC 3.00 8.00
93 Lou Nanne 3.00 8.00
94 Checklist 1-176 DP 10.00 25.00
95 Red Berenson DP 3.00 8.00
96 Bob Plager 3.00 8.00
97 Jim Rutherford RC 3.00 8.00
98 Rick Foley DP RC 3.00 8.00
99 Pit Martin DP 3.00 8.00
100 Bobby Orr DP 30.00 80.00
101 Stan Gilbertson 3.00 8.00
102 Barry Wilkins 3.00 8.00
103 Terry Crisp DP 3.00 8.00
104 Cesare Maniago DP 3.00 8.00
105 Marc Tardif 3.00 8.00
106 Don Luce DP 3.00 8.00
107 Mike Pelyk 3.00 8.00
108 Juha Widing DP 3.00 8.00
109 Phil Myre DP RC 3.00 8.00
110 Vic Hadfield 3.00 8.00
111 Arnie Brown DP 3.00 8.00
112 Ross Lonsberry DP 3.00 8.00
113 Dick Redmond 3.00 8.00
114 Gary Smith 3.00 8.00
115 Bill Goldsworthy 3.00 8.00
116 Bryan Watson 3.00 8.00
117 Dave Balon DP 3.00 8.00
118 Bill Mikkelson DP RC 3.00 8.00
119 Terry Harper DP 3.00 8.00
120 Gilbert Perreault DP 5.00 12.00
121 Tony Esposito AS1 4.00 10.00
122 Bobby Orr AS1 20.00 50.00
123 Brad Park AS1 3.00 8.00
124 Phil Esposito AS1 3.00 8.00
125 Rod Gilbert AS1 3.00 8.00
126 Bobby Hull AS1 6.00 15.00
127 Ken Dryden AS2 DP 5.00 12.00
128 Bill White AS2 DP 3.00 8.00
129 Pat Stapleton AS2 DP 3.00 8.00
130 Jean Ratelle AS2 DP 3.00 8.00
131 Yvan Cournoyer AS2 DP 3.00 8.00
132 Vic Hadfield AS2 DP 3.00 8.00
133 Ralph Backstrom DP 3.00 8.00
134 Bob Baun DP 3.00 8.00
135 Fred Stanfield DP 3.00 8.00
136 Barclay Plager DP 3.00 8.00
137 Gilles Villemure 3.00 8.00
138 Ron Harris DP 3.00 8.00
139 Bill Flett DP 3.00 8.00
140 Frank Mahovlich 3.00 8.00
141 Alex Delvecchio DP 3.00 8.00
142 Paul Popiel 3.00 8.00
143 Jean Pronovost DP 3.00 8.00
144 Denis DeJordy DP 3.00 8.00
145 Richard Martin DP 3.00 8.00
146 Ivan Boldirev RC 3.00 8.00
147 Jack Egers RC 3.00 8.00
148 Jim Pappin 3.00 8.00
149 Rod Seiling 3.00 8.00
150 Phil Esposito 10.00 25.00
151 Gary Edwards 3.00 8.00
152 Ron Ellis DP 3.00 8.00
153 Jude Drouin 3.00 8.00
154 Ernie Hicke DP 3.00 8.00
155 Mickey Redmond 3.00 8.00
156 Joe Watson DP 3.00 8.00
157 Bryan Hextall 3.00 8.00
158 Andre Boudrias 3.00 8.00
159 Ed Westfall 3.00 8.00
160 Ken Dryden 10.00 25.00
161 Rene Robert DP RC 3.00 8.00
162 Bert Marshall DP 3.00 8.00
163 Gary Sabourin 3.00 8.00
164 Dennis Hull 3.00 8.00
165 Ed Giacomin DP 3.00 8.00
166 Ken Hodge 3.00 8.00
167 Gilles Marotte DP 3.00 8.00
168 Norm Ullman DP 3.00 8.00
169 Barry Gibbs RC 3.00 8.00
170 Art Ross Trophy 3.00 8.00
171 Hart Memorial Trophy 3.00 8.00
172 James Norris Trophy 3.00 8.00
173 Vezina Trophy DP 3.00 8.00
174 Calder Trophy DP 3.00 8.00
175 Lady Byng Trophy DP 3.00 8.00
176 Conn Smythe Trophy DP 3.00 8.00

1973-74 Topps

COMPLETE SET (198) 125.00 200.00
1 P.Espo/MacLeish LL 3.00 8.00
2 P.Espo/B.Clarke LL 3.00 8.00
3 P.Espo/B.Clarke LL 3.00 8.00
4 K.Dryden/T.Espo LL 3.00 8.00
5 D.Schultz/Schoenfeld LL 3.00 8.00
6 P.Espo/MacLeish LL 3.00 8.00
7 Paul Henderson DP 3.00 8.00
8 Gregg Sheppard DP UER 3.00 8.00
9 Rod Seiling DP 3.00 8.00
10 Ken Dryden 10.00 25.00
11 Jean Pronovost DP 3.00 8.00
12 Dick Redmond 3.00 8.00
13 Keith McCreary DP 3.00 8.00
14 Ted Harris DP 3.00 8.00
15 Garry Unger 3.00 8.00
16 Neil Komadoski RC 3.00 8.00
17 Marcel Dionne 6.00 15.00
18 Ernie Hicke DP 3.00 8.00
19 Andre Boudrias 3.00 8.00
20 Bill Flett 3.00 8.00
21 Marshall Johnston 3.00 8.00
22 Gerry Meehan 3.00 8.00
23 Ed Johnston DP 3.00 8.00
24 Serge Savard 3.00 8.00
25 Walt Tkaczuk 3.00 8.00
26 Johnny Bucyk 3.00 8.00
27 Dave Burrows 3.00 8.00
28 Cliff Koroll 3.00 8.00
29 Rey Comeau DP 3.00 8.00
30 Barry Gibbs 3.00 8.00
31 Wayne Stephenson 3.00 8.00
32 Dan Maloney DP 3.00 8.00
33 Henry Boucha DP 3.00 8.00
34 Gerry Hart 3.00 8.00
35 Bobby Schmautz 3.00 8.00
36 Ross Lonsberry DP 3.00 8.00
37 Ted McAneeley 3.00 8.00
38 Don Luce DP 3.00 8.00
39 Jim McKenny DP 3.00 8.00
40 Frank Mahovlich 3.00 8.00
41 Bill Fairbairn 3.00 8.00
42 Dallas Smith 3.00 8.00
43 Bryan Hextall 3.00 8.00
44 Keith Magnuson 3.00 8.00
45 Dan Bouchard 3.00 8.00
46 Jean-Paul Parise DP 3.00 8.00
47 Barclay Plager 3.00 8.00
48 Mike Corrigan 3.00 8.00
49 Nick Libett DP 3.00 8.00
50 Bobby Clarke 8.00 20.00
51 Bert Marshall DP 3.00 8.00
52 Craig Patrick 3.00 8.00
53 Richard Lemieux 3.00 8.00
54 Tracy Pratt DP 3.00 8.00
55 Ron Ellis DP 3.00 8.00
56 Jacques Lemaire 3.00 8.00
57 Steve Vickers DP 3.00 8.00
58 Carol Vadnais 3.00 8.00
59 Jim Rutherford DP 3.00 8.00
60 Dennis Hull 3.00 8.00
61 Pat Quinn DP 3.00 8.00
62 Bill Goldsworthy DP 3.00 8.00
63 Fran Huck RC 3.00 8.00
64 Rogatien Vachon DP 3.00 8.00
65 Gary Bergman DP 3.00 8.00
66 Bernie Parent 3.00 8.00
67 Ed Westfall 3.00 8.00
68 Ivan Boldirev 3.00 8.00
69 Don Tannahill DP 3.00 8.00
70 Gilbert Perreault DP 3.00 8.00
71 Mike Pelyk DP 3.00 8.00
72 Guy Lafleur DP 10.00 25.00
73 Jean Ratelle 3.00 8.00
74 Gilles Gilbert DP RC 3.00 8.00
75 Greg Polis 3.00 8.00
76 Doug Jarrett DP 3.00 8.00
77 Phil Myre DP 3.00 8.00
78 Fred Harvey DP 3.00 8.00
79 Jack Egers 3.00 8.00
80 Terry Harper 3.00 8.00
81 Bill Barber RC 15.00 40.00
82 Roy Edwards DP 3.00 8.00
83 Brian Spencer 3.00 8.00
84 Reggie Leach DP 3.00 8.00
85 Dave Keon 3.00 8.00
86 Jim Schoenfeld 3.00 8.00
87 Henri Richard DP 3.00 8.00
88 Rod Gilbert DP 3.00 8.00
89 Don Marcotte DP 3.00 8.00
90 Tony Esposito 3.00 8.00
91 Joe Watson 3.00 8.00
92 Flames Team 3.00 8.00
93 Bruins Team 3.00 8.00
94 Sabres Team DP 3.00 8.00
95 Golden Seals Team DP 3.00 8.00
96 Blackhawks Team 3.00 8.00
97 Red Wings Team DP 3.00 8.00
98 Kings Team DP 3.00 8.00
99 North Stars Team 3.00 8.00
100 Canadiens Team 3.00 8.00
101 Islanders Teams 3.00 8.00
102 Rangers Team DP 3.00 8.00
103 Flyers Team DP 3.00 8.00
104 Penguins Team 3.00 8.00
105 Blues Team 3.00 8.00
106 Maple Leafs Team 3.00 8.00
107 Canucks Team 3.00 8.00
108 Roger Crozier DP 3.00 8.00
109 Tom Reid 3.00 8.00
110 Hilliard Graves RC 3.00 8.00
111 Don Lever 3.00 8.00
112 Jim Pappin 3.00 8.00
113 Ron Schock DP 3.00 8.00
114 Gerry Desjardins 3.00 8.00
115 Yvan Cournoyer DP 3.00 8.00
116 Checklist Card 5.00 12.00
117 Bob Leiter 3.00 8.00
118 Ab DeMarco 3.00 8.00
119 Doug Favell 3.00 8.00
120 Phil Esposito 8.00 20.00
121 Mike Robitaille 3.00 8.00
122 Real Lemieux 3.00 8.00
123 Jim Neilson 3.00 8.00
124 Tim Ecclestone DP 3.00 8.00
125 Jude Drouin 3.00 8.00
126 Gary Smith DP 3.00 8.00
127 Walt McKechnie 3.00 8.00
128 Lowell MacDonald 3.00 8.00
129 Dale Tallon DP 3.00 8.00
130 Billy Harris RC 3.00 8.00
131 Randy Manery DP 3.00 8.00
132 Darryl Sittler DP 12.00 30.00
133 Ken Hodge 3.00 8.00
134 Bob Plager 3.00 8.00
135 Rick MacLeish 3.00 8.00
136 Dennis Hextall 3.00 8.00
137 Jacques Laperriere DP 3.00 8.00
138 Butch Goring 3.00 8.00
139 Rene Robert 3.00 8.00
140 Ed Giacomin 3.00 8.00
141 Alex Delvecchio DP 3.00 8.00
142 Jocelyn Guevremont 3.00 8.00
143 Joey Johnston 3.00 8.00
144 Bryan Watson DP 3.00 8.00
145 Stan Mikita 4.00 10.00
146 Cesare Maniago 3.00 8.00
147 Craig Cameron 3.00 8.00
148 Norm Ullman DP 3.00 8.00
149 Dave Schultz RC 4.00 10.00
150 Bobby Orr 40.00 100.00
151 Phil Roberto 3.00 8.00
152 Curt Bennett RC 3.00 8.00
153 Gilles Villemure DP 3.00 8.00
154 Chuck Lefley RC 3.00 8.00
155 Richard Martin 3.00 8.00
156 Juha Widing 3.00 8.00
157 Orland Kurtenbach 3.00 8.00
158 Bill Collins DP 3.00 8.00
159 Bob Stewart RC 3.00 8.00
160 Syl Apps 3.00 8.00
161 Danny Grant 3.00 8.00
162 Billy Smith RC 30.00 80.00
163 Brian Glennie 3.00 8.00
164 Pit Martin DP 3.00 8.00
165 Brad Park 3.00 8.00
166 Wayne Cashman DP 3.00 8.00
167 Gary Dornhoefer 3.00 8.00
168 Steve Durbano RC 3.00 8.00
169 Jacques Richard 3.00 8.00
170 Guy Lapointe 3.00 8.00
171 Jim Lorentz 3.00 8.00
172 Bob Berry DP 3.00 8.00
173 Dennis Kearns 3.00 8.00
174 Red Berenson 3.00 8.00
175 Gilles Meloche DP 3.00 8.00
176 Al McDonough 3.00 8.00
177 Dennis O'Brien RC 3.00 8.00
178 Germaine Gagnon UER DP 3.00 8.00
179 Rick Kehoe DP 3.00 8.00
180 Bill White 3.00 8.00
181 Vic Hadfield DP 3.00 8.00
182 Derek Sanderson 3.00 8.00
183 Andre Dupont DP 3.00 8.00
184 Gary Sabourin 3.00 8.00
185 Larry Romanchych RC 3.00 8.00
186 Peter Mahovlich 3.00 8.00
187 Dave Dryden 3.00 8.00
188 Gilles Marotte 3.00 8.00
189 Bobby Lalonde 3.00 8.00
190 Mickey Redmond 3.00 8.00
191 Series A 3.00 8.00
192 Series B 3.00 8.00
193 Series C 3.00 8.00
194 Series D 3.00 8.00
195 Series E 3.00 8.00
196 Series F 3.00 8.00
197 Series G 3.00 8.00
198 Canadiens Champs 3.00 8.00

1973-74 Topps Team Stickers

COMPLETE SET (22) 50.00 100.00
1 Atlanta Flames/Sabres 2.00 5.00
2 Boston Bruins/Penguins 2.00 5.00
3 Boston Bruins/Rangers 2.00 5.00
4 Buffalo Sabres/Islanders 2.00 5.00
5 California Golden Seals/Blues 2.00 5.00
6 Chicago Blackhawks/Flames 2.00 5.00
7 Detroit Red Wings/Golden Seals 2.00 5.00
8 Detroit Red Wings/North Stars 2.00 5.00
9 Los Angeles Kings/Maple Leafs 2.00 5.00
10 Minnesota North Stars/Canadiens 2.00 5.00
11 Montreal Canadiens/Maple Leafs 2.00 5.00
12 Montreal Canadiens/Red Wings 2.00 5.00
13 New York Islanders/Bruins 2.00 5.00
14 New York Rangers/Black Hawks 2.00 5.00
15 New York Rangers/Canucks 2.00 5.00
16 Philadelphia Flyers/Red Wings 2.00 5.00
17 Pittsburgh Penguins/Black Hawks 2.00 5.00
18 St. Louis Blues/Canadiens 2.00 5.00
19 Toronto Maple Leafs/Bruins 2.00 5.00
20 Toronto Maple Leafs/Flyers 2.00 5.00
21 Vancouver Canucks/Rangers 2.00 5.00
22 NHL Logo/Kings 2.00 5.00

1974-75 Topps

COMPLETE SET (264) 125.00 200.00
1 P.Espo/Goldsworthy LL 3.00 8.00
2 B.Orr/D.Hextall LL 3.00 8.00
3 P.Espo/B.Clarke LL 3.00 8.00
4 D.Favell/B.Parent LL 3.00 8.00
5 B.Watson/D.Schultz LL 3.00 8.00
6 M.Redmond/R.Mac LL 3.00 8.00
7 Gary Bromley RC 3.00 8.00
8 Bill Barber 3.00 8.00
9 Emile Francis CO 3.00 8.00
10 Gilles Gilbert 3.00 8.00
11 John Davidson RC 4.00 10.00
12 Ron Ellis 3.00 8.00
13 Syl Apps 3.00 8.00
14 Richard/Lysiak/McCreary TL 3.00 8.00
15 Dan Bouchard 4.00 10.00
16 Ivan Boldirev 3.00 8.00
17 Gary Coalter RC 3.00 8.00
18 Bob Berry 3.00 8.00
19 Red Berenson 4.00 10.00
20 Stan Mikita 3.00 8.00
21 Fred Shero CO RC 3.00 8.00
22 Gary Smith 3.00 8.00
23 Bill Mikkelson 3.00 8.00
24 Jacques Lemaire UER 3.00 8.00
25 Gilbert Perreault 3.00 8.00
26 Cesare Maniago 3.00 8.00
27 Bobby Schmautz 3.00 8.00
28 Espo/Orr/Bucyk TL 8.00 20.00
29 Steve Vickers 3.00 8.00
30 Lowell MacDonald 3.00 8.00
31 Fred Stanfield 3.00 8.00
32 Ed Westfall 4.00 10.00
33 Curt Bennett 3.00 8.00
34 Bep Guidolin CO 3.00 8.00
35 Cliff Koroll 3.00 8.00
36 Gary Croteau 3.00 8.00
37 Mike Corrigan 3.00 8.00
38 Henry Boucha 4.00 10.00
39 Ron Low 3.00 8.00
40 Darryl Sittler 3.00 8.00
41 Tracy Pratt 3.00 8.00
42 R.Martin/R.Robert TL 3.00 8.00
43 Larry Carriere 3.00 8.00
44 Gary Dornhoefer 3.00 8.00
45 Denis Herron RC 3.00 8.00
46 Doug Favell 3.00 8.00
47 Dave Gardner RC 3.00 8.00
48 Morris Mott RC 3.00 8.00
49 Marc Boileau CO 3.00 8.00
50 Brad Park 3.00 8.00
51 Bob Leiter 3.00 8.00
52 Tom Reid 3.00 8.00
53 Serge Savard 3.00 8.00
54 Checklist 1-132 UER 4.00 10.00
55 Terry Harper 3.00 8.00
56 Johnston/McKechnie TL 3.00 8.00
57 Guy Charron 3.00 8.00
58 Pit Martin 3.00 8.00
59 Chris Evans 3.00 8.00
60 Bernie Parent 3.00 8.00
61 Jim Lorentz 3.00 8.00
62 Dave Kryskow RC 3.00 8.00
63 Lou Angotti CO 4.00 10.00
64 Bill Flett 3.00 8.00
65 Vic Hadfield 4.00 10.00
66 Wayne Merrick RC 4.00 10.00
67 Andre Dupont 4.00 10.00
68 Tom Lysiak RC 3.00 8.00
69 Pappin/Mikita/Bord TL 3.00 8.00
70 Guy Lapointe 3.00 8.00
71 Gerry O'Flaherty 3.00 8.00
72 Marcel Dionne 3.00 8.00
73 Butch Deadmarsh RC 4.00 10.00
74 Butch Goring 3.00 8.00
75 Keith Magnuson 3.00 8.00
76 Red Kelly CO 3.00 8.00
77 Pete Stemkowski 3.00 8.00
78 Jim Roberts 3.00 8.00
79 Don Luce 3.00 8.00
80 Don Awrey 3.00 8.00
81 Rick Kehoe 3.00 8.00
82 Billy Smith 3.00 8.00
83 Jean-Paul Parise 3.00 8.00
84 Redmond/Dionne/Hog TL 3.00 8.00
85 Ed Van Impe 3.00 8.00
86 Randy Manery 3.00 8.00
87 Barclay Plager 4.00 10.00
88 Inge Hammarstrom RC 3.00 8.00
89 Ab DeMarco 3.00 8.00
90 Bill White 3.00 8.00
91 Al Arbour CO 3.00 8.00
92 Bob Stewart 3.00 8.00
93 Jack Egers 3.00 8.00
94 Don Lever 3.00 8.00
95 Reggie Leach 3.00 8.00
96 Dennis O'Brien 3.00 8.00
97 Peter Mahovlich 3.00 8.00
98 Goring/St.Marseille/Kozak TL 3.00 8.00
99 Gerry Meehan 3.00 8.00
100 Bobby Orr 25.00 60.00
101 Jean Potvin RC 3.00 8.00
102 Rod Seiling 3.00 8.00
103 Keith McCreary 3.00 8.00
104 Phil Maloney CO RC 3.00 8.00
105 Denis Dupere 3.00 8.00
106 Steve Durbano 3.00 8.00
107 Bob Plager UER 3.00 8.00
108 Chris Oddleifson RC 3.00 8.00
109 Jim Neilson 3.00 8.00
110 Jean Pronovost 3.00 8.00
111 Don Kozak RC 3.00 8.00
112 Goldsworthy/Grant/Hex 3.00 8.00
113 Jim Pappin 3.00 8.00
114 Richard Lemieux 3.00 8.00
115 Dennis Hextall 3.00 8.00
116 Bill Hogaboam 3.00 8.00
117 Canucks Leaders 3.00 8.00
118 Jimmy Anderson CO 3.00 8.00
119 Walt Tkaczuk 3.00 8.00
120 Mickey Redmond 4.00 10.00
121 Jim Schoenfeld 3.00 8.00
122 Jocelyn Guevremont 3.00 8.00
123 Bob Nystrom 3.00 8.00
124 Cour/F.Mahov/Larose TL 3.00 8.00
125 Lew Morrison 4.00 10.00
126 Terry Murray 3.00 8.00
127 Richard Martin AS 3.00 8.00
128 Ken Hodge AS 3.00 8.00
129 Phil Esposito AS 3.00 8.00
130 Bobby Orr AS 15.00 40.00
131 Brad Park AS 4.00 10.00
132 Gilles Gilbert AS 4.00 10.00
133 Lowell MacDonald AS 3.00 8.00
134 Bill Goldsworthy AS 3.00 8.00
135 Bobby Clarke AS 6.00 15.00
136 Bill White AS 4.00 10.00
137 Dave Burrows AS 3.00 8.00
138 Bernie Parent AS 3.00 8.00
139 Jacques Richard 3.00 8.00
140 Yvan Cournoyer 3.00 8.00
141 R.Gilbert/B.Park TL 3.00 8.00
142 Rene Robert 3.00 8.00
143 J. Bob Kelly RC 4.00 10.00
144 Ross Lonsberry 3.00 8.00
145 Jean Ratelle 3.00 8.00
146 Dallas Smith 3.00 8.00
147 Bernie Geoffrion CO 3.00 8.00
148 Ted McAneeley 3.00 8.00
149 Pierre Plante 3.00 8.00
150 Dennis Hull 3.00 8.00
151 Dave Keon 3.00 8.00
152 Dave Dunn RC 3.00 8.00
153 Michel Belhumeur 3.00 8.00
154 B.Clarke/D.Schultz TL 3.00 8.00
155 Ken Dryden 6.00 15.00
156 John Wright RC 3.00 8.00
157 Larry Romanchych 3.00 8.00
158 Ralph Stewart 4.00 10.00
159 Mike Robitaille 3.00 8.00
160 Ed Giacomin 3.00 8.00
161 Don Cherry CO RC 15.00 40.00
162 Checklist 133-264 4.00 10.00
163 Rick MacLeish 3.00 8.00
164 Greg Polis 4.00 10.00
165 Carol Vadnais 3.00 8.00
166 Pete Laframboise 3.00 8.00
167 Ron Schock 3.00 8.00
168 Lanny McDonald RC 12.00 30.00
169 Scouts Emblem 3.00 8.00
170 Tony Esposito 12.00 30.00
171 Pierre Jarry 3.00 8.00
172 Dan Maloney 3.00 8.00
173 Peter McDuffe 3.00 8.00
174 Danny Grant 3.00 8.00
175 John Stewart 3.00 8.00
176 Floyd Smith CO 3.00 8.00
177 Bert Marshall 3.00 8.00
178 Chuck Lefley UER 3.00 8.00
179 Gilles Villemure 3.00 8.00
180 Borje Salming RC 25.00 60.00
181 Doug Mohns 3.00 8.00
182 Barry Wilkins 3.00 8.00
183 L.MacDonald/S.Apps TL 3.00 8.00
184 Gregg Sheppard 3.00 8.00
185 Joey Johnston 3.00 8.00
186 Dick Redmond 3.00 8.00
187 Simon Nolet 3.00 8.00
188 Ron Stackhouse 3.00 8.00
189 Marshall Johnston 3.00 8.00
190 Richard Martin 3.00 8.00
191 Andre Boudrias 3.00 8.00
192 Steve Atkinson 4.00 10.00
193 Nick Libett 3.00 8.00
194 Bob Murdoch RC 3.00 8.00
195 Denis Potvin RC 20.00 50.00
196 Dave Schultz 3.00 8.00
197 G.Unger/P.Plante TL 3.00 8.00
198 Jim McKenny 3.00 8.00
199 Gerry Hart 3.00 8.00
200 Phil Esposito 3.00 8.00
201 Rod Gilbert 3.00 8.00
202 Jacques Laperriere 3.00 8.00
203 Barry Gibbs 3.00 8.00
204 Billy Reay CO 3.00 8.00
205 Gilles Meloche 3.00 8.00
206 Wayne Cashman 3.00 8.00
207 Dennis Ververgaert RC 3.00 8.00
208 Phil Roberto 3.00 8.00
209 Quarter Finals 3.00 8.00
210 Quarter Finals 3.00 8.00
211 Quarter Finals 3.00 8.00
212 Quarter Finals 3.00 8.00
213 Stanley Cup Semifinals 3.00 8.00
214 Stanley Cup Semifinals 3.00 8.00
215 Stanley Cup Finals 3.00 8.00
216 Flyers Champions 3.00 8.00
217 Joe Watson 3.00 8.00
218 Wayne Stephenson 4.00 10.00
219 Sittler/Ullman/Hend TL 3.00 8.00
220 Bill Goldsworthy 3.00 8.00
221 Don Marcotte 3.00 8.00
222 Alex Delvecchio CO 3.00 8.00
223 Stan Gilbertson 3.00 8.00
224 Mike Murphy 3.00 8.00
225 Jim Rutherford 3.00 8.00
226 Phil Russell 3.00 8.00
227 Lynn Powis 3.00 8.00
228 Billy Harris 3.00 8.00
229 Bob Pulford CO 3.00 8.00
230 Ken Hodge 3.00 8.00
231 Bill Fairbairn 3.00 8.00
232 Guy Lafleur 20.00 50.00
233 Harris/Stew/Potvin TL 3.00 8.00
234 Fred Barrett 3.00 8.00
235 Rogatien Vachon 3.00 8.00
236 Norm Ullman 3.00 8.00
237 Garry Unger 4.00 10.00
238 Jack Gordon CO RC 3.00 8.00
239 Johnny Bucyk 3.00 8.00
240 Bob Dailey RC 3.00 8.00
241 Dave Burrows 3.00 8.00
242 Len Frig RC 3.00 8.00
243 Henri Richard Masterson 4.00 10.00
244 Phil Esposito Hart 3.00 8.00
245 Johnny Bucyk Byng 3.00 8.00
246 Phil Esposito Ross 3.00 8.00
247 Prince of Wales Trophy 3.00 8.00
248 Bobby Orr Norris 12.00 30.00
249 Bernie Parent Vezina 3.00 8.00
250 Stanley Cup 3.00 8.00
251 Bernie Parent Smythe 3.00 8.00
252 Denis Potvin Calder 3.00 8.00
253 Flyers Campbell Trophy 3.00 8.00
254 Pierre Bouchard 3.00 8.00
255 Jude Drouin 3.00 8.00
256 Capitals Emblem 3.00 8.00
257 Michel Plasse 3.00 8.00
258 Juha Widing 4.00 10.00
259 Bryan Watson 4.00 10.00
260 Bobby Clarke 6.00 15.00
261 Scotty Bowman CO RC 20.00 50.00
262 Craig Patrick 4.00 10.00
263 Craig Cameron 4.00 10.00
264 Ted Irvine 5.00 12.00

1974-75 Topps Team Cloth Stickers

COMPLETE SET (24) 40.00 80.00
1 Atlanta Flames/Canadiens 1.50 4.00
2 Atlanta Flames/Penguins 1.50 4.00
3 Boston Bruins/Flames 1.50 4.00
4 Boston Bruins/Maple Leafs 1.50 4.00
5 Buffalo Sabres/Canucks 1.50 4.00
6 California Golden Seals Canadiens 1.50 4.00
7 Chicago Blackhawks/Bruins 1.50 4.00
8 Detroit Red Wings/Blues 1.50 4.00
9 Kansas City Scouts/Bruins 1.50 4.00
10 Los Angeles Kings/Black Hawks 1.50 4.00
11 Minnesota North Stars/Black Hawks 1.50 4.00
12 Montreal Canadiens/Flyers 1.50 4.00
13 Montreal Canadiens/Rangers 1.50 4.00
14 New York Islanders/North Stars 1.50 4.00
15 New York Rangers/Capitals 1.50 4.00
16 New York Rangers/Golden Seals 1.50 4.00
17 Philadelphia Flyers/Kings 1.50 4.00
18 Pittsburgh Penguins/Flames 1.50 4.00
19 St. Louis Blues/Islanders 1.50 4.00
20 Toronto Maple Leafs/Rangers 1.50 4.00
21 Toronto Maple Leafs/Red Wings 1.50 4.00
22 Vancouver Canucks/Sabres 1.50 4.00
23 Washington Capitals/Scouts 1.50 4.00
24 NHL Logo/Flyers 1.50 4.00
PUZ1 NHL Crest UL .40 1.00
PUZ2 NHL Crest UCL .40 1.00
PUZ3 NHL Crest UCR .40 1.00
PUZ4 NHL Crest UR .40 1.00
PUZ5 NHL Crest ML .40 1.00
PUZ6 NHL Crest MCL .40 1.00
PUZ7 NHL Crest MCR .40 1.00
PUZ8 NHL Crest MR .40 1.00
PUZ9 NHL Crest LL .40 1.00
PUZ10 NHL Crest LCL .40 1.00
PUZ11 NHL Crest LCR .40 1.00
PUZ12 NHL Crest LR .40 1.00

1975-76 Topps

COMPLETE SET (330) 75.00 150.00
1 Stanley Cup Finals 2.50 6.00
2 Semi-Finals 2.50 6.00
3 Semi-Finals 2.50 6.00
4 Quarter Finals 2.50 6.00
5 Quarter Finals 4.00 10.00
6 Quarter Finals 2.50 6.00
7 Quarter Finals 2.50 6.00
8 Curt Bennett 2.50 6.00
9 Johnny Bucyk 2.50 6.00
10 Gilbert Perreault 2.50 6.00
11 Darryl Edestrand 2.50 6.00
12 Ivan Boldirev 2.50 6.00
13 Nick Libett 2.50 6.00
14 Jim McElmury RC 2.50 6.00
15 Frank St.Marseille 2.50 6.00
16 Blake Dunlop 4.00 10.00
17 Yvon Lambert 2.50 6.00
18 Gerry Hart 2.50 6.00
19 Steve Vickers 2.50 6.00
20 Rick MacLeish 4.00 10.00
21 Bob Paradise 2.50 6.00
22 Red Berenson 2.50 6.00
23 Lanny McDonald 2.50 6.00
24 Mike Robitaille 2.50 6.00
25 Ron Low 2.50 6.00
26 Bryan Hextall 2.50 6.00
27 Carol Vadnais 2.50 6.00
28 Jim Lorentz 2.50 6.00
29 Gary Simmons 4.00 10.00
30 Stan Mikita 2.50 6.00
31 Bryan Watson 2.50 6.00
32 Guy Charron 2.50 6.00
33 Bob Murdoch 2.50 6.00
34 Norm Gratton 2.50 6.00
35 Ken Dryden 8.00 20.00
36 Jean Potvin 2.50 6.00
37 Rick Middleton 4.00 10.00
38 Ed Van Impe 2.50 6.00
39 Rick Kehoe 2.50 6.00
40 Garry Unger 2.50 6.00
41 Ian Turnbull 2.50 6.00
42 Dennis Ververgaert 2.50 6.00
43 Mike Marson RC 2.50 6.00
44 Randy Manery 4.00 10.00
45 Gilles Gilbert 2.50 6.00
46 Rene Robert 2.50 6.00
47 Bob Stewart 2.50 6.00
48 Pit Martin 2.50 6.00
49 Danny Grant 2.50 6.00
50 Peter Mahovlich 4.00 10.00
51 Dennis Patterson RC 2.50 6.00
52 Mike Murphy 2.50 6.00
53 Dennis O'Brien 2.50 6.00
54 Garry Howatt 2.50 6.00
55 Ed Giacomin 2.50 6.00
56 Andre Dupont 4.00 10.00
57 Chuck Arnason 2.50 6.00
58 Bob Gassoff RC 4.00 10.00
59 Ron Ellis 2.50 6.00
60 Andre Boudrias 2.50 6.00
61 Yvon Labre 2.50 6.00
62 Hilliard Graves 2.50 6.00
63 Wayne Cashman 2.50 6.00
64 Danny Gare RC 2.50 6.00
65 Rick Hampton 2.50 6.00
66 Darcy Rota 2.50 6.00
67 Bill Hogaboam 2.50 6.00
68 Denis Herron 2.50 6.00
69 Sheldon Kannegiesser 2.50 6.00
70 Yvan Cournoyer UER 2.50 6.00
71 Ernie Hicke 2.50 6.00
72 Bert Marshall 2.50 6.00
73 Derek Sanderson 2.50 6.00
74 Tom Bladon 2.50 6.00
75 Ron Schock 2.50 6.00
76 Larry Sacharuk RC 2.50 6.00
77 George Ferguson 2.50 6.00
78 Ab DeMarco 2.50 6.00
79 Tom Williams 2.50 6.00
80 Phil Roberto 2.50 6.00
81 Bruins Team CL 2.50 6.00
82 Seals Team CL 2.50 6.00
83 Sabres Team CL UER 2.50 6.00
84 Blackhawks CL UER 2.50 6.00
85 Flames Team CL 2.50 6.00
86 Kings Team CL 2.50 6.00
87 Red Wings Team CL 2.50 6.00
88 Scouts Team CL UER 2.50 6.00
89 North Stars Team CL 2.50 6.00
90 Canadiens Team CL 2.50 6.00
91 Maple Leafs Team CL 2.50 6.00
92 Islanders Team CL 2.50 6.00
93 Penguins Team CL 2.50 6.00
94 Rangers Team CL 2.50 6.00
95 Flyers Team CL UER 2.50 6.00
96 Blues Team CL 2.50 6.00
97 Canucks Team CL 2.50 6.00
98 Capitals Team CL 2.50 6.00
99 Checklist 1-110 4.00 10.00
100 Bobby Orr 15.00 40.00
101 Germaine Gagnon UER 2.50 6.00
102 Phil Russell 2.50 6.00
103 Billy Lochead 2.50 6.00
104 Robin Burns 4.00 10.00
105 Gary Edwards 2.50 6.00
106 Dwight Bialowas 2.50 6.00
107 D. Risebrough UER RC 4.00 10.00
108 Dave Lewis 4.00 10.00
109 Bill Fairbairn 4.00 10.00
110 Ross Lonsberry 2.50 6.00
111 Ron Stackhouse 2.50 6.00
112 Claude Larose 2.50 6.00
113 Don Luce 2.50 6.00
114 Errol Thompson RC 2.50 6.00
115 Gary Smith 2.50 6.00
116 Jack Lynch 2.50 6.00
117 Jacques Richard 4.00 10.00
118 Dallas Smith 4.00 10.00
119 Dave Gardner 2.50 6.00
120 Mickey Redmond 2.50 6.00
121 John Marks 2.50 6.00
122 Dave Hudson 2.50 6.00
123 Bob Nevin 2.50 6.00
124 Fred Barrett 2.50 6.00
125 Gerry Desjardins 4.00 10.00
126 Guy Lafleur UER 4.00 10.00
127 Jean-Paul Parise 2.50 6.00
128 Walt Tkaczuk 2.50 6.00
129 Gary Dornhoefer 2.50 6.00
130 Syl Apps 2.50 6.00
131 Bob Plager 2.50 6.00
132 Stan Weir 2.50 6.00
133 Tracy Pratt 2.50 6.00
134 Jack Egers 2.50 6.00
135 Eric Vail 2.50 6.00
136 Al Sims 2.50 6.00
137 Larry Patey 2.50 6.00
138 Jim Schoenfeld 2.50 6.00
139 Cliff Koroll 2.50 6.00
140 Marcel Dionne 2.50 6.00
141 Jean-Guy Lagace 2.50 6.00
142 Juha Widing 2.50 6.00
143 Lou Nanne 2.50 6.00
144 Serge Savard 2.50 6.00
145 Glenn Resch 2.50 6.00
146 Ron Greschner RC 2.50 6.00
147 Dave Schultz 2.50 6.00
148 Barry Wilkins 2.50 6.00
149 Floyd Thomson 2.50 6.00
150 Darryl Sittler 2.50 6.00
151 Paulin Bordeleau 2.50 6.00
152 Ron Lalonde RC 2.50 6.00
153 Larry Romanchych 2.50 6.00
154 Larry Carriere 2.50 6.00
155 Andre Savard 2.50 6.00
156 Dave Hrechkosy RC 2.50 6.00
157 Bill White 2.50 6.00
158 Dave Kryskow 2.50 6.00
159 Denis Dupere 2.50 6.00
160 Rogatien Vachon 2.50 6.00
161 Doug Rombough 2.50 6.00
162 Murray Wilson 2.50 6.00
163 Bob Bourne RC 2.50 6.00
164 Gilles Marotte 4.00 10.00
165 Vic Hadfield 4.00 10.00
166 Reggie Leach 2.50 6.00
167 Jerry Butler 4.00 10.00
168 Inge Hammarstrom 2.50 6.00
169 Chris Oddleifson 2.50 6.00
170 Greg Joly 2.50 6.00
171 Checklist 111-220 5.00 12.00
172 Pat Quinn 4.00 10.00
173 Dave Forbes 2.50 6.00
174 Len Frig 2.50 6.00
175 Richard Martin 2.50 6.00
176 Keith Magnuson 2.50 6.00
177 Dan Maloney 2.50 6.00
178 Craig Patrick 2.50 6.00
179 Tom Williams 4.00 10.00
180 Bill Goldsworthy 2.50 6.00
181 Steve Shutt 2.50 6.00
182 Ralph Stewart 2.50 6.00
183 John Davidson 2.50 6.00
184 Bob Kelly 2.50 6.00
185 Ed Johnston 2.50 6.00
186 Dave Burrows 2.50 6.00
187 Dave Dunn 2.50 6.00
188 Dennis Kearns 2.50 6.00
189 Bill Clement 2.50 6.00
190 Gilles Meloche 2.50 6.00
191 Bob Leiter 2.50 6.00
192 Jerry Korab 2.50 6.00
193 Joey Johnston 2.50 6.00
194 Walt McKechnie 2.50 6.00
195 Wilf Paiement 2.50 6.00
196 Bob Berry 2.50 6.00
197 Dean Talafous RC 2.50 6.00
198 Guy Lapointe 2.50 6.00
199 Clark Gillies RC 2.50 6.00
200 Phil Esposito 2.50 6.00
201 Greg Polis 2.50 6.00
202 Jimmy Watson 4.00 10.00
203 Gord McRae RC 2.50 6.00
204 Lowell MacDonald 2.50 6.00
205 Barclay Plager 2.50 6.00
206 Don Lever 2.50 6.00
207 Bill Mikkelson 2.50 6.00
208 Espo/Lafleur/Martin LL 2.50 6.00
209 Clarke/Orr/P.Mahov LL 2.50 6.00
210 Orr/Espo/Dionne LL 8.00 20.00
211 Schultz/Dupont/Rusl LL 2.50 6.00
212 Espo/Martin/Grant LL 4.00 10.00
213 Parent/Vach/Dryden LL 4.00 10.00
214 Barry Gibbs 2.50 6.00
215 Ken Hodge 2.50 6.00
216 Jocelyn Guevremont 2.50 6.00
217 Warren Williams RC 2.50 6.00
218 Dick Redmond 2.50 6.00
219 Jim Rutherford 2.50 6.00
220 Simon Nolet 2.50 6.00
221 Butch Goring 2.50 6.00
222 Glen Sather 2.50 6.00
223 Mario Tremblay RC 2.50 6.00
224 Jude Drouin 4.00 10.00
225 Rod Gilbert 2.50 6.00
226 Bill Barber 2.50 6.00
227 Gary Inness RC 2.50 6.00
228 Wayne Merrick 2.50 6.00
229 Rod Seiling 2.50 6.00
230 Tom Lysiak 2.50 6.00
231 Bob Dailey 2.50 6.00
232 Michel Belhumeur 4.00 10.00
233 Bill Hajt RC 2.50 6.00
234 Jim Pappin 2.50 6.00
235 Gregg Sheppard 2.50 6.00
236 Gary Bergman 2.50 6.00
237 Randy Rota 2.50 6.00
238 Neil Komadoski 4.00 10.00
239 Craig Cameron 2.50 6.00
240 Tony Esposito 2.50 6.00
241 Larry Robinson 4.00 10.00
242 Billy Harris 2.50 6.00
243 Jean Ratelle 2.50 6.00
244 Ted Irvine UER 2.50 6.00
245 Bob Neely 2.50 6.00
246 Bobby Lalonde 2.50 6.00
247 Ron Jones RC 2.50 6.00
248 Rey Comeau 2.50 6.00
249 Michel Plasse 2.50 6.00
250 Bobby Clarke 6.00 15.00
251 Bobby Schmautz 2.50 6.00
252 Peter McNab RC 2.50 6.00

Card	Low	High
253 Al MacAdam	2.50	6.00
254 Dennis Hull	2.50	6.00
255 Terry Harper	2.50	6.00
256 Peter McDuffe	2.50	6.00
257 Jean Hamel	4.00	10.00
258 Jacques Lemaire	4.00	10.00
259 Bob Nystrom	2.50	6.00
260 Brad Park	2.50	6.00
261 Cesare Maniago	2.50	6.00
262 Don Saleski	2.50	6.00
263 J. Bob Kelly	2.50	6.00
264 Bob Hess RC	2.50	6.00
265 Blaine Stoughton	2.50	6.00
266 John Gould	2.50	6.00
267 Checklist 221-330	4.00	10.00
268 Dan Bouchard	2.50	6.00
269 Don Marcotte	2.50	6.00
270 Jim Neilson	2.50	6.00
271 Craig Ramsay	2.50	6.00
272 Grant Mulvey RC	2.50	6.00
273 Larry Giroux RC	2.50	6.00
274 Real Lemieux	4.00	10.00
275 Denis Potvin	5.00	12.00
276 Don Kozak	4.00	10.00
277 Tom Reid	2.50	6.00
278 Bob Gainey	2.50	6.00
279 Nick Beverley	4.00	10.00
280 Jean Pronovost	2.50	6.00
281 Joe Watson	4.00	10.00
282 Chuck Lefley	2.50	6.00
283 Borje Salming	2.50	6.00
284 Garnet Bailey	2.50	6.00
285 Gregg Boddy	2.50	6.00
286 Bobby Clarke AS1	2.50	6.00
287 Denis Potvin AS1	2.50	6.00
288 Bobby Orr AS1	8.00	20.00
289 Richard Martin AS1	2.50	6.00
290 Guy Lafleur AS1	2.50	6.00
291 Bernie Parent AS1	2.50	6.00
292 Phil Esposito AS2	2.50	6.00
293 Guy Lapointe AS2	2.50	6.00
294 Borje Salming AS2	2.50	6.00
295 Steve Vickers AS2	2.50	6.00
296 Rene Robert AS2	2.50	6.00
297 Rogatien Vachon AS2	2.50	6.00
298 Buster Harvey RC	2.50	6.00
299 Gary Sabourin	2.50	6.00
300 Bernie Parent	2.50	6.00
301 Terry O'Reilly	2.50	6.00
302 Ed Westfall	2.50	6.00
303 Pete Stemkowski	4.00	10.00
304 Pierre Bouchard	2.50	6.00
305 Pierre Larouche RC	2.50	6.00
306 Lee Fogolin RC	2.50	6.00
307 Gerry O'Flaherty	2.50	6.00
308 Phil Myre	2.50	6.00
309 Pierre Plante	2.50	6.00
310 Dennis Hextall	4.00	10.00
311 Jim McKenny	2.50	6.00
312 Vic Venasky	2.50	6.00
313 Flames Leaders	2.50	6.00
314 Espo/Orr/Bucyk TL	2.50	6.00
315 Sabres Leaders	2.50	6.00
316 Seals Leaders	2.50	6.00
317 S.Mikita/J.Pappin TL	2.50	6.00
318 D.Grant/M.Dionne TL	2.50	6.00
319 Scouts Leaders	2.50	6.00
320 Kings Leaders	2.50	6.00
321 North Stars Leaders	2.50	6.00
322 Lafleur/P.Mahov TL	2.50	6.00
323 Nystrom/Potvin/Gill TL	2.50	6.00
324 Vick/Gilbert/Ratelle TL	4.00	10.00
325 R.Leach/B.Clarke TL	2.50	6.00
326 Penguins Leaders	4.00	10.00
327 Blues Leaders	4.00	10.00
328 Darryl Sittler TL	4.00	10.00
329 Canucks Leaders	2.50	6.00
330 Capitals Leaders	2.50	6.00

1976-77 Topps

Card	Low	High
COMPLETE SET (264)	100.00	200.00
1 Loach/Lafleur/Larou LL	2.50	6.00
2 Clarke/Lafleur/Perr/ LL	2.50	6.00
3 Lafleur/Clarke/Perr LL	2.50	6.00
4 Durbno/Watsn/Schultz LL	2.50	6.00
5 Espo/Lafleur/Potvin LL	2.50	6.00
6 Dryden/Resch/Laroc LL	2.50	6.00
7 Gary Doak	2.50	6.00
8 Jacques Richard	2.50	6.00
9 Wayne Dillon	2.50	6.00
10 Bernie Parent	2.50	6.00
11 Ed Westfall	2.50	6.00
12 Dick Redmond	2.50	6.00
13 Bryan Hextall	2.50	6.00
14 Jean Pronovost	2.50	6.00
15 Peter Mahovlich	2.50	6.00
16 Danny Grant	2.50	6.00
17 Phil Myre	2.50	6.00
18 Wayne Merrick	2.50	6.00
19 Steve Durbano	2.50	6.00
20 Derek Sanderson	2.50	6.00
21 Mike Murphy	2.50	6.00
22 Borje Salming	2.50	6.00
23 Mike Walton	2.50	6.00
24 Randy Manery	2.50	6.00
25 Ken Hodge	2.50	6.00
26 Mel Bridgman RC	2.50	6.00
27 Jerry Korab	2.50	6.00
28 Gilles Gratton	2.50	6.00
29 Andre St.Laurent	2.50	6.00
30 Yvan Cournoyer	2.50	6.00
31 Phil Russell	2.50	6.00
32 Dennis Hextall	2.50	6.00
33 Lowell MacDonald	2.50	6.00
34 Dennis O'Brien	2.50	6.00
35 Gerry Meehan	2.50	6.00
36 Gilles Meloche	2.50	6.00
37 Wilf Paiement	2.50	6.00
38 Bob MacMillan RC	2.50	6.00
39 Ian Turnbull	2.50	6.00
40 Rogatien Vachon	2.50	6.00
41 Nick Beverley	2.50	6.00
42 Rene Robert	2.50	6.00
43 Andre Savard	2.50	6.00
44 Bob Gainey	2.50	6.00
45 Joe Watson	2.50	6.00
46 Billy Smith	2.50	6.00
47 Darcy Rota	2.50	6.00
48 Rick Lapointe RC	2.50	6.00
49 Pierre Jarry	2.50	6.00
50 Syl Apps	2.50	6.00
51 Eric Vail	2.50	6.00
52 Greg Joly	2.50	6.00
53 Don Lever	2.50	6.00
54 Bob Murdoch Seals	2.50	6.00
55 Denis Herron	2.50	6.00
56 Mike Bloom	2.50	6.00
57 Bill Fairbairn	2.50	6.00
58 Fred Stanfield	2.50	6.00
59 Steve Shutt	2.50	6.00
60 Brad Park	2.50	6.00
61 Gilles Villemure	2.50	6.00
62 Bert Marshall	2.50	6.00
63 Chuck Lefley	2.50	6.00
64 Simon Nolet	2.50	6.00
65 Reggie Leach RB	2.50	6.00
66 Darryl Sittler RB	2.50	6.00
67 Bryan Trottier RB	4.00	10.00
68 Garry Unger RB	2.50	6.00
69 Ron Low	2.50	6.00
70 Bobby Clarke	4.00	10.00
71 Michel Bergeron RC	2.50	6.00
72 Ron Stackhouse	2.50	6.00
73 Bill Hogaboam	2.50	6.00
74 Bob Murdoch Kings	2.50	6.00
75 Steve Vickers	2.50	6.00
76 Pit Martin	2.50	6.00
77 Gerry Hart	2.50	6.00
78 Craig Ramsay	2.50	6.00
79 Michel Larocque	2.50	6.00
80 Jean Ratelle	2.50	6.00
81 Don Saleski	2.50	6.00
82 Bill Clement	2.50	6.00
83 Dave Burrows	2.50	6.00
84 Wayne Thomas	2.50	6.00
85 John Gould	2.50	6.00
86 Dennis Maruk RC	2.50	6.00
87 Ernie Hicke	2.50	6.00
88 Jim Rutherford	2.50	6.00
89 Dale Tallon	2.50	6.00
90 Rod Gilbert	2.50	6.00
91 Marcel Dionne	2.50	6.00
92 Chuck Arnason	2.50	6.00
93 Jean Potvin	2.50	6.00
94 Don Luce	2.50	6.00
95 Johnny Bucyk	2.50	6.00
96 Larry Goodenough	2.50	6.00
97 Mario Tremblay	2.50	6.00
98 Nelson Pyatt RC	2.50	6.00
99 Brian Glennie	2.50	6.00
100 Tony Esposito	2.50	6.00
101 Dan Maloney	2.50	6.00
102 Barry Wilkins	2.50	6.00
103 Dean Talafous	2.50	6.00
104 Ed Staniowski RC	2.50	6.00
105 Dallas Smith	2.50	6.00
106 Jude Drouin	2.50	6.00
107 Pat Hickey	2.50	6.00
108 Jocelyn Guevremont	2.50	6.00
109 Doug Risebrough	2.50	6.00
110 Reggie Leach	2.50	6.00
111 Dan Bouchard	2.50	6.00
112 Chris Oddleifson	2.50	6.00
113 Rick Hampton	2.50	6.00
114 John Marks	2.50	6.00
115 Bryan Trottier RC	15.00	40.00
116 Checklist 1-132	4.00	10.00
117 Greg Polis	2.50	6.00
118 Peter McNab	2.50	6.00
119 Jim Roberts	2.50	6.00
120 Gerry Cheevers	2.50	6.00
121 Rick MacLeish	2.50	6.00
122 Billy Lochead	2.50	6.00
123 Tom Reid	2.50	6.00
124 Rick Kohoe	2.50	6.00
125 Keith Magnuson	2.50	6.00
126 Clark Gillies	2.50	6.00
127 Rick Middleton	2.50	6.00
128 Bill Hajt	2.50	6.00
129 Jacques Lemaire	2.50	6.00
130 Terry O'Reilly	2.50	6.00
131 Andre Dupont	2.50	6.00
132 Flames Team CL	2.50	6.00
133 Bruins Team CL	2.50	6.00
134 Sabres Team CL	2.50	6.00
135 Seals Team CL	2.50	6.00
136 Blackhawks Team CL	2.50	6.00
137 Red Wings Team CL	2.50	6.00
138 Scouts Team CL	2.50	6.00
139 Kings Team CL	2.50	6.00
140 North Stars Team CL	2.50	6.00
141 Canadiens Team CL	2.50	6.00
142 Islanders Team CL	2.50	6.00
143 Rangers Team CL	2.50	6.00
144 Flyers Team CL	2.50	6.00
145 Penguins Team CL	2.50	6.00
146 Blues Team CL	2.50	6.00
147 Maple Leafs Team CL	2.50	6.00
148 Canucks Team CL	2.50	6.00
149 Capitals Team CL	2.50	6.00
150 Dave Schultz	2.50	6.00
151 Larry Robinson	4.00	10.00
152 Al Smith	2.50	6.00
153 Bob Nystrom	2.50	6.00
154 Ron Greschner UER	2.50	6.00
155 Gregg Sheppard	2.50	6.00
156 Alain Daigle	2.50	6.00
157 Ed Van Impe	2.50	6.00
158 Tim Young RC	2.50	6.00
159 Gary Bergman	2.50	6.00
160 Ed Giacomin	2.50	6.00
161 Yvon Labre	2.50	6.00
162 Jim Lorentz	2.50	6.00
163 Guy Lafleur	5.00	12.00
164 Tom Bladon	2.50	6.00
165 Wayne Cashman	2.50	6.00
166 Pete Stemkowski	2.50	6.00
167 Grant Mulvey	2.50	6.00
168 Yves Belanger RC	2.50	6.00
169 Bill Goldsworthy	2.50	6.00
170 Denis Potvin	4.00	10.00
171 Nick Libett	2.50	6.00
172 Michel Plasse	2.50	6.00
173 Lou Nanne	2.50	6.00
174 Tom Lysiak	2.50	6.00
175 Dennis Ververgaert	2.50	6.00
176 Gary Simmons	2.50	6.00
177 Pierre Bouchard	2.50	6.00
178 Bill Barber	2.50	6.00
179 Darryl Edestrand	2.50	6.00
180 Gilbert Perreault	2.50	6.00
181 Dave Maloney RC	2.50	6.00
182 Jean-Paul Parise	2.50	6.00
183 Bobby Sheehan	2.50	6.00
184 Pete Lopresti RC	2.50	6.00
185 Don Kozak	2.50	6.00
186 Guy Charron	2.50	6.00
187 Stan Gilbertson	2.50	6.00
188 Bill Nyrop RC	2.50	6.00
189 Bobby Schmautz	2.50	6.00
190 Wayne Stephenson	2.50	6.00
191 Brian Spencer	2.50	6.00
192 Gilles Marotte	2.50	6.00
193 Lorne Henning	2.50	6.00
194 Bob Neely	2.50	6.00
195 Dennis Hull	2.50	6.00
196 Walt McKechnie	2.50	6.00
197 Curt Ridley RC	2.50	6.00
198 Dwight Bialowas	2.50	6.00
199 Pierre Larouche	2.50	6.00
200 Ken Dryden	20.00	50.00
201 Ross Lonsberry	2.50	6.00
202 Curt Bennett	2.50	6.00
203 Hartland Monahan RC	2.50	6.00
204 John Davidson	2.50	6.00
205 Serge Savard	2.50	6.00
206 Garry Howatt	2.50	6.00
207 Darryl Sittler	2.50	6.00
208 J.P. Bordeleau	2.50	6.00
209 Henry Boucha	2.50	6.00
210 Richard Martin	2.50	6.00
211 Vic Venasky	2.50	6.00
212 Buster Harvey	2.50	6.00
213 Bobby Orr	10.00	25.00
214 Martin/Perrlt/Robert	2.50	6.00
215 Barber/Clarke/Leach	2.50	6.00
216 Gillies/Trottier/Harris	2.50	6.00
217 Gainey/Jarvis/Roberts	2.50	6.00
218 MacDon/Apps/Pronvst	2.50	6.00
219 Bob Kelly	2.50	6.00
220 Walt Tkaczuk	2.50	6.00
221 Dave Lewis	2.50	6.00
222 Danny Gare	2.50	6.00
223 Guy Lapointe	2.50	6.00
224 Hank Nowak RC	2.50	6.00
225 Stan Mikita	2.50	6.00
226 Vic Hadfield	2.50	6.00
227 Bernie Wolfe RC	2.50	6.00
228 Bryan Watson	2.50	6.00
229 Ralph Stewart	2.50	6.00
230 Gerry Desjardins	2.50	6.00
231 John Bednarski RC	2.50	6.00
232 Yvon Lambert	2.50	6.00
233 Orest Kindrachuk	2.50	6.00
234 Don Marcotte	2.50	6.00
235 Bill White	2.50	6.00
236 Red Berenson	2.50	6.00
237 Al MacAdam	2.50	6.00
238 Rick Blight RC	2.50	6.00
239 Butch Goring	2.50	6.00
240 Cesare Maniago	2.50	6.00
241 Jim Schoenfeld	2.50	6.00
242 Cliff Koroll	2.50	6.00
243 Mickey Redmond	2.50	6.00
244 Rick Chartraw	2.50	6.00
245 Phil Esposito	2.50	6.00
246 Dave Forbes	2.50	6.00
247 Jimmy Watson	2.50	6.00
248 Ron Schock	2.50	6.00
249 Fred Barrett	2.50	6.00
250 Glenn Resch	2.50	6.00
251 Ivan Boldirev	2.50	6.00
252 Billy Harris	2.50	6.00
253 Lee Fogolin	2.50	6.00
254 Murray Wilson	2.50	6.00
255 Gilles Gilbert	2.50	6.00
256 Gary Dornhoefer	2.50	6.00
257 Carol Vadnais	2.50	6.00
258 Checklist 133-264	4.00	10.00
259 Errol Thompson	2.50	6.00
260 Garry Unger	2.50	6.00
261 J. Bob Kelly	2.50	6.00
262 Terry Harper	2.50	6.00
263 Blake Dunlop	2.50	6.00
264 Canadiens Champs	2.50	6.00

1976-77 Topps Glossy Inserts

Card	Low	High
COMPLETE SET (22)	40.00	80.00
1 Bobby Clarke	2.00	4.00
2 Brad Park	1.25	2.50
3 Tony Esposito	1.50	3.00
4 Marcel Dionne	2.00	4.00
5 Ken Dryden	7.50	15.00
6 Glenn Resch	1.00	2.00
7 Phil Esposito	2.50	5.00
8 Darryl Sittler	1.50	3.00
9 Gilbert Perreault	1.00	2.00
10 Denis Potvin	2.00	4.00
11 Guy Lafleur	4.00	8.00
12 Bill Barber	1.00	2.00
13 Syl Apps	.50	1.00
14 Johnny Bucyk	1.00	2.00
15 Bryan Trottier	7.50	15.00
16 Dennis Hull	.50	1.00
17 Guy Lapointe	.75	1.50
18 Rod Gilbert	1.25	2.50
19 Richard Martin	.75	1.50
20 Bobby Orr	12.50	25.00
21 Reggie Leach	.75	1.50
22 Jean Ratelle	1.25	2.50

1977-78 Topps

Card	Low	High
COMPLETE SET (264)	45.00	90.00
1 Shutt/Lafleur/Dionne LL	2.50	6.00
2 Lafleur/Dionne/Sal LL	2.50	6.00
3 Lafleur/Dionne/Shutt LL	2.50	6.00
4 Williams/Polnch/Gasff LL	2.50	6.00
5 McDonald/Espo/Will LL	2.50	6.00
6 Laroc/Dryden/Resch LL	2.50	6.00
7 Perr/Shutt/Lafleur LL	2.50	6.00
8 Dryden/Vach/Parent LL	2.50	6.00
9 Brian Spencer	2.50	6.00
10 Denis Potvin AS2	2.50	6.00
11 Nick Fotiu	2.50	6.00
12 Bob Murray	2.50	6.00
13 Pete Lopresti	2.50	6.00
14 J. Bob Kelly	2.50	6.00
15 Rick MacLeish	2.50	6.00
16 Terry Harper	2.50	6.00
17 Willi Plett RC	2.50	6.00
18 Peter McNab	2.50	6.00
19 Wayne Thomas	2.50	6.00
20 Pierre Bouchard	2.50	6.00
21 Dennis Maruk	2.50	6.00
22 Mike Murphy	2.50	6.00
23 Cesare Maniago	2.50	6.00
24 Paul Gardner RC	2.50	6.00
25 Rod Gilbert	2.50	6.00
26 Orest Kindrachuk	2.50	6.00
27 Bill Hajt	2.50	6.00
28 John Davidson	2.50	6.00
29 Jean-Paul Parise	2.50	6.00
30 Larry Robinson AS1	2.50	6.00
31 Yvon Labre	2.50	6.00
32 Walt McKechnie	2.50	6.00
33 Rick Kehoe	2.50	6.00
34 Randy Holt RC	2.50	6.00
35 Garry Unger	2.50	6.00
36 Lou Nanne	2.50	6.00
37 Dan Bouchard	2.50	6.00
38 Darryl Sittler	2.50	6.00
39 Bob Murdoch	2.50	6.00
40 Jean Ratelle	2.50	6.00
41 Dave Maloney	2.50	6.00
42 Danny Gare	2.50	6.00
43 Jimmy Watson	2.50	6.00
44 Tom Williams	2.50	6.00
45 Serge Savard	2.50	6.00
46 Derek Sanderson	2.50	6.00
47 John Marks	2.50	6.00
48 Al Cameron RC	2.50	6.00
49 Dean Talafous	2.50	6.00
50 Glenn Resch	2.50	6.00
51 Ron Schock	2.50	6.00
52 Gary Croteau	2.50	6.00
53 Gerry Meehan	2.50	6.00
54 Ed Staniowski	2.50	6.00
55 Phil Esposito	2.50	6.00
56 Dennis Ververgaert	2.50	6.00
57 Rick Wilson	2.50	6.00
58 Jim Lorentz	2.50	6.00
59 Bobby Schmautz	2.50	6.00
60 Guy Lapointe AS2	2.50	6.00
61 Ivan Boldirev	2.50	6.00
62 Bob Nystrom	2.50	6.00
63 Rick Hampton	2.50	6.00
64 Jack Valiquette	2.50	6.00
65 Bernie Parent	2.50	6.00
66 Dave Burrows	2.50	6.00
67 Butch Goring	2.50	6.00
68 Checklist 1-132	4.00	10.00
69 Murray Wilson	2.50	6.00
70 Ed Giacomin	2.50	6.00
71 Flames Team CL	2.50	6.00
72 Bruins Team CL	2.50	6.00
73 Sabres Team CL	2.50	6.00
74 Blackhawks Team CL	2.50	6.00
75 Barons Team CL	2.50	6.00
76 Rockies Team CL	2.50	6.00
77 Red Wings Team CL	2.50	6.00
78 Kings Team CL	2.50	6.00
79 North Stars Team CL	2.50	6.00
80 Canadiens Team CL	2.50	6.00
81 Islanders Team CL	2.50	6.00
82 Rangers Team CL	2.50	6.00
83 Flyers Team CL	2.50	6.00
84 Penguins Team CL	2.50	6.00
85 Blues Team CL	2.50	6.00
86 Maple Leafs Team CL	2.50	6.00
87 Canucks Team CL	2.50	6.00
88 Capitals Team CL	2.50	6.00
89 Keith Magnuson	2.50	6.00
90 Walt Tkaczuk	2.50	6.00
91 Bill Nyrop	2.50	6.00
92 Michel Plasse	2.50	6.00
93 Bob Bourne	2.50	6.00
94 Lee Fogolin	2.50	6.00
95 Gregg Sheppard	2.50	6.00
96 Hartland Monahan	2.50	6.00
97 Curt Bennett	2.50	6.00
98 Bob Dailey	2.50	6.00
99 Bill Goldsworthy	2.50	6.00
100 Ken Dryden AS1	8.00	20.00
101 Grant Mulvey	2.50	6.00
102 Pierre Larouche	2.50	6.00
103 Nick Libett	2.50	6.00
104 Rick Smith	2.50	6.00
105 Bryan Trottier	5.00	12.00
106 Pierre Jarry	2.50	6.00
107 Red Berenson	2.50	6.00
108 Jim Schoenfeld	2.50	6.00
109 Gilles Meloche	2.50	6.00
110 Lanny McDonald AS2	2.50	6.00
111 Don Lever	2.50	6.00
112 Greg Polis	2.50	6.00
113 Gary Sargent RC	2.50	6.00
114 Earl Anderson RC	2.50	6.00
115 Bobby Clarke	2.50	6.00
116 Dave Lewis	2.50	6.00
117 Darcy Rota	2.50	6.00
118 Andre Savard	2.50	6.00
119 Denis Herron	2.50	6.00
120 Steve Shutt AS1	2.50	6.00
121 Mel Bridgman	2.50	6.00
122 Buster Harvey	2.50	6.00
123 Roland Eriksson RC	2.50	6.00
124 Dale Tallon	2.50	6.00
125 Gilles Gilbert	2.50	6.00
126 Billy Harris	2.50	6.00
127 Tom Lysiak	2.50	6.00
128 Jerry Korab	2.50	6.00
129 Bob Gainey	2.50	6.00
130 Wilf Paiement	2.50	6.00
131A Tom Bladon Standing	2.50	6.00
131B Tom Bladon Skating	2.50	6.00
132 Ernie Hicke	2.50	6.00
133 J.P. LeBlanc	2.50	6.00
134 Mike Milbury RC	10.00	25.00
135 Pit Martin	2.50	6.00
136 Steve Vickers	2.50	6.00
137 Don Awrey	2.50	6.00
138A Bernie Wolfe MacAdam	2.50	6.00
138B Bernie Wolfe COR	2.50	6.00
139 Doug Jarvis	2.50	6.00
140 Borje Salming AS1	2.50	6.00
141 Bob MacMillan	2.50	6.00
142 Wayne Stephenson	2.50	6.00
143 Dave Forbes	2.50	6.00
144 Jean Potvin	2.50	6.00
145 Guy Charron	2.50	6.00
146 Cliff Koroll	2.50	6.00
147 Danny Grant	2.50	6.00
148 Bill Hogaboam UER	2.50	6.00
149A Al MacAdam ERR Wolfe	2.50	6.00
149B Al MacAdam COR	2.50	6.00
150 Gerry Desjardins	2.50	6.00
151 Yvon Lambert	2.50	6.00
152A Rick Lapointe ERR	2.50	6.00
152B Rick Lapointe COR	2.50	6.00
153 Ed Westfall	2.50	6.00
154 Carol Vadnais	2.50	6.00
155 Johnny Bucyk	2.50	6.00
156 J.P. Bordeleau	2.50	6.00
157 Ron Stackhouse	2.50	6.00
158 Glen Sharpley RC	2.50	6.00
159 Michel Bergeron	2.50	6.00
160 Rogatien Vachon AS2	2.50	6.00
161 Fred Stanfield	2.50	6.00
162 Gerry Hart	2.50	6.00
163 Mario Tremblay	2.50	6.00
164 Andre Dupont	2.50	6.00
165 Don Marcotte	2.50	6.00
166 Wayne Dillon	2.50	6.00
167 Claude Larose	2.50	6.00
168 Eric Vail	2.50	6.00
169 Tom Edur	2.50	6.00
170 Tony Esposito	2.50	6.00
171 Andre St.Laurent	2.50	6.00
172 Dan Maloney	2.50	6.00
173 Dennis O'Brien	2.50	6.00
174 Blair Chapman RC	2.50	6.00
175 Dennis Kearns	2.50	6.00
176 Wayne Merrick	2.50	6.00
177 Michel Larocque	2.50	6.00
178 Bob Kelly	2.50	6.00
179 Dave Farrish RC	2.50	6.00
180 Richard Martin AS2	2.50	6.00
181 Gary Doak	2.50	6.00
182 Jude Drouin	2.50	6.00
183 Barry Dean RC	2.50	6.00
184 Gary Smith	2.50	6.00
185 Reggie Leach	2.50	6.00
186 Ian Turnbull	2.50	6.00
187 Vic Venasky	2.50	6.00
188 Wayne Bianchin RC	2.50	6.00
189 Doug Risebrough	2.50	6.00
190 Brad Park	2.50	6.00
191 Craig Ramsay	2.50	6.00
192 Ken Hodge	2.50	6.00
193 Phil Myre	2.50	6.00
194 Garry Howatt	2.50	6.00
195 Stan Mikita	2.50	6.00
196 Garnet Bailey	2.50	6.00
197 Dennis Hextall	2.50	6.00
198 Nick Beverley	2.50	6.00
199 Larry Patey	2.50	6.00
200 Guy Lafleur AS1	2.50	6.00
201 Don Edwards RC	2.50	6.00
202 Gary Dornhoefer	2.50	6.00
203 Stan Gilbertson	2.50	6.00
204 Alex Pirus RC	2.50	6.00
205 Peter Mahovlich	2.50	6.00
206 Bert Marshall	2.50	6.00
207 Gilles Gratton	2.50	6.00
208 Alain Daigle	2.50	6.00
209 Chris Oddleifson	2.50	6.00
210 Gilbert Perreault AS2	2.50	6.00
211 Mike Palmateer RC	8.00	20.00
212 Billy Lochead	2.50	6.00
213 Dick Redmond	2.50	6.00
214 Guy Lafleur RB	2.50	6.00
215 Ian Turnbull RB	2.50	6.00
216 Guy Lafleur RB	2.50	6.00
217 Steve Shutt RB	2.50	6.00
218 Guy Lafleur RB	2.50	6.00
219 Lorne Henning	2.50	6.00
220 Terry O'Reilly	2.50	6.00
221 Pat Hickey	2.50	6.00
222 Rene Robert	2.50	6.00
223 Tim Young	2.50	6.00
224 Dunc Wilson	2.50	6.00
225 Dennis Hull	2.50	6.00
226 Rod Seiling	2.50	6.00
227 Bill Barber	2.50	6.00
228 Dennis Polonich RC	2.50	6.00
229 Billy Smith	2.50	6.00
230 Yvan Cournoyer	2.50	6.00
231 Don Luce	2.50	6.00
232 Mike McEwen RC	2.50	6.00
233 Don Saleski	2.50	6.00
234 Wayne Cashman	2.50	6.00
235 Phil Russell	2.50	6.00
236 Mike Corrigan	2.50	6.00
237 Guy Chouinard	2.50	6.00
238 Steve Jensen RC	2.50	6.00
239 Jim Rutherford	2.50	6.00
240 Marcel Dionne AS1	2.50	6.00
241 Rejean Houle	2.50	6.00
242 Jocelyn Guevremont	2.50	6.00
243 Jim Harrison	2.50	6.00
244 Don Murdoch RC	2.50	6.00
245 Rick Green RC	2.50	6.00
246 Rick Middleton	2.50	6.00
247 Joe Watson	2.50	6.00
248 Syl Apps	2.50	6.00
249 Checklist 133-264	4.00	10.00
250 Clark Gillies	2.50	6.00
251 Bobby Orr	12.00	30.00
252 Nelson Pyatt	2.50	6.00
253 Gary McAdam RC	2.50	6.00
254 Jacques Lemaire	2.50	6.00
255 Bill Fairbairn	2.50	6.00
256 Ron Greschner	2.50	6.00
257 Ross Lonsberry	2.50	6.00
258 Dave Gardner	2.50	6.00
259 Rick Blight	2.50	6.00
260 Gerry Cheevers	2.50	6.00
261 Jean Pronovost	2.50	6.00
262 Mon/NYI Semi-Finals	2.50	6.00
263 Bruins Semi-Finals	2.50	6.00
264 Canadiens Champs	2.50	6.00

1977-78 Topps/O-Pee-Chee Glossy

Card	Low	High
COMPLETE SET (22)	7.50	15.00
1 Wayne Cashman	.20	.40
2 Gerry Cheevers	.75	1.50
3 Bobby Clarke	.75	1.50
4 Marcel Dionne	.75	1.50
5 Ken Dryden	2.00	4.00
6 Clark Gillies	.20	.40
7 Guy Lafleur	1.25	2.50
8 Reggie Leach	.18	.35
9 Rick MacLeish	.25	.50
10 Dave Maloney	.13	.25
11 Richard Martin	.20	.40
12 Don Murdoch	.13	.25
13 Brad Park	.38	.75
14 Gilbert Perreault	.50	1.00
15 Denis Potvin	.75	1.50
16 Jean Ratelle	.38	.75
17 Glenn Resch	.38	.75
18 Larry Robinson	.75	1.50
19 Steve Shutt	.38	.75
20 Darryl Sittler	.63	1.25
21 Rogatien Vachon	.38	.75
22 Tim Young	.13	.25

1978-79 Topps

Card	Low	High
COMPLETE SET (264)	40.00	80.00
1 Mike Bossy HL	5.00	12.00
2 Phil Esposito HL	2.50	6.00
3 Guy Lafleur HL	2.50	6.00
4 Darryl Sittler HL	2.50	6.00
5 Garry Unger HL	2.50	6.00
6 Gary Edwards	2.50	6.00
7 Rick Blight	2.50	6.00
8 Larry Patey	2.50	6.00
9 Craig Ramsay	2.50	6.00
10 Bryan Trottier AS1	4.00	10.00
11 Don Murdoch	2.50	6.00
12 Phil Russell	2.50	6.00
13 Doug Jarvis	2.50	6.00
14 Gene Carr	2.50	6.00
15 Bernie Parent	2.50	6.00
16 Perry Miller	2.50	6.00
17 Kent-Erik Andersson RC	2.50	6.00
18 Gregg Sheppard	2.50	6.00
19 Dennis Owchar	2.50	6.00
20 Rogatien Vachon	2.50	6.00
21 Dan Maloney	2.50	6.00
22 Guy Charron	2.50	6.00
23 Dick Redmond	2.50	6.00
24 Checklist 1-132	2.50	6.00
25 Anders Hedberg	2.50	6.00
26 Mel Bridgman	2.50	6.00
27 Lee Fogolin	2.50	6.00
28 Gilles Meloche	2.50	6.00
29 Garry Howatt	2.50	6.00
30 Darryl Sittler AS2	2.50	6.00
31 Curt Bennett	2.50	6.00
32 Andre St.Laurent	2.50	6.00
33 Blair Chapman	2.50	6.00
34 Keith Magnuson	2.50	6.00
35 Pierre Larouche	2.50	6.00
36 Michel Plasse	2.50	6.00
37 Gary Sargent	2.50	6.00
38 Mike Walton	2.50	6.00
39 Robert Picard RC	2.50	6.00
40 Terry O'Reilly AS2	2.50	6.00
41 Dave Farrish	2.50	6.00
42 Gary McAdam	2.50	6.00
43 Joe Watson	2.50	6.00
44 Yves Belanger	2.50	6.00
45 Steve Jensen	2.50	6.00
46 Bob Stewart	2.50	6.00
47 Darcy Rota	2.50	6.00
48 Dennis Hextall	2.50	6.00
49 Bert Marshall	2.50	6.00
50 Ken Dryden AS1	4.00	10.00
51 Peter Mahovlich	2.50	6.00
52 Dennis Ververgaert	2.50	6.00
53 Inge Hammarstrom	2.50	6.00
54 Doug Favell	2.50	6.00
55 Steve Vickers	2.50	6.00
56 Syl Apps	2.50	6.00
57 Errol Thompson	2.50	6.00
58 Don Luce	2.50	6.00
59 Mike Milbury	2.50	6.00
60 Yvan Cournoyer	2.50	6.00
61 Kirk Bowman	2.50	6.00
62 Billy Smith	2.50	6.00
63 Lafleur/Bossy/Shutt LL	2.50	6.00
64 Trott/Lafleur/Sitt LL	2.50	6.00
65 Lafleur/Trott/Sitt LL	2.50	6.00
66 Schltz/Wil/Polnich LL	2.50	6.00
67 Bossy/Espo/Shutt LL	2.50	6.00
68 Dryden/Parent/Gilb LL	2.50	6.00
69 Lafleur/Barber/Sitt LL	2.50	6.00
70 Parent/Dryden/Espo LL	2.50	6.00
71 Bob Kelly	2.50	6.00
72 Ron Stackhouse	2.50	6.00
73 Wayne Dillon	2.50	6.00
74 Jim Rutherford	2.50	6.00
75 Stan Mikita	2.50	6.00
76 Bob Gainey	2.50	6.00
77 Gerry Hart	2.50	6.00
78 Lanny McDonald	2.50	6.00
79 Brad Park	2.50	6.00
80 Richard Martin	2.50	6.00
81 Bernie Wolfe	2.50	6.00
82 Bob MacMillan	2.50	6.00
83 Brad Maxwell RC	2.50	6.00
84 Mike Fidler	2.50	6.00
85 Carol Vadnais	2.50	6.00
86 Don Lever	2.50	6.00
87 Phil Myre	2.50	6.00
88 Paul Gardner	2.50	6.00
89 Bob Murray	2.50	6.00
90 Guy Lafleur AS1	2.50	6.00
91 Bob Murdoch	2.50	6.00
92 Ron Ellis	2.50	6.00
93 Jude Drouin	2.50	6.00
94 Jocelyn Guevremont	2.50	6.00
95 Gilles Gilbert	2.50	6.00
96 Bob Sirois	2.50	6.00
97 Tom Lysiak	2.50	6.00
98 Andre Dupont	2.50	6.00
99 Per-Olov Brasar RC	2.50	6.00
100 Phil Esposito	2.50	6.00
101 J.P. Bordeleau	2.50	6.00
102 Pierre Mondou RC	2.50	6.00
103 Wayne Bianchin	2.50	6.00
104 Dennis O'Brien	2.50	6.00
105 Glenn Resch	2.50	6.00
106 Dennis Polonich	2.50	6.00
107 Kris Manery RC	2.50	6.00
108 Bill Hajt	2.50	6.00
109 Jere Gillis RC	2.50	6.00
110 Garry Unger	2.50	6.00
111 Nick Beverley	2.50	6.00
112 Pat Hickey	2.50	6.00
113 Rick Middleton	2.50	6.00
114 Orest Kindrachuk	2.50	6.00
115 Mike Bossy RC	20.00	50.00
116 Pierre Bouchard	2.50	6.00
117 Alain Daigle	2.50	6.00
118 Terry Martin	2.50	6.00
119 Tom Edur	2.50	6.00
120 Marcel Dionne	2.50	6.00
121 Barry Beck RC	2.50	6.00
122 Billy Lochead	2.50	6.00
123 Paul Harrison	2.50	6.00
124 Wayne Cashman	2.50	6.00
125 Rick MacLeish	2.50	6.00
126 Bob Bourne	2.50	6.00
127 Ian Turnbull	2.50	6.00
128 Gerry Meehan	2.50	6.00
129 Eric Vail	2.50	6.00
130 Gilbert Perreault	2.50	6.00
131 Bob Dailey	2.50	6.00
132 Dale McCourt RC	2.50	6.00
133 John Wensink RC	2.50	6.00
134 Bill Nyrop	2.50	6.00
135 Ivan Boldirev	2.50	6.00
136 Lucien DeBlois RC	2.50	6.00
137 Brian Spencer	2.50	6.00
138 Tim Young	2.50	6.00
139 Ron Sedlbauer	2.50	6.00
140 Gerry Cheevers	2.50	6.00
141 Dennis Maruk	2.50	6.00
142 Barry Dean	2.50	6.00
143 Bernie Federko RC	12.00	30.00
144 Stefan Persson RC	2.50	6.00
145 Wilf Paiement	2.50	6.00
146 Dale Tallon	2.50	6.00
147 Yvon Lambert	2.50	6.00
148 Greg Joly	2.50	6.00
149 Dean Talafous	2.50	6.00
150 Don Edwards AS2	2.50	6.00
151 Butch Goring	2.50	6.00
152 Tom Bladon	2.50	6.00
153 Bob Nystrom	2.50	6.00
154 Ron Greschner	2.50	6.00
155 Jean Ratelle	2.50	6.00
156 Russ Anderson RC	2.50	6.00
157 John Marks	2.50	6.00
158 Michel Larocque	2.50	6.00
159 Paul Woods RC	2.50	6.00
160 Mike Palmateer	2.50	6.00
161 Jim Lorentz	2.50	6.00
162 Dave Lewis	2.50	6.00
163 Harvey Bennett	2.50	6.00
164 Rick Smith	2.50	6.00
165 Reggie Leach	2.50	6.00
166 Wayne Thomas	2.50	6.00
167 Dave Forbes	2.50	6.00
168 Doug Wilson RC	8.00	20.00
169 Dan Bouchard	2.50	6.00
170 Steve Shutt AS2	2.50	6.00
171 Mike Kaszycki RC	2.50	6.00
172 Denis Herron	2.50	6.00
173 Rick Bowness	2.50	6.00
174 Rick Hampton	2.50	6.00
175 Glen Sharpley	2.50	6.00
176 Bill Barber	2.50	6.00
177 Ron Duguay RC	2.50	6.00
178 Jim Schoenfeld	2.50	6.00
179 Pierre Plante	2.50	6.00
180 Jacques Lemaire	2.50	6.00
181 Stan Jonathan	2.50	6.00
182 Billy Harris	2.50	6.00
183 Chris Oddleifson	2.50	6.00
184 Jean Pronovost	2.50	6.00
185 Fred Barrett	2.50	6.00
186 Ross Lonsberry	2.50	6.00
187 Mike McEwen	2.50	6.00
188 Rene Robert	2.50	6.00
189 J. Bob Kelly	2.50	6.00
190 Serge Savard AS2	2.50	6.00
191 Dennis Kearns	2.50	6.00
192 Flames Team CL	2.50	6.00
193 Bruins Team CL	2.50	6.00
194 Sabres Team CL	2.50	6.00
195 Blackhawks Team CL	2.50	6.00
196 Rockies Team CL	2.50	6.00
197 Red Wings Team CL	2.50	6.00
198 Kings Team CL	2.50	6.00
199 North Stars Team CL	2.50	6.00
200 Canadiens Team CL	2.50	6.00
201 Islanders Team CL	2.50	6.00
202 Rangers Team CL	2.50	6.00
203 Flyers Team CL	2.50	6.00
204 Penguins Team CL	2.50	6.00
205 Blues Team CL	2.50	6.00
206 Maple Leafs Team CL	2.50	6.00
207 Canucks Team CL	2.50	6.00
208 Capitals Team CL	2.50	6.00
209 Danny Gare	2.50	6.00
210 Larry Robinson AS1	2.50	6.00
211 John Davidson	2.50	6.00
212 Peter McNab	2.50	6.00
213 Rick Kehoe	2.50	6.00
214 Terry Harper	2.50	6.00
215 Bobby Clarke	2.50	6.00
216 Bryan Maxwell UER	2.50	6.00
217 Ted Bulley	2.50	6.00
218 Red Berenson	2.50	6.00
219 Ron Grahame	2.50	6.00
220 Clark Gillies AS1	2.50	6.00
221 Dave Maloney	2.50	6.00
222 Derek Smith RC	2.50	6.00

223 Wayne Stephenson 2.50 6.00
224 John Van Boxmeer 2.50 6.00
225 Dave Schultz 2.50 6.00
226 Reed Larson RC 2.50 6.00
227 Rejean Houle 2.50 6.00
228 Doug Hicks 2.50 6.00
229 Mike Murphy 2.50 6.00
230 Pete Lopresti 2.50 6.00
231 Jerry Korab 2.50 6.00
232 Ed Westfall 2.50 6.00
233 Greg Malone RC 2.50 6.00
234 Paul Holmgren 2.50 6.00
235 Walt Tkaczuk 2.50 6.00
236 Don Marcotte 2.50 6.00
237 Ron Low 2.50 6.00
238 Rick Chartraw 2.50 6.00
239 Cliff Koroll 2.50 6.00
240 Borje Salming AS1 2.50 6.00
241 Roland Eriksson 2.50 6.00
242 Ric Seiling RC 2.50 6.00
243 Jim Bedard RC 2.50 6.00
244 Peter Lee RC 2.50 6.00
245 Denis Potvin AS2 2.50 6.00
246 Greg Polis 2.50 6.00
247 Jimmy Watson 2.50 6.00
248 Bobby Schmautz 2.50 6.00
249 Doug Risebrough 2.50 6.00
250 Tony Esposito 2.50 6.00
251 Nick Libett 2.50 6.00
252 Ron Zanussi RC 2.50 6.00
253 Andre Savard 2.50 6.00
254 Dave Burrows 2.50 6.00
255 Ulf Nilsson 2.50 6.00
256 Richard Mulhern 2.50 6.00
257 Don Saleski 2.50 6.00
258 Wayne Merrick 2.50 6.00
259 Checklist 133-264 2.50 6.00
260 Guy Lapointe 2.50 6.00
261 Grant Mulvey 2.50 6.00
262 Stanley Cup: Semis 2.50 6.00
263 Stanley Cup: Semis 2.50 6.00
264 Stanley Cup Finals 2.50 6.00

1978-79 Topps Team Stickers

COMPLETE SET (17) 7.50 15.00
1 Atlanta Flames .75 1.50
2A Boston Bruins/Puck .75 1.50
2B Boston Bruins/Stick .75 2.00
3 Buffalo Sabres .50 1.00
4 Chicago Blackhawks .75 1.50
5 Colorado Rockies .75 1.50
6 Detroit Red Wings .75 1.50
7 Los Angeles Kings .50 1.00
8 Minnesota North Stars .50 1.00
9A Montreal Canadiens/Goalie .75 1.50
9B Montreal Canadiens/Puck .75 2.00
10A New York Islanders/Center .50 1.00
10B New York Islanders/Goal! .50 1.00
11A New York Rangers/Goalie .75 1.50
11B New York Rangers/Sticks .75 1.50
12A Philadelphia Flyers/Goalie .50 1.00
12B Philadelphia Flyers/Sticks .50 1.00
13 Pittsburgh Penguins .50 1.00
14 St. Louis Blues .50 1.00
15 Toronto Maple Leafs .75 1.50
16 Vancouver Canucks .50 1.00
17 Washington Capitals .50 1.00

1979-80 Topps

COMPLETE SET (264) 800.00 2000.00
1 Bossy/Dionne/Lafleur LL 2.00 5.00
2 Trott/Lafleur/Dionne LL 2.00 5.00
3 Trott/Dionne/Lafleur LL 2.00 5.00
4 Williams/Holt/Schultz LL 2.00 5.00
5 Bossy/Dionne/Gardner LL 2.00 5.00
6 Dryden/Resch/Parent LL 2.00 5.00
7 Lafleur/Bossy/Trott/ LL 2.00 5.00
8A Dryden/Espo/Par LL ERR 3.00 8.00
8B Dryden/Espo/Par LL COR 2.00 5.00
9 Greg Malone 2.00 5.00
10 Rick Middleton 2.00 5.00
11 Greg Smith 2.00 5.00
12 Rene Robert 2.00 5.00
13 Doug Risebrough 2.00 5.00
14 Bob Kelly 2.00 5.00
15 Walt Tkaczuk 2.00 5.00
16 John Marks 2.00 5.00
17 Willie Huber RC 2.00 5.00
18 Wayne Gretzky RC 800.00 2000.00
19 Ron Sedlbauer 2.00 5.00
20 Glenn Resch AS2 2.00 5.00
21 Blair Chapman 2.00 5.00
22 Ron Zanussi 2.00 5.00
23 Brad Park 2.00 5.00
24 Yvon Lambert 2.00 5.00
25 Andre Savard 2.00 5.00
26 Jimmy Watson 2.00 5.00
27 Hal Philipoff RC 2.00 5.00
28 Dan Bouchard 2.00 5.00
29 Bob Sirois 2.00 5.00
30 Ulf Nilsson 2.00 5.00
31 Mike Murphy 2.00 5.00
32 Stefan Persson 2.00 5.00
33 Garry Unger 2.00 5.00
34 Rejean Houle 2.00 5.00
35 Barry Beck 2.00 5.00
36 Tim Young 2.00 5.00
37 Rick Dudley 2.00 5.00
38 Wayne Stephenson 2.00 5.00
39 Peter McNab 2.00 5.00
40 Borje Salming AS2 2.00 5.00
41 Tom Lysiak 2.00 5.00
42 Don Maloney RC 2.00 5.00
43 Mike Rogers 2.00 5.00
44 Dave Lewis 2.00 5.00
45 Peter Lee 2.00 5.00
46 Marty Howe 2.00 5.00
47 Serge Bernier 2.00 5.00
48 Paul Woods 2.00 5.00
49 Bob Sauve 2.00 5.00
50 Larry Robinson AS1 2.00 5.00
51 Tom Gorence RC 2.00 5.00
52 Gary Sargent 2.00 5.00
53 Thomas Gradin RC 2.00 5.00
54 Dean Talafous 2.00 5.00
55 Bob Murray 2.00 5.00
56 Bob Bourne 2.00 5.00
57 Larry Patey 2.00 5.00
58 Ross Lonsberry 2.00 5.00
59 Rick Smith 2.00 5.00
60 Guy Chouinard 2.00 5.00
61 Danny Gare 2.00 5.00
62 Jim Bedard 2.00 5.00
63 Dale McCourt 2.00 5.00
64 Steve Payne RC 2.00 5.00
65 Pat Hughes RC 2.00 5.00
66 Mike McEwen 2.00 5.00
67 Reg Kerr RC 2.00 5.00
68 Walt McKechnie 2.00 5.00
69 Michel Plasse 2.00 5.00
70 Denis Potvin AS1 2.00 5.00
71 Dave Dryden 2.00 5.00
72 Gary McAdam 2.00 5.00
73 Andre St.Laurent 2.00 5.00
74 Jerry Korab 2.00 5.00
75 Rick MacLeish 2.00 5.00
76 Dennis Kearns 2.00 5.00
77 Jean Pronovost 2.00 5.00
78 Ron Greschner 2.00 5.00
79 Wayne Cashman 2.00 5.00
80 Tony Esposito 2.00 5.00
81 Cup Semi-Finals 2.00 5.00
82 Cup Semi-Finals 2.00 5.00
83 Stanley Cup Finals 2.00 5.00
84 Brian Sutter 2.00 5.00
85 Gerry Cheevers 2.00 5.00
86 Pat Hickey 2.00 5.00
87 Mike Kaszycki 2.00 5.00
88 Grant Mulvey 2.00 5.00
89 Derek Smith 2.00 5.00
90 Steve Shutt 2.00 5.00
91 Robert Picard 2.00 5.00
92 Dan Labraaten 2.00 5.00
93 Glen Sharpley 2.00 5.00
94 Denis Herron 2.00 5.00
95 Reggie Leach 2.00 5.00
96 John Van Boxmeer 2.00 5.00
97 Tiger Williams 2.00 5.00
98 Butch Goring 2.00 5.00
99 Don Marcotte 2.00 5.00
100 Bryan Trottier AS1 2.00 5.00
101 Serge Savard AS2 2.00 5.00
102 Cliff Koroll 2.00 5.00
103 Gary Smith 2.00 5.00
104 Al MacAdam 2.00 5.00
105 Don Edwards 2.00 5.00
106 Errol Thompson 2.00 5.00
107 Andre Lacroix 2.00 5.00
108 Marc Tardif 2.00 5.00
109 Rick Kehoe 2.00 5.00
110 John Davidson 2.00 5.00
111 Behn Wilson RC 2.00 5.00
112 Doug Jarvis 2.00 5.00
113 Tom Rowe RC 2.00 5.00
114 Mike Milbury 2.00 5.00
115 Billy Harris 2.00 5.00
116 Greg Fox RC 2.00 5.00
117 Curt Fraser RC 2.00 5.00
118 Jean-Paul Parise 2.00 5.00
119 Ric Seiling 2.00 5.00
120 Darryl Sittler 2.00 5.00
121 Rick Lapointe 2.00 5.00
122 Jim Rutherford 2.00 5.00
123 Mario Tremblay 2.00 5.00
124 Randy Carlyle 2.00 5.00
125 Bobby Clarke 2.00 5.00
126 Wayne Thomas 2.00 5.00
127 Ivan Boldirev 2.00 5.00
128 Ted Bulley 2.00 5.00
129 Dick Redmond 2.00 5.00
130 Clark Gillies AS1 2.00 5.00
131 Checklist 1-132 15.00 40.00
132 Vaclav Nedomansky 2.00 5.00
133 Richard Mulhern 2.00 5.00
134 Dave Schultz 2.00 5.00
135 Guy Lapointe 2.00 5.00
136 Gilles Meloche 2.00 5.00
137 Randy Pierce RC 2.00 5.00
138 Cam Connor 2.00 5.00
139 George Ferguson 2.00 5.00
140 Bill Barber 2.00 5.00
141 Mike Walton 2.00 5.00
142 Wayne Babych RC 2.00 5.00
143 Phil Russell 2.00 5.00
144 Bobby Schmautz 2.00 5.00
145 Carol Vadnais 2.00 5.00
146 John Tonelli RC 3.00 8.00
147 Peter Marsh RC 2.00 5.00
148 Thommie Bergman 2.00 5.00
149 Richard Martin 2.00 5.00
150 Ken Dryden AS1 10.00 25.00
151 Kris Manery 2.00 5.00
152 Guy Charron 2.00 5.00
153 Lanny McDonald 2.00 5.00
154 Ron Stackhouse 2.00 5.00
155 Stan Mikita 2.00 5.00
156 Paul Holmgren 2.00 5.00
157 Perry Miller 2.00 5.00
158 Gary Croteau 2.00 5.00
159 Dave Maloney 2.00 5.00
160 Marcel Dionne AS2 2.00 5.00
161 Mike Bossy RB 2.00 5.00
162 Don Maloney RB 2.00 5.00
163 Ulf Nilsson RB 2.00 5.00
164 Brad Park RB 2.00 5.00
165 Bryan Trottier RB 2.00 5.00
166 Al Hill RC 2.00 5.00
167 Gary Bromley 2.00 5.00
168 Don Murdoch 2.00 5.00
169 Wayne Merrick 2.00 5.00
170 Bob Gainey 2.00 5.00
171 Jim Schoenfeld 2.00 5.00
172 Gregg Sheppard 2.00 5.00
173 Dan Bolduc RC 2.00 5.00
174 Blake Dunlop 2.00 5.00
175 Gordie Howe 15.00 40.00
176 Richard Brodeur 2.00 5.00
177 Tom Younghans 2.00 5.00
178 Andre Dupont 2.00 5.00
179 Ed Johnstone RC 2.00 5.00
180 Gilbert Perreault 2.00 5.00
181 Bob Lorimer RC 2.00 5.00
182 John Wensink 2.00 5.00
183 Lee Fogolin 2.00 5.00
184 Greg Carroll RC 2.00 5.00
185 Bobby Hull 10.00 25.00
186 Harold Snepsts 2.00 5.00
187 Peter Mahovlich 2.00 5.00
188 Eric Vail 2.00 5.00
189 Phil Myre 2.00 5.00
190 Wilf Paiement 2.00 5.00
191 Charlie Simmer RC 6.00 15.00
192 Per-Olov Brasar 2.00 5.00
193 Lorne Henning 2.00 5.00
194 Don Luce 2.00 5.00
195 Steve Vickers 2.00 5.00
196 Bob Miller RC 2.00 5.00
197 Mike Palmateer 2.00 5.00
198 Nick Libett 2.00 5.00
199 Pat Ribble RC 2.00 5.00
200 Guy Lafleur AS1 2.00 5.00
201 Mel Bridgman 2.00 5.00
202 Morris Lukowich RC 2.00 5.00
203 Don Lever 2.00 5.00
204 Tom Bladon 2.00 5.00
205 Garry Howatt 2.00 5.00
206 Bobby Smith RC 3.00 8.00
207 Craig Ramsay 2.00 5.00
208 Ron Duguay 2.00 5.00
209 Gilles Gilbert 2.00 5.00
210 Bob MacMillan 2.00 5.00
211 Pierre Mondou 2.00 5.00
212 J.P. Bordeleau 2.00 5.00
213 Reed Larson 2.00 5.00
214 Dennis Ververgaert 2.00 5.00
215 Bernie Federko 2.00 5.00
216 Mark Howe 2.00 5.00
217 Bob Nystrom 2.00 5.00
218 Orest Kindrachuk 2.00 5.00
219 Mike Fidler 2.00 5.00
220 Phil Esposito 2.00 5.00
221 Bill Hajt 2.00 5.00
222 Mark Napier 2.00 5.00
223 Dennis Maruk 2.00 5.00
224 Dennis Polonich 2.00 5.00
225 Jean Ratelle 2.00 5.00
226 Bob Dailey 2.00 5.00
227 Alain Daigle 2.00 5.00
228 Ian Turnbull 2.00 5.00
229 Jack Valiquette 2.00 5.00
230 Mike Bossy AS2 4.00 10.00
231 Brad Maxwell 2.00 5.00
232 Dave Taylor 3.00 8.00
233 Pierre Larouche 2.00 5.00
234 Rod Schutt RC 2.00 5.00
235 Rogatien Vachon 2.00 5.00
236 Ryan Walter RC 2.00 5.00
237 Checklist 133-264 20.00 50.00
238 Terry O'Reilly 2.00 5.00
239 Real Cloutier 2.00 5.00
240 Anders Hedberg 2.00 5.00
241 Ken Linseman RC 2.00 5.00
242 Billy Smith 2.00 5.00
243 Rick Chartraw 2.00 5.00
244 Flames Team 2.00 5.00
245 Bruins Team 2.00 5.00
246 Sabres Team 2.00 5.00
247 Blackhawks Team 2.00 5.00
248 Rockies Team 2.00 5.00
249 Red Wings Team 2.00 5.00
250 Kings Team 2.00 5.00
251 North Stars Team 2.00 5.00
252 Canadiens Team 2.00 5.00
253 Islanders Team 2.00 5.00
254 Rangers Team 2.00 5.00
255 Flyers Team 2.00 5.00
256 Penguins Team 2.00 5.00
257 Blues Team 2.00 5.00
258 Maple Leafs Team 2.00 5.00
259 Canucks Team 2.00 5.00
260 Capitals Team 2.00 5.00
261 New NHL Entries CL 20.00 50.00
262 Jean Hamel 2.00 5.00
263 Stan Jonathan 2.00 5.00
264 Russ Anderson 2.00 5.00

1979-80 Topps Team Stickers

COMPLETE SET (22) 10.00 20.00
1 Atlanta Flames .60 1.50
2 Boston Bruins .60 1.50
3 Buffalo Sabres .50 1.25
4 Chicago Blackhawks .60 1.50
5 Colorado Rockies .60 1.50
6 Detroit Red Wings .60 1.50
7 Edmonton Oilers .60 1.50
8 Hartford Whalers .50 1.25
9 Los Angeles Kings .50 1.25
10 Minnesota North Stars .50 1.25
11A Montreal Canadiens goalie .60 1.50
11B Montreal Canadiens score .60 1.50
12 New York Islanders .50 1.25
13 New York Rangers .60 1.50
14 Philadelphia Flyers .50 1.25
15 Pittsburgh Penguins UER .60 1.50
16 Quebec Nordiques .60 1.50
17 St. Louis Blues .50 1.25
18 Toronto Maple Leafs .60 1.50
19 Vancouver Canucks .50 1.25
20 Washington Capitals .50 1.25
21 Winnipeg Jets .50 1.25

1980-81 Topps

COMPLETE SET (264) 100.00 200.00
*SCRATCHED: 20X to .40X
1 Flyers RB .30 .75
2 Ray Bourque RB 15.00 40.00
3 Wayne Gretzky RB 25.00 60.00
4 Charlie Simmer RB .30 .75
5 Billy Smith RB .20 .50
6 Jean Ratelle .20 .50
7 Dave Maloney .15 .40
8 Phil Myre .20 .50
9 Ken Morrow OLY RC .60 1.50
10 Guy Lafleur .60 1.50
11 Bill Derlago RC .15 .40
12 Doug Wilson .30 .75
13 Craig Ramsay .12 .30
14 Pat Boutette .12 .30
15 Eric Vail .12 .30
16 Mike Foligno TL .40 1.00
17 Bobby Smith .40 1.00
18 Rick Kehoe .15 .40
19 Joel Quenneville .12 .30
20 Marcel Dionne .40 1.00
21 Kevin McCarthy .12 .30
22 Jim Craig OLY RC 4.00 10.00
23 Steve Vickers .12 .30
24 Ken Linseman .20 .50
25 Mike Bossy 1.25 3.00
26 Serge Savard .25 .60
27 Grant Mulvey TL .15 .40
28 Pat Hickey .12 .30
29 Peter Sullivan .12 .30
30 Blaine Stoughton .15 .40
31 Mike Liut RC 2.00 5.00
32 Blair MacDonald .12 .30
33 Rick Green .12 .30
34 Al MacAdam .15 .40
35 Robbie Ftorek .12 .30
36 Dick Redmond .12 .30
37 Ron Duguay .15 .40
38 Danny Gare TL .15 .40
39 Brian Propp RC 2.00 5.00
40 Bryan Trottier .50 1.25
41 Rich Preston .12 .30
42 Pierre Mondou .12 .30
43 Reed Larson .12 .30
44 George Ferguson .12 .30
45 Guy Chouinard .20 .50
46 Billy Harris .12 .30
47 Gilles Meloche .20 .50
48 Blair Chapman .12 .30
49 Mike Gartner TL 1.50 4.00
50 Darryl Sittler .25 .60
51 Richard Martin .20 .50
52 Ivan Boldirev .12 .30
53 Craig Norwich RC .12 .30
54 Dennis Polonich .12 .30
55 Bobby Clarke .60 1.50
56 Terry O'Reilly .20 .50
57 Carol Vadnais .12 .30
58 Bob Gainey .25 .60
59 Blaine Stoughton TL .15 .40
60 Billy Smith .20 .50
61 Mike O'Connell RC .12 .30
62 Lanny McDonald .25 .60
63 Lee Fogolin .12 .30
64 Rocky Saganiuk RC .12 .30
65 Rolf Edberg RC .12 .30
66 Paul Shmyr .12 .30
67 Michel Goulet RC 10.00 25.00
68 Dan Bouchard .20 .50
69 Mark Johnson OLY RC .60 1.50
70 Reggie Leach .15 .40
71 Bernie Federko TL .40 1.00
72 Peter Mahovlich .12 .30
73 Anders Hedberg .12 .30
74 Brad Park .15 .40
75 Clark Gillies .20 .50
76 Doug Jarvis .12 .30
77 John Garrett .20 .50
78 Dave Hutchinson .12 .30
79 John Anderson RC .25 .60
80 Gilbert Perreault .20 .50
81 Marcel Dionne AS1 .40 1.00
82 Guy Lafleur AS1 .60 1.50
83 Charlie Simmer AS1 .30 .75
84 Larry Robinson AS1 .20 .50
85 Borje Salming AS1 .20 .50
86 Tony Esposito AS1 .20 .50
87 Wayne Gretzky AS2 25.00 60.00
88 Danny Gare AS2 .15 .40
89 Steve Shutt AS2 .15 .40
90 Barry Beck AS2 .15 .40
91 Mark Howe AS2 .30 .75
92 Don Edwards AS2 .15 .40
93 Tom McCarthy RC .12 .30
94 P.McNab/R.Middleton TL .20 .50
95 Mike Palmateer .20 .50
96 Jim Schoenfeld .20 .50
97 Jordy Douglas .12 .30
98 Keith Brown RC .15 .40
99 Dennis Ververgaert .12 .30
100 Phil Esposito .30 .75
101 Jack Brownschidle .12 .30
102 Bob Nystrom .12 .30
103 Steve Christoff OLY RC .20 .50
104 Rob Palmer .12 .30
105 Tiger Williams .15 .40
106 Kent Nilsson TL .15 .40
107 Morris Lukowich .12 .30
108 Jack Valiquette .12 .30
109 Richie Dunn RC .12 .30
110 Rogatien Vachon .25 .60
111 Mark Napier .12 .30
112 Gordie Roberts .12 .30
113 Stan Jonathan .12 .30
114 Brett Callighen .12 .30
115 Rick MacLeish .12 .30
116 Ulf Nilsson .15 .40
117 Rick Kehoe TL .12 .30
118 Dan Maloney .12 .30
119 Terry Ruskowski .12 .30
120 Denis Potvin .50 1.25
121 Wayne Stephenson .20 .50
122 Rich Leduc .12 .30
123 Checklist 1-132 1.50 4.00
124 Don Lever .12 .30
125 Jim Rutherford .20 .50
126 Ray Allison RC .12 .30
127 Mike Ramsey OLY RC 1.00 2.50
128 Stan Smyl TL .30 .75
129 Al Secord RC 1.00 2.50
130 Denis Herron .20 .50
131 Bob Dailey .12 .30
132 Dean Talafous .12 .30
133 Ian Turnbull .12 .30
134 Ron Sedlbauer .12 .30
135 Tom Bladon .12 .30
136 Bernie Federko .30 .75
137 Dave Taylor .75 2.00
138 Bob Lorimer .12 .30
139 MacAdam/Payne TL .15 .40
140 Ray Bourque RC 40.00 100.00
141 Glen Hanlon .20 .50
142 Willy Lindstrom .12 .30
143 Mike Rogers .12 .30
144 Tony McKegney RC .15 .40
145 Behn Wilson .12 .30
146 Lucien DeBlois .12 .30
147 Dave Burrows .12 .30
148 Paul Woods .12 .30
149 Phil Esposito TL .30 .75
150 Tony Esposito .60 1.50
151 Pierre Larouche .20 .50
152 Brad Maxwell .12 .30
153 Stan Weir .12 .30
154 Ryan Walter .12 .30
155 Dale Hoganson .12 .30
156 Anders Kallur RC .12 .30
157 Paul Reinhart RC .40 1.00
158 Greg Millen .20 .50
159 Ric Seiling .12 .30
160 Mark Howe .60 1.50
161 Goals Leaders
Danny Gare (1)
Charlie Simmer (1)
Blaine Stoughton (1) .30 .75
162 Gretz/Dio/Laf LL 5.00 12.00
163 Gretz/Dio/Laf LL 4.00 10.00
164 Penalty Minutes
Leaders
Jimmy Mann (1)
Dave (Tiger) Williams (2)
Paul Holmgren (3) .20 .50
165 Power Play Goals
Leaders
Charlie Simmer (1)
Marcel Dionne (2)
Danny Gare (2)
Steve Shutt (2)
Darryl Sittler (2) .40 1.00
166 Goals Against Average
Leaders
Bob Sauve (1)
Denis Herron (2)
Don Edwards (3) .20 .50
167 Game-Winning Goals
Leaders
Danny Gare (1)
Peter McNab (2)
Blaine Stoughton (2) .15 .40
168 Espo/Chee/Gar/McN .30 .75
169 Perry Turnbull RC .12 .30
170 Barry Beck .15 .40
171 Charlie Simmer TL .30 .75
172 Paul Shmyr .15 .40
173 Willie Huber .12 .30
174 Tim Young .12 .30
175 Gilles Gilbert .20 .50
176 Dave Christian OLY RC .75 2.00
177 Lars Lindgren RC .12 .30
178 Real Cloutier .15 .40
179 Laurie Boschman RC .15 .40
180 Steve Shutt .15 .40
181 Bob Murray .12 .30
182 Wayne Gretzky TL 15.00 40.00
183 John Van Boxmeer .12 .30
184 Nick Fotiu .20 .50
185 Mike McEwen .12 .30
186 Greg Malone .12 .30
187 Mike Foligno RC 1.25 3.00
188 Dave Langevin RC .12 .30
189 Mel Bridgman .12 .30
190 John Davidson .20 .50
191 Mike Milbury .12 .30
192 Ron Zanussi .12 .30
193 Darryl Sittler TL .25 .60
194 John Marks .12 .30
195 Mike Gartner RC 10.00 25.00
196 Dave Lewis .12 .30
197 Kent Nilsson RC 1.00 2.50
198 Rick Ley .12 .30
199 Derek Smith .12 .30
200 Bill Barber .20 .50
201 Guy Lapointe .20 .50
202 Vaclav Nedomansky .12 .30
203 Don Murdoch .12 .30
204 Mike Bossy TL .60 1.50
205 Pierre Hamel RC .12 .30
206 Mike Eaves RC .12 .30
207 Doug Halward .12 .30
208 Stan Smyl RC .50 1.25
209 Mike Zuke RC .12 .30
210 Borje Salming .20 .50
211 Walt Tkaczuk .20 .50
212 Grant Mulvey .12 .30
213 Rob Ramage RC .40 1.00
214 Tom Rowe .12 .30
215 Don Edwards .15 .40
216 G.Lafleur/P.Larouche TL .60 1.50
217 Dan Labraaten .12 .30
218 Glen Sharpley .12 .30
219 Stefan Persson .12 .30
220 Peter McNab .15 .40
221 Doug Hicks .12 .30
222 Bengt Gustafsson RC .12 .30
223 Michel Dion .20 .50
224 Jimmy Watson .12 .30
225 Wilf Paiement .12 .30
226 Phil Russell .12 .30
227 Morris Lukowich TL .20 .50
228 Ron Stackhouse .12 .30
229 Ted Bulley .12 .30
230 Larry Robinson .20 .50
231 Don Maloney .12 .30
232 Rob McClanahan OLY RC .15 .40
233 Al Sims .12 .30
234 Errol Thompson .12 .30
235 Glenn Resch .20 .50
236 Bob Miller .12 .30
237 Gary Sargent .12 .30
238 Real Cloutier TL .15 .40
239 Rene Robert .25 .60
240 Charlie Simmer .60 1.50
241 Thomas Gradin .12 .30
242 Rick Vaive RC 1.25 3.00
243 Ron Wilson RC .12 .30
244 Brian Sutter .40 1.00
245 Dale McCourt .12 .30
246 Yvon Lambert .12 .30
247 Tom Lysiak .12 .30
248 Ron Greschner .12 .30
249 Reggie Leach TL .15 .40
250 Wayne Gretzky 100.00 250.00
251 Rick Middleton .20 .50
252 Al Smith .12 .30
253 Fred Barrett .12 .30
254 Butch Goring .20 .50
255 Robert Picard .12 .30
256 Marc Tardif .12 .30
257 Checklist 133-264 1.50 4.00
258 Barry Long .12 .30
259 Rene Robert TL .25 .60
260 Danny Gare .15 .40
261 Rejean Houle .12 .30
262 Stanley Cup Semifinals .15 .40
263 Stanley Cup Semifinals .15 .40
264 Stanley Cup Finals .50 1.25

1980-81 Topps Team Posters

COMPLETE SET (16) 12.50 25.00
1 New York Islanders .60 1.50
2 New York Rangers .75 2.00
3 Philadelphia Flyers .60 1.50
4 Boston Bruins 1.00 2.50
5 Whalers w/Howe 1.50 4.00
6 Buffalo Sabres .60 1.50
7 Chicago Blackhawks 1.00 2.50
8 Detroit Red Wings 1.00 2.50
9 Minn. North Stars .75 2.00
10 Toronto Maple Leafs 1.00 2.50
11 Montreal Canadiens 1.00 2.50
12 Colorado Rockies 1.00 2.50
13 Los Angeles Kings 1.25 3.00
14 Vancouver Canucks .60 1.50
15 St. Louis Blues .60 1.50
16 Washington Capitals .60 1.50

1981-82 Topps

COMPLETE SET (198) 20.00 50.00
1 Dave Babych RC .25 .60
2 Bill Barber .12 .30
3 Barry Beck .20 .50
4 Mike Bossy .60 1.50
5 Ray Bourque 8.00 20.00
6 Guy Chouinard .15 .40
7 Dave Christian .12 .30
8 Bill Derlago .12 .30
9 Marcel Dionne .25 .60
10 Brian Engblom .12 .30
11 Tony Esposito .15 .40
12 Bernie Federko .15 .40
13 Bob Gainey .15 .40
14 Danny Gare .12 .30
15 Thomas Gradin .12 .30
16 Wayne Gretzky 20.00 50.00
17 Rick Kehoe .12 .30
18 Jari Kurri RC 10.00 25.00
19 Guy Lafleur .60 1.50
20 Mike Liut .20 .50
21 Dale McCourt .12 .30
22 Rick Middleton .12 .30
23 Mark Napier .12 .30
24 Kent Nilsson .12 .30
25 Wilf Paiement .12 .30
26 Willi Plett .12 .30
27 Denis Potvin .20 .50
28 Paul Reinhart .12 .30
29 Jacques Richard .12 .30
30 Pat Riggin RC .25 .60
31 Larry Robinson .20 .50
32 Mike Rogers .12 .30
33 Borje Salming .20 .50
34 Steve Shutt .12 .30
35 Charlie Simmer .12 .30
36 Darryl Sittler .25 .60
37 Bobby Smith .12 .30
38 Stan Smyl .20 .50
39 Peter Stastny RC 3.00 8.00
40 Dave Taylor .15 .40
41 Bryan Trottier .20 .50
42 Ian Turnbull .12 .30
43 Eric Vail .12 .30
44 Rick Vaive .20 .50
45 Behn Wilson .12 .30
46 Rick Middleton TL .12 .30
47 Danny Gare TL .12 .30
48 Kent Nilsson TL .12 .30
49 Tom Lysiak TL .12 .30
50 Lanny McDonald TL .12 .30
51 Dale McCourt TL .12 .30
52 Wayne Gretzky TL 2.50 6.00
53 Mike Rogers TL .12 .30
54 Marcel Dionne TL .25 .60
55 Bobby Smith TL .12 .30
56 Steve Shutt TL .12 .30
57 Mike Bossy TL .60 1.50
58 Anders Hedberg TL .12 .30
59 Bill Barber TL .12 .30
60 Rick Kehoe TL .12 .30
61 Peter Stastny TL .15 .40
62 Bernie Federko TL .15 .40
63 Wilf Paiement TL .12 .30
64 Thomas Gradin TL .12 .30
65 Dennis Maruk TL .12 .30
66 Dave Christian TL .12 .30
E67 Dwight Foster .12 .30
E68 Steve Kasper RC .40 1.00
E69 Peter McNab .12 .30
E70 Mike O'Connell .15 .40
E71 Terry O'Reilly .15 .40
E72 Brad Park .15 .40
E73 Dick Redmond .12 .30
E74 Rogatien Vachon .20 .50
E75 Don Edwards .12 .30
E76 Tony McKegney .12 .30
E77 Bob Sauve .15 .40
E78 Andre Savard .12 .30
E79 Derek Smith .12 .30
E80 John Van Boxmeer .12 .30
E81 Pat Boutette .25 .60
E82 Mark Howe .20 .50
E83 Dave Keon .20 .50
E84 Warren Miller RC .12 .30
E85 Al Sims .12 .30
E86 Blaine Stoughton .12 .30
E87 Bob Bourne .12 .30
E88 Clark Gillies .20 .50
E89 Butch Goring .12 .30
E90 Anders Kallur .15 .40
E91 Ken Morrow .15 .40
E92 Stefan Persson .12 .30
E93 Billy Smith .20 .50
E94 Mike Allison RC .12 .30
E95 John Davidson .20 .50
E96 Ron Duguay .15 .40
E97 Ron Greschner .12 .30
E98 Anders Hedberg .12 .30
E99 Ed Johnstone .12 .30
E100 Dave Maloney .12 .30
E101 Don Maloney .12 .30
E102 Ulf Nilsson .20 .50
E103 Bobby Clarke .30 .75
E104 Bob Dailey .12 .30
E105 Paul Holmgren .15 .40
E106 Reggie Leach .20 .50
E107 Ken Linseman .20 .50
E108 Rick MacLeish .15 .40
E109 Pete Peeters .20 .50
E110 Brian Propp .20 .50
E111 Checklist 1-132 .40 1.00
E112 Randy Carlyle .20 .50
E113 Paul Gardner .12 .30
E114 Peter Lee .12 .30
E115 Greg Millen .15 .40
E116 Rod Schutt .12 .30
E117 Mike Gartner 2.00 5.00
E118 Rick Green .12 .30
E119 Bob Kelly .12 .30
E120 Dennis Maruk .12 .30
E121 Mike Palmateer .12 .30
E122 Ryan Walter .12 .30
E123 Bill Barber SA .12 .30
E124 Barry Beck SA .20 .50
E125 Mike Bossy SA .60 1.50
E126 Ray Bourque SA 2.00 5.00
E127 Danny Gare SA .12 .30
E128 Rick Kehoe SA .12 .30
E129 Rick Middleton SA .12 .30
E130 Denis Potvin SA .20 .50
E131 Mike Rogers SA .12 .30
E132 Bryan Trottier SA .20 .50
W67 Keith Brown .12 .30
W68 Ted Bulley .12 .30
W69 Tim Higgins RC .12 .30
W70 Reg Kerr .12 .30
W71 Tom Lysiak .12 .30
W72 Grant Mulvey .12 .30
W73 Bob Murray .12 .30
W74 Terry Ruskowski .12 .30
W75 Denis Savard RC 8.00 20.00
W76 Glen Sharpley .12 .30
W77 Darryl Sutter RC .40 1.00
W78 Doug Wilson .15 .40
W79 Lucien DeBlois .12 .30
W80 Paul Gagne RC .12 .30
W81 Merlin Malinowski RC .12 .30
W82 Lanny McDonald .12 .30
W83 Joel Quenneville .12 .30
W84 Rob Ramage .15 .40
W85 Glenn Resch .15 .40
W86 Steve Tambellini .12 .30
W87 Mike Foligno .15 .40
W88 Gilles Gilbert .15 .40
W89 Willie Huber .12 .30
W90 Mark Kirton RC .12 .30
W91 Jim Korn RC .12 .30
W92 Reed Larson .12 .30
W93 Gary McAdam .12 .30
W94 Vaclav Nedomansky .12 .30
W95 John Ogrodnick .12 .30
W96 Billy Harris .12 .30
W97 Jerry Korab .12 .30
W98 Mario Lessard .15 .40
W99 Don Luce .12 .30
W100 Larry Murphy RC 8.00 20.00
W101 Mike Murphy .12 .30
W102 Kent-Erik Andersson .12 .30
W103 Don Beaupre RC 1.50 4.00
W104 Steve Christoff .12 .30
W105 Dino Ciccarelli RC 12.00 30.00
W106 Craig Hartsburg .12 .30
W107 Al MacAdam .12 .30
W108 Tom McCarthy .12 .30
W109 Gilles Meloche .15 .40
W110 Steve Payne .12 .30
W111 Gordie Roberts .12 .30
W112 Greg Smith .12 .30
W113 Tim Young .12 .30
W114 Wayne Babych .12 .30
W115 Blair Chapman .12 .30
W116 Tony Currie .12 .30
W117 Blake Dunlop .12 .30
W118 Ed Kea .12 .30
W119 Rick Lapointe .12 .30
W120 Checklist 1-132 .60 1.50
W121 Jorgen Pettersson RC .12 .30
W122 Brian Sutter .20 .50
W123 Perry Turnbull .12 .30
W124 Mike Zuke .12 .30
W125 Marcel Dionne SA .25 .60
W126 Tony Esposito SA .15 .40
W127 Bernie Federko SA .15 .40
W128 Mike Liut SA .20 .50
W129 Dale McCourt SA .12 .30
W130 Charlie Simmer SA .12 .30
W131 Bobby Smith SA .12 .30
W132 Dave Taylor SA .20 .50

1983 Topps History's Greatest Olympians

COMPLETE SET (99) 12.00 30.00
33 Jim Craig .20 .50
36 Mike Eruzione .30 .75

1984-85 Topps

COMPLETE SET (165) 40.00 100.00
1 Ray Bourque .75 2.00
2 Keith Crowder SP .15 .40
3 Tom Fergus .15 .40
4 Doug Keans RC .20 .50
5 Gord Kluzak SP .15 .40
6 Mike Krushelnyski SP .15 .40
7 Nevin Markwart RC .15 .40
8 Rick Middleton .20 .50
9 Mike O'Connell .15 .40
10 Terry O'Reilly SP .20 .50
11 Barry Pederson .15 .40
12 Pete Peeters .20 .50
13 Dave Andreychuk SP RC 6.00 15.00

14 Tom Barrasso RC 4.00 10.00
15 Real Cloutier SP .15 .40
16 Mike Foligno .20 .50
17 Bill Hajt SP .15 .40
18 Phil Housley SP .20 .50
19 Gilbert Perreault .25 .60
20 Larry Playfair SP .15 .40
21 Craig Ramsay SP .15 .40
22 Mike Ramsey .15 .40
23 Lindy Ruff SP .15 .40
24 Ed Beers .15 .40
25 Rejean Lemelin SP .15 .40
26 Lanny McDonald .20 .50
27 Murray Bannerman .20 .50
28 Keith Brown SP .15 .40
29 Curt Fraser .15 .40
30 Steve Larmer .40 1.00
31 Tom Lysiak .15 .40
32 Bob Murray .15 .40
33 Jack O'Callahan SP RC .20 .50
34 Rich Preston .15 .40
35 Denis Savard .25 .60
36 Darryl Sutter .15 .40
37 Doug Wilson .20 .50
38 Ivan Boldirev .15 .40
39 Colin Campbell SP .15 .40
40 Ron Duguay SP .20 .50
41 Dwight Foster SP .15 .40
42 Danny Gare SP .15 .40
43 Ed Johnstone .15 .40
44 Reed Larson SP .15 .40
45 Eddie Mio SP .20 .50
46 John Ogrodnick .15 .40
47 Brad Park .20 .50
48 Greg Stefan SP RC .20 .50
49 Steve Yzerman RC 25.00 60.00
50 Paul Coffey .40 1.00
51 Wayne Gretzky 15.00 40.00
52 Jari Kurri .50 1.25
53 Bob Crawford RC .15 .40
54 Ron Francis .50 1.25
55 Marty Howe .15 .40
56 Mark Johnson SP .15 .40
57 Greg Malone SP .15 .40
58 Greg Millen SP .20 .50
59 Ray Neufeld .15 .40
60 Joel Quenneville SP .15 .40
61 Risto Siltanen .15 .40
62 Sylvain Turgeon RC .20 .50
63 Mike Zuke SP .15 .40
64 Marcel Dionne .30 .75
65 Brian Engblom SP .15 .40
66 Jim Fox SP .15 .40
67 Bernie Nicholls .50 1.25
68 Terry Ruskowski SP .15 .40
69 Charlie Simmer .15 .40
70 Don Beaupre .20 .50
71 Brian Bellows .20 .50
72 Neal Broten SP .25 .60
73 Dino Ciccarelli .25 .60
74 Paul Holmgren SP .20 .50
75 Al MacAdam SP .15 .40
76 Dennis Maruk .20 .50
77 Brad Maxwell SP .15 .40
78 Tom McCarthy SP .15 .40
79 Gilles Meloche SP .20 .50
80 Steve Payne .15 .40
81 Guy Lafleur .30 .75
82 Larry Robinson .25 .60
83 Bobby Smith .20 .50
84 Mel Bridgman .15 .40
85 Joe Cirella .15 .40
86 Don Lever .15 .40
87 Dave Lewis .15 .40
88 Jan Ludvig RC .15 .40
89 Glenn Resch .20 .50
90 Pat Verbeek RC 2.50 6.00
91 Mike Bossy .25 .60
92 Bob Bourne .15 .40
93 Greg Gilbert RC .20 .50
94 Clark Gillies SP .25 .60
95 Butch Goring SP .20 .50
96 Pat LaFontaine SP RC 5.00 12.00
97 Ken Morrow .15 .40
98 Bob Nystrom SP .15 .40
99 Stefan Persson SP .15 .40
100 Denis Potvin .25 .60
101 Billy Smith SP .25 .60
102 Brent Sutter SP .15 .40
103 John Tonelli .20 .50
104 Bryan Trottier .25 .60
105 Barry Beck .15 .40
106 Glen Hanlon SP .20 .50
107 Anders Hedberg SP .20 .50
108 Pierre Larouche SP .20 .50
109 Don Maloney SP .15 .40
110 Mark Osborne SP .15 .40
111 Larry Patey .15 .40
112 James Patrick RC .25 .60
113 Mark Pavelich SP .15 .40
114 Mike Rogers SP .15 .40
115 Reijo Ruotsalainen SP .15 .40
116 Peter Sundstrom SP RC .20 .50
117 Bob Froese .20 .50
118 Mark Howe .25 .60
119 Tim Kerr SP .15 .40
120 Dave Poulin RC .40 1.00
121 Darryl Sittler SP .30 .75
122 Ron Sutter RC .25 .60
123 Mike Bullard SP .15 .40
124 Ron Flockhart SP .15 .40
125 Rick Kehoe .20 .50
126 Kevin McCarthy SP .15 .40
127 Mark Taylor .15 .40
128 Dan Bouchard SP .20 .50
129 Michel Goulet .20 .50
130 Peter Stastny SP .20 .50
131 Bernie Federko .20 .50
132 Mike Liut .15 .40
133 Joe Mullen SP .40 1.00
134 Rob Ramage .15 .40
135 Brian Sutter .20 .50
136 John Anderson SP .15 .40
137 Dan Daoust .15 .40
138 Rick Vaive .15 .40
139 Darcy Rota SP .15 .40
140 Stan Smyl SP .15 .40
141 Tony Tanti .15 .40
142 Dave Christian SP .15 .40
143 Mike Gartner SP .75 2.00
144 Bengt Gustafsson SP .15 .40
145 Doug Jarvis .15 .40
146 Al Jensen .20 .50
147 Rod Langway .20 .50
148 Pat Riggin .20 .50
149 Scott Stevens SP .75 2.00
150 Dave Babych .15 .40
151 Laurie Boschman .15 .40
152 Dale Hawerchuk .75 2.00
153 Michel Goulet AS .20 .50
154 Wayne Gretzky AS 1.50 4.00
155 Mike Bossy AS .25 .60
156 Rod Langway AS .20 .50
157 Ray Bourque AS .75 2.00
158 Tom Barrasso AS 1.25 3.00
159 Mark Messier AS .50 1.25
160 Bryan Trottier AS .25 .60
161 Jari Kurri AS .50 1.25
162 Denis Potvin AS .25 .60
163 Paul Coffey AS .40 1.00
164 Pat Riggin AS .20 .50
165 Checklist 1-165 SP .60 1.50

1985-86 Topps

COMPLETE SET (165) 125.00 300.00
1 Lanny McDonald .40 1.00
2 Mike O'Connell SP .25 .60
3 Curt Fraser SP .25 .60
4 Steve Penney .25 .60
5 Brian Engblom .25 .60
6 Ron Sutter .25 .60
7 Joe Mullen .25 .60
8 Rod Langway .25 .60
9 Mario Lemieux RC 125.00 300.00
10 Dave Babych .25 .60
11 Bob Nystrom .25 .60
12 Andy Moog SP .75 2.00
13 Dino Ciccarelli .25 .60
14 Dwight Foster SP .25 .60
15 James Patrick SP .25 .60
16 Thomas Gradin SP .25 .60
17 Mike Foligno .25 .60
18 Mario Gosselin RC .25 .60
19 Mike Zuke SP .25 .60
20 John Anderson SP .25 .60
21 Dave Pichette .25 .60
22 Nick Fotiu SP .25 .60
23 Tom Lysiak .20 .50
24 Peter Zezel RC .50 1.25
25 Denis Potvin .25 .60
26 Bob Carpenter .20 .50
27 Murray Bannerman SP .20 .50
28 Gordie Roberts SP .20 .50
29 Steve Yzerman 8.00 20.00
30 Phil Russell .20 .50
31 Peter Stastny .20 .50
32 Craig Ramsay SP .20 .50
33 Terry Ruskowski SP .20 .50
34 Kevin Dineen SP RC 1.00 2.50
35 Mark Howe .25 .60
36 Glenn Resch .20 .50
37 Danny Gare SP .20 .50
38 Doug Bodger RC .20 .50
39 Mike Rogers .25 .60
40 Ray Bourque 1.25 3.00
41 John Tonelli .20 .50
42 Mel Bridgman .25 .60
43 Sylvain Turgeon SP .20 .50
44 Mark Johnson .25 .60
45 Doug Wilson .20 .50
46 Mike Gartner .40 1.00
47 Brent Peterson .25 .60
48 Paul Reinhart SP .20 .50
49 Mike Krushelnyski .25 .60
50 Brian Bellows .20 .50
51 Chris Chelios 1.50 4.00
52 Barry Pederson SP .25 .60
53 Murray Craven SP .20 .50
54 Pierre Larouche SP .20 .50
55 Reed Larson .20 .50
56 Pat Verbeek SP .20 .50
57 Randy Carlyle .20 .50
58 Ray Neufeld SP .20 .50
59 Keith Brown SP .25 .60
60 Bryan Trottier .25 .60
61 Jim Fox SP .25 .60
62 Scott Stevens .40 1.00
63 Phil Housley .20 .50
64 Rick Middleton .20 .50
65 Steve Payne .15 .40
66 Dave Lewis .20 .50
67 Mike Bullard .20 .50
68 Stan Smyl SP .20 .50
69 Mark Pavelich SP .20 .50
70 John Ogrodnick .20 .50
71 Bill Derlago SP .20 .50
72 Brad Marsh SP .20 .50
73 Denis Savard .25 .60
74 Mark Fusco RC .20 .50
75 Pete Peeters .20 .50
76 Doug Gilmour 2.50 6.00
77 Mike Ramsey .20 .50
78 Anton Stastny SP .20 .50
79 Steve Kasper SP .15 .40
80 Bryan Erickson SP RC .20 .50
81 Clark Gillies .25 .60
82 Keith Acton .20 .50
83 Pat Flatley .20 .50
84 Kirk Muller RC 1.00 2.50
85 Paul Coffey 1.25 3.00
86 Ed Olczyk RC .25 .60
87 Charlie Simmer SP .15 .40
88 Mike Liut .15 .40
89 Dave Maloney .25 .60
90 Marcel Dionne .30 .75
91 Tim Kerr .15 .40
92 Ivan Boldirev SP .25 .60
93 Ken Morrow SP .15 .40
94 Don Maloney SP .25 .60
95 Rejean Lemelin .15 .40
96 Curt Giles .25 .60
97 Bob Bourne .15 .40
98 Joe Cirella .25 .60
99 Dave Christian SP .15 .40
100 Darryl Sutter .25 .60
101 Kelly Kisio .25 .60
102 Mats Naslund .25 .60
103 Joel Quenneville SP .25 .60
104 Bernie Federko .20 .50
105 Tom Barrasso .25 .60
106 Rick Vaive .25 .60
107 Brent Sutter .25 .60
108 Wayne Babych .20 .50
109 Dale Hawerchuk .40 1.00
110 Pelle Lindbergh SP 8.00 20.00
111 Dennis Maruk SP .15 .40
112 Reijo Ruotsalainen SP .15 .40
113 Tom Fergus SP .15 .40
114 Bob Murray SP .15 .40
115 Patrik Sundstrom .20 .50
116 Ron Duguay SP .20 .50
117 Alan Haworth SP .15 .40
118 Greg Malone .15 .40
119 Bill Hajt .15 .40
120 Wayne Gretzky 15.00 40.00
121 Craig Redmond .15 .40
122 Kelly Hrudey RC 1.25 3.00
123 Tomas Sandstrom RC 1.25 3.00
124 Neal Broten .20 .50
125 Moe Mantha SP .20 .50
126 Greg Gilbert SP .20 .50
127 Bruce Driver SP RC .25 .60
128 Dave Poulin .20 .50
129 Morris Lukowich SP .20 .50
130 Mike Bossy .25 .60
131 Larry Playfair SP .20 .50
132 Steve Larmer .20 .50
133 Doug Keans SP .20 .50
134 Bob Manno .25 .60
135 Brian Sutter .25 .60
136 Pat Riggin .25 .60
137 Pat LaFontaine .75 2.00
138 Barry Beck SP .25 .60
139 Rich Preston SP .25 .60
140 Ron Francis 1.00 2.50
141 Brian Propp SP .25 .60
142 Don Beaupre .25 .60
143 Dave Andreychuk SP .25 .60
144 Ed Beers .20 .50
145 Paul MacLean .20 .50
146 Troy Murray SP .25 .60
147 Larry Robinson .25 .60
148 Bernie Nicholls .25 .60
149 Glen Hanlon SP .25 .60
150 Michel Goulet .25 .60
151 Doug Jarvis SP .25 .60
152 Warren Young .20 .50
153 Tony Tanti .20 .50
154 Tomas Jonsson SP .20 .50
155 Jari Kurri 1.00 2.50
156 Tony McKegney .20 .50
157 Greg Stefan SP .20 .50
158 Brad McCrimmon SP .20 .50
159 Keith Crowder SP .15 .40
160 Gilbert Perreault .25 .60
161 Tim Bothwell SP .20 .50
162 Bob Crawford SP .20 .50
163 Paul Gagne SP .20 .50
164 Dan Daoust SP .20 .50
165 Checklist 1-165 SP 1.00 2.50

1985-86 Topps Box Bottoms

COMPLETE SET (16) 26.00 65.00
A Brian Bellows .25 .60
B Ray Bourque 1.00 2.50
C Bob Carpenter .15 .40
D Chris Chelios 1.50 4.00
E Marcel Dionne .50 1.25
F Ron Francis 1.00 2.50
G Wayne Gretzky 10.00 25.00
H Tim Kerr .15 .40
I Mario Lemieux 8.00 20.00
J John Ogrodnick .16 .40
K Gilbert Perreault .30 .75
L Glenn Resch .25 .60
M Reijo Ruotsalainen .15 .40
N Brian Sutter .25 .60
O John Tonelli .15 .40
P Doug Wilson .25 .60

1985-86 Topps Sticker Inserts

COMPLETE SET (33) 8.00 20.00
1 John Ogrodnick .10 .25
2 Wayne Gretzky 4.00 10.00
3 Jari Kurri .40 1.00
4 Paul Coffey .60 1.50
5 Ray Bourque .60 1.50
6 Pelle Lindbergh 1.50 4.00
7 John Tonelli .10 .25
8 Dale Hawerchuk .30 .75
9 Mike Bossy .40 1.00
10 Rod Langway .10 .25
11 Doug Wilson .10 .25
12 Tom Barrasso .30 .75
13 Toronto Maple Leafs .15 .40
14 Buffalo Sabres .10 .25
15 Detroit Red Wings .10 .25
16 Pittsburgh Penguins .10 .25
17 New York Rangers .10 .25
18 Calgary Flames .10 .25
19 Winnipeg Jets .10 .25
20 Quebec Nordiques .10 .25
21 Chicago Blackhawks .10 .25
22 Los Angeles Kings .10 .25
23 Montreal Canadiens .15 .40
24 Vancouver Canucks .10 .25
25 Hartford Whalers .15 .40
26 Philadelphia Flyers .10 .25
27 New Jersey Devils .10 .25
28 St. Louis Blues .10 .25
29 Minnesota North Stars .10 .25
30 Washington Capitals .10 .25
31 Boston Bruins .10 .25
32 New York Islanders .10 .25
33 Edmonton Oilers .10 .25

1986-87 Topps

COMPLETE SET (198) 60.00 150.00
1 Ray Bourque 1.00 2.50
2 Pat LaFontaine DP .60 1.50
3 Wayne Gretzky 10.00 25.00
4 Lindy Ruff .05 .15
5 Brad McCrimmon .05 .15
6 Tiger Williams .15 .40
7 Denis Savard DP .15 .40
8 Lanny McDonald .05 .15
9 John Vanbiesbrouck DP RC 2.00 5.00
10 Greg Adams RC .30 .75
11 Steve Yzerman 2.50 6.00
12 Craig Hartsburg .05 .15
13 John Anderson DP .05 .15
14 Bob Bourne DP .05 .15
15 Kjell Dahlin RC .05 .15
16 Dave Andreychuk .30 .75
17 Rob Ramage DP .05 .15
18 Ron Greschner DP .05 .15
19 Bruce Driver .05 .15
20 Peter Stastny .15 .40
21 Dave Christian .05 .15
22 Doug Keans .05 .15
23 Scott Bjugstad RC .05 .15
24 Doug Bodger DP .05 .15
25 Troy Murray DP .05 .15
26 Al Iafrate .30 .75
27 Kelly Hrudey .30 .75
28 Doug Jarvis .05 .15
29 Rich Sutter .05 .15
30 Marcel Dionne .15 .40
31 Curt Fraser .05 .15
32 Doug Lidster .05 .15
33 Brian MacLellan .05 .15
34 Barry Pederson .05 .15
35 Craig Laughlin .05 .15
36 Ilkka Sinisalo DP .05 .15
37 John MacLean RC 1.00 2.50
38 Brian Mullen .05 .15
39 Duane Sutter DP .05 .15
40 Brian Engblom .05 .15
41 Chris Cichocki .05 .15
42 Gordie Roberts .05 .15
43 Ron Francis .60 1.50
44 Joe Mullen .30 .75
45 Moe Mantha DP .05 .15
46 Pat Verbeek .05 .15
47 Clint Malarchuk RC .30 .75
48 Bob Brooke DP .05 .15
49 Darryl Sutter DP .05 .15
50 Stan Smyl DP .05 .15
51 Greg Stefan .15 .40
52 Bill Hajt DP .05 .15
53 Patrick Roy RC 60.00 150.00
54 Gord Kluzak .05 .15
55 Bob Froese DP .05 .15
56 Grant Fuhr 1.00 2.50
57 Mark Hunter DP .05 .15
58 Dana Murzyn RC .15 .40
59 Mike Gartner .30 .75
60 Dennis Maruk .05 .15
61 Rich Preston .05 .15
62 Larry Robinson DP .05 .15
63 Dave Taylor DP .05 .15
64 Bob Murray DP .05 .15
65 Ken Morrow .15 .40
66 Mike Ridley RC .30 .75
67 John Tucker RC .05 .15
68 Miroslav Frycer .05 .15
69 Danny Gare .15 .40
70 Randy Burridge RC .30 .75
71 Dave Poulin .05 .15
72 Brian Sutter .15 .40
73 Dave Babych .05 .15
74 Dale Hawerchuk DP .30 .75
75 Brian Bellows .05 .15
76 Dave Pasin DP RC .05 .15
77 Pete Peeters DP .05 .15
78 Tomas Jonsson DP .05 .15
79 Gilbert Perreault DP .05 .15
80 Glenn Anderson DP .30 .75
81 Don Maloney .05 .15
82 Ed Olczyk DP .05 .15
83 Mike Bullard DP .05 .15
84 Tom Fergus .05 .15
85 Dave Lewis .05 .15
86 Brian Propp .15 .40
87 John Ogrodnick .05 .15
88 Kevin Dineen DP .30 .75
89 Don Beaupre .15 .40
90 Mike Bossy DP .50 1.25
91 Tom Barrasso DP .30 .75
92 Michel Goulet DP .05 .15
93 Doug Gilmour 1.25 3.00
94 Kirk Muller .30 .75
95 Larry Melnyk DP RC .05 .15
96 Bob Gainey DP .30 .75
97 Steve Kasper .05 .15
98 Petr Klima RC .15 .40
99 Neal Broten DP .05 .15
100 Al Secord DP .05 .15
101 Bryan Erickson DP .05 .15
102 Rejean Lemelin .15 .40
103 Sylvain Turgeon .05 .15
104 Bob Nystrom .05 .15
105 Bernie Federko .15 .40
106 Doug Wilson DP .05 .15
107 Alan Haworth .05 .15
108 Jari Kurri .60 1.50
109 Ron Sutter .05 .15
110 Reed Larson DP .05 .15
111 Terry Ruskowski DP .05 .15
112 Mark Johnson DP .05 .15
113 James Patrick .05 .15
114 Paul MacLean .05 .15
115 Mike Ramsey DP .05 .15
116 Kelly Kisio DP .05 .15
117 Brent Sutter .05 .15
118 Joel Quenneville .05 .15
119 Curt Giles DP .05 .15
120 Tony Tanti DP .05 .15
121 Doug Sulliman DP .05 .15
122 Mario Lemieux 25.00 60.00
123 Mark Howe DP .05 .15
124 Bob Sauve .15 .40
125 Anton Stastny .05 .15
126 Scott Stevens DP .30 .75
127 Mike Foligno .05 .15
128 Reijo Ruotsalainen DP .05 .15
129 Denis Potvin .15 .40
130 Keith Crowder .05 .15
131 Bob Janecyk DP .05 .15
132 John Tonelli .05 .15
133 Mike Liut DP .05 .15
134 Tim Kerr DP .05 .15
135 Al Jensen .15 .40
136 Mel Bridgman .05 .15
137 Paul Coffey DP .60 1.50
138 Dino Ciccarelli DP .15 .40
139 Steve Larmer .30 .75
140 Mike O'Connell .05 .15
141 Clark Gillies .15 .40
142 Phil Russell DP .05 .15
143 Dirk Graham DP RC .30 .75
144 Randy Carlyle .05 .15
145 Charlie Simmer .05 .15
146 Ron Flockhart DP .05 .15
147 Tom Laidlaw .05 .15
148 Dave Tippett RC .15 .40
149 Wendel Clark DP RC 12.00 30.00
150 Bob Carpenter DP .05 .15
151 Bill Watson RC .05 .15
152 Roberto Romano DP RC .05 .15
153 Doug Shedden .05 .15
154 Phil Housley .40 .75
155 Bryan Trottier .30 .75
156 Patrik Sundstrom DP .05 .15
157 Rick Middleton DP .05 .15
158 Glenn Resch .15 .40
159 Bernie Nicholls DP .30 .75
160 Ray Ferraro RC 1.00 2.50
161 Mats Naslund DP .05 .15
162 Pat Flatley DP .05 .15
163 Joe Cirella .05 .15
164 Rod Langway DP .05 .15
165 Checklist 1-99 .30 .75
166 Carey Wilson .05 .15
167 Murray Craven .05 .15
168 Paul Gillis RC .05 .15
169 Borje Salming .05 .15
170 Perry Turnbull .05 .15
171 Chris Chelios 1.25 3.00
172 Keith Acton .05 .15
173 Al MacInnis 2.00 5.00
174 Russ Courtnall RC 1.00 2.50
175 Brad Marsh .05 .15
176 Guy Carbonneau .15 .40
177 Ray Neufeld .05 .15
178 Craig MacTavish RC .30 .75
179 Rick Lanz .05 .15
180 Murray Bannerman .15 .40
181 Brent Ashton .05 .15
182 Jim Peplinski .05 .15
183 Mark Napier .05 .15
184 Laurie Boschman .05 .15
185 Larry Murphy .15 .40
186 Mark Messier .30 .75
187 Risto Siltanen .05 .15
188 Bobby Smith .15 .40
189 Gary Suter RC .75 2.00
190 Peter Zezel .05 .15
191 Rick Vaive .05 .15
192 Dale Hunter .15 .40
193 Mike Krushelnyski .05 .15
194 Scott Arniel .05 .15
195 Larry Playfair .05 .15
196 Doug Risebrough .05 .15
197 Kevin Lowe .05 .15
198 Checklist 100-198 .30 .75

1986-87 Topps Box Bottoms

COMPLETE SET (16) 14.00 35.00
A Greg Adams .20 .50
B Mike Bossy .40 1.00
C Dave Christian .08 .25
D Mike Foligno .08 .25
E Michel Goulet .20 .50
F Wayne Gretzky 6.00 15.00
G Tim Kerr .08 .25
H Jari Kurri .60 1.50
I Mario Lemieux 8.00 20.00
J Lanny McDonald .20 .50
K Bernie Nicholls .20 .50
L Mike Ridley .20 .50
M Larry Robinson .20 .50
N Denis Savard .20 .50
O Brian Sutter .08 .25
P Bryan Trottier .30 .75

1986-87 Topps Sticker Inserts

COMPLETE SET (33) 12.00 30.00
1 John Vanbiesbrouck 3.00 8.00
2 Michel Goulet .20 .50
3 Wayne Gretzky 4.00 10.00
4 Mike Bossy .40 1.00
5 Paul Coffey .60 1.50
6 Mark Howe .15 .40
7 Bob Froese .15 .40
8 Mats Naslund .15 .40
9 Mario Lemieux 4.00 10.00
10 Jari Kurri .60 1.50
11 Ray Bourque .75 2.00
12 Larry Robinson .20 .50
13 Toronto Maple Leafs .08 .25
14 Buffalo Sabres .05 .15
15 Detroit Red Wings .08 .25
16 Pittsburgh Penguins .05 .15
17 New York Rangers .08 .25
18 Calgary Flames .05 .15
19 Winnipeg Jets .05 .15
20 Quebec Nordiques .05 .15
21 Chicago Blackhawks .08 .25
22 Los Angeles Kings .05 .15
23 Montreal Canadiens .08 .25
24 Vancouver Canucks .05 .15
25 Hartford Whalers .05 .15
26 Philadelphia Flyers .05 .15
27 New Jersey Devils .05 .15
28 St. Louis Blues .05 .15
29 Minnesota North Stars .05 .15
30 Washington Capitals .05 .15
31 Boston Bruins .08 .25
32 New York Islanders .05 .15
33 Edmonton Oilers .05 .15

1987-88 Topps

COMPLETE SET (198) 30.00 80.00
1 Denis Potvin DP .25 .60
2 Rick Tocchet RC 3.00 8.00
3 Dave Andreychuk .25 .60
4 Stan Smyl .20 .50
5 Dave Babych DP .20 .50
6 Pat Verbeek .20 .50
7 Esa Tikkanen RC 2.00 5.00
8 Mike Ridley .20 .50
9 Randy Carlyle .20 .50
10 Greg Paslawski RC .20 .50
11 Neal Broten .20 .50
12 Wendel Clark DP 1.00 2.50
13 Bill Ranford DP RC 2.00 5.00
14 Doug Wilson .20 .50
15 Mario Lemieux 12.00 30.00
16 Mats Naslund .15 .40
17 Mel Bridgman .20 .50
18 James Patrick DP .20 .50
19 Rollie Melanson .20 .50
20 Lanny McDonald .20 .50
21 Peter Stastny .20 .50
22 Murray Craven .20 .50
23 Ulf Samuelsson DP RC .75 2.00
24 Michael Thelven DP UER
(Misspelled Thelvin .20 .50
25 Scott Stevens .25 .60
26 Petr Klima .20 .50
27 Brent Sutter DP .20 .50
28 Tomas Sandstrom .20 .50
29 Tim Bothwell .20 .50
30 Bob Carpenter DP .20 .50
31 Brian MacLellan DP .20 .50
32 John Chabot .20 .50
33 Phil Housley DP .20 .50
34 Patrik Sundstrom DP .20 .50
35 Dave Ellett .20 .50
36 John Vanbiesbrouck 2.50 6.00
37 Dave Lewis .20 .50
38 Tom McCarthy DP .20 .50
39 Dave Poulin .20 .50
40 Mike Foligno .20 .50
41 Gordie Roberts .20 .50
42 Luc Robitaille RC 12.00 30.00
43 Duane Sutter .20 .50
44 Pete Peeters .20 .50
45 John Anderson .20 .50
46 Aaron Broten .20 .50
47 Keith Brown .20 .50
48 Bobby Smith .20 .50
49 Don Maloney .20 .50
50 Mark Hunter .20 .50
51 Moe Mantha .20 .50
52 Charlie Simmer .15 .40
53 Wayne Gretzky 8.00 20.00
54 Mark Howe .25 .60
55 Bob Gould .20 .50
56 Steve Yzerman DP 2.50 6.00
57 Larry Playfair .20 .50
58 Alain Chevrier .20 .50
59 Steve Larmer .20 .50
60 Bryan Trottier .25 .60
61 Stewart Gavin DP .25 .60
62 Russ Courtnall DP .25 .60
63 Mike Ramsey DP .25 .60
64 Bob Brooke .25 .60
65 Rick Wamsley DP .25 .60
66 Ken Morrow DP .15 .40
67 Gerard Gallant UER RC .25 .60
68 Kevin Hatcher RC .60 1.50
69 Cam Neely .75 2.00
70 Sylvain Turgeon DP .25 .60
71 Peter Zezel .25 .60
72 Al MacInnis 1.00 2.50
73 Terry Ruskowski DP .25 .60
74 Troy Murray .25 .60
75 Jim Fox DP .25 .60
76 Kelly Kisio .25 .60
77 Michel Goulet DP .25 .60
78 Tom Barrasso DP .25 .60
79 Bruce Driver DP .25 .60
80 Craig Simpson DP RC .40 1.00
81 Dino Ciccarelli .25 .60
82 Gary Nylund DP .25 .60
83 Bernie Federko .20 .50
84 John Tonelli DP .25 .60
85 Brad McCrimmon DP .25 .60
86 Dave Tippett DP .25 .60
87 Ray Bourque DP .75 2.00
88 Dave Christian .15 .40
89 Glen Hanlon .25 .60
90 Brian Curran .25 .60
91 Paul MacLean .25 .60
92 Jimmy Carson RC .25 .60
93 Willie Huber .25 .60
94 Brian Bellows .20 .50
95 Doug Jarvis DP .25 .60
96 Clark Gillies .25 .60
97 Tony Tanti .25 .60
98 Pelle Eklund DP RC .25 .60
99 Paul Coffey 1.00 2.50
100 Brent Ashton DP .25 .60
101 Mark Johnson .25 .60
102 Greg Johnston RC .25 .60
103 Ron Flockhart .25 .60
104 Ed Olczyk .25 .60
105 Mike Bossy .25 .60
106 Chris Chelios 1.00 2.50
107 Gilles Meloche .25 .60
108 Rod Langway .25 .60
109 Ray Ferraro DP .25 .60
110 Ron Duguay DP .20 .50
111 Al Secord DP .25 .60
112 Mark Messier .50 1.25
113 Ron Sutter .25 .60
114 Darren Veitch RC .25 .60
115 Rick Middleton DP .25 .60
116 Doug Sulliman .25 .60
117 Dennis Maruk DP .25 .60
118 Dave Taylor .25 .60
119 Kelly Hrudey .25 .60
120 Tom Fergus .15 .40
121 Christian Ruuttu RC .25 .60
122 Brian Benning RC .25 .60
123 Adam Oates RC 10.00 25.00
124 Kevin Dineen .25 .60
125 Doug Bodger DP .25 .60
126 Joe Mullen .25 .60
127 Denis Savard .25 .60
128 Brad Marsh .25 .60
129 Marcel Dionne DP .30 .75
130 Bryan Erickson .25 .60
131 Reed Larson DP .25 .60
132 Don Beaupre .25 .60
133 Larry Murphy DP .20 .50
134 John Ogrodnick DP .25 .60
135 Greg Adams DP .25 .60
136 Pat Flatley .25 .60
137 Scott Arniel DP .15 .40
138 Dana Murzyn .25 .60
139 Greg C. Adams .15 .40
140 Bob Sauve .15 .40
141 Mike O'Connell .15 .40
142 Walt Poddubny DP .15 .40
143 Paul Reinhart .15 .40
144 Tim Kerr DP .15 .40
145 Brian Lawton RC .15 .40
146 Gino Cavallini RC .15 .40
147 Doug Keans DP .15 .40
148 Jari Kurri .15 .40
149 Dale Hawerchuk .30 .75
150 Randy Cunneyworth RC .20 .50
151 Jay Wells .15 .40
152 Mike Liut DP .15 .40
153 Steve Konroyd .15 .40
154 John Tucker .15 .40
155 Rick Vaive DP .15 .40
156 Bob Murray .15 .40
157 Kirk Muller DP .15 .40
158 Brian Propp .15 .40
159 Ron Greschner .15 .40
160 Rob Ramage .15 .40
161 Craig Laughlin .15 .40
162 Steve Kasper DP .15 .40
163 Patrick Roy 8.00 20.00
164 Shawn Burr DP RC .20 .50
165 Craig Hartsburg DP .20 .50
166 Dean Evason RC .20 .50
167 Bob Bourne .15 .40
168 Mike Gartner .30 .75
169 Ron Hextall RC 12.00 30.00
170 Joe Cirella .20 .50
171 Dan Quinn DP .20 .50
172 Tony McKegney .20 .50
173 Pat LaFontaine DP .25 .60
174 Allen Pedersen DP RC .20 .50
175 Doug Gilmour .30 .75
176 Gary Suter DP .20 .50
177 Barry Pederson DP .20 .50
178 Grant Fuhr DP .40 1.00
179 Wayne Presley RC .20 .50
180 Wilf Paiement .20 .50
181 Doug Smail .25 .60
182 Doug Crossman DP .25 .60
183 Bernie Nicholls UER
(Misspelled Nichols
on card front) .25 .60
184 Dirk Graham UER
(Misspelled Dick
on card front) .25 .60
185 Anton Stastny .25 .60
186 Greg Stefan .25 .60
187 Ron Francis .30 .75
188 Steve Thomas DP .25 .60
189 Kelly Miller RC .25 .60
190 Tomas Jonsson .25 .60
191 John MacLean .25 .60
192 Larry Robinson DP .25 .60
193 Doug Wickenheiser DP .20 .50
194 Keith Crowder DP .15 .40
195 Bob Froese .20 .50
196 Jim Johnson .20 .50
197 Checklist 1-99 .30 .75
198 Checklist 100-198 .30 .75

1987-88 Topps Box Bottoms

COMPLETE SET (16) 10.00 25.00
A Wayne Gretzky 4.00 10.00
B Tim Kerr .08 .25
C Steve Yzerman 2.00 5.00
D Luc Robitaille 1.50 4.00
E Doug Gilmour .40 1.00
F Ray Bourque .75 2.00
G Joe Mullen .20 .50
H Larry Murphy .20 .50
I Dale Hawerchuk .25 .60
J Ron Francis .40 1.00
K Walt Poddubny .05 .15
L Mats Naslund .15 .40
M Michel Goulet .20 .50
N Denis Savard .20 .50
O Bryan Trottier .25 .60
P Russ Courtnall .20 .50

1987-88 Topps Sticker Inserts

COMPLETE SET (33) 8.00 20.00
1 Ray Bourque .75 2.00
2 Ron Hextall 1.00 2.50
3 Mark Howe .15 .40
4 Jari Kurri .30 .75
5 Wayne Gretzky 3.00 8.00
6 Michel Goulet .15 .40
7 Larry Murphy .15 .40
8 Mike Liut .15 .40
9 Al MacInnis .20 .50
10 Tim Kerr .08 .25
11 Mario Lemieux 4.00 10.00
12 Luc Robitaille 1.50 4.00
13 Toronto Maple Leafs .08 .25
14 Buffalo Sabres .05 .15
15 Detroit Red Wings .08 .25
16 Pittsburgh Penguins .05 .15
17 New York Rangers .08 .25
18 Calgary Flames .05 .15
19 Winnipeg Jets .05 .15
20 Quebec Nordiques .05 .15
21 Chicago Blackhawks .05 .15
22 Los Angeles Kings .05 .15
23 Montreal Canadiens .08 .25
24 Vancouver Canucks .05 .15
25 Hartford Whalers .05 .15
26 Philadelphia Flyers .05 .15
27 New Jersey Devils .05 .15
28 St. Louis Blues .05 .15
29 Minnesota North Stars .05 .15
30 Washington Capitals .05 .15
31 Boston Bruins .08 .25
32 New York Islanders .05 .15
33 Edmonton Oilers .05 .15

1988-89 Topps

COMPLETE SET (198) 50.00 125.00
1 Mario Lemieux DP 6.00 15.00

Card	Low	High
2 Bob Joyce DP RC	.25	.60
3 Joel Quenneville DP	.20	.50
4 Tony McKegney	.20	.50
5 Stephane Richer DP	.20	.50
6 Mark Howe DP	.25	.60
7 Brent Sutter DP	.20	.50
8 Gilles Meloche DP	.20	.50
9 Jimmy Carson DP	.20	.50
10 John MacLean	.20	.50
11 Gary Leeman	.20	.50
12 Gerard Gallant DP	.20	.50
13 Marcel Dionne	.30	.75
14 Dave Christian DP	.15	.40
15 Gary Nylund	.20	.50
16 Joe Nieuwendyk RC	6.00	15.00
17 Billy Smith DP	.25	.60
18 Christian Ruuttu	.20	.50
19 Randy Cunneyworth	.20	.50
20 Brian Lawton	.20	.50
21 Scott Mellanby DP RC	.75	2.00
22 Peter Stastny DP	.20	.50
23 Gord Kluzak	.15	.40
24 Sylvain Turgeon	.20	.50
25 Clint Malarchuk	.20	.50
26 Denis Savard	.25	.60
27 Craig Simpson	.20	.50
28 Petr Klima	.20	.50
29 Pat Verbeek	.20	.50
30 Moe Mantha	.20	.50
31 Chris Nilan	.15	.40
32 Barry Pederson	.20	.50
33 Randy Burridge	.20	.50
34 Ron Hextall	.50	1.25
35 Gaston Gingras	.20	.50
36 Kevin Dineen DP	.20	.50
37 Tom Laidlaw	.20	.50
38 Paul MacLean DP	.20	.50
39 John Chabot DP	.20	.50
40 Lindy Ruff	.20	.50
41 Dan Quinn DP	.20	.50
42 Don Beaupre	.20	.50
43 Gary Suter	.20	.50
44 Mikko Makela DP RC	.20	.50
45 Mark Johnson DP	.20	.50
46 Dave Taylor	.20	.50
47 Ulf Dahlen DP RC	.20	.50
48 Jeff Sharples RC	.20	.50
49 Chris Chelios	.60	1.50
50 Mike Gartner DP	.30	.75
51 Darren Pang DP RC	.75	2.00
52 Ron Francis	.30	.75
53 Ken Morrow	.15	.40
54 Michel Goulet	.20	.50
55 Ray Sheppard RC	.75	2.00
56 Doug Gilmour	.30	.75
57 David Shaw DP	.20	.50
58 Cam Neely DP	.60	1.50
59 Grant Fuhr DP	.40	1.00
60 Scott Stevens	.25	.60
61 Bob Brooke	.25	.60
62 Dave Hunter	.25	.60
63 Alan Kerr RC	.25	.60
64 Brad Marsh	.25	.60
65 Dale Hawerchuk DP	.30	.75
66 Brett Hull DP RC	10.00	25.00
67 Patrik Sundstrom DP	.25	.60
68 Greg Stefan	.25	.60
69 James Patrick	.25	.60
70 Dale Hunter DP	.25	.60
71 Al Iafrate	.25	.60
72 Bob Carpenter	.20	.50
73 Ray Bourque DP	.75	2.00
74 John Tucker DP	.25	.60
75 Carey Wilson	.25	.60
76 Joe Mullen	.25	.60
77 Rick Vaive	.25	.60
78 Shawn Burr DP	.25	.60
79 Murray Craven DP	.25	.60
80 Clark Gillies	.25	.60
81 Bernie Federko	.20	.50
82 Tony Tanti	.25	.60
83 Greg Gilbert	.25	.60
84 Kirk Muller	.25	.60
85 Dave Tippett	.25	.60
86 Kevin Hatcher DP	.25	.60
87 Rick Middleton DP	.25	.60
88 Bobby Smith	.25	.60
89 Doug Wilson DP	.20	.50
90 Scott Arniel	.15	.40
91 Brian Mullen	.25	.60
92 Mike O'Connell DP	.15	.40
93 Mark Messier DP	.50	1.25
94 Sean Burke RC	1.00	2.50
95 Brian Bellows DP	.20	.50
96 Doug Bodger	.15	.40
97 Bryan Trottier	.25	.60
98 Anton Stastny	.15	.40
99 Checklist 1-99	.20	.60
100 Dave Poulin DP	.15	.40
101 Bob Bourne DP	.15	.40
102 John Vanbiesbrouck	.25	.60
103 Allen Pedersen	.15	.40
104 Mike Ridley	.15	.40
105 Andrew McBain	.15	.40
106 Troy Murray DP	.15	.40
107 Tom Barrasso	.15	.40
108 Tomas Jonsson	.15	.40
109 Rob Brown RC	.15	.40
110 Hakan Loob DP	.15	.40
111 Ilkka Sinisalo DP	.15	.40
112 Dave Archibald RC	.15	.40
113 Doug Halward	.15	.40
114 Ray Ferraro	.15	.40
115 Doug Brown RC	.15	.40
116 Patrick Roy DP	1.50	4.00
117 Greg Millen	.15	.40
118 Ken Linseman	.15	.40
119 Phil Housley DP	.20	.50
120 Wayne Gretzky Sweater	8.00	20.00
121 Tomas Sandstrom	.15	.40
122 Brendan Shanahan RC	8.00	20.00
123 Pat LaFontaine	.25	.60
124 Luc Robitaille DP	1.00	2.50
125 Ed Olczyk DP	.15	.40
126 Ron Sutter	.15	.40
127 Mike Liut	.15	.40
128 Brent Ashton DP	.15	.40
129 Tony Hrkac RC	.15	.40
130 Kelly Miller	.15	.40
131 Alan Haworth	.15	.40
132 Dave McLlwain RC	.15	.40
133 Mike Ramsey	.15	.40
134 Bob Sweeney RC	.20	.50
135 Dirk Graham DP	.20	.50
136 Ulf Samuelsson	.20	.50
137 Petri Skriko	.20	.50
138 Aaron Broten DP	.20	.50
139 Jim Fox	.20	.50
140 Randy Wood DP RC	.20	.50
141 Larry Murphy	.20	.50
142 Daniel Berthiaume DP	.20	.50
143 Kelly Kisio	.20	.50
144 Neal Broten	.20	.50
145 Reed Larson	.20	.50
146 Peter Zezel DP	.20	.50
147 Jari Kurri	.20	.50
148 Jim Johnson	.20	.50
149 Gino Cavallini DP	.20	.50
150 Glen Hanlon DP	.20	.50
151 Bengt Gustafsson	.20	.50
152 Mike Bullard DP	.20	.50
153 John Ogrodnick	.20	.50
154 Steve Larmer	.20	.50
155 Kelly Hrudey	.20	.50
156 Mats Naslund	.15	.40
157 Bruce Driver	.20	.50
158 Randy Hillier	.20	.50
159 Craig Hartsburg	.20	.50
160 Rollie Melanson	.20	.50
161 Adam Oates DP	.50	1.25
162 Greg Adams DP	.15	.40
163 Dave Andreychuk DP	.25	.60
164 Dave Babych	.20	.50
165 Brian Noonan RC	.20	.50
166 Glen Wesley RC	.20	.50
167 Dave Ellett	.20	.50
168 Brian Propp	.20	.50
169 Bernie Nicholls	.20	.50
170 Walt Poddubny	.20	.50
171 Steve Konroyd	.20	.50
172 Doug Sulliman DP	.20	.50
173 Mario Gosselin	.20	.50
174 Brian Benning	.20	.50
175 Dino Ciccarelli	.20	.50
176 Steve Kasper	.15	.40
177 Rick Tocchet	.60	1.50
178 Brad McCrimmon	.20	.50
179 Paul Coffey	.50	1.25
180 Pete Peeters	.20	.50
181 Bob Probert DP RC	10.00	25.00
182 Steve Duchesne DP RC	.60	1.50
183 Russ Courtnall	.20	.50
184 Mike Foligno DP	.20	.50
185 Wayne Presley DP	.20	.50
186 Rejean Lemelin	.15	.40
187 Mark Hunter	.20	.50
188 Joe Cirella	.20	.50
189 Glenn Anderson DP	.20	.50
190 John Anderson	.15	.40
191 Pat Flatley	.15	.40
192 Rod Langway	.15	.40
193 Brian MacLellan	.20	.50
194 Pierre Turgeon RC	8.00	20.00
195 Brian Hayward	.20	.50
196 Steve Yzerman DP	.75	2.00
197 Doug Crossman	.20	.50
198 Checklist 100-198	.25	.60

1988-89 Topps Box Bottoms

Card	Low	High
COMPLETE SET (16)	5.60	14.00
A Ron Francis	.30	.75
B Wayne Gretzky	2.50	6.00
C Pat LaFontaine	.30	.75
D Bobby Smith	.08	.25
E Bernie Federko	.08	.25
F Kirk Muller	.20	.50
G Ed Olczyk	.05	.15
H Denis Savard	.20	.50
I Ray Bourque	.60	1.50
J Murray Craven Brian Propp	.05	.15
K Dale Hawerchuk	.20	.50
L Steve Yzerman	1.25	3.00
M Dave Andreychuk	.15	.40
N Mike Gartner	.20	.50
O Hakan Loob	.08	.25
P Luc Robitaille	.40	1.00

1988-89 Topps Sticker Inserts

Card	Low	High
COMPLETE SET (33)	6.00	15.00
1 Luc Robitaille	.60	1.50
2 Mario Lemieux	1.50	4.00
3 Hakan Loob	.08	.25
4 Scott Stevens	.15	.40
5 Ray Bourque	.30	.75
6 Grant Fuhr	.20	.50
7 Michel Goulet	.15	.40
8 Wayne Gretzky	2.00	5.00
9 Cam Neely	.30	.75
10 Brad McCrimmon	.08	.25
11 Gary Suter	.08	.25
12 Patrick Roy	2.00	5.00
13 Toronto Maple Leafs	.08	.25
14 Buffalo Sabres	.05	.15
15 Detroit Red Wings	.08	.25
16 Pittsburgh Penguins	.05	.15
17 New York Rangers	.08	.25
18 Calgary Flames	.05	.15
19 Winnipeg Jets	.05	.15
20 Quebec Nordiques	.05	.15
21 Chicago Blackhawks	.08	.25
22 Los Angeles Kings	.05	.15
23 Montreal Canadiens	.08	.25
24 Vancouver Canucks	.05	.15
25 Hartford Whalers	.05	.15
26 Philadelphia Flyers	.05	.15
27 New Jersey Devils	.05	.15
28 St. Louis Blues	.05	.15
29 Minnesota North Stars	.05	.15
30 Washington Capitals	.05	.15
31 Boston Bruins	.08	.25
32 New York Islanders	.05	.15
33 Edmonton Oilers	.05	.15

1989-90 Topps

Card	Low	High
1 Mario Lemieux	1.50	4.00
2 Ulf Dahlen DP	.20	.50
3 Terry Carkner RC	.20	.50
4 Tony McKegney	.20	.50
5 Denis Savard	.20	.50
6 Derek King DP RC	.20	.50
7 Lanny McDonald	.20	.50
8 John Tonelli	.20	.50
9 Tom Kurvers DP	.20	.50
10 Dave Archibald	.20	.50
11 Peter Sidorkiewicz RC	.20	.50
12 Esa Tikkanen	.20	.50
13 Dave Barr	.20	.50
14 Brent Sutter	.20	.50
15 Cam Neely	.20	.50
16 Calle Johansson RC	.15	.40
17 Patrick Roy DP	1.00	2.50
18 Dale DeGray DP RC	.15	.40
19 Phil Bourque RC	.15	.40
20 Kevin Dineen	.15	.40
21 Mike Bullard DP	.15	.40
22 Gary Leeman	.15	.40
23 Greg Stefan DP	.15	.40
24 Brian Mullen	.15	.40
25 Pierre Turgeon DP	.40	1.00
26 Bob Rouse DP	.15	.40
27 Peter Zezel	.15	.40
28 Jeff Brown DP	.15	.40
29 Andy Brickley DP RC	.15	.40
30 Mike Gartner	.25	.60
31 Darren Pang	.15	.40
32 Pat Verbeek	.15	.40
33 Petri Skriko DP	.15	.40
34 Tom Laidlaw	.15	.40
35 Randy Wood	.15	.40
36 Tom Barrasso DP	.15	.40
37 John Tucker DP	.15	.40
38 Andrew McBain	.15	.40
39 David Shaw DP	.15	.40
40 Rejean Lemelin	.12	.30
41 Dino Ciccarelli DP	.15	.40
42 Jeff Sharples	.15	.40
43 Jari Kurri	.15	.40
44 Murray Craven DP	.15	.40
45 Cliff Ronning DP RC	.60	1.50
46 Dave Babych	.15	.40
47 Bernie Nicholls DP	.15	.40
48 Jon Casey RC	.15	.40
49 Al MacInnis	.25	.60
50 Bob Errey DP RC	.15	.40
51 Glen Wesley	.15	.40
52 Dirk Graham	.15	.40
53 Guy Carbonneau DP	.15	.40
54 Tomas Sandstrom	.15	.40
55 Rod Langway DP	.15	.40
56 Patrik Sundstrom	.15	.40
57 Michel Goulet	.15	.40
58 Dave Taylor	.15	.40
59 Phil Housley	.15	.40
60 Pat LaFontaine DP	.20	.50
61 Kirk McLean DP RC	.25	.60
62 Ken Linseman	.15	.40
63A Randy Cunneyworth PIT	.15	.40
63B Randy Cunneyworth WIN	.15	.40
64 Tony Hrkac DP	.15	.40
65 Mark Messier DP	.40	1.00
66 Carey Wilson DP	.15	.40
67 Stephen Leach RC	.15	.40
68 Christian Ruuttu	.15	.40
69 Dave Ellett	.15	.40
70 Ray Ferraro	.15	.40
71 Colin Patterson RC	.15	.40
72 Tim Kerr	.12	.30
73 Bob Joyce	.15	.40
74 Doug Gilmour DP	.25	.60
75 Lee Norwood DP	.15	.40
76 Dale Hunter	.15	.40
77 Jim Johnson DP	.15	.40
78 Mike Foligno DP	.20	.50
79 Al Iafrate DP	.20	.50
80 Rick Tocchet DP	.20	.50
81 Greg Hawgood DP RC	.20	.50
82 Steve Thomas	.20	.50
83 Steve Yzerman DP	.50	1.25
84 Mike McPhee	.20	.50
85 David Volek DP RC	.20	.50
86 Brian Benning	.20	.50
87 Neal Broten	.20	.50
88 Luc Robitaille	.20	.50
89 Trevor Linden RC	.60	1.50
90 James Patrick DP	.20	.50
91 Brian Lawton	.20	.50
92 Sean Burke DP	.20	.50
93 Scott Stevens	.20	.50
94 Pat Elynuik DP RC	.20	.50
95 Paul Coffey	.20	.50
96 Jan Erixon DP	.20	.50
97 Mike Liut	.12	.30
98 Wayne Presley	.20	.50
99 Craig Simpson	.20	.50
100 Kjell Samuelsson RC	.20	.50
101 Shawn Burr DP	.20	.50
102 John MacLean	.20	.50
103 Tom Fergus	.12	.30
104 Mike Krushelnyski	.20	.50
105 Gary Nylund	.20	.50
106 Dave Andreychuk	.20	.50
107 Bernie Federko	.15	.40
108 Gary Suter	.15	.40
109 Dave Gagner DP	.20	.50
110 Ray Bourque	.30	.75
111 Geoff Courtnall RC	.40	1.00
112 Doug Wilson	.15	.40
113 Joe Sakic RC	3.00	8.00
114 John Vanbiesbrouck	.20	.50
115 Dave Poulin	.20	.50
116 Rick Meagher	.12	.30
117 Kirk Muller DP	.12	.30
118 Mats Naslund	.12	.30
119 Ray Sheppard	.12	.30
120 Jeff Norton RC	.15	.40
121 Randy Burridge DP	.12	.30
122 Dale Hawerchuk DP	.25	.60
123 Steve Duchesne	.12	.30
124 John Anderson	.12	.30
125 Rick Vaive DP	.12	.30
126 Randy Hillier	.12	.30
127 Jimmy Carson	.12	.30
128 Larry Murphy	.15	.40
129 Paul MacLean DP	.12	.30
130 Joe Cirella	.12	.30
131 Kelly Miller DP	.12	.30
132 Alain Chevrier DP	.12	.30
133 Ed Olczyk	.12	.30
134 Dave Tippett	.12	.30
135 Bob Sweeney	.12	.30
136 Brian Leetch RC	6.00	15.00
137 Greg Millen	.12	.30
138 Joe Nieuwendyk	.15	.40
139 Brian Propp	.12	.30
140 Mike Ramsey	.12	.30
141 Mike Allison	.12	.30
142 Shawn Chambers RC	.12	.30
143 Peter Stastny DP	.15	.40
144 Glen Hanlon	.12	.30
145 John Cullen RC	.15	.40
146 Kevin Hatcher	.15	.40
147 Brendan Shanahan	.20	.50
148 Paul Reinhart	.15	.40
149 Bryan Trottier	.20	.50
150 Dave Manson RC	.15	.40
151 Marc Habscheid DP RC	.15	.40
152 Dan Quinn	.15	.40
153 Stephane Richer DP	.15	.40
154 Doug Bodger DP	.15	.40
155 Ron Hextall	.20	.50
156 Wayne Gretzky	1.25	3.00
157 Steve Tuttle DP RC	.20	.50
158 Charlie Huddy DP	.20	.50
159 Dave Christian DP	.12	.30
160 Andy Moog	.20	.50
161 Tony Granato RC	.20	.50
162 Sylvain Cote RC	.20	.50
163 Mike Vernon	.25	.60
164 Steve Chiasson RC	.15	.40
165 Mike Ridley	.15	.40
166 Kelly Hrudey	.15	.40
167 Bob Carpenter DP	.15	.40
168 Zarley Zalapski RC	.15	.40
169 Derek Laxdal RC	.20	.50
170 Clint Malarchuk DP	.20	.50
171 Kelly Kisio	.20	.50
172 Gerard Gallant	.20	.50
173 Ron Sutter	.20	.50
174 Chris Chelios	.20	.50
175 Ron Francis	.25	.60
176 Gino Cavallini	.15	.40
177 Brian Bellows DP	.15	.40
178 Greg C. Adams DP	.15	.40
179 Steve Larmer	.15	.40
180 Aaron Broten	.15	.40
181 Brent Ashton DP	.15	.40
182 Gerald Diduck DP RC	.15	.40
183 Paul MacDermid RC	.15	.40
184 Walt Poddubny DP	.15	.40
185 Adam Oates	.20	.50
186 Brett Hull	6.00	15.00
187 Scott Arniel	.12	.30
188 Bobby Smith	.15	.40
189 Guy Lafleur	.25	.60
190 Craig Janney RC	.25	.60
191 Mark Howe	.20	.50
192 Grant Fuhr DP	.30	.75
193 Rob Brown	.12	.30
194 Steve Kasper DP	.12	.30
195 Pete Peeters	.12	.30
196 Joe Mullen	.12	.30
197 Checklist 1-99	.30	.75
198 Checklist 100-198 DP	.30	.75

1989-90 Topps Box Bottoms

Card	Low	High
COMPLETE SET (16)	4.00	10.00
A Mario Lemieux	1.50	4.00
B Mike Ridley	.08	.25
C Tomas Sandstrom	.08	.25
D Petri Skriko	.08	.25
E Wayne Gretzky	1.50	4.00
F Brett Hull	.75	2.00
G Tim Kerr	.08	.25
H Mats Naslund	.08	.25
I Jari Kurri	.20	.50
J Steve Larmer	.20	.50
K Cam Neely	.30	.75
L Steve Yzerman	.75	2.00
M Kevin Dineen	.08	.25
N Dave Gagner	.15	.40
O Joe Mullen	.15	.40
P Pierre Turgeon	.30	.75

1989-90 Topps Sticker Inserts

Card	Low	High
COMPLETE SET (33)	4.00	10.00
1 Chris Chelios	.30	.75
2 Gerard Gallant DP	.05	.15
3 Mario Lemieux	2.00	5.00
4 Al MacInnis	.20	.50
5 Joe Mullen DP	.08	.25
6 Patrick Roy	1.50	4.00
7 Ray Bourque	.30	.75
8 Rob Brown	.08	.25
9 Geoff Courtnall DP	.08	.25
10 Steve Duchesne DP	.05	.15
11 Wayne Gretzky	2.00	5.00
12 Mike Vernon	.15	.40
13 Toronto Maple Leafs	.05	.15
14 Buffalo Sabres	.05	.15
15 Detroit Red Wings	.05	.15
16 Pittsburgh Penguins	.05	.15
17 New York Rangers	.05	.15
18 Calgary Flames	.05	.15
19 Winnipeg Jets	.05	.15
20 Quebec Nordiques	.05	.15
21 Chicago Blackhawks	.05	.15
22 Los Angeles Kings	.05	.15
23 Montreal Canadiens	.05	.15
24 Vancouver Canucks	.05	.15
25 Hartford Whalers	.05	.15
26 Philadelphia Flyers	.05	.15
27 New Jersey Devils DP	.02	.10
28 St. Louis Blues DP	.02	.10
29 Minn. North Stars DP	.02	.10
30 Washington Capitals DP	.02	.10
31 Boston Bruins DP	.02	.10
32 New York Islanders DP	.02	.10
33 Edmonton Oilers DP	.02	.10

1990-91 Topps

*TIFFANY: 3X TO 8X BASIC CARDS

Card	Low	High
1 Wayne Gretzky Indy	1.00	2.50
2 Wayne Gretzky Oilers	1.00	2.50
3 Wayne Gretzky LA	1.00	2.50
4 Brett Hull HL	.30	.75
5 Jari Kurri HL UER misspelled Jarri	.20	.50
6 Bryan Trottier HL	.15	.40
7 Jeremy Roenick RC	.75	2.00
8 Brian Propp	.15	.40
9 Jim Hrivnak RC	.15	.40
10 Mick Vukota RC	.15	.40
11 Tom Kurvers	.15	.40
12 Ulf Dahlen	.15	.40
13 Bernie Nicholls	.12	.30
14 Peter Sidorkiewicz	.15	.40
15 Peter Zezel	.15	.40
16 Mike Hartman RC	.15	.40
17 Kings Team	.12	.30
18 Jim Sandlak	.15	.40
19 Rob Brown	.30	.75
20 Paul Ranheim RC	.15	.40
21 Rick Zombo RC	.15	.40
22 Paul Gillis	.12	.30
23 Brian Hayward	.15	.40
24 Brent Ashton	.15	.40
25 Mark Lamb	.15	.40
26 Rick Tocchet	.15	.40
27 Slava Fetisov RC	.30	.75
28 Denis Savard	.15	.40
29 Chris Chelios	.15	.40
30 Janne Ojanen RC	.15	.40
31 Don Maloney	.15	.40
32 Allan Bester	.15	.40
33 Geoff Smith RC	.15	.40
34 Daniel Shank RC	.15	.40
35 Mikael Andersson RC	.15	.40
36 Gino Cavallini	.15	.40
37 Rob Murphy RC	.15	.40
38 Flames Team	.15	.40
39 Laurie Boschman	.12	.30
40 Craig Wolanin RC	.12	.30
41 Phil Bourque	.12	.30
42 Alexander Mogilny RC	.50	1.25
43 Ray Bourque	.25	.60
44 Mike Liut	.10	.25
45 Ron Sutter	.12	.30
46 Bob Kudelski RC	.12	.30
47 Larry Murphy	.12	.30
48 Darren Turcotte RC	.12	.30
49 Paul Ysebaert RC	.12	.30
50 Alan Kerr	.12	.30
51 Randy Carlyle	.12	.30
52 Iiro Jarvi	.12	.30
53 Don Barber RC	.12	.30
54 Carey Wilson	.12	.30
55 Joey Kocur RC	.30	.75
56 Steve Larmer	.12	.30
57 Paul Cavallini	.12	.30
58 Shayne Corson	.12	.30
59 Canucks Team	.12	.30
60 Sergei Makarov RC	.30	.75
61 Kjell Samuelsson	.12	.30
62 Tony Granato	.10	.25
63 Tom Fergus	.10	.25
64 Martin Gelinas RC	.30	.75
65 Tom Barrasso	.12	.30
66 Pierre Turgeon	.12	.30
67 Randy Cunneyworth	.12	.30
68 Michal Pivonka RC	.12	.30
69 Cam Neely	.15	.40
70 Brian Bellows	.12	.30
71 Pat Elynuik	.12	.30
72 Doug Crossman	.12	.30
73 Sylvain Turgeon	.12	.30
74 Shawn Burr	.12	.30
75 John Vanbiesbrouck	.15	.40
76 Steve Bozek	.12	.30
77 Brett Hull	.30	.75
78 Zarley Zalapski	.12	.30
79 Wendel Clark	.25	.60
80 Flyers Team Kjell Samuelsson Wendell Young	.15	.40
81 Kelly Miller	.10	.25
82 Mark Pederson RC	.15	.40
83 Adam Creighton	.10	.25
84 Scott Young	.10	.25
85 Petr Klima	.10	.25
86 Steve Duchesne	.10	.25
87 Joe Nieuwendyk	.12	.30
88 Andy Brickley	.10	.25
89 Phil Housley	.12	.30
90 Neal Broten	.10	.25
91 Al Iafrate	.10	.25
92 Steve Thomas	.10	.25
93 Guy Carbonneau	.10	.25
94 Steve Chiasson	.10	.25
95 Mike Tomlak RC	.15	.40
96 Roger Johansson RC	.15	.40
97 Randy Wood	.10	.25
98 Jim Johnson	.10	.25
99 Bob Sweeney	.10	.25
100 Dino Ciccarelli	.15	.40
101 Rangers Team James Patrick	.15	.40
102 Mike Ramsey	.10	.25
103 Kelly Hrudey	.10	.25
104 Dave Ellett	.10	.25
105 Bob Brooke	.10	.25
106 Greg Adams	.10	.25
107 Joe Cirella	.10	.25
108 Jari Kurri	.20	.50
109 Pete Peeters	.10	.25
110 Paul MacLean	.12	.30
111 Doug Wilson	.12	.30
112 Pat Verbeek	.12	.30
113 Bob Beers RC	.12	.30
114 Mike O'Connell	.12	.30
115 Brian Bradley	.12	.30
116 Paul Coffey	.15	.40
117 Doug Brown	.12	.30
118 Aaron Broten	.12	.30
119 Bob Essensa RC	.25	.60
120 Wayne Gretzky UER	1.00	2.50
121 Vincent Damphousse	.12	.30
122 Nordiques Team Paul Gillis	.12	.30
123 Mike Foligno	.12	.30
124 Russ Courtnall	.15	.40
125 Rick Meagher	.12	.30
126 Craig Fisher RC	.15	.40
127 Al MacInnis	.20	.50
128 Derek King	.15	.40
129 Dale Hunter	.15	.40
130 Mark Messier UER	.30	.75
131 James Patrick UER (Orange border rather than blue)	.15	.40
132 Checklist 1-132	.05	.15
133 Red Wings Team Steve Yzerman	.50	1.25
134 Barry Pederson	.12	.30
135 Gary Leeman	.12	.30
136 Doug Gilmour	.20	.50
137 Mike McPhee	.12	.30
138 Bob Murray	.12	.30
139 Bob Carpenter	.12	.30
140 Sean Burke	.12	.30
141 Dale Hawerchuk	.20	.50
142 Guy Lafleur	.20	.50
143 Lindy Ruff	.12	.30
144 Whalers Team Brad Shaw	.12	.30
145 Glenn Anderson	.12	.30
146 Dave Chyzowski RC	.12	.30
147 Kevin Hatcher	.12	.30
148 Rick Vaive	.12	.30
149 Adam Oates	.15	.40
150 Garth Butcher	.12	.30
151 Basil McRae	.10	.25
152 Ilkka Sinisalo	.12	.30
153 Steve Kasper	.10	.25
154 Greg Paslawski	.12	.30
155 Brad Marsh	.12	.30
156 Esa Tikkanen	.12	.30
157 Tony Tanti	.12	.30
158 Mario Marois	.12	.30
159 Sylvain Lefebvre RC	.12	.30
160 Troy Murray	.12	.30
161 Gary Roberts	.15	.40
162 Randy Ladouceur	.15	.40
163 John Chabot	.15	.40
164 Calle Johansson	.15	.40
165 Bruins Team Ray Bourque	.25	.60
166 Jeff Norton	.15	.40
167 Mike Krushelnyski	.15	.40
168 Dave Gagner	.15	.40
169 Dave Andreychuk	.15	.40
170 Dave Capuano RC	.15	.40
171 Curtis Joseph RC	.50	1.25
172 Bruce Driver	.15	.40
173 Scott Mellanby	.15	.40
174 John Ogrodnick	.15	.40
175 Mario Lemieux	.60	1.50
176 Marc Fortier	.12	.30
177 Vincent Riendeau RC	.15	.40
178 Mark Johnson	.12	.30
179 Dirk Graham	.12	.30
180 Jets Team	.15	.40
181 Robb Stauber RC	.15	.40
182 Christian Ruuttu	.12	.30
183 Dave Tippett	.12	.30
184 Pat LaFontaine	.15	.40
185 Mark Howe	.15	.40
186 Stephane Richer	.15	.40
187 Jan Erixon	.15	.40
188 Neil Sheehy	.15	.40
189 Craig MacTavish	.12	.30
190 Randy Burridge	.12	.30
191 Bernie Federko	.12	.30
192 Shawn Chambers	.12	.30
193 Mark Messier AS1	.30	.75
194 Luc Robitaille AS1	.15	.40
195 Brett Hull AS1	.30	.75
196 Ray Bourque AS1	.25	.60
197 Al MacInnis AS1	.20	.50
198 Patrick Roy AS1	.40	1.00
199 Wayne Gretzky AS2	1.00	2.50
200 Brian Bellows AS2	.12	.30
201 Cam Neely AS2	.15	.40
202 Paul Coffey AS2	.15	.40
203 Doug Wilson AS2	.12	.30
204 Daren Puppa AS2 UER	.12	.30
205 Gary Suter	.10	.25
206 Ed Olczyk	.15	.40
207 Doug Lidster	.15	.40
208 John Cullen	.15	.40
209 Luc Robitaille	.15	.40
210 Tim Kerr	.10	.25
211 Scott Stevens	.15	.40
212 Craig Janney	.15	.40
213 Kevin Dineen	.15	.40
214 Jim Waite RC	.15	.40
215 Benoit Hogue	.15	.40
216 Curtis Leschyshyn RC	.12	.30
217 Brad Lauer	.12	.30
218 Joe Mullen	.12	.30
219 Patrick Roy	.40	1.00
220 Blues Team Jeff Brown	.15	.40
221 Brian Leetch	.20	.50
222 Steve Yzerman	.50	1.25
223 Steph Beauregard RC	.12	.30
224 John MacLean	.12	.30
225 Trevor Linden	.15	.40
226 Bill Ranford	.12	.30
227 Mark Osborne	.12	.30
228 Curt Giles	.12	.30
229 Mikko Makela	.12	.30
230 Bob Errey	.12	.30
231 Jimmy Carson	.12	.30
232 Kay Whitmore RC	.12	.30
233 Gary Nylund	.12	.30
234 Jiri Hrdina RC	.12	.30
235 Stephen Leach	.12	.30
236 Greg Hawgood	.12	.30
237 Jocelyn Lemieux RC	.12	.30
238 Daren Puppa	.12	.30
239 Kelly Kisio	.12	.30
240 Craig Simpson	.12	.30
241 Maple Leafs Team Vincent Damphousse	.12	.30
242 Fredrik Olausson	.12	.30
243 Ron Hextall	.15	.40
244 Sergio Momesso RC	.12	.30
245 Kirk Muller	.12	.30
246 Petr Svoboda	.12	.30
247 Daniel Berthiaume	.12	.30
248 Andrew McBain	.12	.30
249 Jeff Jackson UER	.12	.30
250 Randy Gilhen RC	.10	.25
251 Oilers Team Adam Graves	.30	.75
252 Rick Bennett RC	.10	.25
253 Don Beaupre	.10	.25
254 Pelle Eklund	.10	.25
255 Greg Gilbert	.10	.25
256 Gordie Roberts	.10	.25
257 Kirk McLean	.10	.25
258 Brent Sutter	.12	.30
259 Brendan Shanahan	.15	.40
260 Todd Krygier RC	.12	.30
261 Larry Robinson UER	.15	.40
262 Sabres Team Phil Housley	.12	.30
263 Dave Christian	.10	.25
264 Checklist 133-264	.05	.15
265 Jamie Macoun	.12	.30
266 Glen Hanlon	.12	.30
267 Daniel Marois	.12	.30
268 Doug Smail	.12	.30
269 Jon Casey	.15	.40
270 Brian Skrudland	.12	.30
271 Michel Petit	.12	.30
272 Dan Quinn	.12	.30
273 Geoff Courtnall	.12	.30
274 Mike Bullard	.12	.30
275 Randy Gregg	.12	.30
276 Keith Brown	.12	.30
277 Troy Mallette RC	.12	.30
278 Steve Tuttle	.12	.30
279 Brad Shaw RC	.12	.30
280 Mark Recchi RC	.50	1.25
281 John Tonelli	.12	.30
282 Doug Bodger	.12	.30
283 Thomas Steen	.12	.30
284 Devils Team Chris Terreri	.30	.75
285 Lee Norwood	.12	.30
286 Brian MacLellan	.12	.30
287 Bobby Smith	.12	.30
288 Rob Cimetta RC	.12	.30
289 Rob Zettler RC	.12	.30
290 David Reid RC	.15	.40
291 Bryan Trottier	.15	.40
292 Brian Mullen	.15	.40
293 Paul Reinhart	.15	.40
294 Andy Moog	.15	.40
295 Jeff Brown	.15	.40
296 Ryan Walter	.15	.40
297 Trent Yawney	.15	.40
298 John Druce RC	.15	.40
299 Dave McLlwain UER (Card says shoots right, should be left)	.15	.40
300 David Volek	.15	.40
301 Tomas Sandstrom	.15	.40
302 Gord Murphy RC	.15	.40
303 Lou Franceschetti RC	.15	.40
304 Dana Murzyn	.15	.40
305 North Stars Team Jon Casey	.15	.40
306 Patrik Sundstrom	.12	.30
307 Kevin Lowe	.15	.40
308 Dave Barr	.15	.40
309 Wendell Young RC	.15	.40
310 Darrin Shannon RC	.15	.40
311 Ron Francis	.20	.50
312 Stephane Fiset RC	.30	.75
313 Paul Fenton	.15	.40
314 Dave Taylor	.15	.40
315 Islanders Team Pat LaFontaine	.15	.40
316 Petri Skriko	.15	.40
317 Rob Ramage	.15	.40
318 Murray Craven	.15	.40
319 Gaetan Duchesne	.15	.40
320 Brad McCrimmon	.15	.40
321 Grant Fuhr	.25	.60
322 Gerard Gallant	.10	.25
323 Tommy Albelin	.10	.25
324 Scott Arniel	.10	.25
325 Mike Keane RC	.10	.25
326 Penguins Team Randy Gilhen	.10	.25
327 Mike Ridley	.10	.25
328 Dave Babych	.10	.25
329 Michel Goulet	.10	.25
330 Mike Richter RC	.50	1.25
331 Garry Galley RC	.10	.25
332 Rod Brind'Amour RC	.30	.75
333 Tony McKegney	.10	.25
334 Peter Stastny	.12	.30
335 Greg Millen	.12	.30
336 Ray Ferraro	.12	.30
337 Miloslav Horava RC	.12	.30
338 Paul MacDermid	.12	.30
339 Craig Coxe RC	.12	.30
340 Dave Snuggerud RC	.12	.30
341 Mike Lalor RC	.12	.30
342 Marc Habscheid	.12	.30
343 Rejean Lemelin	.10	.25
344 Charlie Huddy	.12	.30
345 Ken Linseman	.12	.30
346 Canadiens Team Sylvain Lefebvre	.12	.30
347 Troy Loney RC	.15	.40
348 Mike Modano RC	.60	1.50
349 Jeff Reese RC	.15	.40
350 Pat Flatley	.15	.40
351 Mike Vernon	.12	.30
352 Todd Elik RC	.15	.40
353 Rod Langway	.15	.40
354 Moe Mantha	.15	.40
355 Keith Acton	.15	.40
356 Scott Pearson RC	.15	.40
357 Perry Berezan RC	.15	.40
358 Alexei Kasatonov RC	.15	.40
359 Igor Larionov RC	.30	.75

360 Kevin Stevens RC .30 .75
361 Yves Racine RC .15 .40
362 Dave Poulin .15 .40
363 Blackhawks Team
Dave Manson
Doug Wilson .15 .40
364 Yvon Corriveau RC .12 .30
365 Brian Benning .12 .30
366 Hubie McDonough RC .12 .30
367 Ron Tugnutt .12 .30
368 Steve Smith .12 .30
369 Joel Otto .12 .30
370 Dave Lowry RC .12 .30
371 Clint Malarchuk .12 .30
372 Mathieu Schneider RC .12 .30
373 Mike Gartner .20 .50
374 John Tucker .12 .30
375 Chris Terreri RC .30 .75
376 Dean Evason .12 .30
377 Jamie Leach RC .12 .30
378 Jacques Cloutier RC .12 .30
379 Glen Wesley .12 .30
380 Vladimir Krutov RC .30 .75
381 Terry Carkner .12 .30
382 John McIntyre RC .12 .30
383 Ville Siren RC .12 .30
384 Joe Sakic .50 1.25
385 Teppo Numminen RC .30 .75
386 Theo Fleury .20 .50
387 Glen Featherstone RC .12 .30
388 Stephan Lebeau RC .12 .30
389 Kevin McClelland .12 .30
390 Uwe Krupp .15 .40
391 Mark Janssens RC .15 .40
392 Marty McSorley .12 .30
393 Vladimir Ruzicka RC .15 .40
394 Capitals Team
Kirk Muller
Scott Stevens .15 .40
395 Mark Fitzpatrick RC .12 .30
396 Checklist 265-396 .05 .15

1990-91 Topps Box Bottoms

COMPLETE SET (16) 3.00 8.00
A Alexander Mogilny .50 1.25
B Jon Casey .15 .40
C Paul Coffey .25 .60
D Wayne Gretzky 1.00 2.50
E Patrick Roy .60 1.50
F Mike Modano .30 .75
G Mario Lemieux .60 1.50
H Al MacInnis .15 .40
I Ray Bourque .25 .60
J Steve Yzerman .40 1.00
K Darren Turcotte .08 .25
L Mike Vernon .15 .40
M Pierre Turgeon .20 .50
N Doug Wilson .08 .25
O Don Beaupre .15 .40
P Sergei Makarov .08 .25

1990-91 Topps Team Scoring Leaders

COMPLETE SET (21) 3.00 7.50
*TIFFANY: 3X TO 8X BASIC INSERTS
1 Steve Larmer .15 .40
2 Brett Hull .40 1.00
3 Cam Neely .20 .50
4 Stephane Richer .20 .50
5 Paul Reinhart .20 .50
6 Dino Ciccarelli .20 .50
7 Kirk Muller .15 .40
8 Joe Nieuwendyk .15 .40
9 Rick Tocchet .20 .50
10 Pat LaFontaine .20 .50
11 Dale Hawerchuk .25 .60
12 Wayne Gretzky 1.25 3.00
13 Gary Leeman .15 .40
14 Joe Sakic .60 1.50
15 Brian Bellows .15 .40
16 Mark Messier .40 1.00
17 Mario Lemieux .75 2.00
18 John Ogrodnick .20 .50
19 Steve Yzerman .60 1.50
20 Pierre Turgeon .15 .40
21 Ron Francis .25 .60

1991-92 Topps

*O-PEE-CHEE: .4X TO 1X TOPPS
1 Guy Lafleur Tribute .20 .50
2 Guy Lafleur Tribute .20 .50
3 Guy Lafleur Tribute .20 .50
4 Ed Belfour SR .40 1.00
5 Ken Hodge Jr. SR .12 .30
6 Rob Blake SR UER .15 .40
7 Bobby Holik SR .15 .40
8 Sergei Fedorov SR UER .25 .60
9 Jaromir Jagr SR .50 1.25
10 Eric Weinrich SR .15 .40
11 Mike Richter SR .15 .40
12 Mats Sundin SR .15 .40
13 Mike Ricci SR .10 .25
14 Eric Desjardins .15 .40
15 Paul Ranheim .15 .40
16 Joe Sakic .50 1.25
17 Curt Giles .15 .40
18 Mike Foligno .15 .40
19 Brad Marsh .15 .40
20 Ed Belfour .40 1.00
21 Steve Smith .15 .40
22 Kirk Muller .10 .25
23 Kelly Chase .12 .30
24 Jim McKenzie RC .15 .40
25 Mick Vukota .12 .30
26 Tony Amonte RC .40 1.00
27 Danton Cole .10 .25
28 Jay Mazur RC .10 .25
29 Pete Peeters .10 .25
30 Petri Skriko .10 .25
31 Steve Duchesne .10 .25
32 Sabres Team .12 .30
33 Phil Bourque UER .12 .30
34 Tim Bergland .12 .30
35 Tim Cheveldae .12 .30
36 Bill Armstrong RC .12 .30
37 John McIntyre .12 .30
38 Dave Andreychuk .15 .40
39 Curtis Leschyshyn .12 .30
40 Jaromir Jagr .50 1.25
41 Craig Janney .12 .30
42 Doug Brown .12 .30
43 Ken Sabourin .12 .30
44 North Stars Team .12 .30
45 Fredrik Olausson UER .12 .30
46 Mike Gartner UER .20 .50
47 Mark Fitzpatrick .12 .30
48 Joe Murphy .12 .30
49 Doug Wilson .12 .30
50 Brian MacLellan .12 .30
51 Bob Bassen .12 .30
52 Robert Kron .12 .30
53 Roger Johansson .12 .30
54 Guy Carbonneau UER .12 .30
55 Rob Ramage .12 .30
56 Bobby Holik .15 .40
57 Alan May .12 .30
58 Rick Meagher .12 .30
59 Cliff Ronning .10 .25
60 Red Wings Team .12 .30
61 Bob Kudelski .10 .25
62 Wayne McBean .12 .30
63 Craig MacTavish .12 .30
64 Owen Nolan .15 .40
65 Dale Hawerchuk .20 .50
66 Ray Bourque .25 .60
67 Sean Burke .15 .40
68 Frank Musil .12 .30
69 Joe Mullen .12 .30
70 Drake Berehowsky .12 .30
71 Darren Turcotte .12 .30
72 Randy Carlyle .12 .30
73 Paul Cyr .12 .30
74 Dave Gagner .12 .30
75 Steve Larmer .12 .30
76 Petr Svoboda .12 .30
77 Keith Acton .12 .30
78 Dimitri Khristich .12 .30
79 Brad McCrimmon .12 .30
80 Pat LaFontaine UER .15 .40
81 Jeff Reese .12 .30
82 Mario Marois .12 .30
83 Rob Brown .12 .30
84 Grant Fuhr .25 .60
85 Carey Wilson .12 .30
86 Garry Galley .12 .30
87 Troy Murray .12 .30
88 Tony Granato .10 .25
89 Gord Murphy UER .12 .30
90 Brent Gilchrist .12 .30
91 Mike Richter .15 .40
92 Eric Weinrich .15 .40
93 Marc Bureau .12 .30
94 Bob Errey .12 .30
95 Dave McLlwain .12 .30
96 Nordiques Team .12 .30
97 Clint Malarchuk UER .12 .30
98 Shawn Antoski UER .12 .30
99 Bob Sweeney .10 .25
100 Stephen Leach .12 .30
101 Gary Nylund .12 .30
102 Lucien DeBlois .12 .30
103 Oilers Team .12 .30
104 Jimmy Carson .12 .30
105 Rod Langway .12 .30
106 Jeremy Roenick .25 .60
107 Mike Vernon .12 .30
108 Brian Leetch .12 .30
109 Mark Hunter .12 .30
110 Brian Bellows .12 .30
111 Pelle Eklund .12 .30
112 Rob Blake .15 .40
113 Mike Hough .12 .30
114 Frank Pietrangelo .12 .30
115 Christian Ruuttu .12 .30
116 Bryan Marchment RC .12 .30
117 Garry Valk .12 .30
118 Ken Daneyko UER .12 .30
119 Russ Courtnall .12 .30
120 Ron Wilson .12 .30
121 Shayne Stevenson .12 .30
122 Bill Berg .12 .30
123 Maple Leafs Team .12 .30
124 Glenn Anderson .12 .30
125 Kevin Miller .12 .30
126 Calle Johansson .12 .30
127 Jimmy Waite .12 .30
128 Allen Pedersen .10 .25
129 Brian Mullen .12 .30
130 Ron Francis .20 .50
131 Jergus Baca .12 .30
132 Checklist 1-132 .12 .30
133 Tony Tanti .12 .30
134 Wes Walz .12 .30
135 Stephan Lebeau .12 .30
136 Ken Wregget .12 .30
137 Scott Arniel UER .10 .25
138 Dave Taylor .12 .30
139 Steven Finn .10 .25
140 Brendan Shanahan .15 .40
141 Petr Nedved .12 .30
142 Chris Dahlquist .12 .30
143 Rich Sutter .12 .30
144 Joe Reekie .12 .30
145 Peter Ing .12 .30
146 Ken Linseman .12 .30
147 Dave Barr .12 .30
148 Al Iafrate .12 .30
149 Greg Gilbert .12 .30
150 Craig Ludwig .12 .30
151 Gary Suter .10 .25
152 Jan Erixon .12 .30
153 Mario Lemieux .60 1.50
154 Mike Liut UER .10 .25
155 Uwe Krupp .12 .30
156 Darin Kimble .12 .30
157 Shayne Corson .12 .30
158 Jets Team .12 .30
159 Stephane Morin UER .12 .30
160 Rick Tocchet .12 .30
161 John Tonelli UER .12 .30
162 Adrien Plavsic .12 .30
163 Jason Miller .12 .30
164 Tim Kerr .10 .25
165 Brent Sutter .15 .40
166 Michel Petit .12 .30
167 Adam Graves .12 .30
168 Jamie Macoun .12 .30
169 Terry Yake .12 .30
170 Bruins Team .12 .30
171 Alexander Mogilny .12 .30
172 Karl Dykhuis TP .12 .30
173 Tomas Sandstrom .12 .30
174 Bernie Nicholls .12 .30
175 Slava Fetisov .12 .30
176 Andrew Cassels .12 .30
177 Ulf Dahlen .12 .30
178 Brian Hayward .12 .30
179 Doug Lidster .12 .30
180 Dave Lowry .12 .30
181 Ron Tugnutt UER .12 .30
182 Ed Olczyk .12 .30
183 Paul Coffey .15 .40
184 Shawn Burr UER .12 .30
185 Whalers Team .12 .30
186 Mark Janssens .12 .30
187 Mike Craig .12 .30
188 Gary Leeman .12 .30
189 Phil Sykes .12 .30
190 Brett Hull LL .30 .75
191 Devils Team .12 .30
192 Cam Neely .15 .40
193 Petr Klima .12 .30
194 Mike Ricci .10 .25
195 Kelly Hrudey .12 .30
196 Mark Recchi .20 .50
197 Mikael Andersson .12 .30
198 Bob Probert .15 .40
199 Craig Wolanin .12 .30
200 Scott Mellanby .12 .30
201 Wayne Gretzky HL UER 1.00 2.50
202 Laurie Boschman .12 .30
203 Gino Odjick .10 .25
204 Garth Butcher .12 .30
205 Randy Wood .12 .30
206 John Druce .12 .30
207 Doug Bodger .12 .30
208 Doug Gilmour .20 .50
209 John LeClair RC .40 1.00
210 Steve Thomas .12 .30
211 Kjell Samuelsson .12 .30
212 Daniel Marois .12 .30
213 Jiri Hrdina .12 .30
214 Darrin Shannon .12 .30
215 Rangers Team .12 .30
216 Bob McGill .12 .30
217 Dirk Graham UER .12 .30
218 Thomas Steen .12 .30
219 Mats Sundin .15 .40
220 Kevin Lowe UER .12 .30
221 Kirk McLean .12 .30
222 Jeff Brown .12 .30
223 Joe Nieuwendyk .15 .40
224 Wayne Gretzky LL 1.00 2.50
225 Marty McSorley .12 .30
226 John Cullen .12 .30
227 Brian Propp UER .12 .30
228 Yves Racine .12 .30
229 Dale Hunter .12 .30
230 Dennis Vaske .12 .30
231 Sylvain Turgeon .12 .30
232 Ron Sutter .12 .30
233 Chris Chelios .15 .40
234 Brian Bradley .12 .30
235 Scott Young .12 .30
236 Mike Ramsey UER .12 .30
237 Jon Casey .12 .30
238 Nevin Markwart .12 .30
239 John MacLean .12 .30
240 Brent Ashton .12 .30
241 Tony Hrkac .12 .30
242 Canucks Team .12 .30
243 Jeff Norton .12 .30
244 Martin Gelinas .12 .30
245 Mike Ridley .12 .30
246 Pat Jablonski RC .12 .30
247 Flames Team .12 .30
248 Paul Ysebaert .12 .30
249 Sylvain Cote .12 .30
250 Marc Habscheid .12 .30
251 Todd Elik .12 .30
252 Mike McPhee .12 .30
253 James Patrick .12 .30
254 Murray Craven .12 .30
255 Trent Yawney .12 .30
256 Rob Cimetta .12 .30
257 Wayne Gretzky LL 1.00 2.50
258 Wayne Gretzky AS 1.00 2.50
259 Brett Hull AS .30 .75
260 Luc Robitaille AS .15 .40
261 Ray Bourque AS .25 .60
262 Al MacInnis AS .20 .50
263 Ed Belfour AS .40 1.00
264 Checklist 133-264 .12 .30
265 Adam Oates AS .15 .40
266 Cam Neely AS .15 .40
267 Kevin Stevens AS .15 .40
268 Chris Chelios AS .15 .40
269 Brian Leetch AS .12 .30
270 Patrick Roy AS .40 1.00
271 Ed Belfour LL .40 1.00
272 Rob Zettler .12 .30
273 Donald Audette .12 .30
274 Teppo Numminen .12 .30
275 Peter Stastny UER .12 .30
276 Dave Christian .10 .25
277 Larry Murphy .12 .30
278 Johan Garpenlov .12 .30
279 Tom Fitzgerald .12 .30
280 Gerald Diduck .12 .30
281 Gino Cavallini .12 .30
282 Theo Fleury .12 .30
283 Kings Team .12 .30
284 Jeff Beukeboom .12 .30
285 Kevin Dineen .12 .30
286 Jacques Cloutier .12 .30
287 Tom Chorske .12 .30
288 Ed Belfour LL .40 1.00
289 Ray Sheppard .12 .30
290 Olaf Kolzig .15 .40
291 Terry Carkner .12 .30
292 Benoit Hogue .12 .30
293 Mike Peluso .12 .30
294 Bruce Driver .12 .30
295 Jari Kurri .12 .30
296 Peter Sidorkiewicz .12 .30
297 Scott Pearson .12 .30
298 Canadiens Team .12 .30
299 Vincent Damphousse .12 .30
300 John Carter .12 .30
301 Geoff Smith .12 .30
302 Steve Kasper UER .10 .25
303 Brett Hull .30 .75
304 Ray Ferraro .12 .30
305 Geoff Courtnall .12 .30
306 David Shaw .12 .30
307 Bob Essensa .12 .30
308 Mark Tinordi .12 .30
309 Keith Primeau .12 .30
310 Kevin Hatcher .12 .30
311 Chris Nilan .10 .25
312 Trevor Kidd TP .12 .30
313 Daniel Berthiaume .12 .30
314 Adam Creighton .12 .30
315 Everett Sanipass .12 .30
316 Ken Baumgartner .10 .25
317 Sheldon Kennedy .12 .30
318 Dave Capuano .12 .30
319 Don Sweeney .10 .25
320 Gary Roberts .12 .30
321 Wayne Gretzky 1.00 2.50
322 T.Fleury/M.McSorley UER .12 .30
323 Ulf Samuelsson .12 .30
324 Mike Krushelnyski .12 .30
325 Dean Evason .12 .30
326 Pat Elynuik .12 .30
327 Michal Pivonka .12 .30
328 Paul Cavallini .12 .30
329 Flyers Team .12 .30
330 Denis Savard .15 .40
331 Paul Fenton .12 .30
332 Jon Morris .12 .30
333 Daren Puppa .12 .30
334 Doug Small .12 .30
335 Kelly Kisio .12 .30
336 Michel Goulet UER .12 .30
337 Mike Sillinger .12 .30
338 Andy Moog .15 .40
339 Paul Stanton .12 .30
340 Greg Adams .12 .30
341 Doug Crossman UER .12 .30
342 Kelly Miller .12 .30
343 Pat Flatley .12 .30
344 Zarley Zalapski .12 .30
345 Mark Osborne UER .12 .30
346 Mark Messier .30 .75
347 Blues Team .12 .30
348 Neil Wilkinson .12 .30
349 Brian Skrudland .12 .30
350 Lyle Odelein .12 .30
351 Luke Richardson .12 .30
352 Zdeno Ciger .12 .30
353 John Vanbiesbrouck .15 .40
354 Lou Franceschetti .12 .30
355 Alexei Gusarov RC .12 .30
356 Bill Ranford .12 .30
357 Normand Lacombe .12 .30
358 Randy Burridge .12 .30
359 Brian Benning .12 .30
360 Dave Hannan .12 .30
361 Todd Gill .12 .30
362 Peter Bondra .15 .40
363 Mike Hartman .12 .30
364 Trevor Linden .15 .40
365 John Ogrodnick .12 .30
366 Steve Konroyd .12 .30
367 Mike Modano .30 .75
368 Glenn Healy .15 .40
369 Stephane Richer .12 .30
370 Vincent Riendeau .12 .30
371 Randy Moller .12 .30
372 Penguins Team .12 .30
373 Murray Baron .12 .30
374 Troy Crowder .12 .30
375 Rick Tabaracci .12 .30
376 Brent Fedyk .12 .30
377 Randy Velischek .12 .30
378 Esa Tikkanen .12 .30
379 Rich Pilon .12 .30
380 Jeff Lazaro RC .12 .30
381 Dave Ellett .12 .30
382 Jeff Hackett .12 .30
383 Stephane Matteau .12 .30
384 Capitals Team .12 .30
385 Wayne Presley .12 .30
386 Grant Ledyard .12 .30
387 Kip Miller .12 .30
388 Dean Kennedy .12 .30
389 Hubie McDonough .12 .30
390 Anatoli Semenov .12 .30
391 Daryl Reaugh .12 .30
392 Mathieu Schneider .12 .30
393 Dan Quinn .12 .30
394 Claude Lemieux .12 .30
395 Phil Housley .12 .30
396 Checklist 265-396 .12 .30
397 Steve Bozek .12 .30
398 Bobby Smith .12 .30
399 Mark Pederson .12 .30
400 Kevin Todd RC .12 .30
401 Sergei Fedorov .25 .60
402 Tom Barrasso .12 .30
403 Brett Hull HL .30 .75
404 Bob Carpenter UER .12 .30
405 Luc Robitaille .15 .40
406 Mark Hardy .12 .30
407 Neil Sheehy .12 .30
408 Mike McNeil .12 .30
409 Dave Manson .12 .30
410 Mike Tomlak .12 .30
411 Robert Reichel .30 .75
412 Islanders Team .12 .30
413 Patrick Roy .40 1.00
414 Shaun Van Allen RC .12 .30
415 Dale Kushner .12 .30
416 Pierre Turgeon .12 .30
417 Curtis Joseph .20 .50
418 Randy Gilhen .12 .30
419 Jyrki Lumme .12 .30
420 Neal Broten .12 .30
421 Kevin Stevens .12 .30
422 Chris Terreri .12 .30
423 David Reid .10 .25
424 Steve Yzerman .50 1.25
425 Ed Belfour LL .40 1.00
426 Jim Johnson .12 .30
427 Joey Kocur .10 .25
428 Joel Otto .12 .30
429 Dino Ciccarelli .12 .30
430 Blackhawks Team .12 .30
431 Claude Lapointe RC .12 .30
432 Chris Joseph .12 .30
433 Gaetan Duchesne .10 .25
434 Mike Keane .10 .25
435 Dave Chyzowski .10 .25
436 Glen Featherstone .10 .25
437 Jim Paek RC .15 .40
438 Doug Evans .10 .25
439 Alexei Kasatonov UER .10 .25
440 Ken Hodge Jr. .12 .30
441 Dave Snuggerud .10 .25
442 Brad Shaw .10 .25
443 Gerard Gallant .10 .25
444 Jiri Latal .10 .25
445 Peter Zezel .10 .25
446 Troy Gamble .10 .25
447 Craig Coxe .10 .25
448 Adam Oates .15 .40
449 Todd Krygier .12 .30
450 Andre Racicot RC .12 .30
451 Patrik Sundstrom .12 .30
452 Glen Wesley UER .12 .30
453 Jocelyn Lemieux .12 .30
454 Rick Zombo .12 .30
455 Derek King .10 .25
456 J.J. Daigneault .10 .25
457 Rick Vaive .15 .40
458 Larry Robinson .15 .40
459 Rick Wamsley .10 .25
460 Craig Simpson .10 .25
461 Corey Millen RC .15 .40
462 Sergio Momesso .12 .30
463 Paul MacDermid .12 .30
464 Wendel Clark .25 .60
465 Mikhail Tatarinov .15 .40
466 Mark Howe .15 .40
467 Jay Miller .12 .30
468 Grant Jennings .12 .30
469 Paul Gillis .12 .30
470 Ron Hextall .15 .40
471 Alexander Godynyuk RC .15 .40
472 Bryan Trottier .15 .40
473 Kevin Haller RC .15 .40
474 Troy Mallette .12 .30
475 Jim Wiemer .12 .30
476 David Maley .12 .30
477 Moe Mantha UER .12 .30
478 Brad Jones .12 .30
479 Craig Muni .12 .30
480 Igor Larionov .12 .30
481 Scott Stevens .15 .40
482 Sergei Makarov .12 .30
483 Mike Lalor .12 .30
484 Tony McKegney .12 .30
485 Perry Berezan .12 .30
486 Derrick Smith .12 .30
487 Jim Hrivnak .12 .30
488 David Volek .12 .30
489 Sylvain Lefebvre .12 .30
490 Rod Brind'Amour .12 .30
491 Al MacInnis .20 .50
492 Jamie Leach .12 .30
493 Robert Dirk .12 .30
494 Gordie Roberts .12 .30
495 Mike Hudson .12 .30
496 Frank Breault .12 .30
497 Rejean Lemelin .10 .25
498 Kris King .12 .30
499 Pat Verbeek .12 .30
500 Bryan Fogarty .12 .30
501 Perry Anderson .12 .30
502 Joe Cirella .12 .30
503 Mikko Makela .12 .30
504 Paul Coffey HL UER .15 .40
505 Don Beaupre .12 .30
506 Brian Glynn .12 .30
507 Dave Poulin .12 .30
508 Steve Chiasson .12 .30
509 Myles O'Connor RC .12 .30
510 Ilkka Sinisalo .12 .30
511 Nick Kypreos .12 .30
512 Doug Houda UER .12 .30
513 Valeri Kamensky RC .40 1.00
514 Sergei Nemchinov .12 .30
515 Dmitri Mironov .12 .30
516 Brett Hull Hart .30 .75
517 Ray Bourque Norris .25 .60
518 Ed Belfour Calder .40 1.00
519 Ed Belfour Vezina UER .40 1.00
520 Wayne Gretzky Byng 1.00 2.50
521 Dirk Graham Selke .12 .30
522 Wayne Gretzky Ross 1.00 2.50
523 Mario Lemieux Smythe .60 1.50
524 Wayne Gretzky HL 1.00 2.50
525 San Jose Sharks Logo .12 .30
526 T.B.Lightning Logo .12 .30
527 Ottawa Senators Logo .12 .30
528 Checklist 397-528 .12 .30

1991-92 Topps/Bowman Preview Sheet

COMPLETE SET (9) 3.00 8.00
1 Mario Lemieux
(Topps) .75 2.00
2 Wayne Gretzky
(Bowman) 1.25 3.00
3 Joe Sakic
(Topps) .50 1.25
4 Ray Bourque
(Bowman) .30 .75
5 Ed Belfour
(Topps) .30 .75
6 Mark Messier
(Bowman) .40 1.00
7 Pat LaFontaine
(Topps) .20 .50
8 Steve Yzerman
(Bowman) .50 1.25
9 Brett Hull
(Topps) .40 1.00
NNO Uncut Panel 3.00 8.00

1991-92 Topps Team Scoring Leaders

COMPLETE SET (21) 2.50 6.00
1 Pat Verbeek .15 .40
2 Dale Hawerchuk .15 .40
3 Steve Yzerman .60 1.50
4 Brian Leetch .20 .50
5 Mark Recchi .15 .40
6 Esa Tikkanen .02 .10
7 Dave Gagner .02 .10
8 Joe Sakic .40 1.00
9 Vincent Damphousse .15 .40
10 Wayne Gretzky 1.25 3.00
11 Phil Housley .02 .10
12 Pat LaFontaine .15 .40
13 Rick Tocchet .15 .40
14 Theo Fleury UER .15 .40
15 John MacLean .02 .10
16 Kevin Hatcher .02 .10
17 Trevor Linden .15 .40
18 Russ Courtnall .02 .10
19 Ray Bourque .20 .50
20 Brett Hull .25 .60
21 Steve Larmer .02 .10

1992-93 Topps

*GOLD: 1.5X TO 3X BASIC INSERTS
1 Wayne Gretzky 1.00 2.50
2 Brett Hull .30 .75
3 Felix Potvin .30 .75
4 Mark Tinordi .10 .25
5 Paul Coffey HL .15 .40
6 Tony Amonte SR .12 .30
7 Pat Falloon SR .10 .25
8 Pavel Bure SR .15 .40
9 Nicklas Lidstrom SR .12 .30
10 Dominic Roussel SR .12 .30
11 Nelson Emerson SR .10 .25
12 Donald Audette .12 .30
13 Gilbert Dionne SR .12 .30
14 Vladimir Konstantinov .15 .40
15 Kevin Todd .10 .25
16 Steve Leach .10 .25
17 Ed Olczyk .10 .25
18 Jim Hrivnak .10 .25
19 Gilbert Dionne .10 .25
20 Mike Vernon .12 .30
21 Dave Christian .10 .25
22 Ed Belfour .15 .40
23 Andrew Cassels .10 .25
24 Jaromir Jagr .30 .75
25 Arturs Irbe .12 .30
26 Petr Klima .10 .25
27 Randy Gilhen .10 .25
28 Ulf Dahlen .10 .25
29 Kelly Hrudey .12 .30
30 Dave Ellett .10 .25
31 Tom Fitzgerald .10 .25
32 Cam Neely .15 .40
33 Greg Paslawski .10 .25
34 Brad May .10 .25
35 Slava Kozlov .12 .30
36 Mark Hunter .10 .25
37 Steve Chiasson .10 .25
38 Joe Murphy .10 .25
39 Darryl Sydor .12 .30
40 Ron Hextall .15 .40
41 Jim Sandlak .10 .25
42 Dave Lowry .12 .30
43 Claude Lemieux .10 .25
44 Gerald Diduck .10 .25
45 Mike McPhee .10 .25
46 Rod Langway .10 .25
47 Guy Larose .10 .25
48 Craig Billington .12 .30
49 Daniel Marois .10 .25
50 Todd Nelson RC .10 .25
51 Jari Kurri .15 .40
52 Keith Brown .12 .30
53 Valeri Kamensky .12 .30
54 Jim Johnson .10 .25
55 Vincent Damphousse .12 .30
56 Pat Elynuik .10 .25
57 Jeff Beukeboom .10 .25
58 Paul Ysebaert .10 .25
59 Ken Sutton .10 .25
60 Dale Craigwell .10 .25
61 Marc Bergevin .10 .25
62 Stephane Beauregard .12 .30
63 Bob Probert .15 .40
64 Jergus Baca .10 .25
65 Brian Propp .10 .25
66 Jacques Cloutier .10 .25
67 Jim Thomson RC .12 .30
68 Anatoli Semenov .10 .25
69 Stephan Lebeau .10 .25
70 Rick Tocchet .12 .30
71 James Patrick .10 .25
72 Rob Brown .12 .30
73 Peter Ahola .10 .25
74 Bob Corkum .12 .30
75 Brent Sutter .12 .30
76 Neil Wilkinson .10 .25
77 Mark Osborne .10 .25
78 Ron Wilson .10 .25
79 Todd Richards .10 .25
80 Robert Kron .10 .25
81 Cliff Ronning .10 .25
82 Zarley Zalapski .10 .25
83 Randy Burridge .10 .25
84 Jarrod Skalde .10 .25
85 Gary Leeman .10 .25
86 Mike Ricci .10 .25
87 Dennis Vaske .10 .25
88 John LeBlanc RC .10 .25
89 Brad Shaw .10 .25
90 Rod Brind'Amour .12 .30
91 Colin Patterson .12 .30
92 Gerard Gallant .10 .25
93 Per Djoos .10 .25
94 Claude Lapointe .10 .25
95 Bob Errey .10 .25
96 Norm Maciver .10 .25
97 Todd Elik .10 .25
98 Chris Chelios .15 .40
99 Keith Primeau .12 .30
100 Jim Waite .12 .30
101 Luc Robitaille .15 .40
102 Keith Tkachuk .15 .40
103 Benoit Hogue .10 .25
104 Brian Mullen .10 .25
105 Joe Nieuwendyk .12 .30
106 Randy McKay .12 .30
107 Michal Pivonka .10 .25
108 Darcy Wakaluk .10 .25
109 Andy Brickley .10 .25
110 Patrick Roy LL .40 1.00
111 Bob Sweeney .10 .25
112 Guy Hebert RC .25 .60
113 Joe Mullen .12 .30
114 Gord Murphy .12 .30
115 Evgeny Davydov .10 .25
116 Gary Roberts .10 .25
117 Pelle Eklund .12 .30
118 Tom Kurvers .10 .25
119 John Tonelli .12 .30
120 Fredrik Olausson .12 .30
121 Mike Donnelly .12 .30
122 Doug Gilmour .20 .50
123 Wayne Gretzky LL 1.00 2.50
124 Curtis Leschyshyn .12 .30
125 Guy Carbonneau .12 .30
126 Bill Ranford .12 .30
127 Ulf Samuelsson .10 .25
128 Joey Kocur .10 .25
129 Kevin Miller .10 .25
130 Kirk McLean .10 .25
131 Kevin Dineen .10 .25
132 John Cullen .10 .25
133 Al Iafrate .10 .25
134 Craig Janney .10 .25
135 Patrick Flatley .10 .25
136 Dominik Hasek .25 .60
137 Benoit Brunet .10 .25
138 Dave Babych .12 .30
139 Doug Brown .10 .25
140 Mike Lalor .10 .25
141 Thomas Steen .10 .25
142 Frank Musil .10 .25
143 Dan Quinn .10 .25
144 Dmitri Mironov .10 .25
145 Bob Kudelski .10 .25
146 Mike Bullard .10 .25
147 Randy Carlyle .10 .25
148 Kent Manderville .10 .25
149 Kevin Hatcher .10 .25
150 Steve Kasper .10 .25
151 Mikael Andersson .10 .25
152 Alexei Kasatonov .10 .25
153 Jan Erixon .10 .25
154 Craig Ludwig .10 .25
155 Dave Poulin .10 .25
156 Scott Stevens .12 .30
157 Robert Reichel .10 .25
158 Uwe Krupp .10 .25
159 Brian Noonan .10 .25
160 Stephane Richer .12 .30
161 Brent Thompson .12 .30
162 Glenn Anderson .12 .30
163 Joe Cirella .10 .25
164 Dave Andreychuk .15 .40
165 Vladimir Konstantinov .15 .40
166 Mike McNeill .12 .30
167 Darrin Shannon .12 .30
168 Rob Pearson .10 .25
169 John Vanbiesbrouck .15 .40
170 Randy Wood .10 .25
171 Marty McSorley .12 .30
172 Mike Hudson .10 .25
173 Paul Fenton .10 .25
174 Jeff Brown .12 .30
175 Mark Greig .12 .30
176 Gordie Roberts .12 .30
177 Josef Beranek .10 .25
178 Shawn Burr .10 .25
179 Marc Bureau .12 .30
180 Mikhail Tatarinov .10 .25
181 Robert Cimetta .12 .30
182 Paul Coffey UER .15 .40
183 Bob Essensa .12 .30
184 Joe Reekie .10 .25
185 Jeff Hackett .12 .30
186 Tomas Forslund .10 .25
187 Claude Vilgrain .10 .25
188 John Druce .10 .25
189 Patrice Brisebois .10 .25
190 Peter Douris .10 .25
191 Brent Ashton .10 .25
192 Eric Desjardins .12 .30
193 Nick Kypreos .10 .25
194 Dana Murzyn .10 .25
195 Don Beaupre .12 .30
196 Jeff Chychrun .10 .25
197 Dave Barr .10 .25
198 Brian Glynn .10 .25
199 Keith Acton .10 .25
200 Igor Kravchuk .10 .25
201 Shayne Corson .12 .30
202 Curt Giles .10 .25
203 Darren Turcotte .10 .25
204 David Volek .10 .25
205 Ray Whitney RC .25 .60
206 Donald Audette .12 .30
207 Steve Yzerman .40 1.00
208 Craig Berube .10 .25
209 Bob McGill .10 .25
210 Stu Barnes .10 .25
211 Rob Blake .10 .25
212 Mario Lemieux .60 1.50
213 Dominic Roussel .12 .30
214 Sergio Momesso .12 .30
215 Brad Marsh .12 .30
216 Mark Fitzpatrick .12 .30
217 Ken Baumgartner .12 .30
218 Greg Gilbert .12 .30
219 Ric Nattress .10 .25
220 Theo Fleury .25 .60
221 Ray Bourque .25 .60
222 Steve Thomas .12 .30
223 Scott Niedermayer .15 .40
224 Jeff Lazaro .10 .25
225 Cheveldae/K.McLean LL .10 .25

226 Marc Fortier .10 .25
227 Rob Zettler .10 .25
228 Kevin Todd .10 .25
229 Tony Amonte .12 .30
230 Mark Lamb .10 .25
231 Chris Dahlquist .12 .30
232 James Black .10 .25
233 Paul Cavallini .10 .25
234 Gino Cavallini .10 .25
235 Tony Tanti .10 .25
236 Mike Ridley .10 .25
237 Curtis Joseph .20 .50
238 Mike Craig .10 .25
239 Luciano Borsato .10 .25
240 Brian Bellows .12 .30
241 Barry Pederson .10 .25
242 Tony Granato .10 .25
243 Jim Paek .12 .30
244 Tim Bergland .10 .25
245 Jay More .10 .25
246 Laurie Boschman .10 .25
247 Doug Bodger .10 .25
248 Murray Craven .10 .25
249 Kris Draper .10 .25
250 Brian Benning .10 .25
251 Jarmo Myllys .10 .25
252 Sergei Fedorov .25 .60
253 Mathieu Schneider .10 .25
254 Dave Gagner .12 .30
255 Michel Goulet .12 .30
256 Alexander Godynyuk .10 .25
257 Ray Sheppard .10 .25
258 Mark Messier AS .30 .75
259 Kevin Stevens AS .12 .30
260 Brett Hull AS .30 .75
261 Brian Leetch AS .12 .30
262 Ray Bourque AS .25 .60
263 Patrick Roy AS .40 1.00
264 Mike Gartner HL .20 .50
265 Mario Lemieux AS .60 1.50
266 Luc Robitaille AS .15 .40
267 Mark Recchi AS .20 .50
268 Phil Housley AS .12 .30
269 Scott Stevens AS .15 .40
270 Kirk McLean AS .10 .25
271 Steve Duchesne .10 .25
272 Jiri Hrdina .10 .25
273 John MacLean .12 .30
274 Mark Messier .30 .75
275 Geoff Smith .10 .25
276 Russ Courtnall .10 .25
277 Yves Racine .10 .25
278 Tom Draper .10 .25
279 Charlie Huddy .12 .30
280 Trevor Kidd .12 .30
281 Garth Butcher .12 .30
282 Mike Sullivan .10 .25
283 Adam Burt .10 .25
284 Troy Murray .10 .25
285 Stephane Fiset .10 .25
286 Perry Anderson .10 .25
287 Sergei Nemchinov .10 .25
288 Rick Zombo .10 .25
289 Pierre Turgeon .12 .30
290 Kevin Lowe .12 .30
291 Brian Bradley .10 .25
292 Martin Gelinas UER .10 .25
293 Brian Leetch .12 .30
294 Peter Bondra .15 .40
295 Brendan Shanahan .15 .40
296 Dale Hawerchuk .20 .50
297 Mike Hough .12 .30
298 Rollie Melanson .10 .25
299 Brad Jones .10 .25
300 Jocelyn Lemieux .10 .25
301 Brad McCrimmon .10 .25
302 Marty McInnis .10 .25
303 Chris Terreri .12 .30
304 Dean Evason .10 .25
305 Glenn Healy .12 .30
306 Ken Hodge Jr. .10 .25
307 Mike Liut .10 .25
308 Gary Suter .10 .25
309 Neal Broten .12 .30
310 Tim Cheveldae .10 .25
311 Tom Fergus .10 .25
312 Petr Svoboda .12 .30
313 Tom Chorske .12 .30
314 Paul Ysebaert LL .10 .25
315 Steve Smith .10 .25
316 Stephane Morin .10 .25
317 Pat MacLeod .10 .25
318 Dino Ciccarelli .12 .30
319 Peter Zezel .10 .25
320 Chris Lindberg .10 .25
321 Grant Ledyard .10 .25
322 Ron Francis .20 .50
323 Adrien Plavsic .10 .25
324 Ray Ferraro .10 .25
325 Wendel Clark .25 .60
326 Corey Millen .10 .25
327 Mark Pederson .10 .25
328 Patrick Poulin .10 .25
329 Adam Graves .10 .25
330 Bobby Holik .12 .30
331 Kelly Kisio .12 .30
332 Peter Sidorkiewicz .10 .25
333 Vladimir Ruzicka .10 .25
334 J.J. Daigneault .10 .25
335 Troy Mallette .10 .25
336 Craig MacTavish .10 .25
337 Michel Petit .10 .25
338 Claude Loiselle .10 .25
339 Teppo Numminen .10 .25
340 Brett Hull LL .30 .75
341 Sylvain Lefebvre .10 .25
342 Perry Berezan .10 .25
343 Kevin Stevens .12 .30
344 Randy Ladouceur .10 .25
345 Pat LaFontaine .15 .40
346 Glen Wesley .10 .25
347 Michel Goulet HL .12 .30
348 Jamie Macoun .12 .30
349 Owen Nolan .15 .40
350 Grant Fuhr .25 .60
351 Tim Kerr .10 .25
352 Kjell Samuelsson .12 .30
353 Pavel Bure .15 .40
354 Murray Baron .10 .25
355 Paul Broten .10 .25
356 Craig Simpson .10 .25
357 Ken Daneyko .10 .25
358 Greg Hawgood .10 .25
359 Johan Garpenlov .10 .25
360 Garry Galley .10 .25
361 Paul DiPietro .10 .25
362 Jamie Leach .10 .25
363 Clint Malarchuk .10 .25
364 Dan Lambert .10 .25
365 Joe Juneau .10 .25
366 Scott Lachance .10 .25
367 Mike Richter .15 .40
368 Sheldon Kennedy .10 .25
369 John McIntyre .10 .25
370 Glen Murray .12 .30
371 Ron Sutter .10 .25
372 David Williams RC .10 .25
373 Bill Lindsay RC .10 .25
374 Todd Gill .10 .25
375 Sylvain Turgeon .10 .25
376 Dirk Graham .10 .25
377 Brad Schlegel .10 .25
378 Bob Carpenter .12 .30
379 Jon Casey .10 .25
380 Andrei Lomakin .10 .25
381 Kay Whitmore .12 .30
382 Alexander Mogilny .12 .30
383 Garry Valk .10 .25
384 Bruce Driver .10 .25
385 Jeff Reese .10 .25
386 Brent Gilchrist .10 .25
387 Kerry Huffman .10 .25
388 Bobby Smith .12 .30
389 Dave Manson .10 .25
390 Russ Romaniuk .10 .25
391 Paul MacDermid .12 .30
392 Louie DeBrusk .10 .25
393 Dave McLlwain .10 .25
394 Andy Moog .15 .40
395 Tie Domi .12 .30
396 Pat Jablonski .12 .30
397 Troy Loney .10 .25
398 Jimmy Carson .10 .25
399 Eric Weinrich .10 .25
400 Jeremy Roenick .25 .60
401 Brent Fedyk .10 .25
402 Geoff Sanderson .12 .30
403 Doug Lidster .12 .30
404 Mike Gartner .20 .50
405 Derian Hatcher .10 .25
406 Gaetan Duchesne .10 .25
407 Randy Moller .10 .25
408 Brian Skrudland .12 .30
409 Luke Richardson .12 .30
410 Mark Recchi .20 .50
411 Steve Konroyd .12 .30
412 Troy Gamble .10 .25
413 Greg Johnston .10 .25
414 Denis Savard .15 .40
415 Mats Sundin .15 .40
416 Bryan Trottier .15 .40
417 Don Sweeney .10 .25
418 Pat Falloon .10 .25
419 Alexander Semak .10 .25
420 David Shaw .12 .30
421 Tomas Sandstrom .12 .30
422 Petr Nedved .12 .30
423 Peter Ing .10 .25
424 Wayne Presley .10 .25
425 Rick Wamsley .10 .25
426 Rob Zamuner RC .12 .30
427 Claude Boivin .10 .25
428 Sylvain Cote .12 .30
429 Kevin Stevens HL .12 .30
430 Randy Velischek .10 .25
431 Derek King .10 .25
432 Terry Yake .10 .25
433 Philippe Bozon .10 .25
434 Rich Sutter .10 .25
435 Brian Lawton .12 .30
436 Brian Hayward .10 .25
437 Robert Dirk .12 .30
438 Bernie Nicholls .12 .30
439 Michel Picard .12 .30
440 Nicklas Lidstrom .12 .30
441 Mike Modano .40 1.00
442 Phil Bourque .10 .25
443 Wayne McBean .10 .25
444 Scott Mellanby .10 .25
445 Kevin Haller .10 .25
446 Dave Taylor UER .12 .30
447 Larry Murphy .12 .30
448 David Bruce .10 .25
449 Steven Finn .10 .25
450 Mike Krushelnyski .10 .25
451 Adam Creighton .10 .25
452 Al MacInnis .20 .50
453 Rick Tabaracci .10 .25
454 Bob Bassen .10 .25
455 Kelly Buchberger .10 .25
456 Phil Housley .12 .30
457 Daren Puppa .12 .30
458 Slava Fetisov .10 .25
459 Doug Smail .10 .25
460 Paul Stanton .10 .25
461 Steve Weeks .10 .25
462 Valeri Zelepukin .10 .25
463 Stephane Matteau .10 .25
464 Dale Hunter .12 .30
465 Terry Carkner .12 .30
466 Vincent Riendeau .12 .30
467 Sergei Makarov .10 .25
468 Igor Ulanov .10 .25
469 Peter Stastny .12 .30
470 Dimitri Khristich .10 .25
471 Joel Otto .10 .25
472 Geoff Courtnall .10 .25
473 Mike Ramsey .10 .25
474 Yvon Corriveau .10 .25
475 Adam Oates .15 .40
476 Esa Tikkanen .10 .25
477 Doug Weight .30 .75
478 Mike Keane .10 .25
479 Kelly Miller .10 .25
480 Nelson Emerson .10 .25
481 Shawn McEachern .10 .25
482 Doug Wilson .12 .30
483 Jeff Odgers .10 .25
484 Stephane Quintal .10 .25
485 Christian Ruuttu .10 .25
486 Paul Ranheim .10 .25
487 Craig Wolanin .10 .25
488 Rob DiMaio .10 .25
489 Shawn Cronin .10 .25
490 Kirk Muller .10 .25
491 Patrick Roy LL .40 1.00
492 Rich Pilon .10 .25
493 Pat Verbeek .10 .25
494 Ken Wregget .12 .30
495 Joe Sakic .30 .75
496 Zdeno Ciger .10 .25
497 Steve Larmer .10 .25
498 Calle Johansson .10 .25
499 Trevor Linden .15 .40
500 John LeClair .15 .40
501 Bryan Marchment .12 .30
502 Todd Krygier .12 .30
503 Tom Barrasso .12 .30
504 Mario Lemieux LL .60 1.50
505 Daniel Berthiaume UER .12 .30
506 Jamie Baker .10 .25
507 Greg Adams .10 .25
508 Patrick Roy .40 1.00
509 Kris King .10 .25
510 Jyrki Lumme .10 .25
511 Darin Kimble .10 .25
512 Igor Larionov .10 .25
513 Martin Brodeur .40 1.00
514 Denny Felsner RC .12 .30
515 Yanic Dupre .10 .25
516 Bill Guerin RC .30 .75
517 Bret Hedican RC UER .12 .30
518 Mike Hartman .10 .25
519 Steve Heinze UER .10 .25
520 Frantisek Kucera .12 .30
521 David Reid .10 .25
522 Frank Pietrangelo .12 .30
523 Martin Rucinsky .10 .25
524 Tony Hrkac .10 .25
525 Checklist 1-132 .12 .30
526 Checklist 133-264 .12 .30
527 Checklist 265-396 .12 .30
528 Checklist 397-528 UER .12 .30
529 Eric Lindros UER .25 .60

1993-94 Topps Premier Promo Sheet

COMPLETE SET (9) 1.50 4.00
1 Patrick Roy .60 1.50
15 Mike Vernon .15 .40
22 Jamie Baker .08 .25
100 Theo Fleury .15 .40
156 Geoff Sanderson .15 .40
244 Dave Lowry .08 .25
257 Scott Lachance .08 .25
601 Mark Messier .20 .50
602 Ray Bourque .20 .50

1993-94 Topps Premier

*GOLD VETS: 1.5X TO 4X BASIC CARDS
1 Patrick Roy .40 1.00
2 Alexei Zhitnik .10 .25
3 Uwe Krupp .10 .25
4 Todd Gill .10 .25
5 Paul Stanton .10 .25
6 Petr Nedved .10 .25
7 Dale Hawerchuk .20 .50
8 Kevin Miller .10 .25
9 Nicklas Lidstrom .15 .40
10 Joe Sakic .30 .75
11 Thomas Steen .10 .25
12 Peter Bondra .15 .40
13 Brian Noonan .10 .25
14 Glen Featherstone .10 .25
15 Mike Vernon .12 .30
16 Janne Ojanen .10 .25
17 Neil Brady .10 .25
18 Dimitri Yushkevich .10 .25
19 Rob Zamuner .10 .25
20 Zarley Zalapski .10 .25
21 Mike Sullivan .10 .25
22 Jamie Baker .10 .25
23 Craig MacTavish .10 .25
24 Mark Tinordi .10 .25
25 Brian Leetch .12 .30
26 Brian Skrudland .10 .25
27 Keith Tkachuk .15 .40
28 Patrick Flatley .10 .25
29 Doug Bodger .10 .25
30 Felix Potvin .30 .75
31 Shawn Antoski .10 .25
32 Eric Desjardins .12 .30
33 Mike Donnelly .10 .25
34 Kjell Samuelsson .10 .25
35 Nelson Emerson .10 .25
36 Phil Housley .12 .30
37 Mario Lemieux LL .60 1.50
38 Shayne Corson .12 .30
39 Steve Smith .10 .25
40 Bob Kudelski .10 .25
41 Joe Cirella .10 .25
42 Sergei Nemchinov .10 .25
43 Kerry Huffman .10 .25
44 Bob Beers .10 .25
45 Al Iafrate .10 .25
46 Mike Modano .25 .60
47 Pat Verbeek .10 .25
48 Joel Otto .10 .25
49 Dino Ciccarelli .12 .30
50 Adam Oates .15 .40
51 Pat Elynuik .10 .25
52 Bobby Holik .10 .25
53 Johan Garpenlov .10 .25
54 Jeff Beukeboom .10 .25
55 Tommy Soderstrom .12 .30
56 Rob Blake .12 .30
57 Marty McInnis .10 .25
58 Dixon Ward .10 .25
59 Patrice Brisebois .10 .25
60 Ed Belfour .15 .40
61 Donald Audette .10 .25
62 Mike Ricci .10 .25
63 Fredrik Olausson .10 .25
64 Norm Maciver .10 .25
65 Andrew Cassels .10 .25
66 Tim Cheveldae .12 .30
67 David Reid .10 .25
68 Philippe Bozon .10 .25
69 Drake Berehowsky .10 .25
70 Tony Amonte .12 .30
71 Dave Manson .10 .25
72 Rick Tocchet .12 .30
73 Steve Kasper .10 .25
74 Assist Leader .15 .40
75 Ulf Dahlen .10 .25
76 Chris Lindberg .10 .25
77 Doug Wilson .12 .30
78 Mike Ridley .10 .25
79 Viacheslav Butsayev .10 .25
80 Scott Stevens .15 .40
81 Cliff Ronning .10 .25
82 Andrei Lomakin .10 .25
83 Shawn Burr .10 .25
84 Benoit Brunet .10 .25
85 Valeri Kamensky .12 .30
86 Randy Carlyle .10 .25
87 Chris Joseph .10 .25
88 Dirk Graham .10 .25
89 Ken Sutton .10 .25
90 Luc Robitaille AS .15 .40
91 Mario Lemieux AS .60 1.50
92 Teemu Selanne AS .30 .75
93 Ray Bourque AS .25 .60
94 Chris Chelios AS .15 .40
95 Ed Belfour AS .15 .40
96 Keith Jones .10 .25
97 Sylvain Turgeon .10 .25
98 Jim Johnson .10 .25
99 Michael Nylander .10 .25
100 Theo Fleury .10 .25
101 Shawn Chambers .10 .25
102 Alexander Semak .10 .25
103 Ron Sutter .10 .25
104 Glenn Anderson .12 .30
105 Jaromir Jagr .50 1.25
106 Adam Graves .10 .25
107 Nikolai Borschevsky .10 .25
108 Vladimir Konstantinov .12 .30
109 Robb Stauber .10 .25
110 Arturs Irbe .12 .30
111 Felix Potvin LL .30 .75
112 Darius Kasparaitis .10 .25
113 Kirk McLean .12 .30
114 Glen Wesley .10 .25
115 Rod Brind'Amour .12 .30
116 Mike Eagles .10 .25
117 Brian Bradley .10 .25
118 Dave Christian .10 .25
119 Randy Wood .10 .25
120 Craig Janney .12 .30
121 Eric Lindros SR .25 .60
122 Tommy Soderstrom SR .12 .30
123 Shawn McEachern SR .10 .25
124 Andrei Kovalenko SR .10 .25
125 Joe Juneau SR .10 .25
126 Felix Potvin SR .30 .75
127 Dixon Ward SR .10 .25
128 Alexei Zhamnov SR .12 .30
129 Vladimir Malakhov SR .10 .25
130 Teemu Selanne SR .30 .75
131 Neal Broten .12 .30
132 Ulf Samuelsson .10 .25
133 Mark Janssens .10 .25
134 Claude Lemieux .10 .25
135 Mike Richter .15 .40
136 Doug Weight .12 .30
137 Rob Pearson .10 .25
138 Sylvain Cote .10 .25
139 Mike Keane .10 .25
140 Benoit Hogue .10 .25
141 Michel Petit .10 .25
142 Mark Freer .10 .25
143 Doug Zmolek .10 .25
144 Tony Granato .10 .25
145 Paul Coffey .15 .40
146 Ted Donato .10 .25
147 Brent Sutter .10 .25
148 A.Mogilny/T.Selanne LL .30 .75
149 James Patrick .10 .25
150 Mikael Andersson .10 .25
151 Steve Duchesne .10 .25
152 Terry Carkner .10 .25
153 Russ Courtnall .10 .25
154 Brian Mullen .10 .25
155 Martin Straka .10 .25
156 Geoff Sanderson .12 .30
157 Mark Howe .15 .40
158 Stephane Richer .12 .30
159 Doug Crossman .10 .25
160 John Vanbiesbrouck .15 .40
161 Bob Essensa .12 .30
162 Wayne Presley .10 .25
163 Mathieu Schneider .10 .25
164 Jiri Slegr .10 .25
165 Stephane Fiset .12 .30
166 Wendell Young .10 .25
167 Kevin Dineen .10 .25
168 Sandis Ozolinsh .10 .25
169 Mike Krushelnyski .10 .25
170 Kevin Stevens AS .12 .30
171 Pat LaFontaine AS .15 .40
172 Alexander Mogilny AS .12 .30
173 Larry Murphy AS .12 .30
174 Al Iafrate AS .10 .25
175 Tom Barrasso AS .12 .30
176 Derek King .10 .25
177 Bob Probert .15 .40
178 Gary Suter .10 .25
179 David Shaw .10 .25
180 Luc Robitaille .15 .40
181 John LeClair .15 .40
182 Troy Murray .10 .25
183 Dave Gagner .12 .30
184 Darcy Loewen .10 .25
185 Mario Lemieux LL .60 1.50
186 Pat Jablonski .10 .25
187 Alexei Kovalev .12 .30
188 Todd Krygier .10 .25
189 Larry Murphy .12 .30
190 Pierre Turgeon .12 .30
191 Craig Ludwig .10 .25
192 Brad May .12 .30
193 John MacLean .12 .30
194 Ron Wilson .10 .25
195 Eric Weinrich .10 .25
196 Steve Chiasson .10 .25
197 Dmitri Kvartalnov .10 .25
198 Andrei Kovalenko .10 .25
199 Rob Gaudreau RC .15 .40
200 Evgeny Davydov .10 .25
201 Adrien Plavsic .10 .25
202 Brian Bellows .12 .30
203 Doug Evans .10 .25
204 Tom Barrasso .12 .30
205 Joe Nieuwendyk .12 .30
206 Jari Kurri .15 .40
207 Bob Rouse .10 .25
208 Yvon Corriveau .10 .25
209 John Blue .12 .30
210 Dimitri Khristich .10 .25
211 Brent Fedyk .10 .25
212 Jody Hull .10 .25
213 Chris Terreri .12 .30
214 Mike McPhee .10 .25
215 Chris Kontos .10 .25
216 Greg Gilbert .10 .25
217 Sergei Zubov .12 .30
218 Grant Fuhr .25 .60
219 Charlie Huddy .10 .25
220 Mario Lemieux .60 1.50
221 Sheldon Kennedy .10 .25
222 Curtis Joseph .20 .50
223 Brad Dalgarno .10 .25
224 Bret Hedican .10 .25
225 Trevor Linden .15 .40
226 Darryl Sydor .10 .25
227 Jay More .10 .25
228 Dave Poulin .10 .25
229 Frank Musil .10 .25
230 Mark Recchi .20 .50
231 Craig Simpson .10 .25
232 Gino Cavallini .10 .25
233 Vincent Damphousse .12 .30
234 Luciano Borsato .10 .25
235 Dave Andreychuk .15 .40
236 Ken Daneyko .10 .25
237 Chris Chelios .15 .40
238 Andrew McBain .10 .25
239 Rick Tabaracci .10 .25
240 Steve Larmer .12 .30
241 Sean Burke .10 .25
242 Rob DiMaio .10 .25
243 Jim Paek .10 .25
244 Dave Lowry .10 .25
245 Alexander Mogilny .12 .30
246 Darren Turcotte .10 .25
247 Brendan Shanahan .15 .40
248 Peter Taglianetti .10 .25
249 Scott Mellanby .12 .30
250 Guy Carbonneau .10 .25
251 Claude LaPointe .10 .25
252 Pat Conacher .10 .25
253 Roger Johansson .10 .25
254 Cam Neely .15 .40
255 Garry Galley .10 .25
256 Keith Primeau .12 .30
257 Scott Lachance .10 .25
258 Bill Ranford .12 .30
259 Pat Falloon .10 .25
260 Pavel Bure .15 .40
261 Darrin Shannon .10 .25
262 Mike Foligno .10 .25
263 Checklist 1-132 .05 .15
264 Checklist 133-264 .05 .15
265 Peter Douris .10 .25
266 Warren Rychel .10 .25
267 Owen Nolan .15 .40
268 Mark Osborne .10 .25
269 Teppo Numminen .10 .25
270 Rob Niedermayer .12 .30
271 Mark Lamb .10 .25
272 Curtis Joseph .20 .50
273 Joe Murphy .10 .25
274 Bernie Nicholls .12 .30
275 Gord Roberts .10 .25
276 Al MacInnis .20 .50
277 Ken Wregget .10 .25
278 Calle Johansson .10 .25
279 Tom Kurvers .10 .25
280 Steve Yzerman .40 1.00
281 Roman Hamrlik .10 .25
282 Esa Tikkanen .10 .25
283 Darrin Madeley RC .15 .40
284 Robert Dirk .10 .25
285 Derek Plante RC .15 .40
286 Ron Tugnutt .12 .30
287 Frank Pietrangelo .12 .30
288 Paul DiPietro .10 .25
289 Alexander Godynyuk .10 .25
290 Kirk Maltby RC .15 .40
291 Olaf Kolzig .15 .40
292 Vitali Karamnov .10 .25
293 Alexei Gusarov .10 .25
294 Bryan Erickson .10 .25
295 Jocelyn Lemieux .10 .25
296 Bryan Trottier .15 .40
297 Dave Ellett .10 .25
298 Tim Watters .10 .25
299 Joe Juneau .10 .25
300 Steve Thomas .10 .25
301 Mark Greig .10 .25
302 Jeff Reese .10 .25
303 Steven King .10 .25
304 Don Beaupre .12 .30
305 Denis Savard .15 .40
306 Greg Smyth .10 .25
307 Jaroslav Modry RC .15 .40
308 Petr Svoboda .10 .25
309 Mike Craig .10 .25
310 Eric Lindros .25 .60
311 Dana Murzyn .10 .25
312 Sean Hill .10 .25
313 Andre Racicot .10 .25
314 John Vanbiesbrouck .15 .40
315 Doug Lidster .10 .25
316 Garth Butcher .10 .25
317 Alexei Yashin .12 .30
318 Sergei Fedorov .25 .60
319 Louie DeBrusk .10 .25
320 Dominik Hasek CZE .25 .60
321 Michal Pivonka .10 .25
322 Bobby Holik .10 .25
323 Roman Hamrlik CZE .10 .25
324 Petr Svoboda .10 .25
325 Jaromir Jagr CZE .50 1.25
326 Steven Finn .10 .25
327 Stephane Richer .12 .30
328 Claude Loiselle .10 .25
329 Joe Sacco .10 .25
330 Wayne Gretzky 1.00 2.50
331 Sylvain Lefebvre .10 .25
332 Sergei Bautin .10 .25
333 Craig Simpson .10 .25
334 Don Sweeney .10 .25
335 Dominic Roussel .12 .30
336 Scott Thomas RC .15 .40
337 Geoff Courtnall .10 .25
338 Tom Fitzgerald .10 .25
339 Kevin Haller .10 .25
340 Troy Loney .10 .25
341 Ronnie Stern .10 .25
342 Mark Astley RC .15 .40
343 Jeff Daniels .10 .25
344 Marc Bureau .10 .25
345 Micah Aivazoff RC .15 .40
346 Matthew Barnaby .12 .30
347 C.J. Young .10 .25
348 Dale Craigwell .10 .25
349 Ray Ferraro .10 .25
350 Ray Bourque .25 .60
351 Stu Barnes .10 .25
352 Alan Conroy RC .10 .25
353 Shawn McEachern .10 .25
354 Garry Valk .10 .25
355 Christian Ruuttu .10 .25
356 Darren Rumble .10 .25
357 Stu Grimson .10 .25
358 Alexander Karpovtsev .10 .25
359 Wendel Clark .25 .60
360 Michal Pivonka .10 .25
361 Peter Popovic RC .15 .40
362 Kevin Dahl .10 .25
363 Jeff Brown .10 .25
364 Daren Puppa .10 .25
365 Dallas Drake RC .15 .40
366 Dean McAmmond .10 .25
367 Martin Rucinsky .10 .25
368 Shane Churla .10 .25
369 Todd Ewen .10 .25
370 Kevin Stevens .12 .30
371 David Volek .10 .25
372 J.J. Daigneault .10 .25
373 Marc Bergevin .10 .25
374 Craig Billington .12 .30
375 Mike Gartner .20 .50
376 Jimmy Carson .10 .25
377 Bruce Driver .10 .25
378 Steve Heinze .10 .25
379 Patrick Carnback RC .15 .40
380 Wayne Gretzky CAN 1.00 2.50
381 Jeff Brown CAN .10 .25
382 Gary Roberts CAN .10 .25
383 Ray Bourque CAN .25 .60
384 Mike Gartner CAN .20 .50
385 Felix Potvin CAN .30 .75
386 Michel Goulet .10 .25
387 Dave Tippett .10 .25
388 Jim Waite .12 .30
389 Yuri Khmylev .10 .25
390 Doug Gilmour .20 .50
391 Brad McCrimmon .10 .25
392 Brent Severyn RC .15 .40
393 Jocelyn Thibault RC .15 .40
394 Boris Mironov .10 .25
395 Marty McSorley .12 .30
396 Shaun Van Allen .10 .25
397 Gary Leeman .10 .25
398 Ed Olczyk .10 .25
399 Darcy Wakaluk .10 .25
400 Murray Craven .10 .25
401 Martin Brodeur .40 1.00
402 Paul Laus RC .10 .25
403 Bill Houlder .10 .25
404 Robert Reichel .10 .25
405 Alexandre Daigle .10 .25
406 Brent Thompson .10 .25
407 Keith Acton .10 .25
408 Dave Karpa .10 .25
409 Igor Korolev .10 .25
410 Chris Gratton .12 .30
411 Vincent Riendeau .10 .25
412 Darren McCarty RC .25 .60
413 Bob Carpenter .12 .30
414 Joe Cirella .10 .25
415 Stephane Matteau .10 .25
416 Jozef Stumpel .10 .25
417 Rich Pilon .10 .25
418 Mattias Norstrom RC .15 .40
419 Dmitri Moronov .10 .25
420 Alexei Zhamnov .12 .30
421 Bill Guerin .15 .40
422 Greg Hawgood .10 .25
423 Randy Cunneyworth .10 .25
424 Ron Francis .20 .50
425 Brett Hull .30 .75
426 Tim Sweeney .10 .25
427 Mike Rathje .10 .25
428 Dave Babych .10 .25
429 Chris Tancill .10 .25
430 Mark Messier .30 .75
431 Bob Sweeney .10 .25
432 Terry Yake .10 .25
433 Joe Reekie .10 .25
434 Tomas Sandstrom .10 .25
435 Kevin Hatcher .10 .25
436 Bill Lindsay .10 .25
437 Jon Casey .12 .30
438 Dennis Vaske .10 .25
439 Allen Pedersen .10 .25
440 Pavel Bure RUS .15 .40
441 Sergei Fedorov RUS .25 .60
442 Arturs Irbe LAT .12 .30
443 Darius Kasparaitis .10 .25
444 Evgeny Davydov .10 .25
445 Vladimir Malakhov .10 .25
446 Tom Barrasso .12 .30
447 Jeff Norton .10 .25
448 David Emma .10 .25
449 Pelle Eklund .10 .25
450 Jeremy Roenick .25 .60
451 Jesse Belanger .10 .25
452 Vitali Prokhorov .10 .25
453 Arto Blomsten .10 .25
454 Peter Zezel .10 .25
455 Kelly Kisio .10 .25
456 Zdeno Ciger .10 .25
457 Greg Johnson .10 .25
458 Dave Archibald .10 .25
459 Vladimir Vujtek .10 .25
460 Mats Sundin .15 .40
461 Dan Keczmer .10 .25
462 Stephan Lebeau .10 .25
463 Dominik Hasek .25 .60
464 Kevin Lowe .10 .25
465 Gord Murphy .10 .25
466 Bryan Smolinski .10 .25
467 Josef Beranek .10 .25
468 Ron Hextall .15 .40
469 Randy Ladouceur .10 .25
470 Scott Niedermayer .15 .40
471 Kelly Hrudey .12 .30
472 Mike Needham .10 .25
473 John Tucker .10 .25
474 Kelly Miller .10 .25
475 Jyrki Lumme .10 .25
476 Andy Moog .15 .40
477 Glen Murray .12 .30
478 Mark Ferner RC .10 .25
479 John Cullen .10 .25
480 Gilbert Dionne .10 .25
481 Paul Ranheim .10 .25
482 Mike Hough .10 .25
483 Teemu Selanne .30 .75
484 Aaron Ward RC .15 .40
485 Chris Pronger .15 .40
486 Glenn Healy .12 .30
487 Curtis Leschyshyn .10 .25
488 Jim Montgomery RC .15 .40
489 Travis Green .12 .30
490 Pat LaFontaine .15 .40
491 Bobby Dollas RC .10 .25
492 Alexei Kasatonov .10 .25
493 Corey Millen .10 .25
494 Slava Kozlov .12 .30
495 Igor Kravchuk .10 .25
496 Dimitri Filimonov .10 .25
497 Jeff Odgers .10 .25
498 Joe Mullen .12 .30
499 Gary Shuchuk .10 .25
500 Jeremy Roenick USA .25 .60
501 Tom Barrasso USA .12 .30
502 Keith Tkachuk USA .15 .40
503 Phil Housley USA .12 .30
504 Tony Granato USA .10 .25
505 Brian Leetch USA .12 .30
506 Anatoli Semenov .10 .25
507 Steve Leach .10 .25
508 Brian Skrudland .10 .25
509 Kirk Muller .10 .25
510 Gary Roberts .10 .25
511 Gerard Gallant .10 .25
512 Joey Kocur .10 .25
513 Tie Domi .12 .30
514 Kay Whitmore .10 .25
515 Vladimir Malakhov .10 .25
516 Stewart Malgunas RC .15 .40
517 Jamie Macoun .10 .25
518 Alan May .10 .25
519 Guy Hebert .12 .30
520 Derian Hatcher .10 .25
521 Richard Smehlik .10 .25
522 Joby Messier RC .15 .40
523 Trent Klatt .10 .25
524 Tom Chorske .10 .25
525 Iain Fraser RC .15 .40
526 Dan Laperriere .10 .25
527 Checklist .05 .15
528 Checklist .05 .15

1993-94 Topps Premier Black Gold

COMPLETE SET (24) 12.00 30.00
COMP.SERIES 1 (12) 6.00 15.00
COMP.SERIES 2 (12) 6.00 15.00
1 Teemu Selanne .50 1.25
2 Steve Duchesne .20 .50
3 Felix Potvin .50 1.25
4 Shawn McEachern .20 .50
5 Adam Oates .30 .75
6 Paul Coffey .40 1.00
7 Wayne Gretzky 3.00 8.00
8 Alexei Zhamnov .25 .60
9 Mario Lemieux 2.00 5.00
10 Gary Suter .20 .50
11 Tom Barrasso .30 .75
12 Joe Juneau .25 .60
13 Eric Lindros .50 1.25
14 Ed Belfour .40 1.00
15 Ray Bourque .60 1.50
16 Steve Yzerman 2.00 5.00
17 Andrei Kovalenko .20 .50
18 Curtis Joseph .30 .75
19 Phil Housley .25 .60
20 Pierre Turgeon .30 .75
21 Brett Hull .50 1.25
22 Patrick Roy 2.00 5.00
23 Larry Murphy .25 .60
24 Pat LaFontaine .40 1.00
A1 Winner A 1-12 EXCH 1.50 4.00
A2 Winner A 1-12 Prize .20 .50
B1 Winner B 13-24 EXCH 1.50 4.00
B2 Winner B 13-24 Prize .20 .50
AB1 Winner A/B 1-24 EXCH 2.50 6.00
AB2 Winner A/B 1-24 Prize .50 1.25

1993-94 Topps Premier Finest

COMPLETE SET (12) 8.00 20.00
1 Alexandre Daigle .20 .50
2 Roman Hamrlik .40 1.00
3 Eric Lindros .75 2.00
4 Owen Nolan .40 1.00

5 Mats Sundin .75 2.00
6 Mike Modano 1.25 3.00
7 Pierre Turgeon .40 1.00
8 Joe Murphy .20 .50
9 Wendel Clark .40 1.00
10 Mario Lemieux 4.00 10.00
11 Dale Hawerchuk .40 1.00
12 Rob Ramage .20 .50

1993-94 Topps Premier Team USA

COMPLETE SET (23) 10.00 20.00
1 Mike Dunham .75 2.00
2 Ian Moran .40 1.00
3 Peter Laviolette .40 1.00
4 Darby Hendrickson .40 1.00
5 Brian Rolston .75 2.00
6 Mark Beaufait .40 1.00
7 Travis Richards .40 1.00
8 John Lilley .40 1.00
9 Chris Ferraro .75 2.00
10 Jon Hillebrandt .40 1.00
11 Chris Imes .40 1.00
12 Ted Crowley .40 1.00
13 David Sacco .40 1.00
14 Todd Marchant .75 2.00
15 Peter Ferraro .40 1.00
16 David Roberts .40 1.00
17 Jim Campbell .75 2.00
18 Barry Richter .40 1.00
19 Craig Johnson .40 1.00
20 Brett Hauer .40 1.00
21 Jeff Lazaro .40 1.00
22 Jim Storm .40 1.00
23 Matt Martin .40 1.00

1994-95 Topps Premier

1 Mark Messier .30 .75
2 Darren Turcotte .10 .25
3 Mikhail Shtalenkov RC .10 .25
4 Rob Gaudreau .10 .25
5 Tony Amonte .12 .30
6 Stephane Quintal .10 .25
7 Iain Fraser .10 .25
8 Doug Weight .12 .30
9 German Titov .10 .25
10 Larry Murphy .12 .30
11 Danton Cole .10 .25
12 Pat Peake .10 .25
13 Chris Terreri .12 .30
14 Yuri Khmylev .10 .25
15 Paul Coffey .15 .40
16 Brian Savage .10 .25
17 Rod Brind'Amour .12 .30
18 Nathan Lafayette .10 .25
19 Gord Murphy .10 .25
20 Al Iafrate .10 .25
21 Kevin Miller .10 .25
22 Peter Zezel .10 .25
23 Sylvain Turgeon .10 .25
24 Mark Tinordi .10 .25
25 Jari Kurri .12 .30
26 Benoit Hogue .10 .25
27 Jeff Reese .10 .25
28 Brian Noonan .10 .25
29 Denis Tsygurov RC .15 .40
30 James Patrick .10 .25
31 Bob Corkum .10 .25
32 Valeri Kamensky .12 .30
33 Ray Whitney .10 .25
34 Joe Murphy .10 .25
35 Dominik Hasek AS .25 .60
36 Ray Bourque AS .25 .60
37 Brian Leetch AS .12 .30
38 Dave Andreychuk AS .15 .40
39 Pavel Bure AS .15 .40
40 Sergei Fedorov AS .25 .60
41 Bob Beers .10 .25
42 Byron Dafoe RC .50 1.25
43 Lyle Odelein .12 .30
44 Markus Naslund .15 .40
45 Dean Chynoweth RC .10 .25
46 Trent Klatt .10 .25
47 Murray Craven .10 .25
48 Dave Mackey .10 .25
49 Norm Maciver .10 .25
50 Alexander Mogilny .12 .30
51 David Reid .10 .25
52 Nicklas Lidstrom .15 .40
53 Tom Fitzgerald .10 .25
54 Roman Hamrlik .10 .25
55 Wendel Clark .25 .60
56 Dominic Roussel .12 .30
57 Alexei Zhitnik .12 .30
58 Valeri Zelepukin .10 .25
59 Calle Johansson .10 .25
60 Craig Janney .12 .30
61 Randy Wood .10 .25
62 Curtis Leschyshyn .10 .25
63 Stephan Lebeau .10 .25
64 Dallas Drake .10 .25
65 Vincent Damphousse .12 .30
66 Scott Lachance .10 .25
67 Dirk Graham .10 .25
68 Kevin Smyth .10 .25
69 Denis Savard .15 .40
70 Mike Richter .15 .40
71 Ronnie Stern .10 .25
72 Kirk Maltby .10 .25
73 Kjell Samuelsson .10 .25
74 Neal Broten .12 .30
75 Trevor Linden .15 .40
76 Todd Elik .10 .25
77 Andrew McBain .10 .25
78 Alexei Kudashov .10 .25
79 Ken Daneyko .10 .25
80 D.Hasek/G.Fuhr GD .25 .60
81 A.Moog/D.Wakaluk GD .15 .40
82 Vanbiesbrouck/M.Fitz. GD .15 .40
83 M.Brodeur/C.Terreri GD .40 1.00
84 T.Barrasso/K.Wregget GD .12 .30
85 K.McLean/K.Whitmore .12 .30
86 Darryl Sydor .10 .25
87 Chris Osgood .25 .60
88 Ted Donato .10 .25
89 Dave Lowry .10 .25
90 Mark Recchi .20 .50
91 Jim Montgomery .10 .25
92 Bill Houlder .10 .25
93 Richard Smehlik .10 .25
94 Benoit Brunet .10 .25
95 Teemu Selanne .30 .75
96 Paul Ranheim .10 .25
97 Andrei Kovalenko .10 .25
98 Grant Ledyard .10 .25
99 Brent Grieve RC .10 .25
100 Joe Juneau .10 .25
101 Martin Gelinas .10 .25
102 Jamie Macoun .10 .25
103 Craig MacTavish .10 .25
104 Micah Aivazoff .10 .25
105 Stephane Richer .12 .30
106 Eric Weinrich .10 .25
107 Pat Elynuik .10 .25
108 Tomas Sandstrom .10 .25
109 Darrin Madeley .10 .25
110 Al MacInnis .20 .50
111 Cam Stewart .10 .25
112 Dixon Ward .10 .25
113 Vlastimil Kroupa .10 .25
114 Rob DiMaio .10 .25
115 Pierre Turgeon .12 .30
116 Mike Hough .10 .25
117 John LeClair .15 .40
118 Dave Hannan .10 .25
119 Todd Ewen .10 .25
120 NY Rangers Champs .30 .75
121 Dave Manson .10 .25
122 Jocelyn Lemieux .10 .25
123 Jocelyn Thibault .12 .30
124 Scott Pearson .10 .25
125 Patrick Roy AS .40 1.00
126 Scott Stevens AS .15 .40
127 Al MacInnis AS .20 .50
128 Adam Graves AS .10 .25
129 Cam Neely AS .15 .40
130 Wayne Gretzky AS 1.00 2.50
131 Tom Chorske .10 .25
132 John Tucker .10 .25
133 Steve Smith .10 .25
134 Kay Whitmore .10 .25
135 Adam Oates .15 .40
136 Bill Berg .10 .25
137 Wes Walz .10 .25
138 Jeff Beukeboom .10 .25
139 Ron Francis .20 .50
140 Alexandre Daigle .10 .25
141 Josef Beranek .10 .25
142 Tom Pederson .10 .25
143 Jamie McLennan .12 .30
144 Scott Mellanby .12 .30
145 Slava Kozlov .12 .30
146 Marty McSorley .12 .30
147 Tim Sweeney .10 .25
148 Luciano Borsato .10 .25
149 Jason Dawe .10 .25
150 Wayne Gretzky LL 1.00 2.50
151 Pavel Bure LL .15 .40
152 Dominik Hasek LL .25 .60
153 Scott Stevens LL .15 .40
154 Wayne Gretzky LL 1.00 2.50
155 Mike Richter LL .15 .40
156 Dominik Hasek LL .25 .60
157 Ted Drury .10 .25
158 Peter Popovic .10 .25
159 Alexei Kasatonov .10 .25
160 Mats Sundin .15 .40
161 Brad Shaw .10 .25
162 Bret Hedican .10 .25
163 Mike McPhee .10 .25
164 Martin Straka .10 .25
165 Dmitri Mironov .10 .25
166 Andrei Trefilov .10 .25
167 Joe Reekie .10 .25
168 Gary Suter .10 .25
169 Greg Gilbert .10 .25
170 Igor Larionov .10 .25
171 Mike Sillinger .10 .25
172 Igor Kravchuk .10 .25
173 Glen Murray .12 .30
174 Shawn Chambers .10 .25
175 John MacLean .12 .30
176 Yves Racine .10 .25
177 Andrei Lomakin .10 .25
178 Patrick Flatley .10 .25
179 Igor Ulanov .10 .25
180 Pat LaFontaine .15 .40
181 Mathieu Schneider .10 .25
182 Peter Stastny .12 .30
183 Tony Granato .10 .25
184 Peter Douris .10 .25
185 Alexei Kovalev .12 .30
186 Geoff Courtnall .10 .25
187 Richard Matvichuk .10 .25
188 Troy Murray .10 .25
189 Todd Gill .10 .25
190 Martin Brodeur RS .40 1.00
191 Mikael Renberg RS .12 .30
192 Alexei Yashin RS .15 .40
193 Jason Arnott RS .12 .30
194 Derek Plante RS .10 .25
195 Alexandre Daigle RS .10 .25
196 Bryan Smolinski RS .10 .25
197 Jesse Belanger RS .10 .25
198 Chris Pronger RS .15 .40
199 Chris Osgood RS .25 .60
200 Jeremy Roenick .25 .60
201 Johan Garpenlov .10 .25
202 Dave Karpa .10 .25
203 Darren McCarty .10 .25
204 Claude Lemieux .15 .40
205 Geoff Sanderson .12 .30
206 Tom Barrasso .12 .30
207 Kevin Dineen .10 .25
208 Sylvain Cote .10 .25
209 Brent Gretzky .10 .25
210 Shayne Corson .12 .30
211 Darius Kasparaitis .10 .25
212 Peter Andersson .10 .25
213 Robert Reichel .10 .25
214 Jozef Stumpel .10 .25
215 Brendan Shanahan .15 .40
216 Craig Muni .10 .25
217 Alexei Zhamnov .12 .30
218 Robert Lang .10 .25
219 Brian Bellows .12 .30
220 Steven King .10 .25
221 Sergei Zubov .12 .30
222 Kelly Miller .10 .25
223 Ilya Byakin .10 .25
224 Chris Tamer RC .10 .25
225 Doug Gilmour .20 .50
226 Shawn Antoski .10 .25
227 Andrew Cassels .10 .25
228 Craig Wolanin .10 .25
229 Jon Casey .12 .30
230 Mike Modano .25 .60
231 Bill Guerin .15 .40
232 Gaetan Duchesne .10 .25
233 Steve Dubinsky .10 .25
234 Jason Bowen .10 .25
235 Steve Yzerman .40 1.00
236 Dave Poulin .10 .25
237 Michael Nylander .12 .30
238 Felix Potvin FUT .25 .60
239 Sandis Ozolinsh FUT .10 .25
240 Scott Niedermayer FUT .15 .40
241 Eric Lindros FUT .25 .60
242 Keith Tkachuk FUT .15 .40
243 Teemu Selanne FUT .30 .75
244 Marty McInnis .10 .25
245 Bob Kudelski .10 .25
246 Paul Cavallini .10 .25
247 Brian Bradley .10 .25
248 Robb Stauber .10 .25
249 Jay Wells .10 .25
250 Mario Lemieux .60 1.50
251 Tommy Albelin .10 .25
252 Paul DiPietro .10 .25
253 Mike Gartner .20 .50
254 Darrin Shannon .10 .25
255 Alexander Karpovtsev .10 .25
256 Dave Babych .10 .25
257 Greg Johnson .10 .25
258 Frank Musil .10 .25
259 Michal Pivonka .10 .25
260 Arturs Irbe .12 .30
261 Paul Broten .10 .25
262 Don Sweeney .10 .25
263 Doug Brown .10 .25
264 Bobby Dollas .10 .25
265 Brian Skrudland .10 .25
266 Dan Plante RC .10 .25
267 Chad Penney .10 .25
268 Steve Leach .10 .25
269 Damian Rhodes .12 .30
270 Glenn Anderson .12 .30
271 Randy McKay .10 .25
272 Jeff Brown .10 .25
273 Steve Konowalchuk .10 .25
274 Checklist 1-136 .05 .15
275 Checklist 137-275 .05 .15
276 Sergei Fedorov TOTG .25 .60
277 Adam Oates TOTG .15 .40
278 Mark Messier TOTG .30 .75
279 Doug Gilmour TOTG .20 .50
280 Wayne Gretzky TOTG 1.00 2.50
281 Rick Tocchet .12 .30
282 Guy Carbonneau .10 .25
283 Peter Bondra .15 .40
284 Valeri Karpov RC .10 .25
285 Ed Belfour .15 .40
286 Petr Nedved .12 .30
287 Mikael Andersson .10 .25
288 Boris Mironov .10 .25
289 Donald Audette .10 .25
290 Kevin Stevens .12 .30
291 Cliff Ronning .10 .25
292 Bruce Driver .10 .25
293 Mariusz Czerkawski RC .15 .40
294 Mikael Renberg .12 .30
295 Theo Fleury .15 .40
296 Robert Kron .10 .25
297 Wendel Clark .25 .60
298 Dave Gagner .12 .30
299 Ulf Dahlen .10 .25
300 Keith Tkachuk .15 .40
301 Mike Ridley .10 .25
302 Mike Vernon .12 .30
303 Troy Mallette .10 .25
304 Derek King .10 .25
305 Kirk Muller .10 .25
306 Rob Niedermayer .12 .30
307 Ian Laperriere RC .15 .40
308 Mike Donnelly .10 .25
309 Joe Sacco .10 .25
310 Patrick Roy TOTG .40 1.00
311 Tom Barrasso .12 .30
312 Dominik Hasek TOTG .25 .60
313 Felix Potvin TOTG .25 .60
314 Mike Richter .15 .40
315 Bobby Holik .10 .25
316 Patrick Poulin .10 .25
317 Stephane Matteau .10 .25
318 Petr Klima .10 .25
319 Fredrik Olausson .10 .25
320 Dale Hawerchuk .20 .50
321 Jim Dowd .10 .25
322 Chris Therien .10 .25
323 Ravil Gusmanov RC .10 .25
324 Vincent Riendeau .10 .25
325 Pavel Bure .15 .40
326 Jimmy Carson .10 .25
327 Steve Chiasson .10 .25
328 Ken Wregget .12 .30
329 Kenny Jonsson .10 .25
330 Keith Primeau .12 .30
331 Bob Errey .10 .25
332 Derian Hatcher .10 .25
333 Stephane Fiset .12 .30
334 Brent Severyn .10 .25
335 Ray Ferraro .10 .25
336 Pavol Demitra .20 .50
337 Valeri Bure .10 .25
338 Guy Hebert .12 .30
339 Matt Johnson RC .10 .25
340 Curtis Joseph .20 .50
341 Rob Pearson .10 .25
342 Jeff Shantz .10 .25
343 Eric Charron RC .15 .40
344 Jason Smith .12 .30
345 M.Sundin/W.Clark .25 .60
346 R.Tocchet/L.Robitaille .15 .40
347 A.MacInnis/P.Housley .20 .50
348 M.Vernon/S.Chiasson .12 .30
349 Craig Simpson .10 .25
350 Adam Graves .10 .25
351 Kevin Haller .10 .25
352 Nelson Emerson .10 .25
353 Phil Housley .12 .30
354 Shawn McEachern .10 .25
355 Felix Potvin .25 .60
356 Sergio Momesso .15 .40
357 Glen Wesley .10 .25
358 David Shaw .10 .25
359 Terry Carkner .10 .25
360 John Vanbiesbrouck .15 .40
361 Dean Evason .10 .25
362 Michal Sykora .10 .25
363 Troy Loney .10 .25
364 Sylvain Lefebvre .10 .25
365 Alexei Yashin .15 .40
366 Gilbert Dionne .10 .25
367 Rick Tabaracci .12 .30
368 Paul Ysebaert .10 .25
369 Craig Johnson .10 .25
370 Scott Stevens .15 .40
371 Philippe Boucher .10 .25
372 Garry Valk .10 .25
373 Jason Muzzatti .12 .30
374 Chris Joseph .10 .25
375 Wayne Gretzky 1.00 2.50
376 Teppo Numminen .10 .25
377 Oleg Petrov .10 .25
378 Patrik Juhlin RC .10 .25
379 Zarley Zalapski .10 .25
380 Martin Brodeur TOTF .40 1.00
381 Chris Pronger TOTF .15 .40
382 Sergei Zubov TOTF .12 .30
383 Mikael Renberg TOTF .12 .30
384 Brett Lindros TOTF .10 .25
385 Peter Forsberg TOTF .30 .75
386 Brandon Convery .10 .25
387 Steve Heinze .10 .25
388 Glenn Healy .12 .30
389 Brian Benning .10 .25
390 Pat Verbeek .12 .30
391 Ulf Samuelsson .10 .25
392 Turner Stevenson .10 .25
393 Bob Rouse .10 .25
394 Steve Konroyd .10 .25
395 Russ Courtnall .10 .25
396 Sergei Makarov .10 .25
397 Kirk McLean .12 .30
398 Steven Finn .10 .25
399 Yan Kaminsky .10 .25
400 Eric Lindros .25 .60
401 Steve Duchesne .10 .25
402 John Slaney .10 .25
403 Bernie Nicholls .12 .30
404 Kelly Buchberger .10 .25
405 Paul Kariya .15 .40
406 Michel Petit .10 .25
407 Cale Hulse RC .12 .30
408 Sheldon Kennedy .10 .25
409 Brad May .10 .25
410 Daren Puppa .12 .30
411 Janne Laukkanen .12 .30
412 Mats Sundin .15 .40
413 Trevor Kidd .12 .30
414 Greg Adams .10 .25
415 Pavel Bure TOTG .15 .40
416 Teemu Selanne TOTG .30 .75
417 Brett Hull TOTG .30 .75
418 Steve Larmer .12 .30
419 Cam Neely TOTG .15 .40
420 Ray Bourque .25 .60
421 Andrei Nikolishin .10 .25
422 Jim Paek .10 .25
423 John Cullen .10 .25
424 Darcy Wakaluk .12 .30
425 Peter Forsberg .30 .75
426 Yves Racine .10 .25
427 Jody Hull .10 .25
428 Ron Sutter .10 .25
429 Ray Sheppard .12 .30
430 Sandis Ozolinsh .10 .25
431 Brent Grieve .10 .25
432 Shaun Van Allen .10 .25
433 Craig Berube .10 .25
434 Vladislav Boulin RC .15 .40
435 Bill Ranford .12 .30
436 Denny Felsner .10 .25
437 Jamie Storr .12 .30
438 Brian Rolston .12 .30
439 Chris Gratton .10 .25
440 Dominik Hasek .25 .60
441 Garth Butcher .12 .30
442 Jyrki Lumme .10 .25
443 Sergei Nemchinov .10 .25
444 Tie Domi .12 .30
445 Gary Roberts .10 .25
446 Dave McLlwain .10 .25
447 John Gruden RC .10 .25
448 Vladimir Konstantinov .12 .30
449 Adam Deadmarsh .10 .25
450 Brian Leetch TOTG .12 .30
451 Scott Stevens .15 .40
452 Mark Tinordi .10 .25
453 Al Iafrate .10 .25
454 Ray Bourque TOTG .25 .60
455 Patrick Roy .40 1.00
456 Viktor Gordiouk .12 .30
457 Owen Nolan .15 .40
458 Stu Barnes .10 .25
459 Zigmund Palffy .12 .30
460 Jaromir Jagr .50 1.25
461 Andrei Nazarov .10 .25
462 Kelly Hrudey .12 .30
463 Jason Wiemer RC .10 .25
464 Oleg Tverdovsky .12 .30
465 Brett Hull .30 .75
466 Luke Richardson .10 .25
467 Jason Allison .12 .30
468 Dimitri Yushkevich .10 .25
469 Todd Simon RC .10 .25
470 Martin Brodeur .40 1.00
471 Thomas Steen .10 .25
472 Vesa Viitakoski .12 .30
473 Todd Harvey .10 .25
474 Kent Manderville .10 .25
475 Chris Chelios .15 .40
476 Joby Messier .10 .25
477 Jassen Cullimore .10 .25
478 Jamie Pushor .12 .30
479 Bryan Smolinski .10 .25
480 Joe Sakic .30 .75
481 David Wilkie .12 .30
482 Craig Billington .12 .30
483 Pat Neaton .12 .30
484 Chris Pronger .15 .40
485 Brian Leetch POW .12 .30
486 Chris Chelios .15 .40
487 Jeff Brown .10 .25
488 Al MacInnis .20 .50
489 Paul Coffey .15 .40
490 Ray Bourque POW .25 .60
491 Phil Housley .12 .30
492 Larry Murphy .12 .30
493 Sergei Zubov POW .12 .30
494 Scott Stevens .15 .40
495 Steve Thomas .10 .25
496 Jim Waite .10 .25
497 Mike Keane .10 .25
498 Rob Blake .15 .40
499 John Lilley .10 .25
500 Brian Leetch .12 .30
501 Derek Plante .10 .25
502 Tim Cheveldae .12 .30
503 Vladimir Vujtek .10 .25
504 Esa Tikkanen .10 .25
505 Cam Neely .15 .40
506 Dale Hunter .10 .25
507 Marc Bergevin .10 .25
508 Joel Otto .10 .25
509 Brent Fedyk .10 .25
510 Dave Andreychuk .15 .40
511 Andy Moog .15 .40
512 Jaroslav Modry .10 .25
513 Sergei Krivokrasov .10 .25
514 Brett Lindros .10 .25
515 Cory Stillman RC .10 .25
516 Jon Rohloff RC .15 .40
517 Joe Mullen .12 .30
518 Evgeny Davydov .10 .25
519 Scott Young .10 .25
520 Sergei Fedorov .25 .60
521 Pat Falloon .10 .25
522 Bill Lindsay .10 .25
523 Ron Tugnutt .12 .30
524 Anatoli Semenov .10 .25
525 Geoff Courtnall .10 .25
526 Luc Robitaille .15 .40
527 Geoff Sanderson .12 .30
528 Esa Tikkanen .10 .25
529 Brendan Shanahan TOTG .15 .40
530 Jason Arnott .12 .30
531 Michal Grosek RC .10 .25
532 Steve Larmer .12 .30
533 Eric Fichaud RC .15 .40
534 Dimitri Khristich .10 .25
535 Garry Galley .10 .25
536 Aaron Gavey .10 .25
537 Joe Nieuwendyk .12 .30
538 Mike Craig .10 .25
539 Scott Niedermayer .15 .40
540 Luc Robitaille .15 .40
541 Dino Ciccarelli .12 .30
542 Sean Burke .12 .30
543 Jiri Slegr .10 .25
544 Jesse Belanger .10 .25
545 Sean Hill .10 .25
546 Vladimir Malakhov .10 .25
547 Jeff Friesen .10 .25
548 Mike Ricci .10 .25
549 Checklist 276-414 .05 .15
550 Checklist 415-550 .05 .15

1994-95 Topps Premier Special Effects

*SER.1 SE VETS: 4X TO 10X BASIC CARDS
*SER.1 SE ROOKIES: 1.5X TO 4X
*SER.2 SE VETS: 6X TO 15X BASIC CARDS
*SER.2 SE ROOKIES: 3X TO 8X
CL REPLACE (274/275/549/55) .40 1.00

1994-95 Topps Premier Finest Inserts

COMPLETE SET (23) 15.00 40.00
1 Pavel Bure 1.50 4.00
2 Brett Hull 2.00 5.00
3 Sergei Fedorov 1.50 4.00
4 Dave Andreychuk .75 2.00
5 Brendan Shanahan 1.50 4.00
6 Ray Sheppard .40 1.00
7 Adam Graves .40 1.00
8 Cam Neely 1.50 4.00
9 Mike Modano 2.00 5.00
10 Wendel Clark .75 2.00
11 Jeremy Roenick 2.00 5.00
12 Eric Lindros 1.50 4.00
13 Luc Robitaille .75 2.00
14 Steve Thomas .40 1.00
15 Geoff Sanderson .40 1.00
16 Gary Roberts .40 1.00
17 Kevin Stevens .40 1.00
18 Keith Tkachuk .75 2.00
19 Theo Fleury .40 1.00
20 Robert Reichel .40 1.00
21 Mark Recchi .75 2.00
22 Vincent Damphousse .40 1.00
23 Bob Kudelski .40 1.00

1994-95 Topps Premier The Go To Guy

COMPLETE SET (15) 12.00 30.00
1 Wayne Gretzky 5.00 12.00
2 Joe Sakic 1.50 4.00
3 Brett Hull 1.00 2.50
4 Mike Modano 1.25 3.00
5 Pavel Bure .75 2.00
6 Pat LaFontaine .75 2.00
7 Theo Fleury .15 .40
8 Jeremy Roenick 1.00 2.50
9 Sergei Fedorov 1.00 2.50
10 Eric Lindros .75 2.00
11 Kirk Muller .15 .40
12 Steve Yzerman 4.00 10.00
13 Alexander Mogilny .30 .75
14 Doug Gilmour .30 .75
15 Mark Messier .75 2.00

1994-95 Topps Finest Bronze

1 Jaromir Jagr 12.00 30.00
2 Eric Lindros 12.00 30.00
3 Patrick Roy 20.00 50.00
4 Pavel Bure 10.00 25.00
5 Teemu Selanne 10.00 25.00
6 Doug Gilmour 8.00 20.00
7 Sergei Fedorov 10.00 25.00
8 Brett Hull 10.00 25.00
9 Paul Kariya 15.00 40.00
10 Cam Neely 8.00 20.00
11 Mats Sundin 8.00 20.00
12 Martin Brodeur 10.00 25.00
13 Jeremy Roenick 8.00 20.00
14 Brian Leetch 6.00 15.00
15 Mark Messier 8.00 20.00
16 Mario Lemieux 20.00 50.00
17 Peter Forsberg 12.00 30.00
18 Felix Potvin 8.00 20.00
19 Alexander Mogilny 4.00 10.00
20 Ray Bourque 12.00 30.00
21 Ed Jovanovski 6.00 15.00
22 Mikael Renberg 4.00 10.00

1995-96 Topps

1 Eric Lindros MM .25 .60
2 Dominik Hasek MM .25 .60
3 Jeremy Roenick MM .25 .60
4 Paul Coffey MM .15 .40
5 Mark Messier MM .30 .75
6 Peter Bondra MM .15 .40
7 Paul Kariya MM .15 .40
8 Chris Chelios .15 .40
9 Martin Brodeur MM .40 1.00
10 Brett Hull MM .30 .75
11 Mike Vernon MM .12 .30
12 Trevor Linden MM .15 .40
13 Pat LaFontaine MM .15 .40
14 Geoff Sanderson MM .10 .25
15 Cam Neely MM .15 .40
16 Brendan Shanahan MM .15 .40
17 Jason Arnott MM .12 .30
18 Mikael Renberg MM .12 .30
19 Mats Sundin MM .15 .40
20 Pavel Bure MM .15 .40
21 Pierre Turgeon MM .12 .30
22 Alexei Zhamnov MM .15 .40
23 Blaine Lacher .12 .30
24 Brian Holzinger RC .30 .75
25 Theo Fleury .20 .50
26 Eric Daze .30 .75
27 Mike Kennedy .12 .30
28 Darren McCarty .10 .25
29 Todd Marchant .10 .25
30 Andrew Cassels .10 .25
31 Rob Niedermayer .12 .30
32 Eric Lacroix .10 .25
33 Steve Rucchin .12 .30
34 Turner Stevenson .10 .25
35 Sergei Brylin .10 .25
36 Mathieu Schneider .10 .25
37 Pat Verbeek .12 .30
38 Steve Larouche RC .10 .25
39 Rod Brind'Amour .15 .40
40 Luc Robitaille .15 .40
41 Brett Lindros .10 .25
42 Shean Donovan .10 .25
43 David Roberts .10 .25
44 Cory Cross .10 .25
45 Todd Warriner .12 .30
46 Yevgeny Namestnikov .10 .25
47 Sergei Gonchar .10 .25
48 Nikolai Khabibulin .12 .30
49 Alexei Zhitnik .10 .25
50 Ray Bourque .25 .60
51 Paul Kruse .10 .25
52 Murray Craven .10 .25
53 Andy Moog .15 .40
54 Keith Primeau .12 .30
55 Shayne Corson .12 .30
56 Johan Garpenlov .10 .25
57 Marek Malik .10 .25
58 Tony Granato .10 .25
59 Bob Corkum .10 .25
60 Patrick Roy .40 1.00
61 Chris McAlpine RC .12 .30
62 Chris Marinucci RC .12 .30
63 Jeff Beukeboom .10 .25
64 Radek Bonk .10 .25
65 John LeClair .15 .40
66 Len Barrie .10 .25
67 Teppo Numminen .10 .25
68 Ray Whitney .12 .30
69 Jeff Norton .10 .25
70 Chris Gratton .10 .25
71 Benoit Hogue .10 .25
72 Bret Hedican .10 .25
73 Keith Jones .12 .30
74 John Cullen .10 .25
75 Brian Leetch .12 .30
76 Dave Reid .10 .25
77 Dino Ciccarelli .12 .30
78 Gary Roberts .10 .25
79 Tony Amonte .12 .30
80 Mike Modano .25 .60
81 Doug Brown .10 .25
82 Scott Thornton .12 .30
83 Bill Lindsay .10 .25
84 Frantisek Kucera .10 .25
85 Wayne Gretzky 1.00 2.50
86 Joe Sacco .10 .25
87 Benoit Brunet .10 .25
88 Bill Guerin .15 .40
89 Travis Green .12 .30
90 Alexei Kovalev .12 .30
91 Stanislav Neckar .10 .25
92 Rob Dimaio .10 .25
93 Chris Joseph .10 .25
94 Craig Martin RC .10 .25
95 Craig Janney .10 .25
96 Greg Gilbert .10 .25
97 Alexander Semak .10 .25
98 Mike Gartner .20 .50
99 Cliff Ronning .10 .25
100 Mario Lemieux .60 1.50
101 Jassen Cullimore .12 .30
102 Steve Duchesne .10 .25
103 Derek Plante .10 .25
104 John Gruden .10 .25
105 Michal Sykora .10 .25
106 Trent Klatt .10 .25
107 Nicklas Lidstrom .15 .40
108 Luke Richardson .10 .25
109 Steven Rice .10 .25
110 Stu Barnes .10 .25
111 John Druce .12 .30
112 Guy Hebert .12 .30
113 Vladimir Malakhov .10 .25
114 Claude Lemieux .15 .40
115 Kirk Muller .12 .30
116 Darren Langdon RC .30 .75
117 Rob Gaudreau .10 .25
118 Karl Dykhuis .10 .25
119 Richard Park .15 .40
120 Dave Manson .10 .25
121 Andrei Nazarov .12 .30
122 Bernie Nicholls .12 .30
123 Mikael Andersson .12 .30
124 Todd Gill .10 .25
125 Trevor Linden .15 .40
126 Kelly Miller .10 .25
127 Don Sweeney .10 .25
128 Jason Dawe .10 .25
129 Steve Chiasson .10 .25
130 Ed Belfour .12 .30
131 Kerry Huffman .10 .25
132 Tim Taylor .10 .25
133 Kirk Maltby .12 .30
134 Jody Hull .10 .25
135 Sean Burke .10 .25
136 Philippe Boucher .10 .25
137 Valeri Karpov .10 .25
138 Yves Racine .10 .25
139 Patrick Flatley .10 .25
140 John MacLean .12 .30
141 Sergei Nemchinov .10 .25
142 Don Beaupre .12 .30
143 Kevin Dineen .12 .30
144 Ulf Samuelsson .10 .25
145 Al MacInnis .20 .50
146 Igor Korolev .10 .25
147 Pat Falloon .10 .25
148 Brian Bradley .12 .30
149 Josef Beranek .10 .25
150 Mats Sundin .15 .40
151 Sylvain Cote .10 .25
152 Keith Tkachuk .15 .40
153 Mariusz Czerkawski .10 .25
154 Trevor Kidd .12 .30
155 Garry Galley .10 .25
156 Gary Suter .10 .25
157 Grant Ledyard .10 .25
158 Doug Weight .15 .40
159 Jesse Belanger .10 .25
160 Mike Vernon .12 .30
161 Robert Kron .10 .25
162 Marty McSorley .12 .30
163 Todd Krygier .10 .25
164 Scott Niedermayer .15 .40
165 Mark Recchi .20 .50
166 Phil Housley .12 .30
167 Ron Hextall .15 .40
168 Richard Smehlik .12 .30
169 Chris Tamer .10 .25
170 Alexei Yashin .12 .30
171 Sergei Makarov .10 .25
172 Patrice Tardif .12 .30
173 Milos Holan .10 .25
174 J.C. Bergeron .12 .30
175 Dave Andreychuk .15 .40
176 Martin Gelinas .10 .25
177 Dale Hunter .12 .30
178 Kevin Haller .10 .25
179 Jeff Shantz .10 .25
180 Adam Oates .15 .40
181 Ronnie Stern .10 .25
182 Jamie Langenbrunner .10 .25
183 Mark Fitzpatrick .12 .30
184 Adam Burt .10 .25
185 Sergei Fedorov .25 .60
186 Robert Lang .10 .25
187 Craig Conroy RC .12 .30
188 Ken Daneyko .10 .25
189 Marko Tuomainen .10 .25
190 Ken Wregget .12 .30
191 Mike Rathje .12 .30
192 Dimitri Yushkevich .10 .25
193 Roman Hamrlik .10 .25
194 Russ Courtnall .10 .25
195 Teemu Selanne .30 .75
196 Jon Rohloff .10 .25
197 Derian Hatcher .12 .30
198 Mark Tinordi .10 .25
199 Patrice Brisebois .10 .25
200 Jaromir Jagr .50 1.25
201 Randy McKay .10 .25
202 Derek King .12 .30
203 Tony Twist .10 .25
204 Jyrki Lumme .10 .25
205 Steve Smith .10 .25
206 Bob Rouse .10 .25
207 Dave Ellett .10 .25
208 Kevin Dean .10 .25
209 Rusty Fitzgerald RC .10 .25
210 Jim Carey .12 .30
211 Kenny Jonsson .15 .40
212 Mike Richter .15 .40
213 Glen Wesley .10 .25
214 Donald Audette .12 .30
215 Curtis Joseph .20 .50
216 Joe Juneau .10 .25
217 Paul Kariya .15 .40
218 1995 Stanley Cup Champions .02 .10
219 Checklist 1-110 .01 .05
220 Checklist 111-220 .01 .05
221 Cam Neely .15 .40
222 Wayne Primeau RC .10 .25
223 Yanic Perreault .10 .25
224 Pierre Turgeon .12 .30
225 Alexander Mogilny .12 .30

226 Daren Puppa .12 .30
227 Ulf Dahlen .10 .25
228 Tomas Sandstrom .12 .30
229 Shayne Corson .12 .30
230 Chris Chelios .15 .40
231 Stephane Richer .12 .30
232 Paul Ranheim .10 .25
233 Joe Nieuwendyk .12 .30
234 Doug Gilmour .20 .50
235 Jeremy Roenick .25 .60
236 Joel Otto .10 .25
237 Steve Yzerman .40 1.00
238 Petr Klima .10 .25
239 Jari Kurri .15 .40
240 Mark Messier .30 .75
241 Bill Ranford .12 .30
242 Grant Fuhr .25 .60
243 Brent Severyn .10 .25
244 Ron Francis .20 .50
245 Ray Ferraro .10 .25
246 Martin Straka .10 .25
247 Gerald Diduck .10 .25
248 Dimitri Khristich .10 .25
249 Wade Flaherty RC .12 .30
250 Pat LaFontaine .15 .40
251 Darren Turcotte .10 .25
252 John Vanbiesbrouck .15 .40
253 Brian Bellows .12 .30
254 Dave Gagner .10 .25
255 Larry Murphy .12 .30
256 Steve Thomas .12 .30
257 Robert Svehla RC .10 .25
258 Deron Quint .12 .30
259 Kjell Samuelsson .10 .25
260 Scott Mellanby .12 .30
261 Dan Quinn .12 .30
262 Tom Barrasso .12 .30
263 Zarley Zalapski .10 .25
264 Rick Tocchet .12 .30
265 Paul Coffey .15 .40
266 Joe Sakic .30 .75
267 Aki Berg RC .15 .40
268 Jeff Brown .12 .30
269 Wendel Clark .25 .60
270 Vincent Damphousse .12 .30
271 Dale Hawerchuk .20 .50
272 Rhett Warrener RC .10 .25
273 Kevin Hatcher .12 .30
274 Calle Johansson .10 .25
275 Scott Stevens .15 .40
276 Geoff Courtnall .10 .25
277 Kirk McLean .12 .30
278 Steve Heinze .10 .25
279 Sylvain Lefebvre .10 .25
280 Joe Murphy .10 .25
281 Mike Keane .10 .25
282 Kevin Stevens .12 .30
283 Miroslav Satan RC .20 .50
284 Stephane Fiset .12 .30
285 Jeff O'Neill .15 .40
286 Denny Lambert RC .12 .30
287 Marcus Ragnarsson RC .20 .50
288 Adam Deadmarsh .10 .25
289 Eric Weinrich .10 .25
290 Eric Desjardins .12 .30
291 Tim Cheveldae .12 .30
292 Glenn Healy .12 .30
293 Byron Dafoe .12 .30
294 Tom Fitzgerald .10 .25
295 Adam Graves .12 .30
296 Arturs Irbe ERR front Aturs .12 .30
297 Shaun Van Allen .10 .25
298 Kelly Buchberger .10 .25
299 Bob Probert .15 .40
300 Pavel Bure .15 .40
301 Chad Kilger RC .15 .40
302 Dominik Hasek .25 .60
303 Bobby Holik .10 .25
304 Petr Nedved .12 .30
305 Owen Nolan .15 .40
306 Saku Koivu .15 .40
307 Rob Blake .12 .30
308 Chris Pronger .15 .40
309 Kyle McLaren RC .10 .25
310 Peter Bondra .15 .40
311 Nelson Emerson .10 .25
312 Bryan McCabe .15 .40
313 Darcy Wakaluk .10 .25
314 Shane Doan RC .50 1.25
315 Felix Potvin .25 .60
316 Jim Dowd .10 .25
317 Roman Oksiuta .10 .25
318 Geoff Sanderson .10 .25
319 Radek Dvorak RC .20 .50
320 Paul Ysebaert .10 .25
321 Shawn McEachern .10 .25
322 Vyacheslav Kozlov .12 .30
323 Marty McInnis .10 .25
324 Ted Donato .10 .25
325 Martin Brodeur .40 1.00
326 Patrick Poulin .10 .25
327 Eric Lindros .25 .60
328 Dallas Drake .10 .25
329 Sean Hill .10 .25
330 Michal Pivonka .10 .25
331 Alexei Zhamnov .15 .40
332 Cory Stillman .10 .25
333 Sergei Zubov .12 .30
334 Tommy Soderstrom .12 .30
335 Patrik Carnback .10 .25
336 Joe Dziedzic .10 .25
337 Steve Duchesne .10 .25
338 Marty Murray .15 .40
339 Todd Bertuzzi RC .20 .50
340 Jason Arnott .12 .30
341 Niklas Sundstrom .15 .40
342 Alexandre Daigle .10 .25
343 Jocelyn Thibault .12 .30
344 Mikhail Shtalenkov .10 .25
345 Chris Osgood .15 .40
346 Brendan Witt .15 .40
347 Ian Laperriere .10 .25
348 Zigmund Palffy .15 .40
349 Brian Savage .10 .25
350 Mike Peca .12 .30
351 Vitali Yachmenev .15 .40
352 Luc Robitaille .15 .40
353 Mikael Renberg .12 .30
354 Ed Jovanovski .15 .40
355 Jason Doig .15 .40
356 Todd Harvey .10 .25
357 Viktor Kozlov .12 .30
358 Valeri Bure .10 .25
359 Peter Forsberg .30 .75
360 Jeff Friesen .10 .25
361 Andrei Nikolishin .10 .25
362 Brian Rolston .12 .30
363 Jamie Storr .12 .30
364 Chris Therien .10 .25
365 Oleg Tverdovsky .15 .40
366 David Oliver .10 .25
367 Alexander Selivanov .12 .30
368 Alex Stojanov .10 .25
369 Daniel Alfredsson RC .75 2.00
370 Brendan Shanahan .15 .40
371 Yuri Khmylev .10 .25
372 Brett Hull .30 .75
373 Sergei Fedorov MM .25 .60
374 Jaromir Jagr MM .50 1.25
375 Wayne Gretzky MM 1.00 2.50
376 Alexander Mogilny MM .12 .30
377 Patrick Roy MM .40 1.00
378 Ed Belfour MM .12 .30
379 Luc Robitaille MM .15 .40
380 Peter Forsberg MM .30 .75
381 Adam Oates MM .15 .40
382 Theo Fleury MM .20 .50
383 Jim Carey MM .12 .30
384 Checklist 221-304 .01 .05
385 Checklist 305-385 .01 .05

1995-96 Topps O-Pee-Chee Parallel

COMPLETE SET (385)
*VETS: 6X TO 15X BASIC TOPPS
*ROOKIES: 2.5X TO 6X TOPPS
*SP's: 10X TO 25X TOPPS

1995-96 Topps Canadian Gold

COMPLETE SET (10) 30.00 60.00
1CG Patrick Roy 12.50 30.00
2CG Alexei Yashin 2.00 5.00
3CG Jason Arnott 2.00 5.00
4CG Trevor Kidd 2.00 5.00
5CG Pavel Bure 2.50 6.00
6CG Theo Fleury 2.00 5.00
7CG Pierre Turgeon 2.00 5.00
8CG Felix Potvin 2.50 6.00
9CG Teemu Selanne 2.50 6.00
10CG Mats Sundin 2.50 6.00

1995-96 Topps Canadian World Juniors

COMPLETE SET (22) 10.00 20.00
1CJ Wade Redden .60 1.50
2CJ Jamie Storr .60 1.50
3CJ Larry Courville .40 1.00
4CJ Jason Allison .60 1.50
5CJ Alexandre Daigle .40 1.00
6CJ Marty Murray .40 1.00
7CJ Bryan McCabe .60 1.50
8CJ Ryan Smyth .75 2.00
9CJ Lee Sorochan .40 1.00
10CJ Todd Harvey .40 1.00
11CJ Nolan Baumgartner .40 1.00
12CJ Denis Pederson .40 1.00
13CJ Shean Donovan .40 1.00
14CJ Jason Botterill .40 1.00
15CJ Jeff Friesen .40 1.00
16CJ Darcy Tucker .60 1.50
17CJ Chad Allan .40 1.00
18CJ Dan Cloutier .60 1.50
19CJ Eric Daze .40 1.00
20CJ Jeff O'Neill .40 1.00
21CJ Jamie Rivers .40 1.00
22CJ Ed Jovanovski .60 1.50

1995-96 Topps Hidden Gems

COMPLETE SET (15) 8.00 20.00
1HG Theo Fleury .75 2.00
2HG Luc Robitaille .75 2.00
3HG Doug Gilmour .75 2.00
4HG Dominik Hasek 2.00 5.00
5HG Pavel Bure 1.25 3.00
6HG Peter Bondra .75 2.00
7HG Steve Larmer .40 1.00
8HG David Oliver .40 1.00
9HG Gary Suter .40 1.00
10HG Brett Hull 1.25 3.00
11HG Kevin Stevens .40 1.00
12HG Ron Hextall .75 2.00
13HG Kirk McLean .40 1.00
14HG Andy Moog .75 2.00
15HG Rick Tocchet .40 1.00

1995-96 Topps Home Grown Canada

HGC1 Patrick Roy 5.00 12.00
HGC2 Wendel Clark 3.00 8.00
HGC3 Pierre Turgeon 1.50 4.00
HGC4 Doug Gilmour 2.50 6.00
HGC5 Theo Fleury 2.50 6.00
HGC6 Eric Lindros 3.00 8.00
HGC7 Paul Kariya 2.00 5.00
HGC8 Bill Ranford 1.50 4.00
HGC9 Ray Bourque 3.00 8.00
HGC10 Brendan Shanahan 2.00 5.00
HGC11 Paul Coffey 2.00 5.00
HGC12 Trevor Linden 2.00 5.00
HGC13 Trevor Kidd 1.50 4.00
HGC14 Alexandre Daigle 1.25 3.00
HGC15 Chris Pronger 2.00 5.00
HGC16 Steve Yzerman 5.00 12.00
HGC17 Todd Harvey 1.25 3.00
HGC18 Felix Potvin 3.00 8.00
HGC19 Luc Robitaille 2.00 5.00
HGC20 Wayne Gretzky 60.00 150.00
HGC21 Keith Primeau 1.50 4.00
HGC22 Al MacInnis 2.50 6.00
HGC23 Cam Neely 2.00 5.00
HGC24 Ed Belfour 1.50 4.00
HGC25 Joe Juneau 1.25 3.00
HGC26 Adam Graves 1.50 4.00
HGC27 Mark Recchi 2.50 6.00
HGC28 Stephane Richer 1.50 4.00
HGC29 Mark Messier 4.00 10.00
HGC30 Mario Lemieux 8.00 20.00

1995-96 Topps Home Grown USA

HGA1 Brian Leetch 1.50 4.00
HGA2 Jeremy Roenick 3.00 8.00
HGA3 Mike Modano 3.00 8.00
HGA4 Pat LaFontaine 2.00 5.00
HGA5 Keith Tkachuk 2.00 5.00
HGA6 Chris Chelios 2.00 5.00
HGA7 Darren Turcotte 1.25 3.00
HGA8 John Vanbiesbrouck 2.00 5.00
HGA9 John LeClair 2.00 5.00
HGA10 Mike Richter 2.00 5.00

1995-96 Topps Marquee Men Power Boosters

1 Eric Lindros 2.00 5.00
2 Dominik Hasek 1.50 4.00
3 Jeremy Roenick 2.00 5.00
4 Paul Coffey 1.50 4.00
5 Mark Messier 1.50 4.00
6 Peter Bondra .75 2.00
7 Paul Kariya 1.50 4.00
8 Chris Chelios 1.50 4.00
9 Martin Brodeur 2.50 6.00
10 Brett Hull 1.50 4.00
11 Mike Vernon .75 2.00
12 Trevor Linden 1.25 3.00
13 Pat LaFontaine .75 2.00
14 Geoff Sanderson .75 2.00
15 Cam Neely .75 2.00
16 Brendan Shanahan 1.50 4.00
17 Jason Arnott .40 1.00
18 Mikael Renberg .75 2.00
19 Mats Sundin 1.50 4.00
20 Pavel Bure 1.50 4.00
21 Pierre Turgeon .75 2.00
22 Alexei Zhamnov .40 1.00
373 Sergei Fedorov 1.50 4.00
374 Jaromir Jagr 1.50 4.00
375 Wayne Gretzky 8.00 20.00
376 Alexander Mogilny .75 2.00
377 Patrick Roy 6.00 15.00
378 Ed Belfour 1.50 4.00
379 Luc Robitaille .75 2.00
380 Peter Forsberg 1.50 4.00
381 Adam Oates .75 2.00
382 Theo Fleury .40 1.00
383 Jim Carey .40 1.00

1995-96 Topps Mystery Finest

COMPLETE SET (22) 50.00 100.00
*REFRACTORS: 1.5X TO 4X BASIC INSERTS
M1 Wayne Gretzky 8.00 20.00
M2 Mario Lemieux 8.00 20.00
M3 Mark Messier 1.50 4.00
M4 Eric Lindros 2.00 5.00
M5 Sergei Fedorov 2.50 6.00
M6 Joe Sakic 3.00 8.00
M7 Brett Hull 2.00 5.00
M8 Jaromir Jagr 2.50 6.00
M9 Teemu Selanne 1.50 4.00
M10 Brendan Shanahan 1.50 4.00
M11 Cam Neely 1.50 4.00
M12 Mikael Renberg .75 2.00
M13 Paul Kariya 1.50 4.00
M14 Keith Tkachuk 1.50 4.00
M15 Pavel Bure 1.50 4.00
M16 Brian Leetch .75 2.00
M17 Scott Stevens .75 2.00
M18 Chris Chelios 1.50 4.00
M19 Dominik Hasek 3.00 8.00
M20 Patrick Roy 8.00 20.00
M21 Martin Brodeur 4.00 10.00
M22 Felix Potvin 2.00 5.00

1995-96 Topps New To The Game

COMPLETE SET (22) 3.00 8.00
1NG Jim Carey .20 .50
2NG Sergei Brylin .08 .25
3NG Todd Marchant .08 .25
4NG Oleg Tverdovsky .08 .25
5NG Paul Kariya .40 1.00
6NG Adam Deadmarsh .08 .25
7NG Mike Kennedy .08 .25
8NG Roman Oksiuta .08 .25
9NG Kenny Jonsson .08 .25
10NG Peter Forsberg 1.00 2.50
11NG Alexander Selivanov .08 .25
12NG Chris Therien .08 .25
13NG Brian Rolston .08 .25
14NG David Oliver .08 .25
15NG Blaine Lacher .20 .50
16NG Sergei Krivokrasov .08 .25
17NG Todd Harvey .20 .50
18NG Jeff Friesen .08 .25
19NG Mariusz Czerkawski .08 .25
20NG Ian Laperriere .08 .25
21NG Brian Savage .08 .25
22NG Andrei Nikolishin .08 .25

1995-96 Topps Power Lines

COMPLETE SET (10) 4.00 10.00
1PL Lindros/LeClair/Renberg .40 1.00
2PL Tkachuk/Selanne/Zhamnov .40 1.00
3PL Graves/Messier/Verbeek .40 1.00
4PL Poulin/Roenick/Amonte .40 1.00
5PL Stevens/Jagr/Francis .75 2.00
6PL Dawe/LaFon./Mogilny .40 1.00
7PL Oates/Neely/Czerkawski .40 1.00
8PL Kozlov/Fedorov/Brown 1.00 2.50
9PL Damp./Turgeon/Recchi .40 1.00
10PL Peluso/Holik/McKay .40 1.00

1995-96 Topps Profiles

COMPLETE SET (20) 12.00 30.00
PF1 Wayne Gretzky 4.00 10.00
PF2 Brian Leetch .30 .75
PF3 Patrick Roy 2.50 6.00
PF4 Jaromir Jagr 1.00 2.50
PF5 Sergei Fedorov 1.00 2.50
PF6 Martin Brodeur 1.50 4.00
PF7 Eric Lindros .60 1.50
PF8 Jeremy Roenick .75 2.00
PF9 John Vanbiesbrouck .30 .75
PF10 Cam Neely .60 1.50
PF11 Pavel Bure .60 1.50
PF12 Paul Coffey .60 1.50
PF13 Scott Stevens .30 .75
PF14 Dominik Hasek 1.25 3.00
PF15 Mario Lemieux 2.50 6.00
PF16 Ed Belfour .60 1.50
PF17 Doug Gilmour .30 .75
PF18 Teemu Selanne .60 1.50
PF19 Brett Hull .75 2.00
PF20 Joe Sakic 1.25 3.00

1995-96 Topps Rink Leaders

COMPLETE SET (10) 30.00 60.00
1RL Mark Messier 2.00 5.00
2RL Mario Lemieux 8.00 20.00
3RL Ray Bourque 3.00 8.00
4RL Brett Hull 2.50 6.00
5RL Pat LaFontaine 2.00 5.00
6RL Scott Stevens 1.00 2.50
7RL Keith Tkachuk 2.00 5.00
8RL Doug Gilmour 1.00 2.50
9RL Chris Chelios 2.00 5.00
10RL Wayne Gretzky 12.50 30.00

1995-96 Topps Young Stars

COMPLETE SET (15) 12.00 25.00
YS1 Paul Kariya 1.00 2.50
YS2 Martin Brodeur 2.50 6.00
YS3 Mikael Renberg .50 1.25
YS4 Peter Forsberg 2.50 6.00
YS5 Alexei Yashin UER .25 .60
YS6 Jeff Friesen .25 .60
YS7 Oleg Tverdovsky .25 .60
YS8 Jim Carey .50 1.25
YS9 Alexei Kovalev .25 .60
YS10 Jason Arnott .25 .60
YS11 Teemu Selanne 1.00 2.50
YS12 Chris Osgood .50 1.25
YS13 Roman Hamrlik .50 1.25
YS14 Scott Niedermayer .25 .60
YS15 Jaromir Jagr 1.50 4.00

1998-99 Topps

1 Peter Forsberg .40 1.00
2 Petr Sykora .12 .30
3 Byron Dafoe .15 .40
4 Ron Francis .25 .60
5 Alexei Yashin .15 .40
6 Dave Ellett .15 .40
7 Jamie Langenbrunner .12 .30
8 Doug Weight .20 .50
9 Jason Woolley .12 .30
10 Paul Coffey .20 .50
11 Uwe Krupp .12 .30
12 Tomas Sandstrom .12 .30
13 Scott Mellanby .12 .30
14 Vladimir Tsyplakov .12 .30
15 Martin Rucinsky .12 .30
16 Mikael Renberg .15 .40
17 Marco Sturm .12 .30
18 Eric Lindros .30 .75
19 Sean Burke .12 .30
20 Martin Brodeur .50 1.25
21 Boyd Devereaux .12 .30
22 Kelly Buchberger .12 .30
23 Scott Stevens .20 .50
24 Jamie Storr .15 .40
25 Anders Eriksson .12 .30
26 Gary Suter .12 .30
27 Theo Fleury .25 .60
28 Steve Leach .12 .30
29 Felix Potvin .30 .75
30 Brett Hull .40 1.00
31 Mike Grier .12 .30
32 Cale Hulse .12 .30
33 Larry Murphy .15 .40
34 Rick Tocchet .15 .40
35 Eric Desjardins .15 .40
36 Igor Kravchuk .12 .30
37 Rob Niedermayer .12 .30
38 Bryan Smolinski .12 .30
39 Valeri Kamensky .12 .30
40 Ryan Smyth .15 .40
41 Bruce Driver .12 .30
42 Mike Johnson .12 .30
43 Rob Zamuner .12 .30
44 Steve Duchesne .15 .40
45 Martin Straka .12 .30
46 Bill Houlder .12 .30
47 Craig Conroy .12 .30
48 Guy Hebert .15 .40
49 Colin Forbes .12 .30
50 Mike Modano .30 .75
51 Jamie Pushor .12 .30
52 Jarome Iginla .25 .60
53 Paul Kariya .20 .50
54 Mattias Ohlund .12 .30
55 Sergei Berezin .15 .40
56 Peter Zezel .12 .30
57 Teppo Numminen .12 .30
58 Dale Hunter .15 .40
59 Sandy Moger .12 .30
60 John LeClair .20 .50
61 Wade Redden .12 .30
62 Patrik Elias .20 .50
63 Rob Blake .20 .50
64 Todd Marchant .12 .30
65 Claude Lemieux .15 .40
66 Trevor Kidd .12 .30
67 Sergei Fedorov .30 .75
68 Joe Sakic .40 1.00
69 Derek Morris .12 .30
70 Alexei Morozov .12 .30
71 Mats Sundin .20 .50
72 Daymond Langkow .12 .30
73 Kevin Hatcher .12 .30
74 Damian Rhodes .20 .50
75 Brian Leetch .15 .40
76 Saku Koivu .20 .50
77 Rick Tabaracci .12 .30
78 Bernie Nicholls .15 .40
79 Alyn McCauley .12 .30
80 Patrice Brisebois .12 .30
81 Bret Hedican .12 .30
82 Sandy McCarthy .12 .30
83 Viktor Kozlov .15 .40
84 Derek King .12 .30
85 Alexander Selivanov .12 .30
86 Mike Vernon .15 .40
87 Jeff Beukeboom .12 .30
88 Tommy Salo .15 .40
89 Adam Graves .12 .30
90 Randy McKay .15 .40
91 Rich Pilon .12 .30
92 Richard Zednik .12 .30
93 Jeff Hackett .12 .30
94 Michael Peca .12 .30
95 Brent Gilchrist .12 .30
96 Stu Grimson .12 .30
97 Bob Probert .20 .50
98 Stu Barnes .12 .30
99 Ruslan Salei .12 .30
100 Al MacInnis .25 .60
101 Ken Daneyko .12 .30
102 Paul Ranheim .12 .30
103 Marty McInnis .12 .30
104 Marian Hossa .20 .50
105 Darren McCarty .12 .30
106 Guy Carbonneau .12 .30
107 Dallas Drake .12 .30
108 Sergei Samsonov .15 .40
109 Teemu Selanne .40 1.00
110 Checklist .02 .10
111 Jaromir Jagr .60 1.50
112 Joe Thornton .30 .75
113 Jon Klemm .12 .30
114 Grant Fuhr .30 .75
115 Nikolai Khabibulin .20 .50
116 Rod Brind'Amour .20 .50
117 Trevor Linden .20 .50
118 Vincent Damphousse .15 .40
119 Dino Ciccarelli .20 .50
120 Pat Verbeek .12 .30
121 Sandis Ozolinsh .12 .30
122 Garth Snow .15 .40
123 Ed Belfour .20 .50
124 Keith Primeau .15 .40
125 Jason Allison .15 .40
126 Peter Bondra .20 .50
127 Ulf Samuelsson .15 .40
128 Jeff Friesen .12 .30
129 Jason Bonsignore .12 .30
130 Daniel Alfredsson .20 .50
131 Bobby Holik .12 .30
132 Jozef Stumpel .12 .30
133 Brian Bellows .15 .40
134 Chris Osgood .20 .50
135 Alexei Zhamnov .12 .30
136 Mattias Norstrom .12 .30
137 Drake Berehowsky .12 .30
138 Mark Messier .40 1.00
139 Geoff Courtnall .15 .40
140 Marc Bureau .12 .30
141 Don Sweeney .12 .30
142 Wendel Clark .30 .75
143 Scott Niedermayer .20 .50
144 Chris Therien .12 .30
145 Kirk Muller .12 .30
146 Wayne Primeau .12 .30
147 Tony Granato .12 .30
148 Derian Hatcher .12 .30
149 Daniel Briere .15 .40
150 Fredrik Olausson .12 .30
151 Joe Juneau .12 .30
152 Michal Grosek .12 .30
153 Janne Laukkanen .12 .30
154 Keith Tkachuk .20 .50
155 Marty McSorley .15 .40
156 Owen Nolan .20 .50
157 Mark Tinordi .12 .30
158 Steve Washburn .12 .30
159 Luke Richardson .12 .30
160 Kris King .12 .30
161 Joe Nieuwendyk .15 .40
162 Travis Green .12 .30
163 Dominik Hasek .30 .75
164 Dimitri Khristich .12 .30
165 Dave Manson .12 .30
166 Chris Chelios .20 .50
167 Claude LaPointe .12 .30
168 Kris Draper .12 .30
169 Brad Isbister .12 .30
170 Patrick Marleau .20 .50
171 Jeremy Roenick .30 .75
172 Darren Langdon .12 .30
173 Kevin Dineen .12 .30
174 Luc Robitaille .20 .50
175 Steve Yzerman .50 1.25
176 Sergei Zubov .15 .40
177 Ed Jovanovski .15 .40
178 Sami Kapanen .12 .30
179 Adam Oates .20 .50
180 Pavel Bure .20 .50
181 Chris Pronger .20 .50
182 Pat Falloon .12 .30
183 Darcy Tucker .12 .30
184 Zigmund Palffy .20 .50
185 Curtis Brown .12 .30
186 Curtis Joseph .25 .60
187 Valeri Zelepukin .12 .30
188 Russ Courtnall .12 .30
189 Adam Foote .12 .30
190 Patrick Roy .50 1.25
191 Cory Stillman .12 .30
192 Alexei Zhitnik .12 .30
193 Olaf Kolzig .20 .50
194 Mark Fitzpatrick .12 .30
195 Eric Daze .15 .40
196 Zarley Zalapski .12 .30
197 Niklas Sundstrom .12 .30
198 Bryan Berard .15 .40
199 Jason Arnott .15 .40
200 Mike Richter .20 .50
201 Ken Baumgartner .12 .30
202 Jason Dawe .12 .30
203 Nicklas Lidstrom .25 .60
204 Tony Amonte .15 .40
205 Kjell Samuelsson .12 .30
206 Ray Bourque .30 .75
207 Alexander Mogilny .15 .40
208 Pierre Turgeon .15 .40
209 Tom Barrasso .15 .40
210 Richard Matvichuk .12 .30
211 Sergei Krivokrasov .12 .30
212 Ted Drury .12 .30
213 Matthew Barnaby .12 .30
214 Denis Pederson .12 .30
215 John Vanbiesbrouck .20 .50
216 Brendan Shanahan .20 .50
217 Jocelyn Thibault .15 .40
218 Nelson Emerson .12 .30
219 Wayne Gretzky 1.25 3.00
220 Checklist .02 .10
221 Ramzi Abid RC .12 .30
222 Mark Bell RC .12 .30
223 Michael Henrich RC .12 .30
224 Vincent Lecavalier .40 1.00
225 Rico Fata .15 .40
226 Bryan Allen .12 .30
227 Daniel Tkaczuk .12 .30
228 Brad Stuart RC .12 .30
229 Derrick Walser RC .12 .30
230 Jonathan Cheechoo RC 3.00 8.00
231 Sergei Varlamov .12 .30
232 Scott Gomez RC 2.00 5.00
233 Jeff Heerema RC .12 .30
234 David Legwand .12 .30
235 Manny Malhotra .20 .50
236 Michael Rupp RC .15 .40
237 Alex Tanguay .15 .40
238 Mathieu Biron RC .15 .40
239 Bujar Amidovski RC .15 .40
240 Brian Finley RC .12 .30
241 Philippe Sauve RC .75 2.00
242 Jiri Fischer RC .15 .40

1998-99 Topps O-Pee-Chee Parallel

*1-220 VETS: 5X TO 12X BASIC CARDS
*221-242 ROOKIES: 1.5X TO 4X

1998-99 Topps Autographs

A1 Jason Allison 5.00 12.00
A2 Sergei Samsonov 5.00 12.00
A3 John LeClair 6.00 15.00
A4 Mattias Ohlund 4.00 10.00
A5 Jaromir Jagr 30.00 80.00
A6 Keith Tkachuk 6.00 15.00
A7 Patrik Elias 6.00 15.00
A8 Dominik Hasek 25.00 60.00
A9 Brian Leetch 5.00 12.00

1998-99 Topps Blast From The Past

1 Wayne Gretzky 12.00 30.00
2 Mark Messier 4.00 10.00
3 Ray Bourque 3.00 8.00
4 Patrick Roy 5.00 12.00
5 Grant Fuhr 3.00 8.00
6 Brett Hull 4.00 10.00
7 Gordie Howe 6.00 15.00
8 Stan Mikita 4.00 10.00
9 Bobby Hull 4.00 10.00
10 Phil Esposito 4.00 10.00

1998-99 Topps Blast From The Past Autographs

7 Gordie Howe 60.00 150.00
8 Stan Mikita 30.00 80.00
9 Bobby Hull 40.00 100.00
10 Phil Esposito 30.00 80.00

1998-99 Topps Board Members

B1 Chris Pronger 1.25 3.00
B2 Chris Chelios 1.25 3.00
B3 Brian Leetch 1.00 2.50
B4 Ray Bourque 2.00 5.00
B5 Mattias Ohlund .75 2.00
B6 Nicklas Lidstrom 1.50 4.00
B7 Sergei Zubov 1.00 2.50
B8 Scott Niedermayer 1.25 3.00
B9 Larry Murphy 1.00 2.50
B10 Sandis Ozolinsh .75 2.00
B11 Rob Blake 1.25 3.00
B12 Scott Stevens 1.25 3.00
B13 Derian Hatcher .75 2.00
B14 Kevin Hatcher .75 2.00
B15 Wade Redden .75 2.00

1998-99 Topps Ice Age 2000

COMPLETE SET (15) 8.00 15.00
I1 Paul Kariya .60 1.50
I2 Marco Sturm .20 .50
I3 Jarome Iginla .75 2.00
I4 Denis Pederson .20 .50
I5 Wade Redden .20 .50
I6 Jason Allison .20 .50
I7 Chris Pronger .50 1.25
I8 Peter Forsberg 1.50 4.00
I9 Saku Koivu .60 1.50
I10 Eric Lindros .60 1.50
I11 Sergei Samsonov .50 1.25
I12 Mattias Ohlund .50 1.25
I13 Joe Thornton 1.00 2.50
I14 Mike Johnson .20 .50
I15 Nikolai Khabibulin .50 1.25

1998-99 Topps Local Legends

COMPLETE SET (15) 30.00 60.00
L1 Peter Forsberg 2.50 6.00
L2 Mats Sundin 1.00 2.50
L3 Zigmund Palffy .75 2.00
L4 Jaromir Jagr 1.50 4.00
L5 Dominik Hasek 2.00 5.00
L6 Martin Brodeur 2.50 6.00
L7 Wayne Gretzky 8.00 20.00
L8 Patrick Roy 5.00 12.00
L9 Eric Lindros 1.00 2.50
L10 Joe Sakic 2.00 5.00
L11 Mark Messier 1.00 2.50
L12 Mike Modano 1.50 4.00
L13 Sergei Fedorov 1.50 4.00
L14 Pavel Bure 1.00 2.50
L15 Teemu Selanne 1.00 2.50

1998-99 Topps Mystery Finest Bronze

COMPLETE SET (20) 40.00 80.00
*BRONZE REF.: .7X TO 1.5X BASIC INSERTS
*GOLD: .8X TO 2X BASIC INSERTS
*GOLD REF.: 4X TO 8X BASIC INSERTS
*SILVER: .6X TO 1.5X BASIC INSERTS
*SILVER REF.: 1X TO 2.5X BASIC INSERTS
M1 Teemu Selanne 1.50 4.00
M2 Olaf Kolzig 1.25 3.00
M3 Pavel Bure 1.50 4.00
M4 Wayne Gretzky 8.00 20.00
M5 Mike Modano 2.50 6.00
M6 Jaromir Jagr 2.50 6.00
M7 Dominik Hasek 3.00 8.00
M8 Peter Forsberg 4.00 10.00
M9 Eric Lindros 1.50 4.00
M10 John LeClair 1.50 4.00
M11 Zigmund Palffy 1.25 3.00
M12 Martin Brodeur 4.00 10.00
M13 Keith Tkachuk 1.50 4.00
M14 Peter Bondra 1.25 3.00
M15 Nicklas Lidstrom 1.50 4.00
M16 Patrick Roy 6.00 15.00
M17 Chris Chelios 1.25 3.00
M18 Saku Koivu 1.50 4.00
M19 Mark Messier 1.50 4.00
M20 Joe Sakic 3.00 8.00

1998-99 Topps Mystery Finest Gold

M1 Teemu Selanne 2.50 6.00
M2 Olaf Kolzig 2.00 5.00
M3 Pavel Bure 2.50 6.00
M4 Wayne Gretzky 15.00 30.00
M5 Mike Modano 4.00 10.00
M6 Jaromir Jagr 4.00 10.00
M7 Dominik Hasek 5.00 12.00
M8 Peter Forsberg 5.00 12.00
M9 Eric Lindros 2.50 6.00
M10 John LeClair 2.50 6.00
M11 Zigmund Palffy 2.00 5.00
M12 Martin Brodeur 8.00 20.00
M13 Keith Tkachuk 2.50 6.00
M14 Peter Bondra 2.00 5.00
M15 Nicklas Lidstrom 3.00 8.00
M16 Patrick Roy 10.00 25.00
M17 Chris Chelios 2.00 5.00
M18 Saku Koivu 2.50 6.00
M19 Mark Messier 3.00 8.00
M20 Joe Sakic 6.00 15.00

1998-99 Topps Mystery Finest Silver

M1 Teemu Selanne 2.50 6.00
M2 Olaf Kolzig 2.00 5.00
M3 Pavel Bure 2.50 6.00
M4 Wayne Gretzky 15.00 40.00
M5 Mike Modano 3.00 8.00
M6 Jaromir Jagr 3.00 8.00
M7 Dominik Hasek 4.00 10.00
M8 Peter Forsberg 6.00 15.00
M9 Eric Lindros 2.50 6.00
M10 John LeClair 2.50 6.00
M11 Zigmund Palffy 2.00 5.00
M12 Martin Brodeur 8.00 20.00
M13 Keith Tkachuk 2.50 6.00
M14 Peter Bondra 2.00 5.00
M15 Nicklas Lidstrom 2.50 6.00
M16 Patrick Roy 10.00 25.00
M17 Chris Chelios 2.00 5.00
M18 Saku Koivu 2.00 5.00
M19 Mark Messier 2.50 6.00
M20 Joe Sakic 5.00 12.00

1998-99 Topps Season's Best

COMPLETE SET (30) 15.00 40.00
SB1 Dominik Hasek 1.50 4.00
SB2 Martin Brodeur 2.00 5.00
SB3 Ed Belfour .75 2.00
SB4 Curtis Joseph .75 2.00
SB5 Jeff Hackett .60 1.50
SB6 Tom Barrasso .60 1.50
SB7 Mike Johnson .30 .75
SB8 Sergei Samsonov .60 1.50
SB9 Patrik Elias .60 1.50
SB10 Patrick Marleau .60 1.50
SB11 Mattias Ohlund .60 1.50
SB12 Marco Sturm .30 .75
SB13 Teemu Selanne .75 2.00
SB14 Peter Bondra .60 1.50
SB15 Pavel Bure .75 2.00
SB16 John LeClair 1.00 2.50
SB17 Zigmund Palffy .60 1.50
SB18 Keith Tkachuk .75 2.00
SB19 Jaromir Jagr 1.25 3.00
SB20 Wayne Gretzky 4.00 10.00
SB21 Peter Forsberg 1.25 3.00
SB22 Ron Francis .60 1.50
SB23 Adam Oates .60 1.50
SB24 Jozef Stumpel .60 1.50
SB25 Chris Pronger .60 1.50
SB26 Larry Murphy .60 1.50
SB27 Jason Allison .30 .75
SB28 John LeClair .75 2.00
SB29 Randy McKay .30 .75
SB30 Dainius Zubrus .30 .75

1999-00 Topps Arena Giveaways

COMPLETE SET (30) 15.00 30.00
ANALK Ladislav Kohn .20 .50
ANAOT Oleg Tverdovsky .20 .50
ATLMJ Matt Johnson .20 .50
ATLPS Patrik Stefan .40 1.00
BOSJG Jonathan Girard .20 .50
BOSJT Joe Thornton 1.50 4.00
BUFMA Maxim Afinogenov .40 1.00
BUFMB Martin Biron .40 1.00
CALDG Denis Gauthier .20 .50
CALRR Robyn Regehr .20 .50
CARBB Bates Battaglia .20 .50
CARDT David Tanabe .20 .50
CHIED Eric Daze .20 .50
CHIJD J-P Dumont .20 .50
COLAT Alex Tanguay .40 1.00
COLMD Marc Denis .40 1.00
DALBM Brenden Morrow .75 2.00
DALJS Jon Sim .20 .50
DETJF Jiri Fischer .20 .50
DETMD Mathieu Dandenault .20 .50
EDMGL Georges Laraque .40 1.00
EDMPC Paul Comrie .20 .50
FLOIN Ivan Novoseltsev .20 .50
FLOOK Oleg Kvasha .20 .50
LAFK Frantisek Kaberle .20 .50
LAJS Jamie Storr .40 1.00
NASDL David Legwand .20 .50
NASTV Tomas Vokoun .40 1.00
NJPE Patrik Elias .20 .50
NJSG Scott Gomez .20 .50
NYIOJ Olli Jokinen .20 .50
NYIRL Roberto Luongo 2.00 5.00
NYRKJ Kim Johnsson .20 .50

NYRMY Mike York .20 .50
OTTMF Mike Fisher .20 .50
OTTMH Marian Hossa .40 1.00
PHORS Radoslav Suchy .20 .50
PHOTL Trevor Letowski .20 .50
PITAF Andrew Ference .20 .50
PITJH Jan Hrdina .20 .50
SJBS Brad Stuart .20 .50
SJMS Marco Sturm .20 .50
STLJH Jochen Hecht .20 .50
STLTN Tyson Nash .20 .50
TBPM Paul Mara .20 .50
TBVL Vincent Lecavalier 1.25 3.00
TORNA Nikolai Antropov .40 1.00
TORTK Tomas Kaberle .20 .50
VANEJ Ed Jovanovski .20 .50
VANSK Steve Kariya .40 1.00
WASJH Jeff Halpern .20 .50
WASRZ Richard Zednik .20 .50

1999-00 Topps

COMPLETE SET (275) 25.00 50.00
COMP.SET w/MMs (330) 60.00 120.00
1 Joe Sakic .30 .75
2 Alexei Yashin .12 .30
3 Paul Kariya .15 .40
4 Keith Tkachuk .15 .40
5 Jaromir Jagr .50 1.25
6 Mike Modano .25 .60
7 Eric Lindros .25 .60
8 Zigmund Palffy .15 .40
9 Dominik Hasek .25 .60
10 Pavel Bure .15 .40
11 Ray Bourque .25 .60
12 Peter Forsberg .30 .75
13 Al MacInnis .20 .50
14 Steve Yzerman .40 1.00
15 Mats Sundin .15 .40
16 Patrick Roy .40 1.00
17 Teemu Selanne .30 .75
18 Keith Primeau .12 .30
19 John LeClair .15 .40
20 Martin Brodeur .40 1.00
21 Joe Thornton .25 .60
22 Rob Blake .15 .40
23 Ron Francis .20 .50
24 Grant Fuhr .25 .60
25 Nicklas Lidstrom .15 .40
26 Vladimir Orszagh RC .10 .25
27 Glen Wesley .10 .25
28 Adam Deadmarsh .10 .25
29 Zdeno Chara .15 .40
30 Brian Leetch .12 .30
31 Valeri Bure .10 .25
32 Ryan Smyth .12 .30
33 Jean-Sebastien Aubin .12 .30
34 Dave Reid .10 .25
35 Ed Jovanovski .12 .30
36 Anders Eriksson .10 .25
37 Mike Ricci .10 .25
38 Todd Bertuzzi .12 .30
39 Shawn Bates .10 .25
40 Kip Miller .10 .25
41 Jozef Stumpel .10 .25
42 Jeremy Roenick .25 .60
43 Todd Marchant .10 .25
44 Josh Holden .10 .25
45 Rob Niedermayer .10 .25
46 Cory Sarich .10 .25
47 Nikolai Khabibulin .12 .30
48 Marty McInnis .10 .25
49 Marty Reasoner .10 .25
50 Gary Roberts .10 .25
51 Manny Malhotra .12 .30
52 Adam Foote .12 .30
53 Luc Robitaille .15 .40
54 Bryan Marchment .12 .30
55 Mark Janssens .10 .25
56 Steve Heinze .10 .25
57 Cory Stillman .10 .25
58 Guy Hebert .12 .30
59 Mike Richter .15 .40
60 Jamie Langenbrunner .10 .25
61 Wade Redden .10 .25
62 Steve Smith .10 .25
63 Daniil Markov .10 .25
64 Erik Rasmussen .10 .25
65 Glen Murray .10 .25
66 Alexei Kovalev .12 .30
67 Peter Bondra .15 .40
68 Dimitri Khristich .10 .25
69 Sami Kapanen .10 .25
70 Tom Poti .10 .25
71 Trevor Linden .15 .40
72 Tomas Vokoun .15 .40
73 Steve Webb .10 .25
74 Jarome Iginla .20 .50
75 Scott Mellanby .10 .25
76 Mattias Ohlund .10 .25
77 Steve Konowalchuk .10 .25
78 Bryan Berard .10 .25
79 Chris Pronger .15 .40
80 Teppo Numminen .10 .25
81 John MacLean .10 .25
82 Jeff Hackett .12 .30
83 Ray Whitney .10 .25
84 Chris Osgood .15 .40
85 Doug Zmolek .10 .25
86 Curtis Brown .10 .25
87 Reid Simpson .10 .25
88 Milan Hejduk .12 .30
89 Donald Audette .10 .25
90 Saku Koivu .15 .40
91 Martin Straka .10 .25
92 Mark Messier .30 .75
93 Richard Zednik .10 .25
94 Curtis Joseph .20 .50
95 Colin Forbes .10 .25
96 Jeff Friesen .12 .30
97 Eric Brewer .10 .25
98 Darius Kasparaitis .12 .30
99 Marian Hossa .15 .40
100 Petr Sykora .12 .30
101 Vladimir Malakhov .10 .25
102 Jamie Storr .10 .25
103 Doug Gilmour .20 .50
104 Doug Weight .15 .40
105 Derian Hatcher .12 .30
106 Chris Drury .12 .30
107 Arturs Irbe .12 .30
108 Fred Brathwaite .12 .30
109 Jason Allison .12 .30
110 Roman Hamrlik .10 .25
111 Rico Fata .10 .25
112 Janne Niinimaa .10 .25
113 Kenny Jonsson .10 .25
114 Marco Sturm .10 .25
115 Steve Thomas .10 .25
116 Garth Snow .12 .30
117 Rick Tocchet .12 .30
118 Jean-Marc Pelletier .10 .25
119 Bobby Holik .10 .25
120 Sergei Fedorov .25 .60
121 J-P Dumont .10 .25
122 Jason Woolley .10 .25
123 James Patrick .10 .25
124 Blake Sloan .12 .30
125 Marcus Nilsson .10 .25
126 Shayne Corson .10 .25
127 Tom Fitzgerald .12 .30
128 Brian Rolston .12 .30
129 Ron Tugnutt .12 .30
130 Mark Recchi .20 .50
131 Matthew Barnaby .10 .25
132 Olaf Kolzig .15 .40
133 Paul Mara .10 .25
134 Patrick Marleau .15 .40
135 Magnus Arvedson .10 .25
136 Felix Potvin .25 .60
137 Bill Guerin .15 .40
138 Brett Hull .30 .75
139 Vitali Yachmenev .10 .25
140 Ruslan Salei .10 .25
141 Mark Parrish .10 .25
142 Randy Cunneyworth .10 .25
143 Damian Rhodes .10 .25
144 Daniel Briere .12 .30
145 Craig Conroy .10 .25
146 Sergei Gonchar .10 .25
147 Vincent Lecavalier .15 .40
148 Adam Graves .12 .30
149 Doug Bodger .10 .25
150 Jeff O'Neill .10 .25
151 Darby Hendrickson .10 .25
152 Sergei Samsonov .12 .30
153 Ed Belfour .15 .40
154 Robert Svehla .10 .25
155 Cliff Ronning .10 .25
156 Brendan Morrison .12 .30
157 Daniel Alfredsson .15 .40
158 Eric Desjardins .10 .25
159 Mike Vernon .12 .30
160 Vadim Sharifijanov .10 .25
161 Jaroslav Svejkovsky .10 .25
162 Michael Peca .12 .30
163 Shane Willis .10 .25
164 Sandis Ozolinsh .10 .25
165 Mathieu Dandenault .12 .30
166 Martin Rucinsky .10 .25
167 Scott Stevens .15 .40
168 Sami Salo .12 .30
169 Tom Barrasso .15 .40
170 Chris Gratton .10 .25
171 Markus Naslund .15 .40
172 Mike Johnson .12 .30
173 Bob Boughner .10 .25
174 Todd Simpson .12 .30
175 Fredrik Olausson .10 .25
176 Jocelyn Thibault .12 .30
177 Juha Ylonen .10 .25
178 Brad Bombardir .10 .25
179 Jan Hrdina .12 .30
180 Adrian Aucoin .12 .30
181 Mike Eagles .12 .30
182 Petr Nedved .10 .25
183 Rem Murray .10 .25
184 Mikael Renberg .10 .25
185 Mike Eastwood .10 .25
186 Byron Dafoe .12 .30
187 Tony Amonte .12 .30
188 Darren McCarty .10 .25
189 Sergei Krivokrasov .10 .25
190 Dave Lowry .10 .25
191 Michal Handzus .10 .25
192 Tie Domi .12 .30
193 Brian Holzinger .10 .25
194 Jason Arnott .12 .30
195 Jose Theodore .15 .40
196 Brendan Shanahan .15 .40
197 Derek Morris .10 .25
198 Steve Rucchin .10 .25
199 Kevin Hodson .10 .25
200 Oleg Kvasha .10 .25
201 John Vanbiesbrouck .15 .40
202 Adam Oates .15 .40
203 Anson Carter .12 .30
204 Sebastien Bordeleau .10 .25
205 Pavol Demitra .20 .50
206 Owen Nolan .15 .40
207 Pavel Rosa .10 .25
208 Petr Svoboda .12 .30
209 Tomas Kaberle .10 .25
210 Claude Lapointe .12 .30
211 Todd Harvey .10 .25
212 Trent McCleary .10 .25
213 Vyacheslav Kozlov .10 .25
214 Marc Denis .12 .30
215 Joe Nieuwendyk .12 .30
216 Kelly Buchberger .10 .25
217 Tommy Albelin .10 .25
218 Kyle McLaren .10 .25
219 Chris Chelios .15 .40
220 Joel Bouchard .10 .25
221 Mats Lindgren .10 .25
222 Jyrki Lumme .10 .25
223 Pierre Turgeon .12 .30
224 Bill Muckalt .10 .25
225 Antti Aalto .10 .25
226 Jere Lehtinen .12 .30
227 Theo Fleury .20 .50
228 Dmitri Mironov .10 .25
229 Scott Niedermayer .15 .40
230 Sean Burke .20 .50
231 Eric Daze .12 .30
232 Alexei Zhitnik .10 .25
233 Christian Matte .10 .25
234 Patrik Elias .15 .40
235 Alexandre Korolyuk .10 .25
236 Sergei Berezin .10 .25
237 Ray Ferraro .10 .25
238 Rod Brind'Amour .15 .40
239 Darcy Tucker .10 .25
240 Darryl Sydor .12 .30
241 Mike Dunham .10 .25
242 Marc Bergevin .10 .25
243 Ray Sheppard .10 .25
244 Miroslav Satan .12 .30
245 Andreas Dackell .10 .25
246 Mike Grier .10 .25
247 Alexei Zhamnov .10 .25
248 David Legwand .10 .25
249 Daniel Tkaczuk .10 .25
250 Roberto Luongo .25 .60
251 Simon Gagne .15 .40
252 Jamie Lundmark .12 .30
253 Alexandre Giroux RC .10 .25
254 Dusty Jamieson RC .12 .30
255 Jamie Chamberlain RC .12 .30
256 Radim Vrbata RC 1.50 4.00
257 Scott Cameron RC .12 .30
258 Simon LaJeunesse RC .30 .75
259 Tim Connolly .10 .25
260 Kris Beech .10 .25
261 Brian Finley .15 .40
262 Alex Auld RC .30 .75
263 Martin Grenier RC .12 .30
264 Sheldon Keefe RC .30 .75
265 Justin Mapletoft RC .12 .30
266 Edward Hill RC .12 .30
267 Nolan Yonkman RC .15 .40
268 Oleg Saprykin RC .15 .40
269 Branislav Mezei RC .10 .25
270 Chris Kelly RC .12 .30
271 Pavel Brendl RC .75 2.00
272 Brett Lysak RC .12 .30
273 Matt Carkner RC .12 .30
274 Luke Sellars RC .15 .40
275 Brad Ralph RC .12 .30
276A Ray Bourque MM .50 1.25
276B Ray Bourque MM
1996 All-Star MVP .50 1.25
276C Ray Bourque MM
5-time Norris Winner .50 1.25
276D Ray Bourque MM
1000 NHL Points .50 1.25
276E Ray Bourque MM
1980 Calder Trophy .50 1.25
277A Peter Forsberg MM .60 1.50
277B Peter Forsberg MM
3 All-Star Games .60 1.50
277C Peter Forsberg MM
1994 Gold Medal .60 1.50
277D Peter Forsberg MM
1994 Gold Medal Goal .60 1.50
277E Peter Forsberg MM
1996 Stanley Cup .60 1.50
278A Joe Nieuwendyk MM .25 .60
278B Joe Nieuwendyk MM
4 All-Star Games .25 .60
278C Joe Nieuwendyk MM
1999 Stanley Cup .25 .60
278D Joe Nieuwendyk MM
1999 Conn Smythe Trophy .25 .60
278E Joe Nieuwendyk MM
1988 Calder Trophy .25 .60
279A Dominik Hasek MM .50 1.25
279B Dominik Hasek MM
5-time Vezina Winner .50 1.25
279C Dominik Hasek MM
2-time Pearson Winner .50 1.25
279D Dominik Hasek MM
4 All-Star Games .50 1.25
279E Dominik Hasek MM
1998 Gold Medal .50 1.25
280A Jaromir Jagr MM 1.00 2.50
280B Jaromir Jagr MM
1999 Hart Trophy 1.00 2.50
280C Jaromir Jagr MM
8 All-Star Games 1.00 2.50
280D Jaromir Jagr MM
3-time Scoring Leader 1.00 2.50
280E Jaromir Jagr MM
2-time Stanley Cup Winner 1.00 2.50
281A Paul Kariya MM .30 .75
281B Paul Kariya MM
3 All-Star Games .30 .75
281C Paul Kariya MM
50 goals 1995-96 .30 .75
281D Paul Kariya MM
1994 Silver Medal .30 .75
281E Paul Kariya MM
1993 NCAA Champ .30 .75
282A Eric Lindros MM .50 1.25
282B Eric Lindros MM
1992 Silver Medal .50 1.25
282C Eric Lindros MM
1995 Hart Trophy .50 1.25
282D Eric Lindros MM
1995 Pearson Award .50 1.25
282E Eric Lindros MM
5 All-Star Games .50 1.25
283A Mark Messier MM .60 1.50
283B Mark Messier MM
6-time Stanley Cup Winner .60 1.50
283C Mark Messier MM
13 All-Star Games .60 1.50
283D Mark Messier MM
2-time Hart Winner .60 1.50
283E Mark Messier MM
2-time Pearson Winner .60 1.50
284A Patrick Roy MM .75 2.00
284B Patrick Roy MM
8 All-Star Games .75 2.00
284C Patrick Roy MM
3-time Vezina Winner .75 2.00
284D Patrick Roy MM
2-time Conn Smythe Winner .75 2.00
284E Patrick Roy MM
Playoff Wins Leader .75 2.00
285A Joe Sakic MM .60 1.50
285B Joe Sakic MM
7 All-Star Games .60 1.50
285C Joe Sakic MM
1996 Stanley Cup .60 1.50
285D Joe Sakic MM
50 goals 1995-96 .60 1.50
285E Joe Sakic MM
1996 Conn Smythe Trophy .60 1.50
286A Steve Yzerman MM .75 2.00
286B Steve Yzerman MM
8 All-Star Games .75 2.00
286C Steve Yzerman MM
1989 Pearson Award .75 2.00
286D Steve Yzerman MM
1998 Conn Smythe Trophy .75 2.00
286E Steve Yzerman MM
2-time Stanley Cup Winner .75 2.00

1999-00 Topps All-Topps

COMPLETE SET (15) 20.00 40.00
AT1 Dominik Hasek 1.50 4.00
AT2 Martin Brodeur 2.00 5.00
AT3 Ray Bourque 1.25 3.00
AT4 Al MacInnis .75 2.00
AT5 Nicklas Lidstrom .75 2.00
AT6 Brian Leetch .75 2.00
AT7 John LeClair 1.00 2.50
AT8 Paul Kariya .75 2.00
AT9 Keith Tkachuk .75 2.00
AT10 Eric Lindros 1.25 3.00
AT11 Peter Forsberg 2.00 5.00
AT12 Steve Yzerman 4.00 10.00
AT13 Jaromir Jagr 1.25 3.00
AT14 Teemu Selanne .75 2.00
AT15 Pavel Bure 1.00 2.50

1999-00 Topps Autographs

TA1 Joe Sakic 12.00 30.00
TA2 Dominik Hasek 15.00 40.00
TA3 Curtis Joseph 10.00 25.00
TA4 Alexei Yashin 8.00 20.00
TA5 Mats Sundin 15.00 40.00
TA6 Chris Drury 8.00 20.00
TA7 Milan Hejduk 10.00 25.00
TA8 Marian Hossa 10.00 25.00
TA9 Vincent Lecavalier 10.00 25.00
TA10 Joe Thornton 12.00 30.00

1999-00 Topps A-Men

COMPLETE SET (6) 6.00 12.00
AM1 Jaromir Jagr .75 2.00
AM2 Peter Forsberg 1.25 3.00
AM3 Paul Kariya 1.25 3.00
AM4 Teemu Selanne 1.25 3.00
AM5 Joe Sakic 1.00 2.50
AM6 Eric Lindros .75 2.00

1999-00 Topps Fantastic Finishers

COMPLETE SET (6) 3.00 8.00
FF1 Teemu Selanne .50 1.25
FF2 Jaromir Jagr .75 2.00
FF3 Tony Amonte .40 1.00
FF4 Alexei Yashin .40 1.00
FF5 John LeClair .60 1.50
FF6 Joe Sakic 1.00 2.50

1999-00 Topps Ice Futures

COMPLETE SET (6) 1.25 3.00
IF1 Mark Parrish .25 .60
IF2 Chris Drury .50 1.25
IF3 Bill Muckalt .25 .60
IF4 Marian Hossa .25 .60
IF5 Milan Hejduk .50 1.25
IF6 Brendan Morrison .50 1.25

1999-00 Topps Ice Masters

COMPLETE SET (20) 40.00 80.00
IM1 Joe Sakic 2.00 5.00
IM2 Dominik Hasek 2.00 5.00
IM3 Eric Lindros 1.50 4.00
IM4 Jaromir Jagr 1.50 4.00
IM5 John LeClair 1.25 3.00
IM6 Mats Sundin 1.25 3.00
IM7 Ray Bourque 1.50 4.00
IM8 Mike Modano 1.50 4.00
IM9 Peter Forsberg 2.50 6.00
IM10 Brian Leetch 1.25 3.00
IM11 Martin Brodeur 2.50 6.00
IM12 Al MacInnis 1.00 2.50
IM13 Paul Kariya 1.25 3.00
IM14 Alexei Yashin 1.00 2.50
IM15 Steve Yzerman 5.00 12.00
IM16 Ed Belfour 1.25 3.00
IM17 Keith Tkachuk 1.25 3.00
IM18 Patrick Roy 5.00 12.00
IM19 Nicklas Lidstrom 1.25 3.00
IM20 Teemu Selanne 1.25 3.00

1999-00 Topps Now Starring

COMPLETE SET (15) 10.00 20.00
NS1 Anson Carter .75 2.00
NS2 Marian Hossa .75 2.00
NS3 Michael Peca .75 2.00
NS4 Kenny Jonsson .60 1.50
NS5 Petr Sykora .60 1.50
NS6 Chris Drury .60 1.50
NS7 Byron Dafoe .75 2.00
NS8 Wade Redden .60 1.50
NS9 Jeff Friesen .60 1.50
NS10 Jamie Langenbrunner .60 1.50
NS11 Mike Johnson .60 1.50
NS12 Keith Primeau .60 1.50
NS13 Vincent Lecavalier .75 2.00
NS14 Mattias Ohlund .75 2.00
NS15 Pavol Demitra .75 2.00

1999-00 Topps Positive Performers

COMPLETE SET (6) 2.00 5.00
PP1 Alexander Karpovtsev .15 .40
PP2 John LeClair .60 1.50
PP3 Eric Lindros .75 2.00
PP4 Magnus Arvedson .15 .40
PP5 Al MacInnis .40 1.00
PP6 Jere Lehtinen .40 1.00

1999-00 Topps Postmasters

COMPLETE SET (6) 5.00 12.00
PM1 Dominik Hasek 1.00 2.50
PM2 Byron Dafoe .40 1.00
PM3 Nikolai Khabibulin .40 1.00
PM4 Ed Belfour .50 1.25
PM5 Patrick Roy 2.50 6.00
PM6 Martin Brodeur 1.25 3.00

1999-00 Topps Stanley Cup Heroes

COMPLETE SET (20) 50.00 120.00
*REFRACTORS: 1.5X TO 4X BASIC INSERTS
SC1 Mario Lemieux 6.00 15.00
SC2 Mike Bossy 4.00 10.00
SC3 Guy Lafleur 4.00 10.00
SC4 Rocket Richard 6.00 15.00
SC5 Lanny McDonald 2.00 5.00
SC6 Frank Mahovlich 2.00 5.00
SC7 Steve Yzerman 6.00 15.00
SC8 Mark Messier 4.00 10.00
SC9 Patrick Roy 6.00 15.00
SC10 Joe Sakic 4.00 10.00
SC11 Jaromir Jagr 4.00 10.00
SC12 Peter Forsberg 3.00 8.00
SC13 Claude Lemieux 1.50 4.00
SC14 Martin Brodeur 5.00 12.00
SC15 Brian Leetch 2.00 5.00
SC16 Mike Richter 3.00 8.00
SC17 Theo Fleury 2.00 5.00
SC18 Chris Osgood 4.00 10.00
SC19 Ed Belfour 4.00 10.00
SC20 Joe Nieuwendyk 2.00 5.00

1999-00 Topps Stanley Cup Heroes Autographs

COMPLETE SET (6)
SCA1 Mario Lemieux 100.00 200.00
SCA2 Mike Bossy 40.00 80.00
SCA3 Guy Lafleur 40.00 100.00
SCA4 Maurice Richard 150.00 300.00
SCA5 Lanny McDonald 30.00 60.00
SCA6 Frank Mahovlich 30.00 60.00

1999-00 Topps Top of the World

COMPLETE SET (20) 30.00 80.00
TW1 Teemu Selanne 2.50 6.00
TW2 Saku Koivu 1.25 3.00
TW3 Jere Lehtinen 1.25 3.00
TW4 Peter Forsberg 2.50 6.00
TW5 Mats Sundin 1.50 4.00
TW6 Nicklas Lidstrom 2.00 5.00
TW7 Alexei Yashin 1.25 3.00
TW8 Nikolai Khabibulin 1.25 3.00
TW9 Pavel Bure 2.50 6.00
TW10 John LeClair 1.25 3.00
TW11 Keith Tkachuk 1.25 3.00
TW12 Mike Modano 4.00 10.00
TW13 Paul Kariya 1.50 4.00
TW14 Joe Sakic 4.00 10.00
TW15 Martin Brodeur 6.00 15.00
TW16 Dominik Hasek 2.50 6.00
TW17 Jaromir Jagr 4.00 10.00
TW18 Peter Bondra 1.25 3.00
TW19 Olaf Kolzig 1.25 3.00
TW20 Marco Sturm 1.25 3.00

2000 Topps AS Sittler

1 Darryl Sittler 1.20 3.00

2000-01 Topps Promos

COMPLETE SET (6) .60 1.50
PP1 Mariusz Czerkawski .08 .20
PP2 Sami Kapanen .08 .20
PP3 Tommy Salo .20 .50
PP4 Radek Bonk .08 .20
PP5 Pat Verbeek .08 .20
PP6 Luc Robitaille .20 .50

2000-01 Topps

COMPLETE SET (330) 15.00 30.00
1 Jaromir Jagr .50 1.25
2 Patrick Roy .40 1.00
3 Paul Kariya .15 .40
4 Mats Sundin .15 .40
5 Ron Francis .20 .50
6 Pavel Bure .15 .40
7 John LeClair .15 .40
8 Olaf Kolzig .15 .40
9 Chris Pronger .15 .40
10 Jeremy Roenick .25 .60
11 Owen Nolan .15 .40
12 Theo Fleury .20 .50
13 Zigmund Palffy .15 .40
14 Patrik Stefan .12 .30
15 Jarome Iginla .20 .50
16 Joe Thornton .25 .60
17 Tony Amonte .12 .30
18 Mike Modano .25 .60
19 Alexander Mogilny .12 .30
20 Mark Messier .30 .75
21 Dominik Hasek .25 .60
22 Steve Yzerman .40 1.00
23 Marian Hossa .15 .40
24 David Legwand .15 .40
25 Jose Theodore .15 .40
26 Vincent Lecavalier .15 .40
27 Mike Ricci .10 .25
28 Scott Stevens .15 .40
29 Kevin Weekes .10 .25
30 Sean Burke .10 .25
31 Alexei Kovalev .12 .30
32 Trevor Linden .15 .40
33 Joe Juneau .10 .25
34 Niklas Sundstrom .10 .25
35 Dan Cloutier .12 .30
36 Drake Berehowsky .10 .25
37 Jonas Hoglund .10 .25
38 Sami Kapanen .10 .25
39 Matthew Barnaby .10 .25
40 Anson Carter .12 .30
41 Miroslav Satan .10 .25
42 Mark Recchi .20 .50
43 Pavol Demitra .20 .50
44 Peter Bondra .15 .40
45 Mike Richter .15 .40
46 Guy Hebert .12 .30
47 Robert Svehla .10 .25
48 Martin Skoula .12 .30
49 Ed Belfour .15 .40
50 Alexei Zhamnov .10 .25
51 Fred Brathwaite .12 .30
52 Andrew Brunette .10 .25
53 Byron Dafoe .12 .30
54 Claude Lemieux .12 .30
55 Sergei Berezin .10 .25
56 Felix Potvin .25 .60
57 Rod Brind'Amour .15 .40
58 Doug Gilmour .20 .50
59 Brett Hull .30 .75
60 Nicklas Lidstrom .15 .40
61 Mike York .10 .25
62 Al MacInnis .20 .50
63 Brian Boucher .12 .30
64 Teemu Selanne .30 .75
65 Mike Vernon .12 .30
66 Bill Guerin .15 .40
67 Ray Bourque .25 .60
68 Bryan McCabe .10 .25
69 Ray Ferraro .10 .25
70 Stephane Fiset .10 .25
71 Sergei Gonchar .10 .25
72 Mattias Ohlund .10 .25
73 Todd Marchant .10 .25
74 Derek Morris .10 .25
75 Brian Rolston .12 .30
76 Damian Rhodes .10 .25
77 Tom Drury .10 .25
78 Curtis Joseph .20 .50
79 Teppo Numminen .10 .25
80 Petr Nedved .10 .25
81 Doug Weight .15 .40
82 Arturs Irbe .10 .25
83 Chris Osgood .15 .40
84 Chris Gratton .10 .25
85 Jocelyn Thibault .12 .30
86 Oleg Tverdovsky .10 .25
87 Derian Hatcher .12 .30
88 Ray Whitney .10 .25
89 Saku Koivu .15 .40
90 Cliff Ronning .10 .25
91 Claude Lapointe .10 .25
92 Fredrik Modin .10 .25
93 Chris Simon .10 .25
94 Todd Harvey .12 .30
95 Martin Rucinsky .10 .25
96 Valeri Bure .10 .25
97 Brad Isbister .12 .30
98 Daymond Langkow .10 .25
99 Todd Bertuzzi .12 .30
100 Roman Turek .12 .30
101 Kenny Jonsson .10 .25
102 Mike Dunham .10 .25
103 Rob Blake .15 .40
104 Darius Kasparaitis .12 .30
105 Daniel Alfredsson .15 .40
106 Bobby Holik .10 .25
107 Tommy Salo .12 .30
108 Sergei Samsonov .12 .30
109 Joe Sakic .30 .75
110 Bryan Smolinski .10 .25
111 Luc Robitaille .15 .40
112 Ryan Smyth .12 .30
113 Eric Daze .12 .30
114 Mariusz Czerkawski .10 .25
115 Brendan Shanahan .15 .40
116 Brian Rafalski .10 .25
117 Mark Parrish .10 .25
118 Jamie Langenbrunner .10 .25
119 Peter Forsberg .30 .75
120 Phil Housley .12 .30
121 Jeff O'Neill .12 .30
122 Stu Barnes .12 .30
123 Glen Murray .12 .30
124 Jeff Hackett .12 .30
125 Sergei Fedorov .25 .60
126 Kyle McLaren .10 .25
127 Michael Nylander .10 .25
128 Sergei Zubov .12 .30
129 Steve Rucchin .10 .25
130 Nelson Emerson .10 .25
131 Martin Brodeur .40 1.00
132 Mike Grier .10 .25
133 Paul Coffey .15 .40
134 Radek Bonk .12 .30
135 Marc Savard .10 .25
136 Milan Hejduk .12 .30
137 Curtis Brown .10 .25
138 Viktor Kozlov .12 .30
139 Jason Woolley .10 .25
140 Adam Foote .12 .30
141 Radek Dvorak .12 .30
142 Jason Arnott .12 .30
143 German Titov .12 .30
144 Scott Thornton .12 .30
145 Brendan Morrison .12 .30
146 Keith Tkachuk .15 .40
147 Patrik Elias .15 .40
148 Donald Audette .10 .25
149 Jochen Hecht .10 .25
150 Dave Scatchard .10 .25
151 Tom Barrasso .12 .30
152 Adam Deadmarsh .10 .25
153 Brian Leetch .12 .30
154 Sergei Krivokrasov .10 .25
155 Randy Robitaille .10 .25
156 Petr Sykora .12 .30
157 Dave Andreychuk .15 .40
158 Mathieu Biron .10 .25
159 Sergei Zholtok .10 .25
160 Shawn McEachern .10 .25
161 Steve Shields .10 .25
162 Petr Svoboda .10 .25
163 Nikolai Antropov .12 .30
164 Michal Handzus .10 .25
165 Martin Straka .12 .30
166 Shane Doan .12 .30
167 Eric Desjardins .10 .25
168 Peter Schaefer .10 .25
169 Adam Oates .15 .40
170 Scott Niedermayer .15 .40
171 Dallas Drake .10 .25
172 Josh Green .10 .25
173 Mike Sillinger .10 .25
174 Adam Graves .12 .30
175 Lubos Bartecko .12 .30
176 Steve Konowalchuk .10 .25
177 Jozef Stumpel .10 .25
178 Vincent Damphousse .12 .30
179 Tomas Kaberle .10 .25
180 Maxim Afinogenov .10 .25
181 Marty McInnis .12 .30
182 Chris Chelios .15 .40
183 Joe Nieuwendyk .12 .30
184 Petr Buzek .10 .25
185 Calle Johansson .10 .25
186 Jeff Friesen .10 .25
187 Paul Mara .10 .25
188 Markus Naslund .15 .40
189 Scott Young .10 .25
190 Trevor Letowski .10 .25
191 Steve Thomas .10 .25
192 Martin Biron .10 .25
193 Jason Allison .12 .30
194 Bob Probert .15 .40
195 Jere Lehtinen .12 .30
196 Tom Poti .10 .25
197 Eric Lindros .25 .60
198 Rob Niedermayer .12 .30
199 Gary Roberts .10 .25
200 Richard Zednik .10 .25
201 Dainius Zubrus .10 .25
202 Tom Fitzgerald .10 .25
203 Scott Gomez .12 .30
204 Travis Green .10 .25
205 Pierre Turgeon .12 .30
206 Ed Jovanovski .12 .30
207 Trevor Kidd .10 .25
208 Jan Hrdina .10 .25
209 Valeri Zelepukin .10 .25
210 Vaclav Prospal .10 .25
211 Matt Cullen .10 .25
212 Karlis Skrastins .10 .25
213 Robyn Regehr .10 .25
214 Darren McCarty .10 .25
215 John Madden .12 .30
216 Scott Mellanby .10 .25
217 Tim Connolly .10 .25
218 Pat Verbeek .12 .30
219 Richard Matvichuk .10 .25
220 Rick Tocchet .12 .30
221 Jan Hlavac .10 .25
222 Jeff Halpern .10 .25
223 Patrick Marleau .15 .40
224 Robert Lang .10 .25
225 Wade Redden .10 .25
226 Stephane Richer .10 .25
227 Kim Johnsson .10 .25
228 Greg Adams .10 .25
229 Alex Tanguay .12 .30
230 Andre Savage .10 .25
231 Slava Kozlov .10 .25
232 Steve Sullivan .10 .25
233 Alexander Selivanov .10 .25
234 Tommy Westlund .10 .25
235 Darcy Tucker .10 .25
236 Simon Gagne .15 .40
237 Brad Stuart .10 .25
238 Jean-Sebastien Aubin .12 .30
239 Mike Johnson .10 .25
240 Shayne Corson .10 .25
241 Michael Peca .12 .30
242 Keith Primeau .12 .30
243 Martin Lapointe .12 .30
244 Tie Domi .12 .30
245 Janne Niinimaa .10 .25
246 Brenden Morrow .12 .30
247 Sandis Ozolinsh .10 .25
248 Ron Tugnutt .12 .30
249 Andrei Nazarov .10 .25
250 Bates Battaglia .10 .25
251A Dan Sylvester .10 .25
252A Hal Gill .10 .25
253A Vladimir Tsyplakov .10 .25
254A Sean Hill .10 .25
255A Michal Grosek .10 .25
256A Darryl Sydor .12 .30
257A Igor Larionov .15 .40
258A Jaroslav Spacek .10 .25
259A Mattias Norstrom .10 .25
260A Ladislav Kohn .10 .25
261A Patric Kjellberg .10 .25
262A Marty Reasoner .10 .25
263A Zdeno Chara .15 .40
264A Mathieu Schneider .10 .25
265A John Vanbiesbrouck .15 .40
266A Jyrki Lumme .10 .25
267A Janne Laukkanen .10 .25
268A Alexander Korolyuk .10 .25
269A Pavel Kubina .10 .25
270A Ulf Dahlen .10 .25
271 Roberto Luongo .25 .60
272 Harold Druken .10 .25
273 Marc Denis .12 .30
274 Oleg Saprykin .10 .25
275 Glen Metropolit .10 .25
276 Mark Eaton .10 .25
277 Dmitri Yakushin .10 .25
278 Scott Hannan .10 .25
279 Dave Tanabe .10 .25
280 Jiri Fischer .10 .25
281 Dmitri Nabokov .10 .25
282 Ivan Novoseltsev .10 .25
283 Manny Fernandez .10 .25
284 Maxim Balmochnyk .10 .25
285 Brian Campbell .10 .25
286 Sergei Varlamov .10 .25
287 Ville Nieminen RC .10 .25
288 Colin White RC .10 .25
289 Mike Fisher .10 .25
290 Matt Elich RC .12 .30
291 Zenith Komarniski .10 .25
292 Eric Nickulas RC .10 .25
293 Steven McCarthy .10 .25
294 Jason Krog .10 .25
295 Robert Esche .10 .25
296 Adam Mair .10 .25
297 Ladislav Nagy .10 .25
298 S.Vyshedkevich RC .10 .25
299 Steve Begin .10 .25
300 Brad Ference .10 .25
301 Andy Delmore .10 .25
302 Brent Sopel RC .15 .40
303 Evgeni Nabokov .12 .30
304 David Gosselin RC .10 .25
305 Tavis Hansen .10 .25
306 Ray Giroux .10 .25
307 Serge Aubin RC .12 .30
308 Shane Willis .10 .25
309 Vitali Vishnevski .10 .25

310 Richard Jackman .10 .25
311 Petr Schastlivy .10 .25
312 Ryan Bonni .10 .25
313 Alexei Tezikov .10 .25
314 Zac Bierk .10 .25
315 Mike Ribeiro .10 .25
316 Darryl Laplante .10 .25
317 Kyle Calder .10 .25
318 Dimitri Kalinin .10 .25
319 Jean-Sebastien Giguere .15 .40
320 Willie Mitchell RC .15 .40
321 Stephen Valiquette RC .12 .30
322 Brian Willsie .10 .25
323 Jarkko Ruutu .10 .25
324 Jon Sim .10 .25
325 Jonathan Girard .10 .25
326 Martin Brodeur HL .40 1.00
327 Ray Bourque HL .25 .60
328 The Bure Brothers HL .15 .40
329 Steve Yzerman HL .40 1.00
330 Brett Hull HL .30 .75
CL1 Checklist 1 .12 .30
CL2 Checklist 2 .12 .30
CL3 Checklist 3 .12 .30

2000-01 Topps Foil Parallel

*FOIL/100: 15X TO 40X BASIC CARDS
20 Mark Messier 15.00 40.00

2000-01 Topps Autographs

ACP Chris Pronger 6.00 15.00
AFB Fred Brathwaite 6.00 15.00
AJL John LeClair 10.00 25.00
AJT Jose Theodore 12.50 30.00
AMM Mike Modano 15.00 40.00
AMR Mark Recchi 6.00 15.00
ARB Ray Bourque 30.00 80.00
ART Roman Turek 6.00 15.00
ASG Scott Gomez 6.00 15.00

2000-01 Topps Combos

COMPLETE SET (10) 15.00 40.00
*JUMBOS: .5X TO 1.2X BASIC INSERTS
TC1 P.Bure/V.Bure 1.50 4.00
TC2 T.Selanne/P.Kariya 1.25 3.00
TC3 J.LeClair/T.Amonte 1.00 2.50
TC4 C.Joseph/D.Hasek 2.00 5.00
TC5 M.Modano/P.Forsberg 2.00 5.00
TC6 R.Bourque/C.Pronger 2.00 5.00
TC7 V.Lecavalier/J.Thornton 2.00 5.00
TC8 P.Roy/M.Brodeur 4.00 10.00
TC9 S.Yzerman/B.Hull 3.00 8.00
TC10 J.Jagr/M.Lemieux 3.00 8.00

2000-01 Topps Combos Jumbos

*JUMBOS: .5X TO 1.2X BASIC INSERTS

2000-01 Topps Game Worn Sweaters

GWAG Adam Graves 8.00 20.00
GWBH Bobby Holik 8.00 20.00
GWDL David Legwand 8.00 20.00
GWDM Darren McCarty 8.00 20.00
GWJJ Jaromir Jagr 10.00 25.00
GWTD Tie Domi 8.00 20.00

2000-01 Topps Hobby Masters

COMPLETE SET (10) 12.00 30.00
HM1 Martin Brodeur 3.00 8.00
HM2 Pavel Bure 1.25 3.00
HM3 Peter Forsberg 2.50 6.00
HM4 Dominik Hasek 2.00 5.00
HM5 Jaromir Jagr 4.00 10.00
HM6 Curtis Joseph 1.50 4.00
HM7 Paul Kariya 1.25 3.00
HM8 Mike Modano 2.00 5.00
HM9 Patrick Roy 3.00 8.00
HM10 Steve Yzerman 3.00 8.00

2000-01 Topps Lemieux Reprints

COMPLETE SET (23) 50.00 100.00
COMMON CARD (1-23) 3.00 8.00

2000-01 Topps Lemieux Reprints Autographs

COMMON CARD (1-23) 100.00 200.00

2000-01 Topps NHL Draft

COMPLETE SET (14) 20.00 40.00
D1 Vincent Lecavalier 1.25 3.00
D2 Eric Lindros 2.00 5.00
D3 Mike Modano 2.00 5.00
D4 Owen Nolan 1.00 2.50
D5 Patrik Stefan 1.00 2.50
D6 Mats Sundin 1.25 3.00
D7 Joe Thornton 2.00 5.00
D8 Pavel Bure 1.50 4.00
D9 Anson Carter 1.00 2.50
D10 Pavol Demitra 1.00 2.50
D11 Doug Gilmour 1.25 3.00
D12 Dominik Hasek 2.50 6.00
D13 Brett Hull 1.50 4.00
D14 Luc Robitaille 1.00 2.50

2000-01 Topps Own the Game

COMPLETE SET (30) 20.00 50.00
OTG1 Jaromir Jagr 1.50 4.00
OTG2 Pavel Bure 1.00 2.50
OTG3 Mark Recchi .75 2.00
OTG4 Paul Kariya 1.00 2.50
OTG5 Teemu Selanne 1.00 2.50
OTG6 Owen Nolan .75 2.00
OTG7 Tony Amonte .75 2.00
OTG8 Mike Modano 1.25 3.00
OTG9 Joe Sakic 2.00 5.00
OTG10 Steve Yzerman 3.00 8.00
OTG11 Martin Brodeur 2.00 5.00
OTG12 Roman Turek .40 1.00
OTG13 Olaf Kolzig .75 2.00
OTG14 Curtis Joseph 1.00 2.50
OTG15 Arturs Irbe .75 2.00
OTG16 Patrick Roy 4.00 10.00
OTG17 Ed Belfour 1.00 2.50
OTG18 Chris Osgood .75 2.00
OTG19 Guy Hebert .75 2.00
OTG20 Steve Shields .75 2.00
OTG21 Scott Gomez .75 2.00
OTG22 Alex Tanguay .75 2.00
OTG23 Mike York .40 1.00
OTG24 Simon Gagne .75 2.00
OTG25 Jan Hlavac .40 1.00
OTG26 Trevor Letowski .40 1.00
OTG27 Brad Stuart .40 1.00
OTG28 Maxim Afinogenov .40 1.00
OTG29 Tim Connolly .40 1.00
OTG30 Jochen Hecht .40 1.00

2000-01 Topps Stanley Cup Heroes

COMPLETE SET (5) 20.00 40.00
SHBG Bob Gainey 4.00 10.00
SHBP Bernie Parent 5.00 12.00
SHBT Bryan Trottier 5.00 12.00
SHLR Larry Robinson 5.00 12.00
SHTL Ted Lindsay 4.00 10.00

2000-01 Topps Stanley Cup Heroes Autographs

SHBG Bob Gainey 25.00 60.00
SHBP Bernie Parent 20.00 50.00
SHBT Bryan Trottier 15.00 40.00
SHLR Larry Robinson 15.00 40.00
SHTL Ted Lindsay 15.00 40.00

2000-01 Topps 1000 Point Club

COMPLETE SET (16) 25.00 50.00
PC1 Mark Messier 1.50 4.00
PC2 Steve Yzerman 6.00 15.00
PC3 Ron Francis 1.00 2.50
PC4 Paul Coffey 1.25 3.00
PC5 Ray Bourque 2.50 6.00
PC6 Doug Gilmour 1.25 3.00
PC7 Adam Oates 1.00 2.50
PC8 Larry Murphy 1.00 2.50
PC9 Dave Andreychuk 1.00 2.50
PC10 Luc Robitaille 1.00 2.50
PC11 Phil Housley 1.00 2.50
PC12 Brett Hull 1.50 4.00
PC13 Al MacInnis 1.00 2.50
PC14 Pierre Turgeon 1.00 2.50
PC15 Joe Sakic 2.50 6.00
PC16 Pat Verbeek 1.00 2.50

2000-01 Topps Premier Plus Promos

COMPLETE SET (6)
PP1 Scott Gomez .75 2.00
PP2 Joe Sakic 1.25 3.00
PP3 Zigmund Palffy .75 2.00
PP4 Tony Amonte .75 2.00
PP5 David Legwand .75 2.00
PP6 Jeff Farkas .75 2.00

2001-02 Topps

1 Mario Lemieux .75 2.00
2 Steve Yzerman .50 1.25
3 Martin Brodeur .50 1.25
4 Brian Leetch .15 .40
5 Tony Amonte .15 .40
6 Bill Guerin .20 .50
7 Olaf Kolzig .20 .50
8 Pavel Bure .20 .50
9 Patrick Marleau .20 .50
10 Mariusz Czerkawski .12 .30
11 Teemu Selanne .40 1.00
12 Alex Tanguay .15 .40
13 Keith Primeau .15 .40
14 Alexei Yashin Senator .15 .40
14U Alexei Yashin Islander .15 .40
15 Markus Naslund .20 .50
16 Chris Pronger .20 .50
17 Sergei Zubov .15 .40
18 Marian Gaborik .20 .50
19 Mats Sundin .20 .50
20 Kevin Weekes .15 .40
21 J.P. Dumont .12 .30
22 Nicklas Lidstrom .20 .50
23 Ron Francis .25 .60
24 Doug Weight Oilers .20 .50
24U Doug Weight Blues .20 .50
25 Zigmund Palffy .20 .50
26 Jason Allison .15 .40
27 Joe Sakic .40 1.00
28 Paul Kariya .20 .50
29 Marian Hossa .20 .50
30 Owen Nolan .20 .50
31 Jason Arnott .15 .40
32 Jaromir Jagr Pens .60 1.50
32U Jaromir Jagr Caps .60 1.50
33 Justin Williams .15 .40
34 Peter Bondra .20 .50
35 Chris Drury .15 .40
36 Radek Bonk .12 .30
37 Theo Fleury .25 .60
38 Keith Tkachuk .20 .50
39 Rick DiPietro .15 .40
40 Ed Jovanovski .15 .40
41 Scott Stevens .20 .50
42 John LeClair .20 .50
43 Jochen Hecht .12 .30
44 Vincent Lecavalier .20 .50
45 Henrik Sedin .25 .60
46 David Aebischer .15 .40
47 Patrick Roy .50 1.25
48 Valeri Bure .12 .30
49 Dominik Hasek Sabres .30 .75
49U Dominik Hasek Red Wings .30 .75
50 Ray Ferraro .12 .30
51 Milan Hejduk .15 .40
52 Mike Modano .30 .75
53 Sergei Fedorov .30 .75
54 Luc Robitaille .20 .50
55 Mark Messier .40 1.00
56 Sean Burke .12 .30
57 Jeff Friesen .12 .30
58 Alexander Mogilny Devils .15 .40
58U Alexander Mogilny Leafs .15 .40
59 Roman Cechmanek .15 .40
60 Martin Straka .12 .30
61 Pavol Demitra .25 .60
62 Curtis Joseph .25 .60
63 Daniel Sedin .25 .60
64 Brad Richards .20 .50
65 Simon Gagne .20 .50
66 Saku Koivu .20 .50
67 Jamie McLennan .12 .30
68 Roberto Luongo .30 .75
69 Brendan Shanahan .20 .50
70 Espen Knutsen .12 .30
71 Rob Blake .20 .50
72 Steve Sullivan .12 .30
73 Arturs Irbe .15 .40
74 Maxim Afinogenov .12 .30
75 Patrik Stefan .15 .40
76 Scott Gomez .15 .40
77 Brad Isbister .12 .30
78 Robert Lang .12 .30
79 Pierre Turgeon Blues .15 .40
79U Pierre Turgeon Stars .15 .40
80 Gary Roberts .12 .30
81 Adam Oates .20 .50
82 Evgeni Nabokov .15 .40
83 Petr Nedved .15 .40
84 Mike Dunham .15 .40
85 Chris Osgood Red Wings .20 .50
85U Chris Osgood Islanders .20 .50
86 Brett Hull Stars .40 1.00
86U Brett Hull Red Wings .40 1.00
87 Peter Forsberg .40 1.00
88 Joe Thornton .30 .75
89 Ray Bourque .30 .75
90 Ed Belfour .20 .50
91 Patrik Elias .20 .50
92 Michael York .12 .30
93 Martin Havlat .15 .40
94 Jeremy Roenick Coyotes .30 .75
94U Jeremy Roenick Flyers .30 .75
95 Alexei Kovalev .15 .40
96 Al MacInnis .25 .60
97 Marco Sturm .12 .30
98 Jose Theodore .20 .50
99 Joe Nieuwendyk .15 .40
100 Darren McCarty .12 .30
101 Mark Recchi .25 .60
102 Daniel Alfredsson .20 .50
103 Miroslav Satan .15 .40
104 Sergei Samsonov .15 .40
105 Roman Turek Blues .15 .40
105U Roman Turek Flames .15 .40
106 Jarome Iginla .25 .60
107 Jeff O'Neill .15 .40
108 Tommy Salo .15 .40
109 Petr Sykora .12 .30
110 Adam Deadmarsh .12 .30
111 Oleg Tverdovsky .12 .30
112 Damian Rhodes .15 .40
113 Bob Probert .20 .50
114 Jere Lehtinen .15 .40
115 Cale Hulse .12 .30
116 Andy Sutton .12 .30
117 Wade Redden .12 .30
118 Brad Stuart .12 .30
119 Tomas Kaberle .12 .30
120 Sergei Gonchar .12 .30
121 Jean-Sebastien Aubin .15 .40
122 Adam Graves .15 .40
123 Teppo Numminen .12 .30
124 Martin Rucinsky .12 .30
125 Scott Young .12 .30
126 Pat Verbeek .15 .40
127 Michael Nylander .12 .30
128 Marc Savard .12 .30
129 Brian Rolston .15 .40
130 Sandis Ozolinsh .12 .30
131 Mike Grier .12 .30
132 Eric Belanger .12 .30
133 Patrick Lalime .15 .40
134 Steve Thomas .12 .30
135 Viktor Kozlov .12 .30
136 Manny Legace .15 .40
137 Oleg Saprykin .12 .30
138 Sami Kapanen .12 .30
139 Janne Niinimaa .12 .30
140 Scott Hartnell .12 .30
141 Tim Connolly .12 .30
142 Travis Green .12 .30
143 Matthew Barnaby .12 .30
144 Brendan Morrison .15 .40
145 Darcy Tucker .12 .30
146 Gary Suter .12 .30
147 Mattias Ohlund .12 .30
148 Patric Kjellberg .12 .30
149 Lubomir Visnovsky .12 .30
150 Claude Lapointe .12 .30
151 Martin Skoula .15 .40
152 Mike Vernon .15 .40
153 Stu Barnes .15 .40
154 Brenden Morrow .15 .40
155 Jim Dowd .12 .30
156 Shane Doan .15 .40
157 Peter Schaefer .12 .30
158 Jeff Halpern .12 .30
159 Sergei Berezin .12 .30
160 Mike Ricci .12 .30
161 Radek Dvorak .15 .40
162 Brian Savage .12 .30
163 Bryan Smolinski .12 .30
164 Derian Hatcher .12 .30
165 Shane Willis .12 .30
166 Ron Tugnutt .15 .40
167 Peter Worrell .12 .30
168 Richard Zednik .15 .40
169 Todd Marchant .12 .30
170 Andrew Brunette .12 .30
171 Derek Morris .12 .30
172 Kyle Calder .12 .30
173 Felix Potvin .30 .75
174 Bobby Holik .12 .30
175 Manny Fernandez .12 .30
176 Rick Tocchet .12 .30
177 Jonas Hoglund .12 .30
178 Todd Bertuzzi .20 .50
179 Garth Snow .15 .40
180 Cliff Ronning .12 .30
181 Martin Lapointe .12 .30
182 Jason Smith .12 .30
183 Byron Dafoe .15 .40
184 Rob Niedermayer .15 .40
185 Steve Rucchin .12 .30
186 Alexei Zhamnov .15 .40
187 Mike Richter .20 .50
188 Michal Handzus .12 .30
189 Pavel Kubina .12 .30
190 Donald Brashear .12 .30
191 Trevor Letowski .12 .30
192 Randy McKay .12 .30
193 Trevor Linden .20 .50
194 Mike Sillinger .12 .30
195 David Vyborny .12 .30
196 Dave Tanabe .12 .30
197 Scott Niedermayer .20 .50
198 Anson Carter .15 .40
199 Mike Leclerc .12 .30
200 Dave Scatchard .12 .30
201 Jan Hrdina .12 .30
202 Brian Holzinger .12 .30
203 Steve Konowalchuk .12 .30
204 Tie Domi .15 .40
205 Brent Johnson .15 .40
206 Shawn McEachern .12 .30
207 Jozef Stumpel .12 .30
208 Jamie Langenbrunner .12 .30
209 Jocelyn Thibault .15 .40
210 Donald Audette .12 .30
211 Serge Aubin .12 .30
212 Andrew Cassels .12 .30
213 Tyson Nash .12 .30
214 Colin White .12 .30
215 Tom Poti .12 .30
216 Rod Brind'Amour .20 .50
217 Fred Brathwaite .15 .40
218 Marc Denis .15 .40
219 Roman Simicek .12 .30
220 Jan Hlavac .12 .30
221 Darius Kasparaitis .12 .30
222 Vincent Damphousse .15 .40
223 Bob Boughner .12 .30
224 Yanic Perreault .12 .30
225 Chris Simon .12 .30
226 Chris Gratton .12 .30
227 Josef Vasicek .12 .30
228 Slava Kozlov .15 .40
229 Kelly Buchberger .15 .40
230 Jeff Hackett .15 .40
231 Taylor Pyatt .12 .30
232 Niklas Sundstrom .15 .40
233 Dan Cloutier .15 .40
234 Eric Daze .15 .40
235 Ryan Smyth .15 .40
236 Marty McInnis .15 .40
237 John Madden .15 .40
238 Claude Lemieux .15 .40
239 Steve Heinze .12 .30
240 Nikolai Antropov .12 .30
241 Cory Stillman .12 .30
242 Geoff Sanderson .12 .30
243 Trevor Kidd .12 .30
244 David Legwand .15 .40
245 Eric Desjardins .15 .40
246 Fredrik Modin .12 .30
247 Brett Clark .12 .30
248 Bryan Muir .12 .30
249 Ron Sutter .15 .40
250 Ken Klee .12 .30
251 Steve Halko .12 .30
252 Steve McKenna .12 .30
253 Marc Bergevin .12 .30
254 Scott Lachance .12 .30
255 Jamie Rivers .12 .30
256 Dixon Ward .12 .30
257 Gord Murphy .12 .30
258 Bret Hedican .12 .30
259 Bob Corkum .12 .30
260 Brent Sopel .12 .30
261 Todd Simpson .12 .30
262 Reid Simpson .12 .30
263 Chris McAlpine .12 .30
264 Deron Quint .12 .30
265 Josh Holden .12 .30
266 Mike Mottau .12 .30
267 Jakub Cutta .12 .30
268 Maxime Ouellet .20 .50
269 Peter Smrek RC .12 .30
270 Daniel Corso .12 .30
271 Rostislav Klesla .12 .30
272 Mika Noronen .12 .30
273 Kris Beech .12 .30
274 Sheldon Keefe .12 .30
275 Miikka Kiprusoff .20 .50
276 Mathieu Garon .15 .40
277 Jason Chimera RC .12 .30
278 Mark Bell .12 .30
279 Chris Nielsen .12 .30
280 Eric Chouinard .12 .30
281 Pierre Dagenais .12 .30
282 Branislav Mezei .12 .30
283 Milan Kraft .12 .30
284 Tomas Kloucek .12 .30
285 Petr Schastlivy .12 .30
286 Lee Goren .12 .30
287 Daniel Tkaczuk .12 .30
288 Andreas Lilja .12 .30
289 Tomas Divisek RC .15 .40
290 Alexei Ponikarovsky .12 .30
291 Mikael Samuelsson RC .15 .40
292 Petr Svoboda .15 .40
293 Mike Comrie .15 .40
294 Johan Hedberg .15 .40
295 Tyler Moss .12 .30
296 Martin Spanhel RC .12 .30
297 Mike Brown .15 .40
298 Derek Gustafson .12 .30
299 Matt Pettinger .12 .30
300 Mike Commodore .12 .30
301 Antti-Jussi Niemi .12 .30
302 Brad Tapper .12 .30
303 Rick Berry .12 .30
304 Andrew Raycroft .15 .40
305 Bryan Allen .12 .30
306 Ivan Novoseltsev .12 .30
307 Jason Williams .12 .30
308 Gregg Naumenko .12 .30
309 Jiri Bicek .12 .30
310 Mathieu Darche RC .20 .50
311 Brian Campbell .12 .30
312 Jeff Farkas .12 .30
313 Rico Fata .12 .30
314 Kristian Kudroc .12 .30
315 Roman Cechmanek AS .15 .40
316 Nicklas Lidstrom AS .20 .50
317 Ray Bourque AS .30 .75
318 Joe Sakic AS .40 1.00
319 Patrik Elias AS .20 .50
320 Jaromir Jagr AS .60 1.50
321 J. Madden/R. McKay .15 .40
322 Mark Recchi .25 .60
323 Vincent Damphousse .15 .40
324 Patrick Roy .50 1.25
325 Jaromir Jagr .60 1.50
326 Mario Lemieux 2.00 5.00
327 Mario Lemieux 2.00 5.00
328 Mario Lemieux 2.00 5.00
329 Mario Lemieux 2.00 5.00
330 Mario Lemieux 2.00 5.00
331 Ilya Kovalchuk RC 5.00 12.00
332 Dan Blackburn RC 1.25 3.00
333 Vaclav Nedorost RC 1.00 2.50
334 Krys Kolanos RC 1.00 2.50
335 Kristian Huselius RC 1.50 4.00
336 Martin Erat RC 1.25 3.00
337 Timo Parssinen RC 1.25 3.00
338 Scott Nichol RC 1.00 2.50
339 Nick Schultz RC 1.00 2.50
340 Jukka Hentunen RC 1.00 2.50
341 Pascal Dupuis RC 1.50 4.00
342 Radek Martinek RC 1.00 2.50
343 Scott Clemmensen RC 1.00 2.50
344 Jeff Jillson RC 1.00 2.50
345 Brian Sutherby RC 1.00 2.50
346 Nikita Alexeev RC 1.00 2.50
347 Niklas Hagman RC 1.25 3.00
348 Erik Cole RC 2.00 5.00
349 Pavel Datsyuk RC 20.00 50.00
350 Ilja Bryzgalov RC 2.50 6.00
351 Chris Neil RC 1.25 3.00
352 Mark Rycroft RC 1.25 3.00
353 Kamil Piros RC 1.00 2.50
354 Niko Kapanen RC 1.50 4.00
355 Jiri Dopita RC 1.00 2.50
356 Andreas Salomonsson RC 1.00 2.50
357 Ivan Ciernik RC 1.00 2.50
358 Jaroslav Bednar RC 1.00 2.50
359 Ty Conklin RC 1.50 4.00
360 Raffi Torres RC 1.50 4.00

2001-02 Topps 71-72 Heritage Parallel

*SINGLES: 1X TO 2.5X BASIC TOPPS

2001-02 Topps 71-72 Heritage Parallel Limited

*SINGLES/50: 12X TO 30X BASIC TOPPS

2001-02 Topps OPC Parallel

*OPC PARALLEL: 1.5X TO 4X BASIC CARDS
55 Mark Messier 1.50 4.00

2001-02 Topps Autographs

ACD Chris Drury 10.00 25.00
AEN Evgeni Nabokov 10.00 25.00
AGR Gary Roberts 8.00 20.00
AJA Jason Arnott 8.00 20.00
AMY Mike York 8.00 20.00
ARF Ron Francis 8.00 20.00
ASG Simon Gagne 12.00 30.00
AVL Vincent Lecavalier 20.00 50.00
AMHA Martin Havlat 8.00 20.00
AMHE Milan Hejduk 12.00 30.00

2001-02 Topps Captain's Cloth

CC1 Jagr/Sakic/Kariya/Lec. 150.00 300.00
CC2 Pronger/Koivu/Amon/Jagr 100.00 200.00
CC3 Franc/Allis/Kariya/Lecav 100.00 200.00

2001-02 Topps Game-Worn Jersey

JBB Brian Boucher 6.00 15.00
JBH Brett Hull 10.00 25.00
JCD Chris Drury 8.00 20.00
JEB Ed Belfour 8.00 20.00
JJA Jason Arnott 6.00 15.00
JMY Mike York 6.00 15.00
JPK Paul Kariya 8.00 20.00
JRF Ron Francis 6.00 15.00
JSG Simon Gagne 8.00 20.00
JVL Vincent Lecavalier 6.00 15.00

2001-02 Topps Jumbo Jersey Autographs

JJACD Chris Drury 25.00 60.00
JJAJA Jason Arnott 25.00 60.00
JJAMY Mike York 25.00 60.00
JJARF Ron Francis 25.00 60.00
JJASG Simon Gagne 25.00 60.00
JJAVL Vincent Lecavalier 40.00 100.00

2001-02 Topps Mario Lemieux Reprints

COMPLETE SET (10) 15.00 40.00
COMMON CARD (1-10) 2.50 6.00

2001-02 Topps Mario Returns Autographs

COMMON AUTO (1-5) 75.00 150.00

2001-02 Topps Own The Game

COMPLETE SET (30) 15.00 30.00
OTG1 Jaromir Jagr .60 1.50
OTG2 Joe Sakic .75 2.00
OTG3 Patrik Elias .30 .75
OTG4 Jason Allison .12 .30
OTG5 Alexei Kovalev .30 .75
OTG6 Martin Straka .12 .30
OTG7 Pavel Bure .50 1.25
OTG8 Doug Weight .30 .75
OTG9 Peter Forsberg .75 2.00
OTG10 Zigmund Palffy .30 .75
OTG11 Brad Richards .30 .75
OTG12 Shane Willis .12 .30
OTG13 Martin Havlat .30 .75
OTG14 Lubomir Visnovsky .12 .30
OTG15 Marian Gaborik .75 2.00
OTG16 Ruslan Fedotenko .30 .75
OTG17 Steven Reinprecht .12 .30
OTG18 Daniel Sedin .12 .30
OTG19 Karel Rachunek .12 .30
OTG20 David Vyborny .12 .30
OTG21 Martin Brodeur 1.00 2.50
OTG22 Patrick Roy 2.00 5.00
OTG23 Dominik Hasek .75 2.00
OTG24 Olaf Kolzig .30 .75
OTG25 Arturs Irbe .30 .75
OTG26 Patrick Lalime .30 .75
OTG27 Tommy Salo .30 .75
OTG28 Roman Cechmanek .30 .75
OTG29 Ed Belfour .40 1.00
OTG30 Curtis Joseph .40 1.00

2001-02 Topps Promos

COMPLETE SET (6) 1.50 4.00
PP1 Zigmund Palffy .40 1.00
PP2 Randy McKay .20 .50
PP3 Gary Roberts .20 .50
PP4 Manny Fernandez .40 1.00
PP5 Steve Sullivan .20 .50
PP6 Adam Oates .40 1.00

2001-02 Topps Rookie Reprints

COMPLETE SET (4) 10.00 20.00
1 Denis Potvin 2.00 5.00
2 Yvan Cournoyer 2.00 5.00
3 Phil Esposito 2.00 5.00
4 Gerry Cheevers 2.00 5.00

2001-02 Topps Rookie Reprint Autographs

1 Denis Potvin 15.00 40.00
2 Yvan Cournoyer 15.00 40.00
3 Phil Esposito 15.00 40.00
4 Gerry Cheevers 15.00 40.00

2001-02 Topps Shot Masters

COMPLETE SET (18) 15.00 30.00
SM1 Mario Lemieux 2.50 6.00
SM2 Pavel Bure .50 1.25
SM3 Brett Hull .50 1.25
SM4 Joe Sakic .75 2.00
SM5 Jaromir Jagr .60 1.50
SM6 Steve Yzerman 2.00 5.00
SM7 Milan Hejduk .40 1.00
SM8 Tony Amonte .30 .75
SM9 Zigmund Palffy .30 .75
SM10 Paul Kariya .40 1.00
SM11 Bill Guerin .30 .75
SM12 Peter Bondra .40 1.00
SM13 Patrik Elias .30 .75
SM14 Alexei Kovalev .30 .75
SM15 John LeClair .50 1.25
SM16 Alexei Yashin 1.00 2.50
SM17 Teemu Selanne .40 1.00
SM18 Alexander Mogilny .30 .75

2001-02 Topps Stanley Cup Heroes

COMPLETE SET (4) 15.00 30.00
SCHDP Denis Potvin 4.00 10.00
SCHGC Gerry Cheevers 5.00 12.00
SCHPE Phil Esposito 4.00 10.00
SCHYC Yvan Cournoyer 5.00 12.00

2001-02 Topps Stanley Cup Heroes Autographs

SCHADP Denis Potvin 15.00 40.00
SCHAGC Gerry Cheevers 15.00 40.00
SCHAPE Phil Esposito 20.00 50.00
SCHAYC Yvan Cournoyer 15.00 40.00

2001-02 Topps Stars of the Game

COMPLETE SET (10) 8.00 15.00
SG1 Mario Lemieux 2.50 6.00
SG2 Sean Burke .30 .75
SG3 Pavel Bure .50 1.25
SG4 Joe Sakic .75 2.00
SG5 Patrik Elias .30 .75
SG6 Mike Modano .60 1.50
SG7 Curtis Joseph .40 1.00
SG8 Alexei Kovalev .30 .75
SG9 Sergei Fedorov .75 2.00
SG10 Tommy Salo .30 .75

2002-03 Topps

COMPLETE SET (340) 20.00 50.00
COMP.SET w/o ROOK.RED. (330) 15.00 40.00
1 Patrick Roy .50 1.25
2 Mario Lemieux .75 2.00
3 Martin Brodeur .50 1.25
4 Steve Yzerman .50 1.25
5 Jaromir Jagr .60 1.50
6 Chris Pronger .20 .50
7 John LeClair .20 .50
8 Paul Kariya .20 .50
9 Tony Amonte .15 .40
9U Tony Amonte update .15 .40
10 Joe Thornton .30 .75
11 Ilya Kovalchuk .25 .60
12 Jarome Iginla .25 .60
13 Mike Modano .30 .75
14 Vincent Lecavalier .20 .50
15 Michael Peca .15 .40
16 Pavel Bure .20 .50
17 Eric Lindros .30 .75
18 Felix Potvin .30 .75
19 Ron Francis .25 .60
20 Miroslav Satan .20 .50
21 Rostislav Klesla .12 .30
22 Mike Comrie .20 .50
23 Daniel Alfredsson .20 .50
24 Sean Burke .12 .30
25 David Legwand .15 .40
26 Marian Gaborik .20 .50
27 Saku Koivu .20 .50
28 Owen Nolan .20 .50
29 Mats Sundin .20 .50
30 J-P Dumont .12 .30
31 Chris Drury .20 .50
31U Chris Drury update .20 .50
32 Markus Naslund .20 .50
33 Anson Carter .15 .40
34 Dwayne Roloson .12 .30
35 Brad Isbister .12 .30
36 Daniel Briere .15 .40
37 Martin St. Louis .20 .50
38 Shayne Corson .15 .40
39 Keith Tkachuk .20 .50
40 Mark Recchi .25 .60
41 Patrice Brisebois .12 .30
42 Niklas Hagman .12 .30
43 Marc Denis .15 .40
44 Robyn Regehr .12 .30
45 Byron Dafoe .15 .40
46 Sergei Fedorov .30 .75
47 Andrew Brunette .12 .30
48 Denis Arkhipov .12 .30
49 Martin Havlat .15 .40
50 Mike Rathje .12 .30
51 Mattias Ohlund .12 .30
52 Ulf Dahlen .12 .30
53 Tim Connolly .12 .30
54 Valeri Bure .15 .40
55 Brian Boucher .15 .40
56 Pascal Dupuis .12 .30
57 Brian Leetch .15 .40
58 Daniel Sedin .25 .60
59 Kenny Jonsson .12 .30
60 Erik Cole .12 .30
61 Patrick Lalime .15 .40
62 Mike Leclerc .12 .30
63 Patrick Marleau .20 .50
64 Tom Poti .12 .30
65 Lubos Bartecko .12 .30
66 Tom Barrasso .15 .40
67 Ryan Smyth .15 .40
68 Sami Kapanen .12 .30
69 Michal Handzus .15 .40
70 Martin Straka .15 .40
71 Peter Forsberg .40 1.00
72 Marc Savard .12 .30
73 Jeff Friesen .12 .30
73U Jeff Friesen update .12 .30
74 Manny Fernandez .12 .30
75 Jason Smith .12 .30
76 Mike Ribeiro .12 .30
77 Steve Heinze .12 .30
78 Adam Foote .12 .30
79 Sandy McCarthy .12 .30
80 Toni Lydman .12 .30
81 Tie Domi .15 .40
82 Scott Stevens .20 .50
83 Radim Vrbata .12 .30
84 Oleg Petrov .12 .30
85 Marty Turco .20 .50
86 Kristian Huselius .12 .30
87 Jeremy Roenick .30 .75
88 Gary Roberts .12 .30
89 Dean McAmmond .12 .30
90 Chris Chelios .20 .50
91 Andy McDonald .20 .50
92 Brett Hull .40 1.00
93 Danny Markov .12 .30
94 Eric Daze .12 .30
95 Alex Tanguay .15 .40
96 Petr Nedved .12 .30
97 Simon Gagne .20 .50
98 Roman Turek .20 .50
99 Milan Hejduk .15 .40
100 Mariusz Czerkawski .12 .30
100U Mariusz Czerkawski update .12 .30
101 Jaroslav Modry .12 .30
102 Dan Cloutier .15 .40
103 Mark Bell .12 .30
104 Brendan Witt .12 .30
105 Teemu Selanne .40 1.00
106 Johan Hedberg .20 .50
107 Mike Ricci .12 .30
108 Roberto Luongo .30 .75
109 Vaclav Prospal .12 .30
110 Zigmund Palffy .20 .50
111 Ed Jovanovski .15 .40
112 Scott Gomez .15 .40
113 Pierre Turgeon .15 .40
114 Niklas Sundstrom .12 .30
115 Martin Biron .15 .40
116 Keith Primeau .15 .40
117 Jean-Sebastien Giguere .20 .50
118 Filip Kuba .12 .30
119 Dave Tanabe .12 .30
120 Brian Savage .12 .30
121 Alexei Zhamnov .15 .40
122 Brent Johnson .15 .40
123 Dan Blackburn .15 .40
124 Eric Belanger .12 .30
125 Janne Niinimaa .12 .30
126 Jonas Hoglund .12 .30
127 Marian Hossa .20 .50
128 Mike Richter .20 .50
129 Peter Bondra .20 .50
130 Rod Brind'Amour .20 .50
131 Shane Doan .15 .40
132 Viktor Kozlov .12 .30
133 Yanic Perreault .12 .30
134 Sergei Samsonov .15 .40
135 Nikolai Khabibulin .20 .50
136 Rob Ray .12 .30
137 Roman Cechmanek .15 .40
138 Patrik Stefan .15 .40
139 Matt Cullen .12 .30
140 Kim Johnsson .12 .30
141 Jim Dowd .12 .30
142 Glen Murray .15 .40
143 Dominik Hasek .30 .75
144 Brad Richards .20 .50
145 Cory Stillman .12 .30
146 Josef Vasicek .12 .30
147 Alexei Kovalev .15 .40
148 Adam Deadmarsh .12 .30
149 Brendan Morrison .15 .40
150 Eric Brewer .12 .30
151 Jason Arnott .15 .40
152 Brenden Morrow .15 .40
153 Manny Legace .20 .50
154 Michael Nylander .12 .30
155 Pavol Demitra .25 .60
156 Olaf Kolzig .20 .50
157 Sergei Berezin .12 .30
158 Teppo Numminen .12 .30
159 Vladimir Orszagh .12 .30
160 Brian Rafalski .12 .30
161 Doug Gilmour .25 .60
162 Jere Lehtinen .20 .50
163 Mark Parrish .12 .30
164 Petr Sykora .15 .40
164U Petr Sykora update .15 .40
165 Sergei Zholtok .12 .30
166 Wade Redden .12 .30
167 Scott Niedermayer .20 .50
168 Olli Jokinen .20 .50
169 Kyle Calder .12 .30
170 Jamie Langenbrunner .15 .40
171 Darcy Tucker .12 .30
172 Alexei Morozov .12 .30
173 Adam Oates .20 .50
173U Adam Oates update .20 .50
174 Chris Osgood .20 .50
175 Espen Knutsen .12 .30

176 Jochen Hecht .12 .30
177 Maxim Afinogenov .12 .30
178 Radek Dvorak .15 .40
179 Steve Sullivan .12 .30
180 Trevor Linden .20 .50
181 Tomi Kallio .12 .30
182 Robert Lang .12 .30
182U Robert Lang update .12 .30
183 Milan Hnilicka .15 .40
184 Justin Williams .15 .40
185 Greg Johnson .12 .30
186 Craig Conroy .12 .30
187 Alexander Mogilny .15 .40
188 Adrian Aucoin .12 .30
189 Fredrik Modin .12 .30
190 Jose Theodore .20 .50
191 Ray Whitney .15 .40
192 Mikael Renberg .12 .30
193 Mike Sillinger .12 .30
194 Richard Zednik .12 .30
195 Mike Dunham .15 .40
196 Joe Sakic .40 1.00
197 Fred Brathwaite .15 .40
198 Chris Simon .12 .30
199 Al MacInnis .25 .60
200 Georges Laraque .15 .40
201 Jozef Stumpel .12 .30
202 Theo Fleury .25 .60
203 Rob Blake .20 .50
204 Todd White .12 .30
205 Dany Heatley .15 .40
206 Scott Hartnell .12 .30
207 Oleg Tverdovsky .12 .30
208 Krys Kolanos .12 .30
209 Ian Laperriere .15 .40
210 Vincent Damphousse .15 .40
211 Nick Boynton .12 .30
212 Curtis Joseph .25 .60
212U Curtis Joseph update .25 .60
213 Henrik Sedin .25 .60
214 Kris Beech .12 .30
215 Sandis Ozolinsh .12 .30
216 Ron Tugnutt .15 .40
217 Todd Bertuzzi .20 .50
218 Tommy Salo .15 .40
219 Martin Lapointe .15 .40
220 Derian Hatcher .15 .40
221 David Vyborny .12 .30
222 Jocelyn Thibault .15 .40
223 Nicklas Lidstrom .20 .50
224 Marcus Nilsson .12 .30
225 Sergei Zubov .15 .40
226 Bryan McCabe .12 .30
227 Claude Lemieux .15 .40
228 Jean-Luc Grand-Pierre .12 .30
229 Bill Guerin .20 .50
229U Bill Guerin update .20 .50
230 Sergei Brylin .12 .30
231 Bryan Smolinski .15 .40
232 Luc Robitaille .20 .50
233 Alexei Yashin .15 .40
234 Evgeni Nabokov .15 .40
235 Pavel Datsyuk .30 .75
236 Martin Erat .12 .30
237 Stu Barnes .12 .30
238 Derek Morris .12 .30
239 Bates Battaglia .12 .30
240 Jason Allison .15 .40
241 Peter Worrell .12 .30
242 Mark Messier .40 1.00
243 Shawn Bates .12 .30
244 Daymond Langkow .15 .40
245 Ed Belfour .20 .50
245U Ed Belfour update .20 .50
246 Jan Hrdina .12 .30
247 Pavel Kubina .12 .30
248 Scott Young .12 .30
249 Curtis Brown .12 .30
250 Brian Rolston .15 .40
251 Jiri Dopita .12 .30
252 Kimmo Timonen .12 .30
253 Marco Sturm .12 .30
254 Arturs Irbe .15 .40
255 Joe Nieuwendyk .15 .40
256 Sergei Gonchar .15 .40
257 Doug Weight .20 .50
258 Jeff O'Neill .12 .30
259 Mike York .12 .30
260 Radek Bonk .15 .40
261 Patrik Elias .20 .50
262 Phil Housley .15 .40
263 Brendan Shanahan .20 .50
264 Sheldon Keefe .12 .30
265 Rick DiPietro .15 .40
266 J-F Fortin .12 .30
267 Jason Chimera .12 .30
268 Andy Hilbert .12 .30
269 Brian Gionta .12 .30
270 Sergei Varlamov .15 .40
271 Alex Auld .12 .30
272 Pavel Brendl .12 .30
273 Branko Radivojevic .12 .30
274 Kamil Piros .12 .30
275 Steve Gainey .12 .30
276 Mike Mottau .12 .30
277 Jimmie Olvestad .12 .30
278 Jeff Jillson .12 .30
279 Ilja Bryzgalov .15 .40
280 Taylor Pyatt .12 .30
281 Andrew Raycroft .15 .40
282 Christian Berglund .12 .30
283 Patrick DesRochers .12 .30
284 Lukas Krajicek .15 .40
285 Riku Hahl .12 .30
286 Ivan Huml .12 .30
287 Jani Rita .12 .30
288 Kristian Kudroc .12 .30
289 Juraj Kolnik .12 .30
290 John Erskine .12 .30
291 Brian Sutherby .12 .30
292 Bruno St-Jacques .12 .30
293 Nick Schultz .12 .30
294 Pasi Nurminen .12 .30
295 Norm Milley .12 .30
296 Marcel Hossa .12 .30
297 Ales Kotalik .12 .30
298 Bryan Allen .12 .30
299 Mika Noronen .15 .40
300 Tyler Arnason .20 .50
301 Petr Schastlivy .12 .30
302 Mike Van Ryn .12 .30
303 Steve Montador .12 .30
304 Denis Shvidki .12 .30
305 Stephen Weiss .20 .50
306 Nikita Alexeev .12 .30
307 Vaclav Nedorost .12 .30
308 Raffi Torres .12 .30
309 Guillaume Lefebvre .12 .30
310 Sean Avery .15 .40
311 Shane Endicott .12 .30
312 Ty Conklin .15 .40
313 J-F Damphousse .15 .40
314 Jeremy Roenick .30 .75
315 Ron Francis .25 .60
316 Brendan Shanahan .20 .50
317 Patrick Roy .50 1.25
318 Luc Robitaille .20 .50
319 Jose Theodore .20 .50
320 Patrick Roy .50 1.25
321 Sergei Gonchar .15 .40
322 Bryan McCabe .12 .30
323 Chris Chelios .20 .50
324 Nicklas Lidstrom .20 .50
325 Simon Gagne .20 .50
326 Brendan Shanahan .20 .50
327 Jaromir Jagr .60 1.50
328 Jarome Iginla .25 .60
329 Mats Sundin .20 .50
330 Joe Sakic .40 1.00
331 Henrik Zetterberg RC 2.50 6.00
332 P-M Bouchard RC .40 1.00
333 Alexander Frolov RC .60 1.50
334 Alexander Svitov RC .25 .60
335 Jason Spezza RC 1.50 4.00
336 Jay Bouwmeester RC .75 2.00
337 Ales Hemsky RC 1.00 2.50
338 Rick Nash RC 1.50 4.00
339 Chuck Kobasew RC .30 .75
340 Stanislav Chistov RC .25 .60
NNO Rookie Redemption expired .20 .50

2002-03 Topps Factory Set Gold

COMP.BASE SET (330) 15.00 40.00
COMP.FACTORY SET (340) 25.00 50.00
*GOLD VETS: .5X TO 1.2X BASIC TOPPS
*GOLD ROOKIES: .6X TO 1.5X BASE RC
242 Mark Messier .50 1.25

2002-03 Topps O-Pee-Chee Blue

*VETS/500: 3X TO 8X BASIC TOPPS
*ROOKIES/500: 1.5X TO 4X TOPPS RC
242 Mark Messier 3.00 8.00

2002-03 Topps O-Pee-Chee Red

*VETS/100: 8X TO 20X BASIC TOPPS
*ROOKIES/100: 4X TO 10X TOPPS RC
242 Mark Messier 8.00 20.00

2002-03 Topps Captain's Cloth

CC1 Lemieux/Sakic/Francis 75.00 200.00
CC2 Primeau/LeClair/Recchi 60.00 150.00
CC3 Hatcher/Zubov/Modano 75.00 150.00
CC4 Pronger/Kariya/Francis 60.00 125.00
CC5 Koivu/Naslund/Sundin 40.00 100.00
CC6 Lemieux
Sundin
Primeau 60.00 120.00
CC7 Kariya/Koivu/Sakic 60.00 150.00
CC8 Mario Lemieux 20.00 50.00
CC9 Keith Primeau 12.50 30.00
CC10 Markus Naslund 10.00 25.00
CC11 Mats Sundin 12.00 30.00
CC12 Paul Kariya 10.00 25.00
CC13 Joe Sakic 15.00 40.00
CC14 Saku Koivu 12.50 30.00
CC15 Ron Francis 15.00 40.00
CC16 Derian Hatcher 12.50 30.00
CC17 Chris Pronger 15.00 40.00

2002-03 Topps Coast to Coast

COMPLETE SET (10) 10.00 20.00
CC1 Mario Lemieux 4.00 10.00
CC2 Pavel Bure .75 2.00
CC3 Jarome Iginla .75 2.00
CC4 Mats Sundin .60 1.50
CC5 Peter Bondra .60 1.50
CC6 Ilya Kovalchuk .75 2.00
CC7 Joe Thornton 1.00 2.50
CC8 Paul Kariya .60 1.50
CC9 Joe Sakic 1.25 3.00
CC10 Patrik Elias .75 2.00

2002-03 Topps First Round Fabric

DB Dan Blackburn 6.00 15.00
EL Eric Lindros 8.00 20.00
KP Keith Primeau 6.00 15.00
MB Martin Biron 6.00 15.00
MM Mike Modano 10.00 25.00
MN Markus Naslund 10.00 25.00
MS Mats Sundin 10.00 25.00
PM Patrick Marleau 6.00 15.00
RD Radek Dvorak 6.00 15.00
SN Scott Niedermayer 6.00 15.00
JPD J-P Dumont 6.00 15.00

2002-03 Topps First Round Fabric Autographs

KP Keith Primeau 12.50 30.00
MB Martin Biron 12.50 30.00
MM Mike Modano 20.00 50.00
MS Mats Sundin 20.00 50.00
RD Radek Dvorak 12.50 30.00
SN Scott Niedermayer 15.00 40.00

2002-03 Topps Hometown Heroes

COMP.USA SET (20) 15.00 30.00
*FACT.SET: .4X TO 1X BASIC INSERTS
HHU1 Martin Brodeur 1.25 3.00
HHU2 Joe Sakic .75 2.50
HHU3 Mario Lemieux 3.00 8.00
HHU4 Steve Yzerman 2.50 6.00
HHU5 Paul Kariya .50 1.25
HHU6 Mike Modano .75 2.00
HHU7 Brett Hull .60 1.50
HHU8 Bill Guerin .40 1.00
HHU9 Tony Amonte .40 1.00
HHU10 Jeremy Roenick .60 1.50
HHU11 John LeClair .50 1.25
HHU12 Brendan Shanahan .75 2.00
HHU13 Owen Nolan .40 1.00
HHU14 Al MacInnis .40 1.00
HHU15 Chris Pronger .40 1.00
HHU16 Doug Weight .40 1.00
HHU17 Ilya Kovalchuk .60 1.50
HHU18 Joe Thornton .75 2.00
HHU19 Patrick Roy 2.50 6.00
HHU20 Ron Francis .40 1.00

2002-03 Topps Own The Game

COMPLETE SET (20) 5.00 10.00
OTG1 Jarome Iginla .30 .75
OTG2 Markus Naslund .20 .50
OTG3 Todd Bertuzzi .20 .50
OTG4 Mats Sundin .20 .50
OTG5 Jaromir Jagr .30 .75
OTG6 Jarome Iginla .30 .75
OTG7 Mats Sundin .20 .50
OTG8 Bill Guerin .15 .40
OTG9 Glen Murray .15 .40
OTG10 Markus Naslund .20 .50
OTG11 Dany Heatley .25 .60
OTG12 Ilya Kovalchuk .30 .75
OTG13 Kristian Huselius .15 .40
OTG14 Erik Cole .15 .40
OTG15 Pavel Datsyuk .30 .75
OTG16 Dominik Hasek .40 1.00
OTG17 Martin Brodeur .60 1.50
OTG18 Evgeni Nabokov .15 .40
OTG19 Byron Dafoe .15 .40
OTG20 Brent Johnson .15 .40

2002-03 Topps Patrick Roy Reprints

COMMON CARD (1-14) 2.00 5.00
*FACT.SET: .5X TO 1.2X BASIC INSERTS
1 Patrick Roy '86-87 3.00 8.00
2 Patrick Roy 2.00 5.00
3 Patrick Roy 2.00 5.00
4 Patrick Roy 2.00 5.00
5 Patrick Roy 2.00 5.00
6 Patrick Roy 2.00 5.00
7 Patrick Roy 2.00 5.00
8 Patrick Roy 2.00 5.00
9 Patrick Roy 2.00 5.00
10 Patrick Roy 2.00 5.00
11 Patrick Roy 2.00 5.00
12 Patrick Roy 2.00 5.00
13 Patrick Roy 2.00 5.00
14 Patrick Roy 2.00 5.00

2002-03 Topps Patrick Roy Reprints Autographs

COMMON CARD (1-14) 60.00 150.00

2002-03 Topps Rookie Reprints

1 Pat LaFontaine 2.00 5.00
2 Mike Gartner 2.00 5.00
3 Pete Mahovlich 3.00 8.00
4 Andy Bathgate 3.00 8.00
5 Gump Worsley 3.00 8.00
6 Danny Gare 2.00 5.00
7 Harry Howell 2.00 5.00
8 Andy Moog 2.00 5.00
9 Keith Magnuson 2.00 5.00
10 Milt Schmidt 3.00 8.00
11 Glen Sather 2.00 5.00
12 Dick Duff 2.00 5.00
13 Garry Unger 2.00 5.00
14 Darren Pang 2.00 5.00
15 Chico Resch 3.00 8.00

2002-03 Topps Rookie Reprint Autographs

1 Pat LaFontaine 15.00 40.00
2 Mike Gartner 15.00 40.00
3 Pete Mahovlich 30.00 60.00
4 Andy Bathgate 25.00 60.00
5 Gump Worsley 25.00 60.00
6 Danny Gare 15.00 40.00
7 Harry Howell 15.00 40.00
8 Andy Moog 20.00 50.00
9 Keith Magnuson 40.00 100.00
10 Milt Schmidt 30.00 80.00
11 Glen Sather 30.00 80.00
12 Dick Duff 20.00 50.00
13 Garry Unger 30.00 80.00
14 Darren Pang 15.00 40.00
15 Chico Resch 12.00 30.00

2002-03 Topps Signs of the Future

DL David Legwand 10.00 25.00
IK Ilya Kovalchuk 15.00 40.00
KK Krys Kolanos 10.00 25.00
MC Mike Comrie 10.00 25.00
MH Martin Havlat 12.50 30.00
RV Radim Vrbata 10.00 25.00

2002-03 Topps Stanley Cup Heroes

COMPLETE SET (5) 25.00 40.00
SCHDS Derek Sanderson 4.00 10.00
SCHJF John Ferguson 4.00 10.00
SCHRL Reggie Leach 4.00 10.00
SCHRM Rick MacLeish 4.00 10.00
SCHSS Steve Shutt 4.00 10.00

2002-03 Topps Stanley Cup Heroes Autographs

SCHDS Derek Sanderson 15.00 40.00
SCHJF John Ferguson 15.00 40.00
SCHRL Reggie Leach 12.50 30.00
SCHRM Rick MacLeish 20.00 50.00
SCHSS Steve Shutt 12.50 30.00

2002-03 Topps Promos

COMPLETE SET (6) 1.50 4.00
PP1 Simon Gagne .40 1.00
PP2 Jason Allison .40 1.00
PP3 Sergei Gonchar .20 .50
PP4 Wade Redden .20 .50
PP5 Byron Dafoe .40 1.00
PP6 Patrik Elias .40 1.00

2003-04 Topps

COMPLETE SET (340) 30.00 60.00
*GOLD/50: 6X TO 15X BASIC CARDS
1 Joe Thornton .30 .75
2 Chris Osgood .20 .50
3 Brian Rafalski .15 .40
4 Chris Chelios .20 .50
5 Marian Gaborik .20 .50
6 Pavel Bure .20 .50
7 Ladislav Nagy .12 .30
8 Stephen Weiss .12 .30
9 Mike Modano .30 .75
10 Paul Kariya .20 .50
11 Daymond Langkow .12 .30
12 Patrick Lalime .15 .40
13 Alyn McCauley .12 .30
14 Steve Rucchin .12 .30
15 Mike Johnson .12 .30
16 Georges Laraque .15 .40
17 Brian Sutherby .12 .30
18 Petr Sykora .15 .40
19 Joe Sakic .40 1.00
20 Henrik Sedin .25 .60
21 Nikolai Khabibulin .20 .50
22 Kevin Weekes .15 .40
23 Jan Bulis .12 .30
24 Ales Kotalik .12 .30
25 Niko Kapanen .12 .30
26 Jaroslav Modry .12 .30
27 Dan Cloutier .15 .40
28 Olli Jokinen .20 .50
29 Todd Marchant .12 .30
30 Jaromir Jagr .60 1.50
31 Rick Nash .20 .50
32 Sami Kapanen .12 .30
33 Brian Boucher .15 .40
34 P.J. Stock .12 .30
35 Teemu Selanne .40 1.00
36 Ossi Vaananen .12 .30
37 Jan Hlavac .12 .30
38 Ville Nieminen .12 .30
39 Jere Lehtinen .15 .40
40 Markus Naslund .20 .50
41 Anson Carter .15 .40
42 Steve Sullivan .12 .30
43 Dwayne Roloson .15 .40
44 Frantisek Kaberle .12 .30
45 Cory Stillman .12 .30
46 Shawn Horcoff .12 .30
47 Robert Lang .12 .30
48 Barret Jackman .12 .30
49 Joe Nieuwendyk .15 .40
50 Alexei Kovalev .15 .40
51 Niclas Wallin .12 .30
52 Cory Sarich .12 .30
53 Brendan Witt .12 .30
54 Mike Fisher .12 .30
55 Ed Belfour .20 .50
56 Sergei Zubov .15 .40
57 Ryan Miller .20 .50
58 Tyler Arnason .12 .30
59 Matt Cooke .12 .30
60 Brian Leetch .15 .40
61 Pavel Datsyuk .30 .75
62 Miikka Kiprusoff .20 .50
63 Michal Handzus .15 .40
64 Steve Shields .15 .40
65 Jason Arnott .15 .40
66 Miroslav Satan .15 .40
67 Nick Schultz .12 .30
68 Daniel Briere .20 .50
69 Alexei Yashin .15 .40
70 Martin Straka .12 .30
71 Martin Biron .15 .40
72 Michael Peca .15 .40
73 Simon Gagne .20 .50
74 Alexei Morozov .12 .30
75 Owen Nolan .20 .50
76 Niklas Hagman .12 .30
77 Kim Johnsson .12 .30
78 David Legwand .15 .40
79 Mark Parrish .12 .30
80 Marcel Hossa .12 .30
81 Mike Rathje .12 .30
82 Ruslan Fedotenko .12 .30
83 Bryan Berard .15 .40
84 Richard Zednik .12 .30
85 Viktor Kozlov .12 .30
86 John Madden .12 .30
87 Roman Hamrlik .12 .30
88 Eric Lindros .30 .75
89 Patrik Elias .20 .50
90 Sergei Fedorov .30 .75
91 Pavel Kubina .12 .30
92 Chris Phillips .12 .30
93 Marc Savard .12 .30
94 Janne Niinimaa .12 .30
95 Michael Nylander .12 .30
96 Radek Bonk .15 .40
97 Dmitri Bykov .12 .30
98 Dave Scatchard .12 .30
99 Marian Hossa .20 .50
100 Mario Lemieux .75 2.00
101 Mark Messier .40 1.00
102 Tim Connolly .12 .30
103 Henrik Zetterberg .25 .60
104 Brendan Morrison .15 .40
105 Craig Conroy .12 .30
106 Darcy Tucker .15 .40
107 Steve Konowalchuk .12 .30
108 Valeri Bure .12 .30
109 Rod Brind'Amour .20 .50
110 Jeremy Roenick .30 .75
111 Zdeno Chara .20 .50
112 Mathieu Schneider .12 .30
113 Scott Hartnell .12 .30
114 Vincent Damphousse .15 .40
115 Brian Gionta .12 .30
116 Jeff O'Neill .12 .30
117 Pascal Dupuis .12 .30
118 Patrik Stefan .12 .30
119 Eric Daze .15 .40
120 Jose Theodore .20 .50
121 Yanic Perreault .12 .30
122 Shawn McEachern .12 .30
123 Daniel Alfredsson .20 .50
124 Peter Bondra .20 .50
125 Doug Weight .20 .50
126 Chris Drury .15 .40
127 Ed Jovanovski .15 .40
128 Scott Stevens .20 .50
129 Adam Foote .12 .30
130 Curtis Joseph .25 .60
131 Phil Housley .15 .40
132 Philippe Boucher .12 .30
133 Patrice Brisebois .12 .30
134 Josef Vasicek .12 .30
135 Peter Worrell .12 .30
136 Mike Knuble .12 .30
137 Jocelyn Thibault .15 .40
138 Keith Primeau .15 .40
139 Marc Chouinard .12 .30
140 Mats Sundin .20 .50
141 Martin Skoula .12 .30
142 Sergei Gonchar .12 .30
143 Pavol Demitra .25 .60
144 Tie Domi .15 .40
145 Denis Arkhipov .12 .30
146 Oleg Saprykin .12 .30
147 Tommy Salo .15 .40
148 Andrei Markov .20 .50
149 Brent Johnson .15 .40
150 Jarome Iginla .25 .60
151 Darryl Sydor .12 .30
152 Bryan Smolinski .12 .30
153 Roberto Luongo .30 .75
154 Sandis Ozolinsh .12 .30
155 Alexander Svitov .12 .30
156 J.P. Dumont .12 .30
157 Mike York .12 .30
158 Martin Brodeur .50 1.25
159 Scott Gomez .15 .40
160 Peter Forsberg .40 1.00
161 Kimmo Timonen .12 .30
162 Derek Morris .12 .30
163 Justin Williams .15 .40
164 Mike Comrie .15 .40
165 Mattias Weinhandl .12 .30
166 Dimitri Kalinin .12 .30
167 John LeClair .20 .50
168 Evgeni Nabokov .15 .40
169 Alexander Mogilny .15 .40
170 Derian Hatcher .12 .30
171 Adam Deadmarsh .12 .30
172 Alexei Smirnov .12 .30
173 Nikolai Antropov .15 .40
174 Radoslav Suchy .12 .30
175 Nick Boynton .12 .30
176 Marc Denis .15 .40
177 Ivan Huml .12 .30
178 Dan Blackburn .15 .40
179 Roman Cechmanek .15 .40
180 Tony Amonte .15 .40
181 Jason Blake .12 .30
182 Erik Cole .12 .30
183 P-M Bouchard .20 .50
184 Reed Low .12 .30
185 Geoff Sanderson .12 .30
186 Andrei Zyuzin .12 .30
187 Jean-Sebastien Giguere .20 .50
188 Patrick Marleau .20 .50
189 Nicklas Lidstrom .20 .50
190 Ilya Kovalchuk .20 .50
191 Petr Nedved .12 .30
192 Vincent Lecavalier .20 .50
193 Andreas Johansson .12 .30
194 Dennis Seidenberg .12 .30
195 Alex Tanguay .15 .40
196 Slava Kozlov .15 .40
197 Eric Brewer .12 .30
198 Adam Hall .12 .30
199 Steve Reinprecht .12 .30
200 Todd Bertuzzi .20 .50
201 Rob Blake .20 .50
202 Olaf Kolzig .20 .50
203 Roman Turek .15 .40
204 Brian Rolston .15 .40
205 Bill Guerin .20 .50
206 Johan Hedberg .15 .40
207 Vladimir Orszagh .12 .30
208 Jordan Leopold .12 .30
209 Donald Brashear .12 .30
210 Saku Koivu .20 .50
211 Dave Andreychuk .20 .50
212 Luc Robitaille .20 .50
213 Shaun Van Allen .12 .30
214 Trevor Linden .20 .50
215 Jason Allison .15 .40
216 Marty Turco .20 .50
217 Kyle McLaren .12 .30
218 Daniel Sedin .25 .60
219 Eric Belanger .12 .30
220 Mattias Ohlund .12 .30
221 Brad Richards .20 .50
222 Kyle Calder .12 .30
223 Alexander Frolov .15 .40
224 Tomas Kaberle .12 .30
225 Martin Havlat .20 .50
226 Patrick Roy .50 1.25
227 Jamie Lundmark .12 .30
228 Wade Redden .12 .30
229 Mark Recchi .25 .60
230 Tomas Vokoun .15 .40
231 Scott Niedermayer .20 .50
232 Bob Boughner .12 .30
233 Rick DiPietro .15 .40
234 Chris Gratton .12 .30
235 Keith Tkachuk .20 .50
236 Rostislav Klesla .12 .30
237 Ruslan Salei .12 .30
238 Jeff Friesen .12 .30
239 Felix Potvin .30 .75
240 Dany Heatley .15 .40
241 Brad Stuart .12 .30
242 Andrew Cassels .12 .30
243 Ray Whitney .15 .40
244 Chris Pronger .20 .50
245 Garth Snow .15 .40
246 Sean Hill .12 .30
247 Kristian Huselius .12 .30
248 Jamie Langenbrunner .15 .40
249 Martin St. Louis .20 .50
250 Ron Francis .25 .60
251 Tyler Wright .12 .30
252 Doug Gilmour .25 .60
253 Mike Dunham .15 .40
254 Jozef Stumpel .12 .30
255 Andrew Brunette .12 .30
256 Bobby Holik .12 .30
257 Brendan Shanahan .20 .50
258 Martin Gelinas .12 .30
259 Sergei Berezin .12 .30
260 Zigmund Palffy .20 .50
261 Yannick Tremblay .12 .30
262 Pasi Nurminen .15 .40
263 Robyn Regehr .12 .30
264 Espen Knutsen .12 .30
265 Al MacInnis .25 .60
266 Adam Oates .20 .50
267 Ryan Smyth .15 .40
268 Marco Sturm .12 .30
269 Tom Poti .12 .30
270 Brett Hull .40 1.00
271 David Aebischer .15 .40
272 Milan Hejduk .15 .40
273 Steve McKenna .12 .30
274 Dick Tarnstrom .12 .30
275 Kenny Jonsson .12 .30
276 Glen Murray .15 .40
277 Stu Barnes .12 .30
278 Jay Bouwmeester .12 .30
279 Darius Kasparaitis BM .10 .25
280 Scott Stevens BM .15 .40
281 Zdeno Chara BM .15 .40
282 Donald Brashear BM .10 .25
283 Reed Low BM .10 .25
284 Jody Shelley BM .10 .25
285 Eric Cairns BM .10 .25
286 Brendan Witt BM .10 .25
287 Rob Ray BM .10 .25
288 Georges Laraque BM .12 .30
289 Brett Hull SH .30 .75
290 Martin Brodeur SH .40 1.00
291 Jean-Sebastien Giguere SH .15 .40
292 Paul Kariya SH .15 .40
293 New Jersey Devils .15 .40
294 Marty Turco AS .15 .40
295 Patrick Lalime AS .12 .30
296 Paul Kariya AS .15 .40
297 Nicklas Lidstrom AS .15 .40
298 Al MacInnis AS .20 .50
299 Scott Stevens AS .15 .40
300 Marian Gaborik AS .15 .40
301 Dany Heatley AS .12 .30
302 Jaromir Jagr AS .50 1.25
303 Olli Jokinen AS .15 .40
304 Bill Guerin AS .15 .40
305 Todd Bertuzzi AS .15 .40
306 Bruno St. Jacques .12 .30
307 Mathieu Darche .12 .30
308 Mathias Johansson .12 .30
309 Joe DiPenta RC .30 .75
310 Milan Bartovic RC .30 .75
311 Rick Mrozik RC .25 .60
312 Kent McDonell RC .30 .75
313 Fernando Pisani .12 .30
314 Kip Brennan .12 .30
315 Miroslav Zalesak .12 .30
316 Peter Sejna RC .30 .75
317 Matt Stajan RC .40 1.00
318 Ivan Ciernik .12 .30
319 Shaone Morrisonn .12 .30
320 Garnet Exelby .12 .30
321 Ari Ahonen .12 .30
322 Mike Rupp .12 .30
323 Kris Vernarsky .12 .30
324 Tomas Kurka .12 .30
325 Brandon Reid .12 .30
326 Jim Vandermeer .12 .30
327 Jared Aulin .12 .30
328 Cristobal Huet .15 .40
329 Alexei Ponikarovsky .12 .30
330 Alexei Semenov .12 .30
331 Patrice Bergeron RC 10.00 25.00
332 Jiri Hudler RC 1.25 3.00
333 Antti Miettinen RC .75 2.00
334 Eric Staal RC 2.50 6.00
335 Nathan Horton RC 1.25 3.00
336 Joffrey Lupul RC 1.25 3.00
337 Tuomo Ruutu RC .75 2.00
338 Jordin Tootoo RC 1.00 2.50
339 Dustin Brown RC 1.25 3.00
340 Marc-Andre Fleury RC 3.00 8.00
NNO Rookie EXCH expired .20 .50

2003-04 Topps Blue

*1-330 VETS/500: 3X TO 8X BASIC CARDS
*309-317 ROOKIES/500: 1.5X TO 4X BASIC RC
*331-340 ROOKIES/500: .8X TO 2X BASIC RC
101 Mark Messier 3.00 8.00

2003-04 Topps Red

*1-330 VETS/100: 6X TO 15X BASIC CARDS
*309-317 ROOKIES/100: 3X TO 8X BASIC RC
*331-340 ROOKIES/100: 1.5X TO 4X BASIC RC

2003-04 Topps First Overall Fabrics

EL Eric Lindros 20.00 50.00
IL Ilya Kovalchuk 25.00 60.00
JT Joe Thornton 30.00 80.00
ML Mario Lemieux 50.00 125.00
MM Mike Modano 20.00 50.00
MS Mats Sundin 15.00 40.00
RN Rick Nash 20.00 50.00
VL Vincent Lecavalier 20.00 50.00
JTIK J.Thornton/I.Kovalchuk 50.00 125.00
JTVL J.Thornton/V.Lecavalier 60.00 150.00
MLMM M.Lemieux/M.Modano 75.00 200.00
MLRN M.Lemieux/R.Nash 75.00 200.00
MMMS M.Modano/M.Sundin 75.00 200.00
MSEL M.Sundin/E.Lindros 50.00 125.00
RNIK R.Nash/I.Kovalchuk 60.00 150.00
VLEL V.Lecavalier/E.Lindros 50.00 125.00

2003-04 Topps First Round Fabrics

AY Alexei Yashin 6.00 15.00
BG Bill Guerin 6.00 15.00
JB Jay Bouwmeester 6.00 15.00
JI Jarome Iginla 12.50 30.00
JJ Jaromir Jagr 10.00 25.00
JL Jamie Lundmark 6.00 15.00
JP Jason Spezza 10.00 25.00
TB Todd Bertuzzi 6.00 15.00
BGJI B.Guerin/J.Iginla 30.00 80.00
JJJL J.Jagr/J.Lundmark
JSJB J.Spezza/J.Bouwmeester 30.00 80.00
TBAY T.Bertuzzi/A.Yashin 50.00 125.00

2003-04 Topps Idols

CI1 Dany Heatley .50 1.25
CI2 Martin Brodeur 1.50 4.00
CI3 Todd Bertuzzi .60 1.50
CI4 Mario Lemieux 2.50 6.00
CI5 Joe Thornton 1.00 2.50
CI6 Ed Belfour .60 1.50
CI7 Michael Peca .50 1.25
CI8 Jarome Iginla .75 2.00
CI9 Marty Turco .60 1.50
CI10 Steve Yzerman 1.50 4.00
CI11 Patrick Lalime .50 1.25
CI12 Jose Theodore .60 1.50
CI13 Rick Nash .60 1.50
CI14 Joe Sakic 1.25 3.00
CI15 Vincent Lecavalier .60 1.50
CI16 Mark Messier 1.25 3.00
CI17 Brendan Shanahan .60 1.50
CI18 Patrick Roy 1.50 4.00
CI19 Paul Kariya .60 1.50
CI20 Jocelyn Thibault .50 1.25
II1 Marian Gaborik .60 1.50
II2 Alex Kovalev .50 1.25
II3 Patrik Elias .60 1.50
II4 Daniel Alfredsson .60 1.50
II5 Alexei Yashin .50 1.25
II6 Peter Bondra .60 1.50
II7 Milan Hejduk .50 1.25
II8 Sergei Fedorov 1.00 2.50
II9 Alexander Mogilny .50 1.25
II10 Olli Jokinen .60 1.50
II11 Pavel Bure .60 1.50
II12 Jaromir Jagr 2.00 5.00
II13 Nicklas Lidstrom .60 1.50
II14 Ilya Kovalchuk .60 1.50
II15 Teemu Selanne 1.25 3.00
II16 Marian Hossa .60 1.50
II17 Markus Naslund .60 1.50
II18 Peter Forsberg 1.25 3.00
II19 Saku Koivu .60 1.50
II20 Mats Sundin .60 1.50
UI1 Bill Guerin .60 1.50
UI2 Jeremy Roenick 1.00 2.50
UI3 Doug Weight .60 1.50
UI4 Chris Drury .50 1.25
UI5 Mike Modano 1.00 2.50
UI6 Chris Chelios .60 1.50
UI7 Scott Gomez .50 1.25
UI8 Brian Rolston .50 1.25
UI9 Keith Tkachuk .60 1.50
UI10 Mark Parrish .40 1.00
UI11 John LeClair .60 1.50
UI12 Mike Dunham .50 1.25
UI13 Tyler Arnason .40 1.00
UI14 Tony Amonte .50 1.25
UI15 Mike York .40 1.00
UI16 David Legwand .50 1.25
UI17 Brian Leetch .50 1.25
UI18 Brent Johnson .50 1.25
UI19 Erik Cole .40 1.00
UI20 Jamie Langenbrunner .50 1.25

2003-04 Topps Lost Rookies

BH Brett Hull .60 1.50
BS Brendan Shanahan .50 1.25
CJ Curtis Joseph .50 1.25
EB Ed Belfour .50 1.25
JR Jeremy Roenick .60 1.50
JS Joe Sakic 1.00 2.50
ML Mario Lemieux 3.00 8.00
MM Mike Modano .75 2.00
PR Patrick Roy 2.50 6.00
RF Ron Francis .50 1.25
SY Steve Yzerman 2.50 6.00

2003-04 Topps Own the Game

COMPLETE SET (20) 6.00 12.00
OTG1 Peter Forsberg .60 1.50
OTG2 Markus Naslund .20 .50
OTG3 Joe Thornton .30 .75
OTG4 Milan Hejduk .20 .50
OTG5 Todd Bertuzzi .20 .50
OTG6 Henrik Zetterberg .30 .75
OTG7 Tyler Arnason .15 .40
OTG8 Rick Nash .30 .75
OTG9 Ales Kotalik .15 .40
OTG10 Niko Kapanen .15 .40
OTG11 Martin Brodeur .75 2.00
OTG12 Patrick Lalime .15 .40
OTG13 Ed Belfour .20 .50
OTG14 Patrick Roy 1.00 2.50
OTG15 Jean-Sebastien Giguere .15 .40
OTG16 Jody Shelley .15 .40
OTG17 Reed Low .15 .40
OTG18 Matt Johnson .15 .40
OTG19 Wade Belak .15 .40
OTG20 Peter Worrell .15 .40

2003-04 Topps Signs of Toughness

GL Georges Laraque 12.50 30.00
KS Kevin Sawyer 12.50 30.00
PW Peter Worrell 12.50 30.00
RR Rob Ray 20.00 50.00
SM Sandy McCarthy 12.50 30.00
SP Scott Parker 12.50 30.00
PJS P.J. Stock 12.50 30.00

2003-04 Topps Signs of Youth

BG Brian Gionta 5.00 12.00
BR Brad Richards 12.50 30.00
IK Ilya Kovalchuk 12.00 30.00
KH Kristian Huselius 10.00 25.00
RN Rick Nash 20.00 50.00
SW Stephen Weiss 10.00 25.00

2003-04 Topps Stanley Cup Heroes

BC Bobby Clarke 4.00 10.00
BN Bobby Nystrom 4.00 10.00
BS Billy Smith 4.00 10.00
DS Dave Schultz 4.00 10.00
GF Grant Fuhr 5.00 12.00
JL Jacques Lemaire 4.00 10.00
SS Serge Savard 4.00 10.00

2003-04 Topps Stanley Cup Heroes Autographs

BC Bobby Clarke 15.00 40.00
BN Bobby Nystrom 12.50 30.00
BS Billy Smith 12.50 30.00
DS Dave Schultz 12.50 30.00
GF Grant Fuhr 15.00 40.00
JL Jacques Lemaire 12.50 30.00
SS Serge Savard

2003-04 Topps Tough Materials

DL Darren Langdon 6.00 15.00
EC Eric Cairns 6.00 15.00
GL Georges Laraque 8.00 20.00
KS Kevin Sawyer 6.00 15.00
PW Peter Worrell 8.00 20.00
RL Reed Low 6.00 15.00
RR Rob Ray 8.00 20.00
SM Sandy McCarthy 6.00 15.00
SP Scott Parker 6.00 15.00
PJS P.J. Stock 10.00 25.00
GLSP G.Laraque/S.Parker 20.00 50.00
KSRL K.Sawyer/R.Low 12.50 30.00
PSRR P.Stock/R.Ray 20.00 50.00
PWDL P.Worrell/D.Langdon 20.00 50.00
SMEC S.McCarthy/E.Cairns 15.00 40.00

2003-04 Topps Tough Materials Autographs

GL Georges Laraque 15.00 40.00
KS Kevin Sawyer 12.00 30.00
PW Peter Worrell 12.00 30.00
RR Rob Ray 15.00 40.00
SM Sandy McCarthy 12.00 30.00
SP Scott Parker 15.00 40.00
PJS P.J. Stock 12.00 30.00

2003-04 Topps Promos

COMPLETE SET (6) 1.50 4.00
PP1 Marian Hossa .30 .75
PP2 Jaromir Jagr .40 1.00
PP3 Curtis Joseph .30 .75
PP4 Mike Modano .40 1.00
PP5 Markus Naslund .30 .75
PP6 Alexei Yashin .25 .60

2003 Topps All-Star Block Party

COMPLETE SET (6) 12.00
1 Patrick Roy 2.00 5.00
2 Jaromir Jagr .80 2.00
3 Jarome Iginla .40 1.00
4 Henrik Zetterberg 1.60 3.00
5 Rick Nash 1.60 4.00
6 Jay Bouwmeester 1.20 2.00

2004 Topps NHL All-Star FANtasy

COMPLETE SET (6) 6.00 15.00
1 Marian Gaborik .60 1.50
2 Dwayne Roloson .60 1.50
3 Patrice Bergeron 1.50 5.00
4 Marc-Andre Fleury 2.00 5.00
5 Eric Staal 1.00 2.00
6 Tuomo Ruutu 1.25 3.00

2001-02 Topps Archives

COMPLETE SET (81) 30.00 60.00
1 Andy Bathgate .50 1.25
2 Bill Gadsby .50 1.25
3 Tony Esposito .75 2.00
4 Harry Howell .40 1.00
5 Larry Robinson .40 1.00
6 Jacques Plante .75 2.00
7 Pierre Pilote .50 1.25
8 Glenn Hall .50 1.25
9 Dale Hunter .25 .60
10 Guy Lapointe .25 .60
11 Norm Ullman .40 1.00
12 Bryan Trottier .60 1.50
13 Alex Delvecchio .50 1.25
14 Stan Mikita .60 1.50
15 Neal Broten .25 .60
16 Bernie Parent .50 1.25
17 Johnny Bucyk .50 1.25
18 Rick Middleton .40 1.00
19 Bobby Clarke .50 1.25
20 Billy Smith .50 1.25
21 Peter Stastny .40 1.00
22 Tim Kerr .25 .60
23 Gerry Cheevers .60 1.50
24 Andy Moog .40 1.00
25 Dennis Hull .40 1.00
26 Nick Fotiu .25 .60
27 Marcel Dionne .40 1.00
28 Guy Lafleur .60 1.50
29 Yvan Cournoyer .50 1.25
30 Brian Mullen .25 .60
31 Wayne Cashman .25 .60
32 Steve Shutt .40 1.00
33 Grant Fuhr .40 1.00
34 Ed Johnston .40 1.00
35 Clark Gillies .25 .60
36 Rick MacLeish .25 .60
37 Denis Potvin .40 1.00
38 Bill Clement .25 .60
39 Darryl Sittler .50 1.25
40 Pierre Larouche .25 .60
41 Vic Hadfield .25 .60
42 Derek Sanderson .40 1.00
43 Reggie Leach .25 .60
44 Brian Propp .25 .60
45 Barry Melrose .40 1.00
46 Danny Gare .25 .60
47 Darren Pang .40 1.00
48 Dick Duff .25 .60
49 Joel Quenneville .25 .60
50 John Ferguson .40 1.00
51 Ed Westfall .25 .60
52 Johnny Bower .50 1.25
53 Serge Savard .50 1.25
54 Keith Magnuson .25 .60
55 Ken Hodge .25 .60
56 Garry Unger .25 .60
57 Lindy Ruff .25 .60
58 Glenn Resch .40 1.00
59 Gump Worsley .50 1.25
60 Bernie Federko .25 .60
61 Mike Foligno .25 .60
62 Milt Schmidt .40 1.00
63 Mike Bossy .40 1.00
64 Ron Low .40 1.00
65 Jacques Lemaire .50 1.25
66 Dave Schultz .40 1.00
67 Glen Sather .40 1.00
68 Doug Wilson .25 .60
69 Terry Sawchuk 1.00 2.50
70 Mike Milbury .25 .60
71 Terry O'Reilly .40 1.00
72 Red Kelly .50 1.25
73 Peter McNab .25 .60
74 Paul Holmgren .25 .60
75 Ken Linseman .25 .60
76 Tim Horton .50 1.25
77 Bobby Smith .25 .60
78 Bobby Hull .75 2.00
79 Pat LaFontaine .40 1.00
80 Pete Mahovlich .25 .60
81 Mike Gartner .40 1.00

2001-02 Topps Archives Arena Seats

ASAD Alex Delvecchio 6.00 15.00
ASBF Bernie Federko 12.00 30.00
ASBS Bobby Smith 5.00 12.00
ASBT Bryan Trottier 8.00 20.00
ASDH Dennis Hull 5.00 12.00
ASDS Derek Sanderson 6.00 15.00
ASDSI Darryl Sittler 5.00 12.00
ASDWI Doug Wilson 5.00 12.00
ASGC Gerry Cheevers 6.00 15.00
ASGHA Glenn Hall 6.00 15.00
ASGL Guy Lapointe 5.00 12.00
ASGLA Guy Lafleur 8.00 20.00
ASJB John Bucyk 5.00 12.00
ASJL Jacques Lemaire 6.00 15.00
ASKH Ken Hodge 5.00 12.00
ASLR Larry Robinson 5.00 12.00
ASMD Marcel Dionne 6.00 15.00
ASNB Neal Broten 12.00 30.00
ASNU Norm Ullman 5.00 12.00
ASPL Pierre Larouche 5.00 12.00
ASPP Pierre Pilote 5.00 12.00
ASSM Stan Mikita 8.00 20.00
ASSSA Serge Savard 6.00 15.00
ASSSH Steve Shutt 6.00 15.00
ASTE Tony Esposito 6.00 15.00
ASTO Terry O'Reilly 6.00 15.00
ASWC Wayne Cashman 5.00 12.00
ASYC Yvan Cournoyer 6.00 15.00

2001-02 Topps Archives Autographs

1 Gerry Cheevers 10.00 25.00
2 Yvan Cournoyer 10.00 25.00
3 Denis Potvin 10.00 25.00
4 John Bucyk 10.00 25.00
5 Glenn Hall 12.00 30.00
6 Pierre Pilote 10.00 25.00
7 Norm Ullman 10.00 25.00
8 Jacques Lemaire 10.00 25.00
9 Grant Fuhr 12.00 30.00
10 Stan Mikita 25.00 50.00
11 Guy Lafleur 20.00 50.00
12 Tony Esposito SP 25.00 60.00
13 Alex Delvecchio 10.00 25.00
14 Dennis Hull 10.00 25.00
15 Marcel Dionne 10.00 25.00
16 Bobby Clarke 12.00 30.00
17 Darryl Sittler 12.50 30.00
18 Dave Schultz SP 50.00 100.00
19 Bryan Trottier 10.00 25.00
21 Terry O'Reilly SP 25.00 60.00
22 Serge Savard SP 40.00 80.00
23 Vic Hadfield SP 60.00 150.00
24 Rick Middleton SP 100.00 200.00
25 Peter McNab SP 100.00 200.00
26 Peter Stastny SP 75.00 150.00
27 Ken Linseman SP 25.00 60.00
28 Ed Westfall SP 50.00 120.00
29 Clark Gillies SP 25.00 60.00
30 Bobby Hull SP 75.00 150.00

2001-02 Topps Archives Buyback Autoproofs

1 Marcel Dionne '88-89 Top 10.00 25.00
2 Bobby Clarke 8.00 20.00
3 Denis Potvin 50.00 100.00
4 Guy Lafleur 15.00 40.00

2001-02 Topps Archives Relics

JAD Alex Delvecchio J 6.00 15.00
JAM Andy Moog J 5.00 12.00
JBC Bobby Clarke J 12.50 30.00
JBM Brian Mullen J 6.00 15.00
JEW Ed Westfall J 5.00 12.00
JGF Grant Fuhr J 8.00 20.00
JLR Larry Robinson J 6.00 15.00
JMG Mike Gartner J 5.00 12.00
JPM Pete Mahovlich J 5.00 12.00
JSM Stan Mikita J 8.00 20.00
JBIS Billy Smith J 6.00 15.00
JBOS Bobby Smith J 5.00 12.00
SBC Bobby Clarke S 12.50 30.00
SDH Dale Hawerchuk S 8.00 20.00
STE Tony Esposito S 12.50 30.00

2003-04 Topps C55

COMPLETE SET (165) 20.00 50.00
1 Peter Forsberg .50 1.25
1B Peter Forsberg Full Length .50 1.25
2 Brian Leetch .20 .50
3 Jarome Iginla .30 .75
4 Scott Stevens .25 .60
5 Nicklas Lidstrom .25 .60
6 Patrick Lalime .20 .50
7 Henrik Zetterberg .30 .75
7B Henrik Zetterberg Full Length .30 .75
8 Patrick Marleau .25 .60
9 Mike Modano .40 1.00
10 Marian Hossa .25 .60
11 Owen Nolan .25 .60
12 John Madden .15 .40
13 Mats Sundin .25 .60
14 Adam Hall .15 .40
15 Ron Francis .30 .75
16 Peter Bondra .25 .60
17 Ilya Kovalchuk .25 .60
17B Ilya Kovalchuk Full Length .25 .60
18 Miroslav Satan .20 .50
19 Joe Sakic .50 1.25
20 Vincent Lecavalier .25 .60
21 Rick Nash .25 .60
21B Rick Nash Full Length .25 .60
22 Anson Carter .20 .50
23 Doug Weight .25 .60
24 Rick DiPietro .20 .50
25 Tyler Arnason .15 .40
26 Mike Johnson .15 .40
27 Jeremy Roenick .40 1.00
28 Teemu Selanne .50 1.25
29 Roberto Luongo .40 1.00
30 Martin Brodeur .60 1.50
30B Martin Brodeur Full Length .60 1.50
31 Bill Guerin .25 .60
32 Tim Connolly .15 .40
33 Roman Turek .20 .50
34 Olli Jokinen .25 .60
35 Radek Bonk .20 .50
36 Steve Rucchin .15 .40
37 Barret Jackman .15 .40
38 Dominik Hasek .40 1.00
39 Petr Nedved .15 .40
40 Marian Gaborik .25 .60
40B Marian Gaborik Full Length .25 .60
41 Josef Vasicek .15 .40
42 Ladislav Nagy .15 .40
43 Felix Potvin .40 1.00
44 Jay Bouwmeester .15 .40
45 Sergei Gonchar .15 .40
46 Niklas Hagman .15 .40
47 Glen Murray .20 .50
48 Kyle Calder .15 .40
49 Ed Belfour .25 .60
50 Milan Hejduk .20 .50
51 Alex Kovalev .20 .50
52 Petr Sykora .20 .50
53 Scott Hartnell .15 .40
54 Tony Amonte .20 .50
55 Ed Jovanovski .20 .50
56 Sergei Zubov .20 .50
57 Mark Recchi .30 .75
58 Markus Naslund .25 .60
59 Zigmund Palffy .25 .60
60 Marty Turco .25 .60
61 Jocelyn Thibault .20 .50
62 Martin Biron .20 .50
63 Roman Hamrlik .15 .40
64 Stanislav Chistov .15 .40
65 Tomas Kaberle .15 .40
66 Mario Lemieux 1.00 2.50
66B Mario Lemieux Full Length 1.00 2.50
67 Rob Blake .25 .60
68 Jaromir Jagr .75 2.00
69 Nikolai Khabibulin .25 .60
70 Brett Hull .50 1.25
71 Slava Kozlov .20 .50
72 Michael Peca .20 .50
73 Jeff O'Neill .15 .40
74 Joe Nieuwendyk .20 .50
75 Yanic Perreault .15 .40
76 Derian Hatcher .15 .40
77 Chris Gratton .15 .40
78 Olaf Kolzig .25 .60
79 Alexei Yashin .20 .50
80 Martin St. Louis .25 .60
81 Chris Pronger .25 .60
82 Dick Tarnstrom .15 .40
83 Nick Schultz .15 .40
84 Ossi Vaananen .15 .40
85 Tie Domi .20 .50
86 Patrik Elias .25 .60
87 Jim Vandermeer .15 .40
88 Alexei Morozov .15 .40
89 Alexander Mogilny .20 .50
90 Dany Heatley .20 .50
91 Marcel Hossa .15 .40
92 Mike Comrie .20 .50
92B Mike Comrie Full Length .20 .50
93 Niko Kapanen .15 .40
94 David Legwand .20 .50
95 Alex Tanguay .20 .50
96 Alyn McCauley .15 .40
97 Brendan Morrison .20 .50
98 Chris Drury .20 .50
99 Paul Kariya .25 .60
100 Joe Thornton .40 1.00
100B Joe Thornton Full Length .40 1.00
101 Tomas Vokoun .20 .50
102 Tommy Salo .20 .50
103 Brad Richards .25 .60
104 Geoff Sanderson .15 .40
105 Daniel Briere .25 .60
106 Mike Dunham .20 .50
107 Kyle McLaren .15 .40
108 Zdeno Chara .25 .60
109 Curtis Joseph .30 .75
110 Todd Bertuzzi .25 .60
111 Saku Koivu .25 .60
112 Martin Havlat .25 .60
113 Dave Andreychuk .25 .60
114 Dan Cloutier .20 .50
115 Pavol Demitra .30 .75
116 Dave Scatchard .15 .40
117 Ryan Smyth .20 .50
118 Craig Conroy .15 .40
119 Eric Brewer .15 .40
120 Jean-Sebastien Giguere .25 .60
120B J.Giguere Full Length .25 .60
121 Alexander Frolov .20 .50
122 Al MacInnis .30 .75
123 Martin Straka .15 .40
124 Brian Rolston .20 .50
125 Jamie Langenbrunner .20 .50
126 Pierre-Marc Bouchard .25 .60
127 Jan Bulis .15 .40
128 Rostislav Klesla .15 .40
129 Pasi Nurminen .20 .50
130 Jose Theodore .25 .60
131 Tuomo Ruutu RC 1.00 2.50
132 Andrew Peters RC .75 2.00
133 Jordin Tootoo RC 1.25 3.00
134 Joe DiPenta RC .75 2.00
135 Milan Bartovic RC .75 2.00
136 Rick Mrozik RC .60 1.50
137 Kent McDonell RC .75 2.00
138 Antti Miettinen RC 1.00 2.50
139 Alexander Semin RC 2.00 5.00
140 Dustin Brown RC 1.50 4.00
141 Peter Sejna RC .75 2.00
142 Matt Stajan RC 1.00 2.50
143 Brent Burns RC 2.00 5.00
144 Paul Martin RC .75 2.00
145 Antoine Vermette RC 1.25 3.00
146 Sean Bergenheim RC .75 2.00
147 Joni Pitkanen RC 1.00 2.50
148 Patrice Bergeron RC 3.00 8.00
149 Eric Staal RC 3.00 8.00
150 Dan Hamhuis RC .75 2.00
151 Marc-Andre Fleury RC 4.00 10.00
152 Jiri Hudler RC 1.50 4.00
153 David Hale RC .60 1.50
154 Milan Michalek RC 1.25 3.00
155 John-Michael Liles RC .75 2.00

2003-04 Topps C55 Minis

*1-30 VETS: .5X TO 1.2X BASIC CARDS
*131-155 ROOKIES: .5X TO 1.2X BASIC RC

2003-04 Topps C55 Minis American Back

*1-130 VETS: .8X TO 2X BASIC CARDS
*131-155 ROOKIES: .6X TO 1.5X BASIC RC

2003-04 Topps C55 Minis American Back Red

*1-130 VETS: 2X TO 5X BASIC CARDS
*131-155 ROOKIES: 1X TO 2.5X BASIC RC

2003-04 Topps C55 Minis Brooklyn Back

*1-130 VETS: .8X TO 2X BASIC CARDS
*131-155 ROOKIES: .6X TO 1.5X BASIC RC

2003-04 Topps C55 Minis Hat Trick Back

*1-130 VETS: 2X TO 5X BASIC CARDS
*131-155 ROOKIES: 1X TO 2.5X BASIC RC

2003-04 Topps C55 Minis O Canada Back

*1-130 VETS: .8X TO 2X BASIC CARDS
*131-155 ROOKIES: .6X TO 1.5X BASIC RC

2003-04 Topps C55 Minis O Canada Back Red

*1-130 VETS: 2X TO 5X BASIC CARDS
*131-155 ROOKIES: 1X TO 2.5X BASIC RC

2003-04 Topps C55 Minis Stanley Cup Back

*1-300 VETS: .6X TO 1.5X BASIC CARDS
*131-155 ROOKIES: .6X TO 1.5X BASIC RC

2003-04 Topps C55 Autographs

TACD Chris Drury C 6.00 15.00
TAEC Erik Cole A 6.00 15.00
TAHZ Henrik Zetterberg A 10.00 25.00
TAIK Ilya Kovalchuk B 10.00 25.00
TAJG Jean-Sebastien Giguere A 8.00 20.00
TAKH Kristian Huselius A 6.00 15.00
TAMH Marian Hossa A 8.00 20.00
TAPE Patrik Elias C 6.00 15.00
TARN Rick Nash A 6.00 15.00
TARV Radim Vrbata C 6.00 15.00
TASW Stephen Weiss A 6.00 15.00
TATB Todd Bertuzzi C 8.00 20.00

2003-04 Topps C55 Award Winners

1 Mighty Ducks of Anaheim .20 .50
2 New Jersey Devils .20 .50
3 Ottawa Senators .20 .50
4 Barret Jackman .20 .50
5 Brendan Shanahan .25 .60
6 Peter Forsberg .40 1.00
7 Martin Brodeur .50 1.25
8 Alexander Mogilny .20 .50
9 Steve Yzerman .75 2.00
10 Nicklas Lidstrom .25 .60
11 Markus Naslund .25 .60
12 Milan Hejduk .20 .50
13 Peter Forsberg .40 1.00
14 Jere Lehtinen .20 .50
15 Jean-Sebastien Giguere .20 .50
16 Martin Brodeur .50 1.25

2003-04 Topps C55 Relics

TRAH Adam Hall E 3.00 8.00
TRAS Alexander Svitov E 3.00 8.00
TRAY Alexei Yashin E 3.00 8.00
TRBG Bill Guerin E 3.00 8.00
TRBH Brett Hull D 8.00 20.00
TRBM Brendan Morrison D 3.00 8.00
TRBRA Branko Radivojevic E 3.00 8.00
TRBR Brad Richards D 4.00 10.00
TRDA Daniel Alfredsson D 4.00 10.00
TRDH Dany Heatley C 6.00 15.00
TRDL David Legwand C 4.00 10.00
TREB Ed Belfour D 6.00 15.00
TRGL Georges Laraque E 3.00 8.00
TRIK Ilya Kovalchuk D 8.00 20.00
TRJB Jay Bouwmeester E 3.00 8.00
TRJI Jarome Iginla E 6.00 15.00
TRJJ Jaromir Jagr E 8.00 20.00
TRJL Jordan Leopold E 3.00 8.00
TRJS Jason Spezza E 6.00 15.00
TRJT Jose Theodore E 6.00 15.00
TRJTH Joe Thornton E 8.00 20.00
TRMC Mike Comrie B 8.00 20.00
TRMG Marian Gaborik E 8.00 20.00
TRMHE Milan Hejduk D 5.00 12.00
TRMH Marian Hossa E 5.00 12.00
TRML Mario Lemieux A 250.00 400.00
TRMM Mike Modano B 50.00 125.00
TRMN Markus Naslund D 5.00 12.00
TRMS Mats Sundin D 5.00 12.00
TRMT Marty Turco E 4.00 10.00
TRNK Nikolai Khabibulin E 5.00 12.00
TRNS Nick Schultz E 3.00 8.00
TRPB Pavel Bure E 8.00 20.00
TRPK Paul Kariya B 20.00 50.00
TRPL Patrick Lalime D 4.00 10.00
TRRB Rob Blake E 4.00 10.00
TRRL Roberto Luongo C 6.00 15.00
TRRM Ryan Miller E 6.00 15.00
TRRN Rick Nash E 6.00 15.00
TRSK Saku Koivu E 5.00 12.00
TRSN Scott Niedermayer B 20.00 50.00
TRSP Scott Parker E 3.00 8.00
TRTB Todd Bertuzzi E 5.00 12.00
TRTC Tim Connolly B 20.00 50.00
TRVL Vincent Lecavalier B 40.00 100.00

2003-04 Topps C55 Stanley Cup Winners

1 Ottawa Senators .30 .75
2 New York Rangers .30 .75
3 Boston Bruins .30 .75
4 Montreal Canadiens .30 .75
5 Montreal Canadiens .30 .75
6 Toronto Maple Leafs .30 .75
7 New York Rangers .30 .75
8 Chicago Blackhawks .30 .75
9 Montreal Maroons .30 .75
10 Detroit Red Wings .30 .75
11 Detroit Red Wings .30 .75
12 Chicago Blackhawks .30 .75
13 Boston Bruins .30 .75
14 New York Rangers .30 .75
15 Boston Bruins .30 .75
16 Toronto Maple Leafs .30 .75
17 Detroit Red Wings .30 .75
18 Montreal Canadiens .30 .75
19 Toronto Maple Leafs .30 .75
20 Montreal Canadiens .30 .75
21 Toronto Maple Leafs .30 .75
22 Toronto Maple Leafs .30 .75
23 Toronto Maple Leafs .30 .75
24 Detroit Red Wings .30 .75
25 Toronto Maple Leafs .30 .75
26 Detroit Red Wings .30 .75
27 Montreal Canadiens .30 .75
28 Detroit Red Wings .30 .75
29 Detroit Red Wings .30 .75
30 Montreal Canadiens .30 .75
31 Montreal Canadiens .30 .75
32 Montreal Canadiens .30 .75
33 Montreal Canadiens .30 .75
34 Montreal Canadiens .30 .75
35 Chicago Blackhawks .30 .75
36 Toronto Maple Leafs .30 .75
37 Toronto Maple Leafs .30 .75
38 Toronto Maple Leafs .30 .75
39 Montreal Canadiens .30 .75
40 Montreal Canadiens .30 .75
41 Toronto Maple Leafs .30 .75
42 Montreal Canadiens .30 .75
43 Montreal Canadiens .30 .75
44 Boston Bruins .30 .75
45 Montreal Canadiens .30 .75
46 Boston Bruins .30 .75
47 Montreal Canadiens .30 .75
48 Philadelphia Flyers .30 .75
49 Philadelphia Flyers .30 .75
50 Montreal Canadiens .30 .75
51 Montreal Canadiens .30 .75
52 Montreal Canadiens .30 .75
53 Montreal Canadiens .30 .75
54 New York Islanders .30 .75
55 New York Islanders .30 .75
56 New York Islanders .30 .75
57 New York Islanders .30 .75
58 Edmonton Oilers .30 .75
59 Edmonton Oilers .30 .75
60 Montreal Canadiens .30 .75
61 Edmonton Oilers .30 .75
62 Edmonton Oilers .30 .75
63 Calgary Flames .30 .75
64 Edmonton Oilers .30 .75
65 Pittsburgh Penguins .30 .75
66 Pittsburgh Penguins .30 .75
67 Montreal Canadiens .30 .75
68 New York Rangers .30 .75
69 New Jersey Devils .30 .75
70 Colorado Avalanche .30 .75
71 Detroit Red Wings .30 .75
72 Detroit Red Wings .30 .75
73 Dallas Stars .30 .75
74 New Jersey Devils .30 .75
75 Colorado Avalanche .30 .75
76 Detroit Red Wings .30 .75
77 New Jersey Devils .30 .75

1999-00 Topps Chrome

COMPLETE SET (297) 150.00 300.00
COMP.SET w/MMs (341) 200.00 400.00
1 Joe Sakic 1.00 2.50
2 Alexei Yashin .40 1.00
3 Paul Kariya .50 1.25
4 Keith Tkachuk .50 1.25
5 Jaromir Jagr 1.50 4.00
6 Mike Modano .75 2.00
7 Eric Lindros .75 2.00
8 Zigmund Palffy .50 1.25
9 Dominik Hasek .75 2.00
10 Pavel Bure .50 1.25
11 Ray Bourque .75 2.00
12 Peter Forsberg 1.00 2.50
13 Al MacInnis .60 1.50
14 Steve Yzerman 1.25 3.00
15 Mats Sundin .50 1.25
16 Patrick Roy 1.25 3.00
17 Teemu Selanne 1.00 2.50
18 Keith Primeau .40 1.00
19 John LeClair .50 1.25
20 Martin Brodeur 1.25 3.00
21 Joe Thornton .75 2.00
22 Rob Blake .50 1.25
23 Ron Francis .60 1.50
24 Grant Fuhr .75 2.00
25 Nicklas Lidstrom .50 1.25
26 Vladimir Orszagh RC .30 .75
27 Glen Wesley .30 .75
28 Adam Deadmarsh .30 .75
29 Zdeno Chara .50 1.25
30 Brian Leetch .40 1.00
31 Valeri Bure .30 .75
32 Ryan Smyth .40 1.00
33 Jean-Sebastien Aubin .40 1.00
34 Dave Reid .30 .75
35 Ed Jovanovski .40 1.00
36 Anders Eriksson .30 .75
37 Mike Ricci .30 .75
38 Todd Bertuzzi .40 1.00
39 Shawn Bates .30 .75
40 Kip Miller .30 .75
41 Jozef Stumpel .30 .75
42 Jeremy Roenick .75 2.00
43 Todd Marchant .30 .75
44 Josh Holden .30 .75
45 Rob Niedermayer .30 .75
46 Cory Sarich .30 .75
47 Nikolai Khabibulin .40 1.00
48 Marty McInnis .30 .75
49 Marty Reasoner .30 .75
50 Gary Roberts .30 .75
51 Manny Malhotra .40 1.00
52 Adam Foote .40 1.00
53 Luc Robitaille .50 1.25
54 Bryan Marchment .40 1.00
55 Mark Janssens .30 .75
56 Steve Heinze .30 .75
57 Cory Stillman .30 .75
58 Guy Hebert .50 1.25
59 Mike Richter .50 1.25
60 Jamie Langenbrunner .30 .75
61 Wade Redden .30 .75
62 Steve Smith .30 .75
63 Daniil Markov .30 .75
64 Erik Rasmussen .30 .75
65 Glen Murray .40 1.00
66 Alexei Kovalev .40 1.00
67 Peter Bondra .50 1.25
68 Dimitri Khristich .30 .75
69 Sami Kapanen .30 .75
70 Tom Poti .30 .75
71 Trevor Linden .50 1.25
72 Tomas Vokoun .50 1.25
73 Steve Webb .30 .75
74 Jarome Iginla .60 1.50
75 Scott Mellanby .30 .75
76 Mattias Ohlund .30 .75
77 Steve Konowalchuk .30 .75
78 Bryan Berard .30 .75
79 Chris Pronger .50 1.25
80 Teppo Numminen .30 .75
81 John MacLean .40 1.00
82 Jeff Hackett .30 .75
83 Ray Whitney .40 1.00
84 Chris Osgood .50 1.25
85 Doug Zmolek .30 .75
86 Curtis Brown .30 .75
87 Reid Simpson .30 .75
88 Milan Hejduk .40 1.00
89 Donald Audette .30 .75
90 Saku Koivu .50 1.25
91 Martin Straka .30 .75
92 Mark Messier 1.00 2.50
93 Richard Zednik .30 .75
94 Curtis Joseph .60 1.50
95 Colin Forbes .30 .75
96 Jeff Friesen .40 1.00
97 Eric Brewer .30 .75
98 Darius Kasparaitis .40 1.00
99 Marian Hossa .50 1.25
100 Petr Sykora .40 1.00
101 Vladimir Malakhov .30 .75
102 Jamie Storr .30 .75
103 Doug Gilmour .60 1.50
104 Doug Weight .50 1.25
105 Derian Hatcher .40 1.00
106 Chris Drury .40 1.00
107 Arturs Irbe .40 1.00
108 Fred Brathwaite .30 .75
109 Jason Allison .40 1.00
110 Roman Hamrlik .30 .75
111 Rico Fata .30 .75
112 Janne Niinimaa .30 .75
113 Kenny Jonsson .30 .75
114 Marco Sturm .30 .75
115 Steve Thomas .30 .75
116 Garth Snow .40 1.00
117 Rick Tocchet .40 1.00
118 Jean-Marc Pelletier .30 .75
119 Bobby Holik .30 .75
120 Sergei Fedorov .75 2.00
121 J-P Dumont .40 1.00
122 Jason Woolley .30 .75
123 James Patrick .30 .75
124 Blake Sloan .40 1.00
125 Marcus Nilsson .30 .75
126 Shayne Corson .40 1.00
127 Tom Fitzgerald .30 .75
128 Brian Rolston .40 1.00
129 Ron Tugnutt .40 1.00
130 Mark Recchi .60 1.50
131 Matthew Barnaby .30 .75
132 Olaf Kolzig .50 1.25
133 Paul Mara .30 .75
134 Patrick Marleau .50 1.25
135 Magnus Arvedson .30 .75
136 Felix Potvin .75 2.00
137 Bill Guerin .50 1.25
138 Brett Hull 1.00 2.50
139 Vitali Yachmenev .30 .75
140 Ruslan Salei .30 .75
141 Mark Parrish .30 .75
142 Randy Cunneyworth .30 .75
143 Damian Rhodes .30 .75
144 Daniel Briere .40 1.00
145 Craig Conroy .30 .75
146 Sergei Gonchar .30 .75
147 Vincent Lecavalier .50 1.25
148 Adam Graves .40 1.00
149 Doug Bodger .30 .75
150 Jeff O'Neill .30 .75
151 Darby Hendrickson .30 .75
152 Sergei Samsonov .40 1.00
153 Ed Belfour .50 1.25
154 Robert Svehla .30 .75
155 Cliff Ronning .30 .75
156 Brendan Morrison .40 1.00
157 Daniel Alfredsson .50 1.25
158 Eric Desjardins .40 1.00
159 Mike Vernon .40 1.00
160 Vadim Sharifijanov .30 .75
161 Jaroslav Svejkovsky .30 .75
162 Michael Peca .40 1.00
163 Shane Willis .30 .75
164 Sandis Ozolinsh .30 .75
165 Mathieu Dandenault .30 .75
166 Martin Rucinsky .30 .75
167 Scott Stevens .50 1.25
168 Sami Salo .40 1.00
169 Tom Barrasso .50 1.25
170 Chris Gratton .30 .75
171 Markus Naslund .50 1.25
172 Mike Johnson .40 1.00
173 Bob Boughner .30 .75
174 Todd Simpson .30 .75
175 Fredrik Olausson .30 .75
176 Jocelyn Thibault .40 1.00
177 Juha Ylonen .30 .75
178 Brad Bombardir .30 .75
179 Jan Hrdina .30 .75
180 Adrian Aucoin .30 .75
181 Mike Eagles .30 .75
182 Petr Nedved .30 .75
183 Rem Murray .30 .75
184 Mikael Renberg .30 .75
185 Mike Eastwood .30 .75
186 Byron Dafoe .40 1.00
187 Tony Amonte .40 1.00
188 Darren McCarty .30 .75
189 Sergei Krivokrasov .30 .75
190 Dave Lowry .30 .75
191 Michal Handzus .40 1.00
192 Tie Domi .40 1.00
193 Brian Holzinger .30 .75
194 Jason Arnott .40 1.00
195 Jose Theodore .50 1.25
196 Brendan Shanahan .50 1.25
197 Derek Morris .30 .75
198 Steve Rucchin .30 .75
199 Kevin Hodson .30 .75
200 Oleg Kvasha .30 .75
201 John Vanbiesbrouck .50 1.25
202 Adam Oates .50 1.25
203 Anson Carter .40 1.00
204 Sebastien Bordeleau .30 .75
205 Pavol Demitra .60 1.50
206 Owen Nolan .50 1.25
207 Pavel Rosa .30 .75
208 Petr Svoboda .40 1.00
209 Tomas Kaberle .30 .75
210 Claude Lapointe .40 1.00
211 Todd Harvey .30 .75
212 Trent McCleary .30 .75
213 Vyacheslav Kozlov .30 .75
214 Marc Denis .40 1.00
215 Joe Nieuwendyk .40 1.00
216 Kelly Buchberger .30 .75
217 Tommy Albelin .30 .75
218 Kyle McLaren .30 .75
219 Chris Chelios .50 1.25
220 Joel Bouchard .30 .75
221 Mats Lindgren .30 .75
222 Jyrki Lumme .30 .75
223 Pierre Turgeon .40 1.00
224 Bill Muckalt .30 .75
225 Antti Aalto .30 .75
226 Jere Lehtinen .40 1.00
227 Theo Fleury .60 1.50
228 Dmitri Mironov .30 .75
229 Scott Niedermayer .50 1.25
230 Sean Burke .30 .75
231 Eric Daze .40 1.00
232 Alexei Zhitnik .30 .75
233 Christian Matte .30 .75
234 Patrik Elias .50 1.25
235 Alexandre Korolyuk .30 .75
236 Sergei Berezin .30 .75
237 Ray Ferraro .30 .75
238 Rod Brind'Amour .50 1.25
239 Darcy Tucker .30 .75
240 Darryl Sydor .40 1.00
241 Mike Dunham .30 .75
242 Marc Bergevin .30 .75
243 Ray Sheppard .30 .75
244 Miroslav Satan .40 1.00
245 Andreas Dackell .30 .75
246 Mike Grier .30 .75
247 Alexei Zhamnov .30 .75
248 David Legwand .30 .75
249 Daniel Tkaczuk .30 .75
250 Roberto Luongo .75 2.00
251 Simon Gagne .50 1.25
252 Jamie Lundmark .40 1.00
253 Alexandre Giroux RC .40 1.00
254 Dusty Jamieson RC .50 1.25
255 Jamie Chamberlain RC .50 1.25
256 Radim Vrbata RC 2.00 5.00
257 Scott Cameron RC .50 1.25
258 Simon Lajeunesse RC .60 1.50
259 Tim Connolly .30 .75
260 Kris Beech .30 .75
261 Brian Finley .50 1.25
262 Alex Auld RC .60 1.50
263 Martin Grenier RC .50 1.25
264 Sheldon Keefe RC .60 1.50
265 Justin Mapletoft RC .50 1.25
266 Edward Hill RC .50 1.25
267 Nolan Yonkman RC .60 1.50
268 Oleg Saprykin RC .60 1.50
269 Branislav Mezei RC .40 1.00
270 Chris Kelly RC .50 1.25
271 Pavel Brendl RC 1.00 2.50
272 Brett Lysak RC .50 1.25
273 Matt Carkner RC .50 1.25
274 Luke Sellars RC .60 1.50
275 Brad Ralph RC .50 1.25
276A Ray Bourque MM 1.50 4.00
276B Ray Bourque MM 1996 All-Star MVP 1.50 4.00
276C Ray Bourque MM 5-time Norris Winner 1.50 4.00
276D Ray Bourque MM 1000 NHL Points 1.50 4.00
276E Ray Bourque MM 1980 Calder Trophy 1.50 4.00
277A Peter Forsberg MM 2.00 5.00
277B Peter Forsberg MM 3 All-Star Games 2.00 5.00
277C Peter Forsberg MM 1994 Gold Medal 2.00 5.00
277D Peter Forsberg MM 1994 Gold Medal Goal 2.00 5.00
277E Peter Forsberg MM 1996 Stanley Cup 2.00 5.00
278A Joe Nieuwendyk MM .75 2.00
278B Joe Nieuwendyk MM

4 All-Star Games .75 2.00
278C Joe Nieuwendyk MM
1999 Stanley Cup .75 2.00
278D Joe Nieuwendyk MM
1999 Conn Smythe Trophy .75 2.00
278E Joe Nieuwendyk MM
1988 Calder Trophy .75 2.00
279A Dominik Hasek MM 1.50 4.00
279B Dominik Hasek MM
5-time Vezina Winner 1.50 4.00
279C Dominik Hasek MM
2-time Pearson Winner 1.50 4.00
279D Dominik Hasek MM
4 All-Star Games 1.50 4.00
279E Dominik Hasek MM
1998 Gold Medal 1.50 4.00
280A Jaromir Jagr MM 3.00 8.00
280B Jaromir Jagr MM
1999 Hart Trophy 3.00 8.00
280C Jaromir Jagr MM
8 All-Star Games 3.00 8.00
280D Jaromir Jagr MM
3-time Scoring Leader 3.00 8.00
280E Jaromir Jagr MM
2-time Stanley Cup Winner 3.00 8.00
281A Paul Kariya MM 1.00 2.50
281B Paul Kariya MM
3 All-Star Games 1.00 2.50
281C Paul Kariya MM
50 goals 1995-96 1.00 2.50
281D Paul Kariya MM
1994 Silver Medal 1.00 2.50
281E Paul Kariya MM
1993 NCAA Champ 1.00 2.50
282A Eric Lindros MM 1.50 4.00
282B Eric Lindros MM
1992 Silver Medal 1.50 4.00
282C Eric Lindros MM
1995 Hart Trophy 1.50 4.00
282D Eric Lindros MM
1995 Pearson Award 1.50 4.00
282E Eric Lindros MM
5 All-Star Games 1.50 4.00
283A Mark Messier MM 2.00 5.00
283B Mark Messier MM
6-time Stanley Cup Winner 2.00 5.00
283C Mark Messier MM
13 All-Star Games 2.00 5.00
283D Mark Messier MM
2-time Hart Winner 2.00 5.00
283E Mark Messier MM
2-time Pearson Winner 2.00 5.00
284A Patrick Roy MM 2.50 6.00
284B Patrick Roy MM
8 All-Star Games 2.50 6.00
284C Patrick Roy MM
3-time Vezina Winner 2.50 6.00
284D Patrick Roy MM
2-time Conn Smythe Winner 2.50 6.00
284E Patrick Roy MM
Playoff Wins Leader 2.50 6.00
285A Joe Sakic MM 2.00 5.00
285B Joe Sakic MM
7 All-Star Games 2.00 5.00
285C Joe Sakic MM
1996 Stanley Cup 2.00 5.00
285D Joe Sakic MM
50 goals 1995-96 2.00 5.00
285E Joe Sakic MM
1996 Conn Smythe Trophy 2.00 5.00
286A Steve Yzerman MM 2.50 6.00
286B Steve Yzerman MM
8 All-Star Games 2.50 6.00
286C Steve Yzerman MM
1989 Pearson Award 2.50 6.00
286D Steve Yzerman MM
1998 Conn Smythe Trophy 2.50 6.00
286E Steve Yzerman MM
2-time Stanley Cup Winner 2.50 6.00
287 Alex Tanguay .40 1.00
288 Brad Stuart .40 1.00
289 Brian Boucher .50 1.25
290 Steve Kariya RC .60 1.50
291 Scott Gomez .40 1.00
292 Mikko Eloranta RC .50 1.25
293 Patrik Stefan RC .60 1.50
294 John Madden RC .60 1.50
295 Per Svartvadet RC .40 1.00
296 Jiri Fischer .30 .75
297 Nikolai Antropov RC 1.50 4.00

1999-00 Topps Chrome Refractors

*VETERANS: 3X TO 8X BASIC CARDS
*253-297 ROOK: 2.5X TO 6X BASIC RC
*276-286 MM: 1.5X TO 4X BASIC MM
92 Mark Messier 8.00 20.00
283A Mark Messier MM
1984 Conn Smythe Trophy 8.00 20.00
283B Mark Messier MM
6-time Stanley Cup Winner 8.00 20.00
283C Mark Messier MM
13 All-Star Games 8.00 20.00
283D Mark Messier MM
2-time Hart Winner 8.00 20.00
283E Mark Messier MM
2-time Pearson Winner 8.00 20.00

1999-00 Topps Chrome All-Topps

COMPLETE SET (15) 15.00 40.00
*REFRACTORS: 1.2X TO 3X BASIC INSERTS
AT1 Dominik Hasek 2.00 5.00
AT2 Martin Brodeur 2.50 6.00
AT3 Ray Bourque 1.50 4.00
AT4 Al MacInnis .75 2.00
AT5 Nicklas Lidstrom 1.00 2.50
AT6 Brian Leetch .75 2.00
AT7 John LeClair .75 2.00
AT8 Paul Kariya 1.00 2.50
AT9 Keith Tkachuk .75 2.00
AT10 Eric Lindros 1.00 2.50
AT11 Peter Forsberg 1.50 4.00
AT12 Steve Yzerman 4.00 10.00
AT13 Jaromir Jagr 1.50 4.00
AT14 Teemu Selanne 1.00 2.50
AT15 Pavel Bure 1.00 2.50

1999-00 Topps Chrome A-Men

COMPLETE SET (6) 10.00 20.00
*REFRACTORS: 1.2X TO 3X BASIC INSERTS
AM1 Jaromir Jagr 1.50 4.00
AM2 Peter Forsberg 2.50 6.00
AM3 Paul Kariya 1.50 4.00
AM4 Teemu Selanne 1.50 4.00
AM5 Joe Sakic 2.00 5.00
AM6 Eric Lindros 1.50 4.00

1999-00 Topps Chrome Fantastic Finishers

COMPLETE SET (6) 6.00 12.00
*REFRACTORS: 1.2X TO 3X BASIC INSERTS
FF1 Teemu Selanne 1.00 2.50
FF2 Jaromir Jagr 1.50 4.00
FF3 Tony Amonte .75 2.00
FF4 Alexei Yashin .75 2.00
FF5 John LeClair 1.00 2.50
FF6 Joe Sakic 2.00 5.00

1999-00 Topps Chrome Ice Futures

COMPLETE SET (6) 4.00 10.00
*REFRACTORS: 1.2X TO 3X BASIC INSERTS
IF1 Mark Parrish .75 2.00
IF2 Chris Drury 1.00 2.50
IF3 Bill Muckalt .75 2.00
IF4 Marian Hossa 1.25 3.00
IF5 Milan Hejduk 1.00 2.50
IF6 Brendan Morrison .75 2.00

1999-00 Topps Chrome Ice Masters

COMPLETE SET (20) 25.00 50.00
*REFRACTORS: 1.2X TO 3X BASIC INSERTS
IM1 Joe Sakic 1.50 4.00
IM2 Dominik Hasek 1.50 4.00
IM3 Eric Lindros .75 2.00
IM4 Jaromir Jagr 1.25 3.00
IM5 John LeClair .75 2.00
IM6 Mats Sundin .75 2.00
IM7 Ray Bourque 1.25 3.00
IM8 Mike Modano 1.25 3.00
IM9 Peter Forsberg 2.00 5.00
IM10 Brian Leetch .75 2.00
IM11 Martin Brodeur 2.00 5.00
IM12 Al MacInnis .60 1.50
IM13 Paul Kariya .75 2.00
IM14 Alexei Yashin .60 1.50
IM15 Steve Yzerman 4.00 10.00
IM16 Ed Belfour .75 2.00
IM17 Keith Tkachuk .75 2.00
IM18 Patrick Roy 4.00 10.00
IM19 Nicklas Lidstrom .75 2.00
IM20 Teemu Selanne .75 2.00

1999-00 Topps Chrome Positive Performers

COMPLETE SET (6) 3.00 8.00
*REFRACTORS: 1.2X TO 3X BASIC INSERTS
PP1 Alexander Karpovtsev .60 1.50
PP2 John LeClair 1.00 2.50
PP3 Eric Lindros 1.00 2.50
PP4 Magnus Arvedson .60 1.50
PP5 Al MacInnis .75 2.00
PP6 Jere Lehtinen .75 2.00

1999-00 Topps Chrome Postmasters

COMPLETE SET (6) 10.00 20.00
*REFRACTORS: 1.2X TO 3X BASIC INSERTS
PM1 Dominik Hasek 2.00 5.00
PM2 Byron Dafoe .75 2.00
PM3 Nikolai Khabibulin .75 2.00
PM4 Ed Belfour 1.00 2.50
PM5 Patrick Roy 5.00 12.00
PM6 Martin Brodeur 2.50 6.00

2000-01 Topps Chrome

1 Jaromir Jagr 1.00 2.50
2 Patrick Roy .75 2.00
3 Paul Kariya .30 .75
4 Mats Sundin .30 .75
5 Ron Francis .40 1.00
6 Pavel Bure .30 .75
7 John LeClair .30 .75
8 Olaf Kolzig .30 .75
9 Chris Pronger .30 .75
10 Jeremy Roenick .50 1.25
11 Owen Nolan .30 .75
12 Theo Fleury .40 1.00
13 Zigmund Palffy .30 .75
14 Patrik Stefan .25 .60
15 Jarome Iginla .40 1.00
16 Joe Thornton .50 1.25
17 Tony Amonte .25 .60
18 Mike Modano .50 1.25
19 Mark Messier .60 1.50
20 Dominik Hasek .50 1.25
21 Steve Yzerman .75 2.00
22 Marian Hossa .30 .75
23 David Legwand .30 .75
24 Jose Theodore .30 .75
25 Vincent Lecavalier .30 .75
26 Scott Stevens .30 .75
27 Mark Parrish .20 .50
28 Sean Burke .20 .50
29 Alexei Kovalev .25 .60
30 Dan Cloutier .25 .60
31 Sami Kapanen .20 .50
32 Anson Carter .25 .60
33 Miroslav Satan .20 .50
34 Mark Recchi .40 1.00
35 Pavol Demitra .40 1.00
36 Peter Bondra .30 .75
37 Mike Richter .30 .75
38 Guy Hebert .25 .60
39 Martin Skoula .25 .60
40 Ed Belfour .30 .75
41 Fred Brathwaite .25 .60
42 Andrew Brunette .20 .50
43 Byron Dafoe .25 .60
44 Felix Potvin .50 1.25
45 Rod Brind'Amour .30 .75
46 Doug Gilmour .40 1.00
47 Brett Hull .60 1.50
48 Nicklas Lidstrom .30 .75
49 Mike York .20 .50
50 Al MacInnis .40 1.00
51 Brian Boucher .25 .60
52 Teemu Selanne .60 1.50
53 Bill Guerin .30 .75
54 Ray Bourque .50 1.25
55 Ray Ferraro .20 .50
56 Sergei Gonchar .20 .50
57 Mattias Ohlund .20 .50
58 Todd Marchant .20 .50
59 Damian Rhodes .20 .50
60 Chris Drury .25 .60
61 Curtis Joseph .40 1.00
62 Teppo Numminen .20 .50
63 Petr Nedved .25 .60
64 Doug Weight .30 .75
65 Arturs Irbe .25 .60
66 Chris Osgood .30 .75
67 Jocelyn Thibault .25 .60
68 Oleg Tverdovsky .20 .50
69 Derian Hatcher .25 .60
70 Ray Whitney .25 .60
71 Saku Koivu .30 .75
72 Cliff Ronning .20 .50
73 Claude Lapointe .20 .50
74 Chris Simon .20 .50
75 Martin Rucinsky .20 .50
76 Valeri Bure .25 .60
77 Brad Isbister .20 .50
78 Roman Turek .25 .60
79 Kenny Jonsson .20 .50
80 Mike Dunham .20 .50
81 Rob Blake .30 .75
82 Daniel Alfredsson .30 .75
83 Tommy Salo .25 .60
84 Sergei Samsonov .25 .60
85 Joe Sakic .60 1.50
86 Bryan Smolinski .25 .60
87 Luc Robitaille .30 .75
88 Mariusz Czerkawski .20 .50
89 Brendan Shanahan .30 .75
90 Brian Rafalski .20 .50
91 Jamie Langenbrunner .25 .60
92 Peter Forsberg .60 1.50
93 Phil Housley .25 .60
94 Glen Murray .25 .60
95 Jeff Hackett .20 .50
96 Sergei Fedorov .50 1.25
97 Sergei Zubov .25 .60
98 Martin Brodeur .75 2.00
99 Mike Grier .20 .50
100 Paul Coffey .30 .75
101 Radek Bonk .25 .60
102 Milan Hejduk .25 .60
103 Viktor Kozlov .25 .60
104 Jason Arnott .25 .60
105 Brendan Morrison .30 .75
106 Keith Tkachuk .30 .75
107 Patrik Elias .30 .75
108 Jochen Hecht .20 .50
109 Brian Leetch .25 .60
110 Petr Sykora .25 .60
111 Dave Andreychuk .30 .75
112 Steve Shields .20 .50
113 Nikolai Antropov .25 .60
114 Martin Straka .25 .60
115 Eric Desjardins .25 .60
116 Adam Oates .30 .75
117 Adam Graves .25 .60
118 Jozef Stumpel .20 .50
119 Vincent Damphousse .25 .60
120 Maxim Afinogenov .20 .50
121 Chris Chelios .30 .75
122 Joe Nieuwendyk .25 .60
123 Petr Buzek .20 .50
124 Jeff Friesen .20 .50
125 Markus Naslund .30 .75
126 Trevor Letowski .20 .50
127 Steve Thomas .20 .50
128 Jason Allison .25 .60
129 Jere Lehtinen .25 .60
130 Tom Poti .20 .50
131 Eric Lindros .50 1.25
132 Rob Niedermayer .25 .60
133 Gary Roberts .20 .50
134 Scott Gomez .25 .60
135 Pierre Turgeon .25 .60
136 Trevor Kidd .20 .50
137 Jan Hrdina .20 .50
138 John Madden .25 .60
139 Tim Connolly .20 .50
140 Pat Verbeek .25 .60
141 Jeff Halpern .20 .50
142 Patrick Marleau .30 .75
143 Wade Redden .20 .50
144 Alex Tanguay .25 .60
145 Darcy Tucker .20 .50
146 Simon Gagne .30 .75
147 Brad Stuart .25 .60
148 Jean-Sebastien Aubin .25 .60
149 Mike Johnson .20 .50
150 Shayne Corson .25 .60
151 Michael Peca .25 .60
152 Keith Primeau .25 .60
153 Tie Domi .25 .60
154 Brenden Morrow .25 .60
155 Sandis Ozolinsh .20 .50
156 Mike Keane .25 .60
157 Patric Kjellberg .20 .50
158 Patrick Lalime .25 .60
159 John Vanbiesbrouck .30 .75
160 Andrew Cassels .20 .50
161 Scott Stephens HL .25 .60
162 Ed Belfour HL .30 .75
163 Martin Brodeur HL .75 2.00
164 Mike Modano HL .50 1.25
165 Jason Arnott HL .25 .60
166 Roberto Luongo .50 1.25
167 Harold Druken .20 .50
168 Marc Denis .25 .60
169 Oleg Saprykin .20 .50
170 Glen Metropolit .20 .50
171 Daniel Sedin .40 1.00
172 Dmitri Yakushin .20 .50
173 Scott Hannan .20 .50
174 Dave Tanabe .20 .50
175 Jiri Fischer .20 .50
176 Dmitri Nabokov .20 .50
177 Ivan Novoseltsev .20 .50
178 Manny Fernandez .20 .50
179 Maxim Balmochnyk .20 .50
180 Brian Campbell .20 .50
181 Sergei Varlamov .20 .50
182 Ville Nieminen RC .20 .50
183 Colin White RC .20 .50
184 Mike Fisher .20 .50
185 Matt Elich RC .25 .60
186 Zenith Komarniski .20 .50
187 Eric Nickulas RC .20 .50
188 Steven McCarthy .20 .50
189 Jason Krog .20 .50
190 Robert Esche .20 .50
191 Adam Mair .20 .50
192 Ladislav Nagy .20 .50
193 Sergei Vyshedkevich RC .20 .50
194 Steve Begin .20 .50
195 Brad Ference .20 .50
196 Andy Delmore .20 .50
197 Brent Sopel RC .30 .75
198 Evgeni Nabokov .25 .60
199 David Gosselin RC .25 .60
200 Tavis Hansen .20 .50
201 Ray Giroux .20 .50
202 Serge Aubin RC .25 .60
203 Shane Willis .20 .50
204 Vitali Vishnevsky .20 .50
205 Richard Jackman .20 .50
206 Petr Schastlivy .20 .50
207 Ryan Bonni .20 .50
208 Alexei Tezikov .20 .50
209 Henrik Sedin .40 1.00
210 Mike Ribeiro .20 .50
211 Darryl Laplante .20 .50
212 Kyle Calder .20 .50
213 Dimitri Kalinin .20 .50
214 Jean-Sebastien Giguere .30 .75
215 Willie Mitchell RC .30 .75
216 Steve Valiquette RC .25 .60
217 Brian Willsie .20 .50
218 Jarkko Ruutu .20 .50
219 Jon Sim .20 .50
220 Jonathan Girard .20 .50
221 Ron Tugnutt .25 .60
222 Lyle Odelein .20 .50
223 Jean-Luc Grand-Pierre .20 .50
224 Geoff Sanderson .25 .60
225 Robert Kron .20 .50
226 Kevin Dineen .20 .50
227 Kevyn Adams .20 .50
228 Tyler Wright .20 .50
229 Jamie Pushor .20 .50
230 David Vyborny .20 .50
231 Jamie McLennan .20 .50
232 Jeff Nielsen .20 .50
233 Scott Pellerin .20 .50
234 Darby Hendrickson .20 .50
235 Jim Dowd .20 .50
236 Filip Kuba .20 .50
237 Stacy Roest .20 .50
238 Sean O'Donnell .20 .50
239 Aaron Gavey .20 .50
240 Sergei Krivokrasov .20 .50
241 Justin Williams RC 2.50 6.00
242 Marian Gaborik RC 3.00 8.00
243 Marty Turco RC 2.00 5.00
244 David Aebischer RC 2.00 5.00
245 Rostislav Klesla RC 2.50 6.00
246 Petr Hubacek RC 1.00 2.50
247 Scott Hartnell RC 2.50 6.00
248 Martin Havlat RC 3.00 8.00
249 Steven Reinprecht RC 1.50 4.00
250 Andrew Raycroft RC 2.50 6.00
251 Rick DiPietro RC 2.00 5.00

2000-01 Topps Chrome Blue

*BLUE/1250: .4X TO 1X BASE SP/1250

2000-01 Topps Chrome Red

*RED/1250: .4X TO 1X BASE SP/1250

2000-01 Topps Chrome OPC Refractors

*1-240 VETS: 1.5X TO 4X BASIC CARDS
*161-240 ROOKIE: 1X TO 2.5X RC
*241-250 ROOK/35: 1.5X TO 4X RC/1250
19 Mark Messier 4.00 10.00

2000-01 Topps Chrome OPC Refractors Blue

*SP ROOKIE/35: 1.5X TO 4X BASIC SP

2000-01 Topps Chrome OPC Refractors Red

*SP ROOKIE/35: 1.5X TO 4X BASIC SP

2000-01 Topps Chrome Refractors

*1-240 VETS: 2X TO 5X BASIC CARDS
*161-240 ROOKIES: 1.2X TO 3X RC
*241-251 ROOK/25: 2X TO 5X RC/1250
19 Mark Messier 5.00 12.00

2000-01 Topps Chrome Refractors Blue

*SP ROOKIE/25: 2X TO 5X BASIC SP

2000-01 Topps Chrome Refractors Red

*SP ROOKIE/25: 2X TO 5X BASIC SP

2000-01 Topps Chrome Combos

COMPLETE SET (10) 15.00 40.00
TC1 P.Bure/V.Bure 1.00 2.50
TC2 T.Selanne/P.Kariya 1.00 2.50
TC3 J.LeClair/T.Amonte 1.00 2.50
TC4 C.Joseph/D.Hasek 2.00 5.00
TC5 M.Modano/P.Forsberg 3.00 8.00
TC6 R.Bourque/C.Pronger 2.00 5.00
TC7 V.Lecavalier/J.Thornton 1.00 2.50
TC8 P.Roy/M.Brodeur 5.00 12.00
TC9 S.Yzerman/B.Hull 4.00 10.00
TC10 J.Jagr/M.Lemieux 4.00 10.00

2000-01 Topps Chrome Hobby Masters Refractors

COMPLETE SET (10) 75.00 150.00
HM1 Martin Brodeur 10.00 25.00
HM2 Pavel Bure 6.00 15.00
HM3 Peter Forsberg 10.00 25.00
HM4 Dominik Hasek 8.00 20.00
HM5 Jaromir Jagr 6.00 15.00
HM6 Curtis Joseph 5.00 12.00
HM7 Paul Kariya 5.00 12.00
HM8 Mike Modano 5.00 12.00
HM9 Patrick Roy 20.00 50.00
HM10 Steve Yzerman 20.00 50.00

2000-01 Topps Chrome Mario Lemieux Reprints

COMPLETE SET (23) 75.00 150.00
COMMON LEMIEUX (1-23) 5.00 12.00
*REFRACTOR: 1.2X TO 3X BASIC INSERT

2000-01 Topps Chrome Rocket's Flare

COMPLETE SET (10) 10.00 20.00
*REFRACTOR: .8X TO 2X BASIC INSERT
RF1 Pavel Bure 1.00 2.50
RF2 Paul Kariya 1.00 2.50
RF3 John LeClair 1.00 2.50
RF4 Jaromir Jagr 1.50 4.00
RF5 Luc Robitaille .75 2.00
RF6 Milan Hejduk 1.00 2.50
RF7 Tony Amonte .75 2.00
RF8 Patrik Elias .75 2.00
RF9 Miroslav Satan .75 2.00
RF10 Teemu Selanne 1.00 2.50

2000-01 Topps Chrome 1000 Point Club Refractors

1 Mark Messier 5.00 12.00
2 Steve Yzerman 20.00 50.00
3 Ron Francis 3.00 8.00
4 Paul Coffey 4.00 10.00
5 Ray Bourque 8.00 20.00
6 Doug Gilmour 3.00 8.00
7 Adam Oates 3.00 8.00
8 Larry Murphy 3.00 8.00
9 Dave Andreychuk 3.00 8.00
10 Luc Robitaille 3.00 8.00
11 Phil Housley 3.00 8.00
12 Brett Hull 5.00 12.00
13 Al MacInnis 3.00 8.00
14 Pierre Turgeon 3.00 8.00
15 Joe Sakic 10.00 25.00
16 Pat Verbeek 3.00 8.00

2001-02 Topps Chrome

COMPLETE SET (182) 50.00 120.00
1 Mario Lemieux 2.00 5.00
2 Steve Yzerman 1.25 3.00
3 Martin Brodeur 1.25 3.00
4 Brian Leetch .40 1.00
5 Tony Amonte .40 1.00
6 Bill Guerin .50 1.25
7 Olaf Kolzig .50 1.25
8 Pavel Bure .50 1.25
9 Patrick Marleau .50 1.25
10 Mariusz Czerkawski .30 .75
11 Teemu Selanne 1.00 2.50
12 Alex Tanguay .40 1.00
13 Keith Primeau .40 1.00
14 Alexei Yashin .40 1.00
15 Markus Naslund .50 1.25
16 Chris Pronger .50 1.25
17 Sergei Zubov .40 1.00
18 Marian Gaborik .50 1.25
19 Mats Sundin .50 1.25
20 David Legwand .40 1.00
21 J-P Dumont .30 .75
22 Nicklas Lidstrom .50 1.25
23 Ron Francis .60 1.50
24 Doug Weight .50 1.25
25 Zigmund Palffy .50 1.25
26 Jason Allison .40 1.00
27 Joe Sakic 1.00 2.50
28 Paul Kariya .50 1.25
29 Marian Hossa .50 1.25
30 Owen Nolan .50 1.25
31 Jason Arnott .40 1.00
32 Jaromir Jagr 1.50 4.00
33 Claude Lemieux .40 1.00
34 Peter Bondra .50 1.25
35 Chris Drury .40 1.00
36 Radek Bonk .30 .75
37 Theo Fleury .60 1.50
38 Keith Tkachuk .50 1.25
39 Rick DiPietro .40 1.00
40 Ed Jovanovski .40 1.00
41 Scott Stevens .50 1.25
42 John LeClair .50 1.25
43 Ryan Smyth .40 1.00
44 Vincent Lecavalier .50 1.25
45 Henrik Sedin .60 1.50
46 David Aebischer .40 1.00
47 Patrick Roy 1.25 3.00
48 Valeri Bure .30 .75
49 Dominik Hasek .75 2.00
50 Ray Ferraro .30 .75
51 Milan Hejduk .40 1.00
52 Mike Modano .75 2.00
53 Sergei Fedorov .75 2.00
54 Luc Robitaille .50 1.25
55 Mark Messier 1.00 2.50
56 Sean Burke .30 .75
57 Jeff Friesen .30 .75
58 Alexander Mogilny .40 1.00
59 Roman Cechmanek .40 1.00
60 Martin Straka .30 .75
61 Pavol Demitra .60 1.50
62 Curtis Joseph .60 1.50
63 Daniel Sedin .60 1.50
64 Brad Richards .50 1.25
65 Simon Gagne .50 1.25
66 Saku Koivu .50 1.25
67 Eric Daze .40 1.00
68 Roberto Luongo .75 2.00
69 Brendan Shanahan .50 1.25
70 Espen Knutsen .30 .75
71 Rob Blake .50 1.25
72 Steve Sullivan .30 .75
73 Arturs Irbe .40 1.00
74 Maxim Afinogenov .30 .75
75 Dan Cloutier .40 1.00
76 Josef Vasicek .30 .75
77 Vincent Damphousse .40 1.00
78 Robert Lang .30 .75
79 Pierre Turgeon .40 1.00
80 Gary Roberts .30 .75
81 Adam Oates .50 1.25
82 Evgeni Nabokov .40 1.00
83 Petr Nedved .40 1.00
84 Mike Dunham .40 1.00
85 Chris Osgood .50 1.25
86 Brett Hull 1.00 2.50
87 Peter Forsberg 1.00 2.50
88 Joe Thornton .75 2.00
89 Marc Denis .40 1.00
90 Ed Belfour .50 1.25
91 Patrik Elias .50 1.25
92 Michael York .30 .75
93 Martin Havlat .40 1.00
94 Jeremy Roenick .75 2.00
95 Alexei Kovalev .40 1.00
96 Al MacInnis .60 1.50
97 Marco Sturm .30 .75
98 Jose Theodore .50 1.25
99 Joe Nieuwendyk .40 1.00
100 Darren McCarty .30 .75
101 Mark Recchi .60 1.50
102 Daniel Alfredsson .50 1.25
103 Miroslav Satan .40 1.00
104 Sergei Samsonov .40 1.00
105 Roman Turek .40 1.00
106 Jarome Iginla .60 1.50
107 Jeff O'Neill .40 1.00
108 Tommy Salo .40 1.00
109 Petr Sykora .30 .75
110 Adam Deadmarsh .30 .75
111 Oleg Tverdovsky .30 .75
112 Sami Kapanen .30 .75
113 Scott Hartnell .30 .75
114 Jere Lehtinen .40 1.00
115 Darcy Tucker .30 .75
116 Stu Barnes .40 1.00
117 Jim Dowd .30 .75
118 Derek Morris .30 .75
119 Felix Potvin .75 2.00
120 Manny Fernandez .30 .75
121 Jason Smith .30 .75
122 Byron Dafoe .40 1.00
123 Teppo Numminen .30 .75
124 Mike Richter .50 1.25
125 Anson Carter .40 1.00
126 Jocelyn Thibault .40 1.00
127 Dany Heatley .40 1.00
128 Marc Savard .30 .75
129 Brian Rolston .40 1.00
130 Martin Biron .40 1.00
131 Mark Parrish .30 .75
132 Mike Peca .40 1.00
133 Patrick Lalime .40 1.00
134 Eric Lindros .75 2.00
135 Brian Boucher .40 1.00
136 Nikolai Khabibulin .50 1.25
137 John Madden .40 1.00
138 Rostislav Klesla .30 .75
139 Mika Noronen .30 .75
140 Kris Beech .30 .75
141 Miikka Kiprusoff .50 1.25
142 Mathieu Garon .40 1.00
143 Mark Bell .30 .75
144 Jussi Markkanen .30 .75
145 Mike Comrie .40 1.00
146 Johan Hedberg .40 1.00
147 Andrew Raycroft .40 1.00
148 Daniel Corso .30 .75
149 Ilya Kovalchuk RC 5.00 12.00
150 Dan Blackburn RC 1.25 3.00
151 Vaclav Nedorost RC 1.00 2.50
152 Krys Kolanos RC 1.00 2.50
153 Kristian Huselius RC 1.50 4.00
154 Martin Erat RC 1.25 3.00
155 Timo Parssinen RC 1.25 3.00
156 Scott Nichol RC 1.00 2.50
157 Nick Schultz RC 1.00 2.50
158 Jukka Hentunen RC 1.00 2.50
159 Pascal Dupuis RC 1.50 4.00
160 Radek Martinek RC 1.00 2.50
161 Scott Clemmensen RC 1.00 2.50
162 Jeff Jillson RC 1.00 2.50
163 Brian Sutherby RC 1.00 2.50
164 Nikita Alexeev RC 1.00 2.50
165 Niklas Hagman RC 1.25 3.00
166 Erik Cole RC 2.00 5.00
167 Pavel Datsyuk RC 30.00 80.00
168 Ilja Bryzgalov RC 2.50 6.00
169 Chris Neil RC 1.25 3.00
170 Mark Rycroft RC 1.25 3.00
171 Kamil Piros RC 1.00 2.50
172 Niko Kapanen RC 1.50 4.00
173 Jiri Dopita RC 1.00 2.50
174 Andreas Salomonsson RC 1.00 2.50
175 Ivan Ciernik RC 1.00 2.50
176 Jaroslav Bednar RC 1.00 2.50
177 Ty Conklin RC 1.50 4.00
178 Richard Scott RC 1.00 2.50
179 Raffi Torres RC 1.50 4.00
180 Vaclav Pletka RC 1.00 2.50
181 Mikael Samuelsson RC 1.25 3.00
182 Mike Farrell RC 1.00 2.50

2001-02 Topps Chrome Refractors

*1-148 VETS: 1.5X TO 4X BASIC CARDS
*149-182 ROOKIES: .8X TO 2X BASIC RC
55 Mark Messier 4.00 10.00
167 Pavel Datsyuk 150.00 400.00

2001-02 Topps Chrome Black Border Refractors

*1-148 VETS/50: 5X TO 12X BASIC CARDS
*149-182 ROOKIE/50: 1.5X TO 4X BASIC RC
55 Mark Messier 12.00 30.00

2001-02 Topps Chrome Mario Lemieux Reprints

COMPLETE SET (10) 30.00 60.00
COMMON LEMIEUX 3.00 8.00
*REFRACTOR: 1.2X TO 3X BASIC INSERT

2001-02 Topps Chrome Mario Returns

COMPLETE SET (5) 25.00 50.00
COMMON LEMIEUX (MR1-MR5) 4.00 10.00
*REFRACTOR: 1.2X TO 3X BASIC INSERT

2001-02 Topps Chrome Reprints

COMPLETE SET (10) 15.00 40.00
*REFRACTOR: 1.2X TO 3X BASIC INSERTS
1 Billy Smith 2.00 5.00
2 Wayne Cashman 2.00 5.00
3 Barry Melrose 2.00 5.00
4 Bernie Federko 2.00 5.00
5 Neal Broten 2.00 5.00
6 Bill Clement 2.00 5.00
7 Guy Lapointe 2.00 5.00
8 Bernie Parent 2.00 5.00
9 Larry Robinson 2.00 5.00
10 Ken Hodge 2.00 5.00

2001-02 Topps Chrome Reprint Autographs

1 Billy Smith/200 12.50 30.00
2 Wayne Cashman/200 12.50 30.00
3 Barry Melrose/200 15.00 40.00
4 Bernie Federko 12.50 30.00
5 Neal Broten/200 12.50 30.00
6 Bill Clement/200 12.50 30.00
7 Guy Lapointe/200 12.50 30.00
8 Bernie Parent 20.00 50.00
9 Larry Robinson/200 15.00 40.00
10 Ken Hodge 12.50 30.00

2002 Topps Chrome All-Star Fantasy

COMPLETE SET (6) 6.00 15.00
1 Paul Kariya 1.20 3.00
2 Zigmund Palffy .40 1.00
3 Joe Sakic 1.20 3.00
4 Jaromir Jagr 1.20 3.00
5 Dominik Hasek .80 2.00
6 Ilya Kovalchuk 2.00 5.00

2002-03 Topps Chrome

COMPLETE SET (182) 50.00 125.00
COMP.SET w/o SP's (148) 10.00 25.00
1 Patrick Roy 1.25 3.00
2 Mario Lemieux 2.00 5.00
3 Martin Brodeur 1.25 3.00
4 Steve Yzerman 1.25 3.00
5 Jaromir Jagr 1.50 4.00
6 Chris Pronger .50 1.25
7 John LeClair .50 1.25
8 Paul Kariya .50 1.25
9 Tony Amonte .40 1.00
10 Joe Thornton .75 2.00
11 Ilya Kovalchuk .60 1.50
12 Jarome Iginla .60 1.50
13 Mike Modano .75 2.00
14 Vincent Lecavalier .50 1.25
15 Michael Peca .40 1.00
16 Pavel Bure .50 1.25
17 Eric Lindros .75 2.00
18 Felix Potvin .75 2.00
19 Ron Francis .60 1.50
20 Miroslav Satan .50 1.25
21 Rostislav Klesla .30 .75
22 Mike Comrie .50 1.25
23 Daniel Alfredsson .50 1.25
24 Sean Burke .30 .75
25 David Legwand .40 1.00
26 Marian Gaborik .50 1.25
27 Saku Koivu .50 1.25
28 Owen Nolan .50 1.25
29 Mats Sundin .50 1.25
30 J-P Dumont .30 .75
31 Chris Drury .50 1.25
32 Markus Naslund .50 1.25
33 Anson Carter .40 1.00
34 Daniel Briere .40 1.00
35 Keith Tkachuk .50 1.25
36 Mark Recchi .60 1.50
37 Marc Denis .40 1.00
38 Sergei Fedorov .75 2.00
39 Andrew Brunette .30 .75
40 Martin Havlat .40 1.00
41 Brian Leetch .40 1.00
42 Erik Cole .30 .75
43 Patrick Lalime .40 1.00
44 Patrick Marleau .50 1.25
45 Ryan Smyth .40 1.00
46 Sami Kapanen .30 .75
47 Martin Straka .40 1.00
48 Peter Forsberg 1.00 2.50
49 Jeff Friesen .30 .75
50 Manny Fernandez .30 .75
51 Scott Stevens .50 1.25
52 Radim Vrbata .30 .75
53 Marty Turco .50 1.25
54 Kristian Huselius .30 .75
55 Jeremy Roenick .75 2.00
56 Gary Roberts .30 .75
57 Chris Chelios .50 1.25
58 Brett Hull 1.00 2.50
59 Eric Daze .30 .75
60 Alex Tanguay .40 1.00
61 Simon Gagne .50 1.25
62 Roman Turek .50 1.25
63 Milan Hejduk .40 1.00
64 Mariusz Czerkawski .30 .75
65 Dan Cloutier .40 1.00
66 Teemu Selanne 1.00 2.50
67 Johan Hedberg .50 1.25
68 Mike Ricci .30 .75
69 Roberto Luongo .75 2.00
70 Zigmund Palffy .50 1.25
71 Ed Jovanovski .40 1.00
72 Scott Gomez .40 1.00
73 Pierre Turgeon .40 1.00
74 Martin Biron .40 1.00
75 Keith Primeau .40 1.00
76 Jean-Sebastien Giguere .50 1.25
77 Alexei Zhamnov .40 1.00
78 Brent Johnson .40 1.00
79 Dan Blackburn .40 1.00
80 Mike Richter .50 1.25
81 Peter Bondra .50 1.25
82 Rod Brind'Amour .50 1.25
83 Shane Doan .40 1.00
84 Sergei Samsonov .40 1.00
85 Nikolai Khabibulin .50 1.25
86 Roman Cechmanek .40 1.00
87 Glen Murray .40 1.00
88 Brad Richards .50 1.25

89 Alexei Kovalev .40 1.00
90 Adam Deadmarsh .30 .75
91 Brendan Morrison .40 1.00
92 Jason Arnott .40 1.00
93 Brenden Morrow .40 1.00
94 Pavol Demitra .60 1.50
95 Olaf Kolzig .50 1.25
96 Doug Gilmour .60 1.50
97 Jere Lehtinen .50 1.25
98 Petr Sykora .40 1.00
99 Wade Redden .30 .75
100 Adam Oates .50 1.25
101 Chris Osgood .50 1.25
102 Espen Knutsen .30 .75
103 Maxim Afinogenov .30 .75
104 Steve Sullivan .30 .75
105 Robert Lang .30 .75
106 Milan Hnilicka .40 1.00
107 Craig Conroy .30 .75
108 Alexander Mogilny .40 1.00
109 Jose Theodore .50 1.25
110 Mike Dunham .40 1.00
111 Joe Sakic 1.00 2.50
112 Al MacInnis .60 1.50
113 Marian Hossa .50 1.25
114 Rob Blake .50 1.25
115 Dany Heatley .40 1.00
116 Scott Hartnell .30 .75
117 Krys Kolanos .30 .75
118 Vincent Damphousse .40 1.00
119 Curtis Joseph .60 1.50
120 Todd Bertuzzi .50 1.25
121 Tommy Salo .40 1.00
122 Jocelyn Thibault .40 1.00
123 Nicklas Lidstrom .50 1.25
124 Bryan McCabe .30 .75
125 Bill Guerin .50 1.25
126 Luc Robitaille .50 1.25
127 Alexei Yashin .40 1.00
128 Evgeni Nabokov .40 1.00
129 Pavel Datsyuk .75 2.00
130 Stu Barnes .30 .75
131 Derek Morris .30 .75
132 Jason Allison .40 1.00
133 Mark Messier 1.00 2.50
134 Ed Belfour .50 1.25
135 Scott Young .30 .75
136 Marco Sturm .30 .75
137 Arturs Irbe .40 1.00
138 Joe Nieuwendyk .40 1.00
139 Sergei Gonchar .40 1.00
140 Doug Weight .50 1.25
141 Jeff O'Neill .30 .75
142 Mike York .30 .75
143 Patrik Elias .50 1.25
144 Brendan Shanahan .50 1.25
145 Rick DiPietro .40 1.00
146 Jani Rita .30 .75
147 Stephen Weiss .50 1.25
148 Nikita Alexeev .30 .75
149 Micki DuPont RC .75 2.00
150 Ivan Majesky RC .75 2.00
151 Jason Spezza RC 5.00 12.00
152 Eric Godard RC .75 2.00
153 Shawn Thornton RC 1.00 2.50
154 Jeff Paul RC .75 2.00
155 Lasse Pirjeta RC .75 2.00
156 Adam Hall RC .75 2.00
157 Mikael Tellqvist RC .75 2.00
158 Tomi Pettinen RC .75 2.00
159 Radovan Somik RC .75 2.00
160 Jordan Leopold RC 1.25 3.00
161 Dmitri Bykov RC .75 2.00
162 Tim Thomas RC 3.00 8.00
163 Martin Gerber RC 1.25 3.00
164 Tom Koivisto RC .75 2.00
165 Patrick Sharp RC 2.50 6.00
166 Steve Eminger RC .75 2.00
167 Anton Volchenkov RC .75 2.00
168 Scottie Upshall RC 1.00 2.50
169 Ron Hainsey RC .75 2.00
170 Kurt Sauer RC .75 2.00
171 Jeff Taffe RC .75 2.00
172 Dennis Seidenberg RC 1.25 3.00
173 Stanislav Chistov RC .75 2.00
174 Chuck Kobasew RC 1.00 2.50
175 Rick Nash RC 5.00 12.00
176 Ales Hemsky RC 3.00 8.00
177 Jay Bouwmeester RC 2.50 6.00
178 Alexei Smirnov RC 1.00 2.50
179 Alexander Svitov RC .75 2.00
180 P-M Bouchard RC 1.25 3.00
181 Alexander Frolov RC 2.00 5.00
182 Henrik Zetterberg RC 6.00 15.00

2002-03 Topps Chrome Black Border Refractors

*1-148 VETS/100: 4X TO 10X BASIC CARDS
*149-182 ROOK/100: 1.5X TO 4X BASIC RC
133 Mark Messier 10.00 25.00

2002-03 Topps Chrome Refractors

*1-148 VETS: 2X TO 5X BASIC CARDS
*149-182 ROOKIES: 1X TO 2.5X BASIC RC
133 Mark Messier 5.00 12.00

2002-03 Topps Chrome e-Topps Decoy Cards

1 Jarome Iginla .30 .75
2 Pavel Bure .30 .75
3 Patrick Roy .30 .75
4 Mats Sundin .30 .75
5 Jaromir Jagr .30 .75
6 Martin Brodeur .30 .75

2002-03 Topps Chrome Chromographs

CGBG Brian Gionta 6.00 15.00
CGBR Brad Richards 8.00 20.00
CGCJ Curtis Joseph 12.50 30.00
CGEC Erik Cole 5.00 12.00
CGRV Radim Vrbata 6.00 15.00
CGSW Stephen Weiss 5.00 12.00

2002-03 Topps Chrome First Round Fabric Patches

DB Dan Blackburn 12.50 30.00
EL Eric Lindros 15.00 40.00
JP J-P Dumont 12.50 30.00
KP Keith Primeau 12.50 30.00
MB Martin Biron 12.50 30.00
MM Mike Modano 15.00 40.00
MN Markus Naslund 15.00 40.00
MS Mats Sundin 15.00 40.00
PM Patrick Marleau 12.50 30.00
RD Radek Dvorak 12.50 30.00
SN Scott Niedermayer 12.50 30.00

2002-03 Topps Chrome Patrick Roy Reprints

COMPLETE SET (25) 15.00 40.00
1 1986-87 Topps 8.00 20.00
2 1987-88 Topps 1.00 2.50
3 1988-89 Topps 1.00 2.50
4 1989-90 Topps 1.00 2.50
5 1990-91 Topps 1.00 2.50
6 1991-92 Topps 1.00 2.50
7 1992-93 Topps 1.00 2.50
8 1993-94 Premier 1.00 2.50
9 1994-95 Premier 1.00 2.50
10 1995-96 Topps 1.00 2.50
11 1998-99 Topps 1.00 2.50
12 1999-00 Topps 1.00 2.50
13 2000-01 Topps 1.00 2.50
14 2001-02 Topps 1.00 2.50
15 1986-87 OPC 1.00 2.50
16 1987-88 OPC 1.00 2.50
17 1988-89 OPC 1.00 2.50
18 1989-90 OPC 1.00 2.50
19 1990-91 OPC 1.00 2.50
20 1991-92 OPC 1.00 2.50
21 1992-93 OPC 1.00 2.50
22 1998-99 OPC 1.00 2.50
23 1999-00 OPC 1.00 2.50
24 2000-01 OPC 1.00 2.50
25 2001-02 OPC 1.00 2.50

2002-03 Topps Chrome Patrick Roy Reprints Refractors

*REFRACTOR: 4X TO 10X BASIC CARD

2002-03 Topps Chrome Patrick Roy Reprint Autographs

COMMON CARD 40.00 80.00
COA Patrick Roy OPC 50.00 100.00
CTA Patrick Roy TOPPS 40.00 80.00

2002-03 Topps Chrome Patrick Roy Reprint Autograph Refractors

*REFRACTOR: 1.5X TO 4X BASIC AUTOGRAPH
COA Patrick Roy OPC 125.00 300.00
CTA Patrick Roy Topps 125.00 300.00

2002-03 Topps Chrome Patrick Roy Reprint Relics

PRJO1 P.Roy JSY OPC 20.00 50.00
PRJT1 P.Roy JSY TOPPS 25.00 60.00
PRP1 P.Roy PATCH OPC
PRPT1 P.Roy PATCH TOPPS

2002-03 Topps Chrome Patrick Roy Reprint Relics Refractors

PRJO1 Patrick Roy OPC Jersey 60.00 150.00
PRJT1 Patrick Roy Topps Jersey 60.00 150.00

1998-99 Topps Gold Label Class 1

*CLASS I BLACK VETS: 2X TO 5X BASIC CARDS
*CLASS 1 BLACK ROOKIES: 1.2X TO 3X
*CLASS I RED VETS: 10X TO 25X BASIC CARDS
*CLASS 1 RED ROOKIES: 8X TO 20X
1 Brendan Shanahan .50 1.25
2 Mike Modano .75 2.00
3 Chris Chelios .50 1.25
4 Wayne Gretzky 3.00 8.00
5 Jaromir Jagr 1.50 4.00
6 Mark Messier 1.00 2.50
7 Teemu Selanne 1.00 2.50
8 Theo Fleury .60 1.50
9 Ray Bourque .75 2.00
10 Martin Brodeur 1.25 3.00
11 Alexei Yashin .40 1.00
12 Keith Tkachuk .50 1.25
13 Eric Lindros .75 2.00
14 Owen Nolan .50 1.25
15 Al MacInnis .60 1.50
16 Peter Bondra .50 1.25
17 Saku Koivu .50 1.25
18 Doug Weight .50 1.25
19 Robert Reichel .30 .75
20 Sergei Fedorov .75 2.00
21 Peter Forsberg 1.00 2.50
22 Ron Francis .60 1.50
23 Dimitri Khristich .30 .75
24 Ed Belfour .50 1.25
25 Oleg Kvasha RC .50 1.25
26 Ray Whitney .30 .75
27 Kenny Jonsson .30 .75
28 Randy McKay .40 1.00
29 Pavol Demitra .60 1.50
30 Pierre Turgeon .40 1.00
31 Steve Yzerman 1.25 3.00
32 Ryan Smyth .40 1.00
33 Tony Amonte .40 1.00
34 Dominik Hasek .75 2.00
35 Jarome Iginla .60 1.50
36 Sami Kapanen .30 .75
37 Patrik Elias .50 1.25
38 Daniel Cleary .30 .75
39 Curtis Joseph .60 1.50
40 Joe Juneau .30 .75
41 Adam Graves .30 .75
42 Trevor Linden .50 1.25
43 Olli Jokinen .40 1.00
44 Joe Nieuwendyk .40 1.00
45 Sergei Samsonov .40 1.00
46 Rico Fata .40 1.00
47 Mark Recchi .60 1.50
48 Rick Tocchet .40 1.00
49 Chris Pronger .50 1.25
50 Jason Allison .40 1.00
51 Paul Kariya .50 1.25
52 Stu Barnes .30 .75
53 Mats Sundin .50 1.25
54 Mike Richter .50 1.25
55 Cliff Ronning .30 .75
56 Keith Primeau .40 1.00
57 Guy Hebert .40 1.00
58 Nicklas Lidstrom .60 1.50
59 John Vanbiesbrouck .50 1.25
60 Jeff Friesen .30 .75
61 Vincent Lecavalier 1.00 2.50
62 Alexander Mogilny .40 1.00
63 Olaf Kolzig .50 1.25
64 Doug Gilmour .60 1.50
65 Joe Sakic 1.00 2.50
66 Mike Johnson .30 .75
67 Vincent Damphousse .40 1.00
68 Eric Brewer .50 1.25
69 Daniel Alfredsson .50 1.25
70 Nikolai Khabibulin .50 1.25
71 Marco Sturm .30 .75
72 Marty Reasoner .50 1.25
73 Bill Muckalt RC .30 .75
74 Pavel Bure .50 1.25
75 Bill Guerin .50 1.25
76 Chris Osgood .50 1.25
77 Patrick Roy 1.25 3.00
78 Tom Barrasso .40 1.00
79 Alyn McCauley .30 .75
80 Adam Oates .50 1.25
81 Joe Thornton .75 2.00
82 Brendan Morrison .30 .75
83 Mike Dunham .40 1.00
84 Jeremy Roenick .75 2.00
85 Brian Leetch .40 1.00
86 John LeClair .50 1.25
87 Mattias Ohlund .30 .75
88 Wade Redden .30 .75
89 Mark Parrish RC .75 2.00
90 Milan Hejduk RC .75 2.00
91 Michael Peca .30 .75
92 Brett Hull 1.00 2.50
93 Manny Malhotra .50 1.25
94 Patrick Marleau .50 1.25
95 Grant Fuhr .75 2.00
96 Rob Blake .50 1.25
97 Damian Rhodes .50 1.25
98 Eric Daze .40 1.00
99 Rod Brind'Amour .50 1.25
100 Scott Stevens .50 1.25

1998-99 Topps Gold Label Class 2

COMPLETE SET (100) 100.00 200.00
*CLASS 2: 1X TO 2.5X BASIC CLASS 1
*CLASS 2 BLACK: 1.5X TO 4X BASIC CLASS 1
*CLASS 2 RED: 8X TO 20X CLASS 1
*CLASS 2 RED ROOKIES: 6X TO 15X CLASS 1

1998-99 Topps Gold Label Class 3

COMPLETE SET (100) 150.00 300.00
*CLASS 3: 1.5X TO 4X BASIC CLASS 1
*CLASS 3 BLACK: 5X TO 12X BASIC CLASS 1
*CLASS 3 RED: 25X TO 60X BASIC CLASS 1
*CLASS 3 RED ROOKIES: 20X TO 50X CLASS 1

1998-99 Topps Gold Label Goal Race '99

*BLACK: .8X TO 2X BASIC INSERTS
*RED/92: 2.5X TO 6X BASIC INSERTS
GR1 Eric Lindros 1.50 4.00
GR2 John LeClair 1.00 2.50
GR3 Teemu Selanne 2.00 5.00
GR4 Paul Kariya 1.00 2.50
GR5 Jaromir Jagr 3.00 8.00
GR6 Keith Tkachuk 1.00 2.50
GR7 Theo Fleury 1.25 3.00
GR8 Brendan Shanahan 1.00 2.50
GR9 Tony Amonte .75 2.00
GR10 Joe Sakic 2.00 5.00

1999-00 Topps Gold Label Class 1

COMPLETE SET (100) 30.00 60.00
*CLASS 1 BLACK: 2X TO 5X BASIC CARDS
*CLASS 1 RED/100: 6X TO 15X BASIC CARDS
*CLASS 2: .8X TO 2X CLASS 1
*CLASS 2 BLACK: 3X TO 8X CLASS 1
*CLASS 2 RED/50: 10X TO 25X CLASS 1
*CLASS 3: 1.5X TO 4X CLASS 1
*CLASS 3 BLACK: 10X TO 25X CLASS 1
*CLASS 3 RED/25: 20X TO 50X CLASS 1
1 Dominik Hasek .60 1.50
2 Al MacInnis .50 1.25
3 Luc Robitaille .40 1.00
4 Steve Yzerman 1.00 2.50
5 Michael Peca .30 .75
6 Keith Tkachuk .40 1.00
7 Saku Koivu .40 1.00
8 Tony Amonte .30 .75
9 Peter Bondra .40 1.00
10 Pavel Bure .40 1.00
11 Ron Francis .50 1.25
12 Eric Lindros .60 1.50
13 Paul Kariya .40 1.00
14 Theo Fleury .50 1.25
15 Jaromir Jagr 1.25 3.00
16 Patrick Roy 1.00 2.50
17 Zigmund Palffy .40 1.00
18 Ed Belfour .40 1.00
19 Sergei Samsonov .30 .75
20 Nicklas Lidstrom .40 1.00
21 Pavol Demitra .50 1.25
22 Sergei Fedorov .60 1.50
23 Teemu Selanne .75 2.00
24 Martin Brodeur 1.00 2.50
25 John LeClair .40 1.00
26 Ray Bourque .60 1.50
27 Peter Forsberg .75 2.00
28 Doug Weight .40 1.00
29 Brian Leetch .30 .75
30 Mark Recchi .50 1.25
31 Jason Allison .30 .75
32 Rob Blake .40 1.00
33 Scott Niedermayer .40 1.00
34 Chris Pronger .40 1.00
35 Joe Sakic .75 2.00
36 Mark Messier .75 2.00
37 Daniel Alfredsson .40 1.00
38 Guy Hebert .40 1.00
39 Bobby Holik .25 .60
40 Joe Thornton .60 1.50
41 Ron Tugnutt .30 .75
42 Jeff Friesen .30 .75
43 Jeremy Roenick .60 1.50
44 Wade Redden .25 .60
45 Chris Osgood .40 1.00
46 Arturs Irbe .30 .75
47 Valeri Bure .25 .60
48 Chris Drury .30 .75
49 Owen Nolan .40 1.00
50 Kenny Jonsson .25 .60
51 Petr Sykora .30 .75
52 Byron Dafoe .30 .75
53 Brett Hull .75 2.00
54 Mike Richter .40 1.00
55 Brendan Shanahan .40 1.00
56 Mats Sundin .40 1.00
57 Miroslav Satan .30 .75
58 Markus Naslund .40 1.00
59 Rod Brind'Amour .40 1.00
60 Joe Nieuwendyk .30 .75
61 Petr Nedved .25 .60
62 Sergei Berezin .25 .60
63 Trevor Linden .40 1.00
64 Marian Hossa .40 1.00
65 Pierre Turgeon .30 .75
66 Vincent Lecavalier .40 1.00
67 Sami Kapanen .25 .60
68 Andrew Brunette .25 .60
69 Brian Savage .25 .60
70 Derian Hatcher .30 .75
71 Curtis Joseph .50 1.25
72 Scott Stevens .40 1.00
73 Radek Bonk .25 .60
74 Jarome Iginla .50 1.25
75 Adam Graves .30 .75
76 Alexander Selivanov .25 .60
77 Alexander Mogilny .30 .75
78 Cliff Ronning .25 .60
79 Vincent Damphousse .30 .75
80 Alexei Kovalev .30 .75
81 Yanic Perreault .25 .60
82 Alexander Korolyuk .25 .60
83 Jozef Stumpel .25 .60
84 Viktor Kozlov .25 .60
85 Mike Modano .60 1.50
86 David Legwand .25 .60
87 Scott Gomez .30 .75
88 Tim Connolly .25 .60
89 Brad Stuart .30 .75
90 Peter Schaefer .25 .60
91 Alex Tanguay .30 .75
92 Simon Gagne .40 1.00
93 Dave Tanabe .25 .60
94 Roberto Luongo .60 1.50
95 Martin Biron .30 .75
96 Mike Fisher RC .40 1.00
97 Patrik Stefan RC .40 1.00
98 Nikolai Antropov RC 1.00 2.50
99 Jochen Hecht RC .60 1.50
100 Steve Kariya RC .40 1.00

1999-00 Topps Gold Label Class 3

36 Mark Messier 3.00 8.00

1999-00 Topps Gold Label Fresh Gold

COMPLETE SET (20) 15.00 30.00
*BLACK: 1.5X TO 4X BASIC INSERTS
*RED: 10X TO 25X BASIC INSERTS
FG1 Sergei Samsonov .75 2.00
FG2 Joe Thornton 2.00 5.00
FG3 Wade Redden .75 2.00
FG4 Chris Drury .75 2.00
FG5 Petr Sykora .75 2.00
FG6 Patrik Stefan 2.00 5.00
FG7 Anson Carter .75 2.00
FG8 Martin Biron .75 2.00
FG9 Alex Tanguay .75 2.00
FG10 Milan Hejduk 1.25 3.00
FG11 Mark Parrish .75 2.00
FG12 David Legwand .75 2.00
FG13 Brendan Morrison .75 2.00
FG14 Scott Gomez .75 2.00
FG15 Tim Connolly 1.25 3.00
FG16 Marian Hossa 1.25 3.00
FG17 Jan Hrdina .75 2.00
FG18 Steve Kariya .75 2.00
FG19 Jochen Hecht 1.50 4.00
FG20 Vincent Lecavalier 1.25 3.00

1999-00 Topps Gold Label Prime Gold

COMPLETE SET (15) 30.00 60.00
*BLACK: 1.5X TO 4X BASIC CARDS
*RED/25: 10X TO 25X BASIC CARDS
PG1 Dominik Hasek 3.00 8.00
PG2 Paul Kariya 1.50 4.00
PG3 Theo Fleury 1.25 3.00
PG4 Jaromir Jagr 2.50 6.00
PG5 Zigmund Palffy 1.25 3.00
PG6 Nicklas Lidstrom 1.50 4.00
PG7 Teemu Selanne 1.50 4.00
PG8 John LeClair 1.50 4.00
PG9 Ray Bourque 2.50 6.00
PG10 Peter Forsberg 4.00 10.00
PG11 Joe Sakic 3.00 8.00
PG12 Jeremy Roenick 2.00 5.00
PG13 Mike Modano 2.50 6.00
PG14 Pavel Bure 1.50 4.00
PG15 Curtis Joseph 1.50 4.00

1999-00 Topps Gold Label Quest for the Cup

COMPLETE SET (10) 15.00 30.00
*BLACK: 1.5X TO 4X BASIC INSERTS
*RED/25: 20X TO 50X BASIC INSERTS
QC1 Steve Yzerman 4.00 10.00
QC2 Keith Tkachuk .75 2.00
QC3 Eric Lindros .75 2.00
QC4 Patrick Roy 3.00 8.00
QC5 Martin Brodeur 2.00 5.00
QC6 Chris Pronger .60 1.50
QC7 Daniel Alfredsson .60 1.50
QC8 Owen Nolan .60 1.50
QC9 Brett Hull 1.00 2.50
QC10 Mats Sundin .75 2.00

2000-01 Topps Gold Label Class 1

COMPLETE SET (115) 75.00 150.00
*CLS 1 GOLD VETS/399: 1.5X TO 4X CLS 1
*CLS 1 GOLD ROOK/99: .6X TO 1.5X CLS 1
*CLS 2 VETS: 1.2X TO 3X CLS 1
*CLS 2 ROOK/666: .5X TO 1.2X CLS 1
*CLS 2 GLD VETS/299: 2X TO 5X CLS 1
*CLS 2 GLD ROOK/66: .8X TO 2X CLS 1
*CLS 3 VETS: 2X TO 5X CLS 1
*CLS 3 ROOK/333: .6X TO 1.5X CLS 1
*CLS 3 GLD VETS/199: 2.5X TO 6X CLS 1
*CLS 3 GLD ROOK/33: 1.2X TO 3X CLS 1
1 Ray Bourque .60 1.50
2 Brendan Shanahan .40 1.00
3 Mark Recchi .50 1.25
4 Olaf Kolzig .40 1.00
5 Brett Hull .75 2.00
6 Valeri Bure .30 .75
7 Joe Thornton .60 1.50
8 Pavel Bure .40 1.00
9 Jeff Hackett .25 .60
10 Patrik Elias .40 1.00
11 Marian Hossa .40 1.00
12 Patrick Marleau .40 1.00
13 Markus Naslund .40 1.00
14 Jaromir Jagr 1.25 3.00
15 Tim Connolly .25 .60
16 Zigmund Palffy .40 1.00
17 Peter Forsberg .75 2.00
18 Byron Dafoe .30 .75
19 Patrik Stefan .30 .75
20 Arturs Irbe .30 .75
21 Jocelyn Thibault .30 .75
22 Bill Guerin .40 1.00
23 Keith Primeau .30 .75
24 Mats Sundin .40 1.00
25 Adam Oates .40 1.00
26 Owen Nolan .40 1.00
27 Mike Richter .40 1.00
28 Luc Robitaille .40 1.00
29 Chris Drury .30 .75
30 Maxim Afinogenov .25 .60
31 Jarome Iginla .50 1.25
32 Joe Nieuwendyk .30 .75
33 Maxim Sushinski .25 .60
34 Daniel Alfredsson .40 1.00
35 Pierre Turgeon .30 .75
36 Jason Allison .30 .75
37 Mario Lemieux 1.50 4.00
38 Sergei Fedorov .60 1.50
39 Paul Kariya .40 1.00
40 Scott Stevens .40 1.00
41 Keith Tkachuk .40 1.00
42 Curtis Joseph .50 1.25
43 Peter Bondra .40 1.00
44 Roman Turek .30 .75
45 Alexei Kovalev .30 .75
46 Brian Boucher .30 .75
47 Mark Messier .75 2.00
48 Saku Koivu .40 1.00
49 Tommy Salo .30 .75
50 Ron Tugnutt .30 .75
51 Patrick Roy 1.00 2.50
52 Fred Brathwaite .30 .75
53 Donald Audette .30 .75
54 Doug Gilmour .50 1.25
55 Alexander Mogilny .30 .75
56 John LeClair .40 1.00
57 Scott Young .25 .60
58 Jeff Friesen .25 .60
59 Simon Gagne .40 1.00
60 Theo Fleury .50 1.25
61 Scott Gomez .30 .75
62 Guy Hebert .30 .75
63 Roberto Luongo .60 1.50
64 Mike Modano .60 1.50
65 Joe Sakic .75 2.00
66 Dominik Hasek .60 1.50
67 Pavol Demitra .50 1.25
68 Daniel Sedin .50 1.25
69 Vincent Lecavalier .40 1.00
70 Jeremy Roenick .60 1.50
71 Martin Brodeur 1.00 2.50
72 Rob Blake .40 1.00
73 Ed Belfour .40 1.00
74 Tony Amonte .30 .75
75 Miroslav Satan .25 .60
76 Alexei Yashin .30 .75
77 Henrik Sedin .50 1.25
78 David Legwand .40 1.00
79 Steve Yzerman 1.00 2.50
80 Ron Francis .50 1.25
81 Milan Hejduk .30 .75
82 Teemu Selanne .75 2.00
83 Brad Isbister .25 .60
84 Jean-Sebastien Aubin .30 .75
85 Chris Pronger .40 1.00
86 Nicklas Lidstrom .40 1.00
87 Brad Richards .40 1.00
88 Brent Johnson .30 .75
89 Oleg Saprykin .25 .60
90 Anson Carter .30 .75
91 Brian Leetch .30 .75
92 Evgeni Nabokov .30 .75
93 Ian Laperriere .25 .60
94 Peter White .25 .60
95 Wes Walz .25 .60
96 Jason Arnott .30 .75
97 Tommy Albelin .25 .60
98 Jeff Toms .25 .60
99 Brad Brown .30 .75
100 Garry Valk .25 .60
101 Andrew Raycroft RC 3.00 8.00
102 Marian Gaborik RC 12.50 30.00
103 David Aebischer RC 2.50 6.00
104 Scott Hartnell RC 3.00 8.00
105 Marty Turco RC 2.50 6.00
106 Justin Williams RC 3.00 8.00
107 Steven Reinprecht RC 2.00 5.00
108 Josef Vasicek RC 3.00 8.00
109 Martin Havlat RC 8.00 20.00
110 Rostislav Klesla RC 3.00 8.00
111 Jani Hurme RC 1.25 3.00
112 Rick DiPietro RC 2.50 6.00
113 Alexander Kharitonov RC 1.25 3.00
114 Matt Pettinger RC 1.25 3.00
115 Roman Cechmanek RC 1.50 4.00

2000-01 Topps Gold Label Autographs

GLABB Brian Boucher 4.00 10.00
GLABR Brad Richards 6.00 15.00
GLAJW Justin Williams 6.00 15.00
GLAMG Marian Gaborik 12.50 30.00
GLAMK Milan Kraft 4.00 10.00
GLAMT Marty Turco 8.00 20.00
GLAMY Mike York 4.00 10.00
GLARB Ray Bourque 20.00 50.00
GLASG Scott Gomez 4.00 10.00
GLASH Scott Hartnell 8.00 20.00

2000-01 Topps Gold Label Behind the Mask

COMPLETE SET (10) 10.00 20.00
BTM1 Curtis Joseph .75 2.00
BTM2 Ed Belfour .75 2.00
BTM3 Dominik Hasek 1.50 4.00
BTM4 Martin Brodeur 2.00 5.00
BTM5 Brian Boucher .75 2.00
BTM6 Roman Turek .75 2.00
BTM7 Olaf Kolzig .75 2.00
BTM8 Patrick Roy 4.00 10.00
BTM9 Arturs Irbe .75 2.00
BTM10 Mike Richter .75 2.00

2000-01 Topps Gold Label Bullion

COMPLETE SET (10) 30.00 60.00
B1 M.Brodeur/S.Gomez/J.Arnott 4.00 10.00
B2 E.Belfour/M.Modano/B.Hull 3.00 8.00
B3 Yzerman/Shanahan/Fedorov 6.00 12.00
B4 P.Roy/Bourque/Forsberg 6.00 15.00
B5 R.Turek/Pronger/Demitra 2.00 5.00
B6 M.Sundin/C.Joseph/T.Domi 4.00 10.00
B7 Roenick/Tkachuk/Numminen 3.00 8.00
B8 J.Friesen/P.Marleau/O.Nolan 3.00 8.00
B9 M.Messier/Leetch/M.Richter 2.00 5.00
B10 D.Sedin/M.Naslund/H.Sedin 2.00 5.00

2000-01 Topps Gold Label Game-Worn Jerseys

GLJJL John LeClair 5.00 12.00
GLJKT Keith Tkachuk 5.00 12.00
GLJMB Martin Brodeur 10.00 25.00
GLJPF Peter Forsberg 10.00 25.00
GLJPM Patrick Marleau 5.00 12.00
GLJSF Sergei Fedorov 6.00 15.00

2000-01 Topps Gold Label Golden Greats

GG1 Pavel Bure 1.25 3.00
GG2 Paul Kariya 1.00 2.50
GG3 Jaromir Jagr 1.50 4.00
GG4 John LeClair 1.00 2.50
GG5 Steve Yzerman 4.00 10.00
GG6 Brett Hull 1.25 3.00
GG7 Alexander Mogilny .75 2.00
GG8 Joe Sakic 2.00 5.00
GG9 Keith Tkachuk 1.00 2.50
GG10 Teemu Selanne 1.00 2.50
GG11 Sergei Fedorov 2.00 5.00
GG12 Luc Robitaille .75 2.00
GG13 Mike Modano 1.50 4.00
GG14 Brendan Shanahan 1.50 4.00
GG15 Jeremy Roenick 1.25 3.00

2000-01 Topps Gold Label New Generation

NG1 Scott Gomez .75 2.00
NG2 Vincent Lecavalier 1.50 4.00
NG3 Joe Thornton 2.00 5.00
NG4 Alex Tanguay 1.25 3.00
NG5 Marian Hossa 1.50 4.00
NG6 Brad Stuart .75 2.00
NG7 Henrik Sedin .75 2.00
NG8 Marian Gaborik 3.00 8.00
NG9 Roberto Luongo 2.00 5.00
NG10 David Legwand .75 2.00
NG11 Daniel Sedin .75 2.00
NG12 Patrik Stefan .75 2.00
NG13 Brian Boucher 1.25 3.00
NG14 Chris Drury 1.25 3.00
NG15 Tim Connolly .75 2.00

2000-01 Topps Heritage

COMPLETE SET (247) 125.00 250.00
COMP.SET w/o SP's (219) 25.00 50.00
1 Ray Bourque .60 1.50
2 Martin Brodeur 1.00 2.50
3 Jaromir Jagr 1.25 3.00
4 Vincent Lecavalier .40 1.00
5 Olaf Kolzig .40 1.00
6 Alexei Yashin .30 .75
7 Mark Messier .75 2.00
8 Paul Kariya .40 1.00
9 Pavel Bure .40 1.00
10 Steve Yzerman 1.00 2.50
11 Patrik Stefan .30 .75
12 Joe Thornton .60 1.50
13 Mats Sundin .40 1.00
14 Brett Hull .75 2.00
15 Zigmund Palffy .40 1.00
16 Peter Bondra .40 1.00
17 Owen Nolan .40 1.00
18 Tony Amonte .30 .75
19 Henrik Sedin .50 1.25
20 Keith Tkachuk .40 1.00
21 Tim Connolly .25 .60
22 Doug Weight .40 1.00
23 Ed Belfour .40 1.00
24 Patrick Roy 1.00 2.50
25 Brad Richards .40 1.00
26 Dominik Hasek .60 1.50
27 Brendan Shanahan .40 1.00
28 Teemu Selanne .75 2.00
29 Scott Gomez .30 .75
30 John LeClair .40 1.00
31 Chris Pronger .40 1.00
32 Ron Francis .50 1.25
33 Daniel Sedin .50 1.25
34 Curtis Joseph .50 1.25
35 Roman Turek .30 .75
36 Jeremy Roenick .60 1.50
37 Mark Recchi .50 1.25
38 Patrik Elias .40 1.00
39 Saku Koivu .40 1.00
40 Luc Robitaille .40 1.00
41 Sergei Fedorov .60 1.50
42 Peter Forsberg .75 2.00
43 Milan Kraft .25 .60
44 Jason Allison .30 .75
45 Mike Modano .60 1.50
46 Roberto Luongo .60 1.50
47 David Legwand .40 1.00
48 Pierre Turgeon .30 .75
49 Maxime Ouellet .40 1.00
50 Oleg Saprykin .25 .60
51 Pavol Demitra .50 1.25
52 Adam Oates .40 1.00
53 Doug Gilmour .50 1.25
54 Joe Sakic .75 2.00
55 Daniel Alfredsson .40 1.00
56 Brian Leetch .30 .75
57 Bill Guerin .40 1.00
58 Brent Johnson .30 .75
59 Scott Stevens .40 1.00
60 Rob Blake .40 1.00
61 Nicklas Lidstrom .40 1.00
62 Milan Hejduk .30 .75
63 Arturs Irbe .30 .75
64 Maxim Afinogenov .25 .60
65 Taylor Pyatt .25 .60
66 Tommy Salo .30 .75
67 Theo Fleury .50 1.25
68 Marian Hossa .40 1.00
69 Simon Gagne .40 1.00
70 Jarome Iginla .50 1.25
71 Alexander Mogilny .30 .75
72 Chris Drury .30 .75
73 Mario Lemieux 1.50 4.00
74 Petr Hubacek RC 2.00 5.00
75 Marty Turco RC 4.00 10.00
76 Rostislav Klesla RC 5.00 12.00
77 Martin Havlat RC 6.00 15.00
78 David Aebischer RC 4.00 10.00
79 Reto Von Arx RC 2.50 6.00
80 Mike Comrie RC 5.00 12.00
81 Tomas Kloucek RC 2.00 5.00
82 Steven Reinprecht RC 3.00 8.00
83 Brad Tapper RC 2.00 5.00
84 Petr Svoboda RC 2.50 6.00
85 Marian Gaborik RC 10.00 25.00
86 Josef Vasicek RC 5.00 12.00
87 Lubomir Visnovsky RC 4.00 10.00
88 Roman Cechmanek RC 2.50 6.00
89 Reed Low RC 2.00 5.00
90 Jani Hurme RC 2.00 5.00
91 Petteri Nummelin RC 2.00 5.00
92 Colin White RC 2.00 5.00
93 Andrew Raycroft RC 5.00 12.00
94 Greg Classen RC 2.00 5.00
95 Alexander Kharitonov RC 2.50 6.00
96 Rick DiPietro RC 4.00 10.00
97 Justin Williams RC 5.00 12.00
98 Eric Belanger RC 2.50 6.00
99 Scott Hartnell RC 5.00 12.00
100 Michel Riesen RC 2.50 6.00
101 Brian Boucher .30 .75
102 Mike Richter .40 1.00
103 John Vanbiesbrouck .40 1.00
104 Jamie McLennan .25 .60
105 Andrei Markov .50 1.25
106 Ron Tugnutt .30 .75
107 Jean-Sebastien Aubin .30 .75
108 Brad Stuart .30 .75
109 Gary Roberts .25 .60
110 Rod Brind'Amour .40 1.00
111 Keith Primeau .30 .75
112 Jeff Halpern .25 .60
113 Jochen Hecht .25 .60
114 Valeri Bure .30 .75
115 Donald Audette .30 .75
116 Brenden Morrow .30 .75
117 Mike Mottau .25 .60
118 Kevin Weekes .25 .60
119 Jamie Storr .30 .75
120 Shane Willis .25 .60
121 Matt Cooke .25 .60
122 Martin Lapointe .30 .75
123 Alexei Kovalev .30 .75
124 Felix Potvin .60 1.50
125 Sean Burke .25 .60
126 Jeff Hackett .25 .60
127 Brad Isbister .25 .60
128 Derian Hatcher .30 .75
129 Marc Savard .25 .60
130 Sergei Samsonov .30 .75
131 Maxim Sushinski .25 .60
132 Radek Bonk .30 .75
133 Mika Noronen .25 .60
134 Adam Graves .30 .75
135 Sheldon Keefe .25 .60
136 Markus Naslund .40 1.00
137 Trevor Letowski .25 .60
138 Jeff Friesen .25 .60
139 Alex Tanguay .30 .75
140 Byron Dafoe .30 .75
141 Chris Osgood .40 1.00
142 Mike York .25 .60
143 Scott Young .25 .60
144 Sami Kapanen .25 .60
145 Evgeni Nabokov .30 .75
146 Brendan Morrison .40 1.00
147 Joe Nieuwendyk .30 .75
148 Tomi Kallio .25 .60
149 Guy Hebert .30 .75
150 Randy McKay .25 .60
151 Mike Johnson .25 .60
152 Miroslav Satan .25 .60
153 Patrick Marleau .40 1.00
154 Jocelyn Thibault .30 .75
155 Martin Straka .30 .75
156 Fred Brathwaite .30 .75
157 Cliff Ronning .25 .60
158 Denis Shvidki .25 .60
159 Espen Knutsen .25 .60
160 Alexei Zhamnov .30 .75
161 Georges Laraque .30 .75
162 Jose Theodore .40 1.00
163 Rick Tocchet .30 .75
164 Donald Brashear .25 .60

165 Darren Langdon .25 .60
166 Rob Ray .25 .60
167 Matthew Barnaby .25 .60
168 Chris Simon .25 .60
169 Ken Belanger .25 .60
170 Tie Domi .30 .75
171 Roman Hamrlik .25 .60
172 Olli Jokinen .30 .75
173 Steve Rucchin .25 .60
174 Jim Cummins .25 .60
175 Tyson Nash .25 .60
176 Scott Parker .25 .60
177 Matt Johnson .25 .60
178 Sandy McCarthy .25 .60
179 Daniel Cleary .30 .75
180 Michal Handzus .25 .60
181 Nikolai Antropov .25 .60
182 Scott Thornton .30 .75
183 Shane Doan .30 .75
184 Wade Redden .25 .60
185 Ray Whitney .30 .75
186 Teppo Numminen .25 .60
187 Pat Verbeek .30 .75
188 Bobby Holik .25 .60
189 Mike Dunham .25 .60
190 Rob Niedermayer .30 .75
191 Ray Ferraro .25 .60
192 Steve Sullivan .25 .60
193 Sergei Zubov .30 .75
194 Scott Walker .25 .60
195 Geoff Sanderson .30 .75
196 Bob Probert .40 1.00
197 Andrew Brunette .25 .60
198 Marty Murray .25 .60
199 Steve Staios .25 .60
200 Kay Whitmore .25 .60
201 Jonas Hoglund .25 .60
202 Niklas Andersson .25 .60
203 Joaquin Gage .25 .60
204 Mike Ricci .25 .60
205 Bryan Helmer .25 .60
206 Patrick Traverse .25 .60
207 Mike Rucinski .25 .60
208 Brantt Myhres .25 .60
209 Claude Lapointe .25 .60
210 Frank Musil .25 .60
211 Sandis Ozolinsh .25 .60
212 Tomas Vokoun .30 .75
213 Jarrod Skalde .25 .60
214 Sergei Gonchar .25 .60
215 Anson Carter .30 .75
216 Steve Yzerman AS .75 2.00
217 Mike Modano AS .50 1.25
218 Paul Kariya AS .30 .75
219 Brendan Shanahan AS .30 .75
220 Pavel Bure AS .30 .75
221 Jaromir Jagr AS 1.00 2.50
222 Chris Pronger AS .30 .75
223 Nicklas Lidstrom AS .30 .75
224 Rob Blake AS .30 .75
225 Eric Desjardins AS .25 .60
226 Olaf Kolzig AS .30 .75
227 Roman Turek AS .25 .60
228 S.Stevens
C.Pronger LL .30 .75
229 S.Gomez
A.Tanguay LL .25 .60
230 P.Bure
O.Nolan LL .30 .75
231 M.Brodeur
R.Turek LL .75 2.00
232 M.Czerkawski
O.Nolan LL .30 .75
233 J.Theodore
E.Belfour LL .30 .75
234 J.Madden
T.Amonte LL .25 .60
235 J.Jagr
P.Kariya LL 1.00 2.50
236 E.Desjardins
N.Lidstrom LL .30 .75
237 B.Boucher
R.Turek LL .25 .60
238 Steve Yzerman AW .75 2.00
239 Scott Stevens AW .30 .75
240 Scott Gomez AW .25 .60
241 Roman Turek AW .30 .75
242 Pavol Demitra AW .40 1.00
243 Pavel Bure AW .30 .75
245 Jaromir Jagr AW 1.00 2.50
246 Chris Pronger AW .30 .75
247 New Jersey Devils SC .20 .50
244 Olaf Kolzig AW .30 .75

2000-01 Topps Heritage Chrome Parallel

*1-73 VETS/555: 2X TO 5X BASIC CARDS
*74-100 ROOK/555: .3X TO .8X BASE RC
7 Mark Messier 4.00 10.00

2000-01 Topps Heritage Arena Relics

OSAJT Joe Thornton 10.00 25.00
OSAMM Mark Messier 12.50 30.00
OSAMS Mats Sundin 10.00 25.00
OSASK Saku Koivu 10.00 25.00
OSASY Steve Yzerman 12.50 30.00
OSATA Tony Amonte 10.00 25.00
OSABG Bill Gadsby 10.00 25.00
OSAGH Gordie Howe 12.00 30.00
OSALW Gump Worsley 10.00 25.00
OSAMR Maurice Richard 15.00 40.00
OSAMS Milt Schmidt 10.00 25.00
OSATK Ted Kennedy 10.00 25.00
OSA Multi Arena Relic/55 175.00 350.00
HAAGH Gordie Howe AU/25 250.00 400.00
HAALW Gump Worsley AU/25 150.00 250.00

2000-01 Topps Heritage Autographs

HAAG Adam Graves 12.50 30.00
HACJ Curtis Joseph 12.50 30.00
HAJH Jeff Hackett 6.00 15.00
HAJT Joe Thornton 20.00 50.00
HASF Sergei Fedorov 20.00 50.00
HAAB Andy Bathgate 10.00 25.00
HAAD Alex Delvecchio 10.00 25.00
HAGH Gordie Howe 75.00 150.00
HALW Gump Worsley 15.00 40.00
HARK Red Kelly 12.50 30.00
HATL Ted Lindsay 12.50 30.00

2000-01 Topps Heritage Heroes

COMPLETE SET (20) 25.00 50.00
HH1 Ray Bourque 1.50 4.00
HH2 Jaromir Jagr 1.25 3.00
HH3 Steve Yzerman 4.00 10.00
HH4 Mike Modano 1.25 3.00
HH5 Patrick Roy 4.00 10.00
HH6 Martin Brodeur 2.00 5.00
HH7 Mark Messier 1.00 2.50
HH8 Peter Forsberg 2.00 5.00
HH9 Scott Stevens .60 1.50
HH10 Teemu Selanne .75 2.00
HH11 Pavel Bure 1.00 2.50
HH12 Curtis Joseph .75 2.00
HH13 John LeClair 1.00 2.50
HH14 Brett Hull 1.00 2.50
HH15 Keith Tkachuk .75 2.00
HH16 Tony Amonte .60 1.50
HH17 Ed Belfour .75 2.00
HH18 Brendan Shanahan 1.25 3.00
HH19 Dominik Hasek 1.50 4.00
HH20 Paul Kariya .75 2.00

2000-01 Topps Heritage New Tradition

COMPLETE SET (10) 6.00 12.00
NT1 Marian Hossa .50 1.25
NT2 Daniel Sedin .40 1.00
NT3 Milan Hejduk .50 1.25
NT4 Vincent Lecavalier .50 1.25
NT5 Joe Thornton .75 2.00
NT6 Scott Gomez .40 1.00
NT7 Chris Drury .40 1.00
NT8 Brian Boucher .40 1.00
NT9 Henrik Sedin .40 1.00
NT10 Marian Gaborik 2.00 5.00

2000-01 Topps Heritage Original Six Relics

OSJAZ Alexei Zhamnov J 2.50 6.00
OSJCO Chris Osgood J 4.00 10.00
OSJJT Joe Thornton J 6.00 15.00
OSJSK Saku Koivu J 3.00 8.00
OSJTD Tie Domi J 2.50 6.00
OSJTF Theo Fleury J 4.00 10.00
OSSBP Bob Probert S 6.00 15.00
OSSJA Jason Allison S 5.00 12.00
OSSJH Jeff Hackett S 8.00 20.00
OSSMM Mark Messier S 12.00 30.00
OSSMS Mats Sundin S 6.00 15.00
OSSSY Steve Yzerman S 15.00 40.00
OSJ Alexei Zhamnov
Theo Fleury
Chris Osgood
Joe Thornton
Saku Koivu
Tie Domi/55 125.00 250.00
OSJAJH Jeff Hackett JSY AU/25 40.00 80.00
OSJAJT Joe Thornton JSY AU/25 75.00 200.00

2001-02 Topps Heritage

COMPLETE SET (187) 40.00 100.00
1 Mario Lemieux 1.25 3.00
2 Evgeni Nabokov .25 .60
3 Nicklas Lidstrom .30 .75
4 Patrik Elias .40 1.00
5 Olaf Kolzig .30 .75
6 Mats Sundin .30 .75
7 Jason Allison .25 .60
8 Mike Modano .50 1.25
9 Keith Tkachuk .30 .75
10 John LeClair .30 .75
11 Pavel Bure .30 .75
12 Tony Amonte .25 .60
13 Zigmund Palffy .30 .75
14 Mark Messier .60 1.50
15 Sean Burke .20 .50
16 Markus Naslund .30 .75
17 Milan Hejduk .25 .60
18 Teemu Selanne .60 1.50
19 Espen Knutsen .20 .50
20 David Legwand .25 .60
21 Saku Koivu .30 .75
22 Ron Francis .40 1.00
23 Ray Ferraro .20 .50
24 Brendan Shanahan .30 .75
25 Rick DiPietro .25 .60
26 Brad Richards .30 .75
27 Henrik Sedin .40 1.00
28 Marian Hossa .30 .75
29 Marian Gaborik .30 .75
30 Ed Belfour .30 .75
31 Miroslav Satan .20 .50
32 Roberto Luongo .50 1.25
33 Brian Leetch .25 .60
34 Chris Pronger .30 .75
35 Peter Bondra .30 .75
36 Keith Primeau .25 .60
37 Johan Hedberg .25 .60
38 Steve Yzerman .75 2.00
39 Peter Forsberg .60 1.50
40 Jarome Iginla .40 1.00
41 Jose Theodore .30 .75
42 Curtis Joseph .40 1.00
43 Martin Havlat .25 .60
44 Sergei Fedorov .50 1.25
45 Arturs Irbe .25 .60
46 Martin Brodeur .75 2.00
47 Owen Nolan .30 .75
48 Daniel Sedin .40 1.00
49 Mark Recchi .40 1.00
50 Adam Deadmarsh .20 .50
51 Tommy Salo .20 .50
52 Alexei Kovalev .25 .60
53 Steve Sullivan .20 .50
54 Paul Kariya .30 .75
55 Vincent Lecavalier .30 .75
56 Alex Tanguay .25 .60
57 Joe Thornton .50 1.25
58 Brent Johnson .25 .60
59 Roman Cechmanek .25 .60
60 Petr Sykora .20 .50
61 J-P Dumont .20 .50
62 Mike Comrie .25 .60
63 Daniel Alfredsson .30 .75
64 Eric Daze .25 .60
65 Felix Potvin .50 1.25
66 Chris Drury .25 .60
67 Manny Fernandez .20 .50
68 Claude Lemieux .25 .60
69 Rob Blake .30 .75
70 Bill Guerin .30 .75
71 Mike Dunham .25 .60
72 Simon Gagne .30 .75
73 Jeff Friesen .20 .50
74 Joe Sakic .60 1.50
75 Jason Arnott .25 .60
76 Patrick Roy .75 2.00
77 Josef Vasicek .20 .50
78 Marty Turco .30 .75
79 Al MacInnis .40 1.00
80 Anson Carter .25 .60
81 Tomi Kallio .20 .50
82 Eric Belanger .20 .50
83 Patrick Lalime .25 .60
84 Scott Young .20 .50
85 Scott Gomez .25 .60
86 Marc Denis .25 .60
87 Jeff O'Neill .25 .60
88 Sergei Samsonov .25 .60
89 Robert Lang .20 .50
90 Byron Dafoe .25 .60
91 Scott Stevens .30 .75
92 Adam Oates .25 .60
93 Patrick Marleau .30 .75
94 Petr Nedved .25 .60
95 Ryan Smyth .25 .60
96 Adam Foote .20 .50
97 Marc Savard .20 .50
98 Brad Isbister .20 .50
99 Martin Straka .20 .50
100 Joe Nieuwendyk .25 .60
101 Shane Willis .20 .50
102 Pavol Demitra .40 1.00
103 Jeff Halpern .20 .50
104 Sergei Zubov .25 .60
105 David Vyborny .20 .50
106 Gary Roberts .25 .60
107 Martin Biron .25 .60
108 Lubomir Visnovsky .25 .60
109 Fredrik Modin .25 .60
110 Brenden Morrow .25 .60
111 Stanley Cup Champs .40 1.00
112 Nicklas Lidstrom AS .30 .75
113 Jaromir Jagr AS .75 2.00
114 Patrik Elias AS .25 .60
115 Joe Sakic AS .50 1.25
116 Dominik Hasek AS .40 1.00
117 Rob Blake AS .25 .60
118 Scott Stevens AS .25 .60
119 Roman Cechmanek AS .20 .50
120 Mario Lemieux AS 1.00 2.50
121 Pavel Bure AS .25 .60
122 Luc Robitaille AS .25 .60
123 J.Jagr/J.Sakic LL .75 2.00
124 P.Bure/J.Sakic LL .50 1.25
125 P.Elias/J.Sakic LL .50 1.25
126 B.Leetch/N.Lidstrom LL .25 .60
127 A.Irbe/T.Salo LL .20 .50
128 M.Brodeur/P.Roy LL .60 1.50
129 M.Turco/R.Cechmanek LL .25 .60
130 Joe Sakic AW .50 1.25
131 Patrick Roy AW .60 1.50
132 Pavel Bure AW .25 .60
133 Evgeni Nabokov AW .20 .50
134 Nicklas Lidstrom AW .25 .60
135 Dominik Hasek AW .40 1.00
136 John Madden AW .20 .50
137 Jaromir Jagr AW .75 2.00
138 Ilya Kovalchuk RC 6.00 15.00
139 Niko Kapanen RC 2.50 6.00
140 Brian Sutherby RC 1.50 4.00
141 Jeff Jillson RC 1.50 4.00
142 Jiri Dopita RC 1.50 4.00
143 Andreas Salomonsson RC 1.50 4.00
144 Timo Parssinen RC 2.00 5.00
145 Vaclav Nedorost RC 1.50 4.00
146 Kristian Huselius RC 2.50 6.00
147 Dan Blackburn RC 2.00 5.00
148 Nikita Alexeev RC 1.50 4.00
149 Peter Smrek RC 1.50 4.00
150 Krys Kolanos RC 1.50 4.00
151 Pavel Datsyuk RC 20.00 50.00
152 Jaroslav Bednar RC 1.50 4.00
153 Chris Neil RC 2.00 5.00
154 Erik Cole RC 3.00 8.00
155 Niklas Hagman RC 2.00 5.00
156 Jason Chimera RC 1.50 4.00
157 Scott Clemmensen RC 1.50 4.00
158 Andrew Brunette .75 2.00
159 Dominik Hasek 2.00 5.00
160 Jaromir Jagr 4.00 10.00
161 Doug Weight 1.25 3.00
162 Brett Hull 2.50 6.00
163 Pierre Turgeon 1.00 2.50
164 Jeremy Roenick 2.00 5.00
165 Alexander Mogilny 1.00 2.50
166 Luc Robitaille 1.25 3.00
167 Michael Peca 1.00 2.50
168 Roman Turek 1.00 2.50
169 Martin Lapointe .75 2.00
170 Alexei Yashin 1.00 2.50
171 Adam Graves 1.00 2.50
172 Valeri Bure .75 2.00
173 Tim Connolly .75 2.00
174 Kris Beech .75 2.00
175 Donald Audette .75 2.00
176 Jochen Hecht .75 2.00
177 Fred Brathwaite 1.00 2.50
178 Rob Niedermayer 1.00 2.50
179 Eric Lindros 2.00 5.00
180 Bill Muckalt .75 2.00
181 Eric Weinrich .75 2.00
182 Taylor Pyatt .75 2.00
183 Pavel Brendl .75 2.00
184 Craig Berube .75 2.00
185 Dany Heatley 1.00 2.50
186 Ken Sutton .75 2.00
187 Slava Kozlov 1.00 2.50

2001-02 Topps Heritage Refractors

*REFRACTOR/558: 3X TO 8X BASIC

2001-02 Topps Heritage Arena Relics

RBG Bernie Geoffrion 6.00 15.00
RHR Henri Richard 6.00 15.00
RJBE Jean Beliveau 10.00 25.00
RJBU John Bucyk 8.00 20.00
RJBBG J.Bucyk/B.Geoffrion 30.00 80.00
RJBHR J.Bucyk/H.Richard 25.00 60.00
RJBJB J.Bucyk/J.Beliveau 30.00 80.00
ARBG Bernie Geoffrion AU 50.00 125.00
ARHR Henri Richard AU 40.00 100.00
ARJBE Jean Beliveau AU 50.00 120.00
ARJBU John Bucyk AU 40.00 100.00
ARJBBG Bucyk AU/Geoffrion AU 150.00 300.00
ARJBHR Bucyk AU/Richard AU 100.00 250.00
ARJBJB Bucyk AU/Beliveau AU 100.00 250.00

2001-02 Topps Heritage Autographs

AAA Al Arbour 10.00 25.00
ABG Bernie Geoffrion 20.00 50.00
AGH Glenn Hall 12.00 30.00
AHH Harry Howell 10.00 25.00
AHR Henri Richard 12.00 30.00
AIK Ilya Kovalchuk 12.00 30.00
AJBE Jean Beliveau 30.00 60.00
AJBU John Bucyk 15.00 40.00
AJH Johan Hedberg 10.00 25.00
AJW Justin Williams 10.00 25.00
AMG Marian Gaborik 10.00 25.00
AMS Miroslav Satan 10.00 25.00
ANU Norm Ullman 12.00 30.00
AOK Olaf Kolzig 10.00 25.00
APP Pierre Pilote 10.00 25.00
AVL Vincent Lecavalier 10.00 25.00

2001-02 Topps Heritage Captain's Cloth

CCAO Adam Oates 6.00 15.00
CCDH Derian Hatcher 6.00 15.00
CCED Eric Desjardins 8.00 20.00
CCPK Paul Kariya 8.00 20.00
CCSK Saku Koivu 8.00 20.00
CCVL Vincent Lecavalier 6.00 15.00

2001-02 Topps Heritage Jerseys

JBL Brian Leetch 6.00 15.00
JJI Jarome Iginla 8.00 20.00
JJL John LeClair 6.00 15.00
JJT Joe Thornton 8.00 20.00
JMB Martin Brodeur 12.50 30.00
JMS Martin Straka 6.00 15.00
JPF Peter Forsberg 10.00 25.00
JPM Patrick Marleau 6.00 15.00
JRL Robert Lang 6.00 15.00
JSF Sergei Fedorov 8.00 20.00

2001-02 Topps Heritage Salute

COMPLETE SET (9) 1.00 30.00
S1 John Bucyk 2.50 6.00
S2 Al Arbour 2.00 5.00
S3 Glenn Hall 2.50 6.00
S4 Harry Howell 2.00 5.00
S5 Pierre Pilote 2.00 5.00
S6 Norm Ullman 2.00 5.00
S7 Jean Beliveau 2.50 6.00
S8 Henri Richard 2.50 6.00
S9 Bernie Geoffrion 2.50 6.00

2001 Topps Heritage Avalanche NHL All-Star Game

COMPLETE SET (6) 12.00 30.00
1 Ray Bourque 3.20 8.00
2 Patrick Roy 4.00 10.00
3 Peter Forsberg 3.20 8.00
4 Joe Sakic 2.40 6.00
5 Milan Hejduk 1.60 4.00
6 Chris Drury 1.60 4.00

2002-03 Topps Heritage

COMPLETE SET (180) 60.00 150.00
COMP.SET w/o SP's (130) 20.00 50.00
1 Nicklas Lidstrom .30 .75
2 Jarome Iginla .40 1.00
3 Jose Theodore .30 .75
4 Ron Francis .40 1.00
5 Joe Thornton .50 1.25
6 Jaromir Jagr 1.00 2.50
7 Mario Lemieux 1.25 3.00
8 Roberto Luongo .50 1.25
9 Dany Heatley .25 .60
10 Pavel Bure .30 .75
11 Brett Hull .60 1.50
12 Keith Tkachuk .30 .75
13 Mats Sundin .30 .75
14 Pavel Datsyuk .50 1.25
15 Daniel Alfredsson .30 .75
16 Marian Gaborik .30 .75
17 Peter Forsberg .60 1.50
18 Miroslav Satan .30 .75
19 Martin Brodeur .75 2.00
20 Jeremy Roenick .50 1.25
21 Teemu Selanne .60 1.50
22 Todd Bertuzzi .30 .75
23 Erik Cole .20 .50
24 Jason Allison .25 .60
25 Sean Burke .20 .50
26 Eric Daze .20 .50
27 Patrick Roy .75 2.00
28 Simon Gagne .30 .75
29 Nikolai Khabibulin .30 .75
30 Alexei Yashin .25 .60
31 Denis Arkhipov .20 .50
32 Steve Yzerman .75 2.00
33 Mike Modano .50 1.25
34 Joe Sakic .60 1.50
35 Sergei Samsonov .25 .60
36 Saku Koivu .30 .75
37 Paul Kariya .30 .75
38 Doug Weight .30 .75
39 Tie Domi .25 .60
40 Kevin Weekes .25 .60
41 Rostislav Klesla .20 .50
42 Zigmund Palffy .30 .75
43 Chris Osgood .30 .75
44 Owen Nolan .30 .75
45 Markus Naslund .30 .75
46 Martin Biron .25 .60
47 Ryan Smyth .25 .60
48 Mike Dunham .25 .60
49 Martin Havlat .25 .60
50 Patrik Elias .30 .75
51 Peter Bondra .30 .75
52 Craig Conroy .20 .50
53 Rob Blake .30 .75
54 Mike Richter .30 .75
55 Stephen Weiss .30 .75
56 Johan Hedberg .30 .75
57 Brendan Morrison .25 .60
58 Chris Pronger .30 .75
59 Patrick Lalime .25 .60
60 David Legwand .25 .60
61 Jocelyn Thibault .25 .60
62 Mike Comrie .30 .75
63 Sergei Fedorov .50 1.25
64 Michael Peca .25 .60
65 Tommy Salo .25 .60
66 Scott Stevens .30 .75
67 Mark Recchi .40 1.00
68 Vincent Damphousse .25 .60
69 Vincent Lecavalier .30 .75
70 Olaf Kolzig .30 .75
71 Shane Doan .25 .60
72 Marty Turco .30 .75
73 Marian Hossa .30 .75
74 Eric Lindros .50 1.25
75 Brent Johnson .25 .60
76 John LeClair .30 .75
77 Dan Cloutier .25 .60
78 Radim Vrbata .20 .50
79 Ilya Kovalchuk .40 1.00
80 Brendan Shanahan .30 .75
81 Stu Barnes .20 .50
82 Alexander Mogilny .25 .60
83 Felix Potvin .50 1.25
84 Jeff O'Neill .20 .50
85 Glen Murray .25 .60
86 Marc Denis .25 .60
87 Brad Richards .30 .75
88 Roman Cechmanek .25 .60
89 Brian Leetch .25 .60
90 Roman Turek .30 .75
91 Andrew Brunette .20 .50
92 Krys Kolanos .20 .50
93 Alyn McCauley .20 .50
94 Jean-Sebastien Giguere .30 .75
95 Alexei Kovalev .25 .60
96 Peter Worrell .20 .50
97 Alexei Zhamnov .25 .60
98 Evgeni Nabokov .25 .60
99 Pavol Demitra .40 1.00
100 Chris Drury .30 .75
101 Jarome Iginla .40 1.00
102 Patrick Roy .75 2.00
103 Dany Heatley .25 .60
104 Nicklas Lidstrom .30 .75
105 Jose Theodore .30 .75
106 Michael Peca .25 .60
107 Ron Francis .40 1.00
108 J.Iginla/M.Sundin .40 1.00
109 J.Iginla/M.Sundin .40 1.00
110 J.Allison
A.Oates .30 .75
111 P.Datsyuk
D.Heatley .50 1.25
112 C.Chelios
J.Roenick .50 1.25
113 N.Lidstrom
S.Gonchar .30 .75
114 K.Sawyer
P.Worrell .20 .50
115 R.Turek
M.Brodeur .75 2.00
116 P.Roy
J.Theodore .75 2.00
117 P.Roy/R.Cechmanek .75 2.00
118 Joe Sakic .60 1.50
119 Jarome Iginla .40 1.00
120 Markus Naslund .30 .75
121 Nicklas Lidstrom .30 .75
122 Chris Chelios .30 .75
123 Patrick Roy .75 2.00
124 Mats Sundin .30 .75
125 Bill Guerin .30 .75
126 Brendan Shanahan .30 .75
127 Rob Blake .30 .75
128 Sergei Gonchar .25 .60
129 Jose Theodore .30 .75
130 Stanley Cup Champions UER .30 .75
131 Henrik Zetterberg RC 6.00 15.00
132 Martin Gerber RC 1.25 3.00
133 Alexander Frolov RC 2.00 5.00
134 Alexei Smirnov RC 1.00 2.50
135 Stanislav Chistov RC .75 2.00
136 Alexander Svitov RC .75 2.00
137 Adam Hall RC .75 2.00
138 Jay Bouwmeester RC 2.50 6.00
139 Ales Hemsky RC 3.00 8.00
140 Rick Nash RC 5.00 12.00
141 Chuck Kobasew RC 1.00 2.50
142 Shawn Thornton RC 1.00 2.50
143 Dennis Seidenberg RC 1.25 3.00
144 Ron Hainsey RC .75 2.00
145 Kurt Sauer RC .75 2.00
146 Lasse Pirjeta RC .75 2.00
147 Jason Spezza RC 5.00 12.00
148 Tom Koivisto RC .75 2.00
149 P-M Bouchard RC 1.25 3.00
150 Patrick Sharp RC 2.50 6.00
151 Scottie Upshall RC 1.00 2.50
152 Steve Eminger RC .75 2.00
153 Radovan Somik RC .75 2.00
154 Anton Volchenkov RC .75 2.00
155 Dmitri Bykov RC .75 2.00
156 Bobby Holik SP .40 1.00
157 Curtis Joseph SP .60 1.50
158 Jeff Friesen SP .40 1.00
159 Petr Sykora SP .40 1.00
160 Ed Belfour SP .60 1.50
161 Darius Kasparaitis SP .40 1.00
162 Scott Young SP .40 1.00
163 Bill Guerin SP .60 1.50
164 Adam Oates SP .60 1.50
165 Tony Amonte SP .50 1.25
166 Jochen Hecht SP .40 1.00
167 Randy McKay SP .40 1.00
168 Jamie Lundmark SP .50 1.25
169 Mariusz Czerkawski SP .40 1.00
170 Bryan Berard SP .40 1.00
171 Shawn McEachern SP .40 1.00
172 Brian Boucher SP .50 1.25
173 Jiri Dopita SP .40 1.00
174 Erik Rasmussen SP .40 1.00
175 Robert Lang SP .40 1.00
176 Steve Shields SP .50 1.25
177 Kelly Buchberger SP .50 1.25
178 Andrew Cassels SP .40 1.00
179 Oleg Tverdovsky SP .40 1.00
180 Ron Tugnutt SP .50 1.25
CL1 Checklist 1 .10 .30
CL2 Checklist 2 .10 .30
CL3 Checklist 3 .10 .30
CL4 Checklist 4 .10 .30
CL5 Checklist 5 .10 .30
CL6 Checklist 6 .10 .30

2002-03 Topps Heritage Chrome Parallel

*CHROME/667: 2X TO 5X BASIC CARDS

2002-03 Topps Heritage Autographs

AM Al MacInnis 6.00 15.00
BM Bryan McCabe 5.00 12.00
CD Chris Drury 5.00 12.00
EC Erik Cole 5.00 12.00
KK Krys Kolanos 5.00 12.00
MP Mike Peca 5.00 12.00
PE Patrik Elias 5.00 12.00
SW Stephen Weiss 5.00 12.00
TB Todd Bertuzzi 5.00 12.00

2002-03 Topps Heritage Autographs Black

*BLACK: .75X TO 2X BASIC AUTO

2002-03 Topps Heritage Autographs Red

*RED: 1.5X TO 4X BASIC AUTO

2002-03 Topps Heritage Calder Cloth

BL Brian Leetch B 6.00 15.00
CD Chris Drury A 12.50 30.00
DA Daniel Alfredsson B 6.00 15.00
DH Dany Heatley B 15.00 40.00
MB Martin Brodeur A 12.00 30.00
PF Peter Forsberg A 15.00 40.00
SG Scott Gomez B 6.00 15.00
SS Sergei Samsonov A 8.00 20.00

2002-03 Topps Heritage Calder Cloth Patches

*PATCH: 1.25X TO 3X BASIC JERSEY

2002-03 Topps Heritage Crease Piece

BB Brian Boucher 4.00 10.00
BD Byron Dafoe 4.00 10.00
DB Dan Blackburn 4.00 10.00
DC Dan Cloutier 4.00 10.00
FP Felix Potvin 5.00 12.00
ML Manny Legace 4.00 10.00
MT Marty Turco 5.00 12.00
PL Patrick Lalime 4.00 10.00
SB Sean Burke 4.00 10.00

2002-03 Topps Heritage Crease Piece Patches

*PATCH: 1X TO 2.5X BASE HI

2002-03 Topps Heritage Great Skates

AK Alexei Kovalev 5.00 12.00
AT Alex Tanguay 5.00 12.00
DL Brian Leetch 5.00 12.00
BM Brendan Morrison 5.00 12.00
MH Milan Hejduk 6.00 15.00
MR Mark Recchi 5.00 12.00
MS Marco Sturm 5.00 12.00
SG Simon Gagne 6.00 15.00
TA Tony Amonte 5.00 12.00
MHO Marian Hossa 6.00 15.00

2002-03 Topps Heritage Great Skates Patches

*PATCH: 1.25X TO 3X BASE HI

2002-03 Topps Heritage Reprint Autographs

ES Eddie Shack 15.00 40.00
JB Johnny Bower 15.00 40.00
JP Jim Pappin 8.00 20.00
RK Red Kelly 10.00 25.00
RP Bob Pulford 15.00 40.00

2002-03 Topps Heritage Reprint Relics

ES Eddie Shack 10.00 25.00
JB Johnny Bower 10.00 25.00
JP Jim Pappin 8.00 20.00
RK Red Kelly 8.00 20.00
RP Robert Pulford 8.00 20.00
TH Tim Horton 15.00 40.00
TS Terry Sawchuk 20.00 50.00

2002-03 Topps Heritage Reprints

ES Eddie Shack 1.00 2.50
JB Johnny Bower 1.25 3.00
JP Jim Pappin 1.00 2.50
RK Red Kelly 1.25 3.00
RP Robert Pulford 1.00 2.50
TH Tim Horton 1.25 3.00
TS Terry Sawchuk 1.50 4.00

2002-03 Topps Heritage USA Test Parallel

2 Jarome Iginla 1.50 4.00
3 Jose Theodore 1.50 4.00
6 Jaromir Jagr 2.00 5.00
7 Mario Lemieux 8.00 20.00
10 Pavel Bure 1.25 3.00
13 Mats Sundin 1.25 3.00
17 Peter Forsberg 3.00 8.00
27 Patrick Roy 6.00 15.00
32 Steve Yzerman 6.00 15.00
79 Ilya Kovalchuk 1.50 4.00

1983-84 Topps M&M's Olympic Heroes

COMPLETE SET (44) 8.00 20.00
13 Mike Eruzione .30 .75

2022-23 Topps Chrome Stickers

6 Sonny Milano .75 2.00
7 Adam Henrique .75 2.00
8 Trevor Zegras 1.00 2.50
9 Jakob Silfverberg .60 1.50
10 John Gibson 1.00 2.50
11 Troy Terry .75 2.00
12 Cam Fowler 1.00 2.50
13 Mason McTavish 1.00 2.50
14 Sam Steel .75 2.00
15 Jamie Drysdale .75 2.00
16 Max Comtois .75 2.00
17 Zach Aston-Reese .60 1.50
23 Alex Galchenyuk .60 1.50
24 Clayton Keller 1.25 3.00
25 Phil Kessel 1.00 2.50
26 Shayne Gostisbehere 1.00 2.50
27 Anton Stralman .60 1.50
28 Karel Vejmelka .60 1.50
29 Jakob Chychrun 1.00 2.50
30 Travis Boyd .60 1.50
31 Jack McBain 1.00 2.50
32 Andrew Ladd .75 2.00
33 Nick Schmaltz .75 2.00
34 Nathan Smith .75 2.00
40 Patrice Bergeron 1.25 3.00
41 David Pastrnak 2.50 6.00
42 Taylor Hall 1.00 2.50
43 Brad Marchand 2.00 5.00
44 Charlie McAvoy 1.25 3.00
45 Charlie Coyle 1.00 2.50
46 Hampus Lindholm .60 1.50
47 Linus Ullmark 1.00 2.50
48 Matt Grzelcyk .75 2.00
49 Brandon Carlo .75 2.00
50 Marc McLaughlin 1.00 2.50
51 Jeremy Swayman 1.50 4.00
57 Rasmus Dahlin 1.25 3.00
58 Alex Tuch 1.00 2.50
59 Peyton Krebs .75 2.00
60 Kyle Okposo .60 1.50
61 Jeff Skinner 1.00 2.50
62 Will Butcher .75 2.00
63 Casey Fitzgerald .75 2.00
64 Craig Anderson .60 1.50
65 Dylan Cozens 1.00 2.50
66 Owen Power 2.00 5.00
67 Zemgus Girgensons .60 1.50
68 Henri Jokiharju .60 1.50
74 Johnny Gaudreau 1.50 4.00
75 Noah Hanifin 1.00 2.50
76 Blake Coleman .75 2.00
77 Jacob Markstrom 1.00 2.50
78 Christopher Tanev .60 1.50
79 Tyler Toffoli 1.00 2.50
80 Elias Lindholm 1.00 2.50
81 Sean Monahan .60 1.50
82 Milan Lucic .75 2.00
83 Matthew Tkachuk 2.00 5.00
84 Dan Vladar .75 2.00
85 Mikael Backlund .75 2.00
91 Sebastian Aho 1.50 4.00
92 Jesperi Kotkaniemi 1.00 2.50
93 Jesper Fast .60 1.50
94 Jordan Staal .75 2.00
95 Andrei Svechnikov 1.25 3.00
96 Teuvo Teravainen 1.00 2.50
97 Vincent Trocheck 1.00 2.50
98 Brady Skjei .60 1.50
99 Frederik Andersen 1.25 3.00
100 Max Domi 1.00 2.50
101 Seth Jarvis 1.25 3.00
102 Nino Niederreiter .60 1.50
108 Alex DeBrincat 1.25 3.00
109 Patrick Kane 2.00 5.00
110 Jonathan Toews 1.50 4.00
111 Dominik Kubalik 1.00 2.50
112 Dylan Strome 1.25 3.00
113 Tyler Johnson .60 1.50
114 Kevin Lankinen 1.00 2.50
115 Calvin de Haan .60 1.50
116 Seth Jones 1.00 2.50
117 Caleb Jones .60 1.50
118 Connor Murphy .75 2.00
119 Mike Hardman .60 1.50
125 Nathan MacKinnon 4.00 10.00
126 Gabriel Landeskog 1.25 3.00
127 Cale Makar 2.50 6.00
128 Alex Newhook .75 2.00
129 Darcy Kuemper 1.00 2.50
130 Ryan Murray .75 2.00
131 Nazem Kadri 1.25 3.00
132 Mikko Rantanen 2.50 6.00
133 Valeri Nichushkin 1.00 2.50
134 Andre Burakovsky .60 1.50
135 Jack Johnson .60 1.50
136 Artturi Lehkonen .75 2.00
142 Jack Roslovic .60 1.50
143 Patrik Laine 1.25 3.00
144 Boone Jenner 1.00 2.50
145 Zach Werenski 1.50 4.00
146 Oliver Bjorkstrand .75 2.00
147 Gustav Nyquist .60 1.50
148 Jakub Voracek .75 2.00
149 Elvis Merzlikins 1.00 2.50
150 Alexandre Texier .60 1.50
151 Vladislav Gavrikov .60 1.50
152 Yegor Chinakhov .75 2.00
153 Cole Sillinger .75 2.00
159 Jamie Benn 1.00 2.50
160 Tyler Seguin 1.25 3.00
161 Joe Pavelski 1.25 3.00
162 Alexander Radulov 1.00 2.50
163 Miro Heiskanen 1.25 3.00
164 Ryan Suter .75 2.00
165 Braden Holtby 1.25 3.00
166 Roope Hintz 1.25 3.00
167 Vladislav Namestnikov .60 1.50
168 Denis Gurianov 1.25 3.00
169 John Klingberg 1.00 2.50
170 Jake Oettinger 1.50 4.00
176 Dylan Larkin 1.25 3.00

177 Tyler Bertuzzi .75 2.00
178 Oskar Sundqvist .60 1.50
179 Lucas Raymond 1.50 4.00
180 Alex Nedeljkovic .75 2.00
181 Marc Staal .60 1.50
182 Filip Zadina .75 2.00
183 Danny DeKeyser .60 1.50
184 Jakub Vrana .75 2.00
185 Joe Veleno .75 2.00
186 Pius Suter .75 2.00
187 Moritz Seider 1.25 3.00
193 Connor McDavid 5.00 12.00
194 Leon Draisaitl 3.00 8.00
195 Ryan Nugent-Hopkins 1.25 3.00
196 Zach Hyman 1.50 4.00
197 Darnell Nurse .75 2.00
198 Duncan Keith .75 2.00
199 Mike Smith .60 1.50
200 Jesse Puljujarvi 1.00 2.50
201 Cody Ceci .60 1.50
202 Derick Brassard .60 1.50
203 Kailer Yamamoto 1.00 2.50
204 Kris Russell .60 1.50
210 Aleksander Barkov 1.50 4.00
211 Jonathan Huberdeau 1.25 3.00
212 Patric Hornqvist .60 1.50
213 Anthony Duclair .75 2.00
214 Joe Thornton 1.50 4.00
215 Aaron Ekblad 1.25 3.00
216 Sergei Bobrovsky 1.50 4.00
217 Anton Lundell 1.00 2.50
218 Radko Gudas .60 1.50
219 Claude Giroux 1.00 2.50
220 Ben Chiarot .60 1.50
221 Spencer Knight 1.00 2.50
227 Anze Kopitar 1.50 4.00
228 Dustin Brown 1.00 2.50
229 Jonathan Quick 1.25 3.00
230 Drew Doughty 1.25 3.00
231 Adrian Kempe 1.00 2.50
232 Quinton Byfield 1.25 3.00
233 Olli Maatta .60 1.50
234 Alex Iafallo .60 1.50
235 Phillip Danault 1.00 2.50
236 Trevor Moore .60 1.50
237 Tobias Bjornfot .60 1.50
238 Calvin Petersen .60 1.50
244 Kirill Kaprizov 3.00 8.00
245 Matt Boldy 3.00 8.00
246 Jordan Greenway .60 1.50
247 Mats Zuccarello 1.00 2.50
248 Marcus Foligno .75 2.00
249 Jordie Benn .60 1.50
250 Cam Talbot 1.00 2.50
251 Dmitry Kulikov .60 1.50
252 Jared Spurgeon 1.00 2.50
253 Joel Eriksson Ek .75 2.00
254 Marco Rossi 2.50 6.00
255 Marc-Andre Fleury 2.00 5.00
261 Cole Caufield 2.00 5.00
262 Carey Price 2.00 5.00
263 Brendan Gallagher 1.00 2.50
264 Mike Hoffman .60 1.50
265 Nick Suzuki 2.00 5.00
266 Justin Barron .75 2.00
267 Jonathan Drouin .75 2.00
268 Jeff Petry 1.00 2.50
269 Rem Pitlick .60 1.50
270 Jake Allen 1.00 2.50
271 Christian Dvorak .75 2.00
272 Cayden Primeau .75 2.00
278 Matt Duchene 1.00 2.50
279 Filip Forsberg 1.50 4.00
280 Eeli Tolvanen 1.00 2.50
281 Roman Josi 1.00 2.50
282 Juuse Saros 1.25 3.00
283 Mattias Ekholm .75 2.00
284 Ryan Johansen .75 2.00
285 Mikael Granlund .75 2.00
286 Nick Cousins .60 1.50
287 Dante Fabbro .60 1.50
288 Matt Benning .60 1.50
289 Tanner Jeannot .60 1.50
295 Jack Hughes 2.50 6.00
296 Nico Hischier 1.50 4.00
297 Dougie Hamilton .75 2.00
298 Dawson Mercer 1.25 3.00
299 Yegor Sharangovich 1.00 2.50
300 Tomas Tatar .60 1.50
301 Damon Severson .60 1.50
302 Ty Smith 1.00 2.50
303 P.K. Subban 1.25 3.00
304 Alexander Holtz 1.00 2.50
305 Mackenzie Blackwood 1.00 2.50
306 Jesper Bratt 1.00 2.50
312 Mathew Barzal 1.25 3.00
313 Anthony Beauvillier .60 1.50
314 Adam Pelech .60 1.50
315 Ilya Sorokin 1.50 4.00
316 Semyon Varlamov 1.00 2.50
317 Jean-Gabriel Pageau .60 1.50
318 Kyle Palmieri .75 2.00
319 Oliver Wahlstrom .60 1.50
320 Zach Parise 1.00 2.50
321 Zdeno Chara 1.00 2.50
322 Anders Lee .75 2.00
323 Ryan Pulock .75 2.00
329 Chris Kreider 1.25 3.00
330 Artemi Panarin 2.00 5.00
331 Kaapo Kakko .75 2.00
332 Alexis Lafreniere 1.50 4.00
333 Adam Fox 1.25 3.00
334 Igor Shesterkin 2.00 5.00
335 Jacob Trouba .75 2.00
336 Mika Zibanejad 1.25 3.00
337 Ryan Strome 1.00 2.50
338 Filip Chytil .75 2.00
339 K'Andre Miller .75 2.00
340 Andrew Copp .60 1.50
346 Brady Tkachuk 1.50 4.00
347 Tim Stutzle 1.25 3.00
348 Adam Gaudette .75 2.00
349 Colin White .75 2.00
350 Mathieu Joseph .60 1.50
351 Matt Murray 1.00 2.50
352 Connor Brown .75 2.00
353 Anton Forsberg .60 1.50
354 Josh Norris 1.00 2.50
355 Filip Gustavsson 1.00 2.50
356 Artem Zub .60 1.50
357 Thomas Chabot 1.00 2.50
363 Kevin Hayes .75 2.00
364 Cam Atkinson 1.00 2.50
365 Sean Couturier .75 2.00
366 Owen Tippett .60 1.50
367 Carter Hart 1.00 2.50
368 Keith Yandle .60 1.50
369 Ivan Provorov .75 2.00
370 Oskar Lindblom .75 2.00
371 James van Riemsdyk .75 2.00
372 Rasmus Ristolainen .60 1.50
373 Bobby Brink 1.00 2.50
374 Travis Konecny 1.00 2.50
380 Sidney Crosby 4.00 10.00
381 Evgeni Malkin 2.00 5.00
382 Jake Guentzel 1.50 4.00
383 Tristan Jarry 1.00 2.50
384 Jeff Carter .75 2.00
385 Rickard Rakell .75 2.00
386 Brian Boyle .60 1.50
387 Kris Letang 1.25 3.00
388 Brian Dumoulin .60 1.50
389 Bryan Rust 1.00 2.50
390 Jason Zucker 1.00 2.50
391 Kasperi Kapanen .75 2.00
397 Logan Couture 1.25 3.00
398 Tomas Hertl 1.00 2.50
399 Timo Meier 1.00 2.50
400 Brent Burns 1.00 2.50
401 Erik Karlsson 1.25 3.00
402 James Reimer .60 1.50
403 Nick Bonino .60 1.50
404 Alexander Barabanov .60 1.50
405 Mario Ferraro .60 1.50
406 Kaapo Kahkonen 1.00 2.50
407 Nicolas Meloche .75 2.00
408 Jonathan Dahlen .60 1.50
414 Jordan Eberle 1.00 2.50
415 Ryan Donato .75 2.00
416 Philipp Grubauer 1.00 2.50
417 Alex Wennberg .60 1.50
418 Yanni Gourde .75 2.00
419 Brandon Tanev .75 2.00
420 Daniel Sprong .60 1.50
421 Adam Larsson 1.00 2.50
422 Jaden Schwartz .75 2.00
423 Haydn Fleury .60 1.50
424 Matthew Beniers 2.50 6.00
425 Vince Dunn .75 2.00
431 Vladimir Tarasenko 1.25 3.00
432 Ryan O'Reilly 1.00 2.50
433 Jordan Kyrou 1.00 2.50
434 Pavel Buchnevich .75 2.00
435 Brandon Saad .75 2.00
436 Brayden Schenn 1.00 2.50
437 Tyler Bozak .60 1.50
438 Jordan Binnington 1.50 4.00
439 Torey Krug .75 2.00
440 David Perron .75 2.00
441 Justin Faulk .75 2.00
442 Ville Husso .60 1.50
448 Steven Stamkos 2.00 5.00
449 Nikita Kucherov 2.00 5.00
450 Andrei Vasilevskiy 1.50 4.00
451 Brayden Point 1.25 3.00
452 Corey Perry 1.50 4.00
453 Alex Killorn .60 1.50
454 Pat Maroon .60 1.50
455 Ondrej Palat .75 2.00
456 Victor Hedman 1.25 3.00
457 Brandon Hagel .75 2.00
458 Ryan McDonagh .60 1.50
459 Anthony Cirelli .75 2.00
465 Auston Matthews 4.00 10.00
466 John Tavares 1.50 4.00
467 Mitch Marner 1.50 4.00
468 William Nylander 2.00 5.00
469 Jack Campbell 1.00 2.50
470 Mark Giordano 1.00 2.50
471 Jason Spezza 1.00 2.50
472 Jake Muzzin 1.00 2.50
473 Morgan Rielly 1.00 2.50
474 Alexander Kerfoot .75 2.00
475 David Kampf .60 1.50
476 Michael Bunting 1.00 2.50
482 Brock Boeser 1.25 3.00
483 J.T. Miller 1.25 3.00
484 Thatcher Demko 1.25 3.00
485 Bo Horvat 1.25 3.00
486 Elias Pettersson 1.50 4.00
487 Oliver Ekman-Larsson .60 1.50
488 Quinn Hughes 2.50 6.00
489 Jaroslav Halak 1.00 2.50
490 Tyler Myers .60 1.50
491 Jason Dickinson .60 1.50
492 Conor Garland .75 2.00
493 Vasily Podkolzin .60 1.50
499 Mark Stone 1.25 3.00
500 Max Pacioretty 1.00 2.50
501 Jack Eichel 1.50 4.00
502 Evgenii Dadonov .60 1.50
503 Reilly Smith 1.00 2.50
504 William Karlsson 1.25 3.00
505 Jonathan Marchessault 1.25 3.00
506 Robin Lehner .75 2.00
507 Alex Pietrangelo .75 2.00
508 Shea Theodore 1.25 3.00
509 Chandler Stephenson .75 2.00
510 Brayden McNabb .60 1.50
516 Alex Ovechkin 4.00 10.00
517 Evgeny Kuznetsov 1.25 3.00
518 Tom Wilson 1.00 2.50
519 John Carlson 1.00 2.50
520 Dmitry Orlov 1.00 2.50
521 T.J. Oshie 1.00 2.50
522 Lars Eller .60 1.50
523 Carl Hagelin .60 1.50
524 Nicklas Backstrom 1.00 2.50
525 Marcus Johansson .60 1.50
526 Vitek Vanecek 1.00 2.50
527 Ilya Samsonov 1.00 2.50
533 Blake Wheeler 1.00 2.50
534 Paul Stastny .75 2.00
535 Mark Scheifele 1.50 4.00
536 Connor Hellebuyck 2.00 5.00
537 Zach Sanford .60 1.50
538 Kyle Connor 1.50 4.00
539 Josh Morrissey 1.25 3.00
540 Nate Schmidt .60 1.50
541 Nikolaj Ehlers 1.00 2.50
542 Evgeny Svechnikov .60 1.50
543 Cole Perfetti 1.00 2.50
544 Adam Lowry .75 2.00
606 Cole Caufield '71-72 2.00 5.00
607 Dawson Mercer '71-72 1.25 3.00
608 Spencer Knight '71-72 1.00 2.50
609 Jeremy Swayman '71-72 1.50 4.00
610 Trevor Zegras '71-72 1.00 2.50
611 Quinton Byfield '71-72 1.25 3.00
612 Vasily Podkolzin '71-72 .60 1.50
613 Alexander Holtz '71-72 1.00 2.50
614 Jamie Drysdale '71-72 .75 2.00
615 Alex Nedeljkovic '71-72 .75 2.00
616 Alex Newhook '71-72 .75 2.00
617 Moritz Seider '71-72 1.25 3.00
618 Owen Power '71-72 2.00 5.00
619 Lucas Raymond '71-72 1.50 4.00
620 Filip Gustavsson '71-72 1.00 2.50
621 Matthew Beniers '71-72 2.50 6.00

2022-23 Topps Chrome Stickers Gold Refractors

*GOLD REF/50: .75X TO 2X BASIC

2022-23 Topps Chrome Stickers Orange Refractors

*ORANGE REF/25: 1.2X TO 3X BASIC

2022-23 Topps Chrome Stickers Refractors

*REFRACTORS/99: .5X TO 1.2X BASIC

2022-23 Topps Stickers

1 Team Logo FOIL .12 .30
2 Team Highlight .12 .30
3 WILD Wing FOIL .12 .30
4 Jamie Drysdale FOIL .12 .30
5 Trevor Zegras FOIL .15 .40
6 Sonny Milano .12 .30
7 Adam Henrique .12 .30
8 Trevor Zegras .15 .40
9 Jakob Silfverberg .10 .25
10 John Gibson .15 .40
11 Troy Terry .12 .30
12 Cam Fowler .15 .40
13 Mason McTavish .15 .40
14 Sam Steel .12 .30
15 Jamie Drysdale .12 .30
16 Max Comtois .12 .30
17 Zach Aston-Reese .10 .25
18 Team Logo FOIL .12 .30
19 Team Highlight .12 .30
20 Howler FOIL .12 .30
21 Clayton Keller FOIL .20 .50
22 Shayne Gostisbehere FOIL .15 .40
23 Alex Galchenyuk .10 .25
24 Clayton Keller .20 .50
25 Phil Kessel .15 .40
26 Shayne Gostisbehere .15 .40
27 Anton Stralman .10 .25
28 Karel Vejmelka .10 .25
29 Jakob Chychrun .15 .40
30 Travis Boyd .10 .25
31 Jack McBain .15 .40
32 Andrew Ladd .12 .30
33 Nick Schmaltz .12 .30
34 Nathan Smith .12 .30
35 Team Logo FOIL .12 .30
36 Team Highlight .12 .30
37 Blades FOIL .12 .30
38 Patrice Bergeron FOIL .20 .50
39 David Pastrnak FOIL .40 1.00
40 Patrice Bergeron .20 .50
41 David Pastrnak .40 1.00
42 Taylor Hall .15 .40
43 Brad Marchand .30 .75
44 Charlie McAvoy .20 .50
45 Charlie Coyle .15 .40
46 Hampus Lindholm .10 .25
47 Linus Ullmark .15 .40
48 Matt Grzelcyk .12 .30
49 Brandon Carlo .12 .30
50 Marc McLaughlin .15 .40
51 Jeremy Swayman .25 .60
52 Team Logo FOIL .12 .30
53 Team Highlight .12 .30
54 Sabretooth FOIL .12 .30
55 Rasmus Dahlin FOIL .20 .50
56 Owen Power FOIL .30 .75
57 Rasmus Dahlin .20 .50
58 Alex Tuch .15 .40
59 Peyton Krebs .12 .30
60 Kyle Okposo .10 .25
61 Jeff Skinner .15 .40
62 Will Butcher .12 .30
63 Casey Fitzgerald .12 .30
64 Craig Anderson .10 .25
65 Dylan Cozens .15 .40
66 Owen Power .30 .75
67 Zemgus Girgensons .10 .25
68 Henri Jokiharju .10 .25
69 Team Logo FOIL .12 .30
70 Team Highlight .12 .30
71 Harvey the Hound FOIL .12 .30
72 Johnny Gaudreau FOIL .25 .60
73 Matthew Tkachuk FOIL .30 .75
74 Johnny Gaudreau .25 .60
75 Noah Hanifin .15 .40
76 Blake Coleman .12 .30
77 Jacob Markstrom .15 .40
78 Christopher Tanev .10 .25
79 Tyler Toffoli .15 .40
80 Elias Lindholm .15 .40
81 Sean Monahan .10 .25
82 Milan Lucic .12 .30
83 Matthew Tkachuk .30 .75
84 Dan Vladar .12 .30
85 Mikael Backlund .12 .30
86 Team Logo FOIL .12 .30
87 Team Highlight .12 .30
88 Stormy FOIL .12 .30
89 Sebastian Aho FOIL .25 .60
90 Andrei Svechnikov FOIL .20 .50
91 Sebastian Aho .25 .60
92 Jesperi Kotkaniemi .15 .40
93 Jesper Fast .10 .25
94 Jordan Staal .12 .30
95 Andrei Svechnikov .20 .50
96 Teuvo Teravainen .15 .40
97 Vincent Trocheck .15 .40
98 Brady Skjei .10 .25
99 Frederik Andersen .20 .50
100 Max Domi .15 .40
101 Seth Jarvis .20 .50
102 Nino Niederreiter .10 .25
103 Team Logo FOIL .12 .30
104 Team Highlight .12 .30
105 Tommy Hawk FOIL .12 .30
106 Patrick Kane FOIL .30 .75
107 Jonathan Toews FOIL .25 .60
108 Alex DeBrincat .20 .50
109 Patrick Kane .30 .75
110 Jonathan Toews .25 .60
111 Dominik Kubalik .15 .40
112 Dylan Strome .20 .50
113 Tyler Johnson .10 .25
114 Kevin Lankinen .15 .40
115 Calvin de Haan .10 .25
116 Seth Jones .15 .40
117 Caleb Jones .10 .25
118 Connor Murphy .12 .30
119 Mike Hardman .10 .25
120 Team Logo FOIL .12 .30
121 Team Highlight .12 .30
122 Bernie FOIL .12 .30
123 Nathan MacKinnon FOIL .60 1.50
124 Cale Makar FOIL .40 1.00
125 Nathan MacKinnon .60 1.50
126 Gabriel Landeskog .20 .50
127 Cale Makar .40 1.00
128 Alex Newhook .12 .30
129 Darcy Kuemper .15 .40
130 Ryan Murray .12 .30
131 Nazem Kadri .20 .50
132 Mikko Rantanen .40 1.00
133 Valeri Nichushkin .15 .40
134 Andre Burakovsky .10 .25
135 Jack Johnson .10 .25
136 Artturi Lehkonen .12 .30
137 Team Logo FOIL .12 .30
138 Team Highlight .12 .30
139 Stinger FOIL .12 .30
140 Patrik Laine FOIL .20 .50
141 Boone Jenner FOIL .15 .40
142 Jack Roslovic .10 .25
143 Patrik Laine .20 .50
144 Boone Jenner .15 .40
145 Zach Werenski .25 .60
146 Oliver Bjorkstrand .12 .30
147 Gustav Nyquist .10 .25
148 Jakub Voracek .12 .30
149 Elvis Merzlikins .15 .40
150 Alexandre Texier .10 .25
151 Vladislav Gavrikov .10 .25
152 Yegor Chinakhov .12 .30
153 Cole Sillinger .12 .30
154 Team Logo FOIL .12 .30
155 Team Highlight .12 .30
156 Victor E. Green FOIL .12 .30
157 Joe Pavelski FOIL .20 .50
158 Tyler Seguin FOIL .20 .50
159 Jamie Benn .15 .40
160 Tyler Seguin .20 .50
161 Joe Pavelski .20 .50
162 Alexander Radulov .15 .40
163 Miro Heiskanen .20 .50
164 Ryan Suter .12 .30
165 Braden Holtby .20 .50
166 Roope Hintz .20 .50
167 Vladislav Namestnikov .10 .25
168 Denis Gurianov .20 .50
169 John Klingberg .15 .40
170 Jake Oettinger .25 .60
171 Team Logo FOIL .12 .30
172 Team Highlight .12 .30
173 Dylan Larkin FOIL .20 .50
174 Lucas Raymond FOIL .25 .60
175 Moritz Seider FOIL .20 .50
176 Dylan Larkin .20 .50
177 Tyler Bertuzzi .12 .30
178 Oskar Sundqvist .10 .25
179 Lucas Raymond .25 .60
180 Alex Nedeljkovic .12 .30
181 Marc Staal .10 .25
182 Filip Zadina .12 .30
183 Danny DeKeyser .10 .25
184 Jakub Vrana .12 .30
185 Joe Veleno .12 .30
186 Pius Suter .12 .30
187 Moritz Seider .20 .50
188 Team Logo FOIL .12 .30
189 Team Highlight .12 .30
190 Hunter FOIL .12 .30
191 Connor McDavid FOIL .75 2.00
192 Leon Draisaitl FOIL .50 1.25
193 Connor McDavid .75 2.00
194 Leon Draisaitl .50 1.25
195 Ryan Nugent-Hopkins .20 .50
196 Zach Hyman .25 .60
197 Darnell Nurse .12 .30
198 Duncan Keith .12 .30
199 Mike Smith .10 .25
200 Jesse Puljujarvi .15 .40
201 Cody Ceci .10 .25
202 Derick Brassard .10 .25
203 Kailer Yamamoto .15 .40
204 Kris Russell .10 .25
205 Team Logo FOIL .12 .30
206 Team Highlight .12 .30
207 Stanley C. Panther FOIL .12 .30
208 Aleksander Barkov FOIL .25 .60
209 Jonathan Huberdeau FOIL .20 .50
210 Aleksander Barkov .25 .60
211 Jonathan Huberdeau .20 .50
212 Patric Hornqvist .10 .25
213 Anthony Duclair .12 .30
214 Joe Thornton .25 .60
215 Aaron Ekblad .20 .50
216 Sergei Bobrovsky .25 .60
217 Anton Lundell .15 .40
218 Radko Gudas .10 .25
219 Claude Giroux .15 .40
220 Ben Chiarot .10 .25
221 Spencer Knight .15 .40
222 Team Logo FOIL .12 .30
223 Team Highlight .12 .30
224 Bailey FOIL .12 .30
225 Anze Kopitar FOIL .25 .60
226 Quinton Byfield FOIL .20 .50
227 Anze Kopitar .25 .60
228 Dustin Brown .15 .40
229 Jonathan Quick .20 .50
230 Drew Doughty .20 .50
231 Adrian Kempe .15 .40
232 Quinton Byfield .20 .50
233 Olli Maatta .10 .25
234 Alex Iafallo .10 .25
235 Phillip Danault .15 .40
236 Trevor Moore .10 .25
237 Tobias Bjornfot .10 .25
238 Calvin Petersen .10 .25
239 Team Logo FOIL .12 .30
240 Team Highlight .12 .30
241 Nordy FOIL .12 .30
242 Kirill Kaprizov FOIL .50 1.25
243 Mats Zuccarello FOIL .15 .40
244 Kirill Kaprizov .50 1.25
245 Matt Boldy .50 1.25
246 Jordan Greenway .10 .25
247 Mats Zuccarello .15 .40
248 Marcus Foligno .12 .30
249 Jordie Benn .10 .25
250 Cam Talbot .15 .40
251 Dmitry Kulikov .10 .25
252 Jared Spurgeon .15 .40
253 Joel Eriksson Ek .12 .30
254 Marco Rossi .40 1.00
255 Marc-Andre Fleury .30 .75
256 Team Logo FOIL .12 .30
257 Team Highlight .12 .30
258 Youppi! FOIL .12 .30
259 Cole Caufield FOIL .30 .75
260 Carey Price FOIL .30 .75
261 Cole Caufield .30 .75
262 Carey Price .30 .75
263 Brendan Gallagher .15 .40
264 Mike Hoffman .10 .25
265 Nick Suzuki .30 .75
266 Justin Barron .12 .30
267 Jonathan Drouin .12 .30
268 Jeff Petry .15 .40
269 Rem Pitlick .10 .25
270 Jake Allen .15 .40
271 Christian Dvorak .12 .30
272 Cayden Primeau .12 .30
273 Team Logo FOIL .12 .30
274 Team Highlight .12 .30
275 Gnash FOIL .12 .30
276 Roman Josi FOIL .15 .40
277 Filip Forsberg FOIL .25 .60
278 Matt Duchene .15 .40
279 Filip Forsberg .25 .60
280 Eeli Tolvanen .15 .40
281 Roman Josi .15 .40
282 Juuse Saros .20 .50
283 Mattias Ekholm .12 .30
284 Ryan Johansen .12 .30
285 Mikael Granlund .12 .30
286 Nick Cousins .10 .25
287 Dante Fabbro .10 .25
288 Matt Benning .10 .25
289 Tanner Jeannot .10 .25
290 Team Logo FOIL .12 .30
291 Team Highlight .12 .30
292 NJ Devil FOIL .12 .30
293 Jack Hughes FOIL .40 1.00
294 Dougie Hamilton FOIL .12 .30
295 Jack Hughes .40 1.00
296 Nico Hischier .25 .60
297 Dougie Hamilton .12 .30
298 Dawson Mercer .20 .50
299 Yegor Sharangovich .15 .40
300 Tomas Tatar .10 .25
301 Damon Severson .10 .25
302 Ty Smith .15 .40
303 P.K. Subban .20 .50
304 Alexander Holtz .15 .40
305 Mackenzie Blackwood .15 .40
306 Jesper Bratt .15 .40
307 Team Logo FOIL .12 .30
308 Team Highlight .12 .30
309 Sparky FOIL .12 .30
310 Mathew Barzal FOIL .20 .50
311 Adam Pelech FOIL .10 .25
312 Mathew Barzal .20 .50
313 Anthony Beauvillier .10 .25
314 Adam Pelech .10 .25
315 Ilya Sorokin .25 .60
316 Semyon Varlamov .15 .40
317 Jean-Gabriel Pageau .10 .25
318 Kyle Palmieri .12 .30
319 Oliver Wahlstrom .10 .25
320 Zach Parise .15 .40
321 Zdeno Chara .15 .40
322 Anders Lee .12 .30
323 Ryan Pulock .12 .30
324 Team Logo FOIL .12 .30
325 Team Highlight .12 .30
326 Artemi Panarin FOIL .30 .75
327 Adam Fox FOIL .20 .50
328 Igor Shesterkin FOIL .30 .75
329 Chris Kreider .20 .50
330 Artemi Panarin .30 .75
331 Kaapo Kakko .12 .30
332 Alexis Lafreniere .25 .60
333 Adam Fox .20 .50
334 Igor Shesterkin .30 .75
335 Jacob Trouba .12 .30
336 Mika Zibanejad .20 .50
337 Ryan Strome .15 .40
338 Filip Chytil .12 .30
339 K'Andre Miller .12 .30
340 Andrew Copp .10 .25
341 Team Logo FOIL .12 .30
342 Team Highlight .12 .30
343 Spartacat FOIL .12 .30
344 Brady Tkachuk FOIL .25 .60
345 Tim Stutzle FOIL .20 .50
346 Brady Tkachuk .25 .60
347 Tim Stutzle .20 .50
348 Adam Gaudette .12 .30
349 Colin White .12 .30
350 Mathieu Joseph .10 .25
351 Matt Murray .15 .40
352 Connor Brown .12 .30
353 Anton Forsberg .10 .25
354 Josh Norris .15 .40
355 Filip Gustavsson .15 .40
356 Artem Zub .10 .25
357 Thomas Chabot .15 .40
358 Team Logo FOIL .12 .30
359 Team Highlight .12 .30
360 Gritty FOIL .12 .30
361 Carter Hart FOIL .15 .40
362 Cam Atkinson FOIL .15 .40
363 Kevin Hayes .12 .30
364 Cam Atkinson .15 .40
365 Sean Couturier .12 .30
366 Owen Tippett .10 .25
367 Carter Hart .15 .40
368 Keith Yandle .10 .25
369 Ivan Provorov .12 .30
370 Oskar Lindblom .12 .30
371 James van Riemsdyk .12 .30
372 Rasmus Ristolainen .10 .25
373 Bobby Brink .15 .40
374 Travis Konecny .15 .40
375 Team Logo FOIL .12 .30
376 Team Highlight .12 .30
377 Iceburgh FOIL .12 .30
378 Sidney Crosby FOIL .60 1.50
379 Evgeni Malkin FOIL .30 .75
380 Sidney Crosby .60 1.50
381 Evgeni Malkin .30 .75
382 Jake Guentzel .25 .60
383 Tristan Jarry .15 .40
384 Jeff Carter .12 .30
385 Rickard Rakell .12 .30
386 Brian Boyle .10 .25
387 Kris Letang .20 .50
388 Brian Dumoulin .10 .25
389 Bryan Rust .15 .40
390 Jason Zucker .15 .40
391 Kasperi Kapanen .12 .30
392 Team Logo FOIL .12 .30
393 Team Highlight .12 .30
394 S.J. Sharkie FOIL .12 .30
395 Tomas Hertl FOIL .15 .40
396 Erik Karlsson FOIL .20 .50
397 Logan Couture .20 .50
398 Tomas Hertl .15 .40
399 Timo Meier .15 .40
400 Brent Burns .15 .40
401 Erik Karlsson .20 .50
402 James Reimer .10 .25
403 Nick Bonino .10 .25
404 Alexander Barabanov .10 .25
405 Mario Ferraro .10 .25
406 Kaapo Kahkonen .15 .40
407 Nicolas Meloche .12 .30
408 Jonathan Dahlen .10 .25
409 Team Logo FOIL .12 .30
410 Team Highlight .12 .30
411 Jordan Eberle FOIL .15 .40
412 Matthew Beniers FOIL .40 1.00
413 Philipp Grubauer FOIL .15 .40
414 Jordan Eberle .15 .40
415 Ryan Donato .12 .30
416 Philipp Grubauer .15 .40
417 Alex Wennberg .10 .25
418 Yanni Gourde .12 .30
419 Brandon Tanev .12 .30
420 Daniel Sprong .10 .25
421 Adam Larsson .15 .40
422 Jaden Schwartz .12 .30
423 Haydn Fleury .10 .25
424 Matthew Beniers .40 1.00
425 Vince Dunn .12 .30
426 Team Logo FOIL .12 .30
427 Team Highlight .12 .30
428 Louie FOIL .12 .30
429 Vladimir Tarasenko FOIL .20 .50
430 Ryan O'Reilly FOIL .15 .40
431 Vladimir Tarasenko .20 .50
432 Ryan O'Reilly .15 .40
433 Jordan Kyrou .15 .40
434 Pavel Buchnevich .12 .30
435 Brandon Saad .12 .30
436 Brayden Schenn .15 .40
437 Tyler Bozak .10 .25
438 Jordan Binnington .25 .60
439 Torey Krug .12 .30
440 David Perron .12 .30
441 Justin Faulk .12 .30
442 Ville Husso .10 .25
443 Team Logo FOIL .12 .30
444 Team Highlight .12 .30
445 Thunderbug FOIL .12 .30
446 Steven Stamkos FOIL .30 .75
447 Nikita Kucherov FOIL .30 .75
448 Steven Stamkos .30 .75
449 Nikita Kucherov .30 .75
450 Andrei Vasilevskiy .25 .60
451 Brayden Point .20 .50
452 Corey Perry .25 .60
453 Alex Killorn .10 .25
454 Pat Maroon .10 .25
455 Ondrej Palat .12 .30
456 Victor Hedman .20 .50
457 Brandon Hagel .12 .30
458 Ryan McDonagh .10 .25
459 Anthony Cirelli .12 .30
460 Team Logo FOIL .12 .30
461 Team Highlight .12 .30
462 Carlton FOIL .12 .30
463 Auston Matthews FOIL .60 1.50
464 John Tavares FOIL .25 .60
465 Auston Matthews .60 1.50
466 John Tavares .25 .60
467 Mitch Marner .25 .60
468 William Nylander .30 .75
469 Jack Campbell .15 .40
470 Mark Giordano .15 .40
471 Jason Spezza .15 .40
472 Jake Muzzin .15 .40
473 Morgan Rielly .15 .40
474 Alexander Kerfoot .12 .30
475 David Kampf .10 .25
476 Michael Bunting .15 .40
477 Team Logo FOIL .12 .30
478 Team Highlight .12 .30
479 Fin FOIL .12 .30
480 Brock Boeser FOIL .20 .50
481 Quinn Hughes FOIL .40 1.00
482 Brock Boeser .20 .50
483 J.T. Miller .20 .50
484 Thatcher Demko .20 .50
485 Bo Horvat .20 .50
486 Elias Pettersson .25 .60
487 Oliver Ekman-Larsson .10 .25
488 Quinn Hughes .40 1.00
489 Jaroslav Halak .15 .40
490 Tyler Myers .10 .25
491 Jason Dickinson .10 .25
492 Conor Garland .12 .30
493 Vasily Podkolzin .10 .25
494 Team Logo FOIL .12 .30
495 Team Highlight .12 .30
496 Chance FOIL .12 .30
497 Mark Stone FOIL .20 .50
498 Jonathan Marchessault FOIL .20 .50
499 Mark Stone .20 .50
500 Max Pacioretty .15 .40
501 Jack Eichel .25 .60
502 Evgenii Dadonov .10 .25
503 Reilly Smith .15 .40
504 William Karlsson .20 .50
505 Jonathan Marchessault .20 .50
506 Robin Lehner .12 .30
507 Alex Pietrangelo .12 .30
508 Shea Theodore .20 .50
509 Chandler Stephenson .12 .30
510 Brayden McNabb .10 .25
511 Team Logo FOIL .12 .30
512 Team Highlight .12 .30
513 Slapshot FOIL .12 .30
514 Alex Ovechkin FOIL .60 1.50
515 John Carlson FOIL .15 .40
516 Alex Ovechkin .60 1.50
517 Evgeny Kuznetsov .20 .50
518 Tom Wilson .15 .40
519 John Carlson .15 .40
520 Dmitry Orlov .15 .40
521 T.J. Oshie .15 .40
522 Lars Eller .10 .25
523 Carl Hagelin .10 .25
524 Nicklas Backstrom .15 .40
525 Marcus Johansson .10 .25
526 Vitek Vanecek .15 .40
527 Ilya Samsonov .15 .40
528 Team Logo FOIL .12 .30
529 Team Highlight .12 .30
530 Moose FOIL .12 .30
531 Blake Wheeler FOIL .15 .40
532 Connor Hellebuyck FOIL .30 .75
533 Blake Wheeler .15 .40
534 Paul Stastny .12 .30
535 Mark Scheifele .25 .60
536 Connor Hellebuyck .30 .75
537 Zach Sanford .10 .25
538 Kyle Connor .25 .60
539 Josh Morrissey .20 .50
540 Nate Schmidt .10 .25
541 Nikolaj Ehlers .15 .40
542 Evgeny Svechnikov .10 .25
543 Cole Perfetti .15 .40
544 Adam Lowry .12 .30
545 Patrice Bergeron C .20 .50
546 Kyle Okposo C .10 .25
547 Dylan Larkin C .20 .50
548 Aleksander Barkov C .25 .60
549 Shea Weber C .15 .40
550 Brady Tkachuk C .25 .60
551 Steven Stamkos C .30 .75
552 John Tavares C .25 .60
553 Jakob Chychrun C .15 .40
554 Jonathan Toews C .25 .60
555 Gabriel Landeskog C .20 .50
556 Jamie Benn C .15 .40
557 Jared Spurgeon C .15 .40
558 Roman Josi C .15 .40
559 Ryan O'Reilly C .15 .40
560 Blake Wheeler C .15 .40
561 Jordan Staal C .12 .30
562 Boone Jenner C .15 .40
563 Nico Hischier C .25 .60
564 Anders Lee C .12 .30
565 Chris Kreider C .20 .50
566 Sean Couturier C .12 .30
567 Sidney Crosby C .60 1.50
568 Alex Ovechkin C .60 1.50
569 Ryan Getzlaf C .15 .40
570 Matthew Tkachuk C .30 .75
571 Connor McDavid C .75 2.00
572 Anze Kopitar C .25 .60
573 Logan Couture C .20 .50
574 Jordan Eberle C .15 .40
575 Bo Horvat C .20 .50
576 Mark Stone C .20 .50
577 Auston Matthews IV FOIL .60 1.50
578 Connor McDavid IV FOIL .75 2.00
579 Jonathan Huberdeau IV FOIL .20 .50
580 Alex Ovechkin IV FOIL .60 1.50
581 Sidney Crosby IV FOIL .60 1.50
582 Steven Stamkos IV FOIL .30 .75

583 Jordan Kyrou AS .15 .40
584 Zach Werenski AS .25 .60
585 Victor Hedman AS .20 .50
586 Alex Pietrangelo AS .12 .30
587 Sebastian Aho AS .25 .60
588 Jack Hughes AS .40 1.00
589 Jordan Kyrou AS .15 .40
590 Tristan Jarry AS .15 .40
591 Claude Giroux AS .15 .40
592 Claude Giroux '84 AS .15 .40
593 Jack Hughes '84 AS .40 1.00
594 Sebastian Aho '84 AS .25 .60
595 Auston Matthews '84 AS .60 1.50
596 Steven Stamkos '84 AS .30 .75
597 Andrei Vasilevskiy '84 AS .25 .60
598 Patrice Bergeron '84 AS .20 .50
599 Connor McDavid '84 AS .75 2.00
600 Leon Draisaitl '84 AS .50 1.25
601 Kirill Kaprizov '84 AS .50 1.25
602 Joe Pavelski '84 AS .20 .50
603 Johnny Gaudreau '84 AS .25 .60
604 Alex Pietrangelo '84 AS .12 .30
605 Cale Makar '84 AS .40 1.00
606 Cole Caufield '71-72 TOPPS .30 .75
607 Dawson Mercer '71-72 TOPPS .20 .50
608 Spencer Knight '71-72 TOPPS .15 .40
609 Jeremy Swayman '71-72 TOPPS.25 .60
610 Trevor Zegras '71-72 TOPPS .15 .40
611 Quinton Byfield '71-72 TOPPS .20 .50
612 Vasily Podkolzin '71-72 TOPPS.10 .25
613 Alexander Holtz '71-72 TOPPS .15 .40
614 Jamie Drysdale '71-72 TOPPS .12 .30
615 Alex Nedeljkovic '71-72 TOPPS.12 .30
616 Alex Newhook '71-72 TOPPS .12 .30
617 Moritz Seider '71-72 TOPPS .20 .50
618 Owen Power '71-72 TOPPS .30 .75
619 Lucas Raymond '71-72 TOPPS.25 .60
620 Filip Gustavsson '71-72 TOPPS.15 .40
621 Matthew Beniers '71-72 TOPPS.40 1.00
622 Nathan Smith '71-72 TOPPS .12 .30
623 Bobby Brink '71-72 TOPPS .15 .40
624 Matthew Beniers II .40 1.00
625 Jonathan Huberdeau II .20 .50
626 Auston Matthews II .60 1.50
627 David Pastrnak II .40 1.00
628 Lucas Raymond II .25 .60
629 Sidney Crosby II .60 1.50
630 Sebastian Aho II .25 .60
631 Owen Power II .30 .75
632 Jack Hughes II .40 1.00
633 Claude Giroux II .15 .40
634 Nathan MacKinnon II .60 1.50
635 Chris Kreider II .20 .50
636 Steven Stamkos II .30 .75
637 Roman Josi II .15 .40
638 Joe Pavelski II .20 .50
639 Leon Draisaitl II .50 1.25
640 Matthew Tkachuk II .30 .75
641 Jack Eichel II .25 .60
642 Trevor Zegras II .15 .40
643 Quinton Byfield II .20 .50
644 Kirill Kaprizov GO .50 1.25
645 Mats Zuccarello GO .15 .40
646 Vladimir Tarasenko GO .20 .50
647 Jordan Binnington GO .25 .60
648 Steven Stamkos GO .30 .75
649 Nikita Kucherov GO .30 .75
650 Filip Forsberg GO .25 .60
651 Juuse Saros GO .20 .50
652 Peyton Krebs GO .12 .30
653 Auston Matthews GO .60 1.50
654 Trevor Zegras CS .15 .40
655 Jack Hughes CS .40 1.00
656 Alex Ovechkin CS .60 1.50
657 Connor McDavid CS .75 2.00
658 Auston Matthews CS .60 1.50
659 Chris Kreider CS .20 .50
660 Nathan MacKinnon CS .60 1.50
661 Cole Caufield CS .30 .75
662 Matt Boldy CS .50 1.25
663 Vasily Podkolzin CS .10 .25
664 Patrick Kane AD .30 .75
665 Connor McDavid AD .75 2.00
666 Nikita Kucherov AD .30 .75
667 Artemi Panarin AD .30 .75
668 David Pastrnak AD .40 1.00
669 Johnny Gaudreau AD .25 .60
670 Mitch Marner AD .25 .60
671 Mathew Barzal AD .20 .50
672 Kirill Kaprizov AD .50 1.25
673 Sidney Crosby AD .60 1.50
674 Stanley Cup Image 1 FOIL .12 .30
675 Stanley Cup Image 2 FOIL .12 .30
676 Stanley Cup Image 3 FOIL .12 .30
677 Stanley Cup Image 4 FOIL .12 .30
678 Stanley Cup Image 5 FOIL .12 .30
679 Stanley Cup Image 6 FOIL .12 .30

2023-24 Topps Stickers

1 Anaheim Ducks Logo FOIL .12 .30
2 Team Highlights .12 .30
3 Wild Wing FOIL .12 .30
4 Trevor Zegras FOIL .15 .40
5 Mason McTavish FOIL .15 .40
6 Adam Henrique .12 .30
7 Mason McTavish .15 .40
8 Trevor Zegras .15 .40
9 Ryan Strome .15 .40
10 Cam Fowler .15 .40
11 Nikita Nesterenko .15 .40
12 John Gibson .15 .40
13 Troy Terry .12 .30
14 Jakob Silfverberg .10 .25
15 Drew Helleson .15 .40
16 Justin Kirkland .10 .25
17 Pavol Regenda .10 .25
18 Arizona Coyotes Logo FOIL .12 .30
19 Team Highlights .12 .30
20 Howler FOIL .12 .30
21 Clayton Keller FOIL .20 .50
22 Matias Maccelli FOIL .12 .30
23 Clayton Keller .20 .50
24 Karel Vejmelka .10 .25
25 Juuso Valimaki .10 .25
26 Janis Moser .10 .25
27 Barrett Hayton .15 .40
28 Nick Schmaltz .12 .30
29 Jack McBain .10 .25
30 Milos Kelemen .15 .40
31 Travis Boyd .10 .25
32 Matias Maccelli .12 .30
33 Dylan Guenther .20 .50
34 Lawson Crouse .10 .25
35 Boston Bruins Logo FOIL .12 .30
36 Team Highlights .12 .30
37 Blades FOIL .12 .30
38 David Pastrnak FOIL .40 1.00
39 Linus Ullmark FOIL .15 .40
40 Patrice Bergeron
41 Brad Marchand .30 .75
42 David Pastrnak .40 1.00
43 Taylor Hall .15 .40
44 Tyler Bertuzzi .12 .30
45 Joona Koppanen .12 .30
46 Charlie McAvoy .20 .50
47 David Krejci .15 .40
48 Linus Ullmark .15 .40
49 Jakub Lauko .15 .40
50 Matt Grzelcyk .12 .30
51 Dmitry Orlov .15 .40
52 Buffalo Sabres Logo FOIL .12 .30
53 Team Highlights .12 .30
54 Sabretooth FOIL .12 .30
55 Tage Thompson FOIL .20 .50
56 Owen Power FOIL .15 .40
57 Tage Thompson .20 .50
58 Alex Tuch .15 .40
59 Jeff Skinner .15 .40
60 Rasmus Dahlin .20 .50
61 Owen Power .15 .40
62 Peyton Krebs .12 .30
63 Kyle Okposo .10 .25
64 Henri Jokiharju .10 .25
65 Ukko-Pekka Luukkonen .12 .30
66 Jordan Greenway .10 .25
67 Dylan Cozens .15 .40
68 Devon Levi .40 1.00
69 Calgary Flames Logo FOIL .12 .30
70 Team Highlights .12 .30
71 Harvey The Hound FOIL .12 .30
72 Nazem Kadri FOIL .20 .50
73 Jonathan Huberdeau FOIL .20 .50
74 Nazem Kadri .20 .50
75 Jonathan Huberdeau .20 .50
76 Noah Hanifin
77 Milan Lucic .12 .30
78 Dillon Dube .10 .25
79 Tyler Toffoli .15 .40
80 Elias Lindholm .15 .40
81 Mikael Backlund .12 .30
82 Dustin Wolf .50 1.25
83 Jacob Markstrom .15 .40
84 Matt Coronato .25 .60
85 Jakob Pelletier .20 .50
86 Carolina Hurricanes Logo FOIL .12 .30
87 Team Highlights .12 .30
88 Stormy FOIL .12 .30
89 Sebastian Aho FOIL .25 .60
90 Brent Burns FOIL .15 .40
91 Sebastian Aho .25 .60
92 Teuvo Teravainen .15 .40
93 Andrei Svechnikov .20 .50
94 Seth Jarvis .20 .50
95 Antti Raanta .15 .40
96 Brent Burns .15 .40
97 Brady Skjei .10 .25
98 Jesper Fast .10 .25
99 Jordan Staal .12 .30
100 Derek Stepan .10 .25
101 Shayne Gostisbehere .15 .40
102 Frederik Andersen .20 .50
103 Chicago Blackhawks Logo FOIL.12 .30
104 Team Highlights .12 .30
105 Tommy Hawk FOIL .12 .30
106 Seth Jones FOIL .15 .40
107 Jonathan Toews FOIL .25 .60
108 Jonathan Toews .25 .60
109 Lukas Reichel .15 .40
110 Tyler Johnson .10 .25
111 Luke Philp .15 .40
112 Seth Jones .15 .40
113 Connor Murphy .12 .30
114 Andreas Athanasiou .12 .30
115 Filip Roos .10 .25
116 Jaxson Stauber .15 .40
117 Petr Mrazek .12 .30
118 Taylor Raddysh .12 .30
119 Alex Stalock .10 .25
120 Colorado Avalanche Logo FOIL.12 .30
121 Team Highlights .12 .30
122 Bernie FOIL .12 .30
123 Nathan MacKinnon FOIL .60 1.50
124 Cale Makar FOIL .40 1.00
125 Nathan MacKinnon .60 1.50
126 Alex Newhook .12 .30
127 Artturi Lehkonen .12 .30
128 Evan Rodrigues .12 .30
129 Mikko Rantanen .40 1.00
130 Cale Makar .40 1.00
131 Gabriel Landeskog .20 .50
132 Alexandar Georgiev .15 .40
133 Pavel Francouz .12 .30
134 Oskar Olausson .10 .25
135 Jean-Luc Foudy .10 .25
136 Lars Eller .10 .25
137 Columbus Blue Jackets Logo FOIL .12 .30
138 Team Highlights .12 .30
139 Stinger FOIL .12 .30
140 Johnny Gaudreau FOIL .25 .60
141 David Jiricek FOIL .15 .40
142 Johnny Gaudreau .25 .60
143 Patrik Laine .20 .50
144 Boone Jenner .15 .40
145 Kirill Marchenko .20 .50
146 Elvis Merzlikins .15 .40
147 Cole Sillinger .12 .30
148 David Jiricek .15 .40
149 Erik Gudbranson .10 .25
150 Marcus Bjork .10 .25
151 Tim Berni .10 .25
152 Andrew Peeke .10 .25
153 Kent Johnson .15 .40
154 Dallas Stars Logo FOIL .12 .30
155 Team Highlights .12 .30
156 Victor E. Green FOIL .12 .30
157 Jason Robertson FOIL .25 .60
158 Wyatt Johnston FOIL .30 .75
159 Jason Robertson .25 .60
160 Joe Pavelski .20 .50
161 Tyler Seguin .20 .50
162 Miro Heiskanen .20 .50
163 Jake Oettinger .25 .60
164 Mason Marchment .12 .30
165 Ryan Suter .12 .30
166 Wyatt Johnston .30 .75
167 Jamie Benn .15 .40
168 Evgeny Dadonov .10 .25
169 Matej Blumel .10 .25
170 Max Domi .15 .40
171 Detroit Red Wings Logo FOIL .12 .30
172 Team Highlights .12 .30
173 Dylan Larkin FOIL .20 .50
174 Lucas Raymond FOIL .25 .60
175 Moritz Seider FOIL .20 .50
176 Dylan Larkin .20 .50
177 Lucas Raymond .25 .60
178 Andrew Copp .10 .25
179 Ville Husso .10 .25
180 Moritz Seider .20 .50
181 Filip Zadina .12 .30
182 Michael Rasmussen .10 .25
183 Robby Fabbri .10 .25
184 Jake Walman .10 .25
185 Elmer Soderblom .15 .40
186 Marco Kasper .40 1.00
187 Dominik Kubalik .15 .40
188 Edmonton Oilers Logo FOIL .12 .30
189 Team Highlights .12 .30
190 Hunter FOIL .12 .30
191 Connor McDavid FOIL .75 2.00
192 Leon Draisaitl FOIL .50 1.25
193 Connor McDavid .75 2.00
194 Leon Draisaitl .50 1.25
195 Ryan Nugent-Hopkins .20 .50
196 Darnell Nurse .12 .30
197 Jack Campbell .15 .40
198 Derek Ryan .10 .25
199 Zach Hyman .25 .60
200 Vincent Desharnais .20 .50
201 Dylan Holloway .15 .40
202 Mattias Ekholm .12 .30
203 James Hamblin .10 .25
204 Stuart Skinner .20 .50
205 Florida Panthers Logo FOIL .12 .30
206 Team Highlights .12 .30
207 Stanley C. Panther FOIL .12 .30
208 Matthew Tkachuk FOIL .30 .75
209 Aleksander Barkov FOIL .25 .60
210 Aleksander Barkov .25 .60
211 Matthew Tkachuk .30 .75
212 Sergei Bobrovsky .25 .60
213 Aaron Ekblad .20 .50
214 Anton Lundell .15 .40
215 Spencer Knight .15 .40
216 Marc Staal .10 .25
217 Sam Reinhart .30 .75
218 Anton Levtchi .10 .25
219 Colin White .12 .30
220 Eetu Luostarinen .10 .25
221 Gustav Forsling .15 .40
222 Los Angeles Kings Logo FOIL .12 .30
223 Team Highlights .12 .30
224 Bailey FOIL .12 .30
225 Anze Kopitar FOIL .25 .60
226 Brandt Clarke FOIL .15 .40
227 Anze Kopitar .25 .60
228 Quinton Byfield .20 .50
229 Adrian Kempe .15 .40
230 Joonas Korpisalo .15 .40
231 Alex Iafallo .10 .25
232 Kevin Fiala .12 .30
233 Drew Doughty .15 .40
234 Brandt Clarke .15 .40
235 Mikey Anderson .12 .30
236 Phillip Danault .15 .40
237 Viktor Arvidsson .10 .25
238 Pheonix Copley .10 .25
239 Minnesota Wild Logo FOIL .12 .30
240 Team Highlights .12 .30
241 Nordy FOIL .12 .30
242 Kirill Kaprizov FOIL .50 1.25
243 Mats Zuccarello FOIL .15 .40
244 Kirill Kaprizov .50 1.25
245 Ryan Hartman .10 .25
246 Marc-Andre Fleury .30 .75
247 Mats Zuccarello .15 .40
248 Marcus Foligno .12 .30
249 Sam Steel .12 .30
250 Joel Eriksson Ek .12 .30
251 Jacob Middleton .10 .25
252 Jared Spurgeon .15 .40
253 Samuel Walker .10 .25
254 Matt Boldy .25 .60
255 Brock Faber .40 1.00
256 Montreal Canadiens Logo FOIL.12 .30
257 Team Highlights .12 .30
258 Youppi FOIL .12 .30
259 Nick Suzuki FOIL .30 .75
260 Juraj Slafkovsky FOIL .30 .75
261 Cole Caufield .30 .75
262 Nick Suzuki .30 .75
263 Juraj Slafkovsky .30 .75
264 Jake Allen .15 .40
265 Arber Xhekaj .15 .40
266 Justin Barron .12 .30
267 Owen Beck .25 .60
268 David Savard .10 .25
269 Josh Anderson .12 .30
270 Kaiden Guhle .15 .40
271 Rem Pitlick .10 .25
272 Denis Gurianov .20 .50
273 Nashville Predators Logo FOIL .12 .30
274 Team Highlights .12 .30
275 Gnash FOIL .12 .30
276 Juuse Saros FOIL .20 .50
277 Filip Forsberg FOIL .25 .60
278 Filip Forsberg .25 .60
279 Juuse Saros .20 .50
280 Matt Duchene .15 .40
281 Roman Josi .15 .40
282 Ryan McDonagh .10 .25
283 Yaroslav Askarov .40 1.00
284 Luke Evangelista .25 .60
285 Juuso Parssinen .10 .25
286 Zach Sanford .10 .25
287 Ryan Johansen .12 .30
288 Jeremy Lauzon .10 .25
289 Cody Glass .12 .30
290 New Jersey Devils Logo FOIL .12 .30
291 Team Highlights .12 .30
292 NJ Devil FOIL .12 .30
293 Jack Hughes FOIL .40 1.00
294 Nico Hischier FOIL .25 .60
295 Jack Hughes .40 1.00
296 Nico Hischier .25 .60
297 Ondrej Palat .12 .30
298 Tomas Tatar .10 .25
299 Jesper Bratt .15 .40
300 Yegor Sharangovich .15 .40
301 Vitek Vanecek .15 .40
302 Timo Meier .15 .40
303 Dougie Hamilton .12 .30
304 Luke Hughes .50 1.25
305 Damon Severson .10 .25
306 Dawson Mercer .20 .50
307 New York Islanders Logo FOIL .12 .30
308 Team Highlights .12 .30
309 Sparky FOIL .12 .30
310 Mathew Barzal FOIL .20 .50
311 Ilya Sorokin FOIL .25 .60
312 Mathew Barzal .20 .50
313 Bo Horvat .20 .50
314 Brock Nelson .15 .40
315 Ilya Sorokin .25 .60
316 Adam Pelech .10 .25
317 Ryan Pulock .12 .30
318 Zach Parise .15 .40
319 Parker Wotherspoon .10 .25
320 Oliver Wahlstrom .10 .25
321 Simon Holmstrom .10 .25
322 Jean-Gabriel Pageau .10 .25
323 Anders Lee .12 .30
324 New York Rangers Logo FOIL .12 .30
325 Team Highlights .12 .30
326 Igor Shesterkin FOIL .30 .75
327 Adam Fox FOIL .20 .50
328 Artemi Panarin FOIL .30 .75
329 Igor Shesterkin .30 .75
330 Artemi Panarin .30 .75
331 Adam Fox .20 .50
332 Mika Zibanejad .20 .50
333 Chris Kreider .20 .50
334 Jacob Trouba .12 .30
335 William Cuylle .25 .60
336 Kaapo Kakko .12 .30
337 Alexis Lafreniere .25 .60
338 Vincent Trocheck .15 .40
339 Patrick Kane .30 .75
340 Vladimir Tarasenko .20 .50
341 Ottawa Senators Logo FOIL .12 .30
342 Team Highlights .12 .30
343 Spartacat FOIL .12 .30
344 Brady Tkachuk FOIL .25 .60
345 Ridly Greig FOIL .25 .60
346 Brady Tkachuk .25 .60
347 Tim Stutzle .20 .50
348 Cam Talbot .15 .40
349 Derick Brassard .10 .25
350 Alex DeBrincat .20 .50
351 Claude Giroux .15 .40
352 Nick Holden .10 .25
353 Jake Lucchini .10 .25
354 Artem Zub .10 .25
355 Jakob Chychrun .15 .40
356 Ridly Greig .25 .60
357 Jake Sanderson .20 .50
358 Philadelphia Flyers Logo FOIL .12 .30
359 Team Highlights .12 .30
360 Gritty FOIL .12 .30
361 Carter Hart FOIL .15 .40
362 Kevin Hayes FOIL .12 .30
363 Carter Hart .15 .40
364 Kevin Hayes .12 .30
365 Rasmus Ristolainen .10 .25
366 Scott Laughton .10 .25
367 James Van Riemsdyk .12 .30
368 Travis Konecny .15 .40
369 Owen Tippett .10 .25
370 Tony DeAngelo .10 .25
371 Samuel Ersson .15 .40
372 Noah Cates .10 .25
373 Cam Atkinson .15 .40
374 Olle Lycksell .10 .25
375 Pittsburgh Penguins Logo FOIL.12 .30
376 Team Highlights .12 .30
377 Iceburgh FOIL .12 .30
378 Sidney Crosby FOIL .60 1.50
379 Evgeni Malkin FOIL .30 .75
380 Sidney Crosby .60 1.50
381 Evgeni Malkin .30 .75
382 Jake Guentzel .25 .60
383 Tristan Jarry .15 .40
384 Kris Letang .20 .50
385 Rickard Rakell .12 .30
386 Bryan Rust .15 .40
387 Samuel Poulin .10 .25
388 Mikael Granlund .12 .30
389 Brian Dumoulin .10 .25
390 Jonathan Gruden .15 .40
391 Jason Zucker .15 .40
392 San Jose Sharks Logo FOIL .12 .30
393 Team Highlights .12 .30
394 S.J. Sharkie FOIL .12 .30
395 Tomas Hertl FOIL .15 .40
396 Erik Karlsson FOIL .20 .50
397 Tomas Hertl .15 .40
398 Fabian Zetterlund .10 .25
399 Logan Couture .20 .50
400 Erik Karlsson .20 .50
401 James Reimer .10 .25
402 Noah Gregor .10 .25
403 Alexander Barabanov .10 .25
404 William Eklund .20 .50
405 Eetu Makiniemi .10 .25
406 Kaapo Kahkonen .15 .40
407 Nick Cicek .10 .25
408 Oskar Lindblom .12 .30
409 Seattle Kraken Logo FOIL .12 .30
410 Team Highlights .12 .30
411 Buoy FOIL .12 .30
412 Matty Beniers FOIL .20 .50
413 Shane Wright FOIL .20 .50
414 Shane Wright .20 .50
415 Matty Beniers .20 .50
416 Jordan Eberle .15 .40
417 Jared McCann .12 .30
418 Jaden Schwartz .12 .30
419 Martin Jones .12 .30
420 Eeli Tolvanen .15 .40
421 Alex Wennberg .10 .25
422 Adam Larsson .15 .40
423 Vince Dunn .12 .30
424 Jamie Oleksiak .12 .30
425 Yanni Gourde .12 .30
426 St. Louis Blues Logo FOIL .12 .30
427 Team Highlights .12 .30
428 Louie FOIL .12 .30
429 Jordan Binnington FOIL .25 .60
430 Jordan Kyrou FOIL .15 .40
431 Jordan Kyrou .15 .40
432 Jordan Binnington .25 .60
433 Sammy Blais .10 .25
434 Brandon Saad .12 .30
435 Nikita Alexandrov .10 .25
436 Robert Thomas .15 .40
437 Brayden Schenn .15 .40
438 Tyler Tucker .10 .25
439 Pavel Buchnevich .12 .30
440 Ivan Barbashev .12 .30
441 William Bitten .10 .25
442 Torey Krug .12 .30
443 Tampa Bay Lightning Logo FOIL.12 .30
444 Team Highlights .12 .30
445 Thunderbug FOIL .12 .30
446 Nikita Kucherov FOIL .30 .75
447 Steven Stamkos FOIL .30 .75
448 Nikita Kucherov .30 .75
449 Steven Stamkos .30 .75
450 Brayden Point .20 .50
451 Andrei Vasilevskiy .25 .60
452 Victor Hedman .20 .50
453 Alex Killorn .10 .25
454 Anthony Cirelli .12 .30
455 Mikey Eyssimont .10 .25
456 Nicklaus Perbix .10 .25
457 Corey Perry .25 .60
458 Tanner Jeannot .10 .25
459 Cole Koepke .10 .25
460 Toronto Maple Leafs Logo FOIL.12 .30
461 Team Highlights .12 .30
462 Carlton FOIL .12 .30
463 Auston Matthews FOIL .60 1.50
464 John Tavares FOIL .25 .60
465 John Tavares .25 .60
466 Auston Matthews .60 1.50
467 Michael Bunting .15 .40
468 Mitch Marner .25 .60
469 Ryan O'Reilly .15 .40
470 Ilya Samsonov .15 .40
471 Filip Kral .10 .25
472 William Nylander .30 .75
473 Bobby McMann .25 .60
474 Matthew Knies .60 1.50
475 Mark Giordano .15 .40
476 Pontus Holmberg .10 .25
477 Vancouver Canucks Logo FOIL .12 .30
478 Team Highlights .12 .30
479 Fin FOIL .12 .30
480 Andrei Kuzmenko FOIL .15 .40
481 Elias Pettersson FOIL .25 .60
482 Elias Pettersson .25 .60
483 J.T. Miller .20 .50
484 Thatcher Demko .20 .50
485 Brock Boeser .20 .50
486 Quinn Hughes .40 1.00
487 Anthony Beauvillier .10 .25
488 Ethan Bear .10 .25
489 Filip Hronek .10 .25
490 Andrei Kuzmenko .15 .40
491 Spencer Martin .10 .25
492 Vasily Podkolzin .10 .25
493 Nils Aman .10 .25
494 Vegas Golden Knights Logo FOIL.12 .30
495 Team Highlights .12 .30
496 Chance FOIL .12 .30
497 Jack Eichel FOIL .25 .60
498 Logan Thompson FOIL .20 .50
499 Mark Stone .20 .50
500 Jack Eichel .25 .60
501 Jonathan Marchessault .20 .50
502 Logan Thompson .20 .50
503 Alex Pietrangelo .12 .30
504 William Karlsson .20 .50
505 Phil Kessel .15 .40
506 Chandler Stephenson .12 .30
507 Shea Theodore .20 .50
508 William Carrier .10 .25
509 Alec Martinez .10 .25
510 Adin Hill .15 .40
511 Washington Capitals Logo FOIL.12 .30
512 Team Highlights .12 .30
513 Slapshot FOIL .12 .30
514 Alex Ovechkin FOIL .60 1.50
515 T.J. Oshie FOIL .15 .40
516 Alex Ovechkin .60 1.50
517 Nicklas Backstrom .15 .40
518 Dylan Strome .20 .50
519 Conor Sheary .15 .40
520 Evgeny Kuznetsov .20 .50
521 T.J. Oshie .15 .40
522 Darcy Kuemper .15 .40
523 Trevor van Riemsdyk .12 .30
524 John Carlson .15 .40
525 Tom Wilson .15 .40
526 Craig Smith .10 .25
527 Rasmus Sandin .12 .30
528 Winnipeg Jets Logo FOIL .12 .30
529 Team Highlights .12 .30
530 Moose FOIL .12 .30
531 Connor Hellebuyck FOIL .30 .75
532 Kyle Connor FOIL .25 .60
533 Connor Hellebuyck .30 .75
534 Mark Scheifele .25 .60
535 Kyle Connor .25 .60
536 Blake Wheeler .15 .40
537 Karson Kuhlman .10 .25
538 Josh Morrissey .20 .50
539 Neal Pionk .10 .25
540 Adam Lowry .12 .30
541 Saku Maenalanen .10 .25
542 Pierre-Luc Dubois .12 .30
543 Nino Niederreiter .10 .25
544 Nate Schmidt .10 .25
545 Patrice Bergeron C .20 .50
546 Kyle Okposo C .10 .25
547 Dylan Larkin C .20 .50
548 Aleksander Barkov C .25 .60
549 Nick Suzuki C .30 .75
550 Brady Tkachuk C .25 .60
551 Steven Stamkos C .30 .75
552 John Tavares C .25 .60
553 Clayton Keller C .20 .50
554 Seth Jones C .15 .40
555 Gabriel Landeskog C .20 .50
556 Jamie Benn C .15 .40
557 Jared Spurgeon C .15 .40
558 Roman Josi C .15 .40
559 Brayden Schenn C .15 .40
560 Mark Scheifele C .25 .60
561 Jordan Staal C .12 .30
562 Boone Jenner C .15 .40
563 Nico Hischier C .25 .60
564 Anders Lee C .12 .30
565 Jacob Trouba C .12 .30
566 Sean Couturier C .12 .30
567 Sidney Crosby C .60 1.50
568 Alex Ovechkin C .60 1.50
569 Adam Henrique C .12 .30
570 Mikael Backlund C .12 .30
571 Connor McDavid C .75 2.00
572 Anze Kopitar C .25 .60
573 Logan Couture C .20 .50
574 Jordan Eberle C .15 .40
575 Quinn Hughes C .40 1.00
576 Mark Stone C .20 .50
577 Connor McDavid IO FOIL .75 2.00
578 Sidney Crosby IO FOIL .60 1.50
579 Alex Ovechkin IO FOIL .60 1.50
580 Cale Makar IO FOIL .40 1.00
581 Adam Fox IO FOIL .20 .50
582 Linus Ullmark IO FOIL .15 .40
583 Elias Pettersson AS .25 .60
584 Andrei Svechnikov AS .20 .50
585 Brock Nelson AS .15 .40
586 S.Crosby/A.Ovechkin AS .60 1.50
587 J.Saros/S.Skinner AS .20 .50
588 Nathan MacKinnon AS .60 1.50
589 Nick Suzuki AS .30 .75
590 Dylan Larkin AS .20 .50
591 Matthew Tkachuk AS .30 .75
592 Matthew Tkachuk '91-92 AS .30 .75
593 Nikita Kucherov '91-92 AS .30 .75
594 David Pastrnak '91-92 AS .40 1.00
595 Dylan Larkin '91-92 AS .20 .50
596 Brady Tkachuk '91-92 AS .25 .60
597 Jack Hughes '91-92 AS .40 1.00
598 Igor Shesterkin '91-92 AS .30 .75
599 Sidney Crosby '91-92 AS .60 1.50
600 Alex Ovechkin '91-92 AS .60 1.50
601 Johnny Gaudreau '91-92 AS .25 .60
602 Cale Makar '91-92 AS .40 1.00
603 Kirill Kaprizov '91-92 AS .50 1.25
604 Juuse Saros '91-92 AS .20 .50
605 Vladimir Tarasenko '91-92 AS .20 .50
606 Jason Robertson '91-92 AS .25 .60
607 Nazem Kadri '91-92 AS .20 .50
608 Connor McDavid '91-92 AS .75 2.00
609 Matty Beniers '91-92 AS .20 .50
610 Elias Pettersson '91-92 AS .25 .60
611 Erik Karlsson '91-92 AS .20 .50
612 Shane Wright '84-85 TOPPS .20 .50
613 Juraj Slafkovsky '84-85 TOPPS.30 .75
614 Oskar Olausson '84-85 TOPPS .10 .25
615 Jake Sanderson '84-85 TOPPS .20 .50
616 Dylan Guenther '84-85 TOPPS .20 .50
617 Yaroslav Askarov '84-85 TOPPS .40 1.00
618 Aatu Raty '84-85 TOPPS .10 .25
619 Matias Maccelli '84-85 TOPPS .12 .30
620 Kent Johnson '84-85 TOPPS .15 .40
621 Owen Beck '84-85 TOPPS .25 .60
622 Simon Holmstrom '84-85 TOPPS.10 .25
623 Matt Coronato '84-85 TOPPS .25 .60
624 Wyatt Johnston '84-85 TOPPS .30 .75
625 Ridly Greig '84-85 TOPPS .25 .60
626 Kirill Marchenko '84-85 TOPPS.20 .50
627 Brock Faber '84-85 TOPPS .40 1.00
628 Brandt Clarke '84-85 TOPPS .15 .40
629 Devon Levi '84-85 TOPPS .40 1.00
630 Luke Hughes '84-85 TOPPS .50 1.25
631 Matthew Knies '84-85 TOPPS .60 1.50
632 Connor McDavid TST .75 2.00
633 Alex Ovechkin TST .60 1.50
634 Sidney Crosby TST .60 1.50
635 David Pastrnak TST .40 1.00
636 Auston Matthews TST .60 1.50
637 Jack Hughes TST .40 1.00
638 Nikita Kucherov TST .30 .75
639 Andrei Vasilevskiy TST .25 .60
640 Leon Draisaitl TST .50 1.25
641 Matthew Tkachuk TST .30 .75
642 Tage Thompson TST .20 .50
643 Jason Robertson TST .25 .60
644 Kirill Kaprizov TST .50 1.25
645 Igor Shesterkin TST .30 .75
646 Nathan MacKinnon TST .60 1.50
647 Elias Pettersson TST .25 .60
648 Adam Fox TST .20 .50
649 Linus Ullmark TST .15 .40
650 Ryan Nugent-Hopkins TST .20 .50
651 Cale Makar TST .40 1.00
652 Jake DeBrusk GO .15 .40
653 Linus Ullmark GO .15 .40
654 Kasperi Kapanen GO .12 .30
655 Casey DeSmith GO .12 .30
656 Martin Necas GO .25 .60
657 Jesperi Kotkaniemi GO .15 .40
658 Tom Wilson GO .15 .40
659 Darcy Kuemper GO .15 .40
660 Vinnie Hinostroza GO .10 .25
661 Auston Matthews GO .60 1.50
662 Artemi Panarin HH .30 .75
663 Nikita Kucherov HH .30 .75
664 Tage Thompson HH .20 .50
665 William Nylander HH .30 .75
666 Jack Hughes HH .40 1.00
667 Igor Shesterkin HH .30 .75
668 Drew Doughty HH .15 .40
669 Kyle Connor HH .25 .60
670 Trevor Zegras HH .15 .40
671 Connor McDavid SD .75 2.00
672 Andrei Svechnikov SD .20 .50
673 Nathan MacKinnon SD .60 1.50
674 Mathew Barzal SD .20 .50
675 Jack Hughes SD .40 1.00
676 Johnny Gaudreau SD .25 .60
677 Cale Makar SD .40 1.00
678 Taylor Hall SD .15 .40
679 Dylan Larkin SD .20 .50
680 Stanley Cup Image 1 FOIL .12 .30
681 Stanley Cup Image 2 FOIL .12 .30
682 Stanley Cup Image 3 FOIL .12 .30
683 Stanley Cup Image 4 FOIL .12 .30
684 Stanley Cup Image 5 FOIL .12 .30
685 Stanley Cup Image 6 FOIL .12 .30

1999 Topps Pearson Award

1 Jaromir Jagr 6.00 15.00

1996-97 Topps Picks

1 Jaromir Jagr .30 .75
3 Mario Lemieux .40 1.00
5 Peter Forsberg .20 .50
7 Teemu Selanne .20 .50
9 Alexander Mogilny .07 .20
11 Patrick Roy .25 .60
13 Jim Carey .10 .25
15 Pavel Bure .10 .25
17 Sergei Fedorov .15 .40
19 Chris Chelios .10 .25
21 Sandis Ozolinsh .05 .15
23 Doug Weight .10 .25
25 Mark Messier .20 .50
27 Martin Brodeur .25 .60
29 Brett Hull .20 .50
31 Steve Yzerman .25 .60
33 Kevin Hatcher .05 .15
35 Roman Hamrlik .05 .15
37 Petr Nedved .07 .20
39 Valeri Kamensky .07 .20
41 Gary Suter .05 .15
43 Mats Sundin .10 .25
45 Trevor Linden .10 .25
47 Jeremy Roenick .15 .40
49 Al MacInnis .12 .30
51 Mike Modano .15 .40
53 Mathieu Schneider .05 .15
55 Michal Pivonka .05 .15
57 Owen Nolan .10 .25
59 Martin Rucinsky .05 .15
61 Joe Nieuwendyk .07 .20
63 Mark Recchi .12 .30
65 Geoff Sanderson .07 .20
67 Vyacheslav Kozlov .05 .15
69 Pat Verbeek .05 .15
71 Brian Bradley .05 .15
73 Steve Duchesne .05 .15
75 Steve Thomas .05 .15
77 Eric Daze .07 .20
79 Alexei Kovalev .07 .20
81 Kevin Stevens .07 .20
83 Curtis Joseph .12 .30
85 Bill Ranford .07 .20
87 Luc Robitaille .10 .25
89 Claude Lemieux .05 .15
91 Sergei Gonchar .05 .15
93 Eric Desjardins .07 .20
95 Garry Galley .05 .15
97 Oleg Tverdovsky .07 .20
99 Rob Niedermayer .07 .20
101 Scott Mellanby .07 .20
103 Adam Deadmarsh .05 .15
105 Cliff Ronning .05 .15
107 Russ Courtnall .05 .15
109 Keith Primeau .07 .20
111 Rick Tocchet .07 .20
113 Scott Young .05 .15
115 Scott Stevens .10 .25
117 Al Iafrate .05 .15
119 Ray Ferraro .05 .15
121 Todd Bertuzzi .10 .25
123 Alexander Selivanov .05 .15
125 Steve Chiasson .05 .15
127 Dave Andreychuk .10 .25
129 Ray Sheppard .07 .20
131 Bernie Nicholls .07 .20
133 Tony Amonte .07 .20
135 Nelson Emerson .05 .15
137 Cam Neely .10 .25
139 Shayne Corson .07 .20
141 Bill Guerin .10 .25
143 Joe Murphy .05 .15
145 Cory Stillman .05 .15
147 Radek Bonk .05 .15
149 Geoff Courtnall .05 .15
151 Chad Kilger .05 .15
153 Sylvain Cote .05 .15
155 Glen Wesley .05 .15
157 Jeff Norton .07 .20
159 Rob Blake .10 .25
161 Calle Johansson .07 .20
163 Uwe Krupp .05 .15
165 James Patrick .05 .15
167 Dmitri Mironov .05 .15
169 Vladimir Konstantinov .07 .20
171 Mattias Norstrom .05 .15
173 David Wilkie .05 .15
175 Bryan McCabe .05 .15
177 Barry Richter .05 .15
179 Ed Belfour .10 .25
NNO CHECKLIST .02 .10

1996-97 Topps Picks 500 Club

COMPLETE SET (8) 12.00 30.00
FC1 Wayne Gretzky 6.00 15.00
FC2 Mike Gartner .75 2.00
FC3 Jari Kurri .75 2.00
FC4 Dino Ciccarelli .75 2.00
FC5 Mario Lemieux 4.00 10.00
FC6 Mark Messier 1.25 3.00
FC7 Steve Yzerman 3.00 8.00
FC8 Dale Hawerchuk .75 2.00

1996-97 Topps Picks Fantasy Team
COMPLETE SET (22) 20.00 50.00
FT1 Patrick Roy 3.00 8.00
FT2 Chris Osgood .40 1.00
FT3 Martin Brodeur 2.00 5.00
FT4 Ray Bourque 1.25 3.00
FT5 Brian Leetch .75 2.00
FT6 Chris Chelios .75 2.00
FT7 Paul Coffey .75 2.00
FT8 Ed Jovanovski .40 1.00
FT9 Roman Hamrlik .40 1.00
FT10 Wayne Gretzky 4.00 10.00
FT11 Paul Kariya 1.25 3.00
FT12 Brett Hull 1.25 3.00
FT13 Pavel Bure 1.25 3.00
FT14 Jaromir Jagr 1.50 4.00
FT15 Mario Lemieux 3.00 8.00
FT16 Peter Forsberg 1.50 4.00
FT17 Sergei Fedorov 1.25 3.00
FT18 Jeremy Roenick 1.25 3.00
FT19 Alexander Mogilny .75 2.00
FT20 Joe Sakic 2.00 5.00
FT21 Teemu Selanne 1.25 3.00
FT22 Eric Lindros 1.25 3.00

1996-97 Topps Picks Ice D
COMPLETE SET (15) 20.00 40.00
ID1 Brian Leetch 1.25 3.00
ID2 Ray Bourque 2.00 5.00
ID3 Chris Chelios 1.25 3.00
ID4 Scott Stevens 1.00 2.50
ID5 Ed Jovanovski 1.00 2.50
ID6 Martin Brodeur 3.00 8.00
ID7 Patrick Roy 4.00 10.00
ID8 Chris Osgood 1.00 2.50
ID9 Jim Carey 1.25 3.00
ID10 Dominik Hasek 2.50 6.00
ID11 Ron Hextall 1.00 2.50
ID12 John Vanbiesbrouck 1.00 2.50
ID13 Mike Richter 1.25 3.00
ID14 Felix Potvin 1.25 3.00
ID15 Grant Fuhr 1.00 2.50

1996-97 Topps Picks OPC Inserts
*OPC: 4X TO 10X BASIC CARDS

1996-97 Topps Picks Rookie Stars
COMPLETE SET (18) 5.00 10.00
*OPC: 4X TO 10X BASIC INSERTS
RS1 Daniel Alfredsson .20 .50
RS2 Jere Lehtinen .60 1.50
RS3 Vitali Yachmenev .20 .50
RS4 Eric Daze .20 .50
RS5 Saku Koivu .60 1.50
RS6 Petr Sykora .20 .50
RS7 Marcus Ragnarsson .20 .50
RS8 Valeri Bure .20 .50
RS9 Cory Stillman .20 .50
RS10 Todd Bertuzzi .60 1.50
RS11 Ed Jovanovski .40 1.00
RS12 Miroslav Satan .40 1.00
RS13 Kyle McLaren .20 .50
RS14 Byron Dafoe .40 1.00
RS15 Eric Fichaud .20 .50
RS16 Corey Hirsch .20 .50
RS17 Jeff O'Neill .20 .50
RS18 Niklas Sundstrom .20 .50

1996-97 Topps Picks Top Shelf
COMPLETE SET (15) 15.00 40.00
TS1 John LeClair .60 1.50
TS2 Wayne Gretzky 4.00 10.00
TS3 Eric Lindros 1.00 2.50
TS4 Paul Kariya 1.00 2.50
TS5 Mark Messier 1.00 2.50
TS6 Jaromir Jagr 1.50 4.00
TS7 Peter Forsberg 1.50 4.00
TS8 Teemu Selanne 1.00 2.50
TS9 Alexander Mogilny .60 1.50
TS10 Brett Hull 1.25 3.00
TS11 Sergei Fedorov 1.25 3.00
TS12 Joe Sakic 2.00 5.00
TS13 Mats Sundin 1.00 2.50
TS14 Theo Fleury .60 1.50
TS15 Steve Yzerman 2.50 6.00

2009-10 Topps Puck Attax
*BLACK: .6X TO 1.5X BASIC CARDS
*GOLD: 2X TO 5X BASIC CARDS
1 Ryan Getzlaf .20 .50
2 Corey Perry .30 .75
3 Teemu Selanne .40 1.00
4 Scott Niedermayer .20 .50
5 Ryan Whitney .12 .30
6 Jonas Hiller .15 .40
7 Bryan Little .20 .50
8 Ilya Kovalchuk .20 .50
9 Chris Thorburn .12 .30
10 Tobias Enstrom .20 .50
11 Ron Hainsey .12 .30
12 Kari Lehtonen .15 .40
13 Marc Savard .12 .30
14 David Krejci .20 .50
15 Milan Lucic .15 .40
16 Chuck Kobasew .12 .30
17 Zdeno Chara .12 .30
18 Dennis Wideman .12 .30
19 Tim Thomas .20 .50
20 Derek Roy .12 .30
21 Paul Gaustad .15 .40
22 Thomas Vanek .15 .40
23 Craig Rivet .12 .30
24 Toni Lydman .12 .30
25 Ryan Miller .20 .50
26 Olli Jokinen .15 .40
27 Jarome Iginla .25 .60
28 Curtis Glencross .15 .40
29 Dion Phaneuf .15 .40
30 Jay Bouwmeester .12 .30
31 Miikka Kiprusoff .12 .30
32 Eric Staal .25 .60
33 Chad LaRose .12 .30
34 Ray Whitney .15 .40
35 Joe Corvo .12 .30
36 Joni Pitkanen .15 .40
37 Cam Ward .20 .50
38 Jonathan Toews .30 .75
39 Patrick Kane .40 1.00
40 Patrick Sharp .20 .50
41 Brian Campbell .15 .40
42 Duncan Keith .15 .40
43 Cristobal Huet .20 .50
44 Milan Hejduk .15 .40
45 Paul Stastny .15 .40
46 Cody McLeod .12 .30
47 John-Michael Liles .12 .30
48 Ruslan Salei .12 .30
49 Peter Budaj .15 .40
50 Rick Nash .20 .50
51 Kristian Huselius .12 .30
52 R.J. Umberger .15 .40
53 Fedor Tyutin .12 .30
54 Mike Commodore .12 .30
55 Steve Mason .15 .40
56 Mike Ribeiro .12 .30
57 Brad Richards .20 .50
58 Mike Modano .30 .75
59 Matt Niskanen .15 .40
60 Stephane Robidas .12 .30
61 Marty Turco .20 .50
62 Dan Cleary .12 .30
63 Johan Franzen .15 .40
64 Pavel Datsyuk .30 .75
65 Henrik Zetterberg .25 .60
66 Brian Rafalski .12 .30
67 Nicklas Lidstrom .20 .50
68 Niklas Kronwall .15 .40
69 Chris Osgood .20 .50
70 Sam Gagner .15 .40
71 Ethan Moreau .12 .30
72 Ales Hemsky .15 .40
73 Sheldon Souray .12 .30
74 Tom Gilbert .12 .30
75 Denis Grebeshkov .12 .30
76 Nikolai Khabibulin .20 .50
77 Stephen Weiss .12 .30
78 David Booth .12 .30
79 Nathan Horton .20 .50
80 Keith Ballard .12 .30
81 Bryan McCabe .15 .40
82 Tomas Vokoun .15 .40
83 Ryan Smyth .15 .40
84 Anze Kopitar .30 .75
85 Wayne Simmonds .25 .60
86 Drew Doughty .25 .60
87 Matt Greene .12 .30
88 Jonathan Quick .25 .60
89 Martin Havlat .15 .40
90 Mikko Koivu .20 .50
91 Cal Clutterbuck .12 .30
92 Marek Zidlicky .12 .30
93 Brent Burns .20 .50
94 Niklas Backstrom .20 .50
95 Mike Cammalleri .15 .40
96 Maxim Lapierre .12 .30
97 Andrei Kostitsyn .15 .40
98 Brian Gionta .12 .30
99 Scott Gomez .15 .40
100 Jaroslav Spacek .12 .30
101 Andrei Markov .20 .50
102 Carey Price .40 1.00
103 David Legwand .15 .40
104 Joel Ward .12 .30
105 Jason Arnott .15 .40
106 Shea Weber .15 .40
107 Ryan Suter .15 .40
108 Pekka Rinne .20 .50
109 Zach Parise .20 .50
110 Patrik Elias .20 .50
111 Jamie Langenbrunner .12 .30
112 Paul Martin .12 .30
113 John Oduya .15 .40
114 Martin Brodeur .50 1.25
115 Doug Weight .20 .50
116 Frans Nielsen .12 .30
117 Kyle Okposo .12 .30
118 Mark Streit .15 .40
119 Bruno Gervais .12 .30
120 Dwayne Roloson .15 .40
121 Rick DiPietro .15 .40
122 Marian Gaborik .20 .50
123 Brandon Dubinsky .12 .30
124 Chris Drury .15 .40
125 Sean Avery .15 .40
126 Dan Girardi .12 .30
127 Marc Staal .12 .30
128 Henrik Lundqvist .50 1.25
129 Jason Spezza .20 .50
130 Chris Kelly .15 .40
131 Daniel Alfredsson .20 .50
132 Filip Kuba .12 .30
133 Chris Campoli .12 .30
134 Pascal Leclaire .20 .50
135 Jeff Carter .15 .40
136 Mike Richards .15 .40
137 Arron Asham .15 .40
138 Chris Pronger .20 .50
139 Kimmo Timonen .12 .30
140 Braydon Coburn .12 .30
141 Ray Emery .15 .40
142 Matthew Lombardi .12 .30
143 Peter Mueller .15 .40
144 Shane Doan .15 .40
145 Zbynek Michalek .12 .30
146 Ed Jovanovski .12 .30
147 Ilya Bryzgalov .15 .40
148 Jason LaBarbera .15 .40
149 Maxime Talbot .12 .30
150 Evgeni Malkin .40 1.00
151 Sidney Crosby .75 2.00
152 Jordan Staal .15 .40
153 Kris Letang .25 .60
154 Sergei Gonchar .12 .30
155 Marc-Andre Fleury .40 1.00
156 Joe Thornton .30 .75
157 Ryane Clowe .12 .30
158 Devin Setoguchi .15 .40
159 Dan Boyle .12 .30
160 Rob Blake .20 .50
161 Evgeni Nabokov .15 .40
162 Brad Boyes .12 .30
163 Keith Tkachuk .20 .50
164 Jay McClement .12 .30
165 Barret Jackman .12 .30
166 Carlo Colaiacovo .12 .30
167 Chris Mason .15 .40
168 Vincent Lecavalier .20 .50
169 Steven Stamkos .40 1.00
170 Martin St. Louis .20 .50
171 Mattias Ohlund .12 .30
172 Andrej Meszaros .12 .30
173 Mike Smith .20 .50
174 Matt Stajan .12 .30
175 Jason Blake .12 .30
176 Alexei Ponikarovsky .12 .30
177 Luke Schenn .20 .50
178 Mike Komisarek .15 .40
179 Tomas Kaberle .12 .30
180 Vesa Toskala .20 .50
181 Henrik Sedin .25 .60
182 Alexandre Burrows .12 .30
183 Daniel Sedin .25 .60
184 Sami Salo .20 .50
185 Kevin Bieksa .15 .40
186 Roberto Luongo .30 .75
187 Nicklas Backstrom .20 .50
188 Alexander Ovechkin .75 2.00
189 David Steckel .12 .30
190 Mike Green .15 .40
191 Shaone Morrisonn .12 .30
192 Simeon Varlamov .20 .50

2009-10 Topps Puck Attax Platinum Blister
COMPLETE SET (6) 6.00 15.00
1 Mike Modano 1.50 4.00
2 Jarome Iginla 1.25 3.00
3 Ilya Kovalchuk 1.00 2.50
4 Rick Nash 1.00 2.50
5 Vincent Lecavalier 1.00 2.50
6 Henrik Sedin 1.25 3.00

2009-10 Topps Puck Attax Platinum Starter
COMPLETE SET (6) 10.00 25.00
1 Sidney Crosby 4.00 10.00
2 Alexander Ovechkin 4.00 10.00
3 Eric Staal 1.25 3.00
4 Nicklas Lidstrom .60 1.50
5 Andrei Markov 1.00 2.50
6 Henrik Lundqvist 2.50 6.00

1999-00 Topps Premier Plus
COMPLETE SET (140) 30.00 75.00
1 Curtis Joseph .20 .50
2 Peter Bondra .15 .40
3 Theo Fleury .05 .15
4 Steve Yzerman 1.00 2.50
5 Peter Forsberg .50 1.25
6 Ray Bourque .30 .75
7 Dominik Hasek .40 1.00
8 Chris Drury .15 .40
9 Brett Hull .25 .60
10 Chris Osgood .15 .40
11 Luc Robitaille .15 .40
12 Bobby Holik .15 .40
13 John LeClair .15 .40
14 Jeremy Roenick .25 .60
15 Owen Nolan .15 .40
16 Wade Redden .05 .15
17 Teemu Selanne .20 .50
18 Doug Weight .15 .40
19 Vincent Lecavalier .20 .50
20 Pierre Turgeon .15 .40
21 Ron Francis .15 .40
22 Sergei Samsonov .15 .40
23 Patrick Roy 1.00 2.50
24 Mark Messier .20 .50
25 Al MacInnis .15 .40
26 Mark Parrish .05 .15
27 Ron Tugnutt .15 .40
28 Joe Nieuwendyk .15 .40
29 Valeri Bure .05 .15
30 Jason Allison .05 .15
31 Tony Amonte .15 .40
32 Scott Niedermayer .05 .15
33 Kenny Jonsson .05 .15
34 Jaromir Jagr .30 .75
35 Sergei Berezin .15 .40
36 Olaf Kolzig .15 .40
37 Byron Dafoe .15 .40
38 Adam Deadmarsh .05 .15
39 Alexei Zhitnik .05 .15
40 Paul Kariya .20 .50
41 Chris Pronger .15 .40
42 Markus Naslund .20 .50
43 Damian Rhodes .15 .40
44 Marian Hossa .20 .50
45 Adam Graves .05 .15
46 Scott Stevens .05 .15
47 Nicklas Lidstrom .20 .50
48 Ed Belfour .20 .50
49 Miroslav Satan .15 .40
50 Rob Blake .15 .40
51 Petr Nedved .15 .40
52 Mark Recchi .15 .40
53 Jeff Friesen .05 .15
54 Mats Sundin .20 .50
55 Arturs Irbe .15 .40
56 Derian Hatcher .15 .40
57 Mike Modano .30 .75
58 Brendan Shanahan .20 .50
59 Zigmund Palffy .15 .40
60 Saku Koivu .20 .50
61 Brian Leetch .20 .50
62 Rod Brind'Amour .15 .40
63 Keith Tkachuk .20 .50
64 Pavol Demitra .15 .40
65 Magnus Arvedson .05 .15
66 Martin Brodeur .50 1.25
67 Chris Chelios .20 .50
68 Joe Sakic .40 1.00
69 Anson Carter .15 .40
70 Sergei Fedorov .30 .75
71 Pavel Bure .20 .50
72 Petr Sykora .05 .15
73 Daniel Alfredsson .15 .40
74 Guy Hebert .15 .40
75 Jere Lehtinen .15 .40
76 Mike Richter .20 .50
77 Michael Peca .15 .40
78 Sandis Ozolinsh .05 .15
79 Joe Thornton .30 .75
80 Eric Lindros .20 .50
81 Milan Hejduk .20 .50
82 Ladislav Nagy RC 1.00 2.50
83 Francis Bouillon RC .15 .40
84 Mark Eaton RC .15 .40
85 Robert Valicevic RC .15 .40
86 Sami Helenius RC .15 .40
87 Travis Brigley RC .15 .40
88 Glen Metropolit RC .60 1.50
89 Alan Letang RC .15 .40
90 Brad Chartrand RC .15 .40
91 Marc Rodgers RC .15 .40
92 Hans Jonsson RC .15 .40
93 Kim Johnsson RC .15 .40
94 Richard Lintner RC .15 .40
95 Andrew Ference .15 .40
96 Jeff Halpern RC .75 2.00
97 Brad Lukowich RC .15 .40
98 Tyson Nash RC .20 .50
99 Oleg Saprykin RC .75 2.00
100 John Grahame RC .75 2.00
101 Patrik Stefan RC .75 2.00
102 Jason Blake RC .15 .40
103 Kyle Calder RC .20 .50
104 John Madden RC .75 2.00
105 Dan Hinote RC .50 1.25
106 Pavel Patera RC .15 .40
107 Yuri Butsayev RC .15 .40
108 Paul Comrie RC .15 .40
109 Ivan Novoseltsev RC .60 1.50
110 Niclas Havelid RC .20 .50
111 Brian Rafalski RC .60 1.50
112 Jorgen Jonsson RC .15 .40
113 Mike Fisher RC .50 1.25
114 Mika Alatalo RC .15 .40
115 Michal Rozsival RC .15 .40
116 Jochen Hecht RC 1.00 2.50
117 Nikolai Antropov RC 1.00 2.50
118 Steve Kariya RC .60 1.50
119 Brian Campbell RC .15 .40
120 Maxim Afinogenov .05 .15
121 Roberto Luongo .25 .60
122 Petr Buzek .05 .15
123 Per Svartvadet RC .15 .40
124 Dave Tanabe .05 .15
125 Brad Stuart .05 .15
126 Michael York .05 .15
127 Jiri Fischer .05 .15
128 Peter Schaefer .15 .40
129 Martin Biron .15 .40
130 Rico Fata .05 .15
131 J-P Dumont .15 .40
132 Martin Skoula RC .60 1.50
133 Alex Tanguay .15 .40
134 Mike Ribeiro .15 .40
135 David Legwand .15 .40
136 Scott Gomez .05 .15
137 Tim Connolly .05 .15
138 Jan Hlavac .05 .15
139 Simon Gagne .20 .50
140 Brian Boucher .20 .50
CTW1 Chris Drury AU 10.00 20.00
NNO Chris Drury JUMBO CHECKLIST
NNO Curtis Joseph JUMBO CHECKLIST

1999-00 Topps Premier Plus Foil Parallel
*VETS: 12X TO 30X BASIC CARDS
*ROOKIES: 8X TO 20X BASIC CARDS

1999-00 Topps Premier Plus Calling All Calders
COMPLETE SET (10) 12.00 25.00
CAC1 Chris Drury .75 2.00
CAC2 Sergei Samsonov 1.00 2.50
CAC3 Daniel Alfredsson .75 2.00
CAC4 Peter Forsberg 2.50 6.00
CAC5 Martin Brodeur 2.50 6.00
CAC6 Teemu Selanne .75 2.00
CAC7 Pavel Bure 1.25 3.00
CAC8 Ed Belfour .75 2.00
CAC9 Joe Nieuwendyk .75 2.00
CAC10 Brian Leetch 1.00 2.50

1999-00 Topps Premier Plus Club Signings
CS1 Ray Bourque 30.00 60.00
CS2 Cam Neely 20.00 40.00
CS3 Curtis Joseph 12.50 30.00
CS4 Johnny Bower 12.50 30.00
CS5 Jaromir Jagr 25.00 60.00
CS6 Mario Lemieux 40.00 100.00
CSC1 R.Bourque/C.Neely 40.00 100.00
CSC2 C.Joseph/J.Bower 30.00 80.00
CSC3 J.Jagr/M.Lemieux 100.00 250.00

1999-00 Topps Premier Plus Code Red
COMPLETE SET (8) 20.00 40.00
CR1 Keith Tkachuk 1.50 4.00
CR2 Teemu Selanne 1.50 4.00
CR3 Zigmund Palffy 1.50 4.00
CR4 Steve Yzerman 8.00 20.00
CR5 Theo Fleury 1.50 4.00
CR6 Jaromir Jagr 2.50 6.00
CR7 Peter Bondra 1.25 3.00
CR8 Pavel Bure 2.00 5.00

1999-00 Topps Premier Plus Feature Presentations
COMPLETE SET (8) 8.00 15.00
FP1 Joe Sakic 1.25 3.00
FP2 Mark Messier .75 2.00
FP3 Steve Yzerman 3.00 8.00
FP4 Mike Modano 1.00 2.50
FP5 Paul Kariya .75 2.00
FP6 Pavel Bure .75 2.00
FP7 Jaromir Jagr 1.00 2.50
FP8 Ray Bourque 1.00 2.50

1999-00 Topps Premier Plus Game Pieces
GPCD Chris Drury S 40.00 100.00
GPDL David Legwand S 7.50 15.00
GPDW Doug Weight J 7.50 15.00
GPMR Mike Richter S 15.00 40.00
GPNL Nicklas Lidstrom J 7.50 15.00
GPSG Scott Gomez J 7.50 15.00

1999-00 Topps Premier Plus Imperial Guard
COMPLETE SET(8) 20.00 40.00
IG1 Ed Belfour 1.50 4.00
IG2 Patrick Roy 8.00 20.00
IG3 Martin Brodeur 4.00 10.00
IG4 Dominik Hasek 3.00 8.00
IG5 Curtis Joseph 1.50 4.00
IG6 John Vanbiesbrouck 1.25 3.00
IG7 Mike Richter 1.50 4.00
IG8 Byron Dafoe 1.25 3.00

1999-00 Topps Premier Plus Premier Rookies
COMPLETE SET (10) 10.00 20.00
*FOIL/250: 1.5X TO 4X BASIC INSERTS
PR1 Alex Tanguay 1.50 4.00
PR2 Brad Stuart 1.25 3.00
PR3 Peter Schaefer .75 2.00
PR4 Scott Gomez .75 2.00
PR5 Patrik Stefan .75 2.00
PR6 Jochen Hecht 1.25 3.00
PR7 David Legwand 1.50 4.00
PR8 Steve Kariya 1.50 4.00
PR9 J-P Dumont 1.00 2.50
PR10 Simon Gagne 1.50 4.00

1999-00 Topps Premier Plus Premier Team
COMPLETE SET (10) 15.00 30.00
*FOIL/250: 4X TO 10X BASIC INSERTS
PT1 Paul Kariya .75 2.00
PT2 Jaromir Jagr 1.25 3.00
PT3 Eric Lindros .75 2.00
PT4 Mike Modano 1.25 3.00
PT5 Mats Sundin .75 2.00
PT6 Peter Forsberg 2.00 5.00
PT7 Steve Yzerman 4.00 10.00
PT8 Patrick Roy 4.00 10.00
PT9 Martin Brodeur 2.00 5.00
PT10 Dominik Hasek 1.50 4.00

1999-00 Topps Premier Plus Signing Bonus
SB1 David Legwand 5.00 12.00
SB2 Scott Gomez 5.00 12.00
SB3 Peter Schaefer 5.00 12.00
SB4 Patrik Stefan 5.00 12.00
SB5 Alex Tanguay 10.00 25.00

1999-00 Topps Premier Plus The Next Ones
COMPLETE SET (8) 6.00 12.00
TNO1 Vincent Lecavalier 1.00 2.50
TNO2 Marian Hossa 1.00 2.50
TNO3 Chris Drury .75 2.00
TNO4 Joe Thornton 1.50 4.00
TNO5 Steve Kariya .30 .75
TNO6 David Legwand .75 2.00
TNO7 Patrik Stefan .30 .75
TNO8 Milan Hejduk 1.00 2.50

1999-00 Topps Premier Plus Promos
COMPLETE SET (6) 2.00 5.00
PP1 Curtis Joseph .60 1.50
PP2 J.P. Dumont .20 .50
PP3 Marian Hossa .60 1.50
PP4 Saku Koivu .30 .75
PP5 Chris Drury .40 1.00
PP6 Ron Francis .20 .50

2000-01 Topps Premier Plus
COMPLETE SET (140) 30.00 60.00
1 Scott Gomez .15 .40
2 Brian Boucher .15 .40
3 Patrik Stefan .15 .40
4 David Legwand .20 .50
5 Tim Connolly .15 .40
6 Jaromir Jagr .60 1.50
7 Owen Nolan .15 .40
8 Patrick Roy .50 1.25
9 Joe Thornton .30 .75
10 Paul Kariya .20 .50
11 Mark Messier .40 1.00
12 Jeremy Roenick .30 .75
13 Jeff Friesen .15 .40
14 Al MacInnis .25 .60
15 Curtis Joseph .25 .60
16 Olaf Kolzig .20 .50
17 Dominik Hasek .30 .75
18 Arturs Irbe .15 .40
19 Joe Sakic .40 1.00
20 Sergei Fedorov .30 .75
21 Zigmund Palffy .20 .50
22 Jason Arnott .15 .40
23 Marian Hossa .20 .50
24 Pierre Turgeon .15 .40
25 Ron Tugnutt .15 .40
26 Valeri Bure .15 .40
27 Tony Amonte .15 .40
28 Jeff Hackett .15 .40
29 Mariusz Czerkawski .12 .30
30 Wade Redden .12 .30
31 Mark Recchi .25 .60
32 Jean-Sebastien Aubin .15 .40
33 Jason Allison .15 .40
34 Michael Peca .15 .40
35 Teemu Selanne .40 1.00
36 Martin Brodeur .50 1.25
37 Simon Gagne .20 .50
38 Chris Simon .15 .40
39 Doug Weight .20 .50
40 Jocelyn Thibault .15 .40
41 Ed Belfour .20 .50
42 Ray Bourque .20 .50
43 Mike Richter .20 .50
44 Curtis Leschyshyn .12 .30
45 Pavol Demitra .25 .60
46 Alexei Kovalev .12 .30
47 Brad Stuart .15 .40
48 Jarome Iginla .25 .60
49 Ron Francis .25 .60
50 Brendan Shanahan .20 .50
51 Rob Blake .20 .50
52 Miroslav Satan .12 .30
53 Theo Fleury .25 .60
54 John LeClair .20 .50
55 Roman Turek .15 .40
56 Brett Hull .40 1.00
57 Peter Forsberg .40 1.00
58 Steve Yzerman .50 1.25
59 Derian Hatcher .15 .40
60 Pavel Bure .20 .50
61 Patrik Elias .20 .50
62 Daniel Alfredsson .20 .50
63 Adam Oates .20 .50
64 Andrew Brunette .12 .30
65 Chris Pronger .20 .50
66 Mario Lemieux .75 2.00
67 Keith Tkachuk .20 .50
68 Markus Naslund .20 .50
69 Mike Modano .30 .75
70 Nicklas Lidstrom .20 .50
71 Scott Stevens .20 .50
72 Vincent Lecavalier .20 .50
73 Luc Robitaille .20 .50
74 Mats Sundin .20 .50
75 Milan Hejduk .15 .40
76 Rod Brind'amour .20 .50
77 Tommy Salo .15 .40
78 Byron Dafoe .15 .40
79 Doug Gilmour .25 .60
80 Guy Hebert .15 .40
81 Keith Primeau .15 .40
82 Chris Drury .15 .40
83 Saku Koivu .20 .50
84 Alexei Yashin .15 .40
85 Martin St. Louis .20 .50
86 Steve McCarthy .12 .30
87 Henrik Sedin .25 .60
88 Kris Beech .12 .30
89 Dimitri Kalinin .12 .30
90 Maxime Ouellet .20 .50
91 Shawn Heins .12 .30
92 Mika Noronen .20 .50
93 Taylor Pyatt .12 .30
94 Brent Johnson .15 .40
95 Oleg Saprykin .12 .30
96 Daniel Tkaczuk .15 .40
97 Daniel Sedin .25 .60
98 Milan Kraft .12 .30
99 Jeff Farkas .12 .30
100 Denis Shvidki .12 .30
101 Mathieu Garon .12 .30
102 Mike Mottau .12 .30
103 Andrei Markov .25 .60
104 Brad Richards .25 .60
105 Brian Swanson RC .25 .60
106 Josef Vasicek RC .60 1.50
107 Reto Von Arx RC .30 .75
108 Lubomir Sekeras RC .25 .60
109 Ruslan Fedotenko RC .25 .60
110 Roman Simicek RC .25 .60
111 Michel Riesen RC .30 .75
112 Petteri Nummelin RC .25 .60
113 Brad Tapper RC .25 .60
114 Alexander Kharitonov RC .25 .60
115 Andrew Raycroft RC .60 1.50
116 Ossi Vaananen RC .30 .75
117 Tyler Bouck RC .30 .75
118 Steven Reinprecht RC .40 1.00
119 Rostislav Klesla RC .60 1.50
120 Martin Havlat RC 1.00 2.50
121 Scott Hartnell RC .60 1.50
122 David Aebischer RC .75 2.00
123 Bryce Salvador RC .30 .75
124 Jani Hurme RC .25 .60
125 Eric Belanger RC .30 .75
126 Marty Turco RC 1.25 3.00
127 Rick DiPietro RC .50 1.25
128 Justin Williams RC .60 1.50
129 Dale Purinton RC .25 .60
130 Marian Gaborik RC 2.00 5.00
131 Petr Svoboda RC .30 .75
132 Niclas Wallin RC .25 .60
133 Petr Hubacek RC .25 .60
134 Colin White RC .25 .60
135 Greg Classen RC .25 .60
136 Roman Cechmanek RC .30 .75
137 Eric Boulton RC .25 .60
138 Sascha Goc RC .25 .60
139 Lubomir Visnovsky RC .50 1.25
140 Ronald Petrovicky RC .25 .60
NNO Scott Gomez CL .12 .30

2000-01 Topps Premier Plus Blue Ice
*1-104 VETS/250: 4X TO 10X BASIC CARDS
*105-140 ROOK/250: 2X TO 5X BASIC RC
11 Mark Messier 4.00 10.00

2000-01 Topps Premier Plus Aspirations
COMPLETE SET (10) 10.00 20.00
PA1 Scott Gomez .75 2.00
PA2 Vincent Lecavalier 1.25 3.00
PA3 Maxim Afinogenov .75 2.00
PA4 Milan Hejduk 1.25 3.00
PA5 Joe Thornton 2.00 5.00
PA6 Marian Hossa 1.25 3.00
PA7 Oleg Saprykin .75 2.00
PA8 Shane Willis .75 2.00
PA9 David Legwand 1.00 2.50
PA10 Tim Connolly .75 2.00

2000-01 Topps Premier Plus Club Signings
CS1 Billy Smith 8.00 20.00
CS2 John Vanbiesbrouck 10.00 25.00
CS3 John LeClair 8.00 20.00
CS4 Bobby Clarke 12.50 30.00
CS5 Luc Robitaille 8.00 20.00
CS6 Marcel Dionne 8.00 20.00
CSC1 J.V'brouck/B.Smith 30.00 80.00
CSC2 J.LeClair/B.Clarke 30.00 80.00
CSC3 L.Robitaille/M.Dionne 30.00 60.00

2000-01 Topps Premier Plus Game-Used Memorabilia
GPAO Adam Oates S 8.00 20.00
GPEB Ed Belfour S 20.00 50.00
GPJI Jarome Iginla S 12.00 30.00
GPJV John Vanbiesbrouck S 15.00 40.00
GPKB Kris Beech J 4.00 10.00
GPMB Max Balmochnyk J 4.00 10.00
GPMT Marty Turco J 8.00 20.00
GPOS Oleg Saprykin J 4.00 10.00
GPRF Rico Fata J 4.00 10.00
GPTP Taylor Pyatt J 4.00 10.00
GPTS Teemu Selanne S 12.00 30.00
GPVB Valeri Bure J 4.00 10.00
GPAOKB K.Beech/A.Oates 8.00 20.00
GPEBMT M.Turco/E.Belfour 30.00 80.00
GPJIRF R.Fata/J.Iginla 20.00 50.00
GPJVTP T.Pyatt/J.V'brouck 20.00 50.00
GPTSMB Balmoc'/Selanne 12.00 30.00
GPVBOS O.Saprykin/V.Bure 8.00 20.00

2000-01 Topps Premier Plus Masters of the Break
COMPLETE SET (20) 30.00 60.00
MB1 Jaromir Jagr 1.50 4.00
MB2 Teemu Selanne 1.00 2.50
MB3 Pavel Bure 1.25 3.00
MB4 Tony Amonte .75 2.00
MB5 Milan Hejduk 1.00 2.50
MB6 Patrik Elias .75 2.00
MB7 Paul Kariya 1.00 2.50
MB8 Peter Forsberg 2.50 6.00
MB9 Sergei Fedorov 2.00 5.00
MB10 Mike Modano 1.50 4.00
MB11 Martin Brodeur 2.50 6.00
MB12 Patrick Roy 5.00 12.00
MB13 Ed Belfour 1.00 2.50
MB14 Curtis Joseph 1.00 2.50
MB15 Dominik Hasek 2.00 5.00
MB16 Olaf Kolzig .60 1.50
MB17 Roman Turek .60 1.50
MB18 Brian Boucher 1.00 2.50
MB19 Mike Richter 1.00 2.50
MB20 Tommy Salo .60 1.50

2000-01 Topps Premier Plus Private Signings
CTW1 Scott Gomez Calder 5.00 12.00
PSBR Brad Richards 6.00 15.00
PSBS Brad Stuart 5.00 12.00
PSCP Chris Pronger 6.00 15.00
PSDS Daniel Sedin 8.00 20.00
PSEN Evgeni Nabokov 5.00 12.00
PSHS Henrik Sedin 8.00 20.00
PSJW Justin Williams 10.00 25.00
PSMB Martin Brodeur 15.00 40.00
PSMG Marian Gaborik 12.00 30.00
PSMK Milan Kraft 4.00 10.00
PSMT Marty Turco 8.00 20.00
PSSH Scott Hartnell 10.00 25.00

2000-01 Topps Premier Plus Rookies
COMPLETE SET (10) 10.00 20.00
*BLUE ICE/250: 1.2X TO 3X BASIC INSERT
PR1 Marian Gaborik 1.50 4.00
PR2 Henrik Sedin 1.25 3.00
PR3 Rostislav Klesla 1.25 3.00
PR4 Brad Richards 1.00 2.50
PR5 Justin Williams 1.25 3.00
PR6 Josef Vasicek 1.25 3.00
PR7 Daniel Sedin 1.25 3.00
PR8 Maxime Ouellet .75 2.00
PR9 Andrei Markov 1.00 2.50
PR10 Oleg Saprykin .60 1.50

2000-01 Topps Premier Plus Team
COMPLETE SET (10) 8.00 15.00
*BLUE ICE/250: .6X TO 1.5X BASIC INSERT
PT1 Paul Kariya .50 1.25
PT2 Peter Forsberg 1.50 4.00
PT3 John LeClair .50 1.25
PT4 Mike Modano 1.00 2.50
PT5 Martin Brodeur 1.50 4.00
PT6 Pavel Bure .50 1.25
PT7 Curtis Joseph .50 1.25
PT8 Jaromir Jagr 1.00 2.50
PT9 Chris Pronger .50 1.25
PT10 Teemu Selanne .50 1.25

2000-01 Topps Premier Plus Trophy Tribute
COMPLETE SET (15) 15.00 30.00
TT1 Dominik Hasek 1.25 3.00
TT2 Jaromir Jagr 1.00 2.50
TT3 Patrick Roy 3.00 8.00
TT4 Chris Pronger .50 1.25
TT5 Paul Kariya .60 1.50
TT6 Ed Belfour .60 1.50
TT7 Mark Messier .75 2.00
TT8 Ray Bourque 1.25 3.00
TT9 Steve Yzerman 3.00 8.00
TT10 Sergei Fedorov 1.25 3.00
TT11 Brett Hull .75 2.00
TT12 Ron Francis .50 1.25
TT13 Pavel Bure .75 2.00
TT14 Teemu Selanne .60 1.50
TT15 Brian Leetch .50 1.25

2000-01 Topps Premier Plus World Premier
COMPLETE SET (20) 30.00 60.00
WP1 Patrick Roy 5.00 12.00
WP2 Martin Brodeur 2.50 6.00
WP3 Chris Pronger .75 2.00
WP4 Sergei Zubov .60 1.50
WP5 Scott Stevens .75 2.00
WP6 Ray Bourque 2.00 5.00
WP7 Nicklas Lidstrom 1.00 2.50
WP8 Rob Blake .75 2.00
WP9 Paul Kariya 1.00 2.50
WP10 John LeClair 1.00 2.50
WP11 Keith Tkachuk 1.00 2.50
WP12 Brendan Shanahan 1.50 4.00
WP13 Vincent Lecavalier 1.00 2.50
WP14 Steve Yzerman 5.00 12.00
WP15 Mike Modano 1.50 4.00
WP16 Peter Forsberg 2.50 6.00
WP17 Pavel Bure 1.25 3.00
WP18 Teemu Selanne 1.00 2.50
WP19 Brett Hull 1.25 3.00
WP20 Jaromir Jagr 1.00 2.50

2003-04 Topps Pristine
1 Jean-Sebastien Giguere .75 2.00
2 Slava Kozlov .60 1.50
3 Steve Shields .60 1.50
4 Martin Biron .60 1.50
5 Roman Turek .60 1.50

6 Kevin Weekes .60 1.50
7 Kyle Calder .50 1.25
8 Patrik Elias .75 2.00
9 Rob Blake .75 2.00
10 Marty Turco .75 2.00
11 Bill Guerin .75 2.00
12 Nicklas Lidstrom .75 2.00
13 Mike Comrie .60 1.50
14 Roberto Luongo 1.25 3.00
15 Ziggy Palffy .75 2.00
16 Paul Kariya .75 2.00
17 Stanislav Chistov .50 1.25
18 Andrew Brunette .50 1.25
19 Richard Zednik .50 1.25
20 Martin Brodeur 2.00 5.00
21 Alexei Yashin .60 1.50
22 Brian Leetch .60 1.50
23 Patrick Lalime .60 1.50
24 Simon Gagne .75 2.00
25 Mike Johnson .50 1.25
26 Mario Lemieux 3.00 8.00
27 Alyn McCauley .50 1.25
28 Kyle McLaren .50 1.25
29 Brent Johnson .60 1.50
30 Vincent Lecavalier .75 2.00
31 Ed Belfour .75 2.00
32 Todd Bertuzzi .75 2.00
33 Brendan Morrison .60 1.50
34 Olaf Kolzig .75 2.00
35 Ilya Kovalchuk .75 2.00
36 Johan Hedberg .60 1.50
37 Mike Knuble .50 1.25
38 Ales Kotalik .50 1.25
39 Chris Drury .60 1.50
40 Joe Thornton 1.25 3.00
41 Dominik Hasek 1.25 3.00
42 Daniel Alfredsson .75 2.00
43 Marc Denis .60 1.50
44 Mike Modano 1.25 3.00
45 Sergei Fedorov 1.25 3.00
46 Henrik Zetterberg 1.00 2.50
47 Tommy Salo .60 1.50
48 Olli Jokinen .75 2.00
49 Felix Potvin 1.25 3.00
50 Dany Heatley .60 1.50
51 Marian Gaborik .75 2.00
52 Saku Koivu .75 2.00
53 Tomas Vokoun .60 1.50
54 Eric Brewer .50 1.25
55 Rick DiPietro .60 1.50
56 Mike Dunham .60 1.50
57 Marian Hossa .75 2.00
58 Jeremy Roenick 1.25 3.00
59 Brian Boucher .60 1.50
60 Milan Hejduk .60 1.50
61 Patrick Marleau .75 2.00
62 Pavol Demitra 1.00 2.50
63 Al MacInnis 1.00 2.50
64 Nikolai Khabibulin .75 2.00
65 Mats Sundin .75 2.00
66 Miroslav Satan .60 1.50
67 Sergei Gonchar .50 1.25
68 Pasi Nurminen .60 1.50
69 Glen Murray .60 1.50
70 Brett Hull 1.50 4.00
71 Jarome Iginla 1.00 2.50
72 Ron Francis 1.00 2.50
73 Tyler Arnason .50 1.25
74 Joe Sakic 1.50 4.00
75 David Aebischer .60 1.50
76 Geoff Sanderson .50 1.25
77 Derian Hatcher .50 1.25
78 Jocelyn Thibault .60 1.50
79 Curtis Joseph 1.00 2.50
80 Markus Naslund .75 2.00
81 Kristian Huselius .50 1.25
82 Alexander Frolov .60 1.50
83 Petr Sykora .60 1.50
84 Dwayne Roloson .60 1.50
85 Jose Theodore .75 2.00
86 David Legwand .60 1.50
87 Scott Stevens .75 2.00
88 Michael Peca .60 1.50
89 Alex Kovalev .60 1.50
90 Jaromir Jagr 2.50 6.00
91 Tony Amonte .60 1.50
92 Daymond Langkow .50 1.25
93 Martin Straka .50 1.25
94 Evgeni Nabokov .60 1.50
95 Chris Pronger .75 2.00
96 Martin St. Louis .75 2.00
97 Alexander Mogilny .60 1.50
98 Owen Nolan .75 2.00
99 Dan Cloutier .60 1.50
100 Peter Forsberg 1.50 4.00
101 Tuomo Ruutu C RC 2.00 5.00
102 Tuomo Ruutu U 2.50 6.00
103 Tuomo Ruutu R 4.00 10.00
104 Marc-Andre Fleury C RC 8.00 20.00
105 Marc-Andre Fleury U 10.00 25.00
106 Marc-Andre Fleury R 15.00 40.00
107 Patrice Bergeron C RC 6.00 15.00
108 Patrice Bergeron U 8.00 20.00
109 Patrice Bergeron R 12.00 30.00
110 Milan Michalek C RC 2.50 6.00
111 Milan Michalek U 3.00 8.00
112 Milan Michalek R 5.00 12.00
113 Dominic Moore C RC 1.25 3.00
114 Dominic Moore U 1.50 4.00
115 Dominic Moore R 2.50 6.00
116 Dustin Brown C RC 3.00 8.00
117 Dustin Brown U 4.00 10.00
118 Dustin Brown R 6.00 15.00
119 Nathan Horton C RC 3.00 8.00
120 Nathan Horton U 4.00 10.00
121 Nathan Horton R 6.00 15.00
122 Chris Higgins C RC 2.50 6.00
123 Chris Higgins U 3.00 8.00
124 Chris Higgins R 5.00 12.00
125 Antti Miettinen C RC 2.00 5.00
126 Antti Miettinen U 2.50 6.00
127 Antti Miettinen R 4.00 10.00
128 Tom Preissing C RC 1.50 4.00
129 Tom Preissing U 2.00 5.00
130 Tom Preissing R 3.00 8.00
131 Marek Svatos C RC 2.50 6.00
132 Marek Svatos U 3.00 8.00
133 Marek Svatos R 5.00 12.00
134 Peter Sejna C RC 1.50 4.00
135 Peter Sejna U 2.00 5.00
136 Peter Sejna R 3.00 8.00
137 Matt Stajan C RC 2.00 5.00
138 Matt Stajan U 2.50 6.00
139 Matt Stajan R 4.00 10.00
140 Jiri Hudler C RC 3.00 8.00
141 Jiri Hudler U 4.00 10.00
142 Jiri Hudler R 6.00 15.00
143 Joni Pitkanen C RC 2.00 5.00
144 Joni Pitkanen U 2.50 6.00
145 Joni Pitkanen R 4.00 10.00
146 Garnet Exelby C 1.25 3.00
147 Garnet Exelby U 1.50 4.00
148 Garnet Exelby R 2.50 6.00
149 Eric Staal C RC 6.00 15.00
150 Eric Staal U 8.00 20.00
151 Eric Staal R 12.00 30.00
152 Sean Bergenheim C RC 1.50 4.00
153 Sean Bergenheim U 2.00 5.00
154 Sean Bergenheim R 3.00 8.00
155 Gregory Campbell C RC 1.25 3.00
156 Gregory Campbell U 1.50 4.00
157 Gregory Campbell R 2.50 6.00
158 Dan Hamhuis C RC 1.50 4.00
159 Dan Hamhuis U 2.00 5.00
160 Dan Hamhuis R 3.00 8.00
161 Maxim Kondratiev C RC 1.25 3.00
162 Maxim Kondratiev U 1.50 4.00
163 Maxim Kondratiev R 2.50 6.00
164 Matthew Lombardi C RC 1.50 4.00
165 Matthew Lombardi U 2.00 5.00
166 Matthew Lombardi R 3.00 8.00
167 Alexander Semin C RC 6.00 15.00
168 Alexander Semin U 8.00 20.00
169 Alexander Semin R 12.00 30.00
170 John-Michael Liles C RC 1.50 4.00
171 John-Michael Liles U 2.00 5.00
172 John-Michael Liles R 3.00 8.00
173 Andrew Peters C RC 1.50 4.00
174 Andrew Peters U 2.00 5.00
175 Andrew Peters R 3.00 8.00
176 Dan Fritsche C RC 1.25 3.00
177 Dan Fritsche U 1.50 4.00
178 Dan Fritsche R 2.50 6.00
179 Antoine Vermette C RC 2.50 6.00
180 Antoine Vermette U 3.00 8.00
181 Antoine Vermette R 5.00 12.00
182 David Hale C RC 1.25 3.00
183 David Hale U 1.50 4.00
184 David Hale R 2.50 6.00
185 Joffrey Lupul C RC 3.00 8.00
186 Joffrey Lupul U 4.00 10.00
187 Joffrey Lupul R 6.00 15.00
188 Jordin Tootoo C RC 2.50 6.00
189 Jordin Tootoo U 3.00 8.00
190 Jordin Tootoo R 5.00 12.00

2003-04 Topps Pristine Gold Refractor Die Cuts

*1-100 VETS/33: 4X TO 10X BASIC CARDS
*COMMON ROOK/33: 1.5X TO 4X BASIC C
*UNCOMM.ROOK/33: 1.2X TO 3X BASIC U
*RARE ROOKIE/33: .8X TO 2X BASIC R

2003-04 Topps Pristine Refractors

*1-100 VET/59: 2.5X TO 6X BASIC CARDS
*COMMON ROOK/499: .5X TO 1.2X BASIC C
*UNCOMM.ROOK/199: .6X TO 1.5X BASIC U
*RARE ROOKIE/59: .5X TO 1.2X BASIC R

2003-04 Topps Pristine Autographs

*GOLD: 1.5X TO 4X BASIC GRP B-C
*GOLD: 1X TO 2.5X BASIC GRP A
PERN Rick Nash A 12.00 30.00
PEMT Marty Turco C 6.00 15.00
PEMN Markus Naslund B 6.00 15.00
PEJG Jean-Sebastien Giguere A 6.00 15.00
PEMH Milan Hejduk A 6.00 15.00
PEMS Martin St. Louis C 8.00 20.00
PESC Stanislav Chistov C 3.00 8.00

2003-04 Topps Pristine Jersey Portions

*REFRACTOR/25: 2X TO 5X BASIC JSY
PPJBMN Brendan Morrison A 3.00 8.00
PPJBMW Brenden Morrow A 3.00 8.00
PPJBRI Brad Richards A 6.00 15.00
PPJBRO Brian Rolston A 4.00 10.00
PPJDA Daniel Alfredsson A 3.00 8.00
PPJDBL Dan Blackburn A 4.00 10.00
PPJDC Dan Cloutier A 3.00 8.00
PPJDH Dany Heatley A 8.00 20.00
PPJDL David Legwand B 3.00 8.00
PPJED Eric Desjardins A 4.00 10.00
PPJEL Eric Lindros A 6.00 15.00
PPJFP Felix Potvin A 6.00 15.00
PPJIK Ilya Kovalchuk A 5.00 12.00
PPJJD J-P Dumont A 3.00 8.00
PPJJW Justin Williams A 3.00 8.00
PPJKP Keith Primeau A 4.00 10.00
PPJMA Maxim Afinogenov A 3.00 8.00
PPJMB Martin Biron A 4.00 10.00
PPJMG Marian Gaborik B 10.00 25.00
PPJMHE Milan Hejduk A 5.00 12.00
PPJMHO Marian Hossa A 4.00 10.00
PPJML Manny Legace A 6.00 15.00
PPJMSA Miroslav Satan A 4.00 10.00
PPJMSU Mats Sundin A 5.00 12.00
PPJMT Marty Turco B 5.00 12.00
PPJPL Patrick Lalime B 5.00 12.00
PPJPM Patrick Marleau A 3.00 8.00
PPJPR Patrick Roy B 12.00 30.00
PPJRB Rob Blake A 5.00 12.00
PPJRF Ron Francis A 4.00 10.00
PPJRL Roberto Luongo A 5.00 12.00
PPJSK Saku Koivu A 6.00 15.00
PPJTB Todd Bertuzzi B 4.00 10.00
PPJTV Tomas Vokoun A 4.00 10.00
PPJZP Zigmund Palffy A 3.00 8.00

2003-04 Topps Pristine Mini

PMMAF Marc-Andre Fleury 8.00 20.00
PMJTO Jordin Tootoo 2.50 6.00
PMJHU Jiri Hudler 3.00 8.00
PMPS Peter Sejna 1.50 4.00
PMAM Antti Miettinen 2.00 5.00
PMDB Dustin Brown 3.00 8.00
PMKW Kevin Weekes 1.50 4.00
PMSC Sebastien Caron 1.50 4.00
PMDR Dwayne Roloson 1.50 4.00
PMTS Tommy Salo 1.50 4.00
PMMDE Marc Denis 1.50 4.00
PMRE Robert Esche 1.25 3.00
PMTV Tomas Vokoun 1.50 4.00
PMSB Sean Burke 1.25 3.00
PMEN Evgeni Nabokov 1.50 4.00
PMCO Chris Osgood 2.00 5.00
PMPL Patrick Lalime 1.50 4.00
PMJT Jocelyn Thibault 1.50 4.00
PMRD Rick DiPietro 1.50 4.00
PMRC Roman Cechmanek 1.50 4.00
PMMBI Martin Biron 1.50 4.00
PMOK Olaf Kolzig 2.00 5.00
PMMT Marty Turco 2.00 5.00
PMDC Dan Cloutier 1.50 4.00
PMDA David Aebischer 1.50 4.00
PMPN Pasi Nurminen 1.50 4.00
PMRT Roman Turek 1.50 4.00
PMJSG Jean-Sebastien Giguere 2.00 5.00
PMMD Mike Dunham 1.50 4.00
PMRL Roberto Luongo 3.00 8.00
PMJTH Jose Theodore 3.00 8.00
PMFP Felix Potvin 3.00 8.00
PMNK Nikolai Khabibulin 2.00 5.00
PMEB Ed Belfour 2.00 5.00
PMMSO Matt Stajan 2.00 5.00
PMNH Nathan Horton 3.00 8.00
PMMB Martin Brodeur 5.00 12.00
PMDH Dominik Hasek 3.00 8.00
PMES Eric Staal 6.00 15.00
PMJL Joffrey Lupul 3.00 8.00
PMAJG J-S Giguere AU 12.50 30.00

2003-04 Topps Pristine Patches

PPDA Daniel Alfredsson 10.00 25.00
PPMA Maxim Afinogenov 8.00 20.00
PPMB Martin Biron 8.00 20.00
PPMSA Miroslav Satan 8.00 20.00
PPMST Marco Sturm 8.00 20.00
PPJD J-P Dumont 8.00 20.00
PPJW Justin Williams 8.00 20.00
PPBRO Brian Rolston 8.00 20.00
PPKP Keith Primeau 8.00 20.00
PPBM Brendan Morrison 8.00 20.00
PPDL David Legwand 8.00 20.00
PPAT Alex Tanguay 8.00 20.00
PPML Manny Legace 8.00 20.00
PPDB Dan Blackburn 8.00 20.00
PPMC Mike Comrie 10.00 25.00
PPRL Roberto Luongo 12.00 30.00
PPJI Jarome Iginla 15.00 40.00
PPEL Eric Lindros 15.00 40.00
PPTB Todd Bertuzzi 8.00 20.00
PPSG Simon Gagne 12.00 30.00
PPMHO Marian Hossa 12.00 30.00
PPSK Saku Koivu 12.00 30.00
PPMHE Milan Hejduk 10.00 25.00
PPMSU Mats Sundin 12.00 30.00
PPMN Markus Naslund 10.00 25.00
PPJL John LeClair 8.00 20.00
PPFP Felix Potvin 15.00 40.00
PPDH Dany Heatley 15.00 40.00
PPPF Peter Forsberg 15.00 40.00
PPPD Pavel Datsyuk 12.00 30.00
PPIK Ilya Kovalchuk 12.00 30.00
PPPR Patrick Roy 30.00 80.00
PPJS Joe Sakic 15.00 40.00
PPMG Marian Gaborik 20.00 50.00
PPMM Mike Modano 15.00 40.00
PPVL Vincent Lecavalier 15.00 40.00
PPRB Rob Blake 8.00 20.00
PPMT Marty Turco 8.00 20.00
PPKH Kristian Huselius 8.00 20.00
PPZP Zigmund Palffy 8.00 20.00
PPPL Patrick Lalime 8.00 20.00

2003-04 Topps Pristine Popular Demand Relics

*REFRACTOR/25: 1.5X TO 4X BASIC JSY
PDJT Joe Thornton C 8.00 20.00
PDPD Pavel Datsyuk C 6.00 15.00
PDPK Paul Kariya A 8.00 20.00
PDML Mario Lemieux A 20.00 50.00
PDSG Simon Gagne A 12.50 30.00
PDMN Markus Naslund A 6.00 15.00
PDJL John LeClair B 5.00 12.00
PDMM Mike Modano B 6.00 15.00
PDJSP Jason Spezza B 6.00 15.00
PDJJ Jaromir Jagr C 8.00 20.00
PDJI Jarome Iginla B 5.00 12.00
PDAZ Alexei Zhamnov B 4.00 10.00
PDMST Marco Sturm B 3.00 8.00
PDBG Bill Guerin C 4.00 10.00
PDMSK Martin Straka C 4.00 10.00
PDAY Alexei Yashin C 4.00 10.00
PDNK Nikolai Khabibulin C 4.00 10.00
PDTD Tie Domi B 4.00 10.00
PDKH Kristian Huselius C 3.00 8.00
PDTC Tim Connolly A 4.00 10.00
PDSN Scott Niedermayer B 4.00 10.00
PDJB Jay Bouwmeester C 4.00 10.00
PDMR Mark Recchi B 4.00 10.00
PDJTH Jose Theodore C 6.00 15.00
PDPB Pavel Bure C 5.00 12.00

2003-04 Topps Pristine Stick Portions

PPSMM Mark Messier 8.00 20.00
PPSSY Steve Yzerman 20.00 50.00
PPSVB Valeri Bure 3.00 8.00
PPSED Eric Desjardins 4.00 10.00
PPSPS Patrik Stefan 4.00 10.00
PPSAO Adam Oates 5.00 12.00
PPSDA Daniel Alfredsson 5.00 12.00
PPSDW Doug Weight 5.00 12.00
PPSJI Jarome Iginla 6.00 15.00
PPSCJ Curtis Joseph 5.00 12.00
PPSJL John LeClair 5.00 12.00
PPSMS Mats Sundin 5.00 12.00

2001-02 Topps Reserve

COMP.SET w/o SP's (100) 40.00 80.00
1 Joe Sakic .75 2.00
2 Patrik Elias .40 1.00
3 Mario Lemieux 1.50 4.00
4 Chris Pronger .40 1.00
5 Simon Gagne .40 1.00
6 Steve Yzerman 1.00 2.50
7 Bill Guerin .40 1.00
8 Pavel Bure .40 1.00
9 Mark Messier .75 2.00
10 Evgeni Nabokov .30 .75
11 Peter Bondra .40 1.00
12 Martin Havlat .30 .75
13 Mike Dunham .30 .75
14 Mike Comrie .30 .75
15 Ed Belfour .40 1.00
16 Tony Amonte .30 .75
17 Patrik Stefan .30 .75
18 Paul Kariya .40 1.00
19 Patrick Roy 1.00 2.50
20 Sean Burke .25 .60
21 Vincent Lecavalier .40 1.00
22 Henrik Sedin .50 1.25
23 Petr Sykora .25 .60
24 Marian Gaborik .40 1.00
25 Rod Brind'Amour .40 1.00
26 Miroslav Satan .30 .75
27 Zigmund Palffy .40 1.00
28 Sergei Fedorov .60 1.50
29 Ron Tugnutt .30 .75
30 Jason Allison .30 .75
31 Marian Hossa .40 1.00
32 John LeClair .40 1.00
33 Keith Tkachuk .40 1.00
34 Adam Oates .40 1.00
35 Johan Hedberg .30 .75
36 Saku Koivu .40 1.00
37 Peter Forsberg .75 2.00
38 Jarome Iginla .50 1.25
39 Nicklas Lidstrom .40 1.00
40 Martin Brodeur 1.00 2.50
41 Daniel Alfredsson .40 1.00
42 Alexei Kovalev .30 .75
43 Mats Sundin .40 1.00
44 Brian Leetch .30 .75
45 Owen Nolan .40 1.00
46 Cliff Ronning .25 .60
47 Mike Modano .60 1.50
48 Milan Hejduk .30 .75
49 Joe Thornton .60 1.50
50 Ray Ferraro .25 .60
51 Geoff Sanderson .25 .60
52 Roberto Luongo .60 1.50
53 Manny Fernandez .25 .60
54 Mark Recchi .50 1.25
55 Curtis Joseph .50 1.25
56 Philippe Boucher .25 .60
57 Patrick Lalime .30 .75
58 Rick DiPietro .30 .75
59 Adam Deadmarsh .25 .60
60 Pierre Turgeon .30 .75
61 Roman Turek .30 .75
62 Jeff Friesen .25 .60
63 Eric Lindros .60 1.50
64 Martin Straka .25 .60
65 Markus Naslund .40 1.00
66 J-P Dumont .25 .60
67 Daniel Sedin .50 1.25
68 Alexei Yashin .30 .75
69 Felix Potvin .60 1.50
70 Chris Drury .30 .75
71 Martin Biron .30 .75
72 Tommy Salo .30 .75
73 Stanislav Neckar .25 .60
74 Jaromir Jagr 1.25 3.00
75 Brendan Shanahan .40 1.00
76 Jose Theodore .40 1.00
77 Teemu Selanne .75 2.00
78 Alexander Mogilny .30 .75
79 Niclas Havelid .25 .60
80 Colin Forbes .25 .60
81 Michael Peca .30 .75
82 Jason Arnott .30 .75
83 Arturs Irbe .30 .75
84 Garry Valk .25 .60
85 Roman Cechmanek .30 .75
86 Scott Gomez .30 .75
87 Chris McAllister .25 .60
88 Shane Doan .30 .75
89 David Harlock .25 .60
90 Jeff O'Neill .30 .75
91 Rob Blake .40 1.00
92 Dominik Hasek .60 1.50
93 Olaf Kolzig .40 1.00
94 Brent Johnson .30 .75
95 Jeremy Roenick .60 1.50
96 Brad Richards .40 1.00
97 Steve Sullivan .25 .60
98 Alex Tanguay .30 .75
99 Brett Hull .75 2.00
100 Doug Weight .40 1.00
101 Niklas Hagman/1099 RC 2.00 5.00
102 Scott Clemmensen/1099 RC 1.50 4.00
103 Brian Sutherby/1099 RC 1.50 4.00
104 Erik Cole/1599 RC 3.00 8.00
105 Vaclav Nedorost/1599 RC 1.50 4.00
106 Jaroslav Bednar/1099 RC 1.50 4.00
107 Nick Schultz/699 RC 2.00 5.00
108 Jiri Dopita/699 RC 2.00 5.00
109 Krys Kolanos/1599 RC 1.50 4.00
110 Jukka Hentunen/1099 RC 1.50 4.00
111 Niko Kapanen/699 RC 3.00 8.00
112 Timo Parssinen/1099 RC 2.00 5.00
113 Kristian Huselius/1599 RC 2.50 6.00
114 A.Salomonsson RC/699 2.00 5.00
115 Ilya Kovalchuk/1599 RC 8.00 20.00
116 Dan Blackburn/1599 RC 2.00 5.00
117 Pavel Datsyuk/699 RC 15.00 40.00
118 Peter Smrek/699 RC 2.00 5.00
119 Jeff Jillson/1099 RC 1.50 4.00
120 Nikita Alexeev/1599 RC 1.50 4.00
121 Scott Nichol/699 RC 2.00 5.00

2001-02 Topps Reserve Jerseys

*EMBLEMS: 1X TO 2.5X JERSEYS
*NAME PLATES: 1X TO 2.5X JERSEYS
*PATCHES: 1.2X TO 3X JERSEYS
AK Alexei Kovalev 3.00 8.00
AO Adam Oates 3.00 8.00
AZ Alexei Zhamnov 3.00 8.00
BB Brian Boucher 3.00 8.00
BL Brian Leetch 5.00 12.00
CD Chris Drury 4.00 10.00
DH Derian Hatcher 3.00 8.00
DM Darren McCarty 5.00 12.00
DY Dimitri Yushkevich 3.00 8.00
EB Ed Belfour 5.00 12.00
ED Eric Desjardins 3.00 8.00
JH Jeff Hackett 3.00 8.00
JI Jarome Iginla 6.00 15.00
JL John LeClair 4.00 10.00
JS Joe Sakic 6.00 15.00
JT Joe Thornton 8.00 20.00
KJ Kenny Jonsson 3.00 8.00
KO Krzysztof Oliwa 3.00 8.00
MB Martin Brodeur 8.00 20.00
MC Mariusz Czerkawski 3.00 8.00
ML Mario Lemieux 10.00 25.00
MM Mike Mottau 3.00 8.00
MP Matt Pettinger 3.00 8.00
MR Mark Recchi 4.00 10.00
MT Marty Turco 5.00 12.00
MY Mike York 3.00 8.00
OS Oleg Saprykin 3.00 8.00
PB Pavel Bure 8.00 20.00
PF Peter Forsberg 6.00 15.00
PK Paul Kariya 5.00 12.00
PM Patrick Marleau 4.00 10.00
PR Patrick Roy 12.00 30.00
RL Robert Lang 3.00 8.00
SB Sean Burke 3.00 8.00
SF Sergei Fedorov 6.00 15.00
SG Simon Gagne 5.00 12.00
SK Saku Koivu 5.00 12.00
SM Shawn McEachern 3.00 8.00
SS Sergei Samsonov 5.00 12.00
SZ Sergei Zubov 3.00 8.00
TA Tony Amonte 4.00 10.00
TD Tie Domi 5.00 12.00
TF Theo Fleury 4.00 10.00
TK Tomas Kloucek 3.00 8.00
TL Trevor Letowski 3.00 8.00
TV Tomas Vokoun 5.00 12.00
VL Vincent Lecavalier 5.00 12.00
WR Wade Redden 3.00 8.00
DAB Daniel Briere 4.00 10.00
DOB Donald Brashear 4.00 10.00
JAI Jason Allison 4.00 10.00
JAR Jason Arnott 4.00 10.00
MIS Miroslav Satan 4.00 10.00
MSA Marc Savard 4.00 10.00
MST Martin Straka 4.00 10.00
ROF Ron Francis 4.00 10.00

2001-02 Topps Reserve Numbers

*NUMBERS: 1X TO 2.5X JERSEYS
JAH Jan Hlavac 12.50 30.00

2000-01 Topps Stars

COMPLETE SET (150) 15.00 40.00
1 Vincent Lecavalier .25 .60
2 Patrick Roy .60 1.50
3 Scott Gomez .20 .50
4 Steve Yzerman .60 1.50
5 Paul Kariya .25 .60
6 Dominik Hasek .40 1.00
7 Mike Modano .40 1.00
8 Zigmund Palffy .25 .60
9 John LeClair .25 .60
10 Mats Sundin .25 .60
11 Owen Nolan .25 .60
12 Tony Amonte .20 .50
13 Patrik Stefan .20 .50
14 Brett Hull .50 1.25
15 Chris Pronger .25 .60
16 Jeremy Roenick .40 1.00
17 Martin Brodeur .60 1.50
18 Doug Weight .25 .60
19 Ray Bourque .40 1.00
20 Olaf Kolzig .25 .60
21 Jaromir Jagr .75 2.00
22 Daniel Alfredsson .25 .60
23 Jeff Hackett .15 .40
24 Jason Allison .20 .50
25 Joe Sakic .50 1.25
26 Brendan Shanahan .25 .60
27 David Legwand .25 .60
28 Tim Connolly .15 .40
29 Mark Recchi .30 .75
30 Brad Stuart .20 .50
31 Pierre Turgeon .20 .50
32 Ed Belfour .25 .60
33 Valeri Bure .20 .50
34 Pavel Bure .25 .60
35 Teemu Selanne .50 1.25
36 Patrik Elias .25 .60
37 Mattias Ohlund .15 .40
38 Rod Brind'Amour .25 .60
39 Derian Hatcher .20 .50
40 Peter Forsberg .50 1.25
41 Eric Lindros .40 1.00
42 Curtis Joseph .30 .75
43 Keith Tkachuk .25 .60
44 Mike Ricci .15 .40
45 Al MacInnis .30 .75
46 Nicklas Lidstrom .25 .60
47 Rob Blake .25 .60
48 Scott Stevens .25 .60
49 Milan Hejduk .20 .50
50 Theo Fleury .30 .75
51 Joe Thornton .40 1.00
52 Tommy Salo .20 .50
53 Eric Desjardins .20 .50
54 Pavol Demitra .30 .75
55 Adam Oates .25 .60
56 Jeff Friesen .15 .40
57 Mariusz Czerkawski .15 .40
58 Luc Robitaille .25 .60
59 Jeff O'Neill .20 .50
60 Andrew Brunette .15 .40
61 Fred Brathwaite .20 .50
62 Robert Svehla .15 .40
63 Kimmo Timonen .15 .40
64 Teppo Numminen .15 .40
65 Nikolai Antropov .20 .50
66 Marian Hossa .25 .60
67 Joe Nieuwendyk .20 .50
68 Michael Peca .20 .50
69 Saku Koivu .25 .60
70 Alexei Kovalev .20 .50
71 Sergei Gonchar .15 .40
72 Brian Leetch .20 .50
73 Ryan Smyth .20 .50
74 Jarome Iginla .30 .75
75 Byron Dafoe .20 .50
76 Ray Whitney .20 .50
77 Wade Redden .15 .40
78 Pavel Kubina .15 .40
79 Markus Naslund .25 .60
80 Brian Boucher .20 .50
81 Martin Rucinsky .15 .40
82 Roman Turek .20 .50
83 Jocelyn Thibault .20 .50
84 Miroslav Satan .15 .40
85 Cliff Ronning .15 .40
86 Mike Richter .25 .60
87 Chris Chelios .25 .60
88 Arturs Irbe .20 .50
89 Steve Thomas .15 .40
90 Felix Potvin .40 1.00
91 Jason Arnott .20 .50
92 Mark Messier .50 1.25
93 Scott Pellerin .15 .40
94 John Vanbiesbrouck .25 .60
95 Dave Andreychuk .25 .60
96 Paul Coffey .25 .60
97 Ron Tugnutt .20 .50
98 Larry Robinson .25 .60
99 Billy Smith .25 .60
100 Mario Lemieux 1.50 4.00
101 Martin Havlat RC 1.00 2.50
102 Petr Hubacek RC .30 .75
103 Niclas Wallin RC .40 1.00
104 Alexander Khavanov RC .30 .75
105 Roman Cechmanek RC .40 1.00
106 Bryce Salvador RC .40 1.00
107 Jonas Ronnqvist RC .30 .75
108 Rostislav Klesla RC .75 2.00
109 Justin Williams RC .75 2.00
110 Sascha Goc RC .30 .75
111 Andrew Raycroft RC .75 2.00
112 Marty Turco RC .60 1.50
113 Marian Gaborik RC 1.00 2.50
114 Josef Vasicek RC .75 2.00
115 Steven Reinprecht RC .50 1.25
116 Jani Hurme RC .30 .75
117 David Aebischer RC .60 1.50
118 Dale Purinton RC .30 .75
119 Jarno Kultanen RC .30 .75
120 Petr Svoboda RC .40 1.00
121 Eric Belanger RC .40 1.00
122 Petteri Nummelin RC .30 .75
123 Michel Riesen RC .40 1.00
124 Jason Labarbera RC .40 1.00
125 Tyler Bouck RC .30 .75
126 Martin Brodeur SL .60 1.50
127 Pavel Bure SL .25 .60
128 Peter Forsberg SL .50 1.25
129 Scott Gomez SL .20 .50
130 Dominik Hasek SL .40 1.00
131 Brett Hull SL .50 1.25
132 Jaromir Jagr SL .75 2.00
133 Curtis Joseph SL .30 .75
134 Paul Kariya SL .25 .60
135 Chris Pronger SL .25 .60
136 Patrick Roy SL .60 1.50
137 Joe Sakic SL .50 1.25
138 Teemu Selanne SL .50 1.25
139 Steve Yzerman SL .60 1.50
140 Vincent Lecavalier SL .25 .60
141 Samuel Pahlsson SL .15 .40
142 Maxime Ouellet SL .25 .60
143 Kris Beech SL .15 .40
144 Henrik Sedin SL .30 .75
145 Daniel Sedin SL .30 .75
146 Milan Kraft SL .15 .40
147 Marty Turco SL .20 .50
148 Oleg Saprykin SL .15 .40
149 Brent Johnson SL .20 .50
150 Marian Gaborik SL .30 .75

2000-01 Topps Stars Blue

*1-100 VETS/299: 4X TO 10X BASIC CARDS
*101-125 ROOK/299: 2X TO 5X BASIC RC
*126-150 SL/99: 6X TO 15X BASIC SL

2000-01 Topps Stars All-Star Authority

COMPLETE SET (11) 8.00 15.00
ASA1 Ray Bourque .60 1.50
ASA2 Brett Hull .40 1.00
ASA3 Mark Messier .40 1.00
ASA4 Patrick Roy 2.00 5.00
ASA5 Jaromir Jagr .60 1.50
ASA6 Dominik Hasek .60 1.50
ASA7 Teemu Selanne .40 1.00
ASA8 Steve Yzerman 2.00 5.00
ASA9 Joe Sakic .60 1.50
ASA10 Pavel Bure .50 1.25
ASA11 John LeClair .40 1.00

2000-01 Topps Stars Autographs

ABB Brian Boucher 6.00 15.00
ACP Chris Pronger 10.00 25.00
ALR Larry Robinson 10.00 25.00
AML Mario Lemieux 75.00 150.00
AMM Mike Modano 15.00 40.00
AMY Mike York 6.00 15.00
AVL Vincent Lecavalier 10.00 25.00
ABSM Billy Smith 12.00 30.00
ABST Brad Stuart 6.00 15.00

2000-01 Topps Stars Game Gear

GGAG Adam Graves J 3.00 8.00
GGCP Chris Pronger J 4.00 10.00
GGDC Don Cherry Suit 10.00 25.00
GGDCA D.Cherry Suit/AU 40.00 100.00
GGDL David Legwand J 3.00 8.00
GGDM Darren McCarty J 3.00 8.00
GGJA Jason Allison J 3.00 8.00
GGKT Keith Tkachuk S 10.00 25.00
GGMC Mariusz Czerkawski J 3.00 8.00
GGML Martin Lapointe J 3.00 8.00
GGMM Mike Modano S 8.00 20.00
GGMR Mike Richter J 4.00 10.00
GGPH Phil Housley J 3.00 8.00
GGPR Patrick Roy J 15.00 40.00
GGRT Ron Tugnutt S 8.00 20.00
GGSZ Sergei Zubov J 3.00 8.00
GGTA Tony Amonte J 3.00 8.00
GGTS Teemu Selanne J 4.00 10.00
GGZP Zigmund Palffy S 10.00 25.00
GGMR Mark Recchi S 10.00 25.00
GGCP Chris Pronger J/AU 100.00 200.00
GGMM Mike Modano S/AU 150.00 300.00

2000-01 Topps Stars Progression

COMPLETE SET (9) 15.00 40.00
P1 M.Lemieux
Modano
Lecav 3.00 8.00
P2 M.Lemieux
Forsberg
Stefan 3.00 8.00
P3 M.Lemieux
Yzerman
Gomez 3.00 8.00
P4 B.Smith
Roy
Loungo 3.00 8.00
P5 B.Smith
Brodeur
Turco 2.00 5.00
P6 B.Smith
Belfour
Boucher 1.25 3.00
P7 Robinson
S.Stevens
Klesla .75 2.00
P8 Robinson
Bourque
Stuart 2.00 5.00
P9 Robinson
Pronger
Skoula .75 2.00

2000-01 Topps Stars Walk of Fame

COMPLETE SET (10) 10.00 20.00
WF1 Pavel Bure .60 1.50
WF2 Paul Kariya .60 1.50
WF3 Jaromir Jagr .75 2.00
WF4 Peter Forsberg 1.25 3.00
WF5 Mike Modano .60 1.50
WF6 Patrick Roy 2.50 6.00
WF7 Steve Yzerman 2.50 6.00
WF8 Dominik Hasek 1.00 2.50
WF9 John LeClair .60 1.50
WF10 Martin Brodeur 1.25 3.00

2019-20 Topps Stickers

1 Anaheim Ducks FOIL .12 .30
2 Anaheim Ducks HL .12 .30
3 Ryan Getzlaf FOIL .15 .40
4 Jakob Silfverberg FOIL .10 .25
5 Adam Henrique FOIL .12 .30
6 Rickard Rakell .12 .30
7 Nick Ritchie .10 .25
8 Hampus Lindholm .10 .25
9 Cam Fowler .15 .40
10 Ondrej Kase .10 .25
11 Carter Rowney .10 .25
12 Josh Manson .10 .25
13 John Gibson .15 .40
14 Ryan Miller .15 .40
15 Ryan Getzlaf .15 .40
16 Jakob Silfverberg .10 .25
17 Adam Henrique .12 .30
18 Arizona Coyotes FOIL .12 .30
19 Arizona Coyotes HL .12 .30
20 Clayton Keller FOIL .20 .50
21 Oliver Ekman-Larsson FOIL .15 .40
22 Alex Galchenyuk FOIL .10 .25
23 Carl Soderberg .10 .25
24 Phil Kessel .15 .40
25 Vinnie Hinostroza .12 .30
26 Derek Stepan .10 .25
27 Brad Richardson .10 .25
28 Alex Goligoski .12 .30
29 Lawson Crouse .10 .25
30 Darcy Kuemper .15 .40
31 Antti Raanta .15 .40
32 Clayton Keller .20 .50
33 Oliver Ekman-Larsson .15 .40
34 Niklas Hjalmarsson .10 .25
35 Boston Bruins FOIL .12 .30
36 Boston Bruins HL .12 .30
37 David Pastrnak FOIL .40 1.00
38 Patrice Bergeron FOIL .20 .50
39 David Krejci FOIL .15 .40
40 Brad Marchand .30 .75
41 Torey Krug .12 .30
42 Jake DeBrusk .15 .40
43 Danton Heinen .12 .30
44 Charlie McAvoy .20 .50
45 Sean Kuraly .10 .25
46 Zdeno Chara .15 .40
47 Tuukka Rask .20 .50
48 Jaroslav Halak .15 .40
49 David Pastrnak .40 1.00
50 Patrice Bergeron .20 .50
51 David Krejci .15 .40
52 Buffalo Sabres FOIL .12 .30
53 Buffalo Sabres HL .12 .30
54 Jack Eichel FOIL .25 .60
55 Sam Reinhart FOIL .30 .75
56 Rasmus Dahlin FOIL .20 .50
57 Jeff Skinner .15 .40
58 Rasmus Ristolainen .10 .25
59 Conor Sheary .15 .40
60 Kyle Okposo .10 .25
61 Evan Rodrigues .12 .30
62 Casey Mittelstadt .15 .40
63 Carter Hutton .12 .30
64 Linus Ullmark .15 .40
65 Colin Miller .10 .25
66 Jack Eichel .25 .60
67 Sam Reinhart .30 .75
68 Rasmus Dahlin .20 .50
69 Calgary Flames FOIL .12 .30
70 Calgary Flames HL .12 .30
71 Johnny Gaudreau FOIL .25 .60
72 Elias Lindholm FOIL .15 .40
73 Matthew Tkachuk FOIL .30 .75
74 Sean Monahan .10 .25
75 Mark Giordano .15 .40

76 Mikael Backlund .12 .30
77 Michael Frolik .12 .30
78 T.J. Brodie .12 .30
79 Noah Hanifin .15 .40
80 David Rittich .12 .30
81 Milan Lucic .12 .30
82 Johnny Gaudreau .25 .60
83 Elias Lindholm .15 .40
84 Matthew Tkachuk .30 .75
85 Sam Bennett .25 .60
86 Carolina Hurricanes FOIL .12 .30
87 Carolina Hurricanes HL .12 .30
88 Sebastian Aho FOIL .25 .60
89 Teuvo Teravainen FOIL .15 .40
90 Justin Williams FOIL .12 .30
91 Jake Gardiner .10 .25
92 James Reimer .15 .40
93 Dougie Hamilton .12 .30
94 Andrei Svechnikov .20 .50
95 Trevor van Riemsdyk .12 .30
96 Jaccob Slavin .12 .30
97 Brett Pesce .10 .25
98 Jordan Staal .12 .30
99 Petr Mrazek .15 .40
100 Sebastian Aho .25 .60
101 Teuvo Teravainen .15 .40
102 Justin Williams .12 .30
103 Chicago Blackhawks FOIL .12 .30
104 Chicago Blackhawks HL .12 .30
105 Patrick Kane FOIL .30 .75
106 Jonathan Toews FOIL .25 .60
107 Alex DeBrincat FOIL .20 .50
108 Andrew Shaw .10 .25
109 Erik Gustafsson .10 .25
110 Brandon Saad .12 .30
111 Duncan Keith .12 .30
112 Brent Seabrook .10 .25
113 David Kampf .10 .25
114 Corey Crawford .15 .40
115 Collin Delia .10 .25
116 Robin Lehner .12 .30
117 Patrick Kane .30 .75
118 Jonathan Toews .25 .60
119 Alex DeBrincat .20 .50
120 Colorado Avalanche FOIL .12 .30
121 Colorado Avalanche HL .12 .30
122 Nathan MacKinnon FOIL .60 1.50
123 Mikko Rantanen FOIL .40 1.00
124 Gabriel Landeskog FOIL .20 .50
125 Nazem Kadri .20 .50
126 J.T. Compher .10 .25
127 Colin Wilson .12 .30
128 Samuel Girard .10 .25
129 Tyson Jost .12 .30
130 Philipp Grubauer .15 .40
131 Joonas Donskoi .10 .25
132 Nathan MacKinnon .60 1.50
133 Mikko Rantanen .40 1.00
134 Gabriel Landeskog .20 .50
135 Cale Makar .75 2.00
136 Nikita Zadorov .10 .25
137 Columbus Blue Jackets FOIL .12 .30
138 Columbus Blue Jackets HL .12 .30
139 Cam Atkinson FOIL .15 .40
140 Pierre-Luc Dubois FOIL .12 .30
141 Seth Jones FOIL .15 .40
142 Josh Anderson .12 .30
143 Zach Werenski .25 .60
144 Boone Jenner .15 .40
145 Oliver Bjorkstrand .12 .30
146 Nick Foligno .12 .30
147 Alexander Wennberg .10 .25
148 Joonas Korpisalo .15 .40
149 Cam Atkinson .15 .40
150 Pierre-Luc Dubois .12 .30
151 Seth Jones .15 .40
152 Ryan Murray .12 .30
153 Riley Nash .10 .25
154 Dallas Stars FOIL .12 .30
155 Dallas Stars HL .12 .30
156 Tyler Seguin FOIL .20 .50
157 Alexander Radulov FOIL .15 .40
158 Ben Bishop FOIL .12 .30
159 Jamie Benn .15 .40
160 John Klingberg .15 .40
161 Miro Heiskanen .20 .50
162 Esa Lindell .12 .30
163 Radek Faksa .12 .30
164 Mattias Janmark .10 .25
165 Roope Hintz .20 .50
166 Anton Khudobin .15 .40
167 Joe Pavelski .20 .50
168 Tyler Seguin .20 .50
169 Alexander Radulov .15 .40
170 Ben Bishop .12 .30
171 Detroit Red Wings FOIL .12 .30
172 Detroit Red Wings HL .12 .30
173 Dylan Larkin FOIL .20 .50
174 Andreas Athanasiou FOIL .12 .30
175 Anthony Mantha FOIL .12 .30
176 Tyler Bertuzzi .12 .30
177 Frans Nielsen .10 .25
178 Mike Green .12 .30
179 Luke Glendening .10 .25
180 Filip Hronek .10 .25
181 Jimmy Howard .12 .30
182 Jonathan Bernier .12 .30
183 Valtteri Filppula .10 .25
184 Dylan Larkin .20 .50
185 Andreas Athanasiou .12 .30
186 Anthony Mantha .12 .30
187 Justin Abdelkader .12 .30
188 Edmonton Oilers FOIL .12 .30
189 Edmonton Oilers HL .12 .30
190 Connor McDavid FOIL .75 2.00
191 Leon Draisaitl FOIL .50 1.25
192 Ryan Nugent-Hopkins FOIL .20 .50
193 Mike Smith .10 .25
194 Darnell Nurse .12 .30
195 Alex Chiasson .12 .30
196 Oscar Klefbom .15 .40
197 Zack Kassian .10 .25
198 Adam Larsson .12 .30
199 Jesse Puljujarvi .15 .40
200 Mikko Koskinen .10 .25
201 Connor McDavid .75 2.00
202 Leon Draisaitl .50 1.25
203 Ryan Nugent-Hopkins .20 .50
204 Kris Russell .10 .25
205 Florida Panthers FOIL .12 .30
206 Florida Panthers HL .12 .30
207 Aleksander Barkov FOIL .25 .60
208 Jonathan Huberdeau FOIL .20 .50
209 Evgeny Dadonov FOIL .10 .25
210 Mike Hoffman .10 .25
211 Keith Yandle .10 .25
212 Frank Vatrano .12 .30
213 Aaron Ekblad .20 .50
214 Vincent Trocheck .15 .40
215 Mike Matheson .12 .30
216 Brett Connolly .10 .25
217 Sergei Bobrovsky .25 .60
218 Aleksander Barkov .25 .60
219 Jonathan Huberdeau .20 .50
220 Evgenii Dadonov .12 .30
221 Denis Malgin .10 .25
222 Los Angeles Kings FOIL .12 .30
223 Los Angeles Kings HL .12 .30
224 Dustin Brown FOIL .15 .40
225 Drew Doughty FOIL .20 .50
226 Ilya Kovalchuk FOIL .15 .40
227 Anze Kopitar .25 .60
228 Tyler Toffoli .15 .40
229 Alex Iafallo .10 .25
230 Jeff Carter .12 .30
231 Adrian Kempe .15 .40
232 Austin Wagner .10 .25
233 Kyle Clifford .10 .25
234 Jonathan Quick .20 .50
235 Jack Campbell .15 .40
236 Dustin Brown .15 .40
237 Drew Doughty .20 .50
238 Ilya Kovalchuk .15 .40
239 Minnesota Wild FOIL .12 .30
240 Minnesota Wild HL .12 .30
241 Eric Staal FOIL .15 .40
242 Ryan Suter FOIL .12 .30
243 Devan Dubnyk FOIL .12 .30
244 Zach Parise .15 .40
245 Jared Spurgeon .15 .40
246 Jason Zucker .15 .40
247 Mikko Koivu .12 .30
248 Jordan Greenway .10 .25
249 Matt Dumba .12 .30
250 Marcus Foligno .12 .30
251 Alex Stalock .10 .25
252 Eric Staal .15 .40
253 Ryan Suter .12 .30
254 Devan Dubnyk .12 .30
255 Ryan Donato .12 .30
256 Montreal Canadiens FOIL .12 .30
257 Montreal Canadiens HL .12 .30
258 Max Domi FOIL .15 .40
259 Tomas Tatar FOIL .10 .25
260 Jonathan Drouin FOIL .12 .30
261 Carey Price .30 .75
262 Phillip Danault .15 .40
263 Brendan Gallagher .15 .40
264 Jeff Petry .15 .40
265 Jesperi Kotkaniemi .15 .40
266 Shea Weber .15 .40
267 Keith Kinkaid .10 .25
268 Nick Cousins .10 .25
269 Max Domi .15 .40
270 Tomas Tatar .10 .25
271 Jonathan Drouin .12 .30
272 Victor Mete .10 .25
273 Nashville Predators FOIL .12 .30
274 Nashville Predators HL .12 .30
275 Roman Josi FOIL .15 .40
276 Filip Forsberg FOIL .25 .60
277 Pekka Rinne FOIL .15 .40
278 Ryan Johansen .12 .30
279 Viktor Arvidsson .10 .25
280 Mattias Ekholm .12 .30
281 Ryan Ellis .12 .30
282 Craig Smith .10 .25
283 Nick Bonino .10 .25
284 Colton Sissons .10 .25
285 Juuse Saros .20 .50
286 Roman Josi .15 .40
287 Filip Forsberg .25 .60
288 Pekka Rinne .15 .40
289 Kyle Turris .12 .30
290 New Jersey Devils FOIL .12 .30
291 New Jersey Devils HL .12 .30
292 Kyle Palmieri FOIL .12 .30
293 Nico Hischier FOIL .25 .60
294 Taylor Hall FOIL .15 .40
295 P.K. Subban .20 .50
296 Travis Zajac .10 .25
297 Damon Severson .10 .25
298 Blake Coleman .12 .30
299 Jesper Bratt .15 .40
300 Will Butcher .12 .30
301 Pavel Zacha .12 .30
302 Andy Greene .10 .25
303 Cory Schneider .15 .40
304 Kyle Palmieri .12 .30
305 Nico Hischier .25 .60
306 Taylor Hall .15 .40
307 New York Islanders FOIL .12 .30
308 New York Islanders HL .12 .30
309 Mathew Barzal FOIL .20 .50
310 Josh Bailey FOIL .12 .30
311 Anders Lee FOIL .12 .30
312 Semyon Varlamov .15 .40
313 Brock Nelson .15 .40
314 Jordan Eberle .15 .40
315 Ryan Pulock .12 .30
316 Casey Cizikas .10 .25
317 Anthony Beauvillier .10 .25
318 Leo Komarov .10 .25
319 Thomas Greiss .12 .30
320 Mathew Barzal .20 .50
321 Josh Bailey .12 .30
322 Anders Lee .12 .30
323 Nick Leddy .10 .25
324 New York Rangers FOIL .12 .30
325 New York Rangers HL .12 .30
326 Mika Zibanejad FOIL .20 .50
327 Chris Kreider FOIL .20 .50
328 Henrik Lundqvist FOIL .40 1.00
329 Jacob Trouba .12 .30
330 Artemi Panarin .30 .75
331 Pavel Buchnevich .12 .30
332 Ryan Strome .15 .40
333 Brady Skjei .12 .30
334 Jesper Fast .10 .25
335 Lias Andersson .12 .30
336 Filip Chytil .12 .30
337 Alexandar Georgiev .15 .40
338 Mika Zibanejad .20 .50
339 Chris Kreider .20 .50
340 Henrik Lundqvist .40 1.00
341 Ottawa Senators FOIL .12 .30
342 Ottawa Senators HL .12 .30
343 Thomas Chabot FOIL .15 .40
344 Chris Tierney FOIL .12 .30
345 Bobby Ryan FOIL .12 .30
346 Brady Tkachuk .25 .60
347 Colin White .10 .25
348 Mikkel Boedker .10 .25
349 Zack Smith .10 .25
350 Dylan DeMelo .10 .25
351 Craig Anderson .12 .30
352 Anders Nilsson .10 .25
353 Artem Anisimov .10 .25
354 Thomas Chabot .15 .40
355 Chris Tierney .12 .30
356 Bobby Ryan .12 .30
357 Christian Jaros .10 .25
358 Philadelphia Flyers FOIL .12 .30
359 Philadelphia Flyers HL .12 .30
360 Claude Giroux FOIL .15 .40
361 Sean Couturier FOIL .12 .30
362 Jakub Voracek FOIL .12 .30
363 Travis Konecny .15 .40
364 James van Riemsdyk .12 .30
365 Shayne Gostisbehere .15 .40
366 Travis Sanheim .10 .25
367 Oskar Lindblom .12 .30
368 Scott Laughton .10 .25
369 Nolan Patrick .15 .40
370 Carter Hart .15 .40
371 Brian Elliott .12 .30
372 Claude Giroux .15 .40
373 Sean Couturier .12 .30
374 Jakub Voracek .12 .30
375 Pittsburgh Penguins FOIL .12 .30
376 Pittsburgh Penguins HL .12 .30
377 Sidney Crosby FOIL .60 1.50
378 Jake Guentzel FOIL .25 .60
379 Evgeni Malkin FOIL .30 .75
380 Dominik Kahun .10 .25
381 Kris Letang .20 .50
382 Patric Hornqvist .10 .25
383 Bryan Rust .15 .40
384 Dominik Simon .10 .25
385 Justin Schultz .15 .40
386 Matt Murray .15 .40
387 Casey DeSmith .12 .30
388 Sidney Crosby .60 1.50
389 Jake Guentzel .25 .60
390 Evgeni Malkin .30 .75
391 Alex Galchenyuk .10 .25
392 San Jose Sharks FOIL .12 .30
393 San Jose Sharks HL .12 .30
394 Brent Burns FOIL .15 .40
395 Tomas Hertl FOIL .15 .40
396 Timo Meier FOIL .15 .40
397 Logan Couture .20 .50
398 Evander Kane .15 .40
399 Kevin Labanc .10 .25
400 Joe Thornton .25 .60
401 Erik Karlsson .20 .50
402 Martin Jones .12 .30
403 Aaron Dell .10 .25
404 Brent Burns .15 .40
405 Tomas Hertl .15 .40
406 Timo Meier .15 .40
407 Marc-Edouard Vlasic .10 .25
408 Melker Karlsson .10 .25
409 St. Louis Blues FOIL .12 .30
410 St. Louis Blues HL .12 .30
411 Ryan O'Reilly FOIL .15 .40
412 Vladimir Tarasenko FOIL .20 .50
413 Jordan Binnington FOIL .25 .60
414 Brayden Schenn .15 .40
415 David Perron .12 .30
416 Alex Pietrangelo .12 .30
417 Tyler Bozak .10 .25
418 Jaden Schwartz .20 .50
419 Vince Dunn .12 .30
420 Robert Thomas .15 .40
421 Colton Parayko .12 .30
422 Jake Allen .15 .40
423 Ryan O'Reilly .15 .40
424 Vladimir Tarasenko .20 .50
425 Jordan Binnington .25 .60
426 Tampa Bay Lightning FOIL .12 .30
427 Tampa Bay Lightning HL .12 .30
428 Nikita Kucherov FOIL .30 .75
429 Steven Stamkos FOIL .30 .75
430 Victor Hedman FOIL .20 .50
431 Brayden Point .20 .50
432 Yanni Gourde .12 .30
433 Tyler Johnson .10 .25
434 Ryan McDonagh .10 .25
435 Alex Killorn .10 .25
436 Anthony Cirelli .12 .30
437 Andrei Vasilevskiy .25 .60
438 Louis Domingue .12 .30
439 Nikita Kucherov .30 .75
440 Steven Stamkos .30 .75
441 Victor Hedman .20 .50
442 Mikhail Sergachev .12 .30
443 Toronto Maple Leafs FOIL .12 .30
444 Toronto Maple Leafs HL .12 .30
445 Mitch Marner FOIL .12 .30
446 John Tavares FOIL .25 .60
447 Auston Matthews FOIL .60 1.50
448 Morgan Rielly .15 .40
449 Kasperi Kapanen .12 .30
450 Andreas Johnsson .15 .40
451 Zach Hyman .25 .60
452 Frederik Andersen .20 .50
453 Cody Ceci .10 .25
454 Jason Spezza .15 .40
455 Tyson Barrie .10 .25
456 Alexander Kerfoot .12 .30
457 Mitch Marner .12 .30
458 John Tavares .25 .60
459 Auston Matthews .60 1.50
460 Vancouver Canucks FOIL .12 .30
461 Vancouver Canucks HL .12 .30
462 Elias Pettersson FOIL .25 .60
463 Bo Horvat FOIL .20 .50
464 Brock Boeser FOIL .20 .50
465 J.T. Miller .20 .50
466 Tyler Myers .10 .25
467 Micheal Ferland .10 .25
468 Alexander Edler .10 .25
469 Loui Eriksson .10 .25
470 Jake Virtanen .15 .40
471 Quinn Hughes .75 2.00
472 Jacob Markstrom .15 .40
473 Thatcher Demko .20 .50
474 Elias Pettersson .25 .60
475 Bo Horvat .20 .50
476 Brock Boeser .20 .50
477 Vegas Golden Knights FOIL .12 .30
478 Vegas Golden Knights HL .12 .30
479 Jonathan Marchessault FOIL .20 .50
480 William Karlsson FOIL .20 .50
481 Marc-Andre Fleury FOIL .30 .75
482 Garret Sparks .10 .25
483 Reilly Smith .15 .40
484 Alex Tuch .15 .40
485 Paul Stastny .12 .30
486 Cody Eakin .10 .25
487 Max Pacioretty .15 .40
488 Shea Theodore .20 .50
489 Nate Schmidt .12 .30
490 Malcolm Subban .12 .30
491 Jonathan Marchessault .20 .50
492 William Karlsson .20 .50
493 Marc-Andre Fleury .30 .75
494 Washington Capitals FOIL .12 .30
495 Washington Capitals HL .12 .30
496 Alex Ovechkin FOIL .12 .30
497 Nicklas Backstrom FOIL .15 .40
498 Evgeny Kuznetsov FOIL .20 .50
499 John Carlson .15 .40
500 T.J. Oshie .15 .40
501 Jakub Vrana .15 .40
502 Tom Wilson .15 .40
503 Lars Eller .10 .25
504 Dmitry Orlov .15 .40
505 Braden Holtby .20 .50
506 Pheonix Copley .10 .25
507 Richard Panik .10 .25
508 Alex Ovechkin .12 .30
509 Nicklas Backstrom .15 .40
510 Evgeny Kuznetsov .20 .50
511 Winnipeg Jets FOIL .12 .30
512 Winnipeg Jets HL .12 .30
513 Blake Wheeler FOIL .15 .40
514 Mark Scheifele FOIL .25 .60
515 Connor Hellebuyck FOIL .30 .75
516 Kyle Connor .25 .60
517 Patrik Laine .20 .50
518 Bryan Little .12 .30
519 Nikolaj Ehlers .15 .40
520 Mathieu Perreault .10 .25
521 Josh Morrissey .20 .50
522 Laurent Brossoit .10 .25
523 Blake Wheeler .15 .40
524 Mark Scheifele .25 .60
525 Connor Hellebuyck .30 .75
526 Dustin Byfuglien .15 .40
527 Jack Roslovic .10 .25
528 Elias Pettersson RD FOIL .25 .60
529 Michael Rasmussen RD .10 .25
530 Rasmus Dahlin RD .20 .50
531 Miro Heiskanen RD .20 .50
532 Brady Tkachuk RD .25 .60
533 MacKenzie Blackwood RD .15 .40
534 Calvin Petersen RD .12 .30
535 Carter Hart RD .15 .40
536 Andrei Svechnikov RD .20 .50
537 Libor Hajek RD .12 .30
538 Austin Wagner RD .10 .25
539 Jesperi Kotkaniemi RD .15 .40
540 Brett Howden RD .10 .25
541 Quinn Hughes RD .75 2.00
542 Conor Garland RD .12 .30
543 Devon Toews RD .12 .30
544 Erik Cernak RD .12 .30
545 Henri Jokiharju RD .10 .25
546 Teddy Blueger RD .15 .40
547 Max Comtois RD .12 .30
548 Connor McDavid AS .75 2.00
549 Johnny Gaudreau AS .25 .60
550 Elias Pettersson AS .25 .60
551 Brent Burns AS .15 .40
552 Marc-Andre Fleury AS .30 .75
553 Patrick Kane AS .30 .75
554 Ryan O'Reilly AS .15 .40
555 Mark Scheifele AS .25 .60
556 Pekka Rinne AS .15 .40
557 Mikko Rantanen AS .40 1.00
558 Auston Matthews AS .60 1.50
559 Nikita Kucherov AS .30 .75
560 Jack Eichel AS .25 .60
561 Steven Stamkos AS .30 .75
562 Andrei Vasilevskiy AS .25 .60
563 Mathew Barzal AS .20 .50
564 Claude Giroux AS .15 .40
565 John Carlson AS .15 .40
566 Henrik Lundqvist AS .40 1.00
567 Sidney Crosby AS FOIL .60 1.50
568 Quebec Nordiques Logo .12 .30
569 Boston Bruins Logo .12 .30
570 Calgary Flames Logo .12 .30
571 Chicago Blackhawks Logo .12 .30
572 Minnesota North Stars Logo .12 .30
573 Edmonton Oilers Logo .12 .30
574 Los Angeles Kings Logo .12 .30
575 Montreal Canadiens Logo .12 .30
576 New Jersey Devils Logo .12 .30
577 New York Islanders Logo .12 .30
578 New York Rangers Logo .12 .30
579 Philadelphia Flyers Logo .12 .30
580 Pittsburgh Penguins Logo .12 .30
581 Hartford Whalers Logo .12 .30
582 Toronto Maple Leafs Logo .12 .30
583 Vancouver Canucks Logo .12 .30
584 Washington Capitals Logo .12 .30
585 Winnipeg Jets Logo .12 .30
586 Predators/Stars Playoffs .12 .30
587 Jets/Blues Playoffs .12 .30
588 Flames/Avalanche Playoffs .12 .30
589 Sharks/Golden/Knights Playoffs.12 .30
590 Blues/Stars Playoffs .12 .30
591 Sharks/Avalanche Playoffs .12 .30
592 Sharks/Blues Playoffs .12 .30
593 Bruins/Hurricanes Playoffs .12 .30
594 Bruins/Blue Jackets Playoffs .12 .30
595 Islanders/Hurricanes Playoffs .12 .30
596 Lightning/Blue Jackets Playoffs.12 .30
597 Bruins/Maple Leafs Playoffs .12 .30
598 Capitals/Hurricanes Playoffs .12 .30
599 Islanders/Penguins Playoffs .12 .30
600 St. Louis Blues Boston Bruins FOIL .12 .30
601 St. Louis Blues Boston Bruins FOIL .12 .30
602 St. Louis Blues Boston Bruins FOIL .12 .30
603 St. Louis Blues Boston Bruins FOIL .12 .30
604 St. Louis Blues Boston Bruins FOIL .12 .30
605 St. Louis Blues Boston Bruins FOIL .12 .30
606 St. Louis Blues Boston Bruins FOIL .12 .30
607 Ryan O'Reilly Celebrations FOIL.15 .40
608 St. Louis Blues Celebrations FOIL.12 .30
609 St. Louis Blues Logo FOIL .12 .30
610 Conn Smythe Trophy FOIL .12 .30
611 Stanley Cup Trophy FOIL .12 .30
612 St. Louis Blues Puzzle .12 .30
613 St. Louis Blues Puzzle .12 .30
614 St. Louis Blues Puzzle .12 .30
615 St. Louis Blues Puzzle .12 .30
616 St. Louis Blues Puzzle .12 .30
617 St. Louis Blues Puzzle .12 .30
618 Stanley Cup Puzzle FOIL .12 .30
619 Stanley Cup Puzzle FOIL .12 .30
620 Stanley Cup Puzzle FOIL .12 .30
621 Stanley Cup Puzzle FOIL .12 .30
622 Nikita Kucherov AW FOIL .30 .75
623 Andrei Vasilevskiy AW .25 .60
624 Ryan O'Reilly AW .15 .40
625 Robin Lehner AW .12 .30
626 Mark Giordano AW .15 .40
627 Nikita Kucherov AW .30 .75
628 Jason Zucker AW .15 .40
629 Aleksander Barkov AW .25 .60
630 Elias Pettersson AW .25 .60

2020-21 Topps Stickers

1 Anaheim Ducks Logo FOIL .12 .30
2 Anaheim Ducks HL .12 .30
3 Wild Wing FOIL .12 .30
4 Adam Henrique FOIL .12 .30
5 Rickard Rakell FOIL .12 .30
6 Adam Henrique .12 .30
7 Rickard Rakell .12 .30
8 Ryan Getzlaf .15 .40
9 John Gibson .15 .40
10 Jakob Silfverberg .10 .25
11 Cam Fowler .15 .40
12 Hampus Lindholm .10 .25
13 Sam Steel .12 .30
14 Carter Rowney .10 .25
15 Michael Del Zotto .12 .30
16 Nicolas Deslauriers .10 .25
17 Max Jones .10 .25
18 Arizona Coyotes Logo FOIL .12 .30
19 Arizona Coyotes HL .12 .30
20 Taylor Hall FOIL .15 .40
21 Clayton Keller FOIL .20 .50
22 Howler FOIL .12 .30
23 Conor Garland .12 .30
24 Nick Schmaltz .12 .30
25 Clayton Keller .20 .50
26 Antti Raanta .15 .40
27 Christian Dvorak .12 .30
28 Phil Kessel .15 .40
29 Carl Soderberg .10 .25
30 Alex Goligoski .12 .30
31 Oliver Ekman-larsson .15 .40
32 Derek Stepan .10 .25
33 Barrett Hayton .15 .40
34 Taylor Hall .15 .40
35 Boston Bruins Logo FOIL .12 .30
36 Boston Bruins HL .12 .30
37 Blades FOIL .12 .30
38 Patrice Bergeron FOIL .20 .50
39 David Pastrnak FOIL .40 1.00
40 Brad Marchand .30 .75
41 Patrice Bergeron .20 .50
42 David Pastrnak .40 1.00
43 Tuukka Rask .20 .50
44 Torey Krug .12 .30
45 David Krejci .15 .40
46 Charlie Coyle .15 .40
47 Jake DeBrusk .15 .40
48 Charlie McAvoy .20 .50
49 Sean Kuraly .10 .25
50 Matt Grzelcyk .12 .30
51 Anders Bjork .10 .25
52 Buffalo Sabres Logo FOIL .12 .30
53 Buffalo Sabres HL .12 .30
54 Sabretooth FOIL .12 .30
55 Jack Eichel FOIL .25 .60
56 Sam Reinhart FOIL .30 .75
57 Jack Eichel .25 .60
58 Sam Reinhart .30 .75
59 Linus Ullmark .15 .40
60 Victor Olofsson .15 .40
61 Rasmus Dahlin .20 .50
62 Rasmus Ristolainen .10 .25
63 Marcus Johansson .12 .30
64 Jeff Skinner .15 .40
65 Jimmy Vesey .12 .30
66 Zemgus Girgensons .12 .30
67 Kyle Okposo .10 .25
68 Wayne Simmonds .15 .40
69 Calgary Flames Logo FOIL .12 .30
70 Calgary Flames HL .12 .30
71 Harvey the Hound FOIL .12 .30
72 Johnny Gaudreau FOIL .25 .60
73 Mark Giordano FOIL .15 .40
74 Johnny Gaudreau .25 .60
75 Mark Giordano .15 .40
76 David Rittich .12 .30
77 Matt Tkachuk .30 .75
78 Elias Lindholm .15 .40
79 Sean Monahan .10 .25
80 Mikael Backlund .12 .30
81 Andrew Mangiapane .15 .40
82 Derek Ryan .10 .25
83 Noah Hanifin .15 .40
84 Rasmus Andersson .12 .30
85 Milan Lucic .12 .30
86 Carolina Hurricanes Logo FOIL .12 .30
87 Carolina Hurricanes HL .12 .30
88 Stormy FOIL .12 .30
89 Sebastian Aho FOIL .25 .60
90 Teuvo Teravainen FOIL .15 .40
91 Sebastian Aho .25 .60
92 Teuvo Teravainen .15 .40
93 Andrei Svechnikov .20 .50
94 Jake Gardiner .10 .25
94 Jake Gardiner .10 .25
95 Petr Mrazek .15 .40
96 Martin Necas .25 .60
97 Jaccob Slavin .12 .30
98 Warren Foegele .12 .30
99 Nino Niederreiter .10 .25
100 Ryan Dzingel .12 .30
101 Jordan Staal .12 .30
102 Brock McGinn .10 .25
103 Chicago Blackhawks Logo FOIL.12 .30
104 Chicago Blackhawks HL .12 .30
105 Tommy Hawk FOIL .12 .30
106 Patrick Kane FOIL .30 .75
107 Jonathan Toews FOIL .25 .60
108 Patrick Kane .30 .75
109 Jonathan Toews .25 .60
110 Dominik Kubalik .15 .40
111 Corey Crawford .15 .40
112 Alex Debrincat .20 .50
113 Dylan Strome .20 .50
114 Brandon Saad .12 .30
115 Duncan Keith .12 .30
116 Alex Nylander .12 .30
117 Kirby Dach .15 .40
118 Connor Murphy .12 .30
119 Olli Maatta .10 .25
120 Colorado Avalanche Logo FOIL.12 .30
121 Colorado Avalanche HL .12 .30
122 Bernie FOIL .12 .30
123 Nathan MacKinnon FOIL .60 1.50
124 Mikko Rantanen FOIL .40 1.00
125 Nathan MacKinnon .60 1.50
126 Mikko Rantanen .40 1.00
127 Cale Makar .40 1.00
128 Andre Burakovsky .10 .25
129 Gabriel Landeskog .20 .50
130 Nazem Kadri .20 .50
131 Samuel Girard .10 .25
132 Joonas Donskoi .10 .25
133 J.T. Compher .10 .25
134 Philipp Grubauer .15 .40
135 Valeri Nichushkin .15 .40
136 Ryan Graves .12 .30
137 Columbus Blue Jackets Logo FOIL .12 .30
138 Columbus Blue Jackets HL .12 .30
139 Stinger FOIL .12 .30
140 Seth Jones FOIL .15 .40
141 Pierre-Luc Dubois FOIL .12 .30
142 Seth Jones .15 .40
143 Pierre-Luc Dubois .12 .30
144 Joonas Korpisalo .15 .40
145 Gustav Nyquist .10 .25
146 Zach Werenski .25 .60
147 Oliver Bjorkstrand .12 .30
148 Nick Foligno .12 .30
149 Nathan Gerbe .10 .25
150 Cam Atkinson .15 .40
151 Boone Jenner .15 .40
152 Alexander Wennberg .10 .25
153 Emil Bemstrom .10 .25
154 Dallas Stars Logo FOIL .12 .30
155 Dallas Stars HL .12 .30
156 Victor E. Green FOIL .12 .30
157 Tyler Seguin FOIL .20 .50
158 Ben Bishop FOIL .12 .30
159 Tyler Seguin .20 .50
160 Ben Bishop .12 .30
161 Jamie Benn .15 .40
162 Miro Heiskanen .20 .50
163 Alexander Radulov .15 .40
163 Alexander Radulov .15 .40
164 Roope Hintz .20 .50
165 John Klingberg .15 .40
166 Joe Pavelski .20 .50
167 Denis Gurianov .20 .50
168 Esa Lindell .12 .30
169 Jason Dickinson .10 .25
170 Mattias Janmark .10 .25
171 Detroit Red Wings Logo FOIL .12 .30
172 Detroit Red Wings HL .12 .30
173 Dylan Larkin FOIL .20 .50
174 Tyler Bertuzzi FOIL .12 .30
175 Jonathan Bernier FOIL .12 .30
176 Dylan Larkin .20 .50
177 Tyler Bertuzzi .12 .30
178 Jonathan Bernier .12 .30
179 Anthony Mantha .12 .30
180 Robby Fabbri .10 .25
181 Filip Hronek .10 .25
182 Valtteri Filppula .10 .25
183 Madison Bowey .10 .25
184 Darren Helm .10 .25
185 Filip Zadina .12 .30
186 Luke Glendening .10 .25
187 Frans Nielsen .10 .25
188 Edmonton Oilers Logo FOIL .12 .30
189 Edmonton Oilers HL .12 .30
190 Hunter FOIL .12 .30
191 Connor McDavid FOIL .75 2.00
192 Leon Draisaitl FOIL .50 1.25
193 Connor McDavid .75 2.00
194 Zack Kassian .10 .25
195 Mikko Koskinen .10 .25
196 Ryan Nugent-Hopkins .20 .50
197 Oscar Klefbom .15 .40
198 Leon Draisaitl .50 1.25
198 Leon Draisaitl .50 1.25
199 Darnell Nurse .12 .30
200 James Neal .10 .25
201 Kailer Yamamoto .15 .40
202 Alex Chiasson .12 .30
203 Josh Archibald .10 .25
204 Ethan Bear .10 .25
205 Florida Panthers Logo FOIL .12 .30
206 Florida Panthers HL .12 .30
207 Stanley C. Panther FOIL .12 .30
208 Aleksander Barkov FOIL .25 .60
209 Sergei Bobrovsky FOIL .25 .60
210 Aleksander Barkov .25 .60
211 Jonathan Huberdeau .20 .50
212 Mike Hoffman .10 .25
213 Evgenii Dadonov .10 .25
214 Keith Yandle .10 .25
215 Aaron Ekblad .20 .50
216 Sergei Bobrovsky .25 .60
216 Sergei Bobrovsky .25 .60
217 Frank Vatrano .12 .30
218 Brett Connolly .10 .25
219 Noel Acciari .10 .25
220 Mike Matheson .10 .25
221 Anton Stralman .10 .25
222 Los Angeles Kings Logo FOIL .12 .30
223 Los Angeles Kings HL .12 .30
224 Bailey FOIL .12 .30
225 Drew Doughty FOIL .20 .50
226 Anze Kopitar FOIL .25 .60
227 Drew Doughty .20 .50
228 Alex Iafallo .10 .25
229 Anze Kopitar .25 .60
229 Anze Kopitar .25 .60
230 Ben Hutton .10 .25
231 Dustin Brown .15 .40
232 Jonathan Quick .20 .50
233 Adrian Kempe .15 .40
234 Jeff Carter .12 .30
235 Sean Walker .10 .25
236 Blake Lizotte .10 .25
237 Matt Roy .10 .25
238 Michael Amadio .10 .25
239 Minnesota Wild Logo FOIL .12 .30
240 Minnesota Wild HL .12 .30
241 Nordy FOIL .12 .30
242 Kevin Fiala FOIL .12 .30
243 Ryan Suter FOIL .12 .30
244 Kevin Fiala .12 .30
245 Ryan Suter .12 .30
246 Alex Stalock .10 .25
247 Eric Staal .15 .40
248 Zach Parise .15 .40
249 Mats Zuccarello .15 .40
249 Mats Zuccarello .15 .40
250 Jared Spurgeon .15 .40
251 Luke Kunin .10 .25
252 Joel Eriksson Ek .12 .30
253 Jordan Greenway .12 .30
254 Jonas Brodin .10 .25
255 Marcus Foligno .12 .30
256 Montreal Canadiens Logo FOIL.12 .30
257 Montreal Canadiens HL .12 .30
258 Youppi FOIL .12 .30
259 Carey Price FOIL .30 .75
260 Tomas Tatar FOIL .10 .25
261 Carey Price .30 .75
262 Tomas Tatar .10 .25
263 Phillip Danault .15 .40
264 Max Domi .15 .40
265 Brendan Gallagher .15 .40
266 Nick Suzuki .30 .75
267 Jeff Petry .15 .40
268 Shea Weber .15 .40
269 Joel Armia .10 .25
270 Artturi Lehkonen .12 .30
271 Ben Chiarot .10 .25
272 Jordan Weal .10 .25
273 Nashville Predators Logo FOIL .12 .30
274 Nashville Predators HL .12 .30
275 Gnash FOIL .12 .30
276 Roman Josi FOIL .15 .40
277 Juuse Saros FOIL .20 .50
278 Roman Josi .15 .40
279 Juuse Saros .20 .50
280 Filip Forsberg .25 .60
281 Kyle Turris .12 .30
282 Ryan Ellis .12 .30
283 Ryan Johansen .12 .30
284 Matt Duchene .15 .40
284 Matt Duchene .15 .40
285 Nick Bonino .10 .25
286 Calle Jarnkrok .10 .25
287 Mattias Ekholm .12 .30
288 Craig Smith .10 .25
289 Rocco Grimaldi .10 .25
290 New Jersey Devils Logo FOIL .12 .30
291 New Jersey Devils HL .12 .30
292 NJ Devil FOIL .12 .30
293 Kyle Palmieri FOIL .12 .30
294 Nikita Gusev FOIL .12 .30
295 Kyle Palmieri .12 .30
296 Nikita Gusev .12 .30
297 Mackenzie Blackwood .15 .40
298 Nico Hischier .25 .60
299 Jesper Bratt .15 .40
300 Pavel Zacha .12 .30
301 Damon Severson .10 .25
302 Travis Zajac .10 .25
303 Miles Wood .10 .25
304 Jack Hughes .40 1.00
305 Will Butcher .12 .30
306 P.K. Subban .20 .50
307 New York Islanders Logo FOIL .12 .30
308 New York Islanders HL .12 .30
309 Sparky FOIL .12 .30
310 Mathew Barzal FOIL .20 .50
311 Semyon Varlamov FOIL .15 .40
312 Mathew Barzal .20 .50
313 Semyon Varlamov .15 .40
314 Brock Nelson .15 .40
315 Josh Bailey .12 .30
316 Anders Lee .12 .30
316 Anders Lee .12 .30
317 Jordan Eberle .15 .40

318 Anthony Beauvillier .10 .25
319 Ryan Pulock .12 .30
320 Derick Brassard .10 .25
321 Devon Toews .12 .30
322 Nick Leddy .10 .25
323 Jean-Gabriel Pageau .10 .25
324 New York Rangers Logo FOIL .12 .30
325 New York Rangers HL .12 .30
326 Artemi Panarin FOIL .30 .75
327 Henrik Lundqvist FOIL .40 1.00
328 Mika Zibanejad FOIL .20 .50
329 Kaapo Kakko .12 .30
330 Henrik Lundqvist .40 1.00
331 Mika Zibanejad .20 .50
332 Ryan Strome .15 .40
333 Tony DeAngelo .10 .25
334 Pavel Buchnevich .12 .30
335 Artemi Panarin .30 .75
335 Artemi Panarin .30 .75
336 Chris Kreider .20 .50
337 Adam Fox .20 .50
338 Jesper Fast .10 .25
339 Jacob Trouba .12 .30
340 Filip Chytil .12 .30
341 Ottawa Senators Logo FOIL .12 .30
342 Ottawa Senators HL .12 .30
343 SpartaCat FOIL .12 .30
344 Brady Tkachuk FOIL .25 .60
345 Connor Brown FOIL .12 .30
346 Brady Tkachuk .25 .60
347 Connor Brown .12 .30
348 Craig Anderson .12 .30
349 Anthony Duclair .12 .30
350 Thomas Chabot .15 .40
351 Chris Tierney .12 .30
352 Colin White .10 .25
353 Artem Anisimov .10 .25
354 Nick Paul .10 .25
355 Mark Borowiecki .10 .25
356 Ron Hainsey .10 .25
357 Nikita Zaitsev .10 .25
358 Philadelphia Flyers Logo FOIL .12 .30
359 Philadelphia Flyers HL .12 .30
360 Gritty FOIL .12 .30
361 Claude Giroux FOIL .15 .40
362 Travis Konecny FOIL .15 .40
363 Claude Giroux .15 .40
364 Travis Konecny .15 .40
365 Carter Hart .15 .40
366 Sean Couturier .12 .30
367 Jakub Voracek .12 .30
368 Kevin Hayes .12 .30
369 James van Riemsdyk .12 .30
370 Ivan Provorov .12 .30
371 Matt Niskanen .12 .30
372 Scott Laughton .10 .25
373 Travis Sanheim .10 .25
374 Joel Farabee .15 .40
375 Pittsburgh Penguins Logo FOIL .12 .30
376 Pittsburgh Penguins HL .12 .30
377 Iceburgh FOIL .12 .30
378 Sidney Crosby FOIL .60 1.50
379 Evgeni Malkin FOIL .30 .75
380 Sidney Crosby .60 1.50
381 Evgeni Malkin .30 .75
382 Matt Murray .15 .40
383 Bryan Rust .15 .40
384 Kris Letang .20 .50
385 Jake Guentzel .25 .60
386 Jared McCann .12 .30
387 Patric Hornqvist .10 .25
388 John Marino .15 .40
389 Brandon Tanev .12 .30
390 Teddy Blueger .10 .25
391 Patrick Marleau .15 .40
392 San Jose Sharks Logo FOIL .12 .30
393 San Jose Sharks HL .12 .30
394 S.J. Sharkie FOIL .12 .30
395 Brent Burns FOIL .15 .40
396 Erik Karlsson FOIL .20 .50
397 Brent Burns .15 .40
398 Erik Karlsson .20 .50
399 Martin Jones .12 .30
400 Timo Meier .15 .40
401 Evander Kane .15 .40
402 Logan Couture .20 .50
403 Tomas Hertl .15 .40
404 Kevin Labanc .10 .25
405 Joe Thornton .25 .60
406 Marcus Sorensen .12 .30
407 Marc-Edouard Vlasic .10 .25
408 Melker Karlsson .10 .25
409 St. Louis Blues Logo FOIL .12 .30
410 St. Louis Blues HL .12 .30
411 Louie FOIL .12 .30
412 Ryan O'Reilly FOIL .15 .40
413 Vladimir Tarasenko FOIL .20 .50
414 Ryan O'Reilly .15 .40
415 Vladimir Tarasenko .20 .50
416 Jordan Binnington .25 .60
417 David Perron .12 .30
418 Brayden Schenn .15 .40
419 Jaden Schwartz .20 .50
420 Alex Pietrangelo .12 .30
421 Robert Thomas .15 .40
422 Zach Sanford .10 .25
423 Tyler Bozak .10 .25
424 Colton Parayko .12 .30
425 Ivan Barbashev .12 .30
426 Tampa Bay Lightning Logo FOIL .12 .30
427 Tampa Bay Lightning HL .12 .30
428 ThunderBug FOIL .12 .30
429 Nikita Kucherov FOIL .30 .75
430 Victor Hedman FOIL .20 .50
431 Nikita Kucherov .30 .75
432 Victor Hedman .20 .50
433 Andrei Vasilevskiy .25 .60
434 Steven Stamkos .30 .75
435 Brayden Point .20 .50
436 Alex Killorn .10 .25
437 Anthony Cirelli .12 .30
438 Ondrej Palat .15 .40
439 Mikhail Sergachev .12 .30
440 Kevin Shattenkirk .10 .25
441 Tyler Johnson .10 .25
442 Yanni Gourde .12 .30
443 Toronto Maple Leafs Logo FOIL .12 .30
444 Toronto Maple Leafs HL .12 .30
445 Carlton FOIL .12 .30
446 Auston Matthews FOIL .60 1.50
447 Mitch Marner FOIL .25 .60
448 John Tavares .25 .60
449 Mitch Marner .25 .60
450 Frederik Andersen .20 .50
451 Auston Matthews .60 1.50
452 William Nylander .30 .75
453 Tyson Barrie .10 .25
454 Zach Hyman .25 .60
455 Kasperi Kapanen .12 .30
456 Alexander Kerfoot .12 .30
457 Morgan Rielly .15 .40
458 Jason Spezza .15 .40
459 Ilya Mikheyev .12 .30
460 Vancouver Canucks Logo FOIL .12 .30
461 Vancouver Canucks HL .12 .30
462 Fin FOIL .12 .30
463 Elias Pettersson FOIL .25 .60
464 J.T. Miller FOIL .20 .50
465 Elias Pettersson .25 .60
466 J.T. Miller .20 .50
467 Jacob Markstrom .15 .40
468 Bo Horvat .20 .50
469 Quinn Hughes .40 1.00
470 Tanner Pearson .15 .40
471 Brock Boeser .20 .50
472 Jake Virtanen .15 .40
473 Adam Gaudette .12 .30
474 Alexander Edler .10 .25
475 Tyler Myers .10 .25
476 Christopher Tanev .10 .25
477 Vegas Golden Knights Logo FOIL .12 .30
478 Vegas Golden Knights HL .12 .30
479 Chance FOIL .12 .30
480 Mark Stone FOIL .20 .50
481 Marc-Andre Fleury FOIL .30 .75
482 Mark Stone .20 .50
483 Marc-Andre Fleury .30 .75
484 Max Pacioretty .15 .40
485 Reilly Smith .15 .40
486 Jonathan Marchessault .20 .50
487 William Karlsson .20 .50
488 Shea Theodore .20 .50
489 Paul Stastny .12 .30
490 Nate Schmidt .12 .30
491 Chandler Stephenson .12 .30
492 William Carrier .10 .25
493 Alex Tuch .15 .40
494 Washington Capitals Logo FOIL .12 .30
495 Washington Capitals HL .12 .30
496 Slapshot FOIL .12 .30
497 Alex Ovechkin FOIL .60 1.50
498 John Carlson FOIL .15 .40
499 Alex Ovechkin .60 1.50
500 Braden Holtby .20 .50
501 Richard Panik .10 .25
502 Nicklas Backstrom .15 .40
503 Jakub Vrana .15 .40
504 Evgeny Kuznetsov .20 .50
505 John Carlson .15 .40
505 John Carlson .15 .40
506 T.J. Oshie .15 .40
507 Tom Wilson .15 .40
508 Lars Eller .10 .25
509 Dmitry Orlov .15 .40
510 Ilya Kovalchuk .15 .40
511 Winnipeg Jets Logo FOIL .12 .30
512 Winnipeg Jets HL .12 .30
513 Moose FOIL .12 .30
514 Mark Scheifele FOIL .25 .60
515 Blake Wheeler FOIL .15 .40
516 Mark Scheifele .25 .60
517 Blake Wheeler .15 .40
518 Connor Hellebuyck .30 .75
519 Kyle Connor .25 .60
520 Patrik Laine .20 .50
521 Nikolaj Ehlers .15 .40
522 Neal Pionk .10 .25
523 Josh Morrissey .20 .50
524 Jack Roslovic .10 .25
525 Andrew Copp .10 .25
526 Tucker Poolman .10 .25
527 Mathieu Perreault .10 .25
528 Ilya Mikheyev DEBUT .12 .30
529 Cale Makar DEBUT .40 1.00
530 Kaapo Kakko DEBUT .12 .30
531 Adam Fox DEBUT .20 .50
532 Emil Bemstrom DEBUT .10 .25
533 John Marino DEBUT .15 .40
534 Dominik Kubalik DEBUT .15 .40
535 Nick Suzuki DEBUT .30 .75
536 Elvis Merzlikins DEBUT .15 .40
537 Vladislav Gavrikov DEBUT .10 .25
538 Ilya Samsonov DEBUT .15 .40
539 Pierre Engvall DEBUT .10 .25
540 Nikolai Prokhorkin DEBUT .10 .25
541 Carter Verhaeghe DEBUT .15 .40
542 Sam Lafferty DEBUT .10 .25
543 Adam Boqvist DEBUT .12 .30
544 Cody Glass DEBUT .12 .30
545 Joel Farabee DEBUT .15 .40
546 Igor Shesterkin DEBUT .30 .75
547 Kirby Dach DEBUT .15 .40
548 Matthew Tkachuk TT .30 .75
549 Leon Draisaitl TT .50 1.25
550 Elias Pettersson TT .25 .60
551 John Carlson TT .15 .40
552 Kyle Connor TT .25 .60
553 Brent Burns TT .15 .40
554 Travis Konecny TT .15 .40
555 Clayton Keller TT .20 .50
556 Cale Makar TT .40 1.00
557 Bryan Rust TT .15 .40
558 Kyle Palmieri TT .12 .30
559 Evgeni Malkin TT .30 .75
560 Sebastian Aho TT .25 .60
561 Ryan O'Reilly TT .15 .40
562 Anze Kopitar TT .25 .60
563 Zach Werenski TT .25 .60
564 Mathew Barzal TT .20 .50
565 Patrice Bergeron TT .20 .50
566 Anthony Duclair TT .12 .30
567 Ryan Getzlaf TT .15 .40
568 Brad Marchand TT .30 .75
569 Mathew Barzal CLASS .20 .50
570 Kyle Palmieri CLASS .12 .30
571 John Tavares CLASS .25 .60
572 Jack Eichel CLASS .25 .60
573 Ryan O'Reilly CLASS .15 .40
574 David Pastrnak CLASS .40 1.00
575 Tyler Seguin CLASS .20 .50
576 Patrick Kane CLASS .30 .75
577 Mika Zibanejad CLASS .20 .50
578 Alex Ovechkin CLASS .60 1.50
579 Connor McDavid CLASS .75 2.00
580 Elias Pettersson CLASS .25 .60
581 Carey Price CLASS .30 .75
582 Evgeni Malkin CLASS .30 .75
583 Travis Konecny CLASS .15 .40
584 Anze Kopitar CLASS .25 .60
585 Dylan Larkin CLASS .20 .50
586 Nathan Mackinnon CLASS .60 1.50
587 Patrice Bergeron CLASS .20 .50
588 Henrik Lundqvist CLASS .40 1.00
589 Sidney Crosby CLASS .60 1.50
590 Connor McDavid AS .75 2.00
591 Patrick Kane AS .30 .75
592 Mark Giordano AS .15 .40
593 Anze Kopitar AS .25 .60
594 Eric Staal AS .15 .40
595 Nathan MacKinnon AS .60 1.50
596 Leon Draisaitl AS .50 1.25
597 Elias Pettersson AS .25 .60
598 Ryan O'Reilly AS .15 .40
599 Tyler Seguin AS .20 .50
600 Shea Weber AS .15 .40
601 Kris Letang AS .20 .50
602 Victor Hedman AS .20 .50
603 Jack Eichel AS .25 .60
604 Braden Holtby AS .20 .50
605 Seth Jones AS .15 .40
606 David Pastrnak AS .40 1.00
607 Andrei Vasilevskiy AS .25 .60
608 Mathew Barzal AS .20 .50
609 John Carlson AS .15 .40
610 Mascot Puzzle .12 .30
611 Mascot Puzzle .12 .30
612 Mascot Puzzle .12 .30
613 Mascot Puzzle .12 .30
614 Mascot Puzzle .12 .30
615 Mascot Puzzle .12 .30
616 All Stars Winner Puzzle .12 .30
617 All Stars Winner Puzzle .12 .30
618 All Stars Winner Puzzle .12 .30
619 All Stars Winner Puzzle .12 .30
620 All Stars Winner Puzzle .12 .30
621 All Stars Winner Puzzle .12 .30
622 Sidney Crosby TOD .60 1.50
623 Connor McDavid TOD .75 2.00
624 Alex Ovechkin TOD .60 1.50
625 Erik Karlsson TOD .20 .50
626 Henrik Lundqvist TOD .40 1.00
627 Evgeni Malkin TOD .30 .75
628 Patrice Bergeron TOD .20 .50
629 Steven Stamkos TOD .30 .75
630 Patrick Kane TOD .30 .75
631 Anze Kopitar TOD .25 .60
632 Jaroslav Halak TOD .15 .40
633 David Krejci TOD .15 .40
634 Marc Staal TOD .10 .25
635 Patrice Bergeron TOD .20 .50
636 Marian Gaborik TOD .15 .40
637 Corey Perry TOD .25 .60
638 Sidney Crosby TOD .60 1.50
639 Jake Guentzel TOD .25 .60
640 Nicklas Backstrom TOD .15 .40
641 Pat Maroon TOD .15 .40
642 Patrick Kane TOD .30 .75
643 Brad Marchand TOD .30 .75
644 Trevor Lewis TOD .10 .25
645 Jonathan Toews TOD .25 .60
646 Alec Martinez TOD .10 .25
647 Duncan Keith TOD .12 .30
648 Kris Letang TOD .20 .50
649 Sidney Crosby TOD .60 1.50
650 Alex Ovechkin TOD .60 1.50
651 Carl Gunnarsson TOD .10 .25
652 Corey Perry HART .25 .60
653 Evgeni Malkin HART .30 .75
654 Alex Ovechkin HART .60 1.50
655 Sidney Crosby HART .60 1.50
656 Carey Price HART .30 .75
657 Patrick Kane HART .30 .75
658 Connor McDavid HART .75 2.00
659 Taylor Hall HART .15 .40
660 Nikita Kucherov HART .30 .75
661 Stanley Cup Puzzle FOIL .12 .30
662 Stanley Cup Puzzle FOIL .12 .30
663 Stanley Cup Puzzle FOIL .12 .30
664 Stanley Cup Puzzle FOIL .12 .30
665 Stanley Cup Puzzle FOIL .12 .30
666 Stanley Cup Puzzle FOIL .12 .30

2021-22 Topps Stickers

1 Playoffs Round 1 .12 .30
2 Playoffs Round 1 .12 .30
3 Playoffs Round 1 .12 .30
4 Playoffs Round 1 .12 .30
5 Playoffs Round 1 .12 .30
6 Playoffs Round 1 .12 .30
7 Playoffs Round 1 .12 .30
8 Playoffs Round 1 .12 .30
9 Playoffs Round 2 .12 .30
10 Playoffs Round 2 .12 .30
11 Playoffs Round 2 .12 .30
12 Playoffs Round 2 .12 .30
13 Playoffs Round 3 .12 .30
14 Playoffs Round 3 .12 .30
15 Stanley Cup Finals Game 1 .12 .30
16 Stanley Cup Finals Game 2 .12 .30
17 Stanley Cup Finals Game 3 .12 .30
18 Stanley Cup Finals Game 4 .12 .30
19 Stanley Cup Finals Game 5 .12 .30
20 Celebration Image .12 .30
21 Conn Smythe Winner .12 .30
22 Stanley Cup Celebration Image 1 .12 .30
23 Stanley Cup Celebration Image 2 .12 .30
24 Stanley Cup Celebration Image 3 .12 .30
25 Stanley Cup Celebration Image 4 .12 .30
26 Stanley Cup Celebration Image 5 .12 .30
27 Stanley Cup Team on Ice Image 1 .12 .30
28 Stanley Cup Team on Ice Image 2 .12 .30
29 Stanley Cup Team on Ice Image 3 .12 .30
30 Stanley Cup Team on Ice Image 4 .12 .30
31 Stanley Cup Team on Ice Image 5 .12 .30
32 Stanley Cup Team on Ice Image 6 .12 .30
33 Connor McDavid A FOIL .75 2.00
34 Marc-Andre Fleury A FOIL .30 .75
35 Adam Fox A FOIL .20 .50
36 Kirill Kaprizov A FOIL .50 1.25
37 Connor McDavid A FOIL .75 2.00
38 Pekka Rinne A FOIL .15 .40
39 Oskar Lindblom A FOIL .12 .30
40 Aleksander Barkov A FOIL .25 .60
41 Jaccob Slavin A FOIL .12 .30
42 Stanley Cup Image 1 FOIL .12 .30
43 Stanley Cup Image 2 FOIL .12 .30
44 Stanley Cup Image 3 FOIL .12 .30
45 Stanley Cup Image 4 FOIL .12 .30
46 Stanley Cup Image 5 FOIL .12 .30
47 Stanley Cup Image 6 FOIL .12 .30
48 Anaheim Ducks Logo FOIL .12 .30
49 Anaheim Ducks HL .12 .30
50 Wild Wing FOIL .12 .30
51 Nicolas Deslauriers FOIL .10 .25
52 Ryan Getzlaf FOIL .15 .40
53 Adam Henrique .12 .30
54 Rickard Rakell .12 .30
55 Ryan Getzlaf .15 .40
56 John Gibson .15 .40
57 Jakob Silfverberg .10 .25
58 Cam Fowler .15 .40
59 Hampus Lindholm .10 .25
60 Sam Steel .12 .30
61 Max Comtois .12 .30
62 Kevin Shattenkirk .10 .25
63 Nicolas Deslauriers .10 .25
64 Max Jones .10 .25
65 Arizona Coyotes Logo FOIL .12 .30
66 Arizona Coyotes HL .12 .30
67 Howler FOIL .12 .30
68 Jakob Chychrun FOIL .15 .40
69 Phil Kessel FOIL .15 .40
70 Nick Schmaltz .12 .30
71 Clayton Keller .20 .50
72 Travis Boyd .10 .25
73 Jay Beagle .10 .25
74 Jakob Chychrun .15 .40
75 Phil Kessel .15 .40
76 Anton Stralman .10 .25
77 Conor Timmins .10 .25
78 Lawson Crouse .10 .25
79 Johan Larsson .12 .30
80 Barrett Hayton .15 .40
81 Christian Fischer .10 .25
82 Boston Bruins Logo FOIL .12 .30
83 Boston Bruins HL .12 .30
84 Blades FOIL .12 .30
85 Brad Marchand FOIL .30 .75
86 Patrice Bergeron FOIL .20 .50
87 Brad Marchand .30 .75
88 Patrice Bergeron .20 .50
89 David Pastrnak .40 1.00
90 Tuukka Rask .20 .50
91 Connor Clifton .10 .25
92 Taylor Hall .15 .40
93 Charlie Coyle .15 .40
94 Jake DeBrusk .15 .40
95 Charlie McAvoy .20 .50
96 Erik Haula .10 .25
97 Matt Grzelcyk .12 .30
98 Derek Forbort .10 .25
99 Buffalo Sabres Logo FOIL .12 .30
100 Buffalo Sabres HL .12 .30
101 Sabretooth FOIL .12 .30
102 Victor Olofsson FOIL .15 .40
103 Rasmus Dahlin FOIL .20 .50
104 Jack Eichel .25 .60
105 John Hayden .10 .25
106 Anders Bjork .10 .25
107 Will Butcher .12 .30
108 Rasmus Dahlin .20 .50
109 Vinnie Hinostroza .10 .25
110 Victor Olofsson .15 .40
111 Jeff Skinner .15 .40
112 Brandon Davidson .10 .25
113 Cody Eakin .10 .25
114 Kyle Okposo .10 .25
115 Tage Thompson .20 .50
116 Calgary Flames Logo FOIL .12 .30
117 Calgary Flames HL .12 .30
118 Harvey the Hound FOIL .12 .30
119 Johnny Gaudreau FOIL .25 .60
120 Matthew Tkachuk FOIL .30 .75
121 Johnny Gaudreau .25 .60
122 Blake Coleman .12 .30
123 Jacob Markstrom .15 .40
124 Milan Lucic .12 .30
125 Dillon Dube .10 .25
126 Sean Monahan .10 .25
127 Mikael Backlund .12 .30
128 Andrew Mangiapane .15 .40
129 Elias Lindholm .15 .40
130 Noah Hanifin .15 .40
131 Rasmus Andersson .12 .30
132 Matthew Tkachuk .30 .75
133 Carolina Hurricanes Logo FOIL .12 .30
134 Carolina Hurricanes HL .12 .30
135 Stormy FOIL .12 .30
136 Sebastian Aho FOIL .25 .60
137 Teuvo Teravainen FOIL .15 .40
138 Sebastian Aho .25 .60
139 Teuvo Teravainen .15 .40
140 Andrei Svechnikov .20 .50
141 Vincent Trocheck .15 .40
142 Derek Stepan .10 .25
143 Jordan Staal .12 .30
144 Brendan Smith .10 .25
145 Antti Raanta .15 .40
146 Brett Pesce .10 .25
147 Martin Necas .25 .60
148 Jesper Fast .10 .25
149 Jaccob Slavin .12 .30
150 Chicago Blackhawks Logo FOIL .12 .30
151 Chicago Blackhawks HL .12 .30
152 Tommy Hawk FOIL .12 .30
153 Patrick Kane FOIL .30 .75
154 Tyler Johnson FOIL .10 .25
155 Patrick Kane .30 .75
156 Jonathan Toews .25 .60
157 Dominik Kubalik .15 .40
158 Malcolm Subban .12 .30
159 Alex DeBrincat .20 .50
160 Adam Gaudette .12 .30
161 Seth Jones .15 .40
162 Tyler Johnson .10 .25
163 Dylan Strome .20 .50
164 Kirby Dach .15 .40
165 Connor Murphy .12 .30
166 Mike Hardman .15 .40
167 Colorado Avalanche Logo FOIL .12 .30
168 Colorado Avalanche HL .12 .30
169 Bernie FOIL .12 .30
170 Mikko Rantanen FOIL .40 1.00
171 Nathan MacKinnon FOIL .60 1.50
172 Nathan MacKinnon .60 1.50
173 Mikko Rantanen .40 1.00
174 Cale Makar .40 1.00
175 Andre Burakovsky .10 .25
176 Gabriel Landeskog .20 .50
177 Nazem Kadri .20 .50
178 Samuel Girard .10 .25
179 Darren Helm .10 .25
180 Tyson Jost .12 .30
181 Kurtis MacDermid .10 .25
182 Valeri Nichushkin .15 .40
183 Mikhail Maltsev .10 .25
184 Columbus Blue Jackets Logo FOIL .12 .30
185 Columbus Blue Jackets HL .12 .30
186 Stinger FOIL .12 .30
187 Oliver Bjorkstrand FOIL .12 .30
188 Alexandre Texier FOIL .10 .25
189 Nathan Gerbe .10 .25
190 Max Domi .15 .40
191 Joonas Korpisalo .15 .40
192 Emil Bemstrom .10 .25
193 Zach Werenski .25 .60
194 Oliver Bjorkstrand .12 .30
195 Yegor Chinakhov .25 .60
196 Justin Danforth .12 .30
197 Gregory Hofmann .15 .40
198 Boone Jenner .15 .40
199 Alexandre Texier .10 .25
200 Gustav Nyquist .10 .25
201 Dallas Stars Logo FOIL .12 .30
202 Dallas Stars HL .12 .30
203 Victor E. Green FOIL .12 .30
204 Joe Pavelski FOIL .20 .50
205 Tyler Seguin FOIL .20 .50
206 Tyler Seguin .20 .50
207 Ben Bishop .12 .30
208 Jamie Benn .15 .40
209 Miro Heiskanen .20 .50
210 Alexander Radulov .15 .40
211 Roope Hintz .20 .50
212 Blake Comeau .10 .25
213 Joe Pavelski .20 .50
214 Denis Gurianov .20 .50
215 Esa Lindell .12 .30
216 Luke Glendening .10 .25
217 Radek Faksa .12 .30
218 Detroit Red Wings Logo FOIL .12 .30
219 Detroit Red Wings HL .12 .30
220 Dylan Larkin FOIL .20 .50
221 Tyler Bertuzzi FOIL .12 .30
222 Filip Hronek FOIL .10 .25
223 Dylan Larkin .20 .50
224 Tyler Bertuzzi .12 .30
225 Thomas Greiss .12 .30
226 Filip Zadina .12 .30
227 Nick Leddy .10 .25
228 Filip Hronek .10 .25
229 Valtteri Filppula .10 .25
230 Danny DeKeyser .10 .25
231 Mitchell Stephens .10 .25
232 Bobby Ryan .12 .30
233 Adam Erne .10 .25
234 Frans Nielsen .10 .25
235 Edmonton Oilers Logo FOIL .12 .30
236 Edmonton Oilers HL .12 .30
237 Hunter FOIL .12 .30
238 Leon Draisaitl FOIL .50 1.25
239 Connor McDavid FOIL .75 2.00
240 Connor McDavid .75 2.00
241 Zack Kassian .10 .25
242 Mikko Koskinen .10 .25
243 Ryan Nugent-Hopkins .20 .50
244 Oscar Klefbom .15 .40
245 Leon Draisaitl .50 1.25
246 Darnell Nurse .12 .30
247 Jesse Puljujarvi .15 .40
248 Kailer Yamamoto .15 .40
249 Alex Chiasson .12 .30
250 Devin Shore .10 .25
251 Tyson Barrie .10 .25
252 Florida Panthers Logo FOIL .12 .30
253 Florida Panthers HL .12 .30
254 Stanley C. Panther FOIL .12 .30
255 Aleksander Barkov FOIL .25 .60
256 Patric Hornqvist FOIL .10 .25
257 Aleksander Barkov .25 .60
258 Jonathan Huberdeau .20 .50
259 Grigori Denisenko .20 .50
260 Patric Hornqvist .10 .25
261 Joe Thornton .25 .60
262 Aaron Ekblad .20 .50
263 Sergei Bobrovsky .25 .60
264 Frank Vatrano .12 .30
265 Sam Reinhart .30 .75
266 Noel Acciari .10 .25
267 MacKenzie Weegar .12 .30
268 Anthony Duclair .12 .30
269 Los Angeles Kings Logo FOIL .12 .30
270 Los Angeles Kings HL .12 .30
271 Bailey FOIL .12 .30
272 Anze Kopitar FOIL .25 .60
273 Dustin Brown FOIL .15 .40
274 Drew Doughty .20 .50
275 Alex Iafallo .10 .25
276 Anze Kopitar .25 .60
277 Olli Maatta .10 .25
278 Dustin Brown .15 .40
279 Jonathan Quick .20 .50
280 Gabriel Vilardi .15 .40
281 Jaret Anderson-Dolan .10 .25
282 Sean Walker .10 .25
283 Blake Lizotte .10 .25
284 Matt Roy .10 .25
285 Viktor Arvidsson .10 .25
286 Minnesota Wild Logo FOIL .12 .30
287 Minnesota Wild HL .12 .30
288 Nordy FOIL .12 .30
289 Joel Eriksson Ek FOIL .12 .30
290 Mats Zuccarello FOIL .15 .40
291 Kevin Fiala .12 .30
292 Matt Boldy .40 1.00
293 Cam Talbot .15 .40
294 Joseph Cramarossa .10 .25
295 Mats Zuccarello .15 .40
296 Kirill Kaprizov .50 1.25
297 Jared Spurgeon .15 .40
298 Nico Sturm .10 .25
299 Joel Eriksson Ek .12 .30
300 Jordan Greenway .10 .25
301 Matt Dumba .12 .30
302 Alex Goligoski .12 .30
303 Montreal Canadiens Logo FOIL .12 .30
304 Montreal Canadiens HL .12 .30
305 Youppi! FOIL .12 .30
306 Carey Price FOIL .30 .75
307 Jeff Petry FOIL .15 .40
308 Carey Price .30 .75
309 Mike Hoffman .10 .25
310 Chris Wideman .10 .25
311 Jake Evans .10 .25
312 Brendan Gallagher .15 .40
313 Nick Suzuki .30 .75
314 Jeff Petry .15 .40
315 Shea Weber .15 .40
316 Josh Anderson .12 .30
317 Artturi Lehkonen .12 .30
318 Ben Chiarot .10 .25
319 Jonathan Drouin .12 .30
320 Nashville Predators Logo FOIL .12 .30
321 Nashville Predators HL .12 .30
322 Gnash FOIL .12 .30
323 Filip Forsberg FOIL .25 .60
324 Ryan Johansen FOIL .12 .30
325 Roman Josi .15 .40
326 Juuse Saros .20 .50
327 Filip Forsberg .25 .60
328 Eeli Tolvanen .15 .40
329 Cody Glass .12 .30
330 Ryan Johansen .12 .30
331 Matt Duchene .15 .40
332 Colton Sissons .10 .25
333 Mikael Granlund .12 .30
334 Mattias Ekholm .12 .30
335 Matt Luff .10 .25
336 Luke Kunin .10 .25
337 New Jersey Devils Logo FOIL .12 .30
338 New Jersey Devils HL .12 .30
339 NJ Devil FOIL .12 .30
340 Jack Hughes FOIL .40 1.00
341 P.K. Subban FOIL .20 .50
342 Jesper Bratt .15 .40
343 Nikita Gusev .12 .30
344 Mackenzie Blackwood .15 .40
345 Nico Hischier .25 .60
346 Yegor Sharangovich .15 .40
347 Pavel Zacha .12 .30
348 Damon Severson .10 .25
349 Travis Zajac .10 .25
350 Miles Wood .10 .25
351 Jack Hughes .40 1.00
352 A.J. Greer .10 .25
353 P.K. Subban .20 .50
354 New York Islanders Logo FOIL .12 .30
355 New York Islanders HL .12 .30
356 Sparky FOIL .12 .30
357 Anders Lee FOIL .12 .30
358 Mathew Barzal FOIL .20 .50
359 Mathew Barzal .20 .50
360 Semyon Varlamov .15 .40
361 Brock Nelson .15 .40
362 Josh Bailey .12 .30
363 Anders Lee .12 .30
364 Anatoli Golyshev .10 .25
365 Anthony Beauvillier .10 .25
366 Ryan Pulock .12 .30
367 Adam Pelech .10 .25
368 Scott Mayfield .10 .25
369 Cal Clutterbuck .10 .25
370 Jean-Gabriel Pageau .10 .25
371 New York Rangers Logo FOIL .12 .30
372 New York Rangers HL .12 .30
373 Kaapo Kakko FOIL .12 .30
374 Artemi Panarin FOIL .30 .75
375 Alexis Lafreniere FOIL .25 .60
376 Kaapo Kakko .12 .30
377 Igor Shesterkin .30 .75
378 Mika Zibanejad .20 .50
379 Ryan Strome .15 .40
380 Dryden Hunt .10 .25
381 Sammy Blais .10 .25
382 Artemi Panarin .30 .75
383 Chris Kreider .20 .50
384 Adam Fox .20 .50
385 Alexis Lafreniere .25 .60
386 Jacob Trouba .12 .30
387 Filip Chytil .12 .30
388 Ottawa Senators Logo FOIL .12 .30
389 Ottawa Senators HL .12 .30
390 Spartacat FOIL .12 .30
391 Brady Tkachuk FOIL .25 .60
392 Nick Paul FOIL .10 .25
393 Brady Tkachuk .25 .60
394 Connor Brown .12 .30
395 Matt Murray .15 .40
396 Josh Norris .15 .40
397 Thomas Chabot .15 .40
398 Chris Tierney .12 .30
399 Michael Del Zotto .12 .30
400 Artem Anisimov .10 .25
401 Nick Paul .10 .25
402 Victor Mete .10 .25
403 Drake Batherson .15 .40
404 Nikita Zaitsev .10 .25
405 Philadelphia Flyers Logo FOIL .12 .30
406 Philadelphia Flyers HL .12 .30
407 Gritty FOIL .12 .30
408 Claude Giroux FOIL .15 .40
409 Kevin Hayes FOIL .12 .30
410 Claude Giroux .15 .40
411 Travis Konecny .15 .40
412 Carter Hart .15 .40
413 Sean Couturier .12 .30
414 Cam Atkinson .15 .40
415 Kevin Hayes .12 .30
416 James van Riemsdyk .12 .30
417 Ivan Provorov .12 .30
418 Joel Farabee .15 .40
419 Scott Laughton .10 .25
420 Travis Sanheim .10 .25
421 Oskar Lindblom .12 .30
422 Pittsburgh Penguins Logo FOIL .12 .30
423 Pittsburgh Penguins HL .12 .30
424 Iceburgh FOIL .12 .30
425 Sidney Crosby FOIL .60 1.50
426 Evgeni Malkin FOIL .30 .75
427 Sidney Crosby .60 1.50
428 Evgeni Malkin .30 .75
429 Tristan Jarry .15 .40
430 Bryan Rust .15 .40
431 Kris Letang .20 .50
432 Jake Guentzel .25 .60
433 Jeff Carter .12 .30
434 Kasperi Kapanen .12 .30
435 John Marino .15 .40
436 Jason Zucker .15 .40
437 Teddy Blueger .10 .25
438 Mike Matheson .10 .25
439 San Jose Sharks Logo FOIL .12 .30
440 San Jose Sharks HL .12 .30
441 S.J. Sharkie FOIL .12 .30
442 Evander Kane FOIL .15 .40
443 Erik Karlsson FOIL .20 .50
444 Brent Burns .15 .40
445 Erik Karlsson .20 .50
446 Alexander Barabanov .10 .25
447 Timo Meier .15 .40
448 Evander Kane .15 .40
449 Logan Couture .20 .50
450 Tomas Hertl .15 .40
451 Kevin Labanc .10 .25
452 Dylan Gambrell .10 .25
453 Ryan Donato .12 .30
454 Marc-Edouard Vlasic .10 .25
455 Joel Kellman .10 .25
456 St. Louis Blues Logo FOIL .12 .30
457 St. Louis Blues HL .12 .30
458 Louie FOIL .12 .30
459 Vladimir Tarasenko FOIL .20 .50
460 Brayden Schenn FOIL .15 .40
461 Ryan O'Reilly .15 .40
462 Vladimir Tarasenko .20 .50
463 Jordan Binnington .25 .60
464 David Perron .12 .30
465 Brayden Schenn .15 .40
466 Brandon Saad .12 .30
467 Torey Krug .12 .30
468 Pavel Buchnevich .12 .30
469 Zach Sanford .10 .25
470 Tyler Bozak .10 .25
471 Colton Parayko .12 .30
472 Ivan Barbashev .12 .30
473 Tampa Bay Lightning Logo FOIL .12 .30
474 Tampa Bay Lightning HL .12 .30
475 Thunderbug FOIL .12 .30
476 Steven Stamkos FOIL .30 .75
477 Brayden Point FOIL .20 .50
478 Nikita Kucherov .30 .75
479 Victor Hedman .20 .50
480 Andrei Vasilevskiy .25 .60
481 Steven Stamkos .30 .75
482 Brayden Point .20 .50
483 Alex Killorn .10 .25
484 Anthony Cirelli .12 .30
485 Ondrej Palat .12 .30
486 Mikhail Sergachev .12 .30
487 Ryan McDonagh .10 .25
488 Ross Colton .20 .50
489 Mathieu Joseph .10 .25
490 Toronto Maple Leafs Logo FOIL .12 .30
491 Toronto Maple Leafs HL .12 .30
492 Carlton FOIL .12 .30
493 John Tavares FOIL .25 .60
494 Auston Matthews FOIL .60 1.50
495 John Tavares .25 .60
496 Mitch Marner .25 .60
497 Kurtis Gabriel .10 .25
498 Auston Matthews .60 1.50
499 William Nylander .30 .75
500 Jake Muzzin .15 .40
501 Michael Bunting .15 .40
502 Wayne Simmonds .15 .40
503 Michael Amadio .10 .25
504 Morgan Rielly .15 .40
505 Jason Spezza .15 .40
506 David Kampf .10 .25
507 Vancouver Canucks Logo FOIL .12 .30
508 Vancouver Canucks HL .12 .30
509 Fin FOIL .12 .30
510 Tanner Pearson FOIL .15 .40
511 Bo Horvat FOIL .20 .50
512 Elias Pettersson .25 .60
513 J.T. Miller .20 .50
514 Jaroslav Halak .15 .40
515 Bo Horvat .20 .50
516 Quinn Hughes .40 1.00
517 Tanner Pearson .15 .40
518 Brock Boeser .20 .50
519 Nils Hoglander .12 .30
520 Madison Bowey .10 .25
521 Brad Hunt .10 .25
522 Tyler Myers .10 .25
523 Justin Bailey .10 .25
524 Vegas Golden Knights Logo FOIL .12 .30
525 Vegas Golden Knights HL .12 .30
526 Chance FOIL .12 .30
527 Alex Pietrangelo FOIL .12 .30
528 Jonathan Marchessault FOIL .20 .50
529 Mark Stone .20 .50
530 Brett Howden .10 .25
531 Max Pacioretty .15 .40
532 Reilly Smith .15 .40
533 Jonathan Marchessault .20 .50
534 William Karlsson .20 .50
535 Shea Theodore .20 .50
536 Alex Pietrangelo .12 .30

Card	Low	High
537 Alec Martinez	.10	.25
538 Chandler Stephenson	.12	.30
539 William Carrier	.10	.25
540 Alex Tuch	.15	.40
541 Washington Capitals Logo FOIL	.12	.30
542 Washington Capitals HL	.12	.30
543 Slapshot FOIL	.12	.30
544 Alex Ovechkin FOIL	.60	1.50
545 Nicklas Backstrom FOIL	.15	.40
546 Alex Ovechkin	.60	1.50
547 Ilya Samsonov	.15	.40
548 Nic Dowd	.10	.25
549 Nicklas Backstrom	.15	.40
550 Carl Hagelin	.10	.25
551 Evgeny Kuznetsov	.20	.50
552 John Carlson	.15	.40
553 T.J. Oshie	.15	.40
554 Tom Wilson	.15	.40
555 Lars Eller	.10	.25
556 Dmitry Orlov	.15	.40
557 Michal Kempny	.10	.25
558 Winnipeg Jets Logo FOIL	.12	.30
559 Winnipeg Jets HL	.12	.30
560 Moose FOIL	.12	.30
561 Mark Scheifele FOIL	.25	.60
562 Blake Wheeler FOIL	.15	.40
563 Mark Scheifele	.25	.60
564 Blake Wheeler	.15	.40
565 Connor Hellebuyck	.30	.75
566 Kyle Connor	.25	.60
567 Brenden Dillon	.10	.25
568 Nikolaj Ehlers	.15	.40
569 Neal Pionk	.10	.25
570 Josh Morrissey	.20	.50
571 Pierre-Luc Dubois	.12	.30
572 Paul Stastny	.12	.30
573 Dylan DeMelo	.10	.25
574 Andrew Copp	.10	.25
575 Nikita Kucherov BH	.30	.75
576 Miro Heiskanen BH	.20	.50
577 Nathan MacKinnon BH	.60	1.50
578 Josh Bailey BH	.12	.30
579 Brayden Point BH	.20	.50
580 Joe Pavelski BH	.20	.50
581 Alex Tuch BH	.15	.40
582 Brock Nelson BH	.15	.40
583 Bo Horvat BH	.20	.50
584 Victor Hedman BH	.20	.50
585 Alex Ovechkin IT	.60	1.50
586 Max Pacioretty IT	.15	.40
587 Sidney Crosby IT	.60	1.50
588 Connor McDavid IT	.75	2.00
589 Artemi Panarin IT	.30	.75
590 Noel Acciari IT	.10	.25
591 Erik Karlsson IT	.20	.50
592 Jonathan Toews IT	.25	.60
593 Ryan McDonagh IT	.10	.25
594 Kirill Kaprizov '54 FOIL	.50	1.25
595 Ty Smith '54 FOIL	.15	.40
596 Pius Suter '54 FOIL	.12	.30
597 Josh Norris '54 FOIL	.15	.40
598 Gabriel Vilardi '54 FOIL	.15	.40
599 Jake Evans '54 FOIL	.10	.25
600 Liam Foudy '54 FOIL	.12	.30
601 Kaapo Kahkonen '54 FOIL	.15	.40
602 John Leonard '54 FOIL	.10	.25
603 Alexis Lafreniere '54 FOIL	.25	.60
604 Alexander Romanov '54 FOIL	.12	.30
605 Igor Shesterkin '54 FOIL	.30	.75
606 Bowen Byram '54 FOIL	.20	.50
607 Ilya Sorokin '54 FOIL	.25	.60
608 Nils Hoglander '54 FOIL	.12	.30
609 Vitek Vanecek '54 FOIL	.15	.40
610 Tim Stutzle '54 FOIL	.20	.50
611 Dylan Cozens '54 FOIL	.15	.40
612 Philipp Kurashev '54 FOIL	.12	.30
613 Joel Kiviranta '54 FOIL	.10	.25
614 Artturi Lehkonen RETRO	.12	.30
615 Bo Horvat RETRO	.20	.50
616 Matthew Tkachuk RETRO	.30	.75
617 Mark Scheifele RETRO	.25	.60
618 Auston Matthews RETRO	.60	1.50
619 Connor McDavid RETRO	.75	2.00
620 Brady Tkachuk RETRO	.25	.60
621 Nathan MacKinnon RETRO	.60	1.50
622 Vladimir Tarasenko RETRO	.20	.50
623 Phil Kessel RETRO	.15	.40
624 Cam Fowler RETRO	.15	.40
625 Jonathan Marchessault RETRO	.20	.50
626 Anze Kopitar RETRO	.25	.60
627 Evander Kane RETRO	.15	.40
628 Jared Spurgeon RETRO	.15	.40
629 Alex DeBrincat RETRO	.20	.50
630 Alexandre Texier RETRO	.10	.25
631 Sebastian Aho RETRO	.25	.60
632 Steven Stamkos RETRO	.30	.75
633 Patric Hornqvist RETRO	.10	.25
634 Filip Forsberg RETRO	.25	.60
635 Filip Zadina RETRO	.12	.30
636 Miro Heiskanen RETRO	.20	.50
637 Patrice Bergeron RETRO	.20	.50
638 Alex Ovechkin RETRO	.60	1.50
639 Jack Hughes RETRO	.40	1.00
640 Claude Giroux RETRO	.15	.40
641 Anders Lee RETRO	.12	.30
642 Sidney Crosby RETRO	.60	1.50
643 Artemi Panarin RETRO	.30	.75
644 Jack Eichel RETRO	.25	.60
645 Semyon Varlamov NS	.15	.40
646 Connor Hellebuyck NS	.30	.75
647 Andrei Vasilevskiy NS	.25	.60
648 Carey Price NS	.30	.75
649 Jordan Binnington NS	.25	.60
650 Mikko Koskinen NS	.10	.25
651 Carter Hart NS	.15	.40
652 Ilya Samsonov NS	.15	.40
653 Jonathan Quick NS	.20	.50
654 Tuukka Rask NS	.20	.50
655 Kraken Logo 1	.12	.30
656 Kraken Logo 2	.12	.30
657 Kraken Logo 3	.12	.30
658 Kraken Logo 4	.12	.30
659 Kraken Logo 5	.12	.30
660 Kraken Logo 6	.12	.30
661 Kraken Logo 7	.12	.30
662 Kraken Logo 8	.12	.30
663 Kraken Logo 9	.12	.30
664 Kraken Logo 10	.12	.30
665 Kraken Logo 11	.12	.30
666 Kraken Logo 12	.12	.30

1995-96 Topps SuperSkills

Card	Low	High
COMPLETE SET (90)	8.00	20.00
1 Mario Lemieux	.75	2.00
2 Adam Oates	.15	.40
3 Donald Audette	.07	.20
4 Andrew Cassels	.07	.20
5 Pat LaFontaine	.15	.40
6 Mathieu Schneider	.07	.20
7 Scott Stevens	.07	.20
8 Mikael Renberg	.15	.40
9 Pierre Turgeon	.15	.40
10 Steve Yzerman	.75	2.00
11 Russ Courtnall	.07	.20
12 Oleg Tverdovsky	.15	.40
13 Craig Janney	.07	.20
14 Doug Gilmour	.20	.50
15 Wayne Gretzky	1.25	3.00
16 Paul Kariya	.60	1.50
17 Joe Sakic	.40	1.00
18 Peter Forsberg	.40	1.00
19 Brian Leetch	.20	.50
20 Jaromir Jagr	.40	1.00
21 Geoff Sanderson	.07	.20
22 Rob Niedermayer	.15	.40
23 Ray Ferraro	.07	.20
24 Alexandre Daigle	.07	.20
25 Joe Juneau	.15	.40
26 Don Sweeney	.07	.20
27 Scott Niedermayer	.07	.20
28 Mike Gartner	.07	.20
29 Paul Coffey	.15	.40
30 Pavel Bure	.40	1.00
31 Teemu Selanne	.30	.75
32 Mats Sundin	.20	.50
33 Trevor Linden	.15	.40
34 Sergei Fedorov	.30	.75
35 Theo Fleury	.20	.50
36 Alexander Mogilny	.15	.40
37 Garry Galley	.07	.20
38 Stu Barnes	.07	.20
39 Glen Wesley	.07	.20
40 Eric Lindros	.40	1.00
41 Stephane Richer	.07	.20
42 John LeClair	.20	.50
43 Pat Verbeek	.15	.40
44 Bill Guerin	.07	.20
45 Wendel Clark	.15	.40
46 Mike Modano	.20	.50
47 Keith Primeau	.15	.40
48 Brett Hull	.25	.60
49 Al MacInnis	.15	.40
50 Chris Chelios	.20	.50
51 Keith Tkachuk	.20	.50
52 Dave Andreychuk	.07	.20
53 Kevin Hatcher	.07	.20
54 Chris Pronger	.07	.20
55 Brendan Shanahan	.20	.50
56 Luc Robitaille	.15	.40
57 Ray Bourque	.30	.75
58 Mark Recchi	.15	.40
59 Brian Bradley	.07	.20
60 Mark Messier	.25	.60
61 Kevin Stevens	.07	.20
62 John MacLean	.07	.20
63 Cam Neely	.20	.50
64 Rick Tocchet	.07	.20
65 Jeremy Roenick	.20	.50
66 Phil Housley	.07	.20
67 Jason Arnott	.15	.40
68 Todd Harvey	.07	.20
69 Jeff Friesen	.15	.40
70 Alexei Zhamnov	.15	.40
71 David Oliver	.07	.20
72 Bernie Nicholls	.07	.20
73 Jim Carey	.15	.40
74 Mike Richter	.15	.40
75 Dominik Hasek	.30	.75
76 Sean Burke	.07	.20
77 Ron Hextall	.15	.40
78 John Vanbiesbrouck	.20	.50
79 Tom Barrasso	.15	.40
80 Martin Brodeur	.40	1.00
81 Patrick Roy	.75	2.00
82 Trevor Kidd	.15	.40
83 Andy Moog	.15	.40
84 Mike Vernon	.07	.20
85 Felix Potvin	.20	.50
86 Bill Ranford	.15	.40
87 Kelly Hrudey	.15	.40
88 Grant Fuhr	.15	.40
89 Kirk McLean	.15	.40
90 Ed Belfour	.20	.50

1995-96 Topps SuperSkills Platinum

Card	Low	High
COMPLETE SET (90)	15.00	40.00
*PLATINUM: .6X TO 1.5X BASIC CARDS		

1995-96 Topps SuperSkills Super Rookies

Card	Low	High
COMPLETE SET (15)	4.80	12.00
SR1 Ed Jovanovski	.20	.50
SR2 Jason Bonsignore	.08	.25
SR3 Jeff O'Neill	.40	1.00
SR4 Cory Stillman	.08	.25
SR5 Chad Kilger	.20	.50
SR6 Aki Berg	.20	.50
SR7 Todd Bertuzzi	1.25	3.00
SR8 Shane Doan	.40	1.00
SR9 Kyle McLaren	.20	.50
SR10 Radek Dvorak	.20	.50
SR11 Saku Koivu	1.25	3.00
SR12 Daniel Alfredsson	.40	1.00
SR13 Antti Tormanen	.08	.25
SR14 Niklas Sundstrom	.20	.50
SR15 Vitali Yachmenev	.08	.25

2002-03 Topps Total

Card	Low	High
COMPLETE SET (440)	15.00	40.00
1 Nicklas Lidstrom	.15	.40
2 Mikko Eloranta	.10	.25
3 Richard Park	.10	.25
4 Eric Lindros	.25	.60
5 Vincent Lecavalier	.15	.40
6 Dany Heatley	.12	.30
7 Roman Turek	.15	.40
8 Rostislav Klesla	.10	.25
9 Paul Kariya	.15	.40
10 Marian Hossa	.15	.40
11 Patrick Roy	.40	1.00
12 Henrik Sedin	.20	.50
13 Adam Graves	.12	.30
14 Ian Laperriere	.12	.30
15 Jiri Fischer	.10	.25
16 Nick Schultz	.10	.25
17 Steve Sullivan	.10	.25
18 Sandis Ozolinsh	.10	.25
19 Evgeni Nabokov	.12	.30
20 Dimitri Khristich	.10	.25
21 Danny Markov	.10	.25
22 Adam Foote	.10	.25
23 David Vyborny	.10	.25
24 Jocelyn Thibault	.12	.30
25 Mike Leclerc	.10	.25
26 Pavol Demitra	.20	.50
27 Scott Mellanby	.10	.25
28 Brent Sopel	.10	.25
29 Brad Isbister	.10	.25
30 Sami Salo	.10	.25
31 Jose Theodore	.15	.40
32 Simon Gagne	.15	.40
33 Rem Murray	.10	.25
34 Mike Ricci	.10	.25
35 Kim Johnsson	.10	.25
36 Adam Oates	.15	.40
37 Taylor Pyatt	.10	.25
38 Rod Brind'Amour	.15	.40
39 Mike Modano	.25	.60
40 Jason Woolley	.10	.25
41 Dimitri Yushkevich	.10	.25
42 Craig Johnson	.10	.25
43 Tony Hrkac	.10	.25
44 Scott Young	.10	.25
45 Marian Gaborik	.15	.40
46 Patrik Stefan	.12	.30
47 Jon Klemm	.10	.25
48 Andy McDonald	.15	.40
49 Chris Pronger	.15	.40
50 Frantisek Kaberle	.10	.25
51 Jean-Sebastien Giguere	.15	.40
52 Luc Robitaille	.15	.40
53 Scott Stevens	.15	.40
54 Roberto Luongo	.25	.60
55 Teppo Numminen	.10	.25
56 Alyn McCauley	.10	.25
57 John Grahame	.10	.25
58 David Legwand	.12	.30
59 Hal Gill	.10	.25
60 Mattias Ohlund	.10	.25
61 Radim Vrbata	.10	.25
62 Doug Gilmour	.20	.50
63 Vaclav Prospal	.10	.25
64 Brian Leetch	.12	.30
65 Sheldon Keefe	.10	.25
66 Randy McKay	.10	.25
67 Mikael Samuelsson	.10	.25
68 Pavel Bure	.15	.40
69 Zdeno Chara	.15	.40
70 P.J. Stock	.10	.25
71 Shawn McEachern	.10	.25
72 Radek Martinek	.10	.25
73 Mike Rathje	.10	.25
74 Kenny Jonsson	.10	.25
75 Jamie Langenbrunner	.12	.30
76 Chris Phillips	.10	.25
77 Zigmund Palffy	.15	.40
78 Stu Barnes	.10	.25
79 Robert Reichel	.10	.25
80 Jason Allison	.12	.30
81 Dimitri Kalinin	.10	.25
82 Chris Simon	.10	.25
83 Arturs Irbe	.12	.30
84 Tony Amonte	.12	.30
85 Ruslan Salei	.10	.25
86 Pascal Rheaume	.10	.25
87 Marc Denis	.12	.30
88 Marc Chouinard	.10	.25
89 Jim Dowd	.10	.25
90 Claude Lemieux	.12	.30
91 Alexei Zhamnov	.12	.30
92 Al MacInnis	.20	.50
93 Cory Stillman	.10	.25
94 Bob Boughner	.10	.25
95 Kris Draper	.10	.25
96 Mario Lemieux	.60	1.50
97 Sean Burke	.10	.25
98 Wes Walz	.10	.25
99 Brenden Morrow	.12	.30
100 Dave Andreychuk	.15	.40
101 Jaromir Jagr	.50	1.25
102 Markus Naslund	.15	.40
103 Nick Boynton	.10	.25
104 Sean Hill	.10	.25
105 Trevor Linden	.15	.40
106 Bryan Berard	.10	.25
107 Chris Neilson	.10	.25
108 Marco Sturm	.10	.25
109 Oleg Petrov	.10	.25
110 Scott Gomez	.12	.30
111 Luke Richardson	.10	.25
112 Manny Malhotra	.10	.25
113 Valeri Bure	.12	.30
114 Marcel Hossa	.10	.25
115 Todd Marchant	.10	.25
116 Radek Bonk	.12	.30
117 Matt Bradley	.10	.25
118 Jochen Hecht	.10	.25
119 Dan McGillis	.10	.25
120 Adrian Aucoin	.10	.25
121 Eric Belanger	.10	.25
122 Peter Forsberg	.30	.75
123 Alexei Morozov	.10	.25
124 Jimmie Olvestad	.10	.25
125 Ed Jovanovski	.12	.30
126 Chris Drury	.15	.40
127 Alexander Mogilny	.12	.30
128 Stephen Weiss	.15	.40
129 Manny Legace	.15	.40
130 Jarome Iginla	.20	.50
131 Doug Weight	.15	.40
132 Martin St. Louis	.15	.40
133 Alexander Khavanov	.10	.25
134 Chris Chelios	.15	.40
135 Viktor Kozlov	.10	.25
136 Bret Hedican	.10	.25
137 Denis Arkhipov	.10	.25
138 Jere Lehtinen	.15	.40
139 Mathieu Schneider	.10	.25
140 Tomas Kaberle	.10	.25
141 Brian Gionta	.10	.25
142 Janne Niinimaa	.10	.25
143 Mark Parrish	.10	.25
144 Todd White	.10	.25
145 Geoff Sanderson	.12	.30
146 Yanic Perreault	.10	.25
147 Roman Hamrlik	.10	.25
148 Mike Fisher	.10	.25
149 Jiri Dopita	.10	.25
150 Claude Lapointe	.10	.25
151 Vaclav Nedorost	.10	.25
152 Mikael Renberg	.10	.25
153 Jozef Stumpel	.10	.25
154 Felix Potvin	.25	.60
155 Chris Gratton	.10	.25
156 Adam Deadmarsh	.10	.25
157 Sergei Fedorov	.25	.60
158 Mike Sillinger	.10	.25
159 Kris Beech	.10	.25
160 Grant Marshall	.10	.25
161 Brent Johnson	.12	.30
162 Alexei Kovalev	.12	.30
163 Darren McCarty	.12	.30
164 Marc Savard	.10	.25
165 Janne Laukkanen	.10	.25
166 Phil Housley	.12	.30
167 Tomas Holmstrom	.10	.25
168 Bill Guerin	.15	.40
169 Darius Kasparaitis	.10	.25
170 Jaroslav Modry	.10	.25
171 Martin Gelinas	.10	.25
172 Peter Bondra	.15	.40
173 Steven Reinprecht	.10	.25
174 Anson Carter	.12	.30
175 Eric Brewer	.10	.25
176 Magnus Arvedson	.10	.25
177 Patrice Brisebois	.10	.25
178 Sergei Brylin	.10	.25
179 Vitali Vishnevski	.10	.25
180 Marcus Nilsson	.10	.25
181 Niklas Sundstrom	.10	.25
182 Daymond Langkow	.12	.30
183 Craig Conroy	.10	.25
184 Gary Roberts	.10	.25
185 Justin Williams	.12	.30
186 Matt Cooke	.10	.25
187 Pierre Turgeon	.12	.30
188 Steve Konowalchuk	.10	.25
189 Yannick Tremblay	.10	.25
190 Tom Poti	.10	.25
191 Sergei Zholtok	.10	.25
192 Robyn Regehr	.10	.25
193 Mike Richter	.15	.40
194 Shawn Bates	.10	.25
195 Pavel Trnka	.10	.25
196 Martin Straka	.12	.30
197 Jonas Hoglund	.10	.25
198 Filip Kuba	.10	.25
199 Chris Osgood	.15	.40
200 Brad May	.10	.25
201 David Aebischer	.12	.30
202 Fred Brathwaite	.12	.30
203 Lubos Bartecko	.10	.25
204 Marty Turco	.15	.40
205 Petr Nedved	.10	.25
206 Shayne Corson	.12	.30
207 Sergei Samsonov	.12	.30
208 Patrik Elias	.15	.40
209 Martin Erat	.10	.25
210 Krystofer Kolanos	.10	.25
211 Joe Thornton	.25	.60
212 Ivan Novoseltsev	.10	.25
213 Eric Messier	.10	.25
214 Daniel Cleary	.12	.30
215 Alex Tanguay	.12	.30
216 Robert Lang	.10	.25
217 Wade Redden	.10	.25
218 Scott Walker	.10	.25
219 Milan Hejduk	.12	.30
220 Ken Daneyko	.10	.25
221 J-P Dumont	.10	.25
222 Ian Moran	.10	.25
223 Christian Berglund	.10	.25
224 Alexei Yashin	.12	.30
225 Brad Stuart	.10	.25
226 Donald Brashear	.10	.25
227 Curtis Brown	.10	.25
228 John LeClair	.15	.40
229 Manny Fernandez	.10	.25
230 Maxim Afinogenov	.10	.25
231 Roman Cechmanek	.12	.30
232 Tyler Wright	.10	.25
233 Slava Kozlov	.10	.25
234 Tyler Arnason	.15	.40
235 Sandy McCarthy	.10	.25
236 Pascal Dupuis	.10	.25
237 Olaf Kolzig	.15	.40
238 Kyle Calder	.10	.25
239 Jeremy Roenick	.25	.60
240 Mathieu Dandenault	.10	.25
241 Jeff O'Neill	.10	.25
242 Dave Tanabe	.10	.25
243 Calle Johansson	.10	.25
244 Greg deVries	.10	.25
245 Andrew Brunette	.10	.25
246 Dan Hinote	.10	.25
247 Jason Smith	.10	.25
248 Mark Bell	.10	.25
249 Pavel Kubina	.10	.25
250 Teemu Selanne	.30	.75
251 Vladimir Orszagh	.10	.25
252 Brad Ference	.10	.25
253 Darryl Sydor	.10	.25
254 Vitali Yachmenev	.10	.25
255 Scott Hartnell	.10	.25
256 Fredrik Modin	.10	.25
257 Alexei Zhitnik	.12	.30
258 Brett Hull	.30	.75
259 Glen Murray	.12	.30
260 Michael Peca	.12	.30
261 Owen Nolan	.15	.40
262 Tie Domi	.12	.30
263 Ville Nieminen	.10	.25
264 Rob Blake	.15	.40
265 Greg Johnson	.10	.25
266 Andrei Markov	.15	.40
267 Josef Vasicek	.10	.25
268 Ryan Smyth	.12	.30
269 Vincent Damphousse	.12	.30
270 Mark Recchi	.20	.50
271 Rob Niedermayer	.12	.30
272 Mariusz Czerkawski	.10	.25
273 Glen Wesley	.10	.25
274 Brian Boucher	.12	.30
275 Bryan McCabe	.10	.25
276 Ron Tugnutt	.12	.30
277 Daniel Briere	.12	.30
278 Igor Larionov	.15	.40
279 Keith Tkachuk	.15	.40
280 Mats Sundin	.15	.40
281 Dwayne Roloson	.10	.25
282 Andrew Cassels	.10	.25
283 Brendan Morrison	.12	.30
284 Bryan Smolinski	.12	.30
285 Jan Hlavac	.10	.25
286 Jamal Mayers	.10	.25
287 Kevin Weekes	.12	.30
288 Tim Connolly	.10	.25
289 Steve Yzerman	.40	1.00
290 Derek Morris	.10	.25
291 Derian Hatcher	.12	.30
292 Steve Shields	.12	.30
293 Martin Brodeur	.40	1.00
294 Marcus Ragnarsson	.10	.25
295 Scott Thornton	.10	.25
296 Oleg Kvasha	.10	.25
297 Mike York	.10	.25
298 Tomi Kallio	.10	.25
299 Martin Skoula	.10	.25
300 Jeff Halpern	.10	.25
301 Ed Belfour	.15	.40
302 Andrew Ference	.10	.25
303 Nikolai Khabibulin	.15	.40
304 Bryce Salvador	.10	.25
305 Lubomir Visnovsky	.10	.25
306 Dan Cloutier	.12	.30
307 Andy Delmore	.10	.25
308 Martin Lapointe	.12	.30
309 Daniel Sedin	.20	.50
310 Kelly Buchberger	.12	.30
311 Darcy Tucker	.10	.25
312 Sergei Berezin	.10	.25
313 Ruslan Fedotenko	.10	.25
314 Mark Messier	.30	.75
315 Mike Comrie	.15	.40
316 Bobby Holik	.10	.25
317 Shane Doan	.12	.30
318 Michal Handzus	.12	.30
319 Joe Sakic	.30	.75
320 Kristian Huselius	.10	.25
321 Ben Clymer	.10	.25
322 Mattias Norstrom	.10	.25
323 Pavel Datsyuk	.25	.60
324 Richard Matvichuk	.10	.25
325 Dainius Zubrus	.10	.25
326 Craig Rivet	.10	.25
327 Eric Desjardins	.10	.25
328 Patrick Marleau	.15	.40
329 Mike Grier	.10	.25
330 Steve Rucchin	.10	.25
331 Kimmo Timonen	.10	.25
332 Brendan Witt	.10	.25
333 Sami Kapanen	.10	.25
334 Todd Bertuzzi	.15	.40
335 Ilya Kovalchuk	.20	.50
336 Donald Audette	.10	.25
337 Georges Laraque	.12	.30
338 Jason Arnott	.12	.30
339 John Madden	.10	.25
340 Petr Sykora	.12	.30
341 Tommy Salo	.12	.30
342 Daniel Alfredsson	.15	.40
343 Eric Weinrich	.10	.25
344 Radek Dvorak	.12	.30
345 Stephane Yelle	.10	.25
346 Sergei Zubov	.12	.30
347 Milan Hnilicka	.12	.30
348 Lubomir Sekeras	.10	.25
349 Espen Knutsen	.10	.25
350 Travis Green	.10	.25
351 Jan Hrdina	.10	.25
352 Paul Laus	.10	.25
353 Bates Battaglia	.10	.25
354 Miroslav Satan	.15	.40
355 Craig Berube	.10	.25
356 Sean O'Donnell	.10	.25
357 Joe Nieuwendyk	.12	.30
358 Patrick Lalime	.12	.30
359 Brian Rafalski	.10	.25
360 Michael Nylander	.10	.25
361 Jean-Luc Grand Pierre	.10	.25
362 Ron Francis	.20	.50
363 Andrei Nikolishin	.10	.25
364 Dallas Drake	.12	.30
365 Eric Daze	.10	.25
366 Andreas Dackell	.10	.25
367 Scott Niedermayer	.15	.40
368 Chris Clark	.10	.25
369 Brendan Shanahan	.15	.40
370 Tomas Vokoun	.12	.30
371 Johan Hedberg	.15	.40
372 Nikita Alexeev	.10	.25
373 Dave Scatchard	.10	.25
374 Matt Cullen	.10	.25
375 Steve Thomas	.10	.25
376 Brian Rolston	.12	.30
377 Richard Zednik	.10	.25
378 Sergei Gonchar	.12	.30
379 Keith Primeau	.12	.30
380 Jeff Friesen	.10	.25
381 Keith Carney	.10	.25
382 Kirk Maltby	.10	.25
383 Erik Cole	.10	.25
384 Martin Biron	.12	.30
385 Jody Shelley	.10	.25
386 Brad Richards	.15	.40
387 Michal Rozsival	.12	.30
388 Martin Havlat	.12	.30
389 Igor Korolev	.10	.25
390 Ladislav Nagy	.10	.25
391 Curtis Joseph	.20	.50
392 Toni Lydman	.10	.25
393 Antti Laaksonen	.10	.25
394 Jeff Jillson	.10	.25
395 Saku Koivu	.15	.40
396 Trevor Letowski	.10	.25
397 Ray Whitney	.12	.30
398 Olli Jokinen	.15	.40
399 Colin White	.10	.25
400 Mike Dunham	.12	.30
401 Dan Blackburn	.12	.30
402 Ron Hainsey RC	.40	1.00
403 Scottie Upshall RC	.50	1.25
404 Anton Volchenkov RC	.40	1.00
405 Dmitri Bykov RC	.40	1.00
406 Steve Eminger RC	.40	1.00
407 Lasse Pirjeta RC	.40	1.00
408 Tomi Pettinen RC	.40	1.00
409 Ales Hemsky RC	1.50	4.00
410 Chuck Kobasew RC	.50	1.25
411 Jason Spezza RC	2.50	6.00
412 Jeff Paul RC	.40	1.00
413 Adam Hall RC	.40	1.00
414 Rick Nash RC	2.50	6.00
415 Kurt Sauer RC	.40	1.00
416 Alexander Frolov RC	1.00	2.50
417 Patrick Sharp RC	1.25	3.00
418 Alexei Smirnov RC	.50	1.25
419 Tom Koivisto RC	.40	1.00
420 Jay Bouwmeester RC	1.25	3.00
421 Mikael Tellqvist RC	.40	1.00
422 P-M Bouchard RC	.60	1.50
423 Radovan Somik RC	.40	1.00
424 Ivan Majesky RC	.40	1.00
425 Jamie Lundmark	.12	.30
426 Henrik Zetterberg RC	4.00	10.00
427 Dennis Seidenberg RC	.60	1.50
428 Jeff Taffe RC	.40	1.00
429 Martin Gerber RC	.60	1.50
430 Lynn Loyns RC	.40	1.00
431 Micki DuPont RC	.40	1.00
432 Jonathan Cheechoo	.12	.30
433 Eric Godard RC	.40	1.00
434 Stanislav Chistov RC	.40	1.00
435 Alexander Svitov RC	.40	1.00
436 Fedor Fedorov	.10	.25
437 Stephane Veilleux RC	.40	1.00
438 Curtis Sanford RC	.60	1.50
439 Jordan Leopold RC	.60	1.50
440 Carlo Colaiacovo RC	.60	1.50

2002-03 Topps Total Award Winners

Card	Low	High
COMPLETE SET (10)	8.00	15.00
AW1 Jarome Iginla	.75	2.00
AW2 Patrick Roy	2.50	6.00
AW3 Nicklas Lidstrom	.60	1.50
AW4 Jose Theodore	.75	2.00
AW5 Dany Heatley	.75	2.00
AW6 Ron Francis	.50	1.25
AW7 Eric Daze	.50	1.25
AW8 Chris Chelios	.60	1.50
AW9 Saku Koivu	.60	1.50
AW10 Michael Peca	.50	1.25

2002-03 Topps Total Production

Card	Low	High
COMPLETE SET (15)	6.00	12.00
TP1 Jarome Iginla	.40	1.00
TP2 Joe Sakic	.60	1.50
TP3 Mats Sundin	.30	.75
TP4 Peter Forsberg	.75	2.00
TP5 Bill Guerin	.25	.60
TP6 Brendan Shanahan	.50	1.25
TP7 Sergei Fedorov	.60	1.50
TP8 Pavel Bure	.40	1.00
TP9 Jeremy Roenick	.40	1.00
TP10 Tony Amonte	.25	.60
TP11 Teemu Selanne	.30	.75
TP12 Alexander Mogilny	.25	.60
TP13 Markus Naslund	.30	.75
TP14 Todd Bertuzzi	.30	.75
TP15 Jaromir Jagr	.50	1.25

2002-03 Topps Total Signatures

Card	Low	High
TSBG Brian Gionta	8.00	20.00
TSEC Erik Cole	10.00	25.00
TSKK Krystofer Kolanos	10.00	25.00
TSRK Rostislav Klesla	12.00	30.00
TSRV Radim Vrbata	12.00	30.00
TSSW Stephen Weiss	12.00	30.00

2002-03 Topps Total Team Checklists

Card	Low	High
COMPLETE SET (30)	6.00	15.00
TTC1 Ilya Kovalchuk	.40	1.00
TTC2 Joe Thornton	.40	1.00
TTC3 Miroslav Satan	.10	.25
TTC4 Jarome Iginla	.40	1.00
TTC5 Ron Francis	.10	.25
TTC6 Jocelyn Thibault	.10	.25
TTC7 Patrick Roy	1.25	3.00
TTC8 Rick Nash	.40	1.00
TTC9 Mike Modano	.40	1.00
TTC10 Steve Yzerman	.75	2.00
TTC11 Tommy Salo	.10	.25
TTC12 Roberto Luongo	.40	1.00
TTC13 Jason Allison	.10	.25
TTC14 Paul Kariya	.30	.75
TTC15 Marian Gaborik	.40	1.00
TTC16 Jose Theodore	.40	1.00
TTC17 Mike Dunham	.20	.50
TTC18 Martin Brodeur	.75	2.00
TTC19 Michael Peca	.10	.25
TTC20 Pavel Bure	.30	.75
TTC21 Daniel Alfredsson	.20	.50
TTC22 John LeClair	.10	.25
TTC23 Tony Amonte	.10	.25
TTC24 Mario Lemieux	1.25	3.00
TTC25 Owen Nolan	.20	.50
TTC26 Keith Tkachuk	.20	.50
TTC27 Nikolai Khabibulin	.30	.75
TTC28 Mats Sundin	.30	.75
TTC29 Todd Bertuzzi	.10	.25
TTC30 Jaromir Jagr	.60	1.50

2002-03 Topps Total Topps

Card	Low	High
COMPLETE SET (20)	8.00	15.00
TT1 Jarome Iginla	.25	.60
TT2 Patrick Roy	1.00	2.50
TT3 Nicklas Lidstrom	.20	.50
TT4 Jose Theodore	.25	.60
TT5 Joe Sakic	.40	1.00
TT6 Mats Sundin	.20	.50
TT7 Ilya Kovalchuk	.25	.60
TT8 Joe Thornton	.30	.75
TT9 Mike Modano	.30	.75
TT10 Brett Hull	.25	.60
TT11 Steve Yzerman	1.00	2.50
TT12 Curtis Joseph	.20	.50
TT13 Paul Kariya	.20	.50
TT14 Patrik Elias	.12	.30
TT15 Martin Brodeur	.50	1.25
TT16 Eric Lindros	.20	.50
TT17 Daniel Alfredsson	.12	.30
TT18 Mario Lemieux	1.25	3.00
TT19 Owen Nolan	.12	.30
TT20 Jaromir Jagr	.30	.75

2003-04 Topps Traded

Card	Low	High
COMPLETE SET (165)	25.00	50.00
TT1 Felix Potvin	.25	.60
TT2 Chris Drury	.12	.30
TT3 Karel Rachunek	.10	.25
TT4 Miikka Kiprusoff	.15	.40
TT5 Justin Williams	.12	.30
TT6 Bryan Berard	.12	.30
TT7 Jim Vandermeer	.10	.25
TT8 Shayne Corson	.12	.30
TT9 Teemu Selanne	.30	.75
TT10 Peter Worrell	.10	.25
TT11 Darryl Sydor	.10	.25
TT12 Todd Marchant	.10	.25
TT13 Ray Whitney	.12	.30
TT14 Robert Lang	.10	.25
TT15 Adam Oates	.15	.40
TT16 Jozef Stumpel	.10	.25
TT17 Luc Robitaille	.15	.40
TT18 Roman Cechmanek	.12	.30
TT19 Martin Straka	.10	.25
TT20 Sergei Fedorov	.25	.60
TT21 Michael Nylander	.10	.25
TT22 Steve Sullivan	.10	.25
TT23 Steve Konowalchuk	.10	.25
TT24 Valeri Bure	.10	.25
TT25 Jaromir Jagr	.50	1.25
TT26 Peter Bondra	.15	.40
TT27 Mike Grier	.10	.25
TT28 Cory Stillman	.10	.25
TT29 Joe Nieuwendyk	.12	.30
TT30 Brian Leetch	.12	.30
TT31 Johan Hedberg	.12	.30
TT32 Andrew Raycroft	.12	.30
TT33 Chuck Kobasew	.10	.25
TT34 Brett McLean	.10	.25
TT35 Craig Andersson	.15	.40
TT36 Michael Leighton	.10	.25
TT37 Matthew Barnaby	.10	.25
TT38 Philippe Sauve	.12	.30
TT39 Chris Gratton	.10	.25
TT40 Radek Dvorak	.12	.30
TT41 Raffi Torres	.10	.25
TT42 Ossi Vaananen	.10	.25
TT43 Trent Klatt	.10	.25
TT44 Alexander Daigle	.12	.30
TT45 Sergei Gonchar	.10	.25
TT46 Niklas Sundstrom	.10	.25
TT47 Michael Ryder	.12	.30
TT48 Igor Larionov	.15	.40
TT49 Jan Hrdina	.10	.25
TT50 Cliff Ronning	.10	.25
TT51 Trent Hunter	.10	.25
TT52 Alexei Zhamnov	.12	.30
TT53 Tommy Salo	.12	.30
TT54 Danny Markov	.10	.25
TT55 Sean Burke	.10	.25
TT56 Shane Doan	.12	.30
TT57 Konstantin Koltsov	.10	.25
TT58 Mike Danton	.10	.25
TT59 John Grahame	.10	.25
TT60 Dimitry Afanasenkov	.12	.30
TT61 Bryan Marchment	.10	.25
TT62 Mikael Tellqvist	.12	.30
TT63 Jason King	.10	.25
TT64 Anson Carter	.12	.30
TT65 Steve Shields	.12	.30
TT66 Ron Francis	.20	.50
TT67 Petr Nedved	.10	.25
TT68 Alexander Svitov	.10	.25
TT69 Ville Nieminen	.10	.25
TT70 Martin Skoula	.10	.25
TT71 Steve Yzerman	.40	1.00
TT72 Jason Spezza	.15	.40
TT73 Stanislav Chistov	.10	.25
TT74 Pascal Leclaire	.10	.25
TT75 Mike Comrie	.12	.30
TT76 Brent Johnson	.12	.30
TT77 Mike Rupp	.10	.25
TT78 Derek Morris	.10	.25
TT79 Geoff Sanderson	.10	.25
TT80 Martin Rucinsky	.10	.25
TT81 Shaone Morrisonn	.10	.25
TT82 Paul Kariya	.15	.40
TT83 Alex Kovalev	.12	.30
TT84 Jeff Jillson	.10	.25
TT85 Kari Lehtonen RC	1.00	2.50
TT86 Karl Stewart RC	.25	.60
TT87 Sergei Zinovjev RC	.25	.60
TT88 Carl Corazzini RC	.25	.60
TT89 Andrew Peters RC	.30	.75
TT90 Derek Roy RC	.40	1.00
TT91 Matthew Lombardi RC	.30	.75
TT92 Alan Rourke RC	.25	.60
TT93 Pavel Vorobiev RC	.30	.75
TT94 Lasse Kukkonen RC	.25	.60
TT95 Travis Moen RC	.30	.75
TT96 Matt Keith RC	.25	.60
TT97 Marek Svatos RC	.50	1.25
TT98 Cody McCormick RC	.30	.75
TT99 Mike Green RC	.30	.75
TT100 Mikhail Kuleshov RC	.25	.60
TT101 Dan Fritsche RC	.25	.60
TT102 Nikolai Zherdev RC	.50	1.25
TT103 Aaron Johnson RC	.25	.60
TT104 Tim Jackman RC	.30	.75
TT105 Trevor Daley RC	.40	1.00

TT106 Nathan Robinson RC .25 .60
TT107 Niklas Kronwall RC .50 1.25
TT108 Darryl Bootland RC .30 .75
TT109 Tony Salmelainen RC .25 .60
TT110 Mike Bishai RC .25 .60
TT111 Gregory Campbell RC .25 .60
TT112 Tim Gleason RC .30 .75
TT113 Dustin Brown RC .60 1.50
TT114 Noah Clarke RC .25 .60
TT115 Chris Kunitz RC .50 1.25
TT116 Tony Martensson RC .25 .60
TT117 Brent Burns RC .75 2.00
TT118 Chris Higgins RC .50 1.25
TT119 Dan Hamhuis RC .30 .75
TT120 Marek Zidlicky RC .30 .75
TT121 Andrew Hutchinson RC .25 .60
TT122 Paul Martin RC .30 .75
TT123 Aleksandar Suglobov RC .25 .60
TT124 David Hale RC .25 .60
TT125 Sean Bergenheim RC .30 .75
TT126 Jed Ortmeyer RC .25 .60
TT127 Lawrence Nycholat RC .30 .75
TT128 Dominic Moore RC .25 .60
TT129 Fedor Tyutin RC .25 .60
TT130 Garth Murray RC .30 .75
TT131 Antoine Vermette RC .50 1.25
TT132 Joni Pitkanen RC .40 1.00
TT133 Antero Niittymaki RC .60 1.50
TT134 Matthew Spiller RC .30 .75
TT135 Fredrik Sjostrom RC .40 1.00
TT136 Ryan Malone RC .50 1.25
TT137 Matt Murley RC .30 .75
TT138 Andy Chiodo RC .25 .60
TT139 Tom Preissing RC .30 .75
TT140 Wade Brookbank RC .30 .75
TT141 Ryan Kesler RC 1.00 2.50
TT142 Nathan Smith RC .25 .60
TT143 Boyd Gordon RC .30 .75
TT144 Alexander Semin RC .75 2.00
TT145 Rastislav Stana RC .40 1.00
TT146 Cory Larose RC .25 .60
TT147 Rob Scuderi RC .30 .75
TT148 Ryan Barnes RC .25 .60
TT149 Matt Ellison RC .25 .60
TT150 Milan Michalek RC .50 1.25
TT151 Kyle Wellwood RC .40 1.00
TT152 Jame Pollock RC .25 .60
TT153 Dwayne Zinger RC .25 .60
TT154 Dan Ellis RC .30 .75
TT155 Patrick Leahy RC .30 .75
TT156 Jozef Balej RC .25 .60
TT157 Colton Orr RC .30 .75
TT158 Julien Vauclair RC .25 .60
TT159 Darcy Verot RC .25 .60
TT160 Christian Ehrhoff RC .30 .75
TT161 Boyd Kane RC .25 .60
TT162 Tuomas Pihlman RC .30 .75
TT163 John-Michael Liles RC .30 .75
TT164 Anton Babchuk RC .25 .60
TT165 Owen Fussey RC .25 .60

2003-04 Topps Traded Blue

*TT1-TT84 VETS/500: 4X TO 10X
*TT85-TT165 ROOKIE/500: 1.5X TO 4X

2003-04 Topps Traded Gold

*TT1-TT84 VETS/50: 10X TO 25X
*TT85-TT165 ROOKIE/50: 4X TO 10X

2003-04 Topps Traded Red

*TT1-TT84 VETS/100: 8X TO 20X
*TT85-TT165 ROOKIE/100: 3X TO 8X

2003-04 Topps Traded Franchise Fabrics

FFJT Joe Thornton 5.00 12.00
FFIK Ilya Kovalchuk
FFMB Martin Brodeur 15.00 40.00
FFMG Marian Gaborik 5.00 12.00
FFML Mario Lemieux 20.00 50.00
FFJS Joe Sakic 5.00 12.00
FFAY Alexei Yashin 3.00 8.00
FFVL Vincent Lecavalier 5.00 12.00
FFPM Patrick Marleau 4.00 10.00
FFMT Marty Turco 3.00 8.00
FFDA Daniel Alfredsson 3.00 8.00
FFBG Bill Guerin 3.00 8.00
FFTV Tomas Vokoun 3.00 8.00
FFMR Mark Recchi 3.00 8.00
FFZP Zigmund Palffy 3.00 8.00
FFKP Keith Primeau 3.00 8.00
FFJSG Jean-Sebastien Giguere 3.00 8.00
FFTB Todd Bertuzzi
FFRL Roberto Luongo 5.00 12.00
FFJI Jarome Iginla 5.00 12.00
FFRN Rick Nash 5.00 12.00
FFJTH Jose Theodore 5.00 12.00
FFMS Mats Sundin 4.00 10.00

2003-04 Topps Traded Future Phenoms

FPRM Ryan Miller 5.00 12.00
FPMS Matthew Stajan 4.00 10.00
FPDA David Aebischer 4.00 10.00
FPNH Nathan Horton 4.00 10.00
FPAV Antoine Vermette 2.00 5.00
FPPS Peter Sejna 2.00 5.00
FPJOL Joffrey Lupul 4.00 10.00
FPJL Jordan Leopold 2.00 5.00
FPSB Sean Bergenheim 2.00 5.00
FPMR Mike Ribeiro 2.00 5.00
FPJLU Jamie Lundmark 2.00 5.00
FPMW Mattias Weinhandl 2.00 5.00
FPDH Dan Hamhuis 2.00 5.00
FPNB Nick Boynton 2.00 5.00
FPJB Jay Bouwmeester 4.00 10.00
FPJP Joni Pitkanen 2.00 5.00
FPAH Adam Hall 2.00 5.00
FPSC Stanislav Chistov 2.00 5.00
FPAM Antti Miettinen 2.00 5.00
FPSW Stephen Weiss 2.00 5.00
FPRR Robyn Regehr 2.00 5.00
FPAF Alexander Frolov 4.00 10.00
FPBR Brad Richards 5.00 12.00
FPAT Alex Tanguay 4.00 10.00
FPBJ Barret Jackman 2.00 5.00
FPPD Pavel Datsyuk 4.00 10.00

2014 Topps U.S. Olympic Team

COMPLETE SET (100) 10.00 25.00
51 Hilary Knight .60 1.50
53 Jocelyne Lamoureux .15 .40
54 Monique Lamoureux .15 .40
73 Rico Roman .15 .40

2014 Topps U.S. Olympic Team Bronze

*BRONZE: .5X TO 1.2X BASIC CARDS
51 Hilary Knight .75 2.00
53 Jocelyne Lamoureux .20 .50
54 Monique Lamoureux .20 .50
73 Rico Roman .20 .50

2014 Topps U.S. Olympic Team Gold

*GOLD: 1.5X TO 4X BASIC CARDS
51 Hilary Knight 2.50 6.00
53 Jocelyne Lamoureux .60 1.50
54 Monique Lamoureux .60 1.50
73 Rico Roman .60 1.50

2014 Topps U.S. Olympic Team Silver

*SILVER: .6X TO 1.5X BASIC CARDS
51 Hilary Knight 1.00 2.50
53 Jocelyne Lamoureux .25 .60
54 Monique Lamoureux .25 .60
73 Rico Roman .25 .60

2014 Topps U.S. Olympic Team Autographs

51 Hilary Knight 20.00 50.00

2014 Topps U.S. Olympic Team Autographs Bronze

*BRONZE/50: SAME AS BASIC AUTO
51 Hilary Knight 20.00 50.00

2014 Topps U.S. Olympic Team Autographs Gold

*GOLD/15: .6X TO 1.5X BASIC AUTO
51 Hilary Knight 40.00 80.00

2014 Topps U.S. Olympic Team Autographs Silver

*SILVER/30: .5X TO 1.2X BASIC AUTO
51 Hilary Knight 25.00 60.00

2014 Topps U.S. Olympic Team Champions Autographs

UOCJC Jim Craig 20.00 50.00
UOCME Mike Eruzione 35.00 70.00

2014 Topps U.S. Olympic Team Commemorative Pins

USPML Monique Lamoureux 8.00 20.00

2014 Topps U.S. Olympic Team Games of the XXII Olympiad

COMPLETE SET (15) 10.00 25.00
OLYHK Hilary Knight Ice Hockey 4.00 10.00

2014 Topps U.S. Olympic Team Relics

ORHKN Hilary Knight 8.00 20.00

2014 Topps U.S. Olympic Team Relics Bronze

*BRONZE/75: SAME PRICE AS BASIC CARD
ORHKN Hilary Knight 8.00 20.00

2014 Topps U.S. Olympic Team Relics Gold

GOLD/25: .6X TO 1.5X BASIC CARDS
ORHKN Hilary Knight 10.00 25.00

2014 Topps U.S. Olympic Team Relics Silver

*SILVER/50: .5X TO 1.2X BASIC CARDS
ORHKN Hilary Knight 8.00 20.00

2014 Topps U.S. Olympic Team Sochi Patch

USPJL Jocelyne Lamoureux 6.00 15.00
USPML Monique Lamoureux 6.00 15.00
USPRR Rico Roman 6.00 15.00

1963-64 Toronto Star

COMPLETE SET (42) 150.00 300.00
1 George Armstrong TML 4.00 8.00
2 Andy Bathgate NYR 4.00 8.00
3 Bob Baun TML 2.50 5.00
4 Jean Beliveau MC 7.50 15.00
5 Leo Boivin BB 2.50 5.00
6 Johnny Bower TML 5.00 10.00
7 Carl Brewer TML 2.50 5.00
8 Johnny Bucyk BB 4.00 8.00
9 Alex Delvecchio DRW 5.00 10.00
10 Kent Douglas TML 2.00 4.00
11 Dick Duff TML 2.50 5.00
12 Bill Gadsby DRW 3.00 6.00
13 Jean-Guy Gendron BB 2.00 4.00
14 BoomBoom Geoffrion MC 7.50 15.00
15 Glenn Hall CBH 6.00 12.00
16 Doug Harvey NYR 5.00 10.00
17 Bill Hay CBH 2.50 5.00
18 Camille Henry NYR 2.50 5.00
19 Tim Horton TML 7.50 15.00
20 Gordie Howe DRW 25.00 50.00
21 Bobby Hull CBH 15.00 30.00
22 Red Kelly TML 5.00 10.00
23 Dave Keon TML 7.50 15.00
24 Parker MacDonald DRW 2.00 4.00
25 Frank Mahovlich TML 7.50 15.00
26 Stan Mikita CBH 7.50 15.00
27 Dickie Moore MC 5.00 10.00
28 Eric Nesterenko CBH 2.50 5.00
29 Marcel Pronovost DRW 2.50 5.00
30 Claude Provost MC 2.50 5.00
31 Bob Pulford TML 3.00 6.00
32 Henri Richard MC 7.50 15.00
33 Terry Sawchuk DRW 10.00 20.00
34 Eddie Shack TML 5.00 10.00
35 Allan Stanley TML 3.00 6.00
36 Ron Stewart TML 2.00 4.00
37 Jean-Guy Talbot MC 2.50 5.00
38 Gilles Tremblay MC 2.00 4.00
39 J.C. Tremblay MC 2.50 5.00
40 Norm Ullman DRW 4.00 8.00
41 Elmer Vasko CBH 2.00 4.00
42 Ken Wharram CBH 2.50 5.00

1964-65 Toronto Star

COMPLETE SET (48) 150.00 300.00
1 Dave Balon MC 2.00 4.00
2 Andy Bathgate TML 4.00 8.00
3 Bob Baun TML 3.00 6.00
4 Jean Beliveau MC 7.50 15.00
5 Red Berenson MC 2.50 5.00
6 Leo Boivin BB 3.00 6.00
7 Carl Brewer TML 2.50 5.00
8 Alex Delvecchio DRW 4.00 8.00
9 Rod Gilbert NYR 4.00 8.00
10 Ted Green BB 2.50 5.00
11 Glenn Hall CBH 5.00 10.00
12 Billy Harris TML 2.00 4.00
13 Bill Hay CBH 2.00 4.00
14 Paul Henderson DRW 3.00 6.00
15 Wayne Hillman CBH 2.00 4.00
16 Charlie Hodge MC 3.00 6.00
17 Tim Horton TML 7.50 15.00
18 Gordie Howe DRW 20.00 40.00
19 Harry Howell NYR 3.00 6.00
20 Bobby Hull CBH 12.50 25.00
21 Larry Jeffrey DRW 2.00 4.00
22 Tom Johnson BB 3.00 6.00
23 Forbes Kennedy BB 2.00 4.00
24 Dave Keon TML 6.00 12.00
25 Orland Kurtenbach BB 2.50 5.00
26 Jacques Laperriere MC 2.50 5.00
27 Parker MacDonald DRW 2.00 4.00
28 Al MacNeil CBH 2.00 4.00
29 Frank Mahovlich TML 6.00 12.00
30 Chico Maki CBH 2.00 4.00
31 Don McKenney TML 2.00 4.00
32 John McKenzie CBH 2.50 5.00
33 Stan Mikita CBH 6.00 12.00
34 Jim Neilson NYR 2.00 4.00
35 Jim Pappin TML 2.00 4.00
36 Pierre Pilote CBH 3.00 6.00
37 Jacques Plante NYR 10.00 20.00
38 Marcel Pronovost DRW 3.00 6.00
39 Claude Provost MC 2.50 5.00
40 Bob Pulford TML 3.00 6.00
41 Henri Richard MC 6.00 12.00
42 Wayne Rivers BB 2.00 4.00
43 Floyd Smith DRW 2.00 4.00
44 Allan Stanley TML 4.00 8.00
45 Ron Stewart TML 2.00 4.00
46 J.C. Tremblay MC 2.50 5.00
47 Norm Ullman DRW 4.00 8.00
48 Elmer Vasko CBH 2.00 4.00
xx Album
Folder 12.50 25.00

1971-72 Toronto Sun

COMPLETE SET (294) 300.00 600.00
1 Boston Bruins 1.50 3.00
2 Don Awrey .50 1.00
3 Garnet Bailey .50 1.00
4 Ivan Boldirev .50 1.00
5 Johnny Bucyk 3.00 6.00
6 Wayne Cashman .75 1.50
7 Gerry Cheevers 4.00 8.00
8 Phil Esposito 10.00 20.00
9 Ted Green .75 1.50
10 Ken Hodge .75 1.50
11 Ed Johnston 1.50 3.00
12 Reggie Leach 1.50 3.00
13 Don Marcotte .50 1.00
14 John McKenzie .50 1.00
15 Bobby Orr 30.00 60.00
16 Derek Sanderson 4.00 8.00
17 Dallas Smith .50 1.00
18 Richard Allan Smith .50 1.00
19 Fred Stanfield .50 1.00
20 Mike Walton .75 1.50
21 Ed Westfall .75 1.50
22 Buffalo Sabres 1.00 2.00
23 Doug Barrie .50 1.00
24 Roger Crozier 2.00 4.00
25 Dave Dryden 1.00 2.00
26 Dick Duff .75 1.50
27 Phil Goyette .50 1.00
28 Al Hamilton .50 1.00
29 Larry Keenan .50 1.00
30 Danny Lawson .50 1.00
31 Don Luce .50 1.00
32 Richard Martin 1.00 2.00
33 Ray McKay .50 1.00
34 Gerry Meehan .75 1.50
35 Kevin O'Shea .50 1.00
36 Gilbert Perreault 4.00 8.00
37 Tracy Pratt .50 1.00
38 Mike Robitaille .50 1.00
39 Eddie Shack 2.00 4.00
40 Jim Watson .50 1.00
41 Rod Zaine .50 1.00
42 California Seals 1.50 3.00
43 Wayne Carleton .50 1.00
44 Lyle Carter .50 1.00
45 Gary Croteau .50 1.00
46 Norm Ferguson .50 1.00
47 Stan Gilbertson .50 1.00
48 Ernie Hicke .50 1.00
49 Gary Jarrett 1.00 2.00
50 Joey Johnston .50 1.00
51 Marshall Johnston .50 1.00
52 Bert Marshall .50 1.00
53 Walt McKechnie .50 1.00
54 Don O'Donoghue .50 1.00
55 Gerry Pinder .75 1.50
56 Dick Redmond .50 1.00
57 Robert Sheehan .50 1.00
58 Paul Shmyr .50 1.00
59 Ron Stackhouse SP 6.00 12.00
60 Carol Vadnais .50 1.00
61 Tom Williams .50 1.00
62 Chicago Blackhawks 1.50 3.00
63 Lou Angotti .50 1.00
64 Bryan Campbell .50 1.00
65 Tony Esposito 10.00 20.00
66 Bobby Hull 15.00 30.00
67 Dennis Hull 1.00 2.00
68 Doug Jarrett .50 1.00
69 Jerry Korab .50 1.00
70 Cliff Koroll .50 1.00
71 Darryl Maggs .50 1.00
72 Keith Magnuson .75 1.50
73 Chico Maki .75 1.50
74 Dan Maloney .50 1.00
75 Pit Martin .75 1.50
76 Stan Mikita 6.00 12.00
77 Eric Nesterenko .50 1.00
78 Danny O'Shea .50 1.00
79 Jim Pappin .50 1.00
80 Gary Smith 1.00 2.00
81 Pat Stapleton .50 1.00
82 Bill White .50 1.00
83 Detroit Red Wings 1.50 3.00
84 Red Berenson .75 1.50
85 Gary Bergman .75 1.50
86 Arnie Brown .50 1.00
87 Guy Charron .50 1.00
88 Bill Collins .50 1.00
89 Brian Conacher .50 1.00
90 Joe Daley 1.50 3.00
91 Alex Delvecchio 3.00 6.00
92 Marcel Dionne 7.50 15.00
93 Tim Ecclestone .50 1.00
94 Ron Harris .50 1.00
95 Gerry Hart .50 1.00
96 Gordie Howe 25.00 50.00
97 Al Karlander .50 1.00
98 Nick Libett .75 1.50
99 Ab McDonald .50 1.00
100 James Niekamp .50 1.00
101 Mickey Redmond 2.00 4.00
102 Leon Rochefort .50 1.00
103 Al Smith .75 1.50
104 Los Angeles Kings 1.00 2.00
105 Ralph Backstrom .75 1.50
106 Bob Berry .75 1.50
107 Mike Byers .50 1.00
108 Larry Cahan .50 1.00
109 Paul Curtis .50 1.00
110 Dennis DeJordy 1.50 3.00
111 Gary Edwards 1.00 2.00
112 Bill Flett .50 1.00
113 Butch Goring .75 1.50
114 Lucien Grenier .50 1.00
115 Larry Hillman .50 1.00
116 Dale Hoganson .50 1.00
117 Harry Howell 1.50 3.00
118 Eddie Joyal .50 1.00
119 Real Lemieux .50 1.00
120 Ross Lonsberry .50 1.00
121 Al McDonough .50 1.00
122 Jean Potvin .50 1.00
123 Bob Pulford 1.50 3.00
124 Juha Widing .75 1.50
125 Minnesota North Stars 1.00 2.00
126 Fred Barrett .50 1.00
127 Charlie Burns .50 1.00
128 Jude Drouin .50 1.00
129 Barry Gibbs .50 1.00
130 Gilles Gilbert 2.00 4.00
131 Bill Goldsworthy 1.00 2.00
132 Danny Grant .75 1.50
133 Ted Hampson .50 1.00
134 Ted Harris .50 1.00
135 Fred Harvey .50 1.00
136 Cesare Maniago 2.00 4.00
137 Doug Mohns .75 1.50
138 Lou Nanne .75 1.50
139 Bob Nevin .75 1.50
140 Dennis O'Brien .50 1.00
141 Murray Oliver .50 1.00
142 Jean-Paul Parise .75 1.50
143 Dean Prentice .75 1.50
144 Tom Reid .50 1.00
145 Gump Worsley 3.00 6.00
146 Montreal Canadiens 1.50 3.00
147 Pierre Bouchard .50 1.00
148 Yvan Cournoyer 3.00 6.00
149 Ken Dryden 25.00 50.00
150 Terry Harper .75 1.50
151 Rejean Houle .75 1.50
152 Guy Lafleur 15.00 30.00
153 Jacques Laperriere 1.00 2.00
154 Guy Lapointe 1.50 3.00
155 Claude Larose .50 1.00
156 Jacques Lemaire 2.00 4.00
157 Frank Mahovlich 6.00 12.00
158 Pete Mahovlich .75 1.50
159 Phil Myre 1.50 3.00
160 Larry Pleau .75 1.50
161 Henri Richard 6.00 12.00
162 Phil Roberto .50 1.00
163 Serge Savard 1.50 3.00
164 Marc Tardif .75 1.50
165 J.C. Tremblay .75 1.50
166 Rogatien Vachon 3.00 6.00
167 New York Rangers 1.50 3.00
168 Dave Balon .50 1.00
169 Ab DeMarco .50 1.00
170 Jack Egers .50 1.00
171 Bill Fairbairn .50 1.00
172 Ed Giacomin 4.00 8.00
173 Rod Gilbert 2.00 4.00
174 Vic Hadfield .75 1.50
175 Ted Irvine .50 1.00
176 Bruce MacGregor .50 1.00
177 Jim Neilson .50 1.00
178 Brad Park 3.00 6.00
179 Jean Ratelle 2.00 4.00
180 Dale Rolfe .50 1.00
181 Bobby Rousseau .50 1.00
182 Glen Sather 1.50 3.00
183 Rod Seiling .50 1.00
184 Pete Stemkowski .50 1.00
185 Walt Tkaczuk .75 1.50
186 Gilles Villemure 1.50 3.00
187 Philadelphia Flyers 1.50 3.00
188 Barry Ashbee 1.00 2.00
189 Serge Bernier .50 1.00
190 Larry Brown .50 1.00
191 Bobby Clarke 10.00 20.00
192 Gary Dornhoefer .75 1.50
193 Doug Favell 1.50 3.00
194 Bruce Gamble 2.00 4.00
195 Jean-Guy Gendron .50 1.00
196 Larry Hale .50 1.00
197 Wayne Hillman .50 1.00
198 Brent Hughes .50 1.00
199 Jim Johnson .50 1.00
200 Bob Kelly .50 1.00
201 Andre Lacroix .75 1.50
202 Bill Lesuk .50 1.00
203 Rick MacLeish 1.00 2.00
204 Larry Mickey .50 1.00
205 Simon Nolet .50 1.00
206 Pierre Plante .50 1.00
207 Ed Van Impe .50 1.00
208 Joe Watson .50 1.00
209 Pittsburgh Penguins 1.00 2.00
210 Syl Apps .75 1.50
211 Les Binkley 1.50 3.00
212 Wally Boyer .50 1.00
213 Darryl Edestrand .50 1.00
214 Roy Edwards 1.50 3.00
215 Nick Harbaruk .50 1.00
216 Bryan Hextall .75 1.50
217 Bill Hicke .50 1.00
218 Tim Horton 5.00 10.00
219 Sheldon Kannegiesser .50 1.00
220 Bob Leiter .50 1.00
221 Keith McCreary .50 1.00
222 Joe Noris .50 1.00
223 Greg Polis .50 1.00
224 Jean Pronovost .75 1.50
225 Rene Robert .75 1.50
226 Duane Rupp .50 1.00
227 Ken Schinkel .50 1.00
228 Ron Schock .50 1.00
229 Bryan Watson .75 1.50
230 Bob Woytowich .50 1.00
231 St. Louis Blues 1.00 2.00
232 Al Arbour 1.50 3.00
233 John Arbour .50 1.00
234 Chris Bordeleau .50 1.00
235 Carl Brewer .75 1.50
236 Gene Carr .50 1.00
237 Wayne Connelly .50 1.00
238 Terry Crisp .75 1.50
239 Jim Lorentz .50 1.00
240 Peter McDuffe 1.00 2.00
241 George Morrison .50 1.00
242 Michel Parizeau .50 1.00
243 Noel Picard .50 1.00
244 Barclay Plager .75 1.50
245 Bob Plager .75 1.50
246 Jim Roberts .50 1.00
247 Gary Sabourin .50 1.00
248 Jim Shires .50 1.00
249 Frank St.Marseille .50 1.00
250 Bill Sutherland .50 1.00
251 Garry Unger 1.00 2.00
252 Ernie Wakely 1.50 3.00
253 Toronto Maple Leafs 1.50 3.00
254 Bob Baun .75 1.50
255 Jim Dorey .50 1.00
256 Denis Dupere .75 1.50
257 Ron Ellis .75 1.50
258 Brian Glennie .50 1.00
259 Jim Harrison .50 1.00
260 Paul Henderson 1.00 2.00
261 Dave Keon 3.00 6.00
262 Rick Ley .50 1.00
263 Billy MacMillan .50 1.00
264 Don Marshall .50 1.00
265 Jim McKenny .50 1.00
266 Garry Monahan .50 1.00
267 Bernie Parent 6.00 12.00
268 Mike Pelyk .50 1.00
269 Jacques Plante 10.00 20.00
270 Brad Selwood .50 1.00
271 Darryl Sittler 6.00 12.00
272 Brian Spencer 1.00 2.00
273 Guy Trottier .50 1.00
274 Norm Ullman 2.50 5.00
275 Vancouver Canucks 1.00 2.00
276 Andre Boudrias .50 1.00
277 George Gardiner .50 1.00
278 Jocelyn Guevremont .75 1.50
279 Murray Hall .50 1.00
280 Danny Johnson .50 1.00
281 Dennis Kearns .50 1.00
282 Orland Kurtenbach .75 1.50
283 Bobby Lalonde .50 1.00
284 Wayne Maki .50 1.00
285 Rosaire Paiement .75 1.50
286 Paul Popiel .50 1.00
287 Pat Quinn 1.00 2.00
288 John Schella .50 1.00
289 Bobby Schmautz .75 1.50
290 Fred Speck .50 1.00
291 Dale Tallon .75 1.50
292 Ron Ward .50 1.00
293 Barry Wilkins .50 1.00
294 Dunc Wilson 1.50 3.00
xx Binder 12.50 25.00
NNO Introduction Card 2.00 4.00

2017-18 Toronto Maple Leafs Centennial

1 Rick Vaive .40 1.00
2 Ace Bailey .50 1.25
3 Eddie Shack .50 1.25
4 Johnny Bower .50 1.25
5 Rick Kehoe .40 1.00
6 Errol Thompson .40 1.00
7 Glenn Anderson .40 1.00
8 Alyn McCauley .40 1.00
9 Barry Melrose .40 1.00
10 Bob Rouse .40 1.00
11 Auston Matthews 2.00 5.00
12 Bob Neely .40 1.00
13 Ed Belfour .60 1.50
14 John Anderson .40 1.00
15 Brian Glennie .40 1.00
16 Bryan Berard .40 1.00
17 Red Horner .40 1.00
18 Mitch Marner .75 2.00
19 Red Kelly .50 1.25
20 King Clancy .50 1.25
21 Bruce Boudreau .40 1.00
22 Syl Apps .40 1.00
23 Bill Barilko .40 1.00
24 Nick Metz .40 1.00
25 Vincent Damphousse .40 1.00
26 Grant Fuhr .75 2.00
27 Jonas Hoglund .40 1.00
28 Gary Leeman .40 1.00
29 Doug Gilmour .60 1.50
30 Allan Bester .40 1.00
31 Dick Irvin .40 1.00
32 Dan Maloney .40 1.00
33 Dmitry Yushkevich .40 1.00
34 Lanny McDonald .50 1.25
35 Dave Hannan .30 .75
36 Dave Reid .30 .75
37 Bob Baun .50 1.25
38 Daniel Marois .40 1.00
39 Phil Kessel .50 1.25
40 Fredrik Modin .40 1.00
41 Norm Ullman .50 1.25
42 Ken Baumgartner .30 .75
43 Gary Roberts .50 1.25
44 Ian Turnbull .30 .75
45 King Clancy .40 1.00
46 Mike Foligno .40 1.00
47 Jamie Macoun .40 1.00
48 Robert Reichel .40 1.00
49 Jim McKenny .40 1.00
50 Darryl Sittler .60 1.50
51 Jim Morrison .40 1.00
52 Garry Valk .40 1.00
53 Bill Berg .40 1.00
54 Jason Blake .30 .75
55 Nik Antropov .40 1.00
56 Jim Dorey .40 1.00
57 Terry Sawchuk .40 1.00
58 Gordie Drillon .40 1.00
59 James van Riemsdyk .40 1.00
60 Peter Ihnacak .40 1.00
61 Nazem Kadri .60 1.50
62 Morgan Rielly .50 1.25
63 Wilf Paiement .40 1.00
64 Frank Mahovlich .50 1.25
65 Bill Derlago .40 1.00
66 Pete Stemkowski .40 1.00
67 Jake Gardiner .30 .75
68 Wendel Clark .75 2.00
69 Russ Courtnall .40 1.00
70 Howie Meeker .40 1.00
71 Leo Komarov .30 .75
72 Harry Lumley .40 1.00
73 Pat Boutette .40 1.00
74 Mike Krushelnyski .40 1.00
75 Tom Fergus .30 .75
76 Charlie Conacher .40 1.00
77 Todd Warriner .40 1.00
78 Ed Olczyk .40 1.00
79 Terry Martin .40 1.00
80 Frederik Andersen .60 1.50
81 Shayne Corson .40 1.00
82 Felix Potvin .75 2.00
83 Dion Phaneuf .40 1.00
84 Miroslav Frycer .40 1.00
85 Kyle Wellwood .40 1.00
86 Mark Osborne .40 1.00
87 Al Iafrate .40 1.00
88 Don Metz .40 1.00
89 William Nylander 1.00 2.50
90 Borje Salming .50 1.25
91 Dave Andreychuk .50 1.25
92 Mike Gartner .60 1.50
93 Laurie Boschman .40 1.00
94 Sergei Berezin .40 1.00
95 Tyler Bozak .30 .75
96 Mike Walton .40 1.00
97 Tomas Kaberle .40 1.00
98 Ron Ellis .40 1.00
99 Mike Johnson .40 1.00
100 Carlton .40 1.00
101 Charlie Conacher CAP .60 1.50
102 Red Horner CAP .60 1.50
103 Syl Apps CAP .60 1.50
104 Bob Davidson CAP .60 1.50
105 Darryl Sittler CAP 1.00 2.50
106 Rick Vaive CAP .60 1.50
107 Wendel Clark CAP 1.25 3.00
108 Doug Gilmour CAP 1.00 2.50
109 Dion Phaneuf CAP .60 1.50
110 Syl Apps TW .60 1.50
111 Gordie Drillon TW .60 1.50
112 Syl Apps TW .60 1.50
113 Howie Meeker TW .60 1.50
114 Harry Lumley TW .60 1.50
115 Frank Mahovlich TW .75 2.00
116 Red Kelly TW .60 1.50
117 Johnny Bower TW .75 2.00
118 Terry Sawchuk TW .75 2.00
119 Johnny Bower TW .75 2.00
120 Doug Gilmour TW 1.00 2.50
121 Jason Blake TW .50 1.25
122 Auston Matthews TW 3.00 8.00
123 Johnny Bower RN .75 2.00
124 Red Kelly RN .75 2.00
125 Red Kelly RN .60 1.50
126 Ace Bailey RN .75 2.00
127 King Clancy RN .60 1.50
128 Charlie Conacher RN .60 1.50
129 Syl Apps RN .60 1.50
130 Wendel Clark RN 1.25 3.00
131 Borje Salming RN .75 2.00
132 Frank Mahovlich RN .75 2.00
133 Darryl Sittler RN 1.00 2.50
134 Doug Gilmour RN 1.00 2.50
135 Felix Potvin RN 1.25 3.00
136 Ed Belfour RN 1.00 2.50
137 Doug Gilmour RH 1.00 2.50
138 Borje Salming RH .75 2.00
139 Darryl Sittler RH 1.00 2.50
140 Gary Roberts RH .75 2.00
141 Felix Potvin RH 1.25 3.00
142 Rick Vaive RH .60 1.50
143 Darryl Sittler RH 1.00 2.50
144 Felix Potvin RH 1.25 3.00
145 Wendel Clark RH 1.25 3.00
146 Harry Lumley RH .60 1.50
147 Borje Salming RH .75 2.00
148 Mitch Marner RH 1.25 3.00
149 Auston Matthews RH 3.00 8.00
150 King Clancy HOF .60 1.50
151 Dick Irvin HOF .60 1.50
152 Syl Apps HOF .60 1.50
153 Charlie Conacher HOF .60 1.50
154 Red Horner HOF .60 1.50
155 Red Kelly HOF .75 2.00
156 Terry Sawchuk HOF .75 2.00
157 Ace Bailey HOF .75 2.00
158 Gordie Drillon HOF .60 1.50
159 Johnny Bower HOF .75 2.00
160 Harry Lumley HOF .60 1.50
161 Frank Mahovlich HOF .75 2.00
162 Norm Ullman HOF .75 2.00
163 Darryl Sittler HOF 1.00 2.50
164 Lanny McDonald HOF .75 2.00
165 Borje Salming HOF .75 2.00
166 Howie Meeker HOF .60 1.50
167 Doug Gilmour HOF 1.00 2.50
168 Ed Belfour HOF 1.00 2.50
169 Ace Bailey MM .75 2.00
170 Syl Apps MM .60 1.50
171 Howie Meeker MM .60 1.50
172 Howie Meeker MM .60 1.50
173 Don Metz MM .60 1.50
174 Bill Barilko MM .60 1.50
175 Harry Lumley MM .60 1.50
176 Red Kelly MM .75 2.00
177 Bob Baun MM .75 2.00
178 Terry Sawchuk MM .60 1.50
179 Red Kelly MM .75 2.00
180 Norm Ullman MM .75 2.00
181 Darryl Sittler MM 1.00 2.50
182 Darryl Sittler MM 1.00 2.50
183 Ian Turnbull MM .50 1.25
184 Ian Turnbull MM .50 1.25
185 Lanny McDonald MM .75 2.00
186 Rick Vaive MM .60 1.50
187 Wendel Clark MM 1.25 3.00
188 Wendel Clark MM 1.25 3.00
189 Gary Leeman MM .60 1.50
190 Doug Gilmour MM 1.00 2.50
191 Doug Gilmour MM 1.00 2.50
192 Felix Potvin MM 1.25 3.00
193 Dave Andreychuk MM .75 2.00
194 Gary Roberts MM .75 2.00
195 Ed Belfour MM 1.00 2.50
196 Ed Belfour MM 1.00 2.50
197 James van Riemsdyk MM .60 1.50
198 Auston Matthews MM 3.00 8.00
199 Auston Matthews MM 3.00 8.00
200 Auston Matthews MM 3.00 8.00

2017-18 Toronto Maple Leafs Centennial Gold

1 Rick Vaive 5.00 12.00
11 Auston Matthews 30.00 80.00
18 Mitch Marner 20.00 50.00

2017-18 Toronto Maple Leafs Centennial Green

*GREEN/25: 8X TO 20X BASIC CARDS
*SP GREEN: 8X TO 20X BASIC CARDS
11 Auston Matthews 80.00 200.00
122 Auston Matthews TW 80.00 200.00
149 Auston Matthews RH 80.00 200.00
198 Auston Matthews MM 80.00 200.00
199 Auston Matthews MM 80.00 200.00
200 Auston Matthews MM 80.00 200.00

2017-18 Toronto Maple Leafs Centennial AKA Autographs

AKAAI Al Iafrate B 30.00 80.00
AKABB Bob Baun B 40.00 100.00
AKABO Bruce Boudreau B 40.00 100.00
AKADA Dave Andreychuk B 30.00 80.00
AKADG Doug Gilmour A 250.00 450.00
AKAEB Ed Belfour A 200.00 300.00
AKAES Eddie Shack B 25.00 60.00
AKAFP Felix Potvin B 50.00 120.00
AKAPS Pete Stemkowski B 25.00 60.00
AKARV Rick Vaive A 250.00 450.00
AKAWC Wendel Clark B 80.00 200.00

2017-18 Toronto Maple Leafs Centennial Blue Die Cut

*BLUE DIE-CUT: .75X TO 2X BASIC CARDS
11 Auston Matthews 8.00 20.00

2017-18 Toronto Maple Leafs Centennial Championship Banners

COMMON CARD 6.00 15.00
191718 1917-18 Maple Leafs 6.00 15.00
192122 1921-22 Maple Leafs 6.00 15.00
193132 1931-32 Maple Leafs 6.00 15.00
194142 1941-42 Maple Leafs 6.00 15.00
194445 1944-45 Maple Leafs 6.00 15.00
194647 1946-47 Maple Leafs 6.00 15.00
194748 1947-48 Maple Leafs 6.00 15.00
194849 1948-49 Maple Leafs 6.00 15.00
195051 1950-51 Maple Leafs 6.00 15.00
196162 1961-62 Maple Leafs 6.00 15.00
196263 1962-63 Maple Leafs 6.00 15.00
196364 1963-64 Maple Leafs 6.00 15.00
196667 1966-67 Maple Leafs 6.00 15.00

2017-18 Toronto Maple Leafs Centennial Maple Leaf Marks

MLMAB Allan Bester D 8.00 20.00
MLMAI Al Iafrate F 8.00 20.00
MLMAL Alyn McCauley D 8.00 20.00
MLMAM Auston Matthews A 1000.00 1500.00
MLMAN Glenn Anderson C 80.00 200.00
MLMBB Bob Baun G 10.00 25.00
MLMBD Bill Derlago F 8.00 20.00
MLMBE Bryan Berard E 8.00 20.00
MLMBG Brian Glennie F 8.00 20.00
MLMBI Bill Berg G 6.00 15.00
MLMBL Jason Blake G 6.00 15.00
MLMBN Bob Neely E 40.00 100.00
MLMBO Bruce Boudreau F 8.00 20.00
MLMBR Bob Rouse F 8.00 20.00
MLMBS Borje Salming B 150.00 250.00
MLMCB Connor Brown E 8.00 20.00
MLMDA Dave Andreychuk C 80.00 200.00
MLMDG Doug Gilmour A 250.00 400.00
MLMDH Dave Hannan F 6.00 15.00
MLMDM Dan Maloney G 30.00 80.00
MLMDR Dave Reid G 6.00 15.00
MLMDS Darryl Sittler B 150.00 300.00
MLMEB Ed Belfour A 200.00 300.00
MLMEO Ed Olczyk F 8.00 20.00
MLMES Eddie Shack E 15.00 40.00
MLMET Errol Thompson F 8.00 20.00
MLMFA Frederik Andersen F 12.00 30.00
MLMFM Frank Mahovlich B 200.00 300.00

MLMFO Mike Foligno F 8.00 20.00
MLMFP Felix Potvin C 60.00 150.00
MLMFR Fredrik Modin D 8.00 20.00
MLMGF Grant Fuhr A 500.00 700.00
MLMGL Gary Leeman G 8.00 20.00
MLMGR Gary Roberts F 10.00 25.00
MLMGV Garry Valk G 8.00 20.00
MLMHL Larry Hillman G 8.00 20.00
MLMHM Howie Meeker D 150.00 250.00
MLMIT Ian Turnbull F 6.00 15.00
MLMJA John Anderson E 8.00 20.00
MLMJB Johnny Bower B 250.00 400.00
MLMJD Jim Dorey E 8.00 20.00
MLMJH Jonas Hoglund G 8.00 20.00
MLMJI Jim Morrison F 8.00 20.00
MLMJM Jamie Macoun E 8.00 20.00
MLMJV Jack Valiquette F 8.00 20.00
MLMKB Ken Baumgartner F 6.00 15.00
MLMKE Rick Kehoe G 8.00 20.00
MLMKM Kirk Muller E 8.00 20.00
MLMKO Mike Komisarek F 8.00 20.00
MLMLB Laurie Boschman F 8.00 20.00
MLMLM Lanny McDonald B 100.00 200.00
MLMMA Daniel Marois G 8.00 20.00
MLMMC Jim McKenny G 8.00 20.00
MLMME Barry Melrose F 8.00 20.00
MLMMF Miroslav Frycer E 8.00 20.00
MLMMG Mike Gartner E 12.00 30.00
MLMMJ Mike Johnson F 8.00 20.00
MLMMK Mike Krushelnyski G 8.00 20.00
MLMMM Mitch Marner A 350.00 500.00
MLMMO Mark Osborne F 8.00 20.00
MLMMR Morgan Rielly B 80.00 200.00
MLMMU Larry Murphy E 100.00 250.00
MLMMW Mike Walton F 8.00 20.00
MLMNA Nik Antropov F 8.00 20.00
MLMNU Norm Ullman
MLMON Owen Nolan D 80.00 200.00
MLMPB Pat Boutette F 8.00 20.00
MLMPH Pat Hickey F 8.00 20.00
MLMPI Peter Ihnacak F 8.00 20.00
MLMPS Pete Stemkowski G 8.00 20.00
MLMRC Russ Courtnall F 8.00 20.00
MLMRE Ron Ellis G 8.00 20.00
MLMRK Red Kelly A 250.00 400.00
MLMRL Rick Ley F 8.00 20.00
MLMRP Rob Pearson F 8.00 20.00
MLMRR Robert Reichel F 8.00 20.00
MLMRV Rick Vaive D 25.00 60.00
MLMRW Ron Wilson F 8.00 20.00
MLMSB Sergei Berezin F 8.00 20.00
MLMSC Shayne Corson F 8.00 20.00
MLMTF Tom Fergus G 6.00 15.00
MLMTK Tomas Kaberle D 8.00 20.00
MLMTM Terry Martin F 8.00 20.00
MLMTW Todd Warriner F 8.00 20.00
MLMVD Vincent Damphousse D 40.00 100.00
MLMWC Wendel Clark C 150.00 250.00
MLMWE Kyle Wellwood G 8.00 20.00
MLMWP Wilf Paiement F 8.00 20.00

2017-18 Toronto Maple Leafs Centennial Maple Leafs Materials

MLAM Auston Matthews C 50.00 125.00
MLBE Jonathan Bernier D 10.00 25.00
MLCB Connor Brown C 10.00 25.00
MLDG Doug Gilmour A 200.00 400.00
MLDP Dion Phaneuf D 10.00 25.00
MLEB Ed Belfour B 25.00 60.00
MLES Eddie Shack B 15.00 40.00
MLFA Frederik Andersen D 15.00 40.00
MLFP Felix Potvin C 20.00 50.00
MLJB Johnny Bower B 30.00 80.00
MLJG Jake Gardiner C 8.00 20.00
MLJV James van Riemsdyk C 10.00 25.00
MLKU Nikolay Kulemin C 12.00 30.00
MLLM Lanny McDonald A 80.00 150.00
MLMG Mike Gartner C 15.00 40.00
MLMM Mitch Marner C 20.00 50.00
MLMR Morgan Rielly D 12.00 30.00
MLNA Nik Antropov D 10.00 25.00
MLNK Nazem Kadri C 15.00 40.00
MLNZ Nikita Zaitsev C 10.00 25.00
MLPK Phil Kessel D 12.00 30.00
MLRV Rick Vaive C 10.00 25.00
MLTB Tyler Bozak D 8.00 20.00
MLTK Tomas Kaberle C 10.00 25.00
MLWN William Nylander C 15.00 40.00

2017-18 Toronto Maple Leafs Centennial Maple Leafs Materials Duos

ML2AR F.Andersen/M.Rielly 30.00 80.00
ML2BP E.Belfour/F.Potvin 50.00 125.00
ML2BV T.Bozak/J.van Riemsdyk 15.00 40.00
ML2GK J.Gardiner/T.Kaberle 40.00 100.00
ML2KB N.Kadri/C.Brown 30.00 80.00

2017-18 Toronto Maple Leafs Centennial Maple Leafs Materials Trios

ML3BBA Belfour/Bower/Andersen 150.00 250.00
ML3NMM Nylander Matthews/Marner 300.00 450.00
ML3VBK van Riemsdyk/Bozak/Kadri 60.00 150.00

2017-18 Toronto Maple Leafs Centennial Treasured Relics

TRBB Bob Baun/25 100.00 250.00
TRBS Borje Salming/15 80.00 200.00
TRDP Dion Phaneuf/25 80.00 150.00
TRGF Grant Fuhr/25 350.00 450.00
TRNK Nazem Kadri/25 250.00 350.00

2013-14 Totally Certified

1 Taylor Hall .50 1.25
2 Jordan Eberle .50 1.25
3 David Perron .40 1.00
4 Sam Gagner .30 .75
5 Ryan Nugent-Hopkins .60 1.50
6 Roberto Luongo .75 2.00
7 Henrik Sedin .60 1.50
8 Kevin Bieksa .40 1.00
9 Daniel Sedin .60 1.50
10 Chris Tanev .30 .75
11 Curtis Glencross .30 .75
12 Dennis Wideman .30 .75
13 Mike Cammalleri .40 1.00
14 T.J. Brodie .30 .75
15 Mikael Backlund .40 1.00
16 P.K. Subban .60 1.50
17 Andrei Markov .30 .75
18 Carey Price 1.00 2.50
19 Max Pacioretty .50 1.25
20 Tomas Plekanec .30 .75
21 Evander Kane .50 1.25
22 Andrew Ladd .30 .75
23 Zach Bogosian .40 1.00
24 Ondrej Pavelec .50 1.25
25 Al Montoya .30 .75
26 Jason Spezza .50 1.25
27 Milan Michalek .30 .75
28 Erik Karlsson .60 1.50
29 Craig Anderson .50 1.25
30 Kyle Turris .30 .75
31 Phil Kessel .50 1.25
32 Nazem Kadri .60 1.50
33 Joffrey Lupul .30 .75
34 James van Riemsdyk .40 1.00
35 Dion Phaneuf .40 1.00
36 Niklas Backstrom .40 1.00
37 Mikko Koivu .40 1.00
38 Zach Parise .50 1.25
39 Jason Pominville .30 .75
40 Josh Harding .50 1.25
41 Brad Marchand 1.00 2.50
42 Tuukka Rask .60 1.50
43 Patrice Bergeron .60 1.50
44 David Krejci .50 1.25
45 Loui Eriksson .30 .75
46 Drew Stafford .30 .75
47 Tyler Ennis .30 .75
48 Ryan Miller .50 1.25
49 Tyler Myers .30 .75
50 Thomas Vanek .40 1.00
51 John Tavares .75 2.00
52 Kyle Okposo .30 .75
53 Lubomir Visnovsky .30 .75
54 Matt Moulson .30 .75
55 Evgeni Nabokov .50 1.25
56 Martin Brodeur 1.25 3.00
57 Cory Schneider .50 1.25
58 Patrik Elias .50 1.25
59 Jaromir Jagr 1.50 4.00
60 Travis Zajac .30 .75
61 Rick Nash .50 1.25
62 Carl Hagelin .30 .75
63 Ryan Callahan .30 .75
64 Dan Girardi .30 .75
65 Henrik Lundqvist 1.25 3.00
66 Henrik Zetterberg .60 1.50
67 Brendan Smith .30 .75
68 Jimmy Howard .60 1.50
69 Daniel Alfredsson .50 1.25
70 Pavel Datsyuk .75 2.00
71 Jonathan Toews .75 2.00
72 Patrick Sharp .50 1.25
73 Patrick Kane 1.00 2.50
74 Brent Seabrook .30 .75
75 Corey Crawford .60 1.50
76 Evgeni Malkin 1.00 2.50
77 Rob Scuderi .30 .75
78 Sidney Crosby 2.00 5.00
79 Chris Kunitz .50 1.25
80 Marc-Andre Fleury 1.00 2.50
81 Scott Hartnell .30 .75
82 Claude Giroux .50 1.25
83 Sean Couturier .40 1.00
84 Brayden Schenn .50 1.25
85 Braydon Coburn .30 .75
86 Braden Holtby .60 1.50
87 Karl Alzner .30 .75
88 Alex Ovechkin 2.00 5.00
89 Martin Erat .30 .75
90 Nicklas Backstrom .50 1.25
91 Jack Johnson .30 .75
92 Sergei Bobrovsky .75 2.00
93 R.J. Umberger .30 .75
94 Nathan Horton .50 1.25
95 Marian Gaborik .50 1.25
96 Joe Pavelski .60 1.50
97 Antti Niemi .40 1.00
98 Logan Couture .60 1.50
99 Brent Burns .50 1.25
100 Joe Thornton .75 2.00
101 Semyon Varlamov .50 1.25
102 Gabriel Landeskog .60 1.50
103 Paul Stastny .40 1.00
104 Matt Duchene .50 1.25
105 Alex Tanguay .30 .75
106 Alexander Steen .30 .75
107 David Backes .30 .75
108 T.J. Oshie .50 1.25
109 Alex Pietrangelo .40 1.00
110 Kevin Shattenkirk .30 .75
111 Eric Staal .60 1.50
112 Jordan Staal .40 1.00
113 Jeff Skinner .60 1.50
114 Tuomo Ruutu .40 1.00
115 Cam Ward .50 1.25
116 David Legwand .40 1.00
117 Mike Fisher .30 .75
118 Shea Weber .40 1.00
119 Roman Josi .50 1.25
120 Pekka Rinne .50 1.25
121 Dustin Brown .50 1.25
122 Jeff Carter .40 1.00
123 Justin Williams .40 1.00
124 Slava Voynov .40 1.00
125 Jonathan Quick .60 1.50
126 Teemu Selanne 1.00 2.50
127 Ryan Getzlaf .50 1.25
128 Francois Beauchemin .30 .75
129 Jonas Hiller .40 1.00
130 Corey Perry .75 2.00
131 Antoine Vermette .30 .75
132 Mike Ribeiro .30 .75
133 Mike Smith .50 1.25
134 Shane Doan .40 1.00
135 Martin Hanzal .30 .75
136 Jamie Benn .50 1.25
137 Stephane Robidas .30 .75
138 Kari Lehtonen .40 1.00
139 Shawn Horcoff .30 .75
140 Tyler Seguin .60 1.50
141 Martin St. Louis .50 1.25
142 Ryan Malone .30 .75
143 Steven Stamkos 1.00 2.50
144 Anders Lindback .30 .75
145 Ben Bishop .40 1.00
146 Shawn Matthias .30 .75
147 Brian Campbell .30 .75
148 Scottie Upshall .30 .75
149 Erik Gudbranson .30 .75
150 Jacob Markstrom .50 1.25
151 Drew Shore RC .75 2.00
152 Cristopher Nilstorp RC .75 2.00
153 Charlie Coyle RC 1.50 4.00
154 Sami Vatanen RC 1.00 2.50
155 Michael Sgarbossa RC 1.00 2.50
156 Danny DeKeyser RC 1.25 3.00
157 Tyler Toffoli RC 2.00 5.00
158 Ben Street RC .75 2.00
159 Thomas Hickey RC .75 2.00
160 Cory Conacher RC .60 1.50
161 Jack Campbell RC 2.50 6.00
162 Filip Forsberg RC 3.00 8.00
163 Edward Pasquale RC .60 1.50
164 Max Reinhart RC 1.00 2.50
165 Alex Killorn RC 1.50 4.00
166 Calvin Pickard RC 1.25 3.00
167 Jared Staal RC .75 2.00
168 J.T. Miller RC 2.50 6.00
169 Emerson Etem RC 1.00 2.50
170 Ryan Murphy RC 1.00 2.50
171 Nicklas Jensen RC .75 2.00
172 Mikhail Grigorenko RC .60 1.50
173 Nikita Kucherov RC 20.00 50.00
174 Richard Panik RC 1.00 2.50
175 Brock Nelson RC 2.00 5.00
176 Tom Wilson RC 2.00 5.00
177 Michael Caruso RC .60 1.50
178 Justin Schultz RC 1.00 2.50
179 Antoine Roussel RC 1.00 2.50
180 Eric Hartzell RC 1.00 2.50
181 Austin Watson RC .75 2.00
182 Vladimir Tarasenko RC 2.50 6.00
183 Anthony Peluso RC .60 1.50
184 Brendan Gallagher RC 2.50 6.00
185 Michal Jordan RC .60 1.50
186 Petr Mrazek RC 2.00 5.00
187 Stefan Matteau RC .75 2.00
188 Tye McGinn RC 1.00 2.50
189 Jarred Tinordi RC 1.00 2.50
190 Nail Yakupov RC 2.00 5.00
191 Frederik Andersen RC 2.50 6.00
192 Mark Arcobello RC 1.00 2.50
193 Ryan Spooner RC 1.00 2.50
194 Zach Redmond RC .75 2.00
195 Carl Soderberg RC 1.00 2.50
196 Jordan Schroeder RC 1.00 2.50
197 Nick Bjugstad RC 1.25 3.00
198 Philipp Grubauer RC 2.50 6.00
199 Jamie Oleksiak RC .75 2.00
200 Eric Gryba RC .75 2.00
201 Scott Laughton RC 1.25 3.00
202 Dmitrij Jaskin RC 1.00 2.50
203 Quinton Howden RC .75 2.00
204 Nathan Beaulieu RC .60 1.50
205 Mikael Granlund RC 1.50 4.00
206 Jonathan Huberdeau RC 2.50 6.00
207 Tanner Pearson RC 1.00 2.50
208 Viktor Fasth RC 1.00 2.50
209 Jonas Brodin RC 1.25 3.00
210 Brian Flynn RC .75 2.00
211 Rickard Rakell RC 1.00 2.50
212 Nick Petrecki RC .60 1.50
213 Beau Bennett RC 1.25 3.00
214 Brian Lashoff RC .75 2.00
215 Alex Chiasson RC 1.00 2.50
216 Dougie Hamilton RC 1.50 4.00
217 Alex Galchenyuk RC 3.00 8.00
218 Matt Irwin RC .75 2.00
219 Johan Larsson RC 1.25 3.00
220 Christian Thomas RC .75 2.00
221 Michael Kostka RC .75 2.00
222 Kevin Connauton RC .75 2.00
223 Darcy Kuemper RC 2.00 5.00
224 Frank Corrado RC .60 1.50
225 Mark Pysyk RC 1.00 2.50
226 Rasmus Ristolainen RC 1.50 4.00
227 Marek Mazanec RC 1.00 2.50
228 Jon Merrill RC 1.00 2.50
229 Nathan MacKinnon RC 8.00 20.00
230 Zemgus Girgensons RC 1.50 4.00
231 Joakim Nordstrom RC .75 2.00
232 Jacob Trouba RC 1.50 4.00
233 Tomas Hertl RC 2.00 5.00
234 Aleksander Barkov RC 3.00 8.00
235 Jesper Fast RC 1.00 2.50
236 Elias Lindholm RC 2.50 6.00
237 Xavier Ouellet RC 1.00 2.50
238 Matt Nieto RC .75 2.00
239 Olli Maatta RC 5.00 12.00
240 Sean Monahan RC 1.50 4.00
241 Seth Jones RC 2.00 5.00
242 Valeri Nichushkin RC 2.00 5.00
243 Boone Jenner RC 2.00 5.00
244 Ryan Murray RC 1.50 4.00
245 Matt Dumba RC .60 1.50
246 Morgan Rielly RC 2.50 6.00
247 Hampus Lindholm RC 1.50 4.00
248 Magnus Hellberg RC 1.00 2.50
249 Michael Bournival RC 1.00 2.50
250 Nikita Zadorov RC .60 1.50

2013-14 Totally Certified Mirror Platinum Blue

*1-150 VETS/10: 5X TO 12X BASIC CARDS
*151-250 ROOKIE/10: 2.5X TO 6X BASIC RC
75 Corey Crawford 8.00 20.00
90 Nicklas Backstrom 6.00 15.00
229 Nathan MacKinnon 125.00 200.00
239 Olli Maatta 60.00 100.00

2013-14 Totally Certified Mirror Platinum Purple

*1-150 VETS/35: 2.5X TO 6X BASIC CARDS
*151-250 ROOKIE/35: 1.5X TO 4X BASIC RC
75 Corey Crawford 4.00 10.00
90 Nicklas Backstrom 3.00 8.00
173 Nikita Kucherov 50.00 125.00

2013-14 Totally Certified Mirror Platinum Red

*1-150 VETS/25: 3X TO 8X BASIC CARDS
*151-250 ROOKIE/25: 2X TO 5X BASIC RC
75 Corey Crawford 5.00 12.00
90 Nicklas Backstrom 4.00 10.00
173 Nikita Kucherov 60.00 150.00
229 Nathan MacKinnon 75.00 135.00

2013-14 Totally Certified Platinum Blue

*1-150 VETS/50: X TO X BASIC CARDS
*151-250 ROOKIE/50: X TO X BASIC RC
75 Corey Crawford 3.00 8.00
90 Nicklas Backstrom 2.50 6.00
173 Nikita Kucherov 40.00 100.00

2013-14 Totally Certified Platinum Gold

*1-150 VETS/25: 3X TO 8X BASIC CARDS
*151-250 ROOKIE/25: 2X TO 5X BASIC RC
75 Corey Crawford 5.00 12.00
90 Nicklas Backstrom 4.00 10.00
173 Nikita Kucherov 60.00 150.00
229 Nathan MacKinnon 75.00 135.00

2013-14 Totally Certified Platinum Red

*1-150 VETS/100: 1.5X TO 4X BASIC CARDS
*151-250 ROOKIE/100: 1X TO 2.5X BASIC RC
75 Corey Crawford 2.50 6.00
90 Nicklas Backstrom 2.00 5.00
173 Nikita Kucherov 25.00 60.00

2013-14 Totally Certified Clear Cloth Jerseys Prime Blue

*BLUE/25: .8X TO 2X RED JSY/100
*BLUE/25: .6X TO 1.5X RED JSY/50
CLNMK Nathan MacKinnon/25 50.00 100.00

2013-14 Totally Certified Clear Cloth Jerseys Red

CLAB Aleksander Barkov/100 6.00 15.00
CLAF Adam Foote/100 2.50 6.00
CLAG Alex Galchenyuk/100 5.00 12.00
CLAH Adam Henrique/100 2.50 6.00
CLBC Bobby Clarke/50 8.00 20.00
CLBH Brett Hull/100 6.00 15.00
CLBR Bobby Ryan/100 3.00 8.00
CLBS Brendan Shanahan/100 3.00 8.00
CLBW Blake Wheeler/100 3.00 8.00
CLCC Cory Conacher/100 2.00 5.00
CLCN Cam Neely/50 6.00 15.00
CLCP Carey Price/100 8.00 20.00
CLDB David Backes/100 3.00 8.00
CLDG Doug Gilmour/100 5.00 12.00
CLDH Dougie Hamilton/100 3.00 8.00
CLEL Eric Lindros/100 8.00 20.00
CLEM Evgeni Malkin/100 6.00 15.00
CLFF Filip Forsberg/100 10.00 25.00
CLGF Grant Fuhr/100 6.00 15.00
CLHL Henrik Lundqvist/100 5.00 12.00
CLHS Henrik Sedin/100 4.00 10.00
CLHZ Henrik Zetterberg/100 4.00 10.00
CLJB Jonas Brodin/100 4.00 10.00
CLJH Jonathan Huberdeau/100 5.00 12.00
CLJJ Jaromir Jagr/100 6.00 15.00
CLJQ Jonathan Quick/100 5.00 12.00
CLJR Jeremy Roenick/100 5.00 12.00
CLJS Joe Sakic/50 10.00 25.00
CLJT John Tavares/100 5.00 12.00
CLKO Kyle Okposo/100 2.00 5.00
CLKY Keith Yandle/100 2.00 5.00
CLLC Logan Couture/100 4.00 10.00
CLLE Loui Eriksson/100 2.00 5.00
CLLU Roberto Luongo/100 5.00 12.00
CLMB Martin Brodeur/100 8.00 20.00
CLMG Marian Gaborik/100 5.00 12.00
CLMI Mikhail Grigorenko/100 1.25 3.00
CLML Mario Lemieux/100 10.00 25.00
CLMO Mike Modano/100 6.00 15.00
CLMP Max Pacioretty/100 3.00 8.00
CLNK Nazem Kadri/100 4.00 10.00
CLNL Nicklas Lidstrom/100 4.00 10.00
CLNY Nail Yakupov/100 4.00 10.00
CLOM Olli Maatta/100 12.00 30.00
CLPB Pavel Bure/50 6.00 15.00
CLPC Paul Coffey/100 4.00 10.00
CLPK Patrick Kane/100 6.00 15.00
CLRB Ray Bourque/100 6.00 15.00
CLRF Ron Francis/100 5.00 12.00
CLRN Rick Nash/100 3.00 8.00
CLSC Sidney Crosby/100 10.00 25.00
CLSD Shane Doan/100 2.50 6.00
CLSJ Seth Jones/100 4.00 10.00
CLSK Saku Koivu/100 5.00 12.00
CLSM Stan Mikita/100 5.00 12.00
CLSS Steven Stamkos/100 6.00 15.00
CLSW Shea Weber/100 2.50 6.00
CLSY Steve Yzerman/100 8.00 20.00
CLTH Taylor Hall/100 3.00 8.00
CLTS Tyler Seguin/100 4.00 10.00
CLVN Valeri Nichushkin/100 4.00 10.00
CLVT Vladimir Tarasenko/100 5.00 12.00
CLWC Wendel Clark/100 4.00 10.00
CLABU Alexandre Burrows/100 2.00 5.00
CLACO Andrew Cogliano/100 2.00 5.00
CLBHY Braden Holtby/100 4.00 10.00
CLBLI Bryan Little/100 3.00 8.00
CLCGX Claude Giroux/100 5.00 12.00
CLDAL Daniel Alfredsson/100 3.00 8.00
CLJLU Joffrey Lupul/100 2.00 5.00
CLJOS Jordan Staal/100 2.50 6.00
CLJTH Joe Thornton/100 6.00 15.00
CLJTO Jonathan Toews/50 6.00 15.00
CLJTR Jacob Trouba/100 3.00 8.00
CLLEL Lars Eller/100 4.00 10.00
CLLUC Luc Robitaille/100 4.00 10.00
CLMAF Marc-Andre Fleury/100 4.00 10.00
CLMBA Mikael Backlund/100 2.50 6.00
CLMBO Mikkel Boedker/100 2.00 5.00
CLMDB Matt Dumba/100 2.00 5.00
CLMGR Mikael Granlund/100 5.00 12.00
CLMRE Matt Read/100 2.00 5.00
CLMRI Mike Richards/100 4.00 10.00
CLMSL Martin St. Louis/100 3.00 8.00
CLNBO Nick Bonino/100 2.00 5.00
CLNMK Nathan MacKinnon/100 15.00 40.00
CLOVI Alex Ovechkin/50 15.00 40.00
CLPKS P.K. Subban/100 4.00 10.00
CLPLF Pat LaFontaine/100 4.00 10.00
CLPMR Petr Mrazek/100 8.00 20.00
CLRBL Rob Blake/100 4.00 10.00
CLRLY Morgan Rielly/100 5.00 12.00
CLRMP Ryan Murphy/100 3.00 8.00
CLRMR Ryan Murray/100 3.00 8.00
CLRNH Ryan Nugent-Hopkins/50 5.00 12.00
CLTHE Tomas Hertl/100 4.00 10.00
CLTMU Teemu Selanne/100 8.00 20.00
CLTTH Tim Thomas/100 3.00 8.00
CLTVA Thomas Vanek/100 2.50 6.00

2013-14 Totally Certified Certified Competitors Jerseys Red

*BLUE/50: .8X TO 2X RED JSY
*BLUE/25: 1X TO 2.5X RED JSY
*PATCH GOLD/15-25: 1.2X TO 3X JSY RED
CCBL M.Brodeur/Lundqvist 6.00 15.00
CCBP D.Brown/C.Perry 5.00 12.00
CCBT D.Backes/J.Toews 5.00 12.00
CCBY D.Byfuglien/K.Yandle 3.00 8.00
CCEP E.Etem/T.Pearson 3.00 8.00
CCFV A.Foote/Vanbiesbrouck 5.00 12.00
CCGC Granlund/A.Chiasson 3.00 8.00
CCGD R.Getzlaf/S.Doan 3.00 8.00
CCGF C.Giroux/M.Fleury 5.00 12.00
CCGM M.Gaborik/E.Malkin 6.00 15.00
CCGN C.Glencross/RNH 4.00 10.00
CCHC J.Howard/C.Crawford 4.00 10.00
CCKA P.Kessel/C.Anderson 3.00 8.00
CCKB N.Kadri/P.Bergeron 4.00 10.00
CCKN T.Kerr/C.Neely 4.00 10.00
CCKP R.Kesler/J.Pavelski 4.00 10.00
CCKR P.Kane/T.Rask 6.00 15.00
CCKS D.Keith/D.Sedin 4.00 10.00
CCLM E.Lindros/M.Messier 6.00 15.00
CCLS J.LeClair/B.Shanahan 3.00 8.00
CCMB S.Matteau/B.Bennett 2.50 6.00
CCMJ S.Jones/N.MacKinnon 8.00 20.00
CCOK A.Ovechkin/C.Kunitz 12.00 30.00
CCPB D.Potvin/B.Barber 4.00 10.00
CCPH D.Phaneuf/C.Hodgson 2.50 6.00
CCRL P.Rinne/K.Lehtonen 3.00 8.00
CCSB J.Schultz/Beauchemin 2.00 5.00
CCSC Z.Chara/P.Subban 4.00 10.00
CCSG B.Salming/B.Gainey 3.00 8.00
CCSH S.Stamkos/Huberdeau 5.00 12.00
CCSP J.Staal/R.Panik 3.00 8.00
CCTB J.Thornton/J.Benn 5.00 12.00
CCTR J.Tavares/B.Richards 5.00 12.00
CCWJ S.Weber/B.Jackman 2.50 6.00
CCYS S.Yzerman/J.Sakic 5.00 12.00

2013-14 Totally Certified EPIX Memorabilia Red Play

*BLUE/50: .6X TO 1.5X RED PLAY
*GOLD/25: .8X TO 2X RED PLAY
EBH Brett Hull 10.00 25.00
EEL Eric Lindros 8.00 20.00
EHL Henrik Lundqvist 10.00 25.00
EJI Jarome Iginla 5.00 12.00
EJJ Jaromir Jagr 12.00 30.00
EJQ Jonathan Quick 5.00 12.00
EJS Joe Sakic 10.00 25.00
EMB Martin Brodeur 10.00 25.00
EML Mario Lemieux 20.00 50.00
EMM Mark Messier 10.00 25.00
EMRI Mike Richards 3.00 8.00
ENY Nail Yakupov 5.00 12.00
EOVI Alex Ovechkin 15.00 40.00
EPB Pavel Bure 8.00 20.00
EPD Pavel Datsyuk 6.00 15.00
EPK Patrick Kane 6.00 15.00
EPKS P.K. Subban 5.00 12.00
EPR Patrick Roy 12.00 30.00
ERB Ray Bourque 8.00 20.00
ERF Ron Francis 6.00 15.00
ESC Sidney Crosby 15.00 40.00
ESS Steven Stamkos 8.00 20.00
ESY Steve Yzerman 8.00 20.00
ETMU Teemu Selanne 8.00 20.00
EZC Zdeno Chara 4.00 10.00

2013-14 Totally Certified HRX

HGH Gordie Howe 50.00 100.00
HMM Mark Messier 30.00 60.00
HNY Nail Yakupov 60.00 120.00
HRNH Ryan Nugent-Hopkins 25.00 60.00
HOVI Alex Ovechkin 75.00 135.00

2013-14 Totally Certified Jerseys Red

*BLUE/50: .6X TO 1.5X RED JSY
*BLUE/25: .8X TO 2X RED JSY
*GOLD/25: .8X TO 2X RED JSY
TCAGR Adam Graves 3.00 8.00
TCAKO Anze Kopitar 5.00 12.00
TCALA Adam Larsson 3.00 8.00
TCAT Alex Tanguay 2.50 6.00
TCAVO Anton Volchenkov 2.00 5.00
TCBE Brian Elliott 2.50 6.00
TCBLI Bryan Little 3.00 8.00
TCBN Bernie Nicholls 3.00 8.00
TCBRM Brad Marchand 6.00 15.00
TCBW Blake Wheeler 3.00 8.00
TCBY Brandon Yip 2.00 5.00
TCCCH Chris Chelios 3.00 8.00
TCCCR Corey Crawford 4.00 10.00
TCCPE Corey Perry 5.00 12.00
TCCTA Chris Tanev 6.00 15.00
TCDA Dave Andreychuk 4.00 10.00
TCDD Drew Doughty 4.00 10.00
TCDE Dan Ellis 2.50 6.00
TCDHA Dan Hamhuis 2.50 6.00
TCDK Duncan Keith 2.50 6.00
TCDS Daniel Sedin 4.00 10.00
TCDST Derek Stepan 2.00 5.00
TCFB Francois Beauchemin 2.00 5.00
TCFN Frans Nielsen 2.00 5.00
TCGB Gabriel Bourque 2.50 6.00
TCGH Gordie Howe 12.00 30.00
TCGL Gabriel Landeskog 4.00 10.00
TCGRN Mike Green 2.50 6.00
TCIL Igor Larionov 5.00 12.00
TCJBO Jay Bouwmeester 2.00 5.00
TCJEN Jhonas Enroth 3.00 8.00
TCJG Josh Gorges 2.50 6.00
TCJHI Jonas Hiller 2.50 6.00
TCJHO Jimmy Howard 4.00 10.00
TCJLC John LeClair 3.00 8.00
TCJLU Joffrey Lupul 2.00 5.00
TCJN Joe Nieuwendyk 3.00 8.00
TCJPE Justin Peters 2.00 5.00
TCJPO Jason Pominville 2.00 5.00
TCKP Keith Primeau 3.00 8.00
TCMBA Mikael Backlund 2.50 6.00
TCMGI Mark Giordano 3.00 8.00
TCMHO Mark Howe 4.00 10.00
TCMMI Milan Michalek 2.00 5.00
TCMN Michal Neuvirth 2.50 6.00
TCMP Max Pacioretty 3.00 8.00
TCMXT Maxime Talbot 2.00 5.00
TCNH Nathan Horton 3.00 8.00
TCNKR Niklas Kronwall 2.50 6.00
TCOVI Alex Ovechkin 12.00 30.00
TCPAP P.A. Parenteau 2.00 5.00
TCPAS Paul Stastny 2.50 6.00
TCPB Pavel Bure 3.00 8.00
TCPBI Paul Bissonnette 2.00 5.00
TCPC Paul Coffey 4.00 10.00
TCPD Pavel Datsyuk 5.00 12.00
TCPRI Pekka Rinne 3.00 8.00
TCPT Pierre Turgeon 2.50 6.00
TCREB Rene Bourque 2.00 5.00
TCRJO Roman Josi 3.00 8.00
TCSC Sidney Crosby 12.00 30.00
TCSH Shawn Horcoff 2.00 5.00
TCSJN Matt Stajan 2.00 5.00
TCSSO Sheldon Souray 2.00 5.00
TCSTM Steve Mason 3.00 8.00
TCTTH Tim Thomas 3.00 8.00
TCTVA Thomas Vanek 2.50 6.00
TCTZ Travis Zajac 2.00 5.00
TCVFI Valtteri Filppula 2.00 5.00
TCZB Zach Boychuk 2.00 5.00

2013-14 Totally Certified Rookie Autograph Jerseys

*BLUE/25: .6X TO 1.5X BASIC INSERTS
*BLUE/25: .5X TO 1.2X BASIC SP
*PLAT.RED/25: .6X TO 1.5X BASIC INSERTS
*PLAT.RED/25: .5X TO 1.2X BASIC SP
*RED/50: .5X TO 1.2X BASIC INSERTS
*RED/50: .4X TO 1X BASIC SP
151 Drew Shore/250 4.00 10.00
152 Cristopher Nilstorp/250 4.00 10.00
153 Charlie Coyle/250 8.00 20.00
154 Sami Vatanen/250 5.00 12.00
155 Michael Sgarbossa/250 5.00 12.00
156 Danny DeKeyser/250 6.00 15.00
157 Tyler Toffoli/100 10.00 25.00
158 Ben Street/250 4.00 10.00
159 Thomas Hickey/250 4.00 10.00
160 Cory Conacher/250 3.00 8.00
161 Jack Campbell/250 12.00 30.00
162 Filip Forsberg/250 15.00 40.00
163 Edward Pasquale/250 3.00 8.00
164 Max Reinhart/250 5.00 12.00
165 Alex Killorn/100 8.00 20.00
166 Calvin Pickard/250 6.00 15.00
167 Jared Staal/250 4.00 10.00
168 J.T. Miller/100 12.00 30.00
169 Emerson Etem/250 5.00 12.00
170 Ryan Murphy/250 5.00 12.00
171 Nicklas Jensen/250 4.00 10.00
172 Mikhail Grigorenko/250 3.00 8.00
174 Richard Panik/250 5.00 12.00
175 Brock Nelson/250 10.00 25.00
176 Tom Wilson/250 10.00 25.00
177 Michael Caruso/250 3.00 8.00
178 Justin Schultz/250 5.00 12.00
179 Antoine Roussel/250 5.00 12.00
180 Eric Hartzell/250 5.00 12.00
181 Austin Watson/250 4.00 10.00
182 Vladimir Tarasenko/100 12.00 30.00
183 Anthony Peluso/250 3.00 8.00
184 Brendan Gallagher/100 12.00 30.00
185 Michal Jordan/250 3.00 8.00
186 Petr Mrazek/250 10.00 25.00
187 Stefan Matteau/100 4.00 10.00
188 Tye McGinn/250 5.00 12.00
189 Jarred Tinordi/100 5.00 12.00
190 Nail Yakupov/250 10.00 25.00
191 Frederik Andersen/100 12.00 30.00
192 Mark Arcobello/250 5.00 12.00
193 Ryan Spooner/100 5.00 12.00
194 Zach Redmond/250 4.00 10.00
195 Carl Soderberg/100 5.00 12.00
196 Jordan Schroeder/250 5.00 12.00
197 Nick Bjugstad/250 6.00 15.00
198 Philipp Grubauer/250 12.00 30.00
199 Jamie Oleksiak/250 4.00 10.00
200 Eric Gryba/250 4.00 10.00
201 Scott Laughton/250 6.00 15.00
202 Dmitrij Jaskin/250 5.00 12.00
203 Quinton Howden/250 4.00 10.00
204 Nathan Beaulieu/250 3.00 8.00
205 Mikael Granlund/250 8.00 20.00
206 Jonathan Huberdeau/100 12.00 30.00
207 Tanner Pearson/250 5.00 12.00
208 Viktor Fasth/250 5.00 12.00
209 Jonas Brodin/100 6.00 15.00
210 Brian Flynn/250 4.00 10.00
211 Rickard Rakell/250 5.00 12.00
212 Nick Petrecki/250 3.00 8.00
213 Beau Bennett/250 6.00 15.00
214 Brian Lashoff/250 4.00 10.00
215 Alex Chiasson/250 5.00 12.00
216 Dougie Hamilton/250 8.00 20.00
217 Alex Galchenyuk/100 12.00 30.00
218 Matt Irwin/250 4.00 10.00
219 Johan Larsson/250 6.00 15.00
220 Christian Thomas/250 4.00 10.00
221 Michael Kostka/250 4.00 10.00
224 Frank Corrado/250 3.00 8.00
225 Mark Pysyk/250 5.00 12.00
226 Rasmus Ristolainen/100 8.00 20.00
227 Marek Mazanec/250 5.00 12.00
228 Jon Merrill/250 5.00 12.00
229 Nathan MacKinnon/250 25.00 60.00
230 Joakim Nordstrom/250 4.00 10.00
231 Zemgus Girgensons/100 8.00 20.00
232 Jacob Trouba/250 8.00 20.00
233 Tomas Hertl/250 10.00 25.00
234 Aleksander Barkov/250 15.00 40.00
236 Elias Lindholm/250 12.00 30.00
237 Xavier Ouellet/100 5.00 12.00
238 Matt Nieto/250 4.00 10.00
239 Olli Maatta/100 EXCH 8.00 20.00
240 Sean Monahan/250 8.00 20.00
241 Seth Jones/250 10.00 25.00
242 Valeri Nichushkin/250 10.00 25.00
243 Boone Jenner/250 10.00 25.00
244 Ryan Murray/250 8.00 20.00
245 Matt Dumba/250 3.00 8.00
246 Morgan Rielly/250 12.00 30.00
247 Hampus Lindholm/250 8.00 20.00
248 Magnus Hellberg/250 5.00 12.00
249 Michael Bournival/250 5.00 12.00
250 Nikita Zadorov/250 3.00 8.00

2013-14 Totally Certified Rookie Roll Call Jerseys Patch Gold

*GOLD/25: .8X TO 2X RED JSY
RRNMK Nathan MacKinnon 60.00 120.00

2013-14 Totally Certified Rookie Roll Call Jerseys Red

*BLUE/50: .6X TO 1.5X RED JSY
RRAB Aleksander Barkov 6.00 15.00
RRAC Alex Chiasson 3.00 8.00
RRAG Alex Galchenyuk 6.00 15.00
RRAK Alex Killorn 5.00 12.00
RRANP Anthony Peluso 2.00 5.00
RRAR Antoine Roussel 3.00 8.00
RRAW Austin Watson 2.50 6.00
RRBB Beau Bennett 5.00 12.00
RRBG Brendan Gallagher 6.00 15.00
RRBJE Boone Jenner 6.00 15.00
RRBNE Brock Nelson 6.00 15.00
RRBST Ben Street 3.00 8.00
RRCB Chris Brown 2.00 5.00
RRCC Cory Conacher 2.00 5.00
RRCM Connor Murphy 2.50 6.00
RRCOY Charlie Coyle 5.00 12.00
RRCSO Carl Soderberg 3.00 8.00
RRDDK Danny DeKeyser 4.00 10.00
RRDH Dougie Hamilton 5.00 12.00
RREE Emerson Etem 3.00 8.00
RRFF Filip Forsberg 10.00 25.00
RRHLI Hampus Lindholm 4.00 10.00
RRJAS Jared Staal 2.50 6.00
RRJB Jonas Brodin 4.00 10.00
RRJC Jack Campbell 8.00 20.00
RRJH Jonathan Huberdeau 5.00 12.00
RRJTM J.T. Miller 8.00 20.00
RRJTR Jacob Trouba 5.00 12.00
RRJUS Justin Schultz 3.00 8.00
RRMDB Matt Dumba 2.00 5.00
RRMGH Magnus Hellberg 3.00 8.00
RRMGR Mikael Granlund 5.00 12.00
RRMI Matt Irwin 2.50 6.00
RRMIK Mikhail Grigorenko 2.00 5.00
RRMNI Matt Nieto 2.50 6.00
RRNBE Nathan Beaulieu 2.00 5.00
RRNBJ Nick Bjugstad 4.00 10.00
RRNJ Nicklas Jensen 2.50 6.00
RRNMK Nathan MacKinnon 10.00 25.00
RRNP Nick Petrecki 2.00 5.00
RRNY Nail Yakupov 5.00 12.00
RROM Olli Maatta 10.00 25.00
RRPMR Petr Mrazek 6.00 15.00
RRQH Quinton Howden 2.50 6.00
RRRLY Morgan Rielly 5.00 12.00
RRRMP Ryan Murphy 3.00 8.00
RRRMR Ryan Murray 4.00 10.00
RRRR Rickard Rakell 3.00 8.00
RRSJ Seth Jones 5.00 12.00
RRSL Scott Laughton 4.00 10.00
RRSMA Stefan Matteau 2.50 6.00
RRSMO Sean Monahan 5.00 12.00
RRSV Sami Vatanen 3.00 8.00
RRTHE Tomas Hertl 6.00 15.00
RRTHI Thomas Hickey 2.50 6.00
RRTMG Tye McGinn 3.00 8.00
RRTP Tanner Pearson 3.00 8.00
RRTT Tyler Toffoli 6.00 15.00
RRTW Tom Wilson 4.00 10.00
RRVF Viktor Fasth 3.00 8.00
RRVN Valeri Nichushkin 5.00 12.00
RRVT Vladimir Tarasenko 8.00 20.00
RRZG Zemgus Girgensons 5.00 12.00
RRZR Zach Redmond 2.50 6.00

2013-14 Totally Certified Rookie Signatures

TRAB Aleksander Barkov 10.00 25.00
TRALE Anders Lee 5.00 12.00
TRANP Anthony Peluso 2.00 5.00
TRAPE Alex Petrovic 2.50 6.00
TRAR Antoine Roussel 3.00 8.00
TRBG Brendan Gallagher 8.00 20.00
TRBJE Boone Jenner 6.00 15.00
TRCB Chris Brown 2.00 5.00
TRCC Cory Conacher 2.00 5.00
TRCSC Cameron Schilling 2.00 5.00
TRDBA Daniel Bang 2.50 6.00
TRDDK Danny DeKeyser 4.00 10.00
TRDH Dougie Hamilton 5.00 12.00
TRFC Frank Corrado 2.00 5.00
TRFF Filip Forsberg 10.00 25.00
TRHLI Hampus Lindholm 5.00 12.00
TRIB Igor Bobkov 2.50 6.00
TRJCN Joe Cannata 2.50 6.00
TRJMU John Muse 3.00 8.00
TRJOO Joonas Rask 2.00 5.00
TRJSD Jordan Schroeder 3.00 8.00
TRJTM J.T. Miller 8.00 20.00
TRJTR Jacob Trouba 5.00 12.00
TRMDB Matt Dumba 2.00 5.00
TRMGR Mikael Granlund 5.00 12.00
TRMIK Mikhail Grigorenko 2.00 5.00
TRNBJ Nick Bjugstad 4.00 10.00
TRNJ Nicklas Jensen 2.50 6.00
TRNMK Nathan MacKinnon 15.00 40.00
TRNY Nail Yakupov 6.00 15.00
TRPMR Petr Mrazek 10.00 25.00
TRRLY Morgan Rielly 8.00 20.00
TRRMR Ryan Murray 5.00 12.00
TRRR Rickard Rakell 3.00 8.00
TRSEC Sean Collins 2.50 6.00
TRSJ Seth Jones 6.00 15.00
TRSL Scott Laughton 4.00 10.00

TRSMA Stefan Matteau 2.50 6.00
TRTB Taylor Beck 2.50 6.00
TRTHE Tomas Hertl 6.00 15.00
TRTP Tanner Pearson 3.00 8.00
TRTW Tom Wilson 6.00 15.00
TRVF Viktor Fasth 3.00 8.00
TRVN Valeri Nichushkin 6.00 15.00

2013-14 Totally Certified Rookie Slideshow

RSAG Alex Galchenyuk 25.00 50.00
RSAW Austin Watson 4.00 10.00
RSBB Beau Bennett 6.00 15.00
RSBG Brendan Gallagher 15.00 40.00
RSBNE Brock Nelson 10.00 25.00
RSCK Chris Kreider 6.00 15.00
RSCOY Charlie Coyle 8.00 20.00
RSDH Dougie Hamilton 8.00 20.00
RSEE Emerson Etem 5.00 12.00
RSFF Filip Forsberg 10.00 25.00
RSJC Jack Campbell 12.00 30.00
RSJO Jamie Oleksiak 4.00 10.00
RSJSC Jaden Schwartz 6.00 15.00
RSJTI Jarred Tinordi 5.00 12.00
RSJUS Justin Schultz 5.00 12.00
RSMIK Mikhail Grigorenko 3.00 8.00
RSNBE Nathan Beaulieu 3.00 8.00
RSNMK Nathan MacKinnon 25.00 60.00
RSNY Nail Yakupov 10.00 25.00
RSQH Quinton Howden 4.00 10.00
RSRLY Morgan Rielly 12.00 30.00
RSRMP Ryan Murphy 5.00 12.00
RSRMR Ryan Murray 8.00 20.00
RSRSM Reilly Smith 8.00 20.00
RSRSP Ryan Spooner 5.00 12.00
RSSJ Seth Jones 10.00 25.00
RSSL Scott Laughton 10.00 25.00
RSTBA Tyson Barrie 3.00 8.00
RSTT Tyler Toffoli 10.00 25.00
RSVT Vladimir Tarasenko 15.00 40.00

2013-14 Totally Certified Rookie Slideshow Autographs

RSAG Alex Galchenyuk/20 30.00 80.00
RSBG Brendan Gallagher/20 30.00 80.00
RSCK Chris Kreider/20 15.00 40.00
RSCOY Charlie Coyle/20 20.00 50.00
RSDH Dougie Hamilton/20 20.00 50.00
RSEE Emerson Etem/20 12.00 30.00
RSFF Filip Forsberg/20 40.00 100.00
RSJSC Jaden Schwartz/20 15.00 40.00
RSJUS Justin Schultz/20 12.00 30.00
RSMIK Mikhail Grigorenko/20 8.00 20.00
RSNMK Nathan MacKinnon/20 60.00 150.00
RSNY Nail Yakupov/20 25.00 60.00
RSRLY Morgan Rielly/20 30.00 80.00
RSRMP Ryan Murphy/20 12.00 30.00
RSRMR Ryan Murray/20 20.00 50.00
RSRSP Ryan Spooner/20 12.00 30.00
RSSJ Seth Jones/20 25.00 60.00
RSTBA Tyson Barrie/20 8.00 20.00
RSVT Vladimir Tarasenko/20 30.00 80.00

2013-14 Totally Certified Signatures

TSAA Akim Aliu 4.00 10.00
TSAH Adam Henrique 5.00 12.00
TSAL Andrew Ladd 4.00 10.00
TSAN Antti Niemi 5.00 12.00
TSBH Brett Hull 12.00 30.00
TSBM Brenden Morrow 5.00 12.00
TSBR Bobby Ryan 5.00 12.00
TSBSD Brandon Saad 5.00 12.00
TSCHO Cody Hodgson 4.00 10.00
TSCHP Chet Pickard 4.00 10.00
TSCK Chris Kreider 8.00 20.00
TSDBR Daniel Briere 6.00 15.00
TSDCA Daniel Carcillo 4.00 10.00
TSDPH Dion Phaneuf 5.00 12.00
TSEB Ed Belfour 6.00 15.00
TSERS Eric Staal 8.00 20.00
TSGH Gordie Howe 60.00 150.00
TSGL Gabriel Landeskog 8.00 20.00
TSHL Henrik Lundqvist 15.00 40.00
TSJI Jarome Iginla 8.00 20.00
TSJJ Jaromir Jagr 20.00 50.00
TSJP Joe Pavelski 8.00 20.00
TSJQ Jonathan Quick EXCH 8.00 20.00
TSJRE James Reimer 6.00 15.00
TSJSC Jaden Schwartz 8.00 20.00
TSJSI Jakob Silfverberg 4.00 10.00
TSJT John Tavares 10.00 25.00
TSJTB J.T. Brown 4.00 10.00
TSJZU Jason Zucker 6.00 15.00
TSLE Loui Eriksson 4.00 10.00
TSMAF Marc-Andre Fleury 12.00 30.00
TSMBA Mikael Backlund 5.00 12.00
TSMG Marian Gaborik 6.00 15.00
TSMM Mark Messier 12.00 30.00
TSMS Mike Smith 6.00 15.00
TSNL Nicklas Lidstrom 6.00 15.00
TSOVI Alex Ovechkin 25.00 60.00
TSPR Patrick Roy 15.00 40.00
TSRJO Roman Josi 6.00 15.00
TSRK Ryan Kesler 6.00 15.00
TSRNH Ryan Nugent-Hopkins 8.00 20.00
TSSB Sven Baertschi 5.00 12.00
TSSC Sidney Crosby 60.00 150.00
TSSDE Simon Despres 5.00 12.00
TSSWE Stephen Weiss 5.00 12.00
TSTS Tyler Seguin 8.00 20.00
TSVL Vincent Lecavalier 6.00 15.00

1972 Tower Hockey Instructions Booklets

1 Skating Skills 10.00 20.00

1936 Triumph Postcards

COMPLETE SET (11) 650.00 1300.00
1 Lionel Conacher/22/2/36 125.00 250.00
2 Harvey Jackson Toronto Maple Leafs/18/1/36 125.00 250.00
3 Ivan Johnson New York Rangers/8/2/36 62.50 125.00
4 Herbie Lewis/7/3/36 40.00 80.00
5 Sylvio Mantha Montreal Canadiens/18/1/36 62.50 125.00
6 Nick Metz Toronto Maple Leafs/15/2/36 40.00 80.00
7 Baldy Northcott Montreal Maroons/1/2/36 45.00 90.00
8 Eddie Shore Boston Bruins/25/1/36 250.00 500.00
9 Paul Thompson Chicago Blackhawks/29/2/36 40.00 80.00
10 Roy Worters New York Americans/18/1/36 62.50 125.00
11 Charley Conacher 40.00 80.00

1993 UDA Commemorative Cards

99 Wayne Gretzky AU/500 (1993-94 Upper Deck jumbo) 150.00 400.00
G5 Wayne Gretzky/2500 Gordie Howe Selects Jumbo 4.00 10.00

1994 UDA Commemorative Cards

54 Wayne Gretzky AU/500 '94-95 SP 150.00 400.00
WG Wayne Gretzky/10,000 802 goals 3.00 8.00
WGA Wayne Gretzky AU/500 802 goals 150.00 400.00
UDHC Wayne Gretzky/45,000 Happy Holidays 3.00 8.00

1995 UDA Commemorative Cards

WG Wayne Gretzky 2500 points 3.00 8.00
127 Wayne Gretzky AU/500 '95-96 SP 150.00 400.00

1996 UDA Commemorative Cards

AV Avalanche Stanley Cup Champs 5.00
170 Wayne Gretzky AU/500 '96-97 Collector's Choice 150.00 400.00
NH1 Wayne Gretzky AU/250 '96 Upper Deck National Hero 300.00 800.00

1997 UDA Commemorative Cards

COMPLETE SET
144 Wayne Gretzky AU/99 97-98 Black Diamond Double Diamond 500.00 1200.00
NNO Wayne Gretzky AU/99 16 Time All-Star 500.00 1200.00
NNO Wayne Gretzky AU/99 All-Star Then and Now 500.00 1200.00
NNO Wayne Gretzky 16 Time All-Star/5000 3.00 8.00
NNO 1996 Wayne Gretzky The Great One/5000 3.00 8.00

1998 UDA Commemorative Cards

55 Wayne Gretzky AU/99 '98-99 Black Diamond 500.00 1200.00
RW 1997 Red Wings Stanley Cup/5000 2.50 6.00
RW 1997 Red Wings Stanley Cup/200 Steve Yzerman AUTO 40.00 80.00

1999 UDA Commemorative Cards

WG Wayne Gretzky Retires/9900 3.00 8.00

2000 UDA Commemorative Cards

WG Wayne Gretzky HOF/5000 3.00

2004-05 UD All-World

COMPLETE SET (120)
1 Roman Turek .15 .40
2 Jiri Fischer .15 .40
3 Martin Rucinsky .15 .40
4 Ales Hemsky .20 .50
5 Milan Hejduk .15 .40
6 Zigmund Palffy .20 .50
7 Peter Stastny .15 .40
8 Petr Nedved .12 .30
9 Radek Bonk .15 .40
10 Roman Hamrlik .12 .30
11 Martin Havlat .20 .50
12 Jarkko Ruutu .15 .40
13 Matti Hagman .15 .40
14 Tomas Vokoun .16 .40
15 Mika Noronen .15 .40
16 Jari Kurri .20 .50
17 Teemu Selanne .40 1.00
18 Dwayne Roloson .15 .40
19 Saku Koivu .20 .50
20 Erik Cole .12 .30
21 Marco Sturm .12 .30
22 Mike York .12 .30
23 Ryan Malone .12 .30
24 Alex Kovalev .15 .40
25 Brad Richards .20 .50
26 Ilya Kovalchuk .20 .50
27 Nikolai Khabibulin .20 .50
28 Vincent Lecavalier .20 .50
29 Jaromir Jagr .60 1.50
30 Alexander Frolov .15 .40
31 Nikolai Zherdev .15 .40
32 Maxim Afinogenov .12 .30
33 Pavel Datsyuk .30 .75
34 Nikolai Antropov .15 .40
35 Evgeni Nabokov .15 .40
36 Patrik Elias .20 .50
37 Petr Sykora .15 .40
38 Sergei Gonchar .15 .40
39 Michael Nylander .12 .30
40 Fedor Fedorov .15 .40
41 Alexei Zhamnov .15 .40
42 Pavol Demitra .25 .60
43 Miroslav Satan .15 .40
44 Borje Salming .20 .50
45 Ulf Nilsson .15 .40
46 Tyler Arnason .12 .30
47 Mats Naslund .12 .30
48 Jose Theodore .20 .50
49 Marty Turco .20 .50
50 Kent Nilsson .15 .40
51 Marian Gaborik .20 .50
52 Mike Comrie .15 .40
53 Sheldon Souray .12 .30
54 Zdeno Chara .20 .50
55 Hakan Loob .12 .30
56 Thomas Steen .20 .50
57 Daniel Alfredsson .20 .50
58 Jonathan Cheechoo .15 .40
59 Michael Ryder .15 .40
60 Brendan Morrison .15 .40
61 Justin Williams .15 .40
62 Tomas Holmstrom .15 .40
63 Adrian Aucoin .12 .30
64 Daniel Sedin .25 .60
65 Henrik Sedin .25 .60
66 Markus Naslund .20 .50
67 Peter Forsberg .40 1.00
68 Anders Hedberg .12 .30
69 Ladislav Nagy .12 .30
70 Marcel Hossa .12 .30
71 Marian Hossa .20 .50
72 Trent Hunter .12 .30
73 Dick Tarnstrom .12 .30
74 Olli Jokinen .15 .40
75 Fredrik Modin .12 .30
76 Henrik Zetterberg .25 .60
77 Miikka Kiprusoff .20 .50
78 Joe Thornton .30 .75
79 Rick Nash .20 .50
80 Martin St. Louis .20 .50
81 Alex Tanguay .15 .40
82 David Aebischer .15 .40
83 Martin Gelinas .12 .30
84 Daniel Briere .20 .50
85 Dany Heatley .15 .40
86 Niko Kapanen .12 .30
87 Igor Larionov .20 .50
88 Richard Zednik .12 .30
89 Jochen Hecht .12 .30
90 Vladislav Tretiak .15 .40
91 Wayne Gretzky UCP 5.00 12.00
92 Gordie Howe UCP 2.50 6.00
93 Patrick Roy UCP 2.00 5.00
94 Joe Thornton UCP 1.25 3.00
95 Rick Nash UCP .75 2.00
96 Martin Brodeur UCP 2.00 5.00
97 Marty Turco UCP .75 2.00
98 Jarome Iginla UCP 1.00 2.50
99 Joe Sakic UCP 1.50 4.00
100 Peter Forsberg UCP 1.50 4.00
101 Mario Lemieux UCP 3.00 8.00
102 Markus Naslund UCP .75 2.00
103 Martin St. Louis UCP .75 2.00
104 Mike Bossy UCP .75 2.00
105 Jose Theodore UCP .75 2.00
106 Matti Hagman EL .60 1.50
107 Teemu Selanne EL 1.50 4.00
109 Borje Salming EL .75 2.00
110A Ulf Nilsson EL .60 1.50
110B Jari Kurri EL .75 2.00
110C Igor Larionov EL .75 2.00
111 Anders Hedberg EL .50 1.25
112 Vladislav Tretiak EL .60 1.50
113 Mats Naslund EL .50 1.25
114 Peter Stastny EL .60 1.50
115 Thomas Steen EL .75 2.00
116 Hakan Loob EL .50 1.25
117 Kent Nilsson EL .60 1.50
118 Saku Koivu EL .75 2.00
120 Jaromir Jagr EL 2.50 6.00

2004-05 UD All-World Gold

*GOLD/50: 6X TO 15X BASIC CARDS
65 Henrik Sedin 6.00 15.00

2004-05 UD All-World Autographs

1 Roman Turek 6.00 15.00
4 Ales Hemsky 8.00 20.00
5 Milan Hejduk 8.00 20.00
6 Zigmund Palffy SP
7 Peter Stastny 8.00 20.00
11 Martin Havlat 10.00 25.00
12 Jarkko Ruutu 6.00 15.00
13 Matti Hagman 6.00 10.00
15 Mika Noronen 6.00 10.00
16 Jari Kurri 8.00 20.00
18 Dwayne Roloson 12.00 30.00
20 Erik Cole 8.00 15.00
26 Ilya Kovalchuk SP
27 Nikolai Khabibulin SP 40.00 80.00
28 Vincent Lecavalier SP
30 Alexander Frolov 6.00 15.00
31 Nikolai Zherdev 8.00 15.00
32 Maxim Afinogenov 6.00 15.00
44 Borje Salming 12.00 30.00
45 Ulf Nilsson 8.00 20.00
46 Tyler Arnason 6.00 10.00
47 Mats Naslund 15.00 40.00
48 Jose Theodore SP
50 Kent Nilsson 6.00 15.00
51 Marian Gaborik 20.00 50.00
52 Mike Comrie 6.00 15.00
53 Sheldon Souray 6.00 15.00
54 Zdeno Chara 10.00 25.00
55 Hakan Loob 12.00 30.00
56 Thomas Steen 6.00 15.00
57 Daniel Alfredsson SP
58 Jonathan Cheechoo 10.00 25.00
59 Michael Ryder SP 15.00 40.00
60 Brendan Morrison 6.00 15.00
61 Justin Williams 8.00 15.00
66 Markus Naslund SP
68 Anders Hedberg 6.00 15.00
69 Ladislav Nagy 6.00 10.00
70 Marcel Hossa 6.00 10.00
71 Marian Hossa SP
72 Trent Hunter 6.00 15.00
76 Henrik Zetterberg SP 25.00 60.00
78 Joe Thornton 15.00 40.00
79 Rick Nash SP 60.00 150.00
80 Martin St. Louis SP
81 Alex Tanguay SP
82 David Aebischer SP 15.00 40.00
84 Daniel Briere 12.00 30.00
85 Dany Heatley SP
87 Igor Larionov 10.00 25.00
88 Richard Zednik 6.00 15.00
90 Vladislav Tretiak 20.00 50.00

2004-05 UD All-World Dual Autographs

ADHN M.Hagman/M.Noronen 25.00 60.00
ADPS Z.Palffy/P.Stastny 25.00 60.00
ADHH M.Hejduk/A.Hemsky 30.00 80.00
ADAF M.Afinogenov/A. Frolov 20.00 50.00
ADFZ A.Frolov/N.Zherdev 30.00 80.00
ADJA J.Thornton/A.Tanguay 75.00 150.00
ADKK J.Kurri/S.Koivu 100.00 200.00
ADKL J.Kurri/H.Loob 30.00 80.00
ADLK V.Lecavalier/N.Khabibulin 75.00 150.00
ADLS H.Loob/T.Steen 30.00 80.00
ADMM M. Hossa/M. Hossa
ADNN M. Naslund/M.Naslund
ADNT R.Nash/J.Thornton 125.00 250.00
ADSC S.Souray/Z.Chara 25.00 60.00
ADSN B.Salming/K.Nilsson 30.00 80.00

2004-05 UD All-World Triple Autographs

ATCWR Cheech/J.Will/J.Ruutu 40.00 80.00
ATKHK Kurri/Hagm/Koivu
ATKSN Kurri/P.Stats/Naslund 40.00 80.00
ATLTZ Larion/Tretiak/Zherd 100.00 175.00
ATNLN Naslung/Loob/Nilsson
ATRCM Ryder/Cheech/Morrison 50.00 100.00
ATSHH P.Stats/Hejd/Hemsky
ATSLN Steen/Loob/Nilsson 30.00 60.00
ATTAR Theod/Aebis/Roloson 50.00 100.00
ATZFA Zherd/Frolov/Afinog 30.00 60.00

2002-03 UD Artistic Impressions

COMPLETE SET (135) 40.00 100.00
COMP.SET w/o SP's (90) 20.00 40.00
1 Jean-Sebastien Giguere .30 .75
2 Paul Kariya .30 .75
3 Dany Heatley .25 .60
4 Ilya Kovalchuk .40 1.00
5 Ray Bourque .50 1.25
6 Joe Thornton .50 1.25
7 Bobby Orr 1.25 3.00
8 Sergei Samsonov .25 .60
9 Maxim Afinogenov .20 .50
10 Martin Biron .25 .60
11 Miroslav Satan .30 .75
12 Roman Turek .30 .75
13 Jarome Iginla .40 1.00
14 Arturs Irbe .25 .60
15 Ron Francis .40 1.00
16 Jeff O'Neill .20 .50
17 Alexei Zhamnov .25 .60
18 Eric Daze .20 .50
19 Jocelyn Thibault .25 .60
20 Rob Blake .30 .75
21 Patrick Roy .75 2.00
22 Joe Sakic .60 1.50
23 Peter Forsberg .60 1.50
24 Ray Bourque .50 1.25
25 Marc Denis .25 .60
26 Espen Knutsen .20 .50
27 Rostislav Klesla .20 .50
28 Marty Turco .30 .75
29 Bill Guerin .30 .75
30 Mike Modano .50 1.25
31 Steve Yzerman .75 2.00
32 Nicklas Lidstrom .30 .75
33 Sergei Fedorov .50 1.25
34 Curtis Joseph .40 1.00
35 Brendan Shanahan .30 .75
36 Gordie Howe 1.00 2.50
37 Mike Comrie .30 .75
38 Tommy Salo .25 .60
39 Wayne Gretzky 2.00 5.00
40 Roberto Luongo .50 1.25
41 Kristian Huselius .20 .50
42 Zigmund Palffy .30 .75
43 Felix Potvin .50 1.25
44 Jason Allison .25 .60
45 Manny Fernandez .20 .50
46 Marian Gaborik .30 .75
47 Saku Koivu .30 .75
48 Doug Gilmour .40 1.00
49 Jose Theodore .30 .75
50 David Legwand .25 .60
51 Tomas Vokoun .25 .60
52 Martin Brodeur .75 2.00
53 Patrik Elias .30 .75
54 Joe Nieuwendyk .25 .60
55 Alexei Yashin .25 .60
56 Michael Peca .25 .60
57 Chris Osgood .30 .75
58 Eric Lindros .50 1.25
59 Pavel Bure .30 .75
60 Brian Leetch .25 .60
61 Martin Havlat .25 .60
62 Marian Hossa .30 .75
63 Daniel Alfredsson .30 .75
64 John LeClair .30 .75
65 Jeremy Roenick .50 1.25
66 Simon Gagne .30 .75
67 Tony Amonte .25 .60
68 Sean Burke .20 .50
69 Daniel Briere .25 .60
70 Alex Kovalev .25 .60
71 Johan Hedberg .30 .75
72 Mario Lemieux 1.25 3.00
73 Teemu Selanne .60 1.50
74 Evgeni Nabokov .25 .60
75 Owen Nolan .30 .75
76 Chris Pronger .30 .75
77 Doug Weight .30 .75
78 Keith Tkachuk .30 .75
79 Brad Richards .30 .75
80 Nikolai Khabibulin .30 .75
81 Vincent Lecavalier .30 .75
82 Mats Sundin .30 .75
83 Ed Belfour .30 .75
84 Alexander Mogilny .25 .60
85 Todd Bertuzzi .30 .75
86 Dan Cloutier .25 .60
87 Markus Naslund .30 .75
88 Jaromir Jagr 1.00 2.50
89 Peter Bondra .30 .75
90 Olaf Kolzig .30 .75
91 Jonathan Hedstrom RC .50 1.25
92 Henrik Zetterberg RC 5.00 12.00
93 Steve Ott RC .50 1.25
94 Jay Bouwmeester RC 1.50 4.00
95 Rick Nash RC 3.00 8.00
96 Pascal LeClaire RC .60 1.50
97 Jason Spezza RC 3.00 8.00
98 Dick Tarnstrom RC .50 1.25
99 Alexei Smirnov RC .60 1.50
100 Ron Hainsey RC .50 1.25
101 Michael Leighton RC .75 2.00
102 Ian MacNeil RC .50 1.25
103 Anton Volchenkov RC .50 1.25
104 Ales Hemsky RC 2.00 5.00
105 Steve Eminger RC .50 1.25
106 Shaone Morrisonn RC .50 1.25
107 Levente Szuper RC .75 2.00
108 Brooks Orpik RC .50 1.25
109 Curtis Sanford RC .75 2.00
110 Jared Aulin RC .50 1.25
111 Eric Godard RC .50 1.25
112 Jim Fahey RC .50 1.25
113 Rickard Wallin RC .50 1.25
114 Mike Cammalleri RC 1.50 4.00
115 Mikael Tellqvist RC .50 1.25
116 Chuck Kobasew RC .60 1.50
117 Scottie Upshall RC .60 1.50
118 Jerred Smithson RC .50 1.25
119 Jeff Taffe RC .50 1.25
120 Cody Rudkowsky RC .50 1.25
121 Alexander Frolov RC 1.25 3.00
122 Alexander Svitov RC .50 1.25
123 Stanislav Chistov RC .50 1.25
124 P-M Bouchard RC .75 2.00
125 Patrick Sharp RC 1.50 4.00
126 Ryan Miller RC 3.00 8.00
127 Tomas Malec RC .50 1.25
128 Curtis Murphy RC .50 1.25
129 Jordan Leopold RC .75 2.00
130 Carlo Colaiacovo RC .75 2.00
131 Alexei Semenov RC .50 1.25
132 Craig Andersson RC 1.50 4.00
133 Jim Vandermeer RC .50 1.25
134 Ray Emery RC 1.50 4.00
135 Paul Manning RC .50 1.25
SC1 Joe Thornton Sample .75 2.00

2002-03 UD Artistic Impressions Gold

*1-90 VETS/199: 2.5X TO 6X BASIC CARDS
*91-135 ROOK/75: 1.2X TO 3X BASIC RC

2002-03 UD Artistic Impressions Artist's Touch Jerseys

*GOLD/199: .5X TO 1.2X JSY/499
ATBS Brendan Shanahan 3.00 8.00
ATCJ Curtis Joseph 3.00 8.00
ATDH Dany Heatley 4.00 10.00
ATFP Felix Potvin 4.00 10.00
ATIK Ilya Kovalchuk 5.00 12.00
ATJI Jarome Iginla 4.00 10.00
ATJJ Jaromir Jagr 4.00 10.00
ATJR Jeremy Roenick 4.00 10.00
ATJS Joe Sakic 5.00 12.00
ATJT Joe Thornton 5.00 12.00
ATMB Martin Brodeur 8.00 20.00
ATMD Mike Dunham 3.00 8.00
ATML Mario Lemieux 10.00 25.00
ATMM Mike Modano 5.00 12.00
ATMS Mats Sundin 3.00 8.00
ATOK Olaf Kolzig 3.00 8.00
ATPF Peter Forsberg 5.00 12.00
ATPK Paul Kariya 3.00 8.00
ATPR Patrick Roy 10.00 25.00
ATRB Ray Bourque 5.00 12.00
ATSB Sean Burke 3.00 8.00
ATSF Sergei Fedorov 4.00 10.00
ATSG Simon Gagne 4.00 10.00
ATTH Jose Theodore 4.00 10.00
ATZP Zigmund Palffy 3.00 8.00

2002-03 UD Artistic Impressions Artwork Signatures

AI1 Ray Bourque 60.00 150.00
AI2 Martin Brodeur 80.00 200.00
AI3 Pavel Bure 30.00 80.00
AI4 Mike Comrie 20.00 50.00
AI5 Dany Heatley 50.00 100.00
AI6 Gordie Howe SP 200.00 400.00
AI7 Jarome Iginla 30.00 80.00
AI8 Curtis Joseph 50.00 120.00
AI9 Ilya Kovalchuk 60.00 150.00
AI10 John LeClair 25.00 60.00
AI11 Markus Naslund 25.00 60.00
AI12 Bobby Orr SP 300.00 600.00
AI13 Patrick Roy 100.00 250.00
AI14 Sergei Samsonov 25.00 60.00
AI15 Jose Theodore 40.00 100.00
AI16 Joe Thornton 60.00 150.00
AI17 Steve Yzerman 60.00 150.00

2002-03 UD Artistic Impressions UD Promos

*UD PROMOS: .8X TO 2X BASIC CARDS
15 Ron Francis .75 2.00

2002-03 UD Artistic Impressions Common Ground

COMPLETE SET (22) 20.00 40.00
*GOLD/75: 1X TO 2.5X BASIC INSERTS
CG1 P.Roy P.LeClaire 2.00 5.00
CG2 A.Hemsky/J.Jagr 1.50 4.00
CG3 W.Gretzky/J.Spezza 4.00 10.00
CG4 J.Bouwmeester/N.Lidstrom 1.25 3.00
CG5 R.Cechmanek/L.Szuper 1.00 2.50
CG6 R.Nash/M.Lemieux 3.00 8.00
CG7 R.Bourque/J.Bouwmeester 1.50 4.00
CG8 P.Bouchard/S.Koivu 1.25 3.00
CG9 G.Howe/R.Nash 2.00 5.00
CG10 A.Frolov/P.Bure 1.25 3.00
CG11 R.Blake/B.Orpik 1.25 3.00
CG12 H.Zetterberg/M.Sundin 1.50 4.00
CG13 S.Samsonov/S.Chistov 1.00 2.50
CG14 J.Leopold/R.Bourque 1.25 3.00
CG15 B.Guerin/C.Kobasew 1.00 2.50
CG16 A.Svitov/S.Federov 1.50 4.00
CG17 J.Roenick/S.Upshall 1.50 4.00
CG18 C.Colaiacovo/N.Lidstrom 1.25 3.00
CG19 S.Yzerman/S.Ott 1.50 4.00
CG20 J.Taffe/M.Modano 1.25 3.00
CG21 P.Forsberg/H.Zetterberg 2.00 5.00
CG22 P.LeClaire/M.Brodeur 2.00 5.00

2002-03 UD Artistic Impressions Flashbacks

COMPLETE SET (9) 15.00 30.00
*GOLD/75: 1.2X TO 3X BASIC INSERTS
UD1 Joe Sakic 2.00 5.00
UD2 Mike Modano 1.25 3.00
UD3 Mario Lemieux 2.50 6.00
UD4 Brian Leetch .75 2.00
UD5 Ron Francis .75 2.00
UD6 Pavel Bure 1.00 2.50
UD7 Ray Bourque 2.00 5.00
UD8 Sergei Fedorov 1.50 4.00
UD9 Jaromir Jagr 1.50 4.00
UD10 Jeremy Roenick 1.00 2.50
UD11 Gordie Howe 2.50 6.00

2002-03 UD Artistic Impressions Great Depictions

COMPLETE SET (12) 12.00 30.00
*GOLD/75: 1.2X TO 3X BASIC INSERTS
GD1 Wayne Gretzky 3.00 8.00
GD2 Patrick Roy 2.50 6.00
GD3 Martin Brodeur 2.50 6.00
GD4 Bobby Orr 3.00 8.00
GD5 Ilya Kovalchuk 1.00 2.50
GD6 Mario Lemieux 3.00 8.00
GD7 Ray Bourque 2.00 5.00
GD8 Steve Yzerman 2.50 6.00
GD9 Gordie Howe 2.00 5.00
GD10 Pavel Bure .75 2.00
GD11 Marian Gaborik 1.00 2.50
GD12 Joe Thornton 1.00 2.50

2002-03 UD Artistic Impressions Performers Jerseys

*GOLD/75: .5X TO 1.2X BASIC JSY/199
SSJJ Jaromir Jagr 4.00 10.00
SSJL John LeClair 3.00 8.00
SSMB Martin Brodeur 10.00 25.00
SSMM Mark Messier 3.00 8.00
SSPR Patrick Roy 12.00 30.00
SSSY Steve Yzerman 12.00 30.00

2002-03 UD Artistic Impressions Retrospectives

COMPLETE SET (100) 30.00 60.00
*SILVER/99: 2X TO 5X BASIC INSERT
*GOLD/25: 8X TO 20X BASIC INSERT
R1 Jean-Sebastien Giguere .25 .60
R2 Paul Kariya .30 .75
R3 Dany Heatley .40 1.00
R4 Ilya Kovalchuk .40 1.00
R5 Ray Bourque .40 1.00
R6 Joe Thornton .40 1.00
R7 Bobby Orr 1.25 3.00
R8 Sergei Samsonov .25 .60
R9 Maxim Afinogenov .20 .50
R10 Martin Biron .20 .50
R11 Miroslav Satan .25 .60
R12 Roman Turek .25 .60
R13 Jarome Iginla .40 1.00
R14 Arturs Irbe .25 .60
R15 Ron Francis .25 .60
R16 Jeff O'Neill .20 .50
R17 Alexei Zhamnov .25 .60
R18 Eric Daze .20 .50
R19 Jocelyn Thibault .25 .60
R20 Rob Blake .25 .60
R21 Patrick Roy 1.25 3.00
R22 Joe Sakic .40 1.00
R23 Peter Forsberg .30 .75
R24 Ray Bourque .40 1.00
R25 Marc Denis .20 .50
R26 Espen Knutsen .20 .50
R27 Rostislav Klesla .20 .50
R28 Marty Turco .25 .60
R29 Bill Guerin .25 .60
R30 Mike Modano .40 1.00
R31 Steve Yzerman 1.00 2.50
R32 Nicklas Lidstrom .30 .75
R33 Sergei Fedorov .40 1.00
R34 Curtis Joseph .30 .75
R35 Brendan Shanahan .30 .75
R36 Gordie Howe 1.25 3.00
R37 Mike Comrie .20 .50
R38 Tommy Salo .25 .60
R39 Wayne Gretzky 1.50 4.00
R40 Roberto Luongo .50 1.25
R41 Kristian Huselius .20 .50
R42 Zigmund Palffy .25 .60
R43 Felix Potvin .40 1.00
R44 Jason Allison .20 .50
R45 Manny Fernandez .25 .60
R46 Marian Gaborik .30 .75
R47 Saku Koivu .30 .75
R48 Doug Gilmour .25 .60
R49 Jose Theodore .30 .75
R50 David Legwand .20 .50
R51 Tomas Vokoun .25 .60
R52 Martin Brodeur 1.00 2.50
R53 Patrik Elias .25 .60
R54 Joe Nieuwendyk .25 .60
R55 Alexei Yashin .25 .60
R56 Michael Peca .20 .50
R57 Chris Osgood .30 .75
R58 Eric Lindros .30 .75
R59 Pavel Bure .30 .75
R60 Brian Leetch .25 .60
R61 Martin Havlat .25 .60
R62 Marian Hossa .30 .75
R63 Daniel Alfredsson .25 .60
R64 John LeClair .30 .75
R65 Jeremy Roenick .40 1.00
R66 Simon Gagne .30 .75
R67 Tony Amonte .25 .60
R68 Sean Burke .20 .50
R69 Daniel Briere .25 .60
R70 Alexei Kovalev .25 .60
R71 Johan Hedberg .25 .60
R72 Mario Lemieux 1.25 3.00
R73 Teemu Selanne .30 .75
R74 Evgeni Nabokov .25 .60
R75 Owen Nolan .20 .50
R76 Chris Pronger .20 .50
R77 Doug Weight .25 .60
R78 Keith Tkachuk .30 .75
R79 Brad Richards .25 .60
R80 Nikolai Khabibulin .30 .75
R81 Vincent Lecavalier .30 .75
R82 Mats Sundin .30 .75
R83 Ed Belfour .30 .75
R84 Alexander Mogilny .25 .60
R85 Todd Bertuzzi .30 .75
R86 Dan Cloutier .25 .60
R87 Markus Naslund .30 .75
R88 Jaromir Jagr .40 1.00
R89 Peter Bondra .25 .60
R90 Olaf Kolzig .25 .60
R91 Jason Spezza .75 2.00
R92 Rick Nash 1.25 3.00
R93 Jay Bouwmeester .50 1.25
R94 Stanislav Chistov .40 1.00
R95 P-M Bouchard .40 1.00
R96 Pascal LeClaire .40 1.00
R97 Brooks Orpik .40 1.00
R98 Steve Ott .40 1.00
R99 Alexander Frolov .60 1.50
R100 Alexander Svitov .30 .75

2002-03 UD Artistic Impressions Retrospectives Autographs

R3 Dany Heatley
R4 Ilya Kovalchuk 40.00 80.00
R5 Ray Bourque 40.00 80.00
R6 Joe Thornton 30.00 60.00
R7 Bobby Orr 125.00 200.00
R9 Maxim Afinogenov 10.00 25.00
R13 Jarome Iginla 15.00 40.00
R24 Ray Bourque/10
R34 Curtis Joseph 30.00 60.00
R36 Gordie Howe/10
R37 Mike Comrie 15.00 40.00
R39 Wayne Gretzky 150.00 400.00
R49 Jose Theodore 12.00 30.00
R52 Martin Brodeur 75.00 150.00
R87 Markus Naslund/10
R91 Jason Spezza 40.00 80.00
R92 Rick Nash 50.00 100.00
R93 Jay Bouwmeester 10.00 25.00
R94 Stanislav Chistov 15.00 40.00
R95 P-M Bouchard 12.00 30.00
R96 Pascal LeClaire 12.00 30.00
R97 Brooks Orpik 10.00 25.00
R98 Steve Ott 12.00 30.00
R99 Alexander Frolov 15.00 40.00
R100 Alexander Svitov 12.00 30.00

2002-03 UD Artistic Impressions Right Track

*GOLD/175: .5X TO 1.2X BASIC INSERTS
RTAF Alexander Frolov 6.00 15.00
RTDB Daniel Briere 3.00 8.00
RTDH Dany Heatley 3.00 8.00
RTJA Jared Aulin 2.50 6.00
RTJL Jamie Lundmark 3.00 8.00
RTJW Justin Williams 3.00 8.00
RTKC Kyle Calder 2.50 6.00
RTMA Maxim Afinogenov 2.50 6.00
RTME Martin Erat 2.50 6.00
RTSC Stanislav Chistov 2.50 6.00
RTSR Steve Reinprecht 2.50 6.00

2008-09 UD Black

1 Alexander Ovechkin 30.00 80.00
2 Cam Neely 8.00 20.00
3 Saku Koivu 8.00 20.00
4 Dany Heatley 6.00 15.00
5 Dino Ciccarelli 8.00 20.00
6 Dominik Hasek 12.00 30.00
7 Eric Staal 10.00 25.00
8 Evgeni Malkin 15.00 40.00
9 Henrik Lundqvist 20.00 50.00
10 Henrik Zetterberg 10.00 25.00
11 Ilya Kovalchuk 8.00 20.00
12 Peter Forsberg 15.00 40.00
13 Jarome Iginla 10.00 25.00
14 Jaromir Jagr 25.00 60.00
15 Sidney Crosby 30.00 80.00
16 Roberto Luongo 12.00 30.00
17 Joe Sakic 15.00 40.00
18 Joe Thornton 12.00 30.00
19 Jonathan Cheechoo 6.00 15.00
20 Jordan Staal 6.00 15.00
21 Lanny McDonald 8.00 20.00
22 Jason Spezza 8.00 20.00
23 Luc Robitaille 8.00 20.00
24 Marian Gaborik 8.00 20.00
25 Ryan Miller 8.00 20.00
26 Mario Lemieux 30.00 80.00
27 Mark Messier 15.00 40.00
28 Markus Naslund 8.00 20.00
29 Martin Brodeur 20.00 50.00
30 Martin St. Louis 8.00 20.00
31 Mats Sundin 8.00 20.00
32 Michael Ryder 5.00 12.00
33 Miikka Kiprusoff 8.00 20.00
34 Mike Modano 12.00 30.00
35 Nicklas Lidstrom 8.00 20.00
36 Patrice Bergeron 10.00 25.00
37 Simon Gagne 8.00 20.00
38 Patrick Roy 20.00 50.00
39 Paul Kariya 8.00 20.00
40 Vincent Lecavalier 8.00 20.00
41 Ray Bourque 12.00 30.00
42 Daniel Alfredsson 8.00 20.00
43 Derick Brassard AU RC 8.00 20.00
44 Mark Fistric AU RC 6.00 15.00
45 Alex Goligoski AU RC 10.00 25.00
46 Claude Giroux AU RC 15.00 40.00
47 Jon Filewich AU RC 6.00 15.00
48 Robbie Earl AU RC 5.00 12.00
49 Ilya Zubov AU RC 6.00 15.00
50 Steve Mason AU RC 12.00 30.00
51 Brian Boyle AU RC 6.00 15.00
52 Shawn Matthias AU RC 8.00 20.00
53 Ryan Stone AU RC 5.00 12.00
54 Teddy Purcell AU RC 6.00 15.00
55 Tom Cavanagh AU RC EXCH 6.00 15.00
56 Kyle Okposo AU RC 10.00 25.00
57 Marc-Andre Gragnani AU RC 6.00 15.00
58 Jonathan Ericsson AU RC 8.00 20.00
59 Kyle Turris AU RC 12.00 30.00
60 Brian Lee RC 6.00 15.00
61 Justin Abdelkader RC 12.00 30.00
62 Theo Peckham RC 6.00 15.00
63 Adam Pineault RC 6.00 15.00
64 Boris Valabik RC 8.00 20.00
65 Darren Helm RC 8.00 20.00
66 Mike Iggulden RC 6.00 15.00
67 Tim Ramholt RC 6.00 15.00
68 Matt D'Agostini RC 6.00 15.00
69 Andrew Ebbett RC 5.00 12.00
70 Sami Lepisto RC 6.00 15.00
71 Tyler Plante RC 6.00 15.00
72 Niklas Hjalmarsson RC 8.00 20.00
73 Alex Foster RC 6.00 15.00
74 Clay Wilson RC 5.00 12.00
75 Zach Fitzgerald RC 8.00 20.00
76 Kyle Greentree RC 8.00 20.00
77 Joe Jensen RC 8.00 20.00

78 David Brine RC 5.00 12.00
79 B.J. Crombeen RC 5.00 12.00
80 Mike Brown RC 8.00 20.00
81 Jordan Hendry RC 6.00 15.00
82 Corey Locke RC 6.00 15.00
83 Cody McLeod RC 6.00 15.00
84 Jesse Winchester RC 5.00 12.00
85 Lauri Korpikoski RC 5.00 12.00
86 Jack Hillen RC 6.00 15.00
87 Mike Mole RC 6.00 15.00
88 Jordan LaVallee RC 8.00 20.00
89 Erik Ersberg RC 6.00 15.00
90 Darryl Boyce RC 6.00 15.00
91 Tom Sestito RC 8.00 20.00
92 Joey Mormina RC 6.00 15.00
93 Chris Minard RC 8.00 20.00
94 Pascal Pelletier RC 5.00 12.00
95 Tim Conboy RC 6.00 15.00
96 Kevin Doell RC 5.00 12.00
97 Andrew Murray RC 6.00 15.00
98 Brandon Nolan RC 6.00 15.00
99 Colin Stuart RC 6.00 15.00
100 Danny Taylor RC 6.00 15.00
101 Dan LaCosta RC 8.00 20.00
102 Mattias Ritola RC 6.00 15.00
103 Steven Stamkos AU RC 60.00 150.00
104 Nikita Filatov AU RC 15.00 40.00
105 Jakub Voracek AU RC 30.00 80.00
106 Fabian Brunnstrom AU RC 12.00 30.00
107 Michael Frolik AU RC 15.00 40.00
108 Drew Doughty AU RC 100.00 250.00
109 Colton Gillies AU RC 12.00 30.00
110 Patric Hornqvist AU RC 15.00 40.00
111 Petr Vrana AU RC 10.00 25.00
112 Luca Sbisa AU RC 10.00 25.00
113 Mikkel Boedker AU RC 20.00 50.00
114 Viktor Tikhonov AU RC 12.00 30.00
115 T.J. Oshie AU RC 30.00 80.00
116 Patrik Berglund AU RC 12.00 30.00
117 Alex Pietrangelo AU RC 25.00 60.00
118 Nikolai Kulemin AU RC 15.00 40.00
119 Luke Schenn AU RC 20.00 50.00
120 Blake Wheeler AU RC 40.00 100.00
121 Brandon Sutter AU RC 15.00 40.00
122 Zach Bogosian AU RC 20.00 50.00
123 James Neal AU RC 30.00 80.00
124 Zach Boychuk AU RC 15.00 40.00

2008-09 UD Black Autographs Jerseys

BAJAF Alexander Frolov
BAJAH Ales Hemsky
BAJAK Anze Kopitar 30.00 80.00
BAJAM Al MacInnis 15.00 40.00
BAJAO Alexander Ovechkin 50.00 120.00
BAJBL Brian Leetch 15.00 40.00
BAJBS Borje Salming 20.00 50.00
BAJDH Dominik Hasek 30.00 80.00
BAJES Eric Staal 25.00 60.00
BAJHA Dale Hawerchuk 25.00 60.00
BAJHE Dany Heatley 12.00 30.00
BAJHJ Milan Hejduk 15.00 40.00
BAJHZ Henrik Zetterberg 25.00 60.00
BAJIK Ilya Kovalchuk 20.00 50.00
BAJJG Jean-Sebastien Giguere 20.00 50.00
BAJJI Jarome Iginla 25.00 60.00
BAJJJ Jack Johnson 12.00 30.00
BAJJT Jonathan Toews 60.00 120.00
BAJLR Luc Robitaille 20.00 50.00
BAJMB Martin Brodeur 60.00 120.00
BAJMF Marc-Andre Fleury 40.00 80.00
BAJMG Marian Gaborik
BAJMM Mike Modano 30.00 80.00
BAJMN Markus Naslund 20.00 50.00
BAJMR Michael Ryder 12.00 30.00
BAJMS Martin St. Louis 15.00 40.00
BAJMT Marty Turco 20.00 50.00
BAJMU Peter Mueller 15.00 40.00
BAJPB Patrice Bergeron 25.00 60.00
BAJPK Patrick Kane 50.00 100.00
BAJPR Patrick Roy 100.00 200.00
BAJPS Paul Stastny 15.00 40.00
BAJRB Ray Bourque 30.00 80.00
BAJRG Ryan Getzlaf 20.00 50.00
BAJRL Rod Langway 15.00 40.00
BAJRM Ryan Miller 20.00 50.00
BAJRV Alexander Radulov
BAJSC Sidney Crosby 175.00 300.00
BAJSG Simon Gagne 20.00 50.00
BAJST Peter Stastny 40.00 80.00
BAJTH Joe Thornton 30.00 80.00
BAJVL Vincent Lecavalier 15.00 40.00

2008-09 UD Black Game Night Autographs Tickets

GNAO Alexander Ovechkin 75.00 150.00
GNBC Bobby Clarke 30.00 80.00
GNBO Bobby Orr 75.00 150.00
GNCN Cam Neely 15.00 40.00
GNCP Carey Price 100.00 175.00
GNDC Dino Ciccarelli 20.00 50.00
GNDH Dale Hawerchuk 25.00 60.00
GNDS Devin Setoguchi 15.00 40.00
GNEM Evgeni Malkin 40.00 100.00
GNFM Frank Mahovlich 20.00 50.00
GNGF Grant Fuhr 30.00 80.00
GNGH Gordie Howe 100.00 175.00
GNGL Guy Lafleur 25.00 60.00
GNHA Dominik Hasek 60.00 120.00
GNHE Dany Heatley 50.00 100.00
GNIK Ilya Kovalchuk 20.00 50.00
GNJB Johnny Bucyk 20.00 50.00
GNJI Jarome Iginla 30.00 80.00
GNJJ Jack Johnson 12.00 30.00
GNJK Jari Kurri 25.00 60.00
GNJS James Sheppard 12.00 30.00
GNJT Jiri Tlusty 30.00 60.00
GNLM Lanny McDonald 15.00 40.00
GNLR Larry Robinson 20.00 50.00
GNMB Mike Bossy 20.00 50.00
GNMM Mark Messier 60.00 120.00
GNMN Markus Naslund 20.00 50.00
GNMO Mike Modano 30.00 80.00
GNMS Marc Staal 12.00 30.00
GNMT Marty Turco 20.00 50.00
GNNB Nicklas Backstrom 20.00 50.00
GNNF Nick Foligno 20.00 50.00
GNNL Nicklas Lidstrom 40.00 80.00
GNPK Patrick Kane 75.00 150.00
GNPM Peter Mueller 15.00 40.00
GNPS Paul Stastny 15.00 40.00
GNRB Ray Bourque 30.00 80.00
GNRL Rod Langway 15.00 40.00
GNRN Rick Nash 30.00 60.00
GNRO Luc Robitaille 20.00 50.00
GNRS Ryan Smyth 15.00 40.00
GNSC Sidney Crosby 100.00 200.00
GNSG Sam Gagner 30.00 80.00
GNSS Steve Shutt 20.00 50.00
GNST Peter Stastny 30.00 60.00
GNTH Joe Thornton 25.00 60.00
GNTL Ted Lindsay 20.00 50.00
GNTO Jonathan Toews 75.00 150.00
GNVL Vincent Lecavalier 20.00 50.00
GNWG Wayne Gretzky 250.00 600.00

2008-09 UD Black Foursomes Jerseys

UBJ4EHMS Hull/Sav/Wils/Espo 25.00 60.00
UBJ4ENBB Espo/Bcyk/Brq/Cam 20.00 50.00
UBJ4FKAM Messi/Kurri/Fhr/Andr 40.00 80.00
UBJ4HMMH Hwe/Hull/Mahv/Mikt 50.00 100.00
UBJ4IGSK Ignl/St.L/Ggne/Kane
UBJ4KTHN Htly/Nash/Karya/Tng 12.00 30.00
UBJ4LCGM Grtz/Mario/Mssi/Sid 60.00 120.00
UBJ4LDBP Mrio/Dnne/Perrlt/Belv 30.00 60.00
UBJ4LZKM Mess/Ltch/Kvalv/Zbv 25.00 60.00
UBJ4MRTM Mdno/Rnik/Mlln/Tkac 20.00 50.00
UBJ4NBLH Howe/Laflr/Bosy/Nly 40.00 100.00
UBJ4PPBR Brq/Rbnsn/Ptvn/Phnf 20.00 50.00
UBJ4PPJJ Prong/Phnf/Jhnsn/Jhns 12.00 30.00
UBJ4RBFE Roy/Fuhr/Espo/Brodr 30.00 80.00
UBJ4RBLF Roy/Brdur/Flry/Lungo 30.00 80.00
UBJ4RNGW Nder/Wrd/Rchrd/Gig 12.00 30.00
UBJ4SLTS Sakc/Thrnt/Lecv/Spz 25.00 60.00
UBJ4SNAZ Sund/Alfrd/Nslnd/Zett 15.00 40.00
UBJ4SRBH Hull/Bcyk/Robit/Shnh 25.00 50.00
UBJ4TPKG Tws/Kane/Ggnr/Price

2008-09 UD Black Jerseys Duals

*GOLD/25: .5X TO 1.2X BASIC DUAL
BDJ2AS J.Spezza/D.Alfredsson 10.00 25.00
BDJ2BJ B.Shanahan/J.Sakic 20.00 50.00
BDJ2BP M.Brodeur/Z.Parise 12.00 30.00
BDJ2BS E.Staal/R.Brind'Amour 12.00 30.00
BDJ2CG W.Gretzky/S.Crosby 50.00 100.00
BDJ2DD P.Datsyuk/K.Draper 15.00 40.00
BDJ2DZ H.Zetterberg/P.Datsyuk 15.00 40.00
BDJ2FB P.Bergeron/M.Fernandez 15.00 40.00
BDJ2GD R.DiPietro/B.Guerin 10.00 25.00
BDJ2GK M.Gaborik.M.Koivu 10.00 25.00
BDJ2HG M.Gaborik/M.Hossa 10.00 25.00
BDJ2IK M.Kiprusoff/J.Iginla 12.00 30.00
BDJ2JL J.Jagr/H.Lundqvist 30.00 80.00
BDJ2JP J.Sakic/P.Roy 30.00 60.00
BDJ2JR J.Sakic/R.Smyth 20.00 50.00
BDJ2KB P.Kariya/B.Boyes 10.00 25.00
BDJ2KL I.Kovalchuk/K.Lehtonen 12.00 30.00
BDJ2KP D.Phaneuf/M.Kiprusoff 10.00 25.00
BDJ2LC S.Crosby/M.Lemieux 40.00 80.00
BDJ2LK R.Luongo/M.Kiprusoff 15.00 40.00
BDJ2LM M.Lemieux/L.Murphy 20.00 50.00
BDJ2LN R.Luongo/M.Naslund 15.00 40.00
BDJ2LS V.Lecavalier/J.Spezza 10.00 25.00
BDJ2MA M.Sundin/A.Steen 10.00 25.00
BDJ2MH E.Malkin/M.Hossa 20.00 50.00
BDJ2MM L.McDonald/J.Mullen 10.00 25.00
BDJ2MR M.Modano/J.Roenick 15.00 40.00
BDJ2MT J.Thornton/P.Marleau 15.00 40.00
BDJ2NL M.Naslund/T.Linden 10.00 25.00
BDJ2PG J.Giguere/C.Pronger 10.00 25.00
BDJ2PM P.Roy/M.Brodeur 40.00 80.00
BDJ2PN S.Niedermayer/C.Pronger 10.00 25.00
BDJ2RB L.Robitaille/R.Blake 10.00 25.00
BDJ2RH D.Roloson/A.Hemsky 8.00 20.00
BDJ2RP R.Nash/P.Leclaire 10.00 25.00
BDJ2RS R.Langway/S.Shutt 10.00 25.00
BDJ2RT V.Toskala/A.Raycroft 15.00 40.00
BDJ2SN R.Nash/B.Shanahan 10.00 25.00
BDJ2SR L.Robitaille/B.Shanahan 10.00 25.00
BDJ2SS J.Sakic/P.Stastny 20.00 50.00
BDJ2VJ T.Vokoun/O.Jokinen 8.00 20.00
BDJ2VM V.Lecavalier/M.St. Louis 10.00 25.00

2008-09 UD Black Lustrous Materials Autographs Jerseys

LM2AH Ales Hemsky 12.00 30.00
LM2AO Alexander Ovechkin 60.00 150.00
LM2AR Alexander Radulov 15.00 40.00
LM2BC Bobby Clarke 25.00 60.00
LM2BF Bernie Federko 12.00 30.00
LM2BL Brian Leetch 12.00 30.00
LM2CD Chris Drury 12.00 30.00
LM2CN Cam Neely 15.00 40.00
LM2DH Dany Heatley 12.00 30.00
LM2DR Dwayne Roloson 12.00 30.00
LM2EJ Erik Johnson 10.00 25.00
LM2EM Evgeni Malkin 30.00 80.00
LM2ES Eric Staal 20.00 50.00
LM2GA Simon Gagne 15.00 40.00
LM2HZ Henrik Zetterberg 20.00 50.00
LM2IK Ilya Kovalchuk 15.00 40.00
LM2JG Jean-Sebastien Giguere 15.00 40.00
LM2JI Jarome Iginla 20.00 50.00
LM2JJ Jack Johnson 10.00 25.00
LM2JT Jonathan Toews 25.00 60.00
LM2KO Anze Kopitar 25.00 60.00
LM2MB Martin Brodeur 40.00 100.00
LM2MC Mike Cammalleri 12.00 30.00
LM2ME Mark Messier 30.00 80.00
LM2MG Marian Gaborik 15.00 40.00
LM2MM Mike Modano 25.00 60.00
LM2MN Markus Naslund 15.00 40.00
LM2MR Michael Ryder 10.00 25.00
LM2MS Miroslav Satan 15.00 40.00
LM2PK Patrick Kane 30.00 80.00
LM2PM Peter Mueller 12.00 30.00
LM2PR Patrick Roy 40.00 100.00
LM2PS Paul Stastny 12.00 30.00
LM2RB Ray Bourque 25.00 60.00
LM2RG Ryan Getzlaf 15.00 40.00
LM2RN Rick Nash 15.00 40.00
LM2SC Sidney Crosby 60.00 150.00
LM2SG Sam Gagner 10.00 25.00
LM2TH Joe Thornton 25.00 60.00
LM2TV Thomas Vanek 12.00 30.00
LM2VO Tomas Vokoun 12.00 30.00
LM2WG Wayne Gretzky 200.00 500.00

2008-09 UD Black Marks of Obsidian Autographs Patches

MOAM Al MacInnis
MOAO Alexander Ovechkin 60.00 120.00
MOAT Alex Tanguay 8.00 20.00
MOBC Bobby Clarke 20.00 50.00
MOBH Bobby Hull 25.00 60.00
MOBL Brian Leetch 10.00 25.00
MOBO Mike Bossy 12.00 30.00
MOBS Borje Salming 12.00 30.00
MOCN Cam Neely 12.00 30.00
MODC Dino Ciccarelli 12.00 30.00
MODH Dany Heatley 10.00 25.00
MODO Dominik Hasek 20.00 50.00
MOEM Evgeni Malkin 30.00 80.00
MOES Eric Staal 15.00 40.00
MOGF Grant Fuhr 20.00 50.00
MOGL Guy Lafleur 15.00 40.00
MOGP Gilbert Perreault 12.00 30.00
MOHA Dale Hawerchuk 15.00 40.00
MOHE Milan Hejduk 10.00 25.00
MOHZ Henrik Zetterberg 30.00 60.00
MOIK Ilya Kovalchuk 12.00 30.00
MOJB Johnny Bucyk 12.00 30.00
MOJC Jonathan Cheechoo 10.00 25.00
MOJG Jean-Sebastien Giguere 15.00 40.00
MOJK Jari Kurri 15.00 40.00
MOJM Joe Mullen 10.00 25.00
MOJT Joe Thornton 20.00 50.00
MOLM Lanny McDonald 12.00 30.00
MOLR Luc Robitaille 12.00 30.00
MOMB Martin Brodeur 50.00 100.00
MOMD Marcel Dionne 15.00 40.00
MOMG Marian Gaborik
MOMH Marian Hossa 25.00 60.00
MOMM Mike Modano 20.00 50.00
MOMN Markus Naslund 12.00 30.00
MOMR Michael Ryder 8.00 20.00
MOMT Marty Turco 12.00 30.00
MONL Nicklas Lidstrom 15.00 40.00
MOOA Adam Oates 12.00 30.00
MOPK Phil Kessel 12.00 30.00
MOPS Peter Stastny 10.00 25.00
MORB Ray Bourque 20.00 50.00
MORH Ron Hextall 20.00 50.00
MORO Larry Robinson 12.00 30.00
MORS Ryan Smyth 10.00 25.00
MOSC Sidney Crosby 100.00 200.00
MOSG Simon Gagne 15.00 40.00
MOSK Saku Koivu 15.00 40.00
MOSM Stan Mikita 20.00 50.00
MOVL Vincent Lecavalier 25.00 60.00

2008-09 UD Black Marks of Obsidian Autographs Patches Duals

MO2BG Bossy/Gillies 15.00 40.00
MO2BP Bucyk/Perreault 15.00 40.00
MO2CG S.Gagner/A.Cogliano 10.00 25.00
MO2DV M.Dionne/R.Vachon 20.00 50.00
MO2EH B.Hull/T.Esposito 30.00 80.00
MO2EJ E.Staal/J.Staal 12.00 30.00
MO2EO B.Orr/P.Esposito 150.00 250.00
MO2FJ F.Mahovlich/J.Bower 25.00 60.00
MO2FK G.Fuhr/J.Kurri 40.00 80.00
MO2FM E.Malkin/M.Fleury 50.00 100.00
MO2FT Tlusty/Foligno 15.00 40.00
MO2GB M.Gaborik/P.Bouchard 15.00 40.00
MO2GG J.Giguere/R.Getzlaf 15.00 40.00
MO2HN D.Heatley/R.Nash 30.00 80.00
MO2HS Stastny/Nash 12.00 30.00
MO2IT J.Iginla/A.Tanguay 20.00 50.00
MO2JJ J.Johnson/E.Johnson 10.00 25.00
MO2JM J.Staal/M.Staal 12.00 30.00
MO2KK Kurri/S.Koivu 15.00 40.00
MO2LH G.Howe/T.Lindsay 50.00 125.00
MO2LM M.Lemieux/M.Messier 100.00 200.00
MO2LS G.Lafleur/S.Shutt 20.00 50.00
MO2LZ Zetterberg/Lidstrom 40.00 100.00
MO2ML M.Messier/B.Leetch 100.00 200.00
MO2MM M.Modano/J.Mullen 20.00 50.00
MO2MS McDonald/Salming 20.00 50.00
MO2NB R.Bourque/C.Neely 25.00 60.00
MO2NO C.Neely/A.Oates 15.00 40.00
MO2NZ Zetterberg/Naslund 20.00 50.00
MO2OM A.Ovechkin/E.Malkin 100.00 200.00
MO2PH C.Price/J.Harding 125.00 250.00
MO2PP P.Stastny/P.Stastny 50.00 100.00
MO2PR C.Price/T.Rask 100.00 200.00
MO2RB M.Brodeur/P.Roy 125.00 250.00
MO2RC J.Carter/M.Richards 30.00 80.00
MO2RP M.Ryder/C.Price 30.00 80.00
MO2SS D.Sedin/H.Sedin 20.00 50.00
MO2TB J.Toews/Backstrom 60.00 125.00
MO2TC Thornton/Cheechoo 100.00 200.00
MO2TK P.Kane/J.Toews 75.00 175.00

2008-09 UD Black Trios Jerseys

UBP3ASH Heatley/Spezza/Alfrd 10.00 25.00
UBP3ASR Radulv/Arntt/Sullvn 10.00 25.00
UBP3BEP Brodeur/Parise/Elias 25.00 60.00
UBP3BML Lngwy/Bourg/MacIns 15.00 40.00
UBP3BSW Staal/Ward/Brind 12.00 30.00
UBP3CLO Ciccrlli/Lngwy/Oates 10.00 25.00
UBP3DGS DiPtro/Guern/Satan 20.00 50.00
UBP3EBC Bcyk/P.Espo/Chvers 15.00 40.00
UBP3EKL Kvalck/Enstrm/Lhtn 12.00 30.00
UBP3FCM Crosby/Fleury/Malkin 40.00 80.00
UBP3FKM Messier/Fuhr/Kurri 20.00 50.00
UBP3GBC Gagne/Briere/Carter 10.00 25.00
UBP3HDZ Zetter/Hask/Datsyk 15.00 40.00
UBP3IGN Nash/Iginla/Gagne 12.00 30.00
UBP3IHN Nash/Heatley/Iginla 12.00 30.00
UBP3IKP Iginla/Kiprsff/Phneuf 12.00 30.00
UBP3KBT Kariya/Byes/Tkchk 15.00 40.00
UBP3KOM Ovech/Malkin/Kvlck 40.00 100.00
UBP3KRK Koivu/Ryder/Kovlev 12.00 30.00
UBP3LCG Grtzky/Lemux/Crsby 60.00 120.00
UBP3LJS Lecav/Jokin/St.Lou 10.00 25.00
UBP3LKM Messier/Ltch/Kovlv 10.00 25.00
UBP3LSR Lafleur/Robnsn/Sht 12.00 30.00
UBP3MMM McDnld/McIns/Mln 12.00 30.00
UBP3MRM Modano/Rnick/Mln 15.00 40.00
UBP3MSS Sittler/McDnld/Slmg 12.00 30.00
UBP3MTC Thrntn/Marl/Chcho 15.00 40.00
UBP3MTM Modano/Trco/Mrrw 15.00 40.00
UBP3NBO Bourque/Nly/Otes 15.00 40.00
UBP3NGG Gig/Getz/Nieder 15.00 40.00
UBP3NLM Lungo/Nslnd/Mrsn 15.00 40.00
UBP3RBL Roy/Brodr/Lungo 25.00 60.00
UBP3RSB Sakic/Brque/Roy 25.00 60.00
UBP3RVG Grtzky/Rbitle/Vchn 50.00 100.00
UBP3RWH Roy/Hextall/Ward 20.00 50.00
UBP3SBK Bergeron/Kesl/Svrd 12.00 30.00
UBP3SJL Jagr/Shanhn/Lndq 12.00 30.00
UBP3SNA Sundin/Nslnd/Alfrd 15.00 40.00
UBP3SSS Sakic/Stastny/Smyth 20.00 50.00
UBP3STS Sundin/Tuckr/Steen 15.00 40.00

2008-09 UD Black Pride of a Nation Autographs Patches

PNAK Anze Kopitar 30.00 80.00
PNAO Alexander Ovechkin 150.00 300.00
PNAR Alexander Radulov
PNBC Bobby Clarke 50.00 120.00
PNBL Brian Leetch 25.00 60.00
PNBO Bobby Orr 200.00 400.00
PNCP Carey Price 150.00 250.00
PNDH Dominik Hasek 50.00 125.00
PNDR Dwayne Roloson 25.00 60.00
PNDS Devin Setoguchi 25.00 60.00
PNEM Evgeni Malkin 75.00 150.00
PNES Eric Staal 40.00 100.00
PNGH Gordie Howe 125.00 200.00
PNGL Guy Lafleur 40.00 100.00
PNGP Gilbert Perreault 30.00 80.00
PNHA Dale Hawerchuk 40.00 100.00
PNHE Dany Heatley 30.00 80.00
PNHL Henrik Lundqvist
PNHZ Henrik Zetterberg 40.00 100.00
PNIK Ilya Kovalchuk 30.00 80.00
PNJC Jonathan Cheechoo 25.00 60.00
PNJG Jean-Sebastien Giguere 30.00 80.00
PNJI Jarome Iginla 40.00 100.00
PNJK Jari Kurri 30.00 80.00
PNJM Joe Mullen 25.00 60.00
PNJS Jordan Staal 40.00 100.00
PNJT Joe Thornton 50.00 125.00
PNKE Phil Kessel 25.00 60.00
PNLR Larry Robinson 30.00 80.00
PNMB Martin Brodeur 100.00 200.00
PNMF Marc-Andre Fleury 75.00 150.00
PNMG Marian Gaborik
PNMH Marian Hossa 30.00 80.00
PNMI Milan Hejduk 25.00 60.00
PNMN Markus Naslund
PNMO Mike Modano 50.00 125.00
PNMR Mike Richards 75.00 150.00
PNMS Miroslav Satan 60.00 120.00
PNMT Marty Turco 30.00 80.00
PNNB Nicklas Backstrom 30.00 80.00
PNNL Nicklas Lidstrom 30.00 80.00
PNPE Phil Esposito 40.00 100.00
PNPK Patrick Kane 75.00 150.00
PNPS Paul Stastny 25.00 60.00
PNRG Ryan Getzlaf 30.00 80.00
PNRM Ryan Miller 30.00 80.00
PNRN Rick Nash 30.00 80.00
PNRS Ryan Smyth
PNSC Sidney Crosby 200.00 350.00
PNSG Sam Gagner 60.00 120.00
PNSK Saku Koivu 40.00 80.00
PNST Martin St. Louis 30.00 80.00
PNTE Tony Esposito 30.00 80.00
PNTL Jiri Tlusty 20.00 50.00
PNTO Jonathan Toews 100.00 200.00
PNTR Tuukka Rask 50.00 120.00
PNTV Thomas Vanek 25.00 60.00
PNVL Vincent Lecavalier 30.00 80.00
PNVO Tomas Vokoun 25.00 60.00
PNZP Zach Parise

2009-10 UD Black

1 Ilya Kovalchuk 6.00 15.00
2 Cam Neely 6.00 15.00
3 Phil Esposito 10.00 25.00
4 Ray Bourque 10.00 25.00
5 Jarome Iginla 8.00 20.00
6 Miikka Kiprusoff 6.00 15.00
7 Eric Staal 8.00 20.00
8 Tony Esposito 10.00 25.00
9 Jonathan Toews 10.00 25.00
10 Patrick Kane 12.00 30.00
11 Rick Nash 6.00 15.00
12 Marty Turco 6.00 15.00
13 Mike Modano 10.00 25.00
14 Gordie Howe 20.00 50.00
15 Henrik Zetterberg 8.00 20.00
16 Nicklas Lidstrom 4.00 10.00
17 Pavel Datsyuk 10.00 25.00
18 Grant Fuhr 10.00 25.00
19 Jari Kurri 6.00 15.00
20 Wayne Gretzky 40.00 100.00
21 Marian Gaborik 6.00 15.00
22 Carey Price 12.00 30.00
23 Larry Robinson 6.00 15.00
24 Patrick Roy 15.00 40.00
25 Martin Brodeur 15.00 40.00
26 Mike Bossy 6.00 15.00
27 Henrik Lundqvist 15.00 40.00
28 Mark Messier 12.00 30.00
29 Markus Naslund 6.00 15.00
30 Ron Hextall 6.00 15.00
31 Peter Mueller 5.00 12.00
32 Evgeni Malkin 12.00 30.00
33 Sidney Crosby 25.00 60.00
34 Mario Lemieux 25.00 60.00
35 Marc-Andre Fleury 12.00 30.00
36 Joe Thornton 10.00 25.00
37 Vincent Lecavalier 6.00 15.00
38 Borje Salming 6.00 15.00
39 Mats Sundin 6.00 15.00
40 Roberto Luongo 10.00 25.00
41 Alexander Ovechkin 25.00 60.00
42 Dale Hawerchuk 8.00 20.00
43 John Negrin RC 6.00 15.00
44 Tom Wandell RC 6.00 15.00
45 Ray Macias RC 5.00 12.00
46 Jay Beagle RC 8.00 20.00
47 Jakub Petruzalek RC 6.00 15.00
48 Alexander Sulzer RC 4.00 10.00
49 Taylor Chorney RC 6.00 15.00
50 Yannick Weber RC 6.00 15.00
51 Cal O'Reilly RC 5.00 12.00
52 Tim Wallace RC 4.00 10.00
53 Kevin Quick RC 4.00 10.00
54 Jesse Joensuu RC 5.00 12.00
55 Spencer Machacek RC 6.00 15.00
56 T.J. Galiardi RC 6.00 15.00
57 Michael Sauer RC 5.00 12.00
58 Matt Beleskey RC 5.00 12.00
59 Tim Stapleton RC 6.00 15.00
60 Grant Lewis RC 5.00 12.00
61 Mikael Backlund AU RC 12.00 30.00
62 Riku Helenius AU RC 8.00 20.00
63 Ville Leino AU RC 6.00 15.00
64 Michal Neuvirth AU RC 12.00 30.00
65 Artem Anisimov AU RC 10.00 25.00
66 Jhonas Enroth AU RC 12.00 30.00
67 Kris Chucko AU RC 5.00 12.00
68 Luca Caputi AU RC 10.00 25.00
69 Christian Hanson AU RC 8.00 20.00
70 Matt Pelech AU RC 8.00 20.00
71 Brian Salcido AU RC 5.00 12.00
72 Ivan Vishnevskiy AU RC 5.00 12.00
73 John Tavares AU RC 40.00 100.00
74 Matt Duchene AU RC 20.00 50.00
75 Victor Hedman AU RC 30.00 80.00
76 Evander Kane AU RC 20.00 50.00
77 James van Riemsdyk AU RC 20.00 50.00
78 Jonas Gustavsson AU RC 12.00 30.00
79 Logan Couture AU RC 20.00 50.00
80 Brad Marchand AU RC 40.00 100.00
81 Tyler Myers AU RC 15.00 40.00
82 Jamie Benn AU RC 30.00 80.00
83 Colin Wilson AU RC 10.00 25.00
84 Michael Del Zotto AU RC 10.00 25.00
85 Viktor Stalberg AU RC 10.00 25.00
86 Michael Grabner AU RC 10.00 25.00
87 Tyler Bozak AU RC 15.00 40.00
88 Erik Karlsson AU RC 30.00 80.00
89 Matt Gilroy AU RC 10.00 25.00
90 Ryan O'Reilly AU RC 20.00 50.00
91 Dmitry Kulikov AU RC 10.00 25.00
92 Sergei Shirokov AU RC 6.00 15.00
93 Cody Franson AU RC 10.00 25.00

2009-10 UD Black Foursomes Jerseys

T4JBDLM Brod/Lundq/Miller/DiPiet 20.00 50.00
T4JDKOM Malkn/Kovl/Dtsyk/Ovch
T4JDSSB Stmk/Schn/Douty/Boed 20.00 40.00
T4JECMP Perrlt/Mahv/Clrke/Espo 30.00 60.00
T4JHLDZ Datsyk/Zettr/Lids/Hssa 30.00 60.00
T4JISCN St.L/Chech/Ignla/Nash 30.00 60.00
T4JKTKP Kovlv/Koivu/Tng/Price 25.00 50.00
T4JLGHM Messi/Grtz/Howe/Mario 125.00 200.00
T4JRBLF Flry/Luongo/Brodr/Roy 40.00 80.00
T4JSKJK Koivu/Kurri/Jokin/Selan 20.00 50.00
T4JSKTK Shrp/Toews/Khab/Kne 25.00 60.00
T4JSLTC Lecav/Crsby/Skic/Thorn 40.00 80.00

2009-10 UD Black Game Night Ticket Autographs

GNAP Alex Pietrangelo 12.00 30.00
GNBC Bobby Clarke 25.00 50.00
GNBM Brendan Mikkelson 10.00 25.00
GNBO Bobby Orr 125.00 200.00
GNBS Brandon Sutter 15.00 40.00
GNBW Blake Wheeler 15.00 40.00
GNCG Colton Gillies 12.00 30.00
GNCP Carey Price 60.00 120.00
GNCS Cory Schneider 25.00 50.00
GNDD Drew Doughty 30.00 60.00
GNDG Doug Gilmour 30.00 60.00
GNEM Evgeni Malkin 50.00 100.00
GNFB Fabian Brunnstrom 10.00 25.00
GNHL Henrik Lundqvist 20.00 50.00
GNHZ Henrik Zetterberg 40.00 80.00
GNIK Ilya Kovalchuk 20.00 50.00
GNJI Jarome Iginla 40.00 80.00
GNJK Jari Kurri 30.00 60.00
GNJP Justin Pogge 12.00 30.00
GNJS Jordan Staal 25.00 50.00
GNJT Jonathan Toews 40.00 80.00
GNKA Karl Alzner 15.00 40.00
GNLS Luke Schenn 25.00 60.00
GNMB Mike Bossy 25.00 50.00
GNMG Marian Gaborik 25.00 50.00
GNMM Mark Messier 30.00 80.00
GNMP Max Pacioretty 20.00 50.00
GNMR Mike Richards 20.00 50.00
GNNB Nicklas Backstrom 30.00 60.00
GNRH Ron Hextall 35.00 80.00
GNRN Rick Nash 25.00 50.00
GNSC Sidney Crosby 150.00 250.00
GNSM Steve Mason 40.00 80.00
GNSS Steven Stamkos 40.00 80.00
GNTH Joe Thornton 30.00 60.00
GNTK Tim Kennedy 15.00 40.00
GNTV Thomas Vanek 25.00 50.00
GNZB Zach Bogosian 25.00 50.00

2009-10 UD Black Game Night Ticket Autographs Duals

GN2CP B.Clarke/G.Perreault 25.00 60.00
GN2DT P.Datsyuk/J.Toews 25.00 60.00
GN2EB Esposito/Beliveau 50.00 100.00
GN2ES P.Esposito/B.Salming 20.00 50.00
GN2GH Heatley/Giguere 15.00 40.00
GN2KP P.Kessel/C.Price
GN2KS I.Kovalchuk/E.Staal 20.00 50.00
GN2LI J.Iginla/V.Lecavalier 20.00 50.00
GN2LK V.Lecavalier/I.Kovalchuk 20.00 50.00
GN2LM N.Lidstrom/E.Malkin 40.00 100.00
GN2NK Kane/Nash 25.00 60.00
GN2NM Nash/Mueller 25.00 60.00
GN2NT E.Nabokov/M.Turco 25.00 60.00
GN2RB Brodeur/Roy 100.00 200.00
GN2RM E.Malkin/M.Richards 30.00 80.00
GN2TM R.Miller/J.Thornton 40.00 100.00

2009-10 UD Black Generations Jerseys

GLW Left Wingers 60.00 120.00
GCEN Centers 60.00 120.00
GDEF Defensemen 50.00 120.00
GEDM Edmonton 150.00 300.00
GGOL Goalies 100.00 200.00
GSTR Superstars 250.00 500.00

2009-10 UD Black Jerseys Autographs

AJAK Anze Kopitar 20.00 40.00
AJBL Brian Leetch 20.00 40.00
AJBS Borje Salming 20.00 40.00
AJBW Blake Wheeler 25.00 50.00
AJCN Cam Neely 20.00 40.00
AJCP Carey Price 40.00 80.00
AJDD Drew Doughty 25.00 50.00
AJDH Dale Hawerchuk 12.00 30.00
AJDP Dion Phaneuf 20.00 40.00
AJEM Evgeni Malkin 60.00 120.00
AJES Eric Staal 12.00 30.00
AJGP Gilbert Perreault 12.00 30.00
AJHL Henrik Lundqvist 30.00 60.00
AJHZ Henrik Zetterberg 30.00 60.00
AJIK Ilya Kovalchuk 25.00 50.00
AJJI Jarome Iginla 25.00 60.00
AJJN James Neal 25.00 50.00
AJJS Jordan Staal 25.00 50.00
AJJT Jonathan Toews 40.00 80.00
AJLS Luke Schenn 12.00 30.00
AJMG Marian Gaborik 12.00 30.00
AJMH Marian Hossa 20.00 40.00
AJMN Markus Naslund 12.00 30.00
AJNB Nicklas Backstrom 20.00 40.00
AJPK Patrick Kane 25.00 50.00
AJRB Ray Bourque 40.00 80.00
AJRN Rick Nash 25.00 50.00
AJSC Sidney Crosby 125.00 250.00
AJSS Steven Stamkos 30.00 60.00

2009-10 UD Black Jerseys Black Ice

QJAK Alex Kovalev 6.00 15.00
QJAO Alexander Ovechkin 20.00 50.00
QJBL Brian Leetch 6.00 15.00
QJBS Borje Salming 8.00 20.00
QJCN Cam Neely 8.00 20.00
QJCP Carey Price 15.00 40.00
QJEM Evgeni Malkin 15.00 40.00
QJES Eric Staal 10.00 25.00
QJGH Gordie Howe 25.00 60.00
QJGP Gilbert Perreault 8.00 20.00
QJHZ Henrik Zetterberg 10.00 25.00
QJIK Ilya Kovalchuk 8.00 20.00
QJJK Jari Kurri 8.00 20.00
QJJS Jason Spezza 8.00 20.00
QJJT Jonathan Toews 12.00 30.00
QJKL Kari Lehtonen 6.00 15.00
QJKO Anze Kopitar 12.00 30.00
QJLR Larry Robinson 8.00 20.00
QJMB Martin Brodeur 12.00 30.00
QJMG Marian Gaborik 8.00 20.00
QJML Mario Lemieux 12.00 30.00
QJMM Mark Messier 15.00 40.00
QJMS Mats Sundin 8.00 20.00
QJNL Nicklas Lidstrom 5.00 12.00
QJPD Pavel Datsyuk 10.00 25.00
QJPK Paul Kariya 8.00 20.00
QJPM Patrick Marleau
QJPR Patrick Roy 20.00 50.00
QJPS Paul Stastny 6.00 15.00
QJRB Ray Bourque 12.00 30.00
QJRL Roberto Luongo 12.00 30.00
QJRN Rick Nash 8.00 20.00
QJSA Joe Sakic 15.00 40.00
QJSC Sidney Crosby 20.00 50.00
QJSK Saku Koivu 6.00 15.00
QJSS Steven Stamkos 15.00 40.00
QJST Jordan Staal 6.00 15.00
QJTS Teemu Selanne 15.00 40.00
QJVL Vincent Lecavalier 8.00 20.00
QJWG Wayne Gretzky 40.00 80.00
QJZP Zach Parise 8.00 20.00

2009-10 UD Black Jerseys Black Ice Autographs

QJBL Brian Leetch 20.00 40.00
QJBS Borje Salming 20.00 40.00
QJCN Cam Neely 20.00 40.00
QJCP Carey Price 40.00 80.00
QJEM Evgeni Malkin 50.00 100.00
QJES Eric Staal 10.00 25.00
QJGH Gordie Howe 75.00 125.00
QJGP Gilbert Perreault 12.00 30.00
QJHZ Henrik Zetterberg 30.00 60.00
QJIK Ilya Kovalchuk 25.00 50.00
QJJK Jari Kurri 20.00 40.00
QJJT Jonathan Toews 40.00 100.00
QJKO Anze Kopitar 20.00 40.00
QJLR Larry Robinson 12.00 30.00
QJMB Martin Brodeur 40.00 80.00
QJMG Marian Gaborik 25.00 50.00
QJML Mario Lemieux 50.00 100.00
QJMM Mark Messier 40.00 80.00
QJNL Nicklas Lidstrom 20.00 40.00
QJPD Pavel Datsyuk 25.00 50.00
QJPR Patrick Roy
QJPS Paul Stastny 20.00 40.00
QJRB Ray Bourque 30.00 60.00
QJRN Rick Nash 20.00 50.00
QJSC Sidney Crosby 125.00 250.00
QJSK Saku Koivu 20.00 40.00
QJSS Steven Stamkos 30.00 60.00
QJST Jordan Staal 12.00 30.00
QJVL Vincent Lecavalier 12.00 30.00
QJWG Wayne Gretzky 250.00 600.00

2009-10 UD Black Lustrous Materials Jersey Autographs

LMAK Anze Kopitar 15.00 40.00
LMAO Adam Oates 12.00 30.00
LMBL Brian Leetch 15.00 40.00
LMBS Borje Salming 10.00 25.00
LMCD Chris Drury 12.00 30.00
LMCN Cam Neely 20.00 40.00
LMCP Carey Price 40.00 80.00
LMDC Dino Ciccarelli
LMDD Drew Doughty 12.00 30.00
LMDG Doug Gilmour 15.00 40.00
LMDH Dale Hawerchuk 12.00 30.00
LMDP Dion Phaneuf 20.00 40.00
LMEM Evgeni Malkin 30.00 80.00
LMES Eric Staal 12.00 30.00
LMGF Grant Fuhr 20.00 40.00
LMGP Gilbert Perreault 12.00 30.00
LMHE Dany Heatley 12.00 30.00
LMHL Henrik Lundqvist 20.00 50.00
LMHZ Henrik Zetterberg 25.00 50.00
LMIK Ilya Kovalchuk 15.00 40.00
LMJJ Jack Johnson 12.00 30.00
LMJN James Neal 12.00 30.00
LMJS Jordan Staal 15.00 40.00
LMJT Joe Thornton 25.00 50.00
LMLR Larry Robinson 10.00 25.00
LMMG Marian Gaborik 25.00 50.00
LMMM Mike Modano 12.00 30.00
LMMN Markus Naslund 10.00 25.00
LMMR Mike Richards 20.00 40.00
LMMT Marty Turco 12.00 30.00
LMNB Nicklas Backstrom 15.00 40.00
LMPB Patrik Berglund 12.00 30.00
LMPE Patrik Elias 12.00 30.00
LMPM Peter Mueller 10.00 25.00
LMPS Paul Stastny 12.00 30.00
LMRB Ray Bourque 30.00 60.00
LMRG Ryan Getzlaf 15.00 40.00
LMRN Rick Nash 20.00 40.00
LMTO Jonathan Toews 25.00 50.00
LMWG Wayne Gretzky 200.00 500.00

2009-10 UD Black Pride of a Nation Patches Autographs

PNAK Anze Kopitar 30.00 60.00
PNBL Brian Leetch 15.00 40.00
PNBO Bobby Orr 175.00 300.00
PNBR Martin Brodeur 60.00 120.00
PNCD Chris Drury 15.00 40.00
PNCW Cam Ward 25.00 60.00
PNDD Drew Doughty 30.00 80.00
PNDH Dany Heatley 15.00 40.00
PNDP Dion Phaneuf 40.00 80.00
PNEM Evgeni Malkin 50.00 100.00
PNEN Evgeni Nabokov 15.00 40.00
PNFB Fabian Brunnstrom 15.00 40.00
PNGA Simon Gagne 20.00 50.00
PNGH Gordie Howe 100.00 175.00
PNGP Gilbert Perreault 20.00 50.00
PNHZ Henrik Zetterberg 50.00 100.00
PNIK Ilya Kovalchuk 25.00 60.00
PNJI Jarome Iginla 40.00 80.00
PNJS Jordan Staal 15.00 40.00
PNKO Saku Koivu 20.00 50.00
PNLS Luke Schenn 15.00 40.00
PNMB Mikkel Boedker 12.00 30.00
PNME Mark Messier 60.00 120.00
PNMG Marian Gaborik 40.00 80.00
PNMM Mike Modano 25.00 60.00
PNMR Mike Richards 40.00 80.00
PNMT Marty Turco 20.00 50.00
PNNF Nikita Filatov 15.00 40.00
PNPD Pavel Datsyuk 40.00 80.00
PNPE Patrik Elias 20.00 50.00
PNPK Patrick Kane 75.00 150.00
PNSC Sidney Crosby 100.00 200.00
PNSG Scott Gomez 15.00 40.00
PNSM Stan Mikita 25.00 60.00
PNSS Steven Stamkos 100.00 200.00
PNTE Tony Esposito 20.00 50.00
PNTV Thomas Vanek 15.00 40.00

2009-10 UD Black Pride of a Nation Patches Autographs Dual

PN2AD K.Alzner/D.Doughty 50.00 100.00
PN2CP B.Clarke/G.Perreault 30.00 60.00
PN2DM E.Malkin/P.Datsyuk 60.00 120.00
PN2EE P.Esposito/T.Esposito 60.00 120.00
PN2EO B.Orr/P.Esposito 175.00 300.00
PN2FH R.Hextall/G.Fuhr 60.00 120.00
PN2FT V.Tikhonov/N.Filatov 25.00 50.00
PN2FV J.Voracek/M.Frolik 60.00 120.00
PN2HG M.Gaborik/M.Hossa 40.00 80.00
PN2JS S.Koivu/J.Kurri 50.00 100.00
PN2KK P.Kane/P.Kessel 50.00 100.00
PN2LE E.Ersberg/H.Lundqvist 30.00 60.00
PN2LI V.Lecavalier/J.Iginla 50.00 100.00
PN2LS N.Lidstrom/B.Salming 30.00 60.00
PN2MM M.Modano/J.Mullen 30.00 60.00
PN2PM S.Mason/C.Price 60.00 120.00
PN2RB Brodeur/Roy EXCH 150.00 250.00
PN2SP J.Pogge/L.Schenn 25.00 50.00
PN2ZB F.Brunnstrom/H.Zetterberg 30.00 60.00

2009-10 UD Black Rivals 6 on 6 Jerseys

ANALAK Ducks/Kings 60.00 120.00
ANASJS Ducks/Sharks 40.00 80.00
BOSNYR Bruins/Rangers 50.00 100.00
CARNJD Hurricanes/Devils 75.00 150.00
CGYEDM Flames/Oilers 75.00 150.00
CHIDET Hawks/Wings 100.00 200.00
CHISTL Hawks/Blues 75.00 150.00
CLBDET Jackets/Wings 50.00 100.00
COLDET Avs/Wings 125.00 250.00
FLATBL Panthers/Lightning 60.00 120.00
MTLBUF Canadians/Sabres 50.00 100.00
NYINYR Islanders/Rangers 75.00 150.00
NYRNJD Rangers/Devils 60.00 120.00
PITPHI Pens/Flyers 150.00 250.00
PITWAS Pens/Caps 125.00 250.00
SJSLAK Sharks/Kings 40.00 100.00
VANCGY Canucks/Flames 75.00 150.00
WASPHI Caps/Flyers 150.00 250.00
BOSMTL1 Bruins/Canadians 1 75.00 150.00
BOSMTL2 Bruins/Canadians 2 100.00 200.00
TORMTL2 Leafs/Canadians 75.00 150.00

2009-10 UD Black Trios Jerseys

T3JBEP Elias/Parise/Brodeur 20.00 40.00
T3JBGW Bouwmstr/Green/Webr 10.00 25.00
T3JCOM Ovech/Malkin/Crosby 40.00 80.00
T3JDKO Datsyuk/Ovech/Koval 20.00 40.00
T3JFBK Brown/Kopitar/Frolov 15.00 30.00
T3JGRC Gagne/Richards/Carter 15.00 30.00
T3JHDZ Datsyuk/Zetter/Hossa 20.00 40.00
T3JIKP Phaneuf/Kiprusf/Iginla 20.00 40.00
T3JKJS Johnson/Stamkos/Kane 20.00 40.00
T3JKKP Price/Kovalev/Koivu 15.00 30.00
T3JLGF Luongo/Fleury/Giguere 20.00 40.00
T3JLGM Lemieux/Gretz/Mess 40.00 80.00
T3JLSS Stamks/St.Lou/Lecav 15.00 30.00
T3JMCP Clarke/McDonld/Perre 15.00 30.00
T3JMDH Sedin/Sundin/Sedin 15.00 30.00
T3JNBO Oates/Bourque/Neely 15.00 30.00
T3JNLZ Zherdev/Lundq/Naslnd 15.00 30.00
T3JPDS Schenn/Dougty/Phanf 15.00 30.00

Card	Low	High
T3JPKK Parise/Kessel/Kane	12.00	30.00
T3JPMR Robnsn/Maclns/Potvn	10.00	25.00
T3JRBH Brodeur/Roy/Hextall	30.00	60.00
T3JSBK Kessel/Savrd/Bergrn	10.00	25.00
T3JSGH Savard/Hawer/Gilmr	20.00	40.00
T3JSKN Shanahan/Kariya/Nash	20.00	40.00
T3JSNG Nieder/Getzlaf/Selann	10.00	25.00
T3JSSS Staal/Staal/Staal	15.00	30.00
T3JSTT Toews/Sakic/Thorntn	15.00	30.00
T3JTKL Kiprusff/Lehton/Toskl	15.00	30.00

2014-15 UD Black

Card	Low	High
1 Alexander Ovechkin	8.00	20.00
2 Pavel Datsyuk	3.00	8.00
3 Ryan Getzlaf	2.00	5.00
4 Evgeni Malkin	4.00	10.00
5 Duncan Keith	1.50	4.00
6 Anze Kopitar	3.00	8.00
7 Sidney Crosby	8.00	20.00
8 Steven Stamkos	4.00	10.00
9 Jonathan Bernier	1.50	4.00
10 P.K. Subban	2.50	6.00
11 Patrice Bergeron	2.50	6.00
12 Henrik Lundqvist	5.00	12.00
13 Tuukka Rask	2.50	6.00
14 Carey Price	6.00	15.00
15 Jonathan Toews	3.00	8.00
16 Shea Weber	1.50	4.00
17 Matt Duchene	2.00	5.00
18 Taylor Hall	2.00	5.00
19 Claude Giroux	2.00	5.00
20 John Tavares	3.00	8.00
21 Marcel Dionne	2.50	6.00
22 Bobby Orr	8.00	20.00
23 Mark Messier	4.00	10.00
24 Mats Sundin	2.00	5.00
25 Tony Esposito	2.00	5.00
26 Patrick Roy	5.00	12.00
27 Wayne Gretzky	12.00	30.00
28 Jean Beliveau	2.00	5.00
29 Mario Lemieux	8.00	20.00
30 Dominik Hasek	3.00	8.00
31 Adam Lowry RC	3.00	8.00
32 Victor Rask RC	2.00	5.00
33 Bo Horvat RC	5.00	12.00
34 Seth Griffith RC	2.50	6.00
35 William Karlsson RC	6.00	15.00
36 Chris Tierney RC	2.00	5.00
37 Evgeny Kuznetsov RC	5.00	12.00
38 Shayne Gostisbehere RC	4.00	10.00
39 Kevin Hayes RC	5.00	12.00
40 Griffin Reinhart RC	2.00	5.00
41 Damon Severson RC	2.00	5.00
42 Andrei Vasilevskiy RC	40.00	100.00
43 Alexander Wennberg RC	3.00	8.00
44 Marko Dano RC	2.00	5.00
45 Johnny Gaudreau RC	15.00	40.00
46 Teuvo Teravainen RC	3.00	8.00
47 Calle Jarnkrok RC	2.00	5.00
48 Jiri Sekac RC	1.50	4.00
49 Jori Lehtera RC	2.50	6.00
50 Sam Reinhart RC	8.00	20.00
51 Stuart Percy RC	2.00	5.00
52 Vladislav Namestnikov RC	3.00	8.00
53 Darnell Nurse RC	4.00	10.00
54 Derrick Pouliot RC	2.50	6.00
55 Anthony Duclair RC	3.00	8.00
56 Andre Burakovsky RC	3.00	8.00
57 Aaron Ekblad RC	5.00	12.00
58 Leon Draisaitl RC	10.00	25.00
59 Curtis Lazar RC	2.00	5.00
60 Jonathan Drouin RC	4.00	10.00

2014-15 UD Black Lustrous Materials

Card	Low	High
LMAO Alexander Ovechkin	25.00	60.00
LMBH Brett Hull	12.00	30.00
LMCP Carey Price	12.00	30.00
LMMB Mike Bossy	6.00	15.00
LMMG Mike Gartner	8.00	20.00
LMML Mario Lemieux	25.00	60.00
LMMM Mark Messier	12.00	30.00
LMPR Patrick Roy	15.00	40.00
LMRB Rob Blake	6.00	15.00
LMRF Ron Francis	8.00	20.00
LMSC Sidney Crosby	25.00	60.00
LMSY Steve Yzerman	15.00	40.00
LMTA John Tavares	10.00	25.00
LMTH Taylor Hall	6.00	15.00
LMWG Wayne Gretzky	20.00	50.00

2014-15 UD Black Lustrous Rookies Autographs

Card	Low	High
LRBG Brandon Gormley	5.00	12.00
LREK Evgeny Kuznetsov	12.00	30.00
LRJD Jonathan Drouin	10.00	25.00
LRJG Johnny Gaudreau	125.00	300.00
LRLD Leon Draisaitl	80.00	200.00
LRSR Sam Reinhart	15.00	40.00
LRTR Ty Rattie	5.00	12.00
LRTT Teuvo Teravainen	15.00	30.00

2014-15 UD Black Lustrous Signatures

Card	Low	High
BSDS Darryl Sittler/99	12.00	30.00
BSEM Evgeni Malkin/99	30.00	60.00
BSJI Jarome Iginla/99	12.00	30.00
BSJJ Jaromir Jagr/49	30.00	60.00
BSJT John Tavares/99	25.00	50.00
BSML Mario Lemieux/25	60.00	100.00
BSMS Martin St. Louis/49	10.00	25.00
BSPD Pavel Datsyuk/99	20.00	40.00
BSPR Patrick Roy/25	50.00	100.00
BSPS Patrick Sharp/99	10.00	25.00
BSRN Rick Nash/99	12.00	30.00
BSSC Sidney Crosby/49	90.00	150.00
BSTS Teemu Selanne/49	20.00	50.00
BSWG Wayne Gretzky/25	200.00	500.00
BSZP Zach Parise/49	12.00	30.00

2015-16 UD Black

Card	Low	High
1 Ryan Getzlaf	4.00	10.00
2 Oliver Ekman-Larsson	4.00	10.00
3 Tuukka Rask	5.00	12.00
4 Ryan O'Reilly	4.00	10.00
5 Sean Monahan	2.50	6.00
6 Justin Faulk	3.00	8.00
7 Jonathan Toews	6.00	15.00
8 Nathan MacKinnon	15.00	40.00
9 Nick Foligno	3.00	8.00
10 Tyler Seguin	5.00	12.00
11 Henrik Zetterberg	5.00	12.00
12 Taylor Hall	4.00	10.00
13 Aaron Ekblad	5.00	12.00
14 Jonathan Quick	5.00	12.00
15 Zach Parise	4.00	10.00
16 P.K. Subban	5.00	12.00
17 Filip Forsberg	6.00	15.00
18 Cory Schneider	4.00	10.00
19 John Tavares	6.00	15.00
20 Henrik Lundqvist	10.00	25.00
21 Erik Karlsson	5.00	12.00
22 Claude Giroux	4.00	10.00
23 Sidney Crosby	15.00	40.00
24 Joe Pavelski	5.00	12.00
25 Vladimir Tarasenko	5.00	12.00
26 Steven Stamkos	8.00	20.00
27 Nazem Kadri	5.00	12.00
28 Daniel Sedin	5.00	12.00
29 Alexander Ovechkin	15.00	40.00
30 Andrew Ladd	2.50	6.00
31 Wayne Gretzky	25.00	60.00
32 Bobby Orr	15.00	40.00
33 Mario Lemieux	15.00	40.00
34 Steve Yzerman	10.00	25.00
35 Patrick Roy	10.00	25.00
36 Anton Slepyshev AU/299 RC	5.00	12.00
37 Nick Shore AU/299 RC	5.00	12.00
38 Kevin Fiala AU/299 RC	10.00	25.00
39 Ryan Hartman AU/299 RC	10.00	25.00
40 Daniel Sprong AU/299 RC	30.00	80.00
41 Sergei Plotnikov AU/299 RC	5.00	12.00
42 Jared McCann AU/299 RC	10.00	25.00
43 Radek Faksa AU/299 RC	8.00	20.00
44 Matt Puempel AU/299 RC	6.00	15.00
45 Chandler Stephenson AU/299 RC	10.00	25.00
46 Henrik Samuelsson AU/299 RC	5.00	12.00
47 Nikolay Goldobin AU/299 RC	8.00	20.00
48 Connor Hellebuyck AU/299 RC	30.00	80.00
49 Devin Shore AU/299 RC	8.00	20.00
50 Colton Parayko AU/299 RC	12.00	30.00
51 Nick Cousins AU/299 RC	8.00	20.00
52 Oscar Lindberg AU/299 RC	8.00	20.00
53 Antoine Bibeau AU/299 RC	8.00	20.00
54 Brock McGinn AU/299 RC	8.00	20.00
55 Nick Ritchie AU/299 RC	8.00	20.00
56 Jordan Weal AU/299 RC	5.00	12.00
57 Viktor Arvidsson AU/299 RC	8.00	20.00
58 Emile Poirier AU/299 RC	6.00	15.00
59 Malcolm Subban AU/299 RC	12.00	30.00
60 Vincent Hinostroza AU/299 RC	5.00	12.00
61 Hunter Shinkaruk AU/299 RC	8.00	20.00
62 Jacob de la Rose AU/299 RC	8.00	20.00
63 Ronalds Kenins AU/299 RC	5.00	12.00
64 Colin Miller AU/299 RC	6.00	15.00
65 Nicolas Petan AU/299 RC	8.00	20.00
66 Sam Brittain AU/299 RC	8.00	20.00
67 Dylan DeMelo AU/299 RC	6.00	15.00
68 Robby Fabbri AU/299 RC	10.00	25.00
69 Ben Hutton AU/299 RC	8.00	20.00
70 Mattias Janmark AU/299 RC	8.00	20.00
71 Shane Prince AU/299 RC	5.00	12.00
72 Andrew Copp AU/299 RC	8.00	20.00
73 Joel Edmundson AU/299 RC	6.00	15.00
74 Andreas Athanasiou AU/299 RC	20.00	50.00
75 Derek Forbort AU/299 RC	6.00	15.00
76 Artemi Panarin AU/199 RC	25.00	60.00
77 Jack Eichel/199 RC	50.00	125.00
78 Max Domi AU/199 RC	25.00	60.00
79 Sam Bennett AU/199 RC	40.00	100.00
80 Mikko Rantanen AU/199 RC	60.00	150.00
81 Noah Hanifin AU/199 RC	20.00	50.00
82 Dylan Larkin AU/199 RC	40.00	100.00
83 Jake Virtanen AU/199 RC	15.00	40.00
84 Nikolaj Ehlers AU/199 RC	25.00	60.00
85 Connor McDavid AU/199 RC	1500.00	4000.00
86 Matt Murray AU/199 RC	80.00	200.00

2015-16 UD Black Gold Spectrum

*VETS/25: .6X TO 1.5X BASIC CARDS
*RC/25: .6X TO 1.5X BASIC CARDS

Card	Low	High
40 Daniel Sprong AU	30.00	80.00
76 Artemi Panarin AU	80.00	200.00
81 Noah Hanifin AU	20.00	50.00
85 Connor McDavid AU	1500.00	4000.00

2015-16 UD Black Black Ice Signatures

Card	Low	High
BIBB Brent Burns/49	10.00	25.00
BIBC Bobby Clarke/49	15.00	40.00
BICM Connor McDavid/25	1200.00	3000.00
BICP Carey Price/25	50.00	120.00
BIFP Felix Potvin/49	15.00	40.00
BIGH Glenn Hall/25	10.00	25.00
BIGL Guy Lafleur/25	20.00	50.00
BIJA Jake Allen/49	10.00	25.00
BIJV John Vanbiesbrouck/49	10.00	25.00
BIMS Mark Stone/49	12.00	30.00
BINK Nikita Kucherov/49	20.00	50.00
BIRF Robby Fabbri/49	12.00	30.00
BITB Tom Barrasso/49	10.00	25.00
BITF Theoren Fleury/25	12.00	30.00
BITH Taylor Hall/49	10.00	25.00
BIVJ Jakub Voracek/49	8.00	20.00

2015-16 UD Black Cup Coronations Autographs

Card	Low	High
CCDG Doug Gilmour/25	15.00	40.00
CCDK David Krejci/99	12.00	30.00
CCGC Gerry Cheevers/99	12.00	30.00
CCGL Guy Lafleur/25	15.00	40.00
CCJS Joe Sakic/25	25.00	60.00
CCJT Jonathan Toews/25	20.00	50.00
CCLR Larry Robinson/99	12.00	30.00
CCMB Martin Brodeur/25	30.00	80.00
CCMS Martin St. Louis/99	12.00	30.00
CCNL Nicklas Lidstrom/25	12.00	30.00
CCRB Rod Brind'Amour/99	10.00	25.00
CCSC Sidney Crosby/25	100.00	250.00
CCTT Tyler Toffoli/99	12.00	30.00
CCWG Wayne Gretzky/25	250.00	600.00

2015-16 UD Black Lustrous Ink

Card	Low	High
LIAB Aleksander Barkov/50	25.00	60.00
LIAL Andrew Ladd/199	6.00	15.00
LIAO Alexander Ovechkin/25	50.00	120.00
LIBG Brendan Gallagher/50	15.00	40.00
LIBH Bo Horvat/199	12.00	30.00
LIBN Bob Nystrom/199	8.00	20.00
LICM Connor McDavid/35	800.00	2000.00
LIDH Dominik Hasek/50	25.00	60.00
LIGA Glenn Anderson/25	20.00	50.00
LIGH Glenn Hall/25	12.00	30.00
LIJA Jake Allen/199	10.00	25.00
LIJH Jiri Hudler/199	8.00	20.00
LIJI Jarome Iginla/50	20.00	50.00
LIJV Jake Virtanen/199	12.00	30.00
LIKF Kevin Fiala/199	12.00	30.00
LILC Logan Couture/50	20.00	50.00
LIMD Marcel Dionne/50	20.00	50.00
LIMS Martin St. Louis/50	15.00	40.00
LINK Nikita Kucherov/199	20.00	50.00
LINP Nicolas Petan/199	10.00	25.00
LIPD Pavel Datsyuk/25	30.00	80.00
LIPR Patrick Roy/25	75.00	150.00
LIRA Rod Brind'Amour/199	8.00	20.00
LIRB Ray Bourque/25	30.00	80.00
LISM Sean Monahan/199	6.00	15.00
LISY Steve Yzerman/25	75.00	150.00

2015-16 UD Black Lustrous Ink Spectrum Jerseys

*PATCH/35-49: .5X TO 1.25X BASIC INSERTS

Card	Low	High
LIAB Aleksander Barkov/99	15.00	40.00
LIAL Andrew Ladd/99	6.00	15.00
LIBG Brendan Gallagher/99	10.00	25.00
LIBH Bo Horvat/99	12.00	30.00
LIBN Bob Nystrom/99	8.00	20.00
LIGH Glenn Hall/25	10.00	25.00
LIJA Jake Allen/99	10.00	25.00
LIJH Jiri Hudler/99	8.00	20.00
LIJI Jarome Iginla/25	12.00	30.00
LIJV Jake Virtanen/99	12.00	30.00
LIKF Kevin Fiala/99	12.00	30.00
LILC Logan Couture/99	12.00	30.00
LIMD Marcel Dionne/25	12.00	30.00
LIMS Martin St. Louis/25	10.00	25.00
LINK Nikita Kucherov/99	20.00	50.00
LINP Nicolas Petan/99	10.00	25.00
LIPD Pavel Datsyuk/25	15.00	40.00
LISM Sean Monahan/50	6.00	15.00

2015-16 UD Black Pride of a Nation

Card	Low	High
PNAB Aleksander Barkov/99	25.00	60.00
PNAE Aaron Ekblad/99	20.00	50.00
PNAI Arturs Irbe/99	12.00	30.00
PNAK Anze Kopitar/25	80.00	150.00
PNAM Al MacInnis/25	30.00	80.00
PNBO Bobby Orr/25	150.00	300.00
PNCC Chris Chelios/25	15.00	40.00
PNCM Connor McDavid/25	1500.00	4000.00
PNCP Carey Price/25	100.00	250.00
PNGC Gerry Cheevers/99	15.00	40.00
PNGH Glenn Hall/25	40.00	100.00
PNGL Guy Lafleur/25	20.00	50.00
PNJH Jiri Hudler/99	12.00	30.00
PNJK John Klingberg/99	15.00	40.00
PNJP Joe Pavelski/99	20.00	50.00
PNJT Jonathan Toews/25	60.00	150.00
PNJV Jakub Voracek/99	12.00	30.00
PNKH Kevin Hayes/99	12.00	30.00
PNKU Jari Kurri/99	15.00	40.00
PNLA Gabriel Landeskog/99	20.00	50.00
PNMO Mike Modano/25	30.00	80.00
PNMZ Mats Zuccarello/99	15.00	40.00
PNNL Nicklas Lidstrom/25	25.00	60.00
PNOP Ondrej Palat/99	12.00	30.00
PNRI Pekka Rinne/99	15.00	40.00
PNSB Sergei Bobrovsky/99	25.00	60.00
PNTT Tomas Tatar/99	10.00	25.00

2015-16 UD Black Pro Penmanship

Card	Low	High
PENAD Andrew Ladd E	5.00	12.00
PENBH Bo Horvat E	10.00	25.00
PENBL Brian Leetch C	10.00	25.00
PENBO Bobby Orr C	90.00	150.00
PENCM Connor McDavid A	400.00	1000.00
PENCS Cory Schneider D	8.00	20.00
PENDL Dylan Larkin E	25.00	60.00
PENGP Gilbert Perreault D	8.00	20.00
PENJB Jamie Benn C	12.00	30.00
PENJC John Carlson E	12.00	30.00
PENJH Jiri Hudler E	6.00	15.00
PENJP Joe Pavelski D	10.00	25.00
PENJR Jeremy Roenick B	30.00	80.00
PENJT Jonathan Toews B	30.00	80.00
PENKY Keith Yandle E	5.00	12.00
PENML Mario Lemieux B	80.00	200.00
PENMR Morgan Rielly D	8.00	20.00
PENMS Mark Stone D	10.00	25.00
PENNG Nikolay Goldobin D	8.00	20.00
PENNM Nathan MacKinnon C	30.00	80.00
PENOP Ondrej Palat E	6.00	15.00
PENPC Paul Coffey B	20.00	50.00
PENTA John Tavares D	20.00	50.00
PENZP Zach Parise C	12.00	30.00

2015-16 UD Black Pro Penmanship Combos

Card	Low	High
PEN2DL P.Datsyuk/N.Lidstrom/15	40.00	100.00
PEN2FW J.Faulk/C.Ward/49	8.00	20.00
PEN2TH K.Turris/M.Hoffman/49	8.00	20.00

2015-16 UD Black Pro Penmanship Trios

Card	Low	High
PEN31ST McDavid Ekblad/MacKinnon	200.00	500.00
PEN3NYI Tavares/Strome/Lee	25.00	60.00
PEN3RC2 Panarin/Lindberg/McCann	25.00	60.00
PEN3SJS Pavelski/Marleau/Burns	60.00	150.00
PEN3TBL Kucherov/Johnson/Palat	30.00	80.00
PEN3HABS Price/Gallagher Galchenyuk	80.00	200.00

2015-16 UD Black Rookie Coverage Autograph Relics Gold

Card	Low	High
RCOVAB Antoine Bibeau	8.00	20.00
RCOVBM Brock McGinn	8.00	20.00
RCOVCM Connor McDavid	800.00	2000.00
RCOVDL Dylan Larkin	50.00	120.00
RCOVEP Emile Poirier	6.00	15.00
RCOVFA Robby Fabbri	15.00	40.00
RCOVHS Henrik Samuelsson	5.00	12.00
RCOVJD Jacob de la Rose	8.00	20.00
RCOVJE Jack Eichel (No Auto)	30.00	80.00
RCOVJM Jared McCann	10.00	25.00
RCOVJV Jake Virtanen	10.00	25.00
RCOVJW Jordan Weal	5.00	12.00
RCOVKF Kevin Fiala	10.00	25.00
RCOVMJ Mattias Janmark	8.00	20.00
RCOVMS Malcolm Subban	12.00	30.00
RCOVNC Nick Cousins	8.00	20.00
RCOVNE Nikolaj Ehlers	15.00	40.00
RCOVNG Nikolay Goldobin	8.00	20.00
RCOVNH Noah Hanifin	12.00	30.00
RCOVNS Nick Shore	5.00	12.00
RCOVOL Oscar Lindberg	8.00	20.00
RCOVRF Radek Faksa	8.00	20.00
RCOVRH Ryan Hartman	10.00	25.00
RCOVSP Shane Prince	5.00	12.00
RCOVZF Zachary Fucale	6.00	15.00

2015-16 UD Black Rookie Coverage Relics

Card	Low	High
RCOVAB Antoine Bibeau B	3.00	8.00
RCOVAP Artemi Panarin A	12.00	30.00
RCOVBM Brock McGinn A	3.00	8.00
RCOVCM Connor McDavid A	25.00	60.00
RCOVDL Dylan Larkin A	15.00	40.00
RCOVEP Emile Poirier B	2.50	6.00
RCOVFA Robby Fabbri B	4.00	10.00
RCOVHS Henrik Samuelsson B	2.00	5.00
RCOVJD Jacob de la Rose B	3.00	8.00
RCOVJE Jack Eichel A	15.00	40.00
RCOVJM Jared McCann B	4.00	10.00
RCOVJV Jake Virtanen B	4.00	10.00
RCOVJW Jordan Weal B	2.00	5.00
RCOVKF Kevin Fiala B	4.00	10.00
RCOVMD Max Domi B	6.00	15.00
RCOVMJ Mattias Janmark B	3.00	8.00
RCOVMR Mikko Rantanen B	15.00	40.00
RCOVNC Nick Cousins B	3.00	8.00
RCOVNE Nikolaj Ehlers B	6.00	15.00
RCOVNG Nikolay Goldobin B	3.00	8.00
RCOVNH Noah Hanifin B	5.00	12.00
RCOVNR Nick Ritchie B	3.00	8.00
RCOVNS Nick Shore B	2.00	5.00
RCOVOL Oscar Lindberg B	3.00	8.00
RCOVRF Radek Faksa B	3.00	8.00
RCOVRH Ryan Hartman B	4.00	10.00
RCOVSB Sam Bennett B	10.00	25.00
RCOVSP Shane Prince B	2.00	5.00
RCOVZF Zachary Fucale B	2.50	6.00

2015-16 UD Black Rookie Trademarks Relics

Card	Low	High
RTRAB Antoine Bibeau B	5.00	12.00
RTRAP Artemi Panarin A	20.00	50.00
RTRCM Connor McDavid A	80.00	200.00
RTRDF Nick Ritchie B	5.00	12.00
RTRDL Dylan Larkin A	15.00	40.00
RTREP Emile Poirier B	4.00	10.00
RTRFA Robby Fabbri B	6.00	15.00
RTRHS Henrik Samuelsson B	3.00	8.00
RTRJD Jacob de la Rose B	5.00	12.00
RTRJE Jack Eichel A	20.00	50.00
RTRJM Jared McCann B	6.00	15.00
RTRJV Jake Virtanen B	6.00	15.00
RTRJW Jordan Weal B	3.00	8.00
RTRKF Kevin Fiala B	6.00	15.00
RTRMD Max Domi B	10.00	25.00
RTRMJ Mattias Janmark B	5.00	12.00
RTRMR Mikko Rantanen B	25.00	60.00
RTRNC Nick Cousins B	5.00	12.00
RTRNE Nikolaj Ehlers B	10.00	25.00
RTRNG Nikolay Goldobin B	5.00	12.00
RTRNH Noah Hanifin B	8.00	20.00
RTRNS Nick Shore B	3.00	8.00
RTROL Oscar Lindberg B	5.00	12.00
RTRRF Radek Faksa B	5.00	12.00
RTRRH Ryan Hartman B	6.00	15.00
RTRSB Sam Bennett A	15.00	40.00
RTRSP Shane Prince B	3.00	8.00
RTRZF Zachary Fucale B	4.00	10.00

2015-16 UD Black Showcase Relics Patch

Card	Low	High
RSRAH Adam Henrique	6.00	15.00
RSRBC Brett Connolly	5.00	12.00
RSRBG Brendan Gallagher	25.00	60.00
RSRBH Bo Horvat	10.00	25.00
RSRBJ Boone Jenner	8.00	20.00
RSRCK Cody Eakin	5.00	12.00
RSRCM Connor McDavid	80.00	200.00
RSRDH Calvin de Haan	5.00	12.00
RSRDL Dylan Larkin	25.00	60.00
RSRDR David Rundblad	5.00	12.00
RSREB Jordan Eberle	8.00	20.00
RSREP Emile Poirier	6.00	15.00
RSRGB Brandon Gormley	5.00	12.00
RSRGL Gabriel Landeskog	10.00	25.00
RSRJA Jake Allen	8.00	20.00
RSRJE Jack Eichel	30.00	80.00
RSRJF Justin Faulk	6.00	15.00
RSRJG Jake Gardiner	5.00	12.00
RSRJH Jonathan Huberdeau	10.00	25.00
RSRJV Jake Virtanen	10.00	25.00
RSRKS Kevin Shattenkirk	5.00	12.00
RSRMG Mikhail Grigorenko	5.00	12.00
RSRMK Marcus Kruger	5.00	12.00
RSRMP Matt Puempel	6.00	15.00
RSRMS Malcolm Subban	12.00	30.00
RSRMZ Mika Zibanejad	10.00	25.00
RSRNG Nikolay Goldobin	8.00	20.00
RSRNH Noah Hanifin	12.00	30.00
RSRNK Nazem Kadri	10.00	25.00
RSRNM Nathan MacKinnon	30.00	80.00
RSRNP Nicolas Petan	8.00	20.00
RSRNR Nick Ritchie	8.00	20.00
RSRPM Petr Mrazek	8.00	20.00
RSRRE Ryan Ellis	5.00	12.00
RSRRF Robby Fabbri	10.00	25.00
RSRRJ Ryan Johansen	6.00	15.00
RSRRN Ryan Nugent-Hopkins	10.00	25.00
RSRRS Ryan Strome	8.00	20.00
RSRSB Brendan Smith	5.00	12.00
RSRSD Simon Despres	5.00	12.00
RSRSK Slater Koekkoek	5.00	12.00
RSRSM Sean Monahan	5.00	12.00
RSRSP Shane Prince	5.00	12.00
RSRTH Tomas Hertl	12.00	30.00
RSRTP Tanner Pearson	5.00	12.00
RSRTW Tom Wilson	8.00	20.00
RSRZF Zachary Fucale	6.00	15.00
RSRZK Zack Kassian	5.00	12.00

2015-16 UD Black Signature Rookies

Card	Low	High
SRAC Andrew Copp/249	6.00	15.00
SRAP Artemi Panarin/49	30.00	80.00
SRCM Connor McDavid/49	2000.00	5000.00
SRDL Dylan Larkin/149	20.00	50.00
SREP Emile Poirier/249	5.00	12.00
SRJM Jared McCann/149	8.00	20.00
SRNE Nikolaj Ehlers/49	12.00	30.00
SRNG Nikolay Goldobin/149	6.00	15.00
SROL Oscar Lindberg/149	6.00	15.00
SRSP Sergei Plotnikov/249	4.00	10.00
SRVA Viktor Arvidsson/249	6.00	15.00

2015-16 UD Black Sixes Relic Booklets

Card	Low	High
6RG1 Brodeur/Roy/Esposito Hasek/Fuhr/Hall	25.00	60.00
6RG2 Lundqvist/Price/Fleury Holtby/Quick/Rinne	25.00	60.00
6RRC1 McDavid/Eichel/Larkin Domi/Panarin/Bennett	150.00	400.00
6RRC2 Rantanen/McGinn/Sprong Poirier/Petan/Virtanen	50.00	125.00
6RRC3 Ehlers/Fiala/Goldobin Hanifin/Fabbri/Ritchie	20.00	50.00
6RRC4 Bibeau/Hellebuyck/Samuelsson Lindberg/Weal/Subban	40.00	100.00
6RVCCF Naslund/Bure/Sedin Fleury/Iginla/McDonald	12.00	30.00
6RAVALA Colorado	40.00	100.00
6RBLUES St. Louis	12.00	30.00
6RBOLTS Tampa Bay	20.00	50.00
6RBRUIN Boston	25.00	60.00
6RCANES Carolina	12.00	30.00
6RCAPIT Washington	40.00	100.00
6RHAWKS Chicago	20.00	50.00
6RISLAN N.Y. Islanders	15.00	40.00
6RKINGS L.A Kings	15.00	40.00
6RLEGEN Legends	20.00	50.00
6ROILER Edmonton	30.00	80.00
6RPENGU Pittsburgh	20.00	50.00
6RPREDA Nashville	15.00	40.00
6RRANGE N.Y. Rangers	25.00	60.00
6RSHARK San Jose	15.00	40.00
6RSTARS Dallas	12.00	30.00
6RWINGS Detroit	30.00	80.00

2015-16 UD Black Star Coverage Autograph Relics Gold

Card	Low	High
SCOVAB Aleksander Barkov	25.00	60.00
SCOVAK Anze Kopitar	25.00	60.00
SCOVBB Brent Burns	15.00	40.00
SCOVBR Bobby Ryan	12.00	30.00
SCOVCW Cam Ward	15.00	40.00
SCOVDG Doug Gilmour	20.00	50.00
SCOVDH Dale Hawerchuk	20.00	50.00
SCOVDK David Krejci	15.00	40.00
SCOVGH Glenn Hall	15.00	40.00
SCOVJG Johnny Gaudreau	25.00	60.00
SCOVJS Joe Sakic	30.00	80.00
SCOVMB Martin Brodeur	40.00	100.00
SCOVMF Marc-Andre Fleury	30.00	80.00
SCOVNM Nathan MacKinnon	60.00	150.00
SCOVSC Sidney Crosby	60.00	150.00

2016-17 UD Black

Card	Low	High
1 Corey Perry	6.00	15.00
2 Max Domi	4.00	10.00
3 Patrice Bergeron	5.00	12.00
4 Jack Eichel	6.00	15.00
5 Sam Bennett	6.00	15.00
6 Jeff Skinner	5.00	12.00
7 Corey Crawford	5.00	12.00
8 Matt Duchene	4.00	10.00
9 Brandon Saad	3.00	8.00
10 John Klingberg	4.00	10.00
11 Dylan Larkin	5.00	12.00
12 Connor McDavid	20.00	50.00
13 Aleksander Barkov	6.00	15.00
14 Anze Kopitar	6.00	15.00
15 Mikko Koivu	3.00	8.00
16 Shea Weber	3.00	8.00
17 P.K. Subban	5.00	12.00
18 Taylor Hall	4.00	10.00
19 Andrew Ladd	2.50	6.00
20 Mats Zuccarello	4.00	10.00
21 Mark Stone	5.00	12.00
22 Shayne Gostisbehere	4.00	10.00
23 Phil Kessel	4.00	10.00
24 Joe Thornton	6.00	15.00
25 Jake Allen	4.00	10.00
26 Victor Hedman	5.00	12.00
27 Morgan Rielly	4.00	10.00
28 Henrik Sedin	5.00	12.00
29 Braden Holtby	5.00	12.00
30 Mark Scheifele	6.00	15.00
31 Chris Chelios	4.00	10.00
32 Joe Sakic	8.00	20.00
33 Phil Housley	3.00	8.00
34 Igor Larionov	4.00	10.00
35 Teemu Selanne	8.00	20.00
36 Dave Andreychuk	4.00	10.00
37 Pat LaFontaine	4.00	10.00
38 Mark Messier	8.00	20.00
39 Tony Esposito	4.00	10.00
40 Doug Gilmour	5.00	12.00
41 Hudson Fasching AU/299 RC	8.00	20.00
42 Oliver Bjorkstrand AU/299 RC	10.00	25.00
43 Kasperi Kapanen AU/299 RC	12.00	30.00
44 Michael Matheson AU/299 RC	8.00	20.00
45 Sonny Milano AU/299 RC	10.00	25.00
46 Esa Lindell AU/299 RC	8.00	20.00
47 Connor Brown AU/299 RC	12.00	30.00
48 Danton Heinen AU/299 RC	6.00	15.00
49 Tyler Motte AU/299 RC	8.00	20.00
50 Sebastian Aho AU/299 RC	25.00	60.00
51 Christian Dvorak AU/299 RC	10.00	25.00
52 Nick Schmaltz AU/299 RC	10.00	25.00
53 Anthony Beauvillier AU/299 RC	8.00	20.00
54 Artturi Lehkonen AU/299 RC	10.00	25.00
55 Joel Eriksson Ek AU/299 RC	12.00	30.00
56 Brayden Point AU/299 RC	30.00	80.00
57 Zach Werenski AU/299 RC	25.00	60.00
58 Pavel Buchnevich AU/299 RC	12.00	30.00
59 Jakob Chychrun AU/299 RC	15.00	40.00
60 Travis Konecny AU/299 RC	15.00	40.00
61 Mathew Barzal AU/299 RC	40.00	100.00
62 Jimmy Vesey AU/299 RC	12.00	30.00
63 Thomas Chabot AU/299 RC	15.00	40.00
64 Kevin Labanc AU/299 RC	8.00	20.00
65 Matthew Tkachuk AU/299 RC	40.00	100.00
66 Jesse Puljujarvi AU/299 RC	20.00	50.00
67 Pavel Zacha AU/299 RC	12.00	30.00
68 Anthony Mantha AU/299 RC	15.00	40.00
69 Ivan Provorov AU/299 RC	12.00	30.00
70 Kyle Connor AU/299 RC	30.00	80.00
71 William Nylander AU/199 RC	30.00	80.00
72 Dylan Strome AU/199 RC	20.00	50.00
73 Mitch Marner AU/99 RC	150.00	400.00
74 Patrik Laine AU/199 RC	80.00	200.00
75 Auston Matthews AU/99 RC	500.00	1200.00

2016-17 UD Black Black Hole Relic Autographs

Card	Low	High
BHAB Anthony Beauvillier D	8.00	20.00
BHAE Aaron Ekblad C	12.00	30.00
BHAG Alex Galchenyuk C	15.00	40.00
BHAK Anze Kopitar B	12.00	30.00
BHBE Brian Elliott C	6.00	15.00
BHCP Carey Price A	15.00	40.00
BHCS Cory Schneider C	8.00	20.00
BHDS Dylan Strome D	20.00	50.00
BHEM Evgeni Malkin A	15.00	40.00
BHIL Igor Larionov A	20.00	50.00
BHJT John Tavares A	12.00	30.00
BHJV Jimmy Vesey D	12.00	30.00
BHMH Mike Hoffman D	5.00	12.00
BHNK Nikita Kucherov C	12.00	30.00
BHRO Ryan O'Reilly B	8.00	20.00
BHVD Vincent Damphousse C	8.00	20.00

2016-17 UD Black Black Hole Relics

Card	Low	High
BHAB Anthony Beauvillier D	4.00	10.00
BHAE Aaron Ekblad C	5.00	12.00
BHAG Alex Galchenyuk D	2.50	6.00
BHAK Anze Kopitar C	6.00	15.00
BHBB Brent Burns C	4.00	10.00
BHBE Brian Elliott D	3.00	8.00
BHCM Connor McDavid A	30.00	80.00
BHCP Carey Price B	8.00	20.00
BHCS Cory Schneider D	4.00	10.00
BHDS Dylan Strome D	10.00	25.00
BHEM Evgeni Malkin B	8.00	20.00
BHIL Igor Larionov A	4.00	10.00
BHJB Jamie Benn C	4.00	10.00
BHJT John Tavares B	6.00	15.00
BHJV Jimmy Vesey D	6.00	15.00
BHMH Mike Hoffman D	2.50	6.00
BHNK Nikita Kucherov D	8.00	20.00
BHRO Ryan O'Reilly D	4.00	10.00
BHVD Vincent Damphousse D	4.00	10.00

2016-17 UD Black Color Coded Jersey Signatures

Card	Low	High
COAD Anthony DeAngelo/25	15.00	40.00
COAE Aaron Ekblad/25	15.00	40.00
COAG Alex Galchenyuk/25	15.00	40.00
COMG Mark Giordano/25	15.00	40.00
CONK Nikita Kucherov/25	40.00	100.00
COTR Jacob Trouba/25	12.00	30.00

2016-17 UD Black Color Coded Signatures

Card	Low	High
COAD Anthony DeAngelo/99	8.00	20.00
COAE Aaron Ekblad/99	12.00	30.00
COAG Alex Galchenyuk/99	20.00	50.00
COAH Adam Henrique/99	10.00	25.00
COBS Brayden Schenn/99	15.00	40.00
COCS Cory Schneider/99	15.00	40.00
CODS Denis Savard/49	12.00	30.00
COJH Jonathan Huberdeau/99	12.00	30.00
COJP Joe Pavelski/99	15.00	40.00
COLM Larry Murphy/49	12.00	30.00
COMD Matt Duchene/99	12.00	30.00
COMG Mark Giordano/49	15.00	40.00
CONK Nikita Kucherov/99	25.00	60.00
COON Owen Nolan/49	12.00	30.00
COPL Patrik Laine/49	150.00	250.00
COPZ Pavel Zacha/49	20.00	50.00
CORJ Roman Josi/99	15.00	40.00
CORN Rick Nash/49	20.00	50.00
COSM Sean Monahan/99	15.00	40.00
COTA John Tavares/25	20.00	50.00
COTR Jacob Trouba/99	15.00	40.00
COTS Tyler Seguin/25	25.00	60.00

2016-17 UD Black Cup Coronations Autographs

Card	Low	High
CCAK Anze Kopitar/99	8.00	20.00
CCBC Bobby Clarke/99	12.00	30.00
CCHZ Henrik Zetterberg/99	10.00	25.00
CCMF Marc-Andre Fleury/49	20.00	50.00
CCMM Mike Modano/49	15.00	40.00
CCVD Vincent Damphousse/49	8.00	20.00

2016-17 UD Black Fresh Gear Rookie Booklets

Card	Low	High
FGAM Auston Matthews	100.00	250.00
FGCD Christian Dvorak	15.00	40.00
FGDS Dylan Strome	20.00	50.00
FGJV Jimmy Vesey	15.00	40.00
FGKC Kyle Connor	25.00	60.00
FGMM Mitch Marner	40.00	100.00
FGZW Zach Werenski	50.00	120.00

2016-17 UD Black Gold Spectrum

*VETS/35: .50X TO 1.25X BASIC CARDS
*RC/35: .6X TO 1.5X BASIC CARDS

Card	Low	High
12 Connor McDavid	30.00	80.00
35 Teemu Selanne	15.00	40.00
66 Jesse Puljujarvi AU/35	25.00	60.00
74 Patrik Laine AU/35	100.00	200.00

2016-17 UD Black Lustrous INK

Card	Low	High
LIBE Brian Elliott/175	6.00	15.00
LIBH Brett Hull/25	25.00	60.00
LIBJ Boone Jenner/175	8.00	20.00
LIBL Brian Leetch/125	6.00	15.00
LIBS Billy Smith/125	8.00	20.00
LICC Chris Chelios/49	15.00	40.00
LICN Cam Neely/49	20.00	50.00
LIDA Dave Andreychuk/125	8.00	20.00
LIHL Henrik Lundqvist/25	40.00	100.00
LIJV Jimmy Vesey/175	12.00	30.00
LIKL Kevin Labanc/175	8.00	20.00
LILD Leon Draisaitl/175	30.00	80.00
LILE Loui Eriksson/175	5.00	12.00
LIMG Marian Gaborik/175	8.00	20.00
LIMH Mike Hoffman/175	5.00	12.00
LIMP Max Pacioretty/175	8.00	20.00
LIMR Mike Richter/125	8.00	20.00
LINE Nikolaj Ehlers/175	8.00	20.00
LIPB Peter Bondra/175	8.00	20.00
LIPK Patrick Kane/25	60.00	150.00
LIPL Patrik Laine/49	60.00	150.00
LIRJ Roman Josi/175	8.00	20.00
LIRK Ryan Kesler/175	8.00	20.00
LIRL Roberto Luongo/125	12.00	30.00
LITA John Tavares/125	12.00	30.00
LIZP Zach Parise/125	8.00	20.00

2016-17 UD Black Obsidian Signature Combos

Card	Low	High
OS2GP John Gibson Corey Perry B	12.00	30.00
OS2SH Mark Stone Mike Hoffman C	15.00	40.00
OS2TK Jonathan Toews Patrick Kane B	60.00	150.00

2016-17 UD Black Obsidian Signature Jersey Combos

Card	Low	High
OS2GP J.Gibson/C.Perry	12.00	30.00
OS2SH M.Stone/M.Hoffman	20.00	50.00

2016-17 UD Black Obsidian Signature Jerseys

Card	Low	High
OSAH Adam Henrique/50	8.00	20.00
OSAV Andrei Vasilevskiy/50	25.00	60.00
OSHZ Henrik Zetterberg/25	15.00	40.00
OSIP Ivan Provorov/50	20.00	50.00
OSPL Patrik Laine/50	40.00	100.00
OSSE Tyler Seguin/25	10.00	25.00

2016-17 UD Black Obsidian Signatures

Card	Low	High
OSAE Aaron Ekblad D	10.00	25.00
OSAH Adam Henrique D	6.00	15.00
OSAM Auston Matthews A	250.00	350.00
OSAO Alexander Ovechkin C	30.00	80.00
OSAV Andrei Vasilevskiy D	12.00	30.00
OSBO Bobby Orr B	60.00	150.00
OSCM Connor McDavid B	150.00	250.00
OSEM Evgeni Malkin B	15.00	40.00
OSHZ Henrik Zetterberg C	10.00	25.00
OSIP Ivan Provorov D	12.00	30.00
OSJE Joel Eriksson Ek D	12.00	30.00
OSJS Joe Sakic C	20.00	50.00
OSJT Joe Thornton C	12.00	30.00
OSJV Jimmy Vesey D	12.00	30.00
OSPL Patrik Laine D	20.00	50.00
OSRL Roberto Luongo C	12.00	30.00
OSSC Sidney Crosby B	200.00	300.00
OSSE Tyler Seguin C	10.00	25.00
OSTS Teemu Selanne C	15.00	40.00

2016-17 UD Black Pro Penmanship

Card	Low	High
PENAD Anthony DeAngelo F	6.00	15.00
PENAH Adam Henrique E	6.00	15.00
PENAK Anze Kopitar B	30.00	80.00
PENAS Andrew Shaw E	5.00	12.00
PENCN Cam Neely C	15.00	40.00
PENCP Carey Price A	40.00	100.00
PENDG Doug Gilmour A	40.00	100.00
PENDT Dave Taylor E	8.00	20.00
PENEM Evgeni Malkin A	15.00	40.00
PENFA Frederik Andersen E	10.00	25.00
PENGF Grant Fuhr B	12.00	30.00
PENHF Hudson Fasching F	8.00	20.00
PENJG John Gibson F	8.00	20.00
PENKL Kevin Labanc F	8.00	20.00
PENKP Kyle Palmieri F	6.00	15.00
PENLA Patrik Laine D	20.00	50.00
PENLM Larry Murphy C	20.00	50.00
PENLR Luc Robitaille C	20.00	50.00
PENMD Matt Duchene D	8.00	20.00
PENMF Marc-Andre Fleury B	25.00	60.00
PENMH Mike Hoffman E	5.00	12.00
PENMS Mark Scheifele E	12.00	30.00
PENNB Nick Bjugstad F	5.00	12.00
PENNK Nikita Kucherov E	15.00	40.00
PENRJ Ryan Johansen D	6.00	15.00
PENSA Derek Sanderson C	20.00	50.00
PENWG Wayne Gretzky A	250.00	600.00

2016-17 UD Black Pro Penmanship Combos

Card	Low	High
PEN2CL K.Connor/P.Laine/49	80.00	150.00
PEN2HS T.Hall/C.Schneider/49	15.00	40.00
PEN2JJ R.Josi/R.Johansen/49	12.00	30.00
PEN2LH P.LaFontaine D.Hawerchuk/25	100.00	200.00
PEN2LR B.Leetch/M.Richter/25	80.00	150.00

2016-17 UD Black Quad Relics

Card	Low	High
4RACR ACR	12.00	30.00
4RARI ARI	5.00	12.00
4RBUF BUF	10.00	25.00
4RCAL CAL	20.00	50.00
4RCBL CBL	15.00	40.00
4REDM EDM	25.00	60.00
4RFLA FLA	15.00	40.00
4RLAK LAK	8.00	20.00
4RMIN MIN	8.00	20.00
4RMLR MLR	20.00	50.00
4RPEN PEN	10.00	25.00
4RPHI PHI	10.00	25.00
4RRC1 RC1	10.00	25.00
4RSEN SEN	6.00	15.00
4RSJS SJS	8.00	20.00
4RSTL STL	6.00	15.00
4RVAN VAN	6.00	15.00
4RWAS WAS	20.00	50.00
4RWIN WIN	12.00	30.00
4RWJR WJR	15.00	40.00

2016-17 UD Black Rookie Trademarks Relics

Card	Low	High
RTRAM Auston Matthews A	20.00	50.00
RTRCD Christian Dvorak C	4.00	10.00
RTRDS Dylan Strome C	8.00	20.00
RTRIP Ivan Provorov C	5.00	12.00
RTRJE Joel Eriksson Ek C	5.00	12.00
RTRJP Jesse Puljujarvi C	6.00	15.00

RTRJV Jimmy Vesey C 5.00 12.00
RTRKC Kyle Connor C 10.00 25.00
RTRKK Kasperi Kapanen C 5.00 12.00
RTRMB Mathew Barzal C 10.00 25.00
RTRMM Mitch Marner B 10.00 25.00
RTRMT Matthew Tkachuk C 12.00 30.00
RTRNS Nick Schmaltz C 4.00 10.00
RTRPL Patrik Laine A 8.00 20.00
RTRPZ Pavel Zacha C 5.00 12.00
RTRSA Sebastian Aho C 10.00 25.00
RTRTC Thomas Chabot C 6.00 15.00
RTRTK Travis Konecny C 6.00 15.00
RTRWN William Nylander B 12.00 30.00

2016-17 UD Black Signature Rookies

SRAB Anthony Beauvillier/149 15.00 40.00
SRAL Artturi Lehkonen/249 10.00 25.00
SRAM Auston Matthews/25 300.00 400.00
SRDS Dylan Strome/149 10.00 25.00
SRIP Ivan Provorov/249 10.00 25.00
SRJE Joel Eriksson Ek/249 6.00 15.00
SRJP Jesse Puljujarvi/149 25.00 60.00
SRJV Jimmy Vesey/249 10.00 25.00
SRKC Kyle Connor/249 20.00 50.00
SRPL Patrik Laine/149 50.00 120.00

2016-17 UD Black Star Trademarks Relic Autographs

TRAE Aaron Ekblad/35 12.00 30.00
TRHZ Henrik Zetterberg/20 12.00 30.00
TRJG John Gibson/35 12.00 30.00
TRJM Jake Muzzin/35 6.00 15.00
TRLE Loui Eriksson/35 15.00 40.00
TRMG Mark Giordano/20 8.00 20.00
TRRK Ryan Kesler/20 12.00 30.00
TRTB Tyson Barrie/35 6.00 15.00

2016-17 UD Black Star Trademarks Relics

TRAE Aaron Ekblad B 4.00 10.00
TRDH Dale Hawerchuk A 6.00 15.00
TREK Erik Karlsson B 4.00 10.00
TRHZ Henrik Zetterberg B 4.00 10.00
TRJE Jack Eichel B 5.00 12.00
TRJG John Gibson C 3.00 8.00
TRJM Jake Muzzin B 3.00 8.00
TRLE Loui Eriksson C 2.00 5.00
TRMB Martin Brodeur A 12.00 30.00
TRMG Mark Giordano C 3.00 8.00
TRRK Ryan Kesler C 3.00 8.00
TRSC Sidney Crosby A 12.00 30.00
TRSM Sean Monahan C 2.00 5.00
TRTB Tyson Barrie C 2.00 5.00
TRWS Wayne Simmonds C 4.00 10.00

2017-18 UD Black Lustrous Rookies

*ONYX/25: .6X TO 1.5X BASIC INSERTS
LRAB Anders Bjork 4.00 10.00
LRAD Alex DeBrincat 8.00 20.00
LRAK Adrian Kempe 6.00 15.00
LRAN Alexander Nylander 5.00 12.00
LRAT Alex Tuch 8.00 20.00
LRBB Brock Boeser 8.00 20.00
LRCF Christian Fischer 4.00 10.00
LRCK Clayton Keller 8.00 20.00
LRCM Charlie McAvoy 8.00 20.00
LRCW Colin White 4.00 10.00
LRDG Denis Gurianov 8.00 20.00
LRES Evgeny Svechnikov 6.00 15.00
LRFK Jakob Forsbacka-Karlsson 3.00 8.00
LRIB Ivan Barbashev 4.00 10.00
LRJG Jon Gillies 3.00 8.00
LRJH Josh Ho-Sang 4.00 10.00
LRJR Jack Roslovic 4.00 10.00
LRJT J.T. Compher 3.00 8.00
LRLK Luke Kunin 3.00 8.00
LRMB Madison Bowey 2.00 5.00
LRMV Mike Vecchione 2.50 6.00
LRNH Nico Hischier 10.00 25.00
LRNP Nolan Patrick 6.00 15.00
LRNS Nikita Scherbak 4.00 10.00
LROT Owen Tippett 6.00 15.00
LRPD Pierre-Luc Dubois 5.00 12.00
LRTJ Tyson Jost 6.00 15.00
LRTS Travis Sanheim 3.00 8.00
LRVS Vadim Shipachyov 4.00 10.00
LRVZ Valentin Zykov 3.00 8.00

2017-18 UD Black Lustrous Rookies Jerseys

LRAD Alex DeBrincat B 5.00 12.00
LRAK Adrian Kempe C 4.00 10.00
LRAN Alexander Nylander B 3.00 8.00
LRAT Alex Tuch B 5.00 12.00
LRBB Brock Boeser A 5.00 12.00
LRCF Christian Fischer B 2.50 6.00
LRCK Clayton Keller A 5.00 12.00
LRCM Charlie McAvoy A 5.00 12.00
LRCW Colin White B 2.50 6.00
LRES Evgeny Svechnikov A 4.00 10.00
LRIB Ivan Barbashev C 2.50 6.00
LRJG Jon Gillies C 2.00 5.00
LRJH Josh Ho-Sang A 2.50 6.00
LRJR Jack Roslovic C 2.50 6.00
LRMB Madison Bowey C 1.25 3.00
LRNH Nico Hischier A 6.00 15.00
LRNP Nolan Patrick A 4.00 10.00
LRNS Nikita Scherbak C 2.50 6.00
LRPD Pierre-Luc Dubois B 3.00 8.00
LRTJ Tyson Jost A 4.00 10.00
LRTS Travis Sanheim C 2.00 5.00

2017-18 UD Black Lustrous Rookies Jerseys Onyx Patch

LRCM Charlie McAvoy 20.00 50.00

2017-18 UD Black Lustrous Rookies Patch Autographs

LRAD Alex DeBrincat/65 25.00 60.00
LRAK Adrian Kempe/65 20.00 50.00
LRAN Alexander Nylander/65 15.00 40.00
LRBB Brock Boeser/35 100.00 200.00
LRCF Christian Fischer/65 12.00 30.00
LRCK Clayton Keller/35 25.00 60.00
LRCM Charlie McAvoy/35 50.00 125.00
LRCW Colin White/65 12.00 30.00
LRES Evgeny Svechnikov/65 20.00 50.00
LRIB Ivan Barbashev/65 12.00 30.00
LRJG Jon Gillies/65 10.00 25.00
LRJH Josh Ho-Sang/35 12.00 30.00
LRJR Jack Roslovic/65 12.00 30.00
LRMB Madison Bowey/65 6.00 15.00
LRNS Nikita Scherbak/65 12.00 30.00
LRPD Pierre-Luc Dubois/65 15.00 40.00
LRTJ Tyson Jost/35 20.00 50.00
LRTS Travis Sanheim/65 10.00 25.00

2017-18 UD Black Obsidian Material Scripts

OSAK Anze Kopitar/49 10.00 25.00
OSAW Alexander Wennberg/49 4.00 10.00
OSDH Dale Hawerchuk/25 8.00 20.00
OSFP Felix Potvin/49 10.00 25.00
OSJC John Carlson/49 6.00 15.00
OSJP Joe Pavelski/25 8.00 20.00
OSMM Matt Murray/25 10.00 25.00
OSSS Steven Stamkos/25 12.00 30.00

2017-18 UD Black Obsidian Material Scripts Onyx

*ONYX: .6X TO 1.5X BASIC INSERTS
OSMM Matt Murray 25.00 60.00
OSPR Patrick Roy 80.00 150.00
OSWG Wayne Gretzky 200.00 500.00

2017-18 UD Black Obsidian Material Scripts Rookies

OSBB Brock Boeser 25.00 60.00
OSCK Clayton Keller 25.00 60.00
OSCM Charlie McAvoy 25.00 60.00
OSCW Colin White 12.00 30.00
OSJH Josh Ho-Sang 12.00 30.00

2017-18 UD Black Obsidian Scripts

OSAW Alexander Wennberg C 3.00 8.00
OSCS Conor Sheary D 5.00 12.00
OSDH Dale Hawerchuk B 6.00 15.00
OSFP Felix Potvin B 8.00 20.00
OSJC John Carlson D 5.00 12.00
OSJP Joe Pavelski B 6.00 15.00
OSMM Matt Murray C 12.00 30.00
OSNE Nikolaj Ehlers D 5.00 12.00
OSPR Patrick Roy A 12.00 30.00
OSRB Rod Brind'Amour C 5.00 12.00
OSSS Steven Stamkos B 10.00 25.00
OSSY Steve Yzerman A 25.00 60.00
OSTB Tom Barrasso C 4.00 10.00
OSWG Wayne Gretzky A 200.00 500.00

2017-18 UD Black Obsidian Scripts Employee Exclusive

UDBO Bobby Orr 50.00 120.00

2017-18 UD Black Obsidian Scripts Onyx

*ONYX/25: .75X TO 2X BASIC INSERTS
OSPR Patrick Roy 50.00 125.00

2017-18 UD Black Obsidian Scripts Rookies

OSBB Brock Boeser B 25.00 60.00
OSCK Clayton Keller B 15.00 40.00
OSCM Charlie McAvoy A 15.00 40.00
OSCW Colin White B 6.00 15.00
OSJH Josh Ho-Sang A 10.00 25.00

2017-18 UD Black Rookie Trademarks Jerseys

RTAB Anders Bjork 4.00 10.00
RTAD Alex DeBrincat 8.00 20.00
RTAN Alexander Nylander 5.00 12.00
RTBB Brock Boeser 8.00 20.00
RTCK Clayton Keller 8.00 20.00
RTCM Charlie McAvoy 8.00 20.00
RTCW Colin White 4.00 10.00
RTES Evgeny Svechnikov 6.00 15.00
RTFC Filip Chytil 3.00 8.00
RTJH Josh Ho-Sang 4.00 10.00
RTLB Logan Brown 3.00 8.00
RTLK Luke Kunin 3.00 8.00
RTNH Nico Hischier 10.00 25.00
RTNP Nolan Patrick 6.00 15.00
RTOT Owen Tippett 6.00 15.00
RTPD Pierre-Luc Dubois 5.00 12.00
RTTJ Tyson Jost 6.00 15.00
RTTT Tage Thompson 8.00 20.00

2017-18 UD Black Rookie Trademarks Patch Autographs

RTAB Anders Bjork 15.00 40.00
RTAD Alex DeBrincat 30.00 80.00
RTAN Alexander Nylander 20.00 50.00
RTBB Brock Boeser 30.00 80.00
RTCK Clayton Keller 30.00 80.00
RTCM Charlie McAvoy 100.00 250.00
RTCW Colin White 15.00 40.00
RTES Evgeny Svechnikov 25.00 60.00
RTJH Josh Ho-Sang 15.00 40.00
RTLB Logan Brown 12.00 30.00
RTLK Luke Kunin 12.00 30.00
RTOT Owen Tippett 25.00 60.00
RTPD Pierre-Luc Dubois 20.00 50.00
RTTJ Tyson Jost 25.00 60.00
RTTT Tage Thompson 30.00 80.00

2017-18 UD Black Star Trademarks Jerseys

STAM Auston Matthews 8.00 20.00
STAW Alexander Wennberg 1.25 3.00
STCA Craig Anderson 2.00 5.00
STJC Jeff Carter 1.50 4.00
STMB Martin Brodeur 5.00 12.00
STPB Patrice Bergeron 2.50 6.00
STPK Patrick Kane 4.00 10.00
STPL Patrik Laine 2.50 6.00
STRJ Ryan Johansen 1.50 4.00
STTS Tyler Seguin 2.50 6.00

2017-18 UD Black Star Trademarks Patch Autographs

STTS Tyler Seguin/35 15.00 40.00

2018-19 UD Black Lustrous Rookies

LRAC Anthony Cirelli 5.00 12.00
LRAG Adam Gaudette 5.00 12.00
LRAJ Andreas Johnsson 4.00 10.00
LRAS Andrei Svechnikov 8.00 20.00
LRCM Casey Mittelstadt 6.00 15.00
LRDB Daniel Brickley 3.00 8.00
LRDG Dylan Gambrell 3.00 8.00
LRDO Ryan Donato 5.00 12.00
LRDS Dylan Sikura 4.00 10.00
LRDT Dominic Turgeon 3.00 8.00
LREB Ethan Bear 5.00 12.00
LREP Elias Pettersson 10.00 25.00
LRET Eeli Tolvanen 6.00 15.00
LRHB Henrik Borgstrom 5.00 12.00
LRIS Ilya Samsonov 6.00 15.00
LRJG Jordan Greenway 3.00 8.00
LRJK Jordan Kyrou 6.00 15.00
LRJV Juuso Valimaki 3.00 8.00
LRLA Lias Andersson 5.00 12.00
LRMD Michael Dal Colle 3.00 8.00
LRMH Miro Heiskanen 8.00 20.00
LRMM Michael McLeod 2.50 6.00
LRMR Michael Rasmussen 4.00 10.00
LRNJ Noah Juulsen 3.00 8.00
LRRD Rasmus Dahlin 8.00 20.00
LRRT Robert Thomas 6.00 15.00
LRSF Spencer Foo 2.50 6.00
LRSM Samuel Montembeault 6.00 15.00
LRSN Sami Niku 2.50 6.00
LRSS Sam Steel 3.00 8.00
LRTD Travis Dermott 5.00 12.00
LRTH Tomas Hyka 3.00 8.00
LRTT Troy Terry 5.00 12.00
LRVE Victor Ejdsell 2.50 6.00
LRZA Zach Aston-Reese 5.00 12.00

2018-19 UD Black Lustrous Rookies Autographs

LRAC Anthony Cirelli C 12.00 30.00
LRAS Andrei Svechnikov A 20.00 50.00
LRCM Casey Mittelstadt 15.00 40.00
LRDB Daniel Brickley D 8.00 20.00
LRDG Dylan Gambrell D 8.00 20.00
LRDS Dylan Sikura B 10.00 25.00
LRDT Dominic Turgeon D 8.00 20.00
LREB Ethan Bear D 12.00 30.00
LREP Elias Pettersson A 60.00 150.00
LRHB Henrik Borgstrom C 12.00 30.00
LRJG Jordan Greenway C 8.00 20.00
LRJK Jordan Kyrou D 15.00 40.00
LRMH Miro Heiskanen D 20.00 50.00
LRMM Michael McLeod D 6.00 15.00
LRMR Michael Rasmussen B 10.00 25.00
LRNJ Noah Juulsen C 8.00 20.00
LRRT Robert Thomas D 15.00 40.00
LRSF Spencer Foo D 6.00 15.00
LRSS Sam Steel C 8.00 20.00
LRTD Travis Dermott D 12.00 30.00
LRTH Tomas Hyka C 8.00 20.00
LRTT Troy Terry C 15.00 40.00
LRVE Victor Ejdsell D 6.00 15.00
LRZA Zach Aston-Reese C 12.00 30.00

2018-19 UD Black Lustrous Rookies Jerseys

LRAC Anthony Cirelli 3.00 8.00
LRAG Adam Gaudette 3.00 8.00
LRAS Andrei Svechnikov 5.00 12.00
LRCM Casey Mittelstadt 4.00 10.00
LRDG Dylan Gambrell 2.00 5.00
LRDO Ryan Donato 3.00 8.00
LRDS Dylan Sikura 2.50 6.00
LREB Ethan Bear 3.00 8.00
LREP Elias Pettersson 15.00 40.00
LRET Eeli Tolvanen 4.00 10.00
LRHB Henrik Borgstrom 3.00 8.00
LRIS Ilya Samsonov 4.00 10.00
LRJG Jordan Greenway 2.00 5.00
LRJK Jordan Kyrou 4.00 10.00
LRJV Juuso Valimaki 2.00 5.00
LRMD Michael Dal Colle 2.00 5.00
LRMH Miro Heiskanen 5.00 12.00
LRMM Michael McLeod 1.50 4.00
LRMR Michael Rasmussen 2.50 6.00
LRNJ Noah Juulsen 2.00 5.00
LRRD Rasmus Dahlin 5.00 12.00
LRTD Travis Dermott 3.00 8.00
LRTT Troy Terry 3.00 8.00

2018-19 UD Black Lustrous Rookies Patch Autographs

LRAC Anthony Cirelli/65 15.00 40.00
LRAS Andrei Svechnikov/35 30.00 80.00
LRCM Casey Mittelstadt/65 20.00 50.00
LRDG Dylan Gambrell/65 10.00 25.00
LRDS Dylan Sikura/65 12.00 30.00
LREB Ethan Bear/65 15.00 40.00
LREP Elias Pettersson/35 200.00 300.00
LRHB Henrik Borgstrom/65 15.00 40.00
LRJG Jordan Greenway/65 10.00 25.00
LRJK Jordan Kyrou/65 60.00 150.00
LRMH Miro Heiskanen/65 25.00 60.00
LRMM Michael McLeod/65 8.00 20.00
LRMR Michael Rasmussen/65 12.00 30.00
LRNJ Noah Juulsen/65 10.00 25.00
LRTD Travis Dermott/65 15.00 40.00
LRTT Troy Terry/65 60.00 150.00

2018-19 UD Black Marks of Obsidian

MOBH Brett Hull 30.00 80.00
MOBO Bobby Orr 60.00 150.00
MOCH Connor Hellebuyck 30.00 80.00
MOCM Connor McDavid 80.00 200.00
MOJT John Tavares 25.00 60.00
MOMM Mitch Marner 25.00 60.00
MOPR Patrick Roy 40.00 100.00
MOTH Taylor Hall 15.00 40.00
MOWG Wayne Gretzky 200.00 500.00

2018-19 UD Black Obsidian Scripts

OSCC Chris Chelios B 15.00 40.00
OSCM Connor McDavid A 150.00 250.00
OSEK Evgeny Kuznetsov C 20.00 50.00
OSJM Jonathan Marchessault C 20.00 50.00
OSJT John Tavares A 25.00 60.00
OSMB Martin Brodeur A 40.00 100.00
OSNK Nikita Kucherov B 30.00 80.00

2018-19 UD Black Radiant Materials

RMAM Auston Matthews A 12.00 30.00
RMAO Alexander Ovechkin A 12.00 30.00
RMAP Artemi Panarin B 6.00 15.00
RMCG Claude Giroux B 3.00 8.00
RMJE Jack Eichel A 5.00 12.00
RMJG John Gibson B 3.00 8.00
RMPB Patrice Bergeron B 4.00 10.00
RMPS P.K. Subban B 4.00 10.00
RMSC Sidney Crosby A 12.00 30.00
RMTS Tyler Seguin A 4.00 10.00

2019-20 UD Black Lustrous Rookies

LRAF Adam Fox JSY AU/125 80.00 200.00
LRBK Brady Keeper JSY AU/125 8.00 20.00
LRBL Blake Lizotte JSY AU/125 8.00 20.00
LRCG Cody Glass JSY AU/75 30.00 80.00
LRCM Cale Makar JSY AU/75 200.00 500.00
LRDF Dante Fabbro JSY AU/125 12.00 30.00
LREB Erik Brannstrom JSY AU/125 8.00 20.00
LRFZ Filip Zadina JSY AU/75 12.00 30.00
LRGR Carl Grundstrom JSY AU/125 8.00 20.00
LRJF Joel Farabee JSY AU/125 12.00 30.00
LRJH Jack Hughes JSY AU/75 80.00 200.00
LRND Noah Dobson JSY AU/125 15.00 40.00
LRZS Zach Senyshyn JSY AU/125 12.00 30.00

2019-20 UD Black Obsidian Jerseys

OJAB Aleksander Barkov A 5.00 12.00
OJAD Alex DeBrincat A 4.00 10.00
OJAT Alex Tuch B 3.00 8.00
OJBB Brent Burns A 3.00 8.00
OJBE Ben Bishop B 2.50 6.00
OJBO Brock Boeser A 4.00 10.00
OJBP Brayden Point A 4.00 10.00
OJCA Cam Atkinson B 3.00 8.00
OJCM Connor McDavid A 15.00 40.00
OJDS Dylan Strome B 4.00 10.00
OJES Eric Staal B 3.00 8.00
OJJD Jonathan Drouin B 2.50 6.00
OJJK John Klingberg B 3.00 8.00
OJLD Leon Draisaitl A 10.00 25.00
OJMM Matt Murray B 3.00 8.00
OJMS Mark Scheifele A 5.00 12.00
OJMT Matthew Tkachuk A 6.00 15.00
OJRO Ryan O'Reilly B 3.00 8.00
OJSJ Seth Jones A 3.00 8.00
OJVA Viktor Arvidsson B 2.00 5.00

2020-21 UD Black

LPAAA Anthony Angello JSY AU/125 RC 15.00 40.00
LPABE Tyler Benson JSY AU/125 RC 25.00 60.00
LPACF Cal Foote JSY AU/125 RC 20.00 50.00
LPADC Dylan Cozens JSY AU/75 RC 60.00 150.00
LPAGQ Gage Quinney JSY AU/125 RC 12.00 30.00
LPAIS Ilya Sorokin JSY AU/125 RC 80.00 200.00
LPAJE Jake Evans JSY AU/125 RC 25.00 60.00
LPAJN Josh Norris JSY AU/75 RC 50.00 125.00
LPAJR Jason Robertson JSY AU/125 RC 80.00 200.00
LPAKB Kieffer Bellows JSY AU/125 RC 15.00 40.00
LPALF Liam Foudy JSY AU/125 RC 20.00 50.00
LPAMA Mikey Anderson JSY AU/125 RC 20.00 50.00
LPAMG Morgan Geekie JSY AU/125 RC 20.00 50.00
LPAMK Martin Kaut JSY AU/125 RC 20.00 50.00
LPAML Maxim Letunov JSY AU/125 RC 15.00 40.00
LPANR Nick Robertson JSY AU/125 RC 30.00 80.00
LPASB Shane Bowers JSY AU/125 RC 15.00 40.00
LPATD Ty Dellandrea JSY AU/125 RC 20.00 50.00
LPATL Timothy Liljegren JSY AU/125 RC 20.00 50.00
LPATR Alexander True JSY AU/125 RC 15.00 40.00
LPATS Ty Smith JSY AU/125 RC 30.00 80.00

2020-21 UD Black Lustrous Rookie Signatures

LSAL Alexis Lafreniere/199 125.00 300.00
LSAN Anthony Angello/299 8.00 20.00
LSBB Bowen Byram/199 30.00 80.00
LSCF Cal Foote/299 12.00 30.00
LSCM Connor McMichael/299 25.00 60.00
LSCT Calvin Thurkauf/299 8.00 20.00
LSDC Dylan Cozens/199 15.00 40.00
LSGQ Gage Quinney/299 6.00 15.00
LSJE Jake Evans/299 25.00 60.00
LSJH Jani Hakanpaa/299 6.00 15.00
LSJN Josh Norris/199 15.00 40.00
LSKB Kieffer Bellows/299 15.00 40.00
LSKK Kirill Kaprizov/199 200.00 500.00
LSKM K'Andre Miller/299 30.00 80.00
LSLC Lucas Carlsson/299 8.00 20.00
LSLF Liam Foudy/299 10.00 25.00
LSMA Mikey Anderson/299 10.00 25.00
LSMG Morgan Geekie/299 10.00 25.00
LSMK Martin Kaut/299 10.00 25.00
LSML Maxim Letunov/299 8.00 20.00
LSNK Nikolai Knyzhov/299 8.00 20.00
LSNR Nick Robertson/299 15.00 40.00
LSOJ Olli Juolevi/299 10.00 25.00
LSPF Pavel Francouz/299 12.00 30.00
LSTB Tyler Benson/299 10.00 25.00
LSTD Ty Dellandrea/199 10.00 25.00
LSTL Timothy Liljegren/199 10.00 25.00
LSTR Alexander True/299 8.00 20.00
LSTS Ty Smith/299 15.00 40.00

2020-21 UD Black Obsidian Jerseys

*PATCH/25: 1X TO 2.5X BASIC
OJAB Aleksander Barkov 4.00 10.00
OJAM Auston Matthews 10.00 25.00
OJAS Andrei Svechnikov 3.00 8.00
OJAV Andrei Vasilevskiy 4.00 10.00
OJBB Brock Boeser 3.00 8.00
OJBG Brendan Gallagher 2.50 6.00
OJBM Brad Marchand 5.00 12.00
OJBU Brent Burns 2.50 6.00
OJCH Carter Hart 2.50 6.00
OJCM Connor McDavid 12.00 30.00
OJEP Elias Pettersson 4.00 10.00
OJJT John Tavares 4.00 10.00
OJMA Cale Makar 6.00 15.00
OJMS Mark Scheifele 4.00 10.00
OJPK Patrick Kane 5.00 12.00
OJQH Quinn Hughes 6.00 15.00
OJRO Ryan O'Reilly 2.50 6.00
OJSA Sebastian Aho 4.00 10.00
OJSC Sidney Crosby 10.00 25.00
OJWK William Karlsson 3.00 8.00

2020-21 UD Black Obsidian Rookie Jerseys

ORJAA Alexander Alexeyev 2.50 6.00
ORJAK Arthur Kaliyev 5.00 12.00
ORJAL Alexis Lafreniere 50.00 125.00
ORJBB Bowen Byram 6.00 15.00
ORJBH Brandon Hagel 4.00 10.00
ORJCT Calvin Thurkauf 2.50 6.00
ORJGL Gustav Lindstrom 2.50 6.00
ORJGV Gabe Vilardi 5.00 12.00
ORJIS Ilya Sorokin 8.00 20.00
ORJJN Josh Norris 5.00 12.00
ORJJR Jason Robertson 8.00 20.00
ORJKB Kieffer Bellows 2.50 6.00
ORJKK Kirill Kaprizov 50.00 125.00
ORJKM K'Andre Miller 6.00 15.00
ORJLC Lucas Carlsson 2.50 6.00
ORJLF Liam Foudy 3.00 8.00
ORJMA Mikey Anderson 3.00 8.00
ORJMG Morgan Geekie 3.00 8.00
ORJMK Martin Kaut 3.00 8.00
ORJNB Nicolas Beaudin 3.00 8.00
ORJNR Nick Robertson 5.00 12.00
ORJPK Peyton Krebs 5.00 12.00
ORJSB Shane Bowers 2.50 6.00
ORJTB Tyler Benson 3.00 8.00
ORJTD Ty Dellandrea 3.00 8.00
ORJTH Thomas Harley 5.00 12.00
ORJTL Timothy Liljegren 3.00 8.00
ORJTS Tim Stutzle 30.00 80.00
ORJVS Victor Soderstrom 2.50 6.00
ORJVV Vitek Vanecek 5.00 12.00

2020-21 UD Black Obsidian Rookie Jerseys Patch Purple

*PATCH/25: .75X TO 2X BASIC
ORJJR Jason Robertson 25.00 60.00
ORJMG Morgan Geekie 12.00 30.00

2020-21 UD Black Obsidian Rookies

*PURPLE/99: .5X TO 1.25X BASIC
OR1 Alexis Lafreniere 30.00 80.00
OR2 Nils Hoglander 4.00 10.00
OR4 Kirill Kaprizov 80.00 200.00
OR5 Gabe Vilardi 6.00 15.00
OR6 Jason Robertson 10.00 25.00
OR7 Vitali Kravtsov 8.00 20.00
OR8 Liam Foudy 4.00 10.00
OR9 Timothy Liljegren 4.00 10.00
OR10 Josh Norris 6.00 15.00
OR11 Connor McMichael 6.00 15.00
OR12 Ty Smith 6.00 15.00
OR13 Philip Broberg 4.00 10.00
OR14 Alexander Alexeyev 3.00 8.00
OR15 Ty Dellandrea 4.00 10.00
OR16 Tyler Benson 4.00 10.00
OR17 Nicolas Beaudin 4.00 10.00
OR18 Olli Juolevi 4.00 10.00
OR19 Martin Kaut 4.00 10.00
OR20 Ryan McLeod 3.00 8.00
OR21 Shane Bowers 3.00 8.00
OR22 Dylan Coghlan 4.00 10.00
OR23 Lucas Carlsson 3.00 8.00
OR24 Mikey Anderson 4.00 10.00
OR25 Morgan Geekie 4.00 10.00
OR26 Brandon Hagel 5.00 12.00
OR27 Alex Belzile 3.00 8.00
OR28 Keegan Kolesar 3.00 8.00
OR29 Steven Lorentz 3.00 8.00
OR30 Calvin Thurkauf 3.00 8.00
OR31 Maxim Letunov 3.00 8.00
OR32 Alexander Yelesin 3.00 8.00
OR33 Gage Quinney 2.50 6.00
OR34 Gustav Lindstrom 3.00 8.00
OR35 Reid Duke 4.00 10.00
OR36 Kieffer Bellows 3.00 8.00
OR37 Pierre-Olivier Joseph 4.00 10.00
OR38 Philipp Kurashev 5.00 12.00
OR39 Jake Oettinger 10.00 25.00
OR40 K'Andre Miller 8.00 20.00
OR41 Victor Soderstrom 3.00 8.00
OR42 Thomas Harley 6.00 15.00
OR43 Peyton Krebs 6.00 15.00
OR44 Ilya Sorokin 10.00 25.00
OR45 Nick Robertson 6.00 15.00
OR46 Arthur Kaliyev 6.00 15.00
OR47 Bowen Byram 8.00 20.00
OR48 Alexander Romanov 5.00 12.00
OR49 Pius Suter 5.00 12.00
OR50 Tim Stutzle 30.00 80.00

2020-21 UD Black Obsidian Scripts

OSAL Anders Lee 12.00 30.00
OSAS Andrei Svechnikov 20.00 50.00
OSAV Andrei Vasilevskiy 25.00 60.00
OSCP Colton Parayko 12.00 30.00
OSDO Dmitry Orlov 15.00 40.00
OSHE Connor Hellebuyck 30.00 80.00
OSKP Kyle Palmieri 12.00 30.00
OSKY Keith Yandle 10.00 25.00
OSMG Mark Giordano 15.00 40.00
OSPD Phillip Danault 15.00 40.00
OSPR Pekka Rinne 15.00 40.00
OSRS Ryan Suter 12.00 30.00
OSSC Mark Scheifele 25.00 60.00
OSSR Sam Reinhart 30.00 80.00
OSST Shea Theodore 20.00 50.00
OSTH Tomas Hertl 15.00 40.00
OSTS Tyler Seguin 20.00 50.00
OSTT Teuvo Teravainen 15.00 40.00
OSWK William Karlsson 20.00 50.00

2020-21 UD Black Pride of a Nation Patches

PNDP David Pastrnak 10.00 25.00
PNJC John Carlson 4.00 10.00
PNML Mario Lemieux 15.00 40.00
PNMM Mitch Marner 6.00 15.00
PNNM Nathan MacKinnon 15.00 40.00

2020-21 UD Black Pride of a Nation Rookie Patch Autographs

PNABB Bowen Byram/99 25.00 60.00
PNADC Dylan Cozens/99 20.00 50.00
PNAJR Jason Robertson/99 100.00 250.00
PNAKB Kieffer Bellows/99 10.00 25.00
PNALF Liam Foudy/99 12.00 30.00
PNALI Timothy Liljegren/99 12.00 30.00
PNAMK Martin Kaut/99 25.00 60.00
PNATS Ty Smith/99 20.00 50.00

2001-02 UD Challenge for the Cup

COMP.SET w/o SP's (90)
1 Paul Kariya .50 1.25
2 Jeff Friesen .30 .75
3 Dany Heatley .40 1.00
4 Milan Hnilicka .40 1.00
5 Joe Thornton .75 2.00
6 Bill Guerin .50 1.25
7 Miroslav Satan .40 1.00
8 Martin Biron .40 1.00
9 Jarome Iginla .60 1.50
10 Roman Turek .40 1.00
11 Craig Conroy .30 .75
12 Jeff O'Neill .40 1.00
13 Arturs Irbe .40 1.00
14 Tony Amonte .40 1.00
15 Steve Sullivan .30 .75
16 Rob Blake .50 1.25
17 Joe Sakic 1.00 2.50
18 Milan Hejduk .40 1.00
19 Chris Drury .40 1.00
20 Patrick Roy 1.25 3.00
21 Espen Knutsen .30 .75
22 Ray Whitney .30 .75
23 Pierre Turgeon .40 1.00
24 Ed Belfour .50 1.25
25 Mike Modano .75 2.00
26 Sergei Zubov .40 1.00
27 Dominik Hasek .75 2.00
28 Steve Yzerman 1.25 3.00
29 Brendan Shanahan .50 1.25
30 Nicklas Lidstrom .50 1.25
31 Luc Robitaille .50 1.25
32 Mike Comrie .40 1.00
33 Ryan Smyth .40 1.00
34 Tommy Salo .40 1.00
35 Roberto Luongo .75 2.00
36 Valeri Bure .30 .75
37 Pavel Bure .50 1.25
38 Felix Potvin .75 2.00
39 Jason Allison .40 1.00
40 Zigmund Palffy .50 1.25
41 Manny Fernandez .30 .75
42 Marian Gaborik .50 1.25
43 Andrew Brunette .30 .75
44 Brian Savage .30 .75
45 Jeff Hackett .40 1.00
46 Oleg Petrov .30 .75
47 Cliff Ronning .30 .75
48 Mike Dunham .40 1.00
49 Scott Walker .30 .75
50 Martin Brodeur 1.25 3.00
51 Scott Niedermayer .50 1.25
52 Scott Gomez .40 1.00
53 Patrik Elias .50 1.25
54 Alexei Yashin .40 1.00
55 Chris Osgood .50 1.25
56 Mike Peca .40 1.00
57 Mark Messier 1.00 2.50
58 Theo Fleury .60 1.50
59 Eric Lindros .75 2.00
60 Brian Boucher .40 1.00
61 John LeClair .50 1.25
62 Jeremy Roenick .75 2.00
63 Keith Primeau .40 1.00
64 Michal Handzus .30 .75
65 Claude Lemieux .40 1.00
66 Sean Burke .30 .75
67 Alexei Kovalev .40 1.00
68 Mario Lemieux 2.00 5.00
69 Johan Hedberg .40 1.00
70 Martin Straka .30 .75
71 Owen Nolan .50 1.25
72 Evgeni Nabokov .40 1.00
73 Teemu Selanne 1.00 2.50
74 Doug Weight .50 1.25
75 Brent Johnson .40 1.00
76 Pavol Demitra .60 1.50
77 Chris Pronger .50 1.25
78 Keith Tkachuk .50 1.25
79 Vincent Lecavalier .50 1.25
80 Brad Richards .50 1.25
81 Nikolai Khabibulin .50 1.25
82 Curtis Joseph .60 1.50
83 Alexander Mogilny .40 1.00
84 Mats Sundin .50 1.25
85 Trevor Linden .50 1.25
86 Markus Naslund .50 1.25
87 Brendan Morrison .40 1.00
88 Jaromir Jagr 1.50 4.00
89 Olaf Kolzig .50 1.25
90 Peter Bondra .50 1.25
91 Ilja Bryzgalov RC 3.00 8.00
92 Timo Parssinen RC 1.50 4.00
93 Kevin Sawyer RC 1.25 3.00
94 Brian Pothier RC 1.25 3.00
95 Ilya Kovalchuk RC 6.00 15.00
96 Kamil Piros RC 1.25 3.00
97 Ivan Huml RC 1.25 3.00
98 Jukka Hentunen RC 1.25 3.00
99 Scott Nichol RC 1.25 3.00
100 Erik Cole RC 2.50 6.00
101 Jaroslav Obsut RC 1.25 3.00
102 Vaclav Nedorost RC 1.25 3.00
103 Martin Spanhel RC 1.25 3.00
104 Niko Kapanen RC 2.00 5.00
105 Pavel Datsyuk RC 20.00 50.00
106 Ty Conklin RC 2.00 5.00
107 Niklas Hagman RC 1.50 4.00
108 Kristian Huselius RC 2.00 5.00
109 Jaroslav Bednar RC 1.25 3.00
110 Pascal Dupuis RC 2.00 5.00
111 Mike Matteucci RC 1.25 3.00
112 Nick Schultz RC 1.25 3.00
113 Travis Roche RC 1.25 3.00
114 Martti Jarventie 1.25 3.00
115 Martin Erat RC 1.50 4.00
116 Pavel Skrbek RC 1.25 3.00
117 Josef Boumedienne RC 1.25 3.00
118 Andreas Salomonsson RC 1.25 3.00
119 Scott Clemmensen RC 1.25 3.00
120 Mikael Samuelsson RC 1.50 4.00
121 Dan Blackburn RC 1.50 4.00
122 Richard Scott RC 1.25 3.00
123 Radek Martinek RC 1.25 3.00
124 Raffi Torres RC 2.00 5.00
125 Ivan Ciernik RC 1.25 3.00
126 Jiri Dopita RC 1.25 3.00
127 Vaclav Pletka RC 1.25 3.00
128 Krys Kolanos RC 1.25 3.00
129 David Cullen RC 1.25 3.00
130 Jeff Jillson RC 1.25 3.00
131 Mark Rycroft RC 1.50 4.00
132 Ryan Tobler RC 1.50 4.00
133 Nikita Alexeev RC 1.25 3.00
134 Brian Sutherby RC 1.25 3.00
135 Chris Corrinet RC 1.25 3.00

2001-02 UD Challenge for the Cup 500 Game Winner

500PR Patrick Roy/300 60.00 150.00
500PRA Patrick Roy AU/25 400.00 800.00

2001-02 UD Challenge for the Cup Backstops

BB1 Roman Turek 12.00 30.00
BB2 Arturs Irbe 12.00 30.00
BB3 Patrick Roy 40.00 100.00
BB4 Dominik Hasek 25.00 60.00
BB5 Tommy Salo 12.00 30.00
BB6 Martin Brodeur 30.00 80.00
BB7 Roman Cechmanek 12.00 30.00
BB8 Evgeni Nabokov 12.00 30.00
BB9 Curtis Joseph 15.00 40.00
BB10 Olaf Kolzig 12.00 30.00

2001-02 UD Challenge for the Cup Century Men

CM1 Jeremy Roenick 8.00 20.00
CM2 Joe Sakic 10.00 25.00
CM3 Steve Yzerman 12.50 30.00
CM4 Sergei Fedorov 8.00 20.00
CM5 Luc Robitaille 6.00 15.00
CM6 Mark Messier 6.00 15.00
CM7 Jaromir Jagr 10.00 25.00
CM8 Mario Lemieux 15.00 40.00
CM9 Brett Hull 8.00 20.00
CM10 Pavel Bure 6.00 15.00

2001-02 UD Challenge for the Cup Cornerstones

COMPLETE SET (10) 75.00 150.00
CR1 Paul Kariya 1.50 4.00
CR2 Ilya Kovalchuk 8.00 20.00
CR3 Joe Sakic 3.00 8.00
CR4 Mike Modano 2.50 6.00
CR5 Steve Yzerman 6.00 15.00
CR6 Pavel Bure 2.00 5.00
CR7 Mario Lemieux 10.00 25.00
CR8 Chris Pronger 1.25 3.00
CR9 Mats Sundin 1.50 4.00
CR10 Jaromir Jagr 2.50 6.00

2001-02 UD Challenge for the Cup Future Famers

FF1 Joe Sakic 25.00 60.00
FF2 Patrick Roy 50.00 120.00
FF3 Brett Hull 30.00 80.00
FF4 Luc Robitaille 25.00 60.00
FF5 Steve Yzerman 40.00 100.00
FF6 Mark Messier 30.00 80.00

2001-02 UD Challenge for the Cup Jerseys

TCJ Curtis Joseph 4.00 10.00
TCO Chris Osgood 4.00 10.00
TDH Dominik Hasek 8.00 20.00
TEB Ed Belfour 6.00 15.00
TFP Felix Potvin 5.00 12.00
TMB Martin Brodeur 12.00 30.00
TMR Mike Richter 4.00 10.00
TPR Patrick Roy SP 20.00 50.00
TSB Sean Burke 4.00 10.00
TTB Tom Barrasso 4.00 10.00
FPDW Doug Weight 4.00 10.00
FPEL Eric Lindros SP 5.00 12.00
FPJA Jason Allison 5.00 12.00
FPJL John LeClair 5.00 12.00
FPML Mario Lemieux 10.00 25.00
FPNL Nicklas Lidstrom 5.00 12.00
FPPF Peter Forsberg 8.00 20.00
FPRB Ray Bourque 8.00 20.00
FPSY Steve Yzerman 10.00 25.00
FPTA Tony Amonte 4.00 10.00
TNAM Al MacInnis Dual 8.00 20.00
TNBS Brendan Shanahan Dual 8.00 20.00
TNCJ Curtis Joseph Dual 8.00 20.00
TNJS Joe Sakic Dual 10.00 25.00
TNKP Keith Primeau Dual 8.00 20.00
TNPR Patrick Roy Dual 12.00 30.00
TNRB Ray Bourque Dual 10.00 25.00
UCLB J.LeClair/B.Boucher 6.00 15.00
UCLL E.Lindros/B.Leetch 6.00 15.00
UCMB M.Modano/E.Belfour 8.00 20.00
UCPD Z.Palffy/A.Deadmarsh 6.00 15.00
UCSH J.Sakic/M.Hejduk SP 15.00 40.00
UCSJ M.Sundin/C.Joseph 8.00 20.00
UCSY B.Shanahan/S.Yzerman 10.00 25.00

2001-02 UD Challenge for the Cup Jersey Autographs

TBE Ed Belfour 20.00 50.00
TBR Martin Brodeur 40.00 100.00
TJO Curtis Joseph 15.00 40.00
TPO Felix Potvin 15.00 40.00
TPR Patrick Roy 75.00 150.00
TRI Mike Richter 15.00 40.00
FPAL Jason Allison 15.00 40.00
FPBO Ray Bourque 25.00 60.00
FPJI Jarome Iginla 25.00 60.00
FPPB Pavel Bure 60.00 120.00
FPWE Doug Weight 15.00 40.00
FPYZ Steve Yzerman 30.00 80.00
TNBO Ray Bourque Dual 40.00 100.00
TNEB Ed Belfour Dual 40.00 100.00

TNJO Curtis Joseph Dual 30.00 80.00
TNKP Keith Primeau Dual 30.00 80.00
TNMA Al MacInnis Dual 30.00 80.00
UCAP J.Allison/Z.Palffy 60.00 120.00
UCBB R.Bourque/R.Blake 125.00 250.00
UCLG J.LeClair/S.Gagne 40.00 100.00
UCST S.Samsonov/J.Thornton 40.00 100.00

1998-99 UD Choice

COMPLETE SET (310) 15.00 30.00
1 Guy Hebert .08 .25
2 Mikhail Shtalenkov .05 .15
3 Josef Marha .05 .15
4 Paul Kariya .10 .30
5 Travis Green .05 .15
6 Steve Rucchin .05 .15
7 Matt Cullen .05 .15
8 Teemu Selanne .10 .30
9 Antti Aalto .05 .15
10 Byron Dafoe .08 .25
11 Ted Donato .05 .15
12 Dimitri Khristich .05 .15
13 Sergei Samsonov .08 .25
14 Jason Allison .05 .15
15 Ray Bourque .20 .50
16 Kyle McLaren .05 .15
17 Cameron Mann .05 .15
18 Shawn Bates .05 .15
19 Joe Thornton .20 .50
20 Vaclav Varada .05 .15
21 Brian Holzinger .05 .15
22 Miroslav Satan .08 .25
23 Dominik Hasek .25 .60
24 Michael Peca .05 .15
25 Erik Rasmussen .05 .15
26 Alexei Zhitnik .05 .15
27 Geoff Sanderson .08 .25
28 Donald Audette .05 .15
29 Derek Morris .05 .15
30 German Titov .05 .15
31 Valeri Bure .05 .15
32 Michael Nylander .05 .15
33 Cory Stillman .05 .15
34 Theo Fleury .05 .15
35 Jarome Iginla .15 .40
36 Gary Roberts .05 .15
37 Jeff O'Neill .05 .15
38 Bates Battaglia .08 .25
39 Keith Primeau .05 .15
40 Sami Kapanen .05 .15
41 Glen Wesley .05 .15
42 Trevor Kidd .08 .25
43 Nelson Emerson .05 .15
44 Daniel Cleary .05 .15
45 Eric Daze .08 .25
46 Chris Chelios .10 .30
47 Gary Suter .05 .15
48 Alexei Zhamnov .05 .15
49 Jeff Hackett .08 .25
50 Dmitri Nabokov .05 .15
51 Tony Amonte .08 .25
52 Jean-Yves Leroux .05 .15
53 Eric Messier .05 .15
54 Patrick Roy .60 1.50
55 Claude Lemieux .05 .15
56 Peter Forsberg .30 .75
57 Adam Deadmarsh .05 .15
58 Valeri Kamensky .05 .15
59 Joe Sakic .25 .60
60 Sandis Ozolinsh .05 .15
61 Jamie Langenbrunner .05 .15
62 Joe Nieuwendyk .08 .25
63 Ed Belfour .10 .30
64 Juha Lind .05 .15
65 Derian Hatcher .05 .15
66 Sergei Zubov .05 .15
67 Darryl Sydor .05 .15
68 Jere Lehtinen .05 .15
69 Mike Modano .20 .50
70 Larry Murphy .08 .25
71 Igor Larionov .05 .15
72 Darren McCarty .05 .15
73 Steve Yzerman .60 1.50
74 Chris Osgood .08 .25
75 Sergei Fedorov .20 .50
76 Brendan Shanahan .10 .30
77 Nicklas Lidstrom .10 .30
78 Vyacheslav Kozlov .05 .15
79 Dean McAmmond .05 .15
80 Roman Hamrlik .05 .15
81 Curtis Joseph .10 .30
82 Ryan Smyth .08 .25
83 Boris Mironov .05 .15
84 Bill Guerin .08 .25
85 Doug Weight .08 .25
86 Janne Niinimaa .05 .15
87 Ray Whitney .05 .15
88 Robert Svehla .05 .15
89 John Vanbiesbrouck .08 .25
90 Scott Mellanby .05 .15
91 Ed Jovanovski .05 .15
92 Dave Gagner .05 .15
93 Dino Ciccarelli .08 .25
94 Rob Niedermayer .05 .15
95 Rob Blake .08 .25
96 Yanic Perreault .05 .15
97 Stephane Fiset .08 .25
98 Luc Robitaille .08 .25
99 Glen Murray .05 .15
100 Jozef Stumpel .08 .25
101 Vladimir Tsyplakov .05 .15
102 Donald MacLean .05 .15
103 Shayne Corson .05 .15
104 Vladimir Malakhov .05 .15
105 Saku Koivu .10 .30
106 Andy Moog .08 .25
107 Matt Higgins RC .05 .15
108 Dave Manson .05 .15
109 Mark Recchi .08 .25
110 Vincent Damphousse .05 .15
111 Brian Savage .05 .15
112 Petr Sykora .05 .15
113 Scott Stevens .08 .25
114 Patrik Elias .08 .25
115 Bobby Holik .05 .15
116 Martin Brodeur .40 1.00
117 Doug Gilmour .08 .25
118 Jason Arnott .05 .15
119 Scott Niedermayer .05 .15
120 Brendan Morrison .08 .25
121 Zigmund Palffy .08 .25
122 Trevor Linden .08 .25
123 Bryan Berard .08 .25
124 Zdeno Chara .15 .30
125 Kenny Jonsson .05 .15
126 Robert Reichel .05 .15
127 Bryan Smolinski .05 .15
128 Wayne Gretzky .75 2.00
129 Brian Leetch .10 .30
130 Pat Lafontaine .10 .30
131 Dan Cloutier .05 .15
132 Niklas Sundstrom .05 .15
133 Marc Savard .08 .25
134 Adam Graves .05 .15
135 Mike Richter .10 .30
136 Jeff Beukeboom .05 .15
137 Daniel Goneau .05 .15
138 Shawn McEachern .05 .15
139 Damian Rhodes .08 .25
140 Wade Redden .05 .15
141 Alexei Yashin .05 .15
142 Marian Hossa .10 .30
143 Chris Phillips .05 .15
144 Daniel Alfredsson .08 .25
145 Vaclav Prospal .05 .15
146 Andreas Dackell .05 .15
147 Sean Burke .05 .15
148 Alexandre Daigle .05 .15
149 Rod Brind'Amour .08 .25
150 Chris Gratton .08 .25
151 Paul Coffey .10 .30
152 Eric Lindros .10 .30
153 John LeClair .10 .30
154 Chris Therien .05 .15
155 Keith Carney .05 .15
156 Craig Janney .05 .15
157 Teppo Numminen .05 .15
158 Jeremy Roenick .15 .40
159 Oleg Tverdovsky .05 .15
160 Keith Tkachuk .10 .30
161 Brad Isbister .05 .15
162 Nikolai Khabibulin .08 .25
163 Daniel Briere .05 .15
164 Juha Ylonen .05 .15
165 Tom Barrasso .08 .25
166 Alexei Morozov .05 .15
167 Stu Barnes .05 .15
168 Jaromir Jagr .20 .50
169 Ron Francis .08 .25
170 Peter Skudra .05 .15
171 Robert Dome .05 .15
172 Kevin Hatcher .05 .15
173 Patrick Marleau .08 .20
174 Jeff Friesen .05 .15
175 Owen Nolan .08 .25
176 John MacLean .05 .15
177 Mike Vernon .08 .25
178 Marcus Ragnarsson .05 .15
179 Andrei Zyuzin .05 .15
180 Mike Ricci .08 .25
181 Marco Sturm .05 .15
182 Steve Duchesne .05 .15
183 Brett Hull .15 .40
184 Pierre Turgeon .08 .25
185 Chris Pronger .08 .25
186 Pavol Demitra .08 .25
187 Jamie McLennan .05 .15
188 Al MacInnis .08 .25
189 Jim Campbell .05 .15
190 Geoff Courtnall .05 .15
191 Daren Puppa .08 .25
192 Daymond Langkow .08 .25
193 Stephane Richer .08 .25
194 Paul Ysebaert .05 .15
195 Alexander Selivanov .05 .15
196 Rob Zamuner .05 .15
197 Mikael Renberg .08 .25
198 Mathieu Schneider .05 .15
199 Mike Johnson .05 .15
200 Alyn McCauley .05 .15
201 Sergei Berezin .08 .25
202 Wendel Clark .08 .25
203 Mats Sundin .10 .30
204 Tie Domi .08 .25
205 Jyrki Lumme .05 .15
206 Mattias Ohlund .08 .25
207 Garth Snow .08 .25
208 Pavel Bure .10 .30
209 Dave Scatchard .05 .15
210 Alexander Mogilny .08 .25
211 Mark Messier .10 .30
212 Todd Bertuzzi .10 .30
213 Peter Bondra .08 .25
214 Joe Juneau .05 .15
215 Olaf Kolzig .08 .25
216 Jan Bulis .05 .15
217 Adam Oates .08 .25
218 Richard Zednik .05 .15
219 Calle Johansson .05 .15
220 Phil Housley .05 .15
221 Dominik Hasek GM .10 .30
222 Ray Bourque GM .10 .30
223 Chris Chelios GM .08 .25
224 Paul Kariya GM .08 .25
225 Wayne Gretzky GM .40 1.00
226 Jaromir Jagr GM .08 .25
227 Rob Blake GM .05 .15
228 Adam Foote GM .05 .15
229 Peter Forsberg GM .10 .30
230 Joe Sakic GM .08 .25
231 Mark Recchi GM .05 .15
232 Patrick Roy GM .10 .30
233 Nicklas Lidstrom GM .08 .25
234 Rob Blake GM .05 .15
235 John LeClair GM .05 .15
236 Wayne Gretzky GM .40 1.00
237 Eric Lindros GM .10 .30
238 Brian Leetch GM .05 .15
239 Scott Stevens GM .08 .25
240 Paul Kariya GM .10 .30
241 Peter Forsberg GM .10 .30
242 Teemu Selanne GM .10 .30
243 Patrick Roy CRL .10 .30
244 Dominik Hasek CRL .10 .30
245 Martin Brodeur CRL .10 .30
246 Mike Richter CRL .08 .25
247 John Vanbiesbrouck CRL .08 .25
248 Chris Osgood CRL .08 .25
249 Ed Belfour CRL .10 .30
250 Tom Barrasso CRL .05 .15
251 Curtis Joseph CRL .10 .30
252 Sean Burke CRL .05 .15
253 Josh Holden .05 .15
254 Daniel Tkaczuk .05 .15
255 Manny Malhotra .05 .15
256 Eric Brewer .05 .15
257 Alex Tanguay .08 .25
258 Roberto Luongo .30 .75
259 Vincent Lecavalier .15 .40
260 Mathieu Garon .08 .25
261 Brad Ference RC .10 .30
262 Jesse Wallin .05 .15
263 Zenith Komarniski .05 .15
264 Sean Blanchard RC .08 .25
265 Cory Sarich .05 .15
266 Mike Van Ryn .05 .15
267 Steve Begin .05 .15
268 Matt Cooke RC .10 .30
269 Daniel Corso .05 .15
270 Brett McLean .05 .15
271 J-P Dumont .05 .15
272 Jason Ward .05 .15
273 Brian Willsie RC .08 .25
274 Matt Bradley RC .05 .15
275 Olli Jokinen .08 .25
276 Teemu Elomo .05 .15
277 Timo Vertala .05 .15
278 Mika Noronen .08 .25
279 Pasi Petrilainen .05 .15
280 Timo Ahmaoja .05 .15
281 Eero Somervuori .05 .15
282 Maxim Afinogenov .25 .60
283 Maxim Balmochnykh .05 .15
284 Artem Chubarov .05 .15
285 Vitali Vishnevsky .05 .15
286 Denis Shvidki .05 .15
287 Dmitri Vlasenkov .05 .15
288 Magnus Nilsson RC .08 .25
289 Mikael Holmqvist RC .08 .25
290 Mattias Karlin RC .05 .15
291 Pierre Hedin .05 .15
292 Henrik Petre .05 .15
293 Johan Forsander .05 .15
294 Daniel Sedin .15 .40
295 Henrik Sedin .15 .40
296 Marcus Nilsson .05 .15
297 Paul Mara .05 .15
298 Brian Gionta RC .75 2.00
299 Chris Hajt RC .08 .25
300 Mike Mottau RC .12 .30
301 Jean-Marc Pelletier RC .12 .30
302 David Legwand .15 .40
303 Ty Jones .05 .15
304 Nikos Tselios .05 .15
305 Jesse Boulerice .05 .15
306 Jeff Farkas .05 .15
307 Toby Petersen .05 .15
308 Wayne Gretzky CL .10 .30
309 Patrick Roy CL .08 .25
310 Steve Yzerman CL .08 .25

1998-99 UD Choice Blow-Ups

COMPLETE SET (5) 6.00 15.00
1 Patrick Roy 2.00 5.00
2 Steve Yzerman 2.00 5.00
3 John LeClair .75 2.00
4 Martin Brodeur 1.25 3.00
5 Peter Forsberg 1.50 4.00

1998-99 UD Choice Draw Your Own Trading Card

DW1 Wayne Gretzky .20 .50

1998-99 UD Choice Hometeam Heroes

COMPLETE SET(20) 6.00 12.00
RW1 Steve Yzerman 2.00 5.00
RW2 Sergei Fedorov 1.25 3.00
RW3 Nicklas Lidstrom .40 1.00
RW4 Vyacheslav Kozlov .40 1.00
RW5 Chris Osgood .75 2.00
RW6 Darren McCarty .40 1.00
RW7 Brendan Shanahan 1.25 3.00
RW8 Igor Larionov .20 .50
RW9 Martin Lapointe .20 .50
RW10 Doug Brown .20 .50
RW11 Kirk Maltby .20 .50
RW12 Kris Draper .20 .50
RW13 Tomas Holmstrom .20 .50
RW14 Larry Murphy .20 .50
RW15 Slave Fetisov .20 .50
RW16 Anders Eriksson .20 .50
RW17 Brent Gilchrist .20 .50
RW18 Joey Kocur .20 .50
RW19 Mike Knuble .20 .50
RW20 Kevin Hodson .20 .50

1998-99 UD Choice Mini Bobbing Head

COMPLETE SET (30) 10.00 25.00
BH1 Wayne Gretzky 2.00 5.00
BH2 Keith Tkachuk .30 .75
BH3 Ray Bourque .50 1.25
BH4 Brett Hull .40 1.00
BH5 Jaromir Jagr .50 1.25
BH6 John LeClair .30 .75
BH7 Martin Brodeur .75 2.00
BH8 Eric Lindros .30 .75
BH9 Mark Messier .30 .75
BH10 John Vanbiesbrouck .25 .60
BH11 Paul Kariya .30 .75
BH12 Luc Robitaille .25 .60
BH13 Zigmund Palffy .25 .60
BH14 Peter Forsberg .75 2.00
BH15 Teemu Selanne .30 .75
BH16 Mike Modano .50 1.25
BH17 Mats Sundin .30 .75
BH18 Dominik Hasek .60 1.50
BH19 Joe Sakic .60 1.50
BH20 Rob Blake .25 .60
BH21 Patrick Roy 1.50 4.00
BH22 Sergei Samsonov .25 .60
BH23 Chris Chelios .30 .75
BH24 Brendan Shanahan .30 .75
BH25 Theo Fleury .25 .60
BH26 Ed Belfour .30 .75
BH27 Steve Yzerman 1.50 4.00
BH28 Saku Koivu .30 .75
BH29 Brian Leetch .30 .75
BH30 Pavel Bure .30 .75

1998-99 UD Choice Preview

COMPLETE SET (110) 6.00 15.00
1 Guy Hebert .20 .50
3 Josef Marha .07 .20
5 Travis Green .07 .20
7 Matt Cullen .07 .20
9 Antti Aalto .07 .20
11 Ted Donato .07 .20
13 Sergei Samsonov .20 .50
15 Ray Bourque .40 1.00
17 Cameron Mann .07 .20
19 Joe Thornton .40 1.00
21 Brian Holzinger .07 .20
23 Dominik Hasek .50 1.25
25 Erik Rasmussen .07 .20
27 Geoff Sanderson .07 .20
29 Derek Morris .07 .20
31 Valeri Bure .07 .20
33 Cory Stillman .07 .20
35 Jarome Iginla .30 .75
37 Jeff O'Neill .07 .20
39 Keith Primeau .07 .20
41 Glen Wesley .07 .20
43 Nelson Emerson .07 .20
45 Eric Daze .20 .50
47 Gary Suter .07 .20
49 Jeff Hackett .20 .50
51 Tony Amonte .20 .50
53 Eric Messier .07 .20
55 Claude Lemieux .07 .20
57 Adam Deadmarsh .07 .20
59 Joe Sakic .50 1.25
61 Jamie Langenbrunner .07 .20
63 Ed Belfour .25 .60
65 Derian Hatcher .07 .20
67 Daryl Sydor .20 .50
69 Mike Modano .40 1.00
71 Igor Larionov .07 .20
73 Steve Yzerman 1.25 3.00
75 Sergei Fedorov .40 1.00
77 Nicklas Lidstrom .25 .60
78 Slava Kozlov .07 .20
79 Dean McAmmond .07 .20
81 Curtis Joseph .25 .60
83 Boris Mironov .07 .20
85 Doug Weight .20 .50
87 Ray Whitney .07 .20
89 John Vanbiesbrouck .20 .50
90 Scott Mellanby .07 .20
91 Ed Jovanovksi .07 .20
93 Dino Ciccarelli .20 .50
95 Rob Blake .20 .50
97 Stephane Fiset .20 .50
99 Glen Murray .07 .20
101 Vladimir Tsyplakov .07 .20
103 Shayne Corson .07 .20
105 Saku Koivu .25 .60
107 Matt Higgins .07 .20
109 Mark Recchi .20 .50
111 Brian Savage .07 .20
113 Scott Stevens .20 .50
115 Bobby Holik .07 .20
117 Doug Gilmour .20 .50
119 Scott Niedermayer .07 .20
121 Zigmund Palffy .20 .50
123 Bryan Berard .07 .20
125 Kenny Jonsson .07 .20
127 Bryan Smolinski .07 .20
129 Brian Leetch .25 .60
131 Dan Cloutier .20 .50
133 Marc Savard .07 .20
135 Mike Richter .25 .60
137 Daniel Goneau .07 .20
139 Damian Rhodes .20 .50
141 Alexei Yashin .07 .20
143 Chris Phillips .07 .20
147 Sean Burke .20 .50
149 Rod Brind'Amour .20 .50
151 Paul Coffey .25 .60
153 John LeClair .25 .60
157 Teppo Numminen .07 .20
159 Oleg Tverdovsky .07 .20
161 Brad Isbister .07 .20
163 Daniel Briere .07 .20
165 Tom Barrasso .20 .50
167 Stu Barnes .07 .20
169 Ron Francis .07 .20
171 Robert Dome .07 .20
173 Patrick Marleau .25 .60
175 Owen Nolan .20 .50
177 Mike Vernon .20 .50
179 Andrei Zyuzin .07 .20
181 Marco Sturm .07 .20
183 Brett Hull .30 .75
185 Chris Pronger .20 .50
187 Jamie McLennan .20 .50
189 Jim Campbell .07 .20
190 Geoff Courtnall .07 .20
191 Daren Puppa .20 .50
193 Stephane Richer .20 .50
195 Alexander Selivanov .07 .20
197 Mikael Renberg .20 .50
199 Mike Johnson .07 .20
201 Sergei Berezin .20 .50
203 Mats Sundin .25 .60
205 Jyrki Lumme .07 .20
207 Garth Snow .20 .50
209 Dave Scatchard .07 .20
211 Mark Messier .25 .60
213 Peter Bondra .20 .50
215 Olaf Kolzig .07 .20
217 Adam Oates .20 .50
219 Calle Johansson .07 .20

1998-99 UD Choice Prime Choice Reserve

*VETS: 25X TO 60X BASIC CARDS
*ROOKIES: 25X TO 60X

1998-99 UD Choice Reserve

*VETS: 2.5X TO 6X BASIC CARDS
*ROOKIES: 1.5X TO 4X BASIC CARDS

1998-99 UD Choice StarQuest Blue

COMPLETE SET (30) 8.00 15.00
*GREEN: 1X TO 2.5X BLUE
*RED: 2.5X TO 6X BLUE
SQ1 Wayne Gretzky 2.50 6.00
SQ2 Pavel Bure .40 1.00
SQ3 Patrick Roy 1.00 2.50
SQ4 Dominik Hasek .60 1.50
SQ5 Teemu Selanne .75 2.00
SQ6 Sergei Samsonov .30 .75
SQ7 Brian Leetch .30 .75
SQ8 Saku Koivu .30 .75
SQ9 Brendan Shanahan .40 1.00
SQ10 Alexei Yashin .30 .75
SQ11 Joe Sakic .75 2.00
SQ12 Patrik Elias .40 1.00
SQ13 Theo Fleury .50 1.25
SQ14 Peter Bondra .40 1.00
SQ15 John LeClair .40 1.00
SQ16 Jaromir Jagr 1.25 3.00
SQ17 Ed Belfour .40 1.00
SQ18 Steve Yzerman 1.00 2.50
SQ19 Mats Sundin .40 1.00
SQ20 Peter Forsberg .75 2.00
SQ21 Ray Bourque .60 1.50
SQ22 Brett Hull .75 2.00
SQ23 Martin Brodeur 1.00 2.50
SQ24 Mike Modano .60 1.50
SQ25 Paul Kariya .40 1.00
SQ26 Tony Amonte .30 .75
SQ27 Mike Johnson .25 .60
SQ28 Eric Lindros .60 1.50
SQ29 Mark Messier .75 2.00
SQ30 Keith Tkachuk .40 1.00

1998-99 UD Choice StarQuest Gold

*GOLD/100: 400X TO 1000X BLUE
SQ1 Wayne Gretzky 4000.00 10000.00
SQ2 Pavel Bure 800.00 2000.00
SQ27 Mike Johnson 300.00 800.00

2004-05 UD Legendary Signatures

COMPLETE SET (100) 40.00 80.00
1 Al Iafrate .25 .60
2 Butch Goring .20 .50
3 Bernie Federko .20 .50
4 Bernie Geoffrion .30 .75
5 Bill Barber .25 .60
6 Bill White .20 .50
7 Bob Nystrom .20 .50
8 Bobby Clarke .50 1.25
9 Bobby Hull .60 1.50
10 Borje Salming .30 .75
11 Brad Marsh .20 .50
12 Brad Park .25 .60
13 Brian Bellows .20 .50
14 Brian Sutter .20 .50
15 Bryan Trottier .30 .75
16 Cam Neely .30 .75
17 Charlie Simmer .20 .50
18 Clark Gillies .30 .75
19 Craig Hartsburg .20 .50
20 Darryl Sittler .40 1.00
21 Billy Smith .25 .60
22 Dave Schultz .25 .60
23 Dave Taylor .25 .60
24 Tiger Williams .20 .50
25 Denis Potvin .30 .75
26 Dennis Hull .25 .60
27 Denis Savard .30 .75
28 Dino Ciccarelli .25 .60
29 Don Cherry .60 1.50
30 Don Marcotte .20 .50
31 Doug Gilmour .40 1.00
32 Doug Wilson .25 .60
33 Tony Twist .20 .50
34 Errol Thompson .20 .50
35 Frank Mahovlich .30 .75
36 Gerry Cheevers .30 .75
37 Gilbert Perreault .30 .75
38 Glenn Anderson .25 .60
39 Glenn Hall .30 .75
40 Gordie Howe 1.00 2.50
41 Grant Fuhr .50 1.25
42 Guy Lafleur .40 1.00
43 Guy Lapointe .20 .50
44 Henri Richard .30 .75
45 Ian Turnbull .20 .50
46 Jari Kurri .30 .75
47 Jean Beliveau .40 1.00
48 Brian Propp .25 .60
49 Johnny Bower .30 .75
50 Johnny Bucyk .30 .75
51 Ken Hodge .25 .60
52 Ken Morrow .20 .50
53 Lanny McDonald .25 .60
54 Gump Worsley .30 .75
55 Marcel Dionne .40 1.00
56 Mark Howe .30 .75
57 Mike Bossy .30 .75
58 Mike Ramsey .20 .50
59 Neal Broten .20 .50
60 Pat Stapleton .20 .50
61 Richard Brodeur .25 .60
62 Paul Coffey .30 .75
63 Paul Henderson .25 .60
64 Peter Mahovlich .20 .50
65 Phil Esposito .50 1.25
66 Randy Gregg .20 .50
67 Red Berenson .20 .50
68 Reggie Leach .25 .60
69 Rene Robert .20 .50
70 Rick Martin .20 .50
71 Wayne Babych .20 .50
72 Willi Plett .20 .50
73 Rod Seiling .20 .50
74 Ron Ellis .20 .50
75 Ron Duguay .25 .60
76 Rogie Vachon .30 .75
77 Stan Jonathan .25 .60
78 Stan Mikita .40 1.00
79 Steve Larmer .20 .50
80 Steve Shutt .25 .60
81 Stu Grimson .20 .50
82 Ted Lindsay .30 .75
83 Terry O'Reilly .25 .60
84 Tony Esposito .30 .75
85 Tony Tanti .20 .50
86 Vic Hadfield .20 .50
87 Wayne Cashman .20 .50
88 Wayne Gretzky 2.00 5.00
89 Rob McClanahan .20 .50
90 Yvan Cournoyer .30 .75
91 Chris Nilan .20 .50
92 Dave Christian .20 .50
93 Don Awrey .20 .50
94 J.P. Parise .20 .50
95 Jim Craig .30 .75
96 Keith Brown .20 .50
97 Ken Linseman .25 .60
98 Mark Tinordi .20 .50
99 Harold Snepsts .20 .50
100 Michel Goulet .20 .50

2004-05 UD Legendary Signatures AKA Autographs

AKABH B.Hull Golden Jet 75.00 125.00
AKADC D.Cherry Grapes 60.00 125.00
AKAYC Y.Cournoyer Road Runner 50.00 100.00
AKABO J.Bower China Wall 50.00 100.00
AKACN C.Nilan Knuckles 20.00 50.00
AKAJB J.Bucyk Chief 20.00 50.00
AKAHS D.Schultz Hammer 30.00 80.00
AKAMJ M.Johnson 30.00 80.00
AKAGE B.Geoffrion Boom 50.00 100.00
AKARD R.Brodeur King 20.00 50.00
AKAGC G.Cheevers Cheesy 25.00 60.00
AKAGH G.Hall Mr.Goalie 30.00 80.00
AKALW L.Worsley Gump 40.00 80.00
AKAGL G.Lafleur The Flower 40.00 80.00
AKAFM F.Mahovlich Big M 50.00 100.00
AKAAI A.Iafrate Wild Thing 25.00 60.00
AKATO T.O'Reilly Taz 40.00 80.00
AKASG S.Grimson Grim Reaper 20.00 50.00
AKATW T.Twist Twister 20.00 50.00
AKABN B.Nystrom Thor 20.00 50.00
AKAGH G.Howe Mr.Hockey 75.00 150.00
AKATE T.Esposito Tony O 40.00 80.00
AKADG D.Gilmour Killer 50.00 100.00
AKAJE J.Beliveau LeGros Bill 75.00 150.00

2004-05 UD Legendary Signatures Autographs

AI Al Iafrate 10.00 25.00
BB Bill Barber 5.00 12.00
BC Bobby Clarke/34 50.00 120.00
BE Brian Bellows 5.00 12.00
BF Bernie Federko 6.00 15.00
BG Butch Goring 6.00 15.00
BH Bobby Hull/81 50.00 120.00
BI Billy Smith 10.00 25.00
BM Brad Marsh 5.00 12.00
BN Bob Nystrom 5.00 12.00
BO Johnny Bower 8.00 20.00
BP Brian Propp 6.00 15.00
BR Brian Sutter 5.00 12.00
BS Borje Salming 10.00 25.00
BT Bryan Trottier 12.00 30.00
BW Bill White 5.00 12.00
CA Cam Neely 15.00 40.00
CG Clark Gillies 5.00 12.00
CH Craig Hartsburg 5.00 12.00
CI Dino Ciccarelli 15.00 40.00
CN Chris Nilan 6.00 15.00
CS Charlie Simmer 6.00 15.00
DC Don Cherry 20.00 50.00
DE Denis Savard 6.00 15.00
DG Doug Gilmour/84 40.00 100.00
DH Dennis Hull 6.00 15.00
DM Don Marcotte 5.00 12.00
DP Denis Potvin 6.00 15.00
DS Darryl Sittler/91 20.00 50.00
DT Dave Taylor 5.00 12.00
DU Ron Duguay 6.00 15.00
DV Dave Christian 5.00 12.00
DW Doug Wilson 5.00 12.00
ET Errol Thompson 5.00 12.00
FM Frank Mahovlich/41 125.00 250.00
GA Glenn Anderson 6.00 15.00
GC Gerry Cheevers 15.00 40.00
GE Bernie Geoffrion 12.00 30.00
GF Grant Fuhr 15.00 40.00
GH Gordie Howe 50.00 100.00
GL Guy Lafleur/25 300.00 500.00
GP Gilbert Perreault/34 100.00 200.00
HA Glenn Hall 12.50 30.00
HR Henri Richard 10.00 25.00
HS Dave Schultz 6.00 15.00
IT Ian Turnbull 5.00 12.00
JB Johnny Bucyk 8.00 20.00
JC Jim Craig 15.00 40.00
JE Jean Beliveau/98 60.00 120.00
JK Jari Kurri 8.00 20.00
JP J.P. Parise 6.00 15.00
KB Keith Brown 5.00 12.00
KH Ken Hodge 5.00 12.00
KL Ken Linseman 6.00 15.00
KM Ken Morrow 5.00 12.00
LA Guy Lapointe 8.00 20.00
LM Lanny McDonald 8.00 20.00
LW Gump Worsley 20.00 50.00
LY Rod Langway 12.00 30.00
MB Mike Bossy 20.00 50.00
MD Marcel Dionne 10.00 25.00
MG Michel Goulet 5.00 12.00
MH Mark Howe 5.00 12.00
MT Mark Tinordi 5.00 12.00
NB Neal Broten 6.00 15.00
PC Paul Coffey 12.50 30.00
PE Phil Esposito/37 100.00 250.00
PH Paul Henderson 20.00 50.00
PM Peter Mahovlich 6.00 15.00
PS Pat Stapleton 5.00 12.00
RA Mike Ramsey 5.00 12.00
RB Red Berenson 5.00 12.00
RD Richard Brodeur 8.00 20.00
RE Ron Ellis 6.00 15.00
RG Randy Gregg 5.00 12.00
RL Reggie Leach 6.00 15.00
RM Rick Martin 8.00 20.00
RR Rene Robert 6.00 15.00
RS Rod Seiling 5.00 12.00
RV Rogie Vachon 10.00 25.00
SC Steve Shutt 6.00 15.00
SG Stu Grimson 5.00 12.00
SJ Stan Jonathan 6.00 15.00
SL Steve Larmer 5.00 12.00
SM Stan Mikita/91 20.00 50.00
SN Harold Snepsts 5.00 12.00
SS Stan Smyl 5.00 12.00
TE Tony Esposito/62 40.00 100.00
TI Tiger Williams 6.00 15.00
TL Ted Lindsay 12.00 30.00
TO Terry O'Reilly/96 25.00 60.00
TT Tony Tanti 5.00 12.00
TW Tony Twist 5.00 12.00
VH Vic Hadfield 5.00 12.00
VP Brad Park 6.00 15.00
WB Wayne Babych 5.00 12.00
WC Wayne Cashman 6.00 15.00
WG Wayne Gretzky 150.00 400.00
WP Willi Plett 5.00 12.00
YC Yvan Cournoyer 12.00 30.00

2004-05 UD Legendary Signatures Buybacks

8 B.Smith Vin Jsy/38 20.00 50.00
52 D.Polvin UD Leg Miles/22 25.00 50.00
75 G.Cheevers Vin Jsy/27
81 G.Perreault UD Leg Miles/21
159 N.Broten Leg Miles/37 25.00 50.00
178 P.Esposito Vin Jsy/35
179 R.Vachon Vin Jsy/30 40.00 80.00
180 S.Shutt UD Leg Miles/20 40.00 100.00
181 S.Shutt Vin SoH/35 40.00 80.00

2004-05 UD Legendary Signatures HOF Inks

HOFGH Gordie Howe/72 125.00 250.00
HOFBC Bobby Clarke/87 25.00 50.00
HOFMD Marcel Dionne/92 20.00 50.00
HOFHR Henri Richard/79 20.00 50.00
HOFBO Johnny Bower/76 20.00 50.00
HOFGF Grant Fuhr/103 15.00 40.00
HOFDS Darryl Sittler/89 20.00 50.00
HOFTE Tony Esposito/88 20.00 50.00
HOFCG Clarke Gillies/102 15.00 40.00
HOFJB Johnny Bucyk/81 15.00 40.00
HOFGP Gilbert Perreault/90 15.00 40.00
HOFHA Glenn Hall/75 30.00 60.00
HOFMB Mike Bossy/91 15.00 40.00
HOFBI Billy Smith/93 15.00 40.00

2004-05 UD Legendary Signatures Linemates

BBBCRL Barber/Clarke/Leach 75.00 150.00
BENBCI Bellows/Brotn/Cicrlli 40.00 100.00
BRBFWB Sutter/Fedrko/Babych 40.00 100.00
CGBTMB Gillies/Trottier/Bossy 75.00 200.00
CSMDDT Simmer/Dionne/Taylor 75.00 175.00
ETDSLM Thmpsn/Sittlr/McDnld 50.00 125.00
GAWGJK Anderson/Gretzky/Kurri 300.00 800.00
RMGPRR Martin/Perreault/Robert 75.00 200.00
SCPMGL Shutt/P.Mahov/Laflr 40.00 100.00
SJDMTO Jonthn/Marcte/O'Rlly 60.00 120.00
SLDEMG Larmer/Savard/Goulet 40.00 100.00
TISSTT Williams/Smyl/Tanti 40.00 100.00
WCPEKH Cshmn/P.Espo/Hdge 75.00 200.00

2004-05 UD Legendary Signatures Miracle Men

COMPLETE SET (18) 12.00 30.00
USA1 Mike Eruzione 1.50 4.00
USA2 Jim Craig 1.25 3.00
USA3 Rob McClanahan .50 1.25
USA4 Buzz Schneider .50 1.25
USA5 Mark Johnson .75 2.00
USA6 Neal Broten .60 1.50
USA7 Mark Pavelich .50 1.25
USA8 Dave Christian .60 1.50
USA9 Mike Ramsey .50 1.25
USA10 Ken Morrow .60 1.50
USA11 Steve Christoff .50 1.25
USA12 Bill Baker .50 1.25
USA13 Marc Wells .50 1.25
USA14 John Harrington .50 1.25
USA15 Dave Silk .50 1.25
USA16 Steve Janaszak .50 1.25
USA17 Eric Strobel .50 1.25
USA18 Bob Suter .50 1.25

2004-05 UD Legendary Signatures Miracle Men Autographs

USARO Rob McClanahan 20.00 50.00
USASI Dave Silk 20.00 50.00
USAMP Mark Pavelich 40.00 100.00
USAME Mike Eruzione 60.00 150.00
USAJC Jim Craig/73 250.00 600.00
USANB Neal Broten/73 800.00 2000.00
USARA Mike Ramsey/97 200.00 500.00
USADV Dave Christian 80.00 200.00
USAJA Steve Janaszak 15.00 40.00
USAKM Ken Morrow 30.00 80.00
USABZ Buzz Schneider 20.00 50.00
USAES Eric Strobel 40.00 100.00
USAOB Bob Suter 100.00 250.00
USAST Steve Christoff 15.00 40.00
USABI Bill Baker 40.00 100.00
USAJH John Harrington 30.00 80.00
USAMW Marc Wells 25.00 60.00
USAMJ Mark Johnson 40.00 100.00

2004-05 UD Legendary Signatures Rearguard Retrospectives

BMMH B.Marsh/M.Howe 12.50 30.00
BSIT B.Salming/I.Turnbull 15.00 40.00
CHMT C.Hartsburg/M.Tinordi 10.00 25.00
DPKM D.Potvin/K.Morrow 20.00 50.00
DWKB D.Wilson/K.Brown 12.50 30.00
PCRG P.Coffey/R.Gregg 20.00 50.00

2004-05 UD Legendary Signatures Summit Stars

COMPLETE SET (20) 10.00 20.00
CDN1 Phil Esposito 1.00 2.50
CDN2 Paul Henderson .75 2.00
CDN3 Bobby Clarke .60 1.50
CDN4 Yvan Cournoyer .60 1.50
CDN5 Brad Park .50 1.25
CDN6 Dennis Hull .50 1.25
CDN7 J.P. Parise .50 1.25

CDN8 Ron Ellis .50 1.25
CDN9 Gilbert Perreault .60 1.50
CDN10 Frank Mahovlich .60 1.50
CDN11 Peter Mahovlich .50 1.25
CDN12 Bill White .50 1.25
CDN13 Wayne Cashman .50 1.25
CDN14 Stan Mikita .60 1.50
CDN15 Red Berenson .50 1.25
CDN16 Don Awrey .50 1.25
CDN17 Vic Hadfield .50 1.25
CDN18 Rod Seiling .50 1.25
CDN19 Pat Stapleton .50 1.25
CDN20 Tony Esposito .60 1.50

2004-05 UD Legendary Signatures Summit Stars Autographs

CDNBC Bobby Clarke/73 75.00 150.00
CDNPH Paul Henderson 25.00 40.00
CDNTE Tony Esposito/24 250.00 500.00
CDNFM Frank Mahovlich/48 100.00 200.00
CDNGP Gilbert Perreault/48 60.00 150.00
CDNPE Phil Esposito/48 200.00 350.00
CDNSM Stan Mikita/97 50.00 125.00
CDNBP Brad Park 12.50 30.00
CDNYC Yvan Cournoyer 15.00 40.00
CDNJP J.P. Parise 8.00 20.00
CDNDH Dennis Hull 8.00 20.00
CDNRB Red Berenson 8.00 20.00
CDNPM Pete Mahovlich 8.00 20.00
CDNRS Rod Seiling 8.00 20.00
CDNPS Pat Stapleton 8.00 20.00
CDNDA Don Awrey 8.00 20.00
CDNRE Ron Ellis 8.00 20.00
CDNBW Bill White 8.00 20.00
CDNWC Wayne Cashman 8.00 20.00
CDNVH Vic Hadfield 8.00 20.00

2004-05 UD Legends Classics

COMPLETE SET (100) 15.00 40.00
1 Al Iafrate .25 .60
2 Andy Bathgate .30 .75
3 Bernie Geoffrion .30 .75
4 Bill Barber .25 .60
5 Bob Cole .20 .50
6 Bob Nystrom .20 .50
7 Bobby Clarke .50 1.25
8 Bobby Hull .60 1.50
9 Brad Park .25 .60
10 Bryan Trottier .30 .75
11 Butch Goring .20 .50
12 Cam Neely .30 .75
13 Clark Gillies .30 .75
14 Tiger Williams .20 .50
15 Dave Schultz .25 .60
16 Dave Taylor .25 .60
17 Derek Sanderson .30 .75
18 Dickie Moore .20 .50
19 Don Cherry .60 1.50
20 Doug Wilson .25 .60
21 Frank Mahovlich .30 .75
22 Fred Cusick .20 .50
23 Gerry Cheevers .30 .75
24 Gilbert Perreault .30 .75
25 Glenn Anderson .25 .60
26 Glenn Hall .30 .75
27 Gordie Howe 1.00 2.50
28 Grant Fuhr .50 1.25
29 Guy Lafleur .40 1.00
30 Jari Kurri .30 .75
31 Jean Beliveau .40 1.00
32 Johnny Bower .30 .75
33 Johnny Bucyk .30 .75
34 Ken Hodge .25 .60
35 Ken Morrow .20 .50
36 Lanny McDonald .25 .60
37 Larry Murphy .25 .60
38 Gump Worsley .30 .75
39 Marcel Dionne .40 1.00
40 Mike Bossy .30 .75
41 Patrick Roy .75 2.00
42 Paul Coffey .30 .75
43 Paul Henderson .25 .60
44 Phil Esposito .50 1.25
45 Phil Esposito .50 1.25
46 Red Kelly .30 .75
47 Reggie Leach .25 .60
48 Rene Robert .20 .50
49 Rick Martin .20 .50
50 Stan Mikita .40 1.00
51 Ted Lindsay .30 .75
52 Tony Esposito .30 .75
53 Wayne Cashman .20 .50
54 Wayne Gretzky 2.00 5.00
55 Darryl Sittler .40 1.00
56 Gordie Howe 1.00 2.50
57 Gordie Howe 1.00 2.50
58 Paul Henderson .25 .60
59 Darryl Sittler .40 1.00
60 Mike Bossy .30 .75
61 Tiger Williams .20 .50
62 Patrick Roy .75 2.00
63 Paul Coffey .30 .75
64 Marcel Dionne .40 1.00
65 Mike Bossy .30 .75
66 Bobby Hull .60 1.50
67 Jari Kurri .30 .75
68 Bryan Trottier .30 .75
69 Phil Esposito .50 1.25
70 Bobby Clarke .50 1.25
71 Jean Beliveau .40 1.00
72 Stan Mikita .40 1.00
73 Gilbert Perreault .30 .75
74 Glenn Hall .30 .75
75 Guy Lafleur .40 1.00
76 Ken Morrow .20 .50
77 Tony Esposito .30 .75
78 Johnny Bower .30 .75
79 Wayne Gretzky 2.00 5.00
80 Wayne Gretzky 2.00 5.00
81 Gordie Howe 1.00 2.50
82 Wayne Gretzky 2.00 5.00
83 Bobby Hull .60 1.50
84 Bobby Clarke .50 1.25
85 Gilbert Perreault .30 .75
86 Darryl Sittler .40 1.00
87 Guy Lafleur .40 1.00
88 Glenn Hall .30 .75
89 Andy Bathgate .30 .75
90 Red Kelly .30 .75
91 Tony Esposito .30 .75
92 Jean Beliveau .40 1.00
93 Grant Fuhr .50 1.25
94 Frank Mahovlich .30 .75
95 Gerry Cheevers .30 .75
96 Phil Esposito .50 1.25
97 Bryan Trottier .30 .75
98 Dickie Moore .20 .50
99 Stan Mikita .40 1.00
100 Marcel Dionne .40 1.00

2004-05 UD Legends Classics Gold

*GOLD/25: 10X TO 25X BASIC CARDS

2004-05 UD Legends Classics Silver

*SILVER/75: 5X TO 12X BASIC CARDS

2004-05 UD Legends Classics Jacket Redemptions

JK1 Boston Bruins
JK2 Chicago Blackhawks 150.00 300.00
JK3 Detroit Red Wings
JK4 Montreal Canadiens 125.00 250.00
JK5 Toronto Maple Leafs 150.00 300.00

2004-05 UD Legends Classics Jersey Redemptions

JY1 Henri Richard 60.00 150.00
JY2 Jean Beliveau 150.00 300.00
JY3 Maurice Richard 150.00 300.00
JY4 Dickie Moore
JY5 Doug Harvey 60.00 150.00
JY6 Jacques Plante 125.00 250.00
JY7 Bernie Geoffrion 60.00 150.00
JY8 Frank Mahovlich
JY9 T.Sawchuk TOR 175.00 350.00
JY10 Tim Horton 150.00 300.00
JY11 Johnny Bower 60.00 150.00
JY12 Red Kelly 75.00 150.00
JY13 Eddie Shack 60.00 150.00
JY14 Dave Keon 60.00 150.00
JY15 Marcel Pronovost 60.00 150.00
JY16 W.Gretzky EDM 300.00 700.00
JY17 Stan Mikita
JY18 Bobby Orr 250.00 500.00
JY19 Gordie Howe 250.00 500.00
JY20 T.Sawchuk DET 150.00 300.00
JY21 Bobby Clarke 125.00 250.00
JY22 Tony Esposito
JY23 P.Esposito BOS
JY24 P.Esposito NYR
JY25 Guy Lafleur 60.00 150.00
JY26 W.Gretzky AS 350.00 700.00
JY27 Bill Barber
JY28 Tiger Williams
JY29 Dave Schultz 60.00 150.00
JY30 Grant Fuhr 60.00 150.00
JY31 Reggie Leach

2004-05 UD Legends Classics Pennants

P1 The Dynamite Line 20.00 50.00
P2 The Kid Line 12.50 30.00
P3 The Punch Line 10.00 25.00
P4 The Pony Line 12.50 30.00
P5 The Kraut Line 10.00 25.00
P6 The Production Line 20.00 50.00
P7 The Uke Line 15.00 40.00
P8 The LCB Line 10.00 25.00
P9 The Big Three 10.00 25.00
P10 The GAG Line 12.50 30.00
P11 The Triple Crown Line
P12 The French Connection 12.50 30.00
P13 Kansas City Scouts 30.00 80.00
P14 California Golden Seals 20.00 50.00
P15 Colorado Rockies 12.50 30.00
P16 Atlanta Flames 6.00 15.00
P17 Hartford Whalers 15.00 40.00
P18 Quebec Nordiques 10.00 25.00
P19 Winnipeg Jets 15.00 40.00
P20 Boston Bruins 10.00 25.00
P21 NY Rangers 6.00 15.00
P22 Chicago Blackhawks 6.00 15.00
P23 Detroit Red Wings 10.00 25.00
P24 Toronto Maple Leafs 8.00 20.00
P25 Montreal Canadiens 6.00 15.00
P26 Philadelphia Flyers 6.00 15.00
P27 LA Kings 6.00 15.00
P28 St.Louis Blues 8.00 20.00
P29 Minnesota North Stars 10.00 25.00
P30 Pittsburgh Penguins 6.00 15.00
P31 Oakland Seals 6.00 15.00
P32 Detroit Cougars 6.00 15.00
P33 Toronto St.Pats 6.00 15.00

2004-05 UD Legends Classics Signature Moments

M1 Wayne Gretzky 200.00 500.00
M2 Gordie Howe 75.00 150.00
M3 Don Cherry 25.00 50.00
M4 Red Kelly 10.00 25.00
M5 Dickie Moore 12.00 30.00
M6 Andy Bathgate 10.00 25.00
M7 Terry O'Reilly 12.50 30.00
M8 Wayne Cashman 12.00 30.00
M9 Tony Esposito 15.00 40.00
M10 Ted Lindsay 15.00 40.00
M11 Stan Mikita 10.00 25.00
M12 Reggie Leach 8.00 20.00
M13 Rene Robert 8.00 20.00
M14 Rick Martin 10.00 25.00
M15 Phil Esposito 20.00 50.00
M16 Paul Henderson 8.00 20.00
M17 Paul Coffey 12.50 30.00
M18 Mike Bossy 15.00 40.00
M19 Lanny McDonald 12.50 30.00
M20 Gump Worsley 10.00 25.00
M21 Marcel Dionne 10.00 25.00
M22 Ken Morrow 6.00 15.00
M23 Ken Hodge 12.00 30.00
M24 Johnny Bucyk 10.00 25.00
M25 Johnny Bower 15.00 30.00
M26 Jari Kurri 12.50 30.00
M27 Cam Neely 15.00 40.00
M28 Jean Beliveau 30.00 60.00
M29 Guy Lafleur 20.00 50.00
M30 Gerry Cheevers 12.50 30.00
M31 Gilbert Perreault 12.50 30.00
M32 Glenn Anderson 8.00 20.00
M33 Glenn Hall 10.00 25.00
M34 Dave Taylor 6.00 15.00
M35 Grant Fuhr 20.00 50.00
M36 Frank Mahovlich 15.00 40.00
M37 Don Cherry 20.00 50.00
M38 Doug Wilson 8.00 20.00
M39 Dave Schultz 8.00 20.00
M40 Tiger Williams 10.00 25.00
M41 Dave Taylor 6.00 15.00
M42 Clark Gillies 10.00 25.00
M43 Bryan Trottier 12.50 30.00
M44 Butch Goring 6.00 15.00
M45 Bernie Geoffrion 15.00 40.00
M46 Al Iafrate 12.50 30.00
M47 Bill Barber 10.00 25.00
M48 Bob Nystrom 8.00 20.00
M49 Bobby Clarke 15.00 40.00
M50 Bobby Hull 30.00 60.00
M51 Brad Park 8.00 20.00
M52 Patrick Roy 40.00 100.00
M53 Ray Bourque 30.00 60.00
M54 Derek Sanderson 15.00 40.00
M55 Reggie Leach 8.00 20.00
M56 Jari Kurri 12.50 30.00
M57 Marcel Dionne 10.00 25.00
M58 Ken Hodge 12.00 30.00
M59 Dave Schultz 8.00 20.00
M60 Brad Park 8.00 20.00
M61 Gilbert Perreault 15.00 40.00
M62 Ken Morrow 6.00 15.00
M63 Gerry Cheevers 15.00 40.00
M64 Ted Lindsay 10.00 25.00
M65 Dave Taylor 6.00 15.00
M66 Cam Neely 20.00 50.00
M67 Johnny Bucyk 12.00 30.00
M68 Larry Murphy 8.00 20.00
M69 Fred Cusick 8.00 20.00
M70 Bob Cole 8.00 20.00

2004-05 UD Legends Classics Signatures

CS1 Wayne Gretzky XSP 200.00 500.00
CS2 Gordie Howe SSP 75.00 150.00
CS3 Don Cherry 15.00 40.00
CS4 Red Kelly 10.00 25.00
CS5 Dickie Moore 12.00 30.00
CS6 Andy Bathgate 10.00 25.00
CS7 Terry O'Reilly 15.00 40.00
CS8 Wayne Cashman 8.00 20.00
CS9 Tony Esposito XSP 40.00 100.00
CS10 Ted Lindsay XSP 20.00 50.00
CS11 Stan Mikita XSP 25.00 60.00
CS12 Reggie Leach 6.00 15.00
CS13 Rene Robert 8.00 20.00
CS14 Rick Martin 8.00 20.00
CS15 Phil Esposito XSP 75.00 125.00
CS16 Paul Henderson 10.00 25.00
CS17 Paul Coffey SSP 20.00 50.00
CS18 Mike Bossy 10.00 25.00
CS19 Lanny McDonald SP 12.50 30.00
CS20 Gump Worsley 15.00 40.00
CS21 Marcel Dionne SSP 15.00 40.00
CS22 Ken Morrow 6.00 15.00
CS23 Ken Hodge 6.00 15.00
CS24 Johnny Bucyk SP 10.00 25.00
CS25 Johnny Bower 10.00 25.00
CS26 Jari Kurri 10.00 25.00
CS27 Cam Neely SP 15.00 40.00
CS28 Jean Beliveau SSP 50.00 100.00
CS29 Guy Lafleur XSP 40.00 100.00
CS30 Gerry Cheevers 12.50 30.00
CS31 Gilbert Perreault XSP 30.00 80.00
CS32 Glenn Anderson 6.00 15.00
CS33 Glenn Hall 10.00 25.00
CS34 Grant Fuhr XSP 25.00 60.00
CS35 Frank Mahovlich XSP 25.00 60.00
CS36 Doug Wilson 6.00 15.00
CS37 Dave Schultz 8.00 20.00
CS38 Tiger Williams 8.00 20.00
CS39 Dave Taylor 6.00 15.00
CS40 Clark Gillies 6.00 15.00
CS41 Bryan Trottier/56* 15.00 40.00
CS42 Butch Goring 6.00 15.00
CS43 Bernie Geoffrion SP 25.00 60.00
CS44 Al Iafrate 6.00 15.00
CS45 Bill Barber 6.00 15.00
CS46 Bob Nystrom 6.00 15.00
CS47 Bobby Clarke SP 20.00 50.00
CS48 Bobby Hull XSP 50.00 100.00
CS49 Brad Park 10.00 25.00
CS50 Patrick Roy SSP 50.00 100.00
CS51 Ray Bourque/25 150.00 400.00
CS52 Derek Sanderson 12.00 30.00
CS53 Fred Cusick 6.00 15.00
CS54 Bob Cole 6.00 15.00
CS55 Larry Murphy 8.00 20.00
DC1 T.Esposito/P.Esposito 50.00 100.00
DC2 J.Beliveau/G.Lafleur 40.00 100.00
DC3 S.Mikita/B.Hull 30.00 80.00
DC4 R.Bourque/C.Neely 30.00 80.00
DC5 M.Bossy/B.Trottier 30.00 80.00
DC6 D.Sanderson/J.Bucyk 25.00 60.00
DC7 R.Robert/G.Perreault 25.00 60.00
DC8 C.Neely/J.Bucyk 25.00 60.00
DC9 J.Beliveau/D.Moore 40.00 100.00
DC10 B.Park/R.Bourque 40.00 100.00
DC11 D.Sanderson/P.Esposito 25.00 60.00
DC12 T.Esposito/G.Hall 40.00 100.00
DC13 M.Dionne/G.Lafleur 30.00 80.00
DC14 G.Howe/B.Hull 100.00 250.00
DC15 D.Schultz/D.Williams 15.00 40.00
DC16 L.Murphy/D.Taylor 20.00 50.00
DC17 M.Dionne/D.Taylor 15.00 40.00
DC18 B.Clarke/G.Perreault 40.00 100.00
DC19 F.Cusick/B.Cole 15.00 40.00
DC20 B.Clarke/B.Barber 30.00 80.00
DC21 A.Bathgate/J.Bower 40.00 100.00
DC22 S.Mikita/D.Wilson 25.00 60.00
TC1 T.Espo/Worsley/Roy 125.00 250.00
TC2 Mahov/Hndrsn/Bower 100.00 250.00
TC3 Chvers/P.Espo/Sandr 100.00 200.00
TC4 Hall/T.Espo/Cheevers 100.00 200.00
TC5 Gillies/Trottier/Bossy 60.00 150.00
TC6 Barber/Clarke/Leach 75.00 200.00
TC7 Geoffrion/Howe/Beliveau 250.00 500.00
TC8 Hodge/Park/P.Espo 30.00 80.00
TC9 Coffey/Murphy/Bourque 60.00 150.00
TC10 Martin/Perreault/Robert 60.00 150.00
TC11 Anderson/Gretzky/Kurri 400.00 1000.00
TC12 Worsley/Beliveau/Moore 60.00 150.00
TC13 Howe/Kelly/Lindsay 200.00 400.00
TC14 Gretzky/Dionne/Lafleur 500.00 1200.00
TC15 T.Esposito/Mikita/Wilson 75.00 200.00
QC1 Roy/T.Espo /Hall/Chvers
QC2 Howe/Lafleur/Bossy/Kurri
QC3 Hull/Mahvl/Lindsay/Bucyk
QC4 Gretz/Trottier/Perrlt/Dionne
QC5 P.Espo/O'Rlly/Neely/Cshmn EX
QC6 Howe/Clarke/Neely/Gillies

2001-02 UD Mask Collection

COMP.SET w/o SP's (100) 15.00 40.00
1 Paul Kariya .30 .75
2 Jeff Friesen .20 .50
3 Matt Cullen .20 .50
4 Dany Heatley .25 .60
5 Lubos Bartecko .20 .50
6 Tony Hrkac .20 .50
7 Sergei Samsonov .25 .60
8 Joe Thornton .50 1.25
9 Bill Guerin .30 .75
10 P.J. Stock .20 .50
11 Stu Barnes .25 .60
12 Tim Connolly .20 .50
13 Jarome Iginla .40 1.00
14 Craig Conroy .20 .50
15 Sami Kapanen .20 .50
16 Ron Francis .40 1.00
17 Tony Amonte .25 .60
18 Mark Bell .20 .50
19 Steve Sullivan .20 .50
20 Chris Drury .25 .60
21 Milan Hejduk .25 .60
22 Joe Sakic .60 1.50
23 Rob Blake .30 .75
24 Alex Tanguay .25 .60
25 Mike Sillinger .20 .50
26 Ray Whitney .20 .50
27 Rostislav Klesla .20 .50
28 Pierre Turgeon .25 .60
29 Jere Lehtinen .25 .60
30 Mike Modano .50 1.25
31 Sergei Zubov .25 .60
32 Brendan Shanahan .30 .75
33 Steve Yzerman .75 2.00
34 Brett Hull .60 1.50
35 Sergei Fedorov .50 1.25
36 Mike Comrie .25 .60
37 Ryan Smyth .25 .60
38 Anson Carter .25 .60
39 Viktor Kozlov .20 .50
40 Marcus Nilsson .20 .50
41 Sandis Ozolinsh .20 .50
42 Adam Deadmarsh .20 .50
43 Jason Allison .25 .60
44 Zigmund Palffy .30 .75
45 Andrew Brunette .20 .50
46 Marian Gaborik .30 .75
47 Jim Dowd .20 .50
48 Yanic Perreault .20 .50
49 Sergei Berezin .20 .50
50 Donald Audette .20 .50
51 Francois Bouillon .20 .50
52 Karlis Skrastins .20 .50
53 David Legwand .25 .60
54 Scott Hartnell .20 .50
55 Bobby Holik .20 .50
56 Joe Nieuwendyk .25 .60
57 Patrik Elias .30 .75
58 Brian Rafalski .20 .50
59 Mark Parrish .20 .50
60 Michael Peca .25 .60
61 Alexei Yashin .25 .60
62 Petr Nedved .25 .60
63 Theo Fleury .40 1.00
64 Pavel Bure .30 .75
65 Eric Lindros .50 1.25
66 Martin Havlat .25 .60
67 Daniel Alfredsson .30 .75
68 Marian Hossa .30 .75
69 Radek Bonk .20 .50
70 Simon Gagne .30 .75
71 John LeClair .30 .75
72 Jeremy Roenick .50 1.25
73 Mark Recchi .40 1.00
74 Michal Handzus .20 .50
75 Claude Lemieux .25 .60
76 Shane Doan .25 .60
77 Jamie Pushor .20 .50
78 Alexei Kovalev .25 .60
79 Mario Lemieux 1.25 3.00
80 Vincent Damphousse .25 .60
81 Owen Nolan .30 .75
82 Teemu Selanne .60 1.50
83 Keith Tkachuk .30 .75
84 Chris Pronger .30 .75
85 Doug Weight .30 .75
86 Pavol Demitra .40 1.00
87 Fredrik Modin .20 .50
88 Brad Richards .30 .75
89 Vincent Lecavalier .30 .75
90 Darcy Tucker .20 .50
91 Alexander Mogilny .25 .60
92 Mats Sundin .30 .75
93 Brendan Morrison .25 .60
94 Todd Bertuzzi .30 .75
95 Markus Naslund .30 .75
96 Ed Jovanovski .25 .60
97 Drake Berehowsky .20 .50
98 Ulf Dahlen .20 .50
99 Peter Bondra .30 .75
100 Jaromir Jagr 1.00 2.50
101 Jean-Sebastien Giguere MTN 1.00 2.50
102 Milan Hnilicka MTN .75 2.00
103 Byron Dafoe MTN .75 2.00
104 Martin Biron MTN .75 2.00
105 Roman Turek MTN .75 2.00
106 Arturs Irbe MTN .75 2.00
107 Jocelyn Thibault MTN .75 2.00
108 Patrick Roy MTN 2.50 6.00
109 Ron Tugnutt MTN .75 2.00
110 Ed Belfour MTN 1.00 2.50
111 Dominik Hasek MTN 1.50 4.00
112 Tommy Salo MTN .75 2.00
113 Roberto Luongo MTN 1.50 4.00
114 Felix Potvin MTN 1.50 4.00
115 Manny Fernandez MTN .60 1.50
116 Jose Theodore MTN 1.00 2.50
117 Mike Dunham MTN .75 2.00
118 Martin Brodeur MTN 2.50 6.00
119 Chris Osgood MTN 1.00 2.50
120 Mike Richter MTN 1.00 2.50
121 Patrick Lalime MTN .75 2.00
122 Roman Cechmanek MTN .75 2.00
123 Sean Burke MTN .60 1.50
124 Johan Hedberg MTN .75 2.00
125 Evgeni Nabokov MTN .75 2.00
126 Brent Johnson MTN .75 2.00
127 Nikolai Khabibulin MTN 1.00 2.50
128 Curtis Joseph MTN 1.25 3.00
129 Dan Cloutier MTN .75 2.00
130 Olaf Kolzig MTN 1.00 2.50
131 Frederic Cassivi RC 1.50 4.00
132 Ilya Kovalchuk RC 8.00 20.00
133 Pasi Nurminen RC 1.50 4.00
134 Mark Hartigan RC 1.50 4.00
135 Francis Lessard RC 1.50 4.00
136 Ivan Huml RC 1.50 4.00
137 Chris Kelleher RC 1.50 4.00
138 Erik Cole RC 3.00 8.00
139 Mike Peluso RC 1.50 4.00
140 Vaclav Nedorost RC 1.50 4.00
141 Jeff Daw RC 1.50 4.00
142 Andrej Nedorost RC 1.50 4.00
143 Sean Avery RC 1.50 4.00
144 Pavel Datsyuk RC 20.00 50.00
145 Stephen Weiss RC 4.00 10.00
146 Niklas Hagman RC 2.00 5.00
147 Kristian Huselius RC 2.50 6.00
148 Lukas Krajicek RC 1.50 4.00
149 Tony Virta RC 1.50 4.00
150 Olivier Michaud RC 2.50 6.00
151 Marcel Hossa RC 2.50 6.00
152 Martin Erat RC 2.00 5.00
153 Christian Berglund RC 2.00 5.00
154 Raffi Torres RC 2.50 6.00
155 Dan Blackburn RC 2.00 5.00
156 Martin Prusek RC 1.50 4.00
157 Chris Bala RC 1.50 4.00
158 Josh Langfeld RC 1.50 4.00
159 Jiri Dopita RC 1.50 4.00
160 Neil Little RC 1.50 4.00
161 Guillaume Lefebvre RC 1.50 4.00
162 Krys Kolanos RC 1.50 4.00
163 Branko Radivojevic RC 1.50 4.00
164 Shane Endicott RC 1.50 4.00
165 Hannes Hyvonen RC 1.50 4.00
166 Jeff Jillson RC 1.50 4.00
167 Nikita Alexeev RC 1.50 4.00
168 Gaetan Royer RC 1.50 4.00
169 Karel Pilar RC 1.50 4.00
170 Brian Sutherby RC 1.50 4.00
171 Byron Dafoe UW 1.50 4.00
172 Martin Biron UW 1.50 4.00
173 Roman Turek UW 1.50 4.00
174 Arturs Irbe UW 1.50 4.00
175 Patrick Roy UW 5.00 12.00
176 Ed Belfour UW 2.00 5.00
177 Dominik Hasek UW 3.00 8.00
178 Tommy Salo UW 1.50 4.00
179 Felix Potvin UW 3.00 8.00
180 Mike Dunham UW 1.50 4.00
181 Martin Brodeur UW 5.00 12.00
182 Chris Osgood UW 2.00 5.00
183 Mike Richter UW 2.00 5.00
184 Roman Cechmanek UW 1.50 4.00
185 Sean Burke UW 1.25 3.00
186 Johan Hedberg UW 1.50 4.00
187 Evgeni Nabokov UW 1.50 4.00
188 Nikolai Khabibulin UW 2.00 5.00
189 Curtis Joseph UW 2.50 6.00
190 Olaf Kolzig UW 2.00 5.00

2001-02 UD Mask Collection Gold

*1-100 VETS/50: 5X TO 12X BASIC CARDS
*101-130 MTN/50: 2.5X TO 6X BASIC MTN
*131-170 ROOKIE/50: 1.5X TO 4X BASIC RC
*171-190 UW/50: 1.2X TO 3X BASIC UW

2001-02 UD Mask Collection Dual Jerseys

MBBC B.Boucher/R.Cechmanek 10.00 25.00
MBBT M.Brodeur/J.Theodore 15.00 40.00
MBCJ Curtis Joseph Dual 10.00 25.00
MBFP Felix Potvin Dual 10.00 25.00
MBPR Patrick Roy Dual 40.00 80.00
MBRD M.Richter/M.Dunham 10.00 25.00
MBTB J.Thibault/E.Belfour 10.00 25.00
PMAD T.Amonte/M.Dunham 10.00 25.00
PMAJ J.Arnott/C.Joseph 10.00 25.00
PMFT S.Fedorov/J.Thibault 10.00 25.00
PMGB S.Gagne/M.Biron 10.00 25.00
PMMJ M.Modano/B.Johnson 10.00 25.00
PMSB J.Sakic/M.Brodeur 12.50 30.00
PMYR S.Yzerman/P.Roy 25.00 60.00

2001-02 UD Mask Collection Gloves

GGAM Alexander Mogilny 8.00 20.00
GGBD Byron Dafoe 8.00 20.00
GGBH Brett Hull 12.00 30.00
GGBS Brendan Shanahan 10.00 25.00
GGCD Chris Drury 8.00 20.00
GGEB Ed Belfour 10.00 25.00
GGJR Jeremy Roenick 12.00 30.00
GGMM Mark Messier 15.00 40.00
GGRB Ray Bourque 12.00 30.00
GGRD Rick DiPietro 10.00 25.00
GGSF Sergei Fedorov 10.00 25.00
GGSK Sami Kapanen 8.00 20.00
GGTK Keith Tkachuk 10.00 25.00

2001-02 UD Mask Collection Goalie Jerseys

MMBB Brian Boucher MM 4.00 10.00
MMBD Byron Dafoe MM 4.00 10.00
MMDA David Aebischer MM 6.00 15.00
MMJT Jocelyn Thibault MM 4.00 10.00
MMMD Mike Dunham MM 4.00 10.00
MMMT Marty Turco MM 6.00 15.00
MMRT Ron Tugnutt MM 4.00 10.00
MMSB Sean Burke MM 4.00 10.00
SSBD Byron Dafoe SS 6.00 15.00
SSBJ Brent Johnson SS 6.00 15.00
SSFP Felix Potvin SS 10.00 25.00
SSJT Jocelyn Thibault SS 6.00 15.00
SSMB Martin Biron SS 6.00 15.00
SSRL Roberto Luongo SS 10.00 25.00
SSRT Ron Tugnutt SS 6.00 15.00
SSTH Jose Theodore SS 10.00 25.00
SYBB Brian Boucher ST 6.00 15.00
SYDA David Aebischer ST 6.00 15.00
SYEB Ed Belfour ST 12.50 30.00
SYJG Jean-Sebastien Giguere ST 6.00 15.00
SYMD Mike Dunham ST 6.00 15.00
SYMN Mika Noronen ST 6.00 15.00
SYPR Patrick Roy ST 15.00 40.00
SYRC Roman Cechmanek ST 6.00 15.00
VCEB Ed Belfour VC 15.00 40.00
VCFP Felix Potvin VC 10.00 25.00
VCMB Martin Brodeur VC 12.50 30.00
VCMD Mike Dunham VC 6.00 15.00
VCMT Marty Turco VC 8.00 20.00
VCPR Patrick Roy VC 15.00 40.00
VCRC Roman Cechmanek VC 6.00 15.00
VCSB Sean Burke VC 10.00 25.00
CGCJ Curtis Joseph CG 8.00 20.00
CGCO Chris Osgood CG 8.00 20.00
CGDH Dominik Hasek CG 12.50 30.00
CGMB Martin Brodeur CG 12.50 30.00
CGMR Mike Richter CG 8.00 20.00
CGPR Patrick Roy CG 15.00 40.00
CGSB Sean Burke CG 8.00 20.00

2001-02 UD Mask Collection Goalie Pads

GPBD Byron Dafoe 5.00 12.00
GPDH Dominik Hasek 8.00 20.00
GPJH Johan Hedberg 5.00 12.00
GPJT Jose Theodore 6.00 15.00
GPMB Martin Biron 5.00 12.00
GPMD Marc Denis 5.00 12.00
GPOK Olaf Kolzig 5.00 12.00
GPPR Patrick Roy 8.00 20.00

2001-02 UD Mask Collection Jerseys

*DUAL PATCH/500: 2X TO 5X JSY/150
*JSY-PATCH/100: 1X TO 2.5X JSY/150
JAD Adam Deadmarsh 4.00 10.00
JAT Alex Tanguay 4.00 10.00
JBB Brian Boucher 4.00 10.00
JBE Mark Bell 4.00 10.00
JBJ Brent Johnson 4.00 10.00
JBL Rob Blake 4.00 10.00
JBS Brendan Shanahan 6.00 15.00
JCD Chris Drury 4.00 10.00
JDA David Aebischer 6.00 15.00
JDB Daniel Briere 4.00 10.00
JEB Ed Belfour 5.00 12.00
JEK Espen Knutsen 4.00 10.00
JFP Felix Potvin 8.00 20.00
JGS Geoff Sanderson 4.00 10.00
JJA Jason Allison 4.00 10.00
JJD J-P Dumont 4.00 10.00
JJF Jeff Friesen 4.00 10.00
JJG Jean-Sebastien Giguere 4.00 10.00
JJI Jarome Iginla 8.00 20.00
JJJ Jaromir Jagr 8.00 20.00
JJN Joe Nieuwendyk 4.00 10.00
JJT Jocelyn Thibault 4.00 10.00
JJW Justin Williams 4.00 10.00
JKO Slava Kozlov 4.00 10.00
JKP Keith Primeau 4.00 10.00
JMA Maxim Afinogenov 4.00 10.00
JMB Martin Biron 4.00 10.00
JMD Marc Denis 4.00 10.00
JMH Milan Hejduk 6.00 15.00
JML Mario Lemieux 10.00 25.00
JMM Mike Modano 8.00 20.00
JMR Mike Richter 6.00 15.00
JMS Miroslav Satan 4.00 10.00
JMS Mats Sundin 6.00 15.00
JMT Marty Turco 4.00 10.00
JMY Mike York 4.00 10.00
JNL Nicklas Lidstrom 8.00 20.00
JPD Pavol Demitra 4.00 10.00
JPF Peter Forsberg 10.00 25.00
JPK Paul Kariya 6.00 15.00
JPR Patrick Roy 15.00 40.00
JRB Ray Bourque 10.00 25.00
JRF Ruslan Fedotenko 4.00 10.00
JRK Rostislav Klesla 4.00 10.00
JRT Ron Tugnutt 4.00 10.00
JRW Ray Whitney 4.00 10.00
JSA Marc Savard 4.00 10.00
JSD Shane Doan 4.00 10.00
JSF Sergei Fedorov 8.00 20.00
JSG Simon Gagne 6.00 15.00
JSK Saku Koivu 6.00 15.00
JSS Steve Sullivan 4.00 10.00
JSY Steve Yzerman 15.00 40.00
JTA Tony Amonte 4.00 10.00
JTC Tim Connolly 4.00 10.00
JTH Jose Theodore 8.00 20.00
JTL Trevor Linden 4.00 10.00
JTS Teemu Selanne 6.00 15.00
JVN Ville Nieminen 4.00 10.00
JZP Zigmund Palffy 4.00 10.00

2001-02 UD Mask Collection Mini Masks

*CHROME MASK: .6X TO 1.5X
CJ Curtis Joseph 15.00 40.00
EBGD Ed Belfour Gold 25.00 60.00
EBGN Ed Belfour Green 15.00 40.00
EN Evgeni Nabokov 12.00 30.00
JH Johan Hedberg 12.00 30.00
JT Jose Theodore 15.00 40.00
MB Martin Brodeur 20.00 50.00
PRA Patrick Roy Col. 25.00 60.00
PRC Patrick Roy Mon. 50.00 120.00

2001-02 UD Mask Collection Signed Patches

SPBI Martin Biron 100.00 200.00
SPCJ Curtis Joseph 150.00 300.00
SPEB Ed Belfour 150.00 300.00
SPFP Felix Potvin 150.00 300.00
SPJT Jose Theodore 200.00 500.00
SPMB Martin Brodeur 300.00 500.00
SPMR Mike Richter 150.00 300.00
SPPR Patrick Roy 300.00 600.00

2001-02 UD Mask Collection Sticks

SSBB Brian Boucher 8.00 20.00
SSDH Dominik Hasek 15.00 40.00
SSFP Felix Potvin 12.50 30.00
SSJT Jose Theodore 12.50 30.00
SSMB Martin Brodeur 15.00 40.00
SSOK Olaf Kolzig 8.00 20.00
SSTS Tommy Salo 8.00 20.00

2002-03 UD Mask Collection

COMPLETE SET (180)
COMP.SET w/o SP's (90) 8.00 20.00
1 J.Giguere/M.Gerber .25 .60
2 P.Kariya/J.Giguere .25 .60
3 B.Dafoe/M.Hnilicka .20 .50
4 M.Hnilicka/B.Dafoe .20 .50
5 D.Heatley/B.Dafoe .20 .50
6 I.Kovalchuk/B.Dafoe .30 .75
7 P.Nurminen/B.Dafoe .20 .50
8 J.Hackett/S.Shields .20 .50
9 S.Shields/J.Hackett .20 .50
10 J.Thornton/J.Hackett .40 1.00
11 M.Biron/M.Noronen .20 .50
12 M.Noronen/M.Biron .20 .50
13 R.Turek/J.McLennan .25 .60
14 J.McLennan/R.Turek .25 .60
15 C.Drury/R.Turek .25 .60
16 J.Iginla/R.Turek .30 .75
17 K.Weekes/A.Irbe .20 .50
18 A.Irbe/K.Weekes .20 .50
19 J.Thibault/S.Passmore .20 .50
20 S.Passmore/J.Thibault .20 .50
21 P.Roy/D.Aebischer .60 1.50
22 D.Aebischer/P.Roy .60 1.50
23 J.Sakic/P.Roy .60 1.50
24 M.Denis/J.Labbe .20 .50
25 J.Labbe/M.Denis .20 .50
26 M.Turco/R.Tugnutt .25 .60
27 R.Tugnutt/M.Turco .25 .60
28 M.Modano/M.Turco .40 1.00
29 B.Guerin/M.Turco .25 .60
30 C.Joseph/M.Legace .30 .75
31 M.Legace/C.Joseph .30 .75
32 S.Yzerman/C.Joseph .60 1.50
33 B.Shanahan/C.Joseph .30 .75
34 T.Salo/J.Markkanen .20 .50
35 J.Markkanen/T.Salo .20 .50
36 M.Comrie/T.Salo .25 .60
37 R.Luongo/J.Hurme .40 1.00
38 J.Hurme/R.Luongo .40 1.00
39 F.Potvin/J.Storr .40 1.00
40 J.Storr/F.Potvin .40 1.00
41 Z.Palffy/F.Potvin .25 .60
42 M.Fernandez/D.Roloson .15 .40
43 D.Roloson/M.Fernandez .15 .40
44 M.Gaborik/M.Fernandez .25 .60
45 J.Theodore/M.Garon .25 .60
46 M.Garon/J.Theodore .25 .60
47 S.Koivu/J.Theodore .25 .60
48 J.Lasak/T.Vokoun .20 .50
49 T.Vokoun/J.Lasak .20 .50
50 M.Brodeur/C.Schwab .60 1.50
51 C.Schwab/M.Brodeur .60 1.50
52 G.Snow/C.Osgood .25 .60
53 C.Osgood/G.Snow .25 .60
54 M.Dunham/D.Blackburn .20 .50
55 D.Blackburn/M.Dunham .20 .50
56 J.Labarbera/D.Blackburn .20 .50
57 P.Bure/M.Dunham .25 .60
58 P.Lalime/M.Prusek .20 .50
59 M.Prusek/P.Lalime .20 .50
60 R.Cechmanek/R.Esche .20 .50
61 R.Esche/R.Cechmanek .20 .50
62 J.Roenick/R.Cechmanek .40 1.00
63 J.LeClair/R.Cechmanek .25 .60
64 B.Boucher/S.Burke .20 .50
65 S.Burke/B.Boucher .20 .50
66 J.Pelletier/B.Boucher .20 .50
67 T.Amonte/S.Burke .20 .50
68 J.Hedberg/J.Aubin .25 .60
69 J.Aubin/J.Hedberg .25 .60
70 M.Lemieux/J.Hedberg 1.00 2.50
71 S.Caron/J.Hedberg .25 .60
72 E.Nabokov/M.Kiprusoff .25 .60
73 V.Toskala/E.Nabokov .20 .50
74 M.Kiprusoff/E.Nabokov .25 .60
75 B.Johnson/Fred Brathwaite .20 .50
76 T.Barrasso/B.Johnson .20 .50
77 F.Brathwaite/B. Johnson .20 .50
78 R.Divis/B.Johnson .20 .50
79 N.Khabibulin/K.Hodson .25 .60
80 K.Hodson/N.Khabibulin .25 .60
81 E.Konstantinov/N.Khabibulin .25 .60
82 E.Belfour/T.Kidd .25 .60
83 T.Kidd/E.Belfour .25 .60
84 M.Sundin/E.Belfour .25 .60
85 D.Cloutier/P.Skudra .20 .50
86 P.Skudra/D.Cloutier .20 .50
87 J.Jagr/O.Kolzig .75 2.00
88 O.Kolzig/C.Billington .25 .60
89 C.Billington/O.Kolzig .25 .60
90 S.Charpentier/O.Kolzig .25 .60
91 Martin Brodeur/1499 5.00 12.00
92 Patrick Roy/1475 5.00 12.00
93 Curtis Joseph/1096 2.50 6.00
94 Roman Cechmanek/1042 1.50 4.00
95 Marty Turco/590 2.50 6.00
96 Jocelyn Thibault/1439 1.50 4.00
97 Jose Theodore/1836 2.00 5.00
98 Jean-Sebastien Giguere/1260 2.00 5.00
99 Ed Belfour/1305 2.00 5.00
100 Steve Shields/771 2.00 5.00
101 Johan Hedberg/1673 2.00 5.00
102 Martin Biron/1630 1.50 4.00
103 Dan Cloutier/1298 1.50 4.00
104 Evgeni Nabakov/1669 1.50 4.00
105 Sean Burke/1574 1.25 3.00
106 Nikolai Khabibulin/1733 2.00 5.00
107 Olaf Kolzig/1785 2.00 5.00
108 Byron Dafoe/1379 1.50 4.00
109 David Aebischer/501 2.00 5.00
110 Manny Fernandez/1032 1.25 3.00
111 Dan Blackburn/840 2.00 5.00

112 Felix Potvin/1529 3.00 8.00
113 Patrick Lalime/1373 1.50 4.00
114 Brent Johnson/1166 1.50 4.00
115 Marc Denis/1046 1.50 4.00
116 Micki Dupont RC 1.00 2.50
117 Cody Rudkowsky RC 1.00 2.50
118 Shawn Thornton RC 1.25 3.00
119 Lasse Pirjeta RC 1.00 2.50
120 Radovan Somik RC 1.00 2.50
121 Tomi Pettinen RC 1.00 2.50
122 Jonathan Hedstrom RC 1.00 2.50
123 Sylvain Blouin RC 1.00 2.50
124 Stephane Veilleux RC 1.00 2.50
125 Curtis Sanford RC 1.50 4.00
126 Kurt Sauer RC 1.00 2.50
127 Vernon Fiddler RC 1.25 3.00
128 Patrick Sharp RC 3.00 8.00
129 Greg Koehler RC 1.00 2.50
130 Dany Sabourin RC 1.00 2.50
131 Dmitri Bykov RC 1.00 2.50
132 Ivan Majesky RC 1.00 2.50
133 Ray Schultz RC 1.00 2.50
134 Matt Henderson RC 1.00 2.50
135 Tom Koivisto RC 1.00 2.50
136 Ian MacNeil RC 1.00 2.50
137 Eric Godard RC 1.00 2.50
138 Dick Tarnstrom RC 1.00 2.50
139 Jeff Paul RC 1.00 2.50
140 Darren Haydar RC 1.00 2.50
141 Levente Szuper RC 1.50 4.00
142 Dennis Seidenberg RC 1.50 4.00
143 Tim Thomas RC 4.00 10.00
144 Fernando Pisani RC 1.00 2.50
145 Alex Henry RC 1.25 3.00
146 Craig Andersson RC 3.00 8.00
147 Kari Haakana RC 1.00 2.50
148 Jared Aulin RC 1.00 2.50
149 Adam Hall RC 1.00 2.50
150 Carlo Colaiacovo RC 1.50 4.00
151 Martin Gerber RC 1.50 4.00
152 Jamie Hodson RC 1.00 2.50
153 Ray Emery RC 3.00 8.00
154 Ari Ahonen RC 1.00 2.50
155 Michael Leighton RC 1.50 4.00
156 Kris Vernarsky RC 1.00 2.50
157 Jim Vandermeer RC 1.00 2.50
158 Chuck Kobasew RC 1.25 3.00
159 Ron Hainsey RC 1.00 2.50
160 P-M Bouchard RC 1.50 4.00
161 Alexander Frolov RC 2.50 6.00
162 Henrik Zetterberg RC 10.00 25.00
163 Alexander Svitov RC 1.00 2.50
164 Mike Cammalleri RC 3.00 8.00
165 Ryan Miller RC 6.00 15.00
166 Anton Volchenkov RC 1.00 2.50
167 Brooks Orpik RC 1.00 2.50
168 Ales Hemsky RC 4.00 10.00
169 Stanislav Chistov RC 1.00 2.50
170 Shaone Morrisonn RC 1.00 2.50
171 Jason Spezza RC 6.00 15.00
172 Jay Bouwmeester RC 3.00 8.00
173 Jordan Leopold RC 1.50 4.00
174 Jeff Taffe RC 1.00 2.50
175 Pascal LeClaire RC 1.25 3.00
176 Scottie Upshall RC 1.25 3.00
177 Alexei Smirnov RC 1.25 3.00
178 Rick Nash RC 6.00 15.00
179 Mikael Tellqvist RC 1.00 2.50
180 Steve Eminger RC 1.00 2.50

2002-03 UD Mask Collection UD Promos

*UD PROMO: .8X TO 2X BASIC CARDS

2002-03 UD Mask Collection Behind the Mask Jersey

BMAM Andy Moog SP 15.00 40.00
BMBI Martin Biron 6.00 15.00
BMBJ Brent Johnson 6.00 15.00
BMCJ Curtis Joseph 6.00 15.00
BMDU Mike Dunham 6.00 15.00
BMEB Ed Belfour 8.00 20.00
BMFP Felix Potvin 20.00 20.00
BMJG J-S Giguere 6.00 15.00
BMJH Johan Hedberg 6.00 15.00
BMJT Jose Theodore 6.00 15.00
BMMB Martin Brodeur 10.00 25.00
BMMD Marc Denis 6.00 15.00
BMMN Mika Noronen 6.00 15.00
BMMT Marty Turco 6.00 15.00
BMOK Olaf Kolzig 6.00 15.00
BMPR Patrick Roy 12.50 30.00
BMRC Roman Cechmanek 6.00 15.00
BMRD Rick DiPietro 6.00 15.00

2002-03 UD Mask Collection Career Wins Jersey

CWAM Andy Moog/372 8.00 20.00
CWBD Byron Dafoe/162 6.00 15.00
CWCJ Curtis Joseph/346 10.00 25.00
CWCO Chris Osgood/253 8.00 20.00
CWEB Ed Belfour/364 8.00 20.00
CWFP Felix Potvin/237 10.00 25.00
CWJT Jocelyn Thibault/196 8.00 20.00
CWMB Martin Brodeur/324 12.00 30.00
CWMD Mike Dunham/92 6.00 15.00
CWMR Mike Richter/296 10.00 25.00
CWOK Olaf Kolzig/182 8.00 20.00
CWPR Patrick Roy/227 12.00 30.00
CWRT Ron Tugnutt/168 8.00 20.00
CWRY Patrick Roy/289 12.00 30.00
CWSB Sean Burke/281 5.00 12.00
CWTS Tommy Salo/168 6.00 15.00
CWTU Roman Turek/126 8.00 20.00

2002-03 UD Mask Collection Great Gloves

GGBB Brian Boucher 5.00 12.00
GGBR Martin Brodeur 10.00 25.00
GGCJ Curtis Joseph 6.00 15.00
GGDB Dan Blackburn 5.00 12.00
GGDU Mike Dunham 5.00 12.00
GGEB Ed Belfour 6.00 15.00
GGFP Felix Potvin 6.00 15.00
GGJG Jean-Sebastien Giguere 6.00 15.00
GGJT Jose Theodore 6.00 15.00
GGMB Martin Biron 5.00 12.00
GGMD Marc Denis 5.00 12.00
GGMR Mike Richter 6.00 15.00
GGMT Marty Turco 5.00 12.00
GGOK Olaf Kolzig SP 10.00 25.00
GGPR Patrick Roy 12.50 30.00
GGRC Roman Cechmanek 5.00 12.00
GGRL Roberto Luongo 8.00 20.00
GGRT Roman Turek 5.00 12.00

2002-03 UD Mask Collection Instant Offense Jerseys

IOAY Alexei Yashin 4.00 10.00
IOBS Brendan Shanahan 5.00 12.00
IOCD Chris Drury 4.00 10.00
IOED Eric Daze 4.00 10.00
IOEL Eric Lindros 5.00 12.00
IOJA Jason Allison 4.00 10.00
IOJI Jarome Iginla 6.00 15.00
IOJJ Jaromir Jagr 8.00 20.00
IOJR Jeremy Roenick 6.00 15.00
IOJS Joe Sakic 8.00 25.00
IOJT Joe Thornton 8.00 20.00
IOML Mario Lemieux 10.00 25.00
IOMM Mike Modano 8.00 20.00
IOMN Markus Naslund 5.00 12.00
IOMS Miroslav Satan 4.00 10.00
IOPB Pavel Bure 5.00 12.00
IOPE Patrik Elias 4.00 10.00
IOPF Peter Forsberg 10.00 25.00
IOPK Paul Kariya 5.00 12.00
IOSG Simon Gagne 5.00 12.00
IOSK Saku Koivu 5.00 12.00
IOSS Sergei Samsonov 4.00 10.00
IOSU Mats Sundin 5.00 12.00
IOSY Steve Yzerman 12.50 30.00
IOZP Zigmund Palffy 4.00 10.00

2002-03 UD Mask Collection Masked Marvels Jerseys

MMBI Martin Biron 4.00 10.00
MMCO Chris Osgood 4.00 10.00
MMFP Felix Potvin 4.00 10.00
MMJG Jean-Sebastien Giguere 6.00 15.00
MMJH Johan Hedberg 4.00 10.00
MMJT Jocelyn Thibault 4.00 10.00
MMMB Martin Brodeur 6.00 15.00
MMMD Mike Dunham 4.00 10.00
MMMR Mike Richter 6.00 15.00
MMMT Marty Turco 5.00 12.00
MMOK Olaf Kolzig SP 5.00 12.00
MMPR Patrick Roy 12.50 30.00
MMRC Roman Cechmanek 4.00 10.00
MMRL Roberto Luongo 6.00 15.00
MMRM Ryan Miller 8.00 20.00
MMRT Roman Turek 4.00 10.00
MMTH Jose Theodore SP 8.00 20.00

2002-03 UD Mask Collection Mini Masks

*GLITTER: 1.25X TO 3X
AM Andy Moog 20.00 50.00
CJ Curtis Joseph 25.00 60.00
CR Glenn Resch 12.50 30.00
EB Ed Belfour 20.00 50.00
EN Evgeni Nabokov 12.50 30.00
FP Felix Potvin 20.00 50.00
GC Gerry Cheevers 60.00 120.00
GF1 Grant Fuhr Sabres 12.50 30.00
GF2 Grant Fuhr Blues SP 25.00 60.00
JH Johan Hedberg 12.50 30.00
JP1 Jacques Plante Pretzel 15.00 40.00
JP2 Jacques Plante Alien SP 90.00 150.00
JT Jose Theodore 15.00 40.00
MB Martin Brodeur 20.00 50.00
NK Nikolai Khabibulin 25.00 60.00
PR Patrick Roy 25.00 60.00
TE Tony Esposito 20.00 50.00
TS Terry Sawchuk 15.00 40.00

2002-03 UD Mask Collection Mini Masks Autographs

CJ Curtis Joseph 75.00 150.00
EB Ed Belfour 125.00 250.00
EN Evgeni Nabokov 40.00 80.00
GC Gerry Cheevers 30.00 80.00
GF1 Grant Fuhr Sabres 30.00 80.00
GF2 Grant Fuhr Blues SP 50.00 125.00
JT Jose Theodore 40.00 100.00
MB Martin Brodeur 100.00 250.00
NK Nikolai Khabibulin 40.00 100.00
PR Patrick Roy 100.00 250.00
TE Tony Esposito 60.00 150.00

2002-03 UD Mask Collection Nation's Best Jerseys

NDBJ Boucher/Johnson/DiPietro 15.00 40.00
NJBT Turco/Burke/Joseph 10.00 25.00
NLBT Theodore/Luongo/Biron 30.00 80.00
NOBB Osgood/Blackburn/Belfour 12.50 30.00
NRBP Brodeur/Roy/Potvin 30.00 80.00
NRDM Richter/Dunham/Miller 12.50 30.00

2002-03 UD Mask Collection Patches

PGBS Brendan Shanahan/37 40.00 100.00
PGDB Daniel Briere/32 25.00 60.00
PGED Eric Daze/37 25.00 60.00
PGEL Eric Lindros/37 25.00 60.00
PGGM Glen Murray/41 25.00 60.00
PGIK Ilya Kovalchuk/29 40.00 100.00
PGJA Jason Allison/19
PGJI Jarome Iginla/52 40.00 100.00
PGJJ Jaromir Jagr/31 40.00 100.00
PGJS Joe Sakic/26 40.00 100.00
PGMM Mike Modano/34 40.00 100.00
PGMN Markus Naslund/40 25.00 60.00
PGMS Mats Sundin/41 25.00 60.00
PGPB Peter Bondra/39 30.00 80.00
PGPE Patrik Elias/29 25.00 60.00
PGPK Paul Kariya/32 30.00 80.00
PGSF Sergei Fedorov/30 25.00 60.00
PGSG Simon Gagne/33 25.00 60.00
PGSY Steve Yzerman/13
PGZP Zigmund Palffy/31 20.00 50.00
PWBJ Brent Johnson/34 20.00 50.00
PWBR Martin Brodeur/38 60.00 150.00
PWCJ Curtis Joseph/29 40.00 100.00
PWCO Chris Osgood/31 20.00 50.00
PWDB Dan Blackburn/12
PWEB Ed Belfour/21 25.00 60.00
PWFP Felix Potvin/31 25.00 60.00
PWJG Jean-Sebastien Giguere/20 20.00 50.00
PWJH Johan Hedberg/25 20.00 50.00
PWJT Jocelyn Thibault/32 25.00 60.00
PWMB Martin Biron/31 20.00 50.00
PWMD Mike Dunham/23 20.00 50.00
PWMR Mike Richter/24
PWMT Marty Turco/15
PWOK Olaf Kolzig/31 20.00 50.00
PWPR Patrick Roy/32 125.00 250.00
PWRC Roman Cechmanek/24 15.00 40.00
PWRL Roberto Luongo/16
PWRT Roman Turek/30 20.00 50.00
PWSB Sean Burke/33 20.00 50.00
PWTH Jose Theodore/31 60.00 120.00
PWTS Tommy Salo/30 25.00 60.00

2002-03 UD Mask Collection Super Stoppers Jerseys

SSCJ Curtis Joseph 6.00 15.00
SSCO Chris Osgood 5.00 12.00
SSJT Jose Theodore 5.00 12.00
SSMB Martin Brodeur 8.00 20.00
SSOK Olaf Kolzig 5.00 12.00
SSPR Patrick Roy 10.00 25.00
SSRC Roman Cechmanek 4.00 10.00
SSRT Roman Turek 5.00 12.00

2002-03 UD Mask Collection View from the Cage Jerseys

VBI Martin Biron 5.00 12.00
VCJ Curtis Joseph 8.00 20.00
VEB Ed Belfour 6.00 15.00
VJG Jean-Sebastien Giguere 6.00 15.00
VJH Johan Hedberg 6.00 15.00
VJT Jocelyn Thibault 5.00 12.00
VMB Martin Brodeur 10.00 25.00
VMR Mike Richter 6.00 15.00
VMT Marty Turco 6.00 15.00
VOK Olaf Kolzig 6.00 15.00
VPR Patrick Roy 10.00 25.00
VRC Roman Cechmanek 5.00 12.00
VRL Roberto Luongo 10.00 25.00
VRT Roman Turek 6.00 15.00
VSB Sean Burke 4.00 10.00
VTH Jose Theodore 6.00 15.00
VTS Tommy Salo 5.00 12.00

2008-09 UD Masterpieces

COMPLETE SET (87) 20.00 50.00
1 Lord Stanley .50 1.25
2 Lester B. Pearson .40 1.00
3 Lady Byng .30 .75
4 Bill Barilko .30 .75
5 Jari Kurri .50 1.25
6 Syl Apps .75 2.00
7 Patrick Roy 1.25 3.00
8 Ron Hextall .50 1.25
9 Richard Brodeur .40 1.00
10 Mark Messier 1.00 2.50
11 Mario Lemieux 2.00 5.00
12 Mario Lemieux 2.00 5.00
13 Lester Patrick .50 1.25
14 Ray Bourque .75 2.00
15 Ray Bourque .75 2.00
16 Theoren Fleury .60 1.50
17 Wayne Gretzky 3.00 8.00
18 Dale Hawerchuk .60 1.50
19 Darryl Evans .30 .75
20 Wayne Gretzky 3.00 8.00
21 Patrick Roy 1.25 3.00
22 Cam Neely .50 1.25
23 Mike Bossy .50 1.25
24 Pat LaFontaine .50 1.25
25 Lanny McDonald .50 1.25
26 Denis Savard .50 1.25
27 Bobby Hull 1.00 2.50
28 B.Hull/G.Howe 1.50 4.00
29 Georges Vezina .75 2.00
30 George Hainsworth .60 1.50
31 Tony Esposito .50 1.25
32 Phil Esposito .75 2.00
33 Bobby Orr 2.00 5.00
34 Bobby Orr 2.00 5.00
35 Jari Kurri .50 1.25
36 Turk Broda .50 1.25
37 Foster Hewitt .30 .75
38 Wayne Gretzky 3.00 8.00
39 Luc Robitaille .50 1.25
40 Rick Vaive .30 .75
41 Borje Salming .50 1.25
42 Darryl Sittler .60 1.50
43 Clark Gillies .50 1.25
44 Scotty Bowman .50 1.25
45 Glenn Anderson .40 1.00
46 Bobby Hull 1.00 2.50
47 Grant Fuhr .75 2.00
48 Ray Bourque .75 2.00
49 Brian Leetch .40 1.00
50 Joe Mullen .40 1.00
51 Johnny Bower .60 1.50
52 Bob Baun .50 1.25
53 Guy Lafleur .60 1.50
54 Stan Mikita .60 1.50
55 Jean Beliveau .50 1.25
56 Dino Ciccarelli .50 1.25
57 Frank Mahovlich .50 1.25
58 Peter Stastny .60 1.50
59 Marcel Dionne .60 1.50
60 Rod Langway .40 1.00
61 Bobby Clarke .75 2.00
62 Sutter/Sutter/Sutter
Sutter/Sutter/Sutter .50 1.25
63 Steve Shutt .50 1.25
64 Rick McLeish .30 .75
65 Manon Rheaume 1.25 3.00
66 Marty McSorley .40 1.00
67 Alex Delvecchio .60 1.50
68 Dale Hawerchuk .60 1.50
69 Gilbert Perreault .60 1.50
70 Rogie Vachon .60 1.50
71 Doug Wilson .40 1.00
72 Eddie Shack .50 1.25
73 Willie O'Ree .60 1.50
74 Guy Lafleur .60 1.50
75 Bernie Parent .60 1.50
76 Andy Bathgate .50 1.25
77 Craig MacTavish .40 1.00
78 Wayne Gretzky 3.00 8.00
79 Mark Messier 1.00 2.50
80 Gordie Howe 1.50 4.00
81 Mario Lemieux 2.00 5.00
82 Bobby Orr 2.00 5.00
83 Phil Esposito .75 2.00
84 Mark Messier 1.00 2.50
85 Gordie Howe 1.50 4.00
86 Mario Lemieux 2.00 5.00
87 Mark Messier 1.00 2.50

2008-09 UD Masterpieces Blue

*BLUE: 3X TO 8X BASE

2008-09 UD Masterpieces Green

*GREEN: 2.5X TO 6X BASE

2008-09 UD Masterpieces Red

*RED: 5X TO 12X BASE

2008-09 UD Masterpieces 5x7

COMPLETE SET (24) 40.00 100.00
XLBH Bobby Hull 4.00 10.00
XLBP Bernie Parent 2.50 6.00
XLBR Richard Brodeur 1.50 4.00
XLBS Borje Salming 2.00 5.00
XLDC Dino Ciccarelli 2.00 5.00
XLDH Dale Hawerchuk 2.50 6.00
XLDS Darryl Sittler 2.50 6.00
XLFM Frank Mahovlich 2.00 5.00
XLGF Grant Fuhr 3.00 8.00
XLGH Gordie Howe 6.00 15.00
XLGL Guy Lafleur 2.50 6.00
XLGP Gilbert Perreault 2.00 5.00
XLLM Lanny McDonald 2.00 5.00
XLMB Mike Bossy 2.00 5.00
XLML Mario Lemieux 8.00 20.00
XLMM Mark Messier 4.00 10.00
XLPE Phil Esposito 3.00 8.00
XLPR Patrick Roy 5.00 12.00
XLRB Ray Bourque 3.00 8.00
XLRL Rod Langway 1.50 4.00
XLSB Scotty Bowman 2.00 5.00
XLVT Vladislav Tretiak 1.50 4.00
XLWG Wayne Gretzky 12.00 30.00
XLWO Willie O'Ree 2.50 6.00

2008-09 UD Masterpieces 5x7 Autographs

XLABB Bob Baun 20.00 50.00
XLABL Brian Leetch 15.00 40.00
XLABO Ray Bourque
XLACN Cam Neely 25.00 50.00
XLAGA Glenn Anderson 10.00 25.00
XLAHH G.Howe/B.Hull 100.00 200.00
XLAJB Johnny Bower 12.00 30.00
XLAJM Joe Mullen 15.00 40.00
XLALR Luc Robitaille 20.00 50.00
XLAMB Mike Bossy 15.00 40.00
XLAML Mario Lemieux
XLAMM Mark Messier
XLAOR Bobby Orr 75.00 150.00
XLAPR Patrick Roy
XLARH Ron Hextall 15.00 40.00
XLATE Tony Esposito
XLATF Theoren Fleury 15.00 40.00
XLAWG Wayne Gretzky 250.00 600.00

2008-09 UD Masterpieces Brushstrokes Blue

*BLUE: .5X TO 1.2X BROWN
MBDH Dale Hawerchuk 50.00 100.00

2008-09 UD Masterpieces Brushstrokes Brown

MBAB Andy Bathgate 8.00 20.00
MBAD Alex Delvecchio 8.00 20.00
MBAM Al MacInnis 10.00 25.00
MBAO Adam Oates 8.00 20.00
MBBB Bob Bourne 5.00 12.00
MBBC Bobby Clarke 12.00 30.00
MBBD Bill Dineen 8.00 20.00
MBBF Bernie Federko 6.00 15.00
MBBH Bobby Hull 25.00 60.00
MBBK Johnny Bucyk 8.00 20.00
MBBL Brian Leetch 6.00 15.00
MBBN Bernie Nicholls 6.00 15.00
MBBO Bob Baun 8.00 20.00
MBBR Brian Sutter 8.00 20.00
MBBS Borje Salming 12.00 30.00
MBBU Butch Bouchard 15.00 40.00
MBCA Guy Carbonneau 8.00 20.00
MBCG Clark Gillies 8.00 20.00
MBCH Don Cherry 20.00 50.00
MBCN Cam Neely 20.00 50.00
MBDA Darryl Sutter 5.00 12.00
MBDC Dino Ciccarelli 8.00 20.00
MBDD Dick Duff 6.00 15.00
MBDG Doug Gilmour 10.00 25.00
MBDH Dale Hawerchuk
MBDP Denis Potvin 8.00 20.00
MBDU Duane Sutter 5.00 12.00
MBDW Doug Wilson 6.00 15.00
MBEL Ron Ellis 5.00 12.00
MBES Eddie Shack 8.00 20.00
MBFM Frank Mahovlich 60.00 120.00
MBGA Glenn Anderson 6.00 15.00
MBGF Grant Fuhr 8.00 20.00
MBGH Gordie Howe 50.00 100.00
MBGL Guy Lafleur 10.00 25.00
MBGP Gilbert Perreault 8.00 20.00
MBHH Harry Howell 8.00 20.00
MBHO Mark Howe 8.00 20.00
MBHX Ron Hextall 15.00 40.00
MBJB Jean Beliveau 40.00 100.00
MBJK Jari Kurri 8.00 20.00
MBJM Joe Mullen 6.00 15.00
MBJO Johnny Bower 8.00 20.00
MBLA Rod Langway 6.00 15.00
MBLM Lanny McDonald 15.00 40.00
MBLR Larry Robinson 8.00 20.00
MBMB Mike Bossy 8.00 20.00
MBMC Craig MacTavish 6.00 15.00
MBMD Marcel Dionne 10.00 25.00
MBMF Mike Foligno 5.00 12.00
MBML Mario Lemieux
MBMM Marty McSorley 6.00 15.00
MBMS Mark Messier 75.00 150.00
MBOR Bobby Orr 75.00 200.00
MBPE Phil Esposito 30.00 80.00
MBPL Pat LaFontaine
MBPR Patrick Roy 200.00 350.00
MBPS Peter Stastny 6.00 15.00
MBRB Ray Bourque 50.00 100.00
MBRD Ron Duguay 6.00 15.00
MBRG Rod Gilbert
MBRH Manon Rheaume 20.00 50.00
MBRI Richard Brodeur 6.00 15.00
MBRK Red Kelly 8.00 20.00
MBRL Rejean Lemelin 5.00 12.00
MBRM Rick MacLeish 5.00 12.00
MBRO Luc Robitaille 8.00 20.00
MBRS Rich Sutter 5.00 12.00
MBRV Rogie Vachon 10.00 25.00
MBSA Denis Savard 8.00 20.00
MBSB Scotty Bowman 40.00 100.00
MBSC Dave Schultz 8.00 20.00
MBSM Stan Mikita 40.00 80.00
MBSR Ron Sutter 6.00 15.00
MBSS Steve Shutt 8.00 20.00
MBSU Brent Sutter 5.00 12.00
MBTE Tony Esposito 15.00 40.00
MBTF Theoren Fleury 12.50 30.00
MBTL Ted Lindsay 8.00 20.00
MBTO Terry O'Reilly 6.00 15.00
MBVT Vladislav Tretiak 25.00 50.00
MBWG Wayne Gretzky 250.00 600.00
MBWO Willie O'Ree 10.00 25.00
MBWT Walt Tkaczuk 5.00 12.00

2008-09 UD Masterpieces Brushstrokes Green

*GREEN/35: .5X TO 1.2X BROWN
MBDH Dale Hawerchuk 50.00 100.00

2008-09 UD Masterpieces Brushstrokes Brown

*BROWN: 1.2X TO 3X

2008-09 UD Masterpieces Canvas Clippings Brown

*BLUE: .5X TO 1.2X BROWN
*GREEN/85: .4X TO 1X BROWN
CCAM1 Al MacInnis 6.00 15.00
CCAM2 Al MacInnis 6.00 15.00
CCAO1 Adam Oates 5.00 12.00
CCAO2 Adam Oates 5.00 12.00
CCBC Bobby Clarke 8.00 20.00
CCBF Bernie Federko 4.00 10.00
CCBL Brian Leetch 4.00 10.00
CCBN1 Bernie Nicholls 4.00 10.00
CCBN2 Bernie Nicholls 4.00 10.00
CCBO Bob Bourne 3.00 8.00
CCBR Richard Brodeur 4.00 10.00
CCBS Billy Smith 5.00 12.00
CCBT Bryan Trottier 5.00 12.00
CCBU Johnny Bucyk 5.00 12.00
CCCN Cam Neely 5.00 12.00
CCDC1 Dino Ciccarelli 5.00 12.00
CCDC2 Dino Ciccarelli 5.00 12.00
CCDH Dale Hawerchuk 6.00 15.00
CCDS Darryl Sittler 6.00 15.00
CCFM1 Frank Mahovlich 6.00 15.00
CCFM2 Frank Mahovlich 6.00 15.00
CCGA1 Glenn Anderson 4.00 10.00
CCGA2 Glenn Anderson 4.00 10.00
CCGF Grant Fuhr 8.00 20.00
CCGH Gordie Howe 15.00 40.00
CCGP Gilbert Perreault 5.00 12.00
CCJB Jean Beliveau 10.00 25.00
CCJK Jari Kurri 5.00 12.00
CCJM1 Joe Mullen 4.00 10.00
CCJM2 Joe Mullen 4.00 10.00
CCLM1 Lanny McDonald 5.00 12.00
CCLM2 Lanny McDonald 5.00 12.00
CCLR Larry Robinson 5.00 12.00
CCMD Marcel Dionne 6.00 15.00
CCML Mario Lemieux 20.00 50.00
CCMM1 Mark Messier 10.00 25.00
CCMM2 Mark Messier 10.00 25.00
CCMR Mike Richter 5.00 12.00
CCPE1 Phil Esposito 8.00 20.00
CCPE2 Phil Esposito 8.00 20.00
CCPL Pat LaFontaine 5.00 12.00
CCPR1 Patrick Roy 12.00 30.00
CCPR2 Patrick Roy 12.00 30.00
CCPS Peter Stastny 4.00 10.00
CCRB1 Ray Bourque 8.00 20.00
CCRB2 Ray Bourque 8.00 20.00
CCRE Ron Ellis 3.00 8.00
CCRH Ron Hextall 8.00 20.00
CCRL Rod Langway 4.00 10.00
CCRO Luc Robitaille 5.00 12.00
CCRV1 Rogie Vachon 6.00 15.00
CCRV2 Rogie Vachon 6.00 15.00
CCSA1 Denis Savard 6.00 15.00
CCSA2 Denis Savard 6.00 15.00
CCSB1 Scotty Bowman 5.00 12.00
CCSB2 Scotty Bowman 5.00 12.00
CCSB3 Scotty Bowman 5.00 12.00
CCSG Borje Salming 5.00 12.00
CCSM Stan Mikita 6.00 15.00
CCSS Steve Shutt 5.00 12.00
CCSU Brent Sutter 3.00 8.00
CCTE Tony Esposito 5.00 12.00
CCTF Theoren Fleury 6.00 15.00
CCTW Tiger Williams 3.00 8.00
CCWC1 Wendel Clark 8.00 20.00
CCWC2 Wendel Clark 8.00 20.00
CCWG Wayne Gretzky 40.00 80.00

2014-15 UD Masterpieces

1 Corey Perry 1.25 3.00
2 Evander Kane .75 2.00
3 Zdeno Chara .75 2.00
4 Cody Hodgson .50 1.25
5 Mark Scheifele 1.25 3.00
6 Dustin Byfuglien .75 2.00
7 Eric Staal 1.00 2.50
8 Patrick Kane 1.50 4.00
9 Blake Wheeler .75 2.00
10 Matt Duchene .75 2.00
11 Sergei Bobrovsky .75 2.00
12 Tyler Seguin 1.00 2.50
13 Daniel Alfredsson .75 2.00
14 Taylor Hall .75 2.00
15 Ryan Getzlaf .75 2.00
16 Jonathan Quick 1.00 2.50
17 Jason Pominville .50 1.25
18 Max Pacioretty .75 2.00
19 Shea Weber .60 1.50
20 Martin Brodeur 2.00 5.00
21 Kyle Okposo .60 1.50
22 Mats Zuccarello .75 2.00
23 Erik Karlsson 1.00 2.50
24 Kyle Turris .75 2.00
25 Keith Yandle .50 1.25
26 Evgeni Malkin 1.50 4.00
27 Joe Thornton 1.25 3.00
28 Alexander Steen .50 1.25
29 Pekka Rinne .75 2.00
30 James van Riemsdyk .60 1.50
31 Alexander Ovechkin 3.00 8.00
32 Tuukka Rask 1.00 2.50
33 Marian Hossa .75 2.00
34 Valeri Nichushkin .75 2.00
35 Sam Gagner .50 1.25
36 Alex Galchenyuk .50 1.25
37 Brad Richards .75 2.00
38 Marc-Andre Fleury 1.50 4.00
39 Ben Bishop .60 1.50
40 Phil Kessel .75 2.00
41 Nicklas Backstrom .75 2.00
42 Paul Stastny .60 1.50
43 Pavel Datsyuk 1.25 3.00
44 Gabriel Landeskog 1.00 2.50
45 Jonas Hiller .60 1.50
46 Seth Jones .75 2.00
47 Tomas Hertl .75 2.00
48 Zach Parise .75 2.00
49 Jim Howard 1.00 2.50
50 Ryan Johansen .60 1.50
51 Cam Ward .60 1.50
52 Corey Crawford 1.00 2.50
53 Aleksander Barkov 1.25 3.00
54 Patrik Elias .75 2.00
55 Wayne Gretzky 2.50 6.00
56 Ryan Strome .75 2.00
57 Logan Couture 1.00 2.50
58 Jonathan Bernier .60 1.50
59 Rick Nash .75 2.00
60 Tomas Plekanec .50 1.25
61 Ryan Nugent-Hopkins 1.00 2.50
62 Jamie Benn .75 2.00
63 Jeff Skinner 1.00 2.50
64 Duncan Keith .60 1.50
65 Brendan Gallagher .75 2.00
66 Patrick Marleau .75 2.00
67 Scott Laughton .50 1.25
68 Kari Lehtonen .60 1.50
69 Mikko Koivu .60 1.50
70 Anze Kopitar 1.25 3.00
71 David Perron .60 1.50
72 Jason Spezza .75 2.00
73 Shane Doan .60 1.50
74 Scott Hartnell .50 1.25
75 David Backes .50 1.25
76 Wayne Gretzky 2.50 6.00
77 Patrick Sharp .75 2.00
78 Vincent Lecavalier .75 2.00
79 T.J. Oshie .75 2.00
80 Radim Vrbata .50 1.25
81 James Neal .50 1.25
82 Dion Phaneuf .60 1.50
83 Chris Kunitz .75 2.00
84 Adam Henrique .60 1.50
85 Gustav Nyquist .50 1.25
86 Mikael Granlund .60 1.50
87 Bobby Ryan .60 1.50
88 Drew Doughty 1.00 2.50
89 Jonathan Huberdeau 1.00 2.50
90 Tyler Ennis .50 1.25
91 Roberto Luongo SP 1.50 4.00
92 Wayne Gretzky SP 6.00 15.00
93 Peter Forsberg SP 2.00 5.00
94 Bill Guerin SP 1.00 2.50
95 Theoren Fleury SP 1.25 3.00
96 Jarome Iginla SP 1.25 3.00
97 Steven Stamkos SP 2.00 5.00
98 Claude Giroux SP 1.25 3.00
99 Phil Esposito SP 1.50 4.00
100 Sidney Crosby SP 4.00 10.00
101 Guy Carbonneau SP 1.00 2.50
102 Mike Gartner SP 1.25 3.00
103 Bill Barber SP 1.25 3.00
104 Bobby Orr SP 4.00 10.00
105 Patrice Bergeron SP 1.25 3.00
106 Bill Ranford SP 1.25 3.00
107 Mike Bossy SP 1.00 2.50
108 Sean Monahan SP .60 1.50
109 Dale Hawerchuk SP 1.25 3.00
110 Jaromir Jagr SP 3.00 8.00
111 Joe Sakic SP 2.00 5.00
112 Henrik Zetterberg SP 1.25 3.00
113 Jordan Eberle SP 1.00 2.50
114 Grant Fuhr SP 1.50 4.00
115 Dominik Hasek SP 1.50 4.00
116 Brett Hull SP 2.00 5.00
117 Mike Richter SP 1.00 2.50
118 Doug Gilmour SP 1.25 3.00
119 Jonathan Toews SP 1.50 4.00
120 Mario Lemieux SP 4.00 10.00
121 Marcel Dionne SP 1.25 3.00
122 Mats Sundin SP 1.00 2.50
123 Adam Oates SP 1.00 2.50
124 Bobby Hull SP 2.00 5.00
125 Nathan MacKinnon SP 4.00 10.00
126 Guy Lafleur SP 1.25 3.00
127 Jeff Carter SP .75 2.00
128 Jeremy Roenick SP 1.50 4.00
129 Steve Yzerman SP 2.50 6.00
130 Martin St. Louis SP 1.00 2.50
131 Patrick Roy SP 3.00 8.00
132 Ray Bourque SP 1.50 4.00
133 Trevor Linden SP 1.00 2.50
134 Larry Robinson SP 1.00 2.50
135 Joe Pavelski SP 1.25 3.00
136 Pierre Turgeon SP .75 2.00
137 Nicklas Lidstrom SP 1.00 2.50
138 Nail Yakupov SP .60 1.50
139 Bobby Clarke SP 1.50 4.00
140 Stan Mikita SP 1.50 4.00
141 P.K. Subban SP 1.25 3.00
142 John Tavares SP 1.50 4.00
143 Jari Kurri SP 1.00 2.50
144 Mark Messier SP 2.00 5.00
145 Henrik Lundqvist SP 2.50 6.00
146 Jean Beliveau SP 2.00 5.00
147 Carey Price SP 2.00 5.00
148 Pelle Lindbergh SP .75 2.00
149 Chris Chelios SP 1.00 2.50
150 Wayne Gretzky SP 6.00 15.00
151 Bobby Orr BW 5.00 12.00
152 Patrick Kane BW 2.50 6.00
153 Mario Lemieux BW 5.00 12.00
154 Sidney Crosby BW 5.00 12.00
155 Mats Sundin BW 1.25 3.00
156 Alexander Ovechkin BW 5.00 12.00
157 Phil Kessel BW 1.25 3.00
158 Steve Yzerman BW 3.00 8.00
159 Evgeni Malkin BW 2.50 6.00
160 Pavel Datsyuk BW 2.00 5.00
161 Joe Sakic BW 2.50 6.00
162 Nathan MacKinnon BW 5.00 12.00
163 Mark Messier BW 2.50 6.00
164 Terry Sawchuk BW 1.25 3.00
165 Wayne Gretzky BW 8.00 20.00
166 Teuvo Teravainen RC 2.00 5.00
167 Evgeny Kuznetsov RC 3.00 8.00
168 Brandon Gormley RC 1.25 3.00
169 Ty Rattie RC 1.25 3.00
170 Johnny Gaudreau RC 4.00 10.00
171 Jonathan Drouin RC 2.50 6.00
172 Aaron Ekblad RC 3.00 8.00
173 Vladislav Namestnikov RC 2.00 5.00
174 Bo Horvat RC 3.00 8.00
175 Curtis Lazar RC 1.25 3.00
176 Alexander Khokhlachev RC 1.25 3.00
177 Joey Hishon RC 1.50 4.00
178 Calle Jarnkrok RC 1.25 3.00
179 Sam Reinhart RC 5.00 12.00
180 Leon Draisaitl RC 8.00 20.00
181 Guy Lafleur WP 1.50 4.00
182 Steve Shutt WP 1.00 2.50
183 Alex Galchenyuk WP .75 2.00
184 Nathan MacKinnon WP 5.00 12.00
185 Jonathan Toews WP 2.00 5.00
186 Teemu Selanne WP 2.50 6.00
187 Phil Kessel WP 1.25 3.00
188 Martin St. Louis WP 1.25 3.00
189 Joe Pavelski WP 1.50 4.00
190 Alexander Ovechkin WP 5.00 12.00
191 John Tavares WP 2.00 5.00
192 Mike Richter WP 1.25 3.00
193 Sidney Crosby WP 5.00 12.00
194 Wayne Gretzky WP 8.00 20.00
195 Sean Monahan WP .75 2.00
196 Mike Smith WP 1.25 3.00
197 John LeClair WP 1.25 3.00
198 Patrick Sharp WP 1.25 3.00
199 Tyler Seguin WP 1.50 4.00
200 Tomas Hertl WP 1.25 3.00
201 Matt Duchene WP 1.25 3.00
202 Corey Perry WP 2.00 5.00
203 Anze Kopitar WP 2.00 5.00
204 Bobby Orr WP 5.00 12.00
205 Jean Beliveau WP 1.25 3.00
206 Max Pacioretty WP 1.25 3.00
207 T.J. Oshie WP 1.25 3.00
208 Tyler Toffoli WP 1.25 3.00
209 Wayne Gretzky WP 8.00 20.00
210 Logan Couture WP 1.50 4.00
211 Mats Sundin WP 1.25 3.00
212 Bill Guerin WP 1.25 3.00
213 Dave Schultz WP 1.25 3.00
214 Brad Park WP 1.00 2.50
215 Pavel Datsyuk WP 2.00 5.00
216 Blake Wheeler WP 1.25 3.00
217 Doug Gilmour WP 1.50 4.00
218 James van Riemsdyk WP 1.00 2.50
219 Marian Gaborik WP 1.25 3.00
220 Valeri Nichushkin WP 1.25 3.00
221 Pete Peeters WP 1.00 2.50
222 Carey Price WP 2.50 6.00
223 Seth Jones WP 1.25 3.00
224 Ondrej Palat WP 1.00 2.50
225 Sergei Bobrovsky WP 2.00 5.00
226 Ryan O'Reilly WP 1.25 3.00
227 Jaromir Jagr WP 4.00 10.00
228 Brendan Gallagher WP 1.25 3.00
229 John Gibson WP 1.25 3.00
230 Nicklas Lidstrom WP 1.25 3.00
231 B.Gallagher/T.Plekanec WP 1.50 4.00
232 Joe Pavelski/Logan Couture WP 2.00 5.00
233 Martin St. Louis
Brad Richards WP 1.50 4.00
234 J.van Riemsdyk/P.Kessel WP 1.50 4.00
235 Ray Bourque/Rob Blake WP 2.50 6.00
236 Seth Jones/N.MacKinnon WP 6.00 15.00
237 Patrick Kane/Patrick Sharp WP 3.00 8.00
238 Dustin Brown/Anze Kopitar WP 2.50 6.00
239 Guy Lafleur/Steve Shutt WP 2.00 5.00
240 Aaron Ekblad/Sam Reinhart WP 6.00 15.00

2014-15 UD Masterpieces Framed Black Leather

*1-90 BLACK/50: 2X TO 5X BASIC CARDS
*91-150 BLACK/50: 1.5X TO 4X BASIC CARDS
*151-165 BLACK/50: 1.2X TO 3X BASIC CARDS
*166-180 BLACK/50: 1X TO 2.5X BASIC RC
41 Nicklas Backstrom 4.00 10.00
52 Corey Crawford 5.00 12.00
150 Wayne Gretzky 25.00 50.00

2014-15 UD Masterpieces Framed Red Cloth

*RED/100: 1.25X TO 3X BASIC CARDS 1-90
*RED/100: 1X TO 2.5X BASIC CARDS 91-150
*RED/100: .75X TO 2X BASIC CARDS 151-180
41 Nicklas Backstrom 2.50 6.00
52 Corey Crawford 3.00 8.00

2014-15 UD Masterpieces Autographs

1 Corey Perry D 10.00 25.00
4 Cody Hodgson E 4.00 10.00
10 Matt Duchene D 6.00 15.00
11 Sergei Bobrovsky E 10.00 25.00
14 Taylor Hall D 6.00 15.00
17 Jason Pominville E 4.00 10.00
18 Max Pacioretty E 6.00 15.00
19 Shea Weber D 5.00 12.00
20 Martin Brodeur C 15.00 40.00
21 Kyle Okposo E 4.00 10.00
24 Kyle Turris
Issued in '15-16 UD2 6.00 15.00
26 Evgeni Malkin C EXCH 12.00 30.00
31 Alexander Ovechkin B EXCH 25.00 60.00
38 Marc-Andre Fleury D 12.00 30.00

2014-15 UD Masterpieces Autographs

39 Ben Bishop F 5.00 12.00
43 Pavel Datsyuk D 10.00 25.00
46 Seth Jones E 6.00 15.00
47 Tomas Hertl F 6.00 15.00
48 Zach Parise C 6.00 15.00
49 Jim Howard E 8.00 20.00
50 Ryan Johansen
Issued in '15-16 UD2 5.00 12.00
54 Patrik Elias E 6.00 15.00
55 Wayne Gretzky B 250.00 600.00
57 Logan Couture D 8.00 20.00
58 Jonathan Bernier D 5.00 12.00
60 Tomas Plekanec E 4.00 10.00
62 Jamie Benn D 6.00 15.00
63 Jeff Skinner D 8.00 20.00
65 Brendan Gallagher E 6.00 15.00
66 Patrick Marleau D 6.00 15.00
67 Scott Laughton F 4.00 10.00
68 Kari Lehtonen
Issued in '15-16 UD2 5.00 12.00
72 Jason Spezza D 6.00 15.00
74 Scott Hartnell E 4.00 10.00
75 David Backes D 4.00 10.00
76 Wayne Gretzky C 250.00 600.00
83 Chris Kunitz F 6.00 15.00
84 Adam Henrique E 5.00 12.00
85 Gustav Nyquist F 4.00 10.00
86 Mikael Granlund F 5.00 12.00
87 Bobby Ryan D 5.00 12.00
89 Jonathan Huberdeau E 8.00 20.00
92 Wayne Gretzky B 250.00 600.00
94 Bill Guerin F 6.00 15.00
95 Theoren Fleury C 8.00 20.00
96 Jarome Iginla B 8.00 20.00
100 Sidney Crosby B EXCH 25.00 60.00
101 Guy Carbonneau F 6.00 15.00
102 Mike Gartner E 8.00 20.00
104 Bobby Orr E 40.00 100.00
106 Bill Ranford F 6.00 15.00
110 Jaromir Jagr B 20.00 50.00
111 Joe Sakic B 12.00 30.00
114 Grant Fuhr C 10.00 25.00
115 Dominik Hasek B 10.00 25.00
116 Brett Hull B 12.00 30.00
119 Jonathan Toews B 10.00 25.00
120 Mario Lemieux B 25.00 60.00
122 Mats Sundin B 6.00 15.00
123 Adam Oates F 6.00 15.00
125 Nathan MacKinnon C 25.00 60.00
129 Steve Yzerman B 15.00 40.00
130 Martin St. Louis C 6.00 15.00
131 Patrick Roy B 40.00 100.00
133 Trevor Linden D 6.00 15.00
135 Joe Pavelski E 8.00 20.00
136 Pierre Turgeon E 5.00 12.00
137 Nicklas Lidstrom B EXCH 6.00 15.00
138 Nail Yakupov E 4.00 10.00
142 John Tavares E 10.00 25.00
143 Jari Kurri E 6.00 15.00
144 Mark Messier B 12.00 30.00
147 Carey Price B 12.00 30.00
149 Chris Chelios B 6.00 15.00
150 Wayne Gretzky A 250.00 600.00
151 Bobby Orr C 60.00 150.00
153 Mario Lemieux A 60.00 150.00
154 Sidney Crosby A 150.00 250.00
155 Mats Sundin B 6.00 15.00
156 Alexander Ovechkin A 25.00 60.00
158 Steve Yzerman A 30.00 80.00
159 Evgeni Malkin C 12.00 30.00
160 Pavel Datsyuk C 10.00 25.00
161 Joe Sakic A 30.00 80.00
162 Nathan MacKinnon C 25.00 60.00
163 Mark Messier A 30.00 80.00
165 Wayne Gretzky B 250.00 600.00
166 Teuvo Teravainen 10.00 25.00
167 Evgeny Kuznetsov 15.00 40.00
168 Brandon Gormley 6.00 15.00
169 Ty Rattie 6.00 15.00
170 Johnny Gaudreau 100.00 250.00
171 Jonathan Drouin 12.00 30.00
172 Aaron Ekblad 15.00 40.00
173 Vladislav Namestnikov 10.00 25.00
174 Bo Horvat 15.00 40.00
175 Curtis Lazar 6.00 15.00
177 Alexander Khokhlachev 8.00 20.00
178 Joey Hishon 6.00 15.00
179 Sam Reinhart 25.00 60.00
180 Leon Draisaitl 30.00 80.00
183 Alex Galchenyuk WP B 4.00 10.00
184 Nathan MacKinnon WP B EXCH 25.00 60.00
185 Jonathan Toews WP A 30.00 80.00
186 Teemu Selanne WP A 30.00 80.00
188 Martin St. Louis WP B 6.00 15.00
189 Joe Pavelski WP D 8.00 20.00
190 Alexander Ovechkin WP A 25.00 60.00
191 John Tavares WP C 10.00 25.00
193 Sidney Crosby WP A 150.00 250.00
194 Wayne Gretzky WP B 250.00 600.00
195 Sean Monahan WP D 4.00 10.00
197 John LeClair WP B 6.00 15.00
200 Tomas Hertl WP D 6.00 15.00
201 Matt Duchene WP C 6.00 15.00
202 Corey Perry WP B 10.00 25.00
203 Anze Kopitar WP B 10.00 25.00
204 Bobby Orr WP C 60.00 150.00
206 Max Pacioretty WP C 6.00 15.00
208 Tyler Toffoli WP D EXCH 6.00 15.00
209 Wayne Gretzky WP A 250.00 600.00
210 Logan Couture WP C 8.00 20.00
211 Mats Sundin WP A 6.00 15.00
212 Bill Guerin WP D 6.00 15.00
213 Dave Schultz WP D 6.00 15.00
214 Brad Park WP C 5.00 12.00
215 Pavel Datsyuk WP B 10.00 25.00
221 Pete Peeters WP D 5.00 12.00
222 Carey Price WP A 50.00 125.00
223 Seth Jones WP C 6.00 15.00
224 Ondrej Palat WP D 5.00 12.00
225 Sergei Bobrovsky WP C 10.00 25.00
226 Ryan O'Reilly WP D 6.00 15.00
227 Jaromir Jagr WP A 50.00 125.00
228 Brendan Gallagher WP C 6.00 15.00
230 Nicklas Lidstrom WP B EXCH 6.00 15.00
232 L.Couture/J.Pavelski WP 8.00 20.00
235 R.Bourque/R.Blake WP 10.00 25.00
238 D.Brown/A.Kopitar WP 10.00 25.00
240 A.Ekblad/S.Reinhart WP 25.00 60.00

2014-15 UD Masterpieces Autographs Framed Red Cloth

55 Wayne Gretzky/30 250.00 600.00
76 Wayne Gretzky/30 250.00 600.00
170 Johnny Gaudreau/30 EXCH 150.00 400.00

2014-15 UD Masterpieces Gretzky Jumbos

150 Wayne Gretzky 5.00 10.00

2014-15 UD Masterpieces Memorabilia

*RED/35-85: .6X TO 1.5X BASIC INSERTS
*BLACK/25-35: .75X TO 2X BASIC INSERTS
1 Corey Perry B 5.00 12.00
2 Evander Kane C 3.00 8.00
3 Zdeno Chara B 3.00 8.00
4 Cody Hodgson C 2.00 5.00
5 Mark Scheifele C 5.00 12.00
6 Dustin Byfuglien C 3.00 8.00
7 Eric Staal B 4.00 10.00
8 Patrick Kane B 6.00 15.00
9 Blake Wheeler C 3.00 8.00
10 Matt Duchene B 3.00 8.00
11 Sergei Bobrovsky B 5.00 12.00
12 Tyler Seguin B 4.00 10.00
13 Daniel Alfredsson B 3.00 8.00
14 Taylor Hall B 3.00 8.00
15 Ryan Getzlaf B 3.00 8.00
16 Jonathan Quick B 4.00 10.00
17 Jason Pominville C 2.00 5.00
18 Max Pacioretty C 3.00 8.00
19 Shea Weber B 2.50 6.00
20 Martin Brodeur B 8.00 20.00
21 Kyle Okposo C 2.00 5.00
22 Mats Zuccarello C 3.00 8.00
23 Erik Karlsson B 4.00 10.00
24 Kyle Turris C 3.00 8.00
25 Keith Yandle B 2.00 5.00
26 Evgeni Malkin B 6.00 15.00
27 Joe Thornton B 5.00 12.00
29 Pekka Rinne B 3.00 8.00
30 James van Riemsdyk C 2.50 6.00
31 Alexander Ovechkin B 12.00 30.00
32 Tuukka Rask B 4.00 10.00
33 Marian Hossa B 3.00 8.00
34 Valeri Nichushkin C 3.00 8.00
35 Sam Gagner C 2.00 5.00
36 Alex Galchenyuk C 2.00 5.00
37 Brad Richards C 3.00 8.00
38 Marc-Andre Fleury C 6.00 15.00
39 Ben Bishop C 2.50 6.00
40 Phil Kessel B 3.00 8.00
41 Nicklas Backstrom B 3.00 8.00
42 Paul Stastny C 2.50 6.00
43 Pavel Datsyuk B 5.00 12.00
44 Gabriel Landeskog C 4.00 10.00
45 Jonas Hiller C 2.50 6.00
46 Seth Jones B 3.00 8.00
47 Tomas Hertl C 3.00 8.00
48 Zach Parise B 3.00 8.00
49 Jim Howard C 4.00 10.00
50 Ryan Johansen B 2.50 6.00
51 Cam Ward B 3.00 8.00
52 Corey Crawford B 4.00 10.00
53 Aleksander Barkov C 5.00 12.00
55 Wayne Gretzky A 25.00 60.00
56 Ryan Strome C 3.00 8.00
57 Logan Couture B 4.00 10.00
58 Jonathan Bernier B 2.50 6.00
59 Rick Nash B 3.00 8.00
61 Ryan Nugent-Hopkins B 4.00 10.00
62 Jamie Benn B 3.00 8.00
63 Jeff Skinner C 4.00 10.00
64 Duncan Keith B 2.50 6.00
65 Brendan Gallagher C 3.00 8.00
66 Patrick Marleau B 3.00 8.00
67 Scott Laughton C 2.00 5.00
68 Kari Lehtonen C 2.50 6.00
69 Mikko Koivu B 2.50 6.00
70 Anze Kopitar C 5.00 12.00
71 David Perron B 2.50 6.00
72 Jason Spezza C 3.00 8.00
73 Shane Doan C 2.50 6.00
74 Scott Hartnell C 2.00 5.00
75 David Backes C 2.00 5.00
76 Wayne Gretzky A 25.00 60.00
77 Patrick Sharp B 3.00 8.00
78 Vincent Lecavalier B 3.00 8.00
79 T.J. Oshie C 3.00 8.00
81 James Neal B 2.00 5.00
82 Dion Phaneuf C 2.50 6.00
83 Chris Kunitz C 3.00 8.00
85 Gustav Nyquist C 2.00 5.00
86 Mikael Granlund C 2.50 6.00
87 Bobby Ryan B 2.50 6.00
88 Drew Doughty B 4.00 10.00
89 Jonathan Huberdeau C 4.00 10.00
90 Tyler Ennis C 2.00 5.00
91 Roberto Luongo B 5.00 12.00
92 Wayne Gretzky A 25.00 60.00
93 Peter Forsberg B 6.00 15.00
94 Bill Guerin B 3.00 8.00
95 Theoren Fleury B 4.00 10.00
96 Jarome Iginla B 4.00 10.00
97 Steven Stamkos B 6.00 15.00
98 Claude Giroux B 3.00 8.00
99 Phil Esposito B 5.00 12.00
100 Sidney Crosby B 12.00 30.00
101 Guy Carbonneau B 3.00 8.00
102 Mike Gartner B 4.00 10.00
105 Patrice Bergeron C 4.00 10.00
106 Bill Ranford B 3.00 8.00
107 Mike Bossy B 3.00 8.00
108 Sean Monahan C 2.00 5.00
109 Dale Hawerchuk B 4.00 10.00
110 Jaromir Jagr B 10.00 25.00
111 Joe Sakic B 6.00 15.00
112 Henrik Zetterberg B 4.00 10.00
113 Jordan Eberle B 3.00 8.00
114 Grant Fuhr B 5.00 12.00
115 Dominik Hasek B 5.00 12.00
116 Brett Hull B 6.00 15.00
118 Doug Gilmour B 4.00 10.00
119 Jonathan Toews B 5.00 12.00
120 Mario Lemieux B 12.00 30.00
121 Marcel Dionne B 4.00 10.00
122 Mats Sundin B 3.00 8.00
123 Adam Oates B 3.00 8.00
125 Nathan MacKinnon C 12.00 30.00
127 Jeff Carter C 2.50 6.00
128 Jeremy Roenick B 5.00 12.00
129 Steve Yzerman B 8.00 20.00
130 Martin St. Louis C 3.00 8.00
131 Patrick Roy B 8.00 20.00
132 Ray Bourque B 5.00 12.00
133 Trevor Linden B 3.00 8.00
135 Joe Pavelski C 4.00 10.00
136 Pierre Turgeon B 2.50 6.00
137 Nicklas Lidstrom B 3.00 8.00
138 Nail Yakupov C 2.00 5.00
140 Stan Mikita A 4.00 10.00
141 P.K. Subban C 4.00 10.00
142 John Tavares C 5.00 12.00
144 Mark Messier B 6.00 15.00
145 Henrik Lundqvist B 8.00 20.00
147 Carey Price C 6.00 15.00
148 Pelle Lindbergh B 2.50 6.00
149 Chris Chelios B 3.00 8.00
150 Wayne Gretzky A 25.00 60.00
152 Patrick Kane BW B 6.00 15.00
153 Mario Lemieux BW B 12.00 30.00
154 Sidney Crosby BW B 12.00 30.00
155 Mats Sundin BW B 3.00 8.00
156 Alexander Ovechkin BW B 12.00 30.00
157 Phil Kessel BW B 3.00 8.00
158 Steve Yzerman BW B 8.00 20.00
159 Evgeni Malkin BW B 6.00 15.00
160 Pavel Datsyuk BW B 5.00 12.00
162 Nathan MacKinnon BW B 12.00 30.00
163 Mark Messier BW B 6.00 15.00
164 Terry Sawchuk BW B 3.00 8.00
165 Wayne Gretzky BW A 25.00 60.00

2006-07 UD Mini Jersey Collection

COMPLETE SET (130) 40.00 100.00
1 Teemu Selanne .75 2.00
2 Jean-Sebastien Giguere .40 1.00
3 Chris Pronger .40 1.00
4 Ilya Kovalchuk .40 1.00
5 Kari Lehtonen .30 .75
6 Marian Hossa .40 1.00
7 Patrice Bergeron .50 1.25
8 Brad Boyes .25 .60
9 Zdeno Chara .40 1.00
10 Thomas Vanek .30 .75
11 Ryan Miller .40 1.00
12 Chris Drury .30 .75
13 Alex Tanguay .25 .60
14 Miikka Kiprusoff .40 1.00
15 Dion Phaneuf .30 .75
16 Jarome Iginla .50 1.25
17 Eric Staal .50 1.25
18 Cam Ward .40 1.00
19 Erik Cole .25 .60
20 Rod Brind'Amour .40 1.00
21 Martin Havlat .25 .60
22 Nikolai Khabibulin .40 1.00
23 Tuomo Ruutu .40 1.00
24 Joe Sakic .75 2.00
25 Marek Svatos .25 .60
26 Milan Hejduk .30 .75
27 Jose Theodore .40 1.00
28 Fredrik Modin .25 .60
29 Rick Nash .40 1.00
30 Sergei Fedorov .60 1.50
31 Nikolai Zherdev .25 .60
32 Eric Lindros .60 1.50
33 Mike Modano .60 1.50
34 Marty Turco .40 1.00
35 Brenden Morrow .30 .75
36 Henrik Zetterberg .50 1.25
37 Nicklas Lidstrom .40 1.00
38 Dominik Hasek .60 1.50
39 Gordie Howe .75 2.00
40 Pavel Datsyuk .60 1.50
41 Joffrey Lupul .25 .60
42 Fernando Pisani .25 .60
43 Ales Hemsky .30 .75
44 Ryan Smyth .30 .75
45 Dwayne Roloson .30 .75
46 Todd Bertuzzi .40 1.00
47 Olli Jokinen .40 1.00
48 Ed Belfour .40 1.00
49 Rob Blake .40 1.00
50 Alexander Frolov .25 .60
51 Marian Gaborik .40 1.00
52 Manny Fernandez .25 .60
53 Pavol Demitra .50 1.25
54 Saku Koivu .40 1.00
55 Michael Ryder .25 .60
56 Patrick Roy 1.00 2.50
57 Sergei Samsonov .30 .75
58 Paul Kariya .40 1.00
59 Tomas Vokoun .30 .75
60 Martin Brodeur 1.00 2.50
61 Patrik Elias .40 1.00
62 Alexei Yashin .30 .75
63 Miroslav Satan .30 .75
64 Rick DiPietro .30 .75
65 Jaromir Jagr 1.25 3.00
66 Henrik Lundqvist 1.00 2.50
67 Brendan Shanahan .40 1.00
68 Martin Gerber .30 .75
69 Jason Spezza .40 1.00
70 Dany Heatley .30 .75
71 Daniel Alfredsson .40 1.00
72 Mike Richards .30 .75
73 Peter Forsberg .75 2.00
74 Simon Gagne .40 1.00
75 Antero Niittymaki .30 .75
76 Jeff Carter .30 .75
77 Shane Doan .30 .75
78 Jeremy Roenick .60 1.50
79 Curtis Joseph .50 1.25
80 Sidney Crosby 1.50 4.00
81 Marc-Andre Fleury .75 2.00
82 Jonathan Cheechoo .30 .75
83 Vesa Toskala .30 .75
84 Patrick Marleau .40 1.00
85 Joe Thornton .60 1.50
86 Keith Tkachuk .40 1.00
87 Vincent Lecavalier .40 1.00
88 Martin St. Louis .40 1.00
89 Brad Richards .40 1.00
90 Mats Sundin .40 1.00
91 Alexander Steen .25 .60
92 Bryan McCabe .25 .60
93 Andrew Raycroft .30 .75
94 Darcy Tucker .30 .75
95 Markus Naslund .40 1.00
96 Roberto Luongo .60 1.50
97 Henrik Sedin .50 1.25
98 Brendan Morrison .25 .60
99 Olaf Kolzig .40 1.00
100 Alexander Ovechkin 1.50 4.00
101 Yan Stastny RC 2.00 5.00
102 Mark Stuart RC 2.00 5.00
103 Phil Kessel RC 4.00 10.00
104 Ryan Shannon RC 2.00 5.00
105 Tomas Kopecky RC 2.50 6.00
106 M-A Pouliot RC 2.00 5.00
107 K.Pushkarev RC 2.50 6.00
108 Patrick O'Sullivan RC 2.50 6.00
109 Anze Kopitar RC 6.00 15.00
110 Shea Weber RC 5.00 12.00
111 Travis Zajac RC 4.00 10.00
112 G. Latendresse RC 2.00 5.00
113 M-E Vlasic RC 3.00 8.00
114 Ladislav Smid RC 2.00 5.00
115 Loui Eriksson RC 1.50 4.00
116 Kristopher Letang RC 8.00 20.00
117 Jarkko Immonen RC 2.50 6.00
118 Nigel Dawes RC 2.00 5.00
119 Luc Bourdon RC 3.00 8.00
120 Ryan Potulny RC 2.00 5.00
121 Keith Yandle RC 5.00 12.00
122 Patrick Thoresen RC 2.00 5.00
123 Noah Welch RC 2.00 5.00
124 Jordan Staal RC 4.00 10.00
125 Matt Carle RC 2.00 5.00
126 Evgeni Malkin RC 10.00 25.00
127 Brendan Bell RC 2.00 5.00
128 Ian White RC 2.50 6.00
129 Jeremy Williams RC 2.00 5.00
130 Eric Fehr RC 2.00 5.00

2006-07 UD Mini Jersey Collection Home Jerseys

COMPLETE SET (21) 125.00 200.00
*AWAY JERSEY: 1X TO 2.5X HOME JERSEY
*AWAY JERSEY: .6X TO 1.5X HOME JRSY SP
AF Alexander Frolov 1.50 4.00
AO Alexander Ovechkin 10.00 25.00
DH Dany Heatley 2.00 5.00
DP Dion Phaneuf 2.00 5.00
EM Evgeni Malkin 6.00 15.00
ES Eric Staal 3.00 8.00
GH Gordie Howe SP 60.00 100.00
HL Henrik Lundqvist 6.00 15.00
IK Ilya Kovalchuk 2.50 6.00
JS Joe Sakic 5.00 12.00
JT Joe Thornton 4.00 10.00
MN Markus Naslund 2.50 6.00
MR Michael Ryder 1.50 4.00
MS Mats Sundin 2.50 6.00
MT Marty Turco 2.50 6.00
PB Patrice Bergeron 3.00 8.00
PF Peter Forsberg 5.00 12.00
PR Patrick Roy 6.00 15.00
RN Rick Nash 2.50 6.00
SC Sidney Crosby 8.00 20.00
TV Thomas Vanek 2.00 5.00

2006-07 UD Mini Jersey Collection Jersey Autographs

1 Patrice Bergeron SP 50.00 100.00
2 Sidney Crosby SP 300.00 500.00
3 Alexander Frolov 25.00 60.00
4 Dany Heatley SP
5 Gordie Howe SP 250.00 400.00
6 Ilya Kovalchuk SP 75.00 150.00
7 Markus Naslund 25.00 60.00
8 Alexander Ovechkin SP 80.00 200.00
9 Dion Phaneuf 30.00 80.00
10 Michael Ryder 20.00 50.00
11 Eric Staal 40.00 80.00
12 Joe Thornton SP 75.00 150.00
13 Marty Turco 15.00 40.00
14 Thomas Vanek 30.00 60.00

2007-08 UD Mini Jersey Collection

COMPLETE SET (150) 125.00 250.00
COMP.SET w/o SPs (100) 12.00 30.00
1 Jean-Sebastien Giguere .40 1.00
2 Ryan Getzlaf .40 1.00
3 Scott Niedermayer .40 1.00
4 Chris Pronger .40 1.00
5 Ilya Kovalchuk .40 1.00
6 Marian Hossa .40 1.00
7 Kari Lehtonen .30 .75
8 Patrice Bergeron .50 1.25
9 Phil Kessel .40 1.00
10 Zdeno Chara .40 1.00
11 Ryan Miller .40 1.00
12 Thomas Vanek .30 .75
13 Jason Pominville .25 .60
14 Derek Roy .25 .60
15 Miikka Kiprusoff .40 1.00
16 Jarome Iginla .50 1.25
17 Alex Tanguay .30 .75
18 Dion Phaneuf .30 .75
19 Eric Staal .50 1.25
20 Cam Ward .40 1.00
21 Justin Williams .30 .75
22 Martin Havlat .40 1.00
23 Nikolai Khabibulin .40 1.00
24 Duncan Keith .30 .75
25 Joe Sakic .75 2.00
26 Milan Hejduk .30 .75
27 Peter Budaj .30 .75
28 Paul Stastny .30 .75
29 Marty Turco .40 1.00
30 Mike Modano .60 1.50
31 Mike Ribeiro .25 .60
32 Henrik Zetterberg .50 1.25
33 Nicklas Lidstrom .40 1.00
34 Pavel Datsyuk .60 1.50
35 Dominik Hasek .60 1.50
36 Ales Hemsky .30 .75
37 Dwayne Roloson .30 .75
38 Jarret Stoll .30 .75
39 Shawn Horcoff .25 .60
40 Tomas Vokoun .30 .75
41 Olli Jokinen .30 .75
42 Nathan Horton .40 1.00
43 Anze Kopitar .60 1.50
44 Alexander Frolov .25 .60
45 Rob Blake .40 1.00
46 Mike Cammalleri .30 .75
47 Marian Gaborik .40 1.00
48 Niklas Backstrom .40 1.00
49 Pierre-Marc Bouchard .40 1.00
50 Saku Koivu .40 1.00
51 Michael Ryder .25 .60
52 Guillaume Latendresse .30 .75
53 Cristobal Huet .30 .75
54 Alexander Radulov .40 1.00
55 Chris Mason .30 .75
56 Jason Arnott .30 .75
57 Martin Brodeur 1.00 2.50
58 Patrik Elias .40 1.00
59 Zach Parise .40 1.00
60 Miroslav Satan .30 .75
61 Bill Guerin .40 1.00
62 Rick DiPietro .30 .75
63 Jaromir Jagr 1.25 3.00
64 Henrik Lundqvist 1.00 2.50
65 Martin Straka .25 .60
66 Dany Heatley .30 .75
67 Ray Emery .30 .75
68 Daniel Alfredsson .40 1.00
69 Jason Spezza .40 1.00
70 Simon Gagne .40 1.00
71 Jeff Carter .30 .75
72 Martin Biron .30 .75
73 Shane Doan .30 .75
74 Ed Jovanovski .30 .75
75 Keith Ballard .25 .60
76 Sidney Crosby 1.50 4.00
77 Evgeni Malkin .75 2.00
78 Marc-Andre Fleury .75 2.00
79 Jordan Staal .30 .75
80 Joe Thornton .60 1.50
81 Patrick Marleau .40 1.00
82 Jonathan Cheechoo .30 .75
83 Evgeni Nabokov .30 .75
84 Doug Weight .40 1.00
85 Manny Legace .30 .75
86 Brad Boyes .25 .60
87 Vincent Lecavalier .40 1.00
88 Brad Richards .40 1.00
89 Martin St. Louis .40 1.00
90 Mats Sundin .40 1.00
91 Vesa Toskala .30 .75
92 Alexander Steen .25 .60
93 Darcy Tucker .30 .75
94 Roberto Luongo .60 1.50
95 Markus Naslund .40 1.00
96 Henrik Sedin .50 1.25
97 Daniel Sedin .50 1.25
98 Alexander Ovechkin 1.50 4.00
99 Olaf Kolzig .40 1.00
100 Alexander Semin .40 1.00
101 Bobby Ryan RC 2.50 6.00
102 Drew Miller RC 1.25 3.00
103 Bryan Little RC 1.50 4.00
104 Ondrej Pavelec RC 2.00 5.00
105 Tuukka Rask RC 4.00 10.00
106 Vladimir Sobotka RC 1.25 3.00
107 Milan Lucic RC 4.00 10.00
108 Curtis McElhinney RC 1.50 4.00
109 Matt Keetley RC 1.00 2.50
110 Jonathan Toews RC 8.00 20.00
111 Patrick Kane RC 6.00 15.00
112 Tyler Weiman RC 1.25 3.00
113 T.J. Hensick RC 1.25 3.00
114 Kris Russell RC 1.50 4.00
115 Jared Boll RC 1.25 3.00
116 Matt Niskanen RC 1.50 4.00
117 Sam Gagner RC 2.00 5.00
118 Andrew Cogliano RC 1.25 3.00
119 Rob Schremp RC 1.25 3.00
120 Stefan Meyer RC 1.25 3.00
121 Jack Johnson RC 1.25 3.00
122 Jonathan Bernier RC 2.00 5.00
123 Petr Kalus RC 1.00 2.50
124 James Sheppard RC 1.00 2.50
125 Cal Clutterbuck RC 1.50 4.00
126 Carey Price RC 8.00 20.00
127 Kyle Chipchura RC 1.50 4.00
128 Nicklas Bergfors RC 1.00 2.50
129 Andy Greene RC 1.25 3.00
130 Frans Nielsen RC 1.50 4.00
131 Marc Staal RC 1.50 4.00
132 Ryan Callahan RC 2.00 5.00
133 Alexander Nikulin RC 1.00 2.50
134 Nick Foligno RC 2.00 5.00
135 Steve Downie RC 1.25 3.00
136 Peter Mueller RC 1.25 3.00
137 Martin Hanzal RC 1.25 3.00
138 Tyler Kennedy RC 1.00 2.50
139 Thomas Greiss RC 2.00 5.00
140 Devin Setoguchi RC 1.50 4.00
141 Torrey Mitchell RC 1.25 3.00
142 Erik Johnson RC 1.50 4.00
143 David Perron RC 2.00 5.00
144 Matt Smaby RC 1.00 2.50
145 Anton Stralman RC 1.00 2.50
146 Jiri Tlusty RC 1.50 4.00
147 Mason Raymond RC 1.50 4.00
148 Jannik Hansen RC 1.25 3.00
149 Chris Bourque RC 1.25 3.00
150 Nicklas Backstrom RC 3.00 8.00

2007-08 UD Mini Jersey Collection Home Jerseys

COMPLETE SET (30) 75.00 150.00
*AWAY JERSEY: .6X TO 1.5X HOME JERSEY
MINI1 Teemu Selanne 5.00 12.00
MINI2 Kari Lehtonen 2.00 5.00
MINI3 Phil Kessel 2.50 6.00
MINI4 Ryan Miller 2.50 6.00
MINI5 Jarome Iginla 3.00 8.00
MINI6 Cam Ward 2.50 6.00
MINI7 Martin Havlat 2.50 6.00
MINI8 Joe Sakic 5.00 12.00
MINI9 Sergei Fedorov 4.00 10.00
MINI10 Mike Modano 4.00 10.00
MINI11 Henrik Zetterberg 3.00 8.00
MINI12 Dwayne Roloson 2.00 5.00
MINI13 Olli Jokinen 2.00 5.00
MINI14 Anze Kopitar 4.00 10.00
MINI15 Marian Gaborik 2.50 6.00
MINI16 Saku Koivu 2.50 6.00
MINI17 Alexander Radulov 2.50 6.00
MINI18 Martin Brodeur 6.00 15.00
MINI19 Rick DiPietro 2.00 5.00
MINI20 Jaromir Jagr 8.00 20.00
MINI21 Jason Spezza 2.50 6.00
MINI22 Simon Gagne 2.50 6.00
MINI23 Shane Doan 2.00 5.00
MINI24 Sidney Crosby 10.00 25.00
MINI25 Jonathan Cheechoo 1.50 4.00
MINI26 Doug Weight 2.50 6.00
MINI27 Vincent Lecavalier 2.50 6.00
MINI28 Mats Sundin 2.50 6.00
MINI29 Roberto Luongo 4.00 10.00
MINI30 Alexander Ovechkin 10.00 25.00
NNO Checklist Card .05 .15

2007-08 UD Mini Jersey Collection Jerseys Autographs

1 Martin Brodeur 80.00 200.00
2 Jonathan Cheechoo 25.00 60.00
3 Sidney Crosby 125.00 300.00
4 Marian Gaborik
5 Simon Gagne
6 Martin Havlat 25.00 60.00
7 Jarome Iginla 40.00 100.00
8 Phil Kessel 30.00 80.00
9 Saku Koivu
10 Anze Kopitar 50.00 125.00
11 Vincent Lecavalier 40.00 80.00
12 Ryan Miller 30.00 80.00
13 Mike Modano 50.00 125.00
14 Alexander Ovechkin 125.00 300.00
15 Alexander Radulov 25.00 60.00
16 Dwayne Roloson 25.00 60.00
17 Cam Ward 30.00 80.00
18 Checklist Card .30 .75

2002-03 UD Piece of History

COMP.SET w/o SP's (90) 15.00 30.00
1 Paul Kariya .25 .60
2 Jean-Sebastien Giguere .25 .60
3 Ilya Kovalchuk .30 .75
4 Dany Heatley .20 .50
5 Joe Thornton .40 1.00
6 Sergei Samsonov .20 .50
7 Glen Murray .20 .50
8 Miroslav Satan .25 .60
9 Tim Connolly .15 .40
10 Martin Biron .20 .50
11 Jeff O'Neill .15 .40
12 Erik Cole .15 .40
13 Ron Francis .30 .75
14 Arturs Irbe .20 .50
15 Roman Turek .25 .60
16 Marc Savard .15 .40
17 Jarome Iginla .30 .75
18 Eric Daze .15 .40
19 Steve Sullivan .15 .40
20 Jocelyn Thibault .20 .50
21 Espen Knutsen .15 .40
22 Rostislav Klesla .15 .40
23 Marc Denis .20 .50
24 Patrick Roy .60 1.50
25 Chris Drury .25 .60
26 Joe Sakic .50 1.25
27 Peter Forsberg .50 1.25
28 Alex Tanguay .20 .50
29 Mike Modano .40 1.00
30 Marty Turco .25 .60
31 Jason Arnott .20 .50
32 Steve Yzerman .60 1.50
33 Sergei Fedorov .40 1.00
34 Nicklas Lidstrom .25 .60
35 Brett Hull .50 1.25
36 Curtis Joseph .30 .75
37 Brendan Shanahan .25 .60
38 Mike Comrie .25 .60
39 Tommy Salo .20 .50
40 Ryan Smyth .20 .50
41 Roberto Luongo .40 1.00
42 Kristian Huselius .15 .40
43 Jason Allison .20 .50
44 Felix Potvin .40 1.00
45 Zigmund Palffy .25 .60
46 Marian Gaborik .25 .60
47 Manny Fernandez .15 .40
48 Jose Theodore .25 .60
49 Saku Koivu .25 .60
50 Patrik Elias .25 .60
51 Martin Brodeur .60 1.50
52 Joe Nieuwendyk .20 .50
53 Scott Hartnell .15 .40
54 Mike Dunham .20 .50
55 Alexei Yashin .20 .50
56 Chris Osgood .25 .60
57 Michael Peca .20 .50
58 Eric Lindros .40 1.00
59 Mike Richter .25 .60
60 Pavel Bure .25 .60
61 Brian Leetch .20 .50
62 Patrick Lalime .20 .50
63 Marian Hossa .25 .60
64 Daniel Alfredsson .25 .60
65 Jeremy Roenick .40 1.00
66 Simon Gagne .25 .60
67 Roman Cechmanek .20 .50
68 Sean Burke .15 .40
69 Daniel Briere .20 .50
70 Tony Amonte .20 .50
71 Alexei Kovalev .20 .50
72 Mario Lemieux 1.00 2.50
73 Johan Hedberg .25 .60
74 Patrick Marleau .25 .60
75 Owen Nolan .25 .60
76 Evgeni Nabokov .20 .50
77 Keith Tkachuk .25 .60
78 Chris Pronger .25 .60
79 Brent Johnson .20 .50
80 Nikolai Khabibulin .25 .60
81 Vincent Lecavalier .25 .60
82 Alexander Mogilny .20 .50
83 Mats Sundin .25 .60
84 Ed Belfour .25 .60
85 Todd Bertuzzi .25 .60
86 Dan Cloutier .20 .50
87 Markus Naslund .25 .60
88 Olaf Kolzig .25 .60
89 Peter Bondra .25 .60
90 Jaromir Jagr .75 2.00
91 Wayne Gretzky SR 6.00 15.00
92 Wayne Gretzky SR 6.00 15.00
93 Mario Lemieux SR 4.00 10.00
94 Patrick Roy SR 2.50 6.00
95 Steve Yzerman SR 2.50 6.00
96 Gordie Howe SR 3.00 8.00
97 Bobby Orr SR 4.00 10.00
98 Ray Bourque SR 1.50 4.00
99 Brett Hull SR 2.00 5.00
100 Teemu Selanne SR 2.00 5.00
101 Martin Brodeur SR 2.50 6.00
102 Jaromir Jagr SR 3.00 8.00
103 Eric Lindros SR 1.50 4.00
104 Joe Sakic SR 2.00 5.00
105 Mike Richter SR 1.00 2.50
106 Sergei Fedorov SR 1.50 4.00
107 Peter Forsberg SR 2.00 5.00
108 Mark Messier SR 2.00 5.00
109 Wayne Gretzky TG 6.00 15.00
110 Wayne Gretzky TG 6.00 15.00
111 Wayne Gretzky TG 6.00 15.00
112 Gordie Howe TG 3.00 8.00
113 Gordie Howe TG 3.00 8.00
114 Gordie Howe TG 3.00 8.00
115 Bobby Orr TG 4.00 10.00
116 Bobby Orr TG 4.00 10.00
117 Bobby Orr TG 4.00 10.00
118 Ray Bourque TG 1.50 4.00
119 Ray Bourque TG 1.50 4.00
120 Ray Bourque TG 1.50 4.00
121 Stanislav Chistov HM RC .75 2.00
122 Alexei Smirnov HM RC 1.00 2.50
123 Henrik Tallinder HM .75 2.00
124 Micki Dupont HM RC .75 2.00
125 Chuck Kobasew HM RC 1.00 2.50
126 Andrej Nedorost HM .75 2.00
127 Rick Nash HM RC 5.00 12.00
128 Henrik Zetterberg HM RC 8.00 20.00
129 Ales Hemsky HM RC 3.00 8.00
130 Jani Rita HM .75 2.00
131 Stephen Weiss HM 1.25 3.00
132 Jay Bouwmeester HM RC 2.50 6.00
133 Alexander Frolov HM RC 2.00 5.00
134 P-M Bouchard HM RC 1.25 3.00
135 Sylvain Blouin HM RC .75 2.00
136 Ron Hainsey HM RC .75 2.00
137 Adam Hall HM RC .75 2.00
138 Jan Lasak HM 1.00 2.50
139 Ray Schultz HM RC .75 2.00
140 Trent Hunter HM .75 2.00
141 Martin Prusek HM .75 2.00
142 Anton Volchenkov HM RC .75 2.00
143 Patrick Sharp HM RC 2.50 6.00
144 Dennis Seidenberg HM RC 1.25 3.00
145 Branko Radivojevic HM .75 2.00
146 Shane Endicott HM .75 2.00
147 Alexander Svitov HM RC .75 2.00
148 Sebastien Centomo HM .75 2.00
149 Karel Pilar HM .75 2.00
150 Steve Eminger HM RC .75 2.00

2002-03 UD Piece of History Awards Collection

COMPLETE SET (28) 25.00 50.00
AC1 Paul Kariya .50 1.25
AC2 Ray Bourque 1.00 2.50
AC3 Sergei Samsonov .40 1.00
AC4 Jarome Iginla .60 1.50
AC5 Chris Drury .40 1.00
AC6 Joe Sakic 1.00 2.50
AC7 Rob Blake .40 1.00
AC8 Peter Forsberg 1.25 3.00
AC9 Patrick Roy 2.00 5.00
AC10 Luc Robitaille .40 1.00
AC11 Brett Hull .60 1.50
AC12 Steve Yzerman 2.00 5.00
AC13 Dominik Hasek 1.00 2.50
AC14 Nicklas Lidstrom .50 1.25
AC15 Sergei Fedorov 1.00 2.50
AC16 Wayne Gretzky 3.00 8.00
AC17 Joe Nieuwendyk .40 1.00
AC18 Martin Brodeur 1.50 4.00
AC19 Brian Leetch .40 1.00
AC20 Pavel Bure .60 1.50
AC21 Claude Lemieux .40 1.00
AC22 Mario Lemieux 2.50 6.00
AC23 Evgeni Nabokov .40 1.00
AC24 Teemu Selanne .50 1.25
AC25 Chris Pronger .40 1.00
AC26 Al MacInnis .40 1.00
AC27 Jaromir Jagr .75 2.00
AC28 Olaf Kolzig .40 1.00

2002-03 UD Piece of History Exquisite Combos

ECBM P.Bure/M.Messier 12.50 30.00
ECBR R.Blake/P.Roy 10.00 25.00
ECLK M.Lemieux/A.Kovalev 20.00 50.00
ECLM E.Lindros/M.Messier 10.00 25.00
ECNB C.Neely/R.Bourque 12.50 30.00

2002-03 UD Piece of History Heroes Jerseys

HHBS Borje Salming 4.00 10.00
HHGP Gilbert Perreault 3.00 8.00
HHJK Jari Kurri 5.00 12.00
HHMG Mike Gartner 3.00 8.00
HHPS Peter Stastny 3.00 8.00

2002-03 UD Piece of History Historical Swatches Jerseys

HSBS Borje Salming 6.00 15.00
HSBT Bryan Trottier 5.00 12.00
HSCN Cam Neely 12.50 30.00
HSGL Guy Lafleur 5.00 12.00
HSJB Johnny Bucyk 5.00 12.00
HSMB Mike Bossy 5.00 12.00
HSMG Michel Goulet 6.00 15.00
HSMG Mike Gartner 5.00 12.00

HSRB Ray Bourque 15.00 40.00
HSWG Wayne Gretzky 30.00 80.00

2002-03 UD Piece of History Hockey Beginnings

COMPLETE SET (8) 20.00 40.00
HB1 Bobby Orr 2.50 6.00
HB2 Ray Bourque .75 2.00
HB3 Steve Yzerman 2.00 5.00
HB4 Gordie Howe 2.00 5.00
HB5 Wayne Gretzky 2.50 6.00
HB6 Patrick Roy 2.00 5.00
HB7 Mike Bossy .60 1.50
HB8 Wayne Gretzky 2.50 6.00

2002-03 UD Piece of History Marks of Distinction

BO Bobby Orr/24 125.00 200.00
BR Rod Brind'Amour 6.00 15.00
BT Bryan Trottier/25
CN Cam Neely/25
DH Dany Heatley 12.50 30.00
DS Daniel Sedin 8.00 20.00
GA Mike Gartner/25 15.00 40.00
GH Gordie Howe/24 75.00 150.00
GL Guy Lafleur/25 75.00 100.00
GP Gilbert Perreault/25 20.00 40.00
HS Henrik Sedin 8.00 20.00
JB Johnny Bucyk/25
JI Jarome Iginla SP 12.50 30.00
JK Jari Kurri/25 15.00 40.00
JT Joe Thornton/24
MB Mike Bossy/25
MC Mike Comrie SP 12.50 30.00
MG Michel Goulet/25
MN Markus Naslund 8.00 20.00
MR Mike Richter 6.00 15.00
PA Pavel Brendl 6.00 15.00
PB Pavel Bure/24
PR Patrick Roy/24
PS Peter Stastny/25
RA Ray Bourque/24
SG Simon Gagne SP 12.50 30.00
SS Sergei Samsonov SP 12.50 30.00
SY Steve Yzerman 40.00 100.00
TS Teemu Selanne 12.00 30.00
VN Vaclav Nedorost 6.00 15.00
WG Wayne Gretzky/24 400.00 1000.00

2002-03 UD Piece of History Patches

PHBA Rob Blake 20.00 50.00
PHBL Brian Leetch 20.00 50.00
PHBS Brendan Shanahan 20.00 50.00
PHEL Eric Lindros 20.00 50.00
PHFP Felix Potvin 25.00 60.00
PHJS Joe Sakic 50.00 125.00
PHJT Jose Theodore 25.00 60.00
PHKP Keith Primeau 20.00 50.00
PHMA Maxim Afinogenov 20.00 50.00
PHMD Mike Dunham 20.00 50.00
PHMM Mike Modano 30.00 80.00
PHMN Markus Naslund 20.00 50.00
PHMS Mats Sundin 20.00 50.00
PHMT Marty Turco 20.00 50.00
PHPK Paul Kariya 20.00 50.00
PHPR Patrick Roy 75.00 200.00
PHRB Ray Bourque 40.00 100.00
PHRT Ron Tugnutt 20.00 50.00
PHSA Sergei Samsonov 20.00 50.00
PHSB Sean Burke 20.00 50.00
PHSF Sergei Fedorov 30.00 80.00
PHSG Simon Gagne 20.00 50.00
PHSS Steve Sullivan 20.00 50.00
PHSY Steve Yzerman 50.00 120.00
PHTH Joe Thornton 30.00 80.00
PHTS Teemu Selanne 20.00 50.00
PHWG Wayne Gretzky 125.00 300.00
PHZP Zigmund Palffy 20.00 50.00

2002-03 UD Piece of History Simply the Best

COMPLETE SET (6) 20.00 40.00
SB1 Ray Bourque 1.25 3.00
SB2 Bobby Orr 4.00 10.00
SB3 Patrick Roy 3.00 8.00
SB4 Steve Yzerman 3.00 8.00
SB5 Gordie Howe 3.00 8.00
SB6 Wayne Gretzky 4.00 10.00

2002-03 UD Piece of History Stellar Stitches Jerseys

SSJS Joe Sakic 6.00 15.00
SSJT Joe Thornton 8.00 20.00
SSMM Mike Modano 8.00 20.00
SSMS Mats Sundin 8.00 20.00
SSPK Paul Kariya 10.00 25.00
SSSY Steve Yzerman 15.00 40.00

2002-03 UD Piece of History Threads Jerseys

TTCD Chris Drury 4.00 10.00
TTCL Claude Lemieux 5.00 12.00
TTJT Jose Theodore 6.00 15.00
TTSF Sergei Fedorov 8.00 20.00
TTSG Simon Gagne 5.00 12.00
TTSH Scott Hartnell 5.00 12.00

2001-02 UD Playmakers

COMP.SET w/o SP's (100) 8.00 20.00
1 Steve Shields .12 .30
2 Jeff Friesen .10 .25
3 Paul Kariya .15 .40
4 Ray Ferraro .10 .25
5 Milan Hnilicka .12 .30
6 Dany Heatley .12 .30
7 Sergei Samsonov .12 .30
8 Joe Thornton .25 .60
9 Byron Dafoe .12 .30
10 Hal Gill .10 .25
11 Miroslav Satan .12 .30
12 Stu Barnes .12 .30
13 Martin Biron .12 .30
14 Marc Savard .10 .25
15 Roman Turek .12 .30
16 Jarome Iginla .20 .50
17 Jeff O'Neill .12 .30
18 Sami Kapanen .10 .25
19 Arturs Irbe .12 .30
20 Steve Sullivan .10 .25
21 Jocelyn Thibault .12 .30
22 Tony Amonte .12 .30
23 Joe Sakic .30 .75
24 Milan Hejduk .12 .30
25 Chris Drury .12 .30
26 Patrick Roy .40 1.00
27 Rob Blake .15 .40
28 Marc Denis .12 .30
29 Ray Whitney .10 .25
30 Rostislav Klesla .10 .25
31 Ed Belfour .15 .40
32 Pierre Turgeon .12 .30
33 Mike Modano .25 .60
34 Brett Hull .30 .75
35 Dominik Hasek .25 .60
36 Brendan Shanahan .15 .40
37 Luc Robitaille .15 .40
38 Steve Yzerman .40 1.00
39 Mike Comrie .12 .30
40 Tommy Salo .12 .30
41 Ryan Smyth .12 .30
42 Anson Carter .12 .30
43 Valeri Bure .10 .25
44 Roberto Luongo .25 .60
45 Pavel Bure .15 .40
46 Felix Potvin .25 .60
47 Jason Allison .12 .30
48 Zigmund Palffy .15 .40
49 Manny Fernandez .10 .25
50 Marian Gaborik .15 .40
51 Andrew Brunette .10 .25
52 Yanic Perreault .10 .25
53 Jose Theodore .15 .40
54 Brian Savage .10 .25
55 David Legwand .12 .30
56 Mike Dunham .12 .30
57 Cliff Ronning .10 .25
58 Martin Brodeur .40 1.00
59 Patrik Elias .15 .40
60 Jason Arnott .12 .30
61 Alexei Yashin .12 .30
62 Chris Osgood .15 .40
63 Mark Parrish .10 .25
64 Theo Fleury .20 .50
65 Brian Leetch .12 .30
66 Mark Messier .30 .75
67 Eric Lindros .25 .60
68 Radek Bonk .10 .25
69 Marian Hossa .15 .40
70 Martin Havlat .12 .30
71 John LeClair .15 .40
72 Mark Recchi .20 .50
73 Roman Cechmanek .12 .30
74 Jeremy Roenick .25 .60
75 Michal Handzus .10 .25
76 Shane Doan .12 .30
77 Sean Burke .10 .25
78 Alexei Kovalev .12 .30
79 Mario Lemieux .60 1.50
80 Johan Hedberg .12 .30
81 Owen Nolan .15 .40
82 Teemu Selanne .30 .75
83 Evgeni Nabokov .12 .30
84 Chris Pronger .15 .40
85 Pavol Demitra .20 .50
86 Keith Tkachuk .15 .40
87 Doug Weight .15 .40
88 Vincent Lecavalier .15 .40
89 Brad Richards .15 .40
90 Nikolai Khabibulin .15 .40
91 Wade Belak .12 .30
92 Alexander Mogilny .12 .30
93 Mats Sundin .15 .40
94 Curtis Joseph .20 .50
95 Brendan Morrison .12 .30
96 Trevor Linden .15 .40
97 Markus Naslund .15 .40
98 Peter Bondra .15 .40
99 Olaf Kolzig .15 .40
100 Jaromir Jagr .50 1.25
101 Timo Parssinen RC 1.25 3.00
102 Ilja Bryzgalov RC 2.50 6.00
103 Mike Weaver RC 1.00 2.50
104 Ilya Kovalchuk RC 5.00 12.00
105 Ivan Huml RC 1.00 2.50
106 Tony Tuzzolino RC 1.00 2.50
107 Jukka Hentunen RC 1.00 2.50
108 Scott Nichol RC 1.00 2.50
109 Erik Cole RC 2.00 5.00
110 Mike Peluso RC 1.00 2.50
111 Riku Hahl RC 1.00 2.50
112 Vaclav Nedorost RC 1.00 2.50
113 Blake Bellefeuille RC 1.00 2.50
114 Niko Kapanen RC 1.50 4.00
115 John Erskine RC 1.00 2.50
116 Pavel Datsyuk RC 5.00 12.00
117 Ty Conklin RC 1.50 4.00
118 Jason Chimera RC 1.00 2.50
119 Niklas Hagman RC 1.25 3.00
120 Kristian Huselius RC 1.50 4.00
121 Kip Brennan RC 1.00 2.50
122 Pascal Dupuis RC 1.50 4.00
123 Marcel Hossa RC 1.50 4.00
124 Olivier Michaud RC 1.50 4.00
125 Martin Erat RC 1.25 3.00
126 Christian Berglund RC 1.25 3.00
127 Andreas Salomonsson RC 1.00 2.50
128 Raffi Torres RC 1.50 4.00
129 Radek Martinek RC 1.00 2.50
130 Mikael Samuelsson RC 1.25 3.00
131 Dan Blackburn RC 1.25 3.00
132 Toni Dahlman RC 1.00 2.50
133 Bruno St. Jacques RC 1.00 2.50
134 Tomas Divisek RC 1.25 3.00
135 Jiri Dopita RC 1.00 2.50
136 Krys Kolanos RC 1.00 2.50
137 Eric Meloche RC 1.00 2.50
138 Tom Kostopoulos RC 1.00 2.50
139 Jeff Jillson RC 1.00 2.50
140 Mark Rycroft RC 1.25 3.00
141 Josef Boumedienne RC 1.00 2.50
142 Nikita Alexeev RC 1.00 2.50
143 Mike Farrell RC 1.00 2.50
144 Todd Rohloff RC 1.00 2.50
145 Brian Sutherby RC 1.00 2.50

2001-02 UD Playmakers Bobble Heads

CJA Curtis Joseph 5.00 12.00
CJH Curtis Joseph 5.00 12.00
DHA Dominik Hasek 5.00 12.00
DHH Dominik Hasek 5.00 12.00
DWA Doug Weight 5.00 12.00
DWH Doug Weight 5.00 12.00
ELA Eric Lindros 5.00 12.00
ELH Eric Lindros 5.00 12.00
IKA Ilya Kovalchuk 10.00 25.00
IKH Ilya Kovalchuk 10.00 25.00
JJA Jaromir Jagr 5.00 12.00
JJH Jaromir Jagr 5.00 12.00
JSA Joe Sakic 5.00 12.00
JSH Joe Sakic 5.00 12.00
MBA Martin Brodeur 5.00 12.00
MBH Martin Brodeur 5.00 12.00
MMA Mike Modano 5.00 12.00
MMH Mike Modano 5.00 12.00
PBA Pavel Bure 5.00 12.00
PBH Pavel Bure 5.00 12.00
PRA Patrick Roy 10.00 25.00
PRH Patrick Roy 10.00 25.00
SYA Steve Yzerman 10.00 25.00
SYH Steve Yzerman 10.00 25.00

2001-02 UD Playmakers Bobble Heads Autographed

CJA Curtis Joseph 30.00 80.00
CJH Curtis Joseph 30.00 80.00
DWA Doug Weight 12.50 30.00
DWH Doug Weight 12.50 30.00
IKA Ilya Kovalchuk 30.00 80.00
IKH Ilya Kovalchuk 30.00 80.00
MBA Martin Brodeur 40.00 100.00
MBH Martin Brodeur 40.00 100.00
PBA Pavel Bure 25.00 60.00
PBH Pavel Bure 25.00 60.00
SYA Steve Yzerman 30.00 80.00
SYH Steve Yzerman 30.00 80.00

2001-02 UD Playmakers Combo Jerseys

*GOLD/50: .8X TO 2X BASIC COMBO
CJJI Jarome Iginla 12.50 30.00
CJJL John LeClair 10.00 25.00
CJMA Maxim Afinogenov 10.00 25.00
CJMD Mike Dunham 10.00 25.00
CJMH Milan Hejduk 10.00 25.00
CJMR Mark Recchi 10.00 25.00
CJPK Paul Kariya 10.00 25.00
CJPR Patrick Roy 25.00 60.00
CJRB Rob Blake 10.00 25.00
CJSG Simon Gagne 12.50 30.00

2001-02 UD Playmakers Jerseys

*GOLD/100: .6X TO 1.5X BASIC JSY
JJI Jarome Iginla 6.00 15.00
JMA Maxim Afinogenov 5.00 12.00
JMB Martin Brodeur 8.00 20.00
JML Mario Lemieux 12.00 30.00
JMR Mark Recchi 5.00 12.00
JPF Peter Forsberg 6.00 15.00
JRT Ron Tugnutt 5.00 12.00
JSG Simon Gagne 5.00 12.00
JTS Teemu Selanne 5.00 12.00
JZP Zigmund Palffy 5.00 12.00

2001-02 UD Playmakers Practice Jerseys

*GOLD/200: .6X TO 1.5X BASIC JSY
PJEB Ed Belfour 6.00 15.00
PJJI Jarome Iginla 8.00 20.00
PJJL John LeClair 6.00 15.00
PJMH Milan Hejduk 6.00 15.00
PJMO Maxime Ouellet 5.00 12.00
PJMS Miroslav Satan 5.00 12.00
PJRB Rod Brind'Amour 5.00 12.00
PJRF Rico Fata 5.00 12.00
PJSG Simon Gagne 6.00 15.00
PJTB Tyler Bouck 5.00 12.00

2001-02 UD Premier Collection

1 Paul Kariya 1.00 2.50
2 Dany Heatley .75 2.00
3 Joe Thornton 1.50 4.00
4 Ray Bourque 1.50 4.00
5 Bobby Orr 4.00 10.00
6 Sergei Samsonov .75 2.00
7 Tim Connolly .60 1.50
8 Jarome Iginla 1.25 3.00
9 Arturs Irbe .75 2.00
10 Jocelyn Thibault .75 2.00
11 Joe Sakic 2.00 5.00
12 Patrick Roy 2.50 6.00
13 Peter Forsberg 2.00 5.00
14 Chris Drury .75 2.00
15 Milan Hejduk .75 2.00
16 Rostislav Klesla .60 1.50
17 Mike Modano 1.50 4.00
18 Ed Belfour 1.00 2.50
19 Gordie Howe 3.00 8.00
20 Brendan Shanahan 1.00 2.50
21 Steve Yzerman 2.50 6.00
22 Brett Hull 2.00 5.00
23 Dominik Hasek 1.50 4.00
24 Sergei Fedorov 1.50 4.00
25 Wayne Gretzky 6.00 15.00
26 Tommy Salo .75 2.00
27 Roberto Luongo 1.50 4.00
28 Felix Potvin 1.50 4.00
29 Marian Gaborik 1.00 2.50
30 Jose Theodore 1.00 2.50
31 Mike Dunham .75 2.00
32 Martin Brodeur 2.50 6.00
33 Alexei Yashin .75 2.00
34 Eric Lindros 1.50 4.00
35 Pavel Bure 1.00 2.50
36 Marian Hossa 1.00 2.50
37 Jeremy Roenick 1.50 4.00
38 John LeClair 1.00 2.50
39 Simon Gagne 1.00 2.50
40 Sean Burke .60 1.50
41 Mario Lemieux 4.00 10.00
42 Evgeni Nabokov .75 2.00
43 Teemu Selanne 2.00 5.00
44 Keith Tkachuk 1.00 2.50
45 Chris Pronger 1.00 2.50
46 Brad Richards 1.00 2.50
47 Curtis Joseph 1.25 3.00
48 Mats Sundin 1.00 2.50
49 Markus Naslund 1.00 2.50
50 Jaromir Jagr 3.00 8.00
51 Timo Parssinen RC 4.00 10.00
52 Ben Simon RC 4.00 10.00
53 Frederic Cassivi RC 3.00 8.00
54 Ales Kotalik RC 6.00 15.00
55 Mike Peluso RC 3.00 8.00
56 Steve Moore RC 5.00 12.00
57 Martin Spanhel RC 3.00 8.00
58 Matt Davidson RC 3.00 8.00
59 Mathieu Darche RC 5.00 12.00
60 Duvie Westcott RC 3.00 8.00
61 Blake Bellefeuille RC 3.00 8.00
62 Ty Conklin RC 5.00 12.00
63 Stephen Weiss RC 8.00 20.00
64 Jaroslav Bednar RC 3.00 8.00
65 Pascal Dupuis RC 5.00 12.00
66 Nick Schultz RC 3.00 8.00
67 Travis Roche RC 3.00 8.00
68 Nathan Perrott RC 3.00 8.00
69 Scott Clemmensen RC 3.00 8.00
70 Andreas Salomonsson RC 3.00 8.00
71 Stanislav Gron RC 3.00 8.00
72 Radek Martinek RC 3.00 8.00
73 Mikael Samuelsson RC 4.00 10.00
74 Toni Dahlman RC 3.00 8.00
75 Bruno St. Jacques RC 3.00 8.00
76 Tomas Divisek RC 4.00 10.00
77 Vaclav Pletka RC 3.00 8.00
78 Eric Meloche RC 3.00 8.00
79 Tom Kostopoulos RC 3.00 8.00
80 Mark Rycroft RC 4.00 10.00
81 Martin Cibak RC 3.00 8.00
82 Josef Boumedienne RC 3.00 8.00
83 Karel Pilar RC 3.00 8.00
84 Sebastien Centomo RC 3.00 8.00
85 Justin Kurtz RC 5.00 12.00
86 Ivan Ciernik RC 3.00 8.00
87 Chris Corrinet RC 3.00 8.00
88 Ilja Bryzgalov RC 10.00 25.00
89 Pasi Nurminen RC 4.00 10.00
90 Ivan Huml RC 4.00 10.00
91 Erik Cole RC 8.00 20.00
92 Tyler Arnason RC 5.00 12.00
93 Riku Hahl RC 4.00 10.00
94 Niko Kapanen RC 6.00 15.00
95 Pavel Datsyuk RC 100.00 250.00
96 Sean Avery RC 4.00 10.00
97 Niklas Hagman RC 5.00 12.00
98 Olivier Michaud RC 6.00 15.00
99 Marcel Hossa RC 6.00 15.00
100 Martin Erat RC 5.00 12.00
101 Christian Berglund RC 5.00 12.00
102 Lukas Krajicek RC 4.00 10.00
103 Jiri Dopita RC 4.00 10.00
104 Branko Radivojevic RC 4.00 10.00
105 Shane Endicott RC 4.00 10.00
106 Jeff Jillson RC 4.00 10.00
107 Nikita Alexeev RC 4.00 10.00
108 Brian Sutherby RC 4.00 10.00
109 Ilya Kovalchuk AU RC 250.00 400.00
110 Vaclav Nedorost AU RC 8.00 20.00
111 Kristian Huselius AU RC 12.00 30.00
112 Raffi Torres AU RC 12.00 30.00
113 Dan Blackburn AU RC 10.00 25.00
114 Krys Kolanos AU RC 8.00 20.00

2001-02 UD Premier Collection Dual Jerseys

*BLACK/50: .5X TO 1.2X BASIC DUAL
DAT T.Amonte/J.Thibault 8.00 20.00
DBA P.Bure/M.Afinogenov 8.00 20.00
DBB R.Bourque/R.Blake 15.00 40.00
DBP R.Blake/C.Pronger 8.00 20.00
DCB R.Cechmanek/B.Boucher 8.00 20.00
DDM C.Drury/M.Modano 12.00 30.00
DDP A.Deadmarsh/F.Potvin 15.00 40.00
DFB S.Fedorov/P.Bure 12.00 30.00
DFD P.Forsberg/C.Drury 15.00 40.00
DGH W.Gretzky/B.Hull 30.00 80.00
DGK W.Gretzky/P.Kariya 25.00 60.00
DGL W.Gretzky/M.Lemieux 50.00 125.00
DGM W.Gretzky/M.Messier 50.00 125.00
DHC D.Hasek/R.Cechmanek 12.00 30.00
DHG G.Howe/W.Gretzky 50.00 125.00
DHJ M.Hejduk/J.Jagr 12.00 30.00
DJB J. Jagr/P.Bondra 12.00 30.00
DJP C.Joseph/F.Potvin 8.00 20.00
DKI P.Kariya/J.Iginla 12.00 30.00
DKS P.Kariya/J.Sakic 15.00 40.00
DLH N.Lidstrom/D.Hasek 12.00 30.00
DLK M.Lemieux/P.Kariya 15.00 40.00
DLR B.Leetch/M.Richter 8.00 20.00
DMB M.Modano/E.Belfour 12.50 30.00
DRB P.Roy/M.Brodeur 30.00 80.00
DRJ M.Richter/C.Joseph 8.00 20.00
DSN T.Selanne/V.Nieminen 8.00 20.00
DSP T.Selanne/Z.Palffy 8.00 20.00
DSR J.Sakic/P.Roy 20.00 50.00
DST S.Samsonov/J.Thornton 12.00 30.00
DSY B.Shanahan/S.Yzerman 20.00 50.00
DTB J.Thibault/S.Burke 8.00 20.00
DTN J.Thornton/J.Nieuwendyk 12.00 30.00
DBTE M.Brodeur/J.Theodore 15.00 40.00
DBTO R.Bourque/J.Thornton 12.50 30.00

2001-02 UD Premier Collection Jerseys

*BLACK BRNZ/150: .5X TO 1.2X BASIC JSY
*BLACK SILVER/75: .5X TO 1.2X BASIC JSY
BBS Brendan Shanahan B 5.00 12.00
BBU Pavel Bure B 5.00 12.00
BCD Chris Drury B 5.00 12.00
BEB Ed Belfour B 5.00 12.00
BEL Eric Lindros B 5.00 12.00
BIK Ilya Kovalchuk B 8.00 20.00
BJA Jaromir Jagr B 8.00 20.00
BJI Jarome Iginla B 6.00 15.00
BJJ Jaromir Jagr B 8.00 20.00
BJL John LeClair B 5.00 12.00
BJS Joe Sakic B 8.00 20.00
BJT Jose Theodore B 6.00 15.00
BMH Milan Hejduk B 5.00 12.00
BMR Mike Richter B 5.00 12.00
BMS Mats Sundin B 5.00 12.00
BOK Olaf Kolzig B 5.00 12.00
BPB Peter Bondra B 5.00 12.00
BPF Peter Forsberg B 8.00 20.00
BPK Paul Kariya B 5.00 12.00
BPR Patrick Roy B 12.00 30.00
BRB Ray Bourque B 10.00 25.00
BSF Sergei Fedorov B 6.00 15.00
BSG Simon Gagne B 5.00 12.00
BSK Saku Koivu B 5.00 12.00
BSS Sergei Samsonov B 5.00 12.00
BTA Tony Amonte B 5.00 12.00
BTF Theo Fleury B 5.00 12.00
BTS Teemu Selanne B 5.00 12.00
BWG Wayne Gretzky B 25.00 60.00
BZP Zigmund Palffy B 5.00 12.00
SCJ Curtis Joseph S 10.00 25.00
SDH Dominik Hasek S 12.00 30.00
SJS Joe Sakic S 15.00 40.00
SJT Joe Thornton S 12.50 30.00
SMB Martin Brodeur S 15.00 40.00
SMM Mike Modano S 12.50 30.00
SPK Paul Kariya S 12.00 30.00
GBH Bobby Hull G 15.00 40.00
GGH Gordie Howe G 30.00 80.00
GML Mario Lemieux G 30.00 80.00
GPR Patrick Roy G 15.00 40.00
GRB Ray Bourque G 25.00 60.00
GSY Steve Yzerman G 30.00 80.00
GWG Wayne Gretzky G 50.00 125.00

2001-02 UD Premier Collection Signatures

*BLACK BRNZ/100: .6X TO 1.5X BASIC AU
*BLACK SLVR/50: 1X TO 2.5X BASIC AU
AI Arturs Irbe B 4.00 10.00
AK Alexei Kovalev B 4.00 10.00
BI Martin Biron B 4.00 10.00
HO Marian Hossa B 6.00 15.00
JH Johan Hedberg B 4.00 10.00
JT Jose Theodore B 10.00 25.00
MC Mike Comrie B 5.00 12.00
MG Marian Gaborik B 6.00 15.00
MH Martin Havlat B 4.00 10.00
MN Markus Naslund B 6.00 15.00
RK Rostislav Klesla B 4.00 10.00
RT Raffi Torres B 5.00 12.00
SA Tommy Salo B 4.00 10.00
TA Tony Amonte B 4.00 10.00
BL Rob Blake S 6.00 15.00
CN Cam Neely S 15.00 40.00
DH Dany Heatley S 10.00 25.00
DW Doug Weight S 8.00 20.00
FP Felix Potvin S 10.00 25.00
HE Milan Hejduk S 8.00 20.00
JI Jarome Iginla S 10.00 25.00
JL John LeClair S 12.00 30.00
MB Mike Bossy S 10.00 25.00
OK Olaf Kolzig S 6.00 15.00
PB Peter Bondra S 8.00 20.00
SG Simon Gagne S 8.00 20.00
ZP Zigmund Palffy S 6.00 15.00
BH Bobby Hull G 20.00 50.00
BO Bobby Orr G 125.00 250.00
BR D.Blackburn/M.Richter G 10.00 25.00
CJ Curtis Joseph G 10.00 25.00
GH Gordie Howe G 40.00 100.00
GR Wayne Gretzky G 200.00 500.00
IK Ilya Kovalchuk G 10.00 25.00
JS J.Thornton/S.Samsonov G 20.00 50.00
PR Patrick Roy G 40.00 80.00
RB Ray Bourque G 20.00 50.00
SY Steve Yzerman G 30.00 80.00
TS Teemu Selanne G 10.00 25.00
WG Wayne Gretzky G 200.00 500.00

2001-02 UD Premier Collection Tribute to 500

1 Patrick Roy Col./Mon. 75.00 200.00

2002-03 UD Premier Collection

1 Paul Kariya 1.50 4.00
2 Ilya Kovalchuk 2.00 5.00
3 Dany Heatley 1.25 3.00
4 Byron Dafoe 1.25 3.00
5 Joe Thornton 2.50 6.00
6 Jeff Hackett 1.25 3.00
7 Sergei Samsonov 1.25 3.00
8 Miroslav Satan 1.50 4.00
9 Jarome Iginla 2.00 5.00
10 Ron Francis 2.00 5.00
11 Tyler Arnason 1.50 4.00
12 Jocelyn Thibault 1.25 3.00
13 Peter Forsberg 3.00 8.00
14 Joe Sakic 3.00 8.00
15 Patrick Roy 4.00 10.00
16 Milan Hejduk 1.25 3.00
17 Marc Denis 1.25 3.00
18 Mike Modano 2.50 6.00
19 Bill Guerin 1.50 4.00
20 Marty Turco 1.50 4.00
21 Steve Yzerman 4.00 10.00
22 Curtis Joseph 2.00 5.00
23 Brendan Shanahan 1.50 4.00
24 Nicklas Lidstrom 1.50 4.00
25 Mike Comrie 1.50 4.00
26 Stephen Weiss 1.50 4.00
27 Roberto Luongo 2.50 6.00
28 Zigmund Palffy 1.50 4.00
29 Marian Gaborik 1.50 4.00
30 Saku Koivu 1.50 4.00
31 Jose Theodore 1.50 4.00
32 David Legwand 1.25 3.00
33 Martin Brodeur 4.00 10.00
34 Michael Peca 1.25 3.00
35 Alexei Kovalev 1.25 3.00
36 Eric Lindros 2.50 6.00
37 Pavel Bure 1.50 4.00
38 Mike Dunham 1.25 3.00
39 Marian Hossa 1.50 4.00
40 Jeremy Roenick 2.50 6.00
41 John LeClair 1.50 4.00
42 Tony Amonte 1.25 3.00
43 Mario Lemieux 6.00 15.00
44A Sebastien Caron 1.25 3.00
44B Martin Gerber RC 4.00 10.00
45A Evgeni Nabokov 1.25 3.00
45B Tim Thomas RC 10.00 25.00
46A Kyle McLaren 1.00 2.50
46B Ryan Miller RC 15.00 40.00
47A Keith Tkachuk 1.50 4.00
47B Jordan Leopold RC 4.00 10.00
48A Vincent Lecavalier 1.50 4.00
48B Shaone Morrisonn RC 2.50 6.00
49A Nikolai Khabibulin 1.50 4.00
49B Levente Szuper RC 4.00 10.00
50 Mats Sundin 1.50 4.00
51A Ed Belfour 1.50 4.00
51B Jim Fahey RC 2.50 6.00
52A Todd Bertuzzi 1.50 4.00
52B Dmitri Bykov RC 2.50 6.00
53 Markus Naslund 1.50 4.00
54 Jaromir Jagr 5.00 12.00
55 Olaf Kolzig 1.50 4.00
56A Wayne Gretzky/299 8.00 20.00
56B Mike Cammalleri RC 8.00 20.00
57A Bobby Orr/299 12.50 30.00
57B Stephane Veilleux RC 2.50 6.00
58A Gordie Howe/299 5.00 12.00
58B Rickard Wallin RC 2.50 6.00
59A Ray Bourque/299 2.50 6.00
59B Vernon Fiddler RC 3.00 8.00
60A Alexei Semenov RC 2.50 6.00
60B Darren Haydar RC 2.50 6.00
61 Anton Volchenkov RC 2.50 6.00
62 Patrick Sharp RC 8.00 20.00
63 Dennis Seidenberg RC 4.00 10.00
64 Tomas Malec RC 2.50 6.00
65 Craig Andersson RC 8.00 20.00
66 Cody Rudkowsky RC 2.50 6.00
67A Ari Ahonen RC 2.50 6.00
67B Curtis Sanford RC 4.00 10.00
68 Adam Hall RC 2.50 6.00
69 Carlo Colaiacovo RC 4.00 10.00
70A Dick Tarnstrom RC 2.50 6.00
70B Steve Eminger RC 2.50 6.00
71A Jamie Hodson RC 2.50 6.00
71B Alexei Smirnov AU RC 8.00 20.00
72A Jarret Stoll RC 10.00 25.00
72B P-M Bouchard AU RC 12.50 30.00
73 Ron Hainsey AU RC 6.00 15.00
74 Pascal Leclaire AU RC 10.00 25.00
75 Scottie Upshall AU RC 8.00 20.00
76 Jeff Taffe AU RC 6.00 15.00
77 Mikael Tellqvist AU RC 6.00 15.00
78 S.Chistov JSY AU RC 15.00 40.00
79 C.Kobasew JSY AU RC 20.00 50.00
80 Rick Nash JSY AU RC 250.00 450.00
81 H.Zetterberg JSY AU RC 250.00 450.00
82 Bouwmeester JSY AU RC 50.00 125.00
83 J.Spezza JSY AU RC 80.00 200.00
84 A.Svitov JSY AU RC 15.00 40.00
88 Jerred Smithson RC 2.50 6.00
89 Jim Vandermeer RC 2.50 6.00
90 Michael Leighton RC 4.00 10.00
91 Ray Emery RC 8.00 20.00
92 Tomas Zizka RC 2.50 6.00
93 Bobby Allen RC 2.50 6.00
94 Kris Vernarsky RC 2.50 6.00
95 Cristobal Huet RC 5.00 12.00
96 Fernando Pisani RC 2.50 6.00
97 Jonathan Hedstrom RC 2.50 6.00
98 Konstantin Koltsov RC 3.00 8.00
99 Ales Hemsky AU RC 25.00 60.00
100 Steve Ott AU RC 6.00 15.00
101 Alexander Frolov AU RC 20.00 50.00
102 Brooks Orpik AU RC 6.00 15.00
103 Jared Aulin AU RC 6.00 15.00

2002-03 UD Premier Collection Gold

*GOLD: .5X TO 1.2X BASIC RC
*71B,72B/73-77/99-103 AU/25: .6X TO 1.5X
*78-84 JSY AU/15: .6X TO 1.5X

2002-03 UD Premier Collection Jerseys Bronze

AA Ari Ahonen 2.00 5.00
AK Alexei Kovalev 2.00 5.00
AS Alexander Svitov 2.00 5.00
AV Anton Volchenkov 2.00 5.00
AX Alexei Semenov 2.00 5.00
DO Brooks Orpik 3.00 8.00
BS Brendan Shanahan 3.00 8.00
CD Chris Drury 3.00 8.00
CJ Curtis Joseph 6.00 15.00
EL Eric Lindros 4.00 10.00
GM Glen Murray 3.00 8.00
IK Ilya Kovalchuk 6.00 15.00
JG Jaromir Jagr 8.00 20.00
JI Jarome Iginla 6.00 15.00
JJ Jaromir Jagr 8.00 20.00
JK Jeremy Roenick 6.00 15.00
JR Jeremy Roenick 6.00 15.00
JS Joe Sakic 8.00 20.00
JT Jose Theodore 6.00 15.00
MB Martin Brodeur 12.50 30.00
MC Mike Comrie 2.00 5.00
MH Milan Hejduk 4.00 10.00
ML Mario Lemieux 15.00 30.00
MM Mike Modano 6.00 15.00
MO Mike Modano 6.00 15.00
MS Mats Sundin 4.00 10.00
OK Olaf Kolzig 4.00 10.00
PB Pavel Bure 4.00 10.00
PF Peter Forsberg 8.00 20.00
PG Peter Forsberg 8.00 20.00
PK Paul Kariya 4.00 10.00
PL Pascal Leclaire 8.00 20.00
PR Patrick Roy 15.00 30.00
RB Ray Bourque 6.00 15.00
SF Sergei Fedorov 6.00 15.00
SG Simon Gagne 4.00 10.00
SK Saku Koivu 4.00 10.00
SO Steve Ott 2.00 5.00
SS Sergei Samsonov 2.00 5.00
SV Sergei Fedorov 6.00 15.00
SY Steve Yzerman 12.50 30.00
TF Theo Fleury 3.00 8.00
TH Joe Thornton 8.00 20.00
WG Wayne Gretzky 25.00 60.00
BL P.Bure/E.Lindros 10.00 25.00
BR R.Blake/P.Roy 12.50 30.00
FH P.Forsberg/M.Hejduk 12.00 30.00
FJ S.Fedorov/C.Joseph 10.00 25.00
GL W.Gretzky/M.Lemieux 50.00 125.00
JK J.Jagr/O.Kolzig 10.00 25.00
JR J.Spezza/R.Nash 25.00 60.00
KG P.Kariya/J.Giguere 10.00 25.00
PA P.Leclaire/A.Ahonen 10.00 25.00
RG J.Roenick/S.Gagne 10.00 25.00
SR J.Sakic/S.Reinprecht 12.50 30.00
ST S.Samsonov/J.Thornton 10.00 25.00
SY B.Shanahan/S.Yzerman 15.00 40.00
TK J.Theodore/S.Koivu 10.00 25.00

2002-03 UD Premier Collection Jerseys Gold

*SNGL.JSY: .6X TO 1.5X BRONZE
*DUAL JSY: .6X TO 1.5X BRONZE

2002-03 UD Premier Collection Jerseys Silver

*SNGL.JSY: .5X TO 1.25X BRONZE
*DUAL JSY: .5X TO 1.25X BRONZE

2002-03 UD Premier Collection Patches

PBO Ray Bourque 75.00 200.00
PBS Brendan Shanahan 50.00 120.00
PCD Chris Drury 50.00 120.00
PCJ Curtis Joseph 50.00 120.00
PEL Eric Lindros 50.00 120.00
PGR Wayne Gretzky 200.00 350.00
PIK Ilya Kovalchuk 60.00 150.00
PJI Jarome Iginla 60.00 150.00
PJJ Jaromir Jagr 75.00 200.00
PJR Jeremy Roenick 100.00 200.00
PJS Joe Sakic 75.00 200.00
PJT Jose Theodore 60.00 150.00
PMB Martin Brodeur 125.00 300.00
PMC Mike Comrie 50.00 120.00
PMH Milan Hejduk 50.00 120.00
PML Mario Lemieux 150.00 400.00
PMM Mike Modano 60.00 150.00
PMS Mats Sundin 50.00 120.00
POK Olaf Kolzig 50.00 120.00
PPB Pavel Bure 75.00 150.00
PPF Peter Forsberg 75.00 200.00
PPK Paul Kariya 50.00 120.00
PPR Patrick Roy 125.00 300.00
PRB Ray Bourque 75.00 200.00
PSF Sergei Fedorov 60.00 150.00
PSG Simon Gagne 50.00 120.00
PSK Saku Koivu 50.00 120.00
PSS Sergei Samsonov 25.00 60.00
PSY Steve Yzerman 125.00 300.00
PTH Joe Thornton 75.00 200.00
PTS Teemu Selanne 40.00 100.00
PWG Wayne Gretzky 200.00 350.00

2002-03 UD Premier Collection Signatures Bronze

SAH Adam Hall SP 5.00 12.00
SAS Alexei Smirnov 5.00 12.00
SBO Bobby Orr 60.00 120.00
SBR Pavel Brendl 5.00 12.00
SBW Jay Bouwmeester 8.00 20.00
SCK Chuck Kobasew 5.00 12.00
SDH Dany Heatley 8.00 20.00
SEB Ed Belfour 10.00 25.00
SEC Erik Cole 5.00 12.00
SGH Gordie Howe 50.00 125.00
SHZ Henrik Zetterberg 12.00 30.00
SIK Ilya Kovalchuk 12.00 30.00
SJB Jay Bouwmeester 10.00 25.00
SJI Jarome Iginla 8.00 20.00
SJL John LeClair 6.00 15.00
SJT Joe Thornton 8.00 20.00
SJW Justin Williams 5.00 12.00
SMA Maxim Afinogenov 5.00 12.00
SMB Martin Brodeur SP 30.00 80.00
SMC Mike Comrie 5.00 12.00
SMF Manny Fernandez 5.00 12.00
SMH Martin Havlat 5.00 12.00
SMN Markus Naslund 6.00 15.00
SMT Mikael Tellqvist SP 8.00 20.00
SNA Rick Nash 20.00 50.00
SNK Nikolai Khabibulin 6.00 15.00
SPB Pavel Bure SP 6.00 15.00
SPM P-M Bouchard 6.00 15.00
SPR Patrick Roy 40.00 100.00
SRA Ray Bourque 15.00 40.00
SRB Ray Bourque 15.00 40.00
SRH Ron Hainsey SP 5.00 12.00
SRN Rick Nash 15.00 40.00
SSC Stanislav Chistov 5.00 12.00
SSG Simon Gagne 6.00 15.00
SSH Scott Hartnell 6.00 15.00
SSP Jason Spezza 25.00 60.00
SSS Sergei Samsonov 5.00 12.00
SSU Scottie Upshall SP 8.00 20.00
SSV Alexander Svitov 5.00 12.00
SSY Steve Yzerman 25.00 60.00
STA Jeff Taffe SP 5.00 12.00
SWG Wayne Gretzky SP 150.00 400.00
ASJT Joe Thornton 10.00 25.00
ASDH Dany Heatley 10.00 25.00
ASJI Jarome Iginla 8.00 20.00
ASMB Martin Brodeur 30.00 80.00
ASPR Patrick Roy SP 40.00 100.00

2002-03 UD Premier Collection Signatures Gold

*GOLD: .6X TO 1.5X BRONZE

2002-03 UD Premier Collection Signatures Silver

*SILVER: .5X TO 1.2X BRONZE

2003-04 UD Premier Collection

COMP.SET w/o SP's (59) 50.00 100.00
1 Jean-Sebastien Giguere 1.25 3.00
2 Sergei Fedorov 2.00 5.00
3 Dany Heatley 1.00 2.50
4 Ilya Kovalchuk 1.25 3.00
5 Sergei Samsonov 1.00 2.50
6 Joe Thornton 2.00 5.00
7 Andrew Raycroft 1.00 2.50
8 Chris Drury 1.00 2.50
9 Jarome Iginla 1.50 4.00
10 Justin Williams 1.00 2.50
11 Jocelyn Thibault 1.00 2.50
12 Bryan Berard 1.00 2.50
13 David Aebischer 1.00 2.50
14 Joe Sakic 2.50 6.00
15 Paul Kariya 1.25 3.00
16 Peter Forsberg 2.50 6.00

17 Rick Nash 1.25 3.00
18 Marty Turco 1.25 3.00
19 Mike Modano 2.00 5.00
20 Brett Hull 2.50 6.00
21 Pavel Datsyuk 2.00 5.00
22 Steve Yzerman 3.00 8.00
23 Raffi Torres .75 2.00
24 Ales Hemsky 1.25 3.00
25 Roberto Luongo 2.00 5.00
26 Zigmund Palffy 1.25 3.00
27 Marian Gaborik 1.25 3.00
28 Jose Theodore 1.25 3.00
29 Saku Koivu 1.25 3.00
30 Tomas Vokoun 1.00 2.50
31 Scott Stevens 1.25 3.00
32 Martin Brodeur 3.00 8.00
33 Alexei Yashin 1.00 2.50
34 Rick DiPietro 1.00 2.50
35 Jaromir Jagr 4.00 10.00
36 Mark Messier 2.50 6.00
37 Eric Lindros 2.00 5.00
38 Jason Spezza 1.25 3.00
39 Marian Hossa 1.25 3.00
40 Patrick Lalime 1.00 2.50
41 Jeremy Roenick 2.00 5.00
42 Tony Amonte 1.00 2.50
43 Mike Comrie 1.00 2.50
44 Brian Boucher 1.00 2.50
45 Mario Lemieux 5.00 12.00
46 Evgeni Nabokov 1.00 2.50
47 Chris Osgood 1.25 3.00
48 Doug Weight 1.25 3.00
49 Keith Tkachuk 1.25 3.00
50 Nikolai Khabibulin 1.25 3.00
51 Mats Sundin 1.25 3.00
52 Owen Nolan 1.25 3.00
53 Ed Belfour 1.25 3.00
54 Ron Francis 1.50 4.00
55 Ed Jovanovski 1.00 2.50
56 Markus Naslund 1.25 3.00
57 Todd Bertuzzi 1.25 3.00
58 Brendan Morrison 1.00 2.50
59 Olaf Kolzig 1.25 3.00
60 Niklas Kronwall RC 5.00 12.00
61 Derek Roy RC 4.00 10.00
62 Tim Jackman RC 3.00 8.00
63 Timofei Shishkanov RC 2.50 6.00
64 Tomas Plekanec RC 8.00 20.00
65 Aleksander Suglobov RC 2.50 6.00
66 Kyle Wellwood RC 4.00 10.00
67 Mike Smith RC 8.00 20.00
68 Anton Babchuk RC 2.50 6.00
69 Ryan Barnes RC 2.50 6.00
70 Jason Pominville RC 6.00 15.00
71 Pavel Vorobiev RC 3.00 8.00
72 Dustin Brown RC 6.00 15.00
73 Chris Higgins RC 5.00 12.00
74 Dan Hamhuis RC 3.00 8.00
75 Marek Zidlicky RC 2.50 6.00
76 Sean Bergenheim RC 3.00 8.00
77 Antoine Vermette RC 5.00 12.00
78 Milan Michalek RC 5.00 12.00
79 Brad Boyes RC 4.00 10.00
80 Alexander Semin RC 8.00 20.00
81 Carl Corazzini RC 2.50 6.00
82 Sergei Zinovjev RC 2.50 6.00
83 Julien Vauclair RC 2.50 6.00
84 John Pohl RC 2.50 6.00
85 Benoit Dusablon RC 2.50 6.00
86 Tony Salmelainen RC 2.50 6.00
87 Bryce Lampman RC 3.00 8.00
88 Trevor Daley RC 4.00 10.00
89 Dan Ellis RC 3.00 8.00
90 Zbynek Michalek RC 2.50 6.00
91 Goran Bezina RC 2.50 6.00
92 Erik Westrum RC 2.50 6.00
93 Ryan Kesler RC 10.00 25.00
94 Owen Fussey RC 2.50 6.00
95 Josh Olson RC 2.50 6.00
96 Dan Fritsche RC 2.50 6.00
97 Michal Barinka RC 2.50 6.00
98 Kari Lehtonen RC 10.00 25.00
99 Mike Stutzel RC 2.50 6.00
100 Matt Hussey RC 2.50 6.00
101 Roman Tvrdon RC 2.50 6.00
102 Matthew Yeats RC 2.50 6.00
103 Brett Lysak 2.50 6.00
104 Thomas Pock RC 3.00 8.00
105 F.Sjostrom PATCH AU RC 20.00 50.00
106 P.Sejna PATCH AU RC 15.00 40.00
107 M.Stajan PATCH AU RC 20.00 50.00
108 N.Zherdev PATCH AU RC 25.00 60.00
109 P.Bergeron PATCH AU RC 200.00 500.00
110 J.Pitkanen PATCH AU RC 15.00 40.00
111 J.Lupul PATCH AU RC 40.00 80.00
112 J.Tootoo PATCH AU RC 40.00 100.00
113 N.Horton PATCH AU RC 40.00 100.00
114 E.Staal PATCH AU RC 100.00 200.00
115 J.Hudler PATCH AU RC 30.00 80.00
116 T.Ruutu PATCH AU RC 40.00 100.00
117 M.Fleury PATCH AU RC 200.00 500.00
118 Fedor Tyutin RC 2.50 6.00
119 Denis Grebeshkov RC 2.50 6.00
120 Cory Larose RC 2.50 6.00
121 Andy Chiodo RC 2.50 6.00

2003-04 UD Premier Collection Legends Jerseys

PLGL Guy Lafleur 20.00 50.00
PLMB Mike Bossy 15.00 40.00
PLMH Gordie Howe 40.00 100.00
PLPR Patrick Roy 50.00 125.00
PLSB Scotty Bowman 25.00 60.00
PLWG Wayne Gretzky 150.00 250.00

2003-04 UD Premier Collection Matchups Jerseys

PMBT Ed Belfour
Jose Theodore 20.00 50.00
PMGB M.Gaborik/T.Bertuzzi 15.00 40.00
PMHM A.Hemsky/M.Modano 20.00 50.00
PMHR M.Hossa/J.Roenick 20.00 50.00
PMRH P.Roy/D.Hasek 25.00 60.00
PMTB J.Thornton/M.Brodeur 25.00 60.00

2003-04 UD Premier Collection Signatures

PSAC Anson Carter 6.00 15.00
PSAH Ales Hemsky 6.00 15.00
PSBO Pavel Bure SP 30.00 60.00
PSBY Mike Bossy 10.00 25.00
PSCJ Curtis Joseph 8.00 20.00
PSDA David Aebischer 6.00 15.00
PSDC Don Cherry 15.00 40.00
PSEL Eric Lindros 8.00 20.00
PSES Eric Staal 10.00 25.00
PSGL Guy Lafleur SP 20.00 50.00
PSG1 Wayne Gretzky 125.00 300.00
PSHZ Henrik Zetterberg 10.00 25.00
PSIK Ilya Kovalchuk 10.00 25.00
PSJH Jiri Hudler 6.00 15.00
PSJI Jarome Iginla 10.00 25.00
PSJR Jeremy Roenick 8.00 20.00
PSJS Jason Spezza 12.00 30.00
PSJT Joe Thornton 10.00 25.00
PSJSG Jean-Sebastien Giguere 6.00 15.00
PSJTH Jose Theodore 10.00 25.00
PSMB Martin Brodeur 40.00 100.00
PSMG Marian Gaborik 10.00 25.00
PSMH Gordie Howe 50.00 100.00
PSMT Marty Turco 6.00 15.00
PSMAF Marc-Andre Fleury 15.00 40.00
PSMAH Marian Hossa 6.00 15.00
PSMCH Marcel Hossa 6.00 15.00
PSMNH Markus Naslund 6.00 15.00
PSNH Nathan Horton 6.00 15.00
PSON Owen Nolan 6.00 15.00
PSPB Patrice Bergeron SP 50.00 125.00
PSPR Patrick Roy 60.00 125.00
PSRL Roberto Luongo 10.00 25.00
PSRN Rick Nash 12.00 30.00
PSROY Patrick Roy SP 125.00 250.00
PSSK Saku Koivu 10.00 25.00
PSTB Todd Bertuzzi 6.00 15.00
PSTR Tuomo Ruutu 5.00 12.00
PSTOO Jordin Tootoo 10.00 25.00
PSWG Wayne Gretzky 150.00 400.00
PSZP Zigmund Palffy 6.00 15.00

2003-04 UD Premier Collection Skills Jerseys

SKBF M.Brodeur/M.Fleury 25.00 50.00
SKBT T.Bertuzzi/K.Tkachuk 12.00 30.00
SKFT P.Forsberg/J.Thornton 12.00 30.00
SKLT M.Lemieux/J.Thornton 20.00 50.00
SKRR J.Roenick/T.Ruutu 12.00 30.00
SKSY J.Sakic/S.Yzerman 25.00 60.00

2003-04 UD Premier Collection Stars Jerseys

*PATCH/100: 1.2X TO 3X BASIC JSY/250
STAM Alexander Mogilny 3.00 8.00
STBH Brett Hull 4.00 10.00
STDH Dan Hamhuis 3.00 8.00
STDW Doug Weight 3.00 8.00
STES Eric Staal 8.00 20.00
STGM Glenn Murray 3.00 8.00
STIK Ilya Kovalchuk 4.00 10.00
STJH Jiri Hudler 3.00 8.00
STJI Jarome Iginla 4.00 10.00
STJL Joffrey Lupul 3.00 8.00
STJS Joe Sakic 6.00 15.00
STJT Jordin Tootoo 4.00 10.00
STJSG Jean-Sebastien Giguere 3.00 8.00
STLR Luc Robitaille 3.00 8.00
STMD Marc Denis 3.00 8.00
STMF Manny Fernandez 3.00 8.00
STMH Milan Hejduk 3.00 8.00
STMN Markus Naslund 3.00 8.00
STMR Mark Recchi 3.00 8.00
STMR Mike Ribeiro 3.00 8.00
STMS Martin Straka 3.00 8.00
STMAF Marc-Andre Fleury 10.00 25.00
STNH Nathan Horton 3.00 8.00
STNZ Nikolai Zherdev 3.00 8.00
STPB Patrice Bergeron 3.00 8.00
STPD Pavol Demitra 3.00 8.00
STPK Paul Kariya 3.00 8.00
STRC Roman Cechmanek 3.00 8.00
STRL Roberto Luongo 4.00 10.00
STSF Sergei Fedorov 5.00 12.00
STSS Sergei Samsonov 3.00 8.00
STSY Steve Yzerman 6.00 15.00
STTB Todd Bertuzzi 3.00 8.00
STTR Tuomo Ruutu 3.00 8.00
STVL Vincent Lecavalier 3.00 8.00

2003-04 UD Premier Collection Super Stars Jerseys

*PATCH/25: 1.2X TO 3X BASIC JSY/100
SSJS Jason Spezza 12.50 30.00
SSJT Joe Thornton 12.50 30.00
SSMB Martin Brodeur 25.00 60.00
SSMG Marian Gaborik 8.00 20.00
SSML Mario Lemieux 20.00 50.00
SSPF Peter Forsberg 12.50 30.00

2003-04 UD Premier Collection Teammates Jerseys

PTAM J.Giguere/S.Fedorov 8.00 20.00
PTBB1 J.Thornton/S.Samsonov 10.00 25.00
PTBB2 J.Thornton/P.Bergeron 10.00 25.00
PTCB J.Thibault/T.Ruutu 8.00 20.00
PTCH R.Francis/E.Staal 12.50 30.00
PTCA1 P.Forsberg/J.Sakic 12.50 30.00
PTCA2 T.Selanne/P.Kariya 8.00 20.00
PTCB1 R.Nash/M.Denis 8.00 20.00
PTCB2 R.Nash/N.Zherdev 8.00 20.00
PTDR1 S.Yzerman/D.Hasek 15.00 40.00
PTDR2 S.Yzerman/B.Hull 12.00 30.00
PTDS1 M.Modano/M.Turco 8.00 20.00
PTDS2 B.Guerin/M.Modano 8.00 20.00
PTE01 W.Gretzky/M.Messier 60.00 150.00
PTE02 R.Torres/A.Hemsky 8.00 20.00
PTFP R.Luongo/O.Jokinen 10.00 25.00
PTLK Z.Palffy/R.Cechmanek 8.00 20.00
PTMC J.Theodore/S.Koivu 10.00 25.00
PTMW M.Gaborik/M.Fernandez 8.00 20.00
PTND M.Brodeur/S.Stevens 12.50 30.00
PTNR E.Lindros/M.Messier 10.00 25.00
PTOS J.Spezza/M.Hossa 10.00 25.00
PTPP M.Lemieux/M.Fleury 25.00 60.00
PTPF1 J.Roenick/T.Amonte 8.00 20.00
PTPF2 J.Roenick/J.Pitkanen 8.00 20.00
PTSB K.Tkachuk/D.Weight 8.00 20.00
PTTL V.Lecavalier/N.Khabibulin 10.00 25.00
PTTM1 M.Sundin/O.Nolan 8.00 20.00
PTTM2 E.Belfour/M.Sundin 8.00 20.00
PTVC T.Bertuzzi/M.Naslund 10.00 25.00

2003-04 UD Premier Collection Teammates Jerseys Patches

*PATCHES/25: 1.5X TO 4X BASIC JSY

2000-01 UD Reserve

1 Paul Kariya .20 .50
2 Steve Rucchin .12 .30
3 Teemu Selanne .40 1.00
4 Damian Rhodes .12 .30
5 Patrik Stefan .15 .40
6 Byron Dafoe .15 .40
7 Jason Allison .15 .40
8 Joe Thornton .30 .75
9 Doug Gilmour .25 .60
10 Dominik Hasek .30 .75
11 Miroslav Satan .12 .30
12 Jarome Iginla .25 .60
13 Oleg Saprykin .12 .30
14 Valeri Bure .15 .40
15 Sandis Ozolinsh .12 .30
16 Ron Francis .25 .60
17 Sami Kapanen .12 .30
18 Steve Sullivan .12 .30
19 Alexei Zhamnov .15 .40
20 Tony Amonte .15 .40
21 Ray Bourque .30 .75
22 Patrick Roy .50 1.25
23 Peter Forsberg .40 1.00
24 Joe Sakic .40 1.00
25 Ron Tugnutt .15 .40
26 Steve Heinze .12 .30
27 Mike Modano .30 .75
28 Brett Hull .40 1.00
29 Ed Belfour .20 .50
30 Brendan Shanahan .20 .50
31 Sergei Fedorov .30 .75
32 Steve Yzerman .50 1.25
33 Ryan Smyth .15 .40
34 Tommy Salo .15 .40
35 Doug Weight .20 .50
36 Pavel Bure .20 .50
37 Ray Whitney .15 .40
38 Roberto Luongo .30 .75
39 Luc Robitaille .20 .50
40 Zigmund Palffy .20 .50
41 Jamie Storr .15 .40
42 Jamie McLennan .12 .30
43 Jim Dowd .12 .30
44 Brian Savage .12 .30
45 Jose Theodore .20 .50
46 Saku Koivu .20 .50
47 David Legwand .20 .50
48 Cliff Ronning .12 .30
49 Tomas Vokoun .15 .40
50 Scott Gomez .15 .40
51 Patrik Elias .20 .50
52 Martin Brodeur .50 1.25
53 Tim Connolly .12 .30
54 Roman Hamrlik .12 .30
55 John Vanbiesbrouck .20 .50
56 Theo Fleury .25 .60
57 Mark Messier .40 1.00
58 Brian Leetch .15 .40
59 Marian Hossa .20 .50
60 Patrick Lalime .15 .40
61 Alexei Yashin .15 .40
62 John LeClair .20 .50
63 Mark Recchi .25 .60
64 Keith Primeau .15 .40
65 Jeremy Roenick .30 .75
66 Sean Burke .12 .30
67 Keith Tkachuk .20 .50
68 Jaromir Jagr .60 1.50
69 Milan Kraft .12 .30
70 Mario Lemieux .75 2.00
71 Owen Nolan .20 .50
72 Jeff Friesen .12 .30
73 Evgeni Nabokov .15 .40
74 Chris Pronger .20 .50
75 Scott Young .12 .30
76 Roman Turek .15 .40
77 Vincent Lecavalier .20 .50
78 Brad Richards .20 .50
79 Mike Johnson .12 .30
80 Curtis Joseph .25 .60
81 Mats Sundin .20 .50
82 Sergei Berezin .12 .30
83 Markus Naslund .20 .50
84 Daniel Sedin .25 .60
85 Henrik Sedin .25 .60
86 Chris Simon .12 .30
87 Peter Bondra .20 .50
88 Olaf Kolzig .20 .50
89 Andrew Raycroft RC .50 1.25
90 Josef Vasicek RC .50 1.25
91 David Aebischer RC .40 1.00
92 Rostislav Klesla RC .50 1.25
93 Marty Turco RC .40 1.00
94 Tyler Bouck RC .20 .50
95 Shawn Horcoff RC .40 1.00
96 Eric Belanger RC .25 .60
97 Steven Reinprecht RC .30 .75
98 Marian Gaborik RC .60 1.50
99 Peter Bartos RC .25 .60
100 Scott Hartnell RC .50 1.25
101 Greg Classen RC .20 .50
102 Chris Mason RC .40 1.00
103 Willie Mitchell RC .30 .75
104 Rick DiPietro RC .40 1.00
105 Jason Labarbera RC .25 .60
106 Jani Hurme RC .20 .50
107 Martin Havlat RC .60 1.50
108 Ruslan Fedotenko RC .20 .50
109 Justin Williams RC .50 1.25
110 Petr Hubacek RC .20 .50
111 Roman Cechmanek RC .25 .60
112 Mark Smith RC .20 .50
113 Alexander Khavanov RC .20 .50
114 Alexander Kharitonov RC .20 .50
115 Marc-Andre Thinel RC .20 .50
116 Zdenek Blatny RC .20 .50
117 Jordan Krestanovich RC .20 .50
118 Jeff Bateman RC .20 .50
119 Mark Messier CL .40 1.00
120 Curtis Joseph CL .25 .60

2000-01 UD Reserve Buyback Autographs

23 S.Samsonov 99MVPSC/29 8.00 20.00
25 S.Gomez 99MVPSCSS/27 12.50 25.00
37 P.Brendl 99MVPSC/301 15.00 30.00
49 M.Ribiero 97UD/52 6.00 15.00
51 M.Ribiero 99UD/25 25.00 60.00
53 M.Modano 90UD46/56 20.00 50.00
56 M.Modano 92UD305/69 20.00 50.00
63 M.Modano 96UD43/39 40.00 100.00
100 K.Tkachuk 99UD/25 75.00 200.00
103 J.Theodore 99MVPSC/356 6.00 15.00
117 H.Sedin 99MVPSC/330 10.00 25.00
129 D.Sedin 99MVPSC/329 10.00 25.00

2000-01 UD Reserve Gold Strike

COMPLETE SET (10) 10.00 25.00
GS1 Teemu Selanne 2.00 5.00
GS2 Joe Sakic 2.00 5.00
GS3 Mike Modano 1.50 4.00
GS4 Sergei Fedorov 1.50 4.00
GS5 Pavel Bure 1.00 2.50
GS6 Scott Gomez .75 2.00
GS7 Theo Fleury 1.25 3.00
GS8 Mario Lemieux 4.00 10.00
GS9 Mats Sundin 1.00 2.50
GS10 Olaf Kolzig 1.00 2.50

2000-01 UD Reserve Golden Goalies

COMPLETE SET (10) 10.00 20.00
GG1 Guy Hebert .75 2.00
GG2 Dominik Hasek 1.50 4.00
GG3 Patrick Roy 2.50 6.00
GG4 Tommy Salo .75 2.00
GG5 Jose Theodore 1.00 2.50
GG6 Mike Dunham .60 1.50
GG7 Martin Brodeur 2.50 6.00
GG8 John Vanbiesbrouck 1.00 2.50
GG9 Roman Turek .75 2.00
GG10 Curtis Joseph 1.25 3.00

2000-01 UD Reserve On-Ice Success

COMPLETE SET (6) 6.00 12.00
OS1 Paul Kariya .75 2.00
OS2 Tony Amonte .75 2.00
OS3 Joe Sakic 1.50 4.00
OS4 Pavel Bure 1.00 2.50
OS5 Luc Robitaille .75 2.00
OS6 Mark Messier 1.00 2.50

2000-01 UD Reserve Power Portfolios

COMPLETE SET (6) 10.00 20.00
PP1 Patrick Roy 4.00 10.00
PP2 Brett Hull 1.00 2.50
PP3 Steve Yzerman 4.00 10.00
PP4 Martin Brodeur 2.00 5.00
PP5 Mark Messier 1.00 2.50
PP6 Jaromir Jagr 1.25 3.00

2000-01 UD Reserve Practice Session Jerseys

CO Chris Osgood 4.00 10.00
JJ Jaromir Jagr 6.00 15.00
JL John LeClair 4.00 10.00
JT Joe Thornton 6.00 15.00
MA Mark Messier 10.00 25.00
MM Mike Modano 6.00 15.00
MR Mark Recchi 4.00 10.00
PF Peter Forsberg 6.00 15.00
TF Theo Fleury 6.00 15.00
TS Teemu Selanne 5.00 12.00

2000-01 UD Reserve Practice Session Jerseys Autographs

CO Chris Osgood 15.00 40.00
JL John LeClair 15.00 40.00
JT Joe Thornton 20.00 50.00
MA Mark Messier 30.00 80.00
MM Mike Modano 20.00 50.00
MR Mark Recchi 15.00 40.00
TF Theo Fleury 15.00 40.00
TS Teemu Selanne 15.00 40.00

2000-01 UD Reserve The Big Ticket

COMPLETE SET (10) 15.00 30.00
BT1 Paul Kariya .75 2.00
BT2 Dominik Hasek 1.50 4.00
BT3 Ray Bourque 1.50 4.00
BT4 Steve Yzerman 4.00 10.00
BT5 Pavel Bure 1.00 2.50
BT6 Marian Gaborik 3.00 8.00
BT7 Martin Brodeur 2.00 5.00
BT8 John LeClair 1.00 2.50
BT9 Jaromir Jagr 1.25 3.00
BT10 Vincent Lecavalier .75 2.00

2005-06 UD Rookie Class

COMPLETE SET (50) 12.50 30.00
1 Sidney Crosby 15.00 40.00
2 Alexander Ovechkin 40.00 100.00
3 Henrik Lundqvist 1.25 3.00
4 Marek Svatos .20 .50
5 Thomas Vanek .50 1.25
6 Brad Boyes .20 .50
7 Petr Prucha .25 .60
8 Jussi Jokinen .25 .60
9 Dion Phaneuf .40 1.00
10 Alexander Steen .40 1.00
11 Alvaro Montoya .25 .60
12 Keith Ballard .20 .50
13 Jeff Carter .40 1.00
14 Michel Ouellet .20 .50
15 Andrej Meszaros .20 .50
16 Pavel Vorobiev .15 .40
17 Mike Richards .50 1.25
18 Milan Michalek .15 .40
19 Antti Miettinen .15 .40
20 Rene Bourque .25 .60
21 Chris Campoli .15 .40
22 Gilbert Brule .25 .60
23 Andrew Ladd .30 .75
24 R.J. Umberger .25 .60
25 Hannu Toivonen .25 .60
26 Ryan Miller .25 .60
27 Kyle Wellwood .20 .50
28 Fedor Tyutin .15 .40
29 Brent Seabrook .50 1.25
30 Jim Howard .60 1.50
31 Ryan Whitney .25 .60
32 Corey Perry .75 2.00
33 Alexander Perezhogin .20 .50
34 Zach Parise .60 1.50
35 Peter Budaj .30 .75
36 Mikko Koivu .30 .75
37 Rostislav Olesz .20 .50
38 Ryan Getzlaf .60 1.50
39 Yann Danis .20 .50
40 Wojtek Wolski .20 .50
41 Ryan Suter .30 .75
42 Patrick Eaves .25 .60
43 Anthony Stewart .20 .50
44 Brandon Bochenski .25 .60
45 Eric Nystrom .20 .50
46 Antero Niittymaki .20 .50
47 Johan Franzen .40 1.00
48 Andrei Kostitsyn .30 .75
49 Carlo Colaiacovo .15 .40
50 Cam Ward .30 .75

2005-06 UD Rookie Class Commemorative Boxtoppers

CC1 Sidney Crosby 8.00 20.00
CC2 Alexander Ovechkin 50.00 125.00
CC3 Henrik Lundqvist 6.00 15.00
CC4 Thomas Vanek 2.50 6.00
CC5 Dion Phaneuf 2.00 5.00
CC6 Alexander Steen 2.00 5.00
CC7 Jeff Carter 2.00 5.00

2001-02 UD Stanley Cup Champs

1 Phil Esposito 2.00 5.00
2 Bobby Orr 8.00 20.00
3 Glenn Hall 1.00 2.50
4 Bobby Hull 1.50 4.00
5 Ray Bourque 1.50 4.00
6 Gordie Howe 4.00 10.00
7 Ted Lindsay .40 1.00
8 Terry Sawchuk 2.00 5.00
9 Grant Fuhr .60 1.50
10 Wayne Gretzky 5.00 12.00
11 Jari Kurri .75 2.00
12 Bill Ranford .40 1.00
13 Jean Beliveau 1.00 2.50
14 Yvan Cournoyer .75 2.00
15 Guy Lafleur 1.50 4.00
16 Jacques Plante 1.25 3.00
17 Maurice Richard 1.50 4.00
18 Henri Richard .40 1.00
19 Mike Bossy 1.25 3.00
20 Bob Nystrom .40 1.00
21 Ken Morrow .40 1.00
22 Bryan Trottier .40 1.00
23 Bobby Clarke 1.25 3.00
24 Bernie Parent .60 1.50
25 Tim Horton .40 1.00
26 Frank Mahovlich .75 2.00
27 Mike Vernon .60 1.50
28 Theo Fleury .40 1.00
29 Al MacInnis .60 1.50
30 Peter Forsberg 2.00 5.00
31 Dan Hinote .40 1.00
32 Milan Hejduk .75 2.00
33 Alex Tanguay .60 1.50
34 David Aebischer .60 1.50
35 Chris Drury .60 1.50
36 Rob Blake .60 1.50
37 Joe Sakic 1.50 4.00
38 Patrick Roy 4.00 10.00
39 Ville Nieminen .40 1.00
40 Steven Reinprecht .40 1.00
41 Adam Foote .40 1.00
42 Adam Deadmarsh .40 1.00
43 Jon Klemm .40 1.00
44 Sandis Ozolinsh .40 1.00
45 Mike Keane .40 1.00
46 Mike Modano 1.25 3.00
47 Brett Hull 1.00 2.50
48 Joe Nieuwendyk .60 1.50
49 Sergei Zubov .40 1.00
50 Ed Belfour .75 2.00
51 Derian Hatcher .40 1.00
52 Jamie Langenbrunner .40 1.00
53 Grant Marshall .40 1.00
54 Jere Lehtinen .60 1.50
55 Darryl Sydor .40 1.00
56 Sergei Fedorov 1.25 3.00
57 Steve Yzerman 4.00 10.00
58 Nicklas Lidstrom .75 2.00
59 Mathieu Dandenault .40 1.00
60 Slava Kozlov .40 1.00
61 Chris Osgood .60 1.50
62 Darren McCarty .40 1.00
63 Kirk Maltby .40 1.00
64 Brendan Shanahan .75 2.00
65 Tomas Holmstrom .40 1.00
66 John LeClair .75 2.00
67 Patrick Roy 4.00 10.00
68 Eric Desjardins .40 1.00
69 Scott Stevens .60 1.50
70 Patrik Elias .60 1.50
71 Randy McKay .40 1.00
72 Jason Arnott .40 1.00
73 Alexander Mogilny .60 1.50
74 Petr Sykora .40 1.00
75 Scott Gomez .40 1.00
76 Sergei Brylin .40 1.00
77 Bobby Holik .40 1.00
78 Martin Brodeur 2.00 5.00
79 John Madden .40 1.00
80 Scott Niedermayer .40 1.00
81 Claude Lemieux .40 1.00
82 Brian Leetch .60 1.50
83 Mike Richter .75 2.00
84 Mark Messier .75 2.00
85 Jaromir Jagr 1.25 3.00
86 Mario Lemieux 5.00 12.00

2001-02 UD Stanley Cup Champs Jerseys

TBH Brett Hull 12.00 30.00
TBL Brian Leetch 8.00 20.00
TBS Brendan Shanahan 12.00 30.00
TBT Bryan Trottier 10.00 25.00
TEB Ed Belfour 12.00 30.00
TGL Guy Lafleur 10.00 25.00
TJJ Jaromir Jagr 12.00 30.00
TJS Joe Sakic 12.00 30.00
TKM Ken Morrow 10.00 25.00
TMB Mike Bossy 8.00 20.00
TME Mark Messier 12.00 30.00
TML Mario Lemieux 20.00 50.00
TMM Mike Modano 12.00 30.00
TPF Peter Forsberg 12.00 30.00
TPR Patrick Roy 20.00 50.00
TRB Ray Bourque 10.00 25.00
TRO Patrick Roy 20.00 50.00
TSF Sergei Fedorov 15.00 40.00
TSY Steve Yzerman 12.00 30.00
TTF Theo Fleury 12.00 30.00

2001-02 UD Stanley Cup Champs Pieces of Glory

GBG Bill Guerin 15.00 40.00
GBH Brett Hull 30.00 80.00
GBL Brian Leetch 15.00 40.00
GBO Mike Bossy 20.00 50.00
GBR Bill Ranford 15.00 40.00
GBS Brendan Shanahan 15.00 40.00
GBT Bryan Trottier 40.00 100.00
GCL Claude Lemieux 15.00 40.00
GCO Chris Osgood 15.00 40.00
GEB Ed Belfour 15.00 40.00
GGL Guy Lafleur 50.00 125.00
GJJ Jaromir Jagr 20.00 50.00
GJN Joe Nieuwendyk 15.00 40.00
GJS Joe Sakic 40.00 100.00
GLM Lanny McDonald 15.00 40.00
GMA Mark Messier 15.00 40.00
GMB Martin Brodeur 50.00 125.00
GML Mario Lemieux 60.00 150.00
GMM Mike Modano 20.00 50.00
GMR Mike Richter 15.00 40.00
GNL Nicklas Lidstrom 15.00 40.00
GPF Peter Forsberg 25.00 60.00
GPR Patrick Roy 60.00 150.00
GRB Ray Bourque 25.00 60.00
GRO Patrick Roy 40.00 100.00
GSF Sergei Fedorov 20.00 50.00
GSY Steve Yzerman 60.00 150.00
GTF Theo Fleury 15.00 40.00
GWG Wayne Gretzky 100.00 200.00

2001-02 UD Stanley Cup Champs Sticks

SAM Al MacInnis 12.50 30.00
SAT Alex Tanguay 12.50 30.00
SBG Bill Guerin 12.50 30.00
SBH Brett Hull 15.00 40.00
SBK Rob Blake 12.50 30.00
SBL Brian Leetch 12.50 30.00
SBO Mike Bossy 20.00 50.00
SBS Brendan Shanahan 12.50 30.00
SBT Bryan Trottier 12.00 30.00
SCL Claude Lemieux 12.50 30.00
SEB Ed Belfour 12.50 30.00
SGH Gordie Howe 30.00 80.00
SGL Guy Lafleur 15.00 40.00
SJJ Jaromir Jagr 15.00 40.00
SJN Joe Nieuwendyk 12.50 30.00
SJS Joe Sakic 15.00 40.00
SMB Martin Brodeur 20.00 50.00
SML Mario Lemieux 40.00 100.00
SMM Mike Modano 15.00 40.00
SMO Alexander Mogilny 12.50 30.00
SMR Mike Richter 12.50 30.00
SPF Peter Forsberg 15.00 40.00
SPR Patrick Roy 15.00 40.00
SRB Ray Bourque 15.00 40.00
SRO Patrick Roy 20.00 50.00
SSF Sergei Fedorov 15.00 40.00
SSY Steve Yzerman 30.00 80.00
STF Theo Fleury 12.50 30.00
SWG Wayne Gretzky 50.00 100.00

2001-02 UD Top Shelf

COMP.SET w/o SP's (90) 30.00 60.00
1 Paul Kariya .60 1.50
2 Patrik Stefan .50 1.25
3 Joe Thornton 1.00 2.50
4 Miroslav Satan .50 1.25
5 Jarome Iginla .75 2.00
6 Jeff O'Neill .50 1.25
7 Tony Amonte .50 1.25
8 Joe Sakic 1.25 3.00
9 Peter Forsberg 1.25 3.00
10 Ray Bourque 1.00 2.50
11 Milan Hejduk .50 1.25
12 Patrick Roy 1.50 4.00
13 Rostislav Klesla .40 1.00
14 Mike Modano 1.00 2.50
15 Steve Yzerman 1.50 4.00
16 Luc Robitaille .60 1.50
17 Dominik Hasek 1.00 2.50
18 Tommy Salo .50 1.25
19 Pavel Bure .60 1.50
20 Zigmund Palffy .60 1.50
21 Brett Hull 1.25 3.00
22 Marian Gaborik .60 1.50
23 Saku Koivu .60 1.50
24 David Legwand .50 1.25
25 Martin Brodeur 1.50 4.00
26 Patrik Elias .60 1.50
27 Rick DiPietro .50 1.25
28 Eric Lindros 1.00 2.50
29 Marian Hossa .60 1.50
30 Jeremy Roenick 1.00 2.50
31 Roman Cechmanek .50 1.25
32 Sean Burke .40 1.00
33 Alexei Kovalev .50 1.25
34 Mario Lemieux 2.50 6.00
35 Johan Hedberg .50 1.25
36 Evgeni Nabokov .50 1.25
37 Teemu Selanne 1.25 3.00
38 Chris Pronger .60 1.50
39 Keith Tkachuk .60 1.50
40 Vincent Lecavalier .60 1.50
41 Curtis Joseph .75 2.00
42 Mats Sundin .60 1.50
43 Markus Naslund .60 1.50
44 Daniel Sedin .75 2.00
45 Jaromir Jagr 2.00 5.00
46A Mikael Samuelsson RC
(facing left) 2.50 6.00
46B Mikael Samuelsson RC
(facing right) 2.50 6.00
47A Dan Snyder RC
(skating) 2.50 6.00
47B Dan Snyder RC
(facing forward) 2.50 6.00
48A Zdenek Kutlak RC
(skating) 2.00 5.00
48B Zdenek Kutlak RC
(closeup) 2.00 5.00
49A Michel Larocque RC
(puck in glove) 2.00 5.00
49B Michel Larocque RC
(closeup) 2.00 5.00
50A Casey Hankinson RC
(stick to left) 2.00 5.00
50B Casey Hankinson RC
(closeup) 2.00 5.00
51A Bill Bowler RC
(stick to left) 2.00 5.00
51B Bill Bowler RC
(closeup) 2.00 5.00
52A Martin Spanhel RC
(highstick) 2.00 5.00
52B Martin Spanhel RC
(closeup) 2.00 5.00
53A Mathieu Darche RC
(stick to left) 3.00 8.00
53B Mathieu Darche RC 3.00 8.00
54A Jason Chimera RC
(stick to left) 2.00 5.00
54B Jason Chimera RC
(closeup) 2.00 5.00
55A Andrej Podkonicky RC
(stick on knees) 2.00 5.00
55B Andrej Podkonicky RC
(closeup) 2.00 5.00
56A Pascal Dupuis RC
(stick to right) 3.00 8.00
56B Pascal Dupuis RC
(closeup) 3.00 8.00
57A Francis Belanger RC
(stick at waist) 2.50 6.00
57B Francis Belanger RC
(closeup) 2.50 6.00
58A Mike Jefferson RC
(facing forward) 2.00 5.00
58B Mike Jefferson RC
(skating right) 2.00 5.00
59A Stanislav Gron RC#(white jersey) 2.00 5.00
59B Stanislav Gron RC
(red jersey) 2.00 5.00
60A Joel Kwiatkowski RC
(white jersey) 2.00 5.00
60B Joel Kwiatkowski RC
(red jersey) 2.00 5.00
61A Kirby Law RC
(skating right) 2.00 5.00
61B Kirby Law RC
(closeup) 2.00 5.00
62A Tomas Divisek RC
(skating right) 2.50 6.00
62B Tomas Divisek RC#(closeup) 2.50 6.00
63A Billy Tibbetts RC
(skating left) 2.00 5.00
63B Billy Tibbetts RC
(closeup) 2.00 5.00
64A Thomas Ziegler RC
(stick right hand) 2.50 6.00
64B Thomas Ziegler RC
(closeup) 2.50 6.00
65A Mike Brown
(facing forward) 2.50 6.00
65B Mike Brown
(closeup) 2.50 6.00
66A Pat Kavanagh RC
(standing up) 2.50 6.00
66B Pat Kavanagh RC
(closeup) 2.50 6.00
67 Ilja Bryzgalov RC 6.00 15.00
68 Ilya Kovalchuk RC 12.00 30.00
69 Vaclav Nedorost RC 2.50 6.00
70 Niko Kapanen RC 4.00 10.00
71 Kristian Huselius RC 4.00 10.00
72 Dan Blackburn RC 3.00 8.00
73 Krystofer Kolanos RC 2.50 6.00
74 Jiri Dopita RC 2.50 6.00
75 Nikita Alexeev RC 2.50 6.00
76 Brian Sutherby RC 2.50 6.00
77 Dany Heatley .50 1.25
78 Sergei Samsonov .50 1.25
79 Bill Guerin .60 1.50
80 Byron Dafoe .50 1.25
81 Martin Biron .50 1.25
82 Roman Turek .50 1.25
83 Arturs Irbe .50 1.25
84 Steve Sullivan .40 1.00
85 Mark Bell .40 1.00
86 Rob Blake .60 1.50
87 Alex Tanguay .50 1.25
88 Chris Drury .50 1.25
89 Espen Knutsen .40 1.00
90 Ed Belfour .60 1.50
91 Brendan Shanahan .60 1.50
92 Nicklas Lidstrom .60 1.50
93 Sergei Fedorov 1.00 2.50
94 Mike Comrie .50 1.25
95 Roberto Luongo 1.00 2.50
96 Felix Potvin 1.00 2.50
97 Jason Allison .50 1.25
98 Jose Theodore .60 1.50
99 Joe Nieuwendyk .50 1.25
100 Brian Gionta .50 1.25
101 Alexei Yashin .50 1.25
102 Michael Peca .50 1.25
103 Chris Osgood .60 1.50
104 Mark Parrish .40 1.00
105 Juraj Kolnik .40 1.00
106 Theo Fleury .75 2.00
107 Mike Richter .60 1.50
108 Brian Leetch .50 1.25
109 Pavel Bure .60 1.50
110 Martin Havlat .50 1.25
111 Adam Oates .60 1.50
112 John LeClair .60 1.50
113 Keith Primeau .50 1.25
114 Owen Nolan .60 1.50
115 Pavol Demitra .75 2.00

116 Brent Johnson .50 1.25
117 Doug Weight .60 1.50
118 Nikolai Khabibulin .60 1.50
119 Brad Richards .60 1.50
120 Peter Bondra .60 1.50
121 Olaf Kolzig .60 1.50
122 Pasi Nurminen RC 2.00 5.00
123 Ivan Huml RC 2.00 5.00
124 Erik Cole RC 4.00 10.00
125 Mike Peluso RC 2.00 5.00
126 Riku Hahl RC 2.00 5.00
127 Pavel Datsyuk RC 10.00 25.00
128 Niklas Hagman RC 2.50 6.00
129 Olivier Michaud RC 3.00 8.00
130 Marcel Hossa RC 3.00 8.00
131 Martin Erat RC 2.50 6.00
132 Christian Berglund RC 2.50 6.00
133 Raffi Torres RC 3.00 8.00
134 Branko Radivojevic RC 2.00 5.00
135 Jeff Jillson RC 2.00 5.00
136 Mark Hartigan RC 10.00 25.00
137 Stephen Weiss RC 25.00 60.00
138 Jan Lasak RC 10.00 25.00
139 Trent Hunter RC 20.00 50.00
140 Evgeny Konstantinov RC 10.00 25.00
141 Sebastien Charpentier RC 10.00 25.00

2001-02 UD Top Shelf All-Star Nets

NDH Dominik Hasek 25.00 60.00
NEN Evgeni Nabokov 15.00 40.00
NMB Martin Brodeur 25.00 60.00
NPR Patrick Roy 30.00 80.00
NRC Roman Cechmanek 15.00 40.00
NSB Sean Burke 15.00 40.00

2001-02 UD Top Shelf Goalie Gear

BJH Johan Hedberg Blocker 5.00 12.00
SCO Chris Osgood Skate 5.00 12.00
GGJH Johan Hedberg Glove 5.00 12.00
LPBB Brian Boucher Pad 5.00 12.00
LPBD Byron Dafoe Pad 5.00 12.00
LPDH Dominik Hasek Pad 8.00 20.00
LPGC Gerry Cheevers Pad 5.00 12.00
LPJH Johan Hedberg Pad 5.00 12.00
LPJT Jose Theodore Pad 6.00 15.00
LPJV John Vanbiesbrouck Pad 5.00 12.00
LPMB Martin Biron Pad 5.00 12.00
LPRC Roman Cechmanek Pad 5.00 12.00
LPRL Roberto Luongo Pad 6.00 15.00
LPSS Steve Shields Pad 5.00 12.00

2001-02 UD Top Shelf Jerseys

AY Alexei Yashin 4.00 10.00
BH Brett Hull SC 5.00 12.00
BS Brendan Shanahan SC 4.00 10.00
DS Daniel Sedin 4.00 10.00
DW Doug Weight 4.00 10.00
EB Ed Belfour SC 4.00 10.00
HS Henrik Sedin 4.00 10.00
JA Jason Allison 4.00 10.00
JI Jarome Iginla 5.00 12.00
JJ Jaromir Jagr SC 6.00 15.00
JL John LeClair SC 4.00 10.00
JO Jose Theodore 5.00 12.00
JS Joe Sakic SC 8.00 20.00
JT Joe Thornton 5.00 12.00
MH Marian Hossa 4.00 10.00
ML Mario Lemieux SC 20.00 50.00
MM Mike Modano SC 6.00 15.00
MR Mike Richter SC 4.00 10.00
MT Marty Turco 4.00 10.00
PB Peter Bondra 4.00 10.00
PF Peter Forsberg SC 10.00 25.00
PK Paul Kariya 4.00 10.00
PR Patrick Roy SC 12.50 30.00
PS Patrik Stefan 4.00 10.00
RB Ray Bourque SC 10.00 25.00
SF Sergei Fedorov SC 6.00 15.00
SY Steve Yzerman SC 12.50 30.00
TS Teemu Selanne 6.00 15.00
VB Valeri Bure 4.00 10.00
VL Vincent Lecavalier 4.00 10.00
TJBS Brendan Shanahan Upd 4.00 10.00
TJCD Chris Drury Upd 4.00 10.00
TJJI Jarome Iginla Upd 4.00 10.00
TJJW Justin Williams Upd 4.00 10.00
TJMH Milan Hejduk Upd 4.00 10.00
TJMN Markus Naslund Upd 4.00 10.00
TJMS Miroslav Satan Upd 4.00 10.00
TJPD Pavol Demitra Upd 4.00 10.00
TJPK Paul Kariya Upd 8.00 20.00
TJZP Zigmund Palffy Upd 4.00 10.00

2001-02 UD Top Shelf Jersey Autographs

DS Daniel Sedin 15.00 40.00
DW Doug Weight 15.00 40.00
EB Ed Belfour SC 15.00 40.00
HS Henrik Sedin 12.00 30.00
JA Jason Allison 15.00 40.00
JI Jarome Iginla 20.00 50.00
JL John LeClair SC 15.00 40.00
JO Jose Theodore 20.00 50.00
JT Joe Thornton 20.00 50.00
MH Marian Hossa 15.00 40.00
MM Mike Modano SC 25.00 60.00
MT Marty Turco 15.00 40.00
PS Patrik Stefan 15.00 40.00
RB Ray Bourque SC 40.00 100.00
SY Steve Yzerman SC 50.00 120.00
TS Teemu Selanne 25.00 60.00
VL Vincent Lecavalier 15.00 40.00

2001-02 UD Top Shelf Patches

PJJ Jaromir Jagr 15.00 40.00
PMB Martin Brodeur 30.00 80.00
PMM Mike Modano 15.00 40.00
PPF Peter Forsberg 20.00 50.00
PPR Patrick Roy 30.00 80.00
PSY Steve Yzerman 60.00 125.00

2001-02 UD Top Shelf Rookie Redemption

TS1 Stanislav Chistov 10.00 25.00
TS2 Rick Nash 30.00 80.00
TS3 Henrik Zetterberg 30.00 80.00
TS4 Jason Spezza 25.00 60.00

2001-02 UD Top Shelf Sticks

SBH Brett Hull 8.00 20.00
SBS Brendan Shanahan 6.00 15.00
SCP Chris Pronger 6.00 15.00
SDH Dominik Hasek 8.00 20.00
SJL John LeClair 6.00 15.00
SJR Jeremy Roenick 8.00 20.00
SJS Joe Sakic 10.00 25.00
SKT Keith Tkachuk 6.00 15.00
SMB Martin Brodeur 15.00 40.00
SML Mario Lemieux 12.00 30.00
SMM Mark Messier 6.00 15.00
SNL Nicklas Lidstrom 6.00 15.00
SPB Peter Bondra 6.00 15.00
SPF Peter Forsberg 8.00 20.00
SPK Paul Kariya 6.00 15.00
SPR Patrick Roy 15.00 40.00
SRB Ray Bourque 8.00 20.00
SSF Sergei Fedorov 6.00 15.00
SSO Sandis Ozolinsh 6.00 15.00
SSY Steve Yzerman 12.50 30.00
STF Theo Fleury 6.00 15.00
SWG Wayne Gretzky 40.00 80.00
SZP Zigmund Palffy 6.00 15.00
SPBU Pavel Bure 6.00 15.00
BFJ Bure/Forsberg/Jagr 50.00 125.00
BPR Bourque/Pronger/Roy 60.00 150.00
KSF Kariya/Sakic/Fleury 40.00 100.00
LOH Lidstrom/Ozolinsh/Hasek 30.00 80.00
RSF Roy/Sakic/Forsberg 40.00 100.00

2002-03 UD Top Shelf

COMP.SET w/o SP's (90) 15.00 40.00
1 Jean-Sebastien Giguere .50 1.25
2 Jeff Friesen .30 .75
3 Paul Kariya .50 1.25
4 Ilya Kovalchuk .60 1.50
5 Dany Heatley .40 1.00
6 Joe Thornton .75 2.00
7 Sergei Samsonov .40 1.00
8 Bill Guerin .50 1.25
9 Martin Biron .40 1.00
10 Miroslav Satan .50 1.25
11 Maxim Afinogenov .30 .75
12 Jarome Iginla .60 1.50
13 Roman Turek .50 1.25
14 Craig Conroy .30 .75
15 Jeff O'Neill .30 .75
16 Arturs Irbe .40 1.00
17 Sami Kapanen .30 .75
18 Jocelyn Thibault .40 1.00
19 Eric Daze .30 .75
20 Alexei Zhamnov .40 1.00
21 Patrick Roy 1.25 3.00
22 Joe Sakic 1.00 2.50
23 Peter Forsberg 1.00 2.50
24 Marc Denis .40 1.00
25 Espen Knutsen .30 .75
26 Mike Modano .75 2.00
27 Jason Arnott .40 1.00
28 Marty Turco .50 1.25
29 Steve Yzerman 1.25 3.00
30 Sergei Fedorov .75 2.00
31 Dominik Hasek .75 2.00
32 Brendan Shanahan .50 1.25
33 Ryan Smyth .40 1.00
34 Tommy Salo .40 1.00
35 Mike Comrie .50 1.25
36 Roberto Luongo .75 2.00
37 Kristian Huselius .30 .75
38 Sandis Ozolinsh .30 .75
39 Zigmund Palffy .50 1.25
40 Jason Allison .40 1.00
41 Felix Potvin .75 2.00
42 Manny Fernandez .30 .75
43 Marian Gaborik .50 1.25
44 Andrew Brunette .30 .75
45 Jose Theodore .50 1.25
46 Saku Koivu .50 1.25
47 Richard Zednik .30 .75
48 Mike Dunham .40 1.00
49 David Legwand .40 1.00
50 Patrik Elias .50 1.25
51 Joe Nieuwendyk .40 1.00
52 Martin Brodeur 1.25 3.00
53 Scott Niedermayer .50 1.25
54 Alexei Yashin .40 1.00
55 Michael Peca .40 1.00
56 Chris Osgood .50 1.25
57 Mike Richter .50 1.25
58 Pavel Bure .50 1.25
59 Eric Lindros .75 2.00
60 Martin Havlat .40 1.00
61 Patrick Lalime .40 1.00
62 Marian Hossa .50 1.25
63 Jeremy Roenick .75 2.00
64 Roman Cechmanek .40 1.00
65 John LeClair .50 1.25
66 Simon Gagne .50 1.25
67 Ladislav Nagy .30 .75
68 Sean Burke .30 .75
69 Daniel Briere .40 1.00
70 Johan Hedberg .50 1.25
71 Mario Lemieux 2.00 5.00
72 Alexei Kovalev .40 1.00
73 Evgeni Nabokov .40 1.00
74 Owen Nolan .50 1.25
75 Teemu Selanne 1.00 2.50
76 Brent Johnson .40 1.00
77 Keith Tkachuk .50 1.25
78 Chris Pronger .50 1.25
79 Brad Richards .50 1.25
80 Vincent Lecavalier .50 1.25
81 Nikolai Khabibulin .50 1.25
82 Alexander Mogilny .40 1.00
83 Mats Sundin .50 1.25
84 Curtis Joseph .60 1.50
85 Todd Bertuzzi .50 1.25
86 Brendan Morrison .40 1.00
87 Markus Naslund .50 1.25
88 Jaromir Jagr 1.50 4.00
89 Peter Bondra .50 1.25
90 Olaf Kolzig .50 1.25
91 Tim Thomas RC 5.00 12.00
92 Ivan Majesky RC 1.25 3.00
93 Jay Bouwmeester RC 4.00 10.00
94 Ron Hainsey RC 1.25 3.00
95 Ray Schultz RC 1.25 3.00
96 Tomi Pettinen RC 1.25 3.00
97 Eric Godard RC 1.25 3.00
98 Anton Volchenkov RC 1.25 3.00
99 Dennis Seidenberg RC 2.00 5.00
100 Radovan Somik RC 1.25 3.00
101 Patrick Sharp RC 4.00 10.00
102 Carlo Colaiacovo RC 2.00 5.00
103 Mikael Tellqvist RC 1.25 3.00
104 Steve Eminger RC 1.25 3.00
105 Alex Henry RC 1.50 4.00
106 Kurt Sauer RC 1.25 3.00
107 Micki Dupont RC 1.25 3.00
108 Shawn Thornton RC 1.50 4.00
109 Matt Henderson RC 1.25 3.00
110 Jeff Paul RC 1.25 3.00
111 Lasse Pirjeta RC 1.25 3.00
112 Dmitri Bykov RC 1.25 3.00
113 Kari Haakana RC 1.25 3.00
114 Sylvain Blouin RC 1.25 3.00
115 Stephane Veilleux RC 1.25 3.00
116 Greg Koehler RC 1.25 3.00
117 Lynn Loyns RC 1.25 3.00
118 Tom Koivisto RC 1.25 3.00
119 Curtis Sanford RC 2.00 5.00
120 Cody Rudkowsky RC 1.25 3.00
121 Martin Gerber RC 4.00 10.00
122 Alexei Smirnov RC 3.00 8.00
123 Stanislav Chistov RC 2.50 6.00
124 Jordan Leopold RC 4.00 10.00
125 Chuck Kobasew RC 3.00 8.00
126 Rick Nash RC 15.00 40.00
127 Henrik Zetterberg RC 12.00 30.00
128 Ales Hemsky RC 10.00 25.00
129 Alexander Frolov RC 6.00 15.00
130 P-M Bouchard RC 4.00 10.00
131 Adam Hall RC 2.50 6.00
132 Scottie Upshall RC 3.00 8.00
133 Jason Spezza RC 15.00 40.00
134 Jeff Taffe RC 2.50 6.00
135 Alexander Svitov RC 2.50 6.00

2002-03 UD Top Shelf All-Stars Jerseys

ASGR Wayne Gretzky 60.00 120.00
ASJJ Jaromir Jagr 12.00 30.00
ASJS Joe Sakic 15.00 40.00
ASKT Keith Tkachuk 8.00 20.00
ASMS Mats Sundin 8.00 20.00
ASPK Paul Kariya 8.00 20.00
ASSF Sergei Fedorov 12.00 30.00
ASSS Scott Stevens 8.00 20.00
ASTA Tony Amonte 6.00 15.00
ASTF Theo Fleury 10.00 25.00
ASTS Teemu Selanne 10.00 25.00
ASWG Wayne Gretzky 60.00 120.00

2002-03 UD Top Shelf Clutch Performers Jerseys

CPAD Adam Deadmarsh 4.00 10.00
CPAM Al MacInnis 8.00 20.00
CPBG Bill Guerin 6.00 15.00
CPBL Brian Leetch 5.00 12.00
CPBO Peter Bondra 6.00 15.00
CPBS Brendan Shanahan 6.00 15.00
CPCD Chris Drury 6.00 15.00
CPCJ Curtis Joseph 8.00 20.00
CPCL Claude Lemieux 5.00 12.00
CPDW Doug Weight 6.00 15.00
CPEB Ed Belfour 6.00 15.00
CPEL Eric Lindros 10.00 25.00
CPIK Ilya Kovalchuk 8.00 20.00
CPJI Jarome Iginla 8.00 20.00
CPJJ Jaromir Jagr 20.00 50.00
CPJN Joe Nieuwendyk 5.00 12.00
CPJR Jeremy Roenick 10.00 25.00
CPJS Joe Sakic 12.00 30.00
CPJT Joe Thornton 10.00 25.00
CPKT Keith Tkachuk 6.00 15.00
CPLR Luc Robitaille 6.00 15.00
CPMB Martin Brodeur 15.00 40.00
CPMH Milan Hejduk 5.00 12.00
CPML Mario Lemieux 25.00 60.00
CPMM Mike Modano 10.00 25.00
CPMR Mike Richter 6.00 15.00
CPMS Mats Sundin 6.00 15.00
CPNL Nicklas Lidstrom 6.00 15.00
CPPB Pavel Bure 6.00 15.00
CPPK Paul Kariya 6.00 15.00
CPPR Patrick Roy 15.00 40.00
CPRB Ray Bourque 10.00 25.00
CPSB Sean Burke 4.00 10.00
CPSF Sergei Fedorov 10.00 25.00
CPSGA Simon Gagne 6.00 15.00
CPSGO Sergei Gonchar 5.00 12.00
CPSSA Sergei Samsonov 5.00 12.00
CPSSU Steve Sullivan 4.00 10.00
CPSY Steve Yzerman 15.00 40.00
CPTS Teemu Selanne 12.00 30.00
CPWG Wayne Gretzky 40.00 100.00
CPZP Zigmund Palffy 6.00 15.00

2002-03 UD Top Shelf Dual Player Jerseys

RBD M.Denis/E.Belfour 8.00 20.00
RBK P.Bure/I.Kovalchuk 10.00 25.00
RBP R.Blake/C.Pronger 8.00 20.00
RBS S.Samsonov/P.Bure 8.00 20.00
RBZ P.Bondra/Z.Palffy 8.00 20.00
RFA Fedorov/Afinogenov 12.00 30.00
RIW J.Iginla/J.Williams 10.00 25.00
RKG S.Gagne/P.Kariya 8.00 20.00
RLK R.Klesla/N.Lidstrom 8.00 20.00
RMC T.Connolly/M.Modano 12.00 30.00
RNL Legwand/Nieuwendyk 6.00 15.00
RPB F.Potvin/M.Biron 12.00 30.00
RPT J.Thornton/K.Primeau 12.00 30.00
RRT P.Roy/J.Theodore 20.00 50.00
RSF R.Fedotenko/M.Satan 8.00 20.00
RSH S.Hartnell/B.Shanahan 8.00 20.00
RSR Reinprecht/S.Sullivan 5.00 12.00
RYK K.Kolanos/S.Yzerman 20.00 50.00
STAB E.Belanger/J.Allison 6.00 15.00
STBB R.Bourque/R.Blake 12.00 30.00
STBD D.Briere/S.Doan 6.00 15.00
STBE B.Leetch/P.Bure 8.00 20.00
STBJ J.Jagr/P.Bondra 25.00 60.00
STBL R.Luongo/V.Bure 12.00 30.00
STBN M.Biron/M.Noronen 6.00 15.00
STBS M.Brodeur/S.Stevens 15.00 40.00
STBT J.Thornton/R.Bourque 12.00 30.00
STDE M.Erat/M.Dunham 6.00 15.00
STDT E.Daze/J.Thibault 6.00 15.00
STFL N.Lidstrom/S.Fedorov 12.00 30.00
STFP K.Primeau/R.Fedotenko 6.00 15.00
STFR M.Richter/T.Fleury 10.00 25.00
STGB B.Boucher/S.Gagne 8.00 20.00
STGD B.Guerin/B.Dafoe 8.00 20.00
STGK O.Kolzig/S.Gonchar 8.00 20.00
STGM M.Messier/W.Gretzky 50.00 100.00
STGR M.Recchi/S.Gagne 10.00 25.00
STGS J.Giguere/S.Shields 8.00 20.00
STHL D.Legwand/S.Hartnell 6.00 15.00
STHR M.Hejduk/Reinprecht 6.00 15.00
STIS J.Iginla/M.Savard 10.00 25.00
STJK J.Jagr/O.Kolzig 25.00 60.00
STKB K.Kolanos/S.Burke 5.00 12.00
STKF J.Friesen/P.Kariya 8.00 20.00
STKT J.Theodore/S.Koivu 8.00 20.00
STKW R.Whitney/R.Klesla 6.00 15.00
STLD C.Lemieux/S.Doan 6.00 15.00
STMA J. Arnott/M.Modano 12.00 30.00
STMM B.Morrow/M.Modano 12.00 30.00
STNL M.Naslund/T.Linden 10.00 25.00
STPD A.Deadmarsh/Z.Palffy 8.00 20.00
STSA M.Afinogenov/M.Satan 8.00 20.00
STSH D.Hinote/J.Sakic 15.00 40.00
STSM S.Sullivan/T.Amonte 6.00 15.00
STSN O.Nolan/T.Selanne 10.00 25.00
STST J.Thornton/S.Samsonov 12.00 30.00
STTD M.Denis/R.Tugnutt 6.00 15.00
STTG B.Guerin/J.Thornton 12.00 30.00
STYH J.Hecht/M.York 5.00 12.00
STYS B.Shanahan/S.Yzerman 20.00 50.00

2002-03 UD Top Shelf Goal Oriented Jerseys

GOAD Adam Deadmarsh 4.00 10.00
GOAT Alex Tanguay 5.00 12.00
GOBG Bill Guerin 6.00 15.00
GOBO Peter Bondra 6.00 15.00
GODA Denis Arkhipov 4.00 10.00
GODB Daniel Briere 5.00 12.00
GOED Eric Daze 4.00 10.00
GOGM Glen Murray 5.00 12.00
GOIK Ilya Kovalchuk 8.00 20.00
GOJJ Jaromir Jagr 20.00 50.00
GOJS Joe Sakic 12.00 30.00
GOJT Joe Thornton 10.00 25.00
GOMA Mats Sundin 6.00 15.00
GOMH Milan Hejduk 5.00 12.00
GOMM Mike Modano 10.00 25.00
GOMS Miroslav Satan 6.00 15.00
GOMY Mike York 4.00 10.00
GOPB Pavel Bure 8.00 20.00
GOPK Paul Kariya 6.00 15.00
GORD Radek Dvorak 5.00 12.00
GORL Robert Lang 4.00 10.00
GOSF Sergei Fedorov 10.00 25.00
GOSG Simon Gagne 6.00 15.00
GOSR Steven Reinprecht 4.00 10.00
GOSS Sergei Samsonov 5.00 12.00
GOSU Steve Sullivan 4.00 10.00
GOSY Steve Yzerman 15.00 40.00
GOTA Tony Amonte 5.00 12.00
GOTS Teemu Selanne 8.00 20.00
GOZP Zigmund Palffy 6.00 15.00

2002-03 UD Top Shelf Milestones Jerseys

MBBRR Jeremy Roenick
Mark Recchi
Pavel Bure
Peter Bondra 50.00 100.00
MBMBS Brque/Bure/Slnne/Mdno 100.00 200.00
MGDYM Grtz./Drqe/Mess./Yze. 250.00 400.00
MGHLY Grtz./Lem./Hwe/Yze. 250.00 400.00
MHPBJ Brke/Ptvin/Brrsso/Hasek 50.00 100.00
MLNLA Amnte/LClr/Lndrs/Noln 50.00 100.00
MMHYR Mocc./Hull/Robit./Yzo. 200.00 350.00
MRBRJ Roy/Brodr./Cujo/Richt. 150.00 300.00
MSFRM Fleury/Shan./Roe./Mess. 75.00 150.00
MSYVR Shan./Yze./Vbeek/Robit. 125.00 250.00

2002-03 UD Top Shelf Shooting Stars Jerseys

SHAR Jason Arnott 5.00 12.00
SHAT Alex Tanguay 5.00 12.00
SHBG Bill Guerin 6.00 15.00
SHBH Brett Hull 12.00 30.00
SHBL Brian Leetch 5.00 12.00
SHBM Brenden Morrow 5.00 12.00
SHBO Peter Bondra 6.00 15.00
SHBS Brendan Shanahan 6.00 15.00
SHDB Daniel Briere 5.00 12.00
SHEK Espen Knutsen 4.00 10.00
SHGM Glen Murray 5.00 12.00
SHJA Jason Allison 5.00 12.00
SHJJ Jaromir Jagr 20.00 50.00
SHJN Joe Nieuwendyk 5.00 12.00
SHKK Krys Kolanos 4.00 10.00
SHLE Rob Blake 6.00 15.00
SHMA Maxim Afinogenov 4.00 10.00
SHMH Milan Hejduk 5.00 12.00
SHML Mario Lemieux 25.00 60.00
SHMM Mike Modano 10.00 25.00
SHMSA Miroslav Satan 6.00 15.00
SHMSU Mats Sundin 6.00 15.00
SHMY Mike York 4.00 10.00
SHNA Nikolai Antropov 5.00 12.00
SHNL Nicklas Lidstrom 6.00 15.00
SHPB Pavel Bure 6.00 15.00
SHPF Peter Forsberg 12.00 30.00
SHPK Paul Kariya 6.00 15.00
SHRB Ray Bourque 10.00 25.00
SHRL Robert Lang 4.00 10.00
SHSD Shane Doan 5.00 12.00
SHSF Sergei Fedorov 10.00 25.00
SHSG Simon Gagne 6.00 15.00
SHSH Scott Hartnell 4.00 10.00
SHSK Saku Koivu 6.00 15.00
SHSR Steven Reinprecht 4.00 10.00
SHSS Steve Sullivan 4.00 10.00
SHSY Steve Yzerman 15.00 40.00
SHTA Tony Amonte 5.00 12.00
SHTF Theo Fleury 8.00 20.00
SHTS Teemu Selanne 8.00 20.00
SHZP Zigmund Palffy 6.00 15.00

2002-03 UD Top Shelf Signatures

AK Alexei Kovalev 5.00 12.00
BB Brian Boucher SP 8.00 20.00
BG Bill Guerin 5.00 12.00
BL Rob Blake 5.00 12.00
BO Bobby Orr/96 100.00 200.00
DH Dany Heatley 10.00 25.00
DS Daniel Sedin 8.00 20.00
DW Doug Weight/92 12.50 30.00
GH Gordie Howe/27 150.00 300.00
HA Martin Havlat 8.00 20.00
HS Henrik Sedin 8.00 20.00
JA Jason Allison SP 5.00 12.00
JH Johan Hedberg SP 5.00 12.00
JI Jarome Iginla 10.00 25.00
JL John LeClair 6.00 15.00
MB Martin Biron SP 5.00 12.00
MC Mike Comrie 5.00 12.00
MH Milan Hejduk 6.00 15.00
MN Markus Naslund 6.00 15.00
MO Maxime Ouellet 5.00 12.00
PA Pavel Brendl 5.00 12.00
PB Pavel Bure 10.00 25.00
PE Peter Bondra 5.00 12.00
PR Patrick Roy SP 40.00 100.00
RB Ray Bourque SP 12.00 30.00
RD Rick DiPietro 5.00 12.00
RK Rostislav Klesla SP 6.00 15.00
RT Raffi Torres 5.00 12.00
SG Simon Gagne 8.00 20.00
SH Scott Hartnell 6.00 15.00
SS Sergei Samsonov 5.00 12.00
SY Steve Yzerman/53 60.00 120.00
TH Jose Theodore 10.00 25.00
TS Tommy Salo 5.00 12.00
WG Wayne Gretzky/95 250.00 600.00
ZP Zigmund Palffy 5.00 12.00

2002-03 UD Top Shelf Stopper Jerseys

SSBB Brian Boucher 5.00 12.00
SSBD Byron Dafoe 5.00 12.00
SSBI Martin Biron 5.00 12.00
SSBJ Brent Johnson 5.00 12.00
SSCJ Curtis Joseph 8.00 20.00
SSDA David Aebischer 5.00 12.00
SSDB Dan Blackburn 5.00 12.00
SSDH Dominik Hasek 10.00 25.00
SSDU Mike Dunham 5.00 12.00
SSEB Ed Belfour 6.00 15.00
SSFP Felix Potvin 10.00 25.00
SSJGO Jean-Sebastien Giguere 6.00 15.00
SSJTO Jocelyn Thibault 5.00 12.00
SSMB Martin Brodeur 15.00 40.00
SSMD Marc Denis 5.00 12.00
SSMN Mika Noronen 5.00 12.00
SSMR Mike Richter 8.00 20.00
SSOK Olaf Kolzig 6.00 15.00
SSPR Patrick Roy 15.00 40.00
SSRC Roman Cechmanek 5.00 12.00
SSRT Ron Tugnutt 5.00 12.00
SSSB Sean Burke 4.00 10.00
SSSS Steve Shields 5.00 12.00
SSTH Jose Theodore 6.00 15.00

2002-03 UD Top Shelf Sweet Sweaters

SWAD Adam Deadmarsh 5.00 12.00
SWAT Alex Tanguay 6.00 15.00
SWBE Mark Bell 5.00 12.00
SWBG Bill Guerin 8.00 20.00
SWBH Brett Hull 15.00 40.00
SWCD Chris Drury 8.00 20.00
SWCJ Curtis Joseph 10.00 25.00
SWCL Claude Lemieux 6.00 15.00
SWDB Daniel Briere 6.00 15.00
SWDE Marc Denis 6.00 15.00
SWDG Doug Gilmour 10.00 25.00
SWFP Felix Potvin 12.00 30.00
SWJA Jason Allison 6.00 15.00
SWJF Jeff Friesen 5.00 12.00
SWJJ Jaromir Jagr 25.00 60.00
SWJO Joe Thornton 12.00 30.00
SWJS Joe Sakic 15.00 40.00
SWJT Jocelyn Thibault 6.00 15.00
SWKP Keith Primeau 6.00 15.00
SWKT Keith Tkachuk 8.00 20.00
SWMA Maxim Afinogenov 5.00 12.00
SWMB Martin Biron 6.00 15.00
SWMD Mike Dunham 6.00 15.00
SWMM Mike Modano 12.00 30.00
SWMS Mats Sundin 8.00 20.00
SWOK Olaf Kolzig 8.00 20.00
SWPB Pavel Bure 10.00 25.00
SWPK Paul Kariya 8.00 20.00
SWRB Ray Bourque 12.00 30.00
SWRK Rostislav Klesla 5.00 12.00
SWSA Miroslav Satan 8.00 20.00
SWSF Sergei Fedorov 12.00 30.00
SWSK Saku Koivu 8.00 20.00
SWSR Steven Reinprecht 5.00 12.00
SWSS Sergei Samsonov 6.00 15.00
SWSU Steve Sullivan 5.00 12.00
SWSY Steve Yzerman 20.00 50.00
SWTH Jose Theodore 8.00 20.00
SWTS Teemu Selanne 10.00 25.00
SWVN Ville Nieminen 5.00 12.00
SWWG Wayne Gretzky 50.00 125.00
SWZP Zigmund Palffy 8.00 20.00

2002-03 UD Top Shelf Triple Jerseys

HTAPS Amonte/Palffy/Selanne 40.00 100.00
HTBSB Bondra/Bure/Satan 40.00 100.00
HTGHB Guerin/Bondra/Hossa 40.00 100.00
HTGLB Gretzky/Lemieux/Bure 250.00 400.00
HTJHS Hejduk/Jagr/Selanne 40.00 100.00
HTKGF Gagne/Kariya/Fleury 40.00 100.00
HTKYI Iginla/Kariya/Yzerman 150.00 300.00
HTLJT Thornton/Jagr/Lemieux 100.00 200.00
HTLRR Roenick/LeClair/Recchi 75.00 150.00
HTNTH Hejduk/Thornton/Naslund 40.00 100.00
HTSHR Shanahan/Hull/Robitaille 75.00 150.00
HTSIG Sakic/Iginla/Gagne 40.00 100.00

1998-99 UD3

COMPLETE SET (180) 300.00 500.00
1 Sergei Samsonov NE .40 1.00
2 Ryan Johnson NE RC .30 .75
3 Josef Marha NE .30 .75
4 Patrick Marleau NE .30 .75
5 Derek Morris NE .30 .75
6 Jamie Storr NE .40 1.00
7 Richard Zednik NE .30 .75
8 Alyn McCauley NE .30 .75
9 Robert Dome NE .30 .75
10 Patrik Elias NE .40 1.00
11 Olli Jokinen NE .40 1.00
12 Warren Luhning NE .30 .75
13 Chris Phillips NE .30 .75
14 Mattias Ohlund NE .40 1.00
15 Joe Thornton NE .75 2.00
16 Matt Cullen NE .30 .75
17 Bates Battaglia NE .30 .75
18 Andrei Zyuzin NE .30 .75
19 Cameron Mann NE .30 .75
20 Zdeno Chara NE .30 .75
21 Marc Savard NE .30 .75
22 Alexei Morozov NE .30 .75
23 Mike Johnson NE .40 1.00
24 Vaclav Varada NE .30 .75
25 Dan Cloutier NE .30 .75
26 Brad Isbister NE .30 .75
27 Marco Sturm NE .30 .75
28 Anders Eriksson NE .30 .75
29 Jan Bulis NE .30 .75
30 Brendan Morrison NE .40 1.00
31 Wayne Gretzky TSS 2.50 6.00
32 Jaromir Jagr TSS .60 1.50
33 Peter Forsberg TSS 1.00 2.50
34 Paul Kariya TSS .40 1.00
35 Brett Hull TSS .50 1.25
36 Martin Brodeur TSS 1.00 2.50
37 Eric Lindros TSS .50 1.25
38 Peter Bondra TSS .40 1.00
39 Mike Modano TSS .60 1.50
40 Theo Fleury TSS .40 1.00
41 Curtis Joseph TSS .40 1.00
42 Sergei Fedorov TSS .60 1.50
43 Saku Koivu TSS .40 1.00
44 Zigmund Palffy TSS .40 1.00
45 Ed Belfour TSS .40 1.00
46 Patrick Roy TSS 2.00 5.00
47 Brendan Shanahan TSS .40 1.00
48 Mats Sundin TSS .40 1.00
49 Alexei Yashin TR .40 1.00
50 Doug Gilmour TSS .40 1.00
51 Chris Osgood TSS .40 1.00
52 Keith Tkachuk TSS .40 1.00
53 Mark Messier TSS .50 1.25
54 John Vanbiesbrouck TSS .40 1.00
55 Ray Bourque TSS .60 1.50
56 John LeClair TSS .50 1.25
57 Dominik Hasek TSS .75 2.00
58 Teemu Selanne TSS .40 1.00
59 Joe Sakic TSS .75 2.00
60 Steve Yzerman TSS 2.00 5.00
61 Sergei Samsonov NE .40 1.00
62 Ryan Johnson NE .30 .75
63 Josef Marha NE .30 .75
64 Patrick Marleau NE .30 .75
65 Derek Morris NE .30 .75
66 Jamie Storr NE .40 1.00
67 Richard Zednik NE .30 .75
68 Alyn McCauley NE .30 .75
69 Robert Dome NE .30 .75
70 Patrik Elias NE .40 1.00
71 Olli Jokinen NE .40 1.00
72 Warren Luhning NE .30 .75
73 Chris Phillips NE .30 .75
74 Mattias Ohlund NE .40 1.00
75 Joe Thornton NE .75 2.00
76 Matt Cullen NE .30 .75
77 Bates Battaglia NE .30 .75
78 Andrei Zyuzin NE .30 .75
79 Cameron Mann NE .40 1.00
80 Zdeno Chara NE .50 1.25
81 Marc Savard NE .30 .75
82 Alexei Morozov NE .40 1.00
83 Mike Johnson NE .40 1.00
84 Vaclav Varada NE .30 .75
85 Dan Cloutier NE .30 .75
86 Brad Isbister NE .30 .75
87 Marco Sturm NE .40 1.00
88 Anders Eriksson NE .30 .75
89 Jan Bulis NE .30 .75
90 Brendan Morrison NE .40 1.00
91 Wayne Gretzky TSS 4.00 10.00
92 Jaromir Jagr TSS 1.00 2.50
93 Peter Forsberg TSS 1.50 4.00
94 Paul Kariya TSS .75 2.00
95 Brett Hull TSS .75 2.00
96 Martin Brodeur TSS 1.50 4.00
97 Eric Lindros TSS .75 2.00
98 Peter Bondra TSS .75 2.00
99 Mike Modano TSS 1.00 2.50
100 Theo Fleury TSS .60 1.50
101 Curtis Joseph TSS .75 2.00
102 Sergei Fedorov TSS 1.00 2.50
103 Saku Koivu TSS .75 2.00
104 Zigmund Palffy TSS .75 2.00
105 Ed Belfour TSS .75 2.00
106 Patrick Roy TSS 3.00 8.00
107 Brendan Shanahan TSS .75 2.00
108 Mats Sundin TSS .75 2.00
109 Alexei Yashin TSS .60 1.50
110 Doug Gilmour TSS .75 2.00
111 Chris Osgood TSS .75 2.00
112 Keith Tkachuk TSS .75 2.00
113 Mark Messier TSS .75 2.00
114 John Vanbiesbrouck TSS .60 1.50
115 Ray Bourque TSS 1.00 2.50
116 John LeClair TSS .50 1.25
117 Dominik Hasek TSS 1.25 3.00
118 Teemu Selanne TSS .75 2.00
119 Joe Sakic TSS 1.25 3.00
120 Steve Yzerman TSS 3.00 8.00
121 Sergei Samsonov NE 1.25 3.00
122 Ryan Johnson NE 1.00 2.50
123 Josef Marha NE 1.00 2.50
124 Patrick Marleau NE 1.00 2.50
125 Derek Morris NE 1.00 2.50
126 Jamie Storr NE 1.25 3.00
127 Richard Zednik NE 1.00 2.50
128 Alyn McCauley NE 1.00 2.50
129 Robert Dome NE 1.00 2.50
130 Patrik Elias NE 1.25 3.00
131 Olli Jokinen NE 1.25 3.00
132 Warren Luhning NE 1.00 2.50
133 Chris Phillips NE 1.00 2.50
134 Mattias Ohlund NE 1.25 3.00
135 Joe Thornton NE 2.50 6.00
136 Matt Cullen NE 1.00 2.50
137 Bates Battglia NE 1.00 2.50
138 Andrei Zyuzin NE 1.00 2.50
139 Cameron Mann NE 1.00 2.50
140 Zdeno Chara NE 1.00 2.50
141 Marc Savard NE 1.00 2.50
142 Alexei Morozov NE 1.25 3.00
143 Mike Johnson NE 1.25 3.00
144 Vaclav Varada NE 1.00 2.50
145 Dan Cloutier NE 1.00 2.50
146 Brad Isbister NE 1.00 2.50
147 Marco Sturm NE 1.25 3.00
148 Anders Eriksson NE 1.00 2.50
149 Jan Bulis NE 1.00 2.50
150 Brendan Morrison NE 1.50 4.00
151 Wayne Gretzky TSS 25.00 60.00
152 Jaromir Jagr TSS 6.00 15.00
153 Peter Forsberg TSS 5.00 12.00
154 Paul Kariya TSS 4.00 10.00
155 Brett Hull TSS 5.00 12.00
156 Martin Brodeur TSS 15.00 40.00
157 Eric Lindros TSS 4.00 10.00
158 Peter Bondra TSS 4.00 10.00
159 Mike Modano TSS 6.00 15.00
160 Theo Fleury TSS 3.00 8.00
161 Curtis Joseph TSS 4.00 10.00
162 Sergei Fedorov TSS 6.00 15.00
163 Saku Koivu TSS 4.00 10.00
164 Zigmund Palffy TSS 3.00 8.00
165 Ed Belfour TSS 4.00 10.00
166 Patrick Roy TSS 15.00 40.00
167 Brendan Shanahan TSS 4.00 10.00
168 Mats Sundin TSS 4.00 10.00
169 Alexei Yashin TSS 3.00 8.00
170 Doug Gilmour TSS 4.00 10.00
171 Chris Osgood TSS 4.00 10.00
172 Keith Tkachuk TSS 4.00 10.00
173 Mark Messier TSS 5.00 12.00
174 John Vanbiesbrouck TSS 4.00 10.00
175 Ray Bourque TSS 6.00 15.00
176 John LeClair TSS 4.00 10.00
177 Dominik Hasek TSS 8.00 20.00
178 Teemu Selanne TSS 4.00 10.00
179 Joe Sakic TSS 8.00 20.00
180 Steve Yzerman TSS 20.00 50.00

1998-99 UD3 Die-Cuts

*1-30 EMB.DIE-CUT/200: 6X TO 15X
*61-90 DIE-CUT/1000: 2X TO 5X
*91-120 DIE-CUT/1000: 2X TO 5X
*121-150 DIE-CUT/50: 5X TO 15X
*151-180 DIE-CUT/100: 1.5X TO 4X

2004-05 Ultimate Collection

1 Jean-Sebastien Giguere 1.00 2.50
2 Dany Heatley .75 2.00
3 Ilya Kovalchuk 1.00 2.50
4 Joe Thornton 1.50 4.00
5 Chris Drury .75 2.00
6 Jarome Iginla 1.25 3.00
7 Miikka Kiprusoff 1.00 2.50
8 Eric Staal 1.25 3.00
9 Jocelyn Thibault .75 2.00
10 Peter Forsberg 2.00 5.00
11 Joe Sakic 2.00 5.00
12 Rick Nash 1.00 2.50
13 Mike Modano 1.50 4.00
14 Pavel Datsyuk 1.50 4.00
15 Gordie Howe 3.00 8.00
16 Steve Yzerman 2.50 6.00
17 Wayne Gretzky 6.00 15.00
18 Ryan Smyth .75 2.00
19 Roberto Luongo 1.50 4.00
20 Luc Robitaille 1.00 2.50
21 Marian Gaborik 1.00 2.50
22 Patrick Roy 2.50 6.00
23 Jose Theodore 1.00 2.50
24 Tomas Vokoun .75 2.00
25 Martin Brodeur 2.50 6.00
26 Jaromir Jagr 3.00 8.00
27 Mark Messier 2.00 5.00
28 Michael Peca .75 2.00
29 Dominik Hasek 1.50 4.00
30 Jason Spezza 1.00 2.50
31 Jeremy Roenick 1.50 4.00
32 Simon Gagne 1.00 2.50
33 Brett Hull 2.00 5.00
34 Mario Lemieux 4.00 10.00
35 Evgeni Nabokov .75 2.00
36 Keith Tkachuk 1.00 2.50
37 Vincent Lecavalier 1.00 2.50
38 Martin St. Louis 1.00 2.50
39 Mats Sundin 1.00 2.50
40 Ed Belfour 1.00 2.50
41 Markus Naslund 1.00 2.50
42 Olaf Kolzig 1.00 2.50
43 Brad Fast RC .75 2.00
44 Brennan Evans RC .75 2.00
45 Layne Ulmer RC .60 1.50
46 Mel Angelstad RC .60 1.50
47 Garret Stroshein RC .60 1.50
48 Marcel Goc RC 1.00 2.50
49 Alexander Ragulin RC 1.00 2.50
50 Herb Brooks 1.00 2.50
51 Cammie Granato RC 1.00 2.50
52 Foster Hewitt .75 2.00
53 Mike Keenan 1.00 2.50
54 Bob Cole .60 1.50
55 Lord Stanley .75 2.00
56 James Norris .75 2.00
57 Ken Hitchcock .75 2.00
58 Dave Reece 1.50 4.00
59 Mario Lemieux WC 4.00 10.00
60 Joe Thornton WC 1.50 4.00
61 Dany Heatley WC .75 2.00
62 Jarome Iginla WC 1.25 3.00
63 Joe Sakic WC 2.00 5.00
64 Vincent Lecavalier WC 1.00 2.50

65 Martin Brodeur WC 2.50 6.00
66 Jaromir Jagr WC 3.00 8.00
67 Milan Hejduk WC .75 2.00
68 Miikka Kiprusoff WC 1.00 2.50
69 Tuomo Ruutu WC .75 2.00
70 Teemu Selanne WC 2.00 5.00
71 Marco Sturm WC .60 1.50
72 Olaf Kolzig WC 1.00 2.50
73 Ilya Kovalchuk WC 1.00 2.50
74 Sergei Samsonov WC .75 2.00
75 Marian Hossa WC 1.00 2.50
76 Marian Gaborik WC 1.00 2.50
77 Nicklas Lidstrom WC 1.00 2.50
78 Mats Sundin WC 1.00 2.50
79 Peter Forsberg WC 2.00 5.00
80 Robert Esche WC .75 2.00
81 Mike Modano WC 1.50 4.00
82 Bill Guerin WC 1.00 2.50
83 Tony Amonte WC .75 2.00
84 Keith Tkachuk WC 1.00 2.50

2004-05 Ultimate Collection Buybacks

1 A.Tanguay MVP Souv/28 15.00 40.00
4 C.Drury MVP Jsy/32 12.50 30.00
26 J.Spezza Prospects Jsy/51 25.00 60.00
28 J.Bouwmster Prospects Jsy/56 15.00 40.00
37 J.Thornton Ice Jsy/22 25.00 60.00
40 J.Thornton MVP Jsy/24 25.00 60.00
45 J.Theodore Mask Col Pad/23 40.00 100.00
46 J.Theodore Top Shelf Gear/18 40.00 100.00
57 M.Naslund Top Shelf Jsy/17 15.00 40.00
61 M.Turco MVP Souv/26 20.00 50.00
63 M.Noronen SPGU Auth Fab/21
64 M.Noronen Mask Col Jsy/22 12.50 30.00
66 M.Hejduk MVP Jsy/20 12.50 30.00
69 M.Hejduk Top Shelf Jsy/22 15.00 40.00
87 Z.Palffy SPGU Auth Fab/23
92 Z.Palffy UD Phenom Finish/19 15.00 40.00
94 Z.Palffy MVP Souv/26 12.50 30.00
96 Z.Palffy Top Shelf Jsy/23 12.50 30.00

2004-05 Ultimate Collection Jerseys

UGJAT Alex Tanguay 4.00 10.00
UGJBC Bobby Clarke 5.00 12.00
UGJBH Bobby Hull 8.00 20.00
UGJBO Mike Bossy 6.00 15.00
UGJBT Bryan Trottier 4.00 10.00
UGJCJ Curtis Joseph 6.00 15.00
UGJDH Dany Heatley 6.00 15.00
UGJDO Dominik Hasek 8.00 20.00
UGJGH Gordie Howe 12.00 30.00
UGJGL Guy Lafleur 8.00 20.00
UGJHE Milan Hejduk 4.00 10.00
UGJJB Johnny Bucyk 4.00 10.00
UGJJI Jarome Iginla 8.00 20.00
UGJJJ Jaromir Jagr 10.00 25.00
UGJJK Jari Kurri 5.00 12.00
UGJJO Jose Theodore 5.00 12.00
UGJJR Jeremy Roenick 5.00 12.00
UGJJS Joe Sakic 10.00 25.00
UGJJT Joe Thornton 8.00 20.00
UGJMB Martin Brodeur 10.00 25.00
UGJMH Marian Hossa 4.00 10.00
UGJML Mario Lemieux 15.00 40.00
UGJMM Mark Messier 8.00 20.00
UGJMN Markus Naslund 4.00 10.00
UGJMO Mike Modano 5.00 12.00
UGJMS Martin St.Louis 4.00 10.00
UGJNK Nikolai Khabibulin 4.00 10.00
UGJNZ Nikolai Zherdev 4.00 10.00
UGJPF Peter Forsberg 6.00 15.00
UGJPK Paul Kariya 4.00 10.00
UGJRB Ray Bourque 5.00 12.00
UGJRN Rick Nash 5.00 12.00
UGJSK Saku Koivu 4.00 10.00
UGJSP Jason Spezza 6.00 15.00
UGJSU Mats Sundin 5.00 12.00
UGJSY Steve Yzerman 10.00 25.00
UGJVL Vincent Lecavalier 4.00 10.00
UGJPR1 Patrick Roy 10.00 25.00
UGJPR2 Patrick Roy 10.00 25.00
UGJWG1 Wayne Gretzky AS 30.00 80.00
UGJWG2 Wayne Gretzky EDM 20.00 50.00

2004-05 Ultimate Collection Jerseys Gold

*GOLD: .75X TO 2X JSY HI

2004-05 Ultimate Collection Patches

UPMH Marian Hossa 50.00 100.00
UPJT Joe Thornton 50.00 100.00
UPMB Martin Brodeur 100.00 200.00
UPJJ Jaromir Jagr 60.00 120.00
UPJO Jose Theodore 50.00 100.00
UPJR Jeremy Roenick 40.00 80.00
UPJS Joe Sakic 75.00 150.00
UPJG Jean-Sebastien Giguere 60.00 120.00
UPHE Milan Hejduk 40.00 80.00
UPMO Mike Modano 50.00 100.00
UPMS Martin St.Louis 40.00 80.00
UPNK Nikolai Khabibulin 40.00 80.00
UPBH Brett Hull 50.00 100.00
UPBL Brian Leetch 50.00 100.00
UPMM Mark Messier 100.00 200.00
UPSK Saku Koivu 50.00 100.00
UPSP Jason Spezza 100.00 200.00
UPSU Mats Sundin 75.00 200.00
UPML Mario Lemieux 200.00 400.00
UPHA Dominik Hasek 60.00 120.00
UPIK Ilya Kovalchuk 60.00 120.00
UPSY Steve Yzerman 125.00 250.00
UPVL Vincent Lecavalier 50.00 100.00
UPNZ Nikolai Zherdev 40.00 80.00
UPPF Peter Forsberg 60.00 120.00
UPRN Rick Nash 50.00 100.00
UPSF Sergei Fedorov 30.00 60.00
UPBS Brendan Shanahan 50.00 100.00
UPBT Bryan Trottier 50.00 100.00
UPPK Paul Kariya/9
UPCJ Curtis Joseph 60.00 120.00
UPEB Ed Belfour 30.00 80.00
UPTK Keith Tkachuk 40.00 80.00
UPRB1 Ray Bourque BOS 75.00 150.00
UPPR1 Patrick Roy COL 100.00 250.00
UPWG1 W.Gretzky LA/25 300.00 600.00
UPRB2 Ray Bourque COL 75.00 150.00
UPPR2 Patrick Roy MTL 100.00 200.00
UPWG2 W.Gretzky AS/25 250.00 500.00
UPDHA D. Heatley JSY 40.00 80.00
UPDHB D. Heatley PATCH 50.00 100.00
UPMNA M. Naslund JSY 30.00 60.00
UPMNB M. Naslund PATCH 40.00 80.00

2004-05 Ultimate Collection Patch Autographs

UPAAT Alex Tanguay 30.00 80.00
UPABR Brad Richards 25.00 60.00
UPACD Chris Drury 25.00 60.00
UPADH Dany Heatley 60.00 150.00
UPADO Dominik Hasek 75.00 150.00
UPAEJ Ed Jovanovski 30.00 80.00
UPAJB Jay Bouwmeester 25.00 60.00
UPAJI Jarome Iginla 50.00 100.00
UPAJK Jari Kurri 50.00 100.00
UPAJO Jose Theodore 50.00 100.00
UPAJR Jeremy Roenick 30.00 80.00
UPAJT Joe Thornton 60.00 150.00
UPAMB Martin Brodeur 125.00 250.00
UPAMD Marcel Dionne 30.00 80.00
UPAMH Milan Hejduk 25.00 60.00
UPAMN Markus Naslund 25.00 60.00
UPAMS Martin St.Louis 30.00 80.00
UPAMT Marty Turco 15.00 40.00
UPANK Nikolai Khabibulin 50.00 100.00
UPANZ Nikolai Zherdev 20.00 50.00
UPAPR Patrick Roy 150.00 300.00
UPARB Ray Bourque 60.00 150.00
UPARL Roberto Luongo 40.00 100.00
UPARN Rick Nash 60.00 150.00
UPASK Saku Koivu 30.00 80.00
UPASP Jason Spezza 75.00 150.00
UPAVL Vincent Lecavalier 50.00 100.00
UPAWG1 Wayne Gretzky AS 300.00 800.00
UPAWG2 Wayne Gretzky LA 300.00 800.00

2004-05 Ultimate Collection Signatures

USAR Andrew Raycroft 6.00 15.00
USAT Alex Tanguay 6.00 15.00
USBB Brad Boyes 8.00 20.00
USBC Bobby Clarke 12.00 30.00
USBH Bobby Hull SP 30.00 80.00
USBL Brian Leetch 6.00 15.00
USBR Brad Richards 8.00 20.00
USBT Bryan Trottier SP 8.00 20.00
USCD Chris Drury 6.00 15.00
USDH Dany Heatley 6.00 15.00
USEJ Ed Jovanovski 6.00 15.00
USES Eric Staal 10.00 25.00
USGH Gordie Howe 60.00 150.00
USHA Dominik Hasek SP 15.00 40.00
USHZ Henrik Zetterberg 10.00 25.00
USIK Ilya Kovalchuk 8.00 20.00
USJB Jay Bouwmeester 5.00 12.00
USJI Jarome Iginla 10.00 25.00
USJK Jari Kurri 8.00 20.00
USJO Jose Theodore SP 8.00 20.00
USJT Joe Thornton 12.00 30.00
USKD Kris Draper 5.00 12.00
USKL Kari Lehtonen 10.00 25.00
USMA Marc-Andre Fleury 15.00 40.00
USMB Martin Brodeur SP 30.00 80.00
USMH Milan Hejduk 6.00 15.00
USMN Markus Naslund 6.00 15.00
USMR Michael Ryder 6.00 15.00
USMS Martin St. Louis 8.00 20.00
USMT Marty Turco 8.00 20.00
USNH Nathan Horton 8.00 20.00
USNK Nikolai Khabibulin 8.00 20.00
USNZ Nikolai Zherdev 6.00 15.00
USPR1 Patrick Roy SP 80.00 200.00
USRB1 Ray Bourque SP 25.00 60.00
USRL Roberto Luongo SP 12.00 30.00
USRN Rick Nash SP 8.00 20.00
USSK Saku Koivu SP 15.00 40.00
USSP Jason Spezza 8.00 20.00
USVL Vincent Lecavalier SP 8.00 20.00
USWG1 Wayne Gretzky 200.00 500.00
USZP Zigmund Palffy 8.00 20.00

2005-06 Ultimate Collection

1 Teemu Selanne 4.00 10.00
2 Jean-Sebastien Giguere 2.00 5.00
3 Joffrey Lupul 1.25 3.00
4 Ilya Kovalchuk 2.00 5.00
5 Marian Hossa 2.00 5.00
6 Kari Lehtonen 1.50 4.00
7 Andrew Raycroft 1.50 4.00
8 Brad Boyes 1.50 4.00
9 Patrice Bergeron 2.50 6.00
10 Brian Leetch 1.50 4.00
11 Glen Murray 1.50 4.00
12 Chris Drury 1.50 4.00
13 Martin Biron 1.50 4.00
14 Daniel Briere 2.00 5.00
15 Jarome Iginla 2.50 6.00
16 Miikka Kiprusoff 2.00 5.00
17 Doug Weight 2.00 5.00
18 Eric Staal 2.50 6.00
19 Nikolai Khabibulin 2.00 5.00
20 Tuomo Ruutu 2.00 5.00
21 Marek Svatos 1.50 4.00
22 Joe Sakic 4.00 10.00
23 Jose Theodore 2.00 5.00
24 Rob Blake 2.00 5.00
25 Alex Tanguay 2.00 5.00
26 Milan Hejduk 1.50 4.00
27 Rick Nash 2.00 5.00
28 Sergei Fedorov 3.00 8.00
29 Mike Modano 3.00 8.00
30 Bill Guerin 2.00 5.00
31 Marty Turco 2.00 5.00
32 Steve Yzerman 5.00 12.00
33 Nicklas Lidstrom 3.00 8.00
34 Gordie Howe 6.00 15.00
35 Brendan Shanahan 3.00 8.00
36 Pavel Datsyuk 3.00 8.00
37 Henrik Zetterberg 2.50 6.00
38 Ryan Smyth 1.50 4.00
39 Chris Pronger 2.00 5.00
40 Ales Hemsky 1.50 4.00
41 Wayne Gretzky 12.00 30.00
42 Roberto Luongo 3.00 8.00
43 Olli Jokinen 2.00 5.00
44 Jeremy Roenick 3.00 8.00
45 Pavol Demitra 2.50 6.00
46 Luc Robitaille 2.00 5.00
47 Marian Gaborik 2.00 5.00
48 David Aebischer 1.50 4.00
49 Michael Ryder 1.50 4.00
50 Saku Koivu 2.00 5.00
51 Mike Ribeiro 1.25 3.00
52 Tomas Vokoun 1.50 4.00
53 Paul Kariya 2.00 5.00
54 Martin Brodeur 5.00 12.00
55 Patrik Elias 2.00 5.00
56 Rick DiPietro 1.50 4.00
57 Alexei Yashin 1.50 4.00
58 Miroslav Satan 1.50 4.00
59 Jaromir Jagr 6.00 15.00
60 Dominik Hasek 3.00 8.00
61 Dany Heatley 1.50 4.00
62 Jason Spezza 2.00 5.00
63 Martin Havlat 2.00 5.00
64 Daniel Alfredsson 2.00 5.00
65 Peter Forsberg 4.00 10.00
66 Simon Gagne 2.00 5.00
67 Robert Esche 1.50 4.00
68 Keith Primeau 1.50 4.00
69 Curtis Joseph 2.50 6.00
70 Shane Doan 1.50 4.00
71 Mario Lemieux 8.00 20.00
72 Ryan Malone 1.25 3.00
73 Marc-Andre Fleury 4.00 10.00
74 Joe Thornton 3.00 8.00
75 Evgeni Nabokov 1.50 4.00
76 Jonathan Cheechoo 1.50 4.00
77 Patrick Marleau 2.00 5.00
78 Keith Tkachuk 2.00 5.00
79 Brad Richards 2.00 5.00
80 Martin St. Louis 2.00 5.00
81 Vincent Lecavalier 2.00 5.00
82 Bryan McCabe 1.25 3.00
83 Eric Lindros 3.00 8.00
84 Ed Belfour 2.00 5.00
85 Mats Sundin 2.00 5.00
86 Markus Naslund 2.00 5.00
87 Brendan Morrison 1.25 3.00
88 Todd Bertuzzi 2.00 5.00
89 Ed Jovanovski 1.50 4.00
90 Olaf Kolzig 2.00 5.00
91 Sidney Crosby AU RC 400.00 1000.00
92 Alexander Ovechkin AU RC 1500.00 4000.00
93 Gilbert Brule AU RC 10.00 25.00
94 Corey Perry AU RC 15.00 40.00
95 Jeff Carter AU RC 15.00 40.00
96 Alexander Steen AU RC 12.00 30.00
97 Henrik Lundqvist AU RC 40.00 80.00
98 Hannu Toivonen AU RC 10.00 25.00
99 Alexander Perezhogin AU RC 8.00 20.00
100 Thomas Vanek AU RC 15.00 40.00
101 Ryan Getzlaf AU RC 25.00 50.00
102 Braydon Coburn AU RC 10.00 25.00
103 Milan Jurcina AU RC 8.00 20.00
104 Andrew Alberts AU RC 6.00 15.00
105 Dion Phaneuf AU RC 15.00 40.00
106 Eric Nystrom AU RC 8.00 20.00
107 Cam Ward AU RC 15.00 40.00
108 Cam Barker AU RC 8.00 20.00
109 Brent Seabrook AU RC 20.00 50.00
110 Rene Bourque AU RC 10.00 25.00
111 Peter Budaj AU RC 12.00 30.00
112 Wojtek Wolski AU RC 8.00 20.00
113 Jussi Jokinen AU RC 10.00 25.00
114 Jim Howard AU RC 12.00 30.00
115 Johan Franzen AU RC 12.00 30.00
116 Brad Winchester AU RC 10.00 25.00
117 Rostislav Olesz AU RC 8.00 20.00
118 Anthony Stewart AU RC 8.00 20.00
119 Matt Foy AU RC 6.00 15.00
120 Yann Danis AU RC 8.00 20.00
121 Ryan Suter AU RC 12.00 30.00
122 Zach Parise AU RC 30.00 60.00
123 Robert Nilsson AU RC 10.00 25.00
124 Alvaro Montoya AU RC 6.00 15.00
125 Petr Prucha AU RC 10.00 25.00
126 Brandon Bochenski AU RC 10.00 25.00
127 Andrej Meszaros AU RC 8.00 20.00
128 Patrick Eaves AU RC 10.00 25.00
129 Mike Richards AU RC 12.00 30.00
130 Keith Ballard AU RC 8.00 20.00
131 Ryane Clowe AU RC 12.00 30.00
132 Jeff Woywitka AU RC 6.00 15.00
133 Michael Wall RC 3.00 8.00
134 Zenon Konopka RC 2.50 6.00
135 Jim Slater RC 3.00 8.00
136 Adam Berkhoel RC 3.00 8.00
137 Daniel Paille RC 4.00 10.00
138 Jordan Sigalet RC 3.00 8.00
139 Niklas Nordgren RC 4.00 10.00
140 Kevin Nastiuk RC 3.00 8.00
141 Duncan Keith RC 8.00 20.00
142 Jaroslav Balastik RC 2.50 6.00
143 Steven Goertzen RC 2.50 6.00
144 Alexandre Picard RC 2.50 6.00
145 Junior Lessard RC 2.50 6.00
146 Vojtech Polak RC 2.50 6.00
147 Brett Lebda RC 2.50 6.00
148 Valtteri Filppula RC 5.00 12.00
149 Kyle Brodziak RC 2.50 6.00
150 Matt Greene RC 2.50 6.00
151 Derek Boogaard RC 6.00 15.00
152 Brad Richardson RC 4.00 10.00
153 Mark Streit RC 4.00 10.00
154 Chris Campoli RC 2.50 6.00
155 Petteri Nokelainen RC 2.50 6.00
156 Kevin Colley RC 3.00 8.00
157 Ryan Hollweg RC 2.50 6.00
158 Jeremy Colliton RC 2.50 6.00
159 Brian McGrattan RC 2.50 6.00
160 Christoph Schubert RC 2.50 6.00
161 R.J. Umberger RC 4.00 10.00
162 Ben Eager RC 3.00 8.00
163 David Leneveu RC 3.00 8.00
164 Maxime Talbot RC 4.00 10.00
165 Josh Gorges RC 3.00 8.00
166 Dimitri Patzold RC 2.50 6.00
167 Jay McClement RC 2.50 6.00
168 Jeff Hoggan RC 2.50 6.00
169 Lee Stempniak RC 4.00 10.00
170 Andrei Kostitsyn RC 3.00 8.00
171 Timo Helbling RC 2.50 6.00
172 Paul Ranger RC 2.50 6.00
173 Ryan Craig RC 2.50 6.00
174 Evgeny Artyukhin RC 3.00 8.00
175 Andrew Wozniewski RC 3.00 8.00
176 Staffan Kronwall RC 2.50 6.00
177 Yanick Lehoux RC 4.00 10.00
178 Ryan Whitney RC 4.00 10.00
179 Erik Christensen RC 2.50 6.00
180 Andrew Ladd RC 5.00 12.00
181 Rob McVicar RC 3.00 8.00
182 Tomas Fleischmann RC 4.00 10.00
183 Jakub Klepis RC 2.50 6.00
184 Mike Green RC 5.00 12.00
185 Corey Crawford RC 15.00 30.00
186 Mikko Koivu RC 5.00 12.00
187 Steve Bernier RC 4.00 10.00
188 Cam Janssen RC 3.00 8.00
189 Barry Tallackson RC 3.00 8.00
190 Jeff Tambellini RC 2.50 6.00
191 Maxim Lapierre RC 4.00 10.00
192 Danny Richmond RC 2.50 6.00
193 Dustin Penner RC 4.00 10.00
194 Ben Walter RC 2.50 6.00
195 Chris Thorburn RC 3.00 8.00
196 Jiri Novotny RC 3.00 8.00
197 Richie Regehr RC 2.50 6.00
198 Chad Larose RC 2.50 6.00
199 James Wisniewski RC 3.00 8.00
200 Vitaly Kolesnik RC 3.00 8.00
201 Joakim Lindstrom RC 2.50 6.00
202 Ole-Kristian Tollefsen RC 3.00 8.00
203 Kyle Quincey RC 3.00 8.00
204 Danny Syvret RC 2.50 6.00
205 Jean-Francois Jacques RC 2.50 6.00
206 Greg Jacina RC 2.50 6.00
207 Petr Taticek RC 3.00 8.00
208 Rob Globke RC 2.50 6.00
209 George Parros RC 2.50 6.00
210 Petr Kanko RC 3.00 8.00
211 Richard Petiot RC 3.00 8.00
212 Jean-Philippe Cote RC 2.50 6.00
213 Kevin Klein RC 2.50 6.00
214 Pekka Rinne RC 15.00 40.00
215 Jason Ryznar RC 2.50 6.00
216 Bruno Gervais RC 2.50 6.00
217 Alexandre Picard RC 2.50 6.00
218 Stefan Ruzicka RC 2.50 6.00
219 Matt Jones RC 2.50 6.00
220 Colby Armstrong RC 4.00 10.00
221 Doug Murray RC 2.50 6.00
222 Grant Stevenson RC 2.50 6.00
223 Colin Hemingway RC 2.50 6.00
224 Kevin Dallman RC 3.00 8.00
225 Dennis Wideman RC 2.50 6.00
226 Darren Reid RC 2.50 6.00
227 Doug O'Brien RC 2.50 6.00
228 Gerald Coleman RC 3.00 8.00
229 Nick Tarnasky RC 2.50 6.00
230 Jay Harrison RC 3.00 8.00
231 Kevin Bieksa RC 6.00 15.00
232 Tomas Mojzis RC 2.50 6.00

2005-06 Ultimate Collection Gold

*1-90 VETS: 1.5X TO 4X BASIC CARDS
*ROOKIES: .8X TO 2X BASIC RC
1 Teemu Selanne 15.00 40.00
2 Jean-Sebastien Giguere 8.00 20.00
3 Joffrey Lupul 5.00 12.00
4 Ilya Kovalchuk 8.00 20.00
5 Marian Hossa 8.00 20.00
6 Kari Lehtonen 6.00 15.00
7 Andrew Raycroft 6.00 15.00
8 Brad Boyes 6.00 15.00
9 Patrice Bergeron 10.00 25.00
10 Brian Leetch 6.00 15.00
11 Glen Murray 6.00 15.00
12 Chris Drury 6.00 15.00
13 Martin Biron 6.00 15.00
14 Daniel Briere 8.00 20.00
15 Jarome Iginla 10.00 25.00
16 Miikka Kiprusoff 8.00 20.00
17 Doug Weight 8.00 20.00
18 Eric Staal 10.00 25.00
19 Nikolai Khabibulin 8.00 20.00
20 Tuomo Ruutu 8.00 20.00
21 Marek Svatos 6.00 15.00
22 Joe Sakic 15.00 40.00
23 Jose Theodore 8.00 20.00
24 Rob Blake 8.00 20.00
25 Alex Tanguay 8.00 20.00
26 Milan Hejduk 6.00 15.00
27 Rick Nash 8.00 20.00
28 Sergei Fedorov 12.00 30.00
29 Mike Modano 12.00 30.00
30 Bill Guerin 8.00 20.00
31 Marty Turco 8.00 20.00
32 Steve Yzerman 20.00 50.00
33 Nicklas Lidstrom 8.00 20.00
34 Gordie Howe 25.00 60.00
35 Brendan Shanahan 8.00 20.00
36 Pavel Datsyuk 12.00 30.00
37 Henrik Zetterberg 10.00 25.00
38 Ryan Smyth 6.00 15.00
39 Chris Pronger 8.00 20.00
40 Ales Hemsky 6.00 15.00
41 Wayne Gretzky 50.00 125.00
42 Roberto Luongo 12.00 30.00
43 Olli Jokinen 8.00 20.00
44 Jeremy Roenick 12.00 30.00
45 Pavol Demitra 10.00 25.00
46 Luc Robitaille 8.00 20.00
47 Marian Gaborik 8.00 20.00
48 David Aebischer 6.00 15.00
49 Michael Ryder 6.00 15.00
50 Saku Koivu 8.00 20.00
51 Mike Ribeiro 5.00 12.00
52 Tomas Vokoun 6.00 15.00
53 Paul Kariya 8.00 20.00
54 Martin Brodeur 20.00 50.00
55 Patrik Elias 8.00 20.00
56 Rick DiPietro 6.00 15.00
57 Alexei Yashin 6.00 15.00
58 Miroslav Satan 6.00 15.00
59 Jaromir Jagr 25.00 60.00
60 Dominik Hasek 12.00 30.00
61 Dany Heatley 6.00 15.00
62 Jason Spezza 8.00 20.00
63 Martin Havlat 8.00 20.00
64 Daniel Alfredsson 8.00 20.00
65 Peter Forsberg 15.00 40.00
66 Simon Gagne 8.00 20.00
67 Robert Esche 6.00 15.00
68 Keith Primeau 6.00 15.00
69 Curtis Joseph 10.00 25.00
70 Shane Doan 6.00 15.00
71 Mario Lemieux 30.00 80.00
72 Ryan Malone 5.00 12.00
73 Marc-Andre Fleury 15.00 40.00
74 Joe Thornton 12.00 30.00
75 Evgeni Nabokov 6.00 15.00
76 Jonathan Cheechoo 6.00 15.00
77 Patrick Marleau 8.00 20.00
78 Keith Tkachuk 8.00 20.00
79 Brad Richards 8.00 20.00
80 Martin St. Louis 8.00 20.00
81 Vincent Lecavalier 8.00 20.00
82 Bryan McCabe 5.00 12.00
83 Eric Lindros 12.00 30.00
84 Ed Belfour 8.00 20.00
85 Mats Sundin 8.00 20.00
86 Markus Naslund 8.00 20.00
87 Brendan Morrison 5.00 12.00
88 Todd Bertuzzi 8.00 20.00
89 Ed Jovanovski 6.00 15.00
90 Olaf Kolzig 8.00 20.00
133 Michael Wall 6.00 15.00
134 Zenon Konopka 5.00 12.00
135 Jim Slater 6.00 15.00
136 Adam Berkhoel 6.00 15.00
137 Daniel Paille 8.00 20.00
138 Jordan Sigalet 5.00 12.00
139 Niklas Nordgren 8.00 20.00
140 Kevin Nastiuk 6.00 15.00
141 Duncan Keith 20.00 50.00
142 Jaroslav Balastik 5.00 12.00
143 Steven Goertzen 5.00 12.00
144 Alexandre Picard 5.00 12.00
145 Junior Lessard 5.00 12.00
146 Vojtech Polak 5.00 12.00
147 Brett Lebda 5.00 12.00
148 Valtteri Filppula 10.00 25.00
149 Kyle Brodziak 5.00 12.00
150 Matt Greene 5.00 12.00
151 Derek Boogaard 12.00 30.00
152 Brad Richardson 8.00 20.00
153 Mark Streit 8.00 20.00
154 Chris Campoli 5.00 12.00
155 Petteri Nokelainen 5.00 12.00
156 Kevin Colley 6.00 15.00
157 Ryan Hollweg 5.00 12.00
158 Jeremy Colliton 5.00 12.00
159 Brian McGrattan 5.00 12.00
160 Christoph Schubert 5.00 12.00
161 R.J. Umberger 8.00 20.00
162 Ben Eager 6.00 15.00
163 David Leneveu 6.00 15.00
164 Maxime Talbot 8.00 20.00
165 Josh Gorges 6.00 15.00
166 Dimitri Patzold 5.00 12.00
167 Jay McClement 5.00 12.00
168 Jeff Hoggan 5.00 12.00
169 Lee Stempniak 8.00 20.00
170 Andrei Kostitsyn 10.00 25.00
171 Timo Helbling 5.00 12.00
172 Paul Ranger 5.00 12.00
173 Ryan Craig 5.00 12.00
174 Evgeny Artyukhin 6.00 15.00
175 Andrew Wozniewski 6.00 15.00
176 Staffan Kronwall 5.00 12.00
177 Yanick Lehoux 8.00 20.00
178 Ryan Whitney 8.00 20.00
179 Erik Christensen 5.00 12.00
180 Andrew Ladd 10.00 25.00
181 Rob McVicar 6.00 15.00
182 Tomas Fleischmann 8.00 20.00
183 Jakub Klepis 5.00 12.00
184 Mike Green 10.00 25.00
186 Mikko Koivu 10.00 25.00
187 Steve Bernier 8.00 20.00
188 Cam Janssen 6.00 15.00
189 Barry Tallackson 6.00 15.00
190 Jeff Tambellini 5.00 12.00
191 Maxim Lapierre 8.00 20.00
192 Danny Richmond 5.00 12.00
193 Dustin Penner 8.00 20.00
194 Ben Walter 5.00 12.00
195 Chris Thorburn 6.00 15.00
196 Jiri Novotny 6.00 15.00
197 Richie Regehr 5.00 12.00
198 Chad Larose 5.00 12.00
199 James Wisniewski 6.00 15.00
200 Vitaly Kolesnik 6.00 15.00
201 Joakim Lindstrom 5.00 12.00
202 Ole-Kristian Tollefsen 6.00 15.00
203 Kyle Quincey 6.00 15.00
204 Danny Syvret 5.00 12.00
205 Jean-Francois Jacques 5.00 12.00
206 Greg Jacina 5.00 12.00
207 Petr Taticek 6.00 15.00
208 Rob Globke 5.00 12.00
209 George Parros 5.00 12.00
210 Petr Kanko 6.00 15.00
211 Richard Petiot 6.00 15.00
212 Jean-Philippe Cote 5.00 12.00
213 Kevin Klein 5.00 12.00
214 Pekka Rinne 25.00 60.00
215 Jason Ryznar 5.00 12.00
216 Bruno Gervais 5.00 12.00
217 Alexandre Picard 5.00 12.00
218 Stefan Ruzicka 5.00 12.00
219 Matt Jones 5.00 12.00
220 Colby Armstrong 8.00 20.00
221 Doug Murray 5.00 12.00
222 Grant Stevenson 5.00 12.00
223 Colin Hemingway 5.00 12.00
224 Kevin Dallman 6.00 15.00
225 Dennis Wideman 5.00 12.00
226 Darren Reid 5.00 12.00
227 Doug O'Brien 5.00 12.00
228 Gerald Coleman 6.00 15.00
229 Nick Tarnasky 5.00 12.00
230 Jay Harrison 6.00 15.00
231 Kevin Bieksa 12.00 30.00
232 Tomas Mojzis 5.00 12.00

2005-06 Ultimate Collection Autographed Patches

91 Sidney Crosby 800.00 1200.00
92 Alexander Ovechkin 3000.00 8000.00
93 Gilbert Brule 150.00 250.00
94 Corey Perry 75.00 150.00
95 Jeff Carter 40.00 100.00
96 Alexander Steen 30.00 80.00
97 Henrik Lundqvist 125.00 250.00
98 Hannu Toivonen 25.00 60.00
99 Alexander Perezhogin
100 Thomas Vanek 75.00 150.00
101 Ryan Getzlaf 50.00 100.00
102 Braydon Coburn 25.00 60.00
103 Milan Jurcina 20.00 50.00
104 Andrew Alberts 15.00 40.00
105 Dion Phaneuf 150.00 250.00
106 Eric Nystrom
107 Cam Ward 100.00 200.00
108 Cam Barker 20.00 50.00
109 Brent Seabrook 50.00 125.00
110 Rene Bourque 25.00 60.00
111 Peter Budaj 30.00 80.00
112 Wojtek Wolski
113 Jussi Jokinen 25.00 60.00
114 Jim Howard 60.00 120.00
115 Johan Franzen 40.00 100.00
116 Brad Winchester 25.00 60.00
117 Rostislav Olesz 20.00 50.00
119 Matt Foy 15.00 40.00
120 Yann Danis
121 Ryan Suter 30.00 80.00
122 Zach Parise 75.00 150.00
123 Robert Nilsson 25.00 60.00
124 Alvaro Montoya 25.00 60.00
126 Brandon Bochenski 25.00 60.00
127 Andrej Meszaros 20.00 50.00
129 Mike Richards 50.00 100.00
130 Keith Ballard 20.00 50.00
131 Ryane Clowe 30.00 80.00
132 Jeff Woywitka 15.00 40.00

2005-06 Ultimate Collection Endorsed Emblems

EEAT Alex Tanguay 15.00 40.00
EEAY Alexei Yashin 15.00 40.00
EEBC Bobby Clarke 30.00 80.00
EEBI Martin Biron 25.00 60.00
EEBK Rob Blake 25.00 60.00
EEBL Brian Leetch 25.00 60.00
EEBM Brendan Morrison 15.00 40.00
EEBU Johnny Bucyk 25.00 60.00
EEBY Mike Bossy 50.00 100.00
EECD Chris Drury 25.00 60.00
EECN Cam Neely 60.00 125.00
EEDA David Aebischer 20.00 50.00
EEDB Dustin Brown 15.00 40.00
EEDG Doug Gilmour EXCH 75.00 125.00
EEDH Dany Heatley 40.00 100.00
EEDL David Legwand 25.00 60.00
EEDP Denis Potvin 50.00 100.00
EEDR Dwayne Roloson 25.00 60.00
EEDS Darryl Sittler 25.00 60.00
EEDW Doug Weight 15.00 40.00
EEEB Ed Belfour 75.00 150.00
EEES Eric Staal 20.00 50.00
EEGE Martin Gerber 25.00 60.00
EEGF Grant Fuhr 40.00 100.00
EEGL Guy Lafleur 25.00 60.00
EEGM Glen Murray 15.00 40.00
EEHJ Milan Hejduk 20.00 50.00
EEHK Dominik Hasek 75.00 150.00
EEHO Marian Hossa EXCH 40.00 100.00
EEHV Martin Havlat 30.00 80.00
EEHZ Henrik Zetterberg 50.00 125.00
EEIK Ilya Kovalchuk 90.00 150.00
EEJC Jonathan Cheechoo 25.00 60.00
EEJI Jarome Iginla 25.00 60.00
EEJO Joe Thornton 40.00 100.00
EEJP Joni Pitkanen 20.00 50.00
EEJR Jeremy Roenick 25.00 60.00
EEJS Jean-Sebastien Giguere 25.00 60.00
EEJT Jose Theodore 25.00 60.00
EEKL Kari Lehtonen 25.00 60.00
EEKP Keith Primeau 15.00 40.00
EELM Lanny McDonald 30.00 80.00
EELR Luc Robitaille 50.00 100.00
EELU Joffrey Lupul 25.00 60.00
EEMB Martin Brodeur 150.00 300.00
EEMC Bryan McCabe 15.00 40.00
EEML Manny Legace 15.00 40.00
EEMM Mike Modano 50.00 100.00
EEMN Markus Naslund 25.00 60.00
EEMS Matt Stajan 15.00 40.00
EEMT Marty Turco 25.00 60.00
EEMU Larry Murphy 20.00 50.00
EEMW Brenden Morrow 25.00 60.00
EENZ Nikolai Zherdev 15.00 40.00
EEOK Olaf Kolzig 30.00 80.00
EEPA Mark Parrish 15.00 40.00
EEPB Patrice Bergeron 30.00 80.00
EEPM Patrick Marleau 25.00 60.00
EEPR Patrick Roy 125.00 250.00
EERB Ray Bourque 75.00 150.00
EERE Robert Esche 15.00 40.00
EERL Roberto Luongo 50.00 100.00
EERM Ryan Miller 40.00 100.00
EERN Rick Nash 50.00 120.00
EERS Ryan Smyth 15.00 40.00
EERY Michael Ryder 30.00 80.00
EERZ Richard Zednik 15.00 40.00
EESG Simon Gagne 20.00 50.00
EESK Saku Koivu 30.00 80.00
EESL Martin St. Louis 25.00 60.00
EESP Jason Spezza 50.00 100.00
EESV Denis Savard 30.00 80.00
EETC Ty Conklin EXCH 15.00 40.00
EEWG Wayne Gretzky 300.00 800.00

2005-06 Ultimate Collection Jerseys

JAO Alexander Ovechkin 125.00 300.00
JAS Alexander Steen 6.00 15.00
JAY Alexei Yashin 3.00 8.00
JBT Bryan Trottier 4.00 10.00
JCO Corey Perry 4.00 10.00
JCP Chris Pronger 3.00 8.00
JDH Dominik Hasek 6.00 15.00
JDP Dion Phaneuf 10.00 25.00
JDW Doug Weight 3.00 8.00
JEL Eric Lindros 5.00 12.00
JES Eric Staal 4.00 10.00
JGB Gilbert Brule 3.00 8.00
JGH Gordie Howe 15.00 40.00
JHE Dany Heatley 5.00 12.00
JHL Henrik Lundqvist 10.00 25.00
JHT Hannu Toivonen 3.00 8.00
JIK Ilya Kovalchuk 6.00 15.00
JJB Jean Beliveau 8.00 20.00
JJC Jeff Carter 6.00 15.00
JJI Jarome Iginla 5.00 12.00
JJJ Jaromir Jagr/200 6.00 15.00
JJO Joe Thornton 6.00 15.00
JJS Joe Sakic 6.00 15.00
JJT Jose Theodore 5.00 12.00
JKL Kari Lehtonen 3.00 8.00
JLR Luc Robitaille 3.00 8.00
JMA Martin St. Louis 3.00 8.00
JMB Martin Brodeur 8.00 20.00
JMG Marian Gaborik 5.00 12.00
JMH Milan Hejduk 3.00 8.00
JML Mario Lemieux 15.00 40.00
JMM Mike Modano 5.00 12.00
JMN Markus Naslund 3.00 8.00
JMS Mats Sundin 3.00 8.00
JMT Marty Turco 3.00 8.00
JPB Patrice Bergeron 3.00 8.00
JPD Pavel Datsyuk 3.00 8.00
JPE Phil Esposito 5.00 12.00
JPF Peter Forsberg 5.00 12.00
JPK Paul Kariya 3.00 8.00
JPM Patrick Marleau 3.00 8.00
JPR Patrick Roy 12.00 30.00
JRB Ray Bourque 5.00 12.00
JRG Ryan Getzlaf 5.00 12.00
JRL Roberto Luongo 5.00 12.00
JSC Sidney Crosby 40.00 100.00
JSG Simon Gagne 3.00 8.00
JSK Saku Koivu/125 8.00 20.00
JSP Jason Spezza 4.00 10.00
JSY Steve Yzerman 10.00 25.00
JTB Todd Bertuzzi 3.00 8.00
JTS Teemu Selanne 3.00 8.00
JTV Tomas Vokoun 3.00 8.00
JVA Thomas Vanek 6.00 15.00
JVL Vincent Lecavalier 3.00 8.00
JWG Wayne Gretzky 30.00 60.00

2005-06 Ultimate Collection Jerseys Dual

DJAL Allison/Lindros 8.00 20.00
DJBR Bergeron/Raycroft 8.00 20.00
DJCR Carter/Richards 15.00 40.00
DJFP Forsberg/Primeau 10.00 25.00
DJFZ Franzen/Zetterberg 10.00 25.00
DJGC Gretzky/Crosby 75.00 150.00
DJHC Hasek/Chara 10.00 25.00
DJHY Howe/Yzerman 60.00 150.00
DJJD Spezza/Heatley 12.00 30.00
DJJL Joseph/Leneveu
DJKH Kovalchuk/Hossa 10.00 25.00
DJKP Koivu/Perezhogin 8.00 20.00
DJKV Kariya/Vokoun 8.00 20.00
DJLC Lemieux/Crosby 90.00 150.00
DJLS Lupul/Selanne 8.00 20.00
DJML Montoya/Lundqvist 15.00 40.00
DJNB Nash/Brule/30 12.00 30.00
DJOC Ovechkin/Crosby 400.00 1000.00
DJPG Perry/Getzlaf 10.00 25.00
DJPI Phaneuf/Iginla 20.00 50.00
DJRT Roy/Theodore 20.00 50.00
DJSB Seabrook/Barker 6.00 15.00
DJSH Sakic/Hejduk 10.00 25.00
DJSL St. Louis/Lecavalier 10.00 25.00
DJTD Theodore/Danis 8.00 20.00
DJTL Toivonen/Lehtonen 6.00 15.00
DJWN Ward/Nastiuk 12.00 30.00

2005-06 Ultimate Collection Jerseys Triple

TJFGC Forsberg/Gagne/Carter 40.00 80.00
TJGLC Gretzky/Lemieux/Sid 250.00 400.00
TJHSH Heatley/Spezza/Hasek 50.00 100.00
TJKTP Koivu/Theodore/Pere. 20.00 50.00
TJLVR St. L./Lecav/Richards 30.00 60.00
TJNOC Nash/Ovechkin/Crosby 500.00 1200.00
TJPGL Perry/Getzlaf/Lupul 20.00 50.00
TJRTB Roy/Theodore/Brodeur 40.00 80.00
TJSLA Sundin/Lindros/Allison 40.00 80.00

2005-06 Ultimate Collection Marquee Attractions

MA1 Corey Perry 3.00 8.00
MA2 Ryan Getzlaf 3.00 8.00
MA3 Jean-Sebastien Giguere 2.50 6.00
MA4 Ilya Kovalchuk 4.00 10.00
MA5 Marian Hossa 2.50 6.00
MA6 Hannu Toivonen 2.50 6.00
MA7 Patrice Bergeron 3.00 8.00
MA8 Andrew Raycroft 1.50 4.00
MA9 Thomas Vanek 3.00 8.00
MA10 Dion Phaneuf 8.00 20.00
MA11 Jarome Iginla 4.00 10.00
MA12 Eric Staal 3.00 8.00
MA13 Nikolai Khabibulin 2.50 6.00
MA14 Alex Tanguay 1.50 4.00
MA15 Milan Hejduk 2.50 6.00
MA16 Rick Nash 3.00 8.00
MA17 Mike Modano 3.00 8.00
MA18 Brenden Morrow 2.50 6.00
MA19 Marty Turco 2.50 6.00
MA20 Johan Franzen 1.50 4.00
MA21 Henrik Zetterberg 3.00 8.00
MA22 Chris Pronger 1.50 4.00
MA23 Roberto Luongo 4.00 10.00
MA24 Jeremy Roenick 3.00 8.00
MA25 Mikko Koivu 2.50 6.00
MA26 Alexander Perezhogin 1.50 4.00
MA27 Saku Koivu 3.00 8.00
MA28 Jose Theodore 3.00 8.00
MA29 Martin Brodeur 6.00 15.00
MA30 Miroslav Satan 2.50 6.00
MA31 Henrik Lundqvist 8.00 20.00
MA32 Dominik Hasek 4.00 10.00
MA33 Dany Heatley 4.00 10.00
MA34 Jason Spezza 3.00 8.00

MA35 Jeff Carter 4.00 10.00
MA36 Mike Richards 3.00 8.00
MA37 Keith Primeau 1.50 4.00
MA38 Shane Doan 1.50 4.00
MA39 Sidney Crosby 20.00 50.00
MA40 Mark Recchi 1.50 4.00
MA41 Joe Thornton 5.00 12.00
MA42 Martin St. Louis 1.50 4.00
MA43 Vincent Lecavalier 3.00 8.00
MA44 Alexander Steen 4.00 10.00
MA45 Mats Sundin 2.50 6.00
MA46 Ed Belfour 2.50 6.00
MA47 Markus Naslund 2.50 6.00
MA48 Alexander Ovechkin 150.00 400.00
MA49 Gilbert Brule 2.50 6.00
MA50 Olaf Kolzig 3.00 8.00

2005-06 Ultimate Collection National Heroes Jerseys

*PATCH/25: .8X TO 2X BASIC JSY
NHJAF Alexander Frolov 3.00 8.00
NHJAK Alexei Kovalev 5.00 12.00
NHJAL Daniel Alfredsson 5.00 12.00
NHJAO Alexander Ovechkin 100.00 250.00
NHJAY Alexei Yashin 4.00 10.00
NHJBG Bill Guerin 5.00 12.00
NHJBR Brian Rolston 4.00 10.00
NHJCC Chris Chelios 5.00 12.00
NHJCD Chris Drury 4.00 10.00
NHJCP Chris Pronger/200 5.00 12.00
NHJDA David Aebischer 4.00 10.00
NHJDW Doug Weight 5.00 12.00
NHJFO Adam Foote 3.00 8.00
NHJFT Fedor Tyutin 3.00 8.00
NHJGA Marian Gaborik 5.00 12.00
NHJHA Michal Handzus 4.00 10.00
NHJHJ Milan Hejduk 4.00 10.00
NHJHK Dominik Hasek/200 8.00 20.00
NHJHO Marian Hossa 5.00 12.00
NHJHS Marcel Hossa 3.00 8.00
NHJHZ Henrik Zetterberg 6.00 15.00
NHJIK Ilya Kovalchuk 5.00 12.00
NHJJB Jay Bouwmeester 3.00 8.00
NHJJI Jarome Iginla 6.00 15.00
NHJJJ Jaromir Jagr 15.00 40.00
NHJJL Jere Lehtinen 4.00 10.00
NHJJO Joe Thornton 8.00 20.00
NHJJP Joni Pitkanen/200 3.00 8.00
NHJJS Joe Sakic 10.00 25.00
NHJKD Kris Draper 6.00 15.00
NHJKT Keith Tkachuk 5.00 12.00
NHJLE Jordan Leopold 3.00 8.00
NHJMB Martin Brodeur 12.00 30.00
NHJMC Bryan McCabe 3.00 8.00
NHJMG Martin Gerber/200 4.00 10.00
NHJMM Mike Modano 8.00 20.00
NHJMO Mattias Ohlund 3.00 8.00
NHJMP Mark Parrish 3.00 8.00
NHJMS Martin Straka/200 3.00 8.00
NHJMT Marty Turco 5.00 12.00
NHJNA Nik Antropov 4.00 10.00
NHJNL Nicklas Lidstrom 5.00 12.00
NHJOJ Olli Jokinen/200 5.00 12.00
NHJOK Olaf Kolzig 5.00 12.00
NHJPA Pavol Demitra 5.00 12.00
NHJPB Peter Bondra 5.00 12.00
NHJPD Pavel Datsyuk 8.00 20.00
NHJPE Patrik Elias 5.00 12.00
NHJPF Peter Forsberg 10.00 25.00
NHJRA Brian Rafalski/200 4.00 10.00
NHJRB Rob Blake 5.00 12.00
NHJRD Rick DiPietro 4.00 10.00
NHJRE Robert Esche 4.00 10.00
NHJRI Brad Richards 5.00 12.00
NHJRL Roberto Luongo 8.00 20.00
NHJRS Ryan Smyth/200 4.00 10.00
NHJSA Miroslav Satan 4.00 10.00
NHJSG Simon Gagne 5.00 12.00
NHJSO Sandis Ozolinsh 3.00 8.00
NHJSU Mats Sundin 5.00 12.00
NHJSV Marek Svatos/200 4.00 10.00
NHJTB Todd Bertuzzi/200 5.00 12.00
NHJTS Teemu Selanne 10.00 25.00
NHJTV Tomas Vokoun 4.00 10.00
NHJVK Viktor Kozlov 3.00 8.00
NHJVL Vincent Lecavalier 5.00 12.00
NHJWR Wade Redden 3.00 8.00
NHJZC Zdeno Chara 5.00 12.00

2005-06 Ultimate Collection Premium Patches

PPAO Alexander Ovechkin 600.00 1500.00
PPAP Alexander Perezhogin 15.00 40.00
PPAS Alexander Steen 25.00 60.00
PPAY Alexei Yashin 20.00 50.00
PPBS Brendan Shanahan 20.00 50.00
PPCP Chris Pronger 20.00 50.00
PPCW Cam Ward 20.00 50.00
PPDH Dany Heatley/30 25.00 60.00
PPDP Dion Phaneuf 30.00 80.00
PPDW Doug Weight 15.00 40.00
PPEL Eric Lindros 40.00 80.00
PPES Eric Staal 25.00 60.00
PPGB Gilbert Brule 15.00 40.00
PPHK Dominik Hasek 25.00 60.00
PPHL Henrik Lundqvist 40.00 100.00
PPHT Hannu Toivonen 15.00 40.00
PPIK Ilya Kovalchuk 30.00 80.00
PPJC Jeff Carter 30.00 80.00
PPJF Johan Franzen 20.00 50.00
PPJI Jarome Iginla 30.00 80.00
PPJJ Jaromir Jagr 50.00 125.00
PPJO Joe Thornton 30.00 80.00
PPJR Jeremy Roenick 25.00 60.00
PPJS Joe Sakic 60.00 120.00
PPJT Jose Theodore 25.00 60.00
PPKL Kari Lehtonen 25.00 60.00
PPLR Luc Robitaille 20.00 50.00
PPMB Martin Brodeur 75.00 150.00
PPMG Marian Gaborik 50.00 100.00
PPMH Milan Hejduk 25.00 60.00
PPML Mario Lemieux 100.00 200.00
PPMM Mike Modano 30.00 60.00
PPMN Markus Naslund 15.00 40.00
PPMR Mike Richards 50.00 100.00
PPMS Mats Sundin 40.00 100.00
PPMT Marty Turco 15.00 40.00
PPPB Patrice Bergeron 20.00 50.00
PPPD Pavel Datsyuk 20.00 50.00
PPPE Corey Perry 20.00 50.00
PPPF Peter Forsberg 30.00 80.00
PPPK Paul Kariya 20.00 50.00
PPPM Patrick Marleau 20.00 50.00
PPPR Patrick Roy 100.00 200.00
PPPS Jason Spezza 20.00 50.00
PPRB Ray Bourque 30.00 80.00
PPRG Ryan Getzlaf 30.00 80.00
PPRL Roberto Luongo 30.00 80.00
PPRN Rick Nash/15
PPSC Sidney Crosby 125.00 250.00
PPSF Sergei Fedorov 20.00 50.00
PPSG Simon Gagne 20.00 50.00
PPSY Steve Yzerman 75.00 150.00
PPTB Todd Bertuzzi 15.00 40.00
PPTS Teemu Selanne 25.00 60.00
PPTV Thomas Vanek 25.00 60.00
PPVL Vincent Lecavalier 30.00 80.00
PPVO Tomas Vokoun 40.00 100.00
PPWG Wayne Gretzky 75.00 150.00

2005-06 Ultimate Collection Premium Swatches

PSAO Alexander Ovechkin 125.00 300.00
PSAP Alexander Perezhogin 4.00 10.00
PSAS Alexander Steen 10.00 25.00
PSAY Alexei Yashin 3.00 8.00
PSBS Brendan Shanahan 6.00 15.00
PSCP Chris Pronger 3.00 8.00
PSCW Cam Ward 8.00 20.00
PSDH Dany Heatley/35 12.00 30.00
PSDP Dion Phaneuf 10.00 25.00
PSDW Doug Weight 3.00 8.00
PSEL Eric Lindros 8.00 20.00
PSES Eric Staal 6.00 15.00
PSGB Gilbert Brule 5.00 12.00
PSHL Henrik Lundqvist 10.00 25.00
PSHT Hannu Toivonen 4.00 10.00
PSIK Ilya Kovalchuk 8.00 20.00
PSJC Jeff Carter 8.00 20.00
PSJF Johan Franzen 3.00 8.00
PSJI Jarome Iginla 6.00 15.00
PSJJ Jaromir Jagr/50 15.00 30.00
PSJO Joe Thornton 8.00 20.00
PSJR Jeremy Roenick 4.00 10.00
PSJS Joe Sakic 10.00 25.00
PSJT Jose Theodore 6.00 15.00
PSKL Kari Lehtonen 4.00 10.00
PSLR Luc Robitaille 4.00 10.00
PSMB Martin Brodeur/50 15.00 40.00
PSMG Marian Gaborik 6.00 15.00
PSMH Milan Hejduk 4.00 10.00
PSML Mario Lemieux 20.00 50.00
PSMM Mike Modano 4.00 10.00
PSMN Markus Naslund 4.00 10.00
PSMR Mike Richards 4.00 10.00
PSMS Mats Sundin 4.00 10.00
PSMT Marty Turco 4.00 10.00
PSPB Patrice Bergeron 4.00 10.00
PSPD Pavel Datsyuk 6.00 15.00
PSPE Corey Perry 4.00 10.00
PSPF Peter Forsberg 8.00 20.00
PSPM Patrick Marleau 3.00 8.00
PSPR Patrick Roy 20.00 50.00
PSPS Jason Spezza 5.00 12.00
PSRB Ray Bourque 5.00 12.00
PSRG Ryan Getzlaf 8.00 20.00
PSRL Roberto Luongo 6.00 15.00
PSSC Sidney Crosby 40.00 100.00
PSSK Saku Koivu 4.00 10.00
PSSL Martin St. Louis 4.00 10.00
PSSY Steve Yzerman 15.00 40.00
PSTB Todd Bertuzzi 4.00 10.00
PSTS Teemu Selanne 6.00 15.00
PSTV Thomas Vanek 6.00 15.00
PSVL Vincent Lecavalier 4.00 10.00
PSVO Tomas Vokoun 4.00 10.00
PSWG Wayne Gretzky 40.00 100.00

2005-06 Ultimate Collection Ultimate Achievements

UAAR Andrew Raycroft/20 15.00 30.00
UADH Dany Heatley/26 25.00 60.00
UAHZ Henrik Zetterberg/22 25.00 50.00
UAIK Ilya Kovalchuk/41 20.00 50.00
UAJC Jonathan Cheechoo/28 25.00 50.00
UAJG Jean-Sebastien Giguere/15 20.00 50.00
UAJI Jarome Iginla/41 20.00 50.00
UAJT Jose Theodore/23
UARL Roberto Luongo/23 30.00 60.00
UARN Rick Nash/41 15.00 40.00
UASL Martin St. Louis/24 12.50 30.00
UASN Scott Niedermayer/18

2005-06 Ultimate Collection Ultimate Debut Threads Jerseys

DTJAA Andrew Alberts 3.00 8.00
DTJAK Andrei Kostsitsyn 4.00 10.00
DTJAL Andrew Ladd 4.00 10.00
DTJAM Andrej Meszaros 3.00 8.00
DTJAO Alexander Ovechkin 200.00 500.00
DTJAP Alexander Perezhogin 3.00 8.00
DTJAS Alexander Steen 6.00 15.00
DTJBB Brandon Bochenski 3.00 8.00
DTJBC Braydon Coburn 3.00 8.00
DTJBS Brent Seabrook 3.00 8.00
DTJBT Barry Tallackson 3.00 8.00
DTJBW Brad Winchester 3.00 8.00
DTJCB Cam Barker 3.00 8.00
DTJCC Chris Campoli 3.00 8.00
DTJCP Corey Perry 4.00 10.00
DTJCS Christoph Schubert 3.00 8.00
DTJCW Cam Ward 6.00 15.00
DTJDB Derek Boogaard 3.00 8.00
DTJDL David Leneveu 3.00 8.00
DTJDP Dion Phaneuf 10.00 25.00
DTJEA Evgeny Artyukhin 3.00 8.00
DTJEN Eric Nystrom 3.00 8.00
DTJGB Gilbert Brule 4.00 10.00
DTJHL Henrik Lundqvist 10.00 25.00
DTJHT Hannu Toivonen 3.00 8.00
DTJJC Jeff Carter 6.00 15.00
DTJJF Johan Franzen 3.00 8.00
DTJJH Jim Howard 5.00 12.00
DTJJJ Jussi Jokinen 4.00 10.00
DTJJK Jakub Klepis 3.00 8.00
DTJJM Jay McClement 3.00 8.00
DTJJS Jim Slater 3.00 8.00
DTJJT Jeff Tambellini 3.00 8.00
DTJJW Jeff Woywitka 3.00 8.00
DTJKB Keith Ballard 3.00 8.00
DTJMJ Milan Jurcina 3.00 8.00
DTJMK Mikko Koivu 4.00 10.00
DTJML Maxim Lapierre 3.00 8.00
DTJMO Alvaro Montoya 4.00 10.00
DTJMR Mike Richards 4.00 10.00
DTJMT Maxime Talbot 3.00 8.00
DTJPP Petr Prucha 4.00 10.00
DTJRB Rene Bourque 3.00 8.00
DTJRC Ryane Clowe 5.00 12.00
DTJRG Ryan Getzlaf 5.00 12.00
DTJRJ R.J. Umberger 3.00 8.00
DTJRN Robert Nilsson 3.00 8.00
DTJRO Rostislav Olesz 4.00 10.00
DTJRS Ryan Suter 3.00 8.00
DTJRW Ryan Whitney 3.00 8.00
DTJSB Steve Bernier 4.00 10.00
DTJSC Sidney Crosby 40.00 80.00
DTJSI Jordan Sigalet 4.00 10.00
DTJTF Tomas Fleischmann 3.00 8.00
DTJTV Thomas Vanek 8.00 20.00
DTJWW Wojtek Wolski 4.00 10.00
DTJYD Yann Danis 3.00 8.00
DTJZP Zach Parise 4.00 10.00

2005-06 Ultimate Collection Ultimate Debut Threads Jerseys Autographs

DAJAO Alexander Ovechkin 4000.00 10000.00
DAJAS Alexander Steen 25.00 60.00
DAJBB Brandon Bochenski 25.00 60.00
DAJBC Braydon Coburn 15.00 40.00
DAJBS Brent Seabrook 30.00 80.00
DAJBW Brad Winchester 15.00 40.00
DAJCP Corey Perry 40.00 100.00
DAJDP Dion Phaneuf 30.00 80.00
DAJGB Gilbert Brule 15.00 40.00
DAJHL Henrik Lundqvist 100.00 175.00
DAJJC Jeff Carter 30.00 80.00
DAJJJ Jussi Jokinen 15.00 40.00
DAJJS Jim Slater 10.00 25.00
DAJKB Keith Ballard 10.00 25.00
DAJMJ Milan Jurcina 12.00 30.00
DAJMO Alvaro Montoya 10.00 25.00
DAJMR Mike Richards 50.00 100.00
DAJMT Maxime Talbot 12.00 30.00
DAJPB Peter Budaj 20.00 50.00
DAJPE Patrick Eaves 12.00 30.00
DAJRB Rene Bourque 15.00 40.00
DAJRG Ryan Getzlaf 40.00 100.00
DAJSC Sidney Crosby 500.00 800.00
DAJTV Thomas Vanek 30.00 60.00
DAJYD Yann Danis 40.00 80.00

2005-06 Ultimate Collection Ultimate Debut Threads Patches

DTPAA Andrew Alberts 10.00 25.00
DTPAL Andrew Ladd 15.00 40.00
DTPAO Alexander Ovechkin 400.00 1000.00
DTPAP Alexander Perezhogin 15.00 40.00
DTPBB Brandon Bochenski 15.00 40.00
DTPBC Braydon Coburn 15.00 40.00
DTPBS Brent Seabrook 25.00 60.00
DTPBT Barry Tallackson 10.00 25.00
DTPBW Brad Winchester 10.00 25.00
DTPCB Cam Barker 15.00 40.00
DTPCC Chris Campoli/40 15.00 40.00
DTPCP Corey Perry 30.00 80.00
DTPCW Cam Ward 30.00 80.00
DTPDB Derek Boogaard 20.00 50.00
DTPDL David Leneveu 15.00 40.00
DTPDP Dion Phaneuf 50.00 125.00
DTPEA Evgeny Artyukhin/25 25.00 60.00
DTPEN Eric Nystrom 15.00 40.00
DTPGB Gilbert Brule/50 20.00 50.00
DTPHL Henrik Lundqvist 50.00 125.00
DTPHT Hannu Toivonen 20.00 50.00
DTPJC Jeff Carter 15.00 40.00
DTPJF Johan Franzen 10.00 25.00
DTPJH Jim Howard 25.00 60.00
DTPJJ Jussi Jokinen 15.00 40.00
DTPJK Jakub Klepis 10.00 25.00
DTPJM Jay McClement/15
DTPJS Jim Slater 12.00 30.00
DTPJT Jeff Tambellini/30 15.00 40.00
DTPJW Jeff Woywitka 10.00 25.00
DTPKB Keith Ballard 10.00 25.00
DTPMJ Milan Jurcina/30 20.00 50.00
DTPMK Mikko Koivu 15.00 40.00
DTPMO Alvaro Montoya 20.00 50.00
DTPMR Mike Richards 25.00 60.00
DTPMT Maxime Talbot 10.00 25.00
DTPPB Peter Budaj 20.00 50.00
DTPPP Petr Prucha/30 30.00 60.00
DTPRB Rene Bourque 15.00 40.00
DTPRG Ryan Getzlaf 30.00 80.00
DTPRJ R.J. Umberger/35 15.00 40.00
DTPRN Robert Nilsson 15.00 40.00
DTPRO Rostislav Olesz 15.00 40.00
DTPRS Ryan Suter 15.00 40.00
DTPRW Ryan Whitney 15.00 40.00
DTPSB Steve Bernier/25 30.00 80.00
DTPSC Sidney Crosby/1
DTPSI Jordan Sigalet/35 25.00 50.00
DTPTF Tomas Fleischmann 10.00 25.00
DTPTV Thomas Vanek 30.00 80.00
DTPWW Wojtek Wolski 15.00 40.00
DTPYD Yann Danis 15.00 40.00
DTPZP Zach Parise 30.00 80.00

2005-06 Ultimate Collection Ultimate Patches

PAO Alexander Ovechkin 200.00 500.00
PAY Alexei Yashin 10.00 25.00
PBS Brendan Shanahan 12.00 30.00
PBT Bryan Trottier 15.00 40.00
PCO Corey Perry 10.00 25.00
PCP Chris Pronger 10.00 25.00
PDH Dominik Hasek 15.00 40.00
PDP Dion Phaneuf 20.00 50.00
PDW Doug Weight 8.00 20.00
PEL Eric Lindros 10.00 25.00
PES Eric Staal 12.00 30.00
PGB Gilbert Brule 12.00 30.00
PGH Gordie Howe/10
PHE Dany Heatley 15.00 40.00
PHL Henrik Lundqvist 20.00 50.00
PHT Hannu Toivonen 10.00 25.00
PIK Ilya Kovalchuk 15.00 40.00
PJC Jeff Carter 12.00 40.00
PJI Jarome Iginla 15.00 40.00
PJJ Jaromir Jagr 20.00 50.00
PJO Joe Thornton 20.00 50.00
PJR Jeremy Roenick 15.00 40.00
PJS Joe Sakic 20.00 50.00
PJT Jose Theodore 12.00 30.00
PKL Kari Lehtonen 10.00 25.00
PLR Luc Robitaille 10.00 25.00
PMA Martin St. Louis 8.00 20.00
PMB Martin Brodeur 25.00 60.00
PMG Marian Gaborik 15.00 40.00
PMH Milan Hejduk 10.00 25.00
PML Mario Lemieux 30.00 80.00
PMM Mike Modano 15.00 40.00
PMN Markus Naslund 12.00 30.00
PMS Mats Sundin 12.00 30.00
PMT Marty Turco 10.00 25.00
PPB Patrice Bergeron 12.00 30.00
PPD Pavel Datsyuk 20.00 40.00
PPE Phil Esposito 12.00 30.00
PPF Peter Forsberg/35 20.00 50.00
PPK Paul Kariya 10.00 25.00
PPM Patrick Marleau 8.00 20.00
PPR Patrick Roy 30.00 80.00
PRB Ray Bourque 15.00 40.00
PRG Ryan Getzlaf 15.00 40.00
PRL Roberto Luongo 15.00 40.00
PSC Sidney Crosby 75.00 150.00
PSF Sergei Fedorov 10.00 25.00
PSG Simon Gagne 8.00 20.00
PSK Saku Koivu 10.00 25.00
PSP Jason Spezza 12.00 30.00
PSY Steve Yzerman 25.00 50.00
PTB Todd Bertuzzi 10.00 25.00
PTS Teemu Selanne 10.00 25.00
PTV Tomas Vokoun 12.00 30.00
PVA Thomas Vanek 15.00 40.00
PVL Vincent Lecavalier 12.00 30.00

2005-06 Ultimate Collection Ultimate Patches Dual

DPAL Allison/Lindros 20.00 50.00
DPBR Bergeron/Raycroft 25.00 60.00
DPCR Carter/Richards 30.00 80.00
DPFP Forsberg/Primeau
DPFZ Franzen/Zetterberg 25.00 60.00
DPHC Hasek/Chara 30.00 80.00
DPHY Howe/Yzerman 150.00 300.00
DPJD Spezza/Heatley 30.00 80.00
DPJL Joseph/Leneveu 15.00 40.00
DPKH Kovalchuk/Hossa 30.00 80.00
DPKP Koivu/Perezhogin 15.00 40.00
DPKV Kariya/Vokoun 15.00 40.00
DPLC Lemieux/Crosby 175.00 350.00
DPLS Lupul/Selanne 25.00 60.00
DPML Montoya/Lundqvist 30.00 80.00
DPNB Nash/Brule 20.00 50.00
DPOC Ovechkin/Crosby 1000.00 2500.00
DPPG Perry/Getzlaf 40.00 80.00
DPPI Phaneuf/Iginla 60.00 120.00
DPRT Roy/Theodore 100.00 200.00
DPSB Seabrook/Barker 15.00 40.00
DPSH Sakic/Hejduk 25.00 60.00
DPSL St. Louis/Lecavalier 20.00 50.00
DPSY Shanahan/Yzerman 50.00 100.00
DPTD Theodore/Danis 15.00 40.00
DPTL Toivonen/Lehtonen 20.00 50.00
DPWN Ward/Nastiuk 25.00 50.00

2005-06 Ultimate Collection Ultimate Signatures

USAO Alexander Ovechkin 1000.00 2500.00
USAP Alexander Perezhogin 5.00 12.00
USAR Andrew Raycroft 5.00 12.00
USAT Alex Tanguay SP 15.00 40.00
USAY Alexei Yashin 5.00 12.00
USBC Bobby Clarke 12.00 30.00
USBL Brian Leetch 6.00 15.00
USBM Brenden Morrow 5.00 12.00
USBP Bernie Parent 8.00 20.00
USBR Brad Richards 8.00 20.00
USCH Jonathan Cheechoo 6.00 15.00
USCN Cam Neely 12.00 30.00
USCW Cam Ward 6.00 15.00
USDH Dany Heatley SP 20.00 50.00
USDW Doug Weight 5.00 12.00
USEB Ed Belfour 10.00 25.00
USEC Erik Cole 5.00 12.00
USEN Eric Nystrom 5.00 12.00
USES Eric Staal EXCH 10.00 25.00
USGB Gilbert Brule 6.00 15.00
USGH Gordie Howe 40.00 80.00
USGP Gilbert Perreault 6.00 15.00
USHK Dominik Hasek 15.00 40.00
USHL Henrik Lundqvist 40.00 100.00
USHO Marian Hossa 5.00 12.00
USHT Hannu Toivonen 5.00 12.00
USHV Martin Havlat 5.00 12.00
USHZ Henrik Zetterberg 12.00 30.00
USIK Ilya Kovalchuk 15.00 40.00
USJB Jean Beliveau 25.00 50.00
USJC Jeff Carter 8.00 20.00
USJG Jean-Sebastien Giguere 5.00 12.00
USJH Jim Howard 8.00 20.00
USJI Jarome Iginla 8.00 20.00
USJO Joe Thornton 10.00 25.00
USJS Jason Spezza 10.00 25.00
USJT Jose Theodore 6.00 15.00
USKL Kari Lehtonen 6.00 15.00
USLR Luc Robitaille 8.00 20.00
USMB Martin Brodeur 40.00 80.00
USMF Marc-Andre Fleury 12.00 30.00
USMH Milan Hejduk 5.00 12.00
USML Manny Legace 5.00 12.00
USMM Mike Modano 10.00 25.00
USMN Markus Naslund 5.00 12.00
USMS Miroslav Satan 6.00 15.00
USMT Marty Turco 5.00 12.00
USNA Evgeni Nabokov 5.00 12.00
USNK Nikolai Khabibulin 6.00 15.00
USNZ Nikolai Zherdev 5.00 12.00
USON Jeff O'Neill 5.00 12.00
USPB Patrice Bergeron 8.00 20.00
USPE Phil Esposito SP 15.00 40.00
USPR Patrick Roy SP 75.00 150.00
USPY Corey Perry 6.00 15.00
USRB Ray Bourque SP 20.00 50.00
USRG Ryan Getzlaf 8.00 20.00
USRL Roberto Luongo 10.00 25.00
USRN Rick Nash 6.00 15.00
USRO Rostislav Olesz 5.00 12.00
USRS Ryan Suter 5.00 12.00
USRW Ryan Whitney 5.00 12.00
USRY Michael Ryder 5.00 12.00
USSC Sidney Crosby 250.00 500.00
USSG Simon Gagne 5.00 12.00
USSK Saku Koivu 8.00 20.00
USSL Martin St. Louis SP 15.00 40.00
USSM Ryan Smyth 8.00 20.00
USSN Scott Niedermayer 5.00 12.00
USST Alexander Steen 8.00 20.00
USSV Marek Svatos 5.00 12.00
USTB Todd Bertuzzi 5.00 12.00
USTE Tony Esposito 12.00 30.00
USTR Tuomo Ruutu 5.00 12.00
USTV Thomas Vanek 10.00 25.00
USVL Vincent Lecavalier 8.00 20.00
USWG Wayne Gretzky SP 250.00 600.00
USWW Wojtek Wolski 5.00 12.00
USYD Yann Danis 6.00 15.00

2005-06 Ultimate Collection Ultimate Signatures Pairings

UPBO Neely/Bourque 25.00 60.00
UPBR Bourque/Roy 40.00 100.00
UPCP Clarke/Parent 25.00 60.00
UPCR Carter/Richards 60.00 150.00
UPEE P.Esposito/T.Espo 25.00 60.00
UPGN Giguere/Niedermayer 15.00 40.00
UPHE Bob.Hull/T.Esposito 30.00 80.00
UPHG Howe/Gretzky 300.00 800.00
UPHH Hasek/Havlat 25.00 60.00
UPHO Horton/Olesz 15.00 40.00
UPHS Heatley/Spezza 15.00 40.00
UPIN Iginla/Nystrom 20.00 50.00
UPKH Kovalchuk/Hossa 15.00 40.00
UPKN Khabibulin/Nabokov 15.00 40.00
UPKP Koivu/Perezhogin 15.00 40.00
UPLA Roenick/Robitaille 25.00 60.00
UPLH Legace/Howard 40.00 100.00
UPLM Lundqvist/Montoya 80.00 200.00
UPLT Lundqvist/Toivonen 80.00 200.00
UPMM Lanny/J. Mullen 15.00 40.00
UPMT Modano/Turco 25.00 60.00
UPNB Naslund/Bertuzzi 15.00 40.00
UPNC Nabokov/Cheechoo 12.00 30.00
UPPG Perry/Getzlaf 50.00 120.00
UPPS Pronger/Smyth 15.00 40.00
UPPV Perreault/Vanek 30.00 80.00
UPRB Roy/Brodeur 40.00 100.00
UPRG Nash/Brule 15.00 40.00
UPRT Raycroft/Toivonen 15.00 40.00
UPSC Staal/Cole 20.00 50.00
UPSL St. Louis/Lecavalier 15.00 40.00
UPTC Thornton/Cheechoo 25.00 60.00
UPTD Theodore/Danis 15.00 40.00
UPTH Tanguay/Hejduk 15.00 40.00
UPYS Yashin/Satan 12.00 30.00
UPZF Zetterberg/Franzen 25.00 60.00

2006-07 Ultimate Collection

1 Teemu Selanne 4.00 10.00
2 Ilya Kovalchuk 2.00 5.00
3 Kari Lehtonen 1.50 4.00
4 Patrice Bergeron 2.50 6.00
5 Bobby Orr 8.00 20.00
6 Ray Bourque 3.00 8.00
7 Phil Esposito 3.00 8.00
8 Ryan Miller 2.00 5.00
9 Gilbert Perreault 2.00 5.00
10 Miikka Kiprusoff 2.00 5.00
11 Jarome Iginla 2.50 6.00
12 Dion Phaneuf 1.50 4.00
13 Eric Staal 2.50 6.00
14 Cam Ward 2.00 5.00
15 Martin Havlat 1.25 3.00
16 Bobby Hull 4.00 10.00
17 Joe Sakic 4.00 10.00
18 Jose Theodore 2.00 5.00
19 Rick Nash 2.00 5.00
20 Mike Modano 3.00 8.00
21 Marty Turco 2.00 5.00
22 Henrik Zetterberg 2.50 6.00
23 Dominik Hasek 3.00 8.00
24 Nicklas Lidstrom 2.00 5.00
25 Gordie Howe 6.00 15.00
26 Ales Hemsky 1.50 4.00
27 Wayne Gretzky 12.00 30.00
28 Jari Kurri 2.00 5.00
29 Ed Belfour 2.00 5.00
30 Rob Blake 2.00 5.00
31 Marian Gaborik 2.00 5.00
32 Saku Koivu 2.00 5.00
33 Michael Ryder 1.25 3.00
34 Patrick Roy 5.00 12.00
35 Tomas Vokoun 1.50 4.00
36 Paul Kariya 2.00 5.00
37 Martin Brodeur 5.00 12.00
38 Alexei Yashin 1.50 4.00
39 Mike Bossy 2.00 5.00
40 Jaromir Jagr 6.00 15.00
41 Brendan Shanahan 2.00 5.00
42 Henrik Lundqvist 5.00 12.00
43 Dany Heatley 1.50 4.00
44 Jason Spezza 2.00 5.00
45 Peter Forsberg 4.00 10.00
46 Shane Doan 1.50 4.00
47 Sidney Crosby 8.00 20.00
48 Marc-Andre Fleury 4.00 10.00
49 Mario Lemieux 8.00 20.00
50 Joe Thornton 3.00 8.00
51 Jonathan Cheechoo 1.50 4.00
52 Patrick Marleau 2.00 5.00
53 Brad Richards 2.00 5.00
54 Vincent Lecavalier 2.00 5.00
55 Martin St. Louis 2.00 5.00
56 Mats Sundin 2.00 5.00
57 Andrew Raycroft 1.50 4.00
58 Markus Naslund 2.00 5.00
59 Roberto Luongo 3.00 8.00
60 Alexander Ovechkin 8.00 20.00
61 David McKee RC 4.00 10.00
62 Ryan Shannon RC 4.00 10.00
63 Clarke MacArthur RC 5.00 12.00
64 Andrej Sekera RC 5.00 12.00
65 Michael Funk RC 4.00 10.00
66 Adam Dennis RC 4.00 10.00
67 Mike Card RC 4.00 10.00
68 Brandon Prust RC 4.00 10.00
69 Troy Brouwer RC 5.00 12.00
70 Adam Burish RC 6.00 15.00
71 Fredrik Norrena RC 4.00 10.00
72 Stefan Liv RC 4.00 10.00
73 Tomas Kopecky RC 5.00 12.00
74 Jeff Drouin-Deslauriers RC 4.00 10.00
75 David Booth RC 5.00 12.00
76 Janis Sprukts RC 4.00 10.00
77 Barry Brust RC 5.00 12.00
78 Konstantin Pushkarev RC 5.00 12.00
79 Shawn Belle RC 4.00 10.00
80 Niklas Backstrom RC 8.00 20.00
81 Mikhail Grabovski RC 8.00 20.00
82 Johnny Oduya RC 6.00 15.00
83 Blake Comeau RC 6.00 15.00
84 Jarkko Immonen RC 5.00 12.00
85 Josh Hennessy RC 4.00 10.00
86 Kelly Guard RC 5.00 12.00
87 Jussi Timonen RC 5.00 12.00
88 Martin Houle RC 5.00 12.00
89 Michel Ouellet RC 5.00 12.00
90 Yan Stastny RC 4.00 10.00
91 Roman Polak RC 5.00 12.00
92 Marek Schwarz RC 6.00 15.00
93 David Backes RC 15.00 40.00
94 Blair Jones RC 4.00 10.00
95 Karri Ramo RC 4.00 10.00
96 Ian White RC 5.00 12.00
97 Brendan Bell RC 4.00 10.00
98 Kris Newbury RC 4.00 10.00
99 Jean-Francois Racine RC 5.00 12.00
100 Jesse Schultz RC 4.00 10.00
101 Alexander Edler RC 6.00 15.00
102 Daren Machesney RC 4.00 10.00
103 Matt Lashoff AU RC 8.00 20.00
104 Phil Kessel AU/99 RC 50.00 100.00
105 Mark Stuart AU RC 8.00 20.00
106 Michael Blunden AU RC 8.00 20.00
107 Dave Bolland AU RC 12.00 30.00
108 Paul Stastny AU RC 15.00 40.00
109 Loui Eriksson AU RC 15.00 40.00
110 Niklas Grossman AU RC 12.00 30.00
111 Ladislav Smid AU RC 8.00 20.00
112 Patrick Thoresen AU RC 8.00 20.00
113 Marc-Antoine Pouliot AU RC 8.00 20.00
114 Anze Kopitar AU RC 25.00 60.00
115 Patrick O'Sullivan AU RC 12.00 30.00
116 G. Latendresse AU RC 12.00 30.00
117 Alexander Radulov AU RC 15.00 40.00
118 Shea Weber AU RC 20.00 40.00
119 Travis Zajac AU RC 15.00 40.00
120 Nigel Dawes AU RC 8.00 20.00
121 Dustin Boyd AU RC 8.00 20.00
122 Ryan Potulny AU RC 8.00 20.00
123 Benoit Pouliot AU RC 10.00 25.00
124 Keith Yandle AU RC 20.00 50.00
125 Evgeni Malkin AU/99 RC 200.00 400.00
126 Kristopher Letang AU RC 20.00 50.00
127 Jordan Staal AU/99 RC 25.00 60.00
128 Noah Welch AU RC 8.00 20.00
129 Marc-Edouard Vlasic AU RC 12.00 30.00
130 Matt Carle AU RC 8.00 20.00
131 Drew Stafford AU RC 12.00 30.00
132 Eric Fehr AU RC 12.00 30.00

2006-07 Ultimate Collection Autographed Jerseys

AJAF Alexander Frolov 8.00 20.00
AJAH Ales Hemsky 10.00 25.00
AJAR Andrew Raycroft 10.00 25.00
AJBB Brad Boyes 8.00 20.00
AJBH Bobby Hull 20.00 50.00
AJBM Brenden Morrow 10.00 25.00
AJBO Mike Bossy 12.00 30.00
AJBP Brad Park 10.00 25.00
AJBS Billy Smith 12.00 30.00
AJCN Cam Neely 12.00 30.00
AJCW Cam Ward 12.00 30.00
AJDH Dany Heatley 10.00 25.00
AJDP Denis Potvin 12.00 30.00
AJDT Dave Taylor 10.00 25.00
AJEL Patrik Elias 12.00 30.00
AJEM Evgeni Malkin 50.00 100.00
AJES Eric Staal 15.00 40.00
AJGC Gerry Cheevers 12.00 30.00
AJGF Grant Fuhr 20.00 50.00
AJGL Guy Lafleur 15.00 40.00
AJGP Gilbert Perreault 12.00 30.00
AJHA Dominik Hasek 20.00 50.00
AJIK Ilya Kovalchuk 12.00 30.00
AJJB Jean Beliveau 25.00 50.00
AJJG Jean-Sebastien Giguere 12.00 30.00
AJJI Jarome Iginla 12.00 30.00
AJJK Jari Kurri 12.00 30.00
AJJR Jeremy Roenick 20.00 50.00
AJJS Jordan Staal 30.00 60.00
AJJT Joe Thornton 20.00 50.00
AJKL Kari Lehtonen 10.00 25.00
AJLM Lanny McDonald 12.00 30.00
AJLR Larry Robinson 12.00 30.00
AJMB Martin Brodeur 50.00 100.00
AJMG Marian Gaborik 12.00 30.00
AJMK Miikka Kiprusoff 12.00 30.00
AJML Mario Lemieux 50.00 120.00
AJMM Mike Modano 20.00 50.00
AJMT Marty Turco 12.00 30.00
AJNL Nicklas Lidstrom 20.00 50.00
AJPE Phil Esposito 20.00 50.00
AJPH Dion Phaneuf 10.00 25.00
AJPK Phil Kessel 15.00 40.00
AJPM Patrick Marleau 12.00 30.00
AJPR Patrick Roy 60.00 120.00
AJRB Ray Bourque 25.00 60.00
AJRM Ryan Miller 12.00 30.00
AJRN Rick Nash 12.00 30.00
AJRV Rogie Vachon 12.00 30.00
AJRY Michael Ryder 8.00 20.00
AJSA Borje Salming 12.00 30.00
AJSC Sidney Crosby 75.00 150.00
AJSG Simon Gagne 12.00 30.00
AJTE Tony Esposito 12.00 30.00
AJTH Jose Theodore 12.00 30.00
AJTV Tomas Vokoun 10.00 25.00
AJVL Vincent Lecavalier 12.00 30.00
AJWG Wayne Gretzky 200.00 500.00

2006-07 Ultimate Collection Jerseys

*PATCH/75: .8X TO 2X JERSEY/200
*PREM.PATCH/25: 1.2X TO 3X JERSEY/200
UJAO Alexander Ovechkin 10.00 25.00
UJBC Bobby Clarke 8.00 20.00
UJBI Billy Smith 5.00 12.00
UJBR Martin Brodeur 12.00 30.00
UJBS Brendan Shanahan 5.00 12.00
UJCN Cam Neely 5.00 12.00
UJCW Cam Ward 5.00 12.00
UJDA Daniel Alfredsson 5.00 12.00
UJDH Dominik Hasek 8.00 20.00
UJDP Dion Phaneuf 4.00 10.00
UJDT Dave Taylor 4.00 10.00
UJEL Eric Lindros 8.00 20.00
UJEM Evgeni Malkin 12.00 30.00
UJES Eric Staal 6.00 15.00
UJGC Gerry Cheevers 5.00 12.00
UJGF Grant Fuhr 8.00 20.00
UJGL Guy Lafleur 6.00 15.00
UJGP Gilbert Perreault 5.00 12.00
UJGW Gump Worsley 5.00 12.00
UJHE Dany Heatley 4.00 10.00
UJHL Henrik Lundqvist 12.00 30.00
UJHZ Henrik Zetterberg 6.00 15.00
UJIK Ilya Kovalchuk 5.00 12.00
UJJB Jean Beliveau 5.00 12.00
UJJI Jarome Iginla 6.00 15.00
UJJJ Jaromir Jagr 15.00 40.00
UJJK Jari Kurri 5.00 12.00
UJJS Joe Sakic 10.00 25.00
UJJT Joe Thornton 10.00 25.00
UJKL Kari Lehtonen 4.00 10.00
UJLM Lanny McDonald 5.00 12.00
UJLR Larry Robinson 5.00 12.00
UJMB Mike Bossy 5.00 12.00
UJMD Marcel Dionne 6.00 15.00
UJMG Marian Gaborik 5.00 12.00
UJMH Milan Hejduk 4.00 10.00
UJML Mario Lemieux 20.00 50.00
UJMM Mike Modano 8.00 20.00
UJMN Markus Naslund 5.00 12.00
UJMR Michael Ryder 3.00 8.00
UJMS Mats Sundin 5.00 12.00
UJNL Nicklas Lidstrom 5.00 12.00
UJPB Patrice Bergeron 6.00 15.00
UJPF Peter Forsberg 10.00 25.00
UJPK Paul Kariya 5.00 12.00
UJPO Denis Potvin 5.00 12.00
UJPR Patrick Roy 12.00 30.00
UJPS Peter Stastny 4.00 10.00
UJRB Ray Bourque 8.00 20.00
UJRL Roberto Luongo 8.00 20.00
UJRN Rick Nash 5.00 12.00
UJSA Borje Salming 5.00 12.00
UJSC Sidney Crosby 15.00 40.00
UJSM Stan Mikita 6.00 15.00
UJSP Jason Spezza 5.00 12.00
UJSS Scott Stevens 5.00 12.00
UJST Martin St. Louis 5.00 12.00
UJTS Teemu Selanne 10.00 25.00
UJTV Tomas Vokoun 4.00 10.00
UJVL Vincent Lecavalier 5.00 12.00

2006-07 Ultimate Collection Jerseys Dual

UJ2CM S.Crosby/E.Malkin 30.00 80.00
UJ2CP B.Clarke/G.Perreault 15.00 40.00
UJ2DB D.Sittler/B.Salming 8.00 20.00
UJ2DV M.Dionne/R.Vachon 8.00 20.00
UJ2EE P.Esposito/T.Esposito 12.00 30.00
UJ2FG P.Forsberg/S.Gagne 12.00 30.00
UJ2GL M.Lemieux/W.Gretzky 50.00 125.00
UJ2HL D.Hasek/N.Lidstrom 10.00 25.00
UJ2HS R.Smyth/A.Hemsky 8.00 20.00
UJ2JL J.Jagr/H.Lundqvist 20.00 50.00
UJ2KA P.Kariya/J.Arnott 10.00 25.00
UJ2KI J.Iginla/M.Kiprusoff 15.00 40.00
UJ2KS T.Selanne/J.Kurri 8.00 20.00
UJ2LN M.Naslund/R.Luongo 10.00 25.00
UJ2LS V.Lecavalier/M.St. Louis 10.00 25.00
UJ2ME L.McDonald/R.Ellis 6.00 15.00
UJ2ML M.Modano/E.Lindros 10.00 25.00
UJ2MM J.Mullen/A.MacInnis 6.00 15.00
UJ2NB C.Neely/P.Bergeron 12.00 30.00
UJ2NL P.LeClaire/R.Nash 8.00 20.00
UJ2RB P.Roy/R.Bourque 15.00 40.00
UJ2RD J.Roenick/S.Doan 6.00 15.00
UJ2RP D.Potvin/L.Robinson 10.00 25.00
UJ2SH J.Spezza/D.Heatley 10.00 25.00
UJ2SS J.Sakic/P.Stastny 15.00 40.00
UJ2SW E.Staal/C.Ward 8.00 20.00
UJ2TC J.Thornton/J.Cheechoo 12.00 30.00
UJ2TH M.Hejduk/J.Theodore 6.00 15.00
UJ2ZD P.Datsyuk/H.Zetterberg 10.00 25.00

2006-07 Ultimate Collection Jerseys Triple

UJ3CMS Crosby/Malkin/Staal 100.00 200.00
UJ3ENK Esposito/Neely/Kessel 50.00 100.00
UJ3GHL Lemieux/Gretzky/Howe 125.00 250.00
UJ3LRS Lafleur/Shutt/Robinson 25.00 60.00
UJ3OMK Koval/Ovechkin/Malkin 50.00 120.00
UJ3RBL Roy/Brodeur/Luongo 75.00 150.00
UJ3SBG Bossy/Potvin/Smith 40.00 80.00
UJ3SFL Lidstrom/Forsberg/Sundin 30.00 80.00
UJ3SSH Sittler/Salming/Henderson 25.00 60.00
UJ3STS Sakic/Thornton/Staal 50.00 100.00

2006-07 Ultimate Collection Patches Dual

UJ2CM Crosby/Malkin 175.00 300.00
UJ2CP Clarke/Perreault 25.00 60.00
UJ2DB Sittler/Salming 20.00 50.00
UJ2DV Dionne/Vachon/15 30.00 80.00
UJ2EE P.Espo/T.Espo 30.00 80.00
UJ2FG Forsberg/Gagne 20.00 50.00
UJ2GL Lemieux/Gretzky 150.00 300.00
UJ2HL Hasek/Lidstrom 25.00 60.00
UJ2HS Smyth/Hemsky 15.00 40.00
UJ2JL Jagr/Lundqvist 30.00 80.00
UJ2KA Kariya/Arnott 20.00 50.00

UJ2KI Iginla/Kiprusoff 25.00 60.00
UJ2KS Selanne/Kurri 60.00 150.00
UJ2LN Naslund/Luongo 25.00 60.00
UJ2LS Lecavalier/St. Louis 30.00 80.00
UJ2ME McDonald/Ellis 12.00 30.00
UJ2ML Modano/Lindros 25.00 60.00
UJ2MM Mullen/MacInnis 15.00 40.00
UJ2NB Neely/Bergeron 25.00 60.00
UJ2NL LeClaire/Nash 25.00 60.00
UJ2RB Roy/Bourque 60.00 150.00
UJ2RD Roenick/Doan 20.00 50.00
UJ2SH Spezza/Heatley 15.00 40.00
UJ2SS Sakic/Stastny 25.00 60.00
UJ2SW Staal/Ward 12.00 30.00
UJ2TC Thornton/Cheechoo 25.00 60.00
UJ2TH Hejduk/Theodore 15.00 40.00
UJ2ZD Datsyuk/Zetterberg 40.00 100.00

2006-07 Ultimate Collection Premium Swatches

*PREM.PATCH/25: .8X TO 2X SWATCH/50
PSAF Alexander Frolov 6.00 15.00
PSAH Ales Hemsky 8.00 20.00
PSAK Alexei Kovalev 8.00 20.00
PSAM Al MacInnis 12.00 30.00
PSAR Andrew Raycroft 8.00 20.00
PSAS Alexander Steen 6.00 15.00
PSAT Alex Tanguay 6.00 15.00
PSAY Alexei Yashin 8.00 20.00
PSBL Rob Blake 10.00 25.00
PSBO Mike Bossy 10.00 25.00
PSBS Borje Salming 10.00 25.00
PSCD Chris Drury 8.00 20.00
PSCJ Curtis Joseph 12.00 30.00
PSCN Cam Neely 12.00 30.00
PSCW Cam Ward 10.00 25.00
PSDB Daniel Briere 10.00 25.00
PSDG Doug Gilmour 12.00 30.00
PSDH Dominik Hasek 15.00 40.00
PSEL Eric Lindros 15.00 40.00
PSES Eric Staal 12.00 30.00
PSGW Gump Worsley 12.00 30.00
PSHA Martin Havlat 6.00 15.00
PSHE Milan Hejduk 8.00 20.00
PSHT Hannu Toivonen 8.00 20.00
PSIK Ilya Kovalchuk 10.00 25.00
PSJB Jay Bouwmeester 6.00 15.00
PSJG Jean-Sebastien Giguere 10.00 25.00
PSJJ Jaromir Jagr 30.00 80.00
PSJL Jere Lehtinen 6.00 15.00
PSJM Joe Mullen 8.00 20.00
PSJP Joni Pitkanen 6.00 15.00
PSJR Jeremy Roenick 15.00 40.00
PSJT Joe Thornton 15.00 40.00
PSKL Kari Lehtonen 8.00 20.00
PSLM Lanny McDonald 10.00 25.00
PSMA Maxim Afinogenov 6.00 15.00
PSMB Martin Brodeur 25.00 60.00
PSMG Marian Gaborik 10.00 25.00
PSMH Marian Hossa 10.00 25.00
PSMK Miikka Kiprusoff 12.00 30.00
PSMM Mike Modano 15.00 40.00
PSMN Markus Naslund 10.00 25.00
PSMP Michael Peca 8.00 20.00
PSMR Mark Recchi 12.00 30.00
PSMS Miroslav Satan 8.00 20.00
PSMT Marty Turco 10.00 25.00
PSMU Larry Murphy 8.00 20.00
PSOK Olaf Kolzig 10.00 25.00
PSPD Pavel Datsyuk 15.00 40.00
PSPE Patrik Elias 10.00 25.00
PSPL Pascal LeClaire 8.00 20.00
PSPM Patrick Marleau 10.00 25.00
PSRB Ray Bourque 15.00 40.00
PSRE Ron Ellis 6.00 15.00
PSRM Ryan Miller 10.00 25.00
PSRS Ryan Smyth 8.00 20.00
PSSF Sergei Fedorov 15.00 40.00
PSSS Scott Stevens 10.00 25.00
PSSZ Sergei Zubov 8.00 20.00
PSZC Zdeno Chara 10.00 25.00

2006-07 Ultimate Collection Rookies Autographed Patches

103 Matt Lashoff 12.00 30.00
104 Phil Kessel 75.00 150.00
105 Mark Stuart 12.00 30.00
106 Michael Blunden 12.00 30.00
107 Dave Bolland 20.00 50.00
108 Paul Stastny 30.00 80.00
109 Loui Eriksson 25.00 60.00
110 Niklas Grossman 20.00 50.00
111 Ladislav Smid 12.00 30.00
112 Patrick Thoresen 12.00 30.00
113 Marc-Antoine Pouliot 12.00 30.00
114 Anze Kopitar 100.00 200.00
115 Patrick O'Sullivan 20.00 50.00
116 Guillaume Latendresse 20.00 50.00
117 Alexander Radulov 25.00 60.00
118 Shea Weber 30.00 80.00
119 Travis Zajac 25.00 60.00
120 Nigel Dawes 12.00 30.00
121 Dustin Boyd 12.00 30.00
122 Ryan Potulny 12.00 30.00
123 Benoit Pouliot 15.00 40.00
124 Keith Yandle 30.00 80.00
125 Evgeni Malkin 200.00 400.00
126 Kristopher Letang 60.00 120.00
127 Jordan Staal 60.00 120.00
128 Noah Welch 12.00 30.00
129 Marc-Edouard Vlasic 20.00 50.00
130 Matt Carle 12.00 30.00
131 Drew Stafford 20.00 50.00
132 Eric Fehr 20.00 50.00

2006-07 Ultimate Collection Signatures

USAF Alexander Frolov 4.00 10.00
USAH Ales Hemsky 5.00 12.00
USAK Anze Kopitar 12.00 30.00
USAM Al MacInnis 8.00 20.00
USAR Andrew Raycroft 5.00 12.00
USAT Alex Tanguay 4.00 10.00
USBB Brad Boyes 4.00 10.00
USBC Bobby Clarke 8.00 20.00
USBF Bernie Federko 5.00 12.00
USBH Bobby Hull SP 20.00 50.00
USBM Mike Bossy SP 20.00 50.00
USBO Pierre-Marc Bouchard 6.00 15.00
USBP Bernie Parent 10.00 25.00
USBR Richard Brodeur 5.00 12.00
USBU Johnny Bucyk 6.00 15.00
USCA Colby Armstrong 5.00 12.00
USCH Jonathan Cheechoo 5.00 12.00
USCI Dino Ciccarelli 6.00 15.00
USCN Cam Neely 8.00 20.00
USCW Cam Ward 6.00 15.00
USDC Don Cherry 15.00 40.00
USDH Dominik Hasek SP 20.00 50.00
USDR Dwayne Roloson 5.00 12.00
USDS Denis Savard 6.00 15.00
USEM Evgeni Malkin 40.00 80.00
USES Eric Staal 8.00 20.00
USGB Gilbert Brule 5.00 12.00
USGC Gerry Cheevers 10.00 25.00
USGF Grant Fuhr SP 12.00 30.00
USGH Gordie Howe 40.00 80.00
USGL G. Latendresse 6.00 15.00
USGP Gilbert Perreault 6.00 15.00
USHA Dale Hawerchuk 6.00 15.00
USHE D. Heatley SP EXCH 12.50 30.00
USHL Henrik Lundqvist 12.00 30.00
USIK Ilya Kovalchuk 8.00 20.00
USJA Jason Arnott 5.00 12.00
USJB Jean Beliveau SP 50.00 100.00
USJG Jean-Sebastien Giguere 6.00 15.00
USJI Jarome Iginla SP 10.00 25.00
USJK Jari Kurri 6.00 15.00
USJM Joe Mullen 5.00 12.00
USJO Johnny Bower 6.00 15.00
USKL Kari Lehtonen 5.00 12.00
USLR Larry Robinson 8.00 20.00
USMB Martin Brodeur SP 60.00 120.00
USMC Matt Carle 4.00 10.00
USMD Marcel Dionne 12.00 30.00
USMF Marc-Andre Fleury 12.00 30.00
USMG Marian Gaborik 8.00 20.00
USMH Martin Havlat 4.00 10.00
USMI Milan Hejduk 5.00 12.00
USML Mario Lemieux SP 100.00 200.00
USMM Mike Modano 10.00 25.00
USMR Michael Ryder 6.00 15.00
USMS Marek Svatos 4.00 10.00
USMT Marty Turco 6.00 15.00
USNL Nicklas Lidstrom 15.00 30.00
USOR Bobby Orr 60.00 120.00
USPB Patrice Bergeron 8.00 20.00
USPE Patrik Elias 6.00 15.00
USPH Phil Esposito SP 10.00 25.00
USPK Phil Kessel 8.00 20.00
USPM Patrick Marleau SP 8.00 20.00
USPO Denis Potvin 6.00 15.00
USPR Patrick Roy SP 75.00 150.00
USPS Paul Stastny 12.50 30.00
USRA Alexander Radulov 10.00 25.00
USRB Ray Bourque SP 25.00 60.00
USRH Ron Hextall 6.00 15.00
USRM Ryan Miller 8.00 20.00
USRN Rick Nash 10.00 25.00
USRS Ryan Smyth 5.00 12.00
USSB Steve Bernier 4.00 10.00
USSC Sidney Crosby 60.00 120.00
USSG Simon Gagne 6.00 15.00
USSK Saku Koivu SP 25.00 50.00
USSP Peter Stastny 5.00 12.00
USSS Scott Stevens 8.00 20.00
USST Jordan Staal 15.00 40.00
USTE Tony Esposito SP 12.00 30.00
USTH Joe Thornton SP 20.00 50.00
USTL Ted Lindsay 8.00 20.00
USTO Terry O'Reilly 8.00 20.00
USTV Tomas Vokoun 5.00 12.00
USVL Vincent Lecavalier SP 20.00 50.00
USVT Vesa Toskala 5.00 12.00
USWG Wayne Gretzky 150.00 400.00

2006-07 Ultimate Collection Ultimate Achievements Autographs

UABC Bobby Clarke/89 12.00 30.00
UABH Bobby Hull/58 15.00 40.00
UABO Bobby Orr/6
UABP Bernie Parent/47 15.00 40.00
UACN Cam Neely/9
UACW Cam Ward/15 40.00 100.00
UADH Dany Heatley/50 15.00 40.00
UAEM Evgeni Malkin/6
UAES Eric Staal/28 15.00 40.00
UAGF Grant Fuhr/23 30.00 60.00
UAGH Gordie Howe/26 60.00 125.00
UAGL Guy Lafleur/60 20.00 50.00
UAGP Gilbert Perreault/72 10.00 25.00
UAHA Dominik Hasek/41 20.00 50.00
UAIK Ilya Kovalchuk/52 12.00 30.00
UAJB Jean Beliveau/10 75.00 150.00
UAJC Jonathan Cheechoo/56 10.00 25.00
UAJI Jarome Iginla/52 15.00 40.00
UAJK Jari Kurri/68 10.00 25.00
UAJT Joe Thornton/96 12.00 30.00
UALR Luc Robitaille/63 20.00 50.00
UAMB Martin Brodeur/43 50.00 100.00
UAMD Marcel Dionne/53 12.00 30.00
UAMF Marc-Andre Fleury/40 20.00 40.00
UAMG Marian Gaborik/38 20.00 50.00
UAMH Milan Hejduk/50 6.00 15.00
UAMI Mike Bossy/9 125.00 200.00
UAMK Miikka Kiprusoff/42 20.00 50.00
UAML Mario Lemieux/8
UAMM Mike Modano/23 25.00 50.00
UANL Nicklas Lidstrom/80 15.00 40.00
UAPE Phil Esposito/76 12.00 30.00
UAPR Patrick Roy/23 100.00 200.00
UAPS Peter Stastny/70 8.00 20.00
UARN Rick Nash/41 15.00 40.00
UASC Sidney Crosby/39 100.00 200.00
UASK Saku Koivu/71 12.00 30.00
UATV Tomas Vokoun/36 12.00 30.00
UAVL Vincent Lecavalier/78 12.00 30.00
UAWG Wayne Gretzky/10 750.00 2000.00

2006-07 Ultimate Collection Ultimate Debut Threads Jerseys

*PATCH/25: 1.5X TO 4X BASIC JSY
DJAK Anze Kopitar 15.00 40.00
DJAR Alexander Radulov 6.00 15.00
DJBB Brendan Bell 3.00 8.00
DJBO Dave Bolland 5.00 12.00
DJBP Benoit Pouliot 4.00 10.00
DJBT Billy Thompson 3.00 8.00
DJCG Carsen Germyn 3.00 8.00
DJDB Dustin Byfuglien 8.00 20.00
DJDK D.J. King 3.00 8.00
DJDP David Printz 3.00 8.00
DJDS Drew Stafford 5.00 12.00
DJDU Dustin Boyd 3.00 8.00
DJEF Eric Fehr 5.00 12.00
DJEM Evgeni Malkin 50.00 100.00
DJFD Frank Doyle 4.00 10.00
DJFN Filip Novak 3.00 8.00
DJGL Guillaume Latendresse 5.00 12.00
DJIW Ian White 4.00 10.00
DJJI Jarkko Immonen 4.00 10.00
DJJJ Jonas Johansson 3.00 8.00
DJJO John Oduya 5.00 12.00
DJJW Jeremy Williams 3.00 8.00
DJKL Kristopher Letang 12.00 30.00
DJKP Konstantin Pushkarev 4.00 10.00
DJKY Keith Yandle 8.00 20.00
DJLB Luc Bourdon 5.00 12.00
DJLE Loui Eriksson 6.00 15.00
DJLS Ladislav Smid 3.00 8.00
DJMB Michael Blunden 3.00 8.00
DJMC Matt Carle 3.00 8.00
DJMI Mikko Lehtonen 4.00 10.00
DJMK Miroslav Kopriva 3.00 8.00
DJML Matt Lashoff 3.00 8.00
DJMM Masi Marjamaki 3.00 8.00
DJMO Michel Ouellet 4.00 10.00
DJMP Marc-Antoine Pouliot 3.00 8.00
DJMS Mark Stuart 3.00 8.00
DJMV Marc-Edouard Vlasic 5.00 12.00
DJNB Niklas Backstrom 6.00 15.00
DJND Nigel Dawes 3.00 8.00
DJNO Fredrik Norrena 3.00 8.00
DJNW Noah Welch 3.00 8.00
DJON Ben Ondrus 3.00 8.00
DJPK Phil Kessel 10.00 25.00
DJPO Patrick O'Sullivan 5.00 12.00
DJPR Brandon Prust 3.00 8.00
DJPS Paul Stastny 8.00 20.00
DJPT Patrick Thoresen 3.00 8.00
DJRO Roman Polak 4.00 10.00
DJRP Ryan Potulny 3.00 8.00
DJRS Ryan Shannon 3.00 8.00
DJSO Shane O'Brien 3.00 8.00
DJST Jordan Staal 8.00 20.00
DJSW Shea Weber 8.00 20.00
DJTK Tomas Kopecky 4.00 10.00
DJTZ Travis Zajac 6.00 15.00
DJYS Yan Stastny 3.00 8.00

2006-07 Ultimate Collection Ultimate Debut Threads Jerseys Autographs

DJAK Anze Kopitar 50.00 125.00
DJAR Alexander Radulov 20.00 50.00
DJBB Brendan Bell 10.00 25.00
DJBO Dave Bolland 15.00 40.00
DJBP Benoit Pouliot 12.00 30.00
DJBT Billy Thompson 10.00 25.00
DJCG Carsen Germyn 10.00 25.00
DJDB Dustin Byfuglien 25.00 60.00
DJDK D.J. King 10.00 25.00
DJDP David Printz 10.00 25.00
DJDS Drew Stafford 15.00 40.00
DJDU Dustin Boyd 10.00 25.00
DJEF Eric Fehr 15.00 40.00
DJEM Evgeni Malkin 75.00 150.00
DJFD Frank Doyle 12.00 30.00
DJFN Filip Novak 10.00 25.00
DJGL G. Latendresse 15.00 40.00
DJIW Ian White 12.00 30.00
DJJI Jarkko Immonen 12.00 30.00
DJJJ Jonas Johansson 10.00 25.00
DJJO John Oduya 15.00 40.00
DJJW Jeremy Williams 10.00 25.00
DJKL Kristopher Letang 40.00 100.00
DJKP Konstantin Pushkarev 12.00 30.00
DJKY Keith Yandle 15.00 40.00
DJLB Luc Bourdon 15.00 40.00
DJLE Loui Eriksson 20.00 50.00
DJLS Ladislav Smid 10.00 25.00
DJMB Michael Blunden 10.00 25.00
DJMC Matt Carle 10.00 25.00
DJMI Mikko Lehtonen 12.00 30.00
DJMK Miroslav Kopriva 10.00 25.00
DJML Matt Lashoff 10.00 25.00
DJMM Masi Marjamaki 10.00 25.00
DJMO Michel Ouellet 12.00 30.00
DJMP Marc-Antoine Pouliot 10.00 25.00
DJMS Mark Stuart 10.00 25.00
DJMV Marc-Edouard Vlasic 15.00 40.00
DJNB Niklas Backstrom 20.00 50.00
DJND Nigel Dawes 10.00 25.00
DJNO Fredrik Norrena 10.00 25.00
DJNW Noah Welch 10.00 25.00
DJON Ben Ondrus 10.00 25.00
DJPK Phil Kessel 30.00 80.00
DJPO Patrick O'Sullivan 15.00 40.00
DJPR Brandon Prust 10.00 25.00
DJPS Paul Stastny 25.00 60.00
DJPT Patrick Thoresen 10.00 25.00
DJRO Roman Polak 12.00 30.00
DJRP Ryan Potulny 10.00 25.00
DJRS Ryan Shannon 10.00 25.00
DJSO Shane O'Brien 10.00 25.00
DJST Jordan Staal 25.00 60.00
DJSW Shea Weber 25.00 60.00
DJTK Tomas Kopecky 12.00 30.00
DJTZ Travis Zajac 20.00 50.00
DJYS Yan Stastny 10.00 25.00

2007-08 Ultimate Collection

COMP.SET w/o SP's (60) 100.00 200.00
1 Alexander Ovechkin 5.00 12.00
2 Roberto Luongo 2.00 5.00
3 Markus Naslund 1.25 3.00
4 Mats Sundin 1.25 3.00
5 Darcy Tucker 1.00 2.50
6 Darryl Sittler 1.50 4.00
7 Frank Mahovlich 1.25 3.00
8 Vincent Lecavalier 1.25 3.00
9 Martin St. Louis 1.25 3.00
10 Paul Kariya 1.25 3.00
11 Keith Tkachuk 1.25 3.00
12 Joe Thornton 2.00 5.00
13 Jonathan Cheechoo 1.00 2.50
14 Patrick Marleau 1.25 3.00
15 Mario Lemieux 5.00 12.00
16 Sidney Crosby 5.00 12.00
17 Marc-Andre Fleury 2.50 6.00
18 Evgeni Malkin 2.50 6.00
19 Shane Doan 1.00 2.50
20 Ron Hextall 1.25 3.00
21 Simon Gagne 1.25 3.00
22 Daniel Briere 1.25 3.00
23 Dany Heatley 1.00 2.50
24 Jason Spezza 1.25 3.00
25 Ray Emery 1.00 2.50
26 Jaromir Jagr 4.00 10.00
27 Brendan Shanahan 1.25 3.00
28 Henrik Lundqvist 3.00 8.00
29 Mike Bossy 1.25 3.00
30 Rick DiPietro 1.00 2.50
31 Martin Brodeur 3.00 8.00
32 Zach Parise 1.25 3.00
33 Alexander Radulov 1.25 3.00
34 Saku Koivu 1.25 3.00
35 Michael Ryder .75 2.00
36 Larry Robinson 1.25 3.00
37 Marian Gaborik 1.25 3.00
38 Wayne Gretzky 8.00 20.00
39 Anze Kopitar 2.00 5.00
40 Tomas Vokoun 1.00 2.50
41 Mark Messier 2.50 6.00
42 Dwayne Roloson 1.00 2.50
43 Dominik Hasek 2.00 5.00
44 Henrik Zetterberg 1.50 4.00
45 Gordie Howe 4.00 10.00
46 Mike Modano 2.00 5.00
47 Rick Nash 1.25 3.00
48 Joe Sakic 2.50 6.00
49 Patrick Roy 3.00 8.00
50 Paul Stastny 1.00 2.50
51 Bobby Hull 2.50 6.00
52 Eric Staal 1.50 4.00
53 Jarome Iginla 1.50 4.00
54 Miikka Kiprusoff 1.25 3.00
55 Thomas Vanek 1.50 4.00
56 Ryan Miller 1.25 3.00
57 Patrice Bergeron 1.50 4.00
58 Bobby Orr 5.00 12.00
59 Ilya Kovalchuk 1.25 3.00
60 Jean-Sebastien Giguere 1.25 3.00
61 T.J. Hensick RC 4.00 10.00
62 Jannik Hansen RC 4.00 10.00
63 Jaroslav Halak RC 15.00 40.00
64 Tom Gilbert RC 4.00 10.00
65 Jason Jaffray RC 3.00 8.00
66 Ryan O'Byrne RC 5.00 12.00
67 Steve Downie RC 4.00 10.00
68 David Moss RC 5.00 12.00
69 Mike Weber RC 3.00 8.00
70 Tomas Popperle RC 3.00 8.00
71 Daniel Girardi RC 4.00 10.00
72 Matt Keetley RC 3.00 8.00
73 Cal Clutterbuck RC 5.00 12.00
74 Tobias Stephan RC 4.00 10.00
75 Marc Methot RC 3.00 8.00
76 Matt Hunwick RC 3.00 8.00
77 Mike Lundin RC 3.00 8.00
78 Ryan Carter RC 3.00 8.00
79 Casey Borer RC 3.00 8.00
80 Martin Lojek RC 3.00 8.00
81 Mark Mancari RC 3.00 8.00
82 Jared Boll RC 4.00 10.00
83 Thomas Greiss RC 6.00 15.00
84 Bryan Young RC 3.00 8.00
85 Patrick Kaleta RC 3.00 8.00
86 Rod Pelley RC 3.00 8.00
87 Jonas Hiller RC 6.00 15.00
88 Magnus Johansson RC 3.00 8.00
89 Cory Murphy RC 3.00 8.00
90 Cody Bass RC 3.00 8.00
91 Craig Weller RC 3.00 8.00
92 Steve Wagner RC 3.00 8.00
93 Johnny Boychuk RC 5.00 12.00
94 Matt Ellis RC 4.00 10.00
95 Joel Lundqvist RC 3.00 8.00
96 Jonathan Quick RC 60.00 150.00
97 Daniel Winnik RC 4.00 10.00
98 Drew MacIntyre RC 3.00 8.00
99 Daniel Carcillo RC 4.00 10.00
100 John Zeiler RC 3.00 8.00
101 Brandon Dubinsky RC 6.00 15.00
102 Liam Reddox RC 3.00 8.00
103 Tomas Plihal RC 3.00 8.00
104 Frans Nielsen RC 5.00 12.00
105 Chris Conner RC 3.00 8.00
106 Jack Skille RC 4.00 10.00
107 Tyler Kennedy RC 3.00 8.00
108 Matt Moulson RC 5.00 12.00
109 Sergei Kostitsyn RC 4.00 10.00
110 Tanner Glass RC 3.00 8.00
111 Kent Huskins RC 3.00 8.00
112 Riley Cote RC 4.00 10.00
113 Antti Pihlstrom RC 4.00 10.00
114 Chris Bourque RC 4.00 10.00
115 David Jones RC 3.00 8.00
116 Lukas Kaspar RC 3.00 8.00
117 Nathan Guenin RC 4.00 10.00
118 Kris Russell RC 5.00 12.00
119 Tobias Enstrom RC 5.00 12.00
120 Anton Stralman RC 3.00 8.00
121 Bobby Ryan AU RC 12.00 30.00
122 Sam Gagner AU RC 10.00 25.00
123 Nicklas Bergfors AU RC 5.00 12.00
124 Erik Johnson AU RC 8.00 20.00
125 Jack Johnson AU RC 6.00 15.00
126 Jonathan Bernier AU RC 15.00 40.00
127 Bryan Little AU RC 8.00 20.00
129 Matt Niskanen AU RC 8.00 20.00
130 Andrew Cogliano AU RC 6.00 15.00
131 Marc Staal AU RC 8.00 20.00
132 Nick Foligno AU RC 10.00 25.00
133 Brett Sterling AU RC 5.00 12.00
134 Martin Hanzal AU RC 6.00 15.00
135 Matt Smaby AU RC 5.00 12.00
136 Petr Kalus AU RC 5.00 12.00
137 Andy Greene AU RC 6.00 15.00
138 Ondrej Pavelec AU RC 10.00 25.00
139 Rob Schremp AU RC 6.00 15.00
140 Kyle Chipchura AU RC 8.00 20.00
141 Ryan Parent AU RC 5.00 12.00
142 David Krejci AU RC 10.00 25.00
143 Lauri Tukonen AU RC 5.00 12.00
144 James Sheppard AU RC 5.00 12.00
145 Mason Raymond AU RC 8.00 20.00
146 Devin Setoguchi AU RC 8.00 20.00
147 Curtis McElhinney AU RC 8.00 20.00
148 Brian Elliott AU RC 10.00 25.00
149 Drew Miller AU RC 6.00 15.00
150 Ryan Callahan AU RC 10.00 25.00
151 Ville Koistinen AU RC 5.00 12.00
152 Torrey Mitchell AU RC 6.00 15.00
153 David Perron AU RC 10.00 25.00
154 Milan Lucic AU RC 12.00 30.00
155 Jaroslav Hlinka AU RC 6.00 15.00
156 Tyler Weiman AU RC 6.00 15.00
157 Jonathan Toews AU/99 RC 250.00 450.00
158 Carey Price AU/99 RC 250.00 400.00
159 Patrick Kane AU/99 RC 1000.00 2500.00
160 Nicklas Backstrom AU/99 RC 75.00 125.00
161 Peter Mueller AU/99 RC 15.00 40.00
162 Jiri Tlusty AU/99 RC 20.00 50.00

2007-08 Ultimate Collection Autographed Jerseys

AJAK Anze Kopitar/50 20.00 50.00
AJAO Alexander Ovechkin/25 50.00 120.00
AJAT Alex Tanguay/50 10.00 25.00
AJBS Borje Salming/50 12.00 30.00
AJCN Cam Neely/25 12.00 30.00
AJCW Cam Ward/50 12.00 30.00
AJEM Evgeni Malkin/25 25.00 60.00
AJES Eric Staal/50 15.00 40.00
AJGF Grant Fuhr/25 20.00 50.00
AJGL Guy Lafleur/25 15.00 40.00
AJGP Gilbert Perreault/50 12.00 30.00
AJIK Ilya Kovalchuk/50 12.00 30.00
AJJG Jean-Sebastien Giguere/50 12.00 30.00
AJJI Jarome Iginla/25 15.00 40.00
AJJT Joe Thornton/25 20.00 50.00
AJLR Larry Robinson/50 12.00 30.00
AJMB Martin Brodeur/25 30.00 80.00
AJMF Marc-Andre Fleury/50 25.00 60.00
AJMG Marian Gaborik/25 12.00 30.00
AJMH Milan Hejduk/50 10.00 25.00
AJML Mario Lemieux/25 50.00 125.00
AJMM Mark Messier/25 25.00 60.00
AJMN Markus Naslund/50 12.00 30.00
AJMO Mike Modano/50 20.00 50.00
AJMR Michael Ryder/50 8.00 20.00
AJNL Nicklas Lidstrom/50 12.00 30.00
AJPR Patrick Roy/25 30.00 80.00
AJPS Peter Stastny/50 10.00 25.00
AJSC Sidney Crosby/25 80.00 200.00
AJSM Stan Mikita/50 15.00 40.00
AJTV Tomas Vokoun/50 10.00 25.00
AJVL Vincent Lecavalier/50 12.00 30.00
AJWG Wayne Gretzky/25 250.00 600.00

2007-08 Ultimate Collection Autographed Patches

AJAK Anze Kopitar/25 40.00 100.00
AJAT Alex Tanguay/25 15.00 40.00
AJBS Borje Salming/25 20.00 50.00
AJCW Cam Ward/25 30.00 60.00
AJES Eric Staal/25 25.00 50.00
AJGP Gilbert Perreault/25 15.00 40.00
AJIK Ilya Kovalchuk/25 25.00 60.00
AJJG Jean-Sebastien Giguere/25 60.00 120.00
AJLR Larry Robinson/25 20.00 50.00
AJMF Marc-Andre Fleury/25 75.00 150.00
AJMH Milan Hejduk/25 15.00 40.00
AJMM Mike Modano/25 20.00 50.00
AJMN Markus Naslund/25 15.00 40.00
AJMR Michael Ryder/25 15.00 40.00
AJMS Martin St. Louis/25 15.00 40.00
AJNL Nicklas Lidstrom/25 60.00 120.00
AJPS Peter Stastny/25 20.00 50.00
AJRG Ryan Getzlaf/25 12.00 30.00
AJSM Stan Mikita/25 25.00 50.00
AJTV Tomas Vokoun/25 20.00 50.00
AJVL Vincent Lecavalier/25 30.00 80.00

2007-08 Ultimate Collection Jerseys

UJAH Ales Hemsky 4.00 10.00
UJAK Anze Kopitar 8.00 20.00
UJAO Alexander Ovechkin 20.00 50.00
UJAT Alex Tanguay 4.00 10.00
UJBC Bobby Clarke 8.00 20.00
UJBL Brian Leetch 4.00 10.00
UJBO Mike Bossy 5.00 12.00
UJBR Brad Richards 5.00 12.00
UJBS Billy Smith 5.00 12.00
UJCN Cam Neely 5.00 12.00
UJCW Cam Ward 5.00 12.00
UJDA Daniel Alfredsson 5.00 12.00
UJDB Daniel Briere 5.00 12.00
UJDH Dale Hawerchuk 6.00 15.00
UJDS Darryl Sittler 6.00 15.00
UJEM Evgeni Malkin 10.00 25.00
UJES Eric Staal 6.00 15.00
UJGP Gilbert Perreault 5.00 12.00
UJHA Dominik Hasek 8.00 20.00
UJHE Dany Heatley 4.00 10.00
UJHL Henrik Lundqvist 12.00 30.00
UJHZ Henrik Zetterberg 6.00 15.00
UJIK Ilya Kovalchuk 5.00 12.00
UJJC Jonathan Cheechoo 4.00 10.00
UJJG Jean-Sebastien Giguere 5.00 12.00
UJJI Jarome Iginla 6.00 15.00
UJJJ Jaromir Jagr 15.00 40.00
UJJO Joe Sakic 10.00 25.00
UJJS Jason Spezza 5.00 12.00
UJJT Joe Thornton 8.00 20.00
UJKL Kari Lehtonen 4.00 10.00
UJMB Martin Brodeur 12.00 30.00
UJMG Marian Gaborik 5.00 12.00
UJMK Miikka Kiprusoff 5.00 12.00
UJML Mario Lemieux 12.00 30.00
UJMM Mike Modano 8.00 20.00
UJMN Markus Naslund 5.00 12.00
UJMR Michael Ryder 3.00 8.00
UJMS Mats Sundin 5.00 12.00
UJPB Patrice Bergeron 6.00 15.00
UJPD Pavel Datsyuk 8.00 20.00
UJPF Peter Forsberg 10.00 25.00
UJPH Dion Phaneuf 4.00 10.00
UJPK Paul Kariya 5.00 12.00
UJPM Patrick Marleau 5.00 12.00
UJPR Patrick Roy 12.00 30.00
UJRB Ray Bourque 8.00 20.00
UJRL Roberto Luongo 8.00 20.00
UJRN Rick Nash 5.00 12.00
UJRS Ryan Smyth 4.00 10.00
UJSA Borje Salming 5.00 12.00
UJSC Sidney Crosby 25.00 50.00
UJSD Shane Doan 4.00 10.00
UJSG Simon Gagne 5.00 12.00
UJSH Brendan Shanahan 5.00 12.00
UJSK Saku Koivu 5.00 12.00
UJSS Scott Stevens 5.00 12.00
UJVL Vincent Lecavalier 5.00 12.00
UJWG Wayne Gretzky 25.00 50.00

2007-08 Ultimate Collection Jerseys Duos

UJ2BB J.Bucyk/P.Bergeron 5.00 12.00
UJ2BS M.Brodeur/S.Stevens 10.00 25.00
UJ2CG W.Gretzky/S.Crosby 25.00 60.00
UJ2CS S.Crosby/J.Staal 15.00 40.00
UJ2DJ J.Spezza/D.Heatley 4.00 10.00
UJ2FK A.Frolov/A.Kopitar 6.00 15.00
UJ2FR G.Fuhr/D.Roloson 6.00 15.00
UJ2GB S.Gagne/D.Briere 4.00 10.00
UJ2GK M.Gaborik/M.Koivu 4.00 10.00
UJ2HD D.Hasek/P.Datsyuk 6.00 15.00
UJ2HK M.Hossa/I.Kovalchuk 4.00 10.00
UJ2IK J.Iginla/M.Kiprusoff 5.00 12.00
UJ2JL J.Jagr/H.Lundqvist 12.00 30.00
UJ2JP P.Marleau/J.Thornton 6.00 15.00
UJ2KW P.Kariya/D.Weight 4.00 10.00
UJ2LM M.Lemieux/M.Messier 15.00 40.00
UJ2LR G.Lafleur/M.Ryder 5.00 12.00
UJ2LZ N.Lidstrom/H.Zetterberg 5.00 12.00
UJ2ME M.Lemieux/E.Malkin 15.00 40.00
UJ2MH S.Mikita/M.Havlat 5.00 12.00
UJ2MT M.Modano/M.Turco 6.00 15.00
UJ2NF R.Nash/S.Fedorov 6.00 15.00
UJ2NK C.Neely/P.Kessel 4.00 10.00
UJ2NL M.Naslund/R.Luongo 6.00 15.00
UJ2OM A.Ovechkin/E.Malkin 15.00 40.00
UJ2PV G.Perreault/T.Vanek 4.00 10.00
UJ2SH J.Sakic/M.Hejduk 8.00 20.00
UJ2SS M.Sundin/B.Salming 4.00 10.00
UJ2VB V.Lecavalier/B.Richards 4.00 10.00
UJ2VH T.Vokoun/N.Horton 4.00 10.00

2007-08 Ultimate Collection Jerseys Trios

UJ3BCP Clarke/Bucyk/Perrlt 15.00 40.00
UJ3BLS Lafleur/Bossy/Sittler 8.00 20.00
UJ3ISH St.L/Htley/Iginla 8.00 20.00
UJ3LCG Lemx/Crsby/Grtzky 40.00 100.00
UJ3LPB Lidst/Brque/Phanf 10.00 25.00
UJ3OMR Malkin/Ovech/Rdulv 25.00 60.00
UJ3RBF Brodeur/Fleury/Roy 15.00 40.00
UJ3SKK Selanne/Koivu/Kurri 12.00 30.00
UJ3SLT Lecav/Sakc/Thrntn 12.00 30.00
UJ3SNZ Sndin/Zettr/Nslund 8.00 20.00

2007-08 Ultimate Collection Patches

UPAH Ales Hemsky 10.00 25.00
UPAK Anze Kopitar 20.00 50.00
UPAO Alexander Ovechkin 125.00 250.00
UPAR Alexander Radulov 12.00 30.00
UPAS Alexander Steen 8.00 20.00
UPAT Alex Tanguay 10.00 25.00
UPBR Brad Richards 30.00 60.00
UPBS Borje Salming 12.00 30.00
UPCN Cam Neely 12.00 30.00
UPCW Cam Ward 30.00 60.00
UPDA Daniel Alfredsson 20.00 50.00
UPDH Dale Hawerchuk 30.00 60.00
UPDR Dwayne Roloson
UPDW Doug Weight 12.00 30.00
UPES Eric Staal 20.00 50.00
UPHA Dominik Hasek 20.00 50.00
UPHE Dany Heatley 10.00 25.00
UPHL Henrik Lundqvist 30.00 60.00
UPHZ Henrik Zetterberg 15.00 40.00
UPIK Ilya Kovalchuk 20.00 50.00
UPJG Jean-Sebastien Giguere 12.00 30.00
UPJI Jarome Iginla 15.00 40.00
UPJJ Jaromir Jagr 30.00 60.00
UPJS Jason Spezza 12.00 30.00
UPJT Joe Thornton 20.00 50.00
UPKE Phil Kessel 30.00 60.00
UPKL Kari Lehtonen 10.00 25.00
UPLM Lanny McDonald 12.00 30.00
UPLR Larry Robinson 12.00 30.00
UPMB Martin Brodeur 30.00 60.00
UPMG Marian Gaborik 20.00 50.00
UPMH Marian Hossa 20.00 50.00
UPMI Milan Hejduk 10.00 25.00
UPMK Mikko Koivu 10.00 25.00
UPML Mario Lemieux 50.00 100.00
UPMM Mike Modano 20.00 50.00
UPMN Markus Naslund 12.00 30.00
UPMR Mark Recchi 15.00 40.00
UPMS Martin St. Louis 12.00 30.00
UPMT Marty Turco 12.00 30.00
UPNL Nicklas Lidstrom 12.00 30.00
UPPB Patrice Bergeron 20.00 50.00
UPPF Peter Forsberg 25.00 60.00
UPPK Paul Kariya 12.00 30.00
UPPR Patrick Roy 50.00 100.00
UPPS Peter Stastny
UPRB Ray Bourque 20.00 50.00
UPRG Ryan Getzlaf 12.00 30.00
UPRL Roberto Luongo 15.00 30.00
UPRN Rick Nash 30.00 60.00
UPRS Ryan Smyth 10.00 25.00
UPSA Joe Sakic 25.00 60.00
UPSC Sidney Crosby 150.00 300.00
UPSD Shane Doan 10.00 25.00
UPSF Sergei Fedorov 20.00 50.00
UPSG Simon Gagne 12.00 30.00
UPSH Brendan Shanahan 12.00 30.00
UPSK Saku Koivu 12.00 30.00
UPSU Mats Sundin 12.00 30.00
UPVL Vincent Lecavalier 12.00 30.00

2007-08 Ultimate Collection Premium Patches

PSAS Alexander Steen
PSBO Borje Salming 40.00 100.00
PSBS Billy Smith 40.00 80.00
PSBU Johnny Bucyk 20.00 50.00
PSCJ Jonathan Cheechoo 20.00 50.00
PSCN Cam Neely 30.00 60.00
PSCP Chris Pronger 30.00 60.00
PSDA Daniel Alfredsson 50.00 100.00
PSDC Dino Ciccarelli 12.00 30.00
PSDG Doug Gilmour 12.00 30.00
PSDH Dale Hawerchuk
PSEL Patrik Elias 12.00 30.00
PSGF Grant Fuhr 40.00 80.00
PSGP Gilbert Perreault 30.00 60.00
PSHE Dany Heatley 30.00 60.00
PSHL Henrik Lundqvist 40.00 80.00
PSHZ Henrik Zetterberg 30.00 60.00
PSIK Ilya Kovalchuk 50.00 100.00
PSJG Jean-Sebastien Giguere 15.00 40.00
PSJI Jarome Iginla 15.00 40.00
PSJJ Jaromir Jagr 75.00 150.00
PSJM Joe Mullen 15.00 40.00
PSJO Joe Sakic 25.00 60.00
PSJS Jason Spezza 30.00 60.00
PSJT Joe Thornton 20.00 50.00
PSLM Lanny McDonald 12.00 30.00
PSMA Al MacInnis 20.00 50.00
PSMB Martin Brodeur 40.00 80.00
PSMG Marian Gaborik 40.00 80.00
PSMH Marian Hossa 20.00 50.00
PSML Mario Lemieux 60.00 120.00
PSMM Mike Modano 20.00 50.00
PSMN Markus Naslund 15.00 40.00
PSMS Martin St. Louis 15.00 40.00
PSMT Marty Turco 15.00 40.00
PSNL Nicklas Lidstrom 20.00 50.00
PSOV Alexander Ovechkin 60.00 120.00
PSPB Patrice Bergeron 15.00 40.00
PSPD Pavel Datsyuk 50.00 100.00
PSPK Paul Kariya 20.00 50.00
PSPM Patrick Marleau 15.00 40.00
PSPR Patrick Roy 75.00 150.00
PSPS Peter Stastny
PSRB Ray Bourque 25.00 60.00
PSRL Roberto Luongo 30.00 60.00
PSRN Rick Nash 60.00 120.00
PSSC Sidney Crosby 100.00 200.00
PSSG Simon Gagne 20.00 50.00
PSSH Brendan Shanahan 20.00 50.00
PSSI Darryl Sittler 15.00 40.00
PSST Jordan Staal 15.00 40.00
PSSU Mats Sundin 15.00 40.00
PSVL Vincent Lecavalier 20.00 50.00
PSWG Wayne Gretzky 150.00 250.00

2007-08 Ultimate Collection Premium Swatches

PSAS Alexander Steen 5.00 12.00
PSBO Borje Salming 8.00 20.00
PSBS Billy Smith 8.00 20.00
PSBU Johnny Bucyk 8.00 20.00
PSCJ Jonathan Cheechoo 6.00 15.00
PSCN Cam Neely 8.00 20.00
PSCP Chris Pronger 8.00 20.00
PSDA Daniel Alfredsson 8.00 20.00
PSDC Dino Ciccarelli 8.00 20.00
PSDG Doug Gilmour 10.00 25.00
PSDH Dale Hawerchuk
PSDS Denis Savard 8.00 20.00
PSEL Patrik Elias 8.00 20.00
PSGF Grant Fuhr 12.00 30.00
PSGP Gilbert Perreault 8.00 20.00
PSHE Dany Heatley 6.00 15.00
PSHL Henrik Lundqvist 20.00 50.00
PSHZ Henrik Zetterberg 10.00 25.00
PSIK Ilya Kovalchuk 8.00 20.00
PSJB Jean Beliveau 10.00 25.00
PSJG Jean-Sebastien Giguere 8.00 20.00
PSJI Jarome Iginla 12.00 30.00
PSJJ Jaromir Jagr 25.00 60.00
PSJM Joe Mullen 6.00 15.00
PSJO Joe Sakic 15.00 40.00
PSJS Jason Spezza 8.00 20.00
PSJT Joe Thornton 12.00 30.00
PSLM Lanny McDonald 8.00 20.00
PSMA Al MacInnis 10.00 25.00
PSMB Martin Brodeur 15.00 40.00
PSMG Marian Gaborik 8.00 20.00
PSMH Marian Hossa 8.00 20.00
PSML Mario Lemieux 15.00 40.00
PSMM Mike Modano 12.00 30.00
PSMN Markus Naslund 8.00 20.00
PSMS Martin St. Louis 8.00 20.00
PSMT Marty Turco 8.00 20.00
PSNL Nicklas Lidstrom 8.00 20.00
PSOV Alexander Ovechkin 30.00 60.00
PSPB Patrice Bergeron 10.00 25.00
PSPD Pavel Datsyuk 12.00 30.00
PSPK Paul Kariya 8.00 20.00
PSPM Patrick Marleau 8.00 20.00
PSPR Patrick Roy 20.00 50.00
PSPS Peter Stastny 6.00 15.00
PSRB Ray Bourque 12.00 30.00
PSRH Ron Hextall 8.00 20.00
PSRL Roberto Luongo 12.00 30.00
PSRM Ryan Miller 8.00 20.00
PSRN Rick Nash 8.00 20.00
PSRY Michael Ryder 5.00 12.00
PSSC Sidney Crosby 30.00 60.00
PSSG Simon Gagne
PSSH Brendan Shanahan 8.00 20.00
PSSI Darryl Sittler 10.00 25.00
PSSK Saku Koivu 8.00 20.00
PSST Jordan Staal 6.00 15.00
PSSU Mats Sundin 8.00 20.00
PSVL Vincent Lecavalier 8.00 20.00
PSWG Wayne Gretzky 40.00 80.00

2007-08 Ultimate Collection Rookies Autographed Patches

121 Bobby Ryan 30.00 80.00
122 Sam Gagner 25.00 60.00
123 Nicklas Bergfors 12.00 30.00
124 Erik Johnson 20.00 50.00
125 Jack Johnson 15.00 40.00
126 Jonathan Bernier 50.00 125.00

127 Bryan Little 15.00 40.00
128 Tuukka Rask 50.00 125.00
129 Matt Niskanen 20.00 50.00
130 Andrew Cogliano 15.00 40.00
131 Marc Staal 20.00 50.00
132 Nick Foligno 25.00 60.00
133 Brett Sterling 12.00 30.00
134 Martin Hanzal 15.00 40.00
135 Matt Smaby 12.00 30.00
136 Petr Kalus 12.00 30.00
137 Andy Greene 15.00 40.00
138 Ondrej Pavelec 25.00 60.00
139 Rob Schremp 15.00 40.00
140 Kyle Chipchura 20.00 50.00
141 Ryan Parent 12.00 30.00
142 David Krejci 40.00 100.00
143 Lauri Tukonen 12.00 30.00
144 James Sheppard 12.00 30.00
145 Mason Raymond 20.00 50.00
146 Devin Setoguchi 20.00 50.00
147 Curtis McElhinney 20.00 50.00
148 Brian Elliott 25.00 60.00
149 Drew Miller 15.00 40.00
150 Ryan Callahan 25.00 60.00
151 Ville Koistinen 12.00 30.00
152 Torrey Mitchell 15.00 40.00
153 David Perron 25.00 60.00
154 Milan Lucic 60.00 150.00
155 Jaroslav Hlinka 15.00 40.00
156 Tyler Weiman 15.00 40.00
157 Jonathan Toews 120.00 300.00
158 Carey Price 150.00 400.00
159 Patrick Kane 200.00 500.00
160 Nicklas Backstrom 50.00 125.00
161 Peter Mueller 30.00 80.00
162 Jiri Tlusty 20.00 50.00

2007-08 Ultimate Collection Signatures

USAC Andrew Cogliano 5.00 12.00
USAO Alexander Ovechkin 25.00 60.00
USAT Alex Tanguay 5.00 12.00
USBO Bobby Orr 25.00 60.00
USBP Bernie Parent 8.00 20.00
USCP Carey Price 25.00 60.00
USEM Evgeni Malkin 12.00 30.00
USES Eric Staal 8.00 20.00
USGF Grant Fuhr 10.00 25.00
USGH Gordie Howe 20.00 50.00
USIK Ilya Kovalchuk 6.00 15.00
USJG Jean-Sebastien Giguere 6.00 15.00
USJJ Jack Johnson 5.00 12.00
USJK Jari Kurri 6.00 15.00
USJM Joe Mullen 5.00 12.00
USJS James Sheppard 4.00 10.00
USJT Joe Thornton 10.00 25.00
USLM Lanny McDonald 6.00 15.00
USMA Martin St. Louis 6.00 15.00
USMB Martin Brodeur 15.00 40.00
USMF Marc-Andre Fleury 12.00 30.00
USMG Marian Gaborik 6.00 15.00
USML Mario Lemieux 25.00 60.00
USMM Mark Messier 12.00 30.00
USMN Markus Naslund 6.00 15.00
USMR Michael Ryder 4.00 10.00
USMS Marc Staal 6.00 15.00
USNB Nicklas Backstrom 12.00 30.00
USNF Nick Foligno 8.00 20.00
USNL Nicklas Lidstrom 6.00 15.00
USPE Corey Perry 10.00 25.00
USPK Patrick Kane 150.00 400.00
USPM Peter Mueller 5.00 12.00
USPR Patrick Roy 15.00 40.00
USPS Paul Stastny 5.00 12.00
USRB Ray Bourque 10.00 25.00
USRH Ron Hextall 6.00 15.00
USRM Ryan Miller 6.00 15.00
USRN Rick Nash 6.00 15.00
USSC Sidney Crosby 25.00 60.00
USSG Sam Gagner 8.00 20.00
USST Jordan Staal 5.00 12.00
USTO Jonathan Toews 25.00 60.00
USTV Tomas Vokoun 5.00 12.00
USVL Vincent Lecavalier 6.00 15.00
USWG Wayne Gretzky 250.00 600.00

2007-08 Ultimate Collection Ultimate Debut Threads Jerseys

DTAC Andrew Cogliano 5.00 12.00
DTAG Andy Greene 5.00 12.00
DTBA Nicklas Backstrom 8.00 20.00
DTBD Brandon Dubinsky 8.00 20.00
DTBE Brian Elliott 8.00 20.00
DTBL Bryan Little 4.00 10.00
DTBR Bobby Ryan 10.00 25.00
DTBS Brett Sterling 4.00 10.00
DTCM Curtis McElhinney 6.00 15.00
DTCP Carey Price 25.00 60.00
DTDK David Krejci 8.00 20.00
DTDP David Perron 8.00 20.00
DTEJ Erik Johnson 6.00 15.00
DTFN Frans Nielsen 6.00 15.00
DTHA Jannik Hansen 5.00 12.00
DTJB Jonathan Bernier 8.00 20.00
DTJH Jaroslav Hlinka 5.00 12.00
DTJJ Jack Johnson 5.00 12.00
DTJS James Sheppard 4.00 10.00
DTJT Jonathan Toews 20.00 50.00
DTKC Kyle Chipchura 6.00 15.00
DTKR Kris Russell 6.00 15.00
DTMH Martin Hanzal 5.00 12.00
DTML Milan Lucic 15.00 40.00
DTMN Matt Niskanen 6.00 15.00
DTMR Mason Raymond 6.00 15.00
DTMS Marc Staal 6.00 15.00
DTNB Nicklas Bergfors 4.00 10.00
DTNF Nick Foligno 8.00 20.00
DTPK Patrick Kane 15.00 40.00
DTPM Peter Mueller 5.00 12.00
DTRC Ryan Callahan 8.00 20.00
DTRP Ryan Parent 4.00 10.00
DTRS Rob Schremp 6.00 15.00
DTSG Sam Gagner 6.00 15.00
DTSM Matt Smaby 4.00 10.00
DTTM Torrey Mitchell 5.00 12.00
DTTS Tobias Stephan 5.00 12.00
DTTW Tyler Weiman 5.00 12.00

2007-08 Ultimate Collection Ultimate Debut Threads Jerseys Autographs

DTAC Andrew Cogliano 10.00 25.00
DTAG Andy Greene 10.00 25.00
DTBA Nicklas Backstrom 40.00 80.00
DTBD Brandon Dubinsky 15.00 40.00
DTBE Brian Elliott 15.00 40.00
DTBL Bryan Little 10.00 25.00
DTBR Bobby Ryan 20.00 50.00
DTBS Brett Sterling 8.00 20.00
DTCM Curtis McElhinney 12.00 30.00
DTCP Carey Price 75.00 150.00
DTDK David Krejci 25.00 60.00
DTDP David Perron 15.00 40.00
DTEJ Erik Johnson 12.00 30.00
DTFN Frans Nielsen 12.00 30.00
DTHA Jannik Hansen 10.00 25.00
DTJB Jonathan Bernier 40.00 80.00
DTJH Jaroslav Hlinka 10.00 25.00
DTJJ Jack Johnson 30.00 60.00
DTJS James Sheppard 8.00 20.00
DTJT Jonathan Toews 75.00 150.00
DTKC Kyle Chipchura 12.00 30.00
DTLT Lauri Tukonen 8.00 20.00
DTMH Martin Hanzal 10.00 25.00
DTML Milan Lucic 30.00 80.00
DTMN Matt Niskanen 12.00 30.00
DTMR Mason Raymond 12.00 30.00
DTMS Marc Staal 12.00 30.00
DTNB Nicklas Bergfors
DTNF Nick Foligno 15.00 40.00
DTPK Patrick Kane 75.00 150.00
DTPM Peter Mueller 15.00 40.00
DTRC Ryan Callahan 15.00 40.00
DTRP Ryan Parent 8.00 20.00
DTRS Rob Schremp 10.00 25.00
DTSG Sam Gagner 30.00 60.00
DTSM Matt Smaby 8.00 20.00
DTTM Torrey Mitchell
DTTS Tobias Stephan 10.00 25.00
DTTW Tyler Weiman 10.00 25.00

2007-08 Ultimate Collection Ultimate Debut Threads Patches

DTAC Andrew Cogliano 12.00 30.00
DTAG Andy Greene 12.00 30.00
DTBA Nicklas Backstrom 40.00 80.00
DTBD Brandon Dubinsky 20.00 50.00
DTBE Brian Elliott 20.00 50.00
DTBL Bryan Little 8.00 20.00
DTBR Bobby Ryan 25.00 60.00
DTBS Brett Sterling 10.00 25.00
DTCM Curtis McElhinney 15.00 40.00
DTCP Carey Price 80.00 200.00
DTDK David Krejci 20.00 50.00
DTDM Drew Miller 12.00 30.00
DTDP David Perron 20.00 50.00
DTEJ Erik Johnson 12.00 30.00
DTFN Frans Nielsen 15.00 40.00
DTHA Jannik Hansen 12.00 30.00
DTJB Jonathan Bernier 20.00 50.00
DTJH Jaroslav Hlinka 12.00 30.00
DTJJ Jack Johnson 12.00 30.00
DTJS James Sheppard 10.00 25.00
DTJT Jonathan Toews 100.00 200.00
DTKA Petr Kalus 10.00 25.00
DTKC Kyle Chipchura 15.00 40.00
DTKR Kris Russell 15.00 40.00
DTLT Lauri Tukonen 10.00 25.00
DTMH Martin Hanzal 12.00 30.00
DTML Milan Lucic 40.00 80.00
DTMN Matt Niskanen 15.00 40.00
DTMR Mason Raymond 15.00 40.00
DTMS Marc Staal 15.00 40.00
DTNB Nicklas Bergfors 10.00 25.00
DTNF Nick Foligno 20.00 60.00
DTPK Patrick Kane 60.00 150.00
DTPM Peter Mueller 12.00 30.00
DTRC Ryan Callahan 20.00 50.00
DTRP Ryan Parent 10.00 25.00
DTRS Rob Schremp 12.00 30.00
DTSG Sam Gagner 20.00 50.00
DTSM Matt Smaby 10.00 25.00
DTTM Torrey Mitchell 40.00 80.00
DTTS Tobias Stephan 12.00 30.00
DTTW Tyler Weiman 20.00 50.00

2008-09 Ultimate Collection

COMP.SET w/o SPs (42) 100.00 200.00
1 Ilya Kovalchuk 1.50 4.00
2 Bobby Orr 6.00 15.00
3 Thomas Vanek 1.25 3.00
4 Jarome Iginla 2.00 5.00
5 Miikka Kiprusoff 1.50 4.00
6 Eric Staal 2.00 5.00
7 Patrick Kane 3.00 8.00
8 Jonathan Toews 2.50 6.00
9 Joe Sakic 3.00 8.00
10 Paul Stastny 1.25 3.00
11 Rick Nash 1.50 4.00
12 Mike Modano 2.50 6.00
13 Henrik Zetterberg 2.00 5.00
14 Wayne Gretzky 10.00 25.00
15 Mark Messier 3.00 8.00
16 Ray Bourque 2.50 6.00
17 Gordie Howe 5.00 12.00
18 Marian Gaborik 1.50 4.00
19 Carey Price 3.00 8.00
20 Saku Koivu 1.50 4.00
21 Patrick Roy 4.00 10.00
22 Martin Brodeur 4.00 10.00
23 Rick DiPietro 1.25 3.00
24 Markus Naslund 1.50 4.00
25 Henrik Lundqvist 4.00 10.00
26 Dany Heatley 1.25 3.00
27 Jason Spezza 1.50 4.00
28 Mike Richards 1.25 3.00
29 Shane Doan 1.25 3.00
30 Peter Mueller 1.25 3.00
31 Mario Lemieux 6.00 15.00
32 Sidney Crosby 6.00 15.00
33 Marc-Andre Fleury 3.00 8.00
34 Evgeni Malkin 3.00 8.00
35 Joe Thornton 2.50 6.00
36 Paul Kariya 1.50 4.00
37 Vincent Lecavalier 1.50 4.00
38 Martin St. Louis 1.50 4.00
39 Vesa Toskala 2.00 5.00
40 Pavel Datsyuk 2.50 6.00
41 Roberto Luongo 2.50 6.00
42 Alexander Ovechkin 6.00 15.00
43 Max Pacioretty RC 6.00 15.00
44 Justin Pogge RC 2.50 6.00
45 Tim Kennedy RC 3.00 8.00
46 Ben Bishop RC 5.00 12.00
47 Michal Repik RC 3.00 8.00
48 Brian Boyle RC 2.50 6.00
49 Brian Lee RC 2.50 6.00
50 John Curry RC 3.00 8.00
51 Ben Maxwell RC 3.00 8.00
52 Jamie McGinn RC 3.00 8.00
53 Jonas Frogren RC 2.00 5.00
54 Brendan Mikkelson RC 2.00 5.00
55 Ty Wishart RC 2.50 6.00
56 Mark Fistric RC 2.50 6.00
57 Matt D'Agostini RC 2.50 6.00
58 Trevor Lewis RC 3.00 8.00
59 Simeon Varlamov RC 15.00 40.00
60 Wayne Simmonds RC 5.00 12.00
61 Adam Pineault AU RC 5.00 12.00
62 Alex Goligoski AU RC 8.00 20.00
63 Alex Pietrangelo AU RC 10.00 25.00
64 Chris Stewart AU RC 6.00 15.00
65 Brandon Sutter AU RC 6.00 15.00
66 Claude Giroux AU RC 30.00 60.00
67 Colton Gillies AU RC 5.00 12.00
68 Darren Helm AU RC 10.00 25.00
69 Derick Brassard AU RC 6.00 15.00
70 Drew Doughty AU RC 25.00 50.00
71 Kenndal McArdle AU RC 5.00 12.00
72 Josh Bailey AU RC 8.00 20.00
73 James Neal AU RC 12.00 30.00
74 Justin Abdelkader AU RC 10.00 25.00
75 Nathan Gerbe AU RC 6.00 15.00
76 Kyle Okposo AU RC 8.00 20.00
77 Luca Sbisa AU RC 4.00 10.00
78 Luke Schenn AU RC 8.00 20.00
79 Mattias Ritola AU RC 5.00 12.00
80 Michael Frolik AU RC 6.00 15.00
81 Mikkel Boedker AU RC 8.00 20.00
82 Cory Schneider AU RC 15.00 40.00
83 Nikolai Kulemin AU RC 6.00 15.00
84 Oscar Moller AU RC 5.00 12.00
85 Patric Hornqvist AU RC 6.00 15.00
86 Patrik Berglund AU RC 5.00 12.00
87 Petr Vrana AU RC 4.00 10.00
88 Robbie Earl AU RC 4.00 10.00
89 Karl Alzner AU RC 4.00 10.00
90 Shawn Matthias AU RC 6.00 15.00
91 Steve Mason AU RC 15.00 40.00
92 T.J. Oshie AU RC 20.00 50.00
93 Viktor Tikhonov AU RC 5.00 12.00
94 Vladimir Mihalik AU RC 4.00 10.00
95 Zach Bogosian AU RC 8.00 20.00
96 Zach Boychuk AU RC 6.00 15.00
97 Nikita Filatov AU RC/99 12.00 30.00
98 Jakub Voracek AU RC/99 25.00 60.00
99 Brunstrm AU RC/51* blu ink 10.00 25.00
99B Brunstrm AU RC/48* blk ink 10.00 25.00
100 Blake Wheeler AU RC/99 25.00 50.00
101 Kyle Turris AU RC/99 30.00 80.00
102 Steven Stamkos AU RC/99 150.00 400.00

2008-09 Ultimate Collection Debut Threads

*PATCH/50: .8X TO 2X BASIC JSY/200
DTAG Alex Goligoski 5.00 12.00
DTAN Andreas Nodl 2.50 6.00
DTAP Adam Pineault 3.00 8.00
DTBB Brian Boyle 3.00 8.00
DTBO Zach Boychuk 4.00 10.00
DTBP Ben Bishop 5.00 12.00
DTBS Brandon Sutter 4.00 10.00
DTBW Blake Wheeler 10.00 25.00
DTCG Colton Gillies 3.00 8.00
DTDB Derick Brassard 4.00 10.00
DTDD Drew Doughty 10.00 25.00
DTDH Darren Helm 4.00 10.00
DTEE Erik Ersberg 3.00 8.00
DTFB Fabian Brunnstrom 3.00 8.00
DTFR Michael Frolik 4.00 10.00
DTGI Claude Giroux 10.00 25.00
DTIZ Ilya Zubov 3.00 8.00
DTJA Justin Abdelkader 6.00 15.00
DTJE Jonathan Ericsson 4.00 10.00
DTJN James Neal 5.00 12.00
DTJV Jakub Voracek 5.00 12.00
DTKO Kyle Okposo 5.00 12.00
DTKP Kevin Porter 3.00 8.00
DTKT Kyle Turris 6.00 15.00
DTLK Lauri Korpikoski 2.50 6.00
DTLS Luca Sbisa 2.50 6.00
DTMA Shawn Matthias 4.00 10.00
DTMB Mikkel Boedker 5.00 12.00
DTMD Matt D'Agostini 3.00 8.00
DTMF Mark Fistric 3.00 8.00
DTMR Mattias Ritola 3.00 8.00
DTNF Nikita Filatov 4.00 10.00
DTNK Nikolai Kulemin 4.00 10.00
DTNO Nathan Oystrick 4.00 10.00
DTOM Oscar Moller 3.00 8.00
DTPB Patrik Berglund 3.00 8.00
DTPH Patric Hornqvist 4.00 10.00
DTPI Alex Pietrangelo 6.00 15.00
DTPV Petr Vrana 2.50 6.00
DTRE Robbie Earl 2.50 6.00
DTRJ Ryan Jones 4.00 10.00
DTRS Ryan Stone 2.50 6.00
DTSC Luke Schenn 5.00 12.00
DTSM Steve Mason 6.00 15.00
DTSS Steven Stamkos 12.00 30.00
DTTO T.J. Oshie 8.00 20.00
DTTS Tom Sestito 4.00 10.00
DTVM Vladimir Mihalik 2.50 6.00
DTVT Viktor Tikhonov 3.00 8.00
DTZB Zach Bogosian 5.00 12.00

2008-09 Ultimate Collection Debut Threads Autographs

SDTAG Alex Goligoski 12.00 30.00
SDTAN Andreas Nodl 6.00 15.00
SDTAP Adam Pineault 8.00 20.00
SDTBB Brian Boyle 8.00 20.00
SDTBO Zach Boychuk 10.00 25.00
SDTBP Ben Bishop 15.00 40.00
SDTBS Brandon Sutter 10.00 25.00
SDTBW Blake Wheeler 25.00 60.00
SDTCG Colton Gillies 8.00 20.00
SDTDB Derick Brassard 10.00 25.00
SDTDD Drew Doughty 25.00 60.00
SDTDH Darren Helm 10.00 25.00
SDTEE Erik Ersberg 8.00 20.00
SDTFB Fabian Brunnstrom 8.00 20.00
SDTFR Michael Frolik 10.00 25.00
SDTGI Claude Giroux 20.00 50.00
SDTIZ Ilya Zubov 8.00 20.00
SDTJA Justin Abdelkader 15.00 40.00
SDTJE Jonathan Ericsson 10.00 25.00
SDTJN James Neal 20.00 50.00
SDTJV Jakub Voracek 20.00 50.00
SDTKO Kyle Okposo 12.00 30.00
SDTKP Kevin Porter 8.00 20.00
SDTKT Kyle Turris 15.00 40.00
SDTLK Lauri Korpikoski 6.00 15.00
SDTLS Luca Sbisa 6.00 15.00
SDTMA Shawn Matthias 10.00 25.00
SDTMB Mikkel Boedker 12.00 30.00
SDTMD Matt D'Agostini 8.00 20.00
SDTMF Mark Fistric 8.00 20.00
SDTMR Mattias Ritola 8.00 20.00
SDTNF Nikita Filatov 10.00 25.00
SDTNK Nikolai Kulemin 10.00 25.00
SDTNO Nathan Oystrick 10.00 25.00
SDTOM Oscar Moller 8.00 20.00
SDTPB Patrik Berglund 8.00 20.00
SDTPH Patric Hornqvist 10.00 25.00
SDTPI Alex Pietrangelo 15.00 40.00
SDTPV Petr Vrana 6.00 15.00
SDTRE Robbie Earl 6.00 15.00
SDTRJ Ryan Jones 10.00 25.00
SDTRS Ryan Stone 6.00 15.00
SDTSC Luke Schenn 12.00 30.00
SDTSM Steve Mason 15.00 40.00
SDTSS Steven Stamkos 40.00 100.00
SDTTO T.J. Oshie 20.00 50.00
SDTTS Tom Sestito 10.00 25.00
SDTVM Vladimir Mihalik 6.00 15.00
SDTVT Viktor Tikhonov 8.00 20.00
SDTZB Zach Bogosian 12.00 30.00

2008-09 Ultimate Collection Premium Patches

PSAO Alexander Ovechkin 30.00 80.00
PSCP Carey Price 15.00 40.00
PSDH Dale Hawerchuk 10.00 25.00
PSDP Dion Phaneuf 6.00 15.00
PSEM Evgeni Malkin 15.00 40.00
PSHZ Henrik Zetterberg 10.00 25.00
PSIK Ilya Kovalchuk 8.00 20.00
PSJC Jonathan Cheechoo 6.00 15.00
PSJI Jarome Iginla 10.00 25.00
PSJS Joe Sakic 15.00 40.00
PSJT Joe Thornton 12.00 30.00
PSKO Anze Kopitar 12.00 30.00
PSLM Lanny McDonald 8.00 20.00
PSMB Martin Brodeur 20.00 50.00
PSMG Marian Gaborik 8.00 20.00
PSMM Mike Modano 12.00 30.00
PSMR Mike Richards 6.00 15.00
PSMS Marc Savard 5.00 12.00
PSNB Nicklas Backstrom 8.00 20.00
PSNL Nicklas Lidstrom 8.00 20.00
PSOJ Olli Jokinen 6.00 15.00
PSPB Patrice Bergeron 10.00 25.00
PSPD Pavel Datsyuk 12.00 30.00
PSPK Patrick Kane 15.00 40.00
PSPM Peter Mueller 6.00 15.00
PSPS Paul Stastny 6.00 15.00
PSRB Ray Bourque 12.00 30.00
PSRG Ryan Getzlaf 8.00 20.00
PSRM Ryan Miller 8.00 20.00
PSRN Rick Nash 8.00 20.00
PSSC Sidney Crosby 30.00 80.00
PSSD Shane Doan 6.00 15.00
PSSG Simon Gagne 8.00 20.00
PSSK Saku Koivu 8.00 20.00
PSSS Steve Shutt 8.00 20.00
PSSZ Jason Spezza 8.00 20.00
PSTO Jonathan Toews 12.00 30.00
PSTS Teemu Selanne 15.00 40.00
PSTV Thomas Vanek 6.00 15.00
PSVL Vincent Lecavalier 8.00 20.00

2008-09 Ultimate Collection Rookie Patch Autographs

121 Adam Pineault 12.00 30.00
122 Alex Goligoski 20.00 50.00
123 Alex Pietrangelo 25.00 60.00
124 Chris Stewart 20.00 50.00
125 Brandon Sutter
126 Claude Giroux 125.00 200.00
127 Colton Gillies 12.00 30.00
128 Darren Helm 15.00 40.00
129 Derick Brassard 15.00 40.00
130 Drew Doughty 50.00 125.00
131 Kenndal McArdle 12.00 30.00
132 Josh Bailey
133 James Neal 30.00 80.00
134 Justin Abdelkader 25.00 60.00
135 Nathan Gerbe 15.00 40.00
136 Kyle Okposo
137 Luca Sbisa 10.00 25.00
138 Luke Schenn 20.00 50.00
139 Mattias Ritola 12.00 30.00
140 Michael Frolik 15.00 40.00
141 Mikkel Boedker 20.00 50.00
142 Cory Schneider 40.00 100.00
143 Nikolai Kulemin 30.00 80.00
144 Oscar Moller 12.00 30.00
145 Patric Hornqvist 15.00 40.00
146 Patrik Berglund 12.00 30.00
147 Petr Vrana 10.00 25.00
148 Robbie Earl 10.00 25.00
150 Shawn Matthias 15.00 40.00
151 Steve Mason 40.00 100.00
152 T.J. Oshie 30.00 80.00
153 Viktor Tikhonov 12.00 30.00
154 Vladimir Mihalik 10.00 25.00
155 Zach Bogosian 20.00 50.00
156 Zach Boychuk 15.00 40.00
157 Nikita Filatov 15.00 40.00
158 Jakub Voracek 30.00 80.00
159 Fabian Brunnstrom 12.00 30.00
160 Blake Wheeler 40.00 80.00
161 Kyle Turris 25.00 60.00
162 Steven Stamkos 200.00 350.00

2008-09 Ultimate Collection Ultimate Jerseys

*PATCH/25: .6X TO 1.5X BASIC JSY/100
UJAO Alexander Ovechkin 12.00 30.00
UJCN Cam Neely 3.00 8.00
UJCP Carey Price 6.00 15.00
UJEM Evgeni Malkin 6.00 15.00
UJHL Henrik Lundqvist 8.00 20.00
UJHZ Henrik Zetterberg 4.00 10.00
UJIK Ilya Kovalchuk 3.00 8.00
UJJI Jarome Iginla 4.00 10.00
UJJS Joe Sakic 6.00 15.00
UJMB Martin Brodeur 8.00 20.00
UJME Mark Messier 6.00 15.00
UJML Mario Lemieux 12.00 30.00
UJPD Pavel Datsyuk 5.00 12.00
UJPR Patrick Roy 8.00 20.00
UJRB Ray Bourque 5.00 12.00
UJRL Roberto Luongo 5.00 12.00
UJRN Rick Nash 3.00 8.00
UJSC Sidney Crosby 12.00 30.00
UJVL Vincent Lecavalier 3.00 8.00
UJWG Wayne Gretzky 20.00 50.00

2008-09 Ultimate Collection Ultimate Jerseys Autographs

AJAK Anze Kopitar 12.00 30.00
AJAO Adam Oates 8.00 20.00
AJBL Brian Leetch 6.00 15.00
AJBR Martin Brodeur/25 20.00 50.00
AJCN Cam Neely/25 8.00 20.00
AJCP Carey Price 15.00 40.00
AJDH Dale Hawerchuk 10.00 25.00
AJEM Evgeni Malkin/25 15.00 40.00
AJES Eric Staal 10.00 25.00
AJGF Grant Fuhr/25 12.00 30.00
AJGP Gilbert Perreault 8.00 20.00
AJHO Marian Hossa 8.00 20.00
AJHZ Henrik Zetterberg/25 10.00 25.00
AJIK Ilya Kovalchuk/25 8.00 20.00
AJJI Jarome Iginla/25 10.00 25.00
AJJS Jordan Staal 6.00 15.00
AJJT Joe Thornton/25 12.00 30.00
AJLR Larry Robinson 8.00 20.00
AJMF Marc-Andre Fleury 15.00 40.00
AJML Mario Lemieux/25 40.00 100.00
AJMM Mark Messier/25 15.00 40.00
AJMO Mike Modano 12.00 30.00
AJMT Marty Turco 8.00 20.00
AJNL Nicklas Lidstrom 8.00 20.00
AJPB Patrice Bergeron 10.00 25.00
AJPK Patrick Kane 15.00 40.00
AJPR Patrick Roy/25 30.00 80.00
AJRG Ryan Getzlaf 8.00 20.00
AJRN Rick Nash 8.00 20.00
AJSC Sidney Crosby/25 200.00 400.00
AJSG Sam Gagner 5.00 12.00
AJVL Vincent Lecavalier 8.00 20.00
AJWG Wayne Gretzky/25 300.00 800.00

2008-09 Ultimate Collection Ultimate Jerseys Duos

UJ2HD Datsyuk/Zetterberg 5.00 12.00
UJ2IK Iginla/Kiprusoff 4.00 10.00
UJ2KM Kovalchuk/Malkin 6.00 15.00
UJ2LM Lemieux/Malkin 12.00 30.00
UJ2LN Lundqvist/Naslund 8.00 20.00
UJ2LZ Lidstrom/Zetterberg 4.00 10.00
UJ2MT Turco/Modano 5.00 12.00
UJ2OB Ovechkin/Backstrom 12.00 30.00
UJ2RB Roy/Brodeur 8.00 20.00

2008-09 Ultimate Collection Ultimate Jerseys Duos Autographs

2UJBN Bourque/Neely/20 25.00 60.00
2UJDM Doan/Mueller/20 12.00 30.00
2UJHM Hasek/Miller/20 25.00 60.00
2UJMF Malkin/Fleury/20 30.00 80.00
2UJMK Malkin/Kovalchuk/20 30.00 80.00
2UJSS Pa.Stastny/Pe.Stastny/20 12.00 30.00
2UJTB Toews/Backstrom/20 25.00 60.00
2UJZD Zetterberg/Datsyuk/20 25.00 60.00

2008-09 Ultimate Collection Ultimate Jerseys Trios

UJ3FWD Lecav/Thornton/Iginla 12.00 30.00
UJ3HOF Gretzky/Messier/Lemieux 50.00 125.00
UJ3NET Roy/Brodeur/Price 15.00 40.00
UJ3RSN Malkin/Koval/Ovech 30.00 80.00
UJ3SWD Zett/Lids/Lundq 20.00 50.00

2008-09 Ultimate Collection Ultimate Patches Autographs

AJAK Anze Kopitar 30.00 80.00
AJBL Brian Leetch 40.00 80.00
AJCP Carey Price 50.00 100.00
AJDH Dale Hawerchuk 15.00 40.00
AJES Eric Staal 25.00 60.00
AJGF Grant Fuhr 25.00 60.00
AJGP Gilbert Perreault
AJHO Marian Hossa 20.00 50.00
AJJS Jordan Staal 15.00 40.00
AJLR Larry Robinson
AJMF Marc-Andre Fleury 40.00 100.00
AJMO Mike Modano
AJNL Nicklas Lidstrom 40.00 80.00
AJPB Patrice Bergeron
AJPK Patrick Kane 40.00 100.00
AJSG Sam Gagner
AJVL Vincent Lecavalier 20.00 50.00

2008-09 Ultimate Collection Ultimate Patches Duos

UJ2HD Datsyuk/Zetterberg 25.00 60.00
UJ2IK Iginla/Kiprusoff 30.00 80.00
UJ2KM Kovalchuk/Malkin 30.00 80.00
UJ2LM Lemieux/Malkin 60.00 150.00
UJ2LN Lundqvist/Naslund
UJ2LZ Lidstrom/Zetterberg 20.00 50.00
UJ2MT Turco/Modano 25.00 60.00
UJ2OB Ovechkin/Backstrom
UJ2RB Roy/Brodeur 40.00 100.00

2008-09 Ultimate Collection Ultimate Signatures

USBK Mikkel Boedker 8.00 20.00
USBL Brian Leetch 5.00 12.00
USBO Bobby Orr 60.00 120.00
USBR Martin Brodeur 50.00 100.00
USBW Blake Wheeler 15.00 40.00
USCA Carey Price 12.00 30.00
USCG Claude Giroux 12.00 30.00
USDH Dany Heatley 5.00 12.00
USEM Evgeni Malkin 20.00 50.00
USES Eric Staal 8.00 20.00
USFB Fabian Brunnstrom 5.00 12.00
USGH Gordie Howe 50.00 100.00
USJI Jarome Iginla 8.00 20.00
USJM Joe Mullen 5.00 12.00
USJS Jordan Staal 5.00 12.00
USJV Jakub Voracek 10.00 25.00
USKT Kyle Turris 15.00 40.00
USLE Brian Lee 5.00 12.00
USMB Mike Bossy 10.00 25.00
USMG Marian Gaborik 6.00 15.00
USML Mario Lemieux 50.00 100.00
USMM Mark Messier 40.00 80.00
USMS Martin St. Louis 6.00 15.00
USNF Nikita Filatov 8.00 20.00
USNL Nicklas Lidstrom 12.00 30.00
USPK Patrick Kane 15.00 40.00
USPR Patrick Roy 60.00 120.00
USPS Paul Stastny 5.00 12.00
USRB Ray Bourque 15.00 40.00
USRH Ron Hextall 12.00 30.00
USSC Sidney Crosby 75.00 150.00
USSS Steven Stamkos 30.00 60.00
USTH Joe Thornton 10.00 25.00
USVL Vincent Lecavalier 10.00 25.00
USWG Wayne Gretzky 150.00 400.00

2009-10 Ultimate Collection

1 Alexander Ovechkin 6.00 15.00
2 Eric Staal 2.00 5.00
3 Marty Turco 1.50 4.00
4 Jarome Iginla 2.00 5.00
5 Martin St. Louis 1.50 4.00
6 Jonathan Toews 2.50 6.00
7 Thomas Vanek 1.25 3.00
8 Gordie Howe 5.00 12.00
9 Jeff Carter 1.25 3.00
10 Rick Nash 1.50 4.00
11 Jason Spezza 1.50 4.00
12 Carey Price 3.00 8.00
13 Devin Setoguchi 1.25 3.00
14 Tim Thomas 1.50 4.00
15 Paul Stastny 1.25 3.00
16 Mario Lemieux 6.00 15.00
17 Shea Weber 1.25 3.00
18 Zach Parise 1.50 4.00
19 Sam Gagner 1.00 2.50
20 Evgeni Malkin 3.00 8.00
21 Marian Gaborik 1.50 4.00
22 Henrik Zetterberg 2.00 5.00
23 Miikka Kiprusoff 1.50 4.00
24 Mark Messier 3.00 8.00
25 Zdeno Chara 1.50 4.00
26 Mike Richards 1.25 3.00
27 Luke Schenn 1.50 4.00
28 Ilya Kovalchuk 1.50 4.00
29 David Perron 1.25 3.00
30 Marc-Andre Fleury 3.00 8.00
31 Nicklas Lidstrom 1.00 2.50
32 Bobby Orr 6.00 15.00
33 Dany Heatley 1.25 3.00
34 Steven Stamkos 3.00 8.00
35 Roberto Luongo 2.50 6.00
36 Mike Modano 2.50 6.00
37 Bobby Ryan 1.25 3.00
38 Patrick Marleau 1.50 4.00
39 Patrick Roy 4.00 10.00
40 Cam Neely 1.50 4.00
41 Steve Mason 1.25 3.00
42 Vincent Lecavalier 1.50 4.00
43 Andrew Cogliano 1.00 2.50
44 Pavel Datsyuk 2.50 6.00
45 Ryan Miller 1.50 4.00
46 Wayne Gretzky 10.00 25.00
47 Saku Koivu 1.50 4.00
48 Patrick Kane 3.00 8.00
49 Henrik Lundqvist 4.00 10.00
50 Joe Thornton 2.50 6.00
51 Doug Gilmour 2.00 5.00
52 Teemu Selanne 3.00 8.00
53 Phil Kessel 1.50 4.00
54 Steve Yzerman 4.00 10.00
55 T.J. Oshie 1.50 4.00
56 Shane Doan 1.25 3.00
57 Martin Brodeur 4.00 10.00
58 Mike Bossy 1.50 4.00
59 Mikko Koivu 1.50 4.00
60 Sidney Crosby 6.00 15.00
101 Matt Beleskey AU RC 4.00 10.00
102 Sergei Shirokov AU RC 3.00 8.00
103 Logan Couture AU RC 15.00 40.00
104 Matt Gilroy AU RC 5.00 12.00
105 Mikael Backlund AU RC 8.00 20.00
106 Dmitry Kulikov AU RC 5.00 12.00
107 Christian Hanson AU RC 5.00 12.00
108 Kris Chucko AU RC 3.00 8.00
109 Perttu Lindgren AU RC 4.00 10.00
110 Artem Anisimov AU RC 3.00 8.00
111 Tyler Myers AU RC 10.00 25.00
112 Tyler Bozak AU RC 8.00 20.00
113 Yannick Weber AU RC 5.00 12.00
114 Viktor Stalberg AU RC 5.00 12.00
115 Ivan Vishnevskiy AU RC 3.00 8.00
116 Ryan O'Reilly AU RC 20.00 50.00
117 Brad Marchand AU RC 50.00 125.00
118 Cody Franson AU RC 5.00 12.00
119 Michael Del Zotto AU RC 5.00 12.00
120 Ville Leino AU RC 4.00 10.00
121 Jamie Benn AU RC 15.00 40.00
122 Antti Niemi AU RC 8.00 20.00
123 Devan Dubnyk AU RC 10.00 25.00
124 Erik Karlsson AU RC 30.00 60.00
125 Michael Grabner AU RC 12.00 30.00
126 Spencer Machacek AU RC 5.00 12.00
127 Colin Wilson AU RC 5.00 12.00
128 Jakub Kindl AU RC 5.00 12.00
129 Brian Salcido AU RC 3.00 8.00
130 Riku Helenius AU RC 5.00 12.00
131 Matt Pelech AU RC 5.00 12.00
131B Michal Neuvirth RC 5.00 12.00
132 Benn Ferriero AU RC 5.00 12.00
132B Mikko Lehtonen RC 5.00 12.00
133 Bobby Sanguinetti AU RC 3.00 8.00
133B Andrei Loktionov RC 4.00 10.00
134 Matthew Corrente AU RC 4.00 10.00
134B Colin McDonald RC 2.50 6.00
135 Alec Martinez AU RC 6.00 15.00
135B John Carlson RC 6.00 15.00
136 Lars Eller AU RC 5.00 12.00
136B MacGregor Sharp RC 3.00 8.00
137 Matt Duchene AU RC/99 60.00 120.00
137B Tyler Eckford RC 2.50 6.00
138 Victor Hedman AU RC/99 30.00 80.00
138B Daniel Larsson RC 2.50 6.00
139 John Tavares AU RC/99 200.00 350.00
139B Tyler Ennis RC 4.00 10.00
140 J.van Riemsdyk AU RC/99 75.00 150.00
140B Tom Pyatt RC 3.00 8.00
141 Evander Kane AU RC/99 30.00 80.00
141B Peter Olvecky RC 3.00 8.00
142 J.Gustavsson AU RC/99 20.00 50.00
142B Anton Khudobin RC 5.00 12.00
143 Steven Zalewski RC 2.50 6.00
144 T.J. Galiardi RC 3.00 8.00
145 John Negrin RC 3.00 8.00
146 Oskars Bartulis RC 3.00 8.00
147 Carl Gunnarsson RC 2.00 5.00
148 David Laliberte RC 2.50 6.00
149 Scott Parse RC 3.00 8.00
150 Andreas Thuresson RC 2.50 6.00
151 Dan Sexton RC 2.50 6.00
152 James Reimer RC 8.00 20.00
153 Ryan Vesce RC 2.50 6.00
154 James Wright RC 3.00 8.00
155 Mathieu Perreault RC 4.00 10.00
156 Phil Oreskovic RC 3.00 8.00
157 Ryan O'Marra RC 2.00 5.00
158 Vladimir Zharkov RC 3.00 8.00
159 Mario Bliznak RC 3.00 8.00
160 Alexander Salak RC 2.50 6.00
161 Chad Johnson RC 3.00 8.00
162 Danny Irmen RC 2.00 5.00
163 Jesse Joensuu RC 2.50 6.00
164 Ryan Wilson RC 3.00 8.00
165 Frazer McLaren RC 2.50 6.00
166 Mathieu Carle RC 3.00 8.00
167 Teemu Laakso RC 2.00 5.00
168 Braden Holtby RC 12.00 30.00
169 Mike Santorelli RC 3.00 8.00
170 Aaron Gagnon RC 2.00 5.00

2009-10 Ultimate Collection Debut Threads

UDTAA Artem Anisimov 2.00 5.00
UDTAN Antti Niemi 5.00 12.00
UDTBM Brad Marchand 12.00 30.00
UDTCA Luca Caputi 3.00 8.00
UDTCF Cody Franson 3.00 8.00
UDTCH Christian Hanson 3.00 8.00
UDTCW Colin Wilson 3.00 8.00
UDTDE Michael Del Zotto 3.00 8.00
UDTDK Dmitry Kulikov 3.00 8.00
UDTEK Evander Kane 6.00 15.00
UDTGR Michael Grabner 3.00 8.00
UDTIV Ivan Vishnevskiy 2.00 5.00
UDTJB Jamie Benn 10.00 25.00
UDTJE Jhonas Enroth 8.00 20.00
UDTJG Jonas Gustavsson 4.00 10.00
UDTJT John Tavares 12.00 30.00
UDTJV James van Riemsdyk 6.00 15.00
UDTKA Erik Karlsson 10.00 25.00
UDTLC Logan Couture 6.00 15.00
UDTMB Mikael Backlund 5.00 12.00
UDTMD Matt Duchene 6.00 15.00
UDTMG Matt Gilroy 3.00 8.00
UDTPL Perttu Lindgren 2.50 6.00
UDTSS Sergei Shirokov 2.00 5.00
UDTTB Tyler Bozak 5.00 12.00
UDTTM Tyler Myers 5.00 12.00
UDTVH Victor Hedman 8.00 20.00
UDTVL Ville Leino 2.50 6.00
UDTVS Viktor Stalberg 3.00 8.00
UDTYW Yannick Weber 3.00 8.00

2009-10 Ultimate Collection Debut Threads Autographs

SDTAA Artem Anisimov 5.00 12.00
SDTAN Antti Niemi 12.00 30.00
SDTCA Luca Caputi 8.00 20.00
SDTCF Cody Franson 8.00 20.00
SDTCH Christian Hanson 8.00 20.00
SDTCW Colin Wilson 8.00 20.00
SDTDE Michael Del Zotto 8.00 20.00
SDTDK Dmitry Kulikov 8.00 20.00
SDTEK Evander Kane 15.00 40.00
SDTGR Michael Grabner 8.00 20.00
SDTJB Jamie Benn 20.00 50.00
SDTJE Jhonas Enroth 10.00 25.00
SDTJG Jonas Gustavsson 10.00 25.00
SDTJT John Tavares 30.00 80.00
SDTJV James van Riemsdyk 15.00 40.00
SDTKA Erik Karlsson 40.00 80.00
SDTLC Logan Couture 15.00 40.00
SDTMB Mikael Backlund 12.00 30.00
SDTMD Matt Duchene 15.00 40.00
SDTMG Matt Gilroy 8.00 20.00
SDTTB Tyler Bozak 12.00 30.00
SDTTM Tyler Myers 12.00 30.00
SDTVL Ville Leino 6.00 15.00
SDTVS Viktor Stalberg 8.00 20.00
SDTYW Yannick Weber 8.00 20.00

2009-10 Ultimate Collection Debut Threads Patches

*SINGLES: 1X TO 2.5X THREADS
UDTAN Antti Niemi 15.00 40.00
UDTCA Luca Caputi 8.00 20.00

2009-10 Ultimate Collection Debut Threads Patches Autographs

SDTAA Artem Anisimov 30.00 60.00
SDTAN Antti Niemi 20.00 50.00
SDTCA Luca Caputi 12.00 30.00
SDTCF Cody Franson 15.00 40.00

SDTCH Christian Hanson 12.00 30.00
SDTCW Colin Wilson 12.00 30.00
SDTDE Michael Del Zotto 12.00 30.00
SDTDK Dmitry Kulikov 12.00 30.00
SDTEK Evander Kane 25.00 60.00
SDTGR Michael Grabner 50.00 100.00
SDTIV Ivan Vishnevskiy 10.00 25.00
SDTJB Jamie Benn 25.00 60.00
SDTJE Jhonas Enroth 15.00 40.00
SDTJG Jonas Gustavsson 50.00 100.00
SDTJT John Tavares 125.00 250.00
SDTJV James van Riemsdyk 25.00 60.00
SDTKA Erik Karlsson 60.00 120.00
SDTLC Logan Couture 40.00 80.00
SDTMB Mikael Backlund 25.00 60.00
SDTMD Matt Duchene 75.00 150.00
SDTMG Matt Gilroy 12.00 30.00
SDTTB Tyler Bozak 15.00 40.00
SDTTM Tyler Myers 75.00 150.00
SDTVL Ville Leino 25.00 60.00
SDTVS Viktor Stalberg 12.00 30.00
SDTYW Yannick Weber 12.00 30.00

2009-10 Ultimate Collection Premium Patches

PSAC Andrew Cogliano 8.00 20.00
PSAO Alexander Ovechkin 50.00 120.00
PSBC Brian Campbell 10.00 25.00
PSBS Borje Salming 12.00 30.00
PSCN Cam Neely 12.00 30.00
PSDB Derick Brassard 8.00 20.00
PSDD Drew Doughty 30.00 60.00
PSDH Dale Hawerchuk 15.00 40.00
PSDP Dion Phaneuf 10.00 25.00
PSEM Evgeni Malkin 25.00 60.00
PSGA Glenn Anderson 10.00 25.00
PSHZ Henrik Zetterberg 15.00 40.00
PSIK Ilya Kovalchuk 12.00 30.00
PSJB Jay Bouwmeester 8.00 20.00
PSJC Jeff Carter 10.00 25.00
PSJI Jarome Iginla 15.00 40.00
PSJS Jordan Staal 10.00 25.00
PSJT Jonathan Toews 20.00 50.00
PSJV Jakub Voracek 10.00 25.00
PSKA Patrick Kane 30.00 80.00
PSKI Miikka Kiprusoff 12.00 30.00
PSLM Lanny McDonald 12.00 30.00
PSMB Martin Brodeur 30.00 80.00
PSMG Marian Gaborik 12.00 30.00
PSMK Mikko Koivu 12.00 30.00
PSMM Mike Modano 20.00 50.00
PSMR Mike Richards 10.00 25.00
PSNB Nicklas Backstrom 12.00 30.00
PSNL Nicklas Lidstrom 8.00 20.00
PSOJ Olli Jokinen 10.00 25.00
PSPB Patrice Bergeron 15.00 40.00
PSPD Pavel Datsyuk 20.00 50.00
PSPK Phil Kessel 12.00 30.00
PSPS Peter Stastny 10.00 25.00
PSRL Roberto Luongo 20.00 50.00
PSRM Ryan Miller 12.00 30.00
PSRN Rick Nash 12.00 30.00
PSRS Ryan Smyth 10.00 25.00
PSSC Sidney Crosby 30.00 80.00
PSSD Shane Doan 10.00 25.00
PSSG Sam Gagner 8.00 20.00
PSSH Steve Shutt 12.00 30.00
PSSK Saku Koivu 12.00 30.00
PSSP Jason Spezza 12.00 30.00
PSSS Steven Stamkos 25.00 60.00
PSST Paul Stastny 10.00 25.00
PSSY Steve Yzerman 30.00 80.00
PSTH Joe Thornton 20.00 50.00
PSTV Tomas Vokoun 10.00 25.00
PSZP Zach Parise 12.00 30.00

2009-10 Ultimate Collection Premium Swatches

PSAO Alexander Ovechkin 25.00 60.00
PSCN Cam Neely 6.00 15.00
PSDB Derick Brassard 4.00 10.00
PSDD Drew Doughty 8.00 20.00
PSDG Doug Gilmour 8.00 20.00
PSDH Dale Hawerchuk 8.00 20.00
PSEM Evgeni Malkin 12.00 30.00
PSES Eric Staal 8.00 20.00
PSIK Ilya Kovalchuk 6.00 15.00
PSJC Jeff Carter 5.00 12.00
PSJV Jakub Voracek 5.00 12.00
PSKA Patrick Kane 15.00 40.00
PSKI Miikka Kiprusoff 6.00 15.00
PSLM Lanny McDonald 6.00 15.00
PSMB Martin Brodeur 15.00 40.00
PSMG Marian Gaborik 6.00 15.00
PSMM Mike Modano 10.00 25.00
PSMR Mike Richards 5.00 12.00
PSNB Nicklas Backstrom 6.00 15.00
PSNL Nicklas Lidstrom 4.00 10.00
PSPD Pavel Datsyuk 10.00 25.00
PSPK Phil Kessel 6.00 15.00
PSPS Peter Stastny 5.00 12.00
PSRL Roberto Luongo 10.00 25.00
PSRM Ryan Miller 6.00 15.00
PSRN Rick Nash 6.00 15.00
PSRS Ryan Smyth 5.00 12.00
PSSD Shane Doan 5.00 12.00
PSSG Sam Gagner 4.00 10.00
PSSH Steve Shutt 6.00 15.00
PSSK Saku Koivu 6.00 15.00
PSST Paul Stastny 5.00 12.00
PSSY Steve Yzerman 15.00 40.00
PSTV Tomas Vokoun 5.00 12.00
PSVL Vincent Lecavalier 6.00 15.00
PSWG Wayne Gretzky 40.00 100.00
PSZP Zach Parise 6.00 15.00

2009-10 Ultimate Collection Rookie Patch Autographs

101 Matt Beleskey 10.00 25.00
103 Logan Couture 25.00 60.00
104 Matt Gilroy 12.00 30.00
105 Mikael Backlund 20.00 50.00
106 Dmitry Kulikov 12.00 30.00
107 Christian Hanson 12.00 30.00
108 Kris Chucko 8.00 20.00
110 Artem Anisimov 8.00 20.00
111 Tyler Myers 20.00 50.00
112 Tyler Bozak 20.00 50.00
113 Yannick Weber 12.00 30.00
114 Viktor Stalberg 12.00 30.00
115 Ivan Vishnevskiy 8.00 20.00
117 Brad Marchand 100.00 250.00
118 Cody Franson 12.00 30.00
119 Michael Del Zotto 12.00 30.00
120 Ville Leino 10.00 25.00
121 Jamie Benn 30.00 80.00
122 Antti Niemi 30.00 80.00
123 Devan Dubnyk 20.00 50.00
124 Erik Karlsson 100.00 175.00
125 Michael Grabner 12.00 30.00
126 Spencer Machacek 12.00 30.00
127 Colin Wilson 12.00 30.00
128 Jakub Kindl 12.00 30.00
129 Brian Salcido 8.00 20.00
131 Matt Pelech 12.00 30.00
132 Benn Ferriero 12.00 30.00
133 Bobby Sanguinetti 8.00 20.00
134 Matthew Corrente 10.00 25.00
135 Alec Martinez 15.00 40.00
136 Lars Eller 12.00 30.00
137 Matt Duchene 25.00 60.00
138 Victor Hedman 100.00 250.00
139 John Tavares 150.00 300.00
140 James van Riemsdyk 25.00 60.00
141 Evander Kane 25.00 60.00
142 Jonas Gustavsson 15.00 40.00

2009-10 Ultimate Collection Ultimate Achievements

UAAO Alexander Ovechkin 40.00 100.00
UABO Bobby Orr 100.00 200.00
UACN Cam Neely 15.00 40.00
UAEM Evgeni Malkin 40.00 80.00
UAGH Gordie Howe 60.00 120.00
UAJB Jean Beliveau 40.00 80.00
UAJI Jarome Iginla 25.00 60.00
UAJT Jonathan Toews 40.00 80.00
UAMB Martin Brodeur 60.00 120.00
UAMI Mike Bossy 15.00 40.00
UAML Mario Lemieux 60.00 120.00
UAPD Pavel Datsyuk 20.00 50.00
UAPE Phil Esposito 15.00 40.00
UAPR Patrick Roy 50.00 100.00
UARH Ron Hextall 25.00 50.00
UASC Sidney Crosby 100.00 200.00
UASM Steve Mason 12.00 30.00
UASY Steve Yzerman 50.00 125.00
UAWG Wayne Gretzky 200.00 500.00

2009-10 Ultimate Collection Ultimate Jerseys

UJAO Alexander Ovechkin 10.00 25.00
UJBC Bobby Clarke 5.00 12.00
UJBL Brian Leetch 3.00 8.00
UJCN Cam Neely 4.00 10.00
UJCW Cam Ward 4.00 10.00
UJDG Doug Gilmour
UJDH Dany Heatley
UJEM Evgeni Malkin 8.00 20.00
UJES Eric Staal 5.00 12.00
UJGF Grant Fuhr 6.00 15.00
UJGH Gordie Howe 12.00 30.00
UJGP Gilbert Perreault 4.00 10.00
UJHA Dale Hawerchuk 5.00 12.00
UJIK Ilya Kovalchuk 4.00 10.00
UJJB Jean Beliveau 4.00 10.00
UJJC Jeff Carter
UJJK Jari Kurri 4.00 10.00
UJJT Jonathan Toews 6.00 15.00
UJLM Lanny McDonald 4.00 10.00
UJMB Martin Brodeur 10.00 25.00
UJMD Marcel Dionne 5.00 12.00
UJMG Marian Gaborik 4.00 10.00
UJMK Miikka Kiprusoff 4.00 10.00
UJMM Mike Modano 6.00 15.00
UJMR Mike Richards 3.00 8.00
UJMT Marty Turco 4.00 10.00
UJNB Nicklas Backstrom 4.00 10.00
UJPD Pavel Datsyuk 6.00 15.00
UJPE Phil Esposito 6.00 15.00
UJPK Patrick Kane 8.00 20.00
UJPR Patrick Roy 10.00 25.00
UJPS Peter Stastny 3.00 8.00
UJRB Ray Bourque 6.00 15.00
UJRL Roberto Luongo 6.00 15.00
UJRN Rick Nash 4.00 10.00
UJSA Borje Salming 4.00 10.00
UJSC Sidney Crosby 15.00 40.00
UJST Jordan Staal 3.00 8.00
UJSY Steve Yzerman 10.00 25.00
UJTE Tony Esposito 6.00 15.00
UJVL Vincent Lecavalier 4.00 10.00
UJWG Wayne Gretzky 25.00 60.00
UJZP Zach Parise 4.00 10.00

2009-10 Ultimate Collection Ultimate Jerseys Autographs

AJAO Alexander Ovechkin 40.00 100.00
AJBL Brian Leetch 10.00 25.00
AJCN Cam Neely 25.00 50.00
AJCP Carey Price 40.00 80.00
AJCW Cam Ward 12.00 30.00
AJEM Evgeni Malkin EXCH 25.00 60.00
AJGH Gordie Howe 75.00 150.00
AJGP Gilbert Perreault 12.00 30.00
AJHZ Henrik Zetterberg 20.00 50.00
AJJI Jarome Iginla 15.00 40.00
AJJK Jari Kurri 12.00 30.00
AJMB Martin Brodeur 50.00 100.00
AJPD Pavel Datsyuk 25.00 60.00
AJPK Patrick Kane 25.00 60.00
AJPR Patrick Roy 60.00 120.00
AJRB Ray Bourque 20.00 50.00
AJRN Rick Nash 12.00 30.00
AJSC Sidney Crosby 100.00 200.00
AJSY Steve Yzerman 75.00 150.00
AJTE Tony Esposito 40.00 80.00
AJTO Jonathan Toews 20.00 50.00
AJWG Wayne Gretzky 250.00 600.00

2009-10 Ultimate Collection Ultimate Jerseys Duos

UJ2AS Spezza/Alfredsson 8.00 20.00
UJ2BL Brodeur/Luongo 20.00 50.00
UJ2CO Ovechkin/Crosby 20.00 50.00
UJ2DP Dionne/Perreault 8.00 20.00
UJ2EE Esposito/Esposito 12.00 30.00
UJ2EH Emery/Hextall 8.00 20.00
UJ2FC Crosby/Fleury 15.00 40.00
UJ2GL Gaborik/Lundqvist 20.00 50.00
UJ2HN Nash/Heatley 8.00 20.00
UJ2HT Hossa/Toews 12.00 30.00
UJ2KA Anderson/Kurri 6.00 15.00
UJ2KO Kovalchuk/Ovechkin 20.00 50.00
UJ2LM Messier/Leetch 15.00 40.00
UJ2LT Lecavalier/Thornton 12.00 30.00
UJ2LY Lemieux/Yzerman 30.00 80.00
UJ2MP Modano/Parise 12.00 30.00
UJ2PK Parise/Kane 15.00 40.00
UJ2RB Brodeur/Roy 20.00 50.00
UJ2RD Robinson/Doughty 10.00 25.00
UJ2RH Robitaille/Hull 15.00 40.00
UJ2RP Roy/Price 20.00 50.00
UJ2SK Selanne/Koivu 15.00 40.00
UJ2SS Stastny/Stastny 6.00 15.00
UJ2YH Howe/Yzerman 25.00 60.00
UJ2ZB Backstrom/Zetterberg 10.00 25.00

2009-10 Ultimate Collection Ultimate Jerseys Trios

UJ3CRT Toews/Richrds/Crosby 30.00 80.00
UJ3DOM Malkin/Datsyuk/Ovech 40.00 100.00
UJ3ICO Ovech/Crosby/Iginla 40.00 100.00
UJ3LTS Lecav/Spezza/Thrntn 15.00 40.00
UJ3MPK Parise/Modano/Kane 20.00 50.00
UJ3RBL Roy/Brodeur/Luongo 25.00 60.00
UJ3YZH Zettrbrg/Howe/Yzermn 30.00 80.00

2009-10 Ultimate Collection Ultimate Nicknames

UNAO Alexander Ovechkin 75.00 150.00
UNBE Jean Beliveau 40.00 80.00
UNBH Bobby Hull 40.00 80.00
UNCN Cam Neely 25.00 60.00
UNDC Don Cherry 40.00 100.00
UNDG Doug Gilmour 25.00 60.00
UNDH Dale Hawerchuk 15.00 40.00
UNEM Evgeni Malkin 25.00 60.00
UNGH Gordie Howe 75.00 150.00
UNJB Johnny Bucyk 15.00 40.00
UNJI Jarome Iginla 25.00 50.00
UNJT Joe Thornton 20.00 50.00
UNLR Luc Robitaille 12.00 30.00
UNMD Marcel Dionne 15.00 40.00
UNMF Marc-Andre Fleury 20.00 50.00
UNML Mario Lemieux 50.00 100.00
UNPR Patrick Roy 60.00 120.00
UNSC Sidney Crosby 125.00 200.00
UNSY Steve Yzerman 100.00 175.00
UNTE Tony Esposito 25.00 50.00

2009-10 Ultimate Collection Ultimate Patches

UJAO Alexander Ovechkin 40.00 100.00
UJBH Bobby Hull 20.00 50.00
UJBL Brian Leetch 8.00 20.00
UJCW Cam Ward 10.00 25.00
UJDH Dany Heatley 8.00 20.00
UJEM Evgeni Malkin 20.00 50.00
UJHZ Henrik Zetterberg 12.00 30.00
UJIK Ilya Kovalchuk 10.00 25.00
UJJC Jeff Carter 8.00 20.00
UJJI Jarome Iginla 12.00 30.00
UJJK Jari Kurri 10.00 25.00
UJJS Jason Spezza 10.00 25.00
UJJT Jonathan Toews 15.00 40.00
UJKO Mikko Koivu 10.00 25.00
UJMB Martin Brodeur 25.00 60.00
UJME Mark Messier 20.00 50.00
UJMG Marian Gaborik 10.00 25.00
UJMK Miikka Kiprusoff 10.00 25.00
UJML Mario Lemieux 40.00 100.00
UJMM Mike Modano 15.00 40.00
UJMR Mike Richards 8.00 20.00
UJMS Martin St. Louis 10.00 25.00
UJMT Marty Turco 10.00 25.00
UJNB Nicklas Backstrom 10.00 25.00
UJPD Pavel Datsyuk 15.00 40.00
UJPE Phil Esposito 15.00 40.00
UJPK Patrick Kane 20.00 50.00
UJPR Patrick Roy 25.00 60.00
UJPS Peter Stastny 8.00 20.00
UJRB Ray Bourque 15.00 40.00
UJRL Roberto Luongo 10.00 25.00
UJRN Rick Nash 10.00 25.00
UJSA Borje Salming 10.00 25.00
UJSC Sidney Crosby 40.00 100.00
UJSN Scott Niedermayer 10.00 25.00
UJST Jordan Staal 8.00 20.00
UJSY Steve Yzerman 25.00 60.00
UJTH Joe Thornton 15.00 40.00
UJTS Teemu Selanne 12.00 30.00
UJWG Wayne Gretzky 50.00 100.00
UJZP Zach Parise 12.00 30.00

2009-10 Ultimate Collection Ultimate Patches Duos

UJ2AS Spezza/Alfredsson 15.00 40.00
UJ2BL Brodeur/Luongo 40.00 100.00
UJ2CO Ovechkin/Crosby 125.00 200.00
UJ2CR Clarke/Richards 40.00 80.00
UJ2EH Hextall/Emery 25.00 60.00
UJ2FC Crosby/Fleury 60.00 120.00
UJ2GL Gaborik/Lundqvist 20.00 50.00
UJ2HN Nash/Heatley 15.00 40.00
UJ2HT Hossa/Toews 25.00 60.00
UJ2IK Iginla/Kiprusoff 25.00 60.00
UJ2IS Iginla/St. Louis 20.00 50.00
UJ2KA Kurri/Anderson 12.00 30.00
UJ2KO Kovalchuk/Ovechkin 30.00 80.00
UJ2LG Gretzky/Lemieux 100.00 200.00
UJ2LM Messier/Leetch 30.00 80.00
UJ2LT Lecavalier/Thornton 25.00 60.00
UJ2LY Lemieux/Yzerman 60.00 120.00
UJ2MP Modano/Parise 25.00 60.00
UJ2PK Parise/Kane 30.00 80.00
UJ2RB Brodeur/Roy 40.00 100.00
UJ2RD Doughty/Robinson 20.00 50.00
UJ2RH Robitaille/Hull 30.00 80.00
UJ2SK Selanne/Koivu 20.00 50.00
UJ2SS Stastny/Stastny 12.00 30.00
UJ2ZB Backstrom/Zetterberg 40.00 100.00

2009-10 Ultimate Collection Ultimate Signatures

USAA Artem Anisimov 4.00 10.00
USAN Antti Niemi 10.00 25.00
USAO Alexander Ovechkin 30.00 80.00
USBH Bobby Hull 12.00 30.00
USBO Bobby Orr 60.00 120.00
USCF Cody Franson 6.00 15.00
USCP Carey Price 12.00 30.00
USCW Colin Wilson 8.00 20.00
USDE Michael Del Zotto 6.00 15.00
USDH Dany Heatley 11-12 4.00 10.00
USEK Evander Kane 10.00 25.00
USES Eric Staal 6.00 15.00
USGF Grant Fuhr 8.00 20.00
USGH Gordie Howe 90.00 150.00
USHL Henrik Lundqvist 15.00 30.00
USHZ Henrik Zetterberg 10.00 25.00
USJB Jamie Benn 12.00 30.00
USJC Jeff Carter 5.00 12.00
USJI Jarome Iginla 10.00 25.00
USJK Jari Kurri 6.00 15.00
USJT Jonathan Toews 25.00 50.00
USJV James van Riemsdyk 10.00 25.00
USKA Erik Karlsson 12.00 30.00
USMB Martin Brodeur 40.00 100.00
USMB Mikael Backlund 10.00 25.00
USMD Matt Duchene 12.00 30.00
USMF Marc-Andre Fleury 10.00 25.00
USMG Marian Gaborik 20.00 50.00
USMG Michael Grabner 6.00 15.00
USMI Mike Bossy 6.00 15.00
USML Mario Lemieux 50.00 100.00
USMO Mike Modano 8.00 20.00
USMR Mike Richards 11-12 5.00 12.00
USPD Pavel Datsyuk 20.00 50.00
USPE Phil Esposito 15.00 40.00
USPK Phil Kessel 6.00 15.00
USPR Patrick Roy 50.00 100.00
USRM Ryan Miller 8.00 20.00
USRN Rick Nash 6.00 15.00
USRY Bobby Ryan 5.00 12.00
USSC Sidney Crosby 75.00 135.00
USSM Steve Mason 8.00 20.00
USSS Steven Stamkos 30.00 80.00
USSY Steve Yzerman 50.00 100.00
USTA John Tavares 15.00 40.00
USTB Tyler Bozak 8.00 20.00
USTE Tony Esposito 10.00 25.00
USTH Joe Thornton 10.00 25.00
USTM Tyler Myers 10.00 25.00
USVH Victor Hedman 11-12 25.00 60.00
USVL Ville Leino 5.00 12.00
USVS Viktor Stalberg 6.00 15.00
USWG Wayne Gretzky

2010-11 Ultimate Collection

1 Teemu Selanne 3.00 8.00
2 Saku Koivu 1.50 4.00
3 Ryan Getzlaf 1.50 4.00
4 Cam Neely 1.50 4.00
5 Bobby Orr 6.00 15.00
6 Thomas Vanek 1.25 3.00
7 Ryan Miller 1.50 4.00
8 Jarome Iginla 2.00 5.00
9 Eric Staal 2.00 5.00
10 Jonathan Toews 2.50 6.00
11 Bobby Hull 3.00 8.00
12 Tony Esposito 1.50 4.00
13 Phil Esposito 2.50 6.00
14 Patrick Kane 3.00 8.00
15 Matt Duchene 1.50 4.00
16 Ray Bourque 2.50 6.00
17 Paul Stastny 1.25 3.00
18 Rick Nash 1.50 4.00
19 Ted Lindsay 1.50 4.00
20 Igor Larionov 1.50 4.00
21 Pavel Datsyuk 2.50 6.00
22 Terry Sawchuk 2.00 5.00
23 Nicklas Lidstrom 1.50 4.00
24 Wayne Gretzky 10.00 25.00
25 Jari Kurri 1.50 4.00
26 Grant Fuhr 2.50 6.00
27 Gordie Howe 5.00 12.00
28 Luc Robitaille 1.50 4.00
29 Anze Kopitar 2.50 6.00
30 Guy Lafleur 2.00 5.00
31 Carey Price 3.00 8.00
32 Patrick Roy 4.00 10.00
33 Martin Brodeur 4.00 10.00
34 Zach Parise 1.50 4.00
35 Ilya Kovalchuk 1.50 4.00
36 John Tavares 2.50 6.00
37 Mark Messier 3.00 8.00
38 Marian Gaborik 1.50 4.00
39 Jason Spezza 1.50 4.00
40 Ron Hextall 1.50 4.00
41 Jeff Carter 1.25 3.00
42 Mike Richards 1.25 3.00
43 Mario Lemieux 6.00 15.00
44 Marc-Andre Fleury 3.00 8.00
45 Ron Francis 2.00 5.00
46 Evgeni Malkin 3.00 8.00
47 Sidney Crosby 6.00 15.00
48 Joe Sakic 3.00 8.00
49 Dany Heatley 1.25 3.00
50 Jaroslav Halak 1.50 4.00
51 Steven Stamkos 3.00 8.00
52 Martin St. Louis 1.50 4.00
53 Doug Gilmour 2.00 5.00
54 Frank Mahovlich 1.50 4.00
55 Markus Naslund 1.50 4.00
56 Roberto Luongo 2.50 6.00
57 Nicklas Backstrom 1.50 4.00
58 Alexander Ovechkin 6.00 15.00
59 Alexander Semin 1.50 4.00
60 Dale Hawerchuk 2.00 5.00
61 Brandon McMillan RC 2.50 6.00
62 Patrice Cormier RC 3.00 8.00
63 Jamie Arniel RC 2.50 6.00
64 Colby Cohen RC 2.50 6.00
65 Jon Matsumoto RC 2.50 6.00
66 Ben Smith RC 3.00 8.00
67 Brandon Pirri RC 2.50 6.00
68 Jeremy Morin RC 2.50 6.00
69 Mark Olver RC 2.50 6.00
70 Jonas Holos RC 2.50 6.00
71 Richard Bachman RC 3.00 8.00
72 Tomas Tatar RC 6.00 15.00
73 Jan Mursak RC 5.00 12.00
74 Linus Omark RC 3.00 8.00
75 Dean Arsene RC 2.50 6.00
76 Jake Muzzin RC 6.00 15.00
77 Maxim Noreau RC 2.00 5.00
78 Nate Prosser RC 2.50 6.00
79 Matt Hackett RC 4.00 10.00
80 Casey Wellman RC 2.50 6.00
81 Matt Kassian RC 2.50 6.00
82 J.T. Wyman RC 2.50 6.00
83 Linus Klasen RC 2.50 6.00
84 Mark Dekanich RC 2.50 6.00
85 Alexander Vasyunov RC 2.50 6.00
86 Alexander Urbom RC 2.50 6.00
87 Ryan McDonagh RC 6.00 15.00
88 Mats Zuccarello-Aasen RC 5.00 12.00
89 Kevin Poulin RC 3.00 8.00
90 Nathan Lawson RC 2.50 6.00
91 Travis Hamonic RC 3.00 8.00
92 Derek Smith RC 2.50 6.00
93 Kaspars Daugavins RC 3.00 8.00
94 Robin Lehner RC 5.00 12.00
95 Alexander Pechurskiy RC 3.00 8.00
96 Brett MacLean RC 3.00 8.00
97 Ryan Reaves RC 3.00 8.00
98 Ian Cole RC 2.50 6.00
99 Nikita Nikitin RC 2.50 6.00
100 Christopher Tanev RC 6.00 15.00
101 Cam Fowler AU/299 RC 10.00 25.00
102 Kyle Palmieri AU/299 RC 8.00 20.00
103 A.Burmistrov AU/299 RC 4.00 10.00
104 Jordan Caron AU/299 RC 6.00 15.00
105 Zach Hamill AU/299 RC 4.00 10.00
106 Henrik Karlsson AU/299 RC 4.00 10.00
107 Jamie McBain AU/299 RC 4.00 10.00
108 Zac Dalpe AU/299 RC 5.00 12.00
109 Jeff Skinner AU/99 RC 30.00 60.00
110 Nick Leddy AU/299 RC 5.00 12.00
111 Brandon Yip AU/299 RC 4.00 10.00
112 K.Shattenkirk AU/299 RC 8.00 20.00
113 Philip Larsen AU/299 RC 4.00 10.00
114 Alex Plante AU/299 RC 4.00 10.00
115 Magnus Paajarvi AU/299 RC 20.00 50.00
116 Brayden Schenn AU/299 RC 15.00 40.00
117 Kyle Clifford AU/299 RC 5.00 12.00
118 Justin Falk AU/299 RC 3.00 8.00
119 M.Scandella AU/299 RC 4.00 10.00
120 Cody Almond AU/299 RC 4.00 10.00
121 A.Lindback AU/299 RC 4.00 10.00
122 Jacob Josefson AU/299 RC 4.00 10.00
123 Nick Palmieri AU/299 RC 4.00 10.00
124 N.Niederreiter AU/299 RC 6.00 15.00
125 E.Grachev AU/299 RC 4.00 10.00
126 Luke Adam AU/299 RC 4.00 10.00
127 Jared Cowen AU/299 RC 4.00 10.00
128 S.Bobrovsky AU/299 RC 30.00 80.00
129 Ekman-Larsson AU/299 RC 6.00 15.00
130 Eric Wellwood AU/299 RC 5.00 12.00
131 Eric Tangradi AU/299 RC 4.00 10.00
132 Nick Johnson AU/299 RC 3.00 8.00
133 M.Tedenby AU/299 RC 4.00 10.00
134 Dustin Tokarski AU/299 RC 4.00 10.00
135 Dana Tyrell AU/299 RC 4.00 10.00
136 M.Johansson AU/299 RC 6.00 15.00
137 Derek Stepan AU/299 RC 5.00 12.00
138 Nazem Kadri AU/99 RC 30.00 60.00
139 P.K. Subban AU/99 RC 75.00 150.00
140 Jordan Eberle AU/99 RC 100.00 200.00
141 Tyler Seguin AU/99 RC 150.00 250.00
142 Taylor Hall AU/99 RC 150.00 250.00
143 Thomas McCollum AU/99 RC
144 Jacob Markstrom AU/99 RC 20.00 40.00

2010-11 Ultimate Collection Debut Threads

*PATCH/35: 1X TO 2.5X THREADS
DTAL Anders Lindback 2.50 6.00
DTBP Brandon Pirri 2.50 6.00
DTBS Brayden Schenn 6.00 15.00
DTBU Alexander Burmistrov 2.50 6.00
DTBY Brandon Yip 2.50 6.00
DTCA Cody Almond 2.50 6.00
DTCC Colby Cohen 2.50 6.00
DTCF Cam Fowler 6.00 15.00
DTDS Derek Stepan 3.00 8.00
DTDT Dustin Tokarski 2.50 6.00
DTEG Evgeny Grachev 2.50 6.00
DTET Eric Tangradi 2.50 6.00
DTEW Eric Wellwood 3.00 8.00
DTHK Henrik Karlsson 2.50 6.00
DTIC Ian Cole 2.50 6.00
DTJC Jared Cowen 2.50 6.00
DTJE Jordan Eberle 8.00 20.00
DTJF Justin Falk 2.00 5.00
DTJJ Jacob Josefson 2.50 6.00
DTJO Jordan Caron 3.00 8.00
DTJS Jeff Skinner 6.00 15.00
DTKC Kyle Clifford 3.00 8.00
DTKP Kyle Palmieri 5.00 12.00
DTKS Kevin Shattenkirk 5.00 12.00
DTLA Philip Larsen 2.50 6.00
DTLK Luke Adam 2.50 6.00
DTMC Jamie McBain 2.50 6.00
DTMJ Marcus Johansson 4.00 10.00
DTMN Maxim Noreau 2.00 5.00
DTMO Mark Olver 2.50 6.00
DTMP Magnus Paajarvi 3.00 8.00
DTMS Marco Scandella 2.50 6.00
DTMT Mattias Tedenby 2.50 6.00
DTNJ Nick Johnson 2.00 5.00
DTNK Nazem Kadri 5.00 12.00
DTNL Nick Leddy 4.00 10.00
DTNN Nino Niederreiter 4.00 10.00
DTNP Nick Palmieri 2.50 6.00
DTNS Nick Spaling 2.50 6.00
DTOE Oliver Ekman-Larsson 5.00 12.00
DTPL Alex Plante 2.50 6.00
DTPS P.K. Subban 8.00 20.00
DTSB Sergei Bobrovsky 10.00 25.00
DTTB T.J. Brodie 2.50 6.00
DTTH Taylor Hall 12.00 30.00
DTTS Tyler Seguin 8.00 20.00
DTTY Dana Tyrell 2.50 6.00
DTZD Zac Dalpe 3.00 8.00
DTZH Zach Hamill 2.50 6.00

2010-11 Ultimate Collection Debut Threads Autographs

*PATCH/25: .8X TO 2X JSY AU/50
SDTAL Anders Lindback 6.00 15.00
SDTBP Brandon Pirri 6.00 15.00
SDTBS Brayden Schenn 10.00 25.00
SDTBU Alexander Burmistrov 6.00 15.00
SDTBY Brandon Yip 6.00 15.00
SDTCA Cody Almond 6.00 15.00
SDTCC Colby Cohen 6.00 15.00
SDTCF Cam Fowler 15.00 40.00
SDTDS Derek Stepan 12.00 30.00
SDTDT Dustin Tokarski 6.00 15.00
SDTEG Evgeny Grachev 6.00 15.00
SDTET Eric Tangradi 10.00 25.00
SDTEW Eric Wellwood 10.00 25.00
SDTHK Henrik Karlsson 6.00 15.00
SDTIC Ian Cole 6.00 15.00
SDTJC Jared Cowen 6.00 15.00
SDTJE Jordan Eberle 50.00 100.00
SDTJF Justin Falk 5.00 12.00
SDTJJ Jacob Josefson 6.00 15.00
SDTJO Jordan Caron 8.00 20.00
SDTJS Jeff Skinner 15.00 40.00
SDTKC Kyle Clifford 6.00 15.00
SDTKS Kevin Shattenkirk 12.00 30.00
SDTLA Philip Larsen 6.00 15.00
SDTLK Luke Adam 6.00 15.00
SDTMC Jamie McBain 6.00 15.00
SDTMJ Marcus Johansson 10.00 25.00
SDTMN Maxim Noreau 5.00 12.00
SDTMO Mark Olver 6.00 15.00
SDTMP Magnus Paajarvi 12.00 30.00
SDTMS Marco Scandella 6.00 15.00
SDTMT Mattias Tedenby 6.00 15.00
SDTNJ Nick Johnson 5.00 12.00
SDTNK Nazem Kadri 20.00 50.00
SDTNL Nick Leddy 12.00 30.00
SDTNN Nino Niederreiter 10.00 25.00
SDTNP Nick Palmieri 6.00 15.00
SDTNS Nick Spaling 6.00 15.00
SDTOE Oliver Ekman-Larsson 10.00 25.00
SDTPL Alex Plante 6.00 15.00
SDTPS P.K. Subban 40.00 100.00
SDTSB Sergei Bobrovsky 25.00 60.00
SDTTB T.J. Brodie 6.00 15.00
SDTTH Taylor Hall 40.00 100.00
SDTTS Tyler Seguin 40.00 100.00
SDTTY Dana Tyrell 6.00 15.00
SDTZD Zac Dalpe 8.00 20.00
SDTZH Zach Hamill 8.00 20.00

2010-11 Ultimate Collection Debut Threads Patches

DTAL Anders Lindback 6.00 15.00
DTBP Brandon Pirri 6.00 15.00
DTBS Brayden Schenn 15.00 40.00
DTBU Alexander Burmistrov 6.00 15.00
DTBY Brandon Yip 6.00 15.00
DTCA Cody Almond 6.00 15.00
DTCC Colby Cohen 6.00 15.00
DTCF Cam Fowler 15.00 40.00
DTDS Derek Stepan 8.00 20.00
DTDT Dustin Tokarski 6.00 15.00
DTEG Evgeny Grachev 6.00 15.00
DTET Eric Tangradi 6.00 15.00
DTEW Eric Wellwood 8.00 20.00
DTHK Henrik Karlsson 6.00 15.00
DTIC Ian Cole 6.00 15.00
DTJC Jared Cowen 6.00 15.00
DTJE Jordan Eberle 20.00 50.00
DTJF Justin Falk 5.00 12.00
DTJJ Jacob Josefson 6.00 15.00
DTJO Jordan Caron 8.00 20.00
DTJS Jeff Skinner 15.00 40.00
DTKC Kyle Clifford 8.00 20.00
DTKP Kyle Palmieri 12.00 30.00
DTKS Kevin Shattenkirk 15.00 40.00
DTLA Philip Larsen 6.00 15.00
DTLK Luke Adam 6.00 15.00
DTMC Jamie McBain 6.00 15.00
DTMJ Marcus Johansson 10.00 25.00
DTMN Maxim Noreau 5.00 12.00
DTMO Mark Olver 6.00 15.00
DTMP Magnus Paajarvi 8.00 20.00
DTMS Marco Scandella 6.00 15.00
DTMT Mattias Tedenby 6.00 15.00
DTNJ Nick Johnson 5.00 12.00
DTNL Nick Leddy 10.00 25.00
DTNN Nino Niederreiter 10.00 25.00
DTNP Nick Palmieri 6.00 15.00
DTNS Nick Spaling 6.00 15.00
DTOE Oliver Ekman-Larsson 12.00 30.00
DTPL Alex Plante 6.00 15.00
DTPS P.K. Subban 20.00 50.00
DTSB Sergei Bobrovsky 25.00 60.00
DTTB T.J. Brodie 6.00 15.00
DTTH Taylor Hall 25.00 60.00
DTTS Tyler Seguin 20.00 50.00
DTTY Dana Tyrell 15.00 40.00
DTZD Zac Dalpe 8.00 20.00
DTZH Zach Hamill 8.00 20.00

2010-11 Ultimate Collection Debut Threads Patches Autographs

*PATCH/25: .8X TO 2X JSY AU/50
SDTAL Anders Lindback 12.00 30.00
SDTBP Brandon Pirri 12.00 30.00
SDTBS Brayden Schenn 20.00 50.00
SDTBU Alexander Burmistrov 12.00 30.00
SDTBY Brandon Yip 12.00 30.00
SDTCA Cody Almond 12.00 30.00
SDTCC Colby Cohen 12.00 30.00
SDTCF Cam Fowler 25.00 50.00
SDTDS Derek Stepan 25.00 60.00
SDTDT Dustin Tokarski 12.00 30.00
SDTEG Evgeny Grachev 12.00 30.00
SDTET Eric Tangradi 20.00 50.00
SDTEW Eric Wellwood 20.00 50.00
SDTHK Henrik Karlsson 12.00 30.00
SDTIC Ian Cole 12.00 30.00
SDTJC Jared Cowen 12.00 30.00
SDTJE Jordan Eberle 75.00 200.00
SDTJF Justin Falk 10.00 25.00
SDTJJ Jacob Josefson 12.00 30.00
SDTJO Jordan Caron 15.00 40.00
SDTJS Jeff Skinner 30.00 80.00
SDTKC Kyle Clifford 12.00 30.00
SDTKS Kevin Shattenkirk 25.00 50.00
SDTLA Philip Larsen 12.00 30.00
SDTLK Luke Adam 12.00 30.00
SDTMC Jamie McBain 12.00 30.00
SDTMJ Marcus Johansson 20.00 50.00
SDTMN Maxim Noreau 10.00 25.00
SDTMO Mark Olver 12.00 30.00
SDTMP Magnus Paajarvi 25.00 60.00
SDTMS Marco Scandella 12.00 30.00
SDTMT Mattias Tedenby 12.00 30.00
SDTNJ Nick Johnson 10.00 25.00
SDTNL Nick Leddy 25.00 60.00
SDTNN Nino Niederreiter 20.00 50.00
SDTNP Nick Palmieri 12.00 30.00
SDTNS Nick Spaling 12.00 30.00
SDTOE Oliver Ekman-Larsson 20.00 50.00
SDTPL Alex Plante 12.00 30.00
SDTPS P.K. Subban 125.00 250.00
SDTSB Sergei Bobrovsky 100.00 250.00
SDTTB T.J. Brodie 12.00 30.00
SDTTH Taylor Hall 100.00 200.00
SDTTS Tyler Seguin EXCH 100.00 250.00
SDTTY Dana Tyrell 12.00 30.00
SDTZD Zac Dalpe 12.00 30.00
SDTZH Zach Hamill 15.00 40.00

2010-11 Ultimate Collection Premium Patches

PAH Ales Hemsky 40.00 100.00
PAK Anze Kopitar 20.00 50.00
PAO Alexander Ovechkin 40.00 80.00
PBR Brad Richards 12.00 30.00
PCG Claude Giroux 12.00 30.00
PDA Daniel Alfredsson 30.00 60.00
PDC Dino Ciccarelli 12.00 30.00
PDD Drew Doughty 25.00 60.00
PDH Dany Heatley 10.00 25.00
PDK Duncan Keith
PDP Dion Phaneuf 20.00 50.00
PDS Devin Setoguchi 10.00 25.00
PEM Evgeni Malkin 40.00 80.00
PHL Henrik Lundqvist 30.00 80.00
PHO Marian Hossa 20.00 50.00
PHZ Henrik Zetterberg 15.00 40.00
PJA Jakub Voracek 10.00 25.00
PJC Jeff Carter 25.00 60.00
PJG Jean-Sebastien Giguere 15.00 40.00
PJI Jarome Iginla 15.00 40.00
PJS Joe Sakic 25.00 60.00
PJT Joe Thornton 25.00 60.00
PJV James van Riemsdyk 10.00 25.00
PKE Phil Kessel
PKO Mikko Koivu 12.00 30.00
PMB Martin Brodeur 30.00 80.00
PMD Matt Duchene 12.00 30.00
PMG Marian Gaborik 30.00 80.00
PMH Milan Hejduk 15.00 40.00
PMK Miikka Kiprusoff 12.00 30.00
PML Mario Lemieux 40.00 100.00
PMS Martin St. Louis 15.00 40.00
PNB Nicklas Backstrom 12.00 30.00
PNL Nicklas Lidstrom 15.00 40.00
PPD Pavel Datsyuk 40.00 100.00
PPK Patrick Kane 25.00 60.00
PPS Patrick Sharp 12.00 30.00
PRG Ryan Getzlaf 25.00 60.00
PRK Ryan Kesler 12.00 30.00
PRL Roberto Luongo 20.00 50.00
PRM Ryan Miller 40.00 80.00
PRN Rick Nash 25.00 60.00
PSC Sidney Crosby 50.00 125.00
PSD Shane Doan 15.00 40.00
PSP Jason Spezza 15.00 40.00
PSS Steven Stamkos 25.00 60.00
PST Jordan Staal 10.00 25.00
PTA John Tavares 40.00 80.00
PTV Thomas Vanek 20.00 50.00
PVO Tomas Vokoun 10.00 25.00
PYZ Steve Yzerman 30.00 80.00

2010-11 Ultimate Collection Premium Swatches

PAK Anze Kopitar 8.00 20.00
PAO Alexander Ovechkin 20.00 50.00
PBR Brad Richards 5.00 12.00
PCG Claude Giroux 5.00 12.00
PCP Carey Price 10.00 25.00
PDD Drew Doughty 8.00 20.00
PDH Dany Heatley 4.00 10.00
PDP Dion Phaneuf 4.00 10.00
PHL Henrik Lundqvist 12.00 30.00
PHO Marian Hossa 5.00 12.00
PHZ Henrik Zetterberg 10.00 25.00
PJC Jeff Carter 4.00 10.00
PJG Jean-Sebastien Giguere 8.00 20.00
PJI Jarome Iginla 10.00 25.00
PJS Joe Sakic 10.00 25.00
PJT Joe Thornton 12.00 30.00
PJV James van Riemsdyk 4.00 10.00
PKE Phil Kessel 5.00 12.00
PKO Mikko Koivu 5.00 12.00
PMB Martin Brodeur 12.00 30.00
PMD Matt Duchene 5.00 12.00
PMG Marian Gaborik 5.00 12.00
PMH Milan Hejduk 4.00 10.00
PMK Miikka Kiprusoff 5.00 12.00
PML Mario Lemieux/10
PMM Mark Messier 10.00 25.00
PMS Martin St. Louis 5.00 12.00
PNB Nicklas Backstrom 5.00 12.00
PNL Nicklas Lidstrom 5.00 12.00
PPD Pavel Datsyuk 8.00 20.00
PPK Patrick Kane 10.00 25.00
PPS Patrick Sharp 5.00 12.00
PRG Ryan Getzlaf 5.00 12.00
PRK Ryan Kesler 5.00 12.00
PRL Roberto Luongo 8.00 20.00
PRM Ryan Miller
PRN Rick Nash 8.00 20.00
PSC Sidney Crosby 20.00 50.00
PSD Shane Doan 4.00 10.00
PSM Steve Mason 4.00 10.00
PSP Jason Spezza 5.00 12.00
PSS Steven Stamkos 10.00 25.00
PST Jordan Staal 4.00 10.00
PTA John Tavares 12.00 30.00
PTO Jonathan Toews 8.00 20.00
PTV Thomas Vanek
PVO Tomas Vokoun 6.00 15.00
PWG Wayne Gretzky 30.00 80.00
PYZ Steve Yzerman 12.00 30.00
PZP Zach Parise 8.00 20.00

2010-11 Ultimate Collection Rookie Patch Autographs

101 Cam Fowler/35 30.00 80.00
102 Kyle Palmieri/35 25.00 60.00
103 Alexander Burmistrov/35 12.00 30.00
104 Jordan Caron/35 15.00 40.00
105 Zach Hamill/35 12.00 30.00
106 Henrik Karlsson/35 12.00 30.00
107 Jamie McBain/35 12.00 30.00
108 Zac Dalpe/35 15.00 40.00
109 Jeff Skinner/25 75.00 150.00
110 Nick Leddy/35 15.00 40.00
111 Brandon Yip/35 12.00 30.00
112 Kevin Shattenkirk/35 25.00 60.00
113 Philip Larsen/35 12.00 30.00
114 Alex Plante/35 12.00 30.00
115 Magnus Paajarvi/35 15.00 40.00
116 Brayden Schenn/35 30.00 80.00
117 Kyle Clifford/35 15.00 40.00
118 Justin Falk/35 10.00 25.00
119 Marco Scandella/35 12.00 30.00
120 Cody Almond/35 12.00 30.00
121 Anders Lindback/35 12.00 30.00
122 Jacob Josefson/35 12.00 30.00
123 Nick Palmieri/35 12.00 30.00
124 Nino Niederreiter/35 20.00 50.00
125 Evgeny Grachev/35 12.00 30.00
126 Luke Adam/35 12.00 30.00
127 Jared Cowen/35 12.00 30.00
128 Sergei Bobrovsky/35 50.00 125.00
129 Oliver Ekman-Larsson/35 20.00 50.00
130 Eric Wellwood/35 15.00 40.00
131 Eric Tangradi/35 12.00 30.00
132 Nick Johnson/35 10.00 25.00
133 Mattias Tedenby/35 12.00 30.00
134 Dustin Tokarski/35 12.00 30.00
135 Dana Tyrell/35 12.00 30.00
136 Marcus Johansson/35 20.00 50.00
137 Derek Stepan/35 30.00 80.00
138 Nazem Kadri/25 75.00 150.00
139 P.K. Subban/25 75.00 150.00
140 Jordan Eberle/25 200.00 350.00
141 Tyler Seguin/25 125.00 250.00
142 Taylor Hall/25 200.00 400.00
144 Jacob Markstrom/25 30.00 80.00

2010-11 Ultimate Collection Ultimate Achievements Autographs

UAAN Antti Niemi 12.00 30.00
UAAO Alexander Ovechkin 40.00 80.00
UABO Bobby Orr 125.00 250.00
UAEM Evgeni Malkin 25.00 60.00
UAGH Gordie Howe 75.00 150.00
UAGL Guy Lafleur 20.00 50.00
UAJT John Tavares 25.00 60.00
UAMB Martin Brodeur 40.00 80.00
UAML Mario Lemieux 50.00 100.00
UAMM Mark Messier 40.00 80.00
UAPD Pavel Datsyuk 15.00 40.00
UAPE Phil Esposito 15.00 40.00
UAPK Patrick Kane 20.00 50.00
UAPR Patrick Roy 60.00 120.00
UARM Ryan Miller 15.00 40.00
UASC Sidney Crosby 100.00 175.00
UASS Steven Stamkos 40.00 80.00
UATM Tyler Myers
UATO Jonathan Toews 25.00 60.00
UAWG Wayne Gretzky 250.00 600.00

2010-11 Ultimate Collection Ultimate Jerseys

UJAK Alex Kovalev 3.00 8.00
UJAO Alexander Ovechkin 15.00 40.00
UJBL Brian Leetch 3.00 8.00
UJCA Craig Anderson 4.00 10.00
UJCN Cam Neely 4.00 10.00
UJCW Cam Ward 4.00 10.00
UJDB David Backes 2.50 6.00
UJDG Doug Gilmour 5.00 12.00
UJDH Dany Heatley 3.00 8.00
UJDS Daniel Sedin 5.00 12.00
UJEM Evgeni Malkin 8.00 20.00
UJES Eric Staal 5.00 12.00
UJGH Gordie Howe 12.00 30.00
UJHS Henrik Sedin 5.00 12.00
UJIK Ilya Kovalchuk 4.00 10.00
UJJC Jeff Carter 3.00 8.00
UJJH Jaroslav Halak 4.00 10.00
UJJI Jarome Iginla 5.00 12.00
UJJK Jari Kurri 4.00 10.00
UJJS Jason Spezza 4.00 10.00
UJJT Jonathan Toews 6.00 15.00
UJLE Loui Eriksson 2.50 6.00
UJMB Martin Brodeur 10.00 25.00
UJMD Matt Duchene 4.00 10.00
UJMF Marc-Andre Fleury 6.00 15.00
UJMG Marian Gaborik 4.00 10.00
UJMK Miikka Kiprusoff 4.00 10.00
UJML Mario Lemieux 15.00 40.00
UJMM Mike Modano 6.00 15.00
UJMR Mike Richards 3.00 8.00
UJMT Marty Turco 4.00 10.00
UJNB Nicklas Backstrom 4.00 10.00
UJPB Patrice Bergeron 5.00 12.00
UJPD Pavel Datsyuk 6.00 15.00
UJPK Patrick Kane 8.00 20.00
UJPM Patrick Marleau 4.00 10.00
UJPR Patrick Roy 10.00 25.00
UJRB Ray Bourque 6.00 15.00
UJRG Ryan Getzlaf 4.00 10.00
UJRI Brad Richards 4.00 10.00
UJRL Roberto Luongo 6.00 15.00
UJRM Ryan Miller 4.00 10.00
UJRN Rick Nash 4.00 10.00
UJSC Sidney Crosby 15.00 40.00
UJSY Steve Yzerman 10.00 25.00
UJTA John Tavares 6.00 15.00
UJTH Joe Thornton 6.00 15.00
UJVL Vincent Lecavalier 4.00 10.00
UJWG Wayne Gretzky 25.00 60.00
UJZC Zdeno Chara 4.00 10.00
UJZP Zach Parise 4.00 10.00

2010-11 Ultimate Collection Ultimate Jerseys Autographs

UAJAK Anze Kopitar 15.00 40.00
UAJAO Alexander Ovechkin 50.00 100.00
UAJBR Brad Richards 12.00 30.00
UAJDD Drew Doughty 15.00 40.00
UAJDH Dany Heatley 10.00 25.00
UAJJC Jeff Carter 12.00 30.00
UAJJI Jarome Iginla 15.00 40.00
UAJJV James van Riemsdyk 10.00 25.00
UAJMB Martin Brodeur 30.00 80.00
UAJMD Matt Duchene 12.00 30.00
UAJML Mario Lemieux 75.00 150.00
UAJMM Mark Messier 40.00 80.00
UAJMR Mike Richards
UAJNB Nicklas Backstrom 12.00 30.00
UAJPK Patrick Kane 30.00 60.00
UAJPR Patrick Roy 60.00 125.00
UAJRM Ryan Miller 15.00 40.00
UAJSC Sidney Crosby 100.00 175.00
UAJSS Steven Stamkos 30.00 80.00
UAJTA John Tavares 20.00 50.00
UAJTM Tyler Myers
UAJTO Jonathan Toews 20.00 50.00
UAJVL Vincent Lecavalier 12.00 30.00
UAJWG Wayne Gretzky 250.00 600.00

2010-11 Ultimate Collection Ultimate Jerseys Duos

UDJBK M.Koivu/N.Backstrom
UDJBP Z.Parise/M.Brodeur 20.00 50.00
UDJCM S.Crosby/E.Malkin 15.00 40.00
UDJCO S.Crosby/A.Ovechkin 20.00 50.00
UDJCR Z.Chara/T.Rask 10.00 25.00
UDJCS S.Stamkos/S.Crosby
UDJCV J.Carter/J.van Riemsdyk 8.00 20.00
UDJGL M.Gaborik/H.Lundqvist 8.00 20.00
UDJGP J.Giguere/D.Phaneuf 8.00 20.00
UDJGR W.Gretzky/L.Robitaille 50.00 125.00
UDJGV M.Green/S.Varlamov 8.00 20.00
UDJHD M.Duchene/M.Hejduk 8.00 20.00
UDJHP D.Penner/A.Hemsky 6.00 15.00
UDJHT M.Hossa/J.Toews 12.00 30.00
UDJIK J.Iginla/M.Kiprusoff 10.00 25.00
UDJKB R.Kesler/D.Backes
UDJKD A.Kopitar/D.Doughty 12.00 30.00
UDJKK P.Kane/D.Keith
UDJKM J.Kurri/M.Messier 15.00 40.00
UDJLM R.Luongo/R.Miller 12.00 30.00
UDJMH P.Marleau/D.Heatley 8.00 20.00
UDJMV R.Miller/T.Vanek 8.00 20.00
UDJNB R.Bourque/C.Neely 12.00 30.00
UDJNV R.Nash/J.Voracek 8.00 20.00
UDJOB A.Ovechkin/N.Backstrom 30.00 80.00
UDJRG M.Richards/C.Giroux 8.00 20.00
UDJRS P.Roy/J.Sakic 20.00 50.00
UDJSM M.St. Louis/S.Stamkos
UDJSS H.Sedin/D.Sedin 10.00 25.00
UDJTD J.Tavares/M.Duchene 12.00 30.00

2010-11 Ultimate Collection Ultimate Jerseys Trios

UTJ1 Lemieux/Yzerman/Gretzky 60.00 150.00
UTJ2 Yzerman/Lemieux/Messier 40.00 100.00
UTJ3 Green/Backstrom/Ovechkin 40.00 100.00
UTJ4 Phaneuf/Kessel/Giguere
UTJ5 Staal/Malkin/Fleury 20.00 50.00
UTJ6 Roy/Brodeur/Price 25.00 60.00
UTJ7 Kane/Toews/Hossa 40.00 100.00
UTJ8 Lecavalier/St. Louis/Stamkos
UTJ9 Myers/Miller/Vanek 10.00 25.00
UTJ10 Heatley/Marleau/Thornton

2010-11 Ultimate Collection Ultimate Nicknames Autographs

UNAD Alex Delvecchio 10.00 25.00
UNAN Antti Niemi 25.00 50.00
UNAO Alexander Ovechkin 75.00 125.00
UNEM Evgeni Malkin 20.00 50.00
UNGH Gordie Howe 60.00 120.00
UNGJ Bobby Hull 25.00 60.00
UNGL Guy Lafleur 25.00 60.00
UNHZ Henrik Zetterberg
UNJG Jean-Sebastien Giguere 15.00 40.00
UNJH Jaroslav Halak 15.00 40.00
UNJI Jarome Iginla 15.00 40.00
UNJT Jonathan Toews 20.00 50.00
UNMB Martin Brodeur 40.00 80.00
UNMF Marc-Andre Fleury 25.00 60.00
UNML Mario Lemieux 60.00 120.00
UNMM Mark Messier 30.00 60.00
UNNL Nicklas Lidstrom 25.00 60.00
UNPR Patrick Roy 75.00 125.00
UNRM Ryan Miller 30.00 60.00
UNRS Ryan Smyth 30.00 60.00

2010-11 Ultimate Collection Ultimate Patches

UJAK Alex Kovalev 8.00 20.00
UJAO Alexander Ovechkin 40.00 100.00
UJBL Brian Leetch 8.00 20.00
UJCA Craig Anderson 10.00 25.00
UJCN Cam Neely 10.00 25.00
UJCW Cam Ward 10.00 25.00
UJDB David Backes 6.00 15.00
UJDH Dany Heatley 8.00 20.00
UJDS Daniel Sedin 12.00 30.00
UJEM Evgeni Malkin 20.00 50.00
UJES Eric Staal 12.00 30.00
UJHL Henrik Lundqvist 25.00 60.00
UJHS Henrik Sedin 12.00 30.00
UJHZ Henrik Zetterberg 12.00 30.00
UJIK Ilya Kovalchuk 10.00 25.00
UJJC Jeff Carter 8.00 20.00
UJJI Jarome Iginla 12.00 30.00
UJJS Jason Spezza 10.00 25.00
UJJT Jonathan Toews 15.00 40.00
UJKO Mikko Koivu 10.00 25.00
UJLE Loui Eriksson 8.00 20.00
UJLR Luc Robitaille 10.00 25.00
UJMB Martin Brodeur 25.00 60.00
UJMF Marc-Andre Fleury 15.00 40.00
UJMG Marian Gaborik 10.00 25.00
UJMK Miikka Kiprusoff 10.00 25.00
UJML Mario Lemieux 40.00 100.00
UJMM Mike Modano 15.00 40.00
UJMS Martin St. Louis 10.00 25.00
UJMT Marty Turco 10.00 25.00
UJNB Nicklas Backstrom 10.00 25.00
UJPB Patrice Bergeron 12.00 30.00
UJPD Pavel Datsyuk 20.00 50.00
UJPK Patrick Kane 20.00 50.00
UJPM Patrick Marleau 10.00 25.00
UJPR Patrick Roy 25.00 60.00
UJRB Ray Bourque 15.00 40.00
UJRG Ryan Getzlaf 10.00 25.00
UJRI Brad Richards 10.00 25.00
UJRL Roberto Luongo 10.00 25.00
UJRM Ryan Miller 10.00 25.00
UJRN Rick Nash 10.00 25.00
UJSC Sidney Crosby 40.00 100.00
UJSY Steve Yzerman 25.00 60.00
UJTA John Tavares 15.00 40.00
UJVL Vincent Lecavalier 10.00 25.00
UJJT Joe Thornton 15.00 40.00
UJZC Zdeno Chara 10.00 25.00

2010-11 Ultimate Collection Ultimate Patches Duos

UDJBK M.Koivu/N.Backstrom
UDJBP Z.Parise/M.Brodeur
UDJCM S.Crosby/E.Malkin 60.00 150.00
UDJCO S.Crosby/A.Ovechkin 100.00 200.00
UDJCR Z.Chara/T.Rask 25.00 60.00
UDJCS S.Stamkos/S.Crosby
UDJCV J.Carter/J.van Riemsdyk 12.00 30.00
UDJGL M.Gaborik/H.Lundqvist 40.00 100.00
UDJGP J.Giguere/D.Phaneuf 15.00 40.00
UDJGR W.Gretzky/L.Robitaille
UDJHD M.Duchene/M.Hejduk 15.00 40.00
UDJHP D.Penner/A.Hemsky
UDJHT M.Hossa/J.Toews 40.00 100.00
UDJIK J.Iginla/M.Kiprusoff 20.00 50.00
UDJKB R.Kesler/D.Backes 25.00 60.00
UDJKD A.Kopitar/D.Doughty 30.00 80.00
UDJKK P.Kane/D.Keith 30.00 80.00
UDJKM J.Kurri/M.Messier
UDJLM R.Luongo/R.Miller 25.00 60.00
UDJMH P.Marleau/D.Heatley 15.00 40.00
UDJMV R.Miller/T.Vanek 15.00 40.00
UDJNB R.Bourque/C.Neely 25.00 60.00
UDJNV R.Nash/J.Voracek 15.00 40.00
UDJOB A.Ovechkin/N.Backstrom 40.00 100.00
UDJRG M.Richards/C.Giroux
UDJRS P.Roy/J.Sakic 40.00 100.00
UDJSM M.St. Louis/S.Stamkos
UDJSS H.Sedin/D.Sedin 20.00 50.00
UDJTD J.Tavares/M.Duchene 25.00 60.00

2010-11 Ultimate Collection Ultimate Signatures

USAO Alexander Ovechkin 40.00 100.00
USBA Mikael Backlund
USBC Bobby Clarke 12.00 30.00
USBD Brandon Dubinsky 4.00 10.00
USBH Bobby Hull 15.00 40.00
USBO Bobby Orr 60.00 120.00
USBR Bobby Ryan 5.00 12.00
USBS Brayden Schenn 12.00 30.00
USBY Brandon Yip 5.00 12.00
USCS Chris Stewart 5.00 12.00
USDD Drew Doughty 10.00 25.00
USDS Derek Stepan 8.00 20.00
USEG Evgeny Grachev 5.00 12.00
USEK Evander Kane 6.00 15.00
USEM Evgeni Malkin 20.00 50.00
USET Eric Tangradi 5.00 12.00
USGH Gordie Howe 60.00 120.00
USGL Guy Lafleur 20.00 50.00
USGU Guillaume Latendresse 5.00 12.00
USJC Jared Cowen 5.00 12.00
USJE Jordan Eberle 12.00 30.00
USJF Jeff Skinner 12.00 30.00
USJH Jaroslav Halak 6.00 15.00
USJI Jarome Iginla 8.00 20.00
USJK Jari Kurri 12.00 30.00
USJM Jamie McBain 5.00 12.00
USJS Joe Sakic 25.00 60.00
USMB Martin Brodeur 40.00 80.00
USMD Matt Duchene 6.00 15.00
USMH Milan Hejduk 5.00 12.00
USMI Mike Bossy 8.00 20.00
USMJ Marcus Johansson 8.00 20.00
USML Mario Lemieux 60.00 120.00
USMM Mark Messier 40.00 80.00
USMP Magnus Paajarvi
USMT Mattias Tedenby 5.00 12.00
USNF Nick Foligno 5.00 12.00
USNK Nazem Kadri 15.00 40.00
USNL Nicklas Lidstrom 12.00 30.00
USNN Nino Niederreiter 8.00 20.00
USPD Pavel Datsyuk 20.00 50.00
USPE Phil Esposito 15.00 40.00
USPK Patrick Kane 50.00 100.00
USPR Patrick Roy 60.00 120.00
USPS P.K. Subban 8.00 20.00
USRM Ryan Miller 10.00 25.00
USSB Sergei Bobrovsky 8.00 20.00
USSC Sidney Crosby 75.00 150.00
USSS Steven Stamkos 15.00 40.00
USTA John Tavares 15.00 40.00
USTH Taylor Hall 12.00 30.00
USTM Tyler Myers
USTO Jonathan Toews 30.00 60.00
USTS Tyler Seguin 15.00 40.00
USWG Wayne Gretzky 300.00 800.00
USZH Zach Hamill 5.00 12.00
USPEI Brad Richards 6.00 15.00

2011-12 Ultimate Collection

1 Corey Perry 2.50 6.00
2 Ryan Getzlaf 1.50 4.00
3 Cam Neely 1.50 4.00
4 Bobby Orr 6.00 15.00
5 Phil Esposito 2.50 6.00
6 Ray Bourque 2.50 6.00
7 Thomas Vanek 1.25 3.00
8 Ryan Miller 1.50 4.00
9 Jarome Iginla 2.00 5.00
10 Miikka Kiprusoff 1.50 4.00
11 Eric Staal 2.00 5.00
12 Jeff Skinner 2.00 5.00
13 Jonathan Toews 2.50 6.00
14 Bobby Hull 3.00 8.00
15 Patrick Kane 3.00 8.00
16 Matt Duchene 1.50 4.00
17 Joe Sakic 3.00 8.00
18 Rick Nash 1.50 4.00
19 Jeff Carter 1.25 3.00
20 Igor Larionov 1.50 4.00
21 Pavel Datsyuk 2.50 6.00
22 Nicklas Lidstrom 1.00 2.50
23 Jordan Eberle 1.50 4.00
24 Taylor Hall 1.50 4.00
25 Jari Kurri 1.50 4.00
26 Paul Coffey 1.50 4.00
27 Brendan Shanahan 1.50 4.00
28 Ron Francis 2.00 5.00
29 Wayne Gretzky 10.00 25.00
30 Luc Robitaille 1.50 4.00
31 Mike Richards 1.25 3.00
32 P.K. Subban 2.00 5.00
33 Jean Beliveau 2.00 5.00
34 Carey Price 3.00 8.00
35 Patrick Roy 6.00 15.00
36 Martin Brodeur 4.00 10.00
37 Zach Parise 1.50 4.00
38 Ilya Kovalchuk 1.50 4.00
39 John Tavares 2.50 6.00
40 Mark Messier 2.00 5.00
41 Henrik Lundqvist 2.50 6.00
42 Jason Spezza 1.50 4.00
43 Brayden Schenn 1.50 4.00
44 Jaromir Jagr 5.00 12.00
45 Ron Hextall 1.50 4.00
46 Mario Lemieux 6.00 15.00
47 Marc-Andre Fleury 3.00 8.00
48 Evgeni Malkin 3.00 8.00
49 Sidney Crosby 5.00 12.00
50 Patrick Marleau 1.50 4.00
51 Joe Thornton 2.50 6.00
52 Jaroslav Halak 1.50 4.00
53 Steven Stamkos 3.00 8.00
54 Phil Kessel 1.50 4.00
55 Markus Naslund 1.50 4.00
56 Roberto Luongo 2.50 6.00
57 Trevor Linden 1.50 4.00
58 Mike Gartner 2.00 5.00
59 Alexander Ovechkin 6.00 15.00
60 Dale Hawerchuk 2.00 5.00
61 Pat Maroon RC 2.50 6.00
62 Peter Holland RC 2.50 6.00
63 Iiro Tarkki RC 3.00 8.00
64 Marcus Foligno RC 4.00 10.00
65 Corey Tropp RC 2.50 6.00
66 Derek Whitmore RC 6.00 15.00
67 Brayden McNabb RC 2.50 6.00
68 Joe Finley RC 2.50 6.00
69 Riley Nash RC 2.50 6.00
70 Dylan Olsen RC 3.00 8.00
71 Andrew Shaw RC 6.00 15.00
72 Jimmy Hayes RC 5.00 12.00
73 Jordie Benn RC 2.50 6.00
74 Brendan Smith RC 2.50 6.00
75 Joakim Andersson RC 2.50 6.00
76 Milan Kytnar RC 3.00 8.00
77 Bracken Kearns RC 2.50 6.00
78 Jarod Palmer RC 2.50 6.00
79 Kris Fredheim RC 2.50 6.00
80 David McIntyre RC 2.50 6.00
81 Frederic St. Denis RC 2.50 6.00
82 Mattias Ekholm RC 5.00 12.00
83 Ryan Ellis RC 2.50 6.00
84 Roman Josi RC 6.00 15.00
85 Keith Kinkaid RC 2.50 6.00
86 David Ullstrom RC 2.50 6.00
87 Mikko Koskinen RC 3.00 8.00
88 Anders Nilsson RC 2.50 6.00
89 Stu Bickel RC 2.50 6.00
90 Carl Hagelin RC 5.00 12.00
91 Andre Petersson RC 3.00 8.00
92 Mike Hoffman RC 15.00 30.00
93 Zac Rinaldo RC 2.50 6.00
94 Harry Zolnierczyk RC 2.50 6.00
95 Marc-Andre Bourdon RC 2.50 6.00
96 Robert Bortuzzo RC 2.50 6.00
97 Carl Sneep RC 2.50 6.00
98 Cade Fairchild RC 2.00 5.00
99 Kevin Marshall RC 2.50 6.00
100 Dmitry Orlov RC 6.00 15.00
101 Ben Holmstrom RC 2.50 6.00
102 Cam Atkinson RC 6.00 15.00
103 David Rundblad RC 2.50 6.00
104 Erik Gustafsson RC 3.00 8.00
105 Joe Vitale RC 2.50 6.00
106 Patrick Wiercioch RC 2.50 6.00
107 Roman Horak RC 3.00 8.00
108 Roman Wick RC 3.00 8.00
109 Stephane Da Costa RC 2.50 6.00
110 Tomas Vincour RC 2.50 6.00
111 Voynov AU/299 RC 4.00 10.00
112 Gustav Nyquist AU/299 RC 20.00 40.00
113 Brendan Smith AU/299 RC 4.00 10.00
114 Alexei Emelin AU/299 RC 4.00 10.00
115 Harri Sateri AU/299 RC 6.00 15.00
116 Carl Klingberg AU/299 RC 4.00 10.00
117 Raphael Diaz AU/299 RC 4.00 10.00
118 Colin Greening AU/299 RC 4.00 10.00
119 Justin Faulk AU/299 RC 6.00 15.00
120 Tim Erixon AU/299 RC 4.00 10.00
121 Nugent-Hopkins AU/99 RC 150.00 300.00
122 G.Landeskog AU/99 RC 30.00 80.00
123 Anton Lander AU/299 RC 4.00 10.00
124 Devante Smith-Pelly AU/299 RC 5.00 12.00
125 Leland Irving AU/99 RC 10.00 25.00
126 Zack Kassian AU/99 RC 30.00 80.00
127 Marcus Kruger AU/299 RC 6.00 15.00
128 Louis Leblanc AU/99 RC 20.00 50.00
129 Ryan Johansen AU/99 RC 40.00 80.00
130 Hartikainen AU/299 RC 8.00 20.00
131 Lennart Petrell AU/299 RC 6.00 15.00
132 E.Gudbranson AU/99 RC 15.00 40.00
133 Matt Frattin AU/299 RC 4.00 10.00
134 Calvin de Haan AU/99 RC 15.00 40.00
135 Palushaj AU/299 RC EXCH 4.00 10.00
136 Adam Henrique AU/99 RC 50.00 120.00
137 Adam Larsson AU/99 RC 25.00 60.00
138 Mika Zibanejad AU/99 RC 30.00 80.00
139 Sean Couturier AU/99 RC 30.00 80.00
140 Matt Read AU/99 RC 30.00 80.00
141 Blake Geoffrion AU/299 RC 4.00 10.00
142 Andy Miele AU/291 RC 4.00 10.00
143 Cody Eakin AU/99 RC 20.00 50.00
144 Brett Connolly AU/99 RC 15.00 40.00
145 Joe Colborne AU/99 RC 15.00 40.00
146 Jake Gardiner AU/99 RC 40.00 80.00
147 Cody Hodgson AU/99 RC 25.00 60.00
148 Craig Smith AU/99 RC 12.00 30.00
149 Jonathon Blum AU/299 RC 4.00 10.00
150 Mark Scheifele AU/99 RC 30.00 80.00

2011-12 Ultimate Collection 1997 Legends Autographs

AL1 Bobby Hull A 40.00 80.00
AL2 Stan Mikita A 30.00 60.00
AL3 Tony Esposito A 30.00 60.00
AL4 Alex Delvecchio C 10.00 25.00
AL5 Red Kelly C 10.00 25.00
AL6 Ted Lindsay B 15.00 40.00
AL7 Bill Ranford C 10.00 25.00
AL8 Glenn Anderson B 12.00 30.00
AL9 Grant Fuhr B 25.00 60.00
AL10 Jari Kurri C 12.00 30.00
AL11 Marty McSorley C 12.00 30.00
AL12 Mark Messier A 50.00 100.00
AL13 Paul Coffey A 25.00 50.00
AL14 Wayne Gretzky A 500.00 1200.00
AL15 Guy Lafleur A 30.00 60.00
AL16 Jean Beliveau A 100.00 200.00
AL17 Larry Robinson B 20.00 40.00
AL18 Patrick Roy A 125.00 250.00
AL19 Bill Barber C 12.00 30.00
AL20 Bobby Clarke B 20.00 50.00
AL21 Dave Schultz C 10.00 25.00
AL22 Eric Lindros A 50.00 100.00
AL23 Ron Hextall B 20.00 50.00
AL24 Reggie Leach C 10.00 25.00
AL25 Rick MacLeish C 12.00 30.00
AL26 Tim Kerr C 8.00 20.00
AL27 Adam Oates C 15.00 40.00
AL28 Brett Hull A 75.00 150.00
AL29 Doug Gilmour A 75.00 150.00
AL30 Wendel Clark B 25.00 60.00

2011-12 Ultimate Collection Debut Threads Autographs

DTAH Adam Henrique 15.00 40.00
DTAL Anton Lander 5.00 12.00
DTAM Andy Miele 5.00 12.00
DTAP Aaron Palushaj 5.00 12.00
DTAY Alexei Emelin 5.00 12.00
DTBB Brett Bulmer (inserted in 2013-14 Ultimate Collection) 5.00 12.00
DTBC Brett Connolly 5.00 12.00
DTBG Blake Geoffrion 5.00 12.00
DTBS Brendan Smith 5.00 12.00
DTCE Cody Eakin 8.00 20.00
DTCG Colin Greening 5.00 12.00
DTCH Cody Hodgson 8.00 20.00
DTCK Carl Klingberg 5.00 12.00
DTCS Craig Smith 6.00 15.00
DTCV Calvin de Haan 5.00 12.00
DTDS Devante Smith-Pelly 6.00 15.00
DTEG Erik Gudbranson 6.00 15.00
DTFO Marcus Foligno 8.00 20.00
DTGL Gabriel Landeskog 15.00 40.00
DTGN Greg Nemisz 5.00 12.00
DTHS Harri Sateri 5.00 12.00
DTJB Jonathon Blum 5.00 12.00
DTJC Joe Colborne 5.00 12.00
DTJF Justin Faulk 8.00 20.00
DTJG Jake Gardiner 8.00 20.00
DTJV Joe Vitale 5.00 12.00
DTLA Adam Larsson 6.00 15.00
DTLI Leland Irving 5.00 12.00
DTLL Louis Leblanc 5.00 12.00
DTLP Lennart Petrell 6.00 15.00
DTMF Matt Frattin 5.00 12.00
DTMK Marcus Kruger 8.00 20.00
DTMR Matt Read 6.00 15.00
DTMS Mark Scheifele 20.00 50.00
DTMZ Mika Zibanejad 15.00 40.00
DTNY Gustav Nyquist 12.00 30.00
DTPW Patrick Wiercioch 5.00 12.00
DTRD Raphael Diaz 5.00 12.00
DTRE Ryan Ellis 5.00 12.00
DTRJ Ryan Johansen 15.00 40.00
DTRN Ryan Nugent-Hopkins 20.00 50.00
DTSA David Savard 5.00 12.00
DTSC Sean Couturier 10.00 25.00
DTSD Stephane Da Costa 5.00 12.00
DTTE Tim Erixon 5.00 12.00
DTTH Teemu Hartikainen 5.00 12.00
DTVV Viatcheslav Voynov 5.00 12.00
DTZK Zack Kassian 6.00 15.00

2011-12 Ultimate Collection Debut Threads Patches

DTAH Adam Henrique 12.00 30.00
DTAL Anton Lander 5.00 12.00
DTAM Andy Miele 5.00 12.00
DTAP Aaron Palushaj 5.00 12.00
DTAY Alexei Emelin 5.00 12.00
DTBB Brett Bulmer 5.00 12.00
DTBC Brett Connolly 5.00 12.00
DTBG Blake Geoffrion 5.00 12.00
DTBS Brendan Smith 5.00 12.00
DTCE Cody Eakin 8.00 20.00
DTCG Colin Greening 5.00 12.00
DTCH Cody Hodgson 8.00 20.00
DTCS Craig Smith 6.00 15.00
DTCV Calvin de Haan 5.00 12.00
DTDR David Rundblad 5.00 12.00
DTDS Devante Smith-Pelly 6.00 15.00
DTEG Erik Gudbranson 6.00 15.00
DTFO Marcus Foligno 8.00 20.00
DTGL Gabriel Landeskog 15.00 40.00
DTGN Greg Nemisz 5.00 12.00
DTHS Harri Sateri 5.00 12.00
DTJB Jonathon Blum 5.00 12.00
DTJC Joe Colborne 5.00 12.00
DTJF Justin Faulk 8.00 20.00
DTJG Jake Gardiner 8.00 20.00
DTJV Joe Vitale 5.00 12.00
DTLA Adam Larsson 6.00 15.00
DTLI Leland Irving 5.00 12.00
DTLL Louis Leblanc 5.00 12.00
DTLP Lennart Petrell 6.00 15.00
DTMF Matt Frattin 5.00 12.00
DTMK Marcus Kruger 8.00 20.00
DTMR Matt Read 6.00 15.00
DTMZ Mika Zibanejad 15.00 40.00
DTNY Gustav Nyquist 12.00 30.00
DTPW Patrick Wiercioch 5.00 12.00
DTRD Raphael Diaz 5.00 12.00
DTRE Ryan Ellis 5.00 12.00
DTRJ Ryan Johansen 15.00 40.00
DTRN Ryan Nugent-Hopkins 20.00 50.00
DTSA David Savard 5.00 12.00
DTSC Sean Couturier 10.00 25.00
DTSD Stephane Da Costa 5.00 12.00
DTTE Tim Erixon 5.00 12.00
DTTH Teemu Hartikainen 5.00 12.00
DTVV Viatcheslav Voynov 5.00 12.00
DTZK Zack Kassian 6.00 15.00

2011-12 Ultimate Collection Premium Swatches

*PATCH/25: 1.25X TO 3X BASIC INSERTS
PSAK Andrei Kostitsyn 2.50 6.00
PSAM Andrei Markov 2.00 5.00
PSCP Chris Pronger 3.00 8.00
PSDA Daniel Alfredsson 3.00 8.00
PSDB Dustin Brown 3.00 8.00
PSDP David Perron 2.50 6.00
PSDR Derek Roy 2.00 5.00
PSGR Mike Green 2.50 6.00
PSHI Jonas Hiller 2.50 6.00
PSHS Henrik Sedin 4.00 10.00
PSHZ Henrik Zetterberg 4.00 10.00
PSIB Ilya Bryzgalov 3.00 8.00
PSIK Ilya Kovalchuk 3.00 8.00
PSJA Jaromir Jagr 10.00 25.00
PSJC Jeff Carter 2.50 6.00
PSJF Johan Franzen 2.50 6.00
PSJG Jean-Sebastien Giguere 3.00 8.00
PSJH Jim Howard 4.00 10.00
PSJI Jarome Iginla 4.00 10.00
PSJJ Jaromir Jagr 10.00 25.00
PSJO Jordan Staal 2.50 6.00
PSJP Jason Pominville 2.00 5.00
PSJS Jason Spezza 3.00 8.00
PSLE Lars Eller 2.00 5.00
PSLO Linus Omark 3.00 8.00
PSMC Michael Cammalleri 2.50 6.00
PSMD Matt Duchene 3.00 8.00
PSMK Miikka Kiprusoff 3.00 8.00
PSMM Mike Modano 5.00 12.00
PSMR Mike Richards 2.50 6.00
PSMT Matt Moulson 2.00 5.00
PSNB Nicklas Backstrom 3.00 8.00
PSNF Nikita Filatov 2.00 5.00
PSOP Ondrej Pavelec 3.00 8.00
PSPE Dustin Penner 2.50 6.00
PSPH Patric Hornqvist 2.00 5.00
PSPR Pekka Rinne 3.00 8.00
PSRL Roberto Luongo 5.00 12.00
PSRM Ryan Miller 3.00 8.00
PSSE Daniel Sedin 4.00 10.00
PSSM Steve Mason 2.50 6.00
PSSN Scott Niedermayer 3.00 8.00
PSST Drew Stafford 2.00 5.00
PSSV Semyon Varlamov 3.00 8.00
PSSW Shea Weber 2.50 6.00
PSTE Tyler Ennis 2.00 5.00
PSTM Tyler Myers 2.00 5.00
PSTR Tuukka Rask 4.00 10.00
PSTT Tim Thomas 3.00 8.00
PSTV Thomas Vanek 2.50 6.00
PSTY Tyler Seguin 4.00 10.00
PSVF Valtteri Filppula 2.00 5.00
PSWG Wayne Gretzky 20.00 50.00
PSZC Zdeno Chara 3.00 8.00
PSZP Zach Parise 3.00 8.00

2011-12 Ultimate Collection Rookie Patch Autographs

111 Viatcheslav Voynov/35 12.00 30.00
112 Gustav Nyquist/35 30.00 80.00
113 Brendan Smith/35 12.00 30.00
114 Alexei Emelin/35 12.00 30.00
115 Harri Sateri/35 25.00 50.00
116 Carl Klingberg/35 15.00 40.00
117 Raphael Diaz/35 12.00 30.00
118 Colin Greening/35 15.00 40.00
119 Justin Faulk/35 20.00 50.00
120 Tim Erixon/35 12.00 30.00
121 Ryan Nugent-Hopkins/25 125.00 250.00
122 Gabriel Landeskog/25 60.00 120.00
123 Anton Lander/25 25.00 50.00
124 Devante Smith-Pelly/25 15.00 40.00
125 Leland Irving/25 12.00 30.00
126 Zack Kassian/25 15.00 40.00
127 Marcus Kruger/25 15.00 40.00
128 Louis Leblanc/25 20.00 50.00
129 Ryan Johansen/25 40.00 80.00
130 Teemu Hartikainen/25 30.00 60.00
131 Lennart Petrell/25 25.00 50.00
132 Erik Gudbranson/25 15.00 40.00
133 Matt Frattin/25 30.00 60.00
134 Calvin de Haan/25 12.00 30.00
135 Aaron Palushaj/25 12.00 30.00
136 Adam Henrique/25 30.00 80.00
137 Adam Larsson/25 15.00 40.00
138 Mika Zibanejad/25 40.00 80.00
139 Sean Couturier/25 40.00 100.00
140 Matt Read/25 15.00 40.00
141 Blake Geoffrion/25 12.00 30.00
142 Andy Miele/25 20.00 50.00
143 Cody Eakin/25 15.00 40.00
144 Brett Connolly/25 25.00 50.00
145 Joe Colborne/25 12.00 30.00
146 Jake Gardiner/25 30.00 75.00
147 Cody Hodgson/25 30.00 80.00
148 Craig Smith/25 20.00 50.00
149 Jonathon Blum/25 12.00 30.00
150 Mark Scheifele/25 75.00 150.00

2011-12 Ultimate Collection Ultimate Jerseys

*PATCH/35: 1X TO 2.5X JSY/100
UJAK Anze Kopitar 6.00 15.00
UJAO Alexander Ovechkin 5.00 12.00
UJBC Brett Connolly 3.00 8.00
UJCU Sean Couturier 6.00 15.00
UJDD Drew Doughty 5.00 12.00
UJDR Derek Roy 2.50 6.00
UJDS Daniel Sedin 5.00 12.00
UJEL Eric Lindros 8.00 20.00
UJES Eddie Shack 4.00 10.00
UJHL Henrik Lundqvist 10.00 25.00
UJHS Henrik Sedin 5.00 12.00
UJHZ Henrik Zetterberg 5.00 12.00
UJIK Ilya Kovalchuk 4.00 10.00
UJJB Johnny Bower 6.00 15.00
UJJC Jeff Carter 3.00 8.00
UJJK Jari Kurri 4.00 10.00
UJJS Jordan Staal 3.00 8.00
UJLR Luc Robitaille 4.00 10.00
UJMB Martin Brodeur 10.00 25.00
UJMD Matt Duchene 4.00 10.00
UJMF Marc-Andre Fleury 8.00 20.00
UJMK Miikka Kiprusoff 4.00 10.00
UJML Mario Lemieux 10.00 25.00
UJMM Mike Modano 6.00 15.00
UJMR Mike Richards 3.00 8.00
UJNB Nicklas Backstrom 4.00 10.00
UJPD Pavel Datsyuk 6.00 15.00
UJPE Phil Esposito 5.00 12.00
UJPK P.K. Subban 6.00 15.00
UJPM Patrick Marleau 4.00 10.00
UJRJ Ryan Johansen 10.00 25.00
UJRL Roberto Luongo 6.00 15.00
UJRM Ryan Miller 4.00 10.00
UJSC Sidney Crosby 15.00 40.00
UJTO Jonathan Toews 8.00 20.00
UJTT Tim Thomas 4.00 10.00
UJTV Thomas Vanek 3.00 8.00
UJVL Vincent Lecavalier 4.00 10.00
UJWG Wayne Gretzky 25.00 60.00
UJZP Zach Parise 4.00 10.00

2011-12 Ultimate Collection Ultimate Jerseys Autographs

UJAK Anze Kopitar 20.00 50.00
UJBC Brett Connolly 10.00 25.00
UJCU Sean Couturier 25.00 50.00
UJDD Drew Doughty 15.00 40.00
UJDR Derek Roy 8.00 20.00
UJEL Eric Lindros 30.00 60.00
UJHL Henrik Lundqvist 30.00 80.00
UJJB Johnny Bower 30.00 80.00
UJJK Jari Kurri 12.00 30.00
UJJS Jordan Staal 10.00 25.00
UJLR Luc Robitaille 20.00 40.00
UJMB Martin Brodeur 40.00 80.00
UJMD Matt Duchene 15.00 40.00
UJMF Marc-Andre Fleury 25.00 60.00
UJML Mario Lemieux 60.00 120.00
UJMM Mike Modano 15.00 40.00
UJNB Nicklas Backstrom
UJNB Nicklas Backstrom (inserted in 2013-14 Ultimate Collection) 12.00 30.00
UJPD Pavel Datsyuk 15.00 40.00
UJPE Phil Esposito 15.00 40.00
UJPK P.K. Subban 15.00 40.00
UJPM Patrick Marleau 12.00 30.00
UJRJ Ryan Johansen
UJRM Ryan Miller 12.00 30.00
UJSC Sidney Crosby 90.00 150.00
UJTO Jonathan Toews 30.00 60.00
UJTV Thomas Vanek 10.00 25.00
UJVL Vincent Lecavalier 12.00 30.00
UJWG Wayne Gretzky 250.00 600.00

2011-12 Ultimate Collection Ultimate Jerseys Duos

*PATCH/25: .8X TO 2X JSY DUO/50
UDJBF M.Brodeur/M.Fleury 15.00 40.00
UDJCC B.Connolly/S.Couturier 10.00 25.00
UDJEE P.Esposito/T.Esposito 8.00 20.00
UDJEH T.Hall/J.Eberle 6.00 15.00
UDJFS M.Fleury/J.Staal 12.00 30.00
UDJGL W.Gretzky/M.Lemieux 40.00 100.00
UDJGV R.Luongo/M.Kiprusoff 10.00 25.00
UDJIK R.Kesler/J.Iginla 8.00 20.00
UDJJC J.Eberle/C.Hodgson 8.00 20.00
UDJJF J.Jagr/R.Francis 20.00 50.00
UDJKP I.Kovalchuk/Z.Parise 6.00 15.00
UDJLD N.Lidstrom/P.Datsyuk 8.00 20.00
UDJMR R.Miller/D.Roy 6.00 15.00
UDJOG A.Ovechkin/M.Green 8.00 20.00
UDJOS A.Ovechkin/A.Semin 10.00 25.00
UDJSK J.Spezza/E.Karlsson 8.00 20.00
UDJTK J.Toews/P.Kane 12.00 30.00
UDJTZ T.Thomas/Z.Chara 6.00 15.00

2011-12 Ultimate Collection Ultimate Jerseys Trios

U3CCJ Couturr/Connlly/Johnsn 20.00 50.00
U3BEES Thomas/Chara/Krejci 15.00 40.00
U3CAPS Ovchkn/Bckstrm/Semn 30.00 80.00
U3GOLD Toews/Perry/Getzlaf 12.00 30.00
U3PENS Fleury/Malkin/Staal 10.00 25.00
U3HAWKS Toews/Kane/Sharp 15.00 40.00
U3WINGS Shanhn/Lidstrm/Hask 12.00 30.00
U3FLYERS Giroux/Brier/vanRms 8.00 20.00
U3OILERS Hall/Ebrl/Paajarvi 8.00 20.00
U3QGFGOLD Luong/Brodr/Flury 20.00 50.00

2011-12 Ultimate Collection Ultimate Nicknames Autographs

NBH Brett Hull 50.00 100.00
NBM Brad Marchand (inserted in 2013-14 Ultimate Collection) 25.00 60.00
NBO Bobby Orr 150.00 250.00
NDS Dave Schultz 25.00 50.00
NEL Eric Lindros 40.00 80.00
NIL Igor Larionov 12.00 30.00
NJF Johan Franzen 10.00 25.00
NJP Joe Pavelski 15.00 40.00
NJT Jonathan Toews 40.00 80.00
NMM Mark Messier 40.00 80.00
NPR Patrick Roy 60.00 120.00
NRL Reggie Leach 20.00 50.00
NRN Ryan Nugent-Hopkins 175.00 300.00
NSC Sidney Crosby 75.00 150.00

2011-12 Ultimate Collection Ultimate Rookie Jerseys

*PATCH/65: .8X TO 2X BASIC JSY/200
URJAH Adam Henrique 6.00 15.00
URJBC Brett Connolly 2.50 6.00
URJBS Brendan Smith 2.50 6.00
URJCE Cody Eakin 4.00 10.00
URJCH Cody Hodgson 5.00 12.00
URJGL Gabriel Landeskog 8.00 20.00
URJJC Joe Colborne 2.50 6.00
URJJG Jake Gardiner 4.00 10.00

URJLA Adam Larsson 3.00 8.00
URJLL Louis Leblanc 2.50 6.00
URJMF Matt Frattin 2.50 6.00
URJMR Matt Read 5.00 12.00
URJMS Mark Scheifele 10.00 25.00
URJRJ Ryan Johansen 8.00 20.00
URJRN Ryan Nugent-Hopkins 10.00 25.00
URJSC Sean Couturier 5.00 12.00
URJTH Teemu Hartikainen 2.50 6.00
URJZK Zack Kassian 3.00 8.00

2011-12 Ultimate Collection Ultimate Rookie Jerseys Duos

*PATCH/35: .8X TO 2X JSY DUO/100
URJ2CF J.Colborne/M.Frattin 3.00 8.00
URJ2CR S.Couturier/M.Read 6.00 15.00
URJ2HC Hodgson/B.Connolly 5.00 12.00
URJ2HL A.Larsson/Henrique 8.00 20.00
URJ2KS Scheifele/C.Klingberg 12.00 30.00
URJ2LD L.Leblanc/R.Diaz 8.00 20.00
URJ2NL RNH/G.Landeskog 12.00 30.00
URJ2ZG Zibanejad/Greening 15.00 40.00

2011-12 Ultimate Collection Ultimate Rookie Jerseys Trios

*PATCH/15: 1X TO 2.5X JSY TRIO/50
URJ3EDM RNH/Lander/Hartikain 25.00 60.00
URJ3NLL RNH/Landskg/Leblanc 25.00 60.00
URJ3TML Colborne/Frattn/Gardnr 5.00 12.00
URJ3CANF Scheifl/Connlly/Coutur 12.50 30.00

2011-12 Ultimate Collection Ultimate Signatures

USAH Adam Henrique B 12.00 30.00
USAL Adam Larsson B 5.00 12.00
USBC Brett Connolly TBL E 5.00 12.00
USBM Brad Marchand A 6.00 15.00
USBO Bobby Orr D 60.00 100.00
USBR Bobby Ryan E 5.00 12.00
USBS Brayden Schenn E 6.00 15.00
USCH Cody Hodgson E 6.00 15.00
USCN B.Connolly Canada B 15.00 30.00
USCP Carey Price C 12.00 30.00
USCR Sidney Crosby B EXCH 75.00 125.00
USCU S.Couturier Canada B 20.00 40.00
USDH Dany Heatley C 5.00 12.00
USEL Eric Lindros A 25.00 50.00
USEM Evgeni Malkin D 15.00 40.00
USGC Guy Carbonneau D 6.00 15.00
USGL Gabriel Landeskog D 12.00 30.00
USGR W.Gretzky Canada A 400.00 1000.00
USJC Joe Colborne E 6.00 15.00
USJE Jordan Eberle B 10.00 25.00
USJM Jacob Markstrom B 5.00 12.00
USJP Joe Pavelski E 5.00 12.00
USJS Jeff Skinner C 10.00 25.00
USJT John Tavares E 12.00 30.00
USKN Patrick Kane C 15.00 30.00
USLC Logan Couture E 5.00 12.00
USMD Matt Duchene E 6.00 15.00
USMF Matt Frattin E 6.00 15.00
USML Mario Lemieux A 60.00 120.00
USMM Mark Messier A 40.00 80.00
USMS Mark Scheifele Jets E 6.00 15.00
USNH Nathan Horton C 8.00 20.00
USNU Nugent-Hopkins Can B 60.00 120.00
USPK P.K. Subban D 8.00 20.00
USPR Pekka Rinne A 5.00 12.00
USRG Ryan Getzlaf D 5.00 12.00
USRK Ryan Kesler C 8.00 20.00
USRL Reggie Leach E 5.00 12.00
USRM Rick MacLeish E 5.00 12.00
USRN R.Nugent-Hopkins Oilr D 15.00 40.00
USRY Patrick Roy C 40.00 80.00
USSA Joe Sakic A 40.00 80.00
USSC S.Couturier Flyers E 8.00 20.00
USSD Sidney Crosby Can A 100.00 175.00
USSF M.Scheifele Canada B 12.00 30.00
USSS Steven Stamkos A 30.00 80.00
USST Jordan Staal C 5.00 12.00
USTH Taylor Hall C 20.00 40.00
USTO Jonathan Toews C 20.00 40.00
USTS Tyler Seguin D 12.00 30.00
USTV Tomas Vokoun E 5.00 12.00
USWG W.Gretzky Oilers B 250.00 600.00

2012-13 Ultimate Collection

1 Teemu Selanne 3.00 8.00
2 Tyler Seguin 2.00 5.00
3 Thomas Vanek 1.25 3.00
4 Patrick Kane 3.00 8.00
5 Jonathan Toews 2.50 6.00
6 Ryan Nugent-Hopkins 2.00 5.00
7 Wayne Gretzky 10.00 25.00
8 Drew Doughty 2.00 5.00
9 Jonathan Quick 2.00 5.00
10 Zach Parise 1.50 4.00
11 Patrick Roy 4.00 10.00
12 Carey Price 3.00 8.00
13 Pekka Rinne 1.50 4.00
14 Martin Brodeur 4.00 10.00
15 Ilya Kovalchuk 1.50 4.00
16 John Tavares 2.50 6.00
17 Henrik Lundqvist 4.00 10.00
18 Jason Spezza 1.50 4.00
19 Eric Lindros 2.50 6.00
20 Evgeni Malkin 3.00 8.00
21 Sidney Crosby 6.00 15.00
22 Mario Lemieux 6.00 15.00
23 Steven Stamkos 3.00 8.00
24 Mats Sundin 2.50 6.00
25 Pavel Bure 1.50 4.00
26 Alexander Ovechkin 6.00 15.00
27 Ondrej Pavelec 1.50 4.00
28 Maxime Sauve AU RC 6.00 15.00
29 Sven Baertschi AU RC 10.00 25.00
30 Brandon Bollig AU RC 12.00 30.00
31 Tyson Barrie AU RC 20.00 50.00
32 Reilly Smith AU RC 15.00 40.00
33 Scott Glennie AU RC EXCH 10.00 25.00
34 Riley Sheahan AU RC 10.00 25.00
35 Jordan Nolan AU RC 6.00 15.00
36 Jason Zucker AU RC 15.00 40.00
37 Chet Pickard AU RC 8.00 20.00
38 Casey Cizikas AU RC 15.00 30.00
39 Chris Kreider AU RC 40.00 100.00
40 Jakob Silfverberg AU RC 20.00 40.00
41 Mark Stone AU RC 25.00 60.00
42 Jake Allen AU RC 20.00 50.00
43 Jaden Schwartz AU RC 25.00 50.00
44 Carter Ashton AU RC 6.00 15.00
45 Jussi Rynnas AU RC 10.00 25.00

2012-13 Ultimate Collection 1997 Legends Autographs

AL32 Brad Park C 15.00 40.00
AL33 Ray Bourque A 40.00 80.00
AL34 Milt Schmidt C 15.00 40.00
AL36 Phil Esposito A 125.00 225.00
AL37 Bobby Orr C 90.00 150.00
AL38 Brett Hull A 50.00 120.00
AL39 Mike Modano B 30.00 60.00
AL40 Ed Belfour B 30.00 80.00
AL41 Marcel Dionne B 12.00 30.00
AL42 Jari Kurri C 15.00 40.00
AL43 Luc Robitaille B 15.00 40.00
AL44 Wayne Gretzky A 300.00 800.00
AL46 Denis Potvin B 20.00 50.00
AL47 Clark Gillies B 20.00 50.00
AL48 Mike Bossy B 25.00 60.00
AL49 Ron Francis B 20.00 50.00
AL50 Mario Lemieux A 175.00 300.00
AL51 Jaromir Jagr A 60.00 120.00

2012-13 Ultimate Collection Debut Threads Patches

UDTPCA Carter Ashton 5.00 12.00
UDTPCC Casey Cizikas 10.00 25.00
UDTPCG Cody Goloubef 8.00 20.00
UDTPCK Chris Kreider 12.00 30.00
UDTPCP Chet Pickard 6.00 15.00
UDTPJA Jake Allen 15.00 40.00
UDTPJN Jordan Nolan 5.00 12.00
UDTPJR Jussi Rynnas 5.00 12.00
UDTPJS Jakob Silfverberg 10.00 25.00
UDTPJZ Jason Zucker 12.00 30.00
UDTPMS Mark Stone 20.00 50.00
UDTPRS Reilly Smith 15.00 40.00
UDTPSB Sven Baertschi 8.00 20.00
UDTPSC Jaden Schwartz 12.00 30.00
UDTPSG Scott Glennie 6.00 15.00
UDTPSH Riley Sheahan 8.00 20.00
UDTPTB Tyson Barrie 15.00 40.00
UDTPTC Tyler Cuma 5.00 12.00

2012-13 Ultimate Collection Rookie Patch Autographs

28 Maxime Sauve 10.00 25.00
29 Sven Baertschi 15.00 40.00
30 Brandon Bollig (inserted in 2013-14 Ultimate Collection) 15.00 40.00
31 Tyson Barrie 30.00 80.00
32 Reilly Smith 30.00 60.00
34 Riley Sheahan 15.00 40.00
35 Jordan Nolan 10.00 25.00
37 Chet Pickard 12.00 30.00
39 Chris Kreider 30.00 60.00
40 Jakob Silfverberg 20.00 50.00
41 Mark Stone 40.00 100.00
42 Jake Allen 30.00 80.00
43 Jaden Schwartz 30.00 60.00
44 Carter Ashton 12.00 30.00
45 Jussi Rynnas 15.00 40.00

2012-13 Ultimate Collection Ultimate Rookie Patches

URPCA Carter Ashton 8.00 20.00
URPCK Chris Kreider 10.00 25.00
URPCP Chet Pickard 10.00 25.00
URPJA Jake Allen 12.00 30.00
URPJR Jussi Rynnas 4.00 10.00
URPJS Jaden Schwartz 12.00 30.00
URPJZ Jason Zucker 10.00 25.00
URPRS Riley Sheahan 10.00 25.00
URPSB Sven Baertschi 6.00 15.00
URPSG Scott Glennie 5.00 12.00
URPSI Jakob Silfverberg 8.00 20.00
URPTB Tyson Barrie 12.00 30.00

2012-13 Ultimate Collection Ultimate Rookie Patches Duos

DRPAR J.Rynnas/C.Ashton 8.00 20.00
DRPAS J.Schwartz/J.Allen 15.00 40.00
DRPBK C.Kreider/S.Baertschi 20.00 50.00
DRPSK C.Kreider/J.Schwartz 20.00 50.00
DRPSS J.Silfverberg/M.Stone 20.00 50.00

2012-13 Ultimate Collection Ultimate Rookie Patches Trios

TRPBKS Baertschi/Kreider/Silfverberg 20.0050.00
TRPPAR Allen/Rynnas/Pickard 20.00 50.00
TRPSBK Kreider/Baertschi/Schwartz 20.00 50.00

2012-13 Ultimate Collection Ultimate Signature Masterpieces

USMAH Adam Henrique C 10.00 25.00
USMBO Bobby Orr B 75.00 135.00
USMCK Chris Kreider C 20.00 50.00
USMCS Cory Schneider C 8.00 20.00
USMDP Dion Phaneuf B 25.00 50.00
USMJA Jaden Schwartz C 12.00 30.00
USMJJ Jaromir Jagr A 60.00 120.00
USMJS Jeff Skinner C 15.00 40.00
USMMD Matt Duchene C 15.00 40.00
USMML Mario Lemieux A 100.00 175.00
USMOV Alexander Ovechkin A 60.00 120.00
USMSC Sidney Crosby A 150.00 250.00
USMWG Wayne Gretzky A 300.00 800.00

2012-13 Ultimate Collection Ultimate Signatures

USAH Adam Henrique B 6.00 15.00
USBO Bobby Orr C 60.00 150.00
USBS Brayden Schenn A 8.00 20.00
USCH Cody Hodgson B 5.00 12.00
USCK Chris Kreider C 20.00 50.00
USCP Carey Price A 30.00 80.00
USEL Eric Lindros B 25.00 60.00
USGL Guy Lafleur B 20.00 50.00
USGR Wayne Gretzky B 200.00 500.00
USJA Jake Allen B 10.00 25.00
USJJ Jaromir Jagr B 30.00 80.00
USJR Jussi Rynnas C 5.00 12.00
USJS Jakob Silfverberg C 10.00 25.00
USLE Mario Lemieux B 80.00 200.00
USME Mark Messier B 25.00 60.00
USOR Bobby Orr A 60.00 150.00
USPB Pavel Bure A 30.00 80.00
USPI Chet Pickard B 6.00 15.00
USPR Carey Price A 15.00 40.00
USRI Pekka Rinne B 8.00 20.00
USRN Ryan Nugent-Hopkins (inserted in 2016-17 Ultimate Collection) 10.00 25.00
USRO Patrick Roy A 40.00 100.00
USSG Scott Glennie B 6.00 15.00
USSJ Jaden Schwartz B 15.00 40.00
USWG Wayne Gretzky A 250.00 600.00

2013-14 Ultimate Collection

1 Logan Couture 2.00 5.00
2 Pavel Datsyuk 2.50 6.00
3 Jeremy Roenick 2.50 6.00
4 Jonathan Toews 2.50 6.00
5 Joe Sakic 3.00 8.00
6 Jaromir Jagr 5.00 12.00
7 Drew Doughty 2.00 5.00
8 Matt Duchene 1.50 4.00
9 Jari Kurri 1.50 4.00
10 Jim Howard 2.00 5.00
11 Wayne Gretzky 10.00 25.00
12 Jordan Eberle 1.50 4.00
13 Evander Kane 1.50 4.00
14 Chris Kunitz 1.50 4.00
15 David Backes 1.00 2.50
16 Nicklas Backstrom 1.50 4.00
17 Tyler Seguin 2.00 5.00
18 Ryan Nugent-Hopkins 2.00 5.00
19 Matt Moulson 1.00 2.50
20 Tuukka Rask 2.00 5.00
21 Antti Niemi 1.25 3.00
22 Bobby Clarke 2.50 6.00
23 Ryan Kesler 1.50 4.00
24 Bobby Ryan 1.25 3.00
25 Zach Parise 1.50 4.00
26 Henrik Sedin 2.00 5.00
27 Ben Bishop 1.25 3.00
28 Ryan Miller 1.50 4.00
29 Ryan Getzlaf 1.50 4.00
30 Alexander Ovechkin 6.00 15.00
31 Mike Ribeiro 1.00 2.50
32 Mike Bossy 1.50 4.00
33 Steven Stamkos 3.00 8.00
34 Sergei Bobrovsky 2.50 6.00
35 Ron Francis 2.00 5.00
36 Carey Price 3.00 8.00
37 Evgeni Malkin 3.00 8.00
38 Phil Kessel 1.50 4.00
39 David Krejci 1.50 4.00
40 Nazem Kadri 2.00 5.00
41 Jamie Benn 1.50 4.00
42 Marian Gaborik 1.50 4.00
43 Jonathan Quick 2.00 5.00
44 Henrik Lundqvist 4.00 10.00
45 Eric Staal 2.00 5.00
46 Jiri Hudler 1.25 3.00
47 Kyle Okposo 1.00 2.50
48 John Tavares 2.50 6.00
49 Mike Gartner 2.00 5.00
50 Alexander Steen 1.00 2.50
51 P.K. Subban 2.00 5.00
52 Pekka Rinne 1.50 4.00
53 Patrick Kane 3.00 8.00
54 Mario Lemieux 6.00 15.00
55 Adam Henrique 1.25 3.00
56 Marcel Dionne 2.00 5.00
57 Vincent Lecavalier 1.50 4.00
58 Sidney Crosby 6.00 15.00
59 Guy Carbonneau 1.50 4.00
60 Erik Karlsson 2.00 5.00
61 Michael Latta/499 RC 2.50 6.00
62 Ryan Stanton/499 RC 3.00 8.00
63 Carl Soderberg/499 RC 3.00 8.00
64 Darcy Kuemper/499 RC 6.00 15.00
65 Tyler Johnson/499 RC 6.00 15.00
65A Tyler Johnson AU/99 RC 100.00 200.00
66 Jack Campbell/499 RC 8.00 20.00
67 Thomas Hickey/499 RC 2.50 6.00
68 Tomas Jurco/499 RC 4.00 10.00
68A Tomas Jurco AU/99 RC 15.00 40.00
69 Jason Missiaen/499 RC 3.00 8.00
70 Eric Hartzell/499 RC 3.00 8.00
71 Anton Belov/499 RC 3.00 8.00
72 Tye McGinn/499 RC 3.00 8.00
73 Reid Boucher/499 RC 3.00 8.00
74 Josh Leivo/499 RC 2.50 6.00
75 Jordan Szwarz/499 RC 3.00 8.00
76 Jamie Oleksiak/499 RC 2.50 6.00
77 Dylan McIlrath/499 RC 2.00 5.00
78 Jon Merrill/499 RC 3.00 8.00
79 Nikita Zadorov/499 RC 2.00 5.00
80 Zach Redmond/499 RC 2.50 6.00
81 Jamie Devane/499 RC 2.50 6.00
82 Xavier Ouellet/499 RC 3.00 8.00
83 Sami Vatanen/499 RC 3.00 8.00
84 Michael Raffl/499 RC 2.50 6.00
85 Ryan Strome/499 RC 6.00 15.00
85A Ryan Strome AU/99 RC 40.00 80.00
86 Jonas Brodin/499 RC 4.00 10.00
87 Linden Vey/499 RC 2.00 5.00
88 Nathan Beaulieu/499 RC 2.00 5.00
89 Antti Raanta/499 RC 6.00 15.00
90 Spencer Abbott/499 RC 2.50 6.00
91 J.T. Miller/499 RC 8.00 20.00
92 Lucas Lessio/499 RC 2.00 5.00
93 Nick Bjugstad/499 RC 4.00 10.00
94 Austin Watson/499 RC 2.50 6.00
95 Mark Barberio/499 RC 2.00 5.00
96 Brian Lashoff/499 RC 2.50 6.00
97 Antoine Roussel/499 RC 3.00 8.00
98 Dmitrij Jaskin/499 RC 3.00 8.00
99 Marek Mazanec/499 RC 3.00 8.00
100 Drew LeBlanc/499 RC 2.00 5.00
101 Eric Gelinas/499 RC 2.50 6.00
102 Reto Berra/499 RC 3.00 8.00
103 Andrej Sustr/499 RC 2.00 5.00
104 Quinton Howden/499 RC 2.50 6.00
105 Nate Schmidt/499 RC 2.50 6.00
106 Frank Corrado/499 RC 2.00 5.00
107 Eric Gryba/499 RC 2.50 6.00
108 Johan Gustafsson/499 RC 4.00 10.00
109 Jeff Zatkoff/499 RC 3.00 8.00
110 Alex Chiasson/499 RC 3.00 8.00
111 Martin Jones/499 RC 5.00 12.00
112 Stefan Matteau/499 RC 2.50 6.00
113 Joakim Nordstrom/499 RC 2.50 6.00
114 Freddie Hamilton/499 RC 3.00 8.00
115 Jason Akeson/499 RC 2.50 6.00
116 John Gibson/499 RC 8.00 20.00
116A John Gibson AU/99 RC 50.00 100.00
117 Patrick Holland/499 RC 5.00 12.00
118 Ondrej Palat/499 RC 5.00 12.00
118A Ondrej Palat AU/99 RC EXCH 25.00 50.00
119 Cody Ceci/499 RC 2.50 6.00
120 David Broll/499 RC 3.00 8.00
121 Frederik Andersen AU/399 RC 12.00 30.00
122 Brock Nelson AU/399 RC 10.00 25.00
123 Chris Brown AU/399 RC 3.00 8.00
124 Matt Nieto AU/399 RC 4.00 10.00
125 Nicklas Jensen AU/399 RC 4.00 10.00
126 Radko Gudas AU/399 RC 5.00 12.00
127 Mark Arcobello AU/399 RC 4.00 10.00
128 Drew Shore AU/399 RC 4.00 10.00
129 Richard Panik AU/399 RC 5.00 12.00
130 Max Reinhart AU/399 RC 5.00 12.00
131 Scott Laughton AU/399 RC 6.00 15.00
132 Alex Killorn AU/399 RC 8.00 20.00
133 Jordan Schroeder AU/399 RC 6.00 15.00
134 Will Acton AU/399 RC 4.00 10.00
135 Jarred Tinordi AU/399 RC 5.00 12.00
136 Jacob Trouba AU/299 RC 8.00 20.00
137 Matt Irwin AU/299 RC 4.00 10.00
138 Mathew Dumba AU/299 RC 3.00 8.00
139 Olli Maatta AU/299 RC 10.00 25.00
140 Tom Wilson AU/299 RC 10.00 25.00
141 Viktor Fasth AU/299 RC 5.00 12.00
142 Michael Bournival AU/299 RC 5.00 12.00
143 Connor Carrick AU/299 RC 4.00 10.00
144 Mikael Granlund AU/299 RC 8.00 20.00
145 Danny DeKeyser AU/299 RC 6.00 15.00
146 Filip Forsberg AU/299 RC 25.00 60.00
147 Beau Bennett AU/299 RC 8.00 20.00
148 Emerson Etem AU/299 RC 8.00 20.00
149 Justin Fontaine AU/299 RC 5.00 12.00
150 Jesper Fast AU/299 RC 5.00 12.00
151 Tanner Pearson AU/299 RC 12.00 30.00
152 Ryan Murphy AU/299 RC 5.00 12.00
153 Jean-Gabriel Pageau AU/299 RC 5.00 12.00
154 Zemgus Girgensons AU/299 RC 8.00 20.00
155 Tyler Toffoli AU/299 RC 15.00 30.00
156 Damien Brunner AU/99 RC 10.00 25.00
157 Seth Jones AU/99 RC 40.00 80.00
158 Brian Flynn AU/99 RC 10.00 25.00
159 Charlie Coyle AU/99 RC 20.00 50.00
160 Hampus Lindholm AU/99 RC 20.00 50.00
161 Petr Mrazek AU/99 RC 25.00 60.00
162 Morgan Rielly AU/99 RC 40.00 50.00
163 Boone Jenner AU/99 RC 20.00 50.00
164 Rasmus Ristolainen AU/99 RC 20.00 50.00
165 Cory Conacher AU/99 RC 8.00 20.00
166 Valeri Nichushkin AU/99 RC 40.00 100.00
167 Ryan Murray AU/99 RC 20.00 50.00
168 Tomas Hertl AU/99 RC 25.00 60.00
169 Mikhail Grigorenko AU/99 RC 8.00 20.00
170 Justin Schultz AU/99 RC 25.00 60.00
171 Nathan MacKinnon AU/99 RC 250.00 500.00
172 Vladimir Tarasenko AU/99 RC 90.00 150.00
173 Sean Monahan AU/99 RC 50.00 100.00
174 Jonathan Huberdeau AU/99 RC 60.00 150.00
175 Brendan Gallagher AU/99 RC 60.00 120.00
176 Nail Yakupov AU/99 RC 40.00 100.00
177 Alex Galchenyuk AU/99 RC 100.00 200.00
178 Aleksander Barkov AU/99 RC 50.00 100.00
179 Elias Lindholm AU/99 RC 20.00 50.00
180 Dougie Hamilton AU/99 RC 50.00 100.00

2013-14 Ultimate Collection '97 Legends Autographs

AL31 Cam Neely B 12.00 30.00
AL35 Johnny Bucyk B 12.00 30.00
AL45 Michel Goulet C 10.00 25.00
AL52 Doug Wilson D 10.00 25.00
AL53 Denis Savard D 12.00 30.00
AL54 Ray Bourque B 20.00 50.00
AL55 Patrick Roy A 60.00 150.00
AL56 Joe Sakic A 25.00 60.00
AL57 Peter Forsberg A 25.00 60.00
AL58 Nicklas Lidstrom D 12.00 30.00
AL59 Dominik Hasek B 20.00 50.00
AL60 Steve Yzerman A 30.00 80.00
AL61 Vincent Damphousse D 10.00 25.00
AL62 Martin Brodeur B 30.00 80.00
AL64 Glenn Anderson D 10.00 25.00
AL65 Wayne Gretzky A 400.00 1000.00
AL66 Theoren Fleury B 15.00 40.00
AL67 Pavel Bure (inserted in 2015-16 Ultimate Collection) 60.00 150.00
AL68 Brian Leetch B 10.00 25.00
AL69 Markus Naslund D 12.00 30.00
AL70 Mark Messier A 60.00 150.00
AL71 Mike Gartner D 15.00 40.00
AL72 Richard Brodeur D 12.00 30.00
AL74 Paul Coffey B 12.00 30.00
AL75 Joe Sakic A 40.00 100.00
AL76 Mats Sundin A 12.00 30.00
AL77 Wayne Gretzky A 400.00 1000.00
AL78 Chris Pronger A 12.00 30.00
AL79 Mats Sundin A 12.00 30.00
AL80 Pavel Bure (inserted in 2015-16 Ultimate Collection) 60.00 150.00
AL81 Alexander Ovechkin A 50.00 120.00
AL82 Mike Richter 12.00 30.00
AL83 John LeClair B 12.00 30.00
AL84 Jeremy Roenick D 20.00 50.00
AL85 Gilbert Perreault D 12.00 30.00
AL86 Arturs Irbe C 10.00 25.00
AL87 Dale Hawerchuk B 15.00 40.00
AL88 Curtis Joseph C 15.00 40.00
AL89 Grant Fuhr C 15.00 40.00
AL90 Trevor Linden C 12.00 30.00

2013-14 Ultimate Collection Debut Threads Patches

UDTAB Aleksander Barkov 15.00 40.00
UDTAG Alex Galchenyuk 20.00 50.00
UDTAK Alex Killorn 12.00 30.00
UDTBB Beau Bennett 10.00 25.00
UDTBF Brian Flynn 6.00 15.00
UDTBG Brendan Gallagher 20.00 50.00
UDTBJ Boone Jenner 15.00 40.00
UDTBN Brock Nelson 15.00 40.00
UDTCA Connor Carrick 6.00 15.00
UDTCB Chris Brown 5.00 12.00
UDTCC Cory Conacher 5.00 12.00
UDTCO Charlie Coyle 12.00 30.00
UDTDB Damien Brunner 6.00 15.00
UDTDD Danny DeKeyser 10.00 25.00
UDTDH Dougie Hamilton 15.00 40.00
UDTDS Drew Shore 6.00 15.00
UDTEE Emerson Etem 8.00 20.00
UDTEL Elias Lindholm 20.00 50.00
UDTFA Frederik Andersen 20.00 50.00
UDTFF Filip Forsberg 25.00 60.00
UDTGR Mikhail Grigorenko 5.00 12.00
UDTHL Hampus Lindholm 10.00 25.00
UDTJE Jesper Fast 8.00 20.00
UDTJF Justin Fontaine 8.00 20.00
UDTJH Jonathan Huberdeau 15.00 40.00
UDTJP Jean-Gabriel Pageau 8.00 20.00
UDTJS Jordan Schroeder 8.00 20.00
UDTJT Jarred Tinordi 8.00 20.00
UDTMA Mark Arcobello 8.00 20.00
UDTMB Michael Bournival 8.00 20.00
UDTMD Mathew Dumba 5.00 12.00
UDTMG Mikael Granlund 10.00 25.00
UDTMI Matt Irwin 6.00 15.00
UDTMN Matt Nieto 6.00 15.00
UDTMR Max Reinhart 8.00 20.00
UDTMU Ryan Murray 12.00 30.00
UDTNJ Nicklas Jensen 8.00 20.00
UDTNM Nathan MacKinnon 80.00 200.00
UDTNY Nail Yakupov 12.00 30.00
UDTOM Olli Maatta 12.00 30.00
UDTPM Petr Mrazek 12.00 30.00
UDTRG Radko Gudas 10.00 25.00
UDTRI Morgan Rielly 15.00 40.00
UDTRM Ryan Murphy 8.00 20.00
UDTRP Richard Panik 8.00 20.00
UDTRR Rasmus Ristolainen 12.00 30.00
UDTSC Justin Schultz 6.00 15.00
UDTSJ Seth Jones 12.00 30.00
UDTSL Scott Laughton 10.00 25.00
UDTSM Sean Monahan 15.00 40.00
UDTTH Tomas Hertl 15.00 40.00
UDTTP Tanner Pearson 8.00 20.00
UDTTR Jacob Trouba 12.00 30.00
UDTTT Tyler Toffoli 12.00 30.00
UDTTW Tom Wilson 15.00 40.00
UDTVF Viktor Fasth 8.00 20.00
UDTVN Valeri Nichushkin 15.00 40.00
UDTVT Vladimir Tarasenko 25.00 50.00
UDTWA Will Acton 6.00 15.00
UDTZG Zemgus Girgensons 10.00 25.00

2013-14 Ultimate Collection Premium Patches

PSAK Anze Kopitar 20.00 50.00
PSAN Antti Niemi 10.00 25.00
PSBB Brian Boyle 8.00 20.00
PSCC Corey Crawford 25.00 50.00
PSCH Carl Hagelin 8.00 20.00
PSCJ Curtis Joseph 15.00 40.00
PSCP Chris Pronger 12.00 30.00
PSDB Dustin Brown 12.00 30.00
PSDC David Clarkson 8.00 20.00
PSDD Drew Doughty 15.00 40.00
PSDE Devan Dubnyk 10.00 25.00
PSDH Dominik Hasek 20.00 50.00
PSDK David Krejci 12.00 30.00
PSDU Duncan Keith 10.00 25.00
PSEB Ed Belfour 12.00 30.00
PSGL Georges Laraque 10.00 25.00
PSGM Glen Murray 10.00 25.00
PSHS Henrik Sedin 15.00 40.00
PSHZ Henrik Zetterberg 15.00 40.00
PSJE Jordan Eberle 12.00 30.00
PSJQ Jonathan Quick 15.00 40.00
PSJS Jason Spezza 12.00 30.00
PSKA Nazem Kadri 15.00 40.00
PSKL Kari Lehtonen 10.00 25.00
PSKO Kyle Okposo 8.00 20.00
PSLC Logan Couture 15.00 40.00
PSMF Marc-Andre Fleury 25.00 60.00
PSMG Michael Grabner 10.00 25.00
PSML Milan Lucic 12.00 30.00
PSMN Markus Naslund 12.00 30.00
PSNB Nicklas Backstrom 12.00 30.00
PSNK Nikolai Kulemin 8.00 20.00
PSPA Patrick Sharp 12.00 30.00
PSPB Patrik Berglund 8.00 20.00
PSPF Peter Forsberg 25.00 60.00
PSPS Paul Stastny 10.00 25.00
PSPU P.A. Parenteau 8.00 20.00
PSRG Ryan Getzlaf 12.00 30.00
PSRJ Ryan Johansen 10.00 25.00
PSRM Ryan Miller 12.00 30.00
PSRN Ryan Nugent-Hopkins 15.00 40.00
PSST Martin St. Louis 12.00 30.00
PSSW Shea Weber 10.00 25.00
PSSY Steve Yzerman 30.00 80.00
PSTH Taylor Hall 12.00 30.00
PSTM Tyler Myers 8.00 20.00
PSTS Tyler Seguin 15.00 40.00
PSTV Thomas Vanek 10.00 25.00

2013-14 Ultimate Collection Premium Swatches

PSAK Anze Kopitar 10.00 25.00
PSAN Antti Niemi 5.00 12.00
PSBB Brian Boyle 4.00 10.00
PSCC Corey Crawford 8.00 20.00
PSCH Carl Hagelin 4.00 10.00
PSCJ Curtis Joseph 8.00 20.00
PSCN Cam Neely 6.00 15.00
PSDB Dustin Brown 6.00 15.00
PSDC David Clarkson 4.00 10.00
PSDD Drew Doughty 8.00 20.00
PSDE Devan Dubnyk 5.00 12.00
PSDH Dominik Hasek 10.00 25.00
PSDK David Krejci 6.00 15.00
PSDS Derek Stepan 4.00 10.00
PSDU Duncan Keith 5.00 12.00
PSEB Ed Belfour 6.00 15.00
PSGM Glen Murray 5.00 12.00
PSHZ Henrik Zetterberg 8.00 20.00
PSIK Ilya Kovalchuk 6.00 15.00
PSJE Jordan Eberle 5.00 12.00
PSJQ Jonathan Quick 8.00 20.00
PSJS Jason Spezza 6.00 15.00
PSKA Nazem Kadri 8.00 20.00
PSKL Kari Lehtonen 5.00 12.00
PSKO Kyle Okposo 4.00 10.00
PSMB Martin Brodeur 12.00 30.00
PSMF Marc-Andre Fleury 12.00 30.00
PSMG Michael Grabner 5.00 12.00
PSMH Milan Hejduk 5.00 12.00
PSML Milan Lucic 6.00 15.00
PSMN Markus Naslund 6.00 15.00
PSNB Nicklas Backstrom 6.00 15.00
PSNK Nikolai Kulemin 4.00 10.00
PSPA Patrick Sharp 6.00 15.00
PSPB Patrik Berglund 4.00 10.00
PSPU P.A. Parenteau 4.00 10.00
PSRG Ryan Getzlaf 6.00 15.00
PSRN Ryan Nugent-Hopkins 8.00 20.00
PSST Martin St. Louis 6.00 15.00
PSSU P.K. Subban 10.00 25.00
PSSW Shea Weber 5.00 12.00
PSSY Steve Yzerman 15.00 40.00
PSTH Taylor Hall 6.00 15.00
PSTM Tyler Myers 4.00 10.00
PSTS Tyler Seguin 8.00 20.00
PSTV Thomas Vanek 5.00 12.00

2013-14 Ultimate Collection Rookie Patch Autographs

65 Tyler Johnson 25.00 60.00
68 Tomas Jurco 15.00 40.00
85 Ryan Strome 20.00 50.00
116 John Gibson 30.00 80.00
121 Frederik Andersen 30.00 80.00
122 Brock Nelson 25.00 60.00
123 Chris Brown 8.00 20.00
124 Matt Nieto 10.00 25.00
125 Nicklas Jensen 10.00 25.00
126 Radko Gudas 12.00 30.00
127 Mark Arcobello 12.00 30.00
128 Drew Shore 10.00 25.00
129 Richard Panik 12.00 30.00
130 Max Reinhart 12.00 30.00
131 Scott Laughton 15.00 40.00
132 Alex Killorn 20.00 50.00
133 Jordan Schroeder 12.00 30.00
134 Will Acton 10.00 25.00
135 Jarred Tinordi 12.00 30.00
136 Jacob Trouba 20.00 50.00
138 Mathew Dumba 8.00 20.00
139 Olli Maatta 20.00 50.00
140 Tom Wilson 25.00 60.00
141 Viktor Fasth 12.00 30.00
142 Michael Bournival 12.00 30.00
143 Connor Carrick 10.00 25.00
144 Mikael Granlund 20.00 50.00
145 Danny DeKeyser 15.00 40.00
146 Filip Forsberg 40.00 100.00
147 Beau Bennett 15.00 40.00
148 Emerson Etem 12.00 30.00
149 Justin Fontaine 12.00 30.00
150 Jesper Fast 12.00 30.00
151 Tanner Pearson 12.00 30.00
152 Ryan Murphy 12.00 30.00
153 Jean-Gabriel Pageau 12.00 30.00
154 Zemgus Girgensons 20.00 50.00
155 Tyler Toffoli 25.00 60.00
156 Damien Brunner 10.00 25.00
157 Seth Jones 25.00 60.00
158 Brian Flynn 10.00 25.00
159 Charlie Coyle 20.00 50.00
160 Hampus Lindholm 20.00 50.00
161 Petr Mrazek 25.00 60.00
162 Morgan Rielly 30.00 80.00
163 Boone Jenner 25.00 60.00
164 Rasmus Ristolainen 20.00 50.00
165 Cory Conacher 8.00 20.00
166 Valeri Nichushkin 25.00 60.00
167 Ryan Murray EXCH 20.00 50.00
168 Tomas Hertl 25.00 60.00
169 Mikhail Grigorenko 8.00 20.00
170 Justin Schultz 12.00 30.00
171 Nathan MacKinnon 250.00 500.00
172 Vladimir Tarasenko 100.00 250.00
173 Sean Monahan 20.00 50.00
174 Jonathan Huberdeau 30.00 80.00
175 Brendan Gallagher 30.00 80.00
176 Nail Yakupov 25.00 60.00
177 Alex Galchenyuk 30.00 80.00
178 Aleksander Barkov 40.00 100.00
179 Elias Lindholm 30.00 80.00
180 Dougie Hamilton 20.00 50.00

2013-14 Ultimate Collection Ultimate Dual Patch Autographs

UDPAF Marc-Andre Fleury/25 30.00 80.00
UDPAH Adam Henrique/25 8.00 20.00
UDPAN Antti Niemi/25 8.00 20.00
UDPCH Carl Hagelin/25 6.00 15.00
UDPCP Corey Perry/25 15.00 40.00
UDPDB Dustin Brown/25 10.00 25.00
UDPDR Dwayne Roloson/25 6.00 15.00
UDPES Eric Staal/25 12.00 30.00
UDPGC Claude Giroux/25 10.00 25.00
UDPGL Gabriel Landeskog/25 12.00 30.00
UDPGM Glen Murray/25 8.00 20.00
UDPJH Jim Howard/25 12.00 30.00
UDPKL Kris Letang/25 12.00 30.00
UDPMH Milan Hejduk/25 8.00 20.00
UDPRK Ryan Kesler/25 10.00 25.00
UDPST Paul Stastny/25 8.00 20.00
UDPSW Shea Weber/25 8.00 20.00

2013-14 Ultimate Collection Ultimate Duos Jerseys

UDJCP L.Couture/C.Perry 10.00 25.00
UDJCR C.Crawford/T.Rask 8.00 20.00
UDJDV D.Doughty/S.Voynov 8.00 20.00
UDJHH T.Hall/A.Hemsky 6.00 15.00
UDJPS C.Price/P.Subban 10.00 25.00
UDJSK J.Spezza/E.Karlsson 8.00 20.00
UDJVR J.Voracek/M.Read 5.00 12.00

2013-14 Ultimate Collection Ultimate Duos Patches

*PATCH: .8X TO 2X JERSEYS/65
UDJCR Corey Crawford Tuukka Rask 15.00 40.00
UDJEZ Patrik Elias Travis Zajac 12.00 30.00

2013-14 Ultimate Collection Ultimate Jerseys

UJCJ Curtis Joseph B 5.00 12.00
UJCK Chris Kreider B 5.00 12.00
UJCP Carey Price B 8.00 20.00
UJDB Dustin Brown B 4.00 10.00
UJDD Drew Doughty B 5.00 12.00
UJDK Duncan Keith B 3.00 8.00
UJEB Ed Belfour B 4.00 10.00
UJJE Jordan Eberle B 4.00 10.00
UJJS Jason Spezza B 4.00 10.00
UJJV Jakub Voracek B 3.00 8.00
UJLR Luc Robitaille B 4.00 10.00
UJNK Niklas Kronwall B 3.00 8.00
UJPE Corey Perry B 6.00 15.00
UJPF Peter Forsberg A 15.00 40.00
UJPK P.K. Subban B 5.00 12.00
UJPS Paul Stastny A 5.00 12.00
UJSU Mats Sundin B 4.00 10.00
UJSV Slava Voynov B 3.00 8.00

2013-14 Ultimate Collection Ultimate Patches

*PATCH/35: 1X TO 2.5X JERSEY
UJEL Patrik Elias 10.00 25.00
UJPF Peter Forsberg 12.00 30.00
UJSK Jeff Skinner 12.00 30.00
UJSM Steve Mason 8.00 20.00

2013-14 Ultimate Collection Ultimate Quad Jerseys

UJ4TOR Jsph/Blfr/Sndn/Lndrs 15.00 40.00
UJ4BEES Brgrn/Chra/Rsk/Lcc 15.00 30.00
UJ4KINGS Dghty/Vynv/Brwn/Rchrds 15.00 30.00

2013-14 Ultimate Collection Ultimate Rookie Jerseys

*PATCH/75: .6X TO 1.5X JERSEY
URJAB Aleksander Barkov 5.00 12.00
URJAC Alex Chiasson 2.50 6.00
URJAK Alex Killorn 4.00 10.00
URJBJ Boone Jenner 5.00 12.00
URJEL Elias Lindholm 6.00 15.00
URJFA Jesper Fast 2.50 6.00
URJHL Hampus Lindholm 4.00 10.00
URJJF Justin Fontaine 2.50 6.00
URJJG John Gibson 5.00 12.00
URJJN Joakim Nordstrom 2.00 5.00
URJJT Jacob Trouba 4.00 10.00
URJLL Lucas Lessio 1.50 4.00
URJMA Mark Arcobello 2.50 6.00
URJMD Mathew Dumba 1.50 4.00
URJMN Matt Nieto 2.00 5.00
URJMR Morgan Rielly 4.00 10.00
URJNM Nathan MacKinnon 12.00 30.00
URJOM Olli Maatta 5.00 12.00
URJRM Ryan Murray 4.00 10.00
URJRR Rasmus Ristolainen 4.00 10.00
URJSJ Seth Jones 5.00 12.00
URJSM Sean Monahan 5.00 12.00
URJTH Tomas Hertl 5.00 12.00
URJVN Valeri Nichushkin 4.00 10.00
URJZG Zemgus Girgensons 4.00 10.00

2013-14 Ultimate Collection Ultimate Rookie Jerseys Duos

*PATCH/35: .8X TO 2X DUAL JSY/75
URJ2D M.Rielly/S.Jones 8.00 20.00
URJ2TB A.Killorn/T.Johnson 5.00 12.00
URJ21ST N.MacKinnon/N.Yakupov 12.00 30.00
URJ2CBJ B.Jenner/R.Murray 5.00 12.00
URJ2DAL V.Nichushkin/A.Chiasson 8.00 20.00
URJ2FLO A.Barkov/J.Huberdeau 5.00 12.00
URJ2NYR J.Miller/D.McIlrath 10.00 25.00
URJ2BUFF R.Ristolainen/N.Zadorov 6.00 15.00
URJ2WILD J.Brodin/M.Dumba 5.00 12.00

2013-14 Ultimate Collection Ultimate Rookie Jerseys Quad

URJ4RUS Ykv/Nch/Grnk/Trsn 12.00 30.00
URJ4USA Jns/Glchk/Bntt/Mllr 12.00 30.00
URJ4CAND Hmln/Rly/Schlt/Mry 12.00 30.00
URJ4CANO McKn/Glhr/Mhn/Hbr 15.00 40.00

2013-14 Ultimate Collection Ultimate Rookie Jerseys Six

URJ6EAST Bar/Hub/Gal/Rlly/Lin/Cnr 15.00 40.00
URJ6WEST McK/Mn/Yk/Jns/Hrt/Nch 40.00 80.00

2013-14 Ultimate Collection Ultimate Rookie Jerseys Trios

*PATCH/25: .6X TO 1.5X BASIC TRIO/65
URJ3C Brkv/Arcbllo/Jnnr 12.00 30.00
URJ3D Mrry/Jns/Rlly 8.00 20.00
URJ3RW Ykpv/Nchshkn/Gllghr 10.00 25.00
URJ3DEF Rstlnn/Trba/Dmba 6.00 15.00
URJ3FWD McKnnn/Hbrdau/Glchnk 15.00 40.00
URJ32013 McKnnn/Brkv/Jns 15.00 40.00
URJ3GOALS Hrtl/Mnhn/Chssn 8.00 20.00
URJ3WING Nto/Fst/Fntne 4.00 10.00

2013-14 Ultimate Collection Ultimate Rookie Patches Quad

*PATCH/15: .8X TO 2X JERSEY/50
URJ4CANO McKn/Glgh/Mnh/Hbrd 100.00200.00

2013-14 Ultimate Collection Ultimate Rookie Signatures

USRAG Alex Galchenyuk A 15.00 40.00
USRBB Beau Bennett B 4.00 10.00
USRBG Brendan Gallagher B 20.00 50.00
USRBJ Boone Jenner B 5.00 12.00
USRCO Cory Conacher B 4.00 10.00
USRDH Dougie Hamilton B 12.50 25.00
USREE Emerson Etem B 3.00 8.00
USREL Elias Lindholm B 8.00 20.00
USRFF Filip Forsberg B 12.00 30.00
USRJC Jack Campbell A 10.00 25.00
USRJH Jonathan Huberdeau A 12.00 30.00
USRJS Justin Schultz B 3.00 8.00
USRMD Mathew Dumba A 2.50 6.00
USRMR Morgan Rielly A 10.00 25.00
USRNM Nathan MacKinnon A 20.00 50.00
USRNY Nail Yakupov A 12.00 30.00
USRPM Petr Mrazek B 6.00 15.00
USRSC Jordan Schroeder B 3.00 8.00
USRSJ Seth Jones A 8.00 20.00
USRSM Sean Monahan A 6.00 15.00
USRTH Tomas Hertl B 6.00 15.00
USRTT Tyler Toffoli B 8.00 20.00

USRVF Viktor Fasth B 3.00 8.00
USRVN Valeri Nichushkin B 10.00 20.00

2013-14 Ultimate Collection Ultimate Signature Masterpiece

USMAB Alexandre Burrows E 5.00 12.00
USMAG Alex Galchenyuk E 20.00 50.00
USMAP Alex Pietrangelo C 6.00 15.00
USMBC Bobby Clarke E 12.00 30.00
USMBG Brendan Gallagher E 20.00 50.00
USMBH Brett Hull B 15.00 40.00
USMCP Carey Price A 60.00 150.00
USMDH Dominik Hasek B 12.00 30.00
USMEM Evgeni Malkin B 15.00 40.00
USMJB Jamie Benn C 8.00 20.00
USMJH Jonathan Huberdeau E 20.00 50.00
USMJN James Neal E 5.00 12.00
USMJT Jonathan Toews B 12.00 30.00
USMJTA John Tavares D 12.00 30.00
USMMS Mats Sundin B 8.00 20.00
USMNM Nathan MacKinnon E 60.00 150.00
USMNY Nail Yakupov D 15.00 40.00
USMPF Peter Forsberg B 15.00 40.00
USMPK Patrick Kane A 60.00 150.00
USMPR Patrick Roy A 60.00 150.00
USMPV Pavel Bure A 60.00 150.00
USMRI Pekka Rinne C 8.00 20.00
USMRN Ryan Nugent-Hopkins D 10.00 25.00
USMSH Scott Hartnell E 5.00 12.00
USMSJ Seth Jones E 15.00 40.00
USMSW Shea Weber D 6.00 15.00
USMSY Steve Yzerman B 20.00 50.00
USMTF Theoren Fleury B 10.00 25.00
USMTH Taylor Hall D 8.00 20.00
USMTS Tyler Seguin C 10.00 25.00
USMVT Vladimir Tarasenko E 20.00 50.00
USMWG Wayne Gretzky B 250.00 600.00
USMZP Zach Parise D 8.00 20.00

2013-14 Ultimate Collection Ultimate Signatures

USAI Arturs Irbe D 6.00 15.00
USAS Andrew Shaw E 5.00 12.00
USBO Bobby Orr B 30.00 80.00
USCH Cody Hodgson E 5.00 12.00
USCO Chris Osgood C 8.00 20.00
USCP Carey Price A 15.00 40.00
USDW Doug Wilson E 6.00 15.00
USGL Gabriel Landeskog E 10.00 25.00
USGR Wayne Gretzky A 200.00 500.00
USJJ Jaromir Jagr A 25.00 60.00
USJS Jeff Skinner A 10.00 25.00
USJT Jonathan Toews A 12.00 30.00
USLE Loui Eriksson E 5.00 12.00
USMK Mikko Koivu D 6.00 15.00
USOR Bobby Orr B 30.00 80.00
USPB Patrice Bergeron C 10.00 25.00
USPK Patrick Kane C 15.00 40.00
USRE Ryan Ellis E 6.00 15.00
USRI Pekka Rinne 8.00 20.00
USSA Joe Sakic A 15.00 40.00
USSK Saku Koivu D 8.00 20.00
USST Jarret Stoll D 6.00 15.00
USSW Shea Weber C 6.00 15.00
USTH Taylor Hall C 8.00 20.00
USTS Tyler Seguin C 10.00 25.00
USWG Wayne Gretzky B 200.00 500.00

2013-14 Ultimate Collection Ultimate Six Jerseys

UJ6LAK Rds/Bn/Ctr/Dgh/Vn/Kp 20.00 40.00
UJ6NET Qk/Rk/Cfd/Nm/Sch/Hd 10.00 25.00
UJ6STLDET St/Ptg/Hk/Hd/Ztr/Frn 10.00 25.00

2013-14 Ultimate Collection Ultimate Threads Autographs

UATAN Antti Niemi/99 10.00 25.00
UATAO Alexander Ovechkin/25 50.00 125.00
UATBH Brett Hull/25 25.00 60.00
UATBU Pavel Bure/25
(inserted in 2015-16
Ultimate Collection) 12.00 30.00
UATCP Carey Price/25 25.00 60.00
UATCS Cory Schneider/99 12.00 30.00
UATDH Dale Hawerchuk/99 15.00 40.00
UATEK Evander Kane/99 12.00 30.00
UATEM Evgeni Malkin/25 25.00 60.00
UATGL Gabriel Landeskog/99 15.00 40.00
UATJH Jonas Hiller/99 10.00 25.00
UATJS Jeff Skinner/99 15.00 40.00
UATJT Jonathan Toews/25 20.00 50.00
UATMD Matt Duchene/99 12.00 30.00
UATML Mario Lemieux/25 50.00 125.00
UATPB Patrice Bergeron/25 15.00 40.00
UATPE Corey Perry/25 20.00 50.00
UATSA Joe Sakic/25 25.00 60.00
UATSH Scott Hartnell/99 8.00 20.00
UATSU Mats Sundin/25 12.00 30.00
UATSY Steve Yzerman/25 30.00 80.00
UATTF Theoren Fleury/25 15.00 40.00
UATTH Taylor Hall/25 EXCH 12.00 30.00
UATTS Tyler Seguin/25 15.00 40.00
UATWG Wayne Gretzky/25 250.00 600.00

2013-14 Ultimate Collection Ultimate Trios Jerseys

U3LAK Dghty/Rchrds/Brwn 6.00 15.00
U3NET Rsk/Crwfrd/Qck 6.00 15.00
U3BEES Nly/Rsk/Mrry 6.00 15.00
U3WINGS Hwrd/Yzrmn/Zttrbrg 6.00 15.00

2013-14 Ultimate Collection Ultimate Trios Patches

U3NJD Brodeur/Elias/Schndr
U3OTT Karlsn/Spezza/Lehner
U3WEST Couture/Perry/Dghty 30.00 60.00

2014-15 Ultimate Collection

1 Jordan Eberle 2.00 5.00
2 Jamie Benn 2.00 5.00
3 Jiri Hudler 1.50 4.00
4 Nathan MacKinnon 8.00 20.00
5 Drew Doughty 2.50 6.00
6 Jason Spezza 2.00 5.00
7 Ryan Miller 2.00 5.00
8 Jonathan Bernier 1.50 4.00
9 David Backes 1.25 3.00
10 Corey Crawford 2.50 6.00
11 Henrik Sedin 2.50 6.00
12 Aleksander Barkov 3.00 8.00
13 Joe Pavelski 2.50 6.00
14 Kyle Turris 2.00 5.00
15 Tomas Hertl 2.00 5.00
16 Martin St. Louis 2.00 5.00
17 Ryan Nugent-Hopkins 2.50 6.00
18 Jakub Voracek 1.50 4.00
19 Jason Pominville 1.25 3.00
20 Kari Lehtonen 1.50 4.00
21 Jonathan Toews 3.00 8.00
22 Alexander Ovechkin 8.00 20.00
23 Corey Perry 3.00 8.00
24 Evgeni Malkin 4.00 10.00
25 Patrick Sharp 2.00 5.00
26 Max Pacioretty 2.00 5.00
27 Pavel Datsyuk 3.00 8.00
28 Tuukka Rask 2.50 6.00
29 Henrik Zetterberg 2.50 6.00
30 Blake Wheeler 2.00 5.00
31 Shane Doan 1.50 4.00
32 Cody Hodgson 1.25 3.00
33 Sergei Bobrovsky 3.00 8.00
34 Alex Galchenyuk 1.25 3.00
35 Zdeno Chara 2.00 5.00
36 Phil Kessel 2.00 5.00
37 Shea Weber 1.50 4.00
38 Henrik Lundqvist 5.00 12.00
39 Gabriel Landeskog 2.50 6.00
40 Milan Lucic 2.00 5.00
41 Kyle Okposo 1.25 3.00
42 Erik Karlsson 2.50 6.00
43 Eric Staal 2.50 6.00
44 Jonathan Quick 2.50 6.00
45 Seth Jones 2.00 5.00
46 P.K. Subban 2.50 6.00
47 Jaromir Jagr 6.00 15.00
48 Jeff Carter 1.50 4.00
49 Roberto Luongo 3.00 8.00
50 Cory Schneider 2.00 5.00
51 Tyler Seguin JSY 5.00 12.00
52 Rick Nash JSY 4.00 10.00
53 T.J. Oshie JSY 4.00 10.00
54 Charlie Coyle JSY 4.00 10.00
55 Patrice Bergeron JSY 5.00 12.00
56 Pekka Rinne JSY 4.00 10.00
57 Patrick Kane JSY 8.00 20.00
58 Taylor Hall JSY 4.00 10.00
59 John Tavares JSY 6.00 15.00
60 Matt Duchene JSY 4.00 10.00
61 Daniel Sedin JSY 5.00 12.00
62 Claude Giroux JSY 4.00 10.00
63 Steven Stamkos JSY 8.00 20.00
64 Alexander Semin JSY 4.00 10.00
65 Zach Parise JSY 4.00 10.00
66 Nicklas Backstrom JSY 4.00 10.00
67 Sean Monahan JSY 2.50 6.00
68 Sidney Crosby JSY 15.00 40.00
69 Vladimir Tarasenko JSY 5.00 12.00
70 Jonathan Huberdeau JSY 5.00 12.00
71 Zemgus Girgensons JSY 3.00 8.00
72 Ryan Kesler JSY 4.00 10.00
73 Ryan Getzlaf JSY 4.00 10.00
74 Carey Price JSY 8.00 20.00
75 Anze Kopitar JSY 6.00 15.00
76 Bogdan Yakimov AU/299 RC 5.00 12.00
77 Patrick Brown AU/299 RC 5.00 12.00
78 P-E Bellemare AU/299 RC 5.00 12.00
79 Sven Andrighetto AU/299 RC 6.00 15.00
80 Christian Folin AU/299 RC 5.00 12.00
81 John Klingberg AU/299 RC 10.00 25.00
82 Justin Hodgman AU/299 RC 4.00 10.00
83 Rocco Grimaldi AU/299 RC 5.00 12.00
84 Josh Jooris AU/299 RC 5.00 12.00
85 B.Goodrow AU/299 RC 5.00 12.00
86 Joe Morrow AU/299 RC 6.00 15.00
87 David Pastrnak AU/99 RC 200.00 500.00
88 D.Everberg AU/299 RC 5.00 12.00
89 M.Granlund AU/299 RC 8.00 20.00
90 A.Vasilevskiy AU/299 RC 60.00 150.00
91 Brandon Kozun AU/299 RC 4.00 10.00
92 Seth Helgeson AU/299 RC 4.00 10.00
93 Brett Ritchie AU/299 RC 5.00 12.00
94 C.McKenzie AU/299 RC 4.00 10.00
95 Hammond AU/99 RC EXCH 8.00 20.00
96 Kevin Hayes AU/299 RC 12.00 30.00
97 Mirco Mueller AU/299 RC 5.00 12.00
98 T.van Riemsdyk AU/299 RC 8.00 20.00
99 Victor Rask AU/299 RC 5.00 12.00
100 V.Namestnikov AU/299 RC 8.00 20.00
101 W.Karlsson AU/299 RC 15.00 40.00
102 Chris Tierney AU/299 RC 5.00 12.00
103 Curtis Lazar AU/299 RC 5.00 12.00
104 Adam Lowry AU/299 RC 8.00 20.00
105 Ryan Sproul AU/299 RC 5.00 12.00
106 Marko Dano AU/299 RC 5.00 12.00
107 Stuart Percy AU/299 RC 5.00 12.00
108 Darnell Nurse AU/299 RC 10.00 25.00
109 Griffin Reinhart AU/299 RC 5.00 12.00
110 S.Gostisbehere AU/299 RC 10.00 25.00
111 D.Severson AU/299 RC 5.00 12.00
112 Jiri Sekac AU/99 RC 4.00 10.00
113 Seth Griffith AU/299 RC 6.00 15.00
114 A.Wennberg AU/299 RC 8.00 20.00
115 A.Duclair AU/99 RC EXCH 25.00 50.00
116 T.Teravainen AU/99 RC 8.00 20.00
117 Jori Lehtera AU/299 RC 6.00 15.00
118 E.Kuznetsov AU/299 RC 12.00 30.00
119 Bo Horvat AU/99 RC 30.00 80.00
120 A.Burakovsky AU/299 RC 8.00 20.00
121 J.Gaudreau AU/99 RC 125.00 300.00
122 Leon Draisaitl AU/99 RC 200.00 500.00
123 Sam Reinhart AU/99 RC 20.00 50.00
124 Aaron Ekblad AU/99 RC 25.00 60.00
125 Jonathan Drouin AU/99 RC 40.00 100.00

2014-15 Ultimate Collection Blue Spectrum

55 Patrice Bergeron STK 12.00 30.00
57 Patrick Kane STK 20.00 50.00
59 John Tavares GLV 15.00 40.00
60 Matt Duchene STK 10.00 25.00
61 Daniel Sedin STK 12.00 30.00
62 Claude Giroux STK 10.00 25.00
64 Alexander Semin STK 10.00 25.00
66 Nicklas Backstrom STK 10.00 25.00
68 Sidney Crosby STK 40.00 100.00
70 Jonathan Huberdeau STK 12.00 30.00
73 Ryan Getzlaf STK 10.00 25.00
75 Anze Kopitar STK 15.00 40.00

2014-15 Ultimate Collection Gold Spectrum

*51-75 PATCH/35: .8X TO 2X BASIC JSY/99
66 Nicklas Backstrom PATCH 8.00 20.00

2014-15 Ultimate Collection '04-05 Retro

1 Phil Kessel/150 1.50 4.00
2 Joe Pavelski/150 2.00 5.00
3 Chris Kunitz/150 1.25 3.00
4 Jonathan Toews/150 2.00 5.00
5 Sidney Crosby/150 5.00 12.00
6 Nathan MacKinnon/150 5.00 12.00
7 Pavel Datsyuk/150 2.00 5.00
8 Tuukka Rask/150 1.50 4.00
9 Ryan Getzlaf/150 1.25 3.00
10 Matt Duchene/150 1.25 3.00
11 Jaromir Jagr/150 4.00 10.00
12 Patrice Bergeron/150 1.50 4.00
13 Duncan Keith/150 1.00 2.50
14 Henrik Lundqvist/150 3.00 8.00
15 Joe Thornton/150 2.00 5.00
16 Claude Giroux/150 1.25 3.00
17 Patrick Kane/150 2.50 6.00
18 Steven Stamkos/150 2.50 6.00
19 Sergei Bobrovsky/150 2.00 5.00
20 Evgeni Malkin/150 2.50 6.00
21 Taylor Hall/150 1.25 3.00
22 Jarome Iginla/150 1.50 4.00
23 John Tavares/150 2.00 5.00
24 Carey Price/150 2.50 6.00
25 Anze Kopitar/150 2.00 5.00
26 Shea Weber/150 1.00 2.50
27 Max Pacioretty/150 1.25 3.00
28 Martin St. Louis/150 1.25 3.00
29 P.K. Subban/150 1.50 4.00
30 Jason Spezza/150 1.25 3.00
31 Henrik Zetterberg/150 1.50 4.00
32 Jamie Benn/150 1.25 3.00
33 Drew Doughty/150 1.50 4.00
34 Alexander Ovechkin/150 5.00 12.00
35 Tyler Seguin/150 1.50 4.00
36 Mario Lemieux/199 5.00 12.00
37 Pelle Lindbergh/199 1.00 2.50
38 Wayne Gretzky/199 8.00 20.00
39 Terry Sawchuk/199 1.25 3.00
40 Bobby Orr/199 5.00 12.00
41 Curtis Lazar/299 1.25 3.00
42 Anthony Duclair/299 2.00 5.00
43 Evgeny Kuznetsov/299 3.00 8.00
44 Johnny Gaudreau/299 4.00 10.00
45 Bo Horvat/299 3.00 8.00
46 Andre Burakovsky/299 2.00 5.00
47 Aaron Ekblad/299 3.00 8.00
48 Leon Draisaitl/299 15.00 40.00
49 Sam Reinhart/299 5.00 12.00
50 Jonathan Drouin/299 2.50 6.00

2014-15 Ultimate Collection '04-05 Retro Ultimate Memorabilia

*GOLD/25: .75X TO 2X BASIC JSY/99
UGJDS Daniel Sedin 5.00 12.00
UGJJB Jonathan Bernier 3.00 8.00
UGJJE Jordan Eberle 4.00 10.00
UGJJS Jason Spezza 4.00 10.00
UGJJV James van Riemsdyk 3.00 8.00
UGJPR Pekka Rinne 4.00 10.00
UGJPS P.K. Subban 5.00 12.00
UGJRO Patrick Roy 10.00 25.00
UGJSH Patrick Sharp 4.00 10.00
UGJTR Tuukka Rask 5.00 12.00
UGJTS Teemu Selanne 8.00 20.00

2014-15 Ultimate Collection '04-05 Retro Ultimate Signatures

RUSAB Aleksander Barkov C 12.00 30.00
RUSAE Aaron Ekblad B 20.00 50.00
RUSAI Arturs Irbe B 6.00 15.00
RUSAO Alexander Ovechkin A 30.00 80.00
RUSAW Alexander Wennberg D 12.00 30.00
RUSBO Bobby Orr A 60.00 150.00
RUSBR Brett Ritchie D 8.00 20.00
RUSBU Andre Burakovsky C 12.00 30.00
RUSCL Curtis Lazar C 8.00 20.00
RUSCP Carey Price B 15.00 40.00
RUSDS Damon Severson D 8.00 20.00
RUSGJ Johnny Gaudreau C 25.00 60.00
RUSGN Gustav Nyquist C 5.00 12.00
RUSJD Jonathan Drouin C 15.00 40.00
RUSJG John Gibson D 8.00 20.00
RUSJI Jarome Iginla B 10.00 25.00
RUSJP Joe Pavelski D 10.00 25.00
RUSJT Jonathan Toews A 12.00 30.00
RUSJV John Vanbiesbrouck D 8.00 20.00
RUSLD Leon Draisaitl C 125.00 300.00
RUSMB Martin Brodeur A 25.00 60.00
RUSMF Marc-Andre Fleury B 15.00 40.00
RUSML Mario Lemieux A 40.00 100.00
RUSMM Mark Messier A 25.00 60.00
RUSMP Max Pacioretty C 8.00 20.00
RUSPD Pavel Datsyuk D 12.00 30.00
RUSPP Pete Peeters C 6.00 15.00
RUSPR Patrick Roy A 30.00 80.00
RUSRN Rick Nash B 8.00 20.00
RUSSB Sergei Bobrovsky D 12.00 30.00
RUSSC Sidney Crosby A 100.00 200.00
RUSSM Sean Monahan C 5.00 12.00
RUSSR Sam Reinhart D 30.00 80.00
RUSTA John Tavares C 12.00 30.00
RUSTS Tyler Seguin A 10.00 25.00
RUSTT Teuvo Teravainen D 12.00 30.00
RUSVD Vincent Damphousse C 6.00 15.00
RUSWG Wayne Gretzky C 200.00 500.00

2014-15 Ultimate Collection Debut Threads Patches

DTAB Andre Burakovsky 6.00 15.00
DTAE Aaron Ekblad 15.00 40.00
DTAL Adam Lowry 6.00 15.00
DTAV Andrei Vasilevskiy 12.00 30.00
DTAW Alexander Wennberg 6.00 15.00
DTBA Barclay Goodrow 4.00 10.00
DTBH Bo Horvat 15.00 40.00
DTBK Brandon Kozun 3.00 8.00
DTBR Brett Ritchie 4.00 10.00
DTCL Curtis Lazar 4.00 10.00
DTCM Curtis McKenzie 3.00 8.00
DTCT Chris Tierney 4.00 10.00
DTDN Darnell Nurse 8.00 20.00
DTDP Derrick Pouliot 5.00 12.00
DTDS Damon Severson 4.00 10.00
DTEK Evgeny Kuznetsov 10.00 25.00
DTGO Shayne Gostisbehere 8.00 20.00
DTGR Griffin Reinhart 4.00 10.00
DTHE Seth Helgeson 3.00 8.00
DTHO Justin Hodgman 3.00 8.00
DTJB Jordan Binnington 12.00 30.00
DTJD Jonathan Drouin 8.00 20.00
DTJG Johnny Gaudreau 12.00 30.00
DTJK John Klingberg 8.00 20.00
DTJL Jori Lehtera 5.00 12.00
DTKR Kerby Rychel 3.00 8.00
DTLD Leon Draisaitl 40.00 100.00
DTMD Marko Dano 4.00 10.00
DTMM Mirco Mueller 4.00 10.00
DTMO Joe Morrow 5.00 12.00
DTPD Phillip Danault 8.00 20.00
DTPE Pierre-Edouard Bellemare 4.00 10.00
DTRG Rocco Grimaldi 4.00 10.00
DTRI Tobias Rieder 4.00 10.00
DTRZ Rob Zepp 6.00 15.00
DTSA Sven Andrighetto 5.00 12.00
DTSG Seth Griffith 5.00 12.00
DTSM Colin Smith 4.00 10.00
DTSP Stuart Percy 4.00 10.00
DTSR Sam Reinhart 15.00 40.00
DTTP Teemu Pulkkinen 5.00 12.00
DTTT Teuvo Teravainen 6.00 15.00
DTTV Trevor van Riemsdyk 6.00 15.00
DTVN Vladislav Namestnikov 6.00 15.00
DTVR Victor Rask 4.00 10.00

2014-15 Ultimate Collection Memorable Materials Dual Swatch Combos

MM2AK C.Anderson/E.Karlsson 8.00 20.00
MM2BL M.Lucic/P.Bergeron 5.00 12.00
MM2BN J.Benn/V.Nichushkin 4.00 10.00
MM2BT D.Backes/Tarasenko 5.00 12.00
MM2CT J.Toews/C.Crawford 6.00 15.00
MM2DR J.Drouin/S.Reinhart 15.00 40.00
MM2EB Kuznetsov/Burakovsky 10.00 25.00
MM2EN Eberle/Nugent-Hopkins 5.00 12.00
MM2ER A.Ekblad/S.Reinhart 15.00 40.00
MM2GC C.Coyle/M.Granlund 4.00 10.00
MM2HB J.Huberdeau/A.Barkov 6.00 15.00
MM2HD S.Hartnell/B.Dubinsky 2.50 6.00
MM2IL J.Iginla/G.Landeskog 5.00 12.00
MM2JT J.Carter/T.Toffoli 4.00 10.00
MM2KG R.Getzlaf/R.Kesler 4.00 10.00
MM2KM E.Malkin/C.Kunitz 8.00 20.00
MM2KV J.van Rmsdyk/Kessel 4.00 10.00
MM2MH C.Hodgson/M.Moulson 2.50 6.00
MM2OB Ovechkin/N.Backstrom 15.00 40.00
MM2PC L.Couture/J.Pavelski 5.00 12.00
MM2PS M.Pacioretty/P.Subban 5.00 12.00
MM2RD L.Draisaitl/S.Reinhart 20.00 50.00
MM2SC R.Strome/C.Coyle 4.00 10.00
MM2SH S.Stamkos/V.Hedman 8.00 20.00
MM2SM R.Miller/H.Sedin 5.00 12.00
MM2SN R.Nash/M.St. Louis 4.00 10.00
MM2SS J.Skinner/A.Semin 5.00 12.00
MM2VG C.Giroux/J.Voracek 4.00 10.00
MM2WJ S.Weber/S.Jones 4.00 10.00
MM2WS B.Wheeler/M.Scheifele 6.00 15.00

2014-15 Ultimate Collection Obsidian Script

OSAG Alex Galchenyuk F 4.00 10.00
OSEK Evgeny Kuznetsov E 12.00 30.00
OSGN Gustav Nyquist F 4.00 10.00
OSJG Johnny Gaudreau F 80.00 200.00
OSLD Leon Draisaitl D 80.00 200.00
OSMB Matt Beleskey F 4.00 10.00
OSMG Mike Gartner F 8.00 20.00
OSMS Mats Sundin A 6.00 15.00
OSOV Alexander Ovechkin A 25.00 60.00
OSRF Ron Francis B 8.00 20.00
OSRK Ryan Kesler E 6.00 15.00
OSSB Sergei Bobrovsky B 10.00 25.00

2014-15 Ultimate Collection Obsidian Script Inscribed

OSAE Aaron Ekblad D 20.00 50.00
OSAO Adam Oates D 8.00 20.00
OSAW Alexander Wennberg F 12.00 30.00
OSBH Brett Hull B 15.00 40.00
OSCC Chris Chelios C 8.00 20.00
OSCJ Curtis Joseph D 10.00 25.00
OSCL Curtis Lazar F 8.00 20.00
OSDA Damon Severson E 8.00 20.00
OSJD Jonathan Drouin D 15.00 40.00
OSJJ Jaromir Jagr A 25.00 60.00
OSMF Marc-Andre Fleury C 15.00 40.00
OSMM Mark Messier A 15.00 40.00
OSMR Morgan Rielly E 8.00 20.00
OSPM Patrick Marleau C 8.00 20.00
OSSG Shayne Gostisbehere E 15.00 40.00
OSSR Sam Reinhart D 30.00 80.00
OSSY Steve Yzerman A 25.00 60.00
OSTE Teuvo Teravainen E 12.00 30.00
OSWG Wayne Gretzky B 250.00 600.00

2014-15 Ultimate Collection Obsidian Script Materials

OSAE Aaron Ekblad 25.00 60.00
OSAG Alex Galchenyuk 6.00 15.00
OSAO Adam Oates 10.00 25.00
OSAV Andrei Vasilevskiy 100.00 250.00
OSAW Alexander Wennberg 15.00 40.00
OSBH Brett Hull 20.00 50.00
OSCC Chris Chelios 10.00 25.00
OSCJ Curtis Joseph 12.00 30.00
OSCL Curtis Lazar 10.00 25.00
OSDA Damon Severson 10.00 25.00
OSDP Derrick Pouliot 12.00 30.00
OSEK Evgeny Kuznetsov 25.00 60.00
OSGN Gustav Nyquist 6.00 15.00
OSJD Jonathan Drouin 20.00 50.00
OSJG Johnny Gaudreau 200.00 500.00
OSJJ Jaromir Jagr 50.00 125.00
OSJL Jori Lehtera 12.00 30.00
OSLD Leon Draisaitl 60.00 150.00
OSMF Marc-Andre Fleury 20.00 50.00
OSMM Mark Messier 20.00 50.00
OSMR Morgan Rielly 10.00 25.00
OSMS Mats Sundin 10.00 25.00
OSOV Alexander Ovechkin 40.00 100.00
OSRF Ron Francis 12.00 30.00
OSSB Sergei Bobrovsky 15.00 40.00
OSSG Shayne Gostisbehere 20.00 50.00
OSSR Sam Reinhart 40.00 100.00
OSSY Steve Yzerman 40.00 100.00
OSTE Teuvo Teravainen 15.00 40.00
OSTS Tyler Seguin 25.00 60.00
OSWG Wayne Gretzky 250.00 600.00

2014-15 Ultimate Collection Rare Materials

*BLUE/10: 1X TO 2.5X BASIC JSY/99
*GOLD/15: 1X TO 2.5X BASIC JSY/99
RMAS Alexander Semin 4.00 10.00
RMBB Ben Bishop 3.00 8.00
RMBW Blake Wheeler 4.00 10.00
RMCA Craig Anderson 4.00 10.00
RMCS Cory Schneider 4.00 10.00
RMDK David Krejci 4.00 10.00
RMEK Evander Kane 4.00 10.00
RMEM Evgeni Malkin 8.00 20.00
RMHI Jonas Hiller 3.00 8.00
RMHL Henrik Lundqvist 10.00 25.00
RMJG John Gibson 4.00 10.00
RMJH Jonathan Huberdeau 5.00 12.00
RMJJ Jaromir Jagr 12.00 30.00
RMJS Jason Spezza 4.00 10.00
RMJT Jonathan Toews 6.00 15.00
RMMM Matt Moulson 2.50 6.00
RMMS Mike Smith 4.00 10.00
RMNK Niklas Kronwall 3.00 8.00
RMNY Nail Yakupov 2.50 6.00
RMPS Paul Stastny 3.00 8.00
RMRN Rick Nash 4.00 10.00
RMSB Sergei Bobrovsky 6.00 15.00
RMSC Sean Couturier 3.00 8.00
RMSS Steven Stamkos 8.00 20.00
RMTT Tyler Toffoli 4.00 10.00

2014-15 Ultimate Collection Ultimate Foursomes

U4CAR Stl/Lndhlm/Sknnr/Smn 5.00 12.00
U4DEF Wbr/Kth/Dghty/Sbbn 5.00 12.00
U4NET Qck/Prce/Rsk/Bbrvsky 8.00 20.00
U4NYR Nsh/Krdr/St.Ls/Zccrllo 5.00 12.00
U4SOPH McKnn/Hrtl/Mnhn/Plt 15.00 40.00
U4WILD Prse/Cyle/Pmnvlle/Grnlnd 4.00 10.00
U4WINGS Zttrbrg/Dtsyk/Jrco/Nyqst 6.00 15.00

2014-15 Ultimate Collection Ultimate Gear

UGAE Aaron Ekblad B 6.00 15.00
UGBE Jamie Benn B 2.50 6.00
UGBH Brett Hull A 5.00 12.00
UGBR Bobby Ryan B 2.00 5.00
UGCJ Curtis Joseph A 3.00 8.00
UGCL Curtis Lazar A 2.50 6.00
UGDB David Backes B 1.50 4.00
UGDK Duncan Keith B 2.00 5.00
UGDN Darnell Nurse B 5.00 12.00
UGDS Daniel Sedin B 3.00 8.00
UGHL Henrik Lundqvist B 6.00 15.00
UGJB Jonathan Bernier B 2.00 5.00
UGJD Jonathan Drouin B 5.00 12.00
UGJN James Neal B 1.50 4.00
UGJS Jeff Skinner B 3.00 8.00
UGLD Leon Draisaitl B 25.00 60.00
UGMD Marcel Dionne A 3.00 8.00
UGMG Marian Gaborik B 2.50 6.00
UGML Milan Lucic B 2.50 6.00
UGMS Martin St. Louis B 2.50 6.00
UGPS P.K. Subban B 3.00 8.00
UGVT Vladimir Tarasenko B 3.00 8.00

2014-15 Ultimate Collection Ultimate Signature Masterpieces

USMAE Aaron Ekblad C 20.00 50.00
USMAI Arturs Irbe A 6.00 15.00
USMBR Brett Hull A 15.00 40.00
USMBS Brandon Saad C 6.00 15.00
USMCJ Curtis Joseph C 10.00 25.00
USMDB Dustin Brown C 8.00 20.00
USMDS Dave Schultz B 8.00 20.00
USMEK Evgeny Kuznetsov C 20.00 50.00
USMGR Wayne Gretzky A 200.00 500.00
USMHE Tomas Hertl C 8.00 20.00
USMJD Jonathan Drouin C 15.00 40.00
USMJG Johnny Gaudreau C 100.00 250.00
USMLD Leon Draisaitl C 80.00 200.00
USMMB Mike Bossy B 8.00 20.00
USMMF Marc-Andre Fleury B 20.00 50.00
USMMM Mark Messier A 25.00 60.00
USMMP Max Pacioretty C 8.00 20.00
USMNA Rick Nash B 8.00 20.00
USMRS Ryan Strome C 8.00 20.00
USMSA Joe Sakic A 30.00 80.00
USMSR Sam Reinhart B 30.00 80.00
USMST Martin St. Louis B 8.00 20.00
USMTB Tom Barrasso B 8.00 20.00
USMTT Teuvo Teravainen C 12.00 30.00

2014-15 Ultimate Collection Ultimate Signature Patches

USPBL Rob Blake/25 15.00 40.00
USPBR Dustin Brown/25 15.00 40.00
USPCS Cory Schneider/25 15.00 40.00
USPDB David Backes/25 10.00 25.00
USPDK David Krejci/25 15.00 40.00
USPDW Doug Weight/25 15.00 40.00
USPGU Bill Guerin/25 15.00 40.00
USPJB Jonathan Bernier/25 12.00 30.00
USPJI Jarome Iginla/25 20.00 50.00
USPLC Logan Couture/25 20.00 50.00
USPMG Marian Gaborik/25 15.00 40.00
USPMR Morgan Rielly/25 15.00 40.00
USPMS Mats Sundin/25 15.00 40.00
USPNA Rick Nash/25 15.00 40.00
USPTH Tomas Hertl/25 15.00 40.00
USPVD Vincent Damphousse/25 12.00 30.00
USPZP Zach Parise/25 15.00 40.00

2015-16 Ultimate Collection

1 Wayne Gretzky JSY/99 30.00 80.00
2 Taylor Hall JSY/199 5.00 12.00
3 Anthony Duclair JSY/199 4.00 10.00
4 Jakub Voracek JSY/199 4.00 10.00
5 Carey Price JSY/199 10.00 25.00
6 Jarome Iginla JSY/199 6.00 15.00
7 Jaromir Jagr JSY/199 15.00 40.00
8 Anze Kopitar JSY/199 8.00 20.00
9 John Tavares JSY/199 8.00 20.00
10 Joe Sakic JSY/99 20.00 50.00
11 Evgeni Malkin JSY/199 10.00 25.00
12 Jori Lehtera JSY/199 3.00 8.00
13 James van Riemsdyk JSY/199 4.00 10.00
14 P.K. Subban JSY/199 6.00 15.00
15 Henrik Lundqvist JSY/199 12.00 30.00
16 Henrik Zetterberg JSY/199 6.00 15.00
17 Joe Pavelski JSY/199 6.00 15.00
18 David Krejci JSY/199 5.00 12.00
19 Steven Stamkos JSY/199 10.00 25.00
20 Mark Messier JSY/99 20.00 50.00
21 Rick Nash JSY/199 5.00 12.00
22 Nathan MacKinnon JSY/199 20.00 50.00
23 Andrew Ladd JSY/199 3.00 8.00
24 Shea Weber JSY/199 4.00 10.00
25 Ryan Miller JSY/199 5.00 12.00
26 Corey Perry JSY/199 8.00 20.00
27 Jonathan Toews JSY/199 8.00 20.00
28 Jiri Hudler JSY/199 4.00 10.00
29 Jamie Benn JSY/199 5.00 12.00
30 Patrick Roy JSY/99 25.00 60.00
31 Sidney Crosby JSY/199 20.00 50.00
32 Kyle Okposo JSY/199 3.00 8.00
33 Patrick Marleau JSY/199 5.00 12.00
34 Daniel Sedin JSY/199 6.00 15.00
35 Sergei Bobrovsky JSY/199 8.00 20.00
36 Zach Parise JSY/199 5.00 12.00
37 Erik Karlsson JSY/199 6.00 15.00
38 Pekka Rinne JSY/199 5.00 12.00
39 Corey Crawford JSY/199 6.00 15.00
40 Ben Bishop JSY/199 4.00 10.00
41 Eric Staal JSY/199 6.00 15.00
42 Johnny Gaudreau JSY/199 8.00 20.00
43 Alexander Ovechkin JSY/199 20.00 50.00
44 Mike Hoffman JSY/199 3.00 8.00
45 Cory Schneider JSY/199 5.00 12.00
46 Tyler Seguin JSY/199 6.00 15.00
47 Nail Yakupov JSY/199 3.00 8.00
48 Pavel Datsyuk JSY/199 8.00 20.00
49 Matt Moulson JSY/199 3.00 8.00
50 Mike Bossy JSY/99 10.00 25.00
51 Brett Pesce AU/299 RC 6.00 15.00
52 Dylan DeMelo AU/299 RC 6.00 15.00
53 Anton Slepyshev AU/299 RC 5.00 12.00
54 Vincent Hinostroza AU/299 RC 5.00 12.00
55 Henrik Samuelsson AU/299 RC 5.00 12.00
56 Jean-Francois Berube AU/299 RC 6.00 15.00
57 Colin Miller AU/299 RC 6.00 15.00
58 Mike McCarron AU/299 RC 10.00 25.00
59 Mark Alt AU/299 RC 5.00 12.00
60 Joonas Donskoi AU/299 RC 8.00 20.00
61 Frank Vatrano AU/299 RC 10.00 25.00
62 Mackenzie Skapski AU/299 RC 8.00 20.00
63 Anthony Stolarz AU/299 RC 20.00 50.00
64 Derek Forbort AU/299 RC 6.00 15.00
65 Mattias Janmark AU/299 RC 8.00 20.00
66 Brock McGinn AU/299 RC 8.00 20.00
67 Viktor Arvidsson AU/299 RC 8.00 20.00
68 Josh Anderson AU/299 RC 15.00 40.00
69 Chandler Stephenson AU/299 RC 10.00 25.00
70 Matt Puempel AU/299 RC 6.00 15.00
71 Andreas Athanasiou AU/299 RC 20.00 50.00
72 Garret Sparks AU/299 RC 8.00 20.00
73 Antoine Bibeau AU/299 RC 8.00 20.00
74 Linus Ullmark AU/299 RC 15.00 40.00
75 Brendan Gaunce AU/299 RC 10.00 25.00
76 David Musil AU/299 RC 6.00 15.00
77 Brett Kulak AU/299 RC 6.00 15.00
78 Shane Prince AU/299 RC 5.00 12.00
79 Chris Wideman AU/299 RC 8.00 20.00
80 Sergei Plotnikov AU/299 RC 5.00 12.00
81 Devin Shore AU/299 RC 8.00 20.00
82 Ben Hutton AU/299 RC 8.00 20.00
83 Colton Parayko AU/299 RC 12.00 30.00
84 Mike Condon AU/299 RC 8.00 20.00
85 Oscar Lindberg AU/299 RC 8.00 20.00
86 Keegan Lowe AU/299 RC 8.00 20.00
87 Brady Skjei AU/299 RC 6.00 15.00
88 Kyle Baun AU/299 RC 8.00 20.00
89 Chris Driedger AU/299 RC 6.00 15.00
90 Radek Faksa AU/299 RC 8.00 20.00
91 Joel Edmundson AU/299 RC 6.00 15.00
92 Stanislav Galiev AU/299 RC 8.00 20.00
93 Slater Koekkoek AU/299 RC 5.00 12.00
94 Matt O'Connor AU/299 RC 6.00 15.00
95 Ronalds Kenins AU/299 RC 5.00 12.00
96 Charles Hudon AU/299 RC 8.00 20.00
97 Andrew Copp AU/299 RC 8.00 20.00
98 Nick Cousins AU/299 RC 8.00 20.00
99 Connor Brickley AU/299 RC 6.00 15.00
100 Ryan Hartman AU/299 RC 10.00 25.00
101 Nicolas Petan AU/299 RC 8.00 20.00
102 Matt Murray AU/99 RC 80.00 200.00
103 Kevin Fiala AU/299 RC 10.00 25.00
104 Emile Poirier AU/299 RC 6.00 15.00
105 Zachary Fucale AU/299 RC 6.00 15.00
106 Daniel Sprong AU/299 RC 10.00 25.00
107 Mikko Rantanen AU/299 RC 40.00 100.00
108 Nikolay Goldobin AU/299 RC 8.00 20.00
109 Connor McDavid
AU/99 RC 6000.00 12000.00
110 Sam Bennett AU/99 RC 30.00 80.00
111 Robby Fabbri AU/99 RC 25.00 60.00
112 Jared McCann AU/99 RC 12.00 30.00
113 Dylan Larkin AU/99 RC 50.00 125.00
114 Jake Virtanen AU/99 RC 20.00 50.00
115 Noah Hanifin AU/99 RC 15.00 40.00
116 Jacob de la Rose AU/99 RC 10.00 25.00
117 Artemi Panarin AU/99 RC 50.00 125.00
118 Nikolaj Ehlers AU/99 RC 40.00 100.00
119 Max Domi AU/99 RC 15.00 40.00
120A Jack Eichel/99 RC 40.00 100.00
120B Jack Eichel AU/99 RC 60.00 150.00

2015-16 Ultimate Collection Gold

109 Connor McDavid PATCH 300.00 800.00

2015-16 Ultimate Collection '05-06 Ultimate Rookies

05AA Andreas Athanasiou AU/275 8.00 20.00
05BM Brock McGinn AU/275 3.00 8.00
05BS Brady Skjei AU/275 2.50 6.00
05CH Charles Hudon AU/275 3.00 8.00
05CM Connor McDavid AU/175 1200.00 3000.00
05CP Colton Parayko AU/275 5.00 12.00
05CS Chandler Stephenson AU/275 4.00 10.00
05DA Daniel Sprong AU/275 4.00 10.00
05DL Dylan Larkin AU/175 25.00 60.00
05EP Emile Poirier AU/275 2.50 6.00
05FA Radek Faksa AU/275 3.00 8.00
05FV Frank Vatrano AU/275 4.00 10.00
05HS Henrik Samuelsson AU/275 2.00 5.00
05JE Jack Eichel/175 12.00 30.00
05JM Jared McCann AU/275 4.00 10.00
05JV Jake Virtanen AU/175 6.00 15.00
05KF Kevin Fiala AU/275 4.00 10.00
05NC Nick Cousins AU/275 3.00 8.00
05NG Nikolay Goldobin AU/275 6.00 15.00
05NH Noah Hanifin AU/175 6.00 15.00
05NP Nicolas Petan AU/275 3.00 8.00
05OL Oscar Lindberg AU/275 3.00 8.00
05RF Robby Fabbri AU/175 4.00 10.00
05SB Sam Bennett AU/175 10.00 25.00
05ST Shea Theodore AU/275 6.00 15.00

2015-16 Ultimate Collection '05-06 Ultimate Rookies Silver

05AA Andreas Athanasiou JSY 6.00 15.00
05AP Artemi Panarin JSY 10.00 25.00
05BM Brock McGinn JSY 2.50 6.00
05BS Brady Skjei JSY 2.00 5.00
05CH Charles Hudon JSY 2.50 6.00
05CM Connor McDavid JSY 150.00 400.00
05CP Colton Parayko JSY 4.00 10.00
05CS Chandler Stephenson JSY 3.00 8.00
05DA Daniel Sprong JSY 3.00 8.00
05DL Dylan Larkin JSY 8.00 20.00
05EP Emile Poirier JSY 2.00 5.00
05FA Radek Faksa JSY 2.50 6.00
05FV Frank Vatrano JSY 3.00 8.00
05HS Henrik Samuelsson JSY 1.50 4.00
05JE Jack Eichel JSY 10.00 25.00
05JM Jared McCann JSY 3.00 8.00
05JV Jake Virtanen JSY 3.00 8.00
05KF Kevin Fiala JSY 3.00 8.00
05MD Max Domi JSY 5.00 12.00
05MR Mikko Rantanen JSY 12.00 30.00
05NC Nick Cousins JSY 2.50 6.00
05NE Nikolaj Ehlers JSY 5.00 12.00
05NG Nikolay Goldobin JSY 2.50 6.00
05NH Noah Hanifin JSY 4.00 10.00
05NP Nicolas Petan JSY 2.50 6.00
05OL Oscar Lindberg JSY 2.50 6.00
05RF Robby Fabbri JSY 3.00 8.00
05SB Sam Bennett JSY 8.00 20.00
05SP Sergei Plotnikov JSY 1.50 4.00
05ST Shea Theodore JSY 4.00 10.00

2015-16 Ultimate Collection '05-06 Ultimate Rookies Spectrum Silver

*SINGLES: .75X TO 2X BASIC INSERTS
05CM Connor McDavid JSY AU 800.00 2000.00
05DL Dylan Larkin JSY AU 40.00 100.00

2015-16 Ultimate Collection Debut Threads

DTAP Artemi Panarin 8.00 20.00
DTBM Brock McGinn 2.00 5.00
DTCH Charles Hudon 2.00 5.00
DTCM Connor McDavid 125.00 300.00
DTDL Dylan Larkin 6.00 15.00
DTDS Daniel Sprong 2.50 6.00
DTEP Emile Poirier 1.50 4.00
DTFA Robby Fabbri 2.50 6.00
DTHS Henrik Samuelsson 1.25 3.00
DTJD Jacob de la Rose 2.00 5.00
DTJE Jack Eichel 8.00 20.00
DTJM Jared McCann 2.50 6.00
DTJV Jake Virtanen 2.50 6.00
DTJW Jordan Weal 1.25 3.00
DTKF Kevin Fiala 2.50 6.00
DTMC Mike Condon 2.00 5.00
DTMD Max Domi 4.00 10.00
DTMR Mikko Rantanen 10.00 25.00
DTMS Malcolm Subban 3.00 8.00
DTNE Nikolaj Ehlers 4.00 10.00
DTNG Nikolay Goldobin 2.00 5.00
DTNH Noah Hanifin 3.00 8.00
DTNP Nicolas Petan 2.00 5.00
DTNR Nick Ritchie 2.00 5.00
DTOL Oscar Lindberg 2.00 5.00
DTRF Radek Faksa 2.00 5.00
DTRH Ryan Hartman 2.50 6.00
DTSB Sam Bennett 6.00 15.00
DTSH Hunter Shinkaruk 2.00 5.00
DTZF Zachary Fucale 1.50 4.00

2015-16 Ultimate Collection Debut Threads Autographs

ADTBM Brock McGinn 6.00 15.00
ADTCH Charles Hudon 6.00 15.00
ADTCM Connor McDavid 400.00 1000.00
ADTDL Dylan Larkin 25.00 60.00
ADTDO Joonas Donskoi 6.00 15.00
ADTDS Daniel Sprong 8.00 20.00
ADTEP Emile Poirier 5.00 12.00
ADTFA Robby Fabbri 8.00 20.00
ADTHS Henrik Samuelsson 4.00 10.00
ADTJD Jacob de la Rose 6.00 15.00
ADTJM Jared McCann 8.00 20.00
ADTJV Jake Virtanen 8.00 20.00
ADTJW Jordan Weal 4.00 10.00
ADTKF Kevin Fiala 8.00 20.00
ADTMC Mike Condon 6.00 15.00
ADTNE Nikolaj Ehlers 12.00 30.00
ADTNG Nikolay Goldobin 6.00 15.00
ADTNH Noah Hanifin 10.00 25.00
ADTNP Nicolas Petan 6.00 15.00
ADTNR Nick Ritchie 6.00 15.00
ADTOL Oscar Lindberg 6.00 15.00
ADTRF Radek Faksa 6.00 15.00
ADTRH Ryan Hartman 8.00 20.00
ADTSB Sam Bennett 20.00 50.00
ADTSH Hunter Shinkaruk 6.00 15.00
ADTZF Zachary Fucale 5.00 12.00

2015-16 Ultimate Collection Honoured Materials

HMAO Alexander Ovechkin 25.00 60.00
HMBH Brett Hull 12.00 30.00
HMBL Rob Blake 6.00 15.00
HMBO Mike Bossy 6.00 15.00

HMCM Connor McDavid 150.00 400.00
HMCP Carey Price 12.00 30.00
HMDH Dale Hawerchuk 8.00 20.00
HMGF Grant Fuhr 10.00 25.00
HMGL Guy Lafleur 8.00 20.00
HMHL Henrik Lundqvist 15.00 40.00
HMHZ Henrik Zetterberg 8.00 20.00
HMJE Jack Eichel 25.00 60.00
HMJK Jari Kurri 6.00 15.00
HMLR Luc Robitaille 6.00 15.00
HMMB Martin Brodeur 15.00 40.00
HMML Mario Lemieux 25.00 60.00
HMMM Mark Messier 12.00 30.00
HMPR Patrick Roy 15.00 40.00
HMRB Ray Bourque 10.00 25.00
HMRM Ryan Miller 6.00 15.00
HMSC Sidney Crosby 25.00 60.00
HMSS Steven Stamkos 12.00 30.00
HMSY Steve Yzerman 15.00 40.00
HMWG Wayne Gretzky 40.00 100.00

2015-16 Ultimate Collection Iconic Fabrics

IFCM Connor McDavid 60.00 150.00
IFEK Erik Karlsson 5.00 12.00
IFHL Henrik Lundqvist 10.00 25.00
IFJB Jamie Benn 4.00 10.00
IFJE Jack Eichel 15.00 40.00
IFJI Jarome Iginla 5.00 12.00
IFJJ Jaromir Jagr 12.00 30.00
IFJM Jared McCann 5.00 12.00
IFJQ Jonathan Quick 5.00 12.00
IFJT Jonathan Toews 6.00 15.00
IFJV Jake Virtanen 5.00 12.00
IFMR Mikko Rantanen 20.00 50.00
IFNH Noah Hanifin 6.00 15.00
IFNP Nicolas Petan 4.00 10.00
IFPK Patrick Kane 8.00 20.00
IFPS P.K. Subban 5.00 12.00
IFRF Robby Fabbri 5.00 12.00
IFSS Steven Stamkos 8.00 20.00
IFTS Tyler Seguin 5.00 12.00
IFZP Zach Parise 4.00 10.00

2015-16 Ultimate Collection Jumbo Material Autographs

AJMCM Connor McDavid/40 200.00 500.00
AJMCP Corey Perry/40 12.00 30.00
AJMDL Dylan Larkin/40 25.00 60.00
AJMDS Denis Savard/40 8.00 20.00
AJMEM Evgeni Malkin/40 15.00 40.00
AJMJB Jamie Benn/40 8.00 20.00
AJMJI Jarome Iginla/40 10.00 25.00
AJMJJ Jaromir Jagr/40 25.00 60.00
AJMJM Jared McCann/40 10.00 25.00
AJMJP Joe Pavelski/40 10.00 25.00
AJMJT Jonathan Toews/40 12.00 30.00
AJMJV Jake Virtanen/40 10.00 25.00
AJMKF Kevin Fiala/40 10.00 25.00
AJMNM Nathan MacKinnon/40 30.00 80.00
AJMOL Oscar Lindberg/40 8.00 20.00
AJMPD Pavel Datsyuk/40 12.00 30.00
AJMPR Carey Price/40 15.00 40.00
AJMRF Robby Fabbri/40 10.00 25.00
AJMSB Sam Bennett/40 25.00 60.00
AJMSP Daniel Sprong/40 10.00 25.00
AJMTA John Tavares/40 12.00 30.00
AJMTH Taylor Hall/40 (inserted in 2016-17 Ultimate Collection) 8.00 20.00
AJMTS Tyler Seguin/40 10.00 25.00
AJMVO Jakub Voracek/40 6.00 15.00
AJMZF Zachary Fucale/40 6.00 15.00
AJMZP Zach Parise/40 8.00 20.00

2015-16 Ultimate Collection Jumbo Materials

JMAH Adam Henrique 3.00 8.00
JMBH Braden Holtby 5.00 12.00
JMBW Blake Wheeler 4.00 10.00
JMCC Corey Crawford 5.00 12.00
JMCG Claude Giroux 4.00 10.00
JMCM Connor McDavid 60.00 150.00
JMDB Dustin Byfuglien 4.00 10.00
JMDD Drew Doughty 5.00 12.00
JMDK Duncan Keith 3.00 8.00
JMDL Dylan Larkin 12.00 30.00
JMDS Daniel Sedin 5.00 12.00
JMEB Jordan Eberle 4.00 10.00
JMEK Erik Karlsson 5.00 12.00
JMHL Henrik Lundqvist 10.00 25.00
JMHS Henrik Sedin 5.00 12.00
JMHU Brett Hull 8.00 20.00
JMHZ Henrik Zetterberg 5.00 12.00
JMJE Jack Eichel 15.00 40.00
JMJG Johnny Gaudreau 6.00 15.00
JMJQ Jonathan Quick 5.00 12.00
JMKE Phil Kessel 4.00 10.00
JMKL Kris Letang 5.00 12.00
JMMB Martin Brodeur 10.00 25.00
JMMD Max Domi 8.00 20.00
JMMF Marc-Andre Fleury 8.00 20.00
JMMJ Martin Jones 3.00 8.00
JMMP Max Pacioretty 4.00 10.00
JMMR Mikko Rantanen 20.00 50.00
JMNA Rick Nash 4.00 10.00
JMNB Nicklas Backstrom 4.00 10.00
JMNE Nikolaj Ehlers 8.00 20.00
JMNK Nazem Kadri 5.00 12.00
JMNR Nick Ritchie 4.00 10.00
JMPA Patrick Roy 10.00 25.00
JMPB Patrice Bergeron 5.00 12.00
JMPC Paul Coffey 4.00 10.00
JMPK Patrick Kane 8.00 20.00
JMPR Pekka Rinne 4.00 10.00
JMPS P.K. Subban 5.00 12.00
JMRF Robby Fabbri 5.00 12.00
JMRG Ryan Getzlaf 4.00 10.00
JMRJ Roman Josi 4.00 10.00
JMRL Roberto Luongo 6.00 15.00
JMRM Ryan Miller 4.00 10.00
JMRN Ryan Nugent-Hopkins 5.00 12.00
JMRO Ryan O'Reilly 4.00 10.00
JMSA Denis Savard 4.00 10.00
JMSB Sam Bennett 12.00 30.00
JMSS Steven Stamkos 8.00 20.00
JMTR Tuukka Rask 5.00 12.00
JMVH Victor Hedman 5.00 12.00
JMVT Vladimir Tarasenko 5.00 12.00
JMWS Wayne Simmonds 5.00 12.00
JMZF Zachary Fucale 3.00 8.00

2015-16 Ultimate Collection Material Achievements

MABB Bob Bourne 2.50 6.00
MABH Brett Hull 8.00 20.00
MADD Drew Doughty 5.00 12.00
MADH Dale Hawerchuk 5.00 12.00
MADS Denis Savard 4.00 10.00
MAGC Gerry Cheevers 4.00 10.00
MAGF Grant Fuhr 6.00 15.00
MAGL Guy Lafleur 5.00 12.00
MAHA Dominik Hasek 6.00 15.00
MAHL Henrik Lundqvist 10.00 25.00
MAHZ Henrik Zetterberg 5.00 12.00
MALR Luc Robitaille 4.00 10.00
MAMM Mark Messier 8.00 20.00
MAMS Martin St. Louis 4.00 10.00
MAPK Patrick Kane 8.00 20.00
MAPR Patrick Roy 10.00 25.00
MARL Roberto Luongo 6.00 15.00
MARO Larry Robinson 4.00 10.00
MASS Steven Stamkos 8.00 20.00
MASY Steve Yzerman 10.00 25.00

2015-16 Ultimate Collection Material Combos

MC2ANA R.Getzlaf/C.Perry B 5.00 12.00
MC2ARZ M.Domi/A.Duclair D 6.00 15.00
MC2CAL J.Gaudreau/S.Monahan C 5.00 12.00
MC2CAR E.Staal/J.Skinner C 4.00 10.00
MC2CHI J.Toews/M.Hossa A 5.00 12.00
MC2CLB N.Foligno/B.Saad D 2.50 6.00
MC2DET H.Zetterberg/G.Nyquist B 4.00 10.00
MC2EDM R.Nugent-Hopkins/J.Eberle C 4.00 10.00
MC2FLA A.Barkov/J.Jagr A 10.00 25.00
MC2LAK A.Kopitar/M.Gaborik C 5.00 12.00
MC2MIN M.Granlund/Z.Parise C 3.00 8.00
MC2NAS F.Forsberg/J.Neal D 5.00 12.00
MC2NJD M.Cammalleri/A.Henrique D 2.50 6.00
MC2NYI J.Tavares/K.Okposo B 5.00 12.00
MC2OTT K.Turris/M.Hoffman D 2.50 6.00
MC2PEN E.Malkin/P.Kessel B 6.00 15.00
MC2TBL S.Stamkos/T.Johnson B 6.00 15.00
MC2TCG M.Brodeur/R.Luongo A 8.00 20.00
MC2TCL W.Gretzky/J.Sakic A 20.00 50.00
MC2TOR J.van Riemsdyk/N.Kadri D 4.00 10.00
MC2WIN B.Wheeler/M.Scheifele D 5.00 12.00

2015-16 Ultimate Collection Material Quads

MC403DR Fleury/Parise/Getzlaf/Perry 12.00 30.00
MC404DR Ovechkin Malkin/Ladd/Wheeler 25.00 60.00
MC406DR Toews/Backstrom Kessel/Okposo 10.00 25.00
MC409DR Tavares/Hedman Duchene/Ekman-Larsson 10.00 25.00
MC410DR Hall/Seguin Skinner/Tarasenko 8.00 20.00
MC411DR Nugent-Hopkins/Landeskog Huberdeau/Zibanejad 8.00 20.00
MC413DR MacKinnon/Barkov Drouin/Monahan 25.00 60.00
MC414DR Ekblad/Reinhart Draisaitl/Bennett 20.00 50.00
MC415DR McDavid/Eichel Hanifin/Rantanen 100.00 250.00
MC497DR Thornton Marleau/Luongo/Hossa 10.00 25.00

2015-16 Ultimate Collection Material Sixes

MC6SC Keith/Kopitar/Kane/Quick Bergeron/Toews B 15.00 40.00
MC6VT Price/Rask/Bobrovsky/Lundqvist Miller/Brodeur B 20.00 50.00
MC6O6C Pacioretty/Phaneuf/Chara/Zetterberg Toews/McDonagh B 12.00 30.00
MC6O6L Lafleur/Gilmour/Bucyk/Hasek Savard/Messier A 15.00 40.00
MC6O6R Fucale/Sparks/Subban/Larkin Panarin/Lindberg B 30.00 80.00
MC6PRZ Lundqvist/Bergeron/Toews Sedin/Sedin/Ovechkin B 30.00 80.00

2015-16 Ultimate Collection Material Trios

MC3BOS Marchand Bergeron/Eriksson C 12.00 30.00
MC3BUF Kane/Eichel/Reinhart C 25.00 60.00
MC3DAL Benn/Seguin/Sharp B 8.00 20.00
MC3NYR Kreider/Stepan/Hayes C 8.00 20.00
MC3PHI Schenn/Giroux/Simmonds C 8.00 20.00
MC3SJS Marleau Thornton/Pavelski C 10.00 25.00
MC3STL Steen/Stastny/Tarasenko C 8.00 20.00
MC3TCS Toews/Iginla/Getzlaf B 10.00 25.00
MC3WAS Ovechkin Backstrom/Oshie B 25.00 60.00
MC390DR Nolan/Jagr/Brodeur A 20.00 50.00

2015-16 Ultimate Collection Signature Honoured Materials

SHMAK Anze Kopitar/35 10.00 25.00
SHMCP Corey Perry/85 10.00 25.00
SHMDL Dylan Larkin/85 20.00 50.00
SHMEM Evgeni Malkin/35 12.00 30.00
SHMJI Jarome Iginla/35 8.00 20.00
SHMJT John Tavares/35 10.00 25.00
SHMJV Jake Virtanen/85 8.00 20.00
SHMNE Nikolaj Ehlers/85 12.00 30.00
SHMTF Theoren Fleury/35 8.00 20.00
SHMZF Zachary Fucale/85 5.00 12.00

2015-16 Ultimate Collection Signature Iconic Fabrics

SIFCP Carey Price/31 50.00 125.00
SIFDL Dylan Larkin/71 25.00 60.00
SIFNE Nikolaj Ehlers/27 12.00 30.00
SIFPR Patrick Roy/33 50.00 125.00
SIFSB Sam Bennett/93 10.00 25.00
SIFSY Steve Yzerman/19 50.00 125.00

2015-16 Ultimate Collection Signature Material Achievements

SMAAE Aaron Ekblad/40 10.00 25.00
SMAAO Alexander Ovechkin/25 30.00 80.00
SMACP Carey Price/40 15.00 40.00
SMAJB Jamie Benn/40 8.00 20.00
SMAJT Jonathan Toews/40 12.00 30.00
SMAMB Martin Brodeur/25 20.00 50.00
SMATA John Tavares/40 12.00 30.00

2015-16 Ultimate Collection Signature Material Laureates

SMLAE Aaron Ekblad/40 25.00 60.00
SMLCP Carey Price/40 75.00 150.00
SMLDK David Krejci/40 20.00 50.00
SMLDS Denis Savard/40 20.00 50.00
SMLEM Evgeni Malkin/40 40.00 100.00
SMLGF Grant Fuhr/40 30.00 80.00
SMLJB Jamie Benn/40 20.00 50.00
SMLJI Jarome Iginla/40 25.00 60.00
SMLJT John Tavares/40 30.00 80.00
SMLKT Kyle Turris/40 15.00 40.00
SMLMS Martin St. Louis/40 20.00 50.00
SMLPD Pavel Datsyuk/40 30.00 80.00
SMLPE Corey Perry/40 30.00 80.00
SMLZP Zach Parise/40 20.00 50.00

2015-16 Ultimate Collection Ultimate Dozen Relic Booklets

U12ALB Flames/Oilers 250.00 600.00
U12FWY Kings/Ducks 25.00 60.00
U12GOV Panthers/Lightning 50.00 120.00
U12HOF HOF 80.00 200.00
U12KEY Flyers/Penguins 30.00 80.00
U1214SC Kings/Rangers 50.00 120.00
U1215SC Blackhawks/Lightning 40.00 100.00
U12BHRW Blackhawks/RedWings 30.00 80.00
U12BRCA Bruins/Canadiens 40.00 100.00
U12CAFL Flames/Canucks 50.00 125.00
U12NYBR Islanders/Rangers 40.00 100.00
U12OIJE Oilers/Jets 250.00 600.00
U12OSIX Original Six 50.00 125.00
U12ROOK Rookies 250.00 600.00

2015-16 Ultimate Collection Ultimate Rookie Autograph Relic Booklets

RBRAP Artemi Panarin/49 100.00 200.00
RBRBM Brock McGinn/99 15.00 40.00
RBRCM Connor McDavid/49 600.00 1500.00
RBRDL Dylan Larkin/49 75.00 150.00
RBRDS Daniel Sprong/99 20.00 50.00
RBREP Emile Poirier/99 12.00 30.00
RBRHS Henrik Samuelsson/99 10.00 25.00
RBRJM Jared McCann/99 20.00 50.00
RBRJV Jake Virtanen/99 20.00 50.00
RBRKF Kevin Fiala/99 20.00 50.00
RBRMP Matt Puempel/99 12.00 30.00
RBRNP Nicolas Petan/99 15.00 40.00
RBRNR Nick Ritchie/99 15.00 40.00
RBRRF Robby Fabbri/99 20.00 50.00
RBRSB Sam Bennett/49 30.00 80.00
RBRSH Hunter Shinkaruk/99 15.00 40.00
RBRZF Zachary Fucale/99 12.00 30.00

2015-16 Ultimate Collection Ultimate Signatures

USAE Aaron Ekblad C 12.00 30.00
USAO Alexander Ovechkin A 40.00 100.00
USBH Bobby Hull A 20.00 50.00
USBO Bobby Orr B 40.00 100.00
USBS Brady Skjei C 8.00 20.00
USCH Charles Hudon C 10.00 25.00
USCP Carey Price A 20.00 50.00
USDK David Krejci C 10.00 25.00
USDL Dylan Larkin C 30.00 80.00
USEM Evgeni Malkin A 20.00 50.00
USJI Jarome Iginla B 12.00 30.00
USJJ Jaromir Jagr B 50.00 125.00
USJP Joe Pavelski B 12.00 30.00
USJT Jonathan Toews A 15.00 40.00
USJV James van Riemsdyk C 8.00 20.00
USMC Mike McCarron C 12.00 30.00
USML Mario Lemieux A 40.00 100.00
USMM Mark Messier A 20.00 50.00
USMS Mark Stone C 12.00 30.00
USNM Nathan MacKinnon C 40.00 100.00
USPD Pavel Datsyuk B 15.00 40.00
USRF Robby Fabbri C 12.00 30.00
USSB Sam Bennett C 30.00 80.00
USSC Sidney Crosby A 100.00 250.00
USTH Taylor Hall 10.00 25.00
USTJ Tyler Johnson C 6.00 15.00
USTS Tyler Seguin B 12.00 30.00
USVI Jake Virtanen C 12.00 30.00
USWG Wayne Gretzky A 250.00 600.00
USZF Zachary Fucale C 8.00 20.00
USZP Zach Parise B 10.00 25.00

2015-16 Ultimate Collection Ultimate Skills Jumbo Jerseys

USKAE Aaron Ekblad C 6.00 15.00
USKAK Anze Kopitar C 8.00 20.00
USKAO Alexander Ovechkin B 20.00 50.00
USKBB Brent Burns C 5.00 12.00
USKBE Brian Elliott C 4.00 10.00
USKBR Bobby Ryan A 4.00 10.00
USKCC Corey Crawford C 6.00 15.00
USKCG Claude Giroux C 5.00 12.00
USKCP Carey Price C 10.00 25.00
USKDD Drew Doughty C 6.00 15.00
USKDK Duncan Keith A 4.00 10.00
USKJF Justin Faulk C 4.00 10.00
USKJG Johnny Gaudreau C 8.00 20.00
USKJH Jaroslav Halak C 5.00 12.00
USKJS Jiri Sekac C 3.00 8.00
USKJV Jakub Voracek A 4.00 10.00
USKKE Phil Kessel C 5.00 12.00
USKMF Marc-Andre Fleury C 10.00 25.00
USKMG Mark Giordano B 5.00 12.00
USKMH Mike Hoffman C 3.00 8.00
USKOE Oliver Ekman-Larsson C 5.00 12.00
USKPB Patrice Bergeron C 6.00 15.00
USKPE Patrik Elias C 5.00 12.00
USKRJ Ryan Johansen C 4.00 10.00
USKRL Roberto Luongo C 8.00 20.00
USKRV Radim Vrbata C 3.00 8.00
USKTS Tyler Seguin B 6.00 15.00

2016-17 Ultimate Collection

1 John Tavares 3.00 8.00
2 Tyler Seguin 2.50 6.00
3 Mats Zuccarello 2.00 5.00
4 Mark Scheifele 3.00 8.00
5 Cory Schneider 2.00 5.00
6 Alexander Ovechkin 8.00 20.00
7 Mike Hoffman 1.25 3.00
8 Jakub Voracek 1.50 4.00
9 Andrew Ladd 1.25 3.00
10 Tyson Barrie 1.25 3.00
11 Henrik Zetterberg 2.50 6.00
12 Patrice Bergeron 2.50 6.00
13 Jake Muzzin 2.00 5.00
14 Steven Stamkos 4.00 10.00
15 P.K. Subban 2.50 6.00
16 Oliver Ekman-Larsson 2.00 5.00
17 James van Riemsdyk 1.50 4.00
18 Taylor Hall 2.00 5.00
19 David Backes 1.25 3.00
20 Boone Jenner 2.00 5.00
21 Erik Karlsson 2.50 6.00
22 Nikita Kucherov 4.00 10.00
23 Roberto Luongo 3.00 8.00
24 Drew Doughty 2.50 6.00
25 Frederik Andersen 2.50 6.00
26 Alex Galchenyuk 1.25 3.00
27 Loui Eriksson 1.25 3.00
28 Jaromir Jagr 6.00 15.00
29 Connor McDavid 15.00 40.00
30 Nikolaj Ehlers 2.00 5.00
31 Jaden Schwartz 2.50 6.00
32 Jamie Benn 2.00 5.00
33 Carey Price 4.00 10.00
34 Brian Elliott 1.50 4.00
35 Artem Anisimov 1.25 3.00
36 Corey Perry 3.00 8.00
37 Henrik Lundqvist 5.00 12.00
38 Patrick Kane 4.00 10.00
39 Ryan O'Reilly 2.00 5.00
40 Joe Thornton 3.00 8.00
41 Evgeni Malkin 4.00 10.00
42 Claude Giroux 2.00 5.00
43 Ryan Johansen 1.50 4.00
44 Brent Burns 2.00 5.00
45 Braden Holtby 2.50 6.00
46 Sidney Crosby 10.00 25.00
47 John Gibson 2.00 5.00
48 Sam Bennett 3.00 8.00
49 Nino Niederreiter 1.25 3.00
50 Teuvo Teravainen 2.00 5.00
51 Brandon Montour RC 5.00 12.00
52 Josh Morrissey RC 5.00 12.00
53 Jared Coreau RC 2.50 6.00
54 Jakub Vrana RC 2.50 6.00
55 Pontus Aberg RC 2.50 6.00
56 Nic Dowd RC 1.50 4.00
57 Chris Bigras RC 1.50 4.00
58 Jacob Larsson RC 3.00 8.00
59 Troy Stecher RC 2.00 5.00
60 Hudson Fasching RC 2.00 5.00
61 Thatcher Demko RC 5.00 12.00
62 Esa Lindell RC 2.00 5.00
63 Zach Sanford RC 2.00 5.00
64 Nick Baptiste RC 2.00 5.00
65 Alan Quine RC 2.00 5.00
66 Thomas Chabot RC 4.00 10.00
67 Michael Matheson RC 2.00 5.00
68 Matthew Benning RC 2.50 6.00
69 Stephen Johns RC 1.50 4.00
70 Sonny Milano RC 2.50 6.00
71 Mathew Barzal RC 6.00 15.00
72 Artturi Lehkonen RC 2.50 6.00
73 Brayden Point RC 5.00 12.00
74 Christian Dvorak RC 2.50 6.00
75 Connor Brown RC 3.00 8.00
76 Jakob Chychrun RC 4.00 10.00
77 Timo Meier RC 4.00 10.00
78 Nick Schmaltz RC 2.50 6.00
79 Pavel Buchnevich RC 3.00 8.00
80 Nikita Zaitsev RC 2.00 5.00
81 Tyler Motte RC 2.00 5.00
82 Brandon Carlo RC 3.00 8.00
83 Pavel Zacha RC 3.00 8.00
84 Kyle Connor RC 6.00 15.00
85 Anthony Mantha RC 4.00 10.00
86 Joel Eriksson Ek RC 3.00 8.00
87 Ivan Provorov RC 3.00 8.00
88 Anthony Beauvillier RC 2.00 5.00
89 Mikhail Sergachev RC 3.00 8.00
90 Sebastian Aho RC 6.00 15.00
91 Travis Konecny RC 4.00 10.00
92 Zach Werenski RC 6.00 15.00
93 Mitch Marner RC 15.00 40.00
94 Jimmy Vesey RC 8.00 20.00
95 Dylan Strome RC 12.00 30.00
96 Jesse Puljujarvi RC 4.00 10.00
97 William Nylander RC 15.00 40.00
98 Matthew Tkachuk RC 8.00 20.00
99 Patrik Laine RC 20.00 50.00
100 Auston Matthews RC 50.00 120.00
102 Christian Dvorak AU/299 8.00 20.00
104 Pavel Buchnevich AU/299 10.00 25.00
105 Trevor Carrick AU/299 6.00 15.00
106 Dominik Simon AU/299 5.00 12.00
107 Jakob Chychrun AU/299 12.00 30.00
108 Thomas Chabot AU/299 12.00 30.00
110 Anthony Beauvillier AU/299 6.00 15.00
111 Jakub Vrana AU/299 15.00 40.00
112 Ivan Provorov AU/299 10.00 25.00
113 Steven Santini AU/299 5.00 12.00
114 Mathew Barzal AU/299 40.00 100.00
115 Hudson Fasching AU/299 6.00 15.00
116 Timo Meier AU/299 12.00 30.00
117 Zach Werenski AU/299 20.00 50.00
118 Brayden Point AU/299 40.00 100.00
119 Sergey Tolchinsky AU/299 5.00 12.00
121 Oliver Bjorkstrand AU/299 8.00 20.00
123 J.C. Lipon AU/299 6.00 15.00
124 Thatcher Demko AU/299 20.00 50.00
125 Lawson Crouse AU/299 5.00 12.00
126 Mark McNeill AU/299 6.00 15.00
127 Chase De Leo AU/299 6.00 15.00
128 Justin Bailey AU/299 6.00 15.00
129 Esa Lindell AU/299 6.00 15.00
130 Charlie Lindgren AU/299 10.00 25.00
131 Sonny Milano AU/299 8.00 20.00
132 Ryan Pulock AU/299 6.00 15.00
133 Nikita Soshnikov AU/299 4.00 10.00
135 Oskar Sundqvist AU/299 6.00 15.00
136 Danton Heinen AU/299 5.00 12.00
139 Oliver Kylington AU/299 5.00 12.00
140 Dylan Strome AU/299 15.00 40.00
141 Josh Morrissey AU/299 15.00 40.00
142 Tom Kuhnhackl AU/299 5.00 12.00
143 Kasperi Kapanen AU/299 10.00 25.00
144 Tyler Motte AU/299 6.00 15.00
145 Jason Dickinson AU/299 5.00 12.00
147 Mikhail Sergachev AU/299 10.00 25.00
149 Mitch Marner AU/99 150.00 400.00
150 Sebastian Aho AU/99 40.00 100.00
151 Travis Konecny AU/99 30.00 80.00
152 Kyle Connor AU/99 30.00 80.00
153 Jimmy Vesey AU/99 15.00 40.00
154 Matthew Tkachuk AU/99 60.00 150.00
155 Pavel Zacha AU/99 15.00 40.00
156 William Nylander AU/99 80.00 200.00
157 Anthony Mantha AU/99 50.00 125.00
158 Jesse Puljujarvi AU/99 20.00 50.00
159 Patrik Laine AU/99 150.00 250.00
160 Auston Matthews AU/99 800.00 2000.00
161 Jake Guentzel AU/99 80.00 200.00
NNO Rookie Autograph Redemption 40.00 100.00

2016-17 Ultimate Collection Gold

*VETS: 1.25X TO 3X BASIC CARDS
*ROOKIES: .6X TO 1.5X BASIC CARDS
1 John Tavares AU/50 12.00 30.00
2 Tyler Seguin AU/50 12.00 30.00
23 Roberto Luongo AU/50 12.00 30.00
33 Carey Price AU/25 40.00 100.00
37 Henrik Lundqvist AU/25 30.00 80.00
40 Joe Thornton AU/50 12.00 30.00
41 Evgeni Malkin AU/25 30.00 80.00
118 Brayden Point PATCH AU/49 60.00 150.00
140 Dylan Strome PATCH AU/49 40.00 100.00
150 Sebastian Aho PATCH AU/49 40.00 100.00
153 Jimmy Vesey PATCH AU/49 20.00 50.00
154 Matthew Tkachuk PATCH AU/49 40.00 100.00
156 William Nylander PATCH AU/49 80.00 200.00
157 Anthony Mantha PATCH AU/49 80.00 150.00
158 Jesse Puljujarvi PATCH AU/49 50.00 125.00
159 Patrik Laine PATCH AU/49 250.00 600.00
160 Auston Matthews PATCH AU/49 400.00 1000.00

2016-17 Ultimate Collection Silver

COMMON CARD 1.00 3.00
SEMISTARS 1.50 4.00
UNLISTED STARS 2.00 5.00
159 Patrik Laine JSY 15.00 40.00
160 Auston Matthews JSY 60.00 150.00

2016-17 Ultimate Collection '06-07 Retro Rookie Autographs

RRAAB Anthony Beauvillier/199 5.00 12.00
RRAAM Auston Matthews/49 300.00 600.00
RRABP Brayden Point/199 30.00 80.00
RRACD Christian Dvorak/199 6.00 15.00
RRADH Danton Heinen/199 4.00 10.00
RRADS Dylan Strome/199 15.00 40.00
RRAEL Esa Lindell/199 5.00 12.00
RRAHF Hudson Fasching/199 5.00 12.00
RRAIP Ivan Provorov/199 8.00 20.00
RRAJC Jakob Chychrun/199 10.00 25.00
RRAJP Jesse Puljujarvi/199 20.00 50.00
RRAJV Jimmy Vesey/199 8.00 20.00
RRAKC Kyle Connor/199 15.00 40.00
RRAKK Kasperi Kapanen/199 8.00 20.00
RRAKL Kevin Labanc/199 5.00 12.00
RRALC Lawson Crouse/199 4.00 10.00
RRAMA Anthony Mantha/49 50.00 120.00
RRAMB Mathew Barzal/199 15.00 40.00
RRAME Timo Meier/199 10.00 25.00
RRAMM Mitch Marner/49 60.00 150.00
RRAMT Matthew Tkachuk/49 20.00 50.00
RRAOB Oliver Bjorkstrand/199 6.00 15.00
RRAOK Oliver Kylington/199 4.00 10.00
RRAPB Pavel Buchnevich/199 8.00 20.00
RRAPL Patrik Laine/49 80.00 200.00
RRAPZ Pavel Zacha/49 12.00 30.00
RRASS Steven Santini/199 4.00 10.00
RRATC Thomas Chabot/199 10.00 25.00
RRATD Thatcher Demko/199 25.00 60.00
RRATM Tyler Motte/199 5.00 12.00
RRAVR Jakub Vrana/199 6.00 15.00
RRAWN William Nylander/49 60.00 150.00

2016-17 Ultimate Collection '06-07 Retro Rookie Jerseys

RRJAB Anthony Beauvillier 2.00 5.00
RRJAM Auston Matthews 40.00 100.00
RRJBP Brayden Point 5.00 12.00
RRJCD Christian Dvorak 2.50 6.00
RRJDS Dylan Strome 5.00 12.00
RRJEL Esa Lindell 2.00 5.00
RRJHF Hudson Fasching 2.00 5.00
RRJIP Ivan Provorov 3.00 8.00
RRJJC Jakob Chychrun 4.00 10.00
RRJJE Joel Eriksson Ek 3.00 8.00
RRJJH Julius Honka 2.00 5.00
RRJJP Jesse Puljujarvi 4.00 10.00
RRJJV Jimmy Vesey 3.00 8.00
RRJKC Kyle Connor 6.00 15.00
RRJKK Kasperi Kapanen 3.00 8.00
RRJKL Kevin Labanc 2.00 5.00
RRJLC Lawson Crouse 1.50 4.00
RRJMA Anthony Mantha 4.00 10.00
RRJMB Mathew Barzal 6.00 15.00
RRJME Timo Meier 4.00 10.00
RRJMI Michael Matheson 2.00 5.00
RRJMM Mitch Marner 6.00 15.00
RRJMT Matthew Tkachuk 8.00 20.00
RRJMW Miles Wood 1.50 4.00
RRJNS Nick Schmaltz 2.50 6.00
RRJOB Oliver Bjorkstrand 2.50 6.00
RRJOK Oliver Kylington 1.50 4.00
RRJPB Pavel Buchnevich 3.00 8.00
RRJPL Patrik Laine 5.00 12.00
RRJPZ Pavel Zacha 3.00 8.00
RRJSA Sebastian Aho 6.00 15.00
RRJSS Steven Santini 1.50 4.00
RRJTC Thomas Chabot 4.00 10.00
RRJTD Thatcher Demko 5.00 12.00
RRJTK Travis Konecny 4.00 10.00
RRJTM Tyler Motte 2.00 5.00
RRJVR Jakub Vrana 2.50 6.00
RRJWN William Nylander 8.00 20.00
RRJZW Zach Werenski 6.00 15.00

2016-17 Ultimate Collection Debut Threads Patch Autographs

DTAB Anthony Beauvillier/99 12.00 30.00
DTAM Auston Matthews/25 350.00 800.00
DTBP Brayden Point 30.00 80.00
DTCA Trevor Carrick/99 12.00 30.00
DTCD Christian Dvorak/99 15.00 40.00
DTCL Charlie Lindgren/99 20.00 50.00
DTDS Dylan Strome/99 30.00 80.00
DTEL Esa Lindell/99 12.00 30.00
DTHF Hudson Fasching/99 12.00 30.00
DTIP Ivan Provorov/99 20.00 50.00
DTJB Justin Bailey/99 12.00 30.00
DTJC Jakob Chychrun/99 25.00 60.00
DTJL J.C. Lipon/99 12.00 30.00
DTJP Jesse Puljujarvi/99 25.00 60.00
DTJV Jimmy Vesey/99 20.00 50.00
DTKC Kyle Connor/99 40.00 100.00
DTKK Kasperi Kapanen/99 20.00 50.00
DTKU Tom Kuhnhackl/99 10.00 25.00
DTLC Lawson Crouse/99 10.00 25.00
DTMA Anthony Mantha/99 25.00 60.00
DTMB Mathew Barzal/99 40.00 100.00
DTMC Mark McNeill/99 12.00 30.00
DTME Timo Meier/99 25.00 60.00
DTMM Mitch Marner/49 200.00 500.00
DTMR Mike Reilly/99 10.00 25.00
DTMT Matthew Tkachuk/49 30.00 80.00
DTOB Oliver Bjorkstrand/99 15.00 40.00
DTOK Oliver Kylington/99 10.00 25.00
DTPB Pavel Buchnevich/99 20.00 50.00
DTPE Brendan Perlini/99 12.00 30.00
DTPL Patrik Laine/49 200.00 500.00
DTPZ Pavel Zacha/99 20.00 50.00
DTRP Ryan Pulock/99 12.00 30.00
DTSM Sonny Milano/99 15.00 40.00
DTSS Steven Santini/99 10.00 25.00
DTTC Thomas Chabot/99 25.00 60.00
DTTM Tyler Motte/99 12.00 30.00
DTVR Jakub Vrana/99 15.00 40.00
DTWN William Nylander/49 60.00 150.00
DTZW Zach Werenski/99 40.00 100.00

2016-17 Ultimate Collection Keystone Fabrics

KFAK Anze Kopitar 4.00 10.00
KFAO Alexander Ovechkin 10.00 25.00
KFAP Alex Pietrangelo 2.00 5.00
KFBW Blake Wheeler 2.50 6.00
KFCG Claude Giroux 2.50 6.00
KFDD Drew Doughty 3.00 8.00
KFDG Doug Gilmour 3.00 8.00
KFDK Duncan Keith 2.00 5.00
KFDS Daniel Sedin 3.00 8.00
KFEK Erik Karlsson 3.00 8.00
KFEM Evgeni Malkin 5.00 12.00
KFHS Henrik Sedin 3.00 8.00
KFHZ Henrik Zetterberg 3.00 8.00
KFJB Jamie Benn 2.50 6.00
KFJQ Jonathan Quick 3.00 8.00
KFJT Jonathan Toews 4.00 10.00
KFKL Kris Letang 3.00 8.00
KFMB Martin Brodeur 6.00 15.00
KFPB Patrice Bergeron 3.00 8.00
KFPE Patrik Elias 2.50 6.00
KFPM Patrick Marleau 2.50 6.00
KFPR Pekka Rinne 2.50 6.00
KFRG Ryan Getzlaf 2.50 6.00
KFSC Sidney Crosby 10.00 25.00
KFSS Steven Stamkos 5.00 12.00
KFTA John Tavares 4.00 10.00
KFTR Tuukka Rask 3.00 8.00
KFVR Victor Rask 1.50 4.00

2016-17 Ultimate Collection Keystone Fabrics Autographs

SKFCP Carey Price/49 40.00 100.00
SKFDS Denis Savard/99 10.00 25.00
SKFEM Evgeni Malkin/49 30.00 80.00
SKFGC Gerry Cheevers/49 25.00 60.00
SKFHL Henrik Lundqvist/49 40.00 100.00
SKFIL Igor Larionov/15 20.00 50.00
SKFJP Joe Pavelski/99 10.00 25.00
SKFMG Mark Giordano/99 5.00 12.00
SKFML Mario Lemieux/15 90.00 150.00
SKFWS Wayne Simmonds/99 20.00 50.00

2016-17 Ultimate Collection Keystone Fabrics Autographs Gold

SKFCP Carey Price/15 90.00 150.00
SKFDT Dave Taylor/25 40.00 100.00
SKFEM Evgeni Malkin/15 90.00 150.00
SKFHL Henrik Lundqvist/15 80.00 150.00
SKFJP Joe Pavelski/25 20.00 50.00
SKFMG Mark Giordano/25 15.00 40.00
SKFWS Wayne Simmonds/25 60.00 150.00

2016-17 Ultimate Collection Numeric Excellence Materials

NEAM Auston Matthews 40.00 100.00
NEBB Brent Burns 6.00 15.00
NEBH Braden Holtby 8.00 20.00
NEBS Brandon Saad 5.00 12.00
NEDH Dominik Hasek 10.00 25.00
NEJE Jack Eichel 10.00 25.00
NEJG Johnny Gaudreau 10.00 25.00
NEJJ Jaromir Jagr 20.00 50.00
NEJV Jimmy Vesey 10.00 25.00
NEML Mario Lemieux 25.00 60.00
NEMM Mitch Marner 20.00 50.00
NEOE Oliver Ekman-Larsson 6.00 15.00
NEPL Patrik Laine 15.00 40.00
NEPS P.K. Subban 8.00 20.00
NERB Ray Bourque 10.00 25.00
NESC Sidney Crosby 25.00 60.00
NETK Travis Konecny 12.00 30.00
NETS Tyler Seguin 8.00 20.00
NEVH Victor Hedman 8.00 20.00
NEVT Vladimir Tarasenko 8.00 20.00

2016-17 Ultimate Collection Signature Laureates

SLBO Bobby Orr 100.00 200.00
SLCN Cam Neely 20.00 50.00
SLGL Guy Lafleur 25.00 60.00
SLMD Marcel Dionne 20.00 50.00
SLWG Wayne Gretzky 250.00 600.00

2016-17 Ultimate Collection Signature Material Laureates

SMLAL Andrew Ladd/99 6.00 15.00
SMLBE Brian Elliott/99 8.00 20.00
SMLCN Cam Neely/99 10.00 25.00
SMLDB David Backes/99 6.00 15.00
SMLHL Henrik Lundqvist/99 25.00 60.00
SMLJS Jaden Schwartz/99 12.00 30.00
SMLLE Loui Eriksson/99 6.00 15.00
SMLMG Marian Gaborik/99 10.00 25.00
SMLMS Mark Scheifele/99 15.00 40.00
SMLNB Nick Bjugstad/99 6.00 15.00
SMLNN Nino Niederreiter/99 6.00 15.00
SMLRK Ryan Kesler/99 10.00 25.00
SMLTS Tyler Seguin/99 12.00 30.00
SMLWS Wayne Simmonds/99 25.00 60.00

2016-17 Ultimate Collection Signature Material Phenoms

SMPAB Anthony Beauvillier/65 12.00 30.00
SMPCD Christian Dvorak/65 15.00 40.00
SMPHF Hudson Fasching/65 12.00 30.00
SMPMB Mathew Barzal/65 40.00 100.00
SMPME Timo Meier/65 25.00 60.00
SMPTC Thomas Chabot/65 25.00 60.00
SMPTD Thatcher Demko/65 25.00 60.00
SMPTM Tyler Motte/65 12.00 30.00

2016-17 Ultimate Collection Ultimate Performers Material Autographs

UPACC Chris Chelios/50 10.00 25.00
UPAJT Jonathan Toews/50 30.00 80.00
UPATE Tony Esposito/25 25.00 60.00

2016-17 Ultimate Collection Ultimate Performers Materials

UPAO Alexander Ovechkin/99 20.00 50.00
UPBH Brett Hull/99 10.00 25.00
UPIL Igor Larionov/49 5.00 12.00
UPJI Jarome Iginla/99 6.00 15.00
UPJJ Jaromir Jagr/99 15.00 40.00
UPMB Martin Brodeur/99 12.00 30.00
UPMH Marian Hossa/99 5.00 12.00
UPML Mario Lemieux/49 20.00 50.00
UPMM Mark Messier/49 10.00 25.00
UPPC Paul Coffey/99 5.00 12.00
UPPR Patrick Roy/49 12.00 30.00
UPRL Roberto Luongo/99 8.00 20.00
UPSC Sidney Crosby/99 20.00 50.00
UPWG Wayne Gretzky/49 30.00 80.00

2017-18 Ultimate Collection

1 Auston Matthews 5.00 12.00
2 Brad Marchand 2.50 6.00
3 Logan Couture 1.50 4.00
4 Erik Karlsson 1.50 4.00
5 Marc-Andre Fleury 2.50 6.00
6 Kevin Shattenkirk .75 2.00
7 John Tavares 2.00 5.00
8 Jason Pominville .75 2.00
9 Anze Kopitar 2.00 5.00
10 Connor McDavid 6.00 15.00
11 Daniel Sedin 1.50 4.00
12 Steven Stamkos 2.50 6.00
13 Christian Dvorak 1.00 2.50
14 Patrik Laine 1.50 4.00
15 Nathan MacKinnon 5.00 12.00
16 Devan Dubnyk 1.00 2.50
17 Jonathan Drouin 1.00 2.50
18 Tyler Seguin 1.50 4.00
19 Filip Forsberg 2.00 5.00
20 Sidney Crosby 5.00 12.00
21 Jeff Skinner 1.50 4.00
22 Taylor Hall 1.25 3.00
23 Vincent Trocheck 1.25 3.00
24 Wayne Simmonds 1.50 4.00
25 Alexander Ovechkin 5.00 12.00
26 Vladimir Tarasenko 1.50 4.00
27 Rickard Rakell 1.00 2.50
28 Matthew Tkachuk 2.50 6.00
29 Sergei Bobrovsky 2.00 5.00
30 Patrick Kane 2.50 6.00
31 Henrik Zetterberg 1.50 4.00
32 Tuukka Rask 1.50 4.00
33 Nikita Kucherov 2.50 6.00
34 Leon Draisaitl 4.00 10.00
35 Carey Price 2.50 6.00
36 Aleksander Barkov 2.00 5.00
37 Jeff Carter 1.00 2.50
38 Roman Josi 1.25 3.00
39 Mitch Marner 2.00 5.00
40 Henrik Lundqvist 3.00 8.00
41 Johnny Gaudreau 2.00 5.00
42 Duncan Keith 1.00 2.50
43 Jack Eichel 2.00 5.00
44 Jake Guentzel 2.00 5.00
45 Anthony Mantha 1.00 2.50
46 Mark Scheifele 2.00 5.00
47 Cam Atkinson 1.25 3.00
48 Matt Murray 2.00 5.00
49 Patrick Marleau 1.25 3.00
50 Jonathan Toews 2.00 5.00
51 Christian Fischer AU/399 RC 8.00 20.00
52 Haydn Fleury/399 RC 6.00 15.00
53 Evgeny Svechnikov/399 RC 12.00 30.00
54 Jakob Forsbacka-Karlsson AU/399 RC 6.00 15.00
55 Filip Chlapik AU/399 RC 5.00 12.00
56 Samuel Morin AU/399 RC 4.00 10.00
57 Ivan Barbashev/399 RC 8.00 20.00
58 Jack Roslovic AU/399 RC 8.00 20.00
59 Martin Necas AU/399 RC 20.00 50.00
60 Ville Husso AU/399 RC 8.00 20.00
61 Nikita Scherbak AU/399 RC 8.00 20.00
62 J.T. Compher AU/399 RC 6.00 15.00
63 Calle Rosen/399 RC 6.00 15.00
64 Colin White AU/399 RC 8.00 20.00
65 Denis Gurianov AU/399 RC 15.00 40.00
66 Michael Amadio AU/399 RC 6.00 15.00
67 Vladislav Kamenev/399 RC 6.00 15.00

68 Lucas Wallmark/399 RC 6.00 15.00
69 Jon Gillies AU/399 RC 6.00 15.00
70 Vince Dunn AU/399 RC 8.00 20.00
71 Robert Hagg AU/399 RC 6.00 15.00
72 Alex Formenton AU/399 RC 6.00 15.00
73 Riley Barber/399 RC 6.00 15.00
74 Christian Djoos AU/399 RC 6.00 15.00
75 Madison Bowey AU/399 RC 4.00 10.00
76 Filip Chytil AU/399 RC 6.00 15.00
77 Alex Kerfoot AU/299 RC 12.00 30.00
78 Luke Kunin AU/299 RC 6.00 15.00
79 Jake DeBrusk AU/299 RC 15.00 40.00
80 Kailer Yamamoto AU/299 RC 15.00 40.00
81 Tage Thompson AU/299 RC 15.00 40.00
82 Victor Mete AU/299 RC 6.00 15.00
83 Travis Sanheim AU/299 RC 6.00 15.00
84 Logan Brown/299 RC 6.00 15.00
85 Adrian Kempe AU/299 RC 12.00 30.00
86 Anders Bjork/299 RC 8.00 20.00
87 Jesper Bratt AU/299 RC 15.00 40.00
88 Alex Tuch AU/299 RC 15.00 40.00
89 Pierre-Luc Dubois AU/99 RC 150.00 250.00
90 Clayton Keller AU/99 RC 30.00 80.00
91 Alex DeBrincat AU/99 RC 80.00 150.00
92 Tyson Jost AU/99 RC 60.00 150.00
93 Brock Boeser AU/99 RC 30.00 80.00
94 Owen Tippett AU/99 RC 15.00 40.00
95 Charlie McAvoy AU/99 RC 40.00 100.00
96 Josh Ho-Sang AU/99 RC 30.00 80.00
97 Alexander Nylander AU/99 RC 20.00 50.00
98 Will Butcher AU/99 RC 15.00 40.00
99A Nico Hischier/99 RC 12.00 30.00
100 Nolan Patrick/99 RC 40.00 100.00

2017-18 Ultimate Collection '07-08 Retro Debut Threads

RDTAB Anders Bjork 2.50 6.00
RDTAD Alex DeBrincat 5.00 12.00
RDTAK Adrian Kempe 4.00 10.00
RDTAN Alexander Nylander 3.00 8.00
RDTAT Alex Tuch 5.00 12.00
RDTBB Brock Boeser 15.00 40.00
RDTCK Clayton Keller 5.00 12.00
RDTCM Charlie McAvoy 5.00 12.00
RDTFC Filip Chytil 2.00 5.00
RDTJD Jake DeBrusk 5.00 12.00
RDTJH Josh Ho-Sang 2.50 6.00
RDTKY Kailer Yamamoto 5.00 12.00
RDTLB Logan Brown 2.00 5.00
RDTLK Luke Kunin 2.00 5.00
RDTMB Madison Bowey 1.25 3.00
RDTNH Nico Hischier 6.00 15.00
RDTNP Nolan Patrick 4.00 10.00
RDTOT Owen Tippett 4.00 10.00
RDTPD Pierre-Luc Dubois 3.00 8.00
RDTTJ Tyson Jost 4.00 10.00
RDTTT Tage Thompson 5.00 12.00
RDTVD Vince Dunn 2.50 6.00
RDTVM Victor Mete 2.00 5.00
RDTWB Will Butcher 2.50 6.00

2017-18 Ultimate Collection '07-08 Retro Debut Threads Patch Autographs

RDTAD Alex DeBrincat 50.00 125.00
RDTAK Adrian Kempe 40.00 100.00
RDTAN Alexander Nylander 30.00 80.00
RDTAT Alex Tuch 50.00 120.00
RDTBB Brock Boeser 50.00 120.00
RDTCK Clayton Keller 50.00 125.00
RDTCM Charlie McAvoy 80.00 200.00
RDTJD Jake DeBrusk 50.00 120.00
RDTJH Josh Ho-Sang 25.00 60.00
RDTKY Kailer Yamamoto 50.00 125.00
RDTLK Luke Kunin 20.00 50.00
RDTMB Madison Bowey 12.00 30.00
RDTNH Nico Hischier (No Auto) 25.00 60.00
RDTNP Nolan Patrick (No Auto) 40.00 100.00
RDTOT Owen Tippett 40.00 100.00
RDTPD Pierre-Luc Dubois 30.00 80.00
RDTTJ Tyson Jost 40.00 100.00
RDTTT Tage Thompson 50.00 125.00
RDTVD Vince Dunn 25.00 60.00
RDTVM Victor Mete 20.00 50.00
RDTWB Will Butcher 25.00 60.00

2017-18 Ultimate Collection '07-08 Retro Rookie Autographs

RRAAD Alex DeBrincat/199 15.00 40.00
RRAAK Adrian Kempe/299 12.00 30.00
RRAAN Alexander Nylander/299 10.00 25.00
RRAAT Alex Tuch/299 15.00 40.00
RRABB Brock Boeser/199 15.00 40.00
RRACF Christian Fischer/299 8.00 20.00
RRACK Clayton Keller/199 15.00 40.00
RRACM Charlie McAvoy/199 20.00 50.00
RRAJB Jesper Bratt/299 15.00 40.00
RRAJD Jake DeBrusk/299 15.00 40.00
RRAJH Josh Ho-Sang/299 8.00 20.00
RRAJK Janne Kuokkanen/299 6.00 15.00
RRAKY Kailer Yamamoto/299 15.00 40.00
RRALK Luke Kunin/299 6.00 15.00
RRANH Nico Hischier/199 (No Auto) 10.00 25.00
RRANP Nolan Patrick/199 (No Auto) 10.00 25.00
RRAOT Owen Tippett/299 12.00 30.00
RRAPD Pierre-Luc Dubois/199 10.00 25.00
RRATJ Tyson Jost/199 12.00 30.00
RRATT Tage Thompson/299 15.00 40.00
RRAVM Victor Mete/299 6.00 15.00
RRAWB Will Butcher/299 8.00 20.00

2017-18 Ultimate Collection Debut Threads Patch Autographs

DTAAD Alex DeBrincat/49 60.00 150.00
DTAAF Alex Formenton/149 15.00 40.00
DTAAK Adrian Kempe/149 30.00 80.00
DTAAN Alexander Nylander/149 25.00 60.00
DTAAT Alex Tuch/149 40.00 100.00
DTABB Brock Boeser/49 150.00 250.00
DTACF Christian Fischer/149 20.00 50.00
DTACK Clayton Keller/49 30.00 80.00
DTACM Charlie McAvoy/49 40.00 100.00
DTACW Colin White/149 20.00 50.00
DTADG Denis Gurianov/149 40.00 100.00
DTAFC Filip Chlapik/149 12.00 30.00
DTAJB Jesper Bratt/149 30.00 80.00
DTAJC J.T. Compher/149 15.00 40.00
DTAJF Jakob Forsbacka-Karlsson/149 15.0040.00
DTAJG Jon Gillies/149 15.00 40.00
DTAJH Josh Ho-Sang/149 20.00 50.00
DTAJK Janne Kuokkanen/149 15.00 40.00
DTAJR Jack Roslovic/149 20.00 50.00
DTAKY Kailer Yamamoto/149 40.00 100.00
DTALK Luke Kunin/149 15.00 40.00
DTAMB Madison Bowey/149 10.00 25.00
DTANH Nico Hischier/49 (No Auto) 20.00 50.00
DTANP Nolan Patrick/49 (No Auto) 40.00 100.00
DTANS Nikita Scherbak/149 20.00 50.00
DTAOT Owen Tippett/149 30.00 80.00
DTAPD Pierre-Luc Dubois/149 25.00 60.00
DTARE Remi Elie/149 12.00 30.00
DTASM Samuel Morin/149 10.00 25.00
DTATJ Tyson Jost/149 30.00 80.00
DTATP Tucker Poolman/149 12.00 30.00
DTATS Travis Sanheim/149 15.00 40.00
DTATT Tage Thompson/149 40.00 100.00
DTAVD Vince Dunn/149 20.00 50.00
DTAVH Ville Husso/149 20.00 50.00
DTAVM Victor Mete/149 15.00 40.00
DTAVZ Valentin Zykov/149 15.00 40.00
DTAWB Will Butcher/149 20.00 50.00

2017-18 Ultimate Collection Future Legacy Jerseys

FLAB Anders Bjork 3.00 8.00
FLAD Alex DeBrincat 6.00 15.00
FLBB Brock Boeser 6.00 15.00
FLCK Clayton Keller 6.00 15.00
FLCM Charlie McAvoy 6.00 15.00
FLJH Josh Ho-Sang 3.00 8.00
FLNH Nico Hischier 8.00 20.00
FLNP Nolan Patrick 5.00 12.00
FLOT Owen Tippett 5.00 12.00
FLPD Pierre-Luc Dubois 4.00 10.00

2017-18 Ultimate Collection Signature Laureates

SLBO Bobby Orr 50.00 125.00
SLMB Mike Bossy 20.00 50.00
SLMM Mark Messier 25.00 60.00
SLWG Wayne Gretzky 250.00 600.00

2017-18 Ultimate Collection Signature Material Laureates

SMLCP Colton Parayko/99 10.00 25.00
SMLDH Dale Hawerchuk/99 15.00 40.00
SMLGF Grant Fuhr/99 20.00 50.00
SMLJC Jeff Carter/99 10.00 25.00
SMLJD Jonathan Drouin/99 10.00 25.00
SMLJG Jake Guentzel/99 20.00 50.00
SMLJP Jason Pominville/99 8.00 20.00
SMLKS Kevin Shattenkirk/99 8.00 20.00
SMLLC Logan Couture/99 15.00 40.00
SMLNK Nikita Kucherov/99 25.00 60.00
SMLSB Sergei Bobrovsky/99 20.00 50.00

2017-18 Ultimate Collection Signature Material Phenoms

SMPAK Adrian Kempe/65 15.00 40.00
SMPAT Alex Tuch/65 25.00 60.00
SMPKY Kailer Yamamoto/65 20.00 50.00
SMPOT Owen Tippett/65 15.00 40.00
SMPVM Victor Mete/65 8.00 20.00
SMPWB Will Butcher/65 10.00 25.00

2017-18 Ultimate Collection Signature Ultimate Performers Jerseys

SUPHL Henrik Lundqvist 12.00 30.00
SUPJI Jarome Iginla 6.00 15.00
SUPJT John Tavares 8.00 20.00
SUPSS Steven Stamkos 10.00 25.00

2017-18 Ultimate Collection Ultimate Introductions

UI1 Henrik Haapala 2.00 5.00
UI2 J.T. Compher 2.00 5.00
UI3 Haydn Fleury 2.00 5.00
UI4 Nikita Scherbak 2.50 6.00
UI5 Carter Rowney 1.50 4.00
UI6 Vince Dunn 2.50 6.00
UI7 Christian Djoos 2.00 5.00
UI8 Samuel Girard 2.00 5.00
UI9 Calle Rosen 2.00 5.00
UI10 Evgeny Svechnikov 4.00 10.00
UI11 Colin White 2.50 6.00
UI12 Christian Jaros 1.50 4.00
UI13 Eric Comrie 1.50 4.00
UI14 Samuel Blais 2.00 5.00
UI15 Filip Chytil 2.00 5.00
UI16 Robert Hagg 2.00 5.00
UI17 Nick Merkley 2.00 5.00
UI18 Tage Thompson 5.00 12.00
UI19 Alex Tuch 5.00 12.00
UI20 Anders Bjork 2.50 6.00
UI21 Alex Kerfoot 4.00 10.00
UI22 Jesper Bratt 4.00 10.00
UI23 Martin Necas 6.00 15.00
UI24 Travis Sanheim 2.00 5.00
UI25 Luke Kunin 2.00 5.00
UI26 Victor Mete 2.00 5.00
UI27 Logan Brown 2.00 5.00
UI28 Christian Fischer 2.50 6.00
UI29 Tyson Jost 4.00 10.00
UI30 Josh Ho-Sang 2.50 6.00
UI31 Kailer Yamamoto 5.00 12.00
UI32 Alexander Nylander 3.00 8.00
UI33 Will Butcher 2.50 6.00
UI34 Jake DeBrusk 5.00 12.00
UI35 Owen Tippett 4.00 10.00
UI36 Adrian Kempe 4.00 10.00
UI37 Charlie McAvoy 5.00 12.00
UI38 Pierre-Luc Dubois 3.00 8.00
UI39 Brock Boeser 5.00 12.00
UI40 Nolan Patrick 4.00 10.00
UI41 Alex DeBrincat 5.00 12.00
UI42 Clayton Keller 5.00 12.00
UI43 Nico Hischier 6.00 15.00

2017-18 Ultimate Collection Ultimate Introductions Gold Spectrum Autographs

UI2 J.T. Compher 10.00 25.00
UI4 Nikita Scherbak 12.00 30.00
UI6 Vince Dunn 12.00 30.00
UI7 Christian Djoos 10.00 25.00
UI8 Samuel Girard 10.00 25.00
UI11 Colin White 12.00 30.00
UI15 Filip Chytil 10.00 25.00
UI16 Robert Hagg 10.00 25.00
UI17 Nick Merkley 10.00 25.00
UI18 Tage Thompson 25.00 60.00
UI19 Alex Tuch 25.00 60.00
UI21 Alex Kerfoot 20.00 50.00
UI22 Jesper Bratt 20.00 50.00
UI23 Martin Necas 30.00 80.00
UI24 Travis Sanheim 10.00 25.00
UI25 Luke Kunin 10.00 25.00
UI26 Victor Mete 10.00 25.00
UI28 Christian Fischer 12.00 30.00
UI29 Tyson Jost 20.00 50.00
UI30 Josh Ho-Sang 12.00 30.00
UI31 Kailer Yamamoto 25.00 60.00
UI32 Alexander Nylander 15.00 40.00
UI33 Will Butcher 12.00 30.00
UI34 Jake DeBrusk 25.00 60.00
UI35 Owen Tippett 20.00 50.00
UI36 Adrian Kempe 20.00 50.00
UI37 Charlie McAvoy 30.00 80.00
UI39 Brock Boeser 25.00 60.00
UI41 Alex DeBrincat 25.00 60.00
UI42 Clayton Keller 25.00 60.00
UI43 Nico Hischier 20.00 50.00

2017-18 Ultimate Collection Ultimate Legacy Jerseys

ULCP Carey Price C 6.00 15.00
ULEK Erik Karlsson D 4.00 10.00
ULJT Jonathan Toews D 5.00 12.00
ULML Mario Lemieux A 12.00 30.00
ULMM Mark Messier A 6.00 15.00
ULPD Pavel Datsyuk D 5.00 12.00
ULPF Peter Forsberg C 6.00 15.00
ULSC Sidney Crosby A 12.00 30.00
ULSS Steven Stamkos B 6.00 15.00
ULWG Wayne Gretzky A 20.00 50.00

2017-18 Ultimate Collection Ultimate Legacy Signatures

ULSBO Bobby Orr C 60.00 150.00
ULSEB Ed Belfour C 12.00 30.00
ULSHL Henrik Lundqvist B 20.00 50.00
ULSSS Steven Stamkos A 15.00 40.00
ULSWG Wayne Gretzky A 200.00 500.00

2017-18 Ultimate Collection Ultimate Performers Jerseys

UPCP Carey Price/99 6.00 15.00
UPDH Dominik Hasek/99 5.00 12.00
UPDS Daniel Sedin/99 4.00 10.00
UPEM Evgeni Malkin/99 6.00 15.00
UPJS Joe Sakic/99 6.00 15.00
UPJT Jonathan Toews/99 5.00 12.00
UPMB Martin Brodeur/49 12.00 30.00
UPPD Pavel Datsyuk/99 5.00 12.00
UPRB Ray Bourque/99 5.00 12.00
UPSY Steve Yzerman/49 20.00 50.00
UPWG Wayne Gretzky/49 25.00 60.00

2018-19 Ultimate Collection

1 Connor McDavid 6.00 15.00
2 Jonathan Marchessault 1.50 4.00
3 Teuvo Teravainen 1.25 3.00
4 Jonathan Quick 1.50 4.00
5 Jamie Benn 1.25 3.00
6 Brendan Gallagher 1.25 3.00
7 Mathew Barzal 1.50 4.00
8 Clayton Keller 1.50 4.00
9 Andrei Vasilevskiy 2.00 5.00
10 Patrick Kane 2.50 6.00
11 Sean Monahan .75 2.00
12 Erik Karlsson 1.50 4.00
13 Nikolaj Ehlers 1.25 3.00
14 Vincent Trocheck 1.25 3.00
15 Auston Matthews 5.00 12.00
16 Vladimir Tarasenko 1.50 4.00
17 David Pastrnak 3.00 8.00
18 Jack Eichel 2.00 5.00
19 Pekka Rinne 1.25 3.00
20 Sidney Crosby 5.00 12.00
21 Mikko Rantanen 3.00 8.00
22 Morgan Rielly 1.25 3.00
23 Mark Stone 1.50 4.00
24 Claude Giroux 1.25 3.00
25 Brock Boeser 1.50 4.00
26 Mats Zuccarello 1.25 3.00
27 Nico Hischier 2.00 5.00
28 Ryan Getzlaf 1.25 3.00
29 Eric Staal 1.25 3.00
30 Alexander Ovechkin 5.00 12.00
31 Sergei Bobrovsky 2.00 5.00
32 Sebastian Aho 2.00 5.00
33 William Karlsson 1.50 4.00
34 Tomas Hertl 1.25 3.00
35 Nathan MacKinnon 5.00 12.00
36 Alex DeBrincat 1.50 4.00
37 Alexander Radulov 1.25 3.00
38 Connor Hellebuyck 2.50 6.00
39 Brent Burns 1.25 3.00
40 John Tavares 2.00 5.00
41 Anthony Mantha 1.00 2.50
42 Evgeni Malkin 2.50 6.00
43 Evgeny Kuznetsov 1.50 4.00
44 Anders Lee 1.00 2.50
45 Marc-Andre Fleury 2.50 6.00
46 Brayden Schenn 1.25 3.00
47 Ilya Kovalchuk 1.00 2.50
48 Steven Stamkos 2.50 6.00
49 Matthew Tkachuk 2.50 6.00
50 Carey Price 2.50 6.00
51A Maxime Comtois/299 RC 2.00 5.00
52 Dominik Kahun AU/299 RC 2.00 5.00
53 Evan Bouchard AU/299 RC 8.00 20.00
54 Isac Lundestrom AU/299 RC 1.50 4.00
55 Adam Gaudette AU/299 RC 3.00 8.00
56 Robert Thomas AU/299 RC 4.00 10.00
57 Dennis Cholowski AU/299 RC 2.00 5.00
58A Anthony Cirelli/299 RC 3.00 8.00
59A Henrik Borgstrom/299 RC 3.00 8.00
60 Brett Howden AU/299 RC 2.50 6.00
61 Warren Foegele AU/299 RC 2.00 5.00
62 Antti Suomela AU/299 RC 1.50 4.00
63A Noah Juulsen/299 RC 2.00 5.00
64 Tomas Hyka AU/299 RC 2.00 5.00
65 Andreas Johnsson AU/299 RC 2.50 6.00
66 Joey Anderson AU/299 RC 2.00 5.00
67 Henri Jokiharju AU/299 RC 1.50 4.00
68 Drake Batherson AU/299 RC 12.00 30.00
69 Dillon Dube AU/299 RC 2.50 6.00
70 Filip Hronek AU/299 RC 2.00 5.00
71 Lias Andersson AU/299 RC 3.00 8.00
72 Ilya Samsonov/299 RC 4.00 10.00
73 Jordan Greenway AU/299 RC 2.00 5.00
74 Oskar Lindblom/299 RC 3.00 8.00
75 Sam Steel AU/299 RC 2.00 5.00
76 Zach Aston-Reese AU/299 RC 3.00 8.00
77 Jordan Kyrou AU/299 RC 20.00 50.00
78 Maxime Lajoie AU/299 RC 3.00 8.00
79 Cooper Marody AU/299 RC 2.00 5.00
80 Kristian Vesalainen AU/299 RC 2.50 6.00
81 Michael Dal Colle AU/299 RC 2.00 5.00
82A Michael Rasmussen/299 RC 2.50 6.00
83 Michael McLeod AU/299 RC 1.50 4.00
84A Juuso Valimaki/299 RC 2.00 5.00
85 Dylan Sikura AU/299 RC 2.50 6.00
86A Jake Bean/299 RC 2.00 5.00
87A Troy Terry/299 RC 3.00 8.00
88 Travis Dermott AU/299 RC 3.00 8.00
89 Jesperi Kotkaniemi AU/99 RC 10.00 25.00
90 Andrei Svechnikov AU/99 RC 80.00 200.00
91 Casey Mittelstadt AU/99 RC 10.00 25.00
92 Miro Heiskanen AU/99 RC 12.00 30.00
93 Brady Tkachuk AU/99 RC 15.00 40.00
94 Eeli Tolvanen/99 RC 10.00 25.00
95 Carter Hart AU/99 RC 120.00 300.00
96 Ryan Donato AU/99 RC 8.00 20.00
97 Elias Pettersson AU/99 RC 15.00 40.00
98 Rasmus Dahlin/99 RC 12.00 30.00
58B Anthony Cirelli AU/299 XRC 10.00 25.00
87B Troy Terry AU/299 XRC 10.00 25.00

2018-19 Ultimate Collection '08-09 Retro Rookies Patch Autographs

RRPAAG Adam Gaudette 30.00 80.00
RRPAAJ Andreas Johnsson 25.00 60.00
RRPABA Drake Batherson 40.00 100.00
RRPABH Brett Howden 25.00 60.00
RRPABO Evan Bouchard 50.00 125.00
RRPABT Brady Tkachuk 60.00 150.00
RRPACH Carter Hart 40.00 100.00
RRPACM Casey Mittelstadt 40.00 100.00
RRPADD Dillon Dube 25.00 60.00
RRPADS Dylan Sikura 25.00 60.00
RRPAEB Ethan Bear 30.00 80.00
RRPAEP Elias Pettersson 200.00 400.00
RRPAFH Filip Hronek 20.00 50.00
RRPAJG Jordan Greenway 20.00 50.00
RRPAJK Jesperi Kotkaniemi 40.00 100.00
RRPAKV Kristian Vesalainen 25.00 60.00
RRPALA Lias Andersson 30.00 80.00
RRPAMB Mackenzie Blackwood 40.00 100.00
RRPAMH Miro Heiskanen 50.00 125.00
RRPAML Maxime Lajoie 30.00 80.00
RRPART Robert Thomas 40.00 100.00
RRPATD Travis Dermott 30.00 80.00
RRPATT Troy Terry 60.00 150.00

2018-19 Ultimate Collection '97 Ultimate Legends HOF Signatures

LHOFBH Brett Hull A 30.00 80.00
LHOFCC Chris Chelios C 15.00 40.00
LHOFDH Dale Hawerchuk C 20.00 50.00
LHOFDS Darryl Sittler B 20.00 50.00
LHOFLM Lanny McDonald D 15.00 40.00
LHOFLR Larry Robinson D 15.00 40.00
LHOFMB Martin Brodeur B 40.00 100.00
LHOFMB Mike Bossy B 15.00 40.00
LHOFMD Marcel Dionne D 20.00 50.00
LHOFML Mario Lemieux A 60.00 150.00
LHOFNL Nicklas Lidstrom D 15.00 40.00
LHOFPL Pat LaFontaine C 15.00 40.00
LHOFPR Patrick Roy D 40.00 100.00
LHOFWO Willie O'Ree D 20.00 50.00

2018-19 Ultimate Collection '97 Ultimate Legends Signatures

AL95 Frank Mahovlich A 10.00 25.00
AL96 Teemu Selanne A 20.00 50.00
AL101 Pat Lafontaine A 10.00 25.00
AL109 Red Kelly B 10.00 25.00
AL110 Peter Forsberg A 20.00 50.00
AL112 Larry Murphy D 8.00 20.00
AL114 Mike Modano B 20.00 50.00
AL118 Patrick Roy A 25.00 60.00
AL119 Guy Lafleur A 12.00 30.00
AL121 Jarome Iginla A 12.00 30.00
AL123 Brian Propp D 8.00 20.00
AL125 Phil Esposito A 15.00 40.00
AL126 Pierre Turgeon B 8.00 20.00
AL127 Curtis Joseph B 12.00 30.00
AL128 Tom Barrasso B 10.00 25.00
AL129 Tony Amonte D 8.00 20.00
AL130 Shayne Corson D 8.00 20.00
AL133 Bob Baun C 10.00 25.00
AL134 Pavel Datsyuk A 15.00 40.00
AL135 John Vanbiesbrouck D 10.00 25.00
AL136 Chris Chelios A 10.00 25.00
AL137 Felix Potvin C 15.00 40.00
AL138 Rod Brind'Amour D 10.00 25.00
AL139 Mark Messier A 20.00 50.00
AL140 Bobby Orr B 40.00 100.00
AL141 Willie O'Ree D 12.00 30.00
AL142 Pat LaFontaine B 10.00 25.00
AL144 Norm Ullman C 10.00 25.00
AL145 Andy Moog C 10.00 25.00
AL146 Dale Hawerchuk B 12.00 30.00
AL148 Rod Langway D 8.00 20.00
AL149 Brett Hull A 20.00 50.00
AL150 Doug Gilmour A 12.00 30.00
AL152 Paul Coffey A 10.00 25.00
AL153 Lanny McDonald B 10.00 25.00
AL156 Arturs Irbe C 8.00 20.00
AL158 Steve Yzerman A 25.00 60.00
AL159 Mario Lemieux A 40.00 100.00

2018-19 Ultimate Collection Autographs

2 Jonathan Marchessault/50 10.00 25.00
4 Jonathan Quick/25 20.00 50.00
9 Andrei Vasilevskiy/50 12.00 30.00
14 Vincent Trocheck/75 8.00 20.00
21 Mikko Rantanen/50 20.00 50.00
23 Mark Stone/50 10.00 25.00
25 Brock Boeser/50 10.00 25.00
27 Nico Hischier/50 12.00 30.00
29 Eric Staal/75 8.00 20.00
34 Tomas Hertl/75 8.00 20.00
36 Alex DeBrincat/75 10.00 25.00
40 John Tavares/25 25.00 60.00
43 Evgeny Kuznetsov/50 10.00 25.00
44 Anders Lee/75 6.00 15.00
45 Marc-Andre Fleury/25 30.00 80.00
46 Brayden Schenn/75 8.00 20.00
48 Steven Stamkos/25 30.00 80.00
49 Matthew Tkachuk/75 15.00 40.00

2018-19 Ultimate Collection Debut Threads Patch Autographs

DTRD Rasmus Dahlin (No Auto) 40.00 100.00
DTAAG Adam Gaudette 25.00 60.00
DTAAJ Andreas Johnsson 20.00 50.00
DTAAN Antti Suomela 12.00 30.00
DTAAS Andrei Svechnikov 40.00 100.00
DTABH Brett Howden 20.00 50.00
DTABT Brady Tkachuk 50.00 125.00
DTACH Carter Hart 120.00 300.00
DTACM Casey Mittelstadt 30.00 80.00
DTACO Cooper Marody 15.00 40.00
DTADA Daniel Brickley 15.00 40.00
DTADB Drake Batherson 30.00 80.00
DTADC Dennis Cholowski 15.00 40.00
DTADD Dillon Dube 20.00 50.00
DTADS Dylan Sikura 20.00 50.00
DTAEB Ethan Bear 25.00 60.00
DTAEP Elias Pettersson 300.00 400.00
DTAEV Evan Bouchard 40.00 100.00
DTAFH Filip Hronek 15.00 40.00
DTAHJ Henri Jokiharju 12.00 30.00
DTAJA Joey Anderson 15.00 40.00
DTAJG Jordan Greenway 15.00 40.00
DTAJK Jesperi Kotkaniemi 30.00 80.00
DTAJO Jordan Kyrou 30.00 80.00
DTAJZ Jakub Zboril 25.00 60.00
DTAKV Kristian Vesalainen 20.00 50.00
DTALA Lias Andersson 25.00 60.00
DTAMB Mackenzie Blackwood 30.00 80.00
DTAMD Michael Dal Colle 15.00 40.00
DTAMH Miro Heiskanen 40.00 100.00
DTAML Maxime Lajoie 25.00 60.00
DTAMM Michael McLeod 12.00 30.00
DTARD Ryan Donato 25.00 60.00
DTART Robert Thomas 30.00 80.00
DTASS Sam Steel 15.00 40.00
DTATD Travis Dermott 25.00 60.00
DTATH Tomas Hyka 15.00 40.00
DTAWF Warren Foegele 15.00 40.00
DTAZR Zach Aston-Reese 25.00 60.00

2018-19 Ultimate Collection Jerseys

51 Maxime Comtois 2.50 6.00
52 Dominik Kahun 2.50 6.00
53 Evan Bouchard 6.00 15.00
54 Isac Lundestrom 2.00 5.00
55 Adam Gaudette 4.00 10.00
56 Robert Thomas 5.00 12.00
57 Dennis Cholowski 2.50 6.00
58 Anthony Cirelli 4.00 10.00
59 Henrik Borgstrom 4.00 10.00
60 Brett Howden 3.00 8.00
61 Warren Foegele 2.50 6.00
62 Antti Suomela 2.00 5.00
63 Noah Juulsen 2.50 6.00
64 Tomas Hyka 2.50 6.00
65 Andreas Johnsson 3.00 8.00
66 Joey Anderson 2.50 6.00
67 Henri Jokiharju 2.00 5.00
68 Drake Batherson 5.00 12.00
69 Dillon Dube 3.00 8.00
70 Filip Hronek 2.50 6.00
71 Lias Andersson 4.00 10.00
72 Ilya Samsonov 5.00 12.00
73 Jordan Greenway 2.50 6.00
74 Oskar Lindblom 4.00 10.00
75 Sam Steel 2.50 6.00
76 Zach Aston-Reese 4.00 10.00
77 Jordan Kyrou 5.00 12.00
78 Maxime Lajoie 4.00 10.00
79 Cooper Marody 2.50 6.00
80 Kristian Vesalainen 3.00 8.00
81 Michael Dal Colle 2.50 6.00
82 Michael Rasmussen 3.00 8.00
83 Michael McLeod 2.00 5.00
84 Juuso Valimaki 2.50 6.00
85 Dylan Sikura 3.00 8.00
86 Jake Bean 2.50 6.00
87 Troy Terry 4.00 10.00
88 Travis Dermott 4.00 10.00
89 Jesperi Kotkaniemi 5.00 12.00
90 Andrei Svechnikov 6.00 15.00
91 Casey Mittelstadt 5.00 12.00
92 Miro Heiskanen 6.00 15.00
93 Brady Tkachuk 8.00 20.00
94 Eeli Tolvanen 5.00 12.00
95 Carter Hart 5.00 12.00
96 Ryan Donato 4.00 10.00
97 Elias Pettersson 8.00 20.00
98 Rasmus Dahlin 6.00 15.00

2018-19 Ultimate Collection Patches

77 Jordan Kyrou AU/99 60.00 150.00
87 Troy Terry AU/99 25.00 60.00
95 Carter Hart AU/49 100.00 250.00
97 Elias Pettersson AU/49 250.00 350.00

2018-19 Ultimate Collection Signature Laureates

SLBO Bobby Orr/25 60.00 150.00
SLMD Marcel Dionne/49 12.00 30.00
SLMR Mikko Rantanen/49 25.00 60.00
SLSB Scotty Bowman/25 40.00 100.00
SLTW Tom Wilson/99 10.00 25.00

2018-19 Ultimate Collection Signature Masterpieces

USMAL Anders Lee D 10.00 25.00
USMAM Auston Matthews A 50.00 125.00
USMAT Alex Tuch C 12.00 30.00
USMAV Andrei Vasilevskiy B 20.00 50.00
USMBS Brayden Schenn C 12.00 30.00
USMBT Brady Tkachuk C 40.00 100.00
USMCM Connor McDavid A 250.00 350.00
USMDB Drake Batherson D 25.00 60.00
USMDC Dennis Cholowski 12.00 30.00
USMDH Dale Hawerchuk B 15.00 40.00
USMDS Daniel Sedin A 15.00 40.00
USMEP Elias Pettersson B 150.00 250.00
USMES Eric Staal C 12.00 30.00
USMFP Felix Potvin C 20.00 50.00
USMHS Henrik Sedin A 15.00 40.00
USMJK Jesperi Kotkaniemi C 25.00 60.00
USMJM Jonathan Marchessaul Ct 15.00 40.00
USMJT John Tavares A 20.00 50.00
USMJV Jakub Vrana D 12.00 30.00
USMKT Kyle Turris D 10.00 25.00
USMKU Jari Kurri B 12.00 30.00
USMMA Marc-Andre Fleury A 25.00 60.00
USMMB Martin Brodeur A 100.00 200.00
USMMD Marcel Dionne B 15.00 40.00
USMMH Miro Heiskanen D 30.00 80.00
USMMI Casey Mittelstadt D 25.00 60.00
USMMR Mikko Rantanen C 30.00 80.00
USMMS Mark Stone D 15.00 40.00
USMMT Matthew Tkachuk C 25.00 60.00
USMNH Nico Hischier B 20.00 50.00
USMPL Pat LaFontaine B 12.00 30.00
USMPM Patrick Marleau A 12.00 30.00
USMRD Ryan Donato D 20.00 50.00
USMRH Ron Hextall C 12.00 30.00
USMSC Mark Scheifele B 20.00 50.00
USMSS Steven Stamkos A 25.00 60.00
USMTW Tom Wilson C 12.00 30.00
USMVA Viktor Arvidsson D 8.00 20.00

2018-19 Ultimate Collection Signature Material Laureates

SMLBH Brett Hull/25 30.00 80.00
SMLCA Casey Mittelstadt/99 30.00 80.00
SMLDB Drake Batherson/99 30.00 80.00
SMLDS Daniel Sedin/25 20.00 50.00
SMLEP Elias Pettersson/49 60.00 150.00
SMLHL Henrik Lundqvist/25 40.00 100.00
SMLPM Patrick Marleau/49 15.00 40.00
SMLSS Steven Stamkos/25 30.00 80.00
SMLTH Tomas Hertl/99 15.00 40.00

2018-19 Ultimate Collection Ultimate Access Material Autographs

UAAAE Aaron Ekblad 12.00 30.00
UAAAM Auston Matthews 60.00 150.00
UAABB Brock Boeser 12.00 30.00
UAABT Brady Tkachuk 30.00 80.00
UAACA Casey Mittelstadt 20.00 50.00
UAADB Drake Batherson 20.00 50.00
UAAES Eric Staal 10.00 25.00
UAAJG Jake Guentzel 15.00 40.00
UAAJK Jesperi Kotkaniemi 20.00 50.00
UAAJM Jonathan Marchessault 12.00 30.00
UAAMH Miro Heiskanen 25.00 60.00
UAAMR Mikko Rantanen 25.00 60.00
UAAMS Mark Stone 12.00 30.00
UAARD Ryan Donato 15.00 40.00
UAARE Ryan Ellis 8.00 20.00

2018-19 Ultimate Collection Ultimate Access Material Autographs Premium Copper

UAAAE Aaron Ekblad 15.00 40.00
UAAAM Auston Matthews 50.00 125.00
UAAAS Andrei Svechnikov 30.00 80.00
UAABB Brock Boeser 15.00 40.00
UAABT Brady Tkachuk 40.00 100.00
UAACA Casey Mittelstadt 25.00 60.00
UAACM Connor McDavid 60.00 150.00
UAADB Drake Batherson 25.00 60.00
UAAEP Elias Pettersson 125.00 300.00
UAAES Eric Staal 12.00 30.00
UAAJG Jake Guentzel 20.00 50.00
UAAJM Jonathan Marchessault 15.00 40.00
UAAMH Miro Heiskanen 30.00 80.00
UAAMR Mikko Rantanen 30.00 80.00
UAAMS Mark Stone 15.00 40.00
UAARD Ryan Donato 20.00 50.00
UAARE Ryan Ellis 10.00 25.00

2018-19 Ultimate Collection Ultimate Access Materials

UAAE Aaron Ekblad 4.00 10.00
UAAM Auston Matthews 12.00 30.00
UAAR Alexander Radulov 3.00 8.00
UAAS Andrei Svechnikov 8.00 20.00
UABB Brock Boeser 4.00 10.00
UABT Brady Tkachuk 10.00 25.00
UACA Casey Mittelstadt 6.00 15.00
UACH Connor Hellebuyck 6.00 15.00
UACM Connor McDavid 15.00 40.00
UACP Carey Price 6.00 15.00
UADB Drake Batherson 6.00 15.00
UAEP Elias Pettersson 10.00 25.00
UAES Eric Staal 3.00 8.00
UAIS Ilya Samsonov 6.00 15.00
UAJE Jack Eichel 5.00 12.00
UAJG Jake Guentzel 5.00 12.00
UAJK Jesperi Kotkaniemi 6.00 15.00
UAJM Jonathan Marchessault 4.00 10.00
UAJN James Neal 2.00 5.00
UAMH Miro Heiskanen 8.00 20.00
UAMR Mikko Rantanen 8.00 20.00
UAMS Mark Stone 4.00 10.00
UARD Ryan Donato 5.00 12.00
UARE Ryan Ellis 2.50 6.00

2018-19 Ultimate Collection Ultimate Dual Material Autographs

DMBP Brock Boeser
Elias Pettersson 300.00 400.00
DMDD Max Domi
Jonathan Drouin 20.00 50.00
DMFM Marc-Andre Fleury
Matt Murray 40.00 100.00
DMGT Johnny Gaudreau
Matthew Tkachuk 40.00 100.00
DMHC Tomas Hertl
Logan Couture 25.00 60.00
DMKJ Jesperi Kotkaniemi
Noah Juulsen 40.00 100.00
DMKW Evgeny Kuznetsov
Tom Wilson 25.00 60.00
DMMS Casey Mittelstadt
Andrei Svechnikov 50.00 125.00
DMSS Daniel Sedin
Henrik Sedin 25.00 60.00
DMTB Brady Tkachuk
Drake Batherson 60.00 150.00
DMTM John Tavares
Mitch Marner 30.00 80.00
DMTS Vladimir Tarasenko
Brayden Schenn 25.00 60.00

2018-19 Ultimate Collection Ultimate Icons Material Autographs

*COPPER/25: .6X TO 1.5X BASIC INSERTS
UIABH Brett Hull 20.00 50.00
UIADH Dale Hawerchuk 15.00 40.00
UIAGF Grant Fuhr 20.00 50.00
UIAHL Henrik Lundqvist 30.00 80.00
UIAHS Henrik Sedin 15.00 40.00
UIAJQ Jonathan Quick 15.00 40.00
UIALR Larry Robinson 12.00 30.00
UIAMF Marc-Andre Fleury 25.00 60.00
UIAPL Pat LaFontaine 12.00 30.00
UIAPM Patrick Marleau 12.00 30.00
UIASS Steven Stamkos 25.00 60.00
UIATB Tom Barrasso 12.00 30.00

2018-19 Ultimate Collection Ultimate Icons Materials

UIBB Brent Burns 3.00 8.00
UIBH Brett Hull 6.00 15.00
UIBM Brad Marchand 6.00 15.00
UICC Chris Chelios 3.00 8.00
UIDH Dale Hawerchuk 4.00 10.00
UIDK Duncan Keith 2.50 6.00
UIEM Evgeni Malkin 6.00 15.00
UIGF Grant Fuhr 5.00 12.00
UIHL Henrik Lundqvist 8.00 20.00
UIHS Henrik Sedin 4.00 10.00
UIHZ Henrik Zetterberg 4.00 10.00
UIJK Jeff Carter 2.50 6.00
UIJQ Jonathan Quick 4.00 10.00
UIJT John Tavares 5.00 12.00
UILR Larry Robinson 3.00 8.00
UIMF Marc-Andre Fleury 6.00 15.00
UIPK Patrick Kane 6.00 15.00
UIPL Pat LaFontaine 3.00 8.00
UIPM Patrick Marleau 3.00 8.00
UIPR Patrick Roy 8.00 20.00
UISC Sidney Crosby 12.00 30.00
UISS Steven Stamkos 6.00 15.00
UITB Tom Barrasso 3.00 8.00
UIVT Vladimir Tarasenko 4.00 10.00
UIWG Wayne Gretzky 20.00 50.00

2018-19 Ultimate Collection Ultimate Introductions

UI1 Jayce Hawryluk 1.25 3.00
UI2 Robert Thomas 3.00 8.00
UI3 Dennis Cholowski 1.50 4.00
UI4 Cooper Marody 1.50 4.00
UI5 Henri Jokiharju 1.25 3.00
UI6 Juuso Valimaki 1.50 4.00
UI7 Isac Lundestrom 1.25 3.00
UI8 Anthony Cirelli 2.50 6.00
UI9 Michael McLeod 1.25 3.00
UI10 Warren Foegele 1.50 4.00
UI11 Jordan Kyrou 3.00 8.00
UI12 Filip Hronek 1.50 4.00
UI13 Troy Terry 2.50 6.00
UI14 Michael Dal Colle 1.50 4.00
UI15 Jaret Anderson-Dolan 1.25 3.00
UI16 Nicolas Roy 1.00 2.50
UI17 Dylan Gambrell 1.50 4.00
UI18 Dominik Kahun 1.50 4.00
UI19 Ilya Samsonov 3.00 8.00
UI20 Noah Juulsen 1.50 4.00
UI21 Michael Rasmussen 2.00 5.00
UI22 Jordan Greenway 1.50 4.00
UI23 Evan Bouchard 4.00 10.00
UI24 Sam Steel 1.50 4.00
UI25 Maxime Lajoie 2.50 6.00
UI26 Kristian Vesalainen 2.00 5.00
UI27 Lias Andersson 2.50 6.00
UI28 Andreas Johnsson 2.00 5.00
UI29 Maxime Comtois 1.50 4.00
UI30 Miro Heiskanen 4.00 10.00
UI31 Eeli Tolvanen 3.00 8.00
UI32 Adam Gaudette 2.50 6.00
UI33 Brett Howden 2.00 5.00
UI34 Travis Dermott 2.50 6.00
UI35 Dylan Sikura 2.00 5.00
UI36 Drake Batherson 3.00 8.00
UI37 Jesperi Kotkaniemi 3.00 8.00
UI38 Brady Tkachuk 5.00 12.00
UI39 Casey Mittelstadt 3.00 8.00
UI40 Elias Pettersson 5.00 12.00
UI41 Ryan Donato 2.50 6.00
UI42 Carter Hart 3.00 8.00
UI43 Andrei Svechnikov 4.00 10.00
UI44 Rasmus Dahlin 4.00 10.00
UI45 Rasmus Dahlin 4.00 10.00
UI46 Jesperi Kotkaniemi 3.00 8.00
UI47 Brady Tkachuk 5.00 12.00
UI48 Andrei Svechnikov 4.00 10.00
UI49 Carter Hart 3.00 8.00
UI50 Elias Pettersson 5.00 12.00

2018-19 Ultimate Collection Ultimate Introductions Onyx Black

*BLACK/25: 1.5X TO 4X BASIC INSERTS
UI4 Cooper Marody 12.00 30.00
UI9 Michael McLeod 12.00 30.00
UI42 Carter Hart 10.00 25.00
UI49 Carter Hart 10.00 25.00
UI50 Elias Pettersson 50.00 125.00

2018-19 Ultimate Collection Ultimate Introductions Autographs Gold

UI1 Jayce Hawryluk 6.00 15.00
UI2 Robert Thomas 15.00 40.00
UI3 Dennis Cholowski 8.00 20.00
UI4 Cooper Marody 8.00 20.00
UI5 Henri Jokiharju 6.00 15.00
UI9 Michael McLeod 6.00 15.00
UI10 Warren Foegele 8.00 20.00
UI11 Jordan Kyrou 15.00 40.00

UI12 Filip Hronek 8.00 20.00
UI13 Troy Terry 10.00 25.00
UI14 Michael Dal Colle 8.00 20.00
UI15 Jaret Anderson-Dolan 6.00 15.00
UI16 Nicolas Roy 5.00 12.00
UI17 Dylan Gambrell 8.00 20.00
UI18 Dominik Kahun 8.00 20.00
UI22 Jordan Greenway 8.00 20.00
UI23 Evan Bouchard 20.00 50.00
UI24 Sam Steel 8.00 20.00
UI25 Maxime Lajoie 12.00 30.00
UI26 Kristian Vesalainen 10.00 25.00
UI27 Lias Andersson 12.00 30.00
UI28 Andreas Johnsson 10.00 25.00
UI30 Miro Heiskanen 20.00 50.00
UI32 Adam Gaudette 12.00 30.00
UI33 Brett Howden 10.00 25.00
UI34 Travis Dermott 12.00 30.00
UI35 Dylan Sikura 10.00 25.00
UI36 Drake Batherson 15.00 40.00
UI37 Jesperi Kotkaniemi 15.00 40.00
UI38 Brady Tkachuk 25.00 60.00
UI39 Casey Mittelstadt 15.00 40.00
UI40 Elias Pettersson 100.00 200.00
UI42 Carter Hart 15.00 40.00
UI43 Andrei Svechnikov 20.00 50.00
UI46 Jesperi Kotkaniemi 15.00 40.00
UI47 Brady Tkachuk 25.00 60.00
UI48 Andrei Svechnikov 20.00 50.00
UI49 Carter Hart 15.00 40.00
UI50 Elias Pettersson 150.00 250.00

2018-19 Ultimate Collection Ultimate Material Signatures

UMSAV Andrei Vasilevskiy/49 25.00 60.00
UMSBB Brock Boeser/25 20.00 50.00
UMSBT Brady Tkachuk/49 50.00 125.00
UMSEK Evgeny Kuznetsov/49 20.00 50.00
UMSEP Elias Pettersson/25 250.00 350.00
UMSES Eric Staal/49 15.00 40.00
UMSHS Henrik Sedin/25 20.00 50.00
UMSJK Jesperi Kotkaniemi/49 30.00 80.00
UMSJM Jonathan Marchessault/49 20.00 50.00
UMSJQ Jonathan Quick/25 20.00 50.00
UMSMF Marc-Andre Fleury/25 30.00 80.00
UMSMH Miro Heiskanen/49 40.00 100.00
UMSNH Nico Hischier/25 25.00 60.00

2018-19 Ultimate Collection Ultimate Quad Materials

UQMBCRC Ray Bourque
Paul Coffey
Larry Robinson
Chris Chelios 10.00 25.00
UQMBMSR Drake Batherson
Casey Mittelstadt
Andrei Svechnikov
Michael Rasmussen 15.00 40.00
UQMESOP Jack Eichel
Jeff Skinner
Kyle Okposo
Jason Pominville 10.00 25.00
UQMFSMT Marc-Andre Fleury
Reilly Smith
Jonathan Marchessault
Alex Tuch 12.00 30.00
UQMGHLS Doug Gilmour
Dale Hawerchuk
Guy Lafleur
Joe Sakic 25.00 60.00
UQMGLYM Wayne Gretzky
Mario Lemieux
Steve Yzerman
Mark Messier 40.00 100.00
UQMGTMN Johnny Gaudreau
Matthew Tkachuk
Sean Monahan
James Neal 12.00 30.00
UQMJFSR Ryan Johansen
Filip Forsberg
P.K. Subban
Pekka Rinne 10.00 25.00
UQMJSEK Henri Jokiharju
Dylan Sikura
Victor Ejdsell
Dominik Kahun 8.00 20.00
UQMMOTS Connor McDavid
Alexander Ovechkin
John Tavares
Steven Stamkos 40.00 100.00
UQMMPBK Brad Marchand
David Pastrnak
Patrice Bergeron
David Krejci 15.00 40.00
UQMMRLK Nathan MacKinnon
Mikko Rantanen
Gabriel Landeskog
Alex Kerfoot 25.00 60.00
UQMOBCH Alexander Ovechkin
Nicklas Backstrom
John Carlson
Braden Holtby 40.00 100.00
UQMPDTK Elias Pettersson
Rasmus Dahlin
Brady Tkachuk
Jesperi Kotkaniemi 20.00 50.00
UQMPFRL Carey Price
MarcAndre Fleury
Pekka Rinne
Henrik Lundqvist 15.00 40.00
UQMRBHB Patrick Roy
Martin Brodeur
Dominik Hasek
Ed Belfour 40.00 100.00
UQMRCEH Michael Rasmussen
Dennis Cholowski
Christoffer Ehn
Filip Hronek 8.00 20.00
UQMSBSR Tyler Seguin
Jamie Benn
Jason Spezza
Alexander Radulov 8.00 20.00
UQMSKHV Steven Stamkos
Nikita Kucherov
Victor Hedman
Andrei Vasilevskiy 12.00 30.00
UQMTMMK Jonathan Toews
Nathan MacKinnon
Evgeni Malkin
Anze Kopitar 25.00 60.00
UQMTMMR John Tavares
Patrick Marleau
Mitch Marner
Morgan Rielly 10.00 25.00

2019-20 Ultimate Collection

1 Connor McDavid 8.00 20.00
2 Ryan O'Reilly 1.25 3.00
3 John Gibson 1.25 3.00
4 Joe Thornton 2.00 5.00
5 Marc-Andre Fleury 2.50 6.00
6 Jake Guentzel 2.00 5.00
7 Alex DeBrincat 1.50 4.00
8 Brayden Point 1.50 4.00
9 Aleksander Barkov 2.00 5.00
10 John Tavares 2.00 5.00
11 Brady Tkachuk 2.00 5.00
12 Mark Scheifele 2.00 5.00
13 Brad Marchand 2.50 6.00
14 Nico Hischier 2.00 5.00
15 Jonathan Toews 2.00 5.00
16 Jonathan Quick 1.50 4.00
17 Andrei Vasilevskiy 2.00 5.00
18 Eric Staal 1.25 3.00
19 Brock Boeser 1.50 4.00
20 Dylan Larkin 1.50 4.00
21 Sebastian Aho 2.00 5.00
22 Matt Murray 1.25 3.00
23 Joe Pavelski 1.50 4.00
24 Jonathan Drouin 1.00 2.50
25 Auston Matthews 8.00 20.00
26 Miro Heiskanen 1.50 4.00
27 William Karlsson 1.50 4.00
28 David Pastrnak 3.00 8.00
29 Carter Hart 1.25 3.00
30 Steven Stamkos 2.50 6.00
31 Seth Jones 1.25 3.00
32 Tomas Hertl 1.25 3.00
33 Matthew Tkachuk 2.50 6.00
34 Mark Stone 1.50 4.00
35 Artemi Panarin 2.50 6.00
36 Erik Karlsson 1.50 4.00
37 Pierre-Luc Dubois 1.00 2.50
38 Sergei Bobrovsky 2.00 5.00
39 Sean Monahan .75 2.00
40 Patrick Kane 2.50 6.00
41 Nathan MacKinnon 5.00 12.00
42 Patrik Laine 1.50 4.00
43 Ryan Getzlaf 1.25 3.00
44 Evgeni Malkin 2.50 6.00
45 Leon Draisaitl 4.00 10.00
46 Tyler Seguin 1.50 4.00
47 Jacob Trouba 1.00 2.50
48 Mathew Barzal 1.50 4.00
49 Mitch Marner 2.00 5.00
50 Sidney Crosby 8.00 20.00
51 Anze Kopitar 2.00 5.00
52 Taylor Hall 1.25 3.00
53 Anders Lee 1.00 2.50
54 Claude Giroux 1.25 3.00
55 Henrik Lundqvist 3.00 8.00
56 Thomas Chabot 1.25 3.00
57 Mikko Rantanen 3.00 8.00
58 Anthony Mantha 1.00 2.50
59 Johnny Gaudreau 2.00 5.00
60 Jack Eichel 2.00 5.00
61 Nicklas Backstrom 1.25 3.00
62 John Carlson 1.25 3.00
63 Andrei Svechnikov 1.50 4.00
64 Rasmus Dahlin 1.50 4.00
65 Carey Price 2.50 6.00
66 Max Domi 1.25 3.00
67 Phil Kessel 1.25 3.00
68 Matt Duchene 1.25 3.00
69 Viktor Arvidsson .75 2.00
70 Brent Burns 1.25 3.00
71 Pekka Rinne 1.25 3.00
72 Nikita Kucherov 2.50 6.00
73 Zach Werenski 2.00 5.00
74 Elias Pettersson 2.00 5.00
75 Alex Ovechkin 5.00 12.00
76 Ray Bourque 6.00 15.00
77 Doug Gilmour 8.00 20.00
78 Pierre Turgeon 1.50 4.00
79 Henrik Sedin 2.50 6.00
80 Gordie Howe 6.00 15.00
81 Daniel Sedin 2.50 6.00
82 Larry Robinson 2.00 5.00
83 Peter Forsberg 4.00 10.00
84 Jaromir Jagr 6.00 15.00
85 Steve Yzerman 8.00 20.00
86 Phil Esposito 3.00 8.00
87 Keith Tkachuk 2.00 5.00
88 Bobby Hull 5.00 12.00
89 Wendel Clark 3.00 8.00
90 Mario Lemieux 8.00 20.00
91 Patrick Roy 5.00 12.00
92 Guy Lafleur 4.00 10.00
93 Mike Modano 3.00 8.00
94 Chris Chelios 2.00 5.00
95 Bobby Orr 8.00 20.00
96 Martin Brodeur 5.00 12.00
97 Mark Messier 4.00 10.00
98 Teemu Selanne 4.00 10.00
99 Joe Sakic 4.00 10.00
100 Wayne Gretzky 12.00 30.00
101 Trent Frederic AU/299 RC 8.00 20.00
102 Vitaly Abramov/299 RC 2.50 6.00
103 Alexander Volkov/299 RC 2.00 5.00
104 Brady Keeper/299 RC 2.50 6.00
105 Joel Persson/299 RC 2.00 5.00
106 Brandon Gignac AU/299 RC 6.00 15.00
107 Danil Yurtaykin/299 RC 2.00 5.00
108 Jimmy Schuldt AU/299 RC 6.00 15.00
109 Julien Gauthier AU/299 RC 8.00 20.00
110 Max Jones AU/299 RC 8.00 20.00
111 Joey Daccord AU/299 RC 15.00 40.00
112 Sam Lafferty AU/299 RC 6.00 15.00
113 Teddy Blueger AU/299 RC 8.00 20.00
114 German Rubtsov AU/299 RC 6.00 15.00
115 Joel L'Esperance AU/299 RC 8.00 20.00
116 Martin Fehervary/299 RC 2.00 5.00
117 Rem Pitlick AU/299 RC 8.00 20.00
118 Guillaume Brisebois AU/299 RC 8.00 20.00
119 Kaden Fulcher AU/299 RC 8.00 20.00
120 Mario Ferraro AU/299 RC 6.00 15.00
121 Kole Sherwood AU/299 RC 8.00 20.00
122 Lean Bergmann AU/299 RC 6.00 15.00
123 Nico Sturm AU/299 RC 6.00 15.00
124 Libor Hajek AU/299 RC 6.00 15.00
125 Elvis Merzlikins AU/299 RC 15.00 40.00
126 Mackenzie Mac Eachern AU/299 RC 8.00 20.00
127 Matt Roy AU/299 RC 8.00 20.00
128 Max Veronneau AU/299 RC 6.00 15.00
129 Nathan Bastian AU/299 RC 8.00 20.00
130 Karson Kuhlman AU/299 RC 8.00 20.00
131 Riley Stillman AU/299 RC 8.00 20.00
132 Rudolfs Balcers/299 RC 2.50 6.00
133 Ryan Kuffner AU/299 RC 6.00 15.00
134 Ryan Lindgren/299 RC 2.50 6.00
135 Connor Clifton AU/299 RC 8.00 20.00
136 Zach Senyshyn AU/299 RC 8.00 20.00
137 Zack MacEwen AU/299 RC 6.00 15.00
138 Joakim Nygard/299 RC 2.00 5.00
139 Oliver Wahlstrom AU/299 RC 12.00 30.00
140 Carter Verhaeghe AU/299 RC 12.00 30.00
141 Conor Timmins/299 RC 2.50 6.00
142 Igor Shesterkin AU/299 RC 80.00 200.00
143 Givani Smith AU/299 RC 6.00 15.00
144 Eetu Luostarinen AU/299 RC 8.00 20.00
145 Carl Grundstrom AU/299 RC 8.00 20.00
146 Rasmus Asplund AU/299 RC 6.00 15.00
147 Connor Bunnaman/299 RC 2.00 5.00
148 Jake Walman AU/299 RC 10.00 25.00
149 John Marino/299 RC 4.00 10.00
150 Trevor Moore AU/299 RC 6.00 15.00
151 Kale Clague AU/299 RC 6.00 15.00
152 Carsen Twarynski/299 RC 2.00 5.00
153 Colton White/299 RC 2.50 6.00
154 Gaetan Haas/299 RC 2.00 5.00
155 Jonathan Davidsson AU/299 RC 5.00 12.00
156 Noah Gregor AU/299 RC 6.00 15.00
157 Cayden Primeau AU/299 RC 20.00 50.00
158 Kevin Stenlund/299 RC 2.00 5.00
159 Nick Caamano/299 RC 2.00 5.00
160 Nikolai Prokhorkin/299 RC 2.00 5.00
161 Klim Kostin/299 RC 2.50 6.00
162 Cole Bardreau/299 RC 2.00 5.00
163 David Gustafsson AU/299 RC 6.00 15.00
164 Otto Koivula AU/299 RC 5.00 12.00
165 Blake Lizotte AU/299 RC 8.00 20.00
166 CJ Suess/299 RC 2.00 5.00
167 Adam Johnson/299 RC 2.00 5.00
168 Ryan MacInnis AU/299 RC 6.00 15.00
169 Joachim Blichfeld AU/299 RC 8.00 20.00
170 Cameron Hughes/299 RC 2.00 5.00
171 Ville Heinola AU/299 RC 10.00 25.00
172 Philippe Myers/299 RC 2.00 5.00
173 Erik Brannstrom AU/299 RC 8.00 20.00
174 Alexandre Texier AU/299 RC 8.00 20.00
175 Dante Fabbro AU/299 RC 8.00 20.00
176 Dominik Kubalik AU/299 RC 12.00 30.00
177 Emil Bemstrom AU/299 RC 8.00 20.00
178 Jesper Boqvist AU/299 RC 6.00 15.00
179 Filip Zadina AU/299 RC 12.00 30.00
180 Nikita Gusev AU/299 RC 12.00 30.00
181 Barrett Hayton AU/299 RC 15.00 40.00
182 Nicolas Hague AU/299 RC 8.00 20.00
183 Taro Hirose AU/299 RC 8.00 20.00
184 Tobias Bjornfot/299 RC 2.50 6.00
185 Ilya Mikheyev AU/299 RC 12.00 30.00
186 Noah Dobson AU/299 RC 20.00 50.00
187 Adam Fox/299 RC 6.00 15.00
188 Adam Boqvist AU/299 RC 8.00 20.00
189 Quinn Hughes AU/99 RC 100.00 250.00
190 Cale Makar AU/99 RC 300.00 800.00
192 Nick Suzuki AU/99 RC 40.00 100.00
193 Ryan Poehling AU/99 RC 12.00 30.00
194 Victor Olofsson/99 RC 5.00 12.00
196 Cody Glass AU/99 RC 30.00 80.00
197 Joel Farabee AU/99 RC 40.00 100.00
198 Kirby Dach AU/99 RC 80.00 200.00
199 Kaapo Kakko/99 RC 40.00 100.00
200 Jack Hughes AU/99 RC 150.00 400.00

2019-20 Ultimate Collection Autographs

2 Ryan O'Reilly B 8.00 20.00
3 John Gibson B 6.00 15.00
4 Joe Thornton A 10.00 25.00
5 Marc-Andre Fleury A 12.00 30.00
6 Jake Guentzel B 10.00 25.00
7 Alex DeBrincat B 8.00 20.00
9 Aleksander Barkov B 10.00 25.00
10 John Tavares A 10.00 25.00
11 Brady Tkachuk B 10.00 25.00
12 Mark Scheifele B 10.00 25.00
13 Brad Marchand B 12.00 30.00
14 Nico Hischier B 10.00 25.00
17 Andrei Vasilevskiy B 10.00 25.00
18 Eric Staal B 6.00 15.00
19 Brock Boeser A 8.00 20.00
23 Joe Pavelski B 8.00 20.00
27 William Karlsson B 8.00 20.00
29 Carter Hart B 60.00 150.00
32 Tomas Hertl B 6.00 15.00
33 Matthew Tkachuk B 12.00 30.00
34 Mark Stone B 8.00 20.00
37 Pierre-Luc Dubois B 5.00 12.00
38 Sergei Bobrovsky B 10.00 25.00
39 Sean Monahan B 4.00 10.00
45 Leon Draisaitl A 20.00 50.00
46 Tyler Seguin A 8.00 20.00
47 Jacob Trouba B 5.00 12.00
51 Anze Kopitar A 10.00 25.00
53 Anders Lee B 5.00 12.00
55 Henrik Lundqvist A 15.00 40.00
56 Thomas Chabot B 6.00 15.00
63 Andrei Svechnikov B 8.00 20.00
70 Brent Burns A 6.00 15.00
71 Pekka Rinne B 6.00 15.00
77 Doug Gilmour A 15.00 40.00
78 Pierre Turgeon B 6.00 15.00
79 Henrik Sedin A 10.00 25.00
81 Daniel Sedin A 10.00 25.00
82 Larry Robinson B 8.00 20.00
83 Peter Forsberg A 15.00 40.00
85 Steve Yzerman A 20.00 50.00
87 Keith Tkachuk B 8.00 20.00
88 Bobby Hull A 20.00 50.00
89 Wendel Clark A 12.00 30.00
90 Mario Lemieux A 120.00 300.00
93 Mike Modano B 12.00 30.00
94 Chris Chelios A 8.00 20.00
95 Bobby Orr B 60.00 150.00
96 Martin Brodeur A 20.00 50.00
97 Mark Messier A 25.00 60.00
98 Teemu Selanne A 15.00 40.00
99 Joe Sakic A 15.00 40.00
100 Wayne Gretzky A 250.00 600.00

2019-20 Ultimate Collection Debut Threads Patch Autographs

DTAT Alexandre Texier/99 12.00 30.00
DTBE Emil Bemstrom/99 12.00 30.00
DTBH Barrett Hayton/49 25.00 60.00
DTBL Teddy Blueger/99 12.00 30.00
DTCG Cody Glass/49 30.00 80.00
DTCP Cayden Primeau/99 40.00 100.00
DTCR Carl Grundstrom/99 12.00 30.00
DTCV Carter Verhaeghe/99 20.00 50.00
DTDF Dante Fabbro/99 12.00 30.00
DTDK Dominik Kubalik/99 25.00 60.00
DTEB Erik Brannstrom/99 12.00 30.00
DTEM Elvis Merzlikins/99 25.00 60.00
DTFZ Filip Zadina/49 50.00 125.00
DTGR German Rubtsov/99 10.00 25.00
DTIM Ilya Mikheyev/99 20.00 50.00
DTIS Igor Shesterkin/99 100.00 250.00
DTJB Jesper Boqvist/99 10.00 25.00
DTJE Joel L'Esperance/99 12.00 30.00
DTJS Jimmy Schuldt/99 10.00 25.00
DTJW Jake Walman/99 15.00 40.00
DTKD Kirby Dach/49 25.00 60.00
DTKK Karson Kuhlman/99 12.00 30.00
DTKO Klim Kostin/99 12.00 30.00
DTLI Blake Lizotte/99 12.00 30.00
DTMF Mario Ferraro/99 10.00 25.00
DTMJ Max Jones/99 12.00 30.00
DTND Noah Dobson/99 30.00 80.00
DTNG Nikita Gusev/99 20.00 50.00
DTNH Nicolas Hague/99 12.00 30.00
DTOW Oliver Wahlstrom/99 20.00 50.00
DTPI Rem Pitlick/99 12.00 30.00
DTRP Ryan Poehling/49 20.00 50.00
DTRS Rasmus Sandin/99 20.00 50.00
DTST Nico Sturm/99 10.00 25.00
DTTH Taro Hirose/99 12.00 30.00
DTTM Trevor Moore/99 10.00 25.00
DTVH Ville Heinola/99 20.00 50.00

2019-20 Ultimate Collection Jerseys

101 Trent Frederic 2.50 6.00
102 Vitaly Abramov 2.50 6.00
104 Brady Keeper 2.50 6.00
105 Joel Persson 2.00 5.00
106 Brandon Gignac 2.00 5.00
107 Danil Yurtaykin 2.00 5.00
108 Jimmy Schuldt 6.00 15.00
109 Julien Gauthier 2.50 6.00
110 Max Jones 2.50 6.00
111 Joey Daccord 5.00 12.00
112 Sam Lafferty 3.00 10.00
113 Teddy Blueger 2.50 6.00
114 German Rubtsov 2.00 5.00
115 Joel L'Esperance 2.50 6.00
116 Martin Fehervary 2.00 5.00
117 Rem Pitlick 2.50 6.00
118 Guillaume Brisebois 2.50 6.00
119 Kaden Fulcher 2.50 6.00
120 Mario Ferraro 2.00 5.00
121 Kole Sherwood 2.50 6.00
122 Lean Bergmann 2.00 5.00
123 Nico Sturm 2.00 5.00
124 Libor Hajek 2.00 5.00
125 Elvis Merzlikins 5.00 12.00
126 Mackenzie MacEachern 2.50 6.00
127 Matt Roy 2.50 6.00
128 Max Veronneau 2.00 5.00
129 Nathan Bastian 2.50 6.00
130 Karson Kuhlman 2.50 6.00
131 Riley Stillman 2.50 6.00
132 Rudolfs Balcers 2.50 6.00
133 Ryan Kuffner 2.00 5.00
134 Ryan Lindgren 2.50 6.00
136 Zach Senyshyn 2.50 6.00
137 Zack MacEwen 2.00 5.00
139 Oliver Wahlstrom 4.00 10.00
140 Carter Verhaeghe 4.00 10.00
142 Igor Shesterkin 10.00 25.00
143 Givani Smith 2.00 5.00
144 Eetu Luostarinen 2.50 6.00
145 Carl Grundstrom 2.50 6.00
146 Rasmus Asplund 2.00 5.00
148 Jake Walman 3.00 8.00
150 Trevor Moore 2.00 5.00
151 Kale Clague 2.00 5.00
157 Cayden Primeau 5.00 12.00
161 Klim Kostin 2.50 6.00
163 David Gustafsson 2.00 5.00
165 Blake Lizotte 2.50 6.00
168 Ryan MacInnis 2.00 5.00
169 Joachim Blichfeld 2.50 6.00
171 Ville Heinola 3.00 8.00
172 Philippe Myers 2.00 5.00
173 Erik Brannstrom 2.50 6.00
174 Alexandre Texier 2.50 6.00
175 Dante Fabbro 2.50 6.00
176 Dominik Kubalik 10.00 25.00
177 Emil Bemstrom 2.50 6.00
178 Jesper Boqvist 2.00 5.00
179 Filip Zadina 4.00 10.00
180 Nikita Gusev 4.00 10.00
181 Barrett Hayton 5.00 12.00
182 Nicolas Hague 2.50 6.00
183 Taro Hirose 2.50 6.00
184 Tobias Bjornfot 2.50 6.00
185 Ilya Mikheyev 4.00 10.00
186 Adam Boqvist 2.50 6.00
187 Adam Fox 6.00 15.00
188 Adam Boqvist 2.50 6.00
189 Quinn Hughes 12.00 30.00
190 Cale Makar 12.00 30.00
191 Rasmus Sandin 4.00 10.00
192 Nick Suzuki 10.00 25.00
193 Ryan Poehling 4.00 10.00
194 Victor Olofsson 5.00 12.00
195 Morgan Frost 4.00 10.00
196 Cody Glass 4.00 10.00
197 Joel Farabee 4.00 10.00
198 Kirby Dach 5.00 12.00
199 Kaapo Kakko 4.00 10.00
200 Jack Hughes 12.00 30.00

2019-20 Ultimate Collection Patch Autographs

101 Trent Frederic/99 12.00 30.00
106 Brandon Gignac/99 10.00 25.00
108 Jimmy Schuldt/99 10.00 25.00
109 Julien Gauthier/99 15.00 40.00
110 Max Jones/99 12.00 30.00
111 Joey Daccord/99 25.00 60.00
112 Sam Lafferty/99 10.00 25.00
113 Teddy Blueger/99 12.00 30.00
114 German Rubtsov/99 10.00 25.00
115 Joel L'Esperance/99 12.00 30.00
117 Rem Pitlick/99 12.00 30.00
118 Guillaume Brisebois/99 12.00 30.00
120 Mario Ferraro/99 10.00 25.00
121 Kole Sherwood/99 12.00 30.00
122 Lean Bergmann/99 10.00 25.00
123 Nico Sturm/99 10.00 25.00
124 Libor Hajek/99 10.00 25.00
126 Mackenzie MacEachern/99 12.00 30.00
127 Matt Roy/99 12.00 30.00
128 Max Veronneau/99 10.00 25.00
129 Nathan Bastian/99 12.00 30.00
130 Karson Kuhlman/99 12.00 30.00
131 Riley Stillman/99 12.00 30.00
133 Ryan Kuffner/99 10.00 25.00
136 Zach Senyshyn/99 12.00 30.00
137 Zack MacEwen/99 10.00 25.00
139 Oliver Wahlstrom/99 20.00 50.00
140 Carter Verhaeghe/99 20.00 50.00
142 Igor Shesterkin/99 150.00 400.00
143 Givani Smith/99 10.00 25.00
144 Eetu Luostarinen/99 12.00 30.00
145 Carl Grundstrom/99 12.00 30.00
146 Rasmus Asplund/99 10.00 25.00
148 Jake Walman/99 15.00 40.00
150 Trevor Moore/99 10.00 25.00
151 Kale Clague/99 10.00 25.00
157 Cayden Primeau/99 60.00 150.00
161 Klim Kostin/99 12.00 30.00
163 David Gustafsson/99 10.00 25.00
165 Blake Lizotte/99 12.00 30.00
168 Ryan MacInnis/99 10.00 25.00
169 Joachim Blichfeld/99 12.00 30.00
171 Ville Heinola/99 15.00 40.00
173 Erik Brannstrom/99 20.00 50.00
174 Alexandre Texier/99 12.00 30.00
175 Dante Fabbro/99 12.00 30.00
176 Dominik Kubalik/99 30.00 80.00
177 Emil Bemstrom/99 12.00 30.00
178 Jesper Boqvist/99 10.00 25.00
179 Filip Zadina/99 60.00 150.00
180 Nikita Gusev/99 20.00 50.00
181 Barrett Hayton/99 25.00 60.00
182 Nicolas Hague/99 12.00 30.00
183 Taro Hirose/99 12.00 30.00
185 Ilya Mikheyev/99 20.00 50.00
188 Adam Boqvist/49 12.00 30.00
191 Rasmus Sandin/49 20.00 50.00
192 Nick Suzuki/49 120.00 300.00
193 Ryan Poehling/49 40.00 100.00
198 Kirby Dach/49 80.00 200.00
200 Jack Hughes/49 125.00 300.00

2019-20 Ultimate Collection Pro Threads Patch Autographs

PTAB Aleksander Barkov/25 25.00 60.00
PTAL Anders Lee/49 15.00 40.00
PTAV Andrei Vasilevskiy/25 25.00 60.00
PTBM Brad Marchand/25 30.00 80.00
PTBO Brock Boeser/25 20.00 50.00
PTBT Brady Tkachuk/49 25.00 60.00
PTGU Jake Guentzel/49 30.00 80.00
PTHL Henrik Lundqvist/25 40.00 100.00
PTJG John Gibson/49 15.00 40.00
PTLD Leon Draisaitl/25 40.00 100.00
PTMS Mark Scheifele/25 25.00 60.00
PTNH Nico Hischier/49 25.00 60.00
PTRO Ryan O'Reilly/25 15.00 40.00
PTTH Tomas Hertl/49 15.00 40.00
PTTW Tom Wilson/49 15.00 40.00
PTWK William Karlsson/49 20.00 50.00

2019-20 Ultimate Collection Retro Rookie Autographs

RRAAB Adam Boqvist/125 5.00 12.00
RRAAT Alexandre Texier/225 5.00 12.00
RRABH Barrett Hayton/125 10.00 25.00
RRABL Blake Lizotte/225 5.00 12.00
RRABR Erik Brannstrom/125 5.00 12.00
RRACC Connor Clifton/225 5.00 12.00
RRACG Cody Glass/125 8.00 20.00
RRACM Cale Makar/49 80.00 200.00
RRACP Cayden Primeau/225 15.00 40.00
RRACV Carter Verhaeghe/225 6.00 15.00
RRADF Dante Fabbro/225 5.00 12.00
RRADK Dominik Kubalik/225 8.00 20.00
RRAEB Emil Bemstrom/225 5.00 12.00
RRAEM Elvis Merzlikins/225 20.00 50.00
RRAFZ Filip Zadina/125 8.00 20.00
RRAGR Carl Grundstrom/225 5.00 12.00
RRAIM Ilya Mikheyev/125 8.00 20.00
RRAJB Jesper Boqvist/225 4.00 10.00
RRAJH Jack Hughes/49 60.00 150.00
RRAJL Joel L'Esperance/225 5.00 12.00
RRAJW Jake Walman/225 6.00 15.00
RRAKD Kirby Dach/49 30.00 80.00
RRAKK Karson Kuhlman/225 5.00 12.00
RRAKO Klim Kostin/225 5.00 12.00
RRAMF Mario Ferraro/225 6.00 15.00
RRAMJ Max Jones/225 5.00 12.00
RRAND Noah Dobson/225 12.00 30.00
RRANG Nikita Gusev/225 8.00 20.00
RRANH Nicolas Hague/225 5.00 12.00
RRANS Nick Suzuki/49 60.00 150.00
RRAPI Rem Pitlick/225 5.00 12.00
RRARP Ryan Poehling/125 8.00 20.00
RRARS Rasmus Sandin/225 8.00 20.00
RRASL Sam Lafferty/225 6.00 15.00
RRAST Nico Sturm/225 4.00 10.00
RRATH Taro Hirose/225 5.00 12.00
RRATM Trevor Moore/225 4.00 10.00
RRAVH Ville Heinola/225 6.00 15.00

2019-20 Ultimate Collection Rookie Accents Autographs

RAAB Adam Boqvist/99 10.00 25.00
RAAT Alexandre Texier/99 10.00 25.00
RABE Emil Bemstrom/99 10.00 25.00
RABH Barrett Hayton/65 20.00 50.00
RABL Blake Lizotte/99 10.00 25.00
RACC Connor Clifton/99 10.00 25.00
RACG Cody Glass/65 15.00 40.00
RACM Cale Makar/99 150.00 400.00
RACP Cayden Primeau/99 20.00 50.00
RACV Carter Verhaeghe/99 15.00 40.00
RADF Dante Fabbro/99 10.00 25.00
RADK Dominik Kubalik/99 20.00 50.00
RAEB Erik Brannstrom/65 10.00 25.00
RAEM Elvis Merzlikins/99 20.00 50.00
RAFZ Filip Zadina/65 15.00 40.00
RAGR Carl Grundstrom/99 10.00 25.00
RAIM Ilya Mikheyev/65 15.00 40.00
RAIS Igor Shesterkin/65 40.00 100.00
RAJB Jesper Boqvist/65 8.00 20.00
RAJG Julien Gauthier/65 10.00 25.00
RAJH Jack Hughes/35 150.00 400.00
RAJL Joel L'Esperance/99 10.00 25.00
RAJS Jimmy Schuldt/65 8.00 20.00
RAJW Jake Walman/65 12.00 30.00
RAKD Kirby Dach/99 20.00 50.00
RAKK Karson Kuhlman/99 10.00 25.00
RAKO Klim Kostin/99 10.00 25.00
RAMF Mario Ferraro/99 8.00 20.00
RAMJ Max Jones/99 10.00 25.00
RAND Noah Dobson/99 25.00 60.00
RANG Nikita Gusev/99 15.00 40.00
RANH Nicolas Hague/99 10.00 25.00
RANS Nick Suzuki/65 60.00 150.00
RAOW Oliver Wahlstrom/99 15.00 40.00
RAPI Rem Pitlick/99 10.00 25.00
RARP Ryan Poehling/65 15.00 40.00
RARS Rasmus Sandin/65 15.00 40.00
RAST Nico Sturm/99 8.00 20.00
RATE Teddy Blueger/65 10.00 25.00
RATH Taro Hirose/99 10.00 25.00
RATM Trevor Moore/65 8.00 20.00
RAVH Ville Heinola/65 12.00 30.00

2019-20 Ultimate Collection Signature Masterpieces

USMAD Alex DeBrincat A 20.00 50.00
USMBB Brock Boeser A 20.00 50.00
USMCG Cody Glass C 25.00 60.00
USMKD Kirby Dach B 30.00 80.00
USMNG Nikita Gusev B 15.00 40.00
USMNS Nick Suzuki C 60.00 150.00
USMRP Ryan Poehling B 25.00 60.00

2019-20 Ultimate Collection Ultimate Access Jerseys

UAAB Aleksander Barkov B 4.00 10.00
UAAD Alex DeBrincat B 3.00 8.00
UAAM Auston Matthews A 10.00 25.00
UAAP Artemi Panarin B 5.00 12.00
UABB Brock Boeser B 3.00 8.00
UABM Brad Marchand B 5.00 12.00
UABP Brayden Point B 3.00 8.00
UACM Connor McDavid A 12.00 30.00
UACP Carey Price A 5.00 12.00
UADL Dylan Larkin B 3.00 8.00
UAEM Evgeni Malkin B 5.00 12.00
UAHL Henrik Lundqvist B 6.00 15.00
UAJE Jack Eichel B 4.00 10.00
UAJG Jake Guentzel B 4.00 10.00
UAJH Jack Hughes B 12.00 30.00
UAJT John Tavares B 4.00 10.00
UALD Leon Draisaitl B 8.00 20.00
UAMA Cale Makar B 12.00 30.00
UAMF Marc-Andre Fleury B 5.00 12.00
UAMS Mark Scheifele B 4.00 10.00
UAMT Matthew Tkachuk B 5.00 12.00
UAPK Patrick Kane A 5.00 12.00
UARO Ryan O'Reilly B 2.50 6.00
UASC Sidney Crosby A 10.00 25.00
UASS Steven Stamkos B 5.00 12.00

2019-20 Ultimate Collection Ultimate Icons Jersey Autographs

UIAAP Artemi Panarin/65 20.00 50.00
UIAAV Andrei Vasilevskiy/135 15.00 40.00
UIACH Connor Hellebuyck/135 20.00 50.00
UIACP Carey Price/35 20.00 50.00
UIADS Daniel Sedin/35 12.00 30.00
UIAJG Jake Guentzel/135 15.00 40.00
UIAJI Jarome Iginla/65 12.00 30.00
UIAJT Joe Thornton/65 15.00 40.00
UIAMB Martin Brodeur/35 25.00 60.00
UIAMM Mark Messier/35 20.00 50.00
UIAMS Mark Scheifele/135 15.00 40.00
UIAPE Pekka Rinne/135 10.00 25.00
UIARO Ryan O'Reilly/135 10.00 25.00
UIASB Sergei Bobrovsky/99 15.00 40.00
UIASG Scott Gomez/135 8.00 20.00
UIASY Steve Yzerman/35 60.00 150.00

2019-20 Ultimate Collection Ultimate Icons Jerseys

UIAP Artemi Panarin B 8.00 20.00
UIAV Andrei Vasilevskiy B 5.00 12.00
UICH Connor Hellebuyck B 6.00 15.00
UICM Connor McDavid A 15.00 40.00
UICP Carey Price A 6.00 15.00
UIDS Daniel Sedin B 4.00 10.00
UIES Eric Staal B 3.00 8.00
UIJG Jake Guentzel B 5.00 12.00
UIJI Jarome Iginla A 4.00 10.00
UIJT Joe Thornton B 5.00 12.00
UIMB Martin Brodeur A 8.00 20.00
UIMM Mark Messier A 6.00 15.00
UIMS Mark Scheifele B 5.00 12.00
UIMU Matt Murray B 3.00 8.00
UIPE Pekka Rinne B 3.00 8.00
UIPR Patrick Roy A 8.00 20.00
UIRO Ryan O'Reilly B 3.00 8.00
UISB Sergei Bobrovsky B 5.00 12.00
UISG Scott Gomez B 2.50 6.00
UISY Steve Yzerman A 10.00 25.00
UITO Jonathan Toews A 5.00 12.00
UIWG Wayne Gretzky A 20.00 50.00

2019-20 Ultimate Collection Ultimate Introductions

UI1 Jack Hughes 20.00 50.00
UI2 Dominik Kubalik 8.00 20.00
UI3 Emil Bemstrom 4.00 10.00
UI4 Oliver Wahlstrom 6.00 15.00
UI5 Ilya Mikheyev 6.00 15.00
UI6 Jesper Boqvist 3.00 8.00
UI7 Nicolas Hague 4.00 10.00
UI8 Philippe Myers 3.00 8.00
UI9 Rasmus Sandin 6.00 15.00
UI10 Cody Glass 6.00 15.00
UI11 Taro Hirose 4.00 10.00
UI12 Trevor Moore 3.00 8.00
UI13 Ville Heinola 5.00 12.00
UI14 Blake Lizotte 4.00 10.00
UI15 Noah Dobson 10.00 25.00
UI16 Tobias Bjornfot 4.00 10.00
UI17 Cale Fleury 5.00 12.00
UI18 Carl Grundstrom 4.00 10.00
UI19 Carter Verhaeghe 6.00 15.00
UI20 Filip Zadina 6.00 15.00
UI21 Elvis Merzlikins 8.00 20.00
UI22 Joel L'Esperance 4.00 10.00
UI23 Joel Persson 3.00 8.00
UI24 Connor Clifton 4.00 10.00
UI25 Barrett Hayton 8.00 20.00
UI26 Joey Daccord 8.00 20.00
UI27 Mario Ferraro 3.00 8.00
UI28 Martin Fehervary 3.00 8.00
UI29 Max Jones 4.00 10.00
UI30 Victor Olofsson 8.00 20.00
UI31 Karson Kuhlman 4.00 10.00
UI32 Nico Sturm 3.00 8.00
UI33 Rem Pitlick 4.00 10.00
UI34 Sam Lafferty 3.00 8.00
UI35 Erik Brannstrom 4.00 10.00
UI36 Teddy Blueger 4.00 10.00
UI37 Trent Frederic 4.00 10.00
UI38 Vitaly Abramov 4.00 10.00
UI39 Alexander Volkov 3.00 8.00
UI40 Nick Suzuki 15.00 40.00
UI41 Brady Keeper 4.00 10.00
UI42 Brandon Gignac 3.00 8.00
UI43 Danil Yurtaykin 3.00 8.00
UI44 German Rubtsov 3.00 8.00
UI45 Joel Farabee 6.00 15.00
UI46 Guillaume Brisebois 4.00 10.00
UI47 Jimmy Schuldt 3.00 8.00
UI48 Julien Gauthier 4.00 10.00
UI49 Jonathan Davidsson 2.50 6.00
UI50 Kaapo Kakko 6.00 15.00
UI51 Kole Sherwood 4.00 10.00
UI52 Lean Bergmann 3.00 8.00
UI53 Libor Hajek 3.00 8.00
UI54 Mackenzie MacEachern 4.00 10.00
UI55 Adam Fox 10.00 25.00
UI56 Matt Roy 4.00 10.00
UI57 Max Veronneau 3.00 8.00
UI58 Nathan Bastian 4.00 10.00
UI59 Riley Stillman 4.00 10.00
UI60 Ryan Poehling 6.00 15.00
UI61 Rudolfs Balcers 4.00 10.00
UI62 Ryan Kuffner 3.00 8.00
UI63 Ryan Lindgren 4.00 10.00
UI64 Zach Senyshyn 4.00 10.00
UI65 Alexandre Texier 4.00 10.00
UI66 Zack MacEwen 3.00 8.00
UI67 David Gustafsson 3.00 8.00
UI68 Joakim Nygard 3.00 8.00
UI69 Nikolai Prokhorkin 3.00 8.00
UI70 Quinn Hughes 20.00 50.00
UI71 Conor Timmins 4.00 10.00
UI72 Dmytro Timashov 4.00 10.00
UI73 Aleksi Saarela 4.00 10.00
UI74 Eetu Luostarinen 4.00 10.00
UI75 Nikita Gusev 6.00 15.00
UI76 John Marino 8.00 20.00
UI77 Igor Shesterkin 20.00 50.00
UI78 Noah Gregor 3.00 8.00
UI79 Jake Walman 5.00 12.00
UI80 Cale Makar 20.00 50.00
UI81 Yakov Trenin 3.00 8.00
UI82 Cayden Primeau 8.00 20.00
UI83 Joona Luoto 3.00 8.00
UI84 Rasmus Asplund 3.00 8.00
UI85 Kirby Dach 8.00 20.00
UI86 Connor Bunnaman 3.00 8.00
UI87 Klim Kostin 4.00 10.00
UI88 Cameron Hughes 3.00 8.00
UI89 Morgan Frost 6.00 15.00
UI90 Adam Boqvist 4.00 10.00

2019-20 Ultimate Collection Ultimate Quad Materials

UQMAJMW Mtthws/Tvrs Mrnr/Nylndr/49 20.00 50.00
UQMANTE Ovchkn/Bkstrm Osh/Kzntsv/99 10.00 25.00
UQMDBPT Pstrnk/Mrchnd Brgrn/Rsk/99 10.00 25.00
UQMIRNR Mkhyv/Szk/Sndn/Phlng/99 15.0040.00
UQMJJJJ Jaromir Jagr/49 60.00 150.00
UQMJQCK Hghs/Mkr/Hghs/Dch/99 30.00 80.00
UQMMAJB Brzl/Lee/Nlsn/Bly/99 20.00 50.00
UQMMBPC Schfl/Whlr Lne/Hllbyck/99 15.00 40.00
UQMPJDA Kane/Toews/Keith DeBrincat/99 20.00 50.00
UQMRVCA O'Reilly/Tarasenko Parayko/Pietrangelo/99 12.00 30.00

2019-20 Ultimate Collection Ultimate Signatures

USAB Aleksander Barkov C 15.00 40.00
USAL Anders Lee C 8.00 20.00
USAM Auston Matthews B 80.00 200.00
USAP Artemi Panarin B 20.00 50.00
USAV Andrei Vasilevskiy B 15.00 40.00
USBH Bobby Hull B 25.00 60.00
USBM Brad Marchand C 20.00 50.00
USBR Brock Boeser B 12.00 30.00
USBT Brady Tkachuk C 15.00 40.00
USDG Doug Gilmour A 12.00 30.00
USGU Jake Guentzel C 15.00 40.00
USHL Henrik Lundqvist A 25.00 60.00
USJG John Gibson C 10.00 25.00
USJO Joe Sakic B 20.00 50.00

USJP Joe Pavelski B 12.00 30.00
USKT Keith Tkachuk B 10.00 25.00
USLD Leon Draisaitl B 30.00 80.00
USMB Martin Brodeur B 25.00 60.00
USMF Marc-Andre Fleury B 20.00 50.00
USMS Mark Stone C 12.00 30.00
USMT Matthew Tkachuk C 15.00 40.00
USNH Nico Hischier B 15.00 40.00
USRO Ryan O'Reilly C 10.00 25.00
USSB Sergei Bobrovsky B 15.00 40.00
USSY Steve Yzerman A 25.00 60.00
USTA John Tavares B 15.00 40.00
USTH Tomas Hertl C 10.00 25.00
USTS Teemu Selanne A 20.00 50.00
USTT Teuvo Teravainen C 10.00 25.00
USWG Wayne Gretzky B 300.00 800.00

2020-21 Ultimate Collection

*GOLD VETS: 1.25X TO 3X BASIC CARDS
*GOLD LEGS: 1X TO 2.5X BASIC CARDS
1 Colton Parayko 1.00 2.50
2 Jake Guentzel 2.00 5.00
3 Anthony Mantha 1.00 2.50
4 Brock Boeser 1.50 4.00
5 Sam Reinhart 2.50 6.00
6 Dougie Hamilton 1.00 2.50
7 Nikolaj Ehlers 1.25 3.00
8 Carey Price 2.50 6.00
9 Anze Kopitar 2.00 5.00
10 Leon Draisaitl 4.00 10.00
11 Maxime Comtois 1.00 2.50
12 Mark Scheifele 2.00 5.00
13 Roman Josi 1.25 3.00
14 Filip Forsberg 2.00 5.00
15 Zach Parise 1.25 3.00
16 Kasperi Kapanen 1.00 2.50
17 Connor Hellebuyck 2.50 6.00
18 Eric Staal 1.25 3.00
19 Jonathan Drouin 1.00 2.50
20 Nathan MacKinnon 5.00 12.00
21 David Pastrnak 3.00 8.00
22 Jonathan Huberdeau 1.50 4.00
23 Sidney Crosby 5.00 12.00
24 Mathew Barzal 1.50 4.00
25 Carter Hart 1.25 3.00
26 Andrei Vasilevskiy 2.00 5.00
27 Devon Toews 1.00 2.50
28 Ryan Suter 1.00 2.50
29 Roope Hintz 1.50 4.00
30 Alexandre Texier 1.00 2.50
31 Auston Matthews 5.00 12.00
32 Connor McDavid 6.00 15.00
33 Brady Tkachuk 2.00 5.00
34 Mark Stone 1.50 4.00
35 Elias Lindholm 1.25 3.00
36 Quinn Hughes 3.00 8.00
37 Victor Olofsson 1.25 3.00
38 Artemi Panarin 2.50 6.00
39 Jack Eichel 2.00 5.00
40 Jakub Vrana 1.25 3.00
41 Adam Fox 1.50 4.00
42 Robert Thomas 1.25 3.00
43 Matt Murray 1.25 3.00
44 Kevin Hayes 1.00 2.50
45 Andreas Johnsson 1.25 3.00
46 Andrei Svechnikov 1.50 4.00
47 Brent Burns 1.25 3.00
48 Nick Schmaltz 1.00 2.50
49 Brad Marchand 2.50 6.00
50 Noah Dobson 1.50 4.00
51 Elias Pettersson 2.00 5.00
52 Alex Ovechkin 5.00 12.00
53 Miro Heiskanen 1.50 4.00
54 Sergei Bobrovsky 2.00 5.00
55 Cale Makar 3.00 8.00
56 John Gibson 1.25 3.00
57 Filip Zadina 1.00 2.50
58 Clayton Keller 1.50 4.00
59 Tomas Hertl 1.25 3.00
60 Joe Thornton 2.00 5.00
61 Pavel Buchnevich 1.00 2.50
62 Max Pacioretty 1.25 3.00
63 Ryan Nugent-Hopkins 1.50 4.00
64 Ryan O'Reilly 1.25 3.00
65 Dominik Kubalik 1.25 3.00
66 Sebastian Aho 2.00 5.00
67 Dylan Larkin 1.50 4.00
68 Jack Hughes 3.00 8.00
69 Nick Suzuki 2.50 6.00
70 Steven Stamkos 2.50 6.00
71 Matthew Tkachuk 2.50 6.00
72 Patrick Kane 2.50 6.00
73 Adrian Kempe 1.25 3.00
74 Cam Atkinson 1.25 3.00
75 John Tavares 2.00 5.00
76 Rod Brind`Amour 2.00 5.00
77 Glenn Hall 2.00 5.00
78 Lanny McDonald 1.50 4.00
79 Eric Lindros 3.00 8.00
80 Billy Smith 2.00 5.00
81 Brett Hull 4.00 10.00
82 Daniel Sedin 2.50 6.00
83 Mario Lemieux 8.00 20.00
84 Jaromir Jagr 6.00 15.00
85 Martin St. Louis 2.00 5.00
86 Guy Lafleur 2.50 6.00
87 John Vanbiesbrouck 2.00 5.00
88 Mark Messier 4.00 10.00
89 Martin Brodeur 5.00 12.00
90 Wayne Gretzky 12.00 30.00
91 Bill Ranford 1.50 4.00
92 Patrick Roy 5.00 12.00
93 Doug Weight 1.50 4.00
94 Bobby Orr 8.00 20.00
95 Mark Recchi 2.50 6.00
96 Teemu Selanne 4.00 10.00
97 John LeClair 2.00 5.00
98 Dominik Hasek 3.00 8.00
99 Henrik Sedin 2.50 6.00
100 Mike Richter 2.00 5.00
101 Cole Hults RC 8.00 20.00
102 Kodie Curran RC 8.00 20.00
103 Joel Kiviranta RC 10.00 25.00
104 Aleksi Heponiemi RC 12.00 30.00
105 Egor Zamula RC 8.00 20.00
106 Joel Hofer RC 10.00 25.00
107 Kevin Bahl RC 8.00 20.00
108 Nolan Foote RC 10.00 25.00
109 Joseph Woll RC 20.00 50.00
110 Sasha Chmelevski RC 8.00 20.00
111 Artem Zub RC 8.00 20.00
112 Drew O'Connor RC 10.00 25.00
113 Jack Rathbone RC 10.00 25.00
114 Logan Stanley RC 10.00 25.00
115 David Kase RC 8.00 20.00
116 Gilles Senn RC 8.00 20.00
117 Mikhail Berdin RC 10.00 25.00
118 Cam Johnson RC 8.00 20.00
119 Niko Mikkola RC 8.00 20.00
120 Connor Mackey RC 8.00 20.00
121 Alexei Melnichuk RC 6.00 15.00
122 Reese Johnson RC 8.00 20.00
123 Cameron Hillis RC 8.00 20.00
124 Patrick Khodorenko RC 6.00 15.00
125 Austin Strand RC 8.00 20.00
126 Arthur Kaliyev RC 15.00 40.00
127 K'Andre Miller RC 20.00 50.00
128 Alexander Barabanov RC 10.00 25.00
129 Jonas Johansson RC 10.00 25.00
130 Philip Broberg RC 10.00 25.00
131 Alexander Alexeyev RC 8.00 20.00
132 Dylan Coghlan RC 10.00 25.00
133 Mikey Anderson RC 10.00 25.00
134 Philipp Kurashev RC 12.00 30.00
135 Vitek Vanecek RC 15.00 40.00
136 Brandon Hagel RC 12.00 30.00
137 Gustav Lindstrom RC 8.00 20.00
138 Jake Evans RC 10.00 25.00
139 Gage Quinney RC 6.00 15.00
140 MacKenzie Entwistle RC 8.00 20.00
141 Victor Soderstrom RC 8.00 20.00
142 Mikko Lehtonen RC 8.00 20.00
143 Kieffer Bellows RC 8.00 20.00
144 Gabe Vilardi RC 15.00 40.00
145 Yegor Sharangovich RC 15.00 40.00
146 Ian Mitchell RC 8.00 20.00
147 Cal Foote RC 12.00 30.00
148 Shane Bowers RC 8.00 20.00
149 Keegan Kolesar RC 8.00 20.00
150 Ty Smith RC 15.00 40.00
151 Alexander Yelesin RC 8.00 20.00
152 Olli Juolevi RC 10.00 25.00
153 Ty Dellandrea RC 10.00 25.00
154 Nicolas Beaudin RC 10.00 25.00
155 Alexander True RC 8.00 20.00
156 Lucas Carlsson RC 8.00 20.00
157 Jani Hakanpaa RC 6.00 15.00
158 Reid Duke RC 10.00 25.00
159 Pavel Francouz RC 12.00 30.00
160 Pierre-Olivier Joseph RC 10.00 25.00
161 Pius Suter RC 12.00 30.00
162 Liam Foudy RC 10.00 25.00
163 Martin Kaut RC 10.00 25.00
164 Morgan Geekie RC 10.00 25.00
165 Matiss Kivlenieks RC 12.00 30.00
166 Thomas Harley RC 15.00 40.00
167 Alex Belzile RC 8.00 20.00
168 Connor Ingram RC 8.00 20.00
169 Chase Priskie RC 8.00 20.00
170 Nikolai Knyzhov RC 8.00 20.00
171 Jason Robertson RC 50.00 125.00
172 Tyler Benson RC 10.00 25.00
173 Ryan McLeod RC 8.00 20.00
174 Timothy Liljegren RC 10.00 25.00
175 Michael McNiven RC 8.00 20.00
176 Nils Hoglander RC 10.00 25.00
177 Vitali Kravtsov RC 20.00 50.00
178 John Leonard RC 8.00 20.00
179 Anthony Angello RC 8.00 20.00
180 Calvin Thurkauf RC 8.00 20.00
181 Mathias Brome RC 8.00 20.00
182 Maxim Letunov RC 8.00 20.00
183 Alec Regula RC 6.00 15.00
184 Steven Lorentz RC 8.00 20.00
185 Michael DiPietro RC 12.00 30.00
186 Philippe Maillet RC 8.00 20.00
187 Egor Korshkov RC 6.00 15.00
188 Jake Oettinger RC 25.00 60.00
189 Peyton Krebs RC 15.00 40.00
190 Kevin Lankinen RC 15.00 40.00
191 Nick Robertson RC 15.00 40.00
192 Ilya Sorokin RC 80.00 200.00
193 Connor McMichael RC 15.00 40.00
194 Josh Norris RC 50.00 125.00
195 Bowen Byram RC 20.00 50.00
196 Alexander Romanov RC 12.00 30.00
197 Dylan Cozens RC 40.00 100.00
198 Tim Stutzle RC 250.00 450.00
199 Kirill Kaprizov RC 1000.00 1500.00
200 Alexis Lafreniere RC 250.00 450.00

2020-21 Ultimate Collection Autographs

2 Jake Guentzel 10.00 25.00
4 Brock Boeser 8.00 20.00
5 Sam Reinhart 12.00 30.00
6 Dougie Hamilton 5.00 12.00
7 Nikolaj Ehlers 6.00 15.00
8 Carey Price 60.00 150.00
10 Leon Draisaitl 20.00 50.00
11 Maxime Comtois 5.00 12.00
12 Mark Scheifele 10.00 25.00
13 Roman Josi 6.00 15.00
15 Zach Parise 6.00 15.00
17 Connor Hellebuyck 12.00 30.00
18 Eric Staal 6.00 15.00
22 Jonathan Huberdeau 8.00 20.00
23 Sidney Crosby 100.00 250.00
26 Andrei Vasilevskiy 10.00 25.00
27 Devon Toews 5.00 12.00
28 Ryan Suter 5.00 12.00
31 Auston Matthews 100.00 250.00
32 Connor McDavid 30.00 80.00
33 Brady Tkachuk 10.00 25.00
34 Mark Stone 8.00 20.00
35 Elias Lindholm 6.00 15.00
37 Victor Olofsson 6.00 15.00
40 Jakub Vrana 6.00 15.00
42 Robert Thomas 6.00 15.00
47 Brent Burns 6.00 15.00
49 Brad Marchand 12.00 30.00
51 Elias Pettersson 10.00 25.00
53 Miro Heiskanen 8.00 20.00
54 Sergei Bobrovsky 10.00 25.00
55 Cale Makar 15.00 40.00
56 John Gibson 6.00 15.00
59 Tomas Hertl 6.00 15.00
61 Pavel Buchnevich 5.00 12.00
62 Max Pacioretty 6.00 15.00
64 Ryan O'Reilly 6.00 15.00
71 Matthew Tkachuk 12.00 30.00
74 Cam Atkinson 6.00 15.00
75 John Tavares 10.00 25.00
76 Rod Brind'Amour 6.00 15.00
77 Glenn Hall 6.00 15.00
78 Lanny McDonald 5.00 12.00
79 Eric Lindros 10.00 25.00
80 Billy Smith 6.00 15.00
81 Brett Hull 60.00 150.00
82 Daniel Sedin 8.00 20.00
85 Martin St. Louis 6.00 15.00
86 Guy Lafleur 8.00 20.00
88 Mark Messier 12.00 30.00
89 Martin Brodeur 15.00 40.00
90 Wayne Gretzky 300.00 800.00
91 Bill Ranford 5.00 12.00
93 Doug Weight 5.00 12.00
94 Bobby Orr 80.00 200.00
95 Mark Recchi 8.00 20.00
96 Teemu Selanne 12.00 30.00
97 John LeClair 6.00 15.00
98 Dominik Hasek 10.00 25.00
99 Henrik Sedin 8.00 20.00
100 Mike Richter 6.00 15.00

2020-21 Ultimate Collection Jerseys

103 Joel Kiviranta 3.00 8.00
104 Aleksi Heponiemi 4.00 10.00
106 Joel Hofer 3.00 8.00
108 Nolan Foote 3.00 8.00
110 Sasha Chmelevski 2.50 6.00
113 Jack Rathbone 3.00 8.00
114 Logan Stanley 3.00 8.00
116 Gilles Senn 2.50 6.00
126 Arthur Kaliyev 5.00 12.00
127 K'Andre Miller 6.00 15.00
128 Alexander Barabanov 3.00 8.00
129 Jonas Johansson 3.00 8.00
130 Philip Broberg 3.00 8.00
131 Alexander Alexeyev 2.50 6.00
132 Dylan Coghlan 3.00 8.00
133 Mikey Anderson 3.00 8.00
134 Philipp Kurashev 4.00 10.00
135 Vitek Vanecek 5.00 12.00
136 Brandon Hagel 4.00 10.00
137 Gustav Lindstrom 2.50 6.00
138 Jake Evans 3.00 8.00
139 Gage Quinney 2.00 5.00
141 Victor Soderstrom 2.50 6.00
142 Mikko Lehtonen 2.50 6.00
143 Kieffer Bellows 2.50 6.00
144 Gabe Vilardi 5.00 12.00
145 Yegor Sharangovich 5.00 12.00
146 Ian Mitchell 2.50 6.00
147 Cal Foote 4.00 10.00
148 Shane Bowers 2.50 6.00
149 Keegan Kolesar 2.50 6.00
150 Ty Smith 5.00 12.00
151 Alexander Yelesin 2.50 6.00
152 Olli Juolevi 3.00 8.00
153 Ty Dellandrea 3.00 8.00
154 Nicolas Beaudin 3.00 8.00
155 Alexander True 2.50 6.00
156 Lucas Carlsson 2.50 6.00
157 Jani Hakanpaa 2.00 5.00
158 Reid Duke 3.00 8.00
159 Pavel Francouz 4.00 10.00
160 Pierre-Olivier Joseph 3.00 8.00
161 Pius Suter 4.00 10.00
162 Liam Foudy 3.00 8.00
163 Martin Kaut 3.00 8.00
164 Morgan Geekie 3.00 8.00
165 Matiss Kivlenieks 4.00 10.00
166 Thomas Harley 5.00 12.00
167 Alex Belzile 2.50 6.00
168 Connor Ingram 2.50 6.00
169 Chase Priskie 2.50 6.00
170 Nikolai Knyzhov 2.50 6.00
171 Jason Robertson 8.00 20.00
172 Tyler Benson 3.00 8.00
173 Ryan McLeod 2.50 6.00
174 Timothy Liljegren 3.00 8.00
176 Nils Hoglander 3.00 8.00
177 Vitali Kravtsov 6.00 15.00
178 John Leonard 2.50 6.00
179 Anthony Angello 2.50 6.00
180 Calvin Thurkauf 2.50 6.00
181 Mathias Brome 2.50 6.00
182 Maxim Letunov 2.50 6.00
183 Alec Regula 2.00 5.00
184 Steven Lorentz 2.00 5.00
186 Philippe Maillet 2.50 6.00
187 Egor Korshkov 2.00 5.00
188 Jake Oettinger 8.00 20.00
189 Peyton Krebs 5.00 12.00
191 Nick Robertson 5.00 12.00
192 Ilya Sorokin 8.00 20.00
193 Connor McMichael 5.00 12.00
194 Josh Norris 5.00 12.00
195 Bowen Byram 6.00 15.00
196 Alexander Romanov 4.00 10.00
197 Dylan Cozens 5.00 12.00
198 Tim Stutzle 6.00 15.00
199 Kirill Kaprizov 12.00 30.00
200 Alexis Lafreniere 10.00 25.00

2020-21 Ultimate Collection NHL Legacy Bronze Patch Autographs

LABT Brady Tkachuk 30.00 80.00
LACP Carey Price 40.00 100.00
LADS Daniel Sedin 25.00 60.00
LAHS Henrik Sedin 25.00 60.00
LAJS Jordan Staal 15.00 40.00
LAMT Matthew Tkachuk 40.00 100.00
LARH Ron Hextall 20.00 50.00
LARS Ryan Suter 15.00 40.00
LASK Saku Koivu 20.00 50.00
LASR Sam Reinhart 40.00 100.00
LATB Tyler Bertuzzi 15.00 40.00
LAZP Zach Parise 20.00 50.00

2020-21 Ultimate Collection NHL Legacy Jersey Autographs

LABR Brett Hull 25.00 60.00
LABT Brady Tkachuk 20.00 50.00
LACP Carey Price 25.00 60.00
LADS Daniel Sedin 15.00 40.00
LAES Eric Staal 12.00 30.00
LAHS Henrik Sedin 15.00 40.00
LAJS Jordan Staal 10.00 25.00
LAMT Matthew Tkachuk 25.00 60.00
LARS Ryan Suter 10.00 25.00
LASK Saku Koivu 12.00 30.00
LASR Sam Reinhart 25.00 60.00
LATB Tyler Bertuzzi 10.00 25.00
LAZP Zach Parise 12.00 30.00

2020-21 Ultimate Collection NHL Legacy Jerseys

LAM Anthony Mantha 2.00 5.00
LBH Bo Horvat 3.00 8.00
LBJ Boone Jenner 2.50 6.00
LBR Brett Hull 5.00 12.00
LBT Brady Tkachuk 4.00 10.00
LCP Carey Price 5.00 12.00
LDS Daniel Sedin 3.00 8.00
LES Eric Staal 2.50 6.00
LHS Henrik Sedin 3.00 8.00
LJD Jake DeBrusk 2.50 6.00
LJS Jordan Staal 2.00 5.00
LMT Matthew Tkachuk 5.00 12.00
LPE Phil Esposito 4.00 10.00
LPS Paul Stastny 2.00 5.00
LRD Ryan Donato 2.00 5.00
LRS Ryan Suter 2.00 5.00
LSK Saku Koivu 2.50 6.00
LSR Sam Reinhart 5.00 12.00
LTB Tyler Bertuzzi 2.00 5.00
LWN William Nylander 5.00 12.00
LZP Zach Parise 2.50 6.00

2020-21 Ultimate Collection Patch Autographs

191 Nick Robertson 60.00 150.00
192 Ilya Sorokin 60.00 150.00
194 Josh Norris 60.00 150.00
195 Bowen Byram 60.00 150.00
196 Alexander Romanov 60.00 150.00
197 Dylan Cozens 40.00 100.00
198 Tim Stutzle 40.00 100.00
199 Kirill Kaprizov 2000.00 4000.00
200 Alexis Lafreniere 500.00 800.00

2020-21 Ultimate Collection Rookie Accents Autographs

RAAA Anthony Angello 8.00 20.00
RAAB Alexander Barabanov 10.00 25.00
RAAK Arthur Kaliyev 15.00 40.00
RAAL Alexis Lafreniere 200.00 500.00
RAAR Alec Regula 6.00 15.00
RAAT Alexander True 8.00 20.00
RAAV Alexander Alexeyev 8.00 20.00
RABB Bowen Byram 20.00 50.00
RABE Alex Belzile 8.00 20.00
RACF Cal Foote 12.00 30.00
RACT Calvin Thurkauf 8.00 20.00
RADC Dylan Cozens 40.00 100.00
RADO Drew O'Connor 10.00 25.00
RAGQ Gage Quinney 6.00 15.00
RAIM Ian Mitchell 8.00 20.00
RAIS Ilya Sorokin 40.00 100.00
RAJE Jake Evans 10.00 25.00
RAJH Jani Hakanpaa 6.00 15.00
RAJL John Leonard 8.00 20.00
RAJN Josh Norris 40.00 100.00
RAKK Kirill Kaprizov 200.00 500.00
RAKM K'Andre Miller 20.00 50.00
RALC Lucas Carlsson 8.00 20.00
RALF Liam Foudy 10.00 25.00
RAML Maxim Letunov 8.00 20.00
RANH Nils Hoglander 10.00 25.00
RANK Nikolai Knyzhov 8.00 20.00
RANR Nick Robertson 15.00 40.00
RAOJ Olli Juolevi 10.00 25.00
RAPF Pavel Francouz 12.00 30.00
RAPS Pius Suter 12.00 30.00
RARD Reid Duke 10.00 25.00
RARO Alexander Romanov 12.00 30.00
RASC Sasha Chmelevski 8.00 20.00
RASL Steven Lorentz 8.00 20.00
RASM Ty Smith 15.00 40.00
RATD Ty Dellandrea 10.00 25.00
RATS Tim Stutzle 150.00 400.00
RAYS Yegor Sharangovich 15.00 40.00

2020-21 Ultimate Collection Signature Masterpieces

USMAL Alexis Lafreniere 80.00 200.00
USMBM Brad Marchand 40.00 100.00
USMCH Carter Hart 20.00 50.00
USMDG Dirk Graham 15.00 40.00
USMEL Eric Lindros 100.00 250.00
USMEP Elias Pettersson 30.00 80.00
USMGH Glenn Hall 20.00 50.00
USMKK Kirill Kaprizov 100.00 250.00
USMLM Lanny McDonald 15.00 40.00
USMMR Mike Richter 20.00 50.00
USMPB Peter Bondra 20.00 50.00
USMRO Ryan O'Reilly 20.00 50.00
USMSK Saku Koivu 20.00 50.00
USMTL Trevor Linden 20.00 50.00

2020-21 Ultimate Collection Signature Masterpieces Laureates

SMLAV Andrei Vasilevskiy 30.00 80.00
SMLBM Brad Marchand 40.00 100.00
SMLCH Carter Hart 20.00 50.00
SMLCM Cale Makar 50.00 125.00
SMLCP Colton Parayko 15.00 40.00
SMLEP Elias Pettersson 30.00 80.00
SMLMC Connor McDavid 300.00 800.00
SMLMO Josh Morrissey 25.00 60.00
SMLMS Mark Stone 25.00 60.00
SMLNL Nicklas Lidstrom 60.00 150.00
SMLZP Zach Parise 20.00 50.00

2020-21 Ultimate Collection Ultimate Access Bronze Patch Autographs

UAAAK Anze Kopitar 30.00 80.00
UAAAL Alexis Lafreniere 800.00 1500.00
UAAAV Andrei Vasilevskiy 30.00 80.00
UAABS Brayden Schenn 20.00 50.00
UAACH Carter Hart 20.00 50.00
UAACM Connor McDavid 100.00 250.00
UAAHE Connor Hellebuyck 40.00 100.00
UAAJG Jake Guentzel 30.00 80.00
UAAJM J.T. Miller 25.00 60.00
UAAJP Joe Pavelski 25.00 60.00
UAAKK Kirill Kaprizov 1500.00 3500.00
UAAMS Mark Stone 25.00 60.00
UAAPE David Perron 15.00 40.00
UAARJ Roman Josi 20.00 50.00
UAASR Sam Reinhart 40.00 100.00
UAATT Teuvo Teravainen 20.00 50.00
UAATW Tom Wilson 20.00 50.00
UAAWK William Karlsson 25.00 60.00

2020-21 Ultimate Collection Ultimate Introductions

UI1 Alexis Lafreniere 30.00 80.00
UI2 Dylan Cozens 4.00 10.00
UI3 Tim Stutzle 5.00 12.00
UI4 Kirill Kaprizov 30.00 80.00
UI5 Bowen Byram 5.00 12.00
UI6 Ilya Sorokin 6.00 15.00
UI7 Nick Robertson 4.00 10.00
UI8 Nils Hoglander 2.50 6.00
UI9 Peyton Krebs 4.00 10.00
UI10 Alexander Romanov 3.00 8.00
UI11 Liam Foudy 2.50 6.00
UI12 Ty Smith 4.00 10.00
UI13 Gabe Vilardi 4.00 10.00
UI14 Philippe Maillet 2.00 5.00
UI15 Brandon Hagel 3.00 8.00
UI16 Jonas Johansson 2.50 6.00
UI17 Mathias Brome 2.00 5.00
UI18 Alexander Yelesin 2.00 5.00
UI19 Vitek Vanecek 4.00 10.00
UI20 Pius Suter 3.00 8.00
UI21 Calvin Thurkauf 2.00 5.00
UI22 Timothy Liljegren 2.50 6.00
UI23 Lucas Carlsson 2.00 5.00
UI24 Vitali Kravtsov 5.00 12.00
UI25 Jake Oettinger 6.00 15.00
UI26 Joel Kiviranta 2.50 6.00
UI27 Gage Quinney 1.50 4.00
UI28 Cole Smith 2.00 5.00
UI29 Aleksi Heponiemi 3.00 8.00
UI30 Shane Bowers 2.00 5.00
UI31 Egor Korshkov 1.50 4.00
UI32 Mikko Lehtonen 2.00 5.00
UI33 Ty Dellandrea 2.50 6.00
UI34 Maxim Letunov 2.00 5.00
UI35 Yegor Sharangovich 4.00 10.00
UI36 Gustav Lindstrom 2.00 5.00
UI37 Reid Duke 2.50 6.00
UI38 Alexander Alexeyev 2.00 5.00
UI39 Kieffer Bellows 2.00 5.00
UI40 John Leonard 2.00 5.00
UI41 Anthony Angello 2.00 5.00
UI42 Jani Hakanpaa 1.50 4.00
UI43 Alex Belzile 2.00 5.00
UI44 Jake Evans 2.50 6.00
UI45 Keegan Kolesar 2.00 5.00
UI46 Darren Raddysh 1.50 4.00
UI47 Alexander Barabanov 2.50 6.00
UI48 Tyler Benson 2.50 6.00
UI49 Mikey Anderson 2.50 6.00
UI50 Josh Norris 4.00 10.00
UI51 Logan Stanley 2.50 6.00
UI52 Dylan Coghlan 2.50 6.00
UI53 Nicolas Beaudin 2.50 6.00
UI54 Alexander True 2.00 5.00
UI55 Steven Lorentz 2.00 5.00
UI56 Olli Juolevi 2.50 6.00
UI57 Michael McNiven 2.00 5.00
UI58 Alec Regula 1.50 4.00
UI59 Thomas Harley 4.00 10.00
UI60 Pavel Francouz 3.00 8.00
UI61 Victor Soderstrom 2.00 5.00
UI62 Philip Broberg 2.50 6.00
UI63 Morgan Geekie 2.50 6.00
UI64 Ian Mitchell 2.00 5.00
UI65 Connor McMichael 4.00 10.00
UI66 Martin Kaut 2.50 6.00
UI67 Pierre-Olivier Joseph 2.50 6.00
UI68 Matiss Kivlenieks 3.00 8.00
UI69 K'Andre Miller 5.00 12.00
UI70 Ryan McLeod 2.00 5.00
UI71 Michael DiPietro 3.00 8.00
UI72 Philipp Kurashev 3.00 8.00
UI73 Cal Foote 3.00 8.00
UI74 Nikolai Knyzhov 2.00 5.00
UI75 Jason Robertson 6.00 15.00
UI76 Arthur Kaliyev 4.00 10.00
UI77 Connor Ingram 2.00 5.00
UI78 Sasha Chmelevski 2.00 5.00
UI79 Kevin Lankinen 4.00 10.00
UI80 Nolan Foote 2.50 6.00
UI81 Egor Zamula 2.00 5.00
UI82 Kevin Bahl 2.00 5.00
UI83 Joel Hofer 2.50 6.00
UI84 Drew O'Connor 2.50 6.00
UI85 Alexei Melnichuk 1.50 4.00
UI86 Mikhail Maltsev 2.00 5.00
UI87 Austin Strand 2.00 5.00
UI88 Artem Zub 2.00 5.00
UI89 Jalen Chatfield 2.00 5.00
UI90 Joseph Woll 5.00 12.00
UI91 Peyton Krebs 8.00 20.00
UI92 Alexander Romanov 8.00 20.00
UI93 Nils Hoglander 8.00 20.00
UI94 Nick Robertson 8.00 20.00
UI95 Ilya Sorokin 8.00 20.00
UI96 Bowen Byram 10.00 25.00
UI97 Kirill Kaprizov 30.00 80.00
UI98 Tim Stutzle 10.00 25.00
UI99 Dylan Cozens 8.00 20.00
UIAL Alexis Lafreniere Redemption 100.00 250.00
UI100 Alexis Lafreniere 30.00 80.00

2020-21 Ultimate Collection Ultimate Introductions Autographs

UI1 Alexis Lafreniere 40.00 100.00
UI2 Dylan Cozens 20.00 50.00
UI3 Tim Stutzle 25.00 60.00
UI4 Kirill Kaprizov 50.00 125.00
UI5 Bowen Byram 25.00 60.00
UI6 Ilya Sorokin 30.00 80.00
UI7 Nick Robertson 20.00 50.00
UI8 Nils Hoglander 12.00 30.00
UI11 Liam Foudy 12.00 30.00
UI12 Ty Smith 20.00 50.00
UI15 Brandon Hagel 15.00 40.00
UI16 Jonas Johansson 12.00 30.00
UI19 Vitek Vanecek 20.00 50.00
UI20 Pius Suter 15.00 40.00
UI21 Calvin Thurkauf 10.00 25.00
UI23 Lucas Carlsson 10.00 25.00
UI25 Jake Oettinger 30.00 80.00
UI26 Joel Kiviranta 12.00 30.00
UI27 Gage Quinney 8.00 20.00
UI30 Shane Bowers 10.00 25.00
UI32 Mikko Lehtonen 10.00 25.00
UI33 Ty Dellandrea 12.00 30.00
UI34 Maxim Letunov 10.00 25.00
UI35 Yegor Sharangovich 20.00 50.00
UI36 Gustav Lindstrom 10.00 25.00
UI37 Reid Duke 12.00 30.00
UI38 Alexander Alexeyev 10.00 25.00
UI39 Kieffer Bellows 10.00 25.00
UI41 Anthony Angello 10.00 25.00
UI42 Jani Hakanpaa 8.00 20.00
UI43 Alex Belzile 10.00 25.00
UI44 Jake Evans 12.00 30.00
UI45 Keegan Kolesar 10.00 25.00
UI47 Alexander Barabanov 12.00 30.00
UI48 Tyler Benson 12.00 30.00
UI49 Mikey Anderson 12.00 30.00
UI51 Logan Stanley 12.00 30.00
UI52 Dylan Coghlan 12.00 30.00
UI53 Nicolas Beaudin 12.00 30.00
UI54 Alexander True 10.00 25.00
UI55 Steven Lorentz 10.00 25.00
UI56 Olli Juolevi 12.00 30.00
UI58 Alec Regula 8.00 20.00
UI60 Pavel Francouz 15.00 40.00
UI61 Victor Soderstrom 10.00 25.00
UI64 Ian Mitchell 10.00 25.00
UI66 Martin Kaut 12.00 30.00
UI67 Pierre-Olivier Joseph 12.00 30.00
UI69 K'Andre Miller 25.00 60.00
UI70 Ryan McLeod 10.00 25.00
UI72 Philipp Kurashev 15.00 40.00
UI73 Cal Foote 15.00 40.00
UI74 Nikolai Knyzhov 10.00 25.00
UI75 Jason Robertson 40.00 100.00
UI93 Nils Hoglander 12.00 30.00
UI94 Nick Robertson 20.00 50.00
UI95 Ilya Sorokin 30.00 80.00
UI96 Bowen Byram 25.00 60.00
UI97 Kirill Kaprizov 150.00 400.00
UI98 Tim Stutzle 80.00 200.00
UI99 Dylan Cozens 20.00 50.00
UI100 Alexis Lafreniere 80.00 200.00

2021-22 Ultimate Collection

1 Leon Draisaitl 4.00 10.00
2 Jack Roslovic .75 2.00
3 Martin Necas 2.00 5.00
4 Brent Burns 1.25 3.00
5 Conor Garland 1.00 2.50
6 Tim Stutzle 1.50 4.00
7 Brady Tkachuk 2.00 5.00
8 Alex Ovechkin 5.00 12.00
9 Brock Boeser 1.50 4.00
10 Connor Hellebuyck 2.50 6.00
11 Steven Stamkos 2.50 6.00
12 Connor McDavid 6.00 15.00
13 Sam Reinhart 2.50 6.00
14 Taylor Hall 1.25 3.00
15 Jason Zucker 1.25 3.00
16 Mitch Marner 2.00 5.00
17 Joe Pavelski 1.50 4.00
18 Boone Jenner 1.25 3.00
19 Matthew Tkachuk 2.50 6.00
20 Drake Batherson 1.25 3.00
21 Jason Robertson 2.00 5.00
22 Dylan Strome 1.50 4.00
23 Patrick Kane 2.50 6.00
24 Dylan Cozens 1.25 3.00
25 Kris Letang 1.50 4.00
26 Nathan MacKinnon 5.00 12.00
27 Maxime Comtois 1.00 2.50
28 Eeli Tolvanen 1.25 3.00
29 Marc-Andre Fleury 2.50 6.00
30 Adam Fox 1.50 4.00
31 Igor Shesterkin 2.50 6.00
32 Philipp Grubauer 1.25 3.00
33 Alex Nedeljkovic 1.00 2.50
34 Auston Matthews 5.00 12.00
35 Jordan Eberle 1.25 3.00
36 Kirill Kaprizov 4.00 10.00
37 Sean Monahan .75 2.00
38 Troy Terry 1.00 2.50
39 Cam Talbot 1.25 3.00
40 Elias Pettersson 2.00 5.00
41 Jesse Puljujarvi 1.25 3.00
42 Nick Suzuki 2.50 6.00
43 Quinn Hughes 3.00 8.00
44 Henri Jokiharju .75 2.00
45 Cale Makar 3.00 8.00
46 Cal Petersen .75 2.00
47 Thatcher Demko 1.50 4.00
48 Clayton Keller 1.50 4.00
49 Jared McCann 1.00 2.50
50 Filip Hronek .75 2.00
51 Anze Kopitar 2.00 5.00
52 Anthony Cirelli 1.00 2.50
53 Jonathan Huberdeau 1.50 4.00
54 Samuel Girard .75 2.00
55 Rasmus Dahlin 1.50 4.00
56 Seth Jones 1.25 3.00
57 Sebastian Aho 2.00 5.00
58 Josh Morrissey 1.50 4.00
59 Tyler Bertuzzi 1.00 2.50
60 Artemi Panarin 2.50 6.00
61 Mark Stone 1.50 4.00
62 Mathew Barzal 1.50 4.00
63 Brad Marchand 2.50 6.00
64 Charlie Coyle 1.25 3.00
65 Andrei Svechnikov 1.50 4.00
66 Kyle Connor 2.00 5.00
67 Jake Guentzel 2.00 5.00
68 Cam Atkinson 1.25 3.00
69 Andrei Vasilevskiy 2.00 5.00
70 John Tavares 2.00 5.00
71 William Karlsson 1.50 4.00
72 Ryan O'Reilly 1.25 3.00
73 Aleksander Barkov 2.00 5.00
74 Sidney Crosby 5.00 12.00
75 Josh Anderson 1.00 2.50
76 Mike Bossy 1.25 3.00
77 Ray Bourque 2.00 5.00
78 Jarome Iginla 1.50 4.00
79 Dany Heatley 1.00 2.50
80 Shayne Corson 1.00 2.50
81 John LeClair 1.25 3.00
82 Brenden Morrow 1.00 2.50
83 Mike Gartner 1.50 4.00
84 Ron Hextall 1.25 3.00
85 Billy Smith 1.25 3.00
86 Martin St. Louis 1.25 3.00
87 Bernie Nicholls 1.00 2.50
88 Lanny McDonald 1.25 3.00
89 Rod Brind'Amour 1.25 3.00
90 Dave Taylor 1.00 2.50
91 Pat LaFontaine 1.25 3.00
92 Brett Hull 2.00 5.00
93 Jaromir Jagr 4.00 10.00
94 Mark Messier 2.50 6.00
95 Doug Weight 1.25 3.00
96 Martin Brodeur 3.00 8.00
97 Dominik Hasek 2.00 5.00
98 Joe Sakic 2.50 6.00
99 Wayne Gretzky 8.00 20.00
100 Mario Lemieux 5.00 12.00
101 Jamie Drysdale AU/299 RC 12.00 30.00
102 Seth Jarvis AU/299 RC 20.00 50.00
103 Philip Tomasino AU/299 RC 10.00 25.00
104 Scott Perunovich AU/299 RC 8.00 20.00
105 Vasily Podkolzin AU/299 RC 10.00 25.00
106 Benoit-Olivier Groulx/299 RC 4.00 10.00
107 Riley Damiani AU/299 RC 8.00 20.00
108 Nils Lundkvist AU/299 RC 8.00 20.00
109 Adam Beckman AU/299 RC 8.00 20.00
110 Joe Veleno AU/299 RC 10.00 25.00
111 Grigori Denisenko AU/299 RC 10.00 25.00
112 Ukko-Pekka Luukkonen AU/299 RC 12.00 30.00
113 Jan Jenik/299 RC 5.00 12.00
114 Boris Katchouk AU/299 RC 6.00 15.00
115 Calen Addison AU/299 RC 8.00 20.00
116 Wade Allison AU/299 RC 8.00 20.00
117 Zac Jones AU/299 RC 10.00 25.00
118 Daniil Miromanov AU/299 RC 8.00 20.00
119 Cam York/299 RC 4.00 10.00
120 Kole Lind/299 RC 5.00 12.00
121 Brett Leason AU/299 RC 8.00 20.00
122 Jonathan Dahlen/299 RC 4.00 10.00
123 Ivan Prosvetov/299 RC 4.00 10.00
124 Brandon Duhaime AU/299 RC 8.00 20.00
125 Oskar Steen/299 RC 5.00 12.00
126 Arttu Ruotsalainen/299 RC 4.00 10.00
127 Matthew Phillips AU/299 RC 8.00 20.00
128 Joey Keane/299 RC 3.00 8.00
129 Jacob Bryson AU/299 RC 8.00 20.00
130 Tyce Thompson AU/299 RC 8.00 20.00
132 Mike Hardman AU/299 RC 8.00 20.00
133 Pavel Dorofeyev AU/299 RC 10.00 25.00
134 Jesse Ylonen/299 RC 4.00 10.00
135 Morgan Barron AU/299 RC 6.00 15.00
136 Parker Kelly AU/299 RC 8.00 20.00
137 Taylor Raddysh AU/299 RC 12.00 30.00
139 Tanner Laczynski AU/299 RC 8.00 20.00
140 David Farrance/299 RC 4.00 10.00
141 Logan Thompson AU/299 RC 20.00 50.00
142 Jasper Weatherby AU/299 RC 8.00 20.00
143 Lane Pederson/299 RC 4.00 10.00
144 Ross Colton AU/299 RC 10.00 25.00
145 Jacob Bernard-Docker AU/299 RC 8.00 20.00
146 Paul Cotter/299 RC 4.00 10.00
147 Wyatt Kalynuk AU/299 RC 8.00 20.00
148 Aliaksei Protas AU/299 RC 8.00 20.00
149 Jake Neighbours AU/299 RC 15.00 40.00
150 Sampo Ranta AU/299 RC 8.00 20.00
151 Jake Leschyshyn AU/299 RC 8.00 20.00
152 Radim Zohorna/299 RC 4.00 10.00
153 Simon Benoit AU/299 RC 8.00 20.00
154 Rasmus Kupari AU/299 RC 8.00 20.00
155 Shane Pinto AU/299 RC 12.00 30.00
156 Jack Ahcan AU/299 RC 8.00 20.00
157 Garrett Pilon AU/299 RC 10.00 25.00
158 Ryan Merkley AU/299 RC 10.00 25.00
159 Karel Vejmelka AU/299 RC 10.00 25.00
160 Robin Salo/299 RC 4.00 10.00
161 Jacob Peterson/299 RC 4.00 10.00
162 Sean Durzi AU/299 RC 8.00 20.00
163 Tanner Jeannot AU/299 RC 8.00 20.00
164 Riley Tufte AU/299 RC 8.00 20.00
165 Nico Daws AU/299 RC 12.00 30.00
166 Lassi Thomson AU/299 RC 8.00 20.00
167 Kasper Bjorkqvist AU/299 RC 8.00 20.00
168 Justin Barron AU/299 RC 12.00 30.00
169 Daniil Tarasov/299 RC 4.00 10.00
170 Cole Sillinger AU/299 RC 12.00 30.00
171 Mason McTavish AU/299 RC 15.00 40.00
172 Hendrix Lapierre AU/299 RC 8.00 20.00
173 William Eklund AU/299 RC 20.00 50.00
174 Michael Bunting AU/299 RC 8.00 20.00
175 Alex Newhook AU/299 RC 12.00 30.00
176 J.J. Peterka AU/299 RC 15.00 40.00
177 Adam Ruzicka/299 RC 4.00 10.00
178 Yegor Chinakhov/299 RC 6.00 15.00
179 Gabriel Fortier AU/299 RC 8.00 20.00
180 Justus Annunen AU/299 RC 10.00 25.00
181 Thomas Novak/299 RC 4.00 10.00
182 Fabian Zetterlund AU/299 RC 8.00 20.00
183 Connor Dewar AU/299 RC 8.00 20.00
184 Egor Sokolov AU/299 RC 8.00 20.00
185 Felix Sandstrom/299 RC 4.00 10.00
186 Cole Schwindt AU/299 RC 8.00 20.00
187 Jack Drury AU/299 RC 12.00 30.00
188 J.J. Moser AU/299 RC 8.00 20.00

189 Lucas Raymond/99 RC 12.00 30.00
190 Trevor Zegras AU/99 RC 150.00 400.00
191 Moritz Seider AU/99 RC 80.00 200.00
192 Cole Caufield AU/99 RC 200.00 500.00
193 Quinton Byfield AU/99 RC 20.00 50.00
194 Spencer Knight AU/99 RC 15.00 40.00
195 Jeremy Swayman AU/99 RC 25.00 60.00
196 Alex Turcotte AU/99 RC 10.00 25.00
197 Anton Lundell AU/99 RC 40.00 100.00
198 Dawson Mercer AU/99 RC 20.00 50.00
199 Alexander Holtz AU/99 RC 12.00 30.00
200 Cole Perfetti AU/99 RC 25.00 60.00

2021-22 Ultimate Collection Gold

*GOLD/35: 1.2X TO 3X BASIC

2021-22 Ultimate Collection Autographs

*GOLD/35: .6X TO 1.5X BASIC
1 Leon Draisaitl B 25.00 60.00
2 Jack Roslovic D 5.00 12.00
4 Brent Burns C 8.00 20.00
6 Tim Stutzle C 10.00 25.00
7 Brady Tkachuk C 12.00 30.00
9 Brock Boeser C 10.00 25.00
10 Connor Hellebuyck C 15.00 40.00
13 Sam Reinhart D 15.00 40.00
17 Joe Pavelski C 10.00 25.00
18 Boone Jenner D 8.00 20.00
20 Drake Batherson D 8.00 20.00
22 Dylan Strome D 10.00 25.00
24 Dylan Cozens D 8.00 20.00
27 Maxime Comtois D 6.00 15.00
29 Marc-Andre Fleury B 15.00 40.00
31 Igor Shesterkin B 15.00 40.00
32 Philipp Grubauer C 8.00 20.00
33 Alex Nedeljkovic D 6.00 15.00
35 Jordan Eberle C 8.00 20.00
41 Jesse Puljujarvi D 8.00 20.00
42 Nick Suzuki C 15.00 40.00
44 Henri Jokiharju D 5.00 12.00
45 Cale Makar B 20.00 50.00
46 Cal Petersen D 5.00 12.00
49 Jared McCann D 6.00 15.00
50 Filip Hronek D 5.00 12.00
51 Anze Kopitar C 12.00 30.00
53 Jonathan Huberdeau C 10.00 25.00
54 Samuel Girard D 5.00 12.00
57 Sebastian Aho C 12.00 30.00
61 Mark Stone C 10.00 25.00
63 Brad Marchand B 15.00 40.00
64 Charlie Coyle D 8.00 20.00
65 Andrei Svechnikov C 10.00 25.00
66 Kyle Connor C 12.00 30.00
67 Jake Guentzel C 12.00 30.00
68 Cam Atkinson C 8.00 20.00
71 William Karlsson C 10.00 25.00
73 Aleksander Barkov C 12.00 30.00
74 Sidney Crosby A 100.00 250.00
75 Josh Anderson D 6.00 15.00
77 Ray Bourque B 12.00 30.00
78 Jarome Iginla B 10.00 25.00
79 Dany Heatley C 6.00 15.00
80 Shayne Corson C 6.00 15.00
81 John LeClair C 8.00 20.00
82 Brenden Morrow C 6.00 15.00
83 Mike Gartner C 10.00 25.00
84 Ron Hextall C 8.00 20.00
86 Martin St. Louis B 8.00 20.00
87 Bernie Nicholls C 6.00 15.00
88 Lanny McDonald B 8.00 20.00
89 Rod Brind'Amour C 8.00 20.00
90 Dave Taylor C 6.00 15.00
91 Pat LaFontaine B 8.00 20.00
94 Mark Messier A 15.00 40.00
95 Doug Weight C 8.00 20.00
96 Martin Brodeur A 20.00 50.00
97 Dominik Hasek A 12.00 30.00
99 Wayne Gretzky A 300.00 800.00
100 Mario Lemieux A 60.00 150.00

2021-22 Ultimate Collection Debut Threads Patch Autographs

ADTAB Adam Beckman/99 12.00 30.00
ADTAH Jack Ahcan/99 12.00 30.00
ADTAL Anton Lundell/49 25.00 60.00
ADTBD Brandon Duhaime/99 12.00 30.00
ADTBE Jacob Bernard-Docker/99 12.00 30.00
ADTCA Calen Addison/99 12.00 30.00
ADTCD Connor Dewar/99 12.00 30.00
ADTCP Cole Perfetti/49 25.00 60.00
ADTCS Cole Sillinger/99 20.00 50.00
ADTDM Dawson Mercer/49 30.00 80.00
ADTDR Jamie Drysdale/49 40.00 100.00
ADTES Egor Sokolov/99 12.00 30.00
ADTFZ Fabian Zetterlund/99 12.00 30.00
ADTGD Grigori Denisenko/49 15.00 40.00
ADTGF Gabriel Fortier/99 12.00 30.00
ADTHL Hendrix Lapierre/99 12.00 30.00
ADTHO Alexander Holtz/99 20.00 50.00
ADTJA Justus Annunen/99 15.00 40.00
ADTJL Jake Leschyshyn/99 12.00 30.00
ADTJN Jake Neighbours/99 25.00 60.00
ADTJS Jeremy Swayman/99 80.00 200.00
ADTKB Kasper Bjorkqvist/99 12.00 30.00
ADTLT Lassi Thomson/99 12.00 30.00
ADTMB Morgan Barron/99 10.00 25.00
ADTMM Mason McTavish/99 25.00 60.00
ADTND Nico Daws/99 20.00 50.00
ADTNL Nils Lundkvist/99 12.00 30.00
ADTPD Pavel Dorofeyev/99 15.00 40.00
ADTPT Philip Tomasino/49 15.00 40.00
ADTQB Quinton Byfield/49 80.00 200.00
ADTRC Ross Colton/99 15.00 40.00
ADTRD Riley Damiani/99 12.00 30.00
ADTRM Ryan Merkley/99 15.00 40.00
ADTRT Riley Tufte/99 12.00 30.00
ADTSB Simon Benoit/99 12.00 30.00
ADTSJ Seth Jarvis/49 30.00 80.00
ADTSK Spencer Knight/99 25.00 60.00
ADTTH Logan Thompson/99 30.00 80.00
ADTTJ Tanner Jeannot/49 12.00 30.00
ADTTL Tanner Laczynski/99 12.00 30.00
ADTTT Tyce Thompson/99 12.00 30.00
ADTVP Vasily Podkolzin/49 30.00 80.00
ADTWA Wade Allison/99 12.00 30.00
ADTWE William Eklund/49 30.00 80.00
ADTZJ Zac Jones/99 15.00 40.00

2021-22 Ultimate Collection Jerseys

101 Jamie Drysdale/699 4.00 10.00
102 Seth Jarvis/699 6.00 15.00
103 Philip Tomasino/699 3.00 8.00
104 Scott Perunovich/699 2.50 6.00
105 Vasily Podkolzin/699 3.00 8.00
106 Benoit-Olivier Groulx/699 2.50 6.00
107 Riley Damiani/699 2.50 6.00
108 Nils Lundkvist/699 2.50 6.00
109 Adam Beckman/699 2.50 6.00
110 Joe Veleno/699 3.00 8.00
111 Grigori Denisenko/699 3.00 8.00
112 Ukko-Pekka Luukkonen/699 4.00 10.00
113 Jan Jenik/699 3.00 8.00
114 Boris Katchouk/699 2.00 5.00
115 Calen Addison/699 2.50 6.00
116 Wade Allison/699 2.50 6.00
117 Zac Jones/699 3.00 8.00
118 Daniil Miromanov/699 2.50 6.00
119 Cam York/699 2.50 6.00
120 Kole Lind/699 3.00 8.00
121 Brett Leason/699 2.50 6.00
122 Jonathan Dahlen/699 2.50 6.00
123 Ivan Prosvetov/699 2.50 6.00
124 Brandon Duhaime/699 2.50 6.00
125 Oskar Steen/699 3.00 8.00
126 Arttu Ruotsalainen/699 2.50 6.00
127 Matthew Phillips/699 2.50 6.00
128 Joey Keane/699 2.00 5.00
129 Jacob Bryson/699 2.50 6.00
130 Tyce Thompson/699 2.50 6.00
131 Mattias Samuelsson/699 2.50 6.00
132 Mike Hardman/699 2.50 6.00
133 Pavel Dorofeyev/699 3.00 8.00
134 Jesse Ylonen/699 2.50 6.00
135 Morgan Barron/699 2.00 5.00
136 Parker Kelly/699 2.50 6.00
137 Taylor Raddysh/699 4.00 10.00
138 Filip Gustavsson/699 5.00 12.00
139 Tanner Laczynski/699 2.50 6.00
140 David Farrance/699 2.50 6.00
141 Logan Thompson/699 6.00 15.00
142 Jasper Weatherby/699 2.50 6.00
143 Lane Pederson/699 2.50 6.00
144 Ross Colton/699 3.00 8.00
145 Jacob Bernard-Docker/699 2.50 6.00
146 Paul Cotter/699 2.50 6.00
147 Wyatt Kalynuk/699 2.50 6.00
148 Aliaksei Protas/699 2.50 6.00
149 Jake Neighbours/699 5.00 12.00
150 Sampo Ranta/699 2.50 6.00
151 Jake Leschyshyn/699 2.50 6.00
152 Radim Zohorna/699 2.50 6.00
153 Simon Benoit/699 2.50 6.00
154 Rasmus Kupari/699 2.50 6.00
155 Shane Pinto/699 4.00 10.00
156 Jack Ahcan/699 2.50 6.00
157 Garrett Pilon/699 3.00 8.00
158 Ryan Merkley/699 3.00 8.00
159 Karel Vejmelka/699 3.00 8.00
160 Robin Salo/699 2.50 6.00
162 Sean Durzi/699 2.50 6.00
163 Tanner Jeannot/699 2.50 6.00
164 Riley Tufte/699 2.50 6.00
165 Nico Daws/699 4.00 10.00
166 Lassi Thomson/699 2.50 6.00
167 Kasper Bjorkqvist/699 2.50 6.00
168 Justin Barron/699 4.00 10.00
170 Cole Sillinger/699 4.00 10.00
171 Mason McTavish/699 5.00 12.00
172 Hendrix Lapierre/699 2.50 6.00
173 William Eklund/699 6.00 15.00
174 Michael Bunting/699 2.50 6.00
175 Alex Newhook/699 4.00 10.00
176 J.J. Peterka/699 5.00 12.00
179 Gabriel Fortier/699 2.50 6.00
180 Justus Annunen/699 3.00 8.00
181 Thomas Novak/699 2.50 6.00
182 Fabian Zetterlund/699 2.50 6.00
183 Connor Dewar/699 2.50 6.00
184 Egor Sokolov/699 2.50 6.00
186 Cole Schwindt/699 2.50 6.00
187 Jack Drury/699 4.00 10.00
188 J.J. Moser/699 2.50 6.00
189 Lucas Raymond/499 8.00 20.00
190 Trevor Zegras/499 5.00 12.00
191 Moritz Seider/499 6.00 15.00
192 Cole Caufield/499 10.00 25.00
193 Quinton Byfield/499 6.00 15.00
194 Spencer Knight/499 5.00 12.00
195 Jeremy Swayman/499 8.00 20.00
196 Alex Turcotte/499 3.00 8.00
197 Anton Lundell/499 5.00 12.00
198 Dawson Mercer/499 6.00 15.00
199 Alexander Holtz/499 4.00 10.00
200 Cole Perfetti/499 5.00 12.00

2021-22 Ultimate Collection Patch Autographs

101 Jamie Drysdale/99 25.00 60.00
102 Seth Jarvis/99 40.00 100.00
103 Philip Tomasino/99 20.00 50.00
104 Scott Perunovich/99 15.00 40.00
105 Vasily Podkolzin/99 20.00 50.00
107 Riley Damiani/99 15.00 40.00
108 Nils Lundkvist/99 15.00 40.00
109 Adam Beckman/99 15.00 40.00
110 Joe Veleno/99 20.00 50.00
111 Grigori Denisenko/99 20.00 50.00
112 Ukko-Pekka Luukkonen/99 25.00 60.00
114 Boris Katchouk/99 12.00 30.00
115 Calen Addison/99 15.00 40.00
116 Wade Allison/99 15.00 40.00
117 Zac Jones/99 20.00 50.00
118 Daniil Miromanov/99 15.00 40.00
121 Brett Leason/99 15.00 40.00
124 Brandon Duhaime/99 15.00 40.00
127 Matthew Phillips/99 15.00 40.00
129 Jacob Bryson/99 15.00 40.00
130 Tyce Thompson/99 15.00 40.00
132 Mike Hardman/99 15.00 40.00
133 Pavel Dorofeyev/99 20.00 50.00
135 Morgan Barron/99 12.00 30.00
136 Parker Kelly/99 15.00 40.00
137 Taylor Raddysh/99 25.00 60.00
139 Tanner Laczynski/99 15.00 40.00
141 Logan Thompson/99 40.00 100.00
142 Jasper Weatherby/99 15.00 40.00
144 Ross Colton/99 20.00 50.00
145 Jacob Bernard-Docker/99 15.00 40.00
147 Wyatt Kalynuk/99 15.00 40.00
148 Aliaksei Protas/99 15.00 40.00
149 Jake Neighbours/99 30.00 80.00
150 Sampo Ranta/99 15.00 40.00
151 Jake Leschyshyn/99 15.00 40.00
153 Simon Benoit/99 15.00 40.00
154 Rasmus Kupari/99 15.00 40.00
155 Shane Pinto/99 25.00 60.00
156 Jack Ahcan/99 15.00 40.00
157 Garrett Pilon/99 20.00 50.00
158 Ryan Merkley/99 20.00 50.00
162 Sean Durzi/99 15.00 40.00
163 Tanner Jeannot/99 15.00 40.00
164 Riley Tufte/99 15.00 40.00
165 Nico Daws/99 25.00 60.00
166 Lassi Thomson/99 15.00 40.00
167 Kasper Bjorkqvist/99 15.00 40.00
170 Cole Sillinger/99 25.00 60.00
171 Mason McTavish/99 30.00 80.00
172 Hendrix Lapierre/99 15.00 40.00
173 William Eklund/99 80.00 200.00
174 Michael Bunting/99 15.00 40.00
175 Alex Newhook/99 25.00 60.00
176 J.J. Peterka/99 50.00 125.00
179 Gabriel Fortier/99 15.00 40.00
180 Justus Annunen/99 20.00 50.00
182 Fabian Zetterlund/99 15.00 40.00
183 Connor Dewar/99 15.00 40.00
184 Egor Sokolov/99 15.00 40.00
186 Cole Schwindt/99 15.00 40.00
188 J.J. Moser/99 15.00 40.00
191 Moritz Seider/49 40.00 100.00
192 Cole Caufield/49 600.00 1500.00
193 Quinton Byfield/49 80.00 200.00
194 Spencer Knight/49 60.00 150.00
195 Jeremy Swayman/49 50.00 125.00
196 Alex Turcotte/49 30.00 80.00
197 Anton Lundell/49 30.00 80.00
198 Dawson Mercer/49 40.00 100.00
200 Cole Perfetti/49 30.00 80.00

2021-22 Ultimate Collection Pro Threads Patch Autographs

PTAB Anthony Beauvillier/49 10.00 25.00
PTAK Anze Kopitar/25 25.00 60.00
PTAL Alexis Lafreniere/25 25.00 60.00
PTAN Alex Nedeljkovic/49 12.00 30.00
PTBM Brad Marchand/25 30.00 80.00
PTBO Brock Boeser/25 20.00 50.00
PTCC Charlie Coyle/49 15.00 40.00
PTCG Conor Garland/49 12.00 30.00
PTDC Dylan Cozens/49 15.00 40.00
PTDS Dylan Strome/49 20.00 50.00
PTET Eeli Tolvanen/49 15.00 40.00
PTJG Jake Guentzel/25 25.00 60.00
PTJH Jonathan Huberdeau/25 20.00 50.00
PTJM Jared McCann/25 12.00 30.00
PTJR Jack Roslovic/49 10.00 25.00
PTKC Kyle Connor/25 25.00 60.00
PTMC Maxime Comtois/49 12.00 30.00
PTMG Mark Giordano/49 15.00 40.00
PTRH Roope Hintz/49 20.00 50.00
PTSM Sean Monahan/49 10.00 25.00
PTST Mark Stone/25 40.00 100.00
PTTS Tim Stutzle/25 80.00 200.00

2021-22 Ultimate Collection Rookie Accents Autographs

RAAD Calen Addison/99 8.00 20.00
RAAH Alexander Holtz/65 12.00 30.00
RAAL Anton Lundell/35 15.00 40.00
RAAP Aliaksei Protas/99 8.00 20.00
RAAT Alex Turcotte/35 10.00 25.00
RABD Brandon Duhaime/99 8.00 20.00
RABL Brett Leason/99 8.00 20.00
RACD Connor Dewar/99 8.00 20.00
RACP Cole Perfetti/35 15.00 40.00
RADM Dawson Mercer/65 40.00 100.00
RAES Egor Sokolov/99 8.00 20.00
RAGD Grigori Denisenko/35 10.00 25.00
RAGF Gabriel Fortier/65 8.00 20.00
RAGP Garrett Pilon/99 10.00 25.00
RAHL Hendrix Lapierre/99 8.00 20.00
RAJA Justus Annunen/99 10.00 25.00
RAJD Jamie Drysdale/65 12.00 30.00
RAJN Jake Neighbours/99 15.00 40.00
RAJS Jeremy Swayman/65 25.00 60.00
RAKB Kasper Bjorkqvist/99 8.00 20.00
RAKV Karel Vejmelka/99 10.00 25.00
RAMI Daniil Miromanov/99 8.00 20.00
RAMP Matthew Phillips/99 8.00 20.00
RANL Nils Lundkvist/99 8.00 20.00
RAPI Shane Pinto/99 12.00 30.00
RAPT Philip Tomasino/65 10.00 25.00
RAQB Quinton Byfield/35 20.00 50.00
RARD Riley Damiani/99 8.00 20.00
RASB Simon Benoit/99 8.00 20.00
RASK Spencer Knight/65 15.00 40.00
RATJ Tanner Jeannot/65 8.00 20.00
RAVP Vasily Podkolzin/35 10.00 25.00
RAWE William Eklund/65 20.00 50.00

2021-22 Ultimate Collection Rookie Signature Premium Materials

RSPAH Alexander Holtz/65 15.00 40.00
RSPAL Anton Lundell/35 20.00 50.00
RSPAN Alex Newhook/65 15.00 40.00
RSPAT Alex Turcotte/35 12.00 30.00
RSPBD Brandon Duhaime/65 10.00 25.00
RSPDM Dawson Mercer/35 80.00 200.00
RSPGF Gabriel Fortier/65 10.00 25.00
RSPJD Jamie Drysdale/65 15.00 40.00
RSPJL Jake Leschyshyn/65 10.00 25.00
RSPKB Kasper Bjorkqvist/35 10.00 25.00
RSPMB Michael Bunting/65 10.00 25.00
RSPMP Matthew Phillips/35 10.00 25.00
RSPNL Nils Lundkvist/65 10.00 25.00
RSPPT Philip Tomasino/35 12.00 30.00
RSPRD Riley Damiani/65 10.00 25.00
RSPSB Simon Benoit/65 10.00 25.00
RSPTJ Tanner Jeannot/65 10.00 25.00
RSPVP Vasily Podkolzin/35 12.00 30.00

2021-22 Ultimate Collection Signature Masterpieces

USMAL Anton Lundell B
USMAT Alex Turcotte A 12.00 30.00
USMBE Jacob Bernard-Docker C 10.00 25.00
USMDM Dawson Mercer B 25.00 60.00
USMES Egor Sokolov C 10.00 25.00
USMJB Justin Barron C 15.00 40.00
USMJS Jeremy Swayman B 60.00 150.00
USMPI Shane Pinto C 15.00 40.00
USMRD Riley Damiani C 10.00 25.00
USMSK Spencer Knight B 20.00 50.00
USMTJ Tanner Jeannot B 10.00 25.00
USMWE William Eklund A 25.00 60.00

2021-22 Ultimate Collection Stick With Me

SWMAK Anze Kopitar 20.00 50.00
SWMAM Alec Martinez 25.00 60.00
SWMAO Alex Ovechkin 50.00 125.00
SWMAT Alex Tuch 12.00 30.00
SWMAV Andrei Vasilevskiy 20.00 50.00
SWMBH Brett Hull 20.00 50.00
SWMBN Bernie Nicholls 10.00 25.00
SWMCK Chris Kreider 15.00 40.00
SWMCM Connor McDavid 60.00 150.00
SWMCP Carey Price 25.00 60.00
SWMDG Doug Gilmour 15.00 40.00
SWMDH Dany Heatley 10.00 25.00
SWMDL Dylan Larkin 15.00 40.00
SWMDN Darnell Nurse 10.00 25.00
SWMDS Daniel Sedin 15.00 40.00
SWMEL Eric Lindros 20.00 50.00
SWMEM Evgeni Malkin 25.00 60.00
SWMFF Filip Forsberg 20.00 50.00
SWMGL Guy Lafleur 30.00 80.00
SWMHA Dominik Hasek 20.00 50.00
SWMHZ Henrik Zetterberg 15.00 40.00
SWMJH Jonathan Huberdeau 15.00 40.00
SWMJT Jonathan Toews 20.00 50.00
SWMKE Clayton Keller 15.00 40.00
SWMLA Gabriel Landeskog 15.00 40.00
SWMMA Auston Matthews 50.00 125.00
SWMMD Marcel Dionne 15.00 40.00
SWMML Mario Lemieux 50.00 120.00
SWMMS Mark Stone 15.00 40.00
SWMNM Nathan MacKinnon 50.00 125.00
SWMPK Patrick Kane 25.00 60.00
SWMSC Sidney Crosby 50.00 125.00
SWMTS Tyler Seguin 15.00 40.00
SWMVL Vincent Lecavalier 12.00 30.00

2021-22 Ultimate Collection Ulti-Mates Jerseys

UTMAS S.Aho/A.Svechnikov 5.00 12.00
UTMBK B.Burns/E.Karlsson 4.00 10.00
UTMBO A.Ovechkin/N.Backstrom 12.00 30.00
UTMBT B.Tkachuk/T.Stutzle 5.00 12.00
UTMCM S.Crosby/E.Malkin 12.00 30.00
UTMDO R.Dahlin/V.Olofsson 4.00 10.00
UTMEK K.Kaprizov/J.Eriksson Ek 10.00 25.00
UTMES J.Eberle/J.Schwartz 3.00 8.00
UTMGC S.Couturier/C.Giroux 3.00 8.00
UTMHB A.Barkov/J.Huberdeau 5.00 12.00
UTMHH N.Hischier/D.Hamilton 5.00 12.00
UTMJM J.Pavelski/M.Heiskanen 4.00 10.00
UTMJT R.Josi/E.Tolvanen 3.00 8.00
UTMKB Q.Byfield/A.Kopitar 8.00 20.00
UTMKG P.Kessel/S.Gostisbehere 3.00 8.00
UTMKP A.Panarin/C.Kreider 6.00 15.00
UTMLB T.Bertuzzi/D.Larkin
UTMMD C.McDavid/L.Draisaitl 15.00 40.00
UTMMM A.Matthews/M.Marner 12.00 30.00
UTMMP D.Pastrnak/B.Marchand 8.00 20.00
UTMMT M.Tkachuk/S.Monahan 6.00 15.00
UTMNB M.Barzal/B.Nelson 4.00 10.00
UTMNC N.MacKinnon/C.Makar 12.00 30.00
UTMPH E.Pettersson/Q.Hughes 8.00 20.00
UTMPS M.Stone/M.Pacioretty 4.00 10.00
UTMSE M.Scheifele/N.Ehlers 5.00 12.00
UTMSK S.Stamkos/N.Kucherov 6.00 15.00
UTMSO R.O'Reilly/B.Schenn 3.00 8.00
UTMTJ T.Zegras/J.Drysdale 6.00 15.00
UTMTK P.Kane/J.Toews 6.00 15.00
UTMTS N.Suzuki/C.Caufield 12.00 30.00
UTMWL P.Laine/Z.Werenski 5.00 12.00

2021-22 Ultimate Collection Ulti-Mates Jerseys Patch

*PATCH/35: .75X TO 2X BASIC
UTMBO Alex Ovechkin
Nicklas Backstrom 40.00 100.00
UTMLB Tyler Bertuzzi
Dylan Larkin 30.00 80.00
UTMMP David Pastrnak
Brad Marchand 25.00 60.00
UTMTK Patrick Kane
Jonathan Toews 25.00 60.00

2021-22 Ultimate Collection Ultimate Display Jersey Autographs

UDAAB Aleksander Barkov/99 20.00 50.00
UDAAK Anze Kopitar/65 20.00 50.00
UDAAN Alex Nedeljkovic/135 10.00 25.00
UDAAS Andrei Svechnikov/99 15.00 40.00
UDABM Brad Marchand/65 25.00 60.00
UDABO Brock Boeser/65 15.00 40.00
UDABT Brady Tkachuk/65 20.00 50.00
UDABU Brent Burns/65 12.00 30.00
UDACA Cam Atkinson/135 12.00 30.00
UDACC Charlie Coyle/135 12.00 30.00
UDACH Connor Hellebuyck/99 25.00 60.00
UDACM Connor McDavid/35 200.00 500.00
UDACP Cal Petersen/135 8.00 20.00
UDADB Drake Batherson/135 12.00 30.00
UDADC Dylan Cozens/135 12.00 30.00
UDAHJ Henri Jokiharju/135 8.00 20.00
UDAIS Igor Shesterkin/65 40.00 100.00
UDAJA Josh Anderson/135 10.00 25.00
UDAJE Jordan Eberle/99 12.00 30.00
UDAJG Jake Guentzel/65 20.00 50.00
UDAJH Jonathan Huberdeau/99 15.00 40.00
UDAJM Jared McCann/135 10.00 25.00
UDAJP Jesse Puljujarvi/135 12.00 30.00
UDAJR Jack Roslovic/135 8.00 20.00
UDAJS Jeremy Swayman/99 40.00 100.00
UDAKC Kyle Connor/65 20.00 50.00
UDAMC Maxime Comtois/135 10.00 25.00
UDAMF Marc-Andre Fleury/35 25.00 60.00
UDAMM Mason McTavish/135 25.00 60.00
UDAMS Mark Stone/99 15.00 40.00
UDANS Nick Suzuki/99 25.00 60.00
UDAPA Joe Pavelski/99 15.00 40.00
UDAPG Philipp Grubauer/99 12.00 30.00
UDASA Sebastian Aho/99 20.00 50.00
UDATS Tim Stutzle/99 15.00 40.00
UDAWK William Karlsson/65 15.00 40.00

2021-22 Ultimate Collection Ultimate Display Jerseys

*PATCH/25: .75X TO 2X BASIC
UDAM Auston Matthews 15.00 40.00
UDAO Alex Ovechkin 10.00 25.00
UDAP Artemi Panarin 5.00 12.00
UDAV Andrei Vasilevskiy 4.00 10.00
UDBM Brad Marchand 5.00 12.00
UDCK Clayton Keller 3.00 8.00
UDCM Connor McDavid 20.00 50.00
UDEP Elias Pettersson 4.00 10.00
UDJR Jason Robertson 4.00 10.00
UDKC Kyle Connor 4.00 10.00
UDKK Kirill Kaprizov 8.00 20.00
UDLD Leon Draisaitl 8.00 20.00
UDMF Marc-Andre Fleury 5.00 12.00
UDMS Mark Stone 3.00 8.00
UDNM Nathan MacKinnon 10.00 25.00
UDNS Nick Suzuki 5.00 12.00
UDPK Patrick Kane 5.00 12.00
UDRD Rasmus Dahlin 3.00 8.00
UDSA Sebastian Aho 4.00 10.00
UDSC Sidney Crosby 10.00 25.00

2021-22 Ultimate Collection Ultimate Emblems Autographs

*GOLD: .6X TO 1.5X BASIC
UEAB Anthony Beauvillier E 4.00 10.00
UEAK Anze Kopitar B 10.00 25.00
UEAN Josh Anderson D 5.00 12.00
UEAS Mason Appleton E 4.00 10.00
UEBA Aleksander Barkov C 10.00 25.00
UEBB Brent Burns B 6.00 15.00
UEBN Brock Nelson D 6.00 15.00
UECC Charlie Coyle E 6.00 15.00
UEDB Drake Batherson E 6.00 15.00
UEDC Dylan Cozens D 6.00 15.00
UEDS Darryl Sittler B 6.00 15.00
UEFH Filip Hronek D 4.00 10.00
UEHJ Henri Jokiharju E 4.00 10.00
UEJA Jake Allen E 6.00 15.00
UEJC Jack Campbell E 6.00 15.00
UEJE Jordan Eberle C 6.00 15.00
UEJH Jonathan Huberdeau C 8.00 20.00
UEJM Jared McCann D 5.00 12.00
UEJP Jeff Petry E 6.00 15.00
UEJR Jack Roslovic E 4.00 10.00
UEKC Kyle Connor B 10.00 25.00
UEMS Mike Smith D 4.00 10.00
UENE Alex Nedeljkovic D 5.00 12.00
UEPG Philipp Grubauer C 6.00 15.00
UEPR Patrick Roy A 40.00 100.00
UEPU Jesse Puljujarvi E 6.00 15.00
UERH Roope Hintz D 8.00 20.00
UESB Sam Bennett E 10.00 25.00
UESG Samuel Girard E 4.00 10.00
UESW Sean Walker E 4.00 10.00
UETS Tim Stutzle B 30.00 80.00

2021-22 Ultimate Collection Ultimate Emblems Rookie Autographs

*GOLD: .6X TO 1.5X BASIC
UEAH Alexander Holtz B 10.00 25.00
UEAJ Jack Ahcan C 6.00 15.00
UEAP Aliaksei Protas C 6.00 15.00
UEAT Alex Turcotte C 8.00 20.00
UEBD Brandon Duhaime C 6.00 15.00
UEBE Adam Beckman C 6.00 15.00
UEBJ Jacob Bernard-Docker C 6.00 15.00
UECP Cole Perfetti C 12.00 30.00
UEGP Garrett Pilon C 8.00 20.00
UEHL Hendrix Lapierre C 6.00 15.00
UEJB Jacob Bryson C 6.00 15.00
UEJD Jamie Drysdale C 10.00 25.00
UEJL Jake Leschyshyn C 6.00 15.00
UEJS Jeremy Swayman B 30.00 80.00
UEJV Joe Veleno C 8.00 20.00
UEJW Jasper Weatherby C 6.00 15.00
UELU Anton Lundell B 12.00 30.00
UEMP Matthew Phillips C 6.00 15.00
UENL Nils Lundkvist B 6.00 15.00
UEPD Pavel Dorofeyev C 8.00 20.00
UEPK Parker Kelly C 6.00 15.00
UERC Ross Colton C 8.00 20.00
UERD Riley Damiani C 6.00 15.00
UESP Shane Pinto C 10.00 25.00
UESR Sampo Ranta C 6.00 15.00
UETL Tanner Laczynski C 6.00 15.00
UETY Tyce Thompson C 6.00 15.00
UEWA Wade Allison C 6.00 15.00

2021-22 Ultimate Collection Ultimate Introductions

*GOLD/49: .75X TO 2X BASIC
UI1 Lucas Raymond 6.00 15.00
UI2 Trevor Zegras 4.00 10.00
UI3 Moritz Seider 5.00 12.00
UI4 Cole Caufield 8.00 20.00
UI5 Quinton Byfield 5.00 12.00
UI6 Spencer Knight 4.00 10.00
UI7 Jeremy Swayman 6.00 15.00
UI8 Alex Turcotte 2.50 6.00
UI9 Anton Lundell 4.00 10.00
UI10 Dawson Mercer 5.00 12.00
UI11 Jamie Drysdale 3.00 8.00
UI12 Seth Jarvis 5.00 12.00
UI13 Philip Tomasino 2.50 6.00
UI14 Alexander Holtz 3.00 8.00
UI15 Scott Perunovich 2.00 5.00
UI16 Vasily Podkolzin 2.50 6.00
UI17 Benoit-Olivier Groulx 2.00 5.00
UI18 Cole Perfetti 4.00 10.00
UI19 Riley Damiani 2.00 5.00
UI20 Nils Lundkvist 2.00 5.00
UI21 Adam Beckman 2.00 5.00
UI22 Joe Veleno 2.50 6.00
UI23 Grigori Denisenko 2.50 6.00
UI24 Ukko-Pekka Luukkonen 3.00 8.00
UI25 Jan Jenik 2.50 6.00
UI26 Boris Katchouk 1.50 4.00
UI27 Calen Addison 2.00 5.00
UI28 Wade Allison 2.00 5.00
UI29 Zac Jones 2.50 6.00
UI30 Daniil Miromanov 2.00 5.00
UI31 Cam York 2.00 5.00
UI32 Kole Lind 2.50 6.00
UI33 Brett Leason 2.00 5.00
UI34 Jonathan Dahlen 2.00 5.00
UI35 Ivan Prosvetov 2.00 5.00
UI36 Brandon Duhaime 2.00 5.00
UI37 Oskar Steen 2.50 6.00
UI38 Arttu Ruotsalainen 2.00 5.00
UI39 Matthew Phillips 2.00 5.00
UI40 Joey Keane 1.50 4.00
UI41 Jacob Bryson 2.00 5.00
UI42 Tyce Thompson 2.00 5.00
UI43 Mattias Samuelsson 2.00 5.00
UI44 Mike Hardman 2.00 5.00
UI45 Pavel Dorofeyev 2.50 6.00
UI46 Jesse Ylonen 2.00 5.00
UI47 Morgan Barron 1.50 4.00
UI48 Parker Kelly 2.00 5.00
UI49 Taylor Raddysh 3.00 8.00
UI50 Filip Gustavsson 4.00 10.00
UI51 Tanner Laczynski 2.00 5.00
UI52 David Farrance 2.00 5.00
UI53 Logan Thompson 5.00 12.00
UI54 Jasper Weatherby 2.00 5.00
UI55 Lane Pederson 2.00 5.00
UI56 Ross Colton 2.50 6.00
UI57 Jacob Bernard-Docker 2.00 5.00
UI58 Paul Cotter 2.00 5.00
UI59 Wyatt Kalynuk 2.00 5.00
UI60 Aliaksei Protas 2.00 5.00
UI61 Jake Neighbours 4.00 10.00
UI62 Sampo Ranta 2.00 5.00
UI63 Jake Leschyshyn 2.00 5.00
UI64 Radim Zohorna 2.00 5.00
UI65 Simon Benoit 2.00 5.00
UI66 Rasmus Kupari 2.00 5.00
UI67 Shane Pinto 3.00 8.00
UI68 Jack Ahcan 2.00 5.00
UI69 Garrett Pilon 2.50 6.00
UI70 Ryan Merkley 2.50 6.00
UI71 Karel Vejmelka 2.50 6.00
UI72 Robin Salo 2.00 5.00
UI73 Justus Annunen 2.50 6.00
UI74 Jack Drury 3.00 8.00
UI75 Tanner Jeannot 2.00 5.00
UI76 Riley Tufte 2.00 5.00
UI77 Nico Daws 3.00 8.00
UI78 Lassi Thomson 2.00 5.00
UI79 Kasper Bjorkqvist 2.00 5.00
UI80 Justin Barron 3.00 8.00
UI81 Sean Durzi 2.00 5.00
UI82 Cole Sillinger 3.00 8.00
UI83 Mason McTavish 4.00 10.00
UI84 Hendrix Lapierre 2.00 5.00
UI85 William Eklund 5.00 12.00
UI86 Michael Bunting 2.00 5.00
UI87 Alex Newhook 3.00 8.00
UI88 J.J. Peterka 4.00 10.00
UI89 Adam Ruzicka 2.00 5.00
UI90 Yegor Chinakhov 3.00 8.00
UI91 Lucas Raymond SHOW 6.00 15.00
UI92 Trevor Zegras SHOW 4.00 10.00
UI93 Moritz Seider SHOW 5.00 12.00
UI94 Cole Caufield SHOW 8.00 20.00
UI95 Quinton Byfield SHOW 5.00 12.00
UI96 Spencer Knight SHOW 4.00 10.00
UI97 Jeremy Swayman SHOW 6.00 15.00
UI98 Alex Turcotte SHOW 2.50 6.00
UI99 Anton Lundell SHOW 4.00 10.00
UI100 Dawson Mercer SHOW 5.00 12.00

2021-22 Ultimate Collection Ultimate Introductions Black

*BLACK/25: 1.2X TO 3X BASIC
UI2 Trevor Zegras 125.00 300.00
UI4 Cole Caufield 60.00 150.00
UI92 Trevor Zegras SHOW 125.00 300.00
UI94 Cole Caufield SHOW 60.00 150.00

2021-22 Ultimate Collection Ultimate Introductions Autographs

*GOLD: .6X TO 1.5X BASIC
UI3 Moritz Seider A 15.00 40.00
UI5 Quinton Byfield B 15.00 40.00
UI6 Spencer Knight C 12.00 30.00
UI7 Jeremy Swayman C 40.00 100.00
UI8 Alex Turcotte C 8.00 20.00
UI9 Anton Lundell B 12.00 30.00
UI10 Dawson Mercer C 15.00 40.00
UI11 Jamie Drysdale B 10.00 25.00
UI13 Philip Tomasino B 8.00 20.00
UI14 Alexander Holtz C 10.00 25.00
UI16 Vasily Podkolzin B 8.00 20.00
UI18 Cole Perfetti C 12.00 30.00
UI19 Riley Damiani D 6.00 15.00
UI20 Nils Lundkvist D 6.00 15.00
UI21 Adam Beckman E 6.00 15.00
UI22 Joe Veleno D 8.00 20.00
UI23 Grigori Denisenko B 8.00 20.00
UI24 Ukko-Pekka Luukkonen E 10.00 25.00
UI26 Boris Katchouk E 5.00 12.00
UI27 Calen Addison E 6.00 15.00
UI28 Wade Allison E 6.00 15.00
UI29 Zac Jones E 8.00 20.00
UI30 Daniil Miromanov E 6.00 15.00
UI33 Brett Leason E 6.00 15.00
UI36 Brandon Duhaime D 6.00 15.00
UI39 Matthew Phillips E 6.00 15.00
UI41 Jacob Bryson E 6.00 15.00
UI42 Tyce Thompson E 6.00 15.00
UI44 Mike Hardman E 6.00 15.00
UI45 Pavel Dorofeyev E 8.00 20.00
UI47 Morgan Barron E 5.00 12.00
UI48 Parker Kelly E 6.00 15.00
UI49 Taylor Raddysh E 10.00 25.00
UI51 Tanner Laczynski E 6.00 15.00
UI53 Logan Thompson E 15.00 40.00
UI54 Jasper Weatherby D 6.00 15.00
UI56 Ross Colton E 8.00 20.00
UI57 Jacob Bernard-Docker E 6.00 15.00
UI59 Wyatt Kalynuk E 6.00 15.00
UI60 Aliaksei Protas E 6.00 15.00
UI61 Jake Neighbours E 12.00 30.00
UI62 Sampo Ranta E 6.00 15.00
UI63 Jake Leschyshyn D 6.00 15.00
UI65 Simon Benoit E 6.00 15.00
UI66 Rasmus Kupari B 6.00 15.00
UI67 Shane Pinto E 10.00 25.00
UI68 Jack Ahcan E 6.00 15.00
UI69 Garrett Pilon E 8.00 20.00
UI70 Ryan Merkley D 8.00 20.00
UI71 Karel Vejmelka E 8.00 20.00
UI73 Justus Annunen E 8.00 20.00
UI74 Jack Drury E 10.00 25.00
UI75 Tanner Jeannot C 6.00 15.00
UI76 Riley Tufte E 6.00 15.00
UI77 Nico Daws E 10.00 25.00
UI78 Lassi Thomson E 6.00 15.00
UI79 Kasper Bjorkqvist E 6.00 15.00
UI80 Justin Barron E 10.00 25.00
UI82 Cole Sillinger B 10.00 25.00
UI84 Hendrix Lapierre D 6.00 15.00
UI85 William Eklund C 15.00 40.00
UI86 Michael Bunting C 6.00 15.00
UI87 Alex Newhook C 10.00 25.00
UI95 Quinton Byfield SHOW B 15.00 40.00
UI96 Spencer Knight SHOW B 12.00 30.00
UI97 Jeremy Swayman SHOW B 40.00 100.00
UI98 Alex Turcotte SHOW B 8.00 20.00
UI99 Anton Lundell SHOW B 12.00 30.00
UI100 Dawson Mercer SHOW B 15.00 40.00

2021-22 Ultimate Collection Ultimate Material Signatures

UMSAB Aleksander Barkov/49 15.00 40.00
UMSAN Alex Nedeljkovic/99 8.00 20.00
UMSAO Alex Ovechkin/25 150.00 400.00
UMSAS Andrei Svechnikov/49 12.00 30.00
UMSBE Anthony Beauvillier/99 6.00 15.00
UMSBN Brock Nelson/99 10.00 25.00
UMSBO Brock Boeser/25 12.00 30.00
UMSBT Brady Tkachuk/49 15.00 40.00
UMSBU Brent Burns/25 10.00 25.00
UMSCC Charlie Coyle/99 10.00 25.00
UMSDC Dylan Cozens/49 10.00 25.00
UMSDS Dylan Strome/99 12.00 30.00
UMSHJ Henri Jokiharju/99 6.00 15.00
UMSJA Josh Anderson/99 8.00 20.00
UMSJE Jordan Eberle/49 10.00 25.00
UMSJG Jake Guentzel/25 15.00 40.00
UMSJP Jean-Gabriel Pageau/99 6.00 15.00
UMSKC Kyle Connor/49 15.00 40.00
UMSPE Jeff Petry/99 10.00 25.00
UMSPU Jesse Puljujarvi/99 10.00 25.00
UMSRH Roope Hintz/99 25.00 60.00
UMSSA Sebastian Aho/49 15.00 40.00
UMSTS Tim Stutzle/49 80.00 200.00

2021-22 Ultimate Collection Ultimate Premium Materials

UMSAN Alex Nedeljkovic/35 4.00 10.00
UMSBE Anthony Beauvillier/35 3.00 8.00
UMSBJ Boone Jenner/35 5.00 12.00
UMSBN Brock Nelson/35 5.00 12.00
UMSCC Charlie Coyle/35 5.00 12.00
UMSCG Conor Garland/35 4.00 10.00
UMSCM Casey Mittelstadt/35 5.00 12.00
UMSDS Dylan Strome/35 6.00 15.00
UMSHJ Henri Jokiharju/35 3.00 8.00
UMSJA Josh Anderson/35 4.00 10.00
UMSJP Jean-Gabriel Pageau/35 3.00 8.00
UMSKC Kyle Connor/35 8.00 20.00
UMSMG Matt Grzelcyk/35 4.00 10.00
UMSMN Martin Necas/35 8.00 20.00
UMSNE Nikolaj Ehlers/35 5.00 12.00
UMSPE Jeff Petry/35 5.00 12.00
UMSPU Jesse Puljujarvi/35 5.00 12.00
UMSRH Roope Hintz/35 6.00 15.00
UMSSA Sebastian Aho/35 8.00 20.00
UMSTD Thatcher Demko/35 6.00 15.00

2021-22 Ultimate Collection Ultimate Quad Materials

*PATCH/25: .6X TO 1.5X BASIC
QMBCKH Burns/Karlsson
Hertl/Couture/99 5.00 12.00
QMBHEB Huberdeau/Ekblad/Barkov
Bobrovsky/49 6.00 15.00
QMBMPM Pastrnak/Marchand
Bergeron/McAvoy/99 10.00 25.00
QMBNLB Barzal/Nelson/Bailey/Lee/99 5.00 12.00
QMBTNS Tkachuk/Batherson
Stutzle/Norris/99 6.00 15.00
QMFTKD Kane/DeBrincat
Fleury/Toews/49 8.00 20.00
QMGCAF Atkinson/Farabee
Couturier/Giroux/99 4.00 10.00
QMGESG Giordano/Eberle
Schwartz/Grubauer/99 4.00 10.00
QMGFGT Terry/Getzlaf
Fowler/Gibson/99 4.00 10.00
QMJCDO Jokiharju/Dahlin
Olofsson/Cozens/99 5.00 12.00
QMJGST Josi/Granlund
Saros/Tolvanen/99 5.00 12.00
QMKDDK Doughty/Kopitar
Danault/Kempe/99 5.00 12.00
QMKPLF Panarin/Lafreniere
Fox/Kreider/49 8.00 20.00
QMMBPH Miller/Hughes
Pettersson/Boeser/99 10.00 25.00
QMMLGT Gaudreau/Tkachuk/Lindholm
Monahan/99 8.00 20.00
QMMLZG Guentzel/Zucker
Letang/Malkin/99 8.00 20.00
QMPLST Theodore/Stone
Pacioretty/Lehner/49 5.00 12.00
QMSEHC Connor/Scheifele
Ehlers/Hellebuyck/99 8.00 20.00
QMSKHH Hintz/Seguin/Klingberg
Heiskanen/99 5.00 12.00
QMSOTB O'Reilly/Tarasenko/Buchnevich
Schenn/99 5.00 12.00
QMSZCR Seider/Raymond
Zegras/Caufield/49 15.00 40.00
QMTASN Aho/Svechnikov

Teravainen/Necas/49 6.00 15.00
QMVBWL Laine/Voracek Werenski/Bjorkstrand/99 6.00 15.00
QMZFEK Kaprizov/Zuccarello Fiala/Eriksson Ek/49 12.00 30.00

2021-22 Ultimate Collection Ultimate Signatures

USAB Anthony Beauvillier D 5.00 12.00
USAN Alex Nedeljkovic C 6.00 15.00
USBJ Boone Jenner D 8.00 20.00
USBM Brad Marchand A 15.00 40.00
USCH Connor Hellebuyck B 15.00 40.00
USCM Connor McDavid A 250.00 600.00
USCN Cam Neely A 6.00 15.00
USCP Cal Petersen C 5.00 12.00
USDB Drake Batherson D 8.00 20.00
USFH Filip Hronek C 5.00 12.00
USHJ Henri Jokiharju D 5.00 12.00
USJA Jake Allen D 8.00 20.00
USJC Jack Campbell C 8.00 20.00
USJE Jordan Eberle B 8.00 20.00
USJG Jake Guentzel A 12.00 30.00
USJO Josh Anderson D 6.00 15.00
USJP Joe Pavelski B 10.00 25.00
USJR Jack Roslovic B 5.00 12.00
USKC Kyle Connor B 12.00 30.00
USLM Lanny McDonald A 8.00 20.00
USMA Mason Appleton D 5.00 12.00
USMC Maxime Comtois C 6.00 15.00
USMI Mike Smith C 5.00 12.00
USMJ Jared McCann D 6.00 15.00
USMS Martin St. Louis A 8.00 20.00
USPL Pat LaFontaine A 8.00 20.00
USPU Jesse Puljujarvi C 8.00 20.00
USRB Ray Bourque A 12.00 30.00
USRD Ryan Dzingel D 6.00 15.00
USSB Sam Bennett C 12.00 30.00
USSG Samuel Girard C 5.00 12.00
USTS Tim Stutzle B 25.00 60.00
USTW Tony Twist B 5.00 12.00
USWK William Karlsson B 10.00 25.00

2021-22 Ultimate Collection Ultimate Signatures Rookies

USRAB Adam Beckman C 8.00 20.00
USRAH Alexander Holtz B 12.00 30.00
USRAL Anton Lundell A 15.00 40.00
USRAT Alex Turcotte A 10.00 25.00
USRBE Jacob Bernard-Docker C 8.00 20.00
USRDM Dawson Mercer B 20.00 50.00
USRES Egor Sokolov C 8.00 20.00
USRGF Gabriel Fortier C 8.00 20.00
USRGP Garrett Pilon C 10.00 25.00
USRHL Hendrix Lapierre C 8.00 20.00
USRJB Jacob Bryson C 8.00 20.00
USRJD Jamie Drysdale B 12.00 30.00
USRJN Jake Neighbours C 15.00 40.00
USRJS Jeremy Swayman B 30.00 80.00
USRJV Joe Veleno C 10.00 25.00
USRJW Jasper Weatherby C 8.00 20.00
USRJY Jesse Ylonen B 8.00 20.00
USRKV Karel Vejmelka C 10.00 25.00
USRMP Matthew Phillips C 8.00 20.00
USRNL Nils Lundkvist C 8.00 20.00
USRPD Pavel Dorofeyev C 10.00 25.00
USRPI Tanner Jeannot B 8.00 20.00
USRPK Parker Kelly C 8.00 20.00
USRRD Riley Damiani C 8.00 20.00
USRSC Cole Schwindt C 8.00 20.00
USRSJ Seth Jarvis B 20.00 50.00
USRSK Spencer Knight A 15.00 40.00
USRSP Shane Pinto C 12.00 30.00
USRSR Sampo Ranta C 8.00 20.00
USRTT Tyce Thompson C 8.00 20.00
USRWA Wade Allison C 8.00 20.00
USRZJ Zac Jones C 10.00 25.00

2022-23 Ultimate Collection

1 Connor McDavid 6.00 15.00
2 Kyle Connor 2.00 5.00
3 Timo Meier 1.25 3.00
4 Alex DeBrincat 1.50 4.00
5 Alex Ovechkin 5.00 12.00
6 Matt Duchene 1.25 3.00
7 Mathew Barzal 1.50 4.00
8 Cole Caufield 2.50 6.00
9 Roman Josi 1.25 3.00
10 Kevin Fiala 1.00 2.50
11 Auston Matthews 5.00 12.00
12 Steven Stamkos 2.50 6.00
13 Bo Horvat 1.50 4.00
14 Mason McTavish 1.25 3.00
15 Tomas Hertl 1.25 3.00
16 Trevor Zegras 1.25 3.00
17 Johnny Gaudreau 2.00 5.00
18 Darcy Kuemper 1.25 3.00
19 Jared McCann 1.00 2.50
20 Mark Scheifele 2.00 5.00
21 Ilya Sorokin 2.00 5.00
22 Brayden Point 1.50 4.00
23 Jordan Kyrou 1.25 3.00
24 Moritz Seider 1.50 4.00
25 Nathan MacKinnon 5.00 12.00
26 Patrik Laine 1.50 4.00
27 Aaron Ekblad 1.50 4.00
28 Sidney Crosby 5.00 12.00
29 Brad Marchand 2.50 6.00
30 Clayton Keller 1.50 4.00
31 Alexander Holtz 1.25 3.00
32 Kirill Kaprizov 4.00 10.00
33 Andrei Svechnikov 1.50 4.00
34 Matthew Tkachuk 2.50 6.00
35 David Pastrnak 3.00 8.00
36 Joel Eriksson Ek 1.00 2.50
37 Michael Bunting 1.25 3.00
38 Jonathan Toews 2.00 5.00
39 Aleksander Barkov 2.00 5.00
40 Lucas Raymond 2.00 5.00
41 Mitch Marner 2.00 5.00
42 Tim Stutzle 1.50 4.00
43 Taylor Hall 1.25 3.00
44 Igor Shesterkin 2.50 6.00
45 Alexis Lafreniere 2.00 5.00
46 Patrick Kane 2.50 6.00
47 Brady Tkachuk 2.00 5.00
48 Anze Kopitar 2.00 5.00
49 Karel Vejmelka .75 2.00
50 Carter Hart 1.25 3.00
51 Jonathan Huberdeau 1.50 4.00
52 Leon Draisaitl 4.00 10.00
53 Tage Thompson 1.50 4.00
54 James van Riemsdyk 1.00 2.50
55 Tyler Bertuzzi 1.00 2.50
56 Marc-Andre Fleury 2.50 6.00
57 Rasmus Dahlin 1.50 4.00
58 Andrei Vasilevskiy 2.00 5.00
59 Cole Sillinger 1.00 2.50
60 Quinn Hughes 3.00 8.00
61 Nick Suzuki 2.50 6.00
62 Jake Oettinger 2.00 5.00
63 Elias Pettersson 2.00 5.00
64 Cale Makar 3.00 8.00
65 Jack Eichel 2.00 5.00
66 Robert Thomas 1.25 3.00
67 Tyler Toffoli 1.25 3.00
68 Bryan Rust 1.25 3.00
69 Jack Hughes 3.00 8.00
70 Jason Robertson 2.00 5.00
71 Jordan Eberle 1.25 3.00
72 Martin Necas 2.00 5.00
73 Roope Hintz 1.50 4.00
74 Brent Burns 1.25 3.00
75 Mark Stone 1.50 4.00
76 Teemu Selanne 2.50 6.00
77 Ed Belfour 1.25 3.00
78 Luc Robitaille 1.25 3.00
79 Grant Fuhr 2.00 5.00
80 Rob Blake 1.25 3.00
81 Paul Coffey 1.25 3.00
82 Jarome Iginla 1.50 4.00
83 Jari Kurri 1.25 3.00
84 Bernie Nicholls 1.00 2.50
85 Joe Sakic 2.50 6.00
86 Pat LaFontaine 1.25 3.00
87 Doug Gilmour 1.50 4.00
88 Jaromir Jagr 4.00 10.00
89 Pekka Rinne 1.25 3.00
90 Gerry Cheevers 1.25 3.00
91 Peter Forsberg 2.50 6.00
92 Keith Tkachuk 1.25 3.00
93 Eric Lindros 2.00 5.00
94 Shayne Corson 1.00 2.50
95 Wayne Gretzky 8.00 20.00
96 Mark Messier 2.50 6.00
97 Denis Potvin 1.25 3.00
98 John LeClair 1.25 3.00
99 Patrick Roy 3.00 8.00
100 Mario Lemieux 5.00 12.00
101 Elmer Soderblom AU/299 RC 15.00 40.00
102 Nick Blankenburg AU/299 RC 6.00 15.00
103 Pontus Holmberg RC 4.00 10.00
104 Kirill Marchenko AU/299 RC 20.00 50.00
105 Oskar Olausson RC 4.00 10.00
106 Michael Eyssimont AU/299 RC 8.00 20.00
107 Nils Aman AU/299 RC 8.00 20.00
108 Jordan Harris AU/299 RC 10.00 25.00
109 Ben Meyers AU/299 RC 8.00 20.00
110 David Jiricek AU/299 RC 15.00 40.00
111 Samuel Ersson RC 8.00 20.00
112 Jack McBain AU/299 RC 8.00 20.00
113 Tim Berni RC 4.00 10.00
114 Thomas Bordeleau AU/299 RC 8.00 20.00
115 Brayden Pachal RC 3.00 8.00
116 Isaac Ratcliffe AU/299 RC 8.00 20.00
117 Kaiden Guhle AU/299 RC 15.00 40.00
118 Mads Sogaard RC 5.00 12.00
119 Mac Hollowell RC 4.00 10.00
120 Olle Lycksell AU/299 RC 8.00 20.00
121 Bobby Brink AU/299 RC 8.00 20.00
122 Mitchell Chaffee RC 3.00 8.00
123 Marc McLaughlin AU/299 RC 8.00 20.00
124 Semyon Der-Arguchintsev RC 4.00 10.00
125 Pavol Regenda AU/299 RC 8.00 20.00
126 Bokondji Imama RC 3.00 8.00
127 Filip Roos AU/299 RC 6.00 15.00
128 Carson Meyer RC 3.00 8.00
129 Jonatan Berggren AU/299 RC 12.00 30.00
130 Samuel Fagemo RC 3.00 8.00
131 Jacob Moverare AU/299 RC 6.00 15.00
132 Dylan Samberg AU/299 RC 8.00 20.00
133 Jakub Galvas RC 4.00 10.00
134 Johnathan Kovacevic AU/299 RC 8.00 20.00
135 Nick Abruzzese AU/299 RC 8.00 20.00
136 Jakub Lauko AU/299 RC 10.00 25.00
137 Fredrik Olofsson RC 4.00 10.00
138 Vladislav Kolyachonok RC 3.00 8.00
139 Nick DeSimone AU/299 RC 8.00 20.00
140 Matias Maccelli AU/299 RC 12.00 30.00
141 Filip Hallander AU/299 RC 8.00 20.00
142 Ronnie Attard AU/299 RC 8.00 20.00
143 Nikita Alexandrov AU/299 RC 8.00 20.00
144 Lukas Dostal AU/299 RC 15.00 40.00
145 Zack Hayes AU/299 RC 6.00 15.00
146 Brandt Clarke AU/299 RC 15.00 40.00
147 Matej Blumel AU/299 RC 10.00 25.00
148 Reilly Walsh AU/299 RC 8.00 20.00
149 Valtteri Puustinen AU/299 RC 6.00 15.00
150 Hunter Drew AU/299 RC 8.00 20.00
151 Aatu Raty AU/299 RC 8.00 20.00
152 Fredrik Karlstrom AU/299 RC 6.00 15.00
153 Linus Sandin RC 3.00 8.00
154 Jake Christiansen AU/299 RC 8.00 20.00
155 Pyotr Kochetkov RC 8.00 20.00
156 Braden Schneider AU/299 RC 12.00 30.00
157 Arber Xhekaj AU/299 RC 15.00 40.00
158 Cole Koepke AU/299 RC 8.00 20.00
159 Cole Reinhardt RC 4.00 10.00
160 Nick Perbix AU/299 RC 6.00 15.00
161 Alex Vlasic RC 3.00 8.00
162 Nathan Smith AU/299 RC 6.00 15.00
163 Nikita Okhotiuk AU/299 RC 6.00 15.00
164 Brayden Tracey AU/299 RC 6.00 15.00
165 Dylan Guenther AU/299 RC 20.00 50.00
166 Mark Kastelic AU/299 RC 6.00 15.00
167 Dylan Wells RC 4.00 10.00
168 Eetu Makiniemi RC 4.00 10.00
169 Jacob Perreault RC 4.00 10.00
170 Filip Kral RC 5.00 12.00
171 Jeff Malott RC 4.00 10.00
172 Samuel Poulin AU/299 RC 10.00 25.00
173 Adam Raska RC 4.00 10.00
174 Noah Cates AU/299 RC 8.00 20.00
175 Kaedan Korczak AU/299 RC 6.00 15.00
176 Simon Holmstrom RC 4.00 10.00
177 Juuso Parssinen AU/299 RC 8.00 20.00
178 Jean-Luc Foudy AU/299 RC 8.00 20.00
179 William Bitten AU/299 RC 8.00 20.00
180 Erik Kallgren AU/299 RC 8.00 20.00
181 Linus Hogberg RC 3.00 8.00
182 Jordan Spence RC 4.00 10.00
183 Hayden Hodgson AU/299 RC 6.00 15.00
184 Trey Fix-Wolansky RC 4.00 10.00
185 Wyatt Johnston AU/299 RC 60.00 150.00
186 Tyler Tucker RC 4.00 10.00
187 Chase Pearson AU/299 RC 6.00 15.00
188 Declan Chisholm RC 4.00 10.00
190 Owen Power AU/99 RC 15.00 40.00
191 Matty Beniers AU/99 RC 20.00 50.00
192 Matt Boldy AU/99 RC 25.00 60.00
193 Lukas Reichel AU/99 RC 15.00 40.00
194 Andrei Kuzmenko AU/99 RC 15.00 40.00
195 Kent Johnson AU/99 RC 15.00 40.00
196 Jake Sanderson AU/99 RC 20.00 50.00
197 Jack Quinn AU/99 RC 12.00 30.00
198 Shane Wright AU/99 RC 30.00 80.00
199 Dylan Holloway AU/99 RC 15.00 40.00
200 Marco Rossi AU/99 RC 20.00 50.00

2022-23 Ultimate Collection Blue

*BLUE/99: .75X TO 2X BASIC

2022-23 Ultimate Collection Gold

*GOLD/35: 1.2X TO 3X BASIC

2022-23 Ultimate Collection '99-00 Ultimate Victory Retro Autographs

UVAAB Aleksander Barkov 12.00 30.00
UVACP Cole Perfetti 8.00 20.00
UVADK Darcy Kuemper 8.00 20.00
UVAJE Jack Eichel SP 12.00 30.00
UVAJK Jordan Kyrou SP 8.00 20.00
UVAJP Jeff Petry 8.00 20.00
UVANI Nick Schmaltz 6.00 15.00
UVANS Nick Suzuki 15.00 40.00
UVAQH Quinn Hughes 20.00 50.00
UVASL Jaccob Slavin 6.00 15.00

2022-23 Ultimate Collection '99-00 Ultimate Victory Retro Rookie Autographs

UVAAK Andrei Kuzmenko 20.00 50.00
UVAAX Arber Xhekaj 20.00 50.00
UVABB Bobby Brink 10.00 25.00
UVABC Brandt Clarke 20.00 50.00
UVABO Matt Boldy 30.00 80.00
UVADG Dylan Guenther 25.00 60.00
UVADH Dylan Holloway 20.00 50.00
UVADJ David Jiricek 20.00 50.00
UVAES Elmer Soderblom 20.00 50.00
UVAJB Jonatan Berggren 15.00 40.00
UVAJH Jordan Harris 12.00 30.00
UVAJQ Jack Quinn 15.00 40.00
UVAJS Juraj Slafkovsky 50.00 125.00
UVAKJ Kent Johnson 20.00 50.00
UVAKM Kirill Marchenko 25.00 60.00
UVAMB Matty Beniers 25.00 60.00
UVAMR Marco Rossi 25.00 60.00
UVASA Jake Sanderson 25.00 60.00
UVASP Samuel Poulin 12.00 30.00
UVASW Shane Wright 25.00 60.00
UVAWJ Wyatt Johnston 40.00 100.00

2022-23 Ultimate Collection Autographs

*GOLD: .6X TO 1.5X BASIC
1 Connor McDavid SP 125.00 300.00
2 Kyle Connor 12.00 30.00
5 Alex Ovechkin SP 80.00 200.00
9 Roman Josi 8.00 20.00
11 Auston Matthews SP 80.00 200.00
14 Mason McTavish 8.00 20.00
15 Tomas Hertl 8.00 20.00
18 Darcy Kuemper 8.00 20.00
19 Jared McCann 6.00 15.00
23 Jordan Kyrou 8.00 20.00
29 Brad Marchand SP 15.00 40.00
31 Alexander Holtz 8.00 20.00
33 Andrei Svechnikov 10.00 25.00
34 Matthew Tkachuk 15.00 40.00
36 Joel Eriksson Ek 6.00 15.00
37 Michael Bunting 8.00 20.00
39 Aleksander Barkov 12.00 30.00
42 Tim Stutzle 10.00 25.00
45 Alexis Lafreniere SP 12.00 30.00
47 Brady Tkachuk 12.00 30.00
49 Karel Vejmelka 5.00 12.00
50 Carter Hart 8.00 20.00
51 Jonathan Huberdeau 10.00 25.00
52 Leon Draisaitl SP 25.00 60.00
53 Tage Thompson 10.00 25.00
54 James van Riemsdyk 6.00 15.00
55 Tyler Bertuzzi 6.00 15.00
56 Marc-Andre Fleury SP 15.00 40.00
58 Andrei Vasilevskiy SP 12.00 30.00
60 Quinn Hughes SP 20.00 50.00
61 Nick Suzuki SP 15.00 40.00
62 Jake Oettinger 12.00 30.00
64 Cale Makar SP 20.00 50.00
65 Jack Eichel SP 12.00 30.00
68 Bryan Rust 8.00 20.00
71 Jordan Eberle 8.00 20.00
73 Roope Hintz 10.00 25.00
74 Brent Burns SP 8.00 20.00
76 Teemu Selanne SP 15.00 40.00
78 Luc Robitaille SP 8.00 20.00
79 Grant Fuhr SP 12.00 30.00
80 Rob Blake SP 8.00 20.00
83 Jari Kurri 8.00 20.00
84 Bernie Nicholls SP 6.00 15.00
85 Joe Sakic SP 15.00 40.00
87 Doug Gilmour SP 10.00 25.00
89 Pekka Rinne 8.00 20.00
90 Gerry Cheevers 8.00 20.00
91 Peter Forsberg SP 15.00 40.00
92 Keith Tkachuk 8.00 20.00
93 Eric Lindros SP 12.00 30.00
94 Shayne Corson 6.00 15.00
95 Wayne Gretzky SP 150.00 400.00
96 Mark Messier SP 15.00 40.00
98 John LeClair SP 8.00 20.00
99 Patrick Roy SP 20.00 50.00
100 Mario Lemieux SP 40.00 100.00

2022-23 Ultimate Collection Debut Threads Patch Autographs

ADTAK Andrei Kuzmenko/49 25.00 60.00
ADTAX Arber Xhekaj/99 25.00 60.00
ADTBC Brandt Clarke/49 25.00 60.00
ADTBL Matej Blumel/99 15.00 40.00
ADTBO Matt Boldy/49 60.00 150.00
ADTCP Chase Pearson/99 10.00 25.00
ADTDG Dylan Guenther/49 30.00 80.00
ADTDS Dylan Samberg/99 12.00 30.00
ADTEK Erik Kallgren/99 12.00 30.00
ADTES Elmer Soderblom/99 25.00 60.00
ADTFH Filip Hallander/99 12.00 30.00
ADTFK Fredrik Karlstrom/99 10.00 25.00
ADTIR Isaac Ratcliffe/99 12.00 30.00
ADTJB Jonatan Berggren/99 20.00 50.00
ADTJC Jake Christiansen/99 12.00 30.00
ADTJH Jordan Harris/99 15.00 40.00
ADTJK Johnathan Kovacevic/99 12.00 30.00
ADTJL Jakub Lauko/99 15.00 40.00
ADTJM Jack McBain/99 12.00 30.00
ADTJP Juuso Parssinen/99 12.00 30.00
ADTJQ Jack Quinn/49 20.00 50.00
ADTJS Juraj Slafkovsky/49 150.00 400.00
ADTKG Kaiden Guhle/99 25.00 60.00
ADTKJ Kent Johnson/49 25.00 60.00
ADTKK Kaedan Korczak/99 10.00 25.00
ADTKM Kirill Marchenko/99 30.00 80.00
ADTLD Lukas Dostal/99 25.00 60.00
ADTLR Lukas Reichel/49 25.00 60.00
ADTMB Matty Beniers/49 60.00 150.00
ADTME Michael Eyssimont/99 12.00 30.00
ADTMK Mark Kastelic/99 10.00 25.00
ADTMM Marc McLaughlin/99 12.00 30.00
ADTMO Jacob Moverare/99 10.00 25.00
ADTMR Marco Rossi/49 30.00 80.00
ADTNA Nick Abruzzese/99 12.00 30.00
ADTNB Nick Blankenburg/99 10.00 25.00
ADTNC Noah Cates/99 12.00 30.00
ADTND Nick DeSimone/99 12.00 30.00
ADTNO Nikita Okhotiuk/99 10.00 25.00
ADTNP Nick Perbix/99 10.00 25.00
ADTNS Nathan Smith/99 10.00 25.00
ADTOL Olle Lycksell/99 12.00 30.00
ADTOP Owen Power/49 60.00 150.00
ADTPO Samuel Poulin/99 15.00 40.00
ADTPR Pavol Regenda/99 12.00 30.00
ADTRA Ronnie Attard/99 12.00 30.00
ADTRW Reilly Walsh/99 12.00 30.00
ADTSA Jake Sanderson/49 30.00 80.00
ADTSW Shane Wright/49 30.00 80.00
ADTTF Trey Fix-Wolansky/99 12.00 30.00
ADTVP Valtteri Puustinen/99 10.00 25.00
ADTWJ Wyatt Johnston/49 80.00 200.00
ADTZH Zack Hayes/99 10.00 25.00

2022-23 Ultimate Collection Jerseys

101 Elmer Soderblom/799 5.00 12.00
102 Nick Blankenburg/799 2.00 5.00
103 Pontus Holmberg/799 2.50 6.00
104 Kirill Marchenko/799 6.00 15.00
105 Oskar Olausson/799 2.50 6.00
106 Michael Eyssimont/799 2.50 6.00
107 Nils Aman/799 2.50 6.00
108 Jordan Harris/799 3.00 8.00
109 Ben Meyers/799 2.50 6.00
110 David Jiricek/799 5.00 12.00
112 Jack McBain/799 2.50 6.00
114 Thomas Bordeleau/799 2.50 6.00
116 Isaac Ratcliffe/799 2.50 6.00
117 Kaiden Guhle/799 5.00 12.00
118 Mads Sogaard/799 3.00 8.00
120 Olle Lycksell/799 2.50 6.00
121 Bobby Brink/799 2.50 6.00
123 Marc McLaughlin/799 2.50 6.00
124 Semyon Der-Arguchintsev/799 2.50 6.00
125 Pavol Regenda/799 2.50 6.00
127 Filip Roos/799 2.00 5.00
129 Jonatan Berggren/799 4.00 10.00
130 Samuel Fagemo/799 2.00 5.00
131 Jacob Moverare/799 2.00 5.00
132 Dylan Samberg/799 2.50 6.00
134 Johnathan Kovacevic/799 2.50 6.00
135 Nick Abruzzese/799 2.50 6.00
136 Jakub Lauko/799 3.00 8.00
138 Vladislav Kolyachonok/799 2.00 5.00
139 Nick DeSimone/799 2.50 6.00
140 Matias Maccelli/799 4.00 10.00
141 Filip Hallander/799 2.50 6.00
142 Ronnie Attard/799 2.50 6.00
143 Nikita Alexandrov/799 2.50 6.00
144 Lukas Dostal/799 5.00 12.00
145 Zack Hayes/799 2.00 5.00
146 Brandt Clarke/799 5.00 12.00
147 Matej Blumel/799 3.00 8.00
148 Reilly Walsh/799 2.50 6.00
149 Valtteri Puustinen/799 2.00 5.00
152 Fredrik Karlstrom/799 2.00 5.00
154 Jake Christiansen/799 2.50 6.00
155 Pyotr Kochetkov/799 5.00 12.00
156 Braden Schneider/799 4.00 10.00
157 Arber Xhekaj/799 5.00 12.00
158 Cole Koepke/799 2.50 6.00
160 Nick Perbix/799 2.00 5.00
161 Alex Vlasic/799 2.00 5.00
162 Nathan Smith/799 2.00 5.00
163 Nikita Okhotiuk/799 2.00 5.00
164 Brayden Tracey/799 2.00 5.00
165 Dylan Guenther/799 6.00 15.00
166 Mark Kastelic/799 2.00 5.00
169 Jacob Perreault/799 2.50 6.00
172 Samuel Poulin/799 3.00 8.00
174 Noah Cates/799 2.50 6.00
175 Kaedan Korczak/799 2.00 5.00
176 Simon Holmstrom/799 2.50 6.00
177 Juuso Parssinen/799 2.50 6.00
179 William Bitten/799 2.50 6.00
180 Erik Kallgren/799 2.50 6.00
182 Jordan Spence/799 2.50 6.00
183 Hayden Hodgson/799 2.00 5.00
184 Trey Fix-Wolansky/799 2.50 6.00
185 Wyatt Johnston/799 10.00 25.00
187 Chase Pearson/799 2.00 5.00
189 Juraj Slafkovsky/599 12.00 30.00
190 Owen Power/599 5.00 12.00
191 Matty Beniers/599 6.00 15.00
192 Matt Boldy/599 8.00 20.00
193 Lukas Reichel/599 5.00 12.00
194 Andrei Kuzmenko/599 5.00 12.00
195 Kent Johnson/599 5.00 12.00
196 Jake Sanderson/599 6.00 15.00
197 Jack Quinn/599 4.00 10.00
198 Shane Wright/599 6.00 15.00
199 Dylan Holloway/599 5.00 12.00
200 Marco Rossi/599 6.00 15.00

2022-23 Ultimate Collection Patch Autographs

101 Elmer Soderblom/99 30.00 80.00
102 Nick Blankenburg/99 12.00 30.00
104 Kirill Marchenko/99 40.00 100.00
106 Michael Eyssimont/99 15.00 40.00
107 Nils Aman/99 15.00 40.00
108 Jordan Harris/99 20.00 50.00
109 Ben Meyers/99 15.00 40.00
110 David Jiricek/99 30.00 80.00
112 Jack McBain/99 15.00 40.00
114 Thomas Bordeleau/99 15.00 40.00
116 Isaac Ratcliffe/99 15.00 40.00
117 Kaiden Guhle/99 30.00 80.00
120 Olle Lycksell/99 15.00 40.00
121 Bobby Brink/99 15.00 40.00
123 Marc McLaughlin/99 15.00 40.00
125 Pavol Regenda/99 15.00 40.00
127 Filip Roos/99 12.00 30.00
129 Jonatan Berggren/99 25.00 60.00
131 Jacob Moverare/99 12.00 30.00
132 Dylan Samberg/99 15.00 40.00
134 Johnathan Kovacevic/99 15.00 40.00
135 Nick Abruzzese/99 15.00 40.00
136 Jakub Lauko/99 20.00 50.00
139 Nick DeSimone/99 15.00 40.00
140 Matias Maccelli/99 25.00 60.00
141 Filip Hallander/99 15.00 40.00
142 Ronnie Attard/99 15.00 40.00
143 Nikita Alexandrov/99 15.00 40.00
144 Lukas Dostal/99 30.00 80.00
145 Zack Hayes/99 12.00 30.00
146 Brandt Clarke/99 30.00 80.00
147 Matej Blumel/99 20.00 50.00
148 Reilly Walsh/99 15.00 40.00
149 Valtteri Puustinen/99 12.00 30.00
152 Fredrik Karlstrom/99 12.00 30.00
154 Jake Christiansen/99 15.00 40.00
156 Braden Schneider/99 25.00 60.00
157 Arber Xhekaj/99 40.00 100.00
158 Cole Koepke/99 15.00 40.00
160 Nick Perbix/99 12.00 30.00
162 Nathan Smith/99 12.00 30.00
163 Nikita Okhotiuk/99 12.00 30.00
164 Brayden Tracey/99 12.00 30.00
165 Dylan Guenther/99 40.00 100.00
166 Mark Kastelic/99 12.00 30.00
172 Samuel Poulin/99 20.00 50.00
174 Noah Cates/99 15.00 40.00
175 Kaedan Korczak/99 12.00 30.00
177 Juuso Parssinen/99 15.00 40.00
180 Erik Kallgren/99 15.00 40.00
183 Hayden Hodgson/99 12.00 30.00
184 Trey Fix-Wolansky/99 15.00 40.00
185 Wyatt Johnston/99 125.00 300.00
187 Chase Pearson/99 12.00 30.00
189 Juraj Slafkovsky/49 200.00 500.00
190 Owen Power/49 60.00 150.00
191 Matty Beniers/49 60.00 150.00
192 Matt Boldy/49 80.00 200.00
193 Lukas Reichel/49 30.00 80.00
194 Andrei Kuzmenko/49 30.00 80.00
195 Kent Johnson/49 60.00 150.00
196 Jake Sanderson/49 50.00 125.00
198 Shane Wright/49 50.00 125.00
199 Dylan Holloway/49 30.00 80.00
200 Marco Rossi/49 50.00 125.00

2022-23 Ultimate Collection Pro Threads Patch Autographs

PTAS Andrei Svechnikov/25 20.00 50.00
PTBS Brandon Saad/49 12.00 30.00
PTCP Cole Perfetti/49 15.00 40.00
PTCS Cole Sillinger/49 12.00 30.00
PTDM Dawson Mercer/25 20.00 50.00
PTGV Gabe Vilardi/49 15.00 40.00
PTJC Jack Campbell/49 15.00 40.00
PTJM Jared McCann/49 12.00 30.00
PTJS Jeremy Swayman/25 80.00 200.00
PTJV James van Riemsdyk/49 12.00 30.00
PTMB Michael Bunting/49 15.00 40.00
PTMF Marc-Andre Fleury/25 30.00 80.00
PTNS Nick Suzuki/25 60.00 150.00
PTPG Philipp Grubauer/49 15.00 40.00
PTPK Peyton Krebs/49 12.00 30.00
PTRO Ryan O'Reilly/49 15.00 40.00
PTSR Sam Reinhart/49 30.00 80.00
PTYS Yegor Sharangovich/49 15.00 40.00

2022-23 Ultimate Collection Rookie Accents Autographs

RAAK Andrei Kuzmenko/35 15.00 40.00
RAAX Arber Xhekaj/99 15.00 40.00
RABB Bobby Brink/65 8.00 20.00
RABC Brandt Clarke/35 15.00 40.00
RABE Matty Beniers/35 60.00 150.00
RABL Matej Blumel/99 10.00 25.00
RABM Ben Meyers/65 8.00 20.00
RABS Braden Schneider/65 12.00 30.00
RABT Brayden Tracey/65 6.00 15.00
RADG Dylan Guenther/35 20.00 50.00
RADH Dylan Holloway/35 15.00 40.00
RADJ David Jiricek/35 15.00 40.00
RAEK Erik Kallgren/65 8.00 20.00
RAES Elmer Soderblom/65 15.00 40.00
RAFH Filip Hallander/99 8.00 20.00
RAFK Fredrik Karlstrom/99 6.00 15.00
RAIR Isaac Ratcliffe/65 8.00 20.00
RAJB Jonatan Berggren/35 12.00 30.00
RAJC Jake Christiansen/99 8.00 20.00
RAJH Jordan Harris/65 10.00 25.00
RAJM Jack McBain/65 8.00 20.00
RAJP Juuso Parssinen/99 8.00 20.00
RAJS Jake Sanderson/35 20.00 50.00
RAKG Kaiden Guhle/65 15.00 40.00
RAKJ Kent Johnson/35 25.00 60.00
RAKK Kaedan Korczak/65 6.00 15.00
RAKM Kirill Marchenko/35 20.00 50.00
RALD Lukas Dostal/65 15.00 40.00
RAMB Matt Boldy/35 60.00 150.00
RAME Michael Eyssimont/99 8.00 20.00
RAMK Mark Kastelic/99 6.00 15.00
RAMM Marc McLaughlin/65 8.00 20.00
RAMO Jacob Moverare/99 6.00 15.00
RANC Noah Cates/65 8.00 20.00
RANS Nathan Smith/65 6.00 15.00
RAOL Olle Lycksell/99 8.00 20.00
RAOP Owen Power/35 60.00 150.00
RARA Ronnie Attard/99 8.00 20.00
RASL Juraj Slafkovsky/35 125.00 300.00
RASW Shane Wright/35 40.00 100.00
RAVP Valtteri Puustinen/99 6.00 15.00
RAWJ Wyatt Johnston/35 100.00 250.00

2022-23 Ultimate Collection Signature Masterpieces

USMAK Andrei Kuzmenko 20.00 50.00
USMAL Anton Lundell SP 10.00 25.00
USMBE Matty Beniers 80.00 200.00
USMBN Brock Nelson 10.00 25.00
USMBO Matt Boldy 60.00 150.00
USMBT Brady Tkachuk 15.00 40.00
USMCP Cole Perfetti 15.00 40.00
USMJB Jonatan Berggren 15.00 40.00
USMJK Jari Kurri 20.00 50.00
USMJS Jake Sanderson 25.00 60.00
USMKM K'Andre Miller 8.00 20.00
USMMA Kirill Marchenko 25.00 60.00
USMMB Martin Brodeur SP 150.00 400.00
USMOP Owen Power 80.00 200.00
USMRH Roope Hintz 12.00 30.00

2022-23 Ultimate Collection Signature Material Laureates

SMLAE Aaron Ekblad/49 12.00 30.00
SMLAL Alexis Lafreniere/25 15.00 40.00
SMLBJ Boone Jenner/99 10.00 25.00
SMLCH Carter Hart/49 10.00 25.00
SMLDC Dylan Cozens/49 10.00 25.00
SMLEI Jack Eichel/25 15.00 40.00
SMLGV Gabe Vilardi/99 10.00 25.00
SMLJE Jordan Eberle/99 10.00 25.00
SMLJH Jonathan Huberdeau/49 12.00 30.00
SMLJP JJ Peterka/99 30.00 80.00
SMLLD Leon Draisaitl/25 80.00 200.00
SMLMM Mason McTavish/49 15.00 40.00
SMLNS Nick Schmaltz/49 8.00 20.00
SMLST Shea Theodore/49 12.00 30.00
SMLTK Torey Krug/99 8.00 20.00

2022-23 Ultimate Collection Stick With Me

SWMAO Alex Ovechkin 30.00 80.00
SWMAT Alex Tuch 8.00 20.00
SWMCM Connor McDavid 40.00 100.00
SWMEI Jack Eichel 12.00 30.00
SWMGL Gabriel Landeskog 10.00 25.00
SWMJE Jordan Eberle 8.00 20.00
SWMJH Jack Hughes 20.00 50.00
SWMJQ Jonathan Quick 10.00 25.00
SWMJT John Tavares 12.00 30.00
SWMME Mark Messier 15.00 40.00
SWMML Mario Lemieux 30.00 80.00
SWMMM Mike Modano 12.00 30.00
SWMMP Max Pacioretty 8.00 20.00
SWMMS Mark Stone 10.00 25.00
SWMPD Pierre-Luc Dubois 6.00 15.00
SWMPK Patrick Kane 15.00 40.00
SWMPL Pat LaFontaine 8.00 20.00
SWMSC Sidney Crosby 30.00 80.00
SWMSS Steven Stamkos 15.00 40.00
SWMSY Steve Yzerman 20.00 50.00

2022-23 Ultimate Collection Ulti-Mates Jerseys

*PATCH/35: .6X TO 1.5X BASIC
UTMBB M.Barzal/J.Bailey 6.00 15.00
UTMBM P.Bergeron/B.Marchand 10.00 25.00
UTMBO A.Ovechkin/N.Backstrom 20.00 50.00
UTMBS B.Burns/A.Svechnikov 6.00 15.00
UTMEC K.Connor/N.Ehlers 8.00 20.00
UTMEM J.McCann/J.Eberle 5.00 12.00
UTMET M.Tkachuk/A.Ekblad 10.00 25.00
UTMFK K.Fiala/A.Kempe 5.00 12.00
UTMGL J.Gaudreau/P.Laine 8.00 20.00
UTMGT C.Giroux/B.Tkachuk 8.00 20.00
UTMHB B.Horvat/B.Boeser 6.00 15.00
UTMHH J.Hughes/D.Hamilton 12.00 30.00
UTMHL J.Huberdeau/E.Lindholm 6.00 15.00
UTMJF R.Josi/F.Forsberg 8.00 20.00
UTMKJ P.Kane/S.Jones 10.00 25.00
UTMKM E.Karlsson/T.Meier 6.00 15.00
UTMKS C.Keller/N.Schmaltz 6.00 15.00
UTMKT R.Thomas/J.Kyrou 5.00 12.00
UTMKV A.Vasilevskiy/N.Kucherov 10.00 25.00
UTMMF A.Fox/K.Miller 6.00 15.00
UTMMG E.Malkin/J.Guentzel 10.00 25.00
UTMMM N.MacKinnon/C.Makar 20.00 50.00
UTMNB W.Nylander/M.Bunting 10.00 25.00
UTMNN D.Nurse/R.Nugent-Hopkins 6.00 15.00
UTMRS R.Hintz/T.Seguin 6.00 15.00
UTMSC C.Caufield/N.Suzuki 10.00 25.00
UTMSE J.Eichel/M.Stone 8.00 20.00
UTMSK K.Kaprizov/J.Spurgeon 15.00 40.00
UTMSR M.Seider/L.Raymond 8.00 20.00
UTMTD T.Thompson/R.Dahlin 6.00 15.00
UTMTZ T.Zegras/T.Terry 5.00 12.00
UTMVK T.Konecny/J.van Riemsdyk 5.00 12.00

2022-23 Ultimate Collection Ultimate Displays Jersey Autographs

UDAAB Aleksander Barkov/99 20.00 50.00
UDAAE Aaron Ekblad/99 15.00 40.00
UDAAK Andrei Kuzmenko/99 25.00 60.00
UDAAL Alexis Lafreniere/49 40.00 100.00
UDAAS Andrei Svechnikov/49 15.00 40.00
UDAAV Andrei Vasilevskiy/49 20.00 50.00
UDABB Brent Burns/99 12.00 30.00
UDABO Matt Boldy/99 60.00 150.00
UDACH Carter Hart/99 12.00 30.00
UDACS Cole Sillinger/135 10.00 25.00
UDADK Darcy Kuemper/99 12.00 30.00
UDAIS Ilya Sorokin/99 20.00 50.00
UDAJE Joel Eriksson Ek/135 10.00 25.00
UDAJH Jonathan Huberdeau/99 15.00 40.00
UDAJK Jordan Kyrou/135 12.00 30.00
UDAJM Jared McCann/135 10.00 25.00
UDAJO Jake Oettinger/99 20.00 50.00
UDAJS Juraj Slafkovsky/99 100.00 250.00
UDAKC Kyle Connor/49 20.00 50.00
UDAKV Karel Vejmelka/135 8.00 20.00
UDAMB Matty Beniers/99 30.00 80.00
UDAMM Mason McTavish/135 12.00 30.00
UDANZ Nick Suzuki/99 40.00 100.00
UDAQH Quinn Hughes/49 30.00 80.00
UDARJ Roman Josi/49 12.00 30.00
UDATH Tomas Hertl/135 12.00 30.00
UDATS Tim Stutzle/25 15.00 40.00
UDATT Tage Thompson/99 15.00 40.00

2022-23 Ultimate Collection Ultimate Displays Jersey Autographs Patch

*PATCH: .6X TO 1.5X BASIC
UDAJO Jake Oettinger/35 40.00 100.00
UDATH Tomas Hertl/35 30.00 80.00

2022-23 Ultimate Collection Ultimate Emblems Autographs

*GOLD: .6X TO 1.5X BASIC
UEAC Andrew Copp 4.00 10.00
UEBC Blake Coleman 5.00 12.00
UEBE Tyler Bertuzzi SP 5.00 12.00
UEBN Brock Nelson SP 6.00 15.00
UEBU Brent Burns SP 6.00 15.00
UECA Carey Price SP 12.00 30.00
UECC Chris Chelios SP 6.00 15.00
UECF Connor Clifton 4.00 10.00
UECP Cal Petersen 4.00 10.00
UEDC Dylan Cozens SP 6.00 15.00
UEEL Eric Lindros SP 10.00 25.00
UEET Eeli Tolvanen 6.00 15.00
UEFS Felix Sandstrom 4.00 10.00
UEFZ Fabian Zetterlund 4.00 10.00
UEGC Gerry Cheevers 6.00 15.00
UEJM Jacob Markstrom 6.00 15.00
UEJO Jonathan Marchessault 8.00 20.00
UEJV James van Riemsdyk 5.00 12.00
UEKP Keith Primeau 5.00 12.00
UEMF Mario Ferraro 4.00 10.00
UEMG Morgan Geekie 4.00 10.00
UEMI Jacob Middleton 4.00 10.00
UEMO Mike Modano SP 10.00 25.00
UENE Nikolaj Ehlers 6.00 15.00
UENP Neal Pionk 4.00 10.00
UEPA Joe Pavelski 8.00 20.00
UEPB Peter Bondra SP 6.00 15.00
UEPE Jeff Petry 6.00 15.00
UEPG Philipp Grubauer 6.00 15.00
UEPI Shane Pinto 5.00 12.00
UEQB Quinton Byfield SP 8.00 20.00
UERO Larry Robinson SP 6.00 15.00
UESM Sonny Milano 5.00 12.00
UEST Shea Theodore 8.00 20.00
UETC Thomas Chabot 6.00 15.00
UETJ Tristan Jarry 6.00 15.00
UEVP Vasily Podkolzin 4.00 10.00
UEZW Zach Werenski 10.00 25.00

2022-23 Ultimate Collection Ultimate Emblems Rookie Autographs

UEAK Andrei Kuzmenko 12.00 30.00
UEAR Aatu Raty 6.00 15.00
UEAX Arber Xhekaj 12.00 30.00
UEBB Bobby Brink 6.00 15.00
UEBO Matt Boldy SP 30.00 80.00
UEBS Braden Schneider 10.00 25.00
UECL Brandt Clarke 12.00 30.00
UEDJ David Jiricek 12.00 30.00
UEDS Dylan Samberg 6.00 15.00
UEEK Erik Kallgren 6.00 15.00
UEES Elmer Soderblom 12.00 30.00
UEJB Jonatan Berggren 10.00 25.00
UEJH Jordan Harris 8.00 20.00
UEJL Jakub Lauko 8.00 20.00
UEJQ Jack Quinn SP 10.00 25.00
UEJS Juraj Slafkovsky SP 40.00 100.00
UEKG Kaiden Guhle 12.00 30.00
UEKJ Kent Johnson 12.00 30.00
UEKK Kaedan Korczak 5.00 12.00
UEKM Kirill Marchenko 15.00 40.00
UELD Lukas Dostal 12.00 30.00
UEMB Matty Beniers SP 15.00 40.00
UEMC Jack McBain 6.00 15.00
UEME Michael Eyssimont 6.00 15.00
UEMK Mark Kastelic 5.00 12.00
UEMR Marco Rossi 15.00 40.00
UEMS Mads Sogaard 8.00 20.00
UENA Nick Abruzzese 6.00 15.00
UEOP Owen Power SP 12.00 30.00
UEPN Juuso Parssinen 6.00 15.00
UEPO Samuel Poulin 8.00 20.00
UEPU Valtteri Puustinen 5.00 12.00
UERE Pavol Regenda 6.00 15.00
UESA Jake Sanderson 15.00 40.00
UESH Simon Holmstrom 6.00 15.00
UESW Shane Wright SP 15.00 40.00
UETB Thomas Bordeleau 6.00 15.00
UETF Trey Fix-Wolansky 6.00 15.00
UEWJ Wyatt Johnston 40.00 100.00

2022-23 Ultimate Collection Ultimate Emblems Rookie Autographs Gold

*GOLD: .6X TO 1.5X BASIC
UEJS Juraj Slafkovsky/25 125.00 300.00
UEKJ Kent Johnson/25 40.00 100.00
UEWJ Wyatt Johnston/25 125.00 300.00

2022-23 Ultimate Collection Ultimate Introductions

*GOLD/49: .75X TO 2X BASIC
*BLACK/25: 1.2X TO 3X BASIC
UI1 Juraj Slafkovsky 10.00 25.00
UI2 Nick Abruzzese 2.00 5.00
UI3 Dylan Guenther 5.00 12.00
UI4 Owen Power 4.00 10.00
UI5 Matty Beniers 5.00 12.00
UI6 Jack McBain 2.00 5.00
UI7 Ben Meyers 2.00 5.00
UI8 Samuel Ersson 4.00 10.00

UI9 Filip Roos 1.50 4.00
UI10 Marcus Bjork 2.00 5.00
UI11 Nikita Alexandrov 2.00 5.00
UI12 Brayden Tracey 1.50 4.00
UI13 Nick DeSimone 2.00 5.00
UI14 Filip Kral 2.50 6.00
UI15 Noah Cates 2.00 5.00
UI16 Nick Cicek 2.00 5.00
UI17 Olle Lycksell 2.00 5.00
UI18 Matt Boldy 6.00 15.00
UI19 Lukas Reichel 4.00 10.00
UI20 David Jiricek 4.00 10.00
UI21 Andrei Kuzmenko 4.00 10.00
UI22 Johnathan Kovacevic 2.00 5.00
UI23 Carson Meyer 1.50 4.00
UI24 Jakub Lauko 2.50 6.00
UI25 Kirill Marchenko 5.00 12.00
UI26 Hayden Hodgson 1.50 4.00
UI27 Kent Johnson 4.00 10.00
UI28 Linus Hogberg 1.50 4.00
UI29 Hunter Drew 2.00 5.00
UI30 Kaedan Korczak 1.50 4.00
UI31 Lukas Dostal 4.00 10.00
UI32 Jonatan Berggren 3.00 8.00
UI33 Trey Fix-Wolansky 2.00 5.00
UI34 Mads Sogaard 2.50 6.00
UI35 Samuel Fagemo 1.50 4.00
UI36 Mark Kastelic 1.50 4.00
UI37 Ronnie Attard 2.00 5.00
UI38 Jake Sanderson 5.00 12.00
UI39 Oskar Olausson 2.00 5.00
UI40 Jack Quinn 3.00 8.00
UI41 Shane Wright 5.00 12.00
UI42 Nick Blankenburg 1.50 4.00
UI43 Jordan Harris 2.50 6.00
UI44 Thomas Bordeleau 2.00 5.00
UI45 Jacob Perreault 2.00 5.00
UI46 Zack Hayes 1.50 4.00
UI47 Nathan Smith 1.50 4.00
UI48 Chase Pearson 1.50 4.00
UI49 Erik Kallgren 2.00 5.00
UI50 Lucas Johansen 1.50 4.00
UI51 Semyon Der-Arguchintsev 2.00 5.00
UI52 Pavol Regenda 2.00 5.00
UI53 Simon Holmstrom 2.00 5.00
UI54 Jake Christiansen 2.00 5.00
UI55 Pontus Holmberg 2.00 5.00
UI56 Isaac Ratcliffe 2.00 5.00
UI57 Marc McLaughlin 2.00 5.00
UI58 Brandt Clarke 4.00 10.00
UI59 Jacob Moverare 1.50 4.00
UI60 Samuel Poulin 2.50 6.00
UI61 Valtteri Puustinen 1.50 4.00
UI62 Dylan Holloway 4.00 10.00
UI63 Michael Eyssimont 2.00 5.00
UI64 Bobby Brink 2.00 5.00
UI65 Pyotr Kochetkov 4.00 10.00
UI66 Juuso Parssinen 2.00 5.00
UI67 Nick Perbix 1.50 4.00
UI68 Jeff Malott 2.00 5.00
UI69 Arber Xhekaj 4.00 10.00
UI70 Jakub Galvas 2.00 5.00
UI71 Nikita Okhotiuk 1.50 4.00
UI72 Braden Schneider 3.00 8.00
UI73 Filip Hallander 2.00 5.00
UI74 Vladislav Kolyachonok 1.50 4.00
UI75 Fredrik Karlstrom 1.50 4.00
UI76 Mac Hollowell 2.00 5.00
UI77 Marco Rossi 5.00 12.00
UI78 Aatu Raty 2.00 5.00
UI79 Dylan Samberg 2.00 5.00
UI80 Elmer Soderblom 4.00 10.00
UI81 Cole Reinhardt 2.00 5.00
UI82 Matej Blumel 2.50 6.00
UI83 Kaiden Guhle 4.00 10.00
UI84 Alex Vlasic 1.50 4.00
UI85 Jordan Spence 2.00 5.00
UI86 Matias Maccelli 3.00 8.00
UI87 Cole Koepke 2.00 5.00
UI88 Reilly Walsh 2.00 5.00
UI89 Nils Aman 2.00 5.00
UI90 Wyatt Johnston 8.00 20.00
UI91 Juraj Slafkovsky SHOW 10.00 25.00
UI92 Wyatt Johnston SHOW 8.00 20.00
UI93 Jack Quinn SHOW 3.00 8.00
UI94 Shane Wright SHOW 5.00 12.00
UI95 Kent Johnson SHOW 4.00 10.00
UI96 Andrei Kuzmenko SHOW 4.00 10.00
UI97 Matt Boldy SHOW 6.00 15.00
UI98 Owen Power SHOW 4.00 10.00
UI99 Matty Beniers SHOW 5.00 12.00
UI100 Jake Sanderson SHOW 5.00 12.00

2022-23 Ultimate Collection Ultimate Introductions Autographs

*GOLD: .6X TO 1.5X BASIC
UI1 Juraj Slafkovsky SP 80.00 200.00
UI2 Nick Abruzzese 6.00 15.00
UI3 Dylan Guenther 15.00 40.00
UI4 Owen Power SP 25.00 60.00
UI5 Matty Beniers SP 40.00 100.00
UI6 Jack McBain 6.00 15.00
UI7 Ben Meyers 6.00 15.00
UI9 Filip Roos 5.00 12.00
UI10 Marcus Bjork 6.00 15.00
UI11 Nikita Alexandrov 6.00 15.00
UI12 Brayden Tracey 5.00 12.00
UI13 Nick DeSimone 6.00 15.00
UI15 Noah Cates 6.00 15.00
UI17 Olle Lycksell 6.00 15.00
UI18 Matt Boldy SP 30.00 80.00
UI19 Lukas Reichel 12.00 30.00
UI20 David Jiricek 12.00 30.00
UI21 Andrei Kuzmenko 12.00 30.00
UI22 Johnathan Kovacevic 6.00 15.00
UI24 Jakub Lauko 8.00 20.00
UI25 Kirill Marchenko SP 15.00 40.00
UI26 Hayden Hodgson 5.00 12.00
UI27 Kent Johnson 12.00 30.00
UI29 Hunter Drew 6.00 15.00
UI30 Kaedan Korczak 5.00 12.00
UI31 Lukas Dostal 12.00 30.00
UI32 Jonatan Berggren 10.00 25.00
UI33 Trey Fix-Wolansky 6.00 15.00
UI35 Samuel Fagemo 5.00 12.00
UI36 Mark Kastelic 5.00 12.00
UI37 Ronnie Attard 6.00 15.00
UI38 Jake Sanderson SP 15.00 40.00
UI40 Jack Quinn SP 10.00 25.00
UI41 Shane Wright SP 15.00 40.00
UI42 Nick Blankenburg 5.00 12.00
UI43 Jordan Harris 8.00 20.00
UI44 Thomas Bordeleau 6.00 15.00
UI46 Zack Hayes 5.00 12.00
UI47 Nathan Smith 5.00 12.00
UI48 Chase Pearson 5.00 12.00
UI49 Erik Kallgren 6.00 15.00
UI52 Pavol Regenda 6.00 15.00
UI54 Jake Christiansen 6.00 15.00
UI56 Isaac Ratcliffe 6.00 15.00
UI57 Marc McLaughlin 6.00 15.00
UI58 Brandt Clarke 12.00 30.00
UI59 Jacob Moverare 5.00 12.00
UI60 Samuel Poulin 8.00 20.00
UI61 Valtteri Puustinen 5.00 12.00
UI62 Dylan Holloway 12.00 30.00
UI63 Michael Eyssimont 6.00 15.00
UI64 Bobby Brink 6.00 15.00
UI66 Juuso Parssinen 6.00 15.00
UI67 Nick Perbix 5.00 12.00
UI69 Arber Xhekaj 12.00 30.00
UI71 Nikita Okhotiuk 5.00 12.00
UI72 Braden Schneider 10.00 25.00
UI73 Filip Hallander 6.00 15.00
UI75 Fredrik Karlstrom 5.00 12.00
UI78 Aatu Raty 6.00 15.00
UI79 Dylan Samberg 6.00 15.00
UI80 Elmer Soderblom 12.00 30.00
UI82 Matej Blumel 8.00 20.00
UI83 Kaiden Guhle 12.00 30.00
UI86 Matias Maccelli 10.00 25.00
UI87 Cole Koepke 6.00 15.00
UI88 Reilly Walsh 6.00 15.00
UI89 Nils Aman 6.00 15.00
UI90 Wyatt Johnston 60.00 150.00
UI91 Juraj Slafkovsky SHOW 80.00 200.00
UI92 Wyatt Johnston SHOW 60.00 150.00
UI93 Jack Quinn SHOW 10.00 25.00
UI94 Shane Wright SHOW 15.00 40.00
UI95 Kent Johnson SHOW 12.00 30.00
UI96 Andrei Kuzmenko SHOW 12.00 30.00
UI97 Matt Boldy SHOW 30.00 80.00
UI98 Owen Power SHOW 25.00 60.00
UI99 Matty Beniers SHOW 40.00 100.00
UI100 Jake Sanderson SHOW 15.00 40.00

2022-23 Ultimate Collection Ultimate Material Signatures

UMSAB Aleksander Barkov/49 12.00 30.00
UMSAH Alexander Holtz/49 8.00 20.00
UMSAL Anders Lee/99 6.00 15.00
UMSBB Bowen Byram/99 10.00 25.00
UMSBM Brad Marchand/25 15.00 40.00
UMSCC Charlie Coyle/99 8.00 20.00
UMSCH Carter Hart/49 8.00 20.00
UMSCM Cale Makar/25 30.00 80.00
UMSCP Cole Perfetti/49 8.00 20.00
UMSDK Darcy Kuemper/49 8.00 20.00
UMSEK Joel Eriksson Ek/49 6.00 15.00
UMSJE Jack Eichel/25 12.00 30.00
UMSJM Jonathan Marchessault/49 10.00 25.00
UMSJO Jake Oettinger/49 12.00 30.00
UMSJP JJ Peterka/99 8.00 20.00
UMSLD Leon Draisaitl/25 40.00 100.00
UMSMB Michael Bunting/99 8.00 20.00
UMSMM Mason McTavish/49 8.00 20.00
UMSPK Peyton Krebs/99 6.00 15.00
UMSTC Thomas Chabot/99 8.00 20.00
UMSTT Tage Thompson/25 10.00 25.00
UMSVP Vasily Podkolzin/99 5.00 12.00

2022-23 Ultimate Collection Ultimate Power Play Combos Jerseys

*PATCH/20: 1.2X TO 3X BASIC
UPCAJ S.Aho/S.Jarvis 8.00 20.00
UPCDC C.Caufield/K.Dach 10.00 25.00
UPCEM J.Eberle/J.McCann 5.00 12.00
UPCKP C.Kreider/A.Panarin 10.00 25.00
UPCLS M.Seider/D.Larkin 6.00 15.00
UPCMM A.Matthews/M.Marner 10.00 25.00
UPCRM C.Makar/M.Rantanen 10.00 25.00
UPCTD R.Dahlin/T.Thompson 6.00 15.00

2022-23 Ultimate Collection Ultimate Premium Materials

UMSAL Anders Lee/35 5.00 12.00
UMSAN Alex Newhook/35 5.00 12.00
UMSCA Cam Atkinson/35 6.00 15.00
UMSCC Charlie Coyle/35 6.00 15.00
UMSJP JJ Peterka/35 6.00 15.00
UMSMB Michael Bunting/35 6.00 15.00
UMSPK Peyton Krebs/35 5.00 12.00
UMSTC Thomas Chabot/35 6.00 15.00
UMSTE Teuvo Teravainen/35 6.00 15.00
UMSVP Vasily Podkolzin/35 4.00 10.00

2022-23 Ultimate Collection Ultimate Quad Materials

QMBASJ Burns/Aho Svechnikov/Jarvis 10.00 25.00
QMBLBN Barzal/Bailey/Lee/Nelson 8.00 20.00
QMBMMP Pastrnak/Bergeron Marchand/McAvoy 15.00 40.00
QMBPBS Slafkovsky/Power Beniers/Boldy 30.00 80.00
QMBRTL Tkachuk/Barkov Reinhart/Lundell 12.00 30.00
QMBSHR Robertson/Seguin Benn/Heiskanen 10.00 25.00
QMCKHM Meier/Hertl Karlsson/Couture 8.00 20.00
QMCWKO Ovechkin/Wilson Kuznetsov/Carlson 25.00 60.00
QMEGMG McCann/Eberle Gourde/Grubauer 6.00 15.00
QMGDTS Giroux/Tkachuk Stutzle/DeBrincat 10.00 25.00
QMGSKV Keller/Schmaltz Gostisbehere/Vejmelka 8.00 20.00
QMGWLS Gaudreau/Laine Werenski/Sillinger 10.00 25.00
QMHBHH Hughes/Hamilton Holtz/Bratt 15.00 40.00
QMHBPH Hughes/Pettersson Horvat/Boeser 15.00 40.00
QMJFST Josi/Forsberg Tomasino/Saros 10.00 25.00
QMLMRM MacKinnon/Makar/Rantanen Landeskog 25.00 60.00
QMMHTL Huberdeau/Lindholm Toffoli/Markstrom 8.00 20.00
QMMLRG Malkin/Letang Rust/Guentzel 12.00 30.00
QMNNDH Nurse/Draisaitl Hyman/Nugent-Hopkins 20.00 50.00
QMOBKT Kyrou/Thomas O'Reilly/Binnington 10.00 25.00
QMSMTE Eichel/Stone Marchessault/Theodore 10.00 25.00
QMTKJK Kane/Toews/Jones/Kurashev 12.0030.00
QMWEHC Connor/Ehlers Wheeler/Hellebuyck 12.00 30.00
QMZKPF Panarin/Fox Zibanejad/Kreider 12.00 30.00

2022-23 Ultimate Collection Ultimate Quad Materials Patch

*PATCH: .75X TO 2X BASIC
QMBSHR Jason Robertson Tyler Seguin Jamie Benn Miro Heiskanen/25 40.00 100.00
QMSMTE Jack Eichel Mark Stone Jonathan Marchessault Shea Theodore/25 30.00 80.00
QMTKJK Patrick Kane Jonathan Toews Seth Jones Philipp Kurashev/25 60.00 150.00

2022-23 Ultimate Collection Ultimate Signatures

USAC Andrew Copp 5.00 12.00
USAG Adam Graves SP 6.00 15.00
USAK Arthur Kaliyev 8.00 20.00
USAL Anders Lee 6.00 15.00
USBB Brent Burns SP 8.00 20.00
USBS Brandon Saad 6.00 15.00
USCC Charlie Coyle 8.00 20.00
USCP Cal Petersen 5.00 12.00
USCS Cole Sillinger 6.00 15.00
USEK Joel Eriksson Ek 6.00 15.00
USEL Eric Lindros SP 60.00 150.00
USGF Grant Fuhr SP 15.00 40.00
USGV Gabe Vilardi 8.00 20.00
USJE Jordan Eberle 8.00 20.00
USJP Joe Pavelski 10.00 25.00
USKM K'Andre Miller 6.00 15.00
USKP Keith Primeau 6.00 15.00
USMB Michael Bunting 8.00 20.00
USMC Maxime Comtois 6.00 15.00
USMG Morgan Geekie 5.00 12.00
USNE Nikolaj Ehlers 8.00 20.00
USOL Oskar Lindblom 6.00 15.00
USPK Peyton Krebs 6.00 15.00
USRM Rick Middleton 8.00 20.00
USST Shea Theodore 10.00 25.00
USTA Tage Thompson 10.00 25.00
USTI Tim Stutzle 10.00 25.00
USTJ Tristan Jarry 8.00 20.00
USTK Torey Krug 6.00 15.00
USYS Yegor Sharangovich 8.00 20.00

2022-23 Ultimate Collection Ultimate Signatures Rookies

USRAK Andrei Kuzmenko 15.00 40.00
USRAX Arber Xhekaj
USRBB Bobby Brink 8.00 20.00
USRBC Brandt Clarke 15.00 40.00
USRBO Matt Boldy SP 30.00 80.00
USRBS Braden Schneider 12.00 30.00
USRBT Brayden Tracey 6.00 15.00
USRDG Dylan Guenther 20.00 50.00
USRDJ David Jiricek 15.00 40.00
USRDS Dylan Samberg 8.00 20.00
USREK Erik Kallgren 8.00 20.00
USRES Elmer Soderblom 15.00 40.00
USRFK Fredrik Karlstrom 6.00 15.00
USRIR Isaac Ratcliffe 8.00 20.00
USRJB Jonatan Berggren 12.00 30.00
USRJH Jordan Harris 10.00 25.00
USRJL Jakub Lauko 10.00 25.00
USRJM Jack McBain 8.00 20.00
USRJS Juraj Slafkovsky SP 80.00 200.00
USRKG Kaiden Guhle 15.00 40.00
USRKJ Kent Johnson SP 15.00 40.00
USRKK Kaedan Korczak 6.00 15.00
USRKM Kirill Marchenko 20.00 50.00
USRLD Lukas Dostal 15.00 40.00
USRLR Lukas Reichel 15.00 40.00
USRMB Matty Beniers SP 30.00 80.00
USRMK Mark Kastelic 6.00 15.00
USRMR Marco Rossi SP 20.00 50.00
USRNA Nick Abruzzese 8.00 20.00
USRNC Noah Cates 8.00 20.00
USRNO Nikita Okhotiuk 6.00 15.00
USROP Owen Power SP 30.00 80.00
USRPO Samuel Poulin 10.00 25.00
USRSA Jake Sanderson SP 20.00 50.00
USRSW Shane Wright SP 20.00 50.00
USRTB Thomas Bordeleau 8.00 20.00
USRTF Trey Fix-Wolansky 8.00 20.00
USRWJ Wyatt Johnston 40.00 100.00

2022-23 Ultimate Collection Ultimate Tendys Jersey Autographs

*PATCH: .5X TO 1.2X BASIC
UTAAV Andrei Vasilevskiy/25 20.00 50.00
UTACH Carter Hart/99 12.00 30.00
UTAHE Connor Hellebuyck/25 25.00 60.00
UTAIS Ilya Sorokin/99 20.00 50.00
UTAJO Jake Oettinger/25 20.00 50.00
UTAJS Juuse Saros/99 15.00 40.00
UTAPG Philipp Grubauer/99 12.00 30.00
UTAVV Vitek Vanecek/99 12.00 30.00

2022-23 Ultimate Collection Ultimate Tendys Jerseys

*PATCH/20: 2X TO 5X BASIC
UTAV Andrei Vasilevskiy 4.00 10.00
UTCH Connor Hellebuyck 5.00 12.00
UTHA Carter Hart 2.50 6.00
UTIS Ilya Sorokin 4.00 10.00
UTJO Jake Oettinger 4.00 10.00
UTJS Juuse Saros 3.00 8.00
UTPG Philipp Grubauer 2.50 6.00
UTSB Sergei Bobrovsky 4.00 10.00
UTVV Vitek Vanecek 2.50 6.00

2023-24 Ultimate Collection

1 Connor McDavid 6.00 15.00
2 Mason McTavish 1.25 3.00
3 Elias Pettersson 2.00 5.00
4 Matty Beniers 1.50 4.00
5 Rasmus Dahlin 1.50 4.00
6 Mikko Rantanen 3.00 8.00
7 Jonathan Huberdeau 1.50 4.00
8 Cole Caufield 2.50 6.00
9 Alex Ovechkin 5.00 12.00
10 Matt Boldy 2.00 5.00
11 David Pastrnak 3.00 8.00
12 Connor Hellebuyck 2.50 6.00
13 Josh Norris 1.25 3.00
14 Roman Josi 1.25 3.00
15 Brad Marchand 2.50 6.00
16 Nick Suzuki 2.50 6.00
17 Jack Eichel 2.00 5.00
18 Wyatt Johnston 2.50 6.00
19 Andrei Vasilevskiy 2.00 5.00
20 Moritz Seider 1.50 4.00
21 Igor Shesterkin 2.50 6.00
22 Auston Matthews 5.00 12.00
23 Brayden Schenn 1.25 3.00
24 Kyle Connor 2.00 5.00
25 Robert Thomas 1.25 3.00
26 Dylan Larkin 1.50 4.00
27 Dawson Mercer 1.50 4.00
28 Andrei Svechnikov 1.50 4.00
29 Pavel Zacha 1.00 2.50
30 Jake Guentzel 2.00 5.00
31 Mitch Marner 2.00 5.00
32 Brady Tkachuk 2.00 5.00
33 Mark Stone 1.50 4.00
34 Mathew Barzal 1.50 4.00
35 Juuse Saros 1.50 4.00
36 Troy Terry 1.00 2.50
37 Jason Zucker 1.25 3.00
38 Jake Oettinger 2.00 5.00
39 Josh Morrissey 1.50 4.00
40 Ilya Sorokin 2.00 5.00
41 Morgan Frost 1.00 2.50
42 Sebastian Aho 2.00 5.00
43 Brock Nelson 1.25 3.00
44 Pierre-Luc Dubois 1.00 2.50
45 Aleksander Barkov 2.00 5.00
46 Stuart Skinner 1.50 4.00
47 Owen Power 1.25 3.00
48 Leon Draisaitl 4.00 10.00
49 Nikita Kucherov 2.50 6.00
50 Petr Mrazek 1.00 2.50
51 Jack Hughes 3.00 8.00
52 Sam Reinhart 2.50 6.00
53 John Tavares 2.00 5.00
54 Dylan Cozens 1.25 3.00
55 Johnny Gaudreau 2.00 5.00
56 Steven Stamkos 2.50 6.00
57 Quinn Hughes 3.00 8.00
58 Mikael Backlund 1.00 2.50
59 Kirill Kaprizov 4.00 10.00
60 Nick Schmaltz 1.00 2.50
61 Cale Makar 3.00 8.00
62 Artemi Panarin 2.50 6.00
63 Anze Kopitar 2.00 5.00
64 Tage Thompson 1.50 4.00
65 Tim Stutzle 1.50 4.00
66 Brock Boeser 1.50 4.00
67 Nathan MacKinnon 5.00 12.00
68 Tomas Hertl 1.25 3.00
69 Matthew Tkachuk 2.50 6.00
70 Vince Dunn 1.00 2.50
71 Miro Heiskanen 1.50 4.00
72 Boone Jenner 1.25 3.00
73 Sidney Crosby 5.00 12.00
74 Alexis Lafreniere 2.00 5.00
75 Shane Wright 1.50 4.00
76 Bobby Orr 5.00 12.00
77 Shane Doan 1.00 2.50
78 Mario Lemieux 5.00 12.00
79 Tony Amonte 1.00 2.50
80 Nicklas Lidstrom 1.25 3.00
81 Mark Messier 2.50 6.00
82 Rick Nash 1.25 3.00
83 Jaromir Jagr 4.00 10.00
84 Gordie Howe 4.00 10.00
85 Mark Recchi 1.25 3.00
86 Dany Heatley 1.00 2.50
87 Martin Brodeur 3.00 8.00
88 Peter Bondra 1.25 3.00
89 Guy Lafleur 1.50 4.00
90 Maurice Richard 2.50 6.00
91 Mike Modano 2.00 5.00
92 Joe Thornton 2.00 5.00
93 Keith Tkachuk 1.25 3.00
94 Pekka Rinne 1.25 3.00
95 Patrick Roy 3.00 8.00
96 Adam Oates 1.25 3.00
97 Charlie Simmer .75 2.00
98 Mike Gartner 1.50 4.00
99 Wayne Gretzky 8.00 20.00
100 Dominik Hasek 2.00 5.00
101 Connor Bedard AU/99 RC 600.00 1500.00
102 Luke Hughes AU/99 RC 80.00 200.00
103 Connor Zary/299 RC 6.00 15.00
104 Will Cuylle AU/299 RC 12.00 30.00
105 Tyson Foerster AU/299 RC 15.00 40.00
106 Jakob Pelletier/299 RC 4.00 10.00
107 Jiri Kulich AU/299 RC 15.00 40.00
108 Fraser Minten AU/299 RC 15.00 40.00
109 Alex Laferriere AU/299 RC 12.00 30.00
110 Leo Carlsson AU/99 RC 60.00 150.00
111 Sean Farrell AU/299 RC 8.00 20.00
112 Tristan Luneau AU/299 RC 8.00 20.00
113 Adam Fantilli AU/99 RC 80.00 200.00
114 Ryker Evans AU/299 RC 10.00 25.00
115 Owen Beck AU/299 RC 12.00 30.00
116 Devon Levi AU/99 RC 20.00 50.00
117 Linus Karlsson/299 RC 3.00 8.00
118 Matt Murray AU/299 RC 8.00 20.00
119 Mackie Samoskevich/299 RC 5.00 12.00
121 William Dufour AU/299 RC 6.00 15.00
122 Leevi Merilainen AU/299 RC 8.00 20.00
123 Arnaud Durandeau/299 RC 3.00 8.00
124 Matthew Poitras AU/299 RC 15.00 40.00
125 Zach Benson AU/99 RC 12.00 30.00
126 Brock Faber/299 RC 8.00 20.00
127 Aidan McDonough AU/299 RC 6.00 15.00
128 Matthew Knies AU/99 RC 250.00 600.00
129 Ilya Solovyov AU/299 RC 8.00 20.00
130 Justin Sourdif AU/299 RC 8.00 20.00
131 John Beecher AU/299 RC 15.00 40.00
132 Kevin Korchinski AU/299 RC 12.00 30.00
133 Elliot Desnoyers AU/299 RC 8.00 20.00
134 Tyler Kleven/299 RC 3.00 8.00
135 Luke Philp AU/299 RC 8.00 20.00
136 Emil Andrae/299 RC 3.00 8.00
137 Martin Pospisil AU/299 RC 10.00 25.00
138 Samuel Knazko AU/299 RC 8.00 20.00
139 Bobby McMann AU/299 RC 12.00 30.00
139 Bobby McMann/299 RC 5.00 12.00
140 Olle Eriksson Ek/299 RC 3.00 8.00
141 Stanislav Svozil/299 RC 2.50 6.00
142 Arturs Silovs/299 RC 6.00 15.00
143 Simon Nemec AU/99 RC 15.00 40.00
144 Cole Guttman AU/299 RC 8.00 20.00
145 Roby Jarventie/299 RC 3.00 8.00
146 Lukas Rousek AU/299 RC 6.00 15.00
147 Ryan Winterton AU/299 RC 8.00 20.00
148 Marc Del Gaizo/299 RC 3.00 8.00
149 Billy Sweezey AU/299 RC 8.00 20.00
150 Pavel Mintyukov AU/99 RC 12.00 30.00
151 Tyler Angle/299 RC 3.00 8.00
152 Ty Emberson/299 RC 3.00 8.00
153 Lucas Condotta/299 RC 3.00 8.00
154 Simon Edvinsson AU/299 RC 15.00 40.00
155 Akito Hirose AU/299 RC 6.00 15.00
156 Walker Duehr AU/299 RC 6.00 15.00
157 John Ludvig/299 RC 3.00 8.00
158 Michael Kesselring AU/299 RC 8.00 20.00
159 Matthew Coronato AU/299 RC 12.00 30.00
160 Jiri Patera AU/299 RC 12.00 30.00
161 Jackson LaCombe/299 RC 3.00 8.00
162 Hugh McGing AU/299 RC 8.00 20.00
163 Jet Greaves AU/299 RC 12.00 30.00
164 Jonathan Gruden/299 RC 3.00 8.00
165 Tristen Robins AU/299 RC 8.00 20.00
166 Daemon Hunt/299 RC 3.00 8.00
167 Cole McWard AU/299 RC 8.00 20.00
168 Nikita Nesterenko/299 RC 3.00 8.00
169 Marco Kasper AU/299 RC 20.00 50.00
170 Samuel Bolduc/299 RC 3.00 8.00
171 Nikolas Matinpalo/299 RC 3.00 8.00
172 Logan Cooley AU/99 RC 100.00 250.00
173 Joel Teasdale/299 RC 3.00 8.00
175 Ondrej Pavel/299 RC 3.00 8.00
176 Milos Kelemen AU/299 RC 8.00 20.00
177 Wyatt Kaiser AU/299 RC 8.00 20.00
178 Vincent Desharnais/299 RC 4.00 10.00
179 Danil Gushchin AU/299 RC 8.00 20.00
180 Adam Ginning AU/299 RC 8.00 20.00
181 Dustin Wolf AU/299 RC 30.00 80.00
182 Jayden Struble/299 RC 4.00 10.00
183 David Gust AU/299 RC 8.00 20.00
184 Ryan Johnson/299 RC 4.00 10.00
185 Joona Koppanen AU/299 RC 6.00 15.00
186 Isak Rosen AU/299 RC 8.00 20.00
187 Egor Afanasyev/299 RC 3.00 8.00
188 Nick Swaney AU/299 RC 8.00 20.00
189 Hunter McKown/299 RC 3.00 8.00
190 Jake Livingstone AU/299 RC 8.00 20.00
191 Matt Savoie AU/299 RC 15.00 40.00
192 Luke Evangelista AU/299 RC 15.00 40.00
193 Henry Thrun AU/299 RC 8.00 20.00
194 Ridly Greig AU/299 RC 12.00 30.00
195 Vincent Iorio AU/299 RC 8.00 20.00
196 Jaxson Stauber AU/299 RC 8.00 20.00
197 Tye Kartye AU/299 RC 12.00 30.00
198 Raphael Lavoie AU/299 RC 8.00 20.00
199 Matthew Kessel AU/299 RC 6.00 15.00
200 Yaroslav Askarov AU/299 RC 20.00 50.00

2023-24 Ultimate Collection Blue

*BLUE/99: .8X TO 2X BASIC

2023-24 Ultimate Collection Gold

*GOLD/35: 1.2X TO 3X BASIC

2023-24 Ultimate Collection '03-04 Retro Signatures

AFA Adam Fantilli/25 30.00 80.00
AVA Andrei Vasilevskiy/25 15.00 40.00
BTA Brady Tkachuk/49 15.00 40.00
CAA Leo Carlsson/65 30.00 80.00
CBA Connor Bedard/25 600.00 1500.00
CHA Connor Hellebuyck/49 20.00 50.00
COA Matthew Coronato/65 15.00 40.00
DLA Devon Levi/65 25.00 60.00
EBA Evan Bouchard/25 12.00 30.00
FMA Fraser Minten/65 20.00 50.00
JKA Jordan Kyrou/49 10.00 25.00
JTA John Tavares/25 25.00 60.00
JUA Juuse Saros/49 12.00 30.00
KAA Marco Kasper/65 25.00 60.00
KOA Kevin Korchinski/65 15.00 40.00
LCA Logan Cooley/65 30.00 80.00
LDA Leon Draisaitl/25 40.00 100.00
LHA Luke Hughes/65 30.00 80.00
MBA Matt Boldy/49 15.00 40.00
MKA Matthew Knies/65 80.00 200.00
MPA Matthew Poitras/65 20.00 50.00
MSA Matt Savoie/65 20.00 50.00
OBA Owen Beck/65 15.00 40.00
PMA Pavel Mintyukov/65 15.00 40.00
REA Ryker Evans/65 12.00 30.00
RGA Ridly Greig/65 15.00 40.00
SAA Sebastian Aho/49 15.00 40.00
SEA Simon Edvinsson/65 20.00 50.00
SNA Simon Nemec/65 20.00 50.00
TFA Tyson Foerster/65 20.00 50.00
YAA Yaroslav Askarov/65 25.00 60.00
ZBA Zach Benson/65 15.00 40.00

2023-24 Ultimate Collection '03-04 Rookie Retro Material Signatures

03RAF Adam Fantilli/65 40.00 100.00
03RCA Leo Carlsson/99 30.00 80.00
03RCB Connor Bedard/65 300.00 800.00
03RDL Devon Levi/99 25.00 60.00
03RLC Logan Cooley/99 30.00 80.00
03RMK Matthew Knies/99 40.00 100.00
03RMP Matthew Poitras/99 20.00 50.00
03ROB Owen Beck/99 5.00 12.00
03RPM Pavel Mintyukov/99 15.00 40.00
03RWC Will Cuylle/99 15.00 40.00
03RYA Yaroslav Askarov/99 25.00 60.00
03RZB Zach Benson/99 15.00 40.00

2023-24 Ultimate Collection '03-04 Rookie Retro Material Signatures Gold Patch

*PATCH: .6X TO 1.5X BASIC
03RCB Connor Bedard/25 1500.00 4000.00

2023-24 Ultimate Collection Autographs

*GOLD: 1X TO 2.5X BASIC
2 Mason McTavish 6.00 15.00
3 Elias Pettersson SP 10.00 25.00
7 Jonathan Huberdeau 8.00 20.00
10 Matt Boldy 10.00 25.00
12 Connor Hellebuyck 12.00 30.00
16 Nick Suzuki 20.00 50.00
18 Wyatt Johnston 12.00 30.00
19 Andrei Vasilevskiy SP 10.00 25.00
23 Brayden Schenn 6.00 15.00
25 Robert Thomas 6.00 15.00
27 Dawson Mercer 8.00 20.00
28 Andrei Svechnikov 8.00 20.00
29 Pavel Zacha 5.00 12.00
32 Brady Tkachuk 10.00 25.00
33 Mark Stone 8.00 20.00
35 Juuse Saros 8.00 20.00
37 Jason Zucker 6.00 15.00
40 Ilya Sorokin 10.00 25.00
42 Sebastian Aho 10.00 25.00
43 Brock Nelson 6.00 15.00
45 Aleksander Barkov 10.00 25.00
47 Owen Power SP 6.00 15.00
49 Nikita Kucherov SP 12.00 30.00
50 Petr Mrazek 5.00 12.00
52 Sam Reinhart 12.00 30.00
53 John Tavares SP 12.00 30.00
58 Mikael Backlund 5.00 12.00
60 Nick Schmaltz 5.00 12.00
61 Cale Makar SP 15.00 40.00
66 Brock Boeser 8.00 20.00
68 Tomas Hertl 6.00 15.00
70 Vince Dunn 5.00 12.00
71 Miro Heiskanen 8.00 20.00
72 Boone Jenner 6.00 15.00
74 Alexis Lafreniere 10.00 25.00
75 Shane Wright 8.00 20.00
77 Shane Doan 5.00 12.00
79 Tony Amonte 5.00 12.00
80 Nicklas Lidstrom 6.00 15.00
81 Mark Messier SP 12.00 30.00
82 Rick Nash 6.00 15.00
85 Mark Recchi 6.00 15.00
86 Dany Heatley 5.00 12.00
87 Martin Brodeur SP 80.00 200.00
88 Peter Bondra 6.00 15.00
91 Mike Modano SP 20.00 50.00
92 Joe Thornton SP 10.00 25.00
93 Keith Tkachuk 6.00 15.00
95 Patrick Roy SP 50.00 125.00
97 Charlie Simmer 4.00 10.00
98 Mike Gartner 8.00 20.00
100 Dominik Hasek SP 50.00 125.00

2023-24 Ultimate Collection Crease Collection Jersey Autographs

*PATCH/35: .6X TO 1.5X BASIC
CCCH Connor Hellebuyck/49 20.00 50.00
CCDH Dominik Hasek/25 15.00 40.00
CCFP Felix Potvin/25 50.00 125.00
CCHL Henrik Lundqvist/25 30.00 80.00
CCJO Jake Oettinger/49 15.00 40.00
CCJS Juuse Saros/49 12.00 30.00
CCMF Marc-Andre Fleury/25 50.00 125.00
CCPG Philipp Grubauer/99 10.00 25.00
CCSO Ilya Sorokin/49 15.00 40.00

2023-24 Ultimate Collection Debut Threads Autographs

ADTAF Adam Fantilli/49 100.00 250.00
ADTAG Adam Ginning/99 12.00 30.00
ADTAH Akito Hirose/99 10.00 25.00
ADTAL Alex Laferriere/99 20.00 50.00
ADTAM Aidan McDonough/99 10.00 25.00
ADTBM Bobby McMann/99 20.00 50.00
ADTCA Leo Carlsson/49 40.00 100.00
ADTCB Connor Bedard/25 600.00 1500.00
ADTCG Cole Guttman/99 12.00 30.00
ADTCM Cole McWard/99 12.00 30.00
ADTDG Danil Gushchin/99 12.00 30.00
ADTDL Devon Levi/49 30.00 80.00
ADTDW Dustin Wolf/99 40.00 100.00
ADTED Elliot Desnoyers/99 12.00 30.00
ADTFM Fraser Minten/99 25.00 60.00
ADTHM Hugh McGing/99 12.00 30.00
ADTIR Isak Rosen/99 12.00 30.00
ADTJB John Beecher/99 25.00 60.00
ADTJK Jiri Kulich/99 25.00 60.00
ADTJL Jake Livingstone/99 12.00 30.00
ADTKA Marco Kasper/99 30.00 80.00
ADTKE Matthew Kessel/99 10.00 25.00
ADTKK Kevin Korchinski/99 20.00 50.00
ADTKM Milos Kelemen/99 12.00 30.00
ADTKO Joona Koppanen/99 10.00 25.00
ADTLC Logan Cooley/49 125.00 300.00
ADTLH Luke Hughes/25 100.00 250.00
ADTLM Leevi Merilainen/99 12.00 30.00
ADTLP Luke Philp/99 12.00 30.00
ADTLR Lukas Rousek/99 10.00 25.00
ADTMC Matthew Coronato/99 20.00 50.00
ADTMI Michael Kesselring/99 12.00 30.00
ADTMM Matt Murray/99 12.00 30.00
ADTMP Martin Pospisil/99 15.00 40.00
ADTMS Mackie Samoskevich/99 20.00 50.00
ADTNS Nick Swaney/99 12.00 30.00
ADTPA Jiri Patera/99 20.00 50.00
ADTPM Pavel Mintyukov/49 20.00 50.00
ADTPO Matthew Poitras/99 25.00 60.00
ADTRE Ryker Evans/99 15.00 40.00
ADTRG Ridly Greig/99 20.00 50.00
ADTRL Raphael Lavoie/99 12.00 30.00
ADTSF Sean Farrell/99 12.00 30.00
ADTSN Simon Nemec/99 25.00 60.00
ADTSO Justin Sourdif/99 12.00 30.00
ADTTF Tyson Foerster/99 25.00 60.00
ADTTK Tye Kartye/99 20.00 50.00
ADTTL Tristan Luneau/99 12.00 30.00
ADTTR Tristen Robins/99 12.00 30.00
ADTVI Vincent Iorio/99 12.00 30.00
ADTWC Will Cuylle/99 20.00 50.00
ADTWD Walker Duehr/99 10.00 25.00
ADTWK Wyatt Kaiser/99 12.00 30.00
ADTYA Yaroslav Askarov/49 30.00 80.00
ADTZB Zach Benson/49 20.00 50.00

2023-24 Ultimate Collection Jerseys

101 Connor Bedard/349 25.00 60.00
102 Luke Hughes/349 8.00 20.00
103 Connor Zary/599 5.00 12.00
104 Will Cuylle/599 4.00 10.00
105 Tyson Foerster/599 5.00 12.00
106 Jakob Pelletier/599 3.00 8.00
107 Jiri Kulich/599 5.00 12.00
108 Fraser Minten/599 5.00 12.00
109 Alex Laferriere/599 4.00 10.00
110 Leo Carlsson/349 8.00 20.00
111 Sean Farrell/599 2.50 6.00
112 Tristan Luneau/599 2.50 6.00
113 Adam Fantilli/349 8.00 20.00
114 Ryker Evans/599 3.00 8.00
115 Owen Beck/599 4.00 10.00
116 Devon Levi/349 6.00 15.00
118 Matt Murray/599 2.50 6.00
119 Mackie Samoskevich/599 4.00 10.00
121 William Dufour/599 2.00 5.00
122 Leevi Merilainen/599 2.50 6.00
123 Arnaud Durandeau/599 2.50 6.00
124 Matthew Poitras/599 5.00 12.00
125 Zach Benson/349 4.00 10.00
126 Brock Faber/599 6.00 15.00
127 Aidan McDonough/599 2.00 5.00
128 Matthew Knies/349 10.00 25.00
130 Justin Sourdif/599 2.50 6.00
131 John Beecher/599 5.00 12.00
132 Kevin Korchinski/599 4.00 10.00
133 Elliot Desnoyers/599 2.50 6.00
134 Tyler Kleven/599 2.50 6.00
135 Luke Philp/599 2.50 6.00
137 Martin Pospisil/599 3.00 8.00
138 Samuel Knazko/599 2.50 6.00
139 Bobby McMann/599 4.00 10.00
140 Olle Eriksson Ek/599 2.50 6.00
141 Stanislav Svozil/599 2.00 5.00
143 Simon Nemec/349 5.00 12.00
144 Cole Guttman/599 2.50 6.00
146 Lukas Rousek/599 2.00 5.00
149 Billy Sweezey/599 2.50 6.00
150 Pavel Mintyukov/349 4.00 10.00
154 Simon Edvinsson/599 5.00 12.00
155 Akito Hirose/599 2.00 5.00
156 Walker Duehr/599 2.00 5.00
158 Michael Kesselring/599 2.50 6.00
159 Matthew Coronato/599 4.00 10.00
160 Jiri Patera/599 4.00 10.00
161 Jackson LaCombe/599 2.50 6.00
162 Hugh McGing/599 2.50 6.00
163 Jet Greaves/599 4.00 10.00
164 Jonathan Gruden/599 2.50 6.00
165 Tristen Robins/599 2.50 6.00
167 Cole McWard/599 2.50 6.00
168 Nikita Nesterenko/599 2.50 6.00
169 Marco Kasper/599 6.00 15.00
170 Samuel Bolduc/599 2.50 6.00
172 Logan Cooley/349 8.00 20.00
176 Milos Kelemen/599 2.50 6.00
177 Wyatt Kaiser/599 2.50 6.00
178 Vincent Desharnais/599 3.00 8.00
179 Danil Gushchin/599 2.50 6.00
180 Adam Ginning/599 2.50 6.00
181 Dustin Wolf/599 8.00 20.00
182 Jayden Struble/599 3.00 8.00
183 David Gust/599 2.50 6.00
185 Joona Koppanen/599 2.00 5.00
186 Isak Rosen/599 2.50 6.00
187 Egor Afanasyev/599 2.50 6.00
188 Nick Swaney/599 2.50 6.00
189 Hunter McKown/599 2.50 6.00
190 Jake Livingstone/599 2.50 6.00
191 Matt Savoie/599 5.00 12.00
192 Luke Evangelista/599 5.00 12.00
193 Henry Thrun/599 2.50 6.00
194 Ridly Greig/599 4.00 10.00
195 Vincent Iorio/599 2.50 6.00
196 Jaxson Stauber/599 2.50 6.00
197 Tye Kartye/599 4.00 10.00
198 Raphael Lavoie/599 2.50 6.00
199 Matthew Kessel/599 2.00 5.00
200 Yaroslav Askarov/599 6.00 15.00

2023-24 Ultimate Collection Jumbo Jerseys

1 Connor McDavid/149 15.00 40.00
2 Mason McTavish/149 3.00 8.00
3 Elias Pettersson/149 5.00 12.00
4 Matty Beniers/149 4.00 10.00
5 Rasmus Dahlin/149 4.00 10.00
6 Mikko Rantanen/149 8.00 20.00
7 Jonathan Huberdeau/149 4.00 10.00
8 Cole Caufield/149 6.00 15.00
9 Alex Ovechkin/149 12.00 30.00
10 Matt Boldy/149 5.00 12.00
11 David Pastrnak/149 8.00 20.00
12 Connor Hellebuyck/149 6.00 15.00
13 Josh Norris/149 3.00 8.00
14 Roman Josi/149 3.00 8.00
15 Brad Marchand/149 6.00 15.00
16 Nick Suzuki/149 6.00 15.00
17 Jack Eichel/149 5.00 12.00
18 Wyatt Johnston/149 6.00 15.00
19 Andrei Vasilevskiy/149 5.00 12.00
20 Moritz Seider/149 4.00 10.00
21 Igor Shesterkin/149 6.00 15.00
22 Auston Matthews/149 12.00 30.00
23 Brayden Schenn/149 3.00 8.00
24 Kyle Connor/149 5.00 12.00

25 Robert Thomas/149 3.00 8.00
26 Dylan Larkin/149 4.00 10.00
27 Dawson Mercer/149 4.00 10.00
28 Andrei Svechnikov/149 4.00 10.00
30 Jake Guentzel/149 5.00 12.00
31 Mitch Marner/149 5.00 12.00
32 Brady Tkachuk/149 5.00 12.00
33 Mark Stone/149 4.00 10.00
34 Mathew Barzal/149 4.00 10.00
35 Juuse Saros/149 4.00 10.00
36 Troy Terry/149 2.50 6.00
37 Jason Zucker/149 3.00 8.00
38 Jake Oettinger/149 5.00 12.00
39 Josh Morrissey/149 4.00 10.00
40 Ilya Sorokin/149 5.00 12.00
41 Morgan Frost/149 2.50 6.00
42 Sebastian Aho/149 5.00 12.00
43 Brock Nelson/149 3.00 8.00
44 Pierre-Luc Dubois/149 2.50 6.00
45 Aleksander Barkov/149 5.00 12.00
46 Stuart Skinner/149 4.00 10.00
47 Owen Power/149 3.00 8.00
48 Leon Draisaitl/149 10.00 25.00
49 Nikita Kucherov/149 6.00 15.00
50 Petr Mrazek/149 2.50 6.00
51 Jack Hughes/149 8.00 20.00
52 Sam Reinhart/149 6.00 15.00
53 John Tavares/149 5.00 12.00
54 Dylan Cozens/149 3.00 8.00
55 Johnny Gaudreau/149 5.00 12.00
56 Steven Stamkos/149 6.00 15.00
57 Quinn Hughes/149 8.00 20.00
58 Mikael Backlund/149 2.50 6.00
59 Kirill Kaprizov/149 10.00 25.00
60 Nick Schmaltz/149 2.50 6.00
61 Cale Makar/149 8.00 20.00
62 Artemi Panarin/149 6.00 15.00
63 Anze Kopitar/149 5.00 12.00
64 Tage Thompson/149 4.00 10.00
65 Tim Stutzle/149 4.00 10.00
66 Brock Boeser/149 4.00 10.00
67 Nathan MacKinnon/149 12.00 30.00
68 Tomas Hertl/149 3.00 8.00
69 Matthew Tkachuk/149 6.00 15.00
70 Vince Dunn/149 2.50 6.00
71 Miro Heiskanen/149 4.00 10.00
72 Boone Jenner/149 3.00 8.00
73 Sidney Crosby/149 12.00 30.00
74 Alexis Lafreniere/149 5.00 12.00
75 Shane Wright/149 4.00 10.00

2023-24 Ultimate Collection La Collection Ultime Jerseys

*PATCH/35: 1X TO 2.5X BASIC
LCUAL Alexis Lafreniere 6.00 15.00
LCUJM Jonathan Marchessault 5.00 12.00
LCUKL Kris Letang 5.00 12.00
LCULR Luc Robitaille SP 4.00 10.00
LCUMF Marc-Andre Fleury 8.00 20.00
LCUPB Patrice Bergeron SP 5.00 12.00
LCUPR Patrick Roy SP 10.00 25.00
LCURB Ray Bourque SP 6.00 15.00

2023-24 Ultimate Collection Patch Autographs

102 Luke Hughes/49 60.00 150.00
104 Will Cuylle/99 20.00 50.00
105 Tyson Foerster/99 50.00 125.00
108 Fraser Minten/99 25.00 60.00
109 Alex Laferriere/99 20.00 50.00
110 Leo Carlsson/49 80.00 200.00
111 Sean Farrell/99 12.00 30.00
112 Tristan Luneau/99 12.00 30.00
113 Adam Fantilli/49 150.00 400.00
114 Ryker Evans/99 15.00 40.00
116 Devon Levi/49 30.00 80.00
118 Matt Murray/99 12.00 30.00
119 Mackie Samoskevich/99 20.00 50.00
121 William Dufour/99 10.00 25.00
122 Leevi Merilainen/99 12.00 30.00
124 Matthew Poitras/99 25.00 60.00
125 Zach Benson/49 20.00 50.00
127 Aidan McDonough/99 10.00 25.00
128 Matthew Knies/49 125.00 300.00
130 Justin Sourdif/99 12.00 30.00
131 John Beecher/99 25.00 60.00
132 Kevin Korchinski/99 20.00 50.00
133 Elliot Desnoyers/99 12.00 30.00
135 Luke Philp/99 12.00 30.00
137 Martin Pospisil/99 15.00 40.00
138 Samuel Knazko/99 12.00 30.00
139 Bobby McMann/99 20.00 50.00
143 Simon Nemec/49 30.00 80.00
144 Cole Guttman/99 12.00 30.00
146 Lukas Rousek/99 10.00 25.00
149 Billy Sweezey/99 12.00 30.00
150 Pavel Mintyukov/49 20.00 50.00
154 Simon Edvinsson/99 25.00 60.00
155 Akito Hirose/99 10.00 25.00
156 Walker Duehr/99 10.00 25.00
158 Michael Kesselring/99 12.00 30.00
159 Matthew Coronato/99 20.00 50.00
160 Jiri Patera/99 20.00 50.00
162 Hugh McGing/99 12.00 30.00
163 Jet Greaves/99 60.00 150.00
165 Tristen Robins/99 12.00 30.00
167 Cole McWard/99 12.00 30.00
169 Marco Kasper/99 30.00 80.00
176 Milos Kelemen/99 12.00 30.00
177 Wyatt Kaiser/99 12.00 30.00
179 Danil Gushchin/99 12.00 30.00
180 Adam Ginning/99 12.00 30.00
183 David Gust/99 12.00 30.00
185 Joona Koppanen/99 10.00 25.00
186 Isak Rosen/99 12.00 30.00
188 Nick Swaney/99 12.00 30.00
190 Jake Livingstone/99 12.00 30.00
192 Luke Evangelista/99 25.00 60.00
193 Henry Thrun/99 12.00 30.00
194 Ridly Greig/99 20.00 50.00
195 Vincent Iorio/99 12.00 30.00
196 Jaxson Stauber/99 12.00 30.00
197 Tye Kartye/99 20.00 50.00
198 Raphael Lavoie/99 12.00 30.00
199 Matthew Kessel/99 10.00 25.00
200 Yaroslav Askarov/99 60.00 150.00

2023-24 Ultimate Collection Pro Threads Patch Autographs

PTAR Alexander Romanov/99 10.00 25.00
PTAT Alex Tuch/49 12.00 30.00
PTBR Bryan Rust/99 12.00 30.00
PTBS Brayden Schenn/99 12.00 30.00
PTCA John Carlson/49 12.00 30.00
PTCP Colton Parayko/99 10.00 25.00
PTCV Carter Verhaeghe/49 12.00 30.00
PTDM Dawson Mercer/99 15.00 40.00
PTDT Devon Toews/99 10.00 25.00
PTFE Mario Ferraro/99 8.00 20.00
PTJD Jamie Drysdale/99 10.00 25.00
PTJH Jonathan Huberdeau/49 15.00 40.00
PTJP JJ Peterka/99 12.00 30.00
PTJS Jake Sanderson/99 15.00 40.00
PTKH Kevin Hayes/99 10.00 25.00
PTMB Mikael Backlund/99 10.00 25.00
PTMH Miro Heiskanen/49 15.00 40.00
PTMM Matias Maccelli/99 10.00 25.00
PTMR Marco Rossi/99 15.00 40.00
PTMT Matthew Tkachuk/49 25.00 60.00
PTNH Nico Hischier/49 15.00 40.00
PTSG Samuel Girard/99 8.00 20.00
PTSP Jared Spurgeon/99 12.00 30.00
PTSW Shane Wright/99 15.00 40.00
PTTW Tom Wilson/49 12.00 30.00
PTVD Vince Dunn/99 10.00 25.00
PTWJ Wyatt Johnston/49 25.00 60.00
PTWK William Karlsson/99 15.00 40.00

2023-24 Ultimate Collection Rookie Accents Autographs

RAAF Adam Fantilli/35 40.00 100.00
RAAH Akito Hirose/99 6.00 15.00
RAAM Aidan McDonough/99 6.00 15.00
RABM Bobby McMann/99 12.00 30.00
RACB Connor Bedard/35 300.00 800.00
RACO Logan Cooley/35 60.00 150.00
RADG Danil Gushchin/99 8.00 20.00
RADL Devon Levi/35 20.00 50.00
RADW Dustin Wolf/35 40.00 100.00
RAGU David Gust/99 8.00 20.00
RAHM Hugh McGing/99 8.00 20.00
RAHT Henry Thrun/99 8.00 20.00
RAIR Isak Rosen/65 8.00 20.00
RAJB John Beecher/99 15.00 40.00
RAJK Joona Koppanen/99 6.00 15.00
RAJL Jake Livingstone/99 8.00 20.00
RAJS Jaxson Stauber/99 8.00 20.00
RAKK Kevin Korchinski/35 12.00 30.00
RAKN Matthew Knies/35 80.00 200.00
RALC Leo Carlsson/35 40.00 100.00
RALH Luke Hughes/35 25.00 60.00
RAMA Matthew Coronato/65 12.00 30.00
RAMK Marco Kasper/35 20.00 50.00
RAMM Matt Murray/99 8.00 20.00
RAMP Martin Pospisil/99 10.00 25.00
RAMS Mackie Samoskevich/99 12.00 30.00
RAOB Owen Beck/65 12.00 30.00
RAPA Jiri Patera/99 12.00 30.00
RAPM Pavel Mintyukov/35 12.00 30.00
RAPO Matthew Poitras/65 15.00 40.00
RARE Ryker Evans/65 10.00 25.00
RARG Ridly Greig/65 12.00 30.00
RARL Raphael Lavoie/65 8.00 20.00
RASE Simon Edvinsson/35 15.00 40.00
RASN Simon Nemec/35 15.00 40.00
RATF Tyson Foerster/65 15.00 40.00
RAWC Will Cuylle/65 12.00 30.00
RAWD Walker Duehr/99 6.00 15.00
RAYA Yaroslav Askarov/35 80.00 200.00
RAZB Zach Benson/35 12.00 30.00

2023-24 Ultimate Collection Rookie Signature Premium Materials

RSMAL Alex Laferriere/65 20.00 50.00
RSMDL Devon Levi/35 30.00 80.00
RSMDW Dustin Wolf/65 100.00 250.00
RSMFM Fraser Minten/65 25.00 60.00
RSMKK Kevin Korchinski/35 20.00 50.00
RSMMC Matthew Coronato/35 20.00 50.00
RSMMK Marco Kasper/35 30.00 80.00
RSMMP Matthew Poitras/35 30.00 80.00
RSMMS Matt Savoie/35 12.00 30.00
RSMOB Owen Beck/35 20.00 50.00
RSMPA Jiri Patera/65 20.00 50.00
RSMPM Pavel Mintyukov/35 25.00 60.00
RSMRE Ryker Evans/65 15.00 40.00
RSMRG Ridly Greig/35 20.00 50.00
RSMSA Mackie Samoskevich/65 50.00 125.00
RSMSE Simon Edvinsson/35 25.00 60.00
RSMWC Will Cuylle/65 20.00 50.00
RSMYA Yaroslav Askarov/35 30.00 80.00

2023-24 Ultimate Collection Signature Masterpieces

USMAF Adam Fantilli SP 150.00 400.00
USMBM Brandon Montour 12.00 30.00
USMCS Chandler Stephenson 8.00 20.00
USMDH Dominik Hasek SP 80.00 200.00
USMLT Logan Thompson 12.00 30.00
USMMB Martin Brodeur SP 150.00 400.00
USMMR Marco Rossi 12.00 30.00
USMMS Matt Savoie 20.00 50.00
USMNE Nikolaj Ehlers 12.00 30.00
USMSW Shane Wright 12.00 30.00
USMTH Tomas Hertl 10.00 25.00
USMTJ Tristan Jarry 10.00 25.00
USMTS Travis Sanheim 12.00 30.00
USMVT Vladimir Tarasenko 12.00 30.00

2023-24 Ultimate Collection Signature Materials

UMSAL Anton Lundell/99 10.00 25.00
UMSBA Mikael Backlund/99 8.00 20.00
UMSBB Bowen Byram/99 12.00 30.00
UMSBT Brady Tkachuk/49 15.00 40.00
UMSDG Dylan Guenther/99 12.00 30.00
UMSEP Elias Pettersson/25 25.00 60.00
UMSKM Kirill Marchenko/99 12.00 30.00
UMSLD Leon Draisaitl/25 80.00 200.00
UMSMA Mason McTavish/49 10.00 25.00
UMSMI K'Andre Miller/99 8.00 20.00
UMSMT Matthew Tkachuk/49 30.00 80.00
UMSNS Nick Schmaltz/99 8.00 20.00
UMSPK Peyton Krebs/99 8.00 20.00
UMSRT Robert Thomas/99 10.00 25.00
UMSSA Jake Sanderson/99 12.00 30.00
UMSSR Sam Reinhart/99 20.00 50.00
UMSWK William Karlsson/99 12.00 30.00
UMSYS Yegor Sharangovich/99 10.00 25.00

2023-24 Ultimate Collection Signature Materials Gold Patch

*PATCH/35: .6X TO 1.5X BASIC
UMSAL Anton Lundell/35 25.00 60.00

2023-24 Ultimate Collection Ulti-Mates Jerseys

*PATCH/49: 1X TO 2.5X BASIC
UTMBS A.Svechnikov/B.Burns 4.00 10.00
UTMBT P.Buchnevich/R.Thomas 3.00 8.00
UTMCK E.Kuznetsov/J.Carlson 4.00 10.00
UTMCS J.Slafkovsky/C.Caufield 6.00 15.00
UTMDB Q.Byfield/P.Dubois 4.00 10.00
UTMDM M.McTavish/J.Drysdale 3.00 8.00
UTMDP R.Dahlin/O.Power 4.00 10.00
UTMGS T.Stutzle/C.Giroux 4.00 10.00
UTMHB B.Horvat/M.Barzal 4.00 10.00
UTMHE T.Hertl/W.Eklund 4.00 10.00
UTMHM N.Hischier/D.Mercer 4.00 10.00
UTMJK P.Kurashev/S.Jones 3.00 8.00
UTMKB W.Karlsson/I.Barbashev 4.00 10.00
UTMKC L.Cooley/C.Keller 10.00 25.00
UTMKF T.Konecny/J.Farabee 3.00 8.00
UTMKL E.Lindholm/N.Kadri 4.00 10.00
UTMLD D.Larkin/A.DeBrincat 4.00 10.00
UTMLK E.Karlsson/K.Letang 4.00 10.00
UTMMM A.Matthews/M.Marner 12.00 30.00
UTMMP E.Pettersson/J.Miller 5.00 12.00
UTMNH R.Nugent-Hopkins/Z.Hyman 5.00 12.00
UTMOF R.O'Reilly/F.Forsberg 5.00 12.00
UTMPH R.Hintz/J.Pavelski 4.00 10.00
UTMPM D.Pastrnak/C.McAvoy 8.00 20.00
UTMRB M.Boldy/M.Rossi 5.00 12.00
UTMRV S.Reinhart/C.Verhaeghe 6.00 15.00
UTMSJ C.Sillinger/K.Johnson 3.00 8.00
UTMSM J.Morrissey/M.Scheifele 5.00 12.00
UTMSP S.Stamkos/B.Point 6.00 15.00
UTMTB B.Byram/D.Toews 4.00 10.00
UTMWB M.Beniers/S.Wright 4.00 10.00
UTMZP M.Zibanejad/A.Panarin 6.00 15.00

2023-24 Ultimate Collection Ultimate Access Patch Autographs

UAAS Andrei Svechnikov/99 20.00 50.00
UACA Leo Carlsson/49 50.00 125.00
UACM Casey Mittelstadt/99 15.00 40.00
UADM Dawson Mercer/99 20.00 50.00
UAIS Ilya Sorokin/25 25.00 60.00
UAKK Kirill Kaprizov/25 50.00 125.00
UALC Logan Cooley/49 50.00 125.00
UASW Shane Wright/49 30.00 80.00

2023-24 Ultimate Collection Ultimate Displays Materials Manufactured Plaque

*PATCH: 2X TO 5X BASIC
UDAD Alex DeBrincat/65 2.00 5.00
UDAM Auston Matthews/25 6.00 15.00
UDAP Artemi Panarin/65 3.00 8.00
UDBB Brent Burns/125 1.50 4.00
UDBO Brock Boeser/125 2.00 5.00
UDCC Cole Caufield/65 3.00 8.00
UDCK Chris Kreider/125 2.00 5.00
UDCL Clayton Keller/125 2.00 5.00
UDCM Charlie McAvoy/125 2.00 5.00
UDDP David Pastrnak/25 4.00 10.00
UDEM Evgeni Malkin/65 3.00 8.00
UDFF Filip Forsberg/125 2.50 6.00
UDJM Jared McCann/125 1.25 3.00
UDJR Jason Robertson/65 2.50 6.00
UDJS Jaden Schwartz/125 1.25 3.00
UDKC Kyle Connor/125 2.50 6.00
UDKK Kirill Kaprizov/65 5.00 12.00
UDKU Nikita Kucherov/65 3.00 8.00
UDMA Mark Scheifele/125 2.50 6.00
UDMC Connor McDavid/25 25.00 60.00
UDMS Moritz Seider/65 2.00 5.00
UDNK Nazem Kadri/125 2.00 5.00
UDNM Nathan MacKinnon/25 6.00 15.00
UDRD Rasmus Dahlin/65 2.00 5.00
UDRT Robert Thomas/125 1.50 4.00
UDSC Sidney Crosby/25 6.00 15.00
UDSJ Seth Jones/125 1.50 4.00
UDSS Steven Stamkos/125 3.00 8.00
UDTB Tyler Bertuzzi/125 1.25 3.00
UDTK Travis Konecny/125 1.50 4.00
UDTO T.J. Oshie/125 1.50 4.00
UDTZ Trevor Zegras/65 1.50 4.00
UDWE William Nylander/125 3.00 8.00
UDWK William Karlsson/125 2.00 5.00
UDZH Zach Hyman/125 2.50 6.00

2023-24 Ultimate Collection Ultimate Emblems Autographs

*GOLD: .6X TO 1.5X BASIC
UEAF Adam Fantilli SP 20.00 50.00
UEAH Akito Hirose 5.00 12.00
UEAI Aidan McDonough 5.00 12.00
UEAL Alex Laferriere 10.00 25.00
UEAO Alex Ovechkin SP 200.00 500.00
UEBB Bobby Brink 6.00 15.00
UEBJ Boone Jenner 6.00 15.00
UEBM Brandon Montour 8.00 20.00
UEBR Bryan Rust 6.00 15.00
UEBS Brayden Schenn 6.00 15.00
UECA Cale Makar SP 50.00 125.00
UECB Connor Bedard SP 300.00 800.00
UECE Cole McWard 6.00 15.00
UECM Connor McDavid SP 250.00 600.00
UECO Logan Cooley SP 30.00 80.00
UECS Chandler Stephenson 5.00 12.00
UEDL Devon Levi SP 15.00 40.00
UEDT Devon Toews 5.00 12.00
UEDW Dustin Wolf SP 30.00 80.00
UEEB Evan Bouchard 8.00 20.00
UEFM Fraser Minten 12.00 30.00
UEFV Frank Vatrano 5.00 12.00
UEHT Henry Thrun 6.00 15.00
UEIR Isak Rosen 6.00 15.00
UEJA Josh Anderson 5.00 12.00
UEJB John Beecher 12.00 30.00
UEJI Jiri Patera 10.00 25.00
UEJP Joe Pavelski SP 8.00 20.00
UEJT J.T. Compher 4.00 10.00
UEJV Joe Veleno 5.00 12.00
UEJW Joseph Woll 8.00 20.00
UEKC Kyle Connor 10.00 25.00
UEKE Matthew Kessel 5.00 12.00
UEKM Kirill Marchenko 8.00 20.00
UEKO Kevin Korchinski SP 10.00 25.00
UELC Leo Carlsson SP 20.00 50.00
UELE Luke Evangelista SP 12.00 30.00
UELM Leevi Merilainen 6.00 15.00
UELR Lukas Reichel 6.00 15.00
UELT Logan Thompson 8.00 20.00
UELU Anton Lundell 6.00 15.00
UEMC Matthew Coronato 10.00 25.00
UEMI Casey Mittelstadt 6.00 15.00
UEMK Marco Kasper 15.00 40.00
UEML Michael Kesselring 6.00 15.00
UEMP Martin Pospisil 8.00 20.00
UEMR Marco Rossi 8.00 20.00
UENS Nick Schmaltz 5.00 12.00
UEOB Owen Beck 10.00 25.00
UEPG Philipp Grubauer 6.00 15.00
UEPM Pavel Mintyukov 10.00 25.00
UEPO Matthew Poitras 12.00 30.00
UERC Ross Colton 5.00 12.00
UERE Ryker Evans 8.00 20.00
UERG Ridly Greig 10.00 25.00
UERH Roope Hintz 8.00 20.00
UERL Raphael Lavoie 6.00 15.00
UESC William Karlsson 8.00 20.00
UESE Simon Edvinsson 12.00 30.00
UESO Justin Sourdif 6.00 15.00
UETF Tyson Foerster 12.00 30.00
UETK Tye Kartye 10.00 25.00
UETL Tristan Luneau 6.00 15.00
UETM Trevor Moore 4.00 10.00
UETS Travis Sanheim 4.00 10.00
UETW Tom Wilson 6.00 15.00
UEVD Vince Dunn 5.00 12.00
UEWC Will Cuylle 10.00 25.00
UEWD Walker Duehr 5.00 12.00
UEYA Yaroslav Askarov SP 15.00 40.00
UEYS Yegor Sharangovich 6.00 15.00
UEZB Zach Benson 10.00 25.00

2023-24 Ultimate Collection Ultimate Introductions

UI1 Connor Bedard 30.00 80.00
UI2 Adam Fantilli 6.00 15.00
UI3 Logan Cooley 6.00 15.00
UI4 Brock Faber 5.00 12.00
UI5 Matthew Knies 8.00 20.00
UI6 Samuel Bolduc 2.00 5.00
UI7 Ryker Evans 2.50 6.00
UI8 Simon Edvinsson 4.00 10.00
UI9 Devon Levi 5.00 12.00
UI10 Akito Hirose 1.50 4.00
UI11 Marco Kasper 5.00 12.00
UI12 Walker Duehr 1.50 4.00
UI13 Tyson Foerster 4.00 10.00
UI14 Aidan McDonough 1.50 4.00
UI15 Pavel Mintyukov 3.00 8.00
UI16 Lukas Rousek 1.50 4.00
UI17 Will Cuylle 3.00 8.00
UI18 Nikita Nesterenko 2.00 5.00
UI19 Tristan Luneau 2.00 5.00
UI20 Zach Benson 3.00 8.00
UI21 Ryan Winterton 2.00 5.00
UI22 Cole McWard 2.00 5.00
UI23 Justin Sourdif 2.00 5.00
UI24 Owen Beck 3.00 8.00
UI25 Matthew Poitras 4.00 10.00
UI26 Billy Sweezey 2.00 5.00
UI27 Marc Del Gaizo 2.00 5.00
UI28 Tristen Robins 2.00 5.00
UI29 Jiri Patera 3.00 8.00
UI30 Connor Zary 4.00 10.00
UI31 Michael Kesselring 2.00 5.00
UI32 Luke Evangelista 4.00 10.00
UI33 Matthew Kessel 1.50 4.00
UI34 Linus Karlsson 2.00 5.00
UI35 Henry Thrun 2.00 5.00
UI36 Matthew Coronato 3.00 8.00
UI37 Yaroslav Askarov 5.00 12.00
UI38 Ridly Greig 3.00 8.00
UI39 Jakob Pelletier 2.50 6.00
UI40 Vincent Iorio 2.00 5.00
UI41 Jackson LaCombe 2.00 5.00
UI42 Hugh McGing 2.00 5.00
UI43 Matt Murray 2.00 5.00
UI44 Jaxson Stauber 2.00 5.00
UI45 Martin Pospisil 2.50 6.00
UI46 Tye Kartye 3.00 8.00
UI47 Raphael Lavoie 2.00 5.00
UI48 Mackie Samoskevich 3.00 8.00
UI49 Arturs Silovs 4.00 10.00
UI50 Simon Nemec 4.00 10.00
UI51 Adam Ginning 2.00 5.00
UI52 Dustin Wolf 6.00 15.00
UI53 Alex Laferriere 3.00 8.00
UI54 Jayden Struble 2.50 6.00
UI55 Emil Andrae 2.00 5.00
UI56 David Gust 2.00 5.00
UI57 Stanislav Svozil 1.50 4.00
UI58 Sean Farrell 2.00 5.00
UI59 Ryan Johnson 2.50 6.00
UI60 Bobby McMann 3.00 8.00
UI61 Olle Eriksson Ek 2.00 5.00
UI62 Joona Koppanen 1.50 4.00
UI63 William Dufour 1.50 4.00
UI64 Isak Rosen 2.00 5.00
UI65 Luke Philp 2.00 5.00
UI66 Egor Afanasyev 2.00 5.00
UI67 Elliot Desnoyers 2.00 5.00
UI68 Samuel Knazko 2.00 5.00
UI69 Nick Swaney 2.00 5.00
UI70 Dmitri Voronkov 2.50 6.00
UI71 Danil Gushchin 2.00 5.00
UI72 Cole Guttman 2.00 5.00
UI73 John Beecher 4.00 10.00
UI74 Roby Jarventie 2.00 5.00
UI75 Hunter McKown 2.00 5.00
UI76 Jiri Kulich 4.00 10.00
UI77 Jake Livingstone 2.00 5.00
UI78 Tyler Kleven 2.00 5.00
UI79 Jet Greaves 3.00 8.00
UI80 Vincent Desharnais 2.50 6.00
UI81 Arnaud Durandeau 2.00 5.00
UI82 Jonathan Gruden 2.00 5.00
UI83 Wyatt Kaiser 2.00 5.00
UI84 Leevi Merilainen 2.00 5.00
UI85 Milos Kelemen 2.00 5.00
UI86 Fraser Minten 4.00 10.00
UI87 Kevin Korchinski 3.00 8.00
UI88 Leo Carlsson 6.00 15.00
UI89 Matt Savoie 4.00 10.00
UI90 Luke Hughes 6.00 15.00
UI91 Leo Carlsson SHOW 6.00 15.00
UI92 Matthew Knies SHOW 8.00 20.00
UI93 Luke Hughes SHOW 6.00 15.00
UI94 Adam Fantilli SHOW 6.00 15.00
UI95 Pavel Mintyukov SHOW 3.00 8.00
UI96 Logan Cooley SHOW 6.00 15.00
UI97 Devon Levi SHOW 5.00 12.00
UI98 Connor Bedard SHOW 30.00 80.00
UI99 Connor Zary SHOW 4.00 10.00
UI100 Zach Benson SHOW 3.00 8.00

2023-24 Ultimate Collection Ultimate Introductions Gold

*GOLD/49: .8X TO 2X BASIC
UI1 Connor Bedard 80.00 200.00
UI98 Connor Bedard SHOW 80.00 200.00

2023-24 Ultimate Collection Ultimate Introductions Purple

*PURPLE/25: 1X TO 2.5X BASIC
UI5 Matthew Knies 50.00 125.00
UI92 Matthew Knies SHOW 50.00 125.00

2023-24 Ultimate Collection Ultimate Introductions Autographs

UI2 Adam Fantilli SP 60.00 150.00
UI3 Logan Cooley SP 30.00 80.00
UI7 Ryker Evans 8.00 20.00
UI8 Simon Edvinsson 12.00 30.00
UI9 Devon Levi SP 15.00 40.00
UI10 Akito Hirose 5.00 12.00
UI11 Marco Kasper 15.00 40.00
UI12 Walker Duehr 5.00 12.00
UI13 Tyson Foerster 12.00 30.00
UI14 Aidan McDonough 5.00 12.00
UI15 Pavel Mintyukov SP 10.00 25.00
UI16 Lukas Rousek 5.00 12.00
UI17 Will Cuylle SP 10.00 25.00
UI19 Tristan Luneau 6.00 15.00
UI20 Zach Benson 10.00 25.00
UI21 Ryan Winterton 6.00 15.00
UI23 Justin Sourdif 6.00 15.00
UI24 Owen Beck 10.00 25.00
UI25 Matthew Poitras 12.00 30.00
UI26 Billy Sweezey 6.00 15.00
UI28 Tristen Robins 6.00 15.00
UI29 Jiri Patera 10.00 25.00
UI31 Michael Kesselring 6.00 15.00
UI32 Luke Evangelista 12.00 30.00
UI33 Matthew Kessel 5.00 12.00
UI35 Henry Thrun 6.00 15.00
UI36 Matthew Coronato 10.00 25.00
UI37 Yaroslav Askarov SP 15.00 40.00
UI38 Ridly Greig 10.00 25.00
UI40 Vincent Iorio 6.00 15.00
UI42 Hugh McGing 6.00 15.00
UI43 Matt Murray 6.00 15.00
UI44 Jaxson Stauber 6.00 15.00
UI45 Martin Pospisil 8.00 20.00
UI46 Tye Kartye 10.00 25.00
UI47 Raphael Lavoie 6.00 15.00
UI51 Adam Ginning 6.00 15.00
UI52 Dustin Wolf 40.00 100.00
UI53 Alex Laferriere 10.00 25.00
UI56 David Gust 6.00 15.00
UI58 Sean Farrell SP 6.00 15.00
UI60 Bobby McMann 10.00 25.00
UI62 Joona Koppanen 5.00 12.00
UI63 William Dufour 5.00 12.00
UI64 Isak Rosen 6.00 15.00
UI65 Luke Philp 6.00 15.00
UI67 Elliot Desnoyers 6.00 15.00
UI68 Samuel Knazko 6.00 15.00
UI71 Danil Gushchin 6.00 15.00
UI72 Cole Guttman 6.00 15.00
UI73 John Beecher 12.00 30.00
UI78 Tyler Kleven 6.00 15.00
UI83 Wyatt Kaiser 6.00 15.00
UI84 Leevi Merilainen 6.00 15.00
UI85 Milos Kelemen 6.00 15.00
UI86 Fraser Minten 12.00 30.00
UI87 Kevin Korchinski 10.00 25.00
UI88 Leo Carlsson SP 20.00 50.00
UI90 Luke Hughes SP 25.00 60.00
UI91 Leo Carlsson SHOW 20.00 50.00
UI93 Luke Hughes SP SHOW 25.00 60.00
UI94 Adam Fantilli SP SHOW 60.00 150.00
UI95 Pavel Mintyukov SHOW 10.00 25.00
UI96 Logan Cooley SHOW 30.00 80.00
UI97 Devon Levi SHOW 15.00 40.00
UI100 Zach Benson SHOW 10.00 25.00

2023-24 Ultimate Collection Ultimate Introductions Autographs Gold

*GOLD: .6X TO 1.5X BASIC
UI3 Logan Cooley/25 60.00 150.00
UI9 Devon Levi/25 30.00 80.00
UI48 Mackie Samoskevich/50 25.00 60.00
UI97 Devon Levi SHOW/25 30.00 80.00

2023-24 Ultimate Collection Ultimate Planks

PLAG Adam Graves 5.00 12.00
PLAM Al MacInnis 8.00 20.00
PLAO Alex Ovechkin 25.00 60.00
PLBT Bryan Trottier 6.00 15.00
PLCC Chris Chelios 6.00 15.00
PLCM Connor McDavid 30.00 80.00
PLDA Dave Andreychuk 6.00 15.00
PLDP David Pastrnak 15.00 40.00
PLEM Evgeni Malkin 12.00 30.00
PLHZ Henrik Zetterberg 8.00 20.00
PLJG John Gibson 6.00 15.00
PLJM Josh Morrissey 8.00 20.00
PLJN Joe Nieuwendyk 5.00 12.00
PLJT John Tavares 10.00 25.00
PLKT Keith Tkachuk 6.00 15.00
PLMB Martin Brodeur 20.00 50.00
PLMM Mike Modano 10.00 25.00
PLMR Mark Recchi 6.00 15.00
PLMS Martin St. Louis 6.00 15.00
PLMV Mike Vernon 5.00 12.00
PLOB Oliver Bjorkstrand 5.00 12.00
PLPC Paul Coffey 6.00 15.00
PLRB Rob Blake 6.00 15.00
PLST Mark Stone 8.00 20.00
PLSW Shane Wright 8.00 20.00
PLTL Trevor Linden 6.00 15.00
PLTS Tim Stutzle 8.00 20.00

2023-24 Ultimate Collection Ultimate Planks Legacy

LSPLBE Jean Beliveau/49 25.00 60.00
LSPLFM Frank Mahovlich/49 25.00 60.00
LSPLJB Johnny Bucyk/49 25.00 60.00
LSPLMR Maurice Richard/25 60.00 150.00
LSPLPE Phil Esposito/49 40.00 100.00
LSPLSM Stan Mikita/49 25.00 60.00

2023-24 Ultimate Collection Ultimate Planks Legends

LPLDH Dominik Hasek/25 50.00 125.00
LPLEL Eric Lindros/25 30.00 80.00
LPLGH Gordie Howe/10
LPLLR Luc Robitaille/25 30.00 80.00
LPLMM Mark Messier/25 60.00 150.00
LPLPE Phil Esposito/25 50.00 125.00
LPLPR Patrick Roy/15
LPLSY Steve Yzerman/15
LPLWG Wayne Gretzky/10

2023-24 Ultimate Collection Ultimate Quad Materials

*PATCH: .8X TO 2X BASIC
QMBLUE Thomas/Kyrou Buchnevich/Neighbours 6.00 15.00
QMBOST Pastrnak/Marchand Ullmark/Swayman 15.00 40.00
QMBUFF Thompson/Dahlin Tuch/Skinner 8.00 20.00
QMCALG Lindholm/Huberdeau Kadri/Markstrom 8.00 20.00
QMCAPS Ovechkin/Kuznetsov Oshie/Kuemper 25.00 60.00
QMCBBJ Gaudreau/Laine Johnson/Sillinger 10.00 25.00
QMDEVL Hughes/Hughes Hischier/Mercer 20.00 50.00
QMDUCK Zegras/McTavish Strome/Terry 6.00 15.00
QMFLOR Barkov/Reinhart Ekblad/Bobrovsky 12.00 30.00
QMGOLD Eichel/Stone Marchessault/Stephenson 10.00 25.00
QMHURR Aho/Svechnikov Necas/Burns 10.00 25.00
QMISLE Barzal/Sorokin/Horvat/Lee 10.00 25.00
QMJETS Connor/Perfetti Scheifele/Hellebuyck 12.00 30.00
QMKING Kopitar/Byfield/Kempe/Fiala 10.0025.00
QMKRAK Beniers/McCann Schwartz/Gourde 8.00 20.00
QMMAPL Matthews/Marner Tavares/Nylander 25.00 60.00
QMNASH O'Reilly/Forsberg Josi/Saros 10.00 25.00
QMNJDV Meier/Holtz/Bratt/Hamilton 6.00 15.00
QMOILR Nugent-Hopkins Kane/Hyman/Skinner 10.00 25.00
QMPENG Malkin/Guentzel Karlsson/Letang 12.00 30.00
QMPHIL Brink/Couturier Farabee/Konecny 6.00 15.00
QMRANG Panarin/Shesterkin Lafreniere/Kreider 12.00 30.00
QMROOK Bedard/Cooley Fantilli/Carlsson 40.00 100.00
QMSENS Stutzle/Tkachuk Giroux/Sanderson 10.00 25.00
QMSTAR Robertson/Hintz Heiskanen/Johnston 12.00 30.00
QMTAMP Kucherov/Hedman Stamkos/Vasilevskiy 12.00 30.00
QMVANC Pettersson/Hughes Boeser/Miller 15.00 40.00
QMWILD Kaprizov/Zuccarello Eriksson Ek/Fleury 20.00 50.00
QMWING Larkin/DeBrincat Raymond/Seider 10.00 25.00
QMYOTE Keller/Schmaltz Maccelli/Guenther 8.00 20.00

2023-24 Ultimate Collection Ultimate Rookie Signatures

URSAF Adam Fantilli SP 25.00 60.00
URSAG Adam Ginning 8.00 20.00
URSAL Alex Laferriere 12.00 30.00
URSBS Billy Sweezey 8.00 20.00
URSCM Cole McWard 8.00 20.00
URSCO Logan Cooley SP 25.00 60.00
URSDL Devon Levi SP 20.00 50.00
URSDW Dustin Wolf SP 25.00 60.00
URSIR Isak Rosen 8.00 20.00
URSKE Matthew Kessel 6.00 15.00
URSKK Kevin Korchinski SP 12.00 30.00
URSKN Matthew Knies SP 80.00 200.00
URSLC Leo Carlsson SP 25.00 60.00
URSLH Luke Hughes SP 30.00 80.00
URSLM Leevi Merilainen 8.00 20.00
URSLR Lukas Rousek 6.00 15.00
URSMC Matthew Coronato 12.00 30.00
URSMI Michael Kesselring 8.00 20.00
URSMK Marco Kasper 20.00 50.00
URSMP Matthew Poitras 15.00 40.00
URSMS Matt Savoie SP 15.00 40.00
URSNS Nick Swaney 8.00 20.00
URSOB Owen Beck 12.00 30.00
URSPM Pavel Mintyukov 12.00 30.00
URSRE Ryker Evans 10.00 25.00
URSRG Ridly Greig 12.00 30.00
URSRL Raphael Lavoie 8.00 20.00
URSSE Simon Edvinsson 15.00 40.00
URSSK Samuel Knazko 8.00 20.00
URSSN Simon Nemec SP 15.00 40.00
URSSO Justin Sourdif 8.00 20.00
URSTF Tyson Foerster 15.00 40.00
URSTK Tye Kartye 12.00 30.00
URSTR Tristen Robins 8.00 20.00
URSWC Will Cuylle SP 12.00 30.00
URSWD William Dufour 6.00 15.00
URSYA Yaroslav Askarov SP 20.00 50.00
URSZB Zach Benson 12.00 30.00

2023-24 Ultimate Collection Ultimate Signatures

USAM Al MacInnis SP 12.00 30.00
USBB Brock Boeser SP 10.00 25.00
USBJ Boone Jenner 8.00 20.00
USBN Brock Nelson 8.00 20.00
USBT Bryan Trottier SP 8.00 20.00
USBU Johnny Bucyk SP 12.00 30.00
USCM Casey Mittelstadt 8.00 20.00
USCO J.T. Compher 5.00 12.00
USCP Cole Perfetti 8.00 20.00
USCS Cole Sillinger 6.00 15.00
USCV Carter Verhaeghe 8.00 20.00
USDG Doug Gilmour SP 25.00 60.00
USDM Dawson Mercer 10.00 25.00
USDP Denis Potvin SP 12.00 30.00
USDT Devon Toews 6.00 15.00
USEP Elias Pettersson SP 12.00 30.00
USGF Grant Fuhr SP 12.00 30.00
USJC John Carlson 8.00 20.00
USJE Jordan Eberle 8.00 20.00
USJK Joonas Korpisalo 8.00 20.00
USJM Jacob Middleton 5.00 12.00
USJO Jonathan Marchessault 10.00 25.00
USJP JJ Peterka 8.00 20.00
USJS Jake Sanderson 10.00 25.00
USLD Lukas Dostal 8.00 20.00
USMA Auston Matthews SP 80.00 200.00
USMR Mark Recchi SP 8.00 20.00
USOP Owen Power SP 8.00 20.00
USPA Joe Pavelski 10.00 25.00
USPM Petr Mrazek 6.00 15.00
USPZ Pavel Zacha 6.00 15.00
USRH Ron Hextall SP 12.00 30.00
USSD Shane Doan SP 6.00 15.00
USSG Samuel Girard 5.00 12.00
USSP Jared Spurgeon 8.00 20.00
USSW Shane Wright 10.00 25.00
USTH Tomas Hertl 8.00 20.00
USVD Vince Dunn 6.00 15.00
USWE William Eklund 10.00 25.00

1991-92 Ultimate Original Six

COMPLETE SET (100) 2.50 6.00
*FRENCH: .4X TO 1X BASIC CARDS
1 Montreal Canadiens .02 .10
2 New York Rangers .01 .05
3 Toronto Maple Leafs .01 .05
4 Boston Bruins .01 .05
5 Chicago Blackhawks .01 .05
6 Detroit Red Wings .01 .05
7 Ralph Backstrom .01 .05
8 Butch Bouchard .05 .15
9 John Ferguson .02 .10
10 Boom Boom Geoffrion .25 .60
11 Phil Goyette .01 .05
12 Doug Harvey .15 .40
13 Don Marshall .02 .10
14 Henri Richard .20 .50
15 Dollard St.Laurent .01 .05
16 Jean-Guy Talbot .02 .10
17 Gump Worsley .15 .40
18 Andy Bathgate .07 .20
19 Lou Fontinato .01 .05
20 Ed Giacomin .07 .20
21 Vic Hadfield .02 .10
22 Camille Henry .01 .05
23 Harry Howell .05 .15
24 Orland Kurtenbach .02 .10
25 Jim Neilson .01 .05
26 Bob Nevin .01 .05
27 Dean Prentice .02 .10
28 Leo Reise Jr. .01 .05
29 George Sullivan .01 .05
30 Bob Baun .08 .20
31 Gus Bodnar .01 .05
32 Johnny Bower .07 .20
33 Bob Davidson .01 .05
34 Ron Ellis .02 .10
35 Billy Harris .01 .05
36 Larry Hillman .01 .05
37 Tim Horton .30 .75
38 Red Kelly .10 .30
39 Dave Keon .07 .20
40 Frank Mahovlich .20 .50
41 Eddie Shack .07 .20
42 Tod Sloan .01 .05
43 Sid Smith .02 .10
44 Allan Stanley .07 .20
45 Gaye Stewart .01 .05
46 Harry Watson .05 .15
47 Wayne Carleton .01 .05
48 Fern Flaman .02 .10
49 Ken Hodge UER .02 .10
50 Leo Labine .01 .05
51 Harry Lumley .07 .20
52 John McKenzie .02 .10
53 Doug Mohns .02 .10
54 Fred Stanfield .01 .05
55 Jerry Toppazzini .01 .05
56 Ed Westfall .02 .10
57 Bobby Hull .40 1.00
58 Ed Litzenberger .01 .05
59 Gilles Marotte .01 .05
60 Ab McDonald .01 .05
61 Bill Mosienko .05 .15
62 Jim Pappin .01 .05
63 Pierre Pilote .05 .15
64 Elmer Vasko .01 .05
65 Johnny Wilson .01 .05
66 Sid Abel .07 .20
67 Gary Bergman .01 .05
68 Alex Delvecchio .10 .30
69 Bill Gadsby .07 .20
70 Ted Lindsay .15 .40
71 Marcel Pronovost .05 .15
72 Norm Ullman .07 .20
73 Boom Boom Geoffrion .25 .60
74 Andy Bathgate .07 .20
75 Allan Stanley .07 .20
76 Fern Flaman .05 .15

77 Bobby Hull .40 1.00
78 Norm Ullman .07 .20
79 Red Kelly .10 .30
80 Johnny Bower .10 .30
81 Henri Richard .20 .50
82 Bobby Hull .40 1.00
83 Boom Boom Geoffrion .25 .60
84 Tim Horton .30 .75
85 Bill Friday REF .01 .05
86 Bruce Hood REF .01 .05
87 Ron Wicks REF .01 .05
88 Bobby Hull
Electric Slap Shot .20 .50
89 Bobby Hull
The Point Race .20 .50
90 Bobby Hull
1960-61 Stanley Cup .20 .50
91 Bobby Hull
The Curse of Muldoon
is lifted .20 .50
92 Bobby Hull
Million Dollar Man .20 .50
93 Bobby Baun
Baun's Heroics .01 .05
94 Ted Lindsay
Lindsay's comeback .05 .15
95 Henri Richard
Richard's 99-year record .05 .15
96 Bobby Hull
Hull breaks 50 goal
barrier .20 .50
97 Tim Horton Tribute .08 .25
98 Keith McCreary .01 .05
99 Checklist 1 .01 .05
100 Checklist 2 .01 .05
NNO Bobby Hull Hologram 4.00 10.00

1991-92 Ultimate Original Six Box Bottoms

COMPLETE SET (4) .60 1.50
1 Ed Giacomin .20 .50
2 Bobby Hull
The Golden Jet .40 1.00
3 Marcel Pronovost .08 .25
4 Eddie Shack .08 .25

1999-00 Ultimate Victory

COMPLETE SET (120) 60.00 125.00
COMP.SET w/o SP's (90) 10.00 20.00
1 Paul Kariya .25 .60
2 Teemu Selanne .25 .60
3 Jason Marshall .08 .25
4 David Harlock .08 .25
5 Ray Ferraro .08 .25
6 Kelly Buchberger .08 .25
7 Sergei Samsonov .20 .50
8 Ray Bourque .40 1.00
9 Darren Van Impe .08 .25
10 Dominik Hasek .50 1.25
11 Miroslav Satan .20 .50
12 Geoff Sanderson .20 .50
13 Valeri Bure .08 .25
14 Cale Hulse .08 .25
15 Cory Stillman .08 .25
16 Ron Francis .20 .50
17 Andrei Kovalenko .08 .25
18 Sami Kapanen .08 .25
19 Tony Amonte .20 .50
20 Steve Sullivan .08 .25
21 Doug Gilmour .20 .50
22 Milan Hejduk .25 .60
23 Joe Sakic .50 1.25
24 Patrick Roy 1.25 3.00
25 Chris Drury .20 .50
26 Peter Forsberg .60 1.50
27 Mike Modano .40 1.00
28 Brett Hull .30 .75
29 Ed Belfour .25 .60
30 Blake Sloan .08 .25
31 Steve Yzerman 1.25 3.00
32 Chris Osgood .20 .50
33 Brendan Shanahan .25 .60
34 Larry Murphy .20 .50
35 Doug Weight .20 .50
36 Christian Laflamme .08 .25
37 Alexander Selivanov .08 .25
38 Pavel Bure .25 .60
39 Jaroslav Spacek .08 .25
40 Viktor Kozlov .20 .50
41 Luc Robitaille .20 .50
42 Zigmund Palffy .20 .50
43 Rob Blake .20 .50
44 Saku Koivu .25 .60
45 Patrick Poulin .08 .25
46 Brian Savage .08 .25
47 David Legwand .20 .50
48 Sergei Krivokrasov .08 .25
49 Rob Valicevic RC .08 .25
50 Martin Brodeur .60 1.50
51 Scott Stevens .20 .50
52 Krzysztof Oliwa .08 .25
53 Jamie Heward .08 .25
54 Mariusz Czerkawski .08 .25
55 Kenny Jonsson .08 .25
56 Mike Richter .25 .60
57 Theo Fleury .08 .25
58 Tim Taylor .08 .25
59 Brian Leetch .25 .60
60 Andreas Dackell .08 .25
61 Marian Hossa .25 .60
62 Ron Tugnutt .20 .50
63 Craig Berube .08 .25
64 Eric Lindros .25 .60
65 John LeClair .25 .60
66 Dallas Drake .08 .25
67 Keith Tkachuk .25 .60
68 Jeremy Roenick .30 .75
69 Jaromir Jagr .40 1.00
70 Martin Straka .08 .25
71 Rob Brown .08 .25
72 Marcus Ragnarsson .08 .25
73 Steve Shields .20 .50
74 Owen Nolan .20 .50
75 Jeff Friesen .08 .25
76 Pavol Demitra .20 .50
77 Roman Turek .20 .50
78 Mike Eastwood .08 .25
79 Vincent Lecavalier .25 .60
80 Dan Cloutier .20 .50
81 Stan Drulia .08 .25
82 Mats Sundin .25 .60
83 Igor Korolev .08 .25
84 Curtis Joseph .25 .60
85 Mark Messier .25 .60
86 Harry York .20 .50
87 Peter Schaefer .08 .25
88 Olaf Kolzig .20 .50
89 Steve Konowalchuk .08 .25
90 Peter Bondra .25 .60
91 Patrik Stefan SP RC 1.25 3.00
92 Brian Campbell SP RC 1.25 3.00
93 Mikko Eloranta SP RC 1.25 3.00
94 Oleg Saprykin SP RC 1.25 3.00
95 Kyle Calder SP RC 1.50 4.00
96 Jon Sim SP RC 1.25 3.00
97 Marc Rodgers SP RC 1.25 3.00
98 Paul Comrie SP RC 1.25 3.00
99 Ivan Novoseltsev SP RC 1.25 3.00
100 Jason Blake SP RC 1.25 3.00
101 Brian Rafalski SP RC 2.00 5.00
102 Jorgen Jonsson SP RC 1.25 3.00
103 Nikolai Antropov SP RC 2.00 5.00
104 Steve Kariya SP RC 1.50 4.00
105 Glen Metropolit SP RC 1.25 3.00
106 Jochen Hecht SP RC 2.00 5.00
107 Sheldon Keefe SP RC 1.25 3.00
108 Branislav Mezei SP RC 1.25 3.00
109 Pavel Brendl SP RC 1.25 3.00
110 Milan Kraft SP RC 1.25 3.00
111 Wayne Gretzky 1.50 4.00
112 Wayne Gretzky 1.50 4.00
113 Wayne Gretzky 1.50 4.00
114 Wayne Gretzky 1.50 4.00
115 Wayne Gretzky 1.50 4.00
116 Wayne Gretzky 1.50 4.00
117 Wayne Gretzky 1.50 4.00
118 Wayne Gretzky 1.50 4.00
119 Wayne Gretzky 1.50 4.00
120 Wayne Gretzky 1.50 4.00

1999-00 Ultimate Victory Foil Parallel

*VETS 1-90/111-120: 1.2X TO 3X BASIC CARDS
*ROOKIES 91-110: .6X TO 1.5X BASIC SP RC

1999-00 Ultimate Victory Parallel 100

*VETS 1-90/111-120: 5X TO 12X BASIC CARDS
*ROOKIES 91-110: 2X TO 5X BASIC SP RC

1999-00 Ultimate Victory Frozen Fury

COMPLETE SET (10) 12.00 25.00
FF1 Eric Lindros 1.25 3.00
FF2 Paul Kariya .75 2.00
FF3 Pavel Bure 1.00 2.50
FF4 Steve Kariya .40 1.00
FF5 Mike Modano 1.25 3.00
FF6 Patrik Stefan .40 1.00
FF7 Martin Brodeur 2.00 5.00
FF8 Jaromir Jagr 1.25 3.00
FF9 Joe Sakic 1.50 4.00
FF10 Steve Yzerman 4.00 10.00

1999-00 Ultimate Victory Legendary Fabrics

BOS Bobby Orr/4 AU
LFBO Bobby Orr/99 100.00 250.00
LFWG Wayne Gretzky/99 100.00 250.00
UFS W.Gretzky/B.Orr/10 AU
UF W.Gretzky/B.Orr/99 250.00 600.00

1999-00 Ultimate Victory Net Work

COMPLETE SET (10) 12.00 25.00
NW1 Dominik Hasek 1.50 4.00
NW2 Patrick Roy 5.00 12.00
NW3 Chris Osgood .75 2.00
NW4 Ed Belfour 1.00 2.50
NW5 Mike Richter 1.00 2.50
NW6 Roman Turek .75 2.00
NW7 Steve Shields .75 2.00
NW8 Curtis Joseph .75 2.00
NW9 Guy Hebert .75 2.00
NW10 Martin Brodeur 2.00 5.00

1999-00 Ultimate Victory Smokin Guns

COMPLETE SET (12) 8.00 15.00
SG1 Jaromir Jagr .75 2.00
SG2 Paul Kariya .50 1.25
SG3 Sergei Fedorov 1.00 2.50
SG4 Steve Kariya .30 .75
SG5 Peter Forsberg 1.25 3.00
SG6 Marian Hossa .50 1.25
SG7 Theo Fleury .50 1.25
SG8 Patrik Stefan .75 2.00
SG9 Pavel Bure .60 1.50
SG10 Eric Lindros .75 2.00
SG11 Brett Hull .60 1.50
SG12 Teemu Selanne .50 1.25

1999-00 Ultimate Victory Stature

COMPLETE SET (12) 6.00 12.00
S1 Paul Kariya .30 .75
S2 Joe Sakic .60 1.50
S3 Peter Forsberg .75 2.00
S4 Mike Modano .50 1.25
S5 Brendan Shanahan .50 1.25
S6 Pavel Bure .40 1.00
S7 Martin Brodeur .75 2.00
S8 Theo Fleury .30 .75
S9 Eric Lindros .50 1.25
S10 Keith Tkachuk .30 .75
S11 Jaromir Jagr .50 1.25
S12 Ray Bourque .50 1.25

1999-00 Ultimate Victory The Victors

COMPLETE SET (8) 10.00 20.00
V1 Mark Messier .75 2.00
V2 Brett Hull .75 2.00
V3 Steve Yzerman 3.00 8.00
V4 Jaromir Jagr 1.00 2.50
V5 Patrick Roy 3.00 8.00
V6 Martin Brodeur 1.50 4.00
V7 Peter Forsberg 1.50 4.00
V8 Theo Fleury .60 1.50

1999-00 Ultimate Victory UV Extra

COMPLETE SET (8) 12.00 25.00
UV1 Jaromir Jagr 1.00 2.50
UV2 Patrick Roy 3.00 8.00
UV3 Pavel Bure .60 1.50
UV4 Bobby Orr 4.00 10.00
UV5 Paul Kariya 1.25 3.00
UV6 Peter Forsberg 1.50 4.00
UV7 Steve Yzerman 3.00 8.00
UV8 Eric Lindros 1.00 2.50

1992-93 Ultra

1 Brent Ashton .10 .25
2 Ray Bourque .25 .60
3 Steve Heinze .10 .25
4 Joe Juneau .10 .25
5 Stephen Leach .10 .25
6 Andy Moog .15 .40
7 Cam Neely .15 .40
8 Adam Oates .15 .40
9 Dave Poulin .10 .25
10 Vladimir Ruzicka .10 .25
11 Glen Wesley .10 .25
12 Dave Andreychuk .15 .40
13 Keith Carney RC .30 .75
14 Tom Draper .10 .25
15 Dale Hawerchuk .20 .50
16 Pat LaFontaine .15 .40
17 Brad May .10 .25
18 Alexander Mogilny .12 .30
19 Mike Ramsey .10 .25
20 Ken Sutton .10 .25
21 Theo Fleury .25 .60
22 Gary Leeman .10 .25
23 Al MacInnis .20 .50
24 Sergei Makarov .10 .25
25 Joe Nieuwendyk .12 .30
26 Joel Otto .10 .25
27 Paul Ranheim .10 .25
28 Robert Reichel .10 .25
29 Gary Roberts .10 .25
30 Gary Suter .10 .25
31 Mike Vernon .12 .30
32 Ed Belfour .15 .40
33 Rob Brown .10 .25
34 Chris Chelios .15 .40
35 Michel Goulet .12 .30
36 Dirk Graham .10 .25
37 Mike Hudson .10 .25
38 Igor Kravchuk .10 .25
39 Steve Larmer .10 .25
40 Dean McAmmond RC .10 .25
41 Jeremy Roenick .25 .60
42 Steve Smith .10 .25
43 Brent Sutter .10 .25
44 Shawn Burr .10 .25
45 Jimmy Carson .10 .25
46 Tim Cheveldae .10 .25
47 Dino Ciccarelli .12 .30
48 Sergei Fedorov .25 .60
49 Vladimir Konstantinov .15 .40
50 Slava Kozlov .12 .30
51 Nicklas Lidstrom .12 .30
52 Brad McCrimmon .10 .25
53 Bob Probert .15 .40
54 Paul Ysebaert .10 .25
55 Steve Yzerman .40 1.00
56 Josef Beranek .10 .25
57 Shayne Corson .12 .30
58 Brian Glynn .10 .25
59 Petr Klima .10 .25
60 Kevin Lowe .12 .30
61 Norm Maciver .10 .25
62 Dave Manson .10 .25
63 Joe Murphy .10 .25
64 Bernie Nicholls .12 .30
65 Bill Ranford .12 .30
66 Craig Simpson .10 .25
67 Esa Tikkanen .10 .25
68 Sean Burke .12 .30
69 Adam Burt .10 .25
70 Andrew Cassels .10 .25
71 Murray Craven .10 .25
72 John Cullen .10 .25
73 Randy Cunneyworth .10 .25
74 Tim Kerr .10 .25
75 Geoff Sanderson .12 .30
76 Eric Weinrich .10 .25
77 Zarley Zalapski .10 .25
78 Peter Ahola .10 .25
79 Rob Blake .12 .30
80 Paul Coffey .15 .40
81 Mike Donnelly .10 .25
82 Tony Granato .10 .25
83 Wayne Gretzky 1.00 2.50
84 Kelly Hrudey .12 .30
85 Jari Kurri .15 .40
86 Corey Millen .10 .25
87 Luc Robitaille .15 .40
88 Tomas Sandstrom .12 .30
89 Neal Broten .12 .30
90 Jon Casey .10 .25
91 Russ Courtnall .10 .25
92 Ulf Dahlen .10 .25
93 Todd Elik .10 .25
94 Dave Gagner .12 .30
95 Jim Johnson .12 .30
96 Mike Modano UER .40 1.00
97 Bobby Smith .12 .30
98 Mark Tinordi .10 .25
99 Darcy Wakaluk .12 .30
100 Brian Bellows .12 .30
101 Benoit Brunet .10 .25
102 Guy Carbonneau .12 .30
103 Vincent Damphousse .12 .30
104 Eric Desjardins .12 .30
105 Gilbert Dionne .10 .25
106 Mike Keane .10 .25
107 Kirk Muller .10 .25
108 Patrick Roy .40 1.00
109 Denis Savard .15 .40
110 Mathieu Schneider .10 .25
111 Brian Skrudland .12 .30
112 Tom Chorske .12 .30
113 Zdeno Ciger .10 .25
114 Claude Lemieux .10 .25
115 John MacLean .12 .30
116 Scott Niedermayer .15 .40
117 Stephane Richer .12 .30
118 Peter Stastny .12 .30
119 Scott Stevens .15 .40
120 Chris Terreri .12 .30
121 Kevin Todd .10 .25
122 Valeri Zelepukin .10 .25
123 Ray Ferraro .10 .25
124 Mark Fitzpatrick .12 .30
125 Patrick Flatley .12 .30
126 Glenn Healy .12 .30
127 Benoit Hogue .10 .25
128 Derek King .10 .25
129 Uwe Krupp .10 .25
130 Scott Lachance .10 .25
131 Steve Thomas .12 .30
132 Pierre Turgeon .12 .30
133 Tony Amonte .12 .30
134 Paul Broten .10 .25
135 Mike Gartner .20 .50
136 Adam Graves .10 .25
137 Alexei Kovalev .12 .30
138 Brian Leetch .12 .30
139 Mark Messier .30 .75
140 Sergei Nemchinov .10 .25
141 James Patrick .10 .25
142 Mike Richter .15 .40
143 Darren Turcotte .10 .25
144 John Vanbiesbrouck .15 .40
145 Dominic Lavoie .12 .30
146 Lonnie Loach RC .10 .25
147 Andrew McBain .12 .30
148 Darren Rumble .10 .25
149 Sylvain Turgeon .10 .25
150 Peter Sidorkiewicz .10 .25
151 Brian Benning .10 .25
152 Rod Brind'Amour .10 .25
153 Viacheslav Butsayev RC .10 .25
154 Kevin Dineen .10 .25
155 Pelle Eklund .12 .30
156 Garry Galley .10 .25
157 Eric Lindros .25 .60
158 Mark Recchi .20 .50
159 Dominic Roussel .12 .30
160 Tommy Soderstrom RC .12 .30
161 Dimitri Yushkevich RC .10 .25
162 Tom Barrasso .12 .30
163 Ron Francis .20 .50
164 Jaromir Jagr .30 .75
165 Mario Lemieux .60 1.50
166 Joe Mullen .12 .30
167 Larry Murphy .12 .30
168 Jim Paek .12 .30
169 Kjell Samuelsson .12 .30
170 Ulf Samuelsson .10 .25
171 Kevin Stevens .12 .30
172 Rick Tocchet .12 .30
173 Alexei Gusarov .10 .25
174 Ron Hextall .15 .40
175 Mike Hough .12 .30
176 Claude Lapointe .10 .25
177 Owen Nolan .15 .40
178 Mike Ricci .10 .25
179 Joe Sakic .30 .75
180 Mats Sundin .15 .40
181 Mikhail Tatarinov .10 .25
182 Bob Bassen .10 .25
183 Jeff Brown .12 .30
184 Garth Butcher .12 .30
185 Paul Cavallini .10 .25
186 Brett Hull .30 .75
187 Craig Janney .12 .30
188 Curtis Joseph .20 .50
189 Brendan Shanahan .15 .40
190 Ron Sutter .10 .25
191 David Bruce .10 .25
192 Dale Craigwell .10 .25
193 Dean Evason .10 .25
194 Pat Falloon .10 .25
195 Jeff Hackett .12 .30
196 Kelly Kisio .12 .30
197 Brian Lawton .12 .30
198 Neil Wilkinson .10 .25
199 Doug Wilson .12 .30
200 Marc Bergevin .12 .30
201 Roman Hamrlik RC .30 .75
202 Pat Jablonski .12 .30
203 Michel Mongeau .12 .30
204 Peter Taglianetti .12 .30
205 Steve Tuttle .12 .30
206 Wendell Young .12 .30
207 Glenn Anderson .12 .30
208 Wendel Clark .25 .60
209 Dave Ellett .10 .25
210 Grant Fuhr .25 .60
211 Doug Gilmour .20 .50
212 Jamie Macoun .12 .30
213 Felix Potvin .30 .75
214 Bob Rouse .12 .30
215 Joe Sacco .10 .25
216 Peter Zezel .10 .25
217 Greg Adams .10 .25
218 Dave Babych .12 .30
219 Pavel Bure .15 .40
220 Geoff Courtnall .10 .25
221 Doug Lidster .12 .30
222 Trevor Linden .15 .40
223 Jyrki Lumme .10 .25
224 Kirk McLean .10 .25
225 Sergio Momesso .10 .25
226 Petr Nedved .12 .30
227 Cliff Ronning .10 .25
228 Jim Sandlak .10 .25
229 Don Beaupre .12 .30
230 Peter Bondra .15 .40
231 Kevin Hatcher .10 .25
232 Dale Hunter .12 .30
233 Al Iafrate .12 .30
234 Calle Johansson .10 .25
235 Dimitri Khristich .10 .25
236 Kelly Miller .10 .25
237 Michal Pivonka .10 .25
238 Mike Ridley .10 .25
239 Luciano Borsato .10 .25
240 Bob Essensa .12 .30
241 Phil Housley .12 .30
242 Troy Murray .10 .25
243 Teppo Numminen .10 .25
244 Fredrik Olausson .10 .25
245 Ed Olczyk .10 .25
246 Darrin Shannon .10 .25
247 Thomas Steen .10 .25
248 Checklist 1 .10 .25
249 Checklist 2 .10 .25
250 Checklist 3 .10 .25
251 Ted Donato .10 .25
252 Dmitri Kvartalnov RC .10 .25
253 Gord Murphy .12 .30
254 Gregori Panteleyev RC .10 .25
255 Gordie Roberts .12 .30
256 David Shaw .12 .30
257 Don Sweeney .10 .25
258 Doug Bodger .10 .25
259 Gord Donnelly .12 .30
260 Yuri Khmylev RC .10 .25
261 Daren Puppa .12 .30
262 Richard Smehlik RC .10 .25
263 Petr Svoboda .12 .30
264 Bob Sweeney .10 .25
265 Randy Wood .10 .25
266 Kevin Dahl RC .10 .25
267 Chris Dahlquist .12 .30
268 Roger Johansson .12 .30
269 Chris Lindberg .10 .25
270 Frank Musil .12 .30
271 Ronnie Stern .12 .30
272 Carey Wilson .12 .30
273 Dave Christian .10 .25
274 Karl Dykhuis .10 .25
275 Greg Gilbert .12 .30
276 Sergei Krivokrasov .10 .25
277 Frantisek Kucera .12 .30
278 Bryan Marchment .12 .30
279 Stephane Matteau .10 .25
280 Brian Noonan .10 .25
281 Christian Ruuttu .10 .25
282 Steve Chiasson .10 .25
283 Dino Ciccarelli .12 .30
284 Gerard Gallant .10 .25
285 Mark Howe .15 .40
286 Keith Primeau .12 .30
287 Yves Racine .10 .25
288 Vincent Riendeau .12 .30
289 Ray Sheppard .10 .25
290 Mike Sillinger .10 .25
291 Kelly Buchberger .10 .25
292 Shayne Corson .12 .30
293 Brent Gilchrist .10 .25
294 Craig MacTavish .10 .25
295 Scott Mellanby .10 .25
296 Craig Muni .12 .30
297 Luke Richardson .12 .30
298 Ron Tugnutt .12 .30
299 Shaun Van Allen .12 .30
300 Steve Konroyd .12 .30
301 Nick Kypreos .10 .25
302 Robert Petrovicky RC .10 .25
303 Frank Pietrangelo .12 .30
304 Patrick Poulin .10 .25
305 Pat Verbeek .10 .25
306 Eric Weinrich .10 .25
307 Jim Hiller RC .10 .25
308 Charlie Huddy .12 .30
309 Lonnie Loach .10 .25
310 Marty McSorley .12 .30
311 Robb Stauber .12 .30
312 Darryl Sydor .10 .25
313 Dave Taylor .12 .30
314 Alexei Zhitnik .10 .25
315 Shane Churla .12 .30
316 Russ Courtnall .10 .25
317 Mike Craig .10 .25
318 Gaetan Duchesne .10 .25
319 Derian Hatcher .10 .25
320 Craig Ludwig .12 .30
321 Richard Matvichuk RC .12 .30
322 Mike McPhee .10 .25
323 Tommy Sjodin RC .10 .25
324 Brian Bellows .12 .30
325 Patrice Brisebois .10 .25
326 J.J.Daigneault .10 .25
327 Kevin Haller .10 .25
328 Sean Hill RC .10 .25
329 Stephan Lebeau .10 .25
330 John LeClair .15 .40
331 Lyle Odelein .12 .30
332 Andre Racicot .12 .30
333 Ed Ronan RC .10 .25
334 Craig Billington .12 .30
335 Ken Daneyko .10 .25
336 Bruce Driver .10 .25
337 Slava Fetisov .10 .25
338 Bill Guerin RC .30 .75
339 Bobby Holik .12 .30
340 Alexei Kasatonov .10 .25
341 Alexander Semak .10 .25
342 Tom Fitzgerald .10 .25
343 Travis Green RC .12 .30
344 Darius Kasparaitis .10 .25
345 Danny Lorenz RC .12 .30
346 Vladimir Malakhov .10 .25
347 Marty McInnis .10 .25
348 Brian Mullen .10 .25
349 Jeff Norton .12 .30
350 David Volek .10 .25
351 Jeff Beukeboom .10 .25
352 Phil Bourque .10 .25
353 Paul Broten .10 .25
354 Mark Hardy .12 .30
355 Steven King RC .10 .25
356 Kevin Lowe .12 .30
357 Ed Olczyk .10 .25
358 Doug Weight .30 .75
359 Sergei Zubov RC .25 .60
360 Jamie Baker .10 .25
361 Daniel Berthiaume .12 .30
362 Chris Luongo RC .10 .25
363 Norm Maciver .10 .25
364 Brad Marsh .12 .30
365 Mike Peluso .12 .30
366 Brad Shaw .10 .25
367 Peter Sidorkiewicz .10 .25
368 Keith Acton .12 .30
369 Stephane Beauregard .12 .30
370 Terry Carkner .12 .30
371 Brent Fedyk .10 .25
372 Andrei Lomakin .10 .25
373 Ryan McGill RC .10 .25
374 Ric Nattress .12 .30
375 Greg Paslawski .10 .25
376 Peter Ahola .10 .25
377 Jeff Daniels .10 .25
378 Troy Loney .10 .25
379 Shawn McEachern .10 .25
380 Mike Needham RC .10 .25
381 Paul Stanton .10 .25
382 Martin Straka RC .30 .75
383 Ken Wregget .12 .30
384 Steve Duchesne .10 .25
385 Ron Hextall .15 .40
386 Kerry Huffman .10 .25
387 Andrei Kovalenko RC .25 .60
388 Bill Lindsay RC .10 .25
389 Mike Ricci .10 .25
390 Martin Rucinsky .10 .25
391 Scott Young .10 .25
392 Philippe Bozon .10 .25
393 Nelson Emerson .10 .25
394 Guy Hebert RC .25 .60
395 Igor Korolev RC .10 .25
396 Kevin Miller .10 .25
397 Vitali Prokhorov RC .10 .25
398 Rich Sutter .10 .25
399 John Carter .12 .30
400 Johan Garpenlov .10 .25
401 Arturs Irbe .12 .30
402 Sandis Ozolinsh .10 .25
403 Tom Pederson RC .12 .30
404 Michel Picard .12 .30
405 Doug Zmolek RC .10 .25
406 Mikael Andersson .10 .25
407 Bob Beers .10 .25
408 Brian Bradley .10 .25
409 Adam Creighton .10 .25
410 Doug Crossman .12 .30
411 Ken Hodge Jr. .10 .25
412 Chris Kontos RC .10 .25
413 Rob Ramage .10 .25
414 John Tucker .10 .25
415 Rob Zamuner RC .12 .30
416 Ken Baumgartner .10 .25
417 Drake Berehowsky .10 .25
418 Nikolai Borschevsky RC .10 .25
419 John Cullen .10 .25
420 Mike Foligno .12 .30
421 Mike Krushelnyski .10 .25
422 Dmitri Mironov .10 .25
423 Rob Pearson .10 .25
424 Gerald Diduck .12 .30
425 Robert Dirk .12 .30
426 Tom Fergus .10 .25
427 Gino Odjick .10 .25
428 Adrien Plavsic .10 .25
429 Anatoli Semenov .10 .25
430 Jiri Slegr .10 .25
431 Dixon Ward RC .12 .30
432 Paul Cavallini .10 .25
433 Sylvain Cote .12 .30
434 Pat Elynuik .10 .25
435 Jim Hrivnak .12 .30
436 Keith Jones RC .15 .40
437 Steve Konowalchuk RC .12 .30
438 Todd Krygier .12 .30
439 Paul MacDermid .12 .30
440 Sergei Bautin RC .10 .25
441 Evgeny Davydov .10 .25
442 John Druce .10 .25
443 Troy Murray .10 .25
444 Teemu Selanne .30 .75
445 Rick Tabaracci .10 .25
446 Keith Tkachuk .15 .40
447 Alexei Zhamnov .12 .30
448 Checklist 4 .10 .25
449 Checklist 5 .10 .25
450 Checklist 6 .30 .75
NNO Jeremy Roenick
Harding Promo .25 .60

1992-93 Ultra All-Stars

COMPLETE SET (12) 8.00 20.00
1 Paul Coffey UER .50 1.25
2 Ray Bourque .75 2.00
3 Patrick Roy 1.50 4.00
4 Mario Lemieux 1.50 4.00
5 Kevin Stevens UER .15 .40
6 Jaromir Jagr .75 2.00
7 Chris Chelios .50 1.25
8 Al MacInnis .30 .75
9 Ed Belfour .50 1.25
10 Wayne Gretzky 2.00 5.00
11 Luc Robitaille .30 .75
12 Brett Hull .75 2.00

1992-93 Ultra Award Winners

COMPLETE SET (10) 6.00 15.00
1 Mark Messier .60 1.50
2 Brian Leetch .50 1.25
3 Guy Carbonneau .30 .75
4 Patrick Roy 1.50 4.00
5 Mario Lemieux 1.50 4.00
6 Wayne Gretzky 2.00 5.00
7 Mark Fitzpatrick .30 .75
8 Ray Bourque .60 1.50
9 Pavel Bure .50 1.25
10 Mark Messier .60 1.50

1992-93 Ultra Imports

COMPLETE SET (25) 8.00 20.00
1 Nikolai Borschevsky .20 .50
2 Pavel Bure 1.00 2.50
3 Sergei Fedorov 1.00 2.50
4 Roman Hamrlik .20 .50
5 Arturs Irbe .50 1.25
6 Jaromir Jagr 1.25 3.00
7 Dimitri Khristich .20 .50
8 Petr Klima .20 .50
9 Andrei Kovalenko .20 .50
10 Alexei Kovalev .40 1.00
11 Jari Kurri .75 2.00
12 Dmitri Kvartalnov .20 .50
13 Nicklas Lidstrom .75 2.00
14 Vladimir Malakhov .20 .50
15 Dmitri Mironov .20 .50
16 Alexander Mogilny .50 1.25
17 Petr Nedved .20 .50
18 Fredrik Olausson .20 .50
19 Sandis Ozolinsh .20 .50
20 Ulf Samuelsson .20 .50
21 Teemu Selanne 2.00 5.00
22 Richard Smehlik .20 .50
23 Tommy Soderstrom .20 .50
24 Peter Stastny .40 1.00
25 Mats Sundin 1.00 2.50

1992-93 Ultra Jeremy Roenick

COMPLETE SET (10) 10.00 20.00
COMMON ROENICK (1-10) .75 2.00
COMMON MAIL-IN (11-12) 1.25 3.00
13 Jeremy Roenick AU 30.00 80.00

1992-93 Ultra Rookies

COMPLETE SET (8) 5.00 10.00
1 Tony Amonte .40 1.00
2 Donald Audette .40 1.00
3 Pavel Bure .75 2.00
4 Gilbert Dionne .40 1.00
5 Nelson Emerson .40 1.00
6 Pat Falloon .40 1.00
7 Nicklas Lidstrom .75 2.00
8 Kevin Todd .40 1.00

1993-94 Ultra

1 Ray Bourque UER .15 .40
2 Andy Moog .10 .25
3 Brian Benning .05 .15
4 Brian Bellows .07 .20
5 Claude Lemieux .05 .15
6 Jamie Baker .05 .15
7 Steve Duchesne .05 .15
8 Ed Courtenay .05 .15
9 Glenn Anderson .07 .20
10 Sergei Bautin .05 .15
11 Al Iafrate .05 .15
12 Gary Shuchuk .05 .15
13 Matthew Barnaby .07 .20
14 Tim Cheveldae .07 .20
15 Sean Burke .05 .15
16 Ray Ferraro .05 .15
17 Josef Beranek .05 .15
18 Bob Beers .05 .15
19 Greg Adams .05 .15
20 John Cullen .05 .15
21 Kirk Muller .05 .15
22 Ed Belfour .10 .25
23 Kevin Dahl .05 .15
24 Rob Blake .07 .20
25 Mike Gartner .12 .30
26 Tom Barrasso .07 .20
27 Garth Butcher .05 .15
28 Don Beaupre .07 .20
29 Kirk McLean .07 .20
30 Felix Potvin .20 .50
31 Doug Bodger .05 .15
32 Dino Ciccarelli .07 .20
33 Andrew Cassels .05 .15
34 Patrick Flatley .05 .15
35 Jason Bowen RC .10 .25
36 Brian Bradley .05 .15
37 Pavel Bure .10 .25
38 Dave Ellett .05 .15
39 Patrick Roy .25 .60
40 Chris Chelios .10 .25
41 Theo Fleury .05 .15
42 Jimmy Carson .05 .15
43 Adam Graves .05 .15
44 Ron Francis .12 .30
45 Nelson Emerson .05 .15
46 Peter Bondra .10 .25
47 Sergio Momesso .05 .15
48 Teemu Selanne .20 .50
49 Joe Juneau .05 .15
50 Russ Courtnall .05 .15
51 Shayne Corson .07 .20
52 Patrice Brisebois .05 .15
53 John MacLean .07 .20
54 Daniel Berthiaume .05 .15
55 Stephane Fiset .07 .20
56 Pat Falloon .05 .15
57 Dave Andreychuk .10 .25
58 Evgeny Davydov .05 .15
59 Dimitri Khristich .05 .15
60 Darryl Sydor .05 .15
61 Dirk Graham .05 .15
62 Chris Lindberg .05 .15
63 Tony Granato .05 .15
64 Corey Hirsch .07 .20
65 Jaromir Jagr .30 .75
66 Bret Hedican .05 .15
67 Pat Elynuik .05 .15
68 Petr Nedved .05 .15
69 Thomas Steen .05 .15
70 Philippe Boucher .05 .15
71 Paul Coffey .10 .25
72 Mike Lenarduzzi RC .05 .15
73 Iain Fraser RC .10 .25
74 Rod Brind'Amour .07 .20
75 Shawn Chambers .05 .15
76 Geoff Courtnall .05 .15
77 Todd Gill .05 .15
78 Mathieu Schneider .05 .15
79 Vincent Damphousse .07 .20
80 Igor Kravchuk .05 .15
81 Ulf Dahlen .05 .15
82 Dmitri Kvartalnov .05 .15
83 Johan Garpenlov .05 .15
84 Valeri Kamensky .07 .20
85 Bob Kudelski .05 .15
86 Bernie Nicholls .07 .20
87 Alexei Zhitnik .05 .15
88 Kelly Miller .05 .15
89 Bob Essensa .07 .20
90 Drake Berehowsky .05 .15
91 Jon Casey .07 .20
92 Dave Gagner .07 .20
93 Dave Manson .05 .15
94 Eric Desjardins .07 .20
95 Scott Niedermayer .10 .25
96 Chris Luongo .05 .15

97 Dave Karpa .05 .15
98 Rob Gaudreau RC .10 .25
99 Nikolai Borschevsky .05 .15
100 Phil Housley .07 .20
101 Michal Pivonka .05 .15
102 Dixon Ward .05 .15
103 Grant Fuhr .15 .40
104 Dallas Drake RC .10 .25
105 Michael Nylander .05 .15
106 Glenn Healy .07 .20
107 Kevin Dineen .05 .15
108 Roman Hamrlik .05 .15
109 Trevor Linden .10 .25
110 Doug Gilmour .12 .30
111 Keith Tkachuk .10 .25
112 Sergei Krivokrasov .05 .15
113 Al MacInnis .12 .30
114 Wayne Gretzky .60 1.50
115 Alexei Kovalev .07 .20
116 Mario Lemieux .40 1.00
117 Brett Hull .20 .50
118 Kevin Hatcher .05 .15
119 Cliff Ronning .05 .15
120 Viktor Gordiouk .05 .15
121 Sergei Fedorov .15 .40
122 Patrick Poulin .05 .15
123 Benoit Hogue .05 .15
124 Garry Galley .05 .15
125 Pat Jablonski .05 .15
126 Jyrki Lumme .05 .15
127 Dimitri Mironov .05 .15
128 Alexei Zhamnov .07 .20
129 Steve Larmer .07 .20
130 Joe Nieuwendyk .07 .20
131 Kelly Hrudey .07 .20
132 Brian Leetch .07 .20
133 Shawn McEachern .05 .15
134 Craig Janney .07 .20
135 Dale Hunter .07 .20
136 Jiri Slegr .05 .15
137 Mats Sundin .10 .25
138 Cam Neely .10 .25
139 Derian Hatcher .05 .15
140 Shjon Podein RC .10 .25
141 Gilbert Dionne .05 .15
142 Scott Pellerin RC .10 .25
143 Norm Maciver .05 .15
144 Andrei Kovalenko .05 .15
145 Arturs Irbe .07 .20
146 Wendel Clark .15 .40
147 Fredrik Olausson .05 .15
148 Mike Ridley .05 .15
149 Dale Hawerchuk .12 .30
150 Vladimir Konstantinov .07 .20
151 Geoff Sanderson .07 .20
152 Stephane Richer .07 .20
153 Darren Rumble .05 .15
154 Owen Nolan .10 .25
155 Kelly Kisio .05 .15
156 Adam Oates .10 .25
157 Trent Klatt .05 .15
158 Bill Ranford .07 .20
159 Paul DiPietro .05 .15
160 Darius Kasparaitis .05 .15
161 Eric Lindros .15 .40
162 Chris Kontos .05 .15
163 Joe Murphy .05 .15
164 Robert Reichel .05 .15
165 Jari Kurri .10 .25
166 Alexander Semak .05 .15
167 Brad Shaw .05 .15
168 Mike Ricci .05 .15
169 Sandis Ozolinsh .05 .15
170 Joby Messier RC .10 .25
171 Joe Mullen .07 .20
172 Curtis Joseph .12 .30
173 Yuri Khmylev .05 .15
174 Slava Kozlov .07 .20
175 Pat Verbeek .05 .15
176 Derek King .05 .15
177 Ryan McGill .05 .15
178 Chris LiPuma RC .05 .15
179 Grigori Pantaleyev .05 .15
180 Richard Matvichuk .05 .15
181 Steven Rice .05 .15
182 Sean Hill .05 .15
183 Mark Messier .20 .50
184 Larry Murphy .07 .20
185 Igor Korolev .05 .15
186 Jeremy Roenick .15 .40
187 Gary Roberts .05 .15
188 Robert Lang .07 .20
189 Scott Stevens .10 .25
190 Sylvain Turgeon .05 .15
191 Martin Rucinsky .05 .15
192 J.F. Quintin .05 .15
193 Dave Poulin .05 .15
194 Mike Modano .15 .40
195 Doug Weight .07 .20
196 Mike Keane .05 .15
197 Pierre Turgeon .07 .20
198 Dimitri Yushkevich .05 .15
199 Rob Zamuner .05 .15
200 Richard Smehlik .05 .15
201 Steve Yzerman .25 .60
202 Tony Amonte .07 .20
203 Sergei Nemchinov .05 .15
204 Ulf Samuelsson .05 .15
205 Kevin Miehm .05 .15
206 Brent Sutter .05 .15
207 Mike Vernon .07 .20
208 Luc Robitaille .10 .25
209 Chris Terreri .07 .20
210 Philippe Bozon .05 .15
211 John Tucker .05 .15
212 Jozef Stumpel .05 .15
213 Mark Tinordi .05 .15
214 Bruce Driver .05 .15
215 John LeClair .10 .25
216 Steve Thomas .05 .15
217 Tommy Soderstrom .07 .20
218 Kevin Miller .05 .15
219 Pat LaFontaine .10 .25
220 Nicklas Lidstrom .10 .25
221 Terry Yake .05 .15
222 Valeri Zelepukin .05 .15
223 Jeff Brown .05 .15
224 Chris Simon RC .10 .25
225 Rick Tocchet .07 .20
226 Gary Suter .05 .15
227 Marty McSorley .07 .20
228 Mike Richter .10 .25
229 Kevin Stevens .07 .20
230 Doug Wilson .07 .20
231 Steve Smith .05 .15
232 Bryan Smolinski .05 .15
233 Tommy Sjodin .05 .15
234 Zarley Zalapski .05 .15
235 Vladimir Malakhov .05 .15
236 Mark Recchi .12 .30
237 David Littman RC .05 .15
238 Alexander Mogilny .10 .25
239 Keith Primeau .07 .20
240 Tyler Wright .05 .15
241 Stephan Lebeau .05 .15
242 Joe Sakic .20 .50
243 Sergei Zubov .07 .20
244 Martin Straka .05 .15
245 Brendan Shanahan .10 .25
246 Tomas Sandstrom .05 .15
247 Milan Tichy RC .05 .15
248 C.J. Young .05 .15
249 Eric Lindros CL .15 .40
250 Teemu Selanne CL .20 .50
251 Patrick Carnback RC .10 .25
252 Todd Ewen .05 .15
253 Stu Grimson .05 .15
254 Guy Hebert .07 .20
255 Sean Hill .05 .15
256 Bill Houlder .05 .15
257 Alexei Kasatonov .05 .15
258 Steven King .05 .15
259 Troy Loney .05 .15
260 Joe Sacco .05 .15
261 Anatoli Semenov .05 .15
262 Tim Sweeney .05 .15
263 Ron Tugnutt .07 .20
264 Shaun Van Allen .05 .15
265 Terry Yake .05 .15
266 Jon Casey .07 .20
267 Ted Donato .05 .15
268 Steve Leach .05 .15
269 David Reid .05 .15
270 Cam Stewart RC .10 .25
271 Don Sweeney .05 .15
272 Glen Wesley .05 .15
273 Donald Audette .05 .15
274 Dominik Hasek .15 .40
275 Sergei Petrenko .05 .15
276 Derek Plante RC .10 .25
277 Craig Simpson .05 .15
278 Bob Sweeney .05 .15
279 Randy Wood .05 .15
280 Ted Drury .05 .15
281 Trevor Kidd .07 .20
282 Kelly Kisio .05 .15
283 Frank Musil .05 .15
284 Jason Muzzatti RC .10 .25
285 Joel Otto .05 .15
286 Paul Ranheim .05 .15
287 Wes Walz .05 .15
288 Ivan Droppa RC .05 .15
289 Michel Goulet .05 .15
290 Stephane Matteau .05 .15
291 Brian Noonan .05 .15
292 Patrick Poulin .05 .15
293 Rich Sutter .05 .15
294 Kevin Todd .05 .15
295 Eric Weinrich .05 .15
296 Neal Broten .05 .15
297 Mike Craig .05 .15
298 Dean Evason .05 .15
299 Grant Ledyard .05 .15
300 Mike McPhee .05 .15
301 Andy Moog .10 .25
302 Jarkko Varvio .05 .15
303 Micah Aivazoff RC .10 .25
304 Terry Carkner .05 .15
305 Steve Chiasson .05 .15
306 Greg Johnson .05 .15
307 Darren McCarty RC .15 .40
308 Chris Osgood RC .60 1.50
309 Bob Probert .10 .25
310 Ray Sheppard .07 .20
311 Mike Sillinger .05 .15
312 Jason Arnott RC .20 .50
313 Fred Brathwaite RC .10 .25
314 Kelly Buchberger .05 .15
315 Zdeno Ciger .05 .15
316 Craig MacTavish .05 .15
317 Dean McAmmond .05 .15
318 Luke Richardson .05 .15
319 Vladimir Vujtek .05 .15
320 Jesse Belanger .05 .15
321 Brian Benning .05 .15
322 Keith Brown .05 .15
323 Evgeny Davydov .05 .15
324 Tom Fitzgerald .05 .15
325 Alexander Godynyuk .05 .15
326 Scott Levins RC .10 .25
327 Andrei Lomakin .05 .15
328 Scott Mellanby .07 .20
329 Gord Murphy .05 .15
330 Rob Niedermayer .07 .20
331 Brent Severyn RC .10 .25
332 Brian Skrudland .05 .15
333 John Vanbiesbrouck .10 .25
334 Mark Greig .05 .15
335 Bryan Marchment .05 .15
336 James Patrick .05 .15
337 Robert Petrovicky .05 .15
338 Frank Pietrangelo .07 .20
339 Chris Pronger .10 .25
340 Brian Propp .05 .15
341 Darren Turcotte .05 .15
342 Pat Conacher .05 .15
343 Mark Hardy .05 .15
344 Charlie Huddy .05 .15
345 Shawn McEachern .05 .15
346 Warren Rychel .05 .15
347 Robb Stauber .05 .15
348 Dave Taylor .05 .15
349 Benoit Brunet .05 .15
350 Guy Carbonneau .05 .15
351 J.J. Daigneault .05 .15
352 Kevin Haller .05 .15
353 Gary Leeman .05 .15
354 Lyle Odelein .05 .15
355 Andre Racicot .05 .15
356 Ron Wilson .05 .15
357 Martin Brodeur .25 .60
358 Ken Daneyko .05 .15
359 Bill Guerin .10 .25
360 Bobby Holik .05 .15
361 Corey Millen .05 .15
362 Jaroslav Modry RC .10 .25
363 Jason Smith RC .05 .15
364 Brad Dalgarno .05 .15
365 Travis Green .07 .20
366 Ron Hextall .10 .25
367 Steve Junker .10 .25
368 Tom Kurvers .05 .15
369 Scott Lachance .05 .15
370 Marty McInnis .05 .15
371 Glenn Healy .07 .20
372 Alexander Karpovtsev .05 .15
373 Steve Larmer .07 .20
374 Doug Lidster .05 .15
375 Kevin Lowe .05 .15
376 Mattias Norstrom RC .10 .25
377 Esa Tikkanen .05 .15
378 Craig Billington .07 .20
379 Robert Burakovsky RC .10 .25
380 Alexandre Daigle .05 .15
381 Dmitri Filimonov .05 .15
382 Darrin Madeley RC .10 .25
383 Vladimir Ruzicka .05 .15
384 Alexei Yashin .07 .20
385 Viacheslav Butsayev .05 .15
386 Pelle Eklund .05 .15
387 Brent Fedyk .05 .15
388 Greg Hawgood .05 .15
389 Milos Holan RC .10 .25
390 Stewart Malgunas RC .10 .25
391 Mikael Renberg .10 .25
392 Dominic Roussel .07 .20
393 Doug Brown .05 .15
394 Marty McSorley .07 .20
395 Markus Naslund .10 .25
396 Mike Ramsey .05 .15
397 Peter Taglianetti .05 .15
398 Bryan Trottier .10 .25
399 Ken Wregget .07 .20
400 Iain Fraser .10 .25
401 Martin Gelinas .05 .15
402 Kerry Huffman .05 .15
403 Claude Lapointe .05 .15
404 Curtis Leschyshyn .05 .15
405 Chris Lindberg .05 .15
406 Jocelyn Thibault RC .10 .25
407 Murray Baron .05 .15
408 Bob Bassen .05 .15
409 Phil Housley .07 .20
410 Jim Hrivnak .05 .15
411 Tony Hrkac .05 .15
412 Vitali Karamnov .05 .15
413 Jim Montgomery RC .10 .25
414 Vlastimil Kroupa RC .10 .25
415 Igor Larionov .05 .15
416 Sergei Makarov .05 .15
417 Jeff Norton .05 .15
418 Mike Rathje .05 .15
419 Jim Waite .07 .20
420 Ray Whitney .05 .15
421 Mikael Andersson .05 .15
422 Donald Dufresne .05 .15
423 Chris Gratton .07 .20
424 Brent Gretzky RC .10 .25
425 Petr Klima .05 .15
426 Bill McDougall RC .10 .25
427 Daren Puppa .05 .15
428 Denis Savard .10 .25
429 Ken Baumgartner .05 .15
430 Sylvain Lefebvre .05 .15
431 Jamie Macoun .05 .15
432 Matt Martin RC .10 .25
433 Mark Osborne .05 .15
434 Rob Pearson .05 .15
435 Damian Rhodes RC .10 .25
436 Peter Zezel .05 .15
437 Shawn Antoski .05 .15
438 Jose Charbonneau .05 .15
439 Murray Craven .05 .15
440 Gerald Diduck .05 .15
441 Dana Murzyn .05 .15
442 Gino Odjick .05 .15
443 Kay Whitmore .05 .15
444 Randy Burridge .05 .15
445 Sylvain Cote .05 .15
446 Keith Jones .05 .15
447 Olaf Kolzig .10 .25
448 Todd Krygier .05 .15
449 Pat Peake .05 .15
450 Dave Poulin .05 .15
451 Stephane Beauregard .05 .15
452 Luciano Borsato .05 .15
453 Nelson Emerson .05 .15
454 Boris Mironov .05 .15
455 Teppo Numminen .05 .15
456 Stephane Quintal .05 .15
457 Paul Ysebaert .05 .15
458 Adrian Aucoin RC .10 .25
459 Todd Brost RC .10 .25
460 Martin Gendron RC .07 .20
461 David Harlock .05 .15
462 Corey Hirsch .07 .20
463 Todd Hlushko RC .07 .20
464 Fabian Joseph RC .07 .20
465 Paul Kariya 2.00 5.00
466 Brett Lindros RC .15 .40
467 Ken Lovsin RC .07 .20
468 Jason Marshall .07 .20
469 Derek Mayer RC .05 .15
470 Dwayne Norris RC .05 .15
471 Russ Romaniuk .05 .15
472 Brian Savage RC .10 .25
473 Trevor Sim RC .10 .25
474 Chris Therien RC .05 .15
475 Brad Turner RC .07 .20
476 Todd Warriner RC .05 .15
477 Craig Woodcroft RC .10 .25
478 Mark Beaufait RC .10 .25
479 Jim Campbell .07 .20
480 Ted Crowley RC .10 .25
481 Mike Dunham .07 .20
482 Chris Ferraro RC .07 .20
483 Peter Ferraro .07 .20
484 Brett Hauer RC .07 .20
485 Darby Hendrickson RC .07 .20
486 Chris Imes RC .07 .20
487 Craig Johnson RC .07 .20
488 Peter Laviolette RC .07 .20
489 Jeff Lazaro .07 .20
490 John Lilley RC .07 .20
491 Todd Marchant .07 .20
492 Ian Moran RC .07 .20
493 Travis Richards RC .07 .20
494 Barry Richter RC .07 .20
495 David Roberts RC .07 .20
496 Brian Rolston .07 .20
497 David Sacco RC .07 .20
498 Checklist Card .05 .15
499 Checklist Card .05 .15
500 Checklist Card .05 .15
C3C Wayne Gretzky 2/10 6.00 15.00

1993-94 Ultra Adam Oates

COMPLETE SET (10) 1.50 4.00
COMMON OATES (1-10) .20 .50
COMMON MAIL-IN (11-12) .75 2.00
NNO Adam Oates AU 12.00 30.00

1993-94 Ultra All-Rookies

1 Philippe Boucher 3.00 8.00
2 Viktor Gordiouk 3.00 8.00
3 Corey Hirsch 5.00 12.00
4 Chris LiPuma 3.00 8.00
5 David Littman 3.00 8.00
6 Joby Messier 3.00 8.00
7 Chris Simon 3.00 8.00
8 Bryan Smolinski 3.00 8.00
9 Jozef Stumpel 3.00 8.00
10 Milan Tichy 3.00 8.00

1993-94 Ultra All-Stars

COMPLETE SET (18) 10.00 25.00
1 Patrick Roy 2.50 6.00
2 Ray Bourque .75 2.00
3 Pierre Turgeon .25 .60
4 Pat LaFontaine .50 1.25
5 Alexander Mogilny .25 .60
6 Kevin Stevens .15 .40
7 Adam Oates .25 .60
8 Al Iafrate .15 .40
9 Kirk Muller .15 .40
10 Ed Belfour .50 1.25
11 Teemu Selanne .50 1.25
12 Steve Yzerman 2.50 6.00
13 Luc Robitaille .25 .60
14 Chris Chelios .50 1.25
15 Wayne Gretzky 3.00 8.00
16 Doug Gilmour .25 .60
17 Pavel Bure .50 1.25
18 Phil Housley .25 .60

1993-94 Ultra Award Winners

COMPLETE SET (6) 3.00 8.00
1 Ed Belfour .60 1.50
2 Chris Chelios .60 1.50
3 Doug Gilmour .30 .75
4 Mario Lemieux 2.00 5.00
5 Dave Poulin .20 .50
6 Teemu Selanne .60 1.50

1993-94 Ultra Premier Pivots

COMPLETE SET (10) 8.00 20.00
1 Doug Gilmour .20 .50
2 Wayne Gretzky 2.50 6.00
3 Pat LaFontaine .40 1.00
4 Mario Lemieux 2.00 5.00
5 Eric Lindros .40 1.00
6 Mark Messier .40 1.00
7 Adam Oates .20 .50
8 Jeremy Roenick .50 1.25
9 Pierre Turgeon .20 .50
10 Steve Yzerman 2.00 5.00

1993-94 Ultra Promo Sheet

NNO Uncut Panel
Joe Juneau
Sergei Fedorov
Mats Sundin
Mark Recchi
Cover Card
Jeremy Roenick
Felix Potvin
Alexei Kovalev
Doug Gilmour 2.00 5.00

1993-94 Ultra Prospects

COMPLETE SET (10) 5.00 10.00
1 Iain Fraser .40 1.00
2 Rob Gaudreau .40 1.00
3 Dave Karpa .40 1.00
4 Trent Klatt .40 1.00
5 Mike Lenarduzzi .40 1.00
6 Kevin Miehm .40 1.00
7 Michael Nylander .75 2.00
8 J.F. Quintin .40 1.00
9 Gary Shuchuk .40 1.00
10 Tyler Wright .40 1.00

1993-94 Ultra Red Light Specials

COMPLETE SET (10) 6.00 15.00
1 Dave Andreychuk .40 1.00
2 Pavel Bure .75 2.00
3 Mike Gartner .40 1.00
4 Brett Hull 1.00 2.50
5 Jaromir Jagr 1.25 3.00
6 Mario Lemieux 2.00 5.00
7 Alexander Mogilny .40 1.00
8 Mark Recchi .40 1.00
9 Luc Robitaille .40 1.00
10 Teemu Selanne .75 2.00

1993-94 Ultra Scoring Kings

COMPLETE SET (6) 10.00 25.00
1 Pat LaFontaine 1.00 2.50
2 Wayne Gretzky 3.00 8.00
3 Brett Hull 1.50 4.00
4 Mario Lemieux 2.50 6.00
5 Pierre Turgeon 1.00 2.50
6 Steve Yzerman 3.00 8.00

1993-94 Ultra Speed Merchants

COMPLETE SET (10) 15.00 40.00
1 Pavel Bure 2.00 5.00
2 Russ Courtnall .75 2.00
3 Sergei Fedorov 2.00 5.00
4 Mike Gartner .75 2.00
5 Al Iafrate .75 2.00
6 Pat LaFontaine 1.50 4.00
7 Alexander Mogilny 1.50 4.00
8 Rob Niedermayer .75 2.00
9 Geoff Sanderson .75 2.00
10 Teemu Selanne 2.00 5.00

1993-94 Ultra Wave of the Future

COMPLETE SET (20) 6.00 15.00
1 Jason Arnott .40 1.00
2 Martin Brodeur 2.00 5.00
3 Alexandre Daigle .20 .50
4 Ted Drury .20 .50
5 Chris Gratton .20 .50
6 Milos Holan .20 .50
7 Greg Johnson .20 .50
8 Boris Mironov .20 .50
9 Jaroslav Modry .20 .50
10 Markus Naslund .60 1.50
11 Rob Niedermayer .40 1.00
12 Chris Osgood .75 2.00
13 Derek Plante .20 .50
14 Chris Pronger .60 1.50
15 Mike Rathje .20 .50
16 Mikael Renberg .40 1.00
17 Jason Smith .20 .50
18 Jocelyn Thibault .60 1.50
19 Jarkko Varvio .20 .50
20 Alexei Yashin .20 .50

1994-95 Ultra

1 Bob Corkum .05 .15
2 Todd Ewen .05 .15
3 Guy Hebert .07 .20
4 Bill Houlder .05 .15
5 Stephan Lebeau .05 .15
6 Joe Sacco .05 .15
7 Anatoli Semenov .05 .15
8 Tim Sweeney .05 .15
9 Terry Yake .05 .15
10 Ray Bourque .15 .40
11 Mariusz Czerkawski RC .10 .25
12 Ted Donato .05 .15
13 Cam Neely .10 .25
14 Adam Oates .10 .25
15 Vincent Riendeau .05 .15
16 Bryan Smolinski .05 .15
17 Don Sweeney .05 .15
18 Glen Wesley .05 .15
19 Donald Audette .05 .15
20 Doug Bodger .05 .15
21 Jason Dawe .05 .15
22 Dominik Hasek .15 .40
23 Dale Hawerchuk .12 .30
24 Pat LaFontaine .10 .25
25 Brad May .05 .15
26 Alexander Mogilny .07 .20
27 Derek Plante .05 .15
28 Richard Smehlik .05 .15
29 Theo Fleury .10 .25
30 Trevor Kidd .07 .20
31 Frank Musil .05 .15
32 Michael Nylander .07 .20
33 James Patrick .05 .15
34 Robert Reichel .05 .15
35 Gary Roberts .05 .15
36 German Titov .05 .15
37 Wes Walz .05 .15
38 Zarley Zalapski .05 .15
39 Ed Belfour .10 .25
40 Chris Chelios .10 .25
41 Dirk Graham .05 .15
42 Bernie Nicholls .07 .20
43 Patrick Poulin .05 .15
44 Jeremy Roenick .15 .40
45 Steve Smith .05 .15
46 Gary Suter .05 .15
47 Brent Sutter .07 .20
48 Neal Broten .07 .20
49 Paul Cavallini .05 .15
50 Dean Evason .05 .15
51 Dave Gagner .07 .20
52 Derian Hatcher .05 .15
53 Trent Klatt .05 .15
54 Grant Ledyard .05 .15
55 Mike Modano .15 .40
56 Andy Moog .10 .25
57 Mark Tinordi .05 .15
58 Dino Ciccarelli .07 .20
59 Paul Coffey .10 .25
60 Sergei Fedorov .15 .40
61 Vladimir Konstantinov .07 .20
62 Nicklas Lidstrom .10 .25
63 Darren McCarty .07 .20
64 Chris Osgood .15 .40
65 Keith Primeau .07 .20
66 Ray Sheppard .07 .20
67 Steve Yzerman .25 .60
68 Jason Arnott .07 .20
69 Bob Beers .05 .15
70 Ilya Byakin .05 .15
71 Zdeno Ciger .05 .15
72 Igor Kravchuk .05 .15
73 Boris Mironov .05 .15
74 Fredrik Olausson .05 .15
75 Scott Pearson .05 .15
76 Bill Ranford .07 .20
77 Doug Weight .07 .20
78 Stu Barnes .05 .15
79 Jesse Belanger .05 .15
80 Bob Kudelski .05 .15
81 Andrei Lomakin .05 .15
82 Dave Lowry .05 .15
83 Gord Murphy .05 .15
84 Rob Niedermayer .07 .20
85 Brian Skrudland .05 .15
86 John Vanbiesbrouck .10 .25
87 Sean Burke .07 .20
88 Ted Drury .05 .15
89 Alexander Godynyuk .05 .15
90 Robert Kron .05 .15
91 Chris Pronger .10 .25
92 Brian Propp .05 .15
93 Geoff Sanderson .07 .20
94 Darren Turcotte .05 .15
95 Pat Verbeek .07 .20
96 Rob Blake .10 .25
97 Mike Donnelly .05 .15
98 John Druce .07 .20
99 Kelly Hrudey .07 .20
100 Jari Kurri .07 .20
101 Robert Lang .05 .15
102 Marty McSorley .07 .20
103 Luc Robitaille .10 .25
104 Alexei Zhitnik .07 .20
105 Brian Bellows .07 .20
106 Patrice Brisebois .05 .15
107 Vincent Damphousse .07 .20
108 Eric Desjardins .07 .20
109 Gilbert Dionne .05 .15
110 Mike Keane .05 .15
111 John LeClair .10 .25
112 Lyle Odelein .07 .20
113 Patrick Roy .25 .60
114 Mathieu Schneider .05 .15
115 Martin Brodeur .25 .60
116 Jim Dowd .05 .15
117 Bill Guerin .10 .25
118 Claude Lemieux .10 .25
119 John MacLean .07 .20
120 Corey Millen .05 .15
121 Scott Niedermayer .10 .25
122 Stephane Richer .07 .20
123 Scott Stevens .10 .25
124 Valeri Zelepukin .05 .15
125 Patrick Flatley .05 .15
126 Travis Green .07 .20
127 Ron Hextall .10 .25
128 Benoit Hogue .05 .15
129 Darius Kasparaitis .05 .15
130 Vladimir Malakhov .05 .15
131 Marty McInnis .05 .15
132 Steve Thomas .05 .15
133 Pierre Turgeon .07 .20
134 Dennis Vaske .05 .15
135 Glenn Anderson .07 .20
136 Jeff Beukeboom .05 .15
137 Adam Graves .05 .15
138 Steve Larmer .07 .20
139 Brian Leetch .07 .20
140 Mark Messier .20 .50
141 Petr Nedved .07 .20
142 Sergei Nemchinov .05 .15
143 Mike Richter .10 .25
144 Sergei Zubov .07 .20
145 Craig Billington .07 .20
146 Alexandre Daigle .05 .15
147 Evgeny Davydov .05 .15
148 Scott Levins .05 .15
149 Norm Maciver .05 .15
150 Troy Mallette .05 .15
151 Brad Shaw .05 .15
152 Alexei Yashin .10 .25
153 Josef Beranek .05 .15
154 Jason Bowen .05 .15
155 Rod Brind'Amour .07 .20
156 Kevin Dineen .05 .15
157 Garry Galley .05 .15
158 Mark Recchi .12 .30
159 Mikael Renberg .07 .20
160 Tommy Soderstrom .07 .20
161 Dimitri Yushkevich .05 .15
162 Tom Barrasso .07 .20
163 Ron Francis .12 .30
164 Jaromir Jagr .30 .75
165 Mario Lemieux .40 1.00
166 Shawn McEachern .05 .15
167 Joe Mullen .07 .20
168 Larry Murphy .07 .20
169 Ulf Samuelsson .05 .15
170 Kevin Stevens .07 .20
171 Martin Straka .05 .15
172 Wendel Clark .15 .40
173 Stephane Fiset .07 .20
174 Iain Fraser .05 .15
175 Andrei Kovalenko .05 .15
176 Sylvain Lefebvre .05 .15
177 Owen Nolan .10 .25
178 Mike Ricci .05 .15
179 Martin Rucinsky .05 .15
180 Joe Sakic .20 .50
181 Scott Young .05 .15
182 Steve Duchesne .05 .15
183 Brett Hull .20 .50
184 Curtis Joseph .12 .30
185 Al MacInnis .12 .30
186 Kevin Miller .05 .15
187 Jim Montgomery .05 .15
188 Vitali Prokhorov .05 .15
189 Brendan Shanahan .10 .25
190 Peter Stastny .07 .20
191 Esa Tikkanen .05 .15
192 Ulf Dahlen .05 .15
193 Todd Elik .05 .15
194 Johan Garpenlov .05 .15
195 Arturs Irbe .07 .20
196 Vlastimil Kroupa .05 .15
197 Igor Larionov .05 .15
198 Sergei Makarov .05 .15
199 Jeff Norton .05 .15
200 Sandis Ozolinsh .05 .15
201 Mike Rathje .05 .15
202 Brian Bradley .05 .15
203 Shawn Chambers .05 .15
204 Danton Cole .05 .15
205 Chris Gratton .05 .15
206 Roman Hamrlik .05 .15
207 Chris Joseph .05 .15
208 Petr Klima .05 .15
209 Daren Puppa .07 .20
210 John Tucker .05 .15
211 Dave Andreychuk .10 .25
212 Ken Baumgartner .05 .15
213 Dave Ellett .05 .15
214 Mike Gartner .12 .30
215 Todd Gill .05 .15
216 Doug Gilmour .12 .30
217 Jamie Macoun .05 .15
218 Dmitri Mironov .05 .15
219 Felix Potvin .15 .40
220 Mats Sundin .10 .25
221 Jeff Brown .05 .15
222 Pavel Bure .10 .25
223 Murray Craven .05 .15
224 Bret Hedican .05 .15
225 Nathan Lafayette .05 .15
226 Trevor Linden .10 .25
227 Jyrki Lumme .05 .15
228 Kirk McLean .07 .20
229 Gino Odjick .05 .15
230 Cliff Ronning .05 .15
231 Peter Bondra .10 .25
232 Sylvain Cote .05 .15
233 Kevin Hatcher .05 .15
234 Dale Hunter .05 .15
235 Calle Johansson .05 .15
236 Dimitri Khristich .05 .15
237 Pat Peake .05 .15
238 Michal Pivonka .05 .15
239 Rick Tabaracci .07 .20
240 Tim Cheveldae .07 .20
241 Dallas Drake .05 .15
242 Nelson Emerson .05 .15
243 Dave Manson .05 .15
244 Teppo Numminen .05 .15
245 Stephane Quintal .05 .15
246 Teemu Selanne .20 .50
247 Keith Tkachuk .10 .25
248 Checklist .05 .15
249 Checklist .07 .20
250 Checklist .05 .15
251 John Lilley .05 .15
252 Mikhail Shtalenkov .05 .15
253 Garry Valk .05 .15
254 John Gruden RC .05 .15
255 Brent Hughes .05 .15
256 Al Iafrate .05 .15
257 Alexei Kasatonov .05 .15
258 Mikko Makela .05 .15
259 Marc Potvin .05 .15
260 Jon Rohloff RC .10 .25
261 Jozef Stumpel .05 .15
262 Grant Fuhr .15 .40
263 Viktor Gordiouk .07 .20
264 Yuri Khmylev .05 .15
265 Craig Muni .05 .15
266 Craig Simpson .05 .15
267 Denis Tsygurov RC .10 .25
268 Steve Chiasson .05 .15
269 Phil Housley .07 .20
270 Joel Otto .05 .15
271 Andrei Trefilov .05 .15
272 Vesa Viitakoski .07 .20
273 Tony Amonte .07 .20
274 Brent Grieve .05 .15
275 Bernie Nicholls .07 .20
276 Christian Soucy RC .07 .20
277 Paul Ysebaert .05 .15
278 Shane Churla .05 .15
279 Russ Courtnall .05 .15
280 Craig Ludwig .05 .15
281 Jarkko Varvio .05 .15
282 Darcy Wakaluk .07 .20
283 Greg Johnson .05 .15
284 Slava Kozlov .07 .20
285 Martin Lapointe .05 .15
286 Tim Taylor RC .10 .25
287 Mike Vernon .07 .20
288 Jason York RC .05 .15
289 Fred Brathwaite .05 .15
290 Kelly Buchberger .05 .15
291 Shayne Corson .07 .20
292 Dean McAmmond .05 .15
293 Vladimir Vujtek .05 .15
294 Doug Barrault .05 .15
295 Keith Brown .05 .15
296 Mark Fitzpatrick .07 .20
297 Mike Hough .05 .15
298 Scott Mellanby .07 .20
299 Jimmy Carson .05 .15
300 Andrew Cassels .05 .15
301 Andrei Nikolishin .05 .15
302 Steven Rice .05 .15
303 Glen Wesley .05 .15
304 Rob Brown .05 .15
305 Tony Granato .05 .15
306 Wayne Gretzky .60 1.50
307 Dan Quinn .07 .20
308 Darryl Sydor .05 .15
309 Rick Tocchet .07 .20
310 Donald Brashear RC .05 .15
311 Valeri Bure .05 .15
312 Jim Montgomery .05 .15
313 Kirk Muller .05 .15
314 Oleg Petrov .05 .15
315 Peter Popovic .05 .15
316 Yves Racine .05 .15
317 Turner Stevenson .05 .15
318 Ken Daneyko .05 .15
319 David Emma .05 .15
320 Brian Rolston .07 .20
321 Alexander Semak .05 .15
322 Jason Smith .05 .15
323 Chris Terreri .07 .20
324 Ray Ferraro .05 .15
325 Derek King .05 .15
326 Scott Lachance .05 .15
327 Brett Lindros .05 .15
328 Jamie McLennan .07 .20
329 Zigmund Palffy .07 .20
330 Corey Hirsch .07 .20
331 Alexei Kovalev .07 .20
332 Stephane Matteau .05 .15
333 Petr Nedved .07 .20
334 Mattias Norstrom .05 .15
335 Mark Osborne .05 .15
336 Randy Cunneyworth .05 .15
337 Pavol Demitra .12 .30
338 Pat Elynuik .05 .15
339 Sean Hill .05 .15
340 Darrin Madeley .05 .15
341 Sylvain Turgeon .05 .15
342 Vladislav Boulin RC .10 .25
343 Ron Hextall .10 .25
344 Patrik Juhlin RC .05 .15

345 Eric Lindros .15 .40
346 Shjon Podein .05 .15
347 Chris Therien .05 .15
348 John Cullen .05 .15
349 Markus Naslund .10 .25
350 Luc Robitaille .10 .25
351 Kjell Samuelsson .05 .15
352 Tomas Sandstrom .05 .15
353 Ken Wregget .07 .20
354 Wendel Clark .15 .40
355 Adam Deadmarsh .05 .15
356 Peter Forsberg .20 .50
357 Valeri Kamensky .07 .20
358 Uwe Krupp .05 .15
359 Janne Laukkanen .07 .20
360 Sylvain Lefebvre .05 .15
361 Jocelyn Thibault .07 .20
362 Bill Houlder .05 .15
363 Craig Janney .07 .20
364 Pat Falloon .05 .15
365 Jeff Friesen .05 .15
366 Viktor Kozlov .05 .15
367 Andrei Nazarov .05 .15
368 Jeff Odgers .05 .15
369 Michal Sykora .05 .15
370 Mikael Andersson .05 .15
371 Eric Charron RC .10 .25
372 Chris LiPuma .05 .15
373 Denis Savard .10 .25
374 Jason Wiemer RC .05 .15
375 Nikolai Borschevsky .05 .15
376 Eric Fichaud RC .10 .25
377 Kenny Jonsson .05 .15
378 Mike Ridley .05 .15
379 Mats Sundin .10 .25
380 Greg Adams .05 .15
381 Shawn Antoski .05 .15
382 Geoff Cournall .05 .15
383 Martin Gelinas .05 .15
384 Sergio Momesso .10 .25
385 Jiri Slegr .05 .15
386 Jason Allison .07 .20
387 Don Beaupre .07 .20
388 Joe Juneau .05 .15
389 Steve Konowalchuk .05 .15
390 Kelly Miller .05 .15
391 Dave Poulin .05 .15
392 Tie Domi .07 .20
393 Michal Grosek RC .05 .15
394 Russ Romaniuk .05 .15
395 Darrin Shannon .05 .15
396 Thomas Steen .05 .15
397 Igor Ulanov .05 .15
398 Alexei Zhamnov .07 .20
399 Checklist .05 .15
400 Checklist .05 .15

1994-95 Ultra All-Rookies

COMPLETE SET (10) 15.00 40.00
1 Jason Arnott 1.25 3.00
2 Martin Brodeur 5.00 12.00
3 Alexandre Daigle 1.25 3.00
4 Chris Gratton .60 1.50
5 Boris Mironov .60 1.50
6 Derek Plante .60 1.50
7 Chris Pronger 1.25 3.00
8 Mikael Renberg .60 1.50
9 Bryan Smolinski .60 1.50
10 Alexei Yashin 1.25 3.00

1994-95 Ultra All-Stars

COMPLETE SET (12) 4.00 10.00
1 Ray Bourque .30 .75
2 Brian Leetch .20 .50
3 Eric Lindros .30 .75
4 Mark Messier .20 .50
5 Alexander Mogilny .20 .50
6 Patrick Roy .75 2.00
7 Pavel Bure .20 .50
8 Chris Chelios .20 .50
9 Paul Coffey .20 .50
10 Wayne Gretzky 1.25 3.00
11 Brett Hull .30 .75
12 Felix Potvin .25 .60

1994-95 Ultra Award Winners

COMPLETE SET (8) 5.00 12.00
1 Ray Bourque .60 1.50
2 Martin Brodeur 1.00 2.50
3 Sergei Fedorov .60 1.50
4 Adam Graves .10 .30
5 Wayne Gretzky 2.50 6.00
6 Dominik Hasek .75 2.00
7 Brian Leetch .40 1.00
8 Cam Neely .40 1.00

1994-95 Ultra Global Greats

COMPLETE SET (10) 25.00 50.00
1 Sergei Fedorov 6.00 15.00
2 Dominik Hasek 6.00 15.00
3 Arturs Irbe 1.25 3.00
4 Jaromir Jagr 6.00 15.00
5 Jari Kurri 3.00 8.00
6 Alexander Mogilny 1.25 3.00
7 Petr Nedved 1.25 3.00
8 Mikael Renberg 1.25 3.00
9 Teemu Selanne 8.00 20.00
10 Alexei Yashin 1.25 3.00

1994-95 Ultra Power

COMPLETE SET (10) 3.00 8.00
1 Dave Andreychuk .30 .75
2 Jason Arnott .20 .50
3 Chris Gratton .20 .50
4 Adam Graves .20 .50
5 Eric Lindros .60 1.50
6 Cam Neely .60 1.50
7 Mikael Renberg .30 .75
8 Jeremy Roenick .60 1.50
9 Brendan Shanahan .60 1.50
10 Keith Tkachuk .60 1.50

1994-95 Ultra Premier Pad Men

COMPLETE SET (6) 10.00 20.00
1 Dominik Hasek 2.00 5.00
2 Arturs Irbe 1.00 2.50
3 Curtis Joseph 1.25 3.00
4 Felix Potvin 1.50 4.00
5 Mike Richter 1.25 3.00
6 Patrick Roy 5.00 12.00

1994-95 Ultra Premier Pivots

COMPLETE SET (10) 6.00 12.00
1 Jason Arnott .10 .30
2 Sergei Fedorov .60 1.50
3 Doug Gilmour .20 .50
4 Wayne Gretzky 2.50 6.00
5 Pat LaFontaine .40 1.00
6 Eric Lindros .60 1.50
7 Mark Messier .40 1.00
8 Mike Modano .60 1.50
9 Adam Oates .20 .50
10 Steve Yzerman 2.00 5.00

1994-95 Ultra Prospects

COMPLETE SET (10) 12.00 25.00
1 Peter Forsberg 5.00 12.00
2 Todd Harvey .75 2.00
3 Paul Kariya 2.00 5.00
4 Viktor Kozlov .75 2.00
5 Brett Lindros .75 2.00
6 Mike Peca .75 2.00
7 Brian Rolston .75 2.00
8 Jamie Storr 1.25 3.00
9 Oleg Tverdovsky .75 2.00
10 Jason Wiemer .75 2.00

1994-95 Ultra Red Light Specials

COMPLETE SET (10) 1.50 4.00
1 Dave Andreychuk .10 .30
2 Pavel Bure .25 .60
3 Mike Gartner .10 .30
4 Adam Graves .07 .20
5 Brett Hull .30 .75
6 Cam Neely .25 .60
7 Gary Roberts .07 .20
8 Teemu Selanne .25 .60
9 Brendan Shanahan .25 .60
10 Kevin Stevens .07 .20

1994-95 Ultra Scoring Kings

COMPLETE SET (7) 5.00 10.00
1 Pavel Bure .25 .60
2 Sergei Fedorov .40 1.00
3 Doug Gilmour .10 .30
4 Wayne Gretzky 1.50 4.00
5 Mario Lemieux 1.25 3.00
6 Eric Lindros .25 .60
7 Steve Yzerman 1.25 3.00

1994-95 Ultra Sergei Fedorov

COMPLETE SET (10) 5.00 10.00
COMMON FEDOROV (1-10) .60 1.50
COMMON FEDOROV AUTO 25.00 60.00
COMMON MAIL-IN (11-12) .75 2.00

1994-95 Ultra Speed Merchants

COMPLETE SET (10) 2.50 6.00
1 Pavel Bure .20 .50
2 Russ Courtnall .05 .15
3 Sergei Fedorov .40 1.00
4 Al Iafrate .05 .15
5 Pat LaFontaine .20 .50
6 Brian Leetch .20 .50
7 Mike Modano .40 1.00
8 Alexander Mogilny .08 .25
9 Jeremy Roenick .25 .60
10 Geoff Sanderson .08 .25

1995-96 Ultra

COMPLETE SET (400) 20.00 50.00
COMP.SERIES 1 (200) 10.00 25.00
COMP.SERIES 2 (200) 10.00 25.00
1 Guy Hebert .05 .15
2 Milos Holan .02 .10
3 Paul Kariya .10 .30
4 Denny Lambert RC .02 .10
5 Stephan Lebeau .02 .10
6 Oleg Tverdovsky .02 .10
7 Shaun Van Allen .02 .10
8 Ray Bourque .20 .50
9 Mariusz Czerkawski .02 .10
10 Blaine Lacher .05 .15
11 Sandy Moger RC .02 .10
12 Cam Neely .10 .30
13 Adam Oates .05 .15
14 Bryan Smolinski .02 .10
15 Donald Audette .02 .10
16 Jason Dawe .02 .10
17 Garry Galley .02 .10
18 Dominik Hasek .25 .60
19 Brian Holzinger RC .05 .15
20 Pat Lafontaine .10 .30
21 Alexander Mogilny .05 .15
22 Alexei Zhitnik .02 .10
23 Steve Chiasson .02 .10
24 Theo Fleury .02 .10
25 Phil Housley .05 .15
26 Trevor Kidd .05 .15
27 Joel Otto .02 .10
28 Gary Roberts .02 .10
29 Zarley Zalapski .02 .10
30 Ed Belfour .10 .30
31 Chris Chelios .10 .30
32 Eric Daze .05 .15
33 Sergei Krivokrasov .02 .10
34 Bernie Nicholls .02 .10
35 Jeremy Roenick .15 .40
36 Gary Suter .02 .10
37 Todd Harvey .05 .15
38 Derian Hatcher .02 .10
39 Mike Kennedy .02 .10
40 Grant Ledyard .02 .10
41 Mike Modano .20 .50
42 Andy Moog .10 .30
43 Mike Torchia RC .05 .15
44 Paul Coffey .10 .30
45 Sergei Fedorov .20 .50
46 Vladimir Konstantinov .05 .15
47 Slava Kozlov .05 .15
48 Keith Primeau .02 .10
49 Ray Sheppard .02 .10
50 Mike Vernon .05 .15
51 Steve Yzerman .60 1.50
52 Jason Arnott .02 .10
53 Shayne Corson .02 .10
54 Igor Kravchuk .02 .10
55 Todd Marchant .02 .10
56 David Oliver .02 .10
57 Bill Ranford .05 .15
58 Doug Weight .05 .15
59 Stu Barnes .02 .10
60 Jesse Belanger .02 .10
61 Gord Murphy .02 .10
62 Rob Niedermayer .05 .15
63 Brian Skrudland .02 .10
64 John Vanbiesbrouck .05 .15
65 Sean Burke .05 .15
66 Andrew Cassels .02 .10
67 Frantisek Kucera .02 .10
68 Andrei Nikolishin .02 .10
69 Chris Pronger .10 .30
70 Geoff Sanderson .02 .10
71 Kevin Smyth .02 .10
72 Darren Turcotte .02 .10
73 Rob Blake .05 .15
74 Wayne Gretzky .75 2.00
75 Kelly Hrudey .05 .15
76 Marty McSorley .02 .10
77 Jamie Storr .05 .15
78 Darryl Sydor .05 .15
79 Rick Tocchet .05 .15
80 Vincent Damphousse .02 .10
81 Vladimir Malakhov .02 .10
82 Mark Recchi .05 .15
83 Patrick Roy .60 1.50
84 Brian Savage .02 .10
85 Pierre Turgeon .05 .15
86 Martin Brodeur .30 .75
87 Neal Broten .05 .15
88 Sergei Brylin .02 .10
89 John MacLean .05 .15
90 Scott Niedermayer .02 .10
91 Stephane Richer .05 .15
92 Scott Stevens .05 .15
93 Ray Ferraro .02 .10
94 Scott Lachance .02 .10
95 Brett Lindros .02 .10
96 Kirk Muller .02 .10
97 Zigmund Palffy .05 .15
98 Tommy Salo RC .20 .50
99 Mathieu Schneider .02 .10
100 Tommy Soderstrom .05 .15
101 Glenn Healy .05 .15
102 Darren Langdon RC .02 .10
103 Steve Larmer .05 .15
104 Brian Leetch .05 .15
105 Mark Messier .10 .30
106 Mattias Norstrom .02 .10
107 Pat Verbeek .02 .10
108 Sergei Zubov .02 .10
109 Don Beaupre .05 .15
110 Radek Bonk .02 .10
111 Alexandre Daigle .02 .10
112 Steve Larouche RC .02 .10
113 Stanislav Neckar .02 .10
114 Alexei Yashin .02 .10
115 Rod Brind'Amour .05 .15
116 Eric Desjardins .05 .15
117 Ron Hextall .05 .15
118 John LeClair .10 .30
119 Eric Lindros .10 .30
120 Mikael Renberg .05 .15
121 Chris Therien .02 .10
122 Ron Francis .05 .15
123 Jaromir Jagr .20 .50
124 Joe Mullen .05 .15
125 Larry Murphy .05 .15
126 Ulf Samuelsson .02 .10
127 Kevin Stevens .02 .10
128 Ken Wregget .05 .15
129 Wendel Clark .05 .15
130 Adam Deadmarsh .02 .10
131 Stephane Fiset .05 .15
132 Peter Forsberg .30 .75
133 Curtis Leschyshyn .02 .10
134 Owen Nolan .05 .15
135 Mike Ricci .05 .15
136 Joe Sakic .25 .60
137 Denis Chasse .02 .10
138 Steve Duchesne .02 .10
139 Brett Hull .15 .40
140 Curtis Joseph .10 .30
141 Ian Laperriere .02 .10
142 Brendan Shanahan .10 .30
143 Esa Tikkanen .02 .10
144 Ulf Dahlen .02 .10
145 Jeff Friesen .02 .10
146 Arturs Irbe .05 .15
147 Craig Janney .02 .10
148 Sergei Makarov .02 .10
149 Sandis Ozolinsh .02 .10
150 Ray Whitney .05 .15
151 Chris Gratton .02 .10
152 Roman Hamrlik .05 .15
153 Petr Klima .02 .10
154 Brantt Myhres RC .02 .10
155 Daren Puppa .05 .15
156 Jason Wiemer .02 .10
157 Paul Ysebaert .02 .10
158 Dave Andreychuk .05 .15
159 Tie Domi .05 .15
160 Doug Gilmour .05 .15
161 Kenny Jonsson .02 .10
162 Felix Potvin .10 .30
163 Mike Ridley .02 .10
164 Mats Sundin .10 .30
165 Jeff Brown .02 .10
166 Pavel Bure .10 .30
167 Geoff Courtnall .02 .10
168 Russ Courtnall .02 .10
169 Trevor Linden .05 .15
170 Kirk McLean .05 .15
171 Roman Oksiuta .02 .10
172 Peter Bondra .05 .15
173 Jim Carey .05 .15
174 Martin Gendron .02 .10
175 Dale Hunter .05 .15
176 Calle Johansson .02 .10
177 Michal Pivonka .02 .10
178 Mark Tinordi .02 .10
179 Nelson Emerson .02 .10
180 Nikolai Khabibulin .05 .15
181 Dave Manson .02 .10
182 Teppo Numminen .02 .10
183 Teemu Selanne .10 .30
184 Keith Tkachuk .10 .30
185 Alexei Zhamnov .05 .15
186 Martin Brodeur SC .30 .75
187 Neal Broten .05 .15
188 Bob Carpenter .02 .10
189 Ken Daneyko .02 .10
190 Bruce Driver .02 .10
191 Bill Guerin .05 .15
192 Claude Lemieux .02 .10
193 John MacLean .05 .15
194 Scott Niedermayer .02 .10
195 Stephane Richer .05 .15
196 Scott Stevens .05 .15
197 Stanley Cup Presentation .05 .15
198 Checklist (1-83) .02 .10
199 Checklist (84-169) .02 .10
200 Checklist (170-200) .02 .10
201 Todd Krygier .02 .10
202 Steve Rucchin .05 .15
203 Mike Sillinger .02 .10
204 Ted Donato .02 .10
205 Shawn McEachern .02 .10
206 Joe Mullen .05 .15
207 Kevin Stevens .02 .10
208 Don Sweeney .02 .10
209 Mark Astley .02 .10
210 Randy Burridge .02 .10
211 Jason Dawe .02 .10
212 Mike Peca .05 .15
213 Michael Nylander .02 .10
214 Cory Stillman .02 .10
215 Pavel Torgajev RC .02 .10
216 Tony Amonte .05 .15
217 Joe Murphy .02 .10
218 Bob Probert .05 .15
219 Denis Savard .05 .15
220 Stephane Fiset .05 .15
221 Valeri Kamensky .05 .15
222 Sylvain Lefebvre .02 .10
223 Claude Lemieux .02 .10
224 Sandis Ozolinsh .02 .10
225 Patrick Roy .60 1.50
226 Scott Young .02 .10
227 Greg Adams .02 .10
228 Guy Carbonneau .10 .30
229 Dave Gagner .02 .10
230 Kevin Hatcher .02 .10
231 Darcy Wakaluk .05 .15
232 Dino Ciccarelli .05 .15
233 Greg Johnson .02 .10
234 Igor Larionov .02 .10
235 Darren McCarty .02 .10
236 Chris Osgood .05 .15
237 Zdeno Ciger .02 .10
238 Bryan Marchment .02 .10
239 Boris Mironov .02 .10
240 Peter White .02 .10
241 Jody Hull .02 .10
242 Scott Mellanby .02 .10
243 Gord Murphy .02 .10
244 Jason Woolley .02 .10
245 Gerald Diduck .02 .10
246 Nelson Emerson .02 .10
247 Brendan Shanahan .10 .30
248 Glen Wesley .02 .10
249 Tony Granato .02 .10
250 Dimitri Khristich .02 .10
251 Jari Kurri .10 .30
252 Eric Lacroix .02 .10
253 Yanic Perreault .02 .10
254 Patrice Brisebois .02 .10
255 Benoit Brunet .02 .10
256 Valeri Bure .02 .10
257 Stephane Quintal .02 .10
258 Jocelyn Thibault .10 .30
259 Shawn Chambers .02 .10
260 Jim Dowd .02 .10
261 Bill Guerin .05 .15
262 Bobby Holik .02 .10
263 Steve Thomas .05 .15
264 Esa Tikkanen .02 .10
265 Wendel Clark .05 .15
266 Travis Green .05 .15
267 Brett Lindros .02 .10
268 Kirk Muller .02 .10
269 Zigmund Palffy .05 .15
270 Mathieu Schneider .02 .10
271 Alexander Semak .02 .10
272 Dennis Vaske .02 .10
273 Ray Ferraro .02 .10
274 Adam Graves .02 .10
275 Alexei Kovalev .02 .10
276 Mike Richter .10 .30
277 Luc Robitaille .05 .15
278 Ulf Samuelsson .02 .10
279 Steve Duchesne .02 .10
280 Trent McCleary RC .02 .10
281 Dan Quinn .02 .10
282 Martin Straka .02 .10
283 Karl Dykhuis .02 .10
284 Pat Falloon .02 .10
285 Joel Otto .02 .10
286 Kjell Samuelsson .02 .10
287 Garth Snow .05 .15
288 Mario Lemieux .60 1.50
289 Norm Maciver .02 .10
290 Dmitri Mironov .02 .10
291 Markus Naslund .10 .30
292 Petr Nedved .05 .15
293 Tomas Sandstrom .02 .10
294 Bryan Smolinski .02 .10
295 Sergei Zubov .02 .10
296 Shayne Corson .02 .10
297 Geoff Courtnall .02 .10
298 Grant Fuhr .10 .30
299 Dale Hawerchuk .10 .30
300 Al MacInnis .05 .15
301 Brian Noonan .02 .10
302 Chris Pronger .10 .30
303 Andrei Nazarov .02 .10
304 Owen Nolan .05 .15
305 Ray Sheppard .02 .10
306 Chris Terreri .05 .15
307 Brian Bellows .02 .10
308 Brian Bradley .02 .10
309 John Cullen .02 .10
310 Alexander Selivanov .02 .10
311 Mike Gartner .05 .15
312 Benoit Hogue .02 .10
313 Sergio Momesso .02 .10
314 Larry Murphy .05 .15
315 Dave Babych .02 .10
316 Bret Hedican .02 .10
317 Alexander Mogilny .05 .15
318 Mike Ridley .02 .10
319 Peter Bondra .05 .15
320 Jim Carey .05 .15
321 Sylvain Cote .02 .10
322 Sergei Gonchar .02 .10
323 Joe Juneau .02 .10
324 Steve Konowalchuk .02 .10
325 Pat Peake .02 .10
326 Dallas Drake .02 .10
327 Igor Korolev .02 .10
328 Darren Turcotte .02 .10
329 Daniel Alfredsson RC .50 1.25
330 Aki Berg RC .05 .15
331 Todd Bertuzzi RC .75 2.00
332 Jason Bonsignore .02 .10
333 Curtis Brown RC .10 .30
334 Byron Dafoe .05 .15
335 Eric Daze .05 .15
336 Shane Doan RC .30 .75
337 Jason Doig .02 .10
338 Radek Dvorak RC .20 .50
339 Joe Dziedzic .02 .10
340 Darby Hendrickson .02 .10
341 Brian Holzinger RC .10 .30
342 Ed Jovanovski .05 .15
343 Chad Kilger RC .02 .10
344 Saku Koivu .10 .30
345 Darren Langdon .02 .10
346 Jamie Langenbrunner .02 .10
347 Jere Lehtinen .05 .15
348 Bryan McCabe .02 .10
349 Kyle McLaren RC .02 .10
350 Marty Murray .02 .10
351 Jeff O'Neill .02 .10
352 Deron Quint .02 .10
353 Marcus Ragnarsson RC .05 .15
354 Tommy Salo .20 .50
355 Miroslav Satan RC .50 1.25
356 Jamie Storr .05 .15
357 Niklas Sundstrom .05 .15
358 Robert Svehla RC .02 .10
359 Denis Pederson .02 .10
360 Antti Tormanen .02 .10
361 Brendan Witt .02 .10
362 Vitali Yachmenev .02 .10
363 Stephane Yelle .02 .10
364 Tom Barrasso NE .05 .15
365 Ed Belfour NE .10 .30
366 Martin Brodeur NE .30 .75
367 Sean Burke NE .05 .15
368 Jim Carey NE .02 .10
369 Stephane Fiset NE .05 .15
370 Dominik Hasek NE .25 .60
371 Ron Hextall NE .05 .15
372 Nikolai Khabibulin NE .05 .15
373 Kirk McLean NE .05 .15
374 Chris Osgood NE .05 .15
375 Felix Potvin NE .05 .15
376 Daren Puppa NE .05 .15
377 Patrick Roy NE .60 1.50
378 John Vanbiesbrouck NE .05 .15
379 Pavel Bure UC .10 .30
380 Chris Chelios UC .10 .30
381 Sergei Fedorov UC .20 .50
382 Theo Fleury UC .02 .10
383 Peter Forsberg UC .30 .75
384 Ron Francis UC .05 .15
385 Wayne Gretzky UC .75 2.00
386 Brett Hull UC .15 .40
387 Jaromir Jagr UC .20 .50
388 Paul Kariya UC .10 .30
389 Pat LaFontaine UC .05 .15
390 Brian Leetch UC .05 .15
391 Mario Lemieux UC .60 1.50
392 Eric Lindros UC .20 .50
393 Mark Messier UC .10 .30
394 Mike Modano UC .10 .30
395 Adam Oates UC .05 .15
396 Jeremy Roenick UC .15 .40
397 Joe Sakic UC .25 .60
398 Alexei Zhamnov UC .05 .15
399 Checklist .02 .10
400 Checklist .02 .10

1995-96 Ultra Gold Medallion

*VETS: 2.5X TO 6X BASIC CARDS
*ROOKIES: 1.2X TO 3X

1995-96 Ultra All-Rookie

COMPLETE SET (10) 6.00 15.00
*GOLD MED: .8X TO 2X BASIC INSERTS
1 Jim Carey .40 1.00
2 Mariusz Czerkawski .40 1.00
3 Peter Forsberg 2.00 5.00
4 Jeff Friesen .40 1.00
5 Paul Kariya 1.50 4.00
6 Blaine Lacher .40 1.00
7 Ian Laperriere .40 1.00
8 Todd Marchant .40 1.00
9 Roman Oksiuta .40 1.00
10 David Oliver .40 1.00

1995-96 Ultra Crease Crashers

COMPLETE SET (20) 30.00 80.00
1 Jason Arnott 2.00 5.00
2 Rod Brind'Amour 2.00 5.00
3 Theo Fleury 3.00 8.00
4 Todd Harvey 2.00 5.00
5 John LeClair 2.50 6.00
6 Claude Lemieux 2.50 6.00
7 Trevor Linden 2.50 6.00
8 Eric Lindros 5.00 12.00
9 Darren McCarty 2.00 5.00
10 Scott Mellanby 2.00 5.00
11 Mark Messier 3.00 8.00
12 Cam Neely 3.00 8.00
13 Owen Nolan 2.00 5.00
14 Keith Primeau 2.00 5.00
15 Jeremy Roenick 4.00 10.00
16 Tomas Sandstrom 2.00 5.00
17 Brendan Shanahan 2.50 6.00
18 Kevin Stevens 2.00 5.00
19 Rick Tocchet 2.00 5.00
20 Keith Tkachuk 2.50 6.00

1995-96 Ultra Extra Attackers

COMPLETE SET (20) 40.00 80.00
1 Peter Bondra 1.25 3.00
2 Eric Daze 1.25 3.00
3 Radek Dvorak 1.25 3.00
4 Sergei Fedorov 2.50 6.00
5 Peter Forsberg 3.00 8.00
6 Ron Francis 1.25 3.00
7 Wayne Gretzky 10.00 25.00
8 Brett Hull 2.00 5.00
9 Jaromir Jagr 3.00 8.00
10 Ed Jovanovski 1.25 3.00
11 Paul Kariya 1.50 4.00
12 Saku Koivu 1.50 4.00
13 Mario Lemieux 8.00 20.00
14 Mike Modano 2.50 6.00
15 Alexander Mogilny 2.00 5.00
16 Adam Oates 1.25 3.00
17 Joe Sakic 4.00 10.00
18 Niklas Sundstrom 1.25 3.00
19 Mats Sundin 1.50 4.00
20 Steve Yzerman 8.00 20.00

1995-96 Ultra High Speed

COMPLETE SET (20) 10.00 20.00
1 Daniel Alfredsson .75 2.00
2 Jason Arnott .20 .50
3 Todd Bertuzzi .75 2.00
4 Radek Bonk .20 .50
5 Martin Brodeur 2.00 5.00
6 Alexandre Daigle .20 .50
7 Shane Doan .40 1.00
8 Peter Forsberg 1.50 4.00
9 Roman Hamrlik .20 .50
10 Todd Harvey .20 .50
11 Paul Kariya .75 2.00
12 Travis Green .20 .50
13 Chris Osgood .40 1.00
14 Zigmund Palffy .40 1.00
15 Marcus Ragnarsson .20 .50
16 Mikael Renberg .20 .50
17 Brian Savage .20 .50
18 Robert Svehla .20 .50
19 Jocelyn Thibault .40 1.00
20 Brendan Witt .20 .50

1995-96 Ultra Premier Pad Men

COMPLETE SET (12) 30.00 60.00
*GOLD MED: 3X TO 6X BASIC INSERTS
1 Ed Belfour 2.50 6.00
2 Martin Brodeur 6.00 15.00
3 Sean Burke 2.00 5.00
4 Jim Carey 2.00 5.00
5 Dominik Hasek 3.00 8.00
6 Curtis Joseph 3.00 8.00
7 Blaine Lacher 2.00 5.00
8 Andy Moog 3.00 8.00
9 Felix Potvin 3.00 8.00
10 Patrick Roy 6.00 15.00
11 John Vanbiesbrouck 4.00 10.00
12 Mike Vernon 3.00 8.00

1995-96 Ultra Premier Pivots

COMPLETE SET (10) 6.00 12.00
*GOLD MED: .8X TO 2X BASIC INSERTS
1 Sergei Fedorov .60 1.50
2 Ron Francis .20 .50
3 Wayne Gretzky 2.50 6.00
4 Eric Lindros .40 1.00
5 Mark Messier .40 1.00
6 Adam Oates .20 .50
7 Jeremy Roenick .50 1.25
8 Joe Sakic .75 2.00
9 Mats Sundin .40 1.00
10 Alexei Zhamnov .20 .50

1995-96 Ultra Red Light Specials

COMPLETE SET (10) 1.25 3.00
*GOLD MED: .75X TO 2X BASIC INSERTS
1 Peter Bondra .20 .50
2 Theo Fleury .15 .40
3 Brett Hull .30 .75
4 Jaromir Jagr .40 1.00
5 John LeClair .25 .60
6 Eric Lindros .30 .75
7 Cam Neely .25 .60
8 Owen Nolan .20 .50
9 Ray Sheppard .15 .40
10 Alexei Zhamnov .20 .50

1995-96 Ultra Rising Stars

COMPLETE SET (10) .75 2.00
*GOLD MED: .8X TO 2X BASIC INSERTS
1 Jason Arnott .15 .40
2 Alexandre Daigle .15 .40
3 Roman Hamrlik .20 .50
4 Trevor Kidd .20 .50
5 Scott Niedermayer .15 .40
6 Keith Primeau .15 .40
7 Mikael Renberg .20 .50
8 Jocelyn Thibault .30 .75
9 Alexei Yashin .15 .40
10 Alexei Zhitnik .15 .40

1995-96 Ultra Ultraview

COMPLETE SET (10) 20.00 40.00
*HOT PACK: .2X TO .5X BASIC INSERTS
1 Sergei Fedorov 1.25 3.00
2 Wayne Gretzky 6.00 15.00
3 Dominik Hasek 2.00 5.00
4 Jaromir Jagr 1.50 4.00
5 Brian Leetch .75 2.00
6 Mario Lemieux 5.00 12.00
7 Eric Lindros 1.00 2.50
8 Jeremy Roenick 1.25 3.00
9 Joe Sakic 2.00 5.00
10 Alexei Zhamnov .75 2.00

1996-97 Ultra

1 Guy Hebert .15 .40
2 Paul Kariya .20 .50
3 Jari Kurri .20 .50
4 Roman Oksiuta .12 .30
5 Ruslan Salei RC .20 .50
6 Teemu Selanne .40 1.00
7 Darren Van Impe .12 .30
8 Ray Bourque .30 .75
9 Kyle McLaren .12 .30
10 Adam Oates .20 .50
11 Bill Ranford .15 .40
12 Rick Tocchet .15 .40
13 Donald Audette .12 .30
14 Curtis Brown .12 .30
15 Jason Dawe .12 .30
16 Dominik Hasek .30 .75
17 Pat LaFontaine .20 .50
18 Jay McKee RC .12 .30
19 Derek Plante .12 .30
20 Wayne Primeau .12 .30
21 Theo Fleury .40 1.00
22 Dave Gagner .20 .50
23 Jonas Hoglund .12 .30
24 Jarome Iginla .25 .60
25 Trevor Kidd .12 .30
26 Robert Reichel .12 .30
27 German Titov .12 .30
28 Tony Amonte .15 .40
29 Ed Belfour .20 .50
30 Chris Chelios .20 .50
31 Eric Daze .15 .40
32 Ethan Moreau RC .20 .50
33 Gary Suter .12 .30
34 Adam Deadmarsh .12 .30
35 Peter Forsberg .40 1.00
36 Valeri Kamensky .15 .40
37 Claude Lemieux .12 .30
38 Sandis Ozolinsh .12 .30
39 Patrick Roy .50 1.25
40 Joe Sakic .40 1.00
41 Landon Wilson .12 .30
42 Derian Hatcher .12 .30
43 Jamie Langenbrunner .12 .30
44 Mike Modano .30 .75
45 Andy Moog .20 .50
46 Joe Nieuwendyk .15 .40
47 Pat Verbeek .12 .30
48 Sergei Zubov .15 .40
49 Anders Eriksson .12 .30
50 Sergei Fedorov .30 .75
51 Vladimir Konstantinov .15 .40
52 Slava Kozlov .12 .30
53 Nicklas Lidstrom .25 .60
54 Chris Osgood .20 .50
55 Brendan Shanahan .20 .50
56 Steve Yzerman .50 1.25
57 Jason Arnott .15 .40
58 Mike Grier RC .25 .60
59 Curtis Joseph .25 .60
60 Rem Murray RC .20 .50
61 Jeff Norton .15 .40
62 Miroslav Satan .12 .30
63 Doug Weight .20 .50
64 Radek Dvorak .15 .40
65 Ed Jovanovski .15 .40
66 Scott Mellanby .15 .40
67 Rob Niedermayer .15 .40
68 Ray Sheppard .15 .40
69 Robert Svehla .12 .30
70 John Vanbiesbrouck .20 .50
71 Steve Washburn RC .20 .50
72 Jeff Brown .12 .30
73 Sean Burke .12 .30
74 Hnat Domenichelli .12 .30
75 Keith Primeau .15 .40
76 Geoff Sanderson .15 .40
77 Rob Blake .20 .50
78 Stephane Fiset .15 .40
79 Dimitri Khristich .12 .30
80 Mattias Norstrom .12 .30
81 Ed Olczyk .12 .30
82 Jamie Storr .12 .30
83 Jan Vopat .12 .30
84 Vitali Yachmenev .12 .30
85 Shayne Corson .15 .40
86 Vincent Damphousse .15 .40
87 Saku Koivu .20 .50
88 Mark Recchi .25 .60
89 Stephane Richer .15 .40
90 Jocelyn Thibault .15 .40
91 David Wilkie .12 .30
92 Dave Andreychuk .20 .50
93 Martin Brodeur .50 1.25
94 Scott Niedermayer .20 .50
95 Scott Stevens .20 .50
96 Petr Sykora .12 .30
97 Steve Thomas .12 .30
98 Bryan Berard .20 .50
99 Todd Bertuzzi .20 .50
100 Eric Fichaud .15 .40
101 Travis Green .15 .40
102 Kenny Jonsson .12 .30
103 Zigmund Palffy .20 .50
104 Christian Dube .12 .30
105 Daniel Goneau RC .20 .50
106 Wayne Gretzky 1.25 3.00
107 Alexei Kovalev .15 .40
108 Brian Leetch .15 .40
109 Mark Messier .40 1.00
110 Mike Richter .20 .50
111 Luc Robitaille .20 .50
112 Niklas Sundstrom .12 .30
113 Daniel Alfredsson .20 .50
114 Radek Bonk .12 .30
115 Andreas Dackell RC .20 .50
116 Alexandre Daigle .12 .30
117 Steve Duchesne .12 .30
118 Wade Redden .12 .30
119 Damian Rhodes .15 .40
120 Alexei Yashin .15 .40
121 Rod Brind'Amour .20 .50
122 Paul Coffey .20 .50
123 Eric Desjardins .15 .40
124 Ron Hextall .20 .50
125 John LeClair .20 .50
126 Eric Lindros .30 .75
127 Janne Niinimaa .20 .50
128 Mikael Renberg .15 .40
129 Dainius Zubrus RC .25 .60
130 Mike Gartner .25 .60
131 Craig Janney .15 .40
132 Nikolai Khabibulin .15 .40
133 Dave Manson .12 .30
134 Teppo Numminen .12 .30
135 Jeremy Roenick .30 .75
136 Keith Tkachuk .20 .50
137 Oleg Tverdovsky .15 .40
138 Tom Barrasso .15 .40
139 Ron Francis .25 .60

140 Kevin Hatcher .12 .30
141 Jaromir Jagr .60 1.50
142 Patrick Lalime RC .25 .60
143 Mario Lemieux .75 2.00
144 Jim Campbell .12 .30
145 Grant Fuhr .30 .75
146 Brett Hull .40 1.00
147 Al MacInnis .25 .60
148 Pierre Turgeon .15 .40
149 Harry York RC .20 .50
150 Kelly Hrudey .15 .40
151 Al Iafrate .12 .30
152 Bernie Nicholls .15 .40
153 Owen Nolan .20 .50
154 Darren Turcotte .12 .30
155 Brian Bradley .12 .30
156 Dino Ciccarelli .20 .50
157 Roman Hamrlik .12 .30
158 Daymond Langkow .15 .40
159 Daren Puppa .15 .40
160 Alexander Selivanov .12 .30
161 Sergei Berezin RC .30 .75
162 Wendel Clark .30 .75
163 Doug Gilmour .25 .60
164 Larry Murphy .15 .40
165 Felix Potvin .30 .75
166 Mats Sundin .20 .50
167 Pavel Bure .20 .50
168 Trevor Linden .20 .50
169 Kirk McLean .15 .40
170 Alexander Mogilny .15 .40
171 Esa Tikkanen .12 .30
172 Peter Bondra .20 .50
173 Andrew Brunette RC .25 .60
174 Jim Carey .20 .50
175 Sergei Gonchar .12 .30
176 Phil Housley .15 .40
177 Joe Juneau .12 .30
178 Michal Pivonka .12 .30
179 Checklist (1-143) .20 .50
180 Checklist (143-180 inserts) .20 .50
S125 John LeClair promo .20 .50

1996-97 Ultra Gold Medallion

*VETS: 2.5X TO 6X BASIC CARDS
*ROOKIES: 1.2X TO 3X

1996-97 Ultra Clear the Ice

COMPLETE SET (10) 50.00 125.00
1 Jim Carey 5.00 12.00
2 Peter Forsberg 10.00 25.00
3 Dominik Hasek 8.00 20.00
4 Jaromir Jagr 8.00 20.00
5 John LeClair 5.00 12.00
6 Eric Lindros 8.00 20.00
7 Mark Messier 5.00 12.00
8 Patrick Roy 20.00 50.00
9 Brendan Shanahan 5.00 12.00
10 Keith Tkachuk 5.00 12.00

1996-97 Ultra Mr. Momentum

COMPLETE SET (10) 20.00 40.00
1 Peter Bondra 1.00 2.50
2 Pavel Bure 2.00 5.00
3 Ron Francis 1.00 2.50
4 Brett Hull 2.50 6.00
5 Jaromir Jagr 3.00 8.00
6 Pat LaFontaine 2.00 5.00
7 Eric Lindros 2.00 5.00
8 Mark Messier 2.00 5.00
9 Mats Sundin 2.00 5.00
10 Steve Yzerman 6.00 15.00

1996-97 Ultra Power

COMPLETE SET (16) 25.00 60.00
1 Ray Bourque 2.00 5.00
2 Chris Chelios 1.25 3.00
3 Paul Coffey 1.25 3.00
4 Sergei Fedorov 2.00 5.00
5 Wayne Gretzky 8.00 20.00
6 Roman Hamrlik .60 1.50
7 Ed Jovanovski .60 1.50
8 Paul Kariya 1.25 3.00
9 Vladimir Konstantinov .60 1.50
10 Brian Leetch 1.25 3.00
11 Mario Lemieux 6.00 15.00
12 Nicklas Lidstrom 1.25 3.00
13 Alexander Mogilny .60 1.50
14 Adam Oates .60 1.50
15 Joe Sakic 2.50 6.00
16 Teemu Selanne 1.25 3.00

1996-97 Ultra Power Blue Line

COMPLETE SET (8) 10.00 25.00
1 Ray Bourque 4.00 10.00
2 Chris Chelios 2.50 6.00
3 Paul Coffey 2.50 6.00
4 Roman Hamrlik 1.25 3.00
5 Ed Jovanovski 1.25 3.00
6 Vladimir Konstantinov 1.25 3.00
7 Brian Leetch 2.50 6.00
8 Nicklas Lidstrom 2.50 6.00

1996-97 Ultra Power Red Line

COMPLETE SET (8) 30.00 80.00
1 Sergei Fedorov 4.00 10.00
2 Wayne Gretzky 12.50 30.00
3 Paul Kariya 2.50 6.00
4 Mario Lemieux 12.50 30.00
5 Alexander Mogilny 1.25 3.00
6 Adam Oates 1.25 3.00
7 Joe Sakic 5.00 12.00
8 Teemu Selanne 2.50 6.00

1996-97 Ultra Rookies

COMPLETE SET (20) 8.00 20.00
1 Bryan Berard .40 1.00
2 Sergei Berezin .40 1.00
3 Curtis Brown .40 1.00
4 Jim Campbell .40 1.00
5 Christian Dube .40 1.00
6 Anders Eriksson .40 1.00
7 Eric Fichaud .75 2.00
8 Daniel Goneau .40 1.00
9 Mike Grier .75 2.00
10 Jarome Iginla 3.00 8.00
11 Jamie Langenbrunner .40 1.00
12 Jay McKee .40 1.00
13 Ethan Moreau .40 1.00
14 Rem Murray .40 1.00
15 Janne Niinimaa .40 1.00
16 Wayne Primeau .40 1.00
17 Wade Redden .75 2.00
18 Jamie Storr .75 2.00
19 David Wilkie .40 1.00
20 Landon Wilson .40 1.00

2005-06 Ultra

1 Jean-Sebastien Giguere .30 .75
2 Teemu Selanne .60 1.50
3 Petr Sykora .25 .60
4 Rob Niedermayer .25 .60
5 Scott Niedermayer .30 .75
6 Sandis Ozolinsh .20 .50
7 Joffrey Lupul .20 .50
8 Kari Lehtonen .25 .60
9 Ilya Kovalchuk .30 .75
10 Peter Bondra .30 .75
11 Marian Hossa .30 .75
12 Patrik Stefan .20 .50
13 Bobby Holik .20 .50
14 Marc Savard .20 .50
15 Andrew Raycroft .25 .60
16 Patrice Bergeron .40 1.00
17 Joe Thornton .50 1.25
18 Glen Murray .25 .60
19 Brian Leetch .25 .60
20 Nick Boynton .20 .50
21 Sergei Samsonov .25 .60
22 Shawn McEachern .20 .50
23 Martin Biron .25 .60
24 Chris Drury .25 .60
25 Daniel Briere .30 .75
26 Derek Roy .20 .50
27 Maxim Afinogenov .20 .50
28 J.P. Dumont .20 .50
29 Mika Noronen .25 .60
30 Miikka Kipruosoff .30 .75
31 Jarome Iginla .40 1.00
32 Tony Amonte .25 .60
33 Matthew Lombardi .20 .50
34 Robyn Regehr .20 .50
35 Jordan Leopold .20 .50
36 Chuck Kobasew .20 .50
37 Phillippe Sauve .25 .60
38 Darren McCarty .20 .50
39 Martin Gerber .25 .60
40 Eric Staal .40 1.00
41 Erik Cole .20 .50
42 Justin Williams .25 .60
43 Glen Wesley .20 .50
44 Oleg Tverdovsky .20 .50
45 Cory Stillman .25 .60
46 Rod Brind'Amour .30 .75
47 Nikolai Khabibulin .30 .75
48 Tuomo Ruutu .30 .75
49 Eric Daze .25 .60
50 Tyler Arnason .20 .50
51 Adrian Aucoin .20 .50
52 Kyle Calder .20 .50
53 Mark Bell .20 .50
54 David Aebischer .25 .60
55 Joe Sakic .60 1.50
56 Milan Hejduk .25 .60
57 Alex Tanguay .30 .75
58 Rob Blake .30 .75
59 John-Michael Liles .20 .50
60 Pierre Turgeon .25 .60
61 Marc Denis .25 .60
62 Rick Nash .30 .75
63 Nikolai Zherdev .20 .50
64 Rostislav Klesla .20 .50
65 Bryan Berard .20 .50
66 Sergei Fedorov .50 1.25
67 Marty Turco .30 .75
68 Mike Modano .50 1.25
69 Brenden Morrow .25 .60
70 Bill Guerin .30 .75
71 Sergei Zubov .25 .60
72 Jere Lehtinen .25 .60
73 Manny Legace .30 .75
74 Steve Yzerman .75 2.00
75 Brendan Shanahan .30 .75
76 Pavel Datsyuk .50 1.25
77 Nicklas Lidstrom .30 .75
78 Chris Chelios .30 .75
79 Henrik Zetterberg .40 1.00
80 Ty Conklin .25 .60
81 Michael Peca .25 .60
82 Ryan Smyth .25 .60
83 Raffi Torres .20 .50
84 Chris Pronger .30 .75
85 Ales Hemsky .25 .60
86 Roberto Luongo .50 1.25
87 Joe Nieuwendyk .25 .60
88 Stephen Weiss .20 .50
89 Olli Jokinen .30 .75
90 Jay Bouwmeester .20 .50
91 Nathan Horton .30 .75
92 Mathieu Garon .25 .60
93 Jeremy Roenick .50 1.25
94 Luc Robitaille .30 .75
95 Pavol Demitra .40 1.00
96 Dustin Brown .30 .75
97 Alexander Frolov .20 .50
98 Dwayne Roloson .25 .60
99 Marian Gaborik .30 .75
100 Alexandre Daigle .20 .50
101 Pierre-Marc Bouchard .30 .75
102 Filip Kuba .20 .50
103 Manny Fernandez .20 .50
104 Saku Koivu .30 .75
105 Jose Theodore .30 .75
106 Mike Ribeiro .20 .50
107 Michael Ryder .25 .60
108 Sheldon Souray .20 .50
109 Richard Zednik .20 .50
110 Tomas Vokoun .25 .60
111 Paul Kariya .30 .75
112 Steve Sullivan .20 .50
113 David Legwand .25 .60
114 Kimmo Timonen .20 .50
115 Scott Walker .20 .50
116 Martin Brodeur .75 2.00
117 Scott Gomez .25 .60
118 Patrik Elias .30 .75
119 Alexander Mogilny .25 .60
120 Brian Rafalski .25 .60
121 John Madden .20 .50
122 Rick DiPietro .25 .60
123 Alexei Yashin .25 .60
124 Miroslav Satan .25 .60
125 Trent Hunter .20 .50
126 Brent Sopel .20 .50
127 Mark Parrish .20 .50
128 Kevin Weekes .25 .60
129 Jaromir Jagr 1.00 2.50
130 Marcel Hossa .20 .50
131 Steve Rucchin .20 .50
132 Tom Poti .20 .50
133 Dominik Hasek .50 1.25
134 Jason Spezza .30 .75
135 Dany Heatley .25 .60
136 Martin Havlat .30 .75
137 Wade Redden .20 .50
138 Zdeno Chara .30 .75
139 Daniel Alfredsson .30 .75
140 Robert Esche .25 .60
141 Peter Forsberg .60 1.50
142 Simon Gagne .30 .75
143 Keith Primeau .25 .60
144 Joni Pitkanen .20 .50
145 Kim Johnsson .20 .50
146 Sami Kapanen .20 .50
147 Curtis Joseph .40 1.00
148 Shane Doan .25 .60
149 Jamie Lundmark .20 .50
150 Ladislav Nagy .20 .50
151 Mike Ricci .20 .50
152 Petr Nedved .20 .50
153 Jocelyn Thibault .25 .60
154 Mario Lemieux 1.25 3.00
155 Mark Recchi .40 1.00
156 Zigmund Palffy .30 .75
157 John LeClair .30 .75
158 Ryan Malone .20 .50
159 Marc-Andre Fleury .60 1.50
160 Evgeni Nabokov .25 .60
161 Patrick Marleau .30 .75
162 Jonathan Cheechoo .25 .60
163 Marco Sturm .20 .50
164 Brad Stuart .20 .50
165 Patrick Lalime .25 .60
166 Doug Weight .30 .75
167 Keith Tkachuk .30 .75
168 Mark Rycroft .20 .50
169 Barret Jackman .20 .50
170 Dallas Drake .20 .50
171 Sean Burke .20 .50
172 Martin St. Louis .30 .75
173 Vincent Lecavalier .30 .75
174 Brad Richards .30 .75
175 Ruslan Fedotenko .20 .50
176 Fredrik Modin .20 .50
177 Dave Andreychuk .30 .75
178 Pavel Kubina .20 .50
179 Ed Belfour .30 .75
180 Mats Sundin .30 .75
181 Eric Lindros .50 1.25
182 Jeff O'Neill .20 .50
183 Bryan McCabe .20 .50
184 Tie Domi .25 .60
185 Matt Stajan .20 .50
186 Nik Antropov .25 .60
187 Jason Allison .25 .60
188 Dan Cloutier .25 .60
189 Markus Naslund .30 .75
190 Brendan Morrison .20 .50
191 Todd Bertuzzi .30 .75
192 Ed Jovanovski .25 .60
193 Mattias Ohlund .20 .50
194 Trevor Linden .30 .75
195 Anson Carter .25 .60
196 Ryan Kesler .30 .75
197 Olaf Kolzig .30 .75
198 Jeff Friesen .20 .50
199 Brian Willsie .20 .50
200 Brendan Witt .20 .50
201 Braydon Coburn RC 2.00 5.00
202 Jim Slater RC 1.50 4.00
203 Adam Berkhoel RC 1.50 4.00
204 Andrew Alberts RC 1.25 3.00
205 Kevin Dallman RC 1.50 4.00
206 Milan Jurcina RC 1.50 4.00
207 Niklas Nordgren RC 2.00 5.00
208 Kevin Nastiuk RC 1.25 3.00
209 Brent Seabrook RC 4.00 10.00
210 Rene Bourque RC 2.00 5.00
211 Duncan Keith RC 3.00 8.00
212 Cam Barker RC 1.50 4.00
213 Peter Budaj RC 2.50 6.00
214 Jaroslav Balastik RC 1.25 3.00
215 Jussi Jokinen RC 2.00 5.00
216 Brett Lebda RC 1.25 3.00
217 Johan Franzen RC 3.00 8.00
218 Brad Winchester RC 2.00 5.00
219 Kyle Brodziak RC 1.25 3.00
220 George Parros RC 1.25 3.00
221 Derek Boogaard RC 3.00 8.00
222 Matthew Foy RC 1.25 3.00
223 Yann Danis RC 1.50 4.00
224 Mark Streit RC 1.25 3.00
225 Raitis Ivanans RC 1.25 3.00
226 Ryan Suter RC 2.50 6.00
227 Petteri Nokelainen RC 1.25 3.00
228 Chris Campoli RC 1.25 3.00
229 Ryan Hollweg RC 1.25 3.00
230 Petr Prucha RC 2.00 5.00
231 Al Montoya RC 2.00 5.00
232 Chris Holt RC 1.25 3.00
233 Brandon Bochenski RC 2.00 5.00
234 Andrej Meszaros RC 1.50 4.00
235 Brian McGrattan RC 1.25 3.00
236 Patrick Eaves RC 2.00 5.00
237 Wade Skolney RC 1.25 3.00
238 Keith Ballard RC 1.50 4.00
239 David Leneveu RC 1.50 4.00
240 Maxime Talbot RC 2.00 5.00
241 Ryane Clowe RC 2.50 6.00
242 Josh Gorges RC 1.50 4.00
243 Jay McClement RC 1.25 3.00
244 Jeff Hoggan RC 1.25 3.00
245 Lee Stempniak RC 2.00 5.00
246 Andy Roach RC 1.25 3.00
247 Timo Helbling RC 1.25 3.00
248 Paul Ranger RC 1.25 3.00
249 Andrew Wozniewski RC 1.50 4.00
250 Anthony Stewart RC 1.50 4.00
251 Sidney Crosby RC 100.00 250.00
252 Alexander Ovechkin RC 125.00 300.00
253 Corey Perry RC 6.00 15.00
254 Jeff Carter RC 3.00 8.00
255 Gilbert Brule RC 2.00 5.00
256 Wojtek Wolski RC 1.50 4.00
257 Jeff Woywitka RC 1.25 3.00
258 Hannu Toivonen RC 2.00 5.00
259 Alexander Perezhogin RC 1.50 4.00
260 Zach Parise RC 5.00 12.00
261 Dion Phaneuf RC 3.00 8.00
262 Mike Richards RC 4.00 10.00
263 Cam Ward RC 3.00 8.00
264 Robert Nilsson RC 2.00 5.00
265 Eric Nystrom RC 1.50 4.00
266 Alexander Steen RC 3.00 8.00
267 Ryan Getzlaf RC 5.00 12.00
268 Rostislav Olesz RC 1.50 4.00
269 Henrik Lundqvist RC 10.00 25.00
270 Jim Howard RC 5.00 12.00
271 Thomas Vanek RC 4.00 10.00

2005-06 Ultra Gold

*1-200 VETS: 1.5X TO 4X BASIC CARDS
*201-250 ROOKIES: .3X TO .8X BASIC RC
*251-271 ROOKIES: 1X TO 2.5X BASIC RC
251 Sidney Crosby 125.00 250.00
252 Alexander Ovechkin 300.00 800.00

2005-06 Ultra Difference Makers

COMPLETE SET (12) 20.00 40.00
DM1 Rick Nash .60 1.50
DM2 Pavel Datsyuk 1.00 2.50
DM3 Steve Yzerman 1.25 3.00
DM4 Todd Bertuzzi .60 1.50
DM5 Jeff Carter 1.00 2.50
DM6 Sidney Crosby 6.00 15.00
DM7 Tuomo Ruutu .40 1.00
DM8 Patrice Bergeron .40 1.00
DM9 Alexander Ovechkin 20.00 50.00
DM10 Martin St. Louis .40 1.00
DM11 Jarome Iginla .75 2.00
DM12 Andrew Raycroft .40 1.00

2005-06 Ultra Difference Makers Jerseys

*PATCH/25: 1.5X TO 4X BASIC JSY
DMJAO Alexander Ovechkin 50.00 125.00
DMJAR Andrew Raycroft 4.00 10.00
DMJJC Jeff Carter 5.00 12.00
DMJJI Jarome Iginla 5.00 12.00
DMJPB Patrice Bergeron 4.00 10.00
DMJPD Pavel Datsyuk 4.00 10.00
DMJRN Rick Nash 8.00 20.00
DMJSC Sidney Crosby 15.00 40.00
DMJSL Martin St. Louis 4.00 10.00
DMJSY Steve Yzerman 8.00 20.00
DMJTB Todd Bertuzzi 4.00 10.00
DMJTR Tuomo Ruutu 4.00 10.00

2005-06 Ultra Fresh Ink

FIAM Al Montoya 10.00 25.00
FIAO Alexander Ovechkin 800.00 2000.00
FIAP Alexander Perezhogin 8.00 20.00
FIAR Andrew Raycroft SP 8.00 20.00
FIAS Alexander Steen 15.00 40.00
FIAT Alex Tanguay SP 10.00 25.00
FIAW Andrew Wozniewski 8.00 20.00
FIAY Alexei Yashin 8.00 20.00
FIBG Boyd Gordon 6.00 15.00
FIBL Brett Lebda 6.00 15.00
FIBM Brenden Morrow 8.00 20.00
FIBO Derek Boogaard 15.00 40.00
FICA Mike Cammalleri 10.00 25.00
FICB Cam Barker 8.00 20.00
FICD Chris Drury 8.00 20.00
FICE Christian Ehrhoff 6.00 15.00
FICK Chris Kunitz 10.00 25.00
FICP Corey Perry SP 30.00 80.00
FICW Cam Ward 15.00 40.00
FIDD Dustin Brown 10.00 25.00
FIDL David Leneveu 8.00 20.00
FIDP Dion Phaneuf 15.00 40.00
FIDR Dwayne Roloson 8.00 20.00
FIDW Doug Weight 10.00 25.00
FIEJ Ed Jovanovski 8.00 20.00
FIEN Eric Nystrom 8.00 20.00
FIES Eric Staal SP 12.00 30.00
FIGB Gilbert Brule 10.00 25.00
FIGM Glen Murray 8.00 20.00
FIGP George Parros 6.00 15.00
FIHO Jeff Hoggan 6.00 15.00
FIHT Hannu Toivonen 10.00 25.00
FIHV Martin Havlat SP 10.00 25.00
FIHZ Henrik Zetterberg 12.00 30.00
FIIK Ilya Kovalchuk SP 10.00 25.00
FIIL Ian Laperriere 6.00 15.00
FIJA Jaroslav Balastik 6.00 15.00
FIJB Jay Bouwmeester SP 6.00 15.00
FIJC Jeff Carter 15.00 40.00
FIJG Josh Gorges 8.00 20.00
FIJH Jochen Hecht 6.00 15.00
FIJI Jarome Iginla 12.00 30.00
FIJI Jim Howard 25.00 60.00
FIJL Joffrey Lupul 6.00 15.00
FIJM Jay McClement 6.00 15.00
FIJN Jocelyn Thibault 8.00 20.00
FIJO Jeff O'Neill 6.00 15.00
FIJR Jeremy Roenick SP 15.00 40.00
FIJS Jason Spezza SP 10.00 25.00
FIJT Joe Thornton SP 15.00 40.00
FIJW Jeff Woywitka 6.00 15.00
FIKD Kevin Dallman 8.00 20.00
FIKP Keith Primeau 8.00 20.00
FIKW Kevin Weekes 8.00 20.00
FILN Ladislav Nagy SP 6.00 15.00
FIMB Martin Brodeur SP 25.00 60.00
FIMC Bryan McCabe 6.00 15.00
FIMO Brendan Morrison 6.00 15.00
FIMP Michael Peca 8.00 20.00
FIMR Mike Richards 20.00 50.00
FIMS Matt Stajan 6.00 15.00
FIMT Marty Turco SP 10.00 25.00
FINI Rob Niedermayer 8.00 20.00
FINN Niklas Nordgren 10.00 25.00
FINS Robert Nilsson 10.00 25.00
FINZ Nikolai Zherdev 6.00 15.00
FION Owen Nolan 10.00 25.00
FIPB Patrice Bergeron SP 12.00 30.00
FIPE Mark Popovic SP 6.00 15.00
FIRE Robert Esche 8.00 20.00
FIRF Ruslan Fedotenko 6.00 15.00
FIRG Ryan Getzlaf SP 25.00 60.00
FIRH Ryan Hollweg 6.00 15.00
FIRI Raitis Ivanans 6.00 15.00
FIRK Ryan Kesler 10.00 25.00
FIRL Roberto Luongo 15.00 40.00
FIRN Rick Nash SP 10.00 25.00
FIRO Rostislav Olesz 8.00 20.00
FIRS Ryan Smyth 8.00 20.00
FIRZ Richard Zednik 6.00 15.00
FISA Miroslav Satan 8.00 20.00
FISB Sean Burke 6.00 15.00
FISC Sidney Crosby SP 200.00 500.00
FISD Shane Doan 8.00 20.00
FISG Simon Gagne 10.00 25.00
FISK Saku Koivu SP 10.00 25.00
FISN Scott Niedermayer 10.00 25.00
FISS Sheldon Souray 6.00 15.00
FIST Anthony Stewart 8.00 20.00
FISU Ryan Suter 12.00 30.00
FITH Jose Theodore SP 10.00 25.00
FITI Timo Helbling 6.00 15.00
FITL Trevor Linden 10.00 25.00
FITR Tuomo Ruutu 10.00 25.00
FITS Timofei Shishkanov 6.00 15.00
FITV Thomas Vanek 20.00 50.00
FIVL Vincent Lecavalier 10.00 25.00
FIWW Wojtek Wolski 8.00 20.00
FIYD Yann Danis 8.00 20.00
FIZC Zdeno Chara 10.00 25.00
FIZP Zach Parise 25.00 60.00

2005-06 Ultra Fresh Ink Blue

*BLUE/25: .5X TO 1.2X BASIC
FIAO Alexander Ovechkin 1000.00 2500.00
FISC Sidney Crosby 400.00 1000.00

2005-06 Ultra Ice

*1-200 VETS/100: 4X TO 10X BASIC CARDS
*201-250 ROOKIE/25: 1.5X TO 4X BASIC RC
*251-271 ROOKIE/25: 1.2X TO 3X BASIC RC
251 Sidney Crosby 400.00 650.00
252 Alexander Ovechkin 400.00 1000.00

2005-06 Ultra Rookie Uniformity Jerseys

*PATCH/35: 1.2X TO 3X BASE JSY
RUAA Andrew Alberts 2.50 6.00
RUAM Andrej Meszaros 3.00 8.00
RUAO Alexander Ovechkin 80.00 200.00
RUAP Alexander Perezhogin 3.00 8.00
RUAS Alexander Steen 6.00 15.00
RUAW Andrew Wozniewski 3.00 8.00
RUBB Brandon Bochenski 4.00 10.00
RUBC Braydon Coburn 4.00 10.00
RUBL Brett Lebda 2.50 6.00
RUBS Brent Seabrook 8.00 20.00
RUBW Brad Winchester 4.00 10.00
RUCB Cam Barker 3.00 8.00
RUCP Corey Perry 12.00 30.00
RUCW Cam Ward 6.00 15.00
RUDK Duncan Keith 8.00 20.00
RUDL David Leneveu 3.00 8.00
RUDP Dion Phaneuf 6.00 15.00
RUEN Eric Nystrom 3.00 8.00
RUGB Gilbert Brule 4.00 10.00
RUGP George Parros 2.50 6.00
RUHL Henrik Lundqvist 8.00 20.00
RUHO Jeff Hoggan 2.50 6.00
RUHT Hannu Toivonen 4.00 10.00
RUJB Jaroslav Balastik 2.50 6.00
RUJC Jeff Carter 6.00 15.00
RUJF Johan Franzen 6.00 15.00
RUJG Josh Gorges 3.00 8.00
RUJH Jim Howard 10.00 25.00
RUJJ Jussi Jokinen 4.00 10.00
RUJM Jay McClement 2.50 6.00
RUJS Jim Slater 3.00 8.00
RUJW Jeff Woywitka 2.50 6.00
RUKB Keith Ballard 3.00 8.00
RUKD Kevin Dallman 3.00 8.00
RUKN Kevin Nastiuk 2.50 6.00
RUMF Matthew Foy 2.50 6.00
RUMJ Milan Jurcina 3.00 8.00
RUMO Al Montoya 4.00 10.00
RUMR Mike Richards 8.00 20.00
RUMT Maxime Talbot 4.00 10.00
RUNN Niklas Nordgren 4.00 10.00
RUPB Peter Budaj 5.00 12.00
RUPE Patrick Eaves 4.00 10.00
RUPN Petteri Nokelainen 2.50 6.00
RUPP Petr Prucha 4.00 10.00
RURB Rene Bourque 4.00 10.00
RURC Ryane Clowe 5.00 12.00
RURG Ryan Getzlaf 10.00 25.00
RURH Ryan Hollweg 2.50 6.00
RURI Raitis Ivanans 2.50 6.00
RURN Robert Nilsson 4.00 10.00
RURO Rostislav Olesz 3.00 8.00
RURS Ryan Suter 5.00 12.00
RUSC Sidney Crosby 30.00 80.00
RUST Anthony Stewart 3.00 8.00
RUTH Timo Helbling 2.50 6.00
RUTV Thomas Vanek 8.00 20.00
RUWW Wojtek Wolski 3.00 8.00
RUYD Yann Danis 3.00 8.00
RUZP Zach Parise 10.00 25.00

2005-06 Ultra Rookie Uniformity Jersey Autographs

ARUAA Andrew Alberts 10.00 25.00
ARUAM Andrej Meszaros 12.00 30.00
ARUAM Al Montoya 15.00 40.00
ARUAO Alexander Ovechkin 1000.00 2500.00
ARUAP Alexander Perezhogin 30.00 80.00
ARUAS Alexander Steen 25.00 60.00
ARUAW Andrew Wozniewski 12.00 30.00
ARUBB Brandon Bochenski 15.00 40.00
ARUBC Braydon Coburn 15.00 40.00
ARUBL Brett Lebda 10.00 25.00
ARUBS Brent Seabrook 30.00 80.00
ARUBW Brad Winchester 15.00 40.00
ARUCB Cam Barker 12.00 30.00
ARUCP Corey Perry 40.00 100.00
ARUCW Cam Ward 40.00 80.00
ARUDK Duncan Keith 40.00 80.00
ARUDL David Leneveu 12.00 30.00
ARUDP Dion Phaneuf 75.00 150.00
ARUEN Eric Nystrom 12.00 30.00
ARUGB Gilbert Brule 15.00 40.00
ARUGP George Parros 10.00 25.00
ARUHL Henrik Lundqvist 75.00 150.00
ARUHO Jeff Hoggan 10.00 25.00
ARUHT Hannu Toivonen 15.00 40.00
ARUJB Jaroslav Balastik 10.00 25.00
ARUJC Jeff Carter 25.00 60.00
ARUJF Johan Franzen 25.00 60.00
ARUJG Josh Gorges 12.00 30.00
ARUJH Jim Howard 40.00 80.00
ARUJJ Jussi Jokinen 15.00 40.00
ARUJM Jay McClement 10.00 25.00
ARUJS Jim Slater 12.00 30.00
ARUJW Jeff Woywitka 10.00 25.00
ARUKB Keith Ballard 12.00 30.00
ARUKD Kevin Dallman 12.00 30.00
ARUKN Kevin Nastiuk 10.00 25.00
ARUMF Matthew Foy 10.00 25.00
ARUMJ Milan Jurcina 12.00 30.00
ARUMR Mike Richards 40.00 100.00
ARUMT Maxime Talbot 15.00 40.00
ARUNN Niklas Nordgren 15.00 40.00
ARUPB Peter Budaj 20.00 50.00
ARUPE Patrick Eaves 15.00 40.00
ARUPN Petteri Nokelainen 10.00 25.00
ARUPP Petr Prucha 15.00 40.00
ARURB Rene Bourque 15.00 40.00
ARURC Ryane Clowe 20.00 50.00
ARURG Ryan Getzlaf 30.00 80.00
ARURH Ryan Hollweg 10.00 25.00
ARURI Raitis Ivanans 10.00 25.00
ARURN Robert Nilsson 15.00 40.00
ARURO Rostislav Olesz 12.00 30.00
ARURS Ryan Suter 20.00 50.00
ARUSC Sidney Crosby 400.00 700.00
ARUST Anthony Stewart 12.00 30.00
ARUTH Timo Helbling 10.00 25.00
ARUTV Thomas Vanek 30.00 80.00
ARUWW Wojtek Wolski 12.00 30.00
ARUYD Yann Danis 12.00 30.00
ARUZP Zach Parise 25.00 60.00

2005-06 Ultra Scoring Kings

SK1 Mario Lemieux 3.00 8.00
SK2 Martin St. Louis .75 2.00
SK3 Joe Thornton 1.25 3.00
SK4 Mats Sundin .75 2.00
SK5 Jarome Iginla 1.00 2.50
SK6 Mike Modano 1.25 3.00
SK7 Steve Yzerman 2.00 5.00
SK8 Joe Sakic 1.50 4.00
SK9 Alex Tanguay .75 2.00
SK10 Dany Heatley .60 1.50
SK11 Sidney Crosby 8.00 20.00
SK12 Jeremy Roenick 1.25 3.00
SK13 Jason Spezza .75 2.00
SK14 Patrik Elias .75 2.00
SK15 Jaromir Jagr 2.50 6.00
SK16 Brad Richards .75 2.00
SK17 Markus Naslund .75 2.00
SK18 Alexander Ovechkin 25.00 60.00
SK19 Doug Weight .75 2.00
SK20 Ilya Kovalchuk .75 2.00
SK21 Peter Forsberg 1.50 4.00
SK22 Sergei Fedorov 1.25 3.00
SK23 Marian Hossa .75 2.00
SK24 Milan Hejduk .60 1.50
SK25 Bill Guerin .75 2.00
SK26 Shane Doan .60 1.50
SK27 Mike Ribiero .50 1.25
SK28 Martin Havlat .75 2.00
SK29 Corey Perry 2.50 6.00
SK30 Mike Richards 1.50 4.00
SK31 Ryan Getzlaf 2.00 5.00
SK32 Keith Tkachuk .75 2.00
SK33 Glen Murray .60 1.50
SK34 Brendan Shanahan .75 2.00
SK35 Paul Kariya .75 2.00
SK36 Marian Gaborik .75 2.00
SK37 Luc Robitaille .75 2.00
SK38 Daniel Alfredsson .75 2.00
SK39 Vincent Lecavalier .75 2.00
SK40 Eric Daze .60 1.50

2005-06 Ultra Scoring Kings Jerseys

SKJAO Alexander Ovechkin 60.00 150.00
SKJAT Alex Tanguay 2.00 5.00
SKJBG Bill Guerin 2.00 5.00
SKJBR Brad Richards 2.00 5.00
SKJBS Brendan Shanahan 2.00 5.00
SKJCP Corey Perry 6.00 15.00
SKJDA Daniel Alfredsson 2.00 5.00
SKJDH Dany Heatley 1.50 4.00
SKJDW Doug Weight 2.00 5.00
SKJED Eric Daze 1.50 4.00
SKJGM Glen Murray 1.50 4.00
SKJHO Marian Hossa 2.00 5.00
SKJHV Martin Havlat 2.00 5.00
SKJIK Ilya Kovalchuk 2.00 5.00
SKJJI Jarome Iginla 2.50 6.00
SKJJJ Jaromir Jagr 5.00 12.00
SKJJR Jeremy Roenick 3.00 8.00
SKJJS Jason Spezza 2.00 5.00
SKJJS Joe Sakic 4.00 10.00
SKJJT Joe Thornton 3.00 8.00
SKJKT Keith Tkachuk 2.00 5.00
SKJLR Luc Robitaille 2.00 5.00
SKJMG Marian Gaborik 2.00 5.00
SKJMH Milan Hejduk 1.50 4.00
SKJML Mario Lemieux 8.00 20.00
SKJMM Mike Modano 3.00 8.00
SKJMN Markus Naslund 2.00 5.00
SKJMR Mike Ribeiro 1.25 3.00
SKJMS Mats Sundin 2.00 5.00
SKJPE Patrik Elias 2.00 5.00
SKJPF Peter Forsberg 4.00 10.00
SKJPK Paul Kariya 2.00 5.00
SKJRG Ryan Getzlaf 5.00 12.00
SKJRI Mike Richards 4.00 10.00
SKJSC Sidney Crosby 10.00 25.00
SKJSD Shane Doan 1.50 4.00
SKJSF Sergei Fedorov 3.00 8.00
SKJSL Martin St. Louis 2.00 5.00
SKJSY Steve Yzerman 5.00 12.00
SKJVL Vincent Lecavalier 2.00 5.00

2005-06 Ultra Scoring Kings Jersey Autographs

KAJAO Alexander Ovechkin 1000.00 2500.00
KAJAT Alex Tanguay 12.00 30.00
KAJBR Brad Richards 12.00 30.00
KAJCP Corey Perry 40.00 100.00
KAJDA Daniel Alfredsson 12.00 30.00
KAJDH Dany Heatley 10.00 25.00
KAJDW Doug Weight 12.00 30.00
KAJED Eric Daze 10.00 25.00
KAJGM Glen Murray 10.00 25.00
KAJHO Marian Hossa 12.00 30.00
KAJHV Martin Havlat 12.00 30.00
KAJIK Ilya Kovalchuk 12.00 30.00
KAJJI Jarome Iginla 15.00 40.00
KAJJR Jeremy Roenick 20.00 50.00
KAJJS Jason Spezza 12.00 30.00
KAJJT Joe Thornton 20.00 50.00
KAJMH Milan Hejduk 10.00 25.00
KAJMM Mike Modano 20.00 50.00
KAJMN Markus Naslund 12.00 30.00
KAJMR Mike Ribiero 8.00 20.00
KAJMS Mats Sundin 12.00 30.00
KAJRG Ryan Getzlaf 30.00 80.00
KAJRI Mike Richards 25.00 60.00
KAJSC Sidney Crosby 200.00 300.00
KAJSD Shane Doan 10.00 25.00
KAJSL Martin St. Louis 12.00 30.00
KAJVL Vincent Lecavalier 12.00 30.00

2005-06 Ultra Scoring Kings Patches

*PATCHES: 1.25X TO 3X BASE JSY
SKPAO Alexander Ovechkin 125.00 300.00
SKPSC Sidney Crosby 100.00 250.00

2005-06 Ultra Super Six

COMPLETE SET (8) 10.00 25.00
SS1 Mario Lemieux 2.50 6.00
SS2 Joe Thornton 1.00 2.50
SS3 Martin Brodeur 1.50 4.00
SS4 Ray Bourque 1.00 2.50
SS5 Joe Sakic 1.25 3.00
SS6 Patrick Roy 1.50 4.00
SS7 Ray Bourque 1.00 2.50
SS8 Patrick Roy 1.50 4.00

2005-06 Ultra Super Six Jerseys

SSJJS Joe Sakic 12.00 30.00
SSJJT Joe Thornton 10.00 25.00
SSJMB Martin Brodeur 8.00 20.00
SSJML Mario Lemieux 15.00 30.00
SSJPR1 Patrick Roy 15.00 30.00
SSJPR2 Patrick Roy 15.00 30.00
SSJRB1 Ray Bourque 6.00 15.00
SSJRB2 Ray Bourque 6.00 15.00

2006-07 Ultra

COMPLETE SET (251) 100.00 250.00
COMP.SET w/o SPs (200) 15.00 40.00
1 Jean-Sebastien Giguere .30 .75
2 Chris Pronger .30 .75
3 Andy McDonald .25 .60
4 Corey Perry .50 1.25
5 Teemu Selanne .60 1.50
6 Ryan Getzlaf .30 .75
7 Scott Niedermayer .30 .75
8 Kari Lehtonen .25 .60
9 Steve Rucchin .20 .50
10 Marian Hossa .30 .75
11 Ilya Kovalchuk .30 .75
12 Slava Kozlov .20 .50
13 Bobby Holik .20 .50
14 Patrice Bergeron .40 1.00
15 Brad Boyes .20 .50
16 Marc Savard .20 .50
17 Brad Stuart .20 .50
18 Marco Sturm .20 .50
19 Glen Murray .25 .60
20 Zdeno Chara .30 .75
21 Thomas Vanek .25 .60
22 Ryan Miller .30 .75
23 Maxim Afinogenov .20 .50
24 Ales Kotalik .20 .50
25 Chris Drury .25 .60
26 Martin Biron .25 .60
27 Daniel Briere .30 .75
28 Miikka Kiprusoff .30 .75
29 Jarome Iginla .40 1.00
30 Chuck Kobasew .20 .50
31 Kristian Huselius .20 .50
32 Daymond Langkow .20 .50
33 Dion Phaneuf .25 .60
34 Alex Tanguay .20 .50
35 Cam Ward .30 .75
36 Andrew Ladd .20 .50
37 Eric Staal .40 1.00
38 Justin Williams .25 .60
39 Erik Cole .20 .50
40 Mike Commodore .20 .50
41 Rod Brind`Amour .30 .75
42 Nikolai Khabibulin .30 .75
43 Tuomo Ruutu .30 .75
44 Kyle Calder .20 .50
45 Martin Havlat .20 .50
46 Rene Bourque .20 .50
47 Duncan Keith .25 .60
48 Jose Theodore .30 .75
49 Joe Sakic .60 1.50
50 Milan Hejduk .25 .60
51 Andrew Brunette .20 .50
52 Marek Svatos .20 .50
53 Pierre Turgeon .25 .60
54 Peter Budaj .25 .60
55 Fredrik Modin .20 .50
56 Nikolai Zherdev .20 .50
57 Rick Nash .30 .75
58 Sergei Fedorov .50 1.25
59 Rostislav Klesla .20 .50
60 Bryan Berard .20 .50
61 David Vyborny .20 .50
62 Marty Turco .30 .75
63 Mike Modano .50 1.25
64 Sergei Zubov .25 .60
65 Brenden Morrow .25 .60
66 Jussi Jokinen .25 .60

67 Eric Lindros .50 1.25
68 Jere Lehtinen .20 .50
69 Tomas Holmstrom .25 .60
70 Henrik Zetterberg .40 1.00
71 Nicklas Lidstrom .30 .75
72 Pavel Datsyuk .50 1.25
73 Chris Osgood .30 .75
74 Kris Draper .20 .50
75 Steve Yzerman .75 2.00
76 Ales Hemsky .25 .60
77 Jarret Stoll .25 .60
78 Joffrey Lupul .20 .50
79 Dwayne Roloson .25 .60
80 Ryan Smyth .25 .60
81 Shawn Horcoff .20 .50
82 Fernando Pisani .20 .50
83 Todd Bertuzzi .30 .75
84 Nathan Horton .30 .75
85 Alex Auld .20 .50
86 Olli Jokinen .30 .75
87 Jay Bouwmeester .20 .50
88 Rostislav Olesz .20 .50
89 Joe Nieuwendyk .25 .60
90 Alexander Frolov .20 .50
91 Mathieu Garon .25 .60
92 Mike Cammalleri .20 .50
93 Rob Blake .30 .75
94 Lubomir Visnovsky .20 .50
95 Dustin Brown .30 .75
96 Marian Gaborik .30 .75
97 Manny Fernandez .20 .50
98 Mark Parrish .20 .50
99 Pierre-Marc Bouchard .30 .75
100 Brian Rolston .25 .60
101 Pavol Demitra .40 1.00
102 Saku Koivu .30 .75
103 Cristobal Huet .25 .60
104 Alex Kovalev .25 .60
105 Michael Ryder .20 .50
106 David Aebischer .25 .60
107 Mike Ribeiro .20 .50
108 Chris Higgins .20 .50
109 Tomas Vokoun .25 .60
110 Steve Sullivan .20 .50
111 David Legwand .25 .60
112 Paul Kariya .30 .75
113 Jason Arnott .25 .60
114 Kimmo Timonen .20 .50
115 Martin Brodeur .75 2.00
116 Brian Rafalski .25 .60
117 Patrik Elias .30 .75
118 Brian Gionta .20 .50
119 Scott Gomez .25 .60
120 Zach Parise .30 .75
121 Alexei Yashin .25 .60
122 Rick DiPietro .25 .60
123 Miroslav Satan .25 .60
124 Trent Hunter .20 .50
125 Jason Blake .20 .50
126 Mike Sillinger .20 .50
127 Henrik Lundqvist .75 2.00
128 Martin Straka .20 .50
129 Jaromir Jagr 1.00 2.50
130 Petr Prucha .25 .60
131 Brendan Shanahan .30 .75
132 Matt Cullen .20 .50
133 Martin Gerber .25 .60
134 Jason Spezza .30 .75
135 Wade Redden .20 .50
136 Dany Heatley .25 .60
137 Daniel Alfredsson .30 .75
138 Patrick Eaves .20 .50
139 Ray Emery .25 .60
140 Peter Forsberg .60 1.50
141 Antero Niittymaki .25 .60
142 Joni Pitkanen .20 .50
143 Simon Gagne .30 .75
144 Keith Primeau .25 .60
145 Jeff Carter .25 .60
146 Robert Esche .25 .60
147 Mike Richards .25 .60
148 Ladislav Nagy .20 .50
149 Curtis Joseph .40 1.00
150 Mike Comrie .25 .60
151 Shane Doan .25 .60
152 Ed Jovanovski .25 .60
153 Jeremy Roenick .50 1.25
154 Sidney Crosby 1.25 3.00
155 Marc-Andre Fleury .60 1.50
156 Ryan Malone .20 .50
157 Colby Armstrong .25 .60
158 Ryan Whitney .25 .60
159 John LeClair .30 .75
160 Evgeni Nabokov .25 .60
161 Joe Thornton .50 1.25
162 Patrick Marleau .30 .75
163 Vesa Toskala .25 .60
164 Jonathan Cheechoo .25 .60
165 Steve Bernier .20 .50
166 Mark Bell .20 .50
167 Keith Tkachuk .30 .75
168 Curtis Sanford .25 .60
169 Doug Weight .30 .75
170 Bill Guerin .30 .75
171 Lee Stempniak .20 .50
172 Petr Cajanek .20 .50
173 Evgeni Artyukhin .20 .50
174 Brad Richards .30 .75
175 Martin St. Louis .30 .75
176 Vincent Lecavalier .30 .75
177 Vaclav Prospal .20 .50
178 Marc Denis .25 .60
179 Ruslan Fedotenko .20 .50
180 Andrew Raycroft .25 .60
181 Mats Sundin .30 .75
182 Bryan McCabe .20 .50
183 Alexander Steen .20 .50
184 Kyle Wellwood .25 .60
185 Darcy Tucker .25 .60
186 Tomas Kaberle .20 .50
187 Michael Peca .25 .60
188 Markus Naslund .30 .75
189 Roberto Luongo .50 1.25
190 Henrik Sedin .40 1.00
191 Mattias Ohlund .20 .50
192 Brendan Morrison .20 .50
193 Ryan Kesler .30 .75
194 Daniel Sedin .40 1.00
195 Olaf Kolzig .30 .75
196 Alexander Ovechkin 1.25 3.00
197 Brian Pothier .20 .50
198 Dainius Zubrus .20 .50
199 Chris Clark .20 .50
200 Matt Pettinger .25 .60
201 Yan Stastny RC 1.25 3.00
202 Mark Stuart RC 1.25 3.00
203 Carsen Germyn RC 1.25 3.00
204 Dustin Byfuglien RC 3.00 8.00
205 Dan Jancevski RC 1.25 3.00
206 Tomas Kopecky RC 1.50 4.00
207 Marc-Antoine Pouliot RC 1.25 3.00
208 Konstantin Pushkarev RC 1.50 4.00
209 Erik Reitz RC 1.25 3.00
210 Miroslav Kopriva RC 1.25 3.00
211 Shea Weber RC 3.00 8.00
212 Frank Doyle RC 1.50 4.00
213 Rob Collins RC 1.25 3.00
214 Steve Regier RC 1.25 3.00
215 Ryan Caldwell RC 1.25 3.00
216 Masi Marjamaki RC 1.25 3.00
217 Jarkko Immonen RC 1.50 4.00
218 Billy Thompson RC 1.25 3.00
219 Filip Novak RC 1.25 3.00
220 Ryan Potulny RC 1.25 3.00
221 Bill Thomas RC 1.25 3.00
222 Joel Perrault RC 1.25 3.00
223 Noah Welch RC 1.25 3.00
224 Michel Ouellet RC 1.50 4.00
225 Matt Carle RC 1.25 3.00
226 Ben Ondrus RC 1.25 3.00
227 Brendan Bell RC 1.25 3.00
228 Ian White RC 1.50 4.00
229 Jeremy Williams RC 1.25 3.00
230 Eric Fehr RC 2.00 5.00
231 Patrick Thoreson RC 1.50 4.00
232 Ryan Shannon RC 1.50 4.00
233 Anze Kopitar RC 8.00 20.00
234 Travis Zajac RC 3.00 8.00
235 Nigel Dawes RC 1.50 4.00
236 Kris Letang RC 6.00 15.00
237 Marc Edouard Vlasic RC 2.50 6.00
238 Keith Yandle RC 4.00 10.00
239 Alexei Mikhnov RC 1.50 4.00
240 Ladislav Smid RC 1.50 4.00
241 Loui Eriksson RC 3.00 8.00
242 Luc Bourdon RC 2.50 6.00
243 Alexander Radulov RC 3.00 8.00
244 Alexei Kaigorodov RC 1.50 4.00
245 Enver Lisin RC 1.50 4.00
246 Patrick O'Sullivan RC 2.50 6.00
247 Jordan Staal RC 4.00 10.00
248 Paul Stastny RC 4.00 10.00
249 Guillaume Latendresse RC 2.50 6.00
250 Phil Kessel RC 5.00 12.00
251 Evgeni Malkin RC 10.00 25.00

2006-07 Ultra Gold Medallion

*STARS 2X to 5X BASE HI
*ROOKIES .75X to 2X BASE HI
ROOKIE REDEMPTIONS: 1X to 1.5X HI

2006-07 Ultra Ice Medallion

*STARS: 6X to 15X BASE HI
ROOKIES: 1.5X to 3X BASE HI
ROOKIE REDEMPTIONS 1.5X to 3X HI
75 Steve Yzerman 12.00 30.00
154 Sidney Crosby 30.00 80.00
196 Alexander Ovechkin 20.00 50.00
233 Anze Kopitar 30.00 80.00
247 Jordan Staal 50.00 125.00
249 Guillaume Latendresse 25.00 60.00
251 Evgeni Malkin 150.00 250.00

2006-07 Ultra Action

UA1 Kari Lehtonen .75 2.00
UA2 Jarome Iginla 1.25 3.00
UA3 Dion Phaneuf .75 2.00
UA4 Eric Staal 1.25 3.00
UA5 Joe Sakic 2.00 5.00
UA6 Marek Svatos .60 1.50
UA7 Rick Nash 1.00 2.50
UA8 Mike Modano 1.50 4.00
UA9 Henrik Zetterberg 1.25 3.00
UA10 Brendan Shanahan 1.00 2.50
UA11 Chris Pronger 1.00 2.50
UA12 Roberto Luongo 1.50 4.00
UA13 Marian Gaborik 1.00 2.50
UA14 Saku Koivu 1.00 2.50
UA15 Paul Kariya 1.00 2.50
UA16 Martin Brodeur 2.50 6.00
UA17 Alexei Yashin .75 2.00
UA18 Jaromir Jagr 3.00 8.00
UA19 Dominik Hasek 1.50 4.00
UA20 Dany Heatley .75 2.00
UA21 Peter Forsberg 2.00 5.00
UA22 Shane Doan .75 2.00
UA23 Sidney Crosby 4.00 10.00
UA24 Joe Thornton 1.50 4.00
UA25 Evgeni Nabokov .75 2.00
UA26 Martin St. Louis 1.00 2.50
UA27 Vincent Lecavalier 1.00 2.50
UA28 Alexander Ovechkin 4.00 10.00
UA29 Mats Sundin 1.00 2.50
UA30 Markus Naslund 1.00 2.50

2006-07 Ultra Difference Makers

DM1 Ilya Bryzgalov .75 2.00
DM2 Ilya Kovalchuk .75 2.00
DM3 Patrice Bergeron 1.00 2.50
DM4 Ryan Miller .75 2.00
DM5 Jarome Iginla 1.00 2.50
DM6 Miikka Kiprusoff .75 2.00
DM7 Eric Staal 1.00 2.50
DM8 Markus Naslund .75 2.00
DM9 Alex Tanguay .50 1.25
DM10 Jose Theodore .75 2.00
DM11 Rick Nash .75 2.00
DM12 Marty Turco .75 2.00
DM13 Pavel Datsyuk 1.25 3.00
DM14 Henrik Zetterberg 1.00 2.50
DM15 Chris Pronger .75 2.00
DM16 Roberto Luongo 1.25 3.00
DM17 Michael Ryder .50 1.25
DM18 Saku Koivu .75 2.00
DM19 Mats Sundin .75 2.00
DM20 Martin Brodeur 2.00 5.00
DM21 Jaromir Jagr 2.50 6.00
DM22 Henrik Lundqvist 2.00 5.00
DM23 Daniel Alfredsson .75 2.00
DM24 Dany Heatley .60 1.50
DM25 Jason Spezza .75 2.00
DM26 Peter Forsberg 1.50 4.00
DM27 Alexander Ovechkin 3.00 8.00
DM28 Sidney Crosby 4.00 10.00
DM29 Joe Thornton 1.25 3.00
DM30 Vincent Lecavalier .75 2.00

2006-07 Ultra Fresh Ink

IAL Andrew Ladd SP 6.00 15.00
IAM Al Montoya 10.00 25.00
IAO Alexander Ovechkin SP 40.00 100.00
IBB Brad Boyes SP 6.00 15.00
IBL Brian Leetch SP 8.00 20.00
IBM Brenden Morrow SP 8.00 20.00
IBR Martin Brodeur SP 25.00 60.00
ICD Chris Drury SP 8.00 20.00
ICK Chuck Kobasew 6.00 15.00
ICO Chris Osgood SP 10.00 25.00
IDB Daniel Briere SP 10.00 25.00
IDC Dan Cloutier SP 8.00 20.00
IDL David Leneveu 8.00 20.00
IDR Dwayne Roloson 8.00 20.00
IEN Evgeni Nabokov 8.00 20.00
IGM Glen Murray SP 8.00 20.00
IHE Milan Hejduk SP 8.00 20.00
IJB Jay Bouwmeester SP 6.00 15.00
IJH Jeff Halpern 6.00 15.00
IJI Jarome Iginla SP 12.00 30.00
IJL Jason Labarbera 8.00 20.00
IJO Jeff O'Neill SP 6.00 15.00
IJT Jose Theodore SP 10.00 25.00
IJV Josef Vasicek 6.00 15.00
IMB Martin Biron 8.00 20.00
IMC Mike Cammalleri SP 6.00 15.00
IMG Marian Gaborik SP 10.00 25.00
IMH Michal Handzus 8.00 20.00
IMN Mika Noronen 8.00 20.00
IMR Michael Ryder SP 6.00 15.00
IMS Marc Savard 6.00 15.00
IMT Mikael Tellqvist 10.00 25.00
IMZ Marek Zidlicky SP 6.00 15.00
INA Nikolai Antropov SP 8.00 20.00
IOK Olaf Kolzig SP 10.00 25.00
IPS Philippe Sauve 8.00 20.00
IRF Ruslan Fedotenko SP 6.00 15.00
IRM Ryan Malone SP 6.00 15.00
IRS Ryan Smyth SP 8.00 20.00
ISC Sidney Crosby SP 150.00 300.00
ISG Scott Gomez SP 8.00 20.00
ISH Scott Hartnell SP 6.00 15.00
ISK Saku Koivu SP 10.00 25.00
ISS Sergei Samsonov SP 8.00 20.00
ISU Ryan Suter 8.00 20.00
ITB Todd Bertuzzi SP 10.00 25.00
ITC Ty Conklin SP 8.00 20.00
ITG Tim Gleason 6.00 15.00

2006-07 Ultra Scoring Kings

SK1 Alex Tanguay .50 1.25
SK2 Alexander Ovechkin 3.00 8.00
SK3 Brad Richards .75 2.00
SK4 Brendan Shanahan .75 2.00
SK5 Daniel Alfredsson .75 2.00
SK6 Dany Heatley .60 1.50
SK7 Eric Staal 1.00 2.50
SK8 Henrik Zetterberg 1.00 2.50
SK9 Ilya Kovalchuk .75 2.00
SK10 Jarome Iginla 1.00 2.50
SK11 Jaromir Jagr 2.50 6.00
SK12 Jason Spezza .75 2.00
SK13 Joe Sakic 1.50 4.00
SK14 Joe Thornton 1.25 3.00
SK15 Jonathan Cheechoo .60 1.50
SK16 Ryan Smyth .60 1.50
SK17 Marian Gaborik .75 2.00
SK18 Markus Naslund .75 2.00
SK19 Mats Sundin .75 2.00
SK20 Michael Ryder .50 1.25
SK21 Mike Modano 1.25 3.00
SK22 Patrice Bergeron 1.00 2.50
SK23 Paul Kariya .75 2.00
SK24 Pavel Datsyuk 1.25 3.00
SK25 Peter Forsberg 1.50 4.00
SK26 Rick Nash .75 2.00
SK27 Saku Koivu .75 2.00
SK28 Sidney Crosby 4.00 10.00
SK29 Simon Gagne .75 2.00
SK30 Vincent Lecavalier .75 2.00

2006-07 Ultra Uniformity

*PATCH/25: 1.5X TO 4X BASIC JSY
UAH Ales Hemsky 3.00 8.00
UAO Alexander Ovechkin 10.00 25.00
UBL Rob Blake 3.00 8.00
UBM Brendan Morrison 3.00 8.00
UBR Martin Brodeur 8.00 20.00
UBS Brad Stuart 3.00 8.00
UCC Carlo Colaiacovo 3.00 8.00
UCD Chris Drury 3.00 8.00
UCP Chris Pronger 4.00 10.00
UDE Pavol Demitra 3.00 8.00
UDH Dan Hamhuis 3.00 8.00
UDL David Legwand 3.00 8.00
UDM Darren McCarty 3.00 8.00
UEB Ed Belfour 4.00 10.00
UED Eric Daze 3.00 8.00
UEJ Ed Jovanovski 3.00 8.00
UEL Eric Lindros 4.00 10.00
UEN Evgeni Nabokov 4.00 10.00
UES Eric Staal 4.00 10.00
UFP Fernando Pisani 3.00 8.00
UGE Martin Gerber 3.00 8.00
UHA Dominik Hasek SP 8.00 20.00
UJA Jason Arnott 3.00 8.00
UJG Jean-Sebastien Giguere 3.00 8.00
UJK Jason King 3.00 8.00
UJL Jere Lehtinen 3.00 8.00
UJS Joe Sakic 8.00 20.00
UJT Joe Thornton 6.00 15.00
UJW Justin Williams 3.00 8.00
UKO Mikko Koivu 3.00 8.00
UKT Keith Tkachuk 3.00 8.00
ULN Ladislav Nagy 3.00 8.00
ULR Luc Robitaille 4.00 10.00
UMB Martin Biron 3.00 8.00
UMC Bryan McCabe 3.00 8.00
UMD Marc Denis 3.00 8.00
UMG Marian Gaborik 6.00 15.00
UMK Miikka Kiprusoff 5.00 12.00
UMM Mike Modano 5.00 12.00
UMN Markus Naslund 4.00 10.00
UMP Mark Parrish 3.00 8.00
UMR Michael Ryder 4.00 10.00
UMS Marek Svatos 3.00 8.00
UNA Nikolai Antropov 3.00 8.00
UPB Pierre-Marc Bouchard 3.00 8.00
UPD Pavel Datsyuk 4.00 10.00
UPE Michael Peca 3.00 8.00
UPF Peter Forsberg 6.00 15.00
UPL Patrick Lalime 3.00 8.00
UPP Petr Prucha 3.00 8.00
URB Radek Bonk 3.00 8.00
URE Robert Esche 3.00 8.00
URR Robyn Regehr 3.00 8.00
URZ Richard Zednik 3.00 8.00
USG Simon Gagne 4.00 10.00
USK Saku Koivu 4.00 10.00
UST Martin Straka 3.00 8.00
USU Mats Sundin 4.00 10.00
USW Stephen Weiss 3.00 8.00
UTS Teemu Selanne 4.00 10.00

2006-07 Ultra Uniformity Autographed Jerseys

UAJA Jason Arnott 6.00 15.00
UAJT Joe Thornton 12.00 30.00
UAMK Miikka Kiprusoff 8.00 20.00
UAPB Pierre-Marc Bouchard 8.00 20.00
UAPE Michael Peca 6.00 15.00

2007-08 Ultra

1 Alexander Ovechkin 1.25 3.00
2 Alexander Semin .30 .75
3 Chris Clark .20 .50
4 Matt Pettinger .20 .50
5 Olaf Kolzig .30 .75
6 Markus Naslund .30 .75
7 Roberto Luongo .50 1.25
8 Henrik Sedin .40 1.00
9 Brendan Morrison .20 .50
10 Kevin Bieksa .25 .60
11 Daniel Sedin .40 1.00
12 Andrew Raycroft .25 .60
13 Mats Sundin .30 .75
14 Bryan McCabe .20 .50
15 Alexander Steen .20 .50
16 Kyle Wellwood .25 .60
17 Darcy Tucker .25 .60
18 Tomas Kaberle .20 .50
19 Brad Richards .30 .75
20 Martin St. Louis .30 .75
21 Vincent Lecavalier .30 .75
22 Vaclav Prospal .20 .50
23 Johan Holmqvist .25 .60
24 Ruslan Fedotenko .20 .50
25 Doug Weight .30 .75
26 Brad Boyes .20 .50
27 Manny Legace .25 .60
28 Lee Stempniak .20 .50
29 Evgeni Nabokov .25 .60
30 Joe Thornton .50 1.25
31 Patrick Marleau .30 .75
32 Matt Carle .20 .50
33 Vesa Toskala .25 .60
34 Jonathan Cheechoo .25 .60
35 Steve Bernier .20 .50
36 Bill Guerin .30 .75
37 Sidney Crosby 1.25 3.00
38 Evgeni Malkin .60 1.50
39 Marc-Andre Fleury .60 1.50
40 Ryan Malone .20 .50
41 Colby Armstrong .20 .50
42 Ryan Whitney .25 .60
43 Jordan Staal .25 .60
44 Georges Laraque .25 .60
45 Zbynek Michalek .20 .50
46 Curtis Joseph .40 1.00
47 Keith Ballard .20 .50
48 Shane Doan .25 .60
49 Ed Jovanovski .25 .60
50 Mike Richards .25 .60
51 R.J. Umberger .20 .50
52 Antero Niittymaki .25 .60
53 Joni Pitkanen .20 .50
54 Simon Gagne .30 .75
55 Jeff Carter .25 .60
56 Martin Biron .25 .60
57 Tom Preissing .20 .50
58 Jason Spezza .30 .75
59 Wade Redden .20 .50
60 Dany Heatley .25 .60
61 Daniel Alfredsson .30 .75
62 Andrej Meszaros .20 .50
63 Ray Emery .25 .60
64 Chris Neil .20 .50
65 Henrik Lundqvist .75 2.00
66 Martin Straka .20 .50
67 Jaromir Jagr 1.00 2.50
68 Petr Prucha .20 .50
69 Brendan Shanahan .30 .75
70 Michael Nylander .20 .50
71 Sean Avery .20 .50
72 Rick DiPietro .25 .60
73 Miroslav Satan .25 .60
74 Ryan Smyth .25 .60
75 Jason Blake .20 .50
76 Mike Sillinger .20 .50
77 Alexei Yashin .25 .60
78 Jamie Langenbrunner .20 .50
79 Martin Brodeur .75 2.00
80 Brian Rafalski .25 .60
81 Patrik Elias .30 .75
82 Brian Gionta .20 .50
83 Scott Gomez .25 .60
84 Zach Parise .30 .75
85 Peter Forsberg .60 1.50
86 Tomas Vokoun .25 .60
87 Steve Sullivan .20 .50
88 David Legwand .25 .60
89 Paul Kariya .30 .75
90 J.P. Dumont .20 .50
91 Shea Weber .25 .60
92 Radek Bonk .20 .50
93 Saku Koivu .30 .75
94 Cristobal Huet .25 .60
95 Sheldon Souray .20 .50
96 Michael Ryder .20 .50
97 Guillaume Latendresse .25 .60
98 Tomas Plekanec .20 .50
99 Mikko Koivu .25 .60
100 Niklas Backstrom .30 .75
101 Pierre-Marc Bouchard .30 .75
102 Brian Rolston .25 .60
103 Pavol Demitra .40 1.00
104 Marian Gaborik .30 .75
105 Manny Fernandez .20 .50
106 Alexander Frolov .20 .50
107 Mike Cammalleri .25 .60
108 Rob Blake .30 .75
109 Anze Kopitar .50 1.25
110 Dustin Brown .30 .75
111 Patrick O'Sullivan .25 .60
112 Nathan Horton .30 .75
113 Ed Belfour .30 .75
114 Olli Jokinen .25 .60
115 Jay Bouwmeester .20 .50
116 Noah Welch .20 .50
117 Ales Hemsky .25 .60
118 Jarret Stoll .25 .60
119 Shawn Horcoff .20 .50
120 Dwayne Roloson .25 .60
121 Petr Sykora .25 .60
122 Joffrey Lupul .20 .50
123 Raffi Torres .20 .50
124 Tomas Holmstrom .25 .60
125 Henrik Zetterberg .40 1.00
126 Nicklas Lidstrom .30 .75
127 Pavel Datsyuk .50 1.25
128 Dominik Hasek .50 1.25
129 Todd Bertuzzi .30 .75
130 Robert Lang .20 .50
131 Marty Turco .30 .75
132 Mike Modano .50 1.25
133 Sergei Zubov .25 .60
134 Brenden Morrow .25 .60
135 Jussi Jokinen .20 .50
136 Eric Lindros .50 1.25
137 Jere Lehtinen .20 .50
138 Philippe Boucher .20 .50
139 Fredrik Modin .20 .50
140 Nikolai Zherdev .20 .50
141 Rick Nash .30 .75
142 Sergei Fedorov .50 1.25
143 Gilbert Brule .25 .60
144 Fredrik Norrena .20 .50
145 David Vyborny .20 .50
146 Wojtek Wolski .25 .60
147 Jose Theodore .30 .75
148 Joe Sakic .60 1.50
149 Milan Hejduk .25 .60
150 Andrew Brunette .20 .50
151 Marek Svatos .20 .50
152 Paul Stastny .25 .60
153 Peter Budaj .25 .60
154 Nikolai Khabibulin .30 .75
155 Tuomo Ruutu .30 .75
156 Brent Seabrook .20 .50
157 Martin Havlat .30 .75
158 Patrick Sharp .30 .75
159 Duncan Keith .25 .60
160 Cam Ward .30 .75
161 Ray Whitney .25 .60
162 Eric Staal .40 1.00
163 Justin Williams .25 .60
164 Erik Cole .20 .50
165 Mike Commodore .20 .50
166 Rod Brind'Amour .30 .75
167 Dustin Boyd .20 .50
168 Miikka Kiprusoff .30 .75
169 Jarome Iginla .40 1.00
170 Kristian Huselius .20 .50
171 Daymond Langkow .20 .50
172 Dion Phaneuf .25 .60
173 Alex Tanguay .25 .60
174 Thomas Vanek .25 .60
175 Ryan Miller .30 .75
176 Maxim Afinogenov .20 .50
177 Jason Pominville .20 .50
178 Chris Drury .25 .60
179 Drew Stafford .20 .50
180 Daniel Briere .30 .75
181 Patrice Bergeron .40 1.00
182 Phil Kessel .30 .75
183 Marc Savard .20 .50
184 Glen Murray .25 .60
185 Zdeno Chara .30 .75
186 Tim Thomas .30 .75
187 Marco Sturm .20 .50
188 Kari Lehtonen .25 .60
189 Marian Hossa .30 .75
190 Ilya Kovalchuk .30 .75
191 Slava Kozlov .20 .50
192 Keith Tkachuk .30 .75
193 Jean-Sebastien Giguere .30 .75
194 Chris Pronger .30 .75
195 Andy McDonald .25 .60
196 Corey Perry .50 1.25
197 Chris Kunitz .30 .75
198 Teemu Selanne .60 1.50
199 Ryan Getzlaf .30 .75
200 Scott Niedermayer .30 .75
201 Aaron Rome RC 1.50 4.00
202 Andy Greene RC 1.50 4.00
203 Brandon Dubinsky RC 2.50 6.00
204 Bryan Bickell RC 2.50 6.00
205 Bryan Young RC 1.25 3.00
206 Colin Fraser RC 1.25 3.00
207 Daniel Girardi RC 1.50 4.00
208 Danny Bois RC 1.25 3.00
209 Curtis Glencross RC 2.00 5.00
210 David Clarkson RC 1.25 3.00
211 David Koci RC 1.25 3.00
212 David Krejci RC 4.00 10.00
213 David Moss RC 2.00 5.00
214 Drew Fata RC 1.25 3.00
215 Drew Miller RC 1.50 4.00
216 Duncan Milroy RC 1.25 3.00
217 Frans Nielsen RC 2.00 5.00
218 Gabe Gauthier RC 1.25 3.00
219 Jack Johnson RC 1.50 4.00
220 Jannik Hansen RC 1.50 4.00
221 Jaroslav Halak RC 4.00 10.00
222 Jeff Finger RC 1.25 3.00
223 Jeff Schultz RC 1.50 4.00
224 Joel Lundqvist RC 1.25 3.00
225 Jonathan Sigalet RC 1.25 3.00
226 Kent Huskins RC 1.25 3.00
227 Krys Barch RC 1.50 4.00
228 Lauri Tukonen RC 1.25 3.00
229 Marc Methot RC 1.25 3.00
230 Mark Fraser RC 1.25 3.00
231 Mark Mancari RC 1.25 3.00
232 Mathieu Roy RC 1.25 3.00
233 Matt Ellis RC 1.50 4.00
234 Nathan Guenin RC 1.50 4.00
235 Patrick Kaleta RC 1.25 3.00
236 Petr Kalus RC 1.25 3.00
237 Rich Peverley RC 1.25 3.00
238 Riley Cote RC 1.50 4.00
239 Rob Schremp RC 1.50 4.00
240 Rod Pelley RC 1.25 3.00
241 Ryan Callahan RC 2.50 6.00
242 Ryan Parent RC 1.25 3.00
243 Scott Munroe RC 1.25 3.00
244 Shay Stephenson RC 1.25 3.00
245 Tobias Stephan RC 1.50 4.00
246 Tom Gilbert RC 1.50 4.00
247 Tomas Popperle RC 1.25 3.00
248 Tomi Maki RC 1.25 3.00
249 Yutaka Fukufuji RC 1.50 4.00
250 Zack Stortini RC 1.25 3.00
251 Carey Price RC 12.00 30.00
252 Jonathan Toews RC 12.00 30.00
253 Sam Gagner RC 3.00 8.00
254 Bobby Ryan RC 4.00 10.00
255 Niklas Bergfors RC 1.50 4.00
256 Erik Johnson RC 2.50 6.00
257 Nicklas Backstrom RC 5.00 12.00
258 Jonathan Bernier RC 3.00 8.00
259 Bryan Little RC 2.50 6.00
260 Patrick Kane RC 30.00 80.00
261 Andrew Cogliano RC 2.00 5.00
262 Marc Staal RC 2.50 6.00
263 Nick Foligno RC 3.00 8.00
264 Peter Mueller RC 2.00 5.00
265 Brett Sterling RC 1.50 4.00
266 Devon Setoguchi RC 2.50 6.00
267 David Perron RC 3.00 8.00
268 James Sheppard RC 1.50 4.00
269 Jiri Tlusty RC 2.50 6.00
270 Mason Raymond RC 2.50 6.00
271 Milan Lucic RC 6.00 15.00

2007-08 Ultra Gold Medallion

*1-200 VETS: 1.5X TO 4X BASIC CARDS
*201-250 ROOKIES: .5X TO 1.2X BASIC RC
*251-271 ROOKIES: .6X TO 1.5X BASIC RC

2007-08 Ultra Ice Medallion

*1-200 VETS/100: 5X TO 12X
*201-250 ROOKIES/100: 1.5X TO 4X
*251-271 ROOKIES/100: 1.5X TO 4X 10.00 25.00
251 Carey Price 50.00 125.00
252 Jonathan Toews 60.00 120.00
260 Patrick Kane 60.00 150.00

2007-08 Ultra Oversized

1 Alexander Ovechkin 10.00 25.00
6 Markus Naslund 2.50 6.00
7 Roberto Luongo 4.00 10.00
12 Andrew Raycroft 2.00 5.00
13 Mats Sundin 2.50 6.00
20 Martin St. Louis 2.50 6.00
21 Vincent Lecavalier 2.50 6.00
30 Joe Thornton 4.00 10.00
37 Sidney Crosby 10.00 25.00
38 Evgeni Malkin 5.00 12.00
39 Marc-Andre Fleury 5.00 12.00
54 Simon Gagne 2.50 6.00
58 Jason Spezza 2.50 6.00
60 Dany Heatley 2.00 5.00
65 Henrik Lundqvist 6.00 15.00
67 Jaromir Jagr 8.00 20.00
79 Martin Brodeur 6.00 15.00
85 Peter Forsberg 5.00 12.00
93 Saku Koivu 2.50 6.00
96 Michael Ryder 1.50 4.00
104 Marian Gaborik 2.50 6.00
117 Ales Hemsky 2.00 5.00
120 Dwayne Roloson 2.00 5.00
125 Henrik Zetterberg 3.00 8.00
126 Nicklas Lidstrom 2.50 6.00
127 Pavel Datsyuk 4.00 10.00
131 Marty Turco 2.50 6.00
132 Mike Modano 4.00 10.00
141 Rick Nash 2.50 6.00
148 Joe Sakic 5.00 12.00
162 Eric Staal 3.00 8.00
168 Miikka Kiprusoff 2.50 6.00
169 Jarome Iginla 3.00 8.00
172 Dion Phaneuf 2.00 5.00
174 Thomas Vanek 2.00 5.00
175 Ryan Miller 2.50 6.00
181 Patrice Bergeron 3.00 8.00
189 Marian Hossa 2.50 6.00
190 Ilya Kovalchuk 2.50 6.00
194 Chris Pronger 2.50 6.00
198 Teemu Selanne 5.00 12.00
199 Ryan Getzlaf 2.50 6.00

2007-08 Ultra Action

COMPLETE SET (7) 10.00 25.00
UA1 Sidney Crosby 3.00 8.00
UA2 Joe Thornton 1.25 3.00
UA3 Alexander Ovechkin 3.00 8.00
UA4 Martin Brodeur 2.00 5.00
UA5 Roberto Luongo 1.25 3.00
UA6 Jarome Iginla 1.00 2.50
UA7 Daniel Briere .75 2.00

2007-08 Ultra All-Stars

COMPLETE SET (30) 100.00 200.00
UAS1 Roberto Luongo 5.00 12.00
UAS2 Nicklas Lidstrom 3.00 8.00
UAS3 Jonathan Cheechoo 2.50 6.00
UAS4 Joe Sakic 6.00 15.00
UAS5 Philippe Boucher 2.00 5.00
UAS6 Joe Thornton 5.00 12.00
UAS7 Teemu Selanne 6.00 15.00
UAS8 Patrick Marleau 3.00 8.00
UAS9 Bill Guerin 3.00 8.00
UAS10 Martin Havlat 3.00 8.00
UAS11 Miikka Kiprusoff 3.00 8.00
UAS12 Marty Turco 3.00 8.00
UAS13 Rick Nash 3.00 8.00
UAS14 Dion Phaneuf 2.50 6.00
UAS15 Yanic Perreault 2.00 5.00
UAS16 Alexander Ovechkin 12.00 30.00
UAS17 Ryan Miller 3.00 8.00
UAS18 Sheldon Souray 2.00 5.00
UAS19 Daniel Briere 3.00 8.00
UAS20 Brian Campbell 2.50 6.00
UAS21 Sidney Crosby 12.00 30.00
UAS22 Vincent Lecavalier 3.00 8.00
UAS23 Simon Gagne 3.00 8.00
UAS24 Brendan Shanahan 3.00 8.00
UAS25 Dany Heatley 2.50 6.00
UAS26 Marian Hossa 3.00 8.00
UAS27 Eric Staal 4.00 10.00
UAS28 Martin St. Louis 3.00 8.00
UAS29 Martin Brodeur 8.00 20.00
UAS30 Cristobal Huet 2.50 6.00

2007-08 Ultra Difference Makers

COMPLETE SET (14) 12.00 30.00
DM1 Ryan Miller .75 2.00
DM2 Jarome Iginla 1.00 2.50
DM3 Rick Nash .75 2.00
DM4 Pavel Datsyuk 1.25 3.00
DM5 Roberto Luongo 1.25 3.00
DM6 Saku Koivu .75 2.00
DM7 Mats Sundin .75 2.00
DM8 Martin Brodeur 2.00 5.00
DM9 Jaromir Jagr 2.50 6.00
DM10 Dany Heatley .60 1.50
DM11 Alexander Ovechkin 3.00 8.00
DM12 Sidney Crosby 3.00 8.00
DM13 Joe Thornton 1.25 3.00
DM14 Teemu Selanne 1.50 4.00

2007-08 Ultra Flair Showcase

COMPLETE SET (100) 200.00 350.00
1 Alex Tanguay 1.50 4.00
2 Alexander Steen 1.25 3.00
3 Andrej Meszaros 1.25 3.00
4 Andrew Raycroft 1.50 4.00
5 Bill Guerin 2.00 5.00
6 Brad Richards 2.00 5.00
7 Brendan Shanahan 2.00 5.00
8 Chris Drury 1.50 4.00
9 Chris Pronger 2.00 5.00
10 Daniel Alfredsson 2.00 5.00
11 Daniel Briere 2.00 5.00
12 Daniel Sedin 2.50 6.00
13 Dany Heatley 1.50 4.00
14 Dion Phaneuf 1.50 4.00
15 Doug Weight 2.00 5.00
16 Drew Stafford 1.25 3.00
17 Dwayne Roloson 1.50 4.00
18 Ed Belfour 2.00 5.00
19 Ed Jovanovski 1.50 4.00
20 Eric Staal 2.50 6.00
21 Evgeni Nabokov 1.50 4.00
22 Gilbert Brule 1.50 4.00
23 Guillaume Latendresse 1.50 4.00
24 Henrik Sedin 2.50 6.00
25 Ilya Kovalchuk 2.00 5.00
26 Jaroslav Halak 4.00 10.00
27 Jeff Carter 1.50 4.00
28 Jonathan Cheechoo 1.50 4.00
29 Jordan Staal 1.50 4.00
30 Kari Lehtonen 1.50 4.00
31 Lauri Tukonen 1.25 3.00
32 Manny Fernandez 1.25 3.00
33 Manny Legace 1.50 4.00
34 Marc-Andre Fleury 4.00 10.00
35 Michael Ryder 1.25 3.00
36 Miikka Kiprusoff 2.00 5.00
37 Mike Modano 3.00 8.00
38 Mike Ribeiro 1.25 3.00
39 Milan Hejduk 1.50 4.00
40 Miroslav Satan 1.50 4.00
41 Nicklas Lidstrom 2.00 5.00
42 Nikolai Khabibulin 2.00 5.00
43 Patrice Bergeron 2.50 6.00
44 Patrick Marleau 2.00 5.00
45 Patrik Elias 2.00 5.00
46 Pavel Datsyuk 3.00 8.00
47 Peter Forsberg 4.00 10.00
48 Petr Kalus 1.25 3.00
49 Ryan Parent 1.25 3.00
50 Ryan Smyth 1.50 4.00
51 Scott Niedermayer 2.00 5.00
52 Sergei Fedorov 3.00 8.00
53 Shane Doan 1.50 4.00
54 Eric Lindros 3.00 8.00
55 Thomas Vanek 1.50 4.00
56 Tomas Kaberle 1.25 3.00
57 Tomas Vokoun 1.50 4.00
58 Vincent Lecavalier 2.00 5.00
59 Wade Redden 1.25 3.00
60 Zdeno Chara 2.00 5.00
61 Evgeni Malkin 4.00 10.00
62 Henrik Zetterberg 2.50 6.00
63 Jean-Sebastien Giguere 2.00 5.00
64 Jarome Iginla 2.50 6.00
65 Rick Nash 2.00 5.00
66 Jason Spezza 2.00 5.00
67 Simon Gagne 2.00 5.00
68 Henrik Lundqvist 5.00 12.00
69 Jack Johnson 1.50 4.00
70 Rob Schremp 1.50 4.00
71 Anze Kopitar 3.00 8.00
72 Marian Gaborik 2.00 5.00
73 Marty Turco 2.00 5.00
74 Ales Hemsky 1.50 4.00
75 Olli Jokinen 1.50 4.00
76 Paul Kariya 2.00 5.00
77 Mats Sundin 2.00 5.00
78 Markus Naslund 2.00 5.00
79 Olaf Kolzig 2.00 5.00
80 Martin St. Louis 2.00 5.00
81 Joe Thornton 3.00 8.00
82 Phil Kessel 2.00 5.00
83 Marian Hossa 2.00 5.00
84 Ryan Miller 2.00 5.00
85 Martin Havlat 2.00 5.00
86 Cam Ward 2.00 5.00

87 Teemu Selanne 4.00 10.00
88 Rick DiPietro 1.50 4.00
89 Saku Koivu 2.00 5.00
90 Dominik Hasek 3.00 8.00
91 Gordie Howe 6.00 15.00
92 Bobby Orr 8.00 20.00
93 Mark Messier 4.00 10.00
94 Sidney Crosby 8.00 20.00
95 Mario Lemieux 8.00 20.00
96 Alexander Ovechkin 8.00 20.00
97 Roberto Luongo 3.00 8.00
98 Joe Sakic 4.00 10.00
99 Jaromir Jagr 6.00 15.00
100 Martin Brodeur 5.00 12.00

2007-08 Ultra Fresh Ink

FIAA Adrian Aucoin 2.50 6.00
FIAD Adam Dennis 3.00 8.00
FIAF Alexander Frolov 2.50 6.00
FIAK Andrei Kostitsyn 3.00 8.00
FIAL Andrew Ladd 2.50 6.00
FIAO Alexander Ovechkin 30.00 80.00
FIAP Alexandre Picard 3.00 8.00
FIAR Alexander Radulov 4.00 10.00
FIAT Alex Tanguay 3.00 8.00
FIAY Alexei Yashin 3.00 8.00
FIBB Brendan Bell 2.50 6.00
FIBM Brendan Morrison 2.50 6.00
FIBO Dave Bolland 3.00 8.00
FIBR Brad Richardson 2.50 6.00
FIBW Ben Walter 2.50 6.00
FICC Chris Campoli 2.50 6.00
FICH Chris Higgins 2.50 6.00
FICK Chuck Kobasew 2.50 6.00
FICO Chris Osgood 4.00 10.00
FIDA David Aebischer 3.00 8.00
FIDB Daniel Briere 4.00 10.00
FIDH Dany Heatley 3.00 8.00
FIDP Dion Phaneuf 3.00 8.00
FIDS Drew Stafford 2.50 6.00
FIDT Darcy Tucker 3.00 8.00
FIDW Doug Weight 4.00 10.00
FIEC Erik Christensen 2.50 6.00
FIEM Evgeni Malkin 15.00 40.00
FIEN Eric Nystrom 2.50 6.00
FIER Erik Cole 2.50 6.00
FIES Eric Staal 5.00 12.00
FIGL Guillaume Latendresse 3.00 8.00
FIHA Martin Havlat 4.00 10.00
FIHE Milan Hejduk 3.00 8.00
FIHL Henrik Lundqvist 20.00 50.00
FIHU Cristobal Huet 3.00 8.00
FIHZ Henrik Zetterberg 5.00 12.00
FIJA Jay Bouwmeester 2.50 6.00
FIJB Jaroslav Balastik 2.50 6.00
FIJC Jeff Carter 3.00 8.00
FIJE Jeremy Colliton 2.50 6.00
FIJJ Jussi Jokinen 2.50 6.00
FIJL Joffrey Lupul 2.50 6.00
FIJP Joel Perrault 2.50 6.00
FIJT Joe Thornton 6.00 15.00
FIJW Jeff Woywitka 2.50 6.00
FIKB Kevin Bieksa 3.00 8.00
FIKC Kyle Calder 2.50 6.00
FIKL Kari Lehtonen 3.00 8.00
FIKO Anze Kopitar 6.00 15.00
FILA Maxim Lapierre 2.50 6.00
FILN Ladislav Nagy 2.50 6.00
FIMH Marcel Hossa 2.50 6.00
FIMI Michal Handzus 3.00 8.00
FIMK Miikka Kiprusoff 4.00 10.00
FIML Mario Lemieux 30.00 80.00
FIMN Mika Noronen 2.50 6.00
FIMO Brenden Morrow 3.00 8.00
FIMS Martin St. Louis 4.00 10.00
FINA Evgeni Nabokov 3.00 8.00
FINL Nicklas Lidstrom 4.00 10.00
FINZ Nikolai Zherdev 2.50 6.00
FIPA Joe Pavelski 5.00 12.00
FIPE Michael Peca 3.00 8.00
FIPK Phil Kessel 4.00 10.00
FIPS Paul Stastny 3.00 8.00
FIPT Patrick Thoresen 2.50 6.00
FIRG Ryan Getzlaf 4.00 10.00
FIRH Ryan Hollweg 2.50 6.00
FIRK Rostislav Klesla 2.50 6.00
FIRN Rick Nash 4.00 10.00
FISG Scott Gomez 3.00 8.00
FITA Maxime Talbot 2.50 6.00
FITR Tuomo Ruutu 4.00 10.00
FIVT Vesa Toskala 3.00 8.00
FIWI Jeremy Williams 2.50 6.00
FIYS Yan Stastny 2.50 6.00
FIZC Zdeno Chara 4.00 10.00

2007-08 Ultra Generations

COMPLETE SET (21) 50.00 100.00
G1 Lemieux/Fleury/Malkin 6.00 15.00
G2 Roy/Sakic/Stastny 4.00 10.00
G3 Robitaille/Blake/Kopitar 2.50 6.00
G4 Dionne/Frolov/O'Sullivan 2.00 5.00
G5 Stastny/Hejduk/Svatos 1.25 3.00
G6 Lemieux/Crosby/Staal 6.00 15.00
G7 Lafleur/Koivu/Latendresse 2.00 5.00
G8 Orr/Bergeron/Kessel 6.00 15.00
G9 Perreault/Vanek/Stafford 1.50 4.00
G10 Salming/Sundin/Steen 1.50 4.00
G11 Cheevers/Thomas/Toivonen 1.50 4.00
G12 Clarke/Gagne/Carter 2.50 6.00
G13 Kurri/Hemsky/Schremp 1.50 4.00
G14 Lafleur/Koivu/Kostitsyn 2.00 5.00
G15 Langway/Pothier/Green 1.25 3.00
G16 Howe/Zetterberg/Hudler 5.00 12.00
G17 Howe/Datsyuk/Filppula 5.00 12.00
G18 Stevens/Brodeur/Parise 4.00 10.00
G19 Roy/Huet/Halak 4.00 10.00
G20 Hull/Havlat/Barker 3.00 8.00
G21 McDonald/Iginla/Boyd 2.00 5.00

2007-08 Ultra Hot Gloves

COMPLETE SET (15) 75.00 150.00
HG1 Martin Brodeur 12.00 30.00
HG2 Roberto Luongo 8.00 20.00
HG3 Ryan Miller 5.00 12.00
HG4 Cristobal Huet 4.00 10.00
HG5 Miikka Kiprusoff 5.00 12.00
HG6 Marty Turco 5.00 12.00
HG7 Dominik Hasek 8.00 20.00
HG8 Ray Emery 4.00 10.00
HG9 Jean-Sebastien Giguere 5.00 12.00
HG10 Rick DiPietro 4.00 10.00
HG11 Marc-Andre Fleury 10.00 25.00
HG12 Evgeni Nabokov 4.00 10.00
HG13 Peter Budaj 4.00 10.00
HG14 Tomas Vokoun 4.00 10.00
HG15 Henrik Lundqvist 12.00 30.00

2007-08 Ultra Hot Numbers

COMPLETE SET (15) 100.00 200.00
HN1 Jarome Iginla 6.00 15.00
HN2 Mats Sundin 5.00 12.00
HN3 Martin St. Louis 5.00 12.00
HN4 Martin Brodeur 12.00 30.00
HN5 Dominik Hasek 8.00 20.00
HN6 Roberto Luongo 8.00 20.00
HN7 Daniel Briere 5.00 12.00
HN8 Vincent Lecavalier 5.00 12.00
HN9 Dany Heatley 4.00 10.00
HN10 Teemu Selanne 10.00 25.00
HN11 Evgeni Malkin 10.00 25.00
HN12 Alexander Ovechkin 20.00 50.00
HN13 Joe Thornton 8.00 20.00
HN14 Joe Sakic 10.00 25.00
HN15 Sidney Crosby 20.00 50.00

2007-08 Ultra Scoring Kings

COMPLETE SET (14) 12.00 30.00
SK1 Alexander Ovechkin 3.00 8.00
SK2 Dany Heatley .60 1.50
SK3 Jarome Iginla 1.00 2.50
SK4 Jaromir Jagr 2.50 6.00
SK5 Jason Spezza .75 2.00
SK6 Joe Sakic 1.50 4.00
SK7 Joe Thornton 1.25 3.00
SK8 Sidney Crosby 3.00 8.00
SK9 Vincent Lecavalier .75 2.00
SK10 Evgeni Malkin 1.50 4.00
SK11 Patrice Bergeron 1.00 2.50
SK12 Marian Hossa .75 2.00
SK13 Martin St. Louis .75 2.00
SK14 Thomas Vanek .60 1.50

2007-08 Ultra Season Crowns

COMPLETE SET (7) 6.00 15.00
SC1 Niklas Backstrom .75 2.00
SC2 Sidney Crosby 3.00 8.00
SC3 Martin Brodeur 2.00 5.00
SC4 Thomas Vanek .60 1.50
SC5 Ben Eager .50 1.25
SC6 Vincent Lecavalier .75 2.00
SC7 Joe Thornton 1.25 3.00

2007-08 Ultra Team Leaders

COMPLETE SET (30) 50.00 100.00
TL1 Vincent Lecavalier 2.00 5.00
TL2 Teemu Selanne 4.00 10.00
TL3 Simon Gagne 2.00 5.00
TL4 Sidney Crosby 8.00 20.00
TL5 Shane Doan 1.50 4.00
TL6 Saku Koivu 2.00 5.00
TL7 Ray Whitney 1.50 4.00
TL8 Pavel Datsyuk 3.00 8.00
TL9 Paul Kariya 2.00 5.00
TL10 Patrik Elias 2.00 5.00
TL11 Olli Jokinen 1.50 4.00
TL12 Mike Ribeiro 1.25 3.00
TL13 Mike Cammalleri 1.50 4.00
TL14 Mats Sundin 2.00 5.00
TL15 Martin Havlat 2.00 5.00
TL16 Marian Hossa 2.00 5.00
TL17 Marc Savard 1.25 3.00
TL18 Joe Thornton 3.00 8.00
TL19 Joe Sakic 4.00 10.00
TL20 Jason Blake 1.25 3.00
TL21 Jaromir Jagr 6.00 15.00
TL22 Jarome Iginla 2.50 6.00
TL23 Doug Weight 2.00 5.00
TL24 David Vyborny 1.25 3.00
TL25 Dany Heatley 1.50 4.00
TL26 Daniel Sedin 2.50 6.00
TL27 Daniel Briere 2.00 5.00
TL28 Brian Rolston 1.50 4.00
TL29 Alexander Ovechkin 8.00 20.00
TL30 Ales Hemsky 1.50 4.00

2007-08 Ultra Uniformity

*PATCH/25: 1.5X TO 3X BASIC JSY
UAA Alex Auld 2.50 6.00
UAF Alexander Frolov 2.50 6.00
UAH Ales Hemsky 3.00 8.00
UAK Alex Kovalev 3.00 8.00
UAL Andrew Ladd 2.50 6.00
UAM Andrej Meszaros 2.50 6.00
UAO Alexander Ovechkin 15.00 40.00
UAP Alexander Perezhogin 2.50 6.00
UAR Andrew Raycroft 3.00 8.00
UAS Alexander Steen 2.50 6.00
UAT Alex Tanguay 3.00 8.00
UAY Alexei Yashin 3.00 8.00
UBB Brad Boyes 2.50 6.00
UBG Bill Guerin 4.00 10.00
UBI Brandon Bochenski 2.50 6.00
UDJ Darret Jackman 2.50 6.00
UBM Brendan Morrison 2.50 6.00
UBO Jay Bouwmeester 2.50 6.00
UBR Brad Richards 4.00 10.00
UBS Brendan Shanahan 4.00 10.00
UBT Barry Tallackson 2.50 6.00
UBW Brendan Witt 2.50 6.00
UCH Chris Higgins 2.50 6.00
UCO Chris Osgood 4.00 10.00
UCP Chris Phillips 2.50 6.00
UCS Curtis Sanford 3.00 8.00
UDA Daniel Alfredsson 4.00 10.00
UDB Dustin Brown 4.00 10.00
UDC Dan Cloutier 3.00 8.00
UDH Dany Heatley 3.00 8.00
UDL David Legwand 3.00 8.00
UDM Dominic Moore 2.50 6.00
UDO Dominik Hasek 6.00 15.00
UDP Daniel Paille 2.50 6.00
UDR Dwayne Roloson 3.00 8.00
UDS Daniel Sedin 5.00 12.00
UDW Doug Weight 4.00 10.00
UEB Ed Belfour 4.00 10.00
UEC Erik Cole 2.50 6.00
UEJ Ed Jovanovski 3.00 8.00
UES Eric Staal 5.00 12.00
UFP Fernando Pisani 2.50 6.00
UGL Georges Laraque 3.00 8.00
UGM Glen Murray 3.00 8.00
UGR Gary Roberts 2.50 6.00
UHA Adam Hall 2.50 6.00
UHD Dan Hamhuis 3.00 8.00
UHS Henrik Sedin 5.00 12.00
UHT Hannu Toivonen 3.00 8.00
UIG Jarome Iginla 5.00 12.00
UIK Ilya Kovalchuk 4.00 10.00
UIW Ian White 2.50 6.00
UJA Jason Arnott 3.00 8.00
UJB Jason Blake 2.50 6.00
UJC Jeff Carter 3.00 8.00
UJF Jeff Friesen 2.50 6.00
UJG Jean-Sebastien Giguere 4.00 10.00
UJH Jeff Hoggan 2.50 6.00
UJI Jarkko Immonen 2.50 6.00
UJJ Jaromir Jagr 12.00 30.00
UJK Jakub Klepis 2.50 6.00
UJL Jere Lehtinen 2.50 6.00
UJP Joni Pitkanen 2.50 6.00
UJS Jarret Stoll 3.00 8.00
UJT Joe Thornton 6.00 15.00
UJW Jason Williams 2.50 6.00
UKC Kyle Calder 2.50 6.00
UKL Kari Lehtonen 3.00 8.00
UKO Andrei Kostitsyn 3.00 8.00
ULJ Jamie Lundmark 2.50 6.00
ULU Joffrey Lupul 2.50 6.00
UMB Martin Brodeur 10.00 25.00
UMC Bryan McCabe 2.50 6.00
UMD Marc Denis 3.00 8.00
UMF Manny Fernandez 2.50 6.00
UMG Martin Gerber 3.00 8.00
UMH Marian Hossa 4.00 10.00
UMK Miikka Kiprusoff 4.00 10.00
UMN Markus Naslund 4.00 10.00
UMR Michael Ryder 2.50 6.00
UMS Mats Sundin 4.00 10.00
UMT Marty Turco 4.00 10.00
UON Ben Ondrus 2.50 6.00
UPB Patrice Bergeron 5.00 12.00
UPE Corey Perry 6.00 15.00
UPK Paul Kariya 4.00 10.00
UPR Chris Pronger 4.00 10.00
URA Brian Rafalski 3.00 8.00
URO Brian Rolston 3.00 8.00
USA Joe Sakic 8.00 20.00
USC Sidney Crosby 15.00 40.00
USG Simon Gagne 4.00 10.00
USK Saku Koivu 4.00 10.00
USP Jason Spezza 4.00 10.00
UST Brad Stuart 2.50 6.00
UTH Billy Thompson 2.50 6.00
UTK Keith Tkachuk 4.00 10.00
UTV Tomas Vokoun 3.00 8.00
UWI Justin Williams 3.00 8.00

2008-09 Ultra

COMP.SET w/o EXCH RC (250) 75.00 150.00
COMP.SET w/o RC's (200) 15.00 40.00
1 Ilya Kovalchuk .30 .75
2 Eric Perrin .20 .50
3 Colby Armstrong .20 .50
4 Kari Lehtonen .40 1.00
5 Bryan Little .25 .60
6 Tobias Enstrom .20 .50
7 Patrice Bergeron .40 1.00
8 Marc Savard .20 .50
9 Tim Thomas .30 .75
10 Zdeno Chara .30 .75
11 Marco Sturm .20 .50
12 Phil Kessel .30 .75
13 Glen Murray .25 .60
14 Michael Ryder .20 .50
15 Thomas Vanek .25 .60
16 Ryan Miller .30 .75
17 Derek Roy .20 .50
18 Jason Pominville .20 .50
19 Drew Stafford .20 .50
20 Daniel Paille .20 .50
21 Eric Staal .40 1.00
22 Rod Brind'Amour .30 .75
23 Cam Ward .30 .75
24 Justin Williams .25 .60
25 Ray Whitney .25 .60
26 Joni Pitkanen .20 .50
27 Tomas Vokoun .25 .60
28 Nathan Horton .25 .60
29 David Booth .20 .50
30 Stephen Weiss .20 .50
31 Jay Bouwmeester .20 .50
32 Saku Koivu .30 .75
33 Carey Price .60 1.50
34 Tomas Plekanec .20 .50
35 Alex Tanguay .20 .50
36 Alex Kovalev .25 .60
37 Chris Higgins .20 .50
38 Andrei Markov .30 .75
39 Guillaume Latendresse .20 .50
40 Martin Brodeur .75 2.00
41 Zach Parise .30 .75
42 Patrik Elias .30 .75
43 Brian Gionta .20 .50
44 John Madden .20 .50
45 Travis Zajac .20 .50
46 Rick DiPietro .25 .60
46 Brian Rolston .25 .60
47 Mike Comrie .25 .60
48 Bill Guerin .30 .75
49 Trent Hunter .20 .50
50 Mark Streit .20 .50
51 Wade Redden .20 .50
52 Michal Rozsival .20 .50
53 Henrik Lundqvist .75 2.00
54 Chris Drury .25 .60
55 Scott Gomez .25 .60
56 Markus Naslund .30 .75
57 Marc Staal .20 .50
58 Brandon Dubinsky .20 .50
59 Nikolai Zherdev .20 .50
60 Jason Spezza .30 .75
61 Andrej Meszaros .20 .50
62 Antoine Vermette .20 .50
63 Mike Fisher .20 .50
64 Daniel Alfredsson .30 .75
66 Martin Gerber .25 .60
67 Dany Heatley .25 .60
68 Martin Biron .25 .60
69 Daniel Briere .30 .75
70 Simon Gagne .30 .75
71 Mike Knuble .20 .50
72 Jeff Carter .25 .60
73 Mike Richards .25 .60
74 Sidney Crosby 1.25 3.00
75 Marc-Andre Fleury .60 1.50
76 Miroslav Satan .30 .75
77 Evgeni Malkin .60 1.50
78 Sergei Gonchar .20 .50
79 Ryan Whitney .30 .75
80 Jordan Staal .25 .60
81 Ryan Malone .20 .50
82 Vincent Lecavalier .30 .75
83 Mike Smith .30 .75
84 Jussi Jokinen .20 .50
85 Martin St. Louis .30 .75
86 Paul Ranger .20 .50
87 Karri Ramo .25 .60
88 Olaf Kolzig .30 .75
89 Mats Sundin .30 .75
90 Vesa Toskala .40 1.00
91 Alexander Steen .20 .50
92 Tomas Kaberle .20 .50
93 Nikolai Antropov .25 .60
94 Matt Stajan .20 .50
95 Jiri Tlusty .20 .50
96 Alexander Ovechkin 1.25 3.00
97 Jose Theodore .30 .75
98 Nicklas Backstrom .30 .75
99 Sergei Fedorov .50 1.25
100 Mike Green .25 .60
101 Alexander Semin .30 .75
102 Ryan Getzlaf .30 .75
103 Jean-Sebastien Giguere .30 .75
104 Corey Perry .50 1.25
105 Teemu Selanne .60 1.50
106 Chris Pronger .30 .75
107 Chris Kunitz .30 .75
108 Scott Niedermayer .30 .75
109 Miikka Kiprusoff .30 .75
110 Jarome Iginla .40 1.00
111 Daymond Langkow .20 .50
112 Dion Phaneuf .25 .60
114 Todd Bertuzzi .30 .75
115 Matthew Lombardi .20 .50
116 Mike Cammalleri .25 .60
117 Patrick Kane .60 1.50
118 Nikolai Khabibulin .30 .75
119 Patrick Sharp .30 .75
120 Brent Seabrook .20 .50
121 Jonathan Toews .50 1.25
122 Martin Havlat .30 .75
123 Duncan Keith .25 .60
124 Brian Campbell .25 .60
125 Darcy Tucker .25 .60
126 Joe Sakic .60 1.50
127 Milan Hejduk .25 .60
128 Marek Svatos .20 .50
129 Paul Stastny .25 .60
130 Wojtek Wolski .25 .60
131 Peter Forsberg .60 1.50
132 Ryan Smyth .25 .60
132 Pascal Leclaire .25 .60
133 R.J. Umberger .20 .50
134 Rostislav Klesla .20 .50
135 Jared Boll .20 .50
136 Rick Nash .30 .75
137 Brad Richards .30 .75
138 Marty Turco .30 .75
139 Mike Ribeiro .20 .50
140 Brenden Morrow .25 .60
141 Jere Lehtinen .20 .50
142 Mike Modano .50 1.25
142 Marian Hossa .30 .75
143 Johan Franzen .25 .60
144 Nicklas Lidstrom .30 .75
145 Pavel Datsyuk .50 1.25
146 Chris Osgood .30 .75
147 Henrik Zetterberg .40 1.00
148 Dan Cleary .25 .60
149 Tomas Holmstrom .25 .60
150 Valtteri Filppula .20 .50
151 Sam Gagner .20 .50
152 Ales Hemsky .25 .60
153 Mathieu Garon .25 .60
154 Shawn Horcoff .20 .50
155 Dustin Penner .25 .60
156 Andrew Cogliano .20 .50
157 Dwayne Roloson .25 .60
158 Gilbert Brule .20 .50
159 Anze Kopitar .50 1.25
160 Alexander Frolov .20 .50
161 Dustin Brown .30 .75
162 Jonathan Bernier .25 .60
163 Patrick O'Sullivan .25 .60
164 Marian Gaborik .30 .75
165 Niklas Backstrom .30 .75
166 Pierre-Marc Bouchard .30 .75
168 Josh Harding .30 .75
169 Mikko Koivu .25 .60
170 Alexander Radulov .30 .75
171 Jason Arnott .25 .60
172 Dan Ellis .20 .50
173 Martin Erat .20 .50
174 J.P. Dumont .20 .50
175 David Legwand .25 .60
176 Peter Mueller .25 .60
177 Shane Doan .25 .60
178 Ilya Bryzgalov .25 .60
179 Ed Jovanovski .25 .60
180 Olli Jokinen .25 .60
181 Martin Hanzal .25 .60
182 Daniel Carcillo .20 .50
183 Evgeni Nabokov .25 .60
184 Jonathan Cheechoo .25 .60
185 Milan Michalek .20 .50
186 Rob Blake .30 .75
187 Patrick Marleau .30 .75
188 Joe Thornton .50 1.25
189 Manny Legace .30 .75
190 Erik Johnson .20 .50
191 Brad Boyes .20 .50
192 Lee Stempniak .20 .50
193 Keith Tkachuk .30 .75
194 Paul Kariya .30 .75
195 Daniel Sedin .40 1.00
196 Steve Bernier .20 .50
197 Ryan Kesler .30 .75
198 Alexander Edler .20 .50
199 Roberto Luongo .50 1.25
200 Henrik Sedin .40 1.00
201 Derick Brassard RC 2.00 5.00
202 Mark Fistric RC 1.50 4.00
203 Alex Goligoski RC 2.50 6.00
204 Claude Giroux RC 4.00 10.00
205 Jon Filewich RC 1.50 4.00
206 Robbie Earl RC 1.25 3.00
207 Ilya Zubov RC 1.50 4.00
208 Steve Mason RC 3.00 8.00
209 Brian Boyle RC 1.50 4.00
210 Shawn Matthias RC 2.00 5.00
211 Ryan Stone RC 1.25 3.00
212 Teddy Purcell RC 1.50 4.00
213 Mike Iggulden RC 1.50 4.00
214 Justin Abdelkader RC 3.00 8.00
215 Marc-Andre Gragnani RC 1.50 4.00
216 Jonathan Ericsson RC 2.00 5.00
217 Kyle Okposo RC 2.50 6.00
218 Kyle Turris RC 3.00 8.00
219 Brian Lee RC 1.50 4.00
220 Theo Peckham RC 1.50 4.00
221 Adam Pineault RC 1.50 4.00
222 Boris Valabik RC 2.00 5.00
223 Matt D'Agostini RC 1.50 4.00
224 Andrew Ebbett RC 1.25 3.00
225 Sami Lepisto RC 1.50 4.00
226 Mattias Ritola RC 1.50 4.00
227 Dan LaCosta RC 2.00 5.00
228 Danny Taylor RC 1.50 4.00
229 Cody McLeod RC 1.50 4.00
230 Corey Locke RC 1.50 4.00
231 Jordan Hendry RC 1.50 4.00
232 Mike Brown RC 2.00 5.00
233 B.J. Crombeen RC 1.25 3.00
234 David Brine RC 1.25 3.00
235 Joe Jensen RC 2.00 5.00
236 Kyle Greentree RC 2.00 5.00
237 Zack Fitzgerald RC 2.00 5.00
238 Clay Wilson RC 1.25 3.00
239 Alex Foster RC 1.50 4.00
240 Tom Cavanagh RC 1.50 4.00
241 Erik Ersberg RC 1.50 4.00
242 Tim Conboy RC 1.50 4.00
243 Jordan LaVallee RC 2.00 5.00
244 Mike Mole RC 1.50 4.00
245 Jesse Winchester RC 1.25 3.00
246 Garrett Stafford RC 2.00 5.00
247 Darryl Boyce RC 1.50 4.00
248 Chris Minard RC 2.00 5.00
249 Jack Hillen RC 1.50 4.00
250 Colin Stuart RC 1.50 4.00
251 Steven Stamkos RC 8.00 20.00
252 Fabian Brunnstrom RC 2.00 5.00
253 Jakub Voracek RC 5.00 12.00
254 Blake Wheeler RC 6.00 15.00
255 Brandon Sutter RC 2.50 6.00
256 Zach Boychuk RC 2.50 6.00
257 Alex Pietrangelo RC 4.00 10.00
258 Zach Bogosian RC 3.00 8.00
259 Drew Doughty RC 6.00 15.00
260 Luke Schenn RC 3.00 8.00
261 T.J. Oshie RC 5.00 12.00
262 Mikkel Boedker RC 3.00 8.00
263 Nikita Filatov RC 2.50 6.00
264 James Neal RC 5.00 12.00
265 Colton Gillies RC 2.00 5.00
266 Petr Vrana RC 1.50 4.00
267 Luca Sbisa RC 1.50 4.00
268 Patric Hornqvist RC 2.50 6.00
269 Andreas Nodl RC 1.50 4.00
270 Nikolai Kulemin RC 2.50 6.00
271 Michael Frolik RC 2.50 6.00

2008-09 Ultra Gold Medallion

*GOLD: 1X TO 2.5X BASE
*GOLD RCs: .6X TO 1.5X BASE RCs
*251-271 GOLD: .8X TO 2X BASE
98 Nicklas Backstrom .75 2.00

2008-09 Ultra Ice Medallion

*ICE: 4X TO 10X BASE
*ICE RCs: 1.5X TO 4X BASE
*ICE EXCH: .8X TO 2X BASE
98 Nicklas Backstrom 3.00 8.00

2008-09 Ultra All-Star Royalty

COMPLETE SET (21) 25.00 60.00
ASR1 Alexander Ovechkin 5.00 12.00
ASR2 Roberto Luongo 2.00 5.00
ASR3 Mats Sundin 1.25 3.00
ASR4 Vincent Lecavalier 1.25 3.00
ASR5 Martin St. Louis 1.25 3.00
ASR6 Joe Thornton 2.00 5.00
ASR7 Sidney Crosby 5.00 12.00
ASR8 Evgeni Malkin 2.50 6.00
ASR9 Dany Heatley 1.00 2.50
ASR10 Martin Brodeur 3.00 8.00
ASR11 Saku Koivu 1.25 3.00
ASR12 Marian Gaborik 1.25 3.00
ASR13 Anze Kopitar 2.00 5.00
ASR14 Nicklas Lidstrom 1.25 3.00
ASR15 Rick Nash 1.25 3.00
ASR16 Joe Sakic 2.50 6.00
ASR17 Eric Staal 1.50 4.00
ASR18 Miikka Kiprusoff 1.25 3.00
ASR19 Jarome Iginla 1.50 4.00
ASR20 Ilya Kovalchuk 1.25 3.00
ASR21 Ryan Getzlaf 1.25 3.00

2008-09 Ultra Difference Makers

COMPLETE SET 15.00 40.00
DM1 Martin Brodeur 1.50 4.00
DM2 Alexander Ovechkin 2.50 6.00
DM3 Teemu Selanne 1.25 3.00
DM4 Paul Stastny .50 1.25
DM5 Nicklas Lidstrom .60 1.50
DM6 Ryan Miller .60 1.50
DM7 Joe Thornton 1.00 2.50
DM8 Peter Mueller .50 1.25
DM9 Miikka Kiprusoff .60 1.50
DM10 Martin St. Louis .60 1.50
DM11 Sidney Crosby 2.50 6.00
DM12 Patrick Kane 1.25 3.00
DM13 Jarome Iginla .75 2.00
DM14 Pavel Datsyuk 1.00 2.50
DM15 Peter Forsberg 1.25 3.00
DM16 Carey Price 1.25 3.00
DM17 Patrice Bergeron .75 2.00
DM18 Roberto Luongo 1.00 2.50
DM19 Evgeni Malkin 1.25 3.00
DM20 Mats Sundin .60 1.50

2008-09 Ultra EX Essential Credentials

COMPLETE SET 60.00 120.00
1 Alexander Ovechkin 5.00 12.00
2 Roberto Luongo 2.00 5.00
3 Mats Sundin 1.25 3.00
4 Vincent Lecavalier 1.25 3.00
5 Martin St. Louis 1.25 3.00
6 Paul Kariya 1.25 3.00
7 Joe Thornton 2.00 5.00
8 Sidney Crosby 5.00 12.00
9 Evgeni Malkin 2.50 6.00
10 Peter Mueller 1.00 2.50
11 Simon Gagne 1.25 3.00
12 Dany Heatley 1.00 2.50
13 Daniel Alfredsson 1.25 3.00
14 Jaromir Jagr 4.00 10.00
15 Brendan Shanahan 1.25 3.00
16 Martin Brodeur 3.00 8.00
17 Alexander Radulov 1.25 3.00
18 Carey Price 2.50 6.00
19 Saku Koivu 1.25 3.00
20 Marian Gaborik 1.25 3.00
21 Anze Kopitar 2.00 5.00
22 Tomas Vokoun 1.00 2.50
23 Sam Gagner .75 2.00
24 Henrik Zetterberg 1.50 4.00
25 Dominik Hasek 2.00 5.00
26 Nicklas Lidstrom 1.25 3.00
27 Mike Modano 2.00 5.00
28 Marty Turco 1.25 3.00
29 Rick Nash 1.25 3.00
30 Peter Forsberg 4.00 10.00
31 Joe Sakic 2.50 6.00
32 Paul Stastny 1.00 2.50
33 Patrick Kane 2.50 6.00
34 Jonathan Toews 2.00 5.00
35 Eric Staal 1.50 4.00
36 Jarome Iginla 1.50 4.00
37 Miikka Kiprusoff 1.25 3.00
38 Ryan Miller 1.25 3.00
39 Patrice Bergeron 1.50 4.00
40 Ilya Kovalchuk 1.25 3.00
41 Ryan Getzlaf 1.25 3.00
42 Teemu Selanne 2.50 6.00

2008-09 Ultra EX Essential Credentials Green

*GREEN: 1.2X TO 3X
1 Alexander Ovechkin/92 20.00 50.00
2 Roberto Luongo/99 8.00 20.00
3 Mats Sundin/87 5.00 12.00
4 Vincent Lecavalier/96 5.00 12.00
5 Martin St. Louis/74 5.00 12.00
6 Paul Kariya/91 5.00 12.00
7 Joe Thornton/81 8.00 20.00
9 Evgeni Malkin/29 10.00 25.00
11 Simon Gagne/88 5.00 12.00
12 Dany Heatley/85 4.00 10.00
13 Daniel Alfredsson/89 5.00 12.00
14 Jaromir Jagr/32 15.00 40.00
15 Brendan Shanahan/86 5.00 12.00
16 Martin Brodeur/70 12.00 30.00
17 Alexander Radulov/53 5.00 12.00
18 Carey Price/69 40.00 100.00
19 Saku Koivu/89 5.00 12.00
20 Marian Gaborik/90 5.00 12.00
21 Anze Kopitar/89 8.00 20.00
22 Tomas Vokoun/71 4.00 10.00
24 Henrik Zetterberg/60 6.00 15.00
25 Dominik Hasek/61 8.00 20.00
26 Nicklas Lidstrom/95 5.00 12.00
27 Mike Modano/91 40.00 100.00
28 Marty Turco/65 5.00 12.00
29 Rick Nash/39 5.00 12.00
30 Peter Forsberg/79 10.00 25.00
31 Joe Sakic/81 10.00 25.00
32 Paul Stastny/74 4.00 10.00
34 Jonathan Toews/81 8.00 20.00
35 Eric Staal/88 6.00 15.00
36 Jarome Iginla/88 6.00 15.00
37 Miikka Kiprusoff/66 5.00 12.00
38 Ryan Miller/70 5.00 12.00
39 Patrice Bergeron/63 50.00 125.00
40 Ilya Kovalchuk/83 5.00 12.00
41 Ryan Getzlaf/85 5.00 12.00
42 Teemu Selanne/92 10.00 25.00

2008-09 Ultra EX Essential Credentials Red

*RED: 1.2X TO 3X BASIC
5 Martin St. Louis/26 4.00 10.00
7 Joe Thornton/19 15.00 40.00
8 Sidney Crosby/87 15.00 40.00
9 Evgeni Malkin/71 8.00 20.00
10 Peter Mueller/88 3.00 8.00
14 Jaromir Jagr/68 12.00 30.00
16 Martin Brodeur/30 10.00 25.00
17 Alexander Radulov/47 4.00 10.00
18 Carey Price/31 80.00 200.00
22 Tomas Vokoun/29 3.00 8.00
23 Sam Gagner/89 2.50 6.00
24 Henrik Zetterberg/40 5.00 12.00
25 Dominik Hasek/39 6.00 15.00
28 Marty Turco/35 4.00 10.00
29 Rick Nash/61 4.00 10.00
30 Peter Forsberg/21 25.00 60.00
32 Paul Stastny/26 3.00 8.00
33 Patrick Kane/88 8.00 20.00
34 Jonathan Toews/19 150.00 400.00
37 Miikka Kiprusoff/34 4.00 10.00
38 Ryan Miller/30 4.00 10.00
39 Patrice Bergeron/37 80.00 200.00

2008-09 Ultra EX Jambalaya

JAM1 Wayne Gretzky 60.00 150.00
JAM2 Bobby Orr 40.00 100.00
JAM3 Gordie Howe 30.00 80.00
JAM4 Mark Messier 125.00 300.00
JAM5 Mario Lemieux 40.00 100.00
JAM6 Teemu Selanne 20.00 50.00
JAM7 Joe Sakic 20.00 50.00
JAM8 Mike Modano 15.00 40.00
JAM9 Sidney Crosby 40.00 100.00
JAM10 Alexander Ovechkin 40.00 100.00
JAM11 Evgeni Malkin 20.00 50.00
JAM12 Ilya Kovalchuk 10.00 25.00
JAM13 Vincent Lecavalier 10.00 25.00
JAM14 Jarome Iginla 12.00 30.00
JAM15 Marian Gaborik 10.00 25.00
JAM16 Dany Heatley 8.00 20.00
JAM17 Simon Gagne 10.00 25.00
JAM18 Jaromir Jagr 30.00 80.00
JAM19 Mats Sundin 10.00 25.00
JAM20 Jonathan Toews 15.00 40.00

2008-09 Ultra Franchise Players

COMPLETE SET (10) 10.00 25.00
FP1 Jarome Iginla .75 2.00
FP2 Joe Thornton 1.00 2.50
FP3 Roberto Luongo 1.00 2.50
FP4 Patrick Kane 1.25 3.00
FP5 Joe Sakic 1.25 3.00
FP6 Martin Brodeur 1.50 4.00
FP7 Mats Sundin .60 1.50
FP8 Carey Price 1.25 3.00
FP9 Vincent Lecavalier .60 1.50
FP10 Sidney Crosby 2.50 6.00

2008-09 Ultra Fresh Ink

FIBB Brad Boyes 6.00 15.00
FIBD Brandon Dubinsky 10.00 25.00
FIBE Brendan Bell 5.00 12.00
FIBR Bobby Ryan 8.00 20.00
FICA Colby Armstrong 5.00 12.00
FICB Casey Borer 8.00 20.00
FICS Cory Stillman 5.00 12.00
FIDB David Booth 8.00 20.00
FIDM Drew Miller 6.00 15.00
FIDP Daniel Paille 8.00 20.00
FIEC Erik Christensen 5.00 12.00
FIES Eric Staal 40.00 80.00
FIFN Fredrik Norrena 8.00 20.00
FIGE Martin Gerber 6.00 15.00
FIHM Martin Havlat 5.00 12.00
FIHO Tomas Holmstrom 5.00 12.00
FIJH Jannik Hansen 6.00 15.00
FIJL John-Michael Liles 6.00 15.00
FIJO Joe Pavelski 5.00 12.00
FIJT Jiri Tlusty 15.00 40.00
FIJW Justin Williams 25.00 50.00
FIKC Kyle Calder 6.00 15.00
FIKN Mike Knuble 10.00 25.00
FIKQ Kyle Quincey 20.00 40.00
FIKY Kyle Chipchura 5.00 12.00
FILE Loui Eriksson 15.00 30.00
FIMI Michal Handzus 5.00 12.00
FIML Milan Lucic 20.00 40.00
FIMP Marc-Antoine Pouliot 8.00 20.00
FIMR Mason Raymond 40.00 80.00
FIMS Marek Schwarz 6.00 15.00
FIMT Maxime Talbot 8.00 20.00
FIND Nigel Dawes 6.00 15.00
FINI Nicklas Bergfors 6.00 15.00
FINW Noah Welch 5.00 12.00
FIPE Corey Perry 8.00 20.00
FIPH Chris Phillips 5.00 12.00
FIPK Patrick Kane 40.00 80.00
FIRC Ryane Clowe 12.00 30.00
FIRS Ryan Smyth 6.00 15.00
FISC Sidney Crosby 75.00 150.00
FISM Stefan Meyer 8.00 20.00
FISS Steve Sullivan 6.00 15.00
FISW Shea Weber 8.00 20.00
FITC Ty Conklin 8.00 20.00
FITE Tobias Enstrom 6.00 15.00
FITG Tom Gilbert 8.00 20.00
FITH Joe Thornton 6.00 15.00
FIVF Valtteri Filppula 8.00 20.00

2008-09 Ultra Oversized

COMPLETE SET (42) 40.00 100.00
TRU1 Ilya Kovalchuk 1.00 2.50
TRU2 Patrice Bergeron 1.25 3.00
TRU3 Ryan Miller 1.00 2.50
TRU4 Eric Staal 1.25 3.00
TRU5 Saku Koivu 1.00 2.50
TRU6 Carey Price 2.00 5.00
TRU7 Martin Brodeur 2.50 6.00
TRU8 Rick DiPietro .75 2.00
TRU9 Henrik Lundqvist 2.50 6.00
TRU10 Jason Spezza 1.00 2.50
TRU11 Dany Heatley .75 2.00
TRU12 Mike Richards .75 2.00
TRU13 Sidney Crosby 4.00 10.00
TRU14 Marc-Andre Fleury 2.00 5.00
TRU15 Evgeni Malkin 2.00 5.00
TRU16 Vincent Lecavalier 1.00 2.50
TRU17 Vesa Toskala 1.25 3.00
TRU18 Alexander Steen .60 1.50
TRU19 Alexander Ovechkin 4.00 10.00
TRU20 Ryan Getzlaf 1.00 2.50
TRU21 Jean-Sebastien Giguere 1.00 2.50
TRU22 Miikka Kiprusoff 1.00 2.50
TRU23 Jarome Iginla 1.25 3.00
TRU24 Patrick Kane 2.00 5.00
TRU25 Jonathan Toews 1.50 4.00
TRU26 Joe Sakic 2.00 5.00
TRU27 Peter Forsberg 2.00 5.00
TRU28 Rick Nash 1.00 2.50
TRU29 Marty Turco 1.00 2.50
TRU30 Mike Modano 1.50 4.00
TRU31 Nicklas Lidstrom 1.00 2.50
TRU32 Henrik Zetterberg 1.25 3.00
TRU33 Sam Gagner .60 1.50
TRU34 Andrew Cogliano .60 1.50
TRU35 Anze Kopitar 1.50 4.00
TRU36 Marian Gaborik 1.00 2.50
TRU37 Jason Arnott .75 2.00
TRU38 Peter Mueller .75 2.00
TRU39 Jonathan Cheechoo .75 2.00
TRU40 Joe Thornton 1.50 4.00
TRU41 Paul Kariya 1.00 2.50
TRU42 Roberto Luongo 1.50 4.00

2008-09 Ultra Rookie Sensations

COMPLETE SET (30) 40.00 100.00
RS1 Jon Filewich 1.50 4.00
RS2 Alex Goligoski 2.50 6.00
RS3 Mark Fistric 1.50 4.00

RS4 Jonathan Ericsson 2.00 5.00
RS5 Marc-Andre Gragnani 1.50 4.00
RS6 Brian Lee 1.50 4.00
RS7 Theo Peckham 1.50 4.00
RS8 Ryan Stone 1.25 3.00
RS9 Adam Pineault 1.50 4.00
RS10 Boris Valabik 2.00 5.00
RS11 Darren Helm 2.00 5.00
RS12 Mike Iggulden 1.50 4.00
RS13 Niklas Hjalmarsson 2.00 5.00
RS14 Tom Sestito 2.00 5.00
RS15 Alex Foster 1.50 4.00
RS16 Tom Cavanagh 1.50 4.00
RS17 Jordan Hendry 1.50 4.00
RS18 Cody McLeod 1.50 4.00
RS19 Dan LaCosta 2.00 5.00
RS20 Justin Abdelkader 3.00 8.00
RS21 Steve Mason 3.00 8.00
RS22 Derick Brassard 2.00 5.00
RS23 Claude Giroux 4.00 10.00
RS24 Robbie Earl 1.25 3.00
RS25 Ilya Zubov 1.50 4.00
RS26 Brian Boyle 1.50 4.00
RS27 Shawn Matthias 2.00 5.00
RS28 Kyle Okposo 2.50 6.00
RS29 Kyle Turris 3.00 8.00
RS30 Tyler Plante 1.50 4.00

2008-09 Ultra Scoring Kings

COMPLETE SET (20) 12.00 30.00
SK1 Sidney Crosby 2.50 6.00
SK2 Joe Thornton 1.00 2.50
SK3 Vincent Lecavalier .60 1.50
SK4 Jarome Iginla .75 2.00
SK5 Joe Sakic 1.25 3.00
SK6 Jaromir Jagr 2.00 5.00
SK7 Henrik Zetterberg .75 2.00
SK8 Daniel Alfredsson .60 1.50
SK9 Marc Savard .40 1.00
SK10 Henrik Sedin .75 2.00
SK11 Evgeni Malkin 1.25 3.00
SK12 Ilya Kovalchuk .60 1.50
SK13 Rick Nash .60 1.50
SK14 Marian Gaborik .60 1.50
SK15 Eric Staal .75 2.00
SK16 Mike Modano 1.00 2.50
SK17 Brendan Shanahan .60 1.50
SK18 Dany Heatley .50 1.25
SK19 Peter Forsberg 1.25 3.00
SK20 Alexander Ovechkin 2.50 6.00

2008-09 Ultra Season Crowns

COMPLETE SET (10) 6.00 15.00
SC1 Alexander Ovechkin 3.00 8.00
SC2 Joe Thornton 1.25 3.00
SC3 Alexander Ovechkin 3.00 8.00
SC4 Evgeni Nabokov .60 1.50
SC5 Dan Ellis .50 1.25
SC6 Chris Osgood .75 2.00
SC7 Henrik Lundqvist 2.00 5.00
SC8 Pavel Datsyuk 1.25 3.00
SC9 Daniel Carcillo .50 1.25
SC10 Henrik Zetterberg 1.00 2.50

2008-09 Ultra Team Leaders

COMPLETE SET (30) 40.00 100.00
TL1 Mike Richards 1.25 3.00
TL2 Rick DiPietro 1.25 3.00
TL3 Daniel Alfredsson 1.50 4.00
TL4 Carey Price 3.00 8.00
TL5 Marc Savard 1.00 2.50
TL6 Ryan Miller 1.50 4.00
TL7 Eric Staal 2.00 5.00
TL8 Ilya Kovalchuk 1.50 4.00
TL9 Tomas Vokoun 1.25 3.00
TL10 Henrik Zetterberg 2.00 5.00
TL11 J.P. Dumont 1.00 2.50
TL12 Rick Nash 1.50 4.00
TL13 Patrick Kane 3.00 8.00
TL14 Paul Kariya 1.50 4.00
TL15 Marian Gaborik 1.50 4.00
TL16 Ales Hemsky 1.25 3.00
TL17 Marty Turco 1.50 4.00
TL18 Jean-Sebastien Giguere 1.50 4.00
TL19 Shane Doan 1.25 3.00
TL20 Anze Kopitar 2.50 6.00
TL21 Martin Brodeur 4.00 10.00
TL22 Sidney Crosby 6.00 15.00
TL23 Jaromir Jagr 5.00 12.00
TL24 Mats Sundin 1.50 4.00
TL25 Alexander Ovechkin 6.00 15.00
TL26 Vincent Lecavalier 1.50 4.00
TL27 Jarome Iginla 2.00 5.00
TL28 Roberto Luongo 2.50 6.00
TL29 Paul Stastny 1.25 3.00
TL30 Joe Thornton 2.50 6.00

2008-09 Ultra Total D

COMPLETE SET (21) 25.00 60.00
TD1 Jean-Sebastien Giguere 2.00 5.00
TD2 Kari Lehtonen 2.50 6.00
TD3 Ryan Miller 2.00 5.00
TD4 Miikka Kiprusoff 2.00 5.00
TD5 Cam Ward 2.00 5.00
TD6 Nikolai Khabibulin 2.00 5.00
TD7 Jose Theodore 2.00 5.00
TD8 Pascal Leclaire 1.50 4.00
TD9 Marty Turco 2.00 5.00
TD10 Vesa Toskala 2.50 6.00
TD11 Chris Osgood 2.00 5.00
TD12 Tomas Vokoun 1.50 4.00
TD13 Josh Harding 2.00 5.00
TD14 Carey Price 4.00 10.00
TD15 Martin Brodeur 5.00 12.00
TD16 Henrik Lundqvist 5.00 12.00
TD17 Martin Biron 1.50 4.00
TD18 Marc-Andre Fleury 4.00 10.00
TD19 Evgeni Nabokov 1.50 4.00
TD20 Manny Legace 2.00 5.00
TD21 Roberto Luongo 3.00 8.00

2008-09 Ultra Uniformity

UAAA Arron Asham 2.50 6.00
UAAE Alexander Edler 2.50 6.00
UAAK Alex Kovalev 3.00 8.00
UAAM Andrej Meszaros 2.50 6.00
UAAO Alexander Ovechkin/250* 15.00 40.00
UAAR Andrew Raycroft 3.00 8.00
UAAS Alexander Semin 4.00 10.00
UABB Brad Boyes 2.50 6.00
UABG Bill Guerin 4.00 10.00
UABJ Barret Jackman 2.50 6.00
UABM Brendan Morrison 2.50 6.00
UABO Brandon Bochenski 2.50 6.00
UABR Brad Richardson 2.50 6.00
UACA Colby Armstrong 2.50 6.00
UACC Carlo Colaiacovo 2.50 6.00
UACH Jonathan Cheechoo 3.00 8.00
UACJ Curtis Joseph 5.00 12.00
UACK Chuck Kobasew 2.50 6.00
UACM Matt Carle 2.50 6.00
UACS Cory Stillman 2.50 6.00
UACW Cam Ward 4.00 10.00
UADB Dustin Brown 4.00 10.00
UADO Donald Brashear 2.50 6.00
UADP Daniel Paille 2.50 6.00
UADS Daniel Sedin 5.00 12.00
UADT Darcy Tucker 3.00 8.00
UADV David Vyborny 2.50 6.00
UAEC Erik Cole 2.50 6.00
UAEJ Ed Jovanovski 3.00 8.00
UAEM Evgeni Malkin/250* 8.00 20.00
UAEN Evgeni Nabokov 3.00 8.00
UAES Eric Staal/250* 5.00 12.00
UAFP Fernando Pisani 2.50 6.00
UAGB Gilbert Brule 2.50 6.00
UAGE Martin Gerber 3.00 8.00
UAGI Brian Gionta 2.50 6.00
UAGM Glen Murray 3.00 8.00
UAHL Henrik Lundqvist 10.00 25.00
UAHS Henrik Sedin 5.00 12.00
UAHT Hannu Toivonen 3.00 8.00
UAIK Ilya Kovalchuk/250* 4.00 10.00
UAIW Ian White 2.50 6.00
UAJA Jason Arnott 3.00 8.00
UAJB Jay Bouwmeester 2.50 6.00
UAJC Jeff Carter
UAJI Jarome Iginla/250* 5.00 12.00
UAJJ Jaromir Jagr/250* 12.00 30.00
UAJL Jere Lehtinen 2.50 6.00
UAJO Erik Johnson 2.50 6.00
UAJP Joni Pitkanen 2.50 6.00
UAJR Jeremy Roenick 6.00 15.00
UAJS Joe Sakic/250* 8.00 20.00
UAJT Joe Thornton/250* 6.00 15.00
UAJU Jussi Jokinen 2.50 6.00
UAJW Justin Williams 3.00 8.00
UAKL Kari Lehtonen 5.00 12.00
UAKO Andrei Kostitsyn 3.00 8.00
UAKT Keith Tkachuk 4.00 10.00
UALE Kristopher Letang 5.00 12.00
UALS Lee Stempniak 2.50 6.00
UALU Joffrey Lupul 2.50 6.00
UAMA Martin Straka 2.50 6.00
UAMB Martin Brodeur/250* 10.00 25.00
UAMC Bryan McCabe 2.50 6.00
UAMF Manny Fernandez 2.50 6.00
UAMG Marian Gaborik 4.00 10.00
UAMI Milan Michalek 2.50 6.00
UAMK Mikko Koivu 3.00 8.00
UAML Manny Legace 4.00 10.00
UAMM Mike Modano 6.00 15.00
UAMN Markus Naslund 4.00 10.00
UAMO Brenden Morrow 3.00 8.00
UAMP Marc-Antoine Pouliot 2.50 6.00
UAMR Mark Recchi 5.00 12.00
UAMS Martin St. Louis 4.00 10.00
UAMT Marty Turco 4.00 10.00
UAMZ Marek Zidlicky 2.50 6.00
UANA Nikolai Antropov 3.00 8.00
UANL Nicklas Lidstrom 4.00 10.00
UANZ Nikolai Zherdev 2.50 6.00
UAOJ Olli Jokinen 3.00 8.00
UAON Owen Nolan 4.00 10.00
UAPB Patrice Bergeron 5.00 12.00
UAPD Pavol Demitra 5.00 12.00
UAPH Dion Phaneuf 3.00 8.00
UAPK Phil Kessel 4.00 10.00
UAPM Patrick Marleau 4.00 10.00
UARI Mike Richards 3.00 8.00
UARL Roberto Luongo 6.00 15.00
UARN Rick Nash 4.00 10.00
UARY Michael Ryder 2.50 6.00
UASA Miroslav Satan 4.00 10.00
UASC Sidney Crosby/250* 15.00 40.00
UASJ Jordan Staal 3.00 8.00
UASM Matt Stajan 2.50 6.00
UAST Drew Stafford 2.50 6.00
UASU Mats Sundin 4.00 10.00
UATH Jose Theodore 4.00 10.00
UATI Kimmo Timonen 2.50 6.00
UAWR Wade Redden 2.50 6.00

2009-10 Ultra

COMPLETE SET (250) 75.00 150.00
COMP.SET w/o SPS (200) 12.00 30.00
1 Ryan Getzlaf .30 .75
2 Corey Perry .50 1.25
3 Bobby Ryan .25 .60
4 Jonas Hiller .25 .60
5 Jean-Sebastien Giguere .30 .75
6 Ilya Kovalchuk .30 .75
7 Slava Kozlov .20 .50
8 Bryan Little .30 .75
9 Kari Lehtonen .25 .60
10 Marc Savard .20 .50
11 Patrice Bergeron .40 1.00
12 Tim Thomas .30 .75
13 David Krejci .30 .75
14 Phil Kessel .30 .75
15 Blake Wheeler .30 .75
16 Thomas Vanek .25 .60
17 Derek Roy .20 .50
18 Ryan Miller .30 .75
19 Jason Pominville .20 .50
20 Drew Stafford .20 .50
21 Jarome Iginla .40 1.00
22 Robyn Regehr .25 .60
23 Daymond Langkow .20 .50
24 Dion Phaneuf .25 .60
25 Miikka Kiprusoff .30 .75
26 Olli Jokinen .25 .60
27 Ray Whitney .25 .60
28 Cam Ward .30 .75
29 Eric Staal .40 1.00
30 Rod Brind`Amour .30 .75
31 Patrick Kane .60 1.50
32 Kris Versteeg .20 .50
33 Jonathan Toews .50 1.25
34 Cristobal Huet .30 .75
35 Brian Campbell .25 .60
36 Patrick Sharp .30 .75
37 Ryan Smyth .25 .60
38 Peter Budaj .25 .60
39 Milan Hejduk .25 .60
40 Paul Stastny .25 .60
41 Wojtek Wolski .20 .50
42 Rick Nash .30 .75
43 Steve Mason .25 .60
44 Nikita Filatov .25 .60
45 Derick Brassard .20 .50
46 Jakub Voracek .25 .60
47 Brad Richards .30 .75
48 Loui Eriksson .20 .50
49 Mike Modano .50 1.25
50 James Neal .20 .50
51 Marty Turco .30 .75
52 Pavel Datsyuk .50 1.25
53 Dan Cleary .30 .75
54 Henrik Zetterberg .40 1.00
55 Nicklas Lidstrom .20 .50
56 Valtteri Filppula .20 .50
57 Ty Conklin .25 .60
58 Ales Hemsky .25 .60
59 Sheldon Souray .20 .50
60 Andrew Cogliano .20 .50
61 Ethan Moreau .20 .50
62 Sam Gagner .20 .50
63 David Booth .20 .50
64 Nathan Horton .30 .75
65 Craig Anderson .30 .75
66 Tomas Vokoun .25 .60
67 Michael Frolik .25 .60
68 Anze Kopitar .50 1.25
69 Dustin Brown .30 .75
70 Alexander Frolov .25 .60
71 Drew Doughty .40 1.00
72 Jonathan Quick .40 1.00
73 Mikko Koivu .30 .75
74 Niklas Backstrom .30 .75
75 Antti Miettinen .20 .50
76 Pierre-Marc Bouchard .30 .75
77 Andrew Brunette .20 .50
78 Andrei Markov .30 .75
79 Jaroslav Halak .30 .75
80 Andrei Kostitsyn .25 .60
81 Sergei Kostitsyn .20 .50
82 Carey Price .60 1.50
83 Tomas Plekanec .20 .50
84 J.P. Dumont .20 .50
85 Jason Arnott .25 .60
86 Pekka Rinne .30 .75
87 Shea Weber .25 .60
88 Martin Brodeur .75 2.00
89 Zach Parise .30 .75
90 Patrik Elias .30 .75
91 Travis Zajac .20 .50
92 David Clarkson .25 .60
93 Doug Weight .30 .75
94 Kyle Okposo .20 .50
95 Rick DiPietro .25 .60
96 Josh Bailey .25 .60
97 Henrik Lundqvist .75 2.00
98 Brandon Dubinsky .20 .50
99 Chris Drury .25 .60
100 Nikolai Zherdev .20 .50
101 Scott Gomez .25 .60
102 Daniel Alfredsson .30 .75
103 Dany Heatley .25 .60
104 Jason Spezza .30 .75
105 Brian Elliott .25 .60
106 Jeff Carter .25 .60
107 Mike Richards .25 .60
108 Simon Gagne .30 .75
109 Daniel Carcillo .20 .50
110 Scott Hartnell .20 .50
111 Shane Doan .25 .60
112 Kyle Turris .30 .75
113 Peter Mueller .25 .60
114 Mikkel Boedker .20 .50
115 Ilya Bryzgalov .25 .60
116 Evgeni Malkin .60 1.50
117 Sidney Crosby 1.25 3.00
118 Jordan Staal .25 .60
119 Marc-Andre Fleury .60 1.50
120 Rob Scuderi .20 .50
121 Chris Kunitz .30 .75
122 Joe Thornton .50 1.25
123 Patrick Marleau .30 .75
124 Evgeni Nabokov .25 .60
125 Devin Setoguchi .25 .60
126 Dan Boyle .20 .50
127 Brad Boyes .20 .50
128 Patrik Berglund .20 .50
129 David Perron .25 .60
130 David Backes .20 .50
131 T.J. Oshie .30 .75
132 Martin St. Louis .30 .75
133 Vincent Lecavalier .30 .75
134 Vaclav Prospal .20 .50
135 Steven Stamkos .60 1.50
136 Luke Schenn .30 .75
137 Matt Stajan .20 .50
138 Justin Pogge .30 .75
139 Alexei Ponikarovsky .20 .50
140 Tomas Kaberle .20 .50
141 Pavol Demitra .40 1.00
142 Alexandre Burrows .20 .50
143 Willie Mitchell .20 .50
144 Roberto Luongo .50 1.25
145 Ryan Kesler .30 .75
146 Alexander Ovechkin 1.25 3.00
147 Nicklas Backstrom .30 .75
148 Mike Green .25 .60
149 Alexander Semin .30 .75
150 Jose Theodore .30 .75
151 Simeon Varlamov .30 .75
152 David Steckel .20 .50
153 Steve Bernier .20 .50
154 Kyle Wellwood .25 .60
155 Mikhail Grabovski .20 .50
156 Niklas Hagman .20 .50
157 Ryan Malone .20 .50
158 Chris Mason .25 .60
159 Andy McDonald .25 .60
160 Joe Pavelski .40 1.00
161 Brad Lukowich .20 .50
162 Sergei Gonchar .20 .50
163 Eric Godard .20 .50
164 Steven Reinprecht .20 .50
165 Keith Yandle .20 .50
166 Daniel Carcillo .20 .50
167 Riley Cote .20 .50
168 Filip Kuba .20 .50
169 Mike Fisher .20 .50
170 Sean Avery .25 .60
171 Nik Antropov .25 .60
172 Mark Streit .20 .50
173 Joey MacDonald .25 .60
174 Jamie Langenbrunner .20 .50
175 Scott Clemmensen .25 .60
176 Greg Zanon .20 .50
177 Ryan Suter .25 .60
178 Saku Koivu .30 .75
179 Alex Kovalev .25 .60
180 Brent Burns .30 .75
181 Marian Gaborik .30 .75
182 Jarret Stoll .25 .60
183 Jack Johnson .20 .50
184 Stephen Weiss .20 .50
185 Dustin Penner .20 .50
186 Shawn Horcoff .20 .50
187 Niklas Kronwall .25 .60
188 Tomas Holmstrom .25 .60
189 Brenden Morrow .25 .60
190 Mike Ribeiro .20 .50
191 Antoine Vermette .20 .50
192 Cody McLeod .20 .50
193 Patrick Sharp .30 .75
194 Erik Cole .20 .50
195 Rene Bourque .20 .50
196 Mike Cammalleri .25 .60
197 Tim Connolly .20 .50
198 Milan Lucic .25 .60
199 Todd White .20 .50
200 George Parros .20 .50
201 Alexander Sulzer RC 1.00 2.50
202 Andrew MacDonald RC 1.00 2.50
203 Antti Niemi RC 2.50 6.00
204 Artem Anisimov RC 1.00 2.50
205 Ben Lovejoy RC 1.50 4.00
206 Brandon Segal RC 1.25 3.00
207 Brian Salcido RC 1.00 2.50
208 Bryan Rodney RC 1.25 3.00
209 Byron Bitz RC 1.25 3.00
210 Cal O'Reilly RC 1.25 3.00
211 Chris Durno RC 1.25 3.00
212 David Schlemko RC 1.25 3.00
213 David Van Der Gulik RC 1.25 3.00
214 Davis Drewiske RC 1.50 4.00
215 Derek Peltier RC 1.00 2.50
216 Grant Lewis RC 1.25 3.00
217 Jakub Petruzalek RC 1.50 4.00
218 Jaime Sifers RC 1.25 3.00
219 Jay Beagle RC 2.00 5.00
220 Jesse Joensuu RC 1.25 3.00
221 Jhonas Enroth RC 2.00 5.00
222 Joel Rechlicz RC 1.00 2.50
223 John Scott RC 1.50 4.00
224 Kevin Quick RC 1.00 2.50
225 Kevin Westgarth RC 1.25 3.00
226 Kris Chucko RC 1.00 2.50
227 Kurtis McLean RC 1.25 3.00
228 Luca Caputi RC 1.50 4.00
229 Matt Beleskey RC 1.25 3.00
230 Matt Hendricks RC 1.25 3.00
231 Michael Vernace RC 1.25 3.00
232 Michal Neuvirth RC 2.50 6.00
233 Mikael Backlund RC 2.50 6.00
234 Mike McKenna RC 1.25 3.00
235 Mike Santorelli RC 1.50 4.00
236 Peter Regin RC 1.25 3.00
237 Phil Oreskovic RC 1.50 4.00
238 Riku Helenius RC 1.50 4.00
239 Riley Armstrong RC 1.25 3.00
240 Ryan Vesce RC 1.25 3.00
241 Scott Lehman RC 1.00 2.50
242 Christian Hanson RC 1.50 4.00
243 Spencer Machacek RC 1.50 4.00
244 T.J. Galiardi RC 1.50 4.00
245 Tim Stapleton RC 1.50 4.00
246 Tim Wallace RC 1.00 2.50
247 Tom Wandell RC 1.50 4.00
248 Troy Bodie RC 1.25 3.00
249 Ville Leino RC 1.25 3.00
250 Yannick Weber RC 1.50 4.00
251 John Tavares RC 10.00 25.00
252 Matt Duchene RC 10.00 25.00
253 Victor Hedman RC 6.00 15.00
254 Evander Kane RC 5.00 12.00
255 James van Riemsdyk RC 5.00 12.00
256 Jonas Gustavsson RC 3.00 8.00
257 Jamie Benn RC 8.00 20.00
258 Erik Karlsson RC 8.00 20.00
259 Tyler Myers RC 4.00 10.00
260 Ryan O'Reilly RC 5.00 12.00
261 Matt Gilroy RC 2.50 6.00
262 Michael Del Zotto RC 2.50 6.00
263 Viktor Stalberg RC 2.50 6.00
264 Tyler Bozak RC 4.00 10.00
265 Sergei Shirokov RC 1.50 4.00
266 Colin Wilson RC 2.50 6.00
267 Benn Ferriero RC 2.50 6.00
268 Michael Grabner RC 2.50 6.00
269 Dmitry Kulikov RC 2.50 6.00
270 Cody Franson RC 2.50 6.00

2009-10 Ultra Gold Medallion

COMP.SET w/o SPs (200) 40.00 100.00
*GOLD: 1X TO 2.5X BASIC CARDS
*GOLD ROOKIE 201-250: .6X TO 1.5X
*GOLD ROOKIE 251-270: .6X TO 1.5X
147 Nicklas Backstrom .75 2.00
251 John Tavares 60.00 120.00
252 Matt Duchene 20.00 50.00
259 Tyler Myers 6.00 15.00
262 Michael Del Zotto 12.00 30.00
263 Viktor Stalberg 4.00 10.00

2009-10 Ultra Ice Medallion

*1-200 ICE VETS: 3X TO 8X BASIC CARDS
*201-250 ICE ROOKIES: 1.5X TO 4X BASE RC
*251-270 ICE ROOKIES: 1.5X TO 4X BASE RC
147 Nicklas Backstrom 2.50 6.00

2009-10 Ultra Crowning Achievements

COMPLETE SET (10) 10.00 25.00
CA1 Steve Mason .60 1.50
CA2 Alexander Ovechkin 3.00 8.00
CA3 Sidney Crosby 3.00 8.00
CA4 Mike Green .60 1.50
CA5 Doug Weight .75 2.00
CA6 Keith Tkachuk .75 2.00
CA7 Eric Staal 1.00 2.50
CA8 Martin Brodeur 2.00 5.00
CA9 Jonas Hiller .60 1.50
CA10 Tim Thomas .75 2.00

2009-10 Ultra EX Hockey

COMPLETE SET (42) 40.00 100.00
EX1 Ryan Getzlaf 1.25 3.00
EX2 Ilya Kovalchuk 1.25 3.00
EX3 Phil Kessel 1.25 3.00
EX4 Thomas Vanek 1.00 2.50
EX5 Ryan Miller 1.25 3.00
EX6 Jarome Iginla 1.50 4.00
EX7 Miikka Kiprusoff 1.25 3.00
EX8 Eric Staal 1.50 4.00
EX9 Jonathan Toews 2.00 5.00
EX10 Patrick Kane 2.50 6.00
EX11 Joe Sakic 2.50 6.00
EX12 Paul Stastny 1.00 2.50
EX13 Rick Nash 1.25 3.00
EX14 Steve Mason 1.00 2.50
EX15 Mike Modano 2.00 5.00
EX16 Henrik Zetterberg 1.50 4.00
EX17 Pavel Datsyuk 2.00 5.00
EX18 Andrew Cogliano .75 2.00
EX19 Tomas Vokoun 1.00 2.50
EX20 Anze Kopitar 2.00 5.00
EX21 Drew Doughty 1.50 4.00
EX22 Marian Gaborik 1.25 3.00
EX23 Carey Price 2.50 6.00
EX24 Saku Koivu 1.25 3.00
EX25 Martin Brodeur 3.00 8.00
EX26 Zach Parise 1.25 3.00
EX27 Henrik Lundqvist 3.00 8.00
EX28 Jason Spezza 1.25 3.00
EX29 Mike Richards 1.00 2.50
EX30 Jeff Carter 1.00 2.50
EX31 Peter Mueller 1.00 2.50
EX32 Sidney Crosby 5.00 12.00
EX33 Evgeni Malkin 2.50 6.00
EX34 Joe Thornton 2.00 5.00
EX35 Patrick Marleau 1.25 3.00
EX36 Paul Kariya 1.25 3.00
EX37 Vincent Lecavalier 1.25 3.00
EX38 Martin St. Louis 1.25 3.00
EX39 Luke Schenn 1.25 3.00
EX40 Roberto Luongo 2.00 5.00
EX41 Alexander Ovechkin 5.00 12.00
EX42 Mike Green 1.00 2.50

2009-10 Ultra EX Hockey Jambalaya

JAM1 Alexander Ovechkin 60.00 150.00
JAM2 Roberto Luongo 25.00 60.00
JAM3 Vincent Lecavalier 20.00 50.00
JAM4 Patrick Marleau 20.00 50.00
JAM5 Evgeni Malkin 30.00 80.00
JAM6 Mario Lemieux 80.00 200.00
JAM7 Sidney Crosby 80.00 200.00
JAM8 Henrik Lundqvist 50.00 120.00
JAM9 Martin Brodeur 40.00 100.00
JAM10 Carey Price 30.00 80.00
JAM11 Patrick Roy 30.00 80.00
JAM12 Mark Messier 30.00 80.00
JAM13 Gordie Howe 60.00 150.00
JAM14 Henrik Zetterberg 25.00 60.00
JAM15 Joe Sakic 40.00 100.00
JAM16 Jonathan Toews 30.00 80.00
JAM17 Patrick Kane 40.00 100.00
JAM18 Jarome Iginla 25.00 60.00
JAM19 Bobby Orr 80.00 200.00
JAM20 Ilya Kovalchuk 20.00 50.00

2009-10 Ultra Fresh Ink

FIAC Andrew Cogliano 4.00 10.00
FIBA Josh Bailey 5.00 12.00
FIBL Brian Lee 6.00 15.00
FIBM Ben Maxwell 5.00 12.00
FIBS Brandon Sutter
FIBW Blake Wheeler 6.00 15.00
FICB Casey Borer
FICG Colton Gillies 6.00 15.00
FICK Chris Kunitz 6.00 15.00
FICL David Clarkson 5.00 12.00
FICP Carey Price
FICS Chris Stewart 5.00 12.00
FIDC Dan Cleary 6.00 15.00
FIDD Drew Doughty
FIDH Dany Heatley
FIDJ David Jones
FIDP Dion Phaneuf 5.00 12.00
FIDS Daniel Sedin
FIDU Dustin Penner 4.00 10.00
FIGR Mike Green 25.00 60.00
FIHL Henrik Lundqvist
FIHS Henrik Sedin
FIIK Ilya Kovalchuk 12.00 30.00
FIJD J.P. Dumont
FIJI Jarome Iginla
FIJN James Neal 12.00 30.00
FIJP Justin Pogge 6.00 15.00
FIJS Jack Skille 4.00 10.00
FIJT Joe Thornton
FIKA Karl Alzner 4.00 10.00
FIKE Tim Kennedy 5.00 12.00
FIKM Kenndal McArdle
FIKV Kris Versteeg 30.00 60.00
FILS Luke Schenn
FIMB Mikkel Boedker
FIMG Marian Gaborik
FIMP Max Pacioretty 6.00 15.00
FINF Nikita Filatov 5.00 12.00
FING Nathan Gerbe 5.00 12.00
FIPB Patrik Berglund 4.00 10.00
FIPD Pavel Datsyuk
FIPE Patrik Elias
FISB Steve Bernier 5.00 12.00
FISC Cory Schneider 20.00 50.00
FISG Simon Gagne
FISM Steve Mason
FISS Steven Stamkos 30.00 80.00
FITK Tyler Kennedy 12.00 30.00
FITL Trevor Lewis 4.00 10.00
FITO T.J. Oshie 10.00 25.00
FITP Tomas Plihal
FITW Ty Wishart 5.00 12.00
FIVT Viktor Tikhonov 5.00 12.00
FIZB Zach Bogosian 5.00 12.00

2009-10 Ultra Go To Players

COMPLETE SET (5) 10.00 25.00
GT1 Alexander Ovechkin 3.00 8.00
GT2 Henrik Zetterberg 1.00 2.50
GT3 Ilya Kovalchuk .75 2.00
GT4 Sidney Crosby 3.00 8.00
GT5 Jonathan Toews 1.25 3.00

2009-10 Ultra Rookie Sensations

COMPLETE SET (30) 40.00 100.00
RS1 Alex Goligoski .60 1.50
RS2 Alex Pietrangelo .60 1.50
RS3 Blake Wheeler SP 1.50 4.00
RS4 Bobby Ryan SP 1.25 3.00
RS5 Brandon Sutter .50 1.25
RS6 Claude Giroux .75 2.00
RS7 Cody McLeod .50 1.25
RS8 Colton Gillies .75 2.00
RS9 Derick Brassard SP 1.00 2.50
RS10 Drew Doughty SP 4.00 10.00
RS11 Fabian Brunnstrom .60 1.50
RS12 Jakub Voracek .60 1.50
RS13 James Neal .50 1.25
RS14 Josh Bailey .60 1.50
RS15 Justin Pogge SP 1.50 4.00
RS16 Kris Versteeg SP 1.00 2.50
RS17 Kyle Okposo .50 1.25
RS18 Kyle Turris .75 2.00
RS19 Luke Schenn SP 1.50 4.00
RS20 Max Pacioretty .75 2.00
RS21 Michael Frolik .60 1.50
RS22 Mikkel Boedker SP 3.00 8.00
RS23 Nikita Filatov .60 1.50
RS24 Nikolai Kulemin .50 1.25
RS25 Patrik Berglund .50 1.25
RS26 Shawn Matthias .75 2.00
RS27 Steve Mason SP 1.25 3.00
RS28 Steven Stamkos SP 3.00 8.00
RS29 T.J. Oshie .75 2.00
RS30 Zach Bogosian .60 1.50

2009-10 Ultra Scoring Kings

COMPLETE SET (10) 12.00 30.00
SK1 Alexander Ovechkin 3.00 8.00
SK2 Martin St. Louis .75 2.00
SK3 Joe Thornton 1.25 3.00
SK4 Sidney Crosby 3.00 8.00
SK5 Evgeni Malkin 1.50 4.00
SK6 Zach Parise .75 2.00
SK7 Pavel Datsyuk 1.25 3.00
SK8 Jarome Iginla 1.00 2.50
SK9 Ilya Kovalchuk .75 2.00
SK10 Ryan Getzlaf .75 2.00

2009-10 Ultra Team Leaders

COMPLETE SET (30) 20.00 50.00
TL1 Ryan Getzlaf .75 2.00
TL2 Ilya Kovalchuk .75 2.00
TL3 Tim Thomas SP 1.25 3.00
TL4 Derek Roy .50 1.25
TL5 Jarome Iginla SP 1.50 4.00
TL6 Ray Whitney .60 1.50
TL7 Jonathan Toews SP 2.00 5.00
TL8 Ryan Smyth .60 1.50
TL9 Rick Nash .75 2.00
TL10 Steve Ott .50 1.25
TL11 Pavel Datsyuk SP 2.00 5.00
TL12 Ales Hemsky SP 1.00 2.50
TL13 David Booth .50 1.25
TL14 Anze Kopitar 1.25 3.00
TL15 Mikko Koivu .75 2.00
TL16 Alex Kovalev SP 1.00 2.50
TL17 J.P. Dumont .50 1.25
TL18 Zach Parise .75 2.00
TL19 Mark Streit .50 1.25
TL20 Henrik Lundqvist SP 3.00 8.00
TL21 Daniel Alfredsson .75 2.00
TL22 Jeff Carter SP 1.00 2.50
TL23 Shane Doan .60 1.50
TL24 Evgeni Malkin SP 2.50 6.00
TL25 Joe Thornton 1.25 3.00
TL26 David Backes .50 1.25
TL27 Martin St. Louis .75 2.00
TL28 Jason Blake .50 1.25
TL29 Roberto Luongo SP 2.00 5.00
TL30 Alexander Ovechkin 3.00 8.00

2009-10 Ultra Total O

COMPLETE SET (5) 6.00 15.00
TO1 Sidney Crosby 3.00 8.00
TO2 Alexander Ovechkin 3.00 8.00
TO3 Evgeni Malkin 1.50 4.00
TO4 Vincent Lecavalier .75 2.00
TO5 Pavel Datsyuk 1.25 3.00

2009-10 Ultra Uniformity

UUAF Adam Foote 3.00 8.00
UUAH Adam Hall 3.00 8.00
UUAK Alex Kovalev 4.00 10.00
UUAN Anze Kopitar 8.00 20.00
UUAO Alexander Ovechkin 20.00 50.00
UUAS Alexander Steen 3.00 8.00
UUBL Bryan Little 5.00 12.00
UUBR Dustin Brown 5.00 12.00
UUCP Carey Price 10.00 25.00
UUCS Cory Stillman 4.00 10.00
UUDB David Booth 3.00 8.00
UUDC David Clarkson 4.00 10.00
UUDD Drew Doughty 6.00 15.00
UUDM Dominic Moore 5.00 12.00
UUDP David Perron 4.00 10.00
UUDR Derek Roy 3.00 8.00
UUDS Drew Stafford 3.00 8.00
UUDT Darcy Tucker 4.00 10.00
UUEC Erik Cole 3.00 8.00
UUEM Evgeni Malkin 10.00 25.00
UUES Eric Staal 6.00 15.00
UUFL Marc-Andre Fleury 10.00 25.00
UUIK Ilya Kovalchuk 5.00 12.00
UUJB Jay Bouwmeester 3.00 8.00
UUJC Jonathan Cheechoo 4.00 10.00
UUJG Jean-Sebastien Giguere 5.00 12.00
UUJL Joffrey Lupul 3.00 8.00
UUJN James Neal 3.00 8.00
UUJP Jason Pominville 3.00 8.00
UUJS Jason Spezza 5.00 12.00
UUKL Kari Lehtonen 4.00 10.00
UUKO Andrei Kostitsyn 4.00 10.00
UULE Kristopher Letang 6.00 15.00
UUMF Manny Fernandez 3.00 8.00
UUMG Marian Gaborik 5.00 12.00
UUMI Ryan Miller 5.00 12.00
UUMM Mike Modano 8.00 20.00
UUMP Marc-Antoine Pouliot 4.00 10.00
UUMR Michael Ryder 3.00 8.00
UUMS Marc Savard 3.00 8.00
UUMU Peter Mueller 4.00 10.00
UUNA Nik Antropov 4.00 10.00
UUNB Nicklas Backstrom 5.00 12.00
UUNL Nicklas Lidstrom 3.00 8.00
UUPM Patrick Marleau 5.00 12.00
UUPO Patrick O'Sullivan 4.00 10.00
UUPR Chris Pronger 5.00 12.00
UURD Rick DiPietro 4.00 10.00
UURI Mike Richards 4.00 10.00
UURL Roberto Luongo 8.00 20.00
UURM Ryan Malone 3.00 8.00
UURN Rick Nash 5.00 12.00
UUSC Sidney Crosby 20.00 50.00
UUSD Shane Doan 4.00 10.00
UUSG Sam Gagner 3.00 8.00
UUSK Saku Koivu 5.00 12.00
UUST Marc Staal 3.00 8.00
UUSV Marek Svatos 3.00 8.00
UUSW Shea Weber 4.00 10.00

2014-15 Ultra

COMP.SET w/o SP's (200) 30.00 60.00
*ROOKIE EXCH: .4X TO 1X RC
1 John Gibson .40 1.00
2 Cam Fowler .40 1.00
3 Sami Vatanen .25 .60
4 Andrew Cogliano .25 .60
5A Ryan Getzlaf .40 1.00
5B R.Getzlaf SP org 6.00 15.00
6 Corey Perry .60 1.50
7A Hampus Lindholm .25 .60
7B H.Lindholm SP org 4.00 10.00
8 Daniel Paille .25 .60
9 David Krejci .40 1.00
10 Zdeno Chara .40 1.00
11 Brad Marchand .75 2.00
12 Torey Krug .30 .75
13 Milan Lucic .40 1.00
14 Patrice Bergeron .50 1.25
15 Reilly Smith .40 1.00
16 Tuukka Rask .50 1.25
17 Michal Neuvirth .30 .75
18 Cody Hodgson .25 .60
19 Tyler Ennis .25 .60
20 Johnny Gaudreau RC 2.50 6.00
21 Karri Ramo .30 .75
22 Jiri Hudler .30 .75
23 Sean Monahan .25 .60
24 Alexander Semin .40 1.00
25 Cam Ward .40 1.00
26 Jeff Skinner .50 1.25
27 Eric Staal .50 1.25
28 Teuvo Teravainen RC 1.25 3.00
29 Antti Raanta .40 1.00
30 Brandon Saad .30 .75
31 Marian Hossa .40 1.00
32 Brent Seabrook .25 .60
33 Andrew Shaw .25 .60
34A Patrick Kane .75 2.00
34B P.Kane SP blk 12.00 30.00
35 Duncan Keith .30 .75
36 Corey Crawford .50 1.25
37A Patrick Sharp .40 1.00
37B P.Sharp SP blk 6.00 15.00
38A Jonathan Toews .60 1.50
38B J.Toews SP blk 15.00 30.00
39 Ryan O'Reilly .40 1.00
40 Nathan MacKinnon 1.50 4.00
41 Semyon Varlamov .40 1.00
42 Jean-Sebastien Giguere .40 1.00
43 Erik Johnson .25 .60
44 Matt Duchene .40 1.00
45 Gabriel Landeskog .50 1.25
46 Ryan Johansen .30 .75
47 Jack Johnson .25 .60
48 Sergei Bobrovsky .60 1.50
49 Cody Eakin .25 .60
50 Shawn Horcoff .25 .60
51 Jack Campbell .40 1.00
52 Kari Lehtonen .30 .75
53 Vernon Fiddler .25 .60
54 Rich Peverley .40 1.00
55 Tyler Seguin .50 1.25
56 Valeri Nichushkin .40 1.00
57 Jamie Benn .40 1.00
58 Justin Abdelkader .30 .75
59 Petr Mrazek .40 1.00
60 Gustav Nyquist .25 .60
61 Darren Helm .25 .60
62 Jim Howard .50 1.25
63 Niklas Kronwall .30 .75
64A Henrik Zetterberg .50 1.25
64B H.Zetterberg SP 8.00 20.00
65 Johan Franzen .30 .75
66 Daniel Alfredsson .40 1.00
67A Pavel Datsyuk .60 1.50
67B P.Datsyuk SP 10.00 25.00
68 Ben Scrivens .30 .75
69 Oscar Klefbom RC 1.50 4.00
70 David Perron .30 .75
71 Viktor Fasth .30 .75
72 Nail Yakupov .25 .60
73 Taylor Hall .40 1.00
74 Jordan Eberle .40 1.00
75 Ryan Nugent-Hopkins .50 1.25
76 Tomas Fleischmann .25 .60
77 Jonathan Huberdeau .50 1.25
78 Roberto Luongo .60 1.50
79 Justin Williams .30 .75
80 Mike Richards .30 .75

81 Slava Voynov .40 1.00
82A Dustin Brown .40 1.00
82B Dustin Brown SP
(Grey Jersey) 6.00 15.00
83 Marian Gaborik .40 1.00
84A Jonathan Quick .50 1.25
84B J.Quick SP 8.00 20.00
85 Drew Doughty .50 1.25
86A Anze Kopitar .60 1.50
86B A.Kopitar SP 10.00 25.00
87 Jeff Carter .30 .75
88 Darcy Kuemper .40 1.00
89 Mikael Granlund .30 .75
90 Erik Haula .25 .60
91 Jason Pominville .25 .60
92 Zach Parise .40 1.00
93 Mikko Koivu .30 .75
94 Ryan Suter .30 .75
95 Nino Niederreiter .25 .60
96 David Desharnais .25 .60
97 Tomas Plekanec .25 .60
98 Andrei Markov .25 .60
99 P.K. Subban .50 1.25
100 Carey Price .75 2.00
101 Alex Galchenyuk .25 .60
102 Max Pacioretty .40 1.00
103 Seth Jones .40 1.00
104 Mike Fisher .25 .60
105 Shea Weber .30 .75
106 Pekka Rinne .40 1.00
107 Marek Zidlicky .25 .60
108A Jaromir Jagr 1.25 3.00
108B J.Jagr SP 20.00 50.00
109 Patrik Elias .40 1.00
110 Adam Henrique .30 .75
111 Cory Schneider .40 1.00
112A Martin Brodeur 1.00 2.50
112B M.Brodeur SP 15.00 40.00
113 Ryan Strome .40 1.00
114A Kyle Okposo .25 .60
114B K.Okposo SP 4.00 10.00
115A John Tavares .60 1.50
115B J.Tavares SP 10.00 25.00
116A Chris Kreider .50 1.25
116B C.Kreider SP 8.00 20.00
117 Ryan McDonagh .25 .60
118A Derek Stepan .25 .60
118B D.Stepan SP 4.00 10.00
119A Rick Nash .40 1.00
119B R.Nash SP 6.00 15.00
120 Henrik Lundqvist 1.00 2.50
121A Mats Zuccarello .40 1.00
121B M.Zuccarello SP 8.00 20.00
122 Martin St. Louis .40 1.00
123 Kyle Turris .40 1.00
124 Mika Zibanejad .50 1.25
125 Clarke MacArthur .25 .60
126 Bobby Ryan .30 .75
127A Cody Ceci .25 .60
127B C.Ceci SP 4.00 10.00
128A Craig Anderson .40 1.00
128B C.Anderson SP 6.00 15.00
129A Erik Karlsson .50 1.25
129B E.Karlsson SP 8.00 20.00
130 Brayden Schenn .40 1.00
131 Wayne Simmonds .50 1.25
132 Jakub Voracek .30 .75
133 Steve Mason .30 .75
134 Matt Read .25 .60
135 Andrew MacDonald .25 .60
136 Claude Giroux .40 1.00
137 Vincent Lecavalier .40 1.00
138 Oliver Ekman-Larsson .40 1.00
139 Mike Smith .40 1.00
140 Keith Yandle .25 .60
141 Martin Hanzal .25 .60
142 Antoine Vermette .25 .60
143 Brandon Gormley RC .75 2.00
144 Shane Doan .30 .75
145 Mark Visentin RC .75 2.00
146 Olli Maatta .25 .60
147 Paul Martin .25 .60
148 Pascal Dupuis .25 .60
149A Evgeni Malkin .75 2.00
149B E.Malkin SP 12.00 30.00
150 Chris Kunitz .40 1.00
151 Marc-Andre Fleury .75 2.00
152 Kris Letang .50 1.25
153A Sidney Crosby 1.50 4.00
153B S.Crosby SP 25.00 60.00
154 Joe Pavelski .50 1.25
155 Tomas Hertl .40 1.00
156 Marc-Edouard Vlasic .25 .60
157 Patrick Marleau .40 1.00
158 Joe Thornton .60 1.50
159 Logan Couture .50 1.25
160 Antti Niemi .30 .75
161 T.J. Oshie .40 1.00
162 Jay Bouwmeester .25 .60
163 Brian Elliott .30 .75
164 Patrik Berglund .25 .60
165 Kevin Shattenkirk .25 .60
166 Ty Rattie RC .75 2.00
167 Alexander Steen .25 .60
168 David Backes .25 .60
169 Alex Pietrangelo .30 .75
170 Vladimir Tarasenko .50 1.25
171 Vladislav Namestnikov RC 1.25 3.00
172 Ben Bishop .30 .75
173 Victor Hedman .50 1.25
174 Ondrej Palat .30 .75
175 Steven Stamkos .75 2.00
176 Ryan Callahan .25 .60
177 Dion Phaneuf .30 .75
178 Greg McKegg RC .60 1.50
179 Colton Orr .25 .60
180A James van Riemsdyk .30 .75
180B J.Riemsdyk SP 5.00 12.00
181 Nazem Kadri .50 1.25
182 Phil Kessel .40 1.00
183A Jonathan Bernier .30 .75
183B J.Bernier SP 6.00 15.00
184 Alexander Edler .25 .60
185 Alexandre Burrows .25 .60
186A Eddie Lack .30 .75
186B E.Lack SP 5.00 12.00
187 Daniel Sedin .50 1.25
188 Henrik Sedin .50 1.25
189A Zack Kassian .25 .60
189B Z.Kassian SP 4.00 10.00
190 Joel Ward .25 .60
191 Evgeny Kuznetsov RC 5.00 12.00
192 Mike Green .30 .75
193 Braden Holtby .50 1.25
194 Nicklas Backstrom .40 1.00
195 Alexander Ovechkin 1.50 4.00
196 Blake Wheeler .40 1.00
197 Bryan Little .40 1.00
198 Ondrej Pavelec .40 1.00
199 Andrew Ladd .25 .60
200 Dustin Byfuglien .40 1.00
201 Jonathan Drouin RC 5.00 12.00
202 Aaron Ekblad RC 6.00 15.00
203 Sam Reinhart RC 10.00 25.00
204 Leon Draisaitl RC 12.00 30.00
205 Bo Horvat RC 6.00 15.00
206 Andre Burakovsky RC 4.00 10.00
207 Anthony Duclair RC 4.00 10.00
208 Curtis Lazar RC 2.50 6.00
209 Seth Griffith RC 3.00 8.00
210 Alexander Wennberg RC 4.00 10.00
211 Jiri Sekac RC 2.00 5.00
212 Damon Severson RC 2.50 6.00
213 Griffin Reinhart RC 2.50 6.00
214 Darnell Nurse RC 5.00 12.00
215 Marko Dano RC 2.50 6.00
216 Stuart Percy RC 2.50 6.00
217 Shayne Gostisbehere RC 5.00 12.00
218 Adam Lowry RC 4.00 10.00
219 Teemu Pulkkinen RC 3.00 8.00
220 Brandon Kozun RC 2.00 5.00
221 Jori Lehtera RC 3.00 8.00
222 David Pastrnak RC 6.00 15.00
223 Victor Rask RC 2.50 6.00
224 William Karlsson RC 8.00 20.00
225 Chris Tierney RC 2.50 6.00
226 Mirco Mueller RC 2.50 6.00
227 Josh Jooris RC 2.50 6.00
228 Kevin Hayes RC 6.00 15.00
229 Tobias Rieder RC 2.50 6.00
230 Trevor van Riemsdyk RC 4.00 10.00

2014-15 Ultra Gold Medallion

*VETS: .5X TO 1.2X BASIC CARDS
*ROOKIES: .5X TO 1.2X BASIC CARDS
*ROOKIE RED: .5X TO 1.2X BASIC CARDS
36 Corey Crawford .60 1.50
194 Nicklas Backstrom .50 1.25

2014-15 Ultra Platinum Medallion

*VETS/99: 3X TO 8X BASIC CARDS
*ROOKIES/99: .2X TO 5X BASIC CARDS
*ROOKIE RED/25: 1.2X TO 3X BASIC CARDS
36 Corey Crawford 4.00 10.00
40 Nathan MacKinnon 20.00 40.00
194 Nicklas Backstrom 3.00 8.00

2014-15 Ultra Buckets

BB1 Ryan Getzlaf 2.00 5.00
BB2 Shane Doan 1.50 4.00
BB3 Patrice Bergeron 2.50 6.00
BB4 Cody Hodgson 1.25 3.00
BB5 Sean Monahan 1.25 3.00
BB6 Eric Staal 2.50 6.00
BB7 Jonathan Toews 3.00 8.00
BB8 Matt Duchene 2.00 5.00
BB9 Brandon Dubinsky 1.25 3.00
BB10 Tyler Seguin 2.50 6.00
BB11 Pavel Datsyuk 3.00 8.00
BB12 Taylor Hall 2.00 5.00
BB13 Jonathan Huberdeau 2.50 6.00
BB14 Anze Kopitar 3.00 8.00
BB15 Ryan Suter 1.50 4.00
BB16 P.K. Subban 2.50 6.00
BB17 Shea Weber 1.50 4.00
BB18 Jaromir Jagr 6.00 15.00
BB19 John Tavares 3.00 8.00
BB20 Derek Stepan 1.25 3.00
BB21 Erik Karlsson 2.50 6.00
BB22 Claude Giroux 2.00 5.00
BB23 Sidney Crosby 8.00 20.00
BB24 Joe Pavelski 2.50 6.00
BB25 Alexander Steen 1.25 3.00
BB26 Steven Stamkos 4.00 10.00
BB27 Phil Kessel 2.00 5.00
BB28 Henrik Sedin 2.50 6.00
BB29 Alexander Ovechkin 8.00 20.00
BB30 Blake Wheeler 2.00 5.00

2014-15 Ultra EX

1 Patrick Kane 3.00 8.00
2 Tyler Seguin 2.00 5.00
3 Jaromir Jagr 5.00 12.00
4 Ryan Getzlaf 1.50 4.00
5 Drew Doughty 2.00 5.00
6 Erik Karlsson 2.00 5.00
7 Evgeni Malkin 3.00 8.00
8 Alexander Ovechkin 6.00 15.00
9 Anze Kopitar 2.50 6.00
10 John Tavares 2.50 6.00
11 Phil Kessel 1.50 4.00
12 Steven Stamkos 3.00 8.00
13 Jonathan Bernier 1.25 3.00
14 Tuukka Rask 2.00 5.00
15 Jonathan Quick 2.00 5.00
16 Corey Perry 2.50 6.00
17 Claude Giroux 1.50 4.00
18 Patrice Bergeron 2.00 5.00
19 Duncan Keith 1.25 3.00
20 Carey Price 3.00 8.00
21 Alex Pietrangelo 1.25 3.00
22 Sidney Crosby 6.00 15.00
23 Henrik Lundqvist 4.00 10.00
24 Pavel Datsyuk 2.50 6.00
25 Jonathan Toews 2.50 6.00
26 Taylor Hall 1.50 4.00
27 P.K. Subban 2.00 5.00
28 Mark Messier 6.00 15.00
29 Patrick Roy 8.00 20.00
30 Joe Sakic 6.00 15.00
31 Wayne Gretzky 20.00 50.00
32 Mike Bossy 3.00 8.00
33 Mats Sundin 3.00 8.00
34 Bobby Orr 6.00 15.00
35 Mario Lemieux 12.00 30.00
36 Luc Robitaille 3.00 8.00
37 Calle Jarnkrok 4.00 10.00
38 Brandon Gormley 4.00 10.00
39 Johnny Gaudreau 12.00 30.00
40 Ty Rattie 4.00 10.00
41 Teuvo Teravainen 6.00 15.00
42 Evgeny Kuznetsov 10.00 25.00

2014-15 Ultra EX Essential Credentials Future

*FUTURE/30-42: 1.2X TO 3X BASIC EX
*FUTURE/20-29: 1.5X TO 4X BASIC EX
*FUTURE/16-19: 2X TO 5X BASIC EX

2014-15 Ultra EX Essential Credentials Now

*FUTURE/37-42: .6X TO 1.5X BASIC EX
*FUTURE/28-36: 1.2X TO 3X BASIC EX
*FUTURE/20-27: 1.5X TO 4X BASIC EX
*FUTURE/16-19: 2X TO 5X BASIC EX

2014-15 Ultra EX Jambalaya

1 Jonathan Bernier 8.00 20.00
2 Corey Perry 15.00 40.00
3 Jeff Carter 8.00 20.00
4 Jaromir Jagr 30.00 80.00
5 Nathan MacKinnon 20.00 50.00
6 Ryan Getzlaf 10.00 25.00
7 Steven Stamkos 12.00 30.00
8 Alexander Ovechkin 20.00 50.00
9 Duncan Keith 8.00 20.00
10 Ryan Suter 8.00 20.00
11 Erik Karlsson 12.00 30.00
12 James van Riemsdyk 8.00 20.00
13 Jamie Benn 10.00 25.00
14 Antti Niemi 8.00 20.00
15 Taylor Hall 10.00 25.00
16 Matt Duchene 10.00 25.00
17 Shea Weber 8.00 20.00
18 Nicklas Backstrom 10.00 25.00
19 Max Pacioretty 10.00 25.00
20 Pavel Datsyuk 15.00 40.00
21 Tuukka Rask 12.00 30.00
22 Phil Kessel 10.00 25.00
23 Evgeni Malkin 20.00 50.00
24 Brad Marchand 20.00 50.00
25 Sidney Crosby 40.00 80.00
26 Claude Giroux 15.00 40.00
27 Tyler Seguin 12.00 30.00
28 Drew Doughty 12.00 30.00
29 Anze Kopitar 15.00 40.00
30 Carey Price 25.00 60.00
31 Jonathan Quick 12.00 30.00
32 Patrick Kane 15.00 40.00
33 Pekka Rinne 10.00 25.00
34 John Tavares 15.00 40.00
35 Henrik Zetterberg 12.00 30.00
36 Jonathan Toews 30.00 60.00
37 Patrice Bergeron 12.00 30.00
38 Martin St. Louis 10.00 25.00
39 Zach Parise 10.00 25.00
40 Henrik Lundqvist 25.00 60.00
41 P.K. Subban 12.00 30.00
42 Patrick Sharp 10.00 25.00

2014-15 Ultra Fresh Ink

FIBH Braden Holtby C 5.00 12.00
FIBO Sergei Bobrovsky C 6.00 15.00
FIBS Brandon Sutter D 2.50 6.00
FIBU Johnny Bucyk C 4.00 10.00
FICK Chris Kreider C 5.00 12.00
FIDH Dany Heatley B 3.00 8.00
FIJB J.T. Brown D 2.50 6.00
FIJC Jared Cowen D 2.50 6.00
FIJF Jesper Fast D 2.50 6.00
FIJJ Jaromir Jagr A 40.00 100.00
FIJM Jacob Markstrom D 4.00 10.00
FIJO Jamie Oleksiak D 3.00 8.00
FIJP Joe Pavelski C 5.00 12.00
FIJS Jared Staal D 3.00 8.00
FIJT John Tavares B 6.00 15.00
FIKS Kevin Shattenkirk D 2.50 6.00
FILE Lars Eller D 2.50 6.00
FILR Larry Robinson C 4.00 10.00
FIMH Milan Hejduk B 3.00 8.00
FIMO John Moore D 2.50 6.00
FIMP Mark Pysyk D 2.50 6.00
FIRF Ron Francis B 5.00 12.00
FIRP Richard Panik D 2.50 6.00
FITO Terry O'Reilly C 3.00 8.00
FITW Tom Wilson D 4.00 10.00
FIVL Vincent Lecavalier B 4.00 10.00
FIZK Zenon Konopka D 3.00 8.00

2014-15 Ultra Gongshow Grinders

GG1 P.K. Subban 2.50 6.00
GG2 Zac Rinaldo 1.50 4.00
GG3 Matt Greene 1.25 3.00
GG4 Shea Weber 1.50 4.00
GG5 Niklas Kronwall 1.50 4.00
GG6 Brent Seabrook 1.25 3.00
GG7 Pat Maroon 1.25 3.00
GG8 Luke Schenn 2.00 5.00
GG9 Radko Gudas 1.25 3.00
GG10 Alexander Ovechkin 8.00 20.00
GG11 Ryan Callahan 1.25 3.00
GG12 David Backes 1.25 3.00
GG13 Cody Franson 1.25 3.00
GG14 Milan Lucic 2.00 5.00
GG15 Cal Clutterbuck 1.25 3.00
GG16 Chris Phillips 1.25 3.00
GG17 Jared Cowen 1.25 3.00
GG18 Matt Martin 1.25 3.00
GG19 Dion Phaneuf 1.50 4.00
GG20 Zdeno Chara 2.00 5.00

2014-15 Ultra National Heroes

NHAB Aleksander Barkov 6.00 15.00
NHAO Alexander Ovechkin 15.00 40.00
NHCP Carey Price 8.00 20.00
NHDA Daniel Alfredsson 4.00 10.00
NHDD Drew Doughty 5.00 12.00
NHEK Erik Karlsson 5.00 12.00
NHEM Evgeni Malkin 8.00 20.00
NHGL Gabriel Landeskog 5.00 12.00
NHHL Henrik Lundqvist 10.00 25.00
NHHZ Henrik Zetterberg 5.00 12.00
NHJB Jamie Benn 4.00 10.00
NHJC Jeff Carter 3.00 8.00
NHJP Joe Pavelski 5.00 12.00
NHJQ Jonathan Quick 5.00 12.00
NHJT Jonathan Toews 6.00 15.00
NHJV James van Riemsdyk 3.00 8.00
NHKA Patrick Kane 8.00 20.00
NHMG Mikael Granlund 3.00 8.00
NHMS Martin St. Louis 4.00 10.00
NHNK Niklas Kronwall 3.00 8.00
NHOM Olli Maatta 2.50 6.00
NHPB Patrice Bergeron 5.00 12.00
NHPD Pavel Datsyuk 6.00 15.00
NHPE Corey Perry 6.00 15.00
NHPK Phil Kessel 4.00 10.00
NHPS Patrick Sharp 4.00 10.00
NHRG Ryan Getzlaf 4.00 10.00
NHRS Ryan Suter 3.00 8.00
NHSB Sergei Bobrovsky 6.00 15.00
NHSC Sidney Crosby 15.00 40.00
NHSU P.K. Subban 5.00 12.00
NHSV Slava Voynov 4.00 10.00
NHSW Shea Weber 3.00 8.00
NHTA John Tavares 6.00 15.00
NHTO T.J. Oshie 4.00 10.00
NHTR Tuukka Rask 5.00 12.00
NHTS Teemu Selanne 8.00 20.00
NHVA Sami Vatanen 2.50 6.00
NHVN Valeri Nichushkin 4.00 10.00
NHZP Zach Parise 4.00 10.00

2014-15 Ultra National Heroes Autographs

NHAB Aleksander Barkov 15.00 40.00
NHAO Alexander Ovechkin 40.00 100.00
NHEM Evgeni Malkin 20.00 50.00
NHGL Gabriel Landeskog 12.00 30.00
NHJP Joe Pavelski 12.00 30.00
NHJT Jonathan Toews 15.00 40.00
NHJV James van Riemsdyk 8.00 20.00
NHKA Patrick Kane 20.00 50.00
NHMG Mikael Granlund 8.00 20.00
NHMS Martin St. Louis 10.00 25.00
NHNK Niklas Kronwall 8.00 20.00
NHPD Pavel Datsyuk 15.00 40.00
NHPE Corey Perry 15.00 40.00
NHPK Phil Kessel 10.00 25.00
NHPS Patrick Sharp 10.00 25.00
NHRS Ryan Suter 8.00 20.00
NHSB Sergei Bobrovsky 15.00 40.00
NHTA John Tavares 15.00 40.00
NHZP Zach Parise 10.00 25.00

2014-15 Ultra Photo Vault Film Slide

PVAI1 Arturs Irbe 8.00 20.00
PVAI2 Arturs Irbe 8.00 20.00
PVAI3 Arturs Irbe 8.00 20.00
PVAI4 Arturs Irbe 8.00 20.00
PVAI5 Arturs Irbe 8.00 20.00
PVBH1 Brett Hull 12.00 30.00
PVBH2 Brett Hull 12.00 30.00
PVBH3 Brett Hull 12.00 30.00
PVBH4 Brett Hull 12.00 30.00
PVBH5 Brett Hull 12.00 30.00
PVFP1 Felix Potvin 10.00 25.00
PVFP2 Felix Potvin 10.00 25.00
PVFP3 Felix Potvin 10.00 25.00
PVFP4 Felix Potvin 10.00 25.00
PVFP5 Felix Potvin 10.00 25.00
PVJJ1 Jaromir Jagr 20.00 50.00
PVJJ2 Jaromir Jagr 20.00 50.00
PVJJ3 Jaromir Jagr 20.00 50.00
PVJJ4 Jaromir Jagr 20.00 50.00
PVJJ5 Jaromir Jagr 20.00 50.00
PVJK1 Jari Kurri 6.00 15.00
PVJK2 Jari Kurri 6.00 15.00
PVJK3 Jari Kurri 6.00 15.00
PVJK4 Jari Kurri 6.00 15.00
PVJK5 Jari Kurri 6.00 15.00
PVJR1 Jeremy Roenick 10.00 25.00
PVJR2 Jeremy Roenick 10.00 25.00
PVJR3 Jeremy Roenick 10.00 25.00
PVJR4 Jeremy Roenick 10.00 25.00
PVJR5 Jeremy Roenick 10.00 25.00
PVLR1 Luc Robitaille 6.00 15.00
PVLR2 Luc Robitaille 6.00 15.00
PVLR3 Luc Robitaille 6.00 15.00
PVLR4 Luc Robitaille 6.00 15.00
PVLR5 Luc Robitaille 6.00 15.00
PVMB1 Martin Brodeur 12.00 30.00
PVMB2 Martin Brodeur 12.00 30.00
PVMB3 Martin Brodeur 12.00 30.00
PVMB4 Martin Brodeur 12.00 30.00
PVMB5 Martin Brodeur 12.00 30.00
PVMS1 Mats Sundin 6.00 15.00
PVMS2 Mats Sundin 6.00 15.00
PVMS3 Mats Sundin 6.00 15.00
PVMS4 Mats Sundin 6.00 15.00
PVMS5 Mats Sundin 6.00 15.00
PVPB1 Pavel Bure 6.00 15.00
PVPB2 Pavel Bure 6.00 15.00
PVPB3 Pavel Bure 6.00 15.00
PVPB4 Pavel Bure 6.00 15.00
PVPB5 Pavel Bure 6.00 15.00
PVPR1 Patrick Roy 12.00 30.00
PVPR2 Patrick Roy 12.00 30.00
PVPR3 Patrick Roy 12.00 30.00
PVPR4 Patrick Roy 12.00 30.00
PVPR5 Patrick Roy 12.00 30.00
PVRB1 Ray Bourque 10.00 25.00
PVRB2 Ray Bourque 10.00 25.00
PVRB3 Ray Bourque 10.00 25.00
PVRB4 Ray Bourque 10.00 25.00
PVRB5 Ray Bourque 10.00 25.00
PVSY1 Steve Yzerman 15.00 40.00
PVSY2 Steve Yzerman 15.00 40.00
PVSY3 Steve Yzerman 15.00 40.00
PVSY4 Steve Yzerman 15.00 40.00
PVSY5 Steve Yzerman 15.00 40.00
PVWG1 Wayne Gretzky 20.00 50.00
PVWG2 Wayne Gretzky 20.00 50.00
PVWG3 Wayne Gretzky 20.00 50.00
PVWG4 Wayne Gretzky 20.00 50.00
PVWG5 Wayne Gretzky 20.00 50.00

2014-15 Ultra Premier Pad Men

PP1 Sergei Bobrovsky 6.00 15.00
PP2 Cory Schneider 4.00 10.00
PP3 Pekka Rinne 4.00 10.00
PP4 Semyon Varlamov 4.00 10.00
PP5 Jonathan Bernier 3.00 8.00
PP6 Corey Crawford 5.00 12.00
PP7 Marc-Andre Fleury 8.00 20.00
PP8 Eddie Lack 3.00 8.00
PP9 Craig Anderson 4.00 10.00
PP10 Steve Mason 5.00 12.00
PP11 Philipp Grubauer 4.00 10.00
PP12 Mike Smith 4.00 10.00
PP13 Ben Bishop 3.00 8.00
PP14 Anders Nilsson 4.00 10.00
PP15 Antti Niemi 3.00 8.00
PP16 Ben Scrivens 3.00 8.00
PP17 Cam Ward 4.00 10.00
PP18 Tuukka Rask 5.00 12.00
PP19 Jhonas Enroth 4.00 10.00
PP20 Jim Howard 5.00 12.00
PP21 Karri Ramo 3.00 8.00
PP22 Kari Lehtonen 3.00 8.00
PP23 Brian Elliott 3.00 8.00
PP24 Josh Harding 3.00 8.00
PP25 Roberto Luongo 6.00 15.00
PP26 Henrik Lundqvist 10.00 25.00
PP27 John Gibson 6.00 15.00
PP28 Carey Price 8.00 20.00
PP29 Ondrej Pavelec 4.00 10.00
PP30 Jonathan Quick 5.00 12.00

2014-15 Ultra Red Light Views

RLV1 Wings vs. Leafs 3.00 8.00
RLV2 Devils vs. Rangers 5.00 12.00
RLV3 Hawks vs. Penguins 4.00 10.00
RLV4 Senators vs. Canucks 2.00 5.00
RLV5 Sharks vs. Kings 2.50 6.00
RLV6 Rangers vs. Penguins 5.00 12.00
RLV7 Ducks vs. Kings 2.50 6.00
RLV8 Kings vs. Rangers 5.00 12.00
RLV9 Rangers vs. Kings 2.50 6.00
RLV10 Canadiens vs. Rangers 1.25 3.00

2014-15 Ultra Road to the Championship

RTCADAC1 A.Cogliano R1 (4/16/14) 1.50 4.00
RTCADAC2 A.Cogliano R1 (4/18/14) 1.50 4.00
RTCADAC3 A.Cogliano R1 (4/25/14) 1.50 4.00
RTCADAC4 A.Cogliano R2 (5/3/14) 2.00 5.00
RTCADAC5 A.Cogliano R2 (5/5/14) 2.00 5.00
RTCADAC6 A.Cogliano R2 (5/12/14) 2.00 5.00
RTCADAC7 A.Cogliano R2 (5/16/14) 2.00 5.00
RTCADCF1 C.Fowler R1 (4/16/14) 2.50 6.00
RTCADCF2 C.Fowler R1 (4/18/14) 2.50 6.00
RTCADCF3 C.Fowler R1 (4/25/14) 2.50 6.00
RTCADCF4 C.Fowler R2 (5/3/14) 3.00 8.00
RTCADCF5 C.Fowler R2 (5/5/14) 3.00 8.00
RTCADCF6 C.Fowler R2 (5/12/14) 3.00 8.00
RTCADCF7 C.Fowler R2 (5/16/14) 3.00 8.00
RTCADCP1 C.Perry R1 (4/16/14) 4.00 10.00
RTCADCP2 C.Perry R1 (4/18/14) 4.00 10.00
RTCADCP3 C.Perry R1 (4/25/14) 4.00 10.00
RTCADCP4 C.Perry R2 (5/3/14) 5.00 12.00
RTCADCP5 C.Perry R2 (5/5/14) 5.00 12.00
RTCADCP6 C.Perry R2 (5/12/14) 5.00 12.00
RTCADCP7 C.Perry R2 (5/16/14) 5.00 12.00
RTCADJG1 J.Gibson R2 (5/12/14) 3.00 8.00
RTCADJG2 J.Gibson R2 (5/16/14) 3.00 8.00
RTCADRG1 R.Getzlaf R1 (4/16/14) 2.50 6.00
RTCADRG2 R.Getzlaf R1 (4/18/14) 2.50 6.00
RTCADRG3 R.Getzlaf R1 (4/25/14) 2.50 6.00
RTCADRG4 R.Getzlaf R2 (5/3/14) 3.00 8.00
RTCADRG5 R.Getzlaf R2 (5/5/14) 3.00 8.00
RTCADRG6 R.Getzlaf R2 (5/12/14) 3.00 8.00
RTCADRG7 R.Getzlaf R2 (5/16/14) 3.00 8.00
RTCADTS1 T.Selanne R1 (4/16/14) 5.00 12.00
RTCADTS2 T.Selanne R1 (4/18/14) 5.00 12.00
RTCADTS3 T.Selanne R1 (4/25/14) 5.00 12.00
RTCADTS4 T.Selanne R2 (5/3/14) 6.00 15.00
RTCADTS5 T.Selanne R2 (5/5/14) 6.00 15.00
RTCADTS6 T.Selanne R2 (5/12/14) 6.00 15.00
RTCADTS7 T.Selanne R2 (5/16/14) 6.00 15.00
RTCBBBM1 B.Marchand R1 (4/18/14) 5.00 12.00
RTCBBBM2 B.Marchand R1 (4/20/14) 5.00 12.00
RTCBBBM3 B.Marchand R1 (4/26/14) 5.00 12.00
RTCBBBM4 B.Marchand R2 (5/1/14) 6.00 15.00
RTCBBBM5 B.Marchand R2 (5/3/14) 6.00 15.00
RTCBBBM6 B.Marchand R2 (5/10/14) 6.00 15.00
RTCBBBM7 B.Marchand R2 (5/14/14) 6.00 15.00
RTCBBDK1 D.Krejci R1 (4/18/14) 2.50 6.00
RTCBBDK2 D.Krejci R1 (4/20/14) 2.50 6.00
RTCBBDK3 D.Krejci R1 (4/26/14) 2.50 6.00
RTCBBDK4 D.Krejci R2 (5/1/14) 3.00 8.00
RTCBBDK5 D.Krejci R2 (5/3/14) 3.00 8.00
RTCBBDK6 D.Krejci R2 (5/10/14) 3.00 8.00
RTCBBDK7 D.Krejci R2 (5/14/14) 3.00 8.00
RTCBBJI1 J.Iginla R1 (4/18/14) 3.00 8.00
RTCBBJI2 J.Iginla R1 (4/20/14) 3.00 8.00
RTCBBJI3 J.Iginla R1 (4/26/14) 3.00 8.00
RTCBBJI4 J.Iginla R2 (5/1/14) 4.00 10.00
RTCBBJI5 J.Iginla R2 (5/3/14) 4.00 10.00
RTCBBJI6 J.Iginla R2 (5/10/14) 4.00 10.00
RTCBBJI7 J.Iginla R2 (5/14/14) 4.00 10.00
RTCBBML1 M.Lucic R1 (4/18/14) 2.50 6.00
RTCBBML2 M.Lucic R1 (4/20/14) 2.50 6.00
RTCBBML3 M.Lucic R1 (4/26/14) 2.50 6.00
RTCBBML4 M.Lucic R2 (5/1/14) 3.00 8.00
RTCBBML5 M.Lucic R2 (5/3/14) 3.00 8.00
RTCBBML6 M.Lucic R2 (5/10/14) 3.00 8.00
RTCBBML7 M.Lucic R2 (5/14/14) 3.00 8.00
RTCBBPB1 P.Bergeron R1 (4/18/14) 3.00 8.00
RTCBBPB2 P.Bergeron R1 (4/20/14) 3.00 8.00
RTCBBPB3 P.Bergeron R1 (4/26/14) 3.00 8.00
RTCBBPB4 P.Bergeron R2 (5/1/14) 4.00 10.00
RTCBBPB5 P.Bergeron R2 (5/3/14) 4.00 10.00
RTCBBPB6 P.Bergeron R2 (5/10/14) 4.00 10.00
RTCBBPB7 P.Bergeron R2 (5/14/14) 4.00 10.00
RTCBBRS1 R.Smith R1 (4/18/14) 2.50 6.00
RTCBBRS2 R.Smith R1 (4/20/14) 2.50 6.00
RTCBBRS3 R.Smith R1 (4/26/14) 2.50 6.00
RTCBBRS4 R.Smith R2 (5/1/14) 3.00 8.00
RTCBBRS5 R.Smith R2 (5/3/14) 3.00 8.00
RTCBBRS6 R.Smith R2 (5/10/14) 3.00 8.00
RTCBBRS7 R.Smith R2 (5/14/14) 3.00 8.00
RTCBBTK1 T.Krug R1 (4/18/14) 2.00 5.00
RTCBBTK2 T.Krug R1 (4/20/14) 2.00 5.00
RTCBBTK3 T.Krug R1 (4/26/14) 2.00 5.00
RTCBBTK4 T.Krug R2 (5/1/14) 2.50 6.00
RTCBBTK5 T.Krug R2 (5/3/14) 2.50 6.00
RTCBBTK6 T.Krug R2 (5/10/14) 2.50 6.00
RTCBBTK7 T.Krug R2 (5/14/14) 2.50 6.00
RTCBBTR1 T.Rask R1 (4/18/14) 3.00 8.00
RTCBBTR2 T.Rask R1 (4/20/14) 3.00 8.00
RTCBBTR3 T.Rask R1 (4/26/14) 3.00 8.00
RTCBBTR4 T.Rask R2 (5/1/14) 4.00 10.00
RTCBBTR5 T.Rask R2 (5/3/14) 4.00 10.00
RTCBBTR6 T.Rask R2 (5/10/14) 4.00 10.00
RTCBBTR7 T.Rask R2 (5/14/14) 4.00 10.00
RTCBBZC1 Z.Chara R1 (4/18/14) 2.50 6.00
RTCBBZC2 Z.Chara R1 (4/20/14) 2.50 6.00
RTCBBZC3 Z.Chara R1 (4/26/14) 2.50 6.00
RTCBBZC4 Z.Chara R2 (5/1/14) 3.00 8.00
RTCBBZC5 Z.Chara R2 (5/3/14) 3.00 8.00
RTCBBZC6 Z.Chara R2 (5/10/14) 3.00 8.00
RTCBBZC7 Z.Chara R2 (5/14/14) 3.00 8.00
RTCCAGL1 G.Landeskog R1 (4/17/14) 3.00 8.00
RTCCAGL2 G.Landeskog R1 (4/19/14) 3.00 8.00
RTCCAGL3 G.Landeskog R1 (4/26/14) 3.00 8.00
RTCCAGL4 G.Landeskog R1 (4/30/14) 3.00 8.00
RTCCAMD M.Duchene R1 (4/30/14) 2.50 6.00
RTCCANM1 MacKinnon R1 (4/17/14) 10.0025.00
RTCCANM2 N.MacKinnon
R1 (4/19/14) 10.00 25.00
RTCCANM3 N.MacKinnon
R1 (4/26/14) 10.00 25.00
RTCCANM4 N.MacKinnon
R1 (4/30/14) 10.00 25.00
RTCCAPS1 P.Stastny R1 (4/17/14) 2.00 5.00
RTCCAPS2 P.Stastny R1 (4/19/14) 2.00 5.00
RTCCAPS3 P.Stastny R1 (4/26/14) 2.00 5.00
RTCCAPS4 P.Stastny R1 (4/30/14) 2.00 5.00
RTCCASV1 S.Varlamov R1 (4/17/14) 2.50 6.00
RTCCASV2 S.Varlamov R1 (4/19/14) 2.50 6.00
RTCCASV3 S.Varlamov R1 (4/26/14) 2.50 6.00
RTCCASV4 S.Varlamov R1 (4/30/14) 2.50 6.00
RTCCBBS1 B.Seabrook R1 (4/27/14) 1.50 4.00
RTCCBBS2 B.Seabrook R2 (5/2/14) 2.00 5.00
RTCCBBS3 B.Seabrook R2 (5/4/14) 2.00 5.00
RTCCBBS4 B.Seabrook R2 (5/11/14) 2.00 5.00
RTCCBBS5 B.Seabrook R3 (5/18/14) 4.00 10.00
RTCCBBS6 B.Seabrook R3 (5/21/14) 4.00 10.00
RTCCBBS7 B.Seabrook R3 (5/28/14) 4.00 10.00
RTCCBBS8 B.Seabrook R3 (6/1/14) 4.00 10.00
RTCCBCC1 C.Crawford R1 (4/21/14) 3.00 8.00
RTCCBCC2 C.Crawford R1 (4/23/14) 3.00 8.00
RTCCBCC3 C.Crawford R1 (4/27/14) 3.00 8.00
RTCCBCC4 C.Crawford R2 (5/2/14) 4.00 10.00
RTCCBCC5 C.Crawford R2 (5/4/14) 4.00 10.00
RTCCBCC6 C.Crawford R2 (5/11/14) 4.00 10.00
RTCCBCC7 C.Crawford R3 (5/18/14) 8.00 20.00
RTCCBCC8 C.Crawford R3 (5/21/14) 8.00 20.00
RTCCBCC9 C.Crawford R3 (5/28/14) 8.00 20.00
RTCCBCC10 C.Crawford R3 (6/1/14) 8.00 20.00
RTCCBDK1 D.Keith R1 (4/21/14) 2.00 5.00
RTCCBDK2 D.Keith R1 (4/27/14) 2.00 5.00
RTCCBDK3 D.Keith R2 (5/2/14) 2.00 5.00
RTCCBDK4 D.Keith R2 (5/4/14) 2.50 6.00
RTCCBDK5 D.Keith R2 (5/11/14) 2.50 6.00
RTCCBDK6 D.Keith R3 (5/18/14) 2.50 6.00
RTCCBDK7 D.Keith R3 (5/21/14) 5.00 12.00
RTCCBDK8 D.Keith R3 (5/28/14) 5.00 12.00
RTCCBDK9 D.Keith R3 (6/1/14) 5.00 12.00
RTCCBDK10 D.Keith R1 (4/23/14) 5.00 12.00
RTCCBJBD1 B.Dubinsky R1 (4/21/14) 1.50 4.00
RTCCBJBD2 B.Dubinsky R1 (4/23/14) 1.50 4.00
RTCCBJBD3 B.Dubinsky R1 (4/28/14) 1.50 4.00
RTCCBJRJ1 R.Johansen R1 (4/21/14) 2.00 5.00
RTCCBJRJ2 R.Johansen R1 (4/23/14) 2.00 5.00
RTCCBJRJ3 R.Johansen R1 (4/28/14) 2.00 5.00
RTCCBJSB1 S.Bobrovsky
R1 (4/21/14) 4.00 10.00
RTCCBJSB2 S.Bobrovsky
R1 (4/23/14) 4.00 10.00
RTCCBJSB3 S.Bobrovsky
R1 (4/28/14) 4.00 10.00
RTCCBJT1 J.Toews R1 (4/21/14) 4.00 10.00
RTCCBJT2 J.Toews R1 (4/23/14) 4.00 10.00
RTCCBJT3 J.Toews R1 (4/27/14) 6.00 15.00
RTCCBJT4 J.Toews R2 (5/2/14) 5.00 12.00
RTCCBJT5 J.Toews R2 (5/4/14) 5.00 12.00
RTCCBJT6 J.Toews R2 (5/11/14) 5.00 12.00
RTCCBJT7 J.Toews R3 (5/18/14) 15.00 40.00
RTCCBJT8 J.Toews R3 (5/21/14) 15.00 40.00
RTCCBJT9 J.Toews R3 (5/28/14) 15.00 40.00
RTCCBJT10 J.Toews R3 (6/1/14) 15.00 40.00
RTCCBMH1 M.Hossa R1 (4/21/14) 2.50 6.00
RTCCBMH2 M.Hossa R1 (4/23/14) 2.50 6.00
RTCCBMH3 M.Hossa R1 (4/27/14) 2.50 6.00
RTCCBMH4 M.Hossa R2 (5/2/14) 3.00 8.00
RTCCBMH5 M.Hossa R2 (5/4/14) 3.00 8.00
RTCCBMH6 M.Hossa R2 (5/11/14) 3.00 8.00
RTCCBMH7 M.Hossa R3 (5/18/14) 6.00 15.00
RTCCBMH8 M.Hossa R3 (5/21/14) 6.00 15.00
RTCCBMH9 M.Hossa R3 (5/28/14) 6.00 15.00
RTCCBMH10 M.Hossa R3 (6/1/14) 6.00 15.00
RTCCBPK1 P.Kane R1 (4/21/14) 5.00 12.00
RTCCBPK2 P.Kane R1 (4/23/14) 5.00 12.00
RTCCBPK3 P.Kane R1 (4/27/14) 5.00 12.00
RTCCBPK4 P.Kane R2 (5/2/14) 6.00 15.00
RTCCBPK5 P.Kane R2 (5/4/14) 6.00 15.00
RTCCBPK6 P.Kane R2 (5/11/14) 6.00 15.00
RTCCBPK7 P.Kane R3 (5/18/14) 12.00 30.00
RTCCBPK8 P.Kane R3 (5/21/14) 12.00 30.00
RTCCBPK9 P.Kane R3 (5/28/14) 12.00 30.00
RTCCBPK10 P.Kane R3 (6/1/14) 12.00 30.00
RTCCBPS1 P.Sharp R1 (4/21/14) 2.50 6.00
RTCCBPS2 P.Sharp R1 (4/23/14) 2.50 6.00
RTCCBPS3 P.Sharp R1 (4/27/14) 2.50 6.00
RTCCBPS4 P.Sharp R2 (5/2/14) 3.00 8.00
RTCCBPS5 P.Sharp R2 (5/4/14) 3.00 8.00
RTCCBPS6 P.Sharp R2 (5/11/14) 3.00 8.00
RTCCBPS7 P.Sharp R3 (5/18/14) 6.00 15.00
RTCCBPS8 P.Sharp R3 (5/21/14) 6.00 15.00
RTCCBPS9 P.Sharp R3 (5/28/14) 6.00 15.00
RTCCBPS10 P.Sharp R3 (6/1/14) 6.00 15.00
RTCCBSA1 B.Saad R1 (4/21/14) 2.00 5.00
RTCCBSA2 B.Saad R1 (4/23/14) 2.00 5.00
RTCCBSA3 B.Saad R1 (4/27/14) 2.00 5.00
RTCCBSA4 B.Saad R2 (5/2/14) 2.50 6.00
RTCCBSA5 B.Saad R2 (5/4/14) 2.50 6.00
RTCCBSA6 B.Saad R2 (5/11/14) 2.50 6.00
RTCCBSA7 B.Saad R3 (5/18/14) 5.00 12.00
RTCCBSA8 B.Saad R3 (5/21/14) 5.00 12.00
RTCCBSA9 B.Saad R3 (5/28/14) 5.00 12.00
RTCCBSA10 B.Saad R3 (6/1/14) 5.00 12.00
RTCDRWHZ Zetterberg R1 (4/24/14) 3.00 8.00
RTCDRWJF1 J.Franzen R1 (4/22/14) 2.00 5.00
RTCDRWJF2 J.Franzen R1 (4/24/14) 2.00 5.00
RTCDRWJH J.Howard R1 (4/22/14) 3.00 8.00
RTCDRWNK1 N.Kronwall R1 (4/22/14) 2.00 5.00
RTCDRWNK2 N.Kronwall R1 (4/24/14) 2.00 5.00
RTCDRWPD1 P.Datsyuk R1 (4/22/14) 4.00 10.00
RTCDRWPD2 P.Datsyuk R1 (4/24/14) 4.00 10.00
RTCDSJB1 J.Benn R1 (4/21/14) 2.50 6.00
RTCDSJB2 J.Benn R1 (4/23/14) 2.50 6.00
RTCDSJB3 J.Benn R1 (4/27/14) 2.50 6.00
RTCDSTS1 T.Seguin R1 (4/21/14) 3.00 8.00
RTCDSTS2 T.Seguin R1 (4/23/14) 3.00 8.00
RTCDSTS3 T.Seguin R1 (4/27/14) 3.00 8.00
RTCLAKAK1 A.Kopitar R1 (4/22/14) 4.00 10.00
RTCLAKAK2 A.Kopitar R1 (4/24/14) 4.00 10.00
RTCLAKAK3 A.Kopitar R1 (4/28/14) 4.00 10.00
RTCLAKAK4 A.Kopitar R2 (5/8/14) 5.00 12.00
RTCLAKAK5 A.Kopitar R2 (5/10/14) 5.00 12.00
RTCLAKAK6 A.Kopitar R2 (5/14/14) 5.00 12.00
RTCLAKAK7 A.Kopitar R3 (5/24/14) 10.00 25.00
RTCLAKAK8 A.Kopitar R3 (5/26/14) 10.00 25.00
RTCLAKAK9 A.Kopitar R3 (5/30/14) 10.00 25.00
RTCLAKAK10 A.Kopitar R4 (6/4/14) 20.00 50.00
RTCLAKAK11 A.Kopitar R4 (6/7/14) 20.00 50.00
RTCLAKAK12 A.Kopitar R4 (6/13/14) 20.0050.00
RTCLAKAM1 A.Martinez R1 (4/22/14) 1.50 4.00
RTCLAKAM2 A.Martinez R1 (4/24/14) 1.50 4.00
RTCLAKAM3 A.Martinez R1 (4/28/14) 1.50 4.00
RTCLAKAM4 A.Martinez R2 (5/8/14) 2.00 5.00
RTCLAKAM5 A.Martinez R2 (5/10/14) 2.00 5.00
RTCLAKAM6 A.Martinez R2 (5/14/14) 2.00 5.00
RTCLAKAM7 A.Martinez R3 (5/24/14) 4.00 10.00
RTCLAKAM8 A.Martinez R3 (5/26/14) 4.00 10.00
RTCLAKAM9 A.Martinez R3 (5/30/14) 4.00 10.00
RTCLAKAM10 A.Martinez R4 (6/4/14) 8.00 20.00
RTCLAKAM11 A.Martinez R4 (6/7/14) 8.00 20.00
RTCLAKAM12 A.Martinez
R4 (6/13/14) 8.00 20.00
RTCLAKDB1 D.Brown R1 (4/22/14) 2.50 6.00
RTCLAKDB2 D.Brown R1 (4/24/14) 2.50 6.00
RTCLAKDB3 D.Brown R1 (4/28/14) 2.50 6.00
RTCLAKDB4 D.Brown R2 (5/8/14) 3.00 8.00
RTCLAKDB5 D.Brown R2 (5/10/14) 3.00 8.00
RTCLAKDB6 D.Brown R2 (5/14/14) 3.00 8.00
RTCLAKDB7 D.Brown R3 (5/24/14) 6.00 15.00
RTCLAKDB8 D.Brown R3 (5/26/14) 6.00 15.00
RTCLAKDB9 D.Brown R3 (5/30/14) 6.00 15.00
RTCLAKDB10 D.Brown R4 (6/4/14) 12.00 30.00
RTCLAKDB11 D.Brown R4 (6/7/14) 12.00 30.00
RTCLAKDB12 D.Brown R4 (6/13/14) 12.00 30.00
RTCLAKDD1 D.Doughty R1 (4/22/14) 3.00 8.00
RTCLAKDD2 D.Doughty R1 (4/24/14) 3.00 8.00
RTCLAKDD3 D.Doughty R1 (4/28/14) 3.00 8.00
RTCLAKDD4 D.Doughty R2 (5/8/14) 4.00 10.00
RTCLAKDD5 D.Doughty R2 (5/10/14) 4.00 10.00
RTCLAKDD6 D.Doughty R2 (5/14/14) 4.00 10.00
RTCLAKDD7 D.Doughty R3 (5/24/14) 8.00 20.00
RTCLAKDD8 D.Doughty R3 (5/26/14) 8.00 20.00
RTCLAKDD9 D.Doughty R3 (5/30/14) 8.00 20.00
RTCLAKDD10 D.Doughty R4 (6/4/14) 15.0040.00
RTCLAKDD11 D.Doughty R4 (6/7/14) 15.0040.00
RTCLAKDD12 D.Doughty
R4 (6/13/14) 15.00 40.00
RTCLAKJC1 J.Carter R1 (4/22/14) 2.00 5.00
RTCLAKJC2 J.Carter R1 (4/24/14) 2.00 5.00
RTCLAKJC3 J.Carter R1 (4/28/14) 2.00 5.00
RTCLAKJC4 J.Carter R2 (5/8/14) 2.50 6.00
RTCLAKJC5 J.Carter R2 (5/10/14) 2.50 6.00
RTCLAKJC6 J.Carter R2 (5/14/14) 2.50 6.00
RTCLAKJC7 J.Carter R3 (5/24/14) 5.00 12.00
RTCLAKJC8 J.Carter R3 (5/26/14) 5.00 12.00
RTCLAKJC9 J.Carter R3 (5/30/14) 5.00 12.00
RTCLAKJC10 J.Carter R4 (6/4/14) 10.00 25.00
RTCLAKJC11 J.Carter R4 (6/7/14) 10.00 25.00
RTCLAKJC12 J.Carter R4 (6/13/14) 10.00 25.00
RTCLAKJQ1 J.Quick R1 (4/22/14) 3.00 8.00
RTCLAKJQ2 J.Quick R1 (4/24/14) 3.00 8.00
RTCLAKJQ3 J.Quick R1 (4/28/14) 3.00 8.00
RTCLAKJQ4 J.Quick R2 (5/8/14) 4.00 10.00
RTCLAKJQ5 J.Quick R2 (5/10/14) 4.00 10.00
RTCLAKJQ6 J.Quick R2 (5/14/14) 4.00 10.00
RTCLAKJQ7 J.Quick R3 (5/24/14) 8.00 20.00
RTCLAKJQ8 J.Quick R3 (5/26/14) 8.00 20.00
RTCLAKJQ9 J.Quick R3 (5/30/14) 8.00 20.00
RTCLAKJQ10 J.Quick R4 (6/4/14) 15.00 40.00
RTCLAKJQ11 J.Quick R4 (6/7/14) 15.00 40.00
RTCLAKJQ12 J.Quick R4 (6/13/14) 15.00 40.00
RTCLAKJW1 J.Williams R1 (4/22/14) 2.00 5.00
RTCLAKJW2 J.Williams R1 (4/24/14) 2.00 5.00
RTCLAKJW3 J.Williams R1 (4/28/14) 2.00 5.00
RTCLAKJW4 J.Williams R2 (5/8/14) 2.50 6.00
RTCLAKJW5 J.Williams R2 (5/10/14) 2.50 6.00
RTCLAKJW6 J.Williams R2 (5/14/14) 2.50 6.00
RTCLAKJW7 J.Williams R3 (5/24/14) 5.00 12.00
RTCLAKJW8 J.Williams R3 (5/26/14) 5.00 12.00
RTCLAKJW9 J.Williams R3 (5/30/14) 5.00 12.00
RTCLAKJW10 J.Williams R4 (6/4/14) 10.0025.00
RTCLAKJW11 J.Williams R4 (6/7/14) 10.0025.00
RTCLAKJW12 J.Williams
R4 (6/13/14) 10.00 25.00
RTCLAKMG1 M.Gaborik R1 (4/22/14) 2.50 6.00
RTCLAKMG2 M.Gaborik R1 (4/24/14) 2.50 6.00
RTCLAKMG3 M.Gaborik R1 (4/28/14) 2.50 6.00
RTCLAKMG4 M.Gaborik R2 (5/8/14) 3.00 8.00
RTCLAKMG5 M.Gaborik R2 (5/10/14) 3.00 8.00
RTCLAKMG6 M.Gaborik R2 (5/14/14) 3.00 8.00
RTCLAKMG7 M.Gaborik R3 (5/24/14) 6.00 15.00
RTCLAKMG8 M.Gaborik R3 (5/26/14) 6.00 15.00
RTCLAKMG9 M.Gaborik R3 (5/30/14) 6.00 15.00
RTCLAKMG10 M.Gaborik R4 (6/4/14) 12.0030.00
RTCLAKMG11 M.Gaborik R4 (6/7/14) 12.0030.00
RTCLAKMG12 M.Gaborik
R4 (6/13/14) 12.00 30.00
RTCLAKTP1 T.Pearson R1 (4/22/14) 1.50 4.00
RTCLAKTP2 T.Pearson R1 (4/24/14) 1.50 4.00
RTCLAKTP3 T.Pearson R1 (4/28/14) 1.50 4.00
RTCLAKTP4 T.Pearson R2 (5/8/14) 2.00 5.00
RTCLAKTP5 T.Pearson R2 (5/10/14) 2.00 5.00
RTCLAKTP6 T.Pearson R2 (5/14/14) 2.00 5.00
RTCLAKTP7 T.Pearson R3 (5/24/14) 4.00 10.00
RTCLAKTP8 T.Pearson R3 (5/26/14) 4.00 10.00
RTCLAKTP9 T.Pearson R3 (5/30/14) 4.00 10.00
RTCLAKTP10 T.Pearson R4 (6/4/14) 8.00 20.00
RTCLAKTP11 T.Pearson R4 (6/7/14) 8.00 20.00
RTCLAKTP12 T.Pearson R4 (6/13/14) 8.00 20.00
RTCLAKTT1 T.Toffoli R1 (4/22/14) 2.50 6.00
RTCLAKTT2 T.Toffoli R1 (4/24/14) 2.50 6.00
RTCLAKTT3 T.Toffoli R1 (4/28/14) 2.50 6.00
RTCLAKTT4 T.Toffoli R2 (5/8/14) 3.00 8.00
RTCLAKTT5 T.Toffoli R2 (5/10/14) 3.00 8.00

RTCLAKTT6 T.Toffoli R2 (5/14/14) 3.00 8.00
RTCLAKTT7 T.Toffoli R3 (5/24/14) 6.00 15.00
RTCLAKTT8 T.Toffoli R3 (5/26/14) 6.00 15.00
RTCLAKTT9 T.Toffoli R3 (5/30/14) 6.00 15.00
RTCLAKTT10 T.Toffoli R4 (6/4/14) 12.00 30.00
RTCLAKTT11 T.Toffoli R4 (6/7/14) 12.00 30.00
RTCLAKTT12 T.Toffoli R4 (6/13/14) 12.00 30.00
RTCMCBG1 B.Gallagher R1 (4/20/14) 2.50 6.00
RTCMCBG2 B.Gallagher R1 (4/22/14) 2.50 6.00
RTCMCBG3 B.Gallagher R2 (5/6/14) 3.00 8.00
RTCMCBG4 B.Gallagher R2 (5/8/14) 3.00 8.00
RTCMCBG5 B.Gallagher R2 (5/12/14) 3.00 8.00
RTCMCBG6 Gallagher R3 (5/17/14) 6.00 15.00
RTCMCBG7 B.Gallagher R3 (5/19/14) 6.00 15.00
RTCMCBG8 B.Gallagher R3 (5/27/14) 6.00 15.00
RTCMCCP1 C.Price R1 (4/20/14) 5.00 12.00
RTCMCCP2 C.Price R1 (4/22/14) 5.00 12.00
RTCMCCP3 C.Price R2 (5/6/14) 6.00 15.00
RTCMCCP4 C.Price R2 (5/8/14) 6.00 15.00
RTCMCCP5 C.Price R2 (5/12/14) 6.00 15.00
RTCMCCP6 C.Price R3 (5/17/14) 12.00 30.00
RTCMCDT1 D.Tokarski R3 (5/17/14) 4.00 10.00
RTCMCDT2 D.Tokarski R3 (5/19/14) 4.00 10.00
RTCMCDT3 D.Tokarski R3 (5/27/14) 4.00 10.00
RTCMCLE1 L.Eller R1 (4/20/14) 1.50 4.00
RTCMCLE2 L.Eller R1 (4/22/14) 1.50 4.00
RTCMCLE3 L.Eller R2 (5/6/14) 2.00 5.00
RTCMCLE4 L.Eller R2 (5/8/14) 2.00 5.00
RTCMCLE5 L.Eller R2 (5/12/14) 2.00 5.00
RTCMCLE6 L.Eller R3 (5/17/14) 4.00 10.00
RTCMCLE7 L.Eller R3 (5/19/14) 4.00 10.00
RTCMCLE8 L.Eller R3 (5/27/14) 4.00 10.00
RTCMCMP1 M.Pacioretty R1 (4/20/14) 2.50 6.00
RTCMCMP2 M.Pacioretty R1 (4/22/14) 2.50 6.00
RTCMCMP3 M.Pacioretty R2 (5/6/14) 3.00 8.00
RTCMCMP4 M.Pacioretty R2 (5/8/14) 3.00 8.00
RTCMCMP5 M.Pacioretty R2 (5/12/14) 3.00 8.00
RTCMCMP6 M.Pacioretty R3 (5/17/14) 6.00 15.00
RTCMCMP7 M.Pacioretty R3 (5/19/14) 6.00 15.00
RTCMCMP8 M.Pacioretty R3 (5/27/14) 6.00 15.00
RTCMCPS1 P.Subban R1 (4/20/14) 3.00 8.00
RTCMCPS2 P.Subban R1 (4/22/14) 3.00 8.00
RTCMCPS3 P.Subban R2 (5/6/14) 4.00 10.00
RTCMCPS4 P.Subban R2 (5/8/14) 4.00 10.00
RTCMCPS5 P.Subban R2 (5/12/14) 4.00 10.00
RTCMCPS6 P.Subban R3 (5/17/14) 8.00 20.00
RTCMCPS7 P.Subban R3 (5/19/14) 8.00 20.00
RTCMCPS8 P.Subban R3 (5/27/14) 8.00 20.00
RTCMCTP1 T.Plekanec R1 (4/20/14) 1.50 4.00
RTCMCTP2 T.Plekanec R1 (4/22/14) 1.50 4.00
RTCMCTP3 T.Plekanec R2 (5/6/14) 2.00 5.00
RTCMCTP4 T.Plekanec R2 (5/8/14) 2.00 5.00
RTCMCTP5 T.Plekanec R2 (5/12/14) 2.00 5.00
RTCMCTP6 T.Plekanec R3 (5/17/14) 4.00 10.00
RTCMCTP7 T.Plekanec R3 (5/19/14) 4.00 10.00
RTCMCTP8 T.Plekanec R3 (5/27/14) 4.00 10.00
RTCMCTV1 T.Vanek R1 (4/20/14) 2.00 5.00
RTCMCTV2 T.Vanek R1 (4/22/14) 2.00 5.00
RTCMCTV3 T.Vanek R2 (5/6/14) 2.50 6.00
RTCMCTV4 T.Vanek R2 (5/8/14) 2.50 6.00
RTCMCTV5 T.Vanek R2 (5/12/14) 2.50 6.00
RTCMCTV6 T.Vanek R3 (5/17/14) 5.00 12.00
RTCMCTV7 T.Vanek R3 (5/19/14) 5.00 12.00
RTCMCTV8 T.Vanek R3 (5/27/14) 5.00 12.00
RTCMWDK1 D.Kuemper R1 (4/21/14) 2.50 6.00
RTCMWDK2 D.Kuemper R1 (4/24/14) 2.50 6.00
RTCMWDK3 D.Kuemper R1 (4/28/14) 2.50 6.00
RTCMWJP1 J.Pominville R1 (4/21/14) 1.50 4.00
RTCMWJP2 J.Pominville R1 (4/24/14) 1.50 4.00
RTCMWJP3 J.Pominville R1 (4/28/14) 1.50 4.00
RTCMWJP4 J.Pominville R2 (5/6/14) 2.00 5.00
RTCMWJP5 J.Pominville R2 (5/9/14) 2.00 5.00
RTCMWJP6 J.Pominville R2 (5/13/14) 2.00 5.00
RTCMWMG1 M.Granlund R1 (4/21/14) 2.00 5.00
RTCMWMG2 M.Granlund R1 (4/24/14) 2.00 5.00
RTCMWMG3 M.Granlund R1 (4/28/14) 2.00 5.00
RTCMWMG4 M.Granlund R2 (5/6/14) 2.50 6.00
RTCMWMG5 M.Granlund R2 (5/9/14) 2.50 6.00
RTCMWMG6 M.Granlund R2 (5/13/14) 2.50 6.00
RTCMWMK1 M.Koivu R1 (4/21/14) 2.00 5.00
RTCMWMK2 M.Koivu R1 (4/24/14) 2.00 5.00
RTCMWMK3 M.Koivu R1 (4/28/14) 2.00 5.00
RTCMWMK4 M.Koivu R2 (5/6/14) 2.50 6.00
RTCMWMK5 M.Koivu R2 (5/9/14) 2.50 6.00
RTCMWMK6 M.Koivu R2 (5/13/14) 2.50 6.00
RTCMWNN1 N.Niederreiter R1 (4/21/14) 1.50 4.00
RTCMWNN2 N.Niederreiter R1 (4/24/14) 1.50 4.00
RTCMWNN3 N.Niederreiter R1 (4/28/14) 1.50 4.00
RTCMWNN4 N.Niederreiter R2 (5/6/14) 2.00 5.00
RTCMWNN5 N.Niederreiter R2 (5/9/14) 2.00 5.00
RTCMWNN6 N.Niederreiter R2 (5/13/14) 2.00 5.00
RTCMWRS1 R.Suter R1 (4/21/14) 2.00 5.00
RTCMWRS2 R.Suter R1 (4/24/14) 2.00 5.00
RTCMWRS3 R.Suter R1 (4/28/14) 2.00 5.00
RTCMWRS4 R.Suter R2 (5/6/14) 2.50 6.00
RTCMWRS5 R.Suter R2 (5/9/14) 2.50 6.00
RTCMWRS6 R.Suter R2 (5/13/14) 2.50 6.00
RTCMWZP1 Z.Parise R1 (4/21/14) 4.00 10.00
RTCMWZP2 Z.Parise R1 (4/24/14) 4.00 10.00
RTCMWZP3 Z.Parise R1 (4/28/14) 4.00 10.00
RTCMWZP4 Z.Parise R2 (5/6/14) 5.00 12.00
RTCMWZP5 Z.Parise R2 (5/9/14) 5.00 12.00
RTCMWZP6 Z.Parise R2 (5/13/14) 5.00 12.00
RTCNYRBP1 B.Pouliot R1 (4/17/14) 1.50 4.00
RTCNYRBP2 B.Pouliot R1 (4/20/14) 1.50 4.00
RTCNYRBP3 B.Pouliot R1 (4/27/14) 1.50 4.00
RTCNYRBP4 B.Pouliot R1 (4/30/14) 1.50 4.00
RTCNYRBP5 B.Pouliot R2 (5/5/14) 2.00 5.00
RTCNYRBP6 B.Pouliot R2 (5/7/14) 2.00 5.00
RTCNYRBP7 B.Pouliot R2 (5/11/14) 2.00 5.00
RTCNYRBP8 B.Pouliot R3 (5/22/14) 4.00 10.00
RTCNYRBP9 B.Pouliot R3 (5/25/14) 4.00 10.00
RTCNYRBP10 B.Pouliot R3 (5/29/14) 4.00 10.00
RTCNYRBP11 B.Pouliot R4 (6/9/14) 8.00 20.00
RTCNYRBP12 B.Pouliot R4 (6/11/14) 8.00 20.00
RTCNYRBR1 B.Richards R1 (4/17/14) 2.50 6.00
RTCNYRBR2 B.Richards R1 (4/20/14) 2.50 6.00
RTCNYRBR3 B.Richards R1 (4/27/14) 2.50 6.00
RTCNYRBR4 B.Richards R1 (4/30/14) 2.50 6.00
RTCNYRBR5 B.Richards R2 (5/5/14) 3.00 8.00
RTCNYRBR6 B.Richards R2 (5/7/14) 3.00 8.00
RTCNYRBR7 B.Richards R2 (5/11/14) 3.00 8.00
RTCNYRBR8 B.Richards R3 (5/22/14) 6.00 15.00
RTCNYRBR9 B.Richards R3 (5/25/14) 6.00 15.00
RTCNYRBR10 B.Richards R3 (5/29/14) 6.00 15.00
RTCNYRBR11 B.Richards R4 (6/9/14) 12.0030.00
RTCNYRBR12 B.Richards R4 (6/11/14) 12.00 30.00
RTCNYRCH1 C.Hagelin R1 (4/17/14) 1.50 4.00
RTCNYRCH2 C.Hagelin R1 (4/20/14) 1.50 4.00
RTCNYRCH3 C.Hagelin R1 (4/27/14) 1.50 4.00
RTCNYRCH4 C.Hagelin R1 (4/30/14) 1.50 4.00
RTCNYRCH5 C.Hagelin R2 (5/5/14) 2.00 5.00
RTCNYRCH6 C.Hagelin R2 (5/7/14) 2.00 5.00
RTCNYRCH7 C.Hagelin R2 (5/11/14) 2.00 5.00
RTCNYRCH8 C.Hagelin R3 (5/22/14) 4.00 10.00
RTCNYRCH9 C.Hagelin R3 (5/25/14) 4.00 10.00
RTCNYRCH10 C.Hagelin R3 (5/29/14) 4.0010.00
RTCNYRCH11 C.Hagelin R4 (6/9/14) 8.00 20.00
RTCNYRCH12 C.Hagelin R4 (6/11/14) 8.0020.00
RTCNYRCK1 C.Kreider R2 (5/7/14) 4.00 10.00
RTCNYRCK2 C.Kreider R2 (5/11/14) 4.00 10.00
RTCNYRCK3 C.Kreider R3 (5/22/14) 8.00 20.00
RTCNYRCK4 C.Kreider R3 (5/25/14) 8.00 20.00
RTCNYRCK5 C.Kreider R3 (5/29/14) 8.00 20.00
RTCNYRCK6 C.Kreider R4 (6/9/14) 15.00 40.00
RTCNYRCK7 C.Kreider R4 (6/11/14) 15.00 40.00
RTCNYRDS1 D.Stepan R1 (4/17/14) 1.50 4.00
RTCNYRDS2 D.Stepan R1 (4/20/14) 1.50 4.00
RTCNYRDS3 D.Stepan R1 (4/27/14) 1.50 4.00
RTCNYRDS4 D.Stepan R1 (4/30/14) 1.50 4.00
RTCNYRDS5 D.Stepan R2 (5/5/14) 2.00 5.00
RTCNYRDS6 D.Stepan R2 (5/7/14) 2.00 5.00
RTCNYRDS7 D.Stepan R2 (5/11/14) 2.00 5.00
RTCNYRDS8 D.Stepan R3 (5/22/14) 8.00 20.00
RTCNYRDS9 D.Stepan R3 (5/29/14) 8.00 20.00
RTCNYRDS10 D.Stepan R4 (6/9/14) 8.00 20.00
RTCNYRDS11 D.Stepan R4 (6/11/14) 8.00 20.00
RTCNYRHL1 Lundqvist R1 (4/17/14) 6.00 15.00
RTCNYRHL2 H.Lundqvist R1 (4/20/14) 6.00 15.00
RTCNYRHL3 H.Lundqvist R1 (4/27/14) 6.00 15.00
RTCNYRHL4 H.Lundqvist R1 (4/30/14) 6.00 15.00
RTCNYRHL5 H.Lundqvist R2 (5/5/14) 8.00 20.00
RTCNYRHL6 H.Lundqvist R2 (5/7/14) 8.00 20.00
RTCNYRHL7 H.Lundqvist R2 (5/11/14) 8.00 20.00
RTCNYRHL8 Lundqvist R3 (5/22/14) 15.00 40.00
RTCNYRHL9 H.Lundqvist R3 (5/25/14) 15.00 40.00
RTCNYRHL10 H.Lundqvist R3 (5/29/14) 15.00 40.00
RTCNYRHL11 H.Lundqvist R4 (6/9/14) 30.00 80.00
RTCNYRHL12 H.Lundqvist R4 (6/11/14) 30.00 80.00
RTCNYRMS1 M.St.Louis R1 (4/17/14) 5.0012.00
RTCNYRMS2 M.St.Louis R1 (4/20/14) 2.50 6.00
RTCNYRMS3 M.St.Louis R1 (4/27/14) 2.50 6.00
RTCNYRMS4 M.St.Louis R1 (4/30/14) 2.50 6.00
RTCNYRMS5 M.St.Louis R2 (5/5/14) 3.00 8.00
RTCNYRMS6 M.St.Louis R2 (5/7/14) 3.00 8.00
RTCNYRMS7 M.St.Louis R2 (5/11/14) 3.00 8.00
RTCNYRMS8 M.St.Louis R3 (5/22/14) 6.0015.00
RTCNYRMS9 M.St.Louis R3 (5/25/14) 6.0015.00
RTCNYRMS10 M.St.Louis R3 (5/29/14) 6.00 15.00
RTCNYRMS11 M.St.Louis R4 (6/9/14) 12.00 30.00
RTCNYRMS12 M.St.Louis R4 (6/11/14) 12.00 30.00
RTCNYRMZ1 M.Zuccarello R1 (4/17/14) 2.50 6.00
RTCNYRMZ2 M.Zuccarello R1 (4/20/14) 2.50 6.00
RTCNYRMZ3 M.Zuccarello R1 (4/27/14) 2.50 6.00
RTCNYRMZ4 M.Zuccarello R1 (4/30/14) 2.50 6.00
RTCNYRMZ5 M.Zuccarello R2 (5/5/14) 3.00 8.00
RTCNYRMZ6 M.Zuccarello R2 (5/7/14) 3.00 8.00
RTCNYRMZ7 M.Zuccarello R2 (5/11/14) 3.00 8.00
RTCNYRMZ8 M.Zuccarello R3 (5/22/14) 6.00 15.00
RTCNYRMZ9 M.Zuccarello R3 (5/25/14) 6.00 15.00
RTCNYRMZ10 M.Zuccarello R3 (5/29/14) 6.00 15.00
RTCNYRMZ11 M.Zuccarello R4 (6/9/14) 12.00 30.00
RTCNYRMZ12 M.Zuccarello R4 (6/11/14) 12.00 30.00
RTCNYRRM1 R.McDonagh R1 (4/17/14) 1.50 4.00
RTCNYRRM2 R.McDonagh R1 (4/20/14) 1.50 4.00
RTCNYRRM3 R.McDonagh R1 (4/27/14) 1.50 4.00
RTCNYRRM4 R.McDonagh R1 (4/30/14) 1.50 4.00
RTCNYRRM5 R.McDonagh R2 (5/5/14) 2.00 5.00
RTCNYRRM6 R.McDonagh R2 (5/7/14) 2.00 5.00
RTCNYRRM7 R.McDonagh R2 (5/11/14) 2.00 5.00
RTCNYRRM8 R.McDonagh R3 (5/22/14) 4.00 10.00
RTCNYRRM9 R.McDonagh R3 (5/25/14) 4.00 10.00
RTCNYRRM10 R.McDonagh R3 (5/29/14) 4.00 10.00
RTCNYRRM11 R.McDonagh R4 (6/9/14) 8.00 20.00
RTCNYRRM12 R.McDonagh R4 (6/11/14) 8.00 20.00
RTCNYRRN1 R.Nash R1 (4/17/14) 2.50 6.00
RTCNYRRN2 R.Nash R1 (4/20/14) 2.50 6.00
RTCNYRRN3 R.Nash R1 (4/27/14) 2.50 6.00
RTCNYRRN4 R.Nash R1 (4/30/14) 2.50 6.00
RTCNYRRN5 R.Nash R2 (5/5/14) 3.00 8.00
RTCNYRRN6 R.Nash R2 (5/7/14) 3.00 8.00
RTCNYRRN7 R.Nash R2 (5/11/14) 3.00 8.00
RTCNYRRN8 R.Nash R3 (5/22/14) 6.00 15.00
RTCNYRRN9 R.Nash R3 (5/25/14) 6.00 15.00
RTCNYRRN10 R.Nash R3 (5/29/14) 6.00 15.00
RTCNYRRN11 R.Nash R4 (6/9/14) 12.00 30.00
RTCNYRRN12 R.Nash R4 (6/11/14) 12.00 30.00
RTCPFCG1 C.Giroux R1 (4/22/14) 2.50 6.00
RTCPFCG2 C.Giroux R1 (4/25/14) 2.50 6.00
RTCPFCG3 C.Giroux R1 (4/29/14) 2.50 6.00
RTCPFJV1 J.Voracek R1 (4/22/14) 2.00 5.00
RTCPFJV2 J.Voracek R1 (4/25/14) 2.00 5.00
RTCPFJV3 J.Voracek R1 (4/29/14) 2.00 5.00
RTCPFSM1 S.Mason R1 (4/22/14) 2.00 5.00
RTCPFSM2 S.Mason R1 (4/25/14) 2.00 5.00
RTCPFSM3 S.Mason R1 (4/29/14) 2.00 5.00
RTCPFWS1 W.Simmonds R1 (4/22/14) 3.00 8.00
RTCPFWS2 W.Simmonds R1 (4/25/14) 3.00 8.00
RTCPFWS3 W.Simmonds R1 (4/29/14) 3.00 8.00
RTCPPCK1 C.Kunitz R1 (4/16/14) 2.50 6.00
RTCPPCK2 C.Kunitz R1 (4/19/14) 2.50 6.00
RTCPPCK3 C.Kunitz R1 (4/26/14) 2.50 6.00
RTCPPCK4 C.Kunitz R2 (5/2/14) 3.00 8.00
RTCPPCK5 C.Kunitz R2 (5/4/14) 3.00 8.00
RTCPPCK6 C.Kunitz R2 (5/9/14) 3.00 8.00
RTCPPCK7 C.Kunitz R2 (5/13/14) 3.00 8.00
RTCPPEM1 E.Malkin R1 (4/16/14) 5.00 12.00
RTCPPEM2 E.Malkin R1 (4/19/14) 5.00 12.00
RTCPPEM3 E.Malkin R1 (4/26/14) 5.00 12.00
RTCPPEM4 E.Malkin R2 (5/2/14) 6.00 15.00
RTCPPEM5 E.Malkin R2 (5/4/14) 6.00 15.00
RTCPPEM6 E.Malkin R2 (5/9/14) 6.00 15.00
RTCPPEM7 E.Malkin R2 (5/13/14) 6.00 15.00
RTCPPJJ1 J.Jokinen R1 (4/16/14) 1.50 4.00
RTCPPJJ2 J.Jokinen R1 (4/19/14) 1.50 4.00
RTCPPJJ3 J.Jokinen R1 (4/26/14) 1.50 4.00
RTCPPJJ4 J.Jokinen R2 (5/2/14) 2.00 5.00
RTCPPJJ5 J.Jokinen R2 (5/4/14) 2.00 5.00
RTCPPJJ6 J.Jokinen R2 (5/9/14) 2.00 5.00
RTCPPJJ7 J.Jokinen R2 (5/13/14) 2.00 5.00
RTCPPJN1 J.Neal R1 (4/16/14) 1.50 4.00
RTCPPJN2 J.Neal R1 (4/19/14) 1.50 4.00
RTCPPJN3 J.Neal R1 (4/26/14) 1.50 4.00
RTCPPJN4 J.Neal R2 (5/2/14) 2.00 5.00
RTCPPJN5 J.Neal R2 (5/4/14) 2.00 5.00
RTCPPJN6 J.Neal R2 (5/9/14) 2.00 5.00
RTCPPJN7 J.Neal R2 (5/13/14) 2.00 5.00
RTCPPKL1 K.Letang R1 (4/16/14) 3.00 8.00
RTCPPKL2 K.Letang R1 (4/19/14) 3.00 8.00
RTCPPKL3 K.Letang R1 (4/26/14) 3.00 8.00
RTCPPKL4 K.Letang R2 (5/2/14) 4.00 10.00
RTCPPKL5 K.Letang R2 (5/4/14) 4.00 10.00
RTCPPKL6 K.Letang R2 (5/9/14) 4.00 10.00
RTCPPKL7 K.Letang R2 (5/13/14) 4.00 10.00
RTCPPMF1 M.Fleury R1 (4/16/14) 5.00 12.00
RTCPPMF2 M.Fleury R1 (4/19/14) 5.00 12.00
RTCPPMF3 M.Fleury R1 (4/26/14) 5.00 12.00
RTCPPMF4 M.Fleury R2 (5/2/14) 6.00 15.00
RTCPPMF5 M.Fleury R2 (5/4/14) 6.00 15.00
RTCPPMF6 M.Fleury R2 (5/9/14) 6.00 15.00
RTCPPMF7 M.Fleury R2 (5/13/14) 6.00 15.00
RTCPPOM1 O.Maatta R1 (4/16/14) 1.50 4.00
RTCPPOM2 O.Maatta R1 (4/19/14) 1.50 4.00
RTCPPOM3 O.Maatta R1 (4/26/14) 1.50 4.00
RTCPPOM4 O.Maatta R2 (5/2/14) 2.00 5.00
RTCPPOM5 O.Maatta R2 (5/4/14) 2.00 5.00
RTCPPOM6 O.Maatta R2 (5/9/14) 2.00 5.00
RTCPPOM7 O.Maatta R2 (5/13/14) 2.00 5.00
RTCPPSC1 S.Crosby R1 (4/16/14) 10.00 25.00
RTCPPSC2 S.Crosby R1 (4/19/14) 10.00 25.00
RTCPPSC3 S.Crosby R1 (4/26/14) 10.00 25.00
RTCPPSC4 S.Crosby R2 (5/2/14) 12.00 30.00
RTCPPSC5 S.Crosby R2 (5/4/14) 12.00 30.00
RTCPPSC6 S.Crosby R2 (5/9/14) 12.00 30.00
RTCPPSC7 S.Crosby R2 (5/13/14) 12.00 30.00
RTCSJSAN1 A.Niemi R1 (4/17/14) 2.00 5.00
RTCSJSAN2 A.Niemi R1 (4/20/14) 2.00 5.00
RTCSJSAN3 A.Niemi R1 (4/26/14) 2.00 5.00
RTCSJSAN4 A.Niemi R1 (4/30/14) 2.00 5.00
RTCSJSBB1 B.Burns R1 (4/17/14) 2.50 6.00
RTCSJSBB2 B.Burns R1 (4/20/14) 2.50 6.00
RTCSJSBB3 B.Burns R1 (4/26/14) 2.50 6.00
RTCSJSBB4 B.Burns R1 (4/30/14) 2.50 6.00
RTCSJSJP1 J.Pavelski R1 (4/17/14) 3.00 8.00
RTCSJSJP2 J.Pavelski R1 (4/20/14) 3.00 8.00
RTCSJSJP3 J.Pavelski R1 (4/26/14) 3.00 8.00
RTCSJSJP4 J.Pavelski R1 (4/30/14) 3.00 8.00
RTCSJSJT1 J.Thornton R1 (4/17/14) 4.00 10.00
RTCSJSJT2 J.Thornton R1 (4/20/14) 4.00 10.00
RTCSJSJT3 J.Thornton R1 (4/26/14) 4.00 10.00
RTCSJSJT4 J.Thornton R1 (4/30/14) 4.00 10.00
RTCSJSLC1 L.Couture R1 (4/17/14) 3.00 8.00
RTCSJSLC2 L.Couture R1 (4/20/14) 3.00 8.00
RTCSJSLC3 L.Couture R1 (4/26/14) 3.00 8.00
RTCSJSLC4 L.Couture R1 (4/30/14) 3.00 8.00
RTCSJSPM1 P.Marleau R1 (4/17/14) 2.50 6.00
RTCSJSPM2 P.Marleau R1 (4/20/14) 2.50 6.00
RTCSJSPM3 P.Marleau R1 (4/26/14) 2.50 6.00
RTCSJSPM4 P.Marleau R1 (4/30/14) 2.50 6.00
RTCSJSTH1 T.Hertl R1 (4/17/14) 2.50 6.00
RTCSJSTH2 T.Hertl R1 (4/20/14) 2.50 6.00
RTCSJSTH3 T.Hertl R1 (4/26/14) 2.50 6.00
RTCSJSTH4 T.Hertl R1 (4/30/14) 2.50 6.00
RTCSTLAP1 A.Pietrangelo R1 (4/17/14) 2.00 5.00
RTCSTLAP2 A.Pietrangelo R1 (4/19/14) 2.00 5.00
RTCSTLAP3 A.Pietrangelo R1 (4/25/14) 2.00 5.00
RTCSTLAS1 A.Steen R1 (4/17/14) 1.50 4.00
RTCSTLAS2 A.Steen R1 (4/19/14) 1.50 4.00
RTCSTLAS3 A.Steen R1 (4/25/14) 1.50 4.00
RTCSTLDB1 D.Backes R1 (4/17/14) 1.50 4.00
RTCSTLDB2 D.Backes R1 (4/19/14) 1.50 4.00
RTCSTLDB3 D.Backes R1 (4/25/14) 1.50 4.00
RTCSTLRM1 R.Miller R1 (4/17/14) 2.50 6.00
RTCSTLRM2 R.Miller R1 (4/19/14) 2.50 6.00
RTCSTLRM3 R.Miller R1 (4/25/14) 2.50 6.00
RTCSTLTO1 T.Oshie R1 (4/19/14) 2.50 6.00
RTCSTLTO2 T.Oshie R1 (4/25/14) 2.50 6.00
RTCTBLOP O.Palat R1 (4/16/14) 2.00 5.00
RTCTBLSS1 S.Stamkos R1 (4/16/14) 5.00 12.00
RTCTBLSS2 S.Stamkos R1 (4/18/14) 5.00 12.00

2014-15 Ultra Rookie Buyback Autographs

20 Johnny Gaudreau 80.00 200.00
28 Teuvo Teravainen 15.00 30.00
143 Brandon Gormley 5.00 12.00
145 Mark Visentin 5.00 12.00
166 Ty Rattie 5.00 12.00
171 Vladislav Namestnikov 8.00 20.00
178 Greg McKegg 4.00 10.00
191 Evgeny Kuznetsov 12.00 30.00

2014-15 Ultra Rule 76

F01 J.Tavares/D.Stepan 5.00 12.00
F02 W.Gretzky/M.Lemieux 10.00 25.00
F03 S.Yzerman/J.Sakic 8.00 20.00
F04 C.Giroux/E.Malkin 6.00 15.00
F05 P.Bergeron/T.Plekanec 4.00 10.00
F06 T.Bozak/D.Desharnais 2.00 5.00
F07 N.Kadri/R.Nugent-Hopkins 4.00 10.00
F08 A.Kopitar/R.Getzlaf 5.00 12.00
F09 E.Staal/N.Backstrom 4.00 10.00
F010 J.Toews/D.Backes 5.00 12.00

2021-22 Ultra

251 Lucas Raymond L13 25.00 60.00
252 Anton Lundell L13 15.00 40.00
253 Trevor Zegras L13 200.00 500.00
254 Cole Sillinger L13 12.00 30.00
255 William Eklund L13 20.00 50.00
256 Jamie Drysdale L13 12.00 30.00
257 Spencer Knight L13 15.00 40.00
258 Vasily Podkolzin L13 10.00 25.00
259 Moritz Seider L13 20.00 50.00
260 Seth Jarvis L13 20.00 50.00
261 Alex Turcotte L13 10.00 25.00
262 Mason McTavish L13 40.00 100.00
263 Quinton Byfield L13 40.00 100.00

2021-22 Ultra Silver Foil

1 Auston Matthews 4.00 10.00
2 Tristan Jarry 1.00 2.50
3 Jakob Chychrun 1.00 2.50
4 Quinn Hughes 2.50 6.00
5 Seth Jones 1.00 2.50
6 Robert Thomas 1.00 2.50
7 Pierre-Luc Dubois .75 2.00
8 Leon Draisaitl 3.00 8.00
9 Taylor Hall 1.00 2.50
10 Aleksander Barkov 1.50 4.00
11 Pius Suter .75 2.00
12 Brady Tkachuk 1.50 4.00
13 John Tavares 1.50 4.00
14 Jesper Bratt 1.00 2.50
15 Sean Couturier .75 2.00
16 Tyler Bertuzzi .75 2.00
17 Nick Suzuki 2.00 5.00
18 Thatcher Demko 1.25 3.00
19 Chandler Stephenson .75 2.00
20 Matthew Tkachuk 2.00 5.00
21 Brad Marchand 2.00 5.00
22 Mike Smith .60 1.50
23 Brock Nelson 1.00 2.50
24 Colton Parayko .75 2.00
25 Igor Shesterkin 2.00 5.00
26 Jack Campbell 1.00 2.50
27 Robin Lehner .75 2.00
28 Joel Eriksson Ek .75 2.00
29 Philipp Grubauer 1.00 2.50
30 Tyler Toffoli 1.00 2.50
31 Filip Hronek .60 1.50
32 Johnny Gaudreau 1.50 4.00
33 Ilya Sorokin 1.50 4.00
34 Teuvo Teravainen 1.00 2.50
35 Dougie Hamilton .75 2.00
36 Conor Garland .75 2.00
37 Brent Burns 1.00 2.50
38 Cam Atkinson 1.00 2.50
39 Marc-Andre Fleury 2.00 5.00
40 Anthony Mantha .75 2.00
41 Alexis Lafreniere 1.50 4.00
42 Josh Norris 1.00 2.50
43 Jakub Vrana .75 2.00
44 Victor Olofsson 1.00 2.50
45 Miro Heiskanen 1.25 3.00
46 Jake Guentzel 1.50 4.00
47 John Gibson 1.00 2.50
48 Kyle Connor 1.50 4.00
49 Brock Boeser 1.25 3.00
50 Andrei Svechnikov 1.25 3.00
51 Alex Iafallo .60 1.50
52 Kevin Fiala .75 2.00
53 Dominik Kubalik 1.00 2.50
54 Drake Batherson 1.00 2.50
55 Vladislav Namestnikov .60 1.50
56 Jared McCann .75 2.00
57 Cale Makar 2.50 6.00
58 Jack Roslovic .60 1.50
59 Andrei Vasilevskiy 1.50 4.00
60 Tim Stutzle 1.25 3.00
61 Jason Robertson 1.50 4.00
62 Jacob Markstrom 1.00 2.50
63 Phillip Danault 1.00 2.50
64 Samuel Girard .60 1.50
65 Charlie McAvoy 1.25 3.00
66 Cam Talbot 1.00 2.50
67 Carter Verhaeghe 1.00 2.50
68 Anders Lee .75 2.00
69 Mark Giordano 1.00 2.50
70 Nazem Kadri 1.25 3.00
71 Kirill Kaprizov 3.00 8.00
72 Carter Hart 1.00 2.50
73 Anze Kopitar 1.50 4.00
74 Sam Reinhart 2.00 5.00
75 Troy Terry .75 2.00
76 Alex Nedeljkovic .75 2.00
77 Jonathan Drouin .75 2.00
78 Anthony Cirelli .75 2.00
79 Jonathan Huberdeau 1.25 3.00
80 Zach Hyman 1.50 4.00
81 Mark Stone 1.25 3.00
82 Jean-Gabriel Pageau .60 1.50
83 Adam Fox 1.25 3.00
84 Josh Morrissey 1.25 3.00
85 Maxime Comtois .75 2.00
86 Casey Mittelstadt 1.00 2.50
87 Boone Jenner 1.00 2.50
88 Martin Necas 1.50 4.00
89 Ryan O'Reilly 1.00 2.50
90 Connor Hellebuyck 2.00 5.00
91 Max Pacioretty 1.00 2.50
92 Josh Anderson .75 2.00
93 Jordan Eberle 1.00 2.50
94 Josh Bailey .75 2.00
95 Patrick Kane 2.00 5.00
96 Joe Pavelski 1.25 3.00
97 Nikolaj Ehlers 1.00 2.50
98 Bryan Rust 1.00 2.50
99 Jonathan Marchessault 1.25 3.00
100 Connor McDavid 5.00 12.00
101 Nico Hischier 1.50 4.00
102 Gabriel Landeskog 1.25 3.00
103 Evgeny Kuznetsov 1.25 3.00
104 Brandon Hagel .75 2.00
105 Carey Price 2.00 5.00
106 Connor Brown .75 2.00
107 Marcus Foligno .75 2.00
108 William Nylander 2.00 5.00
109 Dylan Larkin 1.25 3.00
110 Mikko Rantanen 2.50 6.00
111 Artturi Lehkonen .75 2.00
112 Alex DeBrincat 1.25 3.00
113 Andreas Johnsson .75 2.00
114 Kevin Shattenkirk .60 1.50
115 Mark Scheifele 1.50 4.00
116 Kailer Yamamoto 1.00 2.50
117 Viktor Arvidsson .60 1.50
118 Mikael Granlund .75 2.00
119 Artemi Panarin 2.00 5.00
120 Elvis Merzlikins 1.00 2.50
121 Alex Killorn .60 1.50
122 Jaden Schwartz .75 2.00
123 Elias Lindholm 1.00 2.50
124 James Reimer .60 1.50
125 Roope Hintz 1.25 3.00
126 Patrice Bergeron 1.25 3.00
127 Ivan Provorov .75 2.00
128 Zach Werenski 1.50 4.00
129 Ryan Hartman .60 1.50
130 Oliver Kylington .75 2.00
131 Alexander Wennberg .60 1.50
132 Alex Ovechkin 4.00 10.00
133 Sidney Crosby 4.00 10.00
134 Jack Eichel 1.50 4.00
135 Shayne Gostisbehere 1.00 2.50
136 Elias Pettersson 1.50 4.00
137 Jack Hughes 2.50 6.00
138 Kasperi Kapanen .75 2.00
139 Kirby Dach 1.00 2.50
140 Ryan Johansen .75 2.00
141 Sebastian Aho 1.50 4.00
142 Brayden Point 1.25 3.00
143 J.T. Miller 1.25 3.00
144 Ilya Samsonov 1.00 2.50
145 Michael Bunting 1.00 2.50
146 Patrik Laine 1.25 3.00
147 Tyson Barrie .60 1.50
148 Frederik Andersen 1.25 3.00
149 Timo Meier 1.00 2.50
150 Rasmus Dahlin 1.25 3.00
151 Chris Kreider 1.25 3.00
152 Ryan Nugent-Hopkins 1.25 3.00
153 Nikita Kucherov 2.00 5.00
154 Oliver Bjorkstrand .75 2.00
155 Matt Duchene 1.00 2.50
156 Clayton Keller 1.25 3.00
157 Pavel Zacha .75 2.00
158 Darnell Nurse .75 2.00
159 Pavel Buchnevich .75 2.00
160 Tage Thompson 1.25 3.00
161 Jason Spezza 1.00 2.50
162 Jonathan Toews 1.50 4.00
163 MacKenzie Weegar .75 2.00
164 Nathan MacKinnon 4.00 10.00
165 Jeff Skinner 1.00 2.50
166 Erik Karlsson 1.25 3.00
167 Evan Rodrigues .75 2.00
168 Nick Schmaltz .75 2.00
169 Tony DeAngelo .60 1.50
170 John Carlson 1.00 2.50
171 Jordan Kyrou 1.00 2.50
172 Ryan Getzlaf 1.00 2.50
173 Andrew Mangiapane 1.00 2.50
174 Victor Hedman 1.25 3.00
175 Aaron Ekblad 1.25 3.00
176 Thomas Chabot 1.00 2.50
177 Travis Konecny 1.00 2.50
178 Drew Doughty 1.25 3.00
179 Vladimir Tarasenko 1.25 3.00
180 Roman Josi 1.00 2.50
181 Logan Couture 1.25 3.00
182 Sonny Milano .75 2.00
183 Morgan Rielly 1.00 2.50
184 Jonathan Quick 1.25 3.00
185 Claude Giroux 1.00 2.50
186 Anthony Beauvillier .60 1.50
187 Tyler Seguin 1.25 3.00
188 Phil Kessel 1.00 2.50
189 Steven Stamkos 2.00 5.00
190 Tom Wilson 1.00 2.50
191 Mitch Marner 1.50 4.00
192 Mika Zibanejad 1.25 3.00
193 Filip Forsberg 1.50 4.00
194 Kyle Okposo .60 1.50
195 Charlie Coyle 1.00 2.50
196 Tomas Hertl 1.00 2.50
197 Lawson Crouse .60 1.50
198 Juuse Saros 1.25 3.00
199 Jake Oettinger 1.50 4.00
200 David Pastrnak 2.50 6.00
201 Jonathan Dahlen 1.25 3.00
202 Alex Newhook 2.00 5.00
203 Brandon Duhaime 1.25 3.00
204 Vasily Podkolzin 1.50 4.00
205 Alex Barre-Boulet 1.25 3.00
206 Calen Addison 1.25 3.00
207 Jacob Bernard-Docker 1.25 3.00
208 Scott Perunovich 1.25 3.00
209 Rasmus Kupari 1.25 3.00
210 Cam York 1.25 3.00
211 Cole Sillinger 2.00 5.00
212 Jeremy Swayman 4.00 10.00
213 Sampo Ranta 1.25 3.00
214 David Farrance 1.25 3.00
215 Dysin Mayo 1.25 3.00
216 Aliaksei Protas 1.25 3.00
217 Moritz Seider 3.00 8.00
218 Seth Jarvis 3.00 8.00
219 Riley Damiani 1.25 3.00
220 Grigori Denisenko 1.50 4.00
221 Alex Turcotte 1.50 4.00
222 Radim Zohorna 1.25 3.00
223 Mattias Samuelsson 1.25 3.00
224 Mike Hardman 1.25 3.00
225 Philip Tomasino 1.50 4.00
226 Markus Niemelainen 1.25 3.00
227 Zac Jones 1.50 4.00
228 Quinton Byfield 3.00 8.00
229 Wade Allison 1.25 3.00
230 Tyce Thompson 1.25 3.00
231 Logan Thompson 3.00 8.00
232 Trevor Zegras 2.50 6.00
233 Taylor Raddysh 2.00 5.00
234 Karel Vejmelka 1.50 4.00
235 Ukko-Pekka Luukkonen 2.00 5.00
236 Dawson Mercer 3.00 8.00
237 Cole Perfetti 2.50 6.00
238 Joey Keane 1.00 2.50
239 Cole Caufield 5.00 12.00
240 Joe Veleno 1.50 4.00
241 Anton Lundell 2.50 6.00
242 Shane Pinto 2.00 5.00
243 Kole Lind 1.50 4.00
244 Alexander Holtz 2.00 5.00
245 Jamie Drysdale 2.00 5.00
246 Jan Jenik 1.50 4.00
247 Robin Salo 1.25 3.00
248 Kasper Bjorkqvist 1.25 3.00
249 Spencer Knight 2.50 6.00
250 Lucas Raymond 4.00 10.00

2021-22 Ultra Blue Foil

*BLUE/399: .6X TO 1.5X SILVER
**BLUE RC/399: 1X TO 2.5X SILVER

2021-22 Ultra Green Foil

*GREEN/25: 2X TO 5X SILVER
*GREEN RC/25: 3X TO 8X SILVER

2021-22 Ultra Rainbow Foil

*RAINBOW: .5X TO 1.2X SILVER
239 Cole Caufield 20.00 50.00

2021-22 Ultra Red Foil

*RED/91: .75X TO 2X SILVER
*RED RC/91: 1.2X TO 3X SILVER
239 Cole Caufield 30.00 80.00

2021-22 Ultra Speckled Rainbow Foil

*SPECKLED: .75X TO 2X SILVER
*SPECKLED RC: 2.5X TO 6X SILVER
232 Trevor Zegras 40.00 100.00
239 Cole Caufield 60.00 150.00

2021-22 Ultra 30th Anniversary

*GOLD/91: 2.5X TO 6X BASIC
A1 Vitek Vanecek 1.25 3.00
A2 Taylor Hall 1.25 3.00
A3 Carter Verhaeghe 1.25 3.00
A4 Jason Zucker 1.25 3.00
A5 Cal Petersen .75 2.00
A6 Casey Mittelstadt 1.25 3.00
A7 Kevin Fiala 1.00 2.50
A8 Wendel Clark 2.00 5.00
A9 Sean Monahan .75 2.00
A10 Paul Coffey 1.50 4.00
A11 Mike Richter 1.25 3.00
A12 Seth Jones 1.25 3.00
A13 Jeff Petry 1.25 3.00
A14 William Karlsson 1.50 4.00
A15 Ryan Reaves 1.00 2.50
A16 Eeli Tolvanen 1.25 3.00
A17 Cam Talbot 1.25 3.00
A18 Martin Necas 2.00 5.00
A19 Conor Garland 1.00 2.50
A20 Logan Stanley .75 2.00
A21 Mike Gartner 1.50 4.00
A22 Jasper Weatherby 1.25 3.00
A23 Dougie Hamilton 1.00 2.50
A24 Mike Bossy 1.25 3.00
A25 Patrick Maroon .75 2.00
A26 Darryl Sittler 1.25 3.00
A27 Calle Jarnkrok .75 2.00
A28 Cam Atkinson 1.25 3.00
A29 Ryan Suter 1.00 2.50
A30 Maxime Comtois 1.00 2.50
A31 Nick Suzuki 2.50 6.00
A32 Jack Roslovic .75 2.00
A33 Kyle Palmieri 1.00 2.50
A34 Pius Suter 1.00 2.50
A35 Mike Smith .75 2.00
A36 Brett Hull 2.00 5.00
A37 Samuel Girard .75 2.00
A38 Drake Batherson 1.25 3.00
A39 Sam Reinhart 2.50 6.00
A40 Billy Smith 1.25 3.00

2021-22 Ultra Autographs Silver Rainbow Foil

6 Robert Thomas 8.00 20.00
10 Aleksander Barkov 12.00 30.00
11 Pius Suter 6.00 15.00
12 Brady Tkachuk 12.00 30.00
13 John Tavares 12.00 30.00
14 Jesper Bratt 8.00 20.00
16 Tyler Bertuzzi 6.00 15.00
20 Matthew Tkachuk 15.00 40.00
21 Brad Marchand 15.00 40.00
22 Mike Smith 5.00 12.00
23 Brock Nelson 8.00 20.00
29 Philipp Grubauer 8.00 20.00
36 Conor Garland 6.00 15.00
38 Cam Atkinson 8.00 20.00
39 Marc-Andre Fleury 15.00 40.00
41 Alexis Lafreniere 25.00 60.00
48 Kyle Connor 12.00 30.00
49 Brock Boeser 10.00 25.00
50 Andrei Svechnikov 10.00 25.00
52 Kevin Fiala 6.00 15.00
54 Drake Batherson 8.00 20.00
55 Vladislav Namestnikov 5.00 12.00
56 Jared McCann 6.00 15.00
58 Jack Roslovic 5.00 12.00
59 Andrei Vasilevskiy 12.00 30.00
60 Tim Stutzle 20.00 50.00
61 Jason Robertson 12.00 30.00
62 Jacob Markstrom 8.00 20.00
64 Samuel Girard 5.00 12.00
67 Carter Verhaeghe 8.00 20.00
68 Anders Lee 6.00 15.00
73 Anze Kopitar 12.00 30.00
74 Sam Reinhart 15.00 40.00
75 Troy Terry 6.00 15.00
76 Alex Nedeljkovic 6.00 15.00
79 Jonathan Huberdeau 10.00 25.00
81 Mark Stone 10.00 25.00
82 Jean-Gabriel Pageau 5.00 12.00
84 Josh Morrissey 10.00 25.00
85 Maxime Comtois 6.00 15.00
87 Boone Jenner 8.00 20.00
88 Martin Necas 12.00 30.00
89 Ryan O'Reilly 8.00 20.00
90 Connor Hellebuyck 15.00 40.00
93 Jordan Eberle 8.00 20.00
96 Joe Pavelski 10.00 25.00
97 Nikolaj Ehlers 8.00 20.00
201 Jonathan Dahlen 8.00 20.00
202 Alex Newhook 12.00 30.00
203 Brandon Duhaime 8.00 20.00
205 Alex Barre-Boulet 8.00 20.00
206 Calen Addison 8.00 20.00
207 Jacob Bernard-Docker 8.00 20.00
208 Scott Perunovich 8.00 20.00
209 Rasmus Kupari 8.00 20.00
211 Cole Sillinger 12.00 30.00
213 Sampo Ranta 8.00 20.00
216 Aliaksei Protas 8.00 20.00
219 Riley Damiani 8.00 20.00
220 Grigori Denisenko 10.00 25.00
221 Alex Turcotte 10.00 25.00
223 Mattias Samuelsson 8.00 20.00
224 Mike Hardman 8.00 20.00
225 Philip Tomasino 10.00 25.00
227 Zac Jones 10.00 25.00
229 Wade Allison 8.00 20.00
230 Tyce Thompson 8.00 20.00
231 Logan Thompson 20.00 50.00
235 Ukko-Pekka Luukkonen 12.00 30.00
237 Cole Perfetti 15.00 40.00
238 Joey Keane 6.00 15.00
240 Joe Veleno 10.00 25.00
241 Anton Lundell 15.00 40.00
242 Shane Pinto 12.00 30.00
243 Kole Lind 10.00 25.00
244 Alexander Holtz 12.00 30.00
245 Jamie Drysdale 12.00 30.00
246 Jan Jenik 10.00 25.00
247 Robin Salo 8.00 20.00

2021-22 Ultra Exclamation Points

*GOLD: .5X TO 1.2X BASIC
EP1 Sidney Crosby 12.00 30.00
EP2 Quinn Hughes 8.00 20.00
EP3 Connor McDavid 15.00 40.00
EP4 Kirill Kaprizov 10.00 25.00
EP5 Nathan MacKinnon 12.00 30.00
EP6 Sebastian Aho 5.00 12.00
EP7 Johnny Gaudreau 5.00 12.00
EP8 Steven Stamkos 6.00 15.00
EP9 Jonathan Huberdeau 4.00 10.00
EP10 Jack Campbell 3.00 8.00
EP11 Artemi Panarin 6.00 15.00
EP12 Patrick Kane 6.00 15.00
EP13 Alex Ovechkin 12.00 30.00
EP14 Kyle Connor 5.00 12.00
EP15 Brad Marchand 6.00 15.00
EP16 Anze Kopitar 5.00 12.00
EP17 Auston Matthews 12.00 30.00
EP18 Jacob Markstrom 3.00 8.00
EP19 Jack Eichel 5.00 12.00

2021-22 Ultra Fabulous 50's

FF1 Leon Draisaitl 2.50 6.00
FF2 Keith Tkachuk .75 2.00
FF3 Bill Barber .75 2.00
FF4 Ken Hodge .60 1.50
FF5 Bernie Nicholls .60 1.50
FF6 Mike Modano 1.25 3.00
FF7 Steve Shutt .75 2.00
FF8 Teemu Selanne 1.50 4.00
FF9 Joe Mullen .75 2.00
FF10 Evgeni Malkin 1.50 4.00
FF11 Michel Goulet .60 1.50
FF12 Steven Stamkos 1.50 4.00
FF13 Guy Lafleur 1.00 2.50
FF14 Joe Sakic 1.50 4.00
FF15 Glenn Anderson .60 1.50
FF16 Corey Perry 1.25 3.00
FF17 Lanny McDonald .75 2.00
FF18 Jeremy Roenick 1.25 3.00
FF19 Wayne Gretzky 5.00 12.00
FF20 Brian Bellows .75 2.00
FF21 Reggie Leach .75 2.00
FF22 Luc Robitaille .75 2.00
FF23 Bryan Trottier .75 2.00
FF24 Bobby Hull 1.25 3.00
FF25 Jarome Iginla 1.00 2.50
FF26 Stephane Richer .50 1.25
FF27 Adam Graves .60 1.50
FF28 Jari Kurri .75 2.00
FF29 Blaine Stoughton .60 1.50
FF30 Pierre Turgeon .60 1.50
FF31 Gary Roberts .75 2.00
FF32 Dale Hawerchuk 1.00 2.50
FF33 Charlie Simmer .50 1.25
FF34 Alex Ovechkin 3.00 8.00
FF35 Ray Sheppard .50 1.25
FF36 Rick Vaive .60 1.50
FF37 Sidney Crosby 3.00 8.00
FF38 Bobby Carpenter .60 1.50
FF39 Mark Messier 1.50 4.00
FF40 Dave Andreychuk .75 2.00
FF41 Steve Yzerman 2.00 5.00
FF42 Marcel Dionne 1.00 2.50
FF43 Joe Nieuwendyk .60 1.50

FF44 Mark Recchi .75 2.00
FF45 Pat LaFontaine .75 2.00
FF46 Brett Hull 1.25 3.00
FF47 John Ogrodnick .50 1.25
FF48 Jimmy Carson .60 1.50
FF49 Mike Gartner 1.00 2.50
FF50 Mario Lemieux 3.00 8.00

2021-22 Ultra High Profile Fans Autographs

*SP: .5X TO 1.2X BASIC
5000AH Andrew Herr 10.00 25.00
5000DP Dylan Playfair 15.00 40.00
5000KK Kamilla Kowal 15.00 40.00
5000MM Michelle Mylett 80.00 200.00
5000MS Melanie Scrofano 15.00 40.00
5000ND Nathan Dales 12.00 30.00
5000TJ Tyler Johnston 12.00 30.00

2021-22 Ultra Medallions

*GOLD/200: 2X TO 5X BASIC
M1 Victor Hedman 1.00 2.50
M2 Matt Duchene .75 2.00
M3 Jeff Skinner .75 2.00
M4 Connor McDavid 4.00 10.00
M5 Pierre-Luc Dubois .60 1.50
M6 Roope Hintz 1.00 2.50
M7 Kyle Connor 1.25 3.00
M8 Marc-Andre Fleury 1.50 4.00
M9 Moritz Seider 2.00 5.00
M10 Patrik Laine 1.00 2.50
M11 Cam Talbot .75 2.00
M12 Ryan O'Reilly .75 2.00
M13 Auston Matthews 3.00 8.00
M14 Andrei Svechnikov 1.00 2.50
M15 Brayden Point
M16 Johnny Gaudreau 1.25 3.00
M17 John Gibson .75 2.00
M18 Nick Suzuki 1.50 4.00
M19 Jonathan Huberdeau 1.00 2.50
M20 Andrew Mangiapane .75 2.00
M21 Sebastian Aho 1.25 3.00
M22 Artemi Panarin 1.50 4.00
M23 Clayton Keller 1.00 2.50
M24 Claude Giroux .75 2.00
M25 Lucas Raymond 2.50 6.00
M26 Nathan MacKinnon 3.00 8.00
M27 Jake Guentzel 1.25 3.00
M28 Kirill Kaprizov 2.50 6.00
M29 Ilya Sorokin 1.25 3.00
M30 David Pastrnak 2.00 5.00
M31 Sidney Crosby 3.00 8.00
M32 Leon Draisaitl 2.50 6.00
M33 John Tavares 1.25 3.00
M34 Anze Kopitar 1.25 3.00
M35 Steven Stamkos 1.50 4.00
M36 Brady Tkachuk 1.25 3.00
M37 Quinn Hughes 2.00 5.00
M38 Adam Fox 1.00 2.50
M39 Brad Marchand 1.50 4.00
M40 Mark Stone 1.00 2.50
M41 Jordan Eberle .75 2.00
M42 Cale Makar 2.00 5.00
M43 Alex Ovechkin 3.00 8.00
M44 Chris Kreider 1.00 2.50
M45 Jack Hughes 2.00 5.00
M46 Elias Lindholm .75 2.00
M47 Timo Meier .75 2.00
M48 Victor Olofsson .75 2.00
M49 Sergei Bobrovsky 1.25 3.00
M50 Trevor Zegras 1.50 4.00

2021-22 Ultra Medallions Platinum

*PLATINUM/100: 2.5X TO 6X BASIC
M4 Connor McDavid 60.00 150.00
M43 Alex Ovechkin 40.00 100.00

2021-22 Ultra Medallions Ruby Red

*RED/50: 3X TO 8X BASIC
M4 Connor McDavid 60.00 150.00
M8 Marc-Andre Fleury 20.00 50.00
M13 Auston Matthews 40.00 100.00
M28 Kirill Kaprizov 20.00 50.00
M30 David Pastrnak 20.00 50.00
M31 Sidney Crosby 50.00 125.00
M43 Alex Ovechkin 60.00 150.00
M50 Trevor Zegras 40.00 100.00

2021-22 Ultra Medallions Sapphire

*SAPPHIRE/25: 4X TO 10X BASIC
M4 Connor McDavid 100.00 250.00
M8 Marc-Andre Fleury 50.00 125.00
M13 Auston Matthews 60.00 150.00
M28 Kirill Kaprizov 30.00 80.00
M29 Ilya Sorokin 20.00 50.00
M30 David Pastrnak 30.00 80.00
M31 Sidney Crosby 80.00 200.00
M38 Adam Fox 20.00 50.00
M42 Cale Makar 60.00 150.00
M43 Alex Ovechkin 80.00 200.00
M50 Trevor Zegras 50.00 125.00

2021-22 Ultra Meteor Shower

ST1 Sidney Crosby 30.00 80.00
ST2 Martin Brodeur 20.00 50.00
ST3 Steven Stamkos 15.00 40.00
ST4 Jeremy Roenick 12.00 30.00
ST5 Patrick Kane 15.00 40.00
ST6 Alex Newhook 12.00 30.00
ST7 Auston Matthews 30.00 80.00
ST8 Vladimir Tarasenko 10.00 25.00
ST9 Bobby Orr 30.00 80.00
ST10 Alex Ovechkin 30.00 80.00
ST11 Lucas Raymond 25.00 60.00
ST12 Ilya Sorokin 12.00 30.00
ST13 Jordan Eberle 8.00 20.00
ST14 Chris Pronger 8.00 20.00
ST15 Quinn Hughes 20.00 50.00
ST16 Mitch Marner 12.00 30.00
ST17 Dawson Mercer 20.00 50.00
ST18 Brady Tkachuk 12.00 30.00
ST19 Mario Lemieux 30.00 80.00
ST20 Max Pacioretty 8.00 20.00
ST21 Artemi Panarin 15.00 40.00
ST22 Patrick Roy 20.00 50.00
ST23 Roman Josi 8.00 20.00
ST24 Brayden Point 10.00 25.00
ST25 Jamie Drysdale 12.00 30.00
ST26 Aleksander Barkov 12.00 30.00
ST27 Leon Draisaitl 25.00 60.00
ST28 Joe Sakic 15.00 40.00
ST29 David Pastrnak 20.00 50.00
ST30 Moritz Seider 20.00 50.00
ST31 Oliver Bjorkstrand 6.00 15.00
ST32 Nazem Kadri 10.00 25.00
ST34 Tristan Jarry 8.00 20.00
ST35 Kyle Connor 12.00 30.00
ST36 Wayne Gretzky 50.00 125.00
ST37 Jason Robertson 12.00 30.00
ST38 Johnny Gaudreau 12.00 30.00
ST39 Spencer Knight 15.00 40.00
ST40 Kirill Kaprizov 25.00 60.00
ST41 Gordie Howe 25.00 60.00
ST42 Seth Jarvis 20.00 50.00
ST43 Marc-Andre Fleury 15.00 40.00
ST45 Philip Tomasino 10.00 25.00
ST46 Sebastian Aho 12.00 30.00
ST47 Igor Shesterkin 15.00 40.00
ST48 Cole Caufield 50.00 125.00
ST49 Timo Meier 8.00 20.00
ST50 Dominik Hasek 12.00 30.00

2021-22 Ultra Pizzazz

*GOLD/100: 2.5X TO 6X BASIC
PZ1 Kris Letang 1.25 3.00
PZ2 Jonathan Marchessault 1.25 3.00
PZ3 Mark Scheifele 1.50 4.00
PZ4 Jake Allen 1.00 2.50
PZ5 Tyler Bertuzzi .75 2.00
PZ6 Dawson Mercer 2.50 6.00
PZ7 Anthony Duclair .75 2.00
PZ8 Tim Stutzle 1.25 3.00
PZ9 Jake Neighbours 2.00 5.00
PZ10 Mike Smith .60 1.50
PZ11 Kyle Connor 1.50 4.00
PZ12 Trevor Zegras 2.00 5.00
PZ13 Matthew Tkachuk 2.00 5.00
PZ14 Nazem Kadri 1.25 3.00
PZ15 Aliaksei Protas 1.00 2.50
PZ16 Alexander Holtz
PZ17 Mitch Marner 1.50 4.00
PZ18 Roope Hintz 1.25 3.00
PZ19 Anthony Mantha .75 2.00
PZ20 Shane Pinto 1.50 4.00
PZ21 Adam Beckman 1.00 2.50
PZ22 Martin Necas 1.50 4.00
PZ23 Alex Newhook 1.50 4.00
PZ24 Jeremy Swayman 3.00 8.00
PZ25 Jason Robertson 1.50 4.00
PZ26 Brent Burns 1.00 2.50
PZ27 Tyler Toffoli 1.00 2.50
PZ28 Dylan Cozens 1.00 2.50
PZ29 Arthur Kaliyev 1.00 2.50
PZ30 Nils Hoglander .75 2.00

2021-22 Ultra Pop Culture

PC1 Steven Stamkos 3.00 8.00
PC2 Steven Stamkos 3.00 8.00
PC3 Steven Stamkos 3.00 8.00
PC4 Steven Stamkos 3.00 8.00
PC5 Auston Matthews SP 6.00 15.00
PC6 Auston Matthews SP 6.00 15.00
PC7 Auston Matthews SP 6.00 15.00
PC8 Auston Matthews SP 6.00 15.00
PC9 Nathan MacKinnon 6.00 15.00
PC10 Nathan MacKinnon 6.00 15.00
PC11 Nathan MacKinnon 6.00 15.00
PC12 Nathan MacKinnon 6.00 15.00
PC13 Sidney Crosby SP 6.00 15.00
PC14 Sidney Crosby SP 6.00 15.00
PC16 Sidney Crosby SP 6.00 15.00
PC16 Sidney Crosby SP 6.00 15.00
PC17 Leon Draisaitl 5.00 12.00
PC18 Leon Draisaitl 5.00 12.00
PC19 Leon Draisaitl 5.00 12.00
PC20 Leon Draisaitl 5.00 12.00
PC21 David Pastrnak 4.00 10.00
PC22 David Pastrnak 4.00 10.00
PC23 David Pastrnak 4.00 10.00
PC24 David Pastrnak 4.00 10.00
PC25 Alex Ovechkin SP 6.00 15.00
PC26 Alex Ovechkin SP 6.00 15.00
PC27 Alex Ovechkin SP 6.00 15.00
PC28 Alex Ovechkin SP 6.00 15.00
PC29 Kirill Kaprizov SP 5.00 12.00
PC30 Kirill Kaprizov SP 5.00 12.00
PC31 Kirill Kaprizov SP 5.00 12.00
PC32 Kirill Kaprizov SP 5.00 12.00
PC33 Connor McDavid SP 8.00 20.00
PC34 Connor McDavid SP 8.00 20.00
PC35 Connor McDavid SP 8.00 20.00
PC36 Connor McDavid SP 8.00 20.00
PC37 Johnny Gaudreau 2.50 6.00
PC38 Johnny Gaudreau 2.50 6.00
PC39 Johnny Gaudreau 2.50 6.00
PC40 Johnny Gaudreau 2.50 6.00
PC41 Artemi Panarin SP 3.00 8.00
PC42 Artemi Panarin SP 3.00 8.00
PC43 Artemi Panarin SP 3.00 8.00
PC44 Artemi Panarin SP 3.00 8.00

2021-22 Ultra Premier Pad Men

PM1 Gerry Cheevers 8.00 20.00
PM2 Ukko-Pekka Luukkonen 12.00 30.00
PM3 Marc-Andre Fleury 15.00 40.00
PM4 Jordan Binnington 12.00 30.00
PM5 Mikko Koskinen 5.00 12.00
PM6 Igor Shesterkin 15.00 40.00
PM7 Jake Oettinger 12.00 30.00
PM8 Sergei Bobrovsky 12.00 30.00
PM9 Connor Hellebuyck 15.00 40.00
PM10 Darcy Kuemper 8.00 20.00
PM11 Elvis Merzlikins 8.00 20.00
PM12 Juuse Saros 10.00 25.00
PM13 James Reimer 5.00 12.00
PM14 Ilya Sorokin 12.00 30.00
PM15 Martin Brodeur 20.00 50.00
PM16 Tristan Jarry 8.00 20.00
PM17 Philipp Grubauer 8.00 20.00
PM18 John Gibson 8.00 20.00
PM19 Frederik Andersen 10.00 25.00
PM20 Alex Nedeljkovic 6.00 15.00
PM21 Andrei Vasilevskiy 12.00 30.00
PM22 Carter Hart 8.00 20.00
PM23 Robin Lehner 6.00 15.00
PM24 Thatcher Demko 10.00 25.00
PM25 Cam Talbot 8.00 20.00
PM26 Jack Campbell 8.00 20.00
PM27 Mackenzie Blackwood 8.00 20.00
PM28 Jeremy Swayman 25.00 60.00
PM29 Carey Price 15.00 40.00
PM30 Jacob Markstrom 8.00 20.00
PM31 Ilya Samsonov 8.00 20.00
PM32 Jonathan Quick 10.00 25.00
PM33 Karel Vejmelka 10.00 25.00
PM34 Filip Gustavsson 15.00 40.00
PM35 Patrick Roy 20.00 50.00

2021-22 Ultra Pucks

1OF100 Troy Terry 1.50 4.00
2OF100 Ryan Getzlaf 2.00 5.00
3OF100 Trevor Zegras 4.00 10.00
4OF100 Jamie Drysdale 3.00 8.00
5OF100 Shayne Gostisbehere 2.00 5.00
6OF100 Clayton Keller 2.50 6.00
7OF100 Karel Vejmelka 2.50 6.00
8OF100 David Pastrnak 5.00 12.00
9OF100 Charlie McAvoy 2.50 6.00
10OF100 Jeremy Swayman 6.00 15.00
11OF100 Victor Olofsson 2.00 5.00
12OF100 Jeff Skinner 2.00 5.00
13OF100 Arttu Ruotsalainen 2.00 5.00
14OF100 Johnny Gaudreau 3.00 8.00
15OF100 Matthew Tkachuk 4.00 10.00
16OF100 Adam Ruzicka 2.00 5.00
17OF100 Sebastian Aho 3.00 8.00
18OF100 Andrei Svechnikov 2.50 6.00
19OF100 Seth Jarvis 5.00 12.00
20OF100 Patrick Kane 4.00 10.00
21OF100 Marc-Andre Fleury 4.00 10.00
22OF100 Mike Hardman 2.00 5.00
23OF100 Cale Makar 5.00 12.00
24OF100 Mikko Rantanen 5.00 12.00
25OF100 Alex Newhook 3.00 8.00
26OF100 Oliver Bjorkstrand 1.50 4.00
27OF100 Jakub Voracek 1.50 4.00
28OF100 Cole Sillinger 3.00 8.00
29OF100 Jason Robertson 3.00 8.00
30OF100 Miro Heiskanen 2.50 6.00
31OF100 Jacob Peterson 2.00 5.00
32OF100 Dylan Larkin 2.50 6.00
33OF100 Tyler Bertuzzi 1.50 4.00
34OF100 Lucas Raymond 6.00 15.00
35OF100 Moritz Seider 5.00 12.00
36OF100 Leon Draisaitl 6.00 15.00
37OF100 Connor McDavid 10.00 25.00
38OF100 Markus Niemelainen 2.00 5.00
39OF100 Jonathan Huberdeau 2.50 6.00
40OF100 Aaron Ekblad 2.50 6.00
41OF100 Spencer Knight 4.00 10.00
42OF100 Anton Lundell 4.00 10.00
43OF100 Anze Kopitar 3.00 8.00
44OF100 Drew Doughty 2.50 6.00
45OF100 Quinton Byfield 5.00 12.00
46OF100 Rasmus Kupari 2.00 5.00
47OF100 Mats Zuccarello 2.00 5.00
48OF100 Kirill Kaprizov 6.00 15.00
49OF100 Brandon Duhaime 2.00 5.00
50OF100 Nick Suzuki 4.00 10.00
51OF100 Josh Anderson 1.50 4.00
52OF100 Cole Caufield 8.00 20.00
53OF100 Matt Duchene 2.00 5.00
54OF100 Roman Josi 2.00 5.00
55OF100 Philip Tomasino 2.50 6.00
56OF100 Jack Hughes 5.00 12.00
57OF100 Dougie Hamilton 1.50 4.00
58OF100 Dawson Mercer 5.00 12.00
59OF100 Brock Nelson 2.00 5.00
60OF100 Mathew Barzal 2.50 6.00
61OF100 Robin Salo 2.00 5.00
62OF100 Adam Fox 2.50 6.00
63OF100 Mika Zibanejad 2.50 6.00
64OF100 Nils Lundkvist 2.00 5.00
65OF100 Drake Batherson 2.00 5.00
66OF100 Brady Tkachuk 3.00 8.00
67OF100 Lassi Thomson 2.00 5.00
68OF100 Claude Giroux 2.00 5.00
69OF100 Sean Couturier 1.50 4.00
70OF100 Max Willman 1.25 3.00
71OF100 Tristan Jarry 2.00 5.00
72OF100 Sidney Crosby 8.00 20.00
73OF100 Radim Zohorna 2.00 5.00
74OF100 Timo Meier 2.00 5.00
75OF100 Logan Couture 2.50 6.00
76OF100 Jonathan Dahlen 2.00 5.00
77OF100 Jaden Schwartz 1.50 4.00
78OF100 Jordan Eberle 2.00 5.00
79OF100 Kole Lind 2.50 6.00
80OF100 Jordan Kyrou 2.00 5.00
81OF100 Pavel Buchnevich 1.50 4.00
82OF100 Scott Perunovich 2.00 5.00
83OF100 Victor Hedman 2.50 6.00
84OF100 Steven Stamkos 4.00 10.00
85OF100 Taylor Raddysh 3.00 8.00
86OF100 Auston Matthews 8.00 20.00
87OF100 John Tavares 3.00 8.00
88OF100 Kristians Rubins 1.25 3.00
89OF100 J.T. Miller 2.50 6.00
90OF100 Thatcher Demko 2.50 6.00
91OF100 Vasily Podkolzin 2.50 6.00
92OF100 Alex Pietrangelo 1.50 4.00
93OF100 William Karlsson 2.50 6.00
94OF100 Jake Leschyshyn 2.00 5.00
95OF100 John Carlson 2.00 5.00
96OF100 Alex Ovechkin 8.00 20.00
97OF100 Aliaksei Protas 2.00 5.00
98OF100 Pierre-Luc Dubois 1.50 4.00
99OF100 Kyle Connor 3.00 8.00
100OF100 Cole Perfetti 4.00 10.00

2021-22 Ultra Rink Masters

1OF30RM Steve Yzerman 3.00 8.00
2OF30RM Mats Sundin 1.25 3.00
3OF30RM Ryan O'Reilly 1.25 3.00
4OF30RM Mark Scheifele 2.00 5.00
5OF30RM Jarome Iginla 1.50 4.00
6OF30RM Doug Gilmour 1.50 4.00
7OF30RM Sidney Crosby 5.00 12.00
8OF30RM Claude Giroux 1.25 3.00
9OF30RM Mark Messier 2.50 6.00
10OF30RM Matthew Tkachuk 2.50 6.00
11OF30RM Gabriel Landeskog 1.50 4.00
12OF30RM Bobby Clarke 2.00 5.00
13OF30RM Trevor Linden 1.25 3.00
14OF30RM John Tavares 2.00 5.00
15OF30RM Darryl Sutter 1.00 2.50
16OF30RM Patrice Bergeron 1.50 4.00
17OF30RM Nico Hischier 2.00 5.00
18OF30RM Owen Nolan 1.00 2.50
19OF30RM Ray Bourque 2.00 5.00
20OF30RM Aleksander Barkov 2.00 5.00
21OF30RM Chris Chelios 1.25 3.00
22OF30RM Mark Giordano 1.25 3.00
23OF30RM Dylan Larkin 1.50 4.00
24OF30RM Wayne Gretzky 8.00 20.00
25OF30RM Alex Ovechkin 5.00 12.00
26OF30RM Joe Sakic 2.50 6.00
27OF30RM Denis Potvin 1.25 3.00
28OF30RM Gordie Howe 4.00 10.00
29OF30RM Anze Kopitar 2.00 5.00
30OF30RM Connor McDavid 6.00 15.00

2021-22 Ultra Scoring Kings

SK1 Artemi Panarin 12.00 30.00
SK2 Aleksander Barkov 10.00 25.00
SK3 Frank Mahovlich 6.00 15.00
SK4 Patrick Kane 12.00 30.00
SK5 Sebastian Aho 10.00 25.00
SK6 Peter Stastny 5.00 12.00
SK7 Connor McDavid 30.00 80.00
SK8 Brad Marchand 12.00 30.00
SK9 Nazem Kadri 8.00 20.00
SK10 Steven Stamkos 12.00 30.00
SK11 Auston Matthews 25.00 60.00
SK12 Stan Mikita 6.00 15.00
SK13 Alex Ovechkin 25.00 60.00
SK14 Leon Draisaitl 20.00 50.00
SK15 Mario Lemieux 25.00 60.00
SK16 Guy Lafleur 8.00 20.00
SK17 Peter Forsberg 12.00 30.00
SK18 William Nylander 12.00 30.00
SK19 Gordie Howe 20.00 50.00
SK20 Kirill Kaprizov 20.00 50.00
SK21 Anze Kopitar 10.00 25.00
SK22 Nathan MacKinnon 25.00 60.00
SK23 Brayden Point 8.00 20.00
SK24 Adam Fox 8.00 20.00
SK25 Johnny Gaudreau 10.00 25.00
SK26 Kyle Connor 10.00 25.00
SK27 Bobby Orr 25.00 60.00
SK28 Sidney Crosby 25.00 60.00
SK29 Wayne Gretzky 30.00 80.00
SK30 Henri Richard 6.00 15.00

2021-22 Ultra Seeing Double

DT1 Elias Pettersson .75 2.00
DT2 Alex Ovechkin 2.00 5.00
DT3 Kirill Kaprizov 1.50 4.00
DT4 Brad Marchand 1.00 2.50
DT5 Alex Newhook .75 2.00
DT6 Connor McDavid 2.50 6.00
DT7 Cole Caufield 2.00 5.00
DT8 Patrick Kane 1.00 2.50
DT9 Brayden Point .60 1.50
DT10 Nathan MacKinnon 2.00 5.00
DT11 Auston Matthews 2.00 5.00
DT12 Leon Draisaitl 1.50 4.00
DT13 Lucas Raymond 1.50 4.00
DT14 Aleksander Barkov .75 2.00
DT15 Sidney Crosby 2.00 5.00
DT16 Trevor Zegras 1.00 2.50
DT17 Andrei Vasilevskiy .75 2.00
DT18 Sebastian Aho .75 2.00
DT19 Moritz Seider 1.25 3.00
DT20 Connor Hellebuyck 1.00 2.50

2021-22 Ultra Ultra Stars

*GOLD: .6X TO 1.5X BASIC
US1 Adam Fox 3.00 8.00
US2 Mikael Granlund 2.00 5.00
US3 Trevor Zegras 5.00 12.00
US4 Jake Guentzel 4.00 10.00
US5 Brayden Point 3.00 8.00
US6 David Pastrnak 6.00 15.00
US7 Lucas Raymond 8.00 20.00
US8 Gabriel Landeskog 3.00 8.00
US9 Igor Shesterkin 5.00 12.00
US10 Alex DeBrincat 3.00 8.00
US11 Leon Draisaitl 8.00 20.00
US12 Aleksander Barkov 4.00 10.00
US13 Evgeny Kuznetsov 3.00 8.00
US14 Pierre-Luc Dubois 2.00 5.00
US15 Chris Kreider 3.00 8.00
US16 Claude Giroux 2.50 6.00
US17 Cale Makar 6.00 15.00
US18 J.T. Miller 3.00 8.00
US19 William Nylander 5.00 12.00
US20 Andrei Svechnikov 3.00 8.00
US21 John Carlson 2.50 6.00
US22 Mitch Marner 4.00 10.00
US23 Aaron Ekblad 3.00 8.00
US24 Jordan Kyrou 2.50 6.00
US25 Ryan Nugent-Hopkins 3.00 8.00
US26 Seth Jones 2.50 6.00
US27 Nazem Kadri 3.00 8.00
US28 Tristan Jarry 2.50 6.00
US29 Victor Hedman 3.00 8.00

2021-22 Ultra Ultra Team

UT2 Nathan MacKinnon 40.00 100.00
UT3 Kyle Connor 15.00 40.00
UT4 Alex Ovechkin 80.00 200.00
UT5 Steven Stamkos 20.00 50.00
UT6 Anze Kopitar 15.00 40.00
UT7 Lucas Raymond 30.00 80.00
UT8 Jonathan Huberdeau 12.00 30.00
UT9 Adam Fox 12.00 30.00
UT10 Frederik Andersen 12.00 30.00
UT11 Johnny Gaudreau 15.00 40.00
UT12 Roman Josi 10.00 25.00
UT13 Brayden Point 12.00 30.00
UT14 Jack Campbell 10.00 25.00
UT15 Connor McDavid 80.00 200.00
UT16 Trevor Zegras 250.00 600.00
UT17 Brad Marchand 20.00 50.00
UT18 Jake Guentzel 15.00 40.00
UT19 Auston Matthews 40.00 100.00
UT20 Sebastian Aho 15.00 40.00
UT21 Leon Draisaitl 30.00 80.00
UT22 Aleksander Barkov 15.00 40.00
UT23 Moritz Seider 80.00 200.00
UT24 Artemi Panarin 20.00 50.00
UT25 Kirill Kaprizov 30.00 80.00

2021-22 Ultra Ultrabilities

UB1 John Tavares 1.25 3.00
UB2 Carter Hart .75 2.00
UB3 Patrice Bergeron 1.00 2.50
UB4 Joe Pavelski 1.00 2.50
UB5 Brady Tkachuk 1.25 3.00
UB6 Ryan Nugent-Hopkins 1.00 2.50
UB7 Roman Josi .75 2.00
UB8 Dylan Larkin 1.00 2.50
UB9 Conor Garland .60 1.50
UB10 Marc-Andre Fleury 1.50 4.00
UB11 Mark Scheifele 1.25 3.00
UB12 Patrik Laine
UB13 Mika Zibanejad 1.00 2.50
UB14 Morgan Rielly .75 2.00
UB15 Drew Doughty 1.00 2.50
UB16 Tom Wilson .75 2.00
UB17 Nick Suzuki 1.50 4.00
UB18 Jack Hughes 2.00 5.00
UB19 Frederik Andersen 1.00 2.50
UB20 Ryan O'Reilly .75 2.00
UB21 Jason Robertson 1.25 3.00
UB22 Matt Duchene .75 2.00
UB23 Evgeni Malkin 1.50 4.00
UB24 Pavel Buchnevich .60 1.50
UB25 Mikko Rantanen 2.00 5.00
UB26 Sergei Bobrovsky 1.25 3.00
UB27 Moritz Seider 2.00 5.00
UB28 Matthew Tkachuk 1.50 4.00
UB29 Timo Meier .75 2.00
UB30 Troy Terry .60 1.50

1961-62 Union Oil WHL

COMPLETE SET (12) 50.00 100.00
1 Jack Bownass 3.00 6.00
2 Ed Diachuk 3.00 6.00
3 Leo LaBine 5.00 10.00
4 Willie O'Ree 20.00 40.00
5 Bruce Carmichael 3.00 6.00
6 Gordon Haworth 4.00 8.00
7 Fleming Mackell 5.00 10.00
8 Robert Solinger 3.00 6.00
9 Gary Edmundson 3.00 6.00
10 Al Nicholson 3.00 6.00
11 Orland Kurtenbach 7.50 15.00
12 Tom Thurlby 3.00 6.00

1990-91 Upper Deck

*1990 BB HOLO: .5X TO 1.2X
*1990 COMIC BALL HOLO: .5X TO 1.5X
*91-92 HOLO: .5X TO 1.2X
1 David Volek .20 .50
2 Brian Propp .20 .50
3 Wendel Clark .30 .75
4 Adam Creighton .12 .30
5 Mark Osborne .15 .40
6 Murray Craven .20 .50
7 Doug Crossman .15 .40
8 Mario Marois .15 .40
9 Curt Giles .15 .40
10 Rick Wamsley .20 .50
11 Troy Mallette RC .15 .40
12 John Cullen .20 .50
13 Miloslav Horava RC .15 .40
14 Kevin Stevens RC .40 1.00
15 David Shaw .20 .50
16 Randy Wood .12 .30
17 Peter Zezel .20 .50
18 Glenn Healy RC .40 1.00
19 Sergio Momesso RC .15 .40
20 Don Maloney .20 .50
21 Craig Muni .15 .40
22 Phil Housley .15 .40
23 Martin Gelinas RC .40 1.00
24 Alexander Mogilny RC .60 1.50
25 John Byce RC .15 .40
26 Joe Nieuwendyk .15 .40
27 Ron Tugnutt .15 .40
28 Don Barber RC .15 .40
29 Gary Roberts .20 .50
30 Basil McRae .12 .30
31 Phil Bourque .15 .40
32 Mike Richter RC .60 1.50
33 Zarley Zalapski .15 .40
34 Bernie Nicholls .15 .40
35 Bob Corkum RC .12 .30
36 Rod Brind'Amour RC .40 1.00
37 Mark Fitzpatrick RC .15 .40
38 Gino Cavallini .20 .50
39 Mick Vukota RC .20 .50
40 Mike Lalor RC .15 .40
41 Dave Andreychuk .20 .50
42 Bill Ranford .15 .40
43 Pierre Turgeon .15 .40
44 Mark Messier .40 1.00
45 Rob Blake RC .30 .75
46 Mike Modano RC 1.00 2.50
47 Theo Fleury .25 .60
48 Neal Broten .12 .30
49 Paul Gillis .15 .40
50 Doug Bodger UER .15 .40
51 Stephan Lebeau RC .15 .40
52 Larry Robinson .20 .50
53 Dale Hawerchuk .25 .60
54 Wayne Gretzky 1.25 3.00
55 Ed Belfour RC .60 1.50
56 Steve Yzerman .60 1.50
57 Rod Langway .20 .50
58 Bernie Federko .15 .40
59 Mario Lemieux Streak .75 2.00
60 Doug Lidster .20 .50
61 Dave Christian .12 .30
62 Rob Ramage .20 .50
63 Jeremy Roenick RC .60 1.50
64 Ray Bourque .30 .75
65 Jon Morris RC .12 .30
66 Sean Burke .15 .40
67 Ron Francis .25 .60
68 Ron Sutter .15 .40
69 Peter Sidorkiewicz .20 .50
70 Sylvain Turgeon .15 .40
71 Dave Ellett .12 .30
72 Bobby Smith .15 .40
73 Luc Robitaille .20 .50
74 Pat Elynuik .15 .40
75 Jason Soules RC .12 .30
76 Dino Ciccarelli .20 .50
77 Vladimir Krutov RC .40 1.00
78 Lee Norwood .15 .40
79 Brian Bradley .15 .40
80 Michal Pivonka RC .15 .40
81 Mark LaForest RC .12 .30
82 Trent Yawney .20 .50
83 Tom Fergus .12 .30
84 Andy Brickley .12 .30
85 Dave Manson .20 .50
86 Gord Murphy RC .20 .50
87 Scott Young .12 .30
88 Tommy Albelin .12 .30
89 Ken Wregget .20 .50
90 Brad Shaw RC .15 .40
91 Mario Gosselin .15 .40
92 Paul Fenton .20 .50
93 Brian Skrudland .15 .40
94 Thomas Steen .15 .40
95 John Tonelli .15 .40
96 Steve Chiasson UER .12 .30
97 Mike Ridley .12 .30
98 Garth Butcher .15 .40
99 Daniel Shank RC .20 .50
100 Checklist 1-100 .12 .30
101 Jamie Macoun .15 .40
102 Wendell Young RC .20 .50
103 Laurie Boschman .15 .40
104 Paul Ranheim RC .20 .50
105 Doug Smail .15 .40
106 Shawn Chambers .15 .40
107 Steve Weeks .20 .50
108 Gaetan Duchesne .20 .50
109 Kevin Hatcher .15 .40
110 Paul Reinhart .20 .50
111 Shawn Burr .15 .40
112 Troy Murray .15 .40
113 John Chabot .20 .50
114 Jacques Cloutier RC .15 .40
115 Rick Zombo RC .20 .50
116 Kjell Samuelsson .15 .40
117 Tim Watters .12 .30
118 Pat Flatley .20 .50
119 Tom Laidlaw .20 .50
120 Ilkka Sinisalo .15 .40
121 Tom Barrasso .15 .40
122 Bob Essensa RC .30 .75
123 Sergei Makarov RC .40 1.00
124 Paul Coffey .20 .50
125 Bob Beers RC .15 .40
126 Brian Bellows .15 .40
127 Mike Liut .12 .30
128 Igor Larionov RC .40 1.00
129 Craig Simpson .15 .40
130 Kelly Miller .12 .30
131 Dirk Graham .15 .40
132 Jimmy Carson .15 .40
133 Michel Goulet .12 .30
134 Gerard Gallant .12 .30
135 Bruce Hoffort RC .20 .50
136 Steve Duchesne .12 .30
137 Bryan Trottier .20 .50
138 Pelle Eklund .12 .30
139 Gary Nylund .15 .40
140 Steve Kasper .12 .30
141 Joel Otto .15 .40
142 Rob Brown .40 1.00
143 Al MacInnis .25 .60
144 Mario Lemieux .75 2.00
145 Peter Eriksson RC UER .12 .30
146 Jari Kurri .25 .60
147 Petri Skriko .20 .50
148 Steve Smith .15 .40
149 Calle Johansson .20 .50
150 Stewart Gavin .20 .50
151 Randy Ladouceur .20 .50
152 Vincent Riendeau RC .20 .50
153 Patrick Roy .50 1.25
154 Brett Hull .40 1.00
155 Craig Fisher RC .20 .50
156 Cam Neely .20 .50
157 Al Iafrate .12 .30
158 Bob Carpenter .15 .40
159 Doug Brown .15 .40
160 Tom Kurvers .20 .50
161 John MacLean .15 .40
162 Guy Lafleur .25 .60
163 Peter Stastny .15 .40
164 Joe Sakic .60 1.50
165 Robb Stauber RC .20 .50
166 Daren Puppa .15 .40
167 Esa Tikkanen .15 .40
168 Mike Ramsey .12 .30
169 Craig MacTavish .15 .40
170 Christian Ruuttu .15 .40
171 Brian Hayward .20 .50
172 Pat Verbeek .15 .40
173 Adam Oates .20 .50
174 Chris Chelios .20 .50
175 Curtis Joseph RC .60 1.50
176 Slava Fetisov RC .40 1.00
177 Dave Poulin .20 .50
178 Mark Recchi RC .60 1.50
179 Daniel Marois .15 .40
180 Mark Johnson .15 .40
181 Michel Petit .15 .40
182 Brian Mullen .20 .50
183 Chris Terreri RC .40 1.00
184 Tony Hrkac .12 .30
185 James Patrick .20 .50
186 Craig Ludwig .20 .50
187 Uwe Krupp .20 .50
188 Guy Carbonneau .12 .30
189 Dave Snuggerud RC .15 .40
190 Joe Murphy RC .15 .40
191 Jeff Brown .20 .50
192 Dean Evason .15 .40
193 Petr Svoboda .15 .40
194 Dave Babych .12 .30
195 Steve Tuttle .15 .40
196 Randy Burridge .15 .40
197 Tony Tanti .15 .40
198 Bob Sweeney .12 .30
199 Brad Marsh .15 .40
200 Checklist 101-200 .12 .30
201 B.Ranford Conn Smythe .15 .40
202 Sergei Makarov Calder .40 1.00
203 Brett Hull Byng .40 1.00
204 Ray Bourque Norris .30 .75
205 Wayne Gretzky Ross 1.25 3.00
206 Mark Messier Hart .40 1.00
207 Patrick Roy Vezina .50 1.25
208 Rick Meagher Selke .15 .40
209 William Jennings Trophy
Andy Moog
Reggie Lemelin .20 .50
210 Aaron Broten .15 .40
211 John Carter RC .15 .40
212 Marty McSorley .15 .40
213 Greg Millen .15 .40
214 Dave Taylor .20 .50
215 Rejean Lemelin .12 .30
216 Dave McLlwain .20 .50
217 Don Beaupre .12 .30
218 Paul MacDermid .15 .40
219 Dale Hunter .20 .50
220 Brent Ashton .20 .50
221 Steve Thomas .12 .30
222 Ed Olczyk .20 .50
223 Doug Wilson .15 .40
224 Vincent Damphousse .15 .40
225 Rob DiMaio RC .20 .50
226 Hubie McDonough RC .15 .40
227 Ron Hextall .20 .50
228 Dave Chyzowski RC .15 .40
229 Larry Murphy .15 .40
230 Mike Bullard .15 .40
231 Kelly Hrudey .12 .30
232 Andy Moog .20 .50
233 Todd Elik RC .20 .50
234 Craig Janney .20 .50
235 Peter Lappin RC .15 .40
236 Scott Stevens .20 .50
237 Fredrik Olausson .15 .40
238 Geoff Courtnall .15 .40
239 Greg Paslawski .15 .40
240 Alan May RC .12 .30
241 Allan Bester .20 .50
242 Steve Larmer .15 .40
243 Gary Leeman .15 .40
244 Denis Savard .20 .50
245 Eric Weinrich RC .20 .50
246 Pat LaFontaine .20 .50
247 Tim Kerr .12 .30
248 Dave Gagner .20 .50
249 Brent Sutter .15 .40
250 Claude Vilgrain RC .12 .30
251 Tomas Sandstrom .20 .50
252 Joe Mullen .15 .40
253 Brian Leetch .25 .60
254 Mike Vernon .15 .40
255 Daniel Dore RC .12 .30
256 Trevor Linden .20 .50
257 Dave Barr .20 .50
258 John Ogrodnick .20 .50
259 Russ Courtnall .20 .50
260 Dan Quinn .15 .40
261 Mark Howe .20 .50
262 Kevin Lowe .20 .50
263 Rick Tocchet .20 .50
264 Grant Fuhr .30 .75
265 Andrew Cassels RC .12 .30
266 Kevin Dineen .20 .50
267 Kirk Muller .15 .40
268 Randy Cunneyworth .15 .40
269 Brendan Shanahan .20 .50
270 Dave Tippett .15 .40
271 Doug Gilmour .25 .60
272 Tony Granato .12 .30
273 Gary Suter .12 .30
274 Darren Turcotte RC .15 .40
275 Murray Baron RC .15 .40
276 Stephane Richer .20 .50
277 Mike Gartner .25 .60
278 Kirk McLean .12 .30
279 John Vanbiesbrouck .20 .50
280 Shayne Corson .15 .40
281 Paul Cavallini .15 .40
282 Petr Klima .12 .30
283 Ulf Dahlen .20 .50
284 Glenn Anderson .15 .40
285 Rick Meagher .15 .40
286 Alexei Kasatonov RC .20 .50
287 Ulf Samuelsson .20 .50
288 Patrik Sundstrom .15 .40
289 Ray Ferraro .15 .40
290 Janne Ojanen RC .20 .50
291 Jeff Jackson .15 .40
292 Jiri Hrdina RC .15 .40
293 Joe Cirella .12 .30
294 Brad McCrimmon .20 .50
295 Curtis Leschyshyn RC .15 .40
296 Kelly Kisio .15 .40
297 Jyrki Lumme RC .12 .30
298 Mark Janssens RC .20 .50
299 Stan Smyl .12 .30
300 Checklist 201-300 .12 .30
301 Joe Sakic TC .60 1.50
302 Petri Skriko TC .20 .50
303 Steve Yzerman TC .60 1.50
304 Tim Kerr TC .12 .30
305 Mario Lemieux TC .75 2.00
306 Pat LaFontaine TC .20 .50
307 Wayne Gretzky TC 1.25 3.00
308 Brian Bellows TC .15 .40

Card	Low	High
309 Rod Langway TC	.20	.50
310 Gary Leeman TC	.15	.40
311 Kirk Muller TC	.15	.40
312 Brett Hull TC	.40	1.00
313 Thomas Steen TC	.15	.40
314 Ron Francis TC	.25	.60
315 Brian Leetch TC	.25	.60
316 Jeremy Roenick TC	.60	1.50
317 Patrick Roy TC	.50	1.25
318 Pierre Turgeon TC	.15	.40
319 Al MacInnis TC	.25	.60
320 Ray Bourque TC	.30	.75
321 Mark Messier TC	.40	1.00
322 Jody Hull RC	.20	.50
323 Chris Joseph RC	.12	.30
324 Adam Burt RC	.15	.40
325 Jason Herter RC	.12	.30
326 Geoff Smith ART RC	.20	.50
327 Brad Shaw ART	.15	.40
328 Rich Sutter	.20	.50
329 Barry Pederson	.15	.40
330 Paul MacLean	.15	.40
331 Randy Carlyle	.15	.40
332 Donald Dufresne RC UER	.12	.30
333 Brent Hughes RC	.12	.30
334 Mathieu Schneider RC	.15	.40
335 Jason Miller RC	.12	.30
336 Sergei Makarov ART	.40	1.00
337 Bob Essensa ART	.30	.75
338 Claude Loiselle RC	.12	.30
339 Wayne Presley	.12	.30
340 Tony McKegney	.12	.30
341 Charlie Huddy	.15	.40
342 Greg Adams UER		
Front photo is Igor Larionov	.12	.30
343 Mike Tomlak RC	.20	.50
344 Adam Graves RC	.40	1.00
345 Michel Mongeau RC	.15	.40
346 Mike Modano ART UER	.60	1.50
347 Rod Brind'Amour ART	.40	1.00
348 Dana Murzyn	.20	.50
349 Dave Lowry RC	.15	.40
350 Star Rookie CL	.12	.30
351 Nol/Prim/Nedv/Ric CL	.60	1.50
352 Owen Nolan RC	.60	1.50
353 Petr Nedved RC	.20	.50
354 Keith Primeau RC	.30	.75
355 Mike Ricci RC	.20	.50
356 Jaromir Jagr RC	3.00	8.00
357 Scott Scissons RC	.15	.40
358 Darryl Sydor RC	.20	.50
359 Derian Hatcher RC	.15	.40
360 John Slaney RC	.12	.30
361 Drake Berehowsky RC	.15	.40
362 Luke Richardson	.15	.40
363 Lucien DeBlois	.15	.40
364 Dave Reid RC	.20	.50
365 Mats Sundin RC	.75	2.00
366 Jan Erixon	.20	.50
367 Troy Loney RC	.20	.50
368 Chris Nilan	.12	.30
369 Gord Dineen	.15	.40
370 Jeff Bloemberg RC	.15	.40
371 John Druce RC	.20	.50
372 Brian MacLellan	.15	.40
373 Bruce Driver	.20	.50
374 Marc Habscheid	.15	.40
375 Paul Ysebaert RC	.15	.40
376 Rick Vaive	.15	.40
377 Glen Wesley	.15	.40
378 Mike Foligno	.15	.40
379 Garry Galley RC	.12	.30
380 Dean Kennedy RC	.12	.30
381 Daniel Berthiaume	.15	.40
382 Mike Keane RC	.12	.30
383 Frank Musil	.12	.30
384 Mike McPhee	.15	.40
385 Jon Casey	.20	.50
386 Jeff Norton	.20	.50
387 John Tucker	.15	.40
388 Alan Kerr	.15	.40
389 Bob Rouse	.12	.30
390 Gerald Diduck	.15	.40
391 Greg Hawgood	.15	.40
392 Randy Velischek	.12	.30
393 Tim Cheveldae RC	.15	.40
394 Mike Krushelnyski	.20	.50
395 Glen Hanlon	.15	.40
396 Lou Franceschetti RC	.20	.50
397 Scott Arniel	.12	.30
398 Terry Carkner	.15	.40
399 Clint Malarchuk	.15	.40
400 Checklist 301-400	.12	.30
401 Mikhail Tatarinov RC	.12	.30
402 Benoit Hogue	.20	.50
403 Frank Pietrangelo RC	.12	.30
404 Paul Stanton RC	.20	.50
405 Anatoli Semenov RC	.15	.40
406 Bobby Smith	.15	.40
407 Derek King	.20	.50
408 J.C. Bergeron RC	.20	.50
409 Brian Propp	.20	.50
410 Jiri Latal RC	.20	.50
411 Joey Kocur RC	.40	1.00
412 Daniel Berthiaume	.15	.40
413 Dave Ellett	.12	.30
414 Jay Miller RC	.12	.30
415 Steph Beauregard RC	.15	.40
416 Mark Hardy	.12	.30
417 Todd Krygier RC	.15	.40
418 Randy Moller	.20	.50
419 Doug Crossman	.15	.40
420 Ray Sheppard	.12	.30
421 Sylvain Lefebvre RC	.15	.40
422 Chris Chelios	.20	.50
423 Joe Mullen	.15	.40
424 Pete Peeters	.12	.30
425 Bryan Trottier	.20	.50
426 Denis Savard	.20	.50
427 Ken Daneyko	.12	.30
428 Eric Desjardins RC	.40	1.00
429 Zdeno Ciger RC	.20	.50
430 Brad McCrimmon	.20	.50
431 Ed Olczyk	.20	.50
432 Peter Ing RC	.20	.50
433 Bob Kudelski RC	.15	.40
434 Troy Gamble RC	.20	.50
435 Phil Housley	.15	.40
436 Scott Stevens	.20	.50
437 Normand Rochefort	.12	.30
438 Geoff Courtnall	.15	.40
439 Ken Baumgartner RC	.20	.50
440 Kris King RC	.20	.50
441 Troy Crowder RC	.12	.30
442 Chris Nilan	.12	.30
443 Dale Hawerchuk	.25	.60
444 Kevin Miller RC	.20	.50
445 Keith Acton	.20	.50
446 Jeff Chychrun RC	.15	.40
447 Claude Lemieux	.12	.30
448 Bob Probert	.20	.50
449 Brian Hayward	.20	.50
450 Craig Berube RC	.12	.30
451 Team Canada Juniors	1.25	3.00
452 Mike Sillinger RC	.20	.50
453 Jason Marshall RC	.12	.30
454 Patrice Brisebois RC	.12	.30
455 Brad May RC	.15	.40
456 Pierre Sevigny RC	.12	.30
457 John Slaney	.12	.30
458 Felix Potvin RC	.75	2.00
459 Scott Thornton RC	.12	.30
460 Greg Johnson RC	.12	.30
461 Scott Niedermayer RC	.30	.75
462 Steven Rice RC	.20	.50
463 Trevor Kidd RC	.15	.40
464 Dale Craigwell RC	.12	.30
465 Kent Manderville RC	.12	.30
466 Kris Draper RC	.15	.40
467 Martin Lapointe RC	.20	.50
468 Chris Snell RC	.12	.30
469 Pat Falloon RC	.12	.30
470 David Harlock RC	.12	.30
471 Karl Dykhuis RC	.15	.40
472 Mike Craig RC	.20	.50
473 Canada's Captains	1.25	3.00
474 Brett Hull AS	.40	1.00
475 Darren Turcotte AS	.15	.40
476 Wayne Gretzky AS	1.25	3.00
477 Steve Yzerman AS	.60	1.50
478 Theo Fleury AS	.25	.60
479 Pat LaFontaine AS	.20	.50
480 Trevor Linden AS	.20	.50
481 Jeremy Roenick AS	.60	1.50
482 Scott Stevens AS	.20	.50
483 Adam Oates AS	.20	.50
484 Vincent Damphousse AS	.15	.40
485 Brian Leetch AS	.25	.60
486 Kevin Hatcher AS	.15	.40
487 Mark Recchi AS	.60	1.50
488 Rick Tocchet AS	.20	.50
489 Ray Bourque AS	.30	.75
490 Joe Sakic AS	.60	1.50
491 Chris Chelios AS	.20	.50
492 John Cullen AS	.20	.50
493 Cam Neely AS	.20	.50
494 Mark Messier AS	.40	1.00
495 Mike Vernon AS	.15	.40
496 Patrick Roy AS	.50	1.25
497 Al MacInnis AS	.25	.60
498 Paul Coffey AS	.20	.50
499 Steve Larmer AS	.15	.40
500 Checklist 401-500	.12	.30
501 Heroes Checklist	.12	.30
502 Red Kelly HERO	.20	.50
503 Eric Nesterenko HERO	.20	.50
504 Darryl Sittler HERO	.25	.60
505 Jim Schoenfeld HERO	.20	.50
506 Serge Savard HERO	.20	.50
507 Glenn Resch HERO	.20	.50
508 Lanny McDonald HERO	.20	.50
509 Bobby Clarke HERO	.30	.75
510 Phil Esposito HERO	.30	.75
511 Harry Howell HERO	.20	.50
512 Rod Gilbert HERO	.20	.50
513 Pit Martin HERO	.20	.50
514 Jimmy Watson HERO	.12	.30
515 Denis Potvin HERO	.20	.50
516 Robert Ray RC	.20	.50
517 Danton Cole RC	.20	.50
518 Gino Odjick RC	.12	.30
519 Donald Audette RC	.20	.50
520 Rick Tabaracci RC	.12	.30
521 Young Guns CL/Federov	.40	1.00
522 Kip Miller YG RC	.15	.40
523 Johan Garpenlov YG RC	.20	.50
524 Stephane Morin YG RC	.12	.30
525 Sergei Fedorov YG RC UER	3.00	8.00
526 Pavel Bure YG RC	3.00	8.00
527 Wes Walz YG RC	.20	.50
528 Robert Kron YG RC	.20	.50
529 Ken Hodge Jr. YG RC	.20	.50
530 Garry Valk YG RC	.12	.30
531 Tim Sweeney YG RC	.20	.50
532 Mark Pederson YG RC	.20	.50
533 Robert Reichel YG RC	.20	.50
534 Bobby Holik YG RC	.20	.50
535 Stephane Matteau YG RC	.20	.50
536 Peter Bondra YG RC	.60	1.50
537 Dimitri Khristich RC	.12	.30
538 Vladimir Ruzicka RC	.20	.50
539 Al Iafrate	.12	.30
540 Rick Bennett RC	.12	.30
541 Daryl Reaugh RC	.12	.30
542 Martin Hostak RC	.20	.50
543 Kari Takko RC	.12	.30
544 Jocelyn Lemieux RC	.15	.40
545 W.Gretzky 2000th	1.25	3.00
546 Brett Hull 50/50	.40	1.00
547 Neil Wilkinson RC	.15	.40
548 Bryan Fogarty RC	.12	.30
549 Zamboni Machine	.12	.30
550 Checklist 501-550	.12	.30

1990-91 Upper Deck French

*FRENCH: .2X TO .5X BASIC

1990-91 Upper Deck Holograms

Card	Low	High
1 Wayne Gretzky	1.25	3.00
2 Wayne Gretzky	1.25	3.00
3 Wayne Gretzky	1.25	3.00
4 Brett Hull	.40	1.00
5 Mark Messier	.40	1.00
6 M.Messier/B.Hull	.40	1.00
7 M.Messier/S.Yzerman	.60	1.50
8 Steve Yzerman	.60	1.50
9 Steve Yzerman	.60	1.50

1990-91 Upper Deck Promos

Card	Low	High
COMPLETE SET (2)	20.00	50.00
241A Wayne Gretzky UER		
Wrong height, feet		
and inches reversed)	12.00	30.00
241B Patrick Roy UER		
Wrong height, feet		
and inches reversed)	10.00	25.00

1990-91 Upper Deck Sheets

Card	Low	High
COMPLETE SET (11)	64.00	160.00
1 Toronto Maple Leafs		
vs. Detroit Red Wings		
Nov. 17, 1990 (20,000)		
Al Iafrate		
Ed Olcyzk		
Vincent Damphousse		
Wendel Clark		
Gary Leeman		
Drake Berehowsky	10.00	25.00
2 Detroit Red Wings I		
vs. Boston Bruins		
Dec. 4, 1990 (22,000)		
Keith Primeau		
Shawn Burr		
Steve Yzerman		
Jimmy Carson		
Tim Cheveldae		
Steve Chiasson	6.00	15.00
3 Los Angeles Kings		
vs. Calgary Flames		
Dec. 13, 1990 (19,500)		
Steve Duchesne		
Luc Robitaille		
Rob Blake		
Wayne Gretzky		
Tony Granato		
Tomas Sandstrom	6.00	15.00
4 New York Rangers I		
vs. Hartford Whalers		
Jan. 13, 1991 (25,700)		
Mike Richter		
Ray Sheppard		
Troy Mallette		
Normand Rochefort		
Mark Janssens		
Dennis Vial		
John Ogrodnick		
Lindy Ruff		
Brian Leetch	4.00	10.00
5 New York Rangers II		
vs. Chicago Blackhawks		
Jan. 17, 1991 (25,700)		
David Shaw		
Miloslav Horava		
Darren Turcotte		
Jan Erixon		
Kelly Kisio		
Brian Mullen		
Bernie Nicholls		
John Vanbiesbrouck		
James Patrick	5.00	12.00
6 Campbell All-Stars		
Chicago Stadium		
Jan. 19, 1991 (15,100)		
Wayne Gretzky		
Chris Chelios		
Luc Robitaille		
Brett Hull		
Al MacInnis		
Mike Vernon	12.00	30.00
7 Wales All-Stars		
Chicago Stadium		
Jan. 19, 1991 (15,100)		
Ray Bourque		
Rick Tocchet		
Joe Sakic		
Paul Coffey		
Cam Neely		
Patrick Roy	10.00	25.00
8 St. Louis Blues		
vs. Buffalo Sabres		
Jan. 29, 1991 (21,000)		
Jeff Brown		
Vincent Riendeau		
Brent Hull		
Paul Cavallini		
Curtis Joseph		
Gino Cavallini		
Adam Oates		
Scott Stevens		
Rod Brind'Amour	4.00	10.00
9 Detroit Red Wings II		
vs. Minnesota North Stars		
Feb. 16, 1991 (23,000)		
Joey Kocur		
Rick Zombo		
Sergei Fedorov		
Gerard Gallant		
Johan Garpenlov		
Glen Hanlon		
Dave Barr		
John Chabot		
Bob Probert	5.00	12.00
10 New York Rangers III		
vs. New York Islanders		
Feb. 18, 1991 (25,700)		
Tie Domi		
Randy Moller		
Mike Gartner		
Kevin Miller		
Mark Hardy		
Jody Hull		
Kris King		
Bob Froese		
Paul Broten	4.00	10.00
11 All-Rookie Team		
June 21, 1991 (16,000)		
Eric Weinrich		
Jaromir Jagr		
Ed Belfour		
Sergei Fedorov		
Rob Blake		
Ken Hodge	8.00	20.00

1991-92 Upper Deck

Card	Low	High
1 Vladimir Malakhov SS RC	.15	.40
2 Alexei Zhamnov SS RC	.15	.40
3 Dimitri Filiminov SS RC	.15	.40
4 Alexander Semak SS RC	.20	.50
5 Slava Kozlov RC	.20	.50
6 Sergei Fedorov SS	.30	.75
7 E.Lindros/B.Hull CC CL	.40	1.00
8 Al MacInnis CC	.25	.60
9 Eric Lindros CC	.30	.75
10 Bill Ranford CC	.15	.40
11 Paul Coffey CC	.20	.50
12 Dale Hawerchuk CC	.25	.60
13 Wayne Gretzky CC	1.25	3.00
14 Mark Messier CC	.40	1.00
15 Steve Larmer CC	.15	.40
16 Zigmund Palffy CC RC	.60	1.50
17 Josef Beranek CC RC	.20	.50
18 Jiri Slegr CC RC	.12	.30
19 Martin Rucinsky CC RC	.15	.40
20 Jaromir Jagr CC	.60	1.50
21 Teemu Selanne CC RC	2.50	6.00
22 Janne Laukkanen CC RC	.12	.30
23 Markus Ketterer CC RC	.12	.30
24 Jari Kurri CC	.15	.40
25 Janne Ojanen CC	.12	.30
26 Nicklas Lidstrom CC RC	1.25	3.00
27 Tomas Forslund CC RC	.20	.50
28 Johan Garpenlov CC	.15	.40
29 Niclas Andersson CC RC	.12	.30
30 Tomas Sandstrom CC	.15	.40
31 Mats Sundin CC	.20	.50
32 Mike Modano CC	.40	1.00
33 Brett Hull CC	.40	1.00
34 Mike Richter CC	.20	.50
35 Brian Leetch CC	.15	.40
36 Jeremy Roenick CC	.30	.75
37 Chris Chelios CC	.20	.50
38 Wayne Gretzky 99	1.25	3.00
39 Ed Belfour ART	.50	1.25
40 Sergei Fedorov ART	.30	.75
41 Ken Hodge Jr. ART	.15	.40
42 Jaromir Jagr ART	.60	1.50
43 Rob Blake ART	.20	.50
44 Eric Weinrich ART	.20	.50
45 The 50/50 Club	1.25	3.00
46 Russ Romaniuk RC	.20	.50
47 M.Lemieux/G.Bush	.75	2.00
48 Michel Picard RC	.20	.50
49 Dennis Vaske	.15	.40
50 Eric Murano RC	.12	.30
51 Enrico Ciccone RC	.12	.30
52 Shaun Van Allen RC	.15	.40
53 Stu Barnes	.15	.40
54 Pavel Bure	.20	.50
55 Neil Wilkinson	.15	.40
56 Tony Hrkac	.15	.40
57 Brian Mullen	.15	.40
58 Jeff Hackett	.15	.40
59 Brian Hayward	.15	.40
60 Craig Coxe	.12	.30
61 Rob Zettler	.15	.40
62 Bob McGill	.15	.40
63 Lapointe		
Pushor CL	.15	.40
64 Peter Forsberg RC	2.00	5.00
65 Patrick Poulin RC	.12	.30
66 Martin Lapointe	.15	.40
67 Tyler Wright RC	.12	.30
68 Philippe Boucher RC	.12	.30
69 Glen Murray RC	.20	.50
70 Martin Rucinsky RC	.15	.40
71 Zigmund Palffy RC	.60	1.50
72 Jassen Cullimore RC	.12	.30
73 Jamie Pushor RC	.12	.30
74 Andrew Verner RC	.12	.30
75 Jason Dawe RC	.12	.30
76 Jamie Matthews RC	.12	.30
77 Sandy McCarthy RC	.15	.40
78 Cam Neely		
(Boston Bruins TC)	.20	.50
79 Dale Hawerchuk		
(Buffalo Sabres TC)	.25	.60
80 Theo Fleury TC	.15	.40
81 Ed Belfour TC	.50	1.25
82 Sergei Fedorov TC	.30	.75
83 Esa Tikkanen		
(Edmonton Oilers TC)	.15	.40
84 John Cullen		
(Hartford Whalers TC)	.15	.40
85 Tomas Sandstrom		
(Los Angeles Kings TC)	.15	.40
86 Dave Gagner		
(Minnesota North Stars TC)	.15	.40
87 Russ Courtnall		
(Montreal Canadiens TC)	.15	.40
88 John MacLean		
(New Jersey Devils TC)	.15	.40
89 David Volek		
(New York Islanders TC)	.15	.40
90 Darren Turcotte		
(New York Rangers TC)	.15	.40
91 Rick Tocchet		
(Philadelphia Flyers TC)	.15	.40
92 Mark Recchi TC	.25	.60
93 Mats Sundin TC	.20	.50
94 Adam Oates TC	.20	.50
95 Neil Wilkinson TC	.15	.40
96 Dave Ellett		
(Toronto Maple Leafs TC)	.15	.40
97 Trevor Linden TC	.20	.50
98 Kevin Hatcher		
(Washington Capitals TC)	.15	.40
99 Ed Olczyk		
(Winnipeg Jets TC)	.15	.40
100 Checklist 1-100	.05	.15
101 Bob Essensa	.15	.40
102 Uwe Krupp	.15	.40
103 Pelle Eklund	.15	.40
104 Christian Ruuttu	.15	.40
105 Kevin Dineen	.15	.40
106 Phil Housley	.15	.40
107 Pat Jablonski RC	.15	.40
108 Jarmo Kekalainen RC	.12	.30
109 Pat Elynuik	.15	.40
110 Corey Millen RC	.20	.50
111 Petr Klima	.15	.40
112 Mike Ridley	.15	.40
113 Peter Stastny	.15	.40
114 Jyrki Lumme	.15	.40
115 Chris Terreri	.15	.40
116 Tom Barrasso	.15	.40
117 Bill Ranford	.15	.40
118 Peter Ing	.15	.40
119 John Tanner	.12	.30
120 Troy Gamble	.12	.30
121 Stephane Matteau	.15	.40
122 Rick Tocchet	.15	.40
123 Wes Walz	.15	.40
124 Dave Andreychuk	.20	.50
125 Mike Craig	.15	.40
126 Dale Hawerchuk	.25	.60
127 Dean Evason	.15	.40
128 Craig Janney	.15	.40
129 Tim Cheveldae	.15	.40
130 Rick Wamsley	.12	.30
131 Peter Bondra	.20	.50
132 Scott Stevens	.20	.50
133 Kelly Miller	.15	.40
134 Mats Sundin	.20	.50
135 Mick Vukota	.15	.40
136 Vincent Damphousse	.15	.40
137 Patrick Roy	.50	1.25
138 Hubie McDonough	.15	.40
139 Curtis Joseph	.25	.60
140 Brent Sutter	.15	.40
141 Tomas Sandstrom	.15	.40
142 Kevin Miller	.15	.40
143 Mike Ricci	.12	.30
144 Sergei Fedorov	.30	.75
145 Luc Robitaille	.20	.50
146 Steve Yzerman	.60	1.50
147 Andy Moog	.20	.50
148 Rob Blake	.20	.50
149 Kirk Muller	.12	.30
150 Daniel Berthiaume	.15	.40
151 John Druce	.15	.40
152 Garry Valk	.15	.40
153 Brian Leetch	.15	.40
154 Kevin Stevens	.15	.40
155 Darren Turcotte	.15	.40
156 Mario Lemieux	.75	2.00
157 Dimitri Khristich	.15	.40
158 Brian Glynn	.15	.40
159 Benoit Hogue UER	.15	.40
160 Mike Modano	.40	1.00
161 Jimmy Carson	.15	.40
162 Steve Thomas	.15	.40
163 Mike Vernon	.15	.40
164 Ed Belfour	.50	1.25
165 Joel Otto	.15	.40
166 Jeremy Roenick	.30	.75
167 Johan Garpenlov	.15	.40
168 Russ Courtnall	.15	.40
169 John MacLean	.15	.40
170 J.J. Daigneault	.12	.30
171 Sylvain Lefebvre	.15	.40
172 Tony Granato	.12	.30
173 David Volek	.15	.40
174 Trevor Linden	.20	.50
175 Mike Richter	.20	.50
176 Pierre Turgeon	.15	.40
177 Paul Coffey	.20	.50
178 Jan Erixon	.15	.40
179 Rick Vaive	.12	.30
180 Dave Gagner	.15	.40
181 Thomas Steen	.15	.40
182 Esa Tikkanen	.15	.40
183 Sean Burke	.20	.50
184 Paul Cavallini	.15	.40
185 Alexei Kasatonov	.12	.30
186 Kevin Lowe	.15	.40
187 Gino Cavallini	.15	.40
188 Doug Gilmour	.25	.60
189 Rod Brind'Amour	.15	.40
190 Gary Roberts	.15	.40
191 Kirk McLean	.15	.40
192 Kevin Haller RC	.20	.50
193 Pat Verbeek	.15	.40
194 Dave Snuggerud	.12	.30
195 Gino Odjick	.12	.30
196 Dave Ellett	.15	.40
197 Don Beaupre	.15	.40
198 Rob Brown	.15	.40
199 Marty McSorley	.15	.40
200 Checklist 101-200	.05	.05
201 Joe Mullen	.15	.40
202 Dave Capuano	.15	.40
203 Paul Stanton	.15	.40
204 Terry Carkner	.15	.40
205 Jon Casey	.15	.40
206 Ken Wregget	.15	.40
207 Gaetan Duchesne	.12	.30
208 Cliff Ronning	.12	.30
209 Dale Hunter	.15	.40
210 Danton Cole	.12	.30
211 Jeff Brown	.15	.40
212 Mike Foligno	.20	.50
213 Michel Mongeau	.12	.30
214 Doug Brown	.15	.40
215 Todd Krygier	.15	.40
216 Jon Morris	.15	.40
217 David Reid	.12	.30
218 John McIntyre	.15	.40
219 Guy Lafleur's Farewell	.25	.60
220 Vincent Riendeau	.15	.40
221 Tim Hunter	.15	.40
222 Dave McLlwain	.15	.40
223 Robert Reichel	.40	1.00
224 Glenn Healy	.20	.50
225 Robert Kron	.15	.40
226 Patrick Flatley	.15	.40
227 Petr Nedved	.15	.40
228 Mark Janssens	.15	.40
229 Michal Pivonka	.15	.40
230 Ulf Samuelsson	.15	.40
231 Zarley Zalapski	.15	.40
232 Neal Broten	.15	.40
233 Bobby Holik	.20	.50
234 Cam Neely	.20	.50
235 John Cullen	.15	.40
236 Brian Bellows	.15	.40
237 Chris Nilan	.12	.30
238 Mikael Andersson	.15	.40
239 Bob Probert	.20	.50
240 Teppo Numminen	.15	.40
241 Peter Zezel	.12	.30
242 Denis Savard	.20	.50
243 Al MacInnis	.25	.60
244 Stephane Richer	.15	.40
245 Theo Fleury	.15	.40
246 Mark Messier	.40	1.00
247 Mike Gartner	.25	.60
248 Daren Puppa	.15	.40
249 Louie DeBrusk RC	.20	.50
250 Glenn Anderson	.15	.40
251 Ken Hodge Jr.	.15	.40
252 Adam Oates	.20	.50
253 Pat LaFontaine	.20	.50
254 Adam Creighton	.15	.40
255 Ray Bourque	.30	.75
256 Jaromir Jagr	.60	1.50
257 Steve Larmer	.15	.40
258 Keith Primeau	.15	.40
259 Mike Liut	.12	.30
260 Brian Propp	.15	.40
261 Stephan Lebeau	.15	.40
262 Kelly Hrudey	.15	.40
263 Joe Nieuwendyk	.15	.40
264 Grant Fuhr	.30	.75
265 Guy Carbonneau	.15	.40
266 Martin Gelinas	.15	.40
267 Alexander Mogilny	.15	.40
268 Adam Graves	.15	.40
269 Anatoli Semenov	.15	.40
270 Dave Taylor	.15	.40
271 Dirk Graham	.15	.40
272 Gary Leeman	.15	.40
273 Valeri Kamensky RC	.50	1.25
274 Marc Bureau	.15	.40
275 James Patrick	.15	.40
276 Dino Ciccarelli	.15	.40
277 Ron Tugnutt	.15	.40
278 Paul Ysebaert	.15	.40
279 Laurie Boschman	.15	.40
280 Dave Manson	.15	.40
281 Dave Chyzowski	.12	.30
282 Shayne Corson	.15	.40
283 Steve Chiasson	.15	.40
284 Craig MacTavish	.15	.40
285 Petr Svoboda	.15	.40
286 Craig Simpson	.12	.30
287 Ron Hoover RC	.12	.30
288 Vladimir Ruzicka	.15	.40
289 Randy Wood	.15	.40
290 Doug Lidster	.15	.40
291 Kay Whitmore	.15	.40
292 Bruce Driver	.15	.40
293 Bobby Smith	.15	.40
294 Claude Lemieux	.15	.40
295 Mark Tinordi	.15	.40
296 Mark Osborne	.15	.40
297 Brad Shaw	.12	.30
298 Igor Larionov	.15	.40
299 Ron Francis	.25	.60
300 Checklist 201-300	.05	.05
301 Bob Kudelski	.12	.30
302 Larry Murphy	.15	.40
303 Brent Ashton	.15	.40
304 Brad Jones	.15	.40
305 Gord Donnelly	.15	.40
306 Murray Craven	.15	.40
307 Chris Dahlquist	.15	.40
308 Jim Paek RC	.20	.50
309 Ron Sutter	.15	.40
310 Mike Tomlak	.15	.40
311 Ray Ferraro	.15	.40
312 Dave Hannan	.15	.40
313 Randy McKay	.15	.40
314 Rod Langway	.15	.40
315 Shawn Burr	.15	.40
316 Calle Johansson	.15	.40
317 Rich Sutter	.15	.40
318 Al Iafrate	.15	.40
319 Bob Bassen	.15	.40
320 Mike Krushelnyski	.15	.40
321 Sergei Makarov	.15	.40
322 Darrin Shannon	.15	.40
323 Terry Yake	.15	.40
324 John Vanbiesbrouck	.20	.50
325 Peter Sidorkiewicz	.15	.40
326 Troy Mallette	.15	.40
327 Ron Hextall	.20	.50
328 Mathieu Schneider	.15	.40
329 Bryan Trottier	.20	.50
330 Kris King	.15	.40
331 Daniel Marois	.15	.40
332 Shayne Stevenson	.15	.40
333 Joe Sakic	.60	1.50
334 Petri Skriko	.12	.30
335 Dominik Hasek RC	4.00	10.00
336 Scott Pearson	.15	.40
337 Bryan Fogarty	.15	.40
338 Don Sweeney	.12	.30
339 Rick Tabaracci	.15	.40
340 Steven Finn	.12	.30
341 Gary Suter	.12	.30
342 Troy Crowder	.15	.40
343 Jim Hrivnak	.15	.40
344 Eric Weinrich	.20	.50
345 John LeClair RC	.50	1.25
346 Mark Recchi	.25	.60
347 Dan Currie RC	.12	.30
348 Ulf Dahlen	.15	.40
349 Robert Ray	.12	.30
350 Steve Smith	.20	.50
351 Shawn Antoski	.15	.40
352 Cam Russell	.12	.30
353 Scott Thornton	.15	.40
354 Chris Chelios	.20	.50
355 Sergei Nemchinov FUDC	.15	.40
356 Bernie Nicholls	.15	.40
357 Jeff Norton	.15	.40
358 Dan Quinn	.15	.40
359 Michel Petit	.15	.40
360 Eric Desjardins	.20	.50
361 Kevin Hatcher	.15	.40
362 Jiri Sejba	.15	.40
363 Mark Pederson	.15	.40
364 Jeff Lazaro RC	.15	.40
365 Alexei Gusarov RC	.15	.40
366 Jari Kurri	.15	.40
367 Owen Nolan	.20	.50
368 Clint Malarchuk	.15	.40
369 Patrik Sundstrom	.15	.40
370 Glen Wesley	.15	.40
371 Wayne Presley	.15	.40
372 Craig Muni	.15	.40
373 Brent Fedyk FUDC	.15	.40
374 Michel Goulet	.15	.40
375 Tim Sweeney	.15	.40
376 Gary Shuchuk	.15	.40
377 Andre Racicot RC	.15	.40
378 Jay Mazur RC	.12	.30
379 Andrew Cassels	.15	.40
380 Brian Noonan	.12	.30
381 Sergei Kharin RC	.15	.40
382 Derek King	.12	.30
383 Fredrik Olausson	.15	.40
384 Tom Fergus	.12	.30
385 Zdeno Ciger	.15	.40
386 Wendel Clark	.30	.75
387 Ed Olczyk	.15	.40
388 Basil McRae	.12	.30
389 Tom Fitzgerald	.15	.40
390 Ray Sheppard	.15	.40
391 Bob Sweeney	.12	.30
392 Gord Murphy	.15	.40
393 John Chabot	.12	.30
394 Jeff Beukeboom	.15	.40
395 Rick Zombo	.15	.40
396 Kjell Samuelsson	.15	.40
397 Garth Butcher	.15	.40
398 Phil Bourque	.15	.40
399 Lou Franceschetti	.15	.40
400 Checklist 301-400	.05	.05
401 Kevin Todd RC	.20	.50
402 Ken Baumgartner	.12	.30
403 Peter Douris	.15	.40
404 Jiri Latal	.12	.30
405 Marc Potvin RC	.12	.30
406 Gary Nylund	.15	.40
407 Yvon Corriveau	.12	.30
408 Sheldon Kennedy FUDC	.15	.40
409 David Shaw	.15	.40
410 Slava Fetisov	.15	.40
411 Mario Doyon RC	.12	.30
412 Jamie Macoun	.15	.40
413 Curtis Leschyshyn	.15	.40
414 Mike Peluso	.15	.40
415 Brian Benning	.15	.40
416 Stu Grimson RC	.12	.30
417 Ken Sabourin	.15	.40
418 Luke Richardson	.15	.40
419 Ken Quinney RC	.12	.30
420 Mike Donnelly RC	.20	.50
421 Darcy Loewen RC	.12	.30
422 Brian Skrudland	.15	.40
423 Joel Savage RC	.12	.30
424 Adrien Plavsic	.15	.40
425 Jergus Baca	.15	.40
426 Greg Adams	.15	.40
427 Tom Chorske	.15	.40
428 Scott Scissons	.12	.30
429 Dale Kushner	.15	.40
430 Todd Richards RC	.12	.30
431 Kip Miller	.15	.40
432 Jason Prosofsky RC	.12	.30
433 Stephane Morin	.15	.40
434 Brian McReynolds	.12	.30
435 Ken Daneyko	.15	.40
436 Chris Joseph	.15	.40
437 Wayne Gretzky	1.25	3.00
438 Jocelyn Lemieux	.15	.40
439 Garry Galley	.15	.40
440 Amon/Weig/Rice SR CL	.50	1.25
441 Steven Rice SR	.15	.40
442 Patrice Brisebois SR	.12	.30
443 Jim Waite FUDC	.15	.40
444 Doug Weight SR RC	.50	1.25
445 Nelson Emerson SR	.15	.40
446 Jarrod Skalde SR RC	.15	.40
447 Jamie Leach SR	.15	.40
448 Gilbert Dionne SR RC	.20	.50
449 Trevor Kidd SR	.15	.40
450 Tony Amonte SR RC	.50	1.25
451 Pat Murray SR	.15	.40
452 Stephane Fiset SR	.12	.30
453 Patrick Lebeau RC	.15	.40
454 Chris Taylor RC	.12	.30
455 Chris Tancill RC	.15	.40
456 Mark Greig SR	.15	.40
457 Mike Sillinger	.15	.40
458 Ken Sutton RC	.20	.50
459 Len Barrie RC	.12	.30
460 Felix Potvin SR	.40	1.00
461 Brian Sakic RC	.12	.30
462 Slava Kozlov RC	.20	.50
463 Matt DelGuidice RC	.20	.50
464 Brett Hull	.40	1.00
465 Norm Foster	.12	.30
466 Alexander Godynyuk RC	.20	.50
467 Geoff Courtnall	.15	.40
468 Frantisek Kucera	.15	.40
469 Benoit Brunet RC	.12	.30
470 Mark Vermette	.12	.30
471 Tim Watters	.12	.30
472 Paul Ranheim	.20	.50
473 Martin Hostak	.12	.30
474 Joe Murphy	.15	.40
475 Claude Boivin RC	.12	.30

476 John Ogrodnick .15 .40
477 Doug Bodger .15 .40
478 Shawn Cronin .15 .40
479 Mark Hunter .15 .40
480 Dave Tippett .15 .40
481 Rob DiMaio .15 .40
482 Lyle Odelein .15 .40
483 Joe Reekie .15 .40
484 Randy Velischek .15 .40
485 Myles O'Connor RC .15 .40
486 Craig Wolanin .15 .40
487 Mike McPhee .15 .40
488 Claude Lapointe RC .15 .40
489 Troy Loney .12 .30
490 Bob Beers .12 .30
491 Sylvain Couturier .12 .30
492 Kimbi Daniels .20 .50
493 Darryl Shannon .20 .50
494 Jim McKenzie RC .20 .50
495 Don Gibson RC .12 .30
496 Ralph Barahona RC .12 .30
497 Murray Baron .15 .40
498 Yves Racine .15 .40
499 Larry Robinson .20 .50
500 Checklist 401-500 .05 .05
501 P.Coffey/Gretzky CC CL 1.25 3.00
502 Dirk Graham CC .15 .40
503 Rick Tocchet CC .15 .40
504 Eric Desjardins CC .20 .50
505 Shayne Corson CC .15 .40
506 Theo Fleury CC .15 .40
507 Luc Robitaille CC .20 .50
508 Tony Granato CC .12 .30
509 Eric Weinrich CC .20 .50
510 Gary Suter CC .12 .30
511 Kevin Hatcher CC .15 .40
512 Craig Janney CC .15 .40
513 Darren Turcotte CC .15 .40
514 Chris Winnes RC .15 .40
515 Kelly Kisio .15 .40
516 Joe Day RC .12 .30
517 Ed Courtenay RC .12 .30
518 Andrei Lomakin FUDC .15 .40
519 Kirk Muller .12 .30
520 Rick Lessard RC .15 .40
521 Scott Thornton .15 .40
522 Luke Richardson .15 .40
523 Mike Eagles .15 .40
524 Mike McNeill .15 .40
525 Ken Priestlay .15 .40
526 Louie DeBrusk .20 .50
527 Dave McLlwain .15 .40
528 Gary Leeman .15 .40
529 Adam Foote RC .40 1.00
530 Kevin Dineen .15 .40
531 David Reid .12 .30
532 Arturs Irbe .15 .40
533 Mark Osiecki RC .15 .40
534 Steve Thomas .15 .40
535 Vincent Damphousse .15 .40
536 Stephane Richer .15 .40
537 Jarmo Myllys .15 .40
538 Carey Wilson .15 .40
539 Scott Stevens .20 .50
540 Uwe Krupp .15 .40
541 Dave Christian .12 .30
542 Scott Mellanby .15 .40
543 Peter Ahola RC .20 .50
544 Todd Elik .15 .40
545 Mark Messier .40 1.00
546 Derian Hatcher .15 .40
547 Rod Brind'Amour .15 .40
548 Dave Manson .15 .40
549 Darryl Sydor .15 .40
550 Paul Broten .12 .30
551 Andrew Cassels .15 .40
552 Tom Draper RC .20 .50
553 Grant Fuhr .30 .75
554 Pierre Turgeon .15 .40
555 Pavel Bure .20 .50
556 Pat LaFontaine .20 .50
557 Dave Thomlinson .12 .30
558 Doug Gilmour .25 .60
559 Craig Billington RC .20 .50
560 Dean Evason .15 .40
561 Brendan Shanahan .20 .50
562 Mike Hough .15 .40
563 Dan Quinn .15 .40
564 Jeff Daniels RC .15 .40
565 Troy Murray .15 .40
566 Bernie Nicholls .15 .40
567 Randy Burridge .15 .40
568 Todd Hartje RC .12 .30
569 Charlie Huddy .15 .40
570 Steve Duchesne .12 .30
571 Sergio Momesso .15 .40
572 Brian Lawton .15 .40
573 Ray Sheppard .15 .40
574 Adam Graves .15 .40
575 Rollie Melanson .12 .30
576 Steve Kasper .12 .30
577 Jim Sandlak .15 .40
578 Pat MacLeod RC .20 .50
579 Sylvain Turgeon .15 .40
580 James Black RC .12 .30
581 Darrin Shannon .15 .40
582 Todd Krygier .15 .40
583 Dominic Roussel RC .20 .50
584 Nicklas Lidstrom YG CL .75 2.00
585 Donald Audette .15 .40
586 Tomas Forslund .20 .50
587 Nicklas Lidstrom .75 2.00
588 Geoff Sanderson RC .20 .50
589 Valeri Zelepukin RC .20 .50
590 Igor Ulanov RC .20 .50
591 Corey Foster RC .20 .50
592 Dan Lambert RC .15 .40
593 Pat Falloon .15 .40
594 Vladimir Konstantinov RC .50 1.25
595 Josef Beranek .20 .50
596 Brad May .15 .40
597 Jeff Odgers RC .20 .50
598 Rob Pearson RC .20 .50
599 Luciano Borsato RC .20 .50
600 Checklist 501-600 .05 .05
601 Peter Douris .15 .40
602 Mark Fitzpatrick .15 .40
603 Randy Gilhen .15 .40
604 Corey Millen .20 .50
605 Jason Cirone RC .12 .30
606 Kyosti Karjalainen RC .20 .50
607 Garry Galley .15 .40
608 Brent Thompson RC .12 .30
609 Alexander Godynyuk .20 .50
610 Leetch/Richt/Mess CL .40 1.00
611 Mario Lemieux AS .75 2.00
612 Brian Leetch AS .15 .40
613 Kevin Stevens AS .15 .40
614 Patrick Roy AS .50 1.25
615 Paul Coffey AS .20 .50
616 Joe Sakic AS .60 1.50
617 Jaromir Jagr AS .60 1.50
618 Alexander Mogilny AS .15 .40
619 Owen Nolan AS .20 .50
620 Mark Messier AS .40 1.00
621 Wayne Gretzky AS 1.25 3.00
622 Brett Hull AS .40 1.00
623 Luc Robitaille AS .20 .50
624 Phil Housley AS .15 .40
625 Ed Belfour AS .50 1.25
626 Steve Yzerman AS .60 1.50
627 Adam Oates AS .20 .50
628 Trevor Linden AS .20 .50
629 Jeremy Roenick AS .30 .75
630 Theo Fleury AS .15 .40
631 Sergei Fedorov AS .30 .75
632 Al MacInnis AS .25 .60
633 Ray Bourque AS .30 .75
634 Mike Richter AS .20 .50
635 Al Secord HERO .12 .30
636 Marcel Dionne HERO .25 .60
637 Ken Morrow HERO .12 .30
638 Guy Lafleur HERO .25 .60
639 Ed Mio HERO .12 .30
640 Clark Gillies HERO .20 .50
641 Bob Nystrom HERO .12 .30
642 Pete Peeters HERO .12 .30
643 Ulf Nilsson HERO .12 .30
644 Lebeau Bros. .15 .40
645 Sutter Bros. .15 .40
646 Cavallini Bros. .15 .40
647 Bure Bros. .20 .50
648 Ferraro Bros. .15 .40
649 World Jr. CCCP Team CL .05 .25
650 Darius Kasparaitis RC .20 .50
651 Alexei Yashin RC .30 .75
652 Nikolai Khabibulin RC .50 1.25
653 Denis Metlyuk RC .12 .30
654 Konstantin Korotkov RC .12 .30
655 Alexei Kovalev RC .60 1.50
656 Alexander Kuzminsky RC .12 .30
657 Alexander Cherbayev RC .12 .30
658 Sergei Krivokrasov RC .12 .30
659 Sergei Zholtok RC .12 .30
660 Alexei Zhitnik RC .12 .30
661 Sandis Ozolinsh RC .20 .50
662 Boris Mironov RC .12 .30
663 Pauli Jaks RC .12 .30
664 Gaetan Voisard RC .12 .30
665 Nicola Celio RC .12 .30
666 Marc Weber RC .12 .30
667 Bernhard Schumperli RC .12 .30
668 Laurent Bucher RC .12 .30
669 Michael Blaha RC .12 .30
670 Tiziano Gianini RC .12 .30
671 Marko Kiprusoff RC .12 .30
672 Janne Gronvall RC .12 .30
673 Juha Ylonen RC .12 .30
674 Sami Kapanen RC .20 .50
675 Marko Tuomainen RC .12 .30
676 Jarkko Varvio RC .15 .40
677 Tomas Gronman RC .15 .40
678 Andreas Naumann RC .15 .40
679 Steffen Ziesche RC .15 .40
680 Jens Schwabe RC .15 .40
681 Thomas Schubert RC .15 .40
682 Hans-Jorg Mayer RC .12 .30
683 Marc Seliger RC .15 .40
684 Trevor Kidd .15 .40
685 Martin Lapointe .15 .40
686 Tyler Wright RC .12 .30
687 Kimbi Daniels RC .20 .50
688 Karl Dykhuis .15 .40
689 Jeff Nelson RC .15 .40
690 Jassen Cullimore RC .12 .30
691 Turner Stevenson .12 .30
692 Scott Lachance RC .20 .50
693 Mike Dunham RC .20 .50
694 Brent Bilodeau RC .15 .40
695 Ryan Sittler RC .15 .40
696 Peter Ferraro RC .15 .40
697 Pat Peake RC .15 .40
698 Keith Tkachuk RC .10 .25
699 Brian Rolston RC .20 .50
700 Checklist 601-700 .05 .05
SP1 Gretzky/Hull/Kamensky 1.25 3.00

1991-92 Upper Deck French

COMPLETE SET (700) 20.00 40.00
COMPLETE LO SET (500) 15.00 30.00
COMPLETE HI SET (200) 5.00 12.00
COMPLETE HI FACT.SET (200) 5.00 12.00
*FRENCH VERSION: SAME VALUE

1991-92 Upper Deck Award Winner Holograms

COMPLETE SET (9) 5.00 12.00
AW1 Wayne Gretzky 1.00 2.50
AW2 Ed Belfour .40 1.00
AW3 Brett Hull .40 1.00
AW4 Ed Belfour .40 1.00
AW5A Ray Bourque ERR .40 1.00
AW5B Ray Bourque COR .40 1.00
AW6 Wayne Gretzky 1.00 2.50
AW7 Ed Belfour .40 1.00
AW8 Dirk Graham .30 .75
AW9 Mario Lemieux .75 2:00

1991-92 Upper Deck Box Bottoms

COMPLETE SET (5) 2.00 5.00
1 Wayne Gretzky .75 2.00
2 Brett Hull .25 .60
3 Mark Messier .25 .60
4 Mark Messier .40 1.00
5 Steve Yzerman
Detroit R .60 1.50

1991-92 Upper Deck Brett Hull Heroes

COMPLETE SET (10) 6.00 15.00
COMMON HULL HEROES (1-9) .40 1.00
*FRENCH: .4X TO 1X BASIC INSERTS
9AU Brett Hull AU/2500 100.00 200.00
NNO Hull Header SP 2.00 5.00

1991-92 Upper Deck Czech World Juniors

COMPLETE SET (100) 12.00 30.00
1 Description Card .05 .15
2 Vladislav Boulin .05 .15
3 Ravil Gusmanov .05 .15
4 Denis Vinokurov .05 .15
5 Mikhail Volkov .05 .15
6 Alexei Troschinsky .05 .15
7 Andrei Nikolishin .20 .50
8 Alexander Sverztov .05 .15
9 Artem Kopot .05 .15
10 Ildar Mukhometov .05 .15
11 Darius Kasparaitis .20 .50
12 Alexei Yashin .30 .75
13 Nikolai Khabibulin .60 1.50
14 Denis Metlyuk .05 .15
15 Konstantin Korotkov .05 .15
16 Alexei Kovalev .60 1.50
17 Alexander Kuzminsky .05 .15
18 Alexander Cherbayev .05 .15
19 Sergei Krivokrasov .20 .50
20 Sergei Zholtok .20 .50
21 Alexei Zhitnik .30 .75
22 Sandis Ozolinsh .30 .75
23 Boris Mironov .30 .75
24 Pauli Jaks .05 .15
25 Gaetan Voisard .05 .15
26 Nicola Celio .05 .15
27 Marc Weber .05 .15
28 Bernhard Schumperli .05 .15
29 Laurent Bucher .05 .15
30 Michael Blaha .05 .15
31 Tiziano Gianini .05 .15
32 Tero Lehtera .05 .15
33 Mikko Luovi .05 .15
34 Marko Kiprusoff .05 .15
35 Janne Gronvall .05 .15
36 Juha Ylonen .20 .50
37 Sami Kapanen .20 .50
38 Marko Tuomainen .05 .15
39 Jarkko Varvio .05 .15
40 Tuomas Gronman .05 .15
41 Andreas Naumann .05 .15
42 Steffen Ziesche .05 .15
43 Jens Schwabe .05 .15
44 Thomas Schubert .05 .15
45 Hans-Jorg Mayer .05 .15
46 Marc Seliger .20 .50
47 Ryan Hughes .05 .15
48 Richard Matvichuk .20 .50
49 David St. Pierre .05 .15
50 Paul Kariya 2.00 5.00
51 Patrick Poulin .20 .50
52 Mike Fountain .20 .50
53 Scott Niedermayer .20 .50
54 John Slaney .05 .15
55 Brad Bombardir .05 .15
56 Andy Schneider .05 .15
57 Steve Junker .05 .15
58 Trevor Kidd .40 1.00
59 Martin Lapointe .40 1.00
60 Tyler Wright .20 .50
61 Kimbi Daniels .05 .15
62 Karl Dykhuis .20 .50
63 Jeff Nelson .05 .15
64 Jassen Cullimore .05 .15
65 Turner Stevenson .20 .50
66 Brian Mueller .05 .15
67 Chris Tucker .05 .15
68 Marty Schriner .05 .15
69 Mike Prendergast .05 .15
70 John Lilley .05 .15
71 Jim Campbell .20 .50
72 Brian Holzinger .20 .50
73 Steve Konowalchuk .20 .50
74 Chris Ferraro .05 .15
75 Chris Imes .05 .15
76 Rich Brennan .05 .15
77 Todd Hall .05 .15
78 Brian Rafalski .20 .50
79 Scott Lachance .20 .50
80 Mike Dunham .40 1.00
81 Brent Bilodeau .05 .15
82 Ryan Sittler .05 .15
83 Peter Ferraro .05 .15
84 Pat Peake .05 .15
85 Keith Tkachuk .75 2.00
86 Brian Rolston .40 1.00
87 Milan Hnilicka .20 .50
88 Roman Hamrlik .20 .50
89 Milan Nedoma .05 .15
90 Patrik Luza .05 .15
91 Jan Caloun .20 .50
92 Viktor Ujcik .05 .15
93 Robert Petrovicky .20 .50
94 Roman Meluzin .05 .15
95 Jan Vopat .05 .15
96 Martin Prochazka .20 .50
97 Zigmund Palffy .50 1.25
98 Ivan Droppa .05 .15
99 Martin Straka .20 .50
100 Checklist 1-100 .05 .15
NNO W.Gretzky Hologram 1.50 4.00
NNO W.Gretzky Hologram 1.50 4.00

1991-92 Upper Deck Euro-Stars

COMPLETE SET (18) 5.00 12.00
*FRENCH: .4X TO 1X BASIC INSERTS
E1 Jarmo Kekalainen .08 .25
E2 Alexander Mogilny .30 .75
E3 Bobby Holik .20 .50
E4 Anatoli Semenov .08 .25
E5 Petr Nedved .20 .50
E6 Jaromir Jagr .60 1.50
E7 Tomas Sandstrom .20 .50
E8 Robert Kron .08 .25
E9 Sergei Fedorov .60 1.50
E10 Esa Tikkanen .20 .50
E11 Christian Ruuttu .08 .25
E12 Peter Bondra .30 .75
E13 Mats Sundin .50 1.25
E14 Dominik Hasek 1.25 3.00
E15 Johan Garpenlov .08 .25
E16 Alexander Godynyuk .08 .25
E17 Ulf Samuelsson .08 .25
E18 Igor Larionov .20 .50

1991-92 Upper Deck Sheets

COMPLETE SET (19) 90.00 225.00
1 Los Angeles Kings 6.00 15.00
2 New York Rangers 4.00 10.00
3 St. Louis Blues 4.00 10.00
4 New Jersey Devils 4.00 10.00
5 Calgary Flames 5.00 12.00
6 New York Rangers 4.00 10.00
7 Philadelphia Flyers 4.00 10.00
8 Campbell All-Stars 10.00 25.00
9 Wales All-Stars 10.00 25.00
10 Detroit Red Wings 5.00 12.00
11 Washington Capitals 4.00 10.00
12 Minnesota North Stars 8.00 20.00
13 Pittsburgh Penguins 8.00 20.00
14 New York Rangers 4.00 10.00
15 Edmonton Oilers 5.00 12.00
16 Minnesota North Stars 8.00 20.00
17 Calgary Flames 5.00 12.00
18 Detroit Red Wings 4.00 10.00
19 Philadelphia Flyers 4.00 10.00

1992-93 Upper Deck

1 Andy Moog TC .10 .25
2 Donald Audette TC .07 .20
3 Tomas Forslund TC .05 .15
4 Steve Larmer TC .05 .15
5 Tim Cheveldae TC .05 .15
6 Vincent Damphousse TC .07 .20
7 Pat Verbeek TC .05 .15
8 Luc Robitaille TC .10 .25
9 Mike Modano TC .25 .60
10 Denis Savard TC .10 .25
11 Kevin Todd TC .05 .15
12 Ray Ferraro TC .05 .15
13 Tony Amonte TC .05 .15
14 Peter Sidorkiewicz TC .05 .15
15 Rod Brind'Amour TC .05 .15
16 Jaromir Jagr TC .20 .50
17 Owen Nolan TC .10 .25
18 Nelson Emerson TC .05 .15
19 Pat Falloon TC .05 .15
20 Anatoli Semenov TC .05 .15
21 Doug Gilmour TC .12 .30
22 Kirk McLean TC .05 .15
23 Don Beaupre TC .07 .20
24 Phil Housley TC .07 .20
25 Wayne Gretzky .60 1.50
26 Mario Lemieux .40 1.00
27 Valeri Kamensky .05 .15
28 Jaromir Jagr .20 .50
29 Brett Hull .20 .50
30 Neil Wilkinson .05 .15
31 Dominic Roussel .07 .20
32 Kent Manderville .05 .15
33 Wayne Gretzky 1500 .60 1.50
34 Presidents Trophy
Rangers .20 .50
35 Miller Bros. .05 .15
36 Sakic Bros. .20 .50
37 Gretkzy Bros. .60 1.50
38 Linden Bros. .10 .25
39 Courtnall Bros. .05 .15
40 Dale Craigwell .05 .15
41 Peter Ahola .05 .15
42 Robert Reichel .05 .15
43 Chris Terreri .07 .20
44 John Vanbiesbrouck .10 .25
45 Alexander Semak .05 .15
46 Mike Sullivan .05 .15
47 Bob Sweeney .05 .15
48 Corey Millen .05 .15
49 Murray Craven .05 .15
50 Dennis Vaske .05 .15
51 David Williams RC .05 .15
52 Tom Fitzgerald .05 .15
53 Corey Foster .05 .15
54 Al Iafrate .07 .20
55 John LeClair .10 .25
56 Stephane Richer .07 .20
57 Claude Boivin .05 .15
58 Rick Tabaracci .05 .15
59 Johan Garpenlov .05 .15
60 Checklist 1-110 .05 .15
61 Steve Leach .05 .15
62 Trent Klatt RC .07 .20
63 Darryl Sydor .05 .15
64 Brian Glynn .05 .15
65 Mike Craig .05 .15
66 Gary Leeman .05 .15
67 Jim Waite .07 .20
68 Jason Marshall .05 .15
69 Robert Kron .05 .15
70 Yanic Perreault RC .25 .60
71 Daniel Marois .05 .15
72 Mark Osborne .05 .15
73 Mark Tinordi .05 .15
74 Brad May .05 .15
75 Kimbi Daniels .05 .15
76 Kay Whitmore .07 .20
77 Luciano Borsato .05 .15
78 Kris King .05 .15
79 Felix Potvin .20 .50
80 Benoit Brunet .05 .15
81 Shawn Antoski .05 .15
82 Randy Gilhen .05 .15
83 Dmitri Mironov .05 .15
84 Dave Manson .05 .15
85 Sergio Momesso .05 .15
86 Cam Neely .10 .25
87 Mike Krushelnyski .05 .15
88 Eric Lindros SP .15 .40
89 Wendel Clark .15 .40
90 Enrico Ciccone .05 .15
91 Jarrod Skalde .05 .15
92 Dominik Hasek .15 .40
93 Dave McLlwain .05 .15
94 Russ Courtnall .05 .15
95 Tim Sweeney .05 .15
96 Alexei Kasatonov .05 .15
97 Chris Lindberg .05 .15
98 Steven Rice .05 .15
99 Tie Domi .07 .20
100 Paul Stanton .05 .15
101 Brad Schlegel .05 .15
102 David Bruce .05 .15
103 Mikael Andersson .05 .15
104 Shawn Chambers .05 .15
105 Rob Ramage .05 .15
106 Joe Reekie .05 .15
107 Sylvain Turgeon .05 .15
108 Rob Murphy .05 .15
109 Brad Shaw .05 .15
110 Darren Rumble RC .05 .15
111 Kyosti Karjalainen .05 .15
112 Mike Vernon .07 .20
113 Michel Goulet .07 .20
114 Garry Valk .05 .15
115 Peter Bondra .10 .25
116 Paul Coffey .10 .25
117 Brian Noonan .05 .15
118 John McIntyre .05 .15
119 Scott Mellanby .05 .15
120 Jim Sandlak .05 .15
121 Mats Sundin .10 .25
122 Brendan Shanahan .10 .25
123 Kelly Buchberger .05 .15
124 Doug Smail .05 .15
125 Craig Janney .07 .20
126 Mike Gartner .12 .30
127 Alexei Gusarov .05 .15
128 Joe Nieuwendyk .07 .20
129 Troy Murray .05 .15
130 Jamie Baker .05 .15
131 Dale Hunter .07 .20
132 Darrin Shannon .05 .15
133 Adam Oates .10 .25
134 Trevor Kidd .07 .20
135 Steve Larmer .05 .15
136 Fredrik Olausson .05 .15
137 Jyrki Lumme .05 .15
138 Tony Amonte .07 .20
139 Calle Johansson .05 .15
140 Rob Blake .07 .20
141 Phil Bourque .05 .15
142 Yves Racine .05 .15
143 Rich Sutter .05 .15
144 Joe Mullen .07 .20
145 Mike Richter .10 .25
146 Pat MacLeod .05 .15
147 Claude Lapointe .05 .15
148 Paul Broten .05 .15
149 Patrick Roy .25 .60
150 Doug Wilson .07 .20
151 Jim Hrivnak .07 .20
152 Joe Murphy .05 .15
153 Randy Burridge .05 .15
154 Thomas Steen .05 .15
155 Steve Yzerman .25 .60
156 Pavel Bure .10 .25
157 Sergei Fedorov .15 .40
158 Trevor Linden .10 .25
159 Chris Chelios .10 .25
160 Cliff Ronning .05 .15
161 Jeff Beukeboom .05 .15
162 Denis Savard .10 .25
163 Claude Lemieux .05 .15
164 Mike Keane .05 .15
165 Pat LaFontaine .10 .25
166 Nelson Emerson .05 .15
167 Alexander Mogilny .07 .20
168 Jamie Leach .05 .15
169 Darren Turcotte .05 .15
170 Checklist 111-220 .05 .15
171 Steve Thomas .07 .20
172 Brian Bellows .07 .20
173 Mike Ridley .05 .15
174 Dave Gagner .07 .20
175 Pierre Turgeon .07 .20
176 Paul Ysebaert .05 .15
177 Brian Propp .05 .15
178 Nicklas Lidstrom .07 .20
179 Kelly Miller .05 .15
180 Kirk Muller .05 .15
181 Bob Bassen .05 .15
182 Tony Tanti .05 .15
183 Mikhail Tatarinov .05 .15
184 Ron Sutter .05 .15
185 Tony Granato .05 .15
186 Curtis Joseph .12 .30
187 Uwe Krupp .05 .15
188 Esa Tikkanen .05 .15
189 Ulf Samuelsson .05 .15
190 Jon Casey .05 .15
191 Derek King .05 .15
192 Greg Adams .05 .15
193 Ray Ferraro .05 .15
194 Dave Christian .05 .15
195 Eric Weinrich .05 .15
196 Josef Beranek .05 .15
197 Tim Cheveldae .05 .15
198 Kevin Hatcher .05 .15
199 Brent Sutter .05 .15
200 Bruce Driver .05 .15
201 Tom Draper .05 .15
202 Ted Donato .05 .15
203 Ed Belfour .10 .25
204 Pat Verbeek .05 .15
205 John Druce .05 .15
206 Neal Broten .07 .20
207 Doug Bodger .05 .15
208 Troy Loney .05 .15
209 Mark Pederson .05 .15
210 Todd Elik .05 .15
211 Ed Olczyk .05 .15
212 Paul Cavallini .05 .15
213 Stephan Lebeau .05 .15
214 Dave Ellett .05 .15
215 Doug Gilmour .12 .30
216 Luc Robitaille .10 .25
217 Bob Essensa .07 .20
218 Jari Kurri .10 .25
219 Dimitri Khristich .05 .15
220 Joel Otto .05 .15
221 Checklist 221-280 .05 .15
222 Jonas Hoglund RC .10 .25
223 Rolf Wanhainen RC .05 .15
224 Stefan Klockare RC .05 .15
225 Johan Norgren RC .05 .15
226 Roger Kyro RC .05 .15
227 Niklas Sundblad RC .05 .15
228 Calle Carlsson RC .05 .15
229 Jakob Karlsson RC .05 .15
230 Fredrik Jax RC .05 .15
231 Bjorn Nord RC .05 .15
232 Kristian Gahn RC .05 .15
233 Mikael Renberg RC .25 .60
234 Markus Naslund RC 1.00 2.50
235 Peter Forsberg .20 .50
236 Michael Nylander RC .05 .15
237 Stanley Cup Centennial .05 .15
238 Rick Tocchet .07 .20
239 Igor Kravchuk .05 .15
240 Geoff Courtnall .05 .15
241 Larry Murphy .07 .20
242 Mark Messier .20 .50
243 Tom Barrasso .07 .20
244 Glen Wesley .05 .15
245 Randy Wood .05 .15
246 Gerard Gallant .05 .15
247 Kip Miller .05 .15
248 Bob Probert .10 .25
249 Gary Suter .05 .15
250 Ulf Dahlen .05 .15
251 Dan Lambert .05 .15
252 Bobby Holik .07 .20
253 Jimmy Carson .05 .15
254 Ken Hodge Jr. .05 .15
255 Joe Sakic .20 .50
256 Kevin Dineen .05 .15
257 Al MacInnis .12 .30
258 Vladimir Ruzicka .05 .15
259 Ken Daneyko .05 .15
260 Guy Carbonneau .07 .20
261 Michal Pivonka .05 .15
262 Bill Ranford .07 .20
263 Petr Nedved .07 .20
264 Rod Brind'Amour .05 .15
265 Ray Bourque .15 .40
266 Joe Sacco .05 .15
267 Vladimir Konstantinov .10 .25
268 Eric Desjardins .07 .20
269 Dave Andreychuk .10 .25
270 Kelly Hrudey .07 .20
271 Grant Fuhr .15 .40
272 Dirk Graham .05 .15
273 Frank Pietrangelo .07 .20
274 Jeremy Roenick .15 .40
275 Kevin Stevens .07 .20
276 Phil Housley .07 .20
277 Patrice Brisebois .05 .15
278 Slava Fetisov .05 .15
279 Doug Weight .20 .50
280 Checklist 281-330 .05 .15
281 Dean Evason .05 .15
282 Martin Gelinas .05 .15
283 Philippe Bozon .05 .15
284 Brian Leetch .07 .20
285 Theo Fleury .15 .40
286 Pat Falloon .05 .15
287 Derian Hatcher .05 .15
288 Andrew Cassels .05 .15
289 Gary Roberts .05 .15
290 Bernie Nicholls .07 .20
291 Ron Francis .12 .30
292 Tom Kurvers .05 .15
293 Geoff Sanderson .07 .20
294 Slava Kozlov .07 .20
295 Valeri Zelepukin .05 .15
296 Ray Sheppard .05 .15
297 Scott Stevens .10 .25
298 Sergei Nemchinov .05 .15
299 Kirk McLean .05 .15
300 Igor Ulanov .05 .15
301 Brian Benning .05 .15
302 Dale Hawerchuk .12 .30
303 Kevin Todd .05 .15
304 John Cullen .05 .15
305 Mike Modano .25 .60
306 Donald Audette .07 .20
307 Vincent Damphousse .07 .20
308 Jeff Hackett .07 .20
309 Craig Simpson .05 .15
310 Don Beaupre .07 .20
311 Adam Creighton .05 .15
312 Pat Elynuik .05 .15
313 David Volek .05 .15
314 Sergei Makarov .05 .15
315 Craig Billington .07 .20
316 Zarley Zalapski .05 .15
317 Brian Mullen .05 .15
318 Rob Pearson .05 .15
319 Garry Galley .05 .15
320 James Patrick .05 .15
321 Owen Nolan .10 .25
322 Marty McSorley .07 .20
323 James Black .05 .15
324 Jacques Cloutier .07 .20
325 Benoit Hogue .05 .15
326 Teppo Numminen .05 .15
327 Mark Recchi .12 .30
328 Paul Ranheim .05 .15
329 Andy Moog .10 .25
330 Shayne Corson .07 .20
331 J.J. Daigneault .05 .15
332 Mark Fitzpatrick .07 .20
333 Moscow Dynamo CL .05 .15
334 Alexei Yashin RS .07 .20
335 Darius Kasparaitis RS .05 .15
336 Alexander Yudin RS RC .05 .15
337 Sergei Bautin RS RC .05 .15
338 Igor Korolev RS RC .05 .15
339 Sergei Klimovich RS RC .07 .20
340 Andrei Nikolishin RS RC .05 .15
341 Vitali Karamnov RS RC .05 .15
342 Alex Andriyevski RS RC .05 .15
343 Sergei Sorokin RS RC .05 .15
344 Yan Kaminsky RS RC .05 .15
345 Andrei Trefilov RS RC .05 .15
346 Sergei Petrenko RS RC .05 .15
347 Ravil Khaidarov RS RC .05 .15
348 Dmitri Frolov RS .05 .15
349 Ravil Yakubov RS RC .05 .15
350 Dimitri Yushkevich RS RC .05 .15
351 Alex Karpovtsev RS RC .07 .20
352 Igor Dorofeyev RS RC .05 .15
353 Alex Galchenyuk RS RC .05 .15
354 Joe Juneau RR .05 .15
355 Pat Falloon RR .05 .15
356 Gilbert Dionne RR .05 .15
357 Vladimir Konstantinov RR .10 .25
358 Rick Tabaracci RR .05 .15
359 Tony Amonte RR .05 .15
360 Scott Lachance RR .05 .15
361 Tom Draper RR .05 .15
362 Pavel Bure RR .07 .20
363 Nicklas Lidstrom RR .07 .20
364 Keith Tkachuk RR .10 .25
365 Kevin Todd RR .05 .15
366 Dominik Hasek RR .15 .40
367 Igor Kravchuk RR .05 .15
368 Shawn McEachern RR .05 .15
369 Blomsten/Forsberg CL .20 .50
370 Dieter Hegen RC .05 .15
371 Stefan Ustorf RC .05 .15
372 Ernst Kopf RC .05 .15
373 Raimond Hilger RC .05 .15
374 Mats Sundin .10 .25
375 Peter Forsberg .20 .50
376 Arto Blomsten RC .05 .15
377 Tommy Soderstrom RC .07 .20
378 Michael Nylander RC .05 .15
379 David Jensen RC .05 .15
380 Chris Winnes .05 .15
381 Ray LeBlanc .07 .20
382 Joe Sacco .05 .15
383 Dennis Vaske .05 .15
384 Jorg Eberle RC .05 .15
385 Trevor Kidd .07 .20
386 Pat Falloon .05 .15
387 Rob Brown .05 .15
388 Adam Graves .05 .15
389 Peter Zezel .05 .15
390 Checklist 391-440 .05 .15
391 Don Sweeney .05 .15
392 Sean Hill RC .05 .15
393 Ted Donato .05 .15
394 Marty McInnis .05 .15
395 C.J. Young RC .05 .15
396 Ted Drury RC .05 .15
397 Scott Young .05 .15
398 S.Lachance/K.Tkachuk CL .10 .25
399 Joe Juneau SR .05 .15
400 Steve Heinze SR .05 .15
401 Glen Murray SR .07 .20
402 Keith Carney SR RC .20 .50
403 Dean McAmmond SR RC .05 .15
404 Karl Dykhuis SR .05 .15
405 Martin Lapointe SR .05 .15
406 Scott Niedermayer SR .10 .25
407 Ray Whitney SR RC .15 .40
408 Martin Brodeur SR .25 .60
409 Scott Lachance SR .05 .15
410 Marty McInnis SR .05 .15
411 Bill Guerin SR RC .20 .50
412 Shawn McEachern SR .05 .15
413 Denny Felsner SR RC .07 .20
414 Bret Hedican SR RC .07 .20
415 Drake Berehowsky SR .05 .15
416 Patrick Poulin SR .05 .15
417 Vladimir Vujtek SR RC .05 .15
418 Steve Konowalchuk SR RC .07 .20
419 Keith Tkachuk SR .10 .25
420 Evgeny Davydov SR .05 .15
421 Yanick Dupre SR .05 .15
422 Jason Woolley RC .05 .15
423 B.Hull/W.Gretzky .60 1.50
424 Tomas Sandstrom .07 .20
425 Craig MacTavish .05 .15
426 Stu Barnes .05 .15
427 Gilbert Dionne .05 .15
428 Andrei Lomakin .05 .15
429 Tomas Forslund .05 .15
430 Andre Racicot .07 .20
431 Pavel Bure AW .10 .25
432 Mark Messier AW .20 .50
433 Mario Lemieux AW .40 1.00
434 Brian Leetch AW .07 .20
435 Wayne Gretzky AW .60 1.50
436 Mario Lemieux AW .40 1.00
437 Mark Messier AW .07 .20
438 Patrick Roy AW .25 .60
439 Guy Carbonneau AW .07 .20
440 Patrick Roy AW .25 .60
441 Russ Courtnall .05 .15
442 Jeff Reese .05 .15
443 Brent Fedyk .05 .15
444 Kerry Huffman .05 .15
445 Mark Freer .05 .15
446 Christian Ruuttu .05 .15
447 Nick Kypreos .05 .15
448 Mike Hurlbut RC .05 .15
449 Bob Sweeney .05 .15
450 Checklist 491-540 .05 .15
451 Perry Berezan .05 .15
452 Phil Bourque .05 .15
453 Messier/Amonte/Graves LL .20 .50
454 Lemieux/Stev/Tocch LL .40 1.00
455 Oates/Juneau/Kvartal LL .10 .25
456 LaFont/Andrey/Mogil LL .10 .25
457 Zdeno Ciger .05 .15
458 Pat Jablonski .07 .20
459 Brent Gilchrist .05 .15
460 Yvon Corriveau .05 .15
461 Dino Ciccarelli .07 .20
462 David Emma .05 .15
463 Corey Hirsch RC .10 .25
464 Jamie Baker .05 .15
465 John Cullen .05 .15
466 Lonnie Loach RC .05 .15
467 Louie DeBrusk .05 .15
468 Brian Mullen .05 .15
469 Gaeten Duchesne .05 .15
470 Eric Lindros .15 .40
471 Brian Bellows .07 .20
472 Bill Lindsay RC .05 .15
473 Dave Archibald .05 .15

474 Reggie Savage .05 .15
475 Tommy Soderstrom .07 .20
476 Vincent Damphousse .07 .20
477 Mike Ricci .05 .15
478 Bob Carpenter .07 .20
479 Kevin Haller .05 .15
480 Peter Sidorkiewicz .05 .15
481 Peter Andersson RC .05 .15
482 Kevin Miller .05 .15
483 Jean-Francois Quintin RC .05 .15
484 Philippe Boucher .05 .15
485 Jozef Stumpel .05 .15
486 Vitali Prokhorov RC .05 .15
487 Stan Drulia RC .05 .15
488 Jay More .05 .15
489 Mike Needham RC .05 .15
490 Glenn Mulvenna RC .05 .15
491 Ed Ronan RC .05 .15
492 Grigori Panteleyev RC .05 .15
493 Kevin Dahl RC .05 .15
494 Ryan McGill RC .05 .15
495 Robb Stauber .07 .20
496 Vladimir Vujtek RC .05 .15
497 Tomas Jelinek RC .05 .15
498 Patrik Kjellberg RC .10 .25
499 Sergei Bautin .05 .15
500 Bobby Holik .07 .20
501 Guy Hebert RC .15 .40
502 Chris Kontos RC .05 .15
503 Vyatcheslav Butsayev RC .05 .15
504 Yuri Khymlev RC .05 .15
505 Richard Matvichuk RC .07 .20
506 Dominik Hasek .15 .40
507 Ed Courtenay .05 .15
508 Jeff Daniels .05 .15
509 Doug Zmolek RC .05 .15
510 Vitali Karamnov .05 .15
511 Norm Maciver .05 .15
512 Terry Yake .05 .15
513 Steve Duchesne .05 .15
514 Andrei Trefilov .05 .15
515 Jiri Slegr .05 .15
516 Sergei Zubov RC .15 .40
517 Dave Karpa RC .05 .15
518 Sean Burke .07 .20
519 Adrien Plavsic .05 .15
520 Michael Nylander .05 .15
521 John MacLean .07 .20
522 Jason Ruff RC .05 .15
523 Sean Hill .05 .15
524 Mike Sillinger .05 .15
525 Daniel Laperriere RC .05 .15
526 Peter Ahola .05 .15
527 Guy Larose .05 .15
528 Tommy Sjodin RC .05 .15
529 Rob DiMaio .05 .15
530 Mark Howe .10 .25
531 Greg Paslawski .05 .15
532 Ron Hextall .10 .25
533 Keith Jones RC .10 .25
534 Chris Luongo RC .05 .15
535 Anatoli Semenov .05 .15
536 Stephane Beauregard .07 .20
537 Pat Elynuik .05 .15
538 Mike McPhee .05 .15
539 Jody Hull .05 .15
540 Stephane Matteau .05 .15
541 Shayne Corson .07 .20
542 Mikhail Kravets RC .05 .15
543 Kevin Miehm RC .05 .15
544 Brian Bradley .05 .15
545 Mathieu Schneider .05 .15
546 Steve Chiasson .05 .15
547 Warren Rychel RC .05 .15
548 John Tucker .05 .15
549 Todd Ewen .05 .15
550 Checklist 591-640 .05 .15
551 Petr Klima .05 .15
552 Robert Lang RC .05 .15
553 Eric Weinrich .05 .15
554 Kasparaitis/Malakhov CL .05 .15
555 Roman Hamrlik RC .20 .50
556 Martin Rucinsky YG .05 .15
557 Patrick Poulin YG .05 .15
558 Tyler Wright YG .05 .15
559 Martin Straka YG RC .20 .50
560 Jim Hiller YG RC .05 .15
561 Dmitri Kvartalnov YG RC .05 .15
562 Scott Niedermayer YG .10 .25
563 Darius Kasparaitis YG .05 .15
564 Richard Smehlik RC .05 .15
565 Shawn McEachern YG .05 .15
566 Alexei Zhitnik YG .05 .15
567 Andrei Kovalenko YG RC .15 .40
568 Sandis Ozolinsh YG .05 .15
569 Robert Petrovicky RC .05 .15
570 Dimitri Yushkevich YG .05 .15
571 Scott Lachance YG .05 .15
572 Nikolai Borschevsky YG .05 .15
573 Alexei Kovalev YG .07 .20
574 Teemu Selanne YG .20 .50
575 Steven King RC .05 .15
576 Guy Leveque YG RC .05 .15
577 Vladimir Malakhov YG .05 .15
578 Alexei Zhamnov YG .07 .20
579 Viktor Gordiouk YG RC .05 .15
580 Dixon Ward YG RC .07 .20
581 Igor Korolev YG .05 .15
582 Sergei Krivokrasov YG .05 .15
583 Rob Zamuner RC .07 .20
584 Aucoin/Lapnte/Wright CL .05 .15
585 Manny Legace RC .10 .25
586 Paul Kariya RC 2.50 6.00
587 Alexandre Daigle RC .10 .25
588 Nathan Lafeyette RC .07 .20
589 Mike Rathje RC .05 .15
590 Chris Gratton RC .10 .25
591 Chris Pronger RC 2.00 5.00
592 Brent Tully RC .05 .15
593 Rob Niedermayer RC .10 .25
594 Darcy Werenka RC .05 .15
595 Peter Forsberg .20 .50
596 Kenny Jonsson RC .10 .25
597 Niklas Sundstrom RC .10 .25
598 Reine Rauhala RC .05 .15
599 Daniel Johansson RC .05 .15
600 David Vyborny RC .10 .25
601 Jan Vopat RC .07 .20
602 Pavol Demitra RC .20 .50
603 Michal Cerny RC .05 .15
604 Ondrej Steiner RC .05 .15
605 Jim Campbell RC .07 .20
606 Todd Marchant RC .07 .20
607 Mike Pomichter RC .07 .20
608 John Emmons RC .05 .15
609 Adam Deadmarsh RC .10 .25
610 Nikolai Semin RC .05 .15
611 Igor Alexandrov RC .05 .15
612 Vadim Sharifjanov RC .10 .25
613 Viktor Kozlov RC .10 .25
614 Nikolai Tsulygin RC .05 .15
615 Jere Lehtinen RC .10 .25
616 Ville Peltonen RC .07 .20
617 Saku Koivu RC 1.50 4.00
618 Kimmo Rintanen RC .05 .15
619 Jonni Vauhkonen RC .05 .15
620 Brett Hull PRO .20 .50
621 Wayne Gretzky PRO .60 1.50
622 Jaromir Jagr PRO .20 .50
623 Darius Kasparaitis PRO .05 .15
624 Bernie Nicholls .07 .20
625 Gilbert Dionne .05 .15
626 Ray Bourque .15 .40
627 Mike Ricci .05 .15
628 Phil Housley .07 .20
629 Chris Chelios .10 .25
630 Kevin Stevens PRO .07 .20
631 Roman Hamrlik PRO .20 .50
632 Sergei Fedorov PRO .15 .40
633 Alexei Kovalev PRO .07 .20
634 Shawn McEachern PRO .05 .15
635 Tony Amonte PRO .05 .15
636 Brian Bellows .07 .20
637 Adam Oates .10 .25
638 Denis Savard .10 .25
639 Doug Gilmour PRO .12 .30
640 Brian Leetch PRO .07 .20
SP2 Pavel Bure ART .10 .25
SP3 World Jr.Gold Medal .30 .75

1992-93 Upper Deck All-Rookie Team

COMPLETE SET (7) 6.00 15.00
AR1 Tony Amonte .40 1.00
AR2 Gilbert Dionne .40 1.00
AR3 Kevin Todd .40 1.00
AR4 Nicklas Lidstrom 2.00 5.00
AR5 Vladimir Konstantinov 2.00 5.00
AR6 Dominik Hasek 2.00 5.00
AR7 Team
Photo Checklist .75 2.00

1992-93 Upper Deck All-World Team

COMPLETE SET (6) 8.00 20.00
W1 Wayne Gretzky 4.00 10.00
W2 Brett Hull 1.00 2.50
W3 Jaromir Jagr 1.00 2.50
W4 Nicklas Lidstrom .60 1.50
W5 Vladimir Konstantinov .60 1.50
W6 Patrick Roy 3.00 8.00

1992-93 Upper Deck Ameri/Can Holograms

COMPLETE SET (6) 2.00 5.00
AC1 Joe Juneau .30 .75
AC2 Keith Tkachuk .50 1.25
AC3 Steve Heinze .30 .75
AC4 Scott Lachance .30 .75
AC5 Scott Niedermayer .30 .75
AC6 Dominic Roussel .40 1.00

1992-93 Upper Deck Calder Candidates

COMPLETE SET (20) 10.00 25.00
CC1 Dixon Ward .40 1.00
CC2 Igor Korolev .40 1.00
CC3 Felix Potvin 1.50 4.00
CC4 Rob Zamuner .40 1.00
CC5 Scott Niedermayer .75 2.00
CC6 Eric Lindros 2.00 5.00
CC7 Alexei Zhitnik .40 1.00
CC8 Roman Hamrlik .40 1.00
CC9 Joe Juneau 1.00 2.50
CC10 Teemu Selanne 2.00 5.00
CC11 Alexei Kovalev .75 2.00
CC12 Vladimir Malakhov .40 1.00
CC13 Darius Kasparaitis .40 1.00
CC14 Shawn McEachern .40 1.00
CC15 Keith Tkachuk 1.50 4.00
CC16 Scott Lachance .40 1.00
CC17 Andrei Kovalenko .40 1.00
CC18 Patrick Poulin .40 1.00
CC19 Evgeny Davydov .40 1.00
CC20 Dimitri Yushkevich .40 1.00

1992-93 Upper Deck Euro-Rookie Team

COMPLETE SET (6) 4.00 10.00
ERT1 Pavel Bure .75 2.00
ERT2 Nicklas Lidstrom 1.00 2.50
ERT3 Dominik Hasek 2.00 5.00
ERT4 Peter Ahola .20 .50
ERT5 Alexander Semak .20 .50
ERT6 Tomas Forslund .20 .50

1992-93 Upper Deck Euro-Rookies

COMPLETE SET (20) 4.00 10.00
ER1 Richard Smehlik .20 .50
ER2 Michael Nylander .30 .75
ER3 Igor Korolev .20 .50
ER4 Robert Lang .20 .50
ER5 Sergei Krivokrasov .20 .50
ER6 Teemu Selanne .75 2.00
ER7 Darius Kasparaitis .20 .50
ER8 Alexei Zhamnov .30 .75
ER9 Jiri Slegr .20 .50
ER10 Alexei Kovalev .60 1.50
ER11 Roman Hamrlik .40 1.00
ER12 Dimitri Yushkevich .20 .50
ER13 Alexei Zhitnik .20 .50
ER14 Andrei Kovalenko .20 .50
ER15 Vladimir Malakhov .20 .50
ER16 Sandis Ozolinsh .40 1.00
ER17 Evgeny Davydov .20 .50
ER18 Victor Gordijuk .20 .50
ER19 Martin Straka .30 .75
ER20 Robert Petrovicky .20 .50

1992-93 Upper Deck Euro-Stars

COMPLETE SET (20) 4.00 10.00
E1 Sergei Fedorov .75 2.00
E2 Pavel Bure .40 1.00
E3 Dominik Hasek 1.00 2.50
E4 Vladimir Ruzicka .20 .50
E5 Peter Ahola .20 .50
E6 Kyosti Karjalainen .20 .50
E7 Igor Kravchuk .20 .50
E8 Evgeny Davydov .20 .50
E9 Nicklas Lidstrom .40 1.00
E10 Vlad. Konstantinov .40 1.00
E11 Josef Beranek .20 .50
E12 Valeri Zelepukin .20 .50
E13 Sergei Nemchinov .20 .50
E14 Jaromir Jagr 1.00 2.50
E15 Igor Ulanov .20 .50
E16 Sergei Makarov .20 .50
E17 Andrei Lomakin .20 .50
E18 Mats Sundin .40 1.00
E19 Jarmo Myllys .20 .50
E20 Valeri Kamensky .20 .50

1992-93 Upper Deck Gordie Howe Heroes

COMPLETE SET (10) 8.00 20.00
COMMON HOWE (19-27) 1.00 2.50
NNO G.Howe Header SP 1.00 3.00

1992-93 Upper Deck Gordie Howe Selects

COMPLETE SET (20) 10.00 25.00
G1 Brian Bellows .15 .40
G2 Luc Robitaille .30 .75
G3 Pat LaFontaine .60 1.50
G4 Kevin Stevens .15 .40
G5 Wayne Gretzky 3.00 8.00
G6 Steve Larmer .30 .75
G7 Brett Hull 1.25 3.00
G8 Jeremy Roenick 1.00 2.50
G9 Mario Lemieux 3.00 8.00
G10 Steve Yzerman 3.00 8.00
G11 Joe Juneau .15 .40
G12 Vladimir Malakhov .15 .40
G13 Alexei Kovalev .30 .75
G14 Eric Lindros .75 2.00
G15 Teemu Selanne 1.50 4.00
G16 Patrick Poulin .15 .40
G17 Shawn McEachern .15 .40
G18 Keith Tkachuk .75 2.00
G19 Andrei Kovalenko .15 .40
G20 Ted Donato .15 .40

1992-93 Upper Deck Sheets

COMPLETE SET (17) 60.00 150.00
1 1991-92 All-Rookie Team/17,000
June 1992
Gilbert Dionne
Kevin Todd
Vladimir Konstantinov
Tony Amonte
Nicklas Lidstrom
Dominik Hasek 4.00 10.00
2 New York Rangers/18,000
Defending Season Champs
Peter Andersson
Phil Bourque
Joe Kocur
Doug Weight
Randy Gilhen
John Vanbiesbrouck
Adam Graves
Mark Messier 4.00 10.00
3 Gordie Howe 65th Birthday
Celebration Tour
(Nine Howe Hockey Heroes cards) 4.00 10.00
4 Gordie Howe Birthday
(Hamilton McDonald's) 4.00 10.00
5 Wayne Gretzky
Heroes Mail-In 6.00 15.00
6 New York Rangers/18,000
Quebec Nordiques, Oct. 29, 1992
Paul Broten
Mike Richter
Sergei Nemchinov
Tie Domi
Kris King
Jeff Beukeboom
Brian Leetch Norris
Tony Amonte 2.00 5.00
7 Los Angeles Kings/18,000
Vancouver Canucks, Nov. 12, 1992
Luc Robitaille
Paul Coffey
Tony Granato
Rob Blake
Tomas Sandstrom
Kelly Hrudey 4.00 10.00
8 Minnesota North Stars/16,500
San Jose Sharks, Nov. 28, 1992 6.00 15.00
9 Edmonton Oilers/18,500
Calgary Flames, Dec. 8, 1992
Brian Glynn
Scott Mellanby
Dave Manson
Craig MacTavish
Bernie Nicholls
Bill Ranford 2.00 5.00
10 Philadelphia Flyers/19,000
Pittsburgh Penguins, Dec. 17, 1992
Kevin Dineen
Mark Recchi
Garry Galley
Dominic Roussel
Brian Benning
Rod Brind'Amour 2.00 5.00
11 Minnesota North Stars/16,500
Tampa Bay Lightning, Jan. 30, 1993
Dave Gagner
Neal Broten
Ulf Dahlen
Todd Elik
Tommy Sjodin
Gaetan Duchesne 6.00 15.00
12 Campbell All-Stars
Montreal Forum, Feb. 6, 1993 4.00 10.00
13 Wales All-Stars
Montreal Forum, Feb. 6, 1993
Patrick Roy
Brian Leetch
Ray Bourque
Kevin Stevens
Mario Lemieux
Jaromir Jagr 4.00 10.00
14 Washington Capitals/17,000
St. Louis Blues, Feb. 21, 1993
Jim Hrivnak
Mike Ridley
Peter Bondra
Dale Hunter
Kelly Miller
Don Beaupre 4.00 10.00
15 Los Angeles Kings/18,000
Ottawa Senators, Mar.4, 1993
Jari Kurri
Corey Millen
Marty McSorley
Darryl Sydor
Wayne Gretzky
Robb Stauber 4.00 10.00
16 Quebec Nordiques/15,000
Hartford Whalers, Mar. 8, 1993 6.00 15.00
17 St.Louis Blues/17,500
Vancouver Canucks, Mar. 30, 1993 2.00 5.00

1992-93 Upper Deck Wayne Gretzky Heroes

COMPLETE SET (10) 10.00 25.00
COMMON GRETZKY (10-18) 2.00 5.00
NNO W.Gretzky Header SP 5.00 10.00

1992-93 Upper Deck World Junior Grads

COMPLETE SET (20) 20.00 50.00
WG1 Scott Niedermayer 1.00 2.50
WG2 Slava Kozlov .50 1.25
WG3 Chris Chelios 1.00 2.50
WG4 Jari Kurri 1.25 3.00
WG5 Pavel Bure 1.50 4.00
WG6 Jaromir Jagr 2.00 5.00
WG7 Steve Yzerman 4.00 10.00
WG8 Joe Sakic 1.50 4.00
WG9 Alexei Kovalev 1.00 2.50
WG10 Wayne Gretzky 6.00 15.00
WG11 Mario Lemieux 4.00 10.00
WG12 Eric Lindros 1.50 4.00
WG13 Pat Falloon 1.00 2.50
WG14 Trevor Linden 1.00 2.50
WG15 Brian Leetch 1.00 2.50
WG16 Sergei Fedorov 2.50 6.00
WG17 Mats Sundin 1.00 2.50
WG18 Alexander Mogilny .75 2.00
WG19 Jeremy Roenick 1.25 3.00
WG20 Luc Robitaille .75 2.00

1993 Upper Deck Locker All-Stars

COMPLETE SET (60) 6.00 15.00
1 Peter Bondra .20 .50
2 Steve Duchesne .01 .05
3 Jaromir Jagr .60 1.50
4 Pat LaFontaine .20 .50
5 Brian Leetch .20 .50
6 Mario Lemieux 1.00 2.50
7 Mark Messier .25 .60
8 Alexander Mogilny .08 .25
9 Kirk Muller .01 .05
10 Adam Oates .08 .25
11 Mark Recchi .08 .25
12 Patrick Roy 1.00 2.50
13 Joe Sakic .40 1.00
14 Kevin Stevens .01 .05
15 Scott Stevens .08 .25
16 Rick Tocchet .01 .05
17 Pierre Turgeon .08 .25
18 Zarley Zalapski .01 .05
19 Ed Belfour .20 .50
20 Brian Bradley .01 .05
21 Pavel Bure .40 1.00
22 Chris Chelios .20 .50
23 Paul Coffey .20 .50
24 Doug Gilmour .20 .50
25 Wayne Gretzky 1.25 3.00
26 Phil Housley .08 .25
27 Brett Hull .25 .60
28 Kelly Kisio .01 .05
29 Jari Kurri .20 .50
30 Dave Manson .01 .05
31 Mike Modano .25 .60
32 Gary Roberts .08 .25
33 Luc Robitaille .08 .25
34 Jeremy Roenick .20 .50
35 Teemu Selanne .40 1.00
36 Steve Yzerman .60 1.50
37 Al Iafrate .08 .25
38 Mike Gartner .08 .25
39 Ray Bourque .25 .60
40 Jon Casey .08 .25
41 Bob Gainey .08 .25
42 Gordie Howe .40 1.00
43 Bobby Hull .30 .75
44 Frank Mahovlich .20 .50
45 Lanny McDonald .08 .25
46 Stan Mikita .15 .40
47 Henri Richard .10 .30
48 Larry Robinson .20 .50
49 Glen Sather .08 .25
50 Bryan Trottier .08 .25
51 Tony Amonte .08 .25
52 Pat Falloon .01 .05
53 Joe Juneau .08 .25
54 Alexei Kovalev .08 .25
55 Dmitri Kvartalnov .01 .05
56 Eric Lindros .50 1.25
57 Vladimir Malakhov .01 .05
58 Felix Potvin .20 .50
59 Mats Sundin .20 .50
60 Alexei Zhamnov .08 .25
AU Gordie Howe AU 60.00 125.00

1993-94 Upper Deck

1 Guy Hebert .07 .20
2 Bob Bassen .05 .15
3 Theo Fleury .05 .15
4 Ray Whitney .05 .15
5 Donald Audette .05 .15
6 Martin Rucinsky .05 .15
7 Lyle Odelein .05 .15
8 John Vanbiesbrouck .10 .25
9 Tim Cheveldae .07 .20
10 Jock Callander .05 .15
11 Nick Kypreos .05 .15
12 Jarrod Skalde .05 .15
13 Gary Shuchuk .05 .15
14 Kris King .05 .15
15 Josef Beranek .05 .15
16 Sean Hill .05 .15
17 Bob Kudelski .05 .15
18 Jiri Slegr .05 .15
19 Dmitri Kvartalnov .05 .15
20 Drake Berehowsky .05 .15
21 Jean-Francois Quintin .05 .15
22 Randy Wood .05 .15
23 Jim McKenzie .05 .15
24 Steven King .05 .15
25 Scott Niedermayer .10 .25
26 Alexander Andrijevski .05 .15
27 Alexei Kovalev .07 .20
28 Steve Konowalchuk .05 .15
29 Vladimir Malakhov .05 .15
30 Eric Lindros .15 .40
31 Mathieu Schneider .05 .15
32 Russ Courtnall .05 .15
33 Ron Sutter .05 .15
34 Radek Hamr RC .10 .25
35 Pavel Bure .10 .25
36 Joe Sacco .05 .15
37 Robert Petrovicky .05 .15
38 Anatoli Fedotov RC .10 .25
39 Pat Falloon .05 .15
40 Martin Straka .05 .15
41 Brad Werenka .05 .15
42 Mike Richter .10 .25
43 Mike McPhee .05 .15
44 Sylvain Turgeon .05 .15
45 Tom Barrasso .07 .20
46 Anatoli Semenov .05 .15
47 Joe Murphy .05 .15
48 Rob Pearson .05 .15
49 Patrick Roy .25 .60
50 Dallas Drake RC .10 .25
51 Mark Messier .20 .50
52 Scott Pellerin RC .10 .25
53 Teppo Numminen .05 .15
54 Chris Kontos .05 .15
55 Richard Matvichuk .05 .15
56 Dale Craigwell .05 .15
57 Mike Eastwood .05 .15
58 Bernie Nicholls .07 .20
59 Travis Green .07 .20
60 Shjon Podein RC .10 .25
61 Darrin Madeley RC .10 .25
62 Dixon Ward .05 .15
63 Andre Faust .05 .15
64 Tony Amonte .07 .20
65 Joe Cirella .05 .15
66 Michel Petit .05 .15
67 David Lowry .05 .15
68 Shawn Chambers .05 .15
69 Joe Sakic .20 .50
70 Michael Nylander .05 .15
71 Peter Andersson .05 .15
72 Sandis Ozolinsh .05 .15
73 Joby Messier RC .10 .25
74 John Blue .07 .20
75 Pat Elynuik .05 .15
76 Keith Osborne RC .10 .25
77 Greg Adams .05 .15
78 Chris Gratton .07 .20
79 Louie DeBrusk .05 .15
80 Todd Harkins RC .10 .25
81 Neil Brady .05 .15
82 Philippe Boucher .05 .15
83 Darryl Sydor .05 .15
84 Oleg Petrov .05 .15
85 Andrei Kovalenko .05 .15
86 Dave Andreychuk .10 .25
87 Jeff Daniels .05 .15
88 Kevin Todd .05 .15
89 Mark Tinordi .05 .15
90 Garry Galley .05 .15
91 Shawn Burr .05 .15
92 Tom Pederson .05 .15
93 Warren Rychel .05 .15
94 Stu Barnes .05 .15
95 Peter Bondra .10 .25
96 Brian Skrudland .05 .15
97 Doug MacDonald RC .10 .25
98 Rob Niedermayer .07 .20
99 Wayne Gretzky .60 1.50
100 Peter Taglianetti .05 .15
101 Don Sweeney .05 .15
102 Andrei Lomakin .05 .15
103 Checklist 1-103 .05 .15
104 Sergio Momesso .05 .15
105 Dave Archibald .05 .15
106 Karl Dykhuis .05 .15
107 Scott Mellanby .07 .20
108 Paul DiPietro .05 .15
109 Neal Broten .07 .20
110 Chris Terreri .07 .20
111 Craig MacTavish .05 .15
112 Jody Hull .05 .15
113 Philippe Bozon .05 .15
114 Geoff Courtnall .05 .15
115 Ed Olcyzk .05 .15
116 Ray Bourque .15 .40
117 Gilbert Dionne .05 .15
118 Valeri Kamensky .07 .20
119 Scott Stevens .10 .25
120 Pelle Eklund .05 .15
121 Brian Bradley .05 .15
122 Steve Thomas .05 .15
123 Don Beaupre .07 .20
124 Joel Otto .05 .15
125 Arturs Irbe .07 .20
126 Kevin Stevens .07 .20
127 Dimitri Yushkevich .05 .15
128 Adam Graves .05 .15
129 Chris Chelios .10 .25
130 Jeff Brown .05 .15
131 Paul Ranheim .05 .15
132 Shayne Corson .07 .20
133 Curtis Leschyshyn .05 .15
134 John MacLean .07 .20
135 Dimitri Khristich .05 .15
136 Dino Ciccarelli .07 .20
137 Pat LaFontaine .10 .25
138 Patrick Poulin .05 .15
139 Jaromir Jagr .30 .75
140 Kevin Hatcher .05 .15
141 Christian Ruuttu .05 .15
142 Ulf Samuelsson .05 .15
143 Ted Donato .05 .15
144 Bob Essensa .07 .20
145 Dave Gagner .07 .20
146 Tony Granato .05 .15
147 Ed Belfour .10 .25
148 Kirk Muller .05 .15
149 Rob Gaudreau RC .10 .25
150 Nicklas Lidstrom .10 .25
151 Gary Roberts .05 .15
152 Trent Klatt .05 .15
153 Ray Ferraro .05 .15
154 Michal Pivonka .05 .15
155 Mike Foligno .05 .15
156 Kirk McLean .07 .20
157 Curtis Joseph .12 .30
158 Roman Hamrlik .05 .15
159 Felix Potvin .20 .50
160 Brett Hull .20 .50
161 Alexei Zhitnik .05 .15
162 Alexei Zhamnov .07 .20
163 Grant Fuhr .15 .40
164 Nikolai Borschevsky .05 .15
165 Tomas Jelinek .05 .15
166 Thomas Steen .05 .15
167 John LeClair .10 .25
168 Vladimir Vujtek .05 .15
169 Richard Smehlik .05 .15
170 Alexandre Daigle .05 .15
171 Sergei Fedorov .15 .40
172 Steve Larmer .07 .20
173 Darius Kasparaitis .05 .15
174 Igor Kravchuk .05 .15
175 Owen Nolan .10 .25
176 Rob DiMaio .05 .15
177 Mike Vernon .07 .20
178 Alexander Semak .05 .15
179 Rick Tocchet .07 .20
180 Bill Ranford .07 .20
181 Sergei Zubov .07 .20
182 Tommy Soderstrom .07 .20
183 Al Iafrate .05 .15
184 Eric Desjardins .07 .20
185 Bret Hedican .05 .15
186 Joe Mullen .07 .20
187 Doug Bodger .05 .15
188 Tomas Sandstrom .05 .15
189 Glen Murray .07 .20
190 Chris Pronger .10 .25
191 Mike Craig .05 .15
192 Jim Paek .05 .15
193 Doug Zmolek .05 .15
194 Yves Racine .05 .15
195 Keith Tkachuk .10 .25
196 Chris Lindberg .05 .15
197 Kelly Buchberger .05 .15
198 Mark Janssens .05 .15
199 Peter Zezel .05 .15
200 Bob Probert .10 .25
201 Brad May .07 .20
202 Rob Zamuner .05 .15
203 Stephane Fiset .07 .20
204 Derian Hatcher .05 .15
205 Mike Gartner .12 .30
206 Checklist 104-206 .05 .05
207 Todd Krygier .05 .15
208 Glen Wesley .05 .15
209 Fredrik Olausson .05 .15
210 Patrick Flatley .05 .15
211 Cliff Ronning .05 .15
212 Kevin Dineen .05 .15
213 Zarley Zalapski .05 .15
214 Stephane Matteau .05 .15
215 Dave Ellett .05 .15
216 Kelly Hrudey .07 .20
217 Steve Duchesne .05 .15
218 Bobby Holik .05 .15
219 Brad Dalgarno .05 .15
220 Mats Sundin 100 CL .10 .25
221 Pat LaFontaine 100 .10 .25
222 Mark Recchi 100 .12 .30
223 Joe Sakic 100 .20 .50
224 Pierre Turgeon 100 .07 .20
225 Craig Janney 100 .07 .20
226 Adam Oates 100 .10 .25
227 Steve Yzerman 100 .25 .60
228 Mats Sundin 100 .10 .25
229 Theo Fleury 100 .05 .15
230 Kevin Stevens 100 .07 .20
231 Luc Robitaille 100 .10 .25
232 Brett Hull 100 .20 .50
233 Rick Tocchet 100 .07 .20
234 Alexander Mogilny 100 .07 .20
235 Jeremy Roenick 100 .15 .40
236 G.Leveque/T.Stevenson .05 .15
237 Adam Bennett SR RC .10 .25
238 Dody Wood SR RC .10 .25
239 Niclas Andersson SR .05 .15
240 Jason Bowen SR RC .10 .25
241 Steve Junker SR RC .10 .25
242 Bryan Smolinski SR .05 .15
243 Chris Simon SR RC .10 .25
244 Sergei Zholtok SR .05 .15
245 Dan Ratushny SR RC .10 .25
246 Guy Leveque SR .05 .15
247 Scott Thomas RC .10 .25
248 Turner Stevenson SR .05 .15
249 Dan Keczmer SR .05 .15
250 Alexandre Daigle WJC CL .05 .15
251 Adrian Aucoin WJC RC .10 .25
252 Jason Smith WJC .05 .15
253 Ralph Intranouvo WJC RC .10 .25
254 Jason Dawe WJC .05 .15
255 Jeff Bes WJC RC .10 .25
256 Tyler Wright WJC .05 .15
257 Martin Lapointe WJC .05 .15
258 Jeff Shantz WJC RC .05 .15
259 Martin Gendron WJC RC .07 .20
260 Philippe DeRouville WJC RC .10 .25
261 Frantisek Kaberle WJC RC .10 .25
262 Radim Bicanek WJC RC .10 .25
263 Tomas Klimt WJC RC .10 .25
264 Tomas Nemcicky WJC RC .10 .25
265 Richard Kapus WJC RC .10 .25
266 Patrik Krisak WJC RC .10 .25
267 Roman Kadera WJC RC .10 .25
268 Kimmo Timonen WJC RC .10 .25
269 Jukka Ollila WJC RC .10 .25
270 Tuomas Gronman WJC .05 .15
271 Mikko Luovi WJC RC .10 .25
272 Sergei Gonchar WJC RC .10 .25
273 Maxim Golanov WJC RC .10 .25
274 Oleg Belov WJC RC .10 .25
275 Sergei Klimovich WJC .10 .25
276 Sergei Brylin WJC RC .10 .25
277 Alexei Yashin WJC .07 .20
278 Vitali Tomilin WJC RC .10 .25
279 Alexander Cherbaev WJC .05 .15
280 Eric Lindros ART .15 .40
281 Teemu Selanne ART .20 .50
282 Joe Juneau ART .05 .15
283 Vladimir Malakhov ART .05 .15
284 Scott Niedermayer ART .10 .25
285 Felix Potvin ART .20 .50
286 Adam Oates TL .10 .25
287 Pat LaFontaine TL .10 .25
288 Theo Fleury TL .05 .15
289 Jeremy Roenick TL .15 .40
290 Steve Yzerman TL .25 .60
291 P.Klima/D.Weight TL .05 .15
292 Geoff Sanderson TL .07 .20
293 Luc Robitaille TL .10 .25
294 Mike Modano TL .15 .40
295 Vincent Damphousse TL .07 .20
296 Claude Lemieux TL .05 .15
297 Pierre Turgeon TL .07 .20
298 Mark Messier TL .20 .50
299 Norm Maciver TL .05 .15
300 Mark Recchi TL .12 .30
301 Mario Lemieux TL .40 1.00
302 Mats Sundin TL .10 .25
303 Craig Janney TL .07 .20
304 Kelly Kisio TL .05 .15
305 Brian Bradley TL .05 .15
306 Doug Gilmour TL .12 .30
307 Pavel Bure TL .10 .25
308 Peter Bondra TL .10 .25
309 Teemu Selanne TL .20 .50
310 Checklist 207-310 .05 .05
311 Terry Yake .05 .15
312 Bob Sweeney .05 .15
313 Robert Reichel .05 .15
314 Jeremy Roenick .15 .40
315 Paul Coffey .10 .25
316 Geoff Sanderson .07 .20
317 Rob Blake .07 .20
318 Patrice Brisebois .05 .15
319 Jaroslav Modry RC .10 .25
320 Scott Lachance .05 .15
321 Glenn Healy .07 .20
322 Martin Gelinas .05 .15
323 Craig Janney .07 .20
324 Bill McDougall RC .10 .25
325 Shawn Antoski .05 .15
326 Olaf Kolzig .10 .25
327 Adam Oates .10 .25
328 Dirk Graham .05 .15
329 Brent Gilchrist .05 .15
330 Zdeno Ciger .05 .15
331 Pat Verbeek .05 .15
332 Jari Kurri .10 .25
333 Kevin Haller .05 .15
334 Martin Brodeur .25 .60
335 Norm Maciver .05 .15
336 Dominic Roussel .07 .20
337 Iain Fraser RC .10 .25
338 Vitali Karamnov .05 .15
339 Rene Corbet RC .10 .25
340 Wendel Clark .15 .40
341 Mike Ridley .05 .15
342 Nelson Emerson .05 .15
343 Joe Juneau .05 .15
344 Vesa Viitakoski RC .10 .25
345 Steve Chiasson .05 .15
346 Andrew Cassels .05 .15
347 Pierre Turgeon .07 .20
348 Brian Leetch .07 .20
349 Alexei Yashin .07 .20
350 Mark Recchi .12 .30
351 Ron Francis .12 .30
352 Mike Ricci .05 .15
353 Igor Korolev .05 .15
354 Brent Gretzky RC .10 .25
355 Dave Poulin .05 .15
356 Cam Neely .10 .25
357 Gary Suter .05 .15
358 Dave Manson .05 .15
359 Robert Kron .05 .15
360 Ulf Dahlen .05 .15
361 Rod Brind'Amour .07 .20
362 Alexei Gusarov .05 .15
363 Vitali Prokhorov .05 .15
364 Damian Rhodes RC .10 .25
365 Paul Ysebaert .05 .15
366 Vladimir Konstantinov .07 .20
367 Steven Rice .05 .15
368 Brian Propp .05 .15
369 Valeri Zelepukin .05 .15
370 David Volek .05 .15
371 Sergei Nemchinov .05 .15
372 Pavol Demitra .12 .30
373 Brent Fedyk .05 .15
374 Larry Murphy .07 .20

375 Dave Karpa .05 .15
376 Dave Babych .05 .15
377 Keith Jones .05 .15
378 Neil Wilkinson .05 .15
379 Jozef Stumpel .05 .15
380 Vincent Damphousse .07 .20
381 Tom Kurvers .05 .15
382 Doug Gilmour .12 .30
383 Trevor Linden .10 .25
384 Kelly Miller .05 .15
385 Tim Sweeney .05 .15
386 Mikhail Tatarinov .05 .15
387 Dominik Hasek .15 .40
388 Steve Yzerman .25 .60
389 Scott Pearson .05 .15
390 Brian Bellows .07 .20
391 Claude Lemieux .05 .15
392 Marty McInnis .05 .15
393 Jim Sandlak .05 .15
394 Jocelyn Thibault RC .10 .25
395 John Cullen .05 .15
396 Joe Nieuwendyk .07 .20
397 Mike Modano .15 .40
398 Ray Sheppard .07 .20
399 Trevor Kidd .07 .20
400 Checklist .05 .15
401 Frank Pietrangelo .07 .20
402 Stephan Lebeau .05 .15
403 Stephane Richer .07 .20
404 Greg Gilbert .05 .15
405 Dmitri Filimonov .05 .15
406 Vyacheslav Butsayev .05 .15
407 Mario Lemieux .40 1.00
408 Kevin Miller .05 .15
409 John Tucker .05 .15
410 Murray Craven .05 .15
411 Dale Hawerchuk .12 .30
412 Al MacInnis .12 .30
413 Keith Primeau .07 .20
414 Luc Robitaille .10 .25
415 Benoit Brunet .05 .15
416 Tom Chorske .05 .15
417 Derek King .05 .15
418 Troy Mallette .05 .15
419 Mats Sundin .10 .25
420 Kent Manderville .05 .15
421 Kip Miller .05 .15
422 Jarkko Varvio .05 .15
423 Jason Arnott RC .20 .50
424 Craig Billington .07 .20
425 Stewart Malgunas RC .10 .25
426 Ron Tugnutt .07 .20
427 Alexei Kudashov RC .10 .25
428 Harijs Vitolinsh .05 .15
429 Bill Houlder .05 .15
430 Craig Simpson .05 .15
431 Wes Walz .05 .15
432 Micah Aivazoff RC .10 .25
433 Scott Levins RC .10 .25
434 Ron Hextall .07 .20
435 Fred Brathwaite RC .10 .25
436 Chad Penney RC .10 .25
437 Vlastimil Kroupa RC .10 .25
438 Troy Loney .05 .15
439 Matthew Barnaby .07 .20
440 Kevin Todd .05 .15
441 Paul Cavallini .05 .15
442 Doug Weight .07 .20
443 Egeny Davydov .05 .15
444 Dominic Lavoie .05 .15
445 Peter Popovic RC .10 .25
446 Sergei Makarov .05 .15
447 Matt Martin RC .10 .25
448 Teemu Selanne .20 .50
449 Todd Ewen .05 .15
450 Sergei Petrenko .05 .15
451 Jeff Shantz .05 .15
452 Greg Johnson .05 .15
453 Brent Severyn RC .10 .25
454 Shawn McEachern .05 .15
455 Pierre Sevigny .05 .15
456 Benoit Hogue .05 .15
457 Esa Tikkanen .05 .15
458 Brian Glynn .05 .15
459 Doug Brown .05 .15
460 Mike Rathje .05 .15
461 Rudy Poeschek .05 .15
462 Jason Woolley .05 .15
463 Patrick Carnback RC .10 .25
464 Cam Stewart RC .10 .25
465 Petr Svoboda .05 .15
466 Ted Drury .05 .15
467 Ladislav Karabin RC .10 .25
468 Paul Broten .05 .15
469 Alexander Godynyuk .05 .15
470 Bob Jay RC .10 .25
471 Steve Larmer .07 .20
472 Jim Montgomery RC .10 .25
473 Darren Puppa .05 .15
474 Alexei Kasatonov .05 .15
475 Derek Plante RC .10 .25
476 German Titov RC .10 .25
477 Steve Dubinsky RC .10 .25
478 Andy Moog .07 .20
479 Aaron Ward RC .10 .25
480 Dean McAmmond .05 .15
481 Randy Gilhen .05 .15
482 Jason Muzzatti RC .10 .25
483 Corey Millen .05 .15
484 Alexander Karpovtsev .05 .15
485 Bill Huard RC .10 .25
486 Mikael Renberg .10 .25
487 Marty McSorley .07 .20
488 Alexander Mogilny .07 .20
489 Michal Sykora RC .10 .25
490 Checklist .05 .05
491 Tom Tilley .05 .15
492 Boris Mironov .05 .15
493 Sandy McCarthy .05 .15
494 Mark Astley RC .10 .25
495 Slava Kozlov .07 .20
496 Brian Benning .05 .15
497 Eric Weinrich .05 .15
498 Robert Burakovsky RC .10 .25
499 Patrick Lebeau .05 .15
500 Markus Naslund .10 .25
501 Jimmy Waite .07 .20
502 Denis Savard .10 .25
503 Jose Charbonneau RC .10 .25
504 Randy Burridge .05 .15
505 Arto Blomsten .05 .15
506 Shaun Van Allen .05 .15
507 Jon Casey .07 .20
508 Darren McCarty RC .15 .40
509 Roman Oksiuta RC .10 .25
510 Jody Hull .05 .15
511 Scott Scissons .05 .15
512 Jeff Norton .05 .15
513 Dmitri Mironov .05 .15
514 Sergei Bautin .05 .15
515 Garry Valk .05 .15
516 Keith Carney .05 .15
517 James Black .05 .15
518 Pat Peake .05 .15
519 Chris Osgood RC 1.50 4.00
520 Kirk Maltby RC .10 .25
521 Gord Murphy .05 .15
522 Mattias Norstrom RC .10 .25
523 Milos Holan RC .10 .25
524 Dave McLlwain .05 .15
525 Phil Housley .07 .20
526 Petr Klima .05 .15
527 John McIntyre .05 .15
528 Enrico Ciccone .05 .15
529 Stephane Quintal .05 .15
530 World Juniors CL
Brent Tully .07 .20
531 Anson Carter WJC RC .10 .25
532 Jeff Friesen WJC RC .10 .25
533 Yanick Dube WJC RC .10 .25
534 Jason Botterill WJC RC .10 .25
535 Todd Harvey WJC RC .10 .25
536 Manny Fernandez WJC RC .10 .25
537 Jason Allison WJC RC .10 .25
538 Jamie Storr WJC RC .10 .25
539 Rick Girard WJC RC .10 .25
540 Martin Gendron WJC .07 .20
541 Joel Bouchard WJC RC .10 .25
542 Mike Peca WJC RC .10 .25
543 Nick Stajduhar WJC RC .10 .25
544 Brendan Witt WJC RC .10 .25
545 Aaron Gavey WJC RC .10 .25
546 Chris Armstrong WJC RC .10 .25
547 Curtis Bowen WJC RC .10 .25
548 Brandon Convery WJC RC .10 .25
549 Bryan McCabe WJC RC .10 .25
550 Marty Murray WJC RC .10 .25
551 Ryan Sittler WJC .05 .15
552 Jason McBain WJC RC .10 .25
553 Richard Park WJC RC .10 .25
554 Aaron Ellis WJC RC .10 .25
555 Toby Kvalevog WJC RC .10 .25
556 Jay Pandolfo WJC RC .10 .25
557 John Emmons WJC .05 .15
558 David Wilkie WJC RC .10 .25
559 John Varga WJC RC .10 .25
560 Jason Bonsignore WJC RC .10 .25
561 Deron Quint WJC RC .10 .25
562 Adam Deadmarsh WJC .05 .15
563 Jon Coleman WJC RC .10 .25
564 Bob Lachance WJC RC .10 .25
565 Chris O'Sullivan WJC RC .10 .25
566 J.Langenbrunner WJC RC .10 .25
567 Kevin Hilton WJC RC .10 .25
568 Kevyn Adams WJC RC .10 .25
569 Saku Koivu WJC .10 .25
570 Mats Lindgren WJC RC .10 .25
571 Valeri Bure WJC RC .10 .25
572 Edvin Frylen WJC RC .10 .25
573 Jaroslav Miklenda WJC RC .10 .25
574 Vadim Sharifjanov WJC .07 .20
575 Checklist Card .05 .15
99B1 W.Gretzky 802 Silver 6.00 15.00
99B2 W.Gretzky 802 Gold 4.00 10.00
SP4 Teemu Selanne Hologram .20 .50

1993-94 Upper Deck Award Winners

COMPLETE SET (8) 5.00 12.00
AW1 Mario Lemieux 1.50 4.00
AW2 Teemu Selanne .30 .75
AW3 Ed Belfour .30 .75
AW4 Patrick Roy 1.50 4.00
AW5 Chris Chelios .30 .75
AW6 Doug Gilmour .15 .40
AW7 Pierre Turgeon .15 .40
AW8 Dave Poulin .08 .25

1993-94 Upper Deck Future Heroes

COMPLETE SET (10) 6.00 15.00
28 Felix Potvin .50 1.25
29 Pat Falloon .15 .40
30 Pavel Bure .40 1.00
31 Eric Lindros .40 1.00
32 Teemu Selanne .30 .75
33 Jaromir Jagr .50 1.25
34 Alexander Mogilny .20 .50
35 Joe Juneau .15 .40
36 Checklist 2.00 5.00
NNO Header Card .75 2.00

1993-94 Upper Deck Gretzky's Great Ones

COMPLETE SET (10) 4.00 10.00
GG1 Denis Savard .30 .75
GG2 Chris Chelios .40 1.00
GG3 Brett Hull .50 1.25
GG4 Mario Lemieux 1.25 3.00
GG5 Mark Messier .50 1.25
GG6 Paul Coffey .40 1.00
GG7 Theo Fleury .40 1.00
GG8 Luc Robitaille .30 .75
GG9 Marty McSorley .30 .75
GG10 Grant Fuhr .30 .75

1993-94 Upper Deck Gretzky Box Bottom

1 Wayne Gretzky .40 1.00

1993-94 Upper Deck Gretzky Sheet

1 Wayne Gretzky 8.00 20.00

1993-94 Upper Deck Hat Tricks

COMPLETE SET (20) 2.00 5.00
HT1 Adam Graves .08 .25
HT2 Geoff Sanderson .02 .10
HT3 Gary Roberts .08 .25
HT4 Robert Reichel .02 .10
HT5 Adam Oates .08 .25
HT6 Steve Yzerman 1.00 2.50
HT7 Alexei Kovalev .08 .25
HT8 Vincent Damphousse .02 .10
HT9 Rob Gaudreau .02 .10
HT10 Pat LaFontaine .08 .25
HT11 Pierre Turgeon .08 .25
HT12 Rick Tocchet .08 .25
HT13 Michael Nylander .02 .10
HT14 Steve Larmer .08 .25
HT15 Alexander Mogilny .08 .25
HT16 Owen Nolan .08 .25
HT17 Luc Robitaille .20 .50
HT18 Jeremy Roenick .25 .60
HT19 Kevin Stevens .02 .10
HT20 Mats Sundin .08 .25

1993-94 Upper Deck Next In Line

COMPLETE SET (6) 7.50 15.00
NL1 W.Gretzky/M.Nylander 2.50 6.00
NL2 B.Hull/P.Poulin .75 2.00
NL3 S.Yzerman/J.Sakic 2.50 6.00
NL4 R.Bourque/B.Leetch 2.00 5.00
NL5 D.Gilmour/K.Tkachuk 1.00 2.50
NL6 P.Roy/F.Potvin 1.25 3.00

1993-94 Upper Deck NHL's Best

COMPLETE SET (10) 5.00 10.00
HB1 Alexander Mogilny .10 .30
HB2 Rob Gaudreau .05 .15
HB3 Brett Hull .40 1.00
HB4 Dallas Drake .05 .15
HB5 Pavel Bure .30 .75
HB6 Alexei Kovalev .10 .30
HB7 Mario Lemieux 1.50 4.00
HB8 Eric Lindros .30 .75
HB9 Wayne Gretzky 2.00 5.00
HB10 Joe Juneau .10 .30

1993-94 Upper Deck NHLPA/Roots

COMPLETE SET (30) 16.00 40.00
COMPLETE SERIES 1 (10) 6.00 15.00
COMPLETE SERIES 2 (10) 6.00 15.00
COMPLETE SERIES 3 (10) 6.00 15.00
1 Trevor Linden .50 1.25
2 Patrick Roy
Montreal Ca 4.00 10.00
3 Felix Potvin .75 2.00
4 Steve Yzerman 4.00 10.00
5 Doug Gilmour
Toronto Ma .60 1.50
6 Wendel Clark .50 1.25
7 Kirk McLean .50 1.25
8 Larry Murphy .15 .40
9 Guy Carbonneau .15 .40
10 Mike Ricci .50 1.25
11 Doug Gilmour
Toronto Ma .60 1.50
12 Sergei Fedorov
Detroit 1.25 3.00
13 Shayne Corson .15 .40
14 Alexei Yashin .50 1.25
15 Pavel Bure 1.50 4.00
16 Joe Sakic 1.50 4.00
17 Teemu Selanne
Winnipeg 1.25 3.00
18 Dave Andreychuk
Toronto .50 1.25
19 Al MacInnis
Calgary Fla .50 1.25
20 Rob Blake
Los Angeles K .50 1.25
21 Doug Gilmour .60 1.50
22 Steve Larmer .15 .40
23 Eric Lindros 1.50 4.00
24 Mike Modano .75 2.00
25 Vincent Damphousse .50 1.25
26 Mike Gartner .50 1.25
27 John Vanbiesbrouck .60 1.50
28 Theo Fleury .60 1.50
29 Ken Baumgartner .15 .40
30 Jeremy Roenick .60 1.50

1993-94 Upper Deck Program of Excellence

COMPLETE SET (15) 40.00 80.00
E1 Adam Smith 1.00 2.50
E2 Jason Podollan 1.00 2.50
E3 Jason Wiemer 1.00 2.50
E4 Jeff O'Neill 4.00 10.00
E5 Daniel Goneau 1.00 2.50
E6 Christian Laflamme 1.00 2.50
E7 Daymond Langkow 1.50 4.00
E8 Jeff Friesen 1.50 4.00
E9 Wayne Primeau 1.00 2.50
E10 Paul Kariya 8.00 20.00
E11 Rob Niedermayer 4.00 10.00
E12 Eric Lindros 5.00 12.00
E13 Mario Lemieux 6.00 15.00
E14 Steve Yzerman 8.00 20.00
E15 Alexandre Daigle 1.50 4.00

1993-94 Upper Deck Silver Skates

COMPLETE HOBBY SET (10) 2.50 6.00
COMPLETE RETAIL SET (10) 5.00 12.00
*RETAIL GOLD EXCH: .75X TO 1.5X BASIC INSERTS
H1 Mario Lemieux 1.50 4.00
H2 Pavel Bure .30 .75
H3 Eric Lindros .30 .75
H4 Rob Niedermayer .20 .50
H5 Chris Pronger .08 .25
H6 Adam Oates .08 .25
H7 Pierre Turgeon .20 .50
H8 Alexei Yashin .20 .50
H9 Joe Sakic .60 1.50
H10 Alexander Mogilny .20 .50
R1 Wayne Gretzky 3.00 8.00
R2 Teemu Selanne .30 .75
R3 Alexandre Daigle .08 .25
R4 Chris Gratton .08 .25
R5 Brett Hull .40 1.00
R6 Steve Yzerman 1.50 4.00
R7 Doug Gilmour .08 .25
R8 Jaromir Jagr .50 1.25
R9 Jason Arnott .60 1.50
R10 Jeremy Roenick .40 1.00
EXG W.Gretzky Gold EXCH 20.00 50.00
EXS W.Gretzky Silver EXCH 15.00 40.00

1993-94 Upper Deck SP Inserts

COMPLETE SET (180) 20.00 50.00
1 Sean Hill .12 .30
2 Troy Loney .12 .30
3 Joe Sacco .12 .30
4 Anatoli Semenov .12 .30
5 Ron Tugnutt .30 .75
6 Terry Yake .12 .30
7 Ray Bourque .75 2.00
8 Jon Casey .30 .75
9 Joe Juneau .30 .75
10 Cam Neely .40 1.00
11 Adam Oates .30 .75
12 Bryan Smolinski .12 .30
13 Matthew Barnaby .20 .50
14 Philippe Boucher .12 .30
15 Grant Fuhr .30 .75
16 Dale Hawerchuk .20 .50
17 Pat LaFontaine .40 1.00
18 Alexander Mogilny .20 .50
19 Craig Simpson .12 .30
20 Ted Drury .12 .30
21 Theo Fleury .12 .30
22 Al MacInnis .20 .50
23 Joe Nieuwendyk .20 .50
24 Joel Otto .12 .30
25 Gary Roberts .12 .30
26 Vesa Viitakoski .12 .30
27 Ed Belfour .60 1.50
28 Chris Chelios .40 1.00
29 Joe Murphy .12 .30
30 Patrick Poulin .12 .30
31 Jeremy Roenick .75 2.00
32 Jeff Shantz .12 .30
33 Kevin Todd .12 .30
34 Neal Broten .20 .50
35 Paul Cavallini .12 .30
36 Russ Courtnall .12 .30
37 Derian Hatcher .12 .30
38 Mike Modano 1.00 2.50
39 Andy Moog .20 .50
40 Jarkko Varvio .12 .30
41 Dino Ciccarelli .20 .50
42 Paul Coffey .40 1.00
43 Dallas Drake .12 .30
44 Sergei Fedorov .60 1.50
45 Keith Primeau .12 .30
46 Bob Probert .30 .75
47 Steve Yzerman 2.00 5.00
48 Jason Arnott .30 .75
49 Shayne Corson .12 .30
50 Dave Manson .12 .30
51 Dean McAmmond .12 .30
52 Bill Ranford .30 .75
53 Doug Weight .20 .50
54 Brad Werenka .12 .30
55 Evgeny Davydov .12 .30
56 Scott Levins .12 .30
57 Scott Mellanby .20 .50
58 Rob Niedermayer .20 .50
59 Brian Skrudland .12 .30
60 John Vanbiesbrouck .20 .50
61 Robert Kron .12 .30
62 Michael Nylander .12 .30
63 Robert Petrovicky .12 .30
64 Chris Pronger .20 .50
65 Geoff Sanderson .20 .50
66 Darren Turcotte .12 .30
67 Pat Verbeek .20 .50
68 Rob Blake .20 .50
69 Tony Granato .12 .30
70 Wayne Gretzky 3.00 8.00
71 Kelly Hrudey .20 .50
72 Shawn McEachern .12 .30
73 Luc Robitaille .30 .75
74 Darryl Sydor .12 .30
75 Alexei Zhitnik .12 .30
76 Brian Bellows .12 .30
77 Vincent Damphousse .12 .30
78 Stephan Lebeau .12 .30
79 John LeClair .40 1.00
80 Kirk Muller .12 .30
81 Patrick Roy 2.00 5.00
82 Pierre Sevigny .12 .30
83 Claude Lemieux .12 .30
84 Corey Millen .12 .30
85 Bernie Nicholls .12 .30
86 Scott Niedermayer .12 .30
87 Stephane Richer .20 .50
88 Alexander Semak .12 .30
89 Scott Stevens .20 .50
90 Ray Ferraro .12 .30
91 Darius Kasparaitis .12 .30
92 Scott Lachance .12 .30
93 Vladimir Malakhov .12 .30
94 Marty McInnis .12 .30
95 Steve Thomas .12 .30
96 Pierre Turgeon .20 .50
97 Tony Amonte .20 .50
98 Mike Gartner .30 .75
99 Adam Graves .12 .30
100 Alexander Karpovtsev .12 .30
101 Alexei Kovalev .20 .50
102 Brian Leetch .40 1.00
103 Mark Messier .60 1.50
104 Esa Tikkanen .12 .30
105 Craig Billington .20 .50
106 Robert Burakovsky .12 .30
107 Alexandre Daigle .12 .30
108 Pavol Demitra .20 .50
109 Dmitri Filimonov .12 .30
110 Bob Kudelski .12 .30
111 Norm Maciver .12 .30
112 Alexei Yashin .12 .30
113 Josef Beranek .12 .30
114 Rod Brind'Amour .20 .50
115 Milos Holan .12 .30
116 Eric Lindros .75 2.00
117 Mark Recchi .20 .50
118 Mikael Renberg .20 .50
119 Dimitri Yushkevich .12 .30
120 Tom Barrasso .20 .50
121 Jaromir Jagr 1.25 3.00
122 Mario Lemieux 2.00 5.00
123 Markus Naslund .40 1.00
124 Kevin Stevens .12 .30
125 Martin Straka .12 .30
126 Rick Tocchet .30 .75
127 Martin Gelinas .12 .30
128 Owen Nolan .30 .75
129 Mike Ricci .12 .30
130 Joe Sakic 1.25 3.00
131 Chris Simon .30 .75
132 Mats Sundin .60 1.50
133 Jocelyn Thibault .40 1.00
134 Philippe Bozon .12 .30
135 Jeff Brown .12 .30
136 Phil Housley .30 .75
137 Brett Hull .75 2.00
138 Craig Janney .30 .75
139 Curtis Joseph .60 1.50
140 Brendan Shanahan .60 1.50
141 Pat Falloon .12 .30
142 Johan Garpenlov .12 .30
143 Rob Gaudreau .12 .30
144 Vlastimil Kroupa .12 .30
145 Sergei Makarov .12 .30
146 Sandis Ozolinsh .12 .30
147 Mike Rathje .12 .30
148 Brian Bradley .12 .30
149 Chris Gratton .30 .75
150 Brent Gretzky .12 .30
151 Roman Hamrlik .30 .75
152 Petr Klima .12 .30
153 Denis Savard .30 .75
154 Rob Zamuner .12 .30
155 Dave Andreychuk .30 .75
156 Nikolai Borschevsky .12 .30
157 Dave Ellett .12 .30
158 Doug Gilmour .30 .75
159 Alexei Kudashov .12 .30
160 Felix Potvin .75 2.00
161 Greg Adams .12 .30
162 Pavel Bure .60 1.50
163 Geoff Courtnall .12 .30
164 Trevor Linden .30 .75
165 Kirk McLean .30 .75
166 Jiri Slegr .12 .30
167 Dixon Ward .12 .30
168 Peter Bondra .30 .75
169 Kevin Hatcher .12 .30
170 Al Iafrate .12 .30
171 Dimitri Khristich .12 .30
172 Pat Peake .12 .30
173 Mike Ridley .12 .30
174 Arto Blomsten .12 .30
175 Nelson Emerson .12 .30
176 Boris Mironov .12 .30
177 Teemu Selanne .60 1.50
178 Keith Tkachuk .40 1.00
179 Paul Ysebaert .12 .30
180 Alexei Zhamnov .30 .75

1994 Upper Deck Gretzky 24K Gold

1 Wayne Gretzky
Los Angel 40.00 100.00

1994 Upper Deck NHLPA/Be A Player

COMPLETE SET (45) 12.00 30.00
1 Tony Amonte
New York Ra .20 .50
2 Chris Chelios .30 .75
3 Alexandre Daigle
Ottawa .08 .25
4 Dave Ellett .08 .25
5 Sergei Fedorov
Detroit .60 1.50
6 Chris Gratton
Tampa Bay .08 .25
7 Wayne Gretzky
Los Angel 2.00 5.00
8 Brett Hull
St. Louis Bl .40 1.00
9 Brian Leetch
New York R .30 .75
10 Rob Niedermayer .20 .50
11 Felix Potvin
Toronto Ma .30 .75
12 Luc Robitaille
Los Ange .20 .50
13 Jeremy Roenick
Chicago .30 .75
14 Joe Sakic
Quebec Nordiq .60 1.50
15 Teemu Selanne
Winnipeg .60 1.50
16 Brendan Shanahan .40 1.00
17 Alexei Yashin .20 .50
18 Steve Yzerman
Detroit R 1.50 4.00
19 Jason Arnott
Edmonton O .20 .50
20 Pavel Bure
Vancouver Ca .60 1.50
21 Theo Fleury .30 .75
22 Mike Gartner .20 .50
23 Kevin Haller .08 .25
24 Derian Hatcher .08 .25
25 Mark Howe
Gordie Howe .30 .75
26 Al Iafrate .08 .25
27 Joe Juneau
Boston Bruin .20 .50
28 Pat LaFontaine
Buffalo .20 .50
29 Eric Lindros
Philadelph .60 1.50
30 Dave Manson .08 .25
31 Mike Modano .40 1.00
32 Scott Niedermayer .20 .50
33 Owen Nolan
Quebec Nordi .20 .50
34 Joel Otto .08 .25
35 Chris Pronger
Hartford .20 .50
36 Scott Stevens .20 .50
37 Pierre Turgeon .20 .50
38 Pat Verbeek .08 .25
39 Doug Weight
Edmonton Oi .20 .50
40 Terry Yake .08 .25
41 Doug Gilmour
(Two-Year .30 .75
42 Doug Gilmour
(Nine-Year .30 .75
43 Doug Gilmour
(Standing .30 .75
44 Doug Gilmour
(Sitting O .30 .75
45 Doug Gilmour
(With Fish .30 .75

1994-95 Upper Deck

1 Wayne Gretzky 1.25 3.00
2 German Titov .12 .30
3 Guy Hebert .15 .40
4 Tony Amonte .15 .40
5 Dino Ciccarelli .15 .40
6 Geoff Sanderson .15 .40
7 Alexei Zhamnov .15 .40
8 John MacLean .15 .40
9 Brent Fedyk .12 .30
10 Adam Graves .12 .30
11 Adam Oates .20 .50
12 Ron Francis .25 .60
13 Bobby Dollas .12 .30
14 Ray Ferraro .12 .30
15 Paul Broten .12 .30
16 Ulf Dahlen .12 .30
17 Pat LaFontaine .20 .50
18 Craig Janney .15 .40
19 Garry Galley .12 .30
20 Gary Roberts .12 .30
21 Bill Ranford .15 .40
22 Mario Lemieux .75 2.00
22B Mike Sillinger ERR .12 .30
23 Glen Murray .15 .40
24 Paul Coffey .20 .50
25 Corey Millen .12 .30
26 Chris Chelios .20 .50
27 Ronnie Stern .12 .30
28 Zdeno Ciger .12 .30
29 Tony Granato .12 .30
30 Donald Audette .12 .30
31 Russ Courtnall .12 .30
32 Mike Gartner .25 .60
33 Marty McSorley .15 .40
34 Jeff Brown .12 .30
35 Mark Janssens .12 .30
36 Patrick Poulin .12 .30
37 Sergei Fedorov .30 .75
38 Tim Sweeney .12 .30
39 John Slaney .12 .30
40 Steve Larmer .15 .40
41 Dave Karpa .12 .30
42 Esa Tikkanen .12 .30
43 Joel Otto .12 .30
44 Doug Weight .15 .40
45 Murray Craven .12 .30
46 John Vanbiesbrouck .20 .50
47 Nelson Emerson .12 .30
48 Dean Evason .12 .30
49 Evgeny Davydov .12 .30
50 Craig Simpson .12 .30
51 Mats Sundin .20 .50
52 Chris Pronger .20 .50
53 Stephan Lebeau .12 .30
54 Martin Gelinas .12 .30
55 Bob Rouse .12 .30
56 Christian Ruuttu .12 .30
57 Gilbert Dionne .12 .30
58 Mike Modano .30 .75
59 Derek King .12 .30
60 Peter Stastny .15 .40
61 Ted Donato .12 .30
62 Mark Messier .40 1.00
63 Dave Manson .12 .30
64 Johan Garpenlov .12 .30
65 Igor Larionov .12 .30
65B Sergio Momesso ERR .20 .50
66 Kirk Muller .12 .30
67 Dave Ellett .12 .30
68 Dale Hunter .12 .30
69 Brent Gretzky .12 .30
70 Tom Barrasso .15 .40
71 Philippe Boucher .12 .30
72 Jesse Belanger .12 .30
73 Scott Stevens .20 .50
74 Gary Suter .12 .30
75 Tim Cheveldae .15 .40
76 Dimitri Khristich .12 .30
77 Pierre Turgeon .20 .50
78 Mike Richter .20 .50
79 Michael Nylander .15 .40
80 Sergei Krivokrasov .12 .30
81 Andy Moog UER .20 .50
82 Al Iafrate .12 .30
83 Bernie Nicholls .15 .40
84 Darren Turcotte .12 .30
85 Sergio Momesso .20 .50
85B Igor Larionov ERR .12 .30
86 Petr Klima .12 .30
87 Alexandre Daigle .12 .30
88 Joe Juneau .12 .30
89 Glen Wesley .12 .30
90 Teemu Selanne .40 1.00
91 Curtis Joseph .25 .60
92 Scott Mellanby .15 .40
93 Jaromir Jagr .60 1.50
94 Mark Recchi .25 .60
95 Jiri Slegr .12 .30
96 Martin Brodeur .50 1.25
97 Scott Pearson .12 .30
98 Eric Lindros .30 .75
99 Larry Murphy .15 .40
100 Sergei Zubov .15 .40
101 Mathieu Schneider .12 .30
102 Dale Hawerchuk .25 .60
103 Owen Nolan .20 .50
104 Darryl Sydor .08 .25
105 Anatoli Semenov .12 .30
106 Marty McInnis .12 .30
107 Derek Mayer .12 .30
108 Steve Duchesne .12 .30
109 Geoff Smith .12 .30
110 Zarley Zalapski .12 .30
111 Rod Brind'Amour .15 .40
112 Nicklas Lidstrom .20 .50
113 Teppo Numminen .12 .30
114 Denny Felsner .12 .30
115 Wendel Clark .30 .75
116 Arturs Irbe .15 .40
117 Josef Beranek .12 .30
118 Brian Bradley .12 .30
119 Eric Weinrich .12 .30
120 Kevin Todd .12 .30
121 Patrick Roy .50 1.25
122 Guy Carbonneau .12 .30
123 Tom Kurvers .12 .30
124 Sergei Makarov .12 .30
125 Pat Peake .12 .30
126 Danton Cole .12 .30
127 Derian Hatcher .12 .30
128 Kjell Samuelsson .12 .30
129 Alexei Yashin .20 .50
130 Chris Osgood .30 .75
131 Kent Manderville .12 .30
132 Jim Montgomery .12 .30
133 Kirk McLean .15 .40
134 Kelly Buchberger .12 .30
135 Peter Bondra .20 .50
136 Stephane Matteau .12 .30
137 Oleg Petrov .12 .30
138 Doug Gilmour .25 .60
139 Vladimir Malakhov .12 .30
140 Peter Zezel .12 .30
141 Mike Vernon .15 .40
142 Derek Plante .12 .30
143 Valeri Zelepukin .12 .30
144 Kevin Haller .12 .30
145 Keith Tkachuk .20 .50
146 Claude Boivin .12 .30
147 Jocelyn Thibault .15 .40
148 Jyrki Lumme .12 .30
149 Ray Whitney .12 .30
150 Al MacInnis .25 .60
151 Kelly Miller .12 .30
152 Ray Sheppard .15 .40
153 Aaron Ward .12 .30
154 Damian Rhodes .15 .40
155 Jozef Stumpel .12 .30
156 Sergei Nemchinov .12 .30
157 Richard Matvichuk .12 .30
158 Sean Burke .15 .40
159 Todd Marchant .12 .30
160 Ryan McGill .12 .30
161 Sean Hill .12 .30
162 Iain Fraser .12 .30
163 Shawn McEachern .12 .30
164 Petr Nedved .15 .40
165 John Lilley .12 .30
166 Joe Sacco .12 .30
167 Jason Dawe .12 .30
168 Mike Rathje .12 .30
169 Phil Housley .15 .40
170 Ron Hextall .20 .50
171 Yves Racine .12 .30
172 Boris Mironov .12 .30
173 Vitali Prokhorov .12 .30
174 Roman Hamrlik .12 .30
175 Robert Lang .12 .30
176 Jody Hull .12 .30
177 Mike Ridley .12 .30
178 Dmitri Filimonov .12 .30
179 Rene Corbet .12 .30
180 Rob Pearson .12 .30
181 Richard Smehlik .12 .30
182 Rob Gaudreau .12 .30
183 Bill Houlder .12 .30
184 Igor Korolev .12 .30
185 Chris Joseph .12 .30
186 Shane Churla .12 .30
187 Rick Tabaracci .15 .40
188 Alexander Godynyuk .12 .30
189 Vladimir Konstantinov .15 .40
190 Markus Naslund .20 .50
191 Tom Chorske .12 .30
192 Thomas Steen .12 .30
193 Patrice Brisebois .12 .30
194 Luc Robitaille .20 .50
195 Michal Sykora .12 .30
196 Troy Mallette .12 .30
197 Steve Chiasson .12 .30
198 Jimmy Carson .12 .30
199 Mike Donnelly .12 .30
200 Mike Sillinger .12 .30
200B Mario Lemieux ERR .75 2.00
201 Martin Rucinsky .12 .30
202 Adam Bennett .12 .30
203 Matt Johnson RC .12 .30
204 Daren Puppa .15 .40
205 Ted Drury .12 .30
206 Jon Casey .15 .40
207 Alexei Kovalev .15 .40
208 Alexei Kasatonov .12 .30
209 Ulf Samuelsson .12 .30
210 Justin Hocking RC .12 .30
211 Greg Adams .12 .30
212 Greg Johnson .12 .30
213 Mike Craig .12 .30
214 Steve Konowalchuk .12 .30
215 Luke Richardson .12 .30
216 Pavol Demitra .25 .60
217 Brian Benning .12 .30
218 Corey Hirsch .15 .40
219 Alexander Semak .12 .30
220 Travis Green .15 .40
221 Turner Stevenson .12 .30
222 Dimitri Mironov .12 .30
223 Christian Soucy RC .15 .40
224 Rick Tocchet .15 .40
225 Craig MacTavish .12 .30
226 Wayne Gretzky RB 802 1.25 3.00
227 Pavel Bure SE .20 .50
228 Wayne Gretzky SE 1.25 3.00
229 Brett Hull SE .40 1.00
230 Mike Gartner .12 .30

231 Brian Leetch .15 .40
232 Al MacInnis .25 .60
233 Dominik Hasek SE .30 .75
234 Mark Messier SE .40 1.00
235 Paul Kariya SR .20 .50
236 Jamie Storr SR .15 .40
237 Jeff Friesen SR .12 .30
238 Kenny Jonsson SR .12 .30
239 Mariusz Czerkawski SR RC .20 .50
240 Brett Lindros SR .12 .30
241 Andrei Nikolishin .12 .30
242 Jason Allison SR .12 .30
243 Oleg Tverdovsky SR .15 .40
244 Brian Savage .12 .30
245 Peter Forsberg SR .40 1.00
246 Patrik Juhlin RC .12 .30
247 Jassen Cullimore .12 .30
248 Chris Therien .12 .30
249 Kevin Brown SR RC .20 .50
250 Jeff Nelson .12 .30
251 Janne Laukkanen .15 .40
252 Jamie McLennan .15 .40
253 Craig Johnson .12 .30
254 Ravil Gusmanov SR RC .12 .30
255 Valeri Bure SR .12 .30
256 Valeri Karpov SR RC .12 .30
257 Mike Peca .15 .40
258 Brian Rolston .15 .40
259 Brandon Convery .12 .30
260 Mark Lawrence SR RC .12 .30
261 Adam Deadmarsh .12 .30
262 Jason Wiemer RC .12 .30
263 Alexander Cherbayev .12 .30
264 Sergei Gonchar .12 .30
265 Viktor Kozlov SR .12 .30
266 Vladislav Boulin RC .20 .50
267 Todd Harvey SR .12 .30
268 Cory Stillman SR RC .12 .30
269 David Oliver SR RC .12 .30
270 Andrei Nazarov .12 .30
271 Mikael Renberg .15 .40
272 Andrei Kovalenko .12 .30
273 Neal Broten .15 .40
274 Ed Olczyk .12 .30
275 Steve Thomas .12 .30
276 Joe Nieuwendyk .15 .40
277 Rob Gaudreau .12 .30
278 Pat Verbeek .15 .40
279 Eric Desjardins .15 .40
280 Vincent Damphousse .15 .40
281 John Cullen .12 .30
282 Garry Valk .12 .30
283 Daniel Lacroix .12 .30
284 Mike Ricci .12 .30
285 Dominik Hasek .30 .75
286 Geoff Courtnall .12 .30
287 Rob Niedermayer .15 .40
288 Alexander Karpovtsev .12 .30
289 Martin Straka .12 .30
290 Ed Belfour .20 .50
291 Dave Lowry .12 .30
292 Brendan Shanahan .20 .50
293 Jari Kurri .15 .40
294 Steven Rice .12 .30
295 Scott Levins .12 .30
296 Ray Bourque .30 .75
297 Mikael Andersson .12 .30
298 Darius Kasparaitis .12 .30
299 Chris Simon .12 .30
300 Steve Yzerman .50 1.25
301 Don McSween .12 .30
302 Brian Noonan .12 .30
303 Claude Lemieux .20 .50
304 Radek Bonk RC .12 .30
305 Jason Arnott .15 .40
306 Ian Laperriere RC .20 .50
307 Pat Falloon .12 .30
308 Kris King .12 .30
309 Brian Bellows .15 .40
310 Uwe Krupp .12 .30
311 Paul Cavallini .12 .30
312 Shaun Van Allen .12 .30
313 Dave Andreychuk .20 .50
314 Bobby Holik .12 .30
315 Theo Fleury .20 .50
316 Mark Osborne .12 .30
317 Andrew Cassels .12 .30
318 Chris Tamer .12 .30
319 Trevor Linden .20 .50
320 Tom Fitzgerald .12 .30
321 Ron Tugnutt .15 .40
322 Jeremy Roenick .30 .75
323 Todd Marchant .12 .30
324 Scott Niedermayer .20 .50
325 Tim Taylor RC .20 .50
326 Mike Kennedy RC .20 .50
327 Steve Heinze .12 .30
328 David Sacco .12 .30
329 Sergei Brylin .12 .30
330 John LeClair .20 .50
331 Brian Skrudland .12 .30
332 Kevin Hatcher .12 .30
333 Brett Hull .40 1.00
334 Alexander Mogilny .15 .40
335 Sylvain Lefebvre .12 .30
336 Sylvain Turgeon .12 .30
337 Keith Primeau .15 .40
338 Eric Fichaud RC .20 .50
339 Jeff Beukeboom .12 .30
340 Cory Cross RC .12 .30
341 J.J. Daigneault .12 .30
342 Stephen Leach .12 .30
343 Zigmund Palffy .15 .40
344 Igor Korolev .12 .30
345 Chris Gratton .12 .30
346 Joe Mullen .15 .40
347 Brent Gilchrist .12 .30
348 Adam Creighton .12 .30
349 Dimitri Yushkevich .12 .30
350 Wes Walz .12 .30
351 Shayne Corson .15 .40
352 Eric Lacroix RC .20 .50
353 Maxim Bets .12 .30
354 Sylvain Cote .12 .30
355 Valeri Kamensky .15 .40
356 Shjon Podein .12 .30
357 Robert Reichel .12 .30
358 Cliff Ronning .12 .30
359 Bill Guerin .20 .50
360 Dallas Drake .12 .30
361 Robert Petrovicky .12 .30
362 Ken Wregget .15 .40
363 Todd Elik .12 .30
364 Cam Neely .20 .50
365 Darren McCarty .12 .30
366 Shean Donovan RC .20 .50
367 Felix Potvin .30 .75
368 Yuri Khmylev .12 .30
369 Mark Tinordi .12 .30
370 Craig Billington .15 .40
371 Patrick Flatley .12 .30
372 Jocelyn Lemieux .12 .30
373 Slava Kozlov .15 .40
374 Trent Klatt .12 .30
375 Geoff Sarjeant RC .20 .50
376 Bob Kudelski .12 .30
377 Stanislav Neckar RC .20 .50
378 Jon Rohloff RC .20 .50
379 Jeff Shantz .12 .30
380 Dale Craigwell .12 .30
381 Adrien Plavsic .12 .30
382 Dave Gagner .15 .40
383 Dave Archibald .12 .30
384 Gilbert Dionne .12 .30
385 Troy Loney .12 .30
386 Dean McAmmond .12 .30
387 Pauli Jaks .15 .40
388 Stephane Richer .15 .40
389 Don Beaupre .15 .40
390 Kevin Stevens .15 .40
391 Brad May .12 .30
392 Neil Wilkinson .12 .30
393 Kevin Lowe .12 .30
394 Frederik Olausson .12 .30
395 Trevor Kidd .15 .40
396 Brent Grieve .12 .30
397 Dominic Roussel .15 .40
398 Bret Hedican .12 .30
399 Bryan Smolinski .12 .30
400 Doug Lidster .12 .30
401 Bob Errey .12 .30
402 Pierre Sevigny .12 .30
403 Rob Brown .12 .30
404 Joe Sakic .40 1.00
405 Nikolai Borschevsky .12 .30
406 Martin Lapointe .12 .30
407 Jean-Yves Roy RC .20 .50
408 Robert Kron .12 .30
409 Tie Domi .15 .40
410 Jim Dowd .12 .30
411 Keith Jones .12 .30
412 Scott Lachance .12 .30
413 Bob Corkum .12 .30
414 Denis Chasse RC .20 .50
415 Denis Savard .20 .50
416 Joe Murphy .12 .30
417 Vyacheslav Butsayev .12 .30
418 Mattias Norstrom .12 .30
419 Sergei Zholtok .12 .30
420 Nikolai Khabibulin .15 .40
421 Pat Elynuik .12 .30
422 Doug Brown .12 .30
423 Dave McLlwain .12 .30
424 James Patrick .12 .30
425 Alexander Selivanov RC .15 .40
426 Scott Thornton .12 .30
427 Todd Ewen .12 .30
428 Peter Popovic .12 .30
429 Jarkko Varvio .12 .30
430 Paul Ranheim .12 .30
431 Kevin Dineen .12 .30
432 Kelly Hrudey .15 .40
433 Michal Grosek RC .12 .30
434 Slava Fetisov .12 .30
435 Ivan Droppa .12 .30
436 Benoit Hogue .12 .30
437 Sheldon Kennedy .12 .30
438 Gord Murphy .12 .30
439 Jamie Baker .12 .30
440 Todd Gill .12 .30
441 Mark Recchi .25 .60
442 Ted Crowley .12 .30
443 Ryan Smyth RC .60 1.50
444 Brian Leetch .15 .40
445 Bob Sweeney .12 .30
446 Don Sweeney .12 .30
447 Byron Dafoe RC .60 1.50
448 Nathan Lafayette .12 .30
449 Keith Carney .12 .30
450 Stephane Fiset .15 .40
451 Kevin Miller .12 .30
452 Craig Darby RC .20 .50
453 Vlastimil Kroupa .12 .30
454 Rob Zettler .12 .30
455 Glenn Healy .15 .40
456 Todd Simon .12 .30
457 Mark Fitzpatrick .15 .40
458 Drake Berehowsky .12 .30
459 Darcy Wakaluk .15 .40
460 Enrico Ciccone .12 .30
461 Tomas Sandstrom .12 .30
462 Mikhail Shtalenkov .12 .30
463 Igor Kravchuk .12 .30
464 Jamie Allison RC .20 .50
465 Gino Odjick .12 .30
466 Norm Maciver .12 .30
467 Terry Carkner .12 .30
468 Rob Zamuner .12 .30
469 Pavel Bure .20 .50
470 Patrice Tardif RC .20 .50
471 Andrei Lomakin .12 .30
472 Kirk Maltby .12 .30
473 Jaroslav Modry .12 .30
474 Tommy Soderstrom .15 .40
475 Patrik Carnback .12 .30
476 Jeff Reese .12 .30
477 Todd Krygier .12 .30
478 John McIntyre .12 .30
479 Joey Kocur .12 .30
480 Steve Rucchin RC .60 1.50
481 Bob Bassen .12 .30
482 Marek Malik RC .15 .40
483 Darrin Shannon .12 .30
484 Shawn Burr .12 .30
485 Louie DeBrusk .12 .30
486 Olaf Kolzig .20 .50
487 Cam Stewart .12 .30
488 Craig Reichert RC .20 .50
489 Eric Charron RC .20 .50
490 Sandis Ozolinsh .12 .30
491 Paul Ysebaert .12 .30
492 Kris Draper .12 .30
493 Stu Barnes .12 .30
494 Doug Bodger .12 .30
495 Blaine Lacher RC .15 .40
496 Ed Jovanovski RC .30 .75
497 Eric Daze RC .30 .75
498 Dan Cloutier RC .30 .75
499 Chad Allan RC .20 .50
500 Todd Harvey .12 .30
501 Jamie Rivers RC .20 .50
502 Bryan McCabe .12 .30
503 Darcy Tucker RC .30 .75
504 Wade Redden RC .30 .75
505 Nolan Baumgartner RC .20 .50
506 Marek Malik RC .12 .30
507 Petr Cajanek RC .30 .75
508 Jan Hlavac RC .30 .75
509 Ladislav Kohn RC .20 .50
510 Kimmo Timonen .15 .40
511 Antti Aalto RC .15 .40
512 Tommi Rajamaki RC .15 .40
513 Vitali Yachmenev RC .20 .50
514 Vadim Epantchinsev RC .15 .40
515 Dmitri Klevakin RC .15 .40
516 Nikolai Zavarukhin RC .20 .50
517 Alexander Korolyuk RC .20 .50
518 Anders Eriksson .15 .40
519 Jesper Mattsson RC .15 .40
520 Mattias Ohlund RC .30 .75
521 Anders Soderberg RC .15 .40
522 Bryan Berard RC .30 .75
523 Jason Bonsignore .20 .50
524 Deron Quint .12 .30
525 Richard Park .12 .30
526 Jeff Friesen CC .12 .30
527 Paul Kariya CC .20 .50
528 Peter Forsberg CC .40 1.00
529 Zigmund Palffy CC .12 .30
530 Kenny Jonsson CC .12 .30
531 Jamie Storr CC .12 .30
532 Alexander Selivanov CC .12 .30
533 Mike Peca CC .12 .30
534 Mariusz Czerkawski CC .12 .30
535 Jason Allison CC .12 .30
536 Todd Harvey CC .12 .30
537 Brett Lindros CC .12 .30
538 Radek Bonk CC .12 .30
539 Blaine Lacher CC .12 .30
540 Oleg Tverdovsky CC .15 .40
541 Wayne Gretzky WT 1.25 3.00
542 Radek Bonk WT .12 .30
543 Mariusz Czerkawski WT .12 .30
544 Jaromir Jagr WT .60 1.50
545 Dominik Hasek WT .30 .75
546 Todd Harvey WT .12 .30
547 Mike Peca WT .15 .40
548 Mats Sundin WT .20 .50
549 Doug Weight WT .15 .40
550 Steve Yzerman WT .50 1.25
551 Brett Lindros WT .12 .30
552 Alexander Mogilny WT .15 .40
553 Patrik Juhlin WT .12 .30
554 Alexei Yashin WT .20 .50
555 Peter Forsberg WT .40 1.00
556 Michael Nylander WT .15 .40
557 Teemu Selanne WT .40 1.00
558 Marek Malik WT .12 .30
559 Jari Kurri WT .15 .40
560 Kenny Jonsson WT .12 .30
561 Mikael Renberg WT .15 .40
562 Adam Deadmarsh WT .12 .30
563 Mark Messier WT .40 1.00
564 Rob Blake WT .20 .50
565 Janne Laukkanen WT .15 .40
566 Theo Fleury WT .20 .50
567 Alexei Kovalev WT .15 .40
568 Jamie Storr WT .15 .40
569 Brett Hull WT .40 1.00
570 Valeri Karpov WT .12 .30
1P Wayne Gretzky Jumbo Promo 1.25 3.00

1994-95 Upper Deck Electric Ice

*VETS: 8X TO 20X BASIC CARDS
*ROOKIES: 4X TO 10X BASIC CARDS

1994-95 Upper Deck Ice Gallery

COMPLETE SET (15) 15.00 40.00
IG1 Steve Yzerman 5.00 12.00
IG2 Jason Arnott .30 .75
IG3 Jeremy Roenick 1.25 3.00
IG4 Brendan Shanahan 1.00 2.50
IG5 Scott Stevens .50 1.25
IG6 Scott Niedermayer .30 .75
IG7 Adam Graves .30 .75
IG8 Mike Modano 1.50 4.00
IG9 Kirk Muller .30 .75
IG10 Alexandre Daigle .30 .75
IG11 Martin Brodeur 2.50 6.00
IG12 Garry Valk .30 .75
IG13 Teemu Selanne 1.00 2.50
IG14 Pat LaFontaine 1.00 2.50
IG15 Wayne Gretzky 5.00 12.00

1994-95 Upper Deck Predictor Canadian

COMPLETE SET (35) 30.00 80.00
*GOLD PRIZE: .2X TO .5X BASIC INSERTS
*SILVER PRIZE: .2X TO .5X BASIC INSERTS
C1 Peter Forsberg WIN 3.00 8.00
C2 Paul Kariya 1.25 3.00
C3 Viktor Kozlov .40 1.00
C4 Jason Allison .40 1.00
C5 Mariusz Czerkawski 1.50 4.00
C6 Valeri Karpov .40 1.00
C7 Brett Lindros .40 1.00
C8 Valeri Bure .40 1.00
C9 Andrei Nikolishin .40 1.00
C10 Mike Peca .40 1.00
C11 Kenny Jonsson .40 1.00
C12 Alexander Cherbayev .40 1.00
C13 Brian Rolston .40 1.00
C14 Oleg Tverdovsky .60 1.50
C15 Calder Long Shot WIN .40 1.00
C16 Wayne Gretzky 5.00 12.00
C17 Brett Hull 1.50 4.00
C18 Doug Gilmour .60 1.50
C19 Jeremy Roenick 1.50 4.00
C20 John Vanbiesbrouck .60 1.50
C21 Sergei Fedorov 2.00 5.00
C22 Mark Messier 1.25 3.00
C23 Eric Lindros WIN 1.25 3.00
C24 Jaromir Jagr WIN 2.00 5.00
C25 Pearson Long Shot .40 1.00
C26 Ray Bourque 2.00 5.00
C27 Sandis Ozolinsh .40 1.00
C28 Brian Leetch 1.25 3.00
C29 Chris Chelios WIN 1.25 3.00
C30 Scott Stevens .60 1.50
C31 Paul Coffey WIN 1.25 3.00
C32 Rob Blake .60 1.50
C33 Al MacInnis .60 1.50
C34 Scott Niedermayer .60 1.50
C35 Norris Long Shot .40 1.00

1994-95 Upper Deck Predictor Hobby

COMPLETE SET (35) 40.00 100.00
*GOLD PRIZE: .2X TO .5X BASIC INSERTS
*SILVER PRIZE: .2X TO .5X BASIC INSERTS
H1 Wayne Gretzky 5.00 12.00
H2 Pavel Bure 1.25 3.00
H3 Doug Gilmour .60 1.50
H4 Mark Messier 1.25 3.00
H5 Patrick Roy 4.00 10.00
H6 Sergei Fedorov 2.00 5.00
H7 Chris Chelios 1.25 3.00
H8 Eric Lindros 1.25 3.00
H9 Alexander Mogilny .60 1.50
H10 Peter Forsberg 3.00 8.00
H11 Brian Leetch 1.25 3.00
H12 Martin Brodeur 3.00 8.00
H13 Jeremy Roenick 1.50 4.00
H14 Paul Kariya 1.25 3.00
H15 Hart Long Shot .40 1.00
H16 Wayne Gretzky 5.00 12.00
H17 Joe Sakic 2.50 6.00
H18 Sergei Fedorov 2.00 5.00
H19 Pavel Bure 1.25 3.00
H20 Adam Oates .60 1.50
H21 Doug Gilmour .60 1.50
H22 Steve Yzerman 4.00 10.00
H23 Eric Lindros 1.25 3.00
H24 Jaromir Jagr 2.00 5.00
H25 Art Ross Long Shot .40 1.00
H26 Patrick Roy 4.00 10.00
H27 Ed Belfour 1.25 3.00
H28 Felix Potvin 1.25 3.00
H29 Martin Brodeur 3.00 8.00
H30 Mike Richter 1.25 3.00
H31 Dominik Hasek 2.50 6.00
H32 John Vanbiesbrouck .60 1.50
H33 Curtis Joseph 1.25 3.00
H34 Kirk McLean .60 1.50
H35 Vezina Long Shot .40 1.00

1994-95 Upper Deck Predictor Retail

COMPLETE SET (60) 40.00 100.00
*EXCH.CARDS: .2X TO .5X BASIC INSERTS
R1 Pavel Bure 1.25 3.00
R2 Brett Hull 1.50 4.00
R3 Teemu Selanne 1.25 3.00
R4 Sergei Fedorov 2.00 5.00
R5 Adam Graves .40 1.00
R6 Dave Andreychuk .60 1.50
R7 Brendan Shanahan 1.25 3.00
R8 Jeremy Roenick 1.50 4.00
R9 Eric Lindros 1.25 3.00
R10 Goals Long Shot .40 1.00
R11 Doug Gilmour .60 1.50
R12 Adam Oates .60 1.50
R13 Brian Leetch 1.25 3.00
R14 Ray Bourque 2.00 5.00
R15 Joe Juneau .60 1.50
R16 Craig Janney .60 1.50
R17 Pat LaFontaine 1.25 3.00
R18 Jaromir Jagr 2.00 5.00
R19 Wayne Gretzky 5.00 12.00
R20 Assists Long Shot .40 1.00
R21 Wayne Gretzky 5.00 12.00
R22 Pat LaFontaine 1.25 3.00
R23 Sergei Fedorov 2.00 5.00
R24 Steve Yzerman 4.00 10.00
R25 Pavel Bure 1.25 3.00
R26 Adam Oates .60 1.50
R27 Doug Gilmour .60 1.50
R28 Eric Lindros 1.25 3.00
R29 Jaromir Jagr 2.00 5.00
R30 Points Long Shot .40 1.00
R31 Pavel Bure 1.25 3.00
R32 Brett Hull 1.50 4.00
R33 Cam Neely 1.25 3.00
R34 Mark Messier 1.25 3.00
R35 Dave Andreychuk .60 1.50
R36 Sergei Fedorov 2.00 5.00
R37 Mike Modano 2.00 5.00
R38 Adam Graves .40 1.00
R39 Jaromir Jagr 2.00 5.00
R40 Playoff Goals .40 1.00
R41 Theo Fleury .40 1.00
R42 Wayne Gretzky 5.00 12.00
R43 Steve Yzerman 4.00 10.00
R44 Adam Oates .60 1.50
R45 Brian Leetch 1.25 3.00
R46 Al MacInnis .60 1.50
R47 Paul Coffey 1.25 3.00
R48 Scott Stevens .60 1.50
R49 Doug Gilmour .60 1.50
R50 Playoff Assists .40 1.00
R51 Brian Leetch 1.25 3.00
R52 Sergei Fedorov 2.00 5.00
R53 Pavel Bure 1.25 3.00
R54 Mark Messier 1.25 3.00
R55 Pat LaFontaine 1.25 3.00
R56 Doug Gilmour .60 1.50
R57 Brett Hull 1.50 4.00
R58 Theo Fleury .40 1.00
R59 Wayne Gretzky 5.00 12.00
R60 Playoff Points .40 1.00

1994-95 Upper Deck SP Inserts

*DIE CUTS: 1.2X TO 3X BASIC
SP1 Maxim Bets .20 .50
SP2 Stephan Lebeau .20 .50
SP3 Garry Valk .20 .50
SP4 Ray Bourque .50 1.25
SP5 Mariusz Czerkawski .30 .75
SP6 Cam Neely .30 .75
SP7 Adam Oates .30 .75
SP8 Dominik Hasek .50 1.25
SP9 Dale Hawerchuk .40 1.00
SP10 Alexander Mogilny .25 .60
SP11 Theo Fleury .20 .50
SP12 Trevor Kidd .25 .60
SP13 Joe Nieuwendyk .25 .60
SP14 Gary Roberts .20 .50
SP15 Ed Belfour .30 .75
SP16 Chris Chelios .30 .75
SP17 Jeremy Roenick .50 1.25
SP18 Neal Broten .25 .60
SP19 Russ Courtnall .20 .50
SP20 Derian Hatcher .20 .50
SP21 Mike Modano .50 1.25
SP22 Paul Coffey .30 .75
SP23 Slava Kozlov .25 .60
SP24 Keith Primeau .25 .60
SP25 Steve Yzerman .75 2.00
SP26 Jason Arnott .25 .60
SP27 Bill Ranford .25 .60
SP28 Doug Weight .25 .60
SP29 Bob Kudelski .20 .50
SP30 Rob Niedermayer .25 .60
SP31 John Vanbiesbrouck .30 .75
SP32 Andrew Cassels .20 .50
SP33 Chris Pronger .30 .75
SP34 Geoff Sanderson .25 .60
SP35 Rob Blake .20 .50
SP36 Wayne Gretzky 2.00 5.00
SP37 Jari Kurri .25 .60
SP38 Alexei Zhitnik .25 .60
SP39 Vincent Damphousse .25 .60
SP40 Kirk Muller .20 .50
SP41 Oleg Petrov .20 .50
SP42 Patrick Roy .75 2.00
SP43 Martin Brodeur .75 2.00
SP44 Stephane Richer .25 .60
SP45 Scott Stevens .30 .75
SP46 Darius Kasparaitis .20 .50
SP47 Vladimir Malakhov .20 .50
SP48 Pierre Turgeon .25 .60
SP49 Alexei Kovalev .25 .60
SP50 Brian Leetch .25 .60
SP51 Mark Messier .60 1.50
SP52 Mike Richter .30 .75
SP53 Craig Billington .25 .60
SP54 Alexandre Daigle .20 .50
SP55 Alexei Yashin .30 .75
SP56 Josef Beranek .20 .50
SP57 Rod Brind'Amour .25 .60
SP58 Mark Recchi .40 1.00
SP59 Mikael Renberg .25 .60
SP60 Jaromir Jagr 1.00 2.50
SP61 Mario Lemieux 1.25 3.00
SP62 Kevin Stevens .25 .60
SP63 Owen Nolan .30 .75
SP64 Mike Ricci .20 .50
SP65 Joe Sakic .60 1.50
SP66 Brett Hull .60 1.50
SP67 Craig Janney .25 .60
SP68 Curtis Joseph .40 1.00
SP69 Brendan Shanahan .30 .75
SP70 Ulf Dahlen .20 .50
SP71 Arturs Irbe .25 .60
SP72 Sergei Makarov .20 .50
SP73 Sandis Ozolinsh .20 .50
SP74 Brian Bradley .20 .50
SP75 Chris Gratton .20 .50
SP76 Denis Savard .30 .75
SP77 Dave Andreychuk .30 .75
SP78 Mike Gartner .40 1.00
SP79 Dimitri Mironov .20 .50
SP80 Felix Potvin .50 1.25
SP81 Jeff Brown .20 .50
SP82 Geoff Courtnall .20 .50
SP83 Trevor Linden .30 .75
SP84 Kirk McLean .25 .60
SP85 Peter Bondra .30 .75
SP86 Kevin Hatcher .20 .50
SP87 Dimitri Khristich .20 .50
SP88 Teemu Selanne .60 1.50
SP89 Keith Tkachuk .30 .75
SP90 Alexei Zhamnov .25 .60
SP91 Paul Kariya .30 .75
SP92 Valeri Karpov .20 .50
SP93 Oleg Tverdovsky .25 .60
SP94 Al Iafrate .20 .50
SP95 Blaine Lacher .25 .60
SP96 Bryan Smolinski .20 .50
SP97 Donald Audette .20 .50
SP98 Yuri Khymlev .20 .50
SP99 Pat LaFontaine .25 .60
SP100 Derek Plante .20 .50
SP101 Steve Chiasson .20 .50
SP102 Phil Housley .25 .60
SP103 Michael Nylander .25 .60
SP104 Robert Reichel .20 .50
SP105 Tony Amonte .25 .60
SP106 Bernie Nicholls .25 .60
SP107 Gary Suter .20 .50
SP108 Paul Cavallini .20 .50
SP109 Todd Harvey .20 .50
SP110 Kevin Hatcher .20 .50
SP111 Andy Moog .30 .75
SP112 Dino Ciccarelli .25 .60
SP113 Sergei Fedorov .50 1.25
SP114 Nicklas Lidstrom .30 .75
SP115 Mike Vernon .25 .60
SP116 Shayne Corson .25 .60
SP117 David Oliver .20 .50
SP118 Ryan Smyth 1.00 2.50
SP119 Jesse Belanger .20 .50
SP120 Mark Fitzpatrick .25 .60
SP121 Scott Mellanby .25 .60
SP122 Andrei Nikolishin .20 .50
SP123 Darren Turcotte .20 .50
SP124 Pat Verbeek .25 .60
SP125 Glen Wesley .20 .50
SP126 Tony Granato .20 .50
SP127 Marty McSorley .25 .60
SP128 Jamie Storr .25 .60
SP129 Rick Tocchet .25 .60
SP130 Brian Bellows .25 .60
SP131 Valeri Bure .20 .50
SP132 Turner Stevenson .20 .50
SP133 John MacLean .25 .60
SP134 Scott Niedermayer .30 .75
SP135 Brian Rolston .20 .50
SP136 Brett Lindros .20 .50
SP137 Jamie McLennan .25 .60
SP138 Zigmund Palffy .25 .60
SP139 Steve Thomas .20 .50
SP140 Adam Graves .20 .50
SP141 Petr Nedved .25 .60
SP142 Sergei Zubov .20 .50
SP143 Don Beaupre .25 .60
SP144 Radek Bonk .20 .50
SP145 Pavol Demitra .40 1.00
SP146 Sylvain Turgeon .20 .50
SP147 Ron Hextall .30 .75
SP148 Patrik Juhlin .20 .50
SP149 Eric Lindros .50 1.25
SP150 Ron Francis .40 1.00
SP151 Markus Naslund .30 .75
SP152 Luc Robitaille .30 .75
SP153 Martin Straka .20 .50
SP154 Wendel Clark .50 1.25
SP155 Adam Deadmarsh .20 .50
SP156 Peter Forsberg .60 1.50
SP157 Janne Laukkanen .25 .60
SP158 Steve Duchesne .20 .50
SP159 Al MacInnis .40 1.00
SP160 Esa Tikkanen .20 .50
SP161 Jeff Friesen .20 .50
SP162 Viktor Kozlov .20 .50
SP163 Ray Whitney .20 .50
SP164 Roman Hamrlik .20 .50
SP165 Alexander Selivanov .25 .60
SP166 Jason Wiemer .20 .50
SP167 Doug Gilmour .40 1.00
SP168 Kenny Jonsson .20 .50
SP169 Mike Ridley .20 .50
SP170 Mats Sundin .30 .75
SP171 Pavel Bure .30 .75
SP172 Martin Gelinas .20 .50
SP173 Mike Peca .25 .60
SP174 Jason Allison .25 .60
SP175 Joe Juneau .20 .50
SP176 Pat Peake .20 .50
SP177 Mark Tinordi .20 .50
SP178 Tim Cheveldae .25 .60
SP179 Nelson Emerson .20 .50
SP180 Dave Manson .20 .50

1995 Upper Deck World Junior Alumni

2 Manny Legace .40 1.00
3 Jeff Nelson .08 .25
4 Alexandre Daigle .15 .40
5 Paul Kariya 2.00 5.00
6 Turner Stevenson .08 .25
7 Mike Peca .40 1.00
8 Tyler Wright .08 .25
9 Brent Tully .08 .25
10 Trevor Kidd .20 .50
11 Martin Lapointe .20 .50
12 Scott Niedermayer .20 .50
13 Jeff Friesen .30 .75
14 Todd Harvey .20 .50
15 Jamie Storr .20 .50

1995-96 Upper Deck

1 Cam Neely .10 .25
2 Donald Audette .07 .20
3 Derian Hatcher .07 .20
4 Mike Vernon .07 .20
5 Darryl Sydor .07 .20
6 Patrice Brisebois .05 .15
7 John LeClair .10 .25
8 Luc Robitaille .10 .25
9 Todd Krygier .05 .15
10 Steve Chiasson .05 .15
11 Sergei Krivokrasov .05 .15
12 Marko Tuomainen .05 .15
13 Paul Ranheim .05 .15
14 Brian Rolston .07 .20
15 Alexei Yashin .07 .20
16 Joe Mullen .07 .20
17 Dallas Drake .05 .15
18 Tony Amonte .07 .20
19 Gary Roberts .05 .15
20 Geoff Sanderson .07 .20
21 Gord Murphy .05 .15
22 Dean Evason .05 .15
23 Brantt Myhres RC .05 .15
24 Sergei Makarov .05 .15
25 Joe Juneau .05 .15
26 Greg Adams .05 .15
27 Yuri Khmylev .05 .15
28 Yanic Perreault .05 .15
29 Jason Arnott .07 .20
30 Glenn Healy .07 .20
31 Sergei Brylin .05 .15
32 Ian Laperriere .05 .15
33 Trevor Linden .07 .20
34 Nicklas Lidstrom .10 .25
35 Don Sweeney .05 .15
36 Brian Savage .05 .15
37 Richard Matvichuk .07 .20
38 Dale Hawerchuk .12 .30
39 Patrick Roy .25 .60
40 Alexander Semak .05 .15
41 Kirk Maltby .07 .20
42 Jiri Slegr .05 .15
43 Joe Sacco .05 .15
44 Claude Lemieux .10 .25
45 Eric Weinrich .05 .15
46 Ron Francis .12 .30
47 Jamie Storr .07 .20
48 Felix Potvin .15 .40
49 Steve Duchesne .05 .15
50 Jody Hull .05 .15
51 Dave Manson .05 .15
52 Marty McInnis .05 .15
53 James Patrick .05 .15
54 Joe Sakic .20 .50
55 Andrei Nikolishin .05 .15
56 Adrian Aucoin .05 .15
57 Wade Flaherty RC .07 .20
58 Marek Malik .05 .15
59 Jason Allison .07 .20
60 Stephane Matteau .05 .15
61 Jason Dawe .05 .15
62 Ray Whitney .07 .20
63 Bill Lindsay .05 .15
64 Alexei Zhamnov .10 .25
65 Adam Deadmarsh .05 .15
66 Vincent Damphousse .07 .20
67 Josef Beranek .05 .15
68 Stanislav Neckar .05 .15
69 Alexei Kasatonov .05 .15
70 Jon Casey .07 .20
71 Todd Marchant .05 .15
72 Mike Sillinger .05 .15
73 Markus Naslund .10 .25
74 John MacLean .07 .20
75 Mike Ridley .05 .15
76 Petr Svoboda .05 .15
77 Milos Holan .05 .15
78 John Tucker .05 .15
79 Doug Brown .05 .15
80 Ted Donato .05 .15
81 Dimitri Yushkevich .05 .15
82 Brett Lindros .05 .15
83 Brian Bradley .07 .20
84 Mario Lemieux .40 1.00
85 Nikolai Khabibulin .07 .20
86 Larry Murphy .07 .20
87 Mike Donnelly .05 .15
88 Brian Holzinger RC .20 .50
89 Steve Larouche RC .05 .15
90 Ray Ferraro .05 .15
91 Mikhail Shtalenkov .05 .15
92 Viktor Kozlov .07 .20
93 Jon Klemm .05 .15
94 Mark Tinordi .05 .15
95 Bret Hedican .05 .15
96 Kevin Stevens .05 .15
97 Bernie Nicholls .07 .20
98 Pat Verbeek .05 .15
99 Wayne Gretzky .60 1.50
100 Rene Corbet .05 .15
101 Shayne Corson .07 .20
102 Cliff Ronning .05 .15
103 Olaf Kolzig .05 .15
104 Dominik Hasek .15 .40
105 Corey Millen .05 .15
106 Patrick Flatley .05 .15
107 Chris Therien .05 .15
108 Ken Wregget .07 .20
109 Paul Ysebaert .05 .15
110 Mike Gartner .12 .30
111 Michal Grosek .05 .15
112 Craig Billington .07 .20
113 Steve Yzerman .25 .60
114 Neal Broten .07 .20
115 Tom Barrasso .07 .20
116 Brent Fedyk .05 .15
117 Todd Gill .05 .15
118 Petr Klima .05 .15
119 Dave Karpa .05 .15
120 Geoff Courtnall .05 .15
121 Kelly Buchberger .05 .15
122 Eric LaCroix .05 .15
123 Janne Laukkanen .05 .15
124 Radek Bonk .05 .15
125 Sergio Momesso .05 .15
126 Esa Tikkanen .05 .15
127 Jon Rohloff .05 .15
128 Ken Klee RC .05 .15
129 Johan Garpenlov .05 .15
130 Sean Burke .05 .15
131 Shean Donovan .05 .15
132 Alexei Kovalev .07 .20
133 Sylvain Cote .05 .15
134 Jeff Friesen .05 .15
135 Scott Pearson .05 .15
136 Kirk McLean .07 .20
137 Glen Wesley .05 .15
138 Bob Kudelski .05 .15
139 Craig Johnson .05 .15
140 Zigmund Palffy .10 .25
141 Kris King .05 .15
142 Rusty Fitzgerald RC .05 .15
143 Trevor Kidd .07 .20
144 Dave Ellett .05 .15
145 Kelly Hrudey .07 .20
146 Igor Kravchuk .05 .15
147 Mats Sundin .10 .25
148 Shawn Chambers .05 .15
149 Bob Corkum .05 .15
150 Shjon Podein .05 .15
151 Murray Craven .05 .15
152 Roman Hamrlik .05 .15
153 Lyle Odelein .05 .15
154 Vyacheslav Kozlov .07 .20
155 David Emma .05 .15
156 Benoit Brunet .05 .15
157 Jozef Stumpel .05 .15
158 Darrin Madeley .05 .15
159 Keith Primeau .07 .20
160 Jeff Norton .05 .15
161 Mathieu Schneider .05 .15
162 Trent Klatt .05 .15
163 Pat Peake .05 .15
164 Rob Gaudreau .05 .15
165 Doug Bodger .05 .15
166 Sergei Nemchinov .05 .15
167 David Oliver .05 .15
168 Sandis Ozolinsh .05 .15
169 Mark Messier .20 .50
170 Chris Chelios .10 .25
171 Teemu Selanne .20 .50
172 Robert Svehla RC .05 .15
173 Nikolai Borschevsky .05 .15
174 Chris Pronger .10 .25
175 Dave Lowry .05 .15
176 Owen Nolan .10 .25
177 Sylvain Turgeon .05 .15
178 Nelson Emerson .05 .15
179 Theo Fleury .12 .30
180 Patrik Carnback .05 .15
181 Kevin Smyth .05 .15

182 Jeff Shantz .05 .15
183 Bob Carpenter .07 .20
184 Brendan Shanahan .10 .25
185 Tomas Sandstrom .07 .20
186 Eric Desjardins .07 .20
187 Alexei Zhitnik .05 .15
188 Alexander Mogilny .07 .20
189 Mariusz Czerkawski .05 .15
190 Vladimir Konstantinov .07 .20
191 Andy Moog .10 .25
192 Peter Popovic .05 .15
193 Marty McSorley .07 .20
194 Mikael Renberg .07 .20
195 Alek Stojanov RC .05 .15
196 Rick Tabaracci .07 .20
197 Adam Oates .10 .25
198 Garry Galley .05 .15
199 Todd Harvey .05 .15
200 Martin Lapointe .05 .15
201 Tony Granato .05 .15
202 Turner Stevenson .05 .15
203 Jeff Beukeboom .05 .15
204 Adam Foote .07 .20
205 Daren Puppa .07 .20
206 Paul Kariya .10 .25
207 German Titov .07 .20
208 Patrick Poulin .05 .15
209 Jesse Belanger .05 .15
210 Steven Rice .05 .15
211 Martin Brodeur .25 .60
212 Rob Pearson .05 .15
213 Igor Larionov .05 .15
214 Pavel Bure 5 .10 .25
215 Sergei Fedorov 5 .15 .40
216 Ed Belfour 5 .07 .20
217 Mark Messier 5 .20 .50
218 Steve Yzerman 5 .25 .60
219 Mats Sundin 5 .10 .25
220 Mike Modano .15 .40
221 Alexander Mogilny .07 .20
222 Wayne Gretzky 5 .60 1.50
223 Keith Primeau .07 .20
224 Adam Graves .07 .20
225 Owen Nolan .10 .25
226 Paul Coffey .10 .25
227 Jeremy Roenick 5 .15 .40
228 Felix Potvin 5 .15 .40
229 Trevor Kidd .07 .20
230 Ray Bourque .15 .40
231 Mario Lemieux 5 .40 1.00
232 Peter Bondra .10 .25
233 Brett Hull 5 .20 .50
234 Alexei Zhamnov .10 .25
235 Theo Fleury .12 .30
236 Brian Leetch .07 .20
237 Cam Neely MM .10 .25
238 Chris Chelios .10 .25
239 Adam Graves .07 .20
240 Doug Gilmour MM .12 .30
241 Jeremy Roenick MM .15 .40
242 Joe Sakic MM .20 .50
243 Keith Tkachuk .10 .25
244 Luc Robitaille .10 .25
245 Paul Kariya MM .10 .25
246 Owen Nolan .10 .25
247 John LeClair .10 .25
248 Paul Coffey .10 .25
249 Peter Bondra .10 .25
250 Ray Bourque .15 .40
251 Brett Hull MM .20 .50
252 Wayne Gretzky MM .60 1.50
253 Teemu Selanne MM .20 .50
254 Ray Sheppard .07 .20
255 Ron Francis .12 .30
256 Kevin Hatcher .07 .20
257 Brett Lindros .05 .15
258 Claude Lemieux .10 .25
259 Saku Koivu .10 .25
260 Radek Dvorak RC .12 .30
261 Niklas Sundstrom .10 .25
262 Chad Kilger RC .10 .25
263 Vitali Yachmenev .10 .25
264 Jeff O'Neill .10 .25
265 Brendan Witt .10 .25
266 Jason Bonsignore .05 .15
267 Aki Berg RC .10 .25
268 Eric Daze .10 .25
269 Shane Doan RC .30 .75
270 Daymond Langkow RC .10 .25
271 Alexandre Daigle .05 .15
272 Brian Noonan .05 .15
273 Guy Carbonneau .05 .15
274 Rick Tocchet .07 .20
275 Teppo Numminen .05 .15
276 Brian Skrudland .05 .15
277 Andrei Trefilov .05 .15
278 Joe Murphy .05 .15
279 Sergei Fedorov .15 .40
280 Doug Weight .10 .25
281 Robert Lang .05 .15
282 Darryl Shannon .05 .15
283 Cory Stillman .05 .15
284 Gary Suter .05 .15
285 Joe Nieuwendyk .07 .20
286 Terry Carkner .05 .15
287 Dimitri Khristich .05 .15
288 Alexander Karpovtsev .05 .15
289 Garth Snow .07 .20
290 Al MacInnis .12 .30
291 Doug Gilmour .12 .30
292 Mike Eastwood .05 .15
293 Steve Heinze .05 .15
294 Phil Housley .07 .20
295 Tim Taylor .05 .15
296 Curtis Joseph .12 .30
297 Patrick Roy .25 .60
298 Ted Drury .05 .15
299 Igor Korolev .05 .15
300 Ray Bourque .15 .40
301 Darren McCarty .10 .25
302 Miroslav Satan RC .12 .30
303 Adam Burt .05 .15
304 Valeri Bure .05 .15
305 Sergei Gonchar .05 .15
306 Jason York .05 .15
307 Brent Grieve .05 .15
308 Greg Johnson .05 .15
309 Kevin Hatcher .07 .20
310 Rob Niedermayer .07 .20
311 Nelson Emerson .05 .15
312 Mark Janssens .05 .15
313 Tommy Soderstrom .07 .20
314 Joey Kocur .05 .15
315 Craig Janney .05 .15
316 Alexander Selivanov .07 .20
317 Russ Courtnall .05 .15
318 Petr Sykora RC .25 .60
319 Rick Zombo .05 .15
320 Randy Burridge .05 .15
321 John Vanbiesbrouck .10 .25
322 Dmitri Mironov .05 .15
323 Sean Hill .05 .15
324 Rod Brind'Amour .10 .25
325 Wendel Clark .15 .40
326 Brent Gilchrist .05 .15
327 Tyler Wright .05 .15
328 Scott Daniels RC .05 .15
329 Adam Graves .07 .20
330 Dean Malkoc RC .05 .15
331 Jamie Macoun .05 .15
332 Sandy Moger RC .05 .15
333 Mike Peca .07 .20
334 Greg Johnson .05 .15
335 Jason Woolley .05 .15
336 Rob Dimaio .05 .15
337 Damian Rhodes .07 .20
338 Gino Odjick .05 .15
339 Peter Bondra .10 .25
340 Todd Ewen .05 .15
341 Matthew Barnaby .10 .25
342 Sylvain Lefebvre .05 .15
343 Oleg Petrov .05 .15
344 Jim Carey .07 .20
345 Stu Barnes .05 .15
346 Kelly Miller .05 .15
347 Antti Tormanen RC .05 .15
348 Ray Sheppard .07 .20
349 Igor Larionov .05 .15
350 Kjell Samuelsson .05 .15
351 Benoit Hogue .05 .15
352 Jeff Brown .07 .20
353 Nolan Baumgartner .05 .15
354 Denis Pederson .05 .15
355 Shawn Burr .05 .15
356 Jyrki Lumme .05 .15
357 Kevin Haller .05 .15
358 John Cullen .05 .15
359 Martin Gelinas .05 .15
360 Shawn McEachern .05 .15
361 Sandy McCarthy .05 .15
362 Grant Marshall .05 .15
363 Dean McAmmond .05 .15
364 Kevin Todd .05 .15
365 Bobby Holik .05 .15
366 Joel Otto .05 .15
367 Dave Andreychuk .10 .25
368 Ronnie Stern .05 .15
369 Jocelyn Thibault .07 .20
370 Dave Gagner .05 .15
371 Bryan Marchment .05 .15
372 Jari Kurri .10 .25
373 Bill Guerin .10 .25
374 Eric Lindros .15 .40
375 Adam Creighton .05 .15
376 Dimitri Yushkevich .05 .15
377 Peter Zezel .05 .15
378 Valeri Karpov .05 .15
379 Patrick Labrecque RC .05 .15
380 Mick Vukota .05 .15
381 Ulf Dahlen .05 .15
382 Enrico Ciccone .05 .15
383 Scott Niedermayer .10 .25
384 Ville Peltonen .05 .15
385 Blaine Lacher .07 .20
386 Pat LaFontaine .10 .25
387 Jeff Hackett .07 .20
388 Mike Keane .05 .15
389 Pierre Turgeon .07 .20
390 Scott Lachance .05 .15
391 Jason Wiemer .05 .15
392 Michal Pivonka .05 .15
393 Dennis Bonvie RC .05 .15
394 Glen Murray .07 .20
395 Bobby Dollas .05 .15
396 Paul Coffey .10 .25
397 Stephane Fiset .07 .20
398 Jere Lehtinen .05 .15
399 Scott Mellanby .07 .20
400 Robert Kron .05 .15
401 Doug Lidster .05 .15
402 Don Beaupre .07 .20
403 Arturs Irbe .05 .15
404 Brian Bellows .07 .20
405 Corey Hirsch .07 .20
406 Pavel Bure .10 .25
407 Chris Gratton .05 .15
408 Oleg Tverdovsky .10 .25
409 Derek Plante .05 .15
410 Dan Keczmer .05 .15
411 Donald Brashear .07 .20
412 Andrei Vasilyev RC .05 .15
413 Tommy Salo RC .15 .40
414 Kevin Lowe .07 .20
415 Dody Wood .05 .15
416 Denis Chasse .05 .15
417 Aaron Gavey .05 .15
418 Scott Walker .05 .15
419 Richard Park .10 .25
420 Mike Modano .15 .40
421 Kyle McLaren RC .10 .25
422 Jeremy Roenick .15 .40
423 Mark Fitzpatrick .07 .20
424 Landon Wilson RC .05 .15
425 Steve Rucchin .07 .20
426 Stephane Richer .07 .20
427 Martin Straka .05 .15
428 Ron Hextall .10 .25
429 Joe Dziedzic RC .05 .15
430 Peter Forsberg .20 .50
431 Dino Ciccarelli .05 .15
432 Robert Dirk .05 .15
433 Wayne Primeau RC .05 .15
434 Denis Savard .10 .25
435 Keith Carney .05 .15
436 Tom Fitzgerald .05 .15
437 Cale Hulse .05 .15
438 Mike Richter .10 .25
439 Marcus Ragnarsson RC .12 .30
440 Roman Vopat .05 .15
441 Zdenek Nedved .05 .15
442 Dale Hunter .07 .20
443 Bob Sweeney .05 .15
444 Randy McKay .05 .15
445 Chris Osgood .10 .25
446 Andrei Kovalenko .05 .15
447 Darius Kasparaitis .05 .15
448 Ulf Samuelsson .05 .15
449 Chris Joseph .05 .15
450 Chris Terreri .07 .20
451 Keith Jones .07 .20
452 Tim Cheveldae .07 .20
453 Stephen Leach .05 .15
454 Michael Nylander .05 .15
455 Ed Belfour .07 .20
456 Claude Lemieux .10 .25
457 Mike Ricci .05 .15
458 Shane Churla .05 .15
459 Kris Draper .10 .25
460 Byron Dafoe .07 .20
461 Troy Mallette .05 .15
462 Petr Nedved .07 .20
463 Kenny Jonsson .10 .25
464 Keith Tkachuk .10 .25
465 Jaromir Jagr .30 .75
466 Vladimir Malakhov .10 .25
467 Guy Hebert .07 .20
468 Brad May .05 .15
469 Bob Probert .10 .25
470 Sandis Ozolinsh .05 .15
471 Oleg Mikulchik RC .05 .15
472 Steve Thomas .07 .20
473 Travis Green .07 .20
474 Sergei Zubov .07 .20
475 Bill Houlder .07 .20
476 Roman Oksiuta .05 .15
477 Jamie Rivers .05 .15
478 Rob Blake .07 .20
479 Todd Elik .05 .15
480 Zarley Zalapski .05 .15
481 Darren Turcotte .05 .15
482 Scott Stevens .10 .25
483 Pat Falloon .05 .15
484 Grant Fuhr .15 .40
485 Martin Rucinsky .05 .15
486 Brett Hull .20 .50
487 Brian Leetch .07 .20
488 Shaun Van Allen .05 .15
489 Valeri Kamensky .07 .20
490 Mark Recchi .12 .30
491 Jason Muzzatti .07 .20
492 Andrew Cassels .05 .15
493 Nick Kypreos .05 .15
494 Bryan Smolinski .05 .15
495 Owen Nolan .10 .25
496 Bryan McCabe .10 .25
497 Matthieu Dandenault RC .20 .50
498 Deron Quint .07 .20
499 Jason Doig .10 .25
500 Marty Murray .10 .25
501 Ed Jovanovski .10 .25
502 Stefan Ustorf .05 .15
503 Jamie Langenbrunner .05 .15
504 Daniel Alfredsson RC .50 1.25
505 Darby Hendrickson .05 .15
506 Brett McLean RC .07 .20
507 Daniel Cleary RC .07 .20
508 Todd Robinson .05 .15
509 Arron Asham RC .07 .20
510 Daniel Corso RC .20 .50
511 Darren Van Oene RC .05 .15
512 Trevor Wasyluk RC .10 .25
513 Josh Holden RC .10 .25
514 Etienne Drapeau RC .07 .20
515 Matt Osborne .05 .15
516 Zenith Komarniski RC .07 .20
517 Chris Phillips RC .10 .25
518 Chris Fleury RC .10 .25
519 Cory Sarich RC .07 .20
520 Glenn Crawford RC .05 .15
521 Francois Methot RC .05 .15
522 Geoff Peters RC .05 .15
523 Joey Tetarenko .07 .20
524 Randy Petruk RC .07 .20
525 Mathieu Garon RC .25 .60
526 Daymond Langkow .10 .25
527 Craig Mills RC .05 .15
528 Rhett Warrener .05 .15
529 Marc Denis RC .30 .75
530 Jose Theodore RC .75 2.00
531 Curtis Brown RC .10 .25
532 Chad Allen .05 .15
533 Denis Gauthier RC .05 .15
534 Brad Larsen .05 .15
535 Jamie Wright RC .10 .25
536 Mike Watt RC .10 .25
537 Jason Holland RC .10 .25
538 Robb Gordon RC .10 .25
539 Hnat Domenichelli RC .10 .25
540 Ondrej Kratena RC .10 .25
541 Michal Bros RC .10 .25
542 Marek Posmyk RC .10 .25
543 Marek Melanovsky RC .10 .25
544 Jan Tomajko .10 .25
545 Ales Pisa RC .10 .25
546 Miika Elomo .10 .25
547 Timo Salonen .10 .25
548 Teemu Riihijarvi RC .10 .25
549 Antti-Jussi Niemi .10 .25
550 Pasi Petrilainen RC .10 .25
551 Toni Lydman RC .10 .25
552 Dmitri Nabokov .10 .25
553 Alexei Morozov .10 .25
554 Sergei Samsonov .10 .25
555 Alexei Vasilyev RC .10 .25
556 Andrei Petrunin .10 .25
557 Dimitri Riabykin .10 .25
558 Sergei Zimakov RC .10 .25
559 Peter Nylander RC .10 .25
560 Marcus Nilsson UER RC .20 .50
561 Niklas Anger RC .10 .25
562 Per Anton Lundstrom RC .10 .25
563 Patrik Wallenberg RC .10 .25
564 Per Ragnar Bergkvist RC .10 .25
565 Mike Sylvia .10 .25
566 Marty Reasoner .10 .25
567 Reg Berg RC .10 .25
568 Tom Poti RC .10 .25
569 Chris Drury RC .30 .75
570 Michael McBain .10 .25

1995-96 Upper Deck Electric Ice

*VETS: 4X TO 10X BASIC CARDS
*ROOKIES: 1X TO 2.5X

1995-96 Upper Deck Electric Ice Gold

*VETS: 20X TO 50X BASIC CARDS
*ROOKIES: 8X TO 20X
J171 Teemu Selanne 2.00 5.00

1995-96 Upper Deck All-Star Game Predictors

*REDEEMED CARDS: 2X TO 3X BASIC PREDICTORS
1 Wayne Gretzky 75.00 200.00
2 Sergei Fedorov 20.00 50.00
3 Brett Hull 15.00 40.00
4 Alexander Mogilny 6.00 15.00
5 Joe Sakic 20.00 50.00
6 Paul Kariya 30.00 75.00
7 Teemu Selanne 20.00 50.00
8 Paul Coffey 10.00 25.00
9 Chris Chelios 15.00 40.00
10 Doug Gilmour 10.00 25.00
11 Peter Forsberg 25.00 60.00
12 Jeremy Roenick 15.00 40.00
13 Theo Fleury 10.00 25.00
14 Mike Modano 15.00 40.00
15 Steve Yzerman 50.00 125.00
16 Mario Lemieux 60.00 150.00
17 Jaromir Jagr 25.00 60.00
18 Eric Lindros 20.00 50.00
19 Mark Messier 15.00 40.00
20 Brendan Shanahan 15.00 40.00
21 Ray Bourque 75.00 200.00
22 Cam Neely 15.00 40.00
23 Ron Francis 6.00 15.00
24 John LeClair 15.00 40.00
25 Brian Leetch 10.00 25.00
26 Peter Bondra 10.00 25.00
27 Scott Stevens 6.00 15.00
28 Adam Oates 6.00 15.00
29 Martin Brodeur 25.00 60.00
30 Longshot 2.00 5.00

1995-96 Upper Deck Freeze Frame

COMPLETE SET (20) 25.00 60.00
*JUMBOS: .8X TO 2X BASIC INSERTS
F1 Peter Forsberg 2.50 6.00
F2 Wayne Gretzky 6.00 15.00
F3 Eric Lindros 1.50 4.00
F4 Jaromir Jagr 2.00 5.00
F5 Cam Neely 1.25 3.00
F6 Jeremy Roenick 1.25 3.00
F7 Mark Messier 1.25 3.00
F8 Sergei Fedorov 1.25 3.00
F9 Paul Kariya 1.25 3.00
F10 Pavel Bure 1.25 3.00
F11 Dominik Hasek 2.50 5.00
F12 Theo Fleury .75 2.00
F13 Alexei Zhamnov .40 1.00
F14 Martin Brodeur 3.00 8.00
F15 Brett Hull 1.25 3.00
F16 Mario Lemieux 4.00 10.00
F17 Paul Coffey .60 1.50
F18 Brian Leetch .60 1.50
F19 Ray Bourque 1.25 3.00
F20 Jim Carey .75 1.50

1995-96 Upper Deck Gretzky Collection

COMPLETE SET (24) 60.00 120.00
COMP.CC SET (10) 12.00 30.00
COMP.SP SET (4) 30.00 80.00
COMP.UD SER.1 (5) 15.00 40.00
COMP.UD SER.2 (4) 15.00 40.00
COMMON CC (G1-G9/HDR) 2.00 5.00
COMMON UD (G10-G17/HUD) 4.00 10.00
COMMON SP (G18-G20/HSP) 12.50 30.00
*JUMBOS: .6X TO 1.5X BASIC INSERTS

1995-96 Upper Deck NHL All-Stars

COMPLETE SET (20) 25.00 50.00
*JUMBOS: .4X TO 1X BASIC INSERTS
AS1 R.Bourque/P.Coffey 1.00 2.50
AS2 Stevens/Chelios .75 2.00
AS3 J.Jagr/B.Hull 1.25 3.00
AS4 B.Shanahan/P.Bure .75 2.00
AS5 M.Lemieux/W.Gretzky 8.00 20.00
AS6 M.Brodeur/E.Belfour 2.00 5.00
AS7 Leetch/Lidstrom .75 2.00
AS8 Hamrlik/Suter .75 2.00
AS9 Desjardins/MacInnis .75 2.00
AS10 Neely/Mogilny .75 2.00
AS11 Bondra/Fleury .75 2.00
AS12 D.Alfredsson/T.Selanne .75 2.00
AS13 Verbeek/Nolan .75 2.00
AS14 J.LeClair/P.Kariya 2.00 5.00
AS15 P.Turgeon/S.Fedorov 1.00 2.50
AS16 M.Messier/D.Weight .75 2.00
AS17 E.Lindros/P.Forsberg 2.50 6.00
AS18 Francis/Sundin .75 2.00
AS19 J.Vanbies./C.Osgood .75 2.00
AS20 D.Hasek/F.Potvin 2.00 5.00

1995-96 Upper Deck Predictor Hobby

COMPLETE SET (40) 30.00 80.00
COMP.HART PRIZE SET (10) 6.00 15.00
COMP.VEZINA PRIZE (10) 5.00 12.00
COMP.CALDER PRIZE (10) 2.50 6.00
COMP.NORRIS PRIZE (10) 2.50 6.00
*PRIZE CARDS: .2X TO .5X BASIC INSERTS
H1 Eric Lindros 1.00 2.50
H2 Jaromir Jagr 1.50 4.00
H3 Paul Coffey 1.00 2.50
H4 Mario Lemieux WIN 4.00 10.00
H5 Martin Brodeur 2.50 6.00
H6 Sergei Fedorov 1.00 2.50
H7 Wayne Gretzky 6.00 15.00
H8 Peter Forsberg 1.50 4.00
H9 Mark Messier WIN 1.25 3.00
H10 Hart Long Shot .40 1.00
H11 Martin Brodeur 2.50 6.00
H12 Mike Richter 1.00 2.50
H13 Dominik Hasek 2.00 5.00
H14 Patrick Roy 4.00 10.00
H15 Blaine Lacher .40 1.00
H16 Jim Carey WIN .40 1.00
H17 Felix Potvin 1.25 3.00
H18 Ed Belfour 1.25 3.00
H19 John Vanbiesbrouck .75 2.00
H20 Vezina Long Shot WIN .40 1.00
H21 Vitali Yachmenev .40 1.00
H22 Saku Koivu 1.00 2.50
H23 Daniel Alfredsson WIN 2.00 5.00
H24 Ed Jovanovski .40 1.00
H25 Aki Berg .40 1.00
H26 Radek Dvorak .40 1.00
H27 Shane Doan .75 2.00
H28 Niklas Sundstrom .40 1.00
H29 Eric Daze WIN .40 1.00
H30 Calder Long Shot .40 1.00
H31 Paul Coffey .75 2.00
H32 Ray Bourque WIN 1.25 3.00
H33 Brian Leetch .75 2.00
H34 Chris Chelios WIN 1.25 3.00
H35 Scott Stevens .40 1.00
H36 Nicklas Lidstrom 1.00 2.50
H37 Sergei Zubov .40 1.00
H38 Larry Murphy .40 1.00
H39 Roman Hamrlik .40 1.00
H40 Norris Long Shot .40 1.00

1995-96 Upper Deck Predictor Retail

COMPLETE SET (60) 75.00 200.00
COMP.ASSIST PRIZE (10) 4.00 10.00
COMP.GOAL PRIZE (10) 6.00 15.00
COMP.POINT PRIZE (10) 6.00 15.00
COMP.ROSS PRIZE (10) 8.00 20.00
COMP.PEARSON PRIZE (10) 8.00 20.00
COMP.SMYTHE PRIZE (10) 10.00 25.00
*PRIZE CARDS: .2X TO .5X BASIC INSERTS
R1 Cam Neely 1.25 3.00
R2 Eric Lindros 1.25 3.00
R3 Jaromir Jagr WIN 2.00 5.00
R4 Brendan Shanahan 1.25 3.00
R5 Brett Hull 1.50 4.00
R6 Alexander Mogilny .60 1.50
R7 Owen Nolan .60 1.50
R8 Theo Fleury .40 1.00
R9 Pavel Bure 1.25 3.00
R10 Assists Long Shot WIN .40 1.00
R11 Ron Francis WIN .60 1.50
R12 Paul Coffey 1.25 3.00
R13 Wayne Gretzky 6.00 15.00
R14 Joe Sakic 2.50 6.00
R15 Steve Yzerman 4.00 10.00
R16 Adam Oates .60 1.50
R17 Joe Juneau .40 1.00
R18 Brian Leetch .60 1.50
R19 Pat LaFontaine 1.25 3.00
R20 Goals Long Shot WIN .40 1.00
R21 Eric Lindros 1.25 3.00
R22 Jaromir Jagr WIN 2.00 5.00
R23 Wayne Gretzky 6.00 15.00
R24 Sergei Fedorov 1.50 4.00
R25 Peter Forsberg 2.00 5.00
R26 Pavel Bure 1.25 3.00
R27 Joe Sakic 2.50 6.00
R28 Alexei Zhamnov .40 1.00
R29 Pat LaFontaine 1.25 3.00
R30 Points Long Shot WIN .40 1.00
R31 Wayne Gretzky 6.00 15.00
R32 Mario Lemieux WIN 4.00 10.00
R33 Eric Lindros 1.25 3.00
R34 Sergei Fedorov 1.50 4.00
R35 Alexander Mogilny .60 1.50
R36 Joe Sakic 2.50 6.00
R37 Peter Forsberg 2.00 5.00
R38 Jaromir Jagr WIN 2.00 5.00
R39 Mark Messier 1.25 3.00
R40 Ross Long Shot .40 1.00
R41 Wayne Gretzky 6.00 15.00
R42 Mario Lemieux 4.00 10.00
R43 Paul Kariya 1.25 3.00
R44 Sergei Fedorov 1.50 4.00
R45 Joe Sakic 2.50 6.00
R46 Jaromir Jagr WIN 2.00 5.00
R47 Jeremy Roenick 1.50 4.00
R48 Ray Bourque 1.25 3.00
R49 Teemu Selanne 1.25 3.00
R50 Pearson Long Shot .40 1.00
R51 Wayne Gretzky 6.00 15.00
R52 Eric Lindros 1.25 3.00
R53 Mario Lemieux WIN 4.00 10.00
R54 Peter Forsberg 2.00 5.00
R55 Patrick Roy WIN 5.00 12.00
R56 Mark Messier 1.25 3.00
R57 Martin Brodeur 2.50 6.00
R58 Steve Yzerman 4.00 10.00
R59 Mike Modano 1.50 4.00
R60 Smythe Long Shot WIN .40 1.00

1995-96 Upper Deck Special Edition

COMPLETE SET (180) 20.00 50.00
*GOLDS: 6X TO 15X BASIC INSERTS
SE1 Paul Kariya .25 .60
SE2 Oleg Tverdovsky .07 .20
SE3 Guy Hebert .10 .30
SE4 Ray Bourque .25 .60
SE5 Adam Oates .10 .30
SE6 Mariusz Czerkawski .07 .20
SE7 Blaine Lacher .10 .30
SE8 Garry Galley .07 .20
SE9 Donald Audette .07 .20
SE10 Pat LaFontaine .25 .60
SE11 Alexei Zhitnik .07 .20
SE12 Joe Nieuwendyk .10 .30
SE13 Phil Housley .10 .30
SE14 German Titov .07 .20
SE15 Trevor Kidd .10 .30
SE16 Bernie Nicholls .07 .20
SE17 Chris Chelios .25 .60
SE18 Tony Amonte .10 .30
SE19 Ed Belfour .25 .60
SE20 Jon Klemm .07 .20
SE21 Peter Forsberg .40 1.00
SE22 Adam Deadmarsh .07 .20
SE23 Stephane Fiset .10 .30
SE24 Dave Gagner .07 .20
SE25 Kevin Hatcher .07 .20
SE26 Mike Modano .30 .75
SE27 Keith Primeau .07 .20
SE28 Dino Ciccarelli .07 .20
SE29 Nicklas Lidstrom .25 .60
SE30 Steve Yzerman 1.25 3.00
SE31 Doug Weight .10 .30
SE32 Bill Ranford .10 .30
SE33 Stu Barnes .07 .20
SE34 Bob Kudelski .07 .20
SE35 Rob Niedermayer .10 .30
SE36 Andrew Cassels .07 .20
SE37 Darren Turcotte .07 .20
SE38 Andrei Nikolishin .07 .20
SE39 Sean Burke .10 .30
SE40 Rick Tocchet .10 .30
SE41 Jari Kurri .25 .60
SE42 Rob Blake .10 .30
SE43 Mark Recchi .10 .30
SE44 Pierre Turgeon .10 .30
SE45 Vladimir Malakhov .07 .20
SE46 Valeri Bure .07 .20
SE47 Stephane Richer .10 .30
SE48 Bill Guerin .10 .30
SE49 Scott Stevens .10 .30
SE50 Claude Lemieux .07 .20
SE51 Zigmund Palffy .10 .30
SE52 Kirk Muller .07 .20
SE53 Todd Bertuzzi .07 .20
SE54 Brett Lindros .07 .20
SE55 Brian Leetch .10 .30
SE56 Alexei Kovalev .07 .20
SE57 Adam Graves .07 .20
SE58 Mike Richter .25 .60
SE59 Alexei Yashin .07 .20
SE60 Alexandre Daigle .07 .20
SE61 Don Beaupre .07 .20
SE62 Radek Bonk .07 .20
SE63 John LeClair .25 .60
SE64 Rod Brind'Amour .10 .30
SE65 Ron Hextall .10 .30
SE66 Ron Francis .10 .30
SE67 Markus Naslund .25 .60
SE68 Tom Barrasso .10 .30
SE69 Ian Laperriere .07 .20
SE70 Esa Tikkanen .07 .20
SE71 Al MacInnis .10 .30
SE72 Ulf Dahlen .07 .20
SE73 Craig Janney .07 .20
SE74 Jeff Friesen .07 .20
SE75 Chris Gratton .07 .20
SE76 Roman Hamrlik .07 .20
SE77 Alexander Selivanov .07 .20
SE78 Daren Puppa .10 .30
SE79 Dave Andreychuk .10 .30
SE80 Doug Gilmour .10 .30
SE81 Kenny Jonsson .07 .20
SE82 Trevor Linden .10 .30
SE83 Kirk McLean .10 .30
SE84 Jeff Brown .07 .20
SE85 Keith Jones .07 .20
SE86 Joe Juneau .07 .20
SE87 Jim Carey .10 .30
SE88 Keith Tkachuk .25 .60
SE89 Teemu Selanne .25 .60
SE90 Igor Korolev .07 .20
SE91 Mike Sillinger .07 .20
SE92 Steve Rucchin .10 .30
SE93 Valeri Karpov .07 .20
SE94 Cam Neely .25 .60
SE95 Shawn McEachern .07 .20
SE96 Kevin Stevens .07 .20
SE97 Ted Donato .07 .20
SE98 Dominik Hasek .50 1.25
SE99 Randy Burridge .07 .20
SE100 Jason Dawe .07 .20
SE101 Theo Fleury .07 .20
SE102 Michael Nylander .07 .20
SE103 Rick Tabaracci .10 .30
SE104 Jeremy Roenick .30 .75
SE105 Bob Probert .10 .30
SE106 Patrick Poulin .07 .20
SE107 Gary Suter .07 .20
SE108 Claude Lemieux .07 .20
SE109 Sandis Ozolinsh .07 .20
SE110 Patrick Roy 1.25 3.00
SE111 Joe Sakic .50 1.25
SE112 Derian Hatcher .07 .20
SE113 Greg Adams .07 .20
SE114 Todd Harvey .10 .30
SE115 Sergei Fedorov .40 1.00
SE116 Chris Osgood .10 .30
SE117 Vyacheslav Kozlov .10 .30
SE118 Paul Coffey .25 .60
SE119 Jason Arnott .07 .20
SE120 David Oliver .07 .20
SE121 Todd Marchant .07 .20
SE122 John Vanbiesbrouck .10 .30
SE123 Jody Hull .07 .20
SE124 Jason Woolley .07 .20
SE125 Brendan Shanahan .25 .60
SE126 Nelson Emerson .07 .20
SE127 Geoff Sanderson .07 .20
SE128 Wayne Gretzky 3.00 8.00
SE129 Marty McSorley .07 .20
SE130 Yanic Perreault .07 .20
SE131 Jocelyn Thibault .25 .60
SE132 Brian Savage .07 .20
SE133 Vincent Damphousse .07 .20
SE134 John Mclean .10 .30
SE135 Martin Brodeur 1.50 4.00
SE136 Steve Thomas .07 .20
SE137 Scott Niedermayer .07 .20
SE138 Travis Green .07 .20
SE139 Wendel Clark .10 .30
SE140 Tommy Soderstrom .10 .30
SE141 Mark Messier .25 .60
SE142 Ulf Samuelsson .07 .20
SE143 Ray Ferraro .07 .20
SE144 Luc Robitaille .10 .30
SE145 Daniel Alfredsson 1.00 2.50
SE146 Martin Straka .07 .20
SE147 Steve Duschene .07 .20
SE148 Eric Lindros .25 .60
SE149 Mikael Renberg .10 .30
SE150 Eric Desjardins .10 .30
SE151 Joel Otto .07 .20
SE152 Mario Lemieux 1.25 3.00
SE153 Jaromir Jagr .40 1.00
SE154 Petr Nedved .10 .30
SE155 Sergei Zubov .07 .20
SE156 Tomas Sandstrom .07 .20
SE157 Brett Hull .30 .75
SE158 Grant Fuhr .25 .60
SE159 Shayne Corson .07 .20
SE160 Chris Pronger .25 .60
SE161 Ray Sheppard .07 .20
SE162 Arturs Irbe .10 .30
SE163 Owen Nolan .10 .30
SE164 Andrei Nazarov .07 .20
SE165 Paul Ysebaert .07 .20
SE166 Brian Bradley .07 .20
SE167 Petr Klima .07 .20
SE168 Felix Potvin .25 .60
SE169 Mats Sundin .25 .60
SE170 Larry Murphy .10 .30
SE171 Benoit Hogue .07 .20
SE172 Pavel Bure .25 .60
SE173 Alexander Mogilny .10 .30
SE174 Cliff Ronning .07 .20
SE175 Pat Peake .07 .20
SE176 Sylvain Cote .07 .20
SE177 Peter Bondra .10 .30
SE178 Dallas Drake .07 .20
SE179 Tim Cheveldae .07 .20
SE180 Darren Turcotte .07 .20

1996-97 Upper Deck

1 Paul Kariya .25 .60
2 Guy Hebert .20 .50
3 J.F. Jomphe RC .25 .60
4 Joe Sacco .30 .75
5 Jason York .15 .40
6 Alex Hicks RC .25 .60
7 Mikhail Shtalenkov .15 .40
8 Bill Ranford .20 .50
9 Kyle McLaren .15 .40
10 Rick Tocchet .20 .50
11 Jon Rohloff .15 .40
12 Jozef Stumpel .15 .40
13 Cam Neely .25 .60
14 Ray Bourque .40 1.00
15 Pat LaFontaine .25 .60
16 Brian Holzinger .20 .50
17 Alexei Zhitnik .15 .40
18 Donald Audette .15 .40
19 Jason Dawe .15 .40
20 Wayne Primeau .15 .40
21 Mike Peca .15 .40
22 Theo Fleury .50 1.25
23 Sandy McCarthy .15 .40
24 Zarley Zalapski .15 .40
25 Trevor Kidd .15 .40
26 Steve Chiasson .15 .40
27 Michael Nylander .15 .40
28 Ronnie Stern .15 .40
29 Eric Daze .20 .50
30 Jeff Hackett .20 .50
31 Chris Chelios .25 .60
32 Tony Amonte .20 .50
33 Bob Probert .20 .50
34 Eric Weinrich .15 .40
35 Jeremy Roenick .40 1.00
36 Mike Ricci .15 .40
37 Sandis Ozolinsh .15 .40
38 Patrick Roy .75 2.00
39 Uwe Krupp .15 .40
40 Stephane Yelle .15 .40
41 Adam Deadmarsh .15 .40
42 Scott Young .15 .40
43 Mike Modano .40 1.00
44 Derian Hatcher .15 .40
45 Todd Harvey .15 .40
46 Brent Fedyk .15 .40
47 Grant Marshall .15 .40
48 Jamie Langenbrunner .15 .40
49 Jere Lehtinen .15 .40
50 Steve Yzerman .75 2.00
51 Igor Larionov .25 .60
52 Vladimir Konstantinov .20 .50
53 Chris Osgood .25 .60
54 Jamie Pushor .15 .40
55 Darren McCarty .15 .40
56 Nicklas Lidstrom .30 .75
57 Jason Arnott .20 .50
58 Doug Weight .15 .40
59 Todd Marchant .15 .40
60 David Oliver .15 .40
61 Luke Richardson .15 .40
62 Jason Bonsignore .15 .40
63 John Vanbiesbrouck .25 .60
64 Stu Barnes .15 .40
65 Martin Straka .15 .40
66 Ed Jovanovski .20 .50
67 Robert Svehla .15 .40
68 Gord Murphy .15 .40
69 Tom Fitzgerald .15 .40
70 Jeff O'Neill .15 .40
71 Jason Muzzatti .15 .40
72 Sean Burke .20 .50
73 Jeff Brown .15 .40
74 Andrew Cassels .15 .40
75 Geoff Sanderson .20 .50
76 Dimitri Khristich .15 .40
77 Vitali Yachmenev .15 .40
78 Kevin Stevens .15 .40
79 Yanic Perreault .15 .40
80 Craig Johnson .15 .40
81 John Slaney .15 .40
82 Saku Koivu .25 .60
83 Jocelyn Thibault .20 .50
84 Vladimir Malakhov .15 .40
85 Turner Stevenson .15 .40
86 Vincent Damphousse .20 .50
87 Mark Recchi .30 .75
88 Patrice Brisebois .15 .40
89 Dave Andreychuk .15 .40
90 Bill Guerin .25 .60
91 Martin Brodeur 1.00 2.50

92 Scott Niedermayer .25 .60
93 Petr Sykora .15 .40
94 Stephane Richer .20 .50
95 John MacLean .20 .50
96 Eric Fichaud .20 .50
97 Zigmund Palffy .25 .60
98 Alexander Semak .15 .40
99 Bryan McCabe .15 .40
100 Darby Hendrickson .15 .40
101 Kenny Jonsson .15 .40
102 Marty McInnis .15 .40
103 Alexei Kovalev .20 .50
104 Ulf Samuelsson .15 .40
105 Jeff Beukeboom .15 .40
106 Marty McSorley .20 .50
107 Niklas Sundstrom .15 .40
108 W.Gretzky/M.Messier 1.50 4.00
109 Mike Richter .25 .60
110 Alexei Yashin .20 .50
111 Randy Cunneyworth .15 .40
112 Damian Rhodes .20 .50
113 Daniel Alfredsson .25 .60
114 Antti Tormanen .15 .40
115 Ted Drury .15 .40
116 Janne Laukkanen .15 .40
117 Sean Hill .15 .40
118 John LeClair .25 .60
119 Ron Hextall .25 .60
120 Dale Hawerchuk .30 .75
121 Rod Brind'Amour .25 .60
122 Pat Falloon .15 .40
123 Eric Desjardins .20 .50
124 Joel Otto .15 .40
125 Alexei Zhamnov .20 .50
126 Nikolai Khabibulin .20 .50
127 Craig Janney .20 .50
128 Deron Quint .15 .40
129 Oleg Tverdovsky .20 .50
130 Chad Kilger .15 .40
131 Teppo Numminen .15 .40
132 Tom Barrasso .20 .50
133 Ron Francis .30 .75
134 Petr Nedved .20 .50
135 Ken Wregget .20 .50
136 Joe Dziedzic .15 .40
137 Tomas Sandstrom .15 .40
138 Dmitri Mironov .15 .40
139 Shayne Corson .20 .50
140 Grant Fuhr .40 1.00
141 Al MacInnis .30 .75
142 Stephen Leach .15 .40
143 Murray Baron .15 .40
144 Chris Pronger .25 .60
145 Jamie Rivers .15 .40
146 Owen Nolan .25 .60
147 Chris Terreri .20 .50
148 Marcus Ragnarsson .15 .40
149 Shean Donovan .15 .40
150 Ray Whitney .15 .40
151 Michal Sykora .15 .40
152 Viktor Kozlov .15 .40
153 Roman Hamrlik .15 .40
154 Bill Houlder .15 .40
155 Mikael Andersson .15 .40
156 Petr Klima .15 .40
157 Jason Wiemer .15 .40
158 Rob Zamuner .15 .40
159 Paul Ysebaert .15 .40
160 Mats Sundin .25 .60
161 Larry Murphy UER .20 .50
162 Doug Gilmour .30 .75
163 Todd Warriner .15 .40
164 Dimitri Yushkevich .15 .40
165 Kirk Muller .15 .40
166 Jamie Macoun .15 .40
167 Alexander Mogilny .20 .50
168 Corey Hirsch .20 .50
169 Trevor Linden .25 .60
170 Markus Naslund .25 .60
171 Martin Gelinas .15 .40
172 Jyrki Lumme .15 .40
173 Bret Hedican .15 .40
174 Jim Carey .25 .60
175 Sergei Gonchar .15 .40
176 Joe Juneau .15 .40
177 Brendan Witt .15 .40
178 Dale Hunter .20 .50
179 Steve Konowalchuk .15 .40
180 Peter Bondra .25 .60
181 Jarome Iginla .30 .75
182 Ralph Intranuovo .15 .40
183 Anders Eriksson .15 .40
184 Andrew Brunette RC .30 .75
185 Steve Sullivan RC .20 .50
186 Brandon Convery .15 .40
187 Ethan Moreau RC .25 .60
188 Marko Kiprusoff .15 .40
189 Jason McBain .15 .40
190 Mark Kolesar .15 .40
191 Greg DeVries RC .25 .60
192 Alexei Yegorov RC .25 .60
193 Sebastien Bordeleau RC .25 .60
194 Nick Stajduhar .15 .40
195 Jan Caloun RC .25 .60
196 Dino Ciccarelli TTG .25 .60
197 Ron Hextall TTG .25 .60
198 Murray Baron TTG .15 .40
199 Patrick Roy TTG .60 1.50
200 Scott Mellanby TTG .20 .50
201 Tie Domi TTG .20 .50
202 Glenn Healy TTG .20 .50
203 Keith Primeau .20 .50
204 Joe Sakic TTG .50 1.25
205 Jeremy Roenick TTG .40 1.00
206 Sergei Fedorov TTG .40 1.00
207 Claude Lemieux TTG .15 .40
208 Theo Fleury TTG .50 1.25
209 Checklist (1-104) .10 .25
210 Checklist (105-210) .10 .25
211 Teemu Selanne .50 1.25
212 Jari Kurri .25 .60
213 Darren Van Impe .15 .40
214 Steve Rucchin .15 .40
215 Ruslan Salei RC .25 .60
216 Adam Oates .25 .60
217 Don Sweeney .15 .40
218 Steve Staios RC .25 .60
219 Barry Richter .15 .40
220 Mattias Timander RC .25 .60
221 Ted Donato .15 .40
222 Dominik Hasek .40 1.00
223 Derek Plante .15 .40
224 Vaclav Varada RC .25 .60
225 Andrei Trefilov .15 .40
226 Curtis Brown .15 .40
227 German Titov .15 .40
228 Robert Reichel .15 .40
229 Cory Stillman .15 .40
230 Chris O'Sullivan .15 .40
231 Corey Millen .15 .40
232 Jonas Hoglund .15 .40
233 Alexei Zhamnov .20 .50
234 Ed Belfour .25 .60
235 Gary Suter .15 .40
236 Kevin Miller .15 .40
237 Tuomas Gronman .15 .40
238 Enrico Ciccone .15 .40
239 Peter Forsberg .50 1.25
240 Joe Sakic .50 1.25
241 Valeri Kamensky .20 .50
242 Landon Wilson .15 .40
243 Claude Lemieux .15 .40
244 Eric Lacroix .15 .40
245 Joe Nieuwendyk .20 .50
246 Sergei Zubov .20 .50
247 Benoit Hogue .15 .40
248 Arturs Irbe .20 .50
249 Pat Verbeek .15 .40
250 Sergei Fedorov .40 1.00
251 Vyacheslav Kozlov .15 .40
252 Brendan Shanahan .25 .60
253 Kevin Hodson RC .25 .60
254 Greg Johnson .15 .40
255 Tomas Holmstrom RC .75 2.00
256 Curtis Joseph .30 .75
257 Dean McAmmond .15 .40
258 Ryan Smyth .20 .50
259 Mike Grier RC .30 .75
260 Miroslav Satan .15 .40
261 Rem Murray RC .25 .60
262 Rob Niedermayer .20 .50
263 Ray Sheppard .20 .50
264 Dave Lowry .15 .40
265 Scott Mellanby .20 .50
266 Rhett Warrener .15 .40
267 Per Gustafsson RC .25 .60
268 Paul Coffey .25 .60
269 Nelson Emerson .15 .40
270 Kevin Dineen .15 .40
271 Keith Primeau .20 .50
272 Hnat Domenichelli .15 .40
273 Ray Ferraro .15 .40
274 Stephane Fiset .20 .50
275 Kai Nurminen RC .25 .60
276 Dan Bylsma RC .25 .60
277 Mattias Norstrom .15 .40
278 Rob Blake .25 .60
279 Jose Theodore .30 .75
280 Martin Rucinsky .15 .40
281 Darcy Tucker .15 .40
282 David Wilkie .15 .40
283 Valeri Bure .15 .40
284 Steve Thomas .15 .40
285 Brian Rolston .20 .50
286 Scott Stevens .25 .60
287 Shawn Chambers .15 .40
288 Denis Pederson .15 .40
289 Lyle Odelein .15 .40
290 Travis Green .20 .50
291 Todd Bertuzzi .25 .60
292 Niclas Andersson .15 .40
293 Darius Kasparaitis .15 .40
294 Bryan Berard .25 .60
295 Daniel Goneau RC .25 .60
296 Christian Dube .15 .40
297 Adam Graves .15 .40
298 Sergei Nemchinov .15 .40
299 Mark Messier .50 1.25
300 Brian Leetch .20 .50
301 Radek Bonk .15 .40
302 Alexandre Daigle .15 .40
303 Andreas Dackell RC .25 .60
304 Steve Duchesne .15 .40
305 Wade Redden .15 .40
306 Eric Lindros .40 1.00
307 Mikael Renberg .20 .50
308 Shjon Podein .15 .40
309 Dainius Zubrus RC .30 .75
310 Janne Niinimaa .25 .60
311 Karl Dykhuis .15 .40
312 Jeremy Roenick .40 1.00
313 Keith Tkachuk .25 .60
314 Shane Doan .20 .50
315 Cliff Ronning .15 .40
316 Mike Gartner .30 .75
317 Dave Manson .15 .40
318 Shawn Antoski .15 .40
319 Kevin Hatcher .15 .40
320 Jaromir Jagr .75 2.00
321 Mario Lemieux .75 2.00
322 Bryan Smolinski .15 .40
323 Stefan Bergkvist RC .25 .60
324 Brett Hull .50 1.25
325 Joe Murphy .15 .40
326 Stephane Matteau .15 .40
327 Geoff Courtnall .15 .40
328 Jim Campbell .15 .40
329 Harry York RC .25 .60
330 Kelly Hrudey .20 .50
331 Al Iafrate .15 .40
332 Jeff Friesen .15 .40
333 Darren Turcotte .15 .40
334 Bernie Nicholls .20 .50
335 Ville Peltonen .15 .40
336 Dino Ciccarelli .25 .60
337 Chris Gratton .20 .50
338 Daren Puppa .20 .50
339 Alexander Selivanov .15 .40
340 Daymond Langkow .20 .50
341 Felix Potvin .40 1.00
342 Wendel Clark .40 1.00
343 Mathieu Schneider .15 .40
344 Dave Ellet .15 .40
345 Fredrik Modin RC .25 .60
346 Sergei Berezin RC .40 1.00
347 Pavel Bure .25 .60
348 Kirk McLean .20 .50
349 Mike Sillinger .15 .40
350 Russ Courtnall .15 .40
351 Scott Walker .15 .40
352 Esa Tikkanen .15 .40
353 Pat Peake .15 .40
354 Olaf Kolzig .25 .60
355 Michal Pivonka .15 .40
356 Richard Zednik RC .30 .75
357 Phil Housley .20 .50
358 Anson Carter .20 .50
359 Eric Daze OII .20 .50
360 Felix Potvin OII .40 1.00
361 Wayne Gretzky OII 1.50 4.00
362 Ed Jovanovski OII .20 .50
363 Mike Modano OII .40 1.00
364 Peter Bondra OII .25 .60
365 Patrick Roy OII .60 1.50
366 Ray Bourque OII .40 1.00
367 Roman Hamrlik OII .15 .40
368 John LeClair OII .25 .60
369 Adam Colagiacomo RC .25 .60
370 Joe Thornton RC 5.00 12.00
371 Patrick Desrochers RC .25 .60
372 Pierre-Luc Therrien RC .25 .60
373 Nick Boynton RC .25 .60
374 Andrew Ference RC .25 .60
375 Jean-Francois Fortin RC .25 .60
376 Daniel Tetrault RC .25 .60
377 Luc Theoret RC .25 .60
378 Mike Van Ryn RC .25 .60
379 Scott Barney RC .25 .60
380 Harold Druken RC .25 .60
381 Dylan Gyori RC .25 .60
382 Chris Heron RC .25 .60
383 Chad Hinz RC .25 .60
384 Patrick Marleau RC 6.00 15.00
385 Serge Payer RC .25 .60
386 Jeremy Reich RC .25 .60
387 Daniel Tkaczuk RC .25 .60
388 Jason Ward RC .25 .60
389 Checklist (211-298) .10 .25
390 Checklist (299-390) .10 .25
HK1 Wayne Gretzky 1.50 4.00

1996-97 Upper Deck Game Jerseys

*MULT.COLOR SWATCH: .6X TO 1.5X
GJ1 Steve Yzerman 100.00 200.00
GJ2 Brett Hull 80.00 150.00
GJ3 Doug Gilmour 50.00 120.00
GJ4 Jaromir Jagr 80.00 200.00
GJ5 Ray Bourque 60.00 150.00
GJ6 Mario Lemieux 150.00 300.00
GJ7 John Vanbiesbrouck 50.00 120.00
GJ8 Eric Lindros 50.00 120.00
GJ9 Mike Modano 50.00 100.00
GJ10 Pavel Bure 80.00 150.00
GJ11 Mark Messier 50.00 120.00
GJ12 Theo Fleury 50.00 120.00
GJ13 Mats Sundin UER 30.00 80.00

1996-97 Upper Deck Generation Next

COMPLETE SET (40) 25.00 60.00
X1 P.Kariya/W.Gretzky 5.00 12.00
X2 T.Linden/P.Forsberg 1.50 4.00
X3 J.Sakic/R.Niedermayer 1.25 3.00
X4 C.O'Sullivan/E.Weinrich .40 1.00
X5 J.Thibault/P.Roy 3.00 8.00
X6 B.Hull/D.Alfredsson 1.25 3.00
X7 C.Osgood/J.Vanbiesbrouck .75 2.00
X8 R.Bourque/R.Hamrlik 1.25 3.00
X9 P.Coffey/S.Ozolinsh 1.25 3.00
X10 D.Gilmour/S.Fedorov 1.25 3.00
X11 C.Chelios/E.Jovanovski 1.25 3.00
X12 J.Arnott/J.Roenick 1.25 3.00
X13 D.Weight/S.Yzerman 3.00 8.00
X14 B.Shanahan/T.Bertuzzi 1.25 3.00
X15 W.Clark/K.Tkachuk 1.25 3.00
X16 S.Koivu/T.Selanne 1.25 3.00
X17 J.Jagr/Z.Palffy 1.25 3.00
X18 E.Belfour/M.Brodeur 1.50 4.00
X19 E.Daze/O.Nolan .75 2.00
X20 V.Kamensky/V.Yachmenev .40 1.00
X21 J.Iginla/M.Modano 1.50 4.00
X22 A.Eriksson/N.Lidstrom 1.25 3.00
X23 B.Leetch/B.Berard 1.25 3.00
X24 J.Kurri/N.Sundstrom .40 1.00
X25 A.Deadmarsh/S.Mellanby .40 1.00
X26 P.Bondra/P.Sykora .40 1.00
X27 C.Joseph/E.Fichaud 1.25 3.00
X28 D.Hasek/R.Turek 2.00 5.00
X29 A.Mogilny/V.Bure .40 1.00
X30 D.Langkow/T.Fleury .40 1.00
X31 B.Nicholls/S.Berezin .75 2.00
X32 C.Gratton/R.Tocchet .75 2.00
X33 F.Potvin/G.Fuhr 1.25 3.00
X34 K.Primeau/K.Stevens .40 1.00
X35 R.Blake/W.Redden .40 1.00
X36 C.Pronger/S.Stevens .75 2.00
X37 G.Suter/K.McLaren .40 1.00
X38 J.Hoglund/M.Sundin .75 2.00
X39 L.Murphy/S.Zubov .40 1.00
X40 A.Oates/J.Juneau .75 2.00

1996-97 Upper Deck Hart Hopefuls Bronze

COMPLETE SET (20) 20.00 50.00
SILVER/1000: 1X TO 2.5X BRONZE
*GOLD/100: 4X TO 10X BRONZE
HH1 Wayne Gretzky 5.00 12.00
HH2 Mark Messier 1.50 4.00
HH3 Eric Lindros 2.00 5.00
HH4 Sergei Fedorov 2.50 6.00
HH5 Saku Koivu 1.25 3.00
HH6 John Vanbiesbrouck 1.50 4.00
HH7 Peter Forsberg 1.50 4.00
HH8 Keith Tkachuk 1.25 3.00
HH9 Paul Kariya 1.25 3.00
HH10 Martin Brodeur 2.50 6.00
HH11 Patrick Roy 3.00 8.00
HH12 Alexander Mogilny 1.25 3.00
HH13 Brett Hull 1.50 4.00
HH14 Pavel Bure 2.00 5.00
HH15 Teemu Selanne 1.50 4.00
HH16 Mario Lemieux 4.00 10.00
HH17 Jeremy Roenick 1.50 4.00
HH18 Jaromir Jagr 2.00 5.00
HH19 Steve Yzerman 3.00 8.00
HH20 Joe Sakic 2.00 5.00

1996-97 Upper Deck Lord Stanley's Heroes Quarterfinals

COMPLETE SET (20) 30.00 80.00
*FINALS/100: 5X TO 12X QUARTER/5000
*SEMIFINAL/1000: 1X TO 2.5X QUART/5000
LS1 Wayne Gretzky 8.00 20.00
LS2 Mark Messier 3.00 8.00
LS3 Mario Lemieux 6.00 15.00
LS4 Jaromir Jagr 3.00 8.00
LS5 Martin Brodeur 5.00 12.00
LS6 Patrick Roy 6.00 15.00
LS7 Joe Sakic 4.00 10.00
LS8 Peter Forsberg 3.00 8.00
LS9 Theo Fleury 2.50 6.00
LS10 Paul Coffey 2.00 5.00
LS11 Doug Gilmour 2.00 5.00
LS12 Paul Kariya 2.00 5.00
LS13 Eric Lindros 3.00 8.00
LS14 Sergei Fedorov 2.50 6.00
LS15 Eric Daze 1.50 4.00
LS16 Teemu Selanne 2.50 6.00
LS17 Keith Tkachuk 2.00 5.00
LS18 Pavel Bure 2.50 6.00
LS19 Mats Sundin 2.50 6.00
LS20 Saku Koivu 2.00 5.00

1996-97 Upper Deck Power Performers

COMPLETE SET (30) 15.00 40.00
P1 Brendan Shanahan 1.50 4.00
P2 Mikael Renberg .40 1.00
P3 John LeClair .75 2.00
P4 Keith Primeau .40 1.00
P5 Adam Graves .40 1.00
P6 Jason Arnott .40 1.00
P7 Todd Bertuzzi .75 2.00
P8 Ed Jovanovski .40 1.00
P9 Scott Stevens .40 1.00
P10 Chris Gratton .40 1.00
P11 Bill Guerin .40 1.00
P12 Vladimir Konstantinov .75 2.00
P13 Mike Grier .40 1.00
P14 Theo Fleury .75 2.00
P15 Chris Chelios .75 2.00
P16 Trevor Linden .75 2.00
P17 Claude Lemieux .40 1.00
P18 Owen Nolan .75 2.00
P19 Jarome Iginla 3.00 8.00
P20 Joe Nieuwendyk .75 2.00
P21 Kevin Hatcher .40 1.00
P22 Dino Ciccarelli .40 1.00
P23 Adam Deadmarsh .40 1.00
P24 Chris Pronger .75 2.00
P25 Mike Ricci .40 1.00
P26 Rod Brind'Amour .75 2.00
P27 Derian Hatcher .40 1.00
P28 Mats Sundin 1.50 4.00
P29 Doug Gilmour .75 2.00
P30 Todd Harvey .40 1.00

1996-97 Upper Deck Superstar Showdown

COMPLETE SET (60) 30.00 80.00
SS1A Pavel Bure .60 1.50
SS1B Paul Kariya .60 1.50
SS2A Patrick Roy 3.00 8.00
SS2B John Vanbiesbrouck .40 1.00
SS3A Eric Lindros .60 1.50
SS3B Ed Jovanovski .40 1.00
SS4A Theo Fleury .40 1.00
SS4B Doug Gilmour .40 1.00
SS5A Wayne Gretzky 4.00 10.00
SS5B Mario Lemieux 3.00 8.00
SS6A Keith Tkachuk .60 1.50
SS6B Brendan Shanahan .60 1.50
SS7A Ray Bourque 1.00 2.50
SS7B Brian Leetch .60 1.50
SS8A Peter Forsberg 1.00 2.50
SS8B Sergei Fedorov .60 1.50
SS9A Mark Messier .60 1.50
SS9B Scott Stevens .40 1.00
SS10A Teemu Selanne .60 1.50
SS10B Alexander Mogilny .40 1.00
SS11A Felix Potvin .60 1.50
SS11B Jocelyn Thibault .60 1.50
SS12A Martin Brodeur 1.50 4.00
SS12B Eric Fichaud .40 1.00
SS13A Roman Hamrlik .40 1.00
SS13B Jaromir Jagr 1.00 2.50
SS14A Jim Carey .60 1.50
SS14B Saku Koivu .60 1.50
SS15A Jeremy Roenick .75 2.00
SS15B Brett Hull .75 2.00
SS16A Joe Sakic 1.25 3.00
SS16B Steve Yzerman 3.00 8.00
SS17A Doug Weight .40 1.00
SS17B Pat LaFontaine .60 1.50
SS18A Daniel Alfredsson .40 1.00
SS18B Eric Daze .40 1.00
SS19A Mike Modano .75 2.00
SS19B Jason Arnott .15 .40
SS20A Paul Coffey .60 1.50
SS20B Sandis Ozolinsh .15 .40
SS21A Zigmund Palffy .40 1.00
SS21B Petr Sykora .15 .40
SS22A Ed Belfour .60 1.50
SS22B Ron Hextall .40 1.00
SS23A Mats Sundin .60 1.50
SS23B Mikael Renberg .40 1.00
SS24A Vitali Yachmenev .15 .40
SS24B Alexei Zhamnov .40 1.00
SS25A Oleg Tverdovsky .40 1.00
SS25B Kyle McLaren .15 .40
SS26A Dominik Hasek 1.25 3.00
SS26B Petr Nedved .40 1.00
SS27A Chris Chelios .60 1.50
SS27B Chris Pronger .40 1.00
SS28A Rob Niedermayer .40 1.00
SS28B Scott Niedermayer .15 .40
SS29A Keith Primeau .15 .40
SS29B Bob Probert .40 1.00
SS30A Bill Ranford .40 1.00
SS30B Chris Osgood .40 1.00

1997-98 Upper Deck

COMPLETE SET (420) 30.00 80.00
COMP.SERIES 1 (210) 10.00 20.00
COMP.SERIES 2 (210) 15.00 40.00
1 Teemu Selanne .30 .75
2 Steve Rucchin .12 .30
3 Kevin Todd .10 .25
4 Darren Van Impe .12 .30
5 Mark Janssens .12 .30
6 Guy Hebert .12 .30
7 Sean Pronger .10 .25
8 Jason Allison .12 .30
9 Ray Bourque .25 .60
10 Landon Wilson .10 .25
11 Anson Carter .10 .25
12 Jean-Yves Roy .10 .25
13 Kyle McLaren .10 .25
14 Don Sweeney .10 .25
15 Brian Holzinger .12 .30
16 Matthew Barnaby .10 .25
17 Wayne Primeau .12 .30
18 Steve Shields RC .15 .40
19 Jason Dawe .12 .30
20 Donald Audette .12 .30
21 Dixon Ward .12 .30
22 Hnat Domenichelli .12 .30
23 Trevor Kidd .10 .25
24 Jarome Iginla .20 .50
25 Sandy McCarthy .10 .25
26 Marty McInnis .10 .25
27 Jonas Hoglund .12 .30
28 Aaron Gavey .10 .25
29 Keith Primeau .12 .30
30 Geoff Sanderson .12 .30
31 Sean Burke .10 .25
32 Steven Rice .12 .30
33 Stu Grimson .12 .30
34 Jeff O'Neill .12 .30
35 Curtis Leschyshyn .10 .25
36 Chris Chelios .15 .40
37 Sergei Krivokrasov .10 .25
38 Jeff Hackett .10 .25
39 Bob Probert .15 .40
40 Chris Terreri .10 .25
41 Eric Daze .10 .25
42 Alexei Zhamnov .10 .25
43 Patrick Roy .40 1.00
44 Sandis Ozolinsh .10 .25
45 Eric Messier RC .15 .40
46 Adam Deadmarsh .10 .25
47 Claude Lemieux .12 .30
48 Mike Ricci .10 .25
49 Stephane Yelle .10 .25
50 Joe Nieuwendyk .12 .30
51 Derian Hatcher .12 .30
52 Jere Lehtinen .12 .30
53 Roman Turek .12 .30
54 Darryl Sydor .10 .25
55 Todd Harvey .12 .30
56 Mike Modano .25 .60
57 Steve Yzerman .40 1.00
58 Martin Lapointe .10 .25
59 Darren McCarty .12 .30
60 Mike Vernon .12 .30
61 Kirk Maltby .10 .25
62 Kris Draper .10 .25
63 Vladimir Konstantinov .10 .25
64 Todd Marchant .12 .30
65 Doug Weight .15 .40
66 Jason Arnott .12 .30
67 Mike Grier .12 .30
68 Mats Lindgren .10 .25
69 Bryan Marchment .15 .40
70 Rem Murray .10 .25
71 Radek Dvorak .12 .30
72 John Vanbiesbrouck .15 .40
73 Robert Svehla .12 .30
74 Bill Lindsay .12 .30
75 Paul Laus .12 .30
76 Kirk Muller .10 .25
77 Dave Nemirovsky .10 .25
78 Roman Vopat .12 .30
79 Jan Vopat .10 .25
80 Dimitri Khristich .12 .30
81 Glen Murray .12 .30
82 Mattias Norstrom .12 .30
83 Ian Laperriere .10 .25
84 Mark Recchi .20 .50
85 Jose Theodore .15 .40
86 Vincent Damphousse .12 .30
87 Sebastien Bordeleau .12 .30
88 Darcy Tucker .15 .40
89 Martin Rucinsky .12 .30
90 Jocelyn Thibault .12 .30
91 Doug Gilmour .20 .50
92 Brian Rolston .12 .30
93 Jay Pandolfo .12 .30
94 John MacLean .10 .25
95 Scott Stevens .15 .40
96 Dave Andreychuk .15 .40
97 Denis Pederson .10 .25
98 Bryan Berard .10 .25
99 Zigmund Palffy .15 .40
100 Bryan McCabe .10 .25
101 Rich Pilon .12 .30
102 Eric Fichaud .12 .30
103 Todd Bertuzzi .15 .40
104 Robert Reichel .12 .30
105 Christian Dube .12 .30
106 Niklas Sundstrom .12 .30
107 Mike Richter .15 .40
108 Adam Graves .10 .25
109 Wayne Gretzky 1.00 2.50
110 Bruce Driver .12 .30
111 Esa Tikkanen .10 .25
112 Daniel Alfredsson .15 .40
113 Ron Tugnutt .15 .40
114 Steve Duchesne .10 .25
115 Bruce Gardiner RC .12 .30
116 Sergei Zholtok .12 .30
117 Alexandre Daigle .10 .25
118 Wade Redden .10 .25
119 Mikael Renberg .12 .30
120 Trent Klatt .12 .30
121 Rod Brind'Amour .15 .40
122 Dainius Zubrus .12 .30
123 John LeClair .15 .40
124 Janne Niinimaa .12 .30
125 Vaclav Prospal RC .12 .30
126 Keith Tkachuk .15 .40
127 Jeremy Roenick .25 .60
128 Mike Gartner .20 .50
129 Nikolai Khabibulin .15 .40
130 Chad Kilger .12 .30
131 Shane Doan .12 .30
132 Cliff Ronning .10 .25
133 Patrick Lalime .12 .30
134 Greg Johnson .10 .25
135 Ron Francis .20 .50
136 Darius Kasparaitis .12 .30
137 Petr Nedved .15 .40
138 Jason Woolley .12 .30
139 Fredrik Olausson .12 .30
140 Harry York .12 .30
141 Brett Hull .30 .75
142 Chris Pronger .15 .40
143 Jim Campbell .10 .25
144 Libor Zabransky RC .10 .25
145 Grant Fuhr .25 .60
146 Pavol Demitra .20 .50
147 Owen Nolan .15 .40
148 Stephen Guolla RC .10 .25
149 Marcus Ragnarsson .10 .25
150 Bernie Nicholls .12 .30
151 Todd Gill .12 .30
152 Shean Donovan .12 .30
153 Corey Schwab .12 .30
154 Dino Ciccarelli .15 .40
155 Chris Gratton .10 .25
156 Alexander Selivanov .10 .25
157 Roman Hamrlik .10 .25
158 Daymond Langkow .10 .25
159 Paul Ysebaert .12 .30
160 Steve Sullivan .12 .30
161 Sergei Berezin .12 .30
162 Fredrik Modin .12 .30
163 Todd Warriner .12 .30
164 Wendel Clark .25 .60
165 Jason Podollan .12 .30
166 Darby Hendrickson .10 .25
167 Martin Gelinas .10 .25
168 Pavel Bure .15 .40
169 Trevor Linden .15 .40
170 Mike Sillinger .10 .25
171 Corey Hirsch .12 .30
172 Lonny Bohonos .12 .30
173 Markus Naslund .15 .40
174 Steve Konowalchuk .12 .30
175 Dale Hunter .12 .30
176 Joe Juneau .10 .25
177 Adam Oates .15 .40
178 Bill Ranford .12 .30
179 Pat Peake .12 .30
180 Sergei Gonchar .10 .25
181 Mike Leclerc RC .20 .50
182 Randy Robitaille RC .20 .50
183 Paxton Schafer RC .10 .25
184 Rumun Ndur RC .15 .40
185 Christian Laflamme RC .15 .40
186 Wade Belak RC .15 .40
187 Mike Knuble RC .15 .40
188 Steve Kelly .12 .30
189 Patrik Elias RC 1.50 4.00
190 Ken Belanger RC .15 .40
191 Colin Forbes RC .15 .40
192 Juha Ylonen .12 .30
193 David Cooper RC .15 .40
194 D.J. Smith RC .15 .40
195 Jaroslav Svejkovsky .12 .30
196 Tie Domi .12 .30
197 Bob Probert .15 .40
198 Doug Gilmour .20 .50
199 Dino Ciccarelli .15 .40
200 Martin Gelinas .10 .25
201 Tony Twist .12 .30
202 Claude Lemieux .12 .30
203 Vladimir Konstantinov .10 .25
204 Ulf Samuelsson .15 .40
205 Chris Simon .12 .30
206 Gino Odjick .10 .25
207 Mike Grier .12 .30
208 Tony Amonte .12 .30
209 Wayne Gretzky CL 1.00 2.50
210 Patrick Roy CL .40 1.00
211 Paul Kariya .15 .40
212 J.J. Daigneault .12 .30
213 Dmitri Mironov .12 .30
214 Joe Sacco .12 .30
215 Richard Park .10 .25
216 Espen Knutsen RC .15 .40
217 Dave Karpa .10 .25
218 Joe Thornton .25 .60
219 Sergei Samsonov .12 .30
220 P.J. Axelsson RC .15 .40
221 Ted Donato .10 .25
222 Dean Chynoweth .12 .30
223 Rob Tallas RC .15 .40
224 Mattias Timander .12 .30
225 Dominik Hasek .25 .60
226 Erik Rasmussen .12 .30
227 Mike Peca .12 .30
228 Rob Ray .10 .25
239B Vaclav Varada .10 .25
230 Curtis Brown .10 .25
231 Jay McKee .10 .25
232 Theo Fleury .20 .50
233 Derek Morris RC .15 .40
234 Chris Dingman RC .15 .40
235 Chris O'Sullivan .12 .30
236 Rick Tabaracci .12 .30
237 Tommy Albelin .12 .30
238 Todd Simpson .12 .30
239A Sami Kapanen .12 .30
240 Gary Roberts .12 .30
241 Kevin Dineen .12 .30
242 Kevin Haller .12 .30
243 Nelson Emerson .12 .30
244 Glen Wesley .10 .25
245 Tony Amonte .12 .30
246 Eric Weinrich .10 .25
247 Daniel Cleary .12 .30
248 Jeff Shantz .12 .30
249 Jean-Yves Leroux RC .15 .40
250 Ethan Moreau .10 .25
251 Craig Mills .10 .25
252 Peter Forsberg .30 .75
253 Joe Sakic .30 .75
254 Valeri Kamensky .12 .30
255 Adam Foote .10 .25
256 Josef Marha .10 .25
257 Christian Matte RC .15 .40
258 Aaron Miller .10 .25
259 Ed Belfour .15 .40
260 Jamie Langenbrunner .12 .30
261 Juha Lind RC .15 .40
262 Pat Verbeek .12 .30
263 Sergei Zubov .12 .30
264 Dave Reid .10 .25
265 Greg Adams .12 .30
266 Sergei Fedorov .25 .60
267 Nicklas Lidstrom .15 .40
268 Brendan Shanahan .15 .40
269 Chris Osgood .15 .40
270 Aaron Ward .10 .25
271 Vyacheslav Kozlov .12 .30
272 Kevin Hodson .12 .30
273 Curtis Joseph .20 .50
274 Ryan Smyth .12 .30
275 Dean McAmmond .10 .25
276 Boris Mironov .10 .25
277 Dennis Bonvie .10 .25
278 Kelly Buchberger .12 .30
279 Kevin Lowe .10 .25
280 Ray Sheppard .12 .30
281 Rob Niedermayer .10 .25
282 Scott Mellanby .12 .30
283 Terry Carkner .12 .30
284 Ed Jovanovski .10 .25
285 Gord Murphy .10 .25
286 Tom Fitzgerald .10 .25
287 Jamie Storr .12 .30
288 Olli Jokinen RC .20 .50
289 Vladimir Tsyplakov .12 .30
290 Luc Robitaille .15 .40
291 Vitali Yachmenev .12 .30
292 Donald MacLean RC .15 .40
293 Saku Koivu .15 .40
294 Andy Moog .15 .40
295 Patrice Brisebois .12 .30
296 Brad Brown RC .15 .40
297 Turner Stevenson .12 .30
298 Shayne Corson .12 .30
299 Brian Savage .10 .25
300 Martin Brodeur .40 1.00
301 Scott Niedermayer .15 .40
302 Krzysztof Oliwa RC .15 .40
303 Valeri Zelepukin .12 .30
304 Bobby Holik .10 .25
305 Ken Daneyko .12 .30
306 Lyle Odelein .10 .25
307 Travis Green .12 .30
308 Steve Webb RC .15 .40
309 Dan Plante .12 .30
310 Bryan Smolinski .12 .30
311 Claude Lapointe .12 .30
312 Kenny Jonsson .12 .30
313 Ulf Samuelsson .15 .40
314 Jeff Beukeboom .12 .30
315 Mike Keane .10 .25
316 Brian Leetch .12 .30
317 Shane Chrula .12 .30
318 Pat LaFontaine .15 .40
319 Alexei Kovalev .12 .30
320 Radek Bonk .10 .25
321 Alexei Yashin .12 .30
322 Damian Rhodes .12 .30
323 Andreas Dackell .12 .30
324 Magnus Arvedson RC .15 .40
325 Chris Phillips .15 .40
326 Marian Hossa RC 3.00 8.00
327 Chris Gratton .10 .25
328 Shjon Podein .10 .25
329 Paul Coffey .15 .40
330 Luke Richardson .10 .25
331 Eric Lindros .25 .60
332 Eric Desjardins .10 .25
333 Joel Otto .10 .25
334 Craig Janney .10 .25
335 Oleg Tverdovsky .12 .30
336 Teppo Numminen .10 .25
337 Jim McKenzie .12 .30
338 Dallas Drake .12 .30
339 Rick Tocchet .10 .25
340 Brad Isbister .12 .30
341 Alexei Morozov .12 .30
342 Jaromir Jagr .50 1.25
343 Kevin Hatcher .10 .25
344 Ken Wregget .10 .25
345 Chris Tamer .10 .25
346 Robert Dome .10 .25
347 Neil Wilkinson .10 .25
348 Chris McAlpine .10 .25
349 Joe Murphy .12 .30
350 Robert Petrovicky .12 .30
351 Marc Bergevin .12 .30
352 Al MacInnis .20 .50
353 Pierre Turgeon .12 .30
354 Patrick Marleau .15 .40
355 Marco Sturm RC .15 .40
356 Mike Vernon .12 .30
357 Al Iafrate .12 .30
358 Jeff Friesen .12 .30
359 Viktor Kozlov .12 .30
360 Tony Granato .10 .25
361 Mikael Renberg .12 .30
362 Daren Puppa .12 .30
363 Roman Hamrlik .10 .25
364 Rob Zamuner .10 .25
365 Cory Cross .10 .25
366 Patrick Poulin .10 .25
367 Felix Potvin .25 .60
368 Tie Domi .12 .30
369 Mats Sundin .15 .40
370 Jeff Ware .10 .25
371 Alyn McCauley .12 .30
372 Mathieu Schneider .12 .30
373 Craig Wolanin .12 .30
374 Mark Messier .30 .75
375 Kirk McLean .12 .30

376 Donald Brashear .12 .30
377 Arturs Irbe .12 .30
378 Jyrki Lumme .12 .30
379 Gino Odjick .10 .25
380 Mattias Ohlund .12 .30
381 Jan Bulis RC .15 .40
382 Andrew Brunette .12 .30
383 Calle Johansson .12 .30
384 Brendan Witt .12 .30
385 Mark Tinordi .12 .30
386 Ken Klee .12 .30
387 Chris Simon .12 .30
388 Richard Zednik .12 .30
389 Ed Jovanovski .10 .25
390 Darren McCarty .12 .30
391 Darius Kasparaitis .12 .30
392 Bryan Marchment .15 .40
393 Matthew Barnaby .10 .25
394 Chris Chelios .15 .40
395 Ulf Samuelsson .15 .40
396 Scott Stevens .15 .40
397 Derian Hatcher .12 .30
398 Chris Pronger .15 .40
399 Mathieu Chouinard RC .15 .40
400 Jake McCracken RC .20 .50
401 Bryan Allen RC .15 .40
402 Christian Chartier RC .20 .50
403 Jonathan Girard RC .15 .40
404 Abe Herbst RC .15 .40
405 Stephen Peat RC .15 .40
406 Robyn Regehr RC .15 .40
407 Blair Betts RC .15 .40
408 Eric Chouinard RC .20 .50
409 Brett DeCecco RC .15 .40
410 Rico Fata RC .20 .50
411 Simon Gagne RC 2.50 6.00
412 Vincent Lecavalier RC 3.00 8.00
413 Manny Malhotra RC .20 .50
414 Norm Milley RC .20 .50
415 Justin Papineau RC .20 .50
416 Garrett Prosofsky RC .15 .40
417 Mike Ribeiro RC .60 1.50
418 Brad Richards RC 1.50 4.00
419 Wayne Gretzky CL 1.00 2.50
420 Patrick Roy CL .40 1.00

1997-98 Upper Deck Jumbos 3x5

COMPLETE SET (20) 15.00 40.00
1A Wayne Gretzky 4.00 10.00
2A Steve Yzerman 3.00 8.00
3A Bryan Berard .40 1.00
4A Owen Nolan .40 1.00
5A Pavel Bure .60 1.50
6A Patrick Roy 3.00 8.00
7A Teemu Selanne .60 1.50
8A Brett Hull .75 2.00
9A Keith Tkachuk .60 1.50
10A John Vanbiesbrouck .40 1.00
1B Paul Kariya .60 1.50
2B Joe Thornton 1.50 4.00
3B Joe Sakic 1.25 3.00
4B Martin Brodeur 1.50 4.00
5B Slava Kozlov .40 1.00
6B Mark Messier .60 1.50
7B Jaromir Jagr 1.00 2.50
8B Eric Lindros .60 1.50
9B Peter Forsberg 1.50 4.00
10B Sergei Samsonov .40 1.00

1997-98 Upper Deck Jumbos 5x7

COMPLETE SET (14) 10.00 25.00
1A Mark Messier .60 1.50
1B Patrick Roy 3.00 8.00
1C Paul Kariya .75 2.00
2A Jaromir Jagr 1.50 4.00
2B Teemu Selanne 1.25 3.00
3A Joe Sakic 1.25 3.00
3B Eric Lindros 1.00 2.50
4A Peter Forsberg 1.50 4.00
4B Martin Brodeur 1.50 4.00
4C Keith Tkachuk .75 2.00
5A Sergei Samsonov .60 1.50
5B Pavel Bure 1.25 3.00
5C Slava Kozlov .60 1.50
5D John Vanbiesbrouck .60 1.50

1997-98 Upper Deck Game Dated Moments Parallel

*GAME DATED: 60X TO 150X BASIC CARDS
135 Ron Francis 15.00 40.00

1997-98 Upper Deck Game Jerseys

GJ1 Patrick Roy HOME 100.00 250.00
GJ2 Patrick Roy AWAY 100.00 250.00
GJ3 Dominik Hasek 60.00 150.00
GJ4 Jarome Iginla 50.00 125.00
GJ5 Sergei Fedorov 60.00 150.00
GJ6 Tony Amonte 30.00 80.00
GJ7 Joe Sakic 80.00 200.00
GJ8 Wayne Gretzky 250.00 600.00
GJ9 Saku Koivu 40.00 100.00
GJ11 Mike Richter 40.00 100.00
GJ12 Doug Weight 40.00 100.00
GJ13 Brendan Shanahan 40.00 100.00
GJ14 Brian Leetch 30.00 80.00
GJ1AU Patrick Roy AU/33 350.00 600.00
GJ8AU Wayne Gretzky AU/99 600.00 1500.00

1997-98 Upper Deck Sixth Sense Masters

COMPLETE SET (30) 125.00 250.00
*WIZARD/100: 2.5X TO 6X BASIC INSERTS
SS1 Wayne Gretzky 12.50 30.00
SS2 Jaromir Jagr 5.00 12.00
SS3 Sergei Fedorov 4.00 10.00
SS4 Brett Hull 4.00 10.00
SS5 Brian Leetch 2.00 5.00
SS6 Joe Thornton 5.00 12.00
SS7 Ray Bourque 4.00 10.00
SS8 Teemu Selanne 3.00 8.00
SS9 Paul Kariya 3.00 8.00
SS10 Doug Weight 2.00 5.00
SS11 Mark Messier 3.00 8.00
SS12 Adam Oates 2.00 5.00
SS13 Mats Sundin 3.00 8.00
SS14 Brendan Shanahan 3.00 8.00
SS15 Saku Koivu 3.00 8.00
SS16 Doug Gilmour 2.00 5.00
SS17 Eric Lindros 3.00 8.00
SS18 Tony Amonte 2.00 5.00
SS19 Joe Sakic 6.00 15.00
SS20 Steve Yzerman 10.00 25.00
SS21 Peter Forsberg 5.00 12.00
SS22 Geoff Sanderson 2.00 5.00
SS23 Keith Tkachuk 2.00 5.00
SS24 Pavel Bure 4.00 10.00
SS25 Ron Francis 2.00 5.00
SS26 Zigmund Palffy 2.00 5.00
SS27 Daniel Alfredsson 2.00 5.00
SS28 Bryan Berard 2.00 5.00
SS29 Mike Modano 5.00 12.00
SS30 Patrick Roy 10.00 25.00

1997-98 Upper Deck Smooth Grooves

COMPLETE SET (60) 30.00 80.00
SG1 Wayne Gretzky 5.00 12.00
SG2 Patrick Roy 4.00 10.00
SG3 Patrick Marleau 1.25 3.00
SG4 Martin Brodeur 2.00 5.00
SG5 Zigmund Palffy .50 1.25
SG6 Joe Thornton 2.00 5.00
SG7 Chris Chelios .75 2.00
SG8 Teemu Selanne .75 2.00
SG9 Paul Kariya .75 2.00
SG10 Tony Amonte .50 1.25
SG11 Mark Messier .75 2.00
SG12 Jarome Iginla 1.00 2.50
SG13 Mats Sundin .75 2.00
SG14 Brendan Shanahan .75 2.00
SG15 Ed Jovanovski .50 1.25
SG16 Brett Hull 1.00 2.50
SG17 Brian Rolston .20 .50
SG18 Saku Koivu .75 2.00
SG19 Steve Yzerman 4.00 10.00
SG20 Doug Weight .50 1.25
SG21 Peter Forsberg 2.00 5.00
SG22 Brian Leetch .75 2.00
SG23 Alexei Yashin .50 1.25
SG24 Owen Nolan .50 1.25
SG25 Mike Grier .20 .50
SG26 Jere Lehtinen .20 .50
SG27 Vaclav Prospal .75 2.00
SG28 Sandis Ozolinsh .20 .50
SG29 Mike Modano 1.25 3.00
SG30 Sergei Samsonov .50 1.25
SG31 Curtis Joseph .75 2.00
SG32 Daymond Langkow .50 1.25
SG33 Doug Gilmour .50 1.25
SG34 Bryan Berard .50 1.25
SG35 Joe Sakic 1.50 4.00
SG36 Wade Redden .20 .50
SG37 Keith Tkachuk .75 2.00
SG38 Jaromir Jagr 1.25 3.00
SG39 Dominik Hasek 1.50 4.00
SG40 Patrick Lalime .50 1.25
SG41 Janne Niinimaa .20 .50
SG42 Oleg Tverdovsky .20 .50
SG43 Vitali Yachmenev .20 .50
SG44 Rob Niedermayer .20 .50
SG45 Nicklas Lidstrom .75 2.00
SG46 Jim Campbell .20 .50
SG47 Roman Hamrlik .50 1.25
SG48 Eric Lindros .75 2.00
SG49 Brian Holzinger .20 .50
SG50 John LeClair .75 2.00
SG51 Sergei Berezin .20 .50
SG52 Jaroslav Svejkovsky .50 1.25
SG53 Mike Richter .75 2.00
SG54 John Vanbiesbrouck .50 1.25
SG55 Keith Primeau .20 .50
SG56 Adam Oates .50 1.25
SG57 Jeremy Roenick 1.00 2.50
SG58 Pavel Bure .75 2.00
SG59 Dainius Zubrus .75 2.00
SG60 Jose Theodore 1.00 2.50

1997-98 Upper Deck The Specialists

COMPLETE SET (30) 40.00 100.00
S1 Wayne Gretzky 5.00 12.00
S2 Patrick Roy 4.00 10.00
S3 Jaromir Jagr 2.00 5.00
S4 Joe Sakic 2.50 6.00
S5 Mark Messier 1.25 3.00
S6 Eric Lindros 1.25 3.00
S7 John Vanbiesbrouck 1.00 2.50
S8 Teemu Selanne 1.25 3.00
S9 Paul Kariya 1.25 3.00
S10 Pavel Bure 1.25 3.00
S11 Sergei Fedorov 2.00 5.00
S12 Peter Bondra 1.00 2.50
S13 Mats Sundin 1.25 3.00
S14 Brendan Shanahan 1.25 3.00
S15 Keith Tkachuk 1.25 3.00
S16 Brett Hull 1.50 4.00
S17 Jeremy Roenick 1.50 4.00
S18 Dominik Hasek 2.50 6.00
S19 Steve Yzerman 4.00 10.00
S20 John LeClair 1.25 3.00
S21 Peter Forsberg 3.00 8.00
S22 Zigmund Palffy 1.00 2.50
S23 Tony Amonte 1.00 2.50
S24 Jarome Iginla 1.25 3.00
S25 Curtis Joseph 1.25 3.00
S26 Mike Modano 2.00 5.00
S27 Ray Bourque 2.00 5.00
S28 Brian Leetch 1.25 3.00
S29 Bryan Berard 1.00 2.50
S30 Martin Brodeur 3.00 8.00

1997-98 Upper Deck Three Star Selects

COMPLETE SET (60) 30.00 80.00
T1A Eric Lindros .75 2.00
T1B Wayne Gretzky 5.00 12.00
T1C Peter Forsberg 2.00 5.00
T2A Dominik Hasek 1.50 4.00
T2B Patrick Roy 3.00 8.00
T2C John Vanbiesbrouck .75 2.00
T3A Joe Sakic 1.50 4.00
T3B Steve Yzerman 3.00 8.00
T3C Paul Kariya .75 2.00
T4A Bryan Berard .20 .50
T4B Brian Leetch .40 1.00
T4C Chris Chelios .40 1.00
T5A Teemu Selanne .75 2.00
T5B Jaromir Jagr 1.25 3.00
T5C Pavel Bure .75 2.00
T6A Owen Nolan .40 1.00
T6B Brendan Shanahan .75 2.00
T6C Keith Tkachuk .40 1.00
T7A Sergei Fedorov 1.00 2.50
T7B Niklas Sundstrom .20 .50
T7C Mike Peca .20 .50
T8A Janne Niinimaa .20 .50
T8B Saku Koivu .75 2.00
T8C Jere Lehtinen .20 .50
T9A Tony Amonte .40 1.00
T9B John LeClair .40 1.00
T9C Brett Hull 1.00 2.50
T10A Martin Brodeur 2.00 5.00
T10B Curtis Joseph .75 2.00
T10C Mike Richter .75 2.00
T11A Ray Bourque 1.00 2.50
T11B Mark Messier .75 2.00
T11C Scott Stevens .20 .50
T12A Patrick Lalime .40 1.00
T12B Marc Denis .40 1.00
T12C Jose Theodore 1.00 2.50
T13A Adam Deadmarsh .20 .50
T13B Doug Weight .40 1.00
T13C Bill Guerin .20 .50
T14A Daniel Alfredsson .40 1.00
T14B Mats Sundin .75 2.00
T14C Nicklas Lidstrom .75 2.00
T15A Jim Campbell .20 .50
T15B Dainius Zubrus .40 1.00
T15C Daymond Langkow .20 .50
T16A Mike Grier .20 .50
T16B Mike Modano 1.25 3.00
T16C Jeremy Roenick 1.00 2.50
T17A Jason Arnott .20 .50
T17B Trevor Linden .40 1.00
T17C Rod Brind'Amour .40 1.00
T18A Adam Oates .40 1.00
T18B Doug Gilmour .40 1.00
T18C Joe Juneau .20 .50
T19A Sergei Berezin .20 .50
T19B Alexander Mogilny .40 1.00
T19C Alexei Zhamnov .20 .50
T20A Derian Hatcher .20 .50
T20B Wade Redden .20 .50
T20C Sandis Ozolinsh .20 .50

1997 Upper Deck Crash the All-Star Game

1 Tony Amonte 8.00 20.00
2 Paul Kariya 50.00 125.00
3 Brett Hull 15.00 40.00
4 Teemu Selanne 25.00 60.00
5 Steve Yzerman 40.00 100.00
6 Owen Nolan 8.00 20.00
7 Mats Sundin 12.00 30.00
8 Pavel Bure 30.00 80.00
9 Brendan Shanahan 25.00 60.00
10 Sandis Ozolinsh 8.00 20.00
11 Keith Tkachuk 12.00 30.00
12 Ray Bourque 15.00 40.00
13 Eric Lindros 30.00 80.00
14 Mark Messier 15.00 40.00
15 John LeClair 20.00 50.00
16 Jaromir Jagr 40.00 100.00
17 Dino Ciccarelli 8.00 20.00
18 Peter Bondra 12.00 30.00
19 Brian Leetch 15.00 40.00
20 Wayne Gretzky 75.00 200.00
AR1 Tony Amonte 4.00 10.00
AR2 Paul Kariya 20.00 50.00
AR3 Brett Hull 6.00 15.00
AR4 Teemu Selanne 10.00 25.00
AR5 Steve Yzerman 15.00 40.00
AR6 Owen Nolan 6.00 15.00
AR7 Mats Sundin 8.00 20.00
AR8 Pavel Bure 10.00 25.00
AR9 Brendan Shanahan 10.00 25.00
AR10 Sandis Ozolinsh 4.00 10.00
AR11 Keith Tkachuk 6.00 15.00
AR12 Ray Bourque 4.00 10.00
AR13 Eric Lindros 20.00 50.00
AR14 Mark Messier 6.00 15.00
AR15 John LeClair 8.00 20.00
AR16 Jaromir Jagr 15.00 40.00
AR17 Dino Ciccarelli 4.00 10.00
AR18 Peter Bondra 5.00 12.00
AR19 Brian Leetch 5.00 12.00
AR20 Wayne Gretzky 30.00 80.00

1998-99 Upper Deck

COMPLETE SET (420) 75.00 150.00
1 Antti Aalto SR .30 .75
2 Cameron Mann SR .30 .75
3 Norm Maracle SR RC .40 1.00
4 Daniel Cleary SR .30 .75
5 Brendan Morrison SR RC .30 .75
6 Marian Hossa SR .50 1.25
7 Daniel Briere SR .40 1.00
8 Mike Crowley SR RC .40 1.00
9 Darryl Laplante SR RC .40 1.00
10 Sven Butenschon SR .40 1.00
11 Yan Golubovsky SR RC .40 1.00
12 Olli Jokinen SR .40 1.00
13 Jean-Sebastien Giguere SR .40 1.00
14 Mike Watt SR .30 .75
15 Ryan Johnson SR RC .30 .75
16 Teemu Selanne RR 1.00 2.50
17 Paul Kariya RR .50 1.25
18 Pavel Bure RR .50 1.25
19 Joe Thornton RR 1.50 4.00
20 Dominik Hasek RR 1.00 2.50
21 Bryan Berard RR .40 1.00
22 Chris Phillips RR .30 .75
23 Sergei Fedorov RR 1.00 2.50
24 Sergei Samsonov RR .40 1.00
25 Marc Denis RR .40 1.00
26 Patrick Marleau RR .50 1.25
27 Jaromir Jagr RR 1.50 4.00
28 Saku Koivu RR .50 1.25
29 Peter Forsberg RR 2.00 5.00
30 Mike Modano RR 1.00 2.50
31 Paul Kariya .20 .50
32 Matt Cullen .12 .30
33 Josef Marha .12 .30
34 Teemu Selanne .40 1.00
35 Pavel Trnka .12 .30
36 Tom Askey RC .15 .40
37 Tim Taylor .12 .30
38 Ray Bourque .30 .75
39 Sergei Samsonov .15 .40
40 Don Sweeney .12 .30
41 Jason Allison .15 .40
42 Steve Heinze .12 .30
43 Erik Rasmussen .12 .30
44 Dominik Hasek .30 .75
45 Geoff Sanderson .12 .30
46 Michael Peca .12 .30
47 Brian Holzinger .12 .30
48 Vaclav Varada .12 .30
49 Steve Begin .12 .30
50 Dennis Gauthier .12 .30
51 Derek Morris .12 .30
52 Valeri Bure .12 .30
53 Hnat Domenichelli .12 .30
54 Cory Stillman .12 .30
55 Jarome Iginla .25 .60
56 Tyler Moss .12 .30
57 Sami Kapanen .12 .30
58 Trevor Kidd .12 .30
59 Glen Wesley .12 .30
60 Nelson Emerson .12 .30
61 Jeff O'Neill .12 .30
62 Bates Battaglia .12 .30
63 Doug Gilmour .25 .60
64 Christian LaFlamme .12 .30
65 Chris Chelios .20 .50
66 Paul Coffey .20 .50
67 Eric Weinrich .12 .30
68 Eric Daze .15 .40
69 Peter Forsberg .40 1.00
70 Eric Messier .12 .30
71 Eric Lacroix .12 .30
72 Adam Deadmarsh .12 .30
73 Claude Lemieux .15 .40
74 Patrick Roy .50 1.25
75 Marc Denis .15 .40
76 Brett Hull .40 1.00
77 Mike Keane .12 .30
78 Joe Nieuwendyk .15 .40
79 Darryl Sydor .12 .30
80 Ed Belfour .20 .50
81 Jamie Langenbrunner .12 .30
82 Petr Buzek .12 .30
83 Nicklas Lidstrom .25 .60
84 Mathieu Dandenault .12 .30
85 Steve Yzerman .50 1.25
86 Martin Lapointe .12 .30
87 Brendan Shanahan .20 .50
88 Anders Eriksson .12 .30
89 Tomas Holmstrom .12 .30
90 Doug Weight .20 .50
91 Janne Niinimaa .12 .30
92 Bill Guerin .20 .50
93 Kelly Buchberger .12 .30
94 Mike Grier .12 .30
95 Craig Millar .12 .30
96 Roman Hamrlik .12 .30
97 Ray Whitney .12 .30
98 Viktor Kozlov .15 .40
99 Peter Worrell RC .15 .40
100 Kevin Weekes .15 .40
101 Ed Jovanovski .15 .40
102 Bill Lindsay .12 .30
103 Jozef Stumpel .12 .30
104 Luc Robitaille .20 .50
105 Yanic Perreault .12 .30
106 Donald MacLean .12 .30
107 Jamie Storr .15 .40
108 Ian Laperriere .12 .30
109 Jason Morgan RC .12 .30
110 Vincent Damphousse .15 .40
111 Mark Recchi .25 .60
112 Vladimir Malakhov .12 .30
113 Dave Manson .12 .30
114 Jose Theodore .20 .50
115 Brian Savage .12 .30
116 Jonas Hoglund .12 .30
117 Krzysztof Oliwa .12 .30
118 Martin Brodeur .50 1.25
119 Patrik Elias .20 .50
120 Jason Arnott .15 .40
121 Scott Stevens .20 .50
122 Sheldon Souray RC .25 .60
123 Brian Rolston .12 .30
124 Trevor Linden .20 .50
125 Warren Luhning .12 .30
126 Zdeno Chara .20 .50
127 Bryan Berard .15 .40
128 Bryan Smolinski .12 .30
129 Jason Dawe .12 .30
130 Kevin Stevens .15 .40
131 P.J. Stock RC .40 1.00
132 Marc Savard .12 .30
133 Pat LaFontaine .20 .50
134 Dan Cloutier .15 .40
135 Wayne Gretzky 1.25 3.00
136 Niklas Sundstrom .12 .30
137 Damian Rhodes .20 .50
138 Magnus Arvedson .12 .30
139 Alexei Yashin .15 .40
140 Chris Phillips .12 .30
141 Janne Laukkanen .12 .30
142 Shawn McEachern .12 .30
143 John LeClair .20 .50
144 Alexandre Daigle .12 .30
145 Dainius Zubrus .12 .30
146 Joel Otto .12 .30
147 Mike Sillinger .12 .30
148 John Vanbiesbrouck .20 .50
149 Chris Gratton .15 .40
150 Eric Desjardins .15 .40
151 Juha Ylonen .12 .30
152 Brad Isbister .12 .30
153 Oleg Tverdovsky .20 .50
154 Keith Tkachuk .20 .50
155 Teppo Numminen .12 .30
156 Cliff Ronning .12 .30
157 Nikolai Khabibulin .20 .50
158 Alexei Morozov .20 .50
159 Kevin Hatcher .12 .30
160 Darius Kasparaitis .12 .30
161 Jaromir Jagr .60 1.50
162 Tom Barrasso .15 .40
163 Tuomas Gronman .12 .30
164 Robert Dome .12 .30
165 Peter Skudra .12 .30
166 Marcus Ragnarsson .12 .30
167 Mike Vernon .15 .40
168 Andrei Zyuzin .12 .30
169 Marco Sturm .12 .30
170 Mike Ricci .12 .30
171 Patrick Marleau .15 .40
172 Pierre Turgeon .15 .40
173 Pavol Demitra .25 .60
174 Chris Pronger .20 .50
175 Pascal Rheaume .12 .30
176 Al MacInnis .25 .60
177 Tony Twist .12 .30
178 Jim Campbell .12 .30
179 Mikael Renberg .15 .40
180 Jason Bonsignore .12 .30
181 Zac Bierk RC .25 .60
182 Alexander Selivanov .12 .30
183 Stephane Richer .12 .30
184 Sandy McCarthy .12 .30
185 Alyn McCauley .12 .30
186 Sergei Berezin .15 .40
187 Mike Johnson .12 .30
188 Wendel Clark .30 .75
189 Tie Domi .15 .40
190 Yannick Tremblay .12 .30
191 Curtis Joseph .25 .60
192 Fredrik Modin .12 .30
193 Pavel Bure .20 .50
194 Todd Bertuzzi .20 .50
195 Mark Messier .40 1.00
196 Bret Hedican .12 .30
197 Mattias Ohlund .12 .30
198 Garth Snow .15 .40
199 Adam Oates .20 .50
200 Peter Bondra .20 .50
201 Sergei Gonchar .12 .30
202 Jan Bulis .12 .30
203 Joe Juneau .12 .30
204 Brian Bellows .15 .40
205 Olaf Kolzig .20 .50
206 Richard Zednik .12 .30
207 Wayne Gretzky CL 1.25 3.00
208 Patrick Roy CL .50 1.25
209 Steve Yzerman CL .50 1.25
210 Mike Dunham .15 .40
211 Johan Davidsson .12 .30
212 Guy Hebert .15 .40
213 Mike Leclerc .12 .30
214 Steve Rucchin .12 .30
215 Travis Green .12 .30
216 Josef Marha .12 .30
217 Ted Donato .12 .30
218 Joe Thornton .30 .75
219 Kyle McLaren .12 .30
220 Peter Nordstrom RC .15 .40
221 Byron Dafoe .15 .40
222 Jonathon Girard .12 .30
223 Antti Laaksonen RC .40 1.00
224 Jason Holland .12 .30
225 Miroslav Satan .15 .40
226 Alexei Zhitnik .12 .30
227 Donald Audette .12 .30
228 Matthew Barnaby .12 .30
229 Rumun Ndur .12 .30
230 Ken Wregget .15 .40
231 Andrew Cassels .12 .30
232 Theo Fleury .25 .60
233 Phil Housley .15 .40
234 Martin St. Louis RC 4.00 10.00
235 Mike Rucinski RC .15 .40
236 Gary Roberts .12 .30
237 Keith Primeau .15 .40
238 Martin Gelinas .12 .30
239 Nolan Pratt RC .12 .30
240 Ray Sheppard .12 .30
241 Ron Francis .25 .60
242 Ty Jones .12 .30
243 Tony Amonte .15 .40
244 Chad Kilger .12 .30
245 Alexei Zhamnov .12 .30
246 Remi Royer RC .12 .30
247 Milan Hejduk RC 1.00 2.50
248 Joe Sakic .40 1.00
249 Valeri Kamensky .12 .30
250 Sandis Ozolinsh .12 .30
251 Shean Donovan .12 .30
252 Wade Belak .12 .30
253 Jamie Wright .12 .30
254 Sergei Zubov .12 .30
255 Richard Matvichuk .12 .30
256 Mike Modano .30 .75
257 Pat Verbeek .12 .30
258 Jere Lehtinen .15 .40
259 Derian Hatcher .12 .30
260 Jason Botterill .12 .30
261 Igor Larionov .20 .50
262 Sergei Fedorov .30 .75
263 Chris Osgood .20 .50
264 Vyacheslav Kozlov .15 .40
265 Larry Murphy .12 .30
266 Darren McCarty .12 .30
267 Doug Brown .12 .30
268 Kris Draper .12 .30
269 Uwe Krupp .12 .30
270 Fredrik Lindquist RC .20 .50
271 Dean McAmmond .12 .30
272 Ryan Smyth .15 .40
273 Boris Mironov .12 .30
274 Tom Poti .12 .30
275 Todd Marchant .12 .30
276 Sean Brown .12 .30
277 Rob Niedermayer .12 .30
278 Robert Svehla .12 .30
279 Scott Mellanby .12 .30
280 Radek Dvorak .12 .30
281 Jaroslav Spacek RC .20 .50
282 Mark Parrish RC .30 .75
283 Ryan Johnson .12 .30
284 Glen Murray .15 .40
285 Rob Blake .20 .50
286 Steve Duchesne .12 .30
287 Vladimir Tsyplakov .12 .30
288 Stephane Fiset .15 .40
289 Mattias Norstrom .12 .30
290 Saku Koivu .20 .50
291 Shayne Corson .15 .40
292 Brad Brown .12 .30
293 Patrice Brisebois .12 .30
294 Terry Ryan .12 .30
295 Jocelyn Thibault .15 .40
296 Miroslav Guren .12 .30
297 Darren Turcotte .15 .40
298 Sebastien Bordeleau .12 .30
299 Jan Vopat .12 .30
300 Blair Atcheynum .12 .30
301 Andrew Brunette .15 .40
302 Sergei Krivokrasov .12 .30
303 Marian Cisar .12 .30
304 Patrick Cote .12 .30
305 J.J. Daigneault .12 .30
306 Greg Johnson .12 .30
307 Chris Terreri .15 .40
308 Scott Niedermayer .20 .50
309 Vadim Sharifijanov .12 .30
310 Petr Sykora .12 .30
311 Sergei Brylin .12 .30
312 Denis Pederson .12 .30
313 Bobby Holik .12 .30
314 Bryan Muir RC .12 .30
315 Zigmund Palffy .20 .50
316 Mike Watt .12 .30
317 Tommy Salo .15 .40
318 Kenny Jonsson .12 .30
319 Dmitri Nabokov .12 .30
320 John MacLean .12 .30
321 Zarley Zalapski .12 .30
322 Brian Leetch .15 .40
323 Todd Harvey .12 .30
324 Mike Richter .20 .50
325 Mike Knuble .12 .30
326 Jeff Beukeboom .12 .30
327 Daniel Alfredsson .20 .50
328 Vaclav Prospal .12 .30
329 Wade Redden .12 .30
330 Igor Kravchuk .12 .30
331 Andreas Dackell .12 .30
332 Mike Maneluk RC .12 .30
333 Eric Lindros .30 .75
334 Rod Brind'Amour .20 .50
335 Colin Forbes .12 .30
336 Dimitri Tertyshny RC .12 .30
337 Shjon Podein .12 .30
338 Chris Therien .12 .30
339 Jeremy Roenick .30 .75
340 Jyrki Lumme .12 .30
341 Rick Tocchet .15 .40
342 Dallas Drake .12 .30
343 Keith Carney .12 .30
344 Greg Adams .12 .30
345 Jan Hrdina RC .25 .60
346 German Titov .12 .30
347 Stu Barnes .12 .30
348 Kevin Hatcher .12 .30
349 Martin Straka .12 .30
350 Jean-Sebastien Aubin RC .30 .75
351 Jeff Friesen .12 .30
352 Tony Granato .12 .30
353 Scott Hannan RC .12 .30
354 Owen Nolan .20 .50
355 Stephane Matteau .12 .30
356 Bryan Marchment .12 .30
357 Geoff Courtnall .12 .30
358 Brent Johnson RC .25 .60
359 Jamie Rivers .12 .30
360 Terry Yake .12 .30
361 Jamie McLennan .15 .40
362 Grant Fuhr .30 .75
363 Michal Handzus RC .25 .60
364 Bill Ranford .15 .40
365 John Cullen .12 .30
366 Craig Janney .12 .30
367 Daren Puppa .15 .40
368 Pavel Kubina RC .30 .75
369 Wendel Clark .30 .75
370 Mats Sundin .20 .50
371 Felix Potvin .30 .75
372 Daniil Markov RC .15 .40
373 Derek King .12 .30
374 Steve Thomas .12 .30
375 Tomas Kaberle RC .25 .60
376 Alexander Mogilny .15 .40
377 Bill Muckalt RC .15 .40
378 Brian Noonan .12 .30
379 Markus Naslund .20 .50
380 Brad May .12 .30
381 Matt Cooke RC .12 .30
382 Calle Johansson .12 .30
383 Dale Hunter .15 .40
384 Jaroslav Svejkovsky .12 .30
385 Dmitri Mironov .12 .30
386 Matt Herr RC .12 .30
387 Nolan Baumgartner .12 .30
388 Wayne Gretzky CL 1.25 3.00
389 Steve Yzerman CL .50 1.25
390 Wayne Gretzky CL 1.25 3.00
391 Brian Finley PE RC .30 .75
392 Maxime Ouellet PE RC .40 1.00
393 Kurtis Foster PE RC .40 1.00
394 Barret Jackman PE RC .60 1.50
395 Ross Lupaschuk PE RC .40 1.00
396 Steven McCarthy PE RC .40 1.00
397 Peter Reynolds PE RC .40 1.00
398 Bart Rushmer PE RC .40 1.00
399 Jonathan Zion PE RC .40 1.00
400 Kris Beech PE RC .40 1.00
401 Brandin Cote PE RC .40 1.00
402 Scott Kelman PE RC .40 1.00
403 Jamie Lundmark PE RC .40 1.00
404 Derek MacKenzie PE RC .40 1.00
405 Rory McDade PE RC .40 1.00
406 David Morisset PE RC .40 1.00
407 Mirko Murovic PE RC .40 1.00
408 Taylor Pyatt PE RC .40 1.00
409 Charlie Stephens PE .40 1.00
410 Kyle Wanvig PE RC .40 1.00
411 Krzystof Wieckowski PE RC .40 1.00
412 Michael Zigomanis PE RC .40 1.00
413 Rico Fata CC .40 1.00
414 Vincent Lecavalier CC 1.00 2.50
415 Chris Drury CC .60 1.50
416 Oleg Kvasha CC RC .50 1.25
417 Eric Brewer CC .50 1.25
418 Josh Green CC RC .50 1.25
419 Marty Reasoner CC .50 1.25
420 Manny Malhotra CC .50 1.25

1998-99 Upper Deck Exclusives

*1-30 SR/RR: 5X TO 12X BASIC CARDS
*1-30 SR/RR RCs: 4X TO 10X BASIC CARDS
*31-390 VETS: 25X TO 60X BASIC CARDS
*31-390 ROOKIES: 15X TO 30X
*391-412 PE: 3X TO 8X BASIC CARDS
*413-420 CC: 3X TO 8X BASIC CARDS

1998-99 Upper Deck Jumbos 5x7

85 Steve Yzerman Upper Deck 3.00 8.00
P3 Steve Yzerman Profiles 3.00 8.00
FF20 Steve Yzerman Fantastic Finishers 3.00 8.00
FT1 Steve Yzerman Frozen in Time 3.00 8.00
LS14 Steve Yzerman Lord Stanley's Heroes 3.00 8.00

1998-99 Upper Deck Fantastic Finishers

COMPLETE SET (30) 50.00 100.00
*QUANTUM ONE/1500: .8X TO 2X BASIC INSERTS
*QUANTUM TWO/50: 8X TO 20X BASIC INSERTS
FF1 Wayne Gretzky 6.00 15.00
FF2 Peter Bondra .75 2.00
FF3 Sergei Samsonov .75 2.00
FF4 Jaromir Jagr 1.50 4.00
FF5 Brendan Shanahan 1.00 2.50
FF6 Joe Sakic 2.00 5.00
FF7 Brett Hull 1.50 4.00
FF8 Paul Kariya 1.00 2.50
FF9 Keith Tkachuk 1.00 2.50
FF10 Zigmund Palffy .75 2.00
FF11 Eric Lindros 1.00 2.50
FF12 Mike Modano 1.50 4.00
FF13 Pavel Bure 1.00 2.50
FF14 Mats Sundin .75 2.00
FF15 Patrik Elias .75 2.00
FF16 Tony Amonte .75 2.00
FF17 Peter Forsberg 2.50 6.00
FF18 Alexei Yashin .75 2.00
FF19 Mark Recchi .75 2.00
FF20 Steve Yzerman 4.00 10.00
FF21 Doug Weight .75 2.00
FF22 Jeremy Roenick 1.25 3.00
FF23 Teemu Selanne 1.00 2.50
FF24 Owen Nolan .75 2.00
FF25 John LeClair 1.00 2.50
FF26 Jason Allison .75 2.00
FF27 Mike Johnson .75 2.00
FF28 Theo Fleury .75 2.00
FF29 Nicklas Lidstrom 1.00 2.50
FF30 Joe Nieuwendyk .75 2.00

1998-99 Upper Deck Frozen In Time

COMPLETE SET (30) 50.00 100.00
*QUANTUM ONE/1000: .6X TO 1.5X BASIC INSERTS
*QUANTUM TWO/25: 5X TO 12X BASIC INSERTS
FT1 Steve Yzerman 4.00 10.00
FT2 Peter Forsberg 2.50 6.00
FT3 Sergei Samsonov 1.25 3.00
FT4 Martin Brodeur 2.50 6.00
FT5 Theo Fleury .75 2.00
FT6 Paul Kariya 1.50 4.00
FT7 Rob Blake 1.25 3.00
FT8 Jari Kurri .75 2.00
FT9 Eric Lindros 1.50 4.00
FT10 Dominik Hasek 2.00 5.00
FT11 Patrick Roy 4.00 10.00
FT12 Saku Koivu 1.50 4.00
FT13 Mike Modano 1.50 4.00
FT14 Alexei Morozov .75 2.00
FT15 Chris Osgood 1.25 3.00
FT16 Doug Gilmour 1.25 3.00
FT17 Owen Nolan 1.25 3.00
FT18 Mike Johnson 1.25 3.00
FT19 Keith Tkachuk 1.50 4.00
FT20 Adam Oates 1.25 3.00
FT21 Chris Chelios 1.50 4.00
FT22 Brendan Shanahan 1.50 4.00
FT23 Joe Sakic 2.00 5.00
FT24 Pavel Bure 1.50 4.00
FT25 Ray Bourque 2.00 5.00
FT26 Ed Belfour 1.50 4.00
FT27 John LeClair 1.50 4.00
FT28 Teemu Selanne 1.50 4.00
FT29 Jaromir Jagr 1.50 4.00
FT30 Wayne Gretzky 6.00 15.00

1998-99 Upper Deck Game Jerseys

GJ1 Wayne Gretzky 40.00 100.00
GJ2 Vincent Lecavalier 15.00 40.00
GJ3 Bobby Hull 15.00 40.00
GJ4 Curtis Joseph 12.00 30.00
GJ5 Roberto Luongo 12.00 30.00
GJ6 Martin Brodeur 15.00 40.00
GJ8 Ed Belfour 12.00 30.00
GJ9 Al MacInnis 8.00 20.00
GJ10 Derian Hatcher 5.00 12.00
GJ11 Daniel Tkaczuk 5.00 12.00
GJ12 Manny Malhotra 6.00 15.00
GJ13 Eric Brewer 5.00 12.00
GJ14 Alex Tanguay 5.00 12.00
GJ15 Brendan Shanahan 12.00 30.00
GJ16 Jaromir Jagr 15.00 40.00
GJ16 Chris Osgood 12.00 30.00
GJ17 Dominik Hasek 25.00 60.00
GJ18 Doug Gilmour 10.00 25.00
GJ19 Mats Sundin 10.00 25.00
GJ20 Darryl Sydor 5.00 12.00
GJ21 Chris Therien 5.00 12.00
GJ22 Darius Kasparaitis 6.00 15.00
GJ23 Alexei Zhamnov 5.00 12.00
GJ24 Joe Nieuwendyk 6.00 15.00
GJA2 W.Gretzky AU/99 400.00 1000.00
GJA3 V.Lecavalier AU/100 60.00 150.00
GJA4 Gretzky JSY AU/99 500.00 1200.00

1998-99 Upper Deck Generation Next

COMPLETE SET (30) 30.00 60.00
*QUANTUM ONE/1000: .6X TO 1.5
*QUANTUM ONE/500: 1.2X TO 3X
*QUANTUM ONE/250: 2X TO 5X
*QUANTUM TWO/75: 8X TO 20X
*QUANTUM TWO/25: 20X TO 50X
*QUANTUM TWO/10: 25X TO 60X
GN1 W.Gretzky/S.Samsonov 2.00 5.00
GN2 W.Gretzky/M.Hossa 2.00 5.00
GN3 W.Gretzky/V.Lecavalier 2.00 5.00
GN4 S.Yzerman/B.Morrison 1.00 2.50
GN5 S.Yzerman/M.Reasoner 1.50 4.00
GN6 S.Yzerman/M.Malhotra 1.50 4.00
GN7 P.Roy/Jean-Sebastien Giguere 1.50 4.00
GN8 P.Roy/J.Theodore 2.00 5.00
GN9 P.Roy/M.Denis 1.50 4.00
GN10 E.Lindros/P.Marleau .60 1.50
GN11 E.Lindros/B.Isbister .60 1.50
GN12 E.Lindros/J.Thornton .60 1.50
GN13 B.Shanahan/J.Green .60 1.50
GN14 B.Shanahan/T.Jones .60 1.50
GN15 B.Shanahan/M.Watt .60 1.50
GN16 R.Bourque/M.Ohlund .60 1.50
GN17 R.Bourque/T.Poti .60 1.50
GN18 R.Bourque/E.Brewer .75 2.00
GN19 P.Kariya/D.Briere .60 1.50
GN20 P.Kariya/R.Fata .60 1.50
GN21 P.Kariya/C.Drury .60 1.50
GN22 J.Jagr/R.Dome .60 1.50
GN23 J.Jagr/R.Zednik .60 1.50
GN24 J.Jagr/O.Kvasha .60 1.50
GN25 P.Forsberg/O.Jokinen 1.25 3.00
GN26 P.Forsberg/N.Sundstrom 1.00 2.50
GN27 P.Forsberg/B.Morrison 1.00 2.50
GN28 P.Bure/V.Sharifijanov .60 1.50
GN29 P.Bure/D.Nabokov .60 1.50
GN30 P.Bure/S.Samsonov .60 1.50

1998-99 Upper Deck Lord Stanley's Heroes

COMPLETE SET (30) 30.00 60.00
*QUANTUM ONE/2000: .6X TO 1.5X BASIC INSERTS
*QUANTUM TWO/100: 8X TO 20X BASIC INSERTS
LS1 Wayne Gretzky 4.00 10.00
LS2 Joe Sakic 1.25 3.00
LS3 Jaromir Jagr .75 2.00
LS4 Brendan Shanahan .60 1.50
LS5 Martin Brodeur 1.50 4.00
LS6 Theo Fleury .60 1.50
LS7 Doug Gilmour .40 1.00
LS8 Ron Francis .40 1.00
LS9 Sergei Fedorov 1.00 2.50
LS10 Patrick Roy 3.00 8.00
LS11 Mark Messier .60 1.50
LS12 Peter Forsberg 1.50 4.00
LS13 Brian Leetch .60 1.50
LS14 Steve Yzerman 3.00 8.00
LS15 Sergei Samsonov .40 1.00
LS16 Eric Lindros .60 1.50
LS17 Paul Kariya .60 1.50
LS18 Saku Koivu .60 1.50
LS19 Bryan Berard .40 1.00
LS20 Chris Pronger .40 1.00
LS21 Keith Tkachuk .60 1.50
LS22 Doug Weight .40 1.00
LS23 Ed Belfour .60 1.50
LS24 Mats Sundin .60 1.50
LS25 John LeClair .60 1.50
LS26 Pavel Bure .60 1.50
LS27 Dominik Hasek 1.25 3.00
LS28 Mike Modano 1.00 2.50
LS29 Curtis Joseph .60 1.50
LS30 Teemu Selanne .60 1.50

1998-99 Upper Deck Profiles

COMPLETE SET (30) 20.00 50.00
*QUANTUM ONE/1500: .6X TO 1.5X BASIC INSERTS
*QUANTUM TWO/50: 10X TO 25X BASIC INSERTS
P1 Marty Reasoner .50 1.25
P2 Brett Hull 1.00 2.50
P3 Steve Yzerman 4.00 10.00
P4 Eric Lindros .75 2.00
P5 Eric Brewer .60 1.50
P6 Martin Brodeur 2.00 5.00
P7 John Vanbiesbrouck .50 1.25
P8 Teemu Selanne .75 2.00
P9 Wayne Gretzky 5.00 12.00
P10 Jaromir Jagr 1.25 3.00
P11 Peter Forsberg 2.00 5.00
P12 Manny Malhotra .50 1.25
P13 Sergei Samsonov .50 1.25
P14 Brendan Shanahan .75 2.00
P15 Doug Gilmour .50 1.25
P16 Vincent Lecavalier .75 2.00
P17 Dominik Hasek 1.50 4.00
P18 Mike Modano 1.25 3.00
P19 Saku Koivu .75 2.00
P20 Curtis Joseph .75 2.00
P21 Paul Kariya .75 2.00
P22 Doug Weight .60 1.50
P23 Ray Bourque 1.50 4.00
P24 Patrick Roy 4.00 10.00
P25 John LeClair .75 2.00
P26 Chris Drury .50 1.25
P27 Theo Fleury .60 1.50
P28 Mats Sundin .60 1.50
P29 Sergei Fedorov 1.00 2.50
P30 Rico Fata .60 1.50

1998-99 Upper Deck Wayne Gretzky Game Jersey Autographs

COMMON CARD 200.00 500.00

1998-99 Upper Deck Year of the Great One

COMPLETE SET (30) 20.00 50.00
COMMON GRETZKY (G01-G030) 1.50 4.00
*QUANTUM ONE/199: 1.5X TO 4X BASIC INSERTS
*QUANTUM TWO/99: 6X TO 15X BASIC INSERTS

1998-99 Upper Deck Arena Giveaway Pittsburgh Penguins

COMPLETE SET (4)

1998 Upper Deck Willie O'Ree Commemorative Card

22 Willie O'Ree 5.00 10.00

1999-00 Upper Deck

COMPLETE SET (335) 40.00 100.00
1 Wayne Gretzky .75 2.00
2 Wayne Gretzky .75 2.00
3 Wayne Gretzky .75 2.00
4 Wayne Gretzky .75 2.00
5 Wayne Gretzky .75 2.00
6 Wayne Gretzky .75 2.00
7 Wayne Gretzky .75 2.00
8 Wayne Gretzky .75 2.00
9 Wayne Gretzky .75 2.00
10 Wayne Gretzky .75 2.00
11 Paul Kariya .20 .50
12 Matt Cullen .12 .30
13 Steve Rucchin .12 .30
14 Fredrik Olausson .12 .30
15 Damian Rhodes .12 .30
16 Jody Hull .12 .30
17 Ray Bourque .30 .75
18 Joe Thornton .30 .75
19 Jonathan Girard .12 .30
20 Shawn Bates .12 .30
21 Byron Dafoe .15 .40
22 Dominik Hasek .30 .75
23 Michael Peca .15 .40
24 Miroslav Satan .15 .40
25 Dixon Ward .12 .30
26 Valeri Bure .12 .30
27 Derek Morris .12 .30
28 Jarome Iginla .25 .60
29 Rico Fata .12 .30
30 Jean-Sebastien Giguere .20 .50
31 Arturs Irbe .15 .40
32 Sami Kapanen .12 .30
33 Gary Roberts .12 .30
34 Bates Battaglia .12 .30
35 J-P Dumont .15 .40
36 Ty Jones .12 .30
37 Tony Amonte .15 .40
38 Anders Eriksson .12 .30
39 Peter Forsberg .40 1.00
40 Adam Foote .15 .40
41 Chris Drury .15 .40
42 Milan Hejduk .15 .40
43 Brett Hull .40 1.00
44 Ed Belfour .20 .50
45 Jamie Langenbrunner .12 .30
46 Derian Hatcher .15 .40
47 Jon Sim RC .20 .50
48 Joe Nieuwendyk .15 .40
49 Steve Yzerman .50 1.25
50 Brendan Shanahan .20 .50
51 Nicklas Lidstrom .20 .50
52 Igor Larionov .20 .50
53 Vyacheslav Kozlov .12 .30
54 Bill Guerin .20 .50
55 Mike Grier .12 .30
56 Tommy Salo .15 .40
57 Tom Poti .12 .30
58 Mark Parrish .12 .30
59 Pavel Bure .20 .50
60 Scott Mellanby .12 .30
61 Chris Allen RC .12 .30
62 Rob Blake .20 .50
63 Pavel Rosa .12 .30
64 Donald Audette .12 .30
65 Vladimir Tsyplakov .12 .30
66 Manny Legace .12 .30
67 Saku Koivu .20 .50
68 Eric Weinrich .12 .30
69 Jeff Hackett .12 .30
70 Arron Asham .12 .30
71 Trevor Linden .20 .50
72 Cliff Ronning .12 .30
73 David Legwand .12 .30
74 Kimmo Timonen .12 .30
75 Sergei Krivokrasov .12 .30
76 Mike Dunham .12 .30
77 Martin Brodeur .50 1.25
78 Patrik Elias .20 .50
79 Petr Sykora .15 .40
80 Vadim Sharifijanov .12 .30
81 John Madden RC .20 .50
82 Eric Brewer .12 .30
83 Dmitri Nabokov .12 .30
84 Kenny Jonsson .12 .30
85 Zdeno Chara .20 .50
86 Wayne Gretzky 1.25 3.00
87 Mike Richter .20 .50
88 Adam Graves .15 .40
89 Manny Malhotra .15 .40
90 Alexei Yashin .15 .40
91 Sami Salo .15 .40
92 Marian Hossa .20 .50
93 Shawn McEachern .12 .30
94 Eric Lindros .30 .75
95 Jean-Marc Pelletier .12 .30
96 Rod Brind'Amour .20 .50
97 Mark Recchi .25 .60
98 Eric Desjardins .15 .40
99 Robert Reichel .12 .30
100 Keith Tkachuk .20 .50
101 Robert Esche RC .20 .50
102 Oleg Tverdovsky .12 .30
103 Trevor Letowski .12 .30
104 Jaromir Jagr .60 1.50
105 Tom Barrasso .20 .50
106 Jan Hrdina .12 .30
107 Matthew Barnaby .12 .30
108 Vincent Damphousse .15 .40
109 Jeff Friesen .15 .40
110 Patrick Marleau .20 .50
111 Mike Ricci .12 .30
112 Scott Hannan .12 .30
113 Pavol Demitra .25 .60
114 Al MacInnis .25 .60
115 Lubos Bartecko .12 .30
116 Jochen Hecht RC .30 .75
117 Vincent Lecavalier .20 .50
118 Paul Mara .12 .30
119 Kevin Hodson .12 .30
120 Dan Cloutier .12 .30
121 Mats Sundin .20 .50
122 Daniil Markov .12 .30
123 Sergei Berezin .12 .30
124 Steve Thomas .12 .30
125 Tomas Kaberle .12 .30
126 Mark Messier .40 1.00
127 Bill Muckalt .12 .30
128 Kevin Weekes .12 .30
129 Josh Holden .12 .30
130 Jaroslav Svejkovsky .12 .30
131 Adam Oates .20 .50
132 Peter Bondra .20 .50
133 Jan Bulis .12 .30
134 Wayne Gretzky CL .75 2.00
135 Wayne Gretzky CL .75 2.00
136 Wayne Gretzky SP 2.00 5.00
137 Eric Lindros SP .50 1.25
138 Jaromir Jagr SP 1.00 2.50
139 Paul Kariya SP .30 .75
140 Steve Yzerman SP .75 2.00
141 Patrick Roy SP .75 2.00
142 Chris Drury SP .25 .60
143 Sergei Samsonov SP .25 .60
144 Brett Hull SP .60 1.50
145 Dominik Hasek SP .50 1.25
146 Keith Tkachuk SP .30 .75
147 Alexei Yashin SP .25 .60
148 Martin Brodeur SP .75 2.00
149 Pavel Bure SP .30 .75
150 Paul Mara SP .20 .50
151 Peter Bondra SP .30 .75
152 Mike Modano SP .50 1.25
153 Teemu Selanne SP .60 1.50
154 Peter Forsberg SP .60 1.50
155 Brendan Shanahan SP .30 .75
156 Ray Bourque SP .50 1.25
157 Saku Koivu SP .30 .75
158 John LeClair SP .30 .75
159 Joe Sakic SP .60 1.50
160 David Legwand SP .20 .50
161 Patrik Stefan YG RC .50 1.25
162 Nick Boynton YG .40 1.00
163 Roberto Luongo YG .75 2.00
164 Rico Fata SP .20 .50
165 Daniel Sedin YG 6.00 15.00
166 Henrik Sedin YG 3.00 8.00
167 Brad Stuart YG .40 1.00
168 Tony Amonte SP .40 1.00
169 Oleg Saprykin YG RC .50 1.25
170 Denis Shvidki YG .40 1.00
171 Guy Hebert .20 .50
172 Niclas Havelid RC .20 .50
173 Oleg Tverdovsky .12 .30
174 Teemu Selanne .40 1.00
175 Damian Rhodes .12 .30
176 Nelson Emerson .12 .30
177 Per Svartvadet RC .12 .30
178 Ray Ferraro .12 .30
179 Kelly Buchberger .12 .30
180 Norm Maracle .12 .30
181 Patrik Stefan .20 .50
182 Dave Andreychuk .20 .50
183 Sergei Samsonov .15 .40
184 John Grahame RC .15 .40
185 Jason Allison .15 .40
186 Kyle McLaren .12 .30
187 Anson Carter .15 .40
188 Martin Biron .15 .40
189 Brian Campbell RC .20 .50
190 Curtis Brown .12 .30
191 Alexei Zhitnik .12 .30
192 David Moravec RC .12 .30
193 Oleg Saprykin .20 .50
194 Grant Fuhr .30 .75
195 Phil Housley .15 .40
196 Marc Savard .12 .30
197 Robyn Regehr .12 .30
198 Martin Gelinas .12 .30
199 Ron Francis .25 .60
200 Jeff O'Neil .12 .30
201 Keith Primeau .15 .40
202 Paul Ranheim .12 .30
203 Kyle Calder RC .15 .40
204 Jocelyn Thibault .15 .40
205 Wendel Clark .30 .75
206 Doug Gilmour .25 .60
207 Josef Marha .12 .30
208 Alexei Zhamnov .12 .30
209 Dan Hinote RC .15 .40
210 Patrick Roy .50 1.25
211 Joe Sakic .40 1.00
212 Alex Tanguay .15 .40
213 Sandis Ozolinsh .12 .30
214 Adam Deadmarsh .12 .30
215 Jere Lehtinen .15 .40
216 Mike Modano .30 .75
217 Darryl Sydor .15 .40
218 Sergei Zubov .15 .40
219 Pavel Patera RC .12 .30
220 Jamie Pushor .12 .30
221 Chris Osgood .20 .50
222 Tomas Holmstrom .12 .30
223 Chris Chelios .20 .50
224 Sergei Fedorov .30 .75
225 Jiri Fischer .12 .30
226 Paul Comrie RC .30 .75
227 Frantisek Musil .12 .30
228 Janne Niinimaa .12 .30
229 Doug Weight .20 .50
230 Trevor Kidd .12 .30
231 Oleg Kvasha .12 .30
232 Victor Kozlov .12 .30
233 Rob Niedermayer .12 .30
234 Luc Robitaille .20 .50
235 Aki Berg .12 .30
236 Bryan Smolinski .12 .30
237 Jozef Stumpel .12 .30
238 Zigmund Palffy .20 .50
239 Stephane Fiset .15 .40
240 Jason Blake RC .15 .40
241 Scott Lachance .12 .30
242 Vladimir Malakhov .12 .30
243 Mike Ribeiro .12 .30
244 Brian Savage .12 .30
245 Tomas Vokoun .20 .50
246 Randy Robitaille .12 .30
247 Sergei Nemchinov .12 .30
248 Brendan Morrison .15 .40
249 Scott Niedermayer .20 .50
250 Scott Stevens .20 .50
251 Scott Gomez .15 .40
252 Mark Lawrence .12 .30
253 Felix Potvin .30 .75
254 Olli Jokinen .15 .40
255 Tim Connolly .12 .30
256 Mariusz Czerkaswki .12 .30
257 Valeri Kamensky .12 .30
258 Brian Leetch .15 .40
259 Petr Nedved .12 .30
260 Theo Fleury .25 .60
261 Kevin Hatcher .12 .30
262 Mike York .12 .30
263 Ron Tugnutt .15 .40
264 Chris Phillips .12 .30
265 Daniel Alfredsson .20 .50
266 Radek Bonk .12 .30
267 Wade Redden .12 .30
268 John Vanbiesbrouck .20 .50
269 John LeClair .20 .50
270 Simon Gagne .20 .50
271 Nikolai Khabibulin .15 .40
272 Daniel Briere .15 .40
273 Jeremy Roenick .30 .75
274 Andrew Ference .12 .30
275 Alexei Kovalev .15 .40
276 Martin Straka .12 .30
277 Alexei Morozov .15 .40
278 Steve Shields .15 .40
279 Marco Sturm .12 .30
280 Niklas Sundstrom .12 .30
281 Brad Stuart .15 .40
282 Owen Nolan .20 .50
283 Roman Turek .15 .40
284 Chris Pronger .20 .50
285 Jim Campbell .12 .30
286 Michal Handzus .15 .40
287 Pierre Turgeon .15 .40
288 Darcy Tucker .12 .30
289 Andrei Zyuzin .12 .30
290 Stephen Guolla .12 .30
291 Curtis Joseph .25 .60
292 Jonas Hoglund .12 .30
293 Bryan Berard .12 .30
294 Mike Johnson .15 .40
295 Garth Snow .15 .40
296 Jason Strudwick .12 .30
297 Steve Kariya RC .20 .50
298 Markus Naslund .20 .50
299 Mattias Ohlund .12 .30
300 Alexander Mogilny .15 .40
301 Olaf Kolzig .20 .50
302 Alexei Tezikov RC .20 .50
303 Alexander Volchkov RC .12 .30
304 Steve Yzerman CL .30 .75
305 Curtis Joseph CL .15 .40
306 Pavel Brendl PRO RC .75 2.00
307 Daniel Sedin PRO 1.25 3.00
308 Henrik Sedin PRO 1.25 3.00
309 Sheldon Keefe PRO RC .50 1.25
310 Ryan Jardine PRO RC .40 1.00
311 Maxime Ouellet PRO .50 1.25
312 Barret Jackman PRO .30 .75
313 Kristian Kudroc PRO RC .30 .75
314 Branislav Mezei PRO RC .30 .75
315 Denis Shvidki PRO .40 1.00
316 Brian Finley PRO .50 1.25
317 Jonathan Cheechoo PRO 1.50 4.00
318 Mark Bell PRO .30 .75
319 Taylor Pyatt PRO .30 .75
320 Norm Milley PRO .30 .75
321 Jamie Lundmark PRO .40 1.00
322 Alexander Buturlin PRO RC .40 1.00
323 Jaroslav Kristek PRO RC .40 1.00
324 Kris Beech PRO .30 .75
325 Scott Kelman PRO .30 .75
326 Milan Kraft PRO RC .40 1.00
327 Mattias Weinhandl PRO .30 .75
328 Alexei Volkov PRO .40 1.00
329 Andrei Shefer PRO RC .40 1.00
330 Mathieu Chouinard PRO .30 .75
331 Justin Papineau PRO .30 .75
332 Mike Van Ryn PRO .30 .75
333 Jeff Heerema PRO .30 .75
334 Michael Zigomanis PRO .30 .75
335 Bryan Kazarian PRO RC .40 1.00

1999-00 Upper Deck Exclusives

*1-305 EXCL/100: 12X TO 30X BASIC CARDS
*136-160 VET/100: 8X TO 20X BASIC SP
*161-170 YG/100: 5X TO 12X BASIC YG
*306-335 PRO/100: 5X TO 12X BASIC PRO

1999-00 Upper Deck A Piece of History 500 Goal Club

500BHA Bobby Hull AU/25 350.00 550.00
500BH Bobby Hull 40.00 100.00
500BTA Bryan Trottier AU/25 200.00 400.00
500BT Bryan Trottier 15.00 40.00
500DCA Dino Ciccarelli AU/25 150.00 300.00
500DC Dino Ciccarelli 25.00 60.00
500GH Gordie Howe 75.00 150.00
500GHA Gordie Howe AU/25 600.00 800.00
500GLA Guy Lafleur AU/25 150.00 350.00
500GL Guy Lafleur 100.00 200.00
500GP Gilbert Perreault 15.00 40.00
500GPA Gilbert Perreault AU/25 400.00 600.00
500JBA Jean Beliveau AU/25 300.00 500.00
500JB Jean Beliveau 100.00 200.00
500LRA Luc Robitaille AU/25 350.00 500.00
500LR Luc Robitaille 15.00 40.00
500MB Mike Bossy 20.00 50.00
500MBA Mike Bossy AU/25 400.00 500.00
500MDAS Marcel Dionne AU/25 125.00 250.00
500MD Marcel Dionne 15.00 40.00
500MGA Michel Goulet AU/25 150.00 300.00
500MG Michel Goulet 15.00 40.00
500MR Maurice Richard 75.00 200.00
500MRA M. Richard AU/25 450.00 700.00
500SM Stan Mikita 25.00 60.00
500SMA Stan Mikita AU/25 200.00 400.00
500SY Steve Yzerman 75.00 150.00
500SYA Steve Yzerman AU/25 500.00 750.00
500BHUA Brett Hull AU/25 250.00 500.00
500BHU Brett Hull 25.00 60.00

1999-00 Upper Deck All-Star Class

COMPLETE SET (20) 30.00 60.00
*SILVER/100: 10X TO 25X BASIC INSERTS
AS1 Dominik Hasek 2.00 5.00
AS2 Patrick Roy 5.00 12.00
AS3 Jaromir Jagr 1.50 4.00
AS4 Paul Kariya 1.00 2.50
AS5 Teemu Selanne 1.00 2.50
AS6 Keith Tkachuk 1.00 2.50
AS7 Pavel Bure 1.00 2.50
AS8 John LeClair 1.00 2.50
AS9 Mats Sundin 1.00 2.50
AS10 Steve Yzerman 5.00 12.00
AS11 Peter Forsberg 2.50 6.00
AS12 Eric Lindros 1.00 2.50
AS13 Steve Kariya 1.25 3.00
AS14 Ed Belfour 1.00 2.50
AS15 Nicklas Lidstrom .75 2.00
AS16 Ray Bourque 1.50 4.00
AS17 Sandis Ozolinsh .75 2.00
AS18 Al MacInnis .75 2.00
AS19 Martin Brodeur 2.50 6.00
AS20 Patrik Stefan 1.50 4.00

1999-00 Upper Deck Crunch Time

COMPLETE SET (30) 15.00 30.00
*SILVER/100: 25X TO 60X BASIC INSERTS
CT1 Vincent Lecavalier .40 1.00
CT2 Steve Yzerman 2.00 5.00
CT3 Peter Bondra .30 .75
CT4 Jean-Marc Pelletier .30 .75
CT5 Brendan Shanahan .40 1.00
CT6 Joe Sakic .75 2.00
CT7 Jean-Sebastien Giguere .30 .75
CT8 Brett Hull .50 1.25
CT9 Jaromir Jagr .60 1.50
CT10 Eric Brewer .30 .75
CT11 Sergei Samsonov .30 .75
CT12 Alexei Yashin .20 .50
CT13 Mats Sundin .40 1.00
CT14 Mike Modano .60 1.50
CT15 Al MacInnis .30 .75
CT16 Paul Mara .20 .50
CT17 David Legwand .30 .75
CT18 Eric Lindros .40 1.00
CT19 Peter Forsberg 1.00 2.50
CT20 Ray Bourque .60 1.50
CT21 Teemu Selanne .40 1.00
CT22 John LeClair .40 1.00
CT23 Dominik Hasek .75 2.00
CT24 Martin Brodeur 1.00 2.50
CT25 Tony Amonte .30 .75
CT26 Keith Tkachuk .40 1.00
CT27 Patrick Roy 2.00 5.00
CT28 Pavel Bure .40 1.00
CT29 Paul Kariya .40 1.00
CT30 Curtis Joseph .40 1.00

1999-00 Upper Deck Fantastic Finishers

COMPLETE SET (15) 12.00 25.00
*SILVER/100: 20X TO 50X BASIC INSERTS
FF1 Brett Hull .60 1.50
FF2 John LeClair .50 1.25
FF3 Eric Lindros .50 1.25
FF4 Jaromir Jagr .75 2.00
FF5 Sergei Samsonov .40 1.00
FF6 Teemu Selanne .50 1.25
FF7 Alexei Yashin .40 1.00
FF8 Keith Tkachuk .50 1.25
FF9 Pavel Bure .50 1.25
FF10 Peter Forsberg 1.25 3.00
FF11 Brendan Shanahan .50 1.25
FF12 Tony Amonte .40 1.00
FF13 Paul Kariya .50 1.25
FF14 Steve Yzerman 2.50 6.00
FF15 Joe Sakic 1.00 2.50

1999-00 Upper Deck Game Jerseys

BH Brett Hull 10.00 25.00
DH Dominik Hasek 12.50 30.00
EL Eric Lindros 8.00 20.00
JJ Jaromir Jagr 12.50 30.00
JL John LeClair 8.00 20.00
JS Joe Sakic 15.00 40.00
MB Martin Brodeur 20.00 50.00
MM Mike Modano 10.00 25.00
PF Peter Forsberg 20.00 50.00
PR Patrick Roy 20.00 50.00
RB Ray Bourque 12.00 30.00
SF Sergei Fedorov 10.00 25.00
SS Sergei Samsonov 8.00 20.00
SY Steve Yzerman 15.00 40.00
TS Teemu Selanne 10.00 25.00
WG1 Wayne Gretzky 30.00 80.00
WG2 Wayne Gretzky Dual/99 300.00 600.00
WG3 Wayne Gretzky Nagano 125.00 300.00
BHS B.Hull AU/25 150.00 300.00
RBS R.Bourque AU/25 150.00 300.00
SYS S.Yzerman AU/25 250.00 500.00
WGS1 W.Gretzky AU/25 600.00 1500.00

1999-00 Upper Deck Game Jerseys Series II

AM Al MacInnis 8.00 20.00
CJ Curtis Joseph 8.00 20.00
DH Dominik Hasek 15.00 40.00
EB Ed Belfour 8.00 20.00
JJ Jaromir Jagr 12.00 30.00
JL John LeClair 8.00 20.00
JR Jeremy Roenick 10.00 25.00
JT Joe Thornton 12.00 30.00
MB Martin Brodeur 20.00 50.00
PF Peter Forsberg 12.00 30.00
PK Paul Kariya 10.00 25.00
PR Patrick Roy 20.00 50.00
SF Sergei Fedorov 10.00 25.00
SY Steve Yzerman 20.00 50.00
TS Teemu Selanne 12.00 30.00
WG Wayne Gretzky 30.00 80.00
CJS C.Joseph AU/25 100.00 200.00
EBS E.Belfour AU/25 100.00 200.00
SYC Steve Yzerman CAN 15.00 40.00
SYS S.Yzerman AU/25 250.00 500.00
WGS W.Gretzky AU/25 600.00 1500.00

1999-00 Upper Deck Game Jersey Patch

WG1P Wayne Gretzky 400.00 800.00
WG2P Wayne Gretzky 400.00 800.00
BHP Brett Hull 125.00 300.00
DHP Dominik Hasek 125.00 300.00
ELP Eric Lindros 75.00 200.00
JJP Jaromir Jagr 125.00 300.00
JLP John LeClair 75.00 200.00
JSP Joe Sakic 125.00 300.00
MBP Martin Brodeur 150.00 400.00
MMP Mike Modano 100.00 250.00
PFP Peter Forsberg 125.00 300.00
PRP Patrick Roy 150.00 400.00
RBP Ray Bourque 125.00 300.00
SFP Sergei Fedorov 125.00 300.00
SSP Sergei Samsonov 75.00 200.00
SYP Steve Yzerman 150.00 400.00
TSP Teemu Selanne 75.00 200.00

1999-00 Upper Deck Game Jersey Patch Series II

CJP Curtis Joseph 100.00 250.00
DHP Dominik Hasek 125.00 300.00
EBP Ed Belfour 100.00 250.00
JJP Jaromir Jagr 125.00 300.00
JLP John LeClair 60.00 150.00
JTP Joe Thornton 100.00 250.00
KTP Keith Tkachuk 60.00 150.00
MBP Martin Brodeur 150.00 350.00
PFP Peter Forsberg 100.00 250.00
PKP Paul Kariya 75.00 200.00
PRP Patrick Roy 150.00 400.00
SFP Sergei Fedorov 75.00 200.00
SYP Steve Yzerman 150.00 400.00
WGP Wayne Gretzky 400.00 800.00

1999-00 Upper Deck Game Pads

CJGP Curtis Joseph 20.00 50.00

1999-00 Upper Deck Gretzky Profiles

COMPLETE SET (10) 20.00 50.00
COMMON GRETZKY (GP1-GP10) 2.50 6.00
*SILVER/100: 2.5X TO 6X BASIC INSERTS

1999-00 Upper Deck Headed for the Hall

COMPLETE SET (15) 20.00 40.00
*SILVER/100: 8X TO 20X BASIC INSERTS
HOF1 Wayne Gretzky 5.00 12.00
HOF2 Dominik Hasek 1.50 4.00
HOF3 Ray Bourque 1.25 3.00
HOF4 Steve Yzerman 4.00 10.00
HOF5 Jaromir Jagr 1.25 3.00
HOF6 Brett Hull 1.00 2.50
HOF7 Eric Lindros .75 2.00
HOF8 Adam Oates .60 1.50
HOF9 Brian Leetch .75 2.00
HOF10 Patrick Roy 4.00 10.00
HOF11 Mark Messier .75 2.00
HOF12 Luc Robitaille .60 1.50
HOF13 Joe Sakic 1.50 4.00
HOF14 Chris Chelios .75 2.00
HOF15 Curtis Joseph .75 2.00

1999-00 Upper Deck Ice Gallery

COMPLETE SET (10) 40.00 80.00
*SILVER/100: 4X TO 10X BASIC INSERTS
IG1 Jaromir Jagr 4.00 10.00
IG2 Paul Kariya 3.00 8.00
IG3 Peter Forsberg 6.00 15.00
IG4 Dominik Hasek 5.00 12.00
IG5 Patrick Roy 12.50 30.00
IG6 Teemu Selanne 3.00 8.00
IG7 Eric Lindros 3.00 8.00
IG8 Patrik Stefan 4.00 10.00
IG9 Steve Kariya 3.00 8.00
IG10 Pavel Bure 3.00 8.00

1999-00 Upper Deck Marquee Attractions

COMPLETE SET (15) 12.00 25.00
*SILVER/100: 20X TO 50X BSIC INSERTS
MA1 Ray Bourque .75 2.00
MA2 Paul Kariya .50 1.25
MA3 Eric Lindros .50 1.25
MA4 Jaromir Jagr .75 2.00
MA5 Dominik Hasek 1.00 2.50
MA6 Patrick Roy 2.50 6.00
MA7 Alexei Yashin .40 1.00
MA8 Mats Sundin .50 1.25
MA9 Steve Yzerman 2.50 6.00
MA10 Pavel Bure .50 1.25
MA11 Vincent Lecavalier .50 1.25
MA12 Teemu Selanne .50 1.25
MA13 Mike Modano .75 2.00
MA14 Keith Tkachuk .50 1.25
MA15 Peter Forsberg 1.25 3.00

1999-00 Upper Deck New Ice Age

COMPLETE SET (20) 20.00 40.00
*SILVER/100: 10X TO 25X BASIC INSERTS
N1 Jaromir Jagr 1.50 4.00
N2 Paul Kariya 1.00 2.50
N3 Sergei Samsonov .75 2.00
N4 Vadim Sharifijanov .40 1.00
N5 Ty Jones .40 1.00
N6 Teemu Selanne 1.00 2.50
N7 Martin Brodeur 2.50 6.00
N8 David Legwand .75 2.00
N9 Vincent Lecavalier 1.00 2.50
N10 Paul Mara .75 2.00
N11 Jean-Marc Pelletier .40 1.00
N12 Jean-Sebastien Giguere .75 2.00
N13 Marian Hossa 1.00 2.50
N14 Milan Hejduk 1.00 2.50
N15 Chris Drury .75 2.00
N16 Rico Fata .40 1.00
N17 Patrik Elias .75 2.00
N18 Eric Brewer .75 2.00
N19 Joe Thornton 1.50 4.00
N20 J-P Dumont .75 2.00

1999-00 Upper Deck NHL Scrapbook

COMPLETE SET (15) 12.00 25.00
*SILVER/100: 10X TO 25X BASIC CARDS
SB1 Patrick Roy 2.50 6.00
SB2 Ray Bourque .75 2.00
SB3 Steve Yzerman 2.50 6.00
SB4 Jaromir Jagr .75 2.00
SB5 Paul Kariya .60 1.50
SB6 Peter Forsberg 1.25 3.00
SB7 Pavel Bure .60 1.50
SB8 Curtis Joseph .60 1.50
SB9 Brett Hull .60 1.50
SB10 Eric Lindros .60 1.50
SB11 Teemu Selanne .60 1.50
SB12 Brendan Shanahan .60 1.50
SB13 John LeClair .60 1.50
SB14 Steve Kariya .60 1.50
SB15 Patrik Stefan .75 2.00

1999-00 Upper Deck PowerDeck Inserts

COMPLETE SET (9) 75.00 150.00
PD1 Dominik Hasek 3.00 8.00
PD2 Paul Kariya 2.00 5.00
PD3 Jaromir Jagr 2.50 6.00
PD4 Steve Yzerman 8.00 20.00
PD5 Patrick Roy 8.00 20.00
PD6 Brett Hull 2.00 5.00
PD7 Wayne Gretzky 12.50 25.00
PD8 Wayne Gretzky SP 30.00 80.00
PD9 Wayne Gretzky SP 30.00 80.00

1999-00 Upper Deck Sixth Sense

COMPLETE SET (20) 10.00 25.00
*SILVER/100: 25X TO 60X BASIC INSERTS
SS1 Paul Kariya .40 1.00
SS2 Patrick Roy 2.00 5.00
SS3 Brett Hull .50 1.25
SS4 Eric Lindros .40 1.00
SS5 Sergei Samsonov .40 1.00
SS6 Peter Forsberg 1.00 2.50
SS7 Patrik Stefan .60 1.50
SS8 Steve Yzerman 2.00 5.00
SS9 Jaromir Jagr .60 1.50
SS10 David Legwand .40 1.00
SS11 Steve Kariya .50 1.25
SS12 Tim Connolly .40 1.00
SS13 Pavel Bure .40 1.00
SS14 Brendan Shanahan .40 1.00
SS15 Martin Brodeur 1.00 2.50
SS16 Dominik Hasek .75 2.00
SS17 Mats Sundin .40 1.00
SS18 Vincent Lecavalier .40 1.00
SS19 Keith Tkachuk .40 1.00
SS20 Mike Modano .60 1.50

1999-00 Upper Deck Ultimate Defense

COMPLETE SET (10) 10.00 20.00
*SILVER/100: 12X TO 30X BASIC INSERTS
UD1 Byron Dafoe .60 1.50
UD2 Dominik Hasek 1.50 4.00
UD3 Patrick Roy 1.25 3.00
UD4 Chris Osgood .60 1.50
UD5 Ed Belfour .75 2.00
UD6 Roman Turek .60 1.50
UD7 Mike Richter .75 2.00
UD8 Nikolai Khabibulin .60 1.50
UD9 Martin Brodeur 2.00 5.00
UD10 Curtis Joseph .60 1.50

1999-00 Upper Deck Sobey's Memorial Cup

COMPLETE SET (16) 16.00 25.00
1 Alexei Volkov .75 2.00
2 Justin Papineau .75 2.00
3 Michael Henrich .40 1.00
4 Kris Beech .75 2.00
5 Mark Bell 1.50 4.00
6 Andrei Shefer .40 1.00
7 Pavel Brendl .75 2.00
8 Blake Robson .40 1.00
9 Ben Knopp .40 1.00
10 Maxime Ouellet 1.50 4.00
11 Thatcher Bell .40 1.00
12 Brian Finley .75 2.00
13 Jared Aulin 1.50 4.00
14 Jared Newman .40 1.00
15 Brad Boyes 4.00 10.00
16 Miguel Delisle .40 1.00

2000-01 Upper Deck

COMPLETE SET (440) 200.00 400.00
COMP.SET w/o YG's (360) 20.00 50.00
COMP.SER.1 (230) 125.00 250.00
COMP.SER.1 w/o YG's (180) 15.00 30.00
COMP.SER.2 (210) 100.00 200.00
COMP.SER.2 w/o YG's (180) 10.00 25.00
1 Paul Kariya .20 .50
2 Steve Rucchin .12 .30
3 Oleg Tverdovsky .12 .30
4 Mike Leclerc .12 .30
5 Ladislav Kohn .12 .30
6 Guy Hebert .15 .40
7 Dean Sylvester .12 .30
8 Andrew Brunette .12 .30
9 Ray Ferraro .12 .30
10 Donald Audette .15 .40
11 Damian Rhodes .12 .30
12 Patrik Stefan .15 .40
13 Joe Thornton .30 .75
14 Brian Rolston .15 .40
15 John Grahame .12 .30
16 Jason Allison .15 .40
17 Kyle McLaren .12 .30
18 Andre Savage .12 .30
19 Martin Biron .15 .40
20 Doug Gilmour .25 .60
21 Chris Gratton .12 .30
22 Miroslav Satan .12 .30
23 Maxim Afinogenov .12 .30
24 Dimitri Kalinin .12 .30
25 Oleg Saprykin .12 .30
26 Valeri Bure .15 .40
27 Derek Morris .12 .30
28 Marc Savard .12 .30
29 Clarke Wilm .12 .30
30 Fred Brathwaite .15 .40
31 Ron Francis .25 .60
32 Sami Kapanen .12 .30
33 Bates Battaglia .12 .30
34 Arturs Irbe .15 .40
35 Dave Tanabe .12 .30

36 Rod Brind'Amour .20 .50
37 Michal Grosek .12 .30
38 Steve Sullivan .12 .30
39 Eric Daze .15 .40
40 Bryan McCabe .12 .30
41 Michael Nylander .12 .30
42 Alexei Zhamnov .15 .40
43 Milan Hejduk .15 .40
44 Ray Bourque .30 .75
45 Patrick Roy .50 1.25
46 Peter Forsberg .40 1.00
47 Martin Skoula .15 .40
48 Shjon Podein .12 .30
49 Aaron Miller .12 .30
50 Espen Knutsen .12 .30
51 Jamie Pushor .12 .30
52 Kevyn Adams .12 .30
53 Marc Denis .15 .40
54 Ron Tugnutt .15 .40
55 Mike Modano .30 .75
56 Joe Nieuwendyk .15 .40
57 Mike Keane .15 .40
58 Darryl Sydor .15 .40
59 Brenden Morrow .15 .40
60 Jere Lehtinen .15 .40
61 Derian Hatcher .15 .40
62 Brendan Shanahan .20 .50
63 Sergei Fedorov .30 .75
64 Darren McCarty .12 .30
65 Tomas Holmstrom .15 .40
66 Chris Osgood .20 .50
67 Nicklas Lidstrom .20 .50
68 Ryan Smyth .15 .40
69 Igor Ulanov .12 .30
70 Tommy Salo .15 .40
71 Ethan Moreau .12 .30
72 Daniel Cleary .15 .40
73 Bill Guerin .20 .50
74 Pavel Bure .20 .50
75 Ray Whitney .15 .40
76 Lance Pitlick .12 .30
77 Trevor Kidd .12 .30
78 Mike Wilson .12 .30
79 Ivan Novoseltsev .12 .30
80 Luc Robitaille .20 .50
81 Stephane Fiset .12 .30
82 Rob Blake .20 .50
83 Jozef Stumpel .12 .30
84 Craig Johnson .12 .30
85 Glen Murray .15 .40
86 Kelly Buchberger .15 .40
87 Manny Fernandez .12 .30
88 Stacy Roest .12 .30
89 Andy Sutton .12 .30
90 Scott Pellerin .12 .30
91 Jim Dowd .12 .30
92 Dainius Zubrus .12 .30
93 Marian Savage .12 .30
94 Martin Rucinsky .12 .30
95 Craig Darby .12 .30
96 Jose Theodore .20 .50
97 David Legwand .20 .50
98 Rob Valicevic .12 .30
99 Randy Robitaille .12 .30
100 Mike Dunham .12 .30
101 Kimmo Timonen .12 .30
102 Scott Gomez .15 .40
103 Petr Sykora .15 .40
104 Alexander Mogilny .15 .40
105 John Madden .15 .40
106 Jason Arnott .15 .40
107 Sergei Brylin .12 .30
108 Scott Stevens .20 .50
109 Tim Connolly .20 .50
110 Mariusz Czerkawski .12 .30
111 Zdeno Chara .20 .50
112 Kenny Jonsson .12 .30
113 Claude Lapointe .12 .30
114 Theo Fleury .25 .60
115 Mike Richter .20 .50
116 Mike York .12 .30
117 Jan Hlavac .12 .30
118 Adam Graves .15 .40
119 Mark Messier .40 1.00
120 Marian Hossa .20 .50
121 Daniel Alfredsson .20 .50
122 Mike Fisher .12 .30
123 Patrick Lalime .15 .40
124 Wade Redden .12 .30
125 Shawn McEachern .12 .30
126 John LeClair .20 .50
127 Mark Recchi .25 .60
128 Brian Boucher .15 .40
129 Simon Gagne .20 .50
130 Eric Desjardins .15 .40
131 Rick Tocchet .15 .40
132 Jeremy Roenick .30 .75
133 Travis Green .12 .30
134 Trevor Letowski .12 .30
135 Teppo Numminen .12 .30
136 Shane Doan .15 .40
137 Mike Sullivan .12 .30
138 Jaromir Jagr .60 1.50
139 Robert Lang .12 .30
140 Jan Hrdina .12 .30
141 Matthew Barnaby .12 .30
142 Jean-Sebastien Aubin .15 .40
143 Jiri Slegr .12 .30
144 Owen Nolan .20 .50
145 Jeff Friesen .12 .30
146 Patrick Marleau .20 .50
147 Brad Stuart .15 .40
148 Steve Shields .12 .30
149 Todd Harvey .15 .40
150 Pavol Demitra .25 .60
151 Chris Pronger .20 .50
152 Scott Young .12 .30
153 Todd Reirden .12 .30
154 Roman Turek .15 .40
155 Marty Reasoner .12 .30
156 Mike Johnson .12 .30
157 Todd Warriner .12 .30
158 Paul Mara .12 .30
159 Dan Cloutier .15 .40
160 Fredrik Modin .12 .30
161 Curtis Joseph .25 .60
162 Steve Thomas .12 .30
163 Darcy Tucker .12 .30
164 Yanic Perreault .12 .30
165 Sergei Berezin .12 .30
166 Dimitri Yushkevich .12 .30
167 Markus Naslund .20 .50
168 Andrew Cassels .12 .30
169 Todd Bertuzzi .15 .40
170 Felix Potvin .30 .75
171 Ed Jovanovski .15 .40
172 Trent Klatt .12 .30
173 Adam Oates .20 .50
174 Chris Simon .12 .30
175 Richard Zednik .12 .30
176 Calle Johansson .12 .30
177 Andrei Nikolishin .12 .30
178 Jeff Halpern .12 .30
179 Steve Yzerman CL .30 .75
180 Curtis Joseph CL .15 .40
181 Eric Nickulas YG RC 1.50 4.00
182 Serge Aubin YG RC 2.00 5.00
183 Keith Aldridge YG RC 1.50 4.00
184 Mike Minard YG RC 2.50 6.00
185 Steven Reinprecht YG RC 2.50 6.00
186 David Gosselin YG RC 2.00 5.00
187 Andrew Berenzweig YG 1.50 4.00
188 Willie Mitchell YG RC 2.50 6.00
189 Colin White YG RC 1.50 4.00
190 Petr Mika YG RC 1.50 4.00
191 Steve Valiquette YG RC 2.00 5.00
192 Kyle Freadrich YG RC 1.50 4.00
193 Rich Parent YG RC 2.00 5.00
194 Greg Andrusak YG RC 2.00 5.00
195 Brent Sopel YG RC 2.50 6.00
196 Matt Pettinger YG RC 1.50 4.00
197 Chris Nielsen YG RC 1.50 4.00
198 Dany Heatley YG RC 8.00 20.00
199 Matt Zultek YG RC 1.50 4.00
200 Dmitri Afanasenkov YG RC 1.50 4.00
201 Tyler Bouck YG RC 1.50 4.00
202 Jonas Andersson YG RC 1.50 4.00
203 Marc-Andre Thinel YG RC 1.50 4.00
204 Jaroslav Svoboda YG RC 1.50 4.00
205 Josef Vasicek YG RC 4.00 10.00
206 Andrew Raycroft YG RC 4.00 10.00
207 Juraj Kolnik YG RC 1.50 4.00
208 Zdenek Blatny YG RC 1.50 4.00
209 Sebastien Caron YG RC 2.00 5.00
210 Michael Ryder YG RC 4.00 10.00
211 Jason Jaspers YG RC 1.50 4.00
212 Pavel Brendl YG 1.50 4.00
213 Milan Kraft YG 1.50 4.00
214 Justin Williams YG RC 12.00 30.00
215 Andreas Karlsson YG 1.50 4.00
216 Herbert Vasiljevs YG RC 1.50 4.00
217 Sergei Vyshedkevich YG RC 1.50 4.00
218 Johnathan Aitken YG RC 1.50 4.00
219 Brandon Smith YG RC 1.50 4.00
220 Jeff Cowan YG RC 1.50 4.00
221 Steve Brule YG RC 1.50 4.00
222 Johan Witehall YG RC 1.50 4.00
223 Jani Hurme YG RC 1.50 4.00
224 Jean-Guy Trudel YG RC 1.50 4.00
225 Kaspars Astashenko YG RC 1.50 4.00
226 Scott Hartnell YG RC 8.00 20.00
227 Dieter Kochan YG RC 1.50 4.00
228 Rostislav Klesla YG RC 4.00 10.00
229 Marian Gaborik YG RC 15.00 40.00
230 Alfie Michaud YG 2.50 6.00
231 Teemu Selanne .40 1.00
232 Matt Cullen .12 .30
233 German Titov .12 .30
234 Vitali Vishnevski .12 .30
235 Pavel Trnka .12 .30
236 Marty McInnis .15 .40
237 Hnat Domenichelli .12 .30
238 Per Svartvadet .12 .30
239 Steve Guolla .12 .30
240 Frantisek Kaberle .12 .30
241 Steve Staios .12 .30
242 Byron Dafoe .15 .40
243 Peter Popovic .12 .30
244 Paul Coffey .20 .50
245 Sergei Samsonov .15 .40
246 Andrei Kovalenko .12 .30
247 Shawn Bates .12 .30
248 Dominik Hasek .30 .75
249 Stu Barnes .15 .40
250 Curtis Brown .12 .30
251 Alexei Zhitnik .15 .40
252 Jay McKee .12 .30
253 Vaclav Varada .12 .30
254 Jarome Iginla .25 .60
255 Phil Housley .15 .40
256 Cory Stillman .12 .30
257 Mike Vernon .15 .40
258 Jeff Shantz .12 .30
259 Brad Werenka .12 .30
260 Jeff O'Neill .15 .40
261 Martin Gelinas .12 .30
262 Tommy Westlund .12 .30
263 Steve Halko .12 .30
264 Sandis Ozolinsh .12 .30
265 Rob DiMaio .12 .30
266 Tony Amonte .15 .40
267 Jocelyn Thibault .15 .40
268 Boris Mironov .12 .30
269 Dean McAmmond .12 .30
270 Jean-Yves Leroux .12 .30
271 Valeri Zelepukin .12 .30
272 Nolan Pratt .12 .30
273 Joe Sakic .40 1.00
274 Chris Drury .15 .40
275 Alex Tanguay .15 .40
276 Adam Deadmarsh .15 .40
277 Stephane Yelle .12 .30
278 Ron Tugnutt .15 .40
279 Geoff Sanderson .15 .40
280 Steve Heinze .12 .30
281 Jean-Luc Grand-Pierre .12 .30
282 Robert Kron .12 .30
283 Kevin Dineen .12 .30
284 Brett Hull .40 1.00
285 Sergei Zubov .15 .40
286 Jamie Langenbrunner .15 .40
287 Ed Belfour .20 .50
288 Roman Lyashenko .12 .30
289 Ted Donato .12 .30
290 Martin LaPointe .15 .40
291 Chris Chelios .20 .50
292 Slava Kozlov .15 .40
293 Steve Yzerman .50 1.25
294 Larry Murphy .15 .40
295 Brent Gilchrist .12 .30
296 Doug Weight .20 .50
297 Eric Brewer .12 .30
298 Todd Marchant .12 .30
299 Tom Poti .12 .30
300 Mike Grier .12 .30
301 Georges Laraque .15 .40
302 Igor Larionov .20 .50
303 Roberto Luongo .30 .75
304 Olli Jokinen .15 .40
305 Viktor Kozlov .15 .40
306 Robert Svehla .12 .30
307 Mike Sillinger .12 .30
308 Jere Karalahti .12 .30
309 Zigmund Palffy .20 .50
310 Mattias Norstrom .12 .30
311 Bryan Smolinski .15 .40
312 Jamie Storr .15 .40
313 Ian Laperriere .12 .30
314 Manny Fernandez .12 .30
315 Sergei Krivokrasov .12 .30
316 Darryl Laplante .12 .30
317 Sean O'Donnell .12 .30
318 Scott Pellerin .12 .30
319 Saku Koivu .20 .50
320 Sergei Zholtok .12 .30
321 Jeff Hackett .12 .30
322 Eric Weinrich .12 .30
323 Karl Dykhuis .12 .30
324 Benoit Brunet .12 .30
325 Cliff Ronning .12 .30
326 Patric Kjellberg .12 .30
327 Drake Berehowsky .12 .30
328 Vitali Yachmenev .12 .30
329 Tomas Vokoun .15 .40
330 Greg Johnson .12 .30
331 Patrik Elias .20 .50
332 Bobby Holik .12 .30
333 Randy McKay .12 .30
334 Brian Rafalski .12 .30
335 Martin Brodeur .50 1.25
336 Sergei Brylin .12 .30
337 Brad Isbister .12 .30
338 Roman Hamrlik .12 .30
339 John Vanbiesbrouck .20 .50
340 Dave Scatchard .12 .30
341 Oleg Kvasha .12 .30
342 Mark Parrish .12 .30
343 Petr Nedved .15 .40
344 Brian Leetch .20 .50
345 Radek Dvorak .15 .40
346 Vladimir Malakhov .12 .30
347 Valeri Kamensky .12 .30
348 Rich Pilon .12 .30
349 Radek Bonk .15 .40
350 Vaclav Prospal .12 .30
351 Jason York .12 .30
352 Andreas Dackell .12 .30
353 Magnus Arvedson .12 .30
354 Rob Zamuner .12 .30
355 Daymond Langkow .12 .30
356 Keith Primeau .15 .40
357 Dan McGillis .12 .30
358 Andy Delmore .12 .30
359 Jody Hull .12 .30
360 Luke Richardson .12 .30
361 Joe Juneau .12 .30
362 Mika Alatalo .12 .30
363 Keith Tkachuk .20 .50
364 Radoslav Suchy .12 .30
365 Louie DeBrusk .12 .30
366 Sean Burke .12 .30
367 Martin Straka .15 .40
368 Alexei Kovalev .15 .40
369 Alexei Morozov .12 .30
370 Josef Beranek .12 .30
371 Milan Kraft .12 .30
372 Darius Kasparaitis .12 .30
373 Vincent Damphousse .15 .40
374 Mike Ricci .12 .30
375 Scott Thornton .15 .40
376 Niklas Sundstrom .12 .30
377 Marco Sturm .12 .30
378 Jeff Norton .12 .30
379 Pierre Turgeon .15 .40
380 Al MacInnis .25 .60
381 Jochen Hecht .12 .30
382 Sean Hill .12 .30
383 Pavol Demitra .12 .30
384 Michal Handzus .12 .30
385 Mike Eastwood .12 .30
386 Vincent Lecavalier .20 .50
387 Brian Holzinger .12 .30
388 Pavel Kubina .12 .30
389 Andrei Zyuzin .12 .30
390 Wayne Primeau .12 .30
391 Mats Sundin .20 .50
392 Gary Roberts .12 .30
393 Igor Korolev .12 .30
394 Shayne Corson .15 .40
395 Tomas Kaberle .12 .30
396 Cory Cross .12 .30
397 Peter Schaefer .12 .30
398 Adrian Aucoin .12 .30
399 Brendan Morrison .20 .50
400 Daniel Sedin .25 .60
401 Donald Brashear .12 .30
402 Henrik Sedin .25 .60
403 Joe Murphy .15 .40
404 Steve Konowalchuk .12 .30
405 Joe Reekie .12 .30
406 Sergei Gonchar .12 .30
407 Peter Bondra .20 .50
408 Olaf Kolzig .20 .50
409 Steve Yzerman CL .30 .75
410 Mark Messier CL .25 .60
411 Rick DiPietro YG RC 3.00 8.00
412 Michel Riesen YG RC 2.00 5.00
413 Reto Von Arx YG RC 2.00 5.00
414 Martin Havlat YG RC 5.00 12.00
415 Matt Elich YG RC 2.00 5.00
416 Jonas Ronnqvist YG RC 1.50 4.00
417 Jason Labarbera YG RC 2.00 5.00
418 Marc Moro YG RC 1.50 4.00
419 Mark Smith YG RC 1.50 4.00
420 Petr Hubacek YG RC 1.50 4.00
421 Niclas Wallin YG RC 2.00 5.00
422 Brian Swanson YG RC 1.50 4.00
423 Petteri Nummelin YG RC 1.50 4.00
424 Alexandre Boikov YG RC 1.50 4.00
425 Ossi Vaananen YG RC 2.00 5.00
426 Roman Simicek YG RC 1.50 4.00
427 Greg Classen YG RC 1.50 4.00
428 Marty Turco YG RC 6.00 15.00
429 Shane Hnidy YG RC 1.50 4.00
430 Lubomir Visnovsky YG RC 3.00 8.00
431 Bryce Salvador YG RC 2.00 5.00
432 Lubomir Sekeras YG RC 1.50 4.00
433 David Aebischer YG RC 3.00 8.00
434 Peter Ratchuk YG RC 2.00 5.00
435 Roman Cechmanek YG RC 2.00 5.00
436 Eric Belanger YG RC 2.00 5.00
437 Alexander Kharitonov YG RC 1.50 4.00
438 Jeff Bateman YG RC 1.50 4.00
439 Damian Surma YG RC 1.50 4.00
440 Jordan Krestanovich YG RC 1.50 4.00

2000-01 Upper Deck Exclusives Tier 1

*VETS/100: 10X TO 25X BASIC CARDS
*YOUNG GUNS/100: 1X TO 2.5X BASIC YG
119 Mark Messier 10.00 25.00
223 Jani Hurme YG 5.00 12.00
229 Marian Gaborik YG 50.00 100.00
230 Alfie Michaud YG 15.00 40.00
410 Mark Messier CL 8.00 20.00

2000-01 Upper Deck Exclusives Tier 2

*VETS/25: 25X TO 60X BASIC CARDS
*YOUNG GUNS/25: 2X TO 5X BASIC YG
119 Mark Messier 25.00 60.00
410 Mark Messier CL 20.00 50.00

2000-01 Upper Deck 500 Goal Club

500DA Dave Andreychuk J 12.00 30.00
500DA D.Andreychuk J AU/25 150.00 300.00
500DH Dale Hawerchuk J 12.00 30.00
500DH D.Hawerchuk J AU/25 150.00 300.00
500FM F. Mahovlich S 20.00 50.00
500FM F. Mahovlich S AU/25 200.00 400.00
500JK Jari Kurri J 30.00 80.00
500JK Jari Kurri J AU/25 400.00 600.00
500JM Joe Mullen J 20.00 50.00
500JM Joe Mullen J AU/25 100.00 250.00
500LM L.McDonald S AU/25 350.00 500.00
500LM Lanny McDonald S 15.00 40.00
500MG Michel Goulet S AU/25 100.00 250.00
500MG Michel Goulet S 12.50 30.00
500ML Mario Lemieux J 100.00 200.00
500ML Mario Lemieux J AU/25 800.00 1200.00
500MM Mark Messier J 30.00 80.00
500MM Mark Messier J AU/25 400.00 600.00
500PE Phil Esposito S 15.00 40.00
500PE Phil Esposito S AU/25 200.00 400.00
500PV Pat Verbeek J 12.50 30.00
500PV Pat Verbeek J AU/25 125.00 250.00
500WG Wayne Gretzky J 75.00 200.00
500WG Wayne Gretzky J AU/25 1500.00 4000.00
500JBU John Bucyk S AU/25 200.00 400.00
500JBU John Bucyk S 12.50 30.00
500MGA Mike Gartner J AU/25 300.00 500.00
500MGA Mike Gartner J 12.50 30.00

2000-01 Upper Deck All-Star Class

COMPLETE SET (10) 8.00 15.00
A1 Teemu Selanne .60 1.50
A2 Valeri Bure .60 1.50
A3 Milan Hejduk .60 1.50
A4 Mike Modano 1.00 2.50
A5 Pavel Bure 1.00 2.50
A6 Marian Hossa .60 1.50
A7 Brian Boucher .60 1.50
A8 Keith Tkachuk .60 1.50
A9 Jaromir Jagr 1.25 3.00
A10 Curtis Joseph .60 1.50

2000-01 Upper Deck Dignitaries

COMPLETE SET (10) 20.00 40.00
D1 Paul Kariya 1.25 3.00
D2 Ray Bourque 2.00 5.00
D3 Patrick Roy 3.00 8.00
D4 Brett Hull 2.50 6.00
D5 Steve Yzerman 3.00 8.00
D6 Pavel Bure 1.25 3.00
D7 Luc Robitaille 1.25 3.00
D8 Brian Leetch 1.00 2.50
D9 Jaromir Jagr 4.00 10.00
D10 Mark Messier 2.50 6.00

2000-01 Upper Deck e-Cards

EC1 Sergei Samsonov .20 .50
EC2 Brett Hull .30 .75
EC3 Steve Yzerman 1.25 3.00
EC4 Pavel Bure .40 1.00
EC5 John LeClair .30 .75
EC6 Curtis Joseph .25 .60
EC7 Martin Brodeur .60 1.50
EC8 Mark Messier .30 .75
EC9 Chris Osgood .20 .50
EC10 Mike Richter .25 .60
EC11 Ray Bourque .50 1.25
EC12 Jeremy Roenick .30 .75

2000-01 Upper Deck e-Card Prizes

ABH Brett Hull AU 20.00 50.00
ACJ Curtis Joseph AU 20.00 50.00
ACO Chris Osgood AU 12.00 30.00
AJL John LeClair AU 10.00 25.00
AJR Jeremy Roenick AU 15.00 40.00
AMB Martin Brodeur AU 25.00 60.00
AMM Mark Messier AU 30.00 80.00
AMR Mike Richter AU 12.00 30.00
APB Pavel Bure AU 15.00 40.00
ARB Ray Bourque AU 15.00 40.00
ASS Sergei Samsonov AU 15.00 40.00
ASY Steve Yzerman AU 30.00 80.00
EBH Brett Hull JSY 10.00 25.00
ECJ Curtis Joseph JSY 10.00 25.00
ECO Chris Osgood JSY 6.00 15.00
EJL John LeClair JSY 6.00 15.00
EJR Jeremy Roenick JSY 6.00 15.00
EMB Martin Brodeur JSY 10.00 25.00
EMR Mike Richter JSY 8.00 20.00
EPB Pavel Bure JSY 10.00 25.00
ERB Ray Bourque JSY 8.00 20.00
ESS Sergei Samsonov JSY 6.00 15.00
ESY Steve Yzerman JSY 15.00 40.00
SRB Ray Bourque GJ/AU 40.00 100.00
SEBH Brett Hull GJ/AU 40.00 100.00
SECJ Curtis oseph GJ/AU 20.00 50.00
SECO Chris Osgood GJ/AU 20.00 50.00
SEJL John LeClair GJ/AU 15.00 40.00
SEJR Jeremy Roenick GJ/AU 20.00 50.00
SEMB Martin Brodeur GJ/AU 50.00 120.00
SEMM Mark Messier GJ/AU 40.00 100.00
SEMR Mike Richter GJ/AU 20.00 50.00
SEPB P.Bure GJ/AU 20.00 50.00
SESS S.Samsonov GJ/AU 15.00 40.00
SESY S.Yzerman GJ/AU 60.00 150.00

2000-01 Upper Deck Fantastic Finishers

COMPLETE SET (11) 15.00 30.00
FF1 Paul Kariya .75 2.00
FF2 Teemu Selanne .75 2.00
FF3 Peter Forsberg 2.00 5.00
FF4 Brett Hull 1.00 2.50
FF5 Steve Yzerman 4.00 10.00
FF6 Pavel Bure 1.00 2.50
FF7 John LeClair 1.00 2.50
FF8 Keith Tkachuk .75 2.00
FF9 Jaromir Jagr 1.25 3.00
FF10 Owen Nolan .60 1.50
FF11 Mats Sundin .75 2.00

2000-01 Upper Deck Frozen in Time

COMPLETE SET (8) 8.00 15.00
FT1 Doug Gilmour .60 1.50
FT2 Ray Bourque 1.25 3.00
FT3 Brett Hull .75 2.00
FT4 Steve Yzerman 3.00 8.00
FT5 Mark Messier .75 2.00
FT6 Jeremy Roenick .75 2.00
FT7 Jaromir Jagr 1.00 2.50
FT8 Curtis Joseph .60 1.50

2000-01 Upper Deck Fun-Damentals

COMPLETE SET (9) 10.00 20.00
F1 Paul Kariya .60 1.50
F2 Dominik Hasek 1.25 3.00
F3 Peter Forsberg 1.50 4.00
F4 Mike Modano 1.00 2.50
F5 Sergei Fedorov 1.25 3.00
F6 Pavel Bure .75 2.00
F7 Marian Hossa .60 1.50
F8 Jaromir Jagr 1.00 2.50
F9 Curtis Joseph .60 1.50

2000-01 Upper Deck Game Jerseys

BS Brendan Shanahan Ser.2 8.00 20.00
BS Brendan Shanahan Ser.1 8.00 20.00
CP Chris Pronger Ser.1 8.00 20.00
JJ Jaromir Jagr Ser.2 12.50 30.00
JJ Jaromir Jagr Ser.1 12.50 30.00
JL John LeClair Ser.1 8.00 20.00
JN Joe Nieuwendyk Ser.1 8.00 20.00
JS Joe Sakic Ser.2 12.50 30.00
JS Joe Sakic Ser.1 12.50 30.00
JT Joe Thornton Ser.1 8.00 20.00
KT Keith Tkachuk Ser.1 8.00 20.00
MB Martin Brodeur Ser.1 20.00 50.00
MS Mats Sundin Ser.2 8.00 20.00
MS Mats Sundin Ser.1 8.00 20.00
PB Pavel Bure Ser.2 8.00 20.00
PE Peter Bondra Ser.1 8.00 20.00
PF Peter Forsberg Ser.2 15.00 40.00
PK Paul Kariya Ser.1 8.00 20.00
PK Paul Kariya Ser.2 8.00 20.00
SF Sergei Fedorov Ser.2 10.00 25.00
SF Sergei Fedorov Ser.1 10.00 25.00
TS Teemu Selanne Ser.2 8.00 20.00
TS Teemu Selanne Ser.1 8.00 20.00
WG Wayne Gretzky Ser.1 25.00 60.00
WG Wayne Gretzky AS Ser.2 25.00 60.00

2000-01 Upper Deck Game Jersey Autographs

HBH Brett Hull Ser.1 40.00 80.00
HCO Chris Osgood Ser.2 10.00 25.00
HJH Jochen Hecht Ser.1 10.00 25.00
HJL John LeClair Ser.2 15.00 40.00
HJR Jeremy Roenick Ser.2 20.00 50.00
HJT Joe Thornton Ser.2 15.00 40.00
HKT Keith Tkachuk Ser.2 12.00 30.00
HMA Martin Biron Ser.1 15.00 40.00
HMR Mike Richter Ser.2 15.00 40.00
HMY Mike York Ser.1 10.00 25.00
HNL Nicklas Lidstrom Ser.1 15.00 40.00
HPB Pavel Bure Ser.1 15.00 40.00
HSG Scott Gomez Ser.1 10.00 25.00
HSS Sergei Samsonov Ser.2 10.00 25.00
HSS Sergei Samsonov Ser.1 10.00 25.00
HSY Steve Yzerman Ser.2 75.00 150.00
HSY Steve Yzerman Ser.1 75.00 150.00
HTC Tim Connolly Ser.1 10.00 25.00

2000-01 Upper Deck Game Jersey Autographs Canadian

CCJ Curtis Joseph Ser.1 15.00 40.00
CJT Jose Theodore Ser.2 25.00 60.00
CMM Mark Messier Ser.2 100.00 250.00
CRL Roberto Luongo Ser.1 10.00 25.00

2000-01 Upper Deck Game Jersey Autographs Exclusives

EBH Brett Hull Ser.1 75.00 150.00
EJH Jochen Hecht Ser.1 20.00 50.00
EJL John LeClair Ser.1 25.00 60.00
EJN Joe Nieuwendyk Ser.1 25.00 60.00
EJS Joe Sakic Ser.1 60.00 120.00
EJT Joe Thornton Ser.1 75.00 150.00
EKT Keith Tkachuk Ser.1 40.00 80.00
EMB Martin Biron Ser.1 25.00 60.00
EMB Martin Brodeur Ser.1 150.00 250.00
EMY Mike York Ser.1 20.00 50.00
ENL Nicklas Lidstrom Ser.1 60.00 120.00
EPB Pavel Bure Ser.1 60.00 120.00
EPE Peter Bondra Ser.1 25.00 60.00
ESF Sergei Fedorov Ser.1 100.00 200.00
ESY Steve Yzerman Ser.1 175.00 300.00
ETC Tim Connolly Ser.1 25.00 60.00
EWG Wayne Gretzky Ser.1 300.00 800.00
ESCO Chris Osgood Ser.2 75.00 150.00
ESJL John LeClair Ser.2 25.00 60.00
ESJR Jeremy Roenick Ser.2 60.00 120.00
ESJT Joe Thornton Ser.2 75.00 150.00
ESKT Keith Tkachuk Ser.2 40.00 80.00
ESMR Mike Richter Ser.2 60.00 120.00
ESPB Pavel Bure Ser.2 60.00 120.00
ESSF Sergei Fedorov Ser.2 100.00 200.00
ESSS Sergei Samsonov Ser.2 25.00 60.00
ESSY Steve Yzerman Ser.2 200.00 300.00
ESWG Wayne Gretzky AS Ser.2 300.00 600.00

2000-01 Upper Deck Game Jersey Combos

DBF R.Bourque/P.Forsberg 50.00 100.00
DBH E.Belfour/D.Hasek 60.00 120.00
DCL T.Connolly/R.Luongo 20.00 50.00
DFB S.Fedorov/P.Bure 20.00 50.00
DGB S.Gomez/M.Brodeur 75.00 150.00
DGH W.Gretzky/B.Hull 100.00 200.00
DGL W.Gretzky/M.Lemieux 125.00 250.00
DGM W.Gretzky/M.Messier 75.00 150.00
DJL J.Jagr/M.Lemieux 50.00 100.00
DLC J.LeClair/B.Clarke 20.00 50.00
DSJ M.Sundin/C.Joseph 20.00 50.00
DSK T.Selanne/P.Kariya 20.00 50.00
DTS J.Thornton/S.Samsonov 15.00 40.00
DYL M.York/B.Leetch 12.00 30.00
DYS S.Yzrmn/B.Shnahan 50.00 100.00

2000-01 Upper Deck Game Jersey Doubles

DBH Brett Hull 20.00 50.00
DBS Brendan Shanahan 15.00 40.00
DDH Dominik Hasek 25.00 60.00
DFP Felix Potvin 15.00 40.00
DJJ Jaromir Jagr 25.00 60.00
DJN Joe Nieuwendyk 12.50 30.00
DJS Joe Sakic 25.00 60.00
DPB Pavel Bure 12.50 30.00
DTS Teemu Selanne 12.50 30.00
DWG Wayne Gretzky AS 60.00 120.00

2000-01 Upper Deck Game Jersey Patches

BHP Brett Hull Ser.1 50.00 120.00
BSP Brendan Shanahan Ser.1 40.00 100.00
CJP Curtis Joseph Ser.1 40.00 100.00
DHP Dominik Hasek Ser.1 50.00 120.00
ELP Eric Lindros Ser.1 40.00 100.00
JHP Jochen Hecht Ser.1 25.00 60.00
JJP Jaromir Jagr Ser.1 50.00 120.00
JLP John LeClair Ser.1 30.00 80.00
JSP Joe Sakic Ser.1 75.00 150.00
JTP Joe Thornton Ser.1 50.00 120.00
KTP Keith Tkachuk Ser.1 25.00 60.00
MBP Martin Brodeur Ser.1 125.00 250.00
MMP Mark Messier Ser.1 40.00 100.00
MYP Mike York Ser.1 25.00 60.00
PBP Pavel Bure Ser.1 40.00 100.00
PBS Brendan Shanahan Ser.2 40.00 100.00
PCO Chris Osgood Ser.2 30.00 80.00
PFP Peter Forsberg Ser.1 30.00 80.00
PJJ Jaromir Jagr Ser.2 50.00 120.00
PJL John LeClair Ser.2 40.00 100.00
PKP Paul Kariya Ser.1 40.00 100.00
PKT Keith Tkachuk Ser.2 40.00 100.00
PPF Peter Forsberg Ser.2 40.00 100.00
PPK Paul Kariya Ser.2 40.00 100.00
PRP Patrick Roy Ser.1 125.00 250.00
PSF Sergei Fedorov Ser.2 50.00 120.00
PSY Steve Yzerman Ser.2 75.00 150.00
PTS Teemu Selanne Ser.2 30.00 80.00
PWG Wayne Gretzky AS Ser.2 200.00 400.00
SFP Sergei Fedorov Ser.1 50.00 120.00
SGP Scott Gomez Ser.1 30.00 80.00
SSP Sergei Samsonov Ser.1 25.00 60.00
SYP Steve Yzerman Ser.1 75.00 150.00
TCP Tim Connolly Ser.1 25.00 60.00
TSP Teemu Selanne Ser.1 30.00 80.00
WGP Wayne Gretzky Ser.1 200.00 350.00

2000-01 Upper Deck Game Jersey Patch Autographs Exclusives

PSWG W.Gretzky AS/99 600.00 1500.00

2000-01 Upper Deck Gate Attractions

COMPLETE SET (11) 15.00 30.00
GA1 Paul Kariya .75 2.00
GA2 Dominik Hasek 1.25 3.00
GA3 Ray Bourque 1.25 3.00
GA4 Patrick Roy 3.00 8.00
GA5 Mike Modano .75 2.00
GA6 Steve Yzerman 3.00 8.00
GA7 Pavel Bure .75 2.00
GA8 Martin Brodeur 1.50 4.00
GA9 John LeClair .75 2.00
GA10 Jaromir Jagr 1.00 2.50
GA11 Curtis Joseph .75 2.00

2000-01 Upper Deck Lord Stanley's Heroes

COMPLETE SET (9) 10.00 20.00
L1 Patrick Roy 3.00 8.00
L2 Joe Sakic 1.25 3.00
L3 Brett Hull .75 2.00
L4 Steve Yzerman 2.50 6.00
L5 Brendan Shanahan 1.00 2.50
L6 Martin Brodeur 1.25 3.00
L7 Scott Gomez .75 2.00
L8 Mark Messier .75 2.00
L9 Jaromir Jagr 1.00 2.50

2000-01 Upper Deck Mario Lemieux Return to Excellence

COMMON CARD 40.00 100.00

2000-01 Upper Deck Number Crunchers

COMPLETE SET (10) 10.00 20.00
NC1 Peter Forsberg 1.50 4.00
NC2 Brendan Shanahan 1.00 2.50
NC3 John LeClair .75 2.00
NC4 Eric Lindros 1.00 2.50
NC5 Keith Tkachuk .60 1.50
NC6 Jeremy Roenick .75 2.00
NC7 Jaromir Jagr 1.00 2.50
NC8 Owen Nolan .60 1.50
NC9 Chris Pronger .60 1.50
NC10 Mark Messier .75 2.00

2000-01 Upper Deck Profiles

COMPLETE SET (10) 12.00 25.00
P1 Dominik Hasek 1.50 4.00
P2 Joe Sakic 1.50 4.00
P3 Mike Modano 1.25 3.00
P4 Brendan Shanahan 1.25 3.00
P5 Pavel Bure 1.00 2.50
P6 Martin Brodeur 2.00 5.00
P7 John LeClair 1.00 2.50
P8 Jaromir Jagr 1.25 3.00
P9 Mats Sundin .75 2.00
P10 Olaf Kolzig .60 1.50

2000-01 Upper Deck Prospects In Depth

COMPLETE SET (10) 10.00 20.00
P1 Patrik Stefan 1.00 2.50
P2 Maxim Afinogenov 1.00 2.50
P3 Alex Tanguay 1.00 2.50
P4 Brenden Morrow 1.00 2.50
P5 Scott Gomez 1.00 2.50
P6 Tim Connolly 1.00 2.50
P7 Mike York 1.00 2.50
P8 Simon Gagne 1.25 3.00
P9 Brian Boucher 1.25 3.00
P10 Jochen Hecht 1.00 2.50

2000-01 Upper Deck Rise to Prominence

COMPLETE SET (8) 5.00 12.00
RP1 Paul Kariya .60 1.50
RP2 Pavel Bure .75 2.00
RP3 Jose Theodore .75 2.00
RP4 Scott Gomez .50 1.25
RP5 Marian Hossa .60 1.50
RP6 Brian Boucher .50 1.25
RP7 Roman Turek .50 1.25
RP8 Vincent Lecavalier .60 1.50

2000-01 Upper Deck Signs of Greatness

SBO Bobby Orr 75.00 150.00
SCJ Curtis Joseph 20.00 40.00
SKT Keith Tkachuk 20.00 40.00
SMB Martin Brodeur 30.00 80.00
SMY Mike York 12.50 30.00
SPB Pavel Brendl 12.50 30.00
SSS Sergei Samsonov 20.00 40.00
SWG Wayne Gretzky 200.00 500.00

2000-01 Upper Deck Skilled Stars

COMPLETE SET (20) 15.00 30.00
SS1 Paul Kariya .50 1.25
SS2 Teemu Selanne .50 1.25
SS3 Dominik Hasek 1.00 2.50
SS4 Valeri Bure .40 1.00
SS5 Patrick Roy 2.50 6.00
SS6 Peter Forsberg 1.25 3.00
SS7 Ed Belfour .50 1.25
SS8 Mike Modano .75 2.00
SS9 Sergei Fedorov 1.00 2.50
SS10 Brendan Shanahan .75 2.00
SS11 Pavel Bure .60 1.50
SS12 Zigmund Palffy .40 1.00
SS13 Martin Brodeur 1.25 3.00
SS14 Tim Connolly .40 1.00
SS15 John LeClair .60 1.50
SS16 Jeremy Roenick .60 1.50
SS17 Jaromir Jagr .75 2.00
SS18 Vincent Lecavalier .50 1.25
SS19 Mats Sundin .50 1.25
SS20 Olaf Kolzig .40 1.00

2000-01 Upper Deck Triple Threat

COMPLETE SET (10) 30.00 80.00
TT1 Kariya/Gomez/Hejduk 4.00 10.00
TT2 Roy/Brodeur/Belfour 10.00 25.00
TT3 Forsberg/Sundin/Sedin 6.00 15.00
TT4 Hull/Roenick/LeClair 4.00 10.00
TT5 Yzerman/Sakic/Modano 10.00 25.00
TT6 Shanahan/Tkachuk/Messier 4.00 10.00
TT7 Bure/Samsonov/Fedorov 3.00 8.00
TT8 Bourque/Pronger/Blake 4.00 10.00
TT9 Jagr/Selanne/Kraft 4.00 10.00
TT10 Turek/Hasek/Kolzig 4.00 10.00

2000-01 Upper Deck UD Flashback

COMPLETE SET (8) 4.00 10.00
UD1 Teemu Selanne .60 1.50
UD2 Tony Amonte .40 1.00
UD3 Milan Hejduk .60 1.50
UD4 Scott Gomez .40 1.00
UD5 Tim Connolly .40 1.00
UD6 John LeClair .75 2.00
UD7 Keith Tkachuk .60 1.50
UD8 Olaf Kolzig .40 1.00

2001 Upper Deck EA Sports

COMPLETE SET (9)
*GOLD: 1.2X TO 3X BASIC CARD
1 Mario Lemieux 4.00 10.00
2 Mario Lemieux 4.00 10.00
3 Owen Nolan .40 1.00
4 Jere Lehtinen .40 1.00
5 Martin Rucinsky .40 1.00
6 Chris Pronger .50 1.25
7 Markus Naslund .40 2.00
8 Peter Forsberg 1.50 4.00
9 Steve Yzerman 4.00 10.00

2001 Upper Deck Pearson Awards

COMPLETE SET (3) 400.00 700.00
LPBJJ Jaromir Jagr 100.00 200.00
LPBML Mario Lemieux 200.00 400.00
LPBJS Joe Sakic 100.00 200.00

2001-02 Upper Deck

COMPLETE SET (441) 300.00 600.00
COMP.SERIES 1 (231) 150.00 300.00
COMP.SER. 1 w/o SP's (180) 15.00 30.00
COMP.SERIES 2 (210) 150.00 300.00
COMP.SER. 2 w/o SP's (180) 15.00 30.00
1 Paul Kariya .25 .60
2 Jeff Friesen .15 .40
3 Mike Leclerc .15 .40
4 Andy McDonald .15 .40
5 Jean-Sebastien Giguere .25 .60
6 Steve Rucchin .15 .40
7 Ray Ferraro .15 .40
8 Milan Hnilicka .20 .50
9 Patrik Stefan .20 .50
10 Jiri Slegr .15 .40
11 Jeff Odgers .15 .40
12 Steve Guolla .15 .40
13 Joe Thornton .40 1.00
14 Sergei Samsonov .20 .50
15 Kyle McLaren .15 .40
16 Jonathan Girard .15 .40
17 Brian Rolston .20 .50
18 Byron Dafoe .20 .50
19 Miroslav Satan .20 .50
20 Curtis Brown .15 .40
21 Stu Barnes .20 .50
22 Maxim Afinogenov .15 .40
23 Vaclav Varada .15 .40
24 Chris Gratton .15 .40
25 Jarome Iginla .30 .75
26 Dave Lowry .15 .40
27 Derek Morris .15 .40
28 Marc Savard .15 .40
29 Oleg Saprykin .15 .40
30 Craig Conroy .15 .40
31 Jeff O'Neill .20 .50
32 Arturs Irbe .20 .50
33 Shane Willis .15 .40
34 Dave Tanabe .15 .40
35 Josef Vasicek .15 .40
36 Sami Kapanen .15 .40
37 Steve Sullivan .15 .40
38 Tony Amonte .20 .50
39 Michael Nylander .15 .40
40 Eric Daze .20 .50
41 Jocelyn Thibault .20 .50
42 Boris Mironov .15 .40
43 Ville Nieminen .15 .40
44 Alex Tanguay .20 .50
45 Milan Hejduk .20 .50
46 Chris Drury .20 .50
47 Peter Forsberg .50 1.25
48 Steven Reinprecht .15 .40
49 Ron Tugnutt .20 .50
50 Ray Whitney .15 .40
51 Geoff Sanderson .15 .40
52 Serge Aubin .15 .40
53 Espen Knutsen .15 .40
54 Rostislav Klesla .15 .40
55 Mike Modano .40 1.00
56 Ed Belfour .25 .60
57 Pierre Turgeon .20 .50
58 Jamie Langenbrunner .15 .40
59 Brenden Morrow .20 .50
60 Donald Audette .15 .40
61 Steve Yzerman .60 1.50
62 Brett Hull .50 1.25
63 Nicklas Lidstrom .25 .60
64 Darren McCarty .15 .40
65 Luc Robitaille .25 .60
66 Dominik Hasek .40 1.00
67 Mike Comrie .20 .50
68 Tommy Salo .20 .50
69 Todd Marchant .15 .40
70 Mike Grier .15 .40
71 Ryan Smyth .20 .50
72 Tom Poti .15 .40
73 Pavel Bure .25 .60
74 Marcus Nilsson .15 .40
75 Roberto Luongo .40 1.00
76 Kevyn Adams .15 .40
77 Dan Boyle .15 .40
78 Robert Svehla .15 .40
79 Zigmund Palffy .25 .60
80 Eric Belanger .15 .40
81 Ian Laperriere .15 .40
82 Bryan Smolinski .15 .40
83 Jozef Stumpel .15 .40
84 Adam Deadmarsh .15 .40
85 Marian Gaborik .25 .60
86 Lubomir Sekeras .15 .40
87 Manny Fernandez .15 .40
88 Darby Hendrickson .15 .40
89 Roman Simicek .15 .40
90 Saku Koivu .25 .60
91 Richard Zednik .20 .50
92 Oleg Petrov .15 .40
93 Patrice Brisebois .15 .40
94 Brian Savage .15 .40
95 Jan Bulis .15 .40
96 David Legwand .20 .50
97 Cliff Ronning .15 .40
98 Mike Dunham .20 .50
99 Greg Johnson .15 .40
100 Kimmo Timonen .15 .40
101 Denis Arkhipov .15 .40
102 Patrik Elias .25 .60
103 Jason Arnott .20 .50
104 Scott Niedermayer .25 .60
105 Scott Gomez .20 .50
106 Scott Stevens .25 .60
107 John Madden .20 .50
108 Rick DiPietro .20 .50
109 Mark Parrish .15 .40
110 Brad Isbister .15 .40
111 Michael Peca .20 .50
112 Kenny Jonsson .15 .40
113 Mariusz Czerkawski .15 .40
114 Mark Messier .50 1.25
115 Theo Fleury .30 .75
116 Radek Dvorak .20 .50
117 Brian Leetch .20 .50
118 Eric Lindros .40 1.00
119 Mike Mottau .15 .40
120 Radek Bonk .15 .40
121 Daniel Alfredsson .25 .60
122 Marian Hossa .25 .60
123 Magnus Arvedson .15 .40
124 Patrick Lalime .20 .50
125 Martin Havlat .20 .50
126 Eric Desjardins .20 .50
127 Keith Primeau .20 .50
128 Mark Recchi .30 .75
129 Justin Williams .20 .50
130 Roman Cechmanek .20 .50
131 Jeremy Roenick .40 1.00
132 Sean Burke .15 .40
133 Shane Doan .20 .50
134 Paul Mara .15 .40
135 Michal Handzus .15 .40
136 Ladislav Nagy .15 .40
137 Mike Johnson .15 .40
138 Mario Lemieux 1.00 2.50
139 Alexei Kovalev .20 .50
140 Robert Lang .15 .40
141 Kevin Stevens .20 .50
142 Andrew Ference .15 .40
143 Johan Hedberg .20 .50
144 Owen Nolan .25 .60
145 Teemu Selanne .50 1.25
146 Scott Thornton .20 .50
147 Patrick Marleau .25 .60
148 Alexander Korolyuk .15 .40
149 Todd Harvey .15 .40
150 Keith Tkachuk .25 .60
151 Pavol Demitra .30 .75
152 Al MacInnis .30 .75
153 Scott Young .15 .40
154 Cory Stillman .15 .40
155 Doug Weight .25 .60
156 Brad Richards .25 .60
157 Nikolai Khabibulin .25 .60
158 Martin St. Louis .25 .60
159 Fredrik Modin .15 .40
160 Matthew Barnaby .15 .40
161 Gary Roberts .15 .40
162 Jonas Hoglund .15 .40
163 Curtis Joseph .30 .75
164 Mats Sundin .25 .60
165 Darcy Tucker .15 .40
166 Shayne Corson .20 .50
167 Markus Naslund .25 .60
168 Daniel Sedin .30 .75
169 Henrik Sedin .30 .75
170 Brendan Morrison .20 .50
171 Peter Schaefer .15 .40
172 Harold Druken .15 .40
173 Peter Bondra .25 .60
174 Olaf Kolzig .25 .60
175 Sergei Gonchar .15 .40
176 Jeff Halpern .15 .40
177 Andrei Nikolishin .15 .40
178 Jaromir Jagr .75 2.00
179 Steve Yzerman CL .40 1.00
180 Pavel Bure CL .15 .40
181 Dan Snyder YG RC 2.50 6.00
182 Zdenek Kutlak YG RC 2.00 5.00
183 Michel Larocque YG RC 2.00 5.00
184 Casey Hankinson YG RC 2.00 5.00
185 Jody Shelley YG RC 2.50 6.00
186 Martin Spanhel YG RC 2.00 5.00
187 Mathieu Darche YG RC 3.00 8.00
188 Matt Davidson YG RC 2.00 5.00
189 Sean Selmser YG RC 2.00 5.00
190 Jason Chimera YG RC 2.00 5.00
191 Andrej Podkonicky YG RC 2.00 5.00
192 Mike Matteucci YG RC 2.00 5.00
193 Pascal Dupuis YG RC 3.00 8.00
194 Francis Belanger YG RC 2.50 6.00
195 Bill Bowler YG RC 2.00 5.00
196 Mike Jefferson YG RC 2.00 5.00
197 Stanislav Gron YG RC 2.00 5.00
198 Mikael Samuelsson YG RC 2.50 6.00
199 Peter Smrek YG RC 2.00 5.00
200 Joel Kwiatkowski YG RC 2.00 5.00
201 Tomas Divisek YG RC 2.50 6.00
202 Kirby Law YG RC 2.00 5.00
203 David Cullen YG RC 2.00 5.00
204 Greg Crozier YG RC 2.00 5.00
205 Billy Tibbetts YG RC 2.00 5.00
206 Dale Clarke YG RC 2.00 5.00
207 Jaroslav Obsut YG RC 2.00 5.00
208 Thomas Ziegler YG RC 2.50 6.00
209 Pat Kavanagh YG RC 2.50 6.00
210 Mike Brown YG 2.50 6.00
211 Ilya Kovalchuk YG RC 15.00 40.00
212 Ray Bourque YGF 4.00 10.00
213 Brett Hull YGF 5.00 12.00
214 Dominik Hasek YGF 4.00 10.00
215 Vaclav Nedorost YG RC 2.50 6.00
216 Steve Yzerman YGF 10.00 25.00
217 Mark Messier YGF 8.00 20.00
218 Mike Modano YGF 6.00 15.00
219 Patrick Roy YGF 10.00 25.00
220A John LeClair YGF 4.00 10.00
220B Jared Aulin YG SP 12.50 30.00
221 Martin Brodeur YGF 10.00 25.00
222 Tony Amonte YGF 3.00 8.00
223 Zigmund Palffy YGF 4.00 10.00
224 Roman Cechmanek YG 2.00 5.00
225 Jeff Jillson YG RC 1.50 4.00
226 Jaromir Jagr YGF 12.00 30.00
227 Nikita Alexeev YG RC 2.50 6.00
228 Krystofer Kolanos YG RC 2.50 6.00
229 Peter Forsberg YGF 8.00 20.00
230 Pavel Bure YGF 4.00 10.00
231 Brian Sutherby YG RC 2.50 6.00
232 Oleg Tverdovsky .15 .40
233 Steve Shields .20 .50
234 Matt Cullen .15 .40
235 Jason York .15 .40
236 Vitali Vishnevsky .15 .40
237 Marty McInnis .20 .50
238 Yannick Tremblay .15 .40
239 Dany Heatley .20 .50
240 Lubos Bartecko .15 .40
241 Damian Rhodes .20 .50
242 Ilya Kovalchuk 5.00 12.00
243 Hnat Domenichelli .15 .40
244 Bill Guerin .25 .60
245 Martin Lapointe .15 .40
246 Scott Pellerin .15 .40
247 Rob Zamuner .15 .40
248 Jozef Stumpel .15 .40
249 Glen Murray .20 .50
250 Martin Biron .20 .50
251 Tim Connolly .15 .40
252 Slava Kozlov .20 .50
253 Jay McKee .15 .40
254 J-P Dumont .15 .40
255 Alexei Zhitnik .15 .40
256 Roman Turek .20 .50
257 Igor Kravchuk .15 .40
258 Clarke Wilm .15 .40
259 Robyn Regehr .15 .40
260 Rob Niedermayer .20 .50
261 Dean McAmmond .15 .40
262 Ron Francis .30 .75
263 Martin Gelinas .15 .40
264 Rod Brind'Amour .25 .60
265 Sandis Ozolinsh .15 .40
266 Bates Battaglia .15 .40
267 Chris Dingman .15 .40
268 Igor Korolev .15 .40
269 Jaroslav Spacek .15 .40
270 Alexei Zhamnov .20 .50
271 Steve Thomas .15 .40
272 Jon Klemm .15 .40
273 Adam Foote .20 .50
274 Joe Sakic .50 1.25
275 Rob Blake .25 .60
276 Patrick Roy .60 1.50
277 Greg deVries .15 .40
278 Dan Hinote .15 .40
279 Marc Denis .20 .50
280 David Vyborny .15 .40
281 Tyler Wright .15 .40
282 Mike Sillinger .15 .40
283 Bruce Gardiner .15 .40
284 Sergei Zubov .20 .50
285 Jere Lehtinen .20 .50
286 Joe Nieuwendyk .20 .50
287 Darryl Sydor .15 .40
288 Rob DiMaio .15 .40
289 Valeri Kamensky .15 .40
290 Brendan Shanahan .25 .60
291 Igor Larionov .25 .60
292 Tomas Holmstrom .15 .40
293 Mathieu Dandenault .15 .40
294 Sergei Fedorov .40 1.00
295 Fredrik Olausson .15 .40
296 Anson Carter .20 .50
297 Jochen Hecht .15 .40
298 Daniel Cleary .20 .50
299 Janne Niinimaa .15 .40
300 Rem Murray .20 .50
301 Eric Brewer .15 .40
302 Valeri Bure .15 .40
303 Viktor Kozlov .15 .40
304 Denis Shvidki .15 .40
305 Olli Jokinen .20 .50
306 Jason Wiemer .15 .40
307 Ryan Johnson .15 .40
308 Felix Potvin .40 1.00
309 Jason Allison .20 .50
310 Mathieu Schneider .15 .40
311 Lubomir Visnovsky .15 .40
312 Mattias Norstrom .15 .40
313 Steve Heinze .15 .40
314 Jim Dowd .15 .40
315 Wes Walz .15 .40
316 Filip Kuba .15 .40
317 Andrew Brunette .15 .40
318 Sergei Zholtok .15 .40
319 Stacy Roest .15 .40
320 Jose Theodore .25 .60
321 Yanic Perreault .15 .40
322 Doug Gilmour .30 .75
323 Andreas Dackell .15 .40
324 Martin Rucinsky .15 .40
325 Chad Kilger .15 .40
326 Scott Walker .15 .40
327 Andy Delmore .15 .40
328 Patric Kjellberg .15 .40
329 Tomas Vokoun .20 .50
330 Vitali Yachmenev .15 .40
331 Bill Houlder .15 .40
332 Martin Brodeur .60 1.50
333 Bobby Holik .15 .40
334 Petr Sykora .15 .40
335 Brian Rafalski .15 .40
336 Sergei Brylin .15 .40
337 Randy McKay .15 .40
338 Alexei Yashin .20 .50
339 Roman Hamrlik .15 .40
340 Michael Peca .20 .50
341 Dave Scatchard .15 .40
342 Claude Lapointe .15 .40
343 Chris Osgood .25 .60
344 Mike Richter .25 .60
345 Mike York .15 .40
346 Eric Lindros .40 1.00
347 Petr Nedved .20 .50
348 Barrett Heisten .15 .40
349 Zdeno Ciger .15 .40
350 Shawn McEachern .15 .40
351 Wade Redden .15 .40
352 Bill Muckalt .15 .40
353 Andre Roy .15 .40
354 Sami Salo .15 .40
355 Todd White .15 .40
356 John LeClair .25 .60
357 Brian Boucher .20 .50
358 Pavel Brendl .15 .40
359 Jan Hlavac .15 .40
360 Dan McGillis .15 .40
361 Simon Gagne .25 .60
362 Daymond Langkow .20 .50
363 Sergei Berezin .15 .40
364 Danny Markov .15 .40
365 Tyler Bouck .15 .40
366 Teppo Numminen .15 .40
367 Trevor Letowski .15 .40
368 Martin Straka .15 .40
369 Jan Hrdina .15 .40
370 Alexei Morozov .15 .40
371 Darius Kasparaitis .15 .40
372 Toby Petersen .15 .40
373 Kris Beech .15 .40
374 Evgeni Nabokov .20 .50
375 Mike Ricci .15 .40
376 Brad Stuart .15 .40
377 Adam Graves .20 .50
378 Vincent Damphousse .20 .50
379 Stephane Matteau .15 .40
380 Chris Pronger .25 .60
381 Brent Johnson .20 .50
382 Fred Brathwaite .20 .50
383 Dallas Drake .15 .40
384 Mike Eastwood .15 .40
385 Daniel Corso .15 .40
386 Brian Holzinger .15 .40
387 Vincent Lecavalier .25 .60
388 Jassen Cullimore .15 .40
389 Vaclav Prospal .15 .40
390 Dave Andreychuk .25 .60
391 Jimmie Olvestad .15 .40
392 Alexander Mogilny .20 .50
393 Tomas Kaberle .15 .40
394 Mikael Renberg .15 .40
395 Travis Green .15 .40
396 Robert Reichel .15 .40
397 Nikolai Antropov .15 .40
398 Andrew Cassels .15 .40
399 Dan Cloutier .20 .50
400 Ed Jovanovski .20 .50
401 Todd Bertuzzi .25 .60
402 Trent Klatt .15 .40
403 Donald Brashear .15 .40
404 Jaromir Jagr .75 2.00
405 Joe Sacco .15 .40
406 Steve Konowalchuk .15 .40
407 Adam Oates .25 .60
408 Dimitri Khristich .15 .40
409 Dainius Zubrus .15 .40
410 John LeClair .25 .60
411 Martin Brodeur .60 1.50
412A Timo Parssinen YG RC (Dodge ad on boards) 2.50 6.00
412B Timo Parssinen YG RC (Stick in right hand) 2.50 6.00
413A Ilja Bryzgalov YG RC (facing his right) 5.00 12.00
413B Ilja Bryzgalov YG RC (facing his left) 5.00 12.00
414A Kevin Sawyer YG RC (facing his right) 2.00 5.00
414B Kevin Sawyer YG RC (facing his left) 2.00 5.00
415A Kamil Piros YG RC (facing forward) 2.00 5.00
415B Kamil Piros YG RC (facing right) 2.00 5.00
416A Ivan Huml YG RC (skating profile) 2.00 5.00
416B Ivan Huml YG RC (facing forward) 2.00 5.00
417A Scott Nichol YG RC (white jersey) 2.00 5.00
417B Scott Nichol YG RC (black jersey) 2.00 5.00
418A Jukka Hentunen YG RC (black jersey) 2.00 5.00
418B Jukka Hentunen YG RC (white jersey) 2.00 5.00
419A Erik Cole YG RC (skating left) 4.00 10.00
419B Erik Cole YG RC (skating right) 4.00 10.00
420A Ben Simon YG RC (skating left) 2.50 6.00
420B Ben Simon YG RC (skating right) 2.50 6.00
421A Niko Kapanen YG RC (facing forward) 3.00 8.00
421B Niko Kapanen YG RC (Staples add on boards) 3.00 8.00
422A Pavel Datsyuk YG RC (purple board in background) 200.00 500.00
422B Pavel Datsyuk YG RC (opponent in background) 150.00 400.00
423A Ty Conklin YG RC (facing left) 3.00 8.00
423B Ty Conklin YG RC (facing right) 3.00 8.00
424A Wayne Gretzky YGF (full body photo) 12.00 30.00
424B Wayne Gretzky YGF (waist up photo) 15.00 40.00
425A Niklas Hagman YG RC (skating right) 2.50 6.00
425B Niklas Hagman YG RC (skating left) 2.50 6.00
426A Kristian Huselius YG RC (facing forward) 3.00 8.00
426B Kristian Huselius YG RC (Panthers logos on boards) 3.00 8.00
427A Jaroslav Bednar YG RC (facing forward) 2.00 5.00
427B Jaroslav Bednar YG RC (facing left) 2.00 5.00
428A Nick Schultz YG RC (green jersey) 2.00 5.00
428B Nick Schultz YG RC (white jersey) 2.00 5.00
429A Travis Roche YG RC (bending) 2.00 5.00
429B Travis Roche YG RC (standing) 2.00 5.00
430A Martin Erat YG RC (white jersey) 2.50 6.00
430B Martin Erat YG RC (blue jersey) 2.50 6.00
431A Andreas Salomonsson YG RC (faceoff) 2.00 5.00
431B Andreas Salomonsson YG RC (skating) 2.00 5.00
432A Josef Boumedienne YG RC (stick at waist) 2.00 5.00
432B Josef Boumedienne YG RC (stick on ice) 2.00 5.00
433A Scott Clemmensen YG RC (mask on) 2.00 5.00
433B Scott Clemmensen YG RC (mask off) 2.00 5.00
434A Dan Blackburn YG RC (white jersey) 2.50 6.00
434B Dan Blackburn YG RC (blue jersey) 2.50 6.00
435A Radek Martinek YG RC (shooting) 2.00 5.00
435B Radek Martinek YG RC 2.00 5.00
436A Raffi Torres YG RC (red logo on boards) 3.00 8.00
436B Raffi Torres YG RC (left hand at knee) 3.00 8.00
437A Ivan Ciernik YG RC (looking right) 2.00 5.00
437B Ivan Ciernik YG RC 2.00 5.00
438A Jiri Dopita YG RC (skating) 2.00 5.00
438B Jiri Dopita YG RC (face close up) 2.00 5.00
439A Mark Rycroft YG RC (blue jersey) 2.50 6.00
439B Mark Rycroft YG RC (white jersey) 2.50 6.00
440A Ryan Tobler YG RC (standing) 2.50 6.00
440B Ryan Tobler YG RC (skating) 2.50 6.00
441A Chris Corrinet YG RC (facing forward) 2.00 5.00
441B Chris Corrinet YG RC (shooting) 2.00 5.00

2001-02 Upper Deck Exclusives

*VETS/100: 10X TO 25X BASIC CARDS
*VET YGF/50: 1.2X TO 3X BASIC YGF
*YG ROOK/50: 2X TO 5X BASIC YG RC
211 Ilya Kovalchuk YG 150.00 300.00
422 Pavel Datsyuk YG 1200.00 3000.00

2001-02 Upper Deck Crunch Timers

COMPLETE SET (15) 15.00 30.00
CT1 Joe Sakic 1.25 3.00
CT2 Milan Hejduk .60 1.50
CT3 Chris Drury .50 1.25
CT4 Mike Modano 1.00 2.50
CT5 Brett Hull .75 2.00
CT6 Steve Yzerman 3.00 8.00
CT7 Zigmund Palffy .50 1.25
CT8 Alexei Yashin .50 1.25
CT9 Jeremy Roenick .75 2.00
CT10 Mark Recchi .50 1.25
CT11 Teemu Selanne .60 1.50
CT12 Keith Tkachuk .60 1.50
CT13 Markus Naslund .60 1.50
CT14 Jaromir Jagr 1.00 2.50
CT15 Peter Bondra .60 1.50

2001-02 Upper Deck Fantastic Finishers

COMPLETE SET (10) 10.00 20.00
FF1 Pavel Bure .75 2.00
FF2 Pavol Demitra .50 1.25
FF3 Markus Naslund .60 1.50
FF4 Mario Lemieux 4.00 10.00
FF5 John LeClair .75 2.00
FF6 Keith Tkachuk .60 1.50
FF7 Marian Hossa .60 1.50
FF8 Teemu Selanne .60 1.50
FF9 Joe Sakic 1.25 3.00
FF10 Zigmund Palffy .50 1.25

2001-02 Upper Deck Franchise Cornerstones

COMPLETE SET (15) 25.00 50.00
FC1 Paul Kariya .60 1.50
FC2 Pavel Bure .75 2.00
FC3 Mario Lemieux 4.00 10.00
FC4 Peter Forsberg 1.50 4.00
FC5 Vincent Lecavalier .50 1.25
FC6 Joe Sakic 1.25 3.00
FC7 Zigmund Palffy .50 1.25
FC8 Martin Brodeur 1.50 4.00
FC9 Patrick Roy 3.00 8.00
FC10 Steve Yzerman 3.00 8.00
FC11 Mike Modano 1.00 2.50
FC12 Tony Amonte .50 1.25
FC13 Teemu Selanne .60 1.50
FC14 John LeClair .75 2.00
FC15 Mats Sundin .60 1.50

2001-02 Upper Deck Game Jerseys

AAM Al MacInnis AS 4.00 10.00
ACC Chris Chelios AS 5.00 12.00
AGL Guy Lafleur AS 4.00 10.00
AJJ Jaromir Jagr AS 8.00 20.00
AJO Joe Sakic AS 10.00 25.00
AMM Mike Modano AS 10.00 20.00
AMS Mats Sundin AS 5.00 12.00
ATF Theo Fleury AS 4.00 10.00
ATS Teemu Selanne AS 5.00 12.00
GJBB Brian Boucher G 10.00 25.00
GJCJ Curtis Joseph G 10.00 25.00
GJDH Dominik Hasek G 12.50 30.00
GJEB Ed Belfour G 10.00 25.00
GJJH Jani Hurme G 10.00 25.00
GJJT Jocelyn Thibault G 10.00 25.00
GJMO Maxime Ouellet G 10.00 25.00
GJMR Mike Richter G 10.00 25.00
GJMT Marty Turco G 10.00 25.00
GJOK Olaf Kolzig G 10.00 25.00
GJPR Patrick Roy G 12.50 30.00
GJRC Roman Cechmanek G 10.00 25.00
GJSB Sean Burke G 10.00 25.00
GJVY Vitali Yeremeyev G 10.00 25.00
NGCB Curtis Brown NG 4.00 10.00
NGDS Daniel Sedin NG 4.00 10.00
NGED Eric Daze NG 4.00 10.00
NGHS Henrik Sedin NG 4.00 10.00
NGJH Jani Hurme NG 4.00 10.00
NGJI Jarome Iginla NG 10.00 25.00
NGJW Justin Williams NG 4.00 10.00
NGMH Marian Hossa NG 5.00 12.00
NGMM Manny Malhotra NG 3.00 8.00
NGMT Marty Turco NG 4.00 10.00
NGMY Mike York NG 4.00 10.00
NGPS Patrik Stefan NG 4.00 10.00
NGRF Ruslan Fedotenko NG 4.00 10.00
NGSD Shane Doan NG 4.00 10.00
NGVL Vincent Lecavalier NG 5.00 12.00
CFR P.Forsberg/P.Roy 15.00 40.00
CHH M.Hossa/J.Hurme 10.00 25.00
CKS P.Kariya/T.Selanne 12.50 30.00
CLJ M.Lemieux/J.Jagr 15.00 40.00
CMN M.Modano/J.Nieuwendyk 15.00 40.00
CPC K.Primeau/R.Cechmanek 12.50 30.00
CSS H.Sedin/D.Sedin 12.50 30.00
FSR Forsberg/Sakic/Roy 20.00 50.00
MNB Modano/Niedyk/Belfour 15.00 40.00
YSF Yzerman/Shanny/Fedorov 15.00 40.00

2001-02 Upper Deck Game Jerseys Series II

FJBS Brendan Shanahan 6.00 15.00
FJCD Chris Drury 4.00 10.00
FJCL Claude Lemieux 4.00 10.00
FJCO Chris Osgood 6.00 15.00
FJEB Ed Belfour 6.00 15.00
FJJL John LeClair 4.00 10.00
FJJN Joe Nieuwendyk 4.00 10.00
FJJS Joe Sakic 10.00 25.00
FJMB Martin Brodeur 12.50 30.00
FJMH Milan Hejduk 6.00 15.00
FJMM Mike Modano 8.00 20.00
FJMS Miroslav Satan 4.00 10.00
FJPF Peter Forsberg 10.00 25.00
FJPR Patrick Roy 12.50 30.00
FJSF Sergei Fedorov 8.00 20.00
FJSS Scott Stevens 4.00 10.00
FJSY Steve Yzerman 12.50 30.00
GNJW Justin Williams 4.00 10.00
GNMB Martin Biron 4.00 10.00
GNMM Manny Malhotra 4.00 10.00
GNMO Maxime Ouellet 4.00 10.00
GNMY Mike York 4.00 10.00
GNPM Patrick Marleau 6.00 15.00
GNRB Radek Bonk 4.00 10.00
GNRF Rico Fata 4.00 10.00
GNSA Serge Aubin 4.00 10.00
GNSG Simon Gagne 6.00 15.00
PFAK Alexei Kovalev 4.00 10.00
PFBS Brendan Shanahan 6.00 15.00
PFJJ Jaromir Jagr 8.00 20.00
PFJL John LeClair 6.00 15.00
PFJS Joe Sakic 10.00 25.00
PFKP Keith Primeau 4.00 10.00
PFML Mario Lemieux 12.00 30.00
PFMN Markus Naslund 4.00 10.00
PFPK Paul Kariya 6.00 15.00
PFZP Zigmund Palffy 4.00 10.00
SSAM Al MacInnis 4.00 10.00
SSCD Chris Drury 6.00 15.00
SSMB Martin Brodeur 12.50 30.00
SSMM Mike Modano 8.00 20.00
SSPF Peter Forsberg 10.00 25.00
SSPK Paul Kariya 6.00 15.00
SSPR Patrick Roy 12.50 30.00
SSRB Ray Bourque 8.00 20.00
SSSY Steve Yzerman 12.50 30.00
SSWG Wayne Gretzky 25.00 60.00
DJBR R.Bourque/P.Roy 15.00 40.00
DJFS S.Fedorov/B.Shanahan 10.00 25.00
DJMN M.Modano/J.Nieuwendyk 10.00 25.00
DJSB S.Stevens/M.Brodeur 20.00 50.00
DJSF J.Sakic/P.Forsberg 25.00 60.00
DJSH M.Satan/D.Hasek 10.00 25.00
DJTD A.Tanguay/C.Drury 10.00 25.00
DJYL S.Yzerman/N.Lidstrom 15.00 40.00
TJNMB Nieuw/Modano/Belfour 15.00 40.00
TJRBH Roy/Sakic/Hejduk 60.00 150.00
TJYFS Yzerman/Fedorov/Shan 25.00 60.00

2001-02 Upper Deck Game Jersey Autographs

SDS Daniel Sedin Ser.1 10.00 25.00
SDW Doug Weight Ser.1 15.00 40.00
SHS Henrik Sedin Ser.1 15.00 40.00
SJL John LeClair Ser.1 10.00 25.00
SMM Mike Modano Ser.1 25.00 60.00
SRB Ray Bourque Ser.1 50.00 100.00
SSY Steve Yzerman Ser.1 100.00 200.00
SJBO Ray Bourque/150 40.00 80.00
SJCJ Curtis Joseph/150 15.00 40.00
SJEB Ed Belfour/150 20.00 50.00
SJJL John LeClair/150 10.00 25.00
SJMB Martin Brodeur/150 50.00 120.00
SJMO Maxime Ouellet/150 10.00 25.00
SJRB Ray Bourque/150 40.00 80.00
SJSG Simon Gagne/150 10.00 25.00
SJSY Steve Yzerman/150 60.00 120.00

2001-02 Upper Deck Gate Attractions

COMPLETE SET (15) 20.00 40.00
GA1 Mark Messier .75 2.00
GA2 Theo Fleury .50 1.25
GA3 Keith Tkachuk .60 1.50
GA4 John LeClair .75 2.00
GA5 Mario Lemieux 4.00 10.00
GA6 Alexei Kovalev .50 1.25
GA7 Chris Drury .50 1.25
GA8 Joe Sakic 1.25 3.00
GA9 Peter Forsberg 1.50 4.00
GA10 Paul Kariya .60 1.50
GA11 Teemu Selanne .60 1.50
GA12 Steve Yzerman 3.00 8.00
GA13 Brendan Shanahan 1.00 2.50
GA14 Mike Modano 1.00 2.50
GA15 Chris Pronger .50 1.25

2001-02 Upper Deck Goalies in Action

COMPLETE SET (10) 12.50 25.00
GL1 Curtis Joseph .75 2.00
GL2 Ed Belfour .75 2.00
GL3 Martin Brodeur 2.00 5.00
GL4 Evgeni Nabokov .60 1.50
GL5 Johan Hedberg .75 2.00
GL6 Patrick Roy 4.00 10.00
GL7 Tommy Salo .60 1.50
GL8 Patrick Lalime .60 1.50
GL9 Olaf Kolzig .60 1.50
GL10 Roberto Luongo 1.00 2.50

2001-02 Upper Deck Goaltender Threads

TTBB Brian Boucher 8.00 20.00
TTCJ Curtis Joseph 8.00 20.00
TTCO Chris Osgood 8.00 20.00
TTJO Jose Theodore 10.00 25.00
TTJT Jocelyn Thibault 8.00 20.00
TTMB Martin Brodeur 12.50 30.00
TTMD Mike Dunham 8.00 20.00
TTMR Mike Richter 8.00 20.00
TTPR Patrick Roy 12.50 30.00
TTRC Roman Cechmanek 8.00 20.00

2001-02 Upper Deck Last Line of Defense

COMPLETE SET (10) 12.50 25.00
LL1 Patrick Roy 4.00 10.00
LL2 Ed Belfour .75 2.00
LL3 Dominik Hasek 1.50 4.00
LL4 Felix Potvin .75 2.00
LL5 Martin Brodeur 2.00 5.00
LL6 Roman Cechmanek .60 1.50
LL7 Johan Hedberg .75 2.00
LL8 Evgeni Nabokov .60 1.50
LL9 Curtis Joseph .75 2.00
LL10 Olaf Kolzig .60 1.50

2001-02 Upper Deck Leaders of the Pack

COMPLETE SET (15) 15.00 30.00
LP1 Paul Kariya .60 1.50
LP2 Tony Amonte .50 1.25
LP3 Joe Sakic 1.25 3.00
LP4 Mike Modano 1.00 2.50
LP5 Steve Yzerman 3.00 8.00
LP6 Pavel Bure .75 2.00
LP7 Scott Stevens .50 1.25
LP8 Mark Messier .75 2.00
LP9 Michael Peca .50 1.25
LP10 Daniel Alfredsson .50 1.25
LP11 Mario Lemieux 4.00 10.00
LP12 Owen Nolan .50 1.25
LP13 Doug Weight .50 1.25
LP14 Chris Pronger .50 1.25
LP15 Mats Sundin .60 1.50

2001-02 Upper Deck Patches

PBS Brendan Shanahan 25.00 60.00
PDW Doug Weight 25.00 60.00
PEB Ed Belfour 30.00 80.00
PJJ Jaromir Jagr 30.00 80.00
PJL John LeClair 25.00 60.00
PJS Joe Sakic 30.00 80.00
PMH Marian Hossa 15.00 40.00
PML Mario Lemieux 60.00 150.00
PMM Mike Modano 25.00 60.00
PMO Mike Modano 25.00 60.00
PMS Mats Sundin 15.00 40.00
PPF Peter Forsberg 40.00 100.00
PPK Paul Kariya 25.00 60.00
PPR Patrick Roy 50.00 120.00
PRB Ray Bourque 40.00 100.00
PSA Joe Sakic 40.00 100.00
PSF Sergei Fedorov 30.00 80.00
PSY Steve Yzerman 50.00 125.00
PTS Teemu Selanne 20.00 50.00

2001-02 Upper Deck Patches Series II

PLJJ Jaromir Jagr 30.00 80.00
PLMB Martin Brodeur 40.00 100.00
PLML Mario Lemieux 40.00 100.00
PLPF Peter Forsberg 40.00 100.00
PLPK Paul Kariya 20.00 50.00
PLPR Patrick Roy 40.00 100.00
PLSF Sergei Fedorov 30.00 80.00
PLSY Steve Yzerman 40.00 100.00
PNBS Brendan Shanahan 20.00 50.00
PNJL John LeClair 20.00 50.00
PNJS Joe Sakic 30.00 80.00
PNML Mario Lemieux 40.00 100.00
PNMM Mike Modano 25.00 60.00
PNPK Paul Kariya 20.00 50.00
PNPR Patrick Roy 40.00 100.00
PNSY Steve Yzerman 40.00 100.00
NABS Brendan Shanahan 40.00 100.00
NAJL John LeClair 40.00 100.00
NAJS Joe Sakic 75.00 200.00
NAML Mario Lemieux 100.00 250.00
NAPF Peter Forsberg 75.00 200.00
NAPR Patrick Roy 100.00 250.00
NASY Steve Yzerman 100.00 250.00
PLMM Mike Modano 60.00 150.00

2001-02 Upper Deck Pride of a Nation

PNBG Bill Guerin 6.00 15.00
PNDH Dominik Hasek 8.00 20.00
PNDW Doug Weight 6.00 15.00
PNJJ Jaromir Jagr 8.00 20.00
PNJS Joe Sakic 10.00 25.00
PNMB Martin Brodeur 12.00 30.00
PNML Mario Lemieux 15.00 40.00
PNPF Peter Forsberg 8.00 20.00
PNPR Patrick Roy 15.00 40.00
PNSF Sergei Fedorov 8.00 20.00
PNSK Saku Koivu 6.00 15.00
PNSY Steve Yzerman 12.00 30.00
PNTA Tony Amonte 6.00 15.00
PNTS Teemu Selanne 6.00 15.00
PNVK Viktor Kozlov 6.00 15.00
DPAG T.Amonte/B.Guerin 12.50 30.00
DPFK S.Fedorov/V.Kozlov 12.50 30.00
DPFS P.Forsberg/M.Sundin 15.00 40.00
DPHJ D.Hasek/J.Jagr 15.00 40.00
DPLK M.Lemieux/P.Kariya 15.00 40.00
DPLM J.LeClair/M.Modano 12.50 30.00
DPRS P.Roy/J.Sakic 30.00 80.00
DPSB S.Stevens/M.Brodeur 12.50 30.00
DPSK T.Selanne/S.Koivu 12.50 30.00
DPYS S.Yzerman/B.Shanahan 25.00 60.00
TPAWL Amonte/Weight/Leetch 20.00 50.00
TPFKK Fedorov/Kovalev/Kozlov 20.00 50.00
TPFSL Forsberg/Sundin/Lidstrom 30.00 80.00
TPHJL Hasek/Jagr/Lang 40.00 100.00
TPYRL Yzerman/Roy/Lemieux 60.00 150.00

2001-02 Upper Deck Pride of the Leafs

MLBJ Borje Salming 40.00 100.00
MLCJ Curtis Joseph 30.00 80.00
MLDG Doug Gilmour 30.00 80.00
MLFP Felix Potvin 40.00 100.00
MLMS Mats Sundin 30.00 80.00
MLNA Nikolai Antropov 25.00 60.00
MLSB Sergei Berezin 20.00 50.00

MLTD Tie Domi 30.00 80.00
MLWC Wendel Clark 50.00 125.00

2001-02 Upper Deck Shooting Stars

COMPLETE SET (20) 15.00 30.00
SS1 Paul Kariya .40 1.00
SS2 Bill Guerin .30 .75
SS3 Joe Sakic .75 2.00
SS4 Milan Hejduk .40 1.00
SS5 Brett Hull .50 1.25
SS6 Brendan Shanahan .60 1.50
SS7 Luc Robitaille .30 .75
SS8 Pavel Bure .60 1.50
SS9 Zigmund Palffy .30 .75
SS10 Patrik Elias .30 .75
SS11 Alexei Yashin .30 .75
SS12 John LeClair .50 1.25
SS13 Alexei Kovalev .30 .75
SS14 Mario Lemieux 2.50 6.00
SS15 Owen Nolan .30 .75
SS16 Teemu Selanne .40 1.00
SS17 Alexander Mogilny .30 .75
SS18 Markus Naslund .40 1.00
SS19 Jaromir Jagr .60 1.50
SS20 Peter Bondra .30 .75

2001-02 Upper Deck Skilled Stars

SS1 Paul Kariya .40 1.00
SS2 Mario Lemieux 1.50 4.00
SS3 Chris Pronger .30 .75
SS4 Teemu Selanne .75 2.00
SS5 Owen Nolan .40 1.00
SS6 Pavel Bure .40 1.00
SS7 Keith Tkachuk .40 1.00
SS8 Mike Modano .60 1.50
SS9 Peter Forsberg .75 2.00
SS10 Zigmund Palffy .40 1.00
SS11 Martin Brodeur 1.00 2.50
SS12 Patrick Roy 1.00 2.50
SS13 Joe Sakic .75 2.00
SS14 Ray Bourque .60 1.50
SS15 Steve Yzerman 1.00 2.50
SS16 Roman Cechmanek .30 .75
SS17 Mark Messier .75 2.00
SS18 Vincent Lecavalier .40 1.00
SS19 John LeClair .40 1.00
SS20 Tony Amonte .30 .75

2001-02 Upper Deck Tandems

COMPLETE SET (10) 20.00 40.00
T1 S.Samsonov/J.Thornton 2.00 5.00
T2 J.Sakic/M.Hejduk 4.00 10.00
T3 B.Shanahan/S.Yzerman 5.00 12.00
T4 V.Bure/P.Bure 1.25 3.00
T5 P.Elias/J.Arnott 1.25 3.00
T6 M.Hossa/R.Bonk 1.25 3.00
T7 J.LeClair/J.Roenick 1.25 3.00
T8 T.Selanne/O.Nolan 1.25 3.00
T9 K.Tkachuk/P.Demitra 1.25 3.00
T10 B.Richards/V.Lecavalier 1.25 3.00

2002 Upper Deck Collectors Club

COMPLETE SET (20) 16.00 40.00
NHL1 Wayne Gretzky 2.00 5.00
NHL2 Gordie Howe 1.20 2.00
NHL3 Bobby Orr 2.00 5.00
NHL4 Ray Bourque .80 2.00
NHL5 Mario Lemieux 1.60 4.00
NHL6 Patrick Roy 1.60 4.00
NHL7 Steve Yzerman 1.60 4.00
NHL8 Jaromir Jagr .80 1.50
NHL9 Dominik Hasek .40 1.00
NHL10 Martin Brodeur .80 2.00
NHL11 Joe Sakic .80 2.00
NHL12 Paul Kariya .80 1.50
NHL13 Teemu Selanne .40 1.00
NHL14 Chris Pronger .20 .50
NHL15 Pavel Bure .40 1.00
NHL16 Peter Forsberg .80 1.50
NHL17 Nicklas Lidstrom .40 1.00
NHL18 Ilya Kovalchuk 2.00 3.00
NHL19 Kristian Huselius .40 .50
NHL20 Dan Blackburn .80 1.00

2002 Upper Deck Collectors Club Jerseys

COMPLETE SET (2) 40.00 100.00
RBJ Ray Bourque 16.00 40.00
SYJ Steve Yzerman 30.00 75.00

2002 Upper Deck Pearson Awards

COMPLETE SET (3) 250.00 500.00
1 Patrick Roy 200.00 400.00
2 Jarome Iginla 75.00 150.00
3 Sean Burke 30.00 75.00

2002 Upper Deck USHL Gordie Howe

1 Gordie Howe AU 200.00 300.00

2002-03 Upper Deck

1 Vitali Vishnevsky .12 .30
2 Jean-Sebastien Giguere .20 .50
3 Steve Rucchin .12 .30
4 Paul Kariya .20 .50
5 Andy McDonald .20 .50
6 Lubos Bartecko .12 .30
7 Ilya Kovalchuk .25 .60
8 Tomi Kallio .12 .30
9 Milan Hnilicka .15 .40
10 Patrik Stefan .15 .40
11 Joe Thornton .30 .75
12 Brian Rolston .15 .40
13 Martin Lapointe .15 .40
14 Nick Boynton .12 .30
15 Andy Hilbert .12 .30
16 Glen Murray .15 .40
17 J-P Dumont .12 .30
18 Tim Connolly .12 .30
19 Miroslav Satan .20 .50
20 Maxim Afinogenov .20 .50
21 Taylor Pyatt .12 .30
22 Jay McKee .12 .30
23 Marc Savard .12 .30
24 Roman Turek .20 .50
25 Dean McAmmond .12 .30
26 Craig Conroy .12 .30
27 Derek Morris .12 .30
28 Rod Brind'Amour .20 .50
29 Josef Vasicek .12 .30
30 Niclas Wallin .12 .30
31 Jaroslav Svoboda .12 .30
32 Sami Kapanen .12 .30
33 Erik Cole .12 .30
34 Jeff O'Neill .12 .30
35 Michael Nylander .12 .30
36 Alexei Zhamnov .15 .40
37 Jon Klemm .12 .30
38 Kyle Calder .12 .30
39 Eric Daze .12 .30
40 Steve Sullivan .12 .30
41 Stephane Yelle .12 .30
42 Rob Blake .20 .50
43 Patrick Roy .50 1.25
44 Radim Vrbata .12 .30
45 Chris Drury .20 .50
46 Milan Hejduk .15 .40
47 Joe Sakic .40 1.00
48 Peter Forsberg .40 1.00
49 Rostislav Klesla .12 .30
50 Marc Denis .15 .40
51 Grant Marshall .12 .30
52 Ray Whitney .15 .40
53 Espen Knutsen .12 .30
54 Mike Sillinger .12 .30
55 Bill Guerin .20 .50
56 Mike Modano .30 .75
57 Sergei Zubov .15 .40
58 Marty Turco .20 .50
59 Jason Arnott .15 .40
60 Jere Lehtinen .12 .30
61 Steve Yzerman .50 1.25
62 Sergei Fedorov .30 .75
63 Nicklas Lidstrom .20 .50
64 Curtis Joseph .25 .60
65 Igor Larionov .12 .30
66 Luc Robitaille .20 .50
67 Tomas Holmstrom .12 .30
68 Brett Hull .40 1.00
69 Mike Comrie .20 .50
70 Marty Reasoner .12 .30
71 Tommy Salo .15 .40
72 Ryan Smyth .15 .40
73 Anson Carter .12 .30
74 Janne Niinimaa .12 .30
75 Sandis Ozolinsh .12 .30
76 Roberto Luongo .30 .75
77 Kristian Huselius .12 .30
78 Valeri Bure .15 .40
79 Brad Ference .12 .30
80 Ian Laperriere .15 .40
81 Mattias Norstrom .12 .30
82 Adam Deadmarsh .12 .30
83 Jason Allison .15 .40
84 Eric Belanger .12 .30
85 Felix Potvin .30 .75
86 Wes Walz .12 .30
87 Darby Hendrickson .12 .30
88 Dwayne Roloson .12 .30
89 Marian Gaborik .20 .50
90 Filip Kuba .12 .30
91 Andrei Markov .20 .50
92 Jose Theodore .20 .50
93 Mike Ribeiro .12 .30
94 Richard Zednik .12 .30
95 Gino Odjick .12 .30
96 Saku Koivu .20 .50
97 Andy Delmore .12 .30
98 Tomas Vokoun .15 .40
99 Martin Erat .12 .30
100 Denis Arkhipov .12 .30
101 Scott Hartnell .12 .30
102 Scott Stevens .20 .50
103 Patrik Elias .20 .50
104 Jamie Langenbrunner .15 .40
105 Brian Gionta .12 .30
106 Joe Nieuwendyk .15 .40
107 Martin Brodeur .50 1.25
108 Roman Hamrlik .12 .30
109 Shawn Bates .12 .30
110 Steve Webb .12 .30
111 Alexei Yashin .15 .40
112 Chris Osgood .20 .50
113 Mark Parrish .12 .30
114 Petr Nedved .12 .30
115 Eric Lindros .30 .75
116 Dan Blackburn .15 .40
117 Radek Dvorak .15 .40
118 Tom Poti .12 .30
119 Pavel Bure .20 .50
120 Todd White .12 .30
121 Patrick Lalime .15 .40
122 Marian Hossa .20 .50
123 Daniel Alfredsson .15 .40
124 Wade Redden .12 .30
125 Mike Fisher .12 .30
126 Keith Primeau .15 .40
127 Jeremy Roenick .30 .75
128 Eric Weinrich .12 .30
129 Roman Cechmanek .15 .40
130 Mark Recchi .25 .60
131 Justin Williams .15 .40
132 Brad May .12 .30
133 Sean Burke .12 .30
134 Paul Mara .12 .30
135 Shane Doan .15 .40
136 Tony Amonte .15 .40
137 Daniel Briere .15 .40
138 Kris Beech .12 .30
139 Martin Straka .15 .40
140 Alexei Kovalev .15 .40
141 Mario Lemieux .75 2.00
142 Andrew Ference .12 .30
143 Johan Hedberg .20 .50
144 Patrick Marleau .20 .50
145 Owen Nolan .20 .50
146 Mike Rathje .12 .30
147 Evgeni Nabokov .15 .40
148 Marco Sturm .12 .30
149 Todd Harvey .12 .30
150 Pavol Demitra .25 .60
151 Doug Weight .20 .50
152 Al MacInnis .25 .60
153 Brent Johnson .15 .40
154 Keith Tkachuk .20 .50
155 Cory Stillman .12 .30
156 Brad Richards .20 .50
157 Pavel Kubina .12 .30
158 Nikolai Khabibulin .20 .50
159 Martin St. Louis .20 .50
160 Vincent Lecavalier .20 .50
161 Bryan McCabe .12 .30
162 Gary Roberts .12 .30
163 Ed Belfour .20 .50
164 Mats Sundin .20 .50
165 Tie Domi .15 .40
166 Alexander Mogilny .15 .40
167 Daniel Sedin .25 .60
168 Todd Bertuzzi .20 .50
169 Mattias Ohlund .12 .30
170 Dan Cloutier .15 .40
171 Markus Naslund .20 .50
172 Jan Hlavac .12 .30
173 Olaf Kolzig .20 .50
174 Peter Bondra .20 .50
175 Sergei Gonchar .15 .40
176 Steve Konowalchuk .12 .30
177 Chris Simon .12 .30
178 Dainius Zubrus .12 .30
179 Patrick Roy CL .40 1.00
180 Steve Yzerman CL .40 1.00
181 Paul Kariya MS .50 1.25
182 Bobby Orr MS 2.00 5.00
183 Jarome Iginla MS .60 1.50
184 Joe Sakic MS 1.00 2.50
185 Patrick Roy MS 1.25 3.00
186 Steve Yzerman MS 1.25 3.00
187 Gordie Howe MS 1.50 4.00
188 Wayne Gretzky MS 3.00 8.00
189 Wayne Gretzky MS 3.00 8.00
190 Martin Brodeur MS 1.25 3.00
191 Mario Lemieux MS 2.00 5.00
192 Brett Hull MS 1.00 2.50
193 Jaromir Jagr MS 1.50 4.00
194 Pavel Bure MS .50 1.25
195 Teemu Selanne MS 1.00 2.50
196 Mark Hartigan YG 1.25 3.00
197 Pasi Nurminen YG 1.25 3.00
198 Henrik Tallinder YG 1.25 3.00
199 Micki Dupont YG RC 1.25 3.00
200 Tyler Arnason YG 2.00 5.00
201 Jordan Krestanovich YG 1.25 3.00
202 Kelly Fairchild YG 1.25 3.00
203 Andrej Nedorost YG 1.25 3.00
204 Sean Avery YG 1.50 4.00
205 Stephen Weiss YG 2.00 5.00
206 Lukas Krajicek YG 1.25 3.00
207 Kyle Rossiter YG 1.25 3.00
208 Eric Beaudoin YG 1.25 3.00
209 Sylvain Blouin YG RC 1.25 3.00
210 Marcel Hossa YG 1.25 3.00
211 Adam Hall YG RC 1.25 3.00
212 Greg Koehler YG RC 1.25 3.00
213 Trent Hunter YG 1.25 3.00
214 Ray Schultz YG RC 1.25 3.00
215 Martin Prusek YG 1.25 3.00
216 Chris Bala YG 1.25 3.00
217 Josh Langfeld YG 1.25 3.00
218 Bruno St. Jacques YG 1.25 3.00
219 Branko Radivojevic YG 1.25 3.00
220 Martin Cibak YG 1.25 3.00
221 Evgeni Konstantinov YG 1.25 3.00
222 Karel Pilar YG 1.25 3.00
223 Sebastien Centomo YG 1.25 3.00
224 Sebastien Charpentier YG 1.25 3.00
225 J-F Fortin YG 1.25 3.00
226 Stanislav Chistov YG RC 5.00 12.00
227 Alexei Smirnov YG RC 6.00 15.00
228 Chuck Kobasew YG RC 6.00 15.00
229 Tony Amonte MS 15.00 40.00
230 Peter Forsberg MS 15.00 40.00
231 Chris Drury MS 20.00 50.00
232 Rick Nash YG RC 80.00 200.00
233 Brendan Shanahan MS 20.00 50.00
234 Henrik Zetterberg YG RC 300.00 600.00
235 Ales Hemsky YG RC 15.00 40.00
236 Jay Bouwmeester YG RC 15.00 40.00
237 Alexei Yashin MS 15.00 40.00
238 Alexander Frolov YG RC 15.00 40.00
239 Pierre-Marc Bouchard YG RC 10.00 25.00
240 Ron Hainsey YG RC 5.00 12.00
241 Sean Burke MS 12.00 30.00
242 Owen Nolan MS 20.00 50.00
243 Chris Pronger MS 20.00 50.00
244 Mats Sundin MS 20.00 50.00
245 Alexander Svitov YG RC 5.00 12.00
246 Steve Eminger YG RC 5.00 12.00
247 Adam Oates .20 .50
248 Petr Sykora .15 .40
249 Fredrik Olausson .12 .30
250 Matt Cullen .12 .30
251 Ruslan Salei .12 .30
252 Slava Kozlov .12 .30
253 Dany Heatley .15 .40
254 Frantisek Kaberle .12 .30
255 Pasi Nurminen .12 .30
256 Shawn McEachern .12 .30
257 Sergei Samsonov .15 .40
258 Steve Shields .15 .40
259 Jonathan Girard .12 .30
260 Jozef Stumpel .12 .30
261 Bryan Berard .12 .30
262 Marty McInnis .12 .30
263 Stu Barnes .12 .30
264 Curtis Brown .12 .30
265 Chris Gratton .12 .30
266 Rhett Warrener .12 .30
267 Jochen Hecht .12 .30
268 James Patrick .12 .30
269 Jarome Iginla .25 .60
270 Martin Gelinas .12 .30
271 Chris Drury .20 .50
272 Stephane Yelle .12 .30
273 Jamie Wright .12 .30
274 Kevin Weekes .15 .40
275 Bret Hedican .12 .30
276 Ron Francis .25 .60
277 Kevyn Adams .12 .30
278 Marek Malik .12 .30
279 Bates Battaglia .12 .30
280 Theo Fleury .25 .60
281 Sergei Berezin .12 .30
282 Mark Bell .12 .30
283 Alexander Karpovtsev .12 .30
284 Steve Passmore .12 .30
285 Bob Probert .20 .50
286 Alex Tanguay .15 .40
287 Steven Reinprecht .12 .30
288 Adam Foote .12 .30
289 David Aebischer .15 .40
290 Greg deVries .12 .30
291 Dan Hinote .12 .30
292 Derek Morris .12 .30
293 Scott Parker .12 .30
294 Geoff Sanderson .15 .40
295 Andrew Cassels .12 .30
296 Jean-Luc Grand-Pierre .12 .30
297 Luke Richardson .12 .30
298 Tyler Wright .12 .30
299 Jody Shelley .12 .30
300 Ron Tugnutt .15 .40
301 Scott Young .12 .30
302 Pierre Turgeon .15 .40
303 Derian Hatcher .15 .40
304 Richard Matvichuk .12 .30
305 Kirk Muller .12 .30
306 Brendan Shanahan .20 .50
307 Chris Chelios .20 .50
308 Mathieu Dandenault .12 .30
309 Pavel Datsyuk .30 .75
310 Kris Draper .12 .30
311 Boyd Devereaux .12 .30
312 Kirk Maltby .12 .30
313 Manny Legace .20 .50
314 Jani Rita .12 .30
315 Todd Marchant .12 .30
316 Daniel Cleary .12 .30
317 Georges Laraque .15 .40
318 Mike York .15 .40
319 Jason Smith .12 .30
320 Viktor Kozlov .12 .30
321 Dimitri Yushkevich .12 .30
322 Olli Jokinen .20 .50
323 Marcus Nilsson .12 .30
324 Ivan Novoseltsev .12 .30
325 Aaron Miller .12 .30
326 Zigmund Palffy .20 .50
327 Jamie Storr .15 .40
328 Bryan Smolinski .15 .40
329 Mathieu Schneider .12 .30
330 Erik Rasmussen .12 .30
331 Andrew Brunette .12 .30
332 Richard Park .12 .30
333 Manny Fernandez .15 .40
334 Matt Johnson .12 .30
335 Ladislav Benysek .12 .30
336 Mariusz Czerkawski .12 .30
337 Sheldon Souray .12 .30
338 Chad Kilger .12 .30
339 Yanic Perreault .12 .30
340 Mathieu Garon .15 .40
341 Craig Rivet .12 .30
342 Mike Dunham .15 .40
343 David Legwand .15 .40
344 Vladimir Orszagh .12 .30
345 Kimmo Timonen .12 .30
346 Cale Hulse .12 .30
347 Oleg Tverdovsky .12 .30
348 Jeff Friesen .12 .30
349 Brian Rafalski .12 .30
350 Sergei Brylin .12 .30
351 John Madden .12 .30
352 Colin White .12 .30
353 Michael Peca .15 .40
354 Eric Cairns .12 .30
355 Dave Scatchard .12 .30
356 Brad Isbister .12 .30
357 Oleg Kvasha .12 .30
358 Mattias Timander .12 .30
359 Matthew Barnaby .12 .30
360 Bobby Holik .12 .30
361 Darius Kasparaitis .12 .30
362 Vladimir Malakhov .12 .30
363 Brian Leetch .15 .40
364 Mark Messier .40 1.00
365 Mike Richter .20 .50
366 Martin Havlat .15 .40
367 Radek Bonk .15 .40
368 Petr Schastlivy .12 .30
369 Zdeno Chara .20 .50
370 Chris Neil .12 .30
371 Magnus Arvedson .12 .30
372 Pavel Brendl .12 .30
373 Donald Brashear .12 .30
374 Michal Handzus .15 .40
375 Kim Johnsson .12 .30
376 John LeClair .20 .50
377 Simon Gagne .20 .50
378 Claude Lemieux .15 .40
379 Brian Boucher .15 .40
380 Teppo Numminen .12 .30
381 Daymond Langkow .15 .40
382 Ladislav Nagy .12 .30
383 Brian Savage .12 .30
384 Ville Nieminen .12 .30
385 Randy Robitaille .12 .30
386 Alexei Morozov .12 .30
387 Jan Hrdina .12 .30
388 Michal Rozsival .15 .40
389 Alexandre Daigle .12 .30
390 Mike Ricci .12 .30
391 Vincent Damphousse .12 .30
392 Teemu Selanne .40 1.00
393 Adam Graves .15 .40
394 Scott Thornton .12 .30
395 Scott Hannan .12 .30
396 Fred Brathwaite .15 .40
397 Jamal Mayers .12 .30
398 Reed Low .12 .30
399 Chris Pronger .20 .50
400 Scott Mellanby .12 .30
401 Alexander Khavanov .12 .30
402 Ruslan Fedotenko .12 .30
403 Fredrik Modin .12 .30
404 Nikita Alexeev .12 .30
405 Shane Willis .12 .30
406 Dave Andreychuk .20 .50
407 Trevor Kidd .12 .30
408 Robert Reichel .12 .30
409 Robert Svehla .12 .30
410 Alyn McCauley .12 .30
411 Tomas Kaberle .12 .30
412 Travis Green .12 .30
413 Henrik Sedin .25 .60
414 Brendan Morrison .15 .40
415 Matt Cooke .12 .30
416 Ed Jovanovski .15 .40
417 Mattias Ohlund .12 .30
418 Trevor Linden .20 .50
419 Jaromir Jagr .60 1.50
420 Robert Lang .12 .30
421 Matt Pettinger .12 .30
422 Ken Klee .12 .30
423 Stephen Peat .12 .30
424 Brian Sutherby .12 .30
425 Joe Thornton .30 .75
426 Wayne Gretzky 1.25 3.00
427 Martin Gerber YG RC 2.50 6.00
428 Kurt Sauer YG RC 1.50 4.00
429 Tim Thomas YG RC 10.00 25.00
430 Jordan Leopold YG RC 2.50 6.00
431 Levente Szuper YG RC 2.50 6.00
432 Shawn Thornton YG RC 2.00 5.00
433 Jeff Paul YG RC 1.50 4.00
434 Lasse Pirjeta YG RC 1.50 4.00
435 Dmitri Bykov YG RC 1.50 4.00
436 Ryan Miller YG RC 25.00 60.00
437 Kari Haakana YG RC 1.50 4.00
438 Ivan Majesky YG RC 1.50 4.00
439 Stephane Veilleux YG RC 1.50 4.00
440 Scottie Upshall YG RC 2.00 5.00
441 Shaone Morrisonn YG RC 1.50 4.00
442 Eric Godard YG RC 1.50 4.00
443 Jason Spezza YG RC 20.00 50.00
444 Anton Volchenkov YG RC 1.50 4.00
445 Dennis Seidenberg YG RC 3.00 8.00
446 Radovan Somik YG RC 1.50 4.00
447 Patrick Sharp YG RC 8.00 20.00
448 Jeff Taffe YG RC 1.50 4.00
449 Lynn Loyns YG RC 1.50 4.00
450 Mike Cammalleri YG RC 8.00 20.00
451 Tom Koivisto YG RC 1.50 4.00
452 Curtis Sanford YG RC 2.50 6.00
453 Cody Rudkowsky YG RC 1.50 4.00
454 Carlo Colaiacovo YG RC 2.50 6.00
455 Mikael Tellqvist YG RC 1.50 4.00
456 Vernon Fiddler YG RC 2.00 5.00

2002-03 Upper Deck Exclusives

*1-180/247-426 VETS/75: 4X TO 10X BASE
*181-195 MS/75: 2X TO 5X BASIC MS
*196-225 YG/75: 2X TO 5X BASIC YG
*226-246 MS/75: .5X TO 1.2X BASIC MS
*226-246 YG/75: .5X TO 1.2X BASIC YG
*427-456 YG/75: 1.5X TO 4X BASIC YG
364 Mark Messier 4.00 10.00
429 Tim Thomas YG 30.00 80.00
436 Ryan Miller YG 40.00 100.00
443 Jason Spezza YG 40.00 100.00
450 Mike Cammalleri YG 20.00 50.00

2002-03 Upper Deck All-Star Jerseys

ASCC Chris Chelios 3.00 8.00
ASEJ Ed Jovanovski 3.00 8.00
ASJS Joe Sakic 6.00 15.00
ASJT Jose Theodore 4.00 10.00
ASMN Markus Naslund 3.00 8.00
ASPK Paul Kariya 3.00 8.00
ASRB Rob Blake 3.00 8.00
ASSB Sean Burke 3.00 8.00
ASSF Sergei Fedorov 5.00 12.00
ASSK Sami Kapanen 3.00 8.00
ASSO Sandis Ozolinsh 3.00 8.00
ASTS Teemu Selanne 3.00 8.00
ASVD Vincent Damphousse 3.00 8.00
ASWG Wayne Gretzky 30.00 80.00

2002-03 Upper Deck All-Star Performers Jerseys

ASEJ Ed Jovanovski 4.00 10.00
AGJT Jose Theodore 5.00 12.00
ASMM Mike Modano 8.00 20.00
ASMN Markus Naslund 3.00 8.00
ASPK Paul Kariya 3.00 8.00
ASPR Patrick Roy 12.00 30.00
ASRB Rob Blake 4.00 10.00
ASSB Sean Burke 4.00 10.00
ASSK Sami Kapanen 4.00 10.00
ASSO Sandis Ozolinsh 4.00 10.00
ASTS Teemu Selanne 3.00 8.00
ASVD Vincent Damphousse 4.00 10.00
ASWG Wayne Gretzky 30.00 80.00

2002-03 Upper Deck UD Promos

*UD PROMOS: .8X TO 2X BASIC CARDS
276 Ron Francis .30 .75

2002-03 Upper Deck Blow-Ups

COMPLETE SET (42) 75.00 150.00
C1 Paul Kariya 4.00 10.00
C2 Ilya Kovalchuk 2.50 6.00
C3 Joe Thornton 2.50 6.00
C4 Roman Turek .75 2.00
C5 Jeff O'Neill .75 2.00
C6 Rob Blake .75 2.00
C7 Patrick Roy 6.00 15.00
C8 Joe Sakic 4.00 10.00
C9 Peter Forsberg 4.00 10.00
C10 Marc Denis 1.25 3.00
C11 Mike Modano 2.50 6.00
C12 Marty Turco 1.50 4.00
C13 Steve Yzerman 6.00 15.00
C14 Curtis Joseph 2.50 6.00
C15 Nicklas Lidstrom 1.50 4.00
C16 Mike Comrie 1.50 4.00
C17 Tommy Salo 1.25 3.00
C18 Roberto Luongo 1.25 3.00
C19 Felix Potvin 1.50 4.00
C20 Marian Gaborik 2.50 6.00
C21 Jose Theodore 1.50 4.00
C22 Saku Koivu 1.50 4.00
C23 Scott Hartnell 1.25 3.00
C24 Scott Stevens .75 2.00
C25 Martin Brodeur 4.00 10.00
C26 Eric Lindros 1.50 4.00
C27 Pavel Bure 2.50 6.00
C28 Marian Hossa 1.50 4.00
C29 Daniel Alfredsson 1.25 3.00
C30 Keith Primeau .75 2.00
C31 Sean Burke 1.25 3.00
C32 Tony Amonte 1.50 4.00
C33 Mario Lemieux 8.00 20.00
C34 Owen Nolan 1.25 3.00
C35 Al MacInnis 1.25 3.00
C36 Matt Cooke 1.25 3.00
C37 Vincent Lecavalier 1.25 3.00
C38 Mats Sundin 1.50 4.00
C39 Ed Belfour 1.50 4.00
C40 Todd Bertuzzi 1.25 3.00
C41 Markus Naslund 1.25 3.00
C42 Olaf Kolzig 1.25 3.00

2002-03 Upper Deck Bright Futures Jerseys

COMMON CARD 4.00 10.00
AM Alexei Morozov 4.00 10.00
BB Brian Boucher 4.00 10.00
DA Denis Arkhipov 4.00 10.00
DL David Legwand 4.00 10.00
IB Ilja Bryzgalov 5.00 12.00
JB Jaroslav Bednar 4.00 10.00
JG Jean-Sebastien Giguere 4.00 10.00
JL Jamie Lundmark 4.00 10.00
ME Martin Erat 4.00 10.00
MM Manny Malhotra 4.00 10.00
MP Matt Pettinger 4.00 10.00
MR Mike Ribeiro 4.00 10.00
MY Mike York 4.00 10.00
PA Timo Parssinen 4.00 10.00
PB Pavel Brendl 4.00 10.00
PS Patrik Stefan 4.00 10.00
RK Rostislav Klesla 4.00 10.00
SG Simon Gagne 5.00 12.00
TC Tim Connolly 4.00 10.00
TP Taylor Pyatt 4.00 10.00
VN Ville Nieminen 4.00 10.00

2002-03 Upper Deck CHL Graduates Jerseys

CGAT Alex Tanguay 3.00 8.00
CGBL Dan Blackburn 3.00 8.00
CGDB Daniel Briere 3.00 8.00
CGDL David Legwand 3.00 8.00
CGED Eric Daze 2.50 6.00
CGEL Eric Lindros 6.00 15.00
CGGM Glen Murray 3.00 8.00
CGJA Jason Arnott 3.00 8.00
CGJF Jeff Friesen 2.50 6.00
CGJS Joe Sakic 8.00 20.00
CGJT Joe Thornton 6.00 15.00
CGKP Keith Primeau 3.00 8.00
CGMD Marc Denis 3.00 8.00
CGML Mario Lemieux 15.00 40.00
CGMM Mike Modano 6.00 15.00
CGMR Mark Recchi 5.00 12.00
CGRT Ron Tugnutt 3.00 8.00
CGSS Steve Sullivan 2.50 6.00
CGSY Steve Yzerman 10.00 25.00
CGTL Trevor Linden 4.00 10.00

2002-03 Upper Deck CHL Graduates Gold

*GOLD: 2X TO 5X BASIC JERSEY

2002-03 Upper Deck Difference Makers Jerseys

BL Brian Leetch 3.00 8.00
BS Brendan Shanahan 3.00 8.00
ED Eric Daze 3.00 8.00
IK Ilya Kovalchuk 5.00 12.00
JA Jason Allison 3.00 8.00
JI Jarome Iginla 4.00 10.00
JJ Jaromir Jagr 6.00 15.00
JT Joe Thornton 8.00 20.00
JT Jose Theodore 4.00 10.00
MD Mike Dunham 3.00 8.00
ML Mario Lemieux 12.50 30.00
MM Mike Modano 6.00 15.00
MS Mats Sundin 3.00 8.00
PK Paul Kariya 3.00 8.00
PR Patrick Roy 12.00 30.00
RB Rob Blake 3.00 8.00
RT Roman Turek 3.00 8.00
SA Miroslav Satan 3.00 8.00
SS Sergei Samsonov 3.00 8.00
SY Steve Yzerman 10.00 25.00
ZP Zigmund Palffy 3.00 8.00

2002-03 Upper Deck Fan Favorites Jerseys

AD Adam Deadmarsh 3.00 8.00
BL Brian Leetch 3.00 8.00
JI Jarome Iginla 4.00 10.00
JJ Jaromir Jagr 6.00 15.00
KP Keith Primeau 3.00 8.00
MB Martin Brodeur 10.00 25.00
MM Mike Modano 8.00 20.00
MN Markus Naslund 3.00 8.00
NL Nicklas Lidstrom 3.00 8.00
PF Peter Forsberg 10.00 25.00
PK Paul Kariya 3.00 8.00
SD Shane Doan 3.00 8.00
SK Saku Koivu 3.00 8.00
SS Sergei Samsonov 3.00 8.00

2002-03 Upper Deck First Class

*GOLD/75: .8X TO 2X BASE JSY
UDJJ Jaromir Jagr 6.00 15.00
UDJS Joe Sakic 10.00 25.00
UDJT Jose Theodore 8.00 20.00
UDML Mario Lemieux 12.50 30.00
UDPK Paul Kariya 6.00 15.00
UDPR Patrick Roy 12.50 30.00
UDSY Steve Yzerman 10.00 25.00

2002-03 Upper Deck Game Jersey Autographs

*GJ AUTO: 3X TO 8X BASE JSY
PR Patrick Roy 75.00 150.00
SY Steve Yzerman 75.00 150.00
WG Wayne Gretzky 250.00 600.00

2002-03 Upper Deck Game Jersey Series II

GJEB Ed Belfour 4.00 10.00
GJHZ Henrik Zetterberg 10.00 25.00
GJIK Ilya Kovalchuk 6.00 15.00
GJJL John LeClair 2.50 6.00
GJJS Joe Sakic 6.00 15.00
GJJT Joe Thornton 6.00 15.00
GJMB Martin Brodeur 12.50 30.00
GJPB Pavel Bure 3.00 8.00
GJPR Patrick Roy 12.50 30.00
GJSG Simon Gagne 4.00 10.00
GJSH Scott Hartnell 4.00 10.00
GJSS Sergei Samsonov 2.50 6.00
GJSY Steve Yzerman 10.00 25.00
GJWG Wayne Gretzky 25.00 60.00

2002-03 Upper Deck Gifted Greats

COMPLETE SET (14) 15.00 30.00
GG1 Paul Kariya .40 1.00
GG2 Bobby Orr 2.50 6.00
GG3 Joe Sakic .60 1.50
GG4 Patrick Roy 1.50 4.00
GG5 Peter Forsberg 1.00 2.50
GG6 Mike Modano .60 1.50
GG7 Dominik Hasek .75 2.00
GG8 Steve Yzerman 1.50 4.00
GG9 Gordie Howe 1.50 4.00
GG10 Martin Brodeur 1.25 3.00
GG11 Wayne Gretzky 3.00 8.00
GG12 Pavel Bure .40 1.00
GG13 Mario Lemieux 2.50 6.00
GG14 Jaromir Jagr .60 1.50

2002-03 Upper Deck Goaltender Threads Jerseys

*GOLD: 2X TO 5X BASE HI
FP Felix Potvin 2.50 6.00
IB Ilja Bryzgalov 3.00 8.00
JG Jean-Sebastien Giguere 2.50 6.00
JT Jose Theodore 3.00 8.00
MB Martin Biron 2.50 6.00
MD Mike Dunham 2.50 6.00
MN Mika Noronen 2.50 6.00
MT Marty Turco 3.00 8.00
OK Olaf Kolzig 2.50 6.00
RC Roman Cechmanek 2.50 6.00
RL Roberto Luongo 4.00 10.00
RT Roman Turek 2.50 6.00
SS Steve Shields 2.50 6.00
TH Jocelyn Thibault 2.50 6.00

2002-03 Upper Deck Good Old Days Jerseys

GOAM Al MacInnis 2.50 6.00
GOBG Bill Guerin 2.00 5.00
GOBH Brett Hull 4.00 10.00
GOBS Brendan Shanahan 2.00 5.00
GOCJ Curtis Joseph 2.50 6.00
GODM Dominik Hasek 3.00 8.00
GOJN Joe Nieuwendyk 1.50 4.00
GOJS Joe Sakic 4.00 10.00
GOKP Keith Primeau 4.00 10.00
GOKT Keith Tkachuk 3.00 8.00
GOMS Mats Sundin 2.00 5.00
GOPB Pavel Bure 6.00 15.00
GOTF Theo Fleury 2.50 6.00
GOTS Teemu Selanne 4.00 10.00

2002-03 Upper Deck Hot Spots Jerseys

HSCL Claude Lemieux 3.00 8.00
HSDA Denis Arkhipov 3.00 8.00
HSDB Daniel Briere 4.00 10.00
HSDL David Legwand 3.00 8.00
HSDU Mike Dunham 3.00 8.00
HSIK Ilya Kovalchuk 5.00 12.00
HSMD Marc Denis 3.00 8.00
HSME Martin Erat 3.00 8.00
HSRK Rostislav Klesla 3.00 8.00
HSRW Ray Whitney 3.00 8.00
HSSD Shane Doan 3.00 8.00
HSSH Scott Hartnell 4.00 10.00

2002-03 Upper Deck Last Line of Defense

COMPLETE SET (14) 10.00 20.00
LL1 Jean-Sebastien Giguere .40 1.00
LL2 Martin Biron .40 1.00
LL3 Patrick Roy 2.00 5.00
LL4 Curtis Joseph .50 1.25
LL5 Tommy Salo .40 1.00
LL6 Roberto Luongo .75 2.00
LL7 Jose Theodore .60 1.50
LL8 Martin Brodeur 1.50 4.00
LL9 Chris Osgood .40 1.00
LL10 Sean Burke .40 1.00
LL11 Evgeni Nabokov .40 1.00
LL12 Nikolai Khabibulin .50 1.25
LL13 Ed Belfour .50 1.25
LL14 Olaf Kolzig .40 1.00

2002-03 Upper Deck Letters of Note Jerseys

*GOLD/50: .6X TO 1.5X BASIC JERSEY
LNCD Chris Drury 6.00 15.00
LNCP Chris Pronger 6.00 15.00
LNJI Jarome Iginla 5.00 12.00
LNJS Joe Sakic 10.00 25.00
LNML Mario Lemieux 20.00 50.00
LNMM Mike Modano 6.00 15.00
LNMN Markus Naslund 6.00 15.00
LNMS Mats Sundin 6.00 15.00
LNON Owen Nolan 6.00 15.00
LNPB Peter Bondra 6.00 15.00
LNPK Paul Kariya 6.00 15.00
LNSK Saku Koivu 6.00 15.00
LNSS Scott Stevens 8.00 20.00
LNSY Steve Yzerman 15.00 40.00

2002-03 Upper Deck Number Crunchers

COMPLETE SET (14) 10.00 20.00
NC1 Joe Thornton .75 2.00
NC2 Theo Fleury .30 .75
NC3 Brenden Morrow .40 1.00
NC4 Gordie Howe 2.00 5.00
NC5 Brendan Shanahan .50 1.25
NC6 Georges Laraque .30 .75
NC7 Scott Hartnell .40 1.00
NC8 Eric Lindros .50 1.25
NC9 Donald Brashear .30 .75
NC10 Keith Primeau .30 .75
NC11 Jeremy Roenick .60 1.50
NC12 Keith Tkachuk .40 1.00

NC13 Ed Jovanovski .40 1.00
NC14 Todd Bertuzzi .40 1.00

2002-03 Upper Deck On the Rise Jerseys

ORBM Brenden Morrow 3.00 8.00
ORDB Dan Blackburn 3.00 8.00
ORIK Ilya Kovalchuk 5.00 12.00
ORKK Krystofer Kolanos 3.00 8.00
ORMB Mark Bell 3.00 8.00
ORRK Rostislav Klesla 3.00 8.00
ORSR Steven Reinprecht 3.00 8.00

2002-03 Upper Deck Patch Card Name Plate

ML Mario Lemieux 75.00 150.00
PF Peter Forsberg 30.00 80.00
SS Sergei Samsonov 30.00 60.00
WG Wayne Gretzky 200.00 300.00

2002-03 Upper Deck Patchwork

PWAK Alexei Kovalev 20.00 50.00
PWBG Bill Guerin 25.00 60.00
PWBS Brendan Shanahan 25.00 60.00
PWCD Chris Drury 25.00 60.00
PWJJ Jaromir Jagr 80.00 200.00
PWJL John LeClair 25.00 60.00
PWJS Joe Sakic 50.00 125.00
PWJT Joe Thornton 40.00 100.00
PWKP Keith Primeau 20.00 50.00
PWMB Martin Brodeur 60.00 150.00
PWMD Mike Dunham 20.00 50.00
PWMH Milan Hejduk 20.00 50.00
PWML Mario Lemieux 100.00 250.00
PWMM Mike Modano 40.00 100.00
PWMN Markus Naslund 25.00 60.00
PWMS Mats Sundin 25.00 60.00
PWMT Marty Turco 25.00 60.00
PWNL Nicklas Lidstrom 25.00 60.00
PWPF Peter Forsberg 50.00 125.00
PWPK Paul Kariya 25.00 60.00
PWPR Patrick Roy 60.00 150.00
PWSF Sergei Fedorov 40.00 100.00
PWSG Simon Gagne 25.00 60.00
PWSK Saku Koivu 25.00 60.00
PWSS Sergei Samsonov 20.00 50.00
PWSY Steve Yzerman 60.00 150.00
PWTA Tony Amonte 20.00 50.00
PWTH Jose Theodore 25.00 60.00
PWZP Zigmund Palffy 25.00 60.00

2002-03 Upper Deck Pinpoint Accuracy Jerseys

PAAT Alex Tanguay 3.00 8.00
PABS Brendan Shanahan 3.00 8.00
PACD Chris Drury 3.00 8.00
PAED Eric Daze 3.00 8.00
PAGS Geoff Sanderson 3.00 8.00
PAJI Jarome Iginla 5.00 12.00
PAJT Joe Thornton 6.00 15.00
PAMH Milan Hejduk 3.00 8.00
PAML Mario Lemieux 12.50 30.00
PAMM Mike Modano 8.00 20.00
PAMR Mark Recchi 3.00 8.00
PAPB Pavel Bure 3.00 8.00
PAPK Paul Kariya 3.00 8.00
PASF Sergei Fedorov 5.00 12.00

2002-03 Upper Deck Reaching Fifty Jerseys

50BH Brett Hull 4.00 10.00
50BO Peter Bondra 3.00 8.00
50JI Jarome Iginla 4.00 10.00
50JJ Jaromir Jagr 5.00 12.00
50JL John LeClair 3.00 8.00
50JS Joe Sakic 6.00 15.00
50KT Keith Tkachuk 3.00 8.00
50ML Mario Lemieux 15.00 40.00
50MM Mike Modano 4.00 10.00
50PB Pavel Bure 3.00 8.00
50PK Paul Kariya 3.00 8.00
50SF Sergei Fedorov 6.00 15.00
50SY Steve Yzerman 10.00 25.00
50WG Wayne Gretzky 25.00 60.00

2002-03 Upper Deck Reaching Fifty Gold

*STARS: 2X TO 5X BASIC JERSEY

2002-03 Upper Deck Saviors Jerseys

SVBB Brian Boucher 3.00 8.00
SVBD Byron Dafoe 3.00 8.00
SVBJ Brent Johnson 3.00 8.00
SVJG Jean-Sebastien Giguere 3.00 8.00
SVJT Jose Theodore SP 5.00 12.00
SVMB Martin Biron 3.00 8.00
SVMD Mike Dunham 3.00 8.00
SVMT Marty Turco 4.00 10.00
SVOK Olaf Kolzig 3.00 8.00
SVPR Patrick Roy SP 25.00 60.00
SVRT Roman Turek 3.00 8.00
SVTH Jocelyn Thibault/100 12.50 30.00
SVTU Ron Tugnutt/100 8.00 20.00

2002-03 Upper Deck Shooting Stars

COMPLETE SET (14) 15.00 30.00
SS1 Paul Kariya .40 1.00
SS2 Jarome Iginla .60 1.50
SS3 Joe Thornton .60 1.50
SS4 Joe Sakic .75 2.00
SS5 Mike Modano .60 1.50
SS6 Gordie Howe 2.00 5.00
SS7 Steve Yzerman 2.00 5.00
SS8 Mike Comrie .30 .75
SS9 Wayne Gretzky 3.00 8.00
SS10 Pavel Bure .40 1.00
SS11 Simon Gagne .50 1.25
SS12 Mario Lemieux 2.50 6.00
SS13 Teemu Selanne .40 1.00
SS14 Jaromir Jagr .60 1.50

2002-03 Upper Deck Sizzling Scorers

COMPLETE SET (14) 8.00 15.00
SS1 Ilya Kovalchuk .60 1.50
SS2 Joe Thornton .60 1.50
SS3 Jarome Iginla .60 1.50
SS4 Ron Francis .40 1.00
SS5 Joe Sakic .75 2.00
SS6 Mike Modano .60 1.50
SS7 Brendan Shanahan .40 1.00
SS8 Mike Comrie .40 1.00
SS9 Marian Gaborik .60 1.50
SS10 Patrik Elias .40 1.00
SS11 Pavel Bure .40 1.00
SS12 Jeremy Roenick .50 1.25
SS13 Mats Sundin .40 1.00
SS14 Todd Bertuzzi .40 1.00

2002-03 Upper Deck Specialists Jerseys

SAZ Alexei Zhamnov 3.00 8.00
SBL Brian Leetch 4.00 10.00
SCD Chris Drury 4.00 10.00
SEB Eric Belanger 3.00 8.00
SJL Jere Lehtinen 3.00 8.00
SMM Mike Modano 6.00 15.00
SMR Mark Recchi 4.00 10.00
SMS Miroslav Satan 3.00 8.00
SPB Peter Bondra 4.00 10.00
SRB Jarome Iginla 6.00 15.00
SRL Robert Lang 3.00 8.00
SSF Sergei Fedorov 5.00 12.00
SSS Sergei Samsonov 4.00 10.00
STM Todd Marchant 3.00 8.00

2002-03 Upper Deck Speed Demons Jerseys

SDDB Daniel Briere 3.00 8.00
SDPB Pavel Bure 3.00 8.00
SDSF Sergei Fedorov 4.00 10.00
SDSG Simon Gagne 4.00 10.00
SDSS Steve Sullivan 3.00 8.00
SDTM Todd Marchant 3.00 8.00
SDZP Zigmund Palffy 3.00 8.00

2002-03 Upper Deck Super Saviors

COMPLETE SET (14) 12.50 25.00
SA1 Martin Biron .40 1.00
SA2 Roman Turek .40 1.00
SA3 Arturs Irbe .40 1.00
SA4 Patrick Roy 2.00 5.00
SA5 Marty Turco .40 1.00
SA6 Dominik Hasek 1.00 2.50
SA7 Jose Theodore 1.00 2.50
SA8 Martin Brodeur 1.50 4.00
SA9 Chris Osgood .40 1.00
SA10 Patrick Lalime .40 1.00
SA11 Sean Burke .40 1.00
SA12 Evgeni Nabokov .40 1.00
SA13 Brent Johnson .40 1.00
SA14 Olaf Kolzig .40 1.00

2003-04 Upper Deck

COMP.SERIES 1 (245) 200.00 400.00
COMP.SER.1 w/o SPs 20.00 40.00
COMP.SERIES 2 (230) 125.00 250.00
COMP.SER.2 w/o SPs 20.00 40.00
1 Petr Sykora .20 .50
2 Steve Rucchin .15 .40
3 Sandis Ozolinsh .15 .40
4 Jason Krog .15 .40
5 Sergei Fedorov .40 1.00
6 Rob Niedermayer .20 .50
7 Jean-Sebastien Giguere .25 .60
8 Dany Heatley .20 .50
9 Slava Kozlov .20 .50
10 Patrik Stefan .15 .40
11 Yannick Tremblay .15 .40
12 Shawn McEachern .15 .40
13 Byron Dafoe .20 .50
14 Joe Thornton .40 1.00
15 Bryan Berard .20 .50
16 P-J Axelsson .15 .40
17 Hal Gill .15 .40
18 P.J. Stock .15 .40
19 Mike Knuble .15 .40
20 Steve Shields .20 .50
21 Daniel Briere .25 .60
22 Ales Kotalik .15 .40
23 Curtis Brown .15 .40
24 JP Dumont .15 .40
25 Alexei Zhitnik .20 .50
26 Maxim Afinogenov .15 .40
27 Martin Biron .20 .50
28 Dean McAmmond .15 .40
29 Jarome Iginla .30 .75
30 Martin Gelinas .15 .40
31 Jordan Leopold .15 .40
32 Chuck Kobasew .15 .40
33 Roman Turek .20 .50
34 Jeff O`Neill .15 .40
35 Ron Francis .30 .75
36 Sean Hill .15 .40
37 Erik Cole .15 .40
38 Pavel Brendl .15 .40
39 Kevin Weekes .20 .50
40 Alexei Zhamnov .20 .50
41 Kyle Calder .15 .40
42 Tyler Arnason .15 .40
43 Igor Radulov .15 .40
44 Jocelyn Thibault .20 .50
45 Peter Forsberg .50 1.25
46 Alex Tanguay .20 .50
47 Derek Morris .15 .40
48 Rob Blake .25 .60
49 Paul Kariya .25 .60
50 Teemu Selanne .50 1.25
51 David Aebischer .20 .50
52 Patrick Roy .60 1.50
53 Pascal Leclaire .15 .40
54 Geoff Sanderson .15 .40
55 Rick Nash .25 .60
56 Rostislav Klesla .15 .40
57 Jody Shelley .15 .40
58 Marc Denis .20 .50
59 Mike Modano .40 1.00
60 Sergei Zubov .20 .50
61 Jere Lehtinen .20 .50
62 Steve Ott .15 .40
63 Niko Kapanen .15 .40
64 Jason Bacashihua .15 .40
65 Marty Turco .25 .60
66 Brett Hull .50 1.25
67 Nicklas Lidstrom .25 .60
68 Mathieu Schneider .15 .40
69 Henrik Zetterberg .30 .75
70 Pavel Datsyuk .40 1.00
71 Derian Hatcher .15 .40
72 Steve Yzerman .60 1.50
73 Manny Legace .15 .40
74 Ryan Smyth .20 .50
75 Mike York .15 .40
76 Ales Hemsky .25 .60
77 Eric Brewer .15 .40
78 Fernando Pisani .15 .40
79 Georges Laraque .20 .50
80 Tommy Salo .20 .50
81 Viktor Kozlov .15 .40
82 Kristian Huselius .15 .40
83 Stephen Weiss .15 .40
84 Jay Bouwmeester .15 .40
85 Roberto Luongo .40 1.00
86 Zigmund Palffy .25 .60
87 Alexander Frolov .20 .50
88 Luc Robitaille .25 .60
89 Ian Laperriere .15 .40
90 Jared Aulin .15 .40
91 Roman Cechmanek .20 .50
92 Marian Gaborik .25 .60
93 Pascal Dupuis .15 .40
94 Andrew Brunette .15 .40
95 Wes Walz .15 .40
96 Pierre-Marc Bouchard .25 .60
97 Willie Mitchell .15 .40
98 Manny Fernandez .15 .40
99 Saku Koivu .25 .60
100 Jan Bulis .15 .40
101 Marcel Hossa .15 .40
102 Michael Komisarek .15 .40
103 Richard Zednik .15 .40
104 Mathieu Garon .15 .40
105 Ron Hainsey .15 .40
106 David Legwand .20 .50
107 Greg Johnson .15 .40
108 Scott Hartnell .15 .40
109 Scottie Upshall .20 .50
110 Tomas Vokoun .20 .50
111 Patrik Elias .25 .60
112 Jeff Friesen .15 .40
113 Joe Nieuwendyk .20 .50
114 Scott Niedermayer .25 .60
115 Grant Marshall .15 .40
116 Scott Stevens .25 .60
117 Martin Brodeur .60 1.50
118 Jason Blake .15 .40
119 Mark Parrish .15 .40
120 Michael Peca .20 .50
121 Adrian Aucoin .15 .40
122 Rick DiPietro .20 .50
123 Eric Godard .15 .40
124 Alex Kovalev .20 .50
125 Anson Carter .20 .50
126 Mark Messier .50 1.25
127 Petr Nedved .15 .40
128 Tom Poti .15 .40
129 Jamie Lundmark .15 .40
130 Mike Dunham .20 .50
131 Marian Hossa .25 .60
132 Martin Havlat .25 .60
133 Zdeno Chara .25 .60
134 Peter Schaefer .15 .40
135 Ray Emery .20 .50
136 Jason Spezza .25 .60
137 Patrick Lalime .20 .50
138 Mark Recchi .30 .75
139 Tony Amonte .20 .50
140 Keith Primeau .20 .50
141 Simon Gagne .25 .60
142 Eric Weinrich .15 .40
143 Jim Vandermeer .15 .40
144 Robert Esche .15 .40
145 Shane Doan .20 .50
146 Chris Gratton .15 .40
147 Jan Hrdina .15 .40
148 Daymond Langkow .15 .40
149 Tyson Nash .15 .40
150 Brian Boucher .20 .50
151 Mario Lemieux 1.00 2.50
152 Aleksey Morozov .15 .40
153 Ramzi Abid .15 .40
154 Dick Tarnstrom .15 .40
155 Rico Fata .15 .40
156 Brooks Orpik .15 .40
157 Vincent Damphousse .20 .50
158 Marco Sturm .15 .40
159 Mike Ricci .15 .40
160 Jim Fahey .15 .40
161 Niko Dimitrakos .15 .40
162 Kyle McLaren .15 .40
163 Evgeni Nabokov .20 .50
164 Al MacInnis .30 .75
165 Scott Mellanby .15 .40
166 Keith Tkachuk .25 .60
167 Barret Jackman .15 .40
168 Reed Low .15 .40
169 Chris Pronger .25 .60
170 Chris Osgood .25 .60
171 Vincent Lecavalier .25 .60
172 Dave Andreychuk .25 .60
173 Brad Richards .25 .60
174 Pavel Kubina .15 .40
175 Alexander Svitov .15 .40
176 John Grahame .15 .40
177 Alexander Mogilny .20 .50
178 Owen Nolan .25 .60
179 Darcy Tucker .20 .50
180 Doug Gilmour .30 .75
181 Tie Domi .20 .50
182 Phil Housley .20 .50
183 Gary Roberts .15 .40
184 Ed Belfour .25 .60
185 Markus Naslund .25 .60
186 Brendan Morrison .20 .50
187 Ed Jovanovski .20 .50
188 Matt Cooke .15 .40
189 Henrik Sedin .30 .75
190 Brandon Reid .15 .40
191 Marek Malik .15 .40
192 Alexander Auld .15 .40
193 Robert Lang .15 .40
194 Sergei Gonchar .15 .40
195 Michael Nylander .15 .40
196 Mike Grier .15 .40
197 Steve Konowalchuk .15 .40
198 Olaf Kolzig .25 .60
199 Joe Thornton CL .30 .75
200 Martin Brodeur CL .50 1.25
201 Garrett Burnett YG RC 1.50 4.00
202 Joffrey Lupul YG RC 4.00 10.00
203 Jiri Hudler YG RC 4.00 10.00
204 Patrice Bergeron YG RC 200.00 500.00
205 Matthew Lombardi YG RC 2.00 5.00
206 Eric Staal YG RC 15.00 40.00
207 Lasse Kukkonen YG RC 1.50 4.00
208 Pavel Vorobiev YG RC 2.00 5.00
209 Travis Moen YG RC 2.00 5.00
210 Tuomo Ruutu YG RC 4.00 10.00
211 Cody McCormick YG RC 2.00 5.00
212 John-Michael Liles YG RC 2.00 5.00
213 Marek Svatos YG RC 3.00 8.00
214 Dan Fritsche YG RC 1.50 4.00
215 Antti Miettinen YG RC 2.50 6.00
216 Nathan Horton YG RC 8.00 20.00
217 Dustin Brown YG RC 8.00 20.00
218 Esa Pirnes YG RC 1.50 4.00
219 Alexander Semin YG RC 6.00 15.00
220 Tim Gleason YG RC 2.00 5.00
221 Brent Burns YG RC 30.00 80.00
222 Christoph Brandner YG RC 2.00 5.00
223 Chris Higgins YG RC 3.00 8.00
224 Dan Hamhuis YG RC 2.00 5.00
225 Jordin Tootoo YG RC 6.00 15.00
226 Marek Zidlicky YG RC 1.50 4.00
227 Wade Brookbank YG RC 2.00 5.00
228 David Hale YG RC 1.50 4.00
229 Paul Martin YG RC 2.00 5.00
230 Sean Bergenheim YG RC 2.00 5.00
231 Antoine Vermette YG RC 3.00 8.00
232 Joni Pitkanen YG RC 2.50 6.00
233 Matthew Spiller YG RC 2.00 5.00
234 Marc-Andre Fleury YG RC 250.00 600.00
235 Matt Murley YG RC 2.00 5.00
236 Ryan Malone YG RC 3.00 8.00
237 Christian Ehrhoff YG RC 2.00 5.00
238 Milan Michalek YG RC 5.00 12.00
239 Andrew Peters YG RC 2.00 5.00
240 Tom Preissing YG RC 2.00 5.00
241 Peter Sejna YG RC 2.00 5.00
242 Matt Stajan YG RC 2.50 6.00
243 Maxim Kondratiev YG RC 1.50 4.00
244 Boyd Gordon YG RC 2.00 5.00
245 Fleury/Staal/Horton CL 2.00 5.00
246 Vaclav Prospal .15 .40
247 Stanislav Chistov .15 .40
248 Mike Leclerc .15 .40
249 Keith Carney .15 .40
250 Martin Gerber .15 .40
251 Sammy Pahlsson .15 .40
252 Ruslan Salei .15 .40
253 Marc Savard .15 .40
254 Ilya Kovalchuk .25 .60
255 Kamil Piros .15 .40
256 Frantisek Kaberle .15 .40
257 Pasi Nurminen .20 .50
258 Sergei Samsonov .20 .50
259 Brian Rolston .20 .50
260 Travis Green .15 .40
261 Glen Murray .20 .50
262 Nick Boynton .15 .40
263 Jeff Jillson .15 .40
264 Felix Potvin .40 1.00
265 Andrew Raycroft .20 .50
266 Jochen Hecht .15 .40
267 Chris Drury .20 .50
268 Miroslav Satan .20 .50
269 Andy Delmore .15 .40
270 Ryan Miller .25 .60
271 Tim Connolly .15 .40
272 Oleg Saprykin .15 .40
273 Craig Conroy .15 .40
274 Steve Reinprecht .15 .40
275 Toni Lydman .15 .40
276 Robyn Regehr .15 .40
277 Jamie McLennan .15 .40
278 Jaroslav Svoboda .15 .40
279 Rod Brind'Amour .25 .60
280 Radim Vrbata .15 .40
281 Bret Hedican .15 .40
282 Danny Markov .15 .40
283 Jamie Storr .20 .50
284 Eric Daze .20 .50
285 Steve Sullivan .15 .40
286 Jon Klemm .15 .40
287 Alexander Karpovtsev .15 .40
288 Michael Leighton .15 .40
289 Joe Sakic .50 1.25
290 Steve Konowalchuk .15 .40
291 Milan Hejduk .20 .50
292 Adam Foote .15 .40
293 Dan Hinote .15 .40
294 Philippe Sauve .20 .50
295 Trevor Letowski .15 .40
296 Andrew Cassels .15 .40
297 Todd Marchant .15 .40
298 David Vyborny .15 .40
299 Darryl Sydor .15 .40
300 Jaroslav Spacek .15 .40
301 Espen Knutsen .15 .40
302 Brenden Morrow .20 .50
303 Jason Arnott .20 .50
304 Pierre Turgeon .20 .50
305 Bill Guerin .25 .60
306 Teppo Numminen .15 .40
307 Ron Tugnutt .20 .50
308 Stu Barnes .15 .40
309 Brendan Shanahan .25 .60
310 Ray Whitney .20 .50
311 Tomas Holmstrom .20 .50
312 Chris Chelios .25 .60
313 Jiri Fischer .15 .40
314 Dominik Hasek .40 1.00
315 Darren McCarty .15 .40
316 Brad Isbister .15 .40
317 Ethan Moreau .15 .40
318 Raffi Torres .15 .40
319 Mike Comrie .20 .50
320 Radek Dvorak .20 .50
321 Jason Smith .15 .40
322 Ty Conklin .20 .50
323 Adam Oates .25 .60
324 Marcus Nilsson .15 .40
325 Olli Jokinen .25 .60
326 Valeri Bure .15 .40
327 Eric Messier .15 .40
328 Branislav Mezei .15 .40
329 Steve Shields .20 .50
330 Matt Cullen .15 .40
331 Adam Deadmarsh .15 .40
332 Jason Allison .20 .50
333 Jozef Stumpel .15 .40
334 Eric Belanger .15 .40
335 Mattias Norstrom .15 .40
336 Cristobal Huet .20 .50
337 Martin Straka .15 .40
338 Antti Laaksonen .15 .40
339 Sergei Zholtok .15 .40
340 Alexandre Daigle .20 .50
341 Filip Kuba .15 .40
342 Dwayne Roloson .20 .50
343 Mike Ribeiro .15 .40
344 Donald Audette .15 .40
345 Michael Ryder .20 .50
346 Andrei Markov .25 .60
347 Jose Theodore .25 .60
348 Yanic Perreault .15 .40
349 Andreas Johansson .15 .40
350 Denis Arkhipov .15 .40
351 Rem Murray .15 .40
352 Scott Walker .15 .40
353 Adam Hall .15 .40
354 Kimmo Timonen .15 .40
355 Jason York .15 .40
356 Sergei Brylin .15 .40
357 John Madden .15 .40
358 Scott Gomez .20 .50
359 Jamie Langenbrunner .20 .50
360 Brian Gionta .15 .40
361 Brian Rafalski .20 .50
362 Corey Schwab .20 .50
363 Igor Larionov .25 .60
364 Oleg Kvasha .15 .40
365 Alexei Yashin .20 .50
366 Mariusz Czerkawski .15 .40
367 Roman Hamrlik .15 .40
368 Janne Niinimaa .15 .40
369 Arron Asham .15 .40
370 Garth Snow .20 .50
371 Jan Hlavac .15 .40
372 Matthew Barnaby .15 .40
373 Eric Lindros .40 1.00
374 Brian Leetch .20 .50
375 Jussi Markkanen .15 .40
376 Mike Fisher .15 .40
377 Radek Bonk .20 .50
378 Bryan Smolinski .15 .40
379 Daniel Alfredsson .25 .60
380 Wade Redden .15 .40
381 Chris Phillips .15 .40
382 Todd White .15 .40
383 Jeremy Roenick .40 1.00
384 Michal Handzus .20 .50
385 Donald Brashear .15 .40
386 John LeClair .25 .60
387 Justin Williams .20 .50
388 Kim Johnsson .15 .40
389 Eric Desjardins .20 .50
390 Jeff Hackett .20 .50
391 Ladislav Nagy .15 .40
392 Brian Savage .15 .40
393 Mike Johnson .15 .40
394 Branko Radivojevic .15 .40
395 Paul Mara .15 .40
396 David Tanabe .15 .40
397 Sean Burke .15 .40
398 Mike Sillinger .15 .40
399 Drake Berehowsky .15 .40
400 Steve McKenna .15 .40
401 Konstantin Koltsov .15 .40
402 Michal Rozsival .15 .40
403 Sebastien Caron .20 .50
404 Patrick Marleau .25 .60
405 Wayne Primeau .15 .40
406 Alexander Korolyuk .15 .40
407 Jonathan Cheechoo .20 .50
408 Mike Rathje .15 .40
409 Brad Stuart .15 .40
410 Scott Thornton .20 .50
411 Pavol Demitra .30 .75
412 Doug Weight .25 .60
413 Eric Boguniecki .15 .40
414 Petr Cajanek .15 .40
415 Brent Johnson .20 .50
416 Dallas Drake .15 .40
417 Cory Stillman .15 .40
418 Fredrik Modin .15 .40
419 Martin St. Louis .25 .60
420 Ruslan Fedotenko .15 .40
421 Dan Boyle .15 .40
422 Nikolai Khabibulin .25 .60
423 Mats Sundin .25 .60
424 Joe Nieuwendyk .20 .50
425 Nik Antropov .20 .50
426 Tomas Kaberle .15 .40
427 Bryan McCabe .15 .40
428 Mikael Tellqvist .20 .50
429 Ken Klee .15 .40
430 Daniel Sedin .30 .75
431 Magnus Arvedson .15 .40
432 Trevor Linden .25 .60
433 Todd Bertuzzi .25 .60
434 Mattias Ohlund .15 .40
435 Dan Cloutier .20 .50
436 Johan Hedberg .20 .50
437 Jason King .15 .40
438 Peter Bondra .25 .60
439 Jeff Halpern .15 .40
440 Jaromir Jagr .75 2.00
441 Steve Eminger .15 .40
442 Sebastien Charpentier .15 .40
443 Dainius Zubrus .15 .40
444 Mario Lemieux 1.00 2.50
445 Jason Spezza .25 .60
446 Brent Krahn YG RC 1.50 4.00
447 Boyd Kane YG RC 1.50 4.00
448 Greg Campbell YG RC 1.50 4.00
449 A.Hutchinson YG RC 1.50 4.00
450 Mike Stuart YG RC 1.50 4.00
451 Nikolai Zherdev YG RC 3.00 8.00
452 Sergei Zinovjev YG RC 1.50 4.00
453 Julien Vauclair YG RC 1.50 4.00
454 Ryan Kesler YG RC 10.00 25.00
455 Fredrik Sjostrom YG RC 2.50 6.00
456 Mikhail Yakubov YG RC 1.50 4.00
457 Nathan Smith YG RC 1.50 4.00
458 Grant McNeill YG RC 1.50 4.00
459 Seamus Kotyk YG RC 1.50 4.00
460 Alan Rourke YG RC 1.50 4.00
461 John Pohl YG RC 1.50 4.00
462 Dominic Moore YG RC 1.50 4.00
463 Tony Salmelainen YG RC 1.50 4.00
464 Rastislav Stana YG RC 2.50 6.00
465 Karl Stewart YG RC 1.50 4.00
466 Darryl Bootland YG RC 2.00 5.00
467 Trevor Daley YG RC 2.50 6.00
468 Peter Sarno YG RC 1.50 4.00
469 Jed Ortmeyer YG RC 1.50 4.00
470 N.Robinson YG RC 1.50 4.00
471 Pat Rissmiller YG RC 2.00 5.00
472 Grtzky/Laflr/Mssier CL 6.00 15.00
473 Jose Theodore HC 4.00 10.00
474 Don Cherry HC 4.00 10.00
475 Salmeln/Moore/Zinov .75 2.00

2003-04 Upper Deck 500 Goal Club

500BS Brendan Shanahan 12.50 30.00
500JJ Jaromir Jagr 15.00 40.00
500JN Joe Nieuwendyk 12.50 30.00
500JS Joe Sakic 20.00 50.00
500RF Ron Francis 12.50 30.00
500JJA Jaromir Jagr AU 250.00 400.00
500JNA Joe Nieuwendyk AU 200.00 300.00
500RFA Ron Francis AU 150.00 300.00

2003-04 Upper Deck All-Star Class

COMPLETE SET (30) 10.00 20.00
AS1 Jean-Sebastien Giguere .20 .50
AS2 Ilya Kovalchuk .40 1.00
AS3 Joe Thornton .40 1.00
AS4 Paul Kariya .20 .50
AS5 Peter Forsberg .60 1.50
AS6 Teemu Selanne .30 .75
AS7 Marty Turco .20 .50
AS8 Mike Modano .50 1.25
AS9 Steve Yzerman 1.25 3.00
AS10 Dominik Hasek .60 1.50
AS11 Nicklas Lidstrom .30 .75
AS12 Jay Bouwmeester .20 .50
AS13 Zigmund Palffy .20 .50
AS14 Marian Gaborik .60 1.50
AS15 Saku Koivu .20 .50
AS16 Martin Brodeur .75 2.00
AS17 Alexei Yashin .20 .50
AS18 Tom Poti .20 .50
AS19 Jason Spezza .30 .75
AS20 Marian Hossa .30 .75
AS21 Jeremy Roenick .40 1.00
AS22 Sean Burke .20 .50
AS23 Mario Lemieux 1.50 4.00
AS24 Patrick Marleau .20 .50
AS25 Chris Pronger .20 .50
AS26 Vincent Lecavalier .20 .50
AS27 Mats Sundin .30 .75
AS28 Ed Belfour .30 .75
AS29 Todd Bertuzzi .30 .75
AS30 Jaromir Jagr .50 1.25

2003-04 Upper Deck All-Star Lineup

COMPLETE SET (10) 40.00 80.00
AS1 Marian Gaborik 3.00 8.00
AS2 Dany Heatley 3.00 8.00
AS3 Joe Thornton 3.00 8.00
AS4 Mario Lemieux 6.00 15.00
AS5 Martin Brodeur 5.00 12.00
AS6 Jason Spezza 2.50 6.00
AS7 Rick Nash 3.00 8.00
AS8 Henrik Zetterberg 2.50 6.00
AS9 Ales Hemsky 2.50 6.00
AS10 Ryan Miller 2.50 6.00

2003-04 Upper Deck Big Playmakers

BPDH Dany Heatley 15.00 40.00
BPIK Ilya Kovalchuk 12.00 30.00
BPJB Jason Blake 10.00 25.00
BPJJ Jaromir Jagr 12.00 30.00
BPJL Jamie Langenbrunner 10.00 25.00
BPJR Jeremy Roenick 20.00 50.00
BPJS Jean-Sebastien Giguere 10.00 25.00
BPJT Joe Thornton 20.00 50.00
BPMB Martin Brodeur 30.00 80.00
BPMG Marian Gaborik 20.00 50.00
BPMH Marian Hossa 12.50 30.00
BPML Mario Lemieux 30.00 80.00
BPMM Mike Modano 20.00 50.00
BPMN Markus Naslund 10.00 25.00
BPMS Mats Sundin 15.00 40.00
BPMT Marty Turco 10.00 25.00
BPON Owen Nolan 10.00 25.00
BPPB Pavel Bure 15.00 40.00
BPPF Peter Forsberg 20.00 50.00
BPPL Pavel Brendl 10.00 25.00
BPPR Patrick Roy 30.00 80.00
BPRL Roberto Luongo 20.00 50.00
BPRN Rick Nash 25.00 60.00
BPSF Sergei Fedorov 20.00 50.00
BPSK Saku Koivu 12.50 30.00
BPTB Todd Bertuzzi 10.00 25.00
BPTH Jocelyn Thibault 10.00 25.00
BPTS Teemu Selanne 15.00 40.00
BPWG Wayne Gretzky 100.00 250.00
BPZP Zigmund Palffy 10.00 25.00

2003-04 Upper Deck Buyback Autographs

7 Joe Thornton 02UD/22 30.00 80.00
8 Markus Naslund 92UD/38 20.00 50.00
18 Markus Naslund 02UD/21 20.00 50.00
24 Todd Bertuzzi 02UD/48 25.00 60.00
25 J.Giguere 02UD/48 15.00 40.00
36 Gordie Howe 02UD/23 60.00 120.00
37 Zigmund Palffy 91UD/28 20.00 50.00
47 Zigmund Palffy 02UD/23 12.00 30.00
48 Jason Spezza 02UD/29 50.00 120.00
54 John LeClair 02UD/23 15.00 40.00
67 Pavel Bure 02UD/48 15.00 40.00
70 Mike Comrie 02UD/30 12.50 30.00
84 Sergei Fedorov 02UD/39 30.00 80.00
96 Ron Francis 02UD/47 20.00 50.00
98 Marian Gaborik 02UD/48 20.00 50.00
104 Marian Hossa 02UD/48 15.00 40.00
109 Curtis Joseph 02UD/48 15.00 40.00
111 Jarome Iginla MS 02UD/47 15.00 40.00
112 Jarome Iginla 02UD/48 15.00 40.00
122 Saku Koivu 02UD/48 20.00 50.00
125 Ilya Kovalchuk 02UD/48 25.00 60.00
138 Joe Nieuwendyk 02UD/48 12.50 30.00
151 Jeremy Roenick 02UD/48 15.00 40.00
165 Patrick Roy 02UD/48 50.00 125.00
166 Patrick Roy MS 02UD/48 50.00 125.00
173 Sergei Samsonov 02UD/48 20.00 50.00
178 Jose Theodore 02UD/48 15.00 40.00
181 Stanislav Chistov 02UD/29 25.00 60.00

2003-04 Upper Deck Canadian Exclusives

*1-200/246-445 VETS/50: 8X TO 20X BASIC
*201-245 YG/50: 1X TO 2.5X BASIC YG
*446-471 YG/25: 1.5X TO 4X BASIC YG
*472-475 CAN/25: 1.5X TO 4X BASIC
221 Brent Burns YG 500.00 1200.00
454 Ryan Kesler YG 50.00 100.00

2003-04 Upper Deck Fan Favorites

COMPLETE SET (10) 12.50 25.00
FF1 Jeremy Roenick 1.25 3.00
FF2 Todd Bertuzzi .75 2.00
FF3 Roberto Luongo 1.25 3.00
FF4 Georges Laraque .75 2.00
FF5 Tie Domi .75 2.00
FF6 Steve Yzerman 3.00 8.00
FF7 Mike Modano 1.50 4.00
FF8 P.J. Stock .75 2.00
FF9 Mario Lemieux 3.00 8.00
FF10 Jean-Sebastien Giguere .75 2.00

2003-04 Upper Deck Franchise Fabrics

FFAY Alexei Yashin 3.00 8.00
FFBL Brian Leetch 3.00 8.00
FFCD Chris Drury 3.00 8.00
FFDH Dany Heatley 5.00 12.00
FFHZ Henrik Zetterberg 3.00 8.00
FFJI Jarome Iginla 6.00 15.00
FFJJ Jaromir Jagr 8.00 20.00
FFJT Joe Thornton 8.00 20.00
FFJT Jose Theodore 6.00 15.00
FFMB Martin Brodeur 10.00 25.00
FFMG Marian Gaborik 6.00 15.00
FFMH Marian Hossa 3.00 8.00
FFML Mario Lemieux 10.00 25.00
FFMN Markus Naslund 3.00 8.00
FFMS Mats Sundin 3.00 8.00
FFMT Marty Turco 3.00 8.00
FFNL Nicklas Lidstrom 4.00 10.00
FFPF Peter Forsberg 6.00 15.00
FFPK Paul Kariya 4.00 10.00
FFRL Roberto Luongo 6.00 15.00
FFRS Ryan Smyth 3.00 8.00
FFSF Sergei Fedorov 6.00 15.00
FFTB Todd Bertuzzi 3.00 8.00
FFVL Vincent Lecavalier 4.00 10.00
FFZP Zigmund Palffy 3.00 8.00

2003-04 Upper Deck Gifted Greats

COMPLETE SET (10) 25.00 60.00
GG1 Wayne Gretzky 6.00 15.00
GG2 Jean-Sebastien Giguere 2.00 5.00
GG3 Joe Thornton 3.00 8.00
GG4 Mario Lemieux 6.00 15.00
GG5 Eric Lindros 2.00 5.00
GG6 Todd Bertuzzi 2.00 5.00
GG7 Marian Gaborik 4.00 10.00
GG8 Dany Heatley 3.00 8.00
GG9 Marian Hossa 2.00 5.00
GG10 Martin Brodeur 5.00 12.00

2003-04 Upper Deck High Gloss Parallel

*1-200/246-445 VETS/25: 10X TO 25X BASIC

2003-04 Upper Deck Highlight Heroes

COMPLETE SET (10) 15.00 30.00
HHAM Alexander Mogilny 2.00 5.00
HHJJ Jaromir Jagr 3.00 8.00
HHJS Jason Spezza 2.00 5.00
HHJT Jocelyn Thibault 2.00 5.00
HHMG Marian Gaborik 3.00 8.00
HHPB Pavel Bure 2.00 5.00
HHRN Rick Nash 2.50 6.00
HHSS Sergei Samsonov 2.00 5.00
HHTA Tony Amonte 2.00 5.00
HHTS Teemu Selanne 2.50 6.00

2003-04 Upper Deck Highlight Heroes Jerseys

HHAM Alexander Mogilny 5.00 12.00
HHJJ Jaromir Jagr 8.00 20.00
HHJS Jason Spezza 6.00 15.00
HHJT Jocelyn Thibault 5.00 12.00
HHMG Marian Gaborik 10.00 25.00
HHPB Pavel Bure 8.00 20.00
HHRN Rick Nash 8.00 20.00
HHSS Sergei Samsonov 5.00 12.00
HHTA Tony Amonte 5.00 12.00
HHTS Teemu Selanne 6.00 15.00

2003-04 Upper Deck Jerseys

GJAK Alex Kovalev Ser. 1 6.00 15.00
GJBG Bill Guerin Ser. 1 6.00 15.00
GJEL Eric Lindros Ser. 1 6.00 15.00
GJIK Ilya Kovalchuk Ser. 1 8.00 20.00
GJJB Owen Nolan Ser. 1 6.00 15.00
GJJG Jean-Sebastien Giguere Ser. 1 6.00 15.00
GJJI Jarome Iginla Ser. 1 8.00 20.00
GJMA Maxim Afinogenov Ser. 1 6.00 15.00
GJMB Martin Brodeur Ser. 1 15.00 40.00
GJMC Mike Comrie Ser. 1 6.00 15.00
GJML Mario Lemieux Ser. 1 15.00 40.00
GJMR Mark Recchi Ser. 1 6.00 15.00
GJMS Martin St. Louis Ser. 1 8.00 20.00

GJSK Saku Koivu Ser. 1 6.00 15.00
GJTB Todd Bertuzzi Ser. 1 6.00 15.00
UDAF Alexander Frolov Ser. 2 6.00 15.00
UDAH Ales Hemsky Ser. 2 6.00 15.00
UDBH Brett Hull Ser. 2 8.00 20.00
UDEJ Ed Jovanovski Ser. 2 6.00 15.00
UDIK Ilya Kovalchuk Ser. 2 8.00 20.00
UDJSG Jean-Sebastien Giguere Ser. 2 6.00 15.00
UDMC Mike Comrie Ser. 2 6.00 15.00
UDMH Marian Hossa Ser. 2 6.00 15.00
UDMK Mike Komisarek Ser. 2 6.00 15.00
UDMS Martin St. Louis Ser. 2 6.00 15.00
UDON Owen Nolan Ser. 2 6.00 15.00
UDRB Rob Blake Ser. 2 6.00 15.00

2003-04 Upper Deck Jersey Autographs

SJAH Ales Hemsky 12.00 30.00
SJCJ Curtis Joseph 15.00 40.00
SJDA David Aebischer 12.00 30.00
SJEL Eric Lindros 15.00 40.00
SJJA Jared Aulin 10.00 25.00
SJJI Jarome Iginla 30.00 80.00
SJJR Jeremy Roenick 15.00 40.00
SJJS Jason Spezza 40.00 100.00
SJJT Joe Thornton 20.00 50.00
SJJSG Jean-Sebastien Giguere 12.00 30.00
SJMH Marian Hossa 20.00 50.00
SJPR Patrick Roy 75.00 200.00
SJRN Rick Nash 40.00 100.00
SJSF Sergei Fedorov 20.00 50.00
SJSH Scott Hartnell 10.00 25.00
SJSK Saku Koivu 15.00 40.00
SJSS Sergei Samsonov 12.00 30.00
SJTB Todd Bertuzzi 12.00 30.00
SJWG Wayne Gretzky 250.00 600.00
SJZP Zigmund Palffy 12.00 30.00

2003-04 Upper Deck Magic Moments

COMPLETE SET (15) 30.00 60.00
MM1 Jean-Sebastien Giguere 1.00 2.50
MM2 Scott Stevens 1.00 2.50
MM3 Jason Spezza 1.25 3.00
MM4 Steve Yzerman 3.00 8.00
MM5 Paul Kariya 1.00 2.50
MM6 Patrick Roy 3.00 8.00
MM7 Joe Thornton 1.25 3.00
MM8 Wayne Gretzky 4.00 10.00
MM9 Marc-Andre Fleury 3.00 8.00
MM10 Milan Hejduk 1.00 2.50
MM11 Dominik Hasek 1.50 4.00
MM12 Martin Brodeur 3.00 8.00
MM13 Peter Forsberg 2.00 5.00
MM14 Sergei Fedorov 1.25 3.00
MM15 Jordin Tootoo 2.00 5.00

2003-04 Upper Deck Memorable Matchups

MMBG T.Bertuzzi
M.Gaborik 5.00 12.00
MMFK S.Fedorov/P.Kariya 8.00 20.00
MMGB J.Giguere/M.Brodeur 12.50 30.00
MMHH B.Hull/D.Hasek 12.50 30.00
MMLS E.Lindros/S.Stevens 8.00 20.00
MMNN R.Niedermayer/S.Niedermayer 5.00 12.00
MMRR J.Roenick/P.Roy 20.00 50.00
MMTH J.Theodore/A.Hemsky 5.00 12.00
MMTT J.Thornton/J.Theodore 8.00 20.00

2003-04 Upper Deck Mr. Hockey

COMPLETE SET (30) 30.00 80.00
COMMON CARD (GH1-GH30) 2.00 5.00

2003-04 Upper Deck NHL's Best

MULT.COLOR SWATCH: .5X TO 1.25X
NBDH Dany Heatley 6.00 15.00
NBGM Glen Murray 5.00 12.00
NBIK Ilya Kovalchuk 6.00 15.00
NBJG Jean-Sebastien Giguere 5.00 12.00
NBJI Jarome Iginla 6.00 15.00
NBJR Jeremy Roenick 6.00 15.00
NBKT Keith Tkachuk 5.00 12.00
NDMD Martin Drodeur 12.50 30.00
NBML Mario Lemieux 12.50 30.00
NBMM Mike Modano 8.00 20.00
NBNL Nicklas Lidstrom 6.00 15.00
NBPR Patrick Roy 15.00 40.00
NBPS Sergei Fedorov 6.00 15.00
NBVL Vincent Lecavalier 5.00 12.00
NBZP Zigmund Palffy 5.00 12.00

2003-04 Upper Deck Patches

LD3 Mario Lemieux Ser.2 100.00 250.00
LD4 Mats Sundin Ser.2 60.00 150.00
LD5 Joe Thornton Ser.2 75.00 200.00
LD6 Ron Francis Ser.2 60.00 125.00
LD7 Markus Naslund Ser.2 40.00 100.00
LD9 Jeremy Roenick Ser.2 60.00 150.00
SP3 Jeremy Roenick Ser.2 60.00 150.00
SP4 Brett Hull Ser.2 75.00 200.00
SP5 Dany Heatley Ser.2 75.00 200.00
SP8 Vincent Lecavalier Ser.2 50.00 125.00
SP9 Bill Guerin Ser.2 30.00 80.00
SP10 Glen Murray Ser.2 40.00 100.00
SV1 Martin Brodeur Ser.2 100.00 200.00
SV2 Roberto Luongo Ser.2 75.00 200.00
SV3 Roman Cechmanek Ser.2 40.00 100.00
SV5 Tommy Salo Ser.2 40.00 100.00
SV7 David Aebischer Ser.2 40.00 100.00
SV8 Patrick Lalime Ser.2 40.00 100.00
SV9 Dominik Hasek Ser.2 50.00 125.00
SV10 Ed Belfour Ser.2 50.00 125.00
PLGJG J-S Giguere Ser.1 40.00 100.00
PLGJS Jason Spezza Ser.1 40.00 100.00
PLGJT Joe Thornton Ser.1 60.00 150.00
PLGMB Martin Brodeur Ser.1 100.00 200.00
PLGMH Marian Hossa Ser.1 40.00 100.00
PLGML Mario Lemieux Ser.1 100.00 200.00
PLGMN Markus Naslund Ser.1 40.00 100.00
PLGPR Patrick Roy Ser.1 150.00 300.00
PLGRN Rick Nash Ser.1 75.00 200.00
PNMJG J-S Giguere Ser.1 40.00 100.00
PNMJS Jason Spezza Ser.1 75.00 200.00
PNMJT Joe Thornton Ser.1 75.00 200.00
PNMMB Martin Brodeur Ser.1 100.00 200.00
PNMMH Marian Hossa Ser.1 40.00 100.00
PNMML Mario Lemieux Ser.1 75.00 200.00
PNMMN Markus Naslund Ser.1 40.00 100.00
PNMPR Patrick Roy Ser.1 150.00 300.00
PNMRN Rick Nash Ser.1 75.00 150.00
PNRJG J-S Giguere Ser.1 75.00 150.00
PNRJS Jason Spezza Ser.1 75.00 200.00
PNRJT Joe Thornton Ser.1 75.00 200.00
PNRMB Martin Brodeur Ser.1 100.00 200.00
PNRMH Marian Hossa Ser.1 40.00 100.00
PNRML Mario Lemieux Ser.1 100.00 250.00
PNRMN Markus Naslund Ser.1 40.00 100.00
PNRPR Patrick Roy Ser.1 150.00 300.00
PNRRN Rick Nash Ser.1 75.00 150.00

2003-04 Upper Deck Performers

COMPLETE SET (15) 20.00 40.00
PS1 Jean-Sebastien Giguere .60 1.50
PS2 Scott Stevens .60 1.50
PS3 Steve Yzerman 2.50 6.00
PS4 Jeremy Roenick .75 2.00
PS5 Peter Forsberg 1.25 3.00
PS6 Jose Theodore .75 2.00
PS7 Marian Gaborik 1.00 2.50
PS8 Martin Brodeur 1.50 4.00
PS9 Ed Belfour .60 1.50
PS10 Mike Modano .75 2.00
PS11 Joe Sakic 1.00 2.50
PS12 Bobby Orr 4.00 10.00
PS13 Mario Lemieux 3.00 8.00
PS14 Wayne Gretzky 4.00 10.00
PS15 Patrick Roy 2.50 6.00

2003-04 Upper Deck Power Zone

COMPLETE SET (10) 10.00 25.00
PZ1 Joe Thornton 1.00 2.50
PZ2 Keith Tkachuk .75 2.00
PZ3 Jeremy Roenick 1.25 3.00
PZ4 Brendan Shanahan 1.00 2.50
PZ5 Todd Bertuzzi .75 2.00
PZ6 Rick Nash 1.25 3.00
PZ7 Peter Forsberg 1.50 4.00
PZ8 Owen Nolan .75 2.00
PZ9 Mario Lemieux 4.00 10.00
PZ10 Eric Lindros 1.00 2.50

2003-04 Upper Deck Rookie Threads Autographs

RT1 Joffrey Lupul 15.00 40.00
RT2 Dustin Brown 15.00 40.00
RT3 Marc-Andre Fleury 50.00 125.00
RT4 Joni Pitkanen 12.50 30.00
RT5 Peter Sejna 12.50 30.00
RT6 Eric Staal 25.00 60.00
RT7 Tuomo Ruutu 15.00 40.00
RT8 Dan Hamhuis 12.50 30.00
RT9 Nathan Horton 20.00 50.00
RT10 Jordin Tootoo 20.00 50.00

2003-04 Upper Deck Shooting Stars

MULT.COLOR SWATCH: .5X TO 1.25X
STAH Ales Hemsky 4.00 10.00
STAS Alexander Svitov 4.00 10.00
STAV Anton Volchenkov 4.00 10.00
STJA Jared Aulin 4.00 10.00
STJB Jay Bouwmeester 5.00 12.00
STJL Jordan Leopold 4.00 10.00
STJS Jason Spezza 8.00 20.00
STJW Justin Williams 5.00 12.00
STMH Marcel Hossa 4.00 10.00
STPM Pierre-Marc Bouchard 5.00 12.00
STRD Rick DiPietro 5.00 12.00
STRM Ryan Miller 6.00 15.00
STRN Rick Nash 12.00 30.00
STSO Steve Ott 5.00 12.00
STSV Alexei Smirnov 4.00 10.00

2003-04 Upper Deck Super Saviors

MULT.COLOR SWATCH: .5X TO 1.25X
SSJG Jean-Sebastien Giguere 6.00 15.00
33MB Martin Brodeur 12.00 30.00
SSMT Marty Turco 8.00 20.00
SSPL Patrick Lalime 6.00 15.00
SSPR Patrick Roy 15.00 40.00
SSRC Roman Cechmanek 6.00 15.00

2003-04 Upper Deck Superstar Spotlight

SS1 Jean-Sebastien Giguere 4.00 10.00
SS2 Joe Thornton 6.00 15.00
SS3 Marian Gaborik 6.00 15.00
SS4 Rick Nash 5.00 12.00
SS5 Steve Yzerman 12.50 30.00
SS6 Martin Brodeur 12.50 30.00
SS7 Jason Spezza 5.00 12.00
SS8 Mike Modano 6.00 15.00
SS9 Mario Lemieux 15.00 40.00
SS10 Jaromir Jagr 6.00 15.00
SS11 Todd Bertuzzi 4.00 10.00
SS12 Dany Heatley 5.00 12.00
SS13 Patrick Roy 15.00 40.00
SS14 Bobby Orr 20.00 50.00
SS15 Gordie Howe 12.50 30.00

2003-04 Upper Deck Team Essentials

UNLISTED STARS 6.00 15.00
TLJS Joe Sakic 10.00 25.00
TLJT Joe Thornton 8.00 20.00
TLML Mario Lemieux 15.00 40.00
TLMN Markus Naslund 6.00 15.00
TLMP Michael Peca 6.00 15.00
TLMS Mats Sundin 6.00 15.00
TLSS Scott Stevens 6.00 15.00
TLSY Steve Yzerman 12.50 30.00
TPAM Al MacInnis 6.00 15.00
TPDA Daniel Alfredsson 6.00 15.00
TPDH Dany Heatley 8.00 20.00
TPJT Joe Thornton 8.00 20.00
TPML Mario Lemieux 10.00 25.00
TPMM Mike Modano 8.00 20.00
TPMS Miroslav Satan 6.00 15.00
TPPF Peter Forsberg 10.00 25.00
TPPK Paul Kariya 6.00 15.00
TPVL Vincent Lecavalier 6.00 15.00
TSDH Dany Heatley 10.00 25.00
TSJJ Jaromir Jagr 12.50 30.00
TSMH Milan Hejduk 8.00 20.00
TSMH Marian Hossa 8.00 20.00
TSPB Pavel Bure 8.00 20.00
TSTB Todd Bertuzzi 6.00 15.00

2003-04 Upper Deck Three Stars

COMPLETE SET (15) 20.00 40.00
TS1 Paul Kariya .60 1.50
TS2 Marian Hossa .60 1.50
TS3 Dany Heatley .75 2.00
TS4 Alexei Yashin .60 1.50
TS5 Jaromir Jagr .75 2.00
TS6 Martin Brodeur 1.50 4.00
TS7 Marian Gaborik 1.00 2.50
TS8 Ziggy Palffy .60 1.50
TS9 Marty Turco .60 1.50
TS10 Mats Sundin .60 1.50
TS11 Jean-Sebastien Giguere .60 1.50
TS12 Mario Lemieux 3.00 8.00
TS13 Jarome Iginla .75 2.00
TS14 Markus Naslund .60 1.50
TS15 Joe Thornton .75 2.00

2003-04 Upper Deck Tough Customers

COMPLETE SET (15) 12.00 25.00
COMMON CARD (TC1-TC15) .75 2.00
TC1 Jody Shelley .75 2.00
TC2 Andrei Nazarov .75 2.00
TC3 Reed Low .75 2.00
TC4 Andrew Peters .75 2.00
TC5 Wade Belak .75 2.00
TC6 Darren McCarty 1.00 2.50
TC7 Krzysztof Oliwa .75 2.00
TC8 P.J. Stock .75 2.00
TC9 Matt Johnson .75 2.00
TC10 Chris Neil .75 2.00
TC11 Garrett Burnett .75 2.00
TC12 Georges Laraque 1.00 2.50
TC13 Tie Domi 1.00 2.50
TC14 Jason Strudwick .75 2.00
TC15 Donald Brashear .75 2.00

2003-04 Upper Deck Exclusives

*246-445 VETS/50: 6X TO 15X BASIC CARDS

2004 Upper Deck Pearson Awards

COMPLETE SET (3) 250.00 400.00
JS Joe Sakic 100.00 200.00
MSL Martin St.Louis 30.00 75.00
RL Roberto Luongo 100.00 200.00

2004-05 Upper Deck

COMPLETE SET (210) 125.00 250.00
COMP.SET w/o SP's (180) 15.00 30.00
1 Petr Sykora .15 .40
2 Andy McDonald .15 .40
3 Sandis Ozolinsh .12 .30
4 Sergei Fedorov .30 .75
5 Joffrey Lupul .12 .30
6 Jean-Sebastien Giguere .20 .50
7 Dany Heatley .15 .40
8 Ilya Kovalchuk .20 .50
9 Patrik Stefan .12 .30
10 Jaroslav Modry .12 .30
11 Serge Aubin .12 .30
12 Kari Lehtonen .25 .60
13 Joe Thornton .30 .75
14 Sergei Gonchar .15 .40
15 Patrice Bergeron .25 .60
16 Nick Boynton .12 .30
17 Sergei Samsonov .15 .40
18 Andrew Raycroft .15 .40
19 Daniel Briere .20 .50
20 Miroslav Satan .15 .40
21 Mika Noronen .15 .40
22 J.P. Dumont .12 .30
23 Maxim Afinogenov .12 .30
24 Martin Biron .15 .40
25 Chris Simon .12 .30
26 Jarome Iginla .25 .60
27 Robyn Regehr .12 .30
28 Jordan Leopold .12 .30
29 Chuck Kobasew .12 .30
30 Miikka Kiprusoff .20 .50
31 Jeff O'Neill .12 .30
32 Ron Francis .25 .60
33 Aaron Ward .12 .30
34 Erik Cole .12 .30
35 Eric Staal .25 .60
36 Martin Gerber .15 .40
37 Matthew Barnaby .12 .30
38 Kyle Calder .12 .30
39 Tyler Arnason .12 .30
40 Eric Daze .15 .40
41 Jocelyn Thibault .15 .40
42 Peter Forsberg .40 1.00
43 Alex Tanguay .15 .40
44 Milan Hejduk .15 .40
45 Rob Blake .20 .50
46 Paul Kariya .20 .50
47 Teemu Selanne .40 1.00
48 David Aebischer .15 .40
49 Luke Richardson .12 .30
50 Rick Nash .20 .50
51 Rostislav Klesla .12 .30
52 Nikolai Zherdev .15 .40
53 Marc Denis .15 .40
54 Mike Modano .30 .75
55 Sergei Zubov .15 .40
56 Bill Guerin .20 .50
57 Jason Arnott .15 .40
58 Niko Kapanen .12 .30
59 Marty Turco .20 .50
60 Kirk Maltby .12 .30
61 Nicklas Lidstrom .20 .50
62 Kris Draper .12 .30
63 Brendan Shanahan .20 .50
64 Pavel Datsyuk .30 .75
65 Robert Lang .12 .30
66 Steve Yzerman .50 1.25
67 Curtis Joseph .25 .60
68 Ryan Smyth .15 .40
69 Jason Smith .12 .30
70 Ales Hemsky .20 .50
71 Eric Brewer .12 .30
72 Raffi Torres .12 .30
73 Ty Conklin .15 .40
74 Mike Van Ryn .12 .30
75 Kristian Huselius .12 .30
76 Stephen Weiss .12 .30
77 Jay Bouwmeester .12 .30
78 Roberto Luongo .30 .75
79 Craig Conroy .12 .30
80 Aaron Miller .12 .30
81 Luc Robitaille .20 .50
82 Martin Straka .12 .30
83 Mattias Norstrom .12 .30
84 Roman Cechmanek .15 .40
85 Marian Gaborik .20 .50
86 Pascal Dupuis .12 .30
87 Alexander Daigle .12 .30
88 Pierre-Marc Bouchard .20 .50
89 Filip Kuba .12 .30
90 Manny Fernandez .12 .30
91 Saku Koivu .20 .50
92 Michael Ryder .15 .40
93 Marcel Hossa .12 .30
94 Mike Ribeiro .12 .30
95 Jose Theodore .20 .50
96 Sheldon Souray .12 .30
97 David Legwand .15 .40
98 Steve Sullivan .12 .30
99 Marek Zidlicky .12 .30
100 Martin Erat .12 .30
101 Tomas Vokoun .15 .40
102 Patrik Elias .20 .50
103 Jeff Friesen .12 .30
104 Brian Rafalski .15 .40
105 Scott Niedermayer .20 .50
106 Scott Stevens .20 .50
107 Martin Brodeur .50 1.25
108 Oleg Kvasha .12 .30
109 Mark Parrish .12 .30
110 Michael Peca .15 .40
111 Adrian Aucoin .12 .30
112 Rick DiPietro .15 .40
113 Trent Hunter .12 .30
114 Eric Lindros .30 .75
115 Tom Poti .12 .30
116 Mark Messier .40 1.00
117 Jaromir Jagr .60 1.50
118 Bobby Holik .12 .30
119 Mike Dunham .15 .40
120 Marian Hossa .20 .50
121 Martin Havlat .20 .50
122 Zdeno Chara .20 .50
123 Daniel Alfredsson .20 .50
124 Jason Spezza .20 .50
125 Dominik Hasek .30 .75
126 Jeremy Roenick .30 .75
127 Tony Amonte .15 .40
128 Keith Primeau .15 .40
129 Simon Gagne .20 .50
130 Danny Markov .12 .30
131 Robert Esche .15 .40
132 Shane Doan .15 .40
133 Mike Comrie .15 .40
134 Ladislav Nagy .12 .30
135 Brett Hull .40 1.00
136 Derek Morris .12 .30
137 Brian Boucher .15 .40
138 Mario Lemieux .75 2.00
139 Mark Recchi .25 .60
140 Ryan Malone .12 .30
141 Dick Tarnstrom .12 .30
142 Rico Fata .12 .30
143 Marc-Andre Fleury .40 1.00
144 Alyn McCauley .12 .30
145 Marco Sturm .12 .30
146 Patrick Marleau .20 .50
147 Scott Hannan .12 .30
148 Kyle McLaren .12 .30
149 Evgeni Nabokov .15 .40
150 Al MacInnis .25 .60
151 Petr Cajanek .12 .30
152 Keith Tkachuk .20 .50
153 Barret Jackman .12 .30
154 Chris Pronger .20 .50
155 Patrick Lalime .15 .40
156 Vincent Lecavalier .20 .50
157 Dave Andreychuk .20 .50
158 Brad Richards .20 .50
159 Pavel Kubina .12 .30
160 Ruslan Fedotenko .12 .30
161 Nikolai Khabibulin .20 .50
162 Alexander Mogilny .15 .40
163 Owen Nolan .20 .50
164 Gary Roberts .12 .30
165 Bryan McCabe .12 .30
166 Ed Belfour .20 .50
167 Joe Nieuwendyk .15 .40
168 Markus Naslund .20 .50
169 Brendan Morrison .15 .40
170 Todd Bertuzzi .20 .50
171 Ed Jovanovski .15 .40
172 Trevor Linden .20 .50
173 Dan Cloutier .15 .40
174 Jeff Halpern .12 .30
175 Dainius Zubrus .12 .30
176 Jason Doig .12 .30
177 Brendan Witt .12 .30
178 Olaf Kolzig .20 .50
179 Wayne Gretzky CL 1.25 3.00
180 Gordie Howe CL .60 1.50
181 Brad Fast YG RC 2.00 5.00
182 Brennan Evans YG RC 2.00 5.00
183 Wayne Gretzky YGR 15.00 40.00
184 Mark Messier YGR 5.00 12.00
185 Peter Forsberg YGR 5.00 12.00
186 Steve Yzerman YGR 6.00 15.00
187 Ron Francis YGR 8.00 20.00
188 Patrick Roy YGR 12.00 30.00
189 Mario Lemieux YGR 15.00 40.00
190 Dave Andreychuk YGR 8.00 20.00
191 Luc Robitaille YGR 8.00 20.00
192 Gordie Howe YGR 8.00 20.00
193 Don Cherry YGR 5.00 12.00
194 Hobey Baker YGL 2.50 6.00
195 Mike Modano YGL 4.00 10.00
196 Denis Brodeur YGL 1.50 4.00
197 Keith Tkachuk YGL 2.00 5.00
198 Bob Goodenow YGL 1.50 4.00
199 Cammi Granato YG RC 2.50 6.00
200 Foster Hewitt YGL 1.50 4.00
201 Mike Keenan YGL 2.00 5.00
202 Dick Irvin Jr. YGL 1.50 4.00
203 Jeremy Roenick YGL 3.00 8.00
204 James Norris YGL 1.50 4.00
205 Alexander Ragulin YG RC 2.50 6.00
206 Brendan Shanahan YGL 2.00 5.00
207 Lord Stanley YGL 1.50 4.00
208 Gary Thorne YGL 1.50 4.00
209 Scott Stevens YGL 2.00 5.00
210 Joe Sakic YGL 4.00 10.00

2004-05 Upper Deck 1997 Game Jerseys

97BB Joe Thornton 15.00 40.00
97BS Brendan Shanahan/100* 25.00 60.00
97JI Jarome Iginla 15.00 40.00
97JS Jason Spezza 10.00 25.00
97MB Martin Brodeur 25.00 60.00
97MM Mike Modano 12.50 30.00
97MS Martin St. Louis 10.00 25.00
97PF Peter Forsberg/50* 25.00 60.00
97PR Patrick Roy/50* 30.00 80.00
97SF Sergei Fedorov 15.00 40.00
97SK Saku Koivu 10.00 25.00
97SU Mats Sundin 10.00 25.00

1999 Wayne Gretzky Living Legend Authentics

COMMON WG PUCK (P1-P6) 15.00 40.00
COMMON WG STICK (S1-S2) 25.00 60.00
C1 Gretzky Jsy-Pck-Stck/99 150.00 300.00
GJ1 Gretzky Jsy/99 150.00 300.00

2004-05 Upper Deck Big Playmakers

BPAT Alex Tanguay 10.00 25.00
BPBH Brett Hull 12.00 30.00
BPEF Sergei Fedorov 12.00 30.00
BPGH Gordie Howe 100.00 200.00
BPHE Milan Hejduk 10.00 25.00
BPHO Marian Hossa 10.00 25.00
BPIK Ilya Kovalchuk 15.00 40.00
BPJI Jarome Iginla 15.00 40.00
BPJJ Jaromir Jagr 20.00 50.00
BPJR Jeremy Roenick 12.00 30.00
BPJS Joe Sakic 20.00 50.00
BPKP Keith Primeau 10.00 25.00
BPKT Keith Tkachuk 10.00 25.00
BPML Mario Lemieux 40.00 100.00
BPMM Mike Modano 12.00 30.00
BPMN Markus Naslund 10.00 25.00
BPMS Martin St. Louis 10.00 25.00
BPPB Pavel Bure 12.00 30.00
BPPD Pavel Datsyuk 12.00 30.00
BPSU Mats Sundin 12.00 30.00
BPTH Joe Thornton 15.00 40.00
BPWG Wayne Gretzky 100.00 200.00

1999 Wayne Gretzky Living Legend Goodwill Ambassador

COMMON GRETZKY (GW1-GW9) 1.50 4.00

2004-05 Upper Deck Canadian Exclusives

*1-180 EXCL/50: 8X TO 20X BASIC CARDS
*181-210 YG EXCL/25: 2X TO 5X BASIC YG
183 Wayne Gretzky YG 75.00 150.00

1999 Wayne Gretzky Living Legend Great Accolades

COMMON GRETZKY (GA1-GA45) 2.50 6.00

2004-05 Upper Deck Clutch Performers

COMPLETE SET (7) 12.50 25.00
CP1 Jarome Iginla 1.50 4.00
CP2 Brad Richards .75 2.00
CP3 Joe Sakic 2.00 5.00
CP4 Joe Thornton 1.50 4.00
CP5 Keith Primeau .75 2.00
CP6 Nikolai Khabibulin 1.25 3.00
CP7 Mario Lemieux 4.00 10.00

1999 Wayne Gretzky Living Legend Great Stats

COMMON GRETZKY (GS1-GS6) 2.00 5.00

2004-05 Upper Deck Hardware Heroes

COMPLETE SET (14) 15.00 30.00
AW1 S.Niedermeyer
Norris .75 2.00
AW2 M.St.Louis/Art Ross .75 2.00
AW3 B.Richards/Conn Smythe .75 2.00
AW4 A.Raycroft/Calder .75 2.00
AW5 M.Brodeur/Vezina 2.50 6.00
AW6 Iginla/Nash/Kova/Richard 2.00 5.00
AW7 M.St.Louis/Hart .75 2.00
AW8 B.Richards/Lady Byng .75 2.00
AW9 K.Draper/Selke .75 2.00
AW10 B.Berard/Masterton .75 2.00
AW11 J.Iginla/Clancy 1.00 2.50
AW12 M.Brodeur/Jennings 2.50 6.00
AW13 Red Wings/President's 2.00 5.00
AW14 Lightning/Stanley Cup 2.50 6.00

1999 Wayne Gretzky Living Legend Magic Moments

COMMON GRETZKY (MM1-MM6) 2.00 5.00

2004-05 Upper Deck Heritage Classic

CCAH Ales Hemsky 12.00 30.00
CCEB Eric Brewer 12.00 30.00
CCGF Grant Fuhr 20.00 50.00
CCJK Jari Kurri 25.00 60.00
CCJT Jose Theodore/75* 30.00 80.00
CCLU Guy Lafleur/82* 40.00 80.00
CCMM Mark Messier/25* 125.00 250.00
CCMR Mike Ribeiro 12.00 30.00
CCPC Paul Coffey/75* 30.00 80.00
CCRS Ryan Smyth 20.00 50.00
CCRT Raffi Torres 12.00 30.00
CCRY Michael Ryder 20.00 50.00
CCSK Saku Koivu 20.00 50.00
CCSS Steve Shutt 12.00 30.00
CCTC Ty Conklin 12.00 30.00

1999 Wayne Gretzky Living Legend More Than a Number

COMMON GRETZKY (1-99) 12.00 30.00

1999 Wayne Gretzky Living Legend The Great One

COMMON GRETZKY (GO1-GO9) .75 2.00

2004-05 Upper Deck Jersey Autographs

GJAAA Arron Asham 15.00 40.00
GJAAF Alexander Frolov 15.00 40.00
GJAAH Adam Hall 15.00 30.00
GJAAL Ales Hemsky 20.00 50.00
GJAAS Alexander Svitov 15.00 40.00
GJAAY Alexei Yashin 15.00 40.00
GJABO Brooks Orpik 15.00 40.00
GJABU Pavel Bure 30.00 80.00
GJACK Chuck Kobasew 15.00 40.00
GJADA David Aebischer 20.00 50.00
GJAGH Gordie Howe 125.00 250.00
GJAHO Marcel Hossa 15.00 30.00
GJAHS Marian Hossa 25.00 60.00
GJAIK Ilya Kovalchuk 60.00 125.00
GJAJG Jean-Sebastien Giguere 15.00 40.00
GJAJI Jarome Iginla 60.00 150.00
GJAJL John LeClair 15.00 40.00
GJAJR Jeremy Roenick 40.00 100.00
GJAJS Jason Spezza 60.00 150.00
GJAMG Marian Gaborik 60.00 125.00
GJAMH Martin Havlat 20.00 50.00
GJAMK Markus Naslund 30.00 80.00
GJAMN Markus Naslund 25.00 60.00
GJAMP Mark Parrish 15.00 40.00
GJAMT Marty Turco 25.00 60.00
GJAPB Pavel Bure 40.00 100.00
GJAPE Michael Peca 15.00 30.00
GJAPH Phil Esposito 25.00 60.00
GJAPR Patrick Roy 150.00 300.00
GJARD Rick DiPietro 25.00 60.00
GJARF Ron Francis 25.00 60.00
GJARL Roberto Luongo 40.00 100.00
GJARN Rick Nash 40.00 100.00
GJASF Sergei Fedorov 30.00 80.00
GJATB Todd Bertuzzi 25.00 60.00
GJATH Joe Thornton 50.00 125.00
GJAWG Wayne Gretzky 300.00 800.00

1999 Wayne Gretzky Living Legend Wearing the Leaf

COMMON GRETZKY (WL1-WL6) 2.00 5.00

2004-05 Upper Deck NHL's Best

NBBL Brian Leetch 6.00 15.00
NBEB Ed Belfour 6.00 15.00
NBJT Jose Theodore 8.00 20.00
NBMB Martin Brodeur 10.00 25.00
NBML Mario Lemieux/50* 30.00 80.00
NBNL Nicklas Lidstrom 6.00 15.00
NBPF Peter Forsberg/75* 15.00 40.00
NBPR Patrick Roy/50* 40.00 100.00
NBRB Rob Blake 6.00 15.00
NBRN Rick Nash 8.00 20.00
NBSG Sergei Gonchar 6.00 15.00
NBSN Scott Niedermayer 6.00 15.00
NBTB Todd Bertuzzi 8.00 15.00
NBWG Wayne Gretzky/25* 150.00 300.00

1999 Wayne Gretzky Living Legend Year of the Great One

COMMON GRETZKY (1-99) 1.50 4.00

2004-05 Upper Deck School of Hard Knocks

COMPLETE SET (7) 8.00 15.00
SHK1 Brendan Shanahan 1.00 2.50
SHK2 Scott Stevens 1.00 2.50
SHK3 Gary Roberts 1.00 2.50
SHK4 Jeremy Roenick 1.50 4.00
SHK5 Zdeno Chara 1.00 2.50
SHK6 Ed Jovanovski 1.00 2.50
SHK7 Todd Bertuzzi 1.00 2.50

2004-05 Upper Deck Swatch of Six

SSAR Andrew Raycroft 8.00 20.00
SSBS Brendan Shanahan 8.00 20.00
SSEB Ed Belfour 8.00 20.00
SSGR Gary Roberts 6.00 15.00
SSJJ Jaromir Jagr/50 15.00 40.00
SSJO Jocelyn Thibault 6.00 15.00
SSJT Jose Theodore 10.00 25.00
SSMM Mark Messier/25 100.00 200.00
SSPD Pavel Datsyuk 8.00 20.00
SSSK Saku Koivu 8.00 20.00
SSSY Steve Yzerman 15.00 40.00
SSTH Joe Thornton 12.50 30.00
SSTR Tuomo Ruutu 8.00 20.00
SSWG Wayne Gretzky/25 150.00 300.00

2004-05 Upper Deck Three Stars

COMPLETE SET (14) 15.00 30.00
AS1 Steve Yzerman 1.50 4.00
AS2 Joe Sakic 1.25 3.00
AS3 Mats Sundin .60 1.50
AS4 Mike Modano .75 2.00
AS5 Jarome Iginla .75 2.00
AS6 Jeremy Roenick .75 2.00
AS7 Martin Brodeur 1.50 4.00
AS8 Vincent Lecavalier .60 1.50
AS9 Markus Naslund .60 1.50
AS10 Jaromir Jagr .75 2.00
AS11 Mario Lemieux 3.00 8.00
AS12 Patrick Roy 1.50 4.00
AS13 Wayne Gretzky 3.00 8.00
AS14 Gordie Howe 1.50 4.00

2004-05 Upper Deck World's Best

COMPLETE SET (30) 12.50 30.00
WB1 Joe Sakic .60 1.50
WB2 Jarome Iginla .40 1.00
WB3 Martin St. Louis .25 .60
WB4 Martin Brodeur 1.25 3.00
WB5 Mario Lemieux 1.50 4.00
WB6 Joe Thornton .50 1.25
WB7 Dany Heatley .40 1.00
WB8 Milan Hejduk .30 .75
WB9 Jaromir Jagr .50 1.25
WB10 Tomas Kaberle .25 .60
WB11 Tomas Vokoun .25 .60
WB12 Saku Koivu .30 .75
WB13 Kari Lehtonen .40 1.00
WB14 Teemu Selanne .30 .75
WB15 Olaf Kolzig .25 .60
WB16 Jochen Hecht .25 .60
WB17 Sergei Gonchar .25 .60
WB18 Ilya Kovalchuk .40 1.00
WB19 Pavel Datsyuk .40 1.00
WB20 Zdeno Chara .25 .60
WB21 Pavel Demitra .25 .60
WB22 Marian Hossa .30 .75
WB23 Marian Gaborik .60 1.50
WB24 Mats Sundin .30 .75
WB25 Peter Forsberg .75 2.00
WB26 Nicklas Lidstrom .30 .75
WB27 Robert Esche .25 .60
WB28 Chris Chelios .30 .75
WB29 Mike Modano .50 1.25
WB30 Keith Tkachuk .30 .75

2004-05 Upper Deck World Cup Tribute

AK Alex Kovalev 4.00 10.00
BB Joe Thornton 10.00 25.00
BG Bill Guerin 3.00 8.00
BH Brett Hull SP 12.00 30.00
BL Brian Leetch 8.00 20.00
BR Brad Richards 3.00 8.00
CC Chris Chelios 4.00 10.00
CD Chris Drury 3.00 8.00
DH Dany Heatley SP 12.00 30.00
HE Milan Hejduk 4.00 10.00
IK Ilya Kovalchuk SP 15.00 40.00
JB Jay Bouwmeester 3.00 8.00
JH Jochen Hecht 3.00 8.00
JI Jarome Iginla 5.00 12.00
JJ Jaromir Jagr 12.00 30.00
JS Joe Sakic 15.00 40.00
MB Martin Brodeur 20.00 50.00
MH Marian Hossa 4.00 10.00
MK Miikka Kiprusoff 10.00 25.00
ML Martin St. Louis 4.00 10.00
MM Mike Modano 8.00 20.00
MS Mats Sundin 4.00 10.00
NL Nicklas Lidstrom 4.00 10.00
OK Olaf Kolzig 3.00 8.00
PD Pavel Datsyuk 5.00 10.00
PE Patrik Elias 3.00 8.00
PF Peter Forsberg SP 15.00 40.00
RD Rick DiPietro 3.00 8.00
RE Robert Esche 3.00 8.00
RL Roberto Luongo 8.00 20.00
SK Saku Koivu SP 10.00 25.00
VL Vincent Lecavalier 5.00 12.00
ZC Zdeno Chara 3.00 8.00
BLBR B.Leetch/B.Ralfalski 8.00 20.00
CCTA C.Chelios/T.Amonte 8.00 20.00
IKAK I.Kovalchuk/A.Kovalev SP 15.00 40.00
JBAF J.Bouwmeester/A.Foote 8.00 20.00
JHOK J.Hecht/O.Kolzig 8.00 20.00
KLMK K.Lehtonen/M.Kiprusoff 12.00 30.00
MBRL M.Brodeur/R.Luongo SP 15.00 40.00
NLMO N.Lidstrom/M.Ohlund 8.00 20.00
RCTV R.Cechmanek/T.Vokoun 8.00 20.00
SNEJ S.Niedermayer/E.Jovanovski 8.00 20.00
WREB W.Redden/E.Brewer 8.00 20.00
ZCMG Z.Chara/M.Gaborik 8.00 20.00
AKAYSS Kovalev/Yashin/Samsonov 20.00 50.00
CCRELDH Chelios/Esche/Leetch 30.00 80.00
DHPMSD Heatley/Marleau/Doan 30.00 80.00
DWMOCD Weight/Modano/Drury 40.00 80.00
EBEJWR Brewer/Jovanoski/Redden 20.00 50.00
JSMLJI Sakic/Lemieux/Iginla 125.00 250.00
KLJPTR Lehtonen/Pitkanen/Ruutu 25.00 60.00
KTDWBH Tkachuk/Weight/Hull 40.00 100.00
MBRLJT Brodeur/Luongo/Theo 125.00 250.00
MGHOMI Gaborik/Hossa/Satan 50.00 125.00
MHSKTV Havlat/Straka/Vokoun 20.00 50.00
MSVLBR St. Louis/Lecav/Richards 75.00 200.00
OJSKTS Jokinen/Koivu/Selanne 50.00 100.00
PBPDZC Bondra/Demitra/Chara 25.00 60.00
PDMAIK Datsyuk/Afinogen/Koval 50.00 100.00
PEJJHE Elias/Jagr/Hejduk 75.00 200.00
PFSLIDA Forsberg/Sundin/Alfred 50.00 100.00
SGTHRS Gagne/Thornton/Smyth 60.00 125.00
TASGBG Amonte/Gomez/Guerin 40.00 80.00
TCRDRE Conklin/DiPietro/Esche 25.00 60.00

2004-05 Upper Deck YoungStars

YSAR Andrew Raycroft 8.00 20.00
YSES Eric Staal 8.00 20.00
YSJC Jonathan Cheechoo 15.00 40.00
YSJL Joffrey Lupul 4.00 10.00
YSMR Michael Ryder 6.00 15.00
YSMS Matt Stajan 5.00 12.00
YSNZ Nikolai Zherdev 6.00 15.00
YSPB Patrice Bergeron 12.50 30.00
YSPS Philippe Sauve 4.00 10.00
YSRT Raffi Torres 4.00 10.00
YSTH Trent Hunter 4.00 10.00
YSTR Tuomo Ruutu 8.00 20.00

2005 Upper Deck Holiday Card

NNO Sidney Crosby 2.50 6.00

2005-06 Upper Deck

COMPLETE SET (487) 400.00 750.00
COMP.SER 1 w/o SP's (200) 12.00 25.00
COMPLETE SERIES 1 (242) 250.00 500.00
COMP.SER 2 w/o SP's (200) 12.00 25.00
COMPLETE SERIES 2 (245) 200.00 400.00
1 Sergei Fedorov .40 1.00
2 Sandis Ozolinsh .15 .40
3 Rob Niedermayer .20 .50
4 Andy McDonald .20 .50
5 Joffrey Lupul .15 .40
6 Jean-Sebastien Giguere .25 .60
7 Ilya Kovalchuk .25 .60
8 Patrik Stefan .15 .40
9 Kari Lehtonen .20 .50
10 Marc Savard .15 .40
11 Andy Sutton .15 .40
12 Niclas Havelid .15 .40
13 Nick Boynton .15 .40
14 Joe Thornton .40 1.00
15 Andrew Raycroft .20 .50
16 P.J. Axelsson .15 .40
17 Patrice Bergeron .30 .75
18 Sergei Samsonov .20 .50
19 Chris Drury .20 .50
20 Derek Roy .15 .40
21 Maxim Afinogenov .15 .40
22 Daniel Briere .25 .60
23 Mika Noronen .20 .50
24 J.P. Dumont .15 .40
25 Jarome Iginla .30 .75

26 Jordan Leopold .15 .40
27 Robyn Regehr .15 .40
28 Marcus Nilson .15 .40
29 Shean Donovan .15 .40
30 Miikka Kiprusoff .25 .60
31 Erik Cole .15 .40
32 Bret Hedican .15 .40
33 Josef Vasicek .15 .40
34 Radim Vrbata .15 .40
35 Niclas Wallin .15 .40
36 Justin Williams .20 .50
37 Mark Bell .15 .40
38 Tuomo Ruutu .25 .60
39 Eric Daze .20 .50
40 Kyle Calder .15 .40
41 Matthew Barnaby .15 .40
42 Tyler Arnason .15 .40
43 Joe Sakic .50 1.25
44 Rob Blake .25 .60
45 Alex Tanguay .25 .60
46 Dan Hinote .15 .40
47 J-M Liles .15 .40
48 Steve Konowalchuk .15 .40
49 David Aebischer .20 .50
50 Riku Hahl .15 .40
51 Rick Nash .25 .60
52 Marc Denis .20 .50
53 Jody Shelley .15 .40
54 David Vyborny .15 .40
55 Manny Malhotra .20 .50
56 Todd Marchant .15 .40
57 Geoff Sanderson .15 .40
58 Bill Guerin .25 .60
59 Brenden Morrow .20 .50
60 Sergei Zubov .20 .50
61 Jaroslav Svoboda .15 .40
62 Steve Ott .15 .40
63 Jason Arnott .20 .50
64 Niko Kapanen .15 .40
65 Stu Barnes .15 .40
66 Steve Yzerman .60 1.50
67 Nicklas Lidstrom .25 .60
68 Robert Lang .15 .40
69 Manny Legace .25 .60
70 Tomas Holmstrom .20 .50
71 Kris Draper .30 .75
72 Jiri Fischer .15 .40
73 Henrik Zetterberg .30 .75
74 Ty Conklin .20 .50
75 Raffi Torres .15 .40
76 Jason Smith .15 .40
77 Radek Dvorak .15 .40
78 Ales Hemsky .20 .50
79 Shawn Horcoff .15 .40
80 Roberto Luongo .40 1.00
81 Mike Van Ryn .15 .40
82 Olli Jokinen .25 .60
83 Jay Bouwmeester .15 .40
84 Nathan Horton .25 .60
85 Niklas Hagman .15 .40
86 Luc Robitaille .25 .60
87 Mathieu Garon .20 .50
88 Lubomir Visnovsky .15 .40
89 Trent Klatt .15 .40
90 Mattias Norstrom .15 .40
91 Dustin Brown .25 .60
92 Dwayne Roloson .20 .50
93 Marian Gaborik .25 .60
94 Pascal Dupuis .15 .40
95 Filip Kuba .15 .40
96 Pierre-Marc Bouchard .25 .60
97 Alexandre Daigle .15 .40
98 Saku Koivu .25 .60
99 Richard Zednik .15 .40
100 Michael Ryder .20 .50
101 Sheldon Souray .15 .40
102 Craig Rivet .15 .40
103 Jan Bulis .15 .40
104 Pierre Dagenais .15 .40
105 Tomas Vokoun .20 .50
106 David Legwand .20 .50
107 Steve Sullivan .15 .40
108 Adam Hall .15 .40
109 Jordin Tootoo .25 .60
110 Denis Arkhipov .15 .40
111 Scott Gomez .20 .50
112 Patrik Elias .25 .60
113 Scott Stevens .25 .60
114 Sergei Brylin .15 .40
115 John Madden .15 .40
116 Jeff Friesen .15 .40
117 Paul Martin .15 .40
118 Alexei Yashin .20 .50
119 Trent Hunter .15 .40
120 Mark Parrish .15 .40
121 Garth Snow .20 .50
122 Jason Blake .15 .40
123 Janne Niinimaa .15 .40
124 Jamie Lundmark .15 .40
125 Tom Poti .15 .40
126 Jaromir Jagr .75 2.00
127 Darius Kasparaitis .15 .40
128 Michael Nylander .15 .40
129 Kevin Weekes .20 .50
130 Daniel Alfredsson .25 .60
131 Dominik Hasek .40 1.00
132 Wade Redden .15 .40
133 Jason Spezza .25 .60
134 Chris Phillips .15 .40
135 Vaclav Varada .15 .40
136 Zdeno Chara .25 .60
137 Simon Gagne .25 .60
138 Joni Pitkanen .15 .40
139 Keith Primeau .20 .50
140 Michal Handzus .20 .50
141 Kim Johnsson .15 .40
142 Sami Kapanen .15 .40
143 Donald Brashear .15 .40
144 Brett Hull .50 1.25
145 Tyson Nash .15 .40
146 Shane Doan .20 .50
147 Derek Morris .15 .40
148 Mike Johnson .15 .40
149 Paul Mara .15 .40
150 Mario Lemieux 1.00 2.50
151 Mark Recchi .30 .75
152 Ryan Malone .15 .40
153 Rico Fata .15 .40
154 Lasse Pirjeta .15 .40
155 Dick Tarnstrom .15 .40
156 Jonathan Cheechoo .20 .50
157 Marco Sturm .15 .40
158 Evgeni Nabokov .20 .50
159 Alyn McCauley .15 .40
160 Kyle McLaren .15 .40
161 Brad Stuart .15 .40
162 Wayne Primeau .15 .40
163 Christian Ehrhoff .15 .40
164 Keith Tkachuk .25 .60
165 Barret Jackman .15 .40
166 Patrick Lalime .20 .50
167 Dallas Drake .15 .40
168 Mark Rycroft .15 .40
169 Christian Backman .15 .40
170 Brad Richards .25 .60
171 Fredrik Modin .15 .40
172 Martin St. Louis .25 .60
173 Ruslan Fedotenko .15 .40
174 Darryl Sydor .15 .40
175 Pavel Kubina .15 .40
176 Tim Taylor .15 .40
177 Mats Sundin .25 .60
178 Matt Stajan .15 .40
179 Bryan McCabe .15 .40
180 Darcy Tucker .20 .50
181 Tomas Kaberle .15 .40
182 Owen Nolan .25 .60
183 Nikolai Antropov .20 .50
184 Ken Klee .15 .40
185 Ed Jovanovski .20 .50
186 Dan Cloutier .20 .50
187 Trevor Linden .25 .60
188 Matt Cooke .15 .40
189 Todd Bertuzzi .25 .60
190 Alex Auld .15 .40
191 Sami Salo .15 .40
192 Mattias Ohlund .15 .40
193 Olaf Kolzig .25 .60
194 Brendan Witt .15 .40
195 Jeff Halpern .15 .40
196 Dainius Zubrus .15 .40
197 Alexander Semin .25 .60
198 Boyd Gordon .15 .40
199 Joe Thornton CL .40 1.00
200 Jarome Iginla CL .30 .75
201 Sidney Crosby YG RC 600.00 1500.00
202 Mike Richards YG RC 5.00 12.00
203 Dion Phaneuf YG RC 4.00 10.00
204 Corey Perry YG RC 12.00 30.00
205 Alexander Steen YG RC 4.00 10.00
206 Zach Parise YG RC 8.00 20.00
207 Rostislav Olesz YG RC 2.00 5.00
208 Matt Foy YG RC 1.50 4.00
209 Brent Seabrook YG RC 6.00 15.00
210 Jeff Hoggan YG RC 1.50 4.00
211 Petteri Nokelainen YG RC 1.50 4.00
212 Andrew Wozniewski YG RC 2.00 5.00
213 Peter Budaj YG RC 3.00 8.00
214 Chris Campoli YG RC 1.50 4.00
215 Jim Howard YG RC 6.00 15.00
216 Henrik Lundqvist YG RC 40.00 100.00
217 David Leneveu YG RC 2.00 5.00
218 George Parros YG RC 1.50 4.00
219 Kevin Dallman YG RC 2.00 5.00
220 Jeff Woywitka YG RC 1.50 4.00
221 Rene Bourque YG RC 2.50 6.00
222 Jim Slater YG RC 2.00 5.00
223 Niklas Nordgren YG RC 2.50 6.00
224 Jay McClement YG RC 1.50 4.00
225 Andrew Alberts YG RC 1.50 4.00
226 A.Perezhogin YG RC 2.00 5.00
227 Yann Danis YG RC 2.00 5.00
228 Andrej Meszaros YG RC 2.00 5.00
229 Cam Ward YG RC 6.00 15.00
230 Duncan Keith YG RC 20.00 50.00
231 Timo Helbling YG RC 1.50 4.00
232 Keith Ballard YG RC 2.00 5.00
233 Braydon Coburn YG RC 2.50 6.00
234 Ryane Clowe YG RC 3.00 8.00
235 Ryan Hollweg YG RC 1.50 4.00
236 Maxime Talbot YG RC 2.50 6.00
237 Brett Lebda YG RC 1.50 4.00
238 Brandon Bochenski YG RC 2.50 6.00
239 Jaroslav Balastik YG RC 1.50 4.00
240 Wojtek Wolski YG RC 2.00 5.00
241 Hannu Toivonen YG RC 2.50 6.00
242 S.Crosby/C.Perry YG CL 12.00 30.00
243 Teemu Selanne .50 1.25
244 Scott Niedermayer .25 .60
245 Ilya Bryzgalov .25 .60
246 Todd Fedoruk .15 .40
247 Chris Kunitz .25 .60
248 Petr Sykora .20 .50
249 Keith Carney .15 .40
250 Marian Hossa .25 .60
251 Peter Bondra .25 .60
252 Bobby Holik .15 .40
253 Mike Dunham .15 .40
254 Vyacheslav Kozlov .15 .40
255 Steve Shields .15 .40
256 Glen Murray .20 .50
257 Brian Leetch .20 .50
258 Brad Boyes .20 .50
259 Jiri Slegr .15 .40
260 Travis Green .15 .40
261 Hal Gill .15 .40
262 Marco Sturm .15 .40
263 Brad Stuart .15 .40
264 Ryan Miller .25 .60
265 Teppo Numminen .15 .40
266 Jochen Hecht .15 .40
267 Martin Biron .20 .50
268 Paul Gaustad .15 .40
269 Ales Kotalik .15 .40
270 Tim Connolly .15 .40
271 Mike Grier .15 .40
272 Tony Amonte .20 .50
273 Philippe Sauve .20 .50
274 Daymond Langkow .15 .40
275 Chuck Kobasew .15 .40
276 Chris Simon .15 .40
277 Matthew Lombardi .15 .40
278 Roman Hamrlik .15 .40
279 Stephane Yelle .15 .40
280 Eric Staal .30 .75
281 Rod Brind'Amour .25 .60
282 Cory Stillman .20 .50
283 Martin Gerber .20 .50
284 Glen Wesley .15 .40
285 Oleg Tverdovsky .15 .40
286 Nikolai Khabibulin .25 .60
287 Pavel Vorobiev .15 .40
288 Martin Lapointe .15 .40
289 Adrian Aucoin .15 .40
290 Matt Ellison .15 .40
291 Jaroslav Spacek .15 .40
292 Milan Hejduk .20 .50
293 Pierre Turgeon .20 .50
294 Ian Laperriere .15 .40
295 Marek Svatos .20 .50
296 Patrice Brisebois .15 .40
297 Antti Laaksonen .15 .40
298 Nikolai Zherdev .15 .40
299 Bryan Berard .15 .40
300 Pascal Leclaire .20 .50
301 Adam Foote .15 .40
302 Sergei Fedorov .40 1.00
303 Trevor Letowski .15 .40
304 Dan Fritsche .15 .40
305 Mike Modano .40 1.00
306 Marty Turco .25 .60
307 Jere Lehtinen .20 .50
308 Johan Hedberg .20 .50
309 Philippe Boucher .15 .40
310 Antti Miettinen .15 .40
311 Trevor Daley .15 .40
312 Brendan Shanahan .25 .60
313 Chris Osgood .25 .60
314 Pavel Datsyuk .40 1.00
315 Chris Chelios .25 .60
316 Jason Williams .15 .40
317 Mikael Samuelsson .15 .40
318 Mathieu Schneider .15 .40
319 Ryan Smyth .20 .50
320 Chris Pronger .25 .60
321 Jussi Markkanen .15 .40
322 Georges Laraque .20 .50
323 Michael Peca .20 .50
324 Marc-Andre Bergeron .15 .40
325 Jarret Stoll .20 .50
326 Jani Rita .15 .40
327 Stephen Weiss .15 .40
328 Joe Nieuwendyk .20 .50
329 Gary Roberts .15 .40
330 Martin Gelinas .15 .40
331 Chris Gratton .15 .40
332 Juraj Kolnik .15 .40
333 Lukas Krajicek .15 .40
334 Jeremy Roenick .40 1.00
335 Alexander Frolov .15 .40
336 Pavol Demitra .30 .75
337 Craig Conroy .15 .40
338 Jason LaBarbera .20 .50
339 Mike Cammalleri .25 .60
340 Tim Gleason .15 .40
341 Manny Fernandez .15 .40
342 Marc Chouinard .15 .40
343 Brian Rolston .20 .50
344 Todd White .15 .40
345 Nick Schultz .15 .40
346 Brent Burns .25 .60
347 Jose Theodore .25 .60
348 Mike Ribeiro .15 .40
349 Steve Begin .15 .40
350 Alex Kovalev .20 .50
351 Tomas Plekanec .15 .40
352 Andrei Markov .25 .60
353 Radek Bonk .15 .40
354 Chris Higgins .15 .40
355 Paul Kariya .25 .60
356 Yanic Perreault .15 .40
357 Scott Hartnell .15 .40
358 Kimmo Timonen .15 .40
359 Scott Walker .15 .40
360 Dan Hamhuis .20 .50
361 Martin Erat .15 .40
362 Martin Brodeur .60 1.50
363 David Hale .15 .40
364 Brian Gionta .15 .40
365 Viktor Kozlov .15 .40
366 Scott Clemmensen .15 .40
367 Jamie Langenbrunner .15 .40
368 Brian Rafalski .20 .50
369 Miroslav Satan .20 .50
370 Rick DiPietro .20 .50
371 Alexei Zhitnik .15 .40
372 Mike York .15 .40
373 Brent Sopel .15 .40
374 Martin Rucinsky .15 .40
375 Martin Straka .15 .40
376 Steve Rucchin .15 .40
377 Marcel Hossa .15 .40
378 Fedor Tyutin .15 .40
379 Dominic Moore .15 .40
380 Dany Heatley .20 .50
381 Martin Havlat .25 .60
382 Peter Schaefer .15 .40
383 Bryan Smolinski .15 .40
384 Antoine Vermette .20 .50
385 Anton Volchenkov .15 .40
386 Peter Forsberg .50 1.25
387 Robert Esche .20 .50
388 Mike Rathje .15 .40
389 Eric Desjardins .20 .50
390 Patrick Sharp .25 .60
391 Mike Knuble .15 .40
392 Curtis Joseph .30 .75
393 Ladislav Nagy .15 .40
394 Geoff Sanderson .15 .40
395 Mike Comrie .20 .50
396 Oleg Saprykin .15 .40
397 Petr Nedved .15 .40
398 Zigmund Palffy .25 .60
399 John LeClair .25 .60
400 Marc-Andre Fleury .50 1.25
401 Sergei Gonchar .15 .40
402 Jocelyn Thibault .20 .50
403 Sebastien Caron .15 .40
404 Patrick Marleau .25 .60
405 Vesa Toskala .20 .50
406 Marcel Goc .20 .50
407 Joe Thornton .40 1.00
408 Milan Michalek .15 .40
409 Niko Dimotrakos .15 .40
410 Doug Weight .25 .60
411 Petr Cajanek .15 .40
412 Reinhard Divis .15 .40
413 Jamal Mayers .15 .40
414 Scott Young .15 .40
415 Eric Brewer .15 .40
416 Vincent Lecavalier .25 .60
417 Sean Burke .15 .40
418 Vaclav Prospal .15 .40
419 Dave Andreychuk .25 .60
420 Cory Sarich .15 .40
421 John Grahame .15 .40
422 Ed Belfour .25 .60
423 Jason Allison .20 .50
424 Jeff O'Neill .15 .40
425 Eric Lindros .40 1.00
426 Tie Domi .20 .50
427 Kyle Wellwood .20 .50
428 Mikael Tellqvist .20 .50
429 Markus Naslund .25 .60
430 Henrik Sedin .30 .75
431 Daniel Sedin .30 .75
432 Ryan Kesler .25 .60
433 Brendan Morrison .15 .40
434 Anson Carter .20 .50
435 Jeff Friesen .15 .40
436 Steve Eminger .15 .40
437 Jamie Heward .15 .40
438 Mike Green RC 3.00 8.00
439 Andrew Cassels .15 .40
440 Shaone Morrisonn .15 .40
441 Peter Forsberg CL .50 1.25
442 Dany Heatley CL .20 .50
443 Alexander Ovechkin YG RC 600.00 1500.00
444 Jeff Carter YG RC 6.00 15.00
445 Cam Barker YG RC 2.00 5.00
446 Gilbert Brule YG RC 2.50 6.00
447 Brad Winchester YG RC 2.50 6.00
448 Eric Nystrom YG RC 2.00 5.00
449 R.J. Umberger YG RC 2.50 6.00
450 Mikko Koivu YG RC 3.00 8.00
451 Robert Nilsson YG RC 2.50 6.00
452 Ryan Getzlaf YG RC 8.00 20.00
453 Anthony Stewart YG RC 2.00 5.00
454 Ryan Suter YG RC 3.00 8.00
455 Al Montoya YG RC 2.50 6.00
456 Johan Franzen YG RC 4.00 10.00
457 Thomas Vanek YG RC 5.00 12.00
458 Patrick Eaves YG RC 2.50 6.00
459 Jussi Jokinen YG RC 2.50 6.00
460 Christoph Schubert YG RC 1.50 4.00
461 Ryan Whitney YG RC 2.50 6.00
462 Evgeny Artyukhin YG RC 2.00 5.00
463 Jordan Sigalet YG RC 1.50 4.00
464 Milan Jurcina YG RC 2.00 5.00
465 Dimitri Patzold YG RC 1.50 4.00
466 Staffan Kronwall YG RC 1.50 4.00
467 Erik Christensen YG RC 1.50 4.00
468 Kyle Brodziak YG RC 1.50 4.00
469 Ryan Craig YG RC 1.50 4.00
470 Steve Bernier YG RC 2.50 6.00
471 Matt Greene YG RC 1.50 4.00
472 Barry Tallackson YG RC 2.00 5.00
473 Jakub Klepis YG RC 1.50 4.00
474 Maxim Lapierre YG RC 2.50 6.00
475 Danny Richmond YG RC 1.50 4.00
476 Tomas Fleischmann YG RC 2.50 6.00
477 Adam Berkhoel YG RC 2.00 5.00
478 Kevin Bieksa YG RC 4.00 10.00
479 Greg Jacina YG RC 1.50 4.00
480 Gerald Coleman YG RC 1.50 4.00
481 Jeremy Colliton YG RC 1.50 4.00
482 Andrei Kostitsyn YG RC 3.00 8.00
483 Valtteri Filppula YG RC 3.00 8.00
484 Dennis Wideman YG RC 1.50 4.00
485 Brad Richardson YG RC 2.50 6.00
486 Jeff Tambellini YG RC 1.50 4.00
487 A.Ovechkin/J.Carter CL 10.00 25.00

2005-06 Upper Deck All-Time Greatest

COMPLETE SET (90) 20.00 50.00
1 Jean-Sebastien Giguere .40 1.00
2 Paul Kariya .40 1.00
3 Ilya Kovalchuk .40 1.00
4 Dany Heatley .30 .75
5 Joe Thornton .60 1.50
6 Cam Neely .40 1.00
7 Dominik Hasek .60 1.50
8 Gilbert Perreault .40 1.00
9 Jarome Iginla .50 1.25
10 Lanny McDonald .40 1.00
11 Rod Brind'Amour .40 1.00
12 Gary Roberts .25 .60
13 Tony Esposito .40 1.00
14 Stan Mikita .50 1.25
15 Joe Sakic .75 2.00
16 Patrick Roy 1.00 2.50
17 Rick Nash .40 1.00
18 Marc Denis .30 .75
19 Mike Modano .60 1.50
20 Ed Belfour .40 1.00
21 Gordie Howe 1.25 3.00
22 Steve Yzerman 1.00 2.50
23 Wayne Gretzky 2.50 6.00
24 Jari Kurri .40 1.00
25 Roberto Luongo .60 1.50
26 Olli Jokinen .40 1.00
27 Wayne Gretzky 2.50 6.00
28 Luc Robitaille .40 1.00
29 Marian Gaborik .40 1.00
30 Dwayne Roloson .30 .75
31 Patrick Roy 1.00 2.50
32 Jose Theodore .40 1.00
33 Steve Sullivan .25 .60
34 Tomas Vokoun .30 .75
35 Martin Brodeur 1.00 2.50
36 Patrik Elias .40 1.00
37 Mike Bossy .40 1.00
38 Alexei Yashin .30 .75
39 Jaromir Jagr 1.25 3.00
40 Brian Leetch .30 .75
41 Daniel Alfredsson .40 1.00
42 Jason Spezza .40 1.00
43 Keith Tkachuk .40 1.00
44 Shane Doan .30 .75
45 Bobby Clarke .60 1.50
46 Ron Hextall .40 1.00
47 Mario Lemieux 1.50 4.00
48 Jaromir Jagr 1.25 3.00
49 Doug Weight .40 1.00
50 Chris Pronger .40 1.00
51 Patrick Marleau .40 1.00
52 Evgeni Nabokov .30 .75
53 Martin St. Louis .40 1.00
54 Vincent Lecavalier .40 1.00
55 Mats Sundin .40 1.00
56 Darryl Sittler .50 1.25
57 Markus Naslund .40 1.00
58 Trevor Linden .40 1.00
59 Olaf Kolzig .40 1.00
60 Peter Bondra .40 1.00
61 Dany Heatley .30 .75
62 Ray Bourque .60 1.50
63 Andrew Raycroft .30 .75
64 Gilbert Perreault .40 1.00
65 Jarome Iginla .50 1.25
66 Tony Esposito .40 1.00
67 Ed Belfour .40 1.00
68 Rick Nash .40 1.00
69 Paul Kariya .40 1.00
70 Gordie Howe 1.25 3.00
71 Steve Yzerman 1.00 2.50
72 Sergei Fedorov .60 1.50
73 Wayne Gretzky 2.50 6.00
74 Luc Robitaille .40 1.00
75 Mike Modano .60 1.50
76 Guy Lafleur .50 1.25
77 Patrick Roy 1.00 2.50
78 Martin Brodeur 1.00 2.50
79 Mike Bossy .40 1.00
80 Brian Leetch .30 .75
81 Daniel Alfredsson .40 1.00
82 Ron Hextall .40 1.00
83 Eric Lindros .60 1.50
84 Sidney Crosby 2.50 6.00
85 Mario Lemieux 1.50 4.00
86 Joe Sakic .75 2.00
87 Peter Forsberg .75 2.00
88 Peter Stastny .30 .75
89 Evgeni Nabokov .30 .75
90 Teemu Selanne .75 2.00

2005-06 Upper Deck Big Playmakers Jerseys

BBMO Bryan McCabe 6.00 15.00
BDAE David Aebischer 8.00 20.00
BDHA Dominik Hasek 15.00 40.00
BDHE Dany Heatley 8.00 20.00
BMBI Mike Bossy 10.00 25.00
BROB Rob Blake 10.00 25.00
BMRE Mark Recchi 12.00 30.00
BMRI Mike Ribeiro 6.00 15.00
BBMC Brendan Morrison 6.00 15.00
BDAR Denis Arkhipov 6.00 15.00
BJEL Jamie Lundmark 6.00 15.00
BJLU Jere Lehtinen 8.00 20.00
BJOL Jordan Leopold 6.00 15.00
BMBO Martin Biron 8.00 20.00
BMDU Mike Dunham 6.00 15.00
BRNI Rob Niedermayer 8.00 20.00
BSST Scott Stevens 10.00 25.00
BMST Martin St. Louis 10.00 25.00
BMAH Marcel Hossa 6.00 15.00
BSSA Sergei Samsonov 8.00 20.00
BMDE Marc Denis 8.00 20.00
BMHA Martin Havlat 10.00 25.00
BJBL Jay Bouwmeester 6.00 15.00
BJBO Jason Blake 6.00 15.00
BMPA Michael Peca 8.00 20.00
BMPE Mark Parrish 6.00 15.00
BMHO Marian Hossa 10.00 25.00
BMSU Mats Sundin 10.00 25.00
BMME Mark Messier 20.00 50.00
BMRY Michael Ryder 8.00 20.00
BPBO Peter Bondra 10.00 25.00
BAC Anson Carter 8.00 20.00
BAF Alexander Frolov 6.00 15.00
BAH Adam Hall 6.00 15.00
BAM Al MacInnis 12.00 30.00
BAT Alexander Mogilny 8.00 20.00
BAT Alex Tanguay 10.00 25.00
BAY Alexei Yashin 8.00 20.00
BBC Bobby Clarke 15.00 40.00
BBG Bill Guerin 10.00 25.00
BBH Brett Hull 20.00 50.00
BBJ Barret Jackman 6.00 15.00
BBS Brendan Shanahan 10.00 25.00
BCC Chris Chelios 10.00 25.00
BCD Chris Drury 8.00 20.00
BCJ Curtis Joseph 12.00 30.00
BCN Cam Neely 10.00 25.00
BCP Chris Pronger 10.00 25.00
BCS Chris Simon 6.00 15.00
BDB Daniel Briere 10.00 25.00
BDC Dan Cloutier 8.00 20.00
BDL David Legwand 8.00 20.00
BDW Doug Weight 10.00 25.00
BEB Ed Belfour 10.00 25.00
BED Eric Daze 8.00 20.00
BEJ Ed Jovanovski 8.00 20.00
BEL Eric Lindros 15.00 40.00
BES Eric Staal 12.00 30.00
BGM Glen Murray 8.00 20.00
BGO Scott Gomez 8.00 20.00
BGS Geoff Sanderson 6.00 15.00
BHJ Milan Hejduk 8.00 20.00
BIK Ilya Kovalchuk 10.00 25.00
BJA Jason Allison 8.00 20.00
BJC Jonathan Cheechoo 8.00 20.00
BJG Jean-Sebastien Giguere 10.00 25.00
BJI Jarome Iginla 12.00 30.00
BJJ Jaromir Jagr 30.00 80.00
BJK Jari Kurri 10.00 25.00
BJL John LeClair 10.00 25.00
BJN Joe Nieuwendyk 8.00 20.00
BJO Jose Theodore 10.00 25.00
BJP Joni Pitkanen 6.00 15.00
BJR Jeremy Roenick 15.00 40.00
BJS Jason Smith 6.00 15.00
BJT Joe Thornton 15.00 40.00
BJW Justin Williams 8.00 20.00
BKP Keith Primeau 8.00 20.00
BKT Keith Tkachuk 10.00 25.00
BLR Luc Robitaille 10.00 25.00
BMA Maxim Afinogenov 6.00 15.00
BMB Martin Brodeur 25.00 60.00
BMF Manny Fernandez 6.00 15.00
BMG Marian Gaborik 10.00 25.00
BML Mario Lemieux 40.00 100.00
BMM Mike Modano 15.00 40.00
BMN Markus Naslund 10.00 25.00
BMO Mattias Ohlund 6.00 15.00
BMS Martin Straka 6.00 15.00
BMT Marty Turco 10.00 25.00
BNA Nik Antropov 8.00 20.00
BNK Nikolai Khabibulin 10.00 25.00
BNL Nicklas Lidstrom 10.00 25.00
BOJ Olli Jokinen 10.00 25.00
BOK Olaf Kolzig 10.00 25.00
BON Owen Nolan 10.00 25.00
BPB Patrice Bergeron 12.00 30.00
BPD Pavel Datsyuk 15.00 40.00
BPE Patrik Elias 10.00 25.00
BPF Peter Forsberg 20.00 50.00
BPK Paul Kariya 10.00 25.00
BPL Patrick Lalime 8.00 20.00
BPM Patrick Marleau 10.00 25.00
BPR Patrick Roy 25.00 60.00
BRB Ray Bourque 15.00 40.00
BRF Ruslan Fedotenko 6.00 15.00
BRH Ron Hextall 10.00 25.00
BRK Rostislav Klesla 6.00 15.00
BRL Roberto Luongo 15.00 40.00
BRN Rick Nash 10.00 25.00
BRS Ryan Smyth 8.00 20.00
BSB Sean Burke 6.00 15.00
BSD Shane Doan 8.00 20.00
BSF Sergei Fedorov 15.00 40.00
BSG Simon Gagne 10.00 25.00
BSH Scott Hartnell 6.00 15.00
BSK Saku Koivu 10.00 25.00
BSO Sandis Ozolinsh 6.00 15.00
BSP Jason Spezza 10.00 25.00
BSY Steve Yzerman 25.00 60.00
BSZ Sergei Zubov 8.00 20.00
BTA Tony Amonte 8.00 20.00
BTB Todd Bertuzzi 10.00 25.00
BTC Ty Conklin 8.00 20.00
BTH Trent Hunter 6.00 15.00
BTP Tom Poti 6.00 15.00
BTR Tuomo Ruutu 10.00 25.00
BTV Tomas Vokoun 8.00 20.00
BVD Vincent Damphousse 8.00 20.00
BVL Vincent Lecavalier 10.00 25.00
BVN Ville Nieminen 6.00 15.00
BWG Wayne Gretzky 60.00 150.00
BZC Zdeno Chara 10.00 25.00

2005-06 Upper Deck Destined for the Hall

COMPLETE SET (7) 12.00 25.00
DH1 Steve Yzerman 4.00 10.00
DH2 Martin Brodeur 4.00 10.00
DH3 Joe Sakic 3.00 8.00
DH4 Dominik Hasek 2.50 6.00
DH5 Jaromir Jagr 5.00 12.00
DH6 Mario Lemieux 6.00 15.00
DH7 Brendan Shanahan 1.50 4.00

2005-06 Upper Deck Diary of a Phenom

COMPLETE SET (30) 15.00 40.00
COMMON CROSBY (DP1-DP30) .50 1.25

2005-06 Upper Deck Goal Celebrations

COMPLETE SET (7) 8.00 20.00
GC1 Ilya Kovalchuk 1.50 4.00
GC2 Dany Heatley 1.25 3.00
GC3 Jaromir Jagr 5.00 12.00
GC4 Jarome Iginla 2.00 5.00
GC5 Martin St. Louis 1.50 4.00
GC6 Rick Nash 1.50 4.00
GC7 Mats Sundin 1.50 4.00

2005-06 Upper Deck Goal Rush

COMPLETE SET (14) 10.00 20.00
GR1 Rick Nash .75 2.00
GR2 Martin St. Louis .75 2.00
GR3 Milan Hejduk .60 1.50
GR4 Steve Yzerman 2.00 5.00
GR5 Joe Sakic 1.50 4.00
GR6 Wayne Gretzky 5.00 12.00
GR7 Mario Lemieux 3.00 8.00
GR8 Ilya Kovalchuk .75 2.00
GR9 Patrice Bergeron 1.00 2.50
GR10 Markus Naslund .75 2.00
GR11 Marian Hossa .75 2.00
GR12 Mike Modano 1.25 3.00
GR13 Jarome Iginla 1.00 2.50
GR14 Dany Heatley .60 1.50

2005-06 Upper Deck Hometown Heroes

COMPLETE SET (28) 20.00 40.00
HH1 Joe Sakic 1.50 4.00
HH2 Martin Brodeur 2.00 5.00
HH3 Joe Thornton 1.25 3.00
HH4 Jarome Iginla 1.00 2.50
HH5 Mats Sundin .75 2.00
HH6 Steve Yzerman 2.00 5.00
HH7 Saku Koivu .75 2.00
HH8 Jaromir Jagr 2.50 6.00
HH9 Ilya Kovalchuk .75 2.00
HH10 Mike Modano 1.25 3.00
HH11 Martin St. Louis .75 2.00
HH12 Mark Messier 1.50 4.00
HH13 Mario Lemieux 3.00 8.00
HH14 Keith Tkachuk .75 2.00
HH15 Daniel Alfredsson .75 2.00
HH16 Evgeni Nabokov .60 1.50
HH17 Jaromir Jagr 2.50 6.00
HH18 Rick Nash .75 2.00
HH19 Peter Forsberg 1.50 4.00
HH20 Paul Kariya .75 2.00
HH21 Jean-Sebastien Giguere .75 2.00
HH22 Nikolai Khabibulin .75 2.00
HH23 Alexei Yashin .60 1.50
HH24 Shane Doan .60 1.50
HH25 Markus Naslund .75 2.00
HH26 Dany Heatley .60 1.50
HH27 Eric Lindros 1.25 3.00
HH28 Olaf Kolzig .75 2.00

2005-06 Upper Deck Jerseys

JBGE Bernie Geoffrion SP 50.00 120.00
JBHU Brett Hull 6.00 15.00
JDSA Denis Savard SP 15.00 40.00
JRHX Ron Hextall SP 15.00 40.00
JRLU Roberto Luongo 5.00 12.00
JGUL Georges Laraque 2.50 6.00
JHSE Henrik Sedin 4.00 10.00
JJAB Jay Bouwmeester 2.00 5.00
JJAR Jason Arnott 2.50 6.00
JJOL Joffrey Lupul 2.00 5.00
JMAH Marcel Hossa 2.00 5.00
JMCA Mike Cammalleri 3.00 8.00
JMGR Mike Grier 2.00 5.00
JMLO Matthew Lombardi 2.00 5.00
JMNI Marcus Nilson 2.00 5.00
JMPA Mark Parrish 2.00 5.00
JMPE Michael Peca 2.50 6.00
JMST Matt Stajan 2.00 5.00
JNIB Nick Boynton 2.00 5.00
JPAS Patrik Stefan 2.00 5.00
JPSY Petr Sykora 2.50 6.00
JMRY Michael Ryder 2.50 6.00
JTRU Tuomo Ruutu 3.00 8.00
JRBK Radek Bonk 2.00 5.00
JRIH Riku Hahl 2.00 5.00
JSGO Scott Gomez 2.50 6.00
JSKA Sami Kapanen 2.00 5.00
JSKO Steve Konowalchuk 2.00 5.00
JSOT Steve Ott 2.00 5.00
JSOZ Sandis Ozolinsh 2.00 5.00
JSTR Steven Reinprecht 2.00 5.00
JBHO Bobby Holik 2.00 5.00
JBMC Bryan McCabe 2.00 5.00
JDAR Denis Arkhipov 2.00 5.00
JDBR Donald Brashear 2.00 5.00
JDSE Daniel Sedin 4.00 10.00
JAHE Ales Hemsky 2.50 6.00
JDAE David Aebischer 2.50 6.00
JJLE Jere Lehtinen 2.50 6.00
JMAD Marc Denis 2.50 6.00
JMBI Martin Biron 2.50 6.00
JMCO Mike Comrie 2.50 6.00
JMGA Mathieu Garon 2.50 6.00
JPDE Pavol Demitra 4.00 10.00
JSSA Sergei Samsonov 2.50 6.00
JSST Scott Stevens 3.00 8.00
JTDO Tie Domi 2.50 6.00
JMHE Milan Hejduk 2.50 6.00
JSGA Simon Gagne 3.00 8.00
JTSE Teemu Selanne 6.00 15.00
JAA Adrian Aucoin 2.00 5.00
JAF Adam Foote 2.00 5.00
JAK Alexei Kovalev 2.50 6.00
JAM Alexander Mogilny 2.50 6.00
JAY Alexei Yashin 2.50 6.00
JBC Bobby Clarke SP 20.00 60.00
JBG Bill Guerin SP 8.00 20.00
JBL Rob Blake 3.00 8.00
JBM Brendan Morrison 2.00 5.00
JBR Dustin Brown 3.00 8.00
JBT Bryan Trottier 3.00 8.00
JBW Brendan Witt 2.00 5.00
JCC Chris Chelios SP 15.00 40.00
JCD Chris Drury 2.50 6.00
JCJ Curtis Joseph 4.00 10.00
JCK Chuck Kobasew 2.00 5.00
JCO Chris Osgood 3.00 8.00
JCP Chris Pronger 3.00 8.00
JDB Daniel Briere 3.00 8.00
JDH Dany Heatley 2.50 6.00
JDL David Legwand 2.50 6.00
JDO Dominik Hasek 5.00 12.00
JDW Doug Weight 3.00 8.00
JEB Ed Belfour 3.00 8.00
JEJ Ed Jovanovski 2.50 6.00
JEL Eric Lindros 5.00 12.00
JGF Grant Fuhr SP 15.00 40.00
JGL Guy Lafleur SP 30.00 80.00
JGM Glen Murray 2.50 6.00
JGR Gary Roberts 2.00 5.00
JHA Dan Hamhuis 2.50 6.00
JJF Jeff Friesen 2.00 5.00
JJG Jean-Sebastien Giguere 3.00 8.00
JJH Jani Hurme 2.50 6.00
JJI Jarome Iginla 4.00 10.00
JJO Jose Theodore 3.00 8.00
JJP Joni Pitkanen SP 2.00 5.00
JJR Jeremy Roenick 5.00 12.00
JJS Joe Sakic SP 10.00 25.00
JJS Jason Smith 2.00 5.00
JJT Joe Thornton 5.00 12.00
JJW Justin Williams 2.50 6.00
JKD Kris Draper 4.00 10.00
JKL Kari Lehtonen SP 8.00 20.00
JKP Keith Primeau 2.50 6.00
JKT Keith Tkachuk 3.00 8.00
JLR Luc Robitaille 3.00 8.00
JMA Maxim Afinogenov 2.00 5.00
JMB Martin Brodeur 8.00 20.00
JMD Mike Dunham 2.00 5.00
JMK Miikka Kiprusoff 3.00 8.00
JML Mario Lemieux SP 15.00 40.00
JMM Mike Modano 5.00 12.00
JMO Mattias Ohlund 2.00 5.00
JMR Mark Recchi 4.00 10.00
JMS Mats Sundin 3.00 8.00
JNA Nik Antropov 2.50 6.00
JNH Nathan Horton 3.00 8.00
JNK Nikolai Khabibulin 3.00 8.00
JNS Nathan Smith 2.00 5.00
JOJ Olli Jokinen 3.00 8.00
JOK Olaf Kolzig 3.00 8.00
JON Owen Nolan 3.00 8.00
JPD Pavel Datsyuk 5.00 12.00
JPF Peter Forsberg 6.00 15.00
JPK Paul Kariya SP 3.00 8.00
JPR Patrick Roy 8.00 20.00
JPT Pierre Turgeon 2.50 6.00
JRB Ray Bourque SP 8.00 20.00
JRE Robert Esche 2.50 6.00
JRM Ryan Miller 3.00 8.00
JRN Rob Niedermayer 2.50 6.00
JRT Raffi Torres 2.00 5.00
JSC Stanislav Chistov 2.00 5.00

JSF Sergei Fedorov 5.00 12.00
JSH Scott Hartnell 2.00 5.00
JSK Saku Koivu 3.00 8.00
JSM Scott Mellanby 2.00 5.00
JSP Jason Spezza 3.00 8.00
JSU Scottie Upshall 2.00 5.00
JSY Steve Yzerman 8.00 20.00
JSZ Sergei Zubov 2.50 6.00
JTA Tony Amonte 2.50 6.00
JTC Ty Conklin 2.50 6.00
JTO Jordin Tootoo 3.00 8.00
JTP Tom Poti 2.00 5.00
JVB Valeri Bure 2.00 5.00
JVK Viktor Kozlov 2.00 5.00
JVL Vincent Lecavalier 3.00 8.00
JVN Ville Nieminen 2.00 5.00
JWG Wayne Gretzky SP 30.00 80.00

2005-06 Upper Deck Jerseys Series II

J2AA Alex Auld 4.00 10.00
J2AC Anson Carter 5.00 12.00
J2AF Alexander Frolov 4.00 10.00
J2AK Alex Kovalev 5.00 12.00
J2AR Andrew Raycroft 5.00 12.00
J2AT Alex Tanguay 6.00 15.00
J2BG Bill Guerin 6.00 15.00
J2BI Martin Biron 5.00 12.00
J2BJ Barrett Jackman 4.00 10.00
J2BL Brian Leetch 5.00 12.00
J2BM Brendan Morrison 4.00 10.00
J2BR Brad Richards 6.00 15.00
J2BS Brendan Shanahan 6.00 15.00
J2CK Matt Cooke 4.00 10.00
J2CM Mike Comrie 5.00 12.00
J2CO Chris Osgood 6.00 15.00
J2CP Chris Pronger 6.00 15.00
J2CS Cory Stillman 5.00 12.00
J2CY Tim Connolly 4.00 10.00
J2DA Daniel Alfredsson 6.00 15.00
J2DC Dan Cloutier 5.00 12.00
J2DM Dominic Moore 4.00 10.00
J2DW Doug Weight 6.00 15.00
J2DY Trevor Daley 4.00 10.00
J2EB Ed Belfour 6.00 15.00
J2EJ Ed Jovanovski 5.00 12.00
J2EL Eric Lindros 10.00 25.00
J2ES Eric Staal 8.00 20.00
J2FT Fedor Tyutin 4.00 10.00
J2GA Simon Gagne 6.00 15.00
J2GE Martin Gerber 5.00 12.00
J2GI Brian Gionta 4.00 10.00
J2GM Glen Murray 5.00 12.00
J2GO Scott Gomez 5.00 12.00
J2HJ Milan Hejduk 5.00 12.00
J2HO Marcel Hossa 4.00 10.00
J2HZ Michal Handzus 5.00 12.00
J2HZ Henrik Zetterberg 8.00 20.00
J2IK Ilya Kovalchuk 6.00 15.00
J2JA Jason Allison 5.00 12.00
J2JB Jay Bouwmeester 4.00 10.00
J2JC Jonathan Cheechoo 8.00 20.00
J2JE Jere Lehtinen 5.00 12.00
J2JG Jean-Sebastien Giguere 6.00 15.00
J2JH Jeff Halpern 4.00 10.00
J2JI Jarome Iginla 8.00 20.00
J2JJ Jaromir Jagr 12.00 30.00
J2JO Jose Theodore 6.00 15.00
J2JP Joni Pitkanen 4.00 10.00
J2JR Jeremy Roenick 10.00 25.00
J2JS Joe Sakic 12.00 30.00
J2JU Justin Williams 5.00 12.00
J2JW Jason Williams 4.00 10.00
J2KC Kyle Calder 4.00 10.00
J2KD Kris Draper 8.00 20.00
J2KL Kari Lehtonen 5.00 12.00
J2KP Keith Primeau 5.00 12.00
J2LE Jordan Leopold 4.00 10.00
J2LO Matthew Lombardi 4.00 10.00
J2LR Luc Robitaille 6.00 15.00
J2LU Joffrey Lupul 4.00 10.00
J2LX Mario Lemieux SP 75.00 150.00
J2MA Maxim Afinogenov 4.00 10.00
J2MB Martin Brodeur 12.00 30.00
J2MC Bryan McCabe 4.00 10.00
J2MG Marian Gaborik 6.00 15.00
J2MH Martin Havlat 6.00 15.00
J2MK Miikka Kiprusoff 6.00 15.00
J2ML Manny Legace 6.00 15.00
J2MM Mike Modano 10.00 25.00
J2MN Markus Naslund 6.00 15.00
J2MO Mattias Ohlund 4.00 10.00
J2MP Michael Peca 5.00 12.00
J2MR Mike Ribeiro 4.00 10.00
J2MS Miroslav Satan 5.00 12.00
J2MT Marty Turco 6.00 15.00
J2MW Brenden Morrow 5.00 12.00
J2NA Nik Antropov 5.00 12.00
J2NB Nick Boynton 4.00 10.00
J2NI Rob Niedermayer 5.00 12.00
J2NK Nikolai Khabibulin SP 40.00 80.00
J2NL Nicklas Lidstrom 6.00 15.00
J2NO Mika Noronen 5.00 12.00
J2NZ Nikolai Zherdev 4.00 10.00
J2OK Olaf Kolzig 6.00 15.00
J2ON Jeff O'Neill 4.00 10.00
J2PA Mark Parrish 4.00 10.00
J2PB Peter Bondra 6.00 15.00
J2PE Patrik Elias 6.00 15.00
J2PF Peter Forsberg 10.00 25.00
J2PK Paul Kariya 6.00 15.00
J2PS Patrick Sharp 6.00 15.00
J2PT Pierre Turgeon 5.00 12.00
J2RD Rick DiPietro 5.00 12.00
J2RE Robert Esche 5.00 12.00
J2RF Ruslan Fedotenko 4.00 10.00
J2RK Brian Rafalski 5.00 12.00
J2RL Roberto Luongo 10.00 25.00
J2RN Rick Nash 6.00 15.00
J2RO Brian Rolston 5.00 12.00
J2RS Ryan Smyth 5.00 12.00
J2RT Raffi Torres 4.00 10.00
J2RY Ryan Miller 6.00 15.00
J2SA Philippe Sauve 5.00 12.00
J2SB Sean Burke 4.00 10.00
J2SD Shane Doan 5.00 12.00
J2SH Shawn Horcoff 4.00 10.00
J2SK Sami Kapanen 4.00 10.00
J2SL Martin St. Louis 6.00 15.00
J2SN Scott Niedermayer 6.00 15.00
J2SO Sandis Ozolinsh 4.00 10.00
J2SP Jason Spezza 6.00 15.00
J2SV Marc Savard 4.00 10.00
J2SS Steve Sullivan 4.00 10.00
J2SU Mats Sundin 6.00 15.00
J2SV Sergei Samsonov 5.00 12.00
J2SW Stephen Weiss 4.00 10.00
J2SY Steve Yzerman SP 50.00 125.00
J2TB Todd Bertuzzi 6.00 15.00
J2TC Ty Conklin 5.00 12.00
J2TD Tie Domi 5.00 12.00
J2TH Trent Hunter 4.00 10.00
J2TL Trevor Linden 6.00 15.00
J2TO Tony Amonte 5.00 12.00
J2TP Tom Poti 4.00 10.00
J2TS Teemu Selanne 12.00 30.00
J2TV Tomas Vokoun 5.00 12.00
J2VK Viktor Kozlov 4.00 10.00
J2VL Vincent Lecavalier 6.00 15.00
J2VP Vaclav Prospal 4.00 10.00
J2WR Wade Redden 4.00 10.00
J2ZC Zdeno Chara 6.00 15.00
J2ZP Zigmund Palffy 6.00 15.00

2005-06 Upper Deck Majestic Materials

MMAF Alexander Frolov 8.00 20.00
MMAO Alexander Ovechkin 400.00 1000.00
MMAP Alexander Perezhogin 10.00 25.00
MMAR Andrew Raycroft 15.00 40.00
MMAS Alexander Steen 15.00 40.00
MMAT Alex Tanguay 12.00 30.00
MMAY Alexei Yashin 15.00 40.00
MMBG Bill Guerin 8.00 20.00
MMBR Brad Richards 20.00 50.00
MMBS Brendan Shanahan 15.00 40.00
MMCH Jonathan Cheechoo 15.00 40.00
MMCP Chris Pronger 12.00 30.00
MMDA Daniel Alfredsson 15.00 40.00
MMDP Dion Phaneuf 20.00 50.00
MMDW Doug Weight 8.00 20.00
MMEB Ed Belfour 15.00 40.00
MMEJ Ed Jovanovski 8.00 20.00
MMEL Eric Lindros 15.00 40.00
MMES Eric Staal 15.00 40.00
MMGB Gilbert Brule 10.00 25.00
MMGI Brian Gionta 15.00 40.00
MMHE Milan Hejduk 8.00 20.00
MMHK Dominik Hasek 20.00 50.00
MMHL Henrik Lundqvist 25.00 60.00
MMHT Hannu Toivonen 10.00 25.00
MMHV Martin Havlat 8.00 20.00
MMHZ Henrik Zetterberg 15.00 40.00
MMIK Ilya Kovalchuk 20.00 50.00
MMJA Jason Allison 12.00 30.00
MMJB Jay Bouwmeester 12.00 30.00
MMJC Jeff Carter 8.00 20.00
MMJG Jean-Sebastien Giguere 8.00 20.00
MMJI Jarome Iginla 30.00 60.00
MMJJ Jaromir Jagr 25.00 60.00
MMJL Joffrey Lupul 8.00 20.00
MMJO Jose Theodore 15.00 40.00
MMJR Jeremy Roenick 15.00 40.00
MMJS Joe Sakic/40 30.00 60.00
MMJT Joe Thornton 15.00 40.00
MMKL Kari Lehtonen 10.00 25.00
MMKP Keith Primeau 8.00 20.00
MMKT Keith Tkachuk 8.00 20.00
MMLE Manny Legace 12.00 30.00
MMLR Luc Robitaille 15.00 40.00
MMMB Martin Brodeur 30.00 80.00
MMMG Marian Gaborik 25.00 60.00
MMML Mario Lemieux 50.00 100.00
MMMM Mike Modano 30.00 60.00
MMMN Markus Naslund 8.00 20.00
MMMP Michael Peca 8.00 20.00
MMMR Michael Ryder 8.00 20.00
MMMS Martin St.Louis 12.00 30.00
MMMT Marty Turco 10.00 25.00
MMMW Brenden Morrow 8.00 20.00
MMNL Nicklas Lidstrom 8.00 20.00
MMNZ Nikolai Zherdev 15.00 40.00
MMOK Olaf Kolzig 12.00 30.00
MMPB Patrice Bergeron 15.00 40.00
MMPD Pavel Datsyuk 12.50 30.00
MMPE Patrik Elias 8.00 20.00
MMPF Peter Forsberg 25.00 60.00
MMPK Paul Kariya 20.00 50.00
MMRB Rob Blake 8.00 20.00
MMRD Rick DiPietro 12.00 30.00
MMRE Mark Recchi 8.00 20.00
MMRI Mike Richards 12.00 30.00
MMRL Roberto Luongo 12.00 30.00
MMRM Ryan Miller 12.00 30.00
MMRN Rick Nash 25.00 60.00
MMRO Mike Ribeiro 8.00 20.00
MMRS Ryan Smyth 15.00 40.00
MMSA Miroslav Satan 10.00 25.00
MMSC Sidney Crosby 125.00 225.00
MMSD Shane Doan 12.00 30.00
MMSG Simon Gagne 20.00 50.00
MMSH Shawn Horcoff 8.00 20.00
MMSK Saku Koivu 15.00 40.00
MMSN Scott Niedermayer 15.00 40.00
MMSP Jason Spezza 20.00 50.00
MMSS Steve Sullivan 8.00 20.00
MMST Matt Stajan 15.00 40.00
MMSW Stephen Weiss 12.00 30.00
MMSY Steve Yzerman 30.00 80.00
MMTB Todd Bertuzzi 10.00 25.00
MMTC Ty Conklin 10.00 25.00
MMTS Teemu Selanne 12.00 30.00
MMTV Tomas Vokoun 15.00 40.00
MMVA Thomas Vanek 12.00 30.00
MMVL Vincent Lecavalier 12.00 30.00
MMZC Zdeno Chara 8.00 20.00
MMZP Zigmund Palffy 15.00 40.00

2005-06 Upper Deck NHL Generations

DAR J. Arnott/M.Ryder 5.00 12.00
DBB R.Bourque/J.Bouwmeest 8.00 20.00
DBT M.Brodeur/J.Theodore 15.00 40.00
DFD S.Fedorov/P.Datsyuk 8.00 20.00
DGB B.Guerin/D.Brown 5.00 12.00
DGL W.Gretzky/M.Lemieux 100.00 200.00
DGR S.Gagne/M.Ribeiro 5.00 12.00
DHV D.Hasek/T.Vokoun 10.00 25.00
DIN J.Iginla/R.Nash 12.00 30.00
DJH J.Jagr/M.Havlat 10.00 25.00
DKS J.Kurri/T.Selanne 15.00 40.00
DKZ I.Kovalchuk/N.Zherdev 6.00 15.00
DLH J.Lehtinen/R.Hahl 5.00 12.00
DML M.Messier/V.Lecavalier 8.00 20.00
DNZ M.Naslund/H.Zetterberg 8.00 20.00
DRB W.Redden/N.Boynton 5.00 12.00
DSC S.Stevens/Z.Chara 5.00 12.00
DST B.Shanahan/J.Thornton 12.50 30.00
DTC M.Turco/T.Conklin 6.00 15.00
DYS S.Yzerman/J.Spezza 15.00 40.00
TBLL Brodeur/Luongo/Leht 20.00 50.00
TCGP Clarke/Gagne/Primeau 15.00 40.00
TFKA Fedorov/Kovalchuk/Afinog 20.00 50.00
TGYS Gretzky/Yzerman/Sakic 225.00 350.00
TLKR LaFleur/Koivu/Ribeiro 15.00 40.00
TMST Messier/Shanahan/Thor 20.00 50.00
TNSN Neely/Shanahan/Nash 20.00 50.00
TRBL Roy/Brodeur/Luongo 60.00 150.00
TSFZ Sundin/Forsberg/Zetter 15.00 40.00
TSHT Sakic/Hejduk/Tanguay 12.00 30.00
TSIR Sakic/Iginla/Ribeiro 20.00 50.00
TSKJ Selanne/Koivu/Jokinen 12.50 30.00
TSTP Sakic/Thornton/Spezza 20.00 50.00

2005-06 Upper Deck Notable Numbers

NBRA Brian Rafalski/28 15.00 40.00
NCCO Carlo Colaiacovo/45 15.00 40.00
NCRC Craig Conroy/22 12.00 30.00
NDUB Dustin Brown/23 20.00 50.00
NJAL Jamie Lundmark/21 15.00 40.00
NJAR Jason Arnott/44 15.00 40.00
NJAR Jani Rita/22 15.00 40.00
NJEO Jeff O'Neill/92 10.00 25.00
NJLI John-Michael Liles/26 20.00 50.00
NJTH Jocelyn Thibault/41 20.00 50.00
NMAS Marco Sturm/19 20.00 50.00
NMBA Matthew Barnaby/38 12.00 30.00
NMBR Martin Brodeur/30 75.00 200.00
NMBY Mike Bossy/22 30.00 60.00
NMDI Marcel Dionne/16 40.00 100.00
NMGE Martin Gerber/29 30.00 80.00
NMNY Michael Nylander/92 8.00 20.00
NMPH Mark Parrish/37 25.00 60.00
NMSA Miroslav Satan/81 10.00 25.00
NNIK Niko Kapanen/39 8.00 20.00
NPLE Pascal Leclaire/31 20.00 50.00
NRBO Ray Bourque/77 40.00 80.00
NTSA Tony Salmelainen/42 15.00 40.00
NPMB P-M Bouchard/96 10.00 25.00
NRON Rob Niedermayer/44 15.00 40.00
NPHS Philippe Sauve/30 15.00 40.00
NAF Marc-Andre Fleury/29 75.00 150.00
NAH Ales Hemsky/83 12.00 30.00
NAN Nikolai Antropov/80 12.00 30.00
NAT Alex Tanguay/18 30.00 80.00
NAY Alexei Yashin/79 10.00 25.00
NBB Brad Boyes/26 20.00 50.00
NBC Bobby Clarke/16 30.00 80.00
NBI Martin Biron/43 15.00 40.00
NBR Brad Richards/19 30.00 80.00
NBY Bryan McCabe/24 30.00 80.00
NCB Christian Backman/55 6.00 15.00
NCD Chris Drury/23 15.00 40.00
NCE Christian Ehrhoff/44 12.00 30.00
NCO Chris Osgood/30 20.00 50.00
NCP Chris Pronger/44 20.00 50.00
NCS Cory Stillman/61 10.00 25.00
NDB Daniel Briere/48 20.00 50.00
NDC Dan Cloutier/39 20.00 50.00
NDF Dan Fritsche/49 10.00 25.00
NDH Dominik Hasek/39 40.00 100.00
NDM Darren McCarty/25 10.00 25.00
NDR Dwayne Roloson/30 20.00 50.00
NDW Doug Weight/39 20.00 50.00
NEB Ed Belfour/20 25.00 60.00
NEC Erik Cole/26 25.00 60.00
NED Eric Daze/55 12.00 30.00
NEJ Ed Jovanovski/55 15.00 40.00
NEN Evgeni Nabokov/20 15.00 40.00
NFR Alexander Frolov/24 25.00 60.00
NFT Fedor Tyutin/51 10.00 25.00
NGC Gerry Cheevers/30 30.00 80.00
NGF Grant Fuhr/31 30.00 80.00
NGI Jean-Sebastien Giguere/35 15.00 40.00
NGL Georges Laraque/27 20.00 50.00
NGM Glen Murray/27 20.00 40.00
NHJ Milan Hejduk/23 15.00 40.00
NHO Marcel Hossa/81 10.00 25.00
NHZ Henrik Zetterberg/40 25.00 60.00
NIK Ilya Kovalchuk/17 40.00 100.00
NIL Ian Laperriere/22 15.00 40.00
NJH Jochen Hecht/55 6.00 15.00
NJK Jari Kurri/17 40.00 100.00
NJL Joffrey Lupul/15 25.00 60.00
NJO Jose Theodore/60 20.00 50.00
NJP Joni Pitkanen/44 20.00 50.00
NJS Jason Spezza/19 50.00 120.00
NJT Joe Thornton/19 40.00 100.00
NJV Josef Vasicek/63 8.00 20.00
NKD Kris Draper/33 15.00 40.00
NKH Kristian Huselius/22 12.00 30.00
NKL Kari Lehtonen/32 25.00 60.00
NKP Keith Primeau/25 20.00 50.00
NKT Kimmo Timonen/44 8.00 20.00
NKW K.Weekes NOT MADE 8.00 20.00
NLM Larry Murphy/55 12.00 30.00
NLN Ladislav Nagy/17 25.00 60.00
NLR Luc Robitaille/20 25.00 60.00
NMA Maxim Afinogenov/61 15.00 40.00
NMC Mike Comrie/89 8.00 20.00
NMH Marian Hossa/18 30.00 80.00
NML Manny Legace/34 20.00 50.00
NMN Markus Naslund/19 20.00 50.00
NMO Olaf Kolzig/37 50.00 100.00
NMP Michael Peca/27 25.00 60.00
NMR Mike Ribeiro/71 12.00 30.00
NMS Martin St. Louis/26 20.00 50.00
NMT Marty Turco/35 20.00 50.00
NNB Nick Boynton/44 8.00 20.00
NNH Nathan Horton/16 30.00 80.00
NNK Nikolai Khabibulin/53 20.00 50.00
NNO Mika Noronen/35 20.00 50.00
NPB Patrice Bergeron/37 20.00 50.00
NPO Mark Popovic/33 10.00 25.00
NPW Peter Worrell/28 15.00 40.00
NRE Robert Esche/42 15.00 40.00
NRF Ruslan Fedotenko/17 25.00 60.00
NRM Ryan Miller/30 15.00 60.00
NRN Rick Nash/61 30.00 80.00
NRO Jeremy Roenick/97 20.00 50.00
NRS Ryan Smyth/94 20.00 50.00
NRV Rogie Vachon/30 30.00 60.00
NRY Michael Ryder/73 15.00 40.00
NSB Sean Burke/41 10.00 25.00
NSD Shane Doan/19 20.00 50.00
NSN Scott Niedermayer/27 20.00 50.00
NSS Sheldon Souray/44 10.00 25.00
NSZ Sergei Zubov/56 6.00 15.00
NTA Tyler Arnason/39 10.00 25.00
NTB Todd Bertuzzi/44 25.00 60.00
NTE Tony Esposito/35 25.00 60.00
NTG Tim Gleason/42 12.00 30.00
NTL Trevor Linden/16 40.00 100.00
NTO Terry O'Reilly/24 30.00 60.00
NTR Tuomo Ruutu/15 25.00 60.00
NTV Steve Sullivan/26 10.00 25.00
NVP Vaclav Prospal/20 15.00 40.00
NVR Mike Van Ryn/26 10.00 25.00
NWG Wayne Gretzky/99 200.00 500.00

2005-06 Upper Deck Playoff Performers

COMPLETE SET (7) 12.00 25.00
PP1 Jarome Iginla 1.00 2.50
PP2 Martin St. Louis .75 2.00
PP3 Peter Forsberg 2.00 5.00
PP4 Wayne Gretzky 4.00 10.00
PP5 Jarome Iginla 1.00 2.50
PP6 Joe Sakic 1.50 4.00
PP7 Mario Lemieux 4.00 10.00

2005-06 Upper Deck Rookie Ink

RIAA Andrew Alberts/41 12.00 30.00
RIAM Andrej Meszaros/14 30.00 80.00
RIAP Alexander Perezhogin/42 12.00 30.00
RIAS Anthony Stewart/57 12.00 30.00
RIAW Andrew Wozniewski/55 12.00 30.00
RIBW Brad Winchester/26 20.00 50.00
RICB Cam Barker/25 12.00 30.00
RICC Chris Campoli/14 12.00 30.00
RICP Corey Perry/61 15.00 40.00
RICW Cam Ward/30 60.00 125.00
RIDL David Leneveu/30 20.00 50.00
RIEN Eric Nystrom/23 25.00 60.00
RIGB Gilbert Brule/17 15.00 40.00
RIGP George Parros/57 12.00 30.00
RIHL Henrik Lundqvist/30 50.00 100.00
RIHO Jeff Hoggan/22 15.00 40.00
RIHT Hannu Toivonen/33 25.00 60.00
RIJB Jaroslav Balastik/29 12.00 30.00
RIJC Jeff Carter/17 40.00 100.00
RIJF Johan Franzen/39 30.00 80.00
RIJH Jim Howard/35 25.00 60.00
RIJJ Jussi Jokinen/36 25.00 60.00
RIJS Jim Slater/23 12.00 30.00
RIJW Jeff Woywitka/29 15.00 40.00
RIKD Kevin Dallman/58 10.00 25.00
RIKN Kevin Nastiuk/35 15.00 40.00
RIMF Matt Foy/83 10.00 25.00
RIMJ Milan Jurcina/68 12.00 30.00
RIMK Mikko Koivu/21 60.00 100.00
RIMO Alvaro Montoya/29 25.00 60.00
RIMR Mike Richards/18 40.00 100.00
RIMT Maxime Talbot/25 25.00 60.00
RIPB Peter Budaj/31 30.00 80.00
RIPN Petteri Nokelainen/29 12.00 30.00
RIPP Petr Prucha/25 40.00 100.00
RIRB Rene Bourque/14 25.00 60.00
RIRC Ryane Clowe/29 15.00 40.00
RIRG Ryan Getzlaf/51 30.00 80.00
RIRH Ryan Hollweg/44 15.00 40.00
RIRN Robert Nilsson/21 25.00 60.00
RIRO Rostislav Olesz/85 12.00 30.00
RIRS Ryan Suter/20 30.00 80.00
RIRU R.J. Umberger/20 20.00 50.00
RIRW Ryan Whitney/19 25.00 60.00
RISC Sidney Crosby/87 225.00 400.00
RITV Thomas Vanek/26 75.00 150.00
RIYD Yann Danis/75 15.00 40.00

2005-06 Upper Deck Rookie Showcase

*BECKETT PROMO: .2X TO .5X
RS1 Corey Perry 15.00 40.00
RS2 Braydon Coburn 5.00 12.00
RS3 Hannu Toivonen 5.00 12.00
RS4 Thomas Vanek 10.00 25.00
RS5 Dion Phaneuf 8.00 20.00
RS6 Cam Ward 8.00 20.00
RS7 Brent Seabrook 10.00 25.00
RS8 Wojtek Wolski 4.00 10.00
RS9 Gilbert Brule 5.00 12.00
RS10 Jussi Jokinen 5.00 12.00
RS11 Jim Howard 12.00 30.00
RS12 Brad Winchester 5.00 12.00
RS13 Rostislav Olesz 4.00 10.00
RS14 George Parros 3.00 8.00
RS15 Matt Foy 3.00 8.00
RS16 Alexander Perezhogin 4.00 10.00
RS17 Ryan Suter 6.00 15.00
RS18 Zach Parise 12.00 30.00
RS19 Robert Nilsson 5.00 12.00
RS20 Henrik Lundqvist 25.00 60.00
RS21 Andrej Meszaros 4.00 10.00
RS22 Jeff Carter 8.00 20.00
RS23 David Leneveu 4.00 10.00
RS24 Sidney Crosby 30.00 80.00
RS25 Ryane Clowe 6.00 15.00
RS26 Jeff Woywitka 3.00 8.00
RS27 Evgeni Artyukhin 4.00 10.00
RS28 Alexander Steen 8.00 20.00
RS29 Rob McVicar 4.00 10.00
RS30 Alexander Ovechkin 80.00 200.00
RS31 Yann Danis 4.00 10.00
RS32 Eric Nystrom 4.00 10.00
RS33 Mike Richards 10.00 25.00
RS34 Ryan Getzlaf 12.00 30.00
RS35 Johan Franzen 8.00 20.00
RS36 Brandon Bochenski 5.00 12.00

2005-06 Upper Deck Rookie Threads

RTAA Andrew Alberts 2.00 5.00
RTAM Andrej Meszaros 2.50 6.00
RTAO Alexander Ovechkin 80.00 200.00
RTAP Alexander Perezhogin 2.50 6.00
RTAS Anthony Stewart 2.50 6.00
RTAW Andrew Wozniewski 2.50 6.00
RTBB Brandon Bochenski 3.00 8.00
RTBC Braydon Coburn 3.00 8.00
RTBL Brett Lebda 2.00 5.00
RTBS Brent Seabrook 6.00 15.00
RTBW Brad Winchester 3.00 8.00
RTCB Cam Barker 2.50 6.00
RTCP Corey Perry 10.00 25.00
RTCW Cam Ward 5.00 12.00
RTDK Duncan Keith 6.00 15.00
RTDL David Leneveu 2.50 6.00
RTDP Dion Phaneuf 5.00 12.00
RTEN Eric Nystrom 2.50 6.00
RTGB Gilbert Brule 3.00 8.00
RTGP George Parros 2.00 5.00
RTHL Henrik Lundqvist 15.00 40.00
RTHO Jim Howard 8.00 20.00
RTHT Hannu Toivonen 3.00 8.00
RTJB Jaroslav Balastik 2.00 5.00
RTJC Jeff Carter 5.00 12.00
RTJF Johan Franzen 5.00 12.00
RTJG Josh Gorges 2.50 6.00
RTJH Jeff Hoggan 2.00 5.00
RTJJ Jussi Jokinen 3.00 8.00
RTJM Jay McClement 2.00 5.00
RTJS Jim Slater 2.50 6.00
RTJW Jeff Woywitka 2.00 5.00
RTKB Keith Ballard 2.50 6.00
RTKD Kevin Dallman 2.50 6.00
RTKN Kevin Nastiuk 2.00 5.00
RTMF Matt Foy 2.00 5.00
RTMJ Milan Jurcina 2.50 6.00
RTMO Alvaro Montoya 3.00 8.00
RTMR Mike Richards 6.00 15.00
RTMT Maxime Talbot 3.00 8.00
RTNN Niklas Nordgren 3.00 8.00
RTPB Peter Budaj 4.00 10.00
RTPE Patrick Eaves 3.00 8.00
RTPN Petteri Nokelainen 2.00 5.00
RTPP Petr Prucha 3.00 8.00
RTRB Rene Bourque 3.00 8.00
RTRC Ryane Clowe 4.00 10.00
RTRG Ryan Getzlaf 8.00 20.00
RTRH Ryan Hollweg 2.00 5.00
RTRI Raitis Ivanans 2.00 5.00
RTRN Robert Nilsson 3.00 8.00
RTRO Rostislav Olesz 2.50 6.00
RTRS Ryan Suter 4.00 10.00
RTSC Sidney Crosby 30.00 80.00
RTST Alexander Steen 5.00 12.00
RTTH Timo Helbling 2.00 5.00
RTTV Thomas Vanek 6.00 15.00
RTWW Wojtek Wolski 2.50 6.00
RTYD Yann Danis 2.50 6.00
RTZP Zach Parise 8.00 20.00

2005-06 Upper Deck Rookie Threads Autographs

ARTAA Andrew Alberts 12.00 30.00
ARTAM Andrej Meszaros 15.00 40.00
ARTAS Anthony Stewart 15.00 40.00
ARTAW Andrew Wozniewski 15.00 40.00
ARTBB Brandon Bochenski 20.00 50.00
ARTBC Braydon Coburn 20.00 50.00
ARTBL Brett Lebda 12.00 30.00
ARTBS Brent Seabrook 40.00 100.00
ARTBW Brad Winchester 20.00 50.00
ARTCW Cam Ward 30.00 80.00
ARTDK Duncan Keith 40.00 100.00
ARTDL David Leneveu 15.00 40.00
ARTDP Dion Phaneuf 30.00 80.00
ARTEN Eric Nystrom 15.00 40.00
ARTGB Gilbert Brule 20.00 50.00
ARTGP George Parros 12.00 30.00
ARTHO Jim Howard 25.00 60.00
ARTHT Hannu Toivonen 20.00 50.00
ARTJB Jaroslav Balastik 12.00 30.00
ARTJF Johan Franzen 20.00 50.00
ARTJG Josh Gorges 15.00 40.00
ARTJH Jeff Hoggan 12.00 30.00
ARTJJ Jussi Jokinen 15.00 40.00
ARTJM Jay McClement 12.00 30.00
ARTJS Jim Slater 15.00 40.00
ARTJW Jeff Woywitka 12.00 30.00
ARTKB Keith Ballard 15.00 40.00
ARTKD Kevin Dallman 15.00 40.00
ARTKN Kevin Nastiuk 12.00 30.00
ARTMF Matt Foy 12.00 30.00
ARTMJ Milan Jurcina 15.00 40.00
ARTMO Alvaro Montoya 20.00 50.00
ARTMT Maxime Talbot 20.00 50.00
ARTNN Niklas Nordgren 20.00 50.00
ARTPB Peter Budaj 25.00 60.00
ARTPE Patrick Eaves 20.00 50.00
ARTPN Petteri Nokelainen 12.00 30.00
ARTPP Petr Prucha 15.00 40.00
ARTRB Rene Bourque 20.00 50.00
ARTRH Ryan Hollweg 12.00 30.00
ARTRI Raitis Ivanans 12.00 30.00
ARTRN Robert Nilsson 20.00 50.00
ARTRO Rostislav Olesz 15.00 40.00
ARTRS Ryan Suter 25.00 60.00
ARTTH Timo Helbling 12.00 30.00
ARTWW Wojtek Wolski 15.00 40.00
ARTYD Yann Danis 15.00 40.00
ARTZP Zach Parise 25.00 60.00

2005-06 Upper Deck School of Hard Knocks

COMPLETE SET (7) 5.00 10.00
HK1 Scott Stevens .75 2.00
HK2 Chris Pronger .75 2.00
HK3 Chris Simon .50 1.25
HK4 Jeremy Roenick 1.25 3.00
HK5 Tie Domi .60 1.50
HK6 Ed Jovanovski .60 1.50
HK7 Brendan Shanahan .75 2.00

2005-06 Upper Deck Scrapbooks

COMPLETE SET (30) 10.00 25.00
HS1 Ilya Kovalchuk .30 .75
HS2 Wayne Gretzky 2.00 5.00
HS3 Joe Thornton .50 1.25
HS4 Kari Lehtonen .25 .60
HS5 Dominik Hasek .50 1.25
HS6 Mario Lemieux 1.25 3.00
HS7 Jose Theodore .30 .75
HS8 Paul Kariya .30 .75
HS9 Mike Modano .50 1.25
HS10 Rick Nash .30 .75
HS11 Mark Messier .60 1.50
HS12 Jarome Iginla .40 1.00
HS13 Peter Forsberg .60 1.50
HS14 Nikolai Khabibulin .30 .75
HS15 Dany Heatley .25 .60
HS16 Brett Hull .60 1.50
HS17 Marian Gaborik .30 .75
HS18 Mats Sundin .30 .75
HS19 Steve Yzerman .75 2.00
HS20 Joe Sakic .60 1.50
HS21 Marian Hossa .30 .75
HS22 Markus Naslund .30 .75
HS23 Jaromir Jagr 1.00 2.50
HS24 Andrew Raycroft .25 .60
HS25 Ed Belfour .30 .75
HS26 Martin St. Louis .30 .75
HS27 Jeremy Roenick .50 1.25
HS28 Brendan Shanahan .30 .75
HS29 Sergei Fedorov .50 1.25
HS30 Martin Brodeur .75 2.00

2005-06 Upper Deck Shooting Stars Jerseys

SAM Alexander Mogilny 3.00 8.00
SBG Bill Guerin 4.00 10.00
SBH Brett Hull 5.00 12.00
SBR Brad Richards 4.00 10.00
SBS Brendan Shanahan 4.00 10.00
SCD Chris Drury 3.00 8.00
SDA Daniel Alfredsson 4.00 10.00
SDH Dany Heatley 6.00 15.00
SEL Eric Lindros 6.00 15.00
SGM Glen Murray 3.00 8.00
SHZ Henrik Zetterberg 5.00 12.00
SIK Ilya Kovalchuk 6.00 15.00
SJI Jarome Iginla 6.00 15.00
SJJ Jaromir Jagr SP 40.00 100.00
SJL John LeClair 4.00 10.00
SJR Jeremy Roenick 6.00 15.00
SJS Joe Sakic 8.00 20.00
SJT Joe Thornton 6.00 15.00
SKP Keith Primeau 3.00 8.00
SKT Keith Tkachuk 4.00 10.00
SLR Luc Robitaille 4.00 10.00
SMG Marian Gaborik 6.00 15.00
SMH Milan Hejduk 3.00 8.00
SMHA Martin Havlat 4.00 10.00
SMHO Marian Hossa 4.00 10.00
SML Mario Lemieux SP 25.00 60.00
SMME Mark Messier 10.00 25.00
SMMO Mike Modano 6.00 15.00
SMN Markus Naslund 4.00 10.00
SMP Michael Peca 3.00 8.00
SMP Mark Parrish 2.50 6.00
SMRI Mike Ribeiro 2.50 6.00
SMRY Michael Ryder 3.00 8.00
SMS Martin St. Louis 4.00 10.00
SMS Mats Sundin 4.00 10.00
SPB Peter Bondra 4.00 10.00
SPE Patrik Elias 4.00 10.00
SPK Paul Kariya 4.00 10.00
SRB Rob Blake 4.00 10.00
SRE Mark Recchi 5.00 12.00
SRS Ryan Smyth 3.00 8.00
SSF Sergei Fedorov 6.00 15.00
SSG Simon Gagne 4.00 10.00
SSS Sergei Samsonov 3.00 8.00
SSY Steve Yzerman 12.00 30.00
STA Tony Amonte 3.00 8.00
SVL Vincent Lecavalier 5.00 12.00
SZP Zigmund Palffy 4.00 10.00

2005-06 Upper Deck Sportsfest

NHL1 Sidney Crosby 10.00 25.00
NHL2 Wayne Gretzky 4.00 10.00

2005-06 Upper Deck Stars in the Making

SM1 Sidney Crosby 10.00 25.00
SM2 Alexander Ovechkin 20.00 50.00
SM3 Jeff Carter 1.25 3.00
SM4 Corey Perry 2.50 6.00
SM5 Thomas Vanek 1.50 4.00
SM6 Henrik Lundqvist 4.00 10.00
SM7 Alexander Perezhogin .60 1.50
SM8 Dion Phaneuf 1.25 3.00
SM9 Hannu Toivonen .75 2.00
SM10 Alexander Steen 1.25 3.00
SM11 Gilbert Brule .75 2.00
SM12 Mike Richards 1.50 4.00
SM13 Zach Parise 2.00 5.00
SM14 Wojtek Wolski .60 1.50

2005-06 Upper Deck Phenomenal Beginnings

COMPLETE SET (20) 15.00 30.00
COMMON CARD (1-20) .60 1.50

2006 Upper Deck Entry Draft

COMPLETE SET (6) 15.00 30.00
DR1 Sidney Crosby 6.00 15.00
DR2 Alexander Ovechkin 4.00 10.00
DR3 Marc-Andre Fleury 1.25 3.00
DR4 Rick Nash 1.50 4.00
DR5 Ilya Kovalchuk 1.50 4.00
DR6 Joe Thornton 1.50 4.00

2006 Upper Deck Rookie Showdown

RSSCAO S.Crosby/A.Ovechkin 3.00 8.00

2006-07 Upper Deck

COMP.SER.1 w/o SPs (200) 12.00 30.00
COMP.SER.2 w/o SPs (200) 12.00 30.00
1 Corey Perry .50 1.25
2 Ilya Bryzgalov .30 .75
3 Teemu Selanne .60 1.50
4 Andy McDonald .25 .60
5 Ryan Getzlaf .30 .75
6 Francois Beauchemin .20 .50
7 Scott Niedermayer .30 .75
8 Kari Lehtonen .25 .60
9 Marian Hossa .30 .75
10 Slava Kozlov .20 .50
11 Jim Slater .20 .50
12 Garnet Exelby .20 .50
13 Bobby Holik .20 .50
14 Niclas Havelid .20 .50
15 Brad Boyes .20 .50
16 Brad Stuart .20 .50
17 Tim Thomas .30 .75
18 Marco Sturm .20 .50
19 Hannu Toivonen .25 .60
20 Glen Murray .25 .60
21 Ryan Miller .30 .75
22 Thomas Vanek .25 .60
23 Chris Drury .25 .60
24 Henrik Tallinder .20 .50
25 Jochen Hecht .20 .50
26 Brian Campbell .25 .60
27 Derek Roy .20 .50
28 Jarome Iginla .40 1.00
29 Dion Phaneuf .25 .60
30 Robyn Regehr .20 .50
31 Jamie Lundmark .20 .50
32 Darren McCarty .20 .50
33 Kristian Huselius .20 .50
34 Chuck Kobasew .20 .50
35 Eric Staal .40 1.00
36 Cam Ward .30 .75
37 Justin Williams .25 .60
38 Glen Wesley .20 .50
39 Mike Commodore .20 .50
40 Cory Stillman .20 .50
41 Ray Whitney .25 .60
42 Tuomo Ruutu .30 .75
43 Radim Vrbata .20 .50
44 Duncan Keith .25 .60
45 Nikolai Khabibulin .30 .75
46 Rene Bourque .20 .50
47 Patrick Sharp .30 .75
48 Jose Theodore .30 .75
49 Milan Hejduk .25 .60
50 Pierre Turgeon .25 .60
51 Andrew Brunette .20 .50
52 Wojtek Wolski .25 .60
53 John-Michael Liles .20 .50
54 Joe Sakic .60 1.50
55 Rick Nash .30 .75
56 Pascal Leclaire .25 .60
57 Adam Foote .20 .50
58 Alexandre Picard .20 .50
59 Bryan Berard .20 .50
60 Sergei Fedorov .50 1.25
61 Marty Turco .30 .75
62 Brenden Morrow .25 .60
63 Jussi Jokinen .25 .60
64 Sergei Zubov .25 .60
65 Jere Lehtinen .20 .50
66 Steve Ott .20 .50
67 Philippe Boucher .20 .50
68 Pavel Datsyuk .50 1.25
69 Mikael Samuelsson .20 .50
70 Tomas Holmstrom .25 .60
71 Kris Draper .20 .50
72 Jason Williams .20 .50
73 Chris Osgood .30 .75
74 Robert Lang .20 .50
75 Ales Hemsky .25 .60
76 Fernando Pisani .20 .50
77 Jarret Stoll .25 .60
78 Marc-Andre Bergeron .20 .50
79 Dwayne Roloson .25 .60
80 Ethan Moreau .20 .50
81 Raffi Torres .20 .50
82 Joe Nieuwendyk .25 .60
83 Jay Bouwmeester .20 .50
84 Nathan Horton .30 .75
85 Rostislav Olesz .20 .50
86 Martin Gelinas .20 .50
87 Stephen Weiss .20 .50
88 Mathieu Garon .25 .60
89 Mike Cammalleri .20 .50
90 Alexander Frolov .20 .50
91 Lubomir Visnovsky .20 .50
92 George Parros .20 .50
93 Dustin Brown .30 .75
94 Marian Gaborik .30 .75
95 Wes Walz .20 .50
96 Pierre-Marc Bouchard .30 .75
97 Nick Schultz .20 .50
98 Derek Boogaard .20 .50
99 Todd White .20 .50
100 Saku Koivu .30 .75
101 Cristobal Huet .25 .60
102 Alex Kovalev .25 .60
103 Chris Higgins .20 .50
104 Andrei Markov .30 .75
105 Alexander Perezhogin .20 .50
106 Mathieu Dandenault .20 .50
107 Steve Sullivan .20 .50
108 Tomas Vokoun .25 .60
109 David Legwand .25 .60
110 Marek Zidlicky .20 .50
111 Kimmo Timonen .20 .50
112 Ryan Suter .25 .60
113 Jordin Tootoo .30 .75
114 Martin Brodeur .75 2.00
115 Brian Gionta .20 .50
116 Zach Parise .30 .75
117 Brian Rafalski .25 .60
118 Jamie Langenbrunner .20 .50
119 John Madden .20 .50
120 Jay Pandolfo .20 .50
121 Miroslav Satan .25 .60
122 Rick DiPietro .25 .60
123 Alexei Zhitnik .20 .50
124 Jeff Tambellini .20 .50
125 Chris Campoli .20 .50
126 Jason Blake .20 .50
127 Trent Hunter .20 .50
128 Jaromir Jagr 1.00 2.50
129 Petr Prucha .25 .60
130 Kevin Weekes .25 .60
131 Sandis Ozolinsh .20 .50
132 Ryan Hollweg .20 .50
133 Darius Kasparaitis .20 .50
134 Martin Straka .20 .50

135 Jason Spezza .30 .75
136 Ray Emery .25 .60
137 Andrej Meszaros .20 .50
138 Patrick Eaves .20 .50
139 Daniel Alfredsson .30 .75
140 Antoine Vermette .25 .60
141 Chris Phillips .20 .50
142 Peter Forsberg .60 1.50
143 Robert Esche .25 .60
144 Mike Knuble .20 .50
145 Joni Pitkanen .20 .50
146 Mike Richards .25 .60
147 R.J. Umberger .20 .50
148 Sami Kapanen .20 .50
149 Shane Doan .25 .60
150 Keith Ballard .20 .50
151 Ladislav Nagy .20 .50
152 Mike Ricci .20 .50
153 Oleg Saprykin .20 .50
154 David Leneveu .25 .60
155 Sidney Crosby 1.25 3.00
156 Colby Armstrong .25 .60
157 John LeClair .30 .75
158 Sergei Gonchar .20 .50
159 Ryan Whitney .25 .60
160 Ryan Malone .20 .50
161 Joe Thornton .50 1.25
162 Vesa Toskala .25 .60
163 Milan Michalek .20 .50
164 Marcel Goc .25 .60
165 Steve Bernier .20 .50
166 Jonathan Cheechoo .25 .60
167 Christian Ehrhoff .20 .50
168 Keith Tkachuk .30 .75
169 Barret Jackman .20 .50
170 Curtis Sanford .25 .60
171 Lee Stempniak .20 .50
172 Petr Cajanek .20 .50
173 Dallas Drake .20 .50
174 Martin St. Louis .30 .75
175 Vaclav Prospal .20 .50
176 Dan Boyle .20 .50
177 Ryan Craig .20 .50
178 Ruslan Fedotenko .20 .50
179 Paul Ranger .20 .50
180 Sean Burke .20 .50
181 Mats Sundin .30 .75
182 Darcy Tucker .25 .60
183 Alexander Steen .20 .50
184 Mikael Tellqvist .30 .75
185 Tomas Kaberle .20 .50
186 Nikolai Antropov .25 .60
187 Bryan McCabe .20 .50
188 Markus Naslund .30 .75
189 Henrik Sedin .40 1.00
190 Mattias Ohlund .20 .50
191 Daniel Sedin .40 1.00
192 Matt Cooke .20 .50
193 Sami Salo .20 .50
194 Ryan Kesler .30 .75
195 Brooks Laich .20 .50
196 Shaone Morrisonn .20 .50
197 Chris Clark .20 .50
198 Alexander Semin .30 .75
199 Sidney Crosby 1.25 3.00
200 Jaromir Jagr 1.00 2.50
201 Shane O'Brien YG RC 2.00 5.00
202 Ryan Shannon YG RC 2.00 5.00
203 Yan Stastny YG RC 2.00 5.00
204 Phil Kessel YG RC 15.00 40.00
205 Carsen Germyn YG RC 2.00 5.00
206 Dustin Byfuglien YG RC 12.00 30.00
207 Paul Stastny YG RC 6.00 15.00
208 Fredrik Norrena YG RC 2.00 5.00
209 Filip Novak YG RC 2.00 5.00
210 Loui Eriksson YG RC 6.00 15.00
211 Tomas Kopecky YG RC 2.50 6.00
212 M-A Pouliot YG RC 2.00 5.00
213 Ladislav Smid YG RC 2.00 5.00
214 Patrick Thoresen YG RC 2.00 5.00
215 Patrick O'Sullivan YG RC 3.00 8.00
216 Anze Kopitar YG RC 30.00 80.00
217 K.Pushkarev YG RC 2.50 6.00
218 Erik Reitz YG RC 2.00 5.00
219 Miroslav Kopriva YG RC 2.00 5.00
220 Niklas Backstrom YG RC 4.00 10.00
221 G.Latendresse YG RC 3.00 8.00
222 Shea Weber YG RC 12.00 30.00
223 Mikko Lehtonen YG RC 2.50 6.00
224 Frank Doyle YG RC 2.50 6.00
225 Travis Zajac YG RC 4.00 10.00
226 John Oduya YG RC 3.00 8.00
227 Ryan Caldwell YG RC 2.00 5.00
228 Masi Marjamaki YG RC 2.00 5.00
229 Matt Koalska YG RC 2.00 5.00
230 Jarkko Immonen YG RC 2.50 6.00
231 Nigel Dawes YG RC 2.00 5.00
232 Ryan Potulny YG RC 2.00 5.00
233 David Printz YG RC 2.00 5.00
234 Bill Thomas YG RC 2.00 5.00
235 Joel Perrault YG RC 2.00 5.00
236 Patrick Fischer YG RC 2.00 5.00
237 Noah Welch YG RC 2.00 5.00
238 Michel Ouellet YG RC 2.50 6.00
239 Jordan Staal YG RC 6.00 15.00
240 Kristopher Letang YG RC 25.00 60.00
241 Matt Carle YG RC 2.00 5.00
242 Marc-Edouard Vlasic YG RC 3.00 8.00
243 D.J. King YG RC 2.00 5.00
244 Ben Ondrus YG RC 2.00 5.00
245 Brendan Bell YG RC 2.00 5.00
246 Ian White YG RC 2.50 6.00
247 Jeremy Williams YG RC 2.00 5.00
248 Luc Bourdon YG RC 3.00 8.00
249 Eric Fehr YG RC 3.00 8.00
250 Phil Kessel YG CL 4.00 10.00
251 Chris Pronger .30 .75
252 Todd Fedoruk .20 .50
253 Chris Kunitz .30 .75
254 Jean-Sebastien Giguere .30 .75
255 Rob Niedermayer .25 .60
256 Todd Marchant .20 .50
257 Samuel Pahlsson .20 .50
258 Ilya Kovalchuk .30 .75
259 Steve Rucchin .20 .50
260 Niko Kapanen .20 .50
261 Greg de Vries .20 .50
262 Johan Hedberg .25 .60
263 Andy Sutton .20 .50
264 Scott Mellanby .20 .50
265 Patrice Bergeron .40 1.00
266 Zdeno Chara .30 .75
267 Andrew Alberts .20 .50
268 P.J. Axelsson .20 .50
269 Marc Savard .20 .50
270 Paul Mara .20 .50
271 Wayne Primeau .20 .50
272 Daniel Briere .30 .75
273 Ales Kotalik .20 .50
274 Jiri Novotny .20 .50
275 Martin Biron .25 .60
276 Jason Pominville .20 .50
277 Maxim Afinogenov .20 .50
278 Jaroslav Spacek .20 .50
279 Alex Tanguay .20 .50
280 Daymond Langkow .20 .50
281 Roman Hamrlik .20 .50
282 Miikka Kiprusoff .30 .75
283 Jeff Friesen .20 .50
284 Andrew Ference .20 .50
285 Stephane Yelle .20 .50
286 Rod Brind'Amour .30 .75
287 Erik Cole .20 .50
288 Andrew Ladd .20 .50
289 John Grahame .20 .50
290 Tim Gleason .20 .50
291 Kevyn Adams .20 .50
292 Martin Havlat .20 .50
293 Brent Seabrook .20 .50
294 Adrian Aucoin .20 .50
295 Brian Boucher .25 .60
296 Bryan Smolinski .20 .50
297 Martin Lapointe .20 .50
298 Michal Handzus .25 .60
299 Marek Svatos .20 .50
300 Mark Rycroft .20 .50
301 Tyler Arnason .20 .50
302 Peter Budaj .20 .50
303 Patrice Brisebois .20 .50
304 Antti Laaksonen .20 .50
305 Ian Laperriere .20 .50
306 Fredrik Modin .20 .50
307 Rostislav Klesla .20 .50
308 Nikolai Zherdev .20 .50
309 Gilbert Brule .25 .60
310 David Vyborny .20 .50
311 Manny Malhotra .20 .50
312 Jody Shelley .20 .50
313 Mike Modano .50 1.25
314 Antti Miettinen .20 .50
315 Jeff Halpern .20 .50
316 Patrik Stefan .20 .50
317 Mike Ribeiro .20 .50
318 Eric Lindros .50 1.25
319 Dominik Hasek .50 1.25
320 Chris Chelios .30 .75
321 Johan Franzen .25 .60
322 Mathieu Schneider .20 .50
323 Henrik Zetterberg .40 1.00
324 Nicklas Lidstrom .30 .75
325 Ryan Smyth .25 .60
326 Steve Staios .20 .50
327 Jussi Markkanen .20 .50
328 Joffrey Lupul .20 .50
329 Jason Smith .20 .50
330 Shawn Horcoff .20 .50
331 Petr Sykora .25 .60
332 Olli Jokinen .30 .75
333 Ed Belfour .30 .75
334 Mike Van Ryn .20 .50
335 Jozef Stumpel .20 .50
336 Alexander Auld .25 .60
337 Todd Bertuzzi .30 .75
338 Gary Roberts .20 .50
339 Rob Blake .30 .75
340 Craig Conroy .20 .50
341 Dan Cloutier .25 .60
342 Mattias Norstrom .20 .50
343 Sean Avery .20 .50
344 Oleg Tverdovsky .20 .50
345 Manny Fernandez .20 .50
346 Brian Rolston .25 .60
347 Mikko Koivu .25 .60
348 Kim Johnsson .20 .50
349 Pavol Demitra .40 1.00
350 Mark Parrish .20 .50
351 Kurtis Foster .20 .50
352 Michael Ryder .20 .50
353 David Aebischer .25 .60
354 Sergei Samsonov .25 .60
355 Sheldon Souray .20 .50
356 Mike Johnson .20 .50
357 Craig Rivet .20 .50
358 Radek Bonk .20 .50
359 Paul Kariya .30 .75
360 Scott Hartnell .20 .50
361 Martin Erat .20 .50
362 Jason Arnott .25 .60
363 Chris Mason .25 .60
364 J.P. Dumont .20 .50
365 Patrik Elias .30 .75
366 Scott Gomez .25 .60
367 Colin White .20 .50
368 Sergei Brylin .20 .50
369 Paul Martin .20 .50
370 Cam Janssen .20 .50
371 Alexei Yashin .25 .60
372 Mike Sillinger .20 .50
373 Arron Asham .20 .50
374 Mike York .20 .50
375 Mike Dunham .20 .50
376 Brendan Witt .20 .50
377 Henrik Lundqvist .75 2.00
378 Adam Hall .20 .50
379 Wayne Gretzky 2.00 5.00
380 Matt Cullen .20 .50
381 Michal Rozsival .20 .50
382 Michael Nylander .20 .50
383 Brendan Shanahan .30 .75
384 Dany Heatley .30 .75
385 Joe Corvo .20 .50
386 Peter Schaefer .20 .50
387 Chris Neil .20 .50
388 Wade Redden .20 .50
389 Martin Gerber .25 .60
390 Mike Fisher .20 .50
391 Simon Gagne .30 .75
392 Jeff Carter .25 .60
393 Antero Niittymaki .25 .60
394 Geoff Sanderson .20 .50
395 Fredrik Meyer .20 .50
396 Kyle Calder .20 .50
397 Curtis Joseph .40 1.00
398 Ed Jovanovski .25 .60
399 Mike Comrie .25 .60
400 Nick Boynton .20 .50
401 Jeremy Roenick .50 1.25
402 Georges Laraque .25 .60
403 Owen Nolan .30 .75
404 Marc-Andre Fleury .60 1.50
405 Nils Ekman .20 .50
406 Jarkko Ruutu .20 .50
407 Mark Eaton .20 .50
408 Dominic Moore .20 .50
409 Mark Recchi .40 1.00
410 Patrick Marleau .30 .75
411 Scott Hannan .20 .50
412 Josh Gorges .20 .50
413 Mike Grier .20 .50
414 Mark Bell .20 .50
415 Evgeni Nabokov .25 .60
416 Doug Weight .30 .75
417 Dennis Wideman .20 .50
418 Jay McClement .20 .50
419 Manny Legace .25 .60
420 Bill Guerin .30 .75
421 Jay McKee .20 .50
422 Vincent Lecavalier .30 .75
423 Marc Denis .25 .60
424 Filip Kuba .20 .50
425 Tim Taylor .20 .50
426 Brad Richards .30 .75
427 Dimitry Afanasenkov .20 .50
428 Andrew Raycroft .25 .60
429 Kyle Wellwood .25 .60
430 Michael Peca .20 .50
431 Alexei Ponikarovsky .20 .50
432 Jeff O'Neill .20 .50
433 Jean-Sebastien Aubin .25 .60
434 Matt Stajan .20 .50
435 Dany Sabourin .20 .50
436 Roberto Luongo .50 1.25
437 Willie Mitchell .20 .50
438 Jan Bulis .20 .50
439 Brendan Morrison .20 .50
440 Trevor Linden .30 .75
441 Lukas Krajicek .20 .50
442 Alexander Ovechkin 1.25 3.00
443 Olaf Kolzig .30 .75
444 Richard Zednik .20 .50
445 Brian Pothier .20 .50
446 Donald Brashear .20 .50
447 Dainius Zubrus .20 .50
448 Ben Clymer .20 .50
449 Miikka Kiprusoff .30 .75
450 Wayne Gretzky 2.00 5.00
451 David McKee YG RC 2.00 5.00
452 Mark Stuart YG RC 2.00 5.00
453 Matt Lashoff YG RC 2.00 5.00
454 Mike Brown YG RC 2.00 5.00
455 Nate Thompson YG RC 2.00 5.00
456 Drew Stafford YG RC 3.00 8.00
457 Adam Dennis YG RC 2.00 5.00
458 Mike Card YG RC 2.00 5.00
459 Michael Funk YG RC 2.00 5.00
460 Michael Ryan YG RC 2.00 5.00
461 Dustin Boyd YG RC 2.00 5.00
462 Brandon Prust YG RC 2.00 5.00
463 Dave Bolland YG RC 4.00 10.00
464 Michael Blunden YG RC 2.00 5.00
465 Adam Burish YG RC 3.00 8.00
466 Stefan Liv YG RC 2.00 5.00
467 Alexei Mikhnov YG RC 2.00 5.00
468 Jeff Deslauriers YG RC 2.00 5.00
469 Jan Hejda YG RC 2.00 5.00
470 David Booth YG RC 2.50 6.00
471 Drew Larman YG RC 2.00 5.00
472 Peter Harrold YG RC 2.00 5.00
473 Barry Brust YG RC 2.50 6.00
474 Karri Ramo YG RC 2.50 6.00
475 Benoit Pouliot YG RC 2.50 6.00
476 Alex Radulov YG RC 10.00 25.00
477 Alex Brooks YG RC 2.00 5.00
478 Alexei Kaigorodov YG RC 2.00 5.00
479 Kelly Guard YG RC 2.50 6.00
480 Jussi Timonen YG RC 2.50 6.00
481 Martin Houle YG RC 2.50 6.00
482 Lars Jonsson YG RC 2.00 5.00
483 Triston Grant YG RC 2.00 5.00
484 Enver Lisin YG RC 2.00 5.00
485 Keith Yandle YG RC 5.00 12.00
486 Evgeni Malkin YG RC 100.00 250.00
487 Joe Pavelski YG RC 25.00 60.00
488 Roman Polak YG RC 2.50 6.00
489 Blair Jones YG RC 2.50 6.00
490 J-F Racine YG RC 2.50 6.00
491 Alexander Edler YG RC 3.00 8.00
492 Jesse Schultz YG RC 2.00 5.00
493 Nathan McIver YG RC 2.00 5.00
494 Patrick Coulombe YG RC 2.00 5.00
495 Evgeni Malkin YG CL 8.00 20.00

2006-07 Upper Deck Exclusives

*VETS/100: 10X TO 25X BASIC CARDS
*YOUNG GUNS/100: 1X TO 2.5X BASIC YG
486 Evgeni Malkin 150.00 300.00

2006-07 Upper Deck All-Time Greatest

COMPLETE SET (28) 15.00 40.00
ATG1 Teemu Selanne 1.50 4.00
ATG2 Ilya Kovalchuk .75 2.00
ATG3 Bobby Orr 4.00 10.00
ATG4 Gilbert Perreault .75 2.00
ATG5 Joe Sakic 1.50 4.00
ATG6 Rick Nash .75 2.00
ATG7 Mike Modano 1.25 3.00
ATG8 Ted Lindsay .75 2.00
ATG9 Wayne Gretzky 4.00 10.00
ATG10 Marcel Dionne 1.00 2.50
ATG11 Marian Gaborik .75 2.00
ATG12 Tomas Vokoun .60 1.50
ATG13 Martin Brodeur 1.50 4.00
ATG14 Andy Bathgate .60 1.50
ATG15 Daniel Alfredsson .75 2.00
ATG16 Bobby Clarke 1.25 3.00
ATG17 Shane Doan .60 1.50
ATG18 Mario Lemieux 2.50 6.00
ATG19 Evgeni Nabokov .60 1.50
ATG20 Martin St. Louis .75 2.00
ATG21 Darryl Sittler 1.00 2.50
ATG22 Alexander Ovechkin 1.50 4.00
ATG23 Tony Esposito .75 2.00
ATG24 Mario Lemieux 2.50 6.00
ATG25 Guy Lafleur 1.00 2.50
ATG26 Gilbert Perreault .75 2.00
ATG27 Wayne Gretzky 4.00 10.00
ATG28 Johnny Bower .75 2.00

2006-07 Upper Deck All World

COMPLETE SET (30) 200.00 350.00
AW1 Mike Modano 5.00 12.00
AW2 Nicklas Lidstrom 3.00 8.00
AW3 Joe Thornton 5.00 12.00
AW4 Teemu Selanne 6.00 15.00
AW5 Kari Lehtonen 2.50 6.00
AW6 Zdeno Chara 3.00 8.00
AW7 Jarome Iginla 4.00 10.00
AW8 Eric Staal 4.00 10.00
AW9 Martin Havlat 2.00 5.00
AW10 Milan Hejduk 2.50 6.00
AW11 Sergei Fedorov 5.00 12.00
AW12 Rick Nash 3.00 8.00
AW13 Henrik Zetterberg 4.00 10.00
AW14 Olli Jokinen 3.00 8.00
AW15 Marian Gaborik 3.00 8.00
AW16 Saku Koivu 3.00 8.00
AW17 Tomas Vokoun 2.50 6.00
AW18 Paul Kariya 3.00 8.00
AW19 Martin Gerber 2.50 6.00
AW20 Markus Naslund 3.00 8.00
AW21 Ilya Kovalchuk SP 12.50 30.00
AW22 Miikka Kiprusoff SP 12.50 30.00
AW23 Joe Sakic SP 25.00 60.00
AW24 Dominik Hasek SP 12.50 30.00
AW25 Martin Brodeur SP 15.00 40.00
AW26 Jaromir Jagr SP 15.00 40.00
AW27 Peter Forsberg SP 10.00 25.00
AW28 Sidney Crosby SP 15.00 40.00
AW29 Mats Sundin SP 10.00 25.00
AW30 Alexander Ovechkin SP 12.50 30.00

2006-07 Upper Deck Award Winners

COMPLETE SET (7) 8.00 20.00
COMMON CARDS .75 2.00
UNLISTED STARS 1.25 3.00
AW1 Joe Thornton 1.50 4.00
AW2 Miikka Kiprusoff 1.25 3.00
AW3 Nicklas Lidstrom .75 2.00
AW4 Alexander Ovechkin 2.00 5.00
AW5 Jaromir Jagr 1.50 4.00
AW6 Rod Brind'Amour .75 2.00
AW7 Cam Ward .75 2.00

2006-07 Upper Deck Biography of a Season

COMPLETE SET (15) 4.00 10.00
BOS1 Eric Staal .40 1.00
BOS2 Brendan Shanahan .30 .75
BOS3 Mats Sundin .30 .75
BOS4 Evgeni Malkin 1.25 3.00
BOS5 Evgeni Malkin 1.25 3.00
BOS6 Ryan Miller .30 .75
BOS7 Patrick Roy .75 2.00
BOS8 Chris Pronger .30 .75
BOS9 Sidney Crosby 1.25 3.00
BOS10 Alexander Ovechkin 1.25 3.00
BOS11 Daniel Briere .30 .75
BOS12 Zach Parise .30 .75
BOS13 Mark Recchi .40 1.00
BOS14 Joe Sakic .60 1.50
BOS15 Sidney Crosby 1.25 3.00

2006-07 Upper Deck Century Marks

COMPLETE SET (7) 10.00 25.00
CM1 Joe Thornton 2.00 5.00
CM2 Alexander Ovechkin 5.00 12.00
CM3 Dany Heatley 1.00 2.50
CM4 Jaromir Jagr 4.00 10.00
CM5 Sidney Crosby 4.00 10.00
CM6 Eric Staal 1.50 4.00
CM7 Daniel Alfredsson 1.25 3.00

2006-07 Upper Deck Diary of a Phenom

COMPLETE SET (25) 15.00 40.00
COMMON MALKIN 1.00 2.50

2006-07 Upper Deck Game Dated Moments

GD1 Sidney Crosby 30.00 80.00
GD2 Alexander Ovechkin 20.00 50.00
GD3 Luc Robitaille 15.00 40.00
GD4 Dion Phaneuf 12.00 30.00
GD5 Miikka Kiprusoff 12.00 30.00
GD6 Jaromir Jagr 15.00 40.00
GD7 Jonathan Cheechoo 10.00 25.00
GD8 Martin Brodeur 20.00 50.00
GD9 Ilya Bryzgalov 6.00 15.00
GD10 Jeffrey Lupul 6.00 15.00
GD11 Ryan Miller 10.00 25.00
GD12 Cam Ward 8.00 20.00
GD13 Teemu Selanne 12.00 30.00
GD14 Pierre Turgeon 6.00 15.00
GD15 Joe Thornton 15.00 40.00
GD16 Brian Leetch 12.00 30.00
GD17 Henrik Lundqvist 12.00 30.00
GD18 Alexander Ovechkin 20.00 50.00
GD19 Sidney Crosby 30.00 80.00
GD20 Ilya Kovalchuk 10.00 25.00
GD21 Sidney Crosby 30.00 80.00
GD22 Alexander Ovechkin 20.00 50.00
GD23 Joe Thornton 15.00 40.00
GD24 Fernando Pisani 6.00 15.00
GD25 Ryan Smyth 10.00 25.00
GD26 Rod Brind'Amour 10.00 25.00
GD27 Shawn Horcoff 6.00 15.00
GD28 Jose Theodore 10.00 25.00
GD29 Patrick Marleau 10.00 25.00
GD30 Daniel Briere 10.00 25.00
GD31 Chris Drury 10.00 25.00
GD32 Cam Ward 10.00 25.00
GD33 Martin Havlat 6.00 15.00
GD34 Michael Ryder 10.00 25.00
GD35 Martin Brodeur 15.00 40.00
GD36 R.J. Umberger 8.00 20.00
GD37 Jarome Iginla 12.00 30.00
GD38 Marian Gaborik 12.00 30.00
GD39 Marek Svatos 6.00 15.00
GD40 Joe Sakic 15.00 40.00
GD41 Cristobal Huet 15.00 40.00
GD42 Patrice Bergeron 10.00 25.00

2006-07 Upper Deck Game Jerseys

JAA Arron Asham 3.00 8.00
JAF Alexander Frolov 4.00 10.00
JAH Ales Hemsky 4.00 10.00
JAK Alex Kovalev 3.00 8.00
JAL Jason Allison 3.00 8.00
JAM Andrej Meszaros 3.00 8.00
JAO Alexander Ovechkin SP 20.00 50.00
JAT Alex Tanguay 6.00 15.00
JAY Alexei Yashin 3.00 8.00
JBA Barret Jackman 3.00 8.00
JBB Brad Boyes 3.00 8.00
JBE Patrice Bergeron 6.00 15.00
JBG Bill Guerin 4.00 10.00
JBI Martin Biron 5.00 12.00
JBL Rob Blake 5.00 12.00
JBM Mark Bell 3.00 8.00
JBR Brian Rolston 3.00 8.00
JBS Brad Stuart 3.00 8.00
JBT Barry Tallackson 3.00 8.00
JBU Peter Budaj 5.00 12.00
JCC Chris Chelios 5.00 12.00
JCD Chris Drury 4.00 10.00
JCJ Curtis Joseph 6.00 15.00
JCO Chris Osgood 5.00 12.00
JCP Corey Perry 5.00 12.00
JCS Curtis Sanford 5.00 12.00
JDA Daniel Alfredsson 5.00 12.00
JDE Pavol Demitra 3.00 8.00
JDK Duncan Keith 3.00 8.00
JDP Daniel Paille 3.00 8.00
JDW Doug Weight 4.00 10.00
JEB Ed Belfour 6.00 15.00
JEJ Ed Jovanovski 3.00 8.00
JEL Eric Lindros 6.00 15.00
JGA Simon Gagne 5.00 12.00
JGL Georges Laraque 3.00 8.00
JHA Martin Havlat 5.00 12.00
JHE Milan Hejduk 5.00 12.00
JHO Marcel Hossa 3.00 8.00
JIK Ilya Kovalchuk SP 20.00 50.00
JJA Jason Arnott 3.00 8.00
JJB Jay Bouwmeester 4.00 10.00
JJC Jonathan Cheechoo 5.00 12.00
JJF Jeff Friesen 3.00 8.00
JJG Jean-Sebastien Giguere 5.00 12.00
JJI Jarome Iginla 8.00 20.00
JJJ Jaromir Jagr 8.00 20.00
JJL Joffrey Lupul 3.00 8.00
JJN Joe Nieuwendyk 5.00 12.00
JJO Jordan Leopold 3.00 8.00
JJS Jason Spezza 6.00 15.00
JJT Joe Thornton 8.00 20.00
JJW Jason Williams 3.00 8.00
JKD Kris Draper 3.00 8.00
JKP Keith Primeau 3.00 8.00
JKS Andrei Kostitsyn 3.00 8.00
JKT Keith Tkachuk 5.00 12.00
JLA Andrew Ladd 3.00 8.00
JLE Jere Lehtinen 4.00 10.00
JLU Jamie Lundmark 3.00 8.00
JLX Mario Lemieux SP 20.00 50.00
JMB Martin Brodeur 10.00 25.00
JMC Mike Comrie 3.00 8.00
JME Martin Erat 3.00 8.00
JMG Marian Gaborik 8.00 20.00
JMH Marian Hossa 6.00 15.00
JMI Mike Komisarek 3.00 8.00
JMK Miikka Kiprusoff 8.00 20.00
JML Manny Legace 3.00 8.00
JMM Mike Modano 8.00 20.00
JMN Markus Naslund 6.00 15.00
JMO Brendan Morrison 3.00 8.00
JMP Michael Peca 4.00 10.00
JMR Mark Recchi 4.00 10.00
JMS Marc Savard 4.00 10.00
JNK Nikolai Khabibulin 5.00 12.00
JPB Peter Bondra 5.00 12.00
JPD Pavel Datsyuk 8.00 20.00
JPF Peter Forsberg 8.00 20.00
JPP Petr Prucha 3.00 8.00
JRB Rod Brind'Amour 5.00 12.00
JRF Ruslan Fedotenko 3.00 8.00
JRH Ryan Hollweg 3.00 8.00
JRI Brad Richards 6.00 15.00
JRM Ryan Miller 6.00 15.00
JRU R.J. Umberger 3.00 8.00
JSC Sidney Crosby SP 200.00 350.00
JSG Scott Gomez 4.00 10.00
JSH Brendan Shanahan 5.00 12.00
JSM Matt Stajan 3.00 8.00
JSN Scott Niedermayer 4.00 10.00
JSS Sergei Samsonov 4.00 10.00
JST Steve Sullivan 3.00 8.00
JSU Scottie Upshall 3.00 8.00
JSW Stephen Weiss 3.00 8.00
JTC Ty Conklin 3.00 8.00
JTL Trevor Linden 6.00 15.00
JTP Tom Poti 3.00 8.00
JVL Vincent Lecavalier SP 15.00 30.00
JWR Wade Redden 3.00 8.00
J2AP Alexander Perezhogin 4.00 10.00
J2AR Andrew Raycroft 6.00 15.00
J2AS Alexander Steen 4.00 10.00
J2BB Brandon Bochenski 3.00 8.00
J2BC Bobby Clarke 5.00 12.00
J2BG Brian Gionta 4.00 10.00
J2BM Brenden Morrow 4.00 10.00
J2BP Brad Park 4.00 10.00
J2BR Bryan McCabe 3.00 8.00
J2BW Brendan Witt 3.00 8.00
J2CA Mike Cammalleri 5.00 12.00
J2CH Cristobal Huet 5.00 12.00
J2CK Chuck Kobasew 3.00 8.00
J2CN Cam Neely 8.00 20.00
J2CP Chris Pronger 4.00 10.00
J2CW Cam Ward 4.00 10.00
J2DB Daniel Briere 4.00 10.00
J2DC Dan Cloutier 3.00 8.00
J2DH Dominik Hasek 8.00 20.00
J2DP Dion Phaneuf 6.00 15.00
J2DR Dwayne Roloson 5.00 12.00
J2DS Daniel Sedin 4.00 10.00
J2DT Darcy Tucker 3.00 8.00
J2DU Ron Duguay 4.00 10.00
J2DW Dave Williams 6.00 15.00
J2EC Erik Cole 3.00 8.00
J2ES Eric Staal 6.00 15.00
J2GM Glen Murray 4.00 10.00
J2GR Gary Roberts 4.00 10.00
J2HE Dany Heatley 5.00 12.00
J2HL Henrik Lundqvist 5.00 12.00
J2HS Henrik Sedin 4.00 10.00
J2HZ Henrik Zetterberg 6.00 15.00
J2JB Jason Bacashihua 4.00 10.00
J2JC Jeff Carter 6.00 15.00
J2JJ Jussi Jokinen 4.00 10.00
J2JK Jakub Klepis 3.00 8.00
J2JP Joni Pitkanen 3.00 8.00
J2JR Jeremy Roenick 6.00 15.00
J2JS Joe Sakic 10.00 25.00
J2JT Jose Theodore 6.00 15.00
J2JW Justin Williams 3.00 8.00
J2KB Kevin Bieksa 3.00 8.00
J2KC Kyle Calder 3.00 8.00
J2KL Kari Lehtonen 6.00 15.00
J2KM Kirk Muller 3.00 8.00
J2KO Saku Koivu 6.00 15.00
J2LA Lanny McDonald 5.00 12.00
J2LM Larry Murphy 3.00 8.00
J2LX Mario Lemieux 15.00 40.00
J2MA Martin St. Louis 5.00 12.00
J2MC Mike Commodore 3.00 8.00
J2MF Manny Fernandez 5.00 12.00
J2MG Mike Grier 3.00 8.00
J2MH Michal Handzus 3.00 8.00
J2MJ Milan Jurcina 3.00 8.00
J2MP Mark Parrish 3.00 8.00
J2MR Michael Ryder 5.00 12.00
J2MS Marek Svatos 3.00 8.00
J2MT Marty Turco 5.00 12.00
J2MY Mike York 3.00 8.00
J2NH Nathan Horton 3.00 8.00
J2NL Nicklas Lidstrom 5.00 12.00
J2OJ Olli Jokinen 3.00 8.00
J2OK Olaf Kolzig 8.00 20.00
J2PE Patrik Elias 8.00 20.00
J2PK Paul Kariya 5.00 12.00
J2PM Patrick Marleau 5.00 12.00
J2PR Bob Probert 5.00 12.00
J2PS Peter Stastny 4.00 10.00
J2RB Ray Bourque 6.00 15.00
J2RD Rick DiPietro 5.00 12.00
J2RE Ron Ellis 3.00 8.00
J2RI Mike Ribeiro 3.00 8.00
J2RK Ryan Kesler 4.00 10.00
J2RL Roberto Luongo 6.00 15.00
J2RN Rick Nash 8.00 20.00
J2RO Patrick Roy 15.00 40.00
J2RS Ryan Smyth 5.00 12.00
J2SA Miroslav Satan 4.00 10.00
J2SB Steve Bernier 4.00 10.00
J2SC Stanislav Chistov 3.00 8.00
J2SD Shane Doan 4.00 10.00
J2SF Sergei Federov 5.00 12.00
J2SH Jody Shelley 4.00 10.00
J2SK Steve Konowalchuk 3.00 8.00
J2SO Sandis Ozolinsh 3.00 8.00
J2SS Sergei Samsonov 5.00 12.00
J2ST Jarret Stoll 3.00 8.00
J2SU Mats Sundin 5.00 12.00
J2SZ Sergei Zubov 3.00 8.00
J2TF Tomas Fleischmann 3.00 8.00
J2TH Tomas Holmstrom 4.00 10.00
J2TS Teemu Selanne 6.00 15.00
J2TT Tim Thomas 5.00 12.00
J2TV Tomas Vokoun 5.00 12.00
J2WG Wayne Gretzky SP 75.00 175.00
J2ZC Zdeno Chara 6.00 15.00

2006-07 Upper Deck Generations Duals

G2BL Brodeur/Luongo 30.00 60.00
G2BP Blake/Phaneuf 12.00 30.00
G2BW Belfour/Ward 10.00 25.00
G2DH Doan/Horton 10.00 25.00
G2EG Elias/Gaborik 10.00 25.00
G2FD Datsyuk/Fedorov 12.00 30.00
G2FK Frolov/Kovalev 8.00 20.00
G2FS Forsberg/Steen 15.00 40.00
G2GB Guerin/Brown 8.00 20.00
G2GC Gretzky/Crosby 75.00 150.00
G2HH Hossa/Hemsky 8.00 20.00
G2HS Hejduk/Svatos 8.00 20.00
G2IL Iginla/Lupul 12.00 30.00
G2JK Jokinen/Koivu 8.00 20.00
G2JO Jagr/Ovechkin 20.00 50.00
G2KD Koivu/Datsyuk 10.00 25.00
G2KL Kipper/Lehtonen 15.00 40.00
G2LP Lidstrom/Pitkanen 12.00 30.00
G2NB S.Nieder/J.Bouw 8.00 20.00
G2NZ Naslund/Zetty 10.00 25.00
G2PG Primeau/Getzlaf 10.00 25.00
G2RM Redden/Meszaros 8.00 20.00
G2SN Shanahan/Nash 10.00 25.00
G2SS Sakic/Spezza 20.00 50.00
G2TS Thornton/Staal 12.50 30.00
G2VH Vokoun/Hasek 12.00 30.00
G2PJD Sakic/Heatley 20.00 50.00
G2PSH Satan/Havlat 10.00 25.00

2006-07 Upper Deck Goal Rush

COMPLETE SET (14) 10.00 25.00
COMMON CARDS .75 2.00
SEMISTARS .75 2.00
UNLISTED STARS 1.00 2.50
GR1 Jonathan Cheechoo .75 2.00
GR2 Jaromir Jagr 3.00 8.00
GR3 Dany Heatley .75 2.00
GR4 Ilya Kovalchuk 1.00 2.50
GR5 Rick Nash 1.00 2.50
GR6 Marian Gaborik 1.00 2.50
GR7 Markus Naslund 1.00 2.50
GR8 Jarome Iginla 1.25 3.00
GR9 Alexander Ovechkin 1.25 3.00
GR10 Simon Gagne 1.00 2.50
GR11 Eric Staal 1.25 3.00
GR12 Teemu Selanne 2.00 5.00
GR13 Brendan Shanahan 1.00 2.50
GR14 Sidney Crosby 2.00 5.00

2006-07 Upper Deck Hometown Heroes

COMPLETE SET (28) 20.00 50.00
COMMON CARD .75 2.00
SEMISTARS .75 2.00
UNLISTED STARS 1.00 2.50
HH29 Teemu Selanne 2.00 5.00
HH30 Patrice Bergeron 1.25 3.00
HH31 Ryan Miller 1.00 2.50
HH32 Miikka Kiprusoff 1.00 2.50
HH33 Eric Staal 1.25 3.00
HH34 Henrik Zetterberg 1.25 3.00
HH35 Michael Ryder .60 1.50
HH36 Henrik Lundqvist 2.50 6.00
HH37 Jason Spezza 1.00 2.50
HH38 Simon Gagne 1.00 2.50
HH39 Sidney Crosby 3.00 8.00
HH40 Jonathan Cheechoo .75 2.00
HH41 Darcy Tucker .75 2.00
HH42 Alexander Ovechkin 4.00 10.00
HH43 Milan Hejduk .75 2.00
HH44 Patrick Marleau 1.00 2.50
HH45 Cristobal Huet .75 2.00
HH46 Cam Ward 1.00 2.50
HH47 Vincent Lecavalier 1.00 2.50
HH48 Kari Lehtonen .75 2.00
HH49 Nicklas Lidstrom 1.00 2.50
HH50 Roberto Luongo 1.50 4.00
HH51 Rob Blake 1.00 2.50
HH52 Marian Gaborik 1.00 2.50
HH53 Alexander Steen .60 1.50
HH54 Doug Weight 1.00 2.50
HH55 Marc-Andre Fleury 2.00 5.00
HH56 Dion Phaneuf .75 2.00

2006-07 Upper Deck Oversized Wal-Mart Exclusives

251 Chris Pronger 1.00 2.50
254 Jean-Sebastien Giguere 1.00 2.50
258 Ilya Kovalchuk 1.00 2.50
265 Patrice Bergeron 1.25 3.00
279 Alex Tanguay .60 1.50
282 Miikka Kiprusoff 1.00 2.50
286 Rod Brind'Amour 1.00 2.50
292 Martin Havlat .60 1.50
299 Marek Svatos .60 1.50
309 Gilbert Brule .75 2.00
313 Mike Modano 1.50 4.00
318 Eric Lindros 1.50 4.00
319 Dominik Hasek 1.50 4.00
323 Henrik Zetterberg 1.25 3.00
324 Nicklas Lidstrom 1.00 2.50
325 Ryan Smyth .75 2.00
333 Ed Belfour 1.00 2.50
337 Todd Bertuzzi 1.00 2.50
339 Rob Blake 1.00 2.50
345 Manny Fernandez .60 1.50
352 Michael Ryder .60 1.50
359 Paul Kariya 1.00 2.50
365 Patrik Elias 1.00 2.50
377 Henrik Lundqvist 2.50 6.00
379 Wayne Gretzky 6.00 15.00
383 Brendan Shanahan 1.00 2.50
384 Dany Heatley .75 2.00
391 Simon Gagne 1.00 2.50
392 Jeff Carter .75 2.00
401 Jeremy Roenick 1.50 4.00
403 Owen Nolan 1.00 2.50
404 Marc-Andre Fleury 2.00 5.00
409 Mark Recchi 1.25 3.00
410 Patrick Marleau 1.00 2.50
415 Evgeni Nabokov .75 2.00
417 Doug Weight 1.00 2.50
422 Vincent Lecavalier 1.00 2.50
426 Brad Richards 1.00 2.50
428 Andrew Raycroft .75 2.00
430 Michael Peca .75 2.00
436 Roberto Luongo 1.50 4.00
442 Alexander Ovechkin 4.00 10.00

2006-07 Upper Deck Rookie Game Dated Moments

RGD1 Ryan Shannon 4.00 10.00
RGD2 Phil Kessel 12.00 30.00
RGD3 Mark Stuart 4.00 10.00
RGD4 Yan Stastny 4.00 10.00
RGD5 Paul Stastny 10.00 25.00
RGD6 Loui Eriksson 8.00 20.00
RGD7 Tomas Kopecky 5.00 12.00
RGD8 Patrick Thoresen 4.00 10.00
RGD9 Ladislav Smid 4.00 10.00
RGD10 Marc-Antoine Pouliot 4.00 10.00
RGD11 Patrick O'Sullivan 6.00 15.00
RGD12 Anze Kopitar 20.00 50.00
RGD13 Guillaume Latendresse 6.00 15.00
RGD14 Shea Weber 10.00 25.00
RGD15 Mikko Lehtonen 5.00 12.00
RGD16 Travis Zajac 8.00 20.00
RGD17 Nigel Dawes 4.00 10.00
RGD18 Alexei Kaigorodov 4.00 10.00
RGD19 Ryan Potulny 4.00 10.00
RGD20 Joel Perrault 4.00 10.00
RGD21 Evgeni Malkin 25.00 60.00
RGD22 Jordan Staal 10.00 25.00
RGD23 Kristopher Letang 15.00 40.00
RGD24 Noah Welch 4.00 10.00
RGD25 Marc-Edouard Vlasic 6.00 15.00
RGD26 Matt Carle 4.00 10.00
RGD27 Ian White 5.00 12.00
RGD28 Ben Ondrus 4.00 10.00
RGD29 Luc Bourdon 6.00 15.00
RGD30 Eric Fehr 6.00 15.00

2006-07 Upper Deck Rookie Headliners

COMPLETE SET (30) 40.00 100.00
RH1 Patrick O'Sullivan 1.50 4.00
RH2 Loui Eriksson 2.00 5.00
RH3 Enver Lisin 1.00 2.50
RH4 Luc Bourdon 1.50 4.00

RH5 Noah Welch 1.00 2.50
RH6 Travis Zajac 2.00 5.00
RH7 Ladislav Smid 1.00 2.50
RH8 Ryan Potulny 1.00 2.50
RH9 Marc-Antoine Pouliot 1.00 2.50
RH10 Dave Bolland 1.50 4.00
RH11 Nigel Dawes 1.00 2.50
RH12 Marc-Edouard Vlasic 1.50 4.00
RH13 Patrick Thoresen 1.00 2.50
RH14 Matt Lashoff 1.00 2.50
RH15 Ian White 1.25 3.00
RH16 Alexei Mikhnov 1.00 2.50
RH17 Tomas Kopecky 1.25 3.00
RH18 Kristopher Letang 4.00 10.00
RH19 Michael Blunden 1.00 2.50
RH20 Brandon Prust 1.00 2.50
RH21 Evgeni Malkin SP 15.00 40.00
RH22 Phil Kessel SP 8.00 20.00
RH23 Jordan Staal SP 6.00 15.00
RH24 G. Latendresse SP 4.00 10.00
RH25 Anze Kopitar SP 12.00 30.00
RH26 Matt Carle SP 2.50 6.00
RH27 Paul Stastny SP 6.00 15.00
RH28 Alexander Radulov SP 5.00 12.00
RH29 Dustin Boyd SP 2.50 6.00
RH30 Drew Stafford SP 4.00 10.00

2006-07 Upper Deck Rookie Materials

*PATCH/15: 1X TO 2.5X BASIC JSY
RMBB Brendan Bell 2.50 6.00
RMBO Ben Ondrus 2.50 6.00
RMBT Billy Thompson 2.50 6.00
RMCG Carsen Germyn 2.50 6.00
RMDB Dustin Byfuglien 6.00 15.00
RMDK D.J. King 2.50 6.00
RMEF Eric Fehr 4.00 10.00
RMEM Evgeni Malkin 15.00 40.00
RMFN Filip Novak 2.50 6.00
RMGL Guillaume Latendresse 4.00 10.00
RMIW Ian White 3.00 8.00
RMJI Jarkko Immonen 3.00 8.00
RMJS Jordan Staal 6.00 15.00
RMJW Jeremy Williams 2.50 6.00
RMKL Kristopher Letang 10.00 25.00
RMKO Anze Kopitar 12.00 30.00
RMKP Konstantin Pushkarev 3.00 8.00
RMKY Keith Yandle 6.00 15.00
RMLB Luc Bourdon 4.00 10.00
RMLE Loui Eriksson 5.00 12.00
RMLS Ladislav Smid 2.50 6.00
RMMC Matt Carle 2.50 6.00
RMMP Marc-Antoine Pouliot 2.50 6.00
RMMS Mark Stuart 2.50 6.00
RMMV Marc-Edouard Vlasic 4.00 10.00
RMNB Niklas Backstrom 5.00 12.00
RMND Nigel Dawes 2.50 6.00
RMNO Fredrik Norrena 2.50 6.00
RMNW Noah Welch 2.50 6.00
RMPK Phil Kessel 8.00 20.00
RMPO Patrick O'Sullivan 4.00 10.00
RMPS Paul Stastny 6.00 15.00
RMPT Patrick Thoresen 2.50 6.00
RMRO Roman Polak 3.00 8.00
RMRP Ryan Potulny 2.50 6.00
RMRS Ryan Shannon 2.50 6.00
RMSO Shane O'Brien 2.50 6.00
RMSW Shea Weber 6.00 15.00
RMTK Tomas Kopecky 3.00 8.00
RMTZ Travis Zajac 5.00 12.00
RMYS Yan Stastny 2.50 6.00

2006-07 Upper Deck Shootout Artists

COMPLETE SET (14) 10.00 25.00
SA1 Jussi Jokinen .60 1.50
SA2 Miroslav Satan .60 1.50
SA3 Brad Richards .75 2.00
SA4 Alexander Ovechkin 2.00 5.00
SA5 Paul Kariya 1.00 2.50
SA6 Ales Hemsky .75 2.00
SA7 Mikko Koivu .75 2.00
SA8 Alexander Frolov .60 1.50
SA9 Jason Williams .60 1.50
SA10 Slava Kozlov .60 1.50
SA11 Brian Gionta .60 1.50
SA12 Vincent Lecavalier 1.00 2.50
SA13 Jaroslav Balastik .30 .75
SA14 Sergei Zubov .60 1.50

2006-07 Upper Deck Signatures

SAO Alexander Ovechkin SP 100.00 250.00
SAP A. Perezhogin 10.00 25.00
SAR Andrew Raycroft 12.00 30.00
SAT Alex Tanguay 10.00 25.00
SBB Brad Boyes 10.00 25.00
SBC Braydon Coburn 10.00 25.00
SBL Brett Lebda 10.00 25.00
SBO J. Bouwmeester 10.00 25.00
SCP Corey Perry SP 25.00 60.00
SCS Cory Stillman 10.00 25.00
SCT Chris Thorburn 10.00 25.00
SDC Dan Cloutier 12.00 30.00
SDH Dany Heatley SP 12.00 30.00
SDL David Legwand SP 12.00 30.00
SDP Daniel Paille 12.00 30.00
SDW Doug Weight SP 15.00 40.00
SEC Erik Cole 10.00 25.00
SEL Enver Lisin 10.00 25.00
SEM Evgeni Malkin 60.00 150.00
SEN Eric Nystrom 10.00 25.00
SES Eric Staal SP 20.00 50.00
SFP Fernando Pisani 10.00 25.00
SGB Gilbert Brule 12.00 30.00
SGH Gordie Howe SP 100.00 200.00
SGL G. Latendresse 15.00 40.00
SGM Glen Murray 12.00 30.00
SHL Henrik Lundqvist 40.00 100.00
SHZ Henrik Zetterberg 20.00 50.00
SJI Jarome Iginla SP 20.00 50.00
SJR Jeremy Roenick 25.00 60.00
SJS Jordan Staal 25.00 60.00
SJT Jeff Tambellini SP 10.00 25.00
SJW Justin Williams 12.00 30.00
SMB Martin Brodeur SP 40.00 100.00
SMG Marian Gaborik SP 15.00 40.00
SMM Mike Modano SP 25.00 60.00
SMN Markus Naslund 15.00 40.00
SMP Michael Peca 12.00 30.00
SMR Mike Ribeiro 10.00 25.00
SMS Martin St. Louis 15.00 40.00
SNK Nikolai Khabibulin 15.00 40.00
SPB Patrice Bergeron 20.00 50.00
SPH Dion Phaneuf 12.00 30.00
SPK Phil Kessel 30.00 80.00
SRH Ryan Hollweg 10.00 25.00
SRK Ryan Kesler 15.00 40.00
SRL Roberto Luongo 25.00 60.00
SSB Steve Bernier 10.00 25.00
SSC Sidney Crosby 150.00 250.00
SSG Simon Gagne 15.00 40.00
SSS Sergei Samsonov 12.00 30.00
SST Matt Stajan 10.00 25.00
STA Tyler Arnason 10.00 25.00
STV Thomas Vanek 12.00 30.00
SVL Vincent Lecavalier SP 15.00 40.00
SWG Wayne Gretzky SP 200.00 500.00
SYD Yann Danis 12.00 30.00
SZP Zach Parise 15.00 40.00

2006-07 Upper Deck Signature Sensations

SSAA Aaron Asham 6.00 15.00
SSAF Alexander Frolov 6.00 15.00
SSAH Adam Hall 6.00 15.00
SSAR Andrew Raycroft 8.00 20.00
SSAS Alexander Steen 10.00 25.00
SSAT Alex Tanguay 6.00 15.00
SSBB Brad Boyes 6.00 15.00
SSBL Brian Leetch 8.00 20.00
SSBO Jay Bouwmeester 6.00 15.00
SSBR Brian Rafalski 8.00 20.00
SSBW Brad Winchester 6.00 15.00
SSCH Chris Higgins 6.00 15.00
SSCK Chris Kunitz 10.00 25.00
SSCP Chris Phillips 6.00 15.00
SSDW Doug Weight 10.00 25.00
SSEJ Ed Jovanovski 8.00 20.00
SSEN Evgeni Nabokov 8.00 20.00
SSFL Marc-Andre Fleury 20.00 50.00
SSFS Fredrik Sjostrom 6.00 15.00
SSGM Glen Murray 8.00 20.00
SSHA Michal Handzus 8.00 20.00
SSHE Milan Hejduk 8.00 20.00
SSHT Hannu Toivonen 8.00 20.00
SSJB Jason Blake 6.00 15.00
SSJP Joni Pitkanen 6.00 15.00
SSJR Jeremy Roenick 15.00 40.00
SSJT Jose Theodore 10.00 25.00
SSKB Keith Ballard 6.00 15.00
SSKL Kari Lehtonen 8.00 20.00
SSKP Keith Primeau 8.00 20.00
SSKT Kimmo Timonen 6.00 15.00
SSMC Mike Comrie 8.00 20.00
SSMG Marian Gaborik 10.00 25.00
SSMH Martin Havlat 6.00 15.00
SSMK Miikka Kiprusoff 10.00 25.00
SSML Mario Lemieux 50.00 125.00
SSMP Mark Parrish 6.00 15.00
SSMS Miroslav Satan 8.00 20.00
SSNK Nikolai Khabibulin 10.00 25.00
SSPB Pierre-Marc Bouchard 10.00 25.00
SSPM Patrick Marleau 10.00 25.00
SSPR Chris Pronger 10.00 25.00
SSRB Rene Bourque 6.00 15.00
SSRF Ruslan Fedotenko 6.00 15.00
SSRN Rick Nash 10.00 25.00
SSRS Ryan Smyth EXCH 8.00 20.00
SSRU R.J. Umberger 6.00 15.00
SSRW Ryan Whitney 8.00 20.00
SSSC Sidney Crosby 60.00 150.00
SSSD Shane Doan 8.00 20.00
SSSG Scott Gomez 8.00 20.00
SSSH Shawn Horcoff 6.00 15.00
SSSS Steve Sullivan 6.00 15.00
SSTA Tyler Arnason 6.00 15.00
SSTL Trevor Linden 10.00 25.00
SSVT Vesa Toskala 8.00 20.00
SSWG Wayne Gretzky SP 200.00 500.00
SSWR Wade Redden 6.00 15.00
SSWW Wojtek Wolski 8.00 20.00

2006-07 Upper Deck Statistical Leaders

COMPLETE SET (7) 10.00 25.00
SL1 Joe Thornton 2.00 5.00
SL2 Jonathan Cheechoo .75 2.00
SL3 Alexander Ovechkin 4.00 10.00
SL4 Wade Redden .75 2.00
SL5 Martin Brodeur 3.00 8.00
SL6 Miikka Kiprusoff 2.00 5.00
SL7 Sean Avery .40 1.00

2006-07 Upper Deck Zero Men

COMPLETE SET (7) 8.00 20.00
ZM1 Martin Brodeur 3.00 8.00
ZM2 Dominik Hasek 2.00 5.00
ZM3 Roberto Luongo 1.25 3.00
ZM4 Miikka Kiprusoff 1.25 3.00
ZM5 Marty Turco 1.00 2.50
ZM6 Cam Ward 1.00 2.50
ZM7 Ed Belfour 1.00 2.50

2007 Upper Deck BAP Draft Redemption Premium

TYSC Sidney Crosby 4.00 10.00

2007-08 Upper Deck

COMP.SER.1 SET w/o SPs (200) 20.00 50.00
COMP.SER.2 SET w/o SPs (200) 20.00 50.00
1 Nicklas Lidstrom .25 .60
2 Dan Cleary .20 .50
3 Kris Draper .15 .40
4 Dominik Hasek .40 1.00
5 Henrik Zetterberg .30 .75
6 Jiri Hudler .20 .50
7 Brett Lebda .15 .40
8 J.P. Dumont .15 .40
9 Steve Sullivan .15 .40
10 Shea Weber .20 .50
11 Martin Erat .15 .40
12 Alexander Radulov .25 .60
13 David Legwand .20 .50
14 Manny Legace .20 .50
15 Lee Stempniak .15 .40
16 Jay McClement .15 .40
17 Eric Brewer .15 .40
18 Brad Boyes .15 .40
19 Barret Jackman .15 .40
20 Rick Nash .25 .60
21 Fredrik Norrena .15 .40
22 Rostislav Klesla .15 .40
23 Gilbert Brule .20 .50
24 David Vyborny .15 .40
25 Manny Malhotra .15 .40
26 Martin Havlat .25 .60
27 Rene Bourque .15 .40
28 Patrick Lalime .20 .50
29 Jason Williams .15 .40
30 Cam Barker .15 .40
31 Patrick Sharp .25 .60
32 Duncan Keith .20 .50
33 Markus Naslund .20 .50
34 Ryan Kesler .25 .60
35 Matt Cooke .15 .40
36 Kevin Bieksa .20 .50
37 Henrik Sedin .30 .75
38 Brendan Morrison .15 .40
39 Mattias Ohlund .15 .40
40 Marian Gaborik .25 .60
41 Stephane Veilleux .15 .40
42 Kim Johnsson .15 .40
43 Niklas Backstrom .25 .60
44 Brian Rolston .20 .50
45 Mikko Koivu .20 .50
46 Derek Boogaard .15 .40
47 Miikka Kiprusoff .25 .60
48 Matthew Lombardi .15 .40
49 Dion Phaneuf .20 .50
50 Craig Conroy .15 .40
51 Alex Tanguay .20 .50
52 Wayne Primeau .15 .40
53 Robyn Regehr .15 .40
54 Joe Sakic .50 1.25
55 Brett Clark .15 .40
56 Ian Laperriere .15 .40
57 Marek Svatos .15 .40
58 Peter Budaj .20 .50
59 John-Michael Liles .15 .40
60 Paul Stastny .20 .50
61 Dwayne Roloson .20 .50
62 Jarret Stoll .20 .50
63 Ladislav Smid .15 .40
64 Raffi Torres .15 .40
65 Marc-Antoine Pouliot .15 .40
66 Ales Hemsky .20 .50
67 Fernando Pisani .15 .40
68 Ryan Getzlaf .25 .60
69 Andy McDonald .15 .40
70 Chris Pronger .25 .60
71 Ilya Bryzgalov .25 .60
72 Chris Kunitz .15 .40
73 Francois Beauchemin .15 .40
74 Dustin Penner .20 .50
75 Joe Thornton .40 1.00
76 Milan Michalek .15 .40
77 Matt Carle .15 .40
78 Evgeni Nabokov .20 .50
79 Steve Bernier .15 .40
80 Mike Grier .15 .40
81 Joe Pavelski .30 .75
82 Mike Modano .40 1.00
83 Sergei Zubov .20 .50
84 Mike Smith .25 .60
85 Mike Ribeiro .15 .40
86 Brenden Morrow .20 .50
87 Jussi Jokinen .15 .40
88 Jeff Halpern .15 .40
89 Anze Kopitar .40 1.00
90 Dan Cloutier .20 .50
91 Dustin Brown .25 .60
92 Mike Cammalleri .20 .50
93 Rob Blake .25 .60
94 Patrick O'Sullivan .20 .50
95 Shane Doan .20 .50
96 Mikael Tellqvist .20 .50
97 Zbynek Michalek .15 .40
98 Keith Ballard .15 .40
99 Kevyn Adams .15 .40
100 Ed Jovanovski .15 .40
101 Patrick Elias .25 .60
102 Travis Zajac .15 .40
103 Jay Pandolfo .15 .40
104 Paul Martin .15 .40
105 Brian Gionta .15 .40
106 John Madden .15 .40
107 Zach Parise .25 .60
108 Sidney Crosby 1.00 2.50
109 Jordan Staal .20 .50
110 Jocelyn Thibault .20 .50
111 Sergei Gonchar .15 .40
112 Gary Roberts .15 .40
113 Erik Christensen .15 .40
114 Evgeni Malkin .50 1.25
115 Jaromir Jagr .75 2.00
116 Petr Prucha .15 .40
117 Marek Malik .15 .40
118 Sean Avery .15 .40
119 Marcel Hossa .15 .40
120 Michal Rozsival .15 .40
121 Ryan Hollweg .15 .40
122 Miroslav Satan .20 .50
123 Trent Hunter .15 .40
124 Mike Sillinger .15 .40
125 Marc-Andre Bergeron .15 .40
126 Rick DiPietro .20 .50
127 Brendan Witt .15 .40
128 Martin Biron .20 .50
129 Jeff Carter .20 .50
130 Ben Eager .15 .40
131 Simon Gagne .25 .60
132 R.J. Umberger .20 .50
133 Scottie Upshall .15 .40
134 Ryan Miller .25 .60
135 Thomas Vanek .20 .50
136 Derek Roy .15 .40
137 Brian Campbell .20 .50
138 Drew Stafford .15 .40
139 Maxim Afinogenov .15 .40
140 Jason Pominville .15 .40
141 Dany Heatley .25 .60
142 Wade Redden .15 .40
143 Chris Kelly .15 .40
144 Ray Emery .20 .50
145 Chris Neil .15 .40
146 Mike Fisher .15 .40
147 Chris Phillips .15 .40
148 Darcy Tucker .20 .50
149 Ian White .15 .40
150 Alexei Ponikarovsky .15 .40
151 Alexander Steen .15 .40
152 Andrew Raycroft .20 .50
153 Bryan McCabe .15 .40
154 Matt Stajan .15 .40
155 Michael Ryder .15 .40
156 Guillaume Latendresse .20 .50
157 Cristobal Huet .20 .50
158 Alex Kovalev .20 .50
159 Mark Streit .15 .40
160 Chris Higgins .15 .40
161 Tomas Plekanec .15 .40
162 Patrice Bergeron .30 .75
163 Hannu Toivonen .20 .50
164 Zdeno Chara .25 .60
165 Phil Kessel .25 .60
166 Chuck Kobasew .15 .40
167 P.J. Axelsson .15 .40
168 Glen Murray .20 .50
169 Ilya Kovalchuk .25 .60
170 Jim Slater .15 .40
171 Johan Hedberg .20 .50
172 Marian Hossa .25 .60
173 Bobby Holik .15 .40
174 Alexei Zhitnik .15 .40
175 Vincent Lecavalier .25 .60
176 Dan Boyle .15 .40
177 Ryan Craig .15 .40
178 Vaclav Prospal .15 .40
179 Marc Denis .20 .50
180 Brad Richards .25 .60
181 Eric Staal .30 .75
182 Rod Brind'Amour .25 .60
183 Cory Stillman .15 .40
184 Mike Commodore .15 .40
185 Erik Cole .15 .40
186 John Grahame .15 .40
187 Olli Jokinen .20 .50
188 Nathan Horton .25 .60
189 Stephen Weiss .15 .40
190 Jay Bouwmeester .20 .50
191 Alex Auld .15 .40
192 Rostislav Olesz .15 .40
193 Alexander Semin .25 .60
194 Chris Clark .15 .40
195 Olaf Kolzig .25 .60
196 Mike Green .20 .50
197 Brian Pothier .15 .40
198 Milan Jurcina .15 .40
199 Nicklas Lidstrom CL .25 .60
200 Sidney Crosby CL 1.00 2.50
201 Drew Miller YG RC 2.50 6.00
202 Bobby Ryan YG RC 12.00 30.00
203 Ryan Carter YG RC 2.00 5.00
204 Jonas Hiller YG RC 4.00 10.00
205 Bryan Little YG RC 3.00 8.00
206 Tobias Enstrom YG RC 3.00 8.00
207 Milan Lucic YG RC 8.00 20.00
208 David Krejci YG RC 10.00 25.00
209 Curtis McElhinney YG RC 3.00 8.00
210 Patrick Kane YG RC 125.00 300.00
211 Magnus Johansson YG RC 2.00 5.00
212 Jaroslav Hlinka YG RC 2.50 6.00
213 Tyler Weiman YG RC 2.50 6.00
214 Kris Russell YG RC 3.00 8.00
215 Jared Boll YG RC 2.50 6.00
216 Matt Niskanen YG RC 3.00 8.00
217 Matt Ellis YG RC 2.00 5.00
218 Sam Gagner YG RC 4.00 10.00
219 Rob Schremp YG RC 2.50 6.00
220 Tom Gilbert YG RC 2.50 6.00
221 Cory Murphy YG RC 2.00 5.00
222 Jack Johnson YG RC 2.50 6.00
223 Jonathan Bernier YG RC 4.00 10.00
224 Lauri Tukonen YG RC 2.00 5.00
225 Brady Murray YG RC 2.00 5.00
226 Petr Kalus YG RC 2.00 5.00
227 Carey Price YG RC 125.00 300.00
228 Jaroslav Halak YG RC 6.00 15.00
229 Ville Koistinen YG RC 2.00 5.00
230 Nicklas Bergfors YG RC 2.00 5.00
231 Andy Greene YG RC 2.50 6.00
232 Frans Nielsen YG RC 2.50 6.00
233 Ryan Callahan YG RC 4.00 10.00
234 Marc Staal YG RC 3.00 8.00
235 Brandon Dubinsky YG RC 4.00 10.00
236 Daniel Girardi YG RC 2.50 6.00
237 Brian Elliott YG RC 4.00 10.00
238 Nick Foligno YG RC 4.00 10.00
239 Denis Tolpeko YG RC 2.00 5.00
240 Peter Mueller YG RC 2.50 6.00
241 Daniel Winnik YG RC 2.50 6.00
242 Torrey Mitchell YG RC 2.50 6.00
243 Erik Johnson YG RC 3.00 8.00
244 Steve Wagner YG RC 2.00 5.00
245 Matt Smaby YG RC 2.00 5.00
246 Mike Lundin YG RC 2.00 5.00
247 Mason Raymond YG RC 3.00 8.00
248 Jannik Hansen YG RC 2.50 6.00
249 Nicklas Backstrom YG RC 15.00 40.00
250 Kane/Price/Jnsn YG CL 6.00 15.00
251 Pavel Datsyuk .40 1.00
252 Chris Osgood .25 .60
253 Brian Rafalski .20 .50
254 Henrik Zetterberg .30 .75
255 Tomas Holmstrom .20 .50
256 Chris Chelios .25 .60
257 Johan Franzen .20 .50
258 Chris Mason .20 .50
259 Dan Hamhuis .20 .50
260 Radek Bonk .15 .40
261 Jordin Tootoo .20 .50
262 Jason Arnott .20 .50
263 Ryan Suter .20 .50
264 Marek Zidlicky .15 .40
265 Paul Kariya .25 .60
266 Christian Backman .15 .40
267 Doug Weight .25 .60
268 Martin Rucinsky .15 .40
269 Jay McKee .15 .40
270 Keith Tkachuk .25 .60
271 Pascal Leclaire .20 .50
272 Nikolai Zherdev .15 .40
273 Jason Chimera .15 .40
274 Adam Foote .15 .40
275 Rick Nash .25 .60
276 Sergei Fedorov .40 1.00
277 Fredrik Modin .15 .40
278 Nikolai Khabibulin .25 .60
279 Yanic Perreault .15 .40
280 Tuomo Ruutu .15 .40
281 Robert Lang .15 .40
282 Brent Sopel .15 .40
283 Brent Seabrook .15 .40
284 Sergei Samsonov .20 .50
285 Roberto Luongo .40 1.00
286 Willie Mitchell .15 .40
287 Taylor Pyatt .15 .40
288 Aaron Miller .15 .40
289 Markus Naslund .25 .60
290 Lukas Krajicek .15 .40
291 Daniel Sedin .30 .75
292 Pavol Demitra .30 .75
293 Kurtis Foster .15 .40
294 Marian Gaborik .25 .60
295 Pierre-Marc Bouchard .25 .60
296 Josh Harding .25 .60
297 Mark Parrish .15 .40
298 Jarome Iginla .30 .75
299 Adrian Aucoin .15 .40
300 Marcus Nilson .15 .40
301 Daymond Langkow .15 .40
302 Cory Sarich .15 .40
303 Kristian Huselius .15 .40
304 Owen Nolan .25 .60
305 Jose Theodore .25 .60
306 Milan Hejduk .20 .50
307 Joe Sakic .50 1.25
308 Scott Hannan .15 .40
309 Wojtek Wolski .20 .50
310 Tyler Arnason .15 .40
311 Ryan Smyth .20 .50
312 Joni Pitkanen .15 .40
313 Ethan Moreau .15 .40
314 Dustin Penner .20 .50
315 Ales Hemsky .20 .50
316 Shawn Horcoff .15 .40
317 Matt Greene .15 .40
318 Geoff Sanderson .15 .40
319 Jean-Sebastien Giguere .25 .60
320 Todd Bertuzzi .25 .60
321 Scott Niedermayer .25 .60
322 Corey Perry .40 1.00
323 Travis Moen .15 .40
324 Mathieu Schneider .15 .40
325 Sean O'Donnell .15 .40
326 Jonathan Cheechoo .20 .50
327 Marc-Edouard Vlasic .15 .40
328 Ryane Clowe .15 .40
329 Craig Rivet .15 .40
330 Joe Thornton .40 1.00
331 Patrick Marleau .25 .60
332 Joe Pavelski .30 .75
333 Marty Turco .25 .60
334 Philippe Boucher .15 .40
335 Loui Eriksson .15 .40
336 Mattias Norstrom .15 .40
337 Mike Modano .40 1.00
338 Jere Lehtinen .15 .40
339 Alexander Frolov .15 .40
340 Lubomir Visnovsky .15 .40
341 Michal Handzus .20 .50
342 Brad Stuart .15 .40
343 Tom Preissing .15 .40
344 Ladislav Nagy .15 .40
345 Niko Kapanen .15 .40
346 Shane Doan .20 .50
347 Nick Boynton .15 .40
348 Fredrik Sjostrom .15 .40
349 Derek Morris .15 .40
350 Steven Reinprecht .15 .40
351 Martin Brodeur .60 1.50
352 Johnny Oduya .20 .50
353 Arron Asham .15 .40
354 Sergei Brylin .15 .40
355 Kevin Weekes .20 .50
356 Dainius Zubrus .15 .40
357 Marc-Andre Fleury .50 1.25
358 Ryan Malone .15 .40
359 Darryl Sydor .15 .40
360 Petr Sykora .20 .50
361 Evgeni Malkin .50 1.25
362 Colby Armstrong .15 .40
363 Mark Recchi .30 .75
364 Henrik Lundqvist .60 1.50
365 Chris Drury .20 .50
366 Colton Orr .15 .40
367 Scott Gomez .20 .50
368 Michal Rozsival .15 .40
369 Brendan Shanahan .25 .60
370 Martin Straka .15 .40
371 Bill Guerin .20 .50
372 Wade Dubielewicz .20 .50
373 Chris Campoli .15 .40
374 Ruslan Fedotenko .15 .40
375 Bruno Gervais .15 .40
376 Mike Comrie .15 .40
377 Daniel Briere .25 .60
378 Mike Richards .25 .60
379 Kimmo Timonen .15 .40
380 Antero Niittymaki .20 .50
381 Simon Gagne .25 .60
382 Joffrey Lupul .15 .40
383 Scott Hartnell .15 .40
384 Tim Connolly .15 .40
385 Daniel Paille .20 .50
386 Jochen Hecht .15 .40
387 Ales Kotalik .15 .40
388 Ryan Miller .25 .60
389 Andrew Peters .15 .40
390 Daniel Alfredsson .25 .60
391 Dany Heatley .25 .60
392 Patrick Eaves .15 .40
393 Antoine Vermette .15 .40
394 Martin Gerber .20 .50
395 Jason Spezza .25 .60
396 Anton Volchenkov .15 .40
397 Vesa Toskala .20 .50
398 Nikolai Antropov .15 .40
399 Tomas Kaberle .15 .40
400 Jason Blake .15 .40
401 Simon Gamache .15 .40
402 Mats Sundin .25 .60
403 Kris Newbury .15 .40
404 Roman Hamrlik .15 .40
405 Bryan Smolinski .15 .40
406 Mike Komisarek .15 .40
407 Saku Koivu .25 .60
408 Andrei Kostitsyn .20 .50
409 Maxim Lapierre .15 .40
410 Josh Gorges .15 .40
411 Manny Fernandez .20 .50
412 Brandon Bochenski .15 .40
413 Patrice Bergeron .30 .75
414 Marco Sturm .15 .40
415 Dennis Wideman .15 .40
416 Tim Thomas .25 .60
417 Marc Savard .15 .40
418 Kari Lehtonen .20 .50
419 Ken Klee .15 .40
420 Ilya Kovalchuk .25 .60
421 Garnet Exelby .15 .40
422 Todd White .15 .40
423 Slava Kozlov .15 .40
424 Johan Holmqvist .20 .50
425 Chris Gratton .15 .40
426 Filip Kuba .15 .40
427 Michel Ouellet .15 .40
428 Paul Ranger .15 .40
429 Martin St. Louis .25 .60
430 Cam Ward .25 .60
431 Ray Whitney .20 .50
432 Eric Staal .30 .75
433 Tim Gleason .15 .40
434 Andrew Ladd .15 .40
435 Glen Wesley .15 .40
436 Justin Williams .20 .50
437 Tomas Vokoun .20 .50
438 Brett McLean .15 .40
439 Noah Welch .15 .40
440 Jozef Stumpel .15 .40
441 Steve Montador .15 .40
442 Mike Van Ryn .15 .40
443 Richard Zednik .15 .40
444 Alexander Ovechkin 1.00 2.50
445 Tom Poti .15 .40
446 Viktor Kozlov .15 .40
447 Donald Brashear .15 .40
448 Michael Nylander .15 .40
449 Joe Thornton .40 1.00
450 Evgeni Malkin .50 1.25
451 Petteri Wirtanen YG RC 2.00 5.00
452 Kent Huskins YG RC 2.00 5.00
453 Ondrej Pavelec YG RC 6.00 15.00
454 Brett Sterling YG RC 2.00 5.00
455 Jonathan Sigalet YG RC 2.00 5.00
456 Tuukka Rask YG RC 30.00 80.00
457 Matt Hunwick YG RC 2.00 5.00
458 Vladimir Sobotka YG RC 2.50 6.00
459 Mark Mancari YG RC 2.00 5.00
460 Mike Weber YG RC 2.00 5.00
461 Matt Keetley YG RC 2.00 5.00
462 Jonathan Toews YG RC 100.00 250.00
463 Petri Kontiola YG RC 2.00 5.00
464 Jake Dowell YG RC 2.00 5.00
465 T.J. Hensick YG RC 2.50 6.00
466 Tomas Popperle YG RC 2.00 5.00
467 Marc Methot YG RC 2.00 5.00
468 Tobias Stephan YG RC 2.50 6.00
469 Chris Conner YG RC 2.00 5.00
470 Andrew Cogliano YG RC 2.50 6.00
471 Bryan Young YG RC 2.00 5.00
472 Zach Stortini YG RC 2.00 5.00
473 Martin Lojek YG RC 2.00 5.00
474 Stefan Meyer YG RC 2.00 5.00
475 Tanner Glass YG RC 2.50 6.00
476 Matt Moulson YG RC 3.00 8.00
477 James Sheppard YG RC 2.50 6.00
478 Cal Clutterbuck YG RC 3.00 8.00
479 Kyle Chipchura YG RC 3.00 8.00
480 Rich Peverley YG RC 2.00 5.00
481 Mark Fraser YG RC 2.00 5.00
482 David Clarkson YG RC 2.00 5.00
483 Rod Pelley YG RC 2.00 5.00
484 Greg Moore YG RC 2.00 5.00
485 Ivan Baranka YG RC 2.50 6.00
486 Alexander Nikulin YG RC 2.00 5.00
487 Steve Downie RC 2.50 6.00
488 Riley Cote YG RC 2.50 6.00
489 Martin Hanzal YG RC 2.50 6.00
490 Craig Weller YG RC 2.00 5.00
491 Daniel Carcillo YG RC 2.50 6.00
492 Tyler Kennedy YG RC 2.00 5.00
493 Devin Setoguchi YG RC 3.00 8.00
494 Lukas Kaspar YG RC 2.00 5.00
495 Thomas Greiss YG RC 4.00 10.00
496 David Perron YG RC 12.00 30.00
497 Jiri Tlusty YG RC 3.00 8.00
498 Anton Stralman YG RC 2.00 5.00
499 Chris Bourque YG RC 2.50 6.00
500 Toews/Tlusty/Setog YG CL 6.00 15.00

2007-08 Upper Deck Exclusives

*VETS/100: 12X TO 30X BASIC CARDS
*YOUNG GUN/100: 1.5X TO 4X BASIC YG
210 Patrick Kane 800.00 2000.00
227 Carey Price 800.00 2000.00
250 Price/Kane/Johnson 50.00 125.00
462 Jonathan Toews 400.00 600.00

2007-08 Upper Deck All-Star Highlights

COMPLETE SET (21) 12.00 30.00
AS1 Zach Parise .60 1.50
AS2 Andy McDonald .50 1.25
AS3 Zdeno Chara .60 1.50
AS4 Roberto Luongo 1.00 2.50
AS5 Daniel Briere .60 1.50
AS6 Sidney Crosby 2.50 6.00
AS7 Alexander Ovechkin 2.50 6.00
AS8 Joe Sakic 1.25 3.00
AS9 Rick Nash .60 1.50
AS10 Brian Rolston .50 1.25
AS11 Dany Heatley .60 1.50
AS12 Marian Hossa .60 1.50
AS13 Dion Phaneuf .50 1.25
AS14 Phil Kessel .60 1.50
AS15 Ryan Getzlaf .60 1.50
AS16 Anze Kopitar 1.00 2.50
AS17 Eric Staal .75 2.00
AS18 Martin Brodeur 1.50 4.00
AS19 Evgeni Malkin 1.25 3.00
AS20 Ryan Miller .60 1.50
AS21 Joe Thornton 1.00 2.50

2007-08 Upper Deck All-World Team

COMPLETE SET (35)
AW1 Jarome Iginla 2.50 6.00
AW2 Martin Brodeur 5.00 12.00
AW3 Joe Thornton 3.00 8.00
AW4 Dany Heatley 1.50 4.00
AW5 Tomas Vokoun 1.50 4.00
AW6 Dominik Hasek 3.00 8.00
AW7 Saku Koivu 2.00 5.00
AW8 Miikka Kiprusoff 2.00 5.00
AW9 Ilya Kovalchuk 2.00 5.00
AW10 Alexander Ovechkin 8.00 20.00
AW11 Marian Gaborik 2.00 5.00
AW12 Henrik Lundqvist 5.00 12.00
AW13 Nicklas Lidstrom 2.00 5.00
AW14 Doug Weight 2.00 5.00
AW15 Ryan Miller 2.00 5.00
AW16 Sidney Crosby SP 25.00 60.00
AW17 Vincent Lecavalier SP 6.00 15.00
AW18 Michael Ryder 1.25 3.00
AW19 Eric Staal SP 8.00 20.00
AW20 Rick Nash SP 6.00 15.00
AW21 Jonathan Cheechoo SP 5.00 12.00
AW22 Patrik Elias 2.00 5.00
AW23 Martin Havlat 2.00 5.00
AW24 Milan Hejduk 1.50 4.00
AW25 Ales Hemsky 1.50 4.00
AW26 Kari Lehtonen 1.50 4.00
AW27 Ilya Kovalchuk SP 6.00 15.00
AW28 Evgeni Malkin SP 12.00 30.00
AW29 Miroslav Satan 1.50 4.00
AW30 Anze Kopitar 3.00 8.00
AW31 Henrik Zetterberg SP 8.00 20.00
AW32 Tomas Holmstrom 1.50 4.00
AW33 Dwayne Roloson 1.50 4.00
AW34 Zach Parise SP 6.00 15.00
AW35 Mike Modano SP 10.00 25.00

2007-08 Upper Deck Big Playmakers

BPAA Alex Auld 8.00 20.00
BPAF Alexander Frolov 8.00 20.00
BPAH Ales Hemsky 10.00 25.00
BPAK Alex Kovalev 10.00 25.00
BPAM Andrej Meszaros 8.00 20.00
BPAN Anze Kopitar 20.00 50.00
BPAO Alexander Ovechkin 50.00 120.00
BPAR Alexander Radulov 12.00 30.00
BPAS Alexander Steen 8.00 20.00
BPAT Alex Tanguay 10.00 25.00
BPAY Alexei Yashin 10.00 25.00
BPBG Bill Guerin 12.00 30.00
BPBI Martin Biron 10.00 25.00
BPBL Rob Blake 12.00 30.00
BPBM Brendan Morrison 8.00 20.00
BPBO Peter Bondra 12.00 30.00
BPBR Brad Richards 12.00 30.00
BPBS Brendan Shanahan 12.00 30.00
BPBU Peter Budaj 10.00 25.00
BPCA Matt Carle 8.00 20.00
BPCH Chris Higgins 8.00 20.00
BPCW Cam Ward 12.00 30.00
BPDA Daniel Alfredsson 12.00 30.00
BPDH Dany Heatley 10.00 25.00
BPDL David Legwand 10.00 25.00
BPDR Dwayne Roloson 10.00 25.00
BPDW Doug Weight 12.00 30.00
BPEJ Ed Jovanovski 8.00 20.00
BPEL Eric Lindros 20.00 50.00
BPEN Evgeni Nabokov 10.00 25.00
BPES Eric Staal 15.00 40.00
BPFL Marc-Andre Fleury 25.00 60.00
BPGA Simon Gagne 10.00 25.00
BPGM Glen Murray 10.00 25.00
BPHA Dominik Hasek 20.00 50.00
BPHL Henrik Lundqvist 30.00 80.00
BPHS Henrik Sedin 15.00 40.00
BPIK Ilya Kovalchuk 12.00 30.00
BPJA Jason Arnott 10.00 25.00
BPJB Jay Bouwmeester 8.00 20.00
BPJC Jeff Carter 10.00 25.00
BPJG Jean-Sebastien Giguere 12.00 30.00
BPJI Jarome Iginla 15.00 40.00
BPJJ Jaromir Jagr 40.00 100.00
BPJL Jere Lehtinen 8.00 20.00
BPJS Jason Spezza 12.00 30.00
BPJT Joe Thornton 20.00 50.00
BPJW Justin Williams 10.00 25.00
BPKC Kyle Calder 8.00 20.00
BPKL Kari Lehtonen 10.00 25.00
BPKO Andrei Kostitsyn 12.00 30.00
BPKT Keith Tkachuk 12.00 30.00
BPLE Mario Lemieux 30.00 80.00
BPLN Ladislav Nagy 8.00 20.00
BPMA Maxim Afinogenov 8.00 20.00
BPMB Martin Brodeur 30.00 80.00
BPMC Bryan McCabe 8.00 20.00
BPMF Manny Fernandez 8.00 20.00
BPMG Marian Gaborik 12.00 30.00
BPMH Marian Hossa 12.00 30.00
BPMI Mikko Koivu 10.00 25.00
BPMK Miikka Kiprusoff 12.00 30.00
BPML Manny Legace 10.00 25.00
BPMM Milan Michalek 8.00 20.00
BPMN Markus Naslund 12.00 30.00
BPMO Mike Modano 20.00 50.00
BPMR Mark Recchi 15.00 40.00
BPMS Marc Savard 8.00 20.00
BPMT Marty Turco 12.00 30.00
BPNL Nicklas Lidstrom 12.00 30.00
BPPB Patrice Bergeron 15.00 40.00
BPPD Pavol Demitra 15.00 40.00
BPPE Patrik Elias 12.00 30.00
BPPF Peter Forsberg 25.00 60.00
BPPK Paul Kariya 12.00 30.00
BPPM Patrick Marleau 12.00 30.00
BPPR Patrick Roy 30.00 80.00
BPRA Andrew Raycroft 15.00 40.00
BPRB Ray Bourque 20.00 50.00
BPRD Rick DiPietro 10.00 25.00

BPRI Mike Ribeiro 8.00 20.00
BPRL Roberto Luongo 20.00 50.00
BPRM Ryan Miller 12.00 30.00
BPRN Rick Nash 12.00 30.00
BPRO Rod Brind'Amour 12.00 30.00
BPRS Ryan Smyth 10.00 25.00
BPSA Joe Sakic 25.00 60.00
BPSC Sidney Crosby 50.00 125.00
BPSD Shane Doan 10.00 25.00
BPSF Sergei Fedorov 20.00 50.00
BPSG Scott Gomez 10.00 25.00
BPSK Saku Koivu 12.00 30.00
BPSM Miroslav Satan 10.00 25.00
BPSN Scott Niedermayer 12.00 30.00
BPSU Mats Sundin 12.00 30.00
BPSV Marek Svatos 8.00 20.00
BPSW Shea Weber 10.00 25.00
BPTB Todd Bertuzzi 12.00 30.00
BPTS Teemu Selanne 25.00 60.00
BPVL Vincent Lecavalier 12.00 30.00

2007-08 Upper Deck Clear Cut Winners

CCW1 Jean-Sebastien Giguere 8.00 20.00
CCW2 Ryan Getzlaf 8.00 20.00
CCW3 Ilya Kovalchuk 8.00 20.00
CCW4 Marian Hossa 8.00 20.00
CCW5 Patrice Bergeron 10.00 25.00
CCW6 Bobby Orr 30.00 80.00
CCW7 Ryan Miller 8.00 20.00
CCW8 Thomas Vanek 6.00 15.00
CCW9 Jarome Iginla 10.00 25.00
CCW10 Miikka Kiprusoff 8.00 20.00
CCW11 Dion Phaneuf 6.00 15.00
CCW12 Eric Staal 10.00 25.00
CCW13 Patrick Roy 30.00 80.00
CCW14 Joe Sakic 15.00 40.00
CCW15 Rick Nash 8.00 20.00
CCW16 Mike Modano 12.00 30.00
CCW17 Nicklas Lidstrom 8.00 20.00
CCW18 Henrik Zetterberg 10.00 25.00
CCW19 Gordie Howe 25.00 60.00
CCW20 Ales Hemsky 6.00 15.00
CCW21 Wayne Gretzky 50.00 125.00
CCW22 Olli Jokinen 6.00 15.00
CCW23 Anze Kopitar 20.00 50.00
CCW24 Marian Gaborik 8.00 20.00
CCW25 Saku Koivu 8.00 20.00
CCW26 Martin Brodeur 20.00 50.00
CCW27 Miroslav Satan 6.00 15.00
CCW28 Jaromir Jagr 25.00 60.00
CCW29 Henrik Lundqvist 20.00 50.00
CCW30 Mark Messier 20.00 50.00
CCW31 Ray Emery 6.00 15.00
CCW32 Dany Heatley 6.00 15.00
CCW33 Simon Gagne 8.00 20.00
CCW34 Shane Doan 6.00 15.00
CCW35 Marc-Andre Fleury 15.00 40.00
CCW36 Sidney Crosby 30.00 80.00
CCW37 Mario Lemieux 30.00 80.00
CCW38 Joe Thornton 12.00 30.00
CCW39 Vincent Lecavalier 8.00 20.00
CCW40 Mats Sundin 8.00 20.00
CCW41 Roberto Luongo 12.00 30.00
CCW42 Alexander Ovechkin 15.00 40.00
CCW43 Chris Pronger 8.00 20.00
CCW44 Scott Niedermayer 8.00 20.00
CCW45 Kari Lehtonen 6.00 15.00
CCW46 Phil Kessel 8.00 20.00
CCW47 Ray Bourque 12.00 30.00
CCW48 Marc Savard 5.00 12.00
CCW49 Jason Pominville 5.00 12.00
CCW50 Gilbert Perreault 8.00 20.00
CCW51 Alex Tanguay 6.00 15.00
CCW52 Cam Ward 8.00 20.00
CCW53 Justin Williams 6.00 15.00
CCW54 Ryan Smyth 6.00 15.00
CCW55 Paul Stastny 6.00 15.00
CCW56 Sergei Fedorov 12.00 30.00
CCW57 Marty Turco 8.00 20.00
CCW58 Pavel Datsyuk 12.00 30.00
CCW59 Dominik Hasek 12.00 30.00
CCW60 Dwayne Roloson 6.00 15.00
CCW61 Tomas Vokoun 6.00 15.00
CCW62 Alexander Frolov 5.00 12.00
CCW63 Mikko Koivu 6.00 15.00
CCW64 Michael Ryder 5.00 12.00
CCW65 Guillaume Latendresse 6.00 15.00
CCW66 Patrik Elias 8.00 20.00
CCW67 Bill Guerin 8.00 20.00
CCW68 Rick DiPietro 6.00 15.00
CCW69 Brendan Shanahan 8.00 20.00
CCW70 Chris Drury 6.00 15.00
CCW71 Jason Spezza 8.00 20.00
CCW72 Daniel Alfredsson 8.00 20.00
CCW73 Daniel Briere 8.00 20.00
CCW74 Jeff Carter 6.00 15.00
CCW75 Ed Jovanovski 6.00 15.00
CCW76 Evgeni Malkin 12.00 30.00
CCW77 Jordan Staal 6.00 15.00
CCW78 Jonathan Cheechoo 6.00 15.00
CCW79 Patrick Marleau 8.00 20.00
CCW80 Vesa Toskala 6.00 15.00
CCW81 Darcy Tucker 6.00 15.00
CCW82 Markus Naslund 8.00 20.00
CCW83 Daniel Sedin 10.00 25.00
CCW84 Alexander Semin 8.00 20.00

2007-08 Upper Deck Clutch Performers

COMPLETE SET (7) 8.00 20.00
CP1 Martin Brodeur 2.50 6.00
CP2 Alexander Ovechkin 4.00 10.00
CP3 Mats Sundin 1.00 2.50
CP4 Dominik Hasek 1.50 4.00
CP5 Jean-Sebastien Giguere 1.00 2.50
CP6 Joe Sakic 2.00 5.00
CP7 Jaromir Jagr 3.00 8.00

2007-08 Upper Deck Fab Four Fabrics

FFBEGP Brod/Elias/Gion/Par 20.00 50.00
FFBLCM Brod/Lid/Cros/Malk 50.00 125.00
FFBNFK Blake/Nag/Fro/Kop 20.00 50.00
FFBRSS Bell/Ray/Staj/Sten 10.00 25.00
FFCAMV Conn/Afino/Mil/Van 12.00 30.00
FFDGBK Dem/Gab/Bouch/Koi 15.00 40.00
FFFCBK Fern/Chara/Berg/Kess 10.00 25.00
FFGBLC Gag/Briere/Lupul/Cart 12.00 30.00
FFGSWD Guer/Sat/Witt/DiPiet 12.00 30.00
FFHLDZ Hasek/Lid/Dats/Zett 20.00 50.00
FFHRKK Hav/Ruut/Keith/Khabi 12.00 30.00
FFITKP Iginla/Tang/Kipr/Phan 15.00 40.00
FFJHHE Jagr/Hasek/Hej/Elias 40.00 100.00
FFKGOK Kolz/Green/Ovech/Klep 50.00 125.00
FFKTHN Kar/Tang/Heat/Nash 12.00 30.00
FFKWTL Kar/Weight/Tkach/Leg 12.00 30.00
FFLCGM Lem/Cros/Gretz/Mess 80.00 200.00
FFLMKB Luon/Morr/Kes/Biek 20.00 50.00
FFLNZF Lecl/Nash/Zher/Fed 20.00 50.00
FFLRSD Lecav/Richs/St. L/Den 12.00 30.00
FFLSWR Legw/Sull/Web/Radu 12.00 30.00
FFMTMJ Mo/Turco/Morr/Jokin 20.00 50.00
FFMWTM Mo/Weight/Tkach/Mill 20.00 50.00
FFNKFO Nab/Koval/Fed/Ovech 20.00 50.00
FFNLSS Nasl/Luongo/Sedins 20.00 50.00
FFRBLG Roy/Brod/Luon/Gig 30.00 80.00
FFRFCM Recc/Fleur/Cros/Malk 50.00 120.00
FFRJDB Roen/Jova/Doan/Bell 20.00 50.00
FFSHRH Stoll/Horc/Rolo/Hems 10.00 25.00
FFSHTS Sakic/Hej/Theo/Smyth 25.00 60.00
FFSJSL Shan/Jagr/Straka/Lund 40.00 100.00
FFSLFA Sund/Lids/Fors/Alf 25.00 60.00
FFSLKJ Selan/Leht/Koivu/Jokin 25.00 60.00
FFSLLS Sakic/Lind/Lecav/Spez 25.00 60.00
FFSNGG Selan/Nied/Gig/Getz 10.00 25.00
FFSSJS Sakic/Shan/Jagr/Sund 40.00 100.00
FFSTMT Sund/Tuck/McCa/Tosk 12.00 30.00
FFTKNL Tosk/Kipr/Niitt/Leht 12.00 30.00
FFTNCM Thorn/Nab/Chee/Mich 20.00 50.00
FFVJBH Vok/Jok/Bouw/Hort 12.00 30.00
FFWBSW Will/Brind/Staal/Ward 15.00 40.00

2007-08 Upper Deck Game Jerseys

JAA Arron Asham 3.00 8.00
JAH Ales Hemsky 4.00 10.00
JAK Alex Kovalev 4.00 10.00
JAM Al MacInnis 6.00 15.00
JAO Alexander Ovechkin 20.00 50.00
JAP Alexander Perezhogin 3.00 8.00
JAR Andrew Raycroft 4.00 10.00
JAS Alexander Steen 3.00 8.00
JAT Alex Tanguay 4.00 10.00
JAY Alexei Yashin 4.00 10.00
JBB Brad Boyes 3.00 8.00
JBF Bernie Federko 4.00 10.00
JBG Bill Guerin 5.00 12.00
JBJ Barret Jackman 3.00 8.00
JBM Brendan Morrison 3.00 8.00
JBO Ray Bourque 8.00 20.00
JBR Bill Ranford 5.00 12.00
JBS Billy Smith 5.00 12.00
JCH Chris Higgins 3.00 8.00
JCI Dino Ciccarelli 5.00 12.00
JCJ Jonathan Cheechoo 4.00 10.00
JCP Chris Pronger 5.00 12.00
JCS Curtis Sanford 4.00 10.00
JCW Cam Ward 5.00 12.00
JDA Daniel Alfredsson 5.00 12.00
JDB Dustin Brown 5.00 12.00
JDC Dan Cloutier 4.00 10.00
JDH Dale Hawerchuk 6.00 15.00
JDK Duncan Keith 4.00 10.00
JDL David Legwand 4.00 10.00
JDP Daniel Paille 3.00 8.00
JDR Dwayne Roloson 4.00 10.00
JDS Daniel Sedin 6.00 15.00
JDW Doug Weight 5.00 12.00
JEJ Ed Jovanovski 4.00 10.00
JEL Eric Lindros 8.00 20.00
JEM Evgeni Malkin 12.00 30.00
JEN Evgeni Nabokov 4.00 10.00
JES Eric Staal 6.00 15.00
JGI Brian Gionta 3.00 8.00
JGM Glen Murray 4.00 10.00
JHA Dominik Hasek 8.00 20.00
JHE Dany Heatley 4.00 10.00
JHL Henrik Lundqvist 12.00 30.00
JHT Hannu Toivonen 4.00 10.00
JIK Ilya Kovalchuk 5.00 12.00
JJA Jay Bouwmeester 3.00 8.00
JJB Jason Bacashihua 4.00 10.00
JJC Jeff Carter 4.00 10.00
JJD J.P. Dumont 3.00 8.00
JJG Jean-Sebastien Giguere 5.00 12.00
JJH Jeff Hoggan 3.00 8.00
JJI Jarome Iginla 6.00 15.00
JJJ Jaromir Jagr 15.00 40.00
JJL Jamie Lundmark 3.00 8.00
JJO Joe Sakic 10.00 25.00
JJS Jarret Stoll 4.00 10.00
JJT Joe Thornton 8.00 20.00
JJW Justin Williams 4.00 10.00
JKC Kyle Calder 3.00 8.00
JKL Kari Lehtonen 4.00 10.00
JKO Andrei Kostitsyn 4.00 10.00
JKT Keith Tkachuk 5.00 12.00
JLR Larry Robinson 5.00 12.00
JLU Joffrey Lupul 3.00 8.00
JMA Mark Stuart 3.00 8.00
JMB Martin Brodeur 12.00 30.00
JMC Bryan McCabe 3.00 8.00
JME Andrej Meszaros 3.00 8.00
JMF Manny Fernandez 3.00 8.00
JMG Marian Gaborik 5.00 12.00
JMH Marian Hossa 5.00 12.00
JMI Milan Michalek 3.00 8.00
JMJ Milan Jurcina 3.00 8.00
JML M. Lemieux waist up 12.00 30.00
JMM Mike Modano 8.00 20.00
JMN Markus Naslund 5.00 12.00
JMO Brenden Morrow 4.00 10.00
JMR Michael Ryder 3.00 8.00
JMS Marek Svatos 3.00 8.00
JMT Marty Turco 5.00 12.00
JNL Nicklas Lidstrom 5.00 12.00
JON Ben Ondrus 3.00 8.00
JPB Patrice Bergeron 6.00 15.00
JPE Corey Perry 8.00 20.00
JPF Peter Forsberg 10.00 25.00
JPK Paul Kariya 5.00 12.00
JPS Patrik Stefan 3.00 8.00
JRB Rod Brind'Amour 5.00 12.00
JRI Brad Richards 5.00 12.00
JRS Ryan Smyth 4.00 10.00
JSA Borje Salming 5.00 12.00
JSC S. Crosby bent waist 12.00 30.00
JSH Brendan Shanahan 5.00 12.00
JSI Darryl Sittler 6.00 15.00
JSK Saku Koivu 5.00 12.00
JSP Jason Spezza 5.00 12.00
JST Brad Stuart 3.00 8.00
JSU Mats Sundin 5.00 12.00
JTW Tiger Williams 3.00 8.00
GJ2AF Alexander Frolov 3.00 8.00
GJ2AK Alex Kovalev 4.00 10.00
GJ2AL Andrew Ladd 3.00 8.00
GJ2BR Brian Rafalski 4.00 10.00
GJ2CC Carlo Colaiacovo 3.00 8.00
GJ2CD Chris Drury 4.00 10.00
GJ2CH Chris Chelios 5.00 12.00
GJ2CJ Curtis Joseph 6.00 15.00
GJ2CO Chris Osgood 5.00 12.00
GJ2DB Daniel Briere 5.00 12.00
GJ2DP Dion Phaneuf 4.00 10.00
GJ2DT Darcy Tucker 4.00 10.00
GJ2GO Scott Gomez 4.00 10.00
GJ2GR Gary Roberts 3.00 8.00
GJ2HS Henrik Sedin 6.00 15.00
GJ2HZ Henrik Zetterberg 6.00 15.00
GJ2JA Jason Arnott 4.00 10.00
GJ2JJ Jaromir Jagr 15.00 40.00
GJ2JL Jere Lehtinen 3.00 8.00
GJ2JP Joni Pitkanen 3.00 8.00
GJ2JS Jordan Staal 4.00 10.00
GJ2KB Kevin Bieksa 4.00 10.00
GJ2KO Anze Kopitar 8.00 20.00
GJ2LN Ladislav Nagy 3.00 8.00
GJ2MA Martin Brodeur 12.00 30.00
GJ2MB Mark Bell 3.00 8.00
GJ2MF Marc-Andre Fleury 10.00 25.00
GJ2ML M. Lemieux knees up 12.00 30.00
GJ2MM Mark Messier 10.00 25.00
GJ2OJ Olli Jokinen 4.00 10.00
GJ2OK Olaf Kolzig 5.00 12.00
GJ2PB Pierre-Marc Bouchard 5.00 12.00
GJ2PD Pavel Datsyuk 8.00 20.00
GJ2PF Peter Forsberg 10.00 25.00
GJ2PK Phil Kessel 5.00 12.00
GJ2PP Petr Prucha 3.00 8.00
GJ2PR Patrick Roy 12.00 30.00
GJ2RB Rob Blake 5.00 12.00
GJ2RD Rick DiPietro 4.00 10.00
GJ2RG Ryan Getzlaf 5.00 12.00
GJ2RL Roberto Luongo 8.00 20.00
GJ2RM Ryan Miller 5.00 12.00
GJ2RN Rick Nash 5.00 12.00
GJ2RS Ryan Smyth 4.00 10.00
GJ2RT Raffi Torres 3.00 8.00
GJ2SC S. Crosby upright 20.00 50.00
GJ2SD Shane Doan 4.00 10.00
GJ2SF Sergei Fedorov 8.00 20.00
GJ2SG Simon Gagne 5.00 12.00
GJ2SN Scott Niedermayer 5.00 12.00
GJ2SS Steve Sullivan 3.00 8.00
GJ2SW Stephen Weiss 3.00 8.00
GJ2TB Todd Bertuzzi 5.00 12.00
GJ2TS Teemu Selanne 10.00 25.00
GJ2TV Tomas Vokoun 4.00 10.00
GJ2VL Vincent Lecavalier 5.00 12.00
GJ2VT Vesa Toskala 4.00 10.00
GJ2WE Shea Weber 4.00 10.00

2007-08 Upper Deck Generation Next

COMPLETE SET (30) 12.00 30.00
GN1 Alexander Ovechkin 3.00 8.00
GN2 Cam Ward .75 2.00
GN3 Corey Perry 1.25 3.00
GN4 Dion Phaneuf .60 1.50
GN5 Evgeni Malkin 1.50 4.00
GN6 Gilbert Brule .60 1.50
GN7 Guillaume Latendresse .60 1.50
GN8 Jordan Staal .60 1.50
GN9 Thomas Vanek .60 1.50
GN10 Phil Kessel .75 2.00
GN11 Ryan Getzlaf .75 2.00
GN12 Kari Lehtonen .60 1.50
GN13 Sidney Crosby 3.00 8.00
GN14 Steve Bernier .50 1.25
GN15 Zach Parise .75 2.00
GN16 Alexander Radulov .75 2.00
GN17 Alexander Semin .75 2.00
GN18 Anze Kopitar 1.25 3.00
GN19 Jack Johnson .60 1.50
GN20 Jeff Carter .60 1.50
GN21 Josh Harding .75 2.00
GN22 Kevin Bieksa .60 1.50
GN23 Lee Stempniak .50 1.25
GN24 Matt Carle .50 1.25
GN25 Mikko Koivu .60 1.50
GN26 Milan Michalek .50 1.25
GN27 Patrick Eaves .50 1.25
GN28 Paul Stastny .60 1.50
GN29 Rob Schremp .60 1.50
GN30 Wojtek Wolski .60 1.50

2007-08 Upper Deck Hometown Heroes

COMPLETE SET (28) 20.00 50.00
HH57 Marian Hossa 1.50 4.00
HH58 Thomas Vanek 1.25 3.00
HH59 Rick DiPietro 1.25 3.00
HH60 Pavel Datsyuk 2.50 6.00
HH61 Evgeni Malkin 3.00 8.00
HH62 Ray Emery 1.25 3.00
HH63 Paul Stastny 1.25 3.00
HH64 Zach Parise 1.50 4.00
HH65 Ryan Getzlaf 1.50 4.00
HH66 Alexander Semin 1.50 4.00
HH67 Dwayne Roloson 1.25 3.00
HH68 Marty Turco 1.50 4.00
HH69 Guillaume Latendresse 1.25 3.00
HH70 Andrew Raycroft 1.25 3.00
HH71 Daniel Briere 1.50 4.00
HH72 Ryan Smyth 1.25 3.00
HH73 Paul Kariya 1.50 4.00
HH74 Tomas Vokoun 1.25 3.00
HH75 Alexander Radulov 1.50 4.00
HH76 Miroslav Satan 1.25 3.00
HH77 Mark Recchi 2.00 5.00
HH78 Phil Kessel 1.50 4.00
HH79 Chris Chelios 1.50 4.00
HH80 Anze Kopitar 2.50 6.00
HH81 Justin Williams 1.25 3.00
HH82 Joe Thornton 2.50 6.00
HH83 Mikko Koivu 1.25 3.00
HH84 Brad Richards 1.50 4.00

2007-08 Upper Deck Lord Stanley's Heroes

COMPLETE SET (7) 5.00 12.00
LSH1 Teemu Selanne 3.00 8.00
LSH2 Jean-Sebastien Giguere 1.50 4.00
LSH3 Chris Pronger 1.50 4.00
LSH4 Scott Niedermayer 1.50 4.00
LSH5 Andy McDonald 1.25 3.00
LSH6 Ryan Getzlaf 1.50 4.00
LSH7 Travis Moen 1.00 2.50

2007-08 Upper Deck NHL's Best

COMPLETE SET (14) 20.00 50.00
B1 Sidney Crosby 6.00 15.00
B2 Martin Brodeur 4.00 10.00
B3 Dany Heatley 1.25 3.00
B4 Alexander Ovechkin 6.00 15.00
B5 Joe Thornton 2.50 6.00
B6 Jarome Iginla 2.00 5.00
B7 Vincent Lecavalier 1.50 4.00
B8 Roberto Luongo 2.50 6.00
B9 Joe Sakic 3.00 8.00
B10 Jaromir Jagr 5.00 12.00
B11 Teemu Selanne 3.00 8.00
B12 Ilya Kovalchuk 1.50 4.00
B13 Ryan Miller 1.50 4.00
B14 Eric Staal 2.00 5.00

2007-08 Upper Deck NHL Award Winners

COMPLETE SET (7) 12.00 30.00
AW1 Sidney Crosby 6.00 15.00
AW2 Martin Brodeur 4.00 10.00
AW3 Nicklas Lidstrom 1.50 4.00
AW4 Evgeni Malkin 3.00 8.00
AW5 Rod Brind'Amour 1.50 4.00
AW6 Pavel Datsyuk 2.50 6.00
AW7 Phil Kessel 1.50 4.00

2007-08 Upper Deck Rookie Headliners

RH1 Jonathan Toews SP 12.00 30.00
RH2 Patrick Kane SP 12.00 30.00
RH3 Carey Price SP 12.00 30.00
RH4 Devin Setoguchi SP 3.00 8.00
RH5 Jiri Tlusty SP 3.00 8.00
RH6 Jack Johnson SP 2.50 6.00
RH7 Bobby Ryan SP 5.00 12.00
RH8 Peter Mueller SP 2.50 6.00
RH9 Bryan Little SP 2.50 6.00
RH10 Sam Gagner SP 4.00 10.00
RH11 Andrew Cogliano 1.00 2.50
RH12 Jonathan Bernier 1.50 4.00
RH13 Nicklas Backstrom 2.50 6.00
RH14 Marc Staal 1.25 3.00
RH15 Erik Johnson 1.25 3.00
RH16 Milan Lucic 3.00 8.00
RH17 James Sheppard .75 2.00
RH18 Nicklas Bergfors .75 2.00
RH19 Nick Foligno 1.50 4.00
RH20 Kyle Chipchura 1.25 3.00

2007-08 Upper Deck Rookie Materials

RMAC Andrew Cogliano 4.00 10.00
RMAG Andy Greene 4.00 10.00
RMAS Anton Stralman 3.00 8.00
RMBA Nicklas Backstrom 10.00 25.00
RMBL Bryan Little 4.00 10.00
RMBR Bobby Ryan 8.00 20.00
RMBS Brett Sterling 3.00 8.00
RMCM Curtis McElhinney 5.00 12.00
RMCP Carey Price 20.00 50.00
RMDK David Krejci 10.00 25.00
RMDM Drew Miller 4.00 10.00
RMDP David Perron 6.00 15.00
RMDS Devin Setoguchi 5.00 12.00
RMEJ Erik Johnson 5.00 12.00
RMFN Frans Nielsen 5.00 12.00
RMJB Jonathan Bernier 8.00 20.00
RMJH Jaroslav Halak 10.00 25.00
RMJJ Jack Johnson 6.00 15.00
RMJS James Sheppard 3.00 8.00
RMJT Jonathan Toews 20.00 50.00
RMKA Petr Kalus 3.00 8.00
RMKC Kyle Chipchura 5.00 12.00
RMMH Martin Hanzal 4.00 10.00
RMML Milan Lucic 12.00 30.00
RMMN Matt Niskanen 5.00 12.00
RMMR Mason Raymond 5.00 12.00
RMMS Marc Staal 5.00 12.00
RMNB Nicklas Bergfors 3.00 8.00
RMNF Nick Foligno 6.00 15.00
RMOP Ondrej Pavelec 6.00 15.00
RMPK Patrick Kane 20.00 50.00
RMPM Peter Mueller 4.00 10.00
RMRC Ryan Callahan 6.00 15.00
RMRP Ryan Parent 3.00 8.00
RMRS Rob Schremp 4.00 10.00
RMSG Sam Gagner 6.00 15.00
RMTL Jiri Tlusty 5.00 12.00
RMTM Torrey Mitchell 4.00 10.00
RMVK Ville Koistinen 3.00 8.00

2007-08 Upper Deck Signature Sensations

SSAK Andrei Kostitsyn 5.00 12.00
SSAO Alex Ovechkin SP 125.00 200.00
SSAR Andrew Raycroft 5.00 12.00
SSBM Brenden Morrow 5.00 12.00
SSBP Benoit Pouliot 4.00 10.00
SSBR Brad Richardson 4.00 10.00
SSBW Ben Walter 4.00 10.00
SSCK Chuck Kobasew 4.00 10.00
SSCT Chris Thorburn 4.00 10.00
SSDK Duncan Keith 5.00 12.00
SSDP Dion Phaneuf 5.00 12.00
SSDS Drew Stafford 4.00 10.00
SSEC Erik Christensen 4.00 10.00
SSEM Evgeni Malkin 12.00 30.00
SSEN Evgeni Nabokov 5.00 12.00
SSES Eric Staal 10.00 25.00
SSFN Filip Novak 4.00 10.00
SSFP Fernando Pisani 4.00 10.00
SSGE Martin Gerber 5.00 12.00
SSGL G. Latendresse 5.00 12.00
SSGO Scott Gomez 5.00 12.00
SSHA Dominik Hasek 25.00 50.00
SSHZ Henrik Zetterberg 8.00 20.00
SSIK Ilya Kovalchuk 6.00 15.00
SSIW Ian White 4.00 10.00
SSJA Jay Bouwmeester 4.00 10.00
SSJC Jonathan Cheechoo 5.00 12.00
SSJF Johan Franzen 5.00 12.00
SSJG Jean-Sebastien Giguere 6.00 15.00
SSJI Jarome Iginla 8.00 20.00
SSJL John-Michael Liles 4.00 10.00
SSJM Jay McClement 4.00 10.00
SSJO Jeff O'Neill 4.00 10.00
SSJT Joe Thornton 10.00 25.00
SSJW Jeremy Williams 4.00 10.00
SSKC Kyle Calder 4.00 10.00
SSKE Ryan Kesler 6.00 15.00
SSKL Kari Lehtonen 5.00 12.00
SSKO Anze Kopitar SP 8.00 20.00
SSLA Maxim Lapierre 4.00 10.00
SSMA Maxim Afinogenov 4.00 10.00
SSME M-E Vlasic 4.00 10.00
SSMG Marian Gaborik 6.00 15.00
SSMH Marcel Hossa 4.00 10.00
SSMI Michal Handzus 5.00 12.00
SSMK Miikka Kiprusoff SP 40.00 80.00
SSML Mario Lemieux SP 60.00 120.00
SSMP Michael Peca 5.00 12.00
SSMS Marek Svatos 4.00 10.00
SSMT Mikael Tellqvist 5.00 12.00
SSNA Nikolai Antropov 5.00 12.00
SSON Ben Ondrus 4.00 10.00
SSPE Patrick Eaves 4.00 10.00
SSPK Phil Kessel 6.00 15.00
SSPR Brandon Prust 4.00 10.00
SSPS Paul Stastny 5.00 12.00
SSRE Robert Esche 5.00 12.00
SSRK Rostislav Klesla 4.00 10.00
SSRM Ryan Malone 4.00 10.00
SSRN Rick Nash 6.00 15.00
SSRS Ryan Smyth 5.00 12.00
SSSC Sidney Crosby SP 100.00 200.00
SSSG Simon Gagne 6.00 15.00
SSSH Shawn Horcoff 4.00 10.00
SSTM Travis Moen 4.00 10.00
SSTR Tuomo Ruutu 6.00 15.00
SSTV Thomas Vanek 5.00 12.00
SSVL Vincent Lecavalier 6.00 15.00
SSWR Wade Redden 4.00 10.00
SSYS Yan Stastny 4.00 10.00

2007-08 Upper Deck Stars In The Making

COMPLETE SET (14) 8.00 20.00
SM1 Zach Parise 1.00 2.50
SM2 Mikko Koivu .75 2.00
SM3 Jordan Staal .75 2.00
SM4 Thomas Vanek .75 2.00
SM5 Phil Kessel 1.00 2.50
SM6 Alexander Semin 1.00 2.50
SM7 Drew Stafford .60 1.50
SM8 Ryan Getzlaf 1.00 2.50
SM9 Alexander Radulov 1.00 2.50
SM10 Steve Bernier .60 1.50
SM11 Dion Phaneuf .75 2.00
SM12 Paul Stastny .75 2.00
SM13 Anze Kopitar 1.50 4.00
SM14 Brent Seabrook .60 1.50

2007-08 Upper Deck Super Snipers

COMPLETE SET (21) 20.00 50.00
SN1 Vincent Lecavalier 1.25 3.00
SN2 Dany Heatley 1.00 2.50
SN3 Jonathan Cheechoo 1.00 2.50
SN4 Martin St. Louis 1.25 3.00
SN5 Ilya Kovalchuk 1.25 3.00
SN6 Joe Sakic 2.50 6.00
SN7 Jaromir Jagr 4.00 10.00
SN8 Jarome Iginla 1.50 4.00
SN9 Marian Hossa 1.25 3.00
SN10 Martin Havlat 1.25 3.00
SN11 Teemu Selanne 2.50 6.00
SN12 Alexander Ovechkin 5.00 12.00
SN13 Jason Spezza 1.25 3.00
SN14 Thomas Vanek 1.00 2.50
SN15 Sidney Crosby 5.00 12.00
SN16 Mike Modano 2.00 5.00
SN17 Henrik Zetterberg 1.50 4.00
SN18 Markus Naslund 1.25 3.00
SN19 Marian Gaborik 1.25 3.00
SN20 Rick Nash 1.25 3.00
SN21 Mats Sundin 1.25 3.00

2007-08 Upper Deck The Men Behind The Mask

COMPLETE SET (15) 25.00 60.00
BM1 Cam Ward 2.50 6.00
BM2 Dominik Hasek 4.00 10.00
BM3 Dwayne Roloson 2.00 5.00
BM4 Henrik Lundqvist 6.00 15.00
BM5 Jean-Sebastien Giguere 2.50 6.00
BM6 Kari Lehtonen 2.00 5.00
BM7 Marc-Andre Fleury 5.00 12.00
BM8 Martin Brodeur 6.00 15.00
BM9 Marty Turco 2.50 6.00
BM10 Miikka Kiprusoff 2.50 6.00
BM11 Ray Emery 2.00 5.00
BM12 Roberto Luongo 4.00 10.00
BM13 Ryan Miller 2.50 6.00
BM14 Tomas Vokoun 2.00 5.00
BM15 Vesa Toskala 2.00 5.00

2007-08 Upper Deck Top Picks

COMPLETE SET (7) 8.00 20.00
TP1 Sidney Crosby 4.00 10.00
TP2 Alexander Ovechkin 4.00 10.00
TP3 Marc-Andre Fleury 2.00 5.00
TP4 Rick Nash 1.00 2.50
TP5 Ilya Kovalchuk 1.00 2.50
TP6 Vincent Lecavalier 1.00 2.50
TP7 Joe Thornton 1.50 4.00

2007-08 Upper Deck UD Signatures

UDSAK Andrei Kostitsyn 8.00 20.00
UDSAM Al Montoya 8.00 20.00
UDSAO Alexander Ovechkin SP 40.00 100.00
UDSBC Blake Comeau 6.00 15.00
UDSBO Bobby Orr SP 40.00 100.00
UDSBP Benoit Pouliot 6.00 15.00
UDSBR Mike Brown 6.00 15.00
UDSCC Chris Campoli 6.00 15.00
UDSCS Cory Stillman SP 6.00 15.00
UDSDB Daniel Briere 10.00 25.00
UDSDH Dominik Hasek SP 15.00 40.00
UDSDS Drew Stafford 6.00 15.00
UDSEM Evgeni Malkin SP 20.00 50.00
UDSGH Gordie Howe SP 30.00 80.00
UDSIK Ilya Kovalchuk SP 10.00 25.00
UDSJB Jaroslav Balastik 6.00 15.00
UDSJC Jeff Carter SP 8.00 20.00
UDSJF Johan Franzen 8.00 20.00
UDSJG Jean-Sebastien Giguere SP 10.00 25.00
UDSJJ Jack Johnson 8.00 20.00
UDSJK Jakub Klepis 6.00 15.00
UDSJM Jay McClement 6.00 15.00
UDSJS Jordan Staal SP 8.00 20.00
UDSJW Jeremy Williams 6.00 15.00
UDSKB Kevin Bieksa 8.00 20.00
UDSKO Anze Kopitar 15.00 40.00
UDSLA Maxim Lapierre 6.00 15.00
UDSLN Ladislav Nagy 6.00 15.00
UDSLT Lauri Tukonen 6.00 15.00
UDSML Mario Lemieux SP 40.00 100.00
UDSMM Mark Messier SP 20.00 50.00
UDSMR Mike Ribeiro SP 6.00 15.00
UDSNB Niklas Backstrom 10.00 25.00
UDSNK Nikolai Khabibulin SP 10.00 25.00
UDSPH Dion Phaneuf 8.00 20.00
UDSPK Phil Kessel SP 10.00 25.00
UDSPM Paul Mara 6.00 15.00
UDSPS Paul Stastny SP 8.00 20.00
UDSRI Mike Richards 8.00 20.00
UDSRK Rostislav Klesla 6.00 15.00
UDSRM Ryan Miller 10.00 25.00
UDSRN Rick Nash SP 10.00 25.00
UDSRO Rob Schremp 8.00 20.00
UDSRS Ryan Smyth SP 8.00 20.00
UDSSC Sidney Crosby SP 40.00 100.00
UDSSS Steve Sullivan SP 6.00 15.00
UDSSW Stephen Weiss 6.00 15.00
UDSTB Todd Bertuzzi SP 10.00 25.00
UDSTV Thomas Vanek 8.00 20.00
UDSWR Wade Redden SP 6.00 15.00
UDSZP Zach Parise 10.00 25.00

2007-08 Upper Deck Young Guns Retro Oversized

COMPLETE SET (14) 60.00 120.00
YG1 Patrick Kane 25.00 60.00
YG2 Carey Price 15.00 40.00
YG3 Erik Johnson 4.00 10.00
YG4 Bobby Ryan 6.00 15.00
YG5 Marc Staal 4.00 10.00
YG6 Nicklas Backstrom 8.00 20.00
YG7 Jonathan Bernier 5.00 12.00
YG8 Bryan Little 3.00 8.00
YG9 Sam Gagner 5.00 12.00
YG10 Nick Foligno 5.00 12.00
YG11 Peter Mueller 3.00 8.00
YG12 Jack Johnson 3.00 8.00
YG13 Nicklas Bergfors 2.50 6.00
YG14 Rob Schremp 3.00 8.00

2007-08 Upper Deck Lucky Shot Arena Giveaways

LA1 Dustin Brown 2.50 6.00
LA2 Mike Cammalleri 2.00 5.00
LA3 Rob Blake 2.50 6.00
LA4 Alexander Frolov 1.50 4.00
LA5 Lubomir Visnovsky 1.50 4.00
LA6 Anze Kopitar 12.00 30.00
NJ1 Travis Zajac 1.50 4.00
NJ2 Jay Pandolfo 1.50 4.00
NJ3 Brian Gionta 1.50 4.00
NJ4 Sergei Brylin 1.50 4.00
NJ5 Dainius Zubrus 1.50 4.00
NJ6 Martin Brodeur 20.00 50.00
SJ1 Joe Pavelski 3.00 8.00
SJ2 Jonathan Cheechoo 2.00 5.00
SJ3 Marc-Edouard Vlasic 1.50 4.00
SJ4 Craig Rivet 1.50 4.00
SJ5 Patrick Marleau 2.50 6.00
SJ6 Joe Thornton 12.00 30.00
TB1 Dan Boyle 1.50 4.00
TB2 Ryan Craig 1.50 4.00
TB3 Vaclav Prospal 1.50 4.00
TB4 Marc Denis 2.00 5.00
TB5 Brad Richards 2.50 6.00
TB6 Vincent Lecavalier 8.00 20.00
ANA1 Andy McDonald 2.00 5.00
ANA2 Chris Pronger 2.50 6.00
ANA3 Chris Kunitz 2.50 6.00
ANA4 Jean-Sebastien Giguere 2.50 6.00
ANA5 Corey Perry 4.00 10.00
ANA6 Ryan Getzlaf 8.00 20.00
ATL1 Ilya Kovalchuk 2.50 6.00
ATL2 Marian Hossa 2.50 6.00
ATL3 Bobby Holik 1.50 4.00
ATL4 Kari Lehtonen 2.00 5.00
ATL5 Slava Kozlov 1.50 4.00
ATL6 Garnet Exelby 5.00 12.00
BOS1 Zdeno Chara 2.50 6.00
BOS2 Phil Kessel 2.50 6.00
BOS3 Glen Murray 2.00 5.00
BOS4 Marco Sturm 1.50 4.00
BOS5 Marc Savard 1.50 4.00
BOS6 Tim Thomas 8.00 20.00
BUF1 Thomas Vanek 2.00 5.00
BUF2 Derek Roy 1.50 4.00
BUF3 Brian Campbell 2.00 5.00
BUF4 Maxim Afinogenov 1.50 4.00
BUF5 Jason Pominville 1.50 4.00
BUF6 Ryan Miller 8.00 20.00
CAR1 Cory Stillman 1.50 4.00
CAR2 Ray Whitney 2.00 5.00
CAR3 Eric Staal 3.00 8.00
CAR4 Glen Wesley 1.50 4.00
CAR5 Justin Williams 2.00 5.00
CAR6 Cam Ward 8.00 20.00
CGY1 Miikka Kiprusoff 2.50 6.00
CGY2 Dion Phaneuf 2.00 5.00
CGY3 Alex Tanguay 2.00 5.00
CGY4 Daymond Langkow 1.50 4.00
CGY5 Kristian Huselius 1.50 4.00
CGY6 Jarome Iginla 10.00 25.00
CHI1 Patrick Kane 10.00 25.00
CHI2 Martin Havlat 2.50 6.00
CHI3 Patrick Sharp 2.50 6.00
CHI4 Nikolai Khabibulin 2.50 6.00
CHI5 Tuomo Ruutu 2.50 6.00
CHI6 Jonathan Toews 15.00 40.00
CLB1 Pascal Leclaire 2.00 5.00
CLB2 Nikolai Zherdev 1.50 4.00
CLB3 Adam Foote 1.50 4.00
CLB4 Sergei Fedorov 4.00 10.00
CLB5 Fredrik Modin 1.50 4.00
CLB6 Rick Nash 8.00 20.00
COL1 Joe Sakic 5.00 12.00
COL2 Ian Laperriere 1.50 4.00
COL3 Milan Hejduk 2.00 5.00
COL4 Scott Hannan 1.50 4.00
COL5 Ryan Smyth 2.00 5.00
COL6 Paul Stastny 6.00 15.00
DAL1 Sergei Zubov 2.00 5.00
DAL2 Mike Ribeiro 1.50 4.00
DAL3 Brenden Morrow 2.00 5.00
DAL4 Marty Turco 2.50 6.00
DAL5 Jere Lehtinen 1.50 4.00
DAL6 Mike Modano 12.00 30.00
DET1 Nicklas Lidstrom 2.50 6.00
DET2 Kris Draper 1.50 4.00
DET3 Pavel Datsyuk 4.00 10.00
DET4 Tomas Holmstrom 2.00 5.00
DET5 Chris Chelios 2.50 6.00
DET6 Henrik Zetterberg 10.00 25.00
EDM1 Dwayne Roloson 2.00 5.00
EDM2 Jarret Stoll 2.00 5.00
EDM3 Dustin Penner 2.00 5.00
EDM4 Shawn Horcoff 1.50 4.00
EDM5 Ethan Moreau 1.50 4.00
EDM6 Ales Hemsky 6.00 15.00
FLA1 Olli Jokinen 2.00 5.00
FLA2 Nathan Horton 2.50 6.00
FLA3 Stephen Weiss 1.50 4.00
FLA4 Jay Bouwmeester 1.50 4.00
FLA5 Tomas Vokoun 2.00 5.00
FLA6 Rostislav Olesz 5.00 12.00
MIN1 Pavol Demitra 3.00 8.00
MIN2 Kurtis Foster 1.50 4.00
MIN3 Pierre-Marc Bouchard 2.50 6.00
MIN4 Josh Harding 2.50 6.00
MIN5 Mark Parrish 1.50 4.00
MIN6 Marian Gaborik 8.00 20.00
MTL1 Guillaume Latendresse 2.00 5.00
MTL2 Cristobal Huet 2.00 5.00
MTL3 Mark Streit 1.50 4.00
MTL4 Chris Higgins 1.50 4.00
MTL5 Roman Hamrlik 1.50 4.00
MTL6 Saku Koivu 8.00 20.00
NAS1 J.P. Dumont 1.50 4.00
NAS2 Martin Erat 1.50 4.00
NAS3 David Legwand 2.00 5.00
NAS4 Chris Mason 2.00 5.00
NAS5 Jason Arnott 2.00 5.00
NAS6 Alexander Radulov 8.00 20.00
NYI1 Mike Sillinger 1.50 4.00
NYI2 Rick DiPietro 2.00 5.00
NYI3 Brendan Witt 1.50 4.00
NYI4 Bill Guerin 2.50 6.00
NYI5 Mike Comrie 2.00 5.00
NYI6 Miroslav Satan 6.00 15.00
NYR1 Jaromir Jagr 8.00 20.00
NYR2 Sean Avery 1.50 4.00
NYR3 Chris Drury 2.00 5.00
NYR4 Scott Gomez 2.00 5.00
NYR5 Brendan Shanahan 2.50 6.00
NYR6 Henrik Lundqvist 20.00 50.00
OTT1 Daniel Alfredsson 2.50 6.00
OTT2 Dany Heatley 2.00 5.00
OTT3 Antoine Vermette 1.50 4.00
OTT4 Jason Spezza 2.50 6.00
OTT5 Anton Volchenkov 1.50 4.00
OTT6 Martin Gerber 6.00 15.00
PHI1 Martin Biron 2.00 5.00
PHI2 Simon Gagne 2.50 6.00
PHI3 Daniel Briere 2.50 6.00
PHI4 Mike Richards 2.00 5.00
PHI5 Kimmo Timonen 1.50 4.00
PHI6 Scottie Upshall 5.00 12.00
PHX1 Zbynek Michalek 1.50 4.00
PHX2 Keith Ballard 1.50 4.00
PHX3 Ed Jovanovski 2.00 5.00
PHX4 Nick Boynton 1.50 4.00
PHX5 Derek Morris 1.50 4.00
PHX6 Shane Doan 6.00 15.00
PIT1 Sidney Crosby 10.00 25.00
PIT2 Sergei Gonchar 1.50 4.00
PIT3 Marc-Andre Fleury 5.00 12.00
PIT4 Petr Sykora 2.00 5.00
PIT5 Evgeni Malkin 5.00 12.00
PIT6 Jordan Staal 6.00 15.00
STL1 Manny Legace 2.00 5.00
STL2 Barret Jackman 1.50 4.00
STL3 Paul Kariya 2.50 6.00
STL4 Doug Weight 2.50 6.00
STL5 Keith Tkachuk 2.50 6.00
STL6 Brad Boyes 5.00 12.00
TOR1 Darcy Tucker 2.00 5.00
TOR2 Bryan McCabe 1.50 4.00
TOR3 Matt Stajan 1.50 4.00
TOR4 Jason Blake 1.50 4.00
TOR5 Mats Sundin 2.50 6.00
TOR6 Tomas Kaberle 5.00 12.00
VAN1 Markus Naslund 2.50 6.00
VAN2 Henrik Sedin 3.00 8.00
VAN3 Mattias Ohlund 1.50 4.00
VAN4 Willie Mitchell 1.50 4.00
VAN5 Daniel Sedin 3.00 8.00
VAN6 Roberto Luongo 12.00 30.00
WAS1 Alexander Semin 2.50 6.00
WAS2 Chris Clark 1.50 4.00
WAS3 Olaf Kolzig 2.50 6.00
WAS4 Alexander Ovechkin 10.00 25.00
WAS5 Michael Nylander 1.50 4.00
WAS6 Donald Brashear 5.00 12.00

2008-09 Upper Deck

COMPLETE SET (500) 200.00 400.00
COMP.SER.1 SET (250) 200.00 350.00
COMP.SER.2 SET (250) 100.00 200.00
COMP.SET w/o SP's (400) 30.00 80.00

Card	Low	High
COMP.SER.1 SET w/o SPs (200)	15.00	40.00
COMP.SER.2 SET w/o SPs (200)	15.00	40.00
1 Nicklas Backstrom	.30	.75
2 Alexander Semin	.30	.75
3 Mike Green	.25	.60
4 Viktor Kozlov	.20	.50
5 Jeff Schultz	.20	.50
6 Boyd Gordon	.20	.50
7 Mattias Ohlund	.20	.50
8 Roberto Luongo	.50	1.25
9 Alexander Edler	.20	.50
10 Mason Raymond	.20	.50
11 Daniel Sedin	.40	1.00
12 Henrik Sedin	.40	1.00
13 Curtis Sanford	.25	.60
14 Ryan Kesler	.30	.75
15 Pavel Kubina	.20	.50
16 Vesa Toskala	.40	1.00
17 Alexander Steen	.20	.50
18 Tomas Kaberle	.20	.50
19 Jiri Tlusty	.20	.50
20 Nik Antropov	.25	.60
21 Ian White	.20	.50
22 Paul Ranger	.20	.50
23 Martin St. Louis	.30	.75
24 Jussi Jokinen	.20	.50
25 Mike Smith	.30	.75
26 Jeff Halpern	.20	.50
27 Mike Lundin	.20	.50
28 Lee Stempniak	.20	.50
29 Paul Kariya	.30	.75
30 Erik Johnson	.20	.50
31 Manny Legace	.30	.75
32 Brad Boyes	.20	.50
33 Andy McDonald	.25	.60
34 David Perron	.25	.60
35 Joe Thornton	.50	1.25
36 Devin Setoguchi	.25	.60
37 Evgeni Nabokov	.25	.60
38 Jonathan Cheechoo	.25	.60
39 Milan Michalek	.20	.50
40 Torrey Mitchell	.20	.50
41 Mike Grier	.20	.50
42 Sidney Crosby	1.25	3.00
43 Marc-Andre Fleury	.60	1.50
44 Kristopher Letang	.40	1.00
45 Tyler Kennedy	.25	.60
46 Jordan Staal	.25	.60
47 Sergei Gonchar	.20	.50
48 Petr Sykora	.25	.60
49 Peter Mueller	.25	.60
50 Ilya Bryzgalov	.25	.60
51 Zbynek Michalek	.20	.50
52 Martin Hanzal	.25	.60
53 Daniel Carcillo	.20	.50
54 Ed Jovanovski	.25	.60
55 Riley Cote	.20	.50
56 Simon Gagne	.30	.75
57 Mike Richards	.25	.60
58 Martin Biron	.25	.60
59 Kimmo Timonen	.20	.50
60 Joffrey Lupul	.20	.50
61 Mike Knuble	.20	.50
62 Daniel Alfredsson	.30	.75
63 Chris Phillips	.20	.50
64 Mike Fisher	.20	.50
65 Antoine Vermette	.20	.50
66 Andrej Meszaros	.20	.50
67 Jason Spezza	.30	.75
68 Chris Neil	.20	.50
69 Stephen Valiquette	.25	.60
70 Nigel Dawes	.20	.50
71 Marc Staal	.20	.50
72 Brandon Dubinsky	.20	.50
73 Scott Gomez	.25	.60
74 Henrik Lundqvist	.75	2.00
75 Bill Guerin	.30	.75
76 Rick DiPietro	.25	.60
77 Blake Comeau	.20	.50
78 Trent Hunter	.20	.50
79 Brendan Witt	.20	.50
80 Mike Sillinger	.20	.50
81 Martin Brodeur	.75	2.00
82 Patrik Elias	.30	.75
83 Johnny Oduya	.25	.60
84 Brian Gionta	.20	.50
85 Paul Martin	.20	.50
86 John Madden	.20	.50
87 Radek Bonk	.20	.50
88 Martin Erat	.20	.50
89 Shea Weber	.25	.60
90 David Legwand	.25	.60
91 Ryan Suter	.25	.60
92 Francis Bouillon	.25	.60
93 Saku Koivu	.30	.75
94 Guillaume Latendresse	.20	.50
95 Carey Price	.60	1.50
96 Tomas Plekanec	.20	.50
97 Mike Komisarek	.20	.50
98 Sergei Kostitsyn	.20	.50
99 Andrei Kostitsyn	.25	.60
100 Josh Harding	.30	.75
101 Marian Gaborik	.30	.75
102 Mikko Koivu	.25	.60
103 James Sheppard	.20	.50
104 Nick Schultz	.20	.50
105 Pierre-Marc Bouchard	.30	.75
106 Benoit Pouliot	.20	.50
107 Anze Kopitar	.50	1.25
108 Jack Johnson	.20	.50
109 Jason LaBarbera	.25	.60
110 Dustin Brown	.30	.75
111 Patrick O'Sullivan	.25	.60
112 Tomas Vokoun	.25	.60
113 Stephen Weiss	.20	.50
114 Nathan Horton	.25	.60
115 Jay Bouwmeester	.20	.50
116 David Booth	.20	.50
117 Rostislav Olesz	.20	.50
118 Fernando Pisani	.20	.50
119 Andrew Cogliano	.20	.50
120 Shawn Horcoff	.20	.50
121 Sheldon Souray	.20	.50
122 Ales Hemsky	.25	.60
123 Mathieu Garon	.25	.60
124 Robert Nilsson	.20	.50
125 Dustin Penner	.25	.60
126 Henrik Zetterberg	.40	1.00
127 Chris Osgood	.30	.75
128 Nicklas Lidstrom	.30	.75
129 Kris Draper	.20	.50
130 Jiri Hudler	.25	.60
131 Niklas Kronwall	.25	.60
132 Tomas Holmstrom	.25	.60
133 Mike Modano	.50	1.25
134 Sergei Zubov	.25	.60
135 Brenden Morrow	.25	.60
136 Brad Richards	.30	.75
137 Trevor Daley	.20	.50
138 Matt Niskanen	.25	.60
139 Steve Ott	.20	.50
140 Rick Nash	.30	.75
141 Pascal Leclaire	.25	.60
142 Jared Boll	.20	.50
143 Rostislav Klesla	.20	.50
144 Kris Russell	.20	.50
145 Michael Peca	.25	.60
146 Ole-Kristian Tollefsen	.20	.50
147 Paul Stastny	.25	.60
148 John-Michael Liles	.20	.50
149 Marek Svatos	.20	.50
150 Peter Budaj	.25	.60
151 Ryan Smyth	.25	.60
152 Milan Hejduk	.25	.60
153 Jordan Leopold	.20	.50
154 Wojtek Wolski	.25	.60
155 Jonathan Toews	.50	1.25
156 Patrick Sharp	.30	.75
157 Adam Burish	.25	.60
158 Cam Barker	.20	.50
159 Martin Havlat	.30	.75
160 Duncan Keith	.25	.60
161 Robert Lang	.20	.50
162 Eric Staal	.40	1.00
163 Tuomo Ruutu	.30	.75
164 Joe Corvo	.20	.50
165 Rod Brind'Amour	.30	.75
166 Matt Cullen	.20	.50
167 Ray Whitney	.25	.60
168 Daymond Langkow	.20	.50
169 Jarome Iginla	.40	1.00
170 Dion Phaneuf	.25	.60
171 Matthew Lombardi	.20	.50
172 Cory Sarich	.20	.50
173 Adrian Aucoin	.20	.50
174 Maxim Afinogenov	.20	.50
175 Ryan Miller	.30	.75
176 Derek Roy	.20	.50
177 Jason Pominville	.20	.50
178 Jaroslav Spacek	.20	.50
179 Drew Stafford	.20	.50
180 Phil Kessel	.30	.75
181 Tim Thomas	.30	.75
182 Zdeno Chara	.30	.75
183 Manny Fernandez	.20	.50
184 Milan Lucic	.50	1.25
185 Mark Stuart	.20	.50
186 Chuck Kobasew	.20	.50
187 Kari Lehtonen	.40	1.00
188 Tobias Enstrom	.20	.50
189 Ilya Kovalchuk	.30	.75
190 Colby Armstrong	.20	.50
191 Todd White	.20	.50
192 Erik Christensen	.20	.50
193 Ryan Getzlaf	.30	.75
194 Chris Kunitz	.30	.75
195 Scott Niedermayer	.30	.75
196 Bobby Ryan	.25	.60
197 Francois Beauchemin	.20	.50
198 Jean-Sebastien Giguere	.30	.75
199 Martin Brodeur CL	.75	2.00
200 Sidney Crosby CL	1.25	3.00
201 Zach Bogosian YG RC	4.00	10.00
202 Blake Wheeler YG RC	10.00	25.00
203 Adam Pardy YG RC	2.50	6.00
204 Brandon Sutter YG RC	3.00	8.00
205 Jakub Voracek YG RC	6.00	15.00
206 Adam Pineault YG RC	2.50	6.00
207 Derick Brassard YG RC	3.00	8.00
208 Steve Mason YG RC	5.00	12.00
209 James Neal YG RC	6.00	15.00
210 Mark Fistric YG RC	2.50	-6.00
211 Justin Abdelkader YG RC	5.00	12.00
212 Jonathan Ericsson YG RC	3.00	8.00
213 Darren Helm YG RC	3.00	8.00
214 Mattias Ritola YG RC	2.50	6.00
215 Tom Sestito YG RC	3.00	8.00
216 Chris Porter YG RC	3.00	8.00
217 Michael Frolik YG RC	3.00	8.00
218 T.J. Oshie YG RC	10.00	25.00
219 Shawn Matthias YG RC	3.00	8.00
220 Drew Doughty YG RC	12.00	30.00
221 Wayne Simmonds YG RC	6.00	15.00
222 Oscar Moller YG RC	2.50	6.00
223 Erik Ersberg YG RC	2.50	6.00
224 Colton Gillies YG RC	2.50	6.00
225 Matt D'Agostini YG RC	2.50	6.00
226 Ryan Jones YG RC	3.00	8.00
227 Patric Hornqvist YG RC	3.00	8.00
228 Anssi Salmela YG RC	3.00	8.00
229 Kyle Okposo YG RC	4.00	10.00
230 Lauri Korpikoski YG RC	2.00	5.00
231 Brian Lee YG RC	2.50	6.00
232 Ilya Zubov YG RC	2.50	6.00
233 Jared Ross YG RC	3.00	8.00
234 Luca Sbisa YG RC	2.00	5.00
235 Claude Giroux YG RC	12.00	30.00
236 Kyle Turris YG RC	5.00	12.00
237 Mikkel Boedker YG RC	4.00	10.00
238 Alex Goligoski YG RC	4.00	10.00
239 Jon Filewich YG RC	2.50	6.00
240 Ryan Stone YG RC	2.00	5.00
241 Alex Pietrangelo YG RC	5.00	12.00
242 Patrik Berglund YG RC	2.50	6.00
243 Vladimir Mihalik YG RC	2.00	5.00
244 Janne Niskala YG RC	3.00	8.00
245 Steven Stamkos YG RC	40.00	100.00
246 John Mitchell YG RC	2.50	6.00
247 Robbie Earl YG RC	2.00	5.00
248 Luke Schenn YG RC	4.00	10.00
249 Mike Brown YG RC	3.00	8.00
250 Dougty/Stamk/Pietrnglo CL	6.00	15.00
251 Teemu Selanne	.60	1.50
252 Chris Pronger	.30	.75
253 Kent Huskins	.20	.50
254 Jonas Hiller	.25	.60
255 Corey Perry	.50	1.25
256 Mathieu Schneider	.20	.50
257 Brett Sterling	.25	.60
258 Johan Hedberg	.25	.60
259 Niclas Havelid	.20	.50
260 Slava Kozlov	.20	.50
261 Bryan Little	.25	.60
262 Jason Williams	.20	.50
263 Ron Hainsey	.20	.50
264 P.J. Axelsson	.20	.50
265 Tuukka Rask	.40	1.00
266 Patrice Bergeron	.40	1.00
267 Dennis Wideman	.20	.50
268 Marc Savard	.20	.50
269 David Krejci	.30	.75
270 Marco Sturm	.20	.50
271 Thomas Vanek	.25	.60
272 Teppo Numminen	.20	.50
273 Jochen Hecht	.20	.50
274 Tim Connolly	.20	.50
275 Toni Lydman	.20	.50
276 Daniel Paille	.20	.50
277 Paul Gaustad	.20	.50
278 Patrick Lalime	.25	.60
279 Craig Rivet	.20	.50
280 Todd Bertuzzi	.30	.75
281 Robyn Regehr	.20	.50
282 Mike Cammalleri	.25	.60
283 Miikka Kiprusoff	.30	.75
284 Cam Ward	.30	.75
285 Patrick Eaves	.20	.50
286 Joni Pitkanen	.20	.50
287 Sergei Samsonov	.25	.60
288 Scott Walker	.20	.50
289 Tim Gleason	.20	.50
290 Patrick Kane	.60	1.50
291 Nikolai Khabibulin	.30	.75
292 Dustin Byfuglien	.30	.75
293 Brent Seabrook	.20	.50
294 Jack Skille	.25	.60
295 Brian Campbell	.25	.60
296 Cristobal Huet	.25	.60
297 Joe Sakic	.60	1.50
298 Peter Forsberg	.60	1.50
299 Ian Laperriere	.20	.50
300 Adam Foote	.20	.50
301 Darcy Tucker	.25	.60
302 Andrew Raycroft	.25	.60
303 Kristian Huselius	.20	.50
304 Fedor Tyutin	.20	.50
305 R.J. Umberger	.20	.50
306 Fredrik Norrena	.20	.50
307 Jason Chimera	.20	.50
308 Fredrik Modin	.20	.50
309 Mike Commodore	.20	.50
310 Jere Lehtinen	.20	.50
311 Mike Ribeiro	.20	.50
312 Philippe Boucher	.20	.50
313 Marty Turco	.30	.75
314 Stephane Robidas	.20	.50
315 Toby Petersen	.20	.50
316 Loui Eriksson	.20	.50
317 Sean Avery	.20	.50
318 Pavel Datsyuk	.50	1.25
319 Chris Chelios	.30	.75
320 Mikael Samuelsson	.20	.50
321 Dan Cleary	.25	.60
322 Johan Franzen	.25	.60
323 Brian Rafalski	.25	.60
324 Valtteri Filppula	.20	.50
325 Marian Hossa	.30	.75
326 Ty Conklin	.25	.60
327 Dwayne Roloson	.25	.60
328 Lubomir Visnovsky	.20	.50
329 Tom Gilbert	.20	.50
330 Sam Gagner	.20	.50
331 Zach Stortini	.20	.50
332 Erik Cole	.20	.50
333 Craig Anderson	.30	.75
334 Richard Zednik	.30	.75
335 Keith Ballard	.20	.50
336 Nick Boynton	.20	.50
337 Brett McLean	.20	.50
338 Cory Murphy	.20	.50
339 Cory Stillman	.20	.50
340 Jarret Stoll	.25	.60
341 Jonathan Bernier	.25	.60
342 Alexander Frolov	.20	.50
343 Kyle Calder	.20	.50
344 Derek Armstrong	.20	.50
345 Michal Handzus	.25	.60
346 Tom Preissing	.20	.50
347 Andrew Brunette	.20	.50
348 Niklas Backstrom	.30	.75
349 Owen Nolan	.30	.75
350 Brent Burns	.30	.75
351 Eric Belanger	.20	.50
352 Derek Boogaard	.20	.50
353 Kim Johnsson	.20	.50
354 Marek Zidlicky	.20	.50
355 Andrei Markov	.30	.75
356 Jaroslav Halak	.30	.75
357 Chris Higgins	.20	.50
358 Alex Kovalev	.25	.60
359 Roman Hamrlik	.20	.50
360 Alex Tanguay	.20	.50
361 Marc Denis	.25	.60
362 Jason Arnott	.25	.60
363 J.P. Dumont	.20	.50
364 Dan Ellis	.20	.50
365 Jordin Tootoo	.30	.75
366 Rich Peverley	.25	.60
367 Bobby Holik	.20	.50
368 Zach Parise	.30	.75
369 Jamie Langenbrunner	.20	.50
370 Dainius Zubrus	.20	.50
371 David Clarkson	.25	.60
372 Travis Zajac	.20	.50
373 Brian Rolston	.25	.60
374 Doug Weight	.30	.75
375 Mark Streit	.20	.50
376 Jeff Tambellini	.20	.50
377 Mike Comrie	.25	.60
378 Chris Campoli	.20	.50
379 Sean Bergenheim	.20	.50
380 Richard Park	.20	.50
381 Chris Drury	.25	.60
382 Aaron Voros	.20	.50
383 Nikolai Zherdev	.20	.50
384 Michal Rozsival	.20	.50
385 Daniel Girardi	.20	.50
386 Wade Redden	.20	.50
387 Dany Heatley	.25	.60
388 Martin Gerber	.25	.60
389 Chris Kelly	.25	.60
390 Chris Phillips	.20	.50
391 Nick Foligno	.30	.75
392 Jeff Carter	.25	.60
393 Antero Niittymaki	.25	.60
394 Braydon Coburn	.20	.50
395 Riley Cote	.20	.50
396 Daniel Briere	.30	.75
397 Scott Hartnell	.20	.50
398 Randy Jones	.20	.50
399 Shane Doan	.25	.60
400 Olli Jokinen	.25	.60
401 Mikael Tellqvist	.25	.60
402 Steven Reinprecht	.20	.50
403 Derek Morris	.20	.50
404 Eric Godard	.20	.50
405 Miroslav Satan	.30	.75
406 Hal Gill	.20	.50
407 Evgeni Malkin	.60	1.50
408 Maxime Talbot	.20	.50
409 Ryan Whitney	.30	.75
410 Patrick Marleau	.30	.75
411 Jeremy Roenick	.50	1.25
412 Mike Grier	.20	.50
413 Rob Blake	.30	.75
414 Brad Winchester	.20	.50
415 Keith Tkachuk	.30	.75
416 Chris Mason	.25	.60
417 David Backes	.20	.50
418 Barret Jackman	.20	.50
419 Yan Stastny	.25	.60
420 Mark Recchi	.40	1.00
421 Radim Vrbata	.20	.50
422 Ryan Malone	.20	.50
423 Vaclav Prospal	.20	.50
424 Vincent Lecavalier	.30	.75
425 Andrej Meszaros	.20	.50
426 Evgeni Artyukhin	.20	.50
427 Gary Roberts	.20	.50
428 Olaf Kolzig	.30	.75
429 Jeff Finger	.20	.50
430 Curtis Joseph	.40	1.00
431 Jason Blake	.20	.50
432 Niklas Hagman	.20	.50
433 Matt Stajan	.20	.50
434 Alexei Ponikarovsky	.20	.50
435 Pavol Demitra	.40	1.00
436 Curtis Sanford	.25	.60
437 Sami Salo	.20	.50
438 Kevin Bieksa	.25	.60
439 Steve Bernier	.20	.50
440 Taylor Pyatt	.20	.50
441 Alexandre Burrows	.20	.50
442 Willie Mitchell	.20	.50
443 Jose Theodore	.30	.75
444 Alexander Ovechkin	1.25	3.00
445 Sergei Fedorov	.50	1.25
446 Tom Poti	.20	.50
447 Michael Nylander	.20	.50
448 Brooks Laich	.20	.50
449 Evgeni Malkin CL	.60	1.50
450 Alexander Ovechkin CL	1.25	3.00
451 Andrew Ebbett YG RC	2.00	5.00
452 Brett Festerling YG RC	2.50	6.00
453 Nathan Oystrick YG RC	3.00	8.00
454 Boris Valabik YG RC	3.00	8.00
455 Nathan Gerbe YG RC	3.00	8.00
456 Justin Peters YG RC	3.00	8.00
457 Zach Boychuk YG RC	3.00	8.00
458 Dwight Helminen YG RC	3.00	8.00
459 Patrick Dwyer YG RC	3.00	8.00
460 Simeon Varlamov YG RC	6.00	15.00
461 Joe Jensen YG RC	3.00	8.00
462 Chris Stewart YG RC	3.00	8.00
463 Dan LaCosta YG RC	3.00	8.00
464 Nikita Filatov YG RC	3.00	8.00
465 Derek Dorsett YG RC	4.00	10.00
466 Andrew Murray YG RC	2.50	6.00
467 Fabian Brunnstrom YG RC	2.50	6.00
468 Steve MacIntyre YG RC	3.00	8.00
469 Theo Peckham YG RC	2.50	6.00
470 Michal Repik YG RC	3.00	8.00
471 Jason Garrison YG RC	3.00	8.00
472 Brian Boyle YG RC	2.50	6.00
473 Teddy Purcell YG RC	2.50	6.00
474 Danny Taylor YG RC	2.50	6.00
475 Matthew Halischuk YG RC	2.00	5.00
476 Petr Vrana YG RC	2.00	5.00
477 Patrick Davis YG RC	2.50	6.00
478 Pierre-Luc Letourneau-Leblond YG RC	2.00	5.00
479 Josh Bailey YG RC	4.00	10.00
480 Brett Skinner YG RC	2.50	6.00
481 Mitch Fritz YG RC	2.50	6.00
482 Jesse Winchester YG RC	2.00	5.00
483 Andreas Nodl YG RC	2.00	5.00
484 Kenndal McArdle YG RC	2.50	6.00
485 Darroll Powe YG RC	3.00	8.00
486 Viktor Tikhonov YG RC	2.50	6.00
487 Kevin Porter YG RC	2.50	6.00
488 Janne Pesonen YG RC	2.50	6.00
489 John Curry YG RC	3.00	8.00
490 Jamie McGinn YG RC	3.00	8.00
491 Brad Staubitz YG RC	2.50	6.00
492 Tom Cavanagh YG RC	2.50	6.00
493 Ben Bishop YG RC	5.00	12.00
494 Justin Pogge YG RC	2.50	6.00
495 Nikolai Kulemin YG RC	3.00	8.00
496 Jonas Frogren YG RC	2.00	5.00
497 Cory Schneider YG RC	8.00	20.00
498 Tyler Sloan YG RC	4.00	10.00
499 Karl Alzner YG RC	2.00	5.00
500 Brunns/Tikhnv/Filatv CL	4.00	10.00

2008-09 Upper Deck Exclusives

*VETS/100: 2.5X TO 6X BASE
*YOUNG GUNS/100: 1X TO 2.5X BASE

Card	Low	High
1 Nicklas Backstrom	3.00	8.00
25 Mike Smith	3.00	8.00
44 Kristopher Letang	4.00	10.00
218 T.J. Oshie YG	60.00	150.00
235 Claude Giroux YG	80.00	200.00
245 Steven Stamkos YG	250.00	600.00

2008-09 Upper Deck All Star Game Montreal

Card	Low	High
COMPLETE SET (10)	15.00	40.00
MTL1 Alex Kovalev	.75	2.00
MTL2 Alexander Ovechkin	4.00	10.00
MTL3 Carey Price	2.00	5.00
MTL4 Guy Lafleur	1.25	3.00
MTL5 Larry Robinson	1.00	2.50
MTL6 Jarome Iginla	1.25	3.00
MTL7 Patrick Roy	2.50	6.00
MTL8 Sidney Crosby	4.00	10.00
MTL9 Saku Koivu	1.00	2.50
MTL10 Jean Beliveau	1.00	2.50

2008-09 Upper Deck All-Stars

Card	Low	High
COMPLETE SET (30)	40.00	100.00
AS1 Tomas Kaberle	.60	1.50
AS2 Daniel Alfredsson	1.00	2.50
AS3 Marian Hossa	1.00	2.50
AS4 Eric Staal	1.25	3.00
AS5 Rick DiPietro	.75	2.00
AS6 Anze Kopitar	1.50	4.00
AS7 Zdeno Chara	1.00	2.50
AS8 Henrik Sedin	1.25	3.00
AS9 Jason Spezza	1.00	2.50
AS10 Shawn Horcoff	.60	1.50
AS11 Marian Gaborik	1.00	2.50
AS12 Andrei Markov	1.00	2.50
AS13 Martin St. Louis	1.00	2.50
AS14 Nicklas Lidstrom	1.00	2.50
AS15 Pavel Datsyuk	1.50	4.00
AS16 Rick Nash	1.00	2.50
AS17 Mike Ribeiro	.60	1.50
AS18 Ryan Getzlaf	1.00	2.50
AS19 Tomas Vokoun	.75	2.00
AS20 Vincent Lecavalier	1.00	2.50
AS21 Joe Thornton SP	5.00	12.00
AS22 Evgeni Nabokov SP	2.50	6.00
AS23 Dion Phaneuf SP	2.50	6.00
AS24 Jarome Iginla SP	4.00	10.00
AS25 Chris Pronger SP	3.00	8.00
AS26 Mike Richards SP	2.50	6.00
AS27 Chris Osgood SP	3.00	8.00
AS28 Evgeni Malkin SP	6.00	15.00
AS29 Alexander Ovechkin SP	12.00	30.00
AS30 Ilya Kovalchuk SP	3.00	8.00

2008-09 Upper Deck All-World Team

Card	Low	High
COMPLETE SET (20)	50.00	100.00
AWT1 Sidney Crosby	5.00	12.00
AWT2 Alexander Ovechkin	5.00	12.00
AWT3 Evgeni Malkin	2.50	6.00
AWT4 Nicklas Lidstrom	1.25	3.00
AWT5 Martin Brodeur	3.00	8.00
AWT6 Henrik Zetterberg	1.50	4.00
AWT7 Jarome Iginla	1.50	4.00
AWT8 Mike Modano	2.00	5.00
AWT9 Ilya Kovalchuk	1.25	3.00
AWT10 Marian Gaborik	1.25	3.00
AWT11 Joe Thornton SP	8.00	20.00
AWT12 Anze Kopitar SP	8.00	20.00
AWT13 Miikka Kiprusoff SP	5.00	12.00
AWT14 Ales Hemsky SP	4.00	10.00
AWT15 Patrick Kane SP	10.00	25.00
AWT16 Michael Ryder SP	3.00	8.00
AWT17 Scott Gomez SP	4.00	10.00
AWT18 Saku Koivu SP	5.00	12.00
AWT19 Evgeni Nabokov SP	4.00	10.00
AWT20 Markus Naslund SP	5.00	12.00

2008-09 Upper Deck Big Game Hunters

Card	Low	High
COMPLETE SET (30)	125.00	250.00
BGHAK Alex Kovalev	3.00	8.00
BGHAO Alexander Ovechkin SP	15.00	40.00
BGHBR Brad Richards	4.00	10.00
BGHCO Chris Osgood	4.00	10.00
BGHCP Chris Pronger	4.00	10.00
BGHDB Daniel Briere	4.00	10.00
BGHDP Dion Phaneuf	3.00	8.00
BGHEM Evgeni Malkin SP	8.00	20.00
BGHES Eric Staal	5.00	12.00
BGHHZ Henrik Zetterberg SP	5.00	12.00
BGHJF Johan Franzen	3.00	8.00
BGHJG Jean-Sebastien Giguere	4.00	10.00
BGHJI Jarome Iginla SP	5.00	12.00
BGHJS Joe Sakic SP	8.00	20.00
BGHJT Joe Thornton SP	6.00	15.00
BGHMB Martin Brodeur SP	10.00	25.00
BGHMG Marian Gaborik	4.00	10.00
BGHMH Marian Hossa	4.00	10.00
BGHMM Mike Modano	6.00	15.00
BGHMT Marty Turco	4.00	10.00
BGHNL Nicklas Lidstrom	4.00	10.00
BGHPE Patrik Elias	4.00	10.00
BGHPR Carey Price	10.00	25.00
BGHSC Sidney Crosby SP	12.00	30.00
BGHSG Scott Gomez	3.00	8.00
BGHSN Scott Niedermayer	4.00	10.00
BGHST Martin St. Louis	4.00	10.00
BGHTO Jonathan Toews SP	6.00	15.00
BGHTS Teemu Selanne	8.00	20.00
BGHVL Vincent Lecavalier SP	4.00	10.00

2008-09 Upper Deck Biography of a Season

Card	Low	High
BS1 Alexander Ovechkin	1.25	3.00
BS2 Henrik Zetterberg	.40	1.00
BS3 Nicklas Lidstrom	.30	.75
BS4 Steven Stamkos	1.25	3.00
BS5 Fabian Brunstrom	1.25	3.00
BS6 H.Lundqvist/M.Staal	.75	2.00
BS7 Sidney Crosby	1.25	3.00
BS8 Carey Price	.60	1.50
BS9 Jordan Staal	.25	.60
BS10 Roberto Luongo	.50	1.25
BS11 Patrick Marleau	.30	.75
BS12 Alexander Ovechkin	1.25	3.00
BS13 Sidney Crosby	1.25	3.00
BS14 Keith Tkachuk	.30	.75
BS15 Thomas Vanek	.25	.60
BS16 Scott Hartnell	.20	.50
BS17 Steve Mason	.50	1.25
BS18 Henrik Zetterberg	.40	1.00
BS19 Doug Weight	.30	.75
BS20 Carey Price	.60	1.50
BS21 Mats Sundin	.30	.75
BS22 Dion Phaneuf	.25	.60
BS23 Blake Wheeler	.75	2.00
BS24 Alex Kovalev	.25	.60
BS25 Martin Brodeur	.75	2.00
BS26 Mike Green	.25	.60
BS27 Jarome Iginla	.40	1.00
BS28 Steven Stamkos	1.25	3.00
BS29 Evgeni Malkin	.60	1.50
BS30 Alexander Ovechkin	1.25	3.00

2008-09 Upper Deck Captains Calling

Card	Low	High
COMPLETE SET (7)	6.00	15.00
CPT1 Sidney Crosby	3.00	8.00
CPT2 Jarome Iginla	1.00	2.50
CPT3 Joe Sakic	1.50	4.00
CPT4 Nicklas Lidstrom	.75	2.00
CPT5 Saku Koivu	.75	2.00
CPT6 Brenden Morrow	.60	1.50
CPT7 Rick Nash	.75	2.00

2008-09 Upper Deck Clear Cut Duos

Card	Low	High
CD1 M.Lemieux/S.Crosby	40.00	100.00
CD2 E.Malkin/J.Staal	20.00	50.00
CD3 W.Gretzky/M.Messier	60.00	150.00
CD4 B.Orr/P.Esposito	40.00	100.00
CD5 R.Getzlaf/J.Giguere	10.00	25.00
CD6 P.Roy/C.Price	25.00	60.00
CD7 T.Selanne/S.Niedermayer	20.00	50.00
CD8 I.Kovalchuk/K.Lehtonen	12.00	30.00
CD9 P.Bergeron/M.Savard	12.00	30.00
CD10 R.Miller/T.Vanek	10.00	25.00
CD11 J.Iginla/M.Kiprusoff	12.00	30.00
CD12 E.Staal/C.Ward	12.00	30.00
CD13 J.Sakic/P.Stastny	20.00	50.00
CD14 R.Nash/S.Mason	15.00	40.00
CD15 J.Toews/P.Kane	20.00	50.00
CD16 M.Modano/M.Turco	15.00	40.00
CD17 H.Zetterberg/P.Datsyuk	15.00	40.00
CD18 S.Gagner/A.Cogliano	6.00	15.00
CD19 T.Vokoun/N.Horton	8.00	20.00
CD20 A.Kopitar/J.Johnson	15.00	40.00
CD21 M.Gaborik/J.Harding	10.00	25.00
CD22 C.Price/S.Koivu	20.00	50.00
CD23 J.Arnott/J.Dumont	8.00	20.00
CD24 M.Brodeur/Z.Parise	25.00	60.00
CD25 G.Howe/H.Zetterberg	30.00	80.00
CD26 H.Lundqvist/C.Drury	25.00	60.00
CD27 M.Messier/B.Leetch	20.00	50.00
CD28 J.Spezza/D.Heatley	10.00	25.00
CD29 S.Gagne/D.Briere	10.00	25.00
CD30 S.Doan/P.Mueller	8.00	20.00
CD31 S.Crosby/E.Malkin	40.00	100.00
CD32 J.Thornton/E.Nabokov	15.00	40.00
CD33 P.Kariya/B.Boyes	10.00	25.00
CD34 V.Lecavalier/M.St. Louis	10.00	25.00
CD35 M.Sundin/A.Steen	10.00	25.00
CD36 R.Luongo/H.Sedin	15.00	40.00
CD37 A.Ovechkin/N.Backstrom	40.00	100.00
CD38 R.Getzlaf/C.Perry	15.00	40.00
CD39 C.Osgood/N.Lidstrom	10.00	25.00
CD40 M.Sundin/T.Kaberle	10.00	25.00
CD41 J.Thornton/P.Marleau	15.00	40.00
CD42 M.Modano/B.Richards	15.00	40.00

2008-09 Upper Deck Clear Cut Rookies

Card	Low	High
CCR1 Ilya Zubov	5.00	12.00
CCR2 Blake Wheeler	25.00	60.00
CCR3 Petr Vrana	4.00	10.00
CCR4 Jakub Voracek	12.00	30.00
CCR5 Kyle Turris	10.00	25.00
CCR6 Viktor Tikhonov	5.00	12.00
CCR7 Brandon Sutter	6.00	15.00
CCR8 Steven Stamkos	40.00	100.00
CCR9 Luke Schenn	25.00	60.00
CCR10 Luca Sbisa	4.00	10.00
CCR11 Mattias Ritola	5.00	12.00
CCR12 Kevin Porter	5.00	12.00
CCR13 Matt D'Agostini	5.00	12.00
CCR14 Alex Pietrangelo	10.00	25.00
CCR15 Nathan Oystrick	6.00	15.00
CCR16 T.J. Oshie	15.00	40.00
CCR17 Kyle Okposo	8.00	20.00
CCR18 Andreas Nodl	4.00	10.00
CCR19 James Neal	12.00	30.00
CCR20 Oscar Moller	5.00	12.00
CCR21 Vladimir Mihalik	4.00	10.00
CCR22 Shawn Matthias	6.00	15.00
CCR23 Steve Mason	40.00	100.00
CCR24 Nikolai Kulemin	6.00	15.00
CCR25 Ryan Jones	6.00	15.00
CCR26 Patric Hornqvist	6.00	15.00
CCR27 Darren Helm	6.00	15.00
CCR28 Alex Goligoski	8.00	20.00
CCR29 Claude Giroux	12.00	30.00
CCR30 Colton Gillies	5.00	12.00
CCR31 Michael Frolik	6.00	15.00
CCR32 Nikita Filatov	6.00	15.00
CCR33 Erik Ersberg	5.00	12.00
CCR34 Robbie Earl	4.00	10.00
CCR35 Drew Doughty	15.00	40.00
CCR36 Fabian Brunnstrom	25.00	60.00
CCR37 Derick Brassard	6.00	15.00
CCR38 Zach Boychuk	6.00	15.00
CCR39 Zach Bogosian	8.00	20.00
CCR40 Mikkel Boedker	8.00	20.00
CCR41 Patrik Berglund	5.00	12.00
CCR42 Justin Abdelkader	10.00	25.00

2008-09 Upper Deck Clear Cut Winners

Card	Low	High
CC1 Alexander Ovechkin	20.00	50.00
CC2 Bobby Orr	20.00	50.00
CC3 Carey Price	10.00	25.00
CC4 Evgeni Malkin	10.00	25.00
CC5 Gordie Howe	15.00	40.00
CC6 Henrik Lundqvist	12.00	30.00
CC7 Henrik Zetterberg	6.00	15.00
CC8 Ilya Kovalchuk	5.00	12.00
CC9 Jarome Iginla	6.00	15.00
CC10 Jason Arnott	4.00	10.00
CC11 Jason Spezza	5.00	12.00
CC12 Joe Sakic	10.00	25.00
CC13 Joe Thornton	8.00	20.00
CC14 Jonathan Toews	8.00	20.00
CC15 Marian Gaborik	5.00	12.00
CC16 Mario Lemieux	20.00	50.00
CC17 Mark Messier	10.00	25.00
CC18 Martin Brodeur	12.00	30.00
CC19 Martin St. Louis	5.00	12.00
CC20 Mats Sundin	5.00	12.00
CC21 Miikka Kiprusoff	5.00	12.00
CC22 Mike Modano	8.00	20.00
CC23 Nicklas Backstrom	5.00	12.00
CC24 Patrick Kane	10.00	25.00
CC25 Patrick Roy	12.00	30.00
CC26 Paul Kariya	5.00	12.00
CC27 Pavel Datsyuk	8.00	20.00
CC28 Peter Mueller	4.00	10.00
CC29 Rick DiPietro	4.00	10.00
CC30 Rick Nash	5.00	12.00
CC31 Roberto Luongo	8.00	20.00
CC32 Ryan Getzlaf	5.00	12.00
CC33 Ryan Miller	5.00	12.00
CC34 Saku Koivu	5.00	12.00
CC35 Sam Gagner	3.00	8.00
CC36 Shane Doan	4.00	10.00
CC37 Sidney Crosby	20.00	50.00
CC38 Simon Gagne	5.00	12.00
CC39 Teemu Selanne	10.00	25.00
CC40 Tomas Vokoun	4.00	10.00
CC41 Vincent Lecavalier	5.00	12.00
CC42 Wayne Gretzky	30.00	80.00

2008-09 Upper Deck Fab Four Fabrics

Card	Low	High
FFANA Selane/GetzlGig/Nieder	15.00	40.00
FFASG Crsby/Sakc/Thrn/Lecv	25.00	60.00
FFATL Kovl/Leht/Armst/Enstrm	10.00	25.00
FFBOS Berg/Svrd/Kessl/Chara	10.00	25.00
FFBUF Vank/Millr/Stffrd/Conly	8.00	20.00
FFCAN Iginl/Ryd/Chch/Ribeiro	10.00	25.00
FFCAR Staal/Ward/Will/Brind	10.00	25.00
FFCEN Staal/Spez/Rich/Berg	10.00	25.00
FFCGY Igin/Phnf/Kiprsf/Caml	10.00	25.00
FFCHI Toews/Kne/Kth/Khab	15.00	40.00
FFCLB Nash/Lecl/Picrd/Peca	8.00	20.00
FFCOL Sakc/Frsb/Stst/Wlski	15.00	40.00
FFCZS Hssa/Hjdk/Elias/Mich	8.00	20.00
FFDAL Modn/Trco/Rich/Morr	12.00	30.00
FFDEF Phnf/Jhns/Jhns/Webr	6.00	15.00
FFDET Zettr/Dtsyk/Lids/Chel	12.00	30.00
FFEDM Ggnr/Hmsk/Brule/Rolo	6.00	15.00
FFFIN Selne/Koivu/Joki/Kvu	15.00	40.00
FFFLA Vokn/Hrtn/Bouw/Weis	6.00	15.00
FFLAK Kopit/Frlv/Jhns/Brwn	12.00	30.00
FFMIN Gabr/Kvu/Bouch/Nln	8.00	20.00
FFMTL Kovl/Tng/Ltnd/Koivu	8.00	20.00
FFNAS Arntt/Wbr/Dmnt/Lgwn	6.00	15.00
FFNET Trco/Lgce/Rlsn/Thms	8.00	20.00
FFNJD Brod/Prse/Gnta/Elias	20.00	50.00
FFNYI DiPtr/Wght/Grin/Cmrie	8.00	20.00
FFNYR Lund/Zhrdv/Gomz/Dru	20.00	50.00
FFOTT Htly/Spez/Alfrd/Phill	8.00	20.00
FFPHI Ggne/Rchr/Brie/Cartr	8.00	20.00
FFPHX Muellr/Doan/Jkin/Jov	6.00	15.00
FFPIT Crsby/Mlkn/Stal/Wht	30.00	80.00
FFQUE Brod/Lngo/Flry/Theod	20.00	50.00
FFRUS Ovch/Mlkn/Kovl/Fedr	30.00	80.00
FFSJS Thrnt/Chech/Marl/Mich	12.00	30.00
FFSTL Krya/Byes/Tkchk/Leg	8.00	20.00
FFSWE Snd/Nasl/Bckstr/Zett	10.00	25.00
FFTBL Lecav/St.L/Rnger/Joki	8.00	20.00
FFTOR Sund/Sten/Blke/Tosk	10.00	25.00
FFUSA Rnck/Mdno/Tkch/Chl	12.00	30.00
FFVAN Lngo/Sdin/Sdin/Bernr	12.00	30.00
FFWAS Ovch/Bck/Semn/Gren	30.00	80.00
FFWNG Nash/Htly/Ggne/St.L	8.00	20.00

2008-09 Upper Deck Favourite Sons

Card	Low	High
COMPLETE SET (14)	12.00	30.00
FS1 Ryan Smyth	.60	1.50
FS2 Brad Richards	.75	2.00
FS3 Jonathan Cheechoo	.60	1.50
FS4 Sidney Crosby	3.00	8.00
FS5 Jason Spezza	.75	2.00
FS6 Shane Doan	.60	1.50
FS7 Devin Setoguchi	.60	1.50
FS8 Brenden Morrow	.60	1.50
FS9 Carey Price	1.50	4.00
FS10 Jonathan Toews	1.25	3.00
FS11 Michael Ryder	.50	1.25
FS12 Martin St. Louis	.75	2.00
FS13 Vincent Lecavalier	.75	2.00
FS14 Patrice Bergeron	1.00	2.50

2008-09 Upper Deck Game Jerseys

Card	Low	High
GJAA Alex Auld	2.50	6.00
GJAE Alexander Edler	2.50	6.00
GJAH Ales Hemsky	3.00	8.00
GJAK Alex Kovalev	3.00	8.00
GJAL Alexander Steen	2.50	6.00
GJAM Andrej Meszaros	2.50	6.00
GJAN Antero Niittymaki	3.00	8.00
GJAO Alexander Ovechkin	8.00	20.00
GJAP Alexandre Picard	2.50	6.00
GJAS Alexander Semin	4.00	10.00
GJAT Alex Tanguay	2.50	6.00
GJBB Brad Boyes	2.50	6.00
GJBE Brendan Bell	2.50	6.00
GJBG Bill Guerin	4.00	10.00
GJBM Brenden Morrow	3.00	8.00
GJBR Brad Richards	4.00	10.00
GJCA Colby Armstrong	2.50	6.00
GJCC Chris Chelios	4.00	10.00
GJCD Chris Drury	3.00	8.00
GJCP Chris Phillips	2.50	6.00
GJCW Cam Ward	4.00	10.00
GJDA Daniel Alfredsson	4.00	10.00
GJDB Daniel Briere	4.00	10.00
GJDH Dany Heatley	3.00	8.00
GJDK Duncan Keith	3.00	8.00
GJDL David Legwand	3.00	8.00
GJDP Dion Phaneuf	3.00	8.00
GJDR Dwayne Roloson	3.00	8.00
GJDS Daniel Sedin	5.00	12.00
GJDT Darcy Tucker	3.00	8.00
GJDW Doug Weight	4.00	10.00
GJEC Erik Cole	2.50	6.00

GJEN Evgeni Nabokov 3.00 8.00
GJES Eric Staal 5.00 12.00
GJGA Marian Gaborik 4.00 10.00
GJGB Gilbert Brule 2.50 6.00
GJGI Brian Gionta 2.50 6.00
GJGM Glen Murray 3.00 8.00
GJGR Gary Roberts 2.50 6.00
GJHT Hannu Toivonen 3.00 8.00
GJHZ Henrik Zetterberg 5.00 12.00
GJIK Ilya Kovalchuk 4.00 10.00
GJIW Ian White 2.50 6.00
GJJA Jason Arnott 3.00 8.00
GJJB Jay Bouwmeester 2.50 6.00
GJJC Jonathan Cheechoo 3.00 8.00
GJJE Jeff Carter 3.00 8.00
GJJG Jean-Sebastien Giguere 4.00 10.00
GJJI Jarome Iginla 5.00 12.00
GJJO Jussi Jokinen 2.50 6.00
GJJP Joni Pitkanen 2.50 6.00
GJJR Jeremy Roenick 6.00 15.00
GJJS Jason Spezza 4.00 10.00
GJJT Joe Thornton 6.00 15.00
GJKA Patrick Kane 8.00 20.00
GJKL Kari Lehtonen 5.00 12.00
GJKO Anze Kopitar 6.00 15.00
GJKT Keith Tkachuk 4.00 10.00
GJLE Manny Legace 4.00 10.00
GJLS Lee Stempniak 2.50 6.00
GJMA Marc Savard 2.50 6.00
GJMB Martin Brodeur 10.00 25.00
GJMC Mike Cammalleri 3.00 8.00
GJMG Mike Green 3.00 8.00
GJMK Miikka Kiprusoff 4.00 10.00
GJML Mario Lemieux 15.00 40.00
GJMM Mark Messier 8.00 20.00
GJMN Markus Naslund 4.00 10.00
GJMO Mike Modano 6.00 15.00
GJMR Mark Recchi 5.00 12.00
GJMS Matt Stajan 2.50 6.00
GJMT Marty Turco 4.00 10.00
GJNZ Nikolai Zherdev 2.50 6.00
GJOJ Olli Jokinen 3.00 8.00
GJPA Patrice Bergeron 5.00 12.00
GJPB Pierre-Marc Bouchard 4.00 10.00
GJPF Peter Forsberg 8.00 20.00
GJPK Paul Kariya 4.00 10.00
GJPL Pascal Leclaire 3.00 8.00
GJPR Patrick Roy 12.50 30.00
GJPS Paul Stastny 3.00 8.00
GJRA Andrew Raycroft 3.00 8.00
GJRB Brian Rafalski 3.00 8.00
GJRI Mike Richards 3.00 8.00
GJRL Roberto Luongo 6.00 15.00
GJRN Rick Nash 4.00 10.00
GJRY Michael Ryder 2.50 6.00
GJSA Joe Sakic 8.00 20.00
GJSC Sidney Crosby 15.00 40.00
GJSM Ladislav Smid 2.50 6.00
GJST Martin St. Louis 4.00 10.00
GJSU Mats Sundin 4.00 10.00
GJTH Jose Theodore 4.00 10.00
GJTI Kimmo Timonen 2.50 6.00
GJTS Teemu Selanne 8.00 20.00
GJTV Thomas Vanek 3.00 8.00
GJWG Wayne Gretzky 25.00 60.00
GJ2AA Arron Asham 2.50 6.00
GJ2AF Maxim Afinogenov 2.50 6.00
GJ2AL Andrew Ladd 2.50 6.00
GJ2AO Alexander Ovechkin 15.00 40.00
GJ2AV Nik Antropov 3.00 8.00
GJ2AW Andrew Wozniewski 2.50 6.00
GJ2BB Brandon Bochenski 2.50 6.00
GJ2BD Martin Brodeur 8.00 20.00
GJ2BL Brian Leetch 3.00 8.00
GJ2BM Brendan Morrison 2.50 6.00
GJ2BS Brad Stuart 2.50 6.00
GJ2CA Matt Carle 2.50 6.00
GJ2CC Chris Campoli 2.50 6.00
GJ2CD Chris Drury 3.00 8.00
GJ2CJ Curtis Joseph 5.00 12.00
GJ2CP Carey Price 8.00 20.00
GJ2CS Curtis Sanford 3.00 8.00
GJ2DB Donald Brashear 2.50 6.00
GJ2DT Darcy Tucker 3.00 8.00
GJ2EC Erik Cole 2.50 6.00
GJ2EJ Ed Jovanovski 3.00 8.00
GJ2EM Evgeni Malkin 8.00 20.00
GJ2ES Eric Staal 5.00 12.00
GJ2FZ Manny Fernandez 2.50 6.00
GJ2HA Martin Havlat 4.00 10.00
GJ2HE Milan Hejduk 3.00 8.00
GJ2HL Henrik Lundqvist 10.00 25.00
GJ2HO Marian Hossa 4.00 10.00
GJ2IK Ilya Kovalchuk 4.00 10.00
GJ2JS Jarret Stoll 3.00 8.00
GJ2JT Jeff Tambellini 2.50 6.00
GJ2JW Justin Williams 3.00 8.00
GJ2KC Kyle Calder 2.50 6.00
GJ2KZ Viktor Kozlov 2.50 6.00
GJ2MA Mark Stuart 2.50 6.00
GJ2MC Bryan McCabe 2.50 6.00
GJ2MD Marc Denis 3.00 8.00
GJ2ME Martin Erat 2.50 6.00
GJ2MF Marc-Andre Fleury 8.00 20.00
GJ2MG Martin Gerber 3.00 8.00
GJ2MK Mikko Koivu 3.00 8.00
GJ2ML Milan Lucic 6.00 15.00
GJ2MM Mark Messier 8.00 20.00
GJ2MN Matt Niskanen 3.00 8.00
GJ2MO Mattias Ohlund 2.50 6.00
GJ2MP Marc-Antoine Pouliot 2.50 6.00
GJ2MR Mark Recchi 5.00 12.00
GJ2MS Marc Savard 2.50 6.00
GJ2MT Marty Turco 4.00 10.00
GJ2OJ Olli Jokinen 3.00 8.00
GJ2PE Michael Peca 3.00 8.00
GJ2PH Chris Phillips 2.50 6.00
GJ2PM Peter Mueller 3.00 8.00
GJ2PY Corey Perry 6.00 15.00
GJ2RB Mike Ribeiro 2.50 6.00
GJ2RO Patrick Roy 10.00 25.00
GJ2RU Tuomo Ruutu 4.00 10.00
GJ2SB Steve Bernier 2.50 6.00
GJ2SE Brent Seabrook 2.50 6.00
GJ2SG Simon Gagne 4.00 10.00
GJ2SH Brendan Shanahan 4.00 10.00
GJ2ST Jordan Staal 3.00 8.00
GJ2SU Mats Sundin 4.00 10.00
GJ2SV Marek Svatos 2.50 6.00
GJ2SW Shea Weber 3.00 8.00
GJ2TO Jonathan Toews 6.00 15.00
GJ2TW Tiger Williams 2.50 6.00
GJ2VL Vincent Lecavalier 4.00 10.00

2008-09 Upper Deck Hat Trick Heroes

COMPLETE SET (14) 6.00 15.00
HT1 Alexander Ovechkin 2.50 6.00
HT2 Teemu Selanne 1.25 3.00
HT3 Jarome Iginla .75 2.00
HT4 Joe Sakic 1.25 3.00
HT5 Thomas Vanek .50 1.25
HT6 Evgeni Malkin 1.25 3.00
HT7 Ilya Kovalchuk .60 1.50
HT8 Vincent Lecavalier .60 1.50
HT9 Henrik Zetterberg .75 2.00
HT10 Dany Heatley .50 1.25
HT11 Rick Nash .60 1.50
HT12 Marian Gaborik .60 1.50
HT13 Marian Hossa .60 1.50
HT14 Eric Staal .75 2.00

2008-09 Upper Deck Hockey Heroes Sidney Crosby

COMPLETE SET (10) 75.00 150.00
COMP.SET w/o SPs (8) 12.00 30.00
COMMON CROSBY (HH1-HH8) 3.00 8.00
HH9 Crosby Painting 10.00 25.00
HHSC Crosby Header Card 15.00 40.00
HHSCA Crosby AU/87 175.00 300.00

2008-09 Upper Deck Masked Men

COMPLETE SET (30) 25.00 60.00
MM1 Martin Brodeur 2.50 6.00
MM2 Miikka Kiprusoff 1.00 2.50
MM3 Roberto Luongo 1.50 4.00
MM4 Chris Osgood 1.00 2.50
MM5 Carey Price 2.00 5.00
MM6 Henrik Lundqvist 2.50 6.00
MM7 Ryan Miller 1.00 2.50
MM8 Vesa Toskala 1.25 3.00
MM9 Jean-Sebastien Giguere 1.00 2.50
MM10 Evgeni Nabokov .75 2.00
MM11 Marty Turco 1.00 2.50
MM12 Manny Legace 1.00 2.50
MM13 Mathieu Garon .75 2.00
MM14 Martin Gerber .75 2.00
MM15 Josh Harding 1.00 2.50
MM16 Tomas Vokoun .75 2.00
MM17 Rick DiPietro .75 2.00
MM18 Kari Lehtonen 1.25 3.00
MM19 Marc-Andre Fleury 2.00 5.00
MM20 Cam Ward 1.00 2.50
MM21 Pascal Leclaire SP 1.00 2.50
MM22 Peter Budaj SP 1.00 2.50
MM23 Martin Biron SP 1.00 2.50
MM24 Tim Thomas SP 1.25 3.00
MM25 Cristobal Huet SP 1.00 2.50
MM26 Mike Smith SP 1.25 3.00
MM27 Chris Mason SP 1.00 2.50
MM28 Nikolai Khabibulin SP 1.25 3.00
MM29 Ilya Bryzgalov SP 1.00 2.50
MM30 Jason LaBarbera SP 1.00 2.50

2008-09 Upper Deck Rookie Impressions

COMPLETE SET (30) 100.00 200.00
RI1 Michael Frolik 3.00 8.00
RI2 Claude Giroux 6.00 15.00
RI3 Oscar Moller 2.50 6.00
RI4 Viktor Tikhonov 2.50 6.00
RI5 Derick Brassard 8.00 20.00
RI6 Kyle Okposo 4.00 10.00
RI7 Zach Boychuk 3.00 8.00
RI8 Patric Hornqvist 3.00 8.00
RI9 Petr Vrana 2.00 5.00
RI10 Luca Sbisa 2.00 5.00
RI11 T.J. Oshie 10.00 25.00
RI12 Nikolai Kulemin 3.00 8.00
RI13 Nikita Filatov 8.00 20.00
RI14 Mikkel Boedker 6.00 15.00
RI15 James Neal 6.00 15.00
RI16 Brian Boyle 2.50 6.00
RI17 Jamie McGinn 3.00 8.00
RI18 Andreas Nodl 2.00 5.00
RI19 Jakub Voracek 6.00 15.00
RI20 Shawn Matthias 3.00 8.00
RI21 Steven Stamkos SP 12.00 30.00
RI22 Kyle Turris SP 5.00 12.00
RI23 Luke Schenn SP 10.00 25.00
RI24 Drew Doughty SP 8.00 20.00
RI25 Colton Gillies SP 2.50 6.00
RI26 Brandon Sutter SP 3.00 8.00
RI27 Blake Wheeler SP 10.00 25.00
RI28 Fabian Brunnstrom SP 10.00 25.00
RI29 Zach Bogosian SP 4.00 10.00
RI30 Alex Pietrangelo SP 5.00 12.00

2008-09 Upper Deck Rookie Materials

*PATCH/15: 1X TO 2.5X BASIC JSY
RMAP Alex Pietrangelo 5.00 12.00
RMBK Zach Boychuk 3.00 8.00
RMBS Brandon Sutter 3.00 8.00
RMBW Blake Wheeler 8.00 20.00
RMCG Claude Giroux 8.00 20.00
RMDB Derick Brassard 3.00 8.00
RMDD Drew Doughty 8.00 20.00
RMFB Fabian Brunnstrom 2.50 6.00
RMGI Colton Gillies 2.50 6.00
RMJA Justin Abdelkader 5.00 12.00
RMJN James Neal 6.00 15.00
RMJV Jakub Voracek 6.00 15.00
RMKO Kyle Okposo 4.00 10.00
RMKP Kevin Porter 2.50 6.00
RMKT Kyle Turris 5.00 12.00
RMLK Lauri Korpikoski 2.00 5.00
RMLS Luca Sbisa 2.00 5.00
RMMA Steve Mason 5.00 12.00
RMMB Mikkel Boedker 4.00 10.00
RMMF Michael Frolik 3.00 8.00
RMNF Nikita Filatov 3.00 8.00
RMNK Nikolai Kulemin 3.00 8.00
RMPB Patrik Berglund 2.50 6.00
RMPH Patric Hornqvist 3.00 8.00
RMSC Luke Schenn 8.00 20.00
RMSM Shawn Matthias 3.00 8.00
RMSS Steven Stamkos 10.00 25.00
RMTO T.J. Oshie 6.00 15.00
RMVT Viktor Tikhonov 2.50 6.00
RMZB Zach Bogosian 4.00 10.00

2008-09 Upper Deck Rookie Playmakers

RPAG Alex Goligoski 8.00 20.00
RPAP Alex Pietrangelo 10.00 25.00
RPBB Brian Boyle 5.00 12.00
RPBG Zach Bogosian 8.00 20.00
RPBL Brian Lee 5.00 12.00
RPBS Brandon Sutter 6.00 15.00
RPBW Blake Wheeler 15.00 40.00
RPCG Colton Gillies 5.00 12.00
RPDB Derick Brassard 6.00 15.00
RPDD Drew Doughty 15.00 40.00
RPEE Erik Ersberg 5.00 12.00
RPFB Fabian Brunnstrom 5.00 12.00
RPFR Michael Frolik 6.00 15.00
RPGI Claude Giroux 10.00 25.00
RPIZ Ilya Zubov 5.00 12.00
RPJA Justin Abdelkader 10.00 25.00
RPJN James Neal 12.00 30.00
RPJV Jakub Voracek 12.00 30.00
RPKO Kyle Okposo 8.00 20.00
RPKP Kevin Porter 5.00 12.00
RPKT Kyle Turris 10.00 25.00
RPLK Lauri Korpikoski 4.00 10.00
RPLS Luca Sbisa 4.00 10.00
RPMA Shawn Matthias 6.00 15.00
RPMB Mikkel Boedker 8.00 20.00
RPMF Mark Fistric 5.00 12.00
RPNF Nikita Filatov 6.00 15.00
RPNK Nikolai Kulemin 6.00 15.00
RPOM Oscar Moller 5.00 12.00
RPPB Patrik Berglund 12.00 30.00
RPPH Patric Hornqvist 6.00 15.00
RPPV Petr Vrana 4.00 10.00
RPRE Robbie Earl 4.00 10.00
RPRS Ryan Stone 4.00 10.00
RPSC Luke Schenn 25.00 60.00
RPSM Steve Mason 25.00 60.00
RPSS Steven Stamkos 30.00 80.00
RPTO T.J. Oshie 12.00 30.00
RPTS Tom Sestito 6.00 15.00
RPVM Vladimir Mihalik 4.00 10.00
RPVT Viktor Tikhonov 5.00 12.00
RPZB Zach Boychuk 6.00 15.00

2008-09 Upper Deck Signature Sensations

SSAC Andrew Cogliano 5.00 12.00
SSBB Brendan Bell Coyotes 5.00 12.00
SSBD Brandon Dubinsky road 10.00 25.00
SSBM Bryan McCabe 5.00 12.00
SSBO Johnny Boychuk 6.00 15.00
SSBR Bobby Ryan skating 6.00 15.00
SSCB Casey Borer 8.00 20.00
SSCL Dan Cleary 15.00 40.00
SSCP Chris Phillips 5.00 12.00
SSCS Cory Stillman home 5.00 12.00
SSDA Daniel Sedin 10.00 25.00
SSDB Dan Boyle 5.00 12.00
SSDC Daniel Carcillo road 5.00 12.00
SSDG Daniel Girardi 10.00 25.00
SSDI Dimitri Patzold 5.00 12.00
SSDJ David Jones 5.00 12.00
SSDL Drew Larman 5.00 12.00
SSDM Drew MacIntyre 8.00 20.00
SSDP Dustin Penner 6.00 15.00
SSDS Drew Stafford 5.00 12.00
SSGH Gordie Howe 60.00 120.00
SSGL Guillaume Latendresse 10.00 25.00
SSGM Greg Moore 5.00 12.00
SSHA Jaroslav Halak 8.00 20.00
SSHE T.J. Hensick 10.00 25.00
SSHI Jonas Hiller 6.00 15.00
SSHJ Jannik Hansen 8.00 20.00
SSHS Henrik Sedin 10.00 25.00
SSJA Jared Boll 5.00 12.00
SSJB Jonathan Bernier skating 6.00 15.00
SSJD Jeff Drouin-Deslauriers 8.00 20.00
SSJH Josh Harding road 8.00 20.00
SSJL John-Michael Liles 5.00 12.00
SSJP Jason Pominville 12.00 30.00
SSJS Jordan Staal 6.00 15.00
SSJT Jonathan Toews 20.00 50.00
SSKN Kevin Nastiuk 5.00 12.00
SSLK Lukas Kaspar 5.00 12.00
SSLT Lauri Tukonen 5.00 12.00
SSLU Joffrey Lupul 5.00 12.00
SSMA Mark Mancari 5.00 12.00
SSME Matt Ellis Kings 5.00 12.00
SSMF Mark Fraser portrait 6.00 15.00
SSMH Michal Handzus 6.00 15.00
SSMI Milan Michalek 12.00 30.00
SSMK Mike Knuble 5.00 12.00
SSML Milan Lucic 8.00 20.00
SSMM Marc Methot 5.00 12.00
SSMN Matt Niskanen face front 6.00 15.00
SSMP Marc-Antoine Pouliot 5.00 12.00
SSMR Mason Raymond 5.00 12.00
SSMS Marek Schwarz profile 8.00 20.00
SSNK Nikolai Khabibulin profile 12.00 30.00
SSPA Ryan Parent 10.00 25.00
SSPD Daniel Paille road 5.00 12.00
SSPE Rod Pelley 5.00 12.00
SSPK Patrick Kane 15.00 40.00
SSPM Peter Mueller 6.00 15.00
SSRB Rene Bourque 5.00 12.00
SSRC Ryane Clowe 10.00 25.00
SSRI Rich Peverley 6.00 15.00
SSRK Rostislav Klesla 5.00 12.00
SSRS Ryan Smyth boards 6.00 15.00
SSSC Sidney Crosby road 75.00 150.00
SSSD Steve Downie 8.00 20.00
SSSE Devin Setoguchi 6.00 15.00
SSSM Stefan Meyer 5.00 12.00
SSST Marco Sturm 5.00 12.00
SSSW Stephen Weiss 5.00 12.00
SSTG Tom Gilbert 10.00 25.00
SSTK Tyler Kennedy 6.00 15.00
SSTL Jiri Tlusty boards w/crowd 5.00 12.00
SSTS Tobias Stephan 15.00 40.00
SSTZ Travis Zajac road 5.00 12.00
SS2AB Adam Burish 10.00 25.00
SS2AG Andy Greene 5.00 12.00
SS2AR Andrew Raycroft 12.00 30.00
SS2BB Brad Boyes 5.00 12.00
SS2BD Brandon Dubinsky home 10.00 25.00
SS2BL Brendan Bell Senators 5.00 12.00
SS2BQ Rene Bourque 5.00 12.00
SS2BR Bobby Ryan standing 6.00 15.00
SS2BS Brett Sterling 6.00 15.00
SS2CB Chris Bourque 6.00 15.00
SS2CH Chuck Kobasew 5.00 12.00
SS2CO Jiri Tlusty boards 5.00 12.00
SS2CS Cory Stillman road 5.00 12.00
SS2DA Daniel Sedin home 10.00 25.00
SS2DC Daniel Carcillo home 5.00 12.00
SS2DP Daniel Paille home 5.00 12.00
SS2DR Dwayne Roloson 6.00 15.00
SS2DS Derek Sanderson 8.00 20.00
SS2DS2 Drew Stafford road 5.00 12.00
SS2DT Darcy Tucker 6.00 15.00
SS2DV David Perron 6.00 15.00
SS2EN Evgeni Nabokov 6.00 15.00
SS2HG Josh Harding home 8.00 20.00
SS2IK Marc-Antoine Pouliot road 5.00 12.00
SS2JB Jonathan Bernier in-goal 6.00 15.00
SS2JG Jean-Sebastien Giguere 25.00 60.00
SS2JH Jannik Hansen 8.00 20.00
SS2JL John-Michael Liles 5.00 12.00
SS2JM Jay McClement 5.00 12.00
SS2JS Jordan Staal home 6.00 15.00
SS2KA Petr Kalus 6.00 15.00
SS2KB Nikolai Khabibulin face 12.00 30.00
SS2KC Kyle Chipchura 6.00 15.00
SS2ME Matt Ellis Sabres 5.00 12.00
SS2MH Milan Hejduk 15.00 40.00
SS2ML Mike Lundin 5.00 12.00
SS2MN Matt Niskanen profile 6.00 15.00
SS2MO Brendan Morrison 6.00 15.00
SS2MS Mark Fraser in-action 6.00 15.00
SS2MY Stefan Meyer 5.00 12.00
SS2NW Noah Welch 5.00 12.00
SS2NZ Nikolai Zherdev 10.00 25.00
SS2OR Bobby Orr 75.00 150.00
SS2PK Phil Kessel 12.00 30.00
SS2PV Rich Peverley 6.00 15.00
SS2PY Ryan Potulny 5.00 12.00
SS2RA Mason Raymond 5.00 12.00
SS2RK Rostislav Klesla 5.00 12.00
SS2RS Ryan Smyth boards w/crowd 6.00 15.00
SS2SC Sidney Crosby home 75.00 150.00
SS2SE Devin Setoguchi road 6.00 15.00
SS2SH James Sheppard 5.00 12.00
SS2SJ Jack Skille road 6.00 15.00
SS2SM Matt Smaby 6.00 15.00
SS2ST Marc Staal 5.00 12.00
SS2SW Marek Schwarz face 8.00 20.00
SS2TE Tobias Enstrom 5.00 12.00
SS2TJ T.J. Hensick 10.00 25.00
SS2TM Torrey Mitchell 5.00 12.00
SS2TP Tomas Popperle 6.00 15.00
SS2TR Tuukka Rask 20.00 50.00
SS2TZ Travis Zajac home 5.00 12.00

2008-09 Upper Deck Sophomore Sensations

COMPLETE SET (7) 8.00 20.00
SS1 Patrick Kane 2.00 5.00
SS2 Jonathan Toews 1.50 4.00
SS3 Carey Price 2.00 5.00
SS4 Marc Staal .60 1.50
SS5 Sam Gagner .60 1.50
SS6 Peter Mueller .75 2.00
SS7 Nicklas Backstrom 1.00 2.50

2008-09 Upper Deck Spectacular Saves

COMPLETE SET (7) 8.00 20.00
SAVE1 Chris Osgood 1.25 3.00
SAVE2 Evgeni Nabokov 1.00 2.50
SAVE3 Henrik Lundqvist 3.00 8.00
SAVE4 Jean-Sebastien Giguere 1.25 3.00
SAVE5 Martin Brodeur 3.00 8.00
SAVE6 Marty Turco 1.25 3.00
SAVE7 Roberto Luongo 2.00 5.00

2008-09 Upper Deck Super Skills

COMPLETE SET (20) 150.00 300.00
SS1 Martin Brodeur 8.00 20.00
SS2 Sidney Crosby 12.00 30.00
SS3 Alexander Ovechkin 12.00 30.00
SS4 Joe Thornton 5.00 12.00
SS5 Jarome Iginla 4.00 10.00
SS6 Martin St. Louis 3.00 8.00
SS7 Ilya Kovalchuk 3.00 8.00
SS8 Jonathan Toews 5.00 12.00
SS9 Evgeni Malkin 6.00 15.00
SS10 Henrik Zetterberg 4.00 10.00
SS11 Rick Nash SP 6.00 15.00
SS12 Carey Price SP 12.00 30.00
SS13 Ryan Getzlaf SP 6.00 15.00
SS14 Mike Richards SP 5.00 12.00
SS15 Paul Stastny SP 5.00 12.00
SS16 Andrew Cogliano SP 4.00 10.00
SS17 Peter Mueller SP 5.00 12.00
SS18 Anze Kopitar SP 10.00 25.00
SS19 Nicklas Backstrom SP 6.00 15.00
SS20 Eric Staal SP 8.00 20.00

2008-09 Upper Deck Tales of the Cup

COMPLETE SET (7) 4.00 10.00
TC1 Peter Forsberg 1.50 4.00
TC2 Mark Messier 1.50 4.00
TC3 Doug Weight .75 2.00
TC4 Ted Lindsay .75 2.00
TC5 Clark Gillies .75 2.00
TC6 Montreal Canadiens .60 1.50
TC7 Ottawa Senators .60 1.50

2008-09 Upper Deck The New Guard

COMPLETE SET (14) 15.00 40.00
NE1 Anze Kopitar 1.50 4.00
NE2 Alexander Ovechkin 4.00 10.00
NE3 Marian Gaborik 1.00 2.50
NE4 Carey Price 2.00 5.00
NE5 Dion Phaneuf .75 2.00
NE6 Evgeni Malkin 2.00 5.00
NE7 Eric Staal 1.25 3.00
NE8 Henrik Lundqvist 2.50 6.00
NE9 Ilya Kovalchuk 1.00 2.50
NE10 Jonathan Toews 1.50 4.00
NE11 Nicklas Backstrom 1.00 2.50
NE12 Patrick Kane 2.00 5.00
NE13 Ryan Getzlaf 1.00 2.50
NE14 Sidney Crosby 4.00 10.00

2008-09 Upper Deck Winter Classic

COMPLETE SET (14) 15.00 40.00
WC1 Sidney Crosby 8.00 20.00
WC2 Ryan Miller 2.00 5.00
WC3 Colby Armstrong 1.25 3.00
WC4 Ales Kotalik 1.25 3.00
WC5 Kristopher Letang 2.50 6.00
WC6 Thomas Vanek 1.50 4.00
WC7 Evgeni Malkin 4.00 10.00
WC8 Brian Campbell 1.50 4.00
WC9 Ty Conklin 1.50 4.00
WC10 Jason Pominville 1.25 3.00
WC11 Ryan Malone 1.25 3.00
WC12 Maxim Afinogenov 1.25 3.00
WC13 Jordan Staal 1.50 4.00
WC14 Tim Connolly 1.25 3.00

2008-09 Upper Deck Winter Classic Highlights Oversized

COMPLETE SET (14) 10.00 25.00
WAL1 Sidney Crosby 5.00 12.00
WAL2 Kristopher Letang 1.50 4.00
WAL3 Colby Armstrong .75 2.00
WAL4 Ryan Malone .75 2.00
WAL5 Jordan Staal 1.00 2.50
WAL6 Thomas Vanek 1.00 2.50
WAL7 Evgeni Malkin 2.50 6.00
WAL8 Brian Campbell 1.00 2.50
WAL9 Ty Conklin 1.00 2.50
WAL10 Ryan Miller 1.25 3.00
WAL11 Ales Kotalik .75 2.00
WAL12 Maxim Afinogenov .75 2.00
WAL13 Jason Pominville .75 2.00
WAL14 Tim Connolly .75 2.00

2008-09 Upper Deck Young Guns Oversized

COMPLETE SET (14) 25.00 60.00
OYG1 Zach Bogosian 1.25 3.00
OYG2 Blake Wheeler 2.50 6.00
OYG3 Brandon Sutter 1.00 2.50
OYG4 Jakub Voracek 2.00 5.00
OYG5 James Neal 2.00 5.00
OYG6 Drew Doughty 2.50 6.00
OYG7 Colton Gillies .75 2.00
OYG8 Kyle Okposo 1.25 3.00
OYG9 Luca Sbisa .60 1.50
OYG10 Mikkel Boedker 1.25 3.00
OYG11 Kyle Turris 1.50 4.00
OYG12 Alex Pietrangelo 1.50 4.00
OYG13 Steven Stamkos 10.00 25.00
OYG14 Luke Schenn 1.25 3.00

2009-10 Upper Deck

COMPLETE SET (500) 300.00 600.00
COMP.SER.1 SET (250) 200.00 350.00
COMP.SER.1 SET w/o SPs (200) 12.00 30.00
COMP.SER.2 SET (250) 125.00 250.00
COMP.SER.2 SET w/o SPs (200) 12.00 30.00
1 Phil Kessel .30 .75
2 David Krejci .30 .75
3 Mark Recchi .40 1.00
4 Zdeno Chara .30 .75
5 Tim Thomas .30 .75
6 Blake Wheeler .30 .75
7 Dennis Wideman .20 .50
8 Tim Connolly .20 .50
9 Ryan Miller .30 .75
10 Craig Rivet .20 .50
11 Derek Roy .20 .50
12 Nathan Gerbe .25 .60
13 Daniel Paille .25 .60
14 Chris Butler .30 .75
15 Andrei Markov .30 .75
16 Maxim Lapierre .20 .50
17 Andrei Kostitsyn .25 .60
18 Carey Price .60 1.50
19 Josh Gorges .20 .50
20 Tomas Plekanec .20 .50
21 Georges Laraque .25 .60
22 Jason Spezza .30 .75
23 Daniel Alfredsson .30 .75
24 Nick Foligno .25 .60
25 Chris Phillips .20 .50
26 Jarkko Ruutu .20 .50
27 Jesse Winchester .25 .60
28 Brian Lee .30 .75
29 Mikhail Grabovski .20 .50
30 Luke Schenn .30 .75
31 Vesa Toskala .30 .75
32 Matt Stajan .20 .50
33 Alexei Ponikarovsky .20 .50
34 Ian White .25 .60
35 Nikolai Kulemin .20 .50
36 Jeff Carter .25 .60
37 Claude Giroux .30 .75
38 Ryan Parent .25 .60
39 Simon Gagne .30 .75
40 Daniel Carcillo .20 .50
41 Matt Carle .25 .60
42 Scott Hartnell .20 .50
43 Sidney Crosby 1.25 3.00
44 Maxime Talbot .20 .50
45 Sergei Gonchar .20 .50
46 Ruslan Fedotenko .20 .50
47 Marc-Andre Fleury .60 1.50
48 Evgeni Malkin .60 1.50
49 Bill Guerin .30 .75
50 Martin Brodeur .75 2.00
51 Paul Martin .20 .50
52 Patrik Elias .30 .75
53 Johnny Oduya .25 .60
54 David Clarkson .25 .60
55 Jamie Langenbrunner .20 .50
56 Josh Bailey .25 .60
57 Rick DiPietro .25 .60
58 Mark Streit .20 .50
59 Kyle Okposo .20 .50
60 Bruno Gervais .20 .50
61 Doug Weight .30 .75
62 Henrik Lundqvist .75 2.00
63 Sean Avery .25 .60
64 Wade Redden .20 .50
65 Chris Drury .25 .60
66 Michal Rozsival .20 .50
67 Brandon Dubinsky .20 .50
68 Marc Staal .20 .50
69 Nathan Horton .30 .75
70 David Booth .20 .50
71 Bryan McCabe .25 .60
72 Stephen Weiss .20 .50
73 Keith Ballard .20 .50
74 Michael Frolik .25 .60
75 Bryan Little .30 .75
76 Zach Bogosian .25 .60
77 Kari Lehtonen .25 .60
78 Todd White .20 .50
79 Tobias Enstrom .30 .75
80 Colby Armstrong .20 .50
81 Rod Brind`Amour .30 .75
82 Eric Staal .40 1.00
83 Joe Corvo .20 .50
84 Chad LaRose .20 .50
85 Jussi Jokinen .20 .50
86 Joni Pitkanen .25 .60
87 Martin St. Louis .30 .75
88 Mike Smith .30 .75
89 Paul Ranger .20 .50
90 Steven Stamkos .60 1.50
91 Ryan Malone .20 .50
92 Noah Welch .20 .50
93 Nicklas Backstrom .30 .75
94 Mike Green .25 .60
95 Simeon Varlamov .30 .75
96 Brooks Laich .20 .50
97 Tom Poti .20 .50
98 Alexander Semin .30 .75
99 Eric Fehr .20 .50
100 Paul Kariya .30 .75
101 Chris Mason .25 .60
102 Jeff Woywitka .20 .50
103 David Perron .25 .60
104 Patrik Berglund .20 .50
105 T.J. Oshie .30 .75
106 Keith Tkachuk .30 .75
107 Jonathan Toews .50 1.25
108 Brian Campbell .25 .60
109 Patrick Sharp .30 .75
110 Cristobal Huet .30 .75
111 Cam Barker .20 .50
112 Dustin Byfuglien .30 .75
113 Kris Versteeg .20 .50
114 Steve Mason .25 .60
115 R.J. Umberger .25 .60
116 Jakub Voracek .25 .60
117 Mike Commodore .20 .50
118 Derick Brassard .20 .50
119 Rick Nash .30 .75
120 Pavel Datsyuk .50 1.25
121 Brian Rafalski .20 .50
122 Johan Franzen .25 .60
123 Chris Osgood .30 .75
124 Darren Helm .20 .50
125 Niklas Kronwall .25 .60
126 Nicklas Lidstrom .20 .50
127 Jason Arnott .25 .60
128 J.P. Dumont .20 .50
129 Steve Sullivan .20 .50
130 Shea Weber .25 .60
131 Jordin Tootoo .30 .75
132 Pekka Rinne .30 .75
133 Anze Kopitar .50 1.25
134 Jack Johnson .20 .50
135 Jonathan Quick .40 1.00
136 Dustin Brown .30 .75
137 Jarret Stoll .25 .60
138 Drew Doughty .40 1.00
139 Mike Modano .50 1.25
140 Stephane Robidas .20 .50
141 Brenden Morrow .25 .60
142 Mike Ribeiro .20 .50
143 Matt Niskanen .25 .60
144 Loui Eriksson .20 .50
145 Teemu Selanne .60 1.50
146 Jonas Hiller .25 .60
147 Bobby Ryan .25 .60
148 Ryan Getzlaf .30 .75
149 Ryan Whitney .20 .50
150 George Parros .20 .50
151 Scott Niedermayer .30 .75
152 Joe Thornton .50 1.25
153 Joe Pavelski .40 1.00
154 Dan Boyle .20 .50
155 Rob Blake .30 .75
156 Torrey Mitchell .30 .75
157 Ryane Clowe .20 .50
158 Evgeni Nabokov .25 .60
159 Peter Mueller .25 .60
160 Keith Yandle .20 .50
161 Mikkel Boedker .20 .50
162 Matthew Lombardi .20 .50
163 Scottie Upshall .20 .50
164 Kyle Turris .30 .75
165 Roberto Luongo .50 1.25
166 Daniel Sedin .40 1.00
167 Kevin Bieksa .25 .60
168 Mason Raymond .20 .50
169 Steve Bernier .20 .50
170 Ryan Kesler .30 .75
171 Alexander Edler .20 .50
172 Jarome Iginla .40 1.00
173 Rene Bourque .20 .50
174 Craig Conroy .20 .50
175 Cory Sarich .20 .50
176 Olli Jokinen .25 .60
177 Daymond Langkow .20 .50
178 Robyn Regehr .25 .60
179 Paul Stastny .25 .60
180 John-Michael Liles .20 .50
181 Peter Budaj .25 .60
182 Cody McLeod .20 .50
183 Darcy Tucker .25 .60
184 Milan Hejduk .25 .60
185 Chris Stewart .25 .60
186 Niklas Backstrom .30 .75
187 Brent Burns .30 .75
188 Owen Nolan .30 .75
189 Mikko Koivu .30 .75
190 Marek Zidlicky .20 .50
191 James Sheppard .20 .50
192 Sam Gagner .20 .50
193 Tom Gilbert .20 .50
194 Ethan Moreau .20 .50
195 Patrick O'Sullivan .25 .60
196 Sheldon Souray .20 .50
197 Shawn Horcoff .20 .50
198 Ales Hemsky .25 .60
199 Roberto Luongo CL .50 1.25
200 Sidney Crosby CL 1.25 3.00
201 John Tavares YG RC 25.00 60.00
202 Victor Hedman YG RC 15.00 40.00
203 Matt Duchene YG RC 8.00 20.00
204 Ville Leino YG RC 2.50 6.00
205 Evander Kane YG RC 8.00 20.00
206 Michael Del Zotto YG RC 3.00 8.00
207 James van Riemsdyk YG RC 6.00 15.00
208 Viktor Stalberg YG RC 3.00 8.00
209 Sergei Shirokov YG RC 2.00 5.00
210 Erik Karlsson YG RC 25.00 60.00
211 Dmitri Kulikov YG RC 3.00 8.00
212 Jamie Benn YG RC 10.00 25.00
213 Ryan O'Reilly YG RC 8.00 20.00
214 Tyler Myers YG RC 5.00 12.00
215 Jason Demers YG RC 5.00 12.00
216 Jay Rosehill YG RC 3.00 8.00
217 Brian Salcido YG RC 2.00 5.00
218 Luca Caputi YG RC 3.00 8.00
219 Spencer Machacek YG RC 3.00 8.00
220 Yannick Weber YG RC 3.00 8.00
221 Artem Anisimov YG RC 2.00 5.00
222 Ivan Vishnevskiy YG RC 2.00 5.00
223 Riku Helenius YG RC 3.00 8.00
224 Peter Regin YG RC 2.50 6.00
225 Antti Niemi YG RC 5.00 12.00
226 Byron Bitz YG RC 2.50 6.00
227 John Negrin YG RC 3.00 8.00
228 Ray Macias YG RC 2.50 6.00
229 Taylor Chorney YG RC 3.00 8.00
230 Mika Pyorala YG RC 2.50 6.00
231 Alec Martinez YG RC 4.00 10.00
232 Grant Lewis YG RC 2.50 6.00
233 Cal O'Reilly YG RC 2.50 6.00
234 Jesse Joensuu YG RC 2.50 6.00
235 Michal Neuvirth YG RC 5.00 12.00
236 John Scott YG RC 3.00 8.00
237 Benn Ferriero YG RC 3.00 8.00
238 Teemu Laakso YG RC 2.00 5.00
239 Jhonas Enroth YG RC 4.00 10.00
240 Matt Beleskey YG RC 2.50 6.00
241 T.J. Galiardi YG RC 3.00 8.00
242 Kris Chucko YG RC 2.00 5.00
243 James Wright YG RC 3.00 8.00
244 Joel Rechlicz YG RC 2.00 5.00
245 Matt Pelech YG RC 3.00 8.00
246 Christian Hanson YG RC 3.00 8.00
247 Matt Hendricks YG RC 2.50 6.00
248 Mike Santorelli YG RC 3.00 8.00
249 Frazer McLaren YG RC 2.50 6.00
250 Duchene/Hedman/Tavares CL 4.00 10.00
251 Milan Lucic .25 .60
252 Patrice Bergeron .40 1.00
253 Michael Ryder .20 .50
254 Andrew Ference .20 .50
255 Marco Sturm .20 .50
256 Marc Savard .20 .50
257 Daniel Paille .25 .60
258 Thomas Vanek .25 .60
259 Jason Pominville .20 .50
260 Mike Grier .20 .50
261 Jochen Hecht .20 .50
262 Henrik Tallinder .20 .50
263 Adam Mair .20 .50
264 Clarke MacArthur .20 .50
265 Scott Gomez .25 .60
266 Mike Cammalleri .25 .60
267 Roman Hamrlik .20 .50
268 Max Pacioretty .30 .75
269 Sergei Kostitsyn .20 .50
270 Guillaume Latendresse .25 .60
271 Brian Gionta .20 .50
272 Alex Kovalev .25 .60
273 Chris Kelly .25 .60
274 Chris Neil .20 .50
275 Pascal Leclaire .30 .75
276 Mike Fisher .20 .50
277 Filip Kuba .20 .50
278 Jonathan Cheechoo .25 .60
279 Jason Blake .20 .50
280 Phil Kessel .30 .75
281 Francois Beauchemin .20 .50
282 John Mitchell .20 .50
283 Tomas Kaberle .20 .50
284 Niklas Hagman .20 .50
285 Mike Komisarek .25 .60
286 Mike Richards .25 .60
287 Chris Pronger .30 .75
288 Ian Laperriere .20 .50
289 Braydon Coburn .20 .50
290 Kimmo Timonen .25 .60
291 Ray Emery .25 .60
292 Daniel Briere .30 .75
293 Evgeni Malkin .60 1.50
294 Pascal Dupuis .20 .50
295 Alex Goligoski .25 .60
296 Chris Kunitz .30 .75
297 Tyler Kennedy .25 .60
298 Brooks Orpik .20 .50
299 Jordan Staal .25 .60
300 Zach Parise .30 .75
301 Travis Zajac .20 .50
302 Andy Greene .20 .50
303 Jay Pandolfo .20 .50
304 Dainius Zubrus .20 .50
305 Rob Niedermayer .20 .50
306 Frederick Meyer .20 .50
307 Sean Bergenheim .20 .50
308 Dwayne Roloson .25 .60
309 Brendan Witt .20 .50
310 Trent Hunter .20 .50
311 Martin Biron .25 .60
312 Marian Gaborik .30 .75
313 Vaclav Prospal .20 .50
314 Daniel Girardi .20 .50
315 Stephen Valiquette .20 .50

316 Donald Brashear .20 .50
317 Aaron Voros .20 .50
318 Chris Higgins .20 .50
319 Tomas Vokoun .25 .60
320 Jordan Leopold .20 .50
321 Rostislav Olesz .20 .50
322 Bryan Allen .20 .50
323 Nick Tarnasky .20 .50
324 Cory Stillman .20 .50
325 Nik Antropov .25 .60
326 Slava Kozlov .20 .50
327 Boris Valabik .30 .75
328 Johan Hedberg .25 .60
329 Jim Slater .20 .50
330 Ilya Kovalchuk .30 .75
331 Cam Ward .30 .75
332 Tuomo Ruutu .20 .50
333 Manny Legace .25 .60
334 Brandon Sutter .20 .50
335 Ray Whitney .25 .60
336 Erik Cole .20 .50
337 Vincent Lecavalier .30 .75
338 Mattias Ohlund .20 .50
339 Antero Niittymaki .30 .75
340 Lukas Krajicek .20 .50
341 Steve Downie .20 .50
342 Alex Tanguay .20 .50
343 Alexander Ovechkin 1.25 3.00
344 Karl Alzner .20 .50
345 Chris Clark .20 .50
346 Jose Theodore .30 .75
347 Michael Nylander .20 .50
348 Mike Knuble .20 .50
349 Brendan Morrison .25 .60
350 Brad Boyes .20 .50
351 Andy McDonald .25 .60
352 Eric Brewer .20 .50
353 Alexander Steen .20 .50
354 Ty Conklin .25 .60
355 Erik Johnson .20 .50
356 David Backes .20 .50
357 Patrick Kane .60 1.50
358 Andrew Ladd .20 .50
359 Dave Bolland .25 .60
360 Duncan Keith .25 .60
361 Marian Hossa .30 .75
362 John Madden .20 .50
363 Brent Seabrook .20 .50
364 Samuel Pahlsson .20 .50
365 Kristian Huselius .20 .50
366 Kris Russell .20 .50
367 Raffi Torres .20 .50
368 Rostislav Klesla .30 .75
369 Fredrik Modin .20 .50
370 Henrik Zetterberg .40 1.00
371 Todd Bertuzzi .30 .75
372 Valtteri Filppula .20 .50
373 Tomas Holmstrom .25 .60
374 Kirk Maltby .20 .50
375 Jason Williams .20 .50
376 Dan Cleary .30 .75
377 Dan Ellis .20 .50
378 David Legwand .25 .60
379 Ryan Suter .25 .60
380 Marcel Goc .25 .60
381 Dan Hamhuis .25 .60
382 Martin Erat .20 .50
383 Ryan Smyth .25 .60
384 Justin Williams .25 .60
385 Oscar Moller .20 .50
386 Wayne Simmonds .40 1.00
387 Raitis Ivanans .20 .50
388 Alexander Frolov .25 .60
389 Marty Turco .30 .75
390 James Neal .20 .50
391 Steve Ott .20 .50
392 Jere Lehtinen .25 .60
393 Fabian Brunnstrom .25 .60
394 Brad Richards .30 .75
395 Saku Koivu .30 .75
396 Luca Sbisa .30 .75
397 Mike Brown .20 .50
398 Joffrey Lupul .20 .50
399 Corey Perry .50 1.25
400 Evgeni Artyukhin .20 .50
401 Jean-Sebastien Giguere .30 .75
402 Patrick Marleau .30 .75
403 Jed Ortmeyer .20 .50
404 Scott Nichol .20 .50
405 Devin Setoguchi .25 .60
406 Jody Shelley .20 .50
407 Marc-Edouard Vlasic .20 .50
408 Dany Heatley .25 .60
409 Shane Doan .25 .60
410 Ed Jovanovski .20 .50
411 Ilya Bryzgalov .25 .60
412 Martin Hanzal .25 .60
413 Vernon Fiddler .20 .50
414 Viktor Tikhonov .25 .60
415 Henrik Sedin .40 1.00
416 Willie Mitchell .20 .50
417 Alexandre Burrows .20 .50
418 Christian Ehrhoff .20 .50
419 Kyle Wellwood .25 .60
420 Sami Salo .30 .75
421 Mathieu Schneider .20 .50
422 Miikka Kiprusoff .30 .75
423 Curtis Glencross .20 .50
424 David Moss .25 .60
425 Dion Phaneuf .25 .60
426 Dustin Boyd .20 .50
427 Fredrik Sjostrom .20 .50
428 Jay Bouwmeester .20 .50
429 Wojtek Wolski .20 .50
430 Craig Anderson .30 .75
431 T.J. Hensick .20 .50
432 Kyle Quincey .20 .50
433 Marek Svatos .20 .50
434 Scott Hannan .20 .50
435 Adam Foote .20 .50
436 Pierre-Marc Bouchard .30 .75
437 Martin Havlat .25 .60
438 Josh Harding .30 .75
439 Antti Miettinen .20 .50
440 Eric Belanger .20 .50
441 Colton Gillies .30 .75
442 Andrew Cogliano .20 .50
443 Steve Staios .20 .50
444 Fernando Pisani .20 .50
445 Lubomir Visnovsky .20 .50
446 Dustin Penner .20 .50
447 Ladislav Smid .20 .50
448 Nikolai Khabibulin .30 .75
449 Evgeni Malkin CL .60 1.50
450 Alexander Ovechkin CL 1.25 3.00
451 MacGregor Sharp YG RC 3.00 8.00
452 Brad Marchand YG RC 100.00 250.00
453 Tyler Ennis YG RC 4.00 10.00
454 Mikael Backlund YG RC 5.00 12.00
455 Ryan Wilson YG RC 3.00 8.00
456 Ryan Stoa YG RC 2.50 6.00
457 Philippe Dupuis YG RC 3.00 8.00
458 Perttu Lindgren YG RC 2.50 6.00
459 Aaron Gagnon YG RC 2.00 5.00
460 Daniel Larsson YG RC 2.50 6.00
461 Ryan O'Marra YG RC 2.00 5.00
462 Devan Dubnyk YG RC 5.00 12.00
463 Colin McDonald YG RC 2.50 6.00
464 Alexander Salak YG RC 2.50 6.00
465 Jakub Kindl YG RC 3.00 8.00
466 Andrei Loktionov YG RC 4.00 10.00
467 Scott Parse YG RC 3.00 8.00
468 Danny Irmen YG RC 2.00 5.00
469 Anton Khudobin YG RC 5.00 12.00
470 David Desharnais YG RC 6.00 15.00
471 Tom Pyatt YG RC 3.00 8.00
472 Mathieu Carle YG RC 3.00 8.00
473 Ryan White YG RC 4.00 10.00
474 Colin Wilson YG RC 3.00 8.00
475 Cody Franson YG RC 3.00 8.00
476 Peter Olvecky YG RC 3.00 8.00
477 Andreas Thuresson YG RC 2.50 6.00
478 Matthew Corrente YG RC 2.50 6.00
479 Vladimir Zharkov YG RC 3.00 8.00
480 Tyler Eckford YG RC 2.50 6.00
481 Matt Gilroy YG RC 3.00 8.00
482 Bobby Sanguinetti YG RC 2.00 5.00
483 Ryan Keller YG RC 3.00 8.00
484 Oskars Bartulis YG RC 3.00 8.00
485 David Laliberte YG RC 2.50 6.00
486 Mark Letestu YG RC 3.00 8.00
487 Logan Couture YG RC 8.00 20.00
488 Steven Zalewski YG RC 2.50 6.00
489 Lars Eller YG RC 5.00 12.00
490 Jonas Gustavsson YG RC 4.00 10.00
491 Tyler Bozak YG RC 5.00 12.00
492 Carl Gunnarsson YG RC 2.00 5.00
493 James Reimer YG RC 8.00 20.00
494 Michael Grabner YG RC 4.00 10.00
495 Mario Bliznak YG RC 3.00 8.00
496 Guillaume Desbiens YG RC 3.00 8.00
497 John Carlson YG RC 10.00 25.00
498 Mathieu Perreault YG RC 6.00 15.00
499 Braden Holtby YG RC 20.00 50.00
500 Gustv/Wilsn/Cture YG CL 6.00 15.00

2009-10 Upper Deck Exclusives

*SINGLES: 3X TO 8X BASIC CARDS
*YG SINGLES: 1.5X TO 4X BASIC CARDS
88 Mike Smith 2.50 6.00
93 Nicklas Backstrom 2.50 6.00
201 John Tavares YG 150.00 250.00
203 Matt Duchene YG 40.00 80.00
205 Evander Kane YG 20.00 50.00
210 Erik Karlsson YG 50.00 120.00
212 Jamie Benn YG 40.00 100.00
452 Brad Marchand YG 150.00 400.00
469 Anton Khudobin YG 20.00 50.00
487 Logan Couture YG 40.00 80.00
499 Braden Holtby YG 60.00 100.00

2009-10 Upper Deck All World

COMPLETE SET (40) 75.00 150.00
COMP.SET w/o SPs (30) 12.00 30.00
AW1 Marian Hossa 1.50 4.00
AW2 Martin Brodeur 4.00 10.00
AW3 Marc-Andre Fleury 3.00 8.00
AW4 Alexander Semin 1.50 4.00
AW5 Mike Green 1.25 3.00
AW6 Johan Franzen 1.25 3.00
AW7 Mikko Koivu 1.50 4.00
AW8 Pavel Datsyuk 2.50 6.00
AW9 Jarome Iginla 2.00 5.00
AW10 Evgeni Nabokov 1.25 3.00
AW11 Zdeno Chara 1.50 4.00
AW12 Henrik Lundqvist 4.00 10.00
AW13 Niklas Backstrom 1.50 4.00
AW14 Jason Spezza 1.50 4.00
AW15 Patrick Kane 3.00 8.00
AW16 Carey Price 3.00 8.00
AW17 Eric Staal 2.00 5.00
AW18 Shea Weber 1.25 3.00
AW19 Anze Kopitar 2.50 6.00
AW20 Pekka Rinne 1.50 4.00
AW21 Jonas Hiller 1.25 3.00
AW22 Martin St. Louis 1.50 4.00
AW23 Ales Hemsky 1.25 3.00
AW24 Miikka Kiprusoff 1.50 4.00
AW25 Mike Richards 1.25 3.00
AW26 Joe Thornton 2.50 6.00
AW27 Jeff Carter 1.25 3.00
AW28 Daniel Sedin 2.00 5.00
AW29 Henrik Sedin 2.00 5.00
AW30 Daniel Alfredsson 1.50 4.00
AW31 Zach Parise SP 2.50 6.00
AW32 Sidney Crosby SP 10.00 25.00
AW33 Evgeni Malkin SP 5.00 12.00
AW34 Ilya Kovalchuk SP 2.50 6.00
AW35 Alexander Ovechkin SP 10.00 25.00
AW36 Tim Thomas SP 2.50 6.00
AW37 Henrik Zetterberg SP 3.00 8.00
AW38 Dany Heatley SP 2.00 5.00
AW39 Rick Nash SP 2.50 6.00
AW40 Jonathan Toews SP 4.00 10.00

2009-10 Upper Deck Ambassadors of the Game

COMPLETE SET (30) 50.00 100.00
COMP.SET w/o SPs (20) 12.00 30.00
AG1 Steve Sullivan 1.25 3.00
AG2 Jason Blake 1.25 3.00
AG3 Phil Kessel 2.00 5.00
AG4 Teemu Selanne 4.00 10.00
AG5 Saku Koivu 2.00 5.00
AG6 Bobby Clarke 3.00 8.00
AG7 Lanny McDonald 2.00 5.00
AG8 Patrice Bergeron 2.50 6.00
AG9 Rod Brind`Amour 2.00 5.00
AG10 Daniel Alfredsson 2.00 5.00
AG11 Shane Doan 1.50 4.00
AG12 Tim Thomas 2.00 5.00
AG13 Vincent Lecavalier 2.00 5.00
AG14 Eric Staal 2.50 6.00
AG15 Rick Nash 2.00 5.00
AG16 Dustin Brown 2.00 5.00
AG17 Marty Turco 2.00 5.00
AG18 Alex Kovalev 1.50 4.00
AG19 Luc Robitaille 2.00 5.00
AG20 Mike Modano 3.00 8.00
AG21 Steve Yzerman SP 6.00 15.00
AG22 Cam Neely SP 2.50 6.00
AG23 Mario Lemieux SP 10.00 25.00
AG24 Jarome Iginla SP 3.00 8.00
AG25 Ray Bourque SP 4.00 10.00
AG26 Alexander Ovechkin SP 10.00 25.00
AG27 Wayne Gretzky SP 10.00 25.00
AG28 Gordie Howe SP 8.00 20.00
AG29 Bobby Orr SP 10.00 25.00
AG30 Bobby Hull SP 5.00 12.00
AG31 Scott Niedermayer 2.00 5.00
AG32 Zdeno Chara 2.00 5.00
AG33 Ryan Miller 2.00 5.00
AG34 Dion Phaneuf 1.50 4.00
AG35 Cam Ward 2.00 5.00
AG36 Kris Versteeg 1.25 3.00
AG37 Kris Draper 1.25 3.00
AG38 Pavel Datsyuk 3.00 8.00
AG39 Sheldon Souray 1.25 3.00
AG40 Ryan Smyth 1.50 4.00
AG41 Georges Laraque 1.50 4.00
AG42 Chris Drury 1.50 4.00
AG43 Don Cherry 2.00 5.00
AG44 Barry Melrose 1.50 4.00
AG45 Jason Spezza 2.00 5.00
AG46 Daniel Alfredsson 2.00 5.00
AG47 Simon Gagne 2.00 5.00
AG48 Marc-Andre Fleury 4.00 10.00
AG49 Paul Kariya 2.00 5.00
AG50 Mike Green 1.50 4.00
AG51 Ilya Kovalchuk SP 2.50 6.00
AG52 Jonathan Toews SP 4.00 10.00
AG53 Tony Esposito SP 2.50 6.00
AG54 Patrick Roy SP 6.00 15.00
AG55 Martin Brodeur SP 6.00 15.00
AG56 John Tavares SP 10.00 25.00
AG57 Mark Messier SP 5.00 12.00
AG58 Mike Richards SP 2.00 5.00
AG59 Jordan Staal SP 2.00 5.00
AG60 Roberto Luongo SP 4.00 10.00

2009-10 Upper Deck Big Playmakers Jerseys

BP96 Wayne Gretzky/25 125.00 200.00
BPAF Alexander Frolov/75 5.00 12.00
BPAK Alex Kovalev/75 5.00 12.00
BPAO Alexander Ovechkin/75 15.00 40.00
BPBC Brian Campbell/25 12.00 30.00
BPBD Brandon Dubinsky/75 4.00 10.00
BPBL Bryan Little/75 6.00 15.00
BPBR Derick Brassard/75 4.00 10.00
BPCH Cristobal Huet/75 6.00 15.00
BPCN Cam Neely/75 6.00 15.00
BPCP Carey Price/75 20.00 40.00
BPCW Cam Ward/75 6.00 15.00
BPDB Dave Bolland/75 5.00 12.00
BPDD Drew Doughty/75 8.00 20.00
BPDM J.P. Dumont/75 4.00 10.00
BPDP David Perron/75 5.00 12.00
BPDR Derek Roy/75 4.00 10.00
BPDU Dustin Brown/75 6.00 15.00
BPEM Evgeni Malkin/75 12.00 30.00
BPES Eric Staal/75 8.00 20.00
BPIK Ilya Kovalchuk/75 6.00 15.00
BPJB Jay Bouwmeester/75 4.00 10.00
BPJO Jordan Staal/75 5.00 12.00
BPJP Jason Pominville/75 4.00 10.00
BPJS Jason Spezza/75 6.00 15.00
BPJV Jakub Voracek/75 5.00 12.00
BPKL Kari Lehtonen/75 5.00 12.00
BPLU Milan Lucic/25 10.00 25.00
BPMB Martin Brodeur/12 100.00 175.00
BPMF Michael Frolik/75 5.00 12.00
BPMG Marian Gaborik/75 6.00 15.00
BPMH Marian Hossa/75 6.00 15.00
BPMI Mikkel Boedker/75 4.00 10.00
BPNB Nicklas Backstrom/75 6.00 15.00
BPNK Nikolai Khabibulin/75 6.00 15.00
BPNL Nicklas Lidstrom/75 4.00 10.00
BPOJ Olli Jokinen/75 5.00 12.00
BPPD Pavel Datsyuk/75 10.00 25.00
BPPE Pekka Rinne/75 8.00 20.00
BPPH Dion Phaneuf/27 12.00 30.00
BPPK Patrick Kane/75 12.00 30.00
BPPL Paul Stastny/100 5.00 12.00
BPPM Peter Mueller/75 5.00 12.00
BPPR Patrick Roy/75 15.00 40.00
BPRB Ray Bourque/75 10.00 25.00
BPRI Mike Richards/75 5.00 12.00
BPRM Ryan Miller/75 6.00 15.00
BPRN Rick Nash/75 6.00 15.00
BPSD Shane Doan/75 5.00 12.00
BPSG Sam Gagner/75 4.00 10.00
BPSP Patrick Sharp/75 6.00 15.00
BPST Drew Stafford/75 4.00 10.00
BPSW Stephen Weiss/75 4.00 10.00
BPTO Jonathan Toews/75 10.00 25.00
BPTP Tomas Plekanec/75 4.00 10.00
BPTV Thomas Vanek/75 5.00 12.00
BPVL Vincent Lecavalier/75 6.00 15.00
BPVO Tomas Vokoun/75 5.00 12.00
BPZP Zach Parise/75 6.00 15.00

2009-10 Upper Deck Biography of a Season

COMPLETE SET (30) 8.00 20.00
BOS1 Sidney Crosby 1.25 3.00
BOS2 Evgeni Malkin .60 1.50
BOS3 Alexander Ovechkin 1.25 3.00
BOS4 John Tavares 1.25 3.00
BOS5 Alexander Ovechkin 1.25 3.00
BOS6 Sidney Crosby 1.25 3.00
BOS7 Brent Seabrook .20 .50
BOS8 Nicklas Lidstrom .20 .50
BOS9 Roberto Luongo .50 1.25
BOS10 Michael Del Zotto .30 .75
BOS11 Phil Kessel .30 .75
BOS12 Steve Yzerman .75 2.00
BOS13 Marian Hossa .30 .75
BOS14 Jarome Iginla .40 1.00
BOS15 Carey Price .60 1.50
BOS16 Martin Brodeur .75 2.00
BOS17 Jonas Gustavsson .40 1.00
BOS18 Scott Niedermayer .30 .75
BOS19 B.Clarke/B.Orr 1.25 3.00
BOS20 Marco Sturm .20 .50
BOS21 Cam Ward .30 .75
BOS22 Alexander Ovechkin 1.25 3.00
BOS23 Ilya Kovalchuk .30 .75
BOS24 Jean-Sebastien Giguere .30 .75
BOS25 Martin Brodeur .75 2.00
BOS26 Ilya Bryzgalov .25 .60
BOS27 Paul Kariya .30 .75
BOS28 Teemu Selanne .60 1.50
BOS29 Steven Stamkos .60 1.50
BOS30 Martin Brodeur .75 2.00

2009-10 Upper Deck Captain's Calling

COMPLETE SET (9) 10.00 25.00
CC1 Sidney Crosby 3.00 8.00
CC2 Jonathan Toews 1.25 3.00
CC3 Jarome Iginla 1.00 2.50
CC4 Roberto Luongo 1.25 3.00
CC5 Rick Nash .75 2.00
CC6 Nicklas Lidstrom .50 1.25
CC7 Vincent Lecavalier .75 2.00
CC8 Ilya Kovalchuk .75 2.00
CC9 Mike Richards .60 1.50

2009-10 Upper Deck Clearcut Trios

CT1 Marleau/Thornton/Setoguchi 15.00 40.00
CT2 Perry/Ryan/Getzlaf 15.00 40.00
CT3 Jokinen/Iginla/Kiprusoff 12.00 30.00
CT4 Toews/Kane/Campbell 20.00 50.00
CT5 Datsyuk/Lidstrom/Zetterberg 15.00 40.00
CT6 Brodeur/Parise/Elias 25.00 60.00
CT7 Crosby/Malkin/Fleury 40.00 100.00
CT8 Anderson/Gretzky/Kurri 60.00 150.00
CT9 Lecavalier/St. Louis/Stamkos 20.00 50.00
CT10 Zetterberg/Howe/Yzerman 30.00 80.00
CT11 Yzerman/Messier/Lemieux 40.00 100.00
CT12 Kulemin/Stajan/Schenn 10.00 25.00
CT13 Luongo/D.Sedin/H.Sedin 15.00 40.00
CT14 Backstrom/Semin/Ovechkin 40.00 100.00
CT15 P.Esposito/Bucyk/Orr 40.00 100.00
CT16 Robinson/Lafleur/Shutt 12.00 30.00
CT17 Kane/Toews/Hull 20.00 50.00
CT18 Vachon/Mahovlich/Beliveau 12.00 30.00
CT19 Roy/Price/Brodeur 30.00 80.00
CT20 Miller/Lundqvist/DiPietro 25.00 60.00
CT21 Kiprusoff/Luongo/Backstrom 15.00 40.00

2009-10 Upper Deck Clearly Canadian

CANAF Adam Foote 6.00 15.00
CANAM Al MacInnis 12.00 30.00
CANBC Bobby Clarke 15.00 40.00
CANBM Brenden Morrow 8.00 20.00
CANBO Bobby Orr 40.00 100.00
CANBR Brad Richards 10.00 25.00
CANCW Cam Ward 10.00 25.00
CANDH Dany Heatley 8.00 20.00
CANDP Denis Potvin 10.00 25.00
CANDR Derek Roy 6.00 15.00
CANES Eric Staal 12.00 30.00
CANFY Marc-Andre Fleury 20.00 50.00
CANGF Grant Fuhr 15.00 40.00
CANGL Guy Lafleur 12.00 30.00
CANGP Gilbert Perreault 10.00 25.00
CANJB Jay Bouwmeester 6.00 15.00
CANJI Jarome Iginla 12.00 30.00
CANJS Joe Sakic 20.00 50.00
CANJT Jonathan Toews 15.00 40.00
CANKD Kris Draper 6.00 15.00
CANLR Luc Robitaille 10.00 25.00
CANMB Martin Brodeur 25.00 60.00
CANMG Mike Green 8.00 20.00
CANML Mario Lemieux 40.00 100.00
CANMM Mark Messier 20.00 50.00
CANMR Mike Richards 8.00 20.00
CANMS Martin St. Louis 10.00 25.00
CANPR Patrick Roy 25.00 60.00
CANPS Patrick Sharp 10.00 25.00
CANRB Ray Bourque 15.00 40.00
CANRG Ryan Getzlaf 10.00 25.00
CANRL Roberto Luongo 15.00 40.00
CANRN Rick Nash 10.00 25.00
CANRR Robyn Regehr 8.00 20.00
CANRS Ryan Smyth 8.00 20.00
CANSC Sidney Crosby 40.00 100.00
CANSG Simon Gagne 10.00 25.00
CANSM Steve Mason 8.00 20.00
CANTH Joe Thornton 15.00 40.00
CANVL Vincent Lecavalier 10.00 25.00
CANWG Wayne Gretzky 40.00 100.00
CANYZ Steve Yzerman 25.00 60.00

2009-10 Upper Deck Draft Day Gems

COMPLETE SET (14) 8.00 20.00
GEM1 Henrik Zetterberg 1.25 3.00
GEM2 Pavel Datsyuk 1.50 4.00
GEM3 Tomas Kaberle .60 1.50
GEM4 Andrei Markov 1.00 2.50
GEM5 Luc Robitaille 1.00 2.50
GEM6 Theoren Fleury 1.50 4.00
GEM7 Ron Hextall 1.00 2.50
GEM8 Dominik Hasek 1.50 4.00
GEM9 Evgeni Nabokov .75 2.00
GEM10 Marty Turco 1.00 2.50
GEM11 Henrik Lundqvist 2.50 6.00
GEM12 Ryan Miller 1.00 2.50
GEM13 Pekka Rinne 1.00 2.50
GEM14 Mark Messier 2.00 5.00
GEM15 Tim Thomas 1.00 2.50
GEM16 Mark Recchi 1.25 3.00
GEM17 Patrick Roy 2.50 6.00
GEM18 Milan Hejduk .75 2.00
GEM19 Cristobal Huet 1.00 2.50
GEM20 Tomas Vokoun .75 2.00
GEM21 Doug Gilmour 1.25 3.00
GEM22 Nikolai Khabibulin 1.00 2.50
GEM23 Michael Ryder .60 1.50
GEM24 Miikka Kiprusoff 1.00 2.50
GEM25 Nicklas Lidstrom .60 1.50
GEM26 Jari Kurri 1.00 2.50
GEM27 Brian Campbell .75 2.00
GEM28 Daniel Alfredsson 1.00 2.50
GEM29 Dustin Byfuglien 1.00 2.50
GEM30 Mark Streit .60 1.50

2009-10 Upper Deck Fab Four Fabrics

BRUN Bergrn/Kssl/Lucic/Ryder 10.00 25.00
CANE Ward/Brind/Ruutu/Staal 10.00 25.00
CAPS Jrcina/Ovch/Morris/Theo 12.00 30.00
CATS Hrtn/Booth/Weiss/Vokn 8.00 20.00
CNKS Bernr/Lngo/Sedin/Sedin 12.00 30.00
DEVL Clarksn/Paris/Brodr/Elias 20.00 50.00
FLAM Ignla/Jokn/Kiprsff/Phnef 10.00 25.00
FLYR Cartr/Rchrds/Emry/Ggne 8.00 20.00
GRTS Mess/Grtzky/Yzer/Crosby 60.00 120.00
HWKS Kane/Toews/Shrp/Cmpb 15.00 40.00
ISLE Okps/Bley/DiPtro/Wght 8.00 20.00
KNGS Brown/Frolv/Dghty/Kpitr 12.00 30.00
LEAF Schn/Kmsk/Hllwg/Tskla 8.00 20.00
FOILR Khab/Cogli/Ggnr/O'Sulli 8.00 20.00
RNGR Gabrk/Drury/Lund/Staal 20.00 50.00
SC00 Gomz/Arntt/Brdeur/Elias 20.00 50.00
SC01 Drury/Roy/Tngy/Brque 20.00 50.00
SC06 Staal/Will/Stllman/Ward 10.00 25.00
SC89 McDn/Mlln/Gilmr/Mclns 10.00 25.00
SC90 Mess/Kurri/Fuhr/Andrsn 15.00 40.00
SENS Spez/Alfrdsn/Htley/Kovl 8.00 20.00
STAR Ribro/Mdno/Lhtin/Turco 12.00 30.00
WING Lidstrm/Zttr/Dtsyk/Hlms 12.00 30.00

2009-10 Upper Deck Face of the Franchise

COMPLETE SET (14) 10.00 25.00
FF1 Sidney Crosby 3.00 8.00
FF2 Alexander Ovechkin 3.00 8.00
FF3 Carey Price 1.50 4.00
FF4 Ales Hemsky .60 1.50
FF5 Roberto Luongo 1.25 3.00
FF6 Marc Savard .50 1.25
FF7 Henrik Lundqvist 2.00 5.00
FF8 Jarome Iginla 1.00 2.50
FF9 Mike Richards .60 1.50
FF10 Jonathan Toews 1.25 3.00
FF11 Jason Spezza .75 2.00
FF12 Luke Schenn .75 2.00
FF13 Joe Thornton 1.25 3.00
FF14 Martin Brodeur 2.00 5.00

2009-10 Upper Deck Game Jerseys

GJAK Anze Kopitar 4.00 10.00
GJAO Alexander Ovechkin 10.00 25.00
GJBB Bob Bourne 1.50 4.00
GJBC Brian Campbell 2.00 5.00
GJBG Butch Goring 2.50 6.00
GJBM Brendan Morrison 2.00 5.00
GJBN Bernie Nicholls 2.00 5.00
GJBO Brooks Orpik 1.50 4.00
GJBP Bob Probert 2.50 6.00
GJBR Brad Richards 2.50 6.00
GJCC Carlo Colaiacovo 1.50 4.00
GJCH Cristobal Huet 2.50 6.00
GJCN Cam Neely 2.50 6.00
GJCO Chris Osgood 2.50 6.00
GJCP Carey Price 5.00 12.00
GJDA David Booth 1.50 4.00
GJDB Dave Bolland 2.00 5.00
GJDC Dino Ciccarelli 2.50 6.00
GJDD Drew Doughty 3.00 8.00
GJDE Derick Brassard 1.50 4.00
GJDH Dale Hawerchuk 3.00 8.00
GJDO Donald Brashear 1.50 4.00
GJDP Dion Phaneuf 2.00 5.00
GJDR Derek Roy 1.50 4.00
GJDS Daniel Sedin 3.00 8.00
GJDU Dustin Brown 2.50 6.00
GJEC Erik Cole 1.50 4.00
GJEM Evgeni Malkin 5.00 12.00
GJES Eric Staal 3.00 8.00
GJFB Francis Bouillon 1.50 4.00
GJFR Michael Frolik 2.00 5.00
GJGA Glenn Anderson 2.00 5.00
GJGC Guy Carbonneau 4.00 10.00
GJGF Grant Fuhr 4.00 10.00
GJGG Simon Gagne 2.50 6.00
GJIK Ilya Kovalchuk 2.50 6.00
GJJB Jay Bouwmeester 1.50 4.00
GJJC Jonathan Cheechoo 2.00 5.00
GJJH Jeff Halpern 1.50 4.00
GJJL Joffrey Lupul 1.50 4.00
GJJO Jordin Tootoo 2.50 6.00
GJJP Jason Pominville 1.50 4.00
GJJS Jason Spezza 2.50 6.00
GJJT Jeff Tambellini 1.50 4.00
GJJV Jakub Voracek 2.00 5.00
GJKL Kari Lehtonen 2.00 5.00
GJKT Kimmo Timonen 2.00 5.00
GJLG Robert Lang 1.50 4.00
GJLM Lanny McDonald 2.50 6.00
GJLX Mario Lemieux 10.00 25.00
GJMA Matt Carle 2.00 5.00
GJMB Martin Brodeur 6.00 15.00
GJMC Bryan McCabe 2.00 5.00
GJMD Marc Denis 1.50 4.00
GJMF Manny Fernandez 1.50 4.00
GJMG Marian Gaborik 2.50 6.00
GJMH Marian Hossa 2.50 6.00
GJML Mike Lundin 1.50 4.00
GJMM Mark Messier 10.00 25.00
GJMP Marc-Antoine Pouliot 2.00 5.00
GJMR Mason Raymond 1.50 4.00
GJMS Marc Staal 1.50 4.00
GJMT Marty Turco 2.50 6.00
GJMU Larry Murphy 2.00 5.00
GJNB Nicklas Backstrom 2.50 6.00
GJNH Nathan Horton 2.50 6.00
GJPA Patrice Brisebois 1.50 4.00
GJPB Patrice Bergeron 3.00 8.00
GJPD Pavel Datsyuk 4.00 10.00
GJPE Peter Stastny 2.00 5.00
GJPK Patrick Kane 5.00 12.00
GJPO Patrick O'Sullivan 2.00 5.00
GJPR Patrick Roy 6.00 15.00
GJPS Patrick Sharp 2.50 6.00
GJRA Paul Ranger 1.50 4.00
GJRB Richard Brodeur 2.50 6.00
GJRI Mike Richards 2.00 5.00
GJRL Roberto Luongo 4.00 10.00
GJRM Ryan Miller 2.50 6.00
GJRN Rick Nash 2.50 6.00
GJSA Borje Salming 2.50 6.00
GJSC Sidney Crosby 10.00 25.00
GJSD Shane Doan 2.00 5.00
GJSG Sam Gagner 1.50 4.00
GJSI Darryl Sittler 3.00 8.00
GJSK Saku Koivu 2.50 6.00
GJSP Paul Stastny 2.00 5.00
GJSS Steve Shutt 2.50 6.00
GJST Drew Stafford 1.50 4.00
GJSU Steve Sullivan 1.50 4.00
GJSW Shea Weber 2.00 5.00
GJSY Steve Yzerman 12.00 30.00
GJTO Jonathan Toews 4.00 10.00
GJTV Thomas Vanek 2.00 5.00
GJTW Tiger Williams 1.50 4.00
GJVO Tomas Vokoun 2.00 5.00
GJVT Vesa Toskala 2.50 6.00
GJWE Stephen Weiss 1.50 4.00
GJWG Wayne Gretzky 75.00 150.00
GJWR Wade Redden 1.50 4.00
GJ2AC Andrew Cogliano 1.50 4.00
GJ2AF Alexander Frolov 2.00 5.00
GJ2AH Adam Hall 1.50 4.00
GJ2AK Anze Kopitar 4.00 10.00
GJ2BA Josh Bailey 2.00 5.00
GJ2BC Brian Campbell 2.00 5.00
GJ2BM Brendan Morrison 2.00 5.00
GJ2BS Borje Salming 2.50 6.00
GJ2CH Jonathan Cheechoo 2.00 5.00
GJ2DH Dale Hawerchuk 3.00 8.00
GJ2DS Devin Setoguchi 2.00 5.00
GJ2DT Dave Taylor 3.00 8.00
GJ2ES Eric Staal 3.00 8.00
GJ2GA Simon Gagne 2.50 6.00
GJ2GH Gordie Howe 80.00 150.00
GJ2HZ Henrik Zetterberg 3.00 8.00
GJ2IK Ilya Kovalchuk 2.50 6.00
GJ2JA Jason Arnott 2.00 5.00
GJ2JC Jeff Carter 2.00 5.00
GJ2JD J.P. Dumont 1.50 4.00
GJ2JI Jarome Iginla 3.00 8.00
GJ2JL Joffrey Lupul 1.50 4.00
GJ2JT Jonathan Toews 4.00 10.00
GJ2KE Phil Kessel 2.50 6.00
GJ2KO Kyle Okposo 1.50 4.00
GJ2LM Lanny McDonald 2.50 6.00
GJ2MC Bryan McCabe 2.00 5.00
GJ2MK Mike Komisarek 2.00 5.00
GJ2ML Milan Lucic 2.00 5.00
GJ2MM Mike Modano 4.00 10.00
GJ2MP Marc-Antoine Pouliot 2.00 5.00
GJ2MR Michael Ryder 1.50 4.00
GJ2MS Marc Staal 1.50 4.00
GJ2OJ Olli Jokinen 2.00 5.00
GJ2PK Paul Kariya 2.50 6.00
GJ2PM Peter Mueller 2.00 5.00
GJ2PS Paul Stastny 2.00 5.00
GJ2RB Rob Blake 2.50 6.00
GJ2RE Ray Emery 2.00 5.00
GJ2RG Ryan Getzlaf 2.50 6.00
GJ2RH Roman Hamrlik 1.50 4.00
GJ2RS Ryan Smyth 2.00 5.00
GJ2SD Shane Doan 2.00 5.00
GJ2SG Scott Gomez 2.00 5.00
GJ2SR Steven Reinprecht 1.50 4.00
GJ2ST Drew Stafford 1.50 4.00
GJ2SY Steve Yzerman 6.00 15.00
GJ2TF Tomas Fleischmann 1.50 4.00
GJ2TH Tomas Holmstrom 2.00 5.00
GJ2TR Tuomo Ruutu 1.50 4.00
GJ2TS Teemu Selanne 5.00 12.00
GJ2VP Vaclav Prospal 1.50 4.00
GJ2VT Vesa Toskala 2.50 6.00

2009-10 Upper Deck Hockey Heroes Mark Messier

HH27 Mark Messier Header 10.00 25.00
HH28 Mark Messier Painted 10.00 25.00
HHMM Mark Messier AU/30 150.00 250.00

2009-10 Upper Deck Hockey Heroes Martin Brodeur

COMPLETE SET (10) 20.00 50.00
COMP.SET w/o SPs (8) 8.00 20.00
COMMON BRODEUR 2.50 6.00
HH18 Martin Brodeur Painting 10.00 25.00
HHMB Martin Brodeur AU/30 150.00 250.00
HHMB Martin Brodeur Header 8.00 20.00

2009-10 Upper Deck Netminders

COMPLETE SET (30) 50.00 100.00
COMP.SET w/o SPs (20) 12.00 30.00
NET1 Marty Turco 1.50 4.00
NET2 Jean-Sebastien Giguere 1.50 4.00
NET3 Nikolai Khabibulin 1.50 4.00
NET4 Chris Mason 1.25 3.00
NET5 Vesa Toskala 1.50 4.00
NET6 Pascal Leclaire 1.50 4.00
NET7 Tomas Vokoun 1.25 3.00
NET8 Mike Smith 1.50 4.00
NET9 Pekka Rinne 1.50 4.00
NET10 Kari Lehtonen 1.25 3.00
NET11 Jonathan Quick 2.00 5.00
NET12 Evgeni Nabokov 1.25 3.00
NET13 Rick DiPietro 1.25 3.00
NET14 Ilya Bryzgalov 1.25 3.00
NET15 Cristobal Huet 1.50 4.00
NET16 Simeon Varlamov 1.50 4.00
NET17 Ray Emery 1.25 3.00
NET18 Niklas Backstrom 1.50 4.00
NET19 Chris Osgood 1.50 4.00
NET20 Peter Budaj 1.25 3.00
NET21 Martin Brodeur SP 5.00 12.00
NET22 Miikka Kiprusoff SP 2.00 5.00
NET23 Roberto Luongo SP 3.00 8.00
NET24 Steve Mason SP 1.50 4.00
NET25 Carey Price SP 4.00 10.00
NET26 Henrik Lundqvist SP 5.00 12.00
NET27 Marc-Andre Fleury SP 4.00 10.00
NET28 Cam Ward SP 2.00 5.00
NET29 Tim Thomas SP 2.00 5.00
NET30 Ryan Miller SP 2.00 5.00

2009-10 Upper Deck Oversize Wal-Mart

COMPLETE SET (42) 15.00 40.00
OS1 Milan Lucic .40 1.00
OS2 Marc Savard .30 .75
OS3 Thomas Vanek .40 1.00
OS4 Jason Pominville .30 .75
OS5 Scott Gomez .40 1.00
OS6 Mike Cammalleri .40 1.00
OS7 Alex Kovalev .40 1.00
OS8 Jonathan Cheechoo .40 1.00
OS9 Phil Kessel .50 1.25
OS10 Tomas Kaberle .30 .75
OS11 Mike Richards .40 1.00
OS12 Chris Pronger .50 1.25
OS13 Evgeni Malkin 1.00 2.50
OS14 Jordan Staal .40 1.00
OS15 Zach Parise .50 1.25
OS16 Marian Gaborik .50 1.25
OS17 Tomas Vokoun .40 1.00
OS18 Ilya Kovalchuk .50 1.25
OS19 Cam Ward .50 1.25
OS20 Vincent Lecavalier .50 1.25
OS21 Alexander Ovechkin 2.00 5.00
OS22 Patrick Kane 1.00 2.50
OS23 Marian Hossa .50 1.25
OS24 Brad Richards .50 1.25
OS25 Henrik Zetterberg .60 1.50
OS26 Jay Bouwmeester .30 .75
OS27 Ryan Smyth .40 1.00
OS28 Marty Turco .50 1.25
OS29 James Neal .30 .75
OS30 Saku Koivu .50 1.25
OS31 Corey Perry .75 2.00
OS32 Patrick Marleau .50 1.25
OS33 Dany Heatley .40 1.00
OS34 Shane Doan .40 1.00
OS35 Henrik Sedin .60 1.50
OS36 Miikka Kiprusoff .50 1.25
OS37 Dion Phaneuf .40 1.00
OS38 Wojtek Wolski .30 .75
OS39 Marek Svatos .30 .75
OS40 Martin Havlat .40 1.00
OS41 Andrew Cogliano .30 .75
OS42 Dustin Penner .30 .75

2009-10 Upper Deck Playoff Performers

COMPLETE SET (16) 12.00 30.00
PP1 Alexander Ovechkin 3.00 8.00
PP2 Cam Ward .75 2.00
PP3 Evgeni Malkin 1.50 4.00
PP4 Henrik Zetterberg 1.00 2.50
PP5 Jarome Iginla 1.00 2.50
PP6 Johan Franzen .60 1.50
PP7 Jonas Hiller .60 1.50
PP8 Marc-Andre Fleury 1.50 4.00
PP9 Martin Brodeur 2.00 5.00
PP10 Patrick Kane 1.50 4.00
PP11 Roberto Luongo 1.25 3.00
PP12 Scott Niedermayer .75 2.00
PP13 Sidney Crosby 3.00 8.00
PP14 Tim Thomas .75 2.00
PP15 Chris Osgood .75 2.00
PP16 Eric Staal 1.00 2.50

2009-10 Upper Deck Rookie Breakouts

RB1 John Tavares 20.00 50.00
RB2 Victor Hedman 12.00 30.00
RB3 Matt Duchene 10.00 25.00
RB4 James van Riemsdyk 10.00 25.00
RB5 Jonas Gustavsson 6.00 15.00
RB6 Evander Kane 10.00 25.00
RB7 Colin Wilson 5.00 12.00
RB8 Michael Grabner 5.00 12.00
RB9 Tyler Myers 8.00 20.00
RB10 Jamie Benn 15.00 40.00
RB11 Dmitry Kulikov 5.00 12.00
RB12 Mikael Backlund 8.00 20.00
RB13 Artem Anisimov 3.00 8.00
RB14 Antti Niemi 8.00 20.00
RB15 Michael Del Zotto 5.00 12.00
RB16 Tyler Bozak 8.00 20.00
RB17 Erik Karlsson 15.00 30.00
RB18 Ryan O'Reilly 10.00 25.00
RB19 Ville Leino 4.00 10.00
RB20 Yannick Weber 5.00 12.00
RB21 Christian Hanson 5.00 12.00
RB22 Cody Franson 5.00 12.00
RB23 Ivan Vishnevskiy 3.00 8.00
RB24 Luca Caputi 5.00 12.00
RB25 Jhonas Enroth 6.00 15.00
RB26 Matt Pelech 5.00 12.00
RB27 Matt Gilroy 5.00 12.00
RB28 Viktor Stalberg 5.00 12.00
RB29 James Wright 5.00 12.00
RB30 Sergei Shirokov 3.00 8.00
RB31 Alec Martinez 6.00 15.00
RB32 Spencer Machacek 5.00 12.00
RB33 T.J. Galiardi 5.00 12.00
RB34 Jason Demers 8.00 20.00

2009-10 Upper Deck Rookie Debuts

COMPLETE SET (9) 15.00 40.00
RD1 John Tavares 3.00 8.00
RD2 James van Riemsdyk 1.50 4.00
RD3 Victor Hedman 2.00 5.00
RD4 Matt Duchene 1.50 4.00
RD5 Jonas Gustavsson 1.00 2.50
RD6 Jamie Benn 2.50 6.00
RD7 Evander Kane 1.50 4.00
RD8 Colin Wilson .75 2.00
RD9 Michael Del Zotto .75 2.00

2009-10 Upper Deck Rookie Headliners

COMPLETE SET (30) 50.00 100.00
COMP.SET w/o SPs (20) 15.00 40.00
RH1 Matt Pelech 1.00 2.50
RH2 Kris Chucko .60 1.50
RH3 Antti Niemi 1.50 4.00
RH4 Ryan O'Reilly 2.00 5.00
RH5 T.J. Galiardi 1.00 2.50
RH6 Perttu Lindgren .75 2.00
RH7 Ivan Vishnevskiy .60 1.50
RH8 Ville Leino .75 2.00

RH9 Dmitry Kulikov 1.00 2.50
RH10 Yannick Weber 1.00 2.50
RH11 Cody Franson 1.00 2.50
RH12 Michael Del Zotto 1.00 2.50
RH13 Matt Gilroy 1.00 2.50
RH14 Artem Anisimov .60 1.50
RH15 Erik Karlsson 3.00 8.00
RH16 Tyler Bozak 1.50 4.00
RH17 Viktor Stalberg 1.00 2.50
RH18 Christian Hanson 1.00 2.50
RH19 Michael Grabner 1.00 2.50
RH20 Sergei Shirokov .60 1.50
RH21 Evander Kane SP 2.50 6.00
RH22 Tyler Myers SP 2.00 5.00
RH23 Mikael Backlund SP 2.00 5.00
RH24 Matt Duchene SP 2.50 6.00
RH25 Jamie Benn SP 4.00 10.00
RH26 Colin Wilson SP 1.25 3.00
RH27 John Tavares SP 5.00 12.00
RH28 James van Riemsdyk SP 2.50 6.00
RH29 Victor Hedman SP 3.00 8.00
RH30 Jonas Gustavsson SP 1.50 4.00

2009-10 Upper Deck Rookie Materials

*PATCH/25: 1.2X TO 3X BASIC JSY
RMAM Alec Martinez 5.00 12.00
RMAN Antti Niemi 6.00 15.00
RMBE Matt Beleskey 3.00 8.00
RMBF Benn Ferriero 4.00 10.00
RMBM Brad Marchand 15.00 40.00
RMBS Brian Salcido 2.50 6.00
RMCB Chris Butler 4.00 10.00
RMCF Cody Franson 4.00 10.00
RMCO Cal O'Reilly 3.00 8.00
RMCW Colin Wilson 4.00 10.00
RMDK Dmitry Kulikov 4.00 10.00
RMDU Matt Duchene 8.00 20.00
RMEK Erik Karlsson 12.00 30.00
RMIV Ivan Vishnevskiy 2.50 6.00
RMJB Jamie Benn 12.00 30.00
RMJD Jason Demers 6.00 15.00
RMJE Jhonas Enroth 5.00 12.00
RMJG Jonas Gustavsson 5.00 12.00
RMJJ Jesse Joensuu 3.00 8.00
RMJS John Scott 4.00 10.00
RMJT John Tavares 15.00 40.00
RMJV James van Riemsdyk 8.00 20.00
RMKA Evander Kane 8.00 20.00
RMKC Kris Chucko 2.50 6.00
RMLC Luca Caputi 4.00 10.00
RMLO Logan Couture 8.00 20.00
RMMA Andrew MacDonald 2.50 6.00
RMMB Mikael Backlund 6.00 15.00
RMMD Michael Del Zotto 4.00 10.00
RMMG Michael Grabner 4.00 10.00
RMMP Matt Pelech 4.00 10.00
RMMS Mike Santorelli 4.00 10.00
RMPL Perttu Lindgren 3.00 8.00
RMRE Joel Rechlicz 2.50 6.00
RMRH Riku Helenius 4.00 10.00
RMRM Ray Macias 3.00 8.00
RMRO Ryan O'Reilly 8.00 20.00
RMSA Michael Sauer 3.00 8.00
RMSM Spencer Machacek 4.00 10.00
RMSS Sergei Shirokov 2.50 6.00
RMTB Tyler Bozak 6.00 15.00
RMTG T.J. Galiardi 4.00 10.00
RMTM Tyler Myers 6.00 15.00
RMVH Victor Hedman 10.00 25.00
RMVL Ville Leino 3.00 8.00
RMYW Yannick Weber 4.00 10.00

2009-10 Upper Deck Season Highlights

COMPLETE SET (7) 6.00 15.00
SH1 Sidney Crosby 1.50 4.00
SH2 Martin Brodeur 1.00 2.50
SH3 Tim Thomas .40 1.00
SH4 Alexander Ovechkin 1.50 4.00
SH5 Henrik Lundqvist 1.00 2.50
SH6 Evgeni Malkin .75 2.00
SH7 Henrik Zetterberg .50 1.25

2009-10 Upper Deck Signatures

UDSAE Andrew Ebbett 5.00 12.00
UDSAM Andrei Markov 8.00 20.00
UDSAP Alex Pietrangelo 6.00 15.00
UDSBM Brendan Mikkelson 5.00 12.00
UDSBO Bobby Orr 150.00 250.00
UDSBR Bobby Ryan 6.00 15.00
UDSBV Boris Valabik 8.00 20.00
UDSBW Blake Wheeler 8.00 20.00
UDSBY Brad Boyes 5.00 12.00
UDSCD Chris Drury 6.00 15.00
UDSCG Claude Giroux 8.00 20.00
UDSCR Sidney Crosby 150.00 250.00
UDSDH Darren Helm 5.00 12.00
UDSDP Dion Phaneuf 6.00 15.00
UDSFB Fabian Brunnstrom 6.00 15.00
UDSFI Mark Fistric 5.00 12.00
UDSFO Nick Foligno 6.00 15.00
UDSGB Gilbert Brule 10.00 25.00
UDSJE Jonathan Ericsson 5.00 12.00
UDSJG Jean-Sebastien Giguere 6.00 15.00
UDSJH Josh Harding 6.00 15.00
UDSJP Justin Pogge 8.00 20.00
UDSKA Karl Alzner 5.00 12.00
UDSLS Luke Schenn 8.00 20.00
UDSMD Matt D'Agostini 6.00 15.00
UDSME Matt Ellis 5.00 12.00
UDSMF Marc-Andre Fleury 25.00 50.00
UDSMI Mike Iggulden 5.00 12.00
UDSMP Max Pacioretty 8.00 20.00
UDSMR Mattias Ritola 6.00 15.00
UDSNF Nikita Filatov 6.00 15.00
UDSNK Nikolai Kulemin 5.00 12.00
UDSOM Oscar Moller 5.00 12.00
UDSPD Pavel Datsyuk 50.00 100.00
UDSPE Michael Peca 25.00 50.00
UDSPK Phil Kessel 15.00 40.00
UDSRO Rostislav Olesz 5.00 12.00
UDSRP Ryan Parent 6.00 15.00
UDSRS Ryan Smyth 25.00 50.00
UDSRY Ryan Potulny 5.00 12.00
UDSSC Cory Schneider 12.00 30.00
UDSSS Steven Stamkos 40.00 80.00
UDSSY Steve Yzerman 125.00 250.00
UDSTK Tim Kennedy 6.00 15.00
UDSTS Tom Sestito 5.00 12.00
UDSTV Thomas Vanek 6.00 15.00
UDSTW Ty Wishart 6.00 15.00
UDSWG Wayne Gretzky 150.00 400.00

2009-10 Upper Deck Signature Sensations

SSAB Adam Burish 10.00 25.00
SSAE Andrew Ebbett 5.00 12.00
SSAM Al MacInnis 30.00 60.00
SSAN Andreas Nodl 6.00 15.00
SSAO Adam Oates 8.00 20.00
SSAP Alexandre Picard 6.00 15.00
SSAT Alex Tanguay 5.00 12.00
SSBB Brian Boyle 5.00 12.00
SSBE Brendan Bell 5.00 12.00
SSCN Cam Neely 25.00 50.00
SSDC Don Cherry 20.00 40.00
SSDH Dominik Hasek 40.00 80.00
SSDL Dan LaCosta 6.00 15.00
SSDN Marcel Dionne 10.00 25.00
SSDP Dimitri Patzold 6.00 15.00
SSEF Eric Fehr 5.00 12.00
SSEL Patrik Elias 8.00 20.00
SSES Phil Esposito 12.00 30.00
SSFN Fredrik Norrena 5.00 12.00
SSGB Gilbert Brule 10.00 25.00
SSGH Gordie Howe 100.00 200.00
SSHA Jannik Hansen 5.00 12.00
SSHZ Henrik Zetterberg 40.00 80.00
SSJB Jean Beliveau 40.00 80.00
SSJE Jonathan Ericsson 5.00 12.00
SSJG Jean-Sebastien Giguere 40.00 80.00
SSJH Josh Hennessy 5.00 12.00
SSJK Jari Kurri 8.00 20.00
SSJL John-Michael Liles 5.00 12.00
SSJS Jarret Stoll 6.00 15.00
SSJT Joe Thornton 12.00 30.00
SSKQ Kyle Quincey 5.00 12.00
SSKT Kyle Turris 8.00 20.00
SSLA Drew Larman 5.00 12.00
SSLR Larry Robinson 8.00 20.00
SSLT Lauri Tukonen 5.00 12.00
SSLU Joffrey Lupul 5.00 12.00
SSMD Matt D'Agostini 6.00 15.00
SSME Matt Ellis 5.00 12.00
SSMF Mark Fistric 5.00 12.00
SSMI Mike Iggulden 5.00 12.00
SSMK Matt Keetley 5.00 12.00
SSML Mike Lundin 5.00 12.00
SSMM Mark Mancari 5.00 12.00
SSMO Mike Modano 40.00 80.00
SSMP Michael Peca 6.00 15.00
SSMR Mattias Ritola 6.00 15.00
SSND Nigel Dawes 5.00 12.00
SSNK Nikolai Khabibulin 8.00 20.00
SSOP Ondrej Pavelec 10.00 25.00
SSOV Alexander Ovechkin 100.00 200.00
SSPA Daniel Paille 6.00 15.00
SSPE Rich Peverley 6.00 15.00
SSPI Adam Pineault 6.00 15.00
SSPR Patrick Roy 100.00 200.00
SSPY Ryan Potulny 5.00 12.00
SSRH Ron Hextall 8.00 20.00
SSRO Rostislav Olesz 5.00 12.00
SSRU R.J. Umberger 6.00 15.00
SSRY Michael Ryder 5.00 12.00
SSSB Scotty Bowman 30.00 60.00
SSSC Sidney Crosby 200.00 300.00
SSSM Stefan Meyer 6.00 15.00
SSST Martin St. Louis 8.00 20.00
SSSW Steve Wagner 5.00 12.00
SSTC Ty Conklin 6.00 15.00
SSTL Jiri Tlusty 5.00 12.00
SSTO Tobias Stephan 5.00 12.00
SSTS Tom Sestito 5.00 12.00
SSTV Thomas Vanek 6.00 15.00
SSTW Tyler Weiman 8.00 20.00
SSVF Valtteri Filppula 5.00 12.00
SSZC Zdeno Chara 20.00 50.00

2009-10 Upper Deck The Champions

COMPLETE SET (40) 40.00 80.00
CHAB Amanda Beard 2.00 5.00
CHAC Alissa Czisny 2.00 5.00
CHAG Alexe Gilles 2.00 5.00
CHAN Miki Ando 2.00 5.00
CHBA Ben Agosto 2.00 5.00
CHBM Bode Miller 2.00 5.00
CHBS Beckie Scott 2.00 5.00
CHBT Jennifer Botterill 2.00 5.00
CHCC Cassie Campbell 2.50 6.00
CHCG Cammie Granato 2.00 5.00
CHCO Sasha Cohen 2.00 5.00
CHDD Derrick Delmore 2.00 5.00
CHGB Gaetan Boucher 2.00 5.00
CHGI Todd Gilles 2.00 5.00
CHGZ Greg Zuerlein 2.00 5.00
CHHW Hayley Wickenheiser 2.00 5.00
CHJA Jeremy Abbott 2.00 5.00
CHJB Jean Luc Brassard 2.00 5.00
CHJC Julie Chu 2.50 6.00
CHJE Jeremy Bloom 2.00 5.00
CHJJ Jojo Starbuck 2.00 5.00
CHJM Julia Mancuso 2.00 5.00
CHKG Kerrin Lee Gartner 2.00 5.00
CHMC Madison Chock 2.00 5.00
CHME Melissa Gregory 2.00 5.00
CHMR Brandon Mroz 2.00 5.00
CHND Natalie Darwitz 2.00 5.00
CHNK Nancy Kerrigan 2.00 5.00
CHNO Nobunari Oda 2.00 5.00
CHPE Denis Petukhov 2.00 5.00
CHPG Piper Gilles 2.00 5.00
CHRF Rachael Flatt 2.00 5.00
CHSB Shae-Lynn Bourne 2.00 5.00
CHSP Kim St. Pierre 2.00 5.00
CHST Jane Summersett 2.00 5.00
CHTB Tanith Belbin 2.00 5.00
CHTG Timothy Goebel 2.00 5.00
CHWE Johnny Weir 2.00 5.00
CHYU Yuka Sato 2.00 5.00
CHZD Zachary Donohue 2.00 5.00

2009-10 Upper Deck The Champions Autographs Gold

*SILVER: .4X TO 1X GOLD AUTO
CHAB Amanda Beard 12.00 30.00
CHAG Alexe Gilles 6.00 15.00
CHAN Miki Ando SP 60.00 120.00
CHBA Ben Agosto 4.00 10.00
CHBM Bode Miller 10.00 25.00
CHBS Beckie Scott SP 30.00 60.00
CHBT Jennifer Botterill 8.00 20.00
CHCC Cassie Campbell 15.00 40.00
CHCG Cammi Granato 8.00 20.00
CHDD Derrick Delmore 5.00 12.00
CHGB Gaetan Boucher 6.00 15.00
CHGI Todd Gilles 5.00 12.00
CHGZ Greg Zuerlein 5.00 12.00
CHHW Haley Wickenheiser 12.00 30.00
CHJA Jeremy Abbott SP 12.00 30.00
CHJB Jeremy Bloom 6.00 15.00
CHJC Julie Chu 6.00 15.00
CHJM Julia Mancuso 12.00 30.00
CHKG Kerrin Lee Gartner 5.00 12.00
CHMC Madison Chock 5.00 12.00
CHME Melissa Gregory 5.00 12.00
CHND Natalie Darwitz 5.00 12.00
CHNK Nancy Kerrigan 10.00 25.00
CHPE Denis Petukhov 6.00 15.00
CHPG Piper Gilles 5.00 12.00
CHRF Rachael Flatt 5.00 12.00
CHRR Ross Rebagliati 6.00 15.00
CHSP Kim St. Pierre 6.00 15.00
CHST Jane Summersett 5.00 12.00
CHTB Tanith Belbin 5.00 12.00
CHTG Timothy Goebel 4.00 10.00
CHWE Johnny Weir 4.00 10.00

2009-10 Upper Deck Top Guns

COMPLETE SET (7) 6.00 15.00
TG1 Alexander Semin .60 1.50
TG2 Zach Parise .60 1.50
TG3 Evgeni Malkin 1.25 3.00
TG4 Eric Staal .75 2.00
TG5 Jarome Iginla .75 2.00
TG6 Thomas Vanek .50 1.25
TG7 Alexander Ovechkin 2.50 6.00

2009-10 Upper Deck Winter Classic Oversized

COMPLETE SET (14) 10.00 25.00
WC1 Dustin Byfuglien 1.25 3.00
WC2 Patrick Kane 2.50 6.00
WC3 Brian Campbell 1.00 2.50
WC4 Patrick Sharp 1.25 3.00
WC5 Jonathan Toews 2.00 5.00
WC6 Kris Versteeg .75 2.00
WC7 Ben Eager 1.00 2.50
WC8 Marian Hossa 1.25 3.00
WC9 Nicklas Lidstrom .75 2.00
WC10 Brian Rafalski .75 2.00
WC11 Ty Conklin 1.00 2.50
WC12 Jiri Hudler 1.00 2.50
WC13 Pavel Datsyuk 2.00 5.00
WC14 Henrik Zetterberg 1.50 4.00

2009-10 Upper Deck Young Guns Oversized

COMPLETE SET (14) 60.00 120.00
XL1 Evander Kane 3.00 8.00
XL2 Tyler Myers 2.50 6.00
XL3 Matt Duchene 3.00 8.00
XL4 Jamie Benn 6.00 15.00
XL5 Ville Leino 1.25 3.00
XL6 Yannick Weber 1.50 4.00
XL7 John Tavares 15.00 40.00
XL8 Michael Del Zotto 1.50 4.00
XL9 Artem Anisimov 1.00 2.50
XL10 Erik Karlsson 5.00 12.00
XL11 James van Riemsdyk 3.00 8.00
XL12 Victor Hedman 4.00 10.00
XL13 Viktor Stalberg 1.50 4.00
XL14 Sergei Shirokov 1.00 2.50

2010-11 Upper Deck

COMPLETE SET (500) 250.00 500.00
COMP.SET w/o SPs (400) 20.00 50.00
COMP.SER.1 SET (250) 125.00 250.00
COMP.SER.1 w/o SPs (200) 10.00 25.00
COMP.SER.2 SET (250) 125.00 250.00
COMP.SER.2 w/o SPs (200) 10.00 25.00
1 Nicklas Backstrom .30 .75
2 Mike Green .25 .60
3 Tomas Fleischmann .20 .50
4 Brooks Laich .20 .50
5 Semyon Varlamov .30 .75
6 Tom Poti .20 .50
7 Henrik Sedin .40 1.00
8 Ryan Kesler .30 .75
9 Alexandre Burrows .20 .50
10 Alexander Edler .20 .50
11 Mikael Samuelsson .20 .50
12 Mason Raymond .20 .50
13 Sami Salo .20 .50
14 Phil Kessel .30 .75
15 Dion Phaneuf .25 .60
16 Jean-Sebastien Giguere .30 .75
17 Mikhail Grabovski .20 .50
18 Francois Beauchemin .20 .50
19 Colton Orr .20 .50
20 John Mitchell .20 .50
21 Steven Stamkos .60 1.50
22 Martin St. Louis .30 .75
23 Steve Downie .20 .50
24 Ryan Malone .20 .50
25 Mattias Ohlund .20 .50
26 Stephane Veilleux .20 .50
27 Mike Smith .30 .75
28 Brad Boyes .20 .50
29 David Backes .20 .50
30 Andy McDonald .25 .60
31 Erik Johnson .20 .50
32 Patrik Berglund .20 .50
33 Jay McClement .20 .50
34 Joe Thornton .50 1.25
35 Dan Boyle .20 .50
36 Joe Pavelski .40 1.00
37 Devin Setoguchi .25 .60
38 Ryane Clowe .20 .50
39 Logan Couture .40 1.00
40 Marc-Edouard Vlasic .20 .50
41 Sidney Crosby 1.25 3.00
42 Jordan Staal .25 .60
43 Maxime Talbot .20 .50
44 Pascal Dupuis .20 .50
45 Brooks Orpik .20 .50
46 Tyler Kennedy .20 .50
47 Alex Goligoski .25 .60
48 Ilya Bryzgalov .25 .60
49 Scottie Upshall .20 .50
50 Radim Vrbata .20 .50
51 Wojtek Wolski .20 .50
52 Martin Hanzal .20 .50
53 Vernon Fiddler .20 .50
54 Derek Morris .20 .50
55 Mike Richards .25 .60
56 Daniel Briere .30 .75
57 Claude Giroux .30 .75
58 Ville Leino .25 .60
59 Scott Hartnell .20 .50
60 Matt Carle .25 .60
61 Brian Boucher .25 .60
62 Jarkko Ruutu .20 .50
63 Daniel Alfredsson .30 .75
64 Mike Fisher .20 .50
65 Filip Kuba .20 .50
66 Erik Karlsson .40 1.00
67 Brian Elliott .25 .60
68 Milan Michalek .20 .50
69 Michal Rozsival .20 .50
70 Marian Gaborik .30 .75
71 Brandon Dubinsky .20 .50
72 Ryan Callahan .20 .50
73 Artem Anisimov .20 .50
74 Marc Staal .20 .50
75 Daniel Girardi .20 .50
76 Trent Hunter .20 .50
77 John Tavares .50 1.25
78 Mark Streit .20 .50
79 Matt Moulson .25 .60
80 Blake Comeau .20 .50
81 Dwayne Roloson .25 .60
82 Dainius Zubrus .20 .50
83 Zach Parise .30 .75
84 Martin Brodeur .75 2.00
85 Jamie Langenbrunner .20 .50
86 Andy Greene .20 .50
87 David Clarkson .20 .50
88 Joel Ward .20 .50
89 Shea Weber .25 .60
90 Martin Erat .20 .50
91 J.P. Dumont .20 .50
92 Pekka Rinne .30 .75
93 Steve Sullivan .20 .50
94 Jaroslav Spacek .20 .50
95 Mike Cammalleri .30 .75
96 Carey Price .60 1.50
97 Brian Gionta .20 .50
98 Josh Gorges .20 .50
99 Tom Pyatt .20 .50
100 Hal Gill .20 .50
101 Kyle Brodziak .20 .50
102 Niklas Backstrom .30 .75
103 Guillaume Latendresse .25 .60
104 Martin Havlat .25 .60
105 Andrew Brunette .20 .50
106 Cal Clutterbuck .20 .50
107 Brent Burns .30 .75
108 Nick Schultz .20 .50
109 Brad Richardson .20 .50
110 Drew Doughty .40 1.00
111 Dustin Brown .30 .75
112 Michal Handzus .25 .60
113 Jonathan Quick .40 1.00
114 Rob Scuderi .20 .50
115 Jarret Stoll .25 .60
116 Cory Stillman .20 .50
117 Tomas Vokoun .25 .60
118 Stephen Weiss .25 .60
119 Michael Frolik .20 .50
120 Bryan McCabe .20 .50
121 Jeff Deslauriers .20 .50
122 Dustin Penner .20 .50
123 Andrew Cogliano .20 .50
124 Shawn Horcoff .20 .50
125 Tom Gilbert .20 .50
126 Gilbert Brule .30 .75
127 Ryan Whitney .20 .50
128 Jonathan Ericsson .20 .50
129 Henrik Zetterberg .40 1.00
130 Johan Franzen .25 .60
131 Brian Rafalski .20 .50
132 Valtteri Filppula .20 .50
133 Brad Stuart .20 .50
134 Darren Helm .20 .50
135 Matt Niskanen .25 .60
136 Brad Richards .30 .75
137 Loui Eriksson .20 .50
138 Brenden Morrow .25 .60
139 Jamie Benn .40 1.00
140 Stephane Robidas .20 .50
141 R.J. Umberger .20 .50
142 Rick Nash .30 .75
143 Antoine Vermette .20 .50
144 Kristian Huselius .20 .50
145 Fedor Tyutin .20 .50
146 Kris Russell .20 .50
147 Cody McLeod .20 .50
148 Matt Duchene .30 .75
149 Craig Anderson .30 .75
150 Chris Stewart .25 .60
151 Ryan O'Reilly .30 .75
152 T.J. Galiardi .25 .60
153 Troy Brouwer .20 .50
154 Jonathan Toews .50 1.25
155 Duncan Keith .25 .60
156 Marian Hossa .30 .75
157 Brent Seabrook .20 .50
158 Dave Bolland .25 .60
159 Brian Campbell .20 .50
160 Sergei Samsonov .25 .60
161 Chad LaRose .20 .50
162 Cam Ward .30 .75
163 Jussi Jokinen .20 .50
164 Joni Pitkanen .25 .60
165 Tuomo Ruutu .25 .60
166 Erik Cole .20 .50
167 Curtis Glencross .20 .50
168 Niklas Hagman .20 .50
169 Jarome Iginla .40 1.00
170 Jay Bouwmeester .20 .50
171 Rene Bourque .20 .50
172 Mark Giordano .30 .75
173 Jochen Hecht .20 .50
174 Chris Butler .20 .50
175 Ryan Miller .30 .75
176 Derek Roy .20 .50
177 Tyler Myers .20 .50
178 Tim Connolly .20 .50
179 Daniel Paille .20 .50
180 Marco Sturm .20 .50
181 Patrice Bergeron .40 1.00
182 Milan Lucic .30 .75
183 Tuukka Rask .40 1.00
184 David Krejci .30 .75
185 Michael Ryder .20 .50
186 Niclas Bergfors .25 .60
187 Ron Hainsey .20 .50
188 Nik Antropov .25 .60
189 Evander Kane .30 .75
190 Rich Peverley .30 .75
191 Tobias Enstrom .20 .50
192 Bryan Little .30 .75
193 George Parros .25 .60
194 Jason Blake .20 .50
195 Corey Perry .50 1.25
196 Bobby Ryan .25 .60
197 Jonas Hiller .25 .60
198 Lubomir Visnovsky .20 .50
199 Toews/Keith/Kane CL .60 1.50
200 Richards/Pronger/Carter CL .30 .75
201 Cam Fowler YG RC 5.00 12.00
202 Nick Bonino YG RC 2.50 6.00
203 Alexander Burmistrov YG RC 2.00 5.00
204 Arturs Kulda YG RC 2.00 5.00
205 Jordan Caron YG RC 2.50 6.00
206 Zach Hamill YG RC 2.00 5.00
207 Jeff Penner YG RC 3.00 8.00
208 Andrew Bodnarchuk YG RC 2.00 5.00
209 Henrik Karlsson YG RC 2.00 5.00
210 T.J. Brodie YG RC 2.00 5.00
211 Jeff Skinner YG RC 12.00 30.00
212 Zac Dalpe YG RC 2.50 6.00
213 Jamie McBain YG RC 2.00 5.00
214 Nick Leddy YG RC 2.50 6.00
215 Brandon Pirri YG RC 2.00 5.00
216 Mark Olver YG RC 2.00 5.00
217 Brandon Yip YG RC 2.00 5.00
218 Philip Larsen YG RC 2.00 5.00
219 Taylor Hall YG RC 12.00 30.00
220 Jordan Eberle YG RC 12.00 30.00
221 Alex Plante YG RC 2.00 5.00
222 Evgeny Dadonov YG RC 2.50 6.00
223 Brayden Schenn YG RC 5.00 12.00
224 Kyle Clifford YG RC 2.50 6.00
225 Jake Muzzin YG RC 5.00 12.00
226 Cody Almond YG RC 2.00 5.00
227 Casey Wellman YG RC 2.00 5.00
228 Clayton Stoner YG RC 2.00 5.00
229 Justin Falk YG RC 1.50 4.00
230 Maxim Noreau YG RC 1.50 4.00
231 P.K. Subban YG RC 12.00 30.00
232 J.T. Wyman YG RC 2.00 5.00
233 Matt Martin YG RC 3.00 8.00
234 Anders Lindback YG RC 2.00 5.00
235 Matt Taormina YG RC 2.00 5.00
236 Alexander Urbom YG RC 2.00 5.00
237 Nick Palmieri YG RC 2.00 5.00
238 Derek Stepan YG RC 2.50 6.00
239 Jared Cowen YG RC 2.00 5.00
240 Sergei Bobrovsky YG RC 25.00 60.00
241 Eric Tangradi YG RC 2.00 5.00
242 Nick Johnson YG RC 1.50 4.00
243 Tommy Wingels YG RC 2.00 5.00
244 Dustin Kohn YG RC 2.00 5.00
245 Dana Tyrell YG RC 2.00 5.00
246 Dustin Tokarski YG RC 2.00 5.00
247 Nazem Kadri YG RC 8.00 20.00
248 Brayden Irwin YG RC 2.00 5.00
249 Marcus Johansson YG RC 3.00 8.00
250 Kadri/Subban/Hall YG CL 2.50 6.00
251 Teemu Selanne .60 1.50
252 Saku Koivu .30 .75
253 Ryan Getzlaf .30 .75
254 Dan Sexton .25 .60
255 Matt Beleskey .25 .60
256 Toni Lydman .20 .50
257 Zach Bogosian .25 .60
258 Dustin Byfuglien .30 .75
259 Ben Eager .20 .50
260 Chris Mason .25 .60
261 Brent Sopel .20 .50
262 Andrew Ladd .20 .50
263 Marc Savard .20 .50
264 Zdeno Chara .30 .75
265 Tim Thomas .30 .75
266 Blake Wheeler .30 .75
267 Mark Recchi .40 1.00
268 Nathan Horton .25 .60
269 Shawn Thornton .20 .50
270 Jason Pominville .20 .50
271 Thomas Vanek .25 .60
272 Drew Stafford .20 .50
273 Craig Rivet .20 .50
274 Jordan Leopold .20 .50
275 Tyler Ennis .20 .50
276 Miikka Kiprusoff .30 .75
277 Brendan Morrison .25 .60
278 Matt Stajan .20 .50
279 Tom Kostopoulos .20 .50
280 Robyn Regehr .20 .50
281 Olli Jokinen .25 .60
282 Alex Tanguay .20 .50
283 Mikael Backlund .25 .60
284 Patrick Dwyer .20 .50
285 Eric Staal .40 1.00
286 Brandon Sutter .20 .50
287 Joe Corvo .20 .50
288 Ian White .25 .60
289 Tim Gleason .20 .50
290 Patrick Sharp .30 .75
291 Patrick Kane .60 1.50
292 Marty Turco .30 .75
293 Niklas Hjalmarsson .20 .50
294 Milan Hejduk .25 .60
295 Paul Stastny .25 .60
296 Peter Mueller .25 .60
297 John-Michael Liles .20 .50
298 Kyle Quincey .20 .50
299 David Jones .20 .50
300 Jakub Voracek .25 .60
301 Steve Mason .25 .60
302 Derick Brassard .20 .50
303 Anton Stralman .20 .50
304 Samuel Pahlsson .20 .50
305 Rostislav Klesla .20 .50
306 Ethan Moreau .20 .50
307 James Neal .20 .50
308 Mike Ribeiro .20 .50
309 Kari Lehtonen .25 .60
310 Steve Ott .20 .50
311 Trevor Daley .20 .50
312 Fabian Brunnstrom .20 .50
313 Mike Modano .50 1.25
314 Jim Howard .40 1.00
315 Nicklas Lidstrom .30 .75
316 Pavel Datsyuk .50 1.25
317 Dan Cleary .30 .75
318 Niklas Kronwall .25 .60
319 Tomas Holmstrom .20 .50
320 Ales Hemsky .25 .60
321 Sam Gagner .20 .50
322 Nikolai Khabibulin .25 .60
323 Kurtis Foster .20 .50
324 Ladislav Smid .20 .50
325 Zach Stortini .20 .50
326 Steve Bernier .20 .50
327 Dennis Wideman .20 .50
328 David Booth .20 .50
329 Radek Dvorak .20 .50
330 Dmitry Kulikov .25 .60
331 Rostislav Olesz .20 .50
332 Bryan Allen .20 .50
333 Steven Reinprecht .20 .50
334 Chris Higgins .20 .50
335 Justin Williams .25 .60
336 Ryan Smyth .25 .60
337 Jack Johnson .20 .50
338 Anze Kopitar .50 1.25
339 Wayne Simmonds .40 1.00
340 Alexei Ponikarovsky .20 .50
341 Matt Greene .20 .50
342 Mikko Koivu .30 .75
343 Antti Miettinen .20 .50
344 Marek Zidlicky .20 .50
345 Cam Barker .20 .50
346 Pierre-Marc Bouchard .30 .75
347 Matt Cullen .20 .50
348 John Madden .20 .50
349 Eric Nystrom .20 .50
350 Scott Gomez .25 .60
351 Tomas Plekanec .20 .50
352 Andrei Markov .30 .75
353 Maxim Lapierre .20 .50
354 Andrei Kostitsyn .25 .60
355 Travis Moen .20 .50
356 Roman Hamrlik .20 .50
357 Ryan Suter .25 .60
358 Patric Hornqvist .20 .50
359 David Legwand .25 .60
360 Cody Franson .20 .50
361 Colin Wilson .25 .60
362 Matthew Lombardi .20 .50
363 Cal O'Reilly .20 .50
364 Jason Arnott .25 .60
365 Brian Rolston .25 .60
366 Travis Zajac .20 .50
367 Patrik Elias .30 .75
368 Ilya Kovalchuk .30 .75
369 Johan Hedberg .25 .60
370 Henrik Tallinder .20 .50
371 Anton Volchenkov .20 .50
372 James Wisniewski .20 .50
373 Kyle Okposo .20 .50
374 Frans Nielsen .20 .50
375 Josh Bailey .25 .60
376 Rob Schremp .20 .50
377 Rick DiPietro .25 .60
378 Doug Weight .30 .75
379 Chris Drury .25 .60
380 Henrik Lundqvist .75 2.00
381 Vaclav Prospal .20 .50
382 Michael Del Zotto .25 .60
383 Sean Avery .25 .60
384 Todd White .20 .50
385 Alexander Frolov .20 .50
386 Jason Spezza .30 .75
387 Alex Kovalev .25 .60
388 Peter Regin .25 .60
389 Chris Kelly .25 .60
390 Chris Phillips .20 .50
391 Sergei Gonchar .20 .50
392 Pascal Leclaire .25 .60
393 James van Riemsdyk .25 .60
394 Chris Pronger .30 .75
395 Jeff Carter .25 .60
396 Kimmo Timonen .20 .50
397 Daniel Carcillo .20 .50
398 Andrej Meszaros .20 .50
399 Michael Leighton .25 .60
400 Ray Whitney .25 .60
401 Eric Belanger .20 .50
402 Shane Doan .25 .60
403 Keith Yandle .20 .50
404 Ed Jovanovski .20 .50
405 Adrian Aucoin .20 .50
406 Lee Stempniak .20 .50
407 Paul Martin .20 .50
408 Chris Kunitz .30 .75
409 Marc-Andre Fleury .60 1.50
410 Evgeni Malkin .60 1.50
411 Kristopher Letang .40 1.00
412 Patrick Marleau .30 .75
413 Dany Heatley .25 .60
414 Doug Murray .20 .50
415 Antero Niittymaki .25 .60
416 Antti Niemi .25 .60
417 T.J. Oshie .30 .75
418 David Perron .25 .60
419 Alexander Steen .20 .50
420 B.J. Crombeen .20 .50
421 Carlo Colaiacovo .20 .50
422 Jaroslav Halak .30 .75
423 Dan Ellis .25 .60
424 Victor Hedman .40 1.00
425 Vincent Lecavalier .30 .75
426 Pavel Kubina .20 .50
427 Sean Bergenheim .20 .50
428 Dominic Moore .20 .50
429 Simon Gagne .30 .75
430 Nikolai Kulemin .20 .50
431 Tyler Bozak .20 .50
432 Mike Komisarek .20 .50
433 Jonas Gustavsson .40 1.00
434 Luca Caputi .25 .60
435 Colby Armstrong .20 .50
436 Kris Versteeg .20 .50
437 Luke Schenn .30 .75
438 Daniel Sedin .40 1.00
439 Roberto Luongo .50 1.25
440 Kevin Bieksa .30 .75
441 Dan Hamhuis .25 .60
442 Keith Ballard .20 .50
443 Alexander Semin .30 .75
444 Alexander Ovechkin 1.25 3.00
445 Eric Fehr .20 .50
446 John Carlson .30 .75
447 Mike Knuble .20 .50
448 Jeff Schultz .20 .50
449 Fleury/Mlkin/Crsby CL 1.25 3.00
450 Bckstm/Ovch/Grn CL 1.25 3.00
451 Brandon McMillan YG RC 2.00 5.00
452 Nick Bonino YG RC 3.00 8.00
453 Kyle Palmieri YG RC 5.00 12.00
454 Jamie Arniel YG RC 2.00 5.00
455 Colby Cohen YG RC 2.00 5.00
456 Tyler Seguin YG RC 30.00 80.00
457 Luke Adam YG RC 2.00 5.00
458 Jon Matsumoto YG RC 2.00 5.00
459 Evan Brophey YG RC 2.00 5.00
460 Ben Smith YG RC 2.50 6.00
461 Jeremy Morin YG RC 2.00 5.00
462 Justin Mercier YG RC 2.00 5.00
463 Jonas Holos YG RC 2.00 5.00
464 Kevin Shattenkirk YG RC 8.00 20.00
465 Nick Holden YG RC 2.00 5.00
466 Magnus Paajarvi YG RC 6.00 15.00
467 Linus Omark YG RC 2.50 6.00
468 Dwight King YG RC 2.00 5.00
469 Nate Prosser YG RC 2.00 5.00
470 Matt Kassian YG RC 2.00 5.00
471 Marco Scandella YG RC 2.00 5.00
472 Jared Spurgeon YG RC 10.00 25.00
473 Linus Klasen YG RC 2.00 5.00
474 Mark Dekanich YG RC 2.00 5.00
475 Stephen Gionta YG RC 2.50 6.00
476 Brad Mills YG RC 2.00 5.00
477 Mark Fayne YG RC 2.00 5.00
478 Alexander Vasyunov YG RC 2.00 5.00
479 Jacob Josefson YG RC 2.00 5.00
480 Mattias Tedenby YG RC 2.00 5.00
481 Olivier Magnan-Grenier YG RC 2.00 5.00
482 Nino Niederreiter YG RC 8.00 20.00
483 Travis Hamonic YG RC 2.50 6.00
484 Matt Zaba YG RC 2.50 6.00
485 Evgeny Grachev YG RC 2.00 5.00
486 Robin Lehner YG RC 15.00 40.00
487 Eric Wellwood YG RC 2.50 6.00
488 Oliver Ekman-Larsson YG RC 8.00 20.00
489 Justin Braun YG RC 2.00 5.00
490 Mike Moore YG RC 2.00 5.00
491 Ian Cole YG RC 2.00 5.00
492 Nikita Nikitin YG RC 2.00 5.00
493 Ryan Reaves YG RC 2.50 6.00
494 Nicholas Drazenovic YG RC 2.50 6.00
495 Stefan Della Rovere YG RC 2.00 5.00
496 Johan Harju YG RC 2.00 5.00
497 Korbinian Holzer YG RC 2.00 5.00
498 Keith Aulie YG RC 2.00 5.00
499 Brian Fahey YG RC 2.00 5.00
500 Seguin/Paajarvi YG CL 4.00 10.00

2010-11 Upper Deck 20th Anniversary Parallel

*1-200/251-450 VETS: 3X TO 8X BASE
*201-250/451-500 YG: .6X TO 1.5X
203 Alexander Burmistrov YG 3.00 8.00
219 Taylor Hall YG 30.00 80.00
220 Jordan Eberle YG 25.00 60.00
250 Eberle/Hall YG CL 20.00 50.00
456 Tyler Seguin YG 20.00 50.00
468 Jared Spurgeon YG 15.00 40.00
500 T.Seguin/M.Paajarvi YG CL 12.00 30.00
501 Wayne Gretzky 40.00 100.00
502 Mark Messier 12.00 30.00
503 Gordie Howe 20.00 50.00
504 Mario Lemieux 12.00 30.00
505 Steve Yzerman 15.00 40.00
506 Bobby Hull 10.00 25.00
507 Tony Esposito 6.00 15.00
508 Brian Leetch 5.00 12.00
509 Bobby Orr 15.00 40.00
510 Bobby Clarke 10.00 25.00
511 Guy Lafleur 12.00 30.00
512 Grant Fuhr 8.00 20.00
513 Patrick Roy 20.00 50.00
514 Ray Bourque 10.00 25.00
515 Cam Neely 6.00 15.00
516 Phil Esposito 8.00 20.00
517 Lanny McDonald 8.00 20.00
518 Marcel Dionne 8.00 20.00
519 Luc Robitaille 6.00 15.00
520 Alex Delvecchio 6.00 15.00
521 Jonathan Toews AW 10.00 25.00
522 Tyler Myers AW 4.00 10.00
523 Martin St. Louis AW 6.00 15.00
524 Duncan Keith AW 5.00 12.00
525 Henrik Sedin AW 8.00 20.00
526 Henrik Sedin AW 8.00 20.00
527 Ryan Miller AW 6.00 15.00
528 Pavel Datsyuk AW 10.00 25.00
529 Martin Brodeur AW 15.00 40.00
530 Jim Howard AW 10.00 25.00
531 Michael Del Zotto ART 10.00 25.00
532 Tyler Myers ART 4.00 10.00
533 Niclas Bergfors ART 5.00 12.00
534 Matt Duchene ART 6.00 15.00
535 John Tavares ART 10.00 25.00
536 Dana Tyrell CWJ 5.00 12.00
537 Keith Aulie CWJ 5.00 12.00
538 Brandon McMillan CWJ 5.00 12.00
539 Dustin Tokarski CWJ 5.00 12.00
540 Travis Hamonic CWJ 6.00 15.00

541 Marco Scandella CWJ 5.00 12.00
542 Stefan Della Rovere CWJ 5.00 12.00
543 Luke Adam CWJ 5.00 12.00
544 Brayden Schenn CWJ 12.00 30.00
545 Jared Cowen CWJ 12.00 30.00
546 Jordan Caron CWJ 6.00 15.00
547 Nazem Kadri CWJ 15.00 40.00
548 P.K. Subban CWJ 25.00 60.00
549 Jordan Eberle CWJ 50.00 100.00
550 Taylor Hall CWJ 50.00 100.00
551 Martin Brodeur YG SP 25.00 60.00
552 Eric Lindros YG SP 50.00 100.00
20ABO Bobby Orr AU/90 200.00 350.00
20ASC Sidney Crosby AU/90 150.00 300.00

2010-11 Upper Deck Exclusives

*1-450 VETS: 6X TO 15X BASE
*YOUNG GUNS: 1.2X TO 3X BASE
211 Jeff Skinner YG 40.00 80.00
219 Taylor Hall YG 80.00 200.00
220 Jordan Eberle YG 25.00 60.00
231 P.K. Subban YG 75.00 135.00
240 Sergei Bobrovsky YG 100.00 250.00
456 Tyler Seguin YG 80.00 200.00
472 Jared Spurgeon YG 30.00 80.00

2010-11 Upper Deck French

COMPLETE SET (250) 250.00 400.00
COMP.SER.1 SET w/o SPs (200) 12.00 30.00
*FRENCH: .4X TO 1X BASE
*FRENCH YG: .4X TO 1X BASE
219 Taylor Hall YG 30.00 80.00
220 Jordan Eberle YG 12.00 30.00
223 Brayden Schenn YG 8.00 20.00
231 P.K. Subban YG 15.00 40.00
240 Sergei Bobrovsky YG 20.00 50.00
247 Nazem Kadri YG 10.00 25.00

2010-11 Upper Deck French Red

*FRENCH RED: 10X TO 25X BASE
*FRENCH RED YG: 2X TO 5X BASE
211 Jeff Skinner YG 60.00 120.00
219 Taylor Hall YG 250.00 400.00
220 Jordan Eberle YG 100.00 200.00
224 Kyle Clifford YG 15.00 40.00
231 P.K. Subban YG 75.00 150.00
240 Sergei Bobrovsky YG 80.00 200.00
250 Kadri/Subban/Hall YG CL 50.00 100.00

2010-11 Upper Deck All World Team

COMP.SET w/o SPs (30) 12.00 30.00
AW1 Patrick Kane 2.50 6.00
AW2 Rick Nash 1.25 3.00
AW3 Patrick Marleau 1.25 3.00
AW4 Zach Parise 1.25 3.00
AW5 Roberto Luongo 2.00 5.00
AW6 Alexander Semin 1.25 3.00
AW7 Mike Richards 1.00 2.50
AW8 Nicklas Backstrom 1.25 3.00
AW9 Jarome Iginla 1.50 4.00
AW10 Anze Kopitar 2.00 5.00
AW11 Dany Heatley 1.00 2.50
AW12 Martin St. Louis 1.25 3.00
AW13 Ilya Bryzgalov 1.00 2.50
AW14 Mikko Koivu 1.25 3.00
AW15 Henrik Zetterberg 1.50 4.00
AW16 Joe Thornton 2.00 5.00
AW17 Jeff Carter 1.00 2.50
AW18 Tomas Vokoun 1.00 2.50
AW19 Ryan Miller 1.25 3.00
AW20 Zdeno Chara 1.25 3.00
AW21 Nicklas Lidstrom 1.25 3.00
AW22 Paul Stastny 1.00 2.50
AW23 Drew Doughty 1.50 4.00
AW24 Teemu Selanne 2.50 6.00
AW25 Phil Kessel 1.25 3.00
AW26 Ryan Getzlaf 1.25 3.00
AW27 Daniel Alfredsson 1.25 3.00
AW28 Eric Staal 1.50 4.00
AW29 Bobby Ryan 1.00 2.50
AW30 Marian Hossa 1.25 3.00
AW31 Jonathan Toews SP 4.00 10.00
AW32 Steven Stamkos SP 6.00 15.00
AW33 Henrik Sedin SP 3.00 8.00
AW34 Marian Gaborik SP 2.50 6.00
AW35 Martin Brodeur SP 6.00 15.00
AW36 Pavel Datsyuk SP 4.00 10.00
AW37 Henrik Lundqvist SP 6.00 15.00
AW38 Alexander Ovechkin SP 10.00 25.00
AW39 Ilya Kovalchuk SP 4.00 10.00
AW40 Sidney Crosby SP 10.00 25.00

2010-11 Upper Deck Ambassadors of the Game

COMP.SET w/o SPs (40) 20.00 50.00
COMP.SER.1 SET w/o SPs (20) 10.00 25.00
COMP.SER.2 SET w/o SPs (20) 12.00 30.00
AG1 Adam Foote .75 2.00
AG2 J.P. Dumont .75 2.00
AG3 Jonathan Toews 2.00 5.00
AG4 Ryan Miller 1.25 3.00
AG5 Jose Theodore 1.25 3.00
AG6 Steve Sullivan .75 2.00
AG7 Phil Kessel 1.25 3.00
AG8 Teemu Selanne 2.50 6.00
AG9 Martin St. Louis 1.25 3.00
AG10 Brad Richards 1.25 3.00
AG11 Marty Turco 1.25 3.00
AG12 Vincent Lecavalier 1.25 3.00
AG13 Dustin Brown 1.25 3.00
AG14 Mike Green 1.00 2.50
AG15 Roberto Luongo 2.00 5.00
AG16 Zdeno Chara 1.25 3.00
AG17 Shane Doan 1.00 2.50
AG18 Nicklas Lidstrom 1.25 3.00
AG19 Jamie Langenbrunner .75 2.00
AG20 Don Cherry 1.25 3.00
AG21 Pavel Datsyuk SP 4.00 10.00
AG22 Jarome Iginla SP 3.00 8.00
AG23 Alexander Ovechkin SP 10.00 25.00
AG24 Bobby Orr SP 10.00 25.00
AG25 Sidney Crosby SP 10.00 25.00
AG26 Bobby Clarke SP 4.00 10.00
AG27 Mario Lemieux SP 10.00 25.00
AG28 Steve Yzerman SP 6.00 15.00
AG29 Mark Messier SP 5.00 12.00
AG30 Wayne Gretzky SP 10.00 25.00
AG31 Corey Perry 2.00 5.00
AG32 Patrick Marleau 1.25 3.00
AG33 Bobby Ryan 1.00 2.50
AG34 Jeff Carter 1.00 2.50
AG35 Paul Stastny 1.00 2.50
AG36 Steven Stamkos 2.50 6.00
AG37 Daniel Sedin 1.50 4.00
AG38 Drew Doughty 1.50 4.00
AG39 Jean-Sebastien Giguere 1.25 3.00
AG40 Brian Gionta .75 2.00
AG41 Henrik Zetterberg 1.50 4.00
AG42 Joe Thornton 2.00 5.00
AG43 Eric Staal 1.50 4.00
AG44 Paul Kariya 1.25 3.00
AG45 Mike Richards 1.00 2.50
AG46 Nicklas Backstrom 1.25 3.00
AG47 Zach Parise 1.25 3.00
AG48 Brenden Morrow 1.00 2.50
AG49 Henrik Lundqvist 3.00 8.00
AG50 Daniel Alfredsson 1.25 3.00
AG51 Rick Nash SP 2.50 6.00
AG52 Jonathan Toews SP 4.00 10.00
AG53 Patrick Roy SP 6.00 15.00
AG54 Henrik Sedin SP 3.00 8.00
AG55 Lanny McDonald SP 2.50 6.00
AG56 Martin Brodeur SP 6.00 15.00
AG57 Ray Bourque SP 4.00 10.00
AG58 Cam Neely SP 2.50 6.00
AG59 Bobby Hull SP 5.00 12.00
AG60 Luc Robitaille SP 2.50 6.00

2010-11 Upper Deck Biography of A Season

COMPLETE SET (30) 8.00 20.00
BOS1 Alexander Ovechkin 1.00 2.50
BOS2 Sidney Crosby 1.00 2.50
BOS3 Henrik Sedin .30 .75
BOS4 Steven Stamkos .50 1.25
BOS5 Mike Cammalleri .25 .60
BOS6 Mike Richards .20 .50
BOS7 Patrick Kane .50 1.25
BOS8 Jonathan Toews .40 1.00
BOS9 Taylor Hall .50 1.25
BOS10 Jaroslav Halak .25 .60
BOS11 Carey Price .50 1.25
BOS12 Steven Stamkos .50 1.25
BOS13 Sergei Bobrovsky .75 2.00
BOS14 Daniel Alfredsson .25 .60
BOS15 Ondrej Pavelec .25 .60
BOS16 Tim Thomas .25 .60
BOS17 Milan Lucic .25 .60
BOS18 Sidney Crosby 1.00 2.50
BOS19 Evgeni Malkin .50 1.25
BOS20 Brandon Dubinsky .15 .40
BOS21 Semyon Varlamov .25 .60
BOS22 Zdeno Chara .25 .60
BOS23 Marian Gaborik .25 .60
BOS24 Patrick Sharp .25 .60
BOS25 Johan Franzen .20 .50
BOS26 Miikka Kiprusoff .25 .60
BOS27 Ryan Callahan .15 .40
BOS28 Jarome Iginla .30 .75
BOS29 P.K. Subban .60 1.50
BOS30 Corey Perry .40 1.00

2010-11 Upper Deck Clear Cut Champions

CCCAM Al MacInnis 12.00 30.00
CCCBC Bobby Clarke 12.00 30.00
CCCBH Bobby Hull 15.00 40.00
CCCBL Brian Leetch 6.00 15.00
CCCBO Bobby Orr 25.00 50.00
CCCBP Bernie Parent 8.00 20.00
CCCBR Brad Richards 8.00 20.00
CCCBU Johnny Bucyk 8.00 20.00
CCCCW Cam Ward 8.00 20.00
CCCDP Denis Potvin 8.00 20.00
CCCEM Evgeni Malkin 15.00 40.00
CCCES Eric Staal 8.00 20.00
CCCFM Frank Mahovlich 8.00 20.00
CCCGF Grant Fuhr 12.00 30.00
CCCGH Gordie Howe 12.00 30.00
CCCGL Guy Lafleur 10.00 25.00
CCCHZ Henrik Zetterberg 8.00 20.00
CCCJB Jean Beliveau 12.00 30.00
CCCJK Jari Kurri 8.00 20.00
CCCJM Joe Mullen 6.00 15.00
CCCJO Johnny Bower 8.00 20.00
CCCJT Jonathan Toews 12.00 30.00
CCCLM Lanny McDonald 8.00 20.00
CCCLR Larry Robinson 8.00 20.00
CCCMB Martin Brodeur 15.00 40.00
CCCMI Mike Bossy 8.00 20.00
CCCML Mario Lemieux 30.00 80.00
CCCMM Mark Messier 12.00 30.00
CCCMO Mike Modano 12.00 30.00
CCCNL Nicklas Lidstrom 8.00 20.00
CCCPE Phil Esposito 12.00 30.00
CCCPK Patrick Kane 15.00 40.00
CCCPR Patrick Roy 20.00 50.00
CCCRB Ray Bourque 12.00 30.00
CCCRG Ryan Getzlaf 8.00 20.00
CCCSC Sidney Crosby 30.00 80.00
CCCSM Stan Mikita 8.00 20.00
CCCSN Scott Niedermayer 8.00 20.00
CCCSY Steve Yzerman 15.00 40.00
CCCTL Ted Lindsay 8.00 20.00
CCCVL Vincent Lecavalier 8.00 20.00
CCCWG Wayne Gretzky 40.00 100.00

2010-11 Upper Deck Clear Cut Hall of Fame

CCHBH J.Beliveau/G.Howe 50.00 125.00
CCHBM F.Mahovlich/J.Bucyk 15.00 40.00
CCHBP D.Potvin/M.Bossy 15.00 40.00
CCHDM M.Dionne/L.McDonald 20.00 50.00
CCHEL G.Lafleur/T.Esposito 20.00 50.00
CCHHM S.Mikita/B.Hull 30.00 80.00
CCHKH D.Hawerchuk/J.Kurri 20.00 50.00
CCHLT B.Trottier/M.Lemieux 30.00 80.00
CCHMM M.Messier/A.MacInnis 30.00 80.00
CCHRF G.Fuhr/P.Roy 40.00 100.00
CCHSG P.Stastny/W.Gretzky 100.00 200.00
CCHYR S.Yzerman/L.Robitaille 25.00 60.00

2010-11 Upper Deck Clear Cut Lineage

CCLBOS Orr/Esposito/Bourque 50.00 125.00
CCLCGY Fleury/MacInnis/Iginla 20.00 50.00
CCLCHI Toews/Hull/Kane 25.00 60.00
CCLDET Yzerman/Howe/Zetter 40.00 100.00
CCLLAK Robitlle/Dionne/Gretzky 80.00 200.00
CCLMTL Cammall/Lafleur/Beliveau 15.00 40.00
CCLPHI Carter/Clarke/Richards 20.00 50.00
CCLPIT Crosby/Malkin/Lemieux 50.00 125.00
CCLTOR Mahov/Gilmour/Kessel 15.00 40.00

2010-11 Upper Deck EA Superstars

COMPLETE SET (15) 15.00 40.00
COMP.SET w/o SPs (10) 8.00 20.00
EA1 Jonathan Toews SP 4.00 10.00
EA2 Patrick Kane SP 5.00 12.00
EA3 Dion Phaneuf SP 2.00 5.00
EA4 Jarome Iginla SP 3.00 8.00
EA5 Chris Pronger SP 2.50 6.00
EA6 Milan Lucic 1.25 3.00
EA7 John Tavares 2.00 5.00
EA8 Eric Staal 1.50 4.00
EA9 Nicklas Backstrom 1.25 3.00
EA10 Mark Streit .75 2.00
EA11 Josh Harding 1.25 3.00
EA12 Mikko Koivu 1.25 3.00
EA13 Henrik Sedin 1.50 4.00
EA14 Daniel Sedin 1.50 4.00
EA15 Zach Stortini .75 2.00

2010-11 Upper Deck Game Jerseys

GJAF Alexander Frolov 2.50 6.00
GJAH Adam Hall 2.50 6.00
GJAK Alex Kovalev 3.00 8.00
GJAN Antero Niittymaki 3.00 8.00
GJAO Adam Oates 3.00 8.00
GJAW Andy Wozniewski 2.50 6.00
GJBG Brian Gionta 2.50 6.00
GJBO David Booth 2.50 6.00
GJBR Derick Brassard 2.50 6.00
GJCA Mike Cammalleri 4.00 10.00
GJCD Chris Drury 3.00 8.00
GJCH Jonathan Cheechoo 3.00 8.00
GJDA Daniel Alfredsson 4.00 10.00
GJDB Daniel Briere 4.00 10.00
GJDC Dino Ciccarelli 3.00 8.00
GJDG Doug Gilmour 4.00 10.00
GJDR Derek Roy 2.50 6.00
GJDS Devin Setoguchi 3.00 8.00
GJDT Darcy Tucker 3.00 8.00
GJDU Dustin Brown 4.00 10.00
GJDW Doug Wilson 2.50 6.00
GJEL Patrik Elias 4.00 10.00
GJEM Evgeni Malkin 8.00 20.00
GJFB Francis Bouillon 2.50 6.00
GJFL Marc-Andre Fleury 8.00 20.00
GJFR Michael Frolik 2.50 6.00
GJGB Gilbert Brule 4.00 10.00
GJGL Guillaume Latendresse 3.00 8.00
GJHL Henrik Lundqvist 10.00 25.00
GJHZ Henrik Zetterberg 5.00 12.00
GJIK Ilya Kovalchuk 4.00 10.00
GJJB Jay Bouwmeester 2.50 6.00
GJJC Jeff Carter 3.00 8.00
GJJG Jean-Sebastien Giguere 4.00 10.00
GJJI Jarome Iginla 5.00 12.00
GJJP Jason Pominville 2.50 6.00
GJJT Jeff Tambellini 2.50 6.00
GJJV Jakub Voracek 3.00 8.00
GJKA Anze Kopitar 6.00 15.00
GJKL Kristopher Letang 5.00 12.00
GJKO Andrei Kostitsyn 3.00 8.00
GJLR Luc Robitaille 3.00 8.00
GJLS Luke Schenn 4.00 10.00
GJMA Martin St. Louis 4.00 10.00
GJMC Matt Carle 3.00 8.00
GJMG Marian Gaborik 4.00 10.00
GJMH Marian Hossa 4.00 10.00
GJMJ Milan Jurcina 2.50 6.00
GJMK Miikka Kiprusoff 4.00 10.00
GJMO Mattias Ohlund 2.50 6.00
GJMP Marc-Antoine Pouliot 3.00 8.00
GJMR Mark Recchi 5.00 12.00
GJMS Marek Svatos 2.50 6.00
GJMT Marty Turco 4.00 10.00
GJNA Nik Antropov 3.00 8.00
GJNB Nicklas Backstrom 4.00 10.00
GJNH Nathan Horton 3.00 8.00
GJNI Rob Niedermayer 2.50 6.00
GJOK Kyle Okposo 2.50 6.00
GJOV Alexander Ovechkin 6.00 15.00
GJPE Patrick Eaves 2.50 6.00
GJPK Patrick Kane 8.00 20.00
GJPM Patrick Marleau 4.00 10.00
GJPS Paul Stastny 3.00 8.00
GJRE Ray Emery 3.00 8.00
GJRG Ryan Getzlaf 4.00 10.00
GJRI Mike Richards 3.00 8.00
GJRL Roberto Luongo 6.00 15.00
GJRM Ryan Miller 4.00 10.00
GJRN Rick Nash 4.00 10.00
GJSA Miroslav Satan 3.00 8.00
GJSC Sidney Crosby 8.00 20.00
GJSG Scott Gomez 3.00 8.00
GJSH Shaone Morrisonn 2.50 6.00
GJSM Steve Mason 3.00 8.00
GJSS Steven Stamkos 8.00 20.00
GJST Drew Stafford 2.50 6.00
GJSV Sergei Samsonov 3.00 8.00
GJSW Shea Weber 3.00 8.00
GJTA John Tavares 6.00 15.00
GJTB Todd Bertuzzi 3.00 8.00
GJTF Tomas Fleischmann 2.50 6.00
GJTH Joe Thornton 6.00 15.00
GJTO Jonathan Toews 6.00 15.00
GJTP Tomas Plekanec 2.50 6.00
GJTR Tuomo Ruutu 3.00 8.00
GJTT Tim Thomas 5.00 12.00
GJTV Thomas Vanek 3.00 8.00
GJVL Vincent Lecavalier 4.00 10.00
GJVO Tomas Vokoun 3.00 8.00
GJWE Stephen Weiss 3.00 8.00
GJWG Wayne Gretzky 20.00 50.00
GJZP Zach Parise 4.00 10.00
GJ2AM Andrei Markov 4.00 10.00
GJ2AO Alexander Ovechkin 8.00 20.00
GJ2BD Brandon Dubinsky 2.50 6.00
GJ2CG Claude Giroux 5.00 12.00
GJ2CO Colton Orr 2.50 6.00
GJ2CP Carey Price 6.00 15.00
GJ2CW Cam Ward 4.00 10.00
GJ2DD Drew Doughty 5.00 12.00
GJ2DH Dany Heatley 3.00 8.00
GJ2DP Dustin Penner 2.50 6.00
GJ2GL Georges Laraque 3.00 8.00
GJ2GP George Parros 3.00 8.00
GJ2HE Milan Hejduk 3.00 8.00
GJ2HL Henrik Lundqvist 5.00 12.00
GJ2JH Jonas Hiller 3.00 8.00
GJ2JL Jamie Langenbrunner 2.50 6.00
GJ2JT John Tavares 6.00 15.00
GJ2JV James van Riemsdyk 5.00 12.00
GJ2KV Kris Versteeg 2.50 6.00
GJ2LA Guillaume Latendresse 3.00 8.00
GJ2LE Loui Eriksson 2.50 6.00
GJ2MB Martin Brodeur 4.00 10.00
GJ2MC Matt Carkner 3.00 8.00
GJ2MD Matt Duchene 4.00 10.00
GJ2MG Marian Gaborik 4.00 10.00
GJ2MH Marian Hossa 4.00 10.00
GJ2MS Martin St. Louis 4.00 10.00
GJ2NB Nicklas Backstrom 4.00 10.00
GJ2NL Nicklas Lidstrom 4.00 10.00
GJ2NZ Nikolai Zherdev 2.50 6.00
GJ2PB Patrice Bergeron 5.00 12.00
GJ2PE Patrik Elias 4.00 10.00
GJ2PS Patrick Sharp 4.00 10.00
GJ2RG Ryan Getzlaf 4.00 10.00
GJ2RK Ryan Kesler 4.00 10.00
GJ2RL Roberto Luongo 6.00 15.00
GJ2SC Sidney Crosby 12.00 30.00
GJ2SD Shane Doan 3.00 8.00
GJ2ST Paul Stastny 3.00 8.00
GJ2SV Semyon Varlamov 4.00 10.00
GJ2TM Tyler Myers 2.50 6.00
GJ2TR Tuukka Rask 5.00 12.00
GJ2ZC Zdeno Chara 4.00 10.00

2010-11 Upper Deck Hockey Heroes Bobby Orr

COMPLETE SET (10) 40.00 80.00
COMP.SET w/o SPs (8) 8.00 20.00
COMMON ORR 2.50 6.00
HH18 Bobby Orr Header 15.00 40.00
HHBO Bobby Orr Art 20.00 50.00
HHBOAU Bobby Orr AU 250.00 400.00

2010-11 Upper Deck Hockey Heroes Steve Yzerman

COMPLETE SET (10) 30.00 80.00
COMP.SET w/o SPs (8) 8.00 20.00
COMMON YZERMAN 2.50 6.00
HH9 Steve Yzerman Header 12.00 30.00
HHYZ Steve Yzerman 10.00 25.00

2010-11 Upper Deck Netminders

COMPLETE SET (30) 15.00 40.00
COMP.SET w/o SPs (20) 12.00 30.00
N1 Rick DiPietro 1.25 3.00
N2 Semyon Varlamov 1.50 4.00
N3 Marty Turco 1.50 4.00
N4 Kari Lehtonen 1.25 3.00
N5 Jonathan Quick 2.00 5.00
N6 Craig Anderson 1.50 4.00
N7 Jim Howard 2.00 5.00
N8 Pekka Rinne 1.50 4.00
N9 Jonas Hiller 1.25 3.00
N10 Niklas Backstrom 1.50 4.00
N11 Tomas Vokoun 1.25 3.00
N12 Tuukka Rask 2.00 5.00
N13 Mike Smith 1.50 4.00
N14 Steve Mason 1.25 3.00
N15 Michael Leighton 1.25 3.00
N16 Carey Price 3.00 8.00
N17 Jean-Sebastien Giguere 1.50 4.00
N18 Brian Elliott 1.25 3.00
N19 Jeff Deslauriers 1.00 2.50
N20 Chris Mason 1.25 3.00
N21 Ryan Miller SP 3.00 8.00
N22 Miikka Kiprusoff SP 3.00 8.00
N23 Cam Ward SP 3.00 8.00
N24 Antti Niemi SP 2.50 6.00
N25 Roberto Luongo SP 5.00 12.00
N26 Henrik Lundqvist SP 8.00 20.00
N27 Ilya Bryzgalov SP 2.50 6.00
N28 Marc-Andre Fleury SP 6.00 15.00
N29 Jaroslav Halak SP 3.00 8.00
N30 Martin Brodeur SP 8.00 20.00

2010-11 Upper Deck Oversized

COMPLETE SET (42) 15.00 40.00
OS1 Bobby Ryan .40 1.00
OS2 Ryan Getzlaf .50 1.25
OS3 Zdeno Chara .50 1.25
OS4 Ryan Miller .50 1.25
OS5 Thomas Vanek .40 1.00
OS6 Jarome Iginla .60 1.50
OS7 Miikka Kiprusoff .50 1.25
OS8 Eric Staal .60 1.50
OS9 Jonathan Toews .75 2.00
OS10 Duncan Keith .40 1.00
OS11 Patrick Kane 1.00 2.50
OS12 Antti Niemi .40 1.00
OS13 Matt Duchene .50 1.25
OS14 Paul Stastny .40 1.00
OS15 Rick Nash .50 1.25
OS16 Brad Richards .50 1.25
OS17 Henrik Zetterberg .60 1.50
OS18 Nicklas Lidstrom .50 1.25
OS19 Pavel Datsyuk .75 2.00
OS20 Dustin Penner .30 .75
OS21 Drew Doughty .60 1.50
OS22 Anze Kopitar .75 2.00
OS23 Brian Gionta .30 .75
OS24 Zach Parise .50 1.25
OS25 Martin Brodeur 1.25 3.00
OS26 Ilya Kovalchuk .50 1.25
OS27 John Tavares .75 2.00
OS28 Marian Gaborik .50 1.25
OS29 Mike Richards .40 1.00
OS30 Jeff Carter .40 1.00
OS31 Shane Doan .40 1.00
OS32 Sidney Crosby 2.00 5.00
OS33 Evgeni Malkin 1.00 2.50
OS34 Joe Thornton .75 2.00
OS35 Dany Heatley .40 1.00
OS36 Steven Stamkos 1.00 2.50
OS37 Phil Kessel .50 1.25
OS38 Henrik Sedin .60 1.50
OS39 Roberto Luongo .75 2.00
OS40 Daniel Sedin .60 1.50
OS41 Nicklas Backstrom .50 1.25
OS42 Alexander Ovechkin 2.00 5.00

2010-11 Upper Deck Rookie Breakouts

RB1 Cam Fowler 12.00 30.00
RB2 Alexander Burmistrov 5.00 12.00
RB3 Zach Hamill 5.00 12.00
RB4 Tyler Seguin 15.00 40.00
RB5 Jordan Caron 6.00 15.00
RB6 Henrik Karlsson 5.00 12.00
RB7 Zac Dalpe 6.00 15.00
RB8 Jeff Skinner 12.00 30.00
RB9 Jamie McBain 5.00 12.00
RB10 Nick Leddy 6.00 15.00
RB11 Kevin Shattenkirk 10.00 25.00
RB12 Brandon Yip 5.00 12.00
RB13 Taylor Hall 30.00 80.00
RB14 Magnus Paajarvi 6.00 15.00
RB15 Jordan Eberle 12.00 30.00
RB16 Brayden Schenn 12.00 30.00
RB17 Mattias Tedenby 5.00 12.00
RB18 P.K. Subban 25.00 60.00
RB19 Anders Lindback 5.00 12.00
RB20 Jacob Josefson 5.00 12.00
RB21 Nino Niederreiter 8.00 20.00
RB22 Derek Stepan 6.00 15.00
RB23 Jared Cowen 5.00 12.00
RB24 Sergei Bobrovsky 12.50 30.00
RB25 Oliver Ekman-Larsson 8.00 20.00
RB26 Eric Tangradi 5.00 12.00
RB27 Dustin Tokarski 5.00 12.00
RB28 Dana Tyrell 5.00 12.00
RB29 Nazem Kadri 15.00 40.00
RB30 Marcus Johansson 8.00 20.00

2010-11 Upper Deck Rookie Headliners

COMPLETE SET (30) 20.00 50.00
COMP.SET w/o SPs (20) 12.00 30.00
RH1 Dustin Tokarski .75 2.00
RH2 Kevin Shattenkirk 1.50 4.00
RH3 Nick Leddy 1.00 2.50
RH4 Dana Tyrell .75 2.00
RH5 Anders Lindback .75 2.00
RH6 Oliver Ekman-Larsson 1.25 3.00
RH7 Zac Dalpe 1.00 2.50
RH8 Jacob Josefson .75 2.00
RH9 Marcus Johansson 1.25 3.00
RH10 Zach Hamill .75 2.00
RH11 Jordan Caron 1.00 2.50
RH12 Cam Fowler 2.00 5.00
RH13 Sergei Bobrovsky 3.00 8.00
RH14 Henrik Karlsson .75 2.00
RH15 Jared Cowen .75 2.00
RH16 Jamie McBain .75 2.00
RH17 Eric Tangradi .75 2.00
RH18 Alexander Burmistrov .75 2.00
RH19 Brandon Yip .75 2.00
RH20 Justin Falk .60 1.50
RH21 Derek Stepan SP 1.25 3.00
RH22 Nino Niederreiter SP 1.50 4.00
RH23 Nazem Kadri SP 3.00 8.00
RH24 P.K. Subban SP 3.00 8.00
RH25 Magnus Paajarvi SP 1.25 3.00
RH26 Brayden Schenn SP 2.50 6.00
RH27 Jeff Skinner SP 2.50 6.00
RH28 Jordan Eberle SP 2.50 6.00
RH29 Tyler Seguin SP 3.00 8.00
RH30 Taylor Hall SP 2.50 6.00

2010-11 Upper Deck Rookie Materials

*PATCH/25: 1.2X TO 3X BASE MATERIALS
RMAB Andrew Bodnarchuk 3.00 8.00
RMAK Arturs Kulda 3.00 8.00
RMAL Anders Lindback 3.00 8.00
RMBS Brayden Schenn 8.00 20.00
RMBU Alexander Burmistrov 3.00 8.00
RMBY Brandon Yip 3.00 8.00
RMCA Cody Almond 3.00 8.00
RMCF Cam Fowler 8.00 20.00
RMCW Casey Wellman 3.00 8.00
RMDS Derek Stepan 6.00 15.00
RMDT Dustin Tokarski 3.00 8.00
RMEG Evgeny Grachev 3.00 8.00
RMET Eric Tangradi 3.00 8.00
RMEW Eric Wellwood 4.00 10.00
RMFA Justin Falk 2.50 6.00
RMHK Henrik Karlsson 3.00 8.00
RMIC Ian Cole 3.00 8.00
RMJC Jared Cowen 3.00 8.00
RMJE Jordan Eberle 6.00 15.00
RMJJ Jacob Josefson 3.00 8.00
RMJO Jordan Caron 4.00 10.00
RMJS Jeff Skinner 12.00 30.00
RMKC Kyle Clifford 4.00 10.00
RMKP Kyle Palmieri 6.00 15.00
RMKS Kevin Shattenkirk 6.00 15.00
RMLA Luke Adam 3.00 8.00
RMLS Philip Larsen 3.00 8.00
RMMC Jamie McBain 3.00 8.00
RMMJ Marcus Johansson 5.00 12.00
RMMN Maxim Noreau 2.50 6.00
RMMO Mark Olver 3.00 8.00
RMMP Magnus Paajarvi 4.00 10.00
RMMS Marco Scandella 3.00 8.00
RMMT Mattias Tedenby 3.00 8.00
RMNJ Nick Johnson 2.50 6.00
RMNK Nazem Kadri 6.00 15.00
RMNL Nick Leddy 4.00 10.00
RMNN Nino Niederreiter 5.00 12.00
RMNP Nick Palmieri 3.00 8.00
RMOE Oliver Ekman-Larsson 5.00 12.00
RMPL Alex Plante 3.00 8.00
RMPS P.K. Subban 15.00 40.00
RMSB Sergei Bobrovsky 8.00 20.00
RMTB T.J. Brodie 3.00 8.00
RMTH Taylor Hall 8.00 20.00
RMTS Tyler Seguin 12.00 30.00
RMTW Tommy Wingels 3.00 8.00
RMTY Dana Tyrell 3.00 8.00
RMZD Zac Dalpe 4.00 10.00
RMZH Zach Hamill 3.00 8.00

2010-11 Upper Deck Signature Sensations

SSAB Justin Abdelkader 5.00 12.00
SSAM Andrew MacDonald 4.00 10.00
SSAN Andreas Nodl 4.00 10.00
SSBA David Backes 4.00 10.00
SSBE Patrik Berglund 4.00 10.00
SSBJ Jamie Benn 8.00 20.00
SSBR Brian Salcido 4.00 10.00
SSBS Bobby Sanguinetti 4.00 10.00
SSCG Claude Giroux 12.00 30.00
SSCH Don Cherry 20.00 40.00
SSDB Derick Brassard 4.00 10.00
SSDG Doug Gilmour 30.00 60.00
SSEK Evander Kane 6.00 15.00
SSEL Patrik Elias 6.00 15.00
SSFB Fabian Brunnstrom 4.00 10.00
SSFR Michael Frolik 8.00 20.00
SSGA Marian Gaborik 6.00 15.00
SSGC Guy Carbonneau 5.00 12.00
SSGH Gordie Howe 50.00 100.00
SSGO Scott Gomez 12.00 30.00
SSHE Matt Hendricks 4.00 10.00
SSIV Ivan Vishnevskiy 4.00 10.00
SSJA Jason Arnott 5.00 12.00
SSJC Jeff Carter 15.00 40.00
SSJG Jean-Sebastien Giguere 10.00 25.00
SSJK Jari Kurri 6.00 15.00
SSJL John-Michael Liles 6.00 15.00
SSJR Joel Rechlicz 4.00 10.00
SSJS John Scott 4.00 10.00
SSJT John Tavares 10.00 25.00
SSJV James van Riemsdyk 5.00 12.00
SSKD Kris Draper 4.00 10.00
SSKL Kari Lehtonen 12.00 30.00
SSLE Trevor Lewis 4.00 10.00
SSMB Mike Brodeur 5.00 12.00
SSMD Matt Duchene 6.00 15.00
SSME Matt Ellis 4.00 10.00
SSMF Mark Fraser 4.00 10.00
SSMG Matt Gilroy 4.00 10.00
SSMH Matthew Halischuk 5.00 12.00
SSMI Stan Mikita 12.00 30.00
SSMM Mike Modano 10.00 25.00
SSMP Matt Pelech 4.00 10.00
SSNE John Negrin 5.00 12.00
SSNF Nick Foligno 5.00 12.00
SSNG Nathan Gerbe 4.00 10.00
SSNH Nathan Horton 5.00 12.00
SSNK Nikolai Kulemin 4.00 10.00
SSPA Pascal Leclaire 5.00 12.00
SSPB Patrice Bergeron 40.00 80.00
SSPE Phil Esposito 6.00 15.00
SSPH Patric Hornqvist 12.00 30.00
SSPK Patrick Kane 12.00 30.00
SSPL Perttu Lindgren 4.00 10.00
SSPM Peter Mueller 5.00 12.00
SSPR Peter Regin 8.00 20.00
SSPS Peter Stastny 12.00 30.00
SSRM Ray Macias 4.00 10.00
SSSA Michael Sauer 4.00 10.00
SSSC Sidney Crosby 100.00 200.00
SSSH James Sheppard 4.00 10.00
SSSK Saku Koivu 25.00 50.00
SSSM Spencer Machacek 4.00 10.00
SSSS Steven Stamkos 40.00 100.00
SSSV Sergei Shirokov 5.00 12.00
SSSW Stephen Weiss 5.00 12.00
SSTC Taylor Chorney 5.00 12.00
SSTE Tony Esposito 12.00 30.00
SSTH Joe Thornton 10.00 25.00
SSTK Tomas Kopecky 5.00 12.00
SSTL Jiri Tlusty 4.00 10.00
SSWE Shea Weber 5.00 12.00
SSWG Wayne Gretzky 200.00 500.00
SSYW Yannick Weber 6.00 15.00

2010-11 Upper Deck Signatures

UDSAL Andrew Ladd 4.00 10.00
UDSAN Antti Niemi 5.00 12.00
UDSAO Alexander Ovechkin 40.00 100.00
UDSBD Brandon Dubinsky 4.00 10.00
UDSBE Matt Beleskey 5.00 12.00
UDSBM Brendan Mikkelson 4.00 10.00
UDSBR Brent Seabrook 4.00 10.00
UDSBS Brandon Sutter 4.00 10.00
UDSBV Boris Valabik 6.00 15.00
UDSBY Brandon Yip 10.00 25.00
UDSCA Colby Armstrong 8.00 20.00
UDSCF Cody Franson 4.00 10.00
UDSCH Chris Higgins 4.00 10.00
UDSCK Chuck Kobasew 4.00 10.00
UDSCS Chris Stewart 5.00 12.00
UDSDA Daniel Carcillo 4.00 10.00
UDSDB Dave Bolland 5.00 12.00
UDSDC Dan Cleary 6.00 15.00
UDSDE Derek Stepan 6.00 15.00
UDSDP David Perron 5.00 12.00
UDSDS Drew Stafford 4.00 10.00
UDSEM Evgeni Malkin 20.00 50.00
UDSFR Michael Frolik 4.00 10.00
UDSGL Guillaume Latendresse 5.00 12.00
UDSHL Henrik Lundqvist 15.00 40.00
UDSHO Tomas Holmstrom 10.00 25.00
UDSIK Ilya Kovalchuk 15.00 40.00
UDSJA Jason Arnott 5.00 12.00
UDSJB Josh Bailey 5.00 12.00
UDSJE Jordan Eberle 12.00 30.00
UDSJG Jean-Sebastien Giguere 25.00 60.00
UDSJH Josh Harding 6.00 15.00
UDSJM Jay McClement 4.00 10.00
UDSJP Jason Pominville 4.00 10.00
UDSJS John Scott 4.00 10.00
UDSJT John Tavares 10.00 25.00
UDSJV Jakub Voracek 5.00 12.00
UDSLC Logan Couture 12.00 30.00
UDSLE Lars Eller 15.00 40.00
UDSMD Michael Del Zotto 5.00 12.00
UDSMF Mark Fraser 4.00 10.00
UDSMG Matt Gilroy 4.00 10.00
UDSMI John Mitchell 4.00 10.00
UDSML Maxim Lapierre 4.00 10.00
UDSMN Michal Neuvirth 5.00 12.00
UDSMP Marc-Antoine Pouliot 6.00 15.00
UDSMS Marc Savard 4.00 10.00
UDSND Nigel Dawes 4.00 10.00
UDSNI Peter Mueller 8.00 20.00
UDSNK Nazem Kadri 15.00 40.00
UDSOP Ondrej Pavelec 6.00 15.00
UDSPA Max Pacioretty 6.00 15.00
UDSPL Matt Niskanen 6.00 15.00
UDSPO Patrick O'Sullivan 4.00 10.00
UDSPS P.K. Subban 15.00 40.00
UDSRI Mike Ribeiro 12.00 30.00
UDSSA Bobby Sanguinetti 4.00 10.00
UDSSC Sidney Crosby 100.00 200.00
UDSSH James Sheppard 4.00 10.00
UDSSM Steve Mason 10.00 25.00
UDSST Marc Staal 4.00 10.00
UDSSW Shea Weber 20.00 50.00
UDSTE Tyler Ennis 4.00 10.00
UDSTG T.J. Galiardi 5.00 12.00
UDSTH Taylor Hall 40.00 80.00
UDSTK Tomas Kopecky 8.00 20.00
UDSTL Jiri Tlusty 4.00 10.00
UDSTR Tuukka Rask 10.00 25.00
UDSTS Tom Sestito 4.00 10.00
UDSTW Ty Wishart 4.00 10.00
UDSVS Viktor Stalberg 5.00 12.00
UDSWG Wayne Gretzky 300.00 800.00

2010-11 Upper Deck Winter Classic Oversized

COMPLETE SET (14) 10.00 25.00
WC1 B.Clarke/B.Orr 5.00 12.00
WC2 Zdeno Chara 1.25 3.00
WC3 Patrice Bergeron 1.50 4.00
WC4 Marco Sturm .75 2.00
WC5 Mark Recchi 1.50 4.00
WC6 Shawn Thornton .75 2.00
WC7 David Krejci 1.25 3.00
WC8 Tim Thomas 1.25 3.00
WC9 Danny Syvret .75 2.00
WC10 Jeff Carter 1.00 2.50
WC11 Scott Hartnell .75 2.00
WC12 Mike Richards 1.00 2.50
WC13 Daniel Carcillo .75 2.00
WC14 Michael Leighton 1.00 2.50

2010-11 Upper Deck Young Guns Oversized

OS1 Jordan Eberle 10.00 25.00
OS2 Brayden Schenn 4.00 10.00
OS3 Derek Stepan 2.00 5.00
OS4 Eric Tangradi 2.50 6.00
OS5 Jamie McBain 2.50 6.00
OS6 Jeff Skinner 8.00 20.00
OS7 Jordan Caron 4.00 10.00
OS8 Alexander Burmistrov 1.50 4.00
OS9 Marcus Johansson 2.50 6.00
OS10 Nazem Kadri 5.00 12.00
OS11 P.K. Subban 8.00 20.00
OS12 Sergei Bobrovsky 12.00 30.00
OS13 Zac Dalpe 2.50 6.00
OS14 Taylor Hall 15.00 40.00

2010-11 Upper Deck Stanley Cup Finals

COMPLETE SET (15) 8.00 20.00
SC1B Patrice Bergeron .50 1.25
SC2B Tim Thomas .40 1.00
SC3B Zdeno Chara .40 1.00
SC4B Brad Marchand .75 2.00
SC5B Milan Lucic .40 1.00
SC1V Ryan Kesler .40 1.00
SC2V Roberto Luongo .60 1.50
SC3V Daniel Sedin .50 1.25
SC4V Henrik Sedin .50 1.25
SC5V Alexandre Burrows .25 .60
SC6 Ray Bourque MM .60 1.50
SC7 Wayne Gretzky MM 2.50 6.00
SC8 Patrick Kane MM .75 2.00
SC9 Bobby Orr MM 1.50 4.00
SC10 Alex Ovechkin MM 1.50 4.00

2011-12 Upper Deck

COMP.SERIES 1 (250) 150.00 300.00
COMP.SERIES 2 (250) 125.00 250.00
COMP.SER.1 w/o SPs (200) 10.00 25.00
COMP.SER.2 w/o SPs (200) 10.00 25.00
1 Dustin Byfuglien .30 .75
2 Patrice Cormier .20 .50
3 Tobias Enstrom .20 .50
4 Evander Kane .30 .75
5 Blake Wheeler .30 .75
6 Ondrej Pavelec .30 .75
7 Alexander Semin .30 .75
8 Alexander Ovechkin 1.25 3.00
9 Mike Knuble .20 .50
10 Mike Green .25 .60
11 Michal Neuvirth .25 .60
12 John Carlson .30 .75
13 Henrik Sedin .40 1.00
14 Daniel Sedin .40 1.00
15 Roberto Luongo .50 1.25
16 Ryan Kesler .30 .75
17 Alexander Edler .20 .50
18 Cory Schneider .30 .75
19 Phil Kessel .30 .75
20 Dion Phaneuf .25 .60
21 James Reimer .30 .75
22 Nazem Kadri .40 1.00
23 Clarke MacArthur .20 .50
24 Nikolai Kulemin .20 .50
25 Luke Schenn .30 .75
26 Steven Stamkos .60 1.50
27 Ryan Malone .20 .50
28 Martin St. Louis .30 .75
29 Dwayne Roloson .25 .60
30 Victor Hedman .40 1.00
31 Steve Downie .20 .50
32 Jaroslav Halak .30 .75
33 David Backes .20 .50
34 Patrik Berglund .20 .50
35 Kevin Shattenkirk .20 .50
36 Chris Stewart .25 .60
37 Alexander Steen .20 .50
38 David Perron .25 .60
39 Joe Thornton .50 1.25
40 Patrick Marleau .30 .75
41 Joe Pavelski .40 1.00
42 Antti Niemi .25 .60
43 Dan Boyle .20 .50
44 Logan Couture .40 1.00
45 Ryane Clowe .20 .50
46 Pascal Dupuis .20 .50
47 Jordan Staal .25 .60
48 Kristopher Letang .40 1.00
49 Chris Kunitz .30 .75
50 Marc-Andre Fleury .60 1.50

51 Matt Cooke .20 .50
52 James Neal .20 .50
53 Shane Doan .25 .60
54 Keith Yandle .20 .50
55 Lauri Korpikoski .20 .50
56 Brett MacLean .20 .50
57 Oliver Ekman-Larsson .30 .75
58 Radim Vrbata .20 .50
59 Claude Giroux .30 .75
60 Kimmo Timonen .20 .50
61 Daniel Briere .30 .75
62 Chris Pronger .30 .75
63 James van Riemsdyk .25 .60
64 Braydon Coburn .20 .50
65 Andreas Nodl .20 .50
66 Jason Spezza .30 .75
67 Daniel Alfredsson .30 .75
68 Erik Karlsson .40 1.00
69 Nick Foligno .25 .60
70 Sergei Gonchar .20 .50
71 Bobby Butler .25 .60
72 Peter Regin .20 .50
73 Henrik Lundqvist .75 2.00
74 Marc Staal .20 .50
75 Derek Stepan .20 .50
76 Ryan Callahan .20 .50
77 Brandon Dubinsky .20 .50
78 Mats Zuccarello-Aasen .30 .75
79 Brian Boyle .20 .50
80 John Tavares .50 1.25
81 Michael Grabner .25 .60
82 P.A. Parenteau .20 .50
83 Blake Comeau .20 .50
84 Kyle Okposo .20 .50
85 Josh Bailey .25 .60
86 Al Montoya .20 .50
87 Martin Brodeur .75 2.00
88 Zach Parise .30 .75
89 Travis Zajac .20 .50
90 Mattias Tedenby .20 .50
91 Anton Volchenkov .20 .50
92 David Clarkson .20 .50
93 Patric Hornqvist .20 .50
94 Ryan Suter .25 .60
95 Sergei Kostitsyn .20 .50
96 Pekka Rinne .30 .75
97 Shea Weber .25 .60
98 Mike Fisher .20 .50
99 Carey Price .60 1.50
100 Andrei Kostitsyn .25 .60
101 Scott Gomez .25 .60
102 P.K. Subban .40 1.00
103 Brian Gionta .20 .50
104 Jaroslav Spacek .20 .50
105 Max Pacioretty .30 .75
106 Mikko Koivu .25 .60
107 Cal Clutterbuck .20 .50
108 Nick Schultz .20 .50
109 Pierre-Marc Bouchard .30 .75
110 Guillaume Latendresse .25 .60
111 Matt Cullen .20 .50
112 Marek Zidlicky .20 .50
113 Drew Doughty .40 1.00
114 Dustin Penner .25 .60
115 Rob Scuderi .20 .50
116 Jarret Stoll .25 .60
117 Justin Williams .25 .60
118 Jonathan Quick .40 1.00
119 Jack Johnson .20 .50
120 David Booth .20 .50
121 Stephen Weiss .25 .60
122 Jacob Markstrom .30 .75
123 Mike Santorelli .20 .50
124 Dmitry Kulikov .20 .50
125 Evgeny Dadonov .20 .50
126 Taylor Hall .30 .75
127 Devan Dubnyk .25 .60
128 Sam Gagner .20 .50
129 Magnus Paajarvi .25 .60
130 Linus Omark .30 .75
131 Ryan Whitney .20 .50
132 Theo Peckham .20 .50
133 Nicklas Lidstrom .20 .50
134 Johan Franzen .25 .60
135 Jim Howard .40 1.00
136 Niklas Kronwall .25 .60
137 Justin Abdelkader .25 .60
138 Henrik Zetterberg .40 1.00
139 Darren Helm .20 .50
140 Brenden Morrow .25 .60
141 Kari Lehtonen .25 .60
142 Alex Goligoski .25 .60
143 Mike Ribeiro .20 .50
144 Jamie Benn .30 .75
145 Steve Ott .20 .50
146 Rick Nash .30 .75
147 Kristian Huselius .20 .50
148 Derick Brassard .20 .50
149 Kris Russell .20 .50
150 Antoine Vermette .20 .50
151 R.J. Umberger .20 .50
152 Anton Stralman .20 .50
153 Erik Johnson .20 .50
154 Paul Stastny .25 .60
155 Jay McClement .20 .50
156 Ryan O'Byrne .20 .50
157 David Jones .20 .50
158 Ryan O'Reilly .30 .75
159 Kevin Porter .20 .50
160 Jonathan Toews .50 1.25
161 Patrick Sharp .30 .75
162 Marian Hossa .30 .75
163 Brent Seabrook .20 .50
164 Dave Bolland .25 .60
165 Corey Crawford .40 1.00
166 Duncan Keith .25 .60
167 Jeff Skinner .40 1.00
168 Jamie McBain .20 .50
169 Eric Staal .40 1.00
170 Cam Ward .30 .75
171 Tuomo Ruutu .25 .60
172 Joni Pitkanen .25 .60
173 Jarome Iginla .40 1.00
174 Miikka Kiprusoff .30 .75
175 Rene Bourque .20 .50
176 Matt Stajan .20 .50
177 Anton Babchuk .20 .50
178 Mark Giordano .30 .75
179 Jay Bouwmeester .20 .50
180 Ryan Miller .30 .75
181 Drew Stafford .20 .50
182 Derek Roy .20 .50
183 Tyler Myers .20 .50
184 Tyler Ennis .20 .50
185 Nathan Gerbe .20 .50
186 Jason Pominville .20 .50
187 Tim Thomas .30 .75
188 Zdeno Chara .30 .75
189 Brad Marchand .60 1.50
190 Nathan Horton .30 .75
191 David Krejci .30 .75
192 Dennis Seidenberg .20 .50
193 Milan Lucic .30 .75
194 Corey Perry .50 1.25
195 Lubomir Visnovsky .20 .50
196 Jonas Hiller .25 .60
197 Ryan Getzlaf .30 .75
198 Cam Fowler .30 .75
199 Sedin/Luongo/Kesler CL .40 1.00
200 Lucic/Thomas/Chara CL .25 .60
201 Devante Smith-Pelly YG RC 2.50 6.00
202 Maxime Macenauer YG RC 2.00 5.00
203 Greg Nemisz YG RC 2.00 5.00
204 Roman Horak YG RC 2.00 5.00
205 Justin Faulk YG RC 3.00 8.00
206 Marcus Kruger YG RC 5.00 12.00
207 Brandon Saad YG RC 8.00 20.00
208 Gabriel Landeskog YG RC 15.00 40.00
209 Cameron Gaunce YG RC 1.50 4.00
210 John Moore YG RC 2.00 5.00
211 David Savard YG RC 2.00 5.00
212 Cam Atkinson YG RC 5.00 12.00
213 Tomas Vincour YG RC 2.00 5.00
214 R.Nugent-Hopkins YG RC 30.00 80.00
215 Anton Lander YG RC 2.00 5.00
216 Teemu Hartikainen YG RC 2.00 5.00
217 Erik Gudbranson YG RC 2.50 6.00
218 Brett Bulmer YG RC 2.00 5.00
219 Aaron Palushaj YG RC 2.00 5.00
220 Alexei Yemelin YG RC 2.00 5.00
221 Raphael Diaz YG RC 2.00 5.00
222 Brendon Nash YG RC 2.00 5.00
223 Jonathon Blum YG RC 2.00 5.00
224 Blake Geoffrion YG RC 2.00 5.00
225 Craig Smith YG RC 2.50 6.00
226 Adam Henrique YG RC 5.00 12.00
227 Adam Larsson YG RC 2.50 6.00
228 Tim Erixon YG RC 2.00 5.00
229 Mika Zibanejad YG RC 15.00 40.00
230 Colin Greening YG RC 2.00 5.00
231 Patrick Wiercioch YG RC 2.00 5.00
232 Erik Condra YG RC 2.00 5.00
233 Stephane Da Costa YG RC 2.00 5.00
234 Sean Couturier YG RC 8.00 20.00
235 Matt Read YG RC 2.50 6.00
236 Erik Gustafsson YG RC 2.50 6.00
237 Joe Vitale YG RC 2.00 5.00
238 Harri Sateri YG RC 2.00 5.00
239 Alex Stalock YG 1.50 4.00
240 Brett Connolly YG RC 2.00 5.00
241 Jake Gardiner YG RC 8.00 20.00
242 Joe Colborne YG RC 2.00 5.00
243 Matt Frattin YG RC 2.00 5.00
244 Ben Scrivens YG RC 2.00 5.00
245 Cody Hodgson YG RC 3.00 8.00
246 Yann Sauve YG RC 2.00 5.00
247 Carl Klingberg YG RC 2.00 5.00
248 Mark Scheifele YG RC 20.00 50.00
249 Paul Postma YG RC 2.00 5.00
250 Ngnt-Hpk/Land/Larsn CL 3.00 8.00
251 Alexander Burmistrov .25 .60
252 Nik Antropov .25 .60
253 Eric Fehr .20 .50
254 Chris Mason .25 .60
255 Jim Slater .20 .50
256 Bryan Little .30 .75
257 Andrew Ladd .20 .50
258 Zach Bogosian .25 .60
259 Tomas Vokoun .25 .60
260 Troy Brouwer .20 .50
261 Nicklas Backstrom .30 .75
262 Brooks Laich .20 .50
263 Marcus Johansson .25 .60
264 Roman Hamrlik .20 .50
265 Joel Ward .20 .50
266 John Erskine .25 .60
267 Alexandre Burrows .20 .50
268 Mason Raymond .20 .50
269 Jannik Hansen .25 .60
270 Dan Hamhuis .25 .60
271 Kevin Bieksa .25 .60
272 David Booth .20 .50
273 Manny Malhotra .25 .60
274 Chris Higgins .20 .50
275 John-Michael Liles .20 .50
276 Mikhail Grabovski .20 .50
277 Jonas Gustavsson .30 .75
278 Joffrey Lupul .20 .50
279 Matthew Lombardi .20 .50
280 Tyler Bozak .20 .50
281 Colton Orr .20 .50
282 Vincent Lecavalier .30 .75
283 Teddy Purcell .20 .50
284 Nate Thompson .20 .50
285 Dominic Moore .20 .50
286 Eric Brewer .20 .50
287 Mathieu Garon .25 .60
288 Andy McDonald .25 .60
289 Brian Elliott .25 .60
290 T.J. Oshie .30 .75
291 Jason Arnott .25 .60
292 Jamie Langenbrunner .20 .50
293 Alex Pietrangelo .25 .60
294 Barret Jackman .20 .50
295 Martin Havlat .25 .60
296 Torrey Mitchell .20 .50
297 Brent Burns .30 .75
298 Benn Ferriero .20 .50
299 Michal Handzus .20 .50
300 Thomas Greiss .25 .60
301 Sidney Crosby 1.25 3.00
302 Evgeni Malkin .60 1.50
303 Tyler Kennedy .20 .50
304 Arron Asham .20 .50
305 Paul Martin .20 .50
306 Brent Johnson .25 .60
307 Steve Sullivan .20 .50
308 Mike Smith .30 .75
309 Jason LaBarbera .25 .60
310 Raffi Torres .20 .50
311 Daymond Langkow .20 .50
312 Ray Whitney .25 .60
313 Boyd Gordon .20 .50
314 Martin Hanzal .20 .50
315 Brayden Schenn .30 .75
316 Jaromir Jagr 1.00 2.50
317 Wayne Simmonds .40 1.00
318 Scott Hartnell .20 .50
319 Jakub Voracek .25 .60
320 Maxime Talbot .20 .50
321 Ilya Bryzgalov .30 .75
322 Milan Michalek .20 .50
323 Zenon Konopka .25 .60
324 Craig Anderson .30 .75
325 Jared Cowen .30 .75
326 Alex Auld .25 .60
327 Filip Kuba .20 .50
328 Brad Richards .30 .75
329 Wojtek Wolski .20 .50
330 Marian Gaborik .30 .75
331 Ruslan Fedotenko .20 .50
332 Artem Anisimov .20 .50
333 Martin Biron .25 .60
334 Brandon Prust .20 .50
335 Andrew MacDonald .20 .50
336 Matt Moulson .20 .50
337 Frans Nielsen .20 .50
338 Nino Niederreiter .20 .50
339 Brian Rolston .25 .60
340 Evgeni Nabokov .25 .60
341 Matt Martin (NYI) .20 .50
342 Mark Streit .20 .50
343 Ilya Kovalchuk .30 .75
344 Dainius Zubrus .20 .50
345 Nick Palmieri .25 .60
346 Patrik Elias .30 .75
347 Johan Hedberg .25 .60
348 Andy Greene .20 .50
349 Martin Erat .20 .50
350 Nicklas Bergfors .25 .60
351 Matthew Halischuk .20 .50
352 Colin Wilson .25 .60
353 Nick Spaling .20 .50
354 David Legwand .25 .60
355 Michael Cammalleri .25 .60
356 Tomas Plekanec .20 .50
357 Erik Cole .20 .50
358 Peter Budaj .25 .60
359 Andrei Markov .20 .50
360 Lars Eller .20 .50
361 Travis Moen .20 .50
362 Devin Setoguchi .25 .60
363 Dany Heatley .25 .60
364 Niklas Backstrom .30 .75
365 Darroll Powe .20 .50
366 Nick Johnson .25 .60
367 Josh Harding .30 .75
368 Mike Richards .25 .60
369 Simon Gagne .30 .75
370 Anze Kopitar .50 1.25
371 Jonathan Bernier .25 .60
372 Dustin Brown .30 .75
373 Kyle Clifford .20 .50
374 Scottie Upshall .20 .50
375 Tomas Fleischmann .20 .50
376 Kris Versteeg .20 .50
377 Marcel Goc .25 .60
378 Jack Skille .25 .60
379 Brian Campbell .20 .50
380 Ed Jovanovski .20 .50
381 Jordan Eberle .30 .75
382 Ales Hemsky .25 .60
383 Ryan Smyth .25 .60
384 Nikolai Khabibulin .25 .60
385 Ben Eager .20 .50
386 Tom Gilbert .20 .50
387 Pavel Datsyuk .50 1.25
388 Dan Cleary .30 .75
389 Jonathan Ericsson .20 .50
390 Tomas Holmstrom .20 .50
391 Ty Conklin .25 .60
392 Valtteri Filppula .20 .50
393 Jakub Kindl .20 .50
394 Loui Eriksson .20 .50
395 Sheldon Souray .20 .50
396 Michael Ryder .20 .50
397 Toby Petersen .20 .50
398 Stephane Robidas .20 .50
399 Andrew Raycroft .25 .60
400 Jeff Carter .25 .60
401 Steve Mason .25 .60
402 Fedor Tyutin .20 .50
403 Vaclav Prospal .20 .50
404 Matt Calvert .20 .50
405 James Wisniewski .20 .50
406 Matt Duchene .30 .75
407 Jean-Sebastien Giguere .30 .75
408 Semyon Varlamov .30 .75
409 Milan Hejduk .25 .60
410 Kyle Quincey .20 .50
411 Patrick Kane .60 1.50
412 Michael Frolik .20 .50
413 Andrew Brunette .20 .50
414 Niklas Hjalmarsson .20 .50
415 Ray Emery .25 .60
416 Anthony Stewart .20 .50
417 Jussi Jokinen .20 .50
418 Zach Boychuk .20 .50
419 Zac Dalpe .20 .50
420 Brandon Sutter .20 .50
421 Jiri Tlusty .20 .50
422 Olli Jokinen .25 .60
423 Mikael Backlund .25 .60
424 David Moss .20 .50
425 Lee Stempniak .20 .50
426 Curtis Glencross .20 .50
427 Henrik Karlsson .25 .60
428 Cory Sarich .20 .50
429 Brad Boyes .20 .50
430 Ville Leino .25 .60
431 Luke Adam .25 .60
432 Thomas Vanek .25 .60
433 Robyn Regehr .20 .50
434 Christian Ehrhoff .20 .50
435 Jordan Leopold .20 .50
436 Tuukka Rask .40 1.00
437 Rich Peverley .30 .75
438 Patrice Bergeron .40 1.00
439 Daniel Paille .20 .50
440 Tyler Seguin .40 1.00
441 Shawn Thornton .20 .50
442 Chris Kelly .25 .60
443 Gregory Campbell .20 .50
444 Bobby Ryan .25 .60
445 Teemu Selanne .60 1.50
446 Andrew Cogliano .20 .50
447 George Parros .25 .60
448 Luca Sbisa .25 .60
449 Rinne/Quick/Backstrom CL .40 1.00
450 Miller/Lundqvist/Vokoun CL .75 2.00
451 Pat Maroon YG RC 8.00 20.00
452 Peter Holland YG RC 2.50 6.00
453 Corey Tropp YG RC 2.50 6.00
454 Brayden McNabb YG RC 2.50 6.00
455 Zack Kassian YG RC 5.00 12.00
456 Marcus Foligno YG RC 6.00 15.00
457 Joe Finley YG RC 2.50 6.00
458 T.J. Brennan YG RC 2.50 6.00
459 Leland Irving YG RC 2.50 6.00
460 Riley Nash YG RC 2.50 6.00
461 Mike Murphy YG RC 2.50 6.00
462 Jimmy Hayes YG RC 3.00 8.00
463 Brad Malone YG RC 2.50 6.00
464 Stefan Elliott YG RC 2.50 6.00
465 Ryan Johansen YG RC 8.00 20.00
466 Jordie Benn YG RC 2.50 6.00
467 Brendan Smith YG RC 2.50 6.00
468 Gustav Nyquist YG RC 6.00 15.00
469 Joakim Andersson YG RC 2.50 6.00
470 Colten Teubert YG RC 2.50 6.00
471 Viatcheslav Voynov YG RC 2.50 6.00
472 Jarod Palmer YG RC 2.50 6.00
473 David McIntyre YG RC 2.50 6.00
474 Kris Fredheim YG RC 2.50 6.00
475 Frederic St. Denis YG RC 2.50 6.00
476 Louis Leblanc YG RC 5.00 12.00
477 Gabriel Bourque YG RC 2.50 6.00
478 Roman Josi YG RC 15.00 40.00
479 Ryan Ellis YG RC 5.00 12.00
480 Mattias Ekholm YG RC 12.00 30.00
481 David Ullstrom YG RC 2.50 6.00
482 Anders Nilsson YG RC 2.50 6.00
483 Calvin de Haan YG RC 2.50 6.00
484 Carl Hagelin YG RC 5.00 12.00
485 Stu Bickel YG RC 2.50 6.00
486 Harry Zolnierczyk YG RC 2.50 6.00
487 Zac Rinaldo YG RC 2.50 6.00
488 Kevin Marshall YG RC 2.50 6.00
489 Marc-Andre Bourdon YG RC 2.50 6.00
490 David Rundblad YG RC 2.50 6.00
491 Andy Miele YG RC 2.50 6.00
492 Carl Sneep YG RC 2.50 6.00
493 Simon Despres YG RC 2.50 6.00
494 Robert Bortuzzo YG RC 2.50 6.00
495 Cade Fairchild YG RC 2.00 5.00
496 Bill Sweatt YG RC 2.50 6.00
497 Eddie Lack YG RC 2.50 6.00
498 Dmitry Orlov YG RC 6.00 15.00
499 Cody Eakin YG RC 5.00 12.00
500 Leblnc/Kass/Johan CL 4.00 10.00

2011-12 Upper Deck Exclusives

*VETS 1-200/251-400: 6X TO 15X BASE
*YG 201-250: 1.2X TO 3X BASE
*YG 401-450: 1X TO 2.5X BASE
165 Corey Crawford 5.00 12.00
208 Gabriel Landeskog YG 80.00 200.00
214 Ryan Nugent-Hopkins YG 100.00 250.00
225 Craig Smith YG 15.00 40.00
226 Adam Henrique YG 20.00 50.00
227 Adam Larsson YG 20.00 50.00
229 Mika Zibanejad YG 40.00 100.00
234 Sean Couturier YG 25.00 60.00
235 Matt Read YG 20.00 50.00
240 Brett Connolly YG 10.00 25.00
245 Cody Hodgson YG 15.00 40.00
247 Carl Klingberg YG 6.00 15.00
248 Mark Scheifele YG 100.00 250.00
261 Nicklas Backstrom 4.00 10.00
453 Corey Tropp YG 6.00 15.00
459 Leland Irving YG 6.00 15.00
464 Stefan Elliott YG 6.00 15.00
468 Gustav Nyquist YG 40.00 80.00
476 Louis Leblanc YG 20.00 50.00
478 Roman Josi YG 125.00 300.00
484 Carl Hagelin YG 20.00 50.00
485 Stu Bickel YG 6.00 15.00

2011-12 Upper Deck All World Team

COMP.SET w/o SPs (30) 12.00 30.00
AW1 Alexander Semin 1.25 3.00
AW2 Antti Niemi 1.00 2.50
AW3 Anze Kopitar 2.00 5.00
AW4 Carey Price 2.50 6.00
AW5 Corey Perry 2.00 5.00
AW6 Daniel Sedin 1.50 4.00
AW7 David Krejci 1.25 3.00
AW8 Drew Doughty 1.50 4.00
AW9 Duncan Keith 1.00 2.50
AW10 Dustin Byfuglien 1.25 3.00
AW11 Henrik Sedin 1.50 4.00
AW12 Henrik Zetterberg 1.50 4.00
AW13 Jaroslav Halak 1.25 3.00
AW14 John Tavares 2.00 5.00
AW15 Jonas Hiller 1.00 2.50
AW16 Jonathan Quick 1.50 4.00
AW17 Marian Gaborik 1.25 3.00
AW18 Marian Hossa 1.25 3.00
AW19 Martin Brodeur 3.00 8.00
AW20 Mats Zuccarello-Aasen 1.25 3.00
AW21 Mikko Koivu 1.00 2.50
AW22 Nicklas Backstrom 1.25 3.00
AW23 Patrick Kane 2.50 6.00
AW24 Patrick Marleau 1.25 3.00
AW25 Paul Stastny 1.00 2.50
AW26 Phil Kessel 1.25 3.00
AW27 Ryan Kesler 1.25 3.00
AW28 Ryan Miller 1.25 3.00
AW29 Shea Weber 1.00 2.50
AW30 Victor Hedman 1.50 4.00
AW31 Zdeno Chara SP 2.50 6.00
AW32 Tim Thomas SP 2.50 6.00
AW33 Steven Stamkos SP 5.00 12.00
AW34 Sidney Crosby SP 10.00 25.00
AW35 Roberto Luongo SP 4.00 10.00
AW36 Nicklas Lidstrom SP 1.50 4.00
AW37 Miikka Kiprusoff SP 2.50 6.00
AW38 Jonathan Toews SP 4.00 10.00
AW39 Henrik Lundqvist SP 6.00 15.00
AW40 Alexander Ovechkin SP 10.00 25.00

2011-12 Upper Deck Biography of A Season

COMPLETE SET (30) 6.00 15.00
BOS1 Tim Thomas .30 .75
BOS2 Ryan Nugent-Hopkins 1.00 2.50
BOS3 Bruins Champions/Z.Chara .30 .75
BOS4 Corey Perry .50 1.25
BOS5 Nicklas Lidstrom .20 .50
BOS6 Jeff Skinner .40 1.00
BOS7 Jaromir Jagr 1.00 2.50
BOS8 Mike Richards .25 .60
BOS9 Mike Modano .50 1.25
BOS10 Back In Winnipeg/N.Antropov.25 .60
BOS11 Phil Kessel .30 .75
BOS12 Jonathan Quick .40 1.00
BOS13 Joffrey Lupul .20 .50
BOS14 Tyler Seguin .40 1.00
BOS15 Ryan Nugent-Hopkins 1.00 2.50
BOS16 Sidney Crosby 1.25 3.00
BOS17 Jonathan Toews .50 1.25
BOS18 Zdeno Chara .30 .75
BOS19 Jimmy Howard .40 1.00
BOS30 Steven Stamkos .60 1.50
BOS29 Evgeni Malkin .60 1.50
BOS28 Ilya Bryzgalov .30 .75
BOS27 Ryan Miller .30 .75
BOS26 Henrik Zetterberg .40 1.00
BOS25 Sam Gagner .20 .50
BOS24 Marian Gaborik .30 .75
BOS23 Shane Doan .25 .60
BOS22 Jarome Iginla .40 1.00
BOS21 Henrik Lundqvist .75 2.00
BOS20 Claude Giroux .30 .75

2011-12 Upper Deck Buyback Autographs

AO A.Ovechkin 05-06 PP/21 75.00 150.00

2011-12 Upper Deck Canvas

COMP.SER.1 w/o SPs (90) 100.00 200.00
C1 Ryan Getzlaf 1.00 2.50
C2 Bobby Ryan .75 2.00
C3 Jonas Hiller .75 2.00
C4 Cam Fowler 1.00 2.50
C5 Zdeno Chara 1.00 2.50
C6 Tuukka Rask 1.25 3.00
C7 Patrice Bergeron 1.25 3.00
C8 Dennis Seidenberg .60 1.50
C9 Brad Marchand 2.00 5.00
C10 Nathan Horton 1.00 2.50
C11 Thomas Vanek .75 2.00
C12 Ryan Miller 1.00 2.50
C13 Tyler Myers .60 1.50
C14 Drew Stafford .60 1.50
C15 Rene Bourque .60 1.50
C16 Jarome Iginla 1.25 3.00
C17 Jay Bouwmeester .60 1.50
C18 Miikka Kiprusoff 1.00 2.50
C19 Matt Stajan .60 1.50
C20 Eric Staal 1.25 3.00
C21 Cam Ward 1.00 2.50
C22 Jussi Jokinen .60 1.50
C23 Jonathan Toews 1.50 4.00
C24 Patrick Kane 2.00 5.00
C25 Marian Hossa 1.00 2.50
C26 Duncan Keith .75 2.00
C27 Matt Duchene 1.00 2.50
C28 Paul Stastny .75 2.00
C29 Rick Nash 1.00 2.50
C30 Steve Mason .75 2.00
C31 Kari Lehtonen .75 2.00
C32 Mike Ribeiro .60 1.50
C33 Brenden Morrow .75 2.00
C34 Jim Howard 1.25 3.00
C35 Henrik Zetterberg 1.25 3.00
C36 Pavel Datsyuk 1.50 4.00
C37 Nicklas Lidstrom .60 1.50
C38 Stephen Weiss .75 2.00
C39 Drew Doughty 1.25 3.00
C40 Jonathan Quick 1.25 3.00
C41 Anze Kopitar 1.50 4.00
C42 Mikko Koivu .75 2.00
C43 Niklas Backstrom 1.00 2.50
C44 Guillaume Latendresse .75 2.00
C45 Tomas Plekanec .60 1.50
C46 Carey Price 2.00 5.00
C47 Michael Cammalleri .75 2.00
C48 Pekka Rinne 1.00 2.50
C49 Patric Hornqvist .60 1.50
C50 Shea Weber .75 2.00
C51 Martin Brodeur 2.50 6.00
C52 Zach Parise 1.00 2.50
C53 Ilya Kovalchuk 1.00 2.50
C54 Kyle Okposo .60 1.50
C55 John Tavares 1.50 4.00
C56 Henrik Lundqvist 2.50 6.00
C57 Marian Gaborik 1.00 2.50
C58 Sean Avery .75 2.00
C59 Jason Spezza 1.00 2.50
C60 Chris Pronger 1.00 2.50
C61 Daniel Briere 1.00 2.50
C62 Scott Hartnell .60 1.50
C63 Claude Giroux 1.00 2.50
C64 Shane Doan .75 2.00
C65 Jordan Staal .75 2.00
C66 Evgeni Malkin 2.00 5.00
C67 Marc-Andre Fleury 2.00 5.00
C68 Joe Thornton 1.50 4.00
C69 Joe Pavelski 1.25 3.00
C70 Patrick Marleau 1.00 2.50
C71 Antti Niemi .75 2.00
C72 Jaroslav Halak 1.00 2.50
C73 Patrik Berglund .60 1.50
C74 David Backes .60 1.50
C75 Kevin Shattenkirk .60 1.50
C76 Steven Stamkos 2.00 5.00
C77 Vincent Lecavalier 1.00 2.50
C78 Dion Phaneuf .75 2.00
C79 Phil Kessel 1.00 2.50
C80 Roberto Luongo 1.50 4.00
C81 Daniel Sedin 1.25 3.00
C82 Henrik Sedin 1.25 3.00
C83 Alexandre Burrows .60 1.50
C84 Michal Neuvirth .75 2.00
C85 Alexander Ovechkin 4.00 10.00
C86 Nicklas Backstrom 1.00 2.50
C87 Mike Green .75 2.00
C88 Dustin Byfuglien 1.00 2.50
C89 Evander Kane 1.00 2.50
C90 Crosby/Ovechkin/Stamkos CL 3.00 8.00
C91 Devante Smith-Pelly YG 5.00 12.00
C92 Greg Nemisz YG 4.00 10.00
C93 Justin Faulk YG 6.00 15.00
C94 Marcus Kruger YG 6.00 15.00
C95 Brandon Saad YG 8.00 20.00
C96 John Moore YG 4.00 10.00
C97 Ryan Johansen YG 12.00 30.00
C98 Ryan Nugent-Hopkins YG 25.00 60.00
C99 Anton Lander YG 4.00 10.00
C100 Teemu Hartikainen YG 4.00 10.00
C101 Brett Bulmer YG 4.00 10.00
C102 Aaron Palushaj YG 4.00 10.00
C103 Raphael Diaz YG 4.00 10.00
C104 Jonathon Blum YG 4.00 10.00
C105 Blake Geoffrion YG 4.00 10.00
C106 Craig Smith YG 6.00 15.00
C107 Adam Henrique YG 10.00 25.00
C108 Mika Zibanejad YG 20.00 50.00
C109 Sean Couturier YG 10.00 25.00
C110 Matt Read YG 5.00 12.00
C111 Erik Gustafsson YG 5.00 12.00
C112 Harri Sateri YG 4.00 10.00
C113 Brett Connolly YG 4.00 10.00
C114 Jake Gardiner YG 6.00 15.00
C115 Joe Colborne YG 4.00 10.00
C116 Matt Frattin YG 4.00 10.00
C117 Cody Hodgson YG 15.00 40.00
C118 Carl Klingberg YG 4.00 10.00
C119 Mark Scheifele YG 25.00 60.00
C120 Ngnt-Hpk/Cnlly/Ctrier CL 10.00 25.00
C121 Corey Perry 1.50 4.00
C122 Teemu Selanne 2.00 5.00
C123 David Krejci 1.00 2.50
C124 Milan Lucic 1.00 2.50
C125 Tim Thomas 1.00 2.50
C126 Tyler Seguin 1.25 3.00
C127 Derek Roy .60 1.50
C128 Luke Adam .75 2.00
C129 Nathan Gerbe .60 1.50
C130 Tyler Ennis .60 1.50
C131 Mark Giordano 1.00 2.50
C132 Rene Bourque .60 1.50
C133 Jamie McBain .60 1.50
C134 Jeff Skinner 1.25 3.00
C135 Tomas Kaberle .60 1.50
C136 Brent Seabrook .60 1.50
C137 Corey Crawford 1.25 3.00
C138 Patrick Sharp 1.00 2.50
C139 Erik Johnson .60 1.50
C140 Antoine Vermette .60 1.50
C141 Derick Brassard .60 1.50
C142 Jeff Carter .75 2.00
C143 Jamie Benn 1.00 2.50
C144 Sheldon Souray .60 1.50
C145 Steve Ott .60 1.50
C146 Dan Cleary 1.00 2.50
C147 Johan Franzen .75 2.00
C148 Valtteri Filppula .60 1.50
C149 Jordan Eberle 1.00 2.50
C150 Magnus Paajarvi .75 2.00
C151 Taylor Hall 2.50 6.00
C152 Jose Theodore 1.00 2.50
C153 Jacob Markstrom 1.00 2.50
C154 Kris Versteeg .60 1.50
C155 Mike Richards .75 2.00
C156 Simon Gagne 1.00 2.50
C157 Cal Clutterbuck .60 1.50
C158 Dany Heatley .75 2.00
C159 Devin Setoguchi .75 2.00
C160 Brian Gionta .60 1.50
C161 P.K. Subban 1.25 3.00
C162 Mike Fisher .60 1.50
C163 Ryan Suter .75 2.00
C164 Sergei Kostitsyn .60 1.50
C165 Mattias Tedenby .60 1.50
C166 Jacob Josefson .60 1.50
C167 Travis Zajac .60 1.50
C168 Al Montoya .60 1.50
C169 Evgeni Nabokov .75 2.00
C170 Michael Grabner .75 2.00
C171 P.A. Parenteau .60 1.50
C172 Brad Richards 1.00 2.50
C173 Ryan Callahan .60 1.50
C174 Daniel Alfredsson 1.00 2.50
C175 Erik Karlsson 1.25 3.00
C176 Robin Lehner .75 2.00
C177 Brayden Schenn 1.00 2.50
C178 Ilya Bryzgalov 1.00 2.50
C179 Jaromir Jagr 3.00 8.00
C180 Maxime Talbot .60 1.50
C181 Lauri Korpikoski .60 1.50
C182 Oliver Ekman-Larsson 1.00 2.50
C183 James Neal .60 1.50
C184 Kristopher Letang 1.25 3.00
C185 Sidney Crosby 4.00 10.00
C186 Brent Burns 1.00 2.50
C187 Dan Boyle .60 1.50
C188 Logan Couture 1.25 3.00
C189 Martin Havlat .75 2.00
C190 Ryane Clowe .60 1.50
C191 Jason Arnott .75 2.00
C192 T.J. Oshie 1.00 2.50
C193 Martin St. Louis 1.00 2.50
C194 Steve Downie .60 1.50
C195 Victor Hedman 1.25 3.00
C196 Colton Orr .60 1.50
C197 James Reimer 1.00 2.50
C198 Nikolai Kulemin .60 1.50
C199 Cory Schneider 1.00 2.50
C200 David Booth .60 1.50
C201 Ryan Kesler 1.00 2.50
C202 Alexander Semin 1.00 2.50
C203 Marcus Johansson .75 2.00
C204 Michal Neuvirth .75 2.00
C205 Nicklas Backstrom 1.00 2.50
C206 Tomas Vokoun .75 2.00
C207 Alexander Burmistrov .75 2.00
C208 Tobias Enstrom .60 1.50
C209 Ondrej Pavelec 1.00 2.50
C210 Lngo/Thms/Prce CL 1.50 4.00
C211 Cody Eakin YG 8.00 20.00
C212 Dmitry Orlov YG 12.00 30.00
C213 Eddie Lack YG 5.00 12.00
C214 Ben Scrivens YG 5.00 12.00
C215 Simon Despres YG 5.00 12.00
C216 David Rundblad YG 5.00 12.00
C217 Andy Miele YG 5.00 12.00
C218 Colin Greening YG 5.00 12.00
C219 Calvin de Haan YG 5.00 12.00
C220 David Ullstrom YG 5.00 12.00
C221 Adam Larsson YG 6.00 15.00
C222 Ryan Ellis YG 10.00 25.00
C223 Louis Leblanc YG 12.00 30.00
C224 Viatcheslav Voynov YG 5.00 12.00
C225 Erik Gudbranson YG 6.00 15.00
C226 Colten Teubert YG 5.00 12.00
C227 Lennart Petrell YG 6.00 15.00
C228 Brendan Smith YG 8.00 20.00
C229 Gustav Nyquist YG 12.50 30.00
C230 Stefan Elliott YG 5.00 12.00
C231 Gabriel Landeskog YG 25.00 60.00
C232 Andrew Shaw YG 15.00 40.00
C233 Riley Nash YG 5.00 12.00
C234 Mike Murphy YG 5.00 12.00
C235 Leland Irving YG 5.00 12.00
C236 Zack Kassian YG 6.00 15.00
C237 Marcus Foligno YG 8.00 20.00
C238 Brayden McNabb YG 5.00 12.00
C239 Peter Holland YG 5.00 12.00
C240 Lnde/Kssn/Leblnc CL 10.00 25.00
C241 Wayne Gretzky RET 40.00 100.00
C242 Mario Lemieux RET 25.00 50.00
C243 Mark Messier RET 25.00 60.00
C244 Patrick Roy RET 25.00 50.00
C245 Paul Coffey RET 12.00 30.00
C246 Pelle Lindbergh RET 15.00 40.00
C247 Bobby Orr RET 25.00 60.00
C248 Eric Lindros RET 20.00 50.00
C249 Joe Sakic RET 10.00 25.00
C250 Jean Beliveau RET 15.00 30.00
C251 Dave Schultz RET 12.00 30.00
C252 Curtis Joseph RET 12.00 30.00
C253 Tony Twist RET 12.00 30.00
C254 Doug Gilmour RET 15.00 40.00
C255 Brett Hull RET 25.00 60.00
C256 Adam Henrique POE 15.00 40.00
C257 Brett Connolly POE 12.00 30.00
C258 Calvin de Haan POE 10.00 25.00
C259 Cody Eakin POE 12.00 30.00
C260 Cody Hodgson POE 12.00 30.00
C261 Colten Teubert POE 10.00 25.00
C262 Erik Gudbranson POE 12.00 30.00
C263 Ryan Ellis POE 20.00 50.00
C264 Louis Leblanc POE 12.00 30.00
C265 Mark Scheifele POE 20.00 50.00
C266 Ryan Johansen POE 12.00 30.00
C267 Ryan Nugent-Hopkins POE 30.00 80.00
C268 Sean Couturier POE 15.00 40.00
C269 Simon Despres POE 12.00 30.00
C270 Zack Kassian POE 12.00 30.00

2011-12 Upper Deck Canvas Autographs

BO Bobby Orr/66 175.00 300.00
CP Carey Price/31 50.00 100.00

2011-12 Upper Deck Clear Cut Foundations

CCF1 R.Getzlaf/C.Perry 30.00 80.00
CCF2 Z.Chara/T.Thomas 40.00 80.00
CCF3 D.Roy/R.Miller 20.00 50.00
CCF4 Kiprusoff/Iginla 25.00 60.00
CCF5 E.Staal/J.Skinner 25.00 60.00
CCF6 J.Toews/P.Kane 40.00 100.00
CCF7 Stastny/Duchene 30.00 80.00
CCF8 S.Mason/R.Nash 20.00 50.00
CCF9 Morrow/Goligoski 15.00 40.00
CCF10 Datsyuk/Zetterberg 25.00 60.00
CCF11 J.Eberle/T.Hall 40.00 100.00
CCF12 Markstrom/Weiss 30.00 80.00
CCF13 Doughty/Kopitar 30.00 80.00
CCF14 Backstrom/M.Koivu 40.00 100.00
CCF15 C.Price/P.Subban 40.00 100.00
CCF16 P.Rinne/S.Weber 25.00 60.00
CCF17 Z.Parise/M.Brodeur 25.00 60.00
CCF18 Tavares/Moulson 25.00 60.00
CCF19 Gaborik/Lundqvist 50.00 120.00
CCF20 J.Spezza/E.Karlsson 30.00 60.00
CCF21 D.Briere/C.Giroux 20.00 50.00
CCF22 Doan/Ekman-Lrssn 25.00 60.00
CCF23 S.Crosby/E.Malkin 80.00 200.00
CCF24 Marleau/Thornton 30.00 80.00
CCF25 J.Halak/D.Backes 20.00 50.00
CCF26 Stamkos/St. Louis 25.00 60.00
CCF27 D.Phaneuf/P.Kessel 25.00 60.00
CCF28 R.Kesler/R.Luongo 40.00 80.00
CCF29 Ovechkin/A.Semin 80.00 200.00
CCF30 D.Byfuglien/E.Kane 40.00 80.00

2011-12 Upper Deck Clear Cut Honoured Members

HOF1 Bobby Orr 40.00 80.00
HOF2 Ray Bourque 12.00 30.00
HOF3 Phil Esposito 12.00 30.00
HOF4 Johnny Bucyk 8.00 20.00
HOF5 Milt Schmidt 6.00 15.00
HOF6 Gilbert Perreault 8.00 20.00
HOF7 Bobby Hull 15.00 40.00
HOF8 Stan Mikita 10.00 25.00
HOF9 Tony Esposito 8.00 20.00
HOF10 Alex Delvecchio 8.00 20.00
HOF11 Igor Larionov 8.00 20.00
HOF12 Gordie Howe 25.00 60.00
HOF13 Ted Lindsay 8.00 20.00
HOF14 Paul Coffey 8.00 20.00
HOF15 Wayne Gretzky 50.00 125.00
HOF16 Jari Kurri 8.00 20.00
HOF17 Grant Fuhr 12.00 30.00
HOF18 Glenn Anderson 6.00 15.00
HOF19 Ron Francis 10.00 25.00
HOF20 Marcel Dionne 10.00 25.00

HOF21 Luc Robitaille 8.00 20.00
HOF22 Dino Ciccarelli 8.00 20.00
HOF23 Patrick Roy 20.00 50.00
HOF24 Jean Beliveau 8.00 20.00
HOF25 Guy Lafleur 10.00 25.00
HOF26 Larry Robinson 8.00 20.00
HOF27 Steve Shutt 8.00 20.00
HOF28 Mike Bossy 8.00 20.00
HOF29 Denis Potvin 8.00 20.00
HOF30 Brian Leetch 6.00 15.00
HOF31 Mark Messier 15.00 40.00
HOF32 Andy Bathgate 8.00 20.00
HOF33 Bobby Clarke 12.00 30.00
HOF34 Bill Barber 8.00 20.00
HOF35 Mario Lemieux 25.00 50.00
HOF36 Brett Hull 15.00 40.00
HOF37 Doug Gilmour 10.00 25.00
HOF38 Darryl Sittler 10.00 25.00
HOF39 Borje Salming 8.00 20.00
HOF40 Johnny Bower 8.00 20.00
HOF41 Red Kelly 8.00 20.00
HOF42 Dale Hawerchuk 10.00 25.00

2011-12 Upper Deck Day With the Cup

DC1 Nathan Horton 50.00 100.00
DC2 Tomas Kaberle 50.00 100.00
DC3 David Krejci 60.00 120.00
DC4 Zdeno Chara 60.00 120.00
DC5 Tuukka Rask 60.00 120.00
DC6 Shawn Thornton 60.00 120.00
DC7 Daniel Paille 60.00 120.00
DC8 Rich Peverley 50.00 100.00
DC9 Gregory Campbell 50.00 100.00
DC10 Tyler Seguin 75.00 150.00
DC11 Marc Savard 50.00 100.00
DC12 Chris Kelly 40.00 80.00
DC13 Patrice Bergeron 150.00 300.00
DC14 Dennis Seidenberg 50.00 100.00
DC15 Cam Neely 50.00 120.00
DC16 Mark Recchi 50.00 100.00
DC17 Milan Lucic 40.00 100.00
DC18 Shane Hnidy 60.00 120.00
DC19 John Boychuk 50.00 100.00
DC20 Tim Thomas 50.00 120.00
DC21 Steve Kampfer 40.00 80.00
DC22 Adam McQuaid 50.00 100.00
DC23 Brad Marchand 50.00 100.00
DC24 Michael Ryder 50.00 100.00
DC25 Andrew Ference 50.00 100.00

2011-12 Upper Deck EA Ultimate Team

COMPLETE SET (15) 8.00 20.00
EA1 Steven Stamkos 3.00 8.00
EA2 Drew Doughty 1.50 4.00
EA3 Daniel Sedin 1.50 4.00
EA4 Henrik Sedin 1.50 4.00
EA5 Jonathan Toews 2.00 5.00
EA6 Patrick Kane 2.50 6.00
EA7 Duncan Keith 1.00 2.50
EA8 Milan Lucic 1.25 3.00
EA9 Corey Perry 2.00 5.00
EA10 Tyler Seguin 1.50 4.00
EA11 Taylor Hall 1.25 3.00
EA12 Dion Phaneuf 1.00 2.50
EA13 Mark Streit .75 2.00
EA14 Jarret Stoll 1.00 2.50
EA15 Jonathan Quick 1.50 4.00

2011-12 Upper Deck Game Jerseys

GJAB Alexandre Burrows E 2.50 6.00
GJAM Andrei Markov F 2.50 6.00
GJAO Alexander Ovechkin 1 B 12.00 30.00
GJAP Alex Pietrangelo F 3.00 8.00
GJAS Alexander Semin E 4.00 10.00
GJBJ Brent Johnson F 4.00 10.00
GJBM Brendan Morrison F 2.50 6.00
GJBO Jay Bouwmeester D 2.50 6.00
GJBR Bobby Ryan E 3.00 8.00
GJBY Dustin Byfuglien E 4.00 10.00
GJCA Craig Anderson F 4.00 10.00
GJCG Claude Giroux E 4.00 10.00
GJCM Clarke MacArthur E 2.50 6.00
GJCP Carey Price C 8.00 20.00
GJCS Chris Stewart 1 F 3.00 8.00
GJDB Daniel Briere E 4.00 10.00
GJDD Drew Doughty E 5.00 12.00
GJDH Dale Hawerchuk F 5.00 12.00
GJDP Dion Phaneuf E 3.00 8.00
GJDS Daniel Sedin F 5.00 12.00
GJDU Dustin Brown 1 C 4.00 10.00
GJEM Evgeni Malkin B 8.00 20.00
GJES Eric Staal D 5.00 12.00
GJHE Milan Hejduk A 50.00 100.00
GJHI Jonas Hiller F 3.00 8.00
GJHL Henrik Lundqvist D 10.00 25.00
GJHS Henrik Sedin B 12.00 30.00
GJIK Ilya Kovalchuk D 4.00 10.00
GJJB Jamie Benn D 4.00 10.00
GJJC Jeff Carter 1 C 3.00 8.00
GJJE Jordan Eberle B 8.00 20.00
GJJF Johan Franzen D 3.00 8.00
GJJG Jean-Sebastien Giguere 1 F 4.00 10.00
GJJH Jim Howard F 5.00 12.00
GJJI Jarome Iginla C 8.00 20.00
GJJO John Carlson D 4.00 10.00
GJJQ Jonathan Quick E 6.00 15.00
GJJS Jason Spezza 1 C 4.00 10.00
GJJT Jonathan Toews 1 B 12.00 30.00
GJVA James van Riemsdyk 1 D 3.00 8.00
GJKE Phil Kessel E 4.00 10.00
GJKL Kristopher Letang D 5.00 12.00
GJKO Anze Kopitar E 6.00 15.00
GJKS Kevin Shattenkirk D 2.50 6.00
GJLE Lars Eller E 2.50 6.00
GJLS Luke Schenn 1 C 4.00 10.00
GJMB Martin Brodeur D 10.00 25.00
GJMC Mike Commodore E 3.00 8.00
GJMD Matt Duchene 1 E 4.00 10.00
GJMF Marc-Andre Fleury C 5.00 12.00
GJMG Mike Green D 3.00 8.00
GJMH Marian Hossa E 4.00 10.00
GJMK Miikka Kiprusoff D 8.00 20.00
GJMR Mike Richards D 3.00 8.00
GJMS Martin St. Louis B 12.00 30.00
GJMW Mike Weber D 2.50 6.00
GJNG Nathan Gerbe 1 D 2.50 6.00
GJNH Nathan Horton E 4.00 10.00
GJNK Nikolai Kulemin E 2.50 6.00
GJNL Nicklas Lidstrom 1 C 8.00 20.00
GJOK Kyle Okposo F 2.50 6.00
GJOP Ondrej Pavelec D 4.00 10.00
GJPA Paul Stastny D 3.00 8.00
GJPB Patrik Berglund D 2.50 6.00
GJPD Dustin Penner B 4.00 10.00
GJPE Corey Perry B 5.00 12.00
GJPF Peter Forsberg F 8.00 20.00
GJPI Pierre-Marc Bouchard D 4.00 10.00
GJPK Patrick Kane D 8.00 20.00
GJPR Chris Pronger 1 F 4.00 10.00
GJPS P.K. Subban B 5.00 12.00
GJRB Rene Bourque F 2.50 6.00
GJRG Ryan Getzlaf D 4.00 10.00
GJRI Brad Richards E 4.00 10.00
GJRK Ryan Kesler D 4.00 10.00
GJRL Roberto Luongo 1 E 6.00 15.00
GJRM Ryan Miller 1 F 4.00 10.00
GJRS Ryan Smyth F 3.00 8.00
GJSB Sergei Bobrovsky E 6.00 15.00
GJSC Sidney Crosby 1 B 15.00 40.00
GJSE Tyler Seguin B 10.00 25.00
GJSG Simon Gagne F 4.00 10.00
GJSH Scott Hartnell 1 E 2.50 6.00
GJSJ Jordan Staal F 3.00 8.00
GJSM Steve Mason F 3.00 8.00
GJSS Steven Stamkos A 50.00 100.00
GJST Drew Stafford 1 F 2.50 6.00
GJSV Semyon Varlamov 1 F 4.00 10.00
GJSW Stephen Weiss E 3.00 8.00
GJTE Tyler Ennis F 2.50 6.00
GJTH Taylor Hall A 40.00 80.00
GJTP Tomas Plekanec E 2.50 6.00
GJTR Tuukka Rask F 5.00 12.00
GJTV Thomas Vanek 1 F 3.00 8.00
GJTZ Travis Zajac 1 E 2.50 6.00
GJVL Vincent Lecavalier F 4.00 10.00
GJVO Tomas Vokoun F 3.00 8.00
GJWG Wayne Gretzky A 125.00 250.00
GJZC Zdeno Chara 1 F 4.00 10.00
GJZP Zach Parise E 4.00 10.00
GJ2AE Alexander Edler C 2.50 6.00
GJ2AH Ales Hemsky B 5.00 12.00
GJ2AO Alexander Ovechkin 2 A 50.00 100.00
GJ2AT Alex Tanguay B 2.50 6.00
GJ2AV Antoine Vermette C 2.50 6.00
GJ2BB Brian Boyle B 4.00 10.00
GJ2BD Brandon Dubinsky B 2.50 6.00
GJ2BR Dustin Brown 2 B 5.00 12.00
GJ2CA Jeff Carter 2 B 3.00 8.00
GJ2CP Chris Pronger 2 B 4.00 10.00
GJ2CS Chris Stewart 2 B 3.00 8.00
GJ2DB Derick Brassard C 2.50 6.00
GJ2DK David Krejci B 4.00 10.00
GJ2DR Derek Roy C 2.50 6.00
GJ2ED Evgeny Dadonov C 2.50 6.00
GJ2GP George Parros C 3.00 8.00
GJ2JA Jason Arnott B 3.00 8.00
GJ2JB Josh Bailey B 3.00 8.00
GJ2JG Jean-Sebastien Giguere 2 C 4.00 10.00
GJ2JJ Jack Johnson B 2.50 6.00
GJ2JL John-Michael Liles C 3.00 8.00
GJ2JP Jason Pominville B 2.50 6.00
GJ2JS Jason Spezza 2 C 4.00 10.00
GJ2JT Jonathan Toews 2 A 75.00 150.00
GJ2JV Jakub Voracek B 3.00 8.00
GJ2KL Kari Lehtonen B 3.00 8.00
GJ2KV Kris Versteeg B 2.50 6.00
GJ2LE Loui Eriksson B 2.50 6.00
GJ2LS Luke Schenn 2 C 4.00 10.00
GJ2MC Matt Carkner B 3.00 8.00
GJ2MD Matt Duchene 2 C 4.00 10.00
GJ2MF Michael Frolik B 2.50 6.00
GJ2MS Marc Staal B 2.50 6.00
GJMT Marty Turco C 4.00 10.00
GJ2NB Nicklas Backstrom C 4.00 10.00
GJ2NF Nikita Filatov C 2.50 6.00
GJ2NG Nathan Gerbe 2 C 2.50 6.00
GJ2NL Nicklas Lidstrom 2 B 2.50 6.00
GJ2HL Roberto Luongo 2 A 75.00 150.00
GJ2RM Ryan Miller 2 B 4.00 10.00
GJ2SC Sidney Crosby 2 A 12.00 30.00
GJ2SE Devin Setoguchi B 3.00 8.00
GJ2SH Scott Hartnell 2 B 2.50 6.00
GJ2SO Steve Ott B 2.50 6.00
GJ2ST Drew Stafford 2 B 2.50 6.00
GJ2SV Semyon Varlamov 2 C 4.00 10.00
GJ2TV Thomas Vanek 2 B 3.00 8.00
GJ2TZ Travis Zajac 2 B 3.00 8.00
GJ2VA James van Riemsdyk 2 B 3.00 8.00
GJ2ZC Zdeno Chara 2 B 4.00 10.00

2011-12 Upper Deck Game Jerseys Patches

*PATCH/15: 1.2X TO 3X BASIC JSY
GJHE Milan Hejduk 25.00 50.00
GJJE Jordan Eberle 25.00 60.00
GJJT Jonathan Toews 25.00 60.00
GJMK Miikka Kiprusoff 15.00 40.00
GJNL Nicklas Lidstrom 20.00 50.00
GJSC Sidney Crosby 40.00 80.00
GJSE Tyler Seguin 30.00 60.00
GJSS Steven Stamkos 25.00 60.00
GJWG Wayne Gretzky 175.00 300.00
GJ2JT Jonathan Toews 25.00 60.00
GJ2NB Nicklas Backstrom 12.00 30.00
GJ2SC Sidney Crosby 40.00 80.00

2011-12 Upper Deck Hockey Heroes

COMP.SER.1 w/o SPs (12) 8.00 20.00
HH1 Johnny Bower 1.00 2.50
HH2 Gump Worsley 1.00 2.50
HH3 Andy Bathgate 1.00 2.50
HH4 Bobby Hull 2.00 5.00
HH5 Johnny Bucyk 1.00 2.50
HH6 Milt Schmidt .75 2.00
HH7 Alex Delvecchio 1.00 2.50
HH8 Terry Sawchuk 1.00 2.50
HH9 Gordie Howe 3.00 8.00
HH10 Red Kelly 1.00 2.50
HH11 Ted Lindsay 1.00 2.50
HH12 Jean Beliveau 1.00 2.50
HH13 Hull/Howe/Bathgt ART 15.00 40.00
HH14 Bobby Hull 2.00 5.00
HH15 Stan Mikita 1.25 3.00
HH16 Phil Esposito 1.50 4.00
HH17 Bobby Orr 4.00 10.00
HH18 Brad Park .75 2.00
HH19 Alex Delvecchio 1.00 2.50
HH20 Red Kelly 1.00 2.50
HH21 Terry Sawchuk 1.00 2.50
HH22 Johnny Bower 1.00 2.50
HH23 Rogie Vachon 1.25 3.00
HH24 Gump Worsley 1.00 2.50
HH25 Jean Beliveau 1.00 2.50
HH26 B.Hull/S.Mikita ART 15.00 30.00
HDR2 Hockey Heroes '60S Header 12.00 30.00
HDR1 Hockey Heroes '50S Header 12.00 30.00

2011-12 Upper Deck Hockey Heroes Autographs

HH1 Johnny Bower 125.00 200.00
HH3 Andy Bathgate 60.00 120.00
HH4 Bobby Hull 75.00 135.00
HH5 Johnny Bucyk 75.00 150.00
HH6 Milt Schmidt 100.00 200.00
HH7 Alex Delvecchio 60.00 120.00
HH9 Gordie Howe 200.00 300.00
HH10 Red Kelly 50.00 100.00
HH11 Ted Lindsay 100.00 200.00
HH12 Jean Beliveau 100.00 200.00
HH15 Stan Mikita/15 50.00 100.00
HH16 Phil Esposito/15 50.00 100.00
HH17 Bobby Orr/15 250.00 400.00
HH19 Alex Delvecchio/15 60.00 100.00
HH20 Red Kelly/15 50.00 100.00
HH22 Johnny Bower/15 40.00 80.00

2011-12 Upper Deck Oversized

OS1 Tim Thomas 1.50 4.00
OS2 Jonathan Toews 2.50 6.00
OS3 Rick Nash 1.50 4.00
OS4 Nicklas Lidstrom 1.00 2.50
OS5 Henrik Zetterberg 2.00 5.00
OS6 Taylor Hall 1.50 4.00
OS7 Carey Price 3.00 8.00
OS8 P.K. Subban 2.00 5.00
OS9 Zach Parise 1.50 4.00
OS10 John Tavares 2.50 6.00
OS11 Henrik Lundqvist 4.00 10.00
OS12 Steven Stamkos 3.00 8.00
OS13 Roberto Luongo 2.50 6.00
OS14 Alexander Ovechkin 6.00 15.00

2011-12 Upper Deck Rookie Breakouts

RBAH Adam Henrique 12.00 30.00
RBAL Adam Larsson 8.00 20.00
RBAP Aaron Palushaj 6.00 15.00
RBBC Brett Connolly 6.00 15.00
RBBG Blake Geoffrion 6.00 15.00
RBCH Cody Hodgson 20.00 50.00
RBCK Carl Klingberg 20.00 50.00
RBCS Craig Smith 8.00 20.00
RBDR David Rundblad 6.00 15.00
RBDS Devante Smith-Pelly 8.00 20.00
RBEG Erik Gudbranson 8.00 20.00
RBGL Gabriel Landeskog 20.00 50.00
RBGN Greg Nemisz 6.00 15.00
RBJC Joe Colborne 6.00 15.00
RBJG Jake Gardiner 10.00 25.00
RBMF Matt Frattin 6.00 15.00
RBMK Marcus Kruger 10.00 25.00
RBMR Matt Read 8.00 20.00
RBMS Mark Scheifele 25.00 60.00
RBMZ Mika Zibanejad 20.00 50.00
RBRJ Ryan Johansen 20.00 50.00
RBRN Ryan Nugent-Hopkins 75.00 150.00
RBSC Sean Couturier 20.00 50.00
RBTH Teemu Hartikainen 6.00 15.00

2011-12 Upper Deck Rookie Materials

*PATCH/25: 1.2X TO 3X BASIC JSY
RMAH Adam Henrique 6.00 15.00
RMAL Adam Larsson 4.00 10.00
RMAP Aaron Palushaj 3.00 8.00
RMBC Brett Connolly 3.00 8.00
RMBG Blake Geoffrion 3.00 8.00
RMBH Ben Holmstrom 3.00 8.00
RMBS Brandon Saad 6.00 15.00
RMCA Cam Atkinson 8.00 20.00
RMCE Cody Eakin 5.00 12.00
RMCG Colin Greening 3.00 8.00
RMCH Cody Hodgson 8.00 20.00
RMDP Simon Despres 3.00 8.00
RMDR David Rundblad 3.00 8.00
RMDS Devante Smith-Pelly 4.00 10.00
RMEG Erik Gudbranson 3.00 8.00
RMGL Gabriel Landeskog 6.00 15.00
RMGN Greg Nemisz 3.00 8.00
RMHS Harri Sateri 3.00 8.00
RMJB Jonathon Blum 3.00 8.00
RMJF Justin Faulk 5.00 12.00
RMJG Jake Gardiner 5.00 12.00
RMJM John Moore 3.00 8.00
RMLA Anton Lander 3.00 8.00
RMLL Louis Leblanc 3.00 8.00
RMLP Lennart Petrell 4.00 10.00
RMMK Marcus Kruger 5.00 12.00
RMMZ Mika Zibanejad 5.00 12.00
RMPW Patrick Wiercioch 3.00 8.00
RMRH Roman Horak 3.00 8.00
RMRJ Ryan Johansen 10.00 25.00
RMRN Ryan Nugent-Hopkins 8.00 20.00
RMSC Sean Couturier 6.00 15.00
RMTE Tim Erixon 3.00 8.00
RMVV Viatcheslav Voynov 3.00 8.00
RMZK Zack Kassian 5.00 12.00

2011-12 Upper Deck Signatures

UDSAL Andrew Ladd C 10.00 25.00
UDSAS Alex Stalock B 5.00 12.00
UDSBA Josh Bailey B 4.00 10.00
UDSBM Brett MacLean A 10.00 25.00
UDSCH Cody Hodgson A 30.00 60.00
UDSCO Cal O'Reilly C 6.00 15.00
UDSDP Dion Phaneuf A 10.00 25.00
UDSGL Gabriel Landeskog A 25.00 50.00
UDSJM Jacob Markstrom A 8.00 20.00
UDSJN James Neal B 12.00 30.00
UDSJO Johnny Oduya C 6.00 15.00
UDSJS James Sheppard C 5.00 12.00
UDSLK Lauri Korpikoski C 5.00 12.00
UDSML Maxim Lapierre C 10.00 25.00
UDSNH Ryan Nugent-Hopkins A 200.00 300.00
UDSPA Daniel Paille A 15.00 40.00
UDSPK Patrick Kane A 20.00 40.00
UDSPO Patrick O'Sullivan B 5.00 12.00
UDSRJ Ryan Jones A 10.00 25.00
UDSTM Thomas McCollum B 5.00 12.00
UDSWG Wayne Gretzky A 200.00 500.00

2011-12 Upper Deck Signature Sensations

SSAC Andrew Cogliano B 4.00 10.00
SSAK Arturs Kulda C 4.00 10.00
SSAN Antti Niemi B 5.00 12.00
SSAO Alexander Ovechkin A 60.00 120.00
SSAS Alex Stalock C 4.00 10.00
SSAT Alex Tanguay A 4.00 10.00
SSBB Butch Bouchard A 10.00 25.00
SSBE Jamie Benn B 8.00 20.00
SSBF Benn Ferriero C 4.00 10.00
SSBJ Johnny Bower B 6.00 15.00
SSBM Brett MacLean C 4.00 10.00
SSBN Brandon Sutter C 4.00 10.00
SSBO Brian Boyle C 4.00 10.00
SSBW Blake Wheeler C 10.00 25.00
SSCH Cody Hodgson B 50.00 100.00
SSCS Chris Stewart B 5.00 12.00
SSDA David Backes B 4.00 10.00
SSDB Dustin Byfuglien B 12.00 30.00
SSDG Doug Gilmour A 60.00 120.00
SSDR Kris Draper B 4.00 10.00
SSEE Erik Ersberg B 4.00 10.00
SSEK Erik Karlsson B 30.00 60.00
SSEN Tyler Ennis B 8.00 20.00
SSFR Mark Fraser B 10.00 25.00
SSGH Gordie Howe A 40.00 80.00
SSGU Jonas Gustavsson B 8.00 20.00
SSHA Taylor Hall A 40.00 80.00
SSIL Igor Larionov A 6.00 15.00
SSJB Jay Bouwmeester B 4.00 10.00
SSJF Johan Franzen B 20.00 40.00
SSJG Jean-Sebastien Giguere A 10.00 25.00
SSJM John Moore B 5.00 12.00
SSJN John Negrin C 5.00 12.00
SSJO Jim O'Brien C 6.00 15.00
SSJP Jason Pominville B 4.00 10.00
SSJS Jordan Staal B 8.00 20.00
SSJT John Tavares A 10.00 25.00
SSKA Evander Kane B 6.00 15.00
SSKD Kaspars Daugavins C 4.00 10.00
SSKS Kevin Shattenkirk C 8.00 20.00
SSKT Kyle Turris B 4.00 10.00
SSLM Lanny McDonald A 12.00 30.00
SSLR Luc Robitaille A 40.00 80.00
SSLS Luke Schenn B 6.00 15.00
SSMA Jacob Markstrom C 12.00 30.00
SSMD Matt Duchene B 6.00 15.00
SSMF Michael Frolik B 4.00 10.00
SSMI Mike Iggulden C 4.00 10.00
SSMM Mark Messier A 60.00 120.00
SSMN Michal Neuvirth B 5.00 12.00
SSMR Mike Ribeiro B 4.00 10.00
SSMT Mattias Tedenby C 4.00 10.00
SSMZ Mats Zuccarello-Aasen B 6.00 15.00
SSNB Niclas Bergfors C 5.00 12.00
SSNH Nathan Horton B 6.00 15.00
SSNK Nazem Kadri B 12.50 30.00
SSPA Patrick Marleau A 10.00 25.00
SSPB Patrice Bergeron A 40.00 80.00
SSPK Patrick Kane A 12.50 30.00
SSPM Peter Mueller B 8.00 20.00
SSPS Peter Stastny A 10.00 25.00
SSRB Richard Brodeur B 20.00 50.00
SSRI Rick MacLeish B 8.00 20.00
SSRK Ryan Kesler B 12.00 30.00
SSRM Ryan McDonagh C 4.00 10.00
SSRY Michael Rydor A 10.00 25.00
SSSB Steve Bernier B 4.00 10.00
SSSC Sidney Crosby A 100.00 200.00
SSSG Scott Gomez B 5.00 12.00
SSSN Scott Niedermayer A 10.00 25.00
SSSS Steven Stamkos A 20.00 40.00
SSSU Brent Sutter B 4.00 10.00
SSSW Shea Weber C 8.00 20.00
SSSY Steve Yzerman A 60.00 120.00
SSTA Maxime Talbot C 4.00 10.00
SSTE Tobias Enstrom C 4.00 10.00
SSTG T.J. Galiardi B 8.00 20.00
SSTH Joe Thornton A 8.00 20.00
SSTM Tyler Myers B 4.00 10.00
SSTP Teddy Purcell B 8.00 20.00
SSTT Tomas Tatar C 4.00 10.00
SSWC Wendel Clark A 40.00 100.00
SSWG Wayne Gretzky A 400.00 1000.00

2011-12 Upper Deck Winter Classic Oversized

COMPLETE SET (14) 15.00 40.00
WC1 Sidney Crosby 5.00 12.00
WC2 Alexander Ovechkin 5.00 12.00
WC3 Evgeni Malkin 2.50 6.00
WC4 Alexander Semin 1.25 3.00
WC5 Jordan Staal 1.00 2.50
WC6 Nicklas Backstrom 1.25 3.00
WC7 Marc-Andre Fleury 2.50 6.00
WC8 Semyon Varlamov 1.25 3.00
WC9 Maxime Talbot .75 2.00
WC10 Mike Knuble .75 2.00
WC11 Kristopher Letang 1.50 4.00
WC12 John Erskine 1.00 2.50
WC13 Michael Rupp .75 2.00
WC14 Eric Fehr .75 2.00

2011-12 Upper Deck Young Guns Oversized

YG1 Devante Smith-Pelly 2.00 5.00
YG2 Greg Nemisz 1.50 4.00
YG3 Brandon Saad 3.00 8.00
YG4 Marcus Kruger 2.50 6.00
YG5 Gabriel Landeskog 15.00 40.00
YG6 Ryan Nugent-Hopkins 25.00 60.00
YG7 Erik Gudbranson 2.00 5.00
YG8 Adam Larsson 2.00 5.00
YG9 Adam Henrique 4.00 10.00
YG10 Mika Zibanejad 5.00 12.00
YG11 Sean Couturier 3.00 8.00
YG12 Brett Connolly 1.50 4.00
YG13 Cody Hodgson 2.50 6.00
YG14 Mark Scheifele 6.00 15.00

2012-13 Upper Deck

COMP.SET w/o RC's (200) 10.00 25.00
1 Saku Koivu .30 .75
2 Teemu Selanne .60 1.50
3 Francois Beauchemin .20 .50
4 Cam Fowler .30 .75
5 Ryan Getzlaf .30 .75
6 Luca Sbisa .25 .60
7 Jonas Hiller .25 .60
8 Zdeno Chara .30 .75
9 David Krejci .30 .75
10 Shawn Thornton .20 .50
11 Tuukka Rask .40 1.00
12 Brad Marchand .60 1.50
13 Tyler Seguin .40 1.00
14 Rich Peverley .30 .75
15 Christian Ehrhoff .20 .50
16 Ville Leino .25 .60
17 Drew Stafford .20 .50
18 Ryan Miller .30 .75
19 Luke Adam .25 .60
20 Tyler Myers .20 .50
21 Jason Pominville .20 .50
22 Miikka Kiprusoff .30 .75
23 Alex Tanguay .25 .60
24 Jay Bouwmeester .20 .50
25 Michael Cammalleri .25 .60
26 Curtis Glencross .20 .50
27 Jarome Iginla .40 1.00
28 Eric Staal .40 1.00
29 Jeff Skinner .40 1.00
30 Cam Ward .30 .75
31 Anthony Stewart .20 .50
32 Joni Pitkanen .25 .60
33 Tuomo Ruutu .25 .60
34 Dave Bolland .25 .60
35 Jonathan Toews .50 1.25
36 Brent Seabrook .20 .50
37 Marian Hossa .30 .75
38 Ray Emery .25 .60
39 Patrick Sharp .30 .75
40 Marcus Kruger .20 .50
41 Ryan O'Reilly .30 .75
42 Milan Hejduk .25 .60
43 Gabriel Landeskog .40 1.00
44 Paul Stastny .25 .60
45 Erik Johnson .20 .50
46 Semyon Varlamov .30 .75
47 R.J. Umberger .20 .50
48 James Wisniewski .20 .50
49 Jack Johnson .20 .50
50 Derek Dorsett .20 .50
51 Nikita Nikitin .20 .50
52 Ryan Johansen .25 .60
53 Kari Lehtonen .25 .60
54 Stephane Robidas .20 .50
55 Alex Goligoski .20 .50
56 Brenden Morrow .25 .60
57 Jamie Benn .30 .75
58 Michael Ryder .20 .50
59 Johan Franzen .25 .60
60 Nicklas Lidstrom .30 .75
61 Valtteri Filppula .20 .50
62 Dan Cleary .30 .75
63 Henrik Zetterberg .40 1.00
64 Niklas Kronwall .25 .60
65 Ian White .25 .60
66 Ryan Nugent-Hopkins .40 1.00
67 Ryan Whitney .20 .50
68 Nikolai Khabibulin .30 .75
69 Shawn Horcoff .20 .50
70 Jordan Eberle .30 .75
71 Ales Hemsky .25 .60
72 Kris Versteeg .20 .50
73 Dmitry Kulikov .20 .50
74 Tomas Fleischmann .20 .50
75 Jose Theodore .30 .75
76 Brian Campbell .20 .50
77 Sean Bergenheim .20 .50
78 Mike Richards .25 .60
79 Jonathan Quick .40 1.00
80 Jeff Carter .25 .60
81 Simon Gagne .30 .75
82 Dwight King .25 .60
83 Drew Doughty .40 1.00
84 Dustin Brown .30 .75
85 Niklas Backstrom .25 .60
86 Matt Cullen .20 .50
87 Mikko Koivu .25 .60
88 Pierre-Marc Bouchard .30 .75
89 Dany Heatley .25 .60
90 Cal Clutterbuck .20 .50
91 Max Pacioretty .30 .75
92 P.K. Subban .40 1.00
93 Lars Eller .20 .50
94 Brian Gionta .20 .50
95 Louis Leblanc .20 .50
96 Tomas Plekanec .20 .50
97 David Desharnais .20 .50
98 Shea Weber .25 .60
99 Patric Hornqvist .20 .50
100 Gabriel Bourque .25 .60
101 Mike Fisher .20 .50
102 Ryan Ellis .20 .50
103 Martin Erat .20 .50
104 Martin Brodeur .75 2.00
105 Ilya Kovalchuk .30 .75
106 Adam Larsson .30 .75
107 Adam Henrique .25 .60
108 Bryce Salvador .20 .50
109 Henrik Tallinder .20 .50
110 Patrik Elias .30 .75
111 Matt Moulson .20 .50
112 Kyle Okposo .20 .50
113 Nino Niederreiter .20 .50
114 Evgeni Nabokov .25 .60
115 Mark Streit .20 .50
116 John Tavares .50 1.25
117 Marian Gaborik .30 .75
118 Carl Hagelin .20 .50
119 Michael Del Zotto .20 .50
120 Ryan Callahan .20 .50
121 Marc Staal .20 .50
122 Henrik Lundqvist .75 2.00
123 Brian Boyle .20 .50
124 Derek Stepan .20 .50
125 Milan Michalek .20 .50
126 Craig Anderson .30 .75
127 Sergei Gonchar .20 .50
128 Daniel Alfredsson .30 .75
129 Kyle Turris .20 .50
130 Erik Karlsson .40 1.00
131 Chris Neil .20 .50
132 Sean Couturier .25 .60
133 Wayne Simmonds .40 1.00
134 Brayden Schenn .30 .75
135 Maxime Talbot .20 .50
136 Daniel Briere .30 .75
137 Claude Giroux .30 .75
138 Scott Hartnell .20 .50
139 Oliver Ekman-Larsson .30 .75
140 Mike Smith .30 .75
141 Antoine Vermette .20 .50
142 Mikkel Boedker .20 .50
143 Keith Yandle .20 .50
144 Martin Hanzal .20 .50
145 Radim Vrbata .20 .50
146 Kris Letang .40 1.00
147 Marc-Andre Fleury .60 1.50
148 Paul Martin .20 .50
149 Chris Kunitz .30 .75
150 Matt Cooke .20 .50
151 Sidney Crosby 1.25 3.00
152 James Neal .20 .50
153 Patrick Marleau .30 .75
154 Ryane Clowe .20 .50
155 Dan Boyle .20 .50
156 Brent Burns .30 .75
157 Michal Handzus .20 .50
158 Martin Havlat .25 .60
159 Joe Pavelski .40 1.00
160 Patrik Berglund .20 .50
161 David Backes .20 .50
162 David Perron .25 .60
163 Kevin Shattenkirk .20 .50
164 Andy McDonald .25 .60
165 Alex Pietrangelo .25 .60
166 Brian Elliott .25 .60
167 Ryan Malone .20 .50
168 Steven Stamkos .60 1.50
169 Marc-Andre Bergeron .20 .50
170 Victor Hedman .40 1.00
171 Mathieu Garon .25 .60
172 Vincent Lecavalier .30 .75
173 Brett Connolly .20 .50
174 James Reimer .30 .75
175 Dion Phaneuf .25 .60
176 Mikhail Grabovski .20 .50
177 Mike Komisarek .25 .60
178 Jake Gardiner .20 .50
179 Phil Kessel .30 .75
180 Alexandre Burrows .20 .50
181 Kevin Bieksa .25 .60
182 Ryan Kesler .30 .75
183 Cory Schneider .30 .75
184 Dan Hamhuis .25 .60
185 David Booth .20 .50
186 Daniel Sedin .40 1.00
187 Karl Alzner .20 .50
188 Braden Holtby .40 1.00
189 John Carlson .30 .75
190 Brooks Laich .20 .50
191 Mike Green .25 .60
192 Marcus Johansson .25 .60
193 Mark Stuart .20 .50
194 Andrew Ladd .20 .50
195 Tobias Enstrom .20 .50
196 Dustin Byfuglien .30 .75
197 Alexander Burmistrov .25 .60
198 Bryan Little .30 .75
199 Parise/Brodeur/Koval CL .75 2.00
200 Kopitar/Quick/Doughty CL .50 1.25
201 Mat Clark YG RC 2.00 5.00
202 Carter Camper YG RC 1.50 4.00
203 Maxime Sauve YG RC 1.50 4.00
204 Lane MacDermid YG RC 2.00 5.00
205 Torey Krug YG RC 5.00 12.00
206 Michael Hutchinson YG RC 2.50 6.00
207 Travis Turnbull YG RC 1.50 4.00
208 Sven Baertschi YG RC 4.00 10.00
209 Akim Aliu YG RC 2.00 5.00
210 Jeremy Welsh YG RC 2.00 5.00
211 Brandon Bollig YG RC 1.50 4.00
212 Tyson Barrie YG RC 8.00 20.00
213 Mike Connolly YG RC 2.00 5.00
214 Dalton Prout YG RC 1.50 4.00
215 Cody Goloubef YG RC 1.50 4.00
216 Shawn Hunwick YG RC 1.50 4.00
217 Andrew Joudrey YG RC 2.00 5.00
218 Ryan Garbutt YG RC 1.50 4.00
219 Reilly Smith YG RC 5.00 12.00
220 Brenden Dillon YG RC 2.00 5.00
221 Scott Glennie YG RC 2.00 5.00
222 Riley Sheahan YG RC 2.50 6.00
223 Philippe Cornet YG RC 2.00 5.00
224 Colby Robak YG RC 1.50 4.00
225 Jordan Nolan YG RC 1.50 4.00
226 Kristopher Foucault YG RC 1.50 4.00
227 Jason Zucker YG RC 4.00 10.00
228 Tyler Cuma YG RC 1.50 4.00
229 Chay Genoway YG RC 1.50 4.00
230 Warren Peters YG RC 2.00 5.00
231 Gabriel Dumont YG RC 2.00 5.00
232 Robert Mayer YG RC 2.50 6.00
233 Chet Pickard YG RC 2.00 5.00
234 Aaron Ness YG RC 1.50 4.00
235 Casey Cizikas YG RC 2.00 5.00
236 Matt Donovan YG RC 2.00 5.00
237 Chris Kreider YG RC 10.00 25.00
238 Jakob Silfverberg YG RC 3.00 8.00
239 Mark Stone YG RC 15.00 40.00
240 Brandon Manning YG RC 2.00 5.00
241 Michael Stone YG RC 2.00 5.00
242 Matt Watkins YG RC 1.50 4.00
243 Tyson Sexsmith YG RC 1.50 4.00
244 Jake Allen YG RC 5.00 12.00
245 Jaden Schwartz YG RC 5.00 12.00
246 J.T. Brown YG RC 2.00 5.00
247 Carter Ashton YG RC 1.50 4.00
248 Ryan Hamilton YG RC 1.50 4.00
249 Jussi Rynnas YG RC 1.50 4.00
250 Krder/Schwrtz/Brtsch YG CL 3.00 8.00
251 Olli Jokinen 1.25 3.00
252 Evander Kane 1.50 4.00
253 Ondrej Pavelec 1.50 4.00
254 Mike Ribeiro 1.00 2.50
255 Alexander Ovechkin 6.00 15.00
256 Jason Garrison 1.00 2.50
257 Zack Kassian 1.00 2.50
258 James van Riemsdyk 1.25 3.00
259 John-Michael Liles 1.00 2.50
260 Anders Lindback 1.00 2.50
261 Brad Stuart 1.00 2.50
262 Joe Thornton 2.50 6.00
263 Evgeni Malkin 3.00 8.00
264 Brandon Sutter 1.00 2.50
265 Tomas Vokoun 1.25 3.00
266 Jarome Iginla 2.00 5.00
267 Luke Schenn 1.50 4.00
268 Guillaume Latendresse 1.25 3.00
269 Jason Spezza 1.50 4.00
270 Rick Nash 1.50 4.00
271 David Clarkson 1.00 2.50
272 Pekka Rinne 1.50 4.00
273 Michael Ryder 1.00 2.50
274 Ryan Suter 1.25 3.00
275 Zach Parise 1.50 4.00
276 Torrey Mitchell 1.00 2.50
277 Anze Kopitar 2.50 6.00
278 George Parros 1.25 3.00
279 Taylor Hall 1.50 4.00
280 Sam Gagner 1.00 2.50
281 Pavel Datsyuk 2.50 6.00
282 Jordin Tootoo 1.25 3.00
283 Derek Roy 1.00 2.50
284 Jaromir Jagr 5.00 12.00
285 Ray Whitney 1.25 3.00
286 Brandon Dubinsky 1.00 2.50
287 Nick Foligno 1.25 3.00
288 P.A. Parenteau 1.00 2.50
289 Marian Gaborik 1.50 4.00
290 Patrick Kane 3.00 8.00
291 Alexander Semin 1.50 4.00
292 Jordan Staal 1.25 3.00
293 Jiri Hudler 1.25 3.00
294 Blake Comeau 1.00 2.50
295 Steve Ott 1.00 2.50
296 Cody Hodgson 1.00 2.50
297 Milan Lucic 1.50 4.00
298 Patrice Bergeron 2.00 5.00
299 Corey Perry 2.50 6.00
300 Crosby/Stamkos/Kane CL 5.00 12.00

2012-13 Upper Deck A Piece of History Game Jerseys

300CJ Curtis Joseph C 12.00 30.00
300CO Chris Osgood C 10.00 25.00
300DH Dominik Hasek D 15.00 40.00
300EB Ed Belfour A 30.00 60.00
300EN Evgeni Nabokov B 15.00 40.00
300MB Martin Brodeur D 20.00 50.00
300MK Miikka Kiprusoff B 12.00 30.00
300NK Nikolai Khabibulin D 12.00 30.00

2012-13 Upper Deck Canvas

C1 Ryan Getzlaf 1.25 3.00
C2 Corey Perry 2.00 5.00
C3 Jonas Hiller 1.00 2.50
C4 Teemu Selanne 2.50 6.00
C5 Shawn Thornton .75 2.00
C6 Tuukka Rask 1.50 4.00
C7 Patrice Bergeron 1.50 4.00
C8 Tyler Seguin 1.50 4.00
C9 Brad Marchand 2.50 6.00
C10 Nathan Horton 1.25 3.00
C11 Thomas Vanek 1.00 2.50
C12 Ryan Miller 1.25 3.00
C13 Jason Pominville .75 2.00
C14 Cody Hodgson .75 2.00
C15 Jarome Iginla 1.50 4.00
C16 Michael Cammalleri 1.00 2.50
C17 Miikka Kiprusoff 1.25 3.00
C18 Jeff Skinner 1.50 4.00
C19 Cam Ward 1.25 3.00
C20 Brent Seabrook .75 2.00
C21 Patrick Kane 2.50 6.00
C22 Corey Crawford 1.50 4.00
C23 Duncan Keith 1.00 2.50
C24 Matt Duchene 1.25 3.00
C25 Gabriel Landeskog 1.50 4.00
C26 Jack Johnson .75 2.00
C27 Kari Lehtonen 1.00 2.50
C28 Jamie Benn 1.25 3.00
C29 Jim Howard 1.50 4.00
C30 Henrik Zetterberg 1.50 4.00
C31 Pavel Datsyuk 2.00 5.00
C32 Johan Franzen 1.00 2.50
C33 Magnus Paajarvi 1.00 2.50
C34 Jordan Eberle 1.25 3.00
C35 Ryan Nugent-Hopkins 1.50 4.00
C36 Stephen Weiss 1.00 2.50
C37 Drew Doughty 1.50 4.00
C38 Jonathan Quick 1.50 4.00
C39 Mike Richards 1.00 2.50
C40 Jeff Carter 1.00 2.50
C41 Mikko Koivu 1.00 2.50
C42 Niklas Backstrom 1.00 2.50
C43 Rene Bourque .75 2.00
C44 Josh Gorges 1.00 2.50
C45 Carey Price 2.50 6.00
C46 P.K. Subban 1.50 4.00
C47 Pekka Rinne 1.25 3.00
C48 Craig Smith .75 2.00
C49 Shea Weber 1.00 2.50
C50 Martin Brodeur 3.00 8.00
C51 David Clarkson .75 2.00
C52 Ilya Kovalchuk 1.25 3.00
C53 Kyle Okposo .75 2.00
C54 John Tavares 2.00 5.00
C55 Henrik Lundqvist 3.00 8.00
C56 Marian Gaborik 1.25 3.00
C57 Brad Richards 1.00 2.50
C58 Daniel Alfredsson 1.25 3.00
C59 Jason Spezza 1.25 3.00
C60 Erik Karlsson 1.50 4.00
C61 Brayden Schenn 1.25 3.00
C62 Daniel Briere 1.25 3.00
C63 Scott Hartnell .75 2.00
C64 Claude Giroux 1.25 3.00
C65 Mike Smith 1.25 3.00

C66 Mikkel Boedker .75 2.00
C67 Sidney Crosby 5.00 12.00
C68 Evgeni Malkin 2.50 6.00
C69 Marc-Andre Fleury 2.50 6.00
C70 Joe Pavelski 1.50 4.00
C71 Antti Niemi 1.00 2.50
C72 Jaroslav Halak 1.25 3.00
C73 David Perron 1.00 2.50
C74 David Backes .75 2.00
C75 Kevin Shattenkirk .75 2.00
C76 Steven Stamkos 2.50 6.00
C77 Martin St. Louis 1.25 3.00
C78 Dion Phaneuf 1.00 2.50
C79 Phil Kessel 1.25 3.00
C80 Cory Schneider 1.25 3.00
C81 Daniel Sedin 1.50 4.00
C82 Ryan Kesler 1.25 3.00
C83 Alexandre Burrows .75 2.00
C84 Alexander Ovechkin 2.50 6.00
C85 Nicklas Backstrom 1.25 3.00
C86 Mike Green 1.00 2.50
C87 Andrew Ladd .75 2.00
C88 Ondrej Pavelec 1.25 3.00
C89 Evander Kane 1.25 3.00
C90 Crosby/Stamkos/Giroux CL 3.00 8.00
C91 Torey Krug YG 10.00 25.00
C92 Maxime Sauve YG 3.00 8.00
C93 Sven Baertschi YG 5.00 12.00
C94 Akim Aliu YG 4.00 10.00
C95 Brandon Bollig YG 3.00 8.00
C96 Tyson Barrie YG 10.00 25.00
C97 Cody Goloubef YG 3.00 8.00
C98 Brenden Dillon YG 4.00 10.00
C99 Reilly Smith YG 10.00 25.00
C100 Scott Glennie YG 4.00 10.00
C101 Riley Sheahan YG 5.00 12.00
C102 Colby Robak YG 3.00 8.00
C103 Jordan Nolan YG 3.00 8.00
C104 Jason Zucker YG 8.00 20.00
C105 Tyler Cuma YG 3.00 8.00
C106 Gabriel Dumont YG 4.00 10.00
C107 Chet Pickard YG 4.00 10.00
C108 Matt Donovan YG 4.00 10.00
C109 Casey Cizikas YG 4.00 10.00
C110 Chris Kreider YG 10.00 25.00
C111 Mark Stone YG 20.00 50.00
C112 Jakob Silfverberg YG 8.00 20.00
C113 Brandon Manning YG 4.00 10.00
C114 Michael Stone YG 4.00 10.00
C115 Jake Allen YG 10.00 25.00
C116 Jaden Schwartz YG 10.00 25.00
C117 J.T. Brown YG 4.00 10.00
C118 Jussi Rynnas YG 3.00 8.00
C119 Carter Ashton YG 3.00 8.00
C120 Kreider/Schwartz YG CL 6.00 15.00

2012-13 Upper Deck Canvas Autographs

CAWG Wayne Gretzky/79 500.00 1200.00

2012-13 Upper Deck Clear Cut Foundations

CCF1 J.Hiller/T.Selanne 20.00 50.00
CCF2 T.Rask/T.Seguin 12.00 30.00
CCF3 T.Myers/R.Miller 10.00 25.00
CCF4 Iginla/Cammalleri 12.00 30.00
CCF5 J.Skinner/C.Ward 12.00 30.00
CCF6 D.Keith/J.Toews 15.00 40.00
CCF7 Duchene/Landeskog 12.00 30.00
CCF8 J.Johnson/S.Mason 8.00 20.00
CCF9 J.Benn/K.Lehtonen 10.00 25.00
CCF10 Datsyuk/Zetterberg 15.00 40.00
CCF11 Hall/Nugent-Hopkins 12.00 30.00
CCF12 Markstrom/Gudbranson 10.00 25.00
CCF13 D.Doughty/A.Kopitar 15.00 40.00
CCF14 Backstrom/Harding 10.00 25.00
CCF15 J.Gorges/P.Subban 12.00 30.00
CCF16 P.Rinne/M.Fisher 10.00 25.00
CCF17 Brodeur/Kovalchuk 25.00 60.00
CCF18 Nabokov/Tavares 15.00 40.00
CCF19 Gaborik/Lundqvist 25.00 60.00
CCF20 E.Karlsson/J.Spezza 12.00 30.00
CCF21 B.Schenn/C.Giroux 10.00 25.00
CCF22 K.Yandle/M.Smith 10.00 25.00
CCF23 M.Fleury/E.Malkin 20.00 50.00
CCF24 A.Niemi/L.Couture 12.00 30.00
CCF25 J.Halak/B.Elliott 10.00 25.00
CCF26 St. Louis/Stamkos 20.00 50.00
CCF27 Kessel/Phaneuf 10.00 25.00
CCF28 Schneider/Burrows 10.00 25.00
CCF29 Ovechkin/Holtby 40.00 100.00
CCF30 E.Kane/O.Pavelec 10.00 25.00

2012-13 Upper Deck Clear Cut Honoured Members

HOF43 Eddie Shore 10.00 25.00
HOF44 King Clancy 10.00 25.00
HOF45 Cam Neely 12.00 30.00
HOF46 Ed Belfour 12.00 30.00
HOF47 Terry Sawchuk 12.00 30.00
HOF48 Howie Morenz 10.00 25.00

2012-13 Upper Deck Clear Cut Pride of Canada

PCA1 Sidney Crosby 30.00 80.00
PCA2 Jonathan Toews 12.00 30.00
PCA3 Steven Stamkos 15.00 40.00
PCA4 Jordan Eberle 8.00 20.00
PCA5 Carey Price 15.00 40.00
PCA6 Claude Giroux 12.00 30.00
PCR1 Wayne Gretzky 50.00 100.00
PCR2 Mario Lemieux 20.00 50.00
PCR3 Bobby Orr 30.00 60.00
PCR4 Mark Messier 20.00 50.00
PCR5 Eric Lindros 25.00 50.00
PCR6 Patrick Roy 20.00 50.00

2012-13 Upper Deck Clear Cut Pride of Finland

FIN1 Pekka Rinne 10.00 25.00
FIN2 Miikka Kiprusoff 10.00 25.00
FIN3 Mikko Koivu 8.00 20.00
FIN4 Saku Koivu 10.00 25.00
FIN5 Teemu Selanne 20.00 50.00
FIN6 Jari Kurri 10.00 25.00

2012-13 Upper Deck Clear Cut Pride of Russia

RUS1 Alexander Ovechkin 40.00 100.00
RUS2 Pavel Datsyuk 12.00 30.00
RUS3 Alexander Semin 10.00 25.00
RUS4 Ilya Kovalchuk 12.00 30.00
RUS5 Evgeni Nabokov 8.00 20.00
RUS6 Igor Larionov 10.00 25.00

2012-13 Upper Deck Clear Cut Pride of Sweden

SWE1 Daniel Sedin 12.00 30.00
SWE2 Henrik Lundqvist 25.00 60.00
SWE3 Nicklas Lidstrom 12.00 30.00
SWE4 Henrik Zetterberg 15.00 40.00
SWE5 Daniel Alfredsson 12.00 30.00
SWE6 Pelle Lindbergh 30.00 60.00

2012-13 Upper Deck Clear Cut Pride of USA

USA1 Jonathan Quick 12.00 30.00
USA2 Zach Parise 12.00 30.00
USA3 Tim Thomas 10.00 25.00
USA4 Ryan Miller 20.00 40.00
USA5 Phil Kessel 10.00 25.00
USA6 Brett Hull 20.00 50.00

2012-13 Upper Deck Day With the Cup

DC1 Viatcheslav Voynov 15.00 40.00
DC2 Andrei Loktionov 12.00 30.00
DC3 Anze Kopitar 25.00 60.00
DC4 Jonathan Bernier 12.00 30.00
DC5 Simon Gagne 15.00 40.00
DC6 Rob Scuderi 12.00 30.00
DC7 Colin Fraser 12.00 30.00
DC8 Darryl Sutter 15.00 40.00
DC9 Jonathan Quick 20.00 50.00
DC10 Dustin Brown 15.00 40.00
DC11 Justin Williams 12.00 30.00
DC12 Matt Greene 12.00 30.00
DC13 Willie Mitchell 12.00 30.00
DC14 Dwight King 12.00 30.00
DC15 Jarret Stoll 12.00 30.00
DC16 Dustin Penner 12.00 30.00
DC17 Mike Richards 12.00 30.00
DC18 Jordan Nolan 10.00 25.00
DC19 Kevin Westgarth 10.00 25.00
DC20 Kyle Clifford 10.00 25.00
DC21 Drew Doughty 20.00 50.00
DC22 Jeff Carter 12.00 30.00
DC23 Brad Richardson 10.00 25.00
DC24 Davis Drewiske 10.00 25.00
DC25 Trevor Lewis 10.00 25.00
DC26 Alec Martinez 12.00 30.00
DC27 Luc Robitaille 15.00 40.00
DC28 Phil Pritchard 10.00 25.00

2012-13 Upper Deck Distributor Promos

*GOLD: .8X TO 2X BASIC CARDS
P1 Alexander Ovechkin 2.50 6.00
P2 Adam Henrique .50 1.25
P3 Taylor Hall .60 1.50
P4 Bobby Orr 2.50 6.00
P5 Phil Kessel .60 1.50
P6 Eric Lindros 1.00 2.50
P7 Dion Phaneuf .50 1.25
P8 Evander Kane .60 1.50
P9 Ryan Nugent-Hopkins .75 2.00
P10 Steven Stamkos 1.25 3.00
P11 Nikolai Kulemin .40 1.00
P12 Jean Beliveau .60 1.50
P13 John Tavares 1.00 2.50
P14 Patrick Kane 1.25 3.00
P15 Thomas Vanek .50 1.25
P16 Chris Kreider 1.25 3.00
P17 Chet Pickard .40 1.00
P18 Jaden Schwartz 1.00 2.50
P19 Jake Allen 1.00 2.50
P20 Jakob Silfverberg .60 1.50
P21 Akim Aliu .40 1.00
P22 Tyson Barrie 1.00 2.50
P23 Jussi Rynnas .30 .75
P24 Sven Baertschi .50 1.25
P25 Scott Glennie .40 1.00
P26 Jason Zucker .75 2.00
P27 Tyler Cuma .30 .75
P28 Casey Cizikas .40 1.00
P29 Carter Ashton .30 .75
P30 Cody Goloubef .30 .75

2012-13 Upper Deck Distributor Promos Autographs

P16 Chris Kreider D 10.00 25.00
P17 Chet Pickard D 3.00 8.00
P18 Jaden Schwartz D 8.00 20.00
P19 Jake Allen D 8.00 20.00
P21 Akim Aliu D 3.00 8.00
P22 Tyson Barrie D 8.00 20.00
P23 Jussi Rynnas D 2.50 6.00
P24 Sven Baertschi D 4.00 10.00
P25 Scott Glennie D 3.00 8.00
P28 Casey Cizikas D 3.00 8.00
P29 Carter Ashton D 2.50 6.00
P30 Cody Goloubef D 2.50 6.00

2012-13 Upper Deck Exclusives

*1-200 VETS/100: 6X TO 15X BASIC CARDS
*201-250 ROOKIE/100: 1X TO 2.5X BASIC RC
*251-300 UPD/100: 1X TO 2.5X BASIC CARDS

2012-13 Upper Deck Game Jerseys

GJAK Andrei Kostitsyn G 3.00 8.00
GJAL Anders Lindback G 3.00 8.00
GJAM Andrei Markov G 2.50 6.00
GJAN Antti Niemi D 5.00 12.00
GJAO Alexander Ovechkin G 15.00 40.00
GJAP Alex Pietrangelo A 125.00 200.00
GJAV Antoine Vermette G 2.50 6.00
GJBJ Brent Johnson E 3.00 8.00
GJBQ Ray Bourque C 6.00 15.00
GJBR Martin Brodeur F 15.00 40.00
GJBS Brent Seabrook D 2.50 6.00
GJBT Bryan Trottier F 4.00 10.00
GJBY Josh Bailey E 3.00 8.00
GJCA Craig Anderson H 3.00 8.00
GJCF Cam Fowler H 4.00 10.00
GJCG Claude Giroux H 5.00 12.00
GJCP Carey Price F 8.00 20.00
GJDA Daniel Alfredsson G 4.00 10.00
GJDB Dustin Brown E 4.00 10.00
GJDD Drew Doughty C 20.00 40.00
GJDE Derick Brassard H 2.50 6.00
GJDR Derek Stepan H 2.50 6.00
GJDS Daniel Sedin F 5.00 12.00
GJDU Brandon Dubinsky F 2.50 6.00
GJDV David Booth F 2.50 6.00
GJEB Jordan Eberle C 8.00 20.00
GJED Evgeny Dadonov H 2.50 6.00
GJEJ Erik Johnson H 2.50 6.00
GJEL Lars Eller H 2.50 6.00
GJGB Michael Grabner H 3.00 8.00
GJGP Gilbert Perreault F 4.00 10.00
GJHK Henrik Karlsson H 3.00 8.00
GJHO Tomas Holmstrom G 2.50 6.00
GJHS Henrik Sedin D 5.00 12.00
GJHZ Henrik Zetterberg D 6.00 15.00
GJIB Ilya Bryzgalov G 4.00 10.00
GJIK Ilya Kovalchuk E 4.00 10.00
GJJA Justin Abdelkader H 3.00 8.00
GJJB Jonathan Bernier H 3.00 8.00
GJJC John Carlson E 4.00 10.00
GJJE Jonathan Ericsson H 2.50 6.00
GJJF Jeff Carter G 3.00 8.00
GJJG Jean-Sebastien Giguere H 4.00 10.00
GJJH Jonas Hiller H 3.00 8.00
GJJI Jarome Iginla G 5.00 12.00
GJJJ Jaromir Jagr F 6.00 15.00
GJJS Jordan Staal H 3.00 8.00
GJJT Jonathan Toews D 6.00 15.00
GJJV James van Riemsdyk H 3.00 8.00
GJKL Kris Letang H 5.00 12.00
GJKO Kyle Okposo H 2.50 6.00
GJKS Kevin Shattenkirk G 2.50 6.00
GJKV Kris Versteeg G 2.50 6.00
GJLE Loui Eriksson F 2.50 6.00
GJLI John-Michael Liles G 3.00 8.00
GJLX Mario Lemieux B 15.00 40.00
GJMA Marc Staal H 2.50 6.00
GJMB Mikkel Boedker D 2.50 6.00
GJMC Michael Cammalleri G 4.00 10.00
GJMD Matt Duchene F 4.00 10.00
GJME Mark Messier D 6.00 15.00
GJMF Marc-Andre Fleury H 8.00 20.00
GJMG Mike Green H 3.00 8.00
GJMI Ryan Miller G 4.00 10.00
GJMM Matt Moulson H 2.50 6.00
GJMP Magnus Paajarvi E 3.00 8.00
GJMR Mike Richards G 3.00 8.00
GJNL Nicklas Lidstrom H 5.00 12.00
GJPH Patric Hornqvist H 2.50 6.00
GJRG Ryan Getzlaf H 4.00 10.00
GJRO Derek Roy H 2.50 6.00
GJRS Ryan Suter H 3.00 8.00
GJRY Bobby Ryan H 3.00 8.00
GJSC Sidney Crosby D 10.00 25.00
GJSE Alexander Semin D 4.00 10.00
GJSF Drew Stafford H 2.50 6.00
GJSG Sam Gagner H 2.50 6.00
GJSH Luke Schenn G 4.00 10.00
GJSK Saku Koivu G 4.00 10.00
GJSM Steve Mason H 3.00 8.00
GJSS Steven Stamkos C 8.00 20.00
GJSV Semyon Varlamov G 4.00 10.00
GJTD Trevor Daley H 2.50 6.00
GJTE Tyler Ennis E 2.50 6.00
GJTH Taylor Hall E 4.00 10.00
GJTR Tuukka Rask H 5.00 12.00
GJTV Thomas Vanek E 3.00 8.00
GJTZ Travis Zajac H 2.50 6.00
GJVH Victor Hedman F 5.00 12.00
GJWE Shea Weber H 3.00 8.00
GJWG Wayne Gretzky AS B 75.00 150.00
GJWS Stephen Weiss H 3.00 8.00

2012-13 Upper Deck Hockey Heroes

HH27 Wayne Gretzky 3.00 8.00
HH28 Bobby Clarke 1.50 4.00
HH29 Bobby Orr 4.00 10.00
HH30 Bryan Trottier 1.00 2.50
HH31 Denis Potvin 1.00 2.50
HH32 Gilbert Perreault 1.00 2.50
HH33 Guy Lafleur 1.25 3.00
HH34 Larry Robinson 1.00 2.50
HH35 Marcel Dionne 1.25 3.00
HH36 Phil Esposito 1.50 4.00
HH37 Borje Salming 1.00 2.50
HH38 Tony Esposito 1.00 2.50
HH39 Laflr/Orr/Clrke ART 15.00 40.00
HDR Header Card 1970s 10.00 25.00

2012-13 Upper Deck Requisite Radiance

RR1 Corey Perry 15.00 40.00
RR2 Teemu Selanne 20.00 50.00
RR3 Tuukka Rask 12.00 30.00
RR4 Zdeno Chara 10.00 25.00
RR5 Patrice Bergeron 12.00 30.00
RR6 Thomas Vanek 8.00 20.00
RR7 Ryan Miller 10.00 25.00
RR8 Jarome Iginla 12.00 30.00
RR9 Miikka Kiprusoff 10.00 25.00
RR10 Jonathan Toews 20.00 50.00
RR11 Patrick Kane 20.00 50.00
RR12 Patrick Sharp 10.00 25.00
RR13 Matt Duchene 10.00 25.00
RR14 Gabriel Landeskog 12.00 30.00
RR15 Loui Eriksson 6.00 15.00
RR16 Nicklas Lidstrom 12.00 30.00
RR17 Pavel Datsyuk 15.00 40.00
RR18 Ryan Nugent-Hopkins 12.00 30.00
RR19 Taylor Hall 10.00 25.00
RR20 Jordan Eberle 10.00 25.00
RR21 Jacob Markstrom 10.00 25.00
RR22 Drew Doughty 12.00 30.00
RR23 Jonathan Quick 12.00 30.00
RR24 Anze Kopitar 15.00 40.00
RR25 Niklas Backstrom 12.00 30.00
RR26 Mikko Koivu 8.00 20.00
RR27 Josh Gorges 8.00 20.00
RR28 P.K. Subban 12.00 30.00
RR29 Carey Price 20.00 50.00
RR30 Louis Leblanc 6.00 15.00
RR31 Pekka Rinne 10.00 25.00
RR32 Ilya Kovalchuk 10.00 25.00
RR33 Martin Brodeur 25.00 60.00
RR34 John Tavares 15.00 40.00
RR35 Henrik Lundqvist 25.00 60.00
RR36 Marian Gaborik 10.00 25.00
RR37 Carl Hagelin 6.00 15.00
RR38 Ilya Bryzgalov 10.00 25.00
RR39 Claude Giroux 10.00 25.00
RR40 Scott Hartnell 6.00 15.00
RR41 Brayden Schenn 10.00 25.00
RR42 Daniel Briere 10.00 25.00
RR43 Keith Yandle 6.00 15.00
RR44 Sidney Crosby 40.00 80.00
RR45 James Neal 6.00 15.00
RR46 Evgeni Malkin 20.00 50.00
RR47 Marc-Andre Fleury 20.00 50.00
RR48 Logan Couture 12.00 30.00
RR49 Brian Elliott 8.00 20.00
RR50 Jaroslav Halak 10.00 25.00
RR51 David Backes 6.00 15.00
RR52 Steven Stamkos 20.00 50.00
RR53 Joffrey Lupul 6.00 15.00
RR54 Phil Kessel 10.00 25.00
RR55 Braden Holtby 12.00 30.00
RR56 Alexander Ovechkin 20.00 50.00
RR57 Nicklas Backstrom 10.00 25.00
RR58 Ondrej Pavelec 15.00 40.00
RR59 Evander Kane 10.00 25.00
RR60 Alexander Burmistrov 8.00 20.00

2012-13 Upper Deck Rookie Trade

R1 Rookie Trade 1/Yakupov 30.00 80.00
R2 Rookie Trade 2/Huberdeau 20.00 50.00
R3 Rookie Trade 3/Galchenyuk 25.00 60.00
TC1 Nail Yakupov 40.00 80.00
TC2 Jonathan Huberdeau 25.00 50.00
TC3 Alex Galchenyuk 30.00 60.00

2012-13 Upper Deck Signature Sensations

SSAB Alexander Burmistrov C 8.00 20.00
SSAC Andrew Cogliano C 6.00 15.00
SSAH Adam Henrique C 8.00 20.00
SSAK Arturs Kulda C 6.00 15.00
SSAL Anders Lindback C 6.00 15.00
SSAM Andrei Markov C 6.00 15.00
SSAO Alexander Ovechkin B 40.00 100.00
SSBC Brett Connolly C 6.00 15.00
SSBE Jamie Benn C 10.00 25.00
SSBF Benn Ferriero D 6.00 15.00
SSBG Blake Geoffrion C 10.00 25.00
SSBH Bobby Hull B 20.00 50.00
SSBI Brayden Irwin D 6.00 15.00
SSBL Brian Lee C 8.00 20.00
SSBM Brett MacLean C 6.00 15.00
SSBO Bobby Orr B 60.00 150.00
SSBR Martin Brodeur B 25.00 60.00
SSBS Brendan Smith C 6.00 15.00
SSBT Bryan Trottier B 10.00 25.00
SSBU Adam Burish C 6.00 15.00
SSBY Mike Bossy B 10.00 25.00
SSCE Cody Eakin C 6.00 15.00
SSCF Cam Fowler C 10.00 25.00
SSCG Claude Giroux B 10.00 25.00
SSCK Carl Klingberg C 6.00 15.00
SSCS Chris Stewart C 8.00 20.00
SSCT Colten Teubert C 6.00 15.00
SSDC Daniel Carcillo C 6.00 15.00
SSDE Stefan Della Rovere D 6.00 15.00
SSDG Daniel Girardi C 6.00 15.00
SSDJ Dustin Jeffrey D 6.00 15.00
SSEB Ed Belfour A 10.00 25.00
SSEL Eric Lindros A 15.00 40.00
SSEN Evgeni Nabokov C 8.00 20.00
SSER Jonathan Ericsson C 6.00 15.00
SSFW Francis Wathier D 8.00 20.00
SSGL Gabriel Landeskog B 12.00 30.00
SSGP Gilbert Perreault B 10.00 25.00
SSGU Guillaume Latendresse C 8.00 20.00
SSHA Travis Hamonic C 8.00 20.00
SSHI Jonas Hiller B 8.00 20.00
SSHM Martin Hanzal D 6.00 15.00
SSHO Tomas Holmstrom C 6.00 15.00
SSHS Harri Sateri D 8.00 20.00
SSHU Brett Hull A 20.00 50.00
SSJA Jason Arnott C 8.00 20.00
SSJB Jonathan Bernier C 8.00 20.00
SSJC John Carlson C 10.00 25.00
SSJE Jordan Eberle B 10.00 25.00
SSJH Josh Harding B 10.00 25.00
SSJJ Jaromir Jagr A 30.00 80.00
SSJR Jay Rosehill D 6.00 15.00
SSJS Joe Sakic A 20.00 50.00
SSJT Jonathan Toews A 15.00 40.00
SSKA Keith Aulie C 6.00 15.00
SSKC Kyle Clifford B 6.00 15.00
SSKU Chris Kunitz B 10.00 25.00
SSLA Maxim Lapierre C 6.00 15.00
SSLS Luke Schenn B 10.00 25.00
SSMA Matt Martin C 6.00 15.00
SSMB Matt Beleskey D 6.00 15.00
SSMC Philip McRae C 6.00 15.00
SSMF Michael Frolik C 6.00 15.00
SSMH Matthew Halischuk D 6.00 15.00
SSMI Brendan Mikkelson D 6.00 15.00
SSML Mario Lemieux A 40.00 100.00
SSMM Mark Messier A 20.00 50.00
SSMN Michal Neuvirth B 8.00 20.00
SSMS Matt Stajan C 6.00 15.00
SSNA Markus Naslund B 10.00 25.00
SSNF Nick Foligno B 8.00 20.00
SSNG Nicklas Grossman C 6.00 15.00
SSPL Pascal Leclaire C 8.00 20.00
SSPM Peter Mueller C 6.00 15.00
SSPR Patrick Roy B 30.00 80.00
SSRA Tuukka Rask C 12.00 30.00
SSRE Ryan Ellis C 6.00 15.00
SSRJ Ryan Jones C 8.00 20.00
SSRN Ryan Nugent-Hopkins B 12.00 30.00
SSRS Ryan Smyth B 8.00 20.00
SSSC Sidney Crosby B 100.00 200.00
SSSD Simon Despres C 8.00 20.00
SSSG Sam Gagner C 6.00 15.00
SSSS Steven Stamkos B 20.00 50.00
SSST Steve Shutt B 8.00 20.00
SSSW Stephen Weiss B 8.00 20.00
SSTH Taylor Hall B 10.00 25.00
SSTL Jiri Tlusty C 6.00 15.00
SSTO T.J. Oshie C 10.00 25.00
SSTR Tuomo Ruutu B 8.00 20.00
SSTS Tim Stapleton C 6.00 15.00
SSTV Tomas Vokoun C 8.00 20.00
SSVA Thomas Vanek B 8.00 20.00
SSVF Valtteri Filppula B 6.00 15.00
SSVS Viktor Stalberg C 6.00 15.00
SSWG Wayne Gretzky B 200.00 500.00
SSWR Wade Redden D 6.00 15.00
SSZB Zach Boychuk D 6.00 15.00
SSZD Zac Dalpe B 6.00 15.00

2012-13 Upper Deck Silver Skates

*SS1-SS30 GOLD: 2.5X TO 6X BASIC INSERTS
*SS31-SS40 GOLD: 1.5X TO 3X BASIC INSERTS
SS1 Corey Perry 2.00 5.00
SS2 Teemu Selanne 2.50 6.00
SS3 Patrice Bergeron 1.50 4.00
SS4 Zdeno Chara 1.25 3.00
SS5 Milan Lucic 1.25 3.00
SS6 Tyler Seguin 1.50 4.00
SS7 Thomas Vanek 1.00 2.50
SS8 Sven Baertschi 1.25 3.00
SS9 Patrick Kane 2.50 6.00
SS10 Jonathan Toews 2.00 5.00
SS11 Riley Sheahan 1.25 3.00
SS12 Henrik Zetterberg 1.50 4.00
SS13 Ryan Nugent-Hopkins 3.00 8.00
SS14 Taylor Hall 3.00 8.00
SS15 Jordan Eberle 1.25 3.00
SS16 P.K. Subban 1.50 4.00
SS17 Adam Henrique 1.00 2.50
SS18 Ilya Kovalchuk 1.25 3.00
SS19 Marian Gaborik 1.25 3.00
SS20 Jakob Silfverberg 2.50 6.00
SS21 Daniel Briere 1.25 3.00
SS22 Claude Giroux 1.25 3.00
SS23 Evgeni Malkin 2.50 6.00
SS24 Jaden Schwartz 2.50 6.00
SS25 Steven Stamkos 2.50 6.00
SS26 Martin St. Louis 1.25 3.00
SS27 Phil Kessel 1.25 3.00
SS28 Henrik Sedin 1.50 4.00
SS29 Daniel Sedin 1.50 4.00
SS30 Nicklas Backstrom 1.25 3.00
SS31 Bobby Orr SP 6.00 15.00
SS32 Chris Kreider SP 6.00 15.00
SS33 Wayne Gretzky SP 20.00 50.00
SS34 Jean Beliveau SP 6.00 15.00
SS35 Mark Messier SP 6.00 15.00
SS36 Eric Lindros SP 8.00 20.00
SS37 Mario Lemieux SP 8.00 20.00
SS38 Sidney Crosby SP 10.00 25.00
SS39 Brett Hull SP 6.00 15.00
SS40 Alexander Ovechkin SP 6.00 15.00

2012-13 Upper Deck Winter Classic Oversized

WC1 Claude Giroux 1.25 3.00
WC2 Scott Hartnell .75 2.00
WC3 Brayden Schenn 1.25 3.00
WC4 Daniel Briere 1.25 3.00
WC5 Sergei Bobrovsky 2.00 5.00
WC6 Matt Carle 1.00 2.50
WC7 Maxime Talbot .75 2.00
WC8 Marian Gaborik 1.25 3.00
WC9 Henrik Lundqvist 3.00 8.00
WC10 Michael Rupp .75 2.00
WC11 Ryan Callahan .75 2.00
WC12 Brad Richards 1.25 3.00
WC13 Brandon Prust .75 2.00
WC14 Ryan McDonagh .75 2.00

2013-14 Upper Deck

COMPLETE SET (500) 350.00 600.00
COMP.SERIES 1 (250) 175.00 300.00
COMP.SERIES 2 (250) 175.00 300.00
COMP.SER.1 w/o RC's (200) 10.00 25.00
COMP.SER.2 w/o RC's (200) 10.00 25.00
1 David Krejci .30 .75
2 Johnny Boychuk .25 .60
3 Torey Krug .25 .60
4 Milan Lucic .30 .75
5 Brad Marchand .60 1.50
6 Dennis Seidenberg .20 .50
7 Patrice Bergeron .40 1.00
8 Gregory Campbell .20 .50
9 Max Pacioretty .30 .75
10 David Desharnais .20 .50
11 Travis Moen .20 .50
12 Brandon Prust .20 .50
13 Andrei Markov .20 .50
14 P.K. Subban .40 1.00
15 Brian Gionta .20 .50
16 Frans Nielsen .20 .50
17 Lubomir Visnovsky .20 .50
18 Josh Bailey .25 .60
19 John Tavares .50 1.25
20 Andrew MacDonald .20 .50
21 Casey Cizikas .20 .50
22 Kyle Okposo .20 .50
23 Ryan McDonagh .20 .50
24 Derick Brassard .20 .50
25 Mats Zuccarello-Aasen .30 .75
26 Rick Nash .30 .75
27 Daniel Girardi .20 .50
28 Henrik Lundqvist .75 2.00
29 Derek Dorsett .20 .50
30 Andy Greene .20 .50
31 Ilya Kovalchuk .30 .75
32 Adam Henrique .25 .60
33 Ryan Carter .20 .50
34 Martin Brodeur .75 2.00
35 Adam Larsson .30 .75
36 Matt Read .20 .50
37 Wayne Simmonds .40 1.00
38 Luke Schenn .30 .75
39 Scott Hartnell .20 .50
40 Jakub Voracek .25 .60
41 Sean Couturier .25 .60
42 Erik Gustafsson .20 .50
43 Craig Anderson .30 .75
44 Mika Zibanejad .40 1.00
45 Chris Neil .20 .50
46 Colin Greening .20 .50
47 Patrick Wiercioch .20 .50
48 Erik Karlsson .40 1.00
49 Karl Alzner .20 .50
50 Nicklas Backstrom .30 .75
51 Braden Holtby .40 1.00
52 Martin Erat .20 .50
53 Troy Brouwer .20 .50
54 John Carlson .30 .75
55 Justin Faulk .25 .60
56 Jiri Tlusty .20 .50
57 Jay Harrison .20 .50
58 Jordan Staal .25 .60
59 Jeff Skinner .40 1.00
60 Alexander Semin .30 .75
61 Steve Ott .20 .50
62 Thomas Vanek .25 .60
63 Jhonas Enroth .30 .75
64 Marcus Foligno .25 .60
65 Tyler Myers .20 .50
66 Tyler Ennis .20 .50
67 Carl Gunnarsson .20 .50
68 Dion Phaneuf .25 .60
69 Ryan O'Byrne .20 .50
70 Joffrey Lupul .20 .50
71 James Reimer .30 .75
72 James van Riemsdyk .25 .60
73 Nikolai Kulemin .20 .50
74 Brooks Orpik .20 .50
75 James Neal .20 .50
76 Kris Letang .40 1.00
77 Tomas Vokoun .25 .60
78 Chris Kunitz .30 .75
79 Matt Niskanen .25 .60
80 Sidney Crosby 1.25 3.00
81 Erik Gudbranson .20 .50
82 Tomas Kopecky .25 .60
83 Jacob Markstrom .30 .75
84 Marcel Goc .25 .60
85 Dmitry Kulikov .20 .50
86 Tomas Fleischmann .20 .50
87 Victor Hedman .40 1.00
88 Anders Lindback .20 .50
89 B.J. Crombeen .20 .50
90 Sami Salo .20 .50
91 Teddy Purcell .20 .50
92 Martin St. Louis .30 .75
93 Fedor Tyutin .20 .50
94 R.J. Umberger .20 .50
95 James Wisniewski .20 .50
96 Marian Gaborik .30 .75
97 Jared Boll .20 .50
98 Mark Letestu .25 .60
99 Sergei Bobrovsky .50 1.25
100 Jonathan Ericsson .20 .50
101 Gustav Nyquist .20 .50
102 Justin Abdelkader .25 .60
103 Brendan Smith .20 .50
104 Pavel Datsyuk .50 1.25
105 Niklas Kronwall .25 .60
106 Jakub Kindl .20 .50
107 David Legwand .25 .60
108 Patric Hornqvist .20 .50
109 Shea Weber .25 .60
110 Craig Smith .20 .50
111 Roman Josi .30 .75
112 Gabriel Bourque .25 .60
113 Corey Crawford .40 1.00
114 Andrew Shaw .20 .50
115 Johnny Oduya .25 .60
116 Brandon Saad .25 .60
117 Jonathan Toews .50 1.25
118 Brent Seabrook .20 .50
119 Patrick Sharp .30 .75
120 Bryan Bickell .20 .50
121 Jay Bouwmeester .20 .50
122 T.J. Oshie .30 .75
123 Alexander Steen .20 .50
124 Kevin Shattenkirk .20 .50
125 Jaroslav Halak .30 .75
126 David Backes .20 .50
127 Barret Jackman .20 .50
128 Jason Pominville .20 .50
129 Mikko Koivu .25 .60
130 Ryan Suter .25 .60
131 Kyle Brodziak .20 .50
132 Niklas Backstrom .25 .60
133 Jared Spurgeon .30 .75
134 Jason Zucker .30 .75
135 Jamie Benn .30 .75
136 Alex Goligoski .20 .50
137 Ray Whitney .25 .60
138 Cody Eakin .20 .50
139 Brenden Dillon .20 .50
140 Kari Lehtonen .25 .60
141 Andrew Ladd .20 .50
142 Tobias Enstrom .20 .50
143 Evander Kane .30 .75
144 Zach Bogosian .25 .60
145 Ondrej Pavelec .30 .75
146 Olli Jokinen .25 .60
147 Matt Duchene .30 .75
148 Tyson Barrie .20 .50
149 Gabriel Landeskog .40 1.00
150 Semyon Varlamov .30 .75
151 P.A. Parenteau .20 .50
152 Matt Hunwick .20 .50
153 Martin Hanzal .20 .50
154 Keith Yandle .20 .50
155 Lauri Korpikoski .20 .50
156 Mikkel Boedker .20 .50
157 Shane Doan .25 .60
158 Derek Morris .20 .50
159 Sam Gagner .20 .50
160 Ladislav Smid .20 .50
161 Taylor Hall .30 .75
162 Jeff Petry .30 .75
163 Ryan Smyth .25 .60
164 Ryan Nugent-Hopkins .40 1.00
165 Mikael Backlund .25 .60
166 Dennis Wideman .20 .50
167 Jiri Hudler .25 .60
168 Michael Cammalleri .25 .60
169 Joey MacDonald .20 .50
170 Sven Baertschi .25 .60
171 Ryan Getzlaf .30 .75
172 Nick Bonino .20 .50
173 Matt Beleskey .20 .50
174 Francois Beauchemin .20 .50
175 Saku Koivu .30 .75
176 Andrew Cogliano .20 .50
177 Teemu Selanne .60 1.50
178 Jarret Stoll .25 .60
179 Matt Greene .20 .50
180 Jeff Carter .25 .60
181 Kyle Clifford .20 .50
182 Jonathan Quick .40 1.00
183 Slava Voynov .25 .60
184 Anze Kopitar .50 1.25
185 Marc-Edouard Vlasic .20 .50
186 Tommy Wingels .20 .50
187 Logan Couture .40 1.00
188 Raffi Torres .20 .50
189 Scott Hannan .20 .50
190 Joe Thornton .50 1.25
191 Dan Boyle .20 .50
192 Zack Kassian .20 .50
193 Dan Hamhuis .25 .60
194 Daniel Sedin .40 1.00
195 Alexander Edler .20 .50
196 Alexandre Burrows .20 .50
197 Jannik Hansen .25 .60
198 Roberto Luongo .50 1.25
199 Chara/Rask/Bergrn CL .40 1.00
200 Sbrk/Crwfrd/Kane CL .60 1.50
201 Carl Soderberg YG RC 2.50 6.00
202 Dougie Hamilton YG RC 6.00 15.00
203 Alex Galchenyuk YG RC 6.00 15.00
204 Brock Nelson YG RC 5.00 12.00
205 J.T. Miller YG RC 15.00 40.00
206 Jesper Fast YG RC 2.50 6.00
207 Nathan Beaulieu YG RC 1.50 4.00
208 Damien Brunner YG RC 2.00 5.00
209 Jean-Gabriel Pageau YG RC 2.50 6.00
210 Cory Conacher YG RC 1.50 4.00
211 Connor Carrick YG RC 2.00 5.00
212 Tom Wilson YG RC 6.00 15.00
213 Michael Latta YG RC 2.00 5.00
214 Ryan Murphy YG RC 2.50 6.00
215 Mikhail Grigorenko YG RC 1.50 4.00
216 Zemgus Girgensons YG RC 4.00 10.00
217 Rasmus Ristolainen YG RC 4.00 10.00
218 Morgan Rielly YG RC 12.00 30.00
219 Beau Bennett YG RC 3.00 8.00
220 Olli Maatta YG RC 4.00 10.00
221 Drew Shore YG RC 2.00 5.00
222 Jonathan Huberdeau YG RC 12.00 30.00
223 Alex Killorn YG RC 4.00 10.00
224 Richard Panik YG RC 2.50 6.00
225 Boone Jenner YG RC 5.00 12.00
226 Ryan Murray YG RC 4.00 10.00
227 Danny DeKeyser YG RC 3.00 8.00
228 Seth Jones YG RC 5.00 12.00
229 Joakim Nordstrom YG RC 2.00 5.00
230 Vladimir Tarasenko YG RC 6.00 15.00
231 Mathew Dumba YG RC 1.50 4.00
232 Justin Fontaine YG RC 2.50 6.00
233 Charlie Coyle YG RC 4.00 10.00
234 Jonas Brodin YG RC 3.00 8.00
235 Alex Chiasson YG RC 2.50 6.00
236 Valeri Nichushkin YG RC 6.00 15.00
237 Jacob Trouba YG RC 4.00 10.00
238 Nathan MacKinnon YG RC 150.00 400.00
239 Lucas Lessio YG RC 1.50 4.00
240 Justin Schultz YG RC 2.50 6.00
241 Nail Yakupov YG RC 5.00 12.00
242 Sean Monahan YG RC 8.00 20.00
243 Sami Vatanen YG RC 2.50 6.00
244 Viktor Fasth YG RC 2.50 6.00
245 Emerson Etem YG RC 2.50 6.00
246 Tyler Toffoli YG RC 6.00 15.00
247 Matt Nieto YG RC 2.00 5.00
248 Tomas Hertl YG RC 5.00 12.00
249 Nicklas Jensen YG RC 2.00 5.00
250 McKn/Jns/Glch YG CL 3.00 8.00
251 Henrik Sedin .40 1.00
252 Jason Garrison .20 .50
253 Brad Richardson .20 .50
254 Mike Santorelli .25 .60
255 Kevin Bieksa .25 .60
256 Ryan Kesler .30 .75
257 Alex Stalock .20 .50
258 Joe Pavelski .40 1.00
259 Brent Burns .30 .75
260 Antti Niemi .25 .60
261 Tyler Kennedy .20 .50
262 Patrick Marleau .30 .75
263 Brad Stuart .20 .50
264 Justin Williams .25 .60
265 Trevor Lewis .20 .50
266 Willie Mitchell .20 .50
267 Mike Richards .25 .60
268 Ben Scrivens .25 .60
269 Drew Doughty .40 1.00
270 Dustin Brown .30 .75
271 Jonas Hiller .25 .60
272 Dustin Penner .25 .60
273 Sheldon Souray .20 .50
274 Jakob Silfverberg .20 .50
275 Corey Perry .50 1.25
276 Daniel Winnik .20 .50
277 Kyle Palmieri .25 .60
278 T.J. Brodie .20 .50
279 David Jones .20 .50
280 Mark Giordano .30 .75
281 Matt Stajan .20 .50
282 Lee Stempniak .20 .50
283 Curtis Glencross .20 .50
284 Devan Dubnyk .25 .60
285 Jordan Eberle .30 .75
286 Philip Larsen .20 .50
287 Andrew Ference .20 .50
288 David Perron .25 .60
289 Ales Hemsky .20 .50
290 Oliver Ekman-Larsson .30 .75
291 Mike Smith .30 .75
292 Kyle Chipchura .20 .50
293 Mike Ribeiro .20 .50
294 Radim Vrbata .20 .50
295 Antoine Vermette .20 .50
296 Ryan O'Reilly .30 .75
297 Alex Tanguay .20 .50
298 Maxime Talbot .20 .50
299 Jamie McGinn .20 .50
300 Erik Johnson .20 .50
301 Paul Stastny .25 .60
302 Dustin Byfuglien .30 .75
303 Blake Wheeler .30 .75
304 Michael Frolik .20 .50
305 Mark Scheifele .50 1.25
306 Grant Clitsome .20 .50
307 Bryan Little .30 .75

308 Devin Setoguchi .25 .60
309 Stephane Robidas .20 .50
310 Shawn Horcoff .20 .50
311 Erik Cole .20 .50
312 Tyler Seguin .40 1.00
313 Trevor Daley .20 .50
314 Rich Peverley .30 .75
315 Sergei Gonchar .20 .50
316 Zach Parise .30 .75
317 Marco Scandella .20 .50
318 Josh Harding .30 .75
319 Matt Cooke .20 .50
320 Dany Heatley .25 .60
321 Nino Niederreiter .20 .50
322 Patrik Berglund .20 .50
323 Alex Pietrangelo .25 .60
324 Chris Stewart .25 .60
325 Jaden Schwartz .40 1.00
326 Derek Roy .20 .50
327 Brian Elliott .25 .60
328 Magnus Paajarvi .25 .60
329 Nick Leddy .20 .50
330 Patrick Kane .60 1.50
331 Marian Hossa .30 .75
332 Niklas Hjalmarsson .20 .50
333 Michal Handzus .20 .50
334 Duncan Keith .25 .60
335 Kris Versteeg .20 .50
336 Colin Wilson .25 .60
337 Pekka Rinne .30 .75
338 Matt Cullen .20 .50
339 Kevin Klein .20 .50
340 Viktor Stalberg .20 .50
341 Mike Fisher .20 .50
342 Matt Hendricks .20 .50
343 Johan Franzen .25 .60
344 Daniel Alfredsson .30 .75
345 Jim Howard .40 1.00
346 Stephen Weiss .25 .60
347 Henrik Zetterberg .40 1.00
348 Joakim Andersson .25 .60
349 Jack Johnson .20 .50
350 Cam Atkinson .30 .75
351 Brandon Dubinsky .20 .50
352 Nick Foligno .25 .60
353 Ryan Johansen .25 .60
354 Artem Anisimov .20 .50
355 Valtteri Filppula .20 .50
356 Ben Bishop .25 .60
357 Steven Stamkos .60 1.50
358 Eric Brewer .20 .50
359 Brett Connolly .20 .50
360 Matt Carle .25 .60
361 Shawn Matthias .20 .50
362 Brian Campbell .20 .50
363 Sean Bergenheim .20 .50
364 Scott Gomez .25 .60
365 Tim Thomas .30 .75
366 Scottie Upshall .20 .50
367 Paul Martin .20 .50
368 Pascal Dupuis .20 .50
369 Evgeni Malkin .60 1.50
370 Marc-Andre Fleury .60 1.50
371 Brandon Sutter .20 .50
372 Rob Scuderi .20 .50
373 Jussi Jokinen .20 .50
374 Tyler Bozak .20 .50
375 David Clarkson .20 .50
376 Cody Franson .20 .50
377 Dave Bolland .20 .50
378 Nazem Kadri .40 1.00
379 Jonathan Bernier .25 .60
380 Phil Kessel .30 .75
381 Jamie McBain .20 .50
382 Drew Stafford .20 .50
383 Ryan Miller .30 .75
384 Matt Moulson .20 .50
385 Cody Hodgson .20 .50
386 Christian Ehrhoff .20 .50
387 Tuomo Ruutu .25 .60
388 Eric Staal .40 1.00
389 Ron Hainsey .20 .50
390 Nathan Gerbe .20 .50
391 Cam Ward .30 .75
392 Andrej Sekera .20 .50
393 Joel Ward .20 .50
394 Jason Chimera .20 .50
395 Alexander Ovechkin 1.25 3.00
396 Mike Green .25 .60
397 Eric Fehr .20 .50
398 Mikhail Grabovski .20 .50
399 Marcus Johansson .25 .60
400 Jason Spezza .30 .75
401 Jared Cowen .20 .50
402 Bobby Ryan .25 .60
403 Kyle Turris .20 .50
404 Chris Phillips .20 .50
405 Milan Michalek .20 .50
406 Clarke MacArthur .20 .50
407 Kimmo Timonen .20 .50
408 Brayden Schenn .30 .75
409 Mark Streit .20 .50
410 Steve Downie .20 .50
411 Claude Giroux .30 .75
412 Braydon Coburn .20 .50
413 Vincent Lecavalier .30 .75
414 Patrik Elias .30 .75
415 Bryce Salvador .20 .50
416 Jaromir Jagr 1.00 2.50
417 Cory Schneider .30 .75
418 Travis Zajac .20 .50
419 Michael Ryder .20 .50
420 Ryane Clowe .20 .50
421 Carl Hagelin .20 .50
422 Marc Staal .20 .50
423 Brad Richards .30 .75
424 Ryan Callahan .20 .50
425 Michael Del Zotto .20 .50
426 Derek Stepan .20 .50
427 Benoit Pouliot .20 .50
428 Cal Clutterbuck .20 .50
429 Pierre-Marc Bouchard .30 .75
430 Travis Hamonic .20 .50
431 Michael Grabner .25 .60
432 Evgeni Nabokov .30 .75
433 Thomas Vanek .25 .60
434 Douglas Murray .20 .50
435 Lars Eller .20 .50
436 Alexei Emelin .20 .50
437 Tomas Plekanec .20 .50
438 Josh Gorges .25 .60
439 Rene Bourque .20 .50
440 Carey Price .60 1.50
441 Daniel Briere .30 .75
442 Adam McQuaid .20 .50
443 Reilly Smith .30 .75
444 Tuukka Rask .40 1.00
445 Jarome Iginla .40 1.00
446 Daniel Paille .20 .50
447 Loui Eriksson .20 .50
448 Zdeno Chara .30 .75
449 Ztrbg/Hwrd/Frnz CL .40 1.00
450 Ksl/Kdri/Frnsn CL .40 1.00
451 Filip Forsberg YG RC 20.00 50.00
452 Dylan McIlrath YG RC 1.50 4.00
453 Michael Bournival YG RC 2.50 6.00
454 Michael Sgarbossa YG RC 2.50 6.00
455 Martin Marincin YG RC 2.00 5.00
456 Ryan Spooner YG RC 2.50 6.00
457 Mark Pysyk YG RC 2.50 6.00
458 Freddie Hamilton YG RC 2.50 6.00
459 Joacim Eriksson YG RC 2.50 6.00
460 Christian Thomas YG RC 2.00 5.00
461 Reto Berra YG RC 2.50 6.00
462 Frederik Andersen YG RC 10.00 25.00
463 Mark Arcobello YG RC 2.50 6.00
464 Jon Merrill YG RC 2.50 6.00
465 Linden Vey YG RC 1.50 4.00
466 Petr Mrazek YG RC 20.00 50.00
467 Philipp Grubauer YG RC 12.00 30.00
468 Marek Mazanec YG RC 2.50 6.00
469 Elias Lindholm YG RC 15.00 40.00
470 Aleksander Barkov YG RC 50.00 125.00
471 Nikita Zadorov YG RC 1.50 4.00
472 Taylor Beck YG RC 2.00 5.00
473 Jack Campbell YG RC 40.00 100.00
474 Mikael Granlund YG RC 6.00 15.00
475 Cody Ceci YG RC 2.00 5.00
476 Tomas Jurco YG RC 3.00 8.00
477 Brendan Gallagher YG RC 25.00 60.00
478 Jarred Tinordi YG RC 2.50 6.00
479 Josh Leivo YG RC 2.00 5.00
480 Rickard Rakell YG RC 2.50 6.00
481 Ondrej Palat YG RC 8.00 20.00
482 Ryan Strome YG RC 4.00 10.00
483 Nikita Kucherov YG RC 125.00 300.00
484 Reid Boucher YG RC 2.50 6.00
485 Martin Jones YG RC 4.00 10.00
486 John Gibson YG RC 8.00 20.00
487 Antti Raanta YG RC 5.00 12.00
488 Nick Bjugstad YG RC 3.00 8.00
489 Scott Laughton YG RC 3.00 8.00
490 Antoine Roussel YG RC 2.50 6.00
491 Thomas Hickey YG RC 2.00 5.00
492 Tyler Johnson YG RC 6.00 15.00
493 Connor Murphy YG RC 2.00 5.00
494 Max Reinhart YG RC 2.50 6.00
495 Jordan Schroeder YG RC 2.50 6.00
496 Matt Irwin YG RC 2.00 5.00
497 Jerry D'Amigo YG RC 2.50 6.00
498 Tanner Pearson YG RC 2.50 6.00
499 Hampus Lindholm YG RC 4.00 10.00
500 Glgr/Mrz/Bkv YG CL 3.00 8.00
ST1 Sam Tageson YG 25.00 50.00

2013-14 Upper Deck Exclusives

*1-450 VETS/100: 6X TO 15X BASIC CARDS
*201-250/451-500 YG/100: 1.5X TO 4X BASIC RC

50 Nicklas Backstrom 4.00 10.00
113 Corey Crawford 5.00 12.00
203 Alex Galchenyuk YG 90.00 150.00
205 J.T. Miller YG 40.00 100.00
220 Olli Maatta YG 12.00 30.00
230 Vladimir Tarasenko YG 60.00 150.00
236 Valeri Nichushkin YG 25.00 60.00
238 Nathan MacKinnon YG 1000.00 2500.00
241 Nail Yakupov YG 50.00 120.00
248 Tomas Hertl YG 25.00 60.00
451 Filip Forsberg YG 80.00 200.00
469 Elias Lindholm YG 40.00 100.00
481 Ondrej Palat YG 25.00 60.00
483 Nikita Kucherov YG 400.00 1000.00
486 John Gibson YG 40.00 100.00
492 Tyler Johnson YG 40.00 100.00

2013-14 Upper Deck A Piece of History 300 Win Club Jerseys

300GF Grant Fuhr B 12.00 30.00
300GW Gump Worsley A 12.00 30.00
300MR Mike Richter B 10.00 25.00
300OK Olaf Kolzig B 12.00 30.00
300PR Patrick Roy B 15.00 40.00
300RL Roberto Luongo A 20.00 50.00
300TE Tony Esposito A 15.00 40.00

2013-14 Upper Deck Buyback Autographs

SC Crosby '09-10 UD1/87 S1 60.00 120.00
535 Tavares '10-11 RtrA/24 S2 60.00 100.00

2013-14 Upper Deck Canvas

C1 Patrice Bergeron 1.50 4.00
C2 Tuukka Rask 1.50 4.00
C3 David Krejci 1.25 3.00
C4 Milan Lucic 1.25 3.00
C5 Max Pacioretty 1.25 3.00
C6 Tomas Plekanec .75 2.00
C7 Carey Price 2.50 6.00
C8 Matt Moulson .75 2.00
C9 Evgeni Nabokov 1.25 3.00
C10 Kyle Okposo .75 2.00
C11 Frans Nielsen .75 2.00
C12 Derek Stepan .75 2.00
C13 Ryan Callahan .75 2.00
C14 Derick Brassard .75 2.00
C15 Brad Richards 1.25 3.00
C16 Patrik Elias 1.25 3.00
C17 Martin Brodeur 3.00 8.00
C18 Adam Henrique 1.00 2.50
C19 Jakub Voracek 1.00 2.50
C20 Wayne Simmonds 1.50 4.00
C21 Brayden Schenn 1.25 3.00
C22 Craig Anderson 1.25 3.00
C23 Kyle Turris .75 2.00
C24 Colin Greening .75 2.00
C25 Alexander Ovechkin 5.00 12.00
C26 Braden Holtby 1.50 4.00
C27 Eric Staal 1.50 4.00
C28 Jiri Tlusty .75 2.00
C29 Thomas Vanek 1.00 2.50
C30 Tyler Ennis .75 2.00
C31 Ryan Miller 1.25 3.00
C32 Phil Kessel 1.25 3.00
C33 James van Riemsdyk 1.00 2.50
C34 Chris Kunitz 1.25 3.00
C35 Pascal Dupuis .75 2.00
C36 James Neal .75 2.00
C37 Evgeni Malkin 2.50 6.00
C38 Marc-Andre Fleury 2.50 6.00
C39 Tomas Fleischmann .75 2.00
C40 Tomas Kopecky 1.00 2.50
C41 Steven Stamkos 2.50 6.00
C42 Teddy Purcell .75 2.00
C43 Sergei Bobrovsky 2.00 5.00
C44 Mark Letestu 1.00 2.50
C45 Jim Howard 1.50 4.00
C46 Johan Franzen 1.00 2.50
C47 Pavel Datsyuk 2.00 5.00
C48 David Legwand 1.00 2.50
C49 Pekka Rinne 1.25 3.00
C50 Patrick Kane 2.50 6.00
C51 Duncan Keith 1.00 2.50
C52 Patrick Sharp 1.25 3.00
C53 Corey Crawford 1.50 4.00
C54 Chris Stewart 1.00 2.50
C55 Alexander Steen .75 2.00
C56 Brian Elliott 1.00 2.50
C57 Kevin Shattenkirk .75 2.00
C58 Dany Heatley 1.00 2.50
C59 Ryan Suter 1.00 2.50
C60 Niklas Backstrom 1.00 2.50
C61 Jamie Benn 1.25 3.00
C62 Kari Lehtonen 1.00 2.50
C63 Evander Kane 1.25 3.00
C64 Andrew Ladd .75 2.00
C65 Matt Duchene 1.25 3.00
C66 Paul Stastny 1.00 2.50
C67 Keith Yandle .75 2.00
C68 Shane Doan 1.00 2.50
C69 Mikkel Boedker .75 2.00
C70 Taylor Hall 1.25 3.00
C71 Jordan Eberle 1.25 3.00
C72 Devan Dubnyk 1.00 2.50
C73 Curtis Glencross .75 2.00
C74 Michael Cammalleri 1.00 2.50
C75 Lee Stempniak .75 2.00
C76 Ryan Getzlaf 1.25 3.00
C77 Jonas Hiller 1.00 2.50
C78 Saku Koivu 1.25 3.00
C79 Teemu Selanne 2.50 6.00
C80 Jonathan Quick 1.50 4.00
C81 Justin Williams 1.00 2.50
C82 Dustin Brown 1.25 3.00
C83 Slava Voynov 1.00 2.50
C84 Joe Thornton 2.00 5.00
C85 Dan Boyle .75 2.00
C86 Antti Niemi 1.00 2.50
C87 Tommy Wingels .75 2.00
C88 Alexandre Burrows .75 2.00
C89 Roberto Luongo 2.00 5.00
C90 Kane/Crwfrd/Keith CL 1.50 4.00
C91 Ryan Spooner YG 4.00 10.00
C92 Dougie Hamilton YG 6.00 15.00
C93 Brendan Gallagher YG 25.00 60.00
C94 Jarred Tinordi YG 4.00 10.00
C95 Michael Bournival YG 4.00 10.00
C96 J.T. Miller YG 15.00 40.00
C97 Damien Brunner YG 6.00 15.00
C98 Connor Carrick YG 3.00 8.00
C99 Elias Lindholm YG 12.00 30.00
C100 Rasmus Ristolainen YG 6.00 15.00
C101 Mikhail Grigorenko YG 2.50 6.00
C102 Olli Maatta YG 6.00 15.00
C103 Nick Bjugstad YG 5.00 12.00
C104 Aleksander Barkov YG 30.00 80.00
C105 Jonathan Huberdeau YG 12.00 30.00
C106 Boone Jenner YG 8.00 20.00
C107 Petr Mrazek YG 8.00 20.00
C108 Seth Jones YG 10.00 25.00
C109 Filip Forsberg YG 15.00 40.00
C110 Mikael Granlund YG 6.00 15.00
C111 Jack Campbell YG 30.00 80.00
C112 Valeri Nichushkin YG 8.00 20.00
C113 Jacob Trouba YG 6.00 15.00
C114 Nathan MacKinnon YG 150.00 400.00
C115 Justin Schultz YG 4.00 10.00
C116 Nail Yakupov YG 12.00 30.00
C117 Viktor Fasth YG 4.00 10.00
C118 Tanner Pearson YG 6.00 15.00
C119 Tomas Hertl YG 10.00 25.00
C120 Yakupv/MacKin YG CL 8.00 20.00
C121 Brad Marchand 2.50 6.00
C122 Loui Eriksson .75 2.00
C123 Zdeno Chara 1.25 3.00
C124 P.K. Subban 1.50 4.00
C125 Lars Eller .75 2.00
C126 David Desharnais .75 2.00
C127 Brian Gionta .75 2.00
C128 John Tavares 2.00 5.00
C129 Thomas Vanek 1.00 2.50
C130 Rick Nash 1.25 3.00
C131 Henrik Lundqvist 3.00 8.00
C132 Carl Hagelin .75 2.00
C133 Jaromir Jagr 4.00 10.00
C134 Cory Schneider 1.25 3.00
C135 Michael Ryder .75 2.00
C136 Travis Zajac .75 2.00
C137 Claude Giroux 1.25 3.00
C138 Vincent Lecavalier 1.25 3.00
C139 Sean Couturier 1.00 2.50
C140 Steve Mason 1.00 2.50
C141 Bobby Ryan 1.00 2.50
C142 Robin Lehner 1.00 2.50
C143 Jason Spezza 1.25 3.00
C144 Mike Green 1.00 2.50
C145 Nicklas Backstrom 1.25 3.00
C146 Jeff Skinner 1.50 4.00
C147 Alexander Semin 1.25 3.00
C148 Jordan Staal 1.00 2.50
C149 Cody Hodgson .75 2.00
C150 Matt Moulson .75 2.00
C151 Nazem Kadri 1.50 4.00
C152 Cody Franson .75 2.00
C153 Jonathan Bernier 1.00 2.50
C154 James Reimer 1.25 3.00
C155 David Clarkson .75 2.00
C156 Sidney Crosby 5.00 12.00
C157 Kris Letang 1.50 4.00
C158 Paul Martin .75 2.00
C159 Jacob Markstrom 1.25 3.00
C160 Brian Campbell .75 2.00
C161 Martin St. Louis 1.25 3.00
C162 Ben Bishop 1.00 2.50
C163 Marian Gaborik 1.25 3.00
C164 Ryan Johansen 1.00 2.50
C165 Jack Johnson .75 2.00
C166 Henrik Zetterberg 1.50 4.00
C167 Daniel Alfredsson 1.25 3.00
C168 Niklas Kronwall 1.00 2.50
C169 Shea Weber 1.00 2.50
C170 Matt Cullen .75 2.00
C171 Jonathan Toews 2.00 5.00
C172 Brent Seabrook .75 2.00
C173 Marian Hossa 1.25 3.00
C174 Andrew Shaw .75 2.00
C175 David Backes .75 2.00
C176 Alex Pietrangelo 1.00 2.50
C177 Jaroslav Halak 1.25 3.00
C178 Zach Parise 1.25 3.00
C179 Mikko Koivu 1.00 2.50
C180 Jason Pominville .75 2.00
C181 Tyler Seguin 1.50 4.00
C182 Ray Whitney 1.00 2.50
C183 Shawn Horcoff .75 2.00
C184 Blake Wheeler 1.25 3.00
C185 Dustin Byfuglien 1.25 3.00
C186 P.A. Parenteau .75 2.00
C187 Gabriel Landeskog 1.50 4.00
C188 Alex Tanguay .75 2.00
C189 Semyon Varlamov 1.25 3.00
C190 Mike Smith 1.25 3.00
C191 Oliver Ekman-Larsson 1.25 3.00
C192 Sam Gagner .75 2.00
C193 Ryan Nugent-Hopkins 1.50 4.00
C194 Ales Hemsky .75 2.00
C195 David Perron 1.00 2.50
C196 Jiri Hudler 1.00 2.50
C197 Matt Stajan .75 2.00
C198 Dennis Wideman .75 2.00
C199 Corey Perry 2.00 5.00
C200 Cam Fowler 1.25 3.00
C201 Jeff Carter 1.00 2.50
C202 Logan Couture 1.50 4.00
C203 Patrick Marleau 1.25 3.00
C204 Marc-Edouard Vlasic .75 2.00
C205 Brent Burns 1.25 3.00
C206 Henrik Sedin 1.50 4.00
C207 Daniel Sedin 1.50 4.00
C208 Ryan Kesler 1.25 3.00
C209 Alexander Edler .75 2.00
C210 Crsby/Tvrs/St.L CL 5.00 12.00
C211 Jordan Schroeder YG 4.00 10.00
C212 Freddie Hamilton YG 4.00 10.00
C213 Matt Nieto YG 3.00 8.00
C214 Martin Jones YG 6.00 15.00
C215 Linden Vey YG 2.50 6.00
C216 Tyler Toffoli YG 8.00 20.00
C217 Emerson Etem YG 4.00 10.00
C218 Sean Monahan YG 6.00 15.00
C219 Mark Arcobello YG 4.00 10.00
C220 Alex Chiasson YG 4.00 10.00
C221 Charlie Coyle YG 6.00 15.00
C222 Jonas Brodin YG 5.00 12.00
C223 Vladimir Tarasenko YG 8.00 20.00
C224 Antti Raanta YG 8.00 20.00
C225 Danny DeKeyser YG 5.00 12.00
C226 Tomas Jurco YG 8.00 20.00
C227 Tyler Johnson YG 6.00 15.00
C228 Alex Killorn YG 6.00 15.00
C229 Beau Bennett YG 6.00 15.00
C230 Morgan Rielly YG 20.00 50.00
C231 Josh Leivo YG 3.00 8.00
C232 Zemgus Girgensons YG 6.00 15.00
C233 Tom Wilson YG 8.00 20.00
C234 Cody Ceci YG 3.00 8.00
C235 Reid Boucher YG 4.00 10.00
C236 Jon Merrill YG 4.00 10.00
C237 Ryan Strome YG 6.00 15.00
C238 Brock Nelson YG 8.00 20.00
C239 Alex Galchenyuk YG 10.00 25.00
C240 Glcnyk/Mnhn YG CL 5.00 12.00
C241 Wayne Gretzky RET 20.00 50.00
C242 Bobby Orr RET 15.00 40.00
C243 Mario Lemieux RET 40.00 100.00
C244 Peter Forsberg RET 20.00 50.00
C245 Dominik Hasek RET 15.00 40.00
C246 Paul Coffey RET 10.00 25.00
C247 Felix Potvin RET 15.00 40.00
C248 Bobby Clarke RET 15.00 40.00
C249 Guy Lafleur RET 12.00 30.00
C250 Arturs Irbe RET 8.00 20.00
C251 Larry Robinson RET 10.00 25.00
C252 Jeremy Roenick RET 15.00 40.00
C253 Steve Yzerman RET 15.00 40.00
C254 Patrick Roy RET 25.00 60.00
C255 Eric Lindros RET 15.00 40.00
C256 Morgan Rielly POE 15.00 40.00
C257 Nathan MacKinnon POE 30.00 80.00
C258 Mathew Dumba POE 10.00 25.00
C259 Brendan Gallagher POE 20.00 50.00
C260 Jonathan Huberdeau POE 15.00 40.00
C261 Ryan Murphy POE 6.00 15.00
C262 Scott Laughton POE 10.00 25.00
C263 Michael Bournival POE 10.00 25.00
C264 Boone Jenner POE 12.00 30.00
C265 Tanner Pearson POE 10.00 25.00
C266 Sean Monahan POE 15.00 40.00
C267 Freddie Hamilton POE 8.00 20.00
C268 Nathan Beaulieu POE 10.00 25.00
C269 Xavier Ouellet POE 12.00 30.00
C270 Dougie Hamilton POE 6.00 15.00

2013-14 Upper Deck Canvas Autographs

CSJT John Tavares/91 2 75.00 125.00

2013-14 Upper Deck Clear Cut Foundations

CCF1 M.Brodeur/P.Elias 50.00 125.00
CCF2 J.Toews/P.Kane 40.00 100.00
CCF3 P.Subban/Pacioretty 25.00 60.00
CCF4 H.Lundqvist/R.Nash 50.00 125.00
CCF5 C.Anderson/K.Turris 20.00 50.00
CCF6 Zetterberg/J.Howard 15.00 40.00
CCF7 D.Byfuglien/A.Ladd 20.00 50.00
CCF8 E.Staal/A.Semin 25.00 60.00
CCF9 Markstrom/Fleischmann 20.00 50.00
CCF10 J.Quick/D.Doughty 25.00 60.00
CCF11 J.Tavares/K.Okposo 30.00 80.00
CCF12 N.Kadri/van Riemsdyk 25.00 60.00
CCF13 Marchand/Bergeron 40.00 100.00
CCF14 T.Hall/J.Eberle 20.00 50.00
CCF15 Gaborik/Bobrovsky 15.00 40.00
CCF16 Backstrom/Ovechkin 80.00 200.00
CCF17 P.Dupuis/C.Kunitz 20.00 50.00
CCF18 P.Hornqvist/S.Weber 15.00 40.00
CCF19 K.Lehtonen/R.Whitney 15.00 40.00
CCF20 R.Kesler/H.Sedin 25.00 60.00
CCF21 R.Suter/Z.Parise 20.00 50.00
CCF22 S.Doan/K.Yandle 15.00 40.00
CCF23 Cammalleri/Stempniak 15.00 40.00
CCF24 T.Vanek/R.Miller 20.00 50.00
CCF25 L.Couture/P.Marleau 25.00 60.00
CCF26 Duchene/Parenteau 15.00 40.00
CCF27 C.Perry/R.Getzlaf 15.00 40.00
CCF28 T.Purcell/S.Stamkos 40.00 100.00
CCF29 B.Elliott/D.Backes 12.00 30.00
CCF30 C.Giroux/J.Voracek 20.00 50.00

2013-14 Upper Deck Clear Cut Honoured Members

HOF49 Adam Oates 8.00 20.00
HOF50 Denis Savard 8.00 20.00
HOF51 Joe Sakic 15.00 40.00
HOF52 Pavel Bure 8.00 20.00
HOF53 Mike Gartner 8.00 20.00
HOF54 Mats Sundin 8.00 20.00

2013-14 Upper Deck Clear Cut Stoppers

CCS1 Dominik Hasek 12.00 30.00
CCS2 Grant Fuhr 10.00 25.00
CCS3 Tuukka Rask 10.00 25.00
CCS4 James Reimer 8.00 20.00
CCS5 Pekka Rinne 8.00 20.00
CCS6 Patrick Roy 20.00 50.00
CCS7 Carey Price 15.00 40.00
CCS8 Steve Mason 6.00 15.00
CCS9 Brian Elliott 6.00 15.00
CCS10 Semyon Varlamov 8.00 20.00
CCS11 Mike Smith 8.00 20.00
CCS12 Roberto Luongo 12.00 30.00
CCS13 Martin Brodeur 20.00 50.00
CCS14 Curtis Joseph 10.00 25.00
CCS15 Rogie Vachon 10.00 25.00
CCS16 Ryan Miller 8.00 20.00
CCS17 Viktor Fasth 5.00 12.00
CCS18 Ondrej Pavelec 8.00 20.00
CCS19 Craig Anderson 8.00 20.00
CCS20 Antti Niemi 6.00 15.00
CCS21 Ed Belfour 8.00 20.00
CCS22 Henrik Lundqvist 20.00 50.00
CCS23 Jim Howard 10.00 25.00
CCS24 Marc-Andre Fleury 15.00 40.00
CCS25 Evgeni Nabokov 8.00 20.00
CCS26 Kari Lehtonen 6.00 15.00
CCS27 Braden Holtby 10.00 25.00
CCS28 Corey Crawford 10.00 25.00
CCS29 Andy Moog 10.00 25.00
CCS30 Bill Ranford 8.00 20.00
CCS31 Jonas Hiller 6.00 15.00
CCS32 Jonathan Quick 10.00 25.00
CCS33 Jaroslav Halak 10.00 25.00
CCS34 Felix Potvin 12.00 30.00
CCS35 Niklas Backstrom 6.00 15.00
CCS36 Tomas Vokoun 6.00 15.00

2013-14 Upper Deck Day With The Cup

DC1 Nick Leddy 1 15.00 40.00
DC2 Ray Emery 2 20.00 50.00
DC3 Daniel Carcillo 1 15.00 40.00
DC4 Ben Smith 2 20.00 50.00
DC5 Andrew Shaw 1 15.00 40.00
DC6 Jonathan Toews 1 50.00 100.00
DC7 Brandon Bollig 2 20.00 50.00
DC8 Dave Bolland 1 15.00 40.00
DC9 Patrick Sharp 1 25.00 60.00
DC10 Michael Frolik 1 20.00 50.00
DC11 Michal Rozsival 2 15.00 40.00
DC12 Michal Handzus 1 15.00 40.00
DC13 Marian Hossa 1 30.00 80.00
DC14 Johnny Oduya 1 20.00 50.00
DC15 Marcus Kruger 1 25.00 60.00
DC16 Viktor Stalberg 1 15.00 40.00
DC17 Niklas Hjalmarsson 1 15.00 40.00
DC18 Jamal Mayers 2 15.00 40.00
DC19 Brandon Saad 1 20.00 50.00
DC20 Patrick Kane 1 60.00 100.00
DC21 Bryan Bickell 1 15.00 40.00
DC22 Ryan Stanton 2 20.00 50.00
DC23 Sheldon Brookbank 2 15.00 40.00
DC24 Brent Seabrook 1 15.00 40.00
DC25 Duncan Keith 2 30.00 80.00
DC26 Corey Crawford 1 30.00 80.00

2013-14 Upper Deck Game Jerseys

GJAH Adam Henrique 1E 2.50 6.00
GJAK Anze Kopitar 2C 5.00 12.00
GJAL Adam Larsson 1D 3.00 8.00
GJAL Anders Lindback 2B 2.00 5.00
GJAN Antti Niemi 2C 2.50 6.00
GJAO Alexander Ovechkin 1C 15.00 40.00
GJBD Brandon Dubinsky 1E 2.00 5.00
GJBH Brett Hull 2C 6.00 15.00
GJBL Brian Leetch 1F 2.50 6.00
GJBM Brad Marchand 1D 6.00 15.00
GJBN Bernie Nicholls 1F 2.50 6.00
GJRB Ray Bourque 1E 5.00 12.00
GJBR Bill Ranford 1F 3.00 8.00
GJBS Borje Salming 1F 3.00 8.00
GJBT Bryan Trottier 1F 3.00 8.00
GJBY Dustin Byfuglien 1D 3.00 8.00
GJCA Craig Anderson 1D 3.00 8.00
GJCF Cam Fowler 2C 3.00 8.00
GJCH Carl Hagelin 2D 2.00 5.00
GJCJ Curtis Joseph 1F 4.00 10.00
GJCL Claude Lemieux 1E 2.50 6.00
GJCP Carey Price 1F 4.00 10.00
GJCP Corey Perry 2B 5.00 12.00
GJCS Chris Stewart 1F 2.50 6.00
GJDC Dino Ciccarelli 1F 3.00 8.00
GJDD Drew Doughty 2D 4.00 10.00
GJDE David Desharnais 2B 2.00 5.00
GJDH Dale Hawerchuk 1F 4.00 10.00
GJDI Marcel Dionne 1F 5.00 12.00
GJDK Duncan Keith 1D 2.50 6.00
GJDP David Perron 2D 2.50 6.00
GJDS Derek Stepan 2B 2.00 5.00
GJDU Dustin Brown 2C 3.00 8.00
GJDW Doug Wilson 1F 2.50 6.00
GJEB Ed Belfour 1F 3.00 8.00
GJEK Evander Kane 1F 3.00 8.00
GJEK Erik Karlsson 2C 4.00 10.00
GJEL Eric Lindros 1A 30.00 60.00
GJES Eric Staal 1E 4.00 10.00
GJFA Justin Faulk 2D 2.50 6.00
GJGA Mathieu Garon 1E 2.50 6.00
GJGC Guy Carbonneau 1F 3.00 8.00
GJGF Grant Fuhr 2C 5.00 12.00
GJGL Gabriel Landeskog 2D 4.00 10.00
GJGO Michel Goulet 1D 2.50 6.00
GJGP Gilbert Perreault 1E 3.00 8.00
GJGR Colin Greening 2B 2.50 6.00
GJHA Dominik Hasek 1F 5.00 12.00
GJHE Ales Hemsky 1D 2.00 5.00
GJHL Henrik Lundqvist 2B 5.00 12.00
GJHS Scott Hartnell 1D 2.00 5.00
GJHS Henrik Sedin 2A 40.00 80.00
GJIK Ilya Kovalchuk 1D 3.00 8.00
GJJB Jamie Benn 2C 3.00 8.00
GJJC Jeff Carter 1E 2.50 6.00
GJJE Jordan Eberle 1E 3.00 8.00
GJJF Johan Franzen 2C 2.50 6.00
GJJG Jean-Sebastien Giguere 1D 3.00 8.00
GJJH Jaroslav Halak 1D 3.00 8.00
GJJH Jonas Hiller 2D 2.50 6.00
GJJJ Jaromir Jagr 1E 4.00 10.00
GJJK Jari Kurri 1E 4.00 10.00
GJJL Jacques Lemaire 1E 2.50 6.00
GJJM Joe Mullen 1F 2.50 6.00
GJJQ Jonathan Quick 2C 4.00 10.00
GJJS Joe Sakic 1C 8.00 20.00
GJJS Jason Spezza 2B 3.00 8.00
GJJT Joe Thornton D 5.00 12.00
GJJV Jakub Voracek 1E 2.50 6.00
GJKE Phil Kessel 2B 3.00 8.00
GJKY Keith Yandle 2C 2.00 5.00
GJLC Logan Couture 2D 4.00 10.00
GJLE Lars Eller 1E 2.00 5.00
GJLI Eric Lindros 1F 5.00 12.00
GJLM Lanny McDonald 1F 3.00 8.00
GJLR Larry Robinson 1D 3.00 8.00
GJLR Luc Robitaille 2D 3.00 8.00
GJLU Milan Lucic 1C 4.00 10.00
GJMA Martin Brodeur AS 1C 10.00 25.00
GJMB Martin Brodeur 1B 10.00 25.00
GJMD Matt Duchene 1E 3.00 8.00
GJMF Marc-Andre Fleury 1C 6.00 15.00
GJMH Michal Handzus 1E 2.00 5.00
GJML Mario Lemieux 1A 40.00 100.00
GJMM Mark Messier 1A 40.00 100.00
GJMN Michal Neuvirth 1D 2.50 6.00
GJMP Michael Peca 1F 2.50 6.00
GJMP Max Pacioretty 2C 3.00 8.00
GJMR1 Mike Richards 1F 2.50 6.00
GJMR2 Mike Richards 2B 2.50 6.00
GJMS Marc Staal 1D 2.00 5.00
GJMS Matt Stajan 2A 12.00 30.00
GJMW Mike Weber 1E 2.00 5.00
GJNB Nicklas Backstrom 1E 3.00 8.00
GJNF Nick Foligno 1E 2.50 6.00
GJNL Nicklas Lidstrom 1F 3.00 8.00
GJOE Oliver Ekman-Larsson 1E 3.00 8.00
GJOP Ondrej Pavelec 1E 3.00 8.00
GJPA Paul Coffey 2B 4.00 10.00
GJPB Patrice Bergeron 1C 5.00 12.00
GJPC Paul Coffey 1F 3.00 8.00
GJPD Pavel Datsyuk 1D 4.00 10.00
GJPF Peter Forsberg 1F 6.00 15.00
GJPM Patrick Marleau 1B 6.00 15.00
GJPR Patrick Roy 1A 50.00 100.00
GJPS P.K. Subban 1C 6.00 15.00
GJRF Ron Francis 1D 4.00 10.00
GJRG Ryan Getzlaf 1F 3.00 8.00
GJRI Pekka Rinne 1D 3.00 8.00
GJRL Roberto Luongo 1F 5.00 12.00
GJRO Robin Lehner 1D 3.00 8.00
GJRY Ryan Miller 1F 3.00 8.00
GJSC Brayden Schenn 1E 3.00 8.00
GJSC Sidney Crosby 2A 20.00 50.00
GJSD Shane Doan 2D 2.50 6.00
GJSG Sam Gagner 1C 2.50 6.00
GJSH Patrick Sharp 1C 4.00 10.00
GJSL Martin St. Louis 2C 3.00 8.00
GJST Jordan Staal 1F 2.50 6.00
GJST Paul Stastny 2D 2.50 6.00
GJSU Mats Sundin 2C 3.00 8.00
GJSV Slava Voynov 2D 2.50 6.00
GJSY Steve Yzerman 2C 8.00 20.00
GJTA Taylor Hall 1E 3.00 8.00
GJTE Tyler Ennis 2D 2.00 5.00
GJTF Theoren Fleury 2B 4.00 10.00
GJTH Jose Theodore 1F 3.00 8.00
GJTM Tyler Myers 1E 2.00 5.00
GJTO Jonathan Toews 1A 40.00 100.00
GJTP Tomas Plekanec 2D 2.00 5.00
GJTR Tuukka Rask 1D 4.00 10.00
GJTV Thomas Vanek 1B 4.00 10.00
GJVD Vincent Damphousse 2B 2.50 6.00
GJWG Wayne Gretzky 1A 60.00 120.00
GJWS Wayne Simmonds 2B 4.00 10.00
GWJMS Mandi Schwartz 1F 50.00 100.00

2013-14 Upper Deck Hockey Heroes

COMP.SER 1 SET (14) 15.00 40.00
COMP. SER 1 w/o SPs (12) 6.00 15.00
HH40 Wayne Gretzky 5.00 12.00
HH41 Paul Coffey .75 2.00
HH42 Mark Messier 1.50 4.00
HH43 Grant Fuhr 1.25 3.00
HH44 Jari Kurri .75 2.00
HH45 Mike Bossy .75 2.00
HH46 Mike Gartner 1.00 2.50
HH47 Ray Bourque 1.25 3.00
HH48 Patrick Roy 2.00 5.00
HH49 Dale Hawerchuk 1.00 2.50
HH50 Mario Lemieux 3.00 8.00
HH51 Peter Stastny .60 1.50
HH52 Bossy/Gretzky ART 5.00 12.00
HH53 Wayne Gretzky 5.00 12.00
HH54 Mats Sundin .75 2.00
HH55 Joe Sakic 1.50 4.00
HH56 Ed Belfour .75 2.00
HH57 Steve Yzerman 2.00 5.00
HH58 Dominik Hasek 1.25 3.00
HH59 Patrick Roy 2.00 5.00
HH60 Ron Francis 1.00 2.50
HH61 Ray Bourque 1.25 3.00
HH62 Mark Messier 1.50 4.00
HH63 Mario Lemieux 3.00 8.00
HH64 Jaromir Jagr 2.50 6.00
HH65 M.Lemieux/P.Roy ART 3.00 8.00
HEADER Header Card 1980s 8.00 20.00
HEADER2 Header Card 1990s 10.00 25.00

2013-14 Upper Deck Lord Stanley's Futures

LSFAG Alex Galchenyuk 40.00 100.00
LSFBB Beau Bennett 15.00 40.00
LSFBG Brendan Gallagher 40.00 100.00
LSFCC Cory Conacher 8.00 20.00
LSFJH Jonathan Huberdeau 25.00 60.00
LSFJM J.T. Miller 30.00 80.00
LSFJS Justin Schultz 12.00 30.00
LSFJT Jarred Tinordi 12.00 30.00
LSFMG Mikael Granlund 20.00 50.00
LSFNB Nathan Beaulieu 8.00 20.00
LSFNY Nail Yakupov 40.00 100.00
LSFVT Vladimir Tarasenko 30.00 80.00

2013-14 Upper Deck Lord Stanley's Heroes

LSH1 Alexander Ovechkin 20.00 50.00
LSH2 Pavel Bure 12.00 30.00
LSH3 Alexandre Burrows 8.00 20.00
LSH4 Roberto Luongo 20.00 50.00
LSH5 Daniel Sedin 15.00 40.00
LSH6 Henrik Sedin 15.00 40.00
LSH7 Mats Sundin 12.00 30.00
LSH8 Steven Stamkos 25.00 60.00
LSH9 Antti Niemi 10.00 25.00
LSH10 Mario Lemieux 30.00 80.00
LSH11 Evgeni Malkin 25.00 60.00
LSH12 Sidney Crosby 60.00 120.00
LSH13 Bobby Clarke 25.00 50.00
LSH14 Eric Lindros 20.00 50.00
LSH15 Mark Messier 15.00 40.00
LSH16 Ilya Kovalchuk 10.00 25.00
LSH17 Martin Brodeur 30.00 80.00
LSH18 Carey Price 25.00 60.00
LSH19 Patrick Roy 40.00 100.00
LSH20 Jeff Carter 10.00 25.00
LSH21 Drew Doughty 15.00 40.00
LSH22 Mike Richards 10.00 25.00
LSH23 Jonathan Quick 15.00 40.00
LSH24 Jari Kurri 12.00 30.00
LSH25 Jordan Eberle 12.00 30.00
LSH26 Ryan Nugent-Hopkins 15.00 40.00
LSH27 Wayne Gretzky 60.00 120.00
LSH28 Taylor Hall 12.00 30.00
LSH29 Nicklas Lidstrom 12.00 30.00
LSH30 Pavel Datsyuk 20.00 50.00
LSH31 Brett Hull 25.00 50.00
LSH32 Milan Hejduk 10.00 25.00
LSH33 Peter Forsberg 25.00 60.00
LSH34 Ray Bourque 20.00 50.00
LSH35 Joe Sakic 25.00 60.00
LSH36 Jonathan Toews 20.00 50.00
LSH37 Patrick Sharp 12.00 30.00
LSH38 Patrick Kane 25.00 60.00
LSH39 Theoren Fleury 15.00 40.00
LSH40 Patrice Bergeron 15.00 40.00
LSH41 Bobby Orr 40.00 100.00
LSH42 Milan Lucic 12.00 30.00
LSH43 Zdeno Chara 12.00 30.00
LSH44 Tyler Seguin 15.00 40.00
LSH45 Brad Marchand 25.00 60.00
LSH46 Jaromir Jagr 40.00 100.00
LSH47 Scott Niedermayer 12.00 30.00
LSH48 Teemu Selanne 25.00 60.00

2013-14 Upper Deck Oversized

7 Patrice Bergeron 1.50 4.00
19 John Tavares 2.00 5.00
43 Craig Anderson 1.25 3.00
62 Thomas Vanek 1.00 2.50
80 Sidney Crosby 5.00 12.00
92 Martin St. Louis 1.25 3.00
109 Shea Weber 1.00 2.50
113 Corey Crawford 1.50 4.00
117 Jonathan Toews 2.00 5.00
143 Evander Kane 1.25 3.00
147 Matt Duchene 1.25 3.00
161 Taylor Hall 1.25 3.00
182 Jonathan Quick 1.50 4.00
187 Logan Couture 1.50 4.00

2013-14 Upper Deck Rookie Breakouts

RB1 Hampus Lindholm 8.00 20.00
RB2 Dougie Hamilton 8.00 20.00
RB3 Ryan Murray 4.00 10.00
RB4 Aleksander Barkov 15.00 40.00
RB5 Olli Maatta 15.00 40.00
RB6 Elias Lindholm 12.00 30.00
RB7 Justin Fontaine 5.00 12.00
RB8 Alex Killorn 6.00 15.00
RB9 Morgan Rielly 12.00 30.00
RB10 Jonathan Huberdeau 12.00 30.00
RB11 Petr Mrazek 10.00 25.00
RB12 Rasmus Ristolainen 8.00 20.00
RB13 Alex Galchenyuk 12.00 30.00
RB14 Alex Chiasson 5.00 12.00
RB15 Danny DeKeyser 6.00 15.00
RB16 Sean Monahan 8.00 20.00
RB17 Nathan MacKinnon 50.00 100.00
RB18 Jacob Trouba 8.00 20.00
RB19 Michael Bournival 5.00 12.00
RB20 Boone Jenner 10.00 25.00
RB21 Seth Jones 10.00 25.00
RB22 Michael Latta 4.00 10.00
RB23 Mark Arcobello 5.00 12.00
RB24 Nail Yakupov 10.00 25.00

RB25 Matt Nieto 4.00 10.00
RB26 Valeri Nichushkin 12.00 30.00
RB27 Sami Vatanen 5.00 12.00
RB28 Tomas Hertl 10.00 25.00

2013-14 Upper Deck Rookie Materials

*PATCH/25: 1X TO 2.5X BASIC JSY
RMAB Aleksander Barkov B 5.00 12.00
RMAC Alex Chiasson C 2.50 6.00
RMAG Alex Galchenyuk A 10.00 25.00
RMBB Beau Bennett C 4.00 10.00
RMBG Brendan Gallagher A 6.00 15.00
RMBJ Boone Jenner C 5.00 12.00
RMBN Brock Nelson C 5.00 12.00
RMCC Charlie Coyle B 4.00 10.00
RMCO Cory Conacher C 3.00 8.00
RMCT Christian Thomas C 2.00 5.00
RMDB Damien Brunner C 2.00 5.00
RMDH Dougie Hamilton A 5.00 12.00
RMEE Emerson Etem B 2.50 6.00
RMEL Elias Lindholm C 6.00 15.00
RMFF Filip Forsberg B 6.00 15.00
RMGR Mikhail Grigorenko A 1.50 4.00
RMHL Hampus Lindholm C 4.00 10.00
RMJF Jesper Fast C 2.50 6.00
RMJH Jonathan Huberdeau A 5.00 12.00
RMJS Justin Schultz B 2.50 6.00
RMJT Jacob Trouba C 4.00 10.00
RMLL Lucas Lessio C 1.50 4.00
RMMD Mathew Dumba C 1.50 4.00
RMMG Mikael Granlund B 4.00 10.00
RMMN Matt Nieto C 2.00 5.00
RMMR Morgan Rielly A 5.00 12.00
RMMU Ryan Murray A 4.00 10.00
RMNJ Nicklas Jensen B 3.00 8.00
RMNM Nathan MacKinnon B 8.00 20.00
RMNY Nail Yakupov A 5.00 12.00
RMOM Olli Maatta B 5.00 12.00
RMPM Petr Mrazek B 5.00 12.00
RMRM Ryan Murphy C 2.50 6.00
RMRR Rasmus Ristolainen C 4.00 10.00
RMSJ Seth Jones B 4.00 10.00
RMSM Sean Monahan B 6.00 15.00
RMTH Tomas Hertl B 8.00 20.00
RMTI Jarred Tinordi B 2.50 6.00
RMTP Tanner Pearson B 2.50 6.00
RMTT Tyler Toffoli B 5.00 12.00
RMTW Tom Wilson C 5.00 12.00
RMVF Viktor Fasth B 2.50 6.00
RMVN Valeri Nichushkin A 5.00 12.00
RMVT Vladimir Tarasenko A 6.00 15.00
RMZG Zemgus Girgensons C 4.00 10.00

2013-14 Upper Deck Shining Stars Centers

COMPLETE SET (10) 12.00 30.00
*RAINBOW VET: 1.5X TO 4X BASIC INSERTS
*RAINBOW ROOK: 1.2X TO 3X BASIC INSERTS
C1 Pavel Datsyuk 2.00 5.00
C2 Jonathan Toews 2.00 5.00
C3 Ryan Nugent-Hopkins 1.50 4.00
C4 Alex Galchenyuk 1.25 3.00
C5 Jonathan Huberdeau 1.25 3.00
C6 John Tavares 2.00 5.00
C7 Evgeni Malkin 2.50 6.00
C8 Sidney Crosby 5.00 12.00
C9 Steven Stamkos 2.50 6.00
C10 Nazem Kadri 1.50 4.00

2013-14 Upper Deck Shining Stars Defense

D1 Ryan Suter 5.00 12.00
D2 Oliver Ekman-Larsson 6.00 15.00
D3 Erik Karlsson 8.00 20.00
D4 Shea Weber 5.00 12.00
D5 Duncan Keith 5.00 12.00
D6 Kris Letang 8.00 20.00
D7 Drew Doughty 8.00 20.00
D8 Niklas Kronwall 5.00 12.00
D9 Zdeno Chara 6.00 15.00
D10 P.K. Subban 8.00 20.00

2013-14 Upper Deck Shining Stars Goalies

*RAINBOW: 1X TO 2.5X BASIC INSERTS
G1 Jim Howard 3.00 8.00
G2 Henrik Lundqvist 6.00 15.00
G3 Jonathan Quick 3.00 8.00
G4 Carey Price 5.00 12.00
G5 Mike Smith 2.50 6.00
G6 Pekka Rinne 2.50 6.00
G7 Martin Brodeur 6.00 15.00
G8 Roberto Luongo 4.00 10.00
G9 Ondrej Pavelec 2.50 6.00
G10 Antti Niemi 2.00 5.00

2013-14 Upper Deck Shining Stars Left Wing

COMPLETE SET (10) 12.00 30.00
*RAINBOW: 1X TO 2.5X BASIC INSERTS
LW1 Thomas Vanek 1.50 4.00
LW2 Evander Kane 2.00 5.00
LW3 James Neal 1.25 3.00
LW4 Daniel Sedin 2.50 6.00
LW5 Chris Kunitz 2.00 5.00
LW6 Rick Nash 2.00 5.00
LW7 Zach Parise 2.00 5.00
LW8 Taylor Hall 2.00 5.00
LW9 Brad Marchand 4.00 10.00
LW10 Milan Lucic 2.00 5.00

2013-14 Upper Deck Shining Stars Right Wing

COMPLETE SET (10) 12.00 30.00
*RAINBOW: 1X TO 2.5X BASIC INSERTS
RW1 Ryan Callahan 1.25 3.00
RW2 Claude Giroux 2.00 5.00
RW3 Patrick Sharp 2.00 5.00
RW4 Patrick Kane 3.00 8.00
RW5 Corey Perry 3.00 8.00
RW6 Nail Yakupov 1.25 3.00
RW7 Jordan Eberle 2.00 5.00
RW8 Chris Stewart 1.50 4.00
RW9 Alexander Ovechkin 8.00 20.00
RW10 Alexandre Burrows 1.25 3.00

2013-14 Upper Deck Signatures

UDSAB Alexander Burmistrov C 5.00 12.00
UDSAH Adam Henrique C 5.00 12.00
UDSAS Andrew Shaw D 4.00 10.00
UDSBD Brandon Dubinsky C 4.00 10.00
UDSBO Bobby Orr B 60.00 150.00
UDSCA Cam Atkinson D 6.00 15.00
UDSCE Cody Eakin D 4.00 10.00
UDSCK Chris Kreider D 8.00 20.00
UDSCN Cam Neely A 6.00 15.00
UDSCO Cal O'Reilly D 4.00 10.00
UDSCS Cory Schneider D 6.00 15.00
UDSDR Derek Roy D 4.00 10.00
UDSFP Felix Potvin C 15.00 40.00
UDSGL Gabriel Landeskog B 8.00 20.00
UDSGM Glen Murray B 5.00 12.00
UDSJR James van Riemsdyk A 5.00 12.00
UDSLC Logan Couture C 8.00 20.00
UDSLR Luc Robitaille A 6.00 15.00
UDSMG Marian Gaborik A 6.00 15.00
UDSMR Mike Richards C 5.00 12.00
UDSPR Pekka Rinne D 6.00 15.00
UDSST Peter Stastny A 5.00 12.00
UDSSW Shea Weber A 5.00 12.00
UDSWG Wayne Gretzky B 150.00 400.00

2013-14 Upper Deck Signature Sensations

SSAE Alexei Emelin E 4.00 10.00
SSAK Arturs Kulda E 4.00 10.00
SSAL Anders Lindback E 4.00 10.00
SSAO Alexander Ovechkin A 30.00 80.00
SSAP Alex Pietrangelo A 5.00 12.00
SSAS Alex Stalock D 4.00 10.00
SSBO Bobby Orr A 60.00 150.00
SSBP Brandon Prust C 4.00 10.00
SSBS Brandon Sutter D 4.00 10.00
SSBU Alexander Burmistrov B 5.00 12.00
SSCF Cam Fowler C 6.00 15.00
SSCG Colin Greening E 4.00 10.00
SSCJ Joe Colborne D 4.00 10.00
SSDE Alex Delvecchio B 6.00 15.00
SSDP Daniel Paille E 4.00 10.00
SSEL Lars Eller C 4.00 10.00
SSGC Grant Clitsome E 4.00 10.00
SSGL Guillaume Latendresse A 5.00 12.00
SSHA Scott Hartnell B 4.00 10.00
SSJE Jonathan Ericsson A 4.00 10.00
SSJF Justin Faulk C 5.00 12.00
SSJH Jonas Hiller E 5.00 12.00
SSJI Jiri Tlusty B 4.00 10.00
SSJM Jacob Markstrom C 6.00 15.00
SSJR Jay Rosehill A 4.00 10.00
SSKP Kyle Palmieri E 5.00 12.00
SSLA Anton Lander C 4.00 10.00
SSLB Lance Bouma D 4.00 10.00
SSMD Michael Del Zotto B 4.00 10.00
SSMG Michael Grabner D 5.00 12.00
SSMH Martin Hanzal E 4.00 10.00
SSMK Marcus Kruger D 4.00 10.00
SSMM Mark Messier A 12.00 30.00
SSMO Jeremy Morin C 5.00 12.00
SSMR Matt Read E 4.00 10.00
SSMS Michael Sauer E 4.00 10.00
SSMT Maxime Talbot D 4.00 10.00
SSMZ Mats Zuccarello-Aasen D 6.00 15.00
SSNF Nick Foligno B 5.00 12.00
SSNL Nick Leddy C 4.00 10.00
SSPB Patrik Berglund C 4.00 10.00
SSPS Paul Stastny A 5.00 12.00
SSRD Raphael Diaz C 4.00 10.00
SSRT Raffi Torres D 4.00 10.00
SSSB Sergei Bobrovsky B 10.00 25.00
SSSC Sidney Crosby A 60.00 150.00
SSSH Andrew Shaw C 4.00 10.00
SSTA John Tavares A 30.00 80.00
SSTB Tyler Bozak C 4.00 10.00
SSTL Trevor Lewis C 4.00 10.00
SSTO T.J. Oshie C 6.00 15.00
SSTR Tuukka Rask B 8.00 20.00
SSTV Tomas Vokoun D 5.00 12.00
SSVA Thomas Vanek B 5.00 12.00
SSVV Slava Voynov E 5.00 12.00
SSWG Wayne Gretzky A 200.00 500.00
SSZD Zac Dalpe E 4.00 10.00
SSZK Zenon Konopka B 5.00 12.00

2013-14 Upper Deck Young Guns Acetate

201 Carl Soderberg 20.00 50.00
202 Dougie Hamilton 50.00 100.00
203 Alex Galchenyuk 175.00 300.00
204 Brock Nelson 40.00 100.00
205 J.T. Miller 50.00 125.00
206 Jesper Fast 20.00 50.00
207 Nathan Beaulieu 12.00 30.00
208 Damien Brunner 15.00 40.00
209 Jean-Gabriel Pageau 20.00 50.00
210 Cory Conacher 12.00 30.00
211 Connor Carrick 15.00 40.00
212 Tom Wilson 40.00 100.00
213 Michael Latta 15.00 40.00
214 Ryan Murphy 25.00 60.00
215 Mikhail Grigorenko 12.00 30.00
216 Zemgus Girgensons 50.00 100.00
217 Rasmus Ristolainen 30.00 80.00
218 Morgan Rielly 60.00 120.00
219 Beau Bennett 40.00 80.00
220 Olli Maatta 75.00 150.00
221 Drew Shore 15.00 40.00
222 Jonathan Huberdeau 60.00 120.00
223 Alex Killorn 30.00 80.00
224 Richard Panik 20.00 50.00
225 Boone Jenner 40.00 100.00
226 Ryan Murray 30.00 80.00
227 Danny DeKeyser 25.00 60.00
228 Seth Jones 40.00 80.00
229 Joakim Nordstrom 15.00 40.00
230 Vladimir Tarasenko 175.00 300.00
231 Mathew Dumba 25.00 60.00
232 Justin Fontaine 20.00 50.00
233 Charlie Coyle 30.00 80.00
234 Jonas Brodin 25.00 60.00
235 Alex Chiasson 20.00 50.00
236 Valeri Nichushkin 75.00 150.00
237 Jacob Trouba 100.00 200.00
238 Nathan MacKinnon 250.00 600.00
239 Lucas Lessio 12.00 30.00
240 Justin Schultz 20.00 50.00
241 Nail Yakupov 100.00 175.00
242 Sean Monahan 75.00 150.00
243 Sami Vatanen 20.00 50.00
244 Viktor Fasth 20.00 50.00
245 Emerson Etem 20.00 50.00
246 Tyler Toffoli 80.00 200.00
247 Matt Nieto 15.00 40.00
248 Tomas Hertl 125.00 200.00
249 Nicklas Jensen 15.00 40.00
451 Filip Forsberg 60.00 150.00
452 Dylan McIlrath 12.00 30.00
453 Michael Bournival 20.00 50.00
454 Michael Sgarbossa 20.00 50.00
455 Martin Marincin 15.00 40.00
456 Ryan Spooner 20.00 50.00
457 Mark Pysyk 20.00 50.00
458 Freddie Hamilton 20.00 50.00
459 Joacim Eriksson 20.00 50.00
460 Christian Thomas 15.00 40.00
461 Reto Berra 20.00 50.00
462 Frederik Andersen 50.00 125.00
463 Mark Arcobello 20.00 50.00
464 Jon Merrill 20.00 50.00
465 Linden Vey 12.00 30.00
466 Petr Mrazek 40.00 100.00
467 Philipp Grubauer 50.00 125.00
468 Marek Mazanec 20.00 50.00
469 Elias Lindholm 50.00 125.00
470 Aleksander Barkov 60.00 150.00
471 Nikita Zadorov 12.00 30.00
472 Taylor Beck 15.00 40.00
473 Jack Campbell 150.00 400.00
474 Mikael Granlund 30.00 80.00
475 Cody Ceci 15.00 40.00
476 Tomas Jurco 25.00 60.00
477 Brendan Gallagher 125.00 200.00
478 Jarred Tinordi 20.00 50.00
479 Josh Leivo 15.00 40.00
480 Rickard Rakell 20.00 50.00
481 Ondrej Palat 30.00 80.00
482 Ryan Strome 75.00 150.00
483 Nikita Kucherov 250.00 600.00
484 Reid Boucher 20.00 50.00
485 Martin Jones 30.00 80.00
486 John Gibson 50.00 125.00
487 Antti Raanta 40.00 100.00
488 Nick Bjugstad 30.00 80.00
489 Scott Laughton 25.00 60.00
490 Antoine Roussel 20.00 50.00
491 Thomas Hickey 15.00 40.00
492 Tyler Johnson 40.00 100.00
493 Connor Murphy 15.00 40.00
494 Max Reinhart 20.00 50.00
495 Jordan Schroeder 20.00 50.00
496 Matthew Irwin 15.00 40.00
497 Jerry D'Amigo 20.00 50.00
498 Tanner Pearson 40.00 80.00
499 Hampus Lindholm 30.00 80.00

2013-14 Upper Deck Young Guns Oversized

202 Dougie Hamilton 2.50 6.00
203 Alex Galchenyuk 4.00 10.00
215 Mikhail Grigorenko 1.00 2.50
222 Jonathan Huberdeau 4.00 10.00
225 Boone Jenner 3.00 8.00
226 Ryan Murray 2.50 6.00
228 Seth Jones 3.00 8.00
230 Vladimir Tarasenko 4.00 10.00
233 Charlie Coyle 2.50 6.00
236 Valeri Nichushkin 3.00 8.00
237 Jacob Trouba 2.50 6.00
238 Nathan MacKinnon 80.00 200.00
240 Justin Schultz 1.50 4.00
242 Sean Monahan 2.50 6.00

2014-15 Upper Deck

1 Ryan Getzlaf .30 .75
2 Cam Fowler .30 .75
3 Andrew Cogliano .20 .50
4 Kyle Palmieri .25 .60
5 Jakob Silfverberg .20 .50
6 Hampus Lindholm .20 .50
7 John Gibson .30 .75
8 Lauri Korpikoski .20 .50
9 Shane Doan .25 .60
10 Antoine Vermette .20 .50
11 Martin Hanzal .20 .50
12 Rob Klinkhammer .20 .50
13 Mike Smith .30 .75
14 Milan Lucic .30 .75
15 Brad Marchand .60 1.50
16 Carl Soderberg .20 .50
17 Torey Krug .25 .60
18 Dougie Hamilton .25 .60
19 Dennis Seidenberg .20 .50
20 David Krejci .30 .75
21 Tyler Ennis .20 .50
22 Zemgus Girgensons .25 .60
23 Tyler Myers .20 .50
24 Marcus Foligno .25 .60
25 Jhonas Enroth .30 .75
26 Mark Giordano .30 .75
27 Jiri Hudler .25 .60
28 Sean Monahan .20 .50
29 T.J. Brodie .20 .50
30 Joe Colborne .20 .50
31 Curtis Glencross .20 .50
32 Jeff Skinner .40 1.00
33 Alexander Semin .30 .75
34 Justin Faulk .25 .60
35 Jiri Tlusty .20 .50
36 Anton Khudobin .30 .75
37 Patrick Sharp .30 .75
38 Jonathan Toews .50 1.25
39 Marian Hossa .30 .75
40 Brent Seabrook .20 .50
41 Kris Versteeg .20 .50
42 Marcus Kruger .20 .50
43 Ben Smith .25 .60
44 Corey Crawford .40 1.00
45 Matt Duchene .30 .75
46 Ryan O'Reilly .30 .75
47 Nathan MacKinnon 1.25 3.00
48 Jamie McGinn .20 .50
49 Erik Johnson .20 .50
50 Nate Guenin .20 .50
51 Semyon Varlamov .30 .75
52 Ryan Johansen .25 .60
53 Brandon Dubinsky .20 .50
54 Nick Foligno .25 .60
55 Mark Letestu .25 .60
56 Jack Johnson .20 .50
57 Sergei Bobrovsky .50 1.25
58 Tyler Seguin .40 1.00
59 Alex Goligoski .20 .50
60 Cody Eakin .20 .50
61 Ryan Garbutt .20 .50
62 Rich Peverley .30 .75
63 Vernon Fiddler .20 .50
64 Erik Cole .20 .50
65 Shawn Horcoff .20 .50
66 Colton Sceviour .20 .50
67 Niklas Kronwall .25 .60
68 Henrik Zetterberg .40 1.00
69 Johan Franzen .25 .60
70 Pavel Datsyuk .50 1.25
71 Danny DeKeyser .20 .50
72 Jim Howard .40 1.00
73 Ben Scrivens .25 .60
74 Jordan Eberle .30 .75
75 Ryan Nugent-Hopkins .40 1.00
76 Justin Schultz .25 .60
77 Jeff Petry .30 .75
78 Andrew Ference .20 .50
79 Anton Belov .30 .75
80 Brian Campbell .20 .50
81 Brad Boyes .20 .50
82 Tomas Fleischmann .20 .50
83 Aleksander Barkov .50 1.25
84 Nick Bjugstad .20 .50
85 Erik Gudbranson .20 .50
86 Mike Richards .25 .60
87 Slava Voynov .30 .75
88 Dwight King .20 .50
89 Jarret Stoll .25 .60
90 Jonathan Quick .40 1.00
91 Tanner Pearson .20 .50
92 Jeff Carter .25 .60
93 Ryan Suter .25 .60
94 Nino Niederreiter .20 .50
95 Matt Cooke .20 .50
96 Zach Parise .30 .75
97 Jonas Brodin .20 .50
98 Jared Spurgeon .30 .75
99 Darcy Kuemper .30 .75
100 Carey Price .60 1.50
101 Max Pacioretty .30 .75
102 David Desharnais .20 .50
103 Andrei Markov .20 .50
104 Brendan Gallagher .30 .75
105 Alex Galchenyuk .20 .50
106 Michael Bournival .25 .60
107 Ryan Ellis .20 .50
108 Carter Hutton .25 .60
109 Mike Fisher .20 .50
110 Matt Cullen .20 .50
111 Roman Josi .30 .75
112 Seth Jones .30 .75
113 Pekka Rinne .30 .75
114 Filip Forsberg .50 1.25
115 Cory Schneider .30 .75
116 Jaromir Jagr 1.00 2.50
117 Travis Zajac .20 .50
118 Marek Zidlicky .20 .50
119 Eric Gelinas .25 .60
120 Damien Brunner .20 .50
121 Travis Hamonic .20 .50
122 John Tavares .50 1.25
123 Josh Bailey .25 .60
124 Brock Nelson .30 .75
125 Cal Clutterbuck .20 .50
126 Thomas Hickey .20 .50
127 Martin St. Louis .30 .75
128 Derek Stepan .20 .50
129 Derick Brassard .20 .50
130 Rick Nash .30 .75
131 Ryan McDonagh .20 .50
132 Henrik Lundqvist .75 2.00
133 Erik Karlsson .40 1.00
134 Kyle Turris .30 .75
135 Bobby Ryan .25 .60
136 Milan Michalek .20 .50
137 Patrick Wiercioch .20 .50
138 Craig Anderson .30 .75
139 Claude Giroux .30 .75
140 Wayne Simmonds .40 1.00
141 Mark Streit .20 .50
142 Matt Read .20 .50
143 Vincent Lecavalier .30 .75
144 Andrew MacDonald .20 .50
145 Ray Emery .25 .60
146 Evgeni Malkin .60 1.50
147 Pascal Dupuis .20 .50
148 Chris Kunitz .30 .75
149 Olli Maatta .20 .50
150 Kris Letang .40 1.00
151 Paul Martin .20 .50
152 Jeff Zatkoff .25 .60
153 Joe Pavelski .40 1.00
154 Logan Couture .40 1.00
155 Tommy Wingels .20 .50
156 Jason Demers .20 .50
157 Marc-Edouard Vlasic .20 .50
158 Matt Nieto .25 .60
159 Matt Irwin .20 .50
160 Alex Stalock .20 .50
161 T.J. Oshie .30 .75
162 Jaden Schwartz .40 1.00
163 Kevin Shattenkirk .20 .50
164 Jay Bouwmeester .20 .50
165 Vladimir Sobotka .20 .50
166 Vladimir Tarasenko .40 1.00
167 Barret Jackman .20 .50
168 Brian Elliott .25 .60
169 Steven Stamkos .60 1.50
170 Valtteri Filppula .20 .50
171 Tyler Johnson .20 .50
172 Alex Killorn .20 .50
173 Matt Carle .20 .50
174 Radko Gudas .20 .50
175 Ondrej Palat .25 .60
176 James van Riemsdyk .25 .60
177 Tyler Bozak .20 .50
178 Joffrey Lupul .20 .50
179 Dion Phaneuf .25 .60
180 Morgan Rielly .30 .75
181 Jonathan Bernier .25 .60
182 David Clarkson .20 .50
183 Daniel Sedin .40 1.00
184 Chris Higgins .20 .50
185 Zack Kassian .20 .50
186 Kevin Bieksa .25 .60
187 Alexander Edler .20 .50
188 Eddie Lack .25 .60
189 Alexander Ovechkin 1.25 3.00
190 Joel Ward .20 .50
191 Troy Brouwer .20 .50
192 Mike Green .25 .60
193 John Carlson .30 .75
194 Blake Wheeler .30 .75
195 Dustin Byfuglien .30 .75
196 Mark Scheifele .50 1.25
197 Jacob Trouba .25 .60
198 Evander Kane .30 .75
199 Quick/Kopitar/Gaborik CL .50 1.25
200 Lundqvist/Nash/St. Louis CL .75 2.00
201 William Karlsson YG RC 8.00 20.00
202 Brandon Gormley YG RC 2.50 6.00
203 Mark Visentin YG RC 2.50 6.00
204 Alexander Khokhlachev YG RC 2.50 6.00
205 Bobby Robins YG RC 2.00 5.00
206 Sam Reinhart YG RC 15.00 40.00
207 Nicolas Deslauriers YG RC 2.50 6.00
208 Jake McCabe YG RC 2.50 6.00
209 Corban Knight YG RC 2.50 6.00
210 Tyler Wotherspoon YG RC 2.50 6.00
211 Johnny Gaudreau YG RC 25.00 60.00
212 Victor Rask YG RC 2.50 6.00
213 Patrick Brown YG RC 2.50 6.00
214 Teuvo Teravainen YG RC 6.00 15.00
215 Trevor van Riemsdyk YG RC 4.00 10.00
216 Joey Hishon YG RC 3.00 8.00
217 Dennis Everberg YG RC 2.50 6.00
218 Alexander Wennberg YG RC 4.00 10.00
219 Patrik Nemeth YG RC 2.50 6.00
220 Ryan Sproul YG RC 2.50 6.00
221 Teemu Pulkkinen YG RC 3.00 8.00
222 Andrej Nestrasil YG RC 2.50 6.00
223 Leon Draisaitl YG RC 200.00 500.00
224 Oscar Klefbom YG RC 8.00 20.00
225 Aaron Ekblad YG RC 8.00 20.00
226 Vincent Trocheck YG RC 5.00 12.00
227 Jonathan Racine YG RC 2.50 6.00
228 Christian Folin YG RC 2.50 6.00
229 Jiri Sekac YG RC 2.00 5.00
230 Calle Jarnkrok YG RC 2.50 6.00
231 Colton Sissons YG RC 2.50 6.00
232 Damon Severson YG RC 2.50 6.00
233 Griffin Reinhart YG RC 2.50 6.00
234 Scott Mayfield YG RC 2.00 5.00
235 Johan Sundstrom YG RC 2.50 6.00
236 Anthony Duclair YG RC 5.00 12.00
237 Curtis Lazar YG RC 2.50 6.00
238 Pierre-Edouard Bellemare YG RC 2.50 6.00
239 Adam Payerl YG RC 2.00 5.00
240 Chris Tierney YG RC 2.50 6.00
241 Jori Lehtera YG RC 3.00 8.00
242 Ty Rattie YG RC 2.50 6.00
243 Vladislav Namestnikov YG RC 4.00 10.00
244 Brandon Kozun YG RC 2.00 5.00
245 Stuart Percy YG RC 2.50 6.00
246 Greg McKegg YG RC 2.00 5.00
247 Michael Zalewski YG RC 2.00 5.00
248 Evgeny Kuznetsov YG RC 6.00 15.00
249 Adam Lowry YG RC 5.00 12.00
250 Ekblad/Reinhart/Draisaitl YG CL 4.00 10.00
251 Ryan Kesler .30 .75
252 Frederik Andersen .40 1.00
253 Devante Smith-Pelly .25 .60
254 Corey Perry .50 1.25
255 Emerson Etem .25 .60
256 Pat Maroon .20 .50
257 Sami Vatanen .20 .50
258 Mikkel Boedker .20 .50
259 Sam Gagner .20 .50
260 Martin Erat .20 .50
261 Keith Yandle .20 .50
262 Oliver Ekman-Larsson .30 .75
263 Michael Stone .20 .50
264 Loui Eriksson .20 .50
265 Patrice Bergeron .40 1.00
266 Daniel Paille .20 .50
267 Zdeno Chara .30 .75
268 Tuukka Rask .40 1.00
269 Ryan Spooner .25 .60
270 Brian Gionta .20 .50
271 Drew Stafford .20 .50
272 Michal Neuvirth .25 .60
273 Chris Stewart .25 .60
274 Cody Hodgson .20 .50
275 Matt Moulson .20 .50
276 Jonas Hiller .25 .60
277 Dennis Wideman .20 .50
278 Matt Stajan .20 .50
279 Sven Baertschi .20 .50
280 Devin Setoguchi .25 .60
281 Mason Raymond .20 .50
282 Elias Lindholm .30 .75
283 Cam Ward .30 .75
284 Ryan Murphy .20 .50
285 Eric Staal .40 1.00
286 Jordan Staal .25 .60
287 Andrew Shaw .20 .50
288 Antti Raanta .30 .75
289 Patrick Kane .60 1.50
290 Brad Richards .30 .75
291 Bryan Bickell .20 .50
292 Duncan Keith .25 .60
293 Niklas Hjalmarsson .20 .50
294 John Mitchell .20 .50
295 Alex Tanguay .20 .50
296 Daniel Briere .25 .60
297 Jarome Iginla .40 1.00
298 Reto Berra .25 .60
299 Gabriel Landeskog .40 1.00
300 Tyson Barrie .20 .50
301 Cam Atkinson .30 .75
302 Scott Hartnell .20 .50
303 Curtis McElhinney .20 .50
304 David Savard .20 .50
305 James Wisniewski .20 .50
306 Jared Boll .20 .50
307 Antoine Roussel .20 .50
308 Jordie Benn .20 .50
309 Jason Spezza .30 .75
310 Trevor Daley .20 .50
311 Kari Lehtonen .25 .60
312 Jamie Benn .30 .75
313 Valeri Nichushkin .30 .75
314 Ales Hemsky .20 .50
315 Tomas Jurco .20 .50
316 Justin Abdelkader .25 .60
317 Tomas Tatar .20 .50
318 Jonas Gustavsson .25 .60
319 Gustav Nyquist .20 .50
320 Riley Sheahan .20 .50
321 Darren Helm .20 .50
322 Benoit Pouliot .20 .50
323 Viktor Fasth .25 .60
324 Nail Yakupov .20 .50
325 Teddy Purcell .20 .50
326 Boyd Gordon .20 .50
327 David Perron .25 .60
328 Taylor Hall .30 .75
329 Sean Bergenheim .20 .50
330 Jonathan Huberdeau .40 1.00
331 Willie Mitchell .20 .50
332 Jussi Jokinen .20 .50
333 Roberto Luongo .50 1.25
334 Dave Bolland .20 .50
335 Justin Williams .25 .60
336 Dustin Brown .30 .75
337 Tyler Toffoli .30 .75
338 Drew Doughty .40 1.00
339 Alec Martinez .20 .50
340 Marian Gaborik .30 .75
341 Anze Kopitar .50 1.25
342 Charlie Coyle .30 .75
343 Niklas Backstrom .25 .60
344 Mikael Granlund .25 .60
345 Erik Haula .20 .50
346 Mikko Koivu .25 .60
347 Thomas Vanek .25 .60
348 Mathew Dumba .20 .50
349 Alexei Emelin .20 .50
350 Tomas Plekanec .20 .50
351 P.K. Subban .40 1.00
352 P.A. Parenteau .20 .50
353 Lars Eller .20 .50
354 Nathan Beaulieu .20 .50
355 Dustin Tokarski .20 .50
356 Shea Weber .25 .60
357 Derek Roy .20 .50
358 Mike Ribeiro .20 .50
359 Colin Wilson .20 .50
360 James Neal .20 .50
361 Craig Smith .20 .50
362 Bryce Salvador .20 .50
363 Stephen Gionta .20 .50
364 Martin Havlat .25 .60
365 Patrik Elias .30 .75
366 Michael Cammalleri .25 .60
367 Adam Henrique .25 .60
368 Andy Greene .20 .50
369 Nick Leddy .20 .50
370 Nikolai Kulemin .20 .50
371 Frans Nielsen .20 .50
372 Jaroslav Halak .30 .75
373 Kyle Okposo .20 .50
374 Ryan Strome .30 .75
375 Johnny Boychuk .25 .60
376 Mikhail Grabovski .20 .50
377 Daniel Girardi .20 .50
378 Chris Kreider .40 1.00
379 Lee Stempniak .20 .50
380 Carl Hagelin .20 .50
381 Marc Staal .20 .50
382 Mats Zuccarello .30 .75
383 Alex Chiasson .25 .60
384 Clarke MacArthur .20 .50
385 Mika Zibanejad .40 1.00
386 Robin Lehner .25 .60
387 Chris Neil .20 .50
388 David Legwand .25 .60
389 Brayden Schenn .30 .75
390 Michael Del Zotto .20 .50
391 Sean Couturier .25 .60
392 Luke Schenn .30 .75
393 Steve Mason .25 .60
394 R.J. Umberger .20 .50
395 Jakub Voracek .25 .60
396 Marc-Andre Fleury .60 1.50
397 Beau Bennett .20 .50
398 Sidney Crosby 1.25 3.00
399 Brandon Sutter .20 .50
400 Christian Ehrhoff .20 .50
401 Patric Hornqvist .20 .50
402 Thomas Greiss .25 .60
403 Brent Burns .30 .75
404 Patrick Marleau .30 .75
405 Antti Niemi .25 .60
406 Tomas Hertl .30 .75
407 Joe Thornton .50 1.25
408 Justin Braun .20 .50
409 Alexander Steen .20 .50
410 David Backes .20 .50
411 Patrik Berglund .20 .50
412 Dmitrij Jaskin .25 .60
413 Jake Allen .30 .75
414 Alex Pietrangelo .25 .60
415 Paul Stastny .25 .60
416 Martin Brodeur .75 2.00
417 Ben Bishop .25 .60
418 J.T. Brown .20 .50
419 Brenden Morrow .25 .60
420 Evgeni Nabokov .25 .60
421 Victor Hedman .40 1.00
422 Ryan Callahan .20 .50
423 Anton Stralman .20 .50
424 Leo Komarov .20 .50
425 James Reimer .30 .75
426 Jake Gardiner .20 .50
427 Phil Kessel .30 .75
428 Peter Holland .20 .50
429 Nazem Kadri .40 1.00
430 Cody Franson .20 .50
431 Henrik Sedin .40 1.00
432 Ryan Miller .30 .75
433 Radim Vrbata .20 .50
434 Luca Sbisa .25 .60
435 Nick Bonino .20 .50
436 Alexandre Burrows .20 .50
437 Matt Niskanen .25 .60
438 Braden Holtby .40 1.00
439 Brooks Orpik .20 .50
440 Marcus Johansson .25 .60
441 Nicklas Backstrom .30 .75
442 Brooks Laich .20 .50
443 Andrew Ladd .20 .50
444 Bryan Little .30 .75
445 Ondrej Pavelec .30 .75
446 Tobias Enstrom .20 .50
447 Zach Bogosian .25 .60
448 Mathieu Perreault .20 .50
449 Price/Subban/Pacioretty CL .60 1.50
450 T.Hall/RNH/Eberle CL .40 1.00
451 Joe Morrow YG RC 3.00 8.00
452 Marko Dano YG RC 2.50 6.00
453 Markus Granlund YG RC 4.00 10.00
454 Rob Zepp YG RC 4.00 10.00
455 Tobias Rieder YG RC 2.50 6.00
456 Scott Harrington YG RC 2.50 6.00
457 Darnell Nurse YG RC 25.00 60.00
458 Laurent Brossoit YG RC 10.00 25.00
459 Colin Smith YG RC 2.50 6.00
460 Joel Armia YG RC 2.50 6.00
461 Jyrki Jokipakka YG RC 2.50 6.00
462 Phillip Danault YG RC 10.00 25.00
463 Cedric Paquette YG RC 2.50 6.00
464 Shayne Gostisbehere YG RC 5.00 12.00
465 Joni Ortio YG RC 3.00 8.00
466 Scott Wilson YG RC 2.00 5.00
467 Andre Burakovsky YG RC 8.00 20.00
468 Melker Karlsson YG RC 2.50 6.00
469 Jordan Binnington YG RC 30.00 80.00
470 Bogdan Yakimov YG RC 2.50 6.00
471 Seth Griffith YG RC 3.00 8.00
472 Seth Helgeson YG RC 2.00 5.00
473 Brendan Shinnimin YG RC 2.00 5.00
474 Borna Rendulic YG RC 2.50 6.00
475 Derrick Pouliot YG RC 3.00 8.00
476 John Klingberg YG RC 10.00 25.00
477 Jonathan Drouin YG RC 10.00 25.00
478 Andrei Vasilevskiy YG RC 100.00 250.00
479 Andrew Agozzino YG RC 2.00 5.00
480 Petteri Lindbohm YG RC 2.00 5.00
481 Adam Clendening YG RC 2.50 6.00
482 Curtis McKenzie YG RC 2.00 5.00
483 Christopher Gibson YG RC 4.00 10.00
484 Mirco Mueller YG RC 2.50 6.00
485 Barclay Goodrow YG RC 4.00 10.00
486 Anton Forsberg YG RC 2.00 5.00
487 Max Friberg YG RC 2.00 5.00
488 Josh Jooris YG RC 2.50 6.00
489 Tyler Graovac YG RC 2.00 5.00
490 Kevin Hayes YG RC 6.00 15.00
491 Chris Wagner YG RC 2.50 6.00
492 Andy Andreoff YG RC 2.50 6.00
493 Sven Andrighetto YG RC 3.00 8.00
494 Bo Horvat YG RC 20.00 50.00
495 David Pastrnak YG RC 200.00 500.00
496 Brett Ritchie YG RC 2.50 6.00
497 Dominik Uher YG RC 2.00 5.00
498 Scott Darling YG RC 5.00 12.00
499 Kerby Rychel YG RC 2.00 5.00
500 Drouin/Pouliot/Horvat YG CL 4.00 10.00
501 Brandon Saad .25 .60
502 Niklas Svedberg .30 .75
503 Mike Santorelli .20 .50
504 Steve Downie .20 .50
505 Michael Hutchinson .20 .50
506 Anders Lee .30 .75
507 Nikita Kucherov .60 1.50
508 Reilly Smith .30 .75
509 Jason Zucker .30 .75
510 Matt Beleskey .20 .50
511 Antoine Vermette .20 .50
512 Jaromir Jagr 1.00 2.50
513 Zach Bogosian .25 .60
514 David Perron .25 .60
515 Devan Dubnyk .25 .60
516 Derek Roy .20 .50
517 Tyler Myers .20 .50
518 Drew Stafford .20 .50
519 Devante Smith-Pelly .25 .60
520 Keith Yandle .20 .50
521 Jesse Blacker YG RC 3.00 8.00
522 Julien Brouillette YG RC 2.00 5.00
523 Miikka Salomaki YG RC 2.00 5.00
524 Adam Clendening YG 2.00 5.00
525 Nikita Nesterov YG RC 2.00 5.00
526 Jiri Sekac YG 1.50 4.00
527 Tyler Gaudet YG RC 1.50 4.00
528 Andrew Hammond YG RC 3.00 8.00
529 Rocco Grimaldi YG RC 2.00 5.00
530 Anthony Duclair YG 3.00 8.00
JB Jean Beliveau Tribute 25.00 60.00

2014-15 Upper Deck Exclusives

*1-200 VETS/100: 6X TO 15X BASIC CARDS
*201-250 YG/100: 1.5X TO 4X BASIC RC
201 William Karlsson YG 30.00 80.00
206 Sam Reinhart YG 60.00 150.00
211 Johnny Gaudreau YG 125.00 300.00
223 Leon Draisaitl YG 300.00 800.00
225 Aaron Ekblad YG 60.00 150.00
226 Vincent Trocheck YG 20.00 50.00
248 Evgeny Kuznetsov YG 25.00 60.00
249 Adam Lowry YG 12.00 30.00
458 Laurent Brossoit YG 25.00 60.00
464 Shayne Gostisbehere YG 60.00 100.00
476 John Klingberg YG 60.00 100.00
477 Jonathan Drouin YG 50.00 125.00
494 Bo Horvat YG 60.00 150.00
495 David Pastrnak YG 300.00 800.00
528 Andrew Hammond YG 50.00 100.00

2014-15 Upper Deck 25th Anniversary Buyback Autographs

32 Mike Richter 25.00 60.00
43 Pierre Turgeon 20.00 50.00
44 Mark Messier 50.00 125.00
46 Mike Modano 40.00 100.00
47 Theoren Fleury 30.00 80.00
52 Larry Robinson 25.00 60.00
54 Wayne Gretzky 300.00 800.00
55 Ed Belfour SR 25.00 60.00
56 Steve Yzerman 60.00 150.00

63 Jeremy Roenick 40.00 100.00
64 Ray Bourque 40.00 100.00
67 Ron Francis 30.00 80.00
73 Luc Robitaille 25.00 60.00
126 Brian Bellows 20.00 50.00
133 Michel Goulet 20.00 50.00
142 Rob Brown 20.00 50.00
143 Al MacInnis 30.00 80.00
144 Mario Lemieux 100.00 250.00
146 Jari Kurri 25.00 60.00
153 Patrick Roy 60.00 150.00
154 Brett Hull 50.00 125.00
156 Cam Neely 25.00 60.00
162 Guy Lafleur 30.00 80.00
164 Joe Sakic 50.00 125.00
173 Adam Oates 25.00 60.00
175 Curtis Joseph SR 30.00 80.00
188 Guy Carbonneau 25.00 60.00
190 Joe Murphy 25.00 60.00
201 Bill Ranford
Conn Smythe Trophy 25.00 60.00
223 Doug Wilson 20.00 50.00
224 Vincent Damphousse 20.00 50.00
227 Ron Hextall 25.00 60.00
232 Andy Moog 25.00 60.00
253 Brian Leetch 20.00 50.00
256 Trevor Linden 25.00 60.00
264 Grant Fuhr 40.00 100.00
271 Doug Gilmour 30.00 80.00
277 Mike Gartner 30.00 80.00
284 Glenn Anderson 20.00 50.00
356 Jaromir Jagr DP 80.00 200.00
365 Mats Sundin 25.00 60.00
422 Chris Chelios 25.00 60.00
426 Denis Savard 25.00 60.00
443 Dale Hawerchuk 30.00 80.00
447 Claude Lemieux 20.00 50.00
458 Felix Potvin WJC 40.00 100.00
483 Adam Oates AS 25.00 60.00
489 Ray Bourque AS 40.00 100.00
493 Cam Neely AS 25.00 60.00
504 Darryl Sittler NH 30.00 80.00
509 Bobby Clarke NH 40.00 100.00
510 Phil Esposito NH 40.00 100.00
526 Pavel Bure YG 25.00 60.00
545 Wayne Gretzky 2000th Pt. 300.00 800.00
546 Brett Hull 50/50 50.00 125.00

2014-15 Upper Deck A Piece of History 1000 Point Club Jerseys

PCAO Adam Oates 1B 20.00 50.00
PCBB Brian Bellows 1C 15.00 40.00
PCBL Brian Leetch 1C 15.00 40.00
PCGP Gilbert Perreault 1B 20.00 50.00
PCJT Joe Thornton 2B 25.00 60.00
PCLR Luc Robitaille 1B 20.00 50.00
PCMB Mike Bossy 2B 15.00 40.00
PCMS Mats Sundin 2B 15.00 40.00
PCNL Nicklas Lidstrom 2A 50.00 100.00
PCPE Phil Esposito 2B 25.00 50.00
PCRB Rod Brind'Amour 2B 12.00 30.00
PCSY Steve Yzerman 1A 80.00 200.00

2014-15 Upper Deck A Piece of History 500 Goal Club Jerseys

GCJI Jarome Iginla 1 40.00 100.00
GCJR Jeremy Roenick 2 50.00 125.00
GCMM Mike Modano 2 50.00 125.00
GCMS Mats Sundin 1 30.00 80.00
GCTS Teemu Selanne 1 60.00 150.00

2014-15 Upper Deck A Piece of History 500 Goal Club Jerseys Autographs

GCJI Jarome Iginla 150.00 250.00

2014-15 Upper Deck Buyback Autographs

20 S.Stamkos 11-12UD/40 20.00 40.00
80 J.Tavares 11-12UD/25 25.00 50.00
133 N.Lidstrom 11-12UD/45 25.00 50.00

2014-15 Upper Deck Canvas

C1 Corey Perry 2.00 5.00
C2 John Gibson 1.25 3.00
C3 Cam Fowler 1.25 3.00
C4 Mike Smith 1.25 3.00
C5 Antoine Vermette .75 2.00
C6 Keith Yandle .75 2.00
C7 Patrice Bergeron 1.50 4.00
C8 Brad Marchand 2.50 6.00
C9 Reilly Smith 1.25 3.00
C10 Loui Eriksson .75 2.00
C11 Zemgus Girgensons 1.00 2.50
C12 Cody Hodgson .75 2.00
C13 Mark Giordano 1.25 3.00
C14 Matt Stajan .75 2.00
C15 Elias Lindholm 1.25 3.00
C16 Alexander Semin 1.25 3.00
C17 Jonathan Toews 2.00 5.00
C18 Duncan Keith 1.00 2.50
C19 Brandon Saad 1.00 2.50
C20 Brent Seabrook .75 2.00
C21 Semyon Varlamov 1.25 3.00
C22 Gabriel Landeskog 1.50 4.00
C23 Nathan MacKinnon 5.00 12.00
C24 Brandon Dubinsky .75 2.00
C25 Ryan Johansen 1.00 2.50
C26 Boone Jenner 1.25 3.00
C27 Valeri Nichushkin 1.25 3.00
C28 Tyler Seguin 1.50 4.00
C29 Antoine Roussel .75 2.00
C30 Henrik Zetterberg 1.50 4.00
C31 Pavel Datsyuk 2.00 5.00
C32 Gustav Nyquist .75 2.00
C33 Taylor Hall 1.25 3.00
C34 Nail Yakupov .75 2.00
C35 Jordan Eberle 1.25 3.00
C36 Roberto Luongo 2.00 5.00
C37 Aleksander Barkov 2.00 5.00
C38 Marian Gaborik 1.25 3.00
C39 Tanner Pearson .75 2.00
C40 Tyler Toffoli 1.25 3.00
C41 Anze Kopitar 2.00 5.00
C42 Jason Pominville .75 2.00
C43 Mikael Granlund 1.00 2.50
C44 Zach Parise 1.25 3.00
C45 Max Pacioretty 1.25 3.00
C46 P.K. Subban 1.50 4.00
C47 Brendan Gallagher 1.25 3.00
C48 Seth Jones 1.25 3.00
C49 Ryan Ellis .75 2.00
C50 Pekka Rinne 1.25 3.00
C51 Jaromir Jagr 4.00 10.00
C52 Eric Gelinas 1.00 2.50
C53 Cory Schneider 1.25 3.00
C54 Kyle Okposo .75 2.00
C55 Ryan Strome 1.25 3.00
C56 John Tavares 2.00 5.00
C57 Henrik Lundqvist 3.00 8.00
C58 Rick Nash 1.25 3.00
C59 Chris Kreider 1.50 4.00
C60 Mika Zibanejad 1.50 4.00
C61 Craig Anderson 1.25 3.00
C62 Jakub Voracek 1.00 2.50
C63 Brayden Schenn 1.25 3.00
C64 Steve Mason 1.00 2.50
C65 Olli Maatta .75 2.00
C66 Chris Kunitz 1.25 3.00
C67 Kris Letang 1.50 4.00
C68 Evgeni Malkin 2.50 6.00
C69 Logan Couture 1.50 4.00
C70 Tomas Hertl 1.25 3.00
C71 Antti Niemi 1.00 2.50
C72 Brian Elliott 1.00 2.50
C73 Alex Pietrangelo 1.00 2.50
C74 Vladimir Tarasenko 1.50 4.00
C75 T.J. Oshie 1.25 3.00
C76 Ryan Callahan .75 2.00
C77 Ben Bishop 1.00 2.50
C78 Ondrej Palat 1.00 2.50
C79 Nazem Kadri 1.50 4.00
C80 Morgan Rielly 1.25 3.00
C81 Phil Kessel 1.25 3.00
C82 Zack Kassian .75 2.00
C83 Henrik Sedin 1.50 4.00
C84 Alexandre Burrows .75 2.00
C85 Alexander Ovechkin 5.00 12.00
C86 Mike Green 1.00 2.50
C87 Philipp Grubauer 1.25 3.00
C88 Dustin Byfuglien 1.25 3.00
C89 Andrew Ladd .75 2.00
C90 Doughty/Brown/Williams CL 1.00 2.50
C91 William Karlsson YG 12.00 30.00
C92 Brandon Gormley YG 4.00 10.00
C93 Alexander Khokhlachev YG 4.00 10.00
C94 Sam Reinhart YG 15.00 40.00
C95 Jake McCabe YG 4.00 10.00
C96 Johnny Gaudreau YG 25.00 60.00
C97 Victor Rask YG 4.00 10.00
C98 Teuvo Teravainen YG 12.00 30.00
C99 Joey Hishon YG 5.00 12.00
C100 Alexander Wennberg YG 6.00 15.00
C101 Marko Dano YG 4.00 10.00
C102 Patrik Nemeth YG 4.00 10.00
C103 Andrej Nestrasil YG 4.00 10.00
C104 Leon Draisaitl YG 250.00 600.00
C105 Aaron Ekblad YG 10.00 25.00
C106 Jiri Sekac YG 3.00 8.00
C107 Calle Jarnkrok YG 4.00 10.00
C108 Damon Severson YG 4.00 10.00
C109 Griffin Reinhart YG 4.00 10.00
C110 Anthony Duclair YG 6.00 15.00
C111 Curtis Lazar YG 4.00 10.00
C112 Chris Tierney YG 4.00 10.00
C113 Mirco Mueller YG 4.00 10.00
C114 Ty Rattie YG 4.00 10.00
C115 Vladislav Namestnikov YG 6.00 15.00
C116 Stuart Percy YG 4.00 10.00
C117 Evgeny Kuznetsov YG 6.00 15.00
C118 Andre Burakovsky YG 8.00 20.00
C119 Adam Lowry YG 6.00 15.00
C120 A.Ekblad/S.Reinhart YG CL 10.00 25.00
C121 Ryan Kesler 1.25 3.00
C122 Ryan Getzlaf 1.25 3.00
C123 Frederik Andersen 1.50 4.00
C124 Shane Doan 1.00 2.50
C125 Sam Gagner .75 2.00
C126 Mikkel Boedker .75 2.00
C127 Zdeno Chara 1.25 3.00
C128 Tuukka Rask 1.50 4.00
C129 Milan Lucic 1.25 3.00
C130 Drew Stafford .75 2.00
C131 Matt Moulson .75 2.00
C132 Tyler Myers .75 2.00
C133 Jiri Hudler 1.00 2.50
C134 Sean Monahan .75 2.00
C135 Eric Staal 1.50 4.00
C136 Jeff Skinner 1.50 4.00
C137 Patrick Sharp 1.25 3.00
C138 Corey Crawford 1.50 4.00
C139 Patrick Kane 2.50 6.00
C140 Jarome Iginla 1.50 4.00
C141 Ryan O'Reilly 1.25 3.00
C142 Matt Duchene 1.25 3.00
C143 Sergei Bobrovsky 2.00 5.00
C144 Jack Johnson .75 2.00
C145 Scott Hartnell .75 2.00
C146 Kari Lehtonen 1.00 2.50
C147 Jamie Benn 1.25 3.00
C148 Jason Spezza 1.25 3.00
C149 Johan Franzen 1.00 2.50
C150 Niklas Kronwall 1.00 2.50
C151 Jim Howard 1.50 4.00
C152 Ben Scrivens 1.00 2.50
C153 Ryan Nugent-Hopkins 1.50 4.00
C154 David Perron 1.00 2.50
C155 Jonathan Huberdeau 1.50 4.00
C156 Nick Bjugstad .75 2.00
C157 Jonathan Quick 1.50 4.00
C158 Jeff Carter 1.00 2.50
C159 Dustin Brown 1.25 3.00
C160 Drew Doughty 1.50 4.00
C161 Ryan Suter 1.00 2.50
C162 Darcy Kuemper 1.25 3.00
C163 Thomas Vanek 1.00 2.50
C164 Alex Galchenyuk .75 2.00
C165 Carey Price 2.50 6.00
C166 Tomas Plekanec .75 2.00
C167 Shea Weber 1.00 2.50
C168 James Neal .75 2.00
C169 Mike Ribeiro .75 2.00
C170 Michael Cammalleri 1.00 2.50
C171 Patrik Elias 1.25 3.00
C172 Jaroslav Halak 1.25 3.00
C173 Brock Nelson 1.25 3.00
C174 Martin St. Louis 1.25 3.00
C175 Ryan McDonagh .75 2.00
C176 Mats Zuccarello 1.25 3.00
C177 Derek Stepan .75 2.00
C178 Marc Staal .75 2.00
C179 Kyle Turris 1.25 3.00
C180 Erik Karlsson 1.50 4.00
C181 Wayne Simmonds 1.50 4.00
C182 Claude Giroux 1.25 3.00
C183 Vincent Lecavalier 1.25 3.00
C184 Marc-Andre Fleury 2.50 6.00
C185 Sidney Crosby 5.00 12.00
C186 Patric Hornqvist .75 2.00
C187 Beau Bennett .75 2.00
C188 Patrick Marleau 1.25 3.00
C189 Joe Pavelski 1.50 4.00
C190 Joe Thornton 2.00 5.00
C191 Paul Stastny 1.00 2.50
C192 Patrik Berglund .75 2.00
C193 Alexander Steen .75 2.00
C194 David Backes .75 2.00
C195 Steven Stamkos 2.50 6.00
C196 Tyler Johnson .75 2.00
C197 Victor Hedman 1.50 4.00
C198 Jonathan Bernier 1.00 2.50
C199 Dion Phaneuf 1.00 2.50
C200 James van Riemsdyk 1.00 2.50
C201 Ryan Miller 1.25 3.00
C202 Daniel Sedin 1.50 4.00
C203 Nick Bonino .75 2.00
C204 Nicklas Backstrom 1.25 3.00
C205 Braden Holtby 1.50 4.00
C206 Brooks Orpik .75 2.00
C207 Matt Niskanen 1.00 2.50
C208 Evander Kane 1.25 3.00
C209 Blake Wheeler 1.25 3.00
C210 Kessel/Bernier/van Riem CL .75 2.00
C211 Phillip Danault YG 10.00 25.00
C212 Markus Granlund YG 6.00 15.00
C213 Colton Sissons YG 4.00 10.00
C214 Jonathan Drouin YG 10.00 25.00
C215 Teemu Pulkkinen YG 5.00 12.00
C216 Josh Jooris YG 4.00 10.00
C217 Sven Andrighetto YG 5.00 12.00
C218 Joe Morrow YG 5.00 12.00
C219 Andy Andreoff YG 4.00 10.00
C220 Tobias Rieder YG 4.00 10.00
C221 Derrick Pouliot YG 5.00 12.00
C222 Barclay Goodrow YG 6.00 15.00
C223 Curtis McKenzie YG 3.00 8.00
C224 Brett Ritchie YG 4.00 10.00
C225 David Pastrnak YG 200.00 500.00
C226 Rocco Grimaldi YG 4.00 10.00
C227 Darnell Nurse YG 30.00 80.00
C228 Jori Lehtera YG 5.00 12.00
C229 Seth Griffith YG 5.00 12.00
C230 Jordan Binnington YG 25.00 60.00
C231 Dennis Everberg YG 4.00 10.00
C232 Ryan Sproul YG 4.00 10.00
C233 Seth Helgeson YG 3.00 8.00
C234 Bo Horvat YG 15.00 40.00
C235 Christian Folin YG 4.00 10.00
C236 Andrei Vasilevskiy YG 100.00 250.00
C237 Trevor van Riemsdyk YG 6.00 15.00
C238 Kevin Hayes YG 10.00 25.00
C239 Shayne Gostisbehere YG 15.00 30.00
C240 Drouin/Horvat YG CL 4.00 10.00
C241 Arturs Irbe RET 8.00 20.00
C242 Chris Chelios RET 10.00 25.00
C243 Cam Neely RET 10.00 25.00
C244 Teemu Selanne RET 20.00 50.00
C245 Darryl Sittler RET 12.00 30.00
C246 Dominik Hasek RET 15.00 40.00
C247 Adam Oates RET 10.00 25.00
C248 John LeClair RET 10.00 25.00
C249 Doug Harvey RET 10.00 25.00
C250 Tony Esposito RET 10.00 25.00
C251 Bobby Orr RET 40.00 100.00
C252 Wendel Clark RET 15.00 40.00
C253 Terry Sawchuk RET 20.00 40.00
C254 Wayne Gretzky RET 30.00 60.00
C255 Mats Sundin RET 10.00 25.00
C256 Mark Visentin POE 8.00 20.00
C257 Brandon Kozun POE 6.00 15.00
C258 Brandon Gormley POE 8.00 20.00
C259 Curtis Lazar POE 10.00 25.00
C260 Ty Rattie POE 8.00 20.00
C261 Griffin Reinhart POE 8.00 20.00
C262 Jonathan Drouin POE 4.00 10.00
C263 Derrick Pouliot POE 12.00 30.00
C264 Anthony Duclair POE 10.00 25.00
C265 Sam Reinhart POE 12.00 30.00
C266 Bo Horvat POE 20.00 50.00
C267 Tyler Wotherspoon POE 8.00 20.00
C268 Aaron Ekblad POE 15.00 40.00
C269 Darnell Nurse POE 12.00 30.00
C270 Brett Ritchie POE 8.00 20.00

2014-15 Upper Deck Canvas Autographs

CAJS Joe Sakic 150.00 250.00
CAJT Jonathan Toews 250.00 400.00

2014-15 Upper Deck Clear Cut Captains

CCCAF Andrew Ference 5.00 12.00
CCCAL Andrew Ladd 5.00 12.00
CCCAO Alexander Ovechkin 30.00 80.00
CCCBA David Backes 5.00 12.00
CCCBE Jean Beliveau 8.00 20.00
CCCBS Bryce Salvador 5.00 12.00
CCCCG Claude Giroux 8.00 20.00
CCCDB Dustin Brown 8.00 20.00
CCCDP Dion Phaneuf 6.00 15.00
CCCES Eric Staal 10.00 25.00
CCCGL Gabriel Landeskog 10.00 25.00
CCCGP Gilbert Perreault 8.00 20.00
CCCHS Henrik Sedin 10.00 25.00
CCCHZ Henrik Zetterberg 10.00 25.00
CCCJB Jamie Benn 8.00 20.00
CCCJT Jonathan Toews 12.00 30.00
CCCMG Mark Giordano 8.00 20.00
CCCMK Mikko Koivu 6.00 15.00
CCCML Mario Lemieux 30.00 80.00
CCCMM Mark Messier 15.00 40.00
CCCPB Pavel Bure 8.00 20.00
CCCRG Ryan Getzlaf 8.00 20.00
CCCSC Sidney Crosby 30.00 80.00
CCCSD Shane Doan 6.00 15.00
CCCSS Steven Stamkos 15.00 40.00
CCCSW Shea Weber 8.00 20.00
CCCTA John Tavares 12.00 30.00
CCCTH Joe Thornton 12.00 30.00
CCCWG Wayne Gretzky 40.00 80.00
CCCZC Zdeno Chara 8.00 20.00

2014-15 Upper Deck Clear Cut Foundations

CCFBM O.Maatta/B.Bennett 8.00 20.00
CCFBR J.Bernier/M.Rielly 12.00 30.00
CCFBS T.Seguin/J.Benn 15.00 40.00
CCFBT Byfuglien/J.Trouba 12.00 30.00
CCFCT J.Carter/T.Toffoli 12.00 30.00
CCFDE Doan/O.Ekman-Lars 12.00 30.00
CCFDJ B.Dubinsky/B.Jenner 12.00 30.00
CCFDM Duchene/MacKinnon 50.00 125.00
CCFDN P.Datsyuk/G.Nyquist 20.00 50.00
CCFGK Kuemper/M.Granlund 12.00 30.00
CCFGM E.Gelinas/J.Merrill 10.00 25.00
CCFGR Ristolainen/Girgensons 10.00 25.00
CCFHB A.Barkov/J.Huberdeau 20.00 50.00
CCFHG P.Grubauer/B.Holtby 15.00 40.00
CCFHM S.Monahan/J.Hudler 10.00 25.00
CCFJP T.Johnson/O.Palat 10.00 25.00
CCFKC E.Karlsson/C.Ceci 15.00 40.00
CCFKJ Z.Kassian/N.Jensen 8.00 20.00
CCFKS T.Krug/R.Smith 12.00 30.00
CCFLG R.Getzlaf/H.Lindholm 12.00 30.00
CCFML E.Lindholm/R.Murphy 12.00 30.00
CCFNY RNH/N.Yakupov 15.00 40.00
CCFPH J.Pavelski/T.Hertl 15.00 40.00
CCFPT C.Price/D.Tokarski 25.00 60.00
CCFSK D.Keith/B.Seabrook 10.00 25.00
CCFSO A.Steen/T.Oshie 12.00 30.00
CCFSR B.Schenn/M.Read 12.00 30.00
CCFTS J.Tavares/R.Strome 20.00 50.00
CCFWJ S.Weber/S.Jones 12.00 30.00
CCFZM McDonagh/Zuccarello 8.00 20.00

2014-15 Upper Deck Clear Cut Stoppers

CCSCC Corey Crawford 8.00 20.00
CCSCJ Curtis Joseph 8.00 20.00
CCSCP Carey Price 12.00 30.00
CCSDH Dominik Hasek 10.00 25.00
CCSEB Ed Belfour 6.00 15.00
CCSHL Henrik Lundqvist 15.00 40.00
CCSJG John Gibson 6.00 15.00
CCSJQ Jonathan Quick 8.00 20.00
CCSMB Martin Brodeur 15.00 40.00
CCSPR Patrick Roy 20.00 50.00
CCSSB Sergei Bobrovsky 10.00 25.00
CCSTR Tuukka Rask 8.00 20.00

2014-15 Upper Deck Day With The Cup

DC1 Tyler Toffoli 30.00 80.00
DC2 Dustin Brown 30.00 80.00
DC3 Jonathan Quick 30.00 80.00
DC4 Marian Gaborik 30.00 80.00
DC5 Anze Kopitar 30.00 80.00
DC6 Slava Voynov 20.00 50.00
DC7 Justin Williams 25.00 60.00
DC8 Tanner Pearson 20.00 50.00
DC9 Drew Doughty 40.00 100.00
DC10 Jake Muzzin 30.00 80.00
DC11 Mike Richards 25.00 60.00
DC12 Jarret Stoll 25.00 60.00
DC13 Robyn Regehr 20.00 50.00
DC14 Jordan Nolan 30.00 80.00
DC15 Matt Greene 20.00 50.00
DC16 Colin Fraser 20.00 50.00
DC17 Willie Mitchell 20.00 50.00
DC18 Martin Jones 25.00 60.00
DC19 Bill Ranford 30.00 80.00
DC20 Alec Martinez 20.00 50.00
DC21 Trevor Lewis 20.00 50.00
DC22 P.Pritchard/C.Campbell 25.00 60.00

2014-15 Upper Deck Day With The Cup Flashback

DCF1 Mario Lemieux 125.00 200.00
DCF2 Ron Francis 40.00 80.00
DCF3 Jaromir Jagr 90.00 150.00
DCF4 Tom Barrasso 30.00 60.00

2014-15 Upper Deck Game Jerseys

GJAG Alex Galchenyuk 1F 2.00 5.00
GJAH Adam Henrique 1F 2.50 6.00
GJAM Andrei Markov 1E 2.00 5.00
GJAN Antti Niemi 1F 2.50 6.00
GJBB Brian Bellows 1E 2.50 6.00
GJBC Braydon Coburn 1F 2.00 5.00
GJBH Brett Hull 2 8.00 20.00
GJBI Bryan Bickell 1F 2.00 5.00
GJBL Rob Blake 2 4.00 10.00
GJBO Ray Bourque 2 6.00 15.00
GJBS Ben Scrivens 1E 2.50 6.00
GJBW Blake Wheeler 2 3.00 8.00
GJCA John Carlson 1F 3.00 8.00
GJCC Corey Crawford 1D 4.00 10.00
GJCC Chris Chelios 2 3.00 8.00
GJCH Cody Hodgson 1E 2.00 5.00
GJCJ Curtis Joseph 1A 12.00 30.00
GJCK Chris Kreider 1F 4.00 10.00
GJCO Sean Couturier 1F 2.50 6.00
GJCP Carey Price 1F 6.00 15.00
GJCS Cory Schneider 1D 3.00 8.00
GJDA Damien Brunner 1F 2.00 5.00
GJDB Dustin Brown 1F 3.00 8.00
GJDD Drew Doughty 1F 4.00 10.00
GJDD2 Drew Doughty TC 2 5.00 12.00
GJDG Doug Gilmour 2 5.00 12.00
GJDH Dominik Hasek Wings 1A 15.00 40.00
GJDH2 Dale Hawerchuk 2 4.00 10.00
GJDK Darcy Kuemper 2 3.00 8.00
GJDS Drew Stafford 1F 2.00 5.00
GJDS Denis Savard 2 3.00 8.00
GJEB Ed Belfour Panth 1B 5.00 12.00
GJEB Ed Belfour Stars 2 4.00 10.00
GJEJ Jhonas Enroth 2 3.00 8.00
GJEK Erik Karlsson 2 4.00 10.00
GJEL Eric Lindros Stars 1B 8.00 20.00
GJEM Evgeni Malkin TC 1D 8.00 20.00
GJER Eric Lindros Flyers 1F 5.00 12.00
GJES Eric Staal 1F 4.00 10.00
GJFO Peter Forsberg Pred 1C 8.00 20.00
GJGE Georges Laraque 1E 2.50 6.00
GJGF Grant Fuhr 1D 5.00 12.00
GJGL Guy Lafleur 2 5.00 12.00
GJGL Gabriel Landeskog 1C 5.00 12.00
GJGM Glen Murray 1F 2.50 6.00
GJGO Michel Goulet 1D 2.50 6.00
GJGR Mikael Granlund 2 2.50 6.00
GJHA Dominik Hasek Sen 2 5.00 12.00
GJHE Dany Heatley TC 1F 3.00 8.00
GJHO Jim Howard 1F 4.00 10.00
GJHZ Henrik Zetterberg 1D 4.00 10.00
GJJA Jake Allen 2 3.00 8.00
GJJC Jeff Carter 1F 2.50 6.00
GJJE Jordan Eberle 2 3.00 8.00
GJJF Johan Franzen 2 2.50 6.00
GJJI Jarome Iginla TC 2 5.00 12.00
GJJL John LeClair 1F 3.00 8.00
GJJO Jamie Oleksiak TC 2 3.00 8.00
GJJQ Jonathan Quick 1F 4.00 10.00
GJJR Jeremy Roenick TC 1D 6.00 15.00
GJJS Joe Sakic TC 2 8.00 20.00
GJJS Jeff Skinner TC 1B 6.00 15.00
GJJT Joe Thornton TC 2 6.00 15.00
GJJT Joe Thornton 1F 5.00 12.00
GJKL Kari Lehtonen 1F 2.50 6.00
GJKT Kyle Turris 1E 3.00 8.00
GJLC Logan Couture 2 4.00 10.00
GJLI Eric Lindros Rngrs 1F 5.00 12.00
GJLM Larry Murphy 1C 3.00 8.00
GJLR Luc Robitaille 1D 3.00 8.00
GJLR Larry Robinson TC 2 4.00 10.00
GJLU Milan Lucic 1C 4.00 10.00
GJMD Matt Duchene 1F 3.00 8.00
GJMF Marc-Andre Fleury TC 1F 8.00 20.00
GJMF Marc-Andre Fleury Pens 2 6.00 15.00
GJMG Mike Gartner 2 4.00 10.00
GJML Mario Lemieux 1A 40.00 100.00
GJMM Mark Messier 1A 20.00 50.00
GJMM Matt Moulson 2 2.00 5.00
GJMN Markus Naslund 1F 3.00 8.00
GJMS Mike Smith 2 3.00 8.00
GJNB Nicklas Backstrom 1D 3.00 8.00
GJNI Nicklas Lidstrom 1F 3.00 8.00
GJNK Niklas Kronwall 1F 2.50 6.00
GJNL Nick Leddy 1F 2.00 5.00
GJNY Nail Yakupov 1D 2.00 5.00
GJOK Olaf Kolzig 1E 3.00 8.00
GJOR Colton Orr 1E 2.00 5.00
GJPB Patrice Bergeron Bruin 1D 4.00 10.00
GJPB Patrice Bergeron TC 2 5.00 12.00
GJPC Paul Coffey TC 1F 4.00 10.00
GJPD Pavel Datsyuk 2 5.00 12.00
GJPF Peter Forsberg Flyers 1D 6.00 15.00
GJPM Patrick Marleau TC 1E 5.00 12.00
GJPR Pekka Rinne 1D 3.00 8.00
GJPS P.K. Subban 1E 4.00 10.00
GJQH Quinton Howden TC 2 2.50 6.00
GJRA Bill Ranford 1C 4.00 10.00
GJRB Richard Brodeur 1E 3.00 8.00
GJRB Rod Brind'Amour 2 2.50 6.00
GJRE Matt Read 1E 2.00 5.00
GJRF Ron Francis 2 4.00 10.00
GJRG Ryan Getzlaf 2 3.00 8.00
GJRH Ron Hextall 1F 3.00 8.00
GJRI Mike Richards 1F 2.50 6.00
GJRL Larry Robinson Kings 1C 4.00 10.00
GJRL Roberto Luongo 2 5.00 12.00
GJRN Rick Nash 1E 3.00 8.00
GJRO Rob Brown 1F 2.50 6.00
GJRS Ryan Strome TC 2 4.00 10.00
GJSA Joe Sakic 1D 6.00 15.00
GJSC Sidney Crosby 1A 40.00 100.00
GJSD Simon Despres 1F 3.00 8.00
GJSE Daniel Sedin 1F 4.00 10.00
GJSK Saku Koivu 1B 5.00 12.00
GJSM Steve Mason 1F 2.50 6.00
GJSV Semyon Varlamov 1F 3.00 8.00
GJTA John Tavares 2 5.00 12.00
GJTH Taylor Hall 1D 3.00 8.00
GJTL Trevor Linden 1F 3.00 8.00
GJTM Tyler Myers 1F 2.00 5.00
GJTS Tyler Seguin 1D 4.00 10.00
GJVD Vincent Damphousse 2 2.50 6.00
GJVO Slava Voynov 1F 3.00 8.00
GJZB Zach Bogosian 1A 10.00 25.00

2014-15 Upper Deck Hockey Heroes

HH66 Steve Yzerman 2.00 5.00
HH67 Sidney Crosby 3.00 8.00
HH68 Jaromir Jagr 2.50 6.00
HH69 Peter Forsberg 1.50 4.00
HH70 Martin Brodeur 2.00 5.00
HH71 Vincent Lecavalier .75 2.00
HH72 Pavel Datsyuk 1.25 3.00
HH73 Nicklas Lidstrom .75 2.00
HH74 Alexander Ovechkin 3.00 8.00
HH75 Joe Sakic 1.50 4.00
HH76 Martin St. Louis .75 2.00
HH77 Jarome Iginla 1.00 2.50
HH78 M.Brodeur/N.Lidstrom ART 15.00 40.00
HH79 John Tavares 1.25 3.00
HH80 Alexander Ovechkin 3.00 8.00
HH81 Phil Kessel .75 2.00
HH82 Evgeni Malkin 1.50 4.00
HH83 Anze Kopitar 1.25 3.00
HH84 Carey Price 1.50 4.00
HH85 Claude Giroux .75 2.00
HH86 Shea Weber .60 1.50
HH87 Sidney Crosby 3.00 8.00
HH88 Patrick Kane 1.50 4.00
HH89 Ryan Getzlaf .75 2.00
HH90 Jonathan Toews 1.25 3.00
HH91 P.Kane/A.Ovechkin ART 12.00 30.00
HEADER Header Card 2000s 10.00 25.00
HEADER2 Header Card 2010s 10.00 25.00

2014-15 Upper Deck NCAA Young Guns

NCAABG Bill Guerin 10.00 25.00
NCAABL Rob Blake 10.00 25.00
NCAABL Brian Leetch 8.00 20.00
NCAACJ Curtis Joseph 12.00 30.00
NCAAMR Mike Richter 10.00 25.00
NCAARB Rod Brind'Amour 8.00 20.00

2014-15 Upper Deck Oversized

1 Ryan Getzlaf 1.25 3.00
38 Jonathan Toews 2.00 5.00
58 Tyler Seguin 1.50 4.00
68 Henrik Zetterberg 1.50 4.00
70 Pavel Datsyuk 2.00 5.00
90 Jonathan Quick 1.50 4.00
100 Carey Price 2.50 6.00
116 Jaromir Jagr 4.00 10.00
122 John Tavares 2.00 5.00
132 Henrik Lundqvist 3.00 8.00
139 Claude Giroux 1.25 3.00
146 Evgeni Malkin 2.50 6.00
169 Steven Stamkos 2.50 6.00
189 Alexander Ovechkin 5.00 12.00

2014-15 Upper Deck Rookie Breakouts

RB1 Leon Draisaitl 60.00 150.00
RB2 William Karlsson 15.00 40.00
RB3 Anthony Duclair 8.00 20.00
RB4 Dennis Everberg 5.00 12.00
RB5 Johnny Gaudreau 30.00 80.00
RB6 Chris Tierney 5.00 12.00
RB7 Vladislav Namestnikov 8.00 20.00
RB8 Kerby Rychel 6.00 15.00
RB9 Jonathan Drouin 25.00 50.00
RB10 Seth Griffith 6.00 15.00
RB11 Stuart Percy 5.00 12.00
RB12 Trevor van Riemsdyk 8.00 20.00
RB13 Jori Lehtera 6.00 15.00
RB14 Evgeny Kuznetsov 12.00 30.00
RB15 Teuvo Teravainen 8.00 20.00
RB16 Aaron Ekblad 12.00 30.00
RB17 Marko Dano 5.00 12.00
RB18 Darnell Nurse 10.00 25.00
RB19 Curtis Lazar 5.00 12.00
RB20 Andre Burakovsky 8.00 20.00
RB21 David Pastrnak 30.00 60.00
RB22 Kevin Hayes 12.00 30.00
RB23 Griffin Reinhart 5.00 12.00
RB24 Sam Reinhart 20.00 50.00
RB25 Victor Rask 5.00 12.00
RB26 Damon Severson 5.00 12.00
RB27 Alexander Wennberg 8.00 20.00
RB28 Jiri Sekac 4.00 10.00

2014-15 Upper Deck Rookie Materials

*PATCH/25: 1X TO 2.5X BASIC JSY
RM1 Damon Severson 2.50 6.00
RM2 Jonathan Drouin 5.00 12.00
RM3 Marko Dano 2.50 6.00
RM4 Aaron Ekblad 5.00 12.00
RM5 Greg McKegg 2.00 5.00
RM6 Alexander Wennberg 4.00 10.00
RM7 Darnell Nurse 5.00 12.00
RM8 Adam Lowry 4.00 10.00
RM9 Jake McCabe 2.50 6.00
RM10 Teuvo Teravainen 4.00 10.00
RM11 Mirco Mueller 2.50 6.00
RM12 Ty Rattie 2.50 6.00
RM14 Ryan Sproul 2.50 6.00
RM16 Leon Draisaitl 12.00 30.00
RM17 Patrik Nemeth 2.50 6.00
RM18 Jiri Sekac 2.00 5.00
RM20 Brandon Kozun 2.00 5.00
RM21 Laurent Brossoit 2.50 6.00
RM22 Sam Reinhart 5.00 12.00
RM23 Bo Horvat 6.00 15.00
RM24 Griffin Reinhart 2.50 6.00
RM25 Alexander Khokhlachev 2.50 6.00
RM26 Colton Sissons 2.50 6.00
RM27 Andre Burakovsky 5.00 12.00
RM28 Vincent Trocheck 5.00 12.00
RM29 Vladislav Namestnikov 4.00 10.00
RM31 Joey Hishon 3.00 8.00
RM32 Curtis McKenzie 2.00 5.00
RM33 Seth Griffith 3.00 8.00
RM34 Stuart Percy 2.50 6.00
RM35 Curtis Lazar 4.00 10.00
RM36 Evgeny Kuznetsov 5.00 12.00
RM37 Mark Visentin 2.50 6.00
RM38 Dennis Everberg 2.50 6.00
RM39 Johnny Gaudreau 10.00 25.00
RM40 William Karlsson 8.00 20.00
RM41 Chris Tierney 2.50 6.00
RM42 Andrej Nestrasil 2.50 6.00

2014-15 Upper Deck Shining Stars

*BLUE: .6X TO 1.5X BASIC INSERTS
SS1 Duncan Keith 1.50 4.00
SS2 Erik Karlsson 2.50 6.00
SS3 P.K. Subban 2.50 6.00
SS4 Alex Pietrangelo 1.50 4.00
SS5 Shea Weber 1.50 4.00
SS6 Ryan McDonagh 1.25 3.00
SS7 Drew Doughty 2.50 6.00
SS8 Jacob Trouba 1.50 4.00
SS9 Mark Giordano 2.00 5.00
SS10 Zdeno Chara 2.00 5.00
SS11 Tuukka Rask 2.50 6.00
SS12 Corey Crawford 2.50 6.00
SS13 Semyon Varlamov 2.00 5.00
SS14 Sergei Bobrovsky 3.00 8.00
SS15 Jonathan Quick 2.50 6.00
SS16 Carey Price 4.00 10.00
SS17 Cory Schneider 2.00 5.00
SS18 Henrik Lundqvist 5.00 12.00
SS19 Ben Bishop 1.50 4.00
SS20 Jonathan Bernier 1.50 4.00
SS21 Ryan Getzlaf 2.00 5.00
SS22 Patrice Bergeron 2.50 6.00
SS23 Jonathan Toews 3.00 8.00
SS24 Tyler Seguin 2.50 6.00
SS25 Anze Kopitar 3.00 8.00
SS26 John Tavares 3.00 8.00
SS27 Claude Giroux 2.00 5.00
SS28 Sidney Crosby 8.00 20.00
SS29 Evgeni Malkin 4.00 10.00
SS30 Steven Stamkos 4.00 10.00
SS31 Corey Perry 3.00 8.00
SS32 Patrick Kane 4.00 10.00
SS33 Alexander Ovechkin 8.00 20.00
SS34 Jamie Benn 2.00 5.00
SS35 Patrick Sharp 2.00 5.00
SS36 Taylor Hall 2.00 5.00
SS37 Max Pacioretty 2.00 5.00
SS38 Martin St. Louis 2.00 5.00
SS39 Alexander Steen 1.25 3.00
SS40 Phil Kessel 2.00 5.00
SS41 Phil Esposito 3.00 8.00
SS42 Steve Yzerman 5.00 12.00
SS43 Mike Bossy 2.00 5.00
SS44 Teemu Selanne 4.00 10.00
SS45 Wayne Gretzky 12.00 30.00
SS46 Mark Messier 4.00 10.00
SS47 Nicklas Lidstrom 2.00 5.00
SS48 Bobby Orr 8.00 20.00
SS49 Peter Forsberg 4.00 10.00
SS50 Mario Lemieux 8.00 20.00

2014-15 Upper Deck Signature Sensations

SSAP Alex Pietrangelo B 5.00 12.00
SSAW Austin Watson E 4.00 10.00
SSBO Bobby Orr A 80.00 200.00
SSBS Brayden Schenn B 6.00 15.00
SSBU Johnny Bucyk A 6.00 15.00
SSCC Charlie Coyle E 6.00 15.00
SSCK Chris Kreider B 8.00 20.00
SSCN Cristopher Nilstorp E 5.00 12.00
SSCT Christian Thomas D 5.00 12.00
SSDB Damien Brunner D 4.00 10.00
SSEL Elias Lindholm E 6.00 15.00
SSGI Jean-Sebastien Giguere A 6.00 15.00
SSJG John Gibson E 6.00 15.00
SSJJ Jaromir Jagr A 50.00 120.00
SSJM Jon Merrill E 4.00 10.00
SSJO Jamie Oleksiak E 5.00 12.00
SSJR Jussi Rynnas E 4.00 10.00
SSJS Jeff Skinner A 8.00 20.00
SSJT John Tavares A 10.00 25.00
SSKT Kyle Turris B 6.00 15.00
SSKU Chris Kunitz A 6.00 15.00
SSLE Lars Eller E 4.00 10.00
SSMB Mike Brown C 5.00 12.00
SSRE Ray Emery E 5.00 12.00
SSRF Ron Francis B 8.00 20.00
SSRM Ryan Murphy E 4.00 10.00
SSRP Richard Panik E 4.00 10.00
SSRR Rickard Rakell E 5.00 12.00
SSRS Riley Sheahan C 4.00 10.00
SSSB Scotty Bowman A 25.00 60.00
SSSH Shawn Horcoff B 4.00 10.00
SSSR Ryan Strome E 6.00 15.00
SSST Jared Staal E 5.00 12.00
SSTO T.J. Oshie C 6.00 15.00
SSTT Tomas Tatar D 4.00 10.00
SSTW Tom Wilson E 6.00 15.00
SSWG Wayne Gretzky A 250.00 600.00

2014-15 Upper Deck Signatures

UDSAP Alex Pietrangelo B 6.00 15.00
UDSBM Brad Marchand C 15.00 40.00
UDSCC Charlie Coyle D 8.00 20.00
UDSCF Cody Franson C 5.00 12.00
UDSCP Chris Pronger B 8.00 20.00
UDSCS Cameron Schilling D 5.00 12.00
UDSEL Elias Lindholm C 8.00 20.00
UDSFP Felix Potvin B 12.00 30.00
UDSJB Jonathan Bernier B 6.00 15.00
UDSJM Jon Merrill D 5.00 12.00
UDSJT Jamie Tardif D 5.00 12.00
UDSLE Lars Eller D 5.00 12.00
UDSLK Lauri Korpikoski D 5.00 12.00
UDSLL Lucas Lessio D 6.00 15.00
UDSLS Luke Schenn C 8.00 20.00
UDSML Michael Latta D 8.00 20.00
UDSMT Marty Turco B 8.00 20.00
UDSNY Nail Yakupov C 5.00 12.00
UDSRM Ryan McDonagh C 5.00 12.00
UDSRS Ryan Strome D 8.00 20.00
UDSSH Scott Hartnell C 5.00 12.00
UDSSP Ryan Spooner D 6.00 15.00
UDSTA John Tavares A 12.00 30.00
UDSTR Tuukka Rask B 10.00 25.00
UDSTV Thomas Vanek C 6.00 15.00
UDSVN Valeri Nichushkin C 8.00 20.00
UDSZG Zemgus Girgensons D 6.00 15.00
UDSZR Zach Redmond D 5.00 12.00

2014-15 Upper Deck UD Portraits

*P46-P60 BLUE/25: 1.5X TO 4X BASIC INSERTS
P1 Drew Doughty 2.00 5.00
P2 Pavel Datsyuk 2.50 6.00
P3 Alexander Ovechkin 6.00 15.00
P4 Martin St. Louis 1.50 4.00
P5 Evgeni Malkin 3.00 8.00
P6 Thomas Vanek 1.25 3.00
P7 Carey Price 3.00 8.00
P8 Claude Giroux 1.50 4.00
P9 T.J. Oshie 1.50 4.00
P10 Joe Thornton 2.50 6.00
P11 Erik Karlsson 2.00 5.00
P12 Duncan Keith 1.25 3.00
P13 Patrick Sharp 1.50 4.00
P14 Shea Weber 1.25 3.00
P15 Jarome Iginla 2.00 5.00
P16 Patrice Bergeron 2.00 5.00
P17 Eric Staal 2.00 5.00
P18 Max Pacioretty 1.50 4.00
P19 P.K. Subban 2.00 5.00
P20 Phil Kessel 1.50 4.00
P21 Joe Pavelski 2.00 5.00
P22 Steven Stamkos 3.00 8.00
P23 John Tavares 2.50 6.00
P24 Jonathan Quick 2.00 5.00
P25 Patrick Kane 3.00 8.00
P26 Zach Parise 1.50 4.00
P27 Matt Duchene 1.50 4.00
P28 Sidney Crosby 6.00 15.00
P29 Jonathan Toews 2.50 6.00
P30 Jamie Benn 1.50 4.00
P31 Jason Spezza 1.50 4.00
P32 Jaromir Jagr 5.00 12.00
P33 Tyler Seguin 2.00 5.00
P34 Taylor Hall 1.50 4.00
P35 Henrik Lundqvist 4.00 10.00
P36 Anze Kopitar 2.50 6.00
P37 Tuukka Rask 2.00 5.00
P38 Nathan MacKinnon 6.00 15.00
P39 Henrik Zetterberg 2.00 5.00
P40 Ryan Getzlaf 1.50 4.00
P41 Wayne Gretzky LEG 12.00 30.00
P42 Terry Sawchuk LEG 2.00 5.00
P43 Steve Yzerman LEG 5.00 12.00
P44 Patrick Roy LEG 5.00 12.00

P45 Joe Sakic LEG 4.00 10.00
P46 Anthony Duclair 2.00 5.00
P47 Griffin Reinhart 1.25 3.00
P48 Curtis Lazar 1.25 3.00
P49 Shayne Gostisbehere 2.50 6.00
P50 Alexander Wennberg 2.00 5.00
P51 Andre Burakovsky 2.00 5.00
P52 Sam Reinhart 5.00 12.00
P53 Johnny Gaudreau 4.00 10.00
P54 Teuvo Teravainen 2.00 5.00
P55 Bo Horvat 4.00 10.00
P56 Aaron Ekblad 3.00 8.00
P57 Jiri Sekac 1.00 2.50
P58 Evgeny Kuznetsov 3.00 8.00
P59 Jonathan Drouin 4.00 10.00
P60 Leon Draisaitl 6.00 15.00

2014-15 Upper Deck UD Portraits Gold

*P1-45 GOLD/25: 1.5X TO 4X BASIC INSERTS
*P46-P60 GOLD/99: 1X TO 2.5X BASIC INSERTS
P41 Wayne Gretzky LEG 40.00 80.00

2014-15 Upper Deck Winter Classic Jumbos

WC1 Pavel Datsyuk 2.00 5.00
WC2 Phil Kessel 1.25 3.00
WC3 Brendan Smith .75 2.00
WC4 Justin Abdelkader 1.00 2.50
WC5 Dion Phaneuf 1.00 2.50
WC6 Henrik Zetterberg 1.50 4.00
WC7 Jay McClement .75 2.00
WC8 Jonathan Bernier 1.00 2.50
WC9 Daniel Alfredsson 1.25 3.00
WC10 Gustav Nyquist .75 2.00
WC11 Tyler Bozak .75 2.00
WC12 Jim Howard 1.50 4.00
WC13 Morgan Rielly 1.25 3.00
WC14 James van Riemsdyk 1.00 2.50

2014-15 Upper Deck Young Guns Acetate

201 William Karlsson 50.00 125.00
202 Brandon Gormley 15.00 40.00
203 Mark Visentin 15.00 40.00
204 Alexander Khokhlachev 15.00 40.00
205 Bobby Robins 12.00 30.00
206 Sam Reinhart 50.00 100.00
207 Nicolas Deslauriers 15.00 40.00
208 Jake McCabe 15.00 40.00
209 Corban Knight 15.00 40.00
210 Tyler Wotherspoon 15.00 40.00
211 Johnny Gaudreau 150.00 400.00
212 Victor Rask 15.00 40.00
213 Patrick Brown 15.00 40.00
214 Teuvo Teravainen 50.00 100.00
215 Trevor van Riemsdyk 20.00 50.00
216 Joey Hishon 20.00 50.00
217 Dennis Everberg 15.00 40.00
218 Alexander Wennberg 25.00 60.00
219 Patrik Nemeth 15.00 40.00
220 Ryan Sproul 15.00 40.00
221 Teemu Pulkkinen 40.00 80.00
222 Andrej Nestrasil 15.00 40.00
223 Leon Draisaitl 80.00 200.00
224 Oscar Klefbom 30.00 80.00
225 Aaron Ekblad 100.00 175.00
226 Vincent Trocheck 30.00 80.00
227 Jonathan Racine 15.00 40.00
228 Christian Folin 15.00 40.00
229 Jiri Sekac 12.00 30.00
230 Calle Jarnkrok 15.00 40.00
231 Colton Sissons 15.00 40.00
232 Damon Severson 15.00 40.00
233 Griffin Reinhart 15.00 40.00
234 Scott Mayfield 12.00 30.00
235 Johan Sundstrom 15.00 40.00
236 Anthony Duclair 25.00 60.00
237 Curtis Lazar 15.00 40.00
238 Pierre-Edouard Bellemare 15.00 40.00
239 Adam Payerl 12.00 30.00
240 Chris Tierney 15.00 40.00
241 Jori Lehtera 20.00 50.00
242 Ty Rattie 15.00 40.00
243 Vladislav Namestnikov 25.00 60.00
244 Brandon Kozun 12.00 30.00
245 Stuart Percy 15.00 40.00
246 Greg McKegg 12.00 30.00
247 Michael Zalewski 12.00 30.00
248 Evgeny Kuznetsov 50.00 100.00
249 Adam Lowry 25.00 50.00
451 Joe Morrow 20.00 50.00
452 Marko Dano 50.00 100.00
453 Markus Granlund 25.00 60.00
454 Rob Zepp 25.00 60.00
455 Tobias Rieder 15.00 40.00
456 Scott Harrington 15.00 40.00
457 Darnell Nurse 40.00 80.00
458 Laurent Brossoit 15.00 40.00
459 Colin Smith 15.00 40.00
460 Joel Armia 15.00 40.00
461 Jyrki Jokipakka 15.00 40.00
462 Phillip Danault 30.00 80.00
463 Cedric Paquette 15.00 40.00
464 Shayne Gostisbehere 30.00 80.00
465 Joni Ortio 20.00 50.00
466 Scott Wilson 12.00 30.00
467 Andre Burakovsky 60.00 120.00
468 Melker Karlsson 15.00 40.00
469 Jordan Binnington 50.00 125.00
470 Bogdan Yakimov 15.00 40.00
471 Seth Griffith 20.00 50.00
472 Seth Helgeson 12.00 30.00
473 Brendan Shinnimin 12.00 30.00
474 Borna Rendulic 15.00 40.00
475 Derrick Pouliot 20.00 50.00
476 John Klingberg 75.00 125.00
477 Jonathan Drouin 100.00 175.00
478 Andrei Vasilevskiy 300.00 800.00
479 Andrew Agozzino 12.00 30.00
480 Petteri Lindbohm 12.00 30.00
481 Adam Clendening 15.00 40.00
482 Curtis McKenzie 12.00 30.00
483 Christopher Gibson 25.00 60.00
484 Mirco Mueller 15.00 40.00
485 Barclay Goodrow 15.00 40.00
486 Anton Forsberg 12.00 30.00
487 Max Friberg 12.00 30.00
488 Josh Jooris 15.00 40.00
489 Tyler Graovac 12.00 30.00
490 Kevin Hayes 40.00 80.00
491 Chris Wagner 15.00 40.00
492 Andy Andreoff 15.00 40.00
493 Sven Andrighetto 20.00 50.00
494 Bo Horvat 125.00 300.00
495 David Pastrnak 500.00 1200.00
496 Brett Ritchie 15.00 40.00
497 Dominik Uher 12.00 30.00
498 Scott Darling 40.00 80.00
499 Kerby Rychel 12.00 30.00
521 Jesse Blacker 15.00 40.00
522 Julien Brouillette 10.00 25.00
523 Miikka Salomaki 10.00 25.00
524 Adam Clendening 10.00 25.00
525 Nikita Nesterov 10.00 25.00
526 Jiri Sekac 8.00 20.00
527 Tyler Gaudet 8.00 20.00
528 Andrew Hammond 40.00 80.00
529 Rocco Grimaldi 10.00 25.00
530 Anthony Duclair 30.00 60.00

2015 Upper Deck Holiday Card

UDHC2015 Connor McDavid 20.00 50.00

2015-16 Upper Deck

COMP.SERIES 1 (250) 300.00 450.00
COMP.SER. 1 w/o RC's (200) 8.00 20.00
COMP.SERIES 2 (250) 150.00 250.00
COMP.SER. 2 w/o RC's (200) 8.00 20.00
1 Cam Fowler .30 .75
2 Frederik Andersen .40 1.00
3 Hampus Lindholm .20 .50
4 Sami Vatanen .20 .50
5 Pat Maroon .20 .50
6 Rickard Rakell .25 .60
7 Ryan Getzlaf .30 .75
8 Martin Hanzal .20 .50
9 Michael Stone .20 .50
10 Mike Smith .30 .75
11 Oliver Ekman-Larsson .30 .75
12 Joe Vitale .20 .50
13 Shane Doan .25 .60
14 Brad Marchand .60 1.50
15 David Krejci .30 .75
16 David Pastrnak .75 2.00
17 Dennis Seidenberg .20 .50
18 Loui Eriksson .20 .50
19 Zdeno Chara .30 .75
20 Tuukka Rask .40 1.00
21 Brian Gionta .20 .50
22 Nicolas Deslauriers .20 .50
23 Zemgus Girgensons .25 .60
24 Marcus Foligno .25 .60
25 Sam Reinhart .60 1.50
26 Tyler Ennis .20 .50
27 Dennis Wideman .20 .50
28 Jiri Hudler .25 .60
29 Joe Colborne .20 .50
30 Johnny Gaudreau .50 1.25
31 Jonas Hiller .25 .60
32 Karri Ramo .25 .60
33 Cam Ward .30 .75
34 Elias Lindholm .30 .75
35 Jeff Skinner .40 1.00
36 Justin Faulk .25 .60
37 Nathan Gerbe .20 .50
38 Andrew Shaw .20 .50
39 Bryan Bickell .20 .50
40 Corey Crawford .40 1.00
41 Duncan Keith .25 .60
42 Marian Hossa .30 .75
43 Niklas Hjalmarsson .20 .50
44 Jonathan Toews .50 1.25
45 Tyson Barrie .20 .50
46 Erik Johnson .20 .50
47 Gabriel Landeskog .40 1.00
48 Matt Duchene .30 .75
49 Semyon Varlamov .30 .75
50 Brandon Dubinsky .20 .50
51 Cam Atkinson .30 .75
52 David Savard .20 .50
53 Jack Johnson .20 .50
54 Matt Calvert .20 .50
55 Scott Hartnell .20 .50
56 Nick Foligno .25 .60
57 Ales Hemsky .20 .50
58 Antoine Roussel .20 .50
59 Alex Goligoski .20 .50
60 John Klingberg .30 .75
61 Kari Lehtonen .25 .60
62 Tyler Seguin .40 1.00
63 Danny DeKeyser .20 .50
64 Darren Helm .20 .50
65 Riley Sheahan .20 .50
66 Jonathan Ericsson .20 .50
67 Niklas Kronwall .25 .60
68 Pavel Datsyuk .50 1.25
69 Tomas Tatar .20 .50
70 Ben Scrivens .25 .60
71 Benoit Pouliot .20 .50
72 Teddy Purcell .20 .50
73 Jordan Eberle .30 .75
74 Matt Hendricks .20 .50
75 Taylor Hall .30 .75
76 Aaron Ekblad .40 1.00
77 Brian Campbell .20 .50
78 Dave Bolland .20 .50
79 Erik Gudbranson .20 .50
80 Jussi Jokinen .20 .50
81 Roberto Luongo .50 1.25
82 Dustin Brown .30 .75
83 Jake Muzzin .30 .75
84 Jeff Carter .25 .60
85 Jonathan Quick .40 1.00
86 Marian Gaborik .30 .75
87 Tanner Pearson .20 .50
88 Trevor Lewis .20 .50
89 Jared Spurgeon .30 .75
90 Jason Zucker .30 .75
91 Devan Dubnyk .25 .60
92 Nino Niederreiter .20 .50
93 Ryan Suter .25 .60
94 Zach Parise .30 .75
95 Andrei Markov .20 .50
96 Tomas Plekanec .20 .50
97 David Desharnais .20 .50
98 Alexei Emelin .20 .50
99 Lars Eller .20 .50
100 Max Pacioretty .30 .75
101 Nathan Beaulieu .20 .50
102 P.K. Subban .40 1.00
103 Carter Hutton .25 .60
104 Eric Nystrom .20 .50
105 Filip Forsberg .50 1.25
106 James Neal .20 .50
107 Seth Jones .30 .75
108 Mike Fisher .20 .50
109 Pekka Rinne .30 .75
110 Shea Weber .25 .60
111 Adam Henrique .25 .60
112 Andy Greene .20 .50
113 Cory Schneider .30 .75
114 Michael Cammalleri .25 .60
115 Patrik Elias .30 .75
116 Travis Zajac .20 .50
117 Frans Nielsen .20 .50
118 Jaroslav Halak .30 .75
119 John Tavares .50 1.25
120 Josh Bailey .25 .60
121 Nikolai Kulemin .20 .50
122 Ryan Strome .30 .75
123 Travis Hamonic .20 .50
124 Keith Yandle .20 .50
125 Derek Stepan .20 .50
126 Chris Kreider .40 1.00
127 Daniel Girardi .20 .50
128 Derick Brassard .20 .50
129 Marc Staal .20 .50
130 Rick Nash .30 .75
131 Ryan McDonagh .20 .50
132 Clarke MacArthur .20 .50
133 Cody Ceci .20 .50
134 Andrew Hammond .40 1.00
135 Erik Karlsson .40 1.00
136 Kyle Turris .25 .60
137 Mika Zibanejad .40 1.00
138 Brayden Schenn .30 .75
139 Claude Giroux .30 .75
140 Mark Streit .20 .50
141 Matt Read .20 .50
142 R.J. Umberger .20 .50
143 Michael Del Zotto .20 .50
144 Derrick Pouliot .20 .50
145 Chris Kunitz .30 .75
146 Marc-Andre Fleury .60 1.50
147 Evgeni Malkin .60 1.50
148 Kris Letang .40 1.00
149 David Perron .25 .60
150 Patric Hornqvist .20 .50
151 Brent Burns .30 .75
152 Joe Thornton .50 1.25
153 Logan Couture .40 1.00
154 Marc-Edouard Vlasic .20 .50
155 Patrick Marleau .30 .75
156 Tomas Hertl .30 .75
157 Alex Pietrangelo .25 .60
158 Alexander Steen .20 .50
159 David Backes .20 .50
160 Jake Allen .30 .75
161 Kevin Shattenkirk .20 .50
162 Patrik Berglund .20 .50
163 Jori Lehtera .20 .50
164 Alex Killorn .20 .50
165 Brian Boyle .20 .50
166 Jonathan Drouin .25 .60
167 Nikita Kucherov .60 1.50
168 Steven Stamkos .60 1.50
169 Tyler Johnson .20 .50
170 Victor Hedman .40 1.00
171 James Reimer .30 .75
172 James van Riemsdyk .25 .60
173 Joffrey Lupul .20 .50
174 Leo Komarov .20 .50
175 Morgan Rielly .30 .75
176 Nazem Kadri .40 1.00
177 Tyler Bozak .20 .50
178 Christopher Tanev .20 .50
179 Bo Horvat .40 1.00
180 Alexandre Burrows .20 .50
181 Henrik Sedin .40 1.00
182 Jannik Hansen .20 .50
183 Derek Dorsett .20 .50
184 Ryan Miller .30 .75
185 Alexander Ovechkin 1.25 3.00
186 Brooks Orpik .20 .50
187 Evgeny Kuznetsov .40 1.00
188 John Carlson .30 .75
189 Matt Niskanen .25 .60
190 Nicklas Backstrom .30 .75
191 Jay Beagle .20 .50
192 Blake Wheeler .30 .75
193 Bryan Little .25 .60
194 Dustin Byfuglien .30 .75
195 Mathieu Perreault .20 .50
196 Ondrej Pavelec .30 .75
197 Tobias Enstrom .20 .50
198 Mark Scheifele .50 1.25
199 F.Forsberg/D.Keith CL .50 1.25
200 R.Nash/P.Subban CL .40 1.00
201 Connor McDavid YG RC 500.00 1200.00
202 Jordan Weal YG RC 1.25 3.00
203 Sergei Plotnikov YG RC 1.25 3.00
204 Max Domi YG RC 4.00 10.00
205 Andrew Copp YG RC 2.00 5.00
206 Mikko Rantanen YG RC 20.00 50.00
207 Joel Edmundson YG RC 1.50 4.00
208 Kevin Fiala YG RC 5.00 12.00
209 Nick Cousins YG RC 2.00 5.00
210 Emile Poirier YG RC 1.50 4.00
211 Malcolm Subban YG RC 3.00 8.00
212 Jacob de la Rose YG RC 2.00 5.00
213 Henrik Samuelsson YG RC 1.25 3.00
214 Connor Hellebuyck YG RC 15.00 40.00
215 Matt Puempel YG RC 1.50 4.00
216 Nick Shore YG RC 1.25 3.00
217 Josh Anderson YG RC 10.00 25.00
218 Shane Prince YG RC 1.25 3.00
219 Jared McCann YG RC 2.50 6.00
220 Stanislav Galiev YG RC 2.00 5.00
221 Artemi Panarin YG RC 10.00 25.00
222 Viktor Arvidsson YG RC 2.00 5.00
223 Nikolaj Ehlers YG RC 5.00 12.00
224 Slater Koekkoek YG RC 1.25 3.00
225 Ronalds Kenins YG RC 1.25 3.00
226 Daniel Sprong YG RC 2.50 6.00
227 Nicolas Petan YG RC 2.50 6.00
228 Dylan Larkin YG RC 12.00 30.00
229 Robby Fabbri YG RC 4.00 10.00
230 Joonas Donskoi YG RC 2.00 5.00
231 Sam Bennett YG RC 6.00 15.00
232 Ben Hutton YG RC 2.00 5.00
233 Matt O'Connor YG RC 1.50 4.00
234 Oscar Lindberg YG RC 2.00 5.00
235 Colton Parayko YG RC 3.00 8.00
236 Stefan Noesen YG RC 1.25 3.00
237 Anton Slepyshev YG RC 1.25 3.00
238 Sergei Kalinin YG RC 1.25 3.00
239 Mike Condon YG RC 2.00 5.00
240 Antoine Bibeau YG RC 2.00 5.00
241 Kyle Baun YG RC 2.00 5.00
242 J-F Berube YG RC 1.50 4.00
243 Joonas Kemppainen YG RC 1.25 3.00
244 Mattias Janmark YG RC 2.00 5.00
245 Evgeny Medvedev YG RC 1.50 4.00
246 Keegan Lowe YG RC 2.00 5.00
247 Colin Miller YG RC 1.50 4.00
248 Brett Kulak YG RC 1.50 4.00
249 Connor Brickley YG RC 1.50 4.00
250 C.McDavid/S.Bennett CL 8.00 20.00
251 Andrew Cogliano .20 .50
252 Jiri Sekac .20 .50
253 Chris Stewart .20 .50
254 Corey Perry .50 1.25
255 Jakob Silfverberg .20 .50
256 Ryan Kesler .30 .75
257 Carl Hagelin .20 .50
258 Antoine Vermette .20 .50
259 Mikkel Boedker .20 .50
260 Steve Downie .20 .50
261 Tobias Rieder .20 .50
262 Anthony Duclair .25 .60
263 Connor Murphy .20 .50
264 Matt Beleskey .20 .50
265 Ryan Spooner .25 .60
266 Torey Krug .25 .60
267 Patrice Bergeron .40 1.00
268 Brett Connolly .20 .50
269 Jimmy Hayes .20 .50
270 Matt Moulson .20 .50
271 David Legwand .25 .60
272 Ryan O'Reilly .30 .75
273 Chad Johnson .25 .60
274 Rasmus Ristolainen .20 .50
275 Evander Kane .30 .75
276 Mikael Backlund .25 .60
277 David Jones .20 .50
278 Mark Giordano .30 .75
279 T.J. Brodie .20 .50
280 Lance Bouma .20 .50
281 Dougie Hamilton .25 .60
282 Michael Frolik .20 .50
283 Sean Monahan .20 .50
284 Jordan Staal .25 .60
285 Riley Nash .20 .50
286 Eric Staal .40 1.00
287 Ron Hainsey .20 .50
288 Ryan Murphy .20 .50
289 Kris Versteeg .20 .50
290 Victor Rask .20 .50
291 Marko Dano .20 .50
292 Scott Darling .25 .60
293 Artem Anisimov .20 .50
294 Trevor Daley .20 .50
295 Teuvo Teravainen .30 .75
296 Brent Seabrook .20 .50
297 Patrick Kane .60 1.50
298 Mikhail Grigorenko .20 .50
299 Francois Beauchemin .20 .50
300 Blake Comeau .20 .50
301 Jarome Iginla .40 1.00
302 Nathan MacKinnon 1.25 3.00
303 Carl Soderberg .20 .50
304 Alex Tanguay .20 .50
305 Nikita Zadorov .20 .50
306 Boone Jenner .30 .75
307 Brandon Saad .25 .60
308 Sergei Bobrovsky .50 1.25
309 Ryan Johansen .25 .60
310 Ryan Murray .20 .50
311 Patrick Sharp .30 .75
312 Jason Spezza .30 .75
313 Johnny Oduya .25 .60
314 Jamie Benn .30 .75
315 Antti Niemi .25 .60
316 Cody Eakin .20 .50
317 Henrik Zetterberg UER
Last name spelled .40 1.00
318 Justin Abdelkader .25 .60
319 Petr Mrazek .30 .75
320 Mike Green .25 .60
321 Tomas Jurco .20 .50
322 Gustav Nyquist .20 .50
323 Brad Richards .30 .75
324 Jim Howard .40 1.00
325 Andrej Sekera .20 .50
326 Justin Schultz .25 .60
327 Nail Yakupov .20 .50
328 Anton Lander .20 .50
329 Cam Talbot .30 .75
330 Ryan Nugent-Hopkins .40 1.00
331 Nick Bjugstad .20 .50
332 Vincent Trocheck .30 .75
333 Jaromir Jagr 1.00 2.50
334 Aleksander Barkov .50 1.25
335 Brandon Pirri .20 .50
336 Reilly Smith .30 .75
337 Jonathan Huberdeau .40 1.00
338 Tyler Toffoli .30 .75
339 Milan Lucic .25 .60
340 Alec Martinez .20 .50
341 Christian Ehrhoff .20 .50
342 Drew Doughty .40 1.00
343 Brayden McNabb .20 .50
344 Anze Kopitar .50 1.25
345 Justin Fontaine .20 .50
346 Mathew Dumba .20 .50
347 Thomas Vanek .25 .60
348 Jason Pominville .20 .50
349 Mikko Koivu .25 .60
350 Charlie Coyle .30 .75
351 Marco Scandella .20 .50
352 Devante Smith-Pelly .25 .60
353 Dale Weise .20 .50
354 Tomas Fleischmann .20 .50
355 Jeff Petry .30 .75
356 Carey Price .60 1.50
357 Brendan Gallagher .30 .75
358 Alex Galchenyuk .20 .50
359 Craig Smith .20 .50
360 Roman Josi .30 .75
361 Calle Jarnkrok .25 .60
362 Mike Ribeiro .20 .50
363 Barret Jackman .20 .50
364 Colin Wilson .20 .50
365 Cody Hodgson .20 .50
366 Jacob Josefson .20 .50
367 Lee Stempniak .20 .50
368 Kyle Palmieri .25 .60
369 John Moore .20 .50
370 Adam Larsson .30 .75
371 Eric Gelinas .20 .50
372 Nick Leddy .20 .50
373 Kyle Okposo .20 .50
374 Marek Zidlicky .20 .50
375 Johnny Boychuk .25 .60
376 Anders Lee .30 .75
377 Brock Nelson .30 .75
378 Antti Raanta .30 .75
379 J.T. Miller .40 1.00
380 Viktor Stalberg .20 .50
381 Kevin Hayes .25 .60
382 Henrik Lundqvist .75 2.00
383 Mats Zuccarello .30 .75
384 Milan Michalek .20 .50
385 Mark Stone .40 1.00
386 Chris Neil .20 .50
387 Craig Anderson .30 .75
388 Bobby Ryan .25 .60
389 Mike Hoffman .20 .50
390 Curtis Lazar .20 .50
391 Jakub Voracek .25 .60
392 Scott Laughton .20 .50
393 Wayne Simmonds .40 1.00
394 Sam Gagner .20 .50
395 Steve Mason .25 .60
396 Sean Couturier .25 .60
397 Michael Raffl .20 .50
398 Sidney Crosby 1.25 3.00
399 Ian Cole .20 .50
400 Phil Kessel .30 .75
401 Olli Maatta .20 .50
402 Nick Bonino .20 .50
403 Beau Bennett .20 .50
404 Martin Jones .25 .60
405 Matt Nieto .20 .50
406 Tommy Wingels .20 .50
407 Joel Ward .20 .50
408 Joe Pavelski .40 1.00
409 Paul Martin .20 .50
410 Jay Bouwmeester .20 .50
411 Dmitrij Jaskin .20 .50
412 Vladimir Tarasenko .40 1.00
413 Paul Stastny .25 .60
414 Jaden Schwartz .40 1.00
415 Troy Brouwer .20 .50
416 Brian Elliott .25 .60
417 Valtteri Filppula .20 .50
418 Ben Bishop .25 .60
419 Anton Stralman .20 .50
420 Ryan Callahan .20 .50
421 Ondrej Palat .25 .60
422 Cedric Paquette .20 .50
423 Peter Holland .20 .50
424 Jake Gardiner .20 .50
425 P.A. Parenteau .20 .50
426 Jonathan Bernier .25 .60
427 Brad Boyes .20 .50
428 Nick Spaling .20 .50
429 Dion Phaneuf .25 .60
430 Daniel Sedin .40 1.00
431 Brandon Sutter .20 .50
432 Radim Vrbata .20 .50
433 Alexander Edler .20 .50
434 Chris Higgins .20 .50
435 Brandon Prust .20 .50
436 Karl Alzner .20 .50
437 Marcus Johansson .25 .60
438 Braden Holtby .40 1.00
439 T.J. Oshie .30 .75
440 Justin Williams .25 .60
441 Andre Burakovsky .20 .50
442 Michael Hutchinson .20 .50
443 Andrew Ladd .20 .50
444 Jacob Trouba .25 .60
445 Tyler Myers .20 .50
446 Drew Stafford .20 .50
447 Alexander Burmistrov .25 .60
448 Adam Lowry .25 .60
449 C.Price/H.Zetterberg CL .60 1.50
450 C.Perry/V.Tarasenko CL .50 1.25
451 Jack Eichel YG RC 20.00 50.00
452 Charles Hudon YG RC 2.00 5.00
453 Nikolay Goldobin YG RC 2.00 5.00
454 Logan Shaw YG RC 2.00 5.00
455 Frank Vatrano YG RC 2.50 6.00
456 Jujhar Khaira YG RC 1.50 4.00
457 Jake Virtanen YG RC 6.00 15.00
458 Andreas Athanasiou YG RC 6.00 15.00
459 Tanner Kero YG RC 2.00 5.00
460 Chris Wideman YG RC 2.00 5.00
461 Zachary Fucale YG RC 5.00 12.00
462 Hunter Shinkaruk YG RC 2.00 5.00
463 Brendan Ranford YG RC 1.50 4.00
464 Juuse Saros YG RC 10.00 25.00
465 Adam Pelech YG RC 1.50 4.00
466 Michael Keranen YG RC 1.50 4.00
467 Dylan DeMelo YG RC 1.50 4.00
468 Mark Alt YG RC 1.25 3.00
469 Jaccob Slavin YG RC 3.00 8.00
470 Alexandre Grenier YG RC 1.50 4.00
471 Louis Domingue YG RC 2.00 5.00
472 Linus Ullmark YG RC 8.00 20.00
473 Derek Forbort YG RC 1.50 4.00
474 Brady Skjei YG RC 1.50 4.00
475 Ryan Hartman YG RC 2.50 6.00
476 Max McCormick YG RC 1.50 4.00
477 Vincent Hinostroza YG RC 1.25 3.00
478 Taylor Leier YG RC 2.00 5.00
479 Radek Faksa YG RC 2.00 5.00
480 Garret Sparks YG RC 3.00 8.00
481 Brendan Gaunce YG RC 2.50 6.00
482 Chris Driedger YG RC 4.00 10.00
483 Joel Vermin YG RC 1.50 4.00
484 Chandler Stephenson YG RC 2.50 6.00
485 David Musil YG RC 1.50 4.00
486 Gustav Olofsson YG RC 2.00 5.00
487 Brett Pesce YG RC 1.50 4.00
488 Anthony Stolarz YG RC 10.00 25.00
489 Devin Shore YG RC 2.00 5.00
490 Petr Straka YG RC 1.25 3.00
491 Mike McCarron YG RC 4.00 10.00
492 Raman Hrabarenka YG RC 1.50 4.00
493 Markus Hannikainen YG RC 1.50 4.00
494 Sam Brittain YG RC 2.00 5.00
495 Shea Theodore YG RC 5.00 12.00
496 Nick Ritchie YG RC 2.00 5.00
497 Brock McGinn YG RC 2.00 5.00
498 Tyler Randell YG RC 2.00 5.00
499 Noah Hanifin YG RC 3.00 8.00
500 J.Eichel/Z.Fucale YG CL 4.00 10.00
501 Ryan Johansen .25 .60
502 Seth Jones .30 .75
503 Richard Panik .20 .50
504 Ben Scrivens .25 .60
505 Trevor Daley .20 .50
506 Zack Kassian .20 .50
507 Vincent Lecavalier .30 .75
508 Landon Ferraro .20 .50
509 Mike Richards .25 .60
510 Mikael Granlund .25 .60
511 Vladislav Namestnikov .20 .50
512 Carl Hagelin .20 .50
513 Jarret Stoll .25 .60
514 Ryan Ellis .20 .50
515 Eric Staal .40 1.00
516 Luke Schenn .30 .75
517 Dion Phaneuf .25 .60
518 Andrew Ladd .20 .50
519 Mikkel Boedker .20 .50
520 David Perron .25 .60
521 Joonas Korpisalo YG RC 15.00 40.00
522 Laurent Dauphin YG RC 2.00 5.00
523 Michael Mersch YG RC 2.00 5.00
524 Daniel Carr YG RC 1.50 4.00
525 Joseph Blandisi YG RC 2.00 5.00
526 Matt Murray YG RC 20.00 50.00
527 Fredrik Claesson YG RC 2.00 5.00
528 Yanni Gourde YG RC 10.00 25.00
529 Phil Di Giuseppe YG RC 2.00 5.00
530 Jordan Weal YG RC 1.25 3.00
SP3 C.McDavid/W.Gretzky 60.00 150.00

2015-16 Upper Deck Exclusives

*1-450 VETS/100: 6X TO 15X BASIC CARDS
*201-250/451-500 YG/100: 2.5X TO 6X YG
201 Connor McDavid YG 5000.00 10000.00
204 Max Domi YG 25.00 60.00
214 Connor Hellebuyck YG 150.00 400.00
217 Josh Anderson YG 40.00 100.00
221 Artemi Panarin YG 150.00 400.00
223 Nikolaj Ehlers YG 40.00 100.00
227 Nicolas Petan YG 15.00 40.00
228 Dylan Larkin YG 150.00 400.00
229 Robby Fabbri YG 25.00 60.00
231 Sam Bennett YG 80.00 200.00
239 Mike Condon YG 50.00 100.00
250 McDavid/S.Bennett CL 50.00 120.00
451 Jack Eichel YG 300.00 500.00
455 Frank Vatrano YG 30.00 80.00
464 Juuse Saros YG 60.00 150.00
472 Linus Ullmark YG 60.00 150.00
488 Anthony Stolarz YG 60.00 150.00
521 Joonas Korpisalo YG 40.00 120.00
528 Yanni Gourde YG 40.00 100.00

2015-16 Upper Deck Silver Foil

*VETERANS: 5X TO 12X BASIC CARDS
*YOUNG GUNS: .75X TO 2X BASIC YG
187 Evgeny Kuznetsov 4.00 10.00
190 Nicklas Backstrom 3.00 8.00
201 Connor McDavid YG 200.00 350.00
204 Max Domi YG 15.00 40.00
221 Artemi Panarin YG 20.00 50.00
228 Dylan Larkin YG 25.00 60.00
451 Jack Eichel YG 100.00 200.00
488 Anthony Stolarz YG 15.00 40.00

2015-16 Upper Deck A Piece of History 1000 Point Club

PCAO Adam Oates 2C 15.00 40.00
PCDG Doug Gilmour 2A 50.00 100.00
PCDH Dale Hawerchuk 2C 15.00 40.00
PCDS Denis Savard 2C 10.00 25.00
PCJI Jarome Iginla 1D 15.00 40.00
PCJJ Jaromir Jagr 2C 25.00 50.00
PCJK Jari Kurri 2C 15.00 40.00
PCJR Jeremy Roenick 2B 30.00 80.00
PCMD Marcel Dionne STK 1C 30.00 60.00
PCMG Mike Gartner 2B 25.00 60.00
PCMM Mike Modano STK 1A 150.00 300.00
PCMS Martin St. Louis 2A 50.00 100.00
PCRB Ray Bourque 2C 15.00 40.00
PCSL Steve Larmer STK 1C 30.00 60.00
PCTS Teemu Selanne 1B 30.00 60.00
PCVD Vincent Damphousse 1D 10.00 25.00

2015-16 Upper Deck A Piece of History 300 Win Club

300HL Henrik Lundqvist B 25.00 50.00
300JV John Vanbiesbrouck STK A 60.00 100.00
300MF Marc-Andre Fleury B 25.00 60.00
300RM Ryan Miller B 12.00 30.00
300TB Tom Barrasso STK A 30.00 60.00
300TS Terry Sawchuk STK A 90.00 150.00

2015-16 Upper Deck Canvas

C211-C240 YG ODDS
1:48H/R, 1:96B SER.2 .75 2.00
C241-C270 RET/POE ODDS 1:192H/R, 1:384B
SER.2 3.00 8.00
C1 Corey Perry 1.50 4.00
C2 Cam Fowler 1.00 2.50
C3 Ryan Kesler 1.00 2.50
C4 Oliver Ekman-Larsson 1.00 2.50
C5 Mike Smith 1.00 2.50
C6 Tuukka Rask 1.25 3.00
C7 Brad Marchand 2.00 5.00
C8 Loui Eriksson .60 1.50
C9 David Pastrnak 2.50 6.00
C10 Zemgus Girgensons .75 2.00
C11 Tyler Ennis .60 1.50
C12 Jiri Hudler .75 2.00
C13 Sean Monahan .60 1.50
C14 Jonas Hiller .75 2.00
C15 Karri Ramo .75 2.00
C16 Cam Ward 1.00 2.50
C17 Elias Lindholm 1.00 2.50
C18 Justin Faulk .75 2.00
C19 Jonathan Toews 1.50 4.00
C20 Duncan Keith .75 2.00
C21 Marian Hossa 1.00 2.50
C22 Corey Crawford 1.25 3.00
C23 Matt Duchene 1.00 2.50
C24 Semyon Varlamov 1.00 2.50
C25 Scott Hartnell .60 1.50
C26 Brandon Dubinsky .60 1.50
C27 Jamie Benn 1.00 2.50
C28 Kari Lehtonen .75 2.00
C29 Henrik Zetterberg 1.25 3.00
C30 Niklas Kronwall .75 2.00
C31 Danny DeKeyser .60 1.50
C32 Tomas Tatar .60 1.50
C33 Ryan Nugent-Hopkins 1.25 3.00
C34 Jordan Eberle 1.00 2.50
C35 Ben Scrivens .75 2.00
C36 Aaron Ekblad 1.25 3.00
C37 Roberto Luongo 1.50 4.00
C38 Jussi Jokinen .60 1.50
C39 Jonathan Quick 1.25 3.00
C40 Marian Gaborik 1.00 2.50
C41 Jeff Carter .75 2.00
C42 Ryan Suter .75 2.00
C43 Zach Parise 1.00 2.50
C44 Carey Price 2.00 5.00
C45 Max Pacioretty 1.00 2.50
C46 Lars Eller .60 1.50
C47 Devante Smith-Pelly .75 2.00
C48 Filip Forsberg 1.50 4.00
C49 Pekka Rinne 1.00 2.50
C50 Shea Weber .75 2.00
C51 Mike Fisher .60 1.50
C52 Cory Schneider 1.00 2.50
C53 Michael Cammalleri .75 2.00
C54 Adam Henrique .75 2.00
C55 John Tavares 1.50 4.00
C56 Jaroslav Halak 1.00 2.50
C57 Ryan Strome 1.00 2.50
C58 Rick Nash 1.00 2.50
C59 Derick Brassard .60 1.50
C60 Keith Yandle .60 1.50
C61 Chris Kreider 1.25 3.00
C62 Clarke MacArthur .60 1.50
C63 Erik Karlsson 1.25 3.00
C64 Kyle Turris .75 2.00
C65 Claude Giroux 1.00 2.50
C66 Wayne Simmonds 1.25 3.00
C67 Matt Read .60 1.50
C68 Sidney Crosby 4.00 10.00
C69 David Perron .75 2.00
C70 Patric Hornqvist .60 1.50
C71 Kris Letang 1.25 3.00
C72 Logan Couture 1.25 3.00
C73 Patrick Marleau 1.00 2.50
C74 Brent Burns 1.00 2.50
C75 David Backes .60 1.50
C76 Alexander Steen .60 1.50
C77 Jake Allen 1.00 2.50
C78 Steven Stamkos 2.00 5.00
C79 Jonathan Drouin .75 2.00
C80 Victor Hedman 1.25 3.00
C81 James van Riemsdyk .75 2.00
C82 Nazem Kadri 1.25 3.00
C83 Morgan Rielly 1.00 2.50
C84 Ryan Miller 1.00 2.50
C85 Henrik Sedin 1.25 3.00
C86 Nicklas Backstrom 1.00 2.50
C87 Evgeny Kuznetsov 1.25 3.00
C88 Ondrej Pavelec 1.00 2.50
C89 Blake Wheeler 1.00 2.50
C90 J.Toews/S.Stamkos CL 1.25 3.00
C91 Jack Eichel YG 20.00 50.00
C92 Emile Poirier YG 3.00 8.00
C93 Colton Parayko YG 6.00 15.00
C94 Joonas Donskoi YG 4.00 10.00
C95 Andrew Copp YG 4.00 10.00
C96 Max Domi YG 5.00 12.00
C97 Kevin Fiala YG 8.00 20.00
C98 Mikko Rantanen YG 20.00 50.00
C99 Mattias Janmark YG 4.00 10.00
C100 Malcolm Subban YG 6.00 15.00
C101 Sam Bennett YG 8.00 20.00
C102 Jacob de la Rose YG 4.00 10.00
C103 Colin Miller YG 3.00 8.00
C104 Connor Hellebuyck YG 15.00 40.00
C105 Nick Shore YG 2.50 6.00
C106 Matt Puempel YG 3.00 8.00
C107 Stanislav Galiev YG 4.00 10.00
C108 Artemi Panarin YG 10.00 25.00
C109 Noah Hanifin YG 10.00 25.00
C110 Daniel Sprong YG 5.00 12.00
C111 Ronalds Kenins YG 2.50 6.00
C112 Dylan Larkin YG 15.00 40.00
C113 Antoine Bibeau YG 4.00 10.00
C114 Jared McCann YG 5.00 12.00
C115 Oscar Lindberg YG 4.00 10.00
C116 Nikolaj Ehlers YG 6.00 15.00
C117 Sergei Plotnikov YG 2.50 6.00
C118 Robby Fabbri YG 5.00 12.00
C119 Nicolas Petan YG 4.00 10.00
C120 J.Eichel/Larkin YG CL 10.00 25.00
C121 Ryan Getzlaf 1.00 2.50
C122 Frederik Andersen 1.25 3.00
C123 Sami Vatanen .60 1.50
C124 Shane Doan .75 2.00
C125 Mikkel Boedker .60 1.50
C126 Patrice Bergeron 1.25 3.00
C127 Zdeno Chara 1.00 2.50
C128 David Krejci 1.00 2.50
C129 Ryan O'Reilly 1.00 2.50
C130 Evander Kane 1.00 2.50
C131 Matt Moulson .60 1.50
C132 Mark Giordano 1.00 2.50
C133 Johnny Gaudreau 1.50 4.00
C134 Michael Frolik .60 1.50

C135 Eric Staal 1.25 3.00
C136 Victor Rask .60 1.50
C137 Teuvo Teravainen 1.00 2.50
C138 Patrick Kane 2.00 5.00
C139 Brent Seabrook .60 1.50
C140 Gabriel Landeskog 1.25 3.00
C141 Jarome Iginla 1.25 3.00
C142 Nathan MacKinnon 4.00 10.00
C143 Brandon Saad .75 2.00
C144 Ryan Johansen .75 2.00
C145 Sergei Bobrovsky 1.50 4.00
C146 Patrick Sharp 1.00 2.50
C147 John Klingberg 1.00 2.50
C148 Tyler Seguin 1.25 3.00
C149 Jason Spezza 1.00 2.50
C150 Pavel Datsyuk 1.50 4.00
C151 Jim Howard 1.25 3.00
C152 Justin Abdelkader .75 2.00
C153 Teddy Purcell .60 1.50
C154 Taylor Hall 1.00 2.50
C155 Nail Yakupov .60 1.50
C156 Nick Bjugstad .60 1.50
C157 Jaromir Jagr 3.00 8.00
C158 Jonathan Huberdeau 1.25 3.00
C159 Milan Lucic .75 2.00
C160 Drew Doughty 1.25 3.00
C161 Anze Kopitar 1.50 4.00
C162 Mikael Granlund .75 2.00
C163 Devan Dubnyk .75 2.00
C164 Mikko Koivu .75 2.00
C165 Jason Pominville .60 1.50
C166 P.K. Subban 1.25 3.00
C167 Brendan Gallagher 1.00 2.50
C168 Tomas Plekanec .60 1.50
C169 Roman Josi 1.00 2.50
C170 Mike Ribeiro .60 1.50
C171 James Neal .60 1.50
C172 Lee Stempniak .60 1.50
C173 Travis Zajac .60 1.50
C174 Nick Leddy .60 1.50
C175 Kyle Okposo .60 1.50
C176 Anders Lee 1.00 2.50
C177 Henrik Lundqvist 2.50 6.00
C178 Ryan McDonagh .60 1.50
C179 Derek Stepan .60 1.50
C180 Mike Hoffman .60 1.50
C181 Mark Stone 1.25 3.00
C182 Bobby Ryan .75 2.00
C183 Andrew Hammond 1.25 3.00
C184 Jakub Voracek .75 2.00
C185 Steve Mason .75 2.00
C186 Marc-Andre Fleury 2.00 5.00
C187 Evgeni Malkin 2.00 5.00
C188 Phil Kessel 1.00 2.50
C189 Joe Thornton 1.50 4.00
C190 Joe Pavelski 1.25 3.00
C191 Brian Elliott .75 2.00
C192 Vladimir Tarasenko 1.25 3.00
C193 Paul Stastny .75 2.00
C194 Ryan Callahan .60 1.50
C195 Ben Bishop .75 2.00
C196 Tyler Johnson .60 1.50
C197 Dion Phaneuf .75 2.00
C198 Tyler Bozak .60 1.50
C199 Jonathan Bernier .75 2.00
C200 Alexandre Burrows .60 1.50
C201 Radim Vrbata .60 1.50
C202 Daniel Sedin 1.25 3.00
C203 Alexander Ovechkin 4.00 10.00
C204 Andre Burakovsky .60 1.50
C205 T.J. Oshie 1.00 2.50
C206 Braden Holtby 1.25 3.00
C207 Andrew Ladd .60 1.50
C208 Bryan Little .75 2.00
C209 Dustin Byfuglien 1.00 2.50
C210 P.Subban/P.Kane CL 1.25 3.00
C211 Connor McDavid YG 500.00 1200.00
C212 Andreas Athanasiou YG 6.00 15.00
C213 Adam Pelech YG 3.00 8.00
C214 Zachary Fucale YG 8.00 20.00
C215 Jake Virtanen YG 8.00 20.00
C216 Brady Skjei YG 3.00 8.00
C217 Linus Ullmark YG 10.00 25.00
C218 Viktor Arvidsson YG 4.00 10.00
C219 Juuse Saros YG 12.00 30.00
C220 Brendan Gaunce YG 5.00 12.00
C221 Brock McGinn YG 4.00 10.00
C222 Chris Wideman YG 4.00 10.00
C223 Connor Brickley YG 3.00 8.00
C224 Hunter Shinkaruk YG 4.00 10.00
C225 Nick Cousins YG 4.00 10.00
C226 Brett Pesce YG 3.00 8.00
C227 Shea Theodore YG 6.00 15.00
C228 Garret Sparks YG 6.00 15.00
C229 Devin Shore YG 4.00 10.00
C230 Mike McCarron YG 5.00 12.00
C231 Jaccob Slavin YG 6.00 15.00
C232 Shane Prince YG 2.50 6.00
C233 Ryan Hartman YG 5.00 12.00
C234 Nick Ritchie YG 4.00 10.00
C235 Gustav Olofsson YG 4.00 10.00
C236 Mike Condon YG 4.00 10.00
C237 Charles Hudon YG 4.00 10.00
C238 Nikolay Goldobin YG 4.00 10.00
C239 Ben Hutton YG 4.00 10.00
C240 C.McDavid/J.Virtanen YG CL 40.00 100.00
C241 Bobby Clarke RET 15.00 40.00
C242 Joe Sakic RET 20.00 50.00
C243 Bobby Hull RET 20.00 50.00
C244 Guy Lafleur RET 12.00 30.00
C245 Phil Esposito RET 15.00 40.00
C246 Patrick Roy RET 12.00 30.00
C247 Martin Brodeur RET 12.00 30.00
C248 Jeremy Roenick RET 15.00 40.00
C249 Wayne Gretzky RET 25.00 50.00
C250 Mark Messier RET 20.00 50.00
C251 Teemu Selanne RET 20.00 50.00
C252 Theoren Fleury RET 12.00 30.00
C253 Bobby Orr RET 40.00 100.00
C254 Doug Gilmour RET 12.00 30.00
C255 Jari Kurri RET 10.00 25.00
C256 Charles Hudon POE 8.00 20.00
C257 Sam Bennett POE 4.00 10.00
C258 Malcolm Subban POE 12.00 30.00
C259 Hunter Shinkaruk POE 8.00 20.00
C260 Max Domi POE 15.00 40.00
C261 Jake Virtanen POE 10.00 25.00
C262 Slater Koekkoek POE 5.00 12.00
C263 Nicolas Petan POE 8.00 20.00
C264 Josh Anderson POE 15.00 40.00
C265 Robby Fabbri POE 10.00 25.00
C266 Zachary Fucale POE 6.00 15.00
C267 Nick Ritchie POE 8.00 20.00
C268 Shea Theodore POE 12.00 30.00
C269 Brendan Gaunce POE 10.00 25.00
C270 Connor McDavid POE 150.00 300.00

2015-16 Upper Deck Canvas Autographs

CABH Brett Hull/16 125.00 200.00
CARN Rick Nash/61 40.00 80.00

2015-16 Upper Deck Clear Cut Foundations

CCF1 C.Perry/J.Silfverberg 25.00 60.00
CCF2 M.Boedker/T.Rieder 10.00 25.00
CCF3 P.Bergeron/D.Pastrnak 40.00 80.00
CCF4 Z.Girgensons/T.Ennis 25.00 50.00
CCF5 J.Hudler/J.Gaudreau 20.00 50.00
CCF6 E.Staal/J.Faulk 20.00 50.00
CCF7 J.Toews/C.Crawford 25.00 60.00
CCF8 N.MacKinnon/T.Barrie 60.00 150.00
CCF9 R.Johansen/N.Foligno 12.00 30.00
CCF10 T.Seguin/C.Eakin 20.00 50.00
CCF11 H.Zetterberg/T.Tatar 20.00 50.00
CCF12 J.Eberle/L.Draisaitl 50.00 125.00
CCF13 J.Jagr/J.Huberdeau 20.00 50.00
CCF14 T.Pearson/T.Toffoli 15.00 40.00
CCF15 D.Dubnyk/M.Dumba 12.00 30.00
CCF16 M.Pacioretty/A.Galchenyuk 15.00 40.00
CCF17 R.Josi/F.Forsberg 25.00 60.00
CCF18 C.Schneider/A.Henrique 12.00 30.00
CCF19 J.Tavares/B.Nelson 25.00 60.00
CCF20 H.Lundqvist/C.Kreider 40.00 100.00
CCF21 E.Karlsson/M.Stone 20.00 50.00
CCF22 C.Giroux/W.Simmonds 20.00 50.00
CCF23 K.Letang/M.Fleury 30.00 80.00
CCF24 L.Couture/B.Burns 12.00 30.00
CCF25 J.Schwartz/V.Tarasenko 20.00 50.00
CCF26 S.Stamkos/T.Johnson 15.00 40.00
CCF27 M.Rielly/J.van Riemsdyk 15.00 40.00
CCF28 B.Horvat/D.Sedin 20.00 50.00
CCF29 A.Ovechkin/M.Johansson 60.00 150.00
CCF30 M.Scheifele/J.Trouba 25.00 60.00

2015-16 Upper Deck Clear Cut Honoured Members

HOF55 Rob Blake 12.00 30.00
HOF56 Chris Chelios 12.00 30.00
HOF57 Mike Modano 20.00 50.00
HOF58 Brad Park 15.00 40.00
HOF59 Steve Yzerman 30.00 80.00
HOF60 Lanny McDonald 12.00 30.00

2015-16 Upper Deck Clear Cut Superstars

CCS1 Patrick Kane 12.00 30.00
CCS2 John Tavares 10.00 25.00
CCS3 Jakub Voracek 8.00 20.00
CCS4 Patrice Bergeron 8.00 20.00
CCS5 Drew Doughty 8.00 20.00
CCS6 Oliver Ekman-Larsson 6.00 15.00
CCS7 Marc-Andre Fleury 10.00 25.00
CCS8 Bobby Orr 25.00 50.00
CCS9 Shea Weber 5.00 12.00
CCS10 Mark Messier 12.00 30.00
CCS11 Vladimir Tarasenko 8.00 20.00
CCS12 Rick Nash 6.00 15.00
CCS13 Jamie Benn 6.00 15.00
CCS14 Johnny Gaudreau 10.00 25.00
CCS15 Aaron Ekblad 8.00 20.00
CCS16 Henrik Zetterberg 8.00 20.00
CCS17 Martin Brodeur 12.00 30.00
CCS18 Henrik Lundqvist 15.00 40.00
CCS19 Erik Karlsson 8.00 20.00
CCS20 James van Riemsdyk 5.00 12.00
CCS21 Brett Hull 12.00 30.00
CCS22 Pavel Datsyuk 10.00 25.00
CCS23 Daniel Sedin 8.00 20.00
CCS24 Wayne Gretzky 25.00 50.00
CCS25 Filip Forsberg 10.00 25.00
CCS26 Duncan Keith 5.00 12.00
CCS27 Alexander Ovechkin 25.00 60.00
CCS28 Steven Stamkos 12.00 30.00
CCS29 Ryan Getzlaf 6.00 15.00
CCS30 Max Pacioretty 6.00 15.00
CCS31 Sidney Crosby 25.00 60.00
CCS32 Carey Price 20.00 40.00
CCS33 Brian Leetch 6.00 15.00
CCS34 Jiri Hudler 6.00 15.00
CCS35 Corey Perry 12.00 30.00
CCS36 Brandon Saad 6.00 15.00
CCS37 Zach Parise 8.00 20.00
CCS38 David Krejci 8.00 20.00
CCS39 Adam Henrique 6.00 15.00
CCS40 Doug Gilmour 10.00 25.00
CCS41 Ryan O'Reilly 8.00 20.00
CCS42 Anthony Duclair 6.00 15.00
CCS43 Alexander Steen 5.00 12.00
CCS44 Connor McDavid 175.00 300.00
CCS45 Nathan MacKinnon 30.00 80.00
CCS46 Tyler Seguin 10.00 25.00
CCS47 Claude Giroux 8.00 20.00
CCS48 Evgeny Kuznetsov 10.00 25.00
CCS49 Roberto Luongo 12.00 30.00
CCS50 Jonathan Toews 12.00 30.00
CCS51 Blake Wheeler 8.00 20.00
CCS52 Kris Versteeg 5.00 12.00
CCS53 Victor Hedman 10.00 25.00
CCS54 Steve Yzerman 20.00 50.00
CCS55 Joe Pavelski 10.00 25.00
CCS56 Ryan Miller 8.00 20.00
CCS57 Patrick Roy 20.00 50.00
CCS58 Mike Bossy 8.00 20.00
CCS59 Jonathan Quick 10.00 25.00
CCS60 Mark Stone 10.00 25.00
CCS61 Pekka Rinne 8.00 20.00
CCS62 Mario Lemieux 30.00 80.00

2015-16 Upper Deck Code to Greatness

CTG00 Connor McDavid 175.00 300.00
CTG0 Connor McDavid 30.00 80.00
CTG1 P.K. Subban 2.50 6.00
CTG2 Alexander Ovechkin 8.00 20.00
CTG3 Patrick Kane 4.00 10.00
CTG4 Jamie Benn 2.00 5.00
CTG5 Wayne Simmonds 2.50 6.00
CTG6 Jaromir Jagr 6.00 15.00
CTG7 Jonathan Bernier 1.50 4.00
CTG8 Tuukka Rask 2.50 6.00
CTG9 Jordan Eberle 2.00 5.00
CTG10 Ryan Johansen 1.50 4.00
CTG11 Pavel Datsyuk 3.00 8.00
CTG12 Evgeni Malkin 4.00 10.00
CTG13 Ryan Getzlaf 2.00 5.00
CTG14 Sidney Crosby 8.00 20.00
CTG15 Steven Stamkos 4.00 10.00
CTG16 Pekka Rinne 2.00 5.00
CTG17 Jonathan Quick 2.50 6.00
CTG18 Henrik Zetterberg 2.50 6.00
CTG19 John Tavares 3.00 8.00
CTG20 Carey Price 4.00 10.00
CTG21 Brett Hull 4.00 10.00
CTG22 Ray Bourque 3.00 8.00
CTG23 Steve Yzerman 5.00 12.00
CTG24 Mario Lemieux 8.00 20.00
CTG25 Wayne Gretzky 12.00 30.00

2015-16 Upper Deck Day With The Cup

DC1 Patrick Sharp 25.00 50.00
DC2 Niklas Hjalmarsson 15.00 40.00
DC3 Jonathan Toews 30.00 60.00
DC4 Brent Seabrook 10.00 25.00
DC5 Antti Raanta 15.00 40.00
DC6 Andrew Desjardins 10.00 25.00
DC7 Daniel Carcillo 12.00 30.00
DC8 Antoine Vermette 10.00 25.00
DC9 Brandon Saad 12.00 30.00
DC10 Brad Richards 15.00 40.00
DC11 Kimmo Timonen 12.00 30.00
DC12 Duncan Keith 12.00 30.00
DC13 Marian Hossa 15.00 40.00
DC14 Teuvo Teravainen 15.00 40.00
DC15 Trevor van Riemsdyk 12.00 30.00
DC16 Johnny Oduya 12.00 30.00
DC17 Marcus Kruger 10.00 25.00
DC18 Corey Crawford 20.00 50.00
DC19 Scott Darling 12.00 30.00
DC20 Patrick Kane 50.00 100.00
DC21 Bryan Bickell 10.00 25.00
DC22 Kris Versteeg 10.00 25.00
DC23 Andrew Shaw 15.00 40.00
DC24 David Rundblad 12.00 30.00
DC25 Kyle Cumiskey 10.00 25.00
DC26 Joakim Nordstrom 10.00 25.00

2015-16 Upper Deck Day With The Cup Flashback

DCF1 Mike Bossy 15.00 40.00
DCF2 Denis Potvin 15.00 40.00
DCF3 Bob Nystrom 12.00 30.00

2015-16 Upper Deck Fusion Rookie Achievement

R1 Connor McDavid 30.00 80.00
R2 Max Domi 4.00 10.00
R3 Zachary Fucale 1.50 4.00
R4 Dylan Larkin 6.00 15.00
R5 Artemi Panarin 8.00 20.00
R6 Noah Hanifin 3.00 8.00
R7 Connor Hellebuyck 8.00 20.00
R8 Robby Fabbri 2.50 6.00
R9 Sam Bennett 6.00 15.00
R10 Jack Eichel 8.00 20.00

2015-16 Upper Deck Game Jerseys

COMPLETE SET (72)
GJAB Aleksander Barkov 2G 5.00 12.00
GJAE Aaron Ekblad 1E 4.00 10.00
GJAG Alex Galchenyuk 1F 2.00 5.00
GJAK Anze Kopitar 2E 5.00 12.00
GJAO Alexander Ovechkin 1B 25.00 60.00
GJBB Brent Burns 1C 4.00 10.00
GJBE Jamie Benn 1E 3.00 8.00
GJBH Brett Hull 2C 20.00 50.00
GJBI Ben Bishop 1F 2.50 6.00
GJBR Bobby Ryan 1G 2.50 6.00
GJBW Blake Wheeler 1C 4.00 10.00
GJCC Charlie Coyle 1F 3.00 8.00
GJCG Claude Giroux 2D 4.00 10.00
GJCK1 Chris Kreider 1F 4.00 10.00
GJCK2 Chris Kreider 2G 4.00 10.00
GJCO Corey Crawford 1E 4.00 10.00
GJCP1 Corey Perry 2F 5.00 12.00
GJCP2 Carey Price 1B 12.00 30.00
GJCR Sidney Crosby 1B 25.00 60.00
GJCW Cam Ward 2G 3.00 8.00
GJDB Dustin Byfuglien 2F 3.00 8.00
GJDD1 Drew Doughty 1F 4.00 10.00
GJDD2 Drew Doughty 2D 5.00 12.00
GJDK David Krejci 1E 3.00 8.00
GJDP Dion Phaneuf 2D 3.00 8.00
GJDS Derek Stepan 2G 2.00 5.00
GJEK1 Erik Karlsson 2F 4.00 10.00
GJEK2 Evgeny Kuznetsov 1D 5.00 12.00
GJEL Elias Lindholm 1G 2.50 6.00
GJEM Evgeni Malkin 1C 4.00 10.00
GJES Eric Staal 2G 4.00 10.00
GJFA Frederik Andersen 2F 4.00 10.00
GJFF Filip Forsberg 2F 5.00 12.00
GJGF Grant Fuhr 2C 15.00 40.00
GJGL Gabriel Landeskog 2F 4.00 10.00
GJGN Gustav Nyquist 1D 2.50 6.00
GJHE Tomas Hertl 1G 3.00 8.00
GJHL1 Henrik Lundqvist 1C 4.00 10.00
GJHL2 Henrik Lundqvist 2F 8.00 20.00
GJHS Henrik Sedin 1E 4.00 10.00
GJHU Jonathan Huberdeau 1E 4.00 10.00
GJHZ Henrik Zetterberg 1C 5.00 12.00
GJJB Jonathan Bernier 1G 2.50 6.00
GJJC John Carlson 2G 2.50 6.00
GJJD Jonathan Drouin 1D 3.00 8.00
GJJE Jordan Eberle 1E 3.00 8.00
GJJG Johnny Gaudreau 1C 6.00 15.00
GJJH Jonas Hiller 1G 2.50 6.00
GJJI Jiri Hudler 1F 2.50 6.00
GJJN James Neal 1E 2.00 5.00
GJJO Roman Josi 2F 3.00 8.00
GJJP1 Joe Pavelski 2E 4.00 10.00
GJJP2 Jason Pominville 1E 2.00 5.00
GJJQ1 Jonathan Quick 1G 4.00 10.00
GJJQ2 Jonathan Quick 2G 4.00 10.00
GJJS Jeff Skinner 2G 4.00 10.00
GJJT1 Jacob Trouba 1F 2.50 6.00
GJJT2 Jacob Trouba 2F 2.50 6.00
GJJV1 James van Riemsdyk 1G 2.50 6.00
GJJV2 Jakub Voracek 2G 2.50 6.00
GJKA Erik Karlsson 1C 5.00 12.00
GJKE Duncan Keith 2F 2.50 6.00
GJKH Kevin Hayes 2F 2.50 6.00
GJKL Kari Lehtonen 2F 2.50 6.00
GJKO Kyle Okposo 1E 2.00 5.00
GJKR Niklas Kronwall 2G 2.50 6.00
GJLC Logan Couture 2F 4.00 10.00
GJLE Kris Letang 2G 4.00 10.00
GJMF Marc-Andre Fleury 2G 6.00 15.00
GJMG Mikael Granlund 2G 2.50 6.00
GJML Milan Lucic 1E 2.50 6.00
GJMP Max Pacioretty 1F 3.00 8.00
GJMS Mark Scheifele 2G 5.00 12.00
GJNB Nicklas Backstrom 1C 4.00 10.00
GJNK Nazem Kadri 1F 4.00 10.00
GJNM Nathan MacKinnon 1E 12.00 30.00
GJOE Oliver Ekman-Larsson 2F 3.00 8.00
GJOL Oliver Ekman-Larsson 1E 3.00 8.00
GJOP Ondrej Palat 1D 3.00 8.00
GJPA Ondrej Pavelec 1G 3.00 8.00
GJPK1 Phil Kessel 2F 3.00 8.00
GJPK2 P.K. Subban 1D 5.00 12.00
GJPM Patrick Marleau 2G 3.00 8.00
GJPR Patrick Roy 1A 50.00 100.00
GJPS1 Patrick Sharp 1E 3.00 8.00
GJPS2 P.K. Subban 2F 4.00 10.00
GJRG Ryan Getzlaf 1D 4.00 10.00
GJRI Pekka Rinne 1E 3.00 8.00
GJRJ Ryan Johansen 2F 2.50 6.00
GJRL Roberto Luongo 2F 5.00 12.00
GJRM Ryan Miller 1E 3.00 8.00
GJRN Rick Nash 1E 3.00 8.00
GJRS Ryan Strome 2F 3.00 8.00
GJSB Sergei Bobrovsky 1F 5.00 12.00
GJSC Sean Couturier 1F 2.50 6.00
GJSD Shane Doan 1G 2.50 6.00
GJSH Scott Hartnell 1F 2.00 5.00
GJSJ Seth Jones 1G 3.00 8.00
GJSM1 Steve Mason 1F 2.50 6.00
GJSM2 Steve Mason 2G 2.50 6.00
GJSP Jason Spezza 2G 3.00 8.00
GJSR Sam Reinhart 1F 6.00 15.00
GJSS Steven Stamkos 1C 4.00 10.00
GJSV Semyon Varlamov 1G 3.00 8.00
GJSY Steve Yzerman 2B 25.00 50.00
GJTA John Tavares 1C 6.00 15.00
GJTF Theoren Fleury 2C 15.00 30.00
GJTH Taylor Hall 1D 4.00 10.00
GJTJ Tomas Jurco 1F 2.00 5.00
GJTO Jonathan Toews 1B 10.00 25.00
GJTR Tuukka Rask 2F 4.00 10.00
GJTS1 Tyler Seguin 1D 5.00 12.00
GJTS2 Tyler Seguin 2E 4.00 10.00
GJTT Tyler Toffoli 1G 3.00 8.00
GJVH Victor Hedman 1D 5.00 12.00
GJVN Valeri Nichushkin 1F 3.00 8.00
GJVT Vladimir Tarasenko 1B 8.00 20.00
GJZC Zdeno Chara 1F 3.00 8.00
GJZG Zemgus Girgensons 1D 3.00 8.00

2015-16 Upper Deck Instant Impressions

II00 Jack Eichel 50.00 100.00
II0 Jack Eichel 5.00 12.00
II1 Malcolm Subban 2.00 5.00
II2 Johnny Gaudreau 2.00 5.00
II3 Mike Hoffman .75 2.00
II4 Vladimir Tarasenko 1.50 4.00
II5 Jonathan Drouin 1.00 2.50
II6 Nathan MacKinnon 5.00 12.00
II7 Seth Jones 1.25 3.00
II8 Sean Monahan .75 2.00
II9 Elias Lindholm 1.25 3.00
II10 Jonathan Huberdeau 1.50 4.00
II11 Ryan Strome 1.25 3.00
II12 Alex Galchenyuk .75 2.00
II13 Jacob Trouba 1.00 2.50
II14 Zemgus Girgensons 1.00 2.50
II15 Nick Bjugstad .75 2.00
II16 Kevin Hayes 1.00 2.50
II17 Mikael Granlund 1.00 2.50
II18 Riley Sheahan .75 2.00
II19 Morgan Rielly 1.25 3.00
II20 Aaron Ekblad 1.50 4.00
II21 Sam Bennett 4.00 10.00
II22 Ryan Hartman 1.50 4.00
II23 Filip Forsberg 2.00 5.00
II24 Nikita Kucherov 2.50 6.00
II25 Jacob de la Rose 1.25 3.00

2015-16 Upper Deck NHL Draft

SP1 Connor McDavid SP 150.00 300.00
SP2 Jack Eichel SP 100.00 200.00
SP1A Connor McDavid AU SP 1200.00 2000.00

2015-16 Upper Deck Oversized

20 Tuukka Rask 2.00 5.00
44 Jonathan Toews 2.50 6.00
62 Tyler Seguin 2.00 5.00
68 Pavel Datsyuk 2.50 6.00
85 Jonathan Quick 2.00 5.00
102 P.K. Subban 2.00 5.00
110 Shea Weber 1.25 3.00
119 John Tavares 2.50 6.00
130 Rick Nash 1.50 4.00
139 Claude Giroux 1.50 4.00
147 Evgeni Malkin 3.00 8.00
168 Steven Stamkos 3.00 8.00
172 James van Riemsdyk 1.25 3.00
185 Alexander Ovechkin 6.00 15.00
201 Connor McDavid YG 40.00 80.00
204 Max Domi YG 3.00 8.00
206 Mikko Rantanen YG 8.00 20.00
208 Kevin Fiala YG 2.00 5.00
210 Emile Poirier YG 1.25 3.00
211 Malcolm Subban YG 2.50 6.00
212 Jacob de la Rose YG 1.50 4.00
214 Connor Hellebuyck YG 6.00 15.00
219 Jared McCann YG 2.00 5.00
221 Artemi Panarin YG 6.00 15.00
223 Nikolaj Ehlers YG 3.00 8.00
228 Dylan Larkin YG 12.50 25.00
229 Robby Fabbri YG 2.00 5.00
231 Sam Bennett YG 5.00 12.00
451 Jack Eichel 6.00 15.00
452 Charles Hudon 1.50 4.00
453 Nikolay Goldobin 1.50 4.00
457 Jake Virtanen 2.00 5.00
458 Andreas Athanasiou 4.00 10.00
461 Zachary Fucale 1.25 3.00
462 Hunter Shinkaruk 1.50 4.00
464 Juuse Saros 4.00 10.00
471 Louis Domingue 1.50 4.00
472 Linus Ullmark 3.00 8.00
480 Garret Sparks 1.50 4.00
495 Shea Theodore 2.50 6.00
496 Nick Ritchie 1.50 4.00
499 Noah Hanifin 2.50 6.00

2015-16 Upper Deck Parkhurst Rookies

*BLUE: .8X TO 2X BASIC INSERTS
PR1 Connor McDavid 20.00 50.00
PR2 Jack Eichel 5.00 12.00
PR3 Sam Bennett 4.00 10.00
PR4 Dylan Larkin 4.00 10.00
PR5 Nikolaj Ehlers 2.50 6.00
PR6 Max Domi 2.50 6.00
PR7 Mikko Rantanen 6.00 15.00
PR8 Robby Fabbri 1.50 4.00
PR9 Jared McCann 1.50 4.00
PR10 Artemi Panarin 5.00 12.00

2015-16 Upper Deck Parkhurst Rookies Red

*RED: 1.5X TO 4X BASIC INSERTS

2015-16 Upper Deck Puck Wizards

COMPLETE SET (6)
PW1 Patrick Kane 6.00 15.00
PW6 Sidney Crosby 12.00 30.00

2015-16 Upper Deck Rookie Breakouts

RB1 Connor McDavid 350.00 500.00
RB2 Mikko Rantanen 40.00 100.00
RB3 Daniel Sprong 10.00 25.00
RB4 Kevin Fiala 10.00 25.00
RB5 Sam Bennett 25.00 60.00
RB6 Oscar Lindberg 8.00 20.00
RB7 Sergei Plotnikov 5.00 12.00
RB8 Nick Shore 5.00 12.00
RB9 Malcolm Subban 20.00 40.00
RB10 Max Domi 30.00 60.00
RB11 Robby Fabbri 20.00 40.00
RB12 Jared McCann 10.00 25.00
RB13 Matt Puempel 6.00 15.00
RB14 Viktor Arvidsson 8.00 20.00
RB15 Emile Poirier 6.00 15.00
RB16 Jordan Weal 5.00 12.00
RB17 Noah Hanifin 12.00 30.00
RB18 Nicolas Petan 8.00 20.00
RB19 Nikolaj Ehlers 20.00 40.00
RB20 Jake Virtanen 20.00 40.00
RB21 Nikolay Goldobin 8.00 20.00
RB22 Joonas Donskoi 8.00 20.00
RB23 Nick Ritchie 8.00 20.00
RB24 Andreas Athanasiou 25.00 50.00
RB25 Jacob de la Rose 8.00 20.00
RB26 Artemi Panarin 40.00 80.00
RB27 Dylan Larkin 60.00 120.00
RB28 Jack Eichel 125.00 200.00

2015-16 Upper Deck Rookie Breakouts Gold

COMPLETE SET (12)

2015-16 Upper Deck Rookie Materials

COMPLETE SET (36)
RMAA Andreas Athanasiou D 4.00 10.00
RMAB Antoine Bibeau D 1.50 4.00
RMAP Artemi Panarin D 6.00 15.00
RMAS Anthony Stolarz D 4.00 10.00
RMBR Brendan Ranford D 1.25 3.00
RMCH Connor Hellebuyck D 6.00 15.00
RMCM Connor McDavid B 60.00 150.00
RMDF Derek Forbort D 1.25 3.00
RMDL Dylan Larkin C 5.00 12.00
RMEP Emile Poirier D 1.25 3.00
RMHS Henrik Samuelsson D 1.00 2.50
RMJA Josh Anderson C 3.00 8.00
RMJD Jacob de la Rose D 1.50 4.00
RMJE Jack Eichel B 6.00 15.00
RMJM Jared McCann A 2.00 5.00
RMJV Jake Virtanen C 2.00 5.00
RMJW Jordan Weal D 1.00 2.50
RMKF Kevin Fiala D 2.00 5.00
RMMD Max Domi C 3.00 8.00
RMMP Matt Puempel D 1.25 3.00
RMMR Mikko Rantanen D 8.00 20.00
RMMS Mackenzie Skapski D 1.50 4.00
RMNC Nick Cousins D 1.50 4.00
RMNE Nikolaj Ehlers C 3.00 8.00
RMNH Noah Hanifin D 2.50 6.00
RMNP Nicolas Petan D 1.50 4.00
RMNS Nick Shore D 1.00 2.50
RMRF Robby Fabbri C 2.00 5.00
RMRH Ryan Hartman D 2.00 5.00
RMRK Ronalds Kenins C 1.00 2.50
RMSB Sam Bennett A 5.00 12.00
RMSK Slater Koekkoek D 1.00 2.50
RMSN Stefan Noesen D 1.00 2.50
RMSP Shane Prince D 1.00 2.50
RMSU Malcolm Subban D 2.50 6.00
RMDS1 Daniel Sprong D 2.00 5.00

2015-16 Upper Deck Shining Stars

*1-10 BLUE: 1.5X TO 4X BASIC INSERTS
*11-20 BLUE: 1.2X TO 3X BASIC INSERTS
*21-50 BLUE: .6X TO 1.5X BASIC INSERTS
SS1 Aaron Ekblad 1.25 3.00
SS2 Alex Pietrangelo .75 2.00
SS3 Drew Doughty 1.25 3.00
SS4 Duncan Keith .75 2.00
SS5 Erik Karlsson 1.25 3.00
SS6 Kris Letang 1.25 3.00
SS7 Mark Giordano 1.00 2.50
SS8 Oliver Ekman-Larsson 1.00 2.50
SS9 P.K. Subban 1.25 3.00
SS10 Shea Weber .75 2.00
SS11 Braden Holtby 1.50 4.00
SS12 Corey Crawford 1.50 4.00
SS13 Carey Price 2.50 6.00
SS14 Henrik Lundqvist 3.00 8.00
SS15 Devan Dubnyk 1.00 2.50
SS16 Jonathan Quick 1.50 4.00
SS17 Marc-Andre Fleury 2.50 6.00
SS18 Pekka Rinne 1.25 3.00
SS19 Roberto Luongo 2.00 5.00
SS20 Tuukka Rask 1.50 4.00
SS21 Evgeni Malkin 1.50 4.00
SS22 Filip Forsberg 1.25 3.00
SS23 Jonathan Toews 1.25 3.00
SS24 Patrice Bergeron 1.00 2.50
SS25 Pavel Datsyuk 1.25 3.00
SS26 Ryan Nugent-Hopkins 1.00 2.50
SS27 Sidney Crosby 3.00 8.00
SS28 Steven Stamkos 1.50 4.00
SS29 John Tavares 1.25 3.00
SS30 Tyler Seguin 1.00 2.50
SS31 Alexander Ovechkin 4.00 10.00
SS32 Corey Perry 1.50 4.00
SS33 Henrik Zetterberg 1.25 3.00
SS34 Johnny Gaudreau 1.50 4.00
SS35 Jakub Voracek .75 2.00
SS36 Marian Hossa 1.00 2.50
SS37 Max Pacioretty 1.00 2.50
SS38 Patrick Kane 2.00 5.00
SS39 Rick Nash 1.00 2.50
SS40 Vladimir Tarasenko 1.25 3.00
SS41 Bobby Hull 2.50 6.00
SS42 Joe Sakic 2.50 6.00
SS43 Grant Fuhr 2.00 5.00
SS44 Martin Brodeur 3.00 8.00
SS45 Mario Lemieux 5.00 12.00
SS46 Mark Messier 2.50 6.00
SS47 Mats Sundin 1.25 3.00
SS48 Patrick Roy 3.00 8.00
SS49 Teemu Selanne 2.50 6.00
SS50 Wayne Gretzky 8.00 20.00

2015-16 Upper Deck Signature Sensations

SSAG Alex Galchenyuk G 3.00 8.00
SSAH Andrew Hammond H 6.00 15.00
SSAK Alex Killorn F 3.00 8.00
SSBB Ben Bishop D 4.00 10.00
SSBD Brenden Dillon F 3.00 8.00
SSBH Bo Horvat H 6.00 15.00
SSBO Bobby Orr B 50.00 125.00
SSBR Brett Ritchie F 3.00 8.00
SSBS Brendan Smith A 20.00 50.00
SSCG Cody Goloubef F 3.00 8.00
SSDE Dennis Everberg H 3.00 8.00
SSDJ Dmitrij Jaskin E 3.00 8.00
SSDS Derek Stepan C 3.00 8.00
SSEL Elias Lindholm E 5.00 12.00
SSES Eric Staal G 6.00 15.00
SSFF Filip Forsberg B 8.00 20.00
SSJB Jordie Benn H 3.00 8.00
SSJC Jared Cowen E 3.00 8.00
SSJP Jason Pominville D 3.00 8.00
SSJS Jaden Schwartz F 6.00 15.00
SSLE Lars Eller G 3.00 8.00
SSLG Luke Glendening H 3.00 8.00
SSLS Luke Schenn F 5.00 12.00
SSNT Nate Thompson G 3.00 8.00
SSPS Paul Stastny F 4.00 10.00
SSRN Riley Nash C 3.00 8.00
SSRS Ryan Strome G 5.00 12.00
SSSB Sergei Bobrovsky E 8.00 20.00
SSSC Sean Couturier G 4.00 10.00
SSSG Seth Griffith G 3.00 8.00
SSSV Semyon Varlamov D 5.00 12.00
SSSW Shea Weber C 4.00 10.00
SSTK Torey Krug H 4.00 10.00
SSTM Tyler Myers C 3.00 8.00
SSTR Tuukka Rask H 6.00 15.00
SSTT Tomas Tatar H 3.00 8.00
SSTY Ty Rattie H 3.00 8.00
SSVN Valeri Nichushkin G 5.00 12.00
SSVR Victor Rask H 3.00 8.00
SSWG Wayne Gretzky A 250.00 600.00
SSZG Zemgus Girgensons H 4.00 10.00

2015-16 Upper Deck Signatures

COMPLETE SET (20)
UDSAD Anthony Duclair E 4.00 10.00
UDSAL Anton Lander C 5.00 12.00
UDSBC Brett Connolly B 8.00 20.00
UDSBG Brandon Gormley C 5.00 12.00
UDSBH Bo Horvat E 8.00 20.00
UDSBS Brandon Sutter D 5.00 12.00
UDSCG Claude Giroux B 15.00 30.00
UDSCJ Calle Jarnkrok E 4.00 10.00
UDSCS Colton Sissons E 3.00 8.00
UDSJA Jake Allen D 8.00 20.00
UDSJH Joey Hishon D 5.00 12.00
UDSKL Kari Lehtonen C 12.50 25.00
UDSPH Patric Hornqvist D 5.00 12.00
UDSRS Ryan Sproul C 6.00 15.00
UDSTT Tomas Tatar E 3.00 8.00
UDSVR Victor Rask E 3.00 8.00
UDSVT Vincent Trocheck E 5.00 12.00

2015-16 Upper Deck Super Snipers

SS1 Sidney Crosby 15.00 40.00
SS2 John Tavares 6.00 15.00
SS3 Steven Stamkos 8.00 20.00
SS4 Jonathan Toews 6.00 15.00
SS5 Rick Nash 4.00 10.00
SS6 Alexander Ovechkin 15.00 40.00

2015-16 Upper Deck UD Portraits

P1 Alexander Ovechkin 3.00 8.00
P2 Oliver Ekman-Larsson .75 2.00
P3 John Tavares 1.25 3.00
P4 Rick Nash .75 2.00
P5 Pavel Datsyuk 1.25 3.00
P6 Corey Crawford 1.00 2.50
P7 Henrik Lundqvist 2.00 5.00
P8 Jonathan Quick 1.00 2.50
P9 Ryan Miller .75 2.00
P10 Marian Hossa .75 2.00
P11 Tuukka Rask 1.00 2.50
P12 Eric Staal 1.00 2.50
P13 Claude Giroux .75 2.00
P14 Ryan Nugent-Hopkins 1.00 2.50
P15 Shea Weber .60 1.50
P16 Erik Karlsson 1.00 2.50
P17 Pekka Rinne .75 2.00
P18 Tyler Johnson .50 1.25
P19 Nicklas Backstrom .75 2.00
P20 Evgeni Malkin 1.50 4.00
P21 Ryan Johansen .60 1.50
P22 Jaromir Jagr 2.50 6.00
P23 Henrik Zetterberg 1.00 2.50
P24 Daniel Sedin 1.00 2.50
P25 Sidney Crosby 3.00 8.00
P26 Kyle Okposo .50 1.25
P27 Marc-Andre Fleury 1.50 4.00
P28 Jakub Voracek .60 1.50
P29 Ryan Getzlaf .75 2.00
P30 Jordan Eberle .75 2.00
P31 Vladimir Tarasenko 1.00 2.50
P32 Jiri Hudler .60 1.50
P33 James van Riemsdyk .60 1.50
P34 Max Pacioretty .75 2.00
P35 P.K. Subban 1.00 2.50
P36 Zach Parise .75 2.00
P37 Johnny Gaudreau 1.25 3.00
P38 Aaron Ekblad 1.00 2.50
P39 Anze Kopitar 1.25 3.00
P40 Adam Henrique .60 1.50
P41 Jonathan Toews 1.25 3.00
P42 Patrick Kane 1.50 4.00
P43 Corey Perry 1.25 3.00
P44 Tyler Seguin 1.00 2.50
P45 Joe Pavelski 1.00 2.50
P46 Patrice Bergeron 1.00 2.50
P47 Carey Price 1.50 4.00
P48 Steven Stamkos 1.50 4.00
P49 Guy Lafleur LEG 1.00 2.50
P50 Wayne Gretzky LEG 5.00 12.00
P51 Phil Esposito LEG 1.25 3.00
P52 Martin Brodeur LEG 2.00 5.00
P53 Mario Lemieux LEG 3.00 8.00
P54 Bobby Hull LEG 1.50 4.00
P55 Malcolm Subban 3.00 8.00
P56 Jacob de la Rose 1.25 3.00
P57 Sam Bennett 4.00 10.00
P58 Kevin Fiala 1.50 4.00
P59 Ryan Hartman 1.50 4.00
P60 Matt Puempel 1.00 2.50
P61 Jack Eichel 5.00 12.00
P62 Nick Cousins 1.25 3.00
P63 Antoine Bibeau 1.25 3.00
P64 Colin Miller 1.00 2.50
P65 Andreas Athanasiou 3.00 8.00
P66 Shane Prince .75 2.00
P67 Henrik Samuelsson .75 2.00
P68 Nick Shore .75 2.00
P69 Ronalds Kenins .75 2.00
P70 Nick Ritchie 1.25 3.00
P71 Emile Poirier 1.00 2.50
P72 Connor Hellebuyck 5.00 12.00
P73 Viktor Arvidsson 1.25 3.00
P74 Sergei Plotnikov .75 2.00
P75 Max Domi 2.50 6.00
P76 Stefan Noesen .75 2.00
P77 Connor Brickley 1.00 2.50
P78 Nikolay Goldobin 1.25 3.00
P79 Hunter Shinkaruk 1.25 3.00
P80 Derek Forbort 1.00 2.50
P81 Noah Hanifin 2.00 5.00
P82 Anton Slepyshev .75 2.00
P83 Jake Virtanen 1.50 4.00
P84 Oscar Lindberg 1.25 3.00
P85 Mike Condon 1.25 3.00
P86 Daniel Sprong 1.50 4.00
P87 Josh Anderson 2.50 6.00
P88 Joonas Donskoi 1.25 3.00
P89 Stanislav Galiev 1.25 3.00
P90 Mikko Rantanen 6.00 15.00
P91 Slater Koekkoek .75 2.00
P92 Kyle Baun 1.25 3.00
P93 Jordan Weal .75 2.00
P94 Andrew Copp 1.25 3.00
P95 Dylan Larkin 4.00 10.00
P96 Dylan DeMelo 1.00 2.50
P97 Mattias Janmark 1.25 3.00
P98 Jean-Francois Berube 1.00 2.50
P99 Colton Parayko 2.00 5.00
P100 Connor McDavid 30.00 80.00
P101 Chandler Stephenson 1.50 4.00
P102 Jared McCann 1.50 4.00
P103 Matt O'Connor 1.00 2.50
P104 Radek Faksa 1.25 3.00
P105 Robby Fabbri 1.50 4.00
P106 Nicolas Petan 1.25 3.00
P107 Nikolaj Ehlers 2.50 6.00
P108 Sam Brittain 1.25 3.00
P109 Brock McGinn 1.25 3.00
P110 Artemi Panarin 5.00 12.00

2015-16 Upper Deck UD Portraits Gold

*P1-P54 GOLD/25: 2.5X TO 6X BASIC INSERTS
*P55-P110 GLD RK/99: .8X TO 2X BASIC INSERTS
P6 Corey Crawford 6.00 15.00
P19 Nicklas Backstrom 5.00 12.00
P59 Ryan Hartman 3.00 8.00
P61 Jack Eichel 20.00 40.00
P100 Connor McDavid 150.00 400.00
P110 Artemi Panarin 20.00 40.00

2015-16 Upper Deck UD Portraits Platinum Blue

*P55-P110 BLU RK/25: 2X TO 5X BASIC INSERTS
P59 Ryan Hartman 8.00 20.00
P61 Jack Eichel 40.00 80.00
P100 Connor McDavid 150.00 400.00
P110 Artemi Panarin 40.00 80.00

2015-16 Upper Deck Winter Classic Jumbos

WC1 Troy Brouwer .60 1.50
WC2 Patrick Sharp 1.00 2.50
WC3 Alexander Ovechkin 4.00 10.00
WC4 Brandon Saad .75 2.00
WC5 Mike Green .75 2.00
WC6 Duncan Keith .75 2.00
WC7 Nicklas Backstrom 1.00 2.50
WC8 Marian Hossa 1.00 2.50
WC9 John Carlson 1.00 2.50

WC10 Patrick Kane 2.00 5.00
WC11 Eric Fehr .60 1.50
WC12 Jonathan Toews 1.50 4.00
WC13 Braden Holtby 1.25 3.00
WC14 Corey Crawford 1.25 3.00

2015-16 Upper Deck Young Guns Acetate

201 Connor McDavid 2500.00 3500.00
202 Jordan Weal 15.00 40.00
203 Sergei Plotnikov 15.00 40.00
204 Max Domi 150.00 250.00
205 Andrew Copp 30.00 80.00
206 Mikko Rantanen 150.00 400.00
207 Joel Edmundson 25.00 60.00
208 Kevin Fiala 40.00 100.00
209 Nick Cousins 30.00 80.00
210 Emile Poirier 25.00 60.00
211 Malcolm Subban 50.00 125.00
212 Jacob de la Rose 30.00 80.00
213 Henrik Samuelsson 20.00 50.00
214 Connor Hellebuyck 150.00 250.00
215 Matt Puempel 25.00 60.00
216 Nick Shore 20.00 50.00
217 Josh Anderson 60.00 150.00
218 Shane Prince 20.00 50.00
219 Jared McCann 60.00 150.00
220 Stanislav Galiev 30.00 80.00
221 Artemi Panarin 300.00 500.00
222 Viktor Arvidsson 30.00 80.00
223 Nikolaj Ehlers 200.00 400.00
224 Slater Koekkoek 20.00 50.00
225 Ronalds Kenins 20.00 50.00
226 Daniel Sprong 40.00 100.00
227 Nicolas Petan 80.00 200.00
228 Dylan Larkin 500.00 1000.00
229 Robby Fabbri 100.00 300.00
230 Joonas Donskoi 30.00 80.00
231 Ben Hutton 30.00 80.00
232 Sam Bennett 150.00 400.00
233 Matt O'Connor 25.00 60.00
234 Oscar Lindberg 30.00 80.00
235 Colton Parayko 50.00 125.00
236 Stefan Noesen 20.00 50.00
237 Anton Slepyshev 20.00 50.00
238 Sergei Kalinin 20.00 50.00
239 Mike Condon 30.00 80.00
240 Antoine Bibeau 30.00 80.00
241 Kyle Baun 30.00 80.00
242 Jean-Francois Berube 25.00 60.00
243 Joonas Kemppainen 20.00 50.00
244 Mattias Janmark 30.00 80.00
245 Evgeny Medvedev 25.00 60.00
246 Keegan Lowe 30.00 80.00
247 Colin Miller 25.00 60.00
248 Brett Kulak 25.00 60.00
249 Connor Brickley 25.00 60.00
451 Jack Eichel 500.00 1000.00
452 Charles Hudon 30.00 80.00
453 Nikolay Goldobin 30.00 80.00
454 Logan Shaw 30.00 80.00
455 Frank Vatrano 60.00 150.00
456 Jujhar Khaira 25.00 60.00
457 Jake Virtanen 200.00 400.00
458 Andreas Athanasiou 100.00 250.00
459 Tanner Kero 30.00 80.00
460 Chris Wideman 30.00 80.00
461 Zachary Fucale 60.00 150.00
462 Hunter Shinkaruk 30.00 80.00
463 Brendan Ranford 25.00 60.00
464 Juuse Saros 80.00 200.00
465 Adam Pelech 25.00 60.00
466 Michael Keranen 25.00 60.00
467 Dylan DeMelo 25.00 60.00
468 Mark Alt 20.00 50.00
469 Jaccob Slavin 50.00 125.00
470 Alexandre Grenier 25.00 60.00
471 Louis Domingue 60.00 150.00
472 Linus Ullmark 60.00 150.00
473 Derek Forbort 25.00 60.00
474 Brady Skjei 25.00 60.00
475 Ryan Hartman 40.00 100.00
476 Max McCormick 25.00 60.00
477 Vincent Hinostroza 20.00 50.00
478 Taylor Leier 30.00 80.00
479 Radek Faksa 30.00 80.00
480 Garret Sparks 30.00 80.00
481 Brendan Gaunce 40.00 100.00
482 Chris Driedger 25.00 60.00
483 Joel Vermin 25.00 60.00
484 Chandler Stephenson 40.00 100.00
485 David Musil 25.00 60.00
486 Gustav Olofsson 30.00 80.00
487 Brett Pesce 25.00 60.00
488 Anthony Stolarz 80.00 200.00
489 Devin Shore 30.00 80.00
490 Petr Straka 20.00 50.00
491 Mike McCarron 40.00 100.00
492 Raman Hrabarenka 25.00 60.00
493 Markus Hannikainen 25.00 60.00
494 Sam Brittain 30.00 80.00
495 Shea Theodore 60.00 150.00
496 Nick Ritchie 30.00 80.00
497 Brock McGinn 30.00 80.00
498 Tyler Randell 30.00 80.00
499 Noah Hanifin 60.00 150.00

2015-16 Upper Deck Biography of a Season

COMPLETE SET (12) 15.00 40.00
COMMON McDAVID 2.00 5.00
COMMON GRETZKY 1.00 2.50

2015-16 Upper Deck Rookie Showcase Moments Fall Expo

COMPLETE SET (6) 20.00 50.00
COMMON McDAVID 4.00 10.00

2016-17 Upper Deck

1 John Gibson .30 .75
2 Cam Fowler .30 .75
3 Jakob Silfverberg .20 .50
4 Andrew Cogliano .20 .50
5 Kevin Bieksa .25 .60
6 Ryan Getzlaf .30 .75
7 Ryan Kesler .30 .75
8 Anthony Duclair .25 .60
9 Shane Doan .25 .60
10 Jordan Martinook .20 .50
11 Martin Hanzal .25 .60
12 Mike Smith .30 .75
13 Oliver Ekman-Larsson .30 .75
14 Brad Marchand .60 1.50
15 David Krejci .30 .75
16 David Pastrnak .75 2.00
17 Jimmy Hayes .20 .50
18 Matt Beleskey .25 .60
19 Ryan Spooner .25 .60
20 Zdeno Chara .30 .75
21 Josh Gorges .20 .50
22 Matt Moulson .20 .50
23 Robin Lehner .25 .60
24 Ryan O'Reilly .30 .75
25 Sam Reinhart .60 1.50
26 Zach Bogosian .25 .60
27 Dougie Hamilton .25 .60
28 Mark Giordano .30 .75
29 Michael Frolik .25 .60
30 Mikael Backlund .25 .60
31 Sam Bennett .50 1.25
32 T.J. Brodie .25 .60
33 Andrej Nestrasil .25 .60
34 Cam Ward .30 .75
35 Elias Lindholm .30 .75
36 Jeff Skinner .40 1.00
37 Justin Faulk .25 .60
38 Noah Hanifin .30 .75
39 Artem Anisimov .20 .50
40 Artemi Panarin .60 1.50
41 Brent Seabrook .20 .50
42 Marcus Kruger .20 .50
43 Marian Hossa .30 .75
44 Patrick Kane .60 1.50
45 Niklas Hjalmarsson .20 .50
46 Carl Soderberg .20 .50
47 Erik Johnson .20 .50
48 Francois Beauchemin .25 .60
49 Gabriel Landeskog .40 1.00
50 Jarome Iginla .40 1.00
51 Matt Duchene .30 .75
52 Alexander Wennberg .20 .50
53 Boone Jenner .30 .75
54 Brandon Dubinsky .20 .50
55 Cam Atkinson .30 .75
56 David Savard .20 .50
57 Nick Foligno .25 .60
58 Scott Hartnell .20 .50
59 Ales Hemsky .25 .60
60 Cody Eakin .20 .50
61 Jamie Benn .30 .75
62 Jason Spezza .30 .75
63 John Klingberg .30 .75
64 Johnny Oduya .25 .60
65 Kari Lehtonen .25 .60
66 Dylan Larkin .40 1.00
67 Henrik Zetterberg .40 1.00
68 Mike Green .25 .60
69 Jonathan Ericsson .20 .50
70 Justin Abdelkader .25 .60
71 Tomas Tatar .20 .50
72 Andrej Sekera .20 .50
73 Benoit Pouliot .25 .60
74 Cam Talbot .30 .75
75 Connor McDavid 1.50 4.00
76 Darnell Nurse .25 .60
77 Oscar Klefbom .50 1.25
78 Leon Draisaitl 1.00 2.50
79 Aaron Ekblad .40 1.00
80 Aleksander Barkov .50 1.25
81 Jaromir Jagr 1.00 2.50
82 Reilly Smith .30 .75
83 Roberto Luongo .50 1.25
84 Vincent Trocheck .30 .75
85 Alec Martinez .20 .50
86 Jeff Carter .25 .60
87 Dwight King .25 .60
88 Jake Muzzin .30 .75
89 Jonathan Quick .40 1.00
90 Kyle Clifford .20 .50
91 Tanner Pearson .25 .60
92 Tyler Toffoli .30 .75
93 Devan Dubnyk .25 .60
94 Erik Haula .20 .50
95 Jason Pominville .20 .50
96 Mikko Koivu .25 .60
97 Nino Niederreiter .20 .50
98 Ryan Suter .25 .60
99 Alex Galchenyuk .20 .50
100 Andrei Markov .20 .50
101 Brendan Gallagher .30 .75
102 Nathan Beaulieu .20 .50
103 Max Pacioretty .30 .75
104 Tomas Plekanec .20 .50
105 Craig Smith .20 .50
106 James Neal .20 .50
107 Mattias Ekholm .25 .60
108 Mike Fisher .20 .50
109 Pekka Rinne .30 .75
110 Ryan Johansen .25 .60
111 Filip Forsberg .50 1.25
112 Adam Henrique .25 .60
113 Kyle Palmieri .25 .60
114 Andy Greene .20 .50
115 Damon Severson .20 .50
116 Michael Cammalleri .25 .60
117 Anders Lee .30 .75
118 Brock Nelson .30 .75
119 Calvin de Haan .20 .50
120 Jaroslav Halak .30 .75
121 John Tavares .50 1.25
122 Nick Leddy .20 .50
123 Daniel Girardi .20 .50
124 Derek Stepan .20 .50
125 Chris Kreider .40 1.00
126 Marc Staal .20 .50
127 Mats Zuccarello .30 .75
128 Rick Nash .30 .75
129 Ryan McDonagh .20 .50
130 Andrew Hammond .25 .60
131 Bobby Ryan .25 .60
132 Curtis Lazar .20 .50
133 Erik Karlsson .40 1.00
134 Mark Stone .40 1.00
135 Kyle Turris .25 .60
136 Claude Giroux .30 .75
137 Mark Streit .25 .60
138 Michael Del Zotto .25 .60
139 Sean Couturier .25 .60
140 Shayne Gostisbehere .30 .75
141 Wayne Simmonds .40 1.00
142 Carl Hagelin .20 .50
143 Kris Letang .40 1.00
144 Matt Murray .50 1.25
145 Phil Kessel .30 .75
146 Sidney Crosby 1.25 3.00
147 Trevor Daley .25 .60
148 Brent Burns .30 .75
149 Chris Tierney .20 .50
150 Joe Pavelski .40 1.00
151 Joel Ward .25 .60
152 Logan Couture .40 1.00
153 Martin Jones .25 .60
154 Paul Martin .25 .60
155 Alex Pietrangelo .25 .60
156 Alexander Steen .20 .50
157 Jake Allen .30 .75
158 Jori Lehtera .20 .50
159 Patrik Berglund .20 .50
160 Paul Stastny .25 .60
161 Robby Fabbri .20 .50
162 Vladimir Tarasenko .40 1.00
163 Anton Stralman .25 .60
164 Ben Bishop .25 .60
165 Ondrej Palat .25 .60
166 Ryan Callahan .20 .50
167 Tyler Johnson .20 .50
168 Victor Hedman .40 1.00
169 Brooks Laich .20 .50
170 James van Riemsdyk .25 .60
171 Joffrey Lupul .20 .50
172 Jake Gardiner .20 .50
173 Leo Komarov .20 .50
174 Peter Holland .20 .50
175 Tyler Bozak .20 .50
176 Alexander Edler .20 .50
177 Bo Horvat .40 1.00
178 Brandon Sutter .20 .50
179 Daniel Sedin .40 1.00
180 Derek Dorsett .20 .50
181 Jake Virtanen .40 1.00
182 Jannik Hansen .20 .50
183 Ryan Miller .30 .75
184 Alexander Ovechkin 1.25 3.00
185 Andre Burakovsky .20 .50
186 Brooks Orpik .20 .50
187 Evgeny Kuznetsov .40 1.00
188 Justin Williams .25 .60
189 Karl Alzner .20 .50
190 Matt Niskanen .25 .60
191 Nicklas Backstrom .30 .75
192 Alexander Burmistrov .20 .50
193 Mark Scheifele .50 1.25
194 Drew Stafford .20 .50
195 Dustin Byfuglien .30 .75
196 Ondrej Pavelec .30 .75
197 Tobias Enstrom .20 .50
198 Tyler Myers .20 .50
199 S.Crosby/J.Pavelski CL 1.25 3.00
200 D.Krejci/A.Galchenyuk CL .30 .75
201 Auston Matthews YG RC 200.00 500.00
202 Lawson Crouse YG RC 2.00 5.00
203 Nick Sorensen YG RC 2.50 6.00
204 Connor Brown YG RC 4.00 10.00
205 Brayden Point YG RC 12.00 30.00
206 Jakob Chychrun YG RC 5.00 12.00
207 Steven Santini YG RC 2.00 5.00
208 Alan Quine YG RC 2.50 6.00
209 Danton Heinen YG RC 6.00 15.00
210 Sebastian Aho YG RC 12.00 30.00
211 Pontus Aberg YG RC 3.00 8.00
212 Kyle Connor YG RC 12.00 30.00
213 Anthony Mantha YG RC 6.00 15.00
214 Ivan Provorov YG RC 4.00 10.00
215 Zach Sanford YG RC 2.50 6.00
216 Tyler Motte YG RC 2.50 6.00
217 Travis Konecny YG RC 5.00 12.00
218 Jimmy Vesey YG RC 4.00 10.00
219 Nick Paul YG RC 3.00 8.00
220 Anthony Beauvillier YG RC 2.50 6.00
221 Nikita Tryamkin YG RC 2.00 5.00
222 Zach Hyman YG RC 10.00 25.00
223 Tom Kuhnhackl YG RC 2.00 5.00
224 Zach Werenski YG RC 8.00 20.00
225 Jesse Puljujarvi YG RC 15.00 40.00
226 Josh Morrissey YG RC 6.00 15.00
227 Pavel Buchnevich YG RC 4.00 10.00
228 Sonny Milano YG RC 3.00 8.00
229 Nick Schmaltz YG RC 3.00 8.00
230 Trevor Carrick YG RC 2.50 6.00
231 Matthew Tkachuk YG RC 20.00 50.00
232 Artturi Lehkonen YG RC 3.00 8.00
233 Denis Malgin YG RC 2.00 5.00
234 Nikita Zaitsev YG RC 2.50 6.00
235 Christian Dvorak YG RC 6.00 15.00
236 Mikhail Sergachev YG RC 4.00 10.00
237 Esa Lindell YG RC 2.50 6.00
238 Noel Acciari YG RC 3.00 8.00
239 Mike Reilly YG RC 2.00 5.00
240 Gustav Forsling YG RC 5.00 12.00
241 Michael Matheson YG RC 2.50 6.00
242 Hudson Fasching YG RC 2.50 6.00
243 Oliver Bjorkstrand YG RC 3.00 8.00
244 Austin Czarnik YG RC 4.00 10.00
245 Chris Bigras YG RC 2.00 5.00
246 Justin Bailey YG RC 2.50 6.00
247 Nic Dowd YG RC 2.00 5.00
248 Pavel Zacha YG RC 4.00 10.00
249 William Nylander YG RC 30.00 80.00
250 A.Matthews YG RC
W.Nylander YG RC CL 8.00 20.00
251 Hampus Lindholm .20 .50
252 Rickard Rakell .25 .60
253 Sami Vatanen .25 .60
254 Corey Perry .50 1.25
255 Antoine Vermette .30 .75
256 Jonathan Bernier .25 .60
257 Tobias Rieder .20 .50
258 Max Domi .30 .75
259 Alex Goligoski .20 .50
260 Radim Vrbata .20 .50
261 Brad Richardson .20 .50
262 Louis Domingue .25 .60
263 Luke Schenn .30 .75
264 Patrice Bergeron .40 1.00
265 Tuukka Rask .40 1.00
266 Torey Krug .25 .60
267 David Backes .20 .50
268 Dominic Moore .20 .50
269 Joe Morrow .25 .60
270 Rasmus Ristolainen .20 .50
271 Zemgus Girgensons .25 .60
272 Brian Gionta .20 .50
273 Evander Kane .30 .75
274 Jack Eichel .50 1.25
275 Tyler Ennis .20 .50
276 Dmitry Kulikov .25 .60
277 Kyle Okposo .20 .50
278 Johnny Gaudreau .50 1.25
279 Sean Monahan .20 .50
280 Dennis Wideman .20 .50
281 Troy Brouwer .20 .50
282 Brian Elliott .25 .60
283 Micheal Ferland .20 .50
284 Lee Stempniak .20 .50
285 Victor Rask .20 .50
286 Jordan Staal .25 .60
287 Ron Hainsey .25 .60
288 Teuvo Teravainen .30 .75
289 Joakim Nordstrom .20 .50
290 Corey Crawford .40 1.00
291 Duncan Keith .25 .60
292 Jonathan Toews .50 1.25
293 Richard Panik .20 .50
294 Trevor van Riemsdyk .25 .60
295 Ryan Hartman .20 .50
296 Joe Colborne .20 .50
297 Mikhail Grigorenko .20 .50
298 Nathan MacKinnon 1.25 3.00
299 Tyson Barrie .20 .50
300 Nikita Zadorov .20 .50
301 Semyon Varlamov .30 .75
302 Blake Comeau .20 .50
303 Seth Jones .30 .75
304 Brandon Saad .25 .60
305 Jack Johnson .20 .50
306 Ryan Murray .20 .50
307 Sergei Bobrovsky .50 1.25
308 Matt Calvert .20 .50
309 Antti Niemi .25 .60
310 Patrick Sharp .25 .60
311 Tyler Seguin .40 1.00
312 Jiri Hudler .25 .60
313 Dan Hamhuis .25 .60
314 Antoine Roussel .20 .50
315 Petr Mrazek .30 .75
316 Riley Sheahan .20 .50
317 Darren Helm .20 .50
318 Gustav Nyquist .20 .50
319 Niklas Kronwall .25 .60
320 Thomas Vanek .25 .60
321 Frans Nielsen .20 .50
322 Andreas Athanasiou .30 .75
323 Kris Russell .20 .50
324 Jordan Eberle .30 .75
325 Patrick Maroon .20 .50
326 Ryan Nugent-Hopkins .40 1.00
327 Milan Lucic .25 .60
328 Adam Larsson .30 .75
329 Zack Kassian .20 .50
330 Jason Demers .20 .50
331 Jonathan Marchessault .40 1.00
332 Jussi Jokinen .30 .75
333 Nick Bjugstad .20 .50
334 James Reimer .30 .75
335 Keith Yandle .20 .50
336 Jared McCann .25 .60
337 Drew Doughty .40 1.00
338 Anze Kopitar .50 1.25
339 Devin Setoguchi .20 .50
340 Dustin Brown .30 .75
341 Nick Shore .20 .50
342 Matt Dumba .20 .50
343 Charlie Coyle .30 .75
344 Mikael Granlund .25 .60
345 Zach Parise .30 .75
346 Eric Staal .40 1.00
347 Jared Spurgeon .30 .75
348 Andrew Shaw .20 .50
349 Carey Price .60 1.50
350 David Desharnais .20 .50
351 Shea Weber .25 .60
352 Alexei Emelin .20 .50
353 Alexander Radulov .30 .75
354 Kevin Fiala .25 .60
355 P.K. Subban .40 1.00
356 Mike Ribeiro .20 .50
357 Roman Josi .30 .75
358 Colin Wilson .30 .75
359 Ryan Ellis .25 .60
360 Taylor Hall .30 .75
361 Cory Schneider .30 .75
362 Travis Zajac .20 .50
363 Devante Smith-Pelly .25 .60
364 John Moore .20 .50
365 P.A. Parenteau .20 .50
366 Andrew Ladd .20 .50
367 Ryan Strome .30 .75
368 Travis Hamonic .20 .50
369 Johnny Boychuk .25 .60
370 Thomas Greiss .25 .60
371 Jason Chimera .20 .50
372 Josh Bailey .25 .60
373 Cal Clutterbuck .20 .50
374 J.T. Miller .40 1.00
375 Henrik Lundqvist .75 2.00
376 Oscar Lindberg .20 .50
377 Kevin Hayes .25 .60
378 Mika Zibanejad .40 1.00
379 Michael Grabner .25 .60
380 Jean-Gabriel Pageau .20 .50
381 Derick Brassard .20 .50
382 Cody Ceci .20 .50
383 Mike Hoffman .20 .50
384 Dion Phaneuf .25 .60
385 Craig Anderson .30 .75
386 Zack Smith .20 .50
387 Brayden Schenn .30 .75
388 Jakub Voracek .25 .60
389 Steve Mason .25 .60
390 Michael Raffl .20 .50
391 Scott Laughton .20 .50
392 Matt Read .25 .60
393 Chris Kunitz .30 .75
394 Marc-Andre Fleury .60 1.50
395 Evgeni Malkin .60 1.50
396 Patric Hornqvist .20 .50
397 Olli Maatta .20 .50
398 Nick Bonino .20 .50
399 Bryan Rust .30 .75
400 Mikkel Boedker .20 .50
401 David Schlemko .20 .50
402 Tomas Hertl .30 .75
403 Joe Thornton .50 1.25
404 Joonas Donskoi .20 .50
405 Marc-Edouard Vlasic .20 .50
406 Patrick Marleau .30 .75
407 Matt Nieto .20 .50
408 David Perron .25 .60
409 Jaden Schwartz .40 1.00
410 Colton Parayko .25 .60
411 Jay Bouwmeester .20 .50
412 Kevin Shattenkirk .20 .50
413 Nail Yakupov .20 .50
414 Nikita Kucherov .60 1.50
415 Vladislav Namestnikov .20 .50
416 Steven Stamkos .60 1.50
417 Andrei Vasilevskiy .50 1.25
418 Valtteri Filppula .20 .50
419 Alex Killorn .20 .50
420 Jonathan Drouin .25 .60
421 Frederik Andersen .40 1.00
422 Morgan Rielly .30 .75
423 Nazem Kadri .40 1.00
424 Jhonas Enroth .30 .75
425 Matt Hunwick .25 .60
426 Matt Martin .20 .50
427 Erik Gudbranson .20 .50
428 Loui Eriksson .20 .50
429 Sven Baertschi .20 .50
430 Alexandre Burrows .20 .50
431 Christopher Tanev .20 .50
432 Henrik Sedin .40 1.00
433 Jacob Markstrom .30 .75
434 Lars Eller .20 .50
435 Dmitry Orlov .30 .75
436 Marcus Johansson .30 .75
437 Braden Holtby .40 1.00
438 John Carlson .30 .75
439 T.J. Oshie .30 .75
440 Tom Wilson .30 .75
441 Brett Connolly .20 .50
442 Shawn Matthias .20 .50
443 Jacob Trouba .25 .60
444 Blake Wheeler .30 .75
445 Bryan Little .25 .60
446 Mathieu Perreault .20 .50
447 Nikolaj Ehlers .30 .75
448 Connor Hellebuyck .60 1.50
449 C.Schneider/B.Holtby CL .40 1.00
450 P.Subban/S.Weber CL .40 1.00
451 Patrik Laine YG RC 20.00 50.00
452 Kasperi Kapanen YG RC 8.00 20.00
453 Miles Wood YG RC 2.00 5.00
454 William Carrier YG RC 2.50 6.00
455 Drake Caggiula YG RC 2.50 6.00
456 Yohann Auvitu YG RC 2.50 6.00
457 Markus Nutivaara YG RC 2.50 6.00
458 Mathew Barzal YG RC 20.00 50.00
459 Joel Eriksson Ek YG RC 10.00 25.00
460 Frederik Gauthier YG RC 2.00 5.00
461 Blake Speers YG RC 2.50 6.00
462 Casey Nelson YG RC 2.50 6.00
463 Anthony DeAngelo YG RC 2.00 5.00
464 Mark McNeill YG RC 2.50 6.00
465 Gemel Smith YG RC 2.50 6.00
466 Tristan Jarry YG RC 10.00 25.00
467 Brandon Tanev YG RC 3.00 8.00
468 Mitch Marner YG RC 60.00 150.00
469 Dominik Simon YG RC 2.00 5.00
470 Rob O'Gara YG RC 2.50 6.00
471 Tyler Bertuzzi YG RC 5.00 12.00
472 Thatcher Demko YG RC 15.00 40.00
473 Charlie Lindgren YG RC 4.00 10.00
474 Kevin Gravel YG RC 3.00 8.00
475 Troy Stecher YG RC 2.50 6.00
476 Brandon Montour YG RC 6.00 15.00
477 Nick Baptiste YG RC 2.50 6.00
478 Aaron Dell YG RC 2.50 6.00
479 Timo Meier YG RC 5.00 12.00
480 Michal Kempny YG RC 2.50 6.00
481 Stephen Johns YG RC 2.00 5.00
482 Brandon Carlo YG RC 4.00 10.00
483 Kyle Rau YG RC 3.00 8.00
484 Nikita Soshnikov YG RC 1.50 4.00
485 Chase De Leo YG RC 2.50 6.00
486 Kevin Labanc YG RC 2.50 6.00
487 Oskar Sundqvist YG RC 2.50 6.00
488 Thomas Chabot YG RC 10.00 25.00
489 Ondrej Kase YG RC 2.50 6.00
490 Ryan Pulock YG RC 2.50 6.00
491 Tobias Lindberg YG RC 4.00 10.00
492 Scott Wedgewood YG RC 4.00 10.00
493 Oliver Kylington YG RC 2.00 5.00
494 Shane Harper YG RC 4.00 10.00
495 Jacob Larsson YG RC 4.00 10.00
496 Zane Mcintyre YG RC 3.00 8.00
497 Jason Dickinson YG RC 2.00 5.00
498 Dylan Strome YG RC 6.00 15.00
499 Brendan Leipsic YG RC 2.00 5.00
500 M.Marner
P.Laine YG CL 4.00 10.00
501 Sam Gagner .20 .50
502 Brandon Pirri .20 .50
503 Markus Granlund .25 .60
504 Carter Hutton .25 .60
505 Jamie McGinn .25 .60
506 Lauri Korpikoski .20 .50
507 Tim Schaller .25 .60
508 Patrick Wiercioch .25 .60
509 Brian Campbell .25 .60
510 Viktor Stalberg .25 .60
511 Alex Chiasson .25 .60
512 Mike Condon .30 .75
513 Rene Bourque .20 .50
514 Dennis Seidenberg .20 .50
515 Colton Sceviour .25 .60
516 A.J. Greer YG RC 3.00 8.00
517 Cole Schneider YG RC 3.00 8.00
518 Joel Hanley YG RC 3.00 8.00
519 Joseph Cramarossa YG RC 3.00 8.00
520 Jakub Vrana YG RC 15.00 40.00
521 Lukas Sedlak YG RC 3.00 8.00
522 Matthew Benning YG RC 4.00 10.00
523 Nick Lappin YG RC 3.00 8.00
524 Roman Lyubimov YG RC 3.00 8.00
525 Jake Guentzel YG RC 20.00 50.00
526 Ryan Getzlaf SH 2.00 5.00
527 Mark Scheifele SH 3.00 8.00
528 Vladimir Tarasenko SH 2.50 6.00
529 Tuukka Rask SH 2.50 6.00
530 Patrik Laine SH 5.00 12.00

2016-17 Upper Deck Exclusives

*VETS: 6X TO 15X BASIC CARDS
*ROOKIES: 2.5X TO 6X BASIC CARDS
201 Auston Matthews YG 1500.00 4000.00
204 Connor Brown YG 40.00 100.00
206 Jakob Chychrun YG 30.00 80.00
210 Sebastian Aho YG 150.00 400.00
212 Kyle Connor YG 100.00 250.00
214 Ivan Provorov YG 40.00 100.00
224 Zach Werenski YG 80.00 200.00
225 Jesse Puljujarvi YG 125.00 300.00
226 Josh Morrissey YG 25.00 60.00
231 Matthew Tkachuk YG 200.00 500.00
249 William Nylander YG 200.00 500.00
250 Auston Matthews YG
William Nylander YG CL 60.00 150.00
451 Patrik Laine YG 80.00 200.00
468 Mitch Marner YG 250.00 600.00
471 Tyler Bertuzzi YG 40.00 100.00
472 Thatcher Demko YG 125.00 300.00
479 Timo Meier YG 300.00 800.00
500 Mitch Marner
Patrik Laine YG CL 40.00 100.00
525 Jake Guentzel YG 150.00 300.00

2016-17 Upper Deck A Piece of History 1000 Point Club

PCJS Joe Sakic B 30.00 80.00
PCLM Larry Murphy B 30.00 80.00
PCMC Lanny McDonald B 10.00 25.00
PCPC Paul Coffey B 15.00 40.00
PCPM Patrick Marleau B 25.00 60.00

2016-17 Upper Deck A Piece of History 500 Goal Club

GCAO Alexander Ovechkin 30.00 80.00
GCMH Marian Hossa 30.00 80.00

2016-17 Upper Deck A Piece of History 300 Win Club

300BS Billy Smith A 30.00 80.00
300GH Glenn Hall A 30.00 80.00

2016-17 Upper Deck Canvas

C1 Ryan Getzlaf 1.00 2.50
C2 John Gibson 1.00 2.50
C3 Jakob Silfverberg .60 1.50
C4 Max Domi 1.00 2.50
C5 Anthony Duclair .75 2.00
C6 Shane Doan .75 2.00
C7 Patrice Bergeron 1.25 3.00
C8 Matt Beleskey .75 2.00
C9 Brad Marchand 2.00 5.00
C10 Jack Eichel 1.50 4.00
C11 Rasmus Ristolainen .60 1.50
C12 Ryan O'Reilly 1.00 2.50
C13 Johnny Gaudreau 1.50 4.00
C14 Dougie Hamilton .75 2.00
C15 Sam Bennett 1.50 4.00
C16 Noah Hanifin 1.00 2.50
C17 Jeff Skinner 1.25 3.00
C18 Jordan Staal .75 2.00
C19 Patrick Kane 2.00 5.00
C20 Brent Seabrook .60 1.50
C21 Artemi Panarin 2.00 5.00
C22 Corey Crawford 1.25 3.00
C23 Nathan MacKinnon 4.00 10.00
C24 Gabriel Landeskog 1.25 3.00
C25 Jarome Iginla 1.25 3.00
C26 Brandon Saad .75 2.00
C27 Seth Jones 1.00 2.50
C28 Boone Jenner 1.00 2.50
C29 Tyler Seguin 1.25 3.00
C30 John Klingberg 1.00 2.50
C31 Jason Spezza 1.00 2.50
C32 Dylan Larkin 1.25 3.00
C33 Tomas Tatar .60 1.50
C34 Mike Green .75 2.00
C35 Connor McDavid 5.00 12.00
C36 Leon Draisaitl 3.00 8.00
C37 Darnell Nurse .75 2.00
C38 Nick Bjugstad .60 1.50
C39 Aleksander Barkov 1.50 4.00
C40 Roberto Luongo 1.50 4.00
C41 Anze Kopitar 1.50 4.00
C42 Tyler Toffoli 1.00 2.50
C43 Drew Doughty 1.25 3.00
C44 Jonathan Quick 1.25 3.00
C45 Devan Dubnyk .75 2.00
C46 Charlie Coyle 1.00 2.50
C47 Nino Niederreiter .60 1.50
C48 Brendan Gallagher 1.00 2.50
C49 Carey Price 2.00 5.00
C50 Ryan Johansen .75 2.00
C51 James Neal .60 1.50
C52 Travis Zajac .60 1.50
C53 Kyle Palmieri .75 2.00
C54 Brock Nelson 1.00 2.50
C55 Anders Lee 1.00 2.50
C56 Henrik Lundqvist 2.50 6.00
C57 Derek Stepan .60 1.50
C58 Erik Karlsson 1.25 3.00
C59 Bobby Ryan .75 2.00
C60 Mark Stone 1.25 3.00
C61 Dion Phaneuf .75 2.00
C62 Jakub Voracek .75 2.00
C63 Shayne Gostisbehere 1.00 2.50
C64 Evgeni Malkin 2.00 5.00
C65 Matt Murray 1.50 4.00
C66 Phil Kessel 1.00 2.50
C67 Carl Hagelin .60 1.50
C68 Joe Pavelski 1.25 3.00
C69 Martin Jones .75 2.00
C70 Joe Thornton 1.50 4.00
C71 Vladimir Tarasenko 1.25 3.00
C72 Alex Pietrangelo .75 2.00
C73 Jake Allen 1.00 2.50
C74 Ben Bishop .75 2.00
C75 Nikita Kucherov 2.00 5.00
C76 Victor Hedman 1.25 3.00
C77 Leo Komarov .60 1.50
C78 Jake Gardiner .60 1.50
C79 Morgan Rielly 1.00 2.50
C80 Daniel Sedin 1.25 3.00
C81 Ryan Miller 1.00 2.50
C82 Jannik Hansen .60 1.50
C83 Braden Holtby 1.25 3.00
C84 John Carlson 1.00 2.50
C85 Alexander Ovechkin 4.00 10.00
C86 Evgeny Kuznetsov 1.25 3.00
C87 Dustin Byfuglien 1.00 2.50
C88 Bryan Little .75 2.00
C89 Mark Scheifele 1.50 4.00
C90 P.Kane/E.Karlsson CL 2.00 5.00
C91 Mitch Marner YG 60.00 150.00
C92 Anthony Mantha YG 8.00 20.00
C93 Esa Lindell YG 4.00 10.00
C94 Sonny Milano YG 5.00 12.00
C95 Connor Brown YG 6.00 15.00
C96 Sebastian Aho YG 15.00 40.00
C97 Brandon Carlo YG 6.00 15.00
C98 Jakob Chychrun YG 8.00 20.00
C99 Brendan Leipsic YG 3.00 8.00
C100 Mikhail Sergachev YG 6.00 15.00
C101 Danton Heinen YG 3.00 8.00
C102 Michael Matheson YG 4.00 10.00
C103 Chris Bigras YG 3.00 8.00
C104 Charlie Lindgren YG 12.00 30.00
C105 Jimmy Vesey YG 6.00 15.00
C106 Patrik Laine YG 20.00 50.00
C107 Mathew Barzal YG 20.00 50.00
C108 Hudson Fasching YG 4.00 10.00
C109 Justin Bailey YG 4.00 10.00
C110 Pavel Zacha YG 6.00 15.00
C111 Oliver Kylington YG 3.00 8.00
C112 Pavel Buchnevich YG 6.00 15.00
C113 Lawson Crouse YG 3.00 8.00
C114 Miles Wood YG 3.00 8.00
C115 Tyler Motte YG 4.00 10.00
C116 Oliver Bjorkstrand YG 5.00 12.00
C117 Anthony Beauvillier YG 4.00 10.00
C118 Gustav Forsling YG 8.00 20.00
C119 Nick Sorensen YG 4.00 10.00
C120 M.Marner YG/P.Laine YG CL 10.00 25.00
C121 Corey Perry 1.50 4.00
C122 Rickard Rakell .75 2.00
C123 Hampus Lindholm .60 1.50
C124 Oliver Ekman-Larsson 1.00 2.50
C125 Martin Hanzal .75 2.00
C126 Tuukka Rask 1.25 3.00
C127 David Krejci 1.00 2.50
C128 David Backes .60 1.50
C129 Sam Reinhart 2.00 5.00
C130 Kyle Okposo .60 1.50
C131 Sean Monahan .60 1.50
C132 Mark Giordano 1.00 2.50
C133 Brian Elliott .75 2.00
C134 Justin Faulk .75 2.00
C135 Victor Rask .60 1.50
C136 Teuvo Teravainen 1.00 2.50
C137 Duncan Keith .75 2.00
C138 Jonathan Toews 1.50 4.00
C139 Artem Anisimov .60 1.50
C140 Matt Duchene 1.00 2.50
C141 Carl Soderberg .60 1.50
C142 Cam Atkinson 1.00 2.50
C143 Alexander Wennberg .60 1.50
C144 Jamie Benn 1.00 2.50
C145 Patrick Sharp .75 2.00
C146 Andreas Athanasiou 1.00 2.50
C147 Henrik Zetterberg 1.25 3.00
C148 Jordan Eberle 1.00 2.50
C149 Milan Lucic .75 2.00
C150 Adam Larsson 1.00 2.50
C151 Jaromir Jagr 3.00 8.00
C152 Aaron Ekblad 1.25 3.00
C153 Vincent Trocheck 1.00 2.50
C154 Jake Muzzin 1.00 2.50
C155 Jeff Carter .75 2.00
C156 Tanner Pearson .75 2.00
C157 Ryan Suter .75 2.00
C158 Zach Parise 1.00 2.50
C159 Mikko Koivu .75 2.00
C160 Eric Staal 1.25 3.00
C161 Shea Weber .75 2.00
C162 Max Pacioretty 1.00 2.50
C163 Alex Galchenyuk .60 1.50
C164 Pekka Rinne 1.00 2.50
C165 Roman Josi 1.00 2.50
C166 Filip Forsberg 1.50 4.00
C167 P.K. Subban 1.25 3.00
C168 Adam Henrique .75 2.00
C169 Cory Schneider 1.00 2.50
C170 Taylor Hall 1.00 2.50
C171 John Tavares 1.50 4.00
C172 Andrew Ladd .60 1.50
C173 Jaroslav Halak 1.00 2.50
C174 Travis Hamonic .60 1.50
C175 Mats Zuccarello 1.00 2.50
C176 J.T. Miller 1.25 3.00
C177 Mika Zibanejad 1.25 3.00
C178 Derick Brassard .60 1.50
C179 Jean-Gabriel Pageau .60 1.50
C180 Mike Hoffman .60 1.50
C181 Claude Giroux 1.00 2.50
C182 Wayne Simmonds 1.25 3.00
C183 Brayden Schenn 1.00 2.50
C184 Kris Letang 1.25 3.00
C185 Patric Hornqvist .60 1.50
C186 Logan Couture 1.25 3.00
C187 Patrick Marleau 1.00 2.50
C188 Mikkel Boedker .60 1.50
C189 Robby Fabbri .60 1.50
C190 Jaden Schwartz 1.25 3.00
C191 David Perron .75 2.00
C192 Ondrej Palat .75 2.00
C193 Alex Killorn .60 1.50
C194 Vladislav Namestnikov .60 1.50
C195 Steven Stamkos 2.00 5.00
C196 Frederik Andersen 1.25 3.00
C197 James van Riemsdyk .75 2.00

C198 Nazem Kadri 1.25 3.00
C199 Loui Eriksson .60 1.50
C200 Henrik Sedin 1.25 3.00
C201 Bo Horvat 1.25 3.00
C202 Sven Baertschi .60 1.50
C203 Nicklas Backstrom 1.00 2.50
C204 Justin Williams .75 2.00
C205 Andre Burakovsky .60 1.50
C206 T.J. Oshie 1.00 2.50
C207 Blake Wheeler 1.00 2.50
C208 Mathieu Perreault .60 1.50
C209 Connor Hellebuyck 2.00 5.00
C210 S.Stamkos/J.Tavares CL 2.00 5.00
C211 Auston Matthews YG 200.00 500.00
C212 Jesse Puljujarvi YG 25.00 60.00
C213 Dylan Strome YG 10.00 25.00
C214 William Nylander YG 30.00 80.00
C215 Brandon Montour YG 8.00 20.00
C216 Kyle Connor YG 15.00 40.00
C217 Joel Eriksson Ek YG 10.00 25.00
C218 Matthew Tkachuk YG 25.00 60.00
C219 Drake Caggiula YG 4.00 10.00
C220 Jacob Larsson YG 6.00 15.00
C221 Nick Baptiste YG 4.00 10.00
C222 Thomas Chabot YG 8.00 20.00
C223 Nikita Zaitsev YG 4.00 10.00
C224 Mike Reilly YG 3.00 8.00
C225 Timo Meier YG 8.00 20.00
C226 Zach Werenski YG 10.00 25.00
C227 Adam Erne YG 5.00 12.00
C228 Kasperi Kapanen YG 12.00 30.00
C229 Nick Schmaltz YG 5.00 12.00
C230 Christian Dvorak YG 10.00 25.00
C231 Josh Morrissey YG 10.00 25.00
C232 Artturi Lehkonen YG 5.00 12.00
C233 Brayden Point YG 15.00 40.00
C234 Travis Konecny YG 8.00 20.00
C235 Jake Guentzel YG 25.00 60.00
C236 Thatcher Demko YG 20.00 50.00
C237 Zach Sanford YG 4.00 10.00
C238 Julius Honka YG 4.00 10.00
C239 Ivan Provorov YG 6.00 15.00
C240 A.Matthews/W.Nylander YG CL 15.00 40.00
C241 Bobby Orr RS 40.00 100.00
C242 Wayne Gretzky RS 60.00 150.00
C243 Mario Lemieux RS 40.00 100.00
C244 Dale Hawerchuk RS 12.00 30.00
C245 Brett Hull RS 20.00 50.00
C246 Norm Ullman RS 10.00 25.00
C247 Trevor Linden RS 10.00 25.00
C248 Mike Richter RS 10.00 25.00
C249 Dominik Hasek RS 15.00 40.00
C250 Mike Modano RS 15.00 40.00
C251 Pat LaFontaine RS 10.00 25.00
C252 Darryl Sittler RS 12.00 30.00
C253 Luc Robitaille RS 10.00 25.00
C254 Steve Yzerman RS 25.00 60.00
C255 Stan Mikita RS 12.00 30.00
C256 Jason Dickinson POE 5.00 12.00
C257 Josh Morrissey POE 15.00 40.00
C258 Ryan Pulock POE 6.00 15.00
C259 Alan Quine POE 6.00 15.00
C260 Anthony Mantha POE 12.00 30.00
C261 Thomas Chabot POE 12.00 30.00
C262 Michael Matheson POE 6.00 15.00
C263 Chris Bigras POE 5.00 12.00
C264 Travis Konecny POE 12.00 30.00
C265 Mitch Marner POE 25.00 60.00
C266 Lawson Crouse POE 5.00 12.00
C267 Brayden Point POE 15.00 40.00
C268 Dylan Strome POE 15.00 40.00
C269 Anthony Beauvillier POE 6.00 15.00
C270 Mathew Barzal POE 20.00 50.00

2016-17 Upper Deck Clear Cut

*VETS: 8X TO 20X BASIC CARDS
*ROOKIES: 2.5X TO 6X BASIC CARDS
201 Auston Matthews YG 1000.00 2500.00
218 Jimmy Vesey YG 8.00 20.00
225 Jesse Puljujarvi YG 60.00 150.00
226 Josh Morrissey YG 20.00 50.00
227 Pavel Buchnevich YG 20.00 50.00
231 Matthew Tkachuk YG 60.00 150.00
244 Austin Czarnik YG 40.00 100.00
249 William Nylander YG 150.00 400.00
458 Mathew Barzal YG 125.00 300.00
468 Mitch Marner YG 200.00 500.00
479 Timo Meier YG 40.00 100.00

2016-17 Upper Deck Clear Cut Foundations

CCF1 R.Getzlaf/J.Gibson 12.00 30.00
CCF2 M.Domi/M.Hanzal 12.00 30.00
CCF3 D.Krejci/B.Marchand 25.00 60.00
CCF4 J.Eichel/R.O'Reilly 20.00 50.00
CCF5 S.Bennett/S.Monahan 20.00 50.00
CCF6 J.Skinner/N.Hanifin 15.00 40.00
CCF7 P.Kane/A.Panarin 25.00 60.00
CCF8 G.Landeskog/J.Iginla 15.00 40.00
CCF9 B.Saad/S.Jones 12.00 30.00
CCF10 J.Benn/J.Klingberg 12.00 30.00
CCF11 N.Kronwall/D.Larkin 15.00 40.00
CCF12 C.McDavid/O.Klefbom 60.00 150.00
CCF13 A.Ekblad/A.Barkov 20.00 50.00
CCF14 J.Carter/D.Doughty 15.00 40.00
CCF15 Z.Parise/N.Niederreiter 12.00 30.00
CCF16 C.Price/B.Gallagher 25.00 60.00
CCF17 R.Johansen/J.Neal 10.00 25.00
CCF18 K.Palmieri/T.Zajac 10.00 25.00
CCF19 J.Halak/C.de Haan 12.00 30.00
CCF20 R.Nash/R.McDonagh 12.00 30.00
CCF21 K.Turris/B.Ryan 10.00 25.00
CCF22 J.Voracek/S.Gostisbehere 12.00 30.00
CCF23 P.Kessel/M.Murray 20.00 50.00
CCF24 J.Pavelski/M.Jones 15.00 40.00
CCF25 R.Fabbri/A.Pietrangelo 10.00 25.00
CCF26 B.Bishop/N.Kucherov 25.00 60.00
CCF27 N.Kadri/L.Komarov 15.00 40.00
CCF28 H.Sedin/J.Virtanen 15.00 40.00
CCF29 E.Kuznetsov/N.Backstrom 15.00 40.00
CCF30 B.Wheeler/D.Byfuglien 12.00 30.00

2016-17 Upper Deck Clear Cut Honoured Members

HOF61 Nicklas Lidstrom 15.00 40.00
HOF62 Dominik Hasek 25.00 60.00
HOF63 Glenn Hall 15.00 40.00
HOF64 Billy Smith 15.00 40.00
HOF65 Gerry Cheevers 15.00 40.00
HOF66 Larry Murphy 12.00 30.00
HOF67 Norm Ullman 15.00 40.00

2016-17 Upper Deck Clear Cut Superstars

CCSAB Aleksander Barkov 15.00 40.00
CCSAK Anze Kopitar 15.00 40.00
CCSAO Alexander Ovechkin 40.00 100.00
CCSBB Brent Burns 10.00 25.00
CCSBH Braden Holtby 12.00 30.00
CCSBW Blake Wheeler 10.00 25.00
CCSCG Claude Giroux 10.00 25.00
CCSCM Connor McDavid 50.00 125.00
CCSCP Carey Price 20.00 50.00
CCSDD Drew Doughty 12.00 30.00
CCSDL Dylan Larkin 12.00 30.00
CCSEK Erik Karlsson 12.00 30.00
CCSEM Evgeni Malkin 20.00 50.00
CCSHL Henrik Lundqvist 25.00 60.00
CCSJB Jamie Benn 10.00 25.00
CCSJE Jack Eichel 15.00 40.00
CCSJG Johnny Gaudreau 15.00 40.00
CCSJI Jarome Iginla 12.00 30.00
CCSJJ Jaromir Jagr 30.00 80.00
CCSJT Jonathan Toews 15.00 40.00
CCSNM Nathan MacKinnon 40.00 100.00
CCSPB Patrice Bergeron 12.00 30.00
CCSPE Corey Perry 15.00 40.00
CCSPK Patrick Kane 20.00 50.00
CCSRG Ryan Getzlaf 10.00 25.00
CCSRS Ryan Suter 8.00 20.00
CCSSC Sidney Crosby 40.00 100.00
CCSSS Steven Stamkos 20.00 50.00
CCSTA John Tavares 15.00 40.00
CCSTH Joe Thornton 15.00 40.00
CCSTS Tyler Seguin 12.00 30.00
CCSVT Vladimir Tarasenko 12.00 30.00

2016-17 Upper Deck Day With The Cup

DC1 Sidney Crosby 100.00 200.00
DC2 Kris Letang 25.00 60.00
DC3 Justin Schultz 15.00 40.00
DC4 Matt Murray 30.00 80.00
DC5 Phil Kessel 30.00 80.00
DC6 Conor Sheary 20.00 50.00
DC7 Matt Cullen 20.00 50.00
DC8 Ian Cole 12.00 30.00
DC9 Eric Fehr 20.00 50.00
DC10 Beau Bennett 15.00 40.00
DC11 Derrick Pouliot 12.00 30.00
DC12 Jeff Zatkoff 20.00 50.00
DC13 Marc-Andre Fleury 40.00 100.00
DC14 Brian Dumoulin 15.00 40.00
DC15 Bryan Rust 20.00 50.00
DC16 Carl Hagelin 12.00 30.00
DC17 Olli Maatta 12.00 30.00
DC18 Trevor Daley 15.00 40.00
DC19 Chris Kunitz 20.00 50.00
DC20 Nick Bonino 12.00 30.00
DC21 Patric Hornqvist 12.00 30.00
DC22 Evgeni Malkin 40.00 100.00
DC23 Ben Lovejoy 12.00 30.00

2016-17 Upper Deck Game Jerseys

GJAD Anthony Duclair F 2.50 6.00
GJAH Andrew Hammond F 2.50 6.00
GJAH Adam Henrique F 2.50 6.00
GJAO Alexander Ovechkin C 12.00 30.00
GJAS Alexander Steen E 2.00 5.00
GJBB Brent Burns C 3.00 8.00
GJBE Matt Beleskey F 2.50 6.00
GJBG Brendan Gallagher G 3.00 8.00
GJBH Braden Holtby G 4.00 10.00
GJBR Brayden Schenn E 3.00 8.00
GJBS Brandon Saad E 2.50 6.00
GJCA Craig Anderson F 3.00 8.00
GJCA John Carlson D 3.00 8.00
GJCC Corey Crawford E 4.00 10.00
GJCG Claude Giroux D 3.00 8.00
GJCM Connor McDavid D 15.00 40.00
GJCP Carey Price C 6.00 15.00
GJCS Cory Schneider G 3.00 8.00
GJDB Dustin Byfuglien D 3.00 8.00
GJDD Drew Doughty E 4.00 10.00
GJDH Dougie Hamilton F 2.50 6.00
GJDH Dale Hawerchuk B 20.00 50.00
GJDK Duncan Keith C 2.50 6.00
GJDO Max Domi F 2.50 6.00
GJDS Daniel Sedin E 4.00 10.00
GJDU Devan Dubnyk F 2.50 6.00
GJEM Evgeni Malkin C 6.00 15.00
GJFF Filip Forsberg G 4.00 10.00
GJGL Gabriel Landeskog D 3.00 8.00
GJHL Henrik Lundqvist C 8.00 20.00
GJHS Henrik Sedin C 4.00 10.00
GJHU Jonathan Huberdeau E 4.00 10.00
GJHZ Henrik Zetterberg C 4.00 10.00
GJJA Jake Allen F 3.00 8.00
GJJB Jamie Benn C 3.00 8.00
GJJC Jeff Carter G 2.50 6.00
GJJE Jack Eichel E 5.00 12.00
GJJF Justin Faulk E 2.50 6.00
GJJG Johnny Gaudreau D 5.00 12.00
GJJH Jaroslav Halak F 3.00 8.00
GJJL John LeClair A 30.00 80.00
GJJP Joe Pavelski D 4.00 10.00
GJJQ Jonathan Quick D 4.00 10.00
GJJS Jordan Staal F 2.50 6.00
GJJS Jeff Skinner F 4.00 10.00
GJKA Nazem Kadri E 4.00 10.00
GJKL John Klingberg G 3.00 8.00
GJKT Kyle Turris F 2.50 6.00
GJKU Evgeny Kuznetsov D 4.00 10.00
GJLE Kris Letang D 4.00 10.00
GJMA Mark Stone E 4.00 10.00
GJMB Martin Brodeur A 50.00 120.00
GJMC Michael Cammalleri F 2.50 6.00
GJMD Matt Duchene G 3.00 8.00
GJMJ Martin Jones E 2.50 6.00
GJMR Morgan Rielly F 3.00 8.00
GJMS Mark Scheifele D 5.00 12.00
GJNA Nathan MacKinnon D 12.00 30.00
GJNB Nick Bjugstad E 2.00 5.00
GJNF Nick Foligno E 2.50 6.00
GJNK Niklas Kronwall F 2.50 6.00
GJNK Nikita Kucherov C 6.00 15.00
GJNL Nick Leddy F 2.00 5.00
GJNN Nino Niederreiter F 2.00 5.00
GJOM Olli Maatta D 2.00 5.00
GJON Owen Nolan B 25.00 60.00
GJOP Ondrej Palat E 2.50 6.00
GJPB Patrice Bergeron E 4.00 10.00
GJPE Corey Perry B 10.00 25.00
GJPK Patrick Kane E 6.00 15.00
GJPM Petr Mrazek F 3.00 8.00
GJRG Ryan Getzlaf C 3.00 8.00
GJRJ Roman Josi C 3.00 8.00
GJRK Ryan Kesler E 3.00 8.00
GJRL Roberto Luongo G 5.00 12.00
GJRN Rick Nash G 3.00 8.00
GJRO Ryan O'Reilly E 3.00 8.00
GJSB Sam Bennett D 5.00 12.00
GJSC Sidney Crosby D 12.00 30.00
GJSI Jakob Silfverberg E 2.00 5.00
GJSM Sean Monahan D 2.00 5.00
GJSP Jason Spezza D 3.00 8.00
GJSR Sam Reinhart E 6.00 15.00
GJST Derek Stepan D 2.00 5.00
GJTA John Tavares C 5.00 12.00
GJTO Tomas Tatar F 2.00 5.00
GJTR Tuukka Rask G 4.00 10.00
GJTT Tyler Toffoli D 3.00 8.00
GJVH Victor Hedman D 4.00 10.00
GJZP Zach Parise E 3.00 8.00

2016-17 Upper Deck Goalie Nightmares

GN1 Corey Perry 1.50 4.00
GN2 Max Domi 1.00 2.50
GN3 Brad Marchand 2.00 5.00
GN4 Jack Eichel 1.50 4.00
GN5 Johnny Gaudreau 1.50 4.00
GN6 Jeff Skinner 1.25 3.00
GN7 Patrick Kane 2.00 5.00
GN8 Matt Duchene 1.00 2.50
GN9 Brandon Saad .75 2.00
GN10 Jamie Benn 1.00 2.50
GN11 Dylan Larkin 1.25 3.00
GN12 Connor McDavid 5.00 12.00
GN13 Aleksander Barkov 1.50 4.00
GN14 Tyler Toffoli 1.00 2.50
GN15 Zach Parise 1.00 2.50
GN16 Alex Galchenyuk .60 1.50
GN17 Filip Forsberg 1.50 4.00
GN18 Kyle Palmieri .75 2.00
GN19 John Tavares 1.50 4.00
GN20 Mats Zuccarello 1.00 2.50
GN21 Mark Stone 1.25 3.00
GN22 Claude Giroux 1.25 3.00
GN23 Sidney Crosby 4.00 10.00
GN24 Joe Pavelski 1.25 3.00
GN25 Vladimir Tarasenko 1.50 4.00
GN26 Nikita Kucherov 2.00 5.00
GN27 James van Riemsdyk .75 2.00
GN28 Daniel Sedin 1.25 3.00
GN29 Alexander Ovechkin 4.00 10.00
GN30 Mark Scheifele 1.50 4.00

2016-17 Upper Deck Oversized

44 Patrick Kane 4.00 10.00
61 Jamie Benn 2.00 5.00
75 Connor McDavid 10.00 25.00
86 Jeff Carter 1.50 4.00
101 Brendan Gallagher 2.00 5.00
133 Erik Karlsson 2.50 6.00
146 Sidney Crosby 8.00 20.00
150 Joe Pavelski 2.00 5.00
162 Vladimir Tarasenko 2.50 6.00
170 James van Riemsdyk 1.50 4.00
179 Daniel Sedin 2.50 6.00
184 Alexander Ovechkin 8.00 20.00
187 Evgeny Kuznetsov 2.50 6.00
195 Dustin Byfuglien 2.00 5.00
201 Auston Matthews YG 40.00 100.00
206 Jakub Chychrun YG 4.00 10.00
212 Kyle Connor YG 6.00 15.00
214 Ivan Provorov YG 4.00 10.00
218 Jimmy Vesey YG 3.00 8.00
224 Zach Werenski YG 6.00 15.00
225 Jesse Puljujarvi YG 4.00 10.00
227 Pavel Buchnevich YG 3.00 8.00
231 Matthew Tkachuk YG 8.00 20.00
235 Christian Dvorak YG 2.50 6.00
236 Mikhail Sergachev YG 3.00 8.00
242 Hudson Fasching YG 2.00 5.00
248 Pavel Zacha YG 3.00 8.00
249 William Nylander YG 8.00 20.00
451 Patrik Laine YG 25.00 60.00
452 Kasperi Kapanen YG 3.00 8.00
458 Mathew Barzal YG 6.00 15.00
459 Joel Eriksson Ek YG 3.00 8.00
463 Anthony DeAngelo YG 1.50 4.00
468 Mitch Marner YG 30.00 80.00
471 Tyler Bertuzzi YG 4.00 10.00
475 Troy Stecher YG 2.00 5.00
482 Brandon Carlo YG 3.00 8.00
484 Nikita Soshnikov YG 1.25 3.00
486 Kevin Labanc YG 2.00 5.00
488 Thomas Chabot YG 4.00 10.00
498 Dylan Strome YG 5.00 12.00
499 Brendan Leipsic YG 1.50 4.00

2016-17 Upper Deck Parkhurst Rookies

PR1 William Nylander 4.00 10.00
PR2 Matthew Tkachuk 4.00 10.00
PR3 Kyle Connor 3.00 8.00
PR4 Sebastian Aho 3.00 8.00
PR5 Ivan Provorov 1.50 4.00
PR6 Christian Dvorak 1.25 3.00
PR7 Mitch Marner 3.00 8.00
PR8 Jesse Puljujarvi 2.00 5.00
PR9 Patrik Laine 5.00 12.00
PR10 Auston Matthews 6.00 15.00

2016-17 Upper Deck Shining Stars

SS1 Brent Burns 1.00 2.50
SS2 Brent Seabrook .60 1.50
SS3 Drew Doughty 1.25 3.00
SS4 Dustin Byfuglien 1.00 2.50
SS5 Erik Karlsson 1.25 3.00
SS6 John Klingberg 1.00 2.50
SS7 Roman Josi 1.00 2.50
SS8 Ryan Suter .75 2.00
SS9 Shayne Gostisbehere 1.00 2.50
SS10 Victor Hedman 1.25 3.00
SS11 Blake Wheeler 1.00 2.50
SS12 Vladimir Tarasenko 1.25 3.00
SS13 James Neal .60 1.50
SS14 Jaromir Jagr 3.00 8.00
SS15 Kyle Palmieri .75 2.00
SS16 Mark Stone 1.25 3.00
SS17 Patrick Kane 2.00 5.00
SS18 Nikita Kucherov 2.00 5.00
SS19 Phil Kessel 1.00 2.50
SS20 Wayne Simmonds 1.25 3.00
SS21 Anze Kopitar 1.50 4.00
SS22 Claude Giroux 1.00 2.50
SS23 Evgeny Kuznetsov 1.25 3.00
SS24 Joe Pavelski 1.25 3.00
SS25 Joe Thornton 1.50 4.00
SS26 Mark Scheifele 1.50 4.00
SS27 Nicklas Backstrom 1.00 2.50
SS28 Ryan Getzlaf 1.00 2.50
SS29 Sean Monahan .60 1.50
SS30 Sidney Crosby 4.00 10.00
SS31 Alexander Ovechkin 8.00 20.00
SS32 Artemi Panarin 4.00 10.00
SS33 Brad Marchand 4.00 10.00
SS34 Brandon Saad 1.50 4.00
SS35 Daniel Sedin 2.50 6.00
SS36 Filip Forsberg 3.00 8.00
SS37 Jamie Benn 2.00 5.00
SS38 Jonathan Huberdeau 2.50 6.00
SS39 Johnny Gaudreau 3.00 8.00
SS40 Zach Parise 2.00 5.00
SS41 Ben Bishop 2.50 6.00
SS42 Braden Holtby 4.00 10.00
SS43 Corey Crawford 4.00 10.00
SS44 Cory Schneider 3.00 8.00
SS45 Jake Allen 3.00 8.00
SS46 John Gibson 3.00 8.00
SS47 Martin Jones 2.50 6.00
SS48 Matt Murray 5.00 12.00
SS49 Petr Mrazek 3.00 8.00
SS50 Thomas Greiss 2.50 6.00

2016-17 Upper Deck Sophomore Sensations

SS1 Jack Eichel 1.25 3.00
SS2 Artemi Panarin 1.50 4.00
SS4 Matt Murray 1.25 3.00
SS5 Dylan Larkin 1.00 2.50
SS6 Connor McDavid 4.00 10.00

2016-17 Upper Deck Super Colossal

SC1 Clayton Stoner 1.50 4.00
SC2 Cody McLeod 1.25 3.00
SC3 Derek Dorsett 1.25 3.00
SC4 Brian Boyle 1.25 3.00
SC5 Chris Neil 1.25 3.00
SC6 Dalton Prout 1.25 3.00
SC7 Matt Hendricks 1.25 3.00
SC8 Chris Thorburn 1.25 3.00
SC9 Brandon Bollig 1.50 4.00
SC10 Alex Petrovic 1.25 3.00
SC11 Antoine Roussel 1.25 3.00
SC12 Kyle Clifford 1.25 3.00
SC13 Shawn Thornton 1.25 3.00
SC14 Tom Wilson 2.00 5.00
SC15 Dustin Byfuglien 2.00 5.00
SC16 Radko Gudas 1.25 3.00
SC17 Wayne Simmonds 2.50 6.00
SC18 Zdeno Chara 2.00 5.00
SC19 Mark Borowiecki 1.25 3.00
SC20 Zac Rinaldo 1.50 4.00

2016-17 Upper Deck Team Triples

DTCA Laine/Matthews/Puljujarvi 20.00 50.00
TTC1 Kylington/Bennett/Shinkaruk 5.00 12.00
TTC2 Monahan/Gaudreau/Giordano 5.00 12.00
TTE1 Draisaitl/McDavid/Nurse 15.00 40.00
TTE2 Eberle/Nugent-Hopkins/Talbot 4.00 10.00
TTM1 Lindgren/Galchenyuk/McCarron 5.00 12.00
TTM2 Pacioretty/Price/Gallagher 6.00 15.00
TTO1 Lazar/Paul/Puempel 4.00 10.00
TTO2 Stone/Karlsson/Turris 4.00 10.00
TTT1 Nylander/Matthews/Leipsic 20.00 50.00
TTT2 Kadri/Rielly/van Riemsdyk 4.00 10.00
TTT3 Kapanen/Brown/Soshnikov 5.00 12.00
TTV1 Horvat/Virtanen/Hutton 4.00 10.00
TTV2 Sedin/Sedin/Edler 4.00 10.00
TTW1 Hellebuyck/Laine/Ehlers 8.00 20.00
TTW2 Wheeler/Scheifele/Byfuglien 5.00 12.00

2016-17 Upper Deck UD Portraits

P1 Seth Jones .75 2.00
P2 Mats Zuccarello .75 2.00
P3 Wayne Simmonds 1.00 2.50
P4 Joe Thornton 1.25 3.00
P5 Pekka Rinne .75 2.00
P6 Evgeny Kuznetsov 1.25 3.00
P7 Mark Scheifele 1.25 3.00
P8 Robby Fabbri .50 1.25
P9 Tyler Toffoli .75 2.00
P10 Noah Hanifin .75 2.00
P11 Matt Murray 1.25 3.00
P12 Braden Holtby 1.25 3.00
P13 Drew Doughty 1.00 2.50
P14 Justin Faulk .60 1.50
P15 Artemi Panarin 1.50 4.00
P16 Aleksander Barkov 1.25 3.00
P17 Jamie Benn .75 2.00
P18 Corey Crawford .75 2.00
P19 Dylan Larkin 1.00 2.50
P20 Roberto Luongo 1.25 3.00
P21 Shayne Gostisbehere .75 2.00
P22 Anthony Duclair .60 1.50
P23 Mark Stone 1.00 2.50
P24 Rickard Rakell .60 1.50
P25 Travis Hamonic .50 1.25
P26 Victor Hedman 1.00 2.50
P27 John Klingberg .75 2.00
P28 Cory Schneider .75 2.00
P29 Henrik Sedin 1.00 2.50
P30 Nathan MacKinnon 3.00 8.00
P31 Jack Eichel 1.25 3.00
P32 Nikita Kucherov 1.50 4.00
P33 Alex Galchenyuk .50 1.25
P34 Ryan Johansen .60 1.50
P35 Sean Monahan .50 1.25
P36 Leon Draisaitl 2.50 6.00
P37 Morgan Rielly .75 2.00
P38 Sam Bennett 1.25 3.00
P39 Martin Jones .60 1.50
P40 Max Domi .75 2.00
P41 Alex Pietrangelo .60 1.50
P42 Brent Burns .75 2.00
P43 Ryan Suter .60 1.50
P44 Blake Wheeler .75 2.00
P45 Brendan Gallagher .75 2.00
P46 Phil Kessel .75 2.00
P47 John Gibson .75 2.00
P48 Brad Marchand 1.50 4.00
P49 Sidney Crosby 5.00 12.00
P50 Patrick Kane 1.50 4.00
P51 Vladimir Tarasenko 1.00 2.50
P52 Erik Karlsson 1.00 2.50
P53 Connor McDavid 4.00 10.00
P54 Alexander Ovechkin 3.00 8.00
P55 Josh Morrissey 2.00 5.00
P56 Anthony Mantha 1.50 4.00
P57 William Nylander 3.00 8.00
P58 Sonny Milano 1.00 2.50
P59 Hudson Fasching .75 2.00
P60 Pavel Zacha 1.25 3.00
P61 Patrik Laine 2.00 5.00
P62 Pontus Aberg 1.00 2.50
P63 Mike Reilly .60 1.50
P64 Steven Santini .60 1.50
P65 Artturi Lehkonen 1.00 2.50
P66 Brandon Carlo 1.25 3.00
P67 Nick Schmaltz 1.00 2.50
P68 Christian Dvorak 1.00 2.50
P69 Kasperi Kapanen 1.25 3.00
P70 Justin Bailey .75 2.00
P71 Anthony Beauvillier .75 2.00
P72 Connor Brown 1.25 3.00
P73 Jakob Chychrun 1.50 4.00
P74 Brendan Leipsic .60 1.50
P75 Travis Konecny 1.50 4.00
P76 Zach Sanford .60 1.50
P77 Joel Eriksson Ek 1.25 3.00
P78 Drake Caggiula .75 2.00
P79 Brayden Point 2.00 5.00
P80 Jake Guentzel 2.50 6.00
P81 Mitch Marner 2.50 6.00
P82 Jacob Larsson 1.25 3.00
P83 Oliver Kylington .60 1.50
P84 Charlie Lindgren 1.25 3.00
P85 Troy Stecher .75 2.00
P86 Ivan Provorov 1.25 3.00
P87 Jesse Puljujarvi 1.50 4.00
P88 Michael Matheson .75 2.00
P89 Zach Werenski 2.50 6.00
P90 Tyler Motte .75 2.00
P91 Dylan Strome 2.00 5.00
P92 Jason Dickinson .60 1.50
P93 Thomas Chabot 1.50 4.00
P94 Kyle Connor 2.50 6.00
P95 Mikhail Sergachev 1.25 3.00
P96 Nikita Zaitsev .75 2.00
P97 Jimmy Vesey 1.25 3.00
P98 Oliver Bjorkstrand 1.00 2.50
P99 Blake Speers .75 2.00
P100 Kevin Labanc .75 2.00
P101 Sebastian Aho 2.50 6.00
P102 Tristan Jarry 1.50 4.00
P103 Miles Wood .60 1.50
P104 Pavel Buchnevich 1.25 3.00
P105 Julius Honka .75 2.00
P106 Mathew Barzal 2.50 6.00
P107 Nick Paul 1.00 2.50
P108 Chris Bigras .60 1.50
P109 Matthew Tkachuk 3.00 8.00
P110 Auston Matthews 5.00 12.00

2016-17 Upper Deck Winter Classic Jumbos

WC1 Brendan Gallagher 1.00 2.50
WC2 Matt Beleskey .75 2.00
WC3 Mike Condon 1.00 2.50
WC4 Zdeno Chara 1.00 2.50
WC5 Tomas Plekanec .60 1.50
WC6 Patrice Bergeron 1.25 3.00
WC7 Paul Byron .75 2.00
WC8 Torey Krug .75 2.00
WC9 Max Pacioretty 1.00 2.50
WC10 Loui Eriksson .60 1.50
WC11 P.K. Subban 1.25 3.00
WC12 Ryan Spooner .75 2.00
WC13 Nathan Beaulieu .60 1.50
WC14 Jimmy Hayes .60 1.50

2016-17 Upper Deck Ceremonial Puck Drop

CDP1 Mario Lemieux 60.00 150.00
CDP2 Rob Blake 15.00 40.00
CDP3 Steve Yzerman 40.00 100.00
CDP4 Brett Hull 30.00 80.00
CDP5 Luc Robitaille 15.00 40.00
CDP6 Nicklas Lidstrom 15.00 40.00
CDP7 Martin Brodeur 40.00 100.00
CDP8 Peter Forsberg 30.00 80.00
CDP9 Wayne Gretzky 100.00 250.00
CDP10 Mike Bossy 15.00 40.00
CDP11 Chris Chelios 15.00 40.00
CDP12 Tony Esposito 15.00 40.00

2016-17 Upper Deck Ceremonial Puck Drop Autograph

CDP4 Brett Hull 60.00 150.00
CDP5 Luc Robitaille 40.00 100.00
CDP6 Nicklas Lidstrom 30.00 80.00
CDP10 Mike Bossy 30.00 80.00
CDP12 Tony Esposito 60.00 150.00

2016-17 Upper Deck Day With The Cup Flashbacks

DCF1 Steve Yzerman 90.00 150.00
DCF2 Igor Larionov 90.00 150.00
DCF4 Larry Murphy 25.00 60.00
DCF5 Chris Osgood 25.00 60.00

2016-17 Upper Deck Rookie Breakouts

RB1 Artturi Lehkonen 10.00 25.00
RB2 William Nylander 30.00 80.00
RB3 Brandon Carlo 12.00 30.00
RB4 Dylan Strome 20.00 50.00
RB5 Travis Konecny 15.00 40.00
RB6 Sebastian Aho 25.00 60.00
RB7 Mathew Barzal 25.00 60.00
RB8 Jimmy Vesey 12.00 30.00
RB9 Hudson Fasching 8.00 20.00
RB10 Christian Dvorak 10.00 25.00
RB11 Mikhail Sergachev 12.00 30.00
RB12 Kyle Connor 25.00 60.00
RB13 Jakub Vrana 10.00 25.00
RB14 Joel Eriksson Ek 12.00 30.00
RB15 Jakob Chychrun 15.00 40.00
RB16 Matthew Tkachuk 30.00 80.00
RB17 Sonny Milano 10.00 25.00
RB18 Nick Schmaltz 10.00 25.00
RB19 Pavel Buchnevich 12.00 30.00
RB20 Ivan Provorov 12.00 30.00
RB21 Pavel Zacha 12.00 30.00
RB22 Zach Werenski 25.00 60.00
RB23 Anthony Beauvillier 8.00 20.00
RB24 Mitch Marner 25.00 60.00
RB25 Anthony Mantha 25.00 60.00
RB26 Jesse Puljujarvi 15.00 40.00

2016-17 Upper Deck Rookie Materials

RMAB Anthony Beauvillier C 3.00 8.00
RMAM Auston Matthews A 20.00 50.00
RMBL Brendan Leipsic D 2.50 6.00
RMBP Brayden Point E 8.00 20.00
RMBR Chris Bigras E 2.50 6.00
RMCB Connor Brown C 5.00 12.00
RMCD Christian Dvorak C 4.00 10.00
RMEL Esa Lindell E 3.00 8.00
RMHF Hudson Fasching C 3.00 8.00
RMIP Ivan Provorov B 5.00 12.00
RMJB Justin Bailey E 3.00 8.00
RMJC Jakob Chychrun B 6.00 15.00
RMJE Joel Eriksson Ek D 5.00 12.00
RMJP Jesse Puljujarvi A 6.00 15.00
RMJV Jimmy Vesey D 5.00 12.00
RMKC Kyle Connor A 10.00 25.00
RMKK Kasperi Kapanen C 5.00 12.00
RMLC Lawson Crouse C 2.50 6.00
RMMA Anthony Mantha C 6.00 15.00
RMMB Mathew Barzal B 10.00 25.00
RMME Michael Matheson E 3.00 8.00
RMMM Mitch Marner A 10.00 25.00
RMMR Mike Reilly E 2.50 6.00
RMMS Mikhail Sergachev A 5.00 12.00
RMMT Matthew Tkachuk A 12.00 30.00
RMNS Nick Schmaltz B 4.00 10.00
RMOB Oliver Bjorkstrand C 4.00 10.00
RMOK Oliver Kylington E 2.50 6.00
RMOS Oskar Sundqvist E 3.00 8.00
RMPB Pavel Buchnevich B 5.00 12.00
RMPL Patrik Laine A 8.00 20.00
RMPZ Pavel Zacha B 5.00 12.00
RMRP Ryan Pulock E 3.00 8.00
RMSA Sebastian Aho C 10.00 25.00
RMSM Sonny Milano B 4.00 10.00
RMSO Nikita Soshnikov E 2.00 5.00
RMTC Thomas Chabot B 6.00 15.00
RMTK Travis Konecny B 6.00 15.00
RMTM Tyler Motte D 3.00 8.00
RMWN William Nylander A 12.00 30.00
RMZW Zach Werenski B 10.00 25.00

2016-17 Upper Deck Rookie Materials Patch

COMMON CARD 6.00 15.00
RMAM Auston Matthews 100.00 200.00
RMMT Matthew Tkachuk 90.00 150.00
RMPL Patrik Laine 60.00 150.00

2016-17 Upper Deck Silver Foil

*VETS: 5X TO 12X BASIC CARDS
*ROOKIES: .6X TO 1.5X BASIC CARDS
187 Evgeny Kuznetsov 4.00 10.00
101 Nicklas Backstrom 3.00 8.00
201 Auston Matthews YG 400.00 500.00
249 William Nylander YG 40.00 100.00
250 A.Matthews YG
RC/W.Nylander YG RC CL 20.00 50.00
290 Corey Crawford 4.00 10.00
420 Jonathan Drouin 2.50 6.00
459 Joel Eriksson Ek YG 20.00 50.00

2017-18 Upper Deck

1 Hampus Lindholm .20 .50
2 Corey Perry .50 1.25
3 Cam Fowler .30 .75
4 Kevin Bieksa .25 .60
5 Rickard Rakell .25 .60
6 Ryan Kesler .30 .75
7 Alex Goligoski .25 .60
8 Christian Dvorak .25 .60
9 Jakob Chychrun .30 .75
10 Max Domi .30 .75
11 Tobias Rieder .20 .50
12 Oliver Ekman-Larsson .30 .75
13 Brad Marchand .60 1.50
14 Brandon Carlo .25 .60
15 David Backes .20 .50
16 Torey Krug .25 .60
17 Tuukka Rask .40 1.00
18 Zdeno Chara .25 .60
19 Jack Eichel .50 1.25
20 Jake McCabe .20 .50
21 Kyle Okposo .20 .50
22 Matt Moulson .20 .50
23 Rasmus Ristolainen .20 .50
24 Zach Bogosian .25 .60
25 Matt Stajan .20 .50
26 Matthew Tkachuk .60 1.50
27 Michael Frolik .20 .50
28 Mikael Backlund .25 .60
29 Sean Monahan .20 .50
30 Troy Brouwer .20 .50
31 T.J. Brodie .25 .60
32 Brett Pesce .25 .60
33 Jaccob Slavin .20 .50
34 Jordan Staal .25 .60
35 Lee Stempniak .20 .50
36 Sebastian Aho .50 1.25
37 Teuvo Teravainen .30 .75
38 Cam Ward .30 .75
39 Brent Seabrook .20 .50
40 Corey Crawford .40 1.00
41 Jonathan Toews .50 1.25
42 Nick Schmaltz .25 .60
43 Richard Panik .20 .50
44 Ryan Hartman .20 .50
45 Blake Comeau .20 .50
46 Semyon Varlamov .30 .75
47 Mikko Rantanen .75 2.00
48 Nathan MacKinnon 1.25 3.00
49 Tyson Barrie .20 .50
50 Carl Soderberg .20 .50
51 Brandon Dubinsky .20 .50
52 David Savard .20 .50
53 Lukas Sedlak .20 .50
54 Sergei Bobrovsky .50 1.25
55 Seth Jones .30 .75
56 Zach Werenski .50 1.25
57 Boone Jenner .30 .75
58 Antoine Roussel .20 .50
59 Radek Faksa .25 .60
60 Dan Hamhuis .20 .50
61 Jason Spezza .30 .75
62 Kari Lehtonen .25 .60
63 Stephen Johns .20 .50
64 Tyler Seguin .40 1.00
65 Anthony Mantha .25 .60
66 Gustav Nyquist .20 .50
67 Henrik Zetterberg .40 1.00
68 Luke Glendening .20 .50
69 Petr Mrazek .30 .75
70 Riley Sheahan .20 .50
71 Darren Helm .20 .50
72 Adam Larsson .30 .75
73 Andrej Sekera .20 .50
74 Drake Caggiula .25 .60
75 Leon Draisaitl 1.00 2.50
76 Mark Letestu .25 .60
77 Matthew Benning .20 .50
78 Patrick Maroon .25 .60
79 Colton Sceviour .20 .50
80 Derek MacKenzie .20 .50
81 Jason Demers .20 .50
82 Jonathan Huberdeau .40 1.00
83 Michael Matheson .25 .60
84 Vincent Trocheck .30 .75
85 Roberto Luongo .50 1.25
86 Alec Martinez .20 .50
87 Anze Kopitar .50 1.25
88 Derek Forbort .20 .50
89 Dustin Brown .30 .75
90 Jonathan Quick .40 1.00
91 Nic Dowd .20 .50
92 Trevor Lewis .20 .50
93 Charlie Coyle .25 .60
94 Eric Staal .40 1.00
95 Jared Spurgeon .30 .75
96 Jason Zucker .25 .60
97 Jonas Brodin .20 .50
98 Matt Dumba .25 .60
99 Zach Parise .30 .75
100 Andrew Shaw .20 .50
101 Artturi Lehkonen .25 .60
102 Carey Price .60 1.50
103 Jeff Petry .30 .75
104 Paul Byron .25 .60
105 Phillip Danault .30 .75
106 Shea Weber .25 .60
107 Viktor Arvidsson .25 .60
108 Calle Jarnkrok .20 .50
109 Filip Forsberg .50 1.25
110 Mattias Ekholm .30 .75
111 P.K. Subban .40 1.00
112 Kevin Fiala .25 .60
113 Pekka Rinne .40 1.00
114 Adam Henrique .25 .60
115 Miles Wood .20 .50
116 Pavel Zacha .25 .60
117 Taylor Hall .30 .75
118 Travis Zajac .20 .50
119 Andy Greene .20 .50
120 Anthony Beauvillier .20 .50
121 Calvin de Haan .20 .50
122 Casey Cizikas .20 .50
123 Josh Bailey .25 .60
124 Nikolay Kulemin .20 .50
125 Thomas Greiss .25 .60
126 Brady Skjei .25 .60
127 J.T. Miller .40 1.00
128 Jimmy Vesey .25 .60
129 Michael Grabner .25 .60
130 Nick Holden .25 .60
131 Rick Nash .30 .75
132 Kevin Hayes .25 .60
133 Clarke MacArthur .20 .50
134 Derick Brassard .20 .50
135 Dion Phaneuf .20 .50
136 Kyle Turris .30 .75
137 Jean-Gabriel Pageau .20 .50
138 Mike Hoffman .20 .50
139 Wayne Simmonds .40 1.00
140 Dale Weise .20 .50
141 Ivan Provorov .25 .60
142 Jakub Voracek .25 .60
143 Travis Konecny .30 .75
144 Valtteri Filppula .20 .50
145 Carl Hagelin .20 .50
146 Evgeni Malkin .60 1.50
147 Ian Cole .20 .50
148 Matt Murray .50 1.25
149 Phil Kessel .30 .75
150 Scott Wilson .20 .50
151 Jake Guentzel .50 1.25
152 Joe Thornton .50 1.25
153 Joel Ward .20 .50
154 Justin Braun .25 .60
155 Marc-Edouard Vlasic .25 .60
156 Mikkel Boedker .20 .50
157 Paul Martin .20 .50
158 Alex Pietrangelo .20 .50
159 Jaden Schwartz .40 1.00
160 Jake Allen .30 .75
161 Kyle Brodziak .20 .50
162 Patrik Berglund .20 .50
163 Paul Stastny .25 .60
164 Alex Killorn .20 .50
165 Andrei Vasilevskiy .50 1.25
166 Anton Stralman .20 .50
167 Brayden Point .40 1.00
168 Nikita Kucherov .60 1.50

169 Ondrej Palat .25 .60
170 Auston Matthews 1.25 3.00
171 Frederik Andersen .40 1.00
172 Leo Komarov .20 .50
173 Matt Martin .20 .50
174 Mitch Marner .50 1.25
175 Nazem Kadri .40 1.00
176 William Nylander .60 1.50
177 Henrik Sedin .40 1.00
178 Jacob Markstrom .30 .75
179 Brandon Sutter .20 .50
180 Markus Granlund .25 .60
181 Sven Baertschi .20 .50
182 Troy Stecher .20 .50
183 Marc-Andre Fleury .60 1.50
184 Jason Garrison .20 .50
185 Brayden McNabb .20 .50
186 Braden Holtby .40 1.00
187 Jay Beagle .20 .50
188 John Carlson .30 .75
189 Lars Eller .20 .50
190 Evgeny Kuznetsov .40 1.00
191 Matt Niskanen .25 .60
192 Nicklas Backstrom .30 .75
193 Adam Lowry .25 .60
194 Blake Wheeler .30 .75
195 Bryan Little .25 .60
196 Josh Morrissey .40 1.00
197 Mathieu Perreault .20 .50
198 Patrik Laine .40 1.00
199 Pekka Rinne
Matt Murray CL .50 1.25
200 Marc-Andre Fleury
Brayden McNabb CL .60 1.50
201 Nico Hischier YG RC 10.00 25.00
202 Kailer Yamamoto YG RC 8.00 20.00
203 Anders Bjork YG RC 4.00 10.00
204 Pierre-Luc Dubois YG RC 8.00 20.00
205 Josh Ho-Sang YG RC 4.00 10.00
206 Jon Gillies YG RC 3.00 8.00
207 Lucas Wallmark YG RC 3.00 8.00
208 Denis Gurianov YG RC 8.00 20.00
209 Alex Kerfoot YG RC 6.00 15.00
210 Adrian Kempe YG RC 6.00 15.00
211 John Hayden YG RC 2.50 6.00
212 Jake DeBrusk YG RC 8.00 20.00
213 Janne Kuokkanen YG RC 3.00 8.00
214 Travis Sanheim YG RC 3.00 8.00
215 Gabriel Carlsson YG RC 2.50 6.00
216 Calle Rosen YG RC 3.00 8.00
217 Logan Brown YG RC 3.00 8.00
218 Rasmus Andersson YG RC 3.00 8.00
219 Alex Formenton YG RC 3.00 8.00
220 Ian McCoshen YG RC 3.00 8.00
221 Alex DeBrincat YG RC 12.00 30.00
222 Alexander Nylander YG RC 5.00 12.00
223 Nathan Walker YG RC 3.00 8.00
224 Evgeny Svechnikov YG RC 6.00 15.00
225 C.J. Smith YG RC 2.50 6.00
226 Samuel Morin YG RC 2.00 5.00
227 Filip Chytil YG RC 3.00 8.00
228 Tage Thompson YG RC 12.00 30.00
229 Andreas Borgman YG RC 3.00 8.00
230 Ivan Barbashev YG RC 4.00 10.00
231 Jonny Brodzinski YG RC 3.00 8.00
232 Robert Hagg YG RC 3.00 8.00
233 Riley Barber YG RC 3.00 8.00
234 Christian Fischer YG RC 4.00 10.00
235 Jakob Forsbacka-Karlsson YG RC 3.00 8.00
236 Haydn Fleury YG RC 3.00 8.00
237 Marcus Sorensen YG RC 2.50 6.00
238 Vladislav Kamenev YG RC 3.00 8.00
239 Jake Dotchin YG RC 2.50 6.00
240 Jack Roslovic YG RC 4.00 10.00
241 Nicolas Kerdiles YG RC 3.00 8.00
242 Charlie McAvoy YG RC 10.00 25.00
243 Carter Rowney YG RC 2.50 6.00
244 Vince Dunn YG RC 4.00 10.00
245 Victor Mete YG RC 3.00 8.00
246 Tyson Jost YG RC 6.00 15.00
247 Brock Boeser YG RC 10.00 25.00
248 Will Butcher YG RC 4.00 10.00
249 Alex Tuch YG RC 8.00 20.00
250 N.Hischier/B.Boeser YG CL 3.00 8.00
251 Ryan Getzlaf .30 .75
252 John Gibson .30 .75
253 Brandon Montour .40 1.00
254 Andrew Cogliano .20 .50
255 Patrick Eaves .25 .60
256 Ryan Miller .30 .75
257 Antti Raanta .30 .75
258 Derek Stepan .20 .50
259 Niklas Hjalmarsson .20 .50
260 Brad Richardson .20 .50
261 Dylan Strome .40 1.00
262 Anthony Duclair .25 .60
263 David Krejci .30 .75
264 Patrice Bergeron .40 1.00
265 David Pastrnak .75 2.00
266 Ryan Spooner .25 .60
267 Riley Nash .20 .50
268 Matt Beleskey .20 .50
269 Frank Vatrano .30 .75
270 Benoit Pouliot .20 .50
271 Ryan O'Reilly .30 .75
272 Sam Reinhart .60 1.50
273 Robin Lehner .25 .60
274 Evander Kane .30 .75
275 Jason Pominville .20 .50
276 Jaromir Jagr 1.00 2.50
277 Dougie Hamilton .25 .60
278 Johnny Gaudreau .50 1.25
279 Mike Smith .30 .75
280 Mark Giordano .30 .75
281 Travis Hamonic .25 .60
282 Justin Williams .25 .60
283 Scott Darling .25 .60
284 Jeff Skinner .40 1.00
285 Victor Rask .20 .50
286 Elias Lindholm .30 .75
287 Trevor van Riemsdyk .25 .60
288 Marcus Kruger .20 .50
289 Patrick Sharp .25 .60
290 Patrick Kane .60 1.50
291 Brandon Saad .25 .60
292 Duncan Keith .25 .60
293 Artem Anisimov .20 .50
294 Connor Murphy .20 .50
295 Nail Yakupov .20 .50
296 Gabriel Landeskog .40 1.00
297 Erik Johnson .20 .50
298 Matt Nieto .20 .50
299 Colin Wilson .25 .60
300 Jonathan Bernier .25 .60
301 Cam Atkinson .30 .75
302 Artemi Panarin .60 1.50
303 Alexander Wennberg .20 .50
304 Ryan Murray .30 .75
305 Nick Foligno .25 .60
306 Jack Johnson .20 .50
307 Marc Methot .20 .50
308 Jamie Benn .30 .75
309 Martin Hanzal .25 .60
310 Ben Bishop .25 .60
311 Alexander Radulov .30 .75
312 Esa Lindell .25 .60
313 Trevor Daley .25 .60
314 Jim Howard .40 1.00
315 Tomas Tatar .20 .50
316 Frans Nielsen .20 .50
317 Dylan Larkin .40 1.00
318 Mike Green .25 .60
319 Michael Cammalleri .25 .60
320 Connor McDavid 1.50 4.00
321 Darnell Nurse .25 .60
322 Cam Talbot .30 .75
323 Oscar Klefbom .25 .60
324 Ryan Nugent-Hopkins .40 1.00
325 Milan Lucic .30 .75
326 Jamie McGinn .20 .50
327 Aleksander Barkov .50 1.25
328 Aaron Ekblad .40 1.00
329 Nick Bjugstad .20 .50
330 Evgeny Dadonov .20 .50
331 James Reimer .30 .75
332 Radim Vrbata .20 .50
333 Jeff Carter .25 .60
334 Darcy Kuemper .30 .75
335 Tyler Toffoli .30 .75
336 Tanner Pearson .25 .60
337 Christian Folin .20 .50
338 Jussi Jokinen .25 .60
339 Ryan Suter .25 .60
340 Devan Dubnyk .25 .60
341 Nino Niederreiter .20 .50
342 Mikael Granlund .25 .60
343 Matt Cullen .25 .60
344 Mikko Koivu .25 .60
345 Tyler Ennis .20 .50
346 Max Pacioretty .30 .75
347 Brendan Gallagher .30 .75
348 Alex Galchenyuk .20 .50
349 Jonathan Drouin .25 .60
350 Karl Alzner .20 .50
351 Ales Hemsky .25 .60
352 Phillip Danault .30 .75
353 Austin Watson .25 .60
354 Nick Bonino .20 .50
355 Roman Josi .30 .75
356 Ryan Johansen .25 .60
357 Craig Smith .20 .50
358 P.K. Subban .40 1.00
359 Scott Hartnell .20 .50
360 John Moore .20 .50
361 Marcus Johansson .25 .60
362 Brian Boyle .20 .50
363 Cory Schneider .30 .75
364 Drew Stafford .20 .50
365 Kyle Palmieri .25 .60
366 John Tavares .50 1.25
367 Jordan Eberle .30 .75
368 Andrew Ladd .20 .50
369 Anders Lee .30 .75
370 Johnny Boychuk .25 .60
371 Brock Nelson .30 .75
372 Henrik Lundqvist .75 2.00
373 Mika Zibanejad .40 1.00
374 Ryan McDonagh .20 .50
375 Brendan Smith .20 .50
376 Chris Kreider .40 1.00
377 David Desharnais .20 .50
378 Kevin Shattenkirk .20 .50
379 Erik Karlsson .40 1.00
380 Craig Anderson .30 .75
381 Johnny Oduya .25 .60
382 Bobby Ryan .25 .60
383 Cody Ceci .20 .50
384 Mark Stone .40 1.00
385 Brian Elliott .25 .60
386 Jori Lehtera .20 .50
387 Shayne Gostisbehere .30 .75
388 Claude Giroux .30 .75
389 Sean Couturier .25 .60
390 Andrew MacDonald .25 .60
391 Sidney Crosby 1.25 3.00
392 Matt Hunwick .20 .50
393 Kris Letang .40 1.00
394 Chad Ruhwedel .20 .50
395 Bryan Rust .30 .75
396 Justin Schultz .30 .75
397 Brent Burns .30 .75
398 Martin Jones .25 .60
399 Paul Martin .20 .50
400 Jannik Hansen .25 .60
401 Tomas Hertl .30 .75
402 Logan Couture .40 1.00
403 Brayden Schenn .30 .75
404 Jaden Schwartz .40 1.00
405 Colton Parayko .25 .60
406 Vladimir Tarasenko .40 1.00
407 Alexander Steen .20 .50
408 Paul Stastny .25 .60
409 Vladimir Sobotka .20 .50
410 Steven Stamkos .60 1.50
411 Ondrej Palat .25 .60
412 Victor Hedman .40 1.00
413 Vladislav Namestnikov .20 .50
414 Tyler Johnson .20 .50
415 Chris Kunitz .30 .75
416 Patrick Marleau .30 .75
417 Morgan Rielly .30 .75
418 Tyler Bozak .20 .50
419 James van Riemsdyk .25 .60
420 Jake Gardiner .20 .50
421 Ron Hainsey .25 .60
422 Daniel Sedin .40 1.00
423 Alexander Edler .20 .50
424 Bo Horvat .40 1.00
425 Michael Del Zotto .20 .50
426 Erik Gudbranson .20 .50
427 Sam Gagner .20 .50
428 Alexander Burmistrov .20 .50
429 Deryk Engelland .20 .50
430 Nate Schmidt .25 .60
431 David Perron .25 .60
432 Reilly Smith .30 .75
433 William Karlsson .40 1.00
434 James Neal .20 .50
435 Jonathan Marchessault .40 1.00
436 Oscar Lindberg .25 .60
437 Alexander Ovechkin 1.25 3.00
438 T.J. Oshie .30 .75
439 Andre Burakovsky .20 .50
440 Tom Wilson .30 .75
441 Dmitry Orlov .30 .75
442 Brett Connolly .20 .50
443 Mark Scheifele .50 1.25
444 Dustin Byfuglien .30 .75
445 Jacob Trouba .25 .60
446 Kyle Connor .50 1.25
447 Nikolaj Ehlers .30 .75
448 Connor Hellebuyck .60 1.50
449 B.Saad/A.Panarin CL .60 1.50
450 A.Ovechkin/S.Stamkos CL 1.25 3.00
451 Christian Djoos YG RC 3.00 8.00
452 Jan Rutta YG RC 3.00 8.00
453 Samuel Blais YG RC 3.00 8.00
454 Adin Hill YG RC 8.00 20.00
455 Nolan Patrick YG RC 12.00 30.00
456 Anton Lindholm YG RC 3.00 8.00
457 Madison Bowey YG RC 2.00 5.00
458 Alex Iafallo YG RC 3.00 8.00
459 MacKenzie Weegar YG RC 4.00 10.00
460 Kalle Kossila YG RC 2.50 6.00
461 Alex Nedeljkovic YG RC 5.00 12.00
462 Christian Jaros YG RC 2.50 6.00
463 Remi Elie YG RC 2.50 6.00
464 Martin Necas YG RC 12.00 30.00
465 Samuel Girard YG RC 3.00 8.00
466 Jesper Bratt YG RC 12.00 30.00
467 Valentin Zykov YG RC 3.00 8.00
468 Kevin Roy YG RC 3.00 8.00
469 Owen Tippett YG RC 6.00 15.00
470 Jordan Schmaltz YG RC 4.00 10.00
471 Peter Cehlarik YG RC 3.00 8.00
472 Filip Chlapik YG RC 2.50 6.00
473 Robbie Russo YG RC 3.00 8.00
474 Paul LaDue YG RC 2.50 6.00
475 Roland McKeown YG RC 3.00 8.00
476 Eric Comrie YG RC 2.50 6.00
477 Clayton Keller YG RC 12.00 30.00
478 Ville Husso YG RC 4.00 10.00
479 Oscar Fantenberg YG RC 3.00 8.00
480 J.T. Compher YG RC 3.00 8.00
481 Mike Vecchione YG RC 2.50 6.00
482 Maxime Lagace YG RC 3.00 8.00
483 Andrew Poturalski YG RC 3.00 8.00
484 Tim Heed YG RC 3.00 8.00
485 Alexandre Carrier YG RC 2.50 6.00
486 Dryden Hunt YG RC 3.00 8.00
487 Brendan Lemieux YG RC 3.00 8.00
488 Dylan Ferguson YG RC 3.00 8.00
489 Jack Rodewald YG RC 3.00 8.00
490 Luke Kunin YG RC 3.00 8.00
491 Michael Amadio YG RC 3.00 8.00
492 Joakim Ryan YG RC 3.00 8.00
493 Colin White YG RC 4.00 10.00
494 Nikita Scherbak YG RC 4.00 10.00
495 Kyle Capobianco YG RC 3.00 8.00
496 Henrik Haapala YG RC 3.00 8.00
497 Andrew Mangiapane YG RC 5.00 12.00
498 Danick Martel YG RC 3.00 8.00
499 Nick Merkley YG RC 3.00 8.00
500 C.Keller/N.Patrick YG CL 2.50 6.00
501 Rick Nash .30 .75
502 Kyle Turris .30 .75
503 Matt Duchene .30 .75
504 Paul Stastny .25 .60
505 Adam Henrique .25 .60
506 Petr Mrazek .30 .75
507 Evander Kane .30 .75
508 Tomas Tatar .20 .50
509 Drew Doughty .40 1.00
510 Kyle Criscuolo YG RC 2.50 6.00
511 Dominic Toninato YG RC 2.50 6.00
512 Casey DeSmith YG RC 10.00 25.00
513 Travis Boyd YG RC 2.50 6.00
514 Alexandar Georgiev YG RC 8.00 20.00
515 Andy Welinski YG RC 2.50 6.00
516 Colby Cave YG RC 2.50 6.00
517 David Kampf YG RC 2.50 6.00
518 Sebastian Aho YG RC 2.50 6.00
519 Vinni Lettieri YG RC 2.50 6.00
520 Tanner Fritz YG RC 2.50 6.00
521 Jeff Glass YG RC 5.00 12.00

2017-18 Upper Deck Exclusives

*VETS/100: 5X TO 12X BASIC CARDS
*YG/100: 2.5X TO 6X BASIC CARDS
201 Nico Hischier YG 100.00 250.00
202 Kailer Yamamoto YG 80.00 150.00
204 Pierre-Luc Dubois YG 60.00 150.00
205 Josh Ho-Sang YG 80.00 150.00
221 Alex DeBrincat YG 125.00 300.00
228 Tage Thompson YG 125.00 300.00
454 Adin Hill YG 50.00 125.00
464 Martin Necas YG 80.00 200.00
466 Jesper Bratt YG 125.00 300.00
477 Clayton Keller YG 100.00 250.00
512 Casey DeSmith YG 40.00 100.00
514 Alexandar Georgiev YG 30.00 80.00

2017-18 Upper Deck Day With The Cup Flashbacks

DC1 Frank Mahovlich 6.00 15.00
DC2 Red Kelly 6.00 15.00
DC3 Mike Walton 5.00 12.00
DC4 Ron Ellis 5.00 12.00
DC5 Pete Stemkowski 5.00 12.00
DC6 Johnny Bower 6.00 15.00

2017-18 Upper Deck A Piece of History 1000 Point Club

PCAD Alex Delvecchio A 250.00 500.00
PCAO Alexander Ovechkin C 80.00 150.00
PCDP Denis Potvin B 50.00 125.00
PCHS Henrik Sedin D 25.00 60.00
PCJB Jean Beliveau B 60.00 150.00
PCSC Sidney Crosby B 200.00 300.00

2017-18 Upper Deck A Piece of History 500 Goal Club

GCPM Patrick Marleau 35.00 80.00

2017-18 Upper Deck Canvas

C1 Ryan Kesler 1.00 2.50
C2 Ryan Getzlaf 1.00 2.50
C3 Cam Fowler 1.00 2.50
C4 Alex Goligoski .75 2.00
C5 Tobias Rieder .60 1.50
C6 Oliver Ekman-Larsson 1.00 2.50
C7 Brad Marchand 2.00 5.00
C8 Ryan Spooner .75 2.00
C9 Torey Krug .75 2.00
C10 Jack Eichel 1.50 4.00
C11 Jake McCabe .60 1.50
C12 Evander Kane 1.00 2.50
C13 Mikael Backlund .75 2.00
C14 T.J. Brodie .75 2.00
C15 Matthew Tkachuk 2.00 5.00
C16 Elias Lindholm 1.00 2.50
C17 Jaccob Slavin .75 2.00
C18 Sebastian Aho 1.50 4.00
C19 Duncan Keith .75 2.00
C20 Ryan Hartman .60 1.50
C21 Jonathan Toews 1.50 4.00
C22 Mikko Rantanen 2.50 6.00
C23 Nathan MacKinnon 4.00 10.00
C24 Zach Werenski 1.50 4.00
C25 Sergei Bobrovsky 1.50 4.00
C26 Brandon Dubinsky .60 1.50
C27 John Klingberg 1.00 2.50
C28 Antoine Roussel .60 1.50
C29 Tyler Seguin 1.25 3.00
C30 Anthony Mantha .75 2.00
C31 Frans Nielsen .60 1.50
C32 Mike Green .75 2.00
C33 Connor McDavid 5.00 12.00
C34 Patrick Maroon .75 2.00
C35 Cam Talbot 1.00 2.50
C36 Vincent Trocheck 1.00 2.50
C37 Jason Demers .60 1.50
C38 Michael Matheson .75 2.00
C39 Jonathan Quick 1.25 3.00
C40 Jeff Carter .75 2.00
C41 Alec Martinez .60 1.50
C42 Jason Zucker 1.00 2.50
C43 Jared Spurgeon 1.00 2.50
C44 Mikko Koivu .75 2.00
C45 Paul Byron .75 2.00
C46 Shea Weber .75 2.00
C47 Carey Price 2.00 5.00
C48 Ryan Ellis .75 2.00
C49 Filip Forsberg 1.50 4.00
C50 Calle Jarnkrok .75 2.00
C51 Andy Greene .60 1.50
C52 Taylor Hall 1.00 2.50
C53 Pavel Zacha .75 2.00
C54 John Tavares 1.50 4.00
C55 Thomas Greiss .75 2.00
C56 Nick Leddy .60 1.50
C57 Kevin Hayes .75 2.00
C58 Rick Nash 1.00 2.50
C59 Jimmy Vesey .75 2.00
C60 Mike Hoffman .60 1.50
C61 Craig Anderson 1.00 2.50
C62 Alexandre Burrows .60 1.50
C63 Claude Giroux 1.00 2.50
C64 Ivan Provorov .75 2.00
C65 Sean Couturier .75 2.00
C66 Sidney Crosby 4.00 10.00
C67 Bryan Rust 1.00 2.50
C68 Kris Letang 1.25 3.00
C69 Brent Burns 1.00 2.50
C70 Marc-Edouard Vlasic .60 1.50
C71 Joel Ward .75 2.00
C72 Alex Pietrangelo .75 2.00
C73 Colton Parayko .75 2.00
C74 Paul Stastny .75 2.00
C75 Brayden Point 1.25 3.00
C76 Andrei Vasilevskiy 1.50 4.00
C77 Nikita Kucherov 2.00 5.00
C78 Tyler Bozak .60 1.50
C79 Auston Matthews 4.00 10.00
C80 Jake Gardiner .60 1.50
C81 Troy Stecher .60 1.50
C82 Jacob Markstrom 1.00 2.50
C83 Markus Granlund .75 2.00
C84 Tom Wilson 1.00 2.50
C85 Nicklas Backstrom 1.00 2.50
C86 Matt Niskanen .75 2.00
C87 Mathieu Perreault .60 1.50
C88 Nikolaj Ehlers 1.00 2.50
C89 Patrik Laine 1.25 3.00
C90 Carey Price
Sergei Bobrovsky CL 2.00 5.00
C91 Nolan Patrick YG 40.00 100.00
C92 Logan Brown YG 6.00 15.00
C93 Tyson Jost YG 12.00 30.00
C94 Adrian Kempe YG 12.00 30.00
C95 Filip Chytil YG 6.00 15.00
C96 Evgeny Svechnikov YG 12.00 30.00
C97 Haydn Fleury YG 6.00 15.00
C98 Pierre-Luc Dubois YG 10.00 25.00
C99 Denis Gurianov YG 15.00 40.00
C100 Tage Thompson YG 12.00 30.00
C101 Jon Gillies YG 6.00 15.00
C102 Kailer Yamamoto YG 12.00 30.00
C103 Christian Fischer YG 8.00 20.00
C104 Calle Rosen YG 6.00 15.00
C105 Charlie McAvoy YG 12.00 30.00
C106 Ivan Barbashev YG 8.00 20.00
C107 Nikita Scherbak YG 8.00 20.00
C108 Jack Roslovic YG 8.00 20.00
C109 Will Butcher YG 8.00 20.00
C110 Clayton Keller YG 12.00 30.00
C111 Alexander Nylander YG 10.00 25.00
C112 Jake DeBrusk YG 15.00 40.00
C113 Janne Kuokkanen YG 6.00 15.00
C114 Alex DeBrincat YG 12.00 30.00
C115 Victor Mete YG 6.00 15.00
C116 Alex Tuch YG 10.00 25.00
C117 Travis Sanheim YG 6.00 15.00
C118 Colin White YG 8.00 20.00
C119 J.T. Compher YG 6.00 15.00
C120 C.Keller/C.McAvoy YG CL 4.00 10.00
C121 Brandon Montour 1.25 3.00
C122 Corey Perry 1.50 4.00
C123 Patrick Eaves .75 2.00
C124 Christian Dvorak .75 2.00
C125 Derek Stepan .60 1.50
C126 Antti Raanta 1.00 2.50
C127 Niklas Hjalmarsson .60 1.50
C128 David Pastrnak 2.50 6.00
C129 Zdeno Chara 1.00 2.50
C130 Patrice Bergeron 1.25 3.00
C131 Mike Smith 1.00 2.50
C132 Travis Hamonic .75 2.00
C133 Kris Versteeg .60 1.50
C134 Justin Williams .75 2.00
C135 Trevor van Riemsdyk .75 2.00
C136 Marcus Kruger .60 1.50
C137 Corey Crawford 1.25 3.00
C138 Brandon Saad .75 2.00
C139 Patrick Sharp .75 2.00
C140 Semyon Varlamov 1.00 2.50
C141 Erik Johnson .60 1.50
C142 Tyson Barrie .60 1.50
C143 Artemi Panarin 2.00 5.00
C144 Jack Johnson .60 1.50
C145 Ryan Murray 1.00 2.50
C146 Alexander Radulov 1.00 2.50
C147 Martin Hanzal .75 2.00
C148 Ben Bishop .75 2.00
C149 Jim Howard 1.25 3.00
C150 Tomas Tatar .60 1.50
C151 Trevor Daley .75 2.00
C152 Drake Caggiula .75 2.00
C153 Ryan Nugent-Hopkins 1.25 3.00
C154 Oscar Klefbom .75 2.00
C155 Jonathan Huberdeau 1.25 3.00
C156 Evgeny Dadonov .60 1.50
C157 Derek MacKenzie .60 1.50
C158 Tyler Toffoli 1.00 2.50
C159 Anze Kopitar 1.50 4.00
C160 Dustin Brown 1.00 2.50
C161 Nino Niederreiter .60 1.50
C162 Eric Staal 1.25 3.00
C163 Tyler Ennis .60 1.50
C164 Jonathan Drouin .75 2.00
C165 Karl Alzner .60 1.50
C166 Alex Galchenyuk .60 1.50
C167 Austin Watson .75 2.00
C168 Viktor Arvidsson .60 1.50
C169 Marcus Johansson .75 2.00
C170 Brian Boyle .60 1.50
C171 Brian Gibbons .60 1.50
C172 Jordan Eberle 1.00 2.50
C173 Calvin de Haan .60 1.50
C174 Johnny Boychuk .75 2.00
C175 Kevin Shattenkirk .60 1.50
C176 Henrik Lundqvist 2.50 6.00
C177 Michael Grabner .60 1.50
C178 Johnny Oduya .75 2.00
C179 Erik Karlsson 1.25 3.00
C180 Derick Brassard .60 1.50
C181 Brian Elliott .75 2.00
C182 Jori Lehtera .60 1.50
C183 Valtteri Filppula .60 1.50
C184 Phil Kessel 1.00 2.50
C185 Conor Sheary 1.00 2.50
C186 Jake Guentzel 1.50 4.00
C187 Brayden Schenn 1.00 2.50
C188 Vladimir Tarasenko 1.25 3.00
C189 Vladimir Sobotka .60 1.50
C190 Victor Hedman 1.25 3.00
C191 Chris Kunitz 1.00 2.50
C192 Ryan Callahan .60 1.50
C193 Mitch Marner 1.50 4.00
C194 Leo Komarov .60 1.50
C195 Nikita Zaitsev .75 2.00
C196 Michael Del Zotto .60 1.50
C197 Alexander Edler .60 1.50
C198 Erik Gudbranson .60 1.50
C199 Marc-Andre Fleury 2.00 5.00
C200 James Neal .60 1.50
C201 Jonathan Marchessault 1.25 3.00
C202 David Perron .75 2.00
C203 Alexander Ovechkin 4.00 10.00
C204 Dmitry Orlov 1.00 2.50
C205 John Carlson 1.00 2.50
C206 Mark Scheifele 1.50 4.00
C207 Steve Mason .75 2.00
C208 Tyler Myers .60 1.50
C209 Shawn Matthias 1.00 2.50
C210 E.Karlsson/V.Hedman CL 1.25 3.00
C211 Nico Hischier YG 30.00 80.00
C212 Jakob Forsbacka-Karlsson YG 6.00 15.00
C213 Filip Chlapik YG 5.00 12.00
C214 Lucas Wallmark YG 6.00 15.00
C215 Robert Hagg YG 6.00 15.00
C216 Vadim Shipachyov YG 8.00 20.00
C217 Michael Amadio YG 6.00 15.00
C218 Eric Comrie YG 5.00 12.00
C219 Nick Merkley YG 6.00 15.00
C220 Alex Formenton YG 6.00 15.00
C221 Josh Ho-Sang YG 8.00 20.00
C222 Christian Jaros YG 5.00 12.00
C223 Brock Boeser YG 20.00 50.00
C224 Jesper Bratt YG 12.00 30.00
C225 Martin Necas YG 12.00 30.00
C226 Alex Iafallo YG 6.00 15.00
C227 Owen Tippett YG 12.00 30.00
C228 Vince Dunn YG 8.00 20.00
C229 Alex Kerfoot YG 12.00 30.00
C230 Luke Kunin YG 6.00 15.00
C231 Henrik Haapala YG 6.00 15.00
C232 Samuel Blais YG 6.00 15.00
C233 Christian Djoos YG 6.00 15.00
C234 Anders Bjork YG 8.00 20.00
C235 John Hayden YG 5.00 12.00
C236 Ville Husso YG 8.00 20.00
C237 Samuel Morin YG 4.00 10.00
C238 Madison Bowey YG 4.00 10.00
C239 Samuel Girard YG 6.00 15.00
C240 N.Hischier/B.Boeser YG CL 5.00 12.00
C241 Jean Beliveau RS 30.00 80.00
C242 Wayne Gretzky RS 60.00 150.00
C243 Pierre Pilote RS 10.00 25.00
C244 Frank Mahovlich RS 15.00 40.00
C245 Brian Propp RS 8.00 20.00
C246 Ed Olczyk RS 8.00 20.00
C247 Rogie Vachon RS 12.00 30.00
C248 Glenn Anderson RS 15.00 40.00
C249 Pavel Bure RS 10.00 25.00
C250 Marcel Dionne RS 12.00 30.00
C251 Tom Barrasso RS 8.00 20.00
C252 Rod Langway RS 10.00 25.00
C253 Alex Delvecchio RS 10.00 25.00
C254 Rod Brind'Amour RS 10.00 25.00
C255 Maurice Richard RS 15.00 40.00
C256 Tyson Jost POE 12.00 30.00
C257 Madison Bowey POE 4.00 10.00
C258 Victor Mete POE 6.00 15.00
C259 Alexandre Carrier POE 5.00 12.00
C260 Josh Ho-Sang POE 8.00 20.00
C261 Samuel Morin POE 4.00 10.00
C262 Chris DiDomenico POE 5.00 12.00
C263 Travis Sanheim POE 6.00 15.00
C264 Haydn Fleury POE 6.00 15.00
C265 Samuel Girard POE 6.00 15.00
C266 Roland McKeown POE 6.00 15.00
C267 Garrett Mitchell POE 6.00 15.00
C268 Pierre-Luc Dubois POE 10.00 25.00
C269 Owen Tippett POE 12.00 30.00
C270 Nolan Patrick POE 12.00 30.00

2017-18 Upper Deck Canvas Autographs

CHL Henrik Lundqvist/30 150.00 300.00

2017-18 Upper Deck Centennial Standouts

CS1 Wayne Gretzky 6.00 15.00
CS2 Duncan Keith .75 2.00
CS3 Patrick Roy 2.50 6.00
CS4 Bobby Orr 4.00 10.00
CS5 Nicklas Lidstrom 1.00 2.50
CS6 Joe Thornton 1.50 4.00
CS7 Paul Coffey 1.00 2.50
CS8 Alexander Ovechkin 4.00 10.00
CS9 Maurice Richard 2.00 5.00
CS10 Darryl Sittler 1.25 3.00
CS11 Mark Messier 2.00 5.00
CS12 Dickie Moore 1.00 2.50
CS13 Grant Fuhr 1.50 4.00
CS14 Jamie Benn 1.00 2.50
CS15 Ryan Getzlaf 1.00 2.50
CS16 Marcel Dionne 1.25 3.00
CS17 Jari Kurri 1.00 2.50
CS18 Phil Esposito 1.50 4.00
CS19 Steve Yzerman 2.50 6.00
CS20 Ed Belfour 1.25 3.00
CS21 Stan Mikita 1.25 3.00
CS22 Daniel Sedin 1.25 3.00
CS23 Henrik Lundqvist 2.50 6.00
CS24 Chris Chelios 1.00 2.50
CS25 Wayne Gretzky 6.00 15.00
CS26 Eddie Shore 1.00 2.50
CS27 Frank Mahovlich 1.00 2.50
CS28 Claude Giroux 1.00 2.50
CS29 Patrik Laine 1.25 3.00
CS30 Martin Brodeur 2.50 6.00
CS31 Carey Price 2.00 5.00
CS32 Jonathan Quick 1.25 3.00
CS33 Henrik Sedin 1.25 3.00
CS34 Auston Matthews 4.00 10.00
CS35 Rod Brind'Amour 1.00 2.50
CS36 Shea Weber .75 2.00
CS37 Syl Apps .75 2.00
CS38 Bobby Orr 4.00 10.00
CS39 Dominik Hasek 1.50 4.00
CS40 Ray Bourque 1.50 4.00
CS41 John Tavares 1.50 4.00
CS42 Syl Apps .75 2.00
CS43 P.K. Subban 1.25 3.00
CS44 Guy Lafleur 1.25 3.00
CS45 Connor McDavid 5.00 12.00
CS46 Patrice Bergeron 1.25 3.00
CS47 Roberto Luongo 1.50 4.00
CS48 Bobby Orr 4.00 10.00
CS49 Jonathan Toews 1.50 4.00
CS50 Maurice Richard 2.00 5.00
CS51 Bill Barilko .75 2.00
CS52 Jarome Iginla 1.25 3.00
CS53 Mark Recchi 1.25 3.00
CS54 Red Kelly 1.00 2.50
CS55 Charlie Conacher .75 2.00
CS56 Jean Beliveau 1.00 2.50
CS57 Drew Doughty 1.25 3.00
CS58 Pierre Pilote 1.00 2.50
CS59 Alex Delvecchio 1.00 2.50
CS60 Steven Stamkos 2.00 5.00
CS61 Corey Perry 1.50 4.00
CS62 Bobby Hull 2.00 5.00
CS63 Nicklas Backstrom 1.00 2.50
CS64 Jean Beliveau 1.00 2.50
CS65 Erik Karlsson 1.25 3.00
CS66 Mario Lemieux 4.00 10.00
CS67 Johnny Bower 1.00 2.50
CS68 Jaromir Jagr 3.00 8.00
CS69 Zdeno Chara 1.00 2.50
CS70 Braden Holtby 1.25 3.00
CS71 Evgeni Malkin 2.00 5.00
CS72 Bobby Clarke 1.50 4.00
CS73 Borje Salming 1.00 2.50
CS74 Denis Potvin 1.00 2.50
CS75 Mario Lemieux 4.00 10.00
CS76 Teemu Selanne 2.00 5.00
CS77 Ray Bourque 1.50 4.00
CS78 Larry Robinson 1.00 2.50
CS79 Guy Lafleur 1.25 3.00
CS80 Mike Gartner 1.25 3.00
CS81 Marian Hossa 1.00 2.50
CS82 Dale Hawerchuk 1.25 3.00
CS83 Mike Bossy 1.00 2.50
CS84 Pat LaFontaine 1.00 2.50
CS85 Brent Burns 1.00 2.50
CS86 Patrick Roy 2.50 6.00
CS87 Sidney Crosby 4.00 10.00
CS88 Patrick Kane 2.00 5.00
CS89 Mike Modano 1.50 4.00
CS90 Brett Hull 2.00 5.00
CS91 Vladimir Tarasenko 1.25 3.00
CS92 Pavel Bure 1.00 2.50
CS93 Doug Gilmour 1.25 3.00
CS94 Mark Messier 2.00 5.00
CS95 Peter Forsberg 2.00 5.00
CS96 Joe Sakic 2.00 5.00
CS97 Connor McDavid 5.00 12.00
CS98 Martin Brodeur 2.50 6.00
CS99 Wayne Gretzky 6.00 15.00
CS100 Mario Lemieux 4.00 10.00

2017-18 Upper Deck Ceremonial Puck Drop

CPD1 Phil Housley 5.00 12.00
CPD2 Ray Bourque 10.00 25.00
CPD3 Igor Larionov 6.00 15.00
CPD4 Mark Recchi 8.00 20.00
CPD5 Mark Messier 12.00 30.00
CPD6 Derek Sanderson 6.00 15.00
CPD7 Bob Probert 6.00 15.00
CPD8 John Vanbiesbrouck 6.00 15.00
CPD9 Maurice Richard 15.00 40.00
CPD10 Bobby Hull
Brett Hull 20.00 50.00
CPD11 M.Lemieux/S.Yzerman 25.00 60.00
CPD12 W.Gretzky/D.Hawerchuk 40.00 100.00

2017-18 Upper Deck Ceremonial Puck Drop Autographs

CPD1 Phil Housley 30.00 80.00
CPD2 Ray Bourque 40.00 100.00
CPD3 Igor Larionov 25.00 60.00
CPD5 Mark Messier 20.00 50.00
CPD6 Derek Sanderson 60.00 150.00

2017-18 Upper Deck Clear Cut

*VETS: 8X TO 20X BASIC CARDS
*YG: 1.5X TO 4X BASIC CARDS
201 Nico Hischier YG 100.00 250.00
202 Kailer Yamamoto YG 150.00 250.00
222 Alexander Nylander YG 80.00 150.00
228 Tage Thompson YG 60.00 150.00
242 Charlie McAvoy YG 100.00 250.00
246 Tyson Jost YG 50.00 125.00
247 Brock Boeser YG 100.00 250.00
250 Nico Hischier
Brock Boeser YG CL 40.00 100.00
454 Adin Hill YG 20.00 50.00
466 Jesper Bratt YG 80.00 200.00
469 Owen Tippett YG 50.00 125.00

2017-18 Upper Deck Clear Cut Foundations

CCF1 R.Rakell/H.Lindholm 10.00 25.00
CCF2 C.Dvorak/O.Ekman-Larsson 12.00 30.00
CCF3 D.Pastrnak/T.Krug 30.00 80.00
CCF4 J.Eichel/R.Ristolainen 20.00 50.00
CCF5 M.Tkachuk/D.Hamilton 25.00 60.00
CCF6 J.Staal/J.Slavin 10.00 25.00
CCF7 C.Crawford/D.Keith 15.00 40.00
CCF8 N.MacKinnon/M.Rantanen 50.00 125.00
CCF9 C.Atkinson/Z.Werenski 20.00 50.00
CCF10 T.Seguin/J.Spezza 15.00 40.00
CCF11 A.Athanasiou/M.Green 12.00 30.00
CCF12 A.Larsson/C.Talbot 12.00 30.00
CCF13 V.Trocheck/J.Huberdeau 15.00 40.00
CCF14 T.Pearson/J.Quick 15.00 40.00
CCF15 E.Staal/D.Dubnyk 15.00 40.00
CCF16 M.Pacioretty/S.Weber 12.00 30.00
CCF17 F.Forsberg/P.Subban 20.00 50.00
CCF18 T.Hall/A.Henrique 12.00 30.00
CCF19 J.Tavares/C.de Haan 20.00 50.00
CCF20 J.Miller/M.Zuccarello 15.00 40.00
CCF21 E.Karlsson/M.Hoffman 15.00 40.00
CCF22 W.Simmonds/I.Provorov 15.00 40.00
CCF23 E.Malkin/K.Letang 25.00 60.00
CCF24 B.Burns/M.Jones 12.00 30.00
CCF25 V.Tarasenko/C.Parayko 15.00 40.00
CCF26 O.Palat/A.Stralman 10.00 25.00
CCF27 A.Matthews/M.Marner 50.00 125.00
CCF28 B.Horvat/J.Markstrom 15.00 40.00
CCF29 T.Oshie/B.Holtby 15.00 40.00
CCF30 P.Laine/N.Ehlers 15.00 40.00

2017-18 Upper Deck Clear Cut Honoured Members

HOF68 Dickie Moore 8.00 20.00
HOF69 Syl Apps 6.00 15.00
HOF70 Phil Housley 15.00 40.00
HOF71 Ace Bailey 8.00 20.00
HOF72 Red Horner 6.00 15.00
HOF73 Pat LaFontaine 15.00 40.00
HOF74 Rogie Vachon 10.00 25.00

2017-18 Upper Deck Clear Cut Superstars

CCSAM Auston Matthews 30.00 80.00
CCSAO Alexander Ovechkin 30.00 80.00
CCSAW Alexander Wennberg 5.00 12.00
CCSBB Brent Burns 8.00 20.00
CCSBM Brad Marchand 15.00 40.00
CCSCM Connor McDavid 40.00 100.00
CCSCP Carey Price 15.00 40.00
CCSCT Cam Talbot 8.00 20.00
CCSDD Devan Dubnyk 6.00 15.00
CCSDK Duncan Keith 6.00 15.00
CCSDP David Pastrnak 20.00 50.00
CCSES Eric Staal 10.00 25.00
CCSHZ Henrik Zetterberg 10.00 25.00
CCSJC Jeff Carter 6.00 15.00
CCSJE Jack Eichel 12.00 30.00
CCSJP Joe Pavelski 10.00 25.00
CCSJV Jakub Voracek 6.00 15.00
CCSLD Leon Draisaitl 25.00 60.00
CCSMG Mikael Granlund 6.00 15.00
CCSMM Mitch Marner 12.00 30.00
CCSMS Mark Scheifele 12.00 30.00
CCSNE Nikolaj Ehlers 8.00 20.00
CCSNK Nikita Kucherov 15.00 40.00
CCSPK Phil Kessel 8.00 20.00
CCSPL Patrik Laine 10.00 25.00
CCSSB Sergei Bobrovsky 12.00 30.00
CCSSC Sidney Crosby 30.00 80.00
CCSSJ Seth Jones 8.00 20.00
CCSSM Sean Monahan 5.00 12.00
CCSTH Taylor Hall 8.00 20.00
CCSTR Tuukka Rask 10.00 25.00
CCSVH Victor Hedman 10.00 25.00

2017-18 Upper Deck Fluorescence

F1 Josh Ho-Sang 4.00 10.00
F2 Tyson Jost 6.00 15.00
F3 Calle Rosen 3.00 8.00
F4 Will Butcher 4.00 10.00
F5 J.T. Compher 3.00 8.00
F6 Colin White 4.00 10.00
F7 Jon Gillies 3.00 8.00
F8 Alex Kerfoot 6.00 15.00
F9 Logan Brown 3.00 8.00
F10 Travis Sanheim 3.00 8.00
F11 Alex Formenton 3.00 8.00
F12 Jake Dotchin 2.50 6.00
F13 Victor Mete 3.00 8.00
F14 Alex Iafallo 3.00 8.00
F15 Nolan Patrick 6.00 15.00
F16 Filip Chytil 3.00 8.00
F17 Luke Kunin 3.00 8.00
F18 Michael Amadio 3.00 8.00
F19 Brock Boeser 8.00 20.00
F20 Vince Dunn 4.00 10.00
F21 Evgeny Svechnikov 6.00 15.00
F22 Kailer Yamamoto 8.00 20.00
F23 Samuel Girard 3.00 8.00
F24 Christian Fischer 4.00 10.00
F25 Haydn Fleury 3.00 8.00
F26 Alex DeBrincat 8.00 20.00
F27 Jakob Forsbacka-Karlsson 3.00 8.00
F28 Martin Necas 10.00 25.00
F29 Samuel Morin 2.00 5.00
F30 Anders Bjork 4.00 10.00
F31 Jack Roslovic 4.00 10.00
F32 Rasmus Andersson 3.00 8.00
F33 Alex Tuch 8.00 20.00
F34 Robert Hagg 3.00 8.00
F35 Janne Kuokkanen 3.00 8.00
F36 Ivan Barbashev 4.00 10.00
F37 Nico Hischier 10.00 25.00
F38 Charlie McAvoy 8.00 20.00
F39 Owen Tippett 6.00 15.00
F40 Christian Djoos 3.00 8.00
F41 Nikita Scherbak 4.00 10.00
F42 Jesper Bratt 6.00 15.00
F43 Tage Thompson 8.00 20.00
F44 Clayton Keller 8.00 20.00
F45 Jake DeBrusk 8.00 20.00
F46 Pierre-Luc Dubois 5.00 12.00
F47 Eric Comrie 2.50 6.00
F48 Madison Bowey 2.00 5.00
F49 Adrian Kempe 6.00 15.00
F50 Alexander Nylander 5.00 12.00

2017-18 Upper Deck Day with The Cup

DC1 Patric Hornqvist 12.00 30.00
DC2 Marc-Andre Fleury 40.00 100.00
DC3 Chad Ruhwedel 12.00 30.00
DC4 Justin Schultz 20.00 50.00
DC5 Jake Guentzel 30.00 80.00
DC6 Trevor Daley 15.00 40.00
DC7 Tom Kuhnhackl 12.00 30.00
DC8 Carter Rowney 15.00 40.00
DC9 Carl Hagelin 12.00 30.00
DC10 Scott Wilson 12.00 30.00
DC11 Olli Maatta 12.00 30.00
DC12 Mark Streit 15.00 40.00
DC13 Kris Letang 25.00 60.00
DC14 Chris Kunitz 20.00 50.00
DC15 Evgeni Malkin 40.00 100.00
DC16 Josh Archibald 12.00 30.00
DC17 Conor Sheary 20.00 50.00
DC18 Bryan Rust 20.00 50.00
DC19 Brian Dumoulin 15.00 40.00
DC20 Matt Murray 30.00 80.00
DC21 Phil Kessel 20.00 50.00
DC22 Ron Hainsey 15.00 40.00
DC23 Matt Cullen 15.00 40.00
DC24 Ian Cole 12.00 30.00
DC25 Nick Bonino 12.00 30.00
DC26 Sidney Crosby 80.00 200.00
DC27 Mario Lemieux 80.00 200.00

2017-18 Upper Deck Game Jerseys

GJAA Artem Anisimov D 2.00 5.00
GJAB Aleksander Barkov E 5.00 12.00
GJAE Aaron Ekblad D 4.00 10.00
GJAG Alex Galchenyuk E 2.00 5.00
GJAH Adam Henrique D 2.50 6.00
GJAK Anze Kopitar D 5.00 12.00
GJAL Andrew Ladd E 2.00 5.00
GJAP Alex Pietrangelo D 2.50 6.00
GJAS Andrew Shaw F 2.00 5.00
GJAT Andreas Athanasiou D 3.00 8.00
GJAV Andrei Vasilevskiy E 5.00 12.00
GJAW Alexander Wennberg F 2.00 5.00
GJBA David Backes F 2.00 5.00
GJBB Brent Burns A 3.00 8.00
GJBH Bo Horvat E 4.00 10.00
GJBJ Boone Jenner F 3.00 8.00
GJBN Brock Nelson E 3.00 8.00
GJBR Derick Brassard E 2.00 5.00
GJBS Brent Seabrook E 2.00 5.00
GJBU Andre Burakovsky F 2.00 5.00
GJBW Blake Wheeler B 3.00 8.00
GJCA Craig Anderson E 3.00 8.00
GJCC Corey Crawford A 4.00 10.00
GJCD Christian Dvorak E 2.50 6.00
GJCP Colton Parayko E 2.50 6.00
GJCS Cory Schneider F 3.00 8.00
GJCT Cam Talbot E 3.00 8.00
GJCW Cam Ward F 3.00 8.00
GJDB Dustin Byfuglien A 3.00 8.00
GJDH Dougie Hamilton C 2.50 6.00
GJDO Louis Domingue E 2.00 5.00
GJDP David Pastrnak D 8.00 20.00
GJEK Evgeny Kuznetsov B 4.00 10.00
GJEL Elias Lindholm F 3.00 8.00
GJES Eric Staal F 4.00 10.00
GJFA Frederik Andersen E 4.00 10.00
GJFN Frans Nielsen E 2.00 5.00
GJGL Gabriel Landeskog E 4.00 10.00
GJIP Ivan Provorov E 2.50 6.00
GJJA Justin Abdelkader E 2.50 6.00
GJJG John Gibson C 3.00 8.00
GJJK John Klingberg D 3.00 8.00
GJJM Jake Muzzin F 3.00 8.00
GJJO Roman Josi E 3.00 8.00
GJJQ Jonathan Quick E 4.00 10.00
GJKL Kris Letang A 20.00 50.00
GJKO Kyle Okposo F 2.00 5.00
GJKP Kyle Palmieri F 2.50 6.00
GJLA Adam Larsson F 3.00 8.00
GJLC Logan Couture F 4.00 10.00
GJLD Leon Draisaitl D 10.00 25.00
GJLE Loui Eriksson B 8.00 20.00
GJMA Max Domi A 25.00 60.00
GJMD Matt Duchene B 8.00 20.00
GJMG Mark Giordano F 3.00 8.00
GJMH Mike Hoffman E 2.00 5.00
GJMJ Martin Jones E 2.50 6.00
GJMK Mikko Koivu E 2.50 6.00
GJML Milan Lucic A 12.00 30.00
GJMM Matt Murray A 12.00 30.00
GJMR Morgan Rielly C 3.00 8.00
GJMS Mark Scheifele D 5.00 12.00
GJMZ Mats Zuccarello B 3.00 8.00
GJNB Nicklas Backstrom B 3.00 8.00
GJNK Nikita Kucherov B 6.00 15.00
GJNL Nick Leddy F 2.00 5.00
GJPK Phil Kessel C 3.00 8.00
GJPR Carey Price B 12.00 30.00
GJRF Robby Fabbri F 2.00 5.00
GJRI Rasmus Ristolainen F 2.00 5.00
GJRJ Ryan Johansen B 2.50 6.00
GJRK Ryan Kesler C 3.00 8.00
GJRR Rickard Rakell D 2.50 6.00
GJRS Ryan Suter E 2.50 6.00
GJSB Sam Bennett F 5.00 12.00
GJSG Shayne Gostisbehere E 3.00 8.00
GJSJ Seth Jones E 3.00 8.00
GJSP Ryan Spooner E 2.50 6.00
GJSR Sam Reinhart E 6.00 15.00
GJSW Shea Weber A 12.00 30.00
GJTA Vladimir Tarasenko D 4.00 10.00
GJTB Tyson Barrie D 2.00 5.00
GJTH Taylor Hall D 3.00 8.00
GJTS Tyler Seguin B 4.00 10.00
GJTT Tyler Toffoli D 3.00 8.00
GJVH Victor Hedman A 12.00 30.00
GJVR Victor Rask F 2.00 5.00
GJVT Vincent Trocheck D 3.00 8.00
GJWS Wayne Simmonds D 4.00 10.00
GJZI Mika Zibanejad F 4.00 10.00

2017-18 Upper Deck NHL Draft

SP1 Nico Hischier 125.00 250.00

2017-18 Upper Deck Oversized

13 Brad Marchand 4.00 10.00
41 Jonathan Toews 3.00 8.00
48 Nathan MacKinnon 8.00 20.00
54 Sergei Bobrovsky 3.00 8.00
75 Leon Draisaitl 6.00 15.00
102 Carey Price 4.00 10.00
146 Evgeni Malkin 4.00 10.00
148 Matt Murray 3.00 8.00
152 Joe Thornton 3.00 8.00
168 Nikita Kucherov 4.00 10.00
170 Auston Matthews 8.00 20.00
183 Marc-Andre Fleury 4.00 10.00
186 Braden Holtby 2.50 6.00
198 Patrik Laine 2.50 6.00
201 Nico Hischier 6.00 15.00
202 Kailer Yamamoto 5.00 12.00
203 Anders Bjork 2.50 6.00
204 Pierre-Luc Dubois 3.00 8.00
205 Josh Ho-Sang 2.50 6.00
206 Jon Gillies 2.00 5.00
207 Lucas Wallmark 2.00 5.00
208 Denis Gurianov 5.00 12.00
210 Adrian Kempe 4.00 10.00
211 John Hayden 1.50 4.00
212 Jake DeBrusk 5.00 12.00
214 Travis Sanheim 2.00 5.00
216 Calle Rosen 2.00 5.00
217 Logan Brown 2.00 5.00
218 Rasmus Andersson 2.00 5.00
221 Alex DeBrincat 5.00 12.00
222 Alexander Nylander 3.00 8.00
224 Evgeny Svechnikov 4.00 10.00
227 Filip Chytil 2.00 5.00
228 Tage Thompson 5.00 12.00
234 Christian Fischer 2.50 6.00
235 Jakob Forsbacka-Karlsson 2.00 5.00
236 Haydn Fleury 2.00 5.00
240 Jack Roslovic 2.50 6.00
245 Victor Mete 2.00 5.00
246 Tyson Jost 4.00 10.00
247 Brock Boeser 15.00 40.00
249 Alex Tuch 5.00 12.00

2017-18 Upper Deck Parkhurst Rookies

PR1 Clayton Keller 2.50 6.00
PR2 Tyson Jost 2.00 5.00
PR3 Nolan Patrick 2.00 5.00
PR4 Charlie McAvoy 2.50 6.00
PR5 Kailer Yamamoto 2.50 6.00
PR6 Nico Hischier 3.00 8.00
PR7 Pierre-Luc Dubois 1.50 4.00
PR8 Filip Chytil 1.00 2.50
PR9 Alex DeBrincat 2.50 6.00
PR10 Josh Ho-Sang 1.25 3.00

2017-18 Upper Deck Rookie Breakouts

RB1 Nico Hischier 30.00 80.00
RB2 Alex Kerfoot 20.00 50.00
RB3 Jesper Bratt 20.00 50.00
RB4 Alex Tuch 25.00 60.00
RB5 Martin Necas 30.00 80.00
RB6 Victor Mete 10.00 25.00
RB7 Luke Kunin 10.00 25.00
RB8 Josh Ho-Sang 12.00 30.00
RB9 Tage Thompson 25.00 60.00
RB10 Haydn Fleury 10.00 25.00
RB11 Alexander Nylander 15.00 40.00
RB12 Brock Boeser 25.00 60.00
RB13 Jake DeBrusk 25.00 60.00
RB14 Adrian Kempe 20.00 50.00
RB15 Charlie McAvoy 25.00 60.00
RB16 Colin White 12.00 30.00
RB17 Will Butcher 12.00 30.00
RB18 Clayton Keller 25.00 60.00
RB19 Nikita Scherbak 12.00 30.00
RB20 Pierre-Luc Dubois 15.00 40.00
RB21 Tyson Jost 20.00 50.00
RB22 Travis Sanheim 10.00 25.00
RB23 Jack Roslovic 12.00 30.00
RB24 Kailer Yamamoto 25.00 60.00
RB25 Logan Brown 10.00 25.00
RB26 Anders Bjork 12.00 30.00
RB27 Alex DeBrincat 25.00 60.00
RB28 Evgeny Svechnikov 20.00 50.00
RB29 Owen Tippett 20.00 50.00
RB30 Nolan Patrick 20.00 50.00

2017-18 Upper Deck Rookie Materials

RMAB Anders Bjork E 4.00 10.00
RMAD Alex DeBrincat C 8.00 20.00
RMAK Adrian Kempe F 6.00 15.00
RMAN Alexander Nylander E 5.00 12.00
RMAT Alex Tuch D 8.00 20.00
RMBB Brock Boeser C 8.00 20.00
RMBR Jesper Bratt D 6.00 15.00
RMCF Christian Fischer D 4.00 10.00
RMCK Clayton Keller C 8.00 20.00
RMCM Charlie McAvoy C 8.00 20.00
RMCW Colin White B 4.00 10.00
RMDG Denis Gurianov D 8.00 20.00
RMES Evgeny Svechnikov E 6.00 15.00
RMGC Gabriel Carlsson F 2.50 6.00
RMHF Haydn Fleury B 3.00 8.00
RMIB Ivan Barbashev D 4.00 10.00
RMJB Jonny Brodzinski F 3.00 8.00
RMJC J.T. Compher D 3.00 8.00
RMJD Jake DeBrusk C 8.00 20.00
RMJF Jakob Forsbacka-Karlsson D 3.00 8.00
RMJG Jon Gillies D 3.00 8.00
RMJH Josh Ho-Sang E 4.00 10.00
RMJK Janne Kuokkanen B 3.00 8.00
RMJR Jack Roslovic B 4.00 10.00
RMJS Jordan Schmaltz F 4.00 10.00
RMKY Kailer Yamamoto A 8.00 20.00
RMLB Logan Brown B 3.00 8.00
RMLW Lucas Wallmark F 3.00 8.00
RMMB Madison Bowey D 2.00 5.00
RMNH Nico Hischier A 10.00 25.00
RMNP Nolan Patrick A 6.00 15.00
RMNS Nikita Scherbak F 4.00 10.00
RMOT Owen Tippett E 6.00 15.00
RMPC Peter Cehlarik F 3.00 8.00
RMPD Pierre-Luc Dubois A 5.00 12.00
RMRB Riley Barber F 3.00 8.00
RMRH Robert Hagg F 3.00 8.00
RMSM Samuel Morin F 2.00 5.00
RMTJ Tyson Jost E 6.00 15.00
RMTS Travis Sanheim F 3.00 8.00
RMTT Tage Thompson E 8.00 20.00
RMVZ Valentin Zykov F 3.00 8.00

2017-18 Upper Deck Shining Stars Centers

SSC1 Auston Matthews 4.00 10.00
SSC2 Alexander Wennberg .60 1.50
SSC3 Connor McDavid 5.00 12.00
SSC4 Jeff Carter .75 2.00
SSC5 Mikael Granlund .75 2.00
SSC6 Mark Scheifele 1.50 4.00
SSC7 Nicklas Backstrom 1.00 2.50
SSC8 Ryan Johansen .75 2.00
SSC9 Sidney Crosby 4.00 10.00
SSC10 Tyler Seguin 1.25 3.00

2017-18 Upper Deck Shining Stars Defensemen

SSD1 Brent Burns 1.00 2.50
SSD2 Dougie Hamilton .75 2.00
SSD3 Duncan Keith .75 2.00
SSD4 Erik Karlsson 1.25 3.00
SSD5 Hampus Lindholm .60 1.50
SSD6 P.K. Subban 1.25 3.00
SSD7 Seth Jones 1.00 2.50
SSD8 Shea Weber .75 2.00
SSD9 Torey Krug .75 2.00
SSD10 Zach Werenski 1.50 4.00

2017-18 Upper Deck Shining Stars Left Wingers

SSL1 Alexander Ovechkin 5.00 12.00
SSL2 Taylor Hall 1.25 3.00
SSL3 Brad Marchand 2.50 6.00
SSL4 Henrik Zetterberg 1.50 4.00
SSL5 James van Riemsdyk 1.00 2.50
SSL6 Johnny Gaudreau 2.00 5.00
SSL7 Jeff Skinner 1.50 4.00
SSL8 Max Pacioretty 1.25 3.00
SSL9 Nikolaj Ehlers 1.25 3.00
SSL10 Viktor Arvidsson .75 2.00

2017-18 Upper Deck Shining Stars Right Wingers

SSR1 Blake Wheeler 1.00 2.50
SSR2 Cam Atkinson 1.00 2.50
SSR3 David Pastrnak 2.50 6.00
SSR4 Jakub Voracek .75 2.00
SSR5 Mats Zuccarello 1.00 2.50
SSR6 Nikita Kucherov 2.00 5.00
SSR7 Nino Niederreiter .60 1.50
SSR8 Patrick Kane 2.00 5.00
SSR9 Patrik Laine 1.25 3.00
SSR10 Vladimir Tarasenko 1.25 3.00

2017-18 Upper Deck Signature Sensations

SSAB Aleksander Barkov B 12.00 30.00
SSAM Anthony Mantha C 6.00 15.00
SSAV Andrei Vasilevskiy A 12.00 30.00
SSBJ Boone Jenner C 8.00 20.00
SSBP Brendan Perlini E 6.00 15.00
SSCA Cam Atkinson B 8.00 20.00
SSCB Connor Brown E 6.00 15.00
SSCD Christian Dvorak E 6.00 15.00
SSCS Conor Sheary E 8.00 20.00
SSEK Evander Kane D 8.00 20.00
SSEL Esa Lindell E 6.00 15.00
SSFV Frank Vatrano E 8.00 20.00
SSGU Jake Guentzel D 15.00 40.00
SSJG John Gibson D 8.00 20.00
SSJM Josh Morrissey D 10.00 25.00
SSMA Michael Matheson D 6.00 15.00
SSMH Mike Hoffman C 5.00 12.00
SSMJ Martin Jones B 12.00 30.00
SSMM Matt Murray A 25.00 60.00
SSMS Mark Scheifele C 15.00 40.00
SSMT Matthew Tkachuk C 15.00 40.00
SSNE Nikolaj Ehlers C 8.00 20.00
SSNN Nino Niederreiter C 5.00 12.00
SSPA Jean-Gabriel Pageau D 5.00 12.00
SSPZ Pavel Zacha E 6.00 15.00
SSRF Radek Faksa E 6.00 15.00
SSRH Ryan Hartman E 5.00 12.00
SSRK Ryan Kesler B 12.00 30.00
SSRP Richard Panik D 5.00 12.00
SSSA Sebastian Aho E 12.00 30.00
SSTH Taylor Hall B 8.00 20.00
SSTS Troy Stecher E 5.00 12.00
SSVA Viktor Arvidsson D 5.00 12.00
SSWS Wayne Simmonds B 10.00 25.00

2017-18 Upper Deck Sophomore Sensations

SOAM Auston Matthews 3.00 8.00
SOJG Jake Guentzel 1.25 3.00
SOMM Mitch Marner 1.25 3.00
SOMT Matthew Tkachuk 1.50 4.00
SOPL Patrik Laine 1.00 2.50
SOWN William Nylander 1.50 4.00

2017-18 Upper Deck Team Triples

TTARI Strome/Keller/Fischer 8.00 20.00
TTAVS Rantanen/Jost/Compher 8.00 20.00
TTBOS Forsbacka-Karlsson McAvoy/Cehlarik 8.00 20.00
TTCGY Andersson/Tkachuk/Gillies 6.00 15.00
TTDET Mantha/Svechnikov/Larkin 6.00 15.00
TTEDM Caggiula/Puljujarvi/Benning 3.00 8.00
TTMTL Lindgren/Scherbak/Lehkonen 4.00 10.00
TTNJD Zacha/Hischier/Wood 10.00 25.00
TTNYI Barzal/Ho-Sang/Beauvillier 4.00 10.00
TTOTT Chabot/White/Englund 4.00 10.00
TTPHI Provorov/Patrick/Konecny 6.00 15.00
TTTOR Marner/Matthews/Nylander 12.00 30.00
TTVAN Stecher/Boeser/Horvat 8.00 20.00
TTJETS Comrie/Laine/Roslovic 4.00 10.00
TTPENS Rowney/Guentzel/Dea 5.00 12.00

2017-18 Upper Deck The Second Six

S61 Bob Baun 8.00 20.00
S62 Charlie Simmer 5.00 12.00
S63 Marcel Dionne 10.00 25.00
S64 Dave Taylor 6.00 15.00
S65 Wayne Gretzky 50.00 125.00
S66 Bob Rouse 6.00 15.00
S67 Larry Murphy 6.00 15.00
S68 Mike Modano 12.00 30.00
S69 Bobby Clarke 12.00 30.00
S610 Rod Brind'Amour 8.00 20.00
S611 Claude Giroux 8.00 20.00
S612 Mario Lemieux 30.00 80.00
S613 Jaromir Jagr 25.00 60.00
S614 Sidney Crosby 30.00 80.00
S615 Evgeni Malkin 15.00 40.00
S616 Brett Hull 15.00 40.00
S617 Alex Pietrangelo 6.00 15.00
S618 Vladimir Tarasenko 10.00 25.00

2017-18 Upper Deck UD Portraits

P1 Nicklas Backstrom .60 1.50
P2 Shea Weber .50 1.25
P3 Daniel Sedin .75 2.00
P4 Max Domi .60 1.50
P5 Artem Anisimov .40 1.00
P6 Rasmus Ristolainen .40 1.00
P7 Gustav Nyquist .40 1.00
P8 Dougie Hamilton .50 1.25
P9 Jack Eichel 1.00 2.50
P10 Marc-Edouard Vlasic .40 1.00
P11 Taylor Hall .60 1.50
P12 Jakub Voracek .50 1.25
P13 Mitch Marner 1.00 2.50
P14 Mike Hoffman .40 1.00
P15 Jaden Schwartz .75 2.00
P16 Patrick Kane 1.25 3.00
P17 Sergei Bobrovsky 1.00 2.50
P18 Jonathan Huberdeau .75 2.00
P19 Jaccob Slavin .50 1.25
P20 Vladimir Tarasenko .75 2.00
P21 Leon Draisaitl 2.00 5.00
P22 Filip Forsberg 1.00 2.50
P23 Eric Staal .75 2.00
P24 Ryan McDonagh .40 1.00
P25 John Tavares 1.00 2.50
P26 P.K. Subban .75 2.00
P27 Vincent Trocheck .60 1.50
P28 Max Pacioretty .60 1.50
P29 Mikko Rantanen 1.50 4.00
P30 J.T. Miller .75 2.00
P31 Patrik Laine .75 2.00
P32 Zach Werenski 1.00 2.50
P33 David Krejci .60 1.50
P34 Hampus Lindholm .40 1.00
P35 Sebastian Aho 1.00 2.50
P36 Josh Bailey .50 1.25
P37 Devan Dubnyk .50 1.25
P38 Erik Karlsson .75 2.00
P39 Ryan Getzlaf .60 1.50
P40 Sean Couturier .50 1.25
P41 Tyler Seguin .75 2.00
P42 Patrick Maroon .50 1.25
P43 Brad Marchand 1.25 3.00
P44 Jonathan Toews 1.00 2.50
P45 Nazem Kadri .75 2.00
P46 Carey Price 1.25 3.00
P47 Jeff Carter .50 1.25
P48 Matthew Tkachuk 1.25 3.00
P49 Brent Burns .60 1.50
P50 Auston Matthews 2.50 6.00
P51 Evgeni Malkin 1.25 3.00
P52 Alexander Ovechkin 2.50 6.00
P53 Connor McDavid 3.00 8.00
P54 Sidney Crosby 2.50 6.00
P55 Tyson Jost 3.00 8.00
P56 Josh Ho-Sang 2.00 5.00
P57 Alexander Nylander 2.50 6.00
P58 Brock Boeser 4.00 10.00
P59 Charlie McAvoy 4.00 10.00
P60 Clayton Keller 4.00 10.00
P61 Nolan Patrick 3.00 8.00
P62 Nikita Scherbak 2.00 5.00
P63 Jon Gillies 1.50 4.00
P64 Denis Gurianov 4.00 10.00
P65 Logan Brown 1.50 4.00
P66 Alex Tuch 4.00 10.00
P67 Ivan Barbashev 2.00 5.00
P68 Riley Barber 1.50 4.00
P69 Will Butcher 2.00 5.00
P70 Pierre-Luc Dubois 2.50 6.00
P71 Tucker Poolman 1.25 3.00
P72 Jake Dotchin 1.25 3.00
P73 Jesper Bratt 3.00 8.00
P74 Jake DeBrusk 4.00 10.00
P75 Samuel Morin 1.00 2.50
P76 Alex Kerfoot 3.00 8.00
P77 Marcus Sorensen 1.25 3.00
P78 Alex Formenton 1.50 4.00
P79 Rasmus Andersson 1.50 4.00
P80 Carter Rowney 1.25 3.00
P81 Nathan Walker 1.50 4.00
P82 Victor Mete 1.50 4.00
P83 Vladislav Kamenev 1.50 4.00
P84 C.J. Smith 1.25 3.00
P85 Colin White 2.00 5.00
P86 Luke Kunin 1.50 4.00
P87 Alex DeBrincat 4.00 10.00
P88 Christian Fischer 2.00 5.00
P89 Giovanni Fiore 1.50 4.00
P90 Haydn Fleury 1.50 4.00
P91 J.T. Compher 1.50 4.00
P92 Tage Thompson 4.00 10.00
P93 Owen Tippett 3.00 8.00
P94 Evgeny Svechnikov 3.00 8.00
P95 Kailer Yamamoto 4.00 10.00
P96 Travis Sanheim 1.50 4.00
P97 Vince Dunn 2.00 5.00
P98 Jack Roslovic 2.00 5.00
P99 Valentin Zykov 1.50 4.00
P100 Adrian Kempe 3.00 8.00
P101 Anders Bjork 2.00 5.00
P102 Calle Rosen 1.50 4.00
P103 Andreas Borgman 1.50 4.00
P104 Eric Comrie 1.25 3.00
P105 Filip Chytil 1.50 4.00
P106 Janne Kuokkanen 1.50 4.00
P107 Martin Necas 5.00 12.00
P108 Robert Hagg 1.50 4.00
P109 Jakob Forsbacka-Karlsson 1.50 4.00
P110 Nico Hischier 5.00 12.00

2017-18 Upper Deck Winter Classic Jumbo

WC1 Vladimir Tarasenko 2.50 6.00
WC2 Artemi Panarin 4.00 10.00
WC3 Robby Fabbri 1.25 3.00
WC4 Duncan Keith 1.50 4.00
WC5 Jake Allen 2.00 5.00
WC6 Patrick Kane 4.00 10.00
WC7 Alex Pietrangelo 1.50 4.00
WC8 Michal Kempny 1.50 4.00
WC9 Jay Bouwmeester 1.25 3.00
WC10 Corey Crawford 2.50 6.00
WC11 Paul Stastny 1.50 4.00
WC12 Jonathan Toews 3.00 8.00
WC13 Colton Parayko 1.50 4.00
WC14 Artem Anisimov 1.25 3.00

2018-19 Upper Deck

1 Adam Henrique .25 .60
2 Ryan Getzlaf .30 .75
3 John Gibson .30 .75
4 Cam Fowler .30 .75
5 Brandon Montour .40 1.00
6 Rickard Rakell .25 .60
7 Clayton Keller .40 1.00
8 Jakob Chychrun .30 .75
9 Oliver Ekman-Larsson .30 .75
10 Antti Raanta .30 .75
11 Christian Dvorak .25 .60
12 Jason Demers .25 .60
13 Charlie McAvoy .40 1.00
14 David Backes .20 .50
15 Jake DeBrusk .30 .75
16 Torey Krug .25 .60
17 Brandon Carlo .25 .60
18 Danton Heinen .25 .60
19 Patrice Bergeron .40 1.00
20 Kyle Okposo .20 .50
21 Sam Reinhart .60 1.50
22 Zemgus Girgensons .25 .60
23 Rasmus Ristolainen .20 .50
24 Jason Pominville .20 .50
25 Jack Eichel .50 1.25
26 Travis Hamonic .25 .60
27 Mike Smith .25 .60
28 Sam Bennett .50 1.25
29 Mikael Backlund .25 .60
30 T.J. Brodie .25 .60
31 Johnny Gaudreau .50 1.25
32 Jaccob Slavin .25 .60
33 Justin Williams .25 .60
34 Haydn Fleury .20 .50
35 Sebastian Aho .50 1.25
36 Victor Rask .20 .50
37 Jordan Staal .25 .60
38 Brandon Saad .25 .60
39 Corey Crawford .25 .60
40 Alex DeBrincat .40 1.00
41 Nick Schmaltz .25 .60
42 Patrick Kane .60 1.50
43 Artem Anisimov .20 .50
44 Colin Wilson .25 .60
45 Erik Johnson .20 .50
46 Alex Kerfoot .25 .60
47 Semyon Varlamov .30 .75
48 Carl Soderberg .20 .50
49 Samuel Girard .20 .50
50 Nathan MacKinnon 1.25 3.00
51 Pierre-Luc Dubois .25 .60
52 Sergei Bobrovsky .50 1.25
53 Seth Jones .30 .75
54 Cam Atkinson .30 .75
55 David Savard .20 .50
56 Sonny Milano .25 .60
57 Nick Foligno .25 .60
58 Jason Spezza .30 .75
59 John Klingberg .30 .75
60 Ben Bishop .25 .60
61 Radek Faksa .25 .60
62 Stephen Johns .20 .50
63 Jamie Benn .30 .75
64 Henrik Zetterberg .40 1.00
65 Danny DeKeyser .20 .50
66 Justin Abdelkader .25 .60
67 Anthony Mantha .25 .60
68 Trevor Daley .25 .60
69 Jim Howard .40 1.00
70 Ryan Nugent-Hopkins .40 1.00
71 Oscar Klefbom .25 .60
72 Jesse Puljujarvi .30 .75
73 Pontus Aberg .20 .50
74 Cam Talbot .30 .75
75 Connor McDavid 1.50 4.00
76 Leon Draisaitl 1.00 2.50
77 Jonathan Huberdeau .40 1.00
78 Evgenii Dadonov .20 .50
79 Nick Bjugstad .20 .50
80 James Reimer .30 .75
81 Aaron Ekblad .40 1.00
82 Michael Matheson .25 .60
83 Dustin Brown .30 .75
84 Alec Martinez .25 .60
85 Adrian Kempe .30 .75
86 Tanner Pearson .25 .60
87 Anze Kopitar .50 1.25
88 Dion Phaneuf .25 .60
89 Jonas Brodin .20 .50
90 Eric Staal .30 .75
91 Mikko Koivu .30 .75
92 Devan Dubnyk .25 .60
93 Zach Parise .30 .75
94 Jared Spurgeon .30 .75
95 Jeff Petry .30 .75
96 Karl Alzner .20 .50
97 Andrew Shaw .20 .50
98 Jonathan Drouin .25 .60
99 Carey Price .60 1.50
100 Brendan Gallagher .30 .75
101 Kyle Turris .25 .60
102 Calle Jarnkrok .20 .50
103 Pekka Rinne .30 .75
104 Roman Josi .30 .75
105 Kevin Fiala .25 .60
106 Mattias Ekholm .25 .60
107 Ryan Johansen .25 .60
108 Brian Boyle .25 .60
109 Sami Vatanen .20 .50
110 Nico Hischier .50 1.25
111 Miles Wood .20 .50
112 Will Butcher .25 .60
113 Pavel Zacha .25 .60
114 Andrew Ladd .20 .50
115 Anthony Beauvillier .20 .50
116 Nick Leddy .20 .50
117 Jordan Eberle .30 .75
118 Mathew Barzal .40 1.00
119 Anders Lee .25 .60
120 Brady Skjei .25 .60
121 Pavel Buchnevich .25 .60
122 Vladislav Namestnikov .20 .50
123 Mats Zuccarello .30 .75
124 Mika Zibanejad .40 1.00
125 Kevin Shattenkirk .20 .50
126 Thomas Chabot .30 .75
127 Mark Stone .40 1.00
128 Jean-Gabriel Pageau .20 .50
129 Craig Anderson .25 .60
130 Zack Smith .20 .50
131 Mark Borowiecki .20 .50
132 Shayne Gostisbehere .30 .75
133 Travis Konecny .30 .75
134 Nolan Patrick .30 .75
135 Sean Couturier .25 .60
136 Ivan Provorov .25 .60
137 Jori Lehtera .20 .50
138 Claude Giroux .30 .75
139 Derick Brassard .20 .50
140 Riley Sheahan .20 .50
141 Evgeni Malkin .60 1.50
142 Patric Hornqvist .20 .50
143 Justin Schultz .25 .60
144 Kris Letang .40 1.00
145 Matt Murray .30 .75
146 Kevin Labanc .20 .50
147 Logan Couture .40 1.00
148 Evander Kane .30 .75
149 Timo Meier .30 .75
150 Marc-Edouard Vlasic .20 .50
151 Martin Jones .25 .60
152 Jaden Schwartz .40 1.00
153 Colton Parayko .25 .60
154 Vladimir Tarasenko .40 1.00
155 Alexander Steen .20 .50
156 Joel Edmundson .20 .50
157 Brayden Schenn .30 .75
158 Dmitrij Jaskin .20 .50
159 Steven Stamkos .60 1.50
160 Andrei Vasilevskiy .50 1.25
161 Ryan McDonagh .20 .50
162 Ondrej Palat .25 .60
163 Brayden Point .40 1.00
164 Mikhail Sergachev .25 .60
165 Anton Stralman .25 .60
166 Morgan Rielly .30 .75
167 Frederik Andersen .40 1.00
168 Patrick Marleau .30 .75
169 Nikita Zaitsev .25 .60
170 Connor Brown .25 .60
171 Mitch Marner .50 1.25
172 Jacob Markstrom .30 .75
173 Alexander Edler .20 .50
174 Erik Gudbranson .20 .50
175 Sven Baertschi .25 .60
176 Michael Del Zotto .25 .60
177 Brock Boeser .40 1.00
178 Alex Tuch .30 .75
179 Jonathan Marchessault .40 1.00
180 Tomas Tatar .20 .50
181 Reilly Smith .30 .75
182 Colin Miller .20 .50
183 Erik Haula .20 .50
184 Marc-Andre Fleury .60 1.50
185 Nicklas Backstrom .30 .75
186 Matt Niskanen .25 .60
187 Braden Holtby .40 1.00
188 Lars Eller .20 .50
189 Dmitry Orlov .30 .75
190 Andre Burakovsky .20 .50
191 Alexander Ovechkin 1.25 3.00
192 Dustin Byfuglien .30 .75
193 Connor Hellebuyck .60 1.50
194 Kyle Connor .50 1.25
195 Jack Roslovic .20 .50
196 Tyler Myers .20 .50
197 Mathieu Perreault .20 .50
198 Blake Wheeler .30 .75
199 M.Fleury/C.Hellebuyck CL .60 1.50
200 S.Stamkos/A.Ovechkin CL 1.25 3.00
201 Rasmus Dahlin YG RC 12.00 30.00
202 Roope Hintz YG RC 8.00 20.00
203 Mikhail Vorobyev YG RC 2.50 6.00
204 Morgan Klimchuk YG RC 3.00 8.00
205 Adam Gaudette YG RC 5.00 12.00
206 Maxim Mamin YG RC 3.00 8.00
207 Dillon Dube YG RC 4.00 10.00
208 Michael Dal Colle YG RC 3.00 8.00
209 Shane Gersich YG RC 2.50 6.00
210 Mackenzie Blackwood YG RC 6.00 15.00
211 Louie Belpedio YG RC 2.50 6.00
212 Neal Pionk YG RC 3.00 8.00
213 Jordan Greenway YG RC 3.00 8.00
214 Filip Hronek YG RC 3.00 8.00
215 Brett Howden YG RC 4.00 10.00
216 Max Comtois YG RC 8.00 20.00
217 Eeli Tolvanen YG RC 6.00 15.00
218 Oskar Lindblom YG RC 5.00 12.00
219 Anthony Cirelli YG RC 5.00 12.00
220 Kiefer Sherwood YG RC 2.50 6.00
221 Evan Bouchard YG RC 12.00 30.00
222 Austin Wagner YG RC 2.50 6.00
223 Max Lajoie YG RC 5.00 12.00
224 Tomas Hyka YG RC 3.00 8.00
225 Ryan Donato YG RC 5.00 12.00
226 Michael Rasmussen YG RC 4.00 10.00
227 Libor Sulak YG RC 2.50 6.00
228 Travis Dermott YG RC 5.00 12.00
229 Marcus Pettersson YG RC 3.00 8.00
230 Henri Jokiharju YG RC 6.00 15.00
231 Dennis Cholowski YG RC 6.00 15.00
232 Dominik Kahun YG RC 3.00 8.00
233 Nick Seeler YG RC 2.50 6.00
234 Christoffer Ehn YG RC 2.50 6.00
235 Trevor Murphy YG RC 2.50 6.00
236 Warren Foegele YG RC 3.00 8.00
237 Zach Whitecloud YG RC 2.50 6.00
238 Antti Suomela YG RC 2.50 6.00
239 Troy Terry YG RC 5.00 12.00
240 Sheldon Dries YG RC 2.50 6.00
241 Jordan Kyrou YG RC 6.00 15.00
242 Samuel Montembeault YG RC 10.00 25.00
243 Par Lindholm YG RC 3.00 8.00
244 Kristian Vesalainen YG RC 4.00 10.00
245 Luke Johnson YG RC 2.50 6.00
246 Miro Heiskanen YG RC 10.00 25.00
247 Igor Ozhiganov YG RC 2.50 6.00
248 Elias Pettersson YG RC 30.00 80.00
249 Jesperi Kotkaniemi YG RC 6.00 15.00
250 R.Dahlin/Elias P.YG CL 4.00 10.00
251 Corey Perry .50 1.25
252 Jakob Silfverberg .20 .50
253 Hampus Lindholm .20 .50
254 Josh Manson .20 .50
255 Ryan Miller .30 .75
256 Andrew Cogliano .20 .50
257 Derek Stepan .20 .50
258 Brad Richardson .20 .50
259 Niklas Hjalmarsson .20 .50
260 Alex Galchenyuk .20 .50
261 Christian Fischer .20 .50
262 Vincent Hinostroza .25 .60
263 Michael Grabner .20 .50
264 Richard Panik .20 .50
265 Brad Marchand .60 1.50
266 David Pastrnak .75 2.00
267 Tuukka Rask .40 1.00
268 David Krejci .30 .75
269 Zdeno Chara .30 .75
270 Zach Bogosian .25 .60
271 Carter Hutton .25 .60
272 Jeff Skinner .40 1.00
273 Patrik Berglund .20 .50
274 Conor Sheary .30 .75
275 Vladimir Sobotka .25 .60
276 Michael Frolik .25 .60
277 Sean Monahan .20 .50
278 Matthew Tkachuk .60 1.50
279 James Neal .20 .50
280 Noah Hanifin .30 .75
281 Mark Giordano .30 .75
282 Elias Lindholm .30 .75
283 Petr Mrazek .30 .75
284 Curtis McElhinney .20 .50
285 Justin Faulk .25 .60
286 Dougie Hamilton .25 .60
287 Teuvo Teravainen .30 .75
288 Calvin de Haan .20 .50
289 Brett Pesce .20 .50
290 Micheal Ferland .20 .50
291 Marcus Kruger .20 .50
292 Brent Seabrook .20 .50
293 Jonathan Toews .50 1.25
294 Duncan Keith .25 .60
295 Chris Kunitz .25 .60
296 Cam Ward .30 .75
297 Tyson Jost .25 .60
298 Gabriel Landeskog .40 1.00
299 Mikko Rantanen .75 2.00
300 Tyson Barrie .20 .50
301 Philipp Grubauer .30 .75
302 Ian Cole .20 .50
303 Oliver Bjorkstrand .25 .60
304 Zach Werenski .50 1.25
305 Artemi Panarin .60 1.50
306 Alexander Wennberg .20 .50
307 Ryan Murray .25 .60
308 Boone Jenner .30 .75
309 Mattias Janmark .20 .50
310 Tyler Seguin .40 1.00
311 Alexander Radulov .30 .75
312 Marc Methot .20 .50
313 Valeri Nichushkin .30 .75
314 Connor Carrick .20 .50
315 Dylan Larkin .40 1.00
316 Andreas Athanasiou .25 .60

317 Jonathan Bernier .25 .60
318 Mike Green .25 .60
319 Niklas Kronwall .25 .60
320 Gustav Nyquist .20 .50
321 Frans Nielsen .20 .50
322 Milan Lucic .25 .60
323 Adam Larsson .30 .75
324 Darnell Nurse .25 .60
325 Mikko Koskinen .20 .50
326 Tobias Rieder .20 .50
327 Ryan Spooner .25 .60
328 Derek MacKenzie .20 .50
329 Mike Hoffman .20 .50
330 Roberto Luongo .50 1.25
331 Aleksander Barkov .50 1.25
332 Keith Yandle .20 .50
333 Vincent Trocheck .30 .75
334 Jeff Carter .25 .60
335 Ilya Kovalchuk .25 .60
336 Jonathan Quick .40 1.00
337 Drew Doughty .40 1.00
338 Jake Muzzin .30 .75
339 Tyler Toffoli .30 .75
340 Joel Eriksson Ek .25 .60
341 Ryan Suter .25 .60
342 Mikael Granlund .25 .60
343 Jason Zucker .30 .75
344 Matt Dumba .20 .50
345 Nino Niederreiter .20 .50
346 Charlie Coyle .30 .75
347 Phillip Danault .30 .75
348 Max Domi .30 .75
349 Artturi Lehkonen .25 .60
350 Tomas Tatar .20 .50
351 Mike Reilly .20 .50
352 Ryan Ellis .25 .60
353 Nick Bonino .20 .50
354 Filip Forsberg .50 1.25
355 P.K. Subban .40 1.00
356 Juuse Saros .40 1.00
357 Viktor Arvidsson .20 .50
358 Marcus Johansson .25 .60
359 Kyle Palmieri .25 .60
360 Blake Coleman .25 .60
361 Taylor Hall .30 .75
362 Travis Zajac .20 .50
363 Cory Schneider .30 .75
364 Keith Kinkaid .20 .50
365 Thomas Greiss .25 .60
366 Robin Lehner .25 .60
367 Valtteri Filppula .20 .50
368 Leo Komarov .20 .50
369 Josh Bailey .25 .60
370 Brock Nelson .30 .75
371 Ryan Pulock .25 .60
372 Adam McQuaid .20 .50
373 Brendan Smith .20 .50
374 Henrik Lundqvist .75 2.00
375 Kevin Hayes .25 .60
376 Chris Kreider .40 1.00
377 Ryan Strome .30 .75
378 Jimmy Vesey .25 .60
379 Colin White .20 .50
380 Ryan Dzingel .25 .60
381 Bobby Ryan .25 .60
382 Cody Ceci .20 .50
383 Matt Duchene .30 .75
384 Mikkel Boedker .20 .50
385 Robert Hagg .20 .50
386 Radko Gudas .25 .60
387 James van Riemsdyk .25 .60
388 Jakub Voracek .25 .60
389 Wayne Simmonds .30 .75
390 Brian Elliott .25 .60
391 Dominik Simon .20 .50
392 Sidney Crosby 1.25 3.00
393 Jack Johnson .20 .50
394 Jake Guentzel .50 1.25
395 Olli Maatta .20 .50
396 Phil Kessel .30 .75
397 Brian Dumoulin .20 .50
398 Erik Karlsson .40 1.00
399 Brent Burns .30 .75
400 Joe Pavelski .40 1.00
401 Joe Thornton .50 1.25
402 Tomas Hertl .30 .75
403 Justin Braun .25 .60
404 Joonas Donskoi .20 .50
405 David Perron .25 .60
406 Ryan O'Reilly .30 .75
407 Tyler Bozak .20 .50
408 Patrick Maroon .25 .60
409 Robby Fabbri .20 .50
410 Alex Pietrangelo .25 .60
411 Jake Allen .30 .75
412 Nikita Kucherov .60 1.50
413 Victor Hedman .40 1.00
414 Tyler Johnson .20 .50
415 J.T. Miller .40 1.00
416 Yanni Gourde .25 .60
417 Alex Killorn .20 .50
418 Auston Matthews 1.25 3.00
419 John Tavares .50 1.25
420 Nazem Kadri .40 1.00
421 Jake Gardiner .20 .50
422 Kasperi Kapanen .25 .60
423 Brandon Sutter .20 .50
424 Jake Virtanen .25 .60
425 Bo Horvat .40 1.00
426 Antoine Roussel .20 .50
427 Jay Beagle .20 .50
428 Christopher Tanev .20 .50
429 Loui Eriksson .20 .50
430 Max Pacioretty .30 .75
431 Paul Stastny .25 .60
432 Brayden McNabb .20 .50
433 William Karlsson .40 1.00
434 Nate Schmidt .25 .60
435 Shea Theodore .40 1.00
436 Cody Eakin .20 .50
437 Evgeny Kuznetsov .40 1.00
438 John Carlson .30 .75
439 Tom Wilson .30 .75
440 T.J. Oshie .30 .75
441 Brett Connolly .20 .50
442 Michal Kempny .30 .75
443 Mark Scheifele .50 1.25
444 Nikolaj Ehlers .30 .75
445 Jacob Trouba .25 .60
446 Patrik Laine .40 1.00
447 Adam Lowry .25 .60
448 Bryan Little .20 .50
449 P.Subban/J.Tavares CL .50 1.25
450 N.Hanifin/D.Hamilton CL .30 .75
451 Andrei Svechnikov YG RC 12.00 30.00
452 Nicolas Aube-Kubel YG RC 2.50 6.00
453 Casey Mittelstadt YG RC 6.00 15.00
454 Jaret Anderson-Dolan YG RC 2.50 6.00
455 Erik Cernak YG RC 2.50 6.00
456 Jeremy Lauzon YG RC 4.00 10.00
457 John Gilmour YG RC 2.00 5.00
458 Sheldon Rempal YG RC 2.50 6.00
459 Eric Robinson YG RC 2.50 6.00
460 Christian Wolanin YG RC 2.50 6.00
461 Henrik Borgstrom YG RC 5.00 12.00
462 Matt Luff YG RC 2.50 6.00
463 Ilya Samsonov YG RC 8.00 20.00
464 Matthew Highmore YG RC 3.00 8.00
465 Jacob MacDonald YG RC 2.50 6.00
466 Isac Lundestrom YG RC 2.50 6.00
467 Gavin Bayreuther YG RC 2.50 6.00
468 Urho Vaakanainen YG RC 6.00 15.00
469 Joe Hicketts YG RC 3.00 8.00
470 Spencer Foo YG RC 2.50 6.00
471 Cal Petersen YG RC 2.50 6.00
472 Robert Thomas YG RC 10.00 25.00
473 Joey Anderson YG RC 3.00 8.00
474 Sami Niku YG RC 2.50 6.00
475 Cooper Marody YG RC 3.00 8.00
476 Nicolas Roy YG RC 2.00 5.00
477 Juuso Valimaki YG RC 3.00 8.00
478 Steven Fogarty YG RC 2.50 6.00
479 Ethan Bear YG RC 5.00 12.00
480 Brett Seney YG RC 2.50 6.00
481 Victor Ejdsell YG RC 2.50 6.00
482 Noah Juulsen YG RC 3.00 8.00
483 Mathieu Joseph YG RC 3.00 8.00
484 Drake Batherson YG RC 8.00 20.00
485 Juho Lammikko YG RC 2.50 6.00
486 Dominic Turgeon YG RC 3.00 8.00
487 Sam Steel YG RC 3.00 8.00
488 Dylan Gambrell YG RC 3.00 8.00
489 Dylan Sikura YG RC 4.00 10.00
490 Alexandre Fortin YG RC 2.50 6.00
491 Carter Hart YG RC 6.00 15.00
492 Andreas Johnsson YG RC 4.00 10.00
493 Dan Vladar YG RC 4.00 10.00
494 Clark Bishop YG RC 2.50 6.00
495 Rourke Chartier YG RC 2.50 6.00
496 Zach Aston-Reese YG RC 5.00 12.00
497 Lias Andersson YG RC 5.00 12.00
498 Jakub Zboril YG RC 5.00 12.00
499 Brady Tkachuk YG RC 25.00 60.00
500 A.Svechnikov/B.Tkachuk YG CL 5.00 12.00
501 Tanner Pearson .25 .60
502 Carl Hagelin .20 .50
503 Nick Schmaltz .25 .60
504 Dylan Strome .40 1.00
505 Brendan Perlini .20 .50
506 Daniel Sprong .20 .50
507 Nino Niederreiter .20 .50
508 Drake Caggiula .25 .60
509 Victor Rask .20 .50
510 Andrew Cogliano .20 .50
511 Nick Bjugstad .20 .50
512 Michael McLeod YG RC 2.50 6.00
513 Jake Bean YG RC 3.00 8.00
514 Josh Mahura YG RC 2.50 6.00
515 Juuso Riikola YG RC 2.50 6.00
516 Mason Appleton YG RC 2.50 6.00
517 Jayce Hawryluk YG RC 2.50 6.00
518 Lawrence Pilut YG RC 2.50 6.00
519 Collin Delia YG RC 3.00 8.00
520 Sidney Crosby AS 8.00 20.00
521 Jack Eichel AS 3.00 8.00
522 Mike Smith AS 1.50 4.00
523 Nikita Kucherov AS 4.00 10.00
524 Pekka Rinne AS 2.00 5.00
525 Connor McDavid AS 10.00 25.00
526 P.K. Subban AS 2.50 6.00
527 Alexander Ovechkin AS 8.00 20.00
528 Brock Boeser AS 2.50 6.00
529 Willie O'Ree AS 2.50 6.00
SM Stan Mikita 3.00 8.00
SP1A Rasmus Dahlin SP 25.00 60.00
SPGRA Gritty 12.00 30.00

2018-19 Upper Deck Exclusives

*VETS/100: 3X TO 8X BASIC CARDS
*ROOKIES: 2.5X TO 6X BASIC CARDS

201 Rasmus Dahlin YG 200.00 500.00
221 Evan Bouchard YG 125.00 300.00
228 Travis Dermott YG 60.00 150.00
231 Dennis Cholowski YG 30.00 80.00
239 Troy Terry YG 40.00 100.00
241 Jordan Kyrou YG 80.00 200.00
246 Miro Heiskanen YG 50.00 125.00
248 Elias Pettersson YG 300.00 800.00
249 Jesperi Kotkaniemi YG 40.00 100.00
451 Andrei Svechnikov YG 125.00 300.00
472 Robert Thomas YG 60.00 150.00
484 Drake Batherson YG 80.00 200.00
491 Carter Hart YG 40.00 100.00
492 Andreas Johnsson YG 50.00 125.00

2018-19 Upper Deck Fanimation

F1 Steven Stamkos 30.00 80.00
F2 Sebastian Aho 20.00 50.00
F3 Vladimir Tarasenko 15.00 40.00
F4 Tyler Seguin 15.00 40.00
F5 Auston Matthews 50.00 125.00
F6 Claude Giroux 12.00 30.00
F7 Aleksander Barkov 20.00 50.00
F8 Brock Boeser 15.00 40.00
F9 Connor McDavid 80.00 200.00
F10 Johnny Gaudreau 20.00 50.00
F11 Jack Eichel 20.00 50.00
F12 Ryan Getzlaf 12.00 30.00
F13 Jonathan Quick 15.00 40.00
F14 P.K. Subban 15.00 40.00
F15 Marc-Andre Fleury 60.00 150.00
F16 Mathew Barzal 15.00 40.00
F17 Nathan MacKinnon 50.00 125.00
F18 Clayton Keller 15.00 40.00
F19 Sergei Bobrovsky 20.00 50.00
F20 Patrice Bergeron 15.00 40.00
F21 Nico Hischier 20.00 50.00
F22 Henrik Lundqvist 30.00 80.00
F23 Sidney Crosby 50.00 125.00
F24 Blake Wheeler 12.00 30.00
F25 Henrik Zetterberg 15.00 40.00
F26 Mikko Koivu 12.00 30.00
F27 Patrick Kane 25.00 60.00
F28 Thomas Chabot 12.00 30.00
F29 Joe Thornton 20.00 50.00
F30 Carey Price 25.00 60.00
F31 Alex Ovechkin 50.00 120.00

2018-19 Upper Deck 25 Under 25

U251 Connor McDavid 2.00 5.00
U252 Mathew Barzal .50 1.25
U253 Nathan MacKinnon 1.50 4.00
U254 Sean Monahan .25 .60
U255 Mikko Rantanen 1.00 2.50
U256 Aleksander Barkov .60 1.50
U257 Leon Draisaitl 1.25 3.00
U258 Jack Eichel .60 1.50
U259 David Pastrnak 1.00 2.50
U2510 Patrik Laine .50 1.25
U2511 Nico Hischier .60 1.50
U2512 Brock Boeser .50 1.25
U2513 Nolan Patrick .40 1.00
U2514 Dylan Larkin .50 1.25
U2515 Nikolaj Ehlers .40 1.00
U2516 Filip Forsberg .60 1.50
U2517 Matthew Tkachuk .75 2.00
U2518 Brayden Point .50 1.25
U2519 Sebastian Aho .60 1.50
U2520 Andrei Vasilevskiy .60 1.50
U2521 Clayton Keller .50 1.25
U2522 Mitch Marner .60 1.50
U2523 Matt Murray .40 1.00
U2524 Charlie McAvoy .50 1.25
U2525 Auston Matthews 1.50 4.00

2018-19 Upper Deck 25 Under 25 Jerseys

U251 Connor McDavid 20.00 50.00
U252 Mathew Barzal 5.00 12.00
U253 Nathan MacKinnon 15.00 40.00
U254 Sean Monahan 2.50 6.00
U255 Mikko Rantanen 10.00 25.00
U256 Aleksander Barkov 6.00 15.00
U257 Leon Draisaitl 12.00 30.00
U258 Jack Eichel 6.00 15.00
U259 David Pastrnak 10.00 25.00
U2510 Patrik Laine 5.00 12.00
U2511 Nico Hischier 6.00 15.00
U2512 Brock Boeser 5.00 12.00
U2513 Nolan Patrick 4.00 10.00
U2514 Dylan Larkin 5.00 12.00
U2515 Nikolaj Ehlers 4.00 10.00
U2516 Filip Forsberg 6.00 15.00
U2517 Matthew Tkachuk 8.00 20.00
U2519 Sebastian Aho 6.00 15.00
U2520 Andrei Vasilevskiy 6.00 15.00
U2521 Clayton Keller 5.00 12.00
U2522 Mitch Marner 6.00 15.00
U2523 Matt Murray 4.00 10.00
U2524 Charlie McAvoy 5.00 12.00
U2525 Auston Matthews 15.00 40.00

2018-19 Upper Deck A Piece of History 1,000 Point Club

PCAM Al MacInnis 15.00 40.00
PCBT Bryan Trottier 12.00 30.00
PCJM Joe Mullen 12.00 30.00
PCMG Michel Goulet 12.00 30.00
PCPS Peter Stastny 10.00 25.00

2018-19 Upper Deck A Piece of History 300 Win Club

300CW Cam Ward 20.00 50.00

2018-19 Upper Deck A Piece of History 500 Goal Club Autographs

GCPM Patrick Marleau 60.00 150.00

2018-19 Upper Deck Canvas

C1 John Gibson .60 1.50
C2 Rickard Rakell .50 1.25
C3 Brendan Perlini .40 1.00
C4 Clayton Keller .75 2.00
C5 Jakob Chychrun .60 1.50
C6 Charlie McAvoy .75 2.00
C7 Jake DeBrusk .60 1.50
C8 Tuukka Rask .75 2.00
C9 Jack Eichel 1.00 2.50
C10 Sam Reinhart 1.25 3.00
C11 Johnny Gaudreau 1.00 2.50
C12 Mark Giordano .60 1.50
C13 Sean Monahan .40 1.00
C14 Brett Pesce .40 1.00
C15 Teuvo Teravainen .60 1.50
C16 Jordan Staal .50 1.25
C17 Patrick Kane 1.25 3.00
C18 Artem Anisimov .40 1.00
C19 Alex DeBrincat .75 2.00
C20 Nathan MacKinnon 2.50 6.00
C21 Gabriel Landeskog .75 2.00
C22 Tyson Jost .50 1.25
C23 Seth Jones .60 1.50
C24 Artemi Panarin 1.25 3.00
C25 Cam Atkinson .60 1.50
C26 Jamie Benn .60 1.50
C27 John Klingberg .60 1.50
C28 Radek Faksa .50 1.25
C29 Dylan Larkin .75 2.00
C30 Anthony Mantha .50 1.25
C31 Henrik Zetterberg .75 2.00
C32 Darnell Nurse .50 1.25
C33 Adam Larsson .60 1.50
C34 Leon Draisaitl 2.00 5.00
C35 Aleksander Barkov 1.00 2.50
C36 Aaron Ekblad .75 2.00
C37 Roberto Luongo 1.00 2.50
C38 Drew Doughty .75 2.00
C39 Tanner Pearson .50 1.25
C40 Adrian Kempe .60 1.50
C41 Zach Parise .60 1.50
C42 Mikael Granlund .50 1.25
C43 Devan Dubnyk .50 1.25
C44 Brendan Gallagher .60 1.50
C45 Carey Price 1.25 3.00
C46 Jeff Petry .60 1.50
C47 P.K. Subban .75 2.00
C48 Kyle Turris .50 1.25
C49 Ryan Johansen .50 1.25
C50 Taylor Hall .60 1.50
C51 Nico Hischier 1.00 2.50
C52 Blake Coleman .50 1.25
C53 Mathew Barzal .75 2.00
C54 Anthony Beauvillier .40 1.00
C55 Mats Zuccarello .60 1.50
C56 Chris Kreider .75 2.00
C57 Pavel Buchnevich .50 1.25
C58 Mark Stone .75 2.00
C59 Thomas Chabot .60 1.50
C60 Claude Giroux .60 1.50
C61 Sean Couturier .50 1.25
C62 Shayne Gostisbehere .60 1.50
C63 Sidney Crosby 2.50 6.00
C64 Evgeni Malkin 1.25 3.00
C65 Matt Murray .60 1.50
C66 Joe Pavelski .75 2.00
C67 Logan Couture .75 2.00
C68 Brent Burns .60 1.50
C69 Jaden Schwartz .75 2.00
C70 Joel Edmundson .40 1.00
C71 Brayden Schenn .60 1.50
C72 Steven Stamkos 1.25 3.00
C73 Ondrej Palat .50 1.25
C74 Brayden Point .75 2.00
C75 Auston Matthews 2.50 6.00
C76 William Nylander 1.25 3.00
C77 Frederik Andersen .75 2.00
C78 Brock Boeser .75 2.00
C79 Bo Horvat .75 2.00
C80 Jacob Markstrom .60 1.50
C81 Nate Schmidt .50 1.25
C82 William Karlsson .75 2.00
C83 Reilly Smith .60 1.50
C84 Braden Holtby .75 2.00
C85 Nicklas Backstrom .60 1.50
C86 Evgeny Kuznetsov .75 2.00
C87 Blake Wheeler .60 1.50
C88 Patrik Laine .75 2.00
C89 Dustin Byfuglien .60 1.50
C90 T.Hall/N.MacKinnon CL 2.50 6.00
C91 Ryan Donato YG 10.00 25.00
C92 Sam Steel YG 6.00 15.00
C93 Dominik Kahun YG 6.00 15.00
C94 Warren Foegele YG 6.00 15.00
C95 Max Comtois YG 6.00 15.00
C96 Andreas Johnsson YG 8.00 20.00
C97 Max Lajoie YG 10.00 25.00
C98 Ethan Bear YG 10.00 25.00
C99 Sami Niku YG 5.00 12.00
C100 Zach Aston-Reese YG 10.00 25.00
C101 Miro Heiskanen YG 10.00 25.00
C102 Henri Jokiharju YG 5.00 12.00
C103 Casey Mittelstadt YG 12.00 30.00
C104 Henrik Borgstrom YG 10.00 25.00
C105 Mikhail Vorobyev YG 5.00 12.00
C106 Austin Wagner YG 5.00 12.00
C107 Travis Dermott YG 10.00 25.00
C108 Lias Andersson YG 10.00 25.00
C109 Michael Rasmussen YG 8.00 20.00
C110 Noah Juulsen YG 6.00 15.00
C111 Kristian Vesalainen YG 8.00 20.00
C112 Juuso Valimaki YG 6.00 15.00
C113 Filip Hronek YG 6.00 15.00
C114 Robert Thomas YG 10.00 25.00
C115 Antti Suomela YG 5.00 12.00
C116 Victor Ejdsell YG 5.00 12.00
C117 Dennis Cholowski YG 6.00 15.00
C118 Mathieu Joseph YG 3.00 8.00
C119 Andrei Svechnikov YG 10.00 25.00
C120 C.Mittelstadt
A.Svechnikov YG CL 6.00 15.00
C121 Adam Henrique .75 2.00
C122 Hampus Lindholm .60 1.50
C123 Oliver Ekman-Larsson 1.00 2.50
C124 Antti Raanta 1.00 2.50
C125 Brad Marchand 2.00 5.00
C126 Patrice Bergeron 1.25 3.00
C127 Torey Krug .75 2.00
C128 Jeff Skinner 1.25 3.00
C129 Rasmus Ristolainen .60 1.50
C130 Conor Sheary 1.00 2.50
C131 Mike Smith .75 2.00
C132 Noah Hanifin 1.00 2.50
C133 James Neal .60 1.50
C134 Sebastian Aho 1.50 4.00
C135 Dougie Hamilton .75 2.00
C136 Calvin de Haan .60 1.50
C137 Jonathan Toews 1.50 4.00
C138 Corey Crawford .75 2.00
C139 Mikko Rantanen 2.50 6.00
C140 Tyson Barrie .60 1.50
C141 Zach Werenski 1.50 4.00
C142 Sergei Bobrovsky 1.50 4.00
C143 Pierre-Luc Dubois .75 2.00
C144 Tyler Seguin 1.25 3.00
C145 Ben Bishop .75 2.00
C146 Alexander Radulov 1.00 2.50
C147 Mike Green .75 2.00
C148 Andreas Athanasiou .75 2.00
C149 Connor McDavid 5.00 12.00
C150 Ryan Nugent-Hopkins 1.25 3.00
C151 Oscar Klefbom .75 2.00
C152 Vincent Trocheck 1.00 2.50
C153 Mike Hoffman .60 1.50
C154 Keith Yandle .60 1.50
C155 Anze Kopitar 1.50 4.00
C156 Jonathan Quick 1.25 3.00
C157 Ilya Kovalchuk .75 2.00
C158 Eric Staal 1.00 2.50
C159 Ryan Suter .75 2.00
C160 Nino Niederreiter .60 1.50
C161 Max Domi 1.00 2.50
C162 Jonathan Drouin .75 2.00
C163 Tomas Tatar .60 1.50
C164 Filip Forsberg 1.50 4.00
C165 Roman Josi 1.00 2.50
C166 Viktor Arvidsson .60 1.50
C167 Sami Vatanen .60 1.50
C168 Kyle Palmieri .75 2.00
C169 Marcus Johansson .75 2.00
C170 Jordan Eberle 1.00 2.50
C171 Anders Lee .75 2.00
C172 Brock Nelson 1.00 2.50
C173 Henrik Lundqvist 2.50 6.00
C174 Jimmy Vesey .75 2.00
C175 Mika Zibanejad 1.25 3.00
C176 Colin White .60 1.50
C177 Mikkel Boedker .60 1.50
C178 Ivan Provorov .75 2.00
C179 Jakub Voracek .75 2.00
C180 Nolan Patrick 1.00 2.50
C181 Matt Murray 1.00 2.50
C182 Kris Letang 1.25 3.00
C183 Phil Kessel 1.00 2.50
C184 Joe Thornton 1.50 4.00
C185 Marc-Edouard Vlasic .60 1.50
C186 Martin Jones .75 2.00
C187 Ryan O'Reilly 1.00 2.50
C188 Vladimir Tarasenko 1.25 3.00
C189 Patrick Maroon .75 2.00
C190 Nikita Kucherov 2.00 5.00
C191 Victor Hedman 1.25 3.00
C192 Andrei Vasilevskiy 1.50 4.00
C193 Mikhail Sergachev .75 2.00
C194 Mitch Marner 1.50 4.00
C195 John Tavares 1.50 4.00
C196 Morgan Rielly 1.00 2.50
C197 Alexander Edler .60 1.50
C198 Sven Baertschi .75 2.00
C199 Christopher Tanev .60 1.50
C200 Jonathan Marchessault 1.25 3.00
C201 Marc-Andre Fleury 2.00 5.00
C202 Paul Stastny .75 2.00
C203 Alexander Ovechkin 4.00 10.00
C204 John Carlson 1.00 2.50
C205 Matt Niskanen .75 2.00
C206 T.J. Oshie 1.00 2.50
C207 Mark Scheifele 1.50 4.00
C208 Kyle Connor 1.50 4.00
C209 Connor Hellebuyck 2.00 5.00
C210 A.Ovechkin/V.Tarasenko CL 4.00 10.00
C211 Elias Pettersson YG 40.00 100.00
C212 Michael McLeod YG 5.00 12.00
C213 Joe Hicketts YG 6.00 15.00
C214 Dillon Dube YG 8.00 20.00
C215 Eeli Tolvanen YG 12.00 30.00
C216 Isac Lundestrom YG 5.00 12.00
C217 Urho Vaakanainen YG 12.00 30.00
C218 Carter Hart YG 12.00 30.00
C219 Joey Anderson YG 6.00 15.00
C220 Brady Tkachuk YG 20.00 50.00
C221 Jaret Anderson-Dolan YG 5.00 12.00
C222 Dylan Gambrell YG 6.00 15.00
C223 Jesperi Kotkaniemi YG 12.00 30.00
C224 Brett Howden YG 8.00 20.00
C225 Jordan Kyrou YG 12.00 30.00
C226 Jordan Greenway YG 6.00 15.00
C227 Ilya Samsonov YG 12.00 30.00
C228 Oskar Lindblom YG 10.00 25.00
C229 Matt Luff YG 5.00 12.00
C230 Drake Batherson YG 10.00 25.00
C231 Cal Petersen YG 5.00 12.00
C232 Jeremy Lauzon YG 8.00 20.00
C233 Troy Terry YG 10.00 25.00
C234 Adam Gaudette YG 10.00 25.00
C235 Jakub Zboril YG 10.00 25.00
C236 Anthony Cirelli YG 6.00 15.00
C237 Dylan Sikura YG 8.00 20.00
C238 Evan Bouchard YG 15.00 40.00
C239 Rasmus Dahlin YG 12.00 30.00
C240 R.Dahlin/E.Pettersson YG CL 20.00 50.00
C241 Bobby Orr RS 25.00 60.00
C242 Mats Sundin RS 6.00 15.00
C243 Peter Stastny RS 5.00 12.00
C244 Brett Hull RS 12.00 30.00
C245 Martin Brodeur RS 15.00 40.00
C246 Wayne Gretzky RS 40.00 100.00
C247 Bryan Trottier RS 6.00 15.00
C248 Stan Mikita RS 6.00 15.00
C249 Mario Lemieux RS 25.00 60.00
C250 Jacques Plante RS 6.00 15.00
C251 Johnny Bower RS 6.00 15.00
C252 Ted Lindsay RS 6.00 15.00
C253 Mike Modano RS 12.00 30.00
C254 Guy Lafleur RS 8.00 20.00
C255 Tim Horton RS 10.00 25.00
C256 Noah Juulsen POE 6.00 15.00
C257 Nicolas Roy POE 4.00 10.00
C258 Anthony Cirelli POE 10.00 25.00
C259 Sam Steel POE 6.00 15.00
C260 Rourke Chartier POE 5.00 12.00
C261 Robert Thomas POE 12.00 30.00
C262 Maxime Comtois POE 6.00 15.00
C263 Samuel Montembeault POE 12.00 30.00
C264 Mathieu Joseph POE 8.00 20.00
C265 Jordan Kyrou POE 12.00 30.00
C266 Travis Dermott POE 10.00 25.00
C267 Dillon Dube POE 8.00 20.00
C268 Brett Howden POE 8.00 20.00
C269 Joe Hicketts POE 6.00 15.00
C270 Dillon Heatherington POE 6.00 15.00

2018-19 Upper Deck Canvas Season Highlights

M1 John Tavares 40.00 100.00
M2 Elias Pettersson 100.00 200.00
M3 Joe Thornton 20.00 50.00

2018-19 Upper Deck Ceremonial Puck Drop

CPD1 Tony Amonte 4.00 10.00
CPD2 Willie O'Ree 6.00 15.00
CPD3 Dominik Hasek 8.00 20.00
CPD4 Phil Esposito 8.00 20.00
CPD5 Ed Belfour 5.00 12.00
CPD6 Wayne Gretzky 12.00 30.00
CPD7 Peter Forsberg 10.00 25.00
CPD8 Larry Robinson 5.00 12.00
CPD9 Martin Brodeur 12.00 30.00
CPD10 Mike Modano 10.00 25.00
CPD11 Ed Olczyk 4.00 10.00
CPD12 Scotty Bowman 5.00 12.00

2018-19 Upper Deck Ceremonial Puck Drop Autographs

CPD2 Willie O'Ree 25.00 60.00
CPD4 Phil Esposito 25.00 60.00
CPD5 Ed Belfour 100.00 200.00
CPD6 Wayne Gretzky 300.00 800.00

2018-19 Upper Deck Clear Cut Parallel

*VETS: 5X TO 12X BASIC CARDS
*ROOKIES: 2X TO 5X BASIC CARDS

201 Rasmus Dahlin YG 100.00 250.00
202 Roope Hintz YG 40.00 100.00
215 Brett Howden YG 30.00 80.00
217 Eeli Tolvanen YG 30.00 80.00
221 Evan Bouchard YG 80.00 200.00
225 Ryan Donato YG 25.00 60.00
226 Michael Rasmussen YG 25.00 60.00
228 Travis Dermott YG 40.00 100.00
231 Dennis Cholowski YG 25.00 60.00
241 Jordan Kyrou YG 40.00 100.00
248 Elias Pettersson YG 150.00 400.00
451 Andrei Svechnikov YG 80.00 200.00
463 Ilya Samsonov YG 30.00 80.00
472 Robert Thomas YG 30.00 80.00
487 Sam Steel YG 25.00 60.00
491 Carter Hart YG 30.00 80.00
499 Brady Tkachuk YG 80.00 150.00

2018-19 Upper Deck Clear Cut Foundations

CCF1 Rakell/Gibson 10.00 25.00
CCF2 Keller/Dvorak 12.00 30.00
CCF3 Rask/Bergeron 12.00 30.00
CCF4 Eichel/Reinhart 20.00 50.00
CCF5 Gaudreau/Giordano 15.00 40.00
CCF6 Aho/Teravainen 15.00 40.00
CCF7 Toews/Saad 15.00 40.00
CCF8 MacKinnon/Landeskog 40.00 100.00
CCF9 Panarin/Jones 20.00 50.00
CCF10 Benn/Bishop 10.00 25.00
CCF11 Mantha/Larkin 12.00 30.00
CCF12 Mcdavid/Draisaitl 50.00 125.00
CCF13 Barkov/Trocheck 15.00 40.00
CCF14 Kopitar/Brown 15.00 40.00
CCF15 Staa/Niederreiter 10.00 25.00
CCF16 Price/Drouin 20.00 50.00
CCF17 Forsberg/Arvidsson 15.00 40.00
CCF18 Hall/Hischier 15.00 40.00
CCF19 Barzal/Eberle 12.00 30.00
CCF20 Lundqvist/Skjei 25.00 60.00
CCF21 Stone/Duchene 12.00 30.00
CCF22 Giroux/Couturier 10.00 25.00
CCF23 Malkin/Kessel 20.00 50.00
CCF24 Couture/Pavelski 12.00 30.00
CCF25 Schenn/Tarasenko 12.00 30.00
CCF26 Kucherov/Hedman 20.00 50.00
CCF27 Matthews/Nylander 40.00 100.00
CCF28 Horvat/Boeser 12.00 30.00
CCF29 Fleury/Marchessault 20.00 50.00
CCF30 Ovechkin/Kuznetsov 40.00 100.00
CCF31 Wheeler/Scheifele 15.00 40.00

2018-19 Upper Deck Clear Cut Honoured Members

HOF75 Peter Forsberg 10.00 25.00
HOF76 Mark Recchi 6.00 15.00
HOF77 Rod Langway 4.00 10.00
HOF78 Bill Barber 5.00 12.00
HOF79 Martin Brodeur 12.00 30.00
HOF80 Dave Andreychuk 5.00 12.00
HOF81 Scotty Bowman 5.00 12.00
HOF82 Pierre Pilote 5.00 12.00
HOF83 Teemu Selanne 10.00 25.00

2018-19 Upper Deck Clear Cut Leaders

CCLGLS Ovechkin/Laine/Karlsson 25.00 60.00
CCLGWG Point/MacKinnon/Monahan 25.0060.00
CCLRGS Connor/Boeser/DeBrincat 10.00 25.00
CCLRPT Barzal/Keller/Gourde 8.00 20.00
CCLSHP Karlsson/Lee/Marchand 12.00 30.00
CCLWIN Hellebuyck
Vasilevskiy/Rinne 12.00 30.00

2018-19 Upper Deck Cup Components

CCPBB B.Clarke/B.Barber 12.00 30.00
CCPBC P.Bergeron/Z.Chara 10.00 25.00
CCPBM B.Barilko/H.Meeker 8.00 20.00
CCPBP M.Bossy/D.Potvin 8.00 20.00
CCPBR R.Bourque/P.Roy 20.00 50.00
CCPBW R.Brind'Amour/C.Ward 8.00 20.00
CCPCB C.Conacher/A.Bailey 8.00 20.00
CCPDQ D.Doughty/J.Quick 10.00 25.00
CCPFM G.Fuhr/A.Moog 12.00 30.00
CCPGK W.Gretzky/J.Kurri 50.00 125.00
CCPGS R.Getzlaf/T.Selanne 15.00 40.00
CCPHM B.Hull/M.Modano 15.00 40.00
CCPKB A.Kopitar/D.Brown 12.00 30.00
CCPKD R.Kelly/A.Delvecchio 8.00 20.00
CCPLJ M.Lemieux/J.Jagr 100.00 200.00
CCPMA M.Messier/G.Anderson 15.00 40.00
CCPMB F.Mahovlich/J.Bower 8.00 20.00
CCPMG L.McDonald/D.Gilmour 10.00 25.00
CCPMH S.Mikita/B.Hull 15.00 40.00
CCPMK E.Malkin/P.Kessel 15.00 40.00
CCPOE B.Orr/P.Esposito 30.00 80.00
CCPRB M.Richard/J.Beliveau 15.00 40.00
CCPRC P.Roy/C.Chelios 20.00 50.00
CCPRL L.Robinson/G.Lafleur 10.00 25.00
CCPSF J.Sakic/P.Forsberg 15.00 40.00
CCPTK J.Toews/P.Kane 15.00 40.00
CCPYL S.Yzerman/N.Lidstrom 20.00 50.00

2018-19 Upper Deck Day With The Cup

DC1 Chandler Stephenson 12.00 30.00
DC2 Alexander Ovechkin 60.00 150.00
DC3 Jakub Vrana 15.00 40.00
DC4 Michal Kempny 15.00 40.00
DC5 Alex Chiasson 12.00 30.00
DC6 Christian Djoos 12.00 30.00
DC7 Matt Niskanen 12.00 30.00
DC8 Braden Holtby 20.00 50.00
DC9 Madison Bowey 10.00 25.00
DC10 Nicklas Backstrom 15.00 40.00
DC11 Brett Connolly 10.00 25.00
DC12 Philipp Grubauer 15.00 40.00
DC13 Lars Eller 10.00 25.00
DC14 Andre Burakovsky 10.00 25.00
DC15 T.J. Oshie 15.00 40.00
DC16 Dmitry Orlov 15.00 40.00
DC17 Brooks Orpik 10.00 25.00
DC18 Evgeny Kuznetsov 20.00 50.00
DC19 Tom Wilson 15.00 40.00
DC20 Jay Beagle 10.00 25.00
DC21 Devante Smith-Pelly 12.00 30.00
DC22 John Carlson 15.00 40.00

2018-19 Upper Deck Day With The Cup Flashbacks

DCF1 Patrick Roy 50.00 125.00
DCF2 Larry Robinson 20.00 50.00
DCF3 Claude Lemieux 20.00 50.00
DCF4 Chris Chelios 20.00 50.00
DCF5 Guy Carbonneau 20.00 50.00

2018-19 Upper Deck Fluorescence

F1 Andrei Svechnikov 8.00 20.00
F2 Dominik Kahun 3.00 8.00
F3 Ilya Samsonov 6.00 15.00
F4 Warren Foegele 3.00 8.00
F5 Drake Batherson 6.00 15.00
F6 Austin Wagner 2.50 6.00
F7 Anthony Cirelli 5.00 12.00
F8 Miro Heiskanen 8.00 20.00
F9 Dennis Cholowski 3.00 8.00
F10 Ryan Donato 5.00 12.00
F11 Michael Rasmussen 4.00 10.00
F12 Brady Tkachuk 10.00 25.00
F13 Andreas Johnsson 4.00 10.00
F14 Jeremy Lauzon 4.00 10.00
F15 Michael Dal Colle 3.00 8.00
F16 Lias Andersson 5.00 12.00
F17 Dillon Dube 4.00 10.00
F18 Eeli Tolvanen 12.00 30.00
F19 Adam Gaudette 5.00 12.00
F20 Jaret Anderson-Dolan 2.50 6.00
F21 Juuso Valimaki 3.00 8.00
F22 Sami Niku 2.50 6.00
F23 Oskar Lindblom 5.00 12.00
F24 Troy Terry 5.00 12.00
F25 Henri Jokiharju 2.50 6.00
F26 Evan Bouchard 8.00 20.00
F27 Maxime Comtois 3.00 8.00
F28 Isac Lundestrom 2.50 6.00
F29 Kristian Vesalainen 4.00 10.00
F30 Antti Suomela 2.50 6.00
F31 Maxime Lajoie 5.00 12.00
F32 Noah Juulsen 3.00 8.00
F33 Robert Thomas 6.00 15.00
F34 Jordan Kyrou 6.00 15.00
F35 Dylan Sikura 4.00 10.00
F36 Sam Steel 3.00 8.00
F37 Brett Howden 4.00 10.00
F38 Henrik Borgstrom 5.00 12.00
F39 Filip Hronek 3.00 8.00
F40 Kiefer Sherwood 2.50 6.00
F41 Travis Dermott 5.00 12.00
F42 Dylan Gambrell 3.00 8.00
F43 Jordan Greenway 3.00 8.00
F44 Cal Petersen 2.50 6.00
F45 Mikhail Vorobyev 2.50 6.00
F46 Zach Aston-Reese 5.00 12.00
F47 Casey Mittelstadt 6.00 15.00
F48 Jesperi Kotkaniemi 6.00 15.00
F49 Elias Pettersson 25.00 60.00
F50 Rasmus Dahlin 8.00 20.00

2018-19 Upper Deck Fluorescence Blue

*BLUE: .6X TO 1.5X BASIC INSERTS

F37 Brett Howden 15.00 40.00
F48 Jesperi Kotkaniemi 10.00 25.00

2018-19 Upper Deck Game Jerseys

GJAB Aleksander Barkov C 5.00 12.00
GJAK Anze Kopitar A 10.00 25.00
GJAL Anders Lee B 2.50 6.00
GJAM Anthony Mantha D 2.50 6.00
GJAO Alexander Ovechkin A 12.00 30.00
GJAR Alexander Radulov C 3.00 8.00
GJAV Andrei Vasilevskiy B 5.00 12.00
GJBH Braden Holtby B 4.00 10.00
GJBI Ben Bishop D 2.50 6.00
GJBO Bo Horvat C 4.00 10.00
GJBR Brayden Schenn C 3.00 8.00
GJBS Brandon Saad B 2.50 6.00
GJBW Blake Wheeler B 3.00 8.00
GJCA Cam Atkinson D 3.00 8.00
GJCC Corey Crawford B 2.50 6.00
GJCD Christian Dvorak C 2.50 6.00
GJCF Cam Fowler D 3.00 8.00
GJCG Claude Giroux B 3.00 8.00
GJCK Chris Kreider C 4.00 10.00
GJCM Charlie McAvoy B 4.00 10.00
GJCP Carey Price B 6.00 15.00
GJCT Cam Talbot D 3.00 8.00
GJDK David Krejci C 3.00 8.00
GJEB Jordan Eberle D 3.00 8.00
GJEM Evgeni Malkin A 6.00 15.00
GJGL Gabriel Landeskog D 4.00 10.00
GJHZ Henrik Zetterberg C 4.00 10.00
GJJD Jonathan Drouin D 2.50 6.00
GJJE Jack Eichel C 5.00 12.00
GJJF Justin Faulk D 2.50 6.00
GJJG Johnny Gaudreau B 5.00 12.00
GJJM Jonathan Marchessault C 4.00 10.00
GJJO Marcus Johansson D 2.50 6.00
GJJP Jason Pominville D 2.00 5.00
GJJQ Jonathan Quick C 4.00 10.00
GJJS Jaden Schwartz C 4.00 10.00
GJKE Clayton Keller B 4.00 10.00
GJKS Kevin Shattenkirk C 2.00 5.00
GJLD Leon Draisaitl C 10.00 25.00
GJMF Marc-Andre Fleury A 12.00 30.00
GJMG Mikael Granlund D 2.50 6.00
GJMJ Martin Jones D 2.50 6.00
GJMM Matt Murray B 3.00 8.00
GJMR Mikko Rantanen C 8.00 20.00
GJMS Mark Scheifele B 5.00 12.00
GJMV Marc-Edouard Vlasic D 2.00 5.00
GJNE Nikolaj Ehlers C 3.00 8.00
GJNK Nazem Kadri B 4.00 10.00
GJPH Patric Hornqvist B 2.00 5.00
GJPK Patrick Kane A 12.00 30.00
GJPM Patrick Marleau C 3.00 8.00
GJRG Ryan Getzlaf C 3.00 8.00
GJRJ Ryan Johansen D 2.50 6.00
GJSA Sebastian Aho D 5.00 12.00
GJSM Mike Smith D 2.50 6.00
GJST Mark Stone C 4.00 10.00

GJSW Shea Weber C 3.00 8.00
GJTH Taylor Hall A 3.00 8.00
GJTJ Tyler Johnson C 2.00 5.00
GJTK Travis Konecny D 3.00 8.00
GJTO T.J. Oshie D 3.00 8.00
GJTR Tuukka Rask D 4.00 10.00
GJTS Troy Stecher D 2.00 5.00
GJVA Viktor Arvidsson D 2.00 5.00
GJVT Vincent Trocheck D 3.00 8.00
GJWN William Nylander B 6.00 15.00
GJZP Zach Parise D 3.00 8.00
GJZW Zach Werenski C 5.00 12.00

2018-19 Upper Deck Jagr Years

JJ1 Jaromir Jagr .60 1.50
JJ2 Jaromir Jagr .60 1.50
JJ3 Jaromir Jagr .60 1.50
JJ4 Jaromir Jagr .60 1.50
JJ5 Jaromir Jagr .60 1.50
JJ6 Jaromir Jagr .60 1.50
JJ7 Jaromir Jagr .60 1.50
JJ8 Jaromir Jagr .60 1.50
JJ9 Jaromir Jagr .60 1.50
NNO Header Card .60 1.50
JJ10 Jaromir Jagr .60 1.50
JJ11 Jaromir Jagr .60 1.50
JJ12 Jaromir Jagr .60 1.50
JJ13 Jaromir Jagr .60 1.50
JJ14 Jaromir Jagr .60 1.50
JJ15 Jaromir Jagr .60 1.50
JJ16 Jaromir Jagr .60 1.50
JJ17 Jaromir Jagr .60 1.50
JJ18 Jaromir Jagr .60 1.50
JJ19 Jaromir Jagr .60 1.50
JJ20 Jaromir Jagr .60 1.50
JJ21 Jaromir Jagr .60 1.50
JJ22 Jaromir Jagr .60 1.50
JJ23 Jaromir Jagr .60 1.50
JJ24 Jaromir Jagr .60 1.50

2018-19 Upper Deck Jagr Years Jerseys

JJ10 Jaromir Jagr 20.00 50.00
JJ12 Jaromir Jagr 20.00 50.00
JJ15 Jaromir Jagr 20.00 50.00
JJ20 Jaromir Jagr 20.00 50.00
JJ23 Jaromir Jagr 20.00 50.00

2018-19 Upper Deck Oversized

201 Rasmus Dahlin 6.00 15.00
207 Dillon Dube 3.00 8.00
217 Eeli Tolvanen 5.00 12.00
219 Anthony Cirelli 4.00 10.00
221 Evan Bouchard 6.00 15.00
225 Ryan Donato 4.00 10.00
226 Michael Rasmussen 3.00 8.00
228 Travis Dermott 4.00 10.00
230 Henri Jokiharju 2.00 5.00
241 Jordan Kyrou 5.00 12.00
244 Kristian Vesalainen 3.00 8.00
246 Miro Heiskanen 6.00 15.00
248 Elias Pettersson 8.00 20.00
249 Jesperi Kotkaniemi 5.00 12.00
451 Andrei Svechnikov 6.00 15.00
453 Casey Mittelstadt 5.00 12.00
461 Henrik Borgstrom 4.00 10.00
463 Ilya Samsonov 5.00 12.00
472 Robert Thomas 5.00 12.00
482 Noah Juulsen 2.50 6.00
483 Mathieu Joseph 3.00 8.00
484 Drake Batherson 5.00 12.00
487 Sam Steel 2.50 6.00
489 Dylan Sikura 3.00 8.00
491 Carter Hart 5.00 12.00
492 Andreas Johnsson 3.00 8.00
497 Lias Andersson 4.00 10.00
499 Brady Tkachuk 8.00 20.00

2018-19 Upper Deck Parkhurst Rookies

*GOLD: .50X TO 1.25X BASIC INSERTS
*COOPER: .6X TO 1.5X BASIC INSERTS
PR1 Casey Mittelstadt 2.50 6.00
PR2 Sam Steel 1.25 3.00
PR3 Ryan Donato 2.00 5.00
PR4 Jesperi Kotkaniemi 2.50 6.00
PR5 Eeli Tolvanen 2.50 6.00
PR6 Michael Rasmussen 1.50 4.00
PR7 Elias Pettersson 4.00 10.00
PR8 Robert Thomas 2.50 6.00
PR9 Andrei Svechnikov 3.00 8.00
PR10 Rasmus Dahlin 3.00 8.00

2018-19 Upper Deck Rookie Breakouts

RB1 Rasmus Dahlin 25.00 60.00
RB2 Jesperi Kotkaniemi 20.00 50.00
RB3 Maxime Lajoie 15.00 40.00
RB4 Dillon Dube 12.00 30.00
RB5 Miro Heiskanen 25.00 60.00
RB6 Lias Andersson 15.00 40.00
RB7 Michael Rasmussen 12.00 30.00
RB8 Casey Mittelstadt 20.00 50.00
RB9 Eeli Tolvanen 20.00 50.00
RB10 Henri Jokiharju 8.00 20.00
RB11 Brady Tkachuk 30.00 80.00
RB12 Brett Howden 12.00 30.00
RB13 Robert Thomas 20.00 50.00
RB14 Ryan Donato 15.00 40.00
RB15 Andrei Svechnikov 25.00 60.00
RB16 Christoffer Ehn 8.00 20.00
RB17 Juuso Valimaki 10.00 25.00
RB18 Jordan Kyrou 20.00 50.00
RB19 Maxime Comtois 10.00 25.00
RB20 Elias Pettersson 80.00 200.00

2018-19 Upper Deck Rookie Commence

RCAS Andrei Svechnikov 2.00 5.00
RCBH Brett Howden 1.00 2.50
RCBT Brady Tkachuk 2.50 6.00
RCCM Casey Mittelstadt 1.50 4.00
RCDO Ryan Donato 1.25 3.00
RCDS Dylan Sikura 1.00 2.50
RCEP Elias Pettersson 2.50 6.00
RCET Eeli Tolvanen 1.50 4.00
RCHB Henrik Borgstrom 1.25 3.00
RCHJ Henri Jokiharju .60 1.50
RCJK Jesperi Kotkaniemi 1.50 4.00
RCLA Lias Andersson 1.25 3.00
RCMC Maxime Comtois .75 2.00
RCMH Miro Heiskanen 2.00 5.00
RCRD Rasmus Dahlin 2.00 5.00

2018-19 Upper Deck Rookie Materials

RMAC Anthony Cirelli D 5.00 12.00
RMAG Adam Gaudette D 5.00 12.00
RMAS Andrei Svechnikov A 8.00 20.00
RMBH Brett Howden C 4.00 10.00
RMBO Evan Bouchard B 8.00 20.00
RMBT Brady Tkachuk A 10.00 25.00
RMCM Casey Mittelstadt B 6.00 15.00
RMDD Dillon Dube D 4.00 10.00
RMDG Dylan Gambrell D 3.00 8.00
RMDO Ryan Donato B 5.00 12.00
RMDS Dylan Sikura D 4.00 10.00
RMDT Dominic Turgeon D 3.00 8.00
RMEB Ethan Bear D 5.00 12.00
RMEP Elias Pettersson A 25.00 60.00
RMET Eeli Tolvanen B 6.00 15.00
RMFH Filip Hronek D 3.00 8.00
RMHB Henrik Borgstrom D 5.00 12.00
RMHJ Henri Jokiharju D 2.50 6.00
RMJG Jordan Greenway D 3.00 8.00
RMJK Jesperi Kotkaniemi A 6.00 15.00
RMJL Jeremy Lauzon D 4.00 10.00
RMJV Juuso Valimaki C 3.00 8.00
RMKY Jordan Kyrou C 6.00 15.00
RMLA Lias Andersson C 5.00 12.00
RMMC Maxime Comtois C 3.00 8.00
RMMD Michael Dal Colle D 3.00 8.00
RMMH Miro Heiskanen B 8.00 20.00
RMML Maxime Lajoie D 5.00 12.00
RMMR Michael Rasmussen C 4.00 10.00
RMNJ Noah Juulsen D 3.00 8.00
RMOL Oskar Lindblom D 5.00 12.00
RMRD Rasmus Dahlin A 8.00 20.00
RMRT Robert Thomas C 6.00 15.00
RMSN Sami Niku D 2.50 6.00
RMSS Sam Steel D 3.00 8.00
RMTD Travis Dermott D 5.00 12.00
RMTH Tomas Hyka D 3.00 8.00
RMTT Troy Terry D 5.00 12.00
RMWF Warren Foegele D 3.00 8.00
RMZA Zach Aston-Reese D 5.00 12.00

2018-19 Upper Deck Rookie Materials Patch

*PATCH/25: 1X TO 2.5X BASIC INSERTS
RMEP Elias Pettersson/25 50.00 125.00
RMNJ Noah Juulsen/25 12.00 30.00
RMRT Robert Thomas/25 20.00 50.00

2018-19 Upper Deck Rookie Photoshoot Flashback Materials

RPFAD Alex DeBrincat B 4.00 10.00
RPFBB Brock Boeser B 4.00 10.00
RPFBP Brayden Point B 4.00 10.00
RPFCK Clayton Keller C 4.00 10.00
RPFCM Connor McDavid A 20.00 50.00
RPFIP Ivan Provorov C 2.50 6.00
RPFJE Jack Eichel A 5.00 12.00
RPFKC Kyle Connor C 5.00 12.00
RPFMB Mathew Barzal A 4.00 10.00
RPFMC Charlie McAvoy C 4.00 10.00
RPFPD Pierre-Luc Dubois C 2.50 6.00
RPFZW Zach Werenski C 5.00 12.00

2018-19 Upper Deck Shooting Stars Centers

*BLACK: .6X TO 1.5X BASIC INSERTS
SSC1 Connor McDavid 4.00 10.00
SSC2 Evgeni Malkin 1.50 4.00
SSC3 William Karlsson 1.00 2.50
SSC4 Steven Stamkos 1.50 4.00
SSC5 Mathew Barzal 1.00 2.50
SSC6 Anze Kopitar 1.25 3.00
SSC7 Claude Giroux .75 2.00
SSC8 Sidney Crosby 3.00 8.00
SSC9 Nathan MacKinnon 3.00 8.00
SSC10 Sean Monahan .50 1.25

2018-19 Upper Deck Shooting Stars Defensemen

SSD1 Seth Jones 2.00 5.00
SSD2 Alex Pietrangelo 1.50 4.00
SSD3 P.K. Subban 2.50 6.00
SSD4 Brent Burns 2.00 5.00
SSD5 John Klingberg 2.00 5.00
SSD6 Cam Fowler 2.00 5.00
SSD7 Shayne Gostisbehere 2.00 5.00
SSD8 John Carlson 2.00 5.00
SSD9 Drew Doughty 2.50 6.00
SSD10 Victor Hedman 2.50 6.00

2018-19 Upper Deck Shooting Stars Goalies

*BLACK: .6X TO 1.5X BASIC INSERTS
SSG1 Connor Hellebuyck 6.00 15.00
SSG2 Mike Smith 2.50 6.00
SSG3 Braden Holtby 4.00 10.00
SSG4 Sergei Bobrovsky 5.00 12.00
SSG5 Jonathan Quick 4.00 10.00
SSG6 Pekka Rinne 3.00 8.00
SSG7 Andrei Vasilevskiy 5.00 12.00
SSG8 Marc-Andre Fleury 6.00 15.00
SSG9 Frederik Andersen 4.00 10.00
SSG10 Ben Bishop 2.50 6.00

2018-19 Upper Deck Shooting Stars Left Wingers

*BLACK: .6X TO 1.5X BASIC INSERTS
SSL1 Filip Forsberg 1.25 3.00
SSL2 Jonathan Huberdeau 1.00 2.50
SSL3 Alexander Ovechkin 3.00 8.00
SSL4 Jaden Schwartz 1.00 2.50
SSL5 Jamie Benn .75 2.00
SSL6 Brad Marchand 1.50 4.00
SSL7 Teuvo Teravainen .75 2.00
SSL8 Artemi Panarin 1.50 4.00
SSL9 Gabriel Landeskog 1.00 2.50
SSL10 Johnny Gaudreau 1.25 3.00

2018-19 Upper Deck Shooting Stars Right Wingers

*BLACK: .6X TO 1.5X BASIC INSERTS
SSR1 Vladimir Tarasenko 1.00 2.50
SSR2 Alexander Radulov .75 2.00
SSR3 Sebastian Aho 1.25 3.00
SSR4 Brock Boeser 1.00 2.50
SSR5 Mikko Rantanen 2.00 5.00
SSR6 Mark Stone 1.00 2.50
SSR7 Patrick Kane 1.50 4.00
SSR8 Josh Bailey .60 1.50
SSR9 Blake Wheeler .75 2.00
SSR10 Nikita Kucherov 1.50 4.00

2018-19 Upper Deck Sibling Sensation

SS0 Henrick Sedin
Daniel Sedin .75 2.00
SS1 Henrick Sedin
Daniel Sedin .75 2.00
SS2 Jamie Benn
Jordie Benn .60 1.50
SS3 William Nylander
Alex Nylander 1.25 3.00
SS4 Mikael Granlund
Markus Granlund .50 1.25
SS5 Malcolm Subban
PK Subban .75 2.00
SS6 James van Riemsdyk
Trevor van Riemsdyk .50 1.25
SS7 Luke Schenn
Brayden Schenn .60 1.50
SS8 Griffin Reinhart
Max Reinhart
Sam Reinhart 1.25 3.00

2018-19 Upper Deck Signature Sensations

SSAD Alex DeBrincat C 12.00 30.00
SSAH Adam Henrique B 6.00 15.00
SSBH Bo Horvat B 10.00 25.00
SSBM Brandon Montour E 10.00 25.00
SSBP Brendan Perlini D 5.00 12.00
SSBR Bobby Ryan A 6.00 15.00
SSBS Brady Skjei E 6.00 15.00
SSCB Connor Brown D 6.00 15.00
SSCH Connor Hellebuyck C 15.00 40.00
SSCM Connor McDavid A 40.00 100.00
SSCP Cedric Paquette C 5.00 12.00
SSDS Derek Stepan B 5.00 12.00
SSEH Erik Haula E 8.00 20.00
SSEK Evgeny Kuznetsov C 10.00 25.00
SSGR Mikael Granlund B 6.00 15.00
SSJA Josh Anderson D 6.00 15.00
SSJH Jonathan Huberdeau B 10.00 25.00
SSJR Jack Roslovic C 5.00 12.00
SSJT Jonathan Toews A 12.00 30.00
SSJV Jakub Vrana C 8.00 20.00
SSJW Jordan Weal D 5.00 12.00
SSKL Kevin Labanc E 5.00 12.00
SSKP Kyle Palmieri C 6.00 15.00
SSMF Marc-Andre Fleury A 60.00 150.00
SSMG Mark Giordano B 8.00 20.00
SSMI Colin Miller D 10.00 25.00
SSMM Mitch Marner A 12.00 30.00
SSMR Mikko Rantanen C 20.00 50.00
SSMT Matthew Tkachuk B 15.00 40.00
SSNE Nikolaj Ehlers C 8.00 20.00
SSOK Oscar Klefbom E 6.00 15.00
SSPD Phillip Danault E 8.00 20.00
SSPL Pierre-Luc Dubois E 12.00 30.00
SSRF Radek Faksa E 6.00 15.00
SSRH Ryan Hartman E 5.00 12.00
SSRM Ryan Murray B 6.00 15.00
SSSI Dominik Simon E 5.00 12.00
SSTH Tomas Hertl B 8.00 20.00
SSTJ Tyson Jost C 12.00 30.00
SSYG Yanni Gourde E 6.00 15.00

2018-19 Upper Deck Stonewalled

SW1 Roberto Luongo 1.25 3.00
SW2 Linus Ullmark .75 2.00
SW3 Ben Bishop .60 1.50
SW4 Darcy Kuemper .75 2.00
SW5 Cory Schneider .75 2.00
SW6 Ryan Miller .75 2.00
SW7 Jacob Markstrom .75 2.00
SW8 Martin Jones .60 1.50
SW9 Jim Howard 1.00 2.50
SW10 Semyon Varlamov .75 2.00
SW11 Pekka Rinne .75 2.00
SW12 Brian Elliott .60 1.50
SW13 Matt Murray .75 2.00
SW14 Jack Campbell .75 2.00
SW15 Devan Dubnyk .60 1.50
SW16 John Gibson .75 2.00
SW17 Corey Crawford .60 1.50
SW18 Frederik Andersen 1.00 2.50
SW19 Andrei Vasilevskiy 1.25 3.00
SW20 Henrik Lundqvist 2.00 5.00
SW21 Jake Allen .75 2.00
SW22 Anton Forsberg .50 1.25
SW23 Aaron Dell .50 1.25
SW24 Braden Holtby 1.00 2.50
SW25 Malcolm Subban .60 1.50
SW26 Cam Talbot .75 2.00
SW27 Carey Price 1.50 4.00
SW28 Scott Darling .60 1.50
SW29 Jonathan Quick 1.00 2.50
SW30 Antti Raanta .75 2.00
SW31 Sergei Bobrovsky 1.25 3.00
SW32 Mike Smith .60 1.50
SW33 Keith Kinkaid .50 1.25
SW34 James Reimer .75 2.00
SW35 Connor Hellebuyck 1.50 4.00
SW36 Juuse Saros 1.00 2.50
SW37 Thomas Greiss .60 1.50
SW38 Craig Anderson .60 1.50
SW39 Tuukka Rask 1.00 2.50
SW40 Marc-Andre Fleury 1.50 4.00
SW41 Dominik Hasek 1.25 3.00
SW42 Ed Belfour .75 2.00
SW43 Felix Potvin 1.25 3.00
SW44 Gerry Cheevers .75 2.00
SW45 Grant Fuhr 1.25 3.00
SW46 Johnny Bower .75 2.00
SW47 Martin Brodeur 2.00 5.00
SW48 Patrick Roy 2.00 5.00
SW49 Ron Hextall .75 2.00
SW50 Tom Barrasso .75 2.00

2018-19 Upper Deck Tricksters

T1 Anze Kopitar 6.00 15.00
T2 Alex DeBrincat 5.00 12.00
T3 William Karlsson 5.00 12.00
T4 Mathew Barzal 5.00 12.00
T5 Brock Boeser 5.00 12.00
T6 Connor McDavid 60.00 150.00
T7 Patrice Bergeron 5.00 12.00
T8 Mark Scheifele 6.00 15.00
T9 Alexander Ovechkin 15.00 40.00
T10 Evgeni Malkin 8.00 20.00
T11 Jamie Benn 4.00 10.00

2018-19 Upper Deck Triple Exposure

2 Ryan Getzlaf 12.00 30.00
25 Jack Eichel 25.00 60.00
31 Johnny Gaudreau 20.00 50.00
42 Patrick Kane 25.00 60.00
53 Seth Jones 12.00 30.00
77 Jonathan Huberdeau 15.00 40.00
87 Anze Kopitar 20.00 50.00
90 Eric Staal 12.00 30.00
104 Roman Josi 12.00 30.00
110 Nico Hischier 20.00 50.00
118 Mathew Barzal 15.00 40.00
138 Claude Giroux 12.00 30.00
141 Evgeni Malkin 25.00 60.00
154 Vladimir Tarasenko 25.00 60.00
171 Mitch Marner 20.00 50.00
177 Brock Boeser 40.00 100.00
178 Alex Tuch 12.00 30.00
198 Blake Wheeler 12.00 30.00
266 David Pastrnak 30.00 80.00
272 Jeff Skinner 15.00 40.00
279 James Neal 8.00 20.00
293 Jonathan Toews 20.00 50.00
299 Mikko Rantanen 30.00 80.00
310 Tyler Seguin 15.00 40.00
337 Drew Doughty 15.00 40.00
374 Henrik Lundqvist 30.00 80.00
392 Sidney Crosby 50.00 125.00
398 Erik Karlsson 15.00 40.00
401 Joe Thornton 20.00 50.00
406 Ryan O'Reilly 12.00 30.00
412 Nikita Kucherov 25.00 60.00
418 Auston Matthews 50.00 125.00
433 William Karlsson 15.00 40.00
437 Evgeny Kuznetsov 15.00 40.00
443 Mark Scheifele 20.00 50.00

2018-19 Upper Deck UD Portraits

P1 Semyon Varlamov .60 1.50
P2 Jonathan Drouin .50 1.25
P3 Mathew Barzal .75 2.00
P4 Marc-Andre Fleury 1.25 3.00
P5 Aaron Ekblad .75 2.00
P6 Brock Boeser .75 2.00
P7 Viktor Arvidsson .40 1.00
P8 Joe Pavelski .75 2.00
P9 Clayton Keller .75 2.00
P10 Alexander Wennberg .40 1.00
P11 Brendan Gallagher .60 1.50
P12 Patrick Marleau .60 1.50
P13 Johnny Gaudreau 1.00 2.50
P14 Dmitry Orlov .60 1.50
P15 Jack Eichel 1.00 2.50
P16 Steven Stamkos 1.25 3.00
P17 Matt Duchene .60 1.50
P18 Teuvo Teravainen .60 1.50
P19 Mikhail Sergachev .50 1.25
P20 Colton Parayko .50 1.25
P21 Artemi Panarin 1.25 3.00
P22 Nino Niederreiter .40 1.00
P23 Connor McDavid 3.00 8.00
P24 David Pastrnak 1.50 4.00
P25 Ivan Provorov .50 1.25
P26 Brandon Montour .75 2.00
P27 Nikolaj Ehlers .60 1.50
P28 Claude Giroux .60 1.50
P29 Ben Bishop .50 1.25
P30 Henrik Lundqvist 1.50 4.00
P31 Tanner Pearson .50 1.25
P32 Nico Hischier 1.00 2.50
P33 Dustin Byfuglien .60 1.50
P34 Auston Matthews 2.50 6.00
P35 Pekka Rinne .60 1.50
P36 Gabriel Landeskog .75 2.00
P37 Brayden Schenn .60 1.50
P38 Alex DeBrincat .75 2.00
P39 Sidney Crosby 2.50 6.00
P40 Henrik Zetterberg .75 2.00
P41 Mike Smith .50 1.25
P42 Jake Guentzel 1.00 2.50
P43 William Karlsson .75 2.00
P44 Alexander Ovechkin 2.50 6.00
P45 Adam Gaudette 1.00 2.50
P46 Ryan Donato 1.00 2.50
P47 Jordan Greenway .60 1.50
P48 Eeli Tolvanen 1.25 3.00
P49 Lias Andersson 1.00 2.50
P50 Casey Mittelstadt 1.25 3.00
P51 Ilya Samsonov 1.25 3.00
P52 Jeremy Lauzon .75 2.00
P53 Mathieu Joseph .75 2.00
P54 Drake Batherson 1.25 3.00
P55 Dennis Cholowski .60 1.50
P56 Warren Foegele .60 1.50
P57 Maxime Lajoie 1.00 2.50
P58 Troy Terry 1.00 2.50
P59 Christian Wolanin .50 1.25
P60 Sami Niku .50 1.25
P61 Jaret Anderson-Dolan .50 1.25
P62 Michael Dal Colle .60 1.50
P63 Victor Ejdsell .50 1.25
P64 Evan Bouchard 1.50 4.00
P65 Dominik Kahun .60 1.50
P66 Robert Thomas 1.25 3.00
P67 Mikhail Vorobyev .50 1.25
P68 Dominic Turgeon .60 1.50
P69 Maxime Comtois .60 1.50
P70 Kristian Vesalainen .75 2.00
P71 Oskar Lindblom 1.00 2.50
P72 Noah Juulsen .60 1.50
P73 Marcus Pettersson .60 1.50
P74 Ethan Bear 1.00 2.50
P75 Travis Dermott 1.00 2.50
P76 Morgan Klimchuk .60 1.50
P77 Brady Tkachuk 2.00 5.00
P78 Brett Howden .75 2.00
P79 Sam Steel .60 1.50
P80 Juuso Valimaki .60 1.50
P81 Isac Lundestrom .50 1.25
P82 Maxim Mamin .60 1.50
P83 Henri Jokiharju .50 1.25
P84 Filip Hronek .60 1.50
P85 Jordan Kyrou 1.25 3.00
P86 Kiefer Sherwood .50 1.25
P87 Antti Suomela .50 1.25
P88 Samuel Montembeault 1.25 3.00
P89 Dillon Dube .75 2.00
P90 Henrik Borgstrom 1.00 2.50
P91 Zach Aston-Reese 1.00 2.50
P92 Dylan Sikura .75 2.00
P93 Michael Rasmussen .75 2.00
P94 Spencer Foo .50 1.25
P95 Neal Pionk .60 1.50
P96 Anthony Cirelli 1.00 2.50
P97 Andreas Johnsson .75 2.00
P98 Jesperi Kotkaniemi 1.25 3.00
P99 Elias Pettersson 2.00 5.00
P100 Rasmus Dahlin 1.50 4.00

2018-19 Upper Deck Winter Classic Jumbo

WC1 J.T. Miller 2.50 6.00
WC2 Robin Lehner 1.50 4.00
WC3 Kevin Hayes 1.50 4.00
WC4 Kyle Okposo 1.25 3.00
WC5 Henrik Lundqvist 5.00 12.00
WC6 Ryan O'Reilly 2.00 5.00
WC7 Kevin Shattenkirk 1.25 3.00
WC8 Rasmus Ristolainen 1.25 3.00
WC9 Mats Zuccarello 2.00 5.00
WC10 Sam Reinhart 4.00 10.00
WC11 Paul Carey 1.25 3.00
WC12 Jack Eichel 3.00 8.00
WC13 Jesper Fast 1.25 3.00
WC14 Marco Scandella 1.25 3.00

2019-20 Upper Deck

1 Auston Matthews 1.25 3.00
2 William Nylander .60 1.50
3 Jake Muzzin .30 .75
4 Zach Hyman .50 1.25
5 Kasperi Kapanen .25 .60
6 Morgan Rielly .30 .75
7 Frederik Andersen .40 1.00
8 Tuukka Rask .40 1.00
9 Charlie Coyle .30 .75
10 Jake DeBrusk .30 .75
11 David Krejci .30 .75
12 Zdeno Chara .30 .75
13 Torey Krug .25 .60
14 Brad Marchand .60 1.50
15 Kyle Okposo .20 .50
16 Conor Sheary .30 .75
17 Casey Mittelstadt .30 .75
18 Sam Reinhart .60 1.50
19 Rasmus Dahlin .40 1.00
20 Zach Bogosian .25 .60
21 Anthony Cirelli .25 .60
22 Nikita Kucherov .60 1.50
23 Yanni Gourde .25 .60
24 Tyler Johnson .20 .50
25 Ondrej Palat .25 .60
26 Alex Killorn .20 .50
27 Victor Hedman .40 1.00
28 Dylan Larkin .40 1.00
29 Frans Nielsen .20 .50
30 Tyler Bertuzzi .25 .60
31 Danny DeKeyser .20 .50
32 Mike Green .25 .60
33 Darren Helm .20 .50
34 Bobby Ryan .25 .60
35 Chris Tierney .25 .60
36 Mikkel Boedker .20 .50
37 Anthony Duclair .25 .60
38 Jean-Gabriel Pageau .20 .50
39 Thomas Chabot .30 .75
40 Aleksander Barkov .50 1.25
41 Mike Hoffman .20 .50
42 Henrik Borgstrom .25 .60
43 Frank Vatrano .25 .60
44 Keith Yandle .20 .50
45 Roberto Luongo .50 1.25
46 Max Domi .30 .75
47 Tomas Tatar .20 .50
48 Jesperi Kotkaniemi .30 .75
49 Phillip Danault .30 .75
50 Jordan Weal .20 .50
51 Shea Weber .30 .75
52 Jeff Petry .30 .75
53 Andrei Svechnikov .40 1.00
54 Teuvo Teravainen .30 .75
55 Warren Foegele .25 .60
56 Nino Niederreiter .20 .50
57 Dougie Hamilton .25 .60
58 Brett Pesce .20 .50
59 Evgeny Kuznetsov .40 1.00
60 Tom Wilson .30 .75
61 T.J. Oshie .30 .75
62 Lars Eller .20 .50
63 Michal Kempny .20 .50
64 John Carlson .30 .75
65 Braden Holtby .40 1.00
66 Cam Atkinson .30 .75
67 Josh Anderson .25 .60
68 Oliver Bjorkstrand .25 .60
69 Alexander Wennberg .20 .50
70 Boone Jenner .30 .75
71 Seth Jones .30 .75
72 Nolan Patrick .30 .75
73 Jakub Voracek .25 .60
74 Sean Couturier .25 .60
75 James van Riemsdyk .25 .60
76 Oskar Lindblom .25 .60
77 Carter Hart .30 .75
78 Taylor Hall .30 .75
79 Kyle Palmieri .25 .60
80 Jesper Bratt .30 .75
81 Blake Coleman .25 .60
82 Damon Severson .20 .50
83 Mackenzie Blackwood .30 .75
84 Chris Kreider .40 1.00
85 Pavel Buchnevich .25 .60
86 Jesper Fast .20 .50
87 Ryan Strome .30 .75
88 Filip Chytil .25 .60
89 Marc Staal .20 .50
90 Henrik Lundqvist .75 2.00
91 Mathew Barzal .40 1.00
92 Josh Bailey .25 .60
93 Casey Cizikas .20 .50
94 Cal Clutterbuck .20 .50
95 Leo Komarov .20 .50
96 Nick Leddy .20 .50
97 Patric Hornqvist .20 .50
98 Nick Bjugstad .20 .50
99 Bryan Rust .30 .75
100 Sidney Crosby 1.25 3.00
101 Dominik Simon .20 .50
102 Justin Schultz .30 .75
103 Matt Murray .30 .75
104 Mark Scheifele .50 1.25
105 Nikolaj Ehlers .30 .75
106 Bryan Little .25 .60
107 Adam Lowry .25 .60
108 Josh Morrissey .40 1.00
109 Connor Hellebuyck .60 1.50
110 Jonathan Toews .50 1.25
111 Dylan Strome .40 1.00
112 Brandon Saad .25 .60
113 Brent Seabrook .20 .50
114 Duncan Keith .25 .60
115 Erik Gustafsson .20 .50
116 Corey Crawford .30 .75
117 Ryan O'Reilly .30 .75
118 Brayden Schenn .30 .75
119 Tyler Bozak .20 .50
120 Robert Thomas .30 .75
121 David Perron .25 .60
122 Alex Pietrangelo .25 .60
123 Jordan Binnington .50 1.25
124 Eric Staal .30 .75
125 Jason Zucker .30 .75
126 Marcus Foligno .25 .60
127 Matt Dumba .20 .50
128 Jared Spurgeon .30 .75
129 Ryan Suter .25 .60
130 Nathan MacKinnon 1.25 3.00
131 Samuel Girard .20 .50
132 Matt Calvert .20 .50
133 Tyson Jost .25 .60
134 J.T. Compher .20 .50
135 Philipp Grubauer .30 .75
136 Filip Forsberg .50 1.25
137 Mikael Granlund .25 .60
138 Viktor Arvidsson .20 .50
139 Nick Bonino .20 .50
140 Kyle Turris .25 .60
141 Mattias Ekholm .25 .60
142 Ryan Ellis .25 .60
143 Tyler Seguin .40 1.00
144 Alexander Radulov .30 .75
145 Radek Faksa .25 .60
146 Roope Hintz .40 1.00
147 John Klingberg .30 .75
148 Esa Lindell .25 .60
149 Ilya Kovalchuk .30 .75
150 Jeff Carter .25 .60
151 Tyler Toffoli .30 .75
152 Kyle Clifford .20 .50
153 Drew Doughty .40 1.00
154 Jonathan Quick .40 1.00
155 Derek Stepan .20 .50
156 Christian Dvorak .25 .60
157 Christian Fischer .20 .50
158 Brad Richardson .20 .50
159 Jakob Chychrun .30 .75
160 Niklas Hjalmarsson .20 .50
161 Logan Couture .40 1.00
162 Evander Kane .30 .75
163 Tomas Hertl .30 .75
164 Marcus Sorensen .25 .60
165 Brent Burns .30 .75
166 Brenden Dillon .20 .50
167 Martin Jones .25 .60
168 Elias Pettersson .50 1.25
169 Bo Horvat .40 1.00
170 Loui Eriksson .20 .50
171 Jake Virtanen .30 .75
172 Antoine Roussel .20 .50
173 Troy Stecher .20 .50
174 Cam Fowler .30 .75
175 Rickard Rakell .25 .60
176 Nick Ritchie .20 .50
177 Jakob Silfverberg .20 .50
178 Daniel Sprong .20 .50
179 Hampus Lindholm .20 .50
180 Johnny Gaudreau .50 1.25
181 Sam Bennett .50 1.25
182 Mikael Backlund .25 .60
183 Elias Lindholm .30 .75
184 Noah Hanifin .30 .75
185 Mark Giordano .30 .75
186 Leon Draisaitl 1.00 2.50
187 Alex Chiasson .25 .60
188 Ryan Nugent-Hopkins .40 1.00
189 Oscar Klefbom .30 .75
190 Darnell Nurse .25 .60
191 Mikko Koskinen .20 .50
192 Mark Stone .40 1.00
193 Max Pacioretty .30 .75
194 Paul Stastny .25 .60
195 Cody Eakin .20 .50
196 Ryan Reaves .20 .50
197 Shea Theodore .40 1.00
198 Marc-Andre Fleury .60 1.50
199 A.Matthews/J.Gaudreau CL 1.25 3.00
200 B.Marchand/R.O'Reilly CL .60 1.50
201 Jack Hughes YG RC 50.00 125.00
202 Blake Lizotte YG RC 3.00 8.00
203 Conor Timmins YG RC 3.00 8.00
204 Ville Heinola YG RC 4.00 10.00
205 Nathan Bastian YG RC 3.00 8.00
206 Jimmy Schuldt YG RC 2.50 6.00
207 Victor Olofsson YG RC 10.00 25.00
208 Connor Bunnaman YG RC 2.50 6.00
209 Cale Fleury YG RC 4.00 10.00
210 Ilya Mikheyev YG RC 8.00 20.00
211 Kevin Stenlund YG RC 2.50 6.00
212 Mackenzie MacEachern YG RC 3.00 8.00
213 Joakim Nygard YG RC 2.50 6.00
214 Carsen Twarynski YG RC 2.50 6.00
215 Taro Hirose YG RC 3.00 8.00
216 Brady Keeper YG RC 3.00 8.00
217 Joel L'Esperance YG RC 3.00 8.00
218 Rudolfs Balcers YG RC 3.00 8.00
219 Nico Sturm YG RC 2.50 6.00
220 Scott Sabourin YG RC 2.50 6.00
221 Philippe Myers YG RC 2.50 6.00
222 Rasmus Sandin YG RC 5.00 12.00
223 Danil Yurtaykin YG RC 2.50 6.00
224 Carter Verhaeghe YG RC 5.00 12.00
225 Alexandre Texier YG RC 6.00 15.00
226 Ryan Poehling YG RC 8.00 20.00
227 Vitaly Abramov YG RC 3.00 8.00
228 Adam Fox YG RC 10.00 25.00
229 Dante Fabbro YG RC 3.00 8.00
230 Mario Ferraro YG RC 2.50 6.00
231 Teddy Blueger YG RC 3.00 8.00
232 Gaetan Haas YG RC 2.50 6.00
233 Jesper Boqvist YG RC 2.50 6.00
234 Zach Senyshyn YG RC 3.00 8.00
235 Matt Roy YG RC 3.00 8.00
236 Martin Fehervary YG RC 2.50 6.00
237 Cody Glass YG RC 5.00 12.00
238 Tobias Bjornfot YG RC 3.00 8.00
239 Brandon Gignac YG RC 2.50 6.00
240 Libor Hajek YG RC 2.50 6.00
241 Vladislav Gavrikov YG RC 2.50 6.00
242 Max Jones YG RC 3.00 8.00
243 Connor Clifton YG RC 3.00 8.00
244 Zack MacEwen YG RC 2.50 6.00
245 Lean Bergmann YG RC 2.50 6.00
246 Dominik Kubalik YG RC 8.00 20.00
247 Josh Brown YG RC 2.50 6.00
248 Karson Kuhlman YG RC 3.00 8.00
249 Quinn Hughes YG RC 50.00 125.00
250 J.Hughes/Q.Hughes YG CL 5.00 12.00
251 John Tavares .50 1.25
252 Alex Kerfoot .25 .60
253 Cody Ceci .20 .50
254 Jason Spezza .30 .75
255 Tyson Barrie .20 .50
256 Mitch Marner .50 1.25
257 Patrice Bergeron .40 1.00
258 Charlie McAvoy .40 1.00
259 Matt Grzelcyk .25 .60
260 Danton Heinen .25 .60
261 Brandon Carlo .25 .60
262 David Backes .20 .50
263 Carter Hutton .25 .60
264 Jack Eichel .50 1.25
265 Jeff Skinner .30 .75
266 Jimmy Vesey .25 .60
267 Brandon Montour .40 1.00
268 Marcus Johansson .25 .60
269 Colin Miller .20 .50
270 Steven Stamkos .60 1.50
271 Brayden Point .40 1.00
272 Andrei Vasilevskiy .50 1.25
273 Ryan McDonagh .20 .50
274 Mikhail Sergachev .25 .60
275 Braydon Coburn .20 .50
276 Kevin Shattenkirk .20 .50
277 Justin Abdelkader .25 .60
278 Andreas Athanasiou .25 .60
279 Madison Bowey .20 .50
280 Jim Howard .40 1.00
281 Anthony Mantha .25 .60
282 Robby Fabbri .20 .50
283 Valtteri Filppula .20 .50
284 Tyler Ennis .20 .50
285 Ron Hainsey .20 .50
286 Artem Anisimov .20 .50
287 Brady Tkachuk .50 1.25
288 Colin White .20 .50
289 Nikita Zaitsev .20 .50
290 Craig Anderson .25 .60
291 Jonathan Huberdeau .40 1.00
292 Vincent Trocheck .30 .75
293 Aaron Ekblad .40 1.00
294 Brett Connolly .20 .50
295 Evgenii Dadonov .20 .50
296 Sergei Bobrovsky .50 1.25
297 Anton Stralman .20 .50
298 Carey Price .60 1.50
299 Jonathan Drouin .25 .60
300 Brendan Gallagher .30 .75
301 Paul Byron .20 .50
302 Joel Armia .20 .50
303 Artturi Lehkonen .25 .60
304 Sebastian Aho .50 1.25
305 Ryan Dzingel .25 .60
306 James Reimer .30 .75
307 Petr Mrazek .30 .75
308 Jordan Staal .25 .60
309 Jaccob Slavin .25 .60
310 Alexander Ovechkin 1.25 3.00
311 Nicklas Backstrom .30 .75
312 Radko Gudas .25 .60
313 Dmitry Orlov .30 .75
314 Carl Hagelin .20 .50
315 Jakub Vrana .30 .75
316 Gustav Nyquist .20 .50
317 Joonas Korpisalo .30 .75
318 Brandon Dubinsky .20 .50
319 Zach Werenski .50 1.25
320 Nick Foligno .25 .60
321 Pierre-Luc Dubois .25 .60
322 Ryan Murray .25 .60
323 Claude Giroux .30 .75
324 Matt Niskanen .25 .60
325 Kevin Hayes .25 .60
326 Shayne Gostisbehere .30 .75
327 Travis Konecny .30 .75
328 Justin Braun .20 .50
329 Brian Elliott .25 .60
330 P.K. Subban .40 1.00
331 Wayne Simmonds .30 .75
332 Will Butcher .25 .60
333 Cory Schneider .30 .75
334 Travis Zajac .20 .50
335 Sami Vatanen .20 .50
336 Nico Hischier .50 1.25
337 Artemi Panarin .60 1.50
338 Mika Zibanejad .40 1.00
339 Brady Skjei .25 .60
340 Lias Andersson .25 .60
341 Anthony DeAngelo .20 .50
342 Brendan Smith .20 .50

343 Jacob Trouba .25 .60
344 Semyon Varlamov .30 .75
345 Anders Lee .25 .60
346 Jordan Eberle .30 .75
347 Matt Martin .20 .50
348 Anthony Beauvillier .20 .50
349 Thomas Greiss .25 .60
350 Evgeni Malkin .60 1.50
351 Jake Guentzel .50 1.25
352 Kris Letang .40 1.00
353 Alex Galchenyuk .20 .50
354 Brian Dumoulin .20 .50
355 Brandon Tanev .25 .60
356 Blake Wheeler .30 .75
357 Mathieu Perreault .20 .50
358 Neal Pionk .20 .50
359 Patrik Laine .40 1.00
360 Kyle Connor .50 1.25
361 Jack Roslovic .20 .50
362 Patrick Kane .60 1.50
363 Alex DeBrincat .40 1.00
364 Robin Lehner .25 .60
365 Andrew Shaw .20 .50
366 Calvin de Haan .20 .50
367 Olli Maatta .20 .50
368 Vladimir Tarasenko .40 1.00
369 Alexander Steen .20 .50
370 Colton Parayko .25 .60
371 Jaden Schwartz .40 1.00
372 Jay Bouwmeester .20 .50
373 Vince Dunn .25 .60
374 Mats Zuccarello .30 .75
375 Ryan Hartman .20 .50
376 Zach Parise .30 .75
377 Devan Dubnyk .25 .60
378 Mikko Koivu .25 .60
379 Kevin Fiala .25 .60
380 Joonas Donskoi .20 .50
381 Nazem Kadri .40 1.00
382 Mikko Rantanen .75 2.00
383 Gabriel Landeskog .40 1.00
384 Andre Burakovsky .20 .50
385 Erik Johnson .20 .50
386 Colin Wilson .20 .50
387 Matt Duchene .30 .75
388 Ryan Johansen .25 .60
389 Roman Josi .30 .75
390 Pekka Rinne .30 .75
391 Colton Sissons .20 .50
392 Craig Smith .20 .50
393 Joe Pavelski .40 1.00
394 Corey Perry .50 1.25
395 Jamie Benn .30 .75
396 Ben Bishop .25 .60
397 Andrej Sekera .20 .50
398 Miro Heiskanen .40 1.00
399 Anze Kopitar .50 1.25
400 Dustin Brown .30 .75
401 Alex Iafallo .20 .50
402 Alec Martinez .20 .50
403 Trevor Lewis .20 .50
404 Adrian Kempe .30 .75
405 Phil Kessel .30 .75
406 Oliver Ekman-Larsson .30 .75
407 Antti Raanta .30 .75
408 Nick Schmaltz .25 .60
409 Clayton Keller .40 1.00
410 Michael Grabner .25 .60
411 Erik Karlsson .40 1.00
412 Timo Meier .30 .75
413 Joe Thornton .50 1.25
414 Kevin Labanc .25 .60
415 Marc-Edouard Vlasic .20 .50
416 Melker Karlsson .20 .50
417 Tyler Myers .20 .50
418 Brock Boeser .40 1.00
419 Jacob Markstrom .30 .75
420 Alexander Edler .20 .50
421 Christopher Tanev .20 .50
422 J.T. Miller .40 1.00
423 Tanner Pearson .30 .75
424 John Gibson .30 .75
425 Ryan Getzlaf .30 .75
426 Adam Henrique .25 .60
427 Ondrej Kase .20 .50
428 Josh Manson .20 .50
429 Ryan Miller .30 .75
430 Matthew Tkachuk .60 1.50
431 David Rittich .25 .60
432 Sean Monahan .25 .60
433 Milan Lucic .25 .60
434 Michael Frolik .25 .60
435 Derek Ryan .20 .50
436 Connor McDavid 1.50 4.00
437 Mike Smith .20 .50
438 James Neal .20 .50
439 Sam Gagner .20 .50
440 Zack Kassian .20 .50
441 Jujhar Khaira .20 .50
442 Adam Larsson .25 .60
443 Alex Tuch .30 .75
444 Nate Schmidt .25 .60
445 William Karlsson .40 1.00
446 Jonathan Marchessault .40 1.00
447 Reilly Smith .30 .75
448 Brayden McNabb .20 .50
449 A.Panarin/S.Bobrovsky CL .60 1.50
450 E.Karlsson/P.Subban CL .40 1.00
451 Kirby Dach YG RC 8.00 20.00
452 Andrew Peeke YG RC 2.00 5.00
453 Aleksi Saarela YG RC 3.00 8.00
454 Cayden Primeau YG RC 15.00 40.00
455 Emil Bemstrom YG RC 3.00 8.00
456 Rem Pitlick YG RC 3.00 8.00
457 Oliver Wahlstrom YG RC 12.00 30.00
458 John Marino YG RC 5.00 12.00
459 Ryan Lindgren YG RC 3.00 8.00
460 Dmytro Timashov YG RC 3.00 8.00
461 David Gustafsson YG RC 2.50 6.00
462 Noah Gregor YG RC 2.50 6.00
463 Barrett Hayton YG RC 6.00 15.00
464 Erik Brannstrom YG RC 3.00 8.00
465 Rhett Gardner YG RC 2.50 6.00
466 Elvis Merzlikins YG RC 4.00 10.00
467 Nikolai Prokhorkin YG RC 2.50 6.00
468 Nikita Gusev YG RC 5.00 12.00
469 Morgan Frost YG RC 5.00 12.00
470 Kaapo Kahkonen YG RC 12.00 30.00
471 Nick Suzuki YG RC 60.00 150.00
472 Trent Frederic YG RC 3.00 8.00
473 Jack Studnicka YG RC 6.00 15.00
474 Givani Smith YG RC 2.50 6.00
475 Rasmus Asplund YG RC 2.50 6.00
476 Pierre Engvall YG RC 2.50 6.00
477 Joey Daccord YG RC 6.00 15.00
478 Filip Zadina YG RC 5.00 12.00
479 Jonathan Davidsson YG RC 2.00 5.00
480 Beck Malenstyn YG RC 3.00 8.00
481 Noah Dobson YG RC 20.00 50.00
482 Max Veronneau YG RC 2.50 6.00
483 Otto Koivula YG RC 2.00 5.00
484 Carl Grundstrom YG RC 3.00 8.00
485 Trevor Moore YG RC 2.50 6.00
486 German Rubtsov YG RC 2.50 6.00
487 Joona Luoto YG RC 2.50 6.00
488 Alexander Volkov YG RC 2.50 6.00
489 Nicolas Hague YG RC 3.00 8.00
490 Eetu Luostarinen YG RC 3.00 8.00
491 Joel Farabee YG RC 10.00 25.00
492 Adam Boqvist YG RC 3.00 8.00
493 Cale Makar YG RC 150.00 400.00
494 Klim Kostin YG RC 3.00 8.00
495 Guillaume Brisebois YG RC 3.00 8.00
496 Sam Lafferty YG RC 2.50 6.00
497 Joel Persson YG RC 2.50 6.00
498 Julien Gauthier YG RC 3.00 8.00
499 Kaapo Kakko YG RC 5.00 12.00
500 K.Dach/K.Kakko YG CL 2.00 5.00
501 David Pastrnak .75 2.00
502 Taylor Hall .30 .75
503 Linus Ullmark .30 .75
504 Connor Brown .25 .60
505 Justin Faulk .25 .60
506 Jason Zucker .30 .75
507 Chandler Stephenson .25 .60
508 Darcy Kuemper .30 .75
509 Blake Coleman .25 .60
510 Tristan Jarry .30 .75
511 Carl Soderberg .20 .50
512 Alec Martinez .20 .50
513 Joel Edmundson .20 .50
514 Tyler Toffoli .30 .75
515 Alexandar Georgiev .30 .75
516 Calle Jarnkrok 2.00 5.00
517 Adam Johnson YG RC 2.50 6.00
518 Nick Caamano YG RC 2.50 6.00
519 David Ayres YG RC 15.00 40.00
520 J.C. Beaudin YG RC 2.50 6.00
521 Yakov Trenin YG RC 2.50 6.00
522 Adam Werner YG RC 2.50 6.00
523 Joachim Blichfeld YG RC 3.00 8.00
524 Mitchell Stephens YG RC 2.00 5.00
525 Kale Clague YG RC 2.50 6.00
526 Adam Brooks YG RC 2.00 5.00
527 Jake Walman YG RC 4.00 10.00
528 Igor Shesterkin YG RC 60.00 150.00
529 Patrick Kane AS .60 1.50
530 Roman Josi AS .30 .75
531 Gabriel Landeskog AS .40 1.00
532 Devan Dubnyk AS .25 .60
533 Johnny Gaudreau AS .50 1.25
534 Braden Holtby AS .40 1.00
535 Steven Stamkos AS .60 1.50
536 Kris Letang AS .40 1.00
537 Cam Atkinson AS .30 .75
538 Cam Atkinson AS .30 .75
539 Henrik Lundqvist AS .75 2.00
540 Sidney Crosby AS 1.25 3.00
541 Mathew Barzal AS .40 1.00
542 Sidney Crosby AS 1.25 3.00
SP1 Jack Hughes SP 30.00 80.00

2019-20 Upper Deck Clear Cut Parallel

*VETS: 6X TO 15X BASIC
*YG: 2X TO 5X BASIC
201 Jack Hughes YG 300.00 800.00
224 Carter Verhaeghe YG 60.00 150.00
225 Alexandre Texier YG 50.00 125.00
226 Ryan Poehling YG 150.00 250.00
228 Adam Fox YG 80.00 200.00
237 Cody Glass YG 25.00 60.00
246 Dominik Kubalik YG 80.00 200.00
249 Quinn Hughes YG 200.00 500.00
451 Kirby Dach 80.00 200.00
454 Cayden Primeau 60.00 150.00
466 Elvis Merzlikins 60.00 150.00
470 Kaapo Kahkonen 100.00 250.00
471 Nick Suzuki 150.00 400.00
473 Jack Studnicka 30.00 80.00
481 Noah Dobson YG 80.00 200.00
491 Joel Farabee 25.00 60.00
493 Cale Makar 500.00 1200.00
499 Kaapo Kakko 30.00 80.00
500 Kirby Dach
Kaapo Kakko YG CL 3.00 8.00

2019-20 Upper Deck Exclusives

*VETS: 3X TO 8X BASIC
*YG: 3X TO 8X BASIC
201 Jack Hughes YG 600.00 1500.00
224 Carter Verhaeghe YG 40.00 100.00
225 Alexandre Texier YG 40.00 100.00
226 Ryan Poehling YG 250.00 350.00
228 Adam Fox YG 150.00 400.00
235 Matt Roy YG 40.00 100.00
236 Martin Fehervary YG 30.00 80.00
246 Dominik Kubalik YG 80.00 200.00
249 Quinn Hughes YG 300.00 800.00
451 Kirby Dach 125.00 300.00
454 Cayden Primeau 125.00 300.00
466 Elvis Merzlikins 125.00 300.00
470 Kaapo Kahkonen 50.00 125.00
471 Nick Suzuki 250.00 600.00
473 Jack Studnicka 60.00 150.00
481 Noah Dobson YG 150.00 400.00
491 Joel Farabee 60.00 150.00
493 Cale Makar 1200.00 3000.00
499 Kaapo Kakko 50.00 125.00
500 Kirby Dach
Kaapo Kakko YG CL 12.00 30.00
519 David Ayres YG 80.00 200.00
528 Igor Shesterkin YG 250.00 600.00

2019-20 Upper Deck '94-95 Rookie Tribute Die Cuts

*RED: .6X TO 1.5X BASIC
1 Cale Makar 3.00 8.00
2 Filip Zadina 1.00 2.50
3 Carl Grundstrom .60 1.50
4 Alexandre Texier .60 1.50
5 Quinn Hughes 3.00 8.00
6 Dante Fabbro .60 1.50
7 Max Jones .60 1.50
8 Zach Senyshyn .60 1.50
9 Vitaly Abramov .60 1.50
10 Ryan Poehling 1.00 2.50
11 Jack Hughes 3.00 8.00
12 Morgan Frost 1.00 2.50
13 Victor Olofsson 1.25 3.00
14 Cody Glass 1.00 2.50
15 Kirby Dach 3.00 8.00
16 Ilya Mikheyev 1.00 2.50
17 Noah Dobson 1.50 4.00
18 Adam Boqvist .60 1.50
19 Nick Suzuki 2.50 6.00
20 Kaapo Kakko 1.00 2.50

2019-20 Upper Deck 30 Years of Upper Deck

UD301 Wayne Gretzky 1.50 4.00
UD302 Wayne Gretzky 1.50 4.00
UD303 Wayne Gretzky 1.50 4.00
UD304 Wayne Gretzky 1.50 4.00
UD305 Wayne Gretzky 1.50 4.00
UD306 Wayne Gretzky 1.50 4.00
UD307 Wayne Gretzky 1.50 4.00
UD308 Wayne Gretzky 1.50 4.00
UD309 Wayne Gretzky 1.50 4.00
UD3010 Wayne Gretzky 1.50 4.00
UD3011 Patrick Roy .60 1.50
UD3012 Patrick Roy .60 1.50
UD3013 Patrick Roy .60 1.50
UD3014 Patrick Roy .60 1.50
UD3015 Patrick Roy .60 1.50
UD3016 Patrick Roy .60 1.50
UD3017 Patrick Roy .60 1.50
UD3018 Patrick Roy .60 1.50
UD3019 Patrick Roy .60 1.50
UD3020 Patrick Roy .60 1.50
UD3021 Connor McDavid 1.25 3.00
UD3022 Connor McDavid 1.25 3.00
UD3023 Connor McDavid 1.25 3.00
UD3024 Connor McDavid 1.25 3.00
UD3025 Connor McDavid 1.25 3.00
UD3026 Connor McDavid 1.25 3.00
UD3027 Connor McDavid 1.25 3.00
UD3028 Connor McDavid 1.25 3.00
UD3029 Connor McDavid 1.25 3.00
UD3030 Connor McDavid 1.25 3.00

2019-20 Upper Deck Canvas

C1 John Tavares 1.00 2.50
C2 Morgan Rielly .60 1.50
C3 Andreas Johnsson .60 1.50
C4 David Pastrnak 1.50 4.00
C5 Patrice Bergeron .75 2.00
C6 Zdeno Chara .60 1.50
C7 Jack Eichel 1.00 2.50
C8 Conor Sheary .50 1.25
C9 Rasmus Ristolainen .40 1.00
C10 Steven Stamkos 1.25 3.00
C11 Andrei Vasilevskiy 1.00 2.50
C12 Ryan McDonagh .40 1.00
C13 Andreas Athanasiou .50 1.25
C14 Tyler Bertuzzi .50 1.25
C15 Brady Tkachuk 1.00 2.50
C16 Mikkel Boedker .40 1.00
C17 Colin White .40 1.00
C18 Jonathan Huberdeau .75 2.00
C19 Vincent Trocheck .60 1.50
C20 Michael Matheson .40 1.00
C21 Jonathan Drouin .50 1.25
C22 Jesperi Kotkaniemi .60 1.50
C23 Shea Weber .60 1.50
C24 Sebastian Aho 1.00 2.50
C25 Jaccob Slavin .50 1.25
C26 Nino Niederreiter .40 1.00
C27 Alexander Ovechkin 2.50 6.00
C28 T.J. Oshie .60 1.50
C29 Nicklas Backstrom .60 1.50
C30 Pierre-Luc Dubois .50 1.25
C31 Brandon Dubinsky .40 1.00
C32 Nick Foligno .50 1.25
C33 Carter Hart .60 1.50
C34 Sean Couturier .50 1.25
C35 Claude Giroux .60 1.50
C36 Nico Hischier 1.00 2.50
C37 Travis Zajac .40 1.00
C38 Miles Wood .40 1.00
C39 Mika Zibanejad .75 2.00
C40 Pavel Buchnevich .50 1.25
C41 Brady Skjei .50 1.25
C42 Brock Nelson .60 1.50
C43 Josh Bailey .50 1.25
C44 Evgeni Malkin 1.25 3.00
C45 Jake Guentzel 1.00 2.50
C46 Kris Letang .75 2.00
C47 Blake Wheeler .60 1.50
C48 Kyle Connor 1.00 2.50
C49 Connor Hellebuyck 1.25 3.00
C50 Patrick Kane 1.25 3.00
C51 Brent Seabrook .40 1.00
C52 Brandon Saad .50 1.25
C53 Vladimir Tarasenko .75 2.00
C54 Colton Parayko .50 1.25
C55 Robert Thomas .60 1.50
C56 Jason Zucker .50 1.25
C57 Mikko Koivu .50 1.25
C58 Eric Staal .60 1.50
C59 Gabriel Landeskog .60 1.50
C60 Mikko Rantanen 1.50 4.00
C61 Samuel Girard .40 1.00
C62 Roman Josi .60 1.50
C63 Mikael Granlund .50 1.25
C64 Pekka Rinne .50 1.25
C65 Jamie Benn .60 1.50
C66 Miro Heiskanen .75 2.00
C67 Ben Bishop .50 1.25
C68 Anze Kopitar 1.00 2.50
C69 Dustin Brown .50 1.25
C70 Ilya Kovalchuk .60 1.50
C71 Clayton Keller .75 2.00
C72 Nick Schmaltz .50 1.25
C73 Tomas Hertl .60 1.50
C74 Evander Kane .60 1.50
C75 Marc-Edouard Vlasic .40 1.00
C76 Brock Boeser .75 2.00
C77 Bo Horvat .75 2.00
C78 Tanner Pearson .60 1.50
C79 Adam Henrique .50 1.25
C80 Ryan Getzlaf .60 1.50
C81 Johnny Gaudreau 1.00 2.50
C82 Matthew Tkachuk 1.25 3.00
C83 Elias Lindholm .60 1.50
C84 Connor McDavid 3.00 8.00
C85 Ryan Nugent-Hopkins .75 2.00
C86 Darnell Nurse .50 1.25
C87 Marc-Andre Fleury 1.25 3.00
C88 Jonathan Marchessault .75 2.00
C89 Mark Stone .75 2.00
C90 C.McDavid/A.Ovechkin CL 3.00 8.00
C91 Kaapo Kakko YG 4.00 10.00
C92 Aleksi Saarela YG 5.00 12.00
C93 Victor Olofsson YG 12.00 30.00
C94 Cale Makar YG 125.00 300.00
C95 Nikita Gusev YG 8.00 20.00
C96 Ville Heinola YG 6.00 15.00
C97 Adam Fox YG 12.00 30.00
C98 Carl Grundstrom YG 5.00 12.00
C99 Cale Fleury YG 4.00 10.00
C100 Mario Ferraro YG 4.00 10.00
C101 Max Veronneau YG 4.00 10.00
C102 Blake Lizotte YG 5.00 12.00
C103 Alexandre Texier YG 5.00 12.00
C104 Filip Zadina YG 8.00 20.00
C105 Nicolas Hague YG 5.00 12.00
C106 Erik Brannstrom YG 5.00 12.00
C107 Karson Kuhlman YG 5.00 12.00
C108 Tobias Bjornfot YG 5.00 12.00
C109 Joey Daccord YG 10.00 25.00
C110 Taro Hirose YG 5.00 12.00
C111 Ilya Mikheyev YG 8.00 20.00
C112 Emil Bemstrom YG 5.00 12.00
C113 Dominik Kubalik YG 6.00 15.00
C114 Joakim Nygard YG 4.00 10.00
C115 Nick Suzuki YG 40.00 100.00
C116 Dmytro Timashov YG 5.00 12.00
C117 Connor Clifton YG 5.00 12.00
C118 Elvis Merzlikins YG 5.00 12.00
C119 Trent Frederic YG 5.00 12.00
C120 K.Kakko/A.Fox YG CL 2.50 6.00
C121 Mitch Marner 1.00 2.50
C122 Auston Matthews 2.50 6.00
C123 Tyson Barrie .40 1.00
C124 Brad Marchand 1.25 3.00
C125 Tuukka Rask .75 2.00
C126 Torey Krug .60 1.50
C127 Jimmy Vesey .50 1.25
C128 Rasmus Dahlin .75 2.00
C129 Jeff Skinner .60 1.50
C130 Nikita Kucherov 1.25 3.00
C131 Victor Hedman .75 2.00
C132 Brayden Point .75 2.00
C133 Dylan Larkin .75 2.00
C134 Frans Nielsen .40 1.00
C135 Anthony Mantha .50 1.25
C136 Thomas Chabot .60 1.50
C137 Artem Anisimov .40 1.00
C138 Bobby Ryan .50 1.25
C139 Sergei Bobrovsky 1.00 2.50
C140 Aleksander Barkov 1.00 2.50
C141 Aaron Ekblad .60 1.50
C142 Carey Price 1.25 3.00
C143 Brendan Gallagher .60 1.50
C144 Max Domi .60 1.50
C145 Andrei Svechnikov .75 2.00
C146 Dougie Hamilton .50 1.25
C147 Ryan Dzingel .50 1.25
C148 Evgeny Kuznetsov .75 2.00
C149 Braden Holtby .75 2.00
C150 John Carlson .60 1.50
C151 Seth Jones .60 1.50
C152 Cam Atkinson .60 1.50
C153 Zach Werenski 1.00 2.50
C154 Jakub Voracek .50 1.25
C155 Kevin Hayes .50 1.25
C156 Travis Konecny .60 1.50
C157 Taylor Hall .60 1.50
C158 P.K. Subban .75 2.00
C159 Kyle Palmieri .50 1.25
C160 Henrik Lundqvist 1.50 4.00
C161 Artemi Panarin 1.25 3.00
C162 Jacob Trouba .50 1.25
C163 Mathew Barzal .75 2.00
C164 Anders Lee .50 1.25
C165 Semyon Varlamov .60 1.50
C166 Sidney Crosby 2.50 6.00
C167 Matt Murray .60 1.50
C168 Alex Galchenyuk .40 1.00
C169 Mark Scheifele 1.00 2.50
C170 Josh Morrissey .75 2.00
C171 Nikolaj Ehlers .60 1.50
C172 Alex DeBrincat .75 2.00
C173 Robin Lehner .50 1.25
C174 Jonathan Toews 1.00 2.50
C175 Jordan Binnington 1.00 2.50
C176 Alex Pietrangelo .50 1.25
C177 Brayden Schenn .60 1.50
C178 Mats Zuccarello .60 1.50
C179 Zach Parise .60 1.50
C180 Devan Dubnyk .50 1.25
C181 Philipp Grubauer .60 1.50
C182 Nathan MacKinnon 2.50 6.00
C183 Nazem Kadri .75 2.00
C184 Matt Duchene .60 1.50
C185 Filip Forsberg 1.00 2.50
C186 Ryan Johansen .60 1.50
C187 John Klingberg .60 1.50
C188 Tyler Seguin .75 2.00
C189 Alexander Radulov .60 1.50
C190 Jonathan Quick .75 2.00
C191 Drew Doughty .75 2.00
C192 Adrian Kempe .60 1.50
C193 Oliver Ekman-Larsson .60 1.50
C194 Phil Kessel .60 1.50
C195 Timo Meier .60 1.50
C196 Erik Karlsson .75 2.00
C197 Brent Burns .60 1.50
C198 J.T. Miller .75 2.00
C199 Elias Pettersson 1.00 2.50
C200 Cam Fowler .60 1.50
C201 John Gibson .60 1.50
C202 Sean Monahan .40 1.00
C203 Mark Giordano .60 1.50
C204 Noah Hanifin .60 1.50
C205 Oscar Klefbom .60 1.50
C206 Leon Draisaitl 2.00 5.00
C207 James Neal .40 1.00
C208 William Karlsson .75 2.00
C209 Max Pacioretty .60 1.50
C210 N.MacKinnon/L.Draisaitl CL 2.50 6.00
C211 Quinn Hughes YG 50.00 125.00
C212 Kale Clague YG 4.00 10.00
C213 Cayden Primeau YG 20.00 50.00
C214 Igor Shesterkin YG 40.00 100.00
C215 Oliver Wahlstrom YG 12.00 30.00
C216 Trevor Moore YG 4.00 10.00
C217 Philippe Myers YG 4.00 10.00
C218 Noah Dobson YG 20.00 50.00
C219 Rasmus Sandin YG 8.00 20.00
C220 Jesper Boqvist YG 4.00 10.00
C221 German Rubtsov YG 4.00 10.00
C222 Barrett Hayton YG 10.00 25.00
C223 Kirby Dach YG 12.00 30.00
C224 Jack Studnicka YG 5.00 12.00
C225 Alexander Volkov YG 4.00 10.00
C226 Ryan Poehling YG 8.00 20.00
C227 Dante Fabbro YG 5.00 12.00
C228 Sam Lafferty YG 4.00 10.00
C229 Otto Koivula YG 3.00 8.00
C230 Joel Farabee YG 12.00 30.00
C231 Cody Glass YG 8.00 20.00
C232 Adam Boqvist YG 5.00 12.00
C233 Klim Kostin YG 5.00 12.00
C234 John Marino YG 8.00 20.00
C235 Martin Fehervary YG 4.00 10.00
C236 David Gustafsson YG 4.00 10.00
C237 Conor Timmins YG 5.00 12.00
C238 Morgan Frost YG 8.00 20.00
C239 Jack Hughes YG 50.00 125.00
C240 J.Hughes/Q.Hughes CL 10.00 25.00
C241 Gordie Howe RS 20.00 50.00
C242 Kirk McLean RS 5.00 12.00
C243 Bernie Nicholls RS 5.00 12.00
C244 Dirk Graham RS 5.00 12.00
C245 Jaromir Jagr RS 20.00 50.00
C246 Curtis Joseph RS 8.00 20.00
C247 Keith Tkachuk RS 6.00 15.00
C248 Daniel Briere RS 5.00 12.00
C249 Guy Carbonneau RS 6.00 15.00
C250 Ray Ferraro RS 5.00 12.00
C251 Bobby Holik RS 5.00 12.00
C252 Eric Daze RS 5.00 12.00
C253 Brian Leetch RS 6.00 15.00
C254 Brendan Shanahan RS 6.00 15.00
C255 Scott Niedermayer RS 6.00 15.00
C256 Conor Timmins POE 6.00 15.00
C257 Barrett Hayton POE 10.00 25.00
C258 Dante Fabbro POE 6.00 15.00
C259 Nicolas Hague POE 6.00 15.00
C260 Cale Makar POE 40.00 100.00
C261 Julien Gauthier POE 6.00 15.00
C262 Morgan Frost POE 10.00 25.00
C263 Kirby Dach POE 12.00 30.00
C264 Jack Studnicka POE 6.00 15.00
C265 Carter Verhaeghe POE 10.00 25.00
C266 Beck Malenstyn POE 6.00 15.00
C267 Noah Dobson POE 15.00 40.00
C268 Cody Glass POE 8.00 20.00
C269 Philippe Myers POE 5.00 12.00
C270 Kale Clague POE 5.00 12.00

2019-20 Upper Deck Canvas Signatures

CAHL Henrik Lundqvist/30 200.00 300.00
CASS D.Sedin/H.Sedin/26 30.00 80.00
CASS2 D.Sedin/H.Sedin/26 30.00 80.00

2019-20 Upper Deck Ceremonial Puck Drop

CPD1 Henri Richard 8.00 20.00
CPD2 Bobby Clarke 12.00 30.00
CPD3 Johnny Bucyk 8.00 20.00
CPD4 Jeremy Roenick 12.00 30.00
CPD5 Dale Hawerchuk 10.00 25.00
CPD6 Marty Turco 8.00 20.00
CPD7 Willie O'Ree 10.00 25.00
CPD8 Olli Jokinen 8.00 20.00

2019-20 Upper Deck Clear Cut Foundations

CCF1 E.Malkin/J.Guentzel 10.00 25.00
CCF2 M.Scheifele/C.Hellebuyck 10.00 25.00
CCF3 B.Tkachuk/T.Chabot 8.00 20.00
CCF4 M.Barzal/J.Bailey 6.00 15.00
CCF5 P.Kane/A.DeBrincat 10.00 25.00
CCF6 S.Aho/A.Svechnikov 8.00 20.00
CCF7 T.Seguin/M.Heiskanen 6.00 15.00
CCF8 D.Larkin/F.Nielsen 6.00 15.00
CCF9 L.Draisaitl/R.Nugent-Hopkins 15.00 40.00
CCF10 A.Ovechkin/J.Carlson 20.00 50.00
CCF11 C.Atkinson/P.Dubois 5.00 12.00
CCF12 J.Huberdeau/K.Yandle 6.00 15.00
CCF13 D.Doughty/I.Kovalchuk 6.00 15.00
CCF14 J.Zucker/V.Rask 5.00 12.00
CCF15 A.Matthews/J.Tavares 20.00 50.00
CCF16 R.O'Reilly/J.Schwartz 6.00 15.00
CCF17 M.Stone/M.Pacioretty 6.00 15.00
CCF18 B.Marchand/J.DeBrusk 10.00 25.00
CCF19 J.Eichel/R.Dahlin 8.00 20.00
CCF20 S.Stamkos/A.Vasilevskiy 10.00 25.00
CCF21 N.Hischier/K.Palmieri 8.00 20.00
CCF22 R.Johansen/P.Rinne 5.00 12.00
CCF23 M.Domi/T.Tatar 5.00 12.00
CCF24 C.Keller/O.Ekman-Larsson 6.00 15.00
CCF25 E.Pettersson/B.Boeser 8.00 20.00
CCF26 A.Henrique/R.Getzlaf 5.00 12.00
CCF27 N.MacKinnon/T.Jost 20.00 50.00
CCF28 H.Lundqvist/M.Zibanejad 12.00 30.00
CCF29 B.Burns/E.Kane 5.00 12.00
CCF30 N.Patrick/C.Hart 5.00 12.00
CCF31 J.Gaudreau/M.Tkachuk 10.00 25.00

2019-20 Upper Deck Clear Cut Honoured Members

HOF84 Martin St. Louis 6.00 15.00
HOF85 Brendan Shanahan 6.00 15.00
HOF86 Scott Niedermayer 6.00 15.00
HOF87 Joe Nieuwendyk 5.00 12.00
HOF88 Mark Howe 6.00 15.00
HOF89 Peter Stastny 5.00 12.00
HOF90 Bryan Trottier 6.00 15.00
HOF91 Tim Horton 10.00 25.00
HOF92 Sid Abel 6.00 15.00

2019-20 Upper Deck Clear Cut Leaders

CCLGAA Bishop/Binnington/Lehner 20.00 50.00
CCLGLS Draisaitl/Ovechkin/Tavares 50.00 120.00
CCLPMR McDonagh/Giordano/Pesce 12.00 30.00
CCLRPT Tkachuk/Pettersson/Dahlin 20.00 50.00
CCLSHU Fleury/Bobrovsky/Bishop 25.00 60.00
CCLSOG Kane/MacKinnon/Ovechkin 50.00 120.00

2019-20 Upper Deck Day With The Cup

DC1 Vladimir Tarasenko 20.00 50.00
DC2 Colton Parayko 12.00 30.00
DC3 Jay Bouwmeester 10.00 25.00
DC4 Jordan Binnington 25.00 60.00
DC5 Michael Del Zotto 12.00 30.00
DC6 Patrick Maroon 15.00 40.00
DC7 Robby Fabbri 10.00 25.00
DC8 Vince Dunn 12.00 30.00
DC9 Brayden Schenn 15.00 40.00
DC10 Robert Bortuzzo 12.00 30.00
DC11 Tyler Bozak 10.00 25.00
DC12 Joel Edmundson 10.00 25.00
DC13 Samuel Blais 10.00 25.00
DC14 Alex Pietrangelo 12.00 30.00
DC15 Robert Thomas 15.00 40.00
DC16 David Perron 12.00 30.00
DC17 Jaden Schwartz 20.00 50.00
DC18 Ivan Barbashev 12.00 30.00
DC19 Oskar Sundqvist 10.00 25.00
DC20 Ryan O'Reilly 15.00 40.00
DC21 Alexander Steen 10.00 25.00
DC22 Jake Allen 15.00 40.00

2019-20 Upper Deck Fanimation

F1 Rasmus Dahlin 40.00 100.00
F2 Mitch Marner 50.00 125.00
F3 Andrei Svechnikov 40.00 100.00
F4 Mikko Rantanen 80.00 200.00
F5 Artemi Panarin 60.00 150.00
F6 Ryan O'Reilly 30.00 80.00
F7 William Karlsson 40.00 100.00
F8 Leon Draisaitl 100.00 250.00
F9 Chris Kreider 40.00 100.00
F10 Elias Pettersson 50.00 125.00
F11 Jamie Benn 30.00 80.00
F12 Brent Burns 30.00 80.00
F13 Zach Parise 30.00 80.00
F14 Oliver Ekman-Larsson 30.00 80.00
F15 Anze Kopitar 50.00 125.00
F16 Carter Hart 30.00 80.00
F17 Brady Tkachuk 50.00 125.00
F18 Jonathan Toews 50.00 125.00
F19 Braden Holtby 40.00 100.00

2019-20 Upper Deck Fluorescence

*BLUE/50: .6X TO 1.5X BASIC INSERTS
F1 Kaapo Kakko 5.00 12.00
F2 Kirby Dach 6.00 15.00
F3 Morgan Frost 5.00 12.00
F4 Dmytro Timashov 3.00 8.00
F5 Max Jones 3.00 8.00
F6 Cale Fleury 4.00 10.00
F7 Alexandre Texier 3.00 8.00
F8 Dante Fabbro 3.00 8.00
F9 Nikita Gusev 5.00 12.00
F10 Ville Heinola 4.00 10.00
F11 Blake Lizotte 3.00 8.00
F12 Joakim Nygard 2.50 6.00
F13 Connor Clifton 3.00 8.00
F14 Cody Glass 5.00 12.00
F15 Filip Zadina 5.00 12.00
F16 Adam Fox 8.00 20.00
F17 Vitaly Abramov 2.50 6.00
F18 Elvis Merzlikins 6.00 15.00
F19 Ilya Mikheyev 6.00 15.00
F20 Dominik Kubalik 6.00 15.00
F21 Nicolas Hague 3.00 8.00
F22 Erik Brannstrom 3.00 8.00
F23 Karson Kuhlman 3.00 8.00
F24 Tobias Bjornfot 3.00 8.00
F25 Barrett Hayton 6.00 15.00
F26 Quinn Hughes 15.00 40.00
F27 Trent Frederic 3.00 8.00
F28 Conor Timmins 3.00 8.00
F29 Noah Dobson 8.00 20.00
F30 Carter Verhaeghe 5.00 12.00
F31 Rasmus Sandin 5.00 12.00
F32 Nick Suzuki 12.00 30.00
F33 Victor Olofsson 6.00 15.00
F34 Zach Senyshyn 3.00 8.00
F35 Taro Hirose 3.00 8.00
F36 Mario Ferraro 2.50 6.00
F37 Ryan Poehling 5.00 12.00
F38 Jesper Boqvist 3.00 8.00
F39 Cale Makar 15.00 40.00
F40 Emil Bemstrom 3.00 8.00
F41 Carl Grundstrom 3.00 8.00
F42 Martin Fehervary 2.50 6.00
F43 Philippe Myers 2.50 6.00
F44 Teddy Blueger 3.00 8.00
F45 Aleksi Saarela 3.00 8.00
F46 Joel L'Esperance 3.00 8.00
F47 Libor Hajek 2.50 6.00
F48 Nico Sturm 2.50 6.00
F49 Rem Pitlick 3.00 8.00
F50 Jack Hughes 15.00 40.00

2019-20 Upper Deck Game Jerseys

GJAA Andreas Athanasiou E 2.50 6.00
GJAB Aleksander Barkov E 5.00 12.00
GJAE Aaron Ekblad E 4.00 10.00
GJAK Anze Kopitar B 5.00 12.00
GJAL Andrew Ladd E 2.00 5.00
GJAM Anthony Mantha D 2.50 6.00
GJAP Alex Pietrangelo E 2.50 6.00
GJAR Alexander Radulov E 3.00 8.00
GJAS Andrei Svechnikov E 4.00 10.00
GJAT Alex Tuch E 3.00 8.00
GJAV Andrei Vasilevskiy E 5.00 12.00
GJBB Brock Boeser A 4.00 10.00
GJBG Brendan Gallagher E 3.00 8.00
GJBH Braden Holtby E 4.00 10.00
GJBM Brad Marchand B 6.00 15.00
GJBO Bo Horvat E 4.00 10.00
GJBP Brayden Point E 4.00 10.00
GJBR Bobby Ryan E 2.50 6.00
GJBS Brent Seabrook E 2.50 6.00
GJBW Blake Wheeler E 3.00 8.00
GJCA Carter Hutton E 2.50 6.00
GJCF Christian Fischer E 2.00 5.00
GJCG Claude Giroux E 3.00 8.00
GJCH Charlie McAvoy E 4.00 10.00
GJCK Chris Kreider E 4.00 10.00
GJCL Clayton Keller E 4.00 10.00
GJCO Connor Hellebuyck E 6.00 15.00
GJCT Cam Atkinson E 3.00 8.00
GJCW Colin White E 2.00 5.00
GJDD Devan Dubnyk E 2.50 6.00
GJDH Dougie Hamilton E 2.50 6.00
GJDK Duncan Keith E 2.50 6.00
GJDP David Perron E 2.50 6.00
GJDR Drew Doughty E 4.00 10.00
GJDS Dylan Strome E 4.00 10.00
GJEK Evgeny Kuznetsov E 4.00 10.00
GJEM Evgeni Malkin B 6.00 15.00
GJGU Jake Guentzel E 5.00 12.00
GJJA Jake Allen E 3.00 8.00
GJJB Jesper Bratt E 3.00 8.00
GJJD Jonathan Drouin E 2.50 6.00
GJJE Jesse Puljujarvi E 3.00 8.00
GJJG John Gibson E 3.00 8.00
GJJK John Klingberg E 3.00 8.00
GJJO Jordan Greenway E 2.00 5.00
GJJP Joe Pavelski D 4.00 10.00
GJJS Jaden Schwartz D 4.00 10.00
GJJV Jake Virtanen E 3.00 8.00
GJKE Alex Kerfoot A 4.00 10.00
GJKF Kevin Fiala E 2.50 6.00
GJKL Leo Komarov E 2.00 5.00
GJKP Kyle Palmieri E 2.50 6.00
GJKR Kris Letang E 4.00 10.00
GJLD Leon Draisaitl E 10.00 25.00
GJLI Elias Lindholm E 2.50 6.00
GJMA Alec Martinez E 2.00 5.00
GJMB Mathew Barzal E 4.00 10.00
GJMF Micheal Ferland E 2.00 5.00
GJMJ Martin Jones E 2.50 6.00
GJML Milan Lucic E 2.50 6.00
GJMM Mitch Marner B 5.00 12.00
GJMR Michael Rasmussen E 2.00 5.00
GJMS Mike Smith D 2.00 5.00
GJMV Marc-Edouard Vlasic C 2.00 5.00
GJNE Nikolaj Ehlers E 3.00 8.00
GJNK Nazem Kadri E 4.00 10.00
GJOB Oliver Bjorkstrand E 2.50 6.00
GJOL Oliver Ekman-Larsson E 2.50 6.00
GJPA Pavel Buchnevich E 2.50 6.00
GJPB Patrice Bergeron C 4.00 10.00
GJPH Phil Kessel E 3.00 8.00
GJPK P.K. Subban E 4.00 10.00
GJPS Paul Stastny E 2.50 6.00
GJRA Rasmus Ristolainen E 2.00 5.00
GJRE Ryan Ellis E 2.50 6.00
GJRF Radek Faksa E 2.50 6.00
GJRH Ryan Nugent-Hopkins E 4.00 10.00
GJRI James van Riemsdyk A 2.50 6.00
GJRJ Roman Josi E 3.00 8.00
GJRK Ryan Kesler E 3.00 8.00
GJRL Roberto Luongo E 5.00 12.00
GJRP Ryan Pulock E 2.50 6.00
GJRR Rickard Rakell D 2.50 6.00
GJRS Reilly Smith D 3.00 8.00
GJSB Sam Bennett E 5.00 12.00
GJSG Shayne Gostisbehere E 3.00 8.00
GJSK Brady Skjei C 2.50 6.00
GJSR Sam Reinhart E 6.00 15.00
GJST Shea Theodore E 4.00 10.00
GJSV Sven Baertschi C 2.00 5.00
GJSW Shea Weber E 3.00 8.00
GJTB Tyson Barrie E 2.00 5.00
GJTC Thomas Chabot E 3.00 8.00
GJTJ T.J. Oshie E 3.00 8.00
GJTY Tyson Jost E 2.50 6.00
GJWB Will Butcher E 2.50 6.00
GJWN William Nylander E 6.00 15.00
GJYG Yanni Gourde E 2.50 6.00
GJZP Zach Parise C 3.00 8.00
GJZW Zach Werenski E 5.00 12.00

2019-20 Upper Deck Generation Next

GN1 Carter Hart 1.25 3.00
GN2 Kyle Connor 2.00 5.00
GN3 Elias Pettersson 2.00 5.00
GN4 Jakub Vrana 1.25 3.00
GN5 Rasmus Dahlin 1.50 4.00
GN6 Timo Meier 1.25 3.00
GN7 Colin White .75 2.00
GN8 Patrik Laine 1.50 4.00
GN9 Brady Tkachuk 2.00 5.00
GN10 Andrei Svechnikov 1.50 4.00
GN11 Charlie McAvoy 1.50 4.00
GN12 Nolan Patrick 1.25 3.00
GN13 Mathew Barzal 1.50 4.00
GN14 Alex DeBrincat 1.50 4.00
GN15 Miro Heiskanen 1.50 4.00
GN16 Pierre-Luc Dubois 1.00 2.50
GN17 Alex Tuch 1.25 3.00
GN18 Brock Boeser 1.50 4.00
GN19 Clayton Keller 1.50 4.00
GN20 Nico Hischier 2.00 5.00

2019-20 Upper Deck Generation Next Jerseys

GN2 Kyle Connor B 5.00 12.00
GN3 Elias Pettersson A 5.00 12.00
GN4 Jakub Vrana B 3.00 8.00
GN5 Rasmus Dahlin A 4.00 10.00
GN7 Colin White B 2.00 5.00
GN8 Patrik Laine A 4.00 10.00
GN9 Brady Tkachuk B 5.00 12.00
GN10 Andrei Svechnikov B 4.00 10.00
GN11 Charlie McAvoy B 4.00 10.00
GN12 Nolan Patrick B 3.00 8.00
GN13 Mathew Barzal A 4.00 10.00
GN14 Alex DeBrincat B 4.00 10.00

GN15 Miro Heiskanen B 4.00 10.00
GN16 Pierre-Luc Dubois B 2.50 6.00
GN17 Alex Tuch B 3.00 8.00
GN18 Brock Boeser A 4.00 10.00
GN19 Clayton Keller B 4.00 10.00
GN20 Nico Hischier A 5.00 12.00

2019-20 Upper Deck Instant Impressions

II1 Elias Pettersson .75 2.00
II2 Mathew Barzal .60 1.50
II3 Rasmus Dahlin .60 1.50
II4 Alex DeBrincat .60 1.50
II5 Carter Hart .50 1.25
II6 Clayton Keller .60 1.50
II7 Nico Hischier .75 2.00
II8 Jesperi Kotkaniemi .50 1.25
II9 Andrei Svechnikov .60 1.50
II10 Jordan Binnington .75 2.00
II11 Miro Heiskanen .60 1.50
II12 Cale Makar 2.50 6.00
II13 Quinn Hughes 2.50 6.00
II14 Filip Zadina .75 2.00
II15 Ryan Poehling .75 2.00

2019-20 Upper Deck OPC Glossy Rookies

*COPPER: .5X TO 1.25X BASIC INSERTS
*GOLD: 6X TO 1.5X BASIC INSERTS
R1 Cale Makar 6.00 15.00
R2 Erik Brannstrom 1.25 3.00
R3 Dante Fabbro 1.25 3.00
R4 Max Jones 1.25 3.00
R5 Filip Zadina 2.00 5.00
R6 Carl Grundstrom 1.25 3.00
R7 Alexandre Texier 1.25 3.00
R8 Ryan Poehling 2.00 5.00
R9 Trent Frederic 1.25 3.00
R10 Quinn Hughes 6.00 15.00

2019-20 Upper Deck Oversized

201 Jack Hughes 12.00 30.00
203 Conor Timmins 2.50 6.00
207 Victor Olofsson 5.00 12.00
209 Cale Fleury 3.00 8.00
215 Taro Hirose 2.50 6.00
221 Philippe Myers 2.00 5.00
222 Rasmus Sandin 4.00 10.00
225 Alexandre Texier 2.50 6.00
226 Ryan Poehling 4.00 10.00
228 Adam Fox 6.00 15.00
229 Dante Fabbro 2.50 6.00
237 Cody Glass 4.00 10.00
243 Connor Clifton 2.50 6.00
249 Quinn Hughes 12.00 30.00
451 Kirby Dach 5.00 12.00
454 Cayden Primeau 5.00 12.00
457 Oliver Wahlstrom 4.00 10.00
463 Barrett Hayton 5.00 12.00
464 Erik Brannstrom 2.50 6.00
468 Nikita Gusev 4.00 10.00
469 Morgan Frost 4.00 10.00
471 Nick Suzuki 20.00 50.00
478 Filip Zadina 4.00 10.00
481 Noah Dobson YG 6.00 15.00
491 Joel Farabee 4.00 10.00
493 Cale Makar 20.00 50.00
494 Klim Kostin 2.50 6.00
499 Kaapo Kakko 4.00 10.00

2019-20 Upper Deck Pure Energy

PE1 Alexander Ovechkin 2.00 5.00
PE2 Brad Marchand 1.00 2.50
PE3 Jack Eichel .75 2.00
PE4 Brent Burns .50 1.25
PE5 Connor McDavid 2.50 6.00
PE6 Max Domi .50 1.25
PE7 Nikita Kucherov 1.00 2.50
PE8 Thomas Chabot .50 1.25
PE9 Johnny Gaudreau .75 2.00
PE10 Anze Kopitar .75 2.00
PE11 Jonathan Marchessault .60 1.50
PE12 Mathew Barzal .60 1.50
PE13 Jonathan Huberdeau .60 1.50
PE14 Claude Giroux .50 1.25
PE15 Sidney Crosby 2.00 5.00
PE16 Mika Zibanejad .60 1.50
PE17 Clayton Keller .60 1.50
PE18 Nathan MacKinnon 2.00 5.00
PE19 Sebastian Aho .75 2.00
PE20 Auston Matthews 2.00 5.00
PE21 Zach Parise .50 1.25
PE22 Vladimir Tarasenko .60 1.50
PE23 Patrik Laine .60 1.50
PE24 Jakob Silfverberg .30 .75
PE25 Patrick Kane 1.00 2.50
PE26 Aleksander Barkov .75 2.00
PE27 Tyler Seguin .60 1.50
PE28 Cam Atkinson .50 1.25
PE29 Dylan Larkin .60 1.50
PE30 Brock Boeser .60 1.50
PE31 Taylor Hall .50 1.25
PE32 David Pastrnak 1.25 3.00
PE33 Gabriel Landeskog .60 1.50
PE34 Nico Hischier .75 2.00
PE35 Evgeni Malkin 1.00 2.50
PE36 Teuvo Teravainen .50 1.25
PE37 Dustin Byfuglien .50 1.25
PE38 Ryan O'Reilly .50 1.25
PE39 Leon Draisaitl 1.50 4.00
PE40 John Tavares .75 2.00
PE41 Logan Couture .60 1.50
PE42 Mark Stone .60 1.50
PE43 Jonathan Drouin .40 1.00
PE44 Evgeny Kuznetsov .60 1.50
PE45 Steven Stamkos 1.00 2.50
PE46 Roman Josi .50 1.25
PE47 Matthew Tkachuk 1.00 2.50
PE48 Jamie Benn .50 1.25
PE49 Drew Doughty .60 1.50
PE50 Jonathan Toews .75 2.00

2019-20 Upper Deck Rookie Breakouts

RB1 Jack Hughes 50.00 125.00
RB2 Kirby Dach 20.00 50.00
RB3 Victor Olofsson 20.00 50.00
RB4 Nick Suzuki 40.00 100.00
RB5 Quinn Hughes 50.00 125.00
RB6 Cody Glass 15.00 40.00
RB7 Filip Zadina 15.00 40.00
RB8 Adam Fox 25.00 60.00
RB9 Cale Makar 50.00 125.00
RB10 Dante Fabbro 10.00 25.00
RB11 Noah Dobson 25.00 60.00
RB12 Erik Brannstrom 10.00 25.00
RB13 Nikita Gusev 15.00 40.00
RB14 Ryan Poehling 15.00 40.00
RB15 Barrett Hayton 20.00 50.00
RB16 Jesper Boqvist 8.00 20.00
RB17 Taro Hirose 10.00 25.00
RB18 Rasmus Sandin 15.00 40.00
RB19 Alexandre Texier 10.00 25.00
RB20 Kaapo Kakko 15.00 40.00

2019-20 Upper Deck Rookie Dual Materials

RDMBA E.Brannstrom/V.Abramov B 3.00 8.00
RDMHG J.Hughes/N.Gusev A 15.00 40.00
RDMHM Q.Hughes/C.Makar A 15.00 40.00
RDMKF K.Kakko/A.Fox A 8.00 20.00
RDMPS R.Poehling/N.Suzuki B 12.00 30.00
RDMSM R.Sandin/I.Mikheyev B 5.00 12.00
RDMZH F.Zadina/T.Hirose B 5.00 12.00

2019-20 Upper Deck Rookie Materials

*PATCH/25: 1.25X TO 3X BASIC INSERTS
RMAB Adam Boqvist A 2.50 6.00
RMAF Adam Fox B 6.00 15.00
RMAT Alexandre Texier B 2.50 6.00
RMBE Emil Bemstrom B 2.50 6.00
RMBH Barrett Hayton A 5.00 12.00
RMBK Brady Keeper C 2.50 6.00
RMBL Blake Lizotte C 2.50 6.00
RMCG Cody Glass A 4.00 10.00
RMCM Cale Makar A 12.00 30.00
RMDF Dante Fabbro B 2.50 6.00
RMEB Erik Brannstrom B 2.50 6.00
RMEM Elvis Merzlikins C 5.00 12.00
RMFZ Filip Zadina A 4.00 10.00
RMGR Carl Grundstrom C 2.50 6.00
RMIM Ilya Mikheyev B 4.00 10.00
RMJB Jesper Boqvist B 2.00 5.00
RMJD Joey Daccord C 5.00 12.00
RMJF Joel Farabee B 4.00 10.00
RMJH Jack Hughes A 12.00 30.00
RMJS Jimmy Schuldt C 2.00 5.00
RMKD Kirby Dach C 5.00 12.00
RMKK Kaapo Kakko A 4.00 10.00
RMKU Karson Kuhlman C 2.50 6.00
RMLH Libor Hajek C 2.00 5.00
RMMJ Max Jones C 2.50 6.00
RMND Noah Dobson B 6.00 15.00
RMNG Nikita Gusev A 4.00 10.00
RMNS Nick Suzuki A 10.00 25.00
RMOW Oliver Wahlstrom B 4.00 10.00
RMPI Rem Pitlick C 2.50 6.00
RMPM Philippe Myers B 2.00 5.00
RMQH Quinn Hughes A 12.00 30.00
RMRP Ryan Poehling B 4.00 10.00
RMRS Rasmus Sandin A 4.00 10.00
RMST Nico Sturm C 2.00 5.00
RMTB Teddy Blueger C 2.50 6.00
RMTF Trent Frederic C 2.50 6.00
RMTH Taro Hirose B 2.50 6.00
RMVA Vitaly Abramov B 2.50 6.00
RMVO Victor Olofsson B 5.00 12.00

2019-20 Upper Deck Shooting Stars Centers

*RED: .6X TO 1.5X BASIC INSERTS
SSC1 Connor McDavid 4.00 10.00
SSC2 Sidney Crosby 3.00 8.00
SSC3 Auston Matthews 3.00 8.00
SSC4 Jonathan Toews 1.25 3.00
SSC5 Nathan MacKinnon 3.00 8.00
SSC6 Steven Stamkos 1.50 4.00
SSC7 Jack Eichel 1.25 3.00
SSC8 Tyler Seguin 1.00 2.50
SSC9 John Tavares 1.25 3.00
SSC10 Elias Pettersson 1.25 3.00

2019-20 Upper Deck Shooting Stars Defenders

*RED: .6X TO 1.5X BASIC INSERTS
SSD1 Brent Burns 2.00 5.00
SSD2 Morgan Rielly 2.00 5.00
SSD3 Roman Josi 2.00 5.00
SSD4 Kris Letang 2.50 6.00
SSD5 Mark Giordano 2.00 5.00
SSD6 Rasmus Dahlin 2.50 6.00
SSD7 Drew Doughty 2.50 6.00
SSD8 Thomas Chabot 2.00 5.00
SSD9 Dustin Byfuglien 2.00 5.00
SSD10 Keith Yandle 1.25 3.00

2019-20 Upper Deck Shooting Stars Right Wingers

*RED: .6X TO 1.5X BASIC INSERTS
SSR1 Patrick Kane 1.50 4.00
SSR2 Vladimir Tarasenko 1.00 2.50
SSR3 Brock Boeser 1.00 2.50
SSR4 Nikita Kucherov 1.50 4.00
SSR5 David Pastrnak 2.00 5.00
SSR6 Mikko Rantanen 2.00 5.00
SSR7 T.J. Oshie .75 2.00
SSR8 Brendan Gallagher .75 2.00
SSR9 Andrei Svechnikov 1.00 2.50
SSR10 Blake Wheeler .75 2.00

2019-20 Upper Deck Team Triples

*GOLD: .6X TO 1.5X BASIC INSERTS
TT1 Alex Ovechkin
Evgeny Kuznetsov
T.J. Oshie 3.00 8.00
TT2 Cale Makar
Nathan MacKinnon
Gabriel Landeskog 4.00 10.00
TT3 Ryan O'Reilly
Vladimir Tarasenko
Jordan Binnington 1.25 3.00
TT4 Nikita Kucherov
Steven Stamkos
Andrei Vasilevskiy 1.50 4.00
TT5 Ryan Poehling
Carey Price
Brendan Gallagher 1.50 4.00
TT6 Mark Stone
Marc-Andre Fleury
Jonathan Marchessault 1.50 4.00
TT7 Claude Giroux
Carter Hart
Nolan Patrick .75 2.00
TT8 Blake Wheeler
Mark Scheifele
Connor Hellebuyck 1.50 4.00
TT9 Jeff Skinner
Jack Eichel
Rasmus Dahlin 1.25 3.00
TT10 Quinn Hughes
Elias Pettersson
Brock Boeser 4.00 10.00
TT11 Sean Monahan
Johnny Gaudreau
Mark Giordano 1.25 3.00
TT12 Bobby Ryan
Brady Tkachuk
Thomas Chabot 1.25 3.00
TT13 Filip Zadina
Dylan Larkin
Anthony Mantha 1.25 3.00
TT14 William Nylander
John Tavares
Morgan Rielly 1.50 4.00
TT15 Brad Marchand
David Pastrnak
Tuukka Rask 2.00 5.00

2019-20 Upper Deck Tricksters

T1 Nikolaj Ehlers 4.00 10.00
T2 Jonathan Toews 6.00 15.00
T3 John Tavares 6.00 15.00
T4 Tomas Hertl 4.00 10.00
T5 Jake Guentzel 6.00 15.00
T6 Johnny Gaudreau 6.00 15.00
T7 James van Riemsdyk 3.00 8.00
T8 Aleksander Barkov 6.00 15.00
T9 Cam Atkinson 4.00 10.00
T10 Alexander Ovechkin 15.00 40.00
T11 David Pastrnak 10.00 25.00
T12 Patrik Laine 5.00 12.00
T13 Jonathan Marchessault 5.00 12.00
T14 Brendan Gallagher 4.00 10.00
T15 Elias Pettersson 6.00 15.00
T16 Viktor Arvidsson 2.50 6.00
T17 Patrick Kane 8.00 20.00
T18 Blake Wheeler 4.00 10.00
T19 Mathew Barzal 5.00 12.00
T20 Mika Zibanejad 5.00 12.00
T21 Brock Boeser 5.00 12.00
T22 Joe Thornton 6.00 15.00

2019-20 Upper Deck UD Portraits

*VETS/25: 1.25X TO 3X BASIC INSERTS
*RC/99: 4X TO 10X BASIC INSERTS
*RC/25: 5X TO 12X BASIC CARDS
P1 Sidney Crosby 2.50 6.00
P2 John Tavares 1.00 2.50
P3 Clayton Keller .75 2.00
P4 Brady Tkachuk 1.00 2.50
P5 Connor McDavid 3.00 8.00
P6 Pierre-Luc Dubois .50 1.25
P7 Carey Price 1.25 3.00
P8 Tyler Seguin .75 2.00
P9 Ryan Getzlaf .60 1.50
P10 Nathan MacKinnon 2.50 6.00
P11 Pekka Rinne .60 1.50
P12 Jack Eichel 1.00 2.50
P13 Connor Hellebuyck 1.25 3.00
P14 Ilya Kovalchuk .60 1.50
P15 Patrick Kane 1.25 3.00
P16 Tomas Hertl .60 1.50
P17 Nikita Kucherov 1.25 3.00
P18 Eric Staal .60 1.50
P19 Dylan Larkin .75 2.00
P20 Henrik Lundqvist 1.50 4.00
P21 Mathew Barzal .75 2.00
P22 Brad Marchand 1.25 3.00
P23 Vladimir Tarasenko .75 2.00
P24 Sebastian Aho 1.00 2.50
P25 Elias Pettersson 1.00 2.50
P26 Jonathan Huberdeau .75 2.00
P27 Taylor Hall .60 1.50
P28 Mark Stone .75 2.00
P29 Johnny Gaudreau 1.00 2.50
P30 Alexander Ovechkin 2.50 6.00
P31 Carter Hart .60 1.50
P32 Leon Draisaitl 2.00 5.00
P33 Tuukka Rask .75 2.00
P34 Andrei Svechnikov .75 2.00
P35 Auston Matthews 2.50 6.00
P36 Kris Letang .75 2.00
P37 Brent Burns .60 1.50
P38 Ryan McDonagh .40 1.00
P39 Max Pacioretty .60 1.50
P40 Max Domi .60 1.50
P41 Filip Zadina 1.00 2.50
P42 Vitaly Abramov .60 1.50
P43 Dante Fabbro .60 1.50
P44 Zach Senyshyn .60 1.50
P45 Quinn Hughes 3.00 8.00
P46 Alexandre Texier .60 1.50
P47 Erik Brannstrom .60 1.50
P48 Ryan Poehling 1.00 2.50
P49 Philippe Myers .50 1.25
P50 Cale Makar 3.00 8.00
P51 Kaapo Kakko 1.00 2.50
P52 Joel Farabee 1.00 2.50
P53 Kirby Dach 1.25 3.00
P54 Emil Bemstrom .60 1.50
P55 Connor Bunnaman .50 1.25
P56 Rasmus Sandin 1.00 2.50
P57 Connor Clifton .60 1.50
P58 Rudolfs Balcers .60 1.50
P59 Noah Dobson 1.50 4.00
P60 Libor Hajek .50 1.25
P61 Eetu Luostarinen .60 1.50
P62 Joakim Nygard .50 1.25
P63 Adam Fox 1.50 4.00
P64 Carl Grundstrom .60 1.50
P65 Tobias Bjornfot .60 1.50
P66 Sam Lafferty .50 1.25
P67 Danil Yurtaykin .50 1.25
P68 Martin Fehervary .50 1.25
P69 Carter Verhaeghe 1.00 2.50
P70 Trent Frederic .60 1.50
P71 John Marino 1.00 2.50
P72 Jonathan Davidsson .40 1.00
P73 Adam Boqvist .60 1.50
P74 Gaetan Haas .50 1.25
P75 Victor Olofsson 1.25 3.00
P76 Nicolas Hague .60 1.50
P77 Alexander Volkov .50 1.25
P78 Trevor Moore .50 1.25
P79 Mackenzie MacEachern .60 1.50
P80 Nick Suzuki 2.50 6.00
P81 Rem Pitlick .60 1.50
P82 Nikita Gusev 1.00 2.50
P83 Dmytro Timashov .60 1.50
P84 Oliver Wahlstrom 1.00 2.50
P85 Max Jones .60 1.50
P86 Ville Heinola .75 2.00
P87 Mario Ferraro .50 1.25
P88 Barrett Hayton 1.25 3.00
P89 Conor Timmins .60 1.50
P90 Cale Fleury .75 2.00
P91 Elvis Merzlikins 1.25 3.00
P92 Ilya Mikheyev 1.00 2.50
P93 Cody Glass 1.00 2.50
P94 Karson Kuhlman .60 1.50
P95 Jesper Boqvist .50 1.25
P96 Taro Hirose .60 1.50
P97 Dominik Kubalik 1.25 3.00
P98 Blake Lizotte .60 1.50
P99 Lean Bergmann .50 1.25
P100 Jack Hughes 3.00 8.00

2020-21 Upper Deck

1 John Gibson .30 .75
2 Danton Heinen .30 .75
3 Hampus Lindholm .20 .50
4 Josh Manson .20 .50
5 Rickard Rakell .25 .60
6 Jakob Silfverberg .20 .50
7 Jakob Chychrun .30 .75
8 Christian Dvorak .25 .60
9 Conor Garland .25 .60
10 Alex Goligoski .25 .60
11 Phil Kessel .30 .75
12 Darcy Kuemper .30 .75
13 Patrice Bergeron .40 1.00
14 Brandon Carlo .25 .60
15 Charlie Coyle .30 .75
16 Charlie McAvoy .40 1.00
17 John Moore .20 .50
18 David Pastrnak .75 2.00
19 Tuukka Rask .40 1.00
20 Rasmus Dahlin .40 1.00
21 Jack Eichel .50 1.25
22 Carter Hutton .25 .60
23 Marcus Johansson .25 .60
24 Colin Miller .20 .50
25 Rasmus Ristolainen .20 .50
26 Mikael Backlund .25 .60
27 Dillon Dube .20 .50
28 Noah Hanifin .30 .75
29 Elias Lindholm .30 .75
30 David Rittich .25 .60
31 Matthew Tkachuk .60 1.50
32 Dougie Hamilton .25 .60
33 Petr Mrazek .30 .75
34 Martin Necas .50 1.25
35 Brady Skjei .25 .60
36 Vincent Trocheck .30 .75
37 Teuvo Teravainen .30 .75
38 Kirby Dach .30 .75
39 Alex DeBrincat .40 1.00
40 Duncan Keith .25 .60
41 Connor Murphy .25 .60
42 Brandon Saad .25 .60
43 Dylan Strome .40 1.00
44 Jonathan Toews .50 1.25
45 J.T. Compher .20 .50
46 Joonas Donskoi .20 .50
47 Samuel Girard .20 .50
48 Philipp Grubauer .30 .75
49 Nazem Kadri .40 1.00
50 Gabriel Landeskog .40 1.00
51 Nathan MacKinnon 1.25 3.00
52 Oliver Bjorkstrand .25 .60
53 Nick Foligno .25 .60
54 Boone Jenner .30 .75
55 Elvis Merzlikins .30 .75
56 Alexander Wennberg .20 .50
57 Zach Werenski .50 1.25
58 Ben Bishop .25 .60
59 John Klingberg .30 .75
60 Esa Lindell .25 .60
61 Joe Pavelski .40 1.00
62 Alexander Radulov .30 .75
63 Tyler Seguin .40 1.00
64 Justin Abdelkader .25 .60
65 Jonathan Bernier .25 .60
66 Filip Hronek .20 .50
67 Dylan Larkin .40 1.00
68 Frans Nielsen .20 .50
69 Filip Zadina .25 .60
70 Zack Kassian .20 .50
71 Oscar Klefbom .30 .75
72 Mikko Koskinen .20 .50
73 Connor McDavid 1.50 4.00
74 James Neal .20 .50
75 Darnell Nurse .25 .60
76 Kailer Yamamoto .30 .75
77 Noel Acciari .20 .50
78 Aleksander Barkov .50 1.25
79 Sergei Bobrovsky .50 1.25
80 Aaron Ekblad .40 1.00
81 Keith Yandle .20 .50
82 Frank Vatrano .25 .60
83 Jeff Carter .25 .60
84 Drew Doughty .40 1.00
85 Alex Iafallo .20 .50
86 Blake Lizotte .20 .50
87 Adrian Kempe .30 .75
88 Anze Kopitar .50 1.25
89 Kevin Fiala .25 .60
90 Zach Parise .30 .75
91 Mats Zuccarello .30 .75
92 Alex Stalock .20 .50
93 Jared Spurgeon .30 .75
94 Ryan Suter .25 .60
95 Phillip Danault .30 .75
96 Jonathan Drouin .25 .60
97 Brendan Gallagher .30 .75
98 Jeff Petry .30 .75
99 Nick Suzuki .60 1.50
100 Tomas Tatar .20 .50
101 Shea Weber .30 .75
102 Matt Duchene .30 .75
103 Ryan Ellis .25 .60
104 Filip Forsberg .50 1.25
105 Rocco Grimaldi .20 .50
106 Calle Jarnkrok .20 .50
107 Juuse Saros .40 1.00
108 Will Butcher .25 .60
109 Nikita Gusev .25 .60
110 Kyle Palmieri .25 .60
111 P.K. Subban .40 1.00
112 Miles Wood .20 .50
113 Pavel Zacha .25 .60
114 Jordan Eberle .30 .75
115 Nick Leddy .20 .50
116 Anders Lee .25 .60
117 Brock Nelson .30 .75
118 Jean-Gabriel Pageau .20 .50
119 Semyon Varlamov .30 .75
120 Tony DeAngelo .20 .50
121 Adam Fox .40 1.00
122 Artemi Panarin .60 1.50
123 Igor Shesterkin .60 1.50
124 Marc Staal .20 .50
125 Jacob Trouba .25 .60
126 Mika Zibanejad .40 1.00
127 Artem Anisimov .20 .50
128 Connor Brown .25 .60
129 Bobby Ryan .25 .60
130 Mike Reilly .20 .50
131 Colin White .20 .50
132 Nikita Zaitsev .20 .50
133 Sean Couturier .25 .60
134 Carter Hart .30 .75
135 Kevin Hayes .25 .60
136 Travis Konecny .30 .75
137 Ivan Provorov .25 .60
138 Travis Sanheim .20 .50
139 Jake Guentzel .50 1.25
140 Patric Hornqvist .20 .50
141 Kris Letang .40 1.00
142 Evgeni Malkin .60 1.50
143 John Marino .30 .75
144 Brandon Tanev .25 .60
145 Jason Zucker .30 .75
146 Erik Karlsson .40 1.00
147 Tomas Hertl .30 .75
148 Martin Jones .25 .60
149 Evander Kane .30 .75
150 Timo Meier .30 .75
151 Marc-Edouard Vlasic .20 .50
152 Jordan Binnington .50 1.25
153 Colton Parayko .25 .60
154 Ryan O'Reilly .30 .75
155 David Perron .25 .60
156 Zach Sanford .20 .50
157 Brayden Schenn .30 .75
158 Robert Thomas .30 .75
159 Blake Coleman .25 .60
160 Yanni Gourde .25 .60
161 Victor Hedman .40 1.00
162 Alex Killorn .20 .50
163 Brayden Point .40 1.00
164 Steven Stamkos .60 1.50
165 Zach Hyman .50 1.25
166 Kasperi Kapanen .25 .60
167 Alex Kerfoot .25 .60
168 Mitch Marner .50 1.25
169 William Nylander .60 1.50
170 Morgan Rielly .30 .75
171 John Tavares .50 1.25
172 Thatcher Demko .40 1.00
173 Brock Boeser .40 1.00
174 Bo Horvat .40 1.00
175 Quinn Hughes .75 2.00
176 J.T. Miller .40 1.00
177 Tyler Myers .20 .50
178 Tanner Pearson .30 .75
179 William Karlsson .40 1.00
180 Jonathan Marchessault .40 1.00
181 Alec Martinez .20 .50
182 Nate Schmidt .25 .60
183 Reilly Smith .30 .75
184 Mark Stone .40 1.00
185 Alex Tuch .30 .75
186 John Carlson .30 .75
187 Nic Dowd .20 .50
188 Lars Eller .20 .50
189 Dmitry Orlov .30 .75
190 T.J. Oshie .30 .75
191 Alex Ovechkin 1.25 3.00
192 Ilya Samsonov .30 .75
193 Nikolaj Ehlers .30 .75
194 Josh Morrissey .40 1.00
195 Mathieu Perreault .20 .50
196 Neal Pionk .20 .50
197 Mark Scheifele .50 1.25
198 Blake Wheeler .30 .75
199 N.MacKinnon/A.Panarin CL 1.25 3.00
200 D.Pastrnak/A.Ovechkin CL 1.25 3.00
201 Alexis Lafreniere YG RC 25.00 60.00
202 Reid Duke YG RC 3.00 8.00
203 Alexander Alexeyev YG RC 2.50 6.00
204 Philip Broberg YG RC 3.00 8.00
205 Bowen Byram YG RC 6.00 15.00
206 Michael DiPietro YG RC 4.00 10.00
207 Joel Kiviranta YG RC 3.00 8.00
208 Joseph Woll YG RC 10.00 25.00
209 Josh Norris YG RC 5.00 12.00
210 Morgan Geekie YG RC 3.00 8.00
211 Vitek Vanecek YG RC 5.00 12.00
212 Lucas Carlsson YG RC 2.50 6.00
213 Ty Dellandrea YG RC 3.00 8.00
214 Dylan Coghlan YG RC 3.00 8.00
215 Gabe Vilardi YG RC 5.00 12.00
216 Pierre-Olivier Joseph YG RC 3.00 8.00
217 Martin Kaut YG RC 3.00 8.00
218 Tyler Benson YG RC 3.00 8.00
219 Egor Korshkov YG RC 2.00 5.00
220 Gustav Lindstrom YG RC 2.50 6.00
221 Victor Soderstrom YG RC 2.50 6.00
222 Olli Juolevi YG RC 3.00 8.00
223 Connor Ingram YG RC 2.50 6.00
224 Liam Foudy YG RC 3.00 8.00
225 Alexander True YG RC 2.50 6.00
226 Nicolas Beaudin YG RC 3.00 8.00
227 Thomas Harley YG RC 5.00 12.00
228 Jonas Johansson YG RC 3.00 8.00
229 Jansen Harkins YG RC 2.50 6.00
230 Alex Belzile YG RC 2.50 6.00
231 Ryan McLeod YG RC 2.50 6.00
232 Egor Zamula YG RC 2.50 6.00
233 Mikey Anderson YG RC 3.00 8.00
234 Connor McMichael YG RC 6.00 15.00
235 Jason Robertson YG RC 12.00 30.00
236 Emil Larmi YG RC 3.00 8.00
237 Nick Robertson YG RC 6.00 15.00
238 Philipp Kurashev YG RC 4.00 10.00
239 Peyton Krebs YG RC 10.00 25.00
240 Shane Bowers YG RC 2.50 6.00
241 Kieffer Bellows YG RC 2.50 6.00
242 Mikhail Berdin YG RC 3.00 8.00
243 Vitali Kravtsov YG RC 6.00 15.00
244 Artem Zagidulin YG RC 3.00 8.00
245 Kirill Ustimenko YG RC 2.50 6.00
246 Jake Oettinger YG RC 10.00 25.00
247 Jake Evans YG RC 3.00 8.00
248 Timothy Liljegren YG RC 3.00 8.00
249 Pavel Francouz YG RC 4.00 10.00
250 A.Lafreniere/V.Kravtsov YG CL 8.00 20.00
251 Cam Fowler .30 .75
252 Ryan Getzlaf .30 .75
253 Adam Henrique .25 .60
254 Carter Rowney .20 .50
255 Sam Steel .25 .60
256 Troy Terry .30 .75
257 Oliver Ekman-Larsson .30 .75
258 Niklas Hjalmarsson .20 .50
259 Clayton Keller .40 1.00
260 Antti Raanta .30 .75
261 Nick Schmaltz .25 .60
262 Derek Stepan .20 .50
263 Anders Bjork .20 .50
264 Zdeno Chara .30 .75
265 Jake DeBrusk .30 .75
266 Jaroslav Halak .30 .75
267 David Krejci .30 .75
268 Sean Kuraly .20 .50
269 Brad Marchand .60 1.50
270 Zemgus Girgensons .25 .60
271 Henri Jokiharju .20 .50
272 Brandon Montour .40 1.00
273 Victor Olofsson .30 .75
274 Sam Reinhart .60 1.50
275 Jeff Skinner .30 .75
276 Rasmus Andersson .25 .60
277 Johnny Gaudreau .50 1.25
278 Mark Giordano .30 .75
279 Milan Lucic .25 .60
280 Andrew Mangiapane .30 .75
281 Sean Monahan .20 .50
282 Derek Ryan .20 .50
283 Sebastian Aho .50 1.25
284 Ryan Dzingel .25 .60
285 Warren Foegele .25 .60
286 Jake Gardiner .20 .50
287 Jaccob Slavin .25 .60
288 Jordan Staal .25 .60
289 Andrei Svechnikov .40 1.00
290 Adam Boqvist .25 .60
291 Calvin de Haan .20 .50
292 David Kampf .20 .50
293 Patrick Kane .60 1.50
294 Dominik Kubalik .30 .75
295 Alexander Nylander .25 .60
296 Malcolm Subban .25 .60
297 Pierre-Edouard Bellemare .20 .50
298 Andre Burakovsky .20 .50
299 Ian Cole .20 .50
300 Ryan Graves .25 .60
301 Cale Makar .75 2.00
302 Valeri Nichushkin .30 .75
303 Mikko Rantanen .75 2.00
304 Cam Atkinson .30 .75
305 Pierre-Luc Dubois .25 .60
306 Vladislav Gavrikov .20 .50
307 Seth Jones .30 .75
308 Joonas Korpisalo .30 .75
309 Gustav Nyquist .20 .50
310 Jamie Benn .30 .75
311 Radek Faksa .25 .60
312 Denis Gurianov .40 1.00
313 Miro Heiskanen .40 1.00
314 Roope Hintz .40 1.00
315 Anton Khudobin .30 .75
316 Corey Perry .50 1.25
317 Tyler Bertuzzi .25 .60
318 Madison Bowey .20 .50
319 Robby Fabbri .20 .50
320 Valtteri Filppula .20 .50
321 Darren Helm .20 .50
322 Anthony Mantha .25 .60
323 Andreas Athanasiou .25 .60
324 Ethan Bear .20 .50
325 Alex Chiasson .25 .60
326 Leon Draisaitl 1.00 2.50
327 Ryan Nugent-Hopkins .40 1.00
328 Mike Smith .20 .50
329 Brett Connolly .20 .50
330 Chris Driedger .20 .50
331 Mike Hoffman .20 .50
332 Jonathan Huberdeau .40 1.00
333 Anton Stralman .20 .50
334 MacKenzie Weegar .25 .60
335 Michael Amadio .20 .50
336 Dustin Brown .30 .75
337 Ben Hutton .20 .50
338 Jonathan Quick .40 1.00
339 Matt Roy .20 .50
340 Sean Walker .20 .50
341 Jonas Brodin .20 .50
342 Joel Eriksson Ek .25 .60
343 Marcus Foligno .25 .60
344 Brad Hunt .20 .50
345 Jordan Greenway .25 .60
346 Ryan Hartman .20 .50
347 Joel Armia .20 .50
348 Paul Byron .20 .50
349 Ben Chiarot .20 .50
350 Jesperi Kotkaniemi .30 .75
351 Artturi Lehkonen .25 .60
352 Victor Mete .20 .50
353 Carey Price .60 1.50
354 Viktor Arvidsson .20 .50
355 Mattias Ekholm .25 .60
356 Dante Fabbro .30 .75
357 Ryan Johansen .25 .60
358 Roman Josi .30 .75
359 Pekka Rinne .30 .75
360 Mackenzie Blackwood .30 .75
361 Jesper Bratt .30 .75
362 Nico Hischier .50 1.25
363 Jack Hughes .75 2.00
364 Damon Severson .20 .50
365 Travis Zajac .20 .50
366 Josh Bailey .25 .60
367 Mathew Barzal .40 1.00
368 Anthony Beauvillier .20 .50
369 Adam Pelech .20 .50
370 Derick Brassard .20 .50
371 Ryan Pulock .25 .60
372 Pavel Buchnevich .25 .60
373 Filip Chytil .25 .60
374 Kaapo Kakko .25 .60
375 Chris Kreider .40 1.00
376 Brendan Lemieux .25 .60
377 Brendan Smith .20 .50
378 Drake Batherson .30 .75
379 Thomas Chabot .30 .75
380 Nick Paul .20 .50
381 Anders Nilsson .20 .50
382 Chris Tierney .25 .60
383 Brady Tkachuk .50 1.25
384 Joel Farabee .30 .75
385 Claude Giroux .30 .75
386 Scott Laughton .20 .50
387 Oskar Lindblom .25 .60
388 James van Riemsdyk .25 .60
389 Jakub Voracek .25 .60
390 Zach Aston-Reese .30 .75
391 Sidney Crosby 1.25 3.00
392 Brian Dumoulin .25 .60
393 Jared McCann .25 .60
394 Marcus Pettersson .20 .50
395 Bryan Rust .30 .75
396 Brent Burns .30 .75
397 Logan Couture .40 1.00
398 Mario Ferraro .20 .50
399 Kevin Labanc .20 .50
400 Marcus Sorensen .25 .60
401 Patrick Marleau .30 .75
402 Ivan Barbashev .25 .60
403 Tyler Bozak .20 .50
404 Vince Dunn .25 .60
405 Justin Faulk .25 .60
406 Jaden Schwartz .40 1.00
407 Oskar Sundqvist .20 .50
408 Vladimir Tarasenko .40 1.00
409 Anthony Cirelli .25 .60
410 Tyler Johnson .20 .50
411 Nikita Kucherov .60 1.50
412 Patrick Maroon .30 .75
413 Ondrej Palat .30 .75
414 Mikhail Sergachev .25 .60
415 Andrei Vasilevskiy .50 1.25
416 Frederik Andersen .40 1.00
417 Travis Dermott .25 .60
418 Justin Holl .20 .50
419 Auston Matthews 1.25 3.00
420 Ilya Mikheyev .25 .60
421 Jake Muzzin .30 .75
422 Jason Spezza .30 .75
423 Jordie Benn .20 .50
424 Alexander Edler .20 .50
425 Adam Gaudette .25 .60
426 Elias Pettersson .50 1.25
427 Antoine Roussel .20 .50
428 Jake Virtanen .30 .75
429 Marc-Andre Fleury .60 1.50
430 Cody Glass .25 .60
431 Robin Lehner .25 .60
432 Max Pacioretty .30 .75
433 Ryan Reaves .20 .50
434 Chandler Stephenson .25 .60
435 Shea Theodore .40 1.00
436 Nicklas Backstrom .30 .75
437 Carl Hagelin .20 .50
438 Michal Kempny .20 .50
439 Evgeny Kuznetsov .40 1.00
440 Richard Panik .20 .50
441 Jakub Vrana .30 .75
442 Tom Wilson .30 .75
443 Kyle Connor .50 1.25
444 Andrew Copp .20 .50
445 Connor Hellebuyck .60 1.50
446 Patrik Laine .40 1.00
447 Tucker Poolman .20 .50
448 Jack Roslovic .20 .50
449 P.Kane/L.Draisaitl CL 1.00 2.50
450 A.Matthews/E.Pettersson CL 1.25 3.00
451 Kirill Kaprizov YG RC 30.00 80.00
452 Jalen Chatfield YG RC 2.50 6.00
453 Gilles Senn YG RC 2.50 6.00
454 Gage Quinney YG RC 2.00 5.00
455 Alexander Romanov YG RC 4.00 10.00
456 Ty Smith YG RC 5.00 12.00
457 Mason Marchment YG RC 3.00 8.00
458 Ian Mitchell YG RC 2.50 6.00
459 Jani Hakanpaa YG RC 2.00 5.00
460 Austin Poganski YG RC 2.50 6.00
461 Ilya Sorokin YG RC 8.00 20.00
462 Nils Hoglander YG RC 10.00 25.00
463 Nicolas Meloche YG RC 2.50 6.00
464 Brandon Crawley YG RC 2.50 6.00
465 Philippe Desrosiers YG RC 2.50 6.00
466 Jordan Gross YG RC 2.50 6.00
467 Calvin Thurkauf YG RC 2.50 6.00
468 Mathias Brome YG RC 2.50 6.00
469 K'Andre Miller YG RC 6.00 15.00
470 Niko Mikkola YG RC 2.50 6.00
471 MacKenzie Entwistle YG RC 2.50 6.00
472 Anthony Angello YG RC 2.50 6.00
473 Chase Priskie YG RC 2.50 6.00
474 John Leonard YG RC 2.50 6.00
475 Brian Pinho YG RC 2.50 6.00
476 Cal Foote YG RC 4.00 10.00

477 Keegan Kolesar YG RC 2.50 6.00
478 Alec Regula YG RC 2.00 5.00
479 William Lagesson YG RC 3.00 8.00
480 Matiss Kivlenieks YG RC 4.00 10.00
481 Cole Smith YG RC 2.50 6.00
482 Tim Stutzle YG RC 15.00 40.00
483 Darren Raddysh YG RC 2.00 5.00
484 Pius Suter YG RC 4.00 10.00
485 Alexander Barabanov YG RC 3.00 8.00
486 Philippe Maillet YG RC 2.50 6.00
487 Maxim Letunov YG RC 2.50 6.00
488 Alexander Yelesin YG RC 2.50 6.00
489 Yegor Sharangovich YG RC 5.00 12.00
490 Lukas Vejdemo YG RC 2.50 6.00
491 Brandon Hagel YG RC 4.00 10.00
492 Nikolai Knyzhov YG RC 2.50 6.00
493 David Kase YG RC 2.50 6.00
494 Steven Lorentz YG RC 2.50 6.00
495 Dylan Cozens YG RC 5.00 12.00
496 Stuart Skinner YG RC 6.00 15.00
497 Kevin Lankinen YG RC 5.00 12.00
498 Joel Kellman YG RC 2.00 5.00
499 Brayden Burke YG RC 2.50 6.00
500 T.Stutzle/D.Cozens YG CL 2.00 5.00
501 Maxime Comtois .25 .60
502 Derek Grant .20 .50
503 Ben Hutton .20 .50
504 Kevin Shattenkirk .20 .50
505 Derick Brassard .20 .50
506 Drake Caggiula .25 .60
507 Johan Larsson .25 .60
508 Tyler Pitlick .20 .50
509 Nick Ritchie .20 .50
510 Craig Smith .20 .50
511 Jack Studnicka .20 .50
512 Chris Wagner .20 .50
513 Cody Eakin .20 .50
514 Taylor Hall .30 .75
515 Tobias Rieder .20 .50
516 Eric Staal .30 .75
517 Josh Leivo .20 .50
518 Jacob Markstrom .30 .75
519 Joakim Nordstrom .20 .50
520 Christopher Tanev .20 .50
521 Juuso Valimaki .20 .50
522 Jesper Fast .20 .50
523 Cedric Paquette .20 .50
524 Nino Niederreiter .20 .50
525 James Reimer .30 .75
526 Mattias Janmark .20 .50
527 Andrew Shaw .20 .50
528 Carl Soderberg .20 .50
529 Lucas Wallmark .20 .50
530 Nikita Zadorov .20 .50
531 Brandon Saad .25 .60
532 Conor Timmins .20 .50
533 Kiefer Sherwood .20 .50
534 Devon Toews .25 .60
535 Michael Del Zotto .25 .60
536 Max Domi .30 .75
537 Patrik Laine .40 1.00
538 Jack Roslovic .20 .50
539 Alexandre Texier .25 .60
540 Nick Caamano .20 .50
541 Andrew Cogliano .20 .50
542 Justin Dowling .20 .50
543 Tanner Kero .20 .50
544 Thomas Greiss .25 .60
545 Taro Hirose .20 .50
546 Vladislav Namestnikov .20 .50
547 Bobby Ryan .25 .60
548 Givani Smith .20 .50
549 Marc Staal .20 .50
550 Troy Stecher .20 .50
551 Tyson Barrie .20 .50
552 Dominik Kahun .20 .50
553 Slater Koekkoek .20 .50
554 Jesse Puljujarvi .30 .75
555 Kyle Turris .25 .60
556 Anthony Duclair .25 .60
557 Radko Gudas .25 .60
558 Patric Hornqvist .20 .50
559 Owen Tippett .25 .60
560 Alexander Wennberg .20 .50
561 Carter Verhaeghe .30 .75
562 Lias Andersson .25 .60
563 Andreas Athanasiou .25 .60
564 Olli Maatta .20 .50
565 Cal Petersen .20 .50
566 Nick Bjugstad .20 .50
567 Nick Bonino .20 .50
568 Ian Cole .20 .50
569 Kaapo Kahkonen .30 .75
570 Cam Talbot .30 .75
571 Jake Allen .30 .75
572 Josh Anderson .25 .60
573 Corey Perry .50 1.25
574 Tyler Toffoli .30 .75
575 Matthew Benning .20 .50
576 Mark Borowiecki .20 .50
577 Nick Cousins .20 .50
578 Erik Haula .20 .50
579 Luke Kunin .20 .50
580 Brad Richardson .20 .50
581 Andreas Johnsson .30 .75
582 Janne Kuokkanen .20 .50
583 Dmitry Kulikov .25 .60
584 Michael McLeod .20 .50
585 Ryan Murray .25 .60
586 Casey Cizikas .20 .50
587 Cal Clutterbuck .20 .50
588 Noah Dobson .40 1.00
589 Matt Martin .20 .50
590 Scott Mayfield .20 .50
591 Cory Schneider .30 .75
592 Phil Di Giuseppe .20 .50
593 Alexandar Georgiev .30 .75
594 Jack Johnson .20 .50
595 Ryan Strome .30 .75
596 Josh Brown .20 .50
597 Braydon Coburn .20 .50
598 Evgenii Dadonov .20 .50
599 Ryan Dzingel .25 .60
600 Erik Gudbranson .20 .50
601 Matt Murray .30 .75
602 Joey Daccord .30 .75
603 Derek Stepan .20 .50
604 Nicolas Aube-Kubel .20 .50
605 Erik Gustafsson .20 .50
606 Nolan Patrick .30 .75
607 Michael Raffl .20 .50
608 Teddy Blueger .20 .50
609 Cody Ceci .20 .50
610 Mark Jankowski .20 .50
611 Kasperi Kapanen .25 .60
612 Colton Sceviour .20 .50
613 Ryan Donato .25 .60
614 Devan Dubnyk .25 .60
615 Dylan Gambrell .20 .50
616 Matt Nieto .20 .50
617 Stefan Noesen .20 .50
618 Kyle Clifford .20 .50
619 Mike Hoffman .20 .50
620 Ville Husso .20 .50
621 Torey Krug .25 .60
622 Jordan Kyrou .30 .75
623 Erik Cernak .20 .50
624 Barclay Goodrow .20 .50
625 Mathieu Joseph .20 .50
626 Ryan McDonagh .20 .50
627 Curtis McElhinney .20 .50
628 Zach Bogosian .25 .60
629 T.J. Brodie .25 .60
630 Alex Galchenyuk .20 .50
631 Wayne Simmonds .30 .75
632 Joe Thornton .50 1.25
633 Jimmy Vesey .25 .60
634 Jay Beagle .20 .50
635 Braden Holtby .40 1.00
636 Tyler Motte .20 .50
637 Nate Schmidt .25 .60
638 Brandon Sutter .20 .50
639 William Carrier .20 .50
640 Tomas Nosek .20 .50
641 Alex Pietrangelo .25 .60
642 Nicolas Roy .20 .50
643 Zach Whitecloud .25 .60
644 Zdeno Chara .30 .75
645 Michael Sgarbossa .25 .60
646 Justin Schultz .30 .75
647 Conor Sheary .30 .75
648 Daniel Sprong .20 .50
649 Trevor van Riemsdyk .25 .60
650 Pierre-Luc Dubois .25 .60
651 Derek Forbort .20 .50
652 Trevor Lewis .20 .50
653 Adam Lowry .25 .60
654 Paul Stastny .25 .60
655 Jordan Binnington AS .50 1.25
656 Connor Hellebuyck AS .60 1.50
657 Roman Josi AS .30 .75
658 Patrick Kane AS .60 1.50
659 Nathan MacKinnon AS 1.25 3.00
660 David Perron AS .25 .60
661 Alex Pietrangelo AS .25 .60
662 Ryan O'Reilly AS .30 .75
663 Mark Scheifele AS .50 1.25
664 Tyler Seguin AS .40 1.00
665 Eric Staal AS .30 .75
666 Mathew Barzal AS .40 1.00
667 John Carlson AS .30 .75
668 Nico Hischier AS .50 1.25
669 Braden Holtby AS .40 1.00
670 Tristan Jarry AS .30 .75
671 Seth Jones AS .30 .75
672 Travis Konecny AS .30 .75
673 Chris Kreider AS .40 1.00
674 Kris Letang AS .40 1.00
675 T.J. Oshie AS .30 .75
676 Jaccob Slavin AS .25 .60
677 Leon Draisaitl AS 1.00 2.50
678 Mark Giordano AS .30 .75
679 Tomas Hertl AS .30 .75
680 Quinn Hughes AS .75 2.00
681 Anze Kopitar AS .50 1.25
682 Jacob Markstrom AS .30 .75
683 Connor McDavid AS 1.50 4.00
684 Max Pacioretty AS .30 .75
685 Elias Pettersson AS .50 1.25
686 David Rittich AS .25 .60
687 Matthew Tkachuk AS .60 1.50
688 Frederik Andersen AS .40 1.00
689 Tyler Bertuzzi AS .25 .60
690 Anthony Duclair AS .25 .60
691 Jack Eichel AS .50 1.25
692 Victor Hedman AS .40 1.00
693 Jonathan Huberdeau AS .40 1.00
694 Mitch Marner AS .50 1.25
695 David Pastrnak AS .75 2.00
696 Brady Tkachuk AS .50 1.25
697 Andrei Vasilevskiy AS .50 1.25
698 Shea Weber AS .30 .75
699 P.Laine/P.Dubois CL .40 1.00
700 C.McDavid/L.Draisaitl AS CL 1.50 4.00
701 Arthur Kaliyev YG RC 8.00 20.00
702 Joel Hofer YG RC 3.00 8.00
703 Logan Stanley YG RC 3.00 8.00
704 Callum Booth YG RC 2.50 6.00
705 Cameron Hillis YG RC 2.50 6.00
706 Jacob Ingham YG RC 2.50 6.00
707 Connor Mackey YG RC 2.50 6.00
708 Kodie Curran YG RC 2.50 6.00
709 Patrick Khodorenko YG RC 2.00 5.00
710 Artem Zub YG RC 2.50 6.00
711 Fredrik Handemark YG RC 2.50 6.00
712 Cam Johnson YG RC 2.50 6.00
713 Jake Bischoff YG RC 2.50 6.00
714 Hayden Verbeek YG RC 2.50 6.00
715 Josef Korenar YG RC 2.50 6.00
716 Aleksi Heponiemi YG RC 4.00 10.00
717 Jack Rathbone YG RC 3.00 8.00
718 Sasha Chmelevski YG RC 2.50 6.00
719 Alex D'Orio YG RC 2.50 6.00
720 Kevin Bahl YG RC 2.50 6.00
721 Mikko Lehtonen YG RC 2.50 6.00
722 Austin Strand YG RC 2.50 6.00
723 Mikhail Maltsev YG RC 2.50 6.00
724 Cole Hults YG RC 2.50 6.00
725 Reese Johnson YG RC 2.50 6.00
726 Glenn Gawdin YG RC 2.50 6.00
727 Michael Bunting YG RC 5.00 12.00
728 Drew O'Connor YG RC 3.00 8.00
729 Nolan Foote YG RC 3.00 8.00
730 A.Heponiemi/A.Kaliyev YG CL 5.00 12.00
SP1 Alexis Lafreniere SP 100.00 250.00
SP1V Alexis Lafreniere SP VAR 200.00 500.00

2020-21 Upper Deck Clear Cut Parallel

*CLR.CUT: 6X TO 15X BASIC
*YG.CLR.CUT: 3X TO 8X BASIC
201 Alexis Lafreniere YG 150.00 400.00
205 Bowen Byram YG 125.00 300.00
208 Joseph Woll YG 40.00 100.00
209 Josh Norris YG 40.00 100.00
234 Connor McMichael YG 30.00 80.00
235 Jason Robertson YG 80.00 200.00
246 Jake Oettinger YG 60.00 150.00
451 Kirill Kaprizov YG 250.00 600.00
456 Ty Smith YG 60.00 150.00
482 Tim Stutzle YG 150.00 400.00
496 Stuart Skinner YG 40.00 100.00
500 Tim Stutzle
Dylan Cozens YG CL 10.00 25.00
701 Arthur Kaliyev YG 80.00 200.00
728 Drew O'Connor YG 25.00 60.00

2020-21 Upper Deck Exclusives

*EXCL: 4X TO 10X BASIC
*YG.EXCL: 4X TO 10X BASIC
201 Alexis Lafreniere YG 300.00 800.00
208 Joseph Woll YG 60.00 150.00
211 Vitek Vanecek YG 60.00 150.00
234 Connor McMichael YG 40.00 100.00
235 Jason Robertson YG 125.00 300.00
243 Vitali Kravtsov YG 100.00 250.00
246 Jake Oettinger YG 125.00 300.00
249 Pavel Francouz YG 60.00 150.00
250 Alexis Lafreniere
Vitali Kravtsov YG CL 100.00 250.00
451 Kirill Kaprizov YG 600.00 1500.00
462 Nils Hoglander YG 150.00 400.00
482 Tim Stutzle YG 300.00 800.00
496 Stuart Skinner YG 80.00 200.00
497 Kevin Lankinen YG 40.00 100.00
701 Arthur Kaliyev YG 150.00 400.00
716 Aleksi Heponiemi YG 40.00 100.00
728 Drew O'Connor YG 60.00 150.00
729 Nolan Foote YG 30.00 80.00

2020-21 Upper Deck French

*FRENCH: 2X TO 5X BASIC
*YG.FRENCH: 1X TO 2.5X BASIC
201 Alexis Lafreniere YG 60.00 150.00
235 Jason Robertson YG 15.00 40.00
246 Jake Oettinger YG 20.00 50.00
250 Alexis Lafreniere
Vitali Kravtsov YG CL 30.00 80.00
451 Kirill Kaprizov YG 60.00 150.00
482 Tim Stutzle YG 15.00 40.00
496 Stuart Skinner YG 15.00 40.00
497 Kevin Lankinen YG 30.00 80.00
701 Arthur Kaliyev YG 25.00 60.00
728 Drew O'Connor YG 12.00 30.00

2020-21 Upper Deck Street Clothes Variation

*STREET: 8X TO 20X BASIC

2020-21 Upper Deck '05-06 Upper Deck Tribute

T1 Maxime Comtois .50 1.25
T2 John Gibson .60 1.50
T3 Conor Garland .50 1.25
T4 Phil Kessel .60 1.50
T5 David Pastrnak 1.50 4.00
T6 Tuukka Rask .75 2.00
T7 Brad Marchand 1.25 3.00
T8 Jack Eichel 1.00 2.50
T9 Taylor Hall .60 1.50
T10 Johnny Gaudreau 1.00 2.50
T11 Matthew Tkachuk 1.25 3.00
T12 Jacob Markstrom .60 1.50
T13 Teuvo Teravainen .60 1.50
T14 Sebastian Aho 1.00 2.50
T15 Andrei Svechnikov .75 2.00
T16 Patrick Kane 1.25 3.00
T17 Alex DeBrincat .75 2.00
T18 Cale Makar 1.50 4.00
T19 Nathan MacKinnon 2.50 6.00
T20 Mikko Rantanen 1.50 4.00
T21 Seth Jones .60 1.50
T22 Zach Werenski 1.00 2.50
T23 Tyler Seguin .75 2.00
T24 Miro Heiskanen .75 2.00
T25 Dylan Larkin .75 2.00
T26 Tyler Bertuzzi .50 1.25
T27 Connor McDavid 3.00 8.00
T28 Leon Draisaitl 2.00 5.00
T29 Ryan Nugent-Hopkins .75 2.00
T30 Aleksander Barkov 1.00 2.50
T31 Jonathan Huberdeau .75 2.00
T32 Anze Kopitar 1.00 2.50
T33 Drew Doughty .75 2.00
T34 Ryan Suter .50 1.25
T35 Jordan Greenway .50 1.25
T36 Carey Price 1.25 3.00
T37 Shea Weber .60 1.50
T38 Nick Suzuki 1.25 3.00
T39 Roman Josi .60 1.50
T40 Filip Forsberg 1.00 2.50
T41 Jack Hughes 1.50 4.00
T42 Nico Hischier 1.00 2.50
T43 Mathew Barzal .75 2.00
T44 Semyon Varlamov .60 1.50
T45 Artemi Panarin 1.25 3.00
T46 Mika Zibanejad .75 2.00
T47 Igor Shesterkin 1.25 3.00
T48 Brady Tkachuk 1.00 2.50
T49 Thomas Chabot .60 1.50
T50 Joel Farabee .60 1.50
T51 Carter Hart .60 1.50
T52 James van Riemsdyk .50 1.25
T53 Jake Guentzel 1.00 2.50
T54 Evgeni Malkin 1.25 3.00
T55 Sidney Crosby 2.50 6.00
T56 Tomas Hertl .60 1.50
T57 Logan Couture .75 2.00
T58 Steven Stamkos 1.25 3.00
T59 Andrei Vasilevskiy 1.00 2.50
T60 Brayden Point .75 2.00
T61 John Tavares 1.00 2.50
T62 Auston Matthews 2.50 6.00
T63 Mitch Marner 1.00 2.50
T64 Elias Pettersson 1.00 2.50
T65 Brock Boeser .75 2.00
T66 Quinn Hughes 1.50 4.00
T67 Robin Lehner .50 1.25
T68 Max Pacioretty .60 1.50
T69 Mark Stone .75 2.00
T70 Alex Ovechkin 2.50 6.00
T71 Nicklas Backstrom .60 1.50
T72 John Carlson .60 1.50
T73 Kyle Connor 1.00 2.50
T74 Mark Scheifele 1.00 2.50
T75 Connor Hellebuyck 1.25 3.00
T76 Alexis Lafreniere YG 30.00 80.00
T77 Ian Mitchell YG 2.50 6.00
T78 Nick Robertson YG 5.00 12.00
T79 Nils Hoglander YG 3.00 8.00
T80 Alexander Romanov YG 4.00 10.00
T81 Tim Stutzle YG 20.00 50.00
T82 Philipp Kurashev YG 4.00 10.00
T83 Vitek Vanecek YG 5.00 12.00
T84 Dylan Cozens YG 5.00 12.00
T85 Cal Foote YG 4.00 10.00
T86 Ty Dellandrea YG 3.00 8.00
T87 Kirill Kaprizov YG 30.00 80.00
T88 Ilya Sorokin YG 8.00 20.00
T89 Kevin Lankinen YG 5.00 12.00
T90 Jake Oettinger YG 8.00 20.00
T91 Liam Foudy YG 3.00 8.00
T92 Josh Norris YG 5.00 12.00
T93 K'Andre Miller YG 6.00 15.00
T94 Pius Suter YG 4.00 10.00
T95 Peyton Krebs YG 5.00 12.00
T96 Gabe Vilardi YG 5.00 12.00
T97 Thomas Harley YG 5.00 12.00
T98 Bowen Byram YG 10.00 25.00
T99 Connor McMichael YG 5.00 12.00
T100 Arthur Kaliyev YG 5.00 12.00

2020-21 Upper Deck '05-06 Upper Deck Tribute Exclusives

*EXCLUSIVES: 4X TO 10X BASIC
T81 Tim Stutzle YG 200.00 500.00
T100 Arthur Kaliyev YG 80.00 200.00

2020-21 Upper Deck '94-95 Rookie Tribute Die Cuts

*RED: .75X TO 2X BASIC
RDT1 Jason Robertson 2.00 5.00
RDT2 Morgan Geekie .75 2.00
RDT3 Kieffer Bellows .60 1.50
RDT4 Gabe Vilardi 1.25 3.00
RDT5 Nicolas Beaudin .75 2.00
RDT6 Maxim Letunov .60 1.50
RDT7 Josh Norris 1.25 3.00
RDT8 Mikey Anderson .75 2.00
RDT9 Timothy Liljegren .75 2.00
RDT10 Tyler Benson .75 2.00
RDT12 Jake Oettinger 2.00 5.00
RDT13 Peyton Krebs 1.25 3.00
RDT14 Bowen Byram 1.50 4.00
RDT15 Nick Robertson 1.25 3.00
RDT16 Philipp Kurashev 1.00 2.50
RDT17 Shane Bowers .60 1.50
RDT18 Connor McMichael 1.25 3.00
RDT19 Vitali Kravtsov 1.50 4.00
RDT20 Victor Soderstrom .60 1.50

2020-21 Upper Deck Box Filler

BF1 Bob Probert 25.00 60.00
BF2 Ryan Reaves 12.00 30.00
BF3 Tom Wilson 20.00 50.00
BF4 Tim Hunter 12.00 30.00
BF5 Chris Chelios 15.00 40.00
BF6 Milan Lucic 15.00 40.00
BF7 Joey Kocur 12.00 30.00
BF8 Paul Bissonnette 12.00 30.00
BF9 Rob Ray 12.00 30.00
BF10 Chris Nilan 12.00 30.00
BF11 Evander Kane 10.00 25.00
BF12 Dave Schultz 15.00 40.00
BF13 Matthew Barnaby 12.00 30.00
BF14 Wendel Clark 20.00 50.00
BF15 Tiger Williams 12.00 30.00
BF16 Dave Brown 12.00 30.00
BF17 Basil McRae 12.00 30.00
BF18 Matthew Tkachuk 12.00 30.00
BF19 Tie Domi 15.00 40.00
BF20 Georges Laraque 15.00 40.00
BF21 Gino Odjick 12.00 30.00
BF22 Marty McSorley 15.00 40.00

2020-21 Upper Deck Canvas

C1 Ryan Getzlaf .60 1.50
C2 Sam Steel .50 1.25
C3 Conor Garland .50 1.25
C4 Oliver Ekman-Larsson .60 1.50
C5 Brad Marchand 1.25 3.00
C6 Tuukka Rask .75 2.00
C7 David Krejci .60 1.50
C8 Rasmus Dahlin .75 2.00
C9 Jeff Skinner .60 1.50
C10 Rasmus Ristolainen .40 1.00
C11 Johnny Gaudreau 1.00 2.50
C12 Elias Lindholm .60 1.50
C13 Mark Giordano .60 1.50
C14 Sebastian Aho 1.00 2.50
C15 Jaccob Slavin .50 1.25
C16 Andrei Svechnikov .75 2.00
C17 Patrick Kane 1.25 3.00
C18 Kirby Dach .60 1.50
C19 Dominik Kubalik .60 1.50
C20 Nathan MacKinnon 2.50 6.00
C21 Andre Burakovsky .40 1.00
C22 Gabriel Landeskog .75 2.00
C23 Seth Jones .60 1.50
C24 Zach Werenski 1.00 2.50
C25 Elvis Merzlikins .60 1.50
C26 Tyler Seguin .75 2.00
C27 Ben Bishop .50 1.25
C28 Miro Heiskanen .75 2.00
C29 Filip Zadina .50 1.25
C30 Tyler Bertuzzi .50 1.25
C31 Jonathan Bernier .50 1.25
C32 Leon Draisaitl 2.00 5.00
C33 Kailer Yamamoto .60 1.50
C34 Zack Kassian .40 1.00
C35 Jonathan Huberdeau .75 2.00
C36 Keith Yandle .40 1.00
C37 Dustin Brown .60 1.50
C38 Jonathan Quick .75 2.00
C39 Anze Kopitar 1.00 2.50
C40 Eric Staal .60 1.50
C41 Mats Zuccarello .60 1.50
C42 Ryan Suter .50 1.25
C43 Carey Price 1.25 3.00
C44 Nick Suzuki 1.25 3.00
C45 Phillip Danault .60 1.50
C46 Ryan Johansen .50 1.25
C47 Roman Josi .60 1.50
C48 Matt Duchene .60 1.50
C49 Jack Hughes 1.50 4.00
C50 Nikita Gusev .50 1.25
C51 Nico Hischier 1.00 2.50
C52 Jean-Gabriel Pageau .40 1.00
C53 Josh Bailey .50 1.25
C54 Igor Shesterkin 1.25 3.00
C55 Pavel Buchnevich .50 1.25
C56 Mika Zibanejad .75 2.00
C57 Chris Kreider .75 2.00
C58 Thomas Chabot .60 1.50
C59 Brady Tkachuk 1.00 2.50
C60 Claude Giroux .60 1.50
C61 Jakub Voracek .50 1.25
C62 James van Riemsdyk .50 1.25
C63 Kris Letang .75 2.00
C64 Sidney Crosby 2.50 6.00
C65 Bryan Rust .60 1.50
C66 Erik Karlsson .75 2.00
C67 Evander Kane .60 1.50
C68 Brent Burns .60 1.50
C69 Ryan O'Reilly .60 1.50
C70 Colton Parayko .50 1.25
C71 Jaden Schwartz .75 2.00
C72 Andrei Vasilevskiy 1.00 2.50
C73 Brayden Point .75 2.00
C74 Nikita Kucherov 1.25 3.00
C75 Auston Matthews 2.50 6.00
C76 Frederik Andersen .75 2.00
C77 Morgan Rielly .60 1.50
C78 Bo Horvat .75 2.00
C79 Elias Pettersson 1.00 2.50
C80 Quinn Hughes 1.50 4.00
C81 Marc-Andre Fleury 1.25 3.00
C82 Jonathan Marchessault .75 2.00
C83 Max Pacioretty .60 1.50
C84 Evgeny Kuznetsov .75 2.00
C85 John Carlson .60 1.50
C86 Jakub Vrana .60 1.50
C87 Patrik Laine .75 2.00
C88 Connor Hellebuyck 1.25 3.00
C89 Kyle Connor 1.00 2.50
C90 E.Pettersson/Q.Hughes CL 1.50 4.00
C91 Alexis Lafreniere YG 25.00 60.00
C92 Jason Robertson YG 12.00 30.00
C93 Morgan Geekie YG 5.00 12.00
C94 Gabe Vilardi YG 8.00 20.00
C95 Philip Broberg YG 5.00 12.00
C96 Pavel Francouz YG 6.00 15.00
C97 Vitali Kravtsov YG 10.00 25.00
C98 Jake Oettinger YG 12.00 30.00
C99 Nicolas Beaudin YG 5.00 12.00
C100 Liam Foudy YG 5.00 12.00
C101 Pierre-Olivier Joseph YG 5.00 12.00
C102 Michael DiPietro YG 6.00 15.00
C103 Victor Soderstrom YG 4.00 10.00
C104 Timothy Liljegren YG 5.00 12.00
C105 Kieffer Bellows YG 4.00 10.00
C106 Ty Dellandrea YG 5.00 12.00
C107 Connor McMichael YG 8.00 20.00
C108 Bowen Byram YG 10.00 25.00
C109 Olli Juolevi YG 5.00 12.00
C110 Egor Zamula YG 4.00 10.00
C111 Josh Norris YG 8.00 20.00
C112 Peyton Krebs YG 10.00 25.00
C113 Tyler Benson YG 5.00 12.00
C114 Mikhail Berdin YG 5.00 12.00
C115 Philipp Kurashev YG 6.00 15.00
C116 Alexander Alexeyev YG 4.00 10.00
C117 Mikey Anderson YG 5.00 12.00
C118 Nick Robertson YG 8.00 20.00
C119 Thomas Harley YG 8.00 20.00
C120 J.Robertson/N.Robertson YG CL 6.00 15.00
C121 John Gibson .60 1.50
C122 Rickard Rakell .50 1.25
C123 Cam Fowler .60 1.50
C124 Nick Schmaltz .50 1.25
C125 Clayton Keller .75 2.00
C126 Darcy Kuemper .60 1.50
C127 Charlie McAvoy .75 2.00
C128 Patrice Bergeron .75 2.00
C129 Jake DeBrusk .60 1.50
C130 Jack Eichel 1.00 2.50
C131 Sam Reinhart 1.25 3.00
C132 Victor Olofsson .60 1.50
C133 Matthew Tkachuk 1.25 3.00
C134 David Rittich .50 1.25
C135 Sean Monahan .40 1.00
C136 Teuvo Teravainen .60 1.50
C137 Dougie Hamilton .50 1.25
C138 Martin Necas 1.00 2.50
C139 Duncan Keith .50 1.25
C140 Jonathan Toews 1.00 2.50
C141 Alex DeBrincat .75 2.00
C142 Cale Makar 1.50 4.00
C143 Mikko Rantanen 1.50 4.00
C144 Philipp Grubauer .60 1.50
C145 Cam Atkinson .60 1.50
C146 Joonas Korpisalo .60 1.50
C147 Pierre-Luc Dubois .50 1.25
C148 Jamie Benn .60 1.50
C149 Roope Hintz .75 2.00
C150 Joe Pavelski .75 2.00
C151 Robby Fabbri .40 1.00
C152 Dylan Larkin .75 2.00
C153 Anthony Mantha .50 1.25
C154 Connor McDavid 3.00 8.00
C155 Andreas Athanasiou .50 1.25
C156 Ryan Nugent-Hopkins .75 2.00
C157 Aleksander Barkov 1.00 2.50
C158 Mike Hoffman .40 1.00
C159 Sergei Bobrovsky 1.00 2.50
C160 Alex Iafallo .40 1.00
C161 Drew Doughty .75 2.00
C162 Matt Dumba .40 1.00
C163 Kevin Fiala .50 1.25
C164 Zach Parise .60 1.50
C165 Tomas Tatar .40 1.00
C166 Brendan Gallagher .60 1.50
C167 Shea Weber .60 1.50
C168 Pekka Rinne .60 1.50
C169 Filip Forsberg 1.00 2.50
C170 Ryan Ellis .50 1.25
C171 Mackenzie Blackwood .60 1.50
C172 P.K. Subban .75 2.00
C173 Kyle Palmieri .50 1.25
C174 Anders Lee .50 1.25
C175 Mathew Barzal .75 2.00
C176 Brock Nelson .60 1.50
C177 Artemi Panarin 1.25 3.00
C178 Adam Fox .75 2.00
C179 Tony DeAngelo .40 1.00
C180 Artem Anisimov .40 1.00
C181 Colin White .40 1.00
C182 Mike Reilly .40 1.00
C183 Travis Konecny .60 1.50
C184 Carter Hart .60 1.50
C185 Sean Couturier .50 1.25
C186 Evgeni Malkin 1.25 3.00
C187 Jake Guentzel 1.00 2.50
C188 Jason Zucker .60 1.50
C189 Kevin Labanc .40 1.00
C190 Logan Couture .75 2.00
C191 Tomas Hertl .60 1.50
C192 Jordan Binnington 1.00 2.50
C193 David Perron .50 1.25
C194 Brayden Schenn .60 1.50
C195 Steven Stamkos 1.25 3.00
C196 Alex Killorn .40 1.00
C197 Victor Hedman .75 2.00
C198 John Tavares 1.00 2.50
C199 Mitch Marner 1.00 2.50
C200 William Nylander 1.25 3.00
C201 Mark Stone .75 2.00
C202 William Karlsson .75 2.00
C203 Shea Theodore .75 2.00
C204 Alex Ovechkin 2.50 6.00
C205 Ilya Samsonov .60 1.50
C206 Nicklas Backstrom .60 1.50
C207 Mark Scheifele 1.00 2.50
C208 Blake Wheeler .60 1.50
C209 Nikolaj Ehlers .60 1.50
C210 M.Tkachuk/B.Tkachuk CL 1.25 3.00
C211 Tim Stutzle YG 15.00 40.00
C212 Ilya Sorokin YG 10.00 25.00
C213 Mathias Brome YG 4.00 10.00
C214 Ty Smith YG 8.00 20.00
C215 Alexander Barabanov YG 5.00 12.00
C216 Jansen Harkins YG 4.00 10.00
C217 Yegor Sharangovich YG 8.00 20.00
C218 Dylan Coghlan YG 5.00 12.00
C219 Martin Kaut YG 5.00 12.00
C220 Brayden Burke YG 4.00 10.00
C221 Brandon Hagel YG 6.00 15.00
C222 Joseph Woll YG 12.00 30.00
C223 Pius Suter YG 6.00 15.00
C224 Jake Evans YG 5.00 12.00
C225 Kirill Kaprizov YG 25.00 60.00
C226 Connor Ingram YG 4.00 10.00
C227 Alexander Romanov YG 6.00 15.00
C228 Joel Kiviranta YG 5.00 12.00
C229 Cal Foote YG 6.00 15.00
C230 Ian Mitchell YG 4.00 10.00
C231 Shane Bowers YG 4.00 10.00
C232 John Leonard YG 4.00 10.00
C233 Dylan Cozens YG 6.00 15.00
C234 Lucas Carlsson YG 4.00 10.00
C235 K'Andre Miller YG 8.00 20.00
C236 Ryan McLeod YG 4.00 10.00
C237 Alex Belzile YG 4.00 10.00
C238 MacKenzie Entwistle YG 4.00 10.00
C239 Nils Hoglander YG 8.00 20.00
C240 K.Kaprizov/I.Sorokin YG CL 12.00 30.00
C241 Peter Bondra RS 5.00 12.00
C242 Gerry Cheevers RS 5.00 12.00
C243 Ken Morrow RS 3.00 8.00
C244 Charlie Simmer RS 3.00 8.00
C245 Owen Nolan RS 5.00 12.00
C246 Nicklas Lidstrom RS 5.00 12.00
C247 Brendan Shanahan RS 5.00 12.00
C248 Joe Nieuwendyk RS 4.00 10.00
C249 Guy Lafleur RS 6.00 15.00
C250 Chris Pronger RS 5.00 12.00
C251 Michel Goulet RS 5.00 12.00
C252 Brett Hull RS 10.00 25.00
C253 Bob Probert RS 5.00 12.00
C254 Denis Savard RS 5.00 12.00
C255 Ed Giacomin RS 4.00 10.00
C256 Alexis Lafreniere POE 30.00 80.00
C257 Thomas Harley POE 10.00 25.00
C258 Ty Dellandrea POE 6.00 15.00
C259 Bowen Byram POE 12.00 30.00
C260 Connor McMichael POE 10.00 25.00
C261 Michael DiPietro POE 8.00 20.00
C262 Shane Bowers POE 5.00 12.00
C263 Dylan Cozens POE 10.00 25.00
C264 Peyton Krebs POE 10.00 25.00
C265 Sidney Crosby POE 30.00 80.00
C266 Jarome Iginla POE 6.00 15.00
C267 Jonathan Toews POE 8.00 20.00
C268 Joe Thornton POE 8.00 20.00
C269 John Tavares POE 8.00 20.00
C270 Taylor Hall POE 5.00 12.00

2020-21 Upper Deck Ceremonial Puck Drop

CPD1 Henrik Zetterberg 10.00 25.00
CPD2 Teemu Selanne 15.00 40.00
CPD3 Federko/MacInnis/Hull 15.00 40.00
CPD4 Chris Phillips 6.00 15.00
CPD5 Markus Naslund 8.00 20.00
CPD6 Dominik Hasek 12.00 30.00
CPD7 Guy Carbonneau 8.00 20.00
CPD8 Bianca Andreescu 30.00 80.00

2020-21 Upper Deck Ceremonial Puck Drop Autographs

CPD1 Henrik Zetterberg 50.00 125.00
CPD8 Bianca Andreescu 150.00 400.00

2020-21 Upper Deck Clear Cut Foundation

CCFBE A.Ekblad/S.Bobrovsky 8.00 20.00
CCFBH J.Hughes/N.Hischier 12.00 30.00
CCFCV J.Carlson/J.Vrana 5.00 12.00
CCFDJ M.Duchene/R.Josi 5.00 12.00
CCFDK D.Kubalik/K.Dach 5.00 12.00
CCFDO V.Olofsson/R.Dahlin 6.00 15.00
CCFDT B.Tkachuk/A.Duclair 8.00 20.00
CCFHC C.Hellebuyck/K.Connor 10.00 25.00
CCFHP Q.Hughes/E.Pettersson 12.00 30.00
CCFKC E.Karlsson/L.Couture 6.00 15.00
CCFKH T.Konecny/C.Hart 5.00 12.00
CCFKI A.Iafallo/A.Kopitar 8.00 20.00
CCFKP B.Point/N.Kucherov 10.00 25.00
CCFKS N.Schmaltz/D.Kuemper 5.00 12.00
CCFMB T.Bertuzzi/A.Mantha 4.00 10.00
CCFML E.Lindholm/S.Monahan 5.00 12.00
CCFMM C.Makar/N.MacKinnon 20.00 50.00
CCFMP D.Pastrnak/B.Marchand 12.00 30.00
CCFND L.Draisaitl/D.Nurse 15.00 40.00
CCFNM M.Marner/W.Nylander 10.00 25.00
CCFNP J.Pageau/B.Nelson 5.00 12.00
CCFNW Z.Werenski/G.Nyquist 8.00 20.00
CCFOB J.Binnington/R.O'Reilly 8.00 20.00
CCFPH M.Heiskanen/J.Pavelski 6.00 15.00
CCFPS A.Panarin/I.Shesterkin 10.00 25.00
CCFSG J.Gibson/J.Silfverberg 5.00 12.00
CCFST T.Tatar/N.Suzuki 10.00 25.00
CCFTK W.Karlsson/S.Theodore 6.00 15.00
CCFTS T.Teravainen/A.Svechnikov 6.00 15.00
CCFZF K.Fiala/M.Zuccarello 5.00 12.00
CCFZG J.Zucker/J.Guentzel 8.00 20.00

2020-21 Upper Deck Clear Cut Honoured Members

HOF93 Michel Goulet 6.00 15.00
HOF94 Willie O'Ree 8.00 20.00
HOF95 Al MacInnis 8.00 20.00
HOF96 Frank Mahovlich 6.00 15.00
HOF97 Bernie Parent 8.00 20.00
HOF98 Jacques Plante 6.00 15.00
HOF99 Ed Giacomin 5.00 12.00
HOF100 Chris Pronger 6.00 15.00
HOF101 Joe Mullen 6.00 15.00

2020-21 Upper Deck Clear Cut Leaders

CCLGAA Rask/Allen/Khudobin 15.00 40.00
CCLGLS Pastrnak
Ovechkin/Matthews 50.00 125.00
CCLGWG Pastrnak/Draisaitl/Eichel 40.00 100.00
CCLRPT Hughes/Makar/Kubalik 30.00 80.00
CCLSOG MacKinnon
Ovechkin/Pacioretty 50.00 120.00
CCLWIN Vasilevskiy
Hellebuyck/Binnington 25.00 60.00

2020-21 Upper Deck Day With The Cup

DC23 Steven Stamkos 25.00 60.00
DC24 Andrei Vasilevskiy 20.00 50.00
DC25 Victor Hedman 15.00 40.00
DC26 Brayden Point 15.00 40.00
DC27 Yanni Gourde 20.00 50.00
DC28 Nikita Kucherov 30.00 80.00

2020-21 Upper Deck Day With The Cup Flashbacks Series 1

DCF1 Wayne Gretzky 60.00 150.00
DCF2 Paul Coffey 15.00 40.00
DCF3 Kevin Lowe 15.00 40.00
DCF4 Mark Messier 40.00 100.00
DCF5 Jari Kurri 15.00 40.00
DCF6 Grant Fuhr 25.00 60.00
DCF7 Steve Larmer 12.00 30.00
DCF8 Adam Graves 12.00 30.00
DCF9 Brian Leetch 25.00 60.00
DCF10 Esa Tikkanen 25.00 60.00
DCF11 Mark Messier 30.00 80.00
DCF12 Mike Richter 20.00 50.00

2020-21 Upper Deck Dazzlers

*GREEN: .75X TO 2X BASIC
*ORANGE: 1.5X TO 4X BASIC
*PINK: 2.5X TO 6X BASIC
DZ1 Rickard Rakell .30 .75
DZ2 Nick Schmaltz .30 .75
DZ3 David Pastrnak 1.00 2.50
DZ4 Brad Marchand .75 2.00
DZ5 Jack Eichel .60 1.50
DZ6 Rasmus Dahlin .50 1.25
DZ7 Matthew Tkachuk .75 2.00
DZ8 Johnny Gaudreau .60 1.50
DZ9 Sebastian Aho .60 1.50
DZ10 Andrei Svechnikov .50 1.25
DZ11 Patrick Kane .75 2.00
DZ12 Nathan MacKinnon 1.50 4.00
DZ13 Cale Makar 1.00 2.50
DZ14 Zach Werenski .60 1.50
DZ15 Tyler Seguin .50 1.25
DZ16 Ben Bishop .30 .75
DZ17 Dylan Larkin .50 1.25
DZ18 Connor McDavid 2.00 5.00
DZ19 Leon Draisaitl 1.25 3.00
DZ20 Jonathan Huberdeau .50 1.25
DZ21 Aleksander Barkov .60 1.50
DZ22 Anze Kopitar .60 1.50
DZ23 Kevin Fiala .30 .75
DZ24 Carey Price .75 2.00
DZ25 Nick Suzuki .75 2.00
DZ26 Matt Duchene .40 1.00
DZ27 Mackenzie Blackwood .40 1.00
DZ28 Mathew Barzal .50 1.25
DZ29 Artemi Panarin .75 2.00
DZ30 Igor Shesterkin .75 2.00
DZ31 Brady Tkachuk .60 1.50
DZ32 Carter Hart .40 1.00
DZ33 Sidney Crosby 1.50 4.00
DZ34 Evgeni Malkin .75 2.00
DZ35 Tomas Hertl .40 1.00
DZ36 Jordan Binnington .60 1.50
DZ37 Ryan O'Reilly .40 1.00
DZ38 Steven Stamkos .75 2.00
DZ39 Andrei Vasilevskiy .60 1.50
DZ40 Nikita Kucherov .75 2.00
DZ41 Mitch Marner .60 1.50
DZ42 Auston Matthews 1.50 4.00
DZ43 Elias Pettersson .60 1.50
DZ44 Quinn Hughes 1.00 2.50
DZ45 Mark Stone .50 1.25
DZ46 Max Pacioretty .40 1.00
DZ47 Alex Ovechkin 1.50 4.00

DZ48 John Carlson .40 1.00
DZ49 Connor Hellebuyck .75 2.00
DZ50 Kyle Connor .60 1.50
DZ51 John Gibson .40 1.00
DZ52 Oliver Ekman-Larsson .40 1.00
DZ53 Victor Soderstrom .40 1.00
DZ54 Patrice Bergeron .50 1.25
DZ55 Tuukka Rask .50 1.25
DZ56 Victor Olofsson .40 1.00
DZ57 Sean Monahan .25 .60
DZ58 Teuvo Teravainen .40 1.00
DZ59 Dominik Kubalik .40 1.00
DZ60 Philipp Kurashev .60 1.50
DZ61 Bowen Byram 1.00 2.50
DZ62 Shane Bowers .40 1.00
DZ63 Liam Foudy .50 1.25
DZ64 Seth Jones .40 1.00
DZ65 Jake Oettinger 1.25 3.00
DZ66 Thomas Harley .75 2.00
DZ67 Ty Dellandrea .50 1.25
DZ68 Anthony Mantha .30 .75
DZ69 Tyler Bertuzzi .30 .75
DZ70 Philip Broberg .50 1.25
DZ71 Keith Yandle .25 .60
DZ72 Gabe Vilardi .75 2.00
DZ73 Zach Parise .40 1.00
DZ74 Shea Weber .40 1.00
DZ75 Connor Ingram .40 1.00
DZ76 Roman Josi .40 1.00
DZ77 Nico Hischier .60 1.50
DZ78 Jack Hughes 1.00 2.50
DZ79 Kieffer Bellows .40 1.00
DZ80 Brock Nelson .40 1.00
DZ81 Alexis Lafreniere 8.00 20.00
DZ82 Vitali Kravtsov 1.00 2.50
DZ83 Josh Norris .75 2.00
DZ84 Travis Konecny .40 1.00
DZ85 Jake Guentzel .60 1.50
DZ86 Brent Burns .40 1.00
DZ87 Brayden Schenn .40 1.00
DZ88 Brayden Point .50 1.25
DZ89 Victor Hedman .50 1.25
DZ90 Timothy Liljegren .50 1.25
DZ91 Nick Robertson .75 2.00
DZ92 Morgan Rielly .40 1.00
DZ93 John Tavares .60 1.50
DZ94 Bo Horvat .50 1.25
DZ95 Olli Juolevi .50 1.25
DZ96 Brock Boeser .50 1.25
DZ97 Peyton Krebs .75 2.00
DZ98 Shea Theodore .50 1.25
DZ99 Connor McMichael .75 2.00
DZ100 Mark Scheifele .60 1.50
DZ101 Ryan Getzlaf .40 1.00
DZ102 Conor Garland .30 .75
DZ103 Charlie McAvoy .50 1.25
DZ104 Dylan Cozens .75 2.00
DZ105 Elias Lindholm .40 1.00
DZ106 Martin Necas .60 1.50
DZ107 Pius Suter .60 1.50
DZ108 Kevin Lankinen .75 2.00
DZ109 Ian Mitchell .40 1.00
DZ110 Mikko Rantanen 1.00 2.50
DZ111 Philipp Grubauer .40 1.00
DZ112 Patrik Laine .50 1.25
DZ113 Miro Heiskanen .50 1.25
DZ114 Jamie Benn .40 1.00
DZ115 Joe Pavelski .50 1.25
DZ116 Filip Zadina .30 .75
DZ117 Ryan Nugent-Hopkins .50 1.25
DZ118 Sergei Bobrovsky .60 1.50
DZ119 Aleksi Heponiemi .60 1.50
DZ120 Drew Doughty .50 1.25
DZ121 Arthur Kaliyev .75 2.00
DZ122 Kirill Kaprizov 12.00 30.00
DZ123 Tyler Toffoli .40 1.00
DZ124 Alexander Romanov .60 1.50
DZ125 Pekka Rinne .40 1.00
DZ126 Ty Smith .75 2.00
DZ127 Ilya Sorokin 1.25 3.00
DZ128 Anders Lee .30 .75
DZ129 K'Andre Miller 1.00 2.50
DZ130 Mika Zibanejad .50 1.25
DZ131 Tim Stutzle 6.00 15.00
DZ132 Joel Farabee .40 1.00
DZ133 Pierre-Olivier Joseph .50 1.25
DZ134 Erik Karlsson .50 1.25
DZ135 Logan Couture .50 1.25
DZ136 David Perron .30 .75
DZ137 Torey Krug .30 .75
DZ138 Cal Foote .60 1.50
DZ139 Mikhail Sergachev .30 .75
DZ140 Joe Thornton .60 1.50
DZ141 Frederik Andersen .50 1.25
DZ142 William Nylander .75 2.00
DZ143 Nils Hoglander .50 1.25
DZ144 Alex Pietrangelo .30 .75
DZ145 William Karlsson .50 1.25
DZ146 Jakub Vrana .40 1.00
DZ147 Nicklas Backstrom .40 1.00
DZ148 Vitek Vanecek .75 2.00
DZ149 Pierre-Luc Dubois .30 .75
DZ150 Blake Wheeler .40 1.00

2020-21 Upper Deck Debut Dates

DD1 Nick Suzuki 3.00 8.00
DD2 Adam Fox 2.00 5.00
DD3 Igor Shesterkin 3.00 8.00
DD4 Cayden Primeau 2.50 6.00
DD5 Kirby Dach 1.50 4.00
DD6 Jack Hughes 4.00 10.00
DD7 Kieffer Bellows 1.50 4.00
DD8 Mario Ferraro 1.00 2.50
DD9 Elvis Merzlikins 1.50 4.00
DD10 Joel Farabee 1.50 4.00
DD11 Ilya Mikheyev 1.25 3.00
DD12 Dominik Kubalik 1.50 4.00
DD13 Noah Dobson 2.00 5.00
DD14 Cody Glass 1.25 3.00
DD15 Nikita Gusev 1.25 3.00
DD16 Ilya Samsonov 1.50 4.00
DD17 Kaapo Kakko 1.25 3.00
DD18 Morgan Frost 1.25 3.00
DD19 Adam Boqvist 1.25 3.00
DD20 John Marino 1.50 4.00

2020-21 Upper Deck Debut Dates Jerseys

*PATCH: 1.5X TO 4X BASIC
DD1 Nick Suzuki 8.00 20.00
DD2 Adam Fox 5.00 12.00
DD3 Igor Shesterkin 8.00 20.00
DD4 Cayden Primeau 6.00 15.00
DD5 Kirby Dach 4.00 10.00
DD6 Jack Hughes 10.00 25.00
DD7 Kieffer Bellows 4.00 10.00
DD8 Mario Ferraro 2.50 6.00
DD9 Elvis Merzlikins 4.00 10.00
DD10 Joel Farabee 4.00 10.00
DD11 Ilya Mikheyev 3.00 8.00
DD12 Dominik Kubalik 4.00 10.00
DD13 Noah Dobson 5.00 12.00
DD14 Cody Glass 3.00 8.00
DD15 Nikita Gusev 3.00 8.00
DD16 Ilya Samsonov 4.00 10.00
DD17 Kaapo Kakko 3.00 8.00
DD18 Morgan Frost 3.00 8.00
DD19 Adam Boqvist 3.00 8.00
DD20 John Marino 4.00 10.00

2020-21 Upper Deck Fluorescence Red

F1 Nick Robertson 5.00 12.00
F2 Liam Foudy 3.00 8.00
F3 Philip Broberg 3.00 8.00
F4 Jansen Harkins 2.50 6.00
F5 Connor McMichael 5.00 12.00
F6 Gabe Vilardi 5.00 12.00
F7 Jason Robertson 8.00 20.00
F8 Nicolas Beaudin 3.00 8.00
F9 Tyler Benson 3.00 8.00
F10 Alexander True 2.50 6.00
F11 Alexis Lafreniere 20.00 50.00
F12 Jake Evans 3.00 8.00
F13 Kieffer Bellows 2.50 6.00
F14 Thomas Harley 5.00 12.00
F15 Gustav Lindstrom 2.50 6.00
F16 Joseph Woll 6.00 15.00
F17 Morgan Geekie 3.00 8.00
F18 Dylan Coghlan 3.00 8.00
F19 Shane Bowers 2.50 6.00
F20 Joel Kiviranta 3.00 8.00
F21 Connor Ingram 2.50 6.00
F22 Egor Zamula 2.50 6.00
F23 Vitali Kravtsov 6.00 15.00
F24 Victor Soderstrom 5.00 12.00
F25 Alexander Alexeyev 2.50 6.00
F26 Martin Kaut 3.00 8.00
F27 Ryan McLeod 2.50 6.00
F28 Timothy Liljegren 3.00 8.00
F29 Josh Norris 5.00 12.00
F30 Ty Dellandrea 3.00 8.00
F31 Alec Regula 2.00 5.00
F32 Peyton Krebs 5.00 12.00
F33 Pierre-Olivier Joseph 3.00 8.00
F34 Mikhail Berdin 3.00 8.00
F35 Michael DiPietro 4.00 10.00
F36 Philipp Kurashev 4.00 10.00
F37 Bowen Byram 6.00 15.00
F38 Olli Juolevi 3.00 8.00
F39 Mikey Anderson 3.00 8.00
F40 Jake Oettinger 8.00 20.00
FAK Arthur Kaliyev 5.00 12.00
FAR Alexander Romanov 15.00 40.00
FDC Dylan Cozens 12.00 30.00
FIS Ilya Sorokin 8.00 20.00
FKK Kirill Kaprizov 12.00 30.00
FTS Tim Stutzle 30.00 80.00

2020-21 Upper Deck Fluorescence Blue

*BLUE: 1.25X TO 3X RED
FKK Kirill Kaprizov 80.00 200.00

2020-21 Upper Deck Fluorescence Gold

*GOLD: .6X TO 1.5X RED
F11 Alexis Lafreniere 60.00 150.00
FAR Alexander Romanov 30.00 80.00
FKK Kirill Kaprizov 40.00 100.00
FTS Tim Stutzle 150.00 400.00

2020-21 Upper Deck Game Jerseys

GJAA Artem Anisimov 1.50 4.00
GJAB Aleksander Barkov 4.00 10.00
GJAE Aaron Ekblad 3.00 8.00
GJAH Adam Henrique 2.00 5.00
GJAK Adrian Kempe 2.50 6.00
GJAL Anders Lee 2.00 5.00
GJAM Anthony Mantha 2.00 5.00
GJAN Anze Kopitar 4.00 10.00
GJAR Alexander Radulov 2.50 6.00
GJAV Andrei Vasilevskiy 4.00 10.00
GJBB Brent Burns 2.50 6.00
GJBC Brett Connolly 1.50 4.00
GJBH Bo Horvat 2.50 6.00
GJBN Brock Nelson 2.50 6.00
GJBS Brayden Schenn 2.50 6.00
GJCD Christian Dvorak 2.00 5.00
GJCF Cam Fowler 2.50 6.00
GJCH Carter Hutton 2.00 5.00
GJCO Connor Hellebuyck 5.00 12.00
GJCP Carey Price 5.00 12.00
GJCW Colin White 1.50 4.00
GJDK Duncan Keith 2.00 5.00
GJDL Dylan Larkin 3.00 8.00
GJDN Darnell Nurse 2.00 5.00
GJDO Max Domi 2.50 6.00
GJDP David Pastrnak 6.00 15.00
GJDS Derek Stepan 1.50 4.00
GJEB Jordan Eberle 2.50 6.00
GJEK Evander Kane 2.50 6.00
GJEL Elias Lindholm 2.50 6.00
GJFA Frederik Andersen 3.00 8.00
GJFF Filip Forsberg 4.00 10.00
GJGL Gabriel Landeskog 3.00 8.00
GJGN Gustav Nyquist 1.50 4.00
GJGU Jake Guentzel 4.00 10.00
GJHE Tomas Hertl 2.50 6.00
GJHO Braden Holtby 3.00 8.00
GJIP Ivan Provorov 2.00 5.00
GJJA Justin Abdelkader 2.00 5.00
GJJB Jamie Benn 2.50 6.00
GJJC Jeff Carter 2.00 5.00
GJJE Joel Eriksson Ek 2.00 5.00
GJJG Johnny Gaudreau 4.00 10.00
GJJH Jonathan Huberdeau 3.00 8.00
GJJM J.T. Miller 3.00 8.00
GJJO Jonathan Quick 3.00 8.00
GJJS Jeff Skinner 2.50 6.00
GJJT Jacob Trouba 2.00 5.00
GJKC Kyle Connor 4.00 10.00
GJKH Kevin Hayes 2.00 5.00
GJKK Kasperi Kapanen 2.00 5.00
GJKL Kris Letang 3.00 8.00
GJKO Kyle Okposo 1.50 4.00
GJKP Kyle Palmieri 2.00 5.00
GJKT Kyle Turris 2.00 5.00
GJKU Evgeny Kuznetsov 3.00 8.00
GJKY Keith Yandle 1.50 4.00
GJLD Leon Draisaitl 8.00 20.00
GJMA Jonathan Marchessault 3.00 8.00
GJMD Matt Dumba 1.50 4.00
GJMR Mikko Rantanen 6.00 15.00
GJMS Mark Scheifele 4.00 10.00
GJMT Matthew Tkachuk 5.00 12.00
GJNB Nicklas Backstrom 2.50 6.00
GJNH Nico Hischier 4.00 10.00
GJNK Nazem Kadri 3.00 8.00
GJOE Oliver Ekman-Larsson 2.50 6.00
GJPB Patrice Bergeron 3.00 8.00
GJPH Patric Hornqvist 1.50 4.00
GJPK Phil Kessel 2.50 6.00
GJPL Patrik Laine 3.00 8.00
GJPR Pekka Rinne 2.50 6.00
GJRD Rasmus Dahlin 3.00 8.00
GJRF Radek Faksa 2.00 5.00
GJRJ Ryan Johansen 2.00 5.00
GJRN Ryan Nugent-Hopkins 3.00 8.00
GJRR Rickard Rakell 2.00 5.00
GJRT Robert Thomas 2.50 6.00
GJSA Sebastian Aho 4.00 10.00
GJSC Sean Couturier 2.00 5.00
GJSS Sam Steel 2.00 5.00
GJST Dylan Strome 3.00 8.00
GJSW Shea Weber 2.50 6.00
GJTH Joe Thornton 4.00 10.00
GJTK Torey Krug 2.00 5.00
GJTR Travis Konecny 2.50 6.00
GJTS Tyler Seguin 2.50 6.00
GJTT Teuvo Teravainen 2.50 6.00
GJVA Viktor Arvidsson 1.50 4.00
GJVH Victor Hedman 3.00 8.00
GJVT Vladimir Tarasenko 3.00 8.00
GJWB Will Butcher 2.00 5.00
GJWK William Karlsson 3.00 8.00
GJWN William Nylander 5.00 12.00
GJZP Zach Parise 2.50 6.00
GJZW Zach Werenski 4.00 10.00

2020-21 Upper Deck HoloGrFx NHL

NHL1 Sidney Crosby 3.00 8.00
NHL2 Artemi Panarin 1.50 4.00
NHL3 Nathan MacKinnon 3.00 8.00
NHL4 Victor Hedman 1.00 2.50
NHL5 Alex Ovechkin 3.00 8.00
NHL6 David Pastrnak 2.00 5.00
NHL7 Pierre-Luc Dubois .60 1.50
NHL8 Auston Matthews 3.00 8.00
NHL9 Cale Makar 2.00 5.00
NHL10 Quinn Hughes 2.00 5.00
NHL11 Sebastian Aho 1.50 4.00
NHL12 Leon Draisaitl 2.50 6.00
NHL13 Patrick Kane 1.50 4.00
NHL14 Matthew Tkachuk 1.50 4.00
NHL15 Jack Eichel 1.25 3.00
NHL16 Jordan Binnington 1.25 3.00
NHL17 Andrei Vasilevskiy 1.25 3.00
NHL18 Brock Boeser 1.00 2.50
NHL19 Brad Marchand 1.50 4.00
NHL20 Connor McDavid 4.00 10.00

2020-21 Upper Deck HoloGrFx Rookies

HG1 Kirill Kaprizov 3.00 8.00
HG2 Dylan Cozens 1.25 3.00
HG3 Tim Stutzle 1.50 4.00
HG4 Nils Hoglander .75 2.00
HG5 Timothy Liljegren .75 2.00
HG6 Thomas Harley 1.25 3.00
HG7 Vitek Vanecek 1.25 3.00
HG8 Pius Suter 1.00 2.50
HG9 Ilya Sorokin 2.00 5.00
HG10 Alexis Lafreniere 2.50 6.00
HG11 Philipp Kurashev 1.00 2.50
HG12 Arthur Kaliyev 1.25 3.00
HG13 Alexander Romanov 1.00 2.50
HG14 Ty Smith 1.25 3.00
HG15 Nick Robertson 1.25 3.00
HG16 K'Andre Miller 1.50 4.00
HG17 Connor McMichael 1.25 3.00
HG18 Ian Mitchell .60 1.50
HG19 Cal Foote 1.00 2.50
HG20 Bowen Byram 1.50 4.00

2020-21 Upper Deck HoloGrFx Rookies Gold

*GOLD: .75X TO 2X BASIC
HG1 Kirill Kaprizov 10.00 25.00

2020-21 Upper Deck McDavid MMXXI

*SILVER/100: 2.5X TO 6X BASIC
*GOLD/25: 10X TO 25X BASIC
CM1 Connor McDavid 1.50 4.00
CM2 Connor McDavid 1.50 4.00
CM3 Connor McDavid 1.50 4.00
CM4 Connor McDavid 1.50 4.00
CM5 Connor McDavid 1.50 4.00
CM6 Connor McDavid 1.50 4.00
CM7 Connor McDavid 1.50 4.00
CM8 Connor McDavid 1.50 4.00
CM9 Connor McDavid 1.50 4.00
CM10 Connor McDavid 1.50 4.00

2020-21 Upper Deck NHL Worldwide

*DIE CUT: 4X TO 10X BASIC
WW1 Leon Draisaitl .75 2.00
WW2 Auston Matthews 1.00 2.50
WW3 Nathan MacKinnon 1.00 2.50
WW4 Sebastian Aho .40 1.00
WW5 Elias Pettersson .40 1.00
WW6 Alex Ovechkin 1.00 2.50
WW7 Connor McDavid 1.25 3.00
WW8 Jakub Voracek .20 .50
WW9 Teuvo Teravainen .25 .60
WW10 Nicklas Backstrom .25 .60
WW11 Evgeni Malkin .50 1.25
WW12 Marc-Andre Fleury .50 1.25
WW13 Zdeno Chara .25 .60
WW14 Tuukka Rask .30 .75
WW15 Tomas Hertl .25 .60
WW16 Patrick Kane .50 1.25
WW17 Philipp Grubauer .25 .60
WW18 Nikita Kucherov .50 1.25
WW19 Oliver Ekman-Larsson .25 .60
WW20 Mats Zuccarello .25 .60
WW21 Jack Eichel .40 1.00
WW22 David Pastrnak .60 1.50
WW23 Henrik Lundqvist .60 1.50
WW24 Elvis Merzlikins .25 .60
WW25 Sidney Crosby 1.00 2.50
WW26 Artemi Panarin .50 1.25
WW27 Aleksander Barkov .40 1.00
WW28 Tomas Tatar .15 .40
WW29 Brad Marchand .50 1.25
WW30 Ben Bishop .20 .50

2020-21 Upper Deck OPC Glossy Rookies

*BRONZE: .6X TO 1.5X BASIC
*GOLD: 1X TO 2.5X BASIC
R1 Gabe Vilardi 1.00 2.50
R2 Jason Robertson 1.50 4.00
R3 Kieffer Bellows .50 1.25
R4 Liam Foudy .60 1.50
R5 Tyler Benson .60 1.50
R6 Morgan Geekie .60 1.50
R7 Martin Kaut .60 1.50
R8 Josh Norris 1.00 2.50
R9 Jake Evans .60 1.50
R10 Nicolas Beaudin .60 1.50
R11 Philipp Kurashev .75 2.00
R12 Vitali Kravtsov 1.25 3.00
R13 Bowen Byram 1.25 3.00
R14 Nick Robertson 1.00 2.50
R15 Alexis Lafreniere 2.00 5.00
R16 Thomas Harley 1.00 2.50
R17 Connor Ingram .50 1.25
R18 Victor Soderstrom .50 1.25
R19 Ty Dellandrea .60 1.50
R20 Connor McMichael 1.00 2.50

2020-21 Upper Deck Ovation

*STANDING: 5X TO 12X BASIC
*STANDING RC: 4X TO 10X BASIC
O31 Tim Stutzle 2.50 6.00
O32 Philipp Kurashev 1.50 4.00
O33 Gabe Vilardi 2.00 5.00
O34 Ty Dellandrea 1.25 3.00
O35 Peyton Krebs 2.00 5.00
O36 Nick Robertson 2.00 5.00
O37 Aleksi Heponiemi 1.50 4.00
O38 Ty Smith 2.00 5.00
O39 Josh Norris 2.00 5.00
O40 Kevin Lankinen 2.00 5.00
O41 Kirill Kaprizov 5.00 12.00
O42 Bowen Byram 2.50 6.00
O43 K'Andre Miller 2.50 6.00
O44 Dylan Cozens 2.50 6.00
O45 Arthur Kaliyev 2.00 5.00
O46 Nils Hoglander 1.25 3.00
O47 Pius Suter 1.50 4.00
O48 Ilya Sorokin 3.00 8.00
O49 Liam Foudy 1.25 3.00
O50 Alexis Lafreniere 4.00 10.00
O1 Alex Ovechkin 2.00 5.00
O2 Auston Matthews 2.00 5.00
O3 Johnny Gaudreau .75 2.00
O4 Brad Marchand 1.00 2.50
O5 Nico Hischier .75 2.00
O6 Bo Horvat .60 1.50
O7 Artemi Panarin 1.00 2.50
O8 Miro Heiskanen .60 1.50
O9 Connor McDavid 2.50 6.00
O10 Steven Stamkos 1.00 2.50
O11 Igor Shesterkin 1.25 3.00
O12 Zach Parise .50 1.25
O13 John Gibson .50 1.25
O14 Oliver Ekman-Larsson .50 1.25
O15 Cale Makar 1.25 3.00
O16 Nick Suzuki 1.25 3.00
O17 Andrei Svechnikov .60 1.50
O18 Mark Scheifele .75 2.00
O19 Elias Pettersson .75 2.00
O20 Aleksander Barkov .75 2.00
O21 John Tavares .75 2.00
O22 Rasmus Dahlin .75 2.00
O23 Patrik Laine .60 1.50
O24 Marc-Andre Fleury .75 2.00
O25 Drew Doughty .60 1.50
O26 Nathan MacKinnon 2.00 5.00
O27 Thomas Chabot .50 1.25
O28 Leon Draisaitl 1.50 4.00
O29 Patrick Kane 1.50 4.00
O30 Sidney Crosby 2.00 5.00

2020-21 Upper Deck Oversized

201 Alexis Lafreniere YG 20.00 50.00
204 Philip Broberg YG 2.50 6.00
205 Bowen Byram YG 5.00 12.00
209 Josh Norris YG 4.00 10.00
215 Gabe Vilardi YG 4.00 10.00
221 Victor Soderstrom YG 2.00 5.00
224 Liam Foudy YG 2.50 6.00
227 Thomas Harley YG 4.00 10.00
234 Connor McMichael YG 4.00 10.00
235 Jason Robertson YG 8.00 20.00
237 Nick Robertson YG 4.00 10.00
238 Philipp Kurashev YG 3.00 8.00
239 Peyton Krebs YG 4.00 10.00
243 Vitali Kravtsov YG 5.00 12.00
455 Alexander Romanov YG 4.00 10.00
456 Ty Smith YG 4.00 10.00
458 Ian Mitchell YG 2.00 5.00
461 Ilya Sorokin YG 6.00 15.00
462 Nils Hoglander YG 2.50 6.00
468 Mathias Brome YG 2.00 5.00
469 K'Andre Miller YG 5.00 12.00
476 Cal Foote YG 3.00 8.00
482 Tim Stutzle YG 5.00 12.00
484 Pius Suter YG 3.00 8.00
485 Alexander Barabanov YG 2.50 6.00
489 Yegor Sharangovich YG 4.00 10.00
495 Dylan Cozens YG 4.00 10.00

2020-21 Upper Deck Predominant

*GOLD: 2X TO 5X BASIC
PR1 David Pastrnak .75 2.00
PR2 Alex Ovechkin 1.25 3.00
PR3 Connor McDavid 1.50 4.00
PR4 Brady Tkachuk .50 1.25
PR5 Sebastian Aho .50 1.25
PR6 Nikita Kucherov .60 1.50
PR7 Tyler Bertuzzi .25 .60
PR8 Sidney Crosby 1.25 3.00
PR9 Darcy Kuemper .30 .75
PR10 Kyle Palmieri .25 .60
PR11 Tomas Tatar .20 .50
PR12 Elias Pettersson .50 1.25
PR13 Matthew Tkachuk .60 1.50
PR14 Joe Thornton .50 1.25
PR15 Drew Doughty .40 1.00
PR16 Tuukka Rask .40 1.00
PR17 Nathan MacKinnon 1.25 3.00
PR18 Artemi Panarin .60 1.50
PR19 Eric Staal .30 .75
PR20 Carter Hart .30 .75
PR21 John Gibson .30 .75
PR22 Roman Josi .30 .75
PR23 Claude Giroux .30 .75
PR24 Ben Bishop .25 .60
PR25 Mark Stone .40 1.00
PR26 Leon Draisaitl 1.00 2.50
PR27 Auston Matthews 1.25 3.00
PR28 Jack Eichel .50 1.25
PR29 Jordan Binnington .50 1.25
PR30 Seth Jones .30 .75
PR31 Kyle Connor .50 1.25
PR32 Patrick Kane .60 1.50
PR33 John Carlson .30 .75
PR34 Jonathan Huberdeau .40 1.00
PR35 Mathew Barzal .40 1.00

2020-21 Upper Deck Rookie Breakouts

RB2 Jake Oettinger 30.00 80.00
RB3 Connor McMichael 20.00 50.00
RB4 Philipp Kurashev 15.00 40.00
RB5 Vitali Kravtsov 25.00 60.00
RB6 Ty Dellandrea 12.00 30.00
RB7 Bowen Byram 25.00 60.00
RB8 Nick Robertson 20.00 50.00
RB9 Liam Foudy 12.00 30.00
RB10 Victor Soderstrom 10.00 25.00
RB11 Thomas Harley 20.00 50.00
RB12 Shane Bowers 10.00 25.00
RB13 Timothy Liljegren 12.00 30.00
RB14 Josh Norris 20.00 50.00
RB15 Peyton Krebs 20.00 50.00
RBIS Ilya Sorokin 30.00 80.00
RBKK Kirill Kaprizov 300.00 800.00

2020-21 Upper Deck Rookie Class SE

*GOLD/75: 3X TO 8X BASIC
RC1 Kirill Kaprizov 4.00 10.00
RC2 Aleksi Heponiemi 1.25 3.00
RC3 Jani Hakanpaa .60 1.50
RC4 Alexander Barabanov 1.00 2.50
RC5 Jake Oettinger 2.50 6.00
RC6 K'Andre Miller 2.00 5.00
RC7 Mikey Anderson 1.00 2.50
RC8 Matiss Kivlenieks 1.25 3.00
RC9 Bowen Byram 2.00 5.00
RC10 Sasha Chmelevski .75 2.00
RC11 Connor McMichael 1.50 4.00
RC12 Dylan Cozens 1.50 4.00
RC13 Egor Zamula .75 2.00
RC14 Nils Hoglander 1.00 2.50
RC15 Mathias Brome .75 2.00
RC16 Thomas Harley 1.50 4.00
RC17 Victor Soderstrom .75 2.00
RC18 Alexander Romanov 1.25 3.00
RC19 Michael DiPietro 1.25 3.00
RC20 Nick Robertson 1.50 4.00
RC21 Gabe Vilardi 1.50 4.00
RC22 Alexis Lafreniere 3.00 8.00
RC23 Ty Smith 1.50 4.00
RC24 Liam Foudy 1.00 2.50
RC25 Tim Stutzle 2.00 5.00
RC26 Kevin Lankinen 1.50 4.00
RC27 Ty Dellandrea 1.00 2.50
RC28 Shane Bowers .75 2.00
RC29 Mikko Lehtonen .75 2.00
RC30 Cal Foote 1.25 3.00
RC31 Peyton Krebs 1.50 4.00
RC32 Ilya Sorokin 2.50 6.00
RC33 Connor Ingram .75 2.00
RC34 Olli Juolevi 1.00 2.50
RC35 Stuart Skinner 2.00 5.00
RC36 Logan Stanley 1.00 2.50
RC37 Pius Suter 1.25 3.00
RC38 Josh Norris 1.50 4.00
RC39 Jason Robertson 2.50 6.00
RC40 Yegor Sharangovich 1.50 4.00
RC41 Kieffer Bellows .75 2.00
RC42 Pierre-Olivier Joseph 1.00 2.50
RC43 Tyler Benson 1.00 2.50
RC44 Arthur Kaliyev 1.50 4.00
RC45 Vitek Vanecek 1.50 4.00

2020-21 Upper Deck Rookie Dual Materials

RDMAJ A.Angello/P.Joseph 4.00 10.00
RDMBB B.Byram/S.Bowers 8.00 20.00
RDMBK N.Beaudin/P.Kurashev 5.00 12.00
RDMFK L.Foudy/M.Kivlenieks 5.00 12.00
RDMGL M.Geekie/S.Lorentz 4.00 10.00
RDMOH T.Harley/J.Oettinger 10.00 25.00
RDMRD J.Robertson/T.Dellandrea 10.00 25.00
RDMRL N.Robertson/T.Liljegren 6.00 15.00
RDMVA G.Vilardi/M.Anderson 6.00 15.00

2020-21 Upper Deck Rookie Materials

RMAA Alexander Alexeyev B 2.00 5.00
RMAL Alexis Lafreniere B 20.00 50.00
RMAN Anthony Angello B 2.00 5.00
RMAT Alexander True B 2.00 5.00
RMBB Bowen Byram B 5.00 12.00
RMCI Connor Ingram B 2.00 5.00
RMCO Dylan Cozens A 12.00 30.00
RMEK Egor Korshkov B 1.50 4.00
RMGQ Gage Quinney B 1.50 4.00
RMGV Gabe Vilardi B 4.00 10.00
RMIS Ilya Sorokin A 25.00 60.00
RMJE Jake Evans B 2.50 6.00
RMJN Josh Norris B 4.00 10.00
RMJO Jake Oettinger B 6.00 15.00
RMJR Jason Robertson B 6.00 15.00
RMKB Kieffer Bellows B 2.00 5.00
RMKI Matiss Kivlenieks B 2.50 6.00
RMKK Kirill Kaprizov A 60.00 150.00
RMKU Philipp Kurashev B 3.00 8.00
RMLC Lucas Carlsson B 2.00 5.00
RMLF Liam Foudy B 2.50 6.00
RMMA Mikey Anderson B 2.50 6.00
RMMG Morgan Geekie B 2.50 6.00
RMMK Martin Kaut B 2.50 6.00
RMML Maxim Letunov B 2.00 5.00
RMNB Nicolas Beaudin B 2.50 6.00
RMNK Nikolai Knyzhov B 2.00 5.00
RMNR Nick Robertson B 4.00 10.00
RMOJ Olli Juolevi B 2.50 6.00
RMPJ Pierre-Olivier Joseph B 2.50 6.00
RMPK Peyton Krebs B 4.00 10.00
RMSB Shane Bowers B 2.00 5.00
RMSL Steven Lorentz B 2.00 5.00
RMTB Tyler Benson B 2.50 6.00
RMTD Ty Dellandrea B 2.50 6.00
RMTH Thomas Harley B 4.00 10.00
RMTL Timothy Liljegren B 2.50 6.00
RMVS Victor Soderstrom B 2.00 5.00

2020-21 Upper Deck Rookie Materials Patch

*PATCH: 1.5X TO 4X BASIC
RMCO Dylan Cozens 60.00 150.00
RMIS Ilya Sorokin 100.00 250.00

2020-21 Upper Deck Rookie Photoshoot Flashback Materials

RPFBB Bowen Byram 6.00 15.00
RPFBT Brady Tkachuk 5.00 12.00
RPFCH Carter Hart 3.00 8.00
RPFIS Igor Shesterkin 6.00 15.00
RPFJF Joel Farabee 3.00 8.00
RPFJO Jake Oettinger 10.00 25.00
RPFKB Kieffer Bellows 3.00 8.00
RPFKD Kirby Dach 3.00 8.00
RPFMH Miro Heiskanen 4.00 10.00
RPFSA Ilya Samsonov 3.00 8.00

2020-21 Upper Deck Rookie Retrospective

RR1 Dominik Kubalik 1.00 2.50
RR2 Victor Olofsson 1.00 2.50
RR3 Quinn Hughes 2.50 6.00
RR4 Kaapo Kakko .75 2.00
RR5 Nick Suzuki 2.50 6.00
RR6 Joel Farabee 1.00 2.50
RR7 Ilya Samsonov 1.00 2.50
RR8 Mackenzie Blackwood 1.00 2.50
RR9 Elvis Merzlikins 1.00 2.50
RR10 Cale Makar 2.50 6.00
RR11 Adam Fox 1.25 3.00
RR12 Martin Necas 1.50 4.00
RR13 Jack Hughes 2.50 6.00
RR14 Igor Shesterkin 2.00 5.00
RR15 Kirby Dach 1.00 2.50

2020-21 Upper Deck Rookie Retrospective Jerseys

*PATCH: 1.5X TO 4X BASIC
RR1 Dominik Kubalik 3.00 8.00
RR2 Victor Olofsson 3.00 8.00
RR3 Quinn Hughes 8.00 20.00
RR4 Kaapo Kakko 2.50 6.00
RR5 Nick Suzuki 6.00 15.00
RR6 Joel Farabee 3.00 8.00
RR7 Ilya Samsonov 3.00 8.00
RR8 Mackenzie Blackwood 3.00 8.00
RR9 Elvis Merzlikins 3.00 8.00
RR10 Cale Makar 8.00 20.00
RR11 Adam Fox 4.00 10.00
RR12 Martin Necas 5.00 12.00
RR13 Jack Hughes 8.00 20.00
RR14 Igor Shesterkin 6.00 15.00
RR15 Kirby Dach 3.00 8.00

2020-21 Upper Deck Signature Sensations

SSAG Adam Gaudette 6.00 15.00
SSAJ Andreas Johnsson 8.00 20.00
SSAM Alec Martinez 5.00 12.00
SSAR Zach Aston-Reese 8.00 20.00
SSAT Alex Tuch 8.00 20.00
SSAV Andrei Vasilevskiy 12.00 30.00
SSBG Brendan Gallagher 8.00 20.00
SSCA Craig Anderson 6.00 15.00
SSCD Chris Driedger 5.00 12.00
SSCK Chris Kreider 10.00 25.00
SSCM Cale Makar 20.00 50.00
SSDG Denis Gurianov 10.00 25.00
SSDH Darren Helm 5.00 12.00
SSDK Dominik Kahun 5.00 12.00
SSDO Dmitry Orlov 8.00 20.00
SSGI Mark Giordano 8.00 20.00
SSGR Andy Greene 5.00 12.00
SSJG Jake Guentzel 12.00 30.00
SSJL Johan Larsson 6.00 15.00
SSJM John Marino 8.00 20.00
SSJS Jaccob Slavin 6.00 15.00
SSJT Jordan Staal 6.00 15.00
SSJV James van Riemsdyk 6.00 15.00
SSJW Jordan Weal 5.00 12.00
SSKK Kasperi Kapanen 6.00 15.00
SSKL Kevin Labanc 5.00 12.00
SSMD Matt Dumba 5.00 12.00
SSMF Morgan Frost 6.00 15.00
SSMG Mikael Granlund 6.00 15.00
SSMJ Martin Jones 6.00 15.00
SSMS Mikhail Sergachev 6.00 15.00
SSNH Niklas Hjalmarsson 5.00 12.00
SSPM Petr Mrazek 8.00 20.00
SSPZ Pavel Zacha 6.00 15.00
SSRB Rudolfs Balcers 5.00 12.00
SSRF Radek Faksa 6.00 15.00
SSRH Roope Hintz 10.00 25.00
SSRL Ryan Lindgren 5.00 12.00
SSRS Ryan Suter 6.00 15.00
SSSS Sam Steel 6.00 15.00
SSST Riley Stillman 5.00 12.00
SSTB Teddy Blueger 5.00 12.00
SSTD Thatcher Demko 10.00 25.00
SSTJ Tyler Johnson 5.00 12.00
SSWK William Karlsson 10.00 25.00
SSYG Yanni Gourde 6.00 15.00

2020-21 Upper Deck SPx Finite

*RADIANCE/299: .75X TO 2X BASIC
*SPECTRUM/99: 1.25X TO 3X BASIC
SF1 Ryan Getzlaf 1.25 3.00
SF2 Nick Schmaltz 1.00 2.50
SF3 David Pastrnak 3.00 8.00
SF4 Jack Eichel 2.00 5.00
SF5 Johnny Gaudreau 2.00 5.00
SF6 Sebastian Aho 2.00 5.00
SF7 Patrick Kane 2.50 6.00
SF8 Nathan MacKinnon 5.00 12.00
SF9 Seth Jones 1.25 3.00
SF10 Miro Heiskanen 1.50 4.00
SF11 Anthony Mantha 1.00 2.50
SF12 Connor McDavid 6.00 15.00
SF13 Aleksander Barkov 2.00 5.00
SF14 Anze Kopitar 2.00 5.00
SF15 Zach Parise 1.25 3.00
SF16 Carey Price 2.50 6.00
SF17 Roman Josi 1.25 3.00
SF18 Jack Hughes 2.00 5.00
SF19 Mathew Barzal 1.50 4.00
SF20 Artemi Panarin 2.50 6.00
SF21 Brady Tkachuk 2.00 5.00
SF22 Carter Hart 1.25 3.00
SF23 Sidney Crosby 5.00 12.00
SF24 Brent Burns 1.25 3.00
SF25 Ryan O'Reilly 1.25 3.00
SF26 Steven Stamkos 2.50 6.00
SF27 Auston Matthews 5.00 12.00
SF28 Elias Pettersson 2.00 5.00
SF29 Mark Stone 1.50 4.00
SF30 Alex Ovechkin 5.00 12.00
SF31 Connor Hellebuyck 2.50 6.00
SF32 Victor Soderstrom 1.25 3.00
SF33 Dylan Cozens 2.50 6.00
SF34 Philipp Kurashev 2.00 5.00
SF35 Pius Suter 2.00 5.00
SF36 Bowen Byram 3.00 8.00
SF37 Jake Oettinger 4.00 10.00
SF38 Aleksi Heponiemi 2.00 5.00
SF39 Arthur Kaliyev 2.50 6.00
SF40 Gabe Vilardi 2.50 6.00
SF41 Kirill Kaprizov 6.00 15.00
SF42 Alexander Romanov 2.00 5.00
SF43 Ty Smith 2.50 6.00
SF44 Ilya Sorokin 4.00 10.00
SF45 Alexis Lafreniere 5.00 12.00
SF46 Josh Norris 2.50 6.00
SF47 Tim Stutzle 3.00 8.00
SF48 Nick Robertson 2.50 6.00
SF49 Connor McMichael 2.50 6.00
SF50 Nils Hoglander 2.00 5.00

2020-21 Upper Deck Team Triples

*GOLD: .6X TO 1.5X BASIC
TTC1 Dube/Andersson/Tkachuk 2.00 5.00
TTC2 Gaudreau/Monahan/Lindholm 1.50 4.00
TTE1 Yamamoto/Bear/Benson 1.25 3.00
TTE2 Draisaitl/Nugent-Hopkins/Nurse 3.00 8.00
TTM1 Suzuki/Primeau/Kotkaniemi 2.00 5.00
TTM2 Price/Tatar/Weber 2.00 5.00
TTO1 Tkachuk/Norris/Brannstrom 2.00 5.00
TTO2 Duclair/White/Chabot 1.00 2.50
TTR1 Hughes/Marner/Tkachuk 2.50 6.00
TTT1 Mikheyev/Sandin/Engvall .75 2.00
TTT2 Andersen/Marner/Matthews 4.00 10.00
TTV1 Demko/Gaudette/Hughes 2.50 6.00
TTV2 Boeser/Pettersson/Horvat 1.50 4.00
TTW1 Niku/Roslovic/Heinola 1.00 2.50
TTW2 Scheifele/Hellebuyck/Connor 2.00 5.00
TTCOL MacKinnon/Landeskog/Makar 4.00 10.00
TTDAL Seguin/Heiskanen/Klingberg 8.00 20.00
TTNYR Panarin/Shesterkin/Zibanejad 4.00 10.00
TTBL Kucherov/Vasilevskiy/Point 2.00 5.00
TTVGK Pacioretty/Stone/Theodore 1.25 3.00
TTWAS Ovechkin/Carlson/Vrana 4.00 10.00

2020-21 Upper Deck Triple Dimensions Reflections

*RUBY/500: .6X TO 1.5X BASIC
*AMETHYST/300: .75X TO 2X BASIC
*EMERALD/100: 1.25X TO 3X BASIC
1 Maxime Comtois .75 2.00
2 Victor Soderstrom 1.00 2.50
3 David Pastrnak 2.50 6.00
4 Brad Marchand 2.00 5.00
5 Dylan Cozens 2.00 5.00
6 Jack Eichel 1.50 4.00
7 Matthew Tkachuk 1.50 4.00
8 Johnny Gaudreau 1.50 4.00
9 Sebastian Aho 1.50 4.00
10 Patrick Kane 2.00 5.00
11 Pius Suter 1.50 4.00
12 Nathan MacKinnon 4.00 10.00
13 Cale Makar 2.50 6.00
14 Bowen Byram 2.50 6.00
15 Patrik Laine 1.25 3.00
16 Dylan Larkin 1.25 3.00
17 Connor McDavid 5.00 12.00
18 Leon Draisaitl 3.00 8.00
19 Aleksander Barkov 1.25 3.00
20 Gabe Vilardi 2.00 5.00
21 Arthur Kaliyev 2.00 5.00
22 Kirill Kaprizov 8.00 20.00
23 Nick Suzuki 2.00 5.00
24 Alexander Romanov 1.50 4.00
25 Roman Josi 1.00 2.50
26 Jack Hughes 2.50 6.00
27 Ty Smith 2.00 5.00
28 Ilya Sorokin 3.00 8.00
29 Mathew Barzal 1.25 3.00
30 Alexis Lafreniere 4.00 10.00
31 Artemi Panarin 2.00 5.00

32 Tim Stutzle 2.50 6.00
33 Josh Norris 2.00 5.00
34 Joel Farabee 1.00 2.50
35 Sidney Crosby 4.00 10.00
36 Logan Couture 1.25 3.00
37 Ryan O'Reilly 1.00 2.50
38 Jordan Binnington 1.50 4.00
39 Steven Stamkos 2.00 5.00
40 Andrei Vasilevskiy 1.50 4.00
41 Auston Matthews 4.00 10.00
42 Mitch Marner 1.50 4.00
43 Quinn Hughes 2.50 6.00
44 Nils Hoglander 1.25 3.00
45 Mark Stone 1.25 3.00
46 Marc-Andre Fleury 2.00 5.00
47 Connor McMichael 2.00 5.00
48 Alex Ovechkin 4.00 10.00
49 Mark Scheifele 1.50 4.00
50 Connor Hellebuyck 2.00 5.00

2020-21 Upper Deck UD Portraits

*PLAT.BLUE.RC/25: 4X TO 10X BASIC
P1 Connor McDavid 3.00 8.00
P2 Roman Josi .60 1.50
P3 Connor Hellebuyck 1.25 3.00
P4 Patrice Bergeron .75 2.00
P5 Alex Ovechkin 2.50 6.00
P6 Thomas Chabot .60 1.50
P7 Tyler Bertuzzi .50 1.25
P8 Ryan O'Reilly .60 1.50
P9 Mika Zibanejad .75 2.00
P10 Andrei Vasilevskiy 1.00 2.50
P11 Tuukka Rask .75 2.00
P12 Nathan MacKinnon 2.50 6.00
P13 Travis Konecny .60 1.50
P14 Max Pacioretty .60 1.50
P15 Max Domi .60 1.50
P16 Elias Pettersson 1.00 2.50
P17 Sidney Crosby 2.50 6.00
P18 Mats Zuccarello .60 1.50
P19 Cale Makar 1.50 4.00
P20 Nikita Kucherov 1.25 3.00
P21 Leon Draisaitl 2.00 5.00
P22 Darcy Kuemper .60 1.50
P23 Marc-Andre Fleury 1.25 3.00
P24 Matthew Tkachuk 1.25 3.00
P25 Brock Nelson .60 1.50
P26 Logan Couture .75 2.00
P27 David Pastrnak 1.50 4.00
P28 Auston Matthews 2.50 6.00
P29 Jack Eichel 1.00 2.50
P30 Ben Bishop .50 1.25
P31 Ryan Getzlaf .60 1.50
P32 Pierre-Luc Dubois .50 1.25
P33 Mitch Marner 1.00 2.50
P34 Sebastian Aho 1.00 2.50
P35 Jack Hughes 1.50 4.00
P36 Quinn Hughes 1.50 4.00
P37 Aleksander Barkov 1.00 2.50
P38 Brayden Schenn .60 1.50
P39 John Carlson .60 1.50
P40 Patrick Kane 1.25 3.00
P41 Gabe Vilardi 1.25 3.00
P42 Kieffer Bellows .60 1.50
P43 Jason Robertson 2.00 5.00
P44 Jake Evans .75 2.00
P45 Martin Kaut .75 2.00
P46 Tyler Benson .75 2.00
P47 Josh Norris 1.25 3.00
P48 Liam Foudy .75 2.00
P49 Nicolas Beaudin .75 2.00
P50 Timothy Liljegren .75 2.00
P51 Alexis Lafreniere 2.50 6.00
P52 Anthony Angello .60 1.50
P53 Chase Priskie .60 1.50
P54 Alexander True .60 1.50
P55 Ty Dellandrea .75 2.00
P56 Steven Lorentz .60 1.50
P57 Egor Zamula .60 1.50
P58 Vitek Vanecek 1.25 3.00
P59 Olli Juolevi .75 2.00
P60 Victor Soderstrom .60 1.50
P61 Egor Korshkov .50 1.25
P62 Connor Ingram .60 1.50
P63 MacKenzie Entwistle .60 1.50
P64 Reid Duke .75 2.00
P65 Joseph Woll 1.50 4.00
P66 Thomas Harley 1.25 3.00
P67 Gustav Lindstrom .60 1.50
P68 Michael DiPietro 1.00 2.50
P69 Pierre-Olivier Joseph .75 2.00
P70 Ryan McLeod .60 1.50
P71 Philipp Kurashev 1.00 2.50
P72 Joel Kiviranta .75 2.00
P73 Shane Bowers .60 1.50
P74 Morgan Geekie .75 2.00
P75 Alexander Alexeyev .60 1.50
P76 Nick Robertson 1.25 3.00
P77 Alec Regula .50 1.25
P78 Brandon Hagel 1.00 2.50
P79 Nikolai Knyzhov .60 1.50
P80 Michael McNiven .60 1.50
P81 Jansen Harkins .60 1.50
P82 Bowen Byram 1.50 4.00
P83 Vitali Kravtsov 1.50 4.00
P84 Mikey Anderson .75 2.00
P85 Alex Belzile .60 1.50
P86 Jake Oettinger 2.00 5.00
P87 Mikhail Berdin .75 2.00
P88 Artem Zagidulin .75 2.00
P89 Philip Broberg .75 2.00
P90 Peyton Krebs 1.25 3.00
P91 Maxim Letunov .60 1.50
P92 Jonas Johansson .75 2.00
P93 Kirill Ustimenko .60 1.50
P94 Matiss Kivlenieks 1.00 2.50
P95 Stuart Skinner 1.50 4.00
P96 Lucas Carlsson .60 1.50
P97 Emil Larmi .75 2.00
P98 Connor McMichael 1.25 3.00
P99 Pavel Francouz 1.00 2.50
P100 Jani Hakanpaa .50 1.25

2020-21 Upper Deck UD Portraits Gold

*GOLD/25: 1.25X TO 3X BASIC
*GOLD.RC/99: 3X TO 8X BASIC
P51 Alexis Lafreniere 40.00 100.00
P82 Bowen Byram 8.00 20.00

2020-21 Upper Deck UD Pros and Prospects

PP1 Leon Draisaitl 6.00 15.00
PP2 Artemi Panarin 4.00 10.00
PP3 Jack Hughes 5.00 12.00
PP4 Sidney Crosby 8.00 20.00
PP5 Patrick Kane 4.00 10.00
PP6 Alex Ovechkin 8.00 20.00
PP7 Mitch Marner 3.00 8.00
PP8 Quinn Hughes 5.00 12.00
PP9 Jonathan Huberdeau 2.50 6.00
PP10 Carey Price 4.00 10.00
PP11 Connor McDavid 10.00 25.00
PP12 Miro Heiskanen 2.50 6.00
PP13 David Pastrnak 5.00 12.00
PP14 Ryan O'Reilly 2.00 5.00
PP15 Cale Makar 5.00 12.00
PP16 Steven Stamkos 4.00 10.00
PP17 Mathew Barzal 2.50 6.00
PP18 Matthew Tkachuk 4.00 10.00
PP19 Mark Stone 2.50 6.00
PP20 Carter Hart 2.00 5.00
PP21 Auston Matthews 8.00 20.00
PP22 Pierre-Luc Dubois 1.50 4.00
PP23 Nathan MacKinnon 8.00 20.00
PP24 Brad Marchand 4.00 10.00
PP25 Elias Pettersson 3.00 8.00
PP26 Tim Stutzle 5.00 12.00
PP27 Gabe Vilardi 4.00 10.00
PP28 Philipp Kurashev 3.00 8.00
PP29 Kirill Kaprizov 20.00 50.00
PP30 Josh Norris 4.00 10.00
PP31 Nils Hoglander 2.50 6.00
PP32 Ilya Sorokin 6.00 15.00
PP33 Peyton Krebs 4.00 10.00
PP34 Alexis Lafreniere 20.00 50.00
PP35 Ty Smith 4.00 10.00
PP36 Bowen Byram 5.00 12.00
PP37 Michael DiPietro 3.00 8.00
PP38 Connor McMichael 4.00 10.00
PP39 Nick Robertson 4.00 10.00
PP40 K'Andre Miller 5.00 12.00
PP41 Ty Dellandrea 2.50 6.00
PP42 Dylan Cozens 4.00 10.00
PP43 Pius Suter 3.00 8.00
PP44 Alexander Romanov 3.00 8.00
PP45 Arthur Kaliyev 4.00 10.00

2020-21 Upper Deck UD Top Shelf Rookies

TS1 Dylan Cozens 8.00 20.00
TS2 Connor McMichael 8.00 20.00
TS3 Josh Norris 8.00 20.00
TS4 Bowen Byram 10.00 25.00
TS5 Alexander Romanov 6.00 15.00
TS6 Tim Stutzle 10.00 25.00
TS7 Nick Robertson 8.00 20.00
TS8 Ilya Sorokin 12.00 30.00
TS9 Kirill Kaprizov 30.00 80.00
TS10 Alexis Lafreniere 30.00 80.00

2020-21 Upper Deck UD3

UD31 Nathan MacKinnon 10.00 25.00
UD32 Brent Burns 2.50 6.00
UD33 Mitch Marner 4.00 10.00
UD34 Brady Tkachuk 4.00 10.00
UD35 Andrei Vasilevskiy 4.00 10.00
UD36 Patrick Kane 5.00 12.00
UD37 Connor McDavid 15.00 40.00
UD38 Carter Hart 2.50 6.00
UD39 Quinn Hughes 6.00 15.00
UD310 Carey Price 5.00 12.00
UD311 Matthew Tkachuk 5.00 12.00
UD312 Sebastian Aho 4.00 10.00
UD313 Sidney Crosby 10.00 25.00
UD314 Connor Hellebuyck 5.00 12.00
UD315 Dylan Larkin 3.00 8.00
UD316 Mathew Barzal 3.00 8.00
UD317 David Pastrnak 6.00 15.00
UD318 Tyler Seguin 3.00 8.00
UD319 Leon Draisaitl 8.00 20.00
UD320 Jack Hughes 6.00 15.00
UD321 Ryan O'Reilly 2.50 6.00
UD322 Auston Matthews 10.00 25.00
UD323 Jack Eichel 4.00 10.00
UD324 Victor Hedman 3.00 8.00
UD325 Jonathan Huberdeau 3.00 8.00
UD326 Anze Kopitar 4.00 10.00
UD327 Roman Josi 2.50 6.00
UD328 Artemi Panarin 5.00 12.00
UD329 Mark Stone 3.00 8.00
UD330 Alex Ovechkin 10.00 25.00
UD331 Alexis Lafreniere 10.00 25.00
UD332 Connor McMichael 5.00 12.00
UD333 Ty Dellandrea 3.00 8.00
UD334 Ilya Sorokin 8.00 20.00
UD335 Tim Stutzle 6.00 15.00
UD336 K'Andre Miller 6.00 15.00
UD337 Nils Hoglander 3.00 8.00
UD338 Ty Smith 5.00 12.00
UD339 Bowen Byram 6.00 15.00
UD340 Kirill Kaprizov 25.00 60.00
UD341 Arthur Kaliyev 5.00 12.00
UD342 Peyton Krebs 5.00 12.00
UD343 Pius Suter 4.00 10.00
UD344 Alexander Romanov 4.00 10.00
UD345 Victor Soderstrom 2.50 6.00
UD346 Nick Robertson 5.00 12.00
UD347 Dylan Cozens 5.00 12.00
UD348 Jake Oettinger 8.00 20.00
UD349 Ian Mitchell 2.50 6.00
UD350 Josh Norris 5.00 12.00

2020-21 Upper Deck UD3 Gold

*GOLD/100: 1X TO 2.5X BASIC
UD37 Connor McDavid 80.00 200.00
UD331 Alexis Lafreniere 60.00 150.00

2020-21 Upper Deck Ultimate Victory

*SILVER/100: 2.5X TO 6X BASIC
UV1 Auston Matthews 1.50 4.00
UV2 Jack Eichel .60 1.50
UV3 Alex Ovechkin 1.50 4.00
UV4 Leon Draisaitl 1.25 3.00
UV5 Joe Pavelski .50 1.25
UV6 Elias Pettersson .60 1.50
UV7 Mika Zibanejad .50 1.25
UV8 Connor McDavid 2.00 5.00
UV9 Nathan MacKinnon 1.50 4.00
UV10 Steven Stamkos .75 2.00
UV11 Mathew Barzal .50 1.25
UV12 John Gibson .40 1.00
UV13 John Carlson .40 1.00
UV14 Sidney Crosby 1.50 4.00
UV15 Dylan Larkin .50 1.25
UV16 Alex Pietrangelo .30 .75
UV17 Mitch Marner .60 1.50
UV18 Anze Kopitar .60 1.50
UV19 Bo Horvat .50 1.25
UV20 Mikko Rantanen 1.00 2.50
UV21 Alexander Romanov .60 1.50
UV22 Peyton Krebs .75 2.00
UV23 Alexander Barabanov .50 1.25
UV24 Ty Dellandrea .50 1.25
UV25 K'Andre Miller 1.00 2.50
UV26 Connor McMichael .75 2.00
UV27 Olli Juolevi .50 1.25
UV28 Philipp Kurashev .60 1.50
UV29 Nick Robertson .75 2.00
UV30 Liam Foudy .50 1.25
UV31 Ty Smith .75 2.00
UV32 Gabe Vilardi .75 2.00
UV33 Ian Mitchell .40 1.00
UV34 Dylan Cozens .75 2.00
UV35 Kirill Kaprizov 2.00 5.00
UV36 Arthur Kaliyev .75 2.00
UV37 Cal Foote .60 1.50
UV38 Ilya Sorokin 1.25 3.00
UV39 Kevin Lankinen .75 2.00
UV40 Jake Oettinger 1.25 3.00
UV41 Victor Soderstrom .40 1.00
UV42 Alexis Lafreniere 1.50 4.00
UV43 Nils Hoglander .50 1.25
UV44 Pius Suter .60 1.50
UV45 Josh Norris .75 2.00

2021-22 Upper Deck

1 Nicolas Deslauriers .20 .50
2 Cam Fowler .30 .75
3 John Gibson .30 .75
4 Adam Henrique .25 .60
5 Jakob Silfverberg .20 .50
6 Troy Terry .25 .60
7 Michael Bunting .30 .75
8 Jakob Chychrun .30 .75
9 Oliver Ekman-Larsson .20 .50
10 Niklas Hjalmarsson .20 .50
11 Clayton Keller .40 1.00
12 Nick Schmaltz .25 .60
13 Patrice Bergeron .40 1.00
14 Charlie Coyle .30 .75
15 Jake DeBrusk .30 .75
16 Matt Grzelcyk .25 .60
17 Brad Marchand .60 1.50
18 Charlie McAvoy .40 1.00
19 Craig Smith .20 .50
20 Dylan Cozens .30 .75
21 Rasmus Dahlin .40 1.00
22 Jack Eichel .50 1.25
23 Rasmus Ristolainen .20 .50
24 Jeff Skinner .30 .75
25 Tage Thompson .40 1.00
26 Rasmus Andersson .25 .60
27 Johnny Gaudreau .50 1.25
28 Noah Hanifin .30 .75
29 Milan Lucic .25 .60
30 Sean Monahan .20 .50
31 Matthew Tkachuk .60 1.50
32 Sebastian Aho .50 1.25
33 Martin Necas .50 1.25
34 Alex Nedeljkovic .25 .60
35 Brett Pesce .25 .60
36 Jacob Slavin .25 .60
37 Jordan Staal .25 .60
38 Adam Boqvist .40 1.00
39 Alex DeBrincat .40 1.00
40 Duncan Keith .25 .60
41 Dominik Kubalik .30 .75
42 Philipp Kurashev .25 .60
43 Kevin Lankinen .30 .75
44 Dylan Strome .40 1.00
45 J.T. Compher .20 .50
46 Joonas Donskoi .20 .50
47 Samuel Girard .20 .50
48 Nazem Kadri .40 1.00
49 Gabriel Landeskog .40 1.00
50 Cale Makar .75 2.00
51 Devon Toews .25 .60
52 Max Domi .30 .75
53 Seth Jones .30 .75
54 Elvis Merzlikins .30 .75
55 Eric Robinson .25 .60
56 Jack Roslovic .25 .60
57 Zach Werenski .50 1.25
58 Miro Heiskanen .40 1.00
59 Denis Gurianov .40 1.00
60 Anton Khudobin .30 .75
61 Alexander Radulov .30 .75
62 Jason Robertson .50 1.25
63 Tyler Seguin .40 1.00
64 Danny DeKeyser .20 .50
65 Thomas Greiss .25 .60
66 Vladislav Namestnikov .20 .50
67 Richard Panik .20 .50
68 Jakub Vrana .25 .60
69 Filip Zadina .25 .60
70 Josh Archibald .20 .50
71 Ethan Bear .20 .50
72 Mikko Koskinen .20 .50
73 Connor McDavid 1.50 4.00
74 Darnell Nurse .25 .60
75 Jesse Puljujarvi .30 .75
76 Sergei Bobrovsky .50 1.25
77 Patric Hornqvist .20 .50
78 Jonathan Huberdeau .40 1.00
79 Carter Verhaeghe .30 .75
80 MacKenzie Weegar .25 .60
81 Keith Yandle .20 .50
82 Drew Doughty .40 1.00
83 Alex Iafallo .20 .50
84 Adrian Kempe .30 .75
85 Trevor Moore .20 .50
86 Cal Petersen .20 .50
87 Sean Walker .20 .50
88 Marcus Foligno .25 .60
89 Jordan Greenway .20 .50
90 Kirill Kaprizov 1.00 2.50
91 Zach Parise .30 .75
92 Jared Spurgeon .30 .75
93 Mats Zuccarello .30 .75
94 Jake Allen .30 .75
95 Josh Anderson .25 .60
96 Joel Edmundson .20 .50
97 Brendan Gallagher .30 .75
98 Jeff Petry .30 .75
99 Tyler Toffoli .30 .75
100 Shea Weber .30 .75
101 Viktor Arvidsson .20 .50
102 Mattias Ekholm .25 .60
103 Filip Forsberg .50 1.25
104 Roman Josi .30 .75
105 Juuse Saros .40 1.00
106 Eeli Tolvanen .30 .75
107 Mackenzie Blackwood .30 .75
108 Jesper Bratt .30 .75
109 Nico Hischier .50 1.25
110 Jack Hughes .75 2.00
111 Ty Smith .30 .75
112 Miles Wood .25 .60
113 Josh Bailey .25 .60
114 Jordan Eberle .30 .75
115 Nick Leddy .20 .50
116 Anders Lee .25 .60
117 Jean-Gabriel Pageau .25 .60
118 Ryan Pulock .25 .60
119 Semyon Varlamov .30 .75
120 Adam Fox .40 1.00
121 Kaapo Kakko .25 .60
122 Chris Kreider .40 1.00
123 Alexis Lafreniere .50 1.25
124 K'Andre Miller .25 .60
125 Artemi Panarin .60 1.50
126 Jacob Trouba .25 .60
127 Thomas Chabot .30 .75
128 Evgenii Dadonov .20 .50
129 Josh Norris .20 .50
130 Tim Stutzle .40 1.00
131 Chris Tierney .25 .60
132 Colin White .25 .60
133 Joel Farabee .30 .75
134 Claude Giroux .30 .75
135 Carter Hart .30 .75
136 Kevin Hayes .25 .60
137 Travis Konecny .30 .75
138 Oskar Lindblom .25 .60
139 Jakub Voracek .25 .60
140 Jeff Carter .25 .60
141 Sidney Crosby 1.25 3.00
142 Jake Guentzel .50 1.25
143 Tristan Jarry .30 .75
144 Kasperi Kapanen .30 .75
145 Jared McCann .25 .60
146 Jason Zucker .30 .75
147 Brent Burns .30 .75
148 Mario Ferraro .20 .50
149 Tomas Hertl .30 .75
150 Martin Jones .25 .60
151 Kevin Labanc .20 .50
152 Timo Meier .30 .75
153 Jordan Binnington .50 1.25
154 Justin Faulk .25 .60
155 Torey Krug .30 .75
156 David Perron .25 .60
157 Brayden Schenn .30 .75
158 Vladimir Tarasenko .40 1.00
159 Anthony Cirelli .25 .60
160 Yanni Gourde .25 .60
161 Victor Hedman .40 1.00
162 Tyler Johnson .20 .50
163 Ondrej Palat .25 .60
164 Mikhail Sergachev .25 .60
165 Andrei Vasilevskiy .50 1.25
166 T.J. Brodie .20 .50
167 Jack Campbell .30 .75
168 Justin Holl .20 .50
169 Alex Kerfoot .25 .60
170 William Nylander .60 1.50
171 Morgan Rielly .30 .75
172 John Tavares .50 1.25
173 Thatcher Demko .40 1.00
174 Nils Hoglander .25 .60
175 Bo Horvat .30 .75
176 J.T. Miller .40 1.00
177 Tyler Myers .20 .50
178 Tanner Pearson .30 .75
179 Elias Pettersson .50 1.25
180 Marc-Andre Fleury .60 1.50
181 Nicolas Hague .20 .50
182 William Karlsson .40 1.00
183 Jonathan Marchessault .40 1.00
184 Reilly Smith .30 .75
185 Chandler Stephenson .25 .60
186 Shea Theodore .40 1.00
187 Nicklas Backstrom .30 .75
188 John Carlson .30 .75
189 Lars Eller .20 .50
190 Evgeny Kuznetsov .40 1.00
191 Justin Schultz .25 .60
192 Vitek Vanecek .30 .75
193 Dylan DeMelo .20 .50
194 Pierre-Luc Dubois .25 .60
195 Adam Lowry .25 .60
196 Josh Morrissey .40 1.00
197 Mark Scheifele .50 1.25
198 Blake Wheeler .30 .75
199 Jason Robertson
Kirill Kaprizov CL 1.00 2.50
200 Jack Hughes
Alexis Lafreniere CL .75 2.00
201 Cole Caufield YG RC 20.00 50.00
202 Ukko-Pekka Luukkonen YG RC 5.00 12.00
203 Olle Alsing YG RC 3.00 8.00
204 Dakota Joshua YG RC 3.00 8.00
205 Jamie Drysdale YG RC 5.00 12.00
206 Kyle Burroughs YG RC 3.00 8.00
207 Tarmo Reunanen YG RC 3.00 8.00
208 Mike Hardman YG RC 3.00 8.00
209 Wade Allison YG RC 3.00 8.00
210 Marian Studenic YG RC 3.00 8.00
211 Keaton Middleton YG RC 3.00 8.00
212 Joe Veleno YG RC 4.00 10.00
213 Wyatt Kalynuk YG RC 3.00 8.00
214 Garrett Pilon YG RC 4.00 10.00
215 Morgan Barron YG RC 2.50 6.00
216 Radim Zohorna YG RC 3.00 8.00
217 Jack Ahcan YG RC 3.00 8.00
218 Joshua Dunne YG RC 3.00 8.00
219 Logan Thompson YG RC 5.00 12.00
220 Brinson Pasichnuk YG RC 3.00 8.00
221 Arttu Ruotsalainen YG RC 3.00 8.00
222 Tanner Jeannot YG RC 4.00 10.00
223 Spencer Knight YG RC 6.00 15.00
224 Ross Colton YG RC 4.00 10.00
225 Filip Gustavsson YG RC 5.00 12.00
226 Jeremy Swayman YG RC 8.00 20.00
227 Calen Addison YG RC 3.00 8.00
228 Simon Benoit YG RC 3.00 8.00
229 Daniel Walcott YG RC 3.00 8.00
230 Mattias Samuelsson YG RC 3.00 8.00
231 Zac Jones YG RC 4.00 10.00
232 Trevor Zegras YG RC 6.00 15.00
233 Jeffrey Viel YG RC 3.00 8.00
234 Lane Pederson YG RC 3.00 8.00
235 Marc Michaelis YG 3.00 8.00
236 Tanner Laczynski YG RC 3.00 8.00
237 Jeremy Davies YG RC 3.00 8.00
238 Jackson Cates YG RC 3.00 8.00
239 Tyce Thompson YG RC 3.00 8.00
240 Parker Kelly YG RC 3.00 8.00
241 Alex Barre-Boulet YG RC 3.00 8.00
242 Rasmus Kupari YG RC 6.00 15.00
243 Cam York YG RC 6.00 15.00
244 Matt Kiersted YG RC 2.50 6.00
245 Michael Houser YG RC 3.00 8.00
246 Shane Pinto YG RC 5.00 12.00
247 Kole Lind YG RC 4.00 10.00
248 Jacob Bryson YG RC 3.00 8.00
249 Joey Keane YG RC 2.50 6.00
250 Cole Caufield
Trevor Zegras YG CL 1.25 3.00
251 Maxime Comtois .25 .60
252 Ryan Getzlaf .30 .75
253 Hampus Lindholm .20 .50
254 Rickard Rakell .25 .60
255 Kevin Shattenkirk .20 .50
256 Sam Steel .25 .60
257 Lawson Crouse .20 .50
258 Christian Fischer .20 .50
259 Barrett Hayton .30 .75
260 Phil Kessel .30 .75
261 Johan Larsson .20 .50
262 Ilya Lyubushkin .20 .50
263 Brandon Carlo .25 .60
264 Connor Clifton .20 .50
265 Trent Frederic .20 .50
266 Taylor Hall .30 .75
267 David Pastrnak .75 2.00
268 Mike Reilly .20 .50
269 Zemgus Girgensons .25 .60
270 Henri Jokiharju .20 .50
271 Colin Miller .20 .50
272 Casey Mittelstadt .30 .75
273 Victor Olofsson .30 .75
274 Kyle Okposo .25 .60
275 Mikael Backlund .25 .60
276 Dillon Dube .20 .50
277 Elias Lindholm .30 .75
278 Andrew Mangiapane .30 .75
279 Jacob Markstrom .30 .75
280 Christopher Tanev .20 .50
281 Juuso Valimaki .20 .50
282 Jesper Fast .20 .50
283 Jake Gardiner .20 .50
284 Nino Niederreiter .20 .50
285 Brady Skjei .20 .50
286 Andrei Svechnikov .40 1.00
287 Teuvo Teravainen .30 .75
288 Vincent Trocheck .30 .75
289 Kirby Dach .30 .75
290 Calvin de Haan .20 .50
291 Brandon Hagel .25 .60
292 Patrick Kane .60 1.50
293 Connor Murphy .25 .60
294 Jonathan Toews .50 1.25
295 Andre Burakovsky .30 .75
296 Bowen Byram .40 1.00
297 Tyson Jost .25 .60
298 Nathan MacKinnon 1.25 3.00
299 Valeri Nichushkin .30 .75
300 Mikko Rantanen .75 2.00
301 Oliver Bjorkstrand .25 .60
302 Vladislav Gavrikov .20 .50
303 Boone Jenner .30 .75
304 Joonas Korpisalo .20 .50
305 Patrik Laine .40 1.00
306 Alexandre Texier .25 .60
307 Jamie Benn .30 .75
308 Radek Faksa .25 .60
309 Roope Hintz .40 1.00
310 Esa Lindell .25 .60
311 John Klingberg .30 .75
312 Joe Pavelski .40 1.00
313 Tyler Bertuzzi .25 .60
314 Robby Fabbri .20 .50
315 Sam Gagner .20 .50
316 Filip Hronek .30 .75
317 Dylan Larkin .40 1.00
318 Michael Rasmussen .20 .50
319 Marc Staal .20 .50
320 Tyson Barrie .20 .50
321 Leon Draisaitl 1.00 2.50
322 Zack Kassian .30 .75
323 Ryan Nugent-Hopkins .40 1.00
324 Mike Smith .20 .50
325 Kailer Yamamoto .30 .75
326 Aleksander Barkov .50 1.25
327 Sam Bennett .50 1.25
328 Anthony Duclair .25 .60
329 Aaron Ekblad .40 1.00
330 Owen Tippett .20 .50
331 Frank Vatrano .25 .60
332 Jaret Anderson-Dolan .20 .50
333 Andreas Athanasiou .20 .50
334 Dustin Brown .30 .75
335 Anze Kopitar .50 1.25
336 Jonathan Quick .40 1.00
337 Gabe Vilardi .30 .75
338 Jonas Brodin .20 .50
339 Matt Dumba .25 .60
340 Joel Eriksson Ek .25 .60
341 Kevin Fiala .25 .60
342 Ryan Hartman .20 .50
343 Cam Talbot .30 .75
344 Joel Armia .20 .50
345 Jonathan Drouin .25 .60
346 Artturi Lehkonen .25 .60
347 Carey Price .60 1.50
348 Alexander Romanov .25 .60
349 Nick Suzuki .60 1.50
350 Nick Cousins .20 .50
351 Matt Duchene .30 .75
352 Dante Fabbro .20 .50
353 Mikael Granlund .25 .60
354 Rocco Grimaldi .20 .50
355 Colton Sissons .20 .50
356 Janne Kuokkanen .20 .50
357 Michael McLeod .20 .50
358 Damon Severson .20 .50
359 Yegor Sharangovich .30 .75
360 P.K. Subban .40 1.00
361 Pavel Zacha .25 .60
362 Mathew Barzal .40 1.00
363 Anthony Beauvillier .20 .50
364 Casey Cizikas .25 .60
365 Brock Nelson .25 .60
366 Ilya Sorokin .50 1.25
367 Oliver Wahlstrom .20 .50
368 Filip Chytil .25 .60
369 Ryan Lindgren .20 .50
370 Kevin Rooney .20 .50
371 Igor Shesterkin .60 1.50
372 Ryan Strome .30 .75
373 Mika Zibanejad .40 1.00
374 Drake Batherson .30 .75
375 Connor Brown .25 .60
376 Matt Murray .30 .75
377 Nick Paul .20 .50
378 Brady Tkachuk .50 1.25
379 Nikita Zaitsev .20 .50
380 Nicolas Aube-Kubel .20 .50
381 Sean Couturier .25 .60
382 Scott Laughton .20 .50
383 Ivan Provorov .25 .60
384 Travis Sanheim .20 .50
385 James van Riemsdyk .25 .60
386 Zach Aston-Reese .25 .60
387 Teddy Blueger .20 .50
388 Kris Letang .40 1.00
389 Evgeni Malkin .60 1.50
390 John Marino .30 .75
391 Bryan Rust .30 .75
392 Alexander Barabanov .20 .50
393 Rudolfs Balcers .20 .50
394 Logan Couture .40 1.00
395 Erik Karlsson .40 1.00
396 John Leonard .20 .50
397 Matt Nieto .25 .60
398 Chris Driedger .20 .50
399 Jordan Eberle .30 .75
400 Haydn Fleury .25 .60
401 Mark Giordano .30 .75
402 Jamie Oleksiak .25 .60
403 Brandon Tanev .25 .60
404 Ivan Barbashev .20 .50
405 Jordan Kyrou .30 .75
406 Ryan O'Reilly .30 .75
407 Colton Parayko .25 .60
408 Marco Scandella .20 .50
409 Robert Thomas .30 .75
410 Mathieu Joseph .20 .50
411 Alex Killorn .20 .50
412 Nikita Kucherov .60 1.50
413 Patrick Maroon .20 .50
414 Ryan McDonagh .30 .75
415 Brayden Point .40 1.00
416 Steven Stamkos .60 1.50
417 Mitch Marner .50 1.25
418 Auston Matthews 1.25 3.00
419 Ilya Mikheyev .25 .60
420 Jake Muzzin .20 .50
421 Wayne Simmonds .30 .75
422 Jason Spezza .30 .75
423 Brock Boeser .40 1.00
424 Travis Hamonic .25 .60
425 Quinn Hughes .75 2.00
426 Matthew Highmore .20 .50
427 Tyler Motte .20 .50
428 Brandon Sutter .20 .50
429 Robin Lehner .25 .60
430 Alec Martinez .20 .50
431 Max Pacioretty .30 .75
432 Alex Pietrangelo .25 .60
433 Mark Stone .40 1.00
434 Brayden McNabb .20 .50
435 Zach Whitecloud .20 .50
436 Anthony Mantha .25 .60
437 Dmitry Orlov .20 .50
438 T.J. Oshie .30 .75
439 Alex Ovechkin 1.25 3.00
440 Ilya Samsonov .30 .75
441 Conor Sheary .30 .75
442 Tom Wilson .30 .75
443 Kyle Connor .50 1.25
444 Andrew Copp .20 .50
445 Nikolaj Ehlers .30 .75
446 Connor Hellebuyck .60 1.50
447 Neal Pionk .20 .50
448 Paul Stastny .25 .60
449 Nathan MacKinnon
Leon Draisaitl CL 1.25 3.00
450 Nikita Kucherov
Alex Ovechkin CL 1.25 3.00
451 Mason McTavish YG RC 10.00 25.00
452 Maksim Sushko YG RC 3.00 8.00
453 Taylor Raddysh YG RC 5.00 12.00
454 Philip Tomasino YG RC 4.00 10.00
455 Brett Murray YG RC 3.00 8.00
456 Nils Lundkvist YG RC 3.00 8.00
457 Sampo Ranta YG RC 3.00 8.00
458 Karel Vejmelka YG RC 4.00 10.00
459 Dawson Mercer YG RC 8.00 20.00
460 Jonas Rondbjerg YG RC 3.00 8.00
461 Alex Newhook YG RC 5.00 12.00
462 Vladimir Tkachev YG RC 3.00 8.00
463 Jan Jenik YG RC 4.00 10.00
464 Lucas Raymond YG RC 10.00 25.00
465 Adam Ruzicka YG RC 3.00 8.00
466 Cole Perfetti YG RC 4.00 12.00
467 Jake Neighbours YG RC 6.00 15.00
468 David Farrance YG RC 3.00 8.00
469 Moritz Seider YG RC 12.00 30.00
470 Mason Geertsen YG RC 3.00 8.00
471 Yegor Chinakhov YG RC 5.00 12.00
472 Hendrix Lapierre YG RC 2.50 6.00
473 Jonathan Dahlen YG RC 3.00 8.00
474 Brandon Duhaime YG RC 3.00 8.00
475 William Eklund YG RC 8.00 20.00
476 Thomas Novak YG RC 3.00 8.00
477 Boris Katchouk YG RC 2.50 6.00
478 Benoit-Olivier Groulx YG RC 3.00 8.00
479 Dysin Mayo YG RC 3.00 8.00
480 Justin Richards YG RC 3.00 8.00
481 Vasily Podkolzin YG RC 4.00 10.00
482 Matthew Phillips YG RC 3.00 8.00
483 Frederic Allard YG RC 3.00 8.00
484 Ivan Prosvetov YG RC 3.00 8.00
485 Jesse Ylonen YG RC 3.00 8.00
486 Gregory Hofmann YG RC 3.00 8.00
487 Jasper Weatherby YG RC 3.00 8.00
488 Quinton Byfield YG RC 8.00 20.00
489 Anton Lundell YG RC 6.00 15.00
490 William Lockwood YG RC 3.00 8.00
491 Grigori Denisenko YG RC 4.00 10.00
492 Jacob Peterson YG RC 3.00 8.00
493 Jake Leschyshyn YG RC 3.00 8.00
494 Oskar Steen YG RC 4.00 10.00
495 Jacob Bernard-Docker YG RC 3.00 8.00
496 Pavel Dorofeyev YG RC 4.00 10.00
497 Maxwell Willman YG RC 3.00 8.00
498 Cole Sillinger YG RC 5.00 12.00
499 Jonah Gadjovich YG RC 3.00 8.00
500 Moritz Seider
Lucas Raymond CL 6.00 15.00
501 Sam Carrick .20 .50
502 Isac Lundestrom .20 .50
503 Sonny Milano .25 .60
504 Greg Pateryn .20 .50
505 Ryan Dzingel .25 .60
506 Loui Eriksson .25 .60
507 Shayne Gostisbehere .30 .75
508 Andrew Ladd .25 .60
509 Antoine Roussel .25 .60
510 Anton Stralman .20 .50
511 Scott Wedgewood .25 .60
512 Nick Foligno .20 .50
513 Derek Forbort .20 .50
514 Erik Haula .30 .75
515 Tomas Nosek .25 .60
516 Tuukka Rask .40 1.00
517 Linus Ullmark .30 .75
518 Craig Anderson .20 .50
519 Will Butcher .25 .60
520 Robert Hagg .20 .50
521 Vincent Hinostroza .20 .50
522 Peyton Krebs .25 .60
523 Mark Pysyk .20 .50
524 Tage Thompson .40 1.00
525 Alex Tuch .30 .75
526 Blake Coleman .25 .60
527 Erik Gudbranson .20 .50
528 Trevor Lewis .20 .50
529 Tyler Pitlick .20 .50
530 Brad Richardson .20 .50
531 Dan Vladar .25 .60
532 Nikita Zadorov .20 .50
533 Frederik Andersen .40 1.00
534 Ethan Bear .20 .50
535 Ian Cole .20 .50
536 Tony DeAngelo .20 .50
537 Jesperi Kotkaniemi .30 .75
538 Antti Raanta .30 .75
539 Derek Stepan .20 .50
540 Marc-Andre Fleury .60 1.50
541 Caleb Jones .20 .50
542 Seth Jones .30 .75
543 Jujhar Khaira .20 .50
544 Sam Lafferty .20 .50
545 Jake McCabe .20 .50
546 Darren Helm .20 .50
547 Darcy Kuemper .30 .75
548 Kurtis MacDermid .25 .60
549 Ryan Murray .25 .60
550 Logan O'Connor .30 .75
551 Jake Bean .20 .50
552 Adam Boqvist .25 .60
553 Sean Kuraly .20 .50
554 Jakub Voracek .25 .60
555 Jani Hakanpaa .25 .60
556 Braden Holtby .40 1.00
557 Luke Glendening .20 .50
558 Michael Raffl .20 .50
559 Ryan Suter .20 .50
560 Nick Leddy .20 .50
561 Alex Nedeljkovic .25 .60
562 Carter Rowney .20 .50
563 Pius Suter .25 .60
564 Evan Bouchard .40 1.00
565 Cody Ceci .20 .50
566 Warren Foegele .20 .50
567 Zach Hyman .50 1.25
568 Evander Kane .30 .75
569 Duncan Keith .25 .60
570 Gustav Forsling .30 .75
571 Mason Marchment .25 .60
572 Brandon Montour .40 1.00
573 Sam Reinhart .60 1.50
574 Joe Thornton .50 1.25
575 Viktor Arvidsson .20 .50
576 Phillip Danault .20 .50
577 Arthur Kaliyev .30 .75
578 Matt Roy .20 .50
579 Frederick Gaudreau .20 .50
580 Alex Goligoski .25 .60
581 Dmitry Kulikov .20 .50
582 Jon Merrill .20 .50
583 Christian Dvorak .25 .60
584 Mike Hoffman .20 .50
585 Samuel Montembeault .30 .75
586 Mathieu Perreault .20 .50
587 David Savard .20 .50
588 Alexandre Carrier .20 .50

589 Luke Kunin .20 .50
590 David Rittich .20 .50
591 Yakov Trenin .20 .50
592 Ryan Graves .20 .50
593 Dougie Hamilton .25 .60
594 Andreas Johnsson .20 .50
595 Tomas Tatar .20 .50
596 Jimmy Vesey .25 .60
597 Zdeno Chara .30 .75
598 Cal Clutterbuck .20 .50
599 Noah Dobson .40 1.00
600 Zach Parise .30 .75
601 Sammy Blais .20 .50
602 Barclay Goodrow .20 .50
603 Dryden Hunt .20 .50
604 Patrik Nemeth .25 .60
605 Ryan Reaves .25 .60
606 Alex Formenton .25 .60
607 Anton Forsberg .20 .50
608 Nick Holden .20 .50
609 Zach Sanford .20 .50
610 Cam Atkinson .30 .75
611 Derick Brassard .20 .50
612 Ryan Ellis .20 .50
613 Martin Jones .25 .60
614 Rasmus Ristolainen .20 .50
615 Nate Thompson .20 .50
616 Keith Yandle .20 .50
617 Teddy Blueger .20 .50
618 Danton Heinen .20 .50
619 Mike Matheson .20 .50
620 Brock McGinn .20 .50
621 Evan Rodrigues .25 .60
622 Nick Bonino .20 .50
623 Andrew Cogliano .20 .50
624 Adin Hill .30 .75
625 Jacob Middleton .20 .50
626 James Reimer .20 .50
627 Colin Blackwell .25 .60
628 Yanni Gourde .25 .60
629 Calle Jarnkrok .20 .50
630 Carson Soucy .20 .50
631 Alexander True .20 .50
632 Tyler Bozak .20 .50
633 Logan Brown .20 .50
634 Pavel Buchnevich .25 .60
635 Brandon Saad .25 .60
636 Pierre-Edouard Bellemare .20 .50
637 Zach Bogosian .20 .50
638 Brian Elliott .20 .50
639 Mathieu Joseph .20 .50
640 Corey Perry .50 1.25
641 Michael Bunting .30 .75
642 David Kampf .20 .50
643 Ondrej Kase .20 .50
644 Petr Mrazek .25 .60
645 Nick Ritchie .20 .50
646 Alex Chiasson .25 .60
647 Jason Dickinson .25 .60
648 Oliver Ekman-Larsson .25 .60
649 Conor Garland .25 .60
650 Jaroslav Halak .30 .75
651 Juho Lammikko .20 .50
652 Tucker Poolman .20 .50
653 Sven Baertschi .20 .50
654 Laurent Brossoit .20 .50
655 Evgenii Dadonov .20 .50
656 Jack Eichel .50 1.25
657 Brett Howden .20 .50
658 Mattias Janmark .20 .50
659 Nolan Patrick .25 .60
660 Nic Dowd .20 .50
661 Garnet Hathaway .20 .50
662 Connor McMichael .30 .75
663 Brenden Dillon .20 .50
664 Nate Schmidt .20 .50
665 Logan Stanley .20 .50
666 Evgeny Svechnikov .20 .50
667 Brad Marchand AS1 .60 1.50
668 Connor McDavid AS1 1.50 4.00
669 Mitch Marner AS1 .50 1.25
670 Adam Fox AS1 .40 1.00
671 Cale Makar AS1 .75 2.00
672 Andrei Vasilevskiy AS1 .50 1.25
673 Jonathan Huberdeau AS2 .40 1.00
674 Auston Matthews AS2 1.25 3.00
675 Mikko Rantanen AS2 .75 2.00
676 Dougie Hamilton AS2 .25 .60
677 Victor Hedman AS2 .40 1.00
678 Marc-Andre Fleury AS2 .60 1.50
679 Adam Larsson .30 .75
680 Alexander Wennberg .20 .50
681 Brandon Tanev .25 .60
682 Chris Driedger .20 .50
683 Haydn Fleury .25 .60
684 Jaden Schwartz .25 .60
685 Jamie Oleksiak .25 .60
686 Jared McCann .25 .60
687 Jeremy Lauzon .20 .50
688 Joonas Donskoi .20 .50
689 Jordan Eberle .30 .75
690 Marcus Johansson .20 .50
691 Mark Giordano .30 .75
692 Mason Appleton .20 .50
693 Morgan Geekie .20 .50
694 Nathan Bastian .20 .50
695 Philipp Grubauer .30 .75
696 Riley Sheahan .20 .50
697 Ryan Donato .25 .60
698 Vince Dunn .25 .60
699 Zach Parise
Zdeno Chara CL .30 .75
700 Seth Jones
Marc-Andre Fleury CL .60 1.50
701 Alexander Holtz YG RC 8.00 20.00
702 Connor Dewar YG RC 3.00 8.00
703 Brett Leason YG RC 3.00 8.00
704 Gabriel Fortier YG RC 3.00 8.00
705 Michael Pezzetta YG RC 3.00 8.00
706 Aliaksei Protas YG RC 3.00 8.00
707 Scott Perunovich YG RC 3.00 8.00
708 Justus Annunen YG RC 4.00 10.00
709 Sean Day YG RC 3.00 8.00
710 Ryan Merkley YG RC 4.00 10.00
711 John-Jason Peterka YG RC 8.00 20.00
712 Janis Moser YG RC 3.00 8.00
713 Riley Tufte YG RC 3.00 8.00
714 Kasper Bjorkqvist YG RC 3.00 8.00
715 Markus Niemelainen YG RC 3.00 8.00
716 Akira Schmid YG RC 3.00 8.00
717 Egor Sokolov YG RC 3.00 8.00
718 Josiah Slavin YG RC 3.00 8.00
719 Alex Turcotte YG RC 4.00 10.00
720 Paul Cotter YG RC 3.00 8.00
721 Cole Schwindt YG RC 3.00 8.00
722 Arvid Soderblom YG RC 3.00 8.00
723 Ben McCartney YG RC 3.00 8.00
724 Sean Durzi YG RC 3.00 8.00
725 Felix Sandstrom YG RC 3.00 8.00
726 Robin Salo YG RC 3.00 8.00
727 Hugo Alnefelt YG RC 3.00 8.00
728 Lassi Thomson YG RC 3.00 8.00
729 Fabian Zetterlund YG RC 3.00 8.00
730 Mason Shaw YG RC 3.00 8.00
731 Jack Drury YG RC 5.00 12.00
732 Cam Dineen YG RC 3.00 8.00
733 Adam Beckman YG RC 3.00 8.00
734 Axel Jonsson-Fjallby YG RC 3.00 8.00
735 Isaak Phillips YG RC 3.00 8.00
736 Daniil Miromanov YG RC 3.00 8.00
737 Alexey Toropchenko YG RC 3.00 8.00
738 Bryce Kindopp YG RC 3.00 8.00
739 Zachary Sawchenko YG RC 2.50 6.00
740 Rafael Harvey-Pinard YG RC 3.00 8.00
741 Riley Damiani YG RC 3.00 8.00
742 Alex Steeves YG RC 4.00 10.00
743 Justin Danforth YG RC 2.50 6.00
744 Justin Barron YG RC 5.00 12.00
745 Seth Jarvis YG RC 10.00 25.00
746 Mattias Norlinder YG RC 3.00 8.00
747 Daniil Tarasov YG RC 3.00 8.00
748 Nico Daws YG RC 5.00 12.00
749 Artemi Kniazev YG RC 3.00 8.00
750 Alex Turcotte
Alexander Holtz YG CL 5.00 12.00

2021-22 Upper Deck Exclusives

*EXCLUSIVES VETS: 3X TO 8X BASIC CARDS
*EXCLUSIVES RC: 3X TO 8X BASIC CARDS
201 Cole Caufield YG 500.00 1200.00
219 Logan Thompson YG 125.00 300.00
223 Spencer Knight YG 100.00 250.00
226 Jeremy Swayman YG 150.00 400.00
232 Trevor Zegras YG 150.00 400.00
451 Mason McTavish 250.00 600.00
459 Dawson Mercer 150.00 400.00
464 Lucas Raymond 400.00 1000.00
466 Cole Perfetti 150.00 400.00
469 Moritz Seider 150.00 400.00
475 William Eklund 150.00 400.00
481 Vasily Podkolzin 60.00 150.00
488 Quinton Byfield 150.00 400.00
711 John-Jason Peterka YG 100.00 250.00
716 Akira Schmid YG 150.00 400.00

2021-22 Upper Deck French

*FRENCH VETS: 2X TO 5X BASIC CARDS
*FRENCH RC: .75X TO 2X BASIC CARDS
201 Cole Caufield YG 40.00 100.00
205 Jamie Drysdale YG 30.00 80.00
223 Spencer Knight YG 12.00 30.00
226 Jeremy Swayman YG 20.00 50.00
232 Trevor Zegras YG 12.00 30.00
246 Shane Pinto YG 15.00 40.00
250 Cole Caufield
Trevor Zegras YG CL 6.00 15.00
451 Mason McTavish 30.00 80.00
464 Lucas Raymond 25.00 60.00
466 Cole Perfetti 25.00 60.00
469 Moritz Seider 30.00 80.00
498 Cole Sillinger 20.00 50.00
711 John-Jason Peterka YG 8.00 20.00

2021-22 Upper Deck Photo Variations

13 Patrice Bergeron 4.00 10.00
17 Brad Marchand 6.00 15.00
22 Jack Eichel 5.00 12.00
31 Matthew Tkachuk 6.00 15.00
32 Sebastian Aho 5.00 12.00
39 Alex DeBrincat 4.00 10.00
50 Cale Makar 8.00 20.00
73 Connor McDavid 15.00 40.00
90 Kirill Kaprizov 10.00 25.00
110 Jack Hughes 8.00 20.00
123 Alexis Lafreniere 5.00 12.00
125 Artemi Panarin 6.00 15.00
130 Tim Stutzle 4.00 10.00
141 Sidney Crosby 12.00 30.00
165 Andrei Vasilevskiy 5.00 12.00
180 Marc-Andre Fleury 6.00 15.00
267 David Pastrnak 8.00 20.00
286 Andrei Svechnikov 4.00 10.00
292 Patrick Kane 6.00 15.00
298 Nathan MacKinnon 12.00 30.00
321 Leon Draisaitl 10.00 25.00
326 Aleksander Barkov 5.00 12.00
335 Anze Kopitar 5.00 12.00
347 Carey Price 6.00 15.00
371 Igor Shesterkin 6.00 15.00
378 Brady Tkachuk 5.00 12.00
389 Evgeni Malkin 6.00 15.00
412 Nikita Kucherov 6.00 15.00
417 Mitch Marner 5.00 12.00
418 Auston Matthews 12.00 30.00
423 Brock Boeser 4.00 10.00
439 Alex Ovechkin 12.00 30.00
516 Tuukka Rask 4.00 10.00
533 Frederik Andersen 4.00 10.00
540 Marc-Andre Fleury 6.00 15.00
542 Seth Jones 3.00 8.00
554 Jakub Voracek 2.50 6.00
559 Ryan Suter 2.50 6.00
569 Duncan Keith 2.50 6.00
574 Joe Thornton 5.00 12.00
597 Zdeno Chara 3.00 8.00
600 Zach Parise 3.00 8.00
610 Cam Atkinson 3.00 8.00
616 Keith Yandle 2.00 5.00
634 Pavel Buchnevich 2.50 6.00
648 Oliver Ekman-Larsson 2.00 5.00
656 Jack Eichel 5.00 12.00
689 Jordan Eberle 3.00 8.00
691 Mark Giordano 3.00 8.00
695 Philipp Grubauer 3.00 8.00

2021-22 Upper Deck '05-06 Black Diamond Retro

*RUBY/100: 1X TO 2.5X BASIC INSERTS
BD1 Jack Hughes 4.00 10.00
BD2 David Pastrnak 4.00 10.00
BD3 Nikita Kucherov 3.00 8.00
BD4 Sebastian Aho 2.50 6.00
BD5 Jake Guentzel 2.50 6.00
BD6 Connor Hellebuyck 3.00 8.00
BD7 Quinn Hughes 4.00 10.00
BD8 Grigori Denisenko 2.00 5.00
BD9 Benoit-Olivier Groulx 1.50 4.00
BD10 Vasily Podkolzin 2.00 5.00
BD11 Philip Tomasino 2.00 5.00
BD12 Alexander Holtz 2.50 6.00
BD13 Cole Perfetti 3.00 8.00
BD14 William Eklund 4.00 10.00
BD15 Jack Eichel 2.50 6.00
BD16 Mitch Marner 2.50 6.00
BD17 Jonathan Huberdeau 2.00 5.00
BD18 Patrick Kane 3.00 8.00
BD19 Brad Marchand 3.00 8.00
BD20 Cale Makar 4.00 10.00
BD21 Marc-Andre Fleury 3.00 8.00
BD22 Dawson Mercer 4.00 10.00
BD23 Cole Sillinger 2.50 6.00
BD24 Seth Jarvis 4.00 10.00
BD25 Mason McTavish 3.00 8.00
BD26 Alex Turcotte 2.00 5.00
BD27 Ukko-Pekka Luukkonen 2.50 6.00
BD28 Spencer Knight 3.00 8.00
BD29 Auston Matthews 6.00 15.00
BD30 Artemi Panarin 3.00 8.00
BD31 Leon Draisaitl 5.00 12.00
BD32 Nathan MacKinnon 6.00 15.00
BD33 Kirill Kaprizov 5.00 12.00
BD34 Andrei Vasilevskiy 2.50 6.00
BD35 Quinton Byfield 12.00 30.00
BD36 Jeremy Swayman 5.00 12.00
BD37 Jamie Drysdale 2.50 6.00
BD38 Anton Lundell 3.00 8.00
BD39 Alex Newhook 2.50 6.00
BD40 Cole Caufield 12.00 30.00
BD41 Connor McDavid 8.00 20.00
BD42 Sidney Crosby 6.00 15.00
BD43 Alex Ovechkin 6.00 15.00
BD44 Moritz Seider 12.00 30.00
BD45 Trevor Zegras 12.00 30.00
BD46 Lucas Raymond 15.00 40.00

2021-22 Upper Deck '05-06 Black Diamond Retro Emerald Autographs

BD9 Benoit-Olivier Groulx/25 12.00 30.00
BD10 Vasily Podkolzin/25 15.00 40.00
BD11 Philip Tomasino/25 15.00 40.00
BD12 Alexander Holtz/25 20.00 50.00
BD13 Cole Perfetti/25 25.00 60.00
BD22 Dawson Mercer/25 30.00 80.00
BD23 Cole Sillinger/25 20.00 50.00
BD25 Mason McTavish/25 25.00 60.00
BD27 Ukko-Pekka Luukkonen/25 20.00 50.00
BD28 Spencer Knight/25 25.00 60.00
BD36 Jeremy Swayman/25 40.00 100.00
BD38 Anton Lundell/25 25.00 60.00
BD44 Moritz Seider/25 30.00 80.00
BD45 Trevor Zegras/25 25.00 60.00
BD46 Lucas Raymond/25 25.00 60.00

2021-22 Upper Deck '06-07 Retro

*GOLD STOCKPILE VETS: 5X TO 12X BASIC CARDS
*GOLD STOCKPILE YGS: 1.25X TO 3X BASIC CARDS
T1 Troy Terry .40 1.00
T2 John Gibson .50 1.25
T3 Phil Kessel .50 1.25
T4 Shayne Gostisbehere .50 1.25
T5 Patrice Bergeron .60 1.50
T6 David Pastrnak 1.25 3.00
T7 Brad Marchand 1.00 2.50
T8 Rasmus Dahlin .60 1.50
T9 Tage Thompson .60 1.50
T10 Matthew Tkachuk 1.00 2.50
T11 Johnny Gaudreau .75 2.00
T12 Jacob Markstrom .50 1.25
T13 Sebastian Aho .75 2.00
T14 Teuvo Teravainen .50 1.25
T15 Marc-Andre Fleury 1.00 2.50
T16 Seth Jones .50 1.25
T17 Patrick Kane 1.00 2.50
T18 Nathan MacKinnon 2.00 5.00
T19 Cale Makar 1.25 3.00
T20 Mikko Rantanen 1.25 3.00
T21 Patrik Laine .60 1.50
T22 Elvis Merzlikins .50 1.25
T23 Miro Heiskanen .60 1.50
T24 Roope Hintz .60 1.50
T25 Joe Pavelski .60 1.50
T26 Tyler Bertuzzi .40 1.00
T27 Dylan Larkin .60 1.50
T28 Connor McDavid 2.50 6.00
T29 Leon Draisaitl 1.50 4.00
T30 Aleksander Barkov .75 2.00
T31 Aaron Ekblad .60 1.50
T32 Jonathan Huberdeau .60 1.50
T33 Anze Kopitar .75 2.00
T34 Drew Doughty .60 1.50
T35 Kirill Kaprizov 1.50 4.00
T36 Kevin Fiala .40 1.00
T37 Jonathan Drouin .40 1.00
T38 Nick Suzuki 1.00 2.50
T39 Roman Josi .50 1.25
T40 Juuse Saros .60 1.50
T41 Jack Hughes 1.25 3.00
T42 Nico Hischier .75 2.00
T43 Anders Lee .40 1.00
T44 Mathew Barzal .60 1.50
T45 Igor Shesterkin 1.00 2.50
T46 Adam Fox .60 1.50
T47 Artemi Panarin 1.00 2.50
T48 Brady Tkachuk .75 2.00
T49 Drake Batherson .50 1.25
T50 Claude Giroux .50 1.25
T51 Cam Atkinson .50 1.25
T52 Sidney Crosby 2.00 5.00
T53 Evgeni Malkin 1.00 2.50
T54 Jake Guentzel .75 2.00
T55 Timo Meier .50 1.25
T56 Tomas Hertl .50 1.25
T57 Philipp Grubauer .50 1.25
T58 Jordan Eberle .50 1.25
T59 Jordan Binnington .75 2.00
T60 Ryan O'Reilly .50 1.25
T61 Jordan Kyrou .50 1.25
T62 Andrei Vasilevskiy .75 2.00
T63 Steven Stamkos 1.00 2.50
T64 Nikita Kucherov 1.00 2.50
T65 Mitch Marner .75 2.00
T66 William Nylander 1.00 2.50
T67 Auston Matthews 2.00 5.00
T68 Brock Boeser .60 1.50
T69 Quinn Hughes 1.25 3.00
T70 Mark Stone .60 1.50
T71 Max Pacioretty .50 1.25
T72 Alex Ovechkin 2.00 5.00
T73 John Carlson .50 1.25
T74 Connor Hellebuyck 1.00 2.50
T75 Kyle Connor .75 2.00
T76 Trevor Zegras YG 10.00 25.00
T77 William Eklund YG 12.00 30.00
T78 Alex Newhook YG 8.00 20.00
T79 Shane Pinto YG 8.00 20.00
T80 Dawson Mercer YG 12.00 30.00
T81 John-Jason Peterka YG 10.00 25.00
T82 Cole Caufield YG 20.00 50.00
T83 Moritz Seider YG 12.00 30.00
T84 Quinton Byfield YG 12.00 30.00
T85 Seth Jarvis YG 12.00 30.00
T86 Anton Lundell YG 10.00 25.00
T87 Scott Perunovich YG 5.00 12.00
T88 Jeremy Swayman YG 15.00 40.00
T89 Vasily Podkolzin YG 6.00 15.00
T90 Hendrix Lapierre YG 5.00 12.00
T91 Jamie Drysdale YG 8.00 20.00
T92 Cole Perfetti YG 10.00 25.00
T93 Philip Tomasino YG 6.00 15.00
T94 Cam York YG 5.00 12.00
T95 Spencer Knight YG 10.00 25.00
T96 Alexander Holtz YG 8.00 20.00
T97 Mason McTavish YG 10.00 25.00
T98 Cole Sillinger YG 8.00 20.00
T99 Alex Turcotte YG 6.00 15.00
T100 Lucas Raymond YG 15.00 40.00

2021-22 Upper Deck '06-07 Retro High Gloss

*VETS/100: .75X TO 2X BASIC INSERTS
*YG/100: .6X TO 1.5X BASIC INSERTS
T99 Alex Turcotte YG 40.00 100.00
T100 Lucas Raymond YG 80.00 200.00

2021-22 Upper Deck '21-22 Rookie Commemorative Class

*RED: .75X TO 2X BASIC INSERTS
RC1 Quinton Byfield 1.25 3.00
RC2 Cam York .50 1.25
RC3 Trevor Zegras 1.00 2.50
RC4 Spencer Knight 1.00 2.50
RC5 Jacob Bernard-Docker .50 1.25
RC6 Wade Allison .50 1.25
RC7 Jeremy Swayman 1.50 4.00
RC8 Ukko-Pekka Luukkonen .75 2.00
RC9 Joe Veleno .60 1.50
RC10 Wyatt Kalynuk .50 1.25
RC11 Jamie Drysdale .75 2.00
RC12 Shane Pinto .75 2.00
RC13 Calen Addison .50 1.25
RC14 Alex Barre-Boulet .50 1.25
RC15 Cole Caufield 2.00 5.00
RC16 Moritz Seider 1.25 3.00
RC17 Mason McTavish 1.00 2.50
RC18 Dawson Mercer 1.25 3.00
RC19 Jan Jenik .60 1.50
RC20 Grigori Denisenko .60 1.50
RC21 Rasmus Kupari .50 1.25
RC22 Zac Jones .60 1.50
RC23 Lucas Raymond 1.50 4.00
RC24 Morgan Barron .40 1.00
RC25 Ross Colton .60 1.50
RC26 Sampo Ranta .50 1.25
RC27 Matthew Phillips .50 1.25
RC28 William Eklund 1.25 3.00
RC29 Filip Gustavsson 1.00 2.50
RC30 Kole Lind .60 1.50

2021-22 Upper Deck '99-00 SPx Retro

*RADIANCE/100: .75X TO 2X BASIC CARDS
SPX1 Sidney Crosby 10.00 25.00
SPX2 Jack Eichel 4.00 10.00
SPX3 Nikita Kucherov 5.00 12.00
SPX4 Andrei Svechnikov 3.00 8.00
SPX5 Brad Marchand 5.00 12.00
SPX6 Artemi Panarin 5.00 12.00
SPX7 Connor McDavid 12.00 30.00
SPX8 Brock Boeser 3.00 8.00
SPX9 Jonathan Huberdeau 3.00 8.00
SPX10 Auston Matthews 10.00 25.00
SPX11 Andrei Vasilevskiy 4.00 10.00
SPX12 Tyler Bertuzzi 2.00 5.00
SPX13 Kirill Kaprizov 8.00 20.00
SPX14 Leon Draisaitl 8.00 20.00
SPX15 Brady Tkachuk 4.00 10.00
SPX16 Patrick Kane 5.00 12.00
SPX17 Mitch Marner 4.00 10.00
SPX18 Connor Hellebuyck 4.00 10.00
SPX19 Cale Makar 6.00 15.00
SPX20 Alex Ovechkin 10.00 25.00
SPX21 Philip Tomasino 3.00 8.00
SPX22 Cam York 2.50 6.00
SPX23 Mason McTavish 5.00 12.00
SPX24 Tanner Jeannot 2.50 6.00
SPX25 William Eklund 6.00 15.00
SPX26 Vasily Podkolzin 3.00 8.00
SPX27 Alex Turcotte 3.00 8.00
SPX28 Alex Newhook 4.00 10.00
SPX29 Spencer Knight 5.00 12.00
SPX30 Quinton Byfield 6.00 15.00
SPX31 Cole Perfetti 5.00 12.00
SPX32 Jeremy Swayman 8.00 20.00
SPX33 Seth Jarvis 6.00 15.00
SPX34 Lucas Raymond 8.00 20.00
SPX35 Calen Addison 2.50 6.00
SPX36 Cole Caufield 10.00 25.00
SPX37 Jamie Drysdale 4.00 10.00
SPX38 Ukko-Pekka Luukkonen 4.00 10.00
SPX39 Jonathan Dahlen 2.50 6.00
SPX40 Justin Barron 4.00 10.00
SPX41 Shane Pinto 4.00 10.00
SPX42 Trevor Zegras 5.00 12.00
SPX43 Dawson Mercer 6.00 15.00
SPX44 John-Jason Peterka 5.00 12.00
SPX45 Alexander Holtz 4.00 10.00
SPX46 Cole Sillinger 4.00 10.00
SPX47 Grigori Denisenko 3.00 8.00
SPX48 Nils Lundkvist 2.50 6.00
SPX49 Benoit-Olivier Groulx 2.50 6.00
SPX50 Moritz Seider 6.00 15.00

2021-22 Upper Deck 25th Anniversary UD Game Jerseys

GJ25AB Aleksander Barkov 5.00 12.00
GJ25AM Auston Matthews 12.00 30.00
GJ25AO Alex Ovechkin 12.00 30.00
GJ25AS Andrei Svechnikov 4.00 10.00
GJ25BB Brent Burns 3.00 8.00
GJ25BM Brad Marchand 6.00 15.00
GJ25BO Brock Boeser 4.00 10.00
GJ25CH Connor Hellebuyck 6.00 15.00
GJ25CP Carey Price 6.00 15.00
GJ25DP David Pastrnak 8.00 20.00
GJ25EM Evgeni Malkin 6.00 15.00
GJ25EP Elias Pettersson 5.00 12.00
GJ25JE Jack Eichel 5.00 12.00
GJ25LD Leon Draisaitl 10.00 25.00
GJ25MB Mathew Barzal 4.00 10.00
GJ25MF Marc-Andre Fleury 6.00 15.00
GJ25MM Mitch Marner 5.00 12.00
GJ25MT Matthew Tkachuk 6.00 15.00
GJ25NM Nathan MacKinnon 12.00 30.00
GJ25PB Patrice Bergeron 4.00 10.00
GJ25PK Patrick Kane 6.00 15.00
GJ25SC Sidney Crosby 12.00 30.00
GJ25SS Steven Stamkos 6.00 15.00

2021-22 Upper Deck '94-95 Rookie Tribute Die Cuts

*RED: 1X TO 2.5X BASIC INSERTS
RDT1 Quinton Byfield 1.50 4.00
RDT2 Cole Caufield 2.50 6.00
RDT3 Spencer Knight 1.25 3.00
RDT4 Alex Newhook 1.00 2.50
RDT5 Trevor Zegras 1.25 3.00
RDT6 Ukko-Pekka Luukkonen 1.00 2.50
RDT7 Jeremy Swayman 2.00 5.00
RDT8 Shane Pinto 1.00 2.50
RDT9 Wade Allison .60 1.50
RDT10 Jamie Drysdale 1.00 2.50
RDT11 Cam York .60 1.50
RDT12 Lucas Raymond 2.00 5.00
RDT13 Cole Sillinger 1.00 2.50
RDT14 Mason McTavish 1.25 3.00
RDT15 Moritz Seider 1.50 4.00
RDT16 Ross Colton .75 2.00
RDT17 Grigori Denisenko .75 2.00
RDT18 David Farrance .60 1.50
RDT19 Wyatt Kalynuk .60 1.50
RDT20 William Eklund 1.50 4.00

2021-22 Upper Deck Autographs

17 Brad Marchand 15.00 40.00
20 Dylan Cozens 8.00 20.00
41 Dominik Kubalik 8.00 20.00
50 Cale Makar 20.00 50.00
56 Joe Veleno 8.00 20.00
58 Miro Heiskanen 10.00 25.00
73 Connor McDavid 40.00 100.00
78 Jonathan Huberdeau 10.00 25.00
97 Brendan Gallagher 8.00 20.00
150 Martin Jones 6.00 15.00
174 Nils Hoglander 6.00 15.00
103 Jonathan Marchessault 10.00 25.00

2021-22 Upper Deck Canvas

*BLACK: .6X TO 1.5X BASIC INSERTS
C1 Maxime Comtois .50 1.25
C2 Rickard Rakell .50 1.25
C3 Kevin Shattenkirk .40 1.00
C4 Conor Garland .50 1.25
C5 Phil Kessel .60 1.50
C6 Patrice Bergeron .75 2.00
C7 Taylor Hall .60 1.50
C8 David Pastrnak 1.50 4.00
C9 Dylan Cozens .60 1.50
C10 Victor Olofsson .60 1.50
C11 Mikael Backlund .50 1.25
C12 Elias Lindholm .60 1.50
C13 Jacob Markstrom .60 1.50
C14 Dougie Hamilton .50 1.25
C15 Andrei Svechnikov .75 2.00
C16 Teuvo Teravainen .60 1.50
C17 Kirby Dach .60 1.50
C18 Patrick Kane 1.25 3.00
C19 Duncan Keith .50 1.25
C20 Philipp Grubauer .60 1.50
C21 Nathan MacKinnon 2.50 6.00
C22 Mikko Rantanen 1.50 4.00
C23 Cam Atkinson .60 1.50
C24 Oliver Bjorkstrand .60 1.50
C25 Patrik Laine .75 2.00
C26 Jamie Benn .60 1.50
C27 Roope Hintz .75 2.00
C28 Joe Pavelski .75 2.00
C29 Tyler Bertuzzi .75 2.00
C30 Filip Hronek .40 1.00
C31 Dylan Larkin .60 1.50
C32 Tyson Barrie .40 1.00
C33 Leon Draisaitl 2.00 5.00
C34 Ryan Nugent-Hopkins .75 2.00
C35 Aleksander Barkov 1.00 2.50
C36 Aaron Ekblad .75 2.00
C37 Dustin Brown .60 1.50
C38 Anze Kopitar 1.00 2.50
C39 Gabe Vilardi .60 1.50
C40 Matt Dumba .50 1.25
C41 Keapo Kahkonen .50 1.25
C42 Ryan Suter .50 1.25
C43 Phillip Danault .40 1.00
C44 Carey Price 1.25 3.00
C45 Nick Suzuki 1.25 3.00
C46 Ryan Ellis .40 1.00
C47 Calle Jarnkrok .40 1.00
C48 Pekka Rinne .60 1.50
C49 P.K. Subban .75 2.00
C50 Pavel Zacha .50 1.25
C51 Mathew Barzal .75 2.00
C52 Brock Nelson .60 1.50
C53 Ilya Sorokin 1.00 2.50
C54 Pavel Buchnevich .50 1.25
C55 Igor Shesterkin 1.25 3.00
C56 Mika Zibanejad .75 2.00
C57 Drake Batherson .60 1.50
C58 Matt Murray .60 1.50
C59 Brady Tkachuk 1.00 2.50
C60 Sean Couturier .50 1.25
C61 Kevin Hayes .50 1.25
C62 James van Riemsdyk .50 1.25
C63 Kris Letang .75 2.00
C64 Evgeni Malkin 1.25 3.00
C65 Bryan Rust .60 1.50
C66 Logan Couture .75 2.00
C67 Evander Kane .60 1.50
C68 Erik Karlsson .75 2.00
C69 David Perron .50 1.25
C70 Ryan O'Reilly .60 1.50
C71 Brayden Schenn .60 1.50
C72 Alex Killorn .40 1.00
C73 Brayden Point .75 2.00
C74 Steven Stamkos 1.25 3.00
C75 Zach Hyman 1.00 2.50
C76 Mitch Marner 1.00 2.50
C77 Auston Matthews 2.50 6.00
C78 Brock Boeser .75 2.00
C79 Braden Holtby .75 2.00
C80 Quinn Hughes 1.50 4.00
C81 Robin Lehner .50 1.25
C82 Max Pacioretty .60 1.50
C83 Mark Stone .75 2.00
C84 Anthony Mantha .50 1.25
C85 T.J. Oshie .60 1.50
C86 Alex Ovechkin 2.50 6.00
C87 Kyle Connor 1.00 2.50
C88 Nikolaj Ehlers .60 1.50
C89 Connor Hellebuyck 1.25 3.00
C90 Auston Matthews
Mitch Marner CL 2.50 6.00
C91 Quinton Byfield YG 8.00 20.00
C92 Zac Jones YG 6.00 15.00
C93 Filip Gustavsson YG 10.00 25.00
C94 Tanner Jeannot YG 8.00 20.00
C95 Wade Allison YG 5.00 12.00
C96 Tyce Thompson YG 5.00 12.00
C97 Jan Jenik YG 6.00 15.00
C98 David Farrance YG 5.00 12.00
C99 Lane Pederson YG 5.00 12.00
C100 Alex Barre-Boulet YG 5.00 12.00
C101 Jacob Bryson YG 5.00 12.00
C102 Oskar Steen YG 6.00 15.00
C103 Shane Pinto YG 8.00 20.00
C104 Ross Colton YG 6.00 15.00
C105 Grigori Denisenko YG 5.00 12.00
C106 Ivan Prosvetov YG 5.00 12.00
C107 Brett Murray YG 5.00 12.00
C108 Calen Addison YG 5.00 12.00
C109 Veini Vehvilainen YG 5.00 12.00
C110 Radim Zohorna YG 5.00 12.00
C111 Kole Lind YG 6.00 15.00
C112 Alex Newhook YG 8.00 20.00
C113 Jacob Bernard-Docker YG 5.00 12.00
C114 Wyatt Kalynuk YG 5.00 12.00
C115 Morgan Barron YG 5.00 12.00
C116 Jeremy Swayman YG 12.00 30.00
C117 Trevor Zegras YG 8.00 20.00
C118 Ivan Chekhovich YG 4.00 10.00
C119 Arttu Ruotsalainen YG 5.00 12.00
C120 Quinton Byfield
Alex Newhook YG CL 6.00 15.00
C121 John Gibson .60 1.50
C122 Cam Fowler .60 1.50
C123 Ryan Getzlaf .60 1.50
C124 Clayton Keller .75 2.00
C125 Jakob Chychrun .60 1.50
C126 Brad Marchand 1.25 3.00
C127 Charlie McAvoy .75 2.00
C128 Craig Smith .40 1.00
C129 Rasmus Dahlin .75 2.00
C130 Kyle Okposo .40 1.00
C131 Johnny Gaudreau 1.00 2.50
C132 Sean Monahan .40 1.00
C133 Matthew Tkachuk 1.25 3.00
C134 Sebastian Aho 1.00 2.50
C135 Martin Necas 1.00 2.50
C136 Jacob Slavin .50 1.25
C137 Alex DeBrincat .75 2.00
C138 Dominik Kubalik .60 1.50
C139 Dylan Strome .50 1.25
C140 Andre Burakovsky .40 1.00
C141 Gabriel Landeskog .75 2.00
C142 Cale Makar 1.50 4.00
C143 Elvis Merzlikins .60 1.50
C144 Jack Roslovic .40 1.00
C145 Zach Werenski 1.00 2.50
C146 Miro Heiskanen .75 2.00
C147 Jason Robertson 1.00 2.50
C148 Tyler Seguin .75 2.00
C149 Jakub Vrana .50 1.25
C150 Filip Zadina .50 1.25
C151 Connor McDavid 3.00 8.00
C152 Darnell Nurse .50 1.25
C153 Jesse Puljujarvi .60 1.50
C154 Sergei Bobrovsky 1.00 2.50
C155 Jonathan Huberdeau .75 2.00
C156 Carter Verhaeghe .60 1.50
C157 Drew Doughty .60 1.50
C158 Cal Petersen .40 1.00
C159 Kevin Fiala .60 1.50
C160 Kirill Kaprizov 2.00 5.00
C161 Mats Zuccarello .60 1.50
C162 Brendan Gallagher .60 1.50
C163 Jeff Petry .60 1.50
C164 Tyler Toffoli .60 1.50
C165 Roman Josi .60 1.50
C166 Juuse Saros .75 2.00
C167 Mackenzie Blackwood .60 1.50
C168 Nico Hischier 1.00 2.50
C169 Jack Hughes 1.50 4.00
C170 Josh Bailey .50 1.25
C171 Ryan Pulock .50 1.25
C172 Semyon Varlamov .60 1.50
C173 Alexis Lafreniere 1.00 2.50
C174 Artemi Panarin 1.25 3.00
C175 Adam Fox .75 2.00
C176 Josh Norris .60 1.50
C177 Tim Stutzle .75 2.00
C178 Joel Farabee .60 1.50
C179 Claude Giroux .60 1.50
C180 Carter Hart .60 1.50
C181 Sidney Crosby 2.50 6.00
C182 Jake Guentzel 1.00 2.50
C183 Tristan Jarry .60 1.50
C184 Brent Burns .60 1.50
C185 Tomas Hertl .60 1.50
C186 Chris Driedger .40 1.00
C187 Jordan Eberle .60 1.50
C188 Mark Giordano .60 1.50
C189 Jordan Binnington 1.00 2.50
C190 Torey Krug .50 1.25
C191 Colton Parayko .50 1.25
C192 Victor Hedman .75 2.00
C193 Nikita Kucherov 1.25 3.00
C194 Andrei Vasilevskiy 1.00 2.50
C195 William Nylander 1.25 3.00
C196 Morgan Rielly .60 1.50
C197 John Tavares 1.00 2.50
C198 Thatcher Demko .75 2.00
C199 Bo Horvat .75 2.00
C200 Elias Pettersson 1.00 2.50
C201 William Karlsson .75 2.00
C202 Jonathan Marchessault .75 2.00
C203 Shea Theodore .75 2.00
C204 Nicklas Backstrom .60 1.50
C205 John Carlson .60 1.50
C206 Evgeny Kuznetsov .75 2.00
C207 Pierre-Luc Dubois .50 1.25
C208 Mark Scheifele 1.00 2.50
C209 Blake Wheeler .60 1.50
C210 Artemi Panarin
Adam Fox 1.25 3.00
C211 Cole Caufield 25.00 60.00
C212 Joe Veleno 6.00 15.00
C213 Boris Katchouk 4.00 10.00
C214 Mattias Samuelsson 5.00 12.00
C215 Parker Kelly 5.00 12.00
C216 Jesse Ylonen 5.00 12.00
C217 Philip Tomasino 6.00 15.00
C218 Jake Leschyshyn 5.00 12.00
C219 Taylor Raddysh 8.00 20.00
C220 Jonathan Dahlen 5.00 12.00
C221 Matthew Phillips 5.00 12.00
C222 Rasmus Kupari 5.00 12.00
C223 Jake Neighbours 10.00 25.00
C224 Cole Sillinger 8.00 20.00
C225 Hendrix Lapierre 5.00 12.00
C226 Lucas Raymond 12.00 30.00
C227 Nils Lundkvist 5.00 12.00
C228 Spencer Knight 10.00 25.00
C229 Mason McTavish 12.00 30.00
C230 Sampo Ranta 5.00 12.00
C231 Anton Lundell 10.00 25.00
C232 Dawson Mercer 10.00 25.00
C233 Cam York 5.00 12.00
C234 William Eklund 12.00 30.00
C235 Vladimir Tkachev 5.00 12.00
C236 Jamie Drysdale 8.00 20.00
C237 Yegor Chinakhov 8.00 20.00
C238 Jasper Weatherby 5.00 12.00
C239 Ukko-Pekka Luukkonen 8.00 20.00
C240 Spencer Knight
Cole Caufield 8.00 20.00
C241 Gordie Howe 15.00 40.00
C242 Tie Domi 5.00 12.00
C243 Teemu Selanne 10.00 25.00
C244 Rob Blake 5.00 12.00
C245 Ed Belfour 5.00 12.00
C246 Mike Liut 3.00 8.00
C247 Pierre Turgeon 4.00 10.00
C248 Terry O'Reilly 4.00 10.00
C249 Clark Gillies 5.00 12.00
C250 Markus Naslund 5.00 12.00
C251 Adam Graves 4.00 10.00
C252 Mike Vernon 4.00 10.00
C253 Al Iafrate 4.00 10.00
C254 Bernie Parent 6.00 15.00
C255 Peter Forsberg 10.00 25.00
C256 Quinton Byfield 12.00 30.00
C257 Mason McTavish 10.00 25.00
C258 Cole Perfetti 10.00 25.00
C259 Philip Tomasino 6.00 15.00
C260 Joe Veleno 6.00 15.00
C261 Alex Newhook 8.00 20.00
C262 Jonah Gadjovich 5.00 12.00
C263 Jamie Drysdale 8.00 20.00
C264 Ty Smith 5.00 12.00
C265 Nick Suzuki 10.00 25.00
C266 Patrice Bergeron 6.00 15.00
C267 Jason Spezza 5.00 12.00
C268 Marc-Andre Fleury 10.00 25.00
C269 Mark Stone 6.00 15.00
C270 Eric Lindros 8.00 20.00
C271 Sonny Milano .50 1.25
C272 Troy Terry .50 1.25
C273 Lawson Crouse .40 1.00
C274 Shayne Gostisbehere .60 1.50
C275 Charlie Coyle .60 1.50
C276 Matt Grzelcyk .50 1.25
C277 Linus Ullmark .50 1.25
C278 Casey Mittelstadt .60 1.50
C279 Jeff Skinner .60 1.50
C280 Tage Thompson .75 2.00
C281 Oliver Kylington .50 1.25
C282 Andrew Mangiapane .60 1.50
C283 Sean Monahan .40 1.00
C284 Frederik Andersen .75 2.00
C285 Tony DeAngelo .40 1.00
C286 Jesperi Kotkaniemi .60 1.50
C287 Marc-Andre Fleury 1.25 3.00
C288 Seth Jones .60 1.50
C289 Jonathan Toews 1.00 2.50
C290 Nazem Kadri .75 2.00
C291 Darcy Kuemper .60 1.50
C292 Devon Toews .60 1.50
C293 Boone Jenner .60 1.50
C294 Jakub Voracek .60 1.50
C295 Braden Holtby .75 2.00
C296 Ryan Suter .50 1.25
C297 Robby Fabbri .40 1.00
C298 Alex Nedeljkovic .50 1.25

C299 Pius Suter .50 1.25
C300 Zach Hyman 1.00 2.50
C301 Evander Kane .60 1.50
C302 Duncan Keith .50 1.25
C303 Anthony Duclair .50 1.25
C304 Sam Reinhart 1.25 3.00
C305 Joe Thornton 1.00 2.50
C306 Viktor Arvidsson .40 1.00
C307 Phillip Danault .60 1.50
C308 Adrian Kempe .60 1.50
C309 Ryan Hartman .40 1.00
C310 Cam Talbot .60 1.50
C311 Jake Allen .60 1.50
C312 Josh Anderson .50 1.25
C313 Jonathan Drouin .50 1.25
C314 Matt Duchene .60 1.50
C315 Filip Forsberg 1.00 2.50
C316 Mikael Granlund .50 1.25
C317 Jesper Bratt .60 1.50
C318 Dougie Hamilton .50 1.25
C319 Andreas Johnsson .50 1.25
C320 Anders Lee .50 1.25
C321 Zach Parise .60 1.50
C322 Oliver Wahlstrom .40 1.00
C323 Kaapo Kakko .50 1.25
C324 Chris Kreider .75 2.00
C325 Jacob Trouba .50 1.25
C326 Connor Brown .50 1.25
C327 Thomas Chabot .60 1.50
C328 Cam Atkinson .60 1.50
C329 Martin Jones .50 1.25
C330 Keith Yandle .40 1.00
C331 Jeff Carter .50 1.25
C332 Evan Rodrigues .50 1.25
C333 Jason Zucker .60 1.50
C334 Alexander Barabanov .40 1.00
C335 Timo Meier .60 1.50
C336 James Reimer .40 1.00
C337 Philipp Grubauer .60 1.50
C338 Jared McCann .50 1.25
C339 Brandon Tanev .50 1.25
C340 Pavel Buchnevich .50 1.25
C341 Jordan Kyrou .60 1.50
C342 Vladimir Tarasenko .75 2.00
C343 Anthony Cirelli .50 1.25
C344 Ondrej Palat .50 1.25
C345 Corey Perry 1.00 2.50
C346 Jack Campbell .60 1.50
C347 Alex Kerfoot .50 1.25
C348 Jason Spezza .60 1.50
C349 Oliver Ekman-Larsson .40 1.00
C350 Conor Garland .50 1.25
C351 J.T. Miller .75 2.00
C352 Alex Pietrangelo .50 1.25
C353 Reilly Smith .60 1.50
C354 Chandler Stephenson .50 1.25
C355 Connor McMichael .60 1.50
C356 Vitek Vanecek .60 1.50
C357 Tom Wilson .50 1.25
C358 Josh Morrissey .75 2.00
C359 Blake Wheeler .60 1.50
C360 Vladimir Tarasenko
Jordan Kyrou CL .75 2.00
C361 Moritz Seider YG 25.00 60.00
C362 Justus Annunen YG 6.00 15.00
C363 Egor Sokolov YG 5.00 12.00
C364 Riley Damiani YG 5.00 12.00
C365 Karel Vejmelka YG 6.00 15.00
C366 Jack Drury YG 8.00 20.00
C367 Aliaksei Protas YG 5.00 12.00
C368 Scott Perunovich YG 5.00 12.00
C369 Brandon Duhaime YG 5.00 12.00
C370 Nico Daws YG 8.00 20.00
C371 Benoit-Olivier Groulx YG 5.00 12.00
C372 Ryan Merkley YG 6.00 15.00
C373 Justin Barron YG 8.00 20.00
C374 Daniil Tarasov YG 5.00 12.00
C375 Riley Tufte YG 5.00 12.00
C376 Seth Jarvis YG 12.00 30.00
C377 Lassi Thomson YG 5.00 12.00
C378 Robin Salo YG 5.00 12.00
C379 Michael Pezzetta YG 5.00 12.00
C380 Sean Durzi YG 5.00 12.00
C381 Alexander Holtz YG 8.00 20.00
C382 Vasily Podkolzin YG 6.00 15.00
C383 Felix Sandstrom YG 5.00 12.00
C384 Adam Beckman YG 5.00 12.00
C385 John-Jason Peterka YG 8.00 20.00
C386 Gabriel Fortier YG 5.00 12.00
C387 Cole Schwindt YG 5.00 12.00
C388 Michael Bunting YG 5.00 12.00
C389 Alex Turcotte YG 6.00 15.00
C390 Moritz Seider
John-Jason Peterka YG CL 12.00 30.00
C391 Wild Wing 15.00 40.00
C392 Howler the Coyote 15.00 40.00
C393 Blades The Bruin 15.00 40.00
C394 Sabretooth 15.00 40.00
C395 Harvey The Hound 15.00 40.00
C396 Stormy 15.00 40.00
C397 Tommy Hawk 15.00 40.00
C398 Bernie the St. Bernard 15.00 40.00
C399 Stinger 15.00 40.00
C400 Victor E. Green 15.00 40.00
C401 Al The Octopus 15.00 40.00
C402 Hunter 15.00 40.00
C403 Stanley C. Panther 15.00 40.00
C404 Bailey 15.00 40.00
C405 Nordy 15.00 40.00
C406 Youppi! 15.00 40.00
C407 Gnash 15.00 40.00
C408 N.J. Devil 15.00 40.00
C409 Sparky the Dragon 15.00 40.00
C410 Spartacat 15.00 40.00
C411 Gritty 15.00 40.00
C412 Iceburgh 15.00 40.00
C413 SJ Sharkie 15.00 40.00
C414 Louie 15.00 40.00
C415 Thunderbug 15.00 40.00
C416 Carlton the Bear 15.00 40.00
C417 Fin The Whale 15.00 40.00
C418 Chance 15.00 40.00
C419 Slapshot 15.00 40.00
C420 Mick E Moose 15.00 40.00

2021-22 Upper Deck Clear Cut Parallel

*CLEAR CUT VET: 6X TO 15X BASIC CARDS
*CLEAR CUT RC: 2.5X TO 6X BASIC CARDS
201 Cole Caufield YG 200.00 500.00
202 Ukko-Pekka Luukkonen YG 30.00 80.00
205 Jamie Drysdale YG 60.00 150.00
222 Tanner Jeannot YG 60.00 150.00
223 Spencer Knight YG 30.00 80.00
226 Jeremy Swayman YG 80.00 200.00
231 Zac Jones YG 60.00 150.00
232 Trevor Zegras YG 40.00 100.00
241 Alex Barre-Boulet YG 30.00 80.00
451 Mason McTavish 100.00 250.00
459 Dawson Mercer 100.00 250.00
464 Lucas Raymond 100.00 250.00
466 Cole Perfetti 80.00 200.00
469 Moritz Seider 125.00 300.00
475 William Eklund 100.00 250.00
481 Vasily Podkolzin 60.00 150.00
488 Quinton Byfield 60.00 150.00
489 Anton Lundell 80.00 200.00
498 Cole Sillinger 80.00 200.00
711 John-Jason Peterka YG 100.00 250.00
745 Seth Jarvis YG 80.00 200.00

2021-22 Upper Deck Clear Cut Foundations

CCFAB Cam Atkinson
Oliver Bjorkstrand 5.00 12.00
CCFBH Jack Hughes
Mackenzie Blackwood 12.00 30.00
CCFBQ Brock Boeser
Quinn Hughes 12.00 30.00
CCFBZ Filip Zadina
Tyler Bertuzzi 4.00 10.00
CCFCD Rasmus Dahlin
Dylan Cozens 6.00 15.00
CCFCF Joel Farabee
Sean Couturier 5.00 12.00
CCFCG Jakob Chychrun
Conor Garland 5.00 12.00
CCFCM Nathan MacKinnon
Cale Makar 20.00 50.00
CCFCO John Carlson
Alex Ovechkin 20.00 50.00
CCFDD Alex DeBrincat
Kirby Dach 6.00 15.00
CCFDZ Jamie Drysdale
Trevor Zegras 10.00 25.00
CCFEJ Eeli Tolvanen
Juuse Saros 6.00 15.00
CCFFK Kirill Kaprizov
Kevin Fiala 15.00 40.00
CCFGT Mark Giordano
Matthew Tkachuk 10.00 25.00
CCFHB Aleksander Barkov
Jonathan Huberdeau 8.00 20.00
CCFHV Victor Hedman
Andrei Vasilevskiy 8.00 20.00
CCFKB Quinton Byfield
Anze Kopitar 12.00 30.00
CCFKH Tomas Hertl
Erik Karlsson 6.00 15.00
CCFLF Alexis Lafreniere
Adam Fox 8.00 20.00
CCFLG Jake Guentzel
Kris Letang 8.00 20.00
CCFMD Leon Draisaitl
Connor McDavid 25.00 60.00
CCFMM Auston Matthews
Mitch Marner 20.00 50.00
CCFNS Tim Stutzle
Josh Norris 6.00 15.00
CCFPM Charlie McAvoy
David Pastrnak 12.00 30.00
CCFRO Jake Oettinger
Jason Robertson 8.00 20.00
CCFSC Nick Suzuki
Cole Caufield 20.00 50.00
CCFSE Mark Scheifele
Nikolaj Ehlers 8.00 20.00
CCFSO Ryan O'Reilly
Brayden Schenn 5.00 12.00
CCFST Mark Stone
Shea Theodore 6.00 15.00
CCFTS Andrei Svechnikov
Teuvo Teravainen 6.00 15.00
CCFVB Semyon Varlamov
Mathew Barzal 6.00 15.00

2021-22 Upper Deck Clear Cut Honoured Members

HOF102 Dick Duff 6.00 15.00
HOF103 Charlie Conacher 6.00 15.00
HOF104 Henri Richard 6.00 15.00
HOF105 Serge Savard 20.00 50.00
HOF106 Guy Carbonneau 6.00 15.00
HOF107 Yvan Cournoyer 6.00 15.00
HOF108 Turk Broda 6.00 15.00
HOF109 Bernie Geoffrion 6.00 15.00
HOF110 Eric Lindros 10.00 25.00

2021-22 Upper Deck Clear Cut Leaders

CCLGAA Alex Nedeljkovic
Philipp Grubauer
Marc-Andre Fleury 30.00 80.00
CCLPIM Tom Wilson
Max Domi
Brendan Smith 15.00 40.00
CCLPPG Leon Draisaitl
Joe Pavelski
T.J. Oshie 50.00 125.00
CCLRPT Kirill Kaprizov
Jason Robertson
Josh Norris 50.00 125.00
CCLSOG Auston Matthews
Brady Tkachuk
Nathan MacKinnon 60.00 150.00
CCLWIN Andrei Vasilevskiy
Philipp Grubauer
Marc-Andre Fleury 30.00 80.00

2021-22 Upper Deck Clear Picks

CP1 Sidney Crosby 50.00 125.00
CP2 Miro Heiskanen 15.00 40.00
CP3 Alexis Lafreniere 20.00 50.00
CP4 Quinton Byfield 30.00 80.00
CP5 Nico Hischier 20.00 50.00
CP6 Kyle Connor 20.00 50.00
CP7 Cole Caufield 50.00 125.00
CP8 Aaron Ekblad 15.00 40.00
CP9 Andrei Svechnikov 15.00 40.00
CP10 Alex Newhook 20.00 50.00
CP11 Auston Matthews 50.00 125.00
CP12 Cam York 12.00 30.00
CP13 Thomas Chabot 12.00 30.00
CP14 Leon Draisaitl 40.00 100.00
CP15 Mathew Barzal 15.00 40.00
CP16 Drew Doughty 15.00 40.00
CP17 Trevor Zegras 25.00 60.00
CP18 Bo Horvat 15.00 40.00
CP19 Steven Stamkos 25.00 60.00
CP20 Joel Farabee 12.00 30.00
CP21 Spencer Knight 25.00 60.00

2021-22 Upper Deck Day With the Cup

DC1 Andrei Vasilevskiy 12.00 30.00
DC2 Nikita Kucherov 15.00 40.00
DC3 Victor Hedman 10.00 25.00
DC4 Steven Stamkos 15.00 40.00
DC5 Mikhail Sergachev 6.00 15.00
DC6 Brayden Point 10.00 25.00

2021-22 Upper Deck Day With The Cup Flashbacks

DCF1 Martin Brodeur 30.00 80.00
DCF2 Tim Horton 20.00 50.00
DCF3 Luc Robitaille 12.00 30.00
DCF4 Rod Brind'Amour 12.00 30.00
DCF5 Dave Andreychuk 12.00 30.00
DCF6 Al MacInnis 15.00 40.00
DCF7 Bobby Clarke 20.00 50.00
DCF8 Bryan Trottier 12.00 30.00
DCF9 Doug Gilmour 15.00 40.00
DCF10 Johnny Bucyk 12.00 30.00
DCF11 Paul Coffey 15.00 40.00
DCF12 Phil Esposito 20.00 50.00
DCF13 Bobby Orr 50.00 125.00
DCF14 Jean Beliveau SP 40.00 100.00
DCF15 Wayne Gretzky SP 60.00 150.00
DCF16 Guy Lafleur SP 40.00 100.00
DCF17 Jacques Plante SP 40.00 100.00
DCF18 Terry Sawchuk SP 40.00 100.00

2021-22 Upper Deck Dazzlers

*GREEN: .6X TO 1.5X BASIC
*ORANGE: 1X TO 2.5X BASIC
*RED: 1X TO 2.5X BASIC
*PURPLE: 1.2X TO 3X BASIC
*PINK: 2.5X TO 6X BASIC
DZ1 Trevor Zegras .75 2.00
DZ2 Jamie Drysdale .60 1.50
DZ3 Jakob Chychrun .40 1.00
DZ4 Jeremy Swayman 1.25 3.00
DZ5 David Pastrnak 1.00 2.50
DZ6 Ukko-Pekka Luukkonen .60 1.50
DZ7 Rasmus Dahlin .50 1.25
DZ8 Elias Lindholm .40 1.00
DZ9 Sebastian Aho .60 1.50
DZ10 Teuvo Teravainen .40 1.00
DZ11 Alex DeBrincat .50 1.25
DZ12 Dominik Kubalik .40 1.00
DZ13 Alex Newhook .60 1.50
DZ14 Cale Makar 1.00 2.50
DZ15 Cam Atkinson .40 1.00
DZ16 Jason Robertson .60 1.50
DZ17 Joe Pavelski .50 1.25
DZ18 Jakub Vrana .30 .75
DZ19 Connor McDavid 2.00 5.00
DZ20 Darnell Nurse .30 .75
DZ21 Spencer Knight .75 2.00
DZ22 Jonathan Huberdeau .50 1.25
DZ23 Quinton Byfield 1.00 2.50
DZ24 Kirill Kaprizov 1.25 3.00
DZ25 Cole Caufield 1.50 4.00
DZ26 Nick Suzuki .75 2.00
DZ27 Juuse Saros .50 1.25
DZ28 Jack Hughes 1.00 2.50
DZ29 Semyon Varlamov .40 1.00
DZ30 Mathew Barzal .50 1.25
DZ31 Artemi Panarin .75 2.00
DZ32 Igor Shesterkin .75 2.00
DZ33 Tim Stutzle .50 1.25
DZ34 Jakub Voracek .30 .75
DZ35 Sidney Crosby 1.50 4.00
DZ36 Jake Guentzel .60 1.50
DZ37 Tomas Hertl .40 1.00
DZ38 David Perron .30 .75
DZ39 Steven Stamkos .75 2.00
DZ40 Brayden Point .50 1.25
DZ41 Mitch Marner .60 1.50
DZ42 Morgan Rielly .40 1.00
DZ43 Brock Boeser .50 1.25
DZ44 J.T. Miller .50 1.25
DZ45 Robin Lehner .30 .75
DZ46 Alex Pietrangelo .30 .75
DZ47 Alex Ovechkin 1.50 4.00
DZ48 Anthony Mantha .30 .75
DZ49 Kyle Connor .60 1.50
DZ50 Connor Hellebuyck .75 2.00
DZ51 Mason McTavish .75 2.00
DZ52 John Gibson .40 1.00
DZ53 Clayton Keller .50 1.25
DZ54 Taylor Hall .40 1.00
DZ55 Charlie McAvoy .50 1.25
DZ56 Victor Olofsson .40 1.00
DZ57 Jacob Markstrom .40 1.00
DZ58 Martin Necas .60 1.50
DZ59 Vincent Trocheck .40 1.00
DZ60 Kirby Dach .40 1.00
DZ61 Mikko Rantanen 1.00 2.50
DZ62 Gabriel Landeskog .50 1.25
DZ63 Cole Sillinger .60 1.50
DZ64 Jack Roslovic .25 .60
DZ65 Roope Hintz .50 1.25
DZ66 Miro Heiskanen .50 1.25
DZ67 Moritz Seider 1.00 2.50
DZ68 Lucas Raymond 1.25 3.00
DZ69 Dylan Larkin .50 1.25
DZ70 Joe Veleno .50 1.25
DZ71 Ryan Nugent-Hopkins .50 1.25
DZ72 Grigori Denisenko .50 1.25
DZ73 Aaron Ekblad .50 1.25
DZ74 Anze Kopitar .60 1.50
DZ75 Calen Addison .40 1.00
DZ76 Tyler Toffoli .40 1.00
DZ77 David Farrance .40 1.00
DZ78 Mackenzie Blackwood .40 1.00
DZ79 Anthony Beauvillier .25 .60
DZ80 Ryan Pulock .30 .75
DZ81 Adam Fox .50 1.25
DZ82 Alexis Lafreniere .60 1.50
DZ83 Brady Tkachuk .60 1.50
DZ84 Joel Farabee .40 1.00
DZ85 Cam York .40 1.00
DZ86 Evgeni Malkin .75 2.00
DZ87 Erik Karlsson .50 1.25
DZ88 Mark Giordano .40 1.00
DZ89 Jordan Eberle .40 1.00
DZ90 Jordan Binnington .60 1.50
DZ91 Victor Hedman .50 1.25
DZ92 Andrei Vasilevskiy .60 1.50
DZ93 Auston Matthews 1.50 4.00
DZ94 Vasily Podkolzin .50 1.25
DZ95 Quinn Hughes 1.00 2.50
DZ96 William Karlsson .50 1.25
DZ97 Jonathan Marchessault .50 1.25
DZ98 T.J. Oshie .40 1.00
DZ99 Nikolaj Ehlers .40 1.00
DZ100 Neal Pionk .25 .60
DZ101 Troy Terry .30 .75
DZ102 Benoit-Olivier Groulx .40 1.00
DZ103 Phil Kessel .40 1.00
DZ104 Tuukka Rask .50 1.25
DZ105 John-Jason Peterka .75 2.00
DZ106 Johnny Gaudreau .60 1.50
DZ107 Frederik Andersen .50 1.25
DZ108 Seth Jarvis 1.00 2.50
DZ109 Marc-Andre Fleury .75 2.00
DZ110 Seth Jones .40 1.00
DZ111 Patrik Laine .50 1.25
DZ112 Tyler Seguin .50 1.25
DZ113 Tyler Bertuzzi .30 .75
DZ114 Leon Draisaitl 1.25 3.00
DZ115 Aleksander Barkov .60 1.50
DZ116 Anton Lundell .75 2.00
DZ117 Drew Doughty .50 1.25
DZ118 Alex Turcotte .50 1.25
DZ119 Cam Talbot .40 1.00
DZ120 Jeff Petry .40 1.00
DZ121 Roman Josi .40 1.00
DZ122 Philip Tomasino .50 1.25
DZ123 Dawson Mercer 1.00 2.50
DZ124 Alexander Holtz .60 1.50
DZ125 Ilya Sorokin .60 1.50
DZ126 Chris Kreider .50 1.25
DZ127 Nils Lundkvist .40 1.00
DZ128 Josh Norris .40 1.00
DZ129 Drake Batherson .40 1.00
DZ130 Cam Atkinson .40 1.00
DZ131 Claude Giroux .40 1.00
DZ132 Kris Letang .50 1.25
DZ133 Tristan Jarry .40 1.00
DZ134 Timo Meier .40 1.00
DZ135 William Eklund 1.00 2.50
DZ136 Philipp Grubauer .40 1.00
DZ137 Jared McCann .30 .75
DZ138 Ryan O'Reilly .40 1.00
DZ139 Jordan Kyrou .40 1.00
DZ140 Nikita Kucherov .75 2.00
DZ141 William Nylander .75 2.00
DZ142 Jack Campbell .40 1.00
DZ143 Elias Pettersson .60 1.50
DZ144 Bo Horvat .50 1.25
DZ145 Shea Theodore .50 1.25
DZ146 Mark Stone .50 1.25
DZ147 Nicklas Backstrom .40 1.00
DZ148 John Carlson .40 1.00
DZ149 Mark Scheifele .60 1.50
DZ150 Cole Perfetti .75 2.00

2021-22 Upper Deck Debut Dates

*GOLD: .75X TO 2X BASIC INSERTS
DD1 Alexis Lafreniere 1.25 3.00
DD2 John Leonard .50 1.25
DD3 Dylan Cozens .75 2.00
DD4 Arthur Kaliyev .75 2.00
DD5 Kevin Lankinen .75 2.00
DD6 K'Andre Miller .60 1.50
DD7 Tim Stutzle 1.00 2.50
DD8 Ty Smith .75 2.00
DD9 Jack Rathbone .60 1.50
DD10 Pierre-Olivier Joseph .50 1.25
DD11 Connor McMichael .75 2.00
DD12 Ty Dellandrea .60 1.50
DD13 Bowen Byram 1.00 2.50
DD14 Peyton Krebs .60 1.50
DD15 Nick Robertson .75 2.00
DD16 Aleksi Heponiemi .75 2.00
DD17 Nils Hoglander .60 1.50
DD18 Alexander Romanov .60 1.50
DD19 Pius Suter .60 1.50
DD20 Jake Oettinger 1.25 3.00
DD21 Yegor Sharangovich .75 2.00
DD22 Ilya Sorokin 1.25 3.00
DD23 Nolan Foote .50 1.25
DD24 Vitali Kravtsov .60 1.50
DD25 Kirill Kaprizov 2.50 6.00

2021-22 Upper Deck Debut Dates Jerseys

DD1 Alexis Lafreniere 5.00 12.00
DD2 John Leonard 2.00 5.00
DD3 Dylan Cozens 3.00 8.00
DD4 Arthur Kaliyev 3.00 8.00
DD5 Kevin Lankinen 3.00 8.00
DD6 K'Andre Miller 2.50 6.00
DD7 Tim Stutzle 4.00 10.00
DD8 Ty Smith 3.00 8.00
DD9 Jack Rathbone 2.50 6.00
DD10 Pierre-Olivier Joseph 2.00 5.00
DD11 Connor McMichael 3.00 8.00
DD12 Ty Dellandrea 2.50 6.00
DD13 Bowen Byram 4.00 10.00
DD14 Peyton Krebs 2.50 6.00
DD15 Nick Robertson 3.00 8.00
DD16 Aleksi Heponiemi 3.00 8.00
DD17 Nils Hoglander 2.50 6.00
DD18 Alexander Romanov 2.50 6.00
DD19 Pius Suter 2.50 6.00
DD20 Jake Oettinger 5.00 12.00
DD21 Yegor Sharangovich 3.00 8.00
DD22 Ilya Sorokin 5.00 12.00
DD23 Nolan Foote 2.00 5.00
DD24 Vitali Kravtsov 2.50 6.00
DD25 Kirill Kaprizov 10.00 25.00

2021-22 Upper Deck Electromagnetic

*GOLD: .75X TO 2X BASIC INSERTS
EM1 Leon Draisaitl 2.50 6.00
EM2 Gabe Vilardi .75 2.00
EM3 Mikko Rantanen 2.00 5.00
EM4 David Perron .60 1.50
EM5 Mitch Marner 1.25 3.00
EM6 Nikolaj Ehlers .75 2.00
EM7 Sebastian Aho 1.25 3.00
EM8 Ilya Sorokin 1.25 3.00
EM9 Dylan Larkin 1.00 2.50
EM10 Joel Farabee .75 2.00
EM11 Maxime Comtois .60 1.50
EM12 Nils Hoglander .60 1.50
EM13 Nick Suzuki 1.50 4.00
EM14 Josh Norris .75 2.00
EM15 Johnny Gaudreau 1.25 3.00
EM16 Evgeni Malkin 1.50 4.00
EM17 Nico Hischier 1.25 3.00
EM18 Miro Heiskanen 1.00 2.50
EM19 Conor Garland .60 1.50
EM20 Alex DeBrincat 1.00 2.50
EM21 Sergei Bobrovsky 1.25 3.00
EM22 Taylor Hall .75 2.00
EM23 Igor Shesterkin 1.50 4.00
EM24 Kirill Kaprizov 2.50 6.00
EM25 Patrik Laine 1.00 2.50
EM26 Shea Theodore 1.00 2.50
EM27 Rasmus Dahlin 1.00 2.50
EM28 Logan Couture 1.00 2.50
EM29 Nikita Kucherov 1.50 4.00
EM30 Nicklas Backstrom .75 2.00

2021-22 Upper Deck Fanimation

F1 Jakob Silfverberg 10.00 25.00
F2 Nick Schmaltz 12.00 30.00
F3 Charlie McAvoy 20.00 50.00
F4 Victor Olofsson 15.00 40.00
F5 Elias Lindholm 15.00 40.00
F6 Jacob Slavin 12.00 30.00
F7 Duncan Keith 12.00 30.00
F8 Cale Makar 40.00 100.00
F9 Cam Atkinson 15.00 40.00
F10 Joe Pavelski 20.00 50.00
F11 Thomas Greiss 12.00 30.00
F12 Darnell Nurse 12.00 30.00
F13 Keith Yandle 10.00 25.00
F14 Dustin Brown 15.00 40.00
F15 Kirill Kaprizov 50.00 125.00
F16 Nick Suzuki 30.00 80.00

2021-22 Upper Deck Game Jerseys

GJAB Adam Boqvist 1.50 4.00
GJAD Alex DeBrincat 3.00 8.00
GJAE Aaron Ekblad 3.00 8.00
GJAH Adam Henrique 2.00 5.00
GJAK Adrian Kempe 2.50 6.00
GJAL Anders Lee 2.00 5.00
GJAR Viktor Arvidsson 1.50 4.00
GJAV Andrei Vasilevskiy 4.00 10.00
GJBA Josh Bailey 2.00 5.00
GJBG Brendan Gallagher 2.50 6.00
GJBH Bo Horvat 3.00 8.00
GJBP Brayden Point 3.00 8.00
GJBS Brayden Schenn 2.50 6.00
GJBU Andre Burakovsky 1.50 4.00
GJBW Blake Wheeler 2.50 6.00
GJCA Cam Atkinson 2.50 6.00
GJCC Charlie Coyle 2.50 6.00
GJCK Clayton Keller 3.00 8.00
GJCM Casey Mittelstadt 2.50 6.00
GJCW Colin White 2.00 5.00
GJDD Drew Doughty 3.00 8.00
GJDK Darcy Kuemper 2.50 6.00
GJDL Dylan Larkin 3.00 8.00
GJDN Darnell Nurse 2.00 5.00
GJEK Evander Kane 2.50 6.00
GJFF Filip Forsberg 4.00 10.00
GJGA Johnny Gaudreau 4.00 10.00
GJJB Jamie Benn 2.50 6.00
GJJC John Carlson 2.50 6.00
GJJF Justin Faulk 2.00 5.00
GJJG John Gibson 2.50 6.00
GJJH Jonathan Huberdeau 3.00 8.00
GJJM Jonathan Marchessault 3.00 8.00
GJJP Jesse Puljujarvi 2.50 6.00
GJJQ Jonathan Quick 3.00 8.00
GJJS Jaden Schwartz 2.00 5.00
GJJT Jacob Trouba 2.00 5.00
GJJV Jakub Voracek 2.00 5.00
GJJZ Jason Zucker 2.50 6.00
GJKF Kevin Fiala 2.00 5.00
GJKL Kris Letang 3.00 8.00
GJKO Anze Kopitar 4.00 10.00
GJKU Evgeny Kuznetsov 3.00 8.00
GJLC Logan Couture 3.00 8.00
GJMD Matt Duchene 2.50 6.00
GJMG Mark Giordano 2.50 6.00
GJMJ Max Jones 1.50 4.00
GJMS Mark Scheifele 4.00 10.00
GJMZ Mika Zibanejad 3.00 8.00
GJNB Nicklas Backstrom 2.50 6.00
GJNK Nikita Kucherov 5.00 12.00
GJNN Nino Niederreiter 1.50 4.00
GJOT Owen Tippett 1.50 4.00
GJPB Pavel Buchnevich 2.00 5.00
GJPS P.K. Subban 3.00 8.00
GJRD Ryan Donato 2.00 5.00
GJRF Robby Fabbri 1.50 4.00
GJRS Reilly Smith 2.50 6.00
GJRT Robert Thomas 2.50 6.00
GJSA Sebastian Aho 4.00 10.00
GJSV Semyon Varlamov 2.50 6.00
GJTA John Tavares 4.00 10.00
GJTC Thomas Chabot 2.50 6.00
GJTG Thomas Greiss 2.00 5.00
GJTJ Tyler Johnson 1.50 4.00
GJTO T.J. Oshie 2.50 6.00
GJVA James van Riemsdyk 2.00 5.00
GJVH Victor Hedman 3.00 8.00
GJVO Victor Olofsson 2.50 6.00
GJWN William Nylander 5.00 12.00

2021-22 Upper Deck Fluorescence Red

*GOLD: .6X TO 1.5X RED
*BLUE: 1.25X TO 3X RED
FL1 Spencer Knight 5.00 12.00
FL2 Mason McTavish 5.00 12.00
FL3 Boris Katchouk 2.00 5.00
FL4 Lucas Raymond 8.00 20.00
FL5 Jake Leschyshyn 2.50 6.00
FL6 Jonathan Dahlen 2.50 6.00
FL7 Nils Lundkvist 2.50 6.00
FL8 Karel Vejmelka 3.00 8.00
FL9 Yegor Chinakhov 4.00 10.00
FL10 Philip Tomasino 3.00 8.00
FL11 Vasily Podkolzin 3.00 8.00
FL12 Jake Neighbours 5.00 12.00
FL13 Vladimir Tkachev 2.50 6.00
FL14 Jasper Weatherby 2.50 6.00
FL15 Morgan Barron 2.00 5.00
FL16 Anton Lundell 5.00 12.00
FL17 William Eklund 6.00 15.00
FL18 Benoit-Olivier Groulx 2.50 6.00
FL19 Moritz Seider 4.00 10.00
FL20 Taylor Raddysh 4.00 10.00
FL21 Sampo Ranta 2.50 6.00
FL22 Cole Sillinger 4.00 10.00
FL23 Jesse Ylonen 2.50 6.00
FL24 Hendrix Lapierre 2.50 6.00
FL25 Dawson Mercer 6.00 15.00
FL26 Cole Perfetti 5.00 12.00
FL27 Wade Allison 2.50 6.00
FL28 Jeremy Swayman 8.00 20.00
FL29 Cam York 2.50 6.00
FL30 Joe Veleno 3.00 8.00
FL31 Kole Lind 3.00 8.00
FL32 Quinton Byfield 6.00 15.00
FL33 Ukko-Pekka Luukkonen 4.00 10.00
FL34 David Farrance 2.50 6.00
FL35 Jacob Bernard-Docker 2.50 6.00
FL36 Zac Jones 3.00 8.00
FL37 Ross Colton 3.00 8.00
FL38 Matthew Phillips 2.50 6.00
FL39 Trevor Zegras 5.00 12.00
FL40 Jan Jenik 3.00 8.00
FL41 Grigori Denisenko 3.00 8.00
FL42 Alex Newhook 4.00 10.00
FL43 Wyatt Kalynuk 2.50 6.00
FL44 Filip Gustavsson 5.00 12.00
FL45 Shane Pinto 4.00 10.00
FL46 Jamie Drysdale 4.00 10.00
FL47 Rasmus Kupari 2.50 6.00
FL48 Calen Addison 1.50 4.00
FL49 Alex Barre-Boulet 2.50 6.00
FL50 Cole Caufield 10.00 25.00

2021-22 Upper Deck HoloGrFx NHL

NHL1 Connor McDavid 5.00 12.00
NHL2 Johnny Gaudreau 1.50 4.00
NHL3 Cale Makar 2.50 6.00
NHL4 Jonathan Huberdeau 1.25 3.00
NHL5 Steven Stamkos 2.00 5.00
NHL6 Brad Marchand 2.00 5.00
NHL7 Sebastian Aho 1.50 4.00
NHL8 Sidney Crosby 4.00 10.00
NHL9 Mathew Barzal 1.25 3.00
NHL10 Mark Stone 1.25 3.00
NHL11 Leon Draisaitl 3.00 8.00
NHL12 Kirill Kaprizov 3.00 8.00
NHL13 Alex DeBrincat 1.25 3.00
NHL14 Igor Shesterkin 2.00 5.00
NHL15 Mitch Marner 1.50 4.00
NHL16 Nathan MacKinnon 4.00 10.00
NHL17 Alex Ovechkin 4.00 10.00
NHL18 Artemi Panarin 2.00 5.00
NHL19 Andrei Vasilevskiy 1.50 4.00
NHL20 Jack Hughes 2.50 6.00

2021-22 Upper Deck HoloGrFx Rookies

*GOLD: .5X TO 1.25X BASIC INSERTS
HG1 Lucas Raymond 5.00 12.00
HG2 Dawson Mercer 4.00 10.00
HG3 Anton Lundell 3.00 8.00
HG4 Cole Perfetti 3.00 8.00
HG5 Tanner Jeannot 1.50 4.00
HG6 Trevor Zegras 3.00 8.00
HG7 Alex Newhook 2.50 6.00
HG8 Alex Turcotte 2.00 5.00
HG9 Seth Jarvis 4.00 10.00
HG10 William Eklund 4.00 10.00
HG11 Vasily Podkolzin 2.00 5.00
HG12 Spencer Knight 3.00 8.00
HG13 Moritz Seider 4.00 10.00
HG14 Quinton Byfield 4.00 10.00
HG15 Nils Lundkvist 1.50 4.00
HG16 Cole Caufield 6.00 15.00
HG17 Jeremy Swayman 5.00 12.00
HG18 Alexander Holtz 2.50 6.00
HG19 Jamie Drysdale 2.50 6.00
HG20 Cole Sillinger 2.50 6.00

2021-22 Upper Deck Honor Roll

*RED: .75X TO 2X BASIC INSERTS
HR1 Nathan MacKinnon 3.00 8.00
HR2 Ryan O'Reilly .75 2.00
HR3 Alex Ovechkin 3.00 8.00
HR4 Alex DeBrincat 1.00 2.50
HR5 Brayden Point 1.00 2.50
HR6 Mark Scheifele 1.25 3.00
HR7 Elias Pettersson 1.25 3.00
HR8 MarcAndre Fleury 1.50 4.00
HR9 Brad Marchand 1.50 4.00
HR10 Brock Boeser 1.00 2.50
HR11 Spencer Knight 1.50 4.00
HR12 Cole Caufield 3.00 8.00
HR13 Patrick Kane 1.50 4.00
HR14 Patrice Bergeron 1.00 2.50
HR15 Sidney Crosby 3.00 8.00
HR16 Igor Shesterkin 1.50 4.00
HR17 Andrei Svechnikov 1.00 2.50
HR18 Connor McDavid 4.00 10.00
HR19 Kyle Connor 1.25 3.00
HR20 John Carlson .75 2.00
HR21 Jack Hughes 2.00 5.00
HR22 Victor Hedman 1.00 2.50
HR23 Cale Makar 2.00 5.00
HR24 Jake Guentzel 1.25 3.00
HR25 Jack Eichel 1.25 3.00
HR26 Mitch Marner 1.25 3.00
HR27 Steven Stamkos 1.50 4.00
HR28 Andrei Vasilevskiy 1.25 3.00
HR29 Sebastian Aho 1.25 3.00
HR30 Alex Newhook 1.25 3.00
HR31 Matthew Tkachuk 1.50 4.00
HR32 Leon Draisaitl 2.50 6.00
HR33 David Pastrnak 2.00 5.00
HR34 John Tavares 1.25 3.00
HR35 Kirill Kaprizov 2.50 6.00
HR36 Quinton Byfield 2.00 5.00
HR37 Artemi Panarin 1.50 4.00
HR38 Connor Hellebuyck 1.50 4.00
HR39 Aleksander Barkov 1.25 3.00
HR40 Quinn Hughes 2.00 5.00
HR41 Mikko Rantanen 2.00 5.00
HR42 Mark Stone 1.00 2.50
HR43 Adam Fox 1.00 2.50
HR44 Semyon Varlamov .75 2.00
HR45 Jonathan Huberdeau 1.00 2.50
HR46 Trevor Zegras 1.50 4.00
HR47 Brady Tkachuk 1.25 3.00
HR48 Jeremy Swayman 2.50 6.00
HR49 Evgeni Malkin 1.50 4.00
HR50 Auston Matthews 3.00 8.00
HR51 Moritz Seider 2.00 5.00
HR52 Boris Katchouk .60 1.50
HR53 Anton Lundell 1.50 4.00
HR54 Yegor Chinakhov 1.25 3.00
HR55 Jake Leschyshyn .75 2.00
HR56 Kole Lind 1.00 2.50
HR57 Vladimir Tkachev .75 2.00
HR58 Vasily Podkolzin 1.00 2.50
HR59 Jake Neighbours 1.50 4.00
HR60 Dawson Mercer 2.00 5.00
HR61 Cole Sillinger 1.25 3.00
HR62 Benoit-Olivier Groulx .75 2.00
HR63 Hendrix Lapierre .75 2.00
HR64 Taylor Raddysh 1.25 3.00
HR65 Lucas Raymond 2.50 6.00
HR66 Mason McTavish 1.50 4.00
HR67 Philip Tomasino 1.00 2.50
HR68 Nils Lundkvist .75 2.00
HR69 William Eklund 2.00 5.00
HR70 Grigori Denisenko 1.00 2.50
HR71 Shane Pinto 1.25 3.00
HR72 Alex Barre-Boulet .75 2.00
HR73 Calen Addison .75 2.00
HR74 Jamie Drysdale 1.25 3.00
HR75 Nikolaj Ehlers .75 2.00
HR76 Tim Stutzle 1.00 2.50
HR77 Roman Josi .75 2.00
HR78 Cam York .75 2.00
HR79 Mathew Barzal 1.00 2.50
HR80 Patrik Laine 1.00 2.50
HR81 Joe Veleno 1.00 2.50
HR82 Morgan Rielly .75 2.00
HR83 Alexis Lafreniere 1.25 3.00
HR84 Johnny Gaudreau 1.25 3.00
HR85 Gabriel Landeskog 1.00 2.50
HR86 Aaron Ekblad 1.00 2.50
HR87 Darnell Nurse .60 1.50
HR88 Brent Burns .75 2.00
HR89 Mika Zibanejad 1.00 2.50
HR90 Phil Kessel .75 2.00
HR91 Anze Kopitar 1.25 3.00
HR92 Anders Lee .60 1.50
HR93 Taylor Hall .75 2.00
HR94 Robin Lehner .60 1.50
HR95 Miro Heiskanen 1.00 2.50
HR96 Tyler Seguin 1.00 2.50
HR97 Nicklas Backstrom .75 2.00
HR98 Tyson Barrie .50 1.25
HR99 Kris Letang 1.00 2.50
HR100 Carey Price 1.50 4.00

2021-22 Upper Deck Honor Roll Rainbow

*RAINBOW/250: 2X TO 5X BASIC INSERTS
HR46 Trevor Zegras 50.00 125.00
HR48 Jeremy Swayman 50.00 125.00

2021-22 Upper Deck Hundo P

*GOLD: .75X TO 2X BASIC INSERTS
HP1 Connor McDavid 4.00 10.00
HP2 Zach Parise .75 2.00
HP3 Brayden Point 1.00 2.50
HP4 Brent Burns .75 2.00
HP5 Sean Couturier .60 1.50
HP6 Alex Pietrangelo .60 1.50
HP7 Milan Lucic .60 1.50
HP8 Brady Tkachuk 1.25 3.00
HP9 Sidney Crosby 3.00 8.00
HP10 Anze Kopitar 1.25 3.00
HP11 Mark Stone 1.00 2.50
HP12 Blake Wheeler .75 2.00
HP13 Duncan Keith .60 1.50
HP14 Adam Fox 1.00 2.50
HP15 Patrice Bergeron 1.00 2.50
HP16 Joe Pavelski 1.00 2.50
HP17 Ryan O'Reilly .75 2.00
HP18 Auston Matthews 3.00 8.00
HP19 Nathan MacKinnon 3.00 8.00
HP20 Phillip Danault .75 2.00
HP21 Seth Jones .75 2.00
HP22 Roman Josi .75 2.00
HP23 Aleksander Barkov 1.25 3.00
HP24 Anders Lee .60 1.50
HP25 Matthew Tkachuk 1.50 4.00

2021-22 Upper Deck NHL Passages

PA1 Connor McDavid 25.00 60.00
PA2 Steven Stamkos 8.00 20.00
PA3 Brent Burns 4.00 10.00
PA4 Carey Price 8.00 20.00
PA5 Patrick Kane 8.00 20.00
PA6 John Tavares 6.00 15.00
PA7 Ryan Getzlaf 4.00 10.00
PA8 Alex Ovechkin 20.00 50.00
PA9 Anze Kopitar 6.00 15.00
PA10 Bo Horvat 5.00 12.00
PA11 Ryan O'Reilly 4.00 10.00
PA12 Nathan MacKinnon 15.00 40.00
PA13 Mark Giordano 4.00 10.00
PA14 Artemi Panarin 8.00 20.00
PA15 Phil Kessel 4.00 10.00
PA16 Joe Thornton 6.00 15.00

PA17 Roman Josi 4.00 10.00
PA18 Joe Pavelski 5.00 12.00
PA19 Blake Wheeler 4.00 10.00
PA20 Taylor Hall 4.00 10.00
PA21 Mark Stone 5.00 12.00
PA22 Sidney Crosby 20.00 50.00

2021-22 Upper Deck NHL Specialists

NS1 Wayne Gretzky 40.00 100.00
NS2 Auston Matthews 25.00 60.00
NS3 Cale Makar 15.00 40.00
NS4 Artemi Panarin 12.00 30.00
NS5 Steve Yzerman 15.00 40.00
NS6 Alex Ovechkin 25.00 60.00
NS7 Mario Lemieux 25.00 60.00
NS8 Connor McDavid 30.00 80.00
NS9 Kirill Kaprizov 20.00 50.00
NS10 Steven Stamkos 12.00 30.00
NS11 Bobby Orr 25.00 60.00
NS12 Aleksander Barkov 10.00 25.00
NS13 Nathan MacKinnon 25.00 60.00
NS14 Leon Draisaitl 20.00 50.00
NS15 Patrick Roy 15.00 40.00
NS16 Quinn Hughes 15.00 40.00
NS17 Brad Marchand 12.00 30.00
NS18 Gordie Howe 20.00 50.00
NS19 Patrick Kane 12.00 30.00
NS20 Sidney Crosby 25.00 60.00

2021-22 Upper Deck Oversized

201 Cole Caufield YG 15.00 40.00
202 Ukko-Pekka Luukkonen YG 4.00 10.00
205 Jamie Drysdale YG 4.00 10.00
209 Wade Allison YG 2.50 6.00
212 Joe Veleno YG 3.00 8.00
213 Wyatt Kalynuk YG 2.50 6.00
223 Spencer Knight YG 5.00 12.00
226 Jeremy Swayman YG 8.00 20.00
227 Calen Addison YG 2.50 6.00
232 Trevor Zegras YG 5.00 12.00
241 Alex Barre-Boulet YG 2.50 6.00
242 Rasmus Kupari YG 2.50 6.00
243 Cam York YG 2.50 6.00
246 Shane Pinto YG 4.00 10.00
451 Mason McTavish YG 5.00 12.00
454 Philip Tomasino YG 3.00 8.00
456 Nils Lundkvist YG 2.50 6.00
461 Alex Newhook YG 4.00 10.00
464 Lucas Raymond YG 8.00 20.00
466 Cole Perfetti YG 5.00 12.00
469 Moritz Seider YG 6.00 15.00
472 Hendrix Lapierre YG 2.50 6.00
475 William Eklund YG 6.00 15.00
478 Benoit-Olivier Groulx YG 2.50 6.00
481 Vasily Podkolzin YG 3.00 8.00
488 Quinton Byfield YG 6.00 15.00
489 Anton Lundell YG 5.00 12.00
498 Cole Sillinger YG 4.00 10.00

2021-22 Upper Deck Portraits

P1 Quinn Hughes 2.00 5.00
P2 Max Pacioretty .75 2.00
P3 Semyon Varlamov .75 2.00
P4 Darnell Nurse .60 1.50
P5 Rasmus Dahlin 1.00 2.50
P6 Alexis Lafreniere 1.25 3.00
P7 Jason Robertson 1.25 3.00
P8 Jack Hughes 2.00 5.00
P9 Andrei Svechnikov 1.00 2.50
P10 Kirill Kaprizov 2.50 6.00
P11 Jakub Voracek .60 1.50
P12 Andrei Vasilevskiy 1.25 3.00
P13 Robin Lehner .60 1.50
P14 Johnny Gaudreau 1.25 3.00
P15 Miro Heiskanen 1.00 2.50
P16 Patrick Kane 1.50 4.00
P17 Alex Ovechkin 3.00 8.00
P18 David Pastrnak 2.00 5.00
P19 Sidney Crosby 3.00 8.00
P20 Tim Stutzle 1.00 2.50
P21 Phil Kessel .75 2.00
P22 Brent Burns .75 2.00
P23 Artemi Panarin 1.50 4.00
P24 Mitch Marner 1.25 3.00
P25 Connor McDavid 4.00 10.00
P26 Kyle Connor 1.25 3.00
P27 Nathan MacKinnon 3.00 8.00
P28 Torey Krug .60 1.50
P29 Auston Matthews 3.00 8.00
P30 Anthony Mantha .60 1.50
P31 Quinton Byfield 2.00 5.00
P32 Spencer Knight 1.50 4.00
P33 Joe Veleno 1.00 2.50
P34 Trevor Zegras 8.00 20.00
P35 Jacob Bernard-Docker .75 2.00
P36 Ukko-Pekka Luukkonen 1.25 3.00
P37 Jamie Drysdale 1.25 3.00
P38 Calen Addison .75 2.00
P39 Alex Barre-Boulet .75 2.00
P40 Cole Caufield 8.00 20.00
P41 Dawson Mercer 2.00 5.00
P42 Jake Neighbours 1.50 4.00
P43 Hendrix Lapierre .75 2.00
P44 Taylor Raddysh 1.25 3.00
P45 Yegor Chinakhov 1.25 3.00
P46 Jake Leschyshyn .75 2.00
P47 Jonathan Dahlen .75 2.00
P48 Nils Lundkvist .75 2.00
P49 Benoit-Olivier Groulx .75 2.00
P50 Jasper Weatherby .75 2.00
P51 Sampo Ranta .75 2.00
P52 Alex Newhook 1.25 3.00
P53 Shane Pinto 1.25 3.00
P54 Cam York .75 2.00
P55 Filip Gustavsson 1.50 4.00
P56 Arttu Ruotsalainen .75 2.00
P57 Grigori Denisenko 1.00 2.50
P58 Ivan Prosvetov .75 2.00
P59 David Farrance .75 2.00
P60 Logan Thompson 2.00 5.00
P61 Wade Allison .75 2.00
P62 Zac Jones 1.00 2.50
P63 Wyatt Kalynuk .75 2.00
P64 Jan Jenik 1.00 2.50
P65 Tanner Jeannot .75 2.00
P66 Lane Pederson .75 2.00
P67 Jesse Ylonen .75 2.00
P68 Matthew Phillips .75 2.00
P69 Marian Studenic .75 2.00
P70 Adam Ruzicka .75 2.00
P71 Cole Sillinger 1.25 3.00
P72 Jeremy Swayman 2.50 6.00
P73 Cole Perfetti 1.50 4.00
P74 Anton Lundell 1.50 4.00
P75 Vasily Podkolzin 1.00 2.50
P77 Moritz Seider 2.00 5.00
P78 Philip Tomasino 1.00 2.50
P79 Lucas Raymond 2.50 6.00
P80 Mason McTavish 1.50 4.00

2021-22 Upper Deck Portraits Black and White

*B&W/250: 1.25X TO 3X BASIC INSERTS
P34 Trevor Zegras 15.00 40.00
P40 Cole Caufield 15.00 40.00

2021-22 Upper Deck Record Collections

*GOLD/250: .75X TO 2X BASIC INSERTS
*PLATINUM/50: 1.25X TO 3X BASIC CARDS
RB1 Mario Lemieux 15.00 40.00
RB2 Brett Hull 6.00 15.00
RB3 Bobby Orr 15.00 40.00
RB4 Alex Ovechkin 15.00 40.00
RB5 Ray Bourque 6.00 15.00
RB6 Teemu Selanne 8.00 20.00
RB7 Marc-Andre Fleury 8.00 20.00
RB8 Mark Messier 8.00 20.00
RB9 Martin Brodeur 10.00 25.00
RB10 Mike Bossy 4.00 10.00
RB11 Patrick Roy 10.00 25.00
RB12 Glenn Hall 4.00 10.00
RB13 Mike Gartner 5.00 12.00
RB14 Keith Yandle 2.50 6.00
RB15 Jaromir Jagr 12.00 30.00
RB16 Gordie Howe 12.00 30.00
RB17 Darryl Sittler 4.00 10.00
RB18 Paul Coffey 5.00 12.00
RB19 Sidney Crosby 15.00 40.00
RB20 Wayne Gretzky 25.00 60.00

2021-22 Upper Deck Rookie Breakouts

RB1 Cole Caufield 40.00 100.00
RB2 Lucas Raymond 30.00 80.00
RB3 Cole Perfetti 20.00 50.00
RB4 Philip Tomasino 12.00 30.00
RB5 Hendrix Lapierre 10.00 25.00
RB6 Vasily Podkolzin 12.00 30.00
RB7 Dawson Mercer 25.00 60.00
RB8 William Eklund 25.00 60.00
RB9 Mason McTavish 20.00 50.00
RB10 Moritz Seider 25.00 60.00
RB11 Cole Sillinger 15.00 40.00
RB12 Jeremy Swayman 30.00 80.00
RB13 Jamie Drysdale 15.00 40.00
RB14 Spencer Knight 20.00 50.00
RB15 Cam York 10.00 25.00
RB16 Alex Newhook 15.00 40.00
RB17 Ross Colton 12.00 30.00
RB18 Trevor Zegras 20.00 50.00
RB19 Quinton Byfield 25.00 60.00
RB20 Joe Veleno 12.00 30.00

2021-22 Upper Deck Rookie Materials

*PATCH/25: .75X TO 2X BASIC INSERTS
RMAN Alex Newhook 3.00 8.00
RMAR Arttu Ruotsalainen 2.00 5.00
RMCA Calen Addison 2.00 5.00
RMCC Cole Caufield 8.00 20.00
RMCP Cole Perfetti 4.00 10.00
RMCY Cam York 2.00 5.00
RMDF David Farrance 2.00 5.00
RMGD Grigori Denisenko 2.50 6.00
RMIP Ivan Prosvetov 2.00 5.00
RMJA Jack Ahcan 2.00 5.00
RMJD Jamie Drysdale 3.00 8.00
RMJJ Jan Jenik 2.50 6.00
RMJK Joey Keane 1.50 4.00
RMJS Jeremy Swayman 6.00 15.00
RMJV Joe Veleno 2.50 6.00
RMJY Jesse Ylonen 2.00 5.00
RMKL Kole Lind 2.50 6.00
RMLR Lucas Raymond 6.00 15.00
RMMH Mike Hardman 2.00 5.00
RMMP Matthew Phillips 2.00 5.00
RMMS Mattias Samuelsson 2.00 5.00
RMPT Philip Tomasino 2.50 6.00
RMQB Quinton Byfield 5.00 12.00
RMRC Ross Colton 2.50 6.00
RMRK Rasmus Kupari 2.00 5.00
RMSE Moritz Seider 5.00 12.00
RMSK Spencer Knight 4.00 10.00
RMSP Shane Pinto 3.00 8.00
RMSR Sampo Ranta 2.00 5.00
RMTL Tanner Laczynski 2.00 5.00
RMTT Tyce Thompson 2.00 5.00
RMTZ Trevor Zegras 4.00 10.00
RMUL Ukko-Pekka Luukkonen 3.00 8.00
RMWA Wade Allison 2.00 5.00
RMWK Wyatt Kalynuk 2.00 5.00
RMZJ Zac Jones 2.50 6.00

2021-22 Upper Deck Rookie Retrospective

RR1 Kirill Kaprizov 3.00 8.00
RR2 Jason Robertson 1.50 4.00
RR3 Mikey Anderson .75 2.00
RR4 Jake Oettinger 1.50 4.00
RR5 Yegor Sharangovich 1.00 2.50
RR6 Gabe Vilardi 1.00 2.50
RR7 Kevin Lankinen 1.00 2.50
RR8 Josh Norris 1.00 2.50
RR9 Nils Hoglander .75 2.00
RR10 Kaapo Kahkonen 1.00 2.50
RR11 Pius Suter .75 2.00
RR12 Eeli Tolvanen 1.00 2.50
RR13 Vitek Vanecek 1.00 2.50
RR14 Ty Smith 1.00 2.50
RR15 Ilya Sorokin 1.50 4.00
RR16 Brandon Hagel .75 2.00
RR17 Tim Stutzle 1.25 3.00
RR18 Alex Nedeljkovic .75 2.00
RR19 K'Andre Miller .75 2.00
RR20 Alexis Lafreniere 1.50 4.00

2021-22 Upper Deck Rookie Retrospective Jerseys

RR1 Kirill Kaprizov 8.00 20.00
RR2 Jason Robertson 4.00 10.00
RR3 Mikey Anderson 2.00 5.00
RR4 Jake Oettinger 4.00 10.00
RR5 Yegor Sharangovich 2.50 6.00
RR6 Gabe Vilardi 2.50 6.00
RR7 Kevin Lankinen 2.50 6.00
RR8 Josh Norris 2.50 6.00
RR9 Nils Hoglander 2.00 5.00
RR10 Kaapo Kahkonen 2.50 6.00
RR11 Pius Suter 2.00 5.00
RR12 Eeli Tolvanen 2.50 6.00
RR13 Vitek Vanecek 2.50 6.00
RR14 Ty Smith 2.50 6.00
RR15 Ilya Sorokin 4.00 10.00
RR16 Brandon Hagel 2.00 5.00
RR17 Tim Stutzle 3.00 8.00
RR18 Alex Nedeljkovic 2.00 5.00
RR19 K'Andre Miller 2.00 5.00
RR20 Alexis Lafreniere 4.00 10.00

2021-22 Upper Deck Rookie Threads Retro

RTAN Alex Newhook 3.00 8.00
RTBT Brady Tkachuk 3.00 8.00
RTCA Calen Addison 2.00 5.00
RTCC Cole Caufield 8.00 20.00
RTCP Cole Perfetti 4.00 10.00
RTCY Cam York 2.00 5.00
RTDF David Farrance 2.00 5.00
RTGD Grigori Denisenko 2.50 6.00
RTHA Mike Hardman 2.00 5.00
RTJA Jack Ahcan 2.00 5.00
RTJD Jamie Drysdale 3.00 8.00
RTJJ Jan Jenik 2.50 6.00
RTJK Joey Keane 1.50 4.00
RTJS Jeremy Swayman 6.00 15.00
RTJV Joe Veleno 2.50 6.00
RTJY Jesse Ylonen 2.00 5.00
RTKL Kole Lind 2.50 6.00
RTLP Lane Pederson 2.00 5.00
RTLR Lucas Raymond 6.00 15.00
RTMP Matthew Phillips 2.00 5.00
RTMS Moritz Seider 5.00 12.00
RTPR Ivan Prosvetov 2.00 5.00
RTPT Philip Tomasino 2.50 6.00
RTQB Quinton Byfield 5.00 12.00
RTRC Ross Colton 2.50 6.00
RTRK Rasmus Kupari 2.00 5.00
RTSK Spencer Knight 4.00 10.00
RTSR Sampo Ranta 2.00 5.00
RTTL Tanner Laczynski 2.00 5.00
RTTT Tyce Thompson 2.00 5.00
RTTZ Trevor Zegras 4.00 10.00
RTUL Ukko-Pekka Luukkonen 3.00 8.00
RTWA Wade Allison 2.00 5.00
RTWK Wyatt Kalynuk 2.00 5.00
RTZJ Zac Jones 2.50 6.00

2021-22 Upper Deck Sophomore Sensations

SO1 Kirill Kaprizov 8.00 20.00
SO2 Tim Stutzle 3.00 8.00
SO3 Alexis Lafreniere 4.00 10.00
SO4 Jason Robertson 4.00 10.00
SO5 Ilya Sorokin 4.00 10.00
SO6 Josh Norris 2.50 6.00

2021-22 Upper Deck SPx Finite

*RADIANCE/799: .75X TO 2X BASIC
*SPECTRUM/99: 1.25X TO 3X BASIC
SF1 Mason McTavish 2.50 6.00
SF2 Trevor Zegras 2.50 6.00
SF3 Jakob Chychrun 1.25 3.00
SF4 Jeremy Swayman 4.00 10.00
SF5 Patrice Bergeron 1.50 4.00
SF6 Ukko-Pekka Luukkonen 2.00 5.00
SF7 Elias Lindholm 1.25 3.00
SF8 Matthew Tkachuk 2.50 6.00
SF9 Andrei Svechnikov 1.50 4.00
SF10 Frederik Andersen 1.50 4.00
SF11 Alex DeBrincat 1.50 4.00
SF12 Patrick Kane 2.50 6.00
SF13 Nathan MacKinnon 5.00 12.00
SF14 Mikko Rantanen 3.00 8.00
SF15 Cole Sillinger 2.00 5.00
SF16 Riley Damiani 1.25 3.00
SF17 Moritz Seider 3.00 8.00
SF18 Lucas Raymond 4.00 10.00
SF19 Connor McDavid 6.00 15.00
SF20 Leon Draisaitl 4.00 10.00
SF21 Jonathan Huberdeau 1.50 4.00
SF22 Anton Lundell 2.50 6.00
SF23 Quinton Byfield 2.50 6.00
SF24 Alex Turcotte 1.50 4.00
SF25 Kirill Kaprizov 4.00 10.00
SF26 Cole Caufield 5.00 12.00
SF27 Juuse Saros 1.50 4.00
SF28 Philip Tomasino 1.50 4.00
SF29 Dawson Mercer 3.00 8.00
SF30 Alexander Holtz 2.00 5.00
SF31 Mathew Barzal 1.50 4.00
SF32 Igor Shesterkin 2.50 6.00
SF33 Adam Fox 1.50 4.00
SF34 Shane Pinto 2.00 5.00
SF35 Cam York 1.25 3.00
SF36 Claude Giroux 1.25 3.00
SF37 Sidney Crosby 5.00 12.00
SF38 Tristan Jarry 1.25 3.00
SF39 William Eklund 3.00 8.00
SF40 Philipp Grubauer 1.25 3.00
SF41 Mark Giordano 1.25 3.00
SF42 Ryan O'Reilly 1.25 3.00
SF43 Steven Stamkos 2.50 6.00
SF44 Victor Hedman 1.50 4.00
SF45 Auston Matthews 5.00 12.00
SF46 John Tavares 2.00 5.00
SF47 Elias Pettersson 2.00 5.00
SF48 Jack Eichel 2.00 5.00
SF49 Alex Ovechkin 5.00 12.00
SF50 Mark Scheifele 2.00 5.00

2021-22 Upper Deck Team Triples

*GOLD: .75X TO 2X BASIC INSERTS
TTBOS David Pastrnak
Brad Marchand
Patrice Bergeron 5.00 12.00
TTBUF Rasmus Dahlin
Ukko-Pekka Luukkonen
Dylan Cozens 3.00 8.00
TTCAL Elias Lindholm
Matthew Tkachuk
Mark Giordano 4.00 10.00
TTCAR Sebastian Aho
Teuvo Teravainen
Andrei Svechnikov 3.00 8.00
TTCHI Patrick Kane
Alex DeBrincat
Dominik Kubalik 4.00 10.00
TTCOL Mikko Rantanen
Cale Makar
Nathan MacKinnon 8.00 20.00
TTEDM Leon Draisaitl
Darnell Nurse
Tyson Barrie 6.00 15.00
TTFLA Spencer Knight
Aleksander Barkov
Jonathan Huberdeau 4.00 10.00
TTLAK Anze Kopitar
Quinton Byfield
Gabe Vilardi 5.00 12.00
TTMON Cole Caufield
Nick Suzuki
Alexander Romanov 8.00 20.00
TTMTL Shea Weber
Carey Price
Tyler Toffoli 4.00 10.00
TTNJD Jack Hughes
Nico Hischier
Mackenzie Blackwood 5.00 12.00
TTNYI Mathew Barzal
Semyon Varlamov
Anders Lee 2.50 6.00
TTNYR Artemi Panarin
Adam Fox
Mika Zibanejad 4.00 10.00
TTOTT Brady Tkachuk
Thomas Chabot
Matt Murray 3.00 8.00
TTPHI Claude Giroux
Jakub Voracek
Sean Couturier 2.00 5.00
TTRDW Moritz Seider
Lucas Raymond
Joe Veleno 6.00 15.00
TTSEA Mark Giordano
Jordan Eberle
Philipp Grubauer 2.00 5.00
TTSEN Shane Pinto
Tim Stutzle
Josh Norris 3.00 8.00
TTSJS William Eklund
Jasper Weatherby
Jonathan Dahlen 5.00 12.00
TTTBL Steven Stamkos
Andrei Vasilevskiy
Victor Hedman 4.00 10.00
TTTML John Tavares
Morgan Rielly
Jack Campbell 3.00 8.00
TTTOR Auston Matthews
Mitch Marner
William Nylander 8.00 20.00
TTVAN Quinn Hughes
Thatcher Demko
Vasily Podkolzin 5.00 12.00
TTVAN Bo Horvat
Brock Boeser
Elias Pettersson 3.00 8.00
TTVGK MarcAndre Fleury
Mark Stone
Max Pacioretty 2.50 6.00
TTWAS Alex Ovechkin
Anthony Mantha
Nicklas Backstrom 8.00 20.00
TTWIN Nikolaj Ehlers
Connor Hellebuyck
Mark Scheifele 4.00 10.00

2021-22 Upper Deck UD3

UD31 Troy Terry 1.50 4.00
UD32 David Pastrnak 5.00 12.00
UD33 Rasmus Dahlin 2.50 6.00
UD34 Matthew Tkachuk 4.00 10.00
UD35 Sebastian Aho 3.00 8.00
UD36 Patrick Kane 4.00 10.00
UD37 Nathan MacKinnon 8.00 20.00
UD38 Jason Robertson 3.00 8.00
UD39 Dylan Larkin 2.50 6.00
UD310 Connor McDavid 10.00 25.00
UD311 Aleksander Barkov 3.00 8.00
UD312 Anze Kopitar 3.00 8.00
UD313 Kirill Kaprizov 6.00 15.00
UD314 Nick Suzuki 4.00 10.00
UD315 Roman Josi 2.00 5.00
UD316 Jack Hughes 5.00 12.00
UD317 Mathew Barzal 2.50 6.00
UD318 Artemi Panarin 4.00 10.00
UD319 Tim Stutzle 2.50 6.00
UD320 Cam Atkinson 2.00 5.00
UD321 Sidney Crosby 8.00 20.00
UD322 Brent Burns 2.00 5.00
UD323 Philipp Grubauer 2.00 5.00
UD324 Jordan Kyrou 2.00 5.00
UD325 Andrei Vasilevskiy 4.00 10.00
UD326 Auston Matthews 8.00 20.00
UD327 Quinn Hughes 5.00 12.00
UD328 Jack Eichel 3.00 8.00
UD329 Alex Ovechkin 8.00 20.00
UD330 Kyle Connor 3.00 8.00
UD331 Trevor Zegras 15.00 40.00
UD332 William Eklund 5.00 12.00
UD333 Anton Lundell 4.00 10.00
UD334 Cole Sillinger 3.00 8.00
UD335 Cole Caufield 15.00 40.00
UD336 Seth Jarvis 5.00 12.00
UD337 Jeremy Swayman 6.00 15.00
UD338 Dawson Mercer 5.00 12.00
UD339 Alex Turcotte 2.50 6.00
UD340 Moritz Seider 15.00 40.00
UD341 Tanner Jeannot 2.00 5.00
UD342 Spencer Knight 4.00 10.00
UD343 Jamie Drysdale 3.00 8.00
UD344 Alexander Holtz 3.00 8.00
UD345 Quinton Byfield 5.00 12.00
UD346 Alex Newhook 3.00 8.00
UD347 Cole Perfetti 4.00 10.00
UD348 Vasily Podkolzin 2.50 6.00
UD349 Mason McTavish 4.00 10.00
UD350 Lucas Raymond 15.00 40.00

2021-22 Upper Deck UD3 Gold

*GOLD/100: 1X TO 2.5X BASIC INSERTS
UD331 Trevor Zegras 50.00 125.00
UD335 Cole Caufield 60.00 150.00
UD340 Moritz Seider 50.00 125.00
UD350 Lucas Raymond 40.00 100.00

2021-22 Upper Deck Work Zone

WZ2 Phil Kessel 1.25 3.00
WZ3 Oliver Ekman-Larsson .75 2.00
WZ4 Brad Marchand 2.50 6.00
WZ5 Charlie McAvoy 1.50 4.00
WZ6 Jack Eichel 2.00 5.00
WZ7 Mark Giordano 1.25 3.00
WZ8 Dougie Hamilton 1.00 2.50
WZ9 Jordan Staal 1.00 2.50
WZ10 Pius Suter 1.00 2.50
WZ11 Kevin Lankinen 1.25 3.00
WZ12 Nathan MacKinnon 5.00 12.00
WZ13 Philipp Grubauer 1.25 3.00
WZ14 Seth Jones 1.25 3.00
WZ15 John Klingberg 1.25 3.00
WZ16 Roope Hintz 1.50 4.00
WZ17 Dylan Larkin 1.50 4.00
WZ18 Tyler Bertuzzi 1.00 2.50
WZ19 Leon Draisaitl 4.00 10.00
WZ20 Darnell Nurse 1.00 2.50
WZ21 Aleksander Barkov 2.00 5.00
WZ22 Keith Yandle .75 2.00
WZ23 Drew Doughty 1.50 4.00
WZ24 Jordan Greenway .75 2.00
WZ25 Shea Weber 1.25 3.00
WZ26 Brendan Gallagher 1.25 3.00
WZ27 Roman Josi 1.25 3.00
WZ28 Mackenzie Blackwood 1.25 3.00
WZ29 Josh Bailey 1.00 2.50
WZ30 Anders Lee 1.00 2.50
WZ31 Alexis Lafreniere 2.00 5.00
WZ32 Brady Tkachuk 2.00 5.00
WZ33 Thomas Chabot 1.25 3.00
WZ34 Claude Giroux 1.25 3.00
WZ35 Ivan Provorov 1.00 2.50
WZ36 Kris Letang 1.50 4.00
WZ37 Logan Couture 1.50 4.00
WZ38 Jordan Binnington 2.00 5.00
WZ39 Anthony Cirelli 1.00 2.50
WZ40 Victor Hedman 1.50 4.00
WZ41 Auston Matthews 5.00 12.00
WZ42 John Tavares 2.00 5.00
WZ43 Thatcher Demko 1.50 4.00
WZ44 Quinn Hughes 3.00 8.00
WZ45 Shea Theodore 1.50 4.00
WZ46 Mark Stone 1.50 4.00
WZ47 Alex Ovechkin 5.00 12.00
WZ48 John Carlson 1.25 3.00
WZ49 Connor Hellebuyck 2.50 6.00
WZ50 Mark Scheifele 2.00 5.00

2022-23 Upper Deck

1 Jamie Drysdale .25 .60
2 Cam Fowler .30 .75
3 Adam Henrique .25 .60
4 Sonny Milano .20 .50
5 Jakob Silfverberg .20 .50
6 Anthony Stolarz .40 1.00
7 Troy Terry .25 .60
8 Lawson Crouse .20 .50
9 Barrett Hayton .30 .75
10 Clayton Keller .40 1.00
11 Nick Schmaltz .25 .60
12 Karel Vejmelka .25 .60
13 Charlie Coyle .30 .75
14 Matt Grzelcyk .25 .60
15 Brad Marchand .60 1.50
16 David Pastrnak .75 2.00
17 Craig Smith .20 .50
18 Linus Ullmark .30 .75
19 Henri Jokiharju .20 .50
20 Casey Mittelstadt .30 .75
21 Kyle Okposo .20 .50
22 Victor Olofsson .30 .75
23 Jeff Skinner .30 .75
24 Alex Tuch .30 .75
25 Rasmus Andersson .25 .60
26 Johnny Gaudreau .50 1.25
27 Oliver Kylington .20 .50
28 Milan Lucic .25 .60
29 Andrew Mangiapane .30 .75
30 Jacob Markstrom .30 .75
31 Tyler Toffoli .30 .75
32 Frederik Andersen .40 1.00
33 Tony DeAngelo .20 .50
34 Jesper Fast .20 .50
35 Martin Necas .50 1.25
36 Brady Skjei .20 .50
37 Andrei Svechnikov .40 1.00
38 Alex DeBrincat .40 1.00
39 Jujhar Khaira .25 .60
40 Philipp Kurashev .25 .60
41 Connor Murphy .25 .60
42 Dylan Strome .40 1.00
43 Jonathan Toews .50 1.25
44 J.T. Compher .25 .60
45 Pavel Francouz .25 .60
46 Samuel Girard .20 .50
47 Erik Johnson .20 .50
48 Gabriel Landeskog .40 1.00
49 Cale Makar .75 2.00
50 Alex Newhook .25 .60
51 Boone Jenner .30 .75
52 Sean Kuraly .20 .50
53 Elvis Merzlikins .30 .75
54 Jack Roslovic .25 .60
55 Cole Sillinger .25 .60
56 Alexandre Texier .20 .50
57 Zach Werenski .50 1.25
58 Denis Gurianov .40 1.00
59 Jani Hakanpaa .25 .60
60 Miro Heiskanen .40 1.00
61 Jason Robertson .50 1.25
62 Ryan Suter .25 .60
63 Filip Hronek .20 .50
64 Dylan Larkin .40 1.00
65 Alex Nedeljkovic .25 .60
66 Lucas Raymond .50 1.25
67 Pius Suter .25 .60
68 Jakub Vrana .25 .60
69 Warren Foegele .20 .50
70 Connor McDavid 1.50 4.00
71 Darnell Nurse .25 .60
72 Stuart Skinner .40 1.00
73 Kailer Yamamoto .30 .75
74 Aleksander Barkov .50 1.25
75 Spencer Knight .30 .75
76 Anton Lundell .30 .75
77 Mason Marchment .25 .60
78 Carter Verhaeghe .30 .75
79 MacKenzie Weegar .25 .60
80 Viktor Arvidsson .20 .50
81 Phillip Danault .30 .75
82 Drew Doughty .40 1.00
83 Sean Durzi .20 .50
84 Trevor Moore .20 .50
85 Cal Petersen .20 .50
86 Jon Merrill .20 .50
87 Jonas Brodin .20 .50
88 Joel Eriksson Ek .25 .60
89 Frederick Gaudreau .20 .50
90 Ryan Hartman .20 .50
91 Cam Talbot .30 .75
92 Mats Zuccarello .30 .75
93 Jake Allen .30 .75
94 Joel Armia .20 .50
95 Cole Caufield .60 1.50
96 Kale Clague .20 .50
97 Jake Evans .20 .50
98 Brendan Gallagher .30 .75
99 Mike Hoffman .30 .75
100 Mattias Ekholm .25 .60
101 Dante Fabbro .20 .50
102 Tanner Jeannot .20 .50
103 Ryan Johansen .25 .60
104 Roman Josi .30 .75
105 Juuse Saros .40 1.00
106 Nathan Bastian .20 .50
107 Jesper Bratt .30 .75
108 Nico Daws .30 .75
109 Nico Hischier .50 1.25
110 Andreas Johnsson .25 .60
111 Damon Severson .20 .50
112 Yegor Sharangovich .30 .75
113 Josh Bailey .25 .60
114 Anthony Beauvillier .25 .60
115 Brock Nelson .30 .75
116 Kyle Palmieri .25 .60
117 Adam Pelech .20 .50
118 Ilya Sorokin .50 1.25
119 Barclay Goodrow .20 .50
120 Chris Kreider .40 1.00
121 Alexis Lafreniere .50 1.25
122 Ryan Reaves .25 .60
123 Igor Shesterkin .60 1.50
124 Jacob Trouba .25 .60
125 Drake Batherson .30 .75
126 Connor Brown .25 .60
127 Alex Formenton .25 .60
128 Anton Forsberg .25 .60
129 Tim Stutzle .40 1.00
130 Artem Zub .20 .50
131 Sean Couturier .25 .60
132 Joel Farabee .30 .75
133 Carter Hart .30 .75
134 Kevin Hayes .25 .60
135 Oskar Lindblom .25 .60
136 Rasmus Ristolainen .20 .50
137 Owen Tippett .20 .50
138 Jeff Carter .25 .60
139 Jake Guentzel .50 1.25
140 Tristan Jarry .30 .75
141 Kasperi Kapanen .25 .60
142 Michael Matheson .20 .50
143 Jonathan Dahlen .20 .50
144 Mario Ferraro .20 .50
145 Kaapo Kahkonen .20 .50
146 Erik Karlsson .40 1.00
147 Timo Meier .30 .75
148 Ryan Donato .25 .60
149 Chris Driedger .25 .60
150 Jared McCann .25 .60
151 Jamie Oleksiak .25 .60
152 Daniel Sprong .20 .50
153 Brandon Tanev .25 .60
154 Alexander Wennberg .20 .50
155 Ivan Barbashev .20 .50
156 Jordan Binnington .50 1.25
157 Pavel Buchnevich .25 .60
158 Justin Faulk .25 .60
159 Jordan Kyrou .30 .75
160 Colton Parayko .25 .60
161 Brandon Saad .25 .60
162 Anthony Cirelli .25 .60
163 Brandon Hagel .25 .60
164 Victor Hedman .40 1.00
165 Alex Killorn .25 .60
166 Brayden Point .40 1.00
167 Mikhail Sergachev .25 .60
168 Alex Kerfoot .25 .60
169 Mitch Marner .50 1.25
170 Jake Muzzin .30 .75
171 William Nylander .60 1.50
172 Morgan Rielly .30 .75
173 Wayne Simmonds .30 .75
174 Thatcher Demko .40 1.00
175 Nils Hoglander .25 .60
176 Quinn Hughes .75 2.00
177 J.T. Miller .40 1.00
178 Tyler Myers .20 .50
179 Tanner Pearson .30 .75
180 Vasily Podkolzin .20 .50
181 William Carrier .20 .50
182 Jack Eichel .50 1.25
183 Robin Lehner .25 .60
184 Chandler Stephenson .25 .60
185 Mark Stone .40 1.00
186 Shea Theodore .40 1.00
187 John Carlson .30 .75
188 Garnet Hathaway .20 .50
189 Anthony Mantha .25 .60
190 T.J. Oshie .30 .75
191 Alex Ovechkin 1.25 3.00
192 Vitek Vanecek .30 .75
193 Mason Appleton .20 .50
194 Morgan Barron .20 .50
195 Kyle Connor .50 1.25
196 Nikolaj Ehlers .30 .75
197 Connor Hellebuyck .60 1.50
198 Neal Pionk .20 .50
199 J.Robertson/I.Shesterkin CL .60 1.50
200 A.Barkov/B.Point CL .50 1.25
201 Matt Boldy YG RC 8.00 20.00
202 Nick Blankenburg YG RC 2.50 6.00
203 Lukas Dostal YG RC 6.00 15.00
204 Jack Quinn YG RC 5.00 12.00
205 Jordan Harris YG RC 4.00 10.00
206 Nathan Smith YG RC 2.50 6.00
207 Hayden Hodgson YG RC 2.50 6.00
208 Erik Kallgren YG RC 3.00 8.00
209 Kent Johnson YG RC 8.00 20.00
210 Thomas Bordeleau YG RC 3.00 8.00
211 Samuel Fagemo YG RC 2.50 6.00
212 Jacob Perreault YG RC 3.00 8.00
213 Matty Beniers YG RC 8.00 20.00
214 Braden Schneider YG RC 5.00 12.00
215 Mark Kastelic YG RC 2.50 6.00
216 Matias Maccelli YG RC 5.00 12.00
217 Linus Sandin YG RC 2.50 6.00
218 Kaedan Korczak YG RC 2.50 6.00
219 Brayden Tracey YG RC 2.50 6.00
220 Marc McLaughlin YG RC 3.00 8.00
221 Jake Christiansen YG RC 3.00 8.00
222 Ben Meyers YG RC 3.00 8.00
223 Johnathan Kovacevic YG RC 3.00 8.00
224 Pyotr Kochetkov YG RC 6.00 15.00
225 Jakub Galvas YG RC 3.00 8.00
226 Jacob Moverare YG RC 2.50 6.00
227 Bobby Brink YG RC 3.00 8.00
228 Owen Power YG RC 6.00 15.00
229 Fredrik Karlstrom YG RC 2.50 6.00
230 Jack McBain YG RC 3.00 8.00
231 Carson Meyer YG RC 2.50 6.00
232 Adam Raska YG RC 3.00 8.00
233 Dylan Samberg YG RC 3.00 8.00
234 Nicholas Abruzzese YG RC 3.00 8.00
235 Lukas Reichel YG RC 6.00 15.00
236 Jack LaFontaine YG RC 3.00 8.00
237 Valtteri Puustinen YG RC 2.50 6.00
238 Jordan Spence YG RC 3.00 8.00
239 Vladislav Kolyachonok YG RC 2.50 6.00
240 Isaac Ratcliffe YG RC 3.00 8.00
241 Trey Fix-Wolansky YG RC 3.00 8.00
242 Zack Hayes YG RC 2.50 6.00
243 Marco Rossi YG RC 8.00 20.00
244 Chase Pearson YG RC 2.50 6.00
245 Mads Sogaard YG RC 4.00 10.00
246 Brayden Pachal YG RC 2.50 6.00
247 Jeff Malott YG RC 2.50 6.00
248 Alex Vlasic YG RC 2.50 6.00
249 Noah Cates YG RC 3.00 8.00
250 M.Boldy/M.Rossi YG CL 6.00 15.00
251 Trevor Zegras .30 .75
252 John Gibson .30 .75
253 Isac Lundestrom .20 .50
254 Sam Carrick .20 .50
255 Derek Grant .20 .50
256 Kevin Shattenkirk .20 .50
257 Shayne Gostisbehere .30 .75
258 Dysin Mayo .20 .50
259 Nick Ritchie .20 .50
260 Travis Boyd .20 .50
261 Janis Moser .20 .50
262 Jakob Chychrun .30 .75
263 Patrice Bergeron .40 1.00
264 Jeremy Swayman .50 1.25
265 Taylor Hall .30 .75
266 Charlie McAvoy .40 1.00
267 Brandon Carlo .25 .60
268 Hampus Lindholm .20 .50
269 Jake DeBrusk .30 .75
270 Peyton Krebs .25 .60
271 Tage Thompson .40 1.00
272 Rasmus Asplund .20 .50
273 Dylan Cozens .30 .75
274 Zemgus Girgensons .20 .50
275 Rasmus Dahlin .40 1.00
276 Trevor Lewis .20 .50
277 Craig Anderson .20 .50
278 Mikael Backlund .20 .50
279 Elias Lindholm .30 .75
280 Noah Hanifin .30 .75
281 Blake Coleman .25 .60
282 Dan Vladar .25 .60
283 Dillon Dube .20 .50
284 Teuvo Teravainen .30 .75
285 Sebastian Aho .50 1.25
286 Jaccob Slavin .30 .75
287 Seth Jarvis .40 1.00
288 Jesperi Kotkaniemi .30 .75
289 Jordan Staal .25 .60
290 Patrick Kane .60 1.50
291 Seth Jones .30 .75
292 Jake McCabe .20 .50
293 Taylor Raddysh .30 .75
294 Caleb Jones .20 .50
295 MacKenzie Entwistle .20 .50
296 Mikko Rantanen .75 2.00
297 Nathan MacKinnon 1.25 3.00
298 Artturi Lehkonen .25 .60
299 Devon Toews .25 .60
300 Bowen Byram .40 1.00
301 Valeri Nichushkin .30 .75
302 Jakub Voracek .25 .60
303 Patrik Laine .40 1.00
304 Gustav Nyquist .20 .50
305 Vladislav Gavrikov .20 .50
306 Tyler Seguin .40 1.00
307 Eric Robertson .25 .60
308 Jamie Benn .30 .75
309 Roope Hintz .40 1.00
310 Joe Pavelski .40 1.00
311 Jake Oettinger .50 1.25
312 Moritz Seider .40 1.00
313 Jacob Peterson .20 .50
314 Robby Fabbri .20 .50
315 Tyler Bertuzzi .25 .60
316 Filip Zadina .25 .60
317 Michael Rasmussen .20 .50

318 Evan Bouchard .40 1.00
319 Leon Draisaitl 1.00 2.50
320 Zach Hyman .50 1.25
321 Evander Kane .30 .75
322 Tyson Barrie .20 .50
323 Jesse Puljujarvi .30 .75
324 Ryan Nugent-Hopkins .40 1.00
325 Sergei Bobrovsky .50 1.25
326 Sam Bennett .50 1.25
327 Anthony Duclair .25 .60
328 Aaron Ekblad .40 1.00
329 Sam Reinhart .60 1.50
330 Brandon Montour .40 1.00
331 Patric Hornqvist .20 .50
332 Adrian Kempe .30 .75
333 Anze Kopitar .50 1.25
334 Matt Roy .20 .50
335 Alex Iafallo .20 .50
336 Arthur Kaliyev .30 .75
337 Quinton Byfield .40 1.00
338 Marcus Foligno .25 .60
339 Jonathan Quick .40 1.00
340 Jordan Greenway .20 .50
341 Kirill Kaprizov 1.00 2.50
342 Marc-Andre Fleury .60 1.50
343 Jared Spurgeon .30 .75
344 Nick Suzuki .60 1.50
345 Matt Dumba .20 .50
346 Justin Barron .25 .60
347 Carey Price .60 1.50
348 Rem Pitlick .20 .50
349 Josh Anderson .25 .60
350 Mikael Granlund .25 .60
351 Paul Byron .20 .50
352 Alexandre Carrier .20 .50
353 Matt Duchene .30 .75
354 Yakov Trenin .20 .50
355 Philip Tomasino .20 .50
356 Dawson Mercer .40 1.00
357 Eeli Tolvanen .30 .75
358 Dougie Hamilton .25 .60
359 Filip Forsberg .50 1.25
360 Jesper Boqvist .20 .50
361 Jack Hughes .75 2.00
362 Anders Lee .25 .60
363 Tomas Tatar .20 .50
364 Ryan Pulock .25 .60
365 Mathew Barzal .40 1.00
366 Noah Dobson .40 1.00
367 Jean-Gabriel Pageau .20 .50
368 Artemi Panarin .60 1.50
369 Semyon Varlamov .30 .75
370 Kaapo Kakko .25 .60
371 Mika Zibanejad .40 1.00
372 K'Andre Miller .25 .60
373 Adam Fox .40 1.00
374 Josh Norris .30 .75
375 Filip Chytil .25 .60
376 Travis Hamonic .25 .60
377 Brady Tkachuk .50 1.25
378 Austin Watson .20 .50
379 Mathieu Joseph .20 .50
380 Travis Konecny .30 .75
381 Thomas Chabot .30 .75
382 Ivan Provorov .25 .60
383 Cam Atkinson .30 .75
384 Scott Laughton .20 .50
385 James van Riemsdyk .25 .60
386 Bryan Rust .30 .75
387 Sidney Crosby 1.25 3.00
388 Kris Letang .40 1.00
389 Teddy Blueger .20 .50
390 Rickard Rakell .25 .60
391 Danton Heinen .20 .50
392 Evgeni Malkin .60 1.50
393 Tomas Hertl .30 .75
394 James Reimer .20 .50
395 Nick Bonino .20 .50
396 Logan Couture .40 1.00
397 William Eklund .40 1.00
398 Alexander Barabanov .20 .50
399 Jordan Eberle .30 .75
400 Adam Larsson .30 .75
401 Jaden Schwartz .25 .60
402 Yanni Gourde .25 .60
403 Vince Dunn .25 .60
404 Vladimir Tarasenko .40 1.00
405 Ryan O'Reilly .30 .75
406 Torey Krug .25 .60
407 Brayden Schenn .30 .75
408 Scott Perunovich .20 .50
409 Nick Leddy .20 .50
410 Robert Thomas .30 .75
411 Andrei Vasilevskiy .50 1.25
412 Steven Stamkos .60 1.50
413 Nikita Kucherov .60 1.50
414 Corey Perry .50 1.25
415 Ross Colton .25 .60
416 Nick Paul .20 .50
417 Auston Matthews 1.25 3.00
418 Erik Cernak .20 .50
419 Michael Bunting .30 .75
420 John Tavares .50 1.25
421 Mark Giordano .30 .75
422 T.J. Brodie .20 .50
423 David Kampf .20 .50
424 Pierre Engvall .20 .50
425 Elias Pettersson .50 1.25
426 Oliver Ekman-Larsson .20 .50
427 Conor Garland .25 .60
428 Bo Horvat .40 1.00
429 Brock Boeser .40 1.00
430 William Karlsson .40 1.00
431 Jonathan Marchessault .40 1.00
432 Alec Martinez .20 .50
433 Alex Pietrangelo .25 .60
434 Nicolas Roy .20 .50
435 Keegan Kolesar .20 .50
436 Reilly Smith .30 .75
437 Evgeny Kuznetsov .40 1.00
438 Conor Sheary .30 .75
439 Tom Wilson .30 .75
440 Nic Dowd .20 .50
441 Lars Eller .20 .50
442 Dmitry Orlov .30 .75
443 Mark Scheifele .50 1.25
444 Pierre-Luc Dubois .25 .60
445 Blake Wheeler .30 .75
446 Josh Morrissey .40 1.00
447 Nate Schmidt .20 .50
448 Adam Lowry .25 .60
449 N.MacKinnon/L.Draisaitl CL 1.25 3.00
450 C.McAvoy/M.Seider CL .40 1.00
451 Juraj Slafkovsky YG RC 20.00 50.00
452 Pavol Regenda YG RC 3.00 8.00
453 Samuel Poulin YG RC 4.00 10.00
454 Nils Aman YG RC 3.00 8.00
455 Brandon Biro YG RC 5.00 12.00
456 Jayden Halbgewachs YG RC 3.00 8.00
457 Michael Eyssimont YG RC 3.00 8.00
458 Cole Reinhardt YG RC 3.00 8.00
459 Wyatt Johnston YG RC 12.00 30.00
460 Brandon Baddock YG RC 3.00 8.00
461 Dylan Holloway YG RC 6.00 15.00
462 Mitchell Chaffee YG RC 2.50 6.00
463 Bokondji Imama YG RC 2.50 6.00
464 Nikita Okhotiuk YG RC 2.50 6.00
465 Andrei Kuzmenko YG RC 4.00 10.00
466 Jake Sanderson YG RC 8.00 20.00
467 Ben Jones YG RC 4.00 10.00
468 Jakub Lauko YG RC 4.00 10.00
469 Filip Roos YG RC 2.50 6.00
470 Brandt Clarke YG RC 6.00 15.00
471 Viktor Lodin YG RC 3.00 8.00
472 David Jiricek YG RC 6.00 15.00
473 Corey Schueneman YG RC 4.00 10.00
474 Olle Lycksell YG RC 3.00 8.00
475 Shane Wright YG RC 8.00 20.00
476 Hunter Drew YG RC 3.00 8.00
477 Filip Hallander YG RC 3.00 8.00
478 Nick Perbix YG RC 2.50 6.00
479 Linus Hogberg YG RC 2.50 6.00
480 Kaiden Guhle YG RC 6.00 15.00
481 Kevin Mandolese YG RC 3.00 8.00
482 Lucas Johansen YG RC 2.50 6.00
483 Reilly Walsh YG RC 3.00 8.00
484 Cole Koepke YG RC 3.00 8.00
485 Grant Hutton YG RC 3.00 8.00
486 Declan Chisholm YG RC 3.00 8.00
487 Dmitri Samorukov YG RC 2.50 6.00
488 Jon Lizotte YG RC 2.50 6.00
489 Elmer Soderblom YG RC 6.00 15.00
490 Arber Xhekaj YG RC 8.00 20.00
491 Michael Carcone YG RC 2.50 6.00
492 Adam Huska YG RC 3.00 8.00
493 Filip Kral YG RC 4.00 10.00
494 Ethan Prow YG RC 3.00 8.00
495 Ronnie Attard YG RC 3.00 8.00
496 Jesper Froden YG RC 3.00 8.00
497 Dylan Guenther YG RC 10.00 25.00
498 Casey Fitzgerald YG RC 2.50 6.00
499 Buoy the Mascot YG 5.00 12.00
500 J.Slafkovsky/S.Wright YG CL 6.00 15.00
501 Frank Vatrano .25 .60
502 John Klingberg .30 .75
503 Dmitry Kulikov .20 .50
504 Ryan Strome .30 .75
505 Simon Benoit .20 .50
506 Maxime Comtois .25 .60
507 Zack Kassian .20 .50
508 Nick Bjugstad .20 .50
509 Josh Brown .25 .60
510 Troy Stecher .20 .50
511 Patrik Nemeth .25 .60
512 Pavel Zacha .25 .60
513 David Krejci .30 .75
514 Anton Stralman .20 .50
515 Nick Foligno .20 .50
516 Trent Frederic .20 .50
517 Ilya Lyubushkin .20 .50
518 Mattias Samuelsson .20 .50
519 Eric Comrie .20 .50
520 Jonathan Huberdeau .40 1.00
521 MacKenzie Weegar .25 .60
522 Nazem Kadri .40 1.00
523 Nicolas Meloche .25 .60
524 Nikita Zadorov .20 .50
525 Brent Burns .30 .75
526 Paul Stastny .25 .60
527 Jordan Martinook .20 .50
528 Antti Raanta .30 .75
529 Calvin de Haan .20 .50
530 Derek Stepan .20 .50
531 Petr Mrazek .25 .60
532 Max Domi .30 .75
533 Andreas Athanasiou .25 .60
534 Colin Blackwell .25 .60
535 Alexandar Georgiev .30 .75
536 Evan Rodrigues .25 .60
537 Josh Manson .20 .50
538 Logan O'Connor .30 .75
539 Andrew Cogliano .20 .50
540 Johnny Gaudreau .50 1.25
541 Erik Gudbranson .20 .50
542 Yegor Chinakhov .25 .60
543 Adam Boqvist .20 .50
544 Mason Marchment .25 .60
545 Colin Miller .20 .50
546 Nils Lundkvist .20 .50
547 Scott Wedgewood .25 .60
548 Luke Glendening .20 .50
549 Ville Husso .20 .50
550 Andrew Copp .20 .50
551 David Perron .25 .60
552 Dominik Kubalik .30 .75
553 Olli Maatta .20 .50
554 Ben Chiarot .20 .50
555 Joe Veleno .25 .60
556 Jack Campbell .30 .75
557 Ryan Murray .25 .60
558 Cody Ceci .20 .50
559 Derek Ryan .20 .50
560 Brett Kulak .20 .50
561 Matthew Tkachuk .60 1.50
562 Marc Staal .20 .50
563 Eric Staal .30 .75
564 Josh Mahura .20 .50
565 Gustav Forsling .30 .75
566 Kevin Fiala .25 .60
567 Gabe Vilardi .30 .75
568 Mikey Anderson .25 .60
569 Filip Gustavsson .30 .75
570 Sam Steel .25 .60
571 Jacob Middleton .20 .50
572 Alex Goligoski .25 .60
573 Mason Shaw .20 .50
574 Kirby Dach .30 .75
575 Evgenii Dadonov .20 .50
576 Michael Matheson .20 .50
577 Sean Monahan .20 .50
578 Ryan McDonagh .20 .50
579 Nino Niederreiter .20 .50
580 Colton Sissons .20 .50
581 Vitek Vanecek .30 .75
582 Ondrej Palat .25 .60
583 Erik Haula .20 .50
584 Brendan Smith .20 .50
585 John Marino .30 .75
586 Fabian Zetterlund .20 .50
587 Alexander Romanov .25 .60
588 Zach Parise .30 .75
589 Oliver Wahlstrom .20 .50
590 Casey Cizikas .25 .60
591 Vincent Trocheck .30 .75
592 Jaroslav Halak .30 .75
593 Ryan Carpenter .20 .50
594 Jimmy Vesey .25 .60
595 Vitali Kravtsov .25 .60
596 Ryan Lindgren .20 .50
597 Alex DeBrincat .40 1.00
598 Cam Talbot .30 .75
599 Claude Giroux .30 .75
600 Tyler Motte .25 .60
601 Derick Brassard .20 .50
602 Erik Brannstrom .20 .50
603 Tony DeAngelo .20 .50
604 Nicolas Deslauriers .20 .50
605 Justin Braun .20 .50
606 Travis Sanheim .20 .50
607 Jan Rutta .20 .50
608 Jeff Petry .30 .75
609 Chad Ruhwedel .20 .50
610 Brock McGinn .20 .50
611 Jason Zucker .30 .75
612 Luke Kunin .20 .50
613 Steven Lorentz .20 .50
614 Oskar Lindblom .25 .60
615 Nico Sturm .20 .50
616 Evgeny Svechnikov .20 .50
617 Oliver Bjorkstrand .25 .60
618 Andre Burakovsky .20 .50
619 Justin Schultz .25 .60
620 Martin Jones .25 .60
621 Daniel Sprong .20 .50
622 Philipp Grubauer .30 .75
623 Morgan Geekie .20 .50
624 Thomas Greiss .25 .60
625 Noel Acciari .20 .50
626 Vladislav Namestnikov .20 .50
627 Patrick Maroon .20 .50
628 Ilya Samsonov .30 .75
629 Calle Jarnkrok .20 .50
630 Matt Murray .30 .75
631 Zach Aston-Reese .20 .50
632 Justin Holl .20 .50
633 Timothy Liljegren .20 .50
634 Rasmus Sandin .25 .60
635 Ilya Mikheyev .25 .60
636 Curtis Lazar .20 .50
637 Dakota Joshua .20 .50
638 Ethan Bear .20 .50
639 Luke Schenn .30 .75
640 Travis Dermott .25 .60
641 Phil Kessel .30 .75
642 Adin Hill .30 .75
643 Ben Hutton .20 .50
644 Darcy Kuemper .30 .75
645 Erik Gustafsson .20 .50
646 Dylan Strome .40 1.00
647 Sonny Milano .25 .60
648 Aliaksei Protas .20 .50
649 Marcus Johansson .20 .50
650 David Rittich .20 .50
651 Sam Gagner .20 .50
652 Axel Jonsson-Fjallby .20 .50
653 David Gustafsson .30 .75
654 Patrice Bergeron AS .40 1.00
655 Rasmus Dahlin AS .40 1.00
656 Dylan Larkin AS .40 1.00
657 Nick Suzuki AS .60 1.50
658 Brady Tkachuk AS .50 1.25
659 Auston Matthews AS 1.25 3.00
660 Steven Stamkos AS .60 1.50
661 Jonathan Huberdeau AS .40 1.00
662 Victor Hedman AS .40 1.00
663 Jack Campbell AS .30 .75
664 Andrei Vasilevskiy AS .50 1.25
665 Clayton Keller AS .40 1.00
666 Kirill Kaprizov AS 1.00 2.50
667 Cale Makar AS .75 2.00
668 Roman Josi AS .30 .75
669 Joe Pavelski AS .40 1.00
670 Juuse Saros AS .40 1.00
671 Kyle Connor AS .50 1.25
672 Jordan Kyrou AS .30 .75
673 Nazem Kadri AS .40 1.00
674 Alex DeBrincat AS .40 1.00
675 Cam Talbot AS .30 .75
676 Frederik Andersen AS .40 1.00
677 Sebastian Aho AS .50 1.25
678 Jack Hughes AS .75 2.00
679 Zach Werenski AS .50 1.25
680 Adam Pelech AS .20 .50
681 Jake Guentzel AS .50 1.25
682 Chris Kreider AS .40 1.00
683 Tristan Jarry AS .30 .75
684 Claude Giroux AS .30 .75
685 Evgeny Kuznetsov AS .40 1.00
686 Tom Wilson AS .30 .75
687 Troy Terry AS .25 .60
688 John Gibson AS .30 .75
689 Connor McDavid AS 1.50 4.00
690 Leon Draisaitl AS 1.00 2.50
691 Adrian Kempe AS .30 .75
692 Timo Meier AS .30 .75
693 Jordan Eberle AS .30 .75
694 Jonathan Marchessault AS .40 1.00
695 Thatcher Demko AS .40 1.00
696 Johnny Gaudreau AS .50 1.25
697 Mark Stone AS .40 1.00
698 Alex Pietrangelo AS .25 .60
699 M.Tkachuk/N.Niederreiter CL .60 1.50
700 N.Kadri/J.Gaudreau CL .50 1.25
701 Nick DeSimone YG RC 3.00 8.00
702 Dylan Wells YG RC 3.00 8.00
703 Marcus Bjork YG RC 3.00 8.00
704 Matej Blumel YG RC 4.00 10.00
705 Jonatan Berggren YG RC 10.00 25.00
706 Juuso Parssinen YG RC 3.00 8.00
707 Nick Cicek YG RC 3.00 8.00
708 Nikita Alexandrov YG RC 3.00 8.00
709 Pontus Holmberg YG RC 3.00 8.00
710 Fredrik Olofsson YG RC 3.00 8.00
711 Tyler Tucker YG RC 3.00 8.00
712 Oskar Olausson YG RC 3.00 8.00
713 Simon Holmstrom YG RC 3.00 8.00
714 Mac Hollowell YG RC 3.00 8.00
715 James Hamblin YG RC 3.00 8.00
716 Jean-Luc Foudy YG RC 3.00 8.00
717 William Bitten YG RC 3.00 8.00
718 Kirill Marchenko YG RC 12.00 30.00
719 Semyon Der-Arguchintsev YG RC 3.00 8.00
720 Tim Berni YG RC 3.00 8.00
721 Callahan Burke YG RC 3.00 8.00
722 Eetu Makiniemi YG RC 3.00 8.00
723 Samuel Walker YG RC 3.00 8.00
724 Jake Lucchini YG RC 3.00 8.00
725 Justin Kirkland YG RC 3.00 8.00
726 Parker Wotherspoon YG RC 3.00 8.00
727 Samuel Ersson YG RC 10.00 25.00
728 Aatu Raty YG RC 3.00 8.00
729 Anton Levtchi YG RC 3.00 8.00
730 J.Berggren/P.Holmberg YG CL 4.00 10.00
731 David Jiricek 1R 2.50 6.00
732 Matty Beniers 1R 3.00 8.00
733 Brandt Clarke 1R 2.50 6.00
734 Marco Rossi 1R 3.00 8.00
735 Kaiden Guhle 1R 2.50 6.00
736 Dylan Holloway 1R 2.50 6.00
737 Braden Schneider 1R 2.00 5.00
738 Samuel Poulin 1R 1.50 4.00
739 Jake Sanderson 1R 3.00 8.00
740 Dylan Guenther 1R 3.00 8.00
741 Lukas Reichel 1R 2.50 6.00
742 Shane Wright 1R 3.00 8.00
743 Kent Johnson 1R 2.50 6.00
744 Jack Quinn 1R 2.00 5.00
745 Matt Boldy 1R 4.00 10.00
746 Oskar Olausson 1R 1.25 3.00
747 Wyatt Johnston 1R 5.00 12.00
748 Simon Holmstrom 1R 1.25 3.00
749 Juraj Slafkovsky 1R 6.00 15.00
750 Owen Power 1R 2.50 6.00

2022-23 Upper Deck Clear Cut Parallel

*CLEAR CUT VETS: 6X TO 15X BASIC
*CLEAR CUT YG/1R: 2.5X TO 6X BASIC
201 Matt Boldy YG 80.00 200.00
204 Jack Quinn YG 30.00 80.00
209 Kent Johnson YG 60.00 150.00
213 Matty Beniers YG 100.00 250.00
224 Pyotr Kochetkov YG 80.00 200.00
228 Owen Power YG 60.00 150.00
243 Marco Rossi YG 100.00 250.00
451 Juraj Slafkovsky YG 150.00 400.00
459 Wyatt Johnston YG 125.00 300.00
461 Dylan Holloway YG 80.00 200.00
465 Andrei Kuzmenko YG 30.00 80.00
466 Jake Sanderson YG 50.00 125.00
475 Shane Wright YG 100.00 250.00
480 Kaiden Guhle YG 40.00 100.00
490 Arber Xhekaj YG 80.00 200.00
497 Dylan Guenther YG 125.00 300.00
499 Buoy the Mascot YG 40.00 100.00
705 Jonatan Berggren YG 80.00 200.00
718 Kirill Marchenko YG 30.00 80.00
727 Samuel Ersson YG 50.00 125.00
730 Jonatan Berggren
Pontus Holmberg CL 15.00 40.00
732 Matty Beniers 1R 50.00 125.00
749 Juraj Slafkovsky 1R 50.00 125.00

2022-23 Upper Deck Exclusives

*EXCL.VETS/YG: 3X TO 8X BASIC
*EXCL.1R: 5X TO 12X BASIC
201 Matt Boldy YG 125.00 300.00
204 Jack Quinn YG 60.00 150.00
209 Kent Johnson YG 150.00 400.00
213 Matty Beniers YG 150.00 400.00
224 Pyotr Kochetkov YG 125.00 300.00
228 Owen Power YG 125.00 300.00
243 Marco Rossi YG 150.00 400.00
451 Juraj Slafkovsky YG 250.00 600.00
459 Wyatt Johnston YG 200.00 500.00
461 Dylan Holloway YG 100.00 250.00
465 Andrei Kuzmenko YG 60.00 150.00
466 Jake Sanderson YG 100.00 250.00
475 Shane Wright YG 150.00 400.00
480 Kaiden Guhle YG 100.00 250.00
490 Arber Xhekaj YG 125.00 300.00
497 Dylan Guenther YG 150.00 400.00
500 Juraj Slafkovsky
Shane Wright YG CL 20.00 50.00
705 Jonatan Berggren YG 50.00 125.00
718 Kirill Marchenko YG 100.00 250.00
730 Jonatan Berggren
Pontus Holmberg CL 20.00 50.00
732 Matty Beniers 1R 15.00 40.00
749 Juraj Slafkovsky 1R 80.00 200.00

2022-23 Upper Deck French

*FRENCH VETS: 2X TO 5X BASIC
*FRENCH YG/1R: .75X TO 2X BASIC
201 Matt Boldy YG 12.00 30.00
204 Jack Quinn YG 10.00 25.00
209 Kent Johnson YG 20.00 50.00
224 Pyotr Kochetkov YG 40.00 100.00
228 Owen Power YG 12.00 30.00
451 Juraj Slafkovsky YG 30.00 80.00
459 Wyatt Johnston YG 25.00 60.00
461 Dylan Holloway YG 15.00 40.00
465 Andrei Kuzmenko YG 12.00 30.00
466 Jake Sanderson YG 15.00 40.00
475 Shane Wright YG 20.00 50.00
480 Kaiden Guhle YG 12.00 30.00
490 Arber Xhekaj YG 25.00 60.00
497 Dylan Guenther YG 15.00 40.00
499 Buoy the Mascot YG 20.00 50.00
500 Juraj Slafkovsky
Shane Wright YG CL 8.00 20.00
705 Jonatan Berggren YG 20.00 50.00
718 Kirill Marchenko YG 20.00 50.00
730 Jonatan Berggren
Pontus Holmberg CL 8.00 20.00
732 Matty Beniers 1R 20.00 50.00

2022-23 Upper Deck '06-07 Black Diamond Retro

*RUBY/100: 2X TO 5X BASIC 1.00 2.50
BD1 Sam Reinhart 2.00 5.00
BD2 Michael Bunting 1.00 2.50
BD3 Jordan Kyrou 1.00 2.50
BD4 Tim Stutzle 1.25 3.00
BD5 Jake Oettinger 1.50 4.00
BD6 Tage Thompson 1.25 3.00
BD7 J.T. Miller 1.25 3.00
BD8 Marco Rossi 2.50 6.00
BD9 David Jiricek 2.00 5.00
BD10 Braden Schneider 1.50 4.00
BD11 Kaiden Guhle 2.00 5.00
BD12 Elmer Soderblom 2.00 5.00
BD13 Thomas Bordeleau 1.00 2.50
BD14 Dylan Holloway 2.00 5.00
BD15 David Pastrnak 2.50 6.00
BD16 Andrei Vasilevskiy 1.50 4.00
BD17 Cole Caufield 2.00 5.00
BD18 Trevor Zegras 1.00 2.50
BD19 Brad Marchand 2.00 5.00
BD20 Alexis Lafreniere 1.50 4.00
BD21 Mikko Rantanen 2.50 6.00
BD22 Lukas Dostal 2.00 5.00
BD23 Jonatan Berggren 1.50 4.00
BD24 Lukas Reichel 2.00 5.00
BD25 Brandt Clarke 2.00 5.00
BD26 Jake Sanderson 2.50 6.00
BD27 Oskar Olausson 1.00 2.50
BD28 Wyatt Johnston 4.00 10.00
BD29 Nathan MacKinnon 4.00 10.00
BD30 Patrick Kane 2.00 5.00
BD31 Jason Robertson 1.50 4.00
BD32 Leon Draisaitl 3.00 8.00
BD33 Cale Makar 2.50 6.00
BD34 Sidney Crosby 4.00 10.00
BD35 Jack Quinn 1.50 4.00
BD36 Andrei Kuzmenko 2.00 5.00
BD37 Dylan Guenther 2.50 6.00
BD38 Kent Johnson 2.00 5.00
BD39 Owen Power 2.00 5.00
BD40 Matt Boldy 3.00 8.00
BD41 Alex Ovechkin 4.00 10.00
BD42 Auston Matthews 4.00 10.00
BD43 Connor McDavid 5.00 12.00
BD44 Shane Wright 2.50 6.00
BD45 Juraj Slafkovsky 5.00 12.00
BD46 Matty Beniers 2.50 6.00

2022-23 Upper Deck '07-08 Upper Deck Retro

T1 Troy Terry .40 1.00
T2 Trevor Zegras .50 1.25
T3 Clayton Keller .60 1.50
T4 Shayne Gostisbehere .50 1.25
T5 David Pastrnak 1.25 3.00
T6 Charlie Coyle .50 1.25
T7 Patrice Bergeron .60 1.50
T8 Tage Thompson .60 1.50
T9 Victor Olofsson .50 1.25
T10 Nazem Kadri .60 1.50
T11 Tyler Toffoli .50 1.25
T12 Jonathan Huberdeau .60 1.50
T13 Sebastian Aho .75 2.00
T14 Martin Necas .75 2.00
T15 Patrick Kane 1.00 2.50
T16 Max Domi .50 1.25
T17 Mikko Rantanen 1.25 3.00
T18 Cale Makar 1.25 3.00
T19 Nathan MacKinnon 2.00 5.00
T20 Johnny Gaudreau .75 2.00
T21 Patrik Laine .60 1.50
T22 Jason Robertson .75 2.00
T23 Roope Hintz .60 1.50
T24 Dylan Larkin .60 1.50
T25 Dominik Kubalik .50 1.25
T26 Connor McDavid 2.50 6.00
T27 Leon Draisaitl 1.50 4.00
T28 Aleksander Barkov .75 2.00
T29 Carter Verhaeghe .50 1.25
T30 Matthew Tkachuk 1.00 2.50
T31 Kevin Fiala .40 1.00
T32 Adrian Kempe .50 1.25
T33 Anze Kopitar .75 2.00
T34 Kirill Kaprizov 1.50 4.00
T35 Mats Zuccarello .50 1.25
T36 Cole Caufield 1.00 2.50
T37 Nick Suzuki 1.00 2.50
T38 Nino Niederreiter .30 .75
T39 Roman Josi .50 1.25
T40 Jack Hughes 1.25 3.00
T41 Nico Hischier .75 2.00
T42 Ilya Sorokin .75 2.00
T43 Mathew Barzal .60 1.50
T44 Igor Shesterkin 1.00 2.50
T45 Artemi Panarin 1.00 2.50
T46 Brady Tkachuk .75 2.00
T47 Tim Stutzle .60 1.50
T48 Carter Hart .50 1.25
T49 Travis Konecny .50 1.25
T50 Sidney Crosby 2.00 5.00
T51 Evgeni Malkin 1.00 2.50
T52 Erik Karlsson .60 1.50
T53 Timo Meier .50 1.25
T54 Andre Burakovsky .30 .75
T55 Jordan Eberle .50 1.25
T56 Jordan Kyrou .50 1.25
T57 Robert Thomas .50 1.25
T58 Vladimir Tarasenko .60 1.50
T59 Steven Stamkos 1.00 2.50
T60 Nikita Kucherov 1.00 2.50
T61 Andrei Vasilevskiy .75 2.00
T62 Auston Matthews 2.00 5.00
T63 Mitch Marner .75 2.00
T64 William Nylander 1.00 2.50
T65 Elias Pettersson .75 2.00
T66 Bo Horvat .60 1.50
T67 Quinn Hughes 1.25 3.00
T68 Logan Thompson .60 1.50
T69 Jack Eichel .75 2.00
T70 Jonathan Marchessault .60 1.50
T71 Alex Ovechkin 2.00 5.00
T72 Dylan Strome .60 1.50
T73 Connor Hellebuyck 1.00 2.50
T74 Mark Scheifele .75 2.00
T75 Kyle Connor .75 2.00
T76 Matias Maccelli YG 5.00 12.00
T77 Dylan Guenther YG 8.00 20.00
T78 Owen Power YG 6.00 15.00
T79 Jack Quinn YG 5.00 12.00
T80 Pyotr Kochetkov YG 6.00 15.00
T81 Lukas Reichel YG 6.00 15.00
T82 Kent Johnson YG 6.00 15.00
T83 David Jiricek YG 6.00 15.00
T84 Wyatt Johnston YG 12.00 30.00
T85 Matej Blumel YG 4.00 10.00
T86 Elmer Soderblom YG 6.00 15.00
T87 Dylan Holloway YG 6.00 15.00
T88 Marco Rossi YG 8.00 20.00
T89 Matt Boldy YG 10.00 25.00
T90 Juraj Slafkovsky YG 15.00 40.00
T91 Kaiden Guhle YG 6.00 15.00
T92 Arber Xhekaj YG 6.00 15.00
T93 Jake Sanderson YG 8.00 20.00
T94 Noah Cates YG 3.00 8.00
T95 Samuel Poulin YG 4.00 10.00
T96 Matty Beniers YG 8.00 20.00
T97 Shane Wright YG 8.00 20.00
T98 Nick Perbix YG 2.50 6.00
T99 Erik Kallgren YG 3.00 8.00
T100 Andrei Kuzmenko YG 6.00 15.00

2022-23 Upper Deck '07-08 Upper Deck Retro Exclusives

*EXCLUSIVES: .75X TO 2X BASIC
*EXCL.YG: 1.2X TO 3X BASIC
T76 Matias Maccelli YG 20.00 50.00
T78 Owen Power YG 50.00 125.00
T79 Jack Quinn YG 15.00 40.00
T80 Pyotr Kochetkov YG 30.00 80.00
T81 Lukas Reichel YG 60.00 150.00
T86 Elmer Soderblom YG 20.00 50.00
T87 Dylan Holloway YG 12.00 30.00
T88 Marco Rossi YG 40.00 100.00
T89 Matt Boldy YG 60.00 150.00
T91 Kaiden Guhle YG 40.00 100.00
T92 Arber Xhekaj YG 50.00 125.00
T93 Jake Sanderson YG 40.00 100.00
T94 Noah Cates YG 12.00 30.00
T95 Samuel Poulin YG 20.00 50.00
T96 Matty Beniers YG 150.00 400.00
T97 Shane Wright YG 40.00 100.00
T98 Nick Perbix YG 40.00 100.00
T100 Andrei Kuzmenko YG 40.00 100.00

2022-23 Upper Deck '22-23 Rookie Class

*RED: .75X TO 2X BASIC
RC1 Matt Boldy 1.50 4.00
RC2 Ben Meyers .50 1.25
RC3 Nathan Smith .40 1.00
RC4 Noah Cates .50 1.25
RC5 Matty Beniers 1.25 3.00
RC6 Jordan Spence .50 1.25
RC7 Thomas Bordeleau .50 1.25
RC8 Marco Rossi 1.25 3.00
RC9 Nick Blankenburg .40 1.00
RC10 Erik Kallgren .50 1.25
RC11 Kent Johnson 1.00 2.50
RC12 Braden Schneider .75 2.00
RC13 Marc McLaughlin .50 1.25
RC14 Lukas Reichel 1.00 2.50
RC15 Owen Power 1.00 2.50
RC16 Shane Wright 1.25 3.00
RC17 Jack Quinn .75 2.00
RC18 Dylan Holloway 1.00 2.50
RC19 Jack McBain .50 1.25
RC20 Wyatt Johnston 2.00 5.00
RC21 Mads Sogaard .60 1.50
RC22 Nick Abruzzese .50 1.25
RC23 Pavol Regenda .50 1.25
RC24 Dylan Guenther 1.25 3.00
RC25 Jordan Harris .60 1.50
RC26 Brandt Clarke 1.00 2.50
RC27 Andrei Kuzmenko 1.00 2.50
RC28 Jake Sanderson 1.25 3.00
RC29 Matias Maccelli .75 2.00
RC30 Juraj Slafkovsky 2.50 6.00

2022-23 Upper Deck '94-95 Rookie Die Cuts

*RED: 1X TO 2.5X BASIC
RDT1 Marco Rossi 1.50 4.00
RDT2 Owen Power 1.25 3.00
RDT3 Matty Beniers 1.50 4.00
RDT4 Kent Johnson 1.25 3.00
RDT5 Lukas Reichel 1.25 3.00
RDT6 Noah Cates .60 1.50
RDT7 Marc McLaughlin .60 1.50
RDT8 Jordan Spence .60 1.50
RDT9 Thomas Bordeleau .60 1.50
RDT10 Matt Boldy 2.00 5.00
RDT11 Jack McBain .60 1.50
RDT12 Andrei Kuzmenko 1.25 3.00
RDT13 Dylan Holloway 1.25 3.00
RDT14 Juraj Slafkovsky 3.00 8.00
RDT15 Jake Sanderson 1.50 4.00
RDT16 Brandt Clarke 1.25 3.00
RDT17 Dylan Guenther 1.50 4.00
RDT18 Wyatt Johnston 2.50 6.00
RDT19 Shane Wright 1.50 4.00
RDT20 Nick Abruzzese .60 1.50

2022-23 Upper Deck '97 Collectors Choice Commemorative

COMMON CARD 1.00 2.50
SEMISTARS 1.25 3.00
UNLISTED STARS 1.50 4.00
CMAK1 Andrei Kuzmenko 3.00 8.00
CMAK2 Andrei Kuzmenko 3.00 8.00
CMAK3 Andrei Kuzmenko 3.00 8.00
CMAM1 Auston Matthews 6.00 15.00
CMAM2 Auston Matthews 6.00 15.00
CMAM3 Auston Matthews 6.00 15.00
CMAO1 Alex Ovechkin 6.00 15.00
CMAO2 Alex Ovechkin 6.00 15.00
CMAO3 Alex Ovechkin 6.00 15.00
CMBE1 Matty Beniers 4.00 10.00
CMBE2 Matty Beniers 4.00 10.00
CMBE3 Matty Beniers 4.00 10.00
CMCM1 Connor McDavid 8.00 20.00
CMCM2 Connor McDavid 8.00 20.00
CMCM3 Connor McDavid 8.00 20.00
CMDP1 David Pastrnak 4.00 10.00
CMDP2 David Pastrnak 4.00 10.00
CMDP3 David Pastrnak 4.00 10.00
CMJR1 Jason Robertson 2.50 6.00
CMJR2 Jason Robertson 2.50 6.00
CMJR3 Jason Robertson 2.50 6.00
CMJS1 Juraj Slafkovsky 8.00 20.00
CMJS2 Juraj Slafkovsky 8.00 20.00
CMJS3 Juraj Slafkovsky 8.00 20.00
CMKK1 Kirill Kaprizov 5.00 12.00
CMKK2 Kirill Kaprizov 5.00 12.00
CMKK3 Kirill Kaprizov 5.00 12.00
CMMA1 Cale Makar 4.00 10.00
CMMA2 Cale Makar 4.00 10.00
CMMA3 Cale Makar 4.00 10.00
CMMB1 Matt Boldy 5.00 12.00
CMMB2 Matt Boldy 5.00 12.00
CMMB3 Matt Boldy 5.00 12.00
CMOP1 Owen Power 3.00 8.00
CMOP2 Owen Power 3.00 8.00
CMOP3 Owen Power 3.00 8.00
CMSC1 Sidney Crosby 6.00 15.00
CMSC2 Sidney Crosby 6.00 15.00
CMSC3 Sidney Crosby 6.00 15.00
CMTT1 Tage Thompson 2.00 5.00
CMTT2 Tage Thompson 2.00 5.00
CMTT3 Tage Thompson 2.00 5.00
CMTZ1 Trevor Zegras 1.50 4.00
CMTZ2 Trevor Zegras 1.50 4.00
CMTZ3 Trevor Zegras 1.50 4.00

2022-23 Upper Deck '97-98 SPx Retro

*BRONZE/250: .75X TO 2X BASIC
*GOLD/250: 1.2X TO 3X BASIC
SPX1 Jeff Skinner 1.25 3.00
SPX2 Elias Lindholm 1.25 3.00
SPX3 Martin Necas 2.00 5.00
SPX4 Jonathan Toews 2.00 5.00
SPX5 Artturi Lehkonen 1.00 2.50
SPX6 Boone Jenner 1.00 2.50
SPX7 Joe Pavelski 1.50 4.00
SPX8 Connor McDavid 6.00 15.00
SPX9 Adrian Kempe 1.25 3.00
SPX10 Joel Eriksson Ek 1.00 2.50
SPX11 Chris Kreider 1.50 4.00
SPX12 Claude Giroux 1.25 3.00
SPX13 Sidney Crosby 5.00 12.00
SPX14 Jake Guentzel 2.00 5.00
SPX15 Tomas Hertl 1.25 3.00
SPX16 Martin Jones 1.00 2.50
SPX17 Auston Matthews 5.00 12.00
SPX18 J.T. Miller 1.50 4.00
SPX19 Mark Stone 1.50 4.00
SPX20 Alex Ovechkin 5.00 12.00
SPX21 Dylan Guenther 3.00 8.00
SPX22 Matias Maccelli 2.00 5.00
SPX23 Jakub Lauko 1.50 4.00
SPX24 Jack Quinn 2.00 5.00
SPX25 Owen Power 2.50 6.00
SPX26 Pyotr Kochetkov 2.50 6.00
SPX27 Kirill Marchenko 3.00 8.00
SPX28 Lukas Reichel 2.50 6.00
SPX29 David Jiricek 2.50 6.00
SPX30 Kent Johnson 2.50 6.00
SPX31 Aatu Raty 1.25 3.00
SPX32 Wyatt Johnston 5.00 12.00
SPX33 Dylan Holloway 2.50 6.00
SPX34 Brandt Clarke 2.50 6.00
SPX35 Marco Rossi 3.00 8.00
SPX36 Matt Boldy 4.00 10.00
SPX37 Juraj Slafkovsky 6.00 15.00
SPX38 Kaiden Guhle 2.50 6.00
SPX39 Arber Xhekaj 2.50 6.00
SPX40 Braden Schneider 2.00 5.00
SPX41 Jake Sanderson 3.00 8.00
SPX42 Mark Kastelic 1.00 2.50
SPX43 Noah Cates 1.25 3.00
SPX44 Samuel Poulin 1.50 4.00
SPX45 Thomas Bordeleau 1.25 3.00
SPX46 Shane Wright 3.00 8.00
SPX47 Matty Beniers 3.00 8.00
SPX48 Nick Perbix 1.00 2.50
SPX49 Erik Kallgren 1.25 3.00
SPX50 Andrei Kuzmenko 2.50 6.00

2022-23 Upper Deck '99-00 Upper Deck Retro History Class

*L1/100: 2X TO 5X BASIC
*L2/25: 3X TO 8X BASIC
HC1 Pavol Regenda 1.00 2.50
HC2 Dylan Guenther 2.50 6.00
HC3 Matias Maccelli 1.50 4.00
HC4 Owen Power 2.00 5.00
HC5 Pyotr Kochetkov 2.00 5.00
HC6 Lukas Reichel 2.00 5.00
HC7 David Jiricek 2.00 5.00
HC8 Kent Johnson 2.00 5.00
HC9 Wyatt Johnston 4.00 10.00
HC10 Dylan Holloway 2.00 5.00
HC11 Brandt Clarke 2.00 5.00
HC12 Matt Boldy 3.00 8.00
HC13 Juraj Slafkovsky 5.00 12.00
HC14 Kaiden Guhle 2.00 5.00
HC15 Juuso Parssinen 1.00 2.50
HC16 Jake Sanderson 2.50 6.00
HC17 Shane Wright 2.50 6.00
HC18 Matty Beniers 2.50 6.00
HC19 Nick Perbix .75 2.00
HC20 Andrei Kuzmenko 2.00 5.00
HC21 Linus Ullmark 1.00 2.50
HC22 Tage Thompson 1.25 3.00
HC23 Patrick Kane 2.00 5.00
HC24 Nathan MacKinnon 4.00 10.00
HC25 Cale Makar 2.50 6.00
HC26 Alexandar Georgiev 1.00 2.50
HC27 Jason Robertson 1.50 4.00
HC28 Connor McDavid 5.00 12.00
HC29 Leon Draisaitl 3.00 8.00
HC30 Matthew Tkachuk 2.00 5.00
HC31 Phillip Danault 1.00 2.50
HC32 Kirill Kaprizov 3.00 8.00
HC33 Nino Niederreiter .60 1.50

HC34 Jesper Bratt 1.00 2.50
HC35 Vitek Vanecek 1.00 2.50
HC36 Artemi Panarin 2.00 5.00
HC37 Mika Zibanejad 1.25 3.00
HC38 Travis Konecny 1.00 2.50
HC39 Sidney Crosby 4.00 10.00
HC40 Evgeni Malkin 2.00 5.00
HC41 Erik Karlsson 1.25 3.00
HC42 Robert Thomas 1.00 2.50
HC43 Nikita Kucherov 2.00 5.00
HC44 Auston Matthews 4.00 10.00
HC45 William Nylander 2.00 5.00
HC46 Bo Horvat 1.25 3.00
HC47 Jack Eichel 1.50 4.00
HC48 Reilly Smith 1.00 2.50
HC49 Alex Ovechkin 4.00 10.00
HC50 Connor Hellebuyck 2.00 5.00

2022-23 Upper Deck Attacking Zone

AZ1 Trevor Zegras 15.00 40.00
AZ2 Auston Matthews 60.00 150.00
AZ3 Matt Duchene 15.00 40.00
AZ4 Gabriel Landeskog 20.00 50.00
AZ5 Jesper Bratt 15.00 40.00
AZ6 Aleksander Barkov 25.00 60.00
AZ7 Cole Caufield 80.00 200.00
AZ8 Johnny Gaudreau 25.00 60.00
AZ9 Dylan Larkin 20.00 50.00
AZ10 David Pastrnak 40.00 100.00
AZ11 Kirill Kaprizov 60.00 150.00
AZ12 Jack Eichel 25.00 60.00
AZ13 Sebastian Aho 25.00 60.00
AZ14 Jason Robertson 25.00 60.00
AZ15 Brayden Point 20.00 50.00
AZ16 Sidney Crosby 60.00 150.00
AZ17 Brady Tkachuk 25.00 60.00
AZ18 Connor McDavid 80.00 200.00
AZ19 Artemi Panarin 30.00 80.00
AZ20 Kyle Connor 25.00 60.00
AZ21 Patrick Kane 30.00 80.00
AZ22 Jordan Kyrou 15.00 40.00
AZ23 Alex Ovechkin 60.00 150.00

2022-23 Upper Deck Black Diamond Dominance

*EMERALD/100: 1.5X TO 4X BASIC
DD1 Trevor Zegras 1.00 2.50
DD2 Matias Maccelli 1.50 4.00
DD3 Dylan Guenther 2.50 6.00
DD4 Brad Marchand 2.00 5.00
DD5 Hampus Lindholm .60 1.50
DD6 Owen Power 2.00 5.00
DD7 Jonathan Huberdeau 1.25 3.00
DD8 Pyotr Kochetkov 2.00 5.00
DD9 Lukas Reichel 2.00 5.00
DD10 Mikko Rantanen 2.50 6.00
DD11 Nathan MacKinnon 4.00 10.00
DD12 Kent Johnson 2.00 5.00
DD13 David Jiricek 2.00 5.00
DD14 Johnny Gaudreau 1.50 4.00
DD15 Wyatt Johnston 4.00 10.00
DD16 Jason Robertson 1.50 4.00
DD17 David Perron .75 2.00
DD18 Dylan Holloway 2.00 5.00
DD19 Connor McDavid 5.00 12.00
DD20 Aleksander Barkov 1.50 4.00
DD21 Brandt Clarke 2.00 5.00
DD22 Marco Rossi 2.50 6.00
DD23 Matt Boldy 3.00 8.00
DD24 Kirill Kaprizov 3.00 8.00
DD25 Juraj Slafkovsky 5.00 12.00
DD26 Matt Duchene 1.00 2.50
DD27 Filip Forsberg 1.50 4.00
DD28 Jesper Bratt 1.00 2.50
DD29 Jack Hughes 2.50 6.00
DD30 Brock Nelson 1.00 2.50
DD31 Braden Schneider 1.50 4.00
DD32 Jake Sanderson 2.50 6.00
DD33 Brady Tkachuk 1.50 4.00
DD34 Noah Cates 1.00 2.50
DD35 Samuel Poulin 1.25 3.00
DD36 Sidney Crosby 4.00 10.00
DD37 Erik Karlsson 1.25 3.00
DD38 Matty Beniers 2.50 6.00
DD39 Shane Wright 2.50 6.00
DD40 Ryan O'Reilly 1.00 2.50
DD41 Brayden Point 1.25 3.00
DD42 Mikhail Sergachev .75 2.00
DD43 Auston Matthews 4.00 10.00
DD44 John Tavares 1.50 4.00
DD45 Andrei Kuzmenko 2.00 5.00
DD46 Chandler Stephenson .75 2.00
DD47 Jack Eichel 1.50 4.00
DD48 Alex Ovechkin 4.00 10.00
DD49 Mark Scheifele 1.50 4.00
DD50 Josh Morrissey 1.25 3.00

2022-23 Upper Deck Calder Candidates

*GOLD: 1.2X TO 3X BASIC
CC1 Matty Beniers 1.25 3.00
CC2 Lukas Reichel 1.00 2.50
CC3 Thomas Bordeleau .50 1.25
CC4 Brandt Clarke 1.00 2.50
CC6 Dylan Guenther 1.25 3.00
CC7 Juraj Slafkovsky 2.50 6.00
CC8 Kent Johnson 1.00 2.50
CC9 Dylan Holloway 1.00 2.50
CC10 Marco Rossi 1.25 3.00
CC11 Owen Power 1.00 2.50
CC12 Jake Sanderson 1.25 3.00
CC13 Shane Wright 1.25 3.00

2022-23 Upper Deck Centre of Attention

*GOLD: .75X TO 2X BASIC
CA1 Nazem Kadri 1.00 2.50
CA2 Roope Hintz 1.00 2.50
CA3 Pierre-Luc Dubois .60 1.50
CA4 Trevor Zegras .75 2.00
CA5 Sidney Crosby 3.00 8.00
CA6 Mika Zibanejad 1.00 2.50
CA7 Ryan O'Reilly .75 2.00
CA8 Elias Lindholm .75 2.00
CA9 Leon Draisaitl 2.50 6.00
CA10 Evgeny Kuznetsov 1.00 2.50
CA11 Ryan Johansen .60 1.50
CA12 Brayden Point 1.00 2.50
CA13 Dylan Larkin 1.00 2.50
CA14 Tim Stutzle 1.00 2.50
CA15 Jack Hughes 2.00 5.00
CA16 Sebastian Aho 1.25 3.00
CA17 Joel Eriksson Ek .60 1.50
CA18 Patrice Bergeron 1.00 2.50
CA19 Jack Eichel 1.25 3.00
CA20 Tomas Hertl .75 2.00
CA21 Aleksander Barkov 1.25 3.00
CA22 Jonathan Toews 1.25 3.00
CA23 J.T. Miller 1.00 2.50
CA24 Anze Kopitar 1.25 3.00
CA25 Auston Matthews 3.00 8.00

2022-23 Upper Deck Clear Cut Foundations

CCFAA S.Aho/F.Andersen 8.00 20.00
CCFAK C.Atkinson/T.Konecny 5.00 12.00
CCFAP J.Anderson/R.Pitlick 4.00 10.00
CCFBK J.Kyrou/P.Buchnevich 5.00 12.00
CCFBM B.Burns/T.Meier 5.00 12.00
CCFBR S.Reinhart/S.Bobrovsky 10.00 25.00
CCFBT D.Batherson/B.Tkachuk 8.00 20.00
CCFBW N.Backstrom/T.Wilson 5.00 12.00
CCFDA V.Arvidsson/P.Danault 5.00 12.00
CCFDP E.Pettersson/T.Demko 8.00 20.00
CCFGK C.Keller/S.Gostisbehere 6.00 15.00
CCFGT J.Gibson/T.Terry 5.00 12.00
CCFHB J.Bratt/D.Hamilton 5.00 12.00
CCFJG J.Guentzel/T.Jarry 8.00 20.00
CCFJJ R.Josi/T.Jeannot 5.00 12.00
CCFJL B.Jenner/P.Laine 6.00 15.00
CCFKB K.Kaprizov/M.Boldy 15.00 40.00
CCFKP B.Point/N.Kucherov 10.00 25.00
CCFKS P.Kane/D.Strome 10.00 25.00
CCFLM E.Lindholm/A.Mangiapane 5.00 12.00
CCFLR M.Rantanen/G.Landeskog 12.00 30.00
CCFME J.Eichel/J.Marchessault 8.00 20.00
CCFMG J.McCann/Y.Gourde 4.00 10.00
CCFMH B.Marchand/T.Hall 10.00 25.00
CCFNH R.Nugent-Hopkins/Z.Hyman 8.00 20.00
CCFNL A.Lee/B.Nelson 5.00 12.00
CCFPH R.Hintz/J.Pavelski 6.00 15.00
CCFPS A.Panarin/I.Shesterkin 10.00 25.00
CCFSR M.Seider/L.Raymond 8.00 20.00
CCFST T.Thompson/J.Skinner 6.00 15.00
CCFTN W.Nylander/J.Tavares 10.00 25.00
CCFWC K.Connor/B.Wheeler 8.00 20.00

2022-23 Upper Deck Clear Cut Honoured Members

HOF111 Sergei Zubov 15.00 40.00
HOF112 Rod Gilbert 20.00 50.00
HOF113 Elmer Lach 15.00 40.00
HOF114 Clark Gillies 20.00 50.00
HOF115 Guy Lapointe 15.00 40.00
HOF116 Bernie Federko 15.00 40.00
HOF117 Jean Ratelle 15.00 40.00

2022-23 Upper Deck Clear Cut League Leaders

CCLBVS Vasilevskiy/Bobrovsky/Saros 25.0060.00
CCLBZR Bunting/Zegras/Raymond 40.00 100.00
CCLKDM Matthews/Draisaitl/Kreider 25.00 60.00
CCLLGT Gaudreau/Lindholm/Tkachuk 20.0050.00
CCLMAS Shesterkin
Andersen/Markstrom 20.00 50.00
CCLMMO Matthews/Ovechkin/Meier 40.00100.00

2022-23 Upper Deck Clear Dominance

CD1 David Pastrnak 6.00 15.00
CD2 Linus Ullmark 2.50 6.00
CD3 Tage Thompson 3.00 8.00
CD4 Andrei Svechnikov 3.00 8.00
CD5 Cale Makar 6.00 15.00
CD6 Nathan MacKinnon 10.00 25.00
CD7 Jason Robertson 4.00 10.00
CD8 Connor McDavid 12.00 30.00
CD9 Leon Draisaitl 8.00 20.00
CD10 Matthew Tkachuk 5.00 12.00
CD11 Kirill Kaprizov 8.00 20.00
CD12 Nick Suzuki 5.00 12.00
CD13 Igor Shesterkin 5.00 12.00
CD14 Sidney Crosby 10.00 25.00
CD15 Steven Stamkos 5.00 12.00
CD16 Nikita Kucherov 5.00 12.00
CD17 Auston Matthews 10.00 25.00
CD18 Jack Eichel 4.00 10.00
CD19 Alex Ovechkin 10.00 25.00
CD20 Connor Hellebuyck 5.00 12.00

2022-23 Upper Deck Clear Dominance Gold Spectrum

*GOLD: 1.5X TO 4X BASIC
CD8 Connor McDavid 125.00 300.00

2022-23 Upper Deck Day with the Cup

DC1 Nikita Kucherov 15.00 40.00
DC2 Carter Verhaeghe 8.00 20.00
DC3 Victor Hedman 10.00 25.00
DC4 Erik Cernak 5.00 12.00
DC5 Barclay Goodrow 5.00 12.00
DC6 Mathieu Joseph 5.00 12.00
DC7 Mikhail Sergachev 6.00 15.00
DC8 Ryan McDonagh 5.00 12.00
DC9 Andrei Vasilevskiy 12.00 30.00
DC10 Brayden Point 10.00 25.00
DC11 Tyler Johnson 5.00 12.00
DC12 Yanni Gourde 6.00 15.00
DC13 Patrick Maroon 5.00 12.00
DC14 Ondrej Palat 6.00 15.00
DC15 Blake Coleman 6.00 15.00
DC16 Steven Stamkos 15.00 40.00
DC17 Nathan MacKinnon 30.00 80.00
DC18 Nazem Kadri 10.00 25.00
DC19 Cale Makar 20.00 50.00
DC20 Gabriel Landeskog 10.00 25.00
DC21 Mikko Rantanen 20.00 50.00
DC22 Samuel Girard 5.00 12.00
DC23 Andre Burakovsky 5.00 12.00
DC24 Erik Johnson 5.00 12.00
DC25 Devon Toews 6.00 15.00
DC26 Josh Manson 5.00 12.00

2022-23 Upper Deck Day With The Cup Flashbacks

DC1 Teemu Selanne 60.00 150.00
DC2 Ray Bourque 30.00 80.00
DC3 Mike Vernon 20.00 50.00
DC4 Scott Niedermayer 25.00 60.00
DC5 Henri Richard 25.00 60.00
DC6 Chris Pronger 25.00 60.00
DC7 Wayne Gretzky 80.00 200.00
DC8 Terry Sawchuk 25.00 60.00

2022-23 Upper Deck Dazzlers Blue

*GREEN: .6X TO 1.5X BASIC
*ORANGE: 1X TO 2.5X BASIC
*RED: .5X TO 1.25X BASIC
DZ1 Auston Matthews 1.50 4.00
DZ2 Brady Tkachuk .60 1.50
DZ3 Carter Hart .40 1.00
DZ4 Josh Anderson .30 .75
DZ5 Ryan Johansen .30 .75
DZ6 Robert Thomas .40 1.00
DZ7 Jakub Voracek .30 .75
DZ8 Marco Rossi 1.00 2.50
DZ9 Brock Nelson .40 1.00
DZ10 Rasmus Andersson .30 .75
DZ11 Ryan Hartman .25 .60
DZ12 Lucas Raymond .60 1.50
DZ13 Evgeny Kuznetsov .50 1.25
DZ14 Patrick Kane .75 2.00
DZ15 Sergei Bobrovsky .60 1.50
DZ16 Victor Hedman .50 1.25
DZ17 Mikael Granlund .30 .75
DZ18 Matty Beniers 8.00 20.00
DZ19 Clayton Keller .50 1.25
DZ20 Tage Thompson .50 1.25
DZ21 Jonathan Marchessault .50 1.25
DZ22 Viktor Arvidsson .25 .60
DZ23 Cam Fowler .40 1.00
DZ24 Andrei Svechnikov .50 1.25
DZ25 Devon Toews .30 .75
DZ26 Matt Duchene .40 1.00
DZ27 Logan Couture .50 1.25
DZ28 Matt Boldy 4.00 10.00
DZ29 Pierre-Luc Dubois .30 .75
DZ30 Jake Oettinger .60 1.50
DZ31 Carter Verhaeghe .40 1.00
DZ32 Zach Hyman .60 1.50
DZ33 Alex Killorn .25 .60
DZ34 Gabriel Landeskog .50 1.25
DZ35 Yegor Sharangovich .40 1.00
DZ36 Alex Kerfoot .30 .75
DZ37 Brad Marchand .75 2.00
DZ38 Yanni Gourde .30 .75
DZ39 Tyler Toffoli .40 1.00
DZ40 Kent Johnson .75 2.00
DZ41 Anthony Duclair .30 .75
DZ42 Andrei Vasilevskiy .60 1.50
DZ43 Quinn Hughes 1.00 2.50
DZ44 Karel Vejmelka .25 .60
DZ45 Mika Zibanejad .50 1.25
DZ46 Jeff Carter .30 .75
DZ47 Jamie Benn .40 1.00
DZ48 Anze Kopitar .60 1.50
DZ49 Andrew Mangiapane .40 1.00
DZ50 Owen Power 3.00 8.00
DZ51 Brandt Clarke .75 2.00
DZ52 Jacob Perreault .40 1.00
DZ53 Braden Schneider .60 1.50
DZ54 Vladislav Kolyachonok .30 .75
DZ55 Pavol Regenda .40 1.00
DZ56 Filip Hallander .40 1.00
DZ57 Thomas Bordeleau .40 1.00
DZ58 Fredrik Karlstrom .30 .75
DZ59 Nikita Okhotiuk .30 .75
DZ60 Marc McLaughlin .40 1.00
DZ61 Linus Hogberg .30 .75
DZ62 Nils Aman .40 1.00
DZ63 Lukas Reichel .75 2.00
DZ64 Shane Wright 4.00 10.00
DZ65 Jack Quinn .60 1.50
DZ66 Cole Koepke .40 1.00
DZ67 Jordan Spence .40 1.00
DZ68 Jack McBain .40 1.00
DZ69 Andrei Kuzmenko .75 2.00
DZ70 Filip Roos .30 .75
DZ71 Nick Blankenburg .30 .75
DZ72 Nick Abruzzese .40 1.00
DZ73 Dylan Guenther 1.00 2.50
DZ74 Ben Meyers .40 1.00
DZ75 Jordan Harris .50 1.25
DZ76 Elmer Soderblom .75 2.00
DZ77 Jake Sanderson 1.00 2.50
DZ78 Reilly Walsh .40 1.00
DZ79 Carson Meyer .30 .75
DZ80 Lukas Dostal .75 2.00
DZ81 Wyatt Johnston 1.50 4.00
DZ82 Matias Maccelli .60 1.50
DZ83 Isaac Ratcliffe .40 1.00
DZ84 Kaiden Guhle .75 2.00
DZ85 Mark Kastelic .30 .75
DZ86 Zack Hayes .30 .75
DZ87 Samuel Fagemo .30 .75
DZ88 Juraj Slafkovsky 6.00 15.00
DZ89 Trey Fix-Wolansky .40 1.00
DZ90 Valtteri Puustinen .30 .75
DZ91 Viktor Lodin .40 1.00
DZ92 Erik Kallgren .40 1.00
DZ93 Bobby Brink .40 1.00
DZ94 Dylan Samberg .40 1.00
DZ95 Pyotr Kochetkov .75 2.00
DZ96 Nathan Smith .30 .75
DZ97 Brayden Tracey .30 .75
DZ98 Jake Christiansen .40 1.00
DZ99 Noah Cates .40 1.00
DZ100 Dylan Holloway .75 2.00
DZ101 Hunter Drew .40 1.00
DZ102 Shayne Gostisbehere .40 1.00
DZ103 Jakub Lauko .50 1.25
DZ104 Rasmus Dahlin .50 1.25
DZ105 Nazem Kadri .50 1.25
DZ106 Sebastian Aho .60 1.50
DZ107 Alex Vlasic .30 .75
DZ108 Jakub Galvas .40 1.00
DZ109 Cale Makar 1.00 2.50
DZ110 David Jiricek .75 2.00
DZ111 Marcus Bjork .40 1.00
DZ112 Matej Blumel .50 1.25
DZ113 Kirill Marchenko 1.00 2.50
DZ114 Jonatan Berggren .60 1.50
DZ115 Connor McDavid 2.00 5.00
DZ116 Leon Draisaitl 1.25 3.00
DZ117 Matthew Tkachuk .75 2.00
DZ118 Jacob Moverare .30 .75
DZ119 Mitchell Chaffee .30 .75
DZ120 Kirill Kaprizov 1.25 3.00
DZ121 Arber Xhekaj .75 2.00
DZ122 Juuso Parssinen .40 1.00
DZ123 Jack Hughes 1.00 2.50
DZ124 Mathew Barzal .50 1.25
DZ125 Ilya Sorokin .60 1.50
DZ126 Artemi Panarin .75 2.00
DZ127 Igor Shesterkin .75 2.00
DZ128 Mads Sogaard .50 1.25
DZ129 Aatu Raty .40 1.00
DZ130 Samuel Ersson .75 2.00
DZ131 Olle Lycksell .40 1.00
DZ132 Ronnie Attard .40 1.00
DZ133 Samuel Poulin .50 1.25
DZ134 Sidney Crosby 1.50 4.00
DZ135 Nick Cicek .40 1.00
DZ136 Andre Burakovsky .25 .60
DZ137 Nikita Alexandrov .40 1.00
DZ138 Tyler Tucker .40 1.00
DZ139 Nick Perbix .30 .75
DZ140 Nikita Kucherov .75 2.00
DZ141 Filip Kral .50 1.25
DZ142 Pontus Holmberg .40 1.00
DZ143 Mitch Marner .60 1.50
DZ144 Elias Pettersson .60 1.50
DZ145 Brayden Pachal .30 .75
DZ146 Kaedan Korczak .30 .75
DZ147 Alex Ovechkin 1.50 4.00
DZ148 Declan Chisholm .40 1.00
DZ149 Johnathan Kovacevic .40 1.00
DZ150 Michael Eyssimont .40 1.00

2022-23 Upper Deck Dazzlers Pink

*PINK: 2.5X TO 6X BASIC
DZ18 Matty Beniers 12.00 30.00
DZ28 Matt Boldy 10.00 25.00
DZ50 Owen Power 8.00 20.00

2022-23 Upper Deck Debut Dates

*GOLD: .75X TO 2X BASIC
DD1 Philip Tomasino .50 1.25
DD2 Vasily Podkolzin .50 1.25
DD3 Anton Lundell .75 2.00
DD4 Nils Lundkvist .50 1.25
DD5 Jamie Drysdale .60 1.50
DD6 Aliaksei Protas .50 1.25
DD7 Alex Newhook .60 1.50
DD8 Lucas Raymond 1.25 3.00
DD9 Quinton Byfield 1.00 2.50
DD10 Jonathan Dahlen .50 1.25
DD11 Jeremy Swayman 1.25 3.00
DD12 Spencer Knight .75 2.00
DD13 Trevor Zegras .75 2.00
DD14 Cole Perfetti .75 2.00
DD15 Cole Sillinger .60 1.50
DD16 Karel Vejmelka .50 1.25
DD17 Scott Perunovich .50 1.25
DD18 Cole Caufield 1.50 4.00
DD19 Michael Bunting .75 2.00
DD20 Dysin Mayo .50 1.25
DD21 Seth Jarvis 1.00 2.50
DD22 Dawson Mercer 1.00 2.50
DD23 Mason McTavish .75 2.00
DD24 Tanner Jeannot .50 1.25
DD25 Moritz Seider 1.00 2.50

2022-23 Upper Deck Defense Mechanism

*GOLD: .75X TO 2X BASIC
DM1 Miro Heiskanen 1.00 2.50
DM2 Roman Josi .75 2.00
DM3 Evan Bouchard 1.00 2.50
DM4 Aaron Ekblad 1.00 2.50
DM5 Morgan Rielly .75 2.00
DM6 Victor Hedman 1.00 2.50
DM7 Drew Doughty 1.00 2.50
DM8 Quinn Hughes 2.00 5.00
DM9 Seth Jones .75 2.00
DM10 Torey Krug .60 1.50
DM11 Rasmus Dahlin 1.00 2.50
DM12 Cam Fowler .75 2.00
DM13 Cale Makar 2.00 5.00
DM14 Dougie Hamilton .60 1.50
DM15 John Carlson .75 2.00
DM16 Thomas Chabot .75 2.00
DM17 Neal Pionk .50 1.25
DM18 Jaccob Slavin .60 1.50
DM19 Jared Spurgeon .75 2.00
DM20 Charlie McAvoy 1.00 2.50
DM21 Zach Werenski 1.25 3.00
DM22 Brent Burns .75 2.00
DM23 Rasmus Andersson .60 1.50
DM24 Moritz Seider 1.00 2.50
DM25 Alex Pietrangelo .60 1.50
DM26 Shayne Gostisbehere .75 2.00
DM27 Adam Fox 1.00 2.50
DM28 Noah Dobson 1.00 2.50
DM29 Vince Dunn .60 1.50
DM30 Travis Sanheim .50 1.25

2022-23 Upper Deck Flourescence Gold

*BLUE/50: .75X TO 2X BASIC
F1 Elmer Soderblom 8.00 20.00
F2 Marc McLaughlin 4.00 10.00
F3 Lukas Reichel 8.00 20.00
F4 Matias Maccelli 6.00 15.00
F5 Fredrik Karlstrom 3.00 8.00
F6 Hayden Hodgson 3.00 8.00
F7 Thomas Bordeleau 4.00 10.00
F8 Jack Quinn 6.00 15.00
F9 Jordan Spence 4.00 10.00
F10 Nick Blankenburg 3.00 8.00
F11 Kaedan Korczak 3.00 8.00
F12 Nils Aman 4.00 10.00
F13 Samuel Fagemo 3.00 8.00
F14 Mads Sogaard 5.00 12.00
F15 Arber Xhekaj 8.00 20.00
F16 Ben Meyers 4.00 10.00
F17 Isaac Ratcliffe 4.00 10.00
F18 Pyotr Kochetkov 8.00 20.00
F19 Braden Schneider 6.00 15.00
F20 Dylan Holloway 8.00 20.00
F21 Juraj Slafkovsky 20.00 50.00
F22 Trey Fix-Wolansky 4.00 10.00
F23 Shane Wright 10.00 25.00
F24 Chase Pearson 3.00 8.00
F25 Wyatt Johnston 15.00 40.00
F26 Matt Boldy 12.00 30.00
F27 Olle Lycksell 4.00 10.00
F28 Kaiden Guhle 8.00 20.00
F29 Nathan Smith 3.00 8.00
F30 Filip Roos 3.00 8.00
F31 Jacob Perreault 4.00 10.00
F32 Kent Johnson 8.00 20.00
F33 Erik Kallgren 4.00 10.00
F34 Owen Power 8.00 20.00
F35 Brandt Clarke 8.00 20.00
F36 Jakub Lauko 5.00 12.00
F37 Lukas Dostal 8.00 20.00
F38 Dylan Samberg 4.00 10.00
F39 Nick Abruzzese 4.00 10.00
F40 Jack McBain 4.00 10.00
F41 Noah Cates 4.00 10.00
F42 Jordan Harris 5.00 12.00
F43 Marco Rossi 10.00 25.00
F44 Cole Koepke 4.00 10.00
F45 Jake Sanderson 10.00 25.00
F46 Michael Eyssimont 4.00 10.00
F47 Andrei Kuzmenko 8.00 20.00
F48 Matty Beniers 10.00 25.00
F49 Pavol Regenda 4.00 10.00
F50 Dylan Guenther 10.00 25.00

2022-23 Upper Deck Freestyles

*BLUE: .6X TO 1.5X BASIC
*GOLD: 1.5X TO 4X BASIC
*RED: .5X TO 1.25X BASIC
FS1 Alex Ovechkin 6.00 15.00
FS2 Jacob Markstrom 1.50 4.00
FS3 Mikko Rantanen 4.00 10.00
FS4 David Pastrnak 4.00 10.00
FS5 Jonathan Huberdeau 2.00 5.00
FS6 Nick Suzuki 3.00 8.00
FS7 Andrei Vasilevskiy 2.50 6.00
FS8 Andrei Svechnikov 2.00 5.00
FS9 Auston Matthews 6.00 15.00
FS10 Jack Hughes 4.00 10.00
FS11 Tage Thompson 2.00 5.00
FS12 Filip Forsberg 2.50 6.00
FS13 Josh Norris 1.50 4.00
FS14 Nathan MacKinnon 6.00 15.00
FS15 Brayden Point 2.00 5.00
FS16 Mitch Marner 2.50 6.00
FS17 Clayton Keller 2.00 5.00
FS18 Elias Lindholm 1.50 4.00
FS19 Steven Stamkos 3.00 8.00
FS20 Troy Terry 1.25 3.00
FS21 Artemi Panarin 3.00 8.00
FS22 Alex DeBrincat 2.00 5.00
FS23 Kyle Connor 2.50 6.00
FS24 Kirill Kaprizov 5.00 12.00
FS25 Patrik Laine 2.00 5.00
FS26 Lucas Raymond 2.50 6.00
FS27 Connor McDavid 8.00 20.00
FS28 Trevor Zegras 1.50 4.00
FS29 Johnny Gaudreau 2.50 6.00
FS30 Anze Kopitar 2.50 6.00
FS31 Timo Meier 1.50 4.00
FS32 Jordan Kyrou 1.50 4.00
FS33 Nikita Kucherov 3.00 8.00
FS34 Jonathan Marchessault 2.00 5.00
FS35 Mathew Barzal 2.00 5.00
FS36 Brad Marchand 3.00 8.00
FS37 Aleksander Barkov 2.50 6.00
FS38 Igor Shesterkin 3.00 8.00
FS39 Sebastian Aho 2.50 6.00
FS40 Victor Hedman 2.00 5.00
FS41 Jared McCann 1.25 3.00
FS42 Cam Atkinson 1.50 4.00
FS43 Leon Draisaitl 5.00 12.00
FS44 Patrick Kane 3.00 8.00
FS45 Jason Robertson 2.50 6.00
FS46 Cale Makar 4.00 10.00
FS47 J.T. Miller 2.00 5.00
FS48 Frederik Andersen 2.00 5.00
FS49 Matthew Tkachuk 3.00 8.00
FS50 Sidney Crosby 6.00 15.00

2022-23 Upper Deck Highlighters

*ORANGE: .4X TO 1.2X BASIC
*PINK: .6X TO 1.5X BASIC
*GREEN: 1X TO 2.5X BASIC
*PURPLE: .6X TO 1.5X BASIC
HL1 Cole Perfetti 3.00 8.00
HL2 Jeff Carter 2.50 6.00
HL3 Craig Anderson 2.00 5.00
HL4 Jason Robertson 5.00 12.00
HL5 Thatcher Demko 4.00 10.00
HL6 Anton Lundell 3.00 8.00
HL7 Jordan Eberle 3.00 8.00
HL8 Sidney Crosby 12.00 30.00
HL9 Logan Couture 4.00 10.00
HL10 Quinton Byfield 4.00 10.00
HL11 Auston Matthews 12.00 30.00
HL12 Scott Wedgewood 2.50 6.00
HL13 Igor Shesterkin 6.00 15.00
HL14 Marc-Andre Fleury 6.00 15.00
HL15 Cole Sillinger 2.50 6.00
HL16 Pierre-Luc Dubois 2.50 6.00
HL17 Robert Thomas 3.00 8.00
HL18 Joonas Donskoi 2.00 5.00
HL19 Jack Hughes 8.00 20.00
HL20 Lucas Raymond 5.00 12.00
HL21 Jordan Kyrou 3.00 8.00
HL22 Chris Kreider 4.00 10.00
HL23 Corey Perry 5.00 12.00
HL24 Karel Vejmelka 2.00 5.00
HL25 Trevor Zegras 3.00 8.00

2022-23 Upper Deck HoloGrFX

*GOLD: .6X TO 1.5X BASIC
HG1 Dylan Guenther 2.50 6.00
HG2 Owen Power 2.00 5.00
HG3 Pyotr Kochetkov 2.00 5.00
HG4 Lukas Reichel 2.00 5.00
HG5 Kent Johnson 2.00 5.00
HG6 Wyatt Johnston 4.00 10.00
HG7 Jonatan Berggren 1.50 4.00
HG8 Brandt Clarke 2.00 5.00
HG9 Matt Boldy 3.00 8.00
HG10 Juraj Slafkovsky 5.00 12.00
HG11 Jake Sanderson 2.50 6.00
HG12 Matty Beniers 2.50 6.00
HG13 Shane Wright 2.50 6.00
HG14 Nick Perbix .75 2.00
HG15 Andrei Kuzmenko 2.00 5.00

2022-23 Upper Deck HoloGrFX Future Fame

FF1 Patrice Bergeron 10.00 25.00
FF2 Patrick Kane 10.00 25.00
FF3 Nathan MacKinnon 12.00 30.00
FF4 Sidney Crosby 25.00 60.00
FF5 Connor McDavid 15.00 40.00
FF6 Auston Matthews 12.00 30.00
FF7 Alex Ovechkin 15.00 40.00
FF8 Marc-Andre Fleury 10.00 25.00
FF9 Evgeni Malkin 10.00 25.00
FF10 Steven Stamkos 10.00 25.00

2022-23 Upper Deck Honor Roll

*RAINBOW/250: 2X TO 5X BASIC
*RED: .75X TO 2X BASIC
HR1 Anze Kopitar 1.25 3.00
HR2 Leon Draisaitl 2.50 6.00
HR3 Frederik Andersen 1.00 2.50
HR4 Lukas Reichel 1.50 4.00
HR5 Auston Matthews 3.00 8.00
HR6 Sam Reinhart 1.50 4.00
HR7 Cam Atkinson .75 2.00
HR8 Mikko Rantanen 2.00 5.00
HR9 Sidney Crosby 3.00 8.00
HR10 Josh Norris .75 2.00
HR11 Marco Rossi 2.00 5.00
HR12 Patrick Kane 1.50 4.00
HR13 Kyle Connor 1.25 3.00
HR14 Morgan Rielly .75 2.00
HR15 Roope Hintz 1.00 2.50
HR16 Tristan Jarry .75 2.00
HR17 Shayne Gostisbehere .75 2.00
HR18 Artemi Panarin 1.50 4.00
HR19 Brad Marchand 1.50 4.00
HR20 Teuvo Teravainen .75 2.00
HR21 Steven Stamkos 1.50 4.00
HR22 Alex DeBrincat 1.00 2.50
HR23 Jesper Bratt .75 2.00
HR24 Jason Robertson 1.25 3.00
HR25 Brady Tkachuk 1.25 3.00
HR26 Matt Boldy 2.50 6.00
HR27 Alex Ovechkin 3.00 8.00
HR28 Lucas Raymond 1.25 3.00
HR29 Oliver Bjorkstrand .60 1.50
HR30 Tage Thompson 1.00 2.50
HR31 J.T. Miller 1.00 2.50
HR32 Timo Meier .75 2.00
HR33 Trevor Zegras .75 2.00
HR34 Jonathan Marchessault 1.00 2.50
HR35 Nick Suzuki 1.50 4.00
HR36 Robert Thomas .75 2.00
HR37 Sebastian Aho 1.25 3.00
HR38 Braden Schneider 1.25 3.00
HR39 Kirill Kaprizov 2.50 6.00
HR40 Jonathan Huberdeau 1.00 2.50
HR41 Brock Nelson .75 2.00
HR42 Matt Duchene .75 2.00
HR43 Jacob Markstrom .75 2.00
HR44 Nikita Kucherov 1.50 4.00
HR45 Roman Josi .75 2.00
HR46 Jared McCann .60 1.50
HR47 Elias Lindholm .75 2.00
HR48 Jordan Kyrou .75 2.00
HR49 Erik Kallgren .75 2.00
HR50 Cale Makar 2.00 5.00
HR51 Nick Blankenburg .60 1.50
HR52 Reilly Walsh .75 2.00
HR53 Jordan Harris 1.00 2.50
HR54 Brayden Tracey .60 1.50
HR55 Elmer Soderblom 1.50 4.00
HR56 Ronnie Attard .75 2.00
HR57 Trey Fix-Wolansky .75 2.00
HR58 Jacob Perreault .75 2.00
HR59 Matty Beniers 2.00 5.00
HR60 Matias Maccelli 1.25 3.00
HR61 Noah Cates .75 2.00
HR62 Mads Sogaard 1.00 2.50
HR63 Filip Hallander .75 2.00
HR64 Brandt Clarke 1.50 4.00
HR65 Owen Power 1.50 4.00
HR66 Ben Meyers .75 2.00
HR67 Jack McBain .75 2.00
HR68 Kaiden Guhle 1.50 4.00
HR69 Nick Abruzzese .75 2.00
HR70 Kaedan Korczak .60 1.50
HR71 Dylan Guenther 2.00 5.00
HR72 Dylan Samberg .75 2.00
HR73 Carson Meyer .60 1.50
HR74 Nathan Smith .60 1.50
HR75 Dylan Holloway 1.50 4.00
HR76 Bobby Brink .75 2.00
HR77 Jordan Spence .75 2.00
HR78 Jake Sanderson 2.00 5.00
HR79 Wyatt Johnston 3.00 8.00
HR80 Valtteri Puustinen .60 1.50
HR81 Fredrik Karlstrom .60 1.50
HR82 Nils Aman .75 2.00
HR83 Kent Johnson 1.50 4.00
HR84 Alex Vlasic .60 1.50
HR85 Cole Koepke .75 2.00
HR86 Andrei Kuzmenko 1.50 4.00
HR87 Jack Quinn 1.25 3.00
HR88 Vladislav Kolyachonok .60 1.50
HR89 Marc McLaughlin .75 2.00
HR90 Michael Eyssimont .75 2.00
HR91 Jakub Galvas .75 2.00
HR92 Chase Pearson .60 1.50
HR93 Pyotr Kochetkov 1.50 4.00
HR94 Shane Wright 2.00 5.00
HR95 Mark Kastelic .60 1.50
HR96 Nikita Okhotiuk .60 1.50
HR97 Hayden Hodgson .60 1.50
HR98 Thomas Bordeleau .75 2.00
HR99 Samuel Fagemo .60 1.50
HR100 Juraj Slafkovsky 4.00 10.00

2022-23 Upper Deck Honor Roll Gold Rainbow

*GOLD/25: 4X TO 10X BASIC
HR11 Marco Rossi 40.00 100.00
HR20 Teuvo Teravainen 12.00 30.00
HR24 Jason Robertson 60.00 150.00
HR43 Jacob Markstrom 20.00 50.00
HR46 Jared McCann 20.00 50.00
HR59 Matty Beniers 125.00 300.00

2022-23 Upper Deck Instant Impressions

*NICKNAME: 1.2X TO 3X BASIC
PZ1 Alex Ovechkin 4.00 10.00
PZ2 Taylor Hall 1.00 2.50
PZ3 J.T. Compher .60 1.50
PZ4 Warren Foegele .60 1.50
PZ5 Pierre-Luc Dubois .75 2.00
PZ6 Joe Pavelski 1.25 3.00
PZ7 Carter Hart 1.00 2.50
PZ8 Cole Caufield 2.00 5.00
PZ9 Ryan O'Reilly 1.00 2.50
PZ10 Kirill Kaprizov 3.00 8.00
PZ11 Anthony Duclair .75 2.00
PZ12 Brian Elliott .60 1.50
PZ13 Patrice Bergeron 1.25 3.00
PZ14 Sebastian Aho 1.50 4.00
PZ15 Andre Burakovsky .60 1.50
PZ16 Brady Tkachuk 1.50 4.00
PZ17 Johnny Gaudreau 1.50 4.00
PZ18 Ryan Nugent-Hopkins 1.25 3.00
PZ19 Jared Spurgeon 1.00 2.50
PZ20 Charlie McAvoy 1.25 3.00
PZ21 Steven Stamkos 2.00 5.00
PZ22 Andrei Svechnikov 1.25 3.00
PZ23 Blake Wheeler 1.00 2.50
PZ24 Dylan Cozens 1.00 2.50
PZ25 Mitch Marner 1.50 4.00
PZ26 Jordan Binnington 1.50 4.00
PZ27 Milan Lucic .75 2.00
PZ28 Jake Guentzel 1.50 4.00
PZ29 Brent Burns 1.00 2.50
PZ30 Blake Coleman .75 2.00
PZ31 Tyler Seguin 1.25 3.00
PZ32 John Tavares 1.50 4.00
PZ33 Corey Perry 1.50 4.00
PZ34 Brad Marchand 2.00 5.00
PZ35 Marc-Andre Fleury 2.00 5.00
PZ36 Dylan Larkin 1.25 3.00
PZ37 Miro Heiskanen 1.25 3.00
PZ38 Juuse Saros 1.25 3.00
PZ39 Anze Kopitar 1.50 4.00
PZ40 Nicklas Backstrom 1.00 2.50
PZ41 Zemgus Girgensons .60 1.50
PZ42 Leon Draisaitl 3.00 8.00
PZ43 Nathan MacKinnon 4.00 10.00
PZ44 David Pastrnak 2.50 6.00
PZ45 Patrick Kane 2.00 5.00
PZ46 Sergei Bobrovsky 1.50 4.00
PZ47 Evgeni Malkin 2.00 5.00
PZ48 Brenden Dillon .60 1.50
PZ49 Tanner Jeannot .60 1.50
PZ50 Artemi Panarin 2.00 5.00

2022-23 Upper Deck Lunch Box Legends

*GOLD: .75X TO 2X BASIC
LB1 Cole Caufield 1.25 3.00
LB2 Trevor Zegras .60 1.50
LB3 Patrick Kane 1.25 3.00
LB4 Elias Pettersson 1.00 2.50
LB5 Alex Ovechkin 2.50 6.00
LB6 Timo Meier .60 1.50
LB7 Mikhail Sergachev .50 1.25
LB8 Clayton Keller .75 2.00
LB9 Charlie McAvoy .75 2.00
LB10 Elias Lindholm .60 1.50
LB11 Cale Makar 1.50 4.00
LB12 Brady Tkachuk 1.00 2.50
LB13 Jordan Kyrou .60 1.50
LB14 Quinton Byfield .75 2.00
LB15 Jason Robertson 1.00 2.50
LB16 Kirill Kaprizov 2.00 5.00
LB17 Jack Eichel 1.00 2.50
LB18 Sebastian Aho 1.00 2.50
LB19 Mitch Marner 1.00 2.50
LB20 Connor McDavid 3.00 8.00
LB21 Tage Thompson .75 2.00
LB22 Jake Guentzel 1.00 2.50
LB23 Aleksander Barkov 1.00 2.50
LB24 Kyle Connor 1.00 2.50
LB25 Jack Hughes 1.50 4.00
LB26 Filip Forsberg 1.00 2.50
LB27 Moritz Seider .75 2.00
LB28 Patrik Laine .75 2.00
LB29 Adam Fox .75 2.00
LB30 Jared McCann .50 1.25

2022-23 Upper Deck O-Pee-Chee Glossy

*BRONZE: .5X TO 1.2X BASIC
*GOLD: .6X TO 1.5X BASIC
R1 Lukas Reichel 2.00 5.00
R2 Noah Cates 1.00 2.50
R3 Kent Johnson 2.00 5.00
R4 Braden Schneider 1.50 4.00
R5 Marc McLaughlin 1.00 2.50
R6 Matt Boldy 3.00 8.00
R7 Owen Power 2.00 5.00
R8 Erik Kallgren 1.00 2.50
R9 Matty Beniers 2.50 6.00
R10 Marco Rossi 2.50 6.00
R11 Dylan Holloway 2.00 5.00
R12 Andrei Kuzmenko 2.00 5.00
R13 Jack McBain 1.00 2.50
R14 Jake Sanderson 2.50 6.00
R15 Thomas Bordeleau 1.00 2.50
R16 Shane Wright 2.50 6.00
R17 Jack Quinn 1.50 4.00
R18 Dylan Guenther 2.50 6.00
R19 Brandt Clarke 2.00 5.00
R20 Juraj Slafkovsky 5.00 12.00

2022-23 Upper Deck Oversized

201 Matt Boldy YG 8.00 20.00
202 Nick Blankenburg YG 2.00 5.00
206 Nathan Smith YG 2.00 5.00
208 Erik Kallgren YG 2.50 6.00
209 Kent Johnson YG 5.00 12.00
210 Thomas Bordeleau YG 2.50 6.00
213 Matty Beniers YG 6.00 15.00
214 Braden Schneider YG 4.00 10.00
220 Marc McLaughlin YG 2.50 6.00
228 Owen Power YG 5.00 12.00
235 Lukas Reichel YG 5.00 12.00
238 Jordan Spence YG 2.50 6.00

243 Marco Rossi YG 6.00 15.00
249 Noah Cates YG 2.50 6.00
451 Juraj Slafkovsky YG 12.00 30.00
453 Samuel Poulin YG 3.00 8.00
459 Wyatt Johnston YG 10.00 25.00
461 Dylan Holloway YG 5.00 12.00
464 Nikita Okhotiuk YG 2.00 5.00
465 Andrei Kuzmenko YG 5.00 12.00
466 Jake Sanderson YG 6.00 15.00
470 Brandt Clarke YG 5.00 12.00
472 David Jiricek YG 5.00 12.00
475 Shane Wright YG 6.00 15.00
484 Cole Koepke YG 2.50 6.00
489 Elmer Soderblom YG 5.00 12.00
490 Arber Xhekaj YG 5.00 12.00
497 Dylan Guenther YG 6.00 15.00

2022-23 Upper Deck Population Count 1000

PC1 Igor Shesterkin 5.00 12.00
PC2 Alex Ovechkin 10.00 25.00
PC3 Dylan Larkin 3.00 8.00
PC4 Tyler Toffoli 2.50 6.00
PC5 Brady Tkachuk 4.00 10.00
PC6 Elias Pettersson 4.00 10.00
PC7 Josh Anderson 2.00 5.00
PC8 Matty Beniers 25.00 60.00
PC9 Sidney Crosby 10.00 25.00
PC10 Marco Rossi 6.00 15.00
PC11 Matt Duchene 2.50 6.00
PC12 Connor Hellebuyck 5.00 12.00
PC13 Alex DeBrincat 3.00 8.00
PC14 Connor McDavid 12.00 30.00
PC15 Pavel Buchnevich 2.00 5.00
PC16 David Pastrnak 6.00 15.00
PC17 Kent Johnson 5.00 12.00
PC18 Drew Doughty 3.00 8.00
PC19 Mikko Rantanen 6.00 15.00
PC20 Clayton Keller 3.00 8.00
PC21 Frederik Andersen 3.00 8.00
PC22 Matt Boldy 8.00 20.00
PC23 Mitch Marner 4.00 10.00
PC24 Ryan Ellis 1.50 4.00
PC25 Sergei Bobrovsky 4.00 10.00
PC26 Jesper Bratt 2.50 6.00
PC27 Nikita Kucherov 5.00 12.00
PC28 Owen Power 5.00 12.00
PC29 John Gibson 2.50 6.00
PC30 Roope Hintz 3.00 8.00
PC31 Braden Schneider 4.00 10.00
PC32 Carson Meyer 2.00 5.00
PC33 Ben Meyers 2.50 6.00
PC34 Jake Sanderson 6.00 15.00
PC35 Marc McLaughlin 2.50 6.00
PC36 Jordan Spence 2.50 6.00
PC37 Pyotr Kochetkov 5.00 12.00
PC38 Valtteri Puustinen 2.00 5.00
PC39 Hayden Hodgson 2.00 5.00
PC40 Kaedan Korczak 2.00 5.00
PC41 Dylan Guenther 6.00 15.00
PC42 Noah Cates 2.50 6.00
PC43 Nick Abruzzese 2.50 6.00
PC44 Matias Maccelli 4.00 10.00
PC45 Lukas Reichel 5.00 12.00
PC46 Nick Blankenburg 2.00 5.00
PC47 Shane Wright 6.00 15.00
PC48 Brandt Clarke 5.00 12.00
PC49 Trey Fix-Wolansky 2.50 6.00
PC50 Kaiden Guhle 5.00 12.00
PC51 Jack Quinn 4.00 10.00
PC52 Dylan Samberg 2.50 6.00
PC53 Juraj Slafkovsky 12.00 30.00
PC54 Jacob Perreault 2.50 6.00
PC55 Dylan Holloway 5.00 12.00
PC56 Cole Koepke 2.50 6.00
PC57 Filip Hallander 2.50 6.00
PC58 Nathan Smith 2.00 5.00
PC59 Thomas Bordeleau 2.50 6.00
PC60 Andrei Kuzmenko 5.00 12.00

2022-23 Upper Deck Population Count 100

*100: 1.2X TO 3X BASIC
PC8 Matty Beniers 100.00 250.00
PC22 Matt Boldy 60.00 150.00
PC28 Owen Power 60.00 150.00

2022-23 Upper Deck Population Count 25

*25: 3X TO 8X BASIC
PC8 Matty Beniers 200.00 500.00
PC22 Matt Boldy 100.00 250.00
PC47 Shane Wright 125.00 300.00
PC53 Juraj Slafkovsky 150.00 400.00

2022-23 Upper Deck Population Count 50

*50: 2.5X TO 6X BASIC
PC8 Matty Beniers 125.00 300.00
PC9 Sidney Crosby 80.00 200.00
PC14 Connor McDavid 100.00 250.00
PC22 Matt Boldy 80.00 200.00

2022-23 Upper Deck Population Count 500

*500: .75X TO 2X BASIC
PC8 Matty Beniers 40.00 100.00

2022-23 Upper Deck Rookie Materials

*PATCH/25: .75X TO 2X BASIC
RMBC Brandt Clarke 4.00 10.00
RMBE Matty Beniers 5.00 12.00
RMBM Ben Meyers 2.00 5.00
RMBR Bobby Brink 2.00 5.00
RMBS Braden Schneider 3.00 8.00
RMDG Dylan Guenther 5.00 12.00
RMDH Dylan Holloway 4.00 10.00
RMDS Dylan Samberg 2.00 5.00
RMFH Filip Hallander 2.00 5.00
RMJH Jordan Harris 2.50 6.00
RMJM Jack McBain 2.00 5.00
RMJP Jacob Perreault 2.00 5.00
RMJQ Jack Quinn 3.00 8.00
RMJS Juraj Slafkovsky 10.00 25.00
RMKJ Kent Johnson 4.00 10.00
RMLD Lukas Dostal 4.00 10.00
RMLR Lukas Reichel 4.00 10.00
RMMB Matt Boldy 6.00 15.00
RMMM Matias Maccelli 3.00 8.00
RMMR Marco Rossi 5.00 12.00
RMMS Mads Sogaard 2.50 6.00
RMNB Nick Blankenburg 1.50 4.00
RMNO Nikita Okhotiuk 1.50 4.00
RMOP Owen Power 4.00 10.00
RMRA Ronnie Attard 2.00 5.00
RMSA Jake Sanderson 5.00 12.00
RMSF Samuel Fagemo 1.50 4.00
RMSW Shane Wright 5.00 12.00
RMTB Thomas Bordeleau 2.00 5.00
RMVK Vladislav Kolyachonok 1.50 4.00

2022-23 Upper Deck Rookie Materials Retro

RTBC Brandt Clarke 10.00 25.00
RTBE Matty Beniers 40.00 100.00
RTBM Ben Meyers 5.00 12.00
RTBR Bobby Brink 5.00 12.00
RTBS Braden Schneider 8.00 20.00
RTDG Dylan Guenther 12.00 30.00
RTDH Dylan Holloway 10.00 25.00
RTDS Dylan Samberg 5.00 12.00
RTFH Filip Hallander 5.00 12.00
RTJH Jordan Harris 6.00 15.00
RTJP Jacob Perreault 5.00 12.00
RTJQ Jack Quinn 8.00 20.00
RTJS Juraj Slafkovsky 25.00 60.00
RTKJ Kent Johnson 10.00 25.00
RTLD Lukas Dostal 10.00 25.00
RTLR Lukas Reichel 10.00 25.00
RTMB Matt Boldy 15.00 40.00
RTMM Matias Maccelli 8.00 20.00
RTMR Marco Rossi 12.00 30.00
RTMS Mads Sogaard 6.00 15.00
RTNB Nick Blankenburg 4.00 10.00
RTNO Nikita Okhotiuk 4.00 10.00
RTOP Owen Power 10.00 25.00
RTRA Ronnie Attard 5.00 12.00
RTSA Jake Sanderson 12.00 30.00
RTSF Samuel Fagemo 4.00 10.00
RTSW Shane Wright 12.00 30.00
RTTB Thomas Bordeleau 5.00 12.00

2022-23 Upper Deck Rookie Retrospective

*GOLD: .75X TO 2X BASIC
RR1 Seth Jarvis 1.25 3.00
RR2 Jonathan Dahlen .60 1.50
RR3 Philip Tomasino .60 1.50
RR4 Jamie Drysdale .75 2.00
RR5 Dawson Mercer 1.25 3.00
RR6 Spencer Knight 1.00 2.50
RR7 Cole Sillinger .75 2.00
RR8 Nico Daws .75 2.00
RR9 Cole Caufield 2.00 5.00
RR10 Jeremy Swayman 1.50 4.00
RR11 Lucas Raymond 1.50 4.00
RR12 Sean Durzi .60 1.50
RR13 Karel Vejmelka .60 1.50
RR14 Trevor Zegras 1.00 2.50
RR15 Anton Lundell 1.00 2.50
RR16 Alex Newhook .75 2.00
RR17 Moritz Seider 1.25 3.00
RR18 Michael Bunting 1.00 2.50
RR19 Vasily Podkolzin .60 1.50
RR20 Tanner Jeannot .60 1.50

2022-23 Upper Deck Smooth Grooves

SG1 Trevor Zegras 1.00 2.50
SG2 Dylan Guenther 2.50 6.00
SG3 Matias Maccelli 1.50 4.00
SG4 David Pastrnak 2.50 6.00
SG5 Owen Power 2.00 5.00
SG6 Jack Quinn 1.50 4.00
SG7 Rasmus Dahlin 1.25 3.00
SG8 Nazem Kadri 1.25 3.00
SG9 Pyotr Kochetkov 2.00 5.00
SG10 Martin Necas 1.50 4.00
SG11 Cale Makar 2.50 6.00
SG12 Nathan MacKinnon 4.00 10.00
SG13 Kent Johnson 2.00 5.00
SG14 Wyatt Johnston 4.00 10.00
SG15 Jake Oettinger 1.50 4.00
SG16 Connor McDavid 5.00 12.00
SG17 Aleksander Barkov 1.50 4.00
SG18 Brandt Clarke 2.00 5.00
SG19 Anze Kopitar 1.50 4.00
SG20 Matt Boldy 3.00 8.00
SG21 Kirill Kaprizov 3.00 8.00
SG22 Juraj Slafkovsky 5.00 12.00
SG23 Cole Caufield 2.00 5.00
SG24 Vitek Vanecek 1.00 2.50
SG25 Jack Hughes 2.50 6.00
SG26 Mathew Barzal 1.25 3.00
SG27 Adam Fox 1.25 3.00
SG28 Artemi Panarin 2.00 5.00
SG29 Jake Sanderson 2.50 6.00
SG30 Jonatan Berggren 1.50 4.00
SG31 Carter Hart 1.00 2.50
SG32 Sidney Crosby 4.00 10.00
SG33 Erik Karlsson 1.25 3.00
SG34 Matty Beniers 2.50 6.00
SG35 Shane Wright 2.50 6.00
SG36 Robert Thomas 1.00 2.50
SG37 Brayden Point 1.25 3.00
SG38 Auston Matthews 4.00 10.00
SG39 Andrei Kuzmenko 2.00 5.00
SG40 Logan Thompson 1.25 3.00

2022-23 Upper Deck Smooth Grooves Gold Spectrum

SG34 Matty Beniers 125.00 300.00

2022-23 Upper Deck Sophomore Sensations

SO1 Matt Boldy 8.00 20.00
SO2 Kent Johnson 5.00 12.00
SO3 Noah Cates 2.50 6.00
SO4 Owen Power 5.00 12.00
SO5 Marco Rossi 6.00 15.00
SO6 Matty Beniers 6.00 15.00

2022-23 Upper Deck UD Canvas

C1 Jamie Drysdale .50 1.25
C2 John Gibson .60 1.50
C3 Troy Terry .50 1.25
C4 Shayne Gostisbehere .60 1.50
C5 Karel Vejmelka .40 1.00
C6 Patrice Bergeron .75 2.00
C7 Charlie Coyle .60 1.50
C8 Jeremy Swayman 1.00 2.50
C9 Dylan Cozens .60 1.50
C10 Peyton Krebs .50 1.25
C11 Kyle Okposo .40 1.00
C12 Jeff Skinner .60 1.50
C13 Blake Coleman .50 1.25
C14 Jacob Markstrom .60 1.50
C15 Frederik Andersen .75 2.00
C16 Seth Jarvis .75 2.00
C17 Martin Necas 1.00 2.50
C18 Teuvo Teravainen .60 1.50
C19 Alex DeBrincat .75 2.00
C20 Patrick Kane 1.25 3.00
C21 Nathan MacKinnon 2.50 6.00
C22 Cale Makar 1.50 4.00
C23 Alex Newhook .50 1.25
C24 Devon Toews .50 1.25
C25 Oliver Bjorkstrand .50 1.25
C26 Elvis Merzlikins .60 1.50
C27 Cole Sillinger .50 1.25
C28 Jason Robertson 1.00 2.50
C29 Tyler Seguin .75 2.00
C30 Dylan Larkin .75 2.00
C31 Alex Nedeljkovic .50 1.25
C32 Moritz Seider .75 2.00
C33 Evan Bouchard .75 2.00
C34 Connor McDavid 3.00 8.00
C35 Jonathan Huberdeau .75 2.00
C36 Anton Lundell .60 1.50
C37 Carter Verhaeghe .60 1.50
C38 Phillip Danault .60 1.50
C39 Alex Iafallo .40 1.00
C40 Anze Kopitar 1.00 2.50
C41 Jon Merrill .40 1.00
C42 Jake Allen .60 1.50
C43 Rem Pitlick .40 1.00
C44 Nick Suzuki 1.25 3.00
C45 Matt Duchene .60 1.50
C46 Mikael Granlund .50 1.25
C47 Tanner Jeannot .40 1.00
C48 Roman Josi .60 1.50
C49 Jack Hughes 1.50 4.00
C50 Andreas Johnsson .50 1.25
C51 Josh Bailey .50 1.25
C52 Brock Nelson .60 1.50
C53 Adam Fox .75 2.00
C54 Chris Kreider .75 2.00
C55 Mika Zibanejad .75 2.00
C56 Drake Batherson .60 1.50
C57 Josh Norris .60 1.50
C58 Rasmus Ristolainen .40 1.00
C59 Sidney Crosby 2.50 6.00
C60 Jake Guentzel 1.00 2.50
C61 Kasperi Kapanen .50 1.25
C62 John Marino .60 1.50
C63 Brent Burns .60 1.50
C64 Jonathan Dahlen .40 1.00
C65 Tomas Hertl .60 1.50
C66 Erik Karlsson .75 2.00
C67 Jared McCann .60 1.50
C68 Pavel Buchnevich .50 1.25
C69 Jordan Kyrou .60 1.50
C70 Brandon Saad .50 1.25
C71 Brandon Hagel .50 1.25
C72 Victor Hedman .75 2.00
C73 Brayden Point .75 2.00
C74 Andrei Vasilevskiy 1.00 2.50
C75 Michael Bunting .60 1.50
C76 Auston Matthews 2.50 6.00
C77 William Nylander 1.25 3.00
C78 John Tavares 1.00 2.50
C79 Thatcher Demko .75 2.00
C80 Oliver Ekman-Larsson .40 1.00
C81 Quinn Hughes 1.50 4.00
C82 Vasily Podkolzin .40 1.00
C83 Jonathan Marchessault .75 2.00
C84 Mark Stone .75 2.00
C85 Nicklas Backstrom .60 1.50
C86 Evgeny Kuznetsov .75 2.00
C87 Tom Wilson .60 1.50
C88 Kyle Connor 1.00 2.50
C89 Pierre-Luc Dubois .50 1.25
C90 J.Hughes/Q.Hughes CL 1.50 4.00
C91 Kent Johnson YG 10.00 25.00
C92 Pyotr Kochetkov YG 15.00 40.00
C93 Matt Boldy YG 10.00 25.00
C94 Matias Maccelli YG 8.00 20.00
C95 Noah Cates YG 5.00 12.00
C96 Marc McLaughlin YG 5.00 12.00
C97 Thomas Bordeleau YG 5.00 12.00
C98 Jacob Perreault YG 5.00 12.00
C99 Jack Quinn YG 8.00 20.00
C100 Matty Beniers YG 12.00 30.00
C101 Trey Fix-Wolansky YG 5.00 12.00
C102 Jack LaFontaine YG 5.00 12.00
C103 Brayden Tracey YG 4.00 10.00
C104 Jakub Galvas YG 5.00 12.00
C105 Braden Schneider YG 8.00 20.00
C106 Erik Kallgren YG 5.00 12.00
C107 Samuel Fagemo YG 4.00 10.00
C108 Valtteri Puustinen YG 4.00 10.00
C109 Jake Christiansen YG 5.00 12.00
C110 Lukas Reichel YG 10.00 25.00
C111 Mark Kastelic YG 4.00 10.00
C112 Isaac Ratcliffe YG 5.00 12.00
C113 Lukas Dostal YG 10.00 25.00
C114 Marco Rossi YG 8.00 20.00
C115 Jordan Spence YG 5.00 12.00
C116 Kaedan Korczak YG 4.00 10.00
C117 Nathan Smith YG 4.00 10.00
C118 Carson Meyer YG 4.00 10.00
C119 Owen Power YG 8.00 20.00
C120 M.Boldy/M.Rossi YG CL 15.00 40.00
C121 Trevor Zegras .60 1.50
C122 Kevin Shattenkirk .40 1.00
C123 Clayton Keller .75 2.00
C124 Nick Ritchie .40 1.00
C125 Dysin Mayo .40 1.00
C126 Brad Marchand 1.25 3.00
C127 Linus Ullmark .60 1.50
C128 Taylor Hall .60 1.50
C129 Alex Tuch .60 1.50
C130 Tage Thompson .75 2.00
C131 Milan Lucic .50 1.25
C132 Tyler Toffoli .50 1.25
C133 Andrew Mangiapane .60 1.50
C134 Elias Lindholm .60 1.50
C135 Andrei Svechnikov .75 2.00
C136 Sebastian Aho 1.00 2.50
C137 Seth Jones .60 1.50
C138 Philipp Kurashev .50 1.25
C139 Gabriel Landeskog .75 2.00
C140 Mikko Rantanen 1.50 4.00
C141 Valeri Nichushkin .60 1.50
C142 Patrik Laine .75 2.00
C143 Jakub Voracek .50 1.25
C144 Zach Werenski 1.00 2.50
C145 Miro Heiskanen .75 2.00
C146 Joe Pavelski .75 2.00
C147 Jake Oettinger 1.00 2.50
C148 Roope Hintz .75 2.00
C149 Lucas Raymond 1.00 2.50
C150 Tyler Bertuzzi .50 1.25
C151 Robby Fabbri .40 1.00
C152 Evander Kane .60 1.50
C153 Leon Draisaitl 2.00 5.00
C154 Zach Hyman 1.00 2.50
C155 Darnell Nurse .50 1.25
C156 Sergei Bobrovsky 1.00 2.50
C157 Sam Bennett 1.00 2.50
C158 Aleksander Barkov 1.00 2.50
C159 Drew Doughty .75 2.00
C160 Viktor Arvidsson .40 1.00
C161 Kirill Kaprizov 2.00 5.00
C162 Joel Eriksson Ek .50 1.25
C163 Ryan Hartman .40 1.00
C164 Marcus Foligno .50 1.25
C165 Mats Zuccarello .60 1.50
C166 Cole Caufield 1.25 3.00
C167 Josh Anderson .50 1.25
C168 Ryan Johansen .50 1.25
C169 Philip Tomasino .40 1.00
C170 Dawson Mercer .75 2.00
C171 Jesper Bratt .60 1.50
C172 Yegor Sharangovich .60 1.50
C173 Anders Lee .50 1.25
C174 Mathew Barzal .75 2.00
C175 Igor Shesterkin 1.25 3.00
C176 Artemi Panarin 1.25 3.00
C177 Alexis Lafreniere 1.00 2.50
C178 Brady Tkachuk 1.00 2.50
C179 Tim Stutzle .75 2.00
C180 Alex Formenton .50 1.25
C181 Carter Hart .60 1.50
C182 Joel Farabee .60 1.50
C183 Travis Konecny .60 1.50
C184 Cam Atkinson .60 1.50
C185 Jeff Carter .50 1.25
C186 Tristan Jarry .60 1.50
C187 Mario Ferraro .40 1.00
C188 Phillip Grubauer .60 1.50
C189 Jaden Schwartz .50 1.25
C190 Jordan Eberle .60 1.50
C191 Alexander Wennberg .40 1.00
C192 Brayden Schenn .60 1.50
C193 Ryan O'Reilly .60 1.50
C194 Ivan Barbashev .50 1.25
C195 Nikita Kucherov 1.25 3.00
C196 Steven Stamkos 1.25 3.00
C197 Mitch Marner 1.00 2.50
C198 Alex Kerfoot .50 1.25
C199 Elias Pettersson 1.00 2.50
C200 Jack Eichel 1.00 2.50
C201 William Karlsson .75 2.00
C202 Chandler Stephenson .50 1.25
C203 Alex Ovechkin 2.50 6.00
C204 T.J. Oshie .60 1.50
C205 Conor Sheary .60 1.50
C206 Mark Scheifele 1.00 2.50
C207 Connor Hellebuyck 1.25 3.00
C208 Nikolaj Ehlers .60 1.50
C209 Blake Wheeler .60 1.50
C210 I.Shesterkin/S.Bobrovsky CL 1.25 3.00
C211 Juraj Slafkovsky YG 25.00 60.00
C212 Pavol Regenda YG 5.00 12.00
C213 Samuel Poulin YG 6.00 15.00
C214 Nils Aman YG 5.00 12.00
C215 Brandon Biro YG 8.00 20.00
C216 Michael Eyssimont YG 5.00 12.00
C217 Cole Reinhardt YG 5.00 12.00
C218 Wyatt Johnston YG 15.00 40.00
C219 Dylan Holloway YG 10.00 25.00
C220 Mitchell Chaffee YG 4.00 10.00
C221 Nikita Okhotiuk YG 4.00 10.00
C222 Andrei Kuzmenko YG 5.00 12.00
C223 Jake Sanderson YG 12.00 30.00
C224 Jakub Lauko YG 6.00 15.00
C225 Filip Roos YG 4.00 10.00
C226 Brandt Clarke YG 8.00 20.00
C227 David Jiricek YG 10.00 25.00
C228 Shane Wright YG 15.00 40.00
C229 Hunter Drew YG 5.00 12.00
C230 Filip Hallander YG 5.00 12.00
C231 Linus Hogberg YG 4.00 10.00
C232 Kaiden Guhle YG 10.00 25.00
C233 Reilly Walsh YG 5.00 12.00
C234 Cole Koepke YG 5.00 12.00
C235 Elmer Soderblom YG 10.00 25.00
C236 Arber Xhekaj YG 10.00 25.00
C237 Filip Kral YG 6.00 15.00
C238 Ronnie Attard YG 5.00 12.00
C239 Dylan Guenther YG 12.00 30.00
C240 D.Guenther/J.Sanderson YG CL 6.00 15.00
C241 King Clancy RET 2.50 6.00
C242 Eric Lindros RET 4.00 10.00
C243 Glenn Hall RET 2.50 6.00
C244 Mike Richter RET 2.50 6.00
C245 Bobby Clarke RET 4.00 10.00
C246 Ray Bourque RET 4.00 10.00
C247 Henri Richard RET 2.50 6.00
C248 Joe Sakic RET 5.00 12.00
C249 Borje Salming RET 2.50 6.00
C250 Luc Robitaille RET 2.50 6.00
C251 Bernie Geoffrion RET 2.50 6.00
C252 Rick Nash RET 2.00 5.00
C253 Mark Messier RET 5.00 12.00
C254 Al MacInnis RET 3.00 8.00
C255 Tony Esposito RET 2.50 6.00
C256 Dylan Guenther POE 6.00 15.00
C257 Kaiden Guhle POE 5.00 12.00
C258 Isaac Ratcliffe POE 2.50 6.00
C259 Brandt Clarke POE 10.00 25.00
C260 Brayden Tracey POE 2.00 5.00
C261 Jordan Spence POE 2.50 6.00
C262 Owen Power POE 5.00 12.00
C263 Braden Schneider POE 4.00 10.00
C264 Wyatt Johnston POE 10.00 25.00
C265 Shane Wright POE 12.00 30.00
C266 Jack Quinn POE 4.00 10.00
C267 Kaedan Korczak POE 2.00 5.00
C268 Dylan Holloway POE 5.00 12.00
C269 Kent Johnson POE 5.00 12.00
C270 Eric Lindros POE 4.00 10.00
C271 Frank Vatrano .50 1.25
C272 Ryan Strome .60 1.50
C273 Mason McTavish .60 1.50
C274 John Klingberg .60 1.50
C275 Lawson Crouse .40 1.00
C276 Travis Boyd .40 1.00
C277 David Krejci .60 1.50
C278 David Pastrnak 1.50 4.00
C279 Jake DeBrusk .60 1.50
C280 Hampus Lindholm .40 1.00
C281 Rasmus Dahlin .75 2.00
C282 Victor Olofsson .60 1.50
C283 Jonathan Huberdeau .75 2.00
C284 Nazem Kadri .75 2.00
C285 Rasmus Andersson .50 1.25
C286 Brent Burns .60 1.50
C287 Jonathan Toews 1.00 2.50
C288 Alexandar Georgiev .60 1.50
C289 Evan Rodrigues .50 1.25
C290 Johnny Gaudreau 1.00 2.50
C291 Boone Jenner .60 1.50
C292 Mason Marchment .50 1.25
C293 Jamie Benn .60 1.50
C294 Dominik Kubalik .60 1.50
C295 Ville Husso .40 1.00
C296 Filip Hronek .40 1.00
C297 Stuart Skinner .75 2.00
C298 Ryan Nugent-Hopkins .75 2.00
C299 Matthew Tkachuk 1.25 3.00
C300 Sam Reinhart 1.25 3.00
C301 Aaron Ekblad .75 2.00
C302 Brandon Montour .75 2.00
C303 Spencer Knight .60 1.50
C304 Gabe Vilardi .60 1.50
C305 Adrian Kempe .60 1.50
C306 Jonathan Quick .75 2.00
C307 Kevin Fiala .60 1.50
C308 Arthur Kaliyev .60 1.50
C309 Marc-Andre Fleury 1.25 3.00
C310 Kirby Dach .60 1.50
C311 Filip Forsberg 1.00 2.50
C312 Nino Niederreiter .40 1.00
C313 Juuse Saros .75 2.00
C314 Nico Hischier 1.00 2.50
C315 Vitek Vanecek .50 1.25
C316 Dougie Hamilton .50 1.25
C317 Noah Dobson .75 2.00
C318 Ilya Sorokin 1.00 2.50
C319 Vincent Trocheck .60 1.50
C320 Jacob Trouba .60 1.50
C321 Alex DeBrincat .75 2.00
C322 Claude Giroux .60 1.50
C323 Shane Pinto .50 1.25
C324 Cam Talbot .60 1.50
C325 Kevin Hayes .60 1.50
C326 Owen Tippett .40 1.00
C327 Nicolas Deslauriers .40 1.00
C328 Evgeni Malkin 1.25 3.00
C329 Jason Zucker .60 1.50
C330 Rickard Rakell .60 1.50
C331 James Reimer .40 1.00
C332 Logan Couture .75 2.00
C333 Timo Meier .75 2.00
C334 Oliver Bjorkstrand .50 1.25
C335 Martin Jones .60 1.50
C336 Andre Burakovsky .40 1.00
C337 Yanni Gourde .50 1.25
C338 Robert Thomas .75 2.00
C339 Vladimir Tarasenko .75 2.00
C340 Jordan Binnington 1.00 2.50
C341 Mikhail Sergachev .50 1.25
C342 Nick Paul .40 1.00
C343 Morgan Rielly .60 1.50
C344 Ilya Samsonov .60 1.50
C345 J.T. Miller .75 2.00
C346 Ilya Mikheyev .50 1.25
C347 Bo Horvat .75 2.00
C348 Logan Thompson .75 2.00
C349 Phil Kessel .60 1.50
C350 Alex Pietrangelo .50 1.25
C351 Reilly Smith .60 1.50
C352 Anthony Mantha .50 1.25
C353 Darcy Kuemper .60 1.50
C354 Dylan Strome .75 2.00
C355 Sonny Milano .60 1.50
C356 Cole Perfetti .60 1.50
C357 Josh Morrissey .75 2.00
C358 Neal Pionk .40 1.00
C359 Adam Lowry .50 1.25
C360 J.Huberdeau/A.DeBrincat CL .75 2.00
C361 Nick DeSimone YG 5.00 12.00
C362 Dylan Wells YG 5.00 12.00
C363 Marcus Bjork YG 5.00 12.00
C364 Matej Blumel YG 6.00 15.00
C365 Jonatan Berggren YG 8.00 20.00
C366 Juuso Parssinen YG 5.00 12.00
C367 Nick Cicek YG 5.00 12.00
C368 Nikita Alexandrov YG 5.00 12.00
C369 Pontus Holmberg YG 5.00 12.00
C370 David Jiricek YG 10.00 25.00
C371 Tyler Tucker YG 5.00 12.00
C372 Oskar Olausson YG 5.00 12.00
C373 Simon Holmstrom YG 5.00 12.00
C374 Mac Hollowell YG 5.00 12.00
C375 James Hamblin YG 5.00 12.00
C376 Jean-Luc Foudy YG 5.00 12.00
C377 William Bitten YG 5.00 12.00
C378 Kirill Marchenko YG 12.00 30.00
C379 Semyon Der-Arguchintsev YG 5.00 12.00
C380 Tim Berni YG 5.00 12.00
C381 Jack McBain YG 5.00 12.00
C382 Aatu Raty YG 5.00 12.00
C383 Samuel Walker YG 5.00 12.00
C384 Nick Perbix YG 4.00 10.00
C385 Jordan Harris YG 6.00 15.00
C386 Nick Blankenburg YG 4.00 10.00
C387 Justin Kirkland YG 5.00 12.00
C388 Fredrik Olofsson YG 5.00 12.00
C389 Anton Levtchi YG 5.00 12.00
C390 J.Harris/J.Parssinen YG CL 6.00 15.00
C391 Howie Morenz 2.50 6.00
C392 Curtis Joseph 3.00 8.00
C393 Denis Potvin 2.50 6.00
C394 Stan Mikita 2.50 6.00
C395 Ron Francis 3.00 8.00
C396 Gordie Howe 8.00 20.00
C397 Wayne Gretzky 20.00 50.00
C398 Jacques Plante 2.50 6.00
C399 Mario Lemieux 10.00 25.00
C400 Adam Oates 2.50 6.00
C401 Henrik Lundqvist 6.00 15.00
C402 Joe Nieuwendyk 2.00 5.00
C403 Igor Larionov 2.50 6.00
C404 Peter Forsberg 5.00 12.00
C405 Tim Horton 4.00 10.00
C406 Auston Matthews AS 10.00 25.00
C407 Zach Werenski AS 4.00 10.00
C408 Clayton Keller AS 3.00 8.00
C409 Thatcher Demko AS 3.00 8.00
C410 Alex Pietrangelo AS 2.00 5.00
C411 Kyle Connor AS 4.00 10.00
C412 Jack Hughes AS 6.00 15.00
C413 Adrian Kempe AS 2.50 6.00
C414 Steven Stamkos AS 5.00 12.00
C415 Juuse Saros AS 3.00 8.00
C416 Kirill Kaprizov AS 8.00 20.00
C417 Chris Kreider AS 3.00 8.00
C418 Jonathan Marchessault AS 3.00 8.00
C419 John Gibson AS 2.50 6.00
C420 Connor McDavid AS 12.00 30.00

2022-23 Upper Deck UD Portraits

P1 Frederik Andersen 1.00 2.50
P2 Lucas Raymond 1.25 3.00
P3 Mikko Rantanen 2.00 5.00
P4 Artemi Panarin 1.50 4.00
P5 Brayden Point 1.00 2.50
P6 Jonathan Marchessault 1.00 2.50
P7 Johnny Gaudreau 1.25 3.00
P8 Patrick Kane 1.50 4.00
P9 Connor McDavid 4.00 10.00
P10 Roman Josi .75 2.00
P11 Jonathan Huberdeau 1.00 2.50
P12 Nikita Kucherov 1.50 4.00
P13 Matthew Tkachuk 1.50 4.00
P14 Sidney Crosby 3.00 8.00
P15 Cale Makar 2.00 5.00
P16 Andrei Svechnikov 1.00 2.50
P17 Auston Matthews 3.00 8.00
P18 J.T. Miller 1.00 2.50
P19 Leon Draisaitl 2.50 6.00
P20 Trevor Zegras .75 2.00
P21 Jason Robertson 1.25 3.00
P22 Kirill Kaprizov 2.50 6.00
P23 Alex Ovechkin 3.00 8.00
P24 Kyle Connor 1.25 3.00
P25 Nathan MacKinnon 3.00 8.00
P26 Aleksander Barkov 1.25 3.00
P27 Steven Stamkos 1.50 4.00
P28 Sebastian Aho 1.25 3.00
P29 Igor Shesterkin 1.50 4.00
P30 Mitch Marner 1.25 3.00
P31 Matt Boldy SP 2.50 6.00
P32 Owen Power SP 1.50 4.00
P33 Erik Kallgren SP .75 2.00
P34 Marc McLaughlin SP .75 2.00
P35 Braden Schneider SP 1.25 3.00
P36 Matty Beniers SP 2.00 5.00
P37 Marco Rossi SP 2.00 5.00
P38 Kent Johnson SP 1.50 4.00
P39 Lukas Reichel SP 1.50 4.00
P40 Noah Cates SP .75 2.00
P41 Nick Abruzzese .75 2.00
P42 Nick Blankenburg SP .60 1.50
P43 Jacob Perreault .75 2.00
P44 Kaedan Korczak .60 1.50
P45 Pyotr Kochetkov 1.50 4.00
P46 Elmer Soderblom 1.50 4.00
P47 Michael Eyssimont .75 2.00
P48 Jordan Spence .75 2.00
P49 Ben Meyers .75 2.00
P50 Mitchell Chaffee .60 1.50
P51 Valtteri Puustinen .60 1.50
P52 Lukas Dostal 1.50 4.00
P53 Nathan Smith .60 1.50
P54 Jake Christiansen .60 1.50
P55 Mark Kastelic .60 1.50
P56 Cole Koepke .75 2.00
P57 Samuel Fagemo .60 1.50
P58 Jordan Harris 1.00 2.50
P59 Carson Meyer .60 1.50
P60 Matias Maccelli 1.25 3.00
P61 Brayden Tracey .60 1.50
P62 Hayden Hodgson .60 1.50
P63 Nikita Okhotiuk .60 1.50
P64 Jacob Moverare .60 1.50
P65 Mads Sogaard 1.00 2.50
P66 Adam Raska .75 2.00
P67 Dylan Samberg .75 2.00
P68 Trey Fix-Wolansky .75 2.00
P69 Jakub Galvas .75 2.00
P70 Bobby Brink .75 2.00
P71 Brandt Clarke SP 1.50 4.00
P72 Thomas Bordeleau SP .75 2.00
P73 Dylan Holloway SP 1.50 4.00
P74 Juraj Slafkovsky SP 4.00 10.00
P75 Wyatt Johnston SP 3.00 8.00
P76 Shane Wright SP 2.00 5.00
P77 Andrei Kuzmenko SP 1.50 4.00
P78 Jack Quinn SP 1.25 3.00
P79 Jake Sanderson SP 2.00 5.00
P80 Dylan Guenther SP 2.00 5.00

2022-23 Upper Deck UD Portraits Gold

*GOLD: 2X TO 5X BASIC
P31 Matt Boldy/25 60.00 150.00

2022-23 Upper Deck UD Portraits Silver

*SILVER: 2X TO 5X BASIC

2022-23 Upper Deck Welcome To

*GOLD: .6X TO 1.5X BASIC
WT1 Anaheim Ducks 1.25 3.00
WT2 Arizona Coyotes 1.25 3.00
WT3 Boston Bruins 1.25 3.00
WT4 Buffalo Sabres 1.25 3.00
WT5 Calgary Flames 1.25 3.00
WT6 Carolina Hurricanes 1.25 3.00
WT7 Chicago Blackhawks 1.25 3.00
WT8 Colorado Avalanche 1.25 3.00
WT9 Columbus Blue Jackets 1.25 3.00
WT10 Dallas Stars 1.25 3.00
WT11 Detroit Red Wings 1.25 3.00
WT12 Edmonton Oilers 1.25 3.00
WT13 Florida Panthers 1.25 3.00
WT14 Los Angeles Kings 1.25 3.00
WT15 Minnesota Wild 1.25 3.00
WT16 Montreal Canadiens 1.25 3.00
WT17 Nashville Predators 1.25 3.00
WT18 New Jersey Devils 1.25 3.00
WT19 New York Islanders 1.25 3.00
WT20 New York Rangers 1.25 3.00
WT21 Ottawa Senators 1.25 3.00
WT22 Philadelphia Flyers 1.25 3.00
WT23 Pittsburgh Penguins 1.25 3.00
WT24 San Jose Sharks 1.25 3.00
WT25 Seattle Kraken 1.25 3.00
WT26 St. Louis Blues 1.25 3.00
WT27 Tampa Bay Lightning 1.25 3.00
WT28 Toronto Maple Leafs 1.25 3.00
WT29 Vancouver Canucks 1.25 3.00
WT30 Vegas Golden Knights 1.25 3.00
WT31 Washington Capitals 1.25 3.00
WT32 Winnipeg Jets 1.25 3.00

2022-23 Upper Deck World Junior Grads

*GOLD: .75X TO 2X BASIC
WG1 Patrik Laine .60 1.50
WG3 Filip Forsberg .75 2.00
WG4 David Pastrnak 1.25 3.00
WG5 Roope Hintz .60 1.50
WG6 Thatcher Demko .60 1.50
WG7 Mikhail Sergachev .40 1.00
WG8 Auston Matthews 2.00 5.00
WG9 Lucas Raymond .75 2.00
WG10 Elias Pettersson .75 2.00
WG11 Andrei Vasilevskiy .75 2.00
WG12 Jordan Kyrou .50 1.25
WG13 Tim Stutzle .60 1.50
WG14 Timo Meier .50 1.25
WG15 Jack Eichel .75 2.00
WG16 Juuse Saros .60 1.50
WG17 Cale Makar 1.25 3.00
WG18 Nikolaj Ehlers .50 1.25
WG19 Martin Necas .75 2.00
WG20 Cole Caufield 1.00 2.50
WG21 Kirill Kaprizov 1.50 4.00
WG22 Moritz Seider .60 1.50
WG23 Miro Heiskanen .60 1.50
WG24 Quinn Hughes 1.25 3.00
WG25 Connor McDavid 2.50 6.00

2023-24 Upper Deck

1 Trevor Zegras .30 .75
2 Mason McTavish .30 .75
3 Frank Vatrano .25 .60
4 Isac Lundestrom .20 .50
5 Lukas Dostal .30 .75
6 Dylan Guenther .40 1.00
7 J.J. Moser .20 .50
8 Juuso Valimaki .20 .50
9 Matias Maccelli .25 .60
10 Jack McBain .20 .50
11 Jake DeBrusk .30 .75
12 Trent Frederic .20 .50
13 Hampus Lindholm .20 .50
14 Charlie McAvoy .40 1.00
15 Jeremy Swayman .50 1.25
16 Taylor Hall .30 .75
17 Tage Thompson .40 1.00
18 Dylan Cozens .30 .75
19 Peyton Krebs .25 .60
20 Owen Power .30 .75
21 Rasmus Dahlin .40 1.00
22 Mattias Samuelsson .20 .50
23 Ukko-Pekka Luukkonen .25 .60
24 Dillon Dube .20 .50
25 Elias Lindholm .30 .75
26 Nazem Kadri .40 1.00
27 Mikael Backlund .25 .60
28 Noah Hanifin .30 .75
29 Dan Vladar .25 .60
30 Sebastian Aho .50 1.25
31 Seth Jarvis .40 1.00
32 Teuvo Teravainen .30 .75
33 Jesperi Kotkaniemi .30 .75
34 Brett Pesce .20 .50
35 Jaccob Slavin .25 .60
36 Lukas Reichel .30 .75
37 Tyler Johnson .20 .50
38 Taylor Raddysh .25 .60
39 Seth Jones .30 .75
40 Petr Mrazek .25 .60
41 Artturi Lehkonen .25 .60
42 Nathan MacKinnon 1.25 3.00
43 Valeri Nichushkin .30 .75
44 Mikko Rantanen .75 2.00
45 Denis Malgin .20 .50
46 Devon Toews .25 .60
47 Bowen Byram .40 1.00
48 Johnny Gaudreau .50 1.25
49 Kirill Marchenko .40 1.00
50 Patrik Laine .40 1.00
51 Andrew Peeke .20 .50
52 Adam Boqvist .20 .50
53 David Jiricek .30 .75
54 Yegor Chinakhov .25 .60
55 Roope Hintz .40 1.00
56 Joe Pavelski .40 1.00
57 Tyler Seguin .40 1.00
58 Jamie Benn .30 .75
59 Radek Faksa .25 .60
60 Jake Oettinger .50 1.25
61 Dominik Kubalik .30 .75
62 David Perron .25 .60
63 Joe Veleno .25 .60
64 Moritz Seider .40 1.00
65 Ben Chiarot .20 .50
66 Robby Fabbri .20 .50
67 Connor McDavid 1.50 4.00

68 Zach Hyman .50 1.25
69 Ryan Nugent-Hopkins .40 1.00
70 Cody Ceci .20 .50
71 Evan Bouchard .40 1.00
72 Jack Campbell .30 .75
73 Evander Kane .30 .75
74 Matthew Tkachuk .60 1.50
75 Sam Reinhart .60 1.50
76 Anthony Duclair .25 .60
77 Aaron Ekblad .40 1.00
78 Brandon Montour .40 1.00
79 Sergei Bobrovsky .50 1.25
80 Sam Bennett .50 1.25
81 Quinton Byfield .40 1.00
82 Anze Kopitar .50 1.25
83 Adrian Kempe .30 .75
84 Alex Iafallo .20 .50
85 Arthur Kaliyev .30 .75
86 Mikey Anderson .25 .60
87 Pheonix Copley .20 .50
88 Kirill Kaprizov 1.00 2.50
89 Matt Boldy .50 1.25
90 Jacob Middleton .20 .50
91 Jared Spurgeon .30 .75
92 Calen Addison .20 .50
93 Marc-Andre Fleury .60 1.50
94 Nick Suzuki .60 1.50
95 Rafael Harvey-Pinard .20 .50
96 Josh Anderson .25 .60
97 Kaiden Guhle .30 .75
98 Kirby Dach .30 .75
99 Juraj Slafkovsky .60 1.50
100 Arber Xhekaj .30 .75
101 Cody Glass .25 .60
102 Matt Duchene .30 .75
103 Alexandre Carrier .20 .50
104 Tyson Barrie .20 .50
105 Juuso Parssinen .20 .50
106 Filip Forsberg .50 1.25
107 Kevin Lankinen .30 .75
108 Dawson Mercer .40 1.00
109 Jack Hughes .75 2.00
110 Jesper Boqvist .20 .50
111 Michael McLeod .20 .50
112 Dougie Hamilton .25 .60
113 Vitek Vanecek .30 .75
114 Bo Horvat .40 1.00
115 Anders Lee .25 .60
116 Ryan Pulock .25 .60
117 Noah Dobson .40 1.00
118 Mathew Barzal .40 1.00
119 Jean-Gabriel Pageau .20 .50
120 Mika Zibanejad .40 1.00
121 Artemi Panarin .60 1.50
122 Filip Chytil .25 .60
123 Kaapo Kakko .25 .60
124 Adam Fox .40 1.00
125 K'Andre Miller .25 .60
126 Brady Tkachuk .50 1.25
127 Claude Giroux .30 .75
128 Shane Pinto .25 .60
129 Mathieu Joseph .20 .50
130 Thomas Chabot .30 .75
131 Jakob Chychrun .30 .75
132 Morgan Frost .25 .60
133 Scott Laughton .20 .50
134 Noah Cates .20 .50
135 Ivan Provorov .25 .60
136 Nick Seeler .20 .50
137 Travis Konecny .30 .75
138 Sidney Crosby 1.25 3.00
139 Bryan Rust .30 .75
140 Mikael Granlund .25 .60
141 Kris Letang .40 1.00
142 Jeff Petry .20 .50
143 William Eklund .40 1.00
144 Tomas Hertl .30 .75
145 Logan Couture .40 1.00
146 Alexander Barabanov .20 .50
147 Kevin Labanc .20 .50
148 Matt Benning .20 .50
149 Matty Beniers .40 1.00
150 Jordan Eberle .25 .60
151 Jaden Schwartz .25 .60
152 Yanni Gourde .25 .60
153 Adam Larsson .20 .50
154 Philipp Grubauer .30 .75
155 Alexey Toropchenko .20 .50
156 Robert Thomas .30 .75
157 Kasperi Kapanen .25 .60
158 Brayden Schenn .30 .75
159 Nick Leddy .20 .50
160 Torey Krug .25 .60
161 Steven Stamkos .60 1.50
162 Nikita Kucherov .60 1.50
163 Nick Paul .20 .50
164 Tanner Jeannot .20 .50
165 Erik Cernak .20 .50
166 Andrei Vasilevskiy .50 1.25
167 Auston Matthews 1.25 3.00
168 John Tavares .50 1.25
169 Sam Lafferty .20 .50
170 T.J. Brodie .20 .50
171 Mark Giordano .30 .75
172 Matt Murray .30 .75
173 Conor Timmins .20 .50
174 Elias Pettersson .50 1.25
175 Anthony Beauvillier .20 .50
176 Brock Boeser .40 1.00
177 Conor Garland .25 .60
178 Sheldon Dries .20 .50
179 Oliver Ekman-Larsson .20 .50
180 Jonathan Marchessault .40 1.00
181 William Karlsson .40 1.00
182 Keegan Kolesar .20 .50
183 Alec Martinez .20 .50
184 Alex Pietrangelo .25 .60
185 Logan Thompson .40 1.00
186 Evgeny Kuznetsov .40 1.00
187 Tom Wilson .30 .75
188 Sonny Milano .25 .60
189 Dylan Strome .40 1.00
190 Nic Dowd .20 .50
191 Darcy Kuemper .30 .75
192 Nick Jensen .20 .50
193 Mark Scheifele .50 1.25
194 Blake Wheeler .30 .75
195 Adam Lowry .25 .60
196 Josh Morrissey .40 1.00
197 Nate Schmidt .20 .50
198 Cole Perfetti .30 .75
199 C.McDavid/S.Stamkos CL 1.50 4.00
200 N.MacKinnon/K.Kaprizov CL 1.25 3.00
201 Matthew Coronato YG RC 5.00 12.00
202 Vincent Desharnais YG RC 4.00 10.00
203 Joona Koppanen YG RC 2.50 6.00
204 Yaroslav Askarov YG RC 12.00 30.00
205 Jonathan Gruden YG RC 3.00 8.00
206 William Dufour YG RC 2.50 6.00
207 Jaxson Stauber YG RC 3.00 8.00
208 Jakob Pelletier YG RC 4.00 10.00
209 Samuel Bolduc YG RC 3.00 8.00
210 Dustin Wolf YG RC 15.00 40.00
211 Milos Kelemen YG RC 3.00 8.00
212 Ridly Greig YG RC 5.00 12.00
213 Will Cuylle YG RC 5.00 12.00
214 Owen Beck YG RC 5.00 12.00
215 Brock Faber YG RC 10.00 25.00
216 Cole Guttman YG RC 3.00 8.00
217 Arnaud Durandeau YG RC 3.00 8.00
218 David Gust YG RC 3.00 8.00
219 Elliot Desnoyers YG RC 3.00 8.00
220 Drew Helleson YG RC 3.00 8.00
221 Luke Evangelista YG RC 5.00 12.00
222 Matthew Knies YG RC 25.00 60.00
223 Tristen Robins YG RC 3.00 8.00
224 Vincent Iorio YG RC 3.00 8.00
225 Tyson Foerster YG RC 6.00 15.00
226 Egor Afanasyev YG RC 3.00 8.00
227 Jiri Patera YG RC 5.00 12.00
228 Simon Edvinsson YG RC 6.00 15.00
229 Wyatt Kaiser YG RC 3.00 8.00
230 Nikita Nesterenko YG RC 3.00 8.00
231 Hunter McKown YG RC 3.00 8.00
232 Aidan McDonough YG RC 2.50 6.00
233 Lukas Rousek YG RC 2.50 6.00
234 Sean Farrell YG RC 3.00 8.00
235 Tyler Kleven YG RC 3.00 8.00
236 Henry Thrun YG RC 3.00 8.00
237 Devon Levi YG RC 12.00 30.00
238 Spencer Stastney YG RC 3.00 8.00
239 Daniil Gushchin YG RC 3.00 8.00
240 Matthew Kessel YG RC 2.50 6.00
241 Marco Kasper YG RC 8.00 20.00
242 Akito Hirose YG RC 2.50 6.00
243 Adam Ginning YG RC 3.00 8.00
244 Cole McWard YG RC 3.00 8.00
245 Jake Livingstone YG RC 3.00 8.00
246 Jet Greaves YG RC 5.00 12.00
247 Leevi Merilainen YG RC 3.00 8.00
248 Luke Hughes YG RC 12.00 30.00
249 Olle Eriksson Ek YG RC 3.00 8.00
250 L.Hughes/M.Knies YG CL 3.00 8.00
251 Jakob Silfverberg .20 .50
252 Troy Terry .25 .60
253 Cam Fowler .30 .75
254 Jamie Drysdale .25 .60
255 Ryan Strome .30 .75
256 Adam Henrique .25 .60
257 John Gibson .30 .75
258 Clayton Keller .40 1.00
259 Barrett Hayton .30 .75
260 Nick Schmaltz .25 .60
261 Lawson Crouse .20 .50
262 Travis Boyd .20 .50
263 Karel Vejmelka .20 .50
264 Brad Marchand .60 1.50
265 David Pastrnak .75 2.00
266 Linus Ullmark .30 .75
267 Charlie Coyle .30 .75
268 Pavel Zacha .25 .60
269 Matt Grzelcyk .25 .60
270 Jeff Skinner .30 .75
271 Jack Quinn .25 .60
272 Casey Mittelstadt .30 .75
273 JJ Peterka .30 .75
274 Victor Olofsson .30 .75
275 Alex Tuch .30 .75
276 Tyler Toffoli .30 .75
277 Andrew Mangiapane .30 .75
278 Jonathan Huberdeau .40 1.00
279 Jacob Markstrom .30 .75
280 Rasmus Andersson .25 .60
281 MacKenzie Weegar .25 .60
282 Andrei Svechnikov .40 1.00
283 Martin Necas .50 1.25
284 Pyotr Kochetkov .30 .75
285 Brent Burns .30 .75
286 Brady Skjei .20 .50
287 Jordan Martinook .20 .50
288 Philipp Kurashev .25 .60
289 Jason Dickinson .20 .50
290 Connor Murphy .25 .60
291 Colin Blackwell .20 .50
292 Nikita Zaitsev .20 .50
293 Logan O'Connor .30 .75
294 Alex Newhook .30 .75
295 Cale Makar .75 2.00
296 Samuel Girard .20 .50
297 Alexandar Georgiev .30 .75
298 Josh Manson .20 .50
299 Boone Jenner .30 .75
300 Kent Johnson .20 .50
301 Jack Roslovic .20 .50
302 Erik Gudbranson .20 .50
303 Elvis Merzlikins .30 .75
304 Zach Werenski .50 1.25
305 Jason Robertson .50 1.25
306 Mason Marchment .25 .60
307 Ty Dellandrea .20 .50
308 Wyatt Johnston .60 1.50
309 Miro Heiskanen .40 1.00
310 Esa Lindell .25 .60
311 Dylan Larkin .40 1.00
312 Lucas Raymond .50 1.25
313 Andrew Copp .20 .50
314 Jonatan Berggren .25 .60
315 Michael Rasmussen .25 .60
316 Ville Husso .20 .50
317 Leon Draisaitl 1.00 2.50
318 Kailer Yamamoto .30 .75
319 Warren Foegele .20 .50
320 Darnell Nurse .25 .60
321 Dylan Holloway .30 .75
322 Stuart Skinner .40 1.00
323 Anton Lundell .30 .75
324 Carter Verhaeghe .30 .75
325 Aleksander Barkov .50 1.25
326 Spencer Knight .30 .75
327 Eetu Luostarinen .20 .50
328 Josh Mahura .20 .50
329 Kevin Fiala .25 .60
330 Phillip Danault .30 .75
331 Viktor Arvidsson .20 .50
332 Gabe Vilardi .30 .75
333 Drew Doughty .30 .75
334 Sean Durzi .20 .50
335 Trevor Moore .20 .50
336 Ryan Hartman .20 .50
337 Mats Zuccarello .30 .75
338 Joel Eriksson Ek .25 .60
339 Sam Steel .25 .60
340 Marcus Foligno .25 .60
341 Filip Gustavsson .30 .75
342 Mike Hoffman .20 .50
343 Denis Gurianov .40 1.00
344 Mike Matheson .20 .50
345 Jordan Harris .20 .50
346 Jake Allen .20 .50
347 Cole Caufield .60 1.50
348 Brendan Gallagher .30 .75
349 Thomas Novak .30 .75
350 Colton Sissons .20 .50
351 Roman Josi .30 .75
352 Ryan McDonagh .20 .50
353 Dante Fabbro .20 .50
354 Juuse Saros .40 1.00
355 Ryan Johansen .25 .60
356 Nico Hischier .50 1.25
357 Timo Meier .30 .75
358 Ondrej Palat .25 .60
359 Jesper Bratt .30 .75
360 Nathan Bastian .20 .50
361 Yegor Sharangovich .20 .50
362 Brock Nelson .30 .75
363 Kyle Palmieri .25 .60
364 Josh Bailey .25 .60
365 Adam Pelech .20 .50
366 Alexander Romanov .25 .60
367 Ilya Sorokin .50 1.25
368 Chris Kreider .40 1.00
369 Vincent Trocheck .30 .75
370 Alexis Lafreniere .50 1.25
371 Igor Shesterkin .60 1.50
372 Braden Schneider .25 .60
373 Jacob Trouba .25 .60
374 Tim Stutzle .40 1.00
375 Alex DeBrincat .40 1.00
376 Drake Batherson .30 .75
377 Artem Zub .20 .50
378 Jake Sanderson .40 1.00
379 Josh Norris .30 .75
380 Joel Farabee .30 .75
381 Owen Tippett .20 .50
382 Nicolas Deslauriers .20 .50
383 Travis Sanheim .20 .50
384 Rasmus Ristolainen .20 .50
385 Carter Hart .30 .75
386 Wade Allison .30 .75
387 Jake Guentzel .50 1.25
388 Rickard Rakell .25 .60
389 Evgeni Malkin .60 1.50
390 Jeff Carter .25 .60
391 Marcus Pettersson .20 .50
392 Fabian Zetterlund .20 .50
393 Nico Sturm .20 .50
394 Steven Lorentz .20 .50
395 Erik Karlsson .40 1.00
396 Mario Ferraro .20 .50
397 Kaapo Kahkonen .20 .50
398 Jared McCann .25 .60
399 Oliver Bjorkstrand .25 .60
400 Eeli Tolvanen .25 .60
401 Daniel Sprong .20 .50
402 Brandon Tanev .25 .60
403 Vince Dunn .20 .50
404 Andre Burakovsky .30 .75
405 Jordan Kyrou .30 .75
406 Pavel Buchnevich .25 .60
407 Brandon Saad .25 .60
408 Colton Parayko .25 .60
409 Justin Faulk .25 .60
410 Jordan Binnington .50 1.25
411 Brayden Point .40 1.00
412 Brandon Hagel .25 .60
413 Anthony Cirelli .25 .60
414 Ross Colton .20 .50
415 Victor Hedman .40 1.00
416 Mikhail Sergachev .25 .60
417 Nick Perbix .20 .50
418 Mitch Marner .50 1.25
419 William Nylander .60 1.50
420 Calle Jarnkrok .20 .50
421 Morgan Rielly .30 .75
422 Ilya Samsonov .30 .75
423 Jake McCabe .20 .50
424 Andrei Kuzmenko .30 .75
425 J.T. Miller .40 1.00
426 Quinn Hughes .75 2.00
427 Ilya Mikheyev .30 .75
428 Thatcher Demko .40 1.00
429 Filip Hronek .20 .50
430 Jack Eichel .50 1.25
431 Mark Stone .30 .75
432 Reilly Smith .30 .75
433 Michael Amadio .20 .50
434 Chandler Stephenson .25 .60
435 Shea Theodore .40 1.00
436 Alex Ovechkin 1.25 3.00
437 Anthony Mantha .25 .60
438 T.J. Oshie .30 .75
439 Nicolas Aube-Kubel .20 .50
440 Martin Fehervary .20 .50
441 John Carlson .30 .75
442 Nicklas Backstrom .30 .75
443 Kyle Connor .50 1.25
444 Nino Niederreiter .20 .50
445 Nikolaj Ehlers .30 .75
446 Morgan Barron .20 .50
447 Neal Pionk .25 .60
448 Connor Hellebuyck .60 1.50
449 E.Karlsson/C.Makar CL .75 2.00
450 W.Johnston/A.Kuzmenko CL .60 1.50
451 Connor Bedard YG RC 100.00 250.00
452 Damien Giroux YG RC 3.00 8.00
453 Tyler Angle YG RC 3.00 8.00
454 Waltteri Merela YG RC 3.00 8.00
455 Maxence Guenette YG RC 3.00 8.00
456 Jackson LaCombe YG RC 3.00 8.00
457 Clay Stevenson YG RC 3.00 8.00
458 Nick Swaney YG RC 3.00 8.00
459 Joel Teasdale YG RC 3.00 8.00
460 Ty Emberson YG RC 3.00 8.00
461 Stanislav Svozil YG RC 2.50 6.00
462 Alex Laferriere YG RC 5.00 12.00
463 Matt Murray YG RC 3.00 8.00
464 Mackie Samoskevich YG RC 5.00 12.00
465 Tye Kartye YG RC 5.00 12.00
466 Emil Andrae YG RC 3.00 8.00
467 Luke Philp YG RC 3.00 8.00
468 Leo Carlsson YG RC 10.00 25.00
469 Hugh McGing YG RC 3.00 8.00
470 Matt Tomkins YG RC 3.00 8.00
471 Justin Sourdif YG RC 3.00 8.00
472 John Beecher YG RC 6.00 15.00
473 Hardy Haman Aktell YG RC 3.00 8.00
474 Zach Benson YG RC 5.00 12.00
475 Walker Duehr YG RC 2.50 6.00
476 Uvis Balinskis YG RC 3.00 8.00
477 Mikael Pyyhtia YG RC 3.00 8.00
478 Matthew Poitras YG RC 6.00 15.00
479 Bobby McMann YG RC 5.00 12.00
480 Tristan Luneau YG RC 3.00 8.00
481 Michael Kesselring YG RC 3.00 8.00
482 Fraser Minten YG RC 6.00 15.00
483 Samuel Knazko YG RC 3.00 8.00
484 Lucas Condotta YG RC 3.00 8.00
485 Arturs Silovs YG RC 6.00 15.00
486 Kevin Korchinski YG RC 5.00 12.00
487 Billy Sweezey YG RC 3.00 8.00
488 Pavel Mintyukov YG RC 5.00 12.00
489 Ryan Shea YG RC 3.00 8.00
490 John Ludvig YG RC 3.00 8.00
491 Hunter Shepard YG RC 3.00 8.00
492 Dmitri Voronkov YG RC 4.00 10.00
493 Ilya Solovyov YG RC 3.00 8.00
494 Daemon Hunt YG RC 3.00 8.00
495 Nikolas Matinpalo YG RC 3.00 8.00
496 Connor Zary YG RC 6.00 15.00
497 Mason Lohrei YG RC 5.00 12.00
498 Marc Del Gaizo YG RC 3.00 8.00
499 Raphael Lavoie YG RC 3.00 8.00
500 Connor Bedard/Leo Carlsson CL 8.00 20.00
501 Radko Gudas .20 .50
502 Alex Killorn .20 .50
503 Ilya Lyubushkin .20 .50
504 Sean Durzi .20 .50
505 Connor Ingram .20 .50
506 Jason Zucker .30 .75
507 Travis Dermott .25 .60
508 Nick Bjugstad .20 .50
509 Alex Kerfoot .25 .60
510 Matt Dumba .20 .50
511 James van Riemsdyk .25 .60
512 Morgan Geekie .20 .50
513 Brandon Carlo .25 .60
514 Kevin Shattenkirk .20 .50
515 Jakub Lauko .30 .75
516 Erik Johnson .20 .50
517 Connor Clifton .20 .50
518 Kyle Okposo .20 .50
519 Zemgus Girgensons .20 .50
520 Yegor Sharangovich .30 .75
521 Blake Coleman .25 .60
522 Adam Ruzicka .25 .60
523 Jordan Staal .20 .50
524 Jesper Fast .20 .50
525 Antti Raanta .30 .75
526 Frederick Andersen .40 1.00
527 Dmitry Orlov .30 .75
528 Michael Bunting .30 .75
529 Tony DeAngelo .20 .50
530 Taylor Hall .30 .75
531 Nick Foligno .20 .50
532 Anthony Beauvillier .20 .50
533 Ryan Donato .25 .60
534 Ryan Johansen .25 .60
535 Ross Colton .25 .60
536 Miles Wood .25 .60
537 Jonathan Drouin .20 .50
538 Andrew Cogliano .20 .50
539 Jack Johnson .20 .50
540 Ivan Provorov .25 .60
541 Damon Severson .20 .50
542 Alexandre Texier .20 .50
543 Evgenii Dadonov .20 .50
544 Craig Smith .20 .50
545 Matt Duchene .30 .75
546 Sam Steel .20 .50
547 Jani Hakanpaa .25 .60
548 Ryan Suter .30 .75
549 Patrick Kane .60 1.50
550 Alex DeBrincat .40 1.00
551 Jeff Petry .20 .50
552 Justin Holl .20 .50
553 Daniel Sprong .20 .50
554 J.T. Compher .20 .50
555 Shayne Gostisbehere .30 .75
556 Connor Brown .25 .60
557 Ryan McLeod .20 .50
558 Mattias Ekholm .25 .60
559 Oliver Ekman-Larsson .20 .50
560 Nick Cousins .20 .50
561 Niko Mikkola .20 .50
562 Dmitry Kulikov .20 .50
563 Steven Lorentz .20 .50
564 Evan Rodrigues .25 .60
565 Pierre-Luc Dubois .25 .60
566 Cam Talbot .30 .75
567 Trevor Lewis .20 .50
568 Trevor Moore .30 .75
569 Patrick Maroon .20 .50
570 Marcus Johansson .20 .50
571 Frederick Gaudreau .20 .50
572 Jujhar Khaira .20 .50
573 Sean Monahan .20 .50
574 Alex Newhook .30 .75
575 Tanner Pearson .30 .75
576 Gustav Lindstrom .20 .50
577 Luke Schenn .30 .75
578 Ryan O'Reilly .30 .75
579 Gustav Nyquist .20 .50
580 Philip Tomasino .20 .50
581 Erik Haula .20 .50
582 Tyler Toffoli .30 .75
583 Tomas Nosek .20 .50
584 John Marino .30 .75
585 Pierre Engvall .20 .50
586 Scott Mayfield .20 .50
587 Semyon Varlamov .30 .75
588 Jonathan Quick .40 1.00
589 Blake Wheeler .30 .75
590 Tyler Pitlick .20 .50
591 Nick Bonino .20 .50
592 Erik Gustafsson .20 .50
593 Erik Brannstrom .20 .50
594 Joonas Korpisalo .30 .75
595 Travis Hamonic .25 .60
596 Dominik Kubalik .30 .75
597 Vladimir Tarasenko .40 1.00
598 Mark Kastelic .25 .60
599 Garnet Hathaway .20 .50
600 Marc Staal .20 .50
601 Cam Atkinson .30 .75
602 Sean Couturier .25 .60
603 Cam York .20 .50
604 Erik Karlsson .40 1.00
605 Reilly Smith .30 .75
606 Matt Nieto .25 .60
607 Noel Acciari .20 .50
608 Tristan Jarry .30 .75
609 Ryan Graves .20 .50
610 Lars Eller .20 .50
611 Mackenzie Blackwood .30 .75
612 Mike Hoffman .20 .50
613 Anthony Duclair .25 .60
614 Filip Zadina .25 .60
615 Mikael Granlund .25 .60
616 Jan Rutta .20 .50
617 Tomas Tatar .20 .50
618 Kailer Yamamoto .30 .75
619 Justin Schultz .25 .60
620 Alexander Wennberg .20 .50
621 William Borgen .20 .50
622 Jamie Oleksiak .25 .60
623 Kevin Hayes .25 .60
624 Jakub Vrana .25 .60
625 Sammy Blais .20 .50
626 Conor Sheary .25 .60
627 Tyler Motte .20 .50
628 Luke Glendening .20 .50
629 Michael Eyssimont .20 .50
630 David Kampf .20 .50
631 Ryan Reaves .25 .60
632 John Klingberg .25 .60
633 Tyler Bertuzzi .25 .60
634 Max Domi .30 .75
635 Timothy Liljegren .20 .50
636 Joseph Woll .40 1.00
637 Sam Lafferty .20 .50
638 Dakota Joshua .25 .60
639 Carson Soucy .20 .50
640 Pius Suter .20 .50
641 Ian Cole .20 .50
642 Tyler Myers .30 .75
643 Ivan Barbashev .20 .50
644 Adin Hill .30 .75
645 Brett Howden .20 .50
646 Nicolas Roy .20 .50
647 Aliaksei Protas .30 .75
648 Trevor van Riemsdyk .25 .60
649 Rasmus Sandin .25 .60
650 Gabe Vilardi .25 .60
651 Alex Iafallo .20 .50
652 Vladislav Namestnikov .30 .75
653 Laurent Brossoit .20 .50
654 Rasmus Kupari .20 .50
655 Aleksander Barkov AS .50 1.25
656 Nikita Kucherov AS .60 1.50
657 Dylan Larkin AS .40 1.00
658 Mitch Marner AS .40 1.00
659 David Pastrnak AS .75 2.00
660 Nick Suzuki AS .60 1.50
661 Brady Tkachuk AS .60 1.50
662 Matthew Tkachuk AS .60 1.50
663 Rasmus Dahlin AS .40 1.00
664 Linus Ullmark AS .30 .75
665 Andrei Vasilevskiy AS .50 1.25
666 Kirill Kaprizov AS 1.00 2.50
667 Clayton Keller AS .40 1.00
668 Nathan MacKinnon AS 1.25 3.00
669 Mikko Rantanen AS .75 2.00
670 Jason Robertson AS .50 1.25
671 Vladimir Tarasenko AS .60 1.50
672 Seth Jones AS .30 .75
673 Cale Makar AS .75 2.00
674 Josh Morrissey AS .40 1.00
675 Connor Hellebuyck AS .60 1.50
676 Juuse Saros AS .40 1.00
677 Sidney Crosby AS 1.25 3.00
678 Johnny Gaudreau AS .50 1.25
679 Kevin Hayes AS .25 .60
680 Jack Hughes AS .75 2.00
681 Brock Nelson AS .30 .75
682 Alex Ovechkin AS 1.25 3.00
683 Artemi Panarin AS .60 1.50
684 Andrei Svechnikov AS .40 1.00
685 Adam Fox AS .40 1.00
686 Igor Shesterkin AS .60 1.50
687 Ilya Sorokin AS .50 1.25
688 Leon Draisaitl AS 1.00 2.50
689 Kevin Fiala AS .25 .60
690 Bo Horvat AS .40 1.00
691 Nazem Kadri AS .40 1.00
692 Connor McDavid AS 1.50 4.00
693 Elias Pettersson AS .50 1.25
694 Chandler Stephenson AS .25 .60
695 Troy Terry AS .25 .60
696 Erik Karlsson AS .40 1.00
697 Stuart Skinner AS .40 1.00
698 Logan Thompson AS .40 1.00
699 P.Dubois/V.Tarasenko CL .40 1.00
700 T.Toffoli/E.Karlsson CL .40 1.00
701 Logan Cooley YG RC 12.00 30.00
702 Ondrej Pavel YG RC 3.00 8.00
703 Adam Edstrom YG RC 3.00 8.00
704 Isak Rosen YG RC 3.00 8.00
705 Roby Jarventie YG RC 3.00 8.00
706 Angus Crookshank YG RC 3.00 8.00
707 Samuel Laberge YG RC 3.00 8.00
708 Ryan Winterton YG RC 3.00 8.00
709 Calle Clang YG RC 3.00 8.00
710 Jiri Kulich YG RC 6.00 15.00
711 Adam Fantilli YG RC 15.00 40.00
712 Magnus Chrona YG RC 3.00 8.00
713 Martin Pospisil YG RC 4.00 10.00
714 Yaniv Perets YG RC 4.00 10.00
715 Jiri Smejkal YG RC 3.00 8.00
716 Sam Malinski YG RC 3.00 8.00
717 Ivan Miroshnichenko YG RC 5.00 12.00
718 Linus Karlsson YG RC 3.00 8.00
719 Ryan Johnson YG RC 4.00 10.00
720 Emil Heineman YG RC 4.00 10.00
721 Louis Crevier YG RC 3.00 8.00
722 Dylan Garand YG RC 5.00 12.00
723 Marc Johnstone YG RC 3.00 8.00
724 Dennis Hildeby YG RC 8.00 20.00
725 Jayden Struble YG RC 4.00 10.00
726 Ryker Evans YG RC 4.00 10.00
727 Simon Nemec YG RC 6.00 15.00
728 Georgii Merkulov YG RC 3.00 8.00
729 Matt Savoie YG RC 6.00 15.00
730 A.Fantilli/L.Cooley YG CL 5.00 12.00
731 Pavel Mintyukov 1R 2.50 6.00
732 John Beecher 1R 3.00 8.00
733 Tyson Foerster 1R 3.00 8.00
734 Marco Kasper 1R 4.00 10.00
735 Ryan Johnson 1R 2.00 5.00
736 Leo Carlsson 1R 5.00 12.00
737 Connor Zary 1R 3.00 8.00
738 Simon Edvinsson 1R 3.00 8.00
739 Zach Benson 1R 2.50 6.00
740 Connor Bedard 1R 12.00 30.00
741 Matthew Coronato 1R 2.50 6.00
742 Adam Fantilli 1R 2.00 5.00
743 Yaroslav Askarov 1R 4.00 10.00
744 Jakob Pelletier 1R 2.00 5.00
745 Matt Savoie 1R 3.00 8.00
746 Ridly Greig 1R 2.50 6.00
747 Mackie Samoskevich 1R 2.50 6.00
748 Logan Cooley 1R 5.00 12.00
749 Kevin Korchinski 1R 2.50 6.00
750 Luke Hughes 1R 5.00 12.00
SP1 Connor Bedard SP 100.00 250.00

2023-24 Upper Deck Clear Cut Parallel

*CLEAR CUT: 4X TO 10X BASIC
*CLEAR CUT YG/1R: 2X TO 5X BASIC
201 Matthew Coronato YG 60.00 150.00
204 Yaroslav Askarov YG 60.00 150.00
208 Jakob Pelletier YG 50.00 125.00
210 Dustin Wolf YG 80.00 200.00
215 Brock Faber YG 80.00 200.00
222 Matthew Knies YG 100.00 250.00
228 Simon Edvinsson YG 40.00 100.00
237 Devon Levi YG 125.00 300.00
248 Luke Hughes YG 100.00 250.00
250 Luke Hughes
Matthew Knies YG CL 20.00 50.00
451 Connor Bedard YG 800.00 2000.00
462 Alex Laferriere YG 25.00 60.00
465 Tye Kartye YG 30.00 80.00
468 Leo Carlsson YG 125.00 300.00
474 Zach Benson YG 20.00 50.00
478 Matthew Poitras YG 60.00 150.00
479 Bobby McMann YG 40.00 100.00
485 Arturs Silovs YG 60.00 150.00
486 Kevin Korchinski YG 40.00 100.00
488 Pavel Mintyukov YG 50.00 125.00
492 Dmitri Voronkov YG 30.00 80.00
496 Connor Zary YG 60.00 150.00
497 Mason Lohrei YG 30.00 80.00
500 Connor Bedard
Leo Carlsson YG CL 30.00 80.00
701 Logan Cooley YG 125.00 300.00
710 Jiri Kulich YG 50.00 125.00
717 Ivan Miroshnichenko YG 60.00 150.00
729 Matt Savoie YG 60.00 150.00

2023-24 Upper Deck Deluxe

*DELUXE/250: 2X TO 5X BASIC
*DELUXE YG/1R: 1.5X TO 4X BASIC
201 Matthew Coronato YG 50.00 125.00
204 Yaroslav Askarov YG 50.00 125.00
208 Jakob Pelletier YG 40.00 100.00
210 Dustin Wolf YG 80.00 200.00
212 Ridly Greig YG 40.00 100.00
213 Will Cuylle YG 50.00 125.00
215 Brock Faber YG 60.00 150.00
222 Matthew Knies YG 125.00 300.00
237 Devon Levi YG 80.00 200.00
241 Marco Kasper YG 50.00 125.00
248 Luke Hughes YG 80.00 200.00
451 Connor Bedard YG 800.00 2000.00
464 Mackie Samoskevich YG 25.00 60.00
465 Tye Kartye YG 40.00 100.00
468 Leo Carlsson YG 125.00 300.00
474 Zach Benson YG 20.00 50.00
478 Matthew Poitras YG 60.00 150.00
479 Bobby McMann YG 25.00 60.00
482 Fraser Minten YG 40.00 100.00
485 Arturs Silovs YG 40.00 100.00
486 Kevin Korchinski YG 50.00 125.00
488 Pavel Mintyukov YG 40.00 100.00
492 Dmitri Voronkov YG 25.00 60.00
496 Connor Zary YG 80.00 200.00
497 Mason Lohrei YG 30.00 80.00
500 Connor Bedard
Leo Carlsson YG CL 20.00 50.00
704 Isak Rosen YG 25.00 60.00
710 Jiri Kulich YG 30.00 80.00
722 Dylan Garand YG 25.00 60.00
729 Matt Savoie YG 50.00 125.00

2023-24 Upper Deck Exclusives

*EXCL/100: 3X TO 8X BASIC
201 Matthew Coronato YG 125.00 300.00
204 Yaroslav Askarov YG 150.00 400.00
208 Jakob Pelletier YG 100.00 250.00
210 Dustin Wolf YG 150.00 400.00
212 Ridly Greig YG 60.00 150.00
213 Will Cuylle YG 40.00 100.00
214 Owen Beck YG 60.00 150.00
215 Brock Faber YG 150.00 400.00
222 Matthew Knies YG 200.00 500.00
228 Simon Edvinsson YG 60.00 150.00
233 Lukas Rousek YG 40.00 100.00
237 Devon Levi YG 150.00 400.00
241 Marco Kasper YG 80.00 200.00
248 Luke Hughes YG 200.00 500.00
451 Connor Bedard YG 2000.00 5000.00
462 Alex Laferriere YG 40.00 100.00
464 Mackie Samoskevich YG 60.00 150.00
465 Tye Kartye YG 80.00 200.00
468 Leo Carlsson YG 250.00 600.00
474 Zach Benson YG 60.00 150.00
478 Matthew Poitras YG 150.00 400.00
479 Bobby McMann YG 80.00 200.00
482 Fraser Minten YG 100.00 250.00
485 Arturs Silovs YG 80.00 200.00
486 Kevin Korchinski YG 150.00 400.00
488 Pavel Mintyukov YG 60.00 150.00
492 Dmitri Voronkov YG 40.00 100.00
496 Connor Zary YG 150.00 400.00
497 Mason Lohrei YG 60.00 150.00
500 Connor Bedard
Leo Carlsson YG CL 125.00 300.00
701 Logan Cooley YG 200.00 500.00
710 Jiri Kulich YG 80.00 200.00
711 Adam Fantilli YG 150.00 400.00
717 Ivan Miroshnichenko YG 80.00 200.00
727 Simon Nemec YG 125.00 300.00
729 Matt Savoie YG 125.00 300.00
740 Connor Bedard 1R 250.00 600.00

2023-24 Upper Deck Outburst Red

*OUT RED/25: 15X TO 40X BASIC
*OUT RED YG/25: 5X TO 12X BASIC
199 Connor McDavid
Steven Stamkos CL 15.00 40.00
201 Matthew Coronato YG 125.00 300.00
202 Vincent Desharnais YG 50.00 125.00
204 Yaroslav Askarov YG 200.00 500.00
208 Jakob Pelletier YG 80.00 200.00
210 Dustin Wolf YG 500.00 1200.00
212 Ridly Greig YG 150.00 400.00
213 Will Cuylle YG 50.00 125.00
215 Brock Faber YG 600.00 1500.00
222 Matthew Knies YG 150.00 400.00
224 Vincent Iorio YG 40.00 100.00
227 Jiri Patera YG 50.00 125.00
228 Simon Edvinsson YG 100.00 250.00
229 Wyatt Kaiser YG 60.00 150.00
234 Sean Farrell YG 60.00 150.00
241 Marco Kasper YG 250.00 600.00
248 Luke Hughes YG 500.00 1200.00
250 Luke Hughes
Matthew Knies YG CL 50.00 125.00
451 Connor Bedard YG 6000.00 15000.00
462 Alex Laferriere YG 80.00 200.00
464 Mackie Samoskevich YG 100.00 250.00
466 Emil Andrae YG 50.00 125.00
468 Leo Carlsson YG 600.00 1500.00
478 Matthew Poitras YG 250.00 600.00
485 Arturs Silovs YG 100.00 200.00
490 John Ludvig YG 30.00 80.00
496 Connor Zary YG 200.00 500.00
500 Connor Bedard
Leo Carlsson YG CL 300.00 800.00
701 Logan Cooley YG 600.00 1500.00
706 Angus Crookshank YG 60.00 150.00
711 Adam Fantilli YG 800.00 2000.00
714 Yaniv Perets YG 60.00 150.00
726 Ryker Evans YG 60.00 150.00
727 Simon Nemec YG 250.00 600.00
728 Georgii Merkulov YG 100.00 250.00
740 Connor Bedard 1R 2000.00 5000.00
742 Adam Fantilli 1R 150.00 400.00

2023-24 Upper Deck Outburst Silver

*OUT SLVR: 2.5X TO 6X BASIC
*OUT SLVR YG/1R: 1X TO 2.5X BASIC
201 Matthew Coronato YG 20.00 50.00
204 Yaroslav Askarov YG 30.00 80.00
208 Jakob Pelletier YG 12.00 30.00
210 Dustin Wolf YG 60.00 150.00
212 Ridly Greig YG 20.00 50.00
215 Brock Faber YG 40.00 100.00
222 Matthew Knies YG 80.00 200.00
228 Simon Edvinsson YG 20.00 50.00
237 Devon Levi YG 50.00 125.00
241 Marco Kasper YG 25.00 60.00
248 Luke Hughes YG 30.00 80.00
250 Luke Hughes
Matthew Knies YG CL 8.00 20.00
451 Connor Bedard YG 300.00 800.00
462 Alex Laferriere YG 15.00 40.00
465 Tye Kartye YG 12.00 30.00
468 Leo Carlsson YG 80.00 200.00
474 Zach Benson YG 15.00 40.00
478 Matthew Poitras YG 30.00 80.00
479 Bobby McMann YG 12.00 30.00
482 Fraser Minten YG 25.00 60.00
485 Arturs Silovs YG 40.00 100.00
486 Kevin Korchinski YG 20.00 50.00
488 Pavel Mintyukov YG 20.00 50.00
492 Dmitri Voronkov YG 15.00 40.00
496 Connor Zary YG 30.00 80.00
497 Mason Lohrei YG 12.00 30.00
500 Connor Bedard
Leo Carlsson YG CL 40.00 100.00
701 Logan Cooley YG 60.00 150.00
704 Isak Rosen YG 12.00 30.00
710 Jiri Kulich YG 25.00 60.00
711 Adam Fantilli YG 60.00 150.00
722 Dylan Garand YG 60.00 150.00
727 Simon Nemec YG 50.00 125.00
729 Matt Savoie YG 50.00 125.00
730 Adam Fantilli
Logan Cooley YG CL 15.00 40.00
736 Leo Carlsson 1R 20.00 50.00
740 Connor Bedard 1R 125.00 300.00
742 Adam Fantilli 1R 8.00 20.00

2023-24 Upper Deck Photo Variations All Star Skills

*AS SKILLS: 3X TO 8X BASIC

2023-24 Upper Deck Photo Variations Snow Spray Autographs
*SPRAY: 20X TO 50X BASIC
636 Joseph Woll 30.00 80.00

2023-24 Upper Deck Photo Variations Swagnificent
*SWAG: 8X TO 20X BASIC

2023-24 Upper Deck '01-02 Upper Deck Retro Young Guns
YG1 Matthew Knies 150.00 400.00
YG2 Connor Bedard 600.00 1500.00
YG3 Logan Cooley 125.00 300.00
YG4 Adam Fantilli 125.00 300.00
YG5 Luke Hughes 125.00 300.00
YG6 Leo Carlsson 125.00 300.00
YG7 Ridly Greig 60.00 150.00
YG8 Matthew Poitras 80.00 200.00

2023-24 Upper Deck '03-04 Beehive
*GOLD/20: 3X TO 8X BASIC
BH1 Sidney Crosby 4.00 10.00
BH2 Brayden Point 1.25 3.00
BH3 Cole Caufield 2.00 5.00
BH4 Ilya Sorokin 1.50 4.00
BH5 Andrei Svechnikov 1.25 3.00
BH6 Trevor Zegras 1.00 2.50
BH7 Auston Matthews 4.00 10.00
BH8 Artemi Panarin 2.00 5.00
BH9 Brady Tkachuk 1.50 4.00
BH10 Connor McDavid 5.00 12.00
BH11 Claude Giroux 1.00 2.50
BH12 Erik Karlsson 1.25 3.00
BH13 Mathew Barzal 1.25 3.00
BH14 Brad Marchand 2.00 5.00
BH15 Anze Kopitar 1.50 4.00
BH16 Tyler Toffoli 1.00 2.50
BH17 Matty Beniers 1.25 3.00
BH18 Matthew Tkachuk 2.00 5.00
BH19 Leon Draisaitl 3.00 8.00
BH20 Nathan MacKinnon 4.00 10.00
BH21 Jack Eichel 1.50 4.00
BH22 Alex Ovechkin 4.00 10.00
BH23 Patrik Laine 1.25 3.00
BH24 Elias Pettersson 1.50 4.00
BH25 Travis Konecny 1.00 2.50
BH26 Kyle Connor 1.50 4.00
BH27 Mitch Marner 1.50 4.00
BH28 Robert Thomas 1.00 2.50
BH29 Jake Oettinger 1.50 4.00
BH30 Rasmus Dahlin 1.25 3.00
BH31 Luke Hughes 3.00 8.00
BH32 Matthew Poitras 2.00 5.00
BH33 Brock Faber 2.50 6.00
BH34 Adam Fantilli 3.00 8.00
BH35 Matthew Knies 4.00 10.00
BH36 Luke Evangelista 1.50 4.00
BH37 Matt Savoie 2.00 5.00
BH38 Leo Carlsson 3.00 8.00
BH39 Ridly Greig 1.50 4.00
BH40 Yaroslav Askarov 2.50 6.00
BH41 Connor Bedard 12.00 30.00
BH42 Tyson Foerster 2.00 5.00
BH43 Zach Benson 1.50 4.00
BH44 Logan Cooley 3.00 8.00
BH45 Matt Murray 1.00 2.50
BH46 Marco Kasper 2.50 6.00
BH47 Pavel Mintyukov 1.50 4.00
BH48 Will Cuylle 1.50 4.00
BH49 Devon Levi 2.50 6.00
BH50 Connor Zary 2.00 5.00

2023-24 Upper Deck '03-04 Beehive Red
*RED/250: 1.2X TO 3X BASIC
BH41 Connor Bedard 125.00 300.00

2023-24 Upper Deck '07-08 Black Diamond Retros
*RUBY/100: 1.2X TO 3X BASIC
BD1 Alex Tuch 1.00 2.50
BD2 Devon Toews .75 2.00
BD3 David Perron .75 2.00
BD4 Filip Gustavsson 1.00 2.50
BD5 Philipp Grubauer 1.00 2.50
BD6 Alex Newhook .75 2.00
BD7 Pavel Zacha .75 2.00
BD8 Mackie Samoskevich 1.50 4.00
BD9 Alex Laferriere 1.50 4.00
BD10 Sean Farrell 1.00 2.50
BD11 Simon Edvinsson 2.00 5.00
BD12 Marco Kasper 2.50 6.00
BD13 Zach Benson 1.50 4.00
BD14 Dustin Wolf 3.00 8.00
BD15 Martin Necas 1.50 4.00
BD16 Ryan Nugent-Hopkins 1.25 3.00
BD17 Carter Verhaeghe 1.25 3.00
BD18 Chandler Stephenson .75 2.00
BD19 Nikolaj Ehlers 1.00 2.50
BD20 Mikael Backlund .75 2.00
BD21 Boone Jenner 1.00 2.50
BD22 Matt Savoie 2.00 5.00
BD23 Devon Levi 2.50 6.00
BD24 Kevin Korchinski 1.50 4.00
BD25 Yaroslav Askarov 2.50 6.00
BD26 Matthew Poitras 2.00 5.00
BD27 Owen Beck 1.50 4.00
BD28 Luke Evangelista 1.50 4.00
BD29 Ilya Sorokin 1.50 4.00
BD30 Brad Marchand 2.00 5.00
BD31 Mitch Marner 1.50 4.00
BD32 Kirill Kaprizov 3.00 8.00
BD33 Kyle Connor 1.50 4.00
BD34 Jack Hughes 2.50 6.00
BD35 Tyson Foerster 2.00 5.00
BD36 Adam Fantilli 3.00 8.00
BD37 Brock Faber 2.50 6.00
BD38 Matthew Knies 4.00 10.00
BD39 Leo Carlsson 3.00 8.00
BD40 Ridly Greig 1.50 4.00
BD41 Connor McDavid 5.00 12.00
BD42 Sidney Crosby 4.00 10.00
BD43 Auston Matthews 4.00 10.00
BD44 Connor Bedard 50.00 125.00
BD45 Luke Hughes 3.00 8.00
BD46 Logan Cooley 3.00 8.00

2023-24 Upper Deck '08-09 Upper Deck Retro
T1 Dylan Larkin .60 1.50
T2 Jordan Kyrou .50 1.25
T3 Kirill Kaprizov 1.50 4.00
T4 Nikita Kucherov 1.00 2.50
T5 Sidney Crosby 2.00 5.00
T6 Jason Robertson .75 2.00
T7 Pierre-Luc Dubois .40 1.00
T8 Tage Thompson .60 1.50
T9 Clayton Keller .60 1.50
T10 Connor McDavid 2.50 6.00
T11 Cale Makar 1.25 3.00
T12 Jack Hughes 1.25 3.00
T13 Auston Matthews 2.00 5.00
T14 Aleksander Barkov .75 2.00
T15 Quinn Hughes 1.25 3.00
T16 Tim Stutzle .60 1.50
T17 Alex Ovechkin 2.00 5.00
T18 David Pastrnak 1.25 3.00
T19 Igor Shesterkin 1.00 2.50
T20 Johnny Gaudreau .75 2.00
T21 William Dufour .75 2.00
T22 Yaroslav Askarov 2.50 6.00
T23 Mackie Samoskevich 1.50 4.00
T24 Owen Beck 1.50 4.00
T25 Ridly Greig 1.50 4.00
T26 Matt Savoie 2.00 5.00
T27 Luke Hughes 3.00 8.00
T28 Will Cuylle 1.50 4.00
T29 Zach Benson 1.50 4.00
T30 Matthew Knies 4.00 10.00
T31 Brock Faber 2.50 6.00
T32 Pavel Mintyukov 1.50 4.00
T33 Luke Evangelista 1.50 4.00
T34 Matt Murray 1.00 2.50
T35 Logan Cooley 3.00 8.00
T36 Matthew Coronato 1.50 4.00
T37 Stanislav Svozil .75 2.00
T38 Simon Edvinsson 2.00 5.00
T39 Tyson Foerster 2.00 5.00
T40 Dustin Wolf 3.00 8.00
T41 Leo Carlsson 3.00 8.00
T42 Alex Laferriere 1.50 4.00
T43 Tye Kartye 1.50 4.00
T44 Kevin Korchinski 1.50 4.00
T45 Devon Levi 2.50 6.00
T46 Marco Kasper 2.50 6.00
T47 Connor Bedard 50.00 125.00
T48 Walker Duehr .75 2.00
T49 Adam Fantilli 3.00 8.00
T50 Matthew Poitras 2.00 5.00

2023-24 Upper Deck '08-09 Upper Deck Retro Exclusives
*EXC/100: 4X TO 10X BASIC
T30 Matthew Knies 50.00 125.00
T32 Pavel Mintyukov 30.00 80.00
T35 Logan Cooley 80.00 200.00
T40 Dustin Wolf 50.00 125.00
T45 Devon Levi 50.00 125.00
T47 Connor Bedard 1200.00 3000.00
T49 Adam Fantilli 150.00 400.00

2023-24 Upper Deck '94-95 Rookie Die Cuts
*RED: 1X TO 2.5X BASIC
RDT1 Jakob Pelletier .75 2.00
RDT2 Luke Hughes 2.00 5.00
RDT3 Luke Evangelista 1.00 2.50
RDT4 Simon Edvinsson 1.25 3.00
RDT5 Ridly Greig 1.00 2.50
RDT6 Matthew Knies 2.50 6.00
RDT7 Yaroslav Askarov 1.50 4.00
RDT8 Dustin Wolf 2.00 5.00
RDT9 Tyson Foerster 1.25 3.00
RDT10 Marco Kasper 1.50 4.00
RDT11 Stanislav Svozil .50 1.25
RDT12 Brock Faber 1.50 4.00
RDT13 Devon Levi 1.50 4.00
RDT14 Cole Guttman .60 1.50
RDT15 Walker Duehr .50 1.25
RDT16 Zach Benson 1.00 2.50
RDT17 Matthew Coronato 1.00 2.50
RDT18 Logan Cooley 2.00 5.00
RDT19 Connor Bedard 30.00 80.00
RDT20 Adam Fantilli 2.00 5.00

2023-24 Upper Deck '97-98 SPx Holoview Retros
*GOLD/50: 2X TO 5X BASIC
SPX1 Matthew Poitras 1.50 4.00
SPX2 Ryan O'Reilly .75 2.00
SPX3 Mathew Barzal 1.00 2.50
SPX4 Leo Carlsson 2.50 6.00
SPX5 Mikko Rantanen 2.00 5.00
SPX6 Brock Boeser 1.00 2.50
SPX7 Matthew Coronato 1.25 3.00
SPX8 Alex Ovechkin 3.00 8.00
SPX9 Cole Caufield 1.50 4.00
SPX10 Matthew Knies 3.00 8.00
SPX11 Pierre-Luc Dubois .60 1.50
SPX12 Adam Fox 1.00 2.50
SPX13 Devon Levi 2.00 5.00
SPX14 Kirill Kaprizov 2.50 6.00
SPX15 Luke Hughes 2.50 6.00
SPX16 Nikita Kucherov 1.50 4.00
SPX17 Sidney Crosby 3.00 8.00
SPX18 Kevin Korchinski 1.50 4.00
SPX19 Clayton Keller 1.00 2.50
SPX20 Rasmus Dahlin 1.00 2.50
SPX21 Brock Faber 2.00 5.00
SPX22 Teuvo Teravainen .75 2.00
SPX23 David Pastrnak 2.00 5.00
SPX24 Simon Edvinsson 1.50 4.00
SPX25 Trevor Zegras .75 2.00
SPX26 Matty Beniers 1.00 2.50
SPX27 Adam Fantilli 2.50 6.00
SPX28 John Tavares 1.25 3.00
SPX29 Jake Sanderson 1.00 2.50
SPX30 Dustin Wolf 2.50 6.00
SPX31 Dylan Larkin 1.00 2.50
SPX32 Jake Oettinger 1.25 3.00
SPX33 Connor Bedard 15.00 40.00
SPX34 Johnny Gaudreau 1.25 3.00
SPX35 Yaroslav Askarov 2.00 5.00
SPX36 Mark Scheifele 1.25 3.00
SPX37 Tomas Hertl .75 2.00
SPX38 Sean Farrell .75 2.00
SPX39 Connor McDavid 4.00 10.00
SPX40 Zach Benson 1.25 3.00
SPX41 Auston Matthews 3.00 8.00
SPX42 Matt Murray .75 2.00
SPX43 Jonathan Marchessault 1.00 2.50
SPX44 Luke Evangelista 1.25 3.00
SPX45 Aleksander Barkov 1.25 3.00
SPX46 Logan Cooley 2.50 6.00
SPX47 Jack Hughes 2.00 5.00
SPX48 Tyson Foerster 1.50 4.00
SPX49 Robert Thomas .75 2.00
SPX50 Ridly Greig 1.25 3.00

2023-24 Upper Deck '97-98 SPx Holoview Retros Red
*RED/250: X TO X BASIC
SPX33 Connor Bedard 100.00 250.00

2023-24 Upper Deck '98-99 UD3
UD31 Simon Edvinsson 1.00 2.50
UD32 Tristan Luneau .50 1.25
UD33 Connor Bedard 6.00 15.00
UD34 Walker Duehr .40 1.00
UD35 Luke Hughes 1.50 4.00
UD36 Leevi Merilainen .50 1.25
UD37 Brock Faber 1.25 3.00
UD38 Matt Savoie 1.00 2.50
UD39 Tyson Foerster 1.00 2.50
UD310 Logan Cooley 1.50 4.00
UD311 Luke Evangelista .75 2.00
UD312 Jackson LaCombe .50 1.25
UD313 Sean Farrell .50 1.25
UD314 Adam Fantilli 1.50 4.00
UD315 Kevin Korchinski .75 2.00
UD316 Mackie Samoskevich .75 2.00
UD317 Ridly Greig .75 2.00
UD318 Matthew Poitras 1.00 2.50
UD319 Alex Laferriere .75 2.00
UD320 Devon Levi 1.25 3.00
UD321 Justin Sourdif .50 1.25
UD322 Pavel Mintyukov .75 2.00
UD323 Dustin Wolf 1.50 4.00
UD324 Owen Beck .75 2.00
UD325 Yaroslav Askarov 1.25 3.00
UD326 Marco Kasper 1.25 3.00
UD327 Matthew Knies 2.00 5.00
UD328 Zach Benson .75 2.00
UD329 Leo Carlsson 1.50 4.00
UD330 Matt Murray .50 1.25

2023-24 Upper Deck '98-99 UD3 Blue
*BLUE/1000: .8X TO 2X BASIC
UD33 Connor Bedard 25.00 60.00

2023-24 Upper Deck '98-99 UD3 Gold
*GOLD/200: 2.5X TO 6X BASIC
UD33 Connor Bedard 50.00 125.00

2023-24 Upper Deck '98-99 UD3 Red
*RED/50: 8X TO 20X BASIC
UD33 Connor Bedard 150.00 400.00

2023-24 Upper Deck 200' x 85'
*GOLD: .6X TO 1.5X BASIC
*RED/99: 1X TO 2.5X BASIC
DM1 Connor McDavid 5.00 12.00
DM2 David Pastrnak 2.50 6.00
DM3 Filip Forsberg 1.50 4.00
DM4 Cole Caufield 2.00 5.00
DM5 Mats Zuccarello 1.00 2.50
DM6 Andrei Kuzmenko 1.00 2.50
DM7 Joona Koppanen .75 2.00
DM8 Jordan Kyrou 1.00 2.50
DM9 Nazem Kadri 1.25 3.00
DM10 Mark Stone 1.25 3.00
DM11 Owen Beck 1.50 4.00
DM12 Ryan Nugent-Hopkins 1.25 3.00
DM13 Robert Thomas 1.00 2.50
DM14 Alex Ovechkin 4.00 10.00
DM15 Erik Karlsson 1.25 3.00
DM16 Andrei Vasilevskiy 1.50 4.00
DM17 Kevin Hayes .75 2.00
DM18 Egor Afanasyev 1.00 2.50
DM19 Mitch Marner 1.50 4.00
DM20 Ilya Sorokin 1.50 4.00
DM21 Tyson Foerster 2.00 5.00
DM22 Cale Makar 2.50 6.00
DM23 Kyle Connor 1.50 4.00
DM24 Vincent Desharnais 1.25 3.00
DM25 Mika Zibanejad 1.25 3.00
DM26 Matthew Knies 4.00 10.00
DM27 Andrei Svechnikov 1.25 3.00
DM28 Roope Hintz 1.25 3.00
DM29 Ridly Greig 1.50 4.00
DM30 Leon Draisaitl 3.00 8.00
DM31 Simon Edvinsson 2.00 5.00
DM32 Matthew Tkachuk 2.00 5.00
DM33 John Tavares 1.50 4.00
DM34 Matty Beniers 1.25 3.00
DM35 Jack Hughes 2.50 6.00
DM36 Nathan MacKinnon 4.00 10.00
DM37 Elias Pettersson 1.50 4.00
DM38 Luke Evangelista 1.50 4.00
DM39 Trevor Zegras 1.00 2.50
DM40 Nick Suzuki 1.50 4.00
DM41 Anze Kopitar 1.50 4.00
DM42 Tyler Toffoli 1.00 2.50
DM43 Johnny Gaudreau 1.50 4.00
DM44 Wyatt Johnston 2.00 5.00
DM45 Owen Power 1.00 2.50
DM46 Tomas Hertl 1.00 2.50
DM47 Brad Marchand 2.00 5.00
DM48 Evgeni Malkin 2.00 5.00
DM49 Jeff Skinner 1.00 2.50
DM50 William Nylander 2.00 5.00
DM51 Dylan Larkin 1.25 3.00
DM52 Martin Necas 1.50 4.00
DM53 Steven Stamkos 2.00 5.00
DM54 Mark Scheifele 1.50 4.00
DM55 Charlie McAvoy 1.25 3.00
DM56 Aleksander Barkov 1.50 4.00
DM57 Moritz Seider 1.25 3.00
DM58 Kevin Fiala .75 2.00
DM59 Josh Morrissey 1.25 3.00
DM60 Quinn Hughes 2.50 6.00
DM61 Cole Guttman 1.00 2.50
DM62 Igor Shesterkin 2.00 5.00
DM63 Kirill Kaprizov 3.00 8.00
DM64 Patrik Laine 1.25 3.00
DM65 Auston Matthews 4.00 10.00
DM66 Tage Thompson 1.25 3.00
DM67 Taylor Raddysh .75 2.00
DM68 Jack Eichel 1.50 4.00
DM69 Jakob Pelletier 1.25 3.00
DM70 Jared McCann .75 2.00
DM71 J.T. Miller 1.25 3.00
DM72 Sidney Crosby 4.00 10.00
DM73 Kent Johnson 1.00 2.50
DM74 Brady Tkachuk 1.50 4.00
DM75 Seth Jones 1.00 2.50
DM76 Yaroslav Askarov 2.50 6.00
DM77 Artemi Panarin 2.00 5.00
DM78 Brock Faber 2.50 6.00
DM79 Mikko Rantanen 2.50 6.00
DM80 Sebastian Aho 1.50 4.00
DM81 Luke Hughes 3.00 8.00
DM82 Bo Horvat 1.25 3.00
DM83 Travis Konecny 1.00 2.50
DM84 Nikita Kucherov 2.00 5.00
DM85 Claude Giroux 1.00 2.50
DM86 Jaxson Stauber 1.00 2.50
DM87 Juraj Slafkovsky 2.00 5.00
DM88 Mathew Barzal 1.25 3.00
DM89 Evgeny Kuznetsov 1.00 2.50
DM90 Nico Hischier 1.50 4.00
DM91 Lawson Crouse .60 1.50
DM92 Connor Hellebuyck 2.00 5.00
DM93 Patrice Bergeron 1.25 3.00
DM94 Troy Terry .75 2.00
DM95 Roman Josi 1.25 3.00
DM96 Jason Robertson 1.50 4.00
DM97 Brayden Point 1.25 3.00
DM98 Tim Stutzle 1.25 3.00
DM99 Linus Ullmark 1.00 2.50
DM100 Clayton Keller 1.25 3.00

2023-24 Upper Deck Commemorative Class
*RED: .75X TO 2X BASIC
CC1 Vincent Desharnais 1.00 2.50
CC2 Ridly Greig 1.25 3.00
CC3 Marco Kasper 2.00 5.00
CC4 Jakob Pelletier 1.00 2.50
CC5 Yaroslav Askarov 2.00 5.00
CC6 Tyson Foerster 1.50 4.00
CC7 Luke Hughes 2.50 6.00
CC8 Owen Beck 1.25 3.00
CC9 Simon Edvinsson 1.50 4.00
CC10 Matthew Knies 3.00 8.00
CC11 Jaxson Stauber .75 2.00
CC12 Luke Evangelista 1.25 3.00
CC13 Brock Faber 2.00 5.00
CC14 Dustin Wolf 2.50 6.00
CC15 Cole Guttman .75 2.00
RC16 Will Cuylle 1.25 3.00
RC17 Logan Cooley 2.50 6.00
RC18 Walker Duehr .60 1.50
RC19 Matthew Coronato 1.25 3.00
RC20 Devon Levi 2.00 5.00
RC21 Connor Bedard 20.00 50.00
RC22 Arnaud Durandeau .75 2.00
RC23 Leevi Merilainen .75 2.00
RC24 Sean Farrell .75 2.00
RC25 Adam Fantilli 2.50 6.00
RC26 Stanislav Svozil .60 1.50
RC27 Danil Gushchin .75 2.00
RC28 William Dufour .60 1.50
RC29 Zach Benson 1.25 3.00
RC30 Maxence Guenette .75 2.00

2023-24 Upper Deck Day With The Cup
DC1 Alec Martinez 60.00 150.00
DC2 Brett Howden 30.00 80.00
DC3 Jonathan Marchessault 80.00 200.00
DC4 Keegan Kolesar 60.00 150.00
DC5 Mark Stone 60.00 150.00
DC6 Paul Cotter 30.00 80.00
DC7 Reilly Smith 50.00 125.00
DC8 Shea Theodore 60.00 150.00
DC9 William Carrier 30.00 80.00
DC10 William Karlsson 60.00 150.00
DC11 Teddy Blueger 30.00 80.00
DC12 Jonathan Quick 80.00 200.00
DC13 Brayden McNabb 50.00 125.00
DC14 Chandler Stephenson 40.00 100.00
DC15 Jack Eichel 80.00 200.00
DC16 Michael Amadio 30.00 80.00
DC17 Nicolas Hague 30.00 80.00
DC18 Alex Pietrangelo 40.00 100.00
DC19 Ben Hutton 30.00 80.00
DC20 Nicolas Roy 30.00 80.00
DC21 Logan Thompson 40.00 100.00
DC22 Zach Whitecloud 30.00 80.00
DC23 Adin Hill 50.00 125.00

2023-24 Upper Deck Dazzlers Blue
*GREEN: .5X TO 1.2X BASIC
*ORANGE: .8X TO 2X BASIC
*PINK: 2X TO 5X BASIC
DZ1 Jake DeBrusk .50 1.25
DZ2 Adam Fox .60 1.50
DZ3 Mason Marchment .40 1.00
DZ4 Mikko Rantanen 1.25 3.00
DZ5 David Perron .40 1.00
DZ6 Sam Reinhart 1.00 2.50
DZ7 Trevor Zegras .50 1.25
DZ8 Jake Guentzel .75 2.00
DZ9 Nino Niederreiter .30 .75
DZ10 Pavel Buchnevich .40 1.00
DZ11 Marc-Andre Fleury 1.00 2.50
DZ12 Yaroslav Askarov 1.25 3.00
DZ13 Chandler Stephenson .40 1.00
DZ14 Darcy Kuemper .50 1.25
DZ15 Evander Kane .50 1.25
DZ16 Jakob Pelletier .60 1.50
DZ17 Nick Suzuki 1.00 2.50
DZ18 Andre Burakovsky .30 .75
DZ19 Roope Hintz .60 1.50
DZ20 Nick Schmaltz .40 1.00
DZ21 Steven Stamkos 1.00 2.50
DZ22 Joel Eriksson Ek .40 1.00
DZ23 Ryan Nugent-Hopkins .60 1.50
DZ24 Mario Ferraro .30 .75
DZ25 Travis Konecny .50 1.25
DZ26 Rickard Rakell .40 1.00
DZ27 Brandon Montour .60 1.50
DZ28 Nikita Kucherov 1.00 2.50
DZ29 Timo Meier .50 1.25
DZ30 Jeff Skinner .50 1.25
DZ31 Anders Lee .40 1.00
DZ32 David Pastrnak 1.25 3.00
DZ33 John Tavares .75 2.00
DZ34 Phillip Danault .50 1.25
DZ35 Jake Sanderson .60 1.50
DZ36 Troy Terry .40 1.00
DZ37 William Nylander 1.00 2.50
DZ38 Drew Doughty .50 1.25
DZ39 Seth Jones .50 1.25
DZ40 Jordan Eberle .50 1.25
DZ41 Alexandar Georgiev .50 1.25
DZ42 Sebastian Aho .75 2.00
DZ43 Jonathan Huberdeau .60 1.50
DZ44 Martin Necas .75 2.00
DZ45 Dylan Strome .60 1.50
DZ46 Johnny Gaudreau .75 2.00
DZ47 Andrei Kuzmenko .50 1.25
DZ48 Juuse Saros .60 1.50
DZ49 Josh Morrissey .60 1.50
DZ50 Moritz Seider .60 1.50
DZ51 Jamie Benn .50 1.25
DZ52 Jordan Kyrou .50 1.25
DZ53 Valeri Nichushkin .50 1.25
DZ54 Luke Evangelista .75 2.00
DZ55 Filip Gustavsson .50 1.25
DZ56 Bo Horvat .60 1.50
DZ57 Cole Caufield 1.00 2.50
DZ58 Noah Cates .30 .75
DZ59 Erik Karlsson .60 1.50
DZ60 Philipp Grubauer .50 1.25
DZ61 Matthew Tkachuk 1.00 2.50
DZ62 Jack Eichel .75 2.00
DZ63 Stuart Skinner .60 1.50
DZ64 Evgeny Kuznetsov .60 1.50
DZ65 Mason McTavish .60 1.50
DZ66 Walker Duehr .40 1.00
DZ67 Dylan Larkin .60 1.50
DZ68 Charlie McAvoy .60 1.50
DZ69 Tage Thompson .60 1.50
DZ70 Adrian Kempe .50 1.25
DZ71 Jason Robertson .75 2.00
DZ72 Dawson Mercer .60 1.50
DZ73 Lucas Raymond .75 2.00
DZ74 Kirill Marchenko .60 1.50
DZ75 Sidney Crosby 2.00 5.00
DZ76 Artemi Panarin 1.00 2.50
DZ77 Jared McCann .40 1.00
DZ78 Carter Verhaeghe .50 1.25
DZ79 Connor Bedard 30.00 80.00
DZ80 Kyle Connor .75 2.00
DZ81 Filip Forsberg .75 2.00
DZ82 Mikhail Sergachev .40 1.00
DZ83 Nico Hischier .75 2.00
DZ84 Tyler Toffoli .50 1.25
DZ85 Mitch Marner .75 2.00
DZ86 Connor McDavid 2.50 6.00
DZ87 Nathan MacKinnon 2.00 5.00
DZ88 Brayden Point .60 1.50
DZ89 Brady Tkachuk .75 2.00
DZ90 Patrik Laine .60 1.50
DZ91 Rasmus Dahlin .60 1.50
DZ92 Tyson Foerster 1.00 2.50
DZ93 Andrei Svechnikov .60 1.50
DZ94 Ilya Sorokin .75 2.00
DZ95 Elias Pettersson .75 2.00
DZ96 Claude Giroux .50 1.25
DZ97 Mats Zuccarello .50 1.25
DZ98 Mika Zibanejad .60 1.50
DZ99 Logan Thompson .60 1.50
DZ100 Clayton Keller .60 1.50
DZ101 Brad Marchand 1.00 2.50
DZ102 Kent Johnson .50 1.25
DZ103 Quinn Hughes 1.25 3.00
DZ104 Roman Josi .60 1.50
DZ105 Matt Boldy .75 2.00
DZ106 Robert Thomas .50 1.25
DZ107 Evgeni Malkin 1.00 2.50
DZ108 Owen Tippett .30 .75
DZ109 Igor Shesterkin 1.00 2.50
DZ110 Morgan Frost .40 1.00
DZ111 Devon Levi 1.25 3.00
DZ112 Zach Hyman .75 2.00
DZ113 Ryan O'Reilly .50 1.25
DZ114 Ivan Barbashev .40 1.00
DZ115 Kevin Korchinski .75 2.00
DZ116 Ryan Johansen .40 1.00
DZ117 Connor Zary 1.00 2.50
DZ118 Pierre-Luc Dubois .40 1.00
DZ119 Logan Cooley 1.50 4.00
DZ120 Jonathan Marchessault .60 1.50
DZ121 Kirill Kaprizov 1.50 4.00
DZ122 Leo Carlsson 1.50 4.00
DZ123 Miro Heiskanen .60 1.50
DZ124 Luke Hughes 1.50 4.00
DZ125 Tim Stutzle .60 1.50
DZ126 Frederik Andersen .60 1.50
DZ127 Jamie Drysdale .40 1.00
DZ128 Reilly Smith .40 1.00
DZ129 Victor Hedman .60 1.50
DZ130 Leon Draisaitl 1.50 4.00
DZ131 Jake Oettinger .75 2.00
DZ132 Aleksander Barkov .75 2.00
DZ133 Mathew Barzal .60 1.50
DZ134 Mikael Granlund .40 1.00
DZ135 Vladimir Tarasenko .60 1.50
DZ136 Pavel Mintyukov .75 2.00
DZ137 Jack Hughes 1.25 3.00
DZ138 Linus Ullmark .50 1.25
DZ139 Mark Scheifele .75 2.00
DZ140 Alex Newhook .40 1.00
DZ141 Alex Tuch .50 1.25
DZ142 Adam Fantilli 1.50 4.00
DZ143 Kevin Fiala .40 1.00
DZ144 Auston Matthews 2.00 5.00
DZ145 Cale Makar 1.25 3.00
DZ146 Alex DeBrincat .60 1.50
DZ147 Matthew Knies 2.00 5.00
DZ148 Andrei Vasilevskiy .75 2.00
DZ149 Alex Ovechkin 2.00 5.00
DZ150 Matthew Poitras 1.00 2.50

2023-24 Upper Deck Dazzlers Black
*BLACK: 3X TO 8X BASIC
DZ79 Connor Bedard 400.00 1000.00

2023-24 Upper Deck Dazzlers Red
*RED: 1.5X TO 4X BASIC
DZ79 Connor Bedard 125.00 300.00

2023-24 Upper Deck Debut Dates
*GOLD: 1X TO 2.5X BASIC
DD1 Jakob Pelletier 1.00 2.50
DD2 Jonathan Gruden .75 2.00
DD3 Luke Evangelista 1.25 3.00
DD4 Will Cuylle 1.25 3.00
DD5 Dustin Wolf 2.50 6.00
DD6 Samuel Bolduc .75 2.00
DD7 Tyson Foerster 1.50 4.00
DD8 Jaxson Stauber .75 2.00
DD9 Vincent Desharnais 1.00 2.50
DD10 Ridly Greig 1.25 3.00
DD11 Matthew Coronato 1.25 3.00
DD12 David Gust .75 2.00
DD13 Yaroslav Askarov 2.00 5.00
DD14 Owen Beck 1.25 3.00
DD15 Brock Faber 2.00 5.00
DD16 Joona Koppanen .60 1.50
DD17 Vincent Iorio .75 2.00
DD18 Matthew Knies 3.00 8.00
DD19 Wyatt Kaiser .75 2.00
DD20 Simon Edvinsson 1.50 4.00
DD21 Arnaud Durandeau .75 2.00
DD22 Cole Guttman .75 2.00
DD23 Devon Levi 2.00 5.00
DD24 Marco Kasper 2.00 5.00
DD25 Luke Hughes 2.50 6.00

2023-24 Upper Deck Deep Roots
DR1 Auston Matthews 2.50 6.00
DR2 Patrice Bergeron 1.00 2.50
DR3 Cam Fowler .75 2.00
DR4 Drew Doughty .75 2.00
DR5 Lawson Crouse .50 1.25
DR6 Nathan MacKinnon 2.50 6.00
DR7 Nikita Kucherov 1.25 3.00
DR8 William Karlsson 1.00 2.50
DR9 Thomas Chabot .75 2.00
DR10 Filip Forsberg 1.25 3.00
DR11 Robert Thomas .75 2.00
DR12 Alex Ovechkin 2.50 6.00
DR13 Aaron Ekblad 1.00 2.50
DR14 Blake Wheeler .75 2.00
DR15 Anze Kopitar 1.00 2.50
DR16 Mathew Barzal 1.00 2.50
DR17 Sidney Crosby 2.50 6.00
DR18 Steven Stamkos 1.25 3.00
DR19 Roman Josi .75 2.00
DR20 Carter Hart .60 1.50
DR21 Aleksander Barkov 1.25 3.00
DR22 Ryan Nugent-Hopkins 1.00 2.50
DR23 William Nylander 1.25 3.00
DR24 Andrei Vasilevskiy 1.25 3.00
DR25 Brendan Gallagher .75 2.00
DR26 Evgeni Malkin 1.25 3.00
DR27 Mikael Backlund .60 1.50
DR28 Morgan Rielly .75 2.00
DR29 Andrew Mangiapane .75 2.00
DR30 Logan Couture .75 2.00
DR31 David Pastrnak 1.50 4.00
DR32 Leon Draisaitl 2.00 5.00
DR33 Mikko Rantanen 1.50 4.00
DR34 Sebastian Aho 1.00 2.50
DR35 Mark Scheifele 1.00 2.50
DR36 Clayton Keller .75 2.00
DR37 Mika Zibanejad .75 2.00
DR38 Brad Marchand 1.25 3.00
DR39 Dylan Larkin .75 2.00
DR40 Mitch Marner 1.00 2.50
DR41 Jamie Benn .75 2.00
DR42 Zach Werenski 1.25 3.00
DR43 Tomas Hertl .75 2.00
DR44 Anders Lee .60 1.50
DR45 Connor McDavid 3.00 8.00
DR46 Tyler Seguin .75 2.00
DR47 Elias Pettersson 1.00 2.50
DR48 Kris Letang 1.00 2.50
DR49 Brayden Point .75 2.00
DR50 John Carlson .75 2.00

2023-24 Upper Deck Deep Roots Purple
*PURPLE: .6X TO 1.5X BASIC
DR1 Auston Matthews 15.00 40.00
DR17 Sidney Crosby 12.00 30.00
DR45 Connor McDavid 15.00 40.00

2023-24 Upper Deck Director of Boards
*SPARKLE: .5X TO 1.2X BASIC
*GOLD SPRKL: 1.5X TO 4X BASIC
DB1 Ryan Reaves 1.50 4.00
DB2 A.J. Greer 1.25 3.00
DB3 Sam Carrick 1.25 3.00
DB4 Michael Pezzetta 1.25 3.00
DB5 Tanner Jeannot 1.25 3.00
DB6 Mathieu Olivier 1.25 3.00
DB7 Liam O'Brien 1.25 3.00
DB8 Marcus Foligno 1.50 4.00
DB9 Zack MacEwen 1.25 3.00
DB10 Arber Xhekaj 2.00 5.00
DB11 Trent Frederic 1.25 3.00
DB12 Austin Watson 1.25 3.00
DB13 Nicolas Deslauriers 1.25 3.00
DB14 Josh Brown 1.25 3.00
DB15 Patrick Maroon 1.25 3.00

2023-24 Upper Deck Ecliptic
*SPARKLE: .5X TO 1.2X BASIC
*GOLD SPRKL: 1.2X TO 3X BASIC
EC1 Jack Hughes 1.50 4.00
EC2 Alex Ovechkin 2.50 6.00
EC3 Elias Pettersson 1.00 2.50
EC4 Jared McCann .50 1.25
EC5 Kirill Kaprizov 2.00 5.00
EC6 Sidney Crosby 2.50 6.00
EC7 Tim Stutzle .75 2.00
EC8 Adrian Kempe .60 1.50
EC9 Cole Caufield 1.25 3.00
EC10 Auston Matthews 2.50 6.00
EC11 Jason Robertson 1.00 2.50
EC12 Brayden Point .75 2.00
EC13 David Pastrnak 1.50 4.00
EC14 Andrei Svechnikov .75 2.00
EC15 Tage Thompson .75 2.00
EC16 Mikko Rantanen 1.50 4.00
EC17 Clayton Keller .75 2.00
EC18 Leon Draisaitl 2.00 5.00
EC19 Artemi Panarin 1.25 3.00
EC20 Bo Horvat .75 2.00

2023-24 Upper Deck Fanimation
FM1 Cale Makar 60.00 150.00
FM2 Kirill Kaprizov 80.00 200.00
FM3 Cole Caufield 50.00 125.00
FM4 Roman Josi 25.00 60.00
FM5 Trevor Zegras 25.00 60.00
FM6 Brent Burns 25.00 60.00
FM7 Tage Thompson 30.00 80.00
FM8 Alex Ovechkin 100.00 250.00
FM9 Jordan Kyrou 25.00 60.00
FM10 Nazem Kadri 30.00 80.00
FM11 Brady Tkachuk 40.00 100.00
FM12 Jack Eichel 40.00 100.00
FM13 Noah Dobson 30.00 80.00
FM14 Jason Robertson 40.00 100.00
FM15 Johnny Gaudreau 40.00 100.00
FM16 Connor McDavid 125.00 300.00
FM17 Auston Matthews 100.00 250.00
FM18 Lucas Raymond 40.00 100.00
FM19 Clayton Keller 30.00 80.00
FM20 Connor Hellebuyck 50.00 125.00
FM21 Anze Kopitar 40.00 100.00
FM22 Matty Beniers 30.00 80.00
FM23 Sidney Crosby 100.00 250.00
FM24 Jack Hughes 60.00 150.00
FM25 Seth Jones 25.00 60.00
FM26 Artemi Panarin 50.00 125.00
FM27 Nikita Kucherov 50.00 125.00
FM28 Elias Pettersson 40.00 100.00
FM29 Tomas Hertl 25.00 60.00
FM30 Carter Hart 25.00 60.00
FM31 Charlie McAvoy 30.00 80.00
FM32 Matthew Tkachuk 50.00 125.00

2023-24 Upper Deck Fluorescence Red
*GOLD/150: 1.2X TO 3X RED
*BLUE/50: 2X TO 5X RED
F1 Jet Greaves 1.50 4.00
F2 Owen Beck 1.50 4.00
F3 Nikita Nesterenko 1.00 2.50
F4 Will Cuylle 1.50 4.00
F5 Tristen Robins 1.00 2.50
F6 Jackson LaCombe 1.00 2.50
F7 Dustin Wolf 3.00 8.00
F8 Vincent Desharnais 1.25 3.00
F9 Egor Afanasyev 1.00 2.50
F10 Adam Ginning 1.00 2.50
F11 Henry Thrun 1.00 2.50
F12 Luke Hughes 3.00 8.00
F13 Matthew Coronato 1.50 4.00
F14 Milos Kelemen 1.00 2.50
F15 Olle Eriksson Ek 1.00 2.50
F16 Aidan McDonough .75 2.00
F17 Bobby McMann 1.50 4.00
F18 Yaroslav Askarov 2.50 6.00
F19 Ridly Greig 1.50 4.00
F20 Marco Kasper 2.50 6.00
F21 Hugh McGing 1.00 2.50
F22 Joona Koppanen .75 2.00
F23 Jakob Pelletier 1.25 3.00
F24 Danil Gushchin 1.00 2.50
F25 Cole Guttman 1.00 2.50
F26 Samuel Bolduc 1.00 2.50
F27 Brock Faber 2.50 6.00
F28 Vincent Iorio 1.00 2.50
F29 Lucas Condotta 1.00 2.50
F30 Hunter McKown 1.00 2.50
F31 Simon Edvinsson 2.00 5.00
F32 Tyler Kleven 1.00 2.50
F33 William Dufour .75 2.00
F34 Tyson Foerster 2.00 5.00
F35 Walker Duehr .75 2.00
F36 Arnaud Durandeau 1.00 2.50
F37 Maxence Guenette 1.00 2.50
F38 Matthew Knies 4.00 10.00
F39 Stanislav Svozil .75 2.00
F40 Jiri Patera 1.50 4.00
F41 Sean Farrell 1.00 2.50
F42 Leevi Merilainen 1.00 2.50
F43 Luke Philp 1.00 2.50
F44 Matt Murray 1.00 2.50
F45 Elliot Desnoyers 1.00 2.50
F46 Jaxson Stauber 1.00 2.50
F47 Tye Kartye 1.50 4.00
F48 Akito Hirose .75 2.00
F49 Devon Levi 2.50 6.00
F50 Luke Evangelista 1.50 4.00

2023-24 Upper Deck Glaring
*GOLD/100: 1.5X TO 4X BASIC
GL1 Alex Ovechkin 4.00 10.00
GL2 Auston Matthews 4.00 10.00
GL3 Kirill Kaprizov 3.00 8.00
GL4 Trevor Zegras 1.00 2.50
GL5 Leon Draisaitl 3.00 8.00
GL6 Chris Kreider 1.25 3.00
GL7 Jason Robertson 1.50 4.00
GL8 Brayden Point 1.25 3.00
GL9 Owen Power 1.00 2.50
GL10 Elias Pettersson 1.50 4.00
GL11 Nazem Kadri 1.25 3.00
GL12 Nathan MacKinnon 4.00 10.00
GL13 Cole Caufield 2.00 5.00
GL14 Drew Doughty 1.00 2.50
GL15 Evander Kane 1.00 2.50
GL16 Sidney Crosby 4.00 10.00
GL17 Erik Karlsson 1.25 3.00
GL18 Filip Forsberg 1.50 4.00

2023-24 Upper Deck Highlighters Yellow
*ORANGE: .5X TO 1.2X YELLOW
*PINK: 1X TO 2.5X YELLOW
*GREEN: 1.5X TO 4X YELLOW
HL1 Linus Ullmark 2.00 5.00
HL2 Andrei Kuzmenko 2.00 5.00
HL3 Phil Kessel 2.00 5.00

HL4 Jake DeBrusk 2.00 5.00
HL5 Matty Beniers 2.50 6.00
HL6 Connor McDavid 10.00 25.00
HL7 Cal Clutterbuck 1.25 3.00
HL8 Erik Karlsson 2.50 6.00
HL9 Claude Giroux 2.00 5.00
HL10 Alex Ovechkin 8.00 20.00
HL11 Joe Pavelski 2.50 6.00
HL12 Martin Necas 3.00 8.00
HL13 Christian Fischer 1.25 3.00
HL14 Steven Stamkos 4.00 10.00
HL15 Tage Thompson 2.50 6.00
HL16 Shane Wright 2.50 6.00
HL17 Ryan Nugent-Hopkins 2.50 6.00
HL18 Sidney Crosby 8.00 20.00
HL19 Matthew Tkachuk 4.00 10.00
HL20 David Pastrnak 5.00 12.00
HL21 Juraj Slafkovsky 4.00 10.00
HL22 Stuart Skinner 2.50 6.00
HL23 Cale Makar 5.00 12.00
HL24 Juuse Saros 2.50 6.00
HL25 Wyatt Johnston 4.00 10.00

2023-24 Upper Deck Hockey Heroes

HH1 Joe Thornton 2.50 6.00
HH2 Sid Abel 1.50 4.00
HH3 David Pastrnak 4.00 10.00
HH4 Matthew Tkachuk 3.00 8.00
HH5 Erik Karlsson 2.00 5.00
HH6 Sebastian Aho 2.50 6.00
HH7 Marian Hossa 1.50 4.00
HH8 Auston Matthews 6.00 15.00
HH9 Steven Stamkos 3.00 8.00
HH10 Mike Modano 2.50 6.00
HH11 Mitch Marner 2.50 6.00
HH12 Jacques Plante 1.50 4.00
HH13 Jack Eichel 2.50 6.00
HH14 Shane Doan 1.25 3.00
HH15 Kirill Kaprizov 5.00 12.00
HH16 Luc Robitaille 1.50 4.00
HH17 Glenn Hall 1.50 4.00
HH18 Connor McDavid 8.00 20.00
HH19 Brady Tkachuk 2.50 6.00
HH20 Peter Bondra 1.50 4.00
HH21 Teemu Selanne 3.00 8.00
HH22 Al MacInnis 2.00 5.00
HH23 Nikita Kucherov 3.00 8.00
HH24 Leon Draisaitl 5.00 12.00
HH25 Matty Beniers 2.00 5.00
HH26 Jack Hughes 4.00 10.00
HH27 Chris Pronger 1.50 4.00
HH28 Eric Lindros 2.50 6.00
HH29 Maurice Richard 3.00 8.00
HH30 Bryan Trottier 1.50 4.00
HH31 Jason Robertson 2.50 6.00
HH32 Pat LaFontaine 1.50 4.00
HH33 Elias Pettersson 2.50 6.00
HH34 Keith Tkachuk 1.50 4.00
HH35 Darryl Sittler 1.50 4.00
HH36 Nathan MacKinnon 6.00 15.00
HH37 Rick Nash 1.50 4.00
HH38 Brad Marchand 3.00 8.00
HH39 Tim Horton 2.50 6.00
HH40 Artemi Panarin 3.00 8.00

2023-24 Upper Deck HoloGrFx Future Fame

FF1 Jonathan Toews 6.00 15.00
FF2 Anze Kopitar 6.00 15.00
FF3 Nikita Kucherov 8.00 20.00
FF4 Joe Pavelski 5.00 12.00
FF5 Jonathan Quick 5.00 12.00
FF6 Alex Pietrangelo 3.00 8.00
FF7 Victor Hedman 5.00 12.00
FF8 Leon Draisaitl 12.00 30.00
FF9 Carey Price 8.00 20.00
FF10 Drew Doughty 4.00 10.00

2023-24 Upper Deck HoloGrFx Rookies

*GOLD: .8X TO 2X BASIC
HG1 Connor Bedard 30.00 80.00
HG2 Leo Carlsson 3.00 8.00
HG3 Adam Fantilli 3.00 8.00
HG4 Matthew Knies 4.00 10.00
HG5 Luke Hughes 3.00 8.00
HG6 Ridly Greig 1.50 4.00
HG7 Luke Evangelista 1.50 4.00
HG8 Brock Faber 2.50 6.00
HG9 Yaroslav Askarov 2.50 6.00
HG10 Pavel Mintyukov 1.50 4.00
HG11 Tyson Foerster 2.00 5.00
HG12 Devon Levi 2.50 6.00
HG13 Logan Cooley 3.00 8.00
HG14 Connor Zary 2.00 5.00
HG15 Matthew Poitras 2.00 5.00

2023-24 Upper Deck Honor Roll

*RED: .75X TO 2X BASIC
*SILVER: 2X TO 5X BASIC
*GOLD/25: 4X TO 10X BASIC
HR1 Johnny Gaudreau 1.25 3.00
HR2 Matty Beniers 1.00 2.50
HR3 Dylan Larkin 1.00 2.50
HR4 David Pastrnak 2.00 5.00
HR5 Adam Fox 1.00 2.50
HR6 Cole Caufield 1.50 4.00
HR7 Pavel Buchnevich .60 1.50
HR8 Tim Stutzle 1.00 2.50
HR9 Aleksander Barkov 1.25 3.00
HR10 Clayton Keller 1.00 2.50
HR11 Nazem Kadri 1.00 2.50
HR12 Elias Pettersson 1.25 3.00
HR13 Mark Scheifele 1.25 3.00
HR14 Alex Ovechkin 3.00 8.00
HR15 Kevin Fiala .60 1.50
HR16 Mitch Marner 1.25 3.00
HR17 Jack Eichel 1.25 3.00
HR18 Bo Horvat 1.00 2.50
HR19 William Nylander 1.50 4.00
HR20 Sidney Crosby 3.00 8.00
HR21 Brayden Point 1.00 2.50
HR22 Kirill Kaprizov 2.50 6.00
HR23 Nathan MacKinnon 3.00 8.00
HR24 Trevor Zegras .75 2.00
HR25 Jack Hughes 2.00 5.00
HR26 Tage Thompson 1.00 2.50
HR27 Seth Jones .75 2.00
HR28 Connor McDavid 4.00 10.00
HR29 Andrei Svechnikov 1.00 2.50
HR30 Matthew Tkachuk 1.50 4.00
HR31 Carter Hart .75 2.00
HR32 Filip Forsberg 1.25 3.00
HR33 Jason Robertson 1.25 3.00
HR34 Leon Draisaitl 2.50 6.00
HR35 Erik Karlsson 1.00 2.50
HR36 Brock Faber 2.00 5.00
HR37 Matthew Coronato 1.25 3.00
HR38 Luke Hughes 2.50 6.00
HR39 Will Cuylle 1.25 3.00
HR40 Luke Evangelista 1.25 3.00
HR41 Simon Edvinsson 1.50 4.00
HR42 Cole Guttman .75 2.00
HR43 Jackson LaCombe .75 2.00
HR44 Jiri Patera 1.25 3.00
HR45 Elliot Desnoyers .75 2.00
HR46 Joona Koppanen .60 1.50
HR47 Matt Murray .75 2.00
HR48 Milos Kelemen .75 2.00
HR49 Stanislav Svozil .60 1.50
HR50 Maxence Guenette .75 2.00
HR51 Sean Farrell .75 2.00
HR52 Jakob Pelletier 1.00 2.50
HR53 Aidan McDonough .60 1.50
HR54 Tyson Foerster 1.50 4.00
HR55 Ridly Greig 1.25 3.00
HR56 Dustin Wolf 2.50 6.00
HR57 Owen Beck 1.25 3.00
HR58 Devon Levi 2.00 5.00
HR59 Bobby McMann 1.25 3.00
HR60 Yaroslav Askarov 2.00 5.00
HR61 Nikita Nesterenko .75 2.00
HR62 Tyler Kleven .75 2.00
HR63 Leevi Merilainen .75 2.00
HR64 William Dufour .60 1.50
HR65 Marco Kasper 2.00 5.00
HR66 Egor Afanasyev .75 2.00
HR67 Matthew Knies 3.00 8.00
HR68 Samuel Bolduc .75 2.00
HR69 Walker Duehr .60 1.50
HR70 Cole McWard .75 2.00

2023-24 Upper Deck Instinctive

*SPARKLE: .5X TO 1.2X BASIC
*GOLD SPRKL: 1.5X TO 4X BASIC
IN1 Ilya Samsonov .60 1.50
IN2 Igor Shesterkin 1.25 3.00
IN3 Connor Hellebuyck 1.25 3.00
IN4 Juuse Saros .75 2.00
IN5 Jake Oettinger 1.00 2.50
IN6 Filip Gustavsson .60 1.50
IN7 Vitek Vanecek .60 1.50
IN8 Stuart Skinner .75 2.00
IN9 Alexandar Georgiev .60 1.50
IN10 Pyotr Kochetkov .60 1.50
IN11 Andrei Vasilevskiy 1.00 2.50
IN12 Karel Vejmelka .40 1.00
IN13 Pheonix Copley .40 1.00
IN14 Kaapo Kahkonen .60 1.50
IN15 Jordan Binnington 1.00 2.50
IN16 Elvis Merzlikins .60 1.50
IN17 Ville Husso .40 1.00
IN18 Jake Allen .40 1.00
IN19 Philipp Grubauer .60 1.50
IN20 John Gibson .60 1.50
IN21 Thatcher Demko .75 2.00
IN22 Jacob Markstrom .60 1.50
IN23 Linus Ullmark .60 1.50
IN24 Carter Hart .60 1.50
IN25 Darcy Kuemper .60 1.50
IN26 Ilya Sorokin 1.00 2.50
IN27 Logan Thompson .75 2.00
IN28 Sergei Bobrovsky 1.00 2.50
IN29 Mads Sogaard .40 1.00
IN30 Tristan Jarry .60 1.50

2023-24 Upper Deck Monster Season

COMMON MCDAVID 1.50 4.00
*GOLD/153: 2.5X TO 6X BASIC

2023-24 Upper Deck OPC Glossy

*GOLD: .5X TO 1.2X BASIC
R1 Brock Faber 2.50 6.00
R2 Jakob Pelletier 1.25 3.00
R3 Mathew Barzal 1.25 3.00
R4 Ridly Greig 1.50 4.00
R5 Nazem Kadri 1.25 3.00
R6 Devon Levi 2.50 6.00
R7 Sidney Crosby 4.00 10.00
R8 Nikita Nesterenko 1.00 2.50
R9 Luke Hughes 3.00 8.00
R10 Dylan Larkin 1.25 3.00
R11 Dustin Wolf 3.00 8.00
R12 Mitch Marner 1.50 4.00
R13 Aidan McDonough .75 2.00
R14 Clayton Keller 1.25 3.00
R15 Yaroslav Askarov 2.50 6.00
R16 Patrice Bergeron 1.25 3.00
R17 Marco Kasper 2.50 6.00
R18 Cale Makar 2.50 6.00
R19 Wyatt Kaiser 1.00 2.50
R20 Quinn Hughes 1.25 3.00
R21 Luke Evangelista 1.50 4.00
R22 Simon Edvinsson 2.00 5.00
R23 Cole Caufield 2.50 6.00
R24 Matthew Knies 4.00 10.00
R25 Tyson Foerster 2.00 5.00
R26 Jack Eichel 1.50 4.00
R27 Walker Duehr .75 2.00
R28 Kirill Kaprizov 3.00 8.00
R29 Owen Beck 1.50 4.00
R30 Matthew Tkachuk 2.00 5.00
R31 Leevi Merilainen 1.00 2.50
R32 Cole Guttman 1.00 2.50
R33 Matty Beniers 1.25 3.00
R34 Jackson LaCombe 1.00 2.50
R35 Luke Philp 1.00 2.50
R36 Nathan MacKinnon 4.00 10.00
R37 Tyler Kleven 1.00 2.50
R38 Elias Pettersson 1.50 4.00
R39 Sean Farrell 1.00 2.50
R40 Stanislav Svozil .75 2.00
R41 Leon Draisaitl 3.00 8.00
R42 Matthew Coronato 1.50 4.00
R43 Jason Robertson 1.50 4.00
R44 Adam Fantilli 3.00 8.00
R45 Logan Cooley 3.00 8.00
R46 Alex Ovechkin 4.00 10.00
R47 Connor Bedard 20.00 50.00
R48 Will Cuylle 1.50 4.00
R49 Trevor Zegras 1.00 2.50
R50 Arnaud Durandeau 1.00 2.50

2023-24 Upper Deck Oversized

204 Yaroslav Askarov YG 6.00 15.00
208 Jakob Pelletier YG 3.00 8.00
210 Dustin Wolf YG 8.00 20.00
228 Simon Edvinsson YG 5.00 12.00
229 Wyatt Kaiser YG 2.50 6.00
230 Nikita Nesterenko YG 2.50 6.00
232 Aidan McDonough YG 2.00 5.00
235 Tyler Kleven YG 2.50 6.00
237 Devon Levi YG 6.00 15.00
239 Daniil Gushchin YG 2.50 6.00
241 Marco Kasper YG 6.00 15.00
243 Adam Ginning YG 2.50 6.00
245 Jake Livingstone YG 2.50 6.00
247 Leevi Merilainen YG 2.50 6.00
451 Connor Bedard YG 80.00 200.00
456 Jackson LaCombe YG 2.50 6.00
462 Alex Laferriere YG 4.00 10.00
463 Matt Murray YG 2.50 6.00
464 Mackie Samoskevich YG 4.00 10.00
465 Tye Kartye YG 4.00 10.00
468 Leo Carlsson YG 8.00 20.00
472 John Beecher YG 5.00 12.00
474 Zach Benson YG 4.00 10.00
475 Walker Duehr YG 2.00 5.00
478 Matthew Poitras YG 5.00 12.00
482 Fraser Minten YG 5.00 12.00
486 Kevin Korchinski YG 4.00 10.00
488 Pavel Mintyukov YG 4.00 10.00

2023-24 Upper Deck PC's

*SPARKLE: .5X TO 1.2X BASIC
*GOLD SPRKL: 1.5X TO 4X BASIC
PC1 Erik Karlsson .75 2.00
PC2 Mathew Barzal .75 2.00
PC3 Clayton Keller .75 2.00
PC4 Nathan MacKinnon 2.50 6.00
PC5 Sidney Crosby 2.50 6.00
PC6 Artemi Panarin 1.25 3.00
PC7 Elias Pettersson 1.25 3.00
PC8 Alex Ovechkin 2.50 6.00
PC9 David Pastrnak 1.50 4.00
PC10 Trevor Zegras .60 1.50
PC11 Connor McDavid 3.00 8.00
PC12 Mitch Marner 1.00 2.50
PC13 Tyler Toffoli .60 1.50
PC14 Jordan Kyrou .60 1.50
PC15 Matthew Tkachuk 1.25 3.00
PC16 Kirill Kaprizov 2.00 5.00
PC17 Cole Caufield 1.25 3.00
PC18 Jack Eichel 1.00 2.50
PC19 Leon Draisaitl 2.00 5.00
PC20 Matty Beniers .75 2.00
PC21 Anze Kopitar 1.00 2.50
PC22 Johnny Gaudreau 1.00 2.50
PC24 Jason Robertson 1.00 2.50
PC25 Tim Stutzle .75 2.00
PC26 Jack Hughes 1.50 4.00
PC27 Dylan Larkin .75 2.00
PC28 Travis Konecny .60 1.50
PC29 Kyle Connor 1.00 2.50
PC30 Patrice Bergeron .75 2.00
PC31 Filip Forsberg 1.00 2.50
PC32 Tage Thompson .75 2.00
PC33 Cale Makar 1.50 4.00
PC34 Sebastian Aho 1.00 2.50
PC35 Auston Matthews 2.50 6.00

2023-24 Upper Deck Population Count 1000

*500: .6X TO 1.5X BASIC
*50: 2.5X TO 6X BASIC
*25: 3X TO 8X BASIC
PC1 Kirill Kaprizov 8.00 20.00
PC2 Travis Konecny 2.50 6.00
PC3 Cole Guttman 2.00 5.00
PC4 Leon Draisaitl 8.00 20.00
PC5 Alex Ovechkin 10.00 25.00
PC6 Martin Necas 4.00 10.00
PC7 Chandler Stephenson 2.00 5.00
PC8 Patrik Laine 3.00 8.00
PC9 Jakob Pelletier 3.00 8.00
PC10 Linus Ullmark 2.50 6.00
PC11 Bo Horvat 3.00 8.00
PC12 Sidney Crosby 10.00 25.00
PC13 Aleksander Barkov 4.00 10.00
PC14 Yaroslav Askarov 6.00 15.00
PC15 Jared McCann 2.00 5.00
PC16 Brady Tkachuk 4.00 10.00
PC17 Elias Pettersson 4.00 10.00
PC18 Robert Thomas 2.50 6.00
PC19 David Pastrnak 6.00 15.00
PC20 Igor Shesterkin 5.00 12.00
PC21 Erik Karlsson 3.00 8.00
PC22 William Nylander 5.00 12.00
PC23 Jonathan Huberdeau 3.00 8.00
PC24 Ridly Greig 4.00 10.00
PC25 Tage Thompson 3.00 8.00
PC26 Nikita Kucherov 5.00 12.00
PC27 Jason Robertson 4.00 10.00
PC28 Jack Hughes 6.00 15.00
PC29 Claude Giroux 2.50 6.00
PC30 Jake DeBrusk 2.50 6.00
PC31 Connor McDavid 12.00 30.00
PC32 Tomas Hertl 2.50 6.00
PC33 Seth Jones 2.50 6.00
PC34 Evgeni Malkin 5.00 12.00
PC35 Cole Caufield 5.00 12.00
PC36 Brayden Point 3.00 8.00
PC37 Mika Zibanejad 3.00 8.00
PC38 Kevin Fiala 2.00 5.00
PC39 Kyle Connor 4.00 10.00
PC40 Matthew Tkachuk 5.00 12.00
PC41 Nick Suzuki 5.00 12.00
PC42 Nathan MacKinnon 10.00 25.00
PC43 Auston Matthews 10.00 25.00
PC44 Johnny Gaudreau 4.00 10.00
PC45 Carter Hart 2.50 6.00
PC46 Luke Evangelista 4.00 10.00
PC47 Trevor Zegras 2.50 6.00
PC48 Charlie McAvoy 3.00 8.00
PC49 Luke Hughes 8.00 20.00
PC50 Mitch Marner 4.00 10.00
PC51 Brock Faber 6.00 15.00
PC52 Clayton Keller 3.00 8.00
PC53 Mathew Barzal 3.00 8.00
PC54 Dylan Larkin 3.00 8.00
PC55 Artemi Panarin 5.00 12.00
PC56 Matty Beniers 3.00 8.00
PC57 Cale Makar 6.00 15.00
PC58 Matthew Knies 10.00 25.00
PC59 Jesper Bratt 2.50 6.00
PC60 Connor Bedard 200.00 500.00
PC61 Moritz Seider 3.00 8.00
PC62 Leo Carlsson 8.00 20.00
PC63 Tim Stutzle 3.00 8.00
PC64 Vladimir Tarasenko 3.00 8.00
PC65 Frederik Andersen 3.00 8.00
PC66 Adam Fox 3.00 8.00
PC67 Jake Oettinger 4.00 10.00
PC68 Quinn Hughes 6.00 15.00
PC69 Mark Stone 3.00 8.00
PC70 Jake Guentzel 4.00 10.00
PC71 Mark Scheifele 4.00 10.00
PC72 Anze Kopitar 4.00 10.00
PC73 Logan Cooley 8.00 20.00
PC74 Shayne Gostisbehere 2.50 6.00
PC75 James van Riemsdyk 2.00 5.00
PC76 Jack Eichel 4.00 10.00
PC77 Ryan O'Reilly 2.50 6.00
PC78 J.T. Miller 3.00 8.00
PC79 Ryan Nugent-Hopkins 3.00 8.00
PC80 Adrian Kempe 2.50 6.00
PC81 Jamie Benn 2.50 6.00
PC82 Tyson Foerster 5.00 12.00
PC83 Troy Terry 2.00 5.00
PC84 John Tavares 4.00 10.00
PC85 Jordan Kyrou 2.50 6.00
PC86 Steven Stamkos 5.00 12.00
PC87 Alex DeBrincat 3.00 8.00
PC88 Tyler Bertuzzi 2.00 5.00
PC89 Adam Fantilli 8.00 20.00
PC90 Mikko Rantanen 6.00 15.00

2023-24 Upper Deck Population Count 100

*100: 1.2X TO 3X BASIC
PC60 Connor Bedard 800.00 2000.00

2023-24 Upper Deck Rookie Retrospective

*GOLD: .75X TO 2X BASIC
RR1 Jack McBain .60 1.50
RR2 Kirill Marchenko 1.25 3.00
RR3 Lukas Dostal 1.00 2.50
RR4 Mark Kastelic .75 2.00
RR5 Owen Power 1.00 2.50
RR6 Juuso Parssinen .60 1.50
RR7 Wyatt Johnston 2.00 5.00
RR8 Samuel Ersson 1.00 2.50
RR9 Dylan Guenther 1.25 3.00
RR10 Kent Johnson 1.00 2.50
RR11 Matty Beniers 1.25 3.00
RR12 Jake Sanderson 1.25 3.00
RR13 Erik Kallgren .60 1.50
RR14 Jonatan Berggren .75 2.00
RR15 Nick Perbix .60 1.50
RR16 Jack Quinn .75 2.00
RR17 Marcus Bjork .60 1.50
RR18 Matias Maccelli .75 2.00
RR19 Pyotr Kochetkov 1.00 2.50
RR20 Noah Cates .60 1.50

2023-24 Upper Deck Seeing Red

SR1 Matty Beniers 1.25 3.00
SR2 Sebastian Aho 1.50 4.00
SR3 Mario Lemieux 4.00 10.00
SR4 Timo Meier 1.00 2.50
SR5 Artemi Panarin 2.00 5.00
SR6 Matthew Knies 4.00 10.00
SR7 Mark Scheifele 1.50 4.00
SR8 Brady Tkachuk 1.50 4.00
SR9 Kevin Fiala .75 2.00
SR10 William Nylander 2.00 5.00
SR11 Owen Nolan 1.00 2.50
SR12 Mika Zibanejad 1.25 3.00
SR13 Andrei Svechnikov 1.25 3.00
SR14 Ryan O'Reilly 1.00 2.50
SR15 Alex DeBrincat 1.25 3.00
SR16 Matthew Tkachuk 2.00 5.00
SR17 Tim Stutzle 1.25 3.00
SR18 Brett Hull 2.00 5.00
SR19 Mitch Marner 1.50 4.00
SR20 Mathew Barzal 1.25 3.00
SR21 Elias Pettersson 1.50 4.00
SR22 Nico Hischier 1.50 4.00
SR23 Brayden Point 1.25 3.00
SR24 Kyle Connor 1.50 4.00
SR25 Nick Suzuki 2.00 5.00
SR26 Johnny Gaudreau 1.50 4.00
SR27 John Tavares 1.50 4.00
SR28 Marcel Dionne 1.25 3.00
SR29 Chris Kreider 1.25 3.00
SR30 Martin Necas 1.50 4.00
SR31 Wyatt Johnston 2.00 5.00
SR32 Tage Thompson 1.25 3.00
SR33 Nikita Kucherov 2.00 5.00
SR34 Claude Giroux 1.00 2.50
SR35 Anze Kopitar 1.50 4.00
SR36 Gordie Howe 3.00 8.00
SR37 Clayton Keller 1.25 3.00
SR38 Jack Hughes 2.50 6.00
SR39 Travis Konecny 1.00 2.50
SR40 Brad Marchand 2.00 5.00
SR41 Matt Boldy 1.50 4.00
SR42 Robert Thomas 1.00 2.50
SR43 Jonathan Marchessault 1.00 2.50
SR44 Jesper Bratt 1.00 2.50
SR45 Connor Bedard 12.00 30.00
SR46 Adrian Kempe 1.00 2.50
SR47 Jason Zucker 1.00 2.50
SR48 Dylan Cozens 1.00 2.50
SR49 Trevor Zegras 1.00 2.50
SR50 Phil Esposito 1.50 4.00
SR51 Tomas Hertl 1.00 2.50
SR52 Dylan Larkin 1.25 3.00
SR53 Vladimir Tarasenko 1.25 3.00
SR54 Wayne Gretzky 6.00 15.00
SR55 Brock Nelson 1.00 2.50
SR56 Evgeni Malkin 2.00 5.00
SR57 Andrei Kuzmenko 1.00 2.50
SR58 Taylor Hall 1.00 2.50
SR59 Roope Hintz 1.25 3.00
SR60 Elias Lindholm 1.00 2.50
SR61 Carter Verhaeghe 1.00 2.50
SR62 Leo Carlsson 3.00 8.00
SR63 Sidney Crosby 4.00 10.00
SR64 Tyler Toffoli 1.00 2.50
SR65 Mark Stone 1.25 3.00
SR66 Owen Tippett .60 1.50
SR67 Ryan Nugent-Hopkins 1.25 3.00
SR68 Aleksander Barkov 1.50 4.00
SR69 Jake Guentzel 1.50 4.00
SR70 Mats Zuccarello 1.00 2.50
SR71 David Pastrnak 2.50 6.00
SR72 Filip Forsberg 1.50 4.00
SR73 Jason Robertson 1.50 4.00
SR74 Mikko Rantanen 2.50 6.00
SR75 Alex Ovechkin 4.00 10.00
SR76 J.T. Miller 1.25 3.00
SR77 Sam Reinhart 2.00 5.00
SR78 Connor Zary 2.00 5.00
SR79 Joe Pavelski 1.25 3.00
SR80 Dylan Strome 1.25 3.00
SR81 Nathan MacKinnon 4.00 10.00
SR82 Alex Tuch 1.00 2.50
SR83 Jack Eichel 1.50 4.00
SR84 Jordan Kyrou 1.00 2.50
SR85 Maurice Richard 2.00 5.00
SR86 Troy Terry .75 2.00
SR87 Kirill Kaprizov 3.00 8.00
SR88 Nazem Kadri 1.25 3.00
SR89 Kirill Marchenko 1.25 3.00
SR90 Jared McCann .75 2.00
SR91 Steven Stamkos 2.00 5.00
SR92 Zach Hyman 1.50 4.00
SR93 Cole Caufield 2.00 5.00
SR94 Bo Horvat 1.25 3.00
SR95 Leon Draisaitl 3.00 8.00
SR96 Adam Fantilli 3.00 8.00
SR97 Connor McDavid 5.00 12.00
SR98 Brandon Hagel .75 2.00
SR99 Auston Matthews 4.00 10.00
SR100 Jeff Skinner 1.00 2.50

2023-24 Upper Deck Seeing Red Gold Foil

*GOLD: .5X TO 1.2X BASIC
SR45 Connor Bedard 40.00 100.00

2023-24 Upper Deck Seeing Red Silver Spectrum

*SILVER: .8X TO 2X BASIC
SR45 Connor Bedard 60.00 150.00

2023-24 Upper Deck Silver Skates

SS1 Dylan Larkin 1.00 2.50
SS2 Tage Thompson 1.00 2.50
SS3 Adam Fantilli 2.50 6.00
SS4 Alexandar Georgiev .75 2.00
SS5 Brayden Point 1.00 2.50
SS6 Elias Pettersson 1.25 3.00
SS7 Sidney Crosby 3.00 8.00
SS8 Trevor Zegras .75 2.00
SS9 Adrian Kempe .75 2.00
SS10 Bo Horvat 1.00 2.50
SS11 Connor Zary 1.50 4.00
SS12 Leon Draisaitl 2.50 6.00
SS13 Jason Robertson 1.25 3.00
SS14 Mitch Marner 1.25 3.00
SS15 Kirill Kaprizov 2.50 6.00
SS16 Brady Tkachuk 1.25 3.00
SS17 Cale Makar 2.00 5.00
SS18 Johnny Gaudreau 1.25 3.00
SS19 Ilya Sorokin 1.25 3.00
SS20 Connor Bedard 12.00 30.00
SS21 Alex Ovechkin 3.00 8.00
SS22 Matty Beniers 1.00 2.50
SS23 Andrei Svechnikov 1.00 2.50
SS24 Cole Caufield 1.50 4.00
SS25 David Pastrnak 2.00 5.00
SS26 Matthew Tkachuk 1.50 4.00
SS27 Connor McDavid 4.00 10.00
SS28 Logan Cooley 2.50 6.00
SS29 Jordan Kyrou .75 2.00
SS30 Auston Matthews 3.00 8.00
SS31 Kyle Connor 1.25 3.00
SS32 Owen Tippett .50 1.25
SS33 Igor Shesterkin 1.50 4.00
SS34 Mark Stone 1.00 2.50
SS35 Roman Josi .75 2.00
SS36 Nathan MacKinnon 3.00 8.00
SS37 Logan Couture 1.00 2.50
SS38 Jack Eichel 1.25 3.00
SS39 Leo Carlsson 2.50 6.00
SS40 Jack Hughes 2.00 5.00

2023-24 Upper Deck Silver Skates Gold

*GOLD: .5X TO 1.2X BASIC
SS20 Connor Bedard 30.00 80.00

2023-24 Upper Deck Silver Skates Red

*RED/100: 1.5X TO 4X BASIC
SS20 Connor Bedard 250.00 600.00

2023-24 Upper Deck Special Forces

SF1 Trevor Zegras 1.25 3.00
SF2 Alex Ovechkin 5.00 12.00
SF3 Luke Hughes 4.00 10.00
SF4 Cale Makar 3.00 8.00
SF5 Sidney Crosby 5.00 12.00
SF6 Adam Fantilli 4.00 10.00
SF7 Auston Matthews 5.00 12.00
SF8 Tim Stutzle 1.50 4.00
SF9 Connor Bedard 60.00 150.00
SF10 Cole Caufield 2.50 6.00
SF11 Clayton Keller 1.50 4.00
SF12 Jack Hughes 3.00 8.00
SF13 Johnny Gaudreau 2.00 5.00
SF14 Matthew Knies 5.00 12.00
SF15 Connor McDavid 6.00 15.00
SF16 Quinn Hughes 3.00 8.00
SF17 Brayden Point 1.50 4.00
SF18 Logan Cooley 4.00 10.00
SF19 Kyle Connor 2.00 5.00
SF20 Leon Draisaitl 4.00 10.00

2023-24 Upper Deck Sophomore Sensations

SO1 Ridly Greig 4.00 10.00
SO2 Luke Evangelista 4.00 10.00
SO3 Tyson Foerster 5.00 12.00
SO4 Cole Guttman 2.50 6.00
SO5 Yaroslav Askarov 6.00 15.00
SO6 Jakob Pelletier 3.00 8.00

2023-24 Upper Deck Special Edition

*RED: 1X TO 2.5X BASIC
SE1 Anze Kopitar 1.50 4.00
SE2 Kyle Connor 1.50 4.00
SE3 Erik Karlsson 1.25 3.00
SE4 Dylan Larkin 1.25 3.00
SE5 Matthew Knies 4.00 10.00
SE6 Sidney Crosby 4.00 10.00
SE7 Jason Robertson 1.50 4.00
SE8 Matty Beniers 1.25 3.00
SE9 Bo Horvat 1.25 3.00
SE10 Simon Edvinsson 2.00 5.00
SE11 Sebastian Aho 1.50 4.00
SE12 Matt Duchene 1.00 2.50
SE13 Jack Hughes 2.50 6.00
SE14 Kirill Kaprizov 3.00 8.00
SE15 Trevor Zegras 1.00 2.50
SE16 Nazem Kadri 1.25 3.00
SE17 Travis Konecny 1.00 2.50
SE18 Ridly Greig 1.50 4.00
SE19 Jack Eichel 1.50 4.00
SE20 Luke Evangelista 1.50 4.00
SE21 Cole Caufield 2.00 5.00
SE22 Clayton Keller 1.25 3.00
SE23 Tyson Foerster 2.00 5.00
SE24 Seth Jones 1.00 2.50
SE25 Artemi Panarin 2.00 5.00
SE26 Connor McDavid 5.00 12.00
SE27 Yaroslav Askarov 2.50 6.00
SE28 Luke Hughes 3.00 8.00
SE29 Alex Ovechkin 4.00 10.00
SE30 Tage Thompson 1.25 3.00
SE31 Matthew Tkachuk 2.00 5.00
SE32 Auston Matthews 4.00 10.00
SE33 Elias Pettersson 1.50 4.00
SE34 Nathan MacKinnon 4.00 10.00
SE35 Jakob Pelletier 1.25 3.00
SE36 Brayden Point 1.25 3.00
SE37 Johnny Gaudreau 1.50 4.00
SE38 David Pastrnak 2.50 6.00
SE39 Jordan Kyrou 1.00 2.50
SE40 Brady Tkachuk 1.50 4.00

2023-24 Upper Deck Special Edition Gold

*GOLD/50: 2X TO 5X BASIC
SE5 Matthew Knies 30.00 80.00
SE10 Simon Edvinsson 30.00 80.00
SE13 Jack Hughes 20.00 50.00
SE21 Cole Caufield 20.00 50.00
SE35 Jakob Pelletier 15.00 40.00

2023-24 Upper Deck Star Surge

*RED: 1.2X TO 3X BASIC
*GOLD/25: 3X TO 8X BASIC
SS1 Tanner Jeannot .60 1.50
SS2 Luke Hughes 3.00 8.00
SS3 Alexis Lafreniere 1.50 4.00
SS4 Juraj Slafkovsky 2.00 5.00
SS5 Moritz Seider 1.25 3.00
SS6 Noah Dobson 1.25 3.00
SS7 Tim Stutzle 1.25 3.00
SS8 Brandt Clarke 1.00 2.50
SS10 Shane Wright 1.25 3.00
SS11 Ridly Greig 1.50 4.00
SS12 Pyotr Kochetkov 1.00 2.50
SS13 Simon Edvinsson 2.00 5.00
SS14 Gabe Vilardi 1.00 2.50
SS15 Matthew Knies 4.00 10.00
SS16 Lukas Reichel 1.00 2.50
SS17 Jakob Pelletier 1.25 3.00
SS18 Andrei Kuzmenko 1.00 2.50
SS19 Jake Sanderson 1.25 3.00
SS20 Matt Boldy 1.50 4.00
SS21 Cole Caufield 2.00 5.00
SS22 Wyatt Johnston 2.00 5.00
SS23 Yaroslav Askarov 2.50 6.00
SS24 Carter Verhaeghe 1.00 2.50
SS25 Lucas Raymond 1.50 4.00
SS26 Matty Beniers 1.25 3.00
SS27 Adam Fox 1.25 3.00
SS28 Dylan Guenther 1.25 3.00
SS29 Seth Jarvis 1.25 3.00
SS30 Kent Johnson 1.00 2.50

2023-24 Upper Deck Star Zone

*RED: .6X TO 1.5X BASIC
*GOLD/50: 1.2X TO 3X BASIC
SZ1 Matthew Tkachuk 1.50 4.00
SZ2 Johnny Gaudreau 1.25 3.00
SZ3 Artemi Panarin 1.50 4.00
SZ4 Steven Stamkos 1.50 4.00
SZ5 Mark Stone 1.00 2.50
SZ6 Joe Pavelski 1.00 2.50
SZ7 Mitch Marner 1.25 3.00
SZ8 Brock Nelson .75 2.00
SZ9 Dougie Hamilton .60 1.50
SZ10 Tyler Toffoli .75 2.00
SZ11 Dylan Larkin 1.00 2.50
SZ12 Erik Karlsson 1.00 2.50
SZ13 Juraj Slafkovsky 1.25 3.00
SZ14 David Pastrnak 2.00 5.00
SZ15 Auston Matthews 3.00 8.00
SZ16 Filip Forsberg 1.25 3.00
SZ17 Brent Burns .75 2.00
SZ18 Mark Scheifele 1.25 3.00
SZ19 Patrice Bergeron 1.00 2.50
SZ20 Leon Draisaitl 2.50 6.00
SZ21 Nathan MacKinnon 3.00 8.00
SZ22 Alex Ovechkin 3.00 8.00
SZ23 John Gibson .75 2.00
SZ24 Mats Zuccarello .75 2.00
SZ25 Brayden Point 1.00 2.50
SZ26 John Tavares 1.25 3.00
SZ27 Elias Pettersson 1.25 3.00
SZ28 Connor McDavid 4.00 10.00
SZ29 Brady Tkachuk 1.25 3.00
SZ30 Sidney Crosby 3.00 8.00

2023-24 Upper Deck Stat Box Fillers

*GOLD: .6X TO 1.5X BASIC
SB1 Nikita Kucherov 1.50 4.00
SB2 Kevin Fiala .60 1.50
SB3 Nathan MacKinnon 3.00 8.00
SB4 Erik Karlsson 1.00 2.50
SB5 Tim Stutzle 1.00 2.50
SB6 Elias Pettersson 1.25 3.00
SB8 Kyle Connor 1.25 3.00
SB9 Alex Ovechkin 3.00 8.00
SB10 Matthew Tkachuk 1.50 4.00
SB11 Leon Draisaitl 2.50 6.00
SB12 Sidney Crosby 3.00 8.00
SB13 Joe Pavelski 1.00 2.50
SB14 Jack Hughes 2.00 5.00
SB15 Hampus Lindholm .50 1.25
SB16 William Nylander 1.50 4.00
SB17 Brady Tkachuk 1.25 3.00
SB18 Mikko Rantanen 2.00 5.00
SB19 Tage Thompson 1.00 2.50
SB20 Kirill Kaprizov 2.50 6.00
SB21 Connor McDavid 4.00 10.00
SB22 Artemi Panarin 1.50 4.00
SB23 Jason Robertson 1.25 3.00
SB24 Auston Matthews 3.00 8.00
SB25 Josh Morrissey 1.00 2.50

2023-24 Upper Deck Teachers Pet

*GOLD: .6X TO 1.5X BASIC
TP1 Alex Ovechkin 2.50 6.00
TP2 Jared McCann .50 1.25
TP3 Scott Laughton .40 1.00
TP4 Mark Scheifele 1.00 2.50
TP5 Roman Josi .60 1.50
TP6 Filip Gustavsson .60 1.50
TP7 Brady Tkachuk 1.00 2.50
TP8 Matthew Tkachuk 1.25 3.00
TP9 Sebastian Aho 1.00 2.50
TP10 Elias Pettersson 1.00 2.50
TP11 Andrei Vasilevskiy 1.00 2.50
TP12 Kevin Fiala .50 1.25
TP13 Boone Jenner .60 1.50
TP14 Mikko Rantanen 1.50 4.00
TP15 Tomas Tatar .40 1.00
TP16 William Carrier .40 1.00
TP17 Jonathan Huberdeau .75 2.00
TP18 Jonathan Toews 1.00 2.50
TP19 Ilya Sorokin 1.00 2.50
TP20 Linus Ullmark .60 1.50
TP21 Igor Shesterkin 1.25 3.00
TP22 Dylan Larkin .75 2.00
TP23 Mitch Marner 1.00 2.50
TP24 Connor McDavid 3.00 8.00
TP25 Erik Karlsson .75 2.00
TP26 Trevor Zegras .60 1.50
TP27 Sidney Crosby 2.50 6.00
TP28 Jack McBain .40 1.00
TP29 Tage Thompson .75 2.00
TP30 Joe Pavelski .75 2.00

2023-24 Upper Deck The NHL Specialists

NS41 Cam Neely 5.00 12.00
NS42 Elias Pettersson 8.00 20.00
NS43 Mark Messier 10.00 25.00
NS44 Kyle Connor 8.00 20.00
NS45 Martin Brodeur 12.00 30.00
NS46 Connor Bedard 80.00 200.00
NS47 Mike Modano 8.00 20.00
NS48 Andrei Vasilevskiy 8.00 20.00
NS49 Bryan Trottier 5.00 12.00
NS50 Cole Caufield 10.00 25.00
NS51 Kevin Lowe 5.00 12.00
NS52 Brady Tkachuk 8.00 20.00
NS53 Luc Robitaille 5.00 12.00
NS54 Mitch Marner 8.00 20.00
NS55 Peter Forsberg 10.00 25.00
NS56 Anze Kopitar 8.00 20.00
NS57 Maurice Richard 10.00 25.00
NS58 Ilya Sorokin 8.00 20.00
NS59 Tiger Williams 3.00 8.00
NS60 Erik Karlsson 6.00 15.00

2023-24 Upper Deck UD Canvas

C1 Troy Terry .50 1.25
C2 Jakob Silfverberg .40 1.00
C3 John Gibson .60 1.50
C4 Clayton Keller .75 2.00
C5 Karel Vejmelka .40 1.00
C6 Brad Marchand 1.25 3.00
C7 Linus Ullmark .60 1.50
C8 Jeff Skinner .60 1.50
C9 Jack Quinn .50 1.25
C10 Victor Olofsson .60 1.50
C11 Tyler Toffoli .60 1.50
C12 MacKenzie Weegar .50 1.25
C13 Rasmus Andersson .50 1.25
C14 Martin Necas 1.00 2.50
C15 Brent Burns .60 1.50
C16 Jason Dickinson .40 1.00
C17 Cale Makar 1.50 4.00
C18 Samuel Girard .40 1.00
C19 Alexandar Georgiev .60 1.50
C20 Kent Johnson .60 1.50
C21 Boone Jenner .60 1.50
C22 Elvis Merzlikins .60 1.50
C23 Mason Marchment .50 1.25
C24 Wyatt Johnston 1.25 3.00
C25 Miro Heiskanen .75 2.00
C26 Lucas Raymond 1.00 2.50
C27 Andrew Copp .40 1.00
C28 Jonatan Berggren .50 1.25
C29 Ville Husso .40 1.00
C30 Leon Draisaitl 2.00 5.00
C31 Warren Foegele .40 1.00
C32 Anton Lundell .60 1.50
C33 Carter Verhaeghe .60 1.50
C34 Kevin Fiala .50 1.25
C35 Phillip Danault .60 1.50
C36 Viktor Arvidsson .40 1.00
C37 Gabe Vilardi .60 1.50
C38 Mats Zuccarello .60 1.50
C39 Filip Gustavsson .60 1.50
C40 Cole Caufield 1.25 3.00
C41 Mike Hoffman .40 1.00
C42 Jake Allen .60 1.50

C43 Brendan Gallagher .60 1.50
C44 Ryan McDonagh .40 1.00
C45 Juuse Saros .75 2.00
C46 Ryan Johansen .50 1.25
C47 Nico Hischier 1.00 2.50
C48 Jesper Bratt .60 1.50
C49 Kyle Palmieri .50 1.25
C50 Ilya Sorokin 1.00 2.50
C51 Vincent Trocheck .60 1.50
C52 Alexis Lafreniere 1.00 2.50
C53 Jimmy Vesey .50 1.25
C54 Jacob Trouba .50 1.25
C55 Alex DeBrincat .75 2.00
C56 Jake Sanderson .75 2.00
C57 Josh Norris .60 1.50
C58 Joel Farabee .60 1.50
C59 Nicolas Deslauriers .40 1.00
C60 Jake Guentzel 1.00 2.50
C61 Rickard Rakell .50 1.25
C62 Jeff Carter .50 1.25
C63 Erik Karlsson .75 2.00
C64 Kaapo Kahkonen .60 1.50
C65 Jared McCann .50 1.25
C66 Oliver Bjorkstrand .50 1.25
C67 Brandon Tanev .50 1.25
C68 Daniel Sprong .40 1.00
C69 Jordan Kyrou .60 1.50
C70 Brandon Saad .50 1.25
C71 Jordan Binnington 1.00 2.50
C72 Brayden Point .75 2.00
C73 Brandon Hagel .50 1.25
C74 Ross Colton .50 1.25
C75 Mikhail Sergachev .50 1.25
C76 William Nylander 1.25 3.00
C77 Morgan Rielly .60 1.50
C78 J.T. Miller .75 2.00
C79 Quinn Hughes 1.50 4.00
C80 Thatcher Demko .75 2.00
C81 Filip Hronek .40 1.00
C82 Jack Eichel 1.00 2.50
C83 Chandler Stephenson .50 1.25
C84 Shea Theodore .75 2.00
C85 Alex Ovechkin 2.50 6.00
C86 T.J. Oshie .60 1.50
C87 Nino Niederreiter .40 1.00
C88 Nikolaj Ehlers .60 1.50
C89 Connor Hellebuyck 1.25 3.00
C90 L.Draisaitl/A.Ovechkin CL 2.50 6.00
C91 Cole Guttman YG 5.00 12.00
C92 Nikita Nesterenko YG 5.00 12.00
C93 Will Cuylle YG 8.00 20.00
C94 Arnaud Durandeau YG 5.00 12.00
C95 Vincent Desharnais YG 6.00 15.00
C96 Egor Afanasyev YG 5.00 12.00
C97 Ridly Greig YG 8.00 20.00
C98 Wyatt Kaiser YG 5.00 12.00
C99 Joona Koppanen YG 4.00 10.00
C100 Tyson Foerster YG 10.00 25.00
C101 Brock Faber YG 23.00 30.00
C102 Owen Beck YG 8.00 20.00
C103 Matthew Knies YG 25.00 60.00
C104 David Gust YG 5.00 12.00
C105 Jakob Pelletier YG 6.00 15.00
C106 Matthew Coronato YG 8.00 20.00
C107 Aidan McDonough YG 4.00 10.00
C108 Luke Evangelista YG 8.00 20.00
C109 Dustin Wolf YG 15.00 40.00
C110 Vincent Iorio YG 5.00 12.00
C111 Yaroslav Askarov YG 12.00 30.00
C112 Samuel Bolduc YG 5.00 12.00
C113 Simon Edvinsson YG 10.00 25.00
C114 Hunter McKown YG 5.00 12.00
C115 Jaxson Stauber YG 5.00 12.00
C116 Tyler Kleven YG 5.00 12.00
C117 Henry Thrun YG 5.00 12.00
C118 Marco Kasper YG 12.00 30.00
C119 Akito Hirose YG 4.00 10.00
C120 Y.Askarov/J.Pelletier YG CL 6.00 15.00
C121 Trevor Zegras .60 1.50
C122 Mason McTavish .60 1.50
C123 Frank Vatrano .50 1.25
C124 Dylan Guenther .75 2.00
C125 Matias Maccelli .50 1.25
C126 Jake DeBrusk .60 1.50
C127 Charlie McAvoy .75 2.00
C128 Jeremy Swayman 1.00 2.50
C129 Taylor Hall .60 1.50
C130 Tage Thompson .75 2.00
C131 Rasmus Dahlin .75 2.00
C132 Elias Lindholm .60 1.50
C133 Nazem Kadri .75 2.00
C134 Mikael Backlund .50 1.25
C135 Sebastian Aho 1.00 2.50
C136 Seth Jarvis .75 2.00
C137 Teuvo Teravainen .60 1.50
C138 Lukas Reichel .60 1.50
C139 Taylor Raddysh .50 1.25
C140 Artturi Lehkonen .50 1.25
C141 Nathan MacKinnon 2.50 6.00
C142 Valeri Nichushkin .60 1.50
C143 Devon Toews .50 1.25
C144 Johnny Gaudreau 1.00 2.50
C145 Kirill Marchenko .75 2.00
C146 Roope Hintz .75 2.00
C147 Joe Pavelski .75 2.00
C148 Tyler Seguin .75 2.00
C149 Jake Oettinger 1.00 2.50
C150 Dominik Kubalik .60 1.50
C151 Moritz Seider .75 2.00
C152 Connor McDavid 3.00 8.00
C153 Ryan Nugent-Hopkins .75 2.00
C154 Evan Bouchard .75 2.00
C155 Evander Kane .60 1.50
C156 Matthew Tkachuk 1.25 3.00
C157 Anthony Duclair .50 1.25
C158 Aaron Ekblad .75 2.00
C159 Sergei Bobrovsky 1.00 2.50
C160 Anze Kopitar 1.00 2.50
C161 Adrian Kempe .60 1.50
C162 Kirill Kaprizov 2.00 5.00
C163 Jared Spurgeon .60 1.50
C164 Marc-Andre Fleury 1.25 3.00
C165 Nick Suzuki 1.25 3.00
C166 Josh Anderson .50 1.25
C167 Tyson Barrie .40 1.00
C168 Filip Forsberg 1.25 3.00
C169 Dawson Mercer .75 2.00
C170 Dougie Hamilton .50 1.25
C171 Vitek Vanecek .60 1.50
C172 Bo Horvat .75 2.00
C173 Mathew Barzal .75 2.00
C174 Mika Zibanejad .75 2.00
C175 Artemi Panarin 1.25 3.00
C176 Brady Tkachuk 1.00 2.50
C177 Claude Giroux .60 1.50
C178 Jakob Chychrun .60 1.50
C179 Morgan Frost .50 1.25
C180 Travis Konecny .60 1.50
C181 Bryan Rust .60 1.50
C182 Mikael Granlund .50 1.25
C183 Kris Letang .75 2.00
C184 Tomas Hertl .60 1.50
C185 Alexander Barabanov .40 1.00
C186 Matty Beniers .75 2.00
C187 Jaden Schwartz .50 1.25
C188 Yanni Gourde .50 1.25
C189 Philipp Grubauer .60 1.50
C190 Robert Thomas .60 1.50
C191 Brayden Schenn .60 1.50
C192 Nikita Kucherov 1.25 3.00
C193 Tanner Jeannot .40 1.00
C194 Andrei Vasilevskiy 1.00 2.50
C195 Auston Matthews 2.50 6.00
C196 Mark Giordano .60 1.50
C197 Matt Murray .60 1.50
C198 Elias Pettersson 1.00 2.50
C199 Anthony Beauvillier .40 1.00
C200 Conor Garland .50 1.25
C201 Jonathan Marchessault .75 2.00
C202 Alex Pietrangelo .50 1.25
C203 Logan Thompson .75 2.00
C204 Tom Wilson .60 1.50
C205 Sonny Milano .50 1.25
C206 Dylan Strome .75 2.00
C207 Darcy Kuemper .60 1.50
C208 Mark Scheifele 1.00 2.50
C209 Josh Morrissey .75 2.00
C210 E.Pettersson
R.Nugent-Hopkins CL 1.00 2.50
C211 Matt Murray YG 5.00 12.00
C212 Arturs Silovs YG 8.00 20.00
C213 Luke Hughes YG 12.00 30.00
C214 Bobby McMann YG 8.00 20.00
C215 Luke Philp YG 5.00 12.00
C216 Billy Sweezey YG 5.00 12.00
C217 Michael Kesselring YG 5.00 12.00
C218 Jackson LaCombe YG 5.00 12.00
C219 Stanislav Svozil YG 4.00 10.00
C220 Walker Duehr YG 4.00 10.00
C221 Tye Kartye YG 8.00 20.00
C222 Sean Farrell YG 5.00 12.00
C223 Tristen Robins YG 5.00 12.00
C224 Leevi Merilainen YG 5.00 12.00
C225 Jet Greaves YG 8.00 20.00
C226 Jiri Patera YG 8.00 20.00
C227 Elliot Desnoyers YG 5.00 12.00
C228 Devon Levi YG 12.00 30.00
C229 Cole McWard YG 5.00 12.00
C230 Danil Gushchin YG 5.00 12.00
C231 Jake Livingstone YG 5.00 12.00
C232 Mackie Samoskevich YG 8.00 20.00
C233 William Dufour YG 4.00 10.00
C234 Hugh McGing YG 5.00 12.00
C235 Maxence Guenette YG 5.00 12.00
C236 Matthew Poitras YG 10.00 25.00
C237 Logan Cooley YG 15.00 40.00
C238 John Beecher YG 10.00 25.00
C239 Zach Benson YG 8.00 20.00
C240 L.Cooley/L.Hughes YG CL 6.00 15.00
C241 Wayne Gretzky 15.00 40.00
C242 Maurice Richard 5.00 12.00
C243 Joe Thornton 4.00 10.00
C244 Derek Sanderson 2.50 6.00
C245 Todd Bertuzzi 2.00 5.00
C246 Jean-Sebastien Giguere 2.50 6.00
C247 Jari Kurri 2.50 6.00
C248 Patrick Roy 6.00 15.00
C249 Jeremy Roenick 4.00 10.00
C250 Rod Gilbert 2.50 6.00
C251 Shane Doan 2.00 5.00
C252 Mike Bossy 2.50 6.00
C253 Doug Gilmour 3.00 8.00
C254 Dominik Hasek 4.00 10.00
C255 Steve Yzerman 6.00 15.00
C256 Devon Levi POE 6.00 15.00
C257 Elliot Desnoyers POE 2.50 6.00
C258 Connor Bedard POE 30.00 80.00
C259 Jakob Pelletier POE 3.00 8.00
C260 Owen Beck POE 4.00 10.00
C261 Ridly Greig POE 4.00 10.00
C262 Tyson Foerster POE 5.00 12.00
C263 Will Cuylle POE 4.00 10.00
C264 William Dufour POE 2.00 5.00
C265 Brendan Morrison POE 2.00 5.00
C266 Brian Campbell POE 2.00 5.00
C267 Simon Gagne POE 2.50 6.00
C268 Todd Harvey POE 2.00 5.00
C269 Bryan McCabe POE 1.50 4.00
C270 Wade Redden POE 2.00 5.00
C271 Andrei Kuzmenko .60 1.50
C272 David Perron .50 1.25
C273 Dmitry Orlov .60 1.50
C274 Gabriel Landeskog .75 2.00
C275 Steven Stamkos 1.25 3.00
C276 Patrick Kane 1.25 3.00
C277 Philipp Kurashev .50 1.25
C278 Adam Fox .75 2.00
C279 Kailer Yamamoto .60 1.50
C280 Luke Schenn .60 1.50
C281 John Tavares 1.00 2.50
C282 Igor Shesterkin 1.25 3.00
C283 Frederick Gaudreau .40 1.00
C284 Mikko Rantanen 1.50 4.00
C285 Timo Meier .60 1.50
C286 Jonathan Quick .75 2.00
C287 Jordan Harris .40 1.00
C288 Torey Krug .50 1.25
C289 Ryan Reaves .50 1.25
C290 Victor Hedman .75 2.00
C291 Logan Couture .75 2.00
C292 Andre Burakovsky .40 1.00
C293 Sean Couturier .50 1.25
C294 Jacob Markstrom .60 1.50
C295 Evgeny Kuznetsov .75 2.00
C296 Erik Karlsson .75 2.00
C297 Owen Power .60 1.50
C298 Drew Doughty .60 1.50
C299 Joonas Korpisalo .60 1.50
C300 Seth Jones .60 1.50
C301 Alex Killorn .40 1.00
C302 John Carlson .60 1.50
C303 Brock Boeser .75 2.00
C304 Ryan Donato .50 1.25
C305 Zach Werenski 1.00 2.50
C306 Matt Boldy 1.00 2.50
C307 Tyler Bertuzzi .50 1.25
C308 Drake Batherson .60 1.50
C309 Jordan Eberle .60 1.50
C310 Vladislav Gavrikov .40 1.00
C311 Jonathan Huberdeau .75 2.00
C312 Anders Lee .50 1.25
C313 Chris Kreider .75 2.00
C314 John Klingberg .60 1.50
C315 Sam Reinhart 1.25 3.00
C316 Mark Stone .75 2.00
C317 Nikita Zadorov .40 1.00
C318 Zach Hyman 1.00 2.50
C319 Adin Hill .60 1.50
C320 Joel Eriksson Ek .50 1.25
C321 Kevin Shattenkirk .40 1.00
C322 Andrei Svechnikov .75 2.00
C323 Jamie Benn .60 1.50
C324 Dylan Larkin .75 2.00
C325 Stuart Skinner .75 2.00
C326 Matt Duchene .60 1.50
C327 Kyle Connor 1.00 2.50
C328 Shane Wright .75 2.00
C329 Patrik Laine .75 2.00
C330 Roman Josi .60 1.50
C331 Michael Bunting .60 1.50
C332 William Karlsson .75 2.00
C333 Evgeni Malkin 1.25 3.00
C334 Frederik Andersen .75 2.00
C335 Juraj Slafkovsky 1.25 3.00
C336 Mitch Marner 1.00 2.50
C337 Travis Dermott .50 1.25
C338 Scott Laughton .40 1.00
C339 Carter Hart .60 1.50
C340 Ivan Barbashev .50 1.25
C341 Blake Wheeler .60 1.50
C342 Aleksander Barkov 1.00 2.50
C343 Cole Perfetti .60 1.50
C344 Owen Tippett .40 1.00
C345 James van Riemsdyk .50 1.25
C346 Jamie Drysdale .50 1.25
C347 Pierre-Luc Dubois .50 1.25
C348 Brock Nelson .60 1.50
C349 Sidney Crosby 2.50 6.00
C350 Jason Robertson 1.00 2.50
C351 Ryan O'Reilly .60 1.50
C352 Pavel Buchnevich .50 1.25
C353 Vladimir Tarasenko .75 2.00
C354 David Pastrnak 1.50 4.00
C355 Kevin Hayes .50 1.25
C356 Tim Stutzle .75 2.00
C357 Tristan Jarry .60 1.50
C358 Mario Ferraro .40 1.00
C359 Jack Hughes 1.50 4.00
C360 J.Robertson/J.Hughes CL 1.50 4.00
C361 Uvis Balinskis YG 5.00 12.00
C362 Leo Carlsson YG 12.00 30.00
C363 Emil Andrae YG 5.00 12.00
C364 Pavel Mintyukov YG 8.00 20.00
C365 Milos Kelemen YG 5.00 12.00
C366 Matt Tomkins YG 5.00 12.00
C367 Kevin Korchinski YG 8.00 20.00
C368 Lukas Rousek YG 4.00 10.00
C369 Joel Teasdale YG 5.00 12.00
C370 Justin Sourdif YG 5.00 12.00
C371 Matthew Kessel YG 4.00 10.00
C372 Hunter Shepard YG 5.00 12.00
C373 Adam Fantilli YG 15.00 40.00
C374 Ryan Shea YG 5.00 12.00
C375 Alex Laferriere YG 8.00 20.00
C376 Spencer Stastney YG 5.00 12.00
C377 Ilya Solovyov YG 5.00 12.00
C378 Tristan Luneau YG 5.00 12.00
C379 Samuel Knazko YG 5.00 12.00
C380 Connor Zary YG 10.00 25.00
C381 Waltteri Merela YG 5.00 12.00
C382 Connor Bedard YG 125.00 300.00
C383 Hardy Haman Aktell YG 5.00 12.00
C384 Ty Emberson YG 5.00 12.00
C385 Adam Ginning YG 5.00 12.00
C386 Fraser Minten YG 10.00 25.00
C387 Lucas Condotta YG 5.00 12.00
C388 Tyler Angle YG 5.00 12.00
C389 John Ludvig YG 5.00 12.00
C390 C.Bedard/A.Fantilli YG CL 12.00 30.00
C391 Jean Ratelle 2.00 5.00
C392 Eric Lindros 4.00 10.00
C393 Alex Delvecchio 2.50 6.00
C394 Rogie Vachon 2.50 6.00
C395 Johnny Bucyk 2.50 6.00
C396 Bill Guerin 2.50 6.00
C397 Tony Amonte 2.00 5.00
C398 Trevor Linden 2.50 6.00
C399 Darryl Sittler 2.50 6.00
C400 Scotty Bowman 2.50 6.00
C401 Henrik Lundqvist 6.00 15.00
C402 Mark Messier 5.00 12.00
C403 Clark Gillies 2.50 6.00
C404 Mario Lemieux 10.00 25.00
C405 Tiger Williams 1.50 4.00
C406 Mitch Marner AS 4.00 10.00
C407 Sidney Crosby AS 10.00 25.00
C408 Connor McDavid AS 12.00 30.00
C409 Kevin Hayes AS 1.50 4.00
C410 Matthew Tkachuk AS 5.00 12.00
C411 David Pastrnak AS 6.00 15.00
C412 Brady Tkachuk AS 4.00 10.00
C413 Linus Ullmark AS 2.50 6.00
C414 Alex Ovechkin AS 10.00 25.00
C415 Josh Morrissey AS 3.00 8.00
C416 Dylan Larkin AS 3.00 8.00
C417 Johnny Gaudreau AS 4.00 10.00
C418 Connor Hellebuyck AS 5.00 12.00
C419 Igor Shesterkin AS 5.00 12.00
C420 Elias Pettersson AS 4.00 10.00

2023-24 Upper Deck UD Canvas Black and White

*B&W: 1.2X TO 3X BASIC
*B&W YG: .6X TO 1.5X BASIC
*B&W RET/POE : 1X TO 2.5X BASIC
C93 Will Cuylle YG 15.00 40.00
C97 Ridly Greig YG 15.00 40.00
C100 Tyson Foerster YG 12.00 30.00
C101 Brock Faber YG 30.00 80.00
C103 Matthew Knies YG 50.00 125.00
C106 Matthew Coronato YG 30.00 80.00
C109 Dustin Wolf YG 30.00 80.00
C111 Yaroslav Askarov YG 30.00 80.00
C113 Simon Edvinsson YG 20.00 50.00
C118 Marco Kasper YG 20.00 50.00
C213 Luke Hughes YG 25.00 60.00
C237 Logan Cooley YG 40.00 100.00
C240 Logan Cooley
Luke Hughes YG CL 10.00 25.00
C256 Devon Levi POE 40.00 100.00
C258 Connor Bedard POE 40.00 100.00
C373 Adam Fantilli YG 30.00 80.00
C382 Connor Bedard YG 150.00 400.00

2023-24 Upper Deck UD Portraits

P1 Robert Thomas .75 2.00
P2 Matt Boldy 1.25 3.00
P3 Johnny Gaudreau 1.25 3.00
P4 Alex Ovechkin 3.00 8.00
P5 Quinn Hughes 2.00 5.00
P6 Andrei Vasilevskiy 1.25 3.00
P7 Nathan MacKinnon 3.00 8.00
P8 Moritz Seider 1.00 2.50
P9 Jake Oettinger 1.25 3.00
P10 Kirill Kaprizov 2.50 6.00
P11 Adam Fox 1.00 2.50
P12 Josh Norris .75 2.00
P13 Kyle Connor 1.25 3.00
P14 Matthew Tkachuk 1.50 4.00
P15 Matty Beniers 1.00 2.50
P16 Andrei Svechnikov 1.00 2.50
P17 Kevin Fiala .60 1.50
P18 Sidney Crosby 3.00 8.00
P19 Brad Marchand 1.50 4.00
P20 Cole Caufield 1.50 4.00
P21 Mark Stone 1.00 2.50
P22 Auston Matthews 3.00 8.00
P23 Jonathan Huberdeau 1.00 2.50
P24 Mitch Marner 1.25 3.00
P25 Leon Draisaitl 2.50 6.00
P26 Tomas Hertl .75 2.00
P27 Joel Eriksson Ek .60 1.50
P28 Shane Wright 1.00 2.50
P29 Connor McDavid 4.00 10.00
P30 Ondrej Palat .60 1.50
P31 Gritty 2.00 5.00
P32 Brady Tkachuk 1.25 3.00
P33 Jack Eichel 1.25 3.00
P34 Nikita Kucherov 1.50 4.00
P35 Yaroslav Askarov 2.00 5.00
P36 Bo Horvat 1.00 2.50
P37 Jordan Kyrou .75 2.00
P38 Seth Jones .75 2.00
P39 Jason Robertson 1.25 3.00
P40 Cale Makar 2.00 5.00
P41 Brent Burns .75 2.00
P42 Linus Ullmark .75 2.00
P43 Matthew Knies 3.00 8.00
P44 Anze Kopitar 1.25 3.00
P45 Elias Pettersson 1.25 3.00
P46 Travis Konecny .75 2.00
P47 Artemi Panarin 1.50 4.00
P48 Clayton Keller 1.00 2.50
P49 Mark Scheifele 1.25 3.00
P50 Jakob Pelletier 1.00 2.50
P51 William Nylander 1.50 4.00
P52 Jack Hughes 2.00 5.00
P53 Nazem Kadri 1.00 2.50
P54 Charlie McAvoy 1.00 2.50
P55 Tage Thompson 1.00 2.50
P56 Trevor Zegras .75 2.00
P57 Luke Hughes 2.50 6.00
P58 Ryan Nugent-Hopkins 1.00 2.50
P59 Filip Forsberg 1.25 3.00
P60 Connor Bedard 6.00 15.00

2023-24 Upper Deck UD Portraits Red Frame

*RED/25: 3X TO 8X BASIC
P31 Gritty 40.00 100.00
P60 Connor Bedard 600.00 1500.00

2023-24 Upper Deck UD Portraits Silver Frame

*SILVER/99: 2X TO 5X BASIC
P31 Gritty 20.00 50.00
P60 Connor Bedard 250.00 600.00

2024-25 Upper Deck

1 Troy Terry .25 .60
2 Jackson LaCombe .20 .50
3 Tristan Luneau .20 .50
4 Pavel Mintyukov .25 .60
5 Frank Vatrano .25 .60
6 Alex Killorn .20 .50
7 Lukas Dostal .30 .75
8 Clayton Keller .40 1.00
9 Alex Kerfoot .25 .60
10 Nick Schmaltz .25 .60
11 Sean Durzi .20 .50
12 Lawson Crouse .20 .50
13 Jack McBain .20 .50
14 Connor Ingram .20 .50
15 Brad Marchand .25 .60
16 Morgan Geekie .20 .50
17 Brandon Carlo .25 .60
18 Linus Ullmark .30 .75
19 Matthew Poitras .30 .75
20 Charlie Coyle .30 .75
21 Pavel Zacha .25 .60
22 Jeff Skinner .30 .75
23 Alex Tuch .30 .75
24 Zach Benson .25 .60
25 Connor Clifton .25 .60
26 Bowen Byram .40 1.00
27 Jack Quinn .25 .60
28 Matt Savoie .30 .75
29 Andrew Mangiapane .30 .75
30 Dustin Wolf .50 1.25
31 Blake Coleman .25 .60
32 Connor Zary .30 .75
33 Yegor Sharangovich .30 .75
34 Jonathan Huberdeau .40 1.00
35 Andrei Kuzmenko .30 .75
36 Brent Burns .30 .75
37 Andrei Svechnikov .40 1.00
38 Pyotr Kochetkov .30 .75
39 Dmitry Orlov .30 .75
40 Jesper Fast .20 .50
41 Martin Necas .50 1.25
42 Connor Bedard 1.00 2.50
43 Nick Foligno .20 .50
44 Kevin Korchinski .25 .60
45 Jason Dickinson .20 .50
46 Alex Vlasic .20 .50
47 Philipp Kurashev .25 .60
48 Cale Makar .75 2.00
49 Samuel Girard .20 .50
50 Ross Colton .25 .60
51 Alexandar Georgiev .30 .75
52 Artturi Lehkonen .25 .60
53 Miles Wood .20 .50
54 Adam Fantilli .50 1.25
55 Boone Jenner .30 .75
56 Dmitri Voronkov .20 .50
57 Yegor Chinakhov .25 .60
58 Cole Sillinger .25 .60
59 Zach Werenski .50 1.25
60 Erik Gudbranson .20 .50
61 Jake Oettinger .50 1.25
62 Jason Robertson .50 1.25
63 Wyatt Johnston .60 1.50
64 Jamie Benn .30 .75
65 Mason Marchment .25 .60
66 Ryan Suter .25 .60
67 Alex DeBrincat .40 1.00
68 Lucas Raymond .50 1.25
69 J.T. Compher .20 .50
70 Joe Veleno .25 .60
71 Alex Lyon .25 .60
72 Andrew Copp .20 .50
73 Jake Walman .20 .50
74 Connor McDavid 1.50 4.00
75 Stuart Skinner .40 1.00
76 Darnell Nurse .25 .60
77 Evander Kane .30 .75
78 Mattias Ekholm .25 .60
79 Raphael Lavoie .20 .50
80 Aleksander Barkov .50 1.25
81 Carter Verhaeghe .30 .75
82 Anton Lundell .30 .75
83 Niko Mikkola .20 .50
84 Sam Bennett .50 1.25
85 Mackie Samoskevich .25 .60
86 Trevor Moore .20 .50
87 Adrian Kempe .30 .75
88 Drew Doughty .30 .75
89 Brandt Clarke .30 .75
90 Alex Laferriere .20 .50
91 Pierre-Luc Dubois .25 .60
92 Brock Faber .40 1.00
93 Joel Eriksson Ek .25 .60
94 Filip Gustavsson .30 .75
95 Ryan Hartman .20 .50
96 Matt Boldy .50 1.25
97 Marco Rossi .40 1.00
98 Cole Caufield .60 1.50
99 Jake Evans .20 .50
100 Brendan Gallagher .30 .75
101 Juraj Slafkovsky .60 1.50
102 Alex Newhook .25 .60
103 Samuel Montembeault .30 .75
104 Ryan O'Reilly .30 .75
105 Thomas Novak .20 .50
106 Luke Evangelista .25 .60
107 Ryan McDonagh .20 .50
108 Roman Josi .30 .75
109 Colton Sissons .20 .50
110 Jesper Bratt .30 .75
111 Simon Nemec .40 1.00
112 Luke Hughes .50 1.25
113 Timo Meier .30 .75
114 Ondrej Palat .25 .60
115 John Marino .30 .75
116 Ilya Sorokin .50 1.25
117 Brock Nelson .30 .75
118 Anders Lee .25 .60
119 Kyle Palmieri .25 .60
120 Pierre Engvall .20 .50
121 Ryan Pulock .25 .60
122 Jacob Trouba .25 .60
123 Jimmy Vesey .25 .60
124 Will Cuylle .25 .60
125 Vincent Trocheck .30 .75
126 Alexis Lafreniere .50 1.25
127 Chris Kreider .40 1.00
128 Tim Stutzle .40 1.00
129 Jake Sanderson .40 1.00
130 Joonas Korpisalo .30 .75
131 Ridly Greig .25 .60
132 Josh Norris .30 .75
133 Drake Batherson .30 .75
134 Jamie Drysdale .25 .60
135 Samuel Ersson .30 .75
136 Joel Farabee .30 .75
137 Tyson Foerster .30 .75
138 Owen Tippett .20 .50
139 Travis Sanheim .20 .50
140 Evgeni Malkin .60 1.50
141 Bryan Rust .25 .60
142 Rickard Rakell .25 .60
143 Kris Letang .40 1.00
144 Marcus Pettersson .20 .50
145 Tristan Jarry .25 .60
146 Mackenzie Blackwood .25 .60
147 Mikael Granlund .25 .60
148 Fabian Zetterlund .20 .50
149 Marc-Edouard Vlasic .20 .50
150 Logan Couture .40 1.00
151 Mario Ferraro .20 .50
152 Jared McCann .25 .60
153 Jaden Schwartz .25 .60
154 Yanni Gourde .25 .60
155 Tye Kartye .25 .60
156 Philipp Grubauer .30 .75
157 Vince Dunn .25 .60
158 Pavel Buchnevich .25 .60
159 Jordan Kyrou .30 .75
160 Jake Neighbours .30 .75
161 Kevin Hayes .25 .60
162 Colton Parayko .25 .60
163 Jordan Binnington .50 1.25
164 Jonas Johansson .30 .75
165 Mikhail Sergachev .25 .60
166 Tanner Jeannot .20 .50
167 Nikita Kucherov .60 1.50
168 Brandon Hagel .25 .60
169 Erik Cernak .20 .50
170 William Nylander .60 1.50
171 Matthew Knies .60 1.50
172 Mitch Marner .50 1.25
173 Calle Jarnkrok .20 .50
174 Jake McCabe .20 .50
175 Joseph Woll .40 1.00
176 Quinn Hughes .75 2.00
177 Thatcher Demko .40 1.00
178 J.T. Miller .40 1.00
179 Ilya Mikheyev .25 .60
180 Pius Suter .25 .60
181 Jack Eichel .50 1.25
182 Adin Hill .30 .75
183 Nicolas Roy .20 .50
184 Ivan Barbashev .25 .60
185 Alex Pietrangelo .25 .60
186 Paul Cotter .20 .50
187 Alex Ovechkin 1.25 3.00
188 John Carlson .30 .75
189 Aliaksei Protas .20 .50
190 Sonny Milano .25 .60
191 Charlie Lindgren .25 .60
192 T.J. Oshie .30 .75
193 Kyle Connor .50 1.25
194 Connor Hellebuyck .60 1.50
195 Gabe Vilardi .30 .75
196 Mason Appleton .20 .50
197 Cole Perfetti .30 .75
198 Neal Pionk .20 .50
199 Q.Hughes/L.Hughes CL .75 2.00
200 N.Kucherov/W.Nylander CL .60 1.50
201 Zachary Bolduc YG RC 6.00 15.00
202 Jesper Wallstedt YG RC 8.00 20.00
203 Landon Slaggert YG RC 3.00 8.00
204 Kyle MacLean YG RC 3.00 8.00
205 Mason Morelli YG RC 3.00 8.00
206 Brennan Othmann YG RC 5.00 12.00
207 Gavin Brindley YG RC 3.00 8.00
208 Bradly Nadeau YG RC 5.00 12.00
209 Zack Ostapchuk YG RC 3.00 8.00
210 Jason Polin YG RC 3.00 8.00
211 Shakir Mukhamadullin YG RC 4.00 10.00
212 Cutter Gauthier YG RC 8.00 20.00
213 Zach Dean YG RC 3.00 8.00
214 Luca Del Bel Belluz YG RC 3.00 8.00
215 Mavrik Bourque YG RC 6.00 15.00
216 Matt Rempe YG RC 6.00 15.00
217 Matt Villalta YG RC 3.00 8.00
218 Maxwell Crozier YG RC 3.00 8.00
219 James Malatesta YG RC 3.00 8.00
220 Ivan Fedotov YG RC 6.00 15.00
221 Ethan Del Mastro YG RC 3.00 8.00
222 Justin Brazeau YG RC 3.00 8.00
223 Collin Graf YG RC 3.00 8.00
224 Graeme Clarke YG RC 3.00 8.00
225 Scott Morrow YG RC 4.00 10.00
226 Brendan Brisson YG RC 4.00 10.00
227 Frank Nazar YG RC 10.00 25.00
228 Brad Lambert YG RC 4.00 10.00
229 Lane Hutson YG RC 50.00 125.00
230 Pierrick Dube YG RC 3.00 8.00
231 Arshdeep Bains YG RC 4.00 10.00
232 Ruslan Iskhakov YG RC 3.00 8.00
233 Josh Doan YG RC 5.00 12.00
234 Jack St. Ivany YG RC 3.00 8.00
235 Yan Kuznetsov YG RC 3.00 8.00
236 Olen Zellweger YG RC 6.00 15.00
237 Marshall Rifai YG RC 3.00 8.00
238 Cameron Crotty YG RC 3.00 8.00
239 Logan Mailloux YG RC 5.00 12.00
240 Sam Colangelo YG RC 3.00 8.00
241 Emil Lilleberg YG RC 3.00 8.00
242 Akil Thomas YG RC 3.00 8.00
243 Marat Khusnutdinov YG RC 3.00 8.00
244 Logan Stankoven YG RC 8.00 20.00
245 Nikita Chibrikov YG RC 3.00 8.00
246 Joshua Roy YG RC 5.00 12.00
247 Gage Goncalves YG RC 4.00 10.00
248 Liam Ohgren YG RC 6.00 15.00
249 Lukas Cormier YG RC 3.00 8.00
250 C.Gauthier/L.Stankoven CL 1.50 4.00
251 Trevor Zegras .30 .75
252 Radko Gudas .20 .50
253 Leo Carlsson .50 1.25
254 John Gibson .30 .75
255 Hampus Lindholm .20 .50
256 Jeremy Swayman .50 1.25
257 Mason Lohrei .25 .60
258 David Pastrnak .75 2.00
259 John Beecher .30 .75
260 Owen Power .30 .75
261 Tage Thompson .40 1.00
262 Peyton Krebs .25 .60
263 Dylan Cozens .30 .75
264 Jordan Greenway .20 .50
265 Mattias Samuelsson .20 .50
266 MacKenzie Weegar .25 .60
267 Martin Pospisil .25 .60
268 Rasmus Andersson .25 .60
269 Dan Vladar .25 .60
270 Walker Duehr .25 .60
271 Nazem Kadri .40 1.00
272 Sebastian Aho .50 1.25
273 Frederik Andersen .40 1.00
274 Jaccob Slavin .25 .60
275 Jordan Staal .25 .60
276 Jesperi Kotkaniemi .25 .60
277 Jack Drury .25 .60
278 Jalen Chatfield .20 .50
279 Ryan Donato .25 .60
280 Taylor Hall .30 .75
281 Petr Mrazek .25 .60
282 Lukas Reichel .25 .60
283 Connor Murphy .25 .60
284 Andreas Athanasiou .25 .60
285 Nathan MacKinnon 1.25 3.00
286 Valeri Nichushkin .30 .75
287 Devon Toews .25 .60
288 Logan O'Connor .30 .75
289 Casey Mittelstadt .30 .75
290 Jonathan Drouin .25 .60
291 Sean Kuraly .20 .50
292 Justin Danforth .20 .50
293 Kent Johnson .30 .75
294 David Jiricek .30 .75
295 Kirill Marchenko .40 1.00
296 Ivan Provorov .25 .60
297 Matt Duchene .30 .75
298 Evgenii Dadonov .20 .50
299 Tyler Seguin .40 1.00
300 Esa Lindell .25 .60
301 Nils Lundkvist .20 .50
302 Sam Steel .25 .60
303 Thomas Harley .30 .75
304 Marco Kasper .30 .75
305 Dylan Larkin .40 1.00
306 Simon Edvinsson .30 .75
307 Michael Rasmussen .20 .50
308 Ville Husso .20 .50
309 Ben Chiarot .20 .50
310 Jeff Petry .30 .75
311 Ryan Nugent-Hopkins .40 1.00
312 Derek Ryan .20 .50
313 Leon Draisaitl 1.00 2.50
314 Adam Henrique .25 .60
315 Corey Perry .50 1.25
316 Mattias Janmark .20 .50
317 Calvin Pickard .30 .75
318 Sam Reinhart .60 1.50
319 Matthew Tkachuk .60 1.50
320 Justin Sourdif .20 .50
321 Eetu Luostarinen .20 .50
322 Uvis Balinskis .20 .50
323 Evan Rodrigues .25 .60
324 Anze Kopitar .50 1.25
325 Mikey Anderson .25 .60
326 Alex Turcotte .20 .50
327 Andreas Englund .20 .50
328 Quinton Byfield .40 1.00
329 Vladislav Gavrikov .20 .50
330 Trevor Lewis .20 .50
331 Kirill Kaprizov 1.00 2.50
332 Frederick Gaudreau .20 .50
333 Marcus Johansson .20 .50
334 Marcus Foligno .25 .60
335 Jacob Middleton .20 .50
336 Jared Spurgeon .30 .75
337 Nick Suzuki .60 1.50
338 Jayden Struble .20 .50
339 Kaiden Guhle .30 .75
340 Arber Xhekaj .30 .75
341 Josh Anderson .25 .60
342 Kirby Dach .30 .75
343 Dante Fabbro .20 .50
344 Gustav Nyquist .20 .50
345 Cole Smith .20 .50
346 Juuse Saros .40 1.00
347 Luke Schenn .30 .75
348 Filip Forsberg .50 1.25
349 Jeremy Lauzon .20 .50
350 Jonas Siegenthaler .20 .50
351 Jack Hughes .75 2.00
352 Erik Haula .20 .50
353 Dawson Mercer .40 1.00
354 Kurtis MacDermid .20 .50
355 Jake Allen .30 .75
356 Mathew Barzal .40 1.00
357 Jean-Gabriel Pageau .20 .50
358 Semyon Varlamov .30 .75
359 Casey Cizikas .25 .60
360 Noah Dobson .40 1.00
361 Adam Pelech .20 .50
362 K'Andre Miller .25 .60
363 Artemi Panarin .60 1.50
364 Kaapo Kakko .25 .60
365 Filip Chytil .25 .60
366 Braden Schneider .25 .60
367 Igor Shesterkin .60 1.50
368 Brady Tkachuk .50 1.25
369 Thomas Chabot .30 .75
370 Shane Pinto .25 .60
371 Anton Forsberg .20 .50
372 Artem Zub .20 .50
373 Sean Couturier .25 .60
374 Bobby Brink .20 .50
375 Garnet Hathaway .20 .50
376 Cam York .20 .50
377 Morgan Frost .25 .60
378 Scott Laughton .20 .50
379 Ryan Graves .20 .50
380 Sidney Crosby 1.25 3.00
381 Lars Eller .20 .50
382 Drew O'Connor .20 .50
383 Valtteri Puustinen .20 .50
384 Michael Bunting .30 .75
385 Nico Sturm .20 .50
386 William Eklund .40 1.00
387 Vitek Vanecek .30 .75
388 Thomas Bordeleau .20 .50
389 Henry Thrun .20 .50
390 Jan Rutta .20 .50
391 Matty Beniers .40 1.00
392 Brandon Tanev .25 .60
393 Jordan Eberle .30 .75
394 Eeli Tolvanen .20 .50
395 Joey Daccord .30 .75
396 Ryker Evans .20 .50
397 Shane Wright .40 1.00
398 Torey Krug .25 .60
399 Robert Thomas .30 .75
400 Scott Perunovich .20 .50
401 Brayden Schenn .25 .60
402 Alexey Toropchenko .20 .50
403 Oskar Sundqvist .20 .50
404 Nick Paul .20 .50
405 Andrei Vasilevskiy .50 1.25
406 Anthony Cirelli .25 .60
407 Brayden Point .40 1.00
408 Luke Glendening .20 .50
409 Michael Eyssimont .20 .50
410 Darren Raddysh .20 .50
411 Auston Matthews 1.25 3.00

412 John Tavares .50 1.25
413 David Kampf .20 .50
414 Max Domi .30 .75
415 Morgan Rielly .30 .75
416 Bobby McMann .25 .60
417 Pontus Holmberg .20 .50
418 Nick Bjugstad .20 .50
419 Logan Cooley .50 1.25
420 Michael Carcone .20 .50
421 Matias Maccelli .25 .60
422 Liam O'Brien .20 .50
423 Michael Kesselring .20 .50
424 Dakota Joshua .20 .50
425 Elias Pettersson .50 1.25
426 Nils Hoglander .25 .60
427 Brock Boeser .40 1.00
428 Teddy Blueger .20 .50
429 Conor Garland .25 .60
430 Tyler Myers .20 .50
431 Mark Stone .40 1.00
432 Nicolas Hague .20 .50
433 Shea Theodore .40 1.00
434 Zach Whitecloud .20 .50
435 Tomas Hertl .30 .75
436 Keegan Kolesar .20 .50
437 Pavel Dorofeyev .20 .50
438 Connor McMichael .30 .75
439 Tom Wilson .30 .75
440 Rasmus Sandin .25 .60
441 Dylan Strome .40 1.00
442 Ethan Bear .20 .50
443 Ivan Miroshnichenko .25 .60
444 Nic Dowd .20 .50
445 Josh Morrissey .40 1.00
446 Mark Scheifele .50 1.25
447 Dylan DeMelo .20 .50
448 Nino Niederreiter .20 .50
449 N.MacKinnon/A.Matthews CL 1.25 3.00
450 S.Aho/B.Tkachuk CL .50 1.25
451 Macklin Celebrini YG RC 80.00 200.00
452 Brian Halonen YG RC 3.00 8.00
453 Patrik Koch YG RC 3.00 8.00
454 Brandon Scanlin YG RC 3.00 8.00
455 Cameron Butler YG RC 3.00 8.00
456 Maksymilian Szuber YG RC 3.00 8.00
457 Georgi Romanov YG RC 4.00 10.00
458 Aku Raty YG RC 3.00 8.00
459 Ethan Cardwell YG RC 2.50 6.00
460 Adam Klapka YG RC 3.00 8.00
461 Oliver Kapanen YG RC 3.00 8.00
462 Nikita Prishchepov YG RC 3.00 8.00
463 Maxim Tsyplakov YG RC 5.00 12.00
464 Victor Mancini YG RC 3.00 8.00
465 Oskar Back YG RC 3.00 8.00
466 Nikolai Kovalenko YG RC 2.50 6.00
467 Declan Carlile YG RC 3.00 8.00
468 Jack Thompson YG RC 3.00 8.00
469 Logan Morrison YG RC 3.00 8.00
470 Jackson Blake YG RC 6.00 15.00
471 Phil Kemp YG RC 3.00 8.00
472 Vasily Ponomarev YG RC 3.00 8.00
473 Devin Cooley YG RC 3.00 8.00
474 Rutger McGroarty YG RC 4.00 10.00
475 Albert Johansson YG RC 3.00 8.00
476 Patrick Giles YG RC 3.00 8.00
477 Calum Ritchie YG RC 4.00 10.00
478 Conor Geekie YG RC 6.00 15.00
479 Daniil Misyul YG RC 3.00 8.00
480 Zachary L'Heureux YG RC 4.00 10.00
481 Ivan Ivan YG RC 3.00 8.00
482 Andre Lee YG RC 3.00 8.00
483 Joel Blomqvist YG RC 4.00 10.00
484 Jett Luchanko YG RC 5.00 12.00
485 Samuel Honzek YG RC 3.00 8.00
486 Matt Stienburg YG RC 3.00 8.00
487 Maveric Lamoureux YG RC 5.00 12.00
488 Drew Commesso YG RC 4.00 10.00
489 Seamus Casey YG RC 4.00 10.00
490 Aleksei Kolosov YG RC 3.00 8.00
491 Nolan Allan YG RC 3.00 8.00
492 Matvei Michkov YG RC 40.00 100.00
493 Brandon Bussi YG RC 3.00 8.00
494 Isaac Poulter YG RC 3.00 8.00
495 Noah Philp YG RC 3.00 8.00
496 M.Michkov/I.Fedotov YG 3.00 8.00
497 L.Mailloux/L.Hutson YG 4.00 10.00
498 O.Zellweger/C.Gauthier YG 3.00 8.00
499 M.Celebrini/W.Smith YG 10.00 25.00
500 M.Celebrini/M.Michkov YG CL 8.00 20.00
501 Robby Fabbri .20 .50
502 Isac Lundestrom .20 .50
503 Ryan Strome .30 .75
504 Mason McTavish .30 .75
505 Brett Leason .20 .50
506 Charlie McAvoy .40 1.00
507 Elias Lindholm .30 .75
508 Trent Frederic .20 .50
509 Nikita Zadorov .20 .50
510 Jason Zucker .30 .75
511 Ukko-Pekka Luukkonen .25 .60
512 JJ Peterka .30 .75
513 Ryan McLeod .20 .50
514 Sam Lafferty .20 .50
515 Rasmus Dahlin .40 1.00
516 Mikael Backlund .25 .60
517 Jakob Pelletier .20 .50
518 Kevin Bahl .20 .50
519 Ryan Lomberg .20 .50
520 William Carrier .20 .50
521 Seth Jarvis .40 1.00
522 Jordan Martinook .20 .50
523 Jack Roslovic .20 .50
524 Shayne Gostisbehere .30 .75
525 Ilya Mikheyev .25 .60
526 Tyler Bertuzzi .25 .60
527 Seth Jones .30 .75
528 Teuvo Teravainen .30 .75
529 Alec Martinez .20 .50
530 Patrick Maroon .20 .50
531 Mikko Rantanen .75 2.00
532 Josh Manson .25 .60
533 Calvin de Haan .20 .50
534 Parker Kelly .20 .50
535 Givani Smith .20 .50
536 James van Riemsdyk .25 .60
537 Elvis Merzlikins .30 .75
538 Sean Monahan .20 .50
539 Damon Severson .20 .50
540 Jordan Harris .20 .50
541 Miro Heiskanen .40 1.00
542 Matt Dumba .20 .50
543 Roope Hintz .40 1.00
544 Casey DeSmith .25 .60
545 Ilya Lyubushkin .20 .50
546 Moritz Seider .40 1.00
547 Patrick Kane .60 1.50
548 Cam Talbot .30 .75
549 Jonatan Berggren .25 .60
550 Vladimir Tarasenko .40 1.00
551 Erik Gustafsson .20 .50
552 Viktor Arvidsson .20 .50
553 Evan Bouchard .40 1.00
554 Jeff Skinner .30 .75
555 Zach Hyman .50 1.25
556 Connor Brown .25 .60
557 Brett Kulak .20 .50
558 Gustav Forsling .30 .75
559 Sergei Bobrovsky .50 1.25
560 Dmitry Kulikov .20 .50
561 Aaron Ekblad .40 1.00
562 Phillip Danault .30 .75
563 Kevin Fiala .25 .60
564 Warren Foegele .20 .50
565 Darcy Kuemper .30 .75
566 Mats Zuccarello .30 .75
567 Zach Bogosian .20 .50
568 Marc-Andre Fleury .60 1.50
569 Jonas Brodin .20 .50
570 Mike Matheson .20 .50
571 Christian Dvorak .25 .60
572 Patrik Laine .40 1.00
573 David Savard .20 .50
574 Joel Armia .20 .50
575 Steven Stamkos .60 1.50
576 Jonathan Marchessault .40 1.00
577 Brady Skjei .20 .50
578 Juuso Parssinen .20 .50
579 Dougie Hamilton .25 .60
580 Jacob Markstrom .30 .75
581 Nico Hischier .50 1.25
582 Brenden Dillon .20 .50
583 Alexander Romanov .25 .60
584 Bo Horvat .40 1.00
585 Scott Mayfield .20 .50
586 Anthony Duclair .25 .60
587 Mika Zibanejad .40 1.00
588 Jonathan Quick .40 1.00
589 Adam Fox .40 1.00
590 Reilly Smith .30 .75
591 Claude Giroux .30 .75
592 David Perron .25 .60
593 Linus Ullmark .30 .75
594 Michael Amadio .20 .50
595 Travis Konecny .30 .75
596 Nicolas Deslauriers .20 .50
597 Noah Cates .20 .50
598 Nick Seeler .20 .50
599 Matt Grzelcyk .25 .60
600 Alex Nedeljkovic .25 .60
601 Erik Karlsson .40 1.00
602 Blake Lizotte .20 .50
603 Barclay Goodrow .20 .50
604 Tyler Toffoli .30 .75
605 Yaroslav Askarov .40 1.00
606 Alexander Wennberg .20 .50
607 Brandon Montour .40 1.00
608 Andre Burakovsky .20 .50
609 Chandler Stephenson .25 .60
610 Oliver Bjorkstrand .25 .60
611 Dylan Holloway .30 .75
612 Justin Faulk .25 .60
613 Philip Broberg .20 .50
614 Brandon Saad .25 .60
615 Alexandre Texier .20 .50
616 Jake Guentzel .50 1.25
617 J.J. Moser .20 .50
618 Cam Atkinson .30 .75
619 Victor Hedman .40 1.00
620 Nick Perbix .20 .50
621 Anthony Stolarz .40 1.00
622 Ryan Reaves .25 .60
623 Christopher Tanev .20 .50
624 Nick Robertson .30 .75
625 Oliver Ekman-Larsson .20 .50
626 Dylan Guenther .40 1.00
627 Karel Vejmelka .20 .50
628 Barrett Hayton .30 .75
629 Ian Cole .20 .50
630 Kevin Stenlund .25 .60
631 Jake DeBrusk .30 .75
632 Filip Hronek .20 .50
633 Vincent Desharnais .20 .50
634 Carson Soucy .20 .50
635 Kiefer Sherwood .20 .50
636 Danton Heinen .20 .50
637 William Karlsson .40 1.00
638 Ilya Samsonov .30 .75
639 Noah Hanifin .30 .75
640 Alexander Holtz .30 .75
641 Brayden McNabb .20 .50
642 Brett Howden .20 .50
643 Taylor Raddysh .25 .60
644 Logan Thompson .40 1.00
645 Jakob Chychrun .30 .75
646 Pierre-Luc Dubois .25 .60
647 Matt Roy .20 .50
648 Brandon Duhaime .20 .50
649 Dylan Samberg .20 .50
650 Alex Iafallo .20 .50
651 Rasmus Kupari .20 .50
652 Eric Comrie .20 .50
653 Morgan Barron .20 .50
654 Nikolaj Ehlers .30 .75
655 Vladislav Namestnikov .20 .50
656 Mitch Marner AS .50 1.25
657 Auston Matthews AS 1.25 3.00
658 William Nylander AS .60 1.50
659 Morgan Rielly AS .30 .75
660 Jake Oettinger AS .50 1.25
661 Vincent Trocheck AS .30 .75
662 Clayton Keller AS .40 1.00
663 Igor Shesterkin AS .60 1.50
664 Mathew Barzal AS .40 1.00
665 Alex DeBrincat AS .40 1.00
666 Filip Forsberg AS .50 1.25
667 Connor McDavid AS 1.50 4.00
668 David Pastrnak AS .75 2.00
669 Leon Draisaitl AS 1.00 2.50
670 Robert Thomas AS .30 .75
671 Rasmus Dahlin AS .40 1.00
672 Sam Reinhart AS .60 1.50
673 Connor Hellebuyck AS .60 1.50
674 Sergei Bobrovsky AS .50 1.25
675 Boone Jenner AS .30 .75
676 Nick Suzuki AS .60 1.50
677 Tomas Hertl AS .30 .75
678 Jeremy Swayman AS .50 1.25
679 Nathan MacKinnon AS 1.25 3.00
680 Sebastian Aho AS .50 1.25
681 Cale Makar AS .75 2.00
682 Tom Wilson AS .30 .75
683 Alexandar Georgiev AS .30 .75
684 Travis Konecny AS .30 .75
685 Sidney Crosby AS 1.25 3.00
686 Elias Lindholm AS .30 .75
687 Kirill Kaprizov AS 1.00 2.50
688 Oliver Bjorkstrand AS .25 .60
689 Quinn Hughes AS .75 2.00
690 Thatcher Demko AS .40 1.00
691 Cam Talbot AS .30 .75
692 Kyle Connor AS .50 1.25
693 Elias Pettersson AS .50 1.25
694 Nikita Kucherov AS .60 1.50
695 Brock Boeser AS .40 1.00
696 Jesper Bratt AS .30 .75
697 J.T. Miller AS .40 1.00
698 Brady Tkachuk AS .50 1.25
699 E.Bouchard/A.Fox CL .40 1.00
700 C.McAvoy/M.Seider CL .40 1.00
701 Will Smith YG RC 30.00 80.00
702 Erik Portillo YG RC 4.00 10.00
703 Owen Pickering YG RC 4.00 10.00
704 Lian Bichsel YG RC 6.00 15.00
705 Brett Berard YG RC 3.00 8.00
706 Jonathan Lekkerimaki YG RC 8.00 20.00
707 Tye Felhaber YG RC 2.50 6.00
708 Sebastian Cossa YG RC 8.00 20.00
709 Trent Miner YG RC 3.00 8.00
710 Denton Mateychuk YG RC 6.00 15.00
711 Isaiah George YG RC 4.00 10.00
712 Chase Bradley YG RC 3.00 8.00
713 Jere Innala YG RC 2.50 6.00
714 Nikita Grebenkin YG RC 4.00 10.00
715 Tyson Kozak YG RC 3.00 8.00
716 Max Sasson YG RC 3.00 8.00
717 Nathan Legare YG RC 3.00 8.00
718 Juha Jaaska YG RC 3.00 8.00
719 Samuel Helenius YG RC 3.00 8.00
720 Adam Wilsby YG RC 3.00 8.00
721 Fabian Lysell YG RC 8.00 20.00
722 Helge Grans YG RC 3.00 8.00
723 Justin Hryckowian YG RC 4.00 10.00
724 Fedor Svechkov YG RC 5.00 12.00
725 Ales Stezka YG RC 4.00 10.00
726 Jakub Dobes YG RC 20.00 50.00
727 Michael Milne YG RC 3.00 8.00
728 Arttu Hyry YG RC 3.00 8.00
729 Nathan Clurman YG RC 3.00 8.00
730 J.Lekkerimaki/W.Smith YG CL 1.50 4.00
731 Frank Nazar 1R 5.00 12.00
732 Owen Pickering 1R 2.00 5.00
733 Cutter Gauthier 1R 4.00 10.00
734 Jesper Wallstedt 1R 4.00 10.00
735 Brennan Othmann 1R 2.50 6.00
736 Sebastian Cossa 1R 4.00 10.00
737 Bradly Nadeau 1R 2.50 6.00
738 Brad Lambert 1R 2.00 5.00
739 Logan Mailloux 1R 2.50 6.00
740 Liam Ohgren 1R 3.00 8.00
741 Mavrik Bourque 1R 3.00 8.00
742 Brendan Brisson 1R 2.00 5.00
743 Macklin Celebrini 1R 8.00 20.00
744 Conor Geekie 1R 3.00 8.00
745 Jonathan Lekkerimaki 1R 4.00 10.00
746 Fedor Svechkov 1R 2.50 6.00
747 Will Smith 1R 5.00 12.00
748 Rutger McGroarty 1R 3.00 8.00
749 Matvei Michkov 1R 6.00 15.00
750 Zachary Bolduc 1R 3.00 8.00

2024-25 Upper Deck Clear Cut Parallel

*CLEAR CUT: 4X TO 10X BASIC
*CLEAR CUT RC: 2X TO 5X BASIC
*CLEAR CUT 1R: 2X TO 5X BASIC
202 Jesper Wallstedt YG 80.00 200.00
208 Bradly Nadeau YG 40.00 100.00
212 Cutter Gauthier YG 60.00 150.00
227 Frank Nazar YG 80.00 200.00
229 Lane Hutson YG 300.00 800.00
236 Olen Zellweger YG 30.00 80.00
239 Logan Mailloux YG 40.00 100.00
244 Logan Stankoven YG 80.00 200.00
451 Macklin Celebrini YG 600.00 1500.00
474 Rutger McGroarty YG 30.00 80.00
492 Matvei Michkov YG 250.00 600.00
496 M.Michkov/I.Fedotov YG 30.00 80.00
497 L.Mailloux/L.Hutson YG 25.00 60.00
498 O.Zellweger/C.Gauthier YG 12.00 30.00
499 M.Celebrini/W.Smith YG 100.00 250.00
500 M.Celebrini/M.Michkov YG CL 60.00 150.00
708 Sebastian Cossa YG 50.00 125.00
743 Macklin Celebrini 1R 80.00 200.00

2024-25 Upper Deck Deluxe

*DELUXE/250: 2X TO 5X BASIC
*DELUXE RC/250: 1.5X TO 4X BASIC
*DELUXE 1R/250: 1.5X TO 4X BASIC
202 Jesper Wallstedt YG 60.00 150.00
208 Bradly Nadeau YG 30.00 80.00
212 Cutter Gauthier YG 40.00 100.00
227 Frank Nazar YG 50.00 125.00
229 Lane Hutson YG 300.00 800.00
236 Olen Zellweger YG 30.00 80.00
239 Logan Mailloux YG 40.00 100.00
244 Logan Stankoven YG 40.00 100.00
451 Macklin Celebrini YG 400.00 1000.00
484 Jett Luchanko YG 30.00 80.00
492 Matvei Michkov YG 200.00 500.00
496 M.Michkov/I.Fedotov YG 25.00 60.00
497 L.Mailloux/L.Hutson YG 30.00 80.00
498 O.Zellweger/C.Gauthier YG 40.00 100.00
499 M.Celebrini/W.Smith YG 80.00 200.00
500 M.Celebrini/M.Michkov YG CL 80.00 200.00
708 Sebastian Cossa YG 30.00 80.00

2024-25 Upper Deck Exclusives

*EXCLUSIVES/100: 3X TO 8X BASIC
201 Zachary Bolduc YG 50.00 125.00
202 Jesper Wallstedt YG 125.00 300.00
208 Bradly Nadeau YG 60.00 150.00
212 Cutter Gauthier YG 200.00 500.00
227 Frank Nazar YG 80.00 200.00
229 Lane Hutson YG 600.00 1500.00
236 Olen Zellweger YG 60.00 150.00
239 Logan Mailloux YG 100.00 250.00
244 Logan Stankoven YG 80.00 200.00
451 Macklin Celebrini YG 1000.00 2500.00
474 Rutger McGroarty YG 80.00 200.00
484 Jett Luchanko YG 80.00 200.00
492 Matvei Michkov YG 800.00 2000.00
496 M.Michkov/I.Fedotov YG 50.00 125.00
497 L.Mailloux/L.Hutson YG 100.00 250.00
498 O.Zellweger/C.Gauthier YG 50.00 125.00
499 M.Celebrini/W.Smith YG 200.00 500.00
500 M.Celebrini/M.Michkov YG CL 150.00400.00
704 Lian Bichsel YG 80.00 200.00
706 Jonathan Lekkerimaki YG 60.00 150.00
708 Sebastian Cossa YG 60.00 150.00
726 Jakub Dobes YG 125.00 300.00
730 J.Lekkerimaki/W.Smith YG CL 12.00 30.00

2024-25 Upper Deck Outburst Red

*OUT RED/25: 15X TO 40X BASIC
*OUT RED RC/25: 5X TO 12X BASIC
*OUT RED 1R/25: 5X TO 12X BASIC
200 N.Kucherov/W.Nylander CL 8.00 20.00
201 Zachary Bolduc YG 100.00 250.00
208 Bradly Nadeau YG 100.00 250.00
212 Cutter Gauthier YG 600.00 1500.00
216 Matt Rempe YG 100.00 250.00
227 Frank Nazar YG 300.00 800.00
229 Lane Hutson YG 2000.00 5000.00
233 Josh Doan YG 80.00 200.00
236 Olen Zellweger YG 150.00 400.00
239 Logan Mailloux YG 200.00 500.00
244 Logan Stankoven YG 300.00 800.00
451 Macklin Celebrini YG 2000.00 5000.00
470 Jackson Blake YG 125.00 300.00
474 Rutger McGroarty YG 150.00 400.00
484 Jett Luchanko YG 150.00 400.00
492 Matvei Michkov YG 1500.00 4000.00
496 M.Michkov/I.Fedotov YG 150.00 400.00
497 L.Mailloux/L.Hutson YG 200.00 500.00
498 O.Zellweger/C.Gauthier YG 80.00 200.00
499 M.Celebrini/W.Smith YG 500.00 1200.00
500 M.Celebrini/M.Michkov YG CL 200.00500.00
706 Jonathan Lekkerimaki YG 150.00 400.00
708 Sebastian Cossa YG 200.00 500.00
710 Denton Mateychuk YG 125.00 300.00
726 Jakub Dobes YG 200.00 500.00
731 Frank Nazar 1R 125.00 300.00
747 Will Smith 1R 100.00 250.00

2024-25 Upper Deck Outburst Silver

*OUT SLVR: 2.5X TO 6X BASIC
*OUT SLVR RC: 1X TO 2.5X BASIC
*OUT SLVR 1R: 1X TO 2.5X BASIC
212 Cutter Gauthier YG 40.00 100.00
227 Frank Nazar YG 60.00 150.00
229 Lane Hutson YG 150.00 400.00
244 Logan Stankoven YG 40.00 100.00
250 Cutter Gauthier
Logan Stankoven CL 8.00 20.00
451 Macklin Celebrini YG 300.00 800.00
474 Rutger McGroarty YG 20.00 50.00
484 Jett Luchanko YG 20.00 50.00
492 Matvei Michkov YG 150.00 400.00
496 M.Michkov/I.Fedotov YG 15.00 40.00
497 L.Mailloux/L.Hutson YG 25.00 60.00
499 M.Celebrini/W.Smith YG 40.00 100.00
500 M.Celebrini/M.Michkov YG CL 40.00 100.00
706 Jonathan Lekkerimaki YG 25.00 60.00
708 Sebastian Cossa YG 25.00 60.00
726 Jakub Dobes YG 60.00 150.00
730 J.Lekkerimaki/W.Smith YG CL 10.00 25.00
743 Macklin Celebrini 1R 40.00 100.00
749 Matvei Michkov 1R 30.00 80.00

2024-25 Upper Deck Photo Variations All-Star Skills

*AS SKILLS: 3X TO 8X BASIC

2024-25 Upper Deck Photo Variations Snow Spray Autographs

*SNOW SPRAY: 15X TO 40X BASIC
105 Thomas Novak 12.00 30.00
374 Bobby Brink 15.00 40.00
583 Alexander Romanov SP 12.00 30.00

2024-25 Upper Deck Photo Variations Special Game

*SPECIAL GAME: 5X TO 12X BASIC

2024-25 Upper Deck Photo Variations Swagnificent

*SWAGNIFICENT: 8X TO 20X BASIC
42 Connor Bedard 50.00 125.00

2024-25 Upper Deck '94-95 Rookie Die Cuts

*RED: 1X TO 2.5X BASIC
RDT1 Cutter Gauthier 1.50 4.00
RDT2 Brennan Othmann 1.00 2.50
RDT3 Logan Stankoven 1.50 4.00
RDT4 Olen Zellweger 1.25 3.00
RDT5 Shakir Mukhamadullin .75 2.00
RDT6 Joshua Roy 1.00 2.50
RDT7 Zachary Bolduc 1.25 3.00
RDT8 Brendan Brisson .75 2.00
RDT9 Jesper Wallstedt 1.50 4.00
RDT10 Matt Rempe 1.25 3.00
RDT11 Brad Lambert .75 2.00
RDT12 Josh Doan 1.00 2.50
RDT16 Liam Ohgren 1.25 3.00
RDT17 Will Smith 2.00 5.00
RDT18 Logan Mailloux 1.25 3.00
RDT19 Mavrik Bourque 1.25 3.00
RDT20 Frank Nazar 2.00 5.00

2024-25 Upper Deck A-Lines

*RED/99: 1X TO 2.5X BASIC
AL1 Zegras/McTavish/Terry 1.25 3.00
AL2 Maccelli/Cooley/Keller 2.00 5.00
AL3 Marchand/Coyle/Pastrnak 3.00 8.00
AL4 Skinner/Thompson/Tuch 1.50 4.00
AL5 Kuzmenko/Kadri/Coleman 1.50 4.00
AL6 Svechnikov/Aho/Necas 2.00 5.00
AL7 Foligno/Bedard/Kurashev 4.00 10.00
AL8 Nichushkin/MacKinnon/Rantanen 5.00 12.00
AL9 Gaudreau/Fantilli/Marchenko 2.00 5.00
AL10 Robertson/Johnston/Seguin 2.50 6.00
AL11 DeBrincat/Larkin/Raymond 2.00 5.00
AL12 Draisaitl/Nugent-
Hopkins/Hyman 4.00 10.00
AL13 Verhaeghe/Barkov/Tkachuk 2.50 6.00
AL14 Byfield/Kopitar/Kempe 2.00 5.00
AL15 Kaprizov/Eriksson Ek/Boldy 4.00 10.00
AL16 Caufield/Suzuki/Slafkovsky 2.50 6.00
AL17 Forsberg/O'Reilly/Nyquist 2.00 5.00
AL18 Meier/Hughes/Bratt 3.00 8.00
AL19 Nelson/Horvat/Barzal 1.50 4.00
AL20 Panarin/Zibanejad/Trocheck 2.50 6.00
AL21 Tkachuk/Stutzle/Giroux 2.00 5.00
AL22 Konecny/Couturier/Farabee 1.25 3.00
AL23 Smith/Malkin/Rakell 2.50 6.00
AL24 Eklund/Couture/Zetterlund 1.50 4.00
AL25 McCann/Beniers/Bjorkstrand 1.50 4.00
AL26 Buchnevich/Thomas/Kyrou 1.25 3.00
AL27 Hagel/Point/Kucherov 2.50 6.00
AL28 Knies/Matthews/Marner 5.00 12.00
AL29 Miller/Pettersson/Boeser 2.00 5.00
AL30 Marchessault/Eichel/Stone 2.00 5.00
AL31 Ovechkin/Strome/Wilson 5.00 12.00
AL32 Connor/Scheifele/Ehlers 2.00 5.00

2024-25 Upper Deck Aimbot

*SPECKLE: .6X TO 1.5X BASIC
*BLACK: .8X TO 2X BASIC
*RED/99: 1.2X TO 3X BASIC
AB1 Alex Ovechkin 2.00 5.00
AB2 Jared McCann .40 1.00
AB3 Nikita Kucherov 1.00 2.50
AB4 Kyle Connor .75 2.00
AB5 Elias Pettersson .75 2.00
AB6 Matthew Tkachuk 1.00 2.50
AB7 Connor McDavid 2.50 6.00
AB8 David Pastrnak 1.25 3.00
AB9 Artemi Panarin 1.00 2.50
AB10 Brayden Point .60 1.50
AB11 Carter Verhaeghe .50 1.25
AB12 Kirill Kaprizov 1.50 4.00
AB13 Jason Robertson .75 2.00
AB14 Nathan MacKinnon 2.00 5.00
AB15 Mark Scheifele .75 2.00
AB16 William Nylander 1.00 2.50
AB17 Jack Hughes 1.25 3.00
AB18 Adrian Kempe .50 1.25
AB19 Tage Thompson .60 1.50
AB20 Leon Draisaitl 1.50 4.00
AB21 Auston Matthews 2.00 5.00
AB22 Sidney Crosby 2.00 5.00
AB23 Mikko Rantanen 1.25 3.00
AB24 Travis Konecny .50 1.25
AB25 Tim Stutzle .60 1.50

2024-25 Upper Deck Bang For Your Puck

*SPECKLE: .5X TO 1.2X BASIC
*BLACK: 1X TO 2.5X BASIC
*RED/99: 1.5X TO 4X BASIC
BP1 Erik Karlsson 1.00 2.50
BP2 Auston Matthews 3.00 8.00
BP3 Filip Hronek .50 1.25
BP4 Josh Morrissey 1.00 2.50
BP5 Victor Hedman 1.00 2.50
BP6 Colton Parayko .60 1.50
BP7 Rasmus Dahlin 1.00 2.50
BP8 Alex Ovechkin 3.00 8.00
BP9 David Pastrnak 2.00 5.00
BP10 Evan Bouchard 1.00 2.50
BP11 Kasperi Kapanen .60 1.50
BP12 J.T. Miller 1.00 2.50
BP13 Travis Sanheim .50 1.25
BP14 Adam Pelech .50 1.25
BP15 Radko Gudas .50 1.25
BP16 John Carlson .75 2.00
BP17 Seth Jones .75 2.00
BP18 Cale Makar 2.00 5.00
BP19 Timo Meier .75 2.00
BP20 Tage Thompson 1.00 2.50
BP21 Tom Wilson .75 2.00
BP22 Elias Pettersson 1.25 3.00
BP23 Arber Xhekaj .75 2.00

2024-25 Upper Deck Beehive

*GOLD: .6X TO 1.5X BASIC
BH1 Cutter Gauthier 2.00 5.00
BH2 Josh Morrissey 1.00 2.50
BH3 Tage Thompson 1.00 2.50
BH4 Filip Forsberg 1.25 3.00
BH5 Will Smith 2.50 6.00
BH6 Connor McDavid 4.00 10.00
BH7 Nick Suzuki 1.50 4.00
BH8 Evgeni Malkin 1.50 4.00
BH9 Logan Stankoven 2.00 5.00
BH10 Victor Hedman 1.00 2.50
BH11 Sebastian Aho 1.25 3.00
BH12 Jason Robertson 1.25 3.00
BH13 Jonathan Lekkerimaki 2.00 5.00
BH14 Chris Kreider 1.00 2.50
BH15 Sebastian Cossa 2.00 5.00
BH16 Connor Bedard 2.50 6.00
BH17 Sidney Crosby 3.00 8.00
BH18 Lane Hutson 4.00 10.00
BH19 Jack Hughes 2.00 5.00
BH20 Frank Nazar 2.50 6.00
BH21 Thatcher Demko 1.00 2.50
BH22 Cale Makar 2.00 5.00
BH23 Alex Ovechkin 3.00 8.00
BH24 Macklin Celebrini 4.00 10.00
BH25 Aleksander Barkov 1.25 3.00
BH26 Denton Mateychuk 1.50 4.00
BH27 Matvei Michkov 3.00 8.00
BH28 David Pastrnak 2.00 5.00
BH29 Tim Stutzle 1.00 2.50
BH30 Auston Matthews 3.00 8.00

2024-25 Upper Deck Breaking News

*RED/99: .8X TO 2X BASIC
BN1 Drew Doughty 1.00 2.50
BN2 Bobby McMann .75 2.00
BN3 Alex Ovechkin 4.00 10.00
BN4 Connor Bedard 3.00 8.00
BN5 Brad Marchand 2.00 5.00
BN6 David Perron .75 2.00
BN7 Tristan Jarry 1.00 2.50
BN8 Kyle Okposo .60 1.50
BN9 Nathan MacKinnon 4.00 10.00
BN10 Nikita Kucherov 2.00 5.00
BN11 John Tavares 1.50 4.00
BN12 Ryan Suter .75 2.00
BN13 Ryan O'Reilly 1.00 2.50
BN14 MacKenzie Weegar .75 2.00
BN15 Cal Clutterbuck .60 1.50
BN16 Trevor Zegras 1.00 2.50
BN17 Kevin Korchinski .75 2.00
BN18 T.J. Oshie 1.00 2.50
BN19 Matt Duchene 1.00 2.50
BN20 Thatcher Demko 1.25 3.00
BN21 Victor Hedman 1.25 3.00
BN22 Marc-Andre Fleury 2.00 5.00
BN23 Leo Carlsson 1.50 4.00
BN24 Joel Hofer .60 1.50
BN25 Connor McDavid 5.00 12.00
BN26 Adam Fantilli 1.50 4.00
BN27 Auston Matthews 4.00 10.00
BN28 Logan Cooley 1.50 4.00
BN29 Leon Draisaitl 3.00 8.00
BN30 Simon Nemec 1.25 3.00
BN31 Anze Kopitar 1.50 4.00
BN32 Joey Daccord 1.00 2.50
BN33 Cale Makar 2.50 6.00
BN34 Matthew Knies 2.00 5.00

2024-25 Upper Deck Checkpoint

*SPECKLE: .8X TO 2X BASIC
*BLACK: 1.5X TO 4X BASIC
*RED/99: 2.5X TO 6X BASIC
CP1 Ethan Bear .40 1.00
CP2 Jesperi Kotkaniemi .60 1.50
CP3 Morgan Geekie .40 1.00
CP4 Nick Cousins .40 1.00
CP5 Brock Faber .75 2.00
CP6 Cole Perfetti .60 1.50
CP7 Evander Kane .60 1.50
CP8 Juraj Slafkovsky 1.25 3.00
CP9 Pavel Mintyukov .50 1.25
CP10 Braden Schneider .50 1.25
CP11 Alex Ovechkin 2.50 6.00
CP12 Vincent Desharnais .40 1.00
CP13 Alexey Toropchenko .40 1.00
CP14 Sidney Crosby 2.50 6.00
CP15 Casey Cizikas .50 1.25
CP16 Arber Xhekaj .60 1.50
CP17 Erik Cernak .40 1.00
CP18 Charlie Coyle .60 1.50
CP19 Jimmy Vesey .50 1.25
CP20 William Borgen .40 1.00
CP21 Brayden McNabb .40 1.00
CP22 Oliver Ekman-Larsson .40 1.00
CP23 Charlie McAvoy .75 2.00
CP24 Esa Lindell .50 1.25
CP25 Austin Watson .40 1.00

2024-25 Upper Deck City Satellites

*SPECKLE: .6X TO 1.5X BASIC
*BLACK: 1X TO 2.5X BASIC
*RED/99: 2.5X TO 6X BASIC
CS1 Sidney Crosby 2.00 5.00
CS2 Elias Pettersson .75 2.00
CS3 Connor McDavid 2.50 6.00
CS4 Alex DeBrincat .60 1.50
CS5 Jack Eichel .75 2.00
CS6 Clayton Keller .60 1.50
CS7 Nazem Kadri .60 1.50
CS8 Kirill Kaprizov 1.50 4.00
CS9 Nikita Kucherov 1.00 2.50
CS10 Nathan MacKinnon 2.00 5.00
CS11 Connor Bedard 1.50 4.00
CS12 Alex Ovechkin 2.00 5.00
CS13 Cole Caufield 1.00 2.50
CS14 Jason Robertson .75 2.00
CS15 David Pastrnak 1.25 3.00
CS16 Jack Hughes 1.25 3.00
CS17 Sebastian Aho .75 2.00
CS18 Artemi Panarin 1.00 2.50
CS19 Matthew Tkachuk 1.00 2.50
CS20 Auston Matthews 2.00 5.00

2024-25 Upper Deck Crossed Up

CU1 Auston Matthews 60.00 150.00
CU2 Connor McDavid 80.00 200.00
CU3 Alex Ovechkin 60.00 150.00
CU4 Sidney Crosby 60.00 150.00
CU5 Nathan MacKinnon 60.00 150.00
CU6 Jack Hughes 40.00 100.00
CU7 Matthew Tkachuk 30.00 80.00
CU8 Jason Robertson 25.00 60.00
CU9 Elias Pettersson 25.00 60.00
CU10 Kirill Kaprizov 60.00 150.00
CU11 David Pastrnak 40.00 100.00
CU12 Leon Draisaitl 50.00 125.00
CU13 Connor Bedard 125.00 300.00
CU14 Nikita Kucherov 60.00 150.00

2024-25 Upper Deck Day With The Cup

DC1 Sam Reinhart 50.00 125.00
DC2 Carter Verhaeghe 50.00 125.00
DC3 Matthew Tkachuk 60.00 150.00
DC4 Aaron Ekblad 60.00 150.00
DC5 Brandon Montour 50.00 125.00
DC6 Sam Bennett 50.00 125.00
DC7 Gustav Forsling 50.00 125.00
DC8 Sergei Bobrovsky 80.00 200.00
DC9 Aleksander Barkov 60.00 150.00
DC10 Anton Lundell 50.00 125.00
DC11 Evan Rodrigues 40.00 100.00
DC12 Vladimir Tarasenko 40.00 100.00
DC13 Nick Cousins 30.00 80.00
DC14 Ryan Lomberg 30.00 80.00
DC15 Steven Lorentz 30.00 80.00
DC16 Anthony Stolarz 60.00 150.00
DC17 Oliver Ekman-Larsson 30.00 80.00
DC18 Jonah Gadjovich 30.00 80.00
DC19 Niko Mikkola 30.00 80.00
DC20 Kevin Stenlund 40.00 100.00
DC21 Dmitry Kulikov 30.00 80.00
DC22 Eetu Luostarinen 30.00 80.00

2024-25 Upper Deck Dazzlers Blue

*GREEN: .5X TO 1.2X BASIC
*ORANGE: .8X TO 2X BASIC
*RED: 1.5X TO 4X BASIC
*PINK: 2X TO 5X BASIC
*BLACK: 3X TO 8X BASIC
DZ1 Gustav Nyquist .30 .75
DZ2 Jordan Kyrou .50 1.25
DZ3 Thatcher Demko .60 1.50
DZ4 William Eklund .60 1.50
DZ5 Joel Farabee .50 1.25
DZ6 Brock Nelson .50 1.25
DZ7 Charlie Coyle .50 1.25
DZ8 Nathan MacKinnon 2.00 5.00
DZ9 Mitch Marner .75 2.00
DZ10 Connor McDavid 2.50 6.00
DZ11 Nazem Kadri .60 1.50
DZ12 Quinton Byfield .60 1.50
DZ13 Connor Bedard 1.50 4.00
DZ14 Jesper Bratt .50 1.25
DZ15 Tristan Jarry .50 1.25
DZ16 Filip Forsberg .75 2.00
DZ17 Sergei Bobrovsky .75 2.00
DZ18 Morgan Rielly .50 1.25
DZ19 Jeremy Swayman .75 2.00
DZ20 Dylan Strome .60 1.50
DZ21 Evan Bouchard .60 1.50
DZ22 Dylan Cozens .50 1.25
DZ23 J.T. Miller .60 1.50
DZ24 Anze Kopitar .75 2.00
DZ25 Shane Pinto .40 1.00
DZ26 Adin Hill .50 1.25
DZ27 Patrick Kane 1.00 2.50
DZ28 Chris Kreider .60 1.50
DZ29 Martin Necas .75 2.00
DZ30 Clayton Keller .60 1.50
DZ31 Drake Batherson .50 1.25
DZ32 Simon Nemec .60 1.50
DZ33 Matthew Tkachuk 1.00 2.50
DZ34 Tyler Seguin .60 1.50
DZ35 Marco Rossi .60 1.50
DZ36 Sidney Crosby 2.00 5.00
DZ37 Vincent Trocheck .50 1.25
DZ38 Dmitri Voronkov .30 .75
DZ39 Jordan Binnington .75 2.00
DZ40 Leo Carlsson .75 2.00
DZ41 Nikolaj Ehlers .50 1.25
DZ42 Juraj Slafkovsky 1.00 2.50
DZ43 Wyatt Johnston 1.00 2.50
DZ44 Nikita Kucherov 1.00 2.50
DZ45 Dylan Larkin .60 1.50
DZ46 Matty Beniers .60 1.50
DZ47 Brandon Hagel .40 1.00
DZ48 Connor Hellebuyck 1.00 2.50
DZ49 Brock Faber .60 1.50
DZ50 Noah Dobson .60 1.50
DZ51 Juuse Saros .60 1.50
DZ52 Zach Hyman .75 2.00
DZ53 Jesper Wallstedt 1.25 3.00
DZ54 Jared McCann .40 1.00
DZ55 Frank Nazar 1.50 4.00
DZ56 Ilya Sorokin .75 2.00
DZ57 John Tavares .75 2.00
DZ58 Mason McTavish .50 1.25
DZ59 Artemi Panarin 1.00 2.50
DZ60 Shakir Mukhamadullin .60 1.50
DZ61 Moritz Seider .60 1.50
DZ62 Quinn Hughes 1.25 3.00
DZ63 Liam Ohgren 1.00 2.50
DZ64 Cale Makar 1.25 3.00
DZ65 Nico Hischier .75 2.00
DZ66 Logan Couture .60 1.50
DZ67 Charlie McAvoy .60 1.50
DZ68 Victor Hedman .60 1.50
DZ69 Logan Mailloux .75 2.00
DZ70 Olen Zellweger 1.00 2.50
DZ71 Brock Boeser .60 1.50
DZ72 Tage Thompson .60 1.50
DZ73 Bo Horvat .60 1.50
DZ74 Vince Dunn .40 1.00
DZ75 Miro Heiskanen .60 1.50
DZ76 Lane Hutson 2.50 6.00
DZ77 Trevor Moore .30 .75
DZ78 John Carlson .50 1.25
DZ79 Brad Marchand 1.00 2.50
DZ80 Owen Tippett .30 .75
DZ81 Cutter Gauthier 1.25 3.00
DZ82 Kris Letang .60 1.50
DZ83 Logan Stankoven 1.25 3.00
DZ84 Kyle Connor .75 2.00
DZ85 Cole Caufield 1.00 2.50
DZ86 MacKenzie Weegar .40 1.00
DZ87 Luke Hughes .75 2.00
DZ88 Brady Tkachuk .75 2.00
DZ89 Auston Matthews 2.00 5.00
DZ90 Josh Doan .75 2.00
DZ91 Jack Eichel .75 2.00
DZ92 Ryan Nugent-Hopkins .60 1.50
DZ93 Andrei Vasilevskiy .75 2.00
DZ94 Owen Power .50 1.25
DZ95 Roman Josi .50 1.25
DZ96 Matt Rempe 1.00 2.50
DZ97 Alex Ovechkin 2.00 5.00
DZ98 Adam Fantilli .75 2.00
DZ99 Jake Neighbours .50 1.25
DZ100 Matt Boldy .75 2.00
DZ101 Nick Suzuki 1.00 2.50
DZ102 Seamus Casey .60 1.50
DZ103 David Pastrnak 1.25 3.00
DZ104 Brennan Othmann .75 2.00
DZ105 William Nylander 1.00 2.50
DZ106 Jason Robertson .75 2.00
DZ107 Logan Cooley .75 2.00
DZ108 Robert Thomas .50 1.25
DZ109 Kirill Kaprizov 1.50 4.00
DZ110 Adam Fox .60 1.50
DZ111 Pierre-Luc Dubois .40 1.00
DZ112 Jonathan Lekkerimaki 1.25 3.00
DZ113 Mathew Barzal .60 1.50
DZ114 Elias Pettersson .75 2.00
DZ115 Kirill Marchenko .60 1.50

DZ116 Tyler Toffoli .50 1.25
DZ117 Steven Stamkos 1.00 2.50
DZ118 Jake Guentzel .75 2.00
DZ119 Taylor Hall .50 1.25
DZ120 Jack Hughes 1.25 3.00
DZ121 Matvei Michkov 4.00 10.00
DZ122 Lucas Raymond .75 2.00
DZ123 Brandon Montour .60 1.50
DZ124 Fedor Svechkov .75 2.00
DZ125 Brad Lambert .60 1.50
DZ126 Rasmus Dahlin .60 1.50
DZ127 Erik Karlsson .60 1.50
DZ128 Macklin Celebrini 8.00 20.00
DZ129 Mark Scheifele .75 2.00
DZ130 Fabian Lysell 1.25 3.00
DZ131 Denton Mateychuk 1.00 2.50
DZ132 Lian Bichsel 1.00 2.50
DZ133 Travis Konecny .50 1.25
DZ134 William Karlsson .60 1.50
DZ135 Trevor Zegras .50 1.25
DZ136 Tim Stutzle .60 1.50
DZ137 Rutger McGroarty 1.00 2.50
DZ138 Mavrik Bourque 1.00 2.50
DZ139 Jett Luchanko 1.00 2.50
DZ140 Will Smith 1.50 4.00
DZ141 Zachary Bolduc 1.00 2.50
DZ142 Jonathan Huberdeau .60 1.50
DZ143 Conor Geekie 1.00 2.50
DZ144 Zach Dean .50 1.25
DZ145 Leon Draisaitl 1.50 4.00
DZ146 Kevin Fiala .40 1.00
DZ147 Jacob Markstrom .50 1.25
DZ148 Brayden Point .60 1.50
DZ149 Mikko Rantanen 1.25 3.00
DZ150 Sam Reinhart 1.00 2.50

2024-25 Upper Deck ElectriCITY
*SPECKLE: .5X TO 1.2X BASIC
*BLACK: 1.2X TO 3X BASIC
EC1 Zach Werenski 1.00 2.50
EC2 Filip Forsberg 1.00 2.50
EC3 Mathew Barzal .75 2.00
EC4 Zach Hyman 1.00 2.50
EC5 Jack Hughes 1.50 4.00
EC6 Clayton Keller .75 2.00
EC7 Connor Bedard 2.00 5.00
EC8 Jared McCann .50 1.25
EC9 Anze Kopitar 1.00 2.50
EC10 Chris Kreider .75 2.00
EC11 Brad Marchand 1.25 3.00
EC12 Elias Pettersson 1.00 2.50
EC13 Lucas Raymond 1.00 2.50
EC14 Robert Thomas .60 1.50
EC15 Sebastian Aho 1.00 2.50
EC16 Alex Ovechkin 2.50 6.00
EC17 Matthew Tkachuk 1.25 3.00
EC18 Evgeni Malkin 1.25 3.00
EC19 Trevor Zegras .60 1.50
EC20 William Nylander 1.25 3.00
EC21 Wyatt Johnston 1.25 3.00
EC22 Mark Stone .75 2.00
EC23 Nazem Kadri .75 2.00
EC24 William Eklund .75 2.00
EC25 Brady Tkachuk 1.00 2.50
EC26 Mikko Rantanen 1.50 4.00
EC27 Brayden Point .75 2.00
EC28 Travis Konecny .60 1.50
EC29 Rasmus Dahlin .75 2.00
EC30 Cole Caufield 1.25 3.00
EC31 Kyle Connor 1.00 2.50
EC32 Matt Boldy 1.00 2.50

2024-25 Upper Deck Encore
*GOLD: .6X TO 1.5X BASIC
E1 Will Smith 2.50 6.00
E2 Travis Konecny .75 2.00
E3 Nathan MacKinnon 3.00 8.00
E4 Steven Stamkos 1.50 4.00
E5 Brad Marchand 1.50 4.00
E6 Aleksander Barkov 1.25 3.00
E7 Nikita Kucherov 2.00 5.00
E8 Macklin Celebrini 4.00 10.00
E9 Connor McDavid 4.00 10.00
E10 Logan Stankoven 2.00 5.00
E11 Lucas Raymond 1.25 3.00
E12 Quinn Hughes 2.00 5.00
E13 Jonathan Lekkerimaki 2.00 5.00
E14 Tyler Toffoli .75 2.00
E15 Lian Bichsel 1.50 4.00
E16 Rasmus Dahlin 1.00 2.50
E17 Auston Matthews 3.00 8.00
E18 Denton Mateychuk 1.50 4.00
E19 Kirill Kaprizov 2.50 6.00
E20 Artemi Panarin 1.50 4.00
E21 Cutter Gauthier 2.00 5.00
E22 Cole Caufield 1.50 4.00
E23 Sidney Crosby 3.00 8.00
E24 Lane Hutson 4.00 10.00
E25 Bo Horvat 1.00 2.50
E26 Matvei Michkov 3.00 8.00
E27 Leon Draisaitl 2.50 6.00
E28 Mitch Marner 1.25 3.00
E29 Frank Nazar 2.50 6.00
E30 Alex Ovechkin 4.00 10.00

2024-25 Upper Deck Fanimation
FM1 Yegor Sharangovich 25.00 60.00
FM2 Moritz Seider 30.00 80.00
FM3 Mats Zuccarello 25.00 60.00
FM4 Bo Horvat 30.00 80.00
FM5 Quinn Hughes 60.00 150.00
FM6 Mason McTavish 25.00 60.00
FM7 Connor Bedard 80.00 200.00
FM8 Jared McCann 20.00 50.00
FM9 Dylan Strome 30.00 80.00
FM10 David Pastrnak 60.00 150.00
FM11 Brayden Point 30.00 80.00
FM12 Tim Stutzle 30.00 80.00
FM13 Patrik Laine 30.00 80.00
FM14 Erik Karlsson 30.00 80.00
FM15 Ryan O'Reilly 25.00 60.00
FM16 Aleksander Barkov 40.00 100.00
FM17 Quinton Byfield 30.00 80.00
FM18 Rasmus Dahlin 30.00 80.00
FM19 Nick Suzuki 50.00 125.00
FM20 Logan Couture 30.00 80.00
FM21 Martin Necas 40.00 100.00
FM22 Mitch Marner 40.00 100.00
FM23 Travis Konecny 25.00 60.00
FM24 Jake Oettinger 40.00 100.00
FM25 Mark Stone 30.00 80.00
FM26 Leon Draisaitl 80.00 200.00
FM27 Jesper Bratt 25.00 60.00
FM28 Robert Thomas 25.00 60.00
FM29 Nathan MacKinnon 100.00 250.00
FM30 Mark Scheifele 30.00 80.00
FM31 Sebastian Aho 40.00 100.00
FM32 Igor Shesterkin 50.00 125.00

2024-25 Upper Deck Fluorescence Red
*BLUE/50: 1.2X TO 3X BASIC
F1 Zach Dean 1.50 4.00
F2 Ethan Cardwell 1.25 3.00
F3 Zack Ostapchuk 1.50 4.00
F4 Maveric Lamoureux 2.50 6.00
F5 Akil Thomas 1.50 4.00
F6 Albert Johansson 1.50 4.00
F7 Brennan Othmann 2.50 6.00
F8 Marat Khusnutdinov 1.50 4.00
F9 Olen Zellweger 3.00 8.00
F10 Matvei Michkov 10.00 25.00
F11 Brad Lambert 2.00 5.00
F12 Oskar Back 1.50 4.00
F13 Mavrik Bourque 3.00 8.00
F14 Logan Mailloux 2.50 6.00
F15 Maxim Tsyplakov 2.50 6.00
F16 Josh Doan 2.50 6.00
F17 Calum Ritchie 2.50 6.00
F18 Cutter Gauthier 4.00 10.00
F19 Zachary L'Heureux 2.00 5.00
F20 Victor Mancini 1.50 4.00
F21 Sam Colangelo 1.50 4.00
F22 Conor Geekie 3.00 8.00
F23 Oliver Kapanen 1.50 4.00
F24 Luca Del Bel Belluz 1.50 4.00
F25 Joel Blomqvist 2.00 5.00
F26 Liam Ohgren 3.00 8.00
F27 Shakir Mukhamadullin 2.00 5.00
F28 Joshua Roy 2.50 6.00
F29 Collin Graf 1.50 4.00
F30 Ruslan Iskhakov 1.50 4.00
F31 Brendan Brisson 2.00 5.00
F32 Jett Luchanko 3.00 8.00
F33 Frank Nazar 5.00 12.00
F34 Samuel Honzek 1.50 4.00
F35 Logan Stankoven 4.00 10.00
F36 Macklin Celebrini 12.00 30.00
F37 Bradly Nadeau 2.50 6.00
F38 Yan Kuznetsov 1.50 4.00
F39 Seamus Casey 2.00 5.00
F40 Scott Morrow 2.00 5.00
F41 Matt Rempe 3.00 8.00
F42 Jesper Wallstedt 4.00 10.00
F43 Jonathan Lekkerimaki 4.00 10.00
F44 Gavin Brindley 1.50 4.00
F46 Nikolai Kovalenko 1.25 3.00
F47 Nolan Allan 1.50 4.00
F48 Lane Hutson 8.00 20.00
F49 Will Smith 5.00 12.00
F50 Rutger McGroarty 3.00 8.00
F90 Zachary Bolduc 2.50 6.00

2024-25 Upper Deck Fluorescence Gold
*GOLD/150: .8X TO 2X BASIC
F10 Matvei Michkov 60.00 150.00
F36 Macklin Celebrini 80.00 200.00
F48 Lane Hutson 50.00 125.00

2024-25 Upper Deck Gaming Co-Op
*SPECKLE: .6X TO 1.5X BASIC
*BLUE: 1X TO 2.5X BASIC
*GREEN/199: 1.5X TO 4X BASIC
*GOLD/25: 2.5X TO 6X BASIC
CGO1 C.McDavid/L.Draisaitl 2.50 6.00
CGO2 D.Pastrnak/B.Marchand 1.25 3.00
CGO3 E.Pettersson/Q.Hughes 1.25 3.00
CGO4 S.Crosby/E.Malkin 2.00 5.00
CGO5 A.Matthews/M.Marner 2.00 5.00
CGO6 C.Bedard/K.Korchinski 1.50 4.00
CGO7 N.Kucherov/B.Point 1.00 2.50
CGO8 N.MacKinnon/C.Makar 2.00 5.00
CGO9 M.Stone/J.Marchessault .60 1.50
CGO10 K.Kaprizov/J.Eriksson Ek 1.50 4.00
CGO11 A.Ovechkin/D.Strome 2.00 5.00
CGO12 B.Tkachuk/T.Stutzle .75 2.00
CGO13 A.Panarin/M.Zibanejad 1.00 2.50
CGO14 A.DeBrincat/D.Larkin .60 1.50
CGO15 J.Kyrou/R.Thomas .50 1.25
CGO16 J.Robertson/R.Hintz .75 2.00
CGO17 M.Tkachuk/C.Verhaeghe 1.00 2.50
CGO18 A.Kopitar/Q.Byfield .75 2.00
CGO19 J.Hughes/J.Bratt 1.25 3.00
CGO20 A.Fantilli/J.Gaudreau .75 2.00
CGO21 M.Barzal/B.Horvat .60 1.50
CGO22 J.McCann/M.Beniers .60 1.50
CGO23 K.Connor/M.Scheifele .75 2.00
CGO24 N.Suzuki/C.Caufield 1.00 2.50
CGO25 S.Aho/A.Svechnikov .75 2.00

2024-25 Upper Deck Gaming FOV
*SPECKLE: .6X TO 1.5X BASIC
*BLUE: .8X TO 2X BASIC
GFOV1 Dylan Larkin .60 1.50
GFOV2 Clayton Keller .60 1.50
GFOV3 Tage Thompson .60 1.50
GFOV4 David Pastrnak 1.25 3.00
GFOV5 Connor Bedard 1.50 4.00
GFOV6 Leon Draisaitl 1.50 4.00
GFOV7 Cole Caufield 1.00 2.50
GFOV8 Kirill Kaprizov 1.50 4.00
GFOV9 Matthew Tkachuk 1.00 2.50
GFOV10 Kirill Marchenko .60 1.50
GFOV11 Auston Matthews 2.00 5.00
GFOV12 Nathan MacKinnon 2.00 5.00
GFOV14 Artemi Panarin 1.00 2.50
GFOV15 Jason Robertson .75 2.00
GFOV16 Filip Forsberg .75 2.00
GFOV17 Aleksander Barkov .75 2.00
GFOV18 Sidney Crosby 2.00 5.00
GFOV19 Nikita Kucherov 1.00 2.50
GFOV20 Connor McDavid 2.50 6.00
GFOV21 Quinn Hughes 1.25 3.00
GFOV22 Anze Kopitar .75 2.00
GFOV23 Robert Thomas .50 1.25
GFOV24 Andrei Svechnikov .60 1.50
GFOV25 Brady Tkachuk .75 2.00

2024-25 Upper Deck Gaming FOV Gold
*GOLD/25: 2.5X TO 6X BASIC
GFOV5 Connor Bedard 20.00 50.00

2024-25 Upper Deck Gaming FOV Green
*GREEN/199: 1X TO 2.5X BASIC
GFOV5 Connor Bedard 8.00 20.00

2024-25 Upper Deck Gaming PVP
*SPECKLE: .5X TO 1.2X BASIC
*BLUE: .8X TO 2X BASIC
*GREEN/199: 1X TO 2.5X BASIC
*GOLD/25: 2.5X TO 6X BASIC
GPVP1 L.Draisaitl/N.Kadri 1.50 4.00
GPVP2 D.Doughty/M.Tkachuk 1.00 2.50
GPVP3 N.Suzuki/B.Marchand 1.00 2.50
GPVP4 M.Marner/C.Caufield 1.00 2.50
GPVP5 C.Bedard/A.DeBrincat 1.50 4.00
GPVP6 E.Malkin/S.Couturier 1.00 2.50
GPVP7 J.Trouba/J.Hughes 1.25 3.00
GPVP8 S.Jones/F.Forsberg .75 2.00
GPVP9 Q.Byfield/T.Zegras .60 1.50
GPVP10 I.Shesterkin/I.Sorokin 1.00 2.50
GPVP11 W.Eklund/T.Terry .60 1.50
GPVP12 N.MacKinnon/D.Larkin 2.00 5.00
GPVP13 C.Makar/K.Kaprizov 1.50 4.00
GPVP14 S.Bobrovsky/A.Vasilevskiy .75 2.00
GPVP15 M.Barzal/K.Letang .60 1.50
GPVP16 A.Ovechkin/E.Karlsson 2.00 5.00
GPVP17 P.Mrazek/J.Binnington .75 2.00
GPVP18 M.Weegar/Q.Hughes 1.25 3.00
GPVP19 F.Zetterlund/J.Eichel .75 2.00
GPVP20 T.Thompson/A.Matthews 2.00 5.00
GPVP21 J.Tavares/T.Stutzle .75 2.00
GPVP22 E.Pettersson/M.Beniers .75 2.00
GPVP23 T.Wilson/S.Aho .75 2.00
GPVP24 M.Seider/A.Fantilli .75 2.00
GPVP25 M.McTavish/C.Keller .60 1.50

2024-25 Upper Deck Gaming XP
*SPECKLE: .5X TO 1.2X BASIC
*GOLD/25: 2.5X TO 6X BASIC
GXP1 Connor Bedard 1.50 4.00
GXP2 Quinton Byfield .60 1.50
GXP3 David Pastrnak 1.25 3.00
GXP4 Nikita Kucherov 1.00 2.50
GXP5 Quinn Hughes 1.25 3.00
GXP6 Wyatt Johnston 1.00 2.50
GXP7 Sidney Crosby 2.00 5.00
GXP8 Clayton Keller .60 1.50
GXP9 Auston Matthews 2.00 5.00
GXP10 Leon Draisaitl 1.50 4.00
GXP11 Jesper Bratt .50 1.25
GXP12 Adam Fantilli .75 2.00
GXP13 Matt Boldy .75 2.00
GXP14 Nathan MacKinnon 2.00 5.00
GXP15 Roman Josi .50 1.25
GXP16 Andrei Svechnikov .60 1.50
GXP17 Sam Reinhart 1.00 2.50
GXP18 William Nylander 1.00 2.50
GXP19 Gabe Vilardi .50 1.25
GXP20 Brady Tkachuk .75 2.00
GXP21 Noah Dobson .60 1.50
GXP22 Dylan Larkin .60 1.50
GXP23 Victor Hedman .60 1.50
GXP24 Cole Caufield 1.00 2.50
GXP25 Connor McDavid 2.50 6.00

2024-25 Upper Deck Gaming XP Blue
*BLUE: .8X TO 2X BASIC
GXP1 Connor Bedard 12.00 30.00

2024-25 Upper Deck Gaming XP Green
*GREEN/199: 1.2X TO 3X BASIC
GXP1 Connor Bedard 15.00 40.00

2024-25 Upper Deck Holotypes
HT1 Kyle Connor 12.00 30.00
HT2 Johnny Gaudreau 12.00 30.00
HT3 Connor Bedard 125.00 300.00
HT4 Kirill Kaprizov 25.00 60.00
HT5 Bo Horvat 10.00 25.00
HT6 Alex Tuch 8.00 20.00
HT7 Sebastian Aho 12.00 30.00
HT8 Mason McTavish 8.00 20.00
HT9 Brayden Point 10.00 25.00
HT10 Nick Suzuki 15.00 40.00
HT11 Sidney Crosby 30.00 80.00
HT12 Jonathan Huberdeau 10.00 25.00
HT13 Leon Draisaitl 25.00 60.00
HT14 Roman Josi 8.00 20.00
HT15 Jason Robertson 12.00 30.00
HT16 Cale Makar 20.00 50.00
HT17 Logan Cooley 12.00 30.00
HT18 Dylan Larkin 10.00 25.00
HT19 John Tavares 12.00 30.00
HT20 Elias Pettersson 12.00 30.00
HT21 Robert Thomas 8.00 20.00
HT22 Matthew Tkachuk 15.00 40.00
HT23 Brad Marchand 15.00 40.00
HT24 Tim Stutzle 15.00 40.00
HT25 Kevin Fiala 6.00 15.00
HT26 Artemi Panarin 15.00 40.00
HT27 Jack Hughes 20.00 50.00
HT28 Mark Stone 10.00 25.00
HT29 Travis Konecny 8.00 20.00
HT30 Matty Beniers 10.00 25.00

2024-25 Upper Deck Incarnations
INC2 Jack Hughes 30.00 80.00
INC3 David Pastrnak 30.00 80.00
INC4 Nikita Kucherov 25.00 60.00
INC5 Leon Draisaitl 40.00 100.00
INC7 Kirill Kaprizov 40.00 100.00
INC8 Josh Doan 20.00 50.00
INC9 Sidney Crosby 100.00 250.00
INC10 Connor Bedard 80.00 200.00
INC11 Wyatt Johnston 25.00 60.00
INC12 Auston Matthews 50.00 125.00
INC13 Logan Stankoven 30.00 80.00
INC14 Quinn Hughes 30.00 80.00
INC15 Nick Suzuki 25.00 60.00
INC16 Jack Eichel 20.00 50.00
INC17 Frank Nazar 40.00 100.00
INC18 Aleksander Barkov 20.00 50.00
INC19 Nathan MacKinnon 50.00 125.00
INC20 Artemi Panarin 25.00 60.00
INC21 Will Smith 60.00 150.00
INC23 William Nylander 25.00 60.00
INC24 Cutter Gauthier 30.00 80.00
INC25 Cale Makar 30.00 80.00

2024-25 Upper Deck O-Pee-Chee Glossy
*GOLD: .5X TO 1.2X BASIC
OG1 Anze Kopitar 1.25 3.00
OG2 Brady Tkachuk 1.25 3.00
OG3 Cale Makar 2.00 5.00
OG4 William Nylander 1.50 4.00
OG5 Alex Ovechkin 3.00 8.00
OG6 Elias Pettersson 1.25 3.00
OG7 Connor Bedard 2.50 6.00
OG8 Nikita Kucherov 1.50 4.00
OG9 Cole Caufield 1.50 4.00
OG10 Tim Stutzle 1.00 2.50
OG11 Auston Matthews 3.00 8.00
OG12 Leon Draisaitl 2.50 6.00
OG13 Artemi Panarin 1.50 4.00
OG14 Jack Hughes 2.00 5.00
OG15 Sidney Crosby 3.00 8.00
OG16 Jason Robertson 1.25 3.00
OG17 David Pastrnak 2.00 5.00
OG18 Quinn Hughes 2.00 5.00
OG19 Mitch Marner 1.25 3.00
OG20 Dylan Larkin 1.00 2.50
OG21 Kirill Kaprizov 2.50 6.00
OG22 Connor McDavid 4.00 10.00
OG23 Matthew Tkachuk 1.50 4.00
OG24 Robert Thomas .75 2.00
OG25 Nathan MacKinnon 3.00 8.00
OPC26 Frank Nazar 2.50 6.00
OPC27 Jack Eichel 1.25 3.00
OPC28 Rutger McGroarty 1.50 4.00
OPC29 Jordan Kyrou .75 2.00
OPC30 Mavrik Bourque 1.50 4.00
OPC31 Sebastian Aho 1.25 3.00
OPC32 Brad Lambert 1.00 2.50
OPC33 Logan Stankoven 2.00 5.00
OPC35 Quinton Byfield 1.00 2.50
OPC36 Brad Marchand 1.50 4.00
OPC37 Brennan Othmann 1.25 3.00
OPC38 Cutter Gauthier 2.00 5.00
OPC39 Brayden Point 1.00 2.50
OPC40 Olen Zellweger 1.50 4.00
OPC41 Moritz Seider 1.00 2.50
OPC42 Logan Mailloux 1.25 3.00
OPC43 Kyle Connor 1.00 2.50
OPC44 Josh Doan 1.25 3.00
OPC45 Will Smith 2.50 6.00
OPC46 Filip Forsberg 1.25 3.00
OPC47 Liam Ohgren 1.50 4.00
OPC48 Mikko Rantanen 2.00 5.00

2024-25 Upper Deck On a Heater
*SPECKLED: .6X TO 1.5X BASIC
*BLACK: 1X TO 2.5X BASIC
*RED/99: 2X TO 5X BASIC
OH1 Patrick Kane 1.25 3.00
OH2 Artemi Panarin 1.25 3.00
OH3 Robert Thomas .60 1.50
OH4 Troy Terry .50 1.25
OH5 Nathan MacKinnon 2.50 6.00
OH6 Jack Eichel 1.00 2.50
OH7 Auston Matthews 2.50 6.00
OH8 Nikita Kucherov 1.25 3.00
OH9 Wyatt Johnston 1.25 3.00
OH10 David Pastrnak 1.50 4.00
OH11 Lucas Raymond 1.00 2.50
OH12 Connor McDavid 3.00 8.00
OH13 Sam Reinhart 1.25 3.00
OH14 William Nylander 1.25 3.00
OH15 Evgeni Malkin 1.25 3.00

2024-25 Upper Deck On Tour
*SPECKLED: .6X TO 1.5X BASIC
*BLACK: 1X TO 2.5X BASIC
*RED/99: 1.2X TO 3X BASIC
OT1 C.Caufield/N.Suzuki 1.25 3.00
OT2 N.MacKinnon/C.Makar 2.50 6.00
OT3 T.Konecny/O.Tippett .60 1.50
OT4 A.Fantilli/K.Johnson 1.00 2.50
OT5 M.Stone/T.Hertl .75 2.00
OT6 F.Forsberg/R.Josi 1.00 2.50
OT7 D.Pastrnak/B.Marchand 1.50 4.00
OT8 W.Eklund/F.Zetterlund .75 2.00
OT9 A.Barkov/M.Tkachuk 1.25 3.00
OT10 K.Connor/J.Morrissey 1.00 2.50
OT11 S.Aho/A.Svechnikov 1.00 2.50
OT12 S.Crosby/E.Malkin 2.50 6.00
OT13 J.Robertson/W.Johnston 1.25 3.00
OT14 B.Horvat/M.Barzal .75 2.00
OT15 J.McCann/M.Beniers .75 2.00
OT16 M.McTavish/T.Zegras .60 1.50
OT17 B.Tkachuk/T.Stutzle 1.00 2.50
OT18 A.Kopitar/T.Moore 1.00 2.50
OT19 N.Kucherov/B.Hagel 1.25 3.00
OT20 N.Kadri/Y.Sharangovich .75 2.00
OT21 R.Thomas/J.Kyrou .60 1.50
OT22 A.Panarin/A.Lafreniere 1.25 3.00
OT23 D.Larkin/L.Raymond 1.00 2.50
OT24 C.Keller/L.Cooley 1.25 3.00
OT25 T.Thompson/R.Dahlin .75 2.00
OT26 E.Pettersson/Q.Hughes 1.50 4.00
OT27 C.McDavid/L.Draisaitl 3.00 8.00
OT28 A.Matthews/M.Marner 2.50 6.00
OT29 J.Hughes/N.Hischier 1.50 4.00
OT30 C.Bedard/T.Hall 2.00 5.00
OT31 A.Ovechkin/T.Wilson 2.50 6.00
OT32 K.Kaprizov/M.Boldy 2.00 5.00

2024-25 Upper Deck Ooh La La
*SPECKLED: .5X TO 1.2X BASIC
*BLACK: .8X TO 2X BASIC
OLL1 Filip Gustavsson .75 2.00
OLL2 Elvis Merzlikins .75 2.00
OLL3 Igor Shesterkin 1.50 4.00
OLL4 Jeremy Swayman 1.25 3.00
OLL5 Connor Hellebuyck 1.50 4.00
OLL6 Vitek Vanecek .75 2.00
OLL7 Petr Mrazek .60 1.50
OLL8 Andrei Vasilevskiy 1.25 3.00
OLL9 Jake Oettinger 1.25 3.00
OLL10 Thatcher Demko 1.00 2.50
OLL11 John Gibson .75 2.00
OLL12 Tristan Jarry .75 2.00
OLL13 Sergei Bobrovsky 1.25 3.00
OLL14 Joey Daccord .75 2.00
OLL15 Dustin Wolf 1.25 3.00
OLL16 Ilya Sorokin 1.25 3.00
OLL17 Jordan Binnington 1.25 3.00
OLL18 Alexandar Georgiev .75 2.00
OLL19 Juuse Saros 1.00 2.50
OLL20 Adin Hill .75 2.00
OLL21 Linus Ullmark .75 2.00
OLL22 Samuel Ersson .75 2.00
OLL23 Stuart Skinner 1.00 2.50
OLL24 Philipp Grubauer .75 2.00
OLL25 Frederik Andersen 1.00 2.50
OLL26 Marc-Andre Fleury 1.50 4.00
OLL27 Joseph Woll 1.00 2.50
OLL28 Ukko-Pekka Luukkonen .60 1.50
OLL29 Charlie Lindgren .60 1.50
OLL30 Samuel Montembeault .75 2.00

2024-25 Upper Deck Outburst Retro
OR1 Patrice Bergeron YG 30.00 80.00
OR2 Sergei Bobrovsky YG 20.00 50.00
OR3 Connor McDavid YG 200.00 500.00
OR4 Nick Suzuki YG 50.00 125.00
OR5 Tim Stutzle YG 30.00 80.00
OR6 Mika Zibanejad YG 12.00 30.00
OR7 Filip Forsberg YG 12.00 30.00
OR8 Nikita Kucherov YG 50.00 125.00
OR9 Jack Hughes YG 60.00 150.00
OR10 Wyatt Johnston YG 50.00 125.00
OR11 Evgeni Malkin YG 50.00 125.00
OR12 Mitch Marner YG 40.00 100.00
OR13 Erik Karlsson YG 30.00 80.00
OR14 Dylan Larkin YG 30.00 80.00
OR15 Quinton Byfield YG 30.00 80.00

2024-25 Upper Deck Outburst Retro Red
*RED/25: 1X TO 2.5X BASIC
OR1 Patrice Bergeron YG 125.00 300.00
OR10 Wyatt Johnston YG 150.00 400.00

2024-25 Upper Deck Oversized
201 Zachary Bolduc YG 4.00 10.00
207 Gavin Brindley YG 2.00 5.00
208 Bradly Nadeau YG 3.00 8.00
212 Cutter Gauthier YG 5.00 12.00
213 Zach Dean YG 2.00 5.00
215 Mavrik Bourque YG 4.00 10.00
226 Brendan Brisson YG 2.50 6.00
227 Frank Nazar YG 6.00 15.00
228 Brad Lambert YG 2.50 6.00
233 Josh Doan YG 3.00 8.00
236 Olen Zellweger YG 4.00 10.00
239 Logan Mailloux YG 3.00 8.00
244 Logan Stankoven YG 5.00 12.00
246 Joshua Roy YG 3.00 8.00
459 Ethan Cardwell YG 1.50 4.00
461 Oliver Kapanen YG 2.00 5.00
474 Rutger McGroarty YG 4.00 10.00
475 Albert Johansson YG 2.00 5.00
477 Calum Ritchie YG 2.50 6.00
478 Conor Geekie YG 3.00 8.00
480 Zachary L'Heureux YG 2.50 6.00
483 Joel Blomqvist YG 2.50 6.00
484 Jett Luchanko YG 4.00 10.00
485 Samuel Honzek YG 2.00 5.00
489 Seamus Casey YG 2.50 6.00
491 Nolan Allan YG 2.00 5.00

2024-25 Upper Deck Playlist
*SPECKLED: .6X TO 1.5X BASIC
*BLACK: .8X TO 2X BASIC
PL1 Nathan MacKinnon 2.00 5.00
PL2 Jason Robertson .75 2.00
PL3 David Pastrnak 1.25 3.00
PL4 Kirill Kaprizov 1.50 4.00
PL5 Connor McDavid 2.50 6.00
PL6 Nikita Kucherov 1.00 2.50
PL7 Sidney Crosby 2.00 5.00
PL8 Cale Makar 1.25 3.00
PL9 Aleksander Barkov .75 2.00
PL10 Auston Matthews 2.00 5.00
PL11 Nick Suzuki 1.00 2.50
PL12 Alex Ovechkin 2.00 5.00
PL13 Sebastian Aho .75 2.00
PL14 Connor Bedard 1.50 4.00
PL15 Jack Eichel .75 2.00
PL16 Leon Draisaitl 1.50 4.00
PL17 Artemi Panarin 1.00 2.50
PL18 Quinn Hughes 1.25 3.00

2024-25 Upper Deck Population Count 1000
PC1 Alex DeBrincat 2.00 5.00
PC2 Owen Tippett 1.00 2.50
PC3 Connor Bedard 5.00 12.00
PC4 Olen Zellweger 3.00 8.00
PC5 Matty Beniers 2.00 5.00
PC6 Sebastian Aho 2.50 6.00
PC7 Sam Reinhart 3.00 8.00
PC8 Adin Hill 1.50 4.00
PC9 Zachary Bolduc 3.00 8.00
PC10 Artemi Panarin 3.00 8.00
PC11 Luke Hughes 2.50 6.00
PC12 Jeremy Swayman 2.50 6.00
PC13 Brayden Point 2.00 5.00
PC14 Rasmus Dahlin 2.00 5.00
PC15 Cutter Gauthier 4.00 10.00
PC16 Nazem Kadri 2.00 5.00
PC17 Tristan Jarry 1.50 4.00
PC18 Clayton Keller 2.00 5.00
PC19 Cale Makar 4.00 10.00
PC20 Cole Caufield 3.00 8.00
PC21 Brennan Othmann 2.50 6.00
PC22 Brady Tkachuk 2.50 6.00
PC23 Thatcher Demko 2.00 5.00
PC24 William Nylander 3.00 8.00
PC25 Connor McDavid 8.00 20.00
PC26 Roope Hintz 2.00 5.00
PC27 Logan Stankoven 4.00 10.00
PC28 Connor Hellebuyck 3.00 8.00
PC29 Mason McTavish 1.50 4.00
PC30 Quinton Byfield 2.00 5.00
PC31 Shakir Mukhamadullin 2.00 5.00
PC32 Frank Nazar 5.00 12.00
PC33 Kirill Kaprizov 5.00 12.00
PC34 Matt Rempe 3.00 8.00
PC35 Alex Ovechkin 6.00 15.00
PC36 Seamus Casey 2.00 5.00
PC37 Auston Matthews 6.00 15.00
PC38 Liam Ohgren 3.00 8.00
PC39 Gavin Brindley 1.50 4.00
PC40 Jason Robertson 2.50 6.00
PC41 Jesper Wallstedt 4.00 10.00
PC42 Macklin Celebrini 30.00 80.00
PC43 Brad Marchand 3.00 8.00
PC44 Zach Dean 1.50 4.00
PC45 Leon Draisaitl 5.00 12.00
PC46 Will Smith 5.00 12.00
PC47 Logan Mailloux 3.00 8.00
PC48 Conor Geekie 2.50 6.00
PC49 Mavrik Bourque 3.00 8.00
PC50 Dylan Larkin 2.00 5.00
PC51 Brad Lambert 2.00 5.00
PC52 Bradly Nadeau 2.50 6.00
PC53 Josh Doan 2.50 6.00
PC54 Jack Hughes 4.00 10.00
PC55 Matvei Michkov 20.00 50.00
PC56 Aleksander Barkov 2.50 6.00
PC57 Brendan Brisson 2.00 5.00
PC58 Lane Hutson 15.00 40.00
PC59 Alexis Lafreniere 2.50 6.00
PC60 Joshua Roy 2.50 6.00

2024-25 Upper Deck Population Count 100
*100: 1.2X TO 3X BASIC
PC3 Connor Bedard 60.00 150.00
PC42 Macklin Celebrini 100.00 250.00
PC46 Will Smith 25.00 60.00

2024-25 Upper Deck Population Count 25
*25: 3X TO 8X BASIC
PC25 Connor McDavid 125.00 300.00
PC42 Macklin Celebrini 300.00 800.00
PC55 Matvei Michkov 200.00 500.00
PC58 Lane Hutson 200.00 500.00

2024-25 Upper Deck Population Count 50
*50: 2X TO 5X BASIC
PC3 Connor Bedard 80.00 200.00
PC42 Macklin Celebrini 200.00 500.00
PC46 Will Smith 30.00 80.00

2024-25 Upper Deck Population Count 500
*500: .6X TO 1.5X BASIC
PC42 Macklin Celebrini 60.00 150.00

2024-25 Upper Deck Pros and Prospects
*GOLD: .5X TO 1.2X BASIC
PP1 Brendan Brisson 1.00 2.50
PP2 Macklin Celebrini 4.00 10.00
PP3 Dylan Larkin 1.00 2.50
PP4 Alex Ovechkin 4.00 10.00
PP5 Frank Nazar 2.50 6.00
PP6 Jack Hughes 2.00 5.00
PP7 Rutger McGroarty 1.50 4.00
PP8 Liam Ohgren 1.50 4.00
PP9 Connor McDavid 4.00 10.00
PP10 Jonathan Lekkerimaki 2.00 5.00
PP11 David Pastrnak 2.00 5.00
PP12 Clayton Keller 1.00 2.50
PP13 Lian Bichsel 1.50 4.00
PP14 Denton Mateychuk 1.50 4.00
PP15 Roman Josi .75 2.00
PP16 Brennan Othmann 1.25 3.00
PP17 Jared McCann .60 1.50
PP18 Olen Zellweger 1.50 4.00
PP19 Fabian Lysell 2.00 5.00
PP20 Connor Bedard 2.00 5.00
PP21 Elias Pettersson 1.25 3.00
PP22 Cutter Gauthier 2.00 5.00
PP23 Nick Suzuki 1.50 4.00
PP24 Lane Hutson 4.00 10.00
PP25 Jake Guentzel 1.25 3.00
PP26 Will Smith 2.50 6.00
PP27 Jesper Wallstedt 2.00 5.00
PP28 Mason McTavish .75 2.00
PP29 Sidney Crosby 3.00 8.00
PP30 Logan Stankoven 2.00 5.00
PP31 Mikko Rantanen 2.00 5.00
PP32 Kirill Kaprizov 2.50 6.00
PP33 Conor Geekie 1.50 4.00
PP34 Mavrik Bourque 1.50 4.00
PP35 Sergei Bobrovsky 1.25 3.00
PP36 Nathan MacKinnon 3.00 8.00
PP37 Josh Doan 1.25 3.00
PP38 Alexis Lafreniere 1.25 3.00
PP39 Matvei Michkov 3.00 8.00
PP40 Auston Matthews 3.00 8.00

2024-25 Upper Deck Rookie Commemorative Class
*RED: .8X TO 2X BASIC
RC1 Bradly Nadeau 1.25 3.00
RC2 Frank Nazar 2.50 6.00
RC3 Matt Rempe 1.50 4.00
RC4 Zach Dean .75 2.00
RC5 Joshua Roy 1.25 3.00
RC6 Gavin Brindley .75 2.00
RC7 Mavrik Bourque 1.50 4.00
RC8 Cutter Gauthier 2.00 5.00
RC9 Brad Lambert 1.00 2.50
RC10 Logan Stankoven 2.00 5.00
RC11 Brendan Brisson 1.00 2.50
RC12 Josh Doan 1.25 3.00
RC13 Zachary Bolduc 1.50 4.00
RC14 Logan Mailloux 1.25 3.00
RC15 Olen Zellweger 1.50 4.00
RC16 Will Smith 2.50 6.00
RC17 Sam Colangelo .75 2.00
RC18 Zack Ostapchuk .75 2.00
RC19 Liam Ohgren 1.50 4.00
RC20 Akil Thomas .75 2.00
RC22 Luca Del Bel Belluz .75 2.00
RC23 Shakir Mukhamadullin 1.00 2.50
RC24 Yan Kuznetsov .75 2.00
RC26 Marat Khusnutdinov .75 2.00
RC28 Scott Morrow 1.00 2.50
RC29 Ivan Fedotov 1.25 3.00
RC30 Jesper Wallstedt 2.00 5.00

2024-25 Upper Deck Rookie Reflections
*GOLD/100: 2X TO 5X BASIC
RR1 Samuel Honzek 1.00 2.50
RR2 Mavrik Bourque 2.00 5.00
RR3 Brad Lambert 1.25 3.00
RR4 Matvei Michkov 4.00 10.00
RR5 Logan Mailloux 1.50 4.00
RR6 Josh Doan 1.50 4.00
RR7 Zach Dean 1.00 2.50
RR8 Calum Ritchie 1.25 3.00
RR9 Logan Stankoven 2.50 6.00
RR10 Rutger McGroarty 2.00 5.00
RR11 Brendan Brisson 1.25 3.00
RR12 Nolan Allan 1.00 2.50
RR13 Brennan Othmann 1.50 4.00
RR14 Will Smith 3.00 8.00
RR15 Jesper Wallstedt 2.50 6.00
RR16 Jett Luchanko 2.00 5.00
RR17 Lane Hutson 5.00 12.00
RR18 Jonathan Lekkerimaki 2.50 6.00
RR19 Liam Ohgren 2.00 5.00
RR20 Shakir Mukhamadullin 1.25 3.00
RR21 Conor Geekie 2.00 5.00
RR22 Bradly Nadeau 1.50 4.00
RR23 Zachary Bolduc 2.00 5.00
RR24 Macklin Celebrini 5.00 12.00
RR25 Olen Zellweger 2.00 5.00
RR26 Fedor Svechkov 1.50 4.00
RR27 Cutter Gauthier 2.50 6.00
RR28 Zachary L'Heureux 1.25 3.00
RR29 Seamus Casey 1.25 3.00
RR30 Matt Rempe 2.00 5.00

2024-25 Upper Deck Silver Skates
*GOLD/250: .6X TO 1.5X BASIC
SS1 Aleksander Barkov 1.50 4.00
SS2 Josh Doan 1.50 4.00
SS3 Matvei Michkov 4.00 10.00
SS4 Jesper Bratt 1.00 2.50
SS5 Owen Power 1.25 3.00
SS6 Nick Suzuki 2.00 5.00
SS7 Macklin Celebrini 5.00 12.00
SS8 Brady Tkachuk 1.50 4.00
SS9 Nathan MacKinnon 4.00 10.00
SS10 Jared McCann .75 2.00
SS11 Logan Stankoven 2.50 6.00
SS12 Leon Draisaitl 3.00 8.00
SS13 Jordan Kyrou 1.00 2.50
SS14 Jonathan Lekkerimaki 2.50 6.00
SS15 Liam Ohgren 2.00 5.00
SS16 Connor Bedard 3.00 8.00
SS17 Mika Zibanejad 1.25 3.00
SS18 Frank Nazar 3.00 8.00
SS19 Sidney Crosby 4.00 10.00
SS20 Seth Jarvis 1.25 3.00
SS21 Quinton Byfield 1.25 3.00
SS22 Brayden Point 1.25 3.00
SS23 Will Smith 3.00 8.00
SS24 Zach Hyman 1.50 4.00
SS25 Quinn Hughes 2.50 6.00
SS26 Brad Marchand 2.00 5.00
SS27 Owen Tippett .60 1.50
SS28 Lucas Raymond 1.50 4.00
SS29 Noah Dobson 1.25 3.00
SS30 Mark Stone 1.25 3.00
SS31 Alex Ovechkin 4.00 10.00
SS32 Adam Fantilli 1.50 4.00
SS33 Lane Hutson 5.00 12.00
SS34 Fedor Svechkov 1.50 4.00
SS35 Steven Stamkos 2.00 5.00
SS36 Roope Hintz 1.25 3.00
SS37 Auston Matthews 4.00 10.00
SS38 Cutter Gauthier 2.50 6.00
SS39 Josh Morrissey 1.25 3.00
SS40 Nazem Kadri 1.25 3.00

2024-25 Upper Deck Sophomore Sensations
SO1 Connor Bedard 8.00 20.00
SO2 Adam Fantilli 4.00 10.00
SO3 Leo Carlsson 4.00 10.00
SO4 Matthew Knies 5.00 12.00
SO5 Luke Hughes 4.00 10.00
SO6 Logan Cooley 4.00 10.00

2024-25 Upper Deck Trilogy Rookie Premiere Level 1
*LEVEL 2/499: .5X TO 1.2X BASIC
T1 Mavrik Bourque 4.00 10.00
T2 Jakub Dobes 10.00 25.00
T3 Frank Nazar 6.00 15.00
T4 Seamus Casey 2.50 6.00
T5 Logan Mailloux 3.00 8.00
T6 Liam Ohgren 4.00 10.00
T7 Owen Pickering 2.50 6.00
T8 Lane Hutson 20.00 50.00
T9 Fedor Svechkov 3.00 8.00
T10 Brendan Brisson 2.50 6.00
T11 Fabian Lysell 5.00 12.00
T12 Cutter Gauthier 5.00 12.00
T13 Macklin Celebrini 20.00 50.00
T14 Jesper Wallstedt 5.00 12.00
T15 Zach Dean 2.00 5.00
T16 Jonathan Lekkerimaki 5.00 12.00
T17 Brad Lambert 2.50 6.00
T18 Olen Zellweger 4.00 10.00
T19 Rutger McGroarty 4.00 10.00
T20 Zachary Bolduc 4.00 10.00
T21 Calum Ritchie 2.50 6.00
T22 Josh Doan 3.00 8.00
T23 Maveric Lamoureux 3.00 8.00
T24 Matvei Michkov 12.00 30.00
T25 Logan Stankoven 5.00 12.00
T26 Conor Geekie 4.00 10.00
T27 Denton Mateychuk 4.00 10.00
T28 Samuel Honzek 2.00 5.00
T29 Nolan Allan 2.00 5.00
T30 Sebastian Cossa 5.00 12.00
T31 Will Smith 6.00 15.00
T32 Jett Luchanko 4.00 10.00
T33 Lian Bichsel 4.00 10.00

2024-25 Upper Deck Trilogy Rookie Premiere Level 3

*LEVEL 3/99: .8X TO 2X BASIC
T8 Lane Hutson 50.00 125.00
T13 Macklin Celebrini 60.00 150.00
T24 Matvei Michkov 100.00 250.00

2024-25 Upper Deck Triple Dimensions Reflections

TDR1 Olen Zellweger 1.50 4.00
TDR2 Will Smith 2.50 6.00
TDR3 Jesper Wallstedt 2.00 5.00
TDR4 Frank Nazar 2.50 6.00
TDR5 Fedor Svechkov 1.25 3.00
TDR6 Lane Hutson 4.00 10.00
TDR7 Matt Rempe 1.50 4.00
TDR8 Matvei Michkov 3.00 8.00
TDR9 Cutter Gauthier 2.00 5.00
TDR10 Rutger McGroarty 1.50 4.00
TDR11 Mavrik Bourque 1.50 4.00
TDR12 Macklin Celebrini 4.00 10.00
TDR13 Logan Mailloux 1.25 3.00
TDR14 Zachary Bolduc 1.50 4.00
TDR15 Jonathan Lekkerimaki 2.00 5.00
TDR16 Logan Stankoven 2.00 5.00
TDR17 Liam Ohgren 1.50 4.00
TDR18 Conor Geekie 1.50 4.00
TDR19 Josh Doan 1.25 3.00
TDR20 Bradly Nadeau 1.25 3.00

2024-25 Upper Deck Triple Dimensions Reflections Amethyst

*AMETHYST/300: .8X TO 2X BASIC
TDR6 Lane Hutson 15.00 40.00
TDR8 Matvei Michkov 15.00 40.00
TDR12 Macklin Celebrini 15.00 40.00

2024-25 Upper Deck Triple Dimensions Reflections Ruby

*RUBY/500: .6X TO 1.5X BASIC
TDR6 Lane Hutson 12.00 30.00
TDR8 Matvei Michkov 10.00 25.00
TDR12 Macklin Celebrini 10.00 25.00

2024-25 Upper Deck UD Canvas

C1 Matthew Knies 1.25 3.00
C2 Dawson Mercer .75 2.00
C3 Alex Ovechkin 2.50 6.00
C4 Bryan Rust .60 1.50
C5 Lucas Raymond 1.00 2.50
C6 Nikita Kucherov 1.25 3.00
C7 Brock Faber .75 2.00
C8 Josh Morrissey .75 2.00
C9 Logan Couture .75 2.00
C10 Robby Fabbri .40 1.00
C11 Adam Fantilli 1.00 2.50
C12 Chris Kreider .75 2.00
C13 Devon Toews .50 1.25
C14 Tim Stutzle .75 2.00
C15 Cole Caufield 1.25 3.00
C16 Devon Levi .75 2.00
C17 Tyler Seguin .75 2.00
C18 Trevor Moore .40 1.00
C19 Cale Makar 1.50 4.00
C20 Jared McCann .50 1.25
C21 Kyle Connor 1.00 2.50
C22 Pavel Buchnevich .50 1.25
C23 Andrei Kuzmenko .60 1.50
C24 Mark Stone .75 2.00
C25 Kaiden Guhle .60 1.50
C26 Noah Dobson .75 2.00
C27 Aleksander Barkov 1.00 2.50
C28 Ivan Barbashev .50 1.25
C29 Connor McDavid 3.00 8.00
C30 Mikael Backlund .50 1.25
C31 Mitch Marner 1.00 2.50
C32 Andre Burakovsky .40 1.00
C33 Tyson Foerster .60 1.50
C34 Ryan O'Reilly .60 1.50
C35 Kirill Marchenko .75 2.00
C36 Zach Hyman 1.00 2.50
C37 Adin Hill .60 1.50
C38 Thomas Novak .40 1.00
C39 Connor Ingram .40 1.00
C40 Quinton Byfield .75 2.00
C41 Claude Giroux .60 1.50
C42 Thatcher Demko .75 2.00
C43 Martin Necas 1.00 2.50
C44 Luke Hughes 1.00 2.50
C45 Pavel Zacha .50 1.25
C46 Adrian Kempe .60 1.50
C47 Dylan Guenther .75 2.00
C48 Matt Boldy 1.00 2.50
C49 Yegor Sharangovich .60 1.50
C50 Conor Garland .50 1.25
C51 Bobby Brink .40 1.00
C52 Charlie Coyle .60 1.50
C53 Petr Mrazek .50 1.25
C54 Juraj Slafkovsky 1.25 3.00
C55 Alex DeBrincat .75 2.00
C56 Jason Robertson 1.00 2.50
C57 Joel Farabee .60 1.50
C58 Clayton Keller .75 2.00
C59 Darcy Kuemper .60 1.50
C60 Alex Tuch .60 1.50
C61 Adam Fox .75 2.00
C62 Sergei Bobrovsky 1.00 2.50
C63 Samuel Girard .40 1.00
C64 Troy Terry .50 1.25
C65 Gabe Vilardi .60 1.50
C66 Sidney Crosby 2.50 6.00
C67 Simon Nemec .75 2.00
C68 Evander Kane .60 1.50
C69 Jordan Kyrou .60 1.50
C70 Jake Oettinger 1.00 2.50
C71 David Pastrnak 1.50 4.00
C72 Connor Bedard 8.00 20.00
C73 Evgeni Malkin 1.25 3.00
C74 Victor Hedman .75 2.00
C75 Seth Jarvis .75 2.00
C76 Jack Eichel 1.00 2.50
C77 Ilya Sorokin 1.00 2.50
C78 Ryan Reaves .50 1.25
C79 Tomas Hertl .60 1.50
C80 Rasmus Dahlin .75 2.00
C81 Mats Zuccarello .60 1.50
C82 Andrei Svechnikov .75 2.00
C83 Mason McTavish .60 1.50
C84 Philip Tomasino .40 1.00
C85 William Nylander 1.25 3.00
C86 Ridly Greig .50 1.25
C87 Quinn Hughes 1.50 4.00
C88 Brock Nelson .60 1.50
C89 Brayden Schenn .60 1.50
C90 C.Caufield/C.Bedard 4.00 10.00
C91 Zack Ostapchuk YG 5.00 12.00
C92 Logan Mailloux YG 8.00 20.00
C93 Mavrik Bourque YG 10.00 25.00
C94 Josh Doan YG 8.00 20.00
C95 Cutter Gauthier YG 10.00 25.00
C96 Gavin Brindley YG 5.00 12.00
C97 Brad Lambert YG 6.00 15.00
C98 Marat Khusnutdinov YG 5.00 12.00
C99 Scott Morrow YG 6.00 15.00
C100 Joshua Roy YG 8.00 20.00
C101 Olen Zellweger YG 10.00 25.00
C102 Brendan Brisson YG 6.00 15.00
C103 Logan Stankoven YG 10.00 25.00
C104 Akil Thomas YG 5.00 12.00
C105 Brennan Othmann YG 8.00 20.00
C106 Luca Del Bel Belluz YG 5.00 12.00
C107 Shakir Mukhamadullin YG 6.00 15.00
C108 Jesper Wallstedt YG 12.00 30.00
C109 Zach Dean YG 5.00 12.00
C110 Sam Colangelo YG 5.00 12.00
C111 Lane Hutson YG 60.00 150.00
C112 Nikita Chibrikov YG 5.00 12.00
C113 Matt Rempe YG 10.00 25.00
C114 Ruslan Iskhakov YG 5.00 12.00
C115 Bradly Nadeau YG 8.00 20.00
C116 Liam Ohgren YG 10.00 25.00
C117 Frank Nazar YG 15.00 40.00
C118 Yan Kuznetsov YG 5.00 12.00
C119 Zachary Bolduc YG 10.00 25.00
C120 J.Doan/O.Zellweger CL 4.00 10.00
C121 Timo Meier .60 1.50
C122 Vince Dunn .50 1.25
C123 Jamie Drysdale .50 1.25
C124 J.T. Miller .75 2.00
C125 Evan Bouchard .75 2.00
C126 Justin Faulk .50 1.25
C127 Charlie Lindgren .50 1.25
C128 Alex Newhook .50 1.25
C129 Fabian Zetterlund .40 1.00
C130 Morgan Rielly .60 1.50
C131 Brad Marchand 1.25 3.00
C132 William Karlsson .75 2.00
C133 Jack Hughes 1.50 4.00
C134 Oliver Bjorkstrand .50 1.25
C135 Nazem Kadri .75 2.00
C136 Leon Draisaitl 2.00 5.00
C137 Cole Perfetti .60 1.50
C138 Mika Zibanejad .75 2.00
C139 Seth Jones .60 1.50
C140 Michael Bunting .60 1.50
C141 Brandon Hagel .50 1.25
C142 JJ Peterka .60 1.50
C143 Owen Tippett .40 1.00
C144 Brock Boeser .75 2.00
C145 Roman Josi .60 1.50
C146 Jonathan Quick .75 2.00
C147 Dylan DeMelo .40 1.00
C148 Gustav Forsling .60 1.50
C149 Kyle Palmieri .50 1.25
C150 Joey Daccord .60 1.50
C151 Drake Batherson .60 1.50
C152 Connor Hellebuyck 1.25 3.00
C153 J.T. Compher .40 1.00
C154 Tristan Jarry .60 1.50
C155 Wyatt Johnston 1.25 3.00
C156 John Carlson .60 1.50
C157 Filip Gustavsson .60 1.50
C158 Alex Pietrangelo .50 1.25
C159 Nico Hischier 1.00 2.50
C160 Bo Horvat .75 2.00
C161 Joseph Woll .75 2.00
C162 Stuart Skinner .75 2.00
C163 Jake Neighbours .60 1.50
C164 Tom Wilson .60 1.50
C165 Michael Matheson .40 1.00
C166 Filip Hronek .40 1.00
C167 Juuse Saros .75 2.00
C168 Auston Matthews 2.50 6.00
C169 Blake Coleman .50 1.25
C170 Travis Konecny .60 1.50
C171 Jordan Binnington 1.00 2.50
C172 Patrick Kane 1.25 3.00
C173 Jacob Trouba .50 1.25
C174 Noah Hanifin .60 1.50
C175 Joel Eriksson Ek .50 1.25
C176 Brayden Point .75 2.00
C177 Shane Pinto .50 1.25
C178 Miro Heiskanen .75 2.00
C179 Erik Karlsson .75 2.00
C180 Jake Sanderson .75 2.00
C181 Alex Vlasic .40 1.00
C182 Alexandar Georgiev .60 1.50
C183 Matthew Tkachuk 1.25 3.00
C184 Boone Jenner .60 1.50
C185 Bowen Byram .75 2.00
C186 Nick Suzuki 1.25 3.00
C187 Brent Burns .60 1.50
C188 Casey Mittelstadt .60 1.50
C189 Charlie McAvoy .75 2.00
C190 Elvis Merzlikins .60 1.50
C191 Frank Vatrano .50 1.25
C192 Anze Kopitar 1.00 2.50
C193 Hampus Lindholm .40 1.00
C194 Jamie Benn .60 1.50
C195 Carter Verhaeghe .60 1.50
C196 Jonathan Huberdeau .75 2.00
C197 Matias Maccelli .50 1.25
C198 William Eklund .75 2.00
C199 Mikko Rantanen 1.50 4.00
C200 Filip Forsberg 1.00 2.50
C201 Moritz Seider .75 2.00
C202 Anders Lee .50 1.25
C203 Nick Schmaltz .50 1.25
C204 Drew Doughty .60 1.50
C205 Radko Gudas .40 1.00
C206 Sebastian Aho 1.00 2.50
C207 Kirill Kaprizov 2.00 5.00
C208 Taylor Hall .60 1.50
C209 Ukko-Pekka Luukkonen .50 1.25
C210 J.Hughes/A.Matthews CL 2.50 6.00
C211 Nolan Allan YG 5.00 12.00
C212 Will Smith YG 25.00 60.00
C213 Maveric Lamoureux YG 8.00 20.00
C214 Albert Johansson YG 5.00 12.00
C215 Jackson Blake YG 10.00 25.00
C216 Ethan Cardwell YG 4.00 10.00
C217 Conor Geekie YG 10.00 25.00
C218 Victor Mancini YG 5.00 12.00
C219 Jett Luchanko YG 6.00 15.00
C220 Andre Lee YG 5.00 12.00
C221 Adam Klapka YG 5.00 12.00
C222 Aleksei Kolosov YG 5.00 12.00
C223 Nikolai Kovalenko YG 4.00 10.00
C224 Vasily Ponomarev YG 5.00 12.00
C225 Calum Ritchie YG 6.00 15.00
C226 Oliver Kapanen YG 5.00 12.00
C227 Nikita Prishchepov YG 5.00 12.00
C228 Rutger McGroarty YG 5.00 12.00
C229 Zachary L'Heureux YG 6.00 15.00
C230 Daniil Misyul YG 5.00 12.00
C231 Devin Cooley YG 5.00 12.00
C232 Jack Thompson YG 5.00 12.00
C233 Oskar Back YG 5.00 12.00
C234 Samuel Honzek YG 5.00 12.00
C235 Noah Philp YG 5.00 12.00
C236 Joel Blomqvist YG 6.00 15.00
C237 Matt Stienburg YG 5.00 12.00
C238 Maxim Tsyplakov YG 8.00 20.00
C239 Seamus Casey YG 6.00 15.00
C240 W.Smith/C.Geekie YG CL 8.00 20.00
C241 Gordie Howe 8.00 20.00
C242 Jean Ratelle 2.00 5.00
C243 Rogie Vachon 2.50 6.00
C244 Joe Nieuwendyk 2.00 5.00
C245 Ed Belfour 2.50 6.00
C246 Joe Sakic 5.00 12.00
C247 Guy Lafleur 3.00 8.00
C248 Teemu Selanne 5.00 12.00
C249 Mario Lemieux 10.00 25.00
C250 Brian Leetch 2.00 5.00
C251 Marian Hossa 2.50 6.00
C252 Alex Delvecchio 2.50 6.00
C253 Darryl Sittler 2.50 6.00
C254 Rick Nash 2.50 6.00
C255 Serge Savard 2.50 6.00
C256 Olen Zellweger POE 5.00 12.00
C256 MacKenzie Weegar (Ext Ser) .40 1.00
C257 Joshua Roy POE 4.00 10.00
C257 Travis Sanheim (Ext Ser) .40 1.00
C258 Brennan Othmann POE 4.00 10.00
C258 Jeff Skinner (Ext Ser) .60 1.50
C259 Macklin Celebrini POE 30.00 80.00
C259 Jason Dickinson (Ext Ser) .40 1.00
C260 Nolan Allan POE 2.50 6.00
C260 Shea Theodore (Ext Ser) .75 2.00
C261 Logan Stankoven POE 6.00 15.00
C261 Artturi Lehkonen (Ext Ser) .50 1.25
C262 Conor Geekie POE 5.00 12.00
C262 Jake Walman (Ext Ser) .40 1.00
C263 Maveric Lamoureux POE 4.00 10.00
C263 Kevin Fiala (Ext Ser) .50 1.25
C264 Mavrik Bourque POE 5.00 12.00
C264 Jake Guentzel (Ext Ser) 1.00 2.50
C265 Zach Dean POE 2.50 6.00
C265 Leo Carlsson (Ext Ser) 1.00 2.50
C266 Ethan Del Mastro POE 2.50 6.00
C266 Brady Skjei (Ext Ser) .40 1.00
C267 Zack Ostapchuk POE 2.50 6.00
C267 Brandon Montour (Ext Ser) .75 2.00
C268 Lukas Cormier POE 2.50 6.00
C268 Owen Power (Ext Ser) .75 2.00
C269 Bobby Clarke POE 4.00 10.00
C269 Jared Spurgeon (Ext Ser) .60 1.50
C270 Mark Messier POE 5.00 12.00
C270 Matt Grzelcyk (Ext Ser) .50 1.25
C271 Alec Martinez .40 1.00
C272 Jonathan Marchessault .75 2.00
C273 Artemi Panarin 1.25 3.00
C274 Nino Niederreiter .40 1.00
C275 Trevor Zegras .60 1.50
C276 Dylan Holloway .60 1.50
C277 Vincent Trocheck .60 1.50
C278 Brandon Saad .50 1.25
C279 Nathan MacKinnon 2.50 6.00
C280 Marc-Andre Fleury 1.25 3.00
C281 Brady Tkachuk 1.00 2.50
C282 Jakob Chychrun .60 1.50
C283 Mikhail Sergachev .50 1.25
C284 Jesper Bratt .60 1.50
C285 Brayden McNabb .40 1.00
C286 Dylan Cozens .60 1.50
C287 Samuel Ersson .60 1.50
C288 Andrei Vasilevskiy 1.00 2.50
C289 Ryan Nugent-Hopkins .75 2.00
C290 Linus Ullmark .60 1.50
C291 Jake DeBrusk .60 1.50
C292 Elias Lindholm .60 1.50
C293 Sam Bennett 1.00 2.50
C294 Kevin Hayes .50 1.25
C295 Christopher Tanev .40 1.00
C296 Kevin Korchinski .50 1.25
C297 Steven Stamkos 1.25 3.00
C298 Igor Shesterkin 1.25 3.00
C299 Zach Werenski 1.00 2.50
C300 Dylan Larkin .75 2.00
C301 Logan Cooley 1.00 2.50
C302 Samuel Montembeault .60 1.50
C303 Kris Letang .75 2.00
C304 Tomas Hertl .60 1.50
C305 Kent Johnson .60 1.50
C306 Sean Monahan .40 1.00
C307 Darcy Kuemper .60 1.50
C308 Dougie Hamilton .50 1.25
C309 John Tavares 1.00 2.50
C310 Jeremy Swayman 1.00 2.50
C311 Dylan Strome .75 2.00
C312 Frederik Andersen .75 2.00
C313 Aaron Ekblad .75 2.00
C314 Arber Xhekaj .60 1.50
C315 Josh Norris .60 1.50
C316 Oliver Ekman-Larsson .40 1.00
C317 Dustin Wolf 1.00 2.50
C318 Anthony Duclair .50 1.25
C319 Matty Beniers .75 2.00
C320 Roope Hintz .75 2.00
C321 Marco Rossi .75 2.00
C322 Jacob Markstrom .60 1.50
C323 Mathew Barzal .75 2.00
C324 Jaccob Slavin .50 1.25
C325 Tyler Toffoli .60 1.50
C326 Colton Parayko .50 1.25
C327 Matt Duchene .60 1.50
C328 Logan Thompson .75 2.00
C329 Cam Talbot .60 1.50
C330 Morgan Frost .50 1.25
C331 Nikolaj Ehlers .60 1.50
C332 Nikita Zadorov .40 1.00
C333 Chandler Stephenson .50 1.25
C334 Brandt Clarke .60 1.50
C335 Alexis Lafreniere 1.00 2.50
C336 Elias Pettersson 1.00 2.50
C337 Connor Zary .60 1.50
C338 Brendan Gallagher .60 1.50
C339 Mark Scheifele 1.00 2.50
C340 Thomas Harley .60 1.50
C341 Pierre-Luc Dubois .50 1.25
C342 Sam Reinhart 1.25 3.00
C343 Robert Thomas .60 1.50
C344 Tage Thompson .75 2.00
C345 N.MacKinnon/B.Tkachuk CL 2.50 6.00
C346 Isaiah George YG 6.00 15.00
C347 Denton Mateychuk YG 10.00 25.00
C348 Owen Pickering YG 6.00 15.00
C349 Tyson Kozak YG 5.00 12.00
C350 Nikita Grebenkin YG 6.00 15.00
C351 Adam Wilsby YG 5.00 12.00
C352 Nathan Clurman YG 5.00 12.00
C353 Matvei Michkov YG 50.00 125.00
C354 Chase Bradley YG 5.00 12.00
C355 Jere Innala YG 4.00 10.00
C356 Ales Stezka YG 6.00 15.00
C357 Justin Hryckowian YG 6.00 15.00
C358 Helge Grans YG 5.00 12.00
C359 Brett Berard YG 5.00 12.00
C360 Macklin Celebrini YG 125.00 300.00
C361 Jakub Dobes YG 25.00 60.00
C362 Fedor Svechkov YG 8.00 20.00
C363 Fabian Lysell YG 12.00 30.00
C364 Jonathan Lekkerimaki YG 12.00 30.00
C365 Sebastian Cossa YG 10.00 25.00
C366 Arttu Hyry YG 5.00 12.00
C367 Trent Miner YG 5.00 12.00
C368 Erik Portillo YG 6.00 15.00
C369 Lian Bichsel YG 10.00 25.00
C370 Samuel Helenius YG 5.00 12.00
C371 Max Sasson YG 5.00 12.00
C372 Nathan Legare YG 5.00 12.00
C373 Tye Felhaber YG 4.00 10.00
C374 Michael Milne YG 5.00 12.00
C375 M.Celebrini/M.Michkov YG CL 15.00 40.00
C376 Bobby Clarke 4.00 10.00
C377 Zdeno Chara 2.50 6.00
C378 Pavel Datsyuk 4.00 10.00
C379 John Vanbiesbrouck 2.50 6.00
C380 Martin St. Louis 2.50 6.00
C381 Tony Esposito 2.50 6.00
C382 Bernie Geoffrion 2.00 5.00
C383 Tim Horton 4.00 10.00
C384 Pat LaFontaine 2.50 6.00
C385 Brett Hull 5.00 12.00
C386 Brendan Shanahan 2.50 6.00
C387 Mats Sundin 2.50 6.00
C388 Evgeni Nabokov 2.00 5.00
C389 Pierre Turgeon 2.00 5.00
C390 Sergei Zubov 2.00 5.00
C391 Nikita Kucherov AS 6.00 15.00
C392 Connor McDavid AS 12.00 30.00
C393 William Nylander AS 5.00 12.00
C394 Mathew Barzal AS 3.00 8.00
C395 Quinn Hughes AS 6.00 15.00
C396 Cale Makar AS 6.00 15.00
C397 Leon Draisaitl AS 8.00 20.00
C398 David Pastrnak AS 6.00 15.00
C399 Auston Matthews AS 10.00 25.00
C400 Nathan MacKinnon AS 10.00 25.00
C401 Elias Pettersson AS 4.00 10.00
C402 J.T. Miller AS 3.00 8.00
C403 Connor Hellebuyck AS 5.00 12.00
C404 Thatcher Demko AS 3.00 8.00
C405 Igor Shesterkin AS 5.00 12.00

2024-25 Upper Deck UD Canvas Black and White

*B&W: 1.2X TO 3X BASIC
*B&W YG: .6X TO 1.5X BASIC
*B&W RET/POE/AS : 1X TO 2.5X BASIC
C95 Cutter Gauthier YG 25.00 60.00
C103 Logan Stankoven YG 20.00 50.00
C111 Lane Hutson YG 80.00 200.00
C212 Will Smith YG 50.00 125.00
C219 Jett Luchanko YG 15.00 40.00
C259 Macklin Celebrini POE 60.00 150.00
C365 Sebastian Cossa YG 20.00 50.00

2024-25 Upper Deck UD Portraits

P1 Elias Pettersson 1.00 2.50
P2 Chris Kreider .75 2.00
P3 Clayton Keller .75 2.00
P4 David Pastrnak 1.50 4.00
P5 Kirill Kaprizov 2.00 5.00
P6 Nathan MacKinnon 2.50 6.00
P7 Noah Dobson .75 2.00
P8 Travis Konecny .60 1.50
P9 Jack Hughes 1.50 4.00
P10 Igor Shesterkin 1.25 3.00
P11 J.T. Miller .75 2.00
P12 Auston Matthews 2.50 6.00
P13 Filip Forsberg 1.00 2.50
P14 Jesper Bratt .60 1.50
P15 Connor Bedard 2.00 5.00
P16 Connor Hellebuyck 1.25 3.00
P17 Sam Reinhart 1.25 3.00
P18 Alex DeBrincat .75 2.00
P19 Thatcher Demko .75 2.00
P20 Sidney Crosby 2.50 6.00
P21 Tim Stutzle .75 2.00
P22 Mitch Marner 1.00 2.50
P23 Sebastian Aho 1.00 2.50
P24 Robert Thomas .60 1.50
P25 Carter Verhaeghe .60 1.50
P26 Jeremy Swayman 1.00 2.50
P27 Victor Hedman .75 2.00
P28 Mark Stone .75 2.00
P29 Jason Robertson 1.00 2.50
P30 Cole Caufield 1.25 3.00
P31 Cale Makar 1.50 4.00
P32 Logan Stankoven 1.50 4.00
P33 Connor McDavid 3.00 8.00
P34 Cutter Gauthier 1.50 4.00
P35 Shakir Mukhamadullin .75 2.00
P36 Charlie McAvoy .75 2.00
P37 Macklin Celebrini 4.00 10.00
P38 Josh Doan 1.00 2.50
P39 Dylan Larkin .75 2.00
P40 Seamus Casey .75 2.00
P41 Olen Zellweger 1.25 3.00
P42 Alex Ovechkin 2.50 6.00
P43 Conor Geekie 1.25 3.00
P44 Lane Hutson 3.00 8.00
P45 Logan Mailloux 1.00 2.50
P46 Frank Nazar 2.00 5.00
P47 Matvei Michkov 2.50 6.00
P48 Rasmus Dahlin .75 2.00
P49 Bradly Nadeau 1.00 2.50
P50 Brad Lambert .75 2.00
P51 Leon Draisaitl 2.00 5.00
P52 Zach Dean .60 1.50
P53 Liam Ohgren 1.25 3.00
P54 Quinn Hughes 1.50 4.00
P55 Zachary Bolduc 1.25 3.00
P56 Brendan Brisson .75 2.00
P57 Nick Suzuki 1.25 3.00
P58 Will Smith 2.00 5.00
P59 Miro Heiskanen .75 2.00
P60 Brennan Othmann 1.00 2.50

2024-25 Upper Deck UD Portraits Black

*BLACK: .8X TO 2X BASIC
P37 Macklin Celebrini 12.00 30.00
P44 Lane Hutson 8.00 20.00
P47 Matvei Michkov 10.00 25.00

2024-25 Upper Deck UD Portraits Red

*RED/99: 2.5X TO 6X BASIC
P37 Macklin Celebrini 40.00 100.00
P44 Lane Hutson 20.00 50.00
P47 Matvei Michkov 25.00 60.00

2024-25 Upper Deck UD Portraits Speckled

*SPECKLED: .5X TO 1.2X BASIC

2024-25 Upper Deck UD3 Future Impact

UD31 Jonathan Lekkerimaki 2.00 5.00
UD32 David Pastrnak 2.00 5.00
UD33 Jack Hughes 2.00 5.00
UD34 Logan Stankoven 2.00 5.00
UD35 Nikita Kucherov 2.00 5.00
UD36 Cale Makar 2.00 5.00
UD37 Anze Kopitar 1.25 3.00
UD38 Matvei Michkov 3.00 8.00
UD39 Evgeni Malkin 1.50 4.00
UD310 Sebastian Aho 1.25 3.00
UD311 Filip Forsberg 1.25 3.00
UD312 Cutter Gauthier 2.00 5.00
UD313 Artemi Panarin 1.50 4.00
UD314 Conor Geekie 1.50 4.00
UD315 Matthew Tkachuk 1.50 4.00
UD316 Mitch Marner 1.25 3.00
UD317 Macklin Celebrini 4.00 10.00
UD318 Elias Pettersson 1.25 3.00
UD319 Rasmus Dahlin 1.00 2.50
UD320 Cole Caufield 1.50 4.00
UD321 Robert Thomas .75 2.00
UD322 Connor McDavid 4.00 10.00
UD323 Bo Horvat 1.00 2.50
UD324 Clayton Keller 1.00 2.50
UD325 Will Smith 2.50 6.00
UD326 Kirill Kaprizov 2.50 0.00
UD327 Lane Hutson 4.00 10.00
UD328 Frank Nazar 2.50 6.00
UD329 Jack Eichel 1.25 3.00
UD330 Moritz Seider 1.00 2.50

2024-25 Upper Deck UD3 Future Impact Gold

*GOLD/333: .8X TO 2X BASIC
UD38 Matvei Michkov 10.00 25.00
UD317 Macklin Celebrini 15.00 40.00
UD325 Will Smith 8.00 20.00
UD327 Lane Hutson 15.00 40.00

2024-25 Upper Deck Welcome Aboard

*SPECKLED: .6X TO 1.5X BASIC
*BLACK: 1X TO 2.5X BASIC
WA1 Liam Ohgren 1.50 4.00
WA2 Olen Zellweger 1.50 4.00
WA3 Logan Stankoven 2.00 5.00
WA4 Jett Luchanko 1.50 4.00
WA5 Jesper Wallstedt 2.00 5.00
WA6 Rutger McGroarty 1.50 4.00
WA7 Cutter Gauthier 2.00 5.00
WA8 Macklin Celebrini 4.00 10.00
WA9 Mavrik Bourque 1.50 4.00
WA10 Brennan Othmann 1.25 3.00
WA11 Josh Doan 1.25 3.00
WA12 Seamus Casey 1.00 2.50
WA13 Frank Nazar 2.50 6.00
WA14 Conor Geekie 1.25 3.00
WA15 Matvei Michkov 3.00 8.00
WA16 Lane Hutson 4.00 10.00
WA17 Zachary Bolduc 1.25 3.00
WA18 Samuel Honzek .75 2.00
WA19 Logan Mailloux 1.50 4.00
WA20 Will Smith 2.50 6.00

2024-25 Upper Deck White House Visit

WH1 Mark Stone 80.00 200.00

2024-25 Upper Deck Young Guns Renewed Series 1

YGR1 Ryan Malone .75 2.00
YGR2 Tuomo Ruutu 1.00 2.50
YGR3 Matt Stajan .75 2.00
YGR4 Tim Thomas 1.25 3.00
YGR5 Patrice Bergeron 1.50 4.00
YGR6 Dustin Brown 1.25 3.00
YGR7 Alexander Semin 1.25 3.00
YGR8 Brent Burns 1.25 3.00
YGR9 Marc-Andre Fleury 2.50 6.00
YGR10 Sidney Crosby 8.00 20.00
YGR11 Henrik Lundqvist 3.00 8.00
YGR12 Cam Ward 1.25 3.00
YGR13 Alex Ovechkin 8.00 20.00
YGR14 Jeff Carter 1.00 2.50
YGR15 Ryan Getzlaf 1.25 3.00
YGR16 Ryan Whitney .75 2.00
YGR17 Anze Kopitar 2.00 5.00
YGR18 Evgeni Malkin 2.50 6.00
YGR19 Joe Pavelski 1.50 4.00
YGR20 Patrick Kane 2.50 6.00
YGR21 Carey Price 2.50 6.00
YGR22 Nicklas Backstrom 1.25 3.00
YGR23 Jonathan Toews 2.00 5.00
YGR24 T.J. Oshie 1.25 3.00
YGR25 Drew Doughty 1.25 3.00
YGR26 Claude Giroux 1.25 3.00
YGR27 Steven Stamkos 2.50 6.00
YGR28 John Tavares 2.00 5.00
YGR29 Victor Hedman 1.50 4.00
YGR30 Erik Karlsson 1.50 4.00
YGR31 Jamie Benn 1.25 3.00
YGR32 Ryan O'Reilly 1.25 3.00
YGR33 Brad Marchand 2.50 6.00
YGR34 Logan Couture 1.50 4.00
YGR35 John Carlson 1.25 3.00
YGR36 Jeff Skinner 1.25 3.00
YGR37 Sergei Bobrovsky 2.00 5.00
YGR38 Nazem Kadri 1.50 4.00
YGR39 Ryan Nugent-Hopkins 1.50 4.00
YGR40 Mika Zibanejad 1.50 4.00
YGR41 Mark Scheifele 2.00 5.00
YGR42 Roman Josi 1.25 3.00
YGR43 Chris Kreider 1.50 4.00
YGR44 Mark Stone 1.50 4.00
YGR45 Brock Nelson 1.25 3.00
YGR46 J.T. Miller 1.50 4.00
YGR47 Jonathan Huberdeau 1.50 4.00
YGR48 Vladimir Tarasenko 1.50 4.00
YGR49 Nathan MacKinnon 5.00 12.00
YGR50 Tyler Toffoli 1.25 3.00

2024-25 Upper Deck Young Guns Renewed Series 1 Exclusives

*EXCLUSIVES/100: 6X TO 15X BASIC
YGR5 Patrice Bergeron 60.00 150.00
YGR9 Marc-Andre Fleury 60.00 150.00
YGR10 Sidney Crosby 150.00 400.00
YGR13 Alex Ovechkin 200.00 500.00
YGR21 Carey Price 100.00 250.00

2024-25 Upper Deck Young Guns Renewed Series 2

201 Connor McDavid 10.00 25.00
201 Auston Matthews 5.00 12.00
201 Cole Caufield 2.50 6.00
201 Jack Hughes 3.00 8.00
201 Nico Hischier 2.00 5.00
202 Roope Hintz 1.50 4.00
205 Brayden Point 1.50 4.00
206 Mikko Rantanen 3.00 8.00
210 Sebastian Aho 2.00 5.00
214 Connor Hellebuyck 2.50 6.00
214 Teuvo Teravainen 1.25 3.00
217 Travis Konecny 1.25 3.00
221 Artemi Panarin 2.50 6.00
221 Alex DeBrincat 1.50 4.00
222 Zach Hyman 2.00 5.00
223 Leon Draisaitl 4.00 10.00
228 Dylan Larkin 1.50 4.00
228 Tage Thompson 1.50 4.00
228 Adam Fox 1.50 4.00
231 Matthew Tkachuk 2.50 6.00
235 Jason Robertson 2.00 5.00
241 Jordan Kyrou 1.25 3.00
242 Charlie McAvoy 1.50 4.00
246 Jake Oettinger 2.00 5.00
247 Brock Boeser 1.50 4.00
248 Elias Pettersson 2.00 5.00
249 William Nylander 2.50 6.00
249 Quinn Hughes 3.00 8.00
451 Jack Eichel 2.00 5.00
451 Filip Forsberg 2.00 5.00
451 Kirill Kaprizov 4.00 10.00
451 Andrei Svechnikov 1.50 4.00
458 Mathew Barzal 1.50 4.00
461 Ilya Sorokin 2.00 5.00
464 Juuse Saros 1.50 4.00
464 Lucas Raymond 2.00 5.00
464 Martin Necas 2.00 5.00
468 Mitch Marner 2.00 5.00
469 Moritz Seider 1.50 4.00
470 Aleksander Barkov 2.00 5.00
471 Nick Suzuki 2.50 6.00
472 Robert Thomas 1.25 3.00
478 Andrei Vasilevskiy 2.00 5.00
482 Tim Stutzle 1.50 4.00
483 Nikita Kucherov 2.50 6.00
493 Cale Makar 3.00 8.00
495 David Pastrnak 3.00 8.00
499 Brady Tkachuk 2.00 5.00
525 Jake Guentzel 2.00 5.00
528 Igor Shesterkin 2.50 6.00

2024-25 Upper Deck Young Guns Renewed Series 2 Exclusives

*EXCLUSIVES/100: 6X TO 15X BASIC
201 Auston Matthews 100.00 250.00
201 Jack Hughes 60.00 150.00
451 Kirill Kaprizov 100.00 250.00
528 Igor Shesterkin 80.00 200.00

2003 Upper Deck All-Star Promos

COMP.SET w/o AUs (15) 12.00 30.00
AS1 Joe Thornton CL .50 1.25
AS2 Rick Nash 4.00 10.00
AS3 Stanislav Chistov 2.00 5.00
AS4 Chuck Kobasew 1.25 3.00
AS5 Stephen Weiss .75 2.00
AS6 Martin Brodeur CL .75 2.00
AS7 Jason Spezza 3.00 8.00
AS8 Alexander Frolov 1.25 3.00
AS9 Carlo Colaiacovo .75 2.00
AS10 Alexander Svitov .75 2.00
AS11 Nikolai Khabibulin CL .40 1.00
AS12 Henrik Zetterberg 4.00 10.00
AS13 Jordan Leopold .75 2.00
AS14 Jay Bouwmeester 2.00 5.00
AS15 Pierre-Marc Bouchard 2.00 5.00
S1 Rick Nash AU 75.00 150.00
S2 Stanislav Chistov AU 15.00 40.00
S3 Jason Spezza AU 30.00 60.00
S4 Alexander Frolov AU 8.00 20.00
S5 Jay Bouwmeester AU 15.00 40.00
S6 Jordan Leopold AU 8.00 20.00

2004 Upper Deck All-Star Promos

COMPLETE SET (15)
BB Brent Burns 4.00 15.00
CB Christoph Brandner 4.00 10.00
ES Eric Staal 6.00 15.00
FS Fredrik Sjostrom 4.00 10.00
GH Gordie Howe 5.00 15.00
JP Joni Pitkanen 4.00 10.00
JS Jason Spezza 5.00 15.00
JT Joe Thornton 6.00 15.00
MF Marc-Andre Fleury 12.50 30.00
MG Marian Gaborik 6.00 15.00
NH Nathan Horton 6.00 12.00
NZ Nikolai Zherdev 8.00 20.00
PB Patrice Bergeron 10.00 30.00
PR Patrick Roy 8.00 30.00
TO Jordin Tootoo 6.00 15.00

2007 Upper Deck All Star Game Redemptions

AS1 Martin Brodeur 4.00 10.00
AS2 Phil Kessel 2.00 5.00
AS3 Eric Lindros 1.50 4.00
AS4 Joe Sakic 3.00 8.00
AS5 Jordan Staal 4.00 10.00
AS6 Marty Turco 1.25 3.00
AS7 Sidney Crosby 8.00 20.00
AS8 Alexander Radulov 2.00 5.00
AS9 Brenden Morrow 1.25 3.00
AS10 Alexander Ovechkin 4.00 10.00
AS11 Evgeni Malkin 6.00 15.00
AS12 Mike Modano 2.00 5.00

2010-11 Upper Deck All Star Game

COMPLETE SET (10) 15.00 40.00
ASG1 Sidney Crosby 4.00 10.00
ASG2 Alexander Ovechkin 4.00 10.00
ASG3 Steven Stamkos 2.00 5.00
ASG4 Wayne Gretzky 6.00 15.00
ASG5 Gordie Howe 3.00 8.00
ASG6 Bobby Orr 4.00 10.00
ASG7 Jeff Skinner 2.00 5.00
ASG8 Eric Staal 1.25 3.00
ASG9 Cam Ward 1.00 2.50
ASG10 Eric Staal
Ron Francis
Cam Ward 1.25 3.00

2015-16 Upper Deck All Star Game

COMPLETE SET (7) 8.00 20.00
FG1 Roman Josi 1.50 4.00
FG2 Pekka Rinne 1.50 4.00
FG3 Shea Weber 1.25 3.00
FG4 P.K. Subban 2.00 5.00
FG5 Alex Ovechkin 6.00 15.00
FG6 Ryan McDonagh 1.00 2.50
NNO Checklist Card .75 2.00

2019-20 Upper Deck Allure

*WHITE.RAINBOW.VET: .6X TO 1.5X BASIC CARDS
*WHITE.RAINBOW.RC: .6X TO 1.5X BASIC CARDS
*RED.RAINBOW.VET: .6X TO 1.5X BASIC CARDS
*RED.RAINBOW.RC: .6X TO 1.5X BASIC CARDS
*YELLOW.TAXI.VET: .6X TO 1.5X BASIC CARDS
*YELLOW.TAXI.RC: .6X TO 1.5X BASIC CARDS
*PEWTER.VETS: 3X TO 8X BASIC CARDS
*PEWTER.RC: 1X TO 2.5X BASIC CARDS
*ORANGE/199: 1.25X TO 3X BASIC CARDS
*ORANGE.RC/199: .6X TO 1.5X BASIC CARDS
*GREEN/99: 1.5X TO 4X BASIC CARDS
*GREEN.RC/99: .6X TO 1.5X BASIC CARDS
*STEEL/50: 3X TO 8X BASIC CARDS
*STEEL.RC/50: 1X TO 2.5X BASIC CARDS
*BLUE/25: 4X TO 10X BASIC CARDS
*BLUE.RC/25: 1.5X TO 4X BASIC CARDS
1 Connor McDavid 1.00 2.50
2 Brayden Point .25 .60
3 Sergei Bobrovsky .30 .75
4 Sebastian Aho .30 .75
5 Auston Matthews .75 2.00
6 Anthony Mantha .15 .40
7 Aleksander Barkov .30 .75
8 Ben Bishop .15 .40
9 John Carlson .20 .50
10 Tomas Hertl .20 .50
11 Carey Price .40 1.00
12 Brady Tkachuk .30 .75
13 Matt Murray .20 .50
14 Brad Marchand .40 1.00
15 Max Domi .20 .50
16 Dylan Larkin .25 .60
17 Claude Giroux .20 .50
18 Cam Atkinson .20 .50
19 Matt Dumba .12 .30
20 Connor Hellebuyck .40 1.00
21 Jake Guentzel .30 .75
22 Teuvo Teravainen .20 .50
23 Matt Duchene .20 .50
24 Nico Hischier .30 .75
25 Erik Karlsson .25 .60
26 Matthew Tkachuk .40 1.00
27 Joe Pavelski .25 .60
28 Alexander Ovechkin .75 2.00
29 Anders Lee .15 .40
30 Mikko Rantanen .50 1.25
31 Ryan O'Reilly .20 .50
32 Jakub Vrana .20 .50
33 Alex Tuch .20 .50
34 Steven Stamkos .40 1.00
35 Seth Jones .20 .50
36 Sidney Crosby .75 2.00
37 Leon Draisaitl .60 1.50
38 Andrei Vasilevskiy .30 .75
39 John Tavares .30 .75
40 Drew Doughty .25 .60

41 Mark Scheifele .30 .75
42 Nathan MacKinnon .75 2.00
43 Brock Boeser .25 .60
44 Artemi Panarin .40 1.00
45 Mark Giordano .20 .50
46 John Gibson .20 .50
47 Oliver Ekman-Larsson .20 .50
48 Jordan Binnington .30 .75
49 Johnny Gaudreau .30 .75
50 Alex DeBrincat .25 .60
51 Mitch Marner .30 .75
52 Colton Parayko .15 .40
53 P.K. Subban .25 .60
54 Phil Kessel .20 .50
55 Patrick Kane .40 1.00
56 Henrik Lundqvist .50 1.25
57 Marc-Andre Fleury .40 1.00
58 Jack Eichel .30 .75
59 Mathew Barzal .25 .60
60 Tyler Seguin .25 .60
61 Jimmy Schuldt RC .50 1.25
62 Joel Farabee RC 1.00 2.50
63 Guillaume Brisebois RC .60 1.50
64 Ilya Mikheyev RC 1.00 2.50
65 Karson Kuhlman RC .60 1.50
66 Quinn Hughes RC 3.00 8.00
67 Rem Pitlick RC .60 1.50
68 Zack MacEwen RC .50 1.25
69 Erik Brannstrom RC .60 1.50
70 Nico Sturm RC .50 1.25
71 Alexandre Texier RC .60 1.50
72 Max Jones RC .60 1.50
73 Carl Grundstrom RC .60 1.50
74 Zach Senyshyn RC .60 1.50
75 Taro Hirose RC .60 1.50
76 Joel L'Esperance RC .60 1.50
77 Max Veronneau RC .50 1.25
78 Dante Fabbro RC .60 1.50
79 Philippe Myers RC .50 1.25
80 Cale Makar RC 3.00 8.00
81 Filip Zadina RC 1.00 2.50
82 Rudolfs Balcers RC .60 1.50
83 Trent Frederic RC .60 1.50
84 Vitaly Abramov RC .60 1.50
85 Nathan Bastian RC .60 1.50
86 Ryan Poehling RC 1.00 2.50
87 Blake Lizotte RC .60 1.50
88 Victor Olofsson RC 1.25 3.00
89 Kirby Dach RC 1.25 3.00
90 Nikita Gusev RC 1.00 2.50
91 Nick Suzuki RC 2.50 6.00
92 Rasmus Sandin RC 1.00 2.50
93 Adam Fox RC 1.50 4.00
94 Cody Glass RC 1.00 2.50
95 Cale Fleury RC .75 2.00
96 Noah Dobson RC 1.50 4.00
97 Barrett Hayton RC 1.25 3.00
98 Oliver Wahlstrom RC 1.00 2.50
99 Kaapo Kakko RC 1.00 2.50
100 Jack Hughes RC 3.00 8.00
101 Quinn Hughes SP 5.00 12.00
102 Cale Makar SP 5.00 12.00
103 Filip Zadina SP 1.50 4.00
104 Ryan Poehling SP 1.50 4.00
105 Barrett Hayton SP 2.00 5.00
106 Cody Glass SP 1.50 4.00
107 Kirby Dach SP 2.00 5.00
108 Nick Suzuki SP 4.00 10.00
109 Kaapo Kakko SP 1.50 4.00
110 Jack Hughes SP 5.00 12.00
111 Rudolfs Balcers SP 1.00 2.50
112 Nikita Gusev SP 1.50 4.00
113 Max Jones SP 1.00 2.50
114 Nathan Bastian SP 1.00 2.50
115 Dante Fabbro SP 1.00 2.50
116 Joel Farabee SP 1.50 4.00
117 Erik Brannstrom SP 1.00 2.50
118 Philippe Myers SP .75 2.00
119 Nico Sturm SP .75 2.00
120 Oliver Wahlstrom SP 1.50 4.00
121 Zach Senyshyn SP 1.00 2.50
122 Taro Hirose SP 1.00 2.50
123 Trent Frederic SP 1.00 2.50
124 Rem Pitlick SP 1.00 2.50
125 Rasmus Sandin SP 1.50 4.00
126 Zack MacEwen SP .75 2.00
127 Ilya Mikheyev SP 1.50 4.00
128 Noah Dobson SP 2.50 6.00
129 Victor Olofsson SP 2.00 5.00
130 Joel L'Esperance SP 1.00 2.50
131 Max Veronneau SP .75 2.00
132 Alexandre Texier SP 1.00 2.50
133 Blake Lizotte SP 1.00 2.50
134 Vitaly Abramov SP 1.00 2.50
135 Carl Grundstrom SP 1.00 2.50

2019-20 Upper Deck Allure Autographs Blue Line

1 Connor McDavid 120.00 300.00
7 Aleksander Barkov 15.00 40.00
8 Ben Bishop 8.00 20.00
10 Tomas Hertl 10.00 25.00
11 Carey Price 20.00 50.00
12 Brady Tkachuk 15.00 40.00
13 Matt Murray 10.00 25.00
14 Brad Marchand 20.00 50.00
15 Max Domi 10.00 25.00
18 Cam Atkinson 10.00 25.00
20 Connor Hellebuyck 20.00 50.00
22 Teuvo Teravainen 10.00 25.00
24 Nico Hischier 15.00 40.00
27 Joe Pavelski 12.00 30.00
29 Anders Lee 8.00 20.00
31 Ryan O'Reilly 10.00 25.00
32 Jakub Vrana 10.00 25.00
37 Leon Draisaitl 30.00 80.00
38 Andrei Vasilevskiy 15.00 40.00
39 John Tavares 15.00 40.00
41 Mark Scheifele 15.00 40.00
46 John Gibson 10.00 25.00
50 Alex DeBrincat 12.00 30.00
51 Mitch Marner 30.00 80.00
55 Patrick Kane 20.00 50.00
56 Henrik Lundqvist 25.00 60.00
57 Marc-Andre Fleury 20.00 50.00
58 Jack Eichel 15.00 40.00
60 Tyler Seguin 12.00 30.00
61 Jimmy Schuldt 8.00 20.00
62 Joel Farabee 15.00 40.00
63 Guillaume Brisebois 10.00 25.00
64 Ilya Mikheyev 15.00 40.00
65 Karson Kuhlman 10.00 25.00
66 Quinn Hughes 50.00 125.00
67 Rem Pitlick 10.00 25.00
68 Zack MacEwen 8.00 20.00
69 Erik Brannstrom 10.00 25.00
70 Nico Sturm 8.00 20.00
71 Alexandre Texier 10.00 25.00
72 Max Jones 10.00 25.00
73 Carl Grundstrom 10.00 25.00
74 Zach Senyshyn 10.00 25.00
75 Taro Hirose 10.00 25.00
76 Joel L'Esperance 10.00 25.00
77 Max Veronneau 8.00 20.00
78 Dante Fabbro 10.00 25.00
79 Philippe Myers 8.00 20.00
80 Cale Makar 50.00 125.00
81 Filip Zadina 15.00 40.00
82 Rudolfs Balcers 10.00 25.00
83 Trent Frederic 10.00 25.00
84 Vitaly Abramov 10.00 25.00
85 Nathan Bastian 10.00 25.00
86 Ryan Poehling 15.00 40.00
87 Blake Lizotte 10.00 25.00
88 Victor Olofsson 20.00 50.00
89 Kirby Dach 20.00 50.00
90 Nikita Gusev 15.00 40.00
91 Nick Suzuki 40.00 100.00
92 Rasmus Sandin 15.00 40.00
93 Adam Fox 25.00 60.00
94 Cody Glass 15.00 40.00
96 Noah Dobson 25.00 60.00
97 Barrett Hayton 20.00 50.00
98 Oliver Wahlstrom 15.00 40.00
100 Jack Hughes 50.00 125.00

2019-20 Upper Deck Allure Autographs Pink Diamond

101 Quinn Hughes 50.00 125.00
102 Cale Makar 50.00 125.00
103 Filip Zadina 15.00 40.00
104 Ryan Poehling 15.00 40.00
105 Barrett Hayton 20.00 50.00
106 Cody Glass 15.00 40.00
107 Kirby Dach 20.00 50.00
108 Nick Suzuki 40.00 100.00
110 Jack Hughes 50.00 125.00
111 Rudolfs Balcers 10.00 25.00
112 Nikita Gusev 15.00 40.00
113 Max Jones 10.00 25.00
114 Nathan Bastian 10.00 25.00
115 Dante Fabbro 10.00 25.00
116 Joel Farabee 15.00 40.00
117 Erik Brannstrom 10.00 25.00
118 Philippe Myers 8.00 20.00
119 Nico Sturm 8.00 20.00
120 Oliver Wahlstrom 15.00 40.00
121 Zach Senyshyn 10.00 25.00
122 Taro Hirose 10.00 25.00
123 Trent Frederic 10.00 25.00
124 Rem Pitlick 10.00 25.00
125 Rasmus Sandin 15.00 40.00
126 Zack MacEwen 8.00 20.00
127 Ilya Mikheyev 15.00 40.00
128 Noah Dobson 25.00 60.00
129 Victor Olofsson 20.00 50.00
130 Joel L'Esperance 10.00 25.00
131 Max Veronneau 8.00 20.00
132 Alexandre Texier 10.00 25.00
133 Blake Lizotte 10.00 25.00
134 Vitaly Abramov 10.00 25.00
135 Carl Grundstrom 10.00 25.00

2019-20 Upper Deck Allure Autographs Red Rainbow

1 Connor McDavid A 80.00 200.00
7 Aleksander Barkov C 10.00 25.00
8 Ben Bishop B 5.00 12.00
10 Tomas Hertl B 6.00 15.00
11 Carey Price A 12.00 30.00
13 Matt Murray B 6.00 15.00
14 Brad Marchand B 12.00 30.00
15 Max Domi A 6.00 15.00
18 Cam Atkinson C 6.00 15.00
20 Connor Hellebuyck C 12.00 30.00
22 Teuvo Teravainen C 6.00 15.00
24 Nico Hischier A 10.00 25.00
27 Joe Pavelski B 8.00 20.00
29 Anders Lee C 5.00 12.00
31 Ryan O'Reilly B 6.00 15.00
32 Jakub Vrana C 6.00 15.00
37 Leon Draisaitl B 20.00 50.00
38 Andrei Vasilevskiy B 10.00 25.00
39 John Tavares A 10.00 25.00
41 Mark Scheifele B 10.00 25.00
50 Alex DeBrincat B 8.00 20.00
51 Mitch Marner A 10.00 25.00
55 Patrick Kane A 12.00 30.00
56 Henrik Lundqvist A 15.00 40.00
57 Marc-Andre Fleury A 12.00 30.00
58 Jack Eichel A 10.00 25.00
61 Jimmy Schuldt/349 5.00 12.00
62 Joel Farabee/349 10.00 25.00
63 Guillaume Brisebois/349 6.00 15.00
64 Ilya Mikheyev/349 10.00 25.00
65 Karson Kuhlman/349 6.00 15.00
66 Quinn Hughes/349 30.00 80.00
67 Rem Pitlick/349 6.00 15.00
69 Erik Brannstrom/349 6.00 15.00
70 Nico Sturm/349 5.00 12.00
71 Alexandre Texier/349 6.00 15.00
72 Max Jones/349 6.00 15.00
73 Carl Grundstrom/349 6.00 15.00
74 Zach Senyshyn/349 6.00 15.00
75 Taro Hirose/349 6.00 15.00
76 Joel L'Esperance/349 6.00 15.00
77 Max Veronneau/349 5.00 12.00
78 Dante Fabbro/349 6.00 15.00
79 Philippe Myers/349 5.00 12.00
80 Cale Makar/249 40.00 100.00
81 Filip Zadina/249 10.00 25.00
82 Rudolfs Balcers/349 6.00 15.00
83 Trent Frederic/349 6.00 15.00
84 Vitaly Abramov/349 6.00 15.00
85 Nathan Bastian/349 6.00 15.00
86 Ryan Poehling/349 10.00 25.00
87 Blake Lizotte/349 6.00 15.00
88 Victor Olofsson/349 12.00 30.00
89 Kirby Dach/349 12.00 30.00
90 Nikita Gusev/349 10.00 25.00
91 Nick Suzuki/349 25.00 60.00
92 Rasmus Sandin/349 10.00 25.00
93 Adam Fox/349 15.00 40.00
94 Cody Glass/349 10.00 25.00
96 Noah Dobson/349 15.00 40.00
97 Barrett Hayton/349 12.00 30.00
98 Oliver Wahlstrom/249 10.00 25.00
100 Jack Hughes/249 30.00 80.00

2019-20 Upper Deck Allure For the Record

FR1 Tuukka Rask .50 1.25
FR2 Nikita Kucherov .75 2.00
FR3 Sidney Crosby 1.50 4.00
FR4 Braden Holtby .50 1.25
FR5 Auston Matthews 1.50 4.00
FR6 Henrik Lundqvist 1.00 2.50
FR7 Blake Wheeler .40 1.00
FR8 Elias Pettersson .60 1.50
FR9 Carey Price .75 2.00
FR10 Alexander Ovechkin 1.50 4.00

2019-20 Upper Deck Allure Iced Out

IOAB Aleksander Barkov .50 1.25
IOAM Auston Matthews 1.25 3.00
IOAO Alexander Ovechkin 1.25 3.00
IOAV Andrei Vasilevskiy .50 1.25
IOBB Brent Burns .30 .75
IOBM Brad Marchand .60 1.50
IOCG Claude Giroux .30 .75
IOCM Connor McDavid 1.50 4.00
IOCP Carey Price .60 1.50
IOEP Elias Pettersson .50 1.25
IOGL Cody Glass .50 1.25
IOJG Johnny Gaudreau .50 1.25
IOJH Jack Hughes 1.50 4.00
IOKK Kaapo Kakko .50 1.25
IOLD Leon Draisaitl 1.00 2.50
IOMA Cale Makar 1.50 4.00
IOMM Mitch Marner .50 1.25
IOMS Mark Scheifele .50 1.25
IONK Nikita Kucherov .60 1.50
IONM Nathan MacKinnon 1.25 3.00
IOPK Patrick Kane .60 1.50
IOQH Quinn Hughes 1.50 4.00
IOSA Sebastian Aho .50 1.25
IOSC Sidney Crosby 1.25 3.00
IOSS Steven Stamkos .60 1.50

2019-20 Upper Deck Allure Iced Out Autographs Purple Diamond

IOAB Aleksander Barkov/25 20.00 50.00
IOAV Andrei Vasilevskiy/50 20.00 50.00
IOBM Brad Marchand/25 25.00 60.00
IOCP Carey Price/25 25.00 60.00
IOEP Elias Pettersson/25 20.00 50.00
IOGL Cody Glass/50 20.00 50.00
IOJH Jack Hughes/50 60.00 150.00
IOLD Leon Draisaitl/50 40.00 100.00
IOMA Cale Makar/50 60.00 150.00
IOMM Mitch Marner/25 20.00 50.00
IOMS Mark Scheifele/25 20.00 50.00
IOQH Quinn Hughes/50 60.00 150.00
IOSA Sebastian Aho/25 20.00 50.00

2019-20 Upper Deck Allure Jersey Autographs Blue Line

1 Connor McDavid 150.00 300.00
3 Sergei Bobrovsky 15.00 40.00
5 Auston Matthews 80.00 200.00
7 Aleksander Barkov 15.00 40.00
8 Ben Bishop 8.00 20.00
10 Tomas Hertl 10.00 25.00
11 Carey Price 20.00 50.00
12 Brady Tkachuk 15.00 40.00
13 Matt Murray 10.00 25.00
14 Brad Marchand 20.00 50.00
15 Max Domi 10.00 25.00
18 Cam Atkinson 10.00 25.00
20 Connor Hellebuyck 20.00 50.00
21 Jake Guentzel 15.00 40.00
22 Teuvo Teravainen 10.00 25.00
24 Nico Hischier 15.00 40.00
27 Joe Pavelski 12.00 30.00
29 Anders Lee 8.00 20.00
31 Ryan O'Reilly 10.00 25.00
32 Jakub Vrana 10.00 25.00
34 Steven Stamkos 20.00 50.00
35 Seth Jones 10.00 25.00
37 Leon Draisaitl 30.00 80.00
38 Andrei Vasilevskiy 15.00 40.00
39 John Tavares 15.00 40.00
41 Mark Scheifele 15.00 40.00
44 Artemi Panarin 20.00 50.00
46 John Gibson 10.00 25.00
50 Alex DeBrincat 12.00 30.00
51 Mitch Marner 15.00 40.00
52 Colton Parayko 8.00 20.00
55 Patrick Kane 20.00 50.00
56 Henrik Lundqvist 25.00 60.00
57 Marc-Andre Fleury 20.00 50.00
58 Jack Eichel 40.00 100.00
60 Tyler Seguin 12.00 30.00
61 Jimmy Schuldt 8.00 20.00
62 Joel Farabee 15.00 40.00
63 Guillaume Brisebois 10.00 25.00
64 Ilya Mikheyev 15.00 40.00
65 Karson Kuhlman 10.00 25.00
66 Quinn Hughes 60.00 150.00
67 Rem Pitlick 10.00 25.00
68 Zack MacEwen 8.00 20.00
69 Erik Brannstrom 10.00 25.00
70 Nico Sturm 8.00 20.00
71 Alexandre Texier 10.00 25.00
72 Max Jones 10.00 25.00
73 Carl Grundstrom 10.00 25.00
74 Zach Senyshyn 10.00 25.00
75 Taro Hirose 10.00 25.00
76 Joel L'Esperance 10.00 25.00
77 Max Veronneau 8.00 20.00
78 Dante Fabbro 10.00 25.00
79 Philippe Myers 8.00 20.00
80 Cale Makar 50.00 125.00
81 Filip Zadina 15.00 40.00
82 Rudolfs Balcers 10.00 25.00
83 Trent Frederic 10.00 25.00
84 Vitaly Abramov 10.00 25.00
85 Nathan Bastian 10.00 25.00
86 Ryan Poehling 15.00 40.00
87 Blake Lizotte 10.00 25.00
88 Victor Olofsson 20.00 50.00
89 Kirby Dach 20.00 50.00
90 Nikita Gusev 15.00 40.00
91 Nick Suzuki 40.00 100.00
92 Rasmus Sandin 15.00 40.00
93 Adam Fox 25.00 60.00
94 Cody Glass 15.00 40.00
96 Noah Dobson 25.00 60.00
97 Barrett Hayton 20.00 50.00
98 Oliver Wahlstrom 15.00 40.00
100 Jack Hughes 50.00 125.00

2019-20 Upper Deck Allure Open Ice

OIAD Alex DeBrincat .40 1.00
OIAM Auston Matthews 1.25 3.00
OIAS Andrei Svechnikov .40 1.00
OIBW Blake Wheeler .30 .75
OICK Clayton Keller .40 1.00
OICM Connor McDavid 1.50 4.00
OIDP David Pastrnak .75 2.00
OIJD Jonathan Drouin .25 .60
OIJH Jack Hughes 1.50 4.00
OIKK Kaapo Kakko .50 1.25
OIMA Cale Makar 1.50 4.00
OIMH Miro Heiskanen .40 1.00
OIMR Mikko Rantanen .75 2.00
OIMT Matthew Tkachuk .60 1.50
OIPD Pierre-Luc Dubois .25 .60
OIQH Quinn Hughes 1.50 4.00
OIRP Ryan Poehling .50 1.25
OISC Sidney Crosby 1.25 3.00
OISS Steven Stamkos .60 1.50
OITC Thomas Chabot .30 .75

2019-20 Upper Deck Allure Pink Diamond

101 Quinn Hughes SP 5.00 12.00
102 Cale Makar SP 5.00 12.00
103 Filip Zadina SP 1.50 4.00
104 Ryan Poehling SP 1.50 4.00
105 Barrett Hayton SP 2.00 5.00
106 Cody Glass SP 1.50 4.00
107 Kirby Dach SP 2.00 5.00
108 Nick Suzuki SP 4.00 10.00
109 Kaapo Kakko SP 1.50 4.00
110 Jack Hughes SP 5.00 12.00
111 Rudolfs Balcers SP 1.00 2.50
112 Nikita Gusev SP 1.50 4.00
113 Max Jones SP 1.00 2.50
114 Nathan Bastian SP 1.00 2.50
115 Dante Fabbro SP 1.00 2.50
116 Joel Farabee SP 1.50 4.00
117 Erik Brannstrom SP 1.00 2.50
118 Philippe Myers SP .75 2.00
119 Nico Sturm SP .75 2.00
120 Oliver Wahlstrom SP 1.50 4.00
121 Zach Senyshyn SP 1.00 2.50
122 Taro Hirose SP 1.00 2.50
123 Trent Frederic SP 1.00 2.50
124 Rem Pitlick SP 1.00 2.50
125 Rasmus Sandin SP 1.50 4.00
126 Zack MacEwen SP .75 2.00
127 Ilya Mikheyev SP 1.50 4.00
128 Noah Dobson SP 2.50 6.00
129 Victor Olofsson SP 2.00 5.00
130 Joel L'Esperance SP 1.00 2.50
131 Max Veronneau SP .75 2.00
132 Alexandre Texier SP 1.00 2.50
133 Blake Lizotte SP 1.00 2.50
134 Vitaly Abramov SP 1.00 2.50
135 Carl Grundstrom SP 1.00 2.50

2019-20 Upper Deck Allure Quartz Autographs

AQAD Alex DeBrincat A 12.00 30.00
AQAE Aaron Ekblad B 12.00 30.00
AQAM Auston Matthews A 40.00 100.00
AQAR Alexander Radulov A 10.00 25.00
AQBT Brady Tkachuk A 15.00 40.00
AQCA Cam Atkinson B 10.00 25.00
AQCM Connor McDavid A 50.00 125.00
AQCP Carey Price B 20.00 50.00
AQDD Devan Dubnyk A 8.00 20.00
AQDE Jake DeBrusk B 10.00 25.00
AQDK David Krejci A 10.00 25.00
AQDL Dylan Larkin A 12.00 30.00
AQDS Dylan Strome B 12.00 30.00
AQEM Evgeni Malkin A 20.00 50.00
AQGU Jake Guentzel A 15.00 40.00
AQJG John Gibson A 10.00 25.00
AQJK Jesperi Kotkaniemi A 10.00 25.00
AQJT Jonathan Toews A 15.00 40.00
AQLD Leon Draisaitl B 30.00 80.00
AQMF Marc-Andre Fleury A 20.00 50.00
AQMI Casey Mittelstadt B 10.00 25.00
AQMM Mitch Marner B 15.00 40.00
AQMP Max Pacioretty A 10.00 25.00
AQNH Noah Hanifin B 10.00 25.00
AQSS Steven Stamkos B 20.00 50.00
AQTC Thomas Chabot B 10.00 25.00
AQTT Teuvo Teravainen B 10.00 25.00

2019-20 Upper Deck Allure Quartz Rookie Autographs

AQRCG Cody Glass 12.00 30.00
AQRCM Cale Makar 40.00 100.00
AQRDF Dante Fabbro 8.00 20.00
AQREB Erik Brannstrom 8.00 20.00
AQRFZ Filip Zadina 12.00 30.00
AQRJH Jack Hughes 40.00 100.00
AQRKD Kirby Dach 15.00 40.00
AQRMJ Max Jones 8.00 20.00
AQRNS Nick Suzuki 30.00 80.00
AQRPM Philippe Myers 6.00 15.00
AQRQH Quinn Hughes 40.00 100.00
AQRRP Ryan Poehling 12.00 30.00
AQRTH Taro Hirose 8.00 20.00
AQRVA Vitaly Abramov 8.00 20.00
AQRVO Victor Olofsson 15.00 40.00

2019-20 Upper Deck Allure Top 50

*BLUE: .50X TO 1.25X BASIC INSERTS
*GREEN/50: 1.25X TO 3X BASIC INSERTS
T501 Kevin Stenlund .20 .50
T502 Kirby Dach .50 1.25
T503 Ryan Kuffner .20 .50
T504 Max Jones .25 .60
T505 Adam Fox .60 1.50
T506 Trent Frederic .25 .60
T507 Carl Grundstrom .25 .60
T508 Barrett Hayton .50 1.25
T509 Cale Makar 1.25 3.00
T5010 Kaapo Kakko .40 1.00
T5011 Taro Hirose .25 .60
T5012 Joey Daccord .50 1.25
T5013 Brandon Gignac .20 .50
T5014 Nikolai Prokhorkin .20 .50
T5015 Max Veronneau .20 .50
T5016 Nathan Bastian .25 .60
T5017 Brady Keeper .25 .60
T5018 Erik Brannstrom .25 .60
T5019 Libor Hajek .20 .50
T5020 Nikita Gusev .40 1.00
T5021 Quinn Hughes 1.25 3.00
T5022 Zach Senyshyn .25 .60
T5023 Dante Fabbro .25 .60
T5024 Blake Lizotte .25 .60
T5025 Cody Glass .40 1.00
T5026 Jimmy Schuldt .20 .50
T5027 Vitaly Abramov .25 .60
T5028 Rem Pitlick .25 .60
T5029 Noah Dobson .60 1.50
T5030 Joel L'Esperance .25 .60
T5031 Zack MacEwen .20 .50
T5032 Oliver Wahlstrom .40 1.00
T5033 Rudolfs Balcers .25 .60
T5034 Filip Zadina .40 1.00
T5035 Karson Kuhlman .25 .60
T5036 Victor Olofsson .50 1.25
T5037 Jack Hughes 1.25 3.00
T5038 Joel Farabee .40 1.00
T5039 Guillaume Brisebois .25 .60
T5040 Alexandre Texier .25 .60
T5041 Philippe Myers .20 .50
T5042 Mackenzie MacEachern .25 .60
T5043 Nico Sturm .20 .50
T5044 Elvis Merzlikins .50 1.25
T5045 Nicolas Hague .25 .60
T5046 Teddy Blueger .25 .60
T5047 Nick Suzuki 1.00 2.50
T5048 Ville Heinola .30 .75
T5049 Rasmus Sandin .40 1.00
T5050 Ryan Poehling .40 1.00

2019-20 Upper Deck Allure Top 50 Autographs Blue

T502 Kirby Dach B 15.00 40.00
T503 Ryan Kuffner D 6.00 15.00
T504 Max Jones D 8.00 20.00
T505 Adam Fox B 20.00 50.00
T506 Trent Frederic D 8.00 20.00
T507 Carl Grundstrom C 8.00 20.00
T508 Barrett Hayton B 15.00 40.00
T509 Cale Makar B 40.00 100.00
T5011 Taro Hirose C 8.00 20.00
T5012 Joey Daccord D 20.00 50.00
T5013 Brandon Gignac D 6.00 15.00
T5015 Max Veronneau C 6.00 15.00
T5016 Nathan Bastian D 8.00 20.00
T5017 Brady Keeper D 8.00 20.00
T5018 Erik Brannstrom D 8.00 20.00
T5019 Libor Hajek D 6.00 15.00
T5020 Nikita Gusev B 12.00 30.00
T5021 Quinn Hughes B 40.00 100.00
T5022 Zach Senyshyn D 8.00 20.00
T5023 Dante Fabbro D 8.00 20.00
T5024 Blake Lizotte D 8.00 20.00
T5025 Cody Glass B 12.00 30.00
T5026 Jimmy Schuldt C 6.00 15.00
T5027 Vitaly Abramov D 8.00 20.00
T5028 Rem Pitlick D 8.00 20.00
T5029 Noah Dobson B 20.00 50.00
T5030 Joel L'Esperance C 8.00 20.00
T5031 Zack MacEwen A 25.00 60.00
T5032 Oliver Wahlstrom D 12.00 30.00
T5033 Rudolfs Balcers D 8.00 20.00
T5034 Filip Zadina B 12.00 30.00
T5035 Karson Kuhlman D 8.00 20.00
T5036 Victor Olofsson D 15.00 40.00
T5037 Jack Hughes B 30.00 80.00
T5038 Joel Farabee B 12.00 30.00
T5039 Guillaume Brisebois D 8.00 20.00
T5040 Alexandre Texier D 8.00 20.00
T5041 Philippe Myers C 6.00 15.00
T5042 Mackenzie MacEachern D 8.00 20.00
T5043 Nico Sturm D 6.00 15.00
T5044 Elvis Merzlikins D 15.00 40.00
T5045 Nicolas Hague D 8.00 20.00
T5046 Teddy Blueger C 8.00 20.00
T5049 Rasmus Sandin C 12.00 30.00
T5050 Ryan Poehling B 12.00 30.00

2019-20 Upper Deck Allure Winter Storm Warning

WSW1 John Tavares .75 2.00
WSW2 Zach Parise .50 1.25
WSW3 Alex Pietrangelo .40 1.00
WSW4 Gabriel Landeskog .60 1.50
WSW5 Brady Tkachuk .50 1.25
WSW6 Dylan Larkin .60 1.50
WSW7 Anders Lee .40 1.00
WSW8 Sean Couturier .40 1.00
WSW9 Evgeni Malkin 1.00 2.50
WSW10 Patrik Laine .60 1.50
WSW11 Brendan Gallagher .50 1.25
WSW12 Taylor Hall .50 1.25
WSW13 Henrik Lundqvist 1.25 3.00
WSW14 Patrice Bergeron .60 1.50
WSW15 Rasmus Dahlin .60 1.50
WSW16 Jonathan Toews .75 2.00
WSW17 Cam Atkinson .50 1.25
WSW18 Sean Monahan .30 .75
WSW19 Bo Horvat .60 1.50
WSW20 Connor McDavid 2.50 6.00

2020-21 Upper Deck Allure

1 Alex Ovechkin .75 2.00
2 Brendan Gallagher .20 .50
3 Jake Guentzel .30 .75
4 Pekka Rinne .20 .50
5 Aleksander Barkov .30 .75
6 Cale Makar .50 1.25
7 David Pastrnak .50 1.25
8 Dustin Brown .20 .50
9 Alex DeBrincat .25 .60
10 Keith Yandle .12 .30
11 Andrei Vasilevskiy .30 .75
12 Carter Hart .20 .50
13 Mark Stone .25 .60
14 Brad Marchand .40 1.00
15 Ryan Suter .15 .40
16 Elvis Merzlikins .20 .50
17 James van Riemsdyk .15 .40
18 John Gibson .20 .50
19 Roman Josi .20 .50
20 Travis Konecny .20 .50
21 Igor Shesterkin .40 1.00
22 Bo Horvat .25 .60
23 Nathan MacKinnon .75 2.00
24 William Karlsson .25 .60
25 Artemi Panarin .40 1.00
26 Dylan Larkin .25 .60
27 Evgeni Malkin .40 1.00
28 Brady Tkachuk .30 .75
29 Nick Suzuki .40 1.00
30 Jean-Gabriel Pageau .12 .30
31 Martin Jones .15 .40
32 Tyler Seguin .25 .60
33 Anders Lee .15 .40
34 Mark Giordano .20 .50
35 Mitch Marner .30 .75
36 Connor Hellebuyck .40 1.00
37 Ryan O'Reilly .20 .50
38 Andrei Svechnikov .25 .60
39 Mathew Barzal .25 .60
40 John Carlson .20 .50
41 Miro Heiskanen .25 .60
42 Victor Olofsson .20 .50
43 Quinn Hughes .50 1.25
44 Nikita Kucherov .40 1.00
45 Tomas Hertl .20 .50
46 Nico Hischier .30 .75
47 Elias Pettersson .30 .75
48 Kyle Palmieri .15 .40
49 Jordan Binnington .30 .75
50 Connor McDavid 1.00 2.50
51 Nick Foligno .15 .40
52 John Tavares .30 .75
53 Zach Parise .20 .50
54 Jakub Vrana .20 .50
55 Carey Price .40 1.00
56 Sebastian Aho .30 .75
57 Steven Stamkos .40 1.00
58 Leon Draisaitl .60 1.50
59 Ryan Getzlaf .20 .50
60 Patrick Kane .40 1.00
61 Mark Scheifele .30 .75
62 Anthony Mantha .15 .40
63 Dylan Strome .25 .60
64 Matthew Tkachuk .40 1.00
65 Jonathan Huberdeau .25 .60
66 Thomas Chabot .20 .50
67 Anze Kopitar .30 .75
68 Jack Eichel .30 .75
69 Auston Matthews .75 2.00
70 Sidney Crosby .75 2.00
71 Alex Belzile RC .50 1.25
72 Kieffer Bellows RC .50 1.25
73 Pavel Francouz RC .75 2.00
74 Morgan Geekie RC .60 1.50
75 Gabe Vilardi RC 1.00 2.50
76 Jake Evans RC .60 1.50
77 Martin Kaut RC .60 1.50
78 Josh Norris RC 1.00 2.50
79 Nicolas Beaudin RC .60 1.50
80 Ty Dellandrea RC .60 1.50
81 Liam Foudy RC .60 1.50
82 Jason Robertson RC 1.50 4.00
83 Mikey Anderson RC .60 1.50
84 Tyler Benson RC .60 1.50
85 Egor Korshkov RC .40 1.00
86 Alexander Alexeyev RC .50 1.25
87 Shane Bowers RC .50 1.25
88 Philipp Kurashev RC .75 2.00
89 Timothy Liljegren RC .60 1.50
90 Victor Soderstrom RC .50 1.25
91 Jake Oettinger RC 1.50 4.00
92 Vitali Kravtsov RC 1.25 3.00
93 Michael DiPietro RC .75 2.00
94 Connor McMichael RC 1.00 2.50
95 Thomas Harley RC 1.00 2.50
96 Peyton Krebs RC 1.00 2.50
97 Egor Zamula RC .50 1.25
98 Bowen Byram RC 1.25 3.00
99 Nick Robertson RC 1.00 2.50
101 Anthony Angello SP RC 1.00 2.50
102 Maxim Letunov SP RC 1.00 2.50
103 Lucas Carlsson SP RC 1.00 2.50
104 Jonas Johansson SP RC 1.25 3.00
105 Jani Hakanpaa SP RC .75 2.00
106 Liam Foudy SP 1.25 3.00
107 Alexander True SP RC 1.00 2.50
108 Tyler Benson SP 1.25 3.00
109 Keegan Kolesar SP RC 1.00 2.50
110 Mikey Anderson SP 1.25 3.00
111 Egor Korshkov SP .75 2.00
112 Jake Evans SP 1.25 3.00
113 Jason Robertson SP 3.00 8.00
114 Timothy Liljegren SP 1.25 3.00
115 Martin Kaut SP 1.25 3.00
116 Gustav Lindstrom SP RC 1.00 2.50
117 Michael DiPietro SP 1.50 4.00
118 Gage Quinney SP RC .75 2.00
119 Morgan Geekie SP 1.25 3.00
120 Alex Belzile SP 1.00 2.50
121 Matiss Kivlenieks SP RC 1.50 4.00
122 Kieffer Bellows SP 1.00 2.50
123 Josh Norris SP 2.00 5.00
124 Gabe Vilardi SP 2.00 5.00
125 Nicolas Beaudin SP 1.25 3.00
126 Olli Juolevi SP RC 1.25 3.00
127 Nick Robertson SP 2.00 5.00
128 Mikhail Berdin SP RC 1.25 3.00
129 Pierre-Olivier Joseph SP RC 1.25 3.00
130 Victor Soderstrom SP 1.00 2.50
131 Connor McMichael SP 2.00 5.00
132 Gilles Senn SP RC 1.00 2.50
133 Jake Oettinger SP 3.00 8.00
134 Philipp Kurashev SP 1.50 4.00
135 Egor Zamula SP 1.00 2.50
136 Shane Bowers SP 1.00 2.50
137 Connor Ingram SP RC 1.00 2.50
138 Philip Broberg SP RC 1.25 3.00
139 Vitali Kravtsov SP 2.50 6.00
140 Ty Dellandrea SP 1.25 3.00
141 MacKenzie Entwistle SP RC 1.00 2.50
142 Peyton Krebs SP 2.00 5.00
143 Pavel Francouz SP 1.50 4.00
144 Joseph Woll SP RC 2.50 6.00
145 Thomas Harley SP 2.00 5.00
146 Alexander Alexeyev SP 1.00 2.50
147 Ryan McLeod SP RC 1.00 2.50
148 Artem Zagidulin SP RC 1.25 3.00
149 Bowen Byram SP 2.50 6.00
150 Alexis Lafreniere SP 4.00 10.00
100A Alexis Lafreniere RC 2.00 5.00
100B Alexis Lafreniere VAR 4.00 10.00
XRCAR Alexander Romanov RC 12.00 30.00
XRCDC Dylan Cozens RC 15.00 40.00
XRCIS Ilya Sorokin RC 25.00 60.00
XRCKK Kirill Kaprizov RC 40.00 100.00
XRCTS Tim Stutzle RC 20.00 50.00

2020-21 Upper Deck Allure 1945 Shield

*1945: 12X TO 30X BASIC
*1945.RC: 8X TO 20X BASIC

2020-21 Upper Deck Allure 2005 Shield

*2005: 4X TO 10X BASIC
*2005.RC: 1.5X TO 4X BASIC
100 Alexis Lafreniere 20.00 50.00

2020-21 Upper Deck Allure Black Rainbow

*BLACK: 3X TO 8X BASIC
*BLACK.RC: 1.2X TO 3X BASIC

2020-21 Upper Deck Allure Blue Line

*BLUE LINE: 15X TO 40X BASIC
*BLUE.LINE.RC: 6X TO 15X BASIC

2020-21 Upper Deck Allure Double Rainbow

*DBL.RAINBOW: .5X TO 1.25X BASIC
150 Alexis Lafreniere SP 25.00 60.00

2020-21 Upper Deck Allure Green Quartz

*GREEN: 6X TO 15X BASIC
*GREEN RC: 4X TO 10X BASIC
*GREEN SP RC: 2X TO 5X BASIC
*GREEN XRC: .5X TO 1.25X BASIC
6 Cale Makar 20.00 50.00
50 Connor McDavid 20.00 50.00
69 Auston Matthews 20.00 50.00
100 Alexis Lafreniere 40.00 100.00
XRCIS Ilya Sorokin 60.00 150.00
XRCKK Kirill Kaprizov 80.00 200.00

2020-21 Upper Deck Allure Leopard

*LEOPARD: 4X TO 10X BASIC
*LEOPARD.RC: 1.5X TO 4X BASIC
100 Alexis Lafreniere 30.00 80.00

2020-21 Upper Deck Allure Orange Slice

*ORANGE: 3X TO 8X BASIC
*ORANGE.RC: 1.25X TO 3X BASIC
*ORANGE.SP.RC: 1X TO 2.5X BASIC
50 Connor McDavid 12.00 30.00
70 Sidney Crosby 15.00 40.00
100 Alexis Lafreniere 12.00 30.00

2020-21 Upper Deck Allure Red Rainbow

*RED: 2X TO 5X BASIC
*RED.RC: .75X TO 2X BASIC
*RED.SP.RC: .6X TO 1.5X BASIC
50 Connor McDavid 12.00 30.00
100 Alexis Lafreniere 12.00 30.00
150 Alexis Lafreniere SP 12.00 30.00

2020-21 Upper Deck Allure Steel

*STEEL: 5X TO 12X BASIC
*STEEL.RC: 2X TO 5X BASIC

2020-21 Upper Deck Allure Yellow Taxi

*YELLOW: 2X TO 5X BASIC
*YELLOW.RC: .75X TO 2X BASIC
50 Connor McDavid 8.00 20.00
100 Alexis Lafreniere 12.00 30.00

2020-21 Upper Deck Allure Autographs Red Rainbow

2 Brendan Gallagher E 10.00 25.00
3 Jake Guentzel D 15.00 40.00
4 Pekka Rinne G 10.00 25.00
5 Aleksander Barkov D 15.00 40.00
8 Dustin Brown F 10.00 25.00
9 Alex DeBrincat F 12.00 30.00
10 Keith Yandle G 6.00 15.00
11 Andrei Vasilevskiy F 15.00 40.00
12 Carter Hart C 10.00 25.00
13 Mark Stone C 12.00 30.00
14 Brad Marchand B 20.00 50.00
15 Ryan Suter G 8.00 20.00
17 James van Riemsdyk D 8.00 20.00
18 John Gibson D 10.00 25.00
19 Roman Josi D 10.00 25.00
20 Travis Konecny F 10.00 25.00
24 William Karlsson G 12.00 30.00
29 Nick Suzuki C 20.00 50.00
30 Jean-Gabriel Pageau F 6.00 15.00
32 Tyler Seguin B 12.00 30.00
33 Anders Lee G 8.00 20.00
34 Mark Giordano G 10.00 25.00
35 Mitch Marner B 15.00 40.00
36 Connor Hellebuyck C 20.00 50.00
37 Ryan O'Reilly C 10.00 25.00

38 Andrei Svechnikov D 12.00 30.00
41 Miro Heiskanen E 12.00 30.00
42 Victor Olofsson F 10.00 25.00
43 Quinn Hughes B 25.00 60.00
45 Tomas Hertl F 10.00 25.00
46 Nico Hischier C 15.00 40.00
47 Elias Pettersson A 15.00 40.00
48 Kyle Palmieri G 8.00 20.00
50 Connor McDavid A 125.00 300.00
51 Nick Foligno F 8.00 20.00
52 John Tavares A 15.00 40.00
53 Zach Parise D 10.00 25.00
54 Jakub Vrana F 10.00 25.00
55 Carey Price B 20.00 50.00
60 Patrick Kane A 20.00 50.00
61 Mark Scheifele D 15.00 40.00
62 Anthony Mantha E 8.00 20.00
63 Dylan Strome E 12.00 30.00
64 Matthew Tkachuk E 20.00 50.00
65 Jonathan Huberdeau E 12.00 30.00
66 Thomas Chabot E 10.00 25.00
67 Anze Kopitar B 15.00 40.00
69 Auston Matthews A 100.00 250.00
71 Alex Belzile/299 5.00 12.00
72 Kieffer Bellows/299 5.00 12.00
74 Morgan Geekie/299 6.00 15.00
75 Gabe Vilardi/299 10.00 25.00
76 Jake Evans/299 6.00 15.00
77 Martin Kaut/299 6.00 15.00
78 Josh Norris/299 10.00 25.00
79 Nicolas Beaudin/299 6.00 15.00
80 Ty Dellandrea/299 6.00 15.00
81 Liam Foudy/299 6.00 15.00
82 Jason Robertson/299 40.00 100.00
83 Mikey Anderson/299 6.00 15.00
84 Tyler Benson/299 6.00 15.00
86 Alexander Alexeyev/199 5.00 12.00
87 Shane Bowers/299 5.00 12.00
88 Philipp Kurashev/299 8.00 20.00
89 Timothy Liljegren/299 6.00 15.00
90 Victor Soderstrom/299 5.00 12.00
91 Jake Oettinger/299 15.00 40.00
96 Peyton Krebs/299 10.00 25.00
98 Bowen Byram/199 20.00 50.00
99 Nick Robertson/199 10.00 25.00
100 Alexis Lafreniere/199 125.00 300.00
101 Anthony Angello D 6.00 15.00
102 Maxim Letunov D 6.00 15.00
103 Lucas Carlsson D 6.00 15.00
104 Jonas Johansson D 8.00 20.00
105 Jani Hakanpaa D 5.00 12.00
106 Liam Foudy D 8.00 20.00
107 Alexander True D 6.00 15.00
108 Tyler Benson D 8.00 20.00
109 Keegan Kolesar D 6.00 15.00
110 Mikey Anderson D 8.00 20.00
112 Jake Evans D 8.00 20.00
113 Jason Robertson B 40.00 100.00
114 Timothy Liljegren C 8.00 20.00
116 Gustav Lindstrom D 6.00 15.00
118 Gage Quinney D 5.00 12.00
119 Morgan Geekie D 8.00 20.00
120 Alex Belzile D 6.00 15.00
121 Matiss Kivlenieks D 10.00 25.00
122 Kieffer Bellows D 6.00 15.00
124 Gabe Vilardi B 12.00 30.00
125 Nicolas Beaudin C 8.00 20.00
126 Olli Juolevi D 8.00 20.00
127 Nick Robertson D 12.00 30.00
129 Pierre-Olivier Joseph D 8.00 20.00
130 Victor Soderstrom C 6.00 15.00
133 Jake Oettinger D 20.00 50.00
134 Philipp Kurashev D 10.00 25.00
136 Shane Bowers D 6.00 15.00
137 Connor Ingram D 6.00 15.00
140 Ty Dellandrea D 8.00 20.00
142 Peyton Krebs D 12.00 30.00
147 Ryan McLeod D 6.00 15.00
149 Bowen Byram C 25.00 60.00
XRCAR Alexander Romanov 15.00 40.00
XRCDC Dylan Cozens 40.00 100.00
XRCIS Ilya Sorokin 30.00 80.00
XRCKK Kirill Kaprizov 125.00 300.00
XRCTS Tim Stutzle 80.00 200.00

2020-21 Upper Deck Allure Autographs Blue Line
*BLUE: .4X TO 1X BASIC
*BLUE.RC: 1.25X TO 3X BASIC
50 Connor McDavid 125.00 300.00
55 Carey Price 80.00 200.00
69 Auston Matthews 125.00 300.00
82 Jason Robertson 100.00 250.00
100 Alexis Lafreniere 250.00 600.00

2020-21 Upper Deck Allure Autographs Magenta
*MAGENTA: .5X TO 1.25X BASIC
113 Jason Robertson 60.00 150.00
150 Alexis Lafreniere 150.00 400.00

2020-21 Upper Deck Allure City Celly
*RED: 1X TO 2.5X BASIC
CC1 Connor McDavid 4.00 10.00
CC2 Sebastian Aho 1.25 3.00
CC3 Bo Horvat 1.00 2.50
CC4 Travis Konecny .75 2.00
CC5 Mark Stone 1.00 2.50
CC6 Jake Guentzel 1.25 3.00
CC7 Steven Stamkos 1.50 4.00
CC8 Evgeny Kuznetsov 1.00 2.50
CC9 Pavel Buchnevich .60 1.50
CC10 Brendan Gallagher .75 2.00
CC11 Mitch Marner 1.25 3.00
CC12 Dylan Strome 1.00 2.50
CC13 Anders Lee .60 1.50
CC14 Joe Pavelski 1.00 2.50
CC15 Cale Makar 2.00 5.00

2020-21 Upper Deck Allure City Celly Seismic Autographs
CC1 Connor McDavid B 200.00 500.00
CC4 Travis Konecny D 6.00 15.00
CC5 Mark Stone D 25.00 60.00
CC6 Jake Guentzel C 30.00 80.00
CC9 Pavel Buchnevich C 8.00 20.00
CC10 Brendan Gallagher C 20.00 50.00
CC11 Mitch Marner B 30.00 80.00
CC12 Dylan Strome C 20.00 50.00
CC13 Anders Lee D 12.00 30.00
CC14 Joe Pavelski D 25.00 60.00
CC15 Cale Makar A 50.00 125.00

2020-21 Upper Deck Allure Diagnostics
*RED: 1X TO 2.5X BASIC
D1 Brent Burns .75 2.00
D2 John Gibson .75 2.00
D3 Nick Suzuki 1.50 4.00
D4 Ryan O'Reilly .75 2.00
D5 Nico Hischier 1.25 3.00
D6 Alex DeBrincat 1.00 2.50
D7 Zach Parise .75 2.00
D8 Andrei Vasilevskiy 1.25 3.00
D9 Matt Murray .75 2.00
D10 Brad Marchand 1.50 4.00
D11 James van Riemsdyk .60 1.50
D12 Quinn Hughes 2.00 5.00
D13 Connor Hellebuyck 1.50 4.00
D14 Artemi Panarin 1.50 4.00
D15 Roman Josi .75 2.00

2020-21 Upper Deck Allure Diagnostics Autographs Black and Green
D1 Brent Burns A 8.00 20.00
D2 John Gibson E 8.00 20.00
D3 Nick Suzuki C 50.00 125.00
D4 Ryan O'Reilly C 8.00 20.00
D5 Nico Hischier B 12.00 30.00
D6 Alex DeBrincat C 10.00 25.00
D7 Zach Parise B 8.00 20.00
D8 Andrei Vasilevskiy D 12.00 30.00
D9 Matt Murray E 8.00 20.00
D10 Brad Marchand A 60.00 150.00
D11 James van Riemsdyk E 6.00 15.00
D13 Connor Hellebuyck D 15.00 40.00
D15 Roman Josi D 8.00 20.00

2020-21 Upper Deck Allure Grand Entrance
*RED: 1.25X TO 3X BASIC
GE1 Tyler Benson .50 1.25
GE2 Timothy Liljegren .50 1.25
GE3 Gabe Vilardi .75 2.00
GE4 Martin Kaut .50 1.25
GE5 Liam Foudy .50 1.25
GE6 Morgan Geekie .50 1.25
GE7 Calvin Thurkauf .40 1.00
GE8 Jake Evans .50 1.25
GE9 Kieffer Bellows .40 1.00
GE10 Brandon Hagel .60 1.50
GE11 Josh Norris .75 2.00
GE12 Jason Robertson 1.25 3.00
GE13 Shane Bowers .40 1.00
GE14 Victor Soderstrom .40 1.00
GE15 Connor McMichael .75 2.00
GE16 Connor Ingram .40 1.00
GE17 Thomas Harley .75 2.00
GE18 Philip Broberg .50 1.25
GE19 Vitali Kravtsov 1.00 2.50
GE20 Bowen Byram 1.00 2.50
GE21 Peyton Krebs .75 2.00
GE22 Jake Oettinger 1.25 3.00
GE23 Nick Robertson .75 2.00
GE24 Alexander Alexeyev .40 1.00
GE25 Alexis Lafreniere 1.50 4.00

2020-21 Upper Deck Allure Grand Entrance Blue
*BLUE: 2X TO 5X BASIC
GE5 Liam Foudy 10.00 25.00
GE25 Alexis Lafreniere 20.00 50.00

2020-21 Upper Deck Allure Grand Entrance Autographs Green
GE1 Tyler Benson D 6.00 15.00
GE2 Timothy Liljegren D 6.00 15.00
GE3 Gabe Vilardi B 20.00 50.00
GE4 Martin Kaut D 6.00 15.00
GE5 Liam Foudy D 6.00 15.00
GE6 Morgan Geekie D 6.00 15.00
GE7 Calvin Thurkauf D 5.00 12.00
GE8 Jake Evans D 6.00 15.00
GE9 Kieffer Bellows D 5.00 12.00
GE10 Brandon Hagel C 8.00 20.00
GE12 Jason Robertson D 60.00 150.00
GE13 Shane Bowers D 5.00 12.00
GE14 Victor Soderstrom D 5.00 12.00
GE16 Connor Ingram D 5.00 12.00
GE20 Bowen Byram D 20.00 50.00
GE21 Peyton Krebs D 10.00 25.00
GE22 Jake Oettinger D 15.00 40.00
GE23 Nick Robertson C 10.00 25.00

2020-21 Upper Deck Allure Iced Out
*RED: 1X TO 2.5X BASIC
IO1 Evgeni Malkin 1.25 3.00
IO2 Miro Heiskanen .75 2.00
IO3 Jakub Vrana .60 1.50
IO4 Victor Olofsson .60 1.50
IO5 Leon Draisaitl 2.00 5.00
IO6 Auston Matthews 2.50 6.00
IO7 Mark Giordano .60 1.50
IO8 Nick Suzuki 1.25 3.00
IO9 Anthony Mantha .50 1.25
IO10 Pekka Rinne .60 1.50
IO11 Andrei Svechnikov .75 2.00
IO12 Yanni Gourde .50 1.25
IO13 Patrick Kane 1.25 3.00
IO14 Carter Hart .60 1.50
IO15 Igor Shesterkin 1.25 3.00
IO16 Nick Robertson 1.25 3.00
IO17 Nicolas Beaudin .75 2.00
IO18 Gabe Vilardi 1.25 3.00
IO19 Timothy Liljegren .75 2.00
IO20 Alexis Lafreniere 2.50 6.00

2020-21 Upper Deck Allure Iced Out Autographs Blue
IO2 Miro Heiskanen C 8.00 20.00
IO3 Jakub Vrana B 6.00 15.00
IO4 Victor Olofsson D 6.00 15.00
IO6 Auston Matthews A 125.00 300.00
IO7 Mark Giordano B 6.00 15.00
IO8 Nick Suzuki C 30.00 80.00
IO9 Anthony Mantha C 10.00 25.00
IO10 Pekka Rinne D 6.00 15.00
IO11 Andrei Svechnikov C 8.00 20.00
IO12 Yanni Gourde D 5.00 12.00
IO13 Patrick Kane A 60.00 150.00
IO14 Carter Hart B 25.00 60.00
IO16 Nick Robertson C 12.00 30.00
IO17 Nicolas Beaudin D 8.00 20.00
IO18 Gabe Vilardi B 12.00 30.00
IO19 Timothy Liljegren C 8.00 20.00

2020-21 Upper Deck Allure Jersey Autographs Blue Line
2 Brendan Gallagher 12.00 30.00
3 Jake Guentzel 15.00 40.00
4 Pekka Rinne 12.00 30.00
5 Aleksander Barkov 20.00 50.00
8 Dustin Brown 15.00 40.00
9 Alex DeBrincat 15.00 40.00
10 Keith Yandle 8.00 20.00
11 Andrei Vasilevskiy 20.00 50.00
12 Carter Hart 60.00 150.00
13 Mark Stone 15.00 40.00
14 Brad Marchand 30.00 80.00
15 Ryan Suter 10.00 25.00
17 James van Riemsdyk 10.00 25.00
18 John Gibson 12.00 30.00
19 Roman Josi 12.00 30.00
20 Travis Konecny 15.00 40.00
24 William Karlsson 20.00 50.00
32 Tyler Seguin 15.00 40.00
33 Anders Lee 10.00 25.00
34 Mark Giordano 12.00 30.00
35 Mitch Marner 20.00 50.00
36 Connor Hellebuyck 25.00 60.00
37 Ryan O'Reilly 12.00 30.00
38 Andrei Svechnikov 15.00 40.00
41 Miro Heiskanen 15.00 40.00
42 Victor Olofsson 12.00 30.00
43 Quinn Hughes 30.00 80.00
45 Tomas Hertl 12.00 30.00
46 Nico Hischier 20.00 50.00
48 Kyle Palmieri 10.00 25.00
50 Connor McDavid 200.00 500.00
51 Nick Foligno 10.00 25.00
52 John Tavares 20.00 50.00
53 Zach Parise 12.00 30.00
54 Jakub Vrana 12.00 30.00
55 Carey Price 25.00 60.00
60 Patrick Kane 40.00 100.00
61 Mark Scheifele 20.00 50.00
63 Dylan Strome 15.00 40.00
64 Matthew Tkachuk 30.00 80.00
66 Thomas Chabot 12.00 30.00
67 Anze Kopitar 20.00 50.00
69 Auston Matthews 100.00 250.00
71 Alex Belzile 10.00 25.00
72 Kieffer Bellows 10.00 25.00
74 Morgan Geekie 10.00 25.00
75 Gabe Vilardi 30.00 80.00
76 Jake Evans 15.00 40.00
77 Martin Kaut 12.00 30.00
78 Josh Norris 20.00 50.00
79 Nicolas Beaudin 12.00 30.00
80 Ty Dellandrea 12.00 30.00
81 Liam Foudy 12.00 30.00
82 Jason Robertson 80.00 200.00
83 Mikey Anderson 12.00 30.00
84 Tyler Benson 12.00 30.00
86 Alexander Alexeyev 10.00 25.00
87 Shane Bowers 10.00 25.00
88 Philipp Kurashev 15.00 40.00
89 Timothy Liljegren 10.00 25.00
90 Victor Soderstrom 10.00 25.00
91 Jake Oettinger 30.00 80.00
94 Connor McMichael 20.00 50.00
95 Thomas Harley 20.00 50.00
96 Peyton Krebs 20.00 50.00
98 Bowen Byram 25.00 60.00
99 Nick Robertson 20.00 50.00
100 Alexis Lafreniere 200.00 500.00

2020-21 Upper Deck Allure Jerseys Red Rainbow
1 Alex Ovechkin 12.00 30.00
2 Brendan Gallagher 3.00 8.00
3 Jake Guentzel 5.00 12.00
4 Pekka Rinne 3.00 8.00
5 Aleksander Barkov 5.00 12.00
6 Cale Makar 8.00 20.00
7 David Pastrnak 8.00 20.00
8 Dustin Brown 3.00 8.00
9 Alex DeBrincat 4.00 10.00
10 Keith Yandle 2.50 6.00
11 Andrei Vasilevskiy 5.00 12.00
12 Carter Hart 3.00 8.00
13 Mark Stone 4.00 10.00
14 Brad Marchand 6.00 15.00
15 Ryan Suter 2.50 6.00
17 James van Riemsdyk 2.50 6.00
18 John Gibson 3.00 8.00
19 Roman Josi 3.00 8.00
20 Travis Konecny 3.00 8.00
22 Bo Horvat 4.00 10.00
23 Nathan MacKinnon 12.00 30.00
24 William Karlsson 4.00 10.00
25 Artemi Panarin 6.00 15.00
26 Dylan Larkin 4.00 10.00
27 Evgeni Malkin 6.00 15.00
28 Brady Tkachuk 5.00 12.00
31 Martin Jones 2.50 6.00
32 Tyler Seguin 4.00 10.00
33 Anders Lee 2.50 6.00
34 Mark Giordano 3.00 8.00
35 Mitch Marner 5.00 12.00
36 Connor Hellebuyck 6.00 15.00
37 Ryan O'Reilly 3.00 8.00
38 Andrei Svechnikov 4.00 10.00
39 Mathew Barzal 4.00 10.00
40 John Carlson 3.00 8.00
41 Miro Heiskanen 4.00 10.00
42 Victor Olofsson 3.00 8.00
43 Quinn Hughes 8.00 20.00
44 Nikita Kucherov 6.00 15.00
45 Tomas Hertl 3.00 8.00
46 Nico Hischier 5.00 12.00
47 Elias Pettersson 5.00 12.00
48 Kyle Palmieri 2.50 6.00
49 Jordan Binnington 5.00 12.00
50 Connor McDavid 15.00 40.00
51 Nick Foligno 2.50 6.00
52 John Tavares 5.00 12.00
53 Zach Parise 3.00 8.00
54 Jakub Vrana 3.00 8.00
55 Carey Price 6.00 15.00
56 Sebastian Aho 5.00 12.00
57 Steven Stamkos 6.00 15.00
58 Leon Draisaitl 10.00 25.00
59 Ryan Getzlaf 3.00 8.00
60 Patrick Kane 6.00 15.00
61 Mark Scheifele 5.00 12.00
63 Dylan Strome 4.00 10.00
64 Matthew Tkachuk 6.00 15.00
65 Jonathan Huberdeau 4.00 10.00
66 Thomas Chabot 3.00 8.00
67 Anze Kopitar 5.00 12.00
68 Jack Eichel 5.00 12.00
69 Auston Matthews 12.00 30.00
70 Sidney Crosby 12.00 30.00
71 Alex Belzile 2.50 6.00
72 Kieffer Bellows 2.50 6.00
74 Morgan Geekie 3.00 8.00
75 Gabe Vilardi 5.00 12.00
76 Jake Evans 3.00 8.00
77 Martin Kaut 3.00 8.00
78 Josh Norris 5.00 12.00
79 Nicolas Beaudin 3.00 8.00
80 Ty Dellandrea 3.00 8.00
81 Liam Foudy 3.00 8.00
82 Jason Robertson 8.00 20.00
83 Mikey Anderson 3.00 8.00
84 Tyler Benson 3.00 8.00
85 Egor Korshkov 2.00 5.00
86 Alexander Alexeyev 2.50 6.00
87 Shane Bowers 2.50 6.00
88 Philipp Kurashev 4.00 10.00
89 Timothy Liljegren 3.00 8.00
90 Victor Soderstrom 2.50 6.00
91 Jake Oettinger 8.00 20.00
92 Vitali Kravtsov 6.00 15.00
94 Connor McMichael 5.00 12.00
95 Thomas Harley 5.00 12.00
96 Peyton Krebs 5.00 12.00
98 Bowen Byram 6.00 15.00
99 Nick Robertson 5.00 12.00
100 Alexis Lafreniere 10.00 25.00

2020-21 Upper Deck Allure Quartz Autographs
AQAV Andrei Vasilevskiy D 12.00 30.00
AQBM Brad Marchand C 15.00 40.00
AQBO Bowen Byram B 20.00 50.00
AQCH Carter Hart D 8.00 20.00
AQGV Gabe Vilardi C 15.00 40.00
AQHE Connor Hellebuyck C 15.00 40.00
AQLF Liam Foudy D 10.00 25.00
AQMA Cale Makar A 20.00 50.00
AQNR Nick Robertson C 15.00 40.00
AQQH Quinn Hughes B 20.00 50.00
AQRJ Roman Josi D 8.00 20.00
AQST Shea Theodore D 10.00 25.00
AQTH Tomas Hertl D 8.00 20.00
AQTL Timothy Liljegren D 10.00 25.00

2021-22 Upper Deck Allure
1 Auston Matthews .75 2.00
2 Dylan Larkin .25 .60
3 Tom Wilson .20 .50
4 Sidney Crosby .75 2.00
5 Adam Fox .25 .60
6 Ryan Nugent-Hopkins .25 .60
7 Brendan Gallagher .20 .50
8 Cale Makar .50 1.25
9 Artemi Panarin .40 1.00
10 Anders Lee .15 .40
11 Sebastian Aho .30 .75
12 Jacob Markstrom .20 .50
13 Phillip Danault .15 .40
14 Anthony Mantha .15 .40
15 Nikita Kucherov .40 1.00
16 Josh Norris .20 .50
17 David Perron .15 .40
18 Brent Burns .20 .50
19 Brady Tkachuk .30 .75
20 John Gibson .20 .50
21 Aleksander Barkov .30 .75
22 Brayden Point .25 .60
23 Dougie Hamilton .15 .40
24 Nathan MacKinnon .75 2.00
25 Maxime Comtois .15 .40
26 J.T. Miller .25 .60
27 Patrice Bergeron .25 .60
28 Roman Josi .20 .50
29 Kailer Yamamoto .20 .50
30 Marc-Andre Fleury .40 1.00
31 Drew Doughty .25 .60
32 Josh Morrissey .25 .60
33 Cam Talbot .20 .50
34 Pavel Buchnevich .15 .40
35 Mark Giordano .20 .50
36 Claude Giroux .20 .50
37 Brad Marchand .40 1.00
38 Max Pacioretty .20 .50
39 Steven Stamkos .40 1.00
40 Kirill Kaprizov .60 1.50
41 Miro Heiskanen .25 .60
42 Sam Reinhart .40 1.00
43 Alex Ovechkin .75 2.00
44 John Tavares .30 .75
45 Quinn Hughes .50 1.25
46 Jason Robertson .30 .75
47 David Pastrnak .50 1.25
48 Patrick Kane .40 1.00
49 Josh Bailey .15 .40
50 Jeff Petry .20 .50
51 Victor Olofsson .20 .50
52 Leon Draisaitl .60 1.50
53 Nico Hischier .30 .75
54 Jonathan Huberdeau .25 .60
55 Colton Parayko .15 .40
56 Cam Atkinson .20 .50
57 Ty Smith .20 .50
58 Carter Hart .20 .50
59 Alexis Lafreniere .30 .75
60 Teuvo Teravainen .20 .50
61 Mark Scheifele .30 .75
62 Elias Pettersson .30 .75
63 Jakub Vrana .15 .40
64 Mitch Marner .30 .75
65 Juuse Saros .25 .60
66 Alex DeBrincat .25 .60
67 Jordan Eberle .20 .50
68 Brock Boeser .25 .60
69 Tristan Jarry .25 .60
70 Jack Eichel .30 .75
71 Carey Price .40 1.00
72 Andrei Svechnikov .25 .60
73 Taylor Hall .20 .50
74 Joe Pavelski .25 .60
75 Nick Suzuki .40 1.00
76 Phil Kessel .20 .50
77 Elias Lindholm .20 .50
78 Jake Guentzel .30 .75
79 Kevin Fiala .15 .40
80 Tim Stutzle .25 .60
81 Alex Nedeljkovic .15 .40
82 Alex Tuch .20 .50
83 Mikko Rantanen .50 1.25
84 Patrik Laine .25 .60
85 Anze Kopitar .30 .75
86 Andrei Vasilevskiy .30 .75
87 Connor Hellebuyck .40 1.00
88 Jakob Chychrun .20 .50
89 Jean-Gabriel Pageau .12 .30
90 Mats Zuccarello .20 .50
91 Nikolaj Ehlers .20 .50
92 Philipp Grubauer .20 .50
93 Ryan O'Reilly .20 .50
94 Matthew Tkachuk .40 1.00
95 Jakub Voracek .15 .40
96 Seth Jones .20 .50
97 Connor McDavid 1.00 2.50
98 Mark Stone .25 .60
99 Tomas Hertl .20 .50
100 Jack Hughes .50 1.25
101 Cole Caufield RC 2.00 5.00
102 William Eklund RC 1.25 3.00
103 Hendrix Lapierre RC .50 1.25
104 Benoit-Olivier Groulx RC .50 1.25
105 Anton Lundell RC 1.00 2.50
106 Nils Lundkvist RC .50 1.25
107 Vasily Podkolzin RC .60 1.50
108 Mason McTavish RC 1.00 2.50
109 Lucas Raymond RC 1.50 4.00
110 Garrett Pilon RC .60 1.50
111 Mike Hardman RC .50 1.25
112 Joey Keane RC .40 1.00
113 Ivan Prosvetov RC .50 1.25
114 Tanner Laczynski RC .50 1.25
115 Jesse Ylonen RC .50 1.25
116 Cole Sillinger RC .75 2.00
117 Wyatt Kalynuk RC .50 1.25
118 Matthew Phillips RC .50 1.25
119 Alex Newhook RC .75 2.00
120 Kole Lind RC .60 1.50
121 Radim Zohorna RC .50 1.25
122 Ukko-Pekka Luukkonen RC .75 2.00
123 Alex Barre-Boulet RC .75 2.00
124 Wade Allison RC .50 1.25
125 Grigori Denisenko RC .60 1.50
126 Arttu Ruotsalainen RC .50 1.25
127 Rasmus Kupari RC .50 1.25
128 Jacob Bernard-Docker RC .50 1.25
129 Tyce Thompson RC .50 1.25
130 Moritz Seider RC 1.25 3.00
131 Joe Veleno RC .60 1.50
132 Philip Tomasino RC .60 1.50
133 Calen Addison RC .60 1.50
134 Mattias Samuelsson RC .50 1.25
135 Spencer Knight RC 1.00 2.50
136 David Farrance RC .50 1.25
137 Jack Ahcan RC .50 1.25
138 Shane Pinto RC .75 2.00
139 Zac Jones RC .60 1.50
140 Jan Jenik RC .60 1.50
141 Sampo Ranta RC .50 1.25
142 Jamie Drysdale RC .75 2.00
143 Cam York RC .60 1.50
144 Ross Colton RC .60 1.50
145 Morgan Barron RC .40 1.00
146 Jeremy Swayman RC 1.50 4.00
147 Cole Perfetti RC 1.00 2.50
148 Filip Gustavsson RC 1.00 2.50
149 Trevor Zegras RC 1.00 2.50
150 Quinton Byfield RC 1.25 3.00

2021-22 Upper Deck Allure '17 Shield
*1917: .6X TO 1.5X BASIC

2021-22 Upper Deck Allure '05 Shield
*2005: 1.2X TO 3X BASIC

2021-22 Upper Deck Allure Black Rainbow
*BLACK.RNBW: 2X TO 5X BASIC
*BLACK.RNBW.RC: 1.5X TO 4X BASIC

2021-22 Upper Deck Allure Blue Line
*BLUE.LINE: 15X TO 40X BASIC
*BLUE.LINE.RC: 6X TO 15X BASIC
130 Moritz Seider 50.00 125.00
146 Jeremy Swayman 40.00 100.00

2021-22 Upper Deck Allure Green Rainbow
*GREEN.RNBW: 6X TO 15X BASIC
*GREEN.RNBW.RC: 4X TO 10X BASIC
101 Cole Caufield 40.00 100.00
109 Lucas Raymond 30.00 80.00
130 Moritz Seider 30.00 80.00
146 Jeremy Swayman 25.00 60.00
149 Trevor Zegras 60.00 150.00

2021-22 Upper Deck Allure Leopard
*LEOPARD: 1.2X TO 3X BASIC

2021-22 Upper Deck Allure Number
*NUMBER: 5X TO 12X BASIC
*NUMBER.RC: 2.5X TO 6X BASIC

2021-22 Upper Deck Allure Orange Slice
*ORANGE.SLICE: 3X TO 8X BASIC
*ORANGE.SLICE.RC: 2.5X TO 6X BASIC

2021-22 Upper Deck Allure Pink Leopard
*PINK.LPRD: 10X TO 25X BASIC
*PINK.LPRD.RC: 5X TO 12X BASIC

2021-22 Upper Deck Allure Red Rainbow
*RED.RNBW: 2.5X TO 6X BASIC
*RED.RNBW.RC: 2X TO 5X BASIC

2021-22 Upper Deck Allure Steel
*STEEL: 5X TO 12X BASIC
*STEEL.RC: 4X TO 10X BASIC

2021-22 Upper Deck Allure Autographs Red Rainbow
3 Tom Wilson D 10.00 25.00
6 Ryan Nugent-Hopkins C 12.00 30.00
8 Cale Makar B 25.00 60.00
10 Anders Lee E 8.00 20.00
11 Sebastian Aho C 15.00 40.00
12 Jacob Markstrom D 10.00 25.00
13 Phillip Danault E 10.00 25.00
14 Anthony Mantha E 8.00 20.00
16 Josh Norris D 10.00 25.00
17 David Perron E 8.00 20.00
18 Brent Burns B 12.00 30.00
19 Brady Tkachuk C 15.00 40.00
20 John Gibson D 12.00 30.00
21 Aleksander Barkov C 15.00 40.00
23 Dougie Hamilton E 8.00 20.00
25 Maxime Comtois E 8.00 20.00
26 J.T. Miller D 12.00 30.00
29 Kailer Yamamoto C 8.00 20.00
30 Marc-Andre Fleury B 20.00 50.00
32 Josh Morrissey E 12.00 30.00
33 Cam Talbot E 10.00 25.00
34 Pavel Buchnevich D 8.00 20.00
37 Brad Marchand B 20.00 50.00
38 Max Pacioretty C 10.00 25.00
41 Miro Heiskanen D 12.00 30.00
42 Sam Reinhart E 20.00 50.00
44 John Tavares B 15.00 40.00
45 Quinn Hughes B 25.00 60.00
46 Jason Robertson E 15.00 40.00
48 Patrick Kane A 20.00 50.00
49 Josh Bailey E 8.00 20.00
50 Jeff Petry E 10.00 25.00
52 Leon Draisaitl A 30.00 80.00
54 Jonathan Huberdeau D 12.00 30.00
55 Colton Parayko E 8.00 20.00
56 Cam Atkinson E 10.00 25.00
57 Ty Smith E 10.00 25.00
58 Carter Hart D 12.00 30.00
59 Alexis Lafreniere B 15.00 40.00
60 Teuvo Teravainen D 10.00 25.00
61 Mark Scheifele C 15.00 40.00
63 Jakub Vrana E 8.00 20.00
64 Mitch Marner B 15.00 40.00
65 Juuse Saros D 12.00 30.00
67 Jordan Eberle E 10.00 25.00
68 Brock Boeser B 12.00 30.00
69 Tristan Jarry E 10.00 25.00
71 Carey Price A 20.00 50.00
72 Andrei Svechnikov C 20.00 50.00
73 Taylor Hall B 12.00 30.00
74 Joe Pavelski C 12.00 30.00
75 Nick Suzuki C 20.00 50.00
78 Jake Guentzel D 15.00 40.00
79 Kevin Fiala E 8.00 20.00
80 Tim Stutzle C 30.00 80.00
81 Alex Nedeljkovic E 8.00 20.00
82 Alex Tuch E 10.00 25.00
83 Mikko Rantanen B 25.00 60.00
85 Anze Kopitar B 15.00 40.00
86 Andrei Vasilevskiy B 15.00 40.00
87 Connor Hellebuyck C 20.00 50.00
89 Jean-Gabriel Pageau E 6.00 15.00
90 Mats Zuccarello D 10.00 25.00
91 Nikolaj Ehlers B 10.00 25.00
92 Philipp Grubauer E 10.00 25.00
93 Ryan O'Reilly C 10.00 25.00
94 Matthew Tkachuk C 20.00 50.00
98 Mark Stone C 12.00 30.00
99 Tomas Hertl D 10.00 25.00
102 William Eklund D 25.00 60.00
103 Hendrix Lapierre E 12.00 30.00
104 Benoit-Olivier Groulx D 10.00 25.00
106 Nils Lundkvist E 10.00 25.00
107 Vasily Podkolzin D 12.00 30.00
109 Lucas Raymond C 30.00 80.00
111 Mike Hardman D 10.00 25.00
113 Ivan Prosvetov E 10.00 25.00
114 Tanner Laczynski E 10.00 25.00
116 Cole Sillinger C 15.00 40.00
118 Matthew Phillips E 10.00 25.00
120 Kole Lind E 12.00 30.00
122 Ukko-Pekka Luukkonen E 15.00 40.00
123 Alex Barre-Boulet D 10.00 25.00
124 Wade Allison E 10.00 25.00
127 Rasmus Kupari E 10.00 25.00
128 Jacob Bernard-Docker E 10.00 25.00
129 Tyce Thompson E 10.00 25.00
130 Moritz Seider C 60.00 150.00
133 Calen Addison E 10.00 25.00
134 Mattias Samuelsson E 10.00 25.00
138 Shane Pinto E 15.00 40.00
139 Zac Jones E 12.00 30.00
140 Jan Jenik E 12.00 30.00
142 Jamie Drysdale D 15.00 40.00
143 Cam York E 10.00 25.00
146 Jeremy Swayman D 30.00 80.00
149 Trevor Zegras A 250.00 600.00
150 Quinton Byfield B 25.00 60.00

2021-22 Upper Deck Allure Autographs Blue Line
*BLUE.LINE: .6X TO 1.5X BASIC
4 Sidney Crosby 125.00 300.00
80 Tim Stutzle 50.00 125.00
97 Connor McDavid 200.00 500.00
130 Moritz Seider 150.00 400.00
146 Jeremy Swayman 125.00 300.00
149 Trevor Zegras 200.00 500.00

2021-22 Upper Deck Allure Breadbaskets
*GREEN.RNBW/99: .75X TO 2X BASIC
BB1 Marc-Andre Fleury 2.00 5.00
BB2 Jordan Binnington 1.50 4.00
BB3 John Gibson 1.00 2.50
BB4 Mackenzie Blackwood 1.00 2.50
BB5 Andrei Vasilevskiy 1.50 4.00
BB6 Sergei Bobrovsky 1.50 4.00
BB7 Alex Nedeljkovic .75 2.00
BB8 Semyon Varlamov 1.00 2.50
BB9 Jacob Markstrom 1.00 2.50
BB10 Igor Shesterkin 2.00 5.00
BB11 Jake Oettinger 1.50 4.00
BB12 Connor Hellebuyck 2.00 5.00
BB13 Robin Lehner .75 2.00
BB14 Juuse Saros 1.25 3.00
BB15 Philipp Grubauer 1.00 2.50
BB16 Cam Talbot 1.00 2.50
BB17 Cal Petersen .60 1.50
BB18 Tristan Jarry 1.00 2.50
BB19 Carey Price 2.00 5.00
BB20 Thatcher Demko 1.25 3.00

2021-22 Upper Deck Allure Breadbaskets Autographs
BB1 Marc-Andre Fleury A 30.00 80.00
BB3 John Gibson B 15.00 40.00
BB5 Andrei Vasilevskiy A 25.00 60.00
BB6 Sergei Bobrovsky B 25.00 60.00
BB7 Alex Nedeljkovic D 12.00 30.00
BB9 Jacob Markstrom C 15.00 40.00
BB11 Jake Oettinger C 25.00 60.00
BB12 Connor Hellebuyck B 30.00 80.00
BB14 Juuse Saros C 40.00 100.00
BB15 Philipp Grubauer B 15.00 40.00
BB16 Cam Talbot C 15.00 40.00
BB17 Cal Petersen C 10.00 25.00
BB18 Tristan Jarry D 15.00 40.00
BB19 Carey Price A 30.00 80.00

2021-22 Upper Deck Allure Control Room
CR1 Spencer Knight 1.50 4.00
CR2 Ross Colton 1.00 2.50
CR3 Ukko-Pekka Luukkonen 1.25 3.00
CR4 Moritz Seider 2.00 5.00
CR5 Filip Gustavsson 1.50 4.00
CR6 Lucas Raymond 2.50 6.00
CR7 Trevor Zegras 1.50 4.00
CR9 Cam York .75 2.00
CR10 Joe Veleno 1.00 2.50
CR11 Grigori Denisenko 1.00 2.50
CR12 Quinton Byfield 2.00 5.00
CR13 Jeremy Swayman 2.50 6.00
CR14 Matthew Phillips .75 2.00
CR15 Calen Addison .75 2.00
CR16 Jamie Drysdale 1.25 3.00
CR17 Mason McTavish 1.50 4.00
CR18 William Eklund 2.00 5.00
CR19 Shane Pinto 1.25 3.00
CR20 Cole Caufield 3.00 8.00

2021-22 Upper Deck Allure Control Room Autographs
CR1 Spencer Knight C 15.00 40.00
CR2 Ross Colton E 10.00 25.00
CR3 Ukko-Pekka Luukkonen E 12.00 30.00
CR4 Moritz Seider B 20.00 50.00
CR5 Filip Gustavsson E 15.00 40.00
CR6 Lucas Raymond B 30.00 80.00
CR8 Alex Newhook E 12.00 30.00
CR9 Cam York D 8.00 20.00
CR10 Joe Veleno D 10.00 25.00
CR11 Grigori Denisenko D 10.00 25.00
CR12 Quinton Byfield A 30.00 80.00
CR13 Jeremy Swayman D 25.00 60.00
CR14 Matthew Phillips E 8.00 20.00
CR15 Calen Addison E 8.00 20.00
CR16 Jamie Drysdale D 12.00 30.00
CR17 Mason McTavish C 15.00 40.00
CR18 William Eklund C 20.00 50.00
CR19 Shane Pinto D 12.00 30.00

2021-22 Upper Deck Allure Full Rainbow Autographs
R1 Quinton Byfield C 25.00 60.00
R2 Nils Lundkvist F 10.00 25.00
R3 Mason McTavish D 20.00 50.00
R4 Vasily Podkolzin E 12.00 30.00
R5 Cole Perfetti E 20.00 50.00
R6 Lucas Raymond C 40.00 100.00
R7 Philip Tomasino G 12.00 30.00
R8 Arttu Ruotsalainen G 10.00 25.00
R9 Jack Ahcan G 10.00 25.00
R10 Garrett Pilon G 12.00 30.00
R11 Logan Thompson G 25.00 60.00
R12 Hendrix Lapierre E 10.00 25.00
R13 Tyce Thompson G 10.00 25.00
R14 Mike Hardman E 10.00 25.00
R15 Joey Keane G 8.00 20.00
R16 Moritz Seider C 25.00 60.00
R17 Spencer Knight E 20.00 50.00
R18 Wyatt Kalynuk G 10.00 25.00
R19 Joe Veleno G 12.00 30.00
R20 Rasmus Kupari F 10.00 25.00
R21 Jacob Bernard-Docker F 10.00 25.00
R22 Jesse Ylonen G 10.00 25.00
R23 Jamie Drysdale G 15.00 40.00
R24 Ukko-Pekka Luukkonen F 15.00 40.00
R25 Ross Colton G 12.00 30.00
R26 Benoit-Olivier Groulx E 10.00 25.00
R27 Shane Pinto F 15.00 40.00
R28 Jan Jenik F 12.00 30.00
R29 Filip Gustavsson G 20.00 50.00
R30 Cam York F 10.00 25.00
R31 Ivan Prosvetov G 10.00 25.00
R32 Kole Lind G 12.00 30.00
R34 Zac Jones G 10.00 25.00
R35 Jeremy Swayman E 40.00 100.00
R36 Alex Newhook F 15.00 40.00
R37 Mattias Samuelsson G 10.00 25.00
R39 Matthew Phillips G 10.00 25.00
R40 Sampo Ranta G 10.00 25.00
R41 Trevor Zegras B 80.00 200.00
R42 Morgan Barron G 8.00 20.00
R43 Wade Allison F 10.00 25.00
R44 Alex Barre-Boulet G 10.00 25.00

Card	Low	High
R45 Grigori Denisenko F	12.00	30.00
R46 Parker Kelly G	10.00	25.00
R47 Lane Pederson G	10.00	25.00
R48 Cole Sillinger C	15.00	40.00
R49 Calen Addison F	10.00	25.00
R53 Alexis Lafreniere B	40.00	100.00
R54 Nils Hoglander F	8.00	20.00
R55 Andrei Svechnikov C	12.00	30.00
R57 Eeli Tolvanen G	10.00	25.00
R58 Alex Nedeljkovic F	8.00	20.00
R59 Cale Makar B	80.00	200.00
R60 Jason Robertson D	15.00	40.00
R61 Ty Smith F	10.00	25.00
R63 Jake Oettinger E	15.00	40.00
R64 Josh Norris E	10.00	25.00
R66 Nick Suzuki D	20.00	50.00
R67 Brady Tkachuk C	15.00	40.00
R69 Miro Heiskanen D	12.00	30.00
R71 Maxime Comtois F	8.00	20.00
R74 Tim Stutzle D	40.00	100.00
R76 Dylan Cozens E	10.00	25.00
R77 Mikko Rantanen D	25.00	60.00
R78 Quinn Hughes B	25.00	60.00
R79 Martin Necas F	15.00	40.00
R80 Kyle Connor E	15.00	40.00
R81 Kirby Dach D	10.00	25.00
R85 Bowen Byram D	12.00	30.00
R89 Andrei Vasilevskiy B	15.00	40.00
R90 Ryan O'Reilly D	10.00	25.00
R91 Brad Marchand B	20.00	50.00
R95 Patrick Kane B	40.00	100.00
R96 Mitch Marner B	40.00	100.00
R98 Matthew Tkachuk C	20.00	50.00
R100 Alex Ovechkin A	150.00	400.00

2021-22 Upper Deck Allure Hustle Hit and Never Quit

Card	Low	High
HH1 Brad Marchand	2.50	6.00
HH2 Duncan Keith	1.00	2.50
HH3 Tom Wilson	1.25	3.00
HH4 Jamie Benn	1.25	3.00
HH5 Anders Lee	1.00	2.50
HH6 Victor Hedman	1.50	4.00
HH7 Ryan Reaves	1.00	2.50
HH8 Wayne Simmonds	1.25	3.00
HH9 Keith Yandle	.75	2.00
HH10 Brent Burns	1.25	3.00
HH11 Matthew Tkachuk	2.50	6.00
HH12 Drew Doughty	1.50	4.00
HH13 Sean Couturier	1.00	2.50
HH14 Brady Tkachuk	2.00	5.00
HH15 Mark Giordano	1.25	3.00

2021-22 Upper Deck Allure Hustle Hit and Never Quit Autographs

Card	Low	High
HH1 Brad Marchand B	40.00	100.00
HH2 Duncan Keith A	15.00	40.00
HH3 Tom Wilson C	20.00	50.00
HH4 Jamie Benn C	20.00	50.00
HH5 Anders Lee D	15.00	40.00
HH7 Ryan Reaves D	25.00	60.00
HH10 Brent Burns C	20.00	50.00
HH11 Matthew Tkachuk B	40.00	100.00
HH14 Brady Tkachuk B	30.00	80.00

2021-22 Upper Deck Allure Iced Out

*GREEN.RNBW/99: 1X TO 2.5X BASIC

Card	Low	High
IO1 Connor McDavid	5.00	12.00
IO2 Quinn Hughes	2.50	6.00
IO3 Brayden Point	1.25	3.00
IO4 Jason Zucker	1.00	2.50
IO5 Nikolaj Ehlers	1.00	2.50
IO6 Jason Robertson	1.50	4.00
IO7 Brock Boeser	1.25	3.00
IO8 Cam Atkinson	1.00	2.50
IO9 Cale Makar	2.50	6.00
IO10 Tomas Hertl	1.00	2.50
IO11 Jack Hughes	2.50	6.00
IO12 Max Pacioretty	1.00	2.50
IO13 Teuvo Teravainen	1.00	2.50
IO14 Mitch Marner	1.50	4.00
IO15 Anthony Mantha	.75	2.00
IO16 Jeremy Swayman	3.00	8.00
IO17 Joe Veleno	1.25	3.00
IO18 Quinton Byfield	2.50	6.00
IO19 Cole Caufield	4.00	10.00
IO20 Spencer Knight	2.00	5.00

2021-22 Upper Deck Allure Iced Out Autographs

Card	Low	High
IO4 Jason Zucker D	10.00	25.00
IO5 Nikolaj Ehlers D	10.00	25.00
IO6 Jason Robertson C	15.00	40.00
IO7 Brock Boeser B	12.00	30.00
IO8 Cam Atkinson D	10.00	25.00
IO10 Tomas Hertl D	10.00	25.00
IO12 Max Pacioretty C	10.00	25.00
IO14 Mitch Marner B	15.00	40.00
IO15 Anthony Mantha D	8.00	20.00
IO16 Jeremy Swayman C	30.00	80.00
IO17 Joe Veleno C	12.00	30.00
IO18 Quinton Byfield B	25.00	60.00
IO20 Spencer Knight B	20.00	50.00

2021-22 Upper Deck Allure Jersey Autographs Blue Line

Card	Low	High
1 Auston Matthews	100.00	250.00
3 Tom Wilson	12.00	30.00
6 Ryan Nugent-Hopkins	15.00	40.00
8 Cale Makar	30.00	80.00
10 Anders Lee	10.00	25.00
11 Sebastian Aho	20.00	50.00
12 Jacob Markstrom	12.00	30.00
14 Anthony Mantha	10.00	25.00
17 David Perron	10.00	25.00
18 Brent Burns	12.00	30.00
19 Brady Tkachuk	20.00	50.00
20 John Gibson	12.00	30.00
21 Aleksander Barkov	20.00	50.00
23 Dougie Hamilton	10.00	25.00
26 J.T. Miller	15.00	40.00
29 Kailer Yamamoto	12.00	30.00
30 Marc-Andre Fleury	25.00	60.00
32 Josh Morrissey	15.00	40.00
33 Cam Talbot	12.00	30.00
34 Pavel Buchnevich	10.00	25.00
37 Brad Marchand	25.00	60.00
38 Max Pacioretty	12.00	30.00
41 Miro Heiskanen	15.00	40.00
42 Sam Reinhart	25.00	60.00
45 Quinn Hughes	30.00	80.00
48 Patrick Kane	25.00	60.00
49 Josh Bailey	10.00	25.00
51 Victor Olofsson	12.00	30.00
52 Leon Draisaitl	40.00	100.00
54 Jonathan Huberdeau	15.00	40.00
55 Colton Parayko	10.00	25.00
56 Cam Atkinson	12.00	30.00
57 Ty Smith	12.00	30.00
58 Carter Hart	12.00	30.00
59 Alexis Lafreniere	20.00	50.00
60 Teuvo Teravainen	12.00	30.00
61 Mark Scheifele	20.00	50.00
63 Jakub Vrana	10.00	25.00
64 Mitch Marner	20.00	50.00
67 Jordan Eberle	12.00	30.00
68 Brock Boeser	15.00	40.00
71 Carey Price	25.00	60.00
72 Andrei Svechnikov	15.00	40.00
74 Joe Pavelski	15.00	40.00
75 Nick Suzuki	25.00	60.00
78 Jake Guentzel	20.00	50.00
79 Kevin Fiala	10.00	25.00
80 Tim Stutzle	15.00	40.00
82 Alex Tuch	12.00	30.00
85 Anze Kopitar	20.00	50.00
86 Andrei Vasilevskiy	20.00	50.00
87 Connor Hellebuyck	25.00	60.00
89 Jean-Gabriel Pageau	8.00	20.00
90 Mats Zuccarello	12.00	30.00
91 Nikolaj Ehlers	12.00	30.00
92 Philipp Grubauer	12.00	30.00
93 Ryan O'Reilly	12.00	30.00
94 Matthew Tkachuk	25.00	60.00
97 Connor McDavid	200.00	500.00
98 Mark Stone	15.00	40.00
99 Tomas Hertl	12.00	30.00
102 William Eklund	25.00	60.00
103 Hendrix Lapierre	10.00	25.00
104 Benoit-Olivier Groulx	10.00	25.00
105 Anton Lundell	20.00	50.00
106 Nils Lundkvist	10.00	25.00
107 Vasily Podkolzin	12.00	30.00
108 Mason McTavish	20.00	50.00
109 Lucas Raymond	30.00	80.00
110 Garrett Pilon	12.00	30.00
111 Mike Hardman	10.00	25.00
112 Joey Keane	8.00	20.00
113 Ivan Prosvetov	10.00	25.00
114 Tanner Laczynski	10.00	25.00
115 Jesse Ylonen	10.00	25.00
116 Cole Sillinger	15.00	40.00
117 Wyatt Kalynuk	10.00	25.00
118 Matthew Phillips	10.00	25.00
119 Alex Newhook	15.00	40.00
120 Kole Lind	12.00	30.00
121 Radim Zohorna	10.00	25.00
122 Ukko-Pekka Luukkonen	15.00	40.00
124 Wade Allison	10.00	25.00
125 Grigori Denisenko	12.00	30.00
126 Arttu Ruotsalainen	10.00	25.00
127 Rasmus Kupari	10.00	25.00
128 Jacob Bernard-Docker	10.00	25.00
129 Tyce Thompson	10.00	25.00
130 Moritz Seider	80.00	200.00
131 Joe Veleno	12.00	30.00
132 Philip Tomasino	12.00	30.00
133 Calen Addison	10.00	25.00
134 Mattias Samuelsson	10.00	25.00
135 Spencer Knight	20.00	50.00
136 David Farrance	10.00	25.00
137 Jack Ahcan	10.00	25.00
138 Shane Pinto	15.00	40.00
139 Zac Jones	12.00	30.00
140 Jan Jenik	12.00	30.00
141 Sampo Ranta	10.00	25.00
142 Jamie Drysdale	15.00	40.00
143 Cam York	10.00	25.00
144 Ross Colton	12.00	30.00
145 Morgan Barron	8.00	20.00
146 Jeremy Swayman	30.00	80.00
147 Cole Perfetti	20.00	50.00
148 Filip Gustavsson	20.00	50.00
150 Quinton Byfield	50.00	125.00

2021-22 Upper Deck Allure Quartz

Card	Low	High
AQAM Auston Matthews	3.00	8.00
AQBB Brock Boeser	1.00	2.50
AQCM Connor McDavid	4.00	10.00
AQCP Carey Price	1.50	4.00
AQJH Jonathan Huberdeau	1.00	2.50
AQJP Joe Pavelski	1.00	2.50
AQJT John Tavares	1.25	3.00
AQKK Kirill Kaprizov	2.50	6.00
AQLD Leon Draisaitl	2.50	6.00
AQNM Nathan MacKinnon	3.00	8.00
AQPK Patrick Kane	1.50	4.00
AQRO Ryan O'Reilly	.75	2.00
AQSC Sidney Crosby	3.00	8.00
AQSS Steven Stamkos	1.50	4.00
AQST Mark Stone	1.00	2.50

2021-22 Upper Deck Allure Quartz Autographs

Card	Low	High
AQBB Brock Boeser C	12.00	30.00
AQJH Jonathan Huberdeau D	12.00	30.00
AQJP Joe Pavelski D	12.00	30.00
AQJT John Tavares B	15.00	40.00
AQLD Leon Draisaitl B	30.00	80.00
AQPK Patrick Kane B	30.00	80.00
AQRO Ryan O'Reilly C	10.00	25.00
AQST Mark Stone D	12.00	30.00

2021-22 Upper Deck Allure Quartz Rookies

Card	Low	High
AQAN Alex Newhook	1.25	3.00
AQCC Cole Caufield	3.00	8.00
AQCY Cam York	.75	2.00
AQJD Jamie Drysdale	1.25	3.00
AQJS Jeremy Swayman	2.50	6.00
AQLR Lucas Raymond	2.50	6.00
AQMS Moritz Seider	2.00	5.00
AQQB Quinton Byfield	2.00	5.00
AQSK Spencer Knight	1.50	4.00
AQTZ Trevor Zegras	1.50	4.00

2021-22 Upper Deck Allure Quartz Rookies Autographs

Card	Low	High
AQAN Alex Newhook C	20.00	50.00
AQCY Cam York C	12.00	30.00
AQJD Jamie Drysdale C	20.00	50.00
AQJS Jeremy Swayman C	40.00	100.00
AQLR Lucas Raymond B	40.00	100.00
AQMS Moritz Seider B	30.00	80.00
AQQB Quinton Byfield A	30.00	80.00
AQSK Spencer Knight C	12.00	30.00

2021-22 Upper Deck Allure Rainbow Red Orange

*ORANGE.YLW: .75X TO 2X BASIC
*YLW.GREEN: 1X TO 2.5X BASIC
*DOUBLE.RNBW: 2X TO 5X BASIC
*GREEN.BLUE/299: 3X TO 8X BASIC
*BLUE.PURPLE/199: 4X TO 10X BASIC

Card	Low	High
R1 Quinton Byfield	2.00	5.00
R2 Nils Lundkvist	.75	2.00
R3 Mason McTavish	1.50	4.00
R4 Vasily Podkolzin	1.00	2.50
R5 Cole Perfetti	1.50	4.00
R6 Lucas Raymond	2.50	6.00
R7 Philip Tomasino	1.00	2.50
R8 Arttu Ruotsalainen	.75	2.00
R9 Jack Ahcan	.75	2.00
R10 Garrett Pilon	1.00	2.50
R11 Logan Thompson	2.00	5.00
R12 Hendrix Lapierre	.75	2.00
R13 Tyce Thompson	.75	2.00
R14 Mike Hardman	.75	2.00
R15 Joey Keane	.60	1.50
R16 Moritz Seider	2.00	5.00
R17 Spencer Knight	1.50	4.00
R18 Wyatt Kalynuk	.75	2.00
R19 Joe Veleno	1.00	2.50
R20 Rasmus Kupari	.75	2.00
R21 Jacob Bernard-Docker	.75	2.00
R22 Jesse Ylonen	.75	2.00
R23 Jamie Drysdale	1.25	3.00
R24 Ukko-Pekka Luukkonen	1.25	3.00
R25 Ross Colton	1.00	2.50
R26 Benoit-Olivier Groulx	.75	2.00
R27 Shane Pinto	1.25	3.00
R28 Jan Jenik	1.00	2.50
R29 Filip Gustavsson	1.50	4.00
R30 Cam York	.75	2.00
R31 Ivan Prosvetov	.75	2.00
R32 Kole Lind	1.00	2.50
R33 David Farrance	.75	2.00
R34 Zac Jones	1.00	2.50
R35 Jeremy Swayman	2.50	6.00
R36 Alex Newhook	1.25	3.00
R37 Mattias Samuelsson	.75	2.00
R38 Radim Zohorna	.75	2.00
R39 Matthew Phillips	.75	2.00
R40 Sampo Ranta	.75	2.00
R41 Trevor Zegras	1.50	4.00
R42 Morgan Barron	.60	1.50
R43 Wade Allison	.75	2.00
R44 Alex Barre-Boulet	.75	2.00
R45 Grigori Denisenko	1.00	2.50
R46 Parker Kelly	.75	2.00
R47 Lane Pederson	.75	2.00
R48 Cole Sillinger	1.25	3.00
R49 Calen Addison	.75	2.00
R50 Cole Caufield	3.00	8.00
R51 Kirill Kaprizov	2.50	6.00
R52 Rasmus Dahlin	1.00	2.50
R53 Alexis Lafreniere	1.25	3.00
R54 Nils Hoglander	.60	1.50
R55 Andrei Svechnikov	1.00	2.50
R56 Ilya Sorokin	1.25	3.00
R57 Eeli Tolvanen	.75	2.00
R58 Alex Nedeljkovic	.60	1.50
R59 Cale Makar	2.00	5.00
R60 Jason Robertson	1.25	3.00
R61 Ty Smith	.75	2.00
R62 Alex DeBrincat	1.00	2.50
R63 Jake Oettinger	1.25	3.00
R64 Josh Norris	.75	2.00
R65 Joel Farabee	.75	2.00
R66 Nick Suzuki	1.50	4.00
R67 Brady Tkachuk	1.25	3.00
R68 Jack Hughes	2.00	5.00
R69 Miro Heiskanen	1.00	2.50
R70 Igor Shesterkin	1.50	4.00
R71 Maxime Comtois	.60	1.50
R72 Adam Fox	1.00	2.50
R73 Charlie McAvoy	1.00	2.50
R74 Tim Stutzle	1.00	2.50
R75 Nico Hischier	1.25	3.00
R76 Dylan Cozens	.75	2.00
R77 Mikko Rantanen	2.00	5.00
R78 Quinn Hughes	2.00	5.00
R79 Martin Necas	1.25	3.00
R80 Kyle Connor	1.25	3.00
R81 Kirby Dach	.75	2.00
R82 Patrik Laine	1.00	2.50
R83 Elias Pettersson	1.25	3.00
R84 Mathew Barzal	1.00	2.50
R85 Bowen Byram	1.00	2.50
R86 Auston Matthews	3.00	8.00
R87 Sidney Crosby	3.00	8.00
R88 Leon Draisaitl	2.50	6.00
R89 Andrei Vasilevskiy	1.25	3.00
R90 Ryan O'Reilly	.75	2.00
R91 Brad Marchand	1.50	4.00
R92 Nathan MacKinnon	3.00	8.00
R93 David Pastrnak	2.00	5.00
R94 Artemi Panarin	1.50	4.00
R95 Patrick Kane	1.50	4.00
R96 Mitch Marner	1.25	3.00
R97 Connor McDavid	4.00	10.00
R98 Matthew Tkachuk	1.50	4.00
R99 Nikita Kucherov	1.50	4.00
R100 Alex Ovechkin	2.00	5.00

2022-23 Upper Deck Allure

Card	Low	High
1 Nathan MacKinnon	.75	2.00
2 Phillip Danault	.20	.50
3 Oliver Bjorkstrand	.15	.40
4 Tim Stutzle	.25	.60
5 Jared Spurgeon	.20	.50
6 Jonathan Huberdeau	.25	.60
7 Sean Couturier	.15	.40
8 Cole Caufield	.40	1.00
9 Matt Duchene	.20	.50
10 Evan Bouchard	.25	.60
11 Juuse Saros	.25	.60
12 Nikolaj Ehlers	.20	.50
13 Mitch Marner	.30	.75
14 Joel Farabee	.20	.50
15 Jake Allen	.20	.50
16 Jesper Bratt	.20	.50
17 Troy Terry	.15	.40
18 Matt Grzelcyk	.15	.40
19 Jordan Greenway	.12	.30
20 Jared McCann	.15	.40
21 Kyle Connor	.30	.75
22 Victor Hedman	.25	.60
23 Shayne Gostisbehere	.20	.50
24 Philipp Grubauer	.20	.50
25 Pavel Buchnevich	.15	.40
26 Kirill Kaprizov	.60	1.50
27 Gabriel Landeskog	.25	.60
28 Elias Pettersson	.30	.75
29 Dylan Larkin	.25	.60
30 Connor McDavid	1.00	2.50
31 Aleksander Barkov	.30	.75
32 Roman Josi	.20	.50
33 Sebastian Aho	.30	.75
34 Boone Jenner	.20	.50
35 Karel Vejmelka	.12	.30
36 Chris Kreider	.25	.60
37 Cam Atkinson	.20	.50
38 Jack Hughes	.50	1.25
39 Jonathan Marchessault	.25	.60
40 Seth Jones	.20	.50
41 Jake Guentzel	.30	.75
42 Jason Robertson	.30	.75
43 Lucas Raymond	.30	.75
44 Timo Meier	.20	.50
45 Evgeny Kuznetsov	.25	.60
46 Joe Pavelski	.25	.60
47 Conor Garland	.15	.40
48 Adam Henrique	.15	.40
49 Nikita Kucherov	.40	1.00
50 Bowen Byram	.25	.60
51 Mark Scheifele	.30	.75
52 Tristan Jarry	.20	.50
53 Yegor Sharangovich	.20	.50
54 Alexis Lafreniere	.30	.75
55 Josh Norris	.20	.50
56 Alex DeBrincat	.25	.60
57 Brad Marchand	.40	1.00
58 Moritz Seider	.25	.60
59 Igor Shesterkin	.40	1.00
60 Trevor Zegras	.20	.50
61 Tom Wilson	.20	.50
62 Dylan Cozens	.20	.50
63 Sam Bennett	.30	.75
64 Casey Mittelstadt	.20	.50
65 Frederik Andersen	.25	.60
66 Auston Matthews	.75	2.00
67 Yanni Gourde	.15	.40
68 Quinton Byfield	.25	.60
69 Brady Tkachuk	.30	.75
70 Cale Makar	.50	1.25
71 Jacob Markstrom	.20	.50
72 William Nylander	.40	1.00
73 Jordan Kyrou	.20	.50
74 Mark Stone	.25	.60
75 Patrick Kane	.40	1.00
76 Tomas Hertl	.20	.50
77 Alex Ovechkin	.75	2.00
78 Jack Roslovic	.12	.30
79 Tage Thompson	.25	.60
80 Jack Eichel	.30	.75
81 Leon Draisaitl	.60	1.50
82 Robert Thomas	.20	.50
83 Josh Anderson	.15	.40
84 Sidney Crosby	.75	2.00
85 Roope Hintz	.25	.60
86 Clayton Keller	.25	.60
87 Brock Nelson	.20	.50
88 Anze Kopitar	.30	.75
89 Brent Burns	.20	.50
90 Artemi Panarin	.40	1.00
91 Tanner Jeannot	.12	.30
92 Anthony Beauvillier	.12	.30
93 Jeremy Swayman	.30	.75
94 Elias Lindholm	.20	.50
95 Viktor Arvidsson	.12	.30
96 Quinn Hughes	.50	1.25
97 Andrei Vasilevskiy	.30	.75
98 Mathew Barzal	.25	.60
99 Andrei Svechnikov	.25	.60
100 Matthew Tkachuk	.40	1.00
101 Owen Power RC	1.00	2.50
102 Mark Kastelic RC	.40	1.00
103 Declan Chisholm RC	.50	1.25
104 Marc McLaughlin RC	.50	1.25
105 Jordan Harris RC	.60	1.50
106 Jake Christiansen RC	.50	1.25
107 Michael Eyssimont RC	.50	1.25
108 Pyotr Kochetkov RC	1.00	2.50
109 Jordan Spence RC	.50	1.25
110 Isaac Ratcliffe RC	.50	1.25
111 Brayden Tracey RC	.40	1.00
112 Filip Hallander RC	.50	1.25
113 Fredrik Karlstrom RC	.40	1.00
114 Matt Boldy RC	1.50	4.00
115 Erik Kallgren RC	.50	1.25
116 Ben Meyers RC	.50	1.25
117 Adam Raska RC	.50	1.25
118 Carson Meyer RC	.40	1.00
119 Lukas Dostal RC	1.00	2.50
120 Matias Maccelli RC	.75	2.00
121 Dylan Holloway RC	1.00	2.50
122 Nick Abruzzese RC	.50	1.25
123 Kaedan Korczak RC	.40	1.00
124 Jack Quinn RC	.75	2.00
125 Jack McBain RC	.50	1.25
126 Samuel Fagemo RC	.40	1.00
127 Lukas Reichel RC	1.00	2.50
128 Nathan Smith RC	.40	1.00
129 Alex Vlasic RC	.40	1.00
130 Jacob Moverare RC	.40	1.00
131 Marco Rossi RC	1.25	3.00
132 Nick Blankenburg RC	.40	1.00
133 Jacob Perreault RC	.50	1.25
134 Nikita Okhotiuk RC	.40	1.00
135 Noah Cates RC	.50	1.25
136 Vladislav Kolyachonok RC	.40	1.00
137 Trey Fix-Wolansky RC	.50	1.25
138 Ronnie Attard RC	.50	1.25
139 Dylan Samberg RC	.50	1.25
140 Mads Sogaard RC	.60	1.50
141 Thomas Bordeleau RC	.50	1.25
142 Brandon Biro RC	.75	2.00
143 Braden Schneider RC	.75	2.00
144 Kent Johnson RC	1.00	2.50
145 Bobby Brink RC	.50	1.25
146 Reilly Walsh RC	.50	1.25
147 Chase Pearson RC	.40	1.00
148 Viktor Lodin RC	.50	1.25
149 Hayden Hodgson RC	.40	1.00
150 Matty Beniers RC	1.25	3.00
151 Shane Wright EXT RC	2.50	6.00
152 Juraj Slafkovsky EXT RC	5.00	12.00
153 Jake Sanderson EXT RC	2.50	6.00
154 Wyatt Johnston EXT RC	4.00	10.00
155 Andrei Kuzmenko EXT RC	2.00	5.00
156 Kirill Marchenko EXT RC	2.50	6.00

2022-23 Upper Deck Allure Black Rainbow

*BLACK RNBW: 2X TO 5X BASIC
*BLACK RNBW RC: 1.5X TO 4X BASIC

2022-23 Upper Deck Allure Blue Line

*BLUE LINE: 12X TO 30X BASIC
*BLUE LINE RC: 5X TO 12X BASIC

2022-23 Upper Deck Allure Glitter Bomb

*GLTR BOMB: 4X TO 10X BASIC
*GLTR BOMB RC: 3X TO 8X BASIC

2022-23 Upper Deck Allure Gold Glitter Bomb

*GOLD GLTR: 5X TO 12X BASIC
*GOLD GLTR RC: 2.5X TO 6X BASIC

2022-23 Upper Deck Allure Green Rainbow Die Cut

*GREEN RNBW: 6X TO 15X BASIC
*GREEN RNBW: 4X TO 10X BASIC

2022-23 Upper Deck Allure Orange Slice Die Cut

*ORANGE: 3X TO 8X BASIC
*ORANGE RC: 2.5X TO 6X BASIC

2022-23 Upper Deck Allure Photo Variations

*PHOTO VAR: 3X TO 8X BASIC
*PHOTO VAR RC: 1.5X TO 4X BASIC

2022-23 Upper Deck Allure Pink Leopard

*PINK LPRD: 10X TO 25X BASIC
*PINK LPRD RC: 5X TO 12X BASIC

2022-23 Upper Deck Allure Red Rainbow

*RED RNBW: 2.5X TO 6X BASIC
*RED RNBW: 2X TO 5X BASIC

2022-23 Upper Deck Allure Steel

*STEEL: 5X TO 12X BASIC
*STEEL RC: 4X TO 10X BASIC

2022-23 Upper Deck Allure White Diamond

*WHITE DMND: 3X TO 8X BASIC
*WHITE DMND RC: 1.5X TO 4X BASIC

2022-23 Upper Deck Allure 16 Bit

Card	Low	High
B1 Wayne Gretzky	250.00	600.00
B2 Sidney Crosby	150.00	400.00
B3 Jonathan Huberdeau	50.00	125.00
B4 Connor McDavid	200.00	500.00
B5 Matty Beniers	100.00	250.00
B6 J.T. Miller	50.00	125.00
B7 Steven Stamkos	80.00	200.00
B8 Matt Boldy	150.00	400.00
B9 Moritz Seider	50.00	125.00
B10 Igor Shesterkin	100.00	250.00
B11 Johnny Gaudreau	60.00	150.00
B12 Alex Ovechkin	150.00	400.00
B13 Frederik Andersen	50.00	125.00
B14 Auston Matthews	150.00	400.00
B15 Owen Power	80.00	200.00
B16 Trevor Zegras	40.00	100.00
B17 Nathan MacKinnon	150.00	400.00
B18 Leon Draisaitl	125.00	300.00
B19 Patrick Kane	100.00	250.00
B20 Shane Wright	100.00	250.00

2022-23 Upper Deck Allure All Time Allure

Card	Low	High
AT1 Wayne Gretzky	50.00	125.00
AT2 Joe Nieuwendyk	6.00	15.00
AT3 Jacques Plante	30.00	80.00
AT4 Jean Ratelle	6.00	15.00
AT5 Mark Messier	15.00	40.00
AT6 Mario Lemieux	30.00	80.00
AT7 Tim Horton	12.00	30.00
AT8 Eric Lindros	12.00	30.00
AT9 Gordie Howe	25.00	60.00
AT10 Patrick Roy	60.00	150.00
AT11 Stan Mikita	8.00	20.00
AT12 Chris Pronger	8.00	20.00
AT13 Dominik Hasek	12.00	30.00
AT14 Bobby Orr	30.00	80.00
AT15 Henri Richard	8.00	20.00
AT16 Martin Brodeur	20.00	50.00
AT17 Mike Bossy	8.00	20.00
AT18 Igor Larionov	8.00	20.00
AT19 Joe Sakic	15.00	40.00
AT20 Jaromir Jagr	15.00	40.00

2022-23 Upper Deck Allure Allure Quartz

Card	Low	High
AQBA Mathew Barzal	1.25	3.00
AQBC Blake Coleman	.75	2.00
AQBJ Boone Jenner	1.00	2.50
AQBM Brad Marchand	2.00	5.00
AQBT Brady Tkachuk	1.50	4.00
AQCP Carey Price	2.00	5.00
AQDS Dylan Strome	1.25	3.00
AQJB Jesper Bratt	1.00	2.50
AQJS Jaccob Slavin	.75	2.00
AQMB Michael Bunting	1.00	2.50
AQMG Matt Grzelcyk	.75	2.00
AQMS Mike Smith	.60	1.50
AQPB Pavel Buchnevich	.75	2.00
AQQB Quinton Byfield	1.25	3.00
AQRH Roope Hintz	1.25	3.00
AQTD Thatcher Demko	1.25	3.00
AQTE Troy Terry	.75	2.00
AQTJ Tanner Jeannot	.60	1.50
AQTT Tage Thompson	1.25	3.00
AQTW Tom Wilson	1.00	2.50

2022-23 Upper Deck Allure Allure Quartz Autographs

Card	Low	High
AQBC Blake Coleman D	8.00	20.00
AQBJ Boone Jenner D	10.00	25.00
AQBM Brad Marchand B	20.00	50.00
AQBT Brady Tkachuk B	15.00	40.00
AQCP Carey Price A	20.00	50.00
AQJS Jaccob Slavin D	8.00	20.00
AQMB Michael Bunting D	10.00	25.00
AQMG Matt Grzelcyk D	8.00	20.00
AQMS Mike Smith C	6.00	15.00
AQRH Roope Hintz C	12.00	30.00
AQTD Thatcher Demko C	12.00	30.00
AQTJ Tanner Jeannot D	6.00	15.00
AQTT Tage Thompson B	12.00	30.00
AQTW Tom Wilson C	10.00	25.00

2022-23 Upper Deck Allure Allure Quartz Rookie Autographs

Card	Low	High
AQBE Matty Beniers B	25.00	60.00
AQBY Matt Boldy B	30.00	80.00
AQIR Isaac Ratcliffe B	10.00	25.00
AQKJ Kent Johnson B	20.00	50.00
AQLR Lukas Reichel B	20.00	50.00
AQMM Marc McLaughlin B	10.00	25.00
AQNC Noah Cates B	10.00	25.00
AQOP Owen Power A	20.00	50.00

2022-23 Upper Deck Allure Allure Quartz Rookies

Card	Low	High
AQBE Matty Beniers	4.00	10.00
AQBY Matt Boldy	5.00	12.00
AQIR Isaac Ratcliffe	1.50	4.00
AQKJ Kent Johnson	3.00	8.00
AQLR Lukas Reichel	3.00	8.00
AQMM Marc McLaughlin	1.50	4.00
AQMR Marco Rossi	4.00	10.00
AQNC Noah Cates	1.50	4.00
AQOP Owen Power	3.00	8.00
AQSP Jordan Spence	1.50	4.00

2022-23 Upper Deck Allure Autographs Red Rainbow

Card	Low	High
4 Tim Stutzle B	8.00	20.00
6 Jonathan Huberdeau A	8.00	20.00
11 Juuse Saros D	8.00	20.00
12 Nikolaj Ehlers E	6.00	15.00
15 Jake Allen E	6.00	15.00
18 Matt Grzelcyk F	5.00	12.00
20 Jared McCann B	5.00	12.00
24 Philipp Grubauer A	6.00	15.00
30 Connor McDavid A	30.00	80.00
31 Aleksander Barkov D	10.00	25.00
34 Boone Jenner E	6.00	15.00
35 Karel Vejmelka F	4.00	10.00
37 Cam Atkinson F	6.00	15.00
46 Joe Pavelski B	8.00	20.00
50 Bowen Byram E	8.00	20.00
53 Yegor Sharangovich F	6.00	15.00
54 Alexis Lafreniere C	10.00	25.00
55 Josh Norris D	6.00	15.00
56 Alex DeBrincat C	8.00	20.00
57 Brad Marchand E	12.00	30.00
62 Dylan Cozens D	6.00	15.00
63 Sam Bennett E	10.00	25.00
64 Casey Mittelstadt F	6.00	15.00
66 Auston Matthews A	25.00	60.00
67 Yanni Gourde D	5.00	12.00
69 Brady Tkachuk C	10.00	25.00
71 Jacob Markstrom F	6.00	15.00
73 Jordan Kyrou C	6.00	15.00
76 Tomas Hertl E	6.00	15.00
77 Alex Ovechkin A	25.00	60.00
78 Jack Roslovic D	4.00	10.00
79 Tage Thompson F	20.00	50.00
81 Leon Draisaitl A	20.00	50.00
82 Robert Thomas D	6.00	15.00
84 Sidney Crosby A	25.00	60.00
85 Roope Hintz D	8.00	20.00
87 Brock Nelson E	6.00	15.00
88 Anze Kopitar B	10.00	25.00
89 Brent Burns A	6.00	15.00
91 Tanner Jeannot F	4.00	10.00
92 Anthony Beauvillier E	4.00	10.00
93 Jeremy Swayman F	20.00	50.00
97 Andrei Vasilevskiy E	10.00	25.00
99 Andrei Svechnikov C	8.00	20.00
100 Matthew Tkachuk A	12.00	30.00
101 Owen Power B	20.00	50.00
104 Marc McLaughlin D	10.00	25.00
105 Jordan Harris D	12.00	30.00
106 Jake Christiansen D	10.00	25.00
107 Michael Eyssimont D	10.00	25.00
108 Pyotr Kochetkov D	20.00	50.00
110 Isaac Ratcliffe D	10.00	25.00
111 Brayden Tracey D	8.00	20.00
114 Matt Boldy B	30.00	80.00
115 Erik Kallgren D	10.00	25.00
116 Ben Meyers C	10.00	25.00
119 Lukas Dostal D	20.00	50.00
120 Matias Maccelli D	15.00	40.00
121 Dylan Holloway C	20.00	50.00
122 Nick Abruzzese D	10.00	25.00
123 Kaedan Korczak D	8.00	20.00
124 Jack Quinn C	15.00	40.00
126 Samuel Fagemo A	8.00	20.00
127 Lukas Reichel C	20.00	50.00
128 Nathan Smith D	8.00	20.00
129 Alex Vlasic D	8.00	20.00
130 Jacob Moverare D	8.00	20.00
132 Nick Blankenburg C	8.00	20.00
133 Jacob Perreault C	10.00	25.00
135 Noah Cates B	10.00	25.00
136 Vladislav Kolyachonok D	8.00	20.00
137 Trey Fix-Wolansky D	10.00	25.00
138 Ronnie Attard A	10.00	25.00
139 Dylan Samberg D	10.00	25.00
140 Mads Sogaard D	12.00	30.00
143 Braden Schneider D	15.00	40.00
144 Kent Johnson C	20.00	50.00
145 Bobby Brink C	10.00	25.00
146 Reilly Walsh D	10.00	25.00
147 Chase Pearson D	8.00	20.00
149 Hayden Hodgson D	8.00	20.00
150 Matty Beniers B	60.00	150.00
151 Shane Wright	30.00	80.00
152 Juraj Slafkovsky	60.00	150.00
153 Jake Sanderson	30.00	80.00
154 Wyatt Johnston	50.00	125.00
155 Andrei Kuzmenko	25.00	60.00
156 Kirill Marchenko	30.00	80.00

2022-23 Upper Deck Allure Autographs Blue Line

*BLUE/35: 1X TO 2.5X BASIC
*BLUE RC/35: .6X TO 1.5X BASIC

Card	Low	High
30 Connor McDavid	250.00	600.00
66 Auston Matthews	80.00	200.00
77 Alex Ovechkin	200.00	500.00
79 Tage Thompson	40.00	100.00
84 Sidney Crosby	150.00	400.00
93 Jeremy Swayman	40.00	100.00
150 Matty Beniers	80.00	200.00

2022-23 Upper Deck Allure Blockers

*RED/299: 1X TO 2.5X BASIC
*GREEN/99: 1.2X TO 3X BASIC

Card	Low	High
BL1 Jacob Markstrom	.75	2.00
BL2 Nico Daws	.60	1.50
BL3 Jonathan Quick	1.00	2.50
BL4 Carter Hart	.75	2.00
BL5 Juuse Saros	1.00	2.50
BL6 Ilya Sorokin	1.25	3.00
BL7 James Reimer	.50	1.25
BL8 Anton Forsberg	.50	1.25
BL9 Carey Price	1.50	4.00
BL10 Ukko-Pekka Luukkonen	.60	1.50
BL11 Logan Thompson	1.00	2.50
BL12 Philipp Grubauer	.75	2.00
BL13 Elvis Merzlikins	.75	2.00
BL14 Marc-Andre Fleury	1.50	4.00
BL15 Spencer Knight	.75	2.00
BL16 Connor Hellebuyck	1.50	4.00
BL17 Jordan Binnington	1.25	3.00
BL18 Tristan Jarry	.75	2.00
BL19 Robin Lehner	.60	1.50
BL20 Igor Shesterkin	1.50	4.00
BL21 John Gibson	.75	2.00
BL22 Jeremy Swayman	1.25	3.00
BL23 Vitek Vanecek	.75	2.00
BL24 Jake Oettinger	1.25	3.00
BL25 Jack Campbell	.75	2.00
BL26 Karel Vejmelka	.50	1.25
BL27 Jake Allen	.75	2.00
BL28 Frederik Andersen	1.00	2.50
BL29 Andrei Vasilevskiy	1.25	3.00
BL30 Cal Petersen	.50	1.25
BL31 Alex Nedeljkovic	.60	1.50
BL32 Cam Talbot	.75	2.00
BL33 Sergei Bobrovsky	1.25	3.00
BL34 Mike Smith	.50	1.25
BL35 Thatcher Demko	1.00	2.50

2022-23 Upper Deck Allure Blockers Autographs

Card	Low	High
BL1 Jacob Markstrom A	10.00	25.00
BL2 Nico Daws D	8.00	20.00
BL5 Juuse Saros C	12.00	30.00
BL9 Carey Price A	20.00	50.00
BL10 Ukko-Pekka Luukkonen D	8.00	20.00
BL11 Logan Thompson D	12.00	30.00
BL13 Elvis Merzlikins B	10.00	25.00
BL14 Marc-Andre Fleury A	20.00	50.00
BL18 Tristan Jarry C	10.00	25.00
BL22 Jeremy Swayman D	15.00	40.00
BL23 Vitek Vanecek D	10.00	25.00
BL25 Jack Campbell C	10.00	25.00
BL27 Jake Allen C	10.00	25.00
BL29 Andrei Vasilevskiy A	15.00	40.00
BL30 Cal Petersen D	6.00	15.00
BL31 Alex Nedeljkovic D	8.00	20.00
BL35 Thatcher Demko B	12.00	30.00

2022-23 Upper Deck Allure Check Please

Card	Low	High
CP1 Tanner Jeannot	1.50	4.00
CP2 Tom Wilson	2.50	6.00
CP3 Ryan Reaves	2.00	5.00
CP4 Brandon Duhaime	1.50	4.00
CP5 Keegan Kolesar	1.50	4.00
CP6 Brad Marchand	5.00	12.00
CP7 Eeli Tolvanen	2.50	6.00
CP8 Pierre-Luc Dubois	2.00	5.00
CP9 Marcus Foligno	2.00	5.00
CP10 Blake Coleman	2.00	5.00

2022-23 Upper Deck Allure Check Please Autographs

Card	Low	High
CP1 Tanner Jeannot	10.00	25.00
CP2 Tom Wilson	15.00	40.00
CP3 Ryan Reaves	12.00	30.00
CP4 Brandon Duhaime	10.00	25.00
CP5 Keegan Kolesar	10.00	25.00
CP6 Brad Marchand	30.00	80.00
CP7 Eeli Tolvanen	15.00	40.00
CP9 Marcus Foligno	20.00	50.00
CP10 Blake Coleman	12.00	30.00

2022-23 Upper Deck Allure Color Flow Autographs Full Rainbow

Card	Low	High
SF3 Yegor Sharangovich F	8.00	20.00
SF4 Jordan Harris F	10.00	25.00
SF6 Alexis Lafreniere C	12.00	30.00
SF7 Alex Vlasic F	6.00	15.00
SF8 Matt Grzelcyk F	6.00	15.00
SF9 Reilly Walsh E	8.00	20.00
SF10 Anders Lee F	6.00	15.00
SF12 Jacob Moverare E	6.00	15.00
SF13 Jack Campbell D	8.00	20.00
SF14 Alex Newhook F	6.00	15.00
SF15 Mads Sogaard F	10.00	25.00
SF17 Brandon Duhaime F	5.00	12.00
SF19 Nick Abruzzese F	8.00	20.00
SF20 Chase Pearson F	6.00	15.00

SF21 Jacob Perreault D 8.00 20.00
SF25 Nathan Smith E 6.00 15.00
SF26 Isaac Ratcliffe F 8.00 20.00
SF28 Dylan Samberg F 8.00 20.00
SF29 Tanner Jeannot F 5.00 12.00
SF31 Braden Schneider F 12.00 30.00
SF33 Spencer Knight F 8.00 20.00
SF34 Owen Power B 30.00 80.00
SF35 Lukas Dostal F 15.00 40.00
SF37 Marco Rossi B 20.00 50.00
SF40 Filip Hallander F 8.00 20.00
SF41 Noah Cates E 8.00 20.00
SF42 Brock Boeser D 10.00 25.00
SF43 Charlie Coyle E 8.00 20.00
SF44 Lukas Reichel F 15.00 40.00
SF48 K'Andre Miller F 6.00 15.00
SF51 Jack McBain F 8.00 20.00
SF52 Michael Bunting C 8.00 20.00
SF53 Bobby Brink F 8.00 20.00
SF55 Kent Johnson B 15.00 40.00
SF57 Zack Hayes F 6.00 15.00
SF58 Brad Marchand A 15.00 40.00
SF59 Peyton Krebs F 6.00 15.00
SF61 Sam Bennett D 12.00 30.00
SF62 Ronnie Attard C 8.00 20.00
SF63 Boone Jenner C 8.00 20.00
SF64 Brayden Tracey F 6.00 15.00
SF65 Andrew Copp E 5.00 12.00
SF67 Michael Eyssimont F 8.00 20.00
SF69 Erik Kallgren F 8.00 20.00
SF70 Kaedan Korczak F 6.00 15.00
SF71 Matt Boldy B 25.00 60.00
SF72 Robin Salo F 5.00 12.00
SF74 Jonathan Dahlen F 5.00 12.00
SF75 Vladislav Kolyachonok E 6.00 15.00
SF76 Thatcher Demko D 10.00 25.00
SF78 Kirby Dach E 8.00 20.00
SF79 Nick Blankenburg E 6.00 15.00
SF80 Tage Thompson E 10.00 25.00
SF81 Samuel Fagemo D 6.00 15.00
SF82 Jesse Puljujarvi B 8.00 20.00
SF83 Hayden Hodgson F 6.00 15.00
SF84 Matias Maccelli F 12.00 30.00
SF86 Ben Meyers E 8.00 20.00
SF87 Trey Fix-Wolansky F 8.00 20.00
SF88 Jeremy Swayman F 12.00 30.00
SF92 Arthur Kaliyev F 8.00 20.00
SF94 Logan Thompson F 10.00 25.00
SF95 Jack Quinn D 12.00 30.00
SF96 Morgan Barron F 5.00 12.00
SF97 Pyotr Kochetkov F 15.00 40.00
SF100 Taylor Hall C 8.00 20.00

2022-23 Upper Deck Allure Color Flow Red Orange

*ORNG YLW: .5X TO 1.2X BASIC
*YLW GRN: .6X TO 1.5X BASIC
*GRN BLU: .75X TO 2X BASIC
*BLU PRPL: 1X TO 2.5X BASIC
*SPEC R-O/100: 1.5X TO 4X BASIC
*SPEC O-Y/85: 2X TO 5X BASIC
*SPEC Y-G/65: 2.5X TO 6X BASIC
*SPEC G-B/50: 3X TO 8X BASIC
*SPEC B-P/35: 4X TO 10X BASIC
SF1 Sebastian Aho .75 2.00
SF2 Torey Krug .40 1.00
SF3 Yegor Sharangovich .50 1.25
SF4 Jordan Harris .60 1.50
SF5 Matty Beniers 1.25 3.00
SF6 Alexis Lafreniere .75 2.00
SF7 Alex Vlasic .40 1.00
SF8 Matt Grzelcyk .40 1.00
SF9 Reilly Walsh .50 1.25
SF10 Anders Lee .40 1.00
SF11 Ross Colton .40 1.00
SF12 Jacob Moverare .40 1.00
SF13 Jack Campbell .50 1.25
SF14 Alex Newhook .40 1.00
SF15 Mads Sogaard .60 1.50
SF16 Ryan Suter .40 1.00
SF17 Brandon Duhaime .30 .75
SF18 Marc McLaughlin .50 1.25
SF19 Nick Abruzzese .50 1.25
SF20 Chase Pearson .40 1.00
SF21 Jacob Perreault .50 1.25
SF22 Scott Perunovich .30 .75
SF23 Adam Raska .50 1.25
SF24 Martin Necas .75 2.00
SF25 Nathan Smith .40 1.00
SF26 Isaac Ratcliffe .50 1.25
SF27 Troy Terry .40 1.00
SF28 Dylan Samberg .50 1.25
SF29 Tanner Jeannot .30 .75
SF30 Roope Hintz .60 1.50
SF31 Braden Schneider .75 2.00
SF32 Dawson Mercer .60 1.50
SF33 Spencer Knight .50 1.25
SF34 Owen Power 1.00 2.50
SF35 Lukas Dostal 1.00 2.50
SF36 Mark Kastelic .40 1.00
SF37 Marco Rossi 1.25 3.00
SF38 Viktor Lodin .50 1.25
SF39 Philip Tomasino .30 .75
SF40 Filip Hallander .50 1.25
SF41 Noah Cates .50 1.25
SF42 Brock Boeser .60 1.50
SF43 Charlie Coyle .50 1.25
SF44 Lukas Reichel 1.00 2.50
SF45 Cole Caufield 1.00 2.50
SF46 Pius Suter .40 1.00
SF47 Carson Meyer .40 1.00
SF48 K'Andre Miller .40 1.00
SF49 Thomas Bordeleau .50 1.25
SF50 Alex Iafallo .30 .75
SF51 Jack McBain .50 1.25
SF52 Michael Bunting .50 1.25
SF53 Bobby Brink .50 1.25
SF54 Kris Letang .60 1.50
SF55 Kent Johnson 1.00 2.50
SF56 Bokondji Imama .40 1.00
SF57 Zack Hayes .40 1.00
SF58 Brad Marchand 1.00 2.50
SF59 Peyton Krebs .40 1.00
SF60 Yanni Gourde .40 1.00
SF61 Sam Bennett .75 2.00
SF62 Ronnie Attard .50 1.25
SF63 Boone Jenner .50 1.25
SF64 Brayden Tracey .40 1.00
SF65 Andrew Copp .30 .75
SF66 Zach Parise .50 1.25
SF67 Michael Eyssimont .50 1.25
SF68 Jakub Galvas .50 1.25
SF69 Erik Kallgren .50 1.25
SF70 Kaedan Korczak .40 1.00
SF71 Matt Boldy 1.50 4.00
SF72 Robin Salo .30 .75
SF73 Jordan Spence .50 1.25
SF74 Jonathan Dahlen .30 .75
SF75 Vladislav Kolyachonok .40 1.00
SF76 Thatcher Demko .60 1.50
SF77 Matthew Tkachuk 1.00 2.50
SF78 Kirby Dach .50 1.25
SF79 Nick Blankenburg .40 1.00
SF80 Tage Thompson .60 1.50
SF81 Samuel Fagemo .40 1.00
SF82 Jesse Puljujarvi .50 1.25
SF83 Hayden Hodgson .40 1.00
SF84 Matias Maccelli .75 2.00
SF85 Nikita Okhotiuk .40 1.00
SF86 Ben Meyers .50 1.25
SF87 Trey Fix-Wolansky .50 1.25
SF88 Jeremy Swayman .75 2.00
SF90 Mike Smith .30 .75
SF91 Fredrik Karlstrom .40 1.00
SF92 Arthur Kaliyev .50 1.25
SF93 Lucas Raymond .75 2.00
SF94 Logan Thompson .60 1.50
SF95 Jack Quinn .75 2.00
SF96 Morgan Barron .30 .75
SF97 Pyotr Kochetkov 1.00 2.50
SF98 Declan Chisholm .40 1.00
SF99 Bowen Byram .60 1.50
SF100 Taylor Hall .50 1.25

2022-23 Upper Deck Allure Doubloons

DB1 Auston Matthews 50.00 125.00
DB2 Quinn Hughes 30.00 80.00
DB3 Jacob Moverare 10.00 25.00
DB4 Isaac Ratcliffe 12.00 30.00
DB5 Igor Shesterkin 25.00 60.00
DB6 Dylan Samberg 12.00 30.00
DB7 Rick Nash 12.00 30.00
DB8 Travis Konecny 12.00 30.00
DB9 Matt Boldy 40.00 100.00
DB10 Ilya Sorokin 20.00 50.00
DB11 Carson Meyer 10.00 25.00
DB12 Tomas Hertl 12.00 30.00
DB13 Evgeny Kuznetsov 15.00 40.00
DB14 Bill Barber 12.00 30.00
DB15 Anze Kopitar 20.00 50.00
DB16 Steven Stamkos 25.00 60.00
DB17 Erik Kallgren 12.00 30.00
DB18 Troy Terry 10.00 25.00
DB19 Kirill Kaprizov 40.00 100.00
DB20 Marc McLaughlin 12.00 30.00
DB21 Jonathan Huberdeau 15.00 40.00
DB22 Matty Beniers 30.00 80.00
DB23 Nathan Smith 10.00 25.00
DB24 Mark Stone 15.00 40.00
DB25 Brady Tkachuk 20.00 50.00
DB26 Adam Oates 12.00 30.00
DB27 Roman Josi 12.00 30.00
DB28 Tim Stutzle 15.00 40.00
DB29 Pyotr Kochetkov 25.00 60.00
DB30 Alex Ovechkin 50.00 120.00
DB31 Jacob Perreault 12.00 30.00
DB32 Elias Lindholm 12.00 30.00
DB33 Lukas Reichel 25.00 60.00
DB34 Brock Nelson 12.00 30.00
DB35 Noah Cates 12.00 30.00
DB36 Juuse Saros 15.00 40.00
DB37 Alex Newhook 10.00 25.00
DB38 Nikita Okhotiuk 10.00 25.00
DB39 Jake Oettinger 20.00 50.00
DB40 Mario Lemieux 50.00 125.00
DB41 Mitch Marner 20.00 50.00
DB42 Boone Jenner 12.00 30.00
DB43 Jack Quinn 20.00 50.00
DB44 Jordan Spence 12.00 30.00
DB45 Connor McDavid 60.00 150.00
DB46 Rob Blake 12.00 30.00
DB47 Lucas Raymond 20.00 50.00
DB48 Marco Rossi 25.00 60.00
DB49 Bobby Brink 12.00 30.00
DB50 Frederik Andersen 15.00 40.00
DB51 Mats Zuccarello 12.00 30.00
DB52 Declan Chisholm 12.00 30.00
DB53 Andrei Svechnikov 15.00 40.00
DB54 Philipp Grubauer 12.00 30.00
DB55 Owen Power 25.00 60.00
DB56 Nathan MacKinnon 50.00 125.00
DB57 David Pastrnak 30.00 80.00
DB58 Mads Sogaard 15.00 40.00
DB59 Moritz Seider 15.00 40.00
DB60 Yvan Cournoyer 12.00 30.00
DB61 Artemi Panarin 25.00 60.00
DB62 Jordan Harris 15.00 40.00
DB63 Clayton Keller 15.00 40.00
DB64 Ronnie Attard 12.00 30.00
DB65 Jack McBain 12.00 30.00
DB66 Robert Thomas 12.00 30.00
DB67 Kent Johnson 25.00 60.00
DB68 Kyle Connor 20.00 50.00
DB69 Braden Schneider 20.00 50.00
DB70 Sidney Crosby 50.00 125.00
DB71 Jack Eichel 20.00 50.00
DB72 Patrick Kane 25.00 60.00
DB73 Wayne Gretzky 80.00 200.00
DB74 Tage Thompson 15.00 40.00
DB75 Andrei Vasilevskiy 20.00 50.00
DB76 Nick Abruzzese 12.00 30.00
DB77 Matthew Tkachuk 25.00 60.00
DB78 Jordan Kyrou 12.00 30.00
DB79 Reilly Walsh 12.00 30.00
DB80 Jake Guentzel 20.00 50.00
DB81 Roope Hintz 15.00 40.00
DB82 Peter Forsberg 25.00 60.00
DB83 Jack Hughes 30.00 80.00
DB84 Cole Caufield 25.00 60.00
DB85 Matias Maccelli 20.00 50.00
DB86 Mark Scheifele 20.00 50.00
DB87 Thomas Bordeleau 12.00 30.00
DB88 Leon Draisaitl 40.00 100.00
DB89 Ben Meyers 12.00 30.00
DB90 Nikita Kucherov 25.00 60.00
DB91 Kaedan Korczak 10.00 25.00
DB92 Brock Boeser 15.00 40.00
DB93 Brian Leetch 10.00 25.00
DB94 Trevor Zegras 12.00 30.00
DB95 Trey Fix-Wolansky 12.00 30.00
DB96 Jared McCann 10.00 25.00
DB97 Carey Price 25.00 60.00
DB98 Nick Blankenburg 10.00 25.00
DB99 Aleksander Barkov 20.00 50.00
DB100 King Clancy 12.00 30.00

2022-23 Upper Deck Allure Game Stills

*RED/299: .6X TO 1.5X BASIC
*GREEN/25: 1X TO 2.5X BASIC
GS1 Auston Matthews 4.00 10.00
GS2 Matt Duchene 1.00 2.50
GS3 Adrian Kempe 1.00 2.50
GS4 Boone Jenner 1.00 2.50
GS5 Anthony Beauvillier .60 1.50
GS6 Alexis Lafreniere 1.50 4.00
GS7 Brock Boeser 1.25 3.00
GS8 Martin Necas 1.50 4.00
GS9 Colton Parayko .75 2.00
GS10 Brayden Point 1.25 3.00
GS11 Troy Terry .75 2.00
GS12 Gabriel Landeskog 1.25 3.00
GS13 Jesper Bratt 1.00 2.50
GS14 Yanni Gourde .75 2.00
GS15 Brady Tkachuk 1.50 4.00
GS16 Jake Guentzel 1.50 4.00
GS17 Brad Marchand 2.00 5.00
GS18 Dylan Cozens 1.00 2.50
GS19 Clayton Keller 1.25 3.00
GS20 Alex Ovechkin 4.00 10.00

2022-23 Upper Deck Allure Iced Out

*RED/299: .6X TO 1.5X BASIC
*GREEN/99: 1X TO 2.5X BASIC
IO1 Kent Johnson 2.00 5.00
IO2 John Gibson 1.00 2.50
IO3 Tyler Bertuzzi .75 2.00
IO4 Matty Beniers 2.50 6.00
IO5 Tanner Jeannot .60 1.50
IO6 Tomas Hertl 1.00 2.50
IO7 Marco Rossi 2.50 6.00
IO8 Sam Bennett 1.50 4.00
IO9 Roope Hintz 1.25 3.00
IO10 Connor McDavid 5.00 12.00
IO11 Quinn Hughes 2.50 6.00
IO12 Mark Scheifele 1.50 4.00
IO13 Chris Kreider 1.25 3.00
IO14 Sam Reinhart 2.00 5.00
IO15 Philipp Grubauer 1.00 2.50
IO16 Joe Pavelski 1.25 3.00
IO17 Matt Boldy 3.00 8.00
IO18 Jonathan Marchessault 1.25 3.00
IO19 Jacob Markstrom 1.00 2.50
IO20 Pius Suter .75 2.00
IO21 Owen Power 2.00 5.00
IO22 Brock Nelson 1.00 2.50
IO23 Nils Hoglander .75 2.00
IO24 Charlie Coyle 1.00 2.50
IO25 Kirill Kaprizov 3.00 8.00

2022-23 Upper Deck Allure Jersey Autographs Blue Line

4 Tim Stutzle/25 50.00 125.00
6 Jonathan Huberdeau/25 15.00 40.00
11 Juuse Saros/25 15.00 40.00
12 Nikolaj Ehlers/25 12.00 30.00
15 Jake Allen/25 12.00 30.00
18 Matt Grzelcyk/25 10.00 25.00
20 Jared McCann/25 10.00 25.00
22 Victor Hedman/25 15.00 40.00
24 Philipp Grubauer/25 12.00 30.00
27 Gabriel Landeskog/25 15.00 40.00
30 Connor McDavid/25 250.00 600.00
31 Aleksander Barkov/25 20.00 50.00
34 Boone Jenner/25 12.00 30.00
37 Cam Atkinson/25 12.00 30.00
46 Joe Pavelski/25 15.00 40.00
47 Conor Garland/25 10.00 25.00
50 Bowen Byram/25 15.00 40.00
52 Tristan Jarry/25 12.00 30.00
53 Yegor Sharangovich/25 12.00 30.00
54 Alexis Lafreniere/25 20.00 50.00
55 Josh Norris/25 12.00 30.00
56 Alex DeBrincat/25 15.00 40.00
57 Brad Marchand/25 25.00 60.00
61 Tom Wilson/25 12.00 30.00
62 Dylan Cozens/25 12.00 30.00
63 Sam Bennett/25 20.00 50.00
64 Casey Mittelstadt/25 10.00 25.00
66 Auston Matthews/25 125.00 300.00
67 Yanni Gourde/25 10.00 25.00
69 Brady Tkachuk/25 20.00 50.00
70 Cale Makar/25 60.00 150.00
71 Jacob Markstrom/25 12.00 30.00
73 Jordan Kyrou/25 12.00 30.00
76 Tomas Hertl/25 12.00 30.00
77 Alex Ovechkin/25 125.00 300.00
78 Jack Roslovic/25 8.00 20.00
79 Tage Thompson/25 15.00 40.00
81 Leon Draisaitl/25 60.00 150.00
82 Robert Thomas/25 12.00 30.00
84 Sidney Crosby/25 125.00 300.00
86 Clayton Keller/25 15.00 40.00
87 Brock Nelson/25 12.00 30.00
88 Anze Kopitar/25 20.00 50.00
89 Brent Burns/25 12.00 30.00
91 Tanner Jeannot/25 8.00 20.00
92 Anthony Beauvillier/25 8.00 20.00
93 Jeremy Swayman/25 20.00 50.00
97 Andrei Vasilevskiy/25 20.00 50.00
99 Andrei Svechnikov/25 15.00 40.00
100 Matthew Tkachuk/25 25.00 60.00
101 Owen Power/75 25.00 60.00
102 Mark Kastelic/75 8.00 20.00
105 Jordan Harris/75 15.00 40.00
106 Jake Christiansen/75 12.00 30.00
107 Michael Eyssimont/75 12.00 30.00
108 Pyotr Kochetkov/75 25.00 60.00
109 Jordan Spence/75 12.00 30.00
110 Isaac Ratcliffe/75 12.00 30.00
111 Brayden Tracey/75 10.00 25.00
112 Filip Hallander/75 12.00 30.00
113 Fredrik Karlstrom/75 10.00 25.00
114 Matt Boldy/75 40.00 100.00
115 Erik Kallgren/75 12.00 30.00
116 Ben Meyers/75 12.00 30.00
119 Lukas Dostal/75 25.00 60.00
120 Matias Maccelli/75 20.00 50.00
121 Dylan Holloway/75 25.00 60.00
122 Nick Abruzzese/75 12.00 30.00
123 Kaedan Korczak/75 10.00 25.00
124 Jack Quinn/75 20.00 50.00
125 Jack McBain/75 12.00 30.00
126 Samuel Fagemo/75 10.00 25.00
127 Lukas Reichel/75 25.00 60.00
128 Nathan Smith/75 10.00 25.00
129 Alex Vlasic/75 10.00 25.00
130 Jacob Moverare/75 10.00 25.00
131 Marco Rossi/75 30.00 80.00
132 Nick Blankenburg/75 10.00 25.00
133 Jacob Perreault/75 12.00 30.00
135 Noah Cates/75 12.00 30.00
136 Vladislav Kolyachonok/75 10.00 25.00
137 Trey Fix-Wolansky/75 12.00 30.00
138 Ronnie Attard/75 12.00 30.00
139 Dylan Samberg/75 12.00 30.00
140 Mads Sogaard/75 15.00 40.00
141 Thomas Bordeleau/35 12.00 30.00
143 Braden Schneider/35 20.00 50.00
144 Kent Johnson/35 25.00 60.00
145 Bobby Brink/35 12.00 30.00
146 Reilly Walsh/35 12.00 30.00
147 Chase Pearson/35 10.00 25.00
149 Hayden Hodgson/35 10.00 25.00
150 Matty Beniers/35 80.00 200.00

2022-23 Upper Deck Allure Runways

*RED/299: .6X TO 1.5X BASIC
*GREEN/99: 1X TO 2.5X BASIC
RW1 Noah Cates 1.00 2.50
RW2 Arthur Kaliyev 1.00 2.50
RW3 Alex Newhook .75 2.00
RW4 Tanner Jeannot .60 1.50
RW5 Owen Power 2.00 5.00
RW6 Kent Johnson 2.00 5.00
RW7 Jack Quinn 1.50 4.00
RW8 Trevor Zegras 1.50 4.00
RW9 Marco Rossi 2.50 6.00
RW10 Jeremy Swayman 1.50 4.00
RW11 Alexis Lafreniere 1.50 4.00
RW12 Spencer Knight 1.00 2.50
RW13 Lucas Raymond 1.50 4.00
RW14 Michael Bunting 1.00 2.50
RW15 Yegor Sharangovich 1.00 2.50
RW16 Jacob Perreault 1.00 2.50
RW17 Matty Beniers 2.50 6.00
RW18 Lukas Reichel 2.00 5.00
RW19 Marc McLaughlin 1.00 2.50
RW20 Matt Boldy 3.00 8.00

2023-24 Upper Deck Allure

1 Erik Karlsson .40 1.00
2 Anton Lundell .30 .75
3 Dylan Larkin .40 1.00
4 Filip Forsberg .50 1.25
5 Mason Marchment .25 .60
6 Igor Shesterkin .60 1.50
7 Mikko Rantanen .75 2.00
8 Blake Coleman .25 .60
9 Elias Pettersson .50 1.25
10 Juraj Slafkovsky .50 1.25
11 Tristan Jarry .30 .75
12 Andrei Svechnikov .40 1.00
13 Leon Draisaitl 1.00 2.50
14 Ilya Sorokin .50 1.25
15 Alex Tuch .30 .75
16 Lucas Raymond .50 1.25
17 Jamie Drysdale .25 .60
18 Evgeny Kuznetsov .40 1.00
19 Artemi Panarin .60 1.50
20 Carter Hart .30 .75
21 Jonathan Huberdeau .40 1.00
22 Brent Burns .30 .75
23 Andrei Kuzmenko .30 .75
24 Mitch Marner .50 1.25
25 Kirill Kaprizov 1.00 2.50
26 Jordan Kyrou .30 .75
27 Nick Suzuki .60 1.50
28 Kirill Marchenko .40 1.00
29 Travis Konecny .30 .75
30 Roope Hintz .40 1.00
31 Cale Makar .75 2.00
32 Ryan Nugent-Hopkins .40 1.00
33 Jack Eichel .50 1.25
34 Quinn Hughes .75 2.00
35 Troy Terry .25 .60
36 Owen Power .40 1.00
37 Cole Perfetti .30 .75
38 Sebastian Aho .50 1.25
39 Anze Kopitar .50 1.25
40 Nikita Kucherov .60 1.50
41 Mathew Barzal .40 1.00
42 Jake Sanderson .40 1.00
43 Johnny Gaudreau .50 1.25
44 Torey Krug .25 .60
45 Darcy Kuemper .30 .75
46 Brady Tkachuk .50 1.25
47 Evan Bouchard .40 1.00
48 Auston Matthews 1.25 3.00
49 Alex Ovechkin 1.25 3.00
50 Nathan MacKinnon 1.25 3.00
51 Jason Robertson .50 1.25
52 Brandon Saad .25 .60
53 Kyle Connor .50 1.25
54 Adam Fox .40 1.00
55 Charlie McAvoy .40 1.00
56 Matty Beniers .40 1.00
57 Mason McTavish .30 .75
58 Robert Thomas .30 .75
59 Andrei Vasilevskiy .50 1.25
60 Jesper Bratt .30 .75
61 Roman Josi .30 .75
62 Jake Oettinger .50 1.25
63 Nazem Kadri .40 1.00
64 Trevor Zegras .30 .75
65 Connor Hellebuyck .60 1.50
66 Sidney Crosby 1.25 3.00
67 Bo Horvat .40 1.00
68 Connor McDavid 1.50 4.00
69 Jared McCann .25 .60
70 Mats Zuccarello .30 .75
71 Dylan Guenther .40 1.00
72 Aleksander Barkov .50 1.25
73 Chandler Stephenson .25 .60
74 Logan Couture .40 1.00
75 Mikey Anderson .25 .60
76 Matthew Tkachuk .60 1.50
77 Seth Jones .30 .75
78 Juuse Saros .40 1.00
79 Tim Stutzle .40 1.00
80 Clayton Keller .40 1.00
81 Josh Morrissey .40 1.00
82 Dawson Mercer .40 1.00
83 Matias Maccelli .25 .60
84 Alex Newhook .25 .60
85 Brayden Point .40 1.00
86 Moritz Seider .40 1.00
87 Joel Eriksson Ek .25 .60
88 Taylor Raddysh .25 .60
89 Tage Thompson .40 1.00
90 Brad Marchand .60 1.50
91 Tomas Hertl .30 .75
92 Jonathan Marchessault .40 1.00
93 Brandon Hagel .25 .60
94 Kevin Fiala .25 .60
95 David Pastrnak .75 2.00
96 Zach Hyman .50 1.25
97 Jack Hughes .75 2.00
98 Philipp Grubauer .30 .75
99 Kent Johnson .30 .75
100 Cole Caufield .60 1.50
101 Will Cuylle RC 1.00 2.50
102 Connor Bedard RC 15.00 40.00
103 Joona Koppanen RC .50 1.25
104 Dustin Wolf RC 2.00 5.00
105 Yaroslav Askarov RC 1.50 4.00
106 Logan Cooley RC 2.00 5.00
107 Cole Guttman RC .60 1.50
108 Danil Gushchin RC .60 1.50
109 Marco Kasper RC 1.50 4.00
110 Adam Fantilli RC 2.00 5.00
111 Jiri Patera RC 1.00 2.50
112 Brock Faber RC 1.50 4.00
113 Nikita Nesterenko RC .60 1.50
114 Leo Carlsson RC 2.00 5.00
115 Zach Benson RC 1.00 2.50
116 Tyson Foerster RC 1.25 3.00
117 Bobby McMann RC 1.00 2.50
118 Walker Duehr RC .50 1.25
119 Jaxson Stauber RC .60 1.50
120 Matthew Poitras RC 1.25 3.00
121 Kevin Korchinski RC 1.00 2.50
122 Matthew Coronato RC 1.00 2.50
123 Simon Nemec RC 1.25 3.00
124 Matthew Kessel RC .50 1.25
125 Aidan McDonough RC .50 1.25
126 Pavel Mintyukov RC 1.00 2.50
127 Matt Murray RC .60 1.50
128 Matt Savoie RC 1.25 3.00
129 Samuel Bolduc RC .60 1.50
130 Leevi Merilainen RC .60 1.50
131 Connor Zary RC 1.25 3.00
132 Tye Kartye RC 1.00 2.50
133 Matthew Knies RC 2.50 6.00
134 Vincent Iorio RC .60 1.50
135 John Beecher RC 1.25 3.00
136 Luke Evangelista RC 1.00 2.50
137 William Dufour RC .50 1.25
138 Isak Rosen RC .60 1.50
139 Luke Hughes RC 2.00 5.00
140 Alex Laferriere RC 1.00 2.50
141 Ridly Greig RC 1.00 2.50
142 Vincent Desharnais RC .75 2.00
143 Sean Farrell RC .60 1.50
144 Devon Levi RC 1.50 4.00
145 Stanislav Svozil RC .50 1.25
146 Akito Hirose RC .50 1.25
147 Simon Edvinsson RC 1.25 3.00
148 Owen Beck RC 1.00 2.50
149 Ryker Evans RC .75 2.00
150 Jonathan Gruden RC .60 1.50

2023-24 Upper Deck Allure Black Rainbow

*BLK RNBW: 1.2X TO 3X BASIC
*BLK RNBW RC: 1X TO 2.5X BASIC
102 Connor Bedard 30.00 80.00

2023-24 Upper Deck Allure Blue Line

*BLUE/35: 8X TO 20X BASIC
*BLUE RC/35: 5X TO 12X BASIC
102 Connor Bedard 500.00 1200.00

2023-24 Upper Deck Allure Confetti

*CONFETTI: 2X TO 5X BASIC
*CONFETTI RC: 1.2X TO 3X BASIC
102 Connor Bedard 125.00 300.00

2023-24 Upper Deck Allure Gold Glitter Bomb

*GOLD/199: 3X TO 8X BASIC
*GOLD RC/199: 2.5X TO 6X BASIC
102 Connor Bedard 200.00 500.00

2023-24 Upper Deck Allure Green Rainbow

*GREEN/99: 4X TO 10X BASIC
*GREEN RC/99: 3X TO 8X BASIC
102 Connor Bedard 200.00 500.00

2023-24 Upper Deck Allure Hypnosis

*HYPNOSIS: 6X TO 15X BASIC
*HYPNOSIS RC: 5X TO 12X BASIC
68 Connor McDavid 60.00 150.00
102 Connor Bedard 400.00 1000.00
114 Leo Carlsson 60.00 150.00
144 Devon Levi 30.00 80.00

2023-24 Upper Deck Allure Orange Slice

*ORANGE: 2X TO 5X BASIC
*ORANGE RC: 1.5X TO 4X BASIC
102 Connor Bedard 60.00 150.00

2023-24 Upper Deck Allure Pink Lemonade

*PINK: 3X TO 8X BASIC
*PINK RC: 4X TO 10X BASIC
102 Connor Bedard 125.00 300.00

2023-24 Upper Deck Allure Red Rainbow

*RED RNBW: 1.5X TO 4X BASIC
*RED RNBW RC: 1.2X TO 3X BASIC
102 Connor Bedard 60.00 150.00

2023-24 Upper Deck Allure Yellow Taxi

*YLW TAXI: 1.5X TO 4X BASIC
*YLW TAXI RC: 1X TO 2.5X BASIC
102 Connor Bedard 60.00 150.00

2023-24 Upper Deck Allure 16 Bit

B1 Brayden Point 50.00 125.00
B2 Cole Caufield 80.00 200.00
B3 Artemi Panarin 80.00 200.00
B4 Alex Ovechkin 200.00 500.00
B5 Connor Bedard 1500.00 4000.00
B6 Connor McDavid 300.00 800.00
B7 Brady Tkachuk 60.00 150.00
B8 Linus Ullmark 60.00 150.00
B9 Tage Thompson 50.00 125.00
B10 Auston Matthews 250.00 600.00
B11 Matthew Tkachuk 80.00 200.00
B12 Erik Karlsson 50.00 125.00
B13 Jason Robertson 60.00 150.00
B14 Nikita Kucherov 80.00 200.00
B15 David Pastrnak 100.00 250.00
B16 Clayton Keller 50.00 125.00
B17 Luke Hughes 150.00 400.00
B18 Mikko Rantanen 100.00 250.00
B19 Matthew Knies 200.00 500.00
B20 Elias Pettersson 60.00 150.00

2023-24 Upper Deck Allure Autographs Red Rainbow

2 Anton Lundell 6.00 15.00
5 Mason Marchment 5.00 12.00
6 Igor Shesterkin SP 12.00 30.00
7 Mikko Rantanen SP 15.00 40.00
8 Blake Coleman 5.00 12.00
9 Elias Pettersson SP 10.00 25.00
10 Juraj Slafkovsky 40.00 100.00
12 Andrei Svechnikov SP 8.00 20.00
13 Leon Draisaitl SP 30.00 80.00
14 Ilya Sorokin SP 10.00 25.00
15 Alex Tuch 6.00 15.00
21 Jonathan Huberdeau 8.00 20.00
22 Brent Burns SP 6.00 15.00
23 Andrei Kuzmenko 6.00 15.00
25 Kirill Kaprizov SP 20.00 50.00
27 Nick Suzuki SP 12.00 30.00
28 Kirill Marchenko 8.00 20.00
29 Travis Konecny SP 6.00 15.00
30 Roope Hintz 8.00 20.00
31 Cale Makar SP 15.00 40.00
32 Ryan Nugent-Hopkins 8.00 20.00
33 Jack Eichel SP 10.00 25.00
34 Quinn Hughes SP 15.00 40.00
36 Owen Power 6.00 15.00
37 Cole Perfetti 6.00 15.00
39 Anze Kopitar SP 10.00 25.00
42 Jake Sanderson 8.00 20.00
45 Darcy Kuemper 6.00 15.00
46 Brady Tkachuk SP 10.00 25.00
47 Evan Bouchard 8.00 20.00
48 Auston Matthews SP 25.00 60.00
49 Alex Ovechkin SP 25.00 60.00
52 Brandon Saad 5.00 12.00
53 Kyle Connor 10.00 25.00
56 Matty Beniers SP 8.00 20.00
57 Mason McTavish 6.00 15.00
58 Robert Thomas 6.00 15.00
59 Andrei Vasilevskiy SP 10.00 25.00
61 Roman Josi 6.00 15.00
62 Jake Oettinger 10.00 25.00
65 Connor Hellebuyck 12.00 30.00
66 Sidney Crosby SP 25.00 60.00
68 Connor McDavid SP 30.00 80.00
69 Jared McCann 5.00 12.00
70 Mats Zuccarello 6.00 15.00
71 Dylan Guenther 8.00 20.00
72 Aleksander Barkov 10.00 25.00
73 Chandler Stephenson 5.00 12.00
75 Mikey Anderson 5.00 12.00
76 Matthew Tkachuk SP 12.00 30.00
78 Juuse Saros 8.00 20.00
79 Tim Stutzle SP 8.00 20.00
81 Josh Morrissey 8.00 20.00
82 Dawson Mercer 8.00 20.00
83 Matias Maccelli 5.00 12.00
87 Joel Eriksson Ek 5.00 12.00
88 Taylor Raddysh 5.00 12.00
90 Brad Marchand SP 12.00 30.00
91 Tomas Hertl 6.00 15.00
92 Jonathan Marchessault 8.00 20.00
94 Kevin Fiala 5.00 12.00
96 Zach Hyman 10.00 25.00
97 Jack Hughes SP 50.00 125.00
98 Philipp Grubauer 6.00 15.00
99 Kent Johnson 6.00 15.00
101 Will Cuylle 10.00 25.00
102 Connor Bedard SP 500.00 1200.00
103 Joona Koppanen 5.00 12.00
104 Dustin Wolf SP 25.00 60.00
105 Yaroslav Askarov SP 15.00 40.00
106 Logan Cooley SP 60.00 150.00
107 Cole Guttman SP 6.00 15.00
108 Danil Gushchin 6.00 15.00
109 Marco Kasper 15.00 40.00
110 Adam Fantilli SP 50.00 125.00
111 Jiri Patera 10.00 25.00
112 Brock Faber 30.00 80.00
113 Nikita Nesterenko 6.00 15.00
114 Leo Carlsson SP 80.00 200.00
115 Zach Benson 25.00 60.00
116 Tyson Foerster 25.00 60.00
117 Bobby McMann 12.00 30.00
118 Walker Duehr 5.00 12.00
119 Jaxson Stauber 6.00 15.00
120 Matthew Poitras 40.00 100.00
121 Kevin Korchinski 10.00 25.00
122 Matthew Coronato SP 10.00 25.00
123 Simon Nemec 12.00 30.00
124 Matthew Kessel 5.00 12.00
125 Aidan McDonough 5.00 12.00
126 Pavel Mintyukov 10.00 25.00
127 Matt Murray 6.00 15.00
128 Matt Savoie SP 20.00 50.00
129 Samuel Bolduc 6.00 15.00
130 Leevi Merilainen 6.00 15.00
131 Connor Zary 12.00 30.00
132 Tye Kartye 10.00 25.00
133 Matthew Knies SP 25.00 60.00
134 Vincent Iorio 6.00 15.00
135 John Beecher 12.00 30.00
136 Luke Evangelista SP 10.00 25.00
137 William Dufour 5.00 12.00
138 Isak Rosen 6.00 15.00
139 Luke Hughes SP 50.00 125.00
140 Alex Laferriere 10.00 25.00
141 Ridly Greig 10.00 25.00
142 Vincent Desharnais 8.00 20.00
143 Sean Farrell SP 6.00 15.00
144 Devon Levi SP 15.00 40.00
145 Stanislav Svozil 5.00 12.00
146 Akito Hirose 5.00 12.00
147 Simon Edvinsson SP 12.00 30.00
148 Owen Beck 10.00 25.00
149 Ryker Evans 8.00 20.00
150 Jonathan Gruden 6.00 15.00

2023-24 Upper Deck Allure Autographs Blue Line

*BLUE/35: 1X TO 2.5X BASIC
48 Auston Matthews 100.00 250.00
49 Alex Ovechkin 200.00 500.00
66 Sidney Crosby 150.00 400.00
68 Connor McDavid 250.00 600.00
102 Connor Bedard 1000.00 2500.00

2023-24 Upper Deck Allure Bar Down

BD1 Teuvo Teravainen 1.00 2.50
BD2 Tage Thompson 1.25 3.00
BD3 Jared McCann .75 2.00
BD4 Andrei Svechnikov 1.25 3.00
BD5 Connor McDavid 5.00 12.00
BD6 Aleksander Barkov 1.50 4.00
BD7 Jack Hughes 2.50 6.00
BD8 Kirill Marchenko 1.25 3.00
BD9 Andrei Kuzmenko 1.25 3.00
BD10 Connor Bedard 10.00 25.00

2023-24 Upper Deck Allure Bar Down Green

*ORANGE/249: .6X TO 1.5X BASIC
BD10 Connor Bedard 60.00 150.00

2023-24 Upper Deck Allure Bar Down Orange

*ORANGE/399: .5X TO 1.2X BASIC
BD10 Connor Bedard 50.00 125.00

2023-24 Upper Deck Allure Bar Down Red

*RED/99: .8X TO 2X BASIC
BD10 Connor Bedard 80.00 200.00

2023-24 Upper Deck Allure Color Flow Red Orange

*ORNG-YLW: .5X TO 1.2X BASIC
*YLW-GRN: .6X TO 1.5X BASIC
CF1 Connor McDavid 2.50 6.00
CF2 Matthew Knies 2.00 5.00
CF3 Arber Xhekaj .50 1.25
CF4 Juuse Saros .60 1.50
CF5 Adam Fantilli 1.50 4.00
CF6 Andrei Svechnikov .60 1.50
CF7 Bryan Rust .50 1.25
CF8 Andrei Kuzmenko .50 1.25
CF9 Alex Tuch .50 1.25
CF10 Alexis Lafreniere .75 2.00
CF11 Shane Wright .60 1.50
CF12 James van Riemsdyk .40 1.00
CF13 Cole Perfetti .50 1.25
CF14 Wyatt Johnston 1.00 2.50
CF15 Cam Atkinson .50 1.25
CF16 Connor Bedard 15.00 40.00
CF17 Elmer Soderblom .50 1.25
CF18 Sidney Crosby 2.00 5.00
CF19 Kirill Marchenko .60 1.50
CF20 Brad Marchand 1.00 2.50
CF21 Chandler Stephenson .40 1.00
CF22 Jake Sanderson .60 1.50
CF23 Gabe Vilardi .50 1.25
CF24 Auston Matthews 2.00 5.00
CF25 Matias Maccelli .40 1.00
CF26 Leon Draisaitl 1.50 4.00
CF27 Mason Marchment .40 1.00
CF28 Luke Hughes 1.50 4.00
CF29 Ilya Sorokin .75 2.00
CF30 Brandon Saad .40 1.00
CF31 Jeremy Swayman .75 2.00
CF32 Tyson Foerster 1.00 2.50
CF33 Brent Burns .50 1.25
CF34 Stanley Cup 10.00 25.00

2023-24 Upper Deck Allure Color Flow Blue Purple

*BLU-PRPL: 1X TO 2.5X BASIC
CF16 Connor Bedard 150.00 400.00
CF34 Stanley Cup 40.00 100.00

2023-24 Upper Deck Allure Color Flow Blue Purple Spectrum

*BLU-PRPL SPEC: 5X TO 12X BASIC
CF1 Connor McDavid/25 80.00 200.00
CF2 Matthew Knies/25 30.00 80.00
CF18 Sidney Crosby/25 40.00 100.00
CF24 Auston Matthews/25 30.00 80.00

2023-24 Upper Deck Allure Color Flow Green Blue

*GRN-BLU: .8X TO 2X BASIC
CF16 Connor Bedard 60.00 150.00

2023-24 Upper Deck Allure Color Flow Green Blue Spectrum

*GRN-BLU SPEC: 4X TO 10X BASIC
CF1 Connor McDavid 60.00 150.00
CF16 Connor Bedard 250.00 600.00
CF28 Luke Hughes 30.00 80.00

2023-24 Upper Deck Allure Color Flow Orange Yellow Spectrum
*ORNG-YLW SPEC: 1.5X TO 4X BASIC
CF16 Connor Bedard 100.00 250.00

2023-24 Upper Deck Allure Color Flow Red Orange Spectrum
*RED-ORNG SPEC: 1.2X TO 3X BASIC
CF16 Connor Bedard/299 80.00 200.00

2023-24 Upper Deck Allure Color Flow Yellow Green Spectrum
*YLW-GRN SPEC: 2X TO 5X BASIC
CF1 Connor McDavid/99 25.00 60.00
CF16 Connor Bedard/99 150.00 400.00
CF34 Stanley Cup/50 100.00 250.00

2023-24 Upper Deck Allure Color Flow Autographs Full Rainbow
CFAAF Adam Fantilli SP 80.00 200.00
CFAAL Anton Lundell 8.00 20.00
CFAAV Andrei Vasilevskiy SP 12.00 30.00
CFABC Blake Coleman 6.00 15.00
CFABG Brendan Gallagher 8.00 20.00
CFABS Braden Schneider 6.00 15.00
CFACB Connor Bedard SP 600.00 1500.00
CFACH Connor Hellebuyck 15.00 40.00
CFACS Chandler Stephenson 6.00 15.00
CFADB Drake Batherson 8.00 20.00
CFADW Dustin Wolf SP 25.00 60.00
CFAFG Filip Gustavsson 8.00 20.00
CFAFZ Fabian Zetterlund 5.00 12.00
CFAGV Gabe Vilardi SP 8.00 20.00
CFAJC Jalen Chatfield 5.00 12.00
CFAJM John Marino 8.00 20.00
CFAJP Jeff Petry 8.00 20.00
CFAKD Kirby Dach 8.00 20.00
CFALC Logan Cooley SP 40.00 100.00
CFALE Luke Evangelista SP 12.00 30.00
CFALH Luke Hughes SP 40.00 100.00
CFAMB Michael Bunting 8.00 20.00
CFAMC Jared McCann 6.00 15.00
CFAMF Mario Ferraro 5.00 12.00
CFAMH Miro Heiskanen 10.00 25.00
CFAMK Matthew Knies SP 30.00 80.00
CFAMM Mason Marchment 6.00 15.00
CFAMO Josh Morrissey 10.00 25.00
CFAND Noah Dobson 10.00 25.00
CFANE Nikolaj Ehlers 8.00 20.00
CFANH Nico Hischier 12.00 30.00
CFAPA Juuso Parssinen 5.00 12.00
CFAPG Philipp Grubauer 8.00 20.00
CFARF Robby Fabbri 5.00 12.00
CFARK Rasmus Kupari 5.00 12.00
CFARN Ryan Nugent-Hopkins SP 10.00 25.00
CFARO Ryan O'Reilly 8.00 20.00
CFASA Brandon Saad 6.00 15.00
CFASE Simon Edvinsson SP 15.00 40.00
CFASK Spencer Knight 8.00 20.00
CFASM Sonny Milano 6.00 15.00
CFASR Sam Reinhart 15.00 40.00
CFAST Shea Theodore 10.00 25.00
CFATF Tyson Foerster SP 20.00 50.00
CFATJ Tanner Jeannot 5.00 12.00
CFATM Timo Meier 8.00 20.00
CFATR Taylor Raddysh 6.00 15.00
CFAYS Yegor Sharangovich 8.00 20.00
CFAZH Zach Hyman 12.00 30.00

2023-24 Upper Deck Allure Color Flow Stanley Cup Autographs Full Rainbow
CFSCJL John LeClair 60.00 150.00
CFSCRO Ryan O'Reilly 30.00 80.00
CFSCWG Wayne Gretzky SP 500.00 1200.00

2023-24 Upper Deck Allure Doubloons
DB1 Brayden Point 15.00 40.00
DB2 Jake Oettinger 20.00 50.00
DB3 Leo Carlsson 80.00 200.00
DB4 Igor Shesterkin 25.00 60.00
DB5 Zach Benson 20.00 50.00
DB6 Pierre-Luc Dubois 10.00 25.00
DB7 Dominik Hasek 20.00 50.00
DB8 Matthew Tkachuk 25.00 60.00
DB9 Ridly Greig 20.00 50.00
DB10 Travis Konecny 12.00 30.00
DB11 Jakob Pelletier 15.00 40.00
DB12 David Pastrnak 30.00 80.00
DB13 Nikita Kucherov 25.00 60.00
DB14 Kevin Korchinski 20.00 50.00
DB15 Nick Suzuki 25.00 60.00
DB16 William Dufour 10.00 25.00
DB17 Sidney Crosby 60.00 150.00
DB18 Alex Ovechkin 50.00 125.00
DB19 Steve Yzerman 30.00 80.00
DB20 Elias Lindholm 12.00 30.00
DB21 Danil Gushchin 12.00 30.00
DB22 Matty Beniers 15.00 40.00
DB23 Bobby McMann 20.00 50.00
DB24 Elias Pettersson 20.00 50.00
DB25 Luke Evangelista 20.00 50.00
DB26 Ilya Sorokin 20.00 50.00
DB27 Teemu Selanne 25.00 60.00
DB28 Kyle Connor 20.00 50.00
DB29 Sean Farrell 12.00 30.00
DB30 Dylan Strome 15.00 40.00
DB31 Walker Duehr 10.00 25.00
DB32 Matt Boldy 20.00 50.00
DB33 Simon Nemec 25.00 60.00
DB34 Jason Robertson 20.00 50.00
DB35 Luke Hughes 40.00 100.00
DB36 Filip Forsberg 20.00 50.00
DB37 Marian Hossa 12.00 30.00
DB38 Jack Eichel 20.00 50.00
DB39 Connor Bedard 500.00 1200.00
DB40 Cole Caufield 25.00 60.00
DB41 Kirill Kaprizov 40.00 100.00
DB42 Dustin Wolf 40.00 100.00
DB43 Cale Makar 30.00 80.00
DB44 Matthew Poitras 25.00 60.00
DB45 Aleksander Barkov 20.00 50.00
DB46 Yaroslav Askarov 30.00 80.00
DB47 Erik Karlsson 15.00 40.00
DB48 Tyson Foerster 25.00 60.00
DB49 Brady Tkachuk 20.00 50.00
DB50 Alex Delvecchio 12.00 30.00
DB51 Trevor Zegras 12.00 30.00
DB52 Matthew Coronato 20.00 50.00
DB53 Mitch Marner 20.00 50.00
DB54 Devon Levi 30.00 80.00
DB55 Dylan Larkin 15.00 40.00
DB56 Adam Fantilli 40.00 100.00
DB57 Connor Hellebuyck 25.00 60.00
DB58 Peter Stastny 10.00 25.00
DB59 Brad Marchand 25.00 60.00
DB60 Jordan Kyrou 12.00 30.00
DB61 Jackson LaCombe 12.00 30.00
DB62 Tim Stutzle 15.00 40.00
DB63 Matthew Knies 50.00 125.00
DB64 Nico Hischier 20.00 50.00
DB65 Tyler Kleven 12.00 30.00
DB66 Andrei Kuzmenko 12.00 30.00
DB67 Martin Necas 20.00 50.00
DB68 Connor Zary 25.00 60.00
DB69 Connor McDavid 80.00 200.00
DB70 Robert Thomas 12.00 30.00
DB71 Simon Edvinsson 25.00 60.00
DB72 Tage Thompson 15.00 40.00
DB73 Marco Kasper 30.00 80.00
DB74 Artemi Panarin 25.00 60.00
DB75 Quinn Hughes 20.00 50.00
DB76 Brock Faber 60.00 150.00
DB77 Andrei Svechnikov 15.00 40.00
DB78 Leevi Merilainen 12.00 30.00
DB79 Bo Horvat 15.00 40.00
DB80 Gordie Howe 80.00 200.00
DB81 Nathan MacKinnon 25.00 60.00
DB82 Stanislav Svozil 10.00 25.00
DB83 Anze Kopitar 20.00 50.00
DB84 Samuel Bolduc 12.00 30.00
DB85 Jonathan Marchessault 15.00 40.00
DB86 Mats Sundin 12.00 30.00
DB87 Logan Couture 15.00 40.00
DB88 Will Cuylle 20.00 50.00
DB89 Jack Hughes 30.00 80.00
DB90 Jared McCann 10.00 25.00
DB91 Owen Beck 20.00 50.00
DB92 Clayton Keller 15.00 40.00
DB94 Johnny Gaudreau 20.00 50.00
DB95 Leon Draisaitl 40.00 100.00
DB96 Tye Kartye 20.00 50.00
DB97 Wyatt Johnston 25.00 60.00
DB98 Logan Cooley 80.00 200.00
DB99 Auston Matthews 80.00 200.00
DB100 Rogie Vachon 12.00 30.00

2023-24 Upper Deck Allure Golden Goalies
*ORANGE/399: .8X TO 2X BASIC
*GREEN/249: 1X TO 2.5X BASIC
*RED/99: 1.5X TO 4X BASIC
GG1 Jonathan Quick 1.25 3.00
GG2 Dan Vladar .75 2.00
GG3 Juuse Saros 1.25 3.00
GG4 Spencer Knight 1.00 2.50
GG5 Ilya Sorokin 1.50 4.00
GG6 Darcy Kuemper 1.00 2.50
GG7 Filip Gustavsson 1.00 2.50
GG8 Alex Nedeljkovic .75 2.00
GG9 Marc-Andre Fleury 2.00 5.00
GG10 Connor Hellebuyck 2.00 5.00
GG11 Andrei Vasilevskiy 1.50 4.00
GG12 Jeremy Swayman 1.50 4.00
GG13 Logan Thompson 1.25 3.00
GG14 Philipp Grubauer 1.00 2.50
GG15 Petr Mrazek .75 2.00

2023-24 Upper Deck Allure Golden Goalies Autographs
GG1 Jonathan Quick 10.00 25.00
GG2 Dan Vladar 6.00 15.00
GG3 Juuse Saros 10.00 25.00
GG4 Spencer Knight 8.00 20.00
GG5 Ilya Sorokin 12.00 30.00
GG6 Darcy Kuemper 8.00 20.00
GG7 Filip Gustavsson 8.00 20.00
GG9 Marc-Andre Fleury SP 15.00 40.00
GG10 Connor Hellebuyck 15.00 40.00
GG11 Andrei Vasilevskiy SP 12.00 30.00
GG12 Jeremy Swayman 12.00 30.00
GG13 Logan Thompson 10.00 25.00
GG14 Philipp Grubauer 8.00 20.00
GG15 Petr Mrazek 6.00 15.00

2023-24 Upper Deck Allure Iced Breakaway
IB1 Shane Wright 1.25 3.00
IB2 Tyson Foerster 2.00 5.00
IB3 Auston Matthews 4.00 10.00
IB4 Anton Lundell 1.00 2.50
IB5 Connor Bedard 8.00 20.00
IB6 Bowen Byram 1.25 3.00
IB7 Arthur Kaliyev 1.00 2.50
IB8 Drake Batherson 1.00 2.50
IB9 Adam Fantilli 3.00 8.00
IB11 Matthew Coronato 1.50 4.00
IB12 Shane Pinto .75 2.00
IB13 Colton Parayko .75 2.00
IB14 William Dufour .75 2.00
IB15 Evgenii Dadonov .60 1.50
IB16 Dylan Guenther 1.25 3.00
IB17 Morgan Barron .60 1.50
IB18 Taylor Raddysh .75 2.00
IB19 Juraj Slafkovsky 2.00 5.00
IB20 Ridly Greig 1.50 4.00
IB21 Peyton Krebs .75 2.00
IB22 Logan Cooley 3.00 8.00
IB23 Joe Veleno .75 2.00
IB24 Matthew Knies 4.00 10.00
IB25 Cole Perfetti 1.00 2.50

2023-24 Upper Deck Allure Iced Breakaway Green
*GREEN/249: 1X TO 2.5X BASIC
IB5 Connor Bedard 60.00 150.00

2023-24 Upper Deck Allure Iced Breakaway Orange
*ORANGE/399: .8X TO 2X BASIC
IB5 Connor Bedard 40.00 100.00

2023-24 Upper Deck Allure Iced Breakaway Red
*RED/99: 1.2X TO 3X BASIC
IB3 Auston Matthews 25.00 60.00
IB5 Connor Bedard 125.00 300.00
IB22 Logan Cooley 25.00 60.00

2023-24 Upper Deck Allure Iced Breakaway Autographs
IB1 Shane Wright 12.00 30.00
IB2 Tyson Foerster 20.00 50.00
IB4 Anton Lundell 10.00 25.00
IB7 Arthur Kaliyev 10.00 25.00
IB9 Adam Fantilli SP 30.00 80.00
IB10 Kirby Dach 10.00 25.00
IB11 Matthew Coronato 15.00 40.00
IB12 Shane Pinto 8.00 20.00
IB13 Colton Parayko 8.00 20.00
IB14 William Dufour 8.00 20.00
IB15 Evgenii Dadonov 6.00 15.00
IB16 Dylan Guenther 12.00 30.00
IB18 Taylor Raddysh 8.00 20.00
IB19 Juraj Slafkovsky SP 20.00 50.00
IB20 Ridly Greig 15.00 40.00
IB21 Peyton Krebs 8.00 20.00
IB22 Logan Cooley SP 30.00 80.00
IB23 Joe Veleno 8.00 20.00
IB24 Matthew Knies SP 40.00 100.00
IB25 Cole Perfetti 10.00 25.00

2023-24 Upper Deck Allure Jersey Autographs Blue Line
2 Anton Lundell/25 12.00 30.00
3 Dylan Larkin/25 15.00 40.00
6 Igor Shesterkin/25 25.00 60.00
7 Mikko Rantanen/25 30.00 80.00
8 Blake Coleman/25 10.00 25.00
9 Elias Pettersson/25 20.00 50.00
10 Juraj Slafkovsky/25 25.00 60.00
11 Tristan Jarry/25 12.00 30.00
12 Andrei Svechnikov/25 15.00 40.00
13 Leon Draisaitl/25 60.00 150.00
14 Ilya Sorokin/25 20.00 50.00
15 Alex Tuch/25 12.00 30.00
21 Jonathan Huberdeau/25 15.00 40.00
22 Brent Burns/25 12.00 30.00
23 Andrei Kuzmenko/25 12.00 30.00
24 Mitch Marner/25 20.00 50.00
25 Kirill Kaprizov/25 40.00 100.00
27 Nick Suzuki/25 25.00 60.00
28 Kirill Marchenko/25 15.00 40.00
29 Travis Konecny/25 12.00 30.00
30 Roope Hintz/25 15.00 40.00
31 Cale Makar/25 80.00 200.00
32 Ryan Nugent-Hopkins/25 15.00 40.00
33 Jack Eichel/25 20.00 50.00
34 Quinn Hughes/25 30.00 80.00
36 Owen Power/25 12.00 30.00
37 Cole Perfetti/25 12.00 30.00
39 Anze Kopitar/25 20.00 50.00
42 Jake Sanderson/25 15.00 40.00
43 Johnny Gaudreau/25 20.00 50.00
44 Torey Krug/25 10.00 25.00
45 Darcy Kuemper/25 12.00 30.00
46 Brady Tkachuk/25 20.00 50.00
48 Auston Matthews/25 125.00 300.00
49 Alex Ovechkin/25 125.00 300.00
52 Brandon Saad/25 10.00 25.00
53 Kyle Connor/25 20.00 50.00
54 Adam Fox/25 15.00 40.00
56 Matty Beniers/25 15.00 40.00
57 Mason McTavish/25 12.00 30.00
58 Robert Thomas/25 12.00 30.00
59 Andrei Vasilevskiy/25 20.00 50.00
61 Roman Josi/25 12.00 30.00
62 Jake Oettinger/25 20.00 50.00
65 Connor Hellebuyck/25 25.00 60.00
66 Sidney Crosby/25 125.00 300.00
68 Connor McDavid/25 250.00 600.00
69 Jared McCann/25 10.00 25.00
71 Dylan Guenther/25 15.00 40.00
72 Aleksander Barkov/25 20.00 50.00
73 Chandler Stephenson/25 10.00 25.00
76 Matthew Tkachuk/25 25.00 60.00
78 Juuse Saros/25 15.00 40.00
79 Tim Stutzle/25 15.00 40.00
80 Clayton Keller/25 15.00 40.00
81 Josh Morrissey/25 15.00 40.00
82 Dawson Mercer/25 15.00 40.00
83 Matias Maccelli/25 10.00 25.00
84 Alex Newhook/25 10.00 25.00
87 Joel Eriksson Ek/25 10.00 25.00
88 Taylor Raddysh/25 10.00 25.00
90 Brad Marchand/25 25.00 60.00
91 Tomas Hertl/25 12.00 30.00
92 Jonathan Marchessault/25 15.00 40.00
94 Kevin Fiala/25 10.00 25.00
96 Zach Hyman/25 20.00 50.00
97 Jack Hughes/25 80.00 200.00
98 Philipp Grubauer/25 12.00 30.00
99 Kent Johnson/25 12.00 30.00
101 Will Cuylle/75 20.00 50.00
103 Joona Koppanen/75 10.00 25.00
104 Dustin Wolf/75 40.00 100.00
105 Yaroslav Askarov/75 30.00 80.00
106 Logan Cooley/35 60.00 150.00
107 Cole Guttman/75 12.00 30.00
108 Danil Gushchin/75 12.00 30.00
109 Marco Kasper/75 30.00 80.00
110 Adam Fantilli/35 80.00 200.00
111 Jiri Patera/75 20.00 50.00
112 Brock Faber/35 80.00 200.00
113 Nikita Nesterenko/75 12.00 30.00
114 Leo Carlsson/35 80.00 200.00
115 Zach Benson/35 20.00 50.00
116 Tyson Foerster/35 25.00 60.00
117 Bobby McMann/75 20.00 50.00
118 Walker Duehr/75 10.00 25.00
119 Jaxson Stauber/75 12.00 30.00
120 Matthew Poitras/75 25.00 60.00
121 Kevin Korchinski/75 20.00 50.00
122 Matthew Coronato/75 20.00 50.00
123 Simon Nemec/75 25.00 60.00
124 Matthew Kessel/75 10.00 25.00
125 Aidan McDonough/75 10.00 25.00
126 Pavel Mintyukov/75 20.00 50.00
127 Matt Murray/75 12.00 30.00
128 Matt Savoie/75 25.00 60.00
129 Samuel Bolduc/75 12.00 30.00
130 Leevi Merilainen/75 12.00 30.00
131 Connor Zary/75 25.00 60.00
132 Tye Kartye/75 20.00 50.00
133 Matthew Knies/35 125.00 300.00
134 Vincent Iorio/75 12.00 30.00
135 John Beecher/75 25.00 60.00
136 Luke Evangelista/75 20.00 50.00
137 William Dufour/75 10.00 25.00
138 Isak Rosen/75 12.00 30.00
139 Luke Hughes/35 80.00 200.00
140 Alex Laferriere/75 20.00 50.00
141 Ridly Greig/75 20.00 50.00
142 Vincent Desharnais/75 15.00 40.00
143 Sean Farrell/75 12.00 30.00
144 Devon Levi/75 30.00 80.00
145 Stanislav Svozil/75 10.00 25.00
146 Akito Hirose/75 10.00 25.00
147 Simon Edvinsson/35 25.00 60.00
148 Owen Beck/75 20.00 50.00
149 Ryker Evans/75 15.00 40.00
150 Jonathan Gruden/75 12.00 30.00

2023-24 Upper Deck Allure Lumber Masters
*ORANGE/399: .6X TO 1.5X BASIC
*GREEN/249: 1X TO 2.5X BASIC
*RED/99: 1.2X TO 3X BASIC
LM1 Matthew Coronato 1.50 4.00
LM2 Mikko Rantanen 2.50 6.00
LM3 Ryan Nugent-Hopkins 1.25 3.00
LM4 Timo Meier 1.00 2.50
LM5 Alex Tuch 1.00 2.50
LM6 Brandon Saad .75 2.00
LM7 Matty Beniers 1.25 3.00
LM8 Bo Horvat 1.25 3.00
LM9 Kent Johnson 1.00 2.50
LM10 Leon Draisaitl 3.00 8.00
LM11 Marco Kasper 2.50 6.00
LM12 Nico Hischier 1.50 4.00
LM13 Nick Suzuki 2.00 5.00
LM14 Wyatt Johnston 2.00 5.00
LM15 Connor McDavid 5.00 12.00
LM16 Bryan Rust 1.00 2.50
LM17 Tim Stutzle 1.25 3.00
LM18 Brandon Hagel .75 2.00
LM19 Matthew Knies 4.00 10.00
LM20 Nikolaj Ehlers 1.00 2.50

2023-24 Upper Deck Allure Lumber Masters Autographs
LM1 Matthew Coronato 12.00 30.00
LM2 Mikko Rantanen SP 20.00 50.00
LM4 Timo Meier 8.00 20.00
LM5 Alex Tuch 8.00 20.00
LM9 Kent Johnson 8.00 20.00
LM11 Marco Kasper 20.00 50.00
LM12 Nico Hischier 12.00 30.00
LM13 Nick Suzuki SP 15.00 40.00
LM14 Wyatt Johnston 40.00 100.00
LM17 Tim Stutzle SP 10.00 25.00
LM19 Matthew Knies SP 30.00 80.00
LM20 Nikolaj Ehlers 8.00 20.00

2023-24 Upper Deck Allure Polished Pros
*ORANGE/399: .6X TO 1.5X BASIC
*GREEN/249: 1X TO 2.5X BASIC
*RED/99: 1.2X TO 3X BASIC
PP1 Cale Makar 2.50 6.00
PP2 Mason Marchment .75 2.00
PP3 Zach Werenski 1.50 4.00
PP4 Evan Bouchard 1.25 3.00
PP5 Mario Ferraro .60 1.50
PP6 K'Andre Miller .75 2.00
PP7 Mikey Anderson .75 2.00
PP8 Alex Ovechkin 4.00 10.00
PP9 Cam Atkinson 1.00 2.50
PP10 Ross Colton .75 2.00
PP11 Jordan Eberle 1.00 2.50
PP12 Brendan Gallagher 1.00 2.50
PP13 Sonny Milano .75 2.00
PP14 David Perron .75 2.00
PP15 Blake Coleman .75 2.00
PP16 Alex Iafallo .60 1.50
PP17 John Marino 1.00 2.50
PP18 Roope Hintz 1.25 3.00
PP19 Evgeny Kuznetsov 1.25 3.00
PP20 Oskar Lindblom .75 2.00
PP21 Anze Kopitar 1.50 4.00
PP22 Brent Burns 1.00 2.50
PP23 Dylan Cozens 1.00 2.50
PP24 Alex Newhook .75 2.00
PP25 Brad Marchand 2.00 5.00
PP26 Travis Sanheim .60 1.50
PP27 Nick Schmaltz .75 2.00
PP28 Zach Hyman 1.50 4.00
PP29 Max Pacioretty 1.00 2.50
PP30 Yegor Sharangovich 1.00 2.50

2023-24 Upper Deck Allure Polished Pros Autographs
PP1 Cale Makar SP 20.00 50.00
PP2 Mason Marchment 6.00 15.00
PP3 Zach Werenski 12.00 30.00
PP4 Evan Bouchard 10.00 25.00
PP5 Mario Ferraro 5.00 12.00
PP6 K'Andre Miller 6.00 15.00
PP7 Mikey Anderson 6.00 15.00
PP10 Ross Colton 6.00 15.00
PP11 Jordan Eberle 8.00 20.00
PP12 Brendan Gallagher 8.00 20.00
PP13 Sonny Milano 6.00 15.00
PP14 David Perron 6.00 15.00
PP15 Blake Coleman 6.00 15.00
PP16 Alex Iafallo 5.00 12.00
PP17 John Marino 8.00 20.00
PP18 Roope Hintz 10.00 25.00
PP20 Tyler Bertuzzi SP 20.00 50.00
PP21 Anze Kopitar SP 12.00 30.00
PP22 Brent Burns SP 8.00 20.00
PP23 Dylan Cozens 8.00 20.00
PP25 Brad Marchand SP 15.00 40.00
PP26 Travis Sanheim 5.00 12.00
PP27 Nick Schmaltz 6.00 15.00
PP28 Zach Hyman 12.00 30.00
PP29 Max Pacioretty 8.00 20.00
PP30 Yegor Sharangovich 8.00 20.00

2024-25 Upper Deck Allure
1 Aleksander Barkov .50 1.25
2 Zach Hyman .50 1.25
3 Charlie McAvoy .40 1.00
4 Tage Thompson .40 1.00
5 Timo Meier .30 .75
6 Matty Beniers .40 1.00
7 Morgan Frost .25 .60
8 Cale Makar .75 2.00
9 Nikita Kucherov .60 1.50
10 Casey Mittelstadt .30 .75
11 Trevor Zegras .30 .75
12 Evgeni Malkin .60 1.50
13 Logan Couture .40 1.00
14 Ryan O'Reilly .30 .75
15 Anton Lundell .30 .75
16 Auston Matthews 1.25 3.00
17 Dylan Larkin .40 1.00
18 Travis Konecny .30 .75
19 Thatcher Demko .40 1.00
20 Leon Draisaitl 1.00 2.50
21 Victor Hedman .40 1.00
22 Luke Hughes .50 1.25
23 Tom Wilson .30 .75
24 Brad Marchand .60 1.50
25 Johnny Gaudreau .50 1.25
26 Leo Carlsson .50 1.25
27 Andrei Svechnikov .40 1.00
28 Matt Boldy .50 1.25
29 Nathan MacKinnon 1.25 3.00
30 Tomas Hertl .30 .75
31 Mason McTavish .30 .75
32 John Tavares .50 1.25
33 Roman Josi .30 .75
34 Bowen Byram .40 1.00
35 Igor Shesterkin .60 1.50
36 Brayden Point .40 1.00
37 Rasmus Dahlin .40 1.00
38 Mitch Marner .50 1.25
39 Cole Caufield .60 1.50
40 Ilya Sorokin .50 1.25
41 Jordan Binnington .50 1.25
42 Logan Cooley .50 1.25
43 Connor Hellebuyck .60 1.50
44 Noah Dobson .40 1.00
45 William Nylander .60 1.50
46 Devon Toews .25 .60
47 Quinn Hughes .75 2.00
48 Juuse Saros .40 1.00
49 Tim Stutzle .40 1.00
50 Jack Eichel .50 1.25
51 Nazem Kadri .40 1.00
52 Jack Hughes .75 2.00
53 Alex Ovechkin 1.25 3.00
54 Jason Robertson .50 1.25
55 Kris Letang .40 1.00
56 Nick Suzuki .60 1.50
57 Dylan Cozens .30 .75
58 Robert Thomas .30 .75
59 Alex DeBrincat .40 1.00
60 Artemi Panarin .60 1.50
61 Nikolaj Ehlers .30 .75
62 Clayton Keller .40 1.00
63 Philipp Kurashev .25 .60
64 William Eklund .40 1.00
65 Kirill Kaprizov 1.00 2.50
66 Mikael Granlund .25 .60
67 Sebastian Aho .50 1.25
68 J.T. Miller .40 1.00
69 Kevin Fiala .25 .60
70 Sidney Crosby 1.25 3.00
71 Josh Morrissey .40 1.00
72 Mikko Rantanen .75 2.00
73 Andrei Vasilevskiy .50 1.25
74 Drew Doughty .30 .75
75 Jared McCann .25 .60
76 Jordan Kyrou .30 .75
77 Jonathan Huberdeau .40 1.00
78 Brady Tkachuk .50 1.25
79 John Carlson .30 .75
80 Moritz Seider .40 1.00
81 Jonathan Marchessault .40 1.00
82 Brock Faber .40 1.00
83 Kyle Connor .50 1.25
84 Adam Fantilli .50 1.25
85 Matthew Tkachuk .60 1.50
86 Chris Kreider .40 1.00
87 Matthew Knies .60 1.50
88 David Pastrnak .75 2.00
89 Mats Zuccarello .30 .75
90 Trevor Moore .20 .50
91 Wyatt Johnston .60 1.50
92 Dylan Holloway .30 .75
93 Mark Stone .40 1.00
94 Connor Bedard 1.00 2.50
95 Vince Dunn .25 .60
96 Anze Kopitar .50 1.25
97 Connor McDavid 1.50 4.00
98 Bo Horvat .40 1.00
99 MacKenzie Weegar .25 .60
100 Elias Pettersson .50 1.25
101 Logan Stankoven RC 1.50 4.00
102 Zachary Bolduc RC 1.00 2.50
103 Matt Rempe RC 1.25 3.00
104 Matt Villalta RC .60 1.50
105 Shakir Mukhamadullin RC .75 2.00
106 Olen Zellweger RC 1.25 3.00
107 Brendan Brisson RC .75 2.00
108 Joshua Roy RC 1.00 2.50
109 Phil Kemp RC .60 1.50
110 Maxwell Crozier RC .60 1.50
111 Jesper Wallstedt RC 1.50 4.00
112 Yan Kuznetsov RC .60 1.50
113 Gage Goncalves RC .75 2.00
114 Graeme Clarke RC .60 1.50
115 Lukas Cormier RC .60 1.50
116 Emil Lilleberg RC .60 1.50
117 Vasily Ponomarev RC .60 1.50
118 Jack Thompson RC .60 1.50
119 Brennan Othmann RC 1.00 2.50
120 Mason Morelli RC .60 1.50
121 Liam Ohgren RC 1.25 3.00
122 James Malatesta RC .60 1.50
123 Logan Morrison RC .60 1.50
124 Cameron Crotty RC .60 1.50
125 Jack St. Ivany RC .60 1.50
126 Zach Dean RC .60 1.50
127 Akil Thomas RC .60 1.50
128 Ivan Fedotov RC 1.00 2.50
129 Josh Doan RC 1.00 2.50
130 Cutter Gauthier RC 1.50 4.00
131 Brad Lambert RC .75 2.00
132 Landon Slaggert RC .60 1.50
133 Devin Cooley RC .60 1.50
134 Marat Khusnutdinov RC .60 1.50
135 Zack Ostapchuk RC .60 1.50
136 Gavin Brindley RC .60 1.50
137 Frank Nazar RC 2.00 5.00
138 Bradly Nadeau RC 1.00 2.50
139 Lane Hutson RC 8.00 20.00
140 Ruslan Iskhakov RC .60 1.50
141 Mavrik Bourque RC 1.25 3.00
142 Nikita Chibrikov RC .60 1.50
143 Jackson Blake RC 1.25 3.00
144 Logan Mailloux RC 1.25 3.00
145 Ethan Del Mastro RC .60 1.50
146 Scott Morrow RC .75 2.00
147 Aku Raty RC .60 1.50
148 Luca Del Bel Belluz RC .60 1.50
149 Adam Klapka RC .60 1.50
150 Sam Colangelo RC .60 1.50
ARJL Jonathan Lekkerimaki EXT RC 12.00 30.00
ARMC Macklin Celebrini EXT RC 40.00 100.00
ARMM Matvei Michkov EXT RC 25.00 60.00
ARRM Rutger McGroarty EXT RC 10.00 25.00
ARWS Will Smith EXT RC 15.00 40.00

2024-25 Upper Deck Allure Black Rainbow
*BLACK: 1X TO 2.5X BASIC
*BLACK RC: .8X TO 2X BASIC
*BLACK EXT: .6X TO 1.5X BASIC
ARMC Macklin Celebrini EXT 60.00 150.00
ARMM Matvei Michkov EXT 40.00 100.00
ARWS Will Smith EXT 25.00 60.00

2024-25 Upper Deck Allure Blue Line
*BLUE/35: 8X TO 20X BASIC
*BLUE RC/35: 5X TO 12X BASIC

2024-25 Upper Deck Allure Flying Puck
*PUCK: 3X TO 8X BASIC
*PUCK RC: 2.5X TO 6X BASIC

2024-25 Upper Deck Allure Glitter Bomb
*GLITTER: 1.5X TO 4X BASIC
*GLITTER RC: 1X TO 2.5X BASIC

2024-25 Upper Deck Allure Gold Glitter Bomb
*GOLD GLTR/199: 3X TO 8X BASIC
*GOLD GLTR RC: 2.5X TO 6X BASIC
139 Lane Hutson 60.00 150.00

2024-25 Upper Deck Allure Green Rainbow
*GREEN/99: 4X TO 10X BASIC
*GREEN RC/99: 3X TO 8X BASIC
139 Lane Hutson 80.00 200.00

2024-25 Upper Deck Allure Orange Slice
*ORANGE: 2X TO 5X BASIC
*ORANGE RC: 1.2X TO 3X BASIC

2024-25 Upper Deck Allure Red Rainbow
*RED RNBW: 1.5X TO 4X BASIC
*RED RNBW RC: 1X TO 2.5X BASIC

2024-25 Upper Deck Allure 16-Bit
B1 John Tavares 60.00 150.00
B2 Mason McTavish 40.00 100.00
B3 Brad Marchand 80.00 200.00
B4 Quinn Hughes 100.00 250.00
B5 Dylan Larkin 50.00 125.00
B6 Kyle Connor 60.00 150.00
B7 Mika Zibanejad 50.00 125.00
B8 Jaromir Jagr 125.00 300.00
B9 Evgeni Malkin 80.00 200.00
B10 Brennan Othmann 60.00 150.00
B11 Olen Zellweger 80.00 200.00
B12 Rasmus Dahlin 50.00 125.00
B13 Brendan Brisson 50.00 125.00
B14 Nick Suzuki 80.00 200.00
B15 Jack Eichel 60.00 150.00
B16 Joshua Roy 60.00 150.00

2024-25 Upper Deck Allure Across the Pond
*ORANGE: .5X TO 1.2X BASIC
*GREEN: .6X TO 1.5X BASIC
*BLUE: .6X TO 1.5X BASIC
*PURPLE: 1X TO 2.5X BASIC
*ORANGE SPEC/199: .8X TO 2X BASIC
*GREEN SPEC/99: 1X TO 2.5X BASIC
*BLUE SPEC/50: 1.5X TO 4X BASIC
*PURPLE SPEC/25: 2X TO 5X BASIC
ATP1 David Pastrnak 2.00 5.00
ATP2 Leo Carlsson 1.25 3.00
ATP3 Mikko Rantanen 2.00 5.00
ATP4 Kirill Kaprizov 2.50 6.00
ATP5 Tomas Hertl .75 2.00
ATP6 Aleksander Barkov 1.25 3.00
ATP7 Ukko-Pekka Luukkonen .60 1.50
ATP8 Simon Nemec 1.00 2.50
ATP9 Miro Heiskanen 1.00 2.50
ATP10 Leon Draisaitl 2.50 6.00

2024-25 Upper Deck Allure Across the Pond Autographs
ATP3 Mikko Rantanen 15.00 40.00
ATP4 Kirill Kaprizov SP 20.00 50.00
ATP6 Aleksander Barkov 10.00 25.00
ATP9 Miro Heiskanen 8.00 20.00
ATP10 Leon Draisaitl SP 20.00 50.00

2024-25 Upper Deck Allure Autographs Red Rainbow
*BLUE/35: 1X TO 2.5X BASIC
1 Aleksander Barkov 10.00 25.00
4 Tage Thompson 8.00 20.00
5 Timo Meier 6.00 15.00
6 Matty Beniers 8.00 20.00
7 Morgan Frost 5.00 12.00
8 Cale Makar SP 30.00 80.00
9 Nikita Kucherov SP 12.00 30.00
10 Casey Mittelstadt 6.00 15.00
14 Ryan O'Reilly 6.00 15.00
16 Auston Matthews SP 50.00 125.00
18 Travis Konecny 6.00 15.00
19 Thatcher Demko 8.00 20.00
20 Leon Draisaitl SP 40.00 100.00
22 Luke Hughes 10.00 25.00
23 Tom Wilson 6.00 15.00
27 Andrei Svechnikov 8.00 20.00
28 Matt Boldy 10.00 25.00
29 Nathan MacKinnon SP 50.00 125.00
30 Tomas Hertl 6.00 15.00
32 John Tavares SP 10.00 25.00
33 Roman Josi 6.00 15.00
34 Bowen Byram 8.00 20.00
35 Igor Shesterkin SP 12.00 30.00
38 Mitch Marner SP 10.00 25.00
40 Ilya Sorokin 10.00 25.00
41 Jordan Binnington 10.00 25.00
42 Logan Cooley 12.00 30.00
43 Connor Hellebuyck 12.00 30.00
44 Noah Dobson 8.00 20.00
46 Devon Toews 5.00 12.00
47 Quinn Hughes SP 15.00 40.00
48 Juuse Saros 8.00 20.00
49 Tim Stutzle SP 8.00 20.00
50 Jack Eichel SP 10.00 25.00
55 Kris Letang 8.00 20.00
56 Nick Suzuki SP 12.00 30.00
57 Dylan Cozens 6.00 15.00
58 Robert Thomas 6.00 15.00
64 William Eklund 8.00 20.00
65 Kirill Kaprizov SP 20.00 50.00
66 Mikael Granlund 5.00 12.00
71 Josh Morrissey SP 8.00 20.00
72 Mikko Rantanen SP 15.00 40.00
73 Andrei Vasilevskiy SP 10.00 25.00
75 Jared McCann 5.00 12.00
77 Jonathan Huberdeau 8.00 20.00
78 Brady Tkachuk 10.00 25.00
79 John Carlson 6.00 15.00
81 Jonathan Marchessault 8.00 20.00
85 Matthew Tkachuk SP 12.00 30.00
87 Matthew Knies 12.00 30.00
90 Trevor Moore 4.00 10.00
91 Wyatt Johnston 12.00 30.00
92 Dylan Holloway 6.00 15.00
93 Mark Stone 8.00 20.00
94 Connor Bedard SP 125.00 300.00
95 Vince Dunn 5.00 12.00
96 Anze Kopitar 10.00 25.00
99 MacKenzie Weegar 5.00 12.00
100 Elias Pettersson SP 10.00 25.00
101 Logan Stankoven SP 20.00 50.00
102 Zachary Bolduc 10.00 25.00
103 Matt Rempe 20.00 50.00
104 Matt Villalta 6.00 15.00
105 Shakir Mukhamadullin 8.00 20.00
106 Olen Zellweger 12.00 30.00
107 Brendan Brisson 8.00 20.00
108 Joshua Roy 10.00 25.00
109 Phil Kemp 6.00 15.00
110 Maxwell Crozier 6.00 15.00
111 Jesper Wallstedt 15.00 40.00
112 Yan Kuznetsov 6.00 15.00
113 Gage Goncalves 8.00 20.00
114 Graeme Clarke 6.00 15.00
115 Lukas Cormier 6.00 15.00
116 Emil Lilleberg 6.00 15.00
117 Vasily Ponomarev 6.00 15.00
118 Jack Thompson 6.00 15.00
119 Brennan Othmann 10.00 25.00
120 Mason Morelli 6.00 15.00
121 Liam Ohgren 12.00 30.00
123 Logan Morrison 6.00 15.00
126 Zach Dean 6.00 15.00
127 Akil Thomas 6.00 15.00
128 Ivan Fedotov 10.00 25.00
129 Josh Doan 10.00 25.00
130 Cutter Gauthier SP 20.00 50.00
133 Devin Cooley 6.00 15.00
134 Marat Khusnutdinov 6.00 15.00
135 Zack Ostapchuk 6.00 15.00
137 Frank Nazar 20.00 50.00
138 Bradly Nadeau 10.00 25.00
139 Lane Hutson SP 100.00 250.00
141 Mavrik Bourque 12.00 30.00
142 Nikita Chibrikov 6.00 15.00
143 Jackson Blake 12.00 30.00
144 Logan Mailloux 12.00 30.00
145 Ethan Del Mastro 6.00 15.00
146 Scott Morrow 8.00 20.00
147 Aku Raty 6.00 15.00
149 Adam Klapka 6.00 15.00
150 Sam Colangelo 6.00 15.00
ARJL Jonathan Lekkerimaki EXT 60.00 150.00
ARMC Macklin Celebrini EXT SP 600.00 1500.00
ARRM Rutger McGroarty EXT 60.00 150.00
ARWS Will Smith EXT SP 80.00 200.00

2024-25 Upper Deck Allure Color Flow Autographs Full Rainbow
CFAAF Anton Forsberg 5.00 12.00
CFAAL Alex Laferriere 5.00 12.00
CFAAP Aliaksei Protas 5.00 12.00
CFAAR Alexander Romanov 6.00 15.00
CFAAT Alex Turcotte 5.00 12.00
CFAAV Andrei Vasilevskiy SP 12.00 30.00
CFAAX Arber Xhekaj 8.00 20.00
CFABA Morgan Barron 5.00 12.00
CFABJ Boone Jenner 8.00 20.00
CFABM Bobby McMann 6.00 15.00
CFABN Brock Nelson 8.00 20.00
CFACC Connor Clifton 5.00 12.00
CFACH Jalen Chatfield 5.00 12.00
CFACL Charlie Lindgren 6.00 15.00
CFACM Casey Mittelstadt 8.00 20.00
CFACP Colton Parayko 6.00 15.00
CFACS Cole Sillinger 6.00 15.00
CFACZ Connor Zary 8.00 20.00
CFADA Joey Daccord 8.00 20.00
CFADC Dylan Cozens 8.00 20.00
CFADG Dylan Guenther 10.00 25.00
CFADJ Dakota Joshua 5.00 12.00
CFADM Dawson Mercer 10.00 25.00
CFADS Dylan Samberg 5.00 12.00
CFADT Devon Toews 6.00 15.00
CFAEP Elias Pettersson SP 12.00 30.00
CFAET Eeli Tolvanen 8.00 20.00
CFAFV Frank Vatrano 6.00 15.00
CFAGV Gabe Vilardi 8.00 20.00
CFAHE Tomas Hertl 8.00 20.00

CFAJA Josh Anderson 6.00 15.00
CFAJB Jordan Binnington SP 12.00 30.00
CFAJC J.T. Compher 5.00 12.00
CFAJD Jack Drury 6.00 15.00
CFAJE Joel Eriksson Ek 6.00 15.00
CFAJN Jake Neighbours 8.00 20.00
CFAJQ Jack Quinn 6.00 15.00
CFAJS Jared Spurgeon 8.00 20.00
CFAKK Kirill Kaprizov SP 25.00 60.00
CFAKM Kirill Marchenko 10.00 25.00
CFAKO Kevin Korchinski 6.00 15.00
CFALA Alexis Lafreniere SP 12.00 30.00
CFALC Logan Cooley 15.00 40.00
CFALR Lukas Reichel 8.00 20.00
CFAMB Matty Beniers SP 10.00 25.00
CFAMC Connor McDavid SP 150.00 400.00
CFAMF Morgan Frost 6.00 15.00
CFAMG Morgan Geekie 5.00 12.00
CFAMI Mikael Backlund 6.00 15.00
CFAMK Matthew Knies 15.00 40.00
CFAMM Mason Marchment 6.00 15.00
CFAMP Matthew Poitras 8.00 20.00
CFAMR Petr Mrazek 6.00 15.00
CFANK Nikita Kucherov SP 15.00 40.00
CFANN Nino Niederreiter 6.00 15.00
CFANS Nick Schmaltz 6.00 15.00
CFAPE Cole Perfetti 8.00 20.00
CFAPM Pavel Mintyukov 6.00 15.00
CFAPZ Pavel Zacha 6.00 15.00
CFARG Ridly Greig 6.00 15.00
CFARN Ryan Nugent-Hopkins 10.00 25.00
CFARR Ryan Reaves 6.00 15.00
CFASD Sean Durzi 5.00 12.00
CFASE Simon Edvinsson 8.00 20.00
CFASG Samuel Girard 5.00 12.00
CFASJ Seth Jarvis 10.00 25.00
CFASP Shane Pinto 6.00 15.00
CFASS Stuart Skinner SP 10.00 25.00
CFASW Shane Wright 10.00 25.00
CFATB Thomas Bordeleau 5.00 12.00
CFATE Teuvo Teravainen 8.00 20.00
CFATK Travis Konecny SP 8.00 20.00
CFATN Thomas Novak 5.00 12.00
CFATT Troy Terry 6.00 15.00
CFATU Alex Tuch 8.00 20.00
CFATW Tom Wilson 8.00 20.00
CFAVD Vince Dunn 6.00 15.00
CFAVV Vitek Vanecek 8.00 20.00
CFAWC Will Cuylle 6.00 15.00
CFAWE William Eklund 10.00 25.00
CFAWJ Wyatt Johnston SP 15.00 40.00
CFAWK William Karlsson 10.00 25.00
CFAYS Yegor Sharangovich SP 8.00 20.00

2024-25 Upper Deck Allure Color Flow Red Orange

*ORANGE YLW: .5X TO 1.2X BASIC
*YELLOW GRN: .5X TO 1.2X BASIC
*GREEN BLUE: .6X TO 1.5X BASIC
*BLUE PURPLE: .8X TO 2X BASIC
*SPEC OR-YL/199: 1.5X TO 4X BASIC
*SPEC RD-OR/150: 2X TO 5X BASIC
*SPEC YL-GR/99: 2.5X TO 6X BASIC
CFL1 Adam Fantilli .75 2.00
CFL2 Adam Fox .60 1.50
CFL3 Adrian Kempe .50 1.25
CFL4 Alex DeBrincat .60 1.50
CFL5 Alex Ovechkin 2.00 5.00
CFL6 Dougie Hamilton .40 1.00
CFL7 Andrei Kuzmenko .50 1.25
CFL8 Artemi Panarin 1.00 2.50
CFL9 Auston Matthews 2.00 5.00
CFL10 Brady Tkachuk .75 2.00
CFL11 Brandon Hagel .40 1.00
CFL12 Brayden Point .60 1.50
CFL13 Brent Burns .50 1.25
CFL14 Bryan Rust .50 1.25
CFL15 Cale Makar 1.25 3.00
CFL16 Cole Caufield 1.00 2.50
CFL17 Connor Bedard 1.50 4.00
CFL18 Connor McDavid 2.50 6.00
CFL19 David Pastrnak 1.25 3.00
CFL20 Elias Pettersson .75 2.00
CFL21 Fabian Zetterlund .30 .75
CFL22 Filip Forsberg .75 2.00
CFL23 Jack Hughes 1.25 3.00
CFL24 Joel Eriksson Ek .40 1.00
CFL25 Josh Doan .75 2.00
CFL26 Kirill Kaprizov 1.50 4.00
CFL27 Leon Draisaitl 1.50 4.00
CFL28 Logan Cooley 1.00 2.50
CFL29 Logan Stankoven 1.25 3.00
CFL30 Luke Hughes .75 2.00
CFL31 Marco Rossi .60 1.50
CFL32 Mark Scheifele .60 1.50
CFL33 Mathew Barzal .60 1.50
CFL34 Matthew Tkachuk 1.00 2.50
CFL35 Miro Heiskanen .60 1.50
CFL36 Mitch Marner .75 2.00
CFL37 Morgan Rielly .50 1.25
CFL38 Moritz Seider .60 1.50
CFL39 Nathan MacKinnon 2.00 5.00
CFL40 Nick Suzuki 1.00 2.50
CFL41 Olen Zellweger 1.00 2.50
CFL42 Owen Power .50 1.25
CFL43 Owen Tippett .30 .75
CFL44 Pavel Buchnevich .40 1.00
CFL45 Quinn Hughes 1.25 3.00
CFL46 Quinton Byfield .60 1.50
CFL47 Rasmus Dahlin .60 1.50
CFL48 Roope Hintz .60 1.50
CFL49 Ryan Nugent-Hopkins .60 1.50
CFL50 Seth Jarvis .60 1.50
CFL51 Shakir Mukhamadullin .60 1.50
CFL52 Shane Pinto .40 1.00
CFL53 Shea Theodore .60 1.50
CFL54 Sidney Crosby 2.00 5.00
CFL55 Travis Sanheim .30 .75
CFL56 Trevor Moore .30 .75
CFL57 Troy Terry .40 1.00
CFL58 Vince Dunn .40 1.00
CFL59 William Karlsson .60 1.50
CFL60 Zachary Bolduc .75 2.00

2024-25 Upper Deck Allure Color Flow Spectrum Blue Purple

*SPEC BL-PU/25: 5X TO 12X BASIC
CFL18 Connor McDavid 80.00 200.00

2024-25 Upper Deck Allure Color Flow Spectrum Green Blue

*SPEC GR-BL/50: 3X TO 8X BASIC
CFL18 Connor McDavid 60.00 150.00

2024-25 Upper Deck Allure Colorful Futures

*ORANGE: .5X TO 1.2X BASIC
*GREEN: .6X TO 1.5X BASIC
*BLUE: .8X TO 2X BASIC
*PURPLE: 1X TO 2.5X BASIC
*SPEC ORG/199: 1X TO 2.5X BASIC
*SPEC GRN/99: 1.2X TO 3X BASIC
*SPEC BLUE/50: 1.5X TO 4X BASIC
*SPEC PURP/25: 2X TO 5X BASIC
CF1 Zach Benson .75 2.00
CF2 Marco Rossi 1.25 3.00
CF3 Jake Neighbours 1.00 2.50
CF4 Cole Caufield 2.00 5.00
CF5 Moritz Seider 1.25 3.00
CF6 Tim Stutzle 1.25 3.00
CF7 Adam Fantilli 1.50 4.00
CF8 Brady Tkachuk 1.50 4.00
CF9 Martin Necas 1.25 3.00
CF10 Connor Bedard 3.00 8.00
CF11 Wyatt Johnston 2.00 5.00
CF12 Evan Bouchard 1.25 3.00
CF13 Lucas Raymond 1.50 4.00
CF14 Matt Boldy 1.50 4.00
CF15 Jack Hughes 2.50 6.00
CF16 Trevor Zegras 1.00 2.50
CF17 Connor Zary 1.00 2.50
CF18 Rasmus Dahlin 1.25 3.00

2024-25 Upper Deck Allure Colorful Futures Autographs

CF2 Marco Rossi 10.00 25.00
CF3 Jake Neighbours 8.00 20.00
CF6 Tim Stutzle SP 10.00 25.00
CF8 Brady Tkachuk 12.00 30.00
CF11 Wyatt Johnston 15.00 40.00
CF14 Matt Boldy 12.00 30.00
CF17 Connor Zary 8.00 20.00

2024-25 Upper Deck Allure Doubloons

DB1 Kirill Kaprizov 40.00 100.00
DB2 Cole Caufield 25.00 60.00
DB3 Victor Hedman 15.00 40.00
DB4 Bobby Orr 50.00 125.00
DB5 Jeremy Swayman 20.00 50.00
DB6 Moritz Seider 15.00 40.00
DB7 Brennan Othmann 20.00 50.00
DB8 Alex Ovechkin 80.00 200.00
DB9 Gordie Howe 40.00 100.00
DB10 Artemi Panarin 25.00 60.00
DB11 Matt Boldy 20.00 50.00
DB12 Leon Draisaitl 40.00 100.00
DB13 Mathew Barzal 15.00 40.00
DB14 Mason McTavish 12.00 30.00
DB15 Tomas Hertl 12.00 30.00
DB16 Jason Robertson 20.00 50.00
DB17 Jesper Wallstedt 30.00 80.00
DB18 William Nylander 25.00 60.00
DB19 Joe Thornton 20.00 50.00
DB20 Sebastian Aho 20.00 50.00
DB21 Nazem Kadri 15.00 40.00
DB22 Sam Reinhart 25.00 60.00
DB23 Sergei Bobrovsky 20.00 50.00
DB24 Alexis Lafreniere 20.00 50.00
DB25 Owen Power 12.00 30.00
DB26 Matthew Knies 25.00 60.00
DB27 Jean Beliveau 12.00 30.00
DB28 Cutter Gauthier 30.00 80.00
DB29 Nathan MacKinnon 50.00 125.00
DB30 Matty Beniers 15.00 40.00
DB31 Brady Tkachuk 20.00 50.00
DB32 Luke Hughes 20.00 50.00
DB33 Zach Hyman 20.00 50.00
DB34 Auston Matthews 50.00 125.00
DB35 Pekka Rinne 12.00 30.00
DB36 Quinn Hughes 30.00 80.00
DB37 Erik Karlsson 15.00 40.00
DB38 Alex Tuch 12.00 30.00
DB39 Shea Theodore 15.00 40.00
DB40 Lane Hutson 150.00 400.00
DB41 Marian Hossa 12.00 30.00
DB42 Adam Fantilli 20.00 50.00
DB43 Jordan Kyrou 12.00 30.00
DB44 Tim Stutzle 15.00 40.00
DB45 Liam Ohgren 25.00 60.00
DB46 Wyatt Johnston 25.00 60.00
DB47 Frank Nazar 40.00 100.00
DB48 Brayden Point 15.00 40.00
DB49 Henrik Lundqvist 30.00 80.00
DB50 Jesper Bratt 12.00 30.00
DB51 Kyle Connor 20.00 50.00
DB52 Evan Bouchard 15.00 40.00
DB53 MacKenzie Weegar 10.00 25.00
DB54 Evgeni Malkin 25.00 60.00
DB55 Mikko Rantanen 30.00 80.00
DB56 Vinco Dunn 10.00 25.00
DB57 Mark Scheifele 20.00 50.00
DB58 Brent Burns 12.00 30.00
DB59 Tom Wilson 12.00 30.00
DB60 Vincent Trocheck 12.00 30.00
DB61 Matthew Tkachuk 25.00 60.00
DB62 Thatcher Demko 15.00 40.00
DB63 Leo Carlsson 20.00 50.00
DB64 John Carlson 12.00 30.00
DB65 Robert Thomas 12.00 30.00
DB66 Nick Suzuki 25.00 60.00
DB67 Scott Niedermayer 12.00 30.00
DB68 Travis Konecny 12.00 30.00
DB69 Zachary Bolduc 20.00 50.00
DB70 Patrick Kane 25.00 60.00
DB71 Juraj Slafkovsky 25.00 60.00
DB72 William Eklund 15.00 40.00
DB73 Charlie McAvoy 15.00 40.00
DB74 Quinton Byfield 15.00 40.00
DB75 Brad Marchand 25.00 60.00
DB76 Owen Tippett 8.00 20.00
DB77 Filip Forsberg 20.00 50.00
DB78 Cale Makar 30.00 80.00
DB79 Mitch Marner 20.00 50.00
DB80 Anze Kopitar 20.00 50.00
DB81 Peter Forsberg 25.00 60.00
DB82 Joel Eriksson Ek 10.00 25.00
DB83 Olen Zellweger 25.00 60.00
DB84 Mark Stone 15.00 40.00
DB85 Clayton Keller 15.00 40.00
DB86 Jack Hughes 30.00 80.00
DB87 Sidney Crosby 50.00 125.00
DB88 David Pastrnak 30.00 80.00
DB89 Josh Doan 20.00 50.00
DB90 Johnny Gaudreau 20.00 50.00
DB91 Kris Letang 15.00 40.00
DB92 Logan Stankoven 30.00 80.00
DB93 Trevor Moore 8.00 20.00
DB94 Rasmus Dahlin 15.00 40.00
DB95 Elias Pettersson 20.00 50.00
DB96 Jake Neighbours 12.00 30.00
DB97 Connor McDavid 80.00 200.00
DB98 Connor Bedard 40.00 100.00
DB99 Wayne Gretzky 80.00 200.00
DB100 Josh Morrissey 15.00 40.00

2024-25 Upper Deck Allure Expressive Intentions

EI1 Nikita Kucherov 50.00 125.00
EI2 Cale Makar 125.00 300.00
EI3 Kirill Kaprizov 80.00 200.00
EI4 Jack Hughes 60.00 150.00
EI5 Artemi Panarin 50.00 125.00
EI7 Connor Bedard 250.00 600.00
EI8 Mitch Marner 40.00 100.00
EI9 Alex Ovechkin 150.00 400.00
EI10 Nick Suzuki 50.00 125.00

2024-25 Upper Deck Allure Protectors of the Ice

*ORANGE: .5X TO 1.2X BASIC
*GREEN: .6X TO 1.5X BASIC
*BLUE: .8X TO 2X BASIC
*PURPLE: 1X TO 2.5X BASIC
*SPEC ORG/199: 1X TO 2.5X BASIC
*SPEC GRN/99: 1.2X TO 3X BASIC
*SPEC BLUE/50: 1.5X TO 4X BASIC
*SPEC PURP/25: 2X TO 5X BASIC
PI1 Adin Hill 1.00 2.50
PI2 Joey Daccord 1.00 2.50
PI3 Jordan Binnington 1.50 4.00
PI4 Jeremy Swayman 1.50 4.00
PI5 Ilya Sorokin 1.50 4.00
PI6 Jake Oettinger 1.50 4.00
PI7 Sergei Bobrovsky 1.50 4.00
PI8 Thatcher Demko 1.25 3.00
PI9 Andrei Vasilevskiy 1.50 4.00
PI10 Igor Shesterkin 2.00 5.00
PI11 Juuse Saros 1.25 3.00
PI12 Connor Hellebuyck 2.00 5.00

2024-25 Upper Deck Allure Protectors of the Ice Autographs

PI1 Adin Hill 10.00 25.00
PI2 Joey Daccord 12.00 30.00
PI3 Jordan Binnington 15.00 40.00
PI4 Jeremy Swayman 15.00 40.00
PI5 Ilya Sorokin SP 15.00 40.00
PI6 Jake Oettinger 15.00 40.00
PI8 Thatcher Demko SP 12.00 30.00
PI9 Andrei Vasilevskiy SP 15.00 40.00
PI10 Igor Shesterkin SP 20.00 50.00
PI11 Juuse Saros 12.00 30.00
PI12 Connor Hellebuyck 20.00 50.00

2001 Upper Deck Avalanche NHL All-Star Game

COMPLETE SET (15) 50.00 125.00
CA1 Ray Bourque 6.00 15.00
CA2 Adam Foote .80 2.00
CA3 Adam Deadmarsh .80 2.00
CA4 Alex Tanguay 4.00 10.00
CA5 Aaron Miller .40 1.00
CA6 Stephane Yelle .40 1.00
HH1 D.Aebischer
P.Roy 8.00 20.00
HH2 M.Hejduk
P.Forsberg 6.00 15.00
HH3 J.Sakic
R.Bourque 6.00 15.00
PP1 Patrick Roy 8.00 20.00
PP2 Joe Sakic 4.80 12.00
PP3 Peter Forsberg 6.00 15.00
PP4 Chris Drury 4.00 10.00
PP5 Milan Hejduk 4.00 10.00
PP6 David Aebischer 4.00 10.00
WG Wayne Gretzky e-Card 2.00 5.00

2001-02 Upper Deck Gretzky Expo e-Card

WG Wayne Gretzky Jsy/200 75.00 150.00
NNO Wayne Gretzky .40 1.00

2002 Upper Deck Gretzky All-Star Game

COMPLETE SET (3) 10.00 25.00
AS1 Wayne Gretzky
All-Time Leading Scorer 4.00 10.00
AS2 Wayne Gretzky
All-Time Leading Goal Scorer 4.00 10.00
AS3 Wayne Gretzky
All-Star Game Goals
in a Period Record 4.00 10.00

2000-01 Upper Deck Jason Spezza Giveaways

1 Jason Spezza AU/300 25.00 60.00
2 Jason Spezza AU/600 15.00 40.00

2014-15 Upper Deck 25th Anniversary Young Guns

UD25AO Adam Oates TSE .75 2.00
UD25BL Brian Leetch NCDU .60 1.50
UD25BP Brad Park TSE .60 1.50
UD25BR Brad Richards TSE .75 2.00
UD25CC Corey Crawford NCDU 1.00 2.50
UD25CJ Curtis Joseph TFE 1.00 2.50
UD25CO1 Chris Osgood NCDU ERR red
(photo is Tim Cheveldae) .75 2.00
UD25CO2 Chris Osgood NCDU COR white
(wearing white jersey) .75 2.00
UD25DA Daniel Alfredsson TFE .75 2.00
UD25DG Doug Gilmour TFE .75 2.00
UD25DH Doug Harvey NCDC .75 2.00
UD25DH Dominik Hasek TFE 1.25 3.00
UD25GC Guy Carbonneau TFE .75 2.00
UD25JB Johnny Boychuk NCDU .60 1.50
UD25JQ Jonathan Quick TFE 1.00 2.50
UD25JW Joel Ward TSE .50 1.25
UD25KV Kris Versteeg TFE .50 1.25
UD25MB Martin Brodeur TFE 2.00 5.00
UD25MG Mike Gartner TSE 1.00 2.50
UD25MS Martin St. Louis TFE .75 2.00
UD25PF Peter Forsberg NCDU 1.50 4.00
UD25PT Pierre Turgeon NCDC .60 1.50
UD25RF Ron Francis NCDC 1.00 2.50
UD25TF Theoren Fleury NCDC 1.00 2.50
UD25TL Trevor Linden TFE 1.00 2.50
UD25VD Vincent Damphousse NCDC .60 1.50

2014-15 Upper Deck 25th Anniversary Young Guns Autographs

PSAK Alexander Khokhlachev/50 Fall 12.00 30.00
PSAL Adam Lowry/20 Spring 20.00 50.00
PSAM Andy Moog/20 Spring 12.00 30.00
PSAO Adam Oates/20 Fall 12.00 30.00
PSAP Alex Pietrangelo/20 Spring 10.00 25.00
PSBB Brent Burns/25 Spring 12.00 30.00
PSBC Brett Connolly/25 Spring 8.00 20.00
PSBG Brandon Gormley/50 Fall 8.00 20.00
PSBK Brandon Kozun/40 Spring 10.00 25.00
PSBR1 Bill Ranford/20 Fall 12.00 30.00
PSBS Brayden Schenn/20 Spring 12.00 30.00
PSCC Cory Conacher/35 Fall 8.00 20.00
PSCH Cody Hodgson/20 Fall 8.00 20.00
PSCK Corban Knight/50 Fall 12.00 30.00
PSCL Claude Lemieux/20 Fall 10.00 25.00
PSDC David Clarkson/25 Spring 8.00 20.00
PSDP1 David Perron/35 Fall 10.00 25.00
PSEK1 Erik Karlsson/25 Spring 12.00 30.00
PSEK2 Evgeny Kuznetsov/35 Fall 30.00 80.00
PSFF Filip Forsberg/25 Spring 20.00 50.00
PSGC Guy Carbonneau/20 Fall 12.00 30.00
PSGM Greg McKegg/50 Fall 10.00 25.00
PSJB Jonathan Bernier/35 Fall 10.00 25.00
PSJC Jared Cowen/25 Fall 8.00 20.00
PSJG Johnny Gaudreau/50 Fall 40.00 100.00
PSJH Jonathan Huberdeau/20 Fall 15.00 40.00
PSJS1 Justin Schultz/35 Fall 10.00 25.00
PSJT2 Jacob Trouba/50 Fall 10.00 25.00
PSKO Kyle Okposo/20 Spring 8.00 20.00
PSKR Kerby Rychel/30 Spring 10.00 25.00
PSKY Keith Yandle/25 Spring 10.00 25.00
PSLL Louis Leblanc/35 Fall 8.00 20.00
PSLS Luke Schenn/20 Fall 12.00 30.00
PSMD1 Marko Dano/40 Spring 12.00 30.00
PSMG2 Markus Granlund/35 Fall 20.00 50.00
PSMV Mark Visentin/40 Spring 12.00 30.00
PSNB Nathan Beaulieu/22 Fall 8.00 20.00
PSNF Nick Foligno/30 Spring 10.00 25.00
PSOK Oscar Klefbom/50 Fall 25.00 60.00
PSRS Ryan Strome/20 Fall 12.00 30.00
PSSA Sven Andrighetto/30 Spring 15.00 40.00
PSSE Jiri Sekac/40 Spring 10.00 25.00
PSSG1 Sam Gagner/50 Fall 8.00 20.00
PSSG2 Shayne Gostisbehere
40 Spring 25.00 60.00
PSSM Sean Monahan/20 Fall 8.00 20.00
PSTG T.J. Galiardi/25 Fall 8.00 20.00
PSTM Tyler Myers/20 Fall 8.00 20.00
PSTR Ty Rattie/50 Fall 12.00 30.00
PSTT Teuvo Teravainen/35 Fall 20.00 50.00
PSVR Victor Rask/40 Spring 12.00 30.00

2020-21 Upper Deck Alexis Lafreniere Collection

1 Alexis Lafreniere 3.00 8.00
2 Alexis Lafreniere 3.00 8.00
3 Alexis Lafreniere 3.00 8.00
4 Alexis Lafreniere 3.00 8.00
5 Alexis Lafreniere 3.00 8.00
6 Alexis Lafreniere 3.00 8.00
7 Alexis Lafreniere 3.00 8.00
8 Alexis Lafreniere 3.00 8.00
9 Alexis Lafreniere 3.00 8.00
10 Alexis Lafreniere 3.00 8.00
11 Alexis Lafreniere 3.00 8.00
12 Alexis Lafreniere 3.00 8.00
13 Alexis Lafreniere 3.00 8.00
14 Alexis Lafreniere 3.00 8.00
15 Alexis Lafreniere 3.00 8.00
16 Alexis Lafreniere 3.00 8.00
17 Alexis Lafreniere 3.00 8.00
18 Alexis Lafreniere 3.00 8.00
19 Alexis Lafreniere 3.00 8.00
20 Alexis Lafreniere 3.00 8.00
21 Alexis Lafreniere 3.00 8.00
22 Alexis Lafreniere 3.00 8.00
23 Alexis Lafreniere 3.00 8.00
24 Alexis Lafreniere 3.00 8.00
25 Alexis Lafreniere 3.00 8.00
26 Alexis Lafreniere M 3.00 8.00
27 Alexis Lafreniere M 3.00 8.00
28 Alexis Lafreniere M 3.00 8.00
29 Alexis Lafreniere M 3.00 8.00
30 Alexis Lafreniere M 3.00 8.00

1999-00 Upper Deck Arena Giveaways

COMPLETE SET (56) 15.00 40.00
AM1 Ladislav Kohn .20 .50
AM2 Mike Leclerc .20 .50
AT1 Patrik Stefan .40 1.00
AT2 Shean Donovan .20 .50
BB1 Jonathan Girard .40 1.00
BB2 Sergei Samsonov 1.25 3.00
BS1 Maxim Afinogenov .75 2.00
BS2 Cory Sarich .20 .50
CA1 Alex Tanguay 1.25 3.00
CA2 Chris Drury 1.25 3.00
CB1 J-P Dumont .40 1.00
CB2 Bryan McCabe .20 .50
CF1 Robyn Regehr .20 .50
CF2 Derek Morris .40 1.00
CH1 Dave Tanabe .20 .50
CH2 Jeff O'Neill .40 1.00
DR1 Jiri Fischer .40 1.00
DR2 Darryl Laplante .20 .50
DS1 Brenden Morrow .75 2.00
DS2 Jamie Langenbrunner .40 1.00
EO1 Paul Comrie .20 .50
EO2 Boyd Devereaux .20 .50
FP1 Ivan Novoseltsev .40 1.00
FP2 Mark Parrish .40 1.00
LK1 Frantisek Kaberle .20 .50
LK2 Aki Berg .20 .50
MC1 Mike Ribeiro .20 .50
MC2 Arron Asham .20 .50
ND1 Scott Gomez .75 2.00
ND2 Sheldon Souray .20 .50
NI1 Roberto Luongo 2.50 6.00
NI2 Tim Connolly .75 2.00
NP1 David Legwand .40 1.00
NP2 Randy Robitaille .20 .50
NR1 Michael York .40 1.00
NR2 Manny Malhotra .20 .50
OS1 Mike Fisher .40 1.00
OS2 Chris Phillips .20 .50
PC1 Trevor Letowski .75 2.00
PC2 Shane Doan .75 2.00
PF1 Simon Gagne 1.25 3.00
PF2 Daymond Langkow .40 1.00
PP1 Andrew Ference .20 .50
PP2 Michal Rozsival .20 .50
SB1 Jochen Hecht .40 1.00
SB2 Michal Handzus .75 2.00
SS1 Brad Stuart .40 1.00
SS2 Jeff Friesen .40 1.00
TL1 Paul Mara .20 .50
TL2 Andrei Zyuzin .20 .50
TM1 Nikolai Antropov .75 2.00
TM2 Danny Markov .20 .50
VC1 Steve Kariya .75 2.00
VC2 Peter Schaefer .20 .50
WC1 Jeff Halpern .40 1.00
WC2 Alexei Tezikov .20 .50

2006-07 Upper Deck Arena Giveaways

ANA1 Corey Perry 4.00 10.00
ANA2 Teemu Selanne 5.00 12.00
ANA3 Andy McDonald 2.00 5.00
ANA4 Scott Niedermayer 2.50 6.00
ANA5 Jean-Sebastien Giguere 2.50 6.00
ANA6 Chris Pronger 2.50 6.00
ATL1 Marian Hossa 2.50 6.00
ATL2 Slava Kozlov 1.50 4.00
ATL3 Bobby Holik 1.50 4.00
ATL4 Ilya Kovalchuk 2.50 6.00
ATL5 Steve Rucchin 1.50 4.00
ATL6 Kari Lehtonen 2.00 5.00
BOS1 Brad Boyes 1.50 4.00
BOS2 Hannu Toivonen 2.00 5.00
BOS3 Patrice Bergeron 3.00 8.00
BOS4 Zdeno Chara 2.50 6.00
BOS5 Marc Savard 1.50 4.00
BOS6 Glen Murray 2.00 5.00
BUF1 Ryan Miller 2.50 6.00
BUF2 Thomas Vanek 2.00 5.00
BUF3 Daniel Briere 2.00 5.00
BUF4 Jason Pominville 1.50 4.00
BUF5 Maxim Afinogenov 1.50 4.00
BUF6 Chris Drury 2.00 5.00
CAR1 Eric Staal 3.00 8.00
CAR2 Cam Ward 2.50 6.00
CAR3 Justin Williams 2.00 5.00
CAR4 Erik Cole 1.50 4.00
CAR5 Andrew Ladd 1.50 4.00
CAR6 Rod Brind'Amour 2.50 6.00
CGY1 Jarome Iginla 3.00 8.00
CGY2 Dion Phaneuf 2.00 5.00
CGY3 Chuck Kobasew 1.50 4.00
CGY4 Alex Tanguay 1.50 4.00
CGY5 Daymond Langkow 1.50 4.00
CGY6 Miikka Kiprusoff 2.50 6.00
CHI1 Tuomo Ruutu 2.50 6.00
CHI2 Martin Havlat 1.50 4.00
CHI3 Brent Seabrook 1.50 4.00
CHI4 Adrian Aucoin 1.50 4.00
CHI5 Bryan Smolinski 1.50 4.00
CHI6 Nikolai Khabibulin 2.50 6.00
CLB1 Rick Nash 2.50 6.00
CLB2 Pascal LeClaire 2.00 5.00
CLB3 Adam Foote 1.50 4.00
CLB4 Fredrik Modin 1.50 4.00
CLB5 Gilbert Brule 2.00 5.00
CLB6 Sergei Fedorov 4.00 10.00
COL1 Jose Theodore 2.00 5.00
COL2 Wojtek Wolski 1.50 4.00
COL3 John-Michael Liles 1.50 4.00
COL4 Joe Sakic 5.00 12.00
COL5 Marek Svatos 1.50 4.00
COL6 Milan Hejduk 2.00 5.00
DAL1 Brenden Morrow 2.00 5.00
DAL1 Brenden Morrow 2.00 5.00
DAL2 Jussi Jokinen 2.00 5.00
DAL2 Jussi Jokinen 2.00 5.00
DAL3 Sergei Zubov 2.00 5.00
DAL3 Sergei Zubov 2.00 5.00
DAL4 Mike Modano 4.00 10.00
DAL4 Mike Modano 4.00 10.00
DAL5 Eric Lindros 4.00 10.00
DAL5 Eric Lindros 4.00 10.00
DAL6 Marty Turco 2.50 6.00
DET1 Kris Draper 1.50 4.00
DET2 Dominik Hasek 4.00 10.00
DET3 Chris Chelios 2.50 6.00
DET4 Henrik Zetterberg 3.00 8.00
DET5 Nicklas Lidstrom 2.50 6.00
DET6 Pavel Datsyuk 4.00 10.00
EDM1 Ales Hemsky 2.00 5.00
EDM2 Fernando Pisani 1.50 4.00
EDM3 Jarret Stoll 2.00 5.00
EDM4 Ryan Smyth 2.00 5.00
EDM5 Jeffrey Lupul 1.50 4.00
EDM6 Dwayne Roloson 2.00 5.00
FLA1 Jay Bouwmeester 1.50 4.00
FLA2 Nathan Horton 2.50 6.00
FLA3 Stephen Weiss 1.50 4.00
FLA4 Olli Jokinen 2.50 6.00
FLA5 Ed Belfour 2.50 6.00
FLA6 Todd Bertuzzi 2.50 6.00
LAK1 Alexander Frolov 1.50 4.00
LAK2 Lubomir Visnovsky 1.50 4.00
LAK3 Dustin Brown 2.50 6.00
LAK4 Rob Blake 2.50 6.00
LAK5 Craig Conroy 1.50 4.00
LAK6 Mike Cammalleri 1.50 4.00
MIN1 Marian Gaborik 2.50 6.00
MIN2 Pierre-Marc Bouchard 2.50 6.00
MIN3 Brian Rolston 2.00 5.00
MIN4 Pavol Demitra 3.00 8.00
MIN5 Mark Parrish 1.50 4.00
MIN6 Manny Fernandez 1.50 4.00
NJD1 Martin Brodeur 6.00 15.00
NJD2 Brian Gionta 1.50 4.00
NJD3 Zach Parise 2.50 6.00
NJD4 Brian Rafalski 2.00 5.00
NJD5 Scott Gomez 2.00 5.00
NJD6 Patrik Elias 2.50 6.00
NSH1 Tomas Vokoun 2.50 6.00
NSH2 David Legwand 2.00 5.00
NSH3 Kimmo Timonen 1.50 4.00
NSH4 Paul Kariya 2.50 6.00
NSH5 Jason Arnott 2.00 5.00
NSH6 Steve Sullivan 1.50 4.00
NYI1 Rick DiPietro 2.00 5.00
NYI2 Jeff Tambellini 1.50 4.00
NYI3 Jason Blake 1.50 4.00
NYI4 Trent Hunter 1.50 4.00
NYI5 Alexei Yashin 2.00 5.00
NYI6 Miroslav Satan 2.00 5.00
NYR1 Jaromir Jagr 8.00 20.00
NYR2 Petr Prucha 2.00 5.00
NYR3 Martin Straka 1.50 4.00
NYR4 Henrik Lundqvist 6.00 15.00
NYR5 Michael Nylander 1.50 4.00
NYR6 Brendan Shanahan 2.50 6.00
OTT1 Jason Spezza 2.50 6.00
OTT2 Chris Phillips 1.50 4.00
OTT3 Dany Heatley 2.00 5.00
OTT4 Wade Redden 1.50 4.00
OTT5 Martin Gerber 2.00 5.00
OTT6 Daniel Alfredsson 2.50 6.00
PHI1 Peter Forsberg 5.00 12.00
PHI2 Robert Esche 2.00 5.00
PHI3 Joni Pitkanen 1.50 4.00
PHI4 Simon Gagne 2.50 6.00
PHI5 Antero Niittymaki 2.00 5.00
PHI6 Jeff Carter 2.00 5.00
PHX1 Shane Doan 2.00 5.00
PHX2 Ladislav Nagy 1.50 4.00
PHX3 Ed Jovanovski 2.00 5.00
PHX4 Jeremy Roenick 4.00 10.00
PHX5 Owen Nolan 2.50 6.00
PHX6 Curtis Joseph 3.00 8.00
PIT1 Sidney Crosby 10.00 25.00
PIT2 Colby Armstrong 2.00 5.00
PIT3 Sergei Gonchar 1.50 4.00
PIT4 Ryan Malone 1.50 4.00
PIT5 Mark Recchi 2.00 5.00
PIT6 Marc-Andre Fleury 5.00 12.00
SJS1 Joe Thornton 4.00 10.00
SJS2 Vesa Toskala 2.00 5.00
SJS3 Steve Bernier 1.50 4.00
SJS4 Patrick Marleau 2.50 6.00
SJS5 Evgeni Nabokov 2.00 5.00
SJS6 Jonathan Cheechoo 2.00 5.00
STL1 Keith Tkachuk 2.50 6.00
STL2 Barret Jackman 1.50 4.00
STL3 Lee Stempniak 1.50 4.00
STL4 Manny Legace 2.00 5.00
STL5 Bill Guerin 2.50 6.00
STL6 Doug Weight 2.50 6.00
TBL1 Martin St. Louis 2.50 6.00
TBL2 Vaclav Prospal 1.50 4.00
TBL3 Ruslan Fedotenko 1.50 4.00
TBL4 Vincent Lecavalier 2.50 6.00
TBL5 Marc Denis 2.00 5.00
TBL6 Brad Richards 2.50 6.00
TOR1 Mats Sundin 2.50 6.00
TOR2 Darcy Tucker 2.00 5.00
TOR3 Alexander Steen 1.50 4.00
TOR4 Andrew Raycroft 2.00 5.00
TOR5 Michael Peca 2.00 5.00
TOR6 Bryan McCabe 1.50 4.00
VAN1 Markus Naslund 2.50 6.00
VAN2 Henrik Sedin 3.00 8.00
VAN3 Roberto Luongo 4.00 10.00
VAN4 Brendan Morrison 1.50 4.00
VAN5 Trevor Linden 2.50 6.00
VAN6 Daniel Sedin 3.00 8.00
WSH1 Shaone Morrisonn 1.50 4.00
WSH2 Alexander Semin 2.50 6.00
WSH3 Alexander Ovechkin 10.00 25.00
WSH4 Richard Zednik 1.50 4.00
WSH5 Dainius Zubrus 1.50 4.00
WSH6 Olaf Kolzig 2.50 6.00

2017-18 Upper Deck Arena Giveaway Buffalo Sabres

BUF1 Jason Pominville 1.25 3.00
BUF2 Ryan O'Reilly 1.25 3.00
BUF3 Rasmus Ristolainen 1.25 3.00
BUF4 Justin Bailey 1.25 3.00
BUF5 Sam Reinhart 1.25 3.00
BUF6 Jack Eichel 1.25 3.00

2010-11 Upper Deck Arena Giveaway Pittsburgh Penguins

COMPLETE SET (7) 3.00 8.00
PIT1 Sidney Crosby 2.00 5.00
PIT2 Jordan Staal .40 1.00
PIT3 Maxime Talbot .30 .75
PIT4 Brooks Orpik .30 .75
PIT5 Marc-Andre Fleury 1.00 2.50
PIT6 Kristopher Letang .60 1.50
PIT7 Evgeni Malkin 1.25 3.00

2023-24 Upper Deck Boston Bruins Centennial

1 Derek Sanderson .60 1.50
2 Steve Heinze .50 1.25
3 Charlie McAvoy .75 2.00
4 Marc Savard .40 1.00
5 Tim Thomas .60 1.50
6 Ken Linseman .60 1.50
7 Chris Nilan .40 1.00
8 Shawn Thornton .40 1.00
9 Bill Ranford .50 1.25
10 Gregg Sheppard .50 1.25
11 Hampus Lindholm .40 1.00
12 Byron Dafoe .50 1.25
13 Al Secord .50 1.25
14 Ed Westfall .50 1.25
15 Norm Leveille .40 1.00
16 Cam Neely .60 1.50
17 Charlie Simmer .40 1.00
18 Rick Middleton .60 1.50
19 Jake DeBrusk .60 1.50
20 Jean Ratelle .50 1.25
21 Keith Crowder .40 1.00
22 Rogie Vachon .60 1.50
23 Ray Bourque 1.00 2.50
24 Dit Clapper .40 1.00
25 Phil Esposito 1.00 2.50
26 Connor Clifton .40 1.00
27 Terry O'Reilly .50 1.25
28 Bill Guerin .60 1.50
29 Joe Thornton 1.00 2.50
30 Rejean Lemelin .40 1.00
31 Dave Christian .40 1.00
32 Dallas Smith .75 2.00
33 Gerry Cheevers .60 1.50
34 Pavel Zacha .50 1.25
35 Adam Oates .60 1.50
36 Kyle McLaren .40 1.00
37 Wayne Cashman .40 1.00
38 Willie O'Ree .75 2.00
39 Dave Forbes .40 1.00
40 Charlie Coyle .60 1.50
41 Gord Kluzak .40 1.00
42 Torey Krug .50 1.25
43 Ed Johnston .60 1.50
44 Glen Murray .50 1.25
45 Brad Marchand 1.25 3.00
46 Milan Lucic .50 1.25
47 Andy Brickley .40 1.00
48 Jason Allison .50 1.25
49 Sergei Samsonov .50 1.25
50 Craig Janney .50 1.25
51 Joe Juneau .40 1.00
52 David Pastrnak 1.50 4.00
53 Jozef Stumpel .40 1.00
54 Steve Kasper .40 1.00
55 Brian Propp .50 1.25
56 Bob Beers .40 1.00
57 Brad Park .50 1.25
58 Hal Gill .40 1.00
59 John Wensink .40 1.00
60 Daniel Paille .40 1.00
61 Allen Pedersen .40 1.00
62 Bobby Orr 2.50 6.00
63 Jakub Lauko .60 1.50
64 Paul Coffey .60 1.50
65 Eddie Shore .60 1.50
66 Don Marcotte .40 1.00
67 Ken Hodge .50 1.25
68 Harry Sinden .40 1.00
69 Bob Sweeney .40 1.00
70 Bobby Carpenter .50 1.25
71 Jacques Plante .60 1.50
72 Ted Donato .40 1.00
73 Andy Moog .60 1.50
74 Brian Leetch .50 1.25
75 Mike Knuble .40 1.00
76 Matt Grzelcyk .50 1.25
77 Zdeno Chara .60 1.50
78 Terry Sawchuk .60 1.50
79 Tom Fergus .40 1.00
80 Ken Hodge Jr. .40 1.00
81 Per-Johan Axelsson .40 1.00
82 Butch Goring .60 1.50
83 Jeremy Swayman 1.00 2.50
84 Reed Larson .50 1.25
85 Randy Burridge .40 1.00
86 Mark Recchi .60 1.50
87 Glen Wesley .40 1.00
88 Andrew Raycroft .50 1.25
89 Patrice Bergeron .75 2.00
90 Lionel Hitchman .40 1.00
91 Johnny Bucyk .60 1.50
92 Don Awrey .40 1.00
93 Marco Sturm .40 1.00
94 Ken Baumgartner .40 1.00
95 Johnny Boychuk .50 1.25
96 Linus Ullmark .60 1.50
97 Rick Nash .60 1.50
98 Mike Milbury .40 1.00
99 Brian Rolston .40 1.00
100 Dave Reid .40 1.00
101 Johnny Bucyk RH 1.25 3.00
102 Lionel Hitchman RN .75 2.00
103 Ray Bourque RN 2.00 5.00
104 Dit Clapper RN .75 2.00
105 Terry O'Reilly RN 1.00 2.50
106 Willie O'Ree RN 1.50 4.00
107 Eddie Shore RN 1.25 3.00
108 Cam Neely RN 1.25 3.00
109 Bobby Orr RN 5.00 12.00
110 Phil Esposito RN 2.00 5.00
111 Terry Sawchuk HOF 1.25 3.00
112 Jean Ratelle HOF 1.00 2.50
113 Brad Park HOF 1.00 2.50
114 Willie O'Ree HOF 1.50 4.00
115 Jacques Plante HOF 1.25 3.00
116 Bobby Orr HOF 5.00 12.00
117 Adam Oates HOF 1.25 3.00
118 Eddie Shore HOF 1.25 3.00
119 Phil Esposito HOF 2.00 5.00
120 Cam Neely HOF 1.25 3.00
121 Ray Bourque RH 2.00 5.00
122 Gerry Cheevers RH 1.25 3.00
123 Charlie Simmer RH .75 2.00
124 Bobby Orr RH 5.00 12.00
125 Tim Thomas RH 1.25 3.00
126 Johnny Bucyk RH 1.25 3.00
127 Brian Rolston RH 1.00 2.50
128 Phil Esposito RH 2.00 5.00
129 Cam Neely RH 1.25 3.00
130 Ed Johnston RH 1.25 3.00
131 Bobby Orr RH 5.00 12.00
132 Terry O'Reilly RH 1.00 2.50
133 Brad Marchand RH 2.50 6.00
134 Phil Esposito RH 2.00 5.00
135 Ray Bourque RH 2.00 5.00
136 Lionel Hitchman MM .75 2.00
137 Eddie Shore MM 1.25 3.00
138 Terry Sawchuk MM 1.25 3.00
139 Willie O'Ree MM 1.50 4.00
140 Bobby Orr MM 5.00 12.00
141 Gerry Cheevers MM 1.25 3.00
142 Bobby Orr MM 5.00 12.00
143 Wayne Cashman MM .75 2.00
144 Jacques Plante MM 1.25 3.00
145 Bobby Orr MM 5.00 12.00
146 Phil Esposito MM 2.00 5.00

147 Johnny Bucyk MM 1.25 3.00
148 Rogie Vachon MM 1.25 3.00
149 Steve Kasper MM .75 2.00
150 Ray Bourque MM 2.00 5.00
151 Cam Neely MM 1.25 3.00
152 A.Moog/R.Lemelin MM 1.25 3.00
153 Joe Juneau MM .75 2.00
154 Norm Leveille MM .75 2.00
155 Zdeno Chara MM 1.25 3.00
156 Brad Marchand MM 2.50 6.00
157 Charlie McAvoy MM 1.50 4.00
158 David Pastrnak MM 3.00 8.00
159 Patrice Bergeron MM 1.50 4.00
160 Linus Ullmark MM 1.25 3.00
161 Brad Marchand C 2.50 6.00
162 Eddie Shore C 1.25 3.00
163 Patrice Bergeron C 1.50 4.00
164 Dit Clapper C .75 2.00
165 Terry O'Reilly C 1.00 2.50
166 Joe Thornton C 2.00 5.00
167 Ray Bourque C 2.00 5.00
168 Johnny Bucyk C 1.25 3.00
169 Rick Middleton C 1.25 3.00
170 Zdeno Chara C 1.25 3.00
171 Derek Sanderson TW 1.25 3.00
172 Sergei Samsonov TW 1.00 2.50
173 Bobby Orr TW 5.00 12.00
174 Zdeno Chara TW 1.25 3.00
175 Tim Thomas TW 1.25 3.00
176 Eddie Shore TW 1.25 3.00
177 Patrice Bergeron TW 1.50 4.00
178 Phil Esposito TW 2.00 5.00
179 Ray Bourque TW 2.00 5.00
180 Linus Ullmark TW 1.25 3.00
181 Terry O'Reilly BBB 1.00 2.50
182 Ken Baumgartner BBB .75 2.00
183 Ray Bourque BBB 2.00 5.00
184 Keith Crowder BBB .75 2.00
185 Brad Marchand BBB 2.50 6.00
186 Al Secord BBB 1.00 2.50
187 Chris Nilan BBB .75 2.00
188 Zdeno Chara BBB 1.25 3.00
189 Bob Sweeney BBB .75 2.00
190 Wayne Cashman BBB .75 2.00
191 Shawn Thornton BBB .75 2.00
192 Derek Sanderson BBB 1.25 3.00
193 Gord Kluzak BBB .75 2.00
194 Mike Milbury BBB .75 2.00
195 Don Awrey BBB .75 2.00
196 Ken Linseman BBB 1.25 3.00
197 Dallas Smith BBB 1.50 4.00
198 Cam Neely BBB 1.25 3.00
199 Eddie Shore BBB 1.25 3.00
200 John Wensink BBB .75 2.00

2023-24 Upper Deck Boston Bruins Centennial Acetate

*ACETATE: .6X TO 1.5X BASIC

2023-24 Upper Deck Boston Bruins Centennial Century

*CENTURY/100: 2.5X TO 6X BASIC
*CENT SUB/100: 1.5X TO 4X BASIC

2023-24 Upper Deck Boston Bruins Centennial Lucky Green

*GREEN/49: 10X TO 25X BASIC
*GREEN SUB/25: 6X TO 15X BASIC

2023-24 Upper Deck Boston Bruins Centennial AKA Autographs

AKAAM Andy Moog/49 40.00 100.00
AKABC Bobby Carpenter/49 30.00 80.00
AKABD Byron Dafoe/49 30.00 80.00
AKABE John Beecher/49 80.00 200.00
AKABG Bill Guerin/49 40.00 100.00
AKABL Brian Leetch/49 30.00 80.00
AKABM Brad Marchand/49 80.00 200.00
AKABO Bobby Orr/49 150.00 400.00
AKABP Brad Park/49 30.00 80.00
AKACC Charlie Coyle/49 40.00 100.00
AKACL Connor Clifton/49 25.00 60.00
AKACN Cam Neely/49 40.00 100.00
AKACS Charlie Simmer/49 25.00 60.00
AKADC Dave Christian/49 25.00 60.00
AKADS Derek Sanderson/49 40.00 100.00
AKAEJ Ed Johnston/49 40.00 100.00
AKAEW Ed Westfall/49 30.00 80.00
AKAFP Felix Potvin/49 60.00 150.00
AKAGC Gerry Cheevers/49 40.00 100.00
AKAJB Johnny Bucyk/49 60.00 150.00
AKAJJ Joe Juneau/49 25.00 60.00
AKAJT Joe Thornton/49 60.00 150.00
AKAJV James van Riemsdyk/49 30.00 80.00
AKAKH Ken Hodge Jr./49 25.00 60.00
AKAKS Kevin Stevens/49 30.00 80.00
AKALA Reed Larson/49 30.00 80.00
AKAMP Matthew Poitras/49 80.00 200.00
AKAMR Mark Recchi/49 40.00 100.00
AKAMS Marco Sturm/49 25.00 60.00
AKAPA Per-Johan Axelsson/49 25.00 60.00
AKAPB Patrice Bergeron/49 50.00 125.00
AKAPR Brian Propp/49 50.00 125.00
AKAPZ Pavel Zacha/49 30.00 80.00
AKARL Rejean Lemelin/49 25.00 60.00
AKARM Rick Middleton/49 40.00 100.00
AKARN Rick Nash/49 40.00 100.00
AKARO Brian Rolston/49 30.00 80.00
AKARV Rogie Vachon/49 40.00 100.00
AKASA Marc Savard/49 25.00 60.00
AKASH Steve Heinze/49 30.00 80.00
AKASK Steve Kasper/49 25.00 60.00
AKASS Sergei Samsonov/49 30.00 80.00
AKAST Shawn Thornton/49 25.00 60.00
AKATO Terry O'Reilly/49 30.00 80.00
AKATT Tim Thomas/49 40.00 100.00

2023-24 Upper Deck Boston Bruins Centennial All-Timers

*GOLD: .8X TO 2X BASIC
1001 Jozef Stumpel 1.00 2.50
1002 Gregg Sheppard 1.25 3.00
1003 Jean Ratelle 1.25 3.00
1004 Ed Westfall 1.25 3.00
1005 Brad Park 1.25 3.00
1006 Ken Hodge 1.25 3.00
1007 Glen Murray 1.25 3.00
1008 Per-Johan Axelsson 1.00 2.50
1009 Torey Krug 1.25 3.00
10010 Ken Linseman 1.50 4.00
10011 Dave Reid 1.00 2.50
10012 Wayne Cashman 1.00 2.50
10013 Rick Middleton 1.50 4.00
10014 Andy Moog 1.50 4.00
10015 Charlie McAvoy 2.00 5.00
10016 Tim Thomas 1.50 4.00
10017 Steve Heinze 1.25 3.00
10018 Byron Dafoe 1.25 3.00
10019 Adam Oates 1.50 4.00
10020 Sergei Samsonov 1.25 3.00
10021 Glen Wesley 1.00 2.50
10022 John Wensink 1.00 2.50
10023 Fred Stanfield 1.00 2.50
10024 Marc Savard 1.00 2.50
10025 Lionel Hitchman 1.00 2.50
10026 Keith Crowder 1.00 2.50
10027 Mike Milbury 1.00 2.50
10028 Don Marcotte 1.00 2.50
10029 Ted Donato 1.00 2.50
10030 Ed Johnston 1.50 4.00
10031 Randy Burridge 1.00 2.50
10032 Willie O'Ree 2.00 5.00
10033 Joe Juneau 1.00 2.50
10034 Steve Kasper 1.00 2.50
10035 Craig Janney 1.25 3.00
10036 Zdeno Chara 1.50 4.00
10037 Terry O'Reilly 1.25 3.00
10038 Joe Thornton 2.50 6.00
10039 Derek Sanderson 1.50 4.00
10040 Gerry Cheevers 1.50 4.00
10041 Dit Clapper SP 1.00 2.50
10042 Cam Neely SP 1.50 4.00
10043 David Pastrnak SP 4.00 10.00
10044 Eddie Shore SP 1.50 4.00
10045 Brad Marchand SP 3.00 8.00
10046 Johnny Bucyk SP 1.50 4.00
10047 Patrice Bergeron SP 2.00 5.00
10048 Phil Esposito SP 2.50 6.00
10049 Ray Bourque SP 2.50 6.00
10050 Bobby Orr SP 6.00 15.00

2023-24 Upper Deck Boston Bruins Centennial Bear Tracks Autographs

BTAB Andy Brickley 15.00 40.00
BTAG A.J. Greer 15.00 40.00
BTAO Adam Oates SP 100.00 250.00
BTAS Al Secord 20.00 50.00
BTAX Per-Johan Axelsson 15.00 40.00
BTBC Bobby Carpenter 20.00 50.00
BTBD Byron Dafoe 20.00 50.00
BTBG Bill Guerin 25.00 60.00
BTBM Brad Marchand SP 125.00 300.00
BTBR Bill Ranford 60.00 150.00
BTCC Charlie Coyle 25.00 60.00
BTCJ Craig Janney 20.00 50.00
BTCL Connor Clifton 15.00 40.00
BTCN Cam Neely SP 150.00 400.00
BTCS Charlie Simmer 15.00 40.00
BTDB David Backes 15.00 40.00
BTDC Dave Christian 15.00 40.00
BTDF Derek Forbort 15.00 40.00
BTDH Danton Heinen 15.00 40.00
BTDM Don Marcotte 15.00 40.00
BTEH Erik Haula 15.00 40.00
BTEJ Ed Johnston 25.00 60.00
BTEW Ed Westfall 20.00 50.00
BTFP Felix Potvin SP 125.00 300.00
BTFV Frank Vatrano 20.00 50.00
BTGC Gerry Cheevers SP 250.00 600.00
BTGE Morgan Geekie 15.00 40.00
BTGW Glen Wesley 15.00 40.00
BTHS Harry Sinden 40.00 100.00
BTJA Jack Ahcan 15.00 40.00
BTJB John Beecher 50.00 125.00
BTJJ Joe Juneau 15.00 40.00
BTJK Joona Koppanen 20.00 50.00
BTJO Johnny Boychuk 20.00 50.00
BTJR Jean Ratelle 40.00 100.00
BTJT Joe Thornton SP 60.00 150.00
BTJV James van Riemsdyk 20.00 50.00
BTJW John Wensink 15.00 40.00
BTKA Jack Studnicka 15.00 40.00
BTKC Keith Crowder 15.00 40.00
BTKH Ken Hodge 20.00 50.00
BTKL Ken Linseman 25.00 60.00
BTKS Kevin Stevens 20.00 50.00
BTLE Rejean Lemelin 15.00 40.00
BTMA Marco Sturm 15.00 40.00
BTML Mason Lohrei 25.00 60.00
BTMP Matthew Poitras SP 150.00 400.00
BTMR Mark Recchi SP 200.00 500.00
BTMS Marc Savard 15.00 40.00
BTNA Noel Acciari 15.00 40.00
BTNF Nick Foligno 15.00 40.00
BTNL Norm Leveille 15.00 40.00
BTPA Brad Park 40.00 100.00
BTPC Paul Coffey SP 80.00 200.00
BTPR Brian Propp 20.00 50.00
BTPZ Pavel Zacha 20.00 50.00
BTRK Kevin Shattenkirk 15.00 40.00
BTRL Reed Larson 20.00 50.00
BTRN Rick Nash 25.00 60.00
BTRO Brian Rolston 20.00 50.00
BTRV Rogie Vachon SP 100.00 250.00
BTSA Derek Sanderson 40.00 100.00
BTSE Sean Kuraly 15.00 40.00
BTSH Steve Heinze 20.00 50.00
BTSK Steve Kasper 15.00 40.00
BTSS Sergei Samsonov 20.00 50.00
BTST Jozef Stumpel 15.00 40.00
BTTD Ted Donato 15.00 40.00
BTTF Trent Frederic 15.00 40.00
BTTH Shawn Thornton 15.00 40.00
BTTK Torey Krug 20.00 50.00
BTTO Terry O'Reilly 50.00 125.00
BTTT Tim Thomas 60.00 150.00
BTWO Willie O'Ree SP 80.00 200.00
BTZC Zdeno Chara 150.00 400.00

2023-24 Upper Deck Boston Bruins Centennial Capturing a Champion

*GOLD: 1X TO 2.5X BASIC
CC1 Ed Johnston 2.00 5.00
CC2 Derek Sanderson 2.00 5.00
CC3 Patrice Bergeron 2.50 6.00
CC4 Bobby Orr 8.00 20.00
CC5 Johnny Boychuk 1.50 4.00
CC6 Ed Westfall 1.50 4.00
CC7 Mark Recchi 2.00 5.00
CC8 Ken Hodge 1.50 4.00
CC9 Phil Esposito 3.00 8.00
CC10 Tim Thomas 2.00 5.00
CC11 Bobby Orr 8.00 20.00
CC12 Wayne Cashman 1.25 3.00
CC13 Zdeno Chara 2.00 5.00
CC14 Gerry Cheevers 2.00 5.00
CC15 Brad Marchand 4.00 10.00
CC16 Don Awrey 1.25 3.00
CC17 Tyler Seguin 2.50 6.00
CC18 Johnny Bucyk 2.00 5.00
CC19 Zdeno Chara 2.00 5.00
CC20 Bobby Orr 8.00 20.00

2023-24 Upper Deck Boston Bruins Centennial Causeway Classics Relics

*PREMIUM/49: 1X TO 2.5X BASIC
CLAO Adam Oates SP 10.00 25.00
CLBM Brad Marchand 20.00 50.00
CLCM Charlie McAvoy 12.00 30.00
CLDH Danton Heinen 6.00 15.00
CLDP David Pastrnak 25.00 60.00
CLGC Gerry Cheevers SP 10.00 25.00
CLHL Hampus Lindholm 6.00 15.00
CLJD Jake DeBrusk 10.00 25.00
CLJS Jeremy Swayman 15.00 40.00
CLLU Linus Ullmark 10.00 25.00
CLMG Matt Grzelcyk 8.00 20.00
CLPB Patrice Bergeron 12.00 30.00
CLPE Phil Esposito SP 15.00 40.00
CLRB Ray Bourque 15.00 40.00
CLTH Taylor Hall 10.00 25.00
CLTK Torey Krug 8.00 20.00
CLTS Tyler Seguin 12.00 30.00
CLTT Tim Thomas 10.00 25.00
CLZC Zdeno Chara 10.00 25.00

2023-24 Upper Deck Boston Bruins Centennial Centennial Cloth Dual Relics

CCR2BB P.Bergeron/R.Bourque 30.00 80.00
CCR2BM P.Bergeron/B.Marchand 40.00 100.00
CCR2CB Z.Chara/R.Bourque 30.00 80.00
CCR2CM C.McAvoy/Z.Chara 25.00 60.00
CCR2CS G.Cheevers/J.Swayman SP 30.00 80.00
CCR2CV F.Vatrano/C.Coyle 20.00 50.00
CCR2HK D.Hamilton/T.Krug 15.00 40.00
CCR2HS T.Hall/T.Seguin 25.00 60.00
CCR2LM B.Leetch/C.McAvoy 25.00 60.00
CCR2MB G.Murray/R.Bourque 30.00 80.00
CCR2MP D.Pastrnak/B.Marchand 50.00 120.00
CCR2NM B.Marchand/C.Neely 40.00 100.00
CCR2PT D.Pastrnak/J.Thornton 50.00 125.00
CCR2RA P.Axelsson/A.Raycroft 15.00 40.00
CCR2TU L.Ullmark/T.Thomas 20.00 50.00

2023-24 Upper Deck Boston Bruins Centennial Centennial Cloth Quad Relics

CCR4BMPD Pastrnak/Marchand Bergeron/DeBrusk 120.00 300.00
CCR4BOMP Bucyk/Marchand Pastrnak/Oates 120.00 300.00
CCR4CTMS Swayman/Moog Cheevers/Thomas 80.00 200.00
CCR4EBOS Bergeron/Esposito Oates/Seguin 80.00 200.00
CCR4GAHV Axelsson/Gagne Hall/Vatrano 50.00 125.00
CCR4HKFM Hamilton/Krug McAvoy/Forbort 60.00 150.00
CCR4LCBP Leetch/Bourque Chara/Park 80.00 200.00
CCR4LMCG McAvoy/Lindholm Grzelcyk/Carlo 60.00 150.00
CCR4NCBB Bourque/Neely Chara/Bergeron 80.00 200.00
CCR4NMPD Pastrnak/Neely Murray/DeBrusk 125.00 300.00

2023-24 Upper Deck Boston Bruins Centennial Centennial Cloth Relics

*PREMIUM/49: 1X TO 2.5X BASIC
CCRAO Adam Oates SP 10.00 25.00
CCRBC Brandon Carlo 8.00 20.00
CCRBL Brian Leetch SP 8.00 20.00
CCRBM Brad Marchand 20.00 50.00
CCRCC Charlie Coyle 10.00 25.00
CCRCM Charlie McAvoy 12.00 30.00
CCRDB David Backes SP 6.00 15.00
CCRDF Derek Forbort 6.00 15.00
CCRDH Danton Heinen 6.00 15.00
CCRDM Dominic Moore 6.00 15.00
CCRDP David Pastrnak 25.00 60.00
CCRFV Frank Vatrano 8.00 20.00
CCRGC Gerry Cheevers SP 10.00 25.00
CCRGH Garnet Hathaway 6.00 15.00
CCRGM Glen Murray 8.00 20.00
CCRHA Dougie Hamilton 8.00 20.00
CCRHL Hampus Lindholm 6.00 15.00
CCRJD Jake DeBrusk 10.00 25.00
CCRJS Jeremy Swayman 15.00 40.00
CCRJT Joe Thornton SP 15.00 40.00
CCRLU Linus Ullmark 10.00 25.00
CCRMG Matt Grzelcyk 8.00 20.00
CCRNF Nick Foligno 6.00 15.00
CCROS Oskar Steen 6.00 15.00
CCRPA Per-Johan Axelsson 6.00 15.00
CCRPB Patrice Bergeron 12.00 30.00
CCRPE Phil Esposito SP 15.00 40.00
CCRRB Ray Bourque SP 15.00 40.00
CCRRD Ryan Donato 8.00 20.00
CCRSG Simon Gagne 10.00 25.00
CCRTH Taylor Hall 10.00 25.00
CCRTK Torey Krug 8.00 20.00
CCRTR Tuukka Rask 12.00 30.00
CCRTS Tyler Seguin 12.00 30.00
CCRTT Tim Thomas 10.00 25.00
CCRZC Zdeno Chara 10.00 25.00

2023-24 Upper Deck Boston Bruins Centennial Centennial Cloth Triple Relics

CCR3BMP Pastrnak Bergeron/Marchand 80.00 200.00
CCR3CBM Marchand Chara/Bergeron 60.00 150.00
CCR3CBP Bourque/Chara/Park 50.00 125.00
CCR3CBS Bergeron/Seguin/Chara 40.00 100.00
CCR3CHS Coyle/Hathaway/Steen 30.00 80.00
CCR3ETP Esposito Thornton/Pastrnak 80.00 200.00
CCR3FGD Forbort/Grzelcyk/DeBrusk 30.00 80.00
CCR3FHL Foligno/Lindholm/Hall 30.00 80.00
CCR3GHP Gagne/Hamilton/Pastrnak 80.00 200.00
CCR3KMV Marchand/Krug/Vatrano 60.00 150.00
CCR3LMC Lindholm/McAvoy/Carlo 40.00 100.00
CCR3MBH Heinen/Moore/Backes 20.00 50.00
CCR3NMB Bourque/Murray/Neely 50.00 125.00
CCR3SRB Raycroft Bourque/Samsonov SP 50.00 125.00
CCR3TUS Thomas Swayman/Ullmark 50.00 125.00

2023-24 Upper Deck Boston Bruins Centennial Next Up

*GOLD: .8X TO 2X BASIC
N1 Mason Lohrei 4.00 10.00
N2 Justin Brazeau 2.00 5.00
N3 Marc McLaughlin 1.50 4.00
N4 David Pastrnak 6.00 15.00
N5 Pavel Zacha 2.00 5.00
N6 Morgan Geekie 1.50 4.00
N7 Jakub Lauko 2.50 6.00
N8 Matthew Poitras 5.00 12.00
N9 Jeremy Swayman 4.00 10.00
N10 John Beecher 5.00 12.00
N11 Charlie McAvoy 3.00 8.00
N12 Georgii Merkulov 2.50 6.00
N13 Brandon Carlo 2.00 5.00
N14 Trent Frederic 1.50 4.00
N15 Parker Wotherspoon 1.50 4.00

2023-24 Upper Deck Boston Bruins Centennial Retro

1 Derek Sanderson 3.00 8.00
2 Steve Heinze 2.50 6.00
3 Charlie McAvoy 4.00 10.00
4 Marc Savard 2.00 5.00
5 Tim Thomas 3.00 8.00
6 Ken Linseman 3.00 8.00
7 Chris Nilan 2.00 5.00
8 Shawn Thornton 2.00 5.00
9 Bill Ranford 2.50 6.00
10 Gregg Sheppard 2.50 6.00
11 Hampus Lindholm 2.00 5.00
12 Byron Dafoe 3.00 8.00
13 Al Secord 2.50 6.00
14 Ed Westfall 2.50 6.00
15 Norm Leveille 2.00 5.00
16 Cam Neely 3.00 8.00
17 Charlie Simmer 2.00 5.00
18 Rick Middleton 3.00 8.00
19 Jake DeBrusk 3.00 8.00
20 Jean Ratelle 2.50 6.00
21 Keith Crowder 2.00 5.00
22 Rogie Vachon 3.00 8.00
23 Ray Bourque 5.00 12.00
24 Dit Clapper 2.00 5.00
25 Phil Esposito 5.00 12.00
26 Connor Clifton 2.00 5.00
27 Terry O'Reilly 2.50 6.00
28 Bill Guerin 3.00 8.00
29 Joe Thornton 5.00 12.00
30 Rejean Lemelin 2.00 5.00
31 Dave Christian 2.00 5.00
32 Dallas Smith 4.00 10.00
33 Gerry Cheevers 3.00 8.00
34 Pavel Zacha 2.50 6.00
35 Adam Oates 3.00 8.00
36 Kyle McLaren 2.00 5.00
37 Wayne Cashman 2.00 5.00
38 Willie O'Ree 4.00 10.00
39 Dave Forbes 2.00 5.00
40 Charlie Coyle 3.00 8.00
41 Gord Kluzak 2.00 5.00
42 Torey Krug 2.50 6.00
43 Ed Johnston 3.00 8.00
44 Glen Murray 2.50 6.00
45 Brad Marchand 6.00 15.00
46 Milan Lucic 2.50 6.00
47 Andy Brickley 2.00 5.00
48 Jason Allison 2.50 6.00
49 Sergei Samsonov 2.50 6.00
50 Craig Janney 2.50 6.00
51 Joe Juneau 2.00 5.00
52 David Pastrnak 8.00 20.00
53 Jozef Stumpel 2.00 5.00
54 Steve Kasper 3.00 8.00
55 Brian Propp 2.50 6.00
56 Bob Beers 2.00 5.00
57 Brad Park 2.50 6.00
58 Hal Gill 2.00 5.00
59 John Wensink 2.00 5.00
60 Daniel Paille 2.00 5.00
61 Allen Pedersen 2.00 5.00
62 Bobby Orr 12.00 30.00
63 Jakub Lauko 3.00 8.00
64 Paul Coffey 3.00 8.00
65 Eddie Shore 3.00 8.00
66 Don Marcotte 2.00 5.00
67 Ken Hodge 2.50 6.00
68 Harry Sinden 2.00 5.00
69 Bob Sweeney 2.00 5.00
70 Bobby Carpenter 2.50 6.00
71 Jacques Plante 3.00 8.00
72 Ted Donato 2.00 5.00
73 Andy Moog 3.00 8.00
74 Brian Leetch 2.50 6.00
75 Mike Knuble 2.00 5.00
76 Matt Grzelcyk 2.50 6.00
77 Zdeno Chara 3.00 8.00
78 Terry Sawchuk 3.00 8.00
79 Tom Fergus 2.00 5.00
80 Ken Hodge Jr. 2.00 5.00
81 Per-Johan Axelsson 3.00 8.00
82 Butch Goring 3.00 8.00
83 Jeremy Swayman 5.00 12.00
84 Reed Larson 2.50 6.00
85 Randy Burridge 2.00 5.00
86 Mark Recchi 3.00 8.00
87 Glen Wesley 2.00 5.00
88 Andrew Raycroft 2.50 6.00
89 Patrice Bergeron 4.00 10.00
90 Lionel Hitchman 2.00 5.00
91 Johnny Bucyk 3.00 8.00
92 Don Awrey 2.00 5.00
93 Marco Sturm 2.00 5.00
94 Ken Baumgartner 2.00 5.00
95 Johnny Boychuk 2.50 6.00
96 Linus Ullmark 3.00 8.00
97 Rick Nash 3.00 8.00
98 Mike Milbury 2.00 5.00
99 Brian Rolston 2.50 6.00
100 Dave Reid 2.00 5.00

2023-24 Upper Deck Boston Bruins Centennial Stoppers

*GOLD: .8X TO 2X BASIC
ST1 Bill Ranford 2.00 5.00
ST2 Tim Thomas 2.50 6.00
ST3 Rogie Vachon 2.50 6.00
ST4 Byron Dafoe 2.00 5.00
ST5 Ron Grahame 2.00 5.00
ST6 Jeremy Swayman 4.00 10.00
ST7 Rejean Lemelin 1.50 4.00
ST8 John Grahame 1.50 4.00
ST9 Felix Potvin 4.00 10.00
ST10 Terry Sawchuk 2.50 6.00
ST11 Andrew Raycroft 2.00 5.00
ST12 Ed Johnston 2.50 6.00
ST13 Jacques Plante 2.50 6.00
ST14 Linus Ullmark 2.50 6.00
ST15 Andy Moog 2.50 6.00

2023-24 Upper Deck Boston Bruins Centennial Box Set

COMP. BASE SET PER BOX
1 Derek Sanderson .50 1.25
2 Steve Heinze .40 1.00
3 Charlie McAvoy .60 1.50
4 Marc Savard .30 .75
5 Tim Thomas .50 1.25
6 Ken Linseman .50 1.25
7 Chris Nilan .30 .75
8 Shawn Thornton .30 .75
9 Bill Ranford .40 1.00
10 Gregg Sheppard .40 1.00
11 Hampus Lindholm .30 .75
12 Byron Dafoe .40 1.00
13 Al Secord .40 1.00
14 Ed Westfall .40 1.00
15 Norm Leveille .30 .75
16 Cam Neely .50 1.25
17 Charlie Simmer .30 .75
18 Rick Middleton .50 1.25
19 Jake DeBrusk .50 1.25
20 Jean Ratelle .40 1.00
21 Keith Crowder .30 .75
22 Rogie Vachon .50 1.25
23 Ray Bourque .75 2.00
24 Dit Clapper .30 .75
25 Phil Esposito .75 2.00
26 Connor Clifton .30 .75
27 Terry O'Reilly .40 1.00
28 Bill Guerin .50 1.25
29 Joe Thornton .75 2.00
30 Rejean Lemelin .30 .75
31 Dave Christian .30 .75
32 Dallas Smith .60 1.50
33 Gerry Cheevers .50 1.25
34 Pavel Zacha .40 1.00
35 Adam Oates .50 1.25
36 Kyle McLaren .30 .75
37 Wayne Cashman .30 .75
38 Willie O'Ree .60 1.50
39 Dave Forbes .30 .75
40 Charlie Coyle .50 1.25
41 Gord Kluzak .30 .75
42 Torey Krug .40 1.00
43 Ed Johnston .50 1.25
44 Glen Murray .40 1.00
45 Brad Marchand 1.00 2.50
46 Milan Lucic .40 1.00
47 Andy Brickley .30 .75
48 Jason Allison .40 1.00
49 Sergei Samsonov .40 1.00
50 Craig Janney .40 1.00
51 Joe Juneau .30 .75
52 David Pastrnak 1.25 3.00
53 Jozef Stumpel .30 .75
54 Steve Kasper .30 .75
55 Brian Propp .40 1.00
56 Bob Beers .30 .75
57 Brad Park .40 1.00
58 Hal Gill .30 .75
59 John Wensink .30 .75
60 Daniel Paille .30 .75
61 Allen Pedersen .30 .75
62 Bobby Orr 2.00 5.00
63 Jakub Lauko .50 1.25
64 Paul Coffey .50 1.25
65 Eddie Shore .50 1.25
66 Don Marcotte .30 .75
67 Ken Hodge .40 1.00
68 Harry Sinden .30 .75
69 Bob Sweeney .30 .75
70 Bobby Carpenter .40 1.00
71 Jacques Plante .50 1.25
72 Ted Donato .30 .75
73 Andy Moog .50 1.25
74 Brian Leetch .40 1.00
75 Mike Knuble .30 .75
76 Matt Grzelcyk .40 1.00
77 Zdeno Chara .50 1.25
78 Terry Sawchuk .50 1.25
79 Tom Fergus .30 .75
80 Ken Hodge Jr. .30 .75
81 P.J. Axelsson .30 .75
82 Butch Goring .50 1.25
83 Jeremy Swayman .75 2.00
84 Reed Larson .40 1.00
85 Randy Burridge .30 .75
86 Mark Recchi .50 1.25
87 Glen Wesley .30 .75
88 Andrew Raycroft .40 1.00
89 Patrice Bergeron .60 1.50
90 Lionel Hitchman .30 .75
91 Johnny Bucyk .50 1.25
92 Don Awrey .30 .75
93 Marco Sturm .30 .75
94 Don Sweeney .30 .75
95 Johnny Boychuk .40 1.00
96 Linus Ullmark .50 1.25
97 Rick Nash .50 1.25
98 Mike Milbury .30 .75
99 Brian Rolston .40 1.00
100 Dave Reid .30 .75

2023-24 Upper Deck Boston Bruins Centennial Box Set Gold Spectrum

*GOLD: 5X TO 12X BASIC

2023-24 Upper Deck Boston Bruins Centennial Box Set Yellow

*YELLOW: 4X TO 10X BASIC

2023-24 Upper Deck Boston Bruins Centennial Box Set Beantown Classics

BC1 Brad Park 5.00 12.00
BC2 Willie O'Ree 8.00 20.00
BC3 Ken Hodge 5.00 12.00
BC4 Brad Marchand 12.00 30.00
BC5 Derek Sanderson 6.00 15.00
BC6 Andy Moog 8.00 20.00
BC7 Rick Middleton 6.00 15.00
BC8 Joe Thornton 10.00 25.00
BC9 Bobby Orr 15.00 40.00
BC10 David Pastrnak 15.00 40.00
BC11 Phil Esposito 10.00 25.00
BC12 Adam Oates 6.00 15.00
BC13 Johnny Bucyk 6.00 15.00
BC14 Ed Johnston 6.00 15.00
BC15 Gerry Cheevers 8.00 20.00
BC16 Cam Neely 6.00 15.00
BC17 Wayne Cashman 4.00 10.00
BC18 Patrice Bergeron 12.00 30.00
BC19 Ray Bourque 10.00 25.00
BC20 Terry O'Reilly 5.00 12.00

2015-16 Upper Deck Buybacks

*GOLD/24: .6X TO 1.5X BASIC CARD/49
1 Sidney Crosby 12.00 30.00
2 Alexander Ovechkin 12.00 30.00
3 Ryan Miller 3.00 8.00
4 Blake Wheeler 3.00 8.00
5 Nazem Kadri 4.00 10.00
6 Steven Stamkos 6.00 15.00
7 Tuukka Rask 4.00 10.00
8 Ryan Getzlaf 3.00 8.00
9 Jonathan Toews 5.00 12.00
10 Henrik Lundqvist 8.00 20.00
11 Jonathan Drouin 2.50 6.00
12 Taylor Hall 3.00 8.00
13 Jaromir Jagr 8.00 20.00
14 Shea Weber 2.50 6.00
15 Carey Price 8.00 20.00
16 Jonathan Quick 4.00 10.00
17 Evgeni Malkin 6.00 15.00
18 Sam Reinhart 6.00 15.00
19 Henrik Zetterberg 4.00 10.00
20 Zach Parise 3.00 8.00
21 Brock Nelson 3.00 8.00
22 Aaron Ekblad 4.00 10.00
23 Claude Giroux 3.00 8.00
24 Marc-Andre Fleury 6.00 15.00
25 Corey Perry 5.00 12.00
26 Nicklas Backstrom 3.00 8.00
27 Wayne Simmonds 4.00 10.00
28 Nathan MacKinnon 12.00 30.00
29 Tyler Seguin 4.00 10.00
30 Sam Gagner 2.00 5.00
31 Vladimir Tarasenko 4.00 10.00
32 Logan Couture 4.00 10.00
33 Erik Karlsson 4.00 10.00
34 Kyle Turris 2.50 6.00
35 Eric Staal 4.00 10.00
36 Anze Kopitar 5.00 12.00
37 P.K. Subban 4.00 10.00
38 Rick Nash 3.00 8.00
39 Daniel Sedin 4.00 10.00
40 James van Riemsdyk 2.50 6.00
41 Johnny Gaudreau 5.00 12.00
42 Joe Pavelski 4.00 10.00
43 Ryan Nugent-Hopkins 4.00 10.00
44 Max Pacioretty 3.00 8.00
45 Sergei Bobrovsky 5.00 12.00
46 Craig Anderson 3.00 8.00
47 Kevin Fiala RC 4.00 10.00
48 Cory Schneider 3.00 8.00
49 Patrick Kane 5.00 12.00
50 Marian Hossa 3.00 8.00
51 Gustav Nyquist 5.00 12.00
52 Jonathan Bernier 2.50 6.00
53 Mark Giordano 3.00 8.00
54 Patrice Bergeron 4.00 10.00
55 Roberto Luongo 5.00 12.00
56 David Pastrnak 5.00 12.00
57 Ryan Strome 3.00 8.00
58 Alex Galchenyuk 2.00 5.00
59 Filip Forsberg 5.00 12.00
60 Pekka Rinne 3.00 8.00
61 Henrik Sedin 4.00 10.00
62 Nail Yakupov 2.00 5.00
63 Devan Dubnyk 2.50 6.00
64 Evgeny Kuznetsov 4.00 10.00
65 Jake Allen 3.00 8.00
66 Cam Ward 3.00 8.00
67 Frederik Andersen 4.00 10.00
68 Jonathan Huberdeau 4.00 10.00
69 Malcolm Subban RC 5.00 12.00
70 Chris Kreider 4.00 10.00
71 John Tavares 5.00 12.00
72 Tyler Johnson 2.00 5.00
73 Jamie Benn 3.00 8.00
74 Ryan Johansen 2.50 6.00
75 Petr Mrazek 6.00 15.00
76 Sean Monahan 2.00 5.00
77 Corey Crawford 4.00 10.00
78 Patrik Elias 3.00 8.00
79 Zemgus Girgensons 2.50 6.00
80 Duncan Keith 2.50 6.00
81 Jaroslav Halak 3.00 8.00
82 Brian Elliott 2.50 6.00
83 Jacob de la Rose RC 3.00 8.00
84 Radim Vrbata 2.00 5.00
85 Jakub Voracek 2.50 6.00
86 Ondrej Pavelec 3.00 8.00
87 Sam Bennett RC 10.00 25.00
88 Oliver Ekman-Larsson 3.00 8.00
89 Gabriel Landeskog 4.00 10.00
90 Tomas Tatar 2.00 5.00
91 Bobby Clarke 6.00 15.00
92 Wayne Gretzky 20.00 40.00
93 Bobby Orr 8.00 20.00
94 Patrick Roy 8.00 20.00
95 Mario Lemieux 15.00 40.00
96 Doug Gilmour 5.00 12.00
97 Grant Fuhr 6.00 15.00
98 Brett Hull 8.00 20.00
99 Steve Yzerman 8.00 20.00
100 Peter Forsberg 8.00 20.00

2015-16 Upper Deck Buybacks Gold

*GOLD/24: .6X TO 1.5X BASIC CARD/49
11 Jonathan Drouin 4.00 10.00
26 Nicklas Backstrom 5.00 12.00
77 Corey Crawford 6.00 15.00

2015-16 Upper Deck Buybacks Autographs '05-06

RUAO Ovechkin ULT RUJ/17 1000.00 2500.00
SM2 A.Ovechkin UD SM/25 800.00 2000.00

2015-16 Upper Deck Buybacks Autographs '09-10

201 J.Tavares YG UD/91 100.00 175.00

2015-16 Upper Deck Buybacks Autographs '10-11

211B J.Skinner YG UD Gld/25 20.00 40.00
253 R.Getzlaf UD 20th/25 20.00 40.00

2015-16 Upper Deck Buybacks Autographs '11-12

208 Landeskog YG UD Gld/25 30.00 60.00
438 J.Tavares OPC/20 40.00 80.00
465 R.Johansen YG UD/24 60.00 100.00
468 G.Nyquist YG UD Gld/25 30.00 60.00

2015-16 Upper Deck Buybacks Autographs '12-13

60 N.Lidstrom UD/36 15.00 40.00
68 N.Lidstrom ART/18 30.00 60.00
69 N.Lidstrom SPGU/20 15.00 30.00
237 C.Kreider YG UD/20 30.00 60.00
585A C.Kreider OPC/20 20.00 40.00
585B C.Kreider OPC R/20 20.00 40.00
C110 C.Kreider YG UD C/20 30.00 60.00

2015-16 Upper Deck Buybacks Autographs '13-14

202B D.Hamilton YG UD/27 30.00 60.00
202C Hamilton YG UD Gld/25 30.00 60.00
203B A.Galchenyuk YG UD/27 100.00 200.00
203C Galchnyk YG UD Gld/25 100.00 200.00
216A Girgensons YG UD/28 25.00 50.00
216B Girgnsns YG UD Gld/25 25.00 50.00
218A M.Rielly YG UD/44 30.00 60.00
218B M. Rielly YG UD/25 30.00 60.00
222B Hubrdeau YG UD Gld/25 40.00 80.00
228B S.Jones YG UD Gld/25 25.00 50.00
237C J.Trouba YG UD Gld/25 15.00 40.00
242A S.Monahan YG UD/23 75.00 135.00
242B Monahan YG UD Gld/25 75.00 135.00
246A T.Toffoli YG UD/73 40.00 80.00
246B T.Toffoli YG UD Gld/25 50.00 100.00
248A T.Hertl YG UD/35 25.00 50.00
248B T.Hertl YG UD Gld/25 25.00 50.00
451B F.Forsbrg YG UD Gld/25 60.00 120.00
462A F.Andersen YG UD/31 25.00 50.00
462B F.Andersn YG UD Gld/25 25.00 50.00
466A P.Mrazek YG UD/34 40.00 80.00
466B P.Mrazek YG UD Gld/25 50.00 100.00
474A M.Granlund YG UD/64 15.00 40.00
474B Granlund YG UD Gld/25 25.00 50.00
476A T.Jurco YG UD/26 15.00 40.00
476B T.Jurco YG UD Gld/25 15.00 40.00
477B Gallagher YG UD Gld/25 75.00 125.00
482B R.Strome YG UD/18 40.00 80.00
482C R.Strome YG UD Gld/25 25.00 50.00
483A N.Kucherov YG UD/86 40.00 80.00
483B Kucherov YG UD Gld/25 40.00 80.00
485A M.Jones YG UD/31 25.00 50.00
485B M.Jones YG UD Gld/25 25.00 50.00
486A J.Gibson YG UD/36 30.00 60.00
486B J.Gibson YG UD Gld/25 30.00 60.00
498A T.Pearson YG UD/70 15.00 40.00
498B Pearson YG UD Gld/25 25.00 50.00

2015-16 Upper Deck Buybacks Autographs '14-15

206 S.Reinhart YG UD/23 40.00 80.00
206G S. Reinhart YG UD Gld/25 30.00 60.00
211G Gaudreau YG UD Gld/25 125.00 200.00
214 Teravainen YG UD/86 50.00 100.00
214G Teravainen YG UD Gld/25 60.00 120.00
223 L.Draisaitl YG UD/29 30.00 60.00
223G Draisaitl YG UD Gld/25 30.00 60.00
229 J.Sekac YG UD/26 20.00 40.00
229G J. Sekac YG UD Gld/25 20.00 40.00
236A A.Duclair YG UD/63 25.00 50.00
236B A. Duclair YG UD Gld/25 30.00 60.00
241G J. Lehtera YG UD Gld/25 20.00 40.00
457 D. Nurse YG UD/25 30.00 60.00
457G D. Nurse YG UD Gld/25 30.00 60.00
464 Gostisbehere YG UD/53 40.00 80.00
464G Gostisbehere YG UD Gld/25 40.00 80.00
467 Burakovsky YG UD/65 20.00 40.00
467G Burakovsky YG UD Gld/25 20.00 40.00
475 D. Pouliot YG UD/51 20.00 40.00
475G D. Pouliot YG UD Gld/25 25.00 50.00
478 Vasilevskiy YG UD/88 25.00 50.00
478G Vasilevskiy YG UD Gld/25 25.00 50.00
490G K. Hayes YG UD Gld/25 20.00 40.00
494 B. Horvat YG UD/53 60.00 100.00
494G B. Horvat YG UD Gld/25 60.00 100.00
498 S. Darling YG UD/33 30.00 60.00
498G S. Darling YG UD Gld/25 30.00 60.00
NHCD16 W.Gretzky NHCD/22 150.00 400.00

2017-18 Upper Deck Buyback Autographs

201 Connor McDavid/97 ('15-16 UD YG) 2750.00 3500.00

2008-09 Upper Deck Champ's

COMPLETE SET (200) 75.00 150.00
COMP.SET w/o SPs 12.00 30.00
1 Ales Hemsky .25 .60
2 Alex Kovalev .25 .60
3 Alex Tanguay .20 .50
4 Alexander Frolov .20 .50
5 Alexander Ovechkin 1.25 3.00
6 Anze Kopitar .50 1.25
7 Bobby Hull .60 1.50
8 Bobby Orr 1.25 3.00
9 Brad Boyes .20 .50
10 Brad Richards .30 .75
11 Brenden Morrow .25 .60
12 Brian Campbell .25 .60
13 Brian Leetch .25 .60
14 Cam Ward .30 .75
15 Carey Price .60 1.50
16 Chris Drury .25 .60
17 Chris Osgood .30 .75
18 Chris Pronger .30 .75
19 Corey Perry .50 1.25
20 Cristobal Huet .25 .60
21 Dan Ellis .20 .50
22 Daniel Alfredsson .30 .75
23 Daniel Briere .30 .75
24 Daniel Sedin .40 1.00
25 Dany Heatley .25 .60
26 Derek Roy .20 .50
27 Dion Phaneuf .25 .60
28 Eric Staal .40 1.00
29 Evgeni Malkin .60 1.50
30 Evgeni Nabokov .25 .60
31 Gordie Howe 1.00 2.50
32 Guy Lafleur .40 1.00
33 Henrik Lundqvist .75 2.00
34 Henrik Sedin .40 1.00
35 Henrik Zetterberg .40 1.00
36 Ilya Kovalchuk .30 .75
37 Jari Kurri .30 .75
38 Jarome Iginla .40 1.00
39 Jason Arnott .25 .60
40 Jason Pominville .20 .50
41 Jason Spezza .30 .75
42 Jean-Sebastien Giguere .30 .75
43 Joe Sakic .60 1.50
44 Joe Thornton .50 1.25
45 Johan Franzen .25 .60
46 Jonathan Toews .50 1.25
47 Jordan Staal .25 .60
48 Kari Lehtonen .40 1.00
49 Marc Savard .20 .50
50 Marc-Andre Fleury .60 1.50
51 Marian Gaborik .30 .75
52 Marian Hossa .30 .75
53 Mario Lemieux 1.25 3.00
54 Mark Messier .60 1.50
55 Martin Brodeur .75 2.00
56 Martin St. Louis .30 .75
57 Marty Turco .30 .75
58 Mats Sundin .30 .75
59 Miikka Kiprusoff .30 .75
60 Mike Bossy .30 .75
61 Mike Modano .50 1.25
62 Mike Ribeiro .20 .50
63 Mike Richards .25 .60
64 Nathan Horton .25 .60
65 Nicklas Backstrom .30 .75
66 Nicklas Lidstrom .30 .75
67 Niklas Backstrom .30 .75
68 Olli Jokinen .25 .60
69 Pascal Leclaire .25 .60
70 Patrick Kane .60 1.50
71 Patrick Roy .75 2.00
72 Patrick Sharp .30 .75
73 Patrik Elias .30 .75
74 Paul Kariya .30 .75
75 Paul Stastny .25 .60
76 Pavel Datsyuk .50 1.25
77 Ryan Smyth .25 .60
78 Peter Mueller .25 .60
79 Phil Esposito .50 1.25
80 Rick DiPietro .25 .60
81 Rick Nash .30 .75
82 Roberto Luongo .50 1.25
83 Rod Brind'Amour .30 .75
84 Ron Hextall .30 .75
85 Ryan Getzlaf .30 .75
86 Ryan Miller .30 .75
87 Saku Koivu .30 .75
88 Scott Niedermayer .30 .75
89 Shane Doan .25 .60
90 Shawn Horcoff .20 .50
91 Sidney Crosby 1.25 3.00
92 Simon Gagne .30 .75
93 Thomas Vanek .25 .60
94 Tomas Kaberle .20 .50
95 Tomas Vokoun .25 .60
96 Tony Esposito .30 .75
97 Vesa Toskala .40 1.00
98 Vincent Lecavalier .30 .75
99 Wayne Gretzky 2.00 5.00
100 Zach Parise .30 .75
101 Ilya Zubov RC 1.50 4.00
102 Ty Wishart RC 1.50 4.00
103 John Mitchell RC 1.50 4.00
104 Boris Valabik RC 2.00 5.00
105 Kyle Turris RC 3.00 8.00
106 Danny Taylor RC 1.50 4.00
107 Brendan Mikkelson RC 1.25 3.00
108 Justin Pogge RC 1.50 4.00
109 Janne Pesonen RC 1.50 4.00
110 Tom Sestito RC 2.00 5.00
111 Mattias Ritola RC 1.50 4.00
112 Kenndal McArdle RC 1.50 4.00
113 Teddy Purcell RC 1.50 4.00
114 Cory Schneider RC 5.00 12.00
115 Adam Pineault RC 1.50 4.00
116 Pascal Pelletier RC 1.50 4.00
117 Theo Peckham RC 1.50 4.00
118 Kyle Okposo RC 2.50 6.00
119 Michal Repik RC 2.00 5.00
120 Andrew Murray RC 1.50 4.00
121 Trevor Smith RC 1.50 4.00
122 Brett Skinner RC 1.50 4.00
123 Patrick Davis RC 1.50 4.00
124 Adam Pardy RC 1.50 4.00
125 Shawn Matthias RC 2.00 5.00
126 Steve Mason RC 3.00 8.00
127 Paul Bissonnette RC 2.50 6.00
128 Sami Lepisto RC 1.50 4.00
129 Brian Lee RC 1.50 4.00
130 Tim Kennedy RC 2.00 5.00
131 Dan LaCosta RC 2.00 5.00
132 Joe Jensen RC 2.00 5.00
133 Anssi Salmela RC 2.00 5.00
134 Niklas Hjalmarsson RC 2.00 5.00
135 Brad Staubitz RC 1.50 4.00
136 Max Pacioretty RC 4.00 10.00
137 Darren Helm RC 2.00 5.00
138 Brett Sutter RC 2.00 5.00
139 Jonas Frogren RC 1.25 3.00
140 Alex Goligoski RC 2.50 6.00
141 Claude Giroux RC 4.00 10.00
142 Simeon Varlamov RC 4.00 10.00
143 Derek Joslin RC 1.50 4.00
144 Mark Fistric RC 1.50 4.00
145 Karl Alzner RC 1.25 3.00
146 Erik Ersberg RC 1.50 4.00
147 Jonathan Ericsson RC 2.00 5.00
148 Andrew Ebbett RC 1.25 3.00
149 Robbie Earl RC 1.25 3.00
150 Tyler Sloan RC 2.50 6.00
151 Matt D'Agostini RC 1.50 4.00
152 Ben Maxwell RC 2.00 5.00
153 Trevor Lewis RC 2.00 5.00
154 Tom Cavanagh RC 1.50 4.00
155 Mike Brown RC 2.00 5.00
156 David Brine RC 1.25 3.00
157 Derick Brassard RC 2.00 5.00
158 Brian Boyle RC 1.50 4.00
159 Darryl Boyce RC 1.50 4.00
160 Justin Abdelkader RC 3.00 8.00
161 Wayne Simmonds RC 3.00 8.00
162 Zach Bogosian RC 2.50 6.00
163 Nathan Oystrick RC 2.00 5.00
164 Blake Wheeler RC 5.00 12.00
165 Zach Boychuk RC 2.00 5.00
166 Brandon Sutter RC 2.00 5.00
167 Nikita Filatov RC 2.00 5.00
168 Jakub Voracek RC 4.00 10.00
169 James Neal RC 4.00 10.00
170 Michael Frolik RC 2.00 5.00
171 Oscar Moller RC 2.00 5.00
172 Colton Gillies RC 1.50 4.00
173 Patric Hornqvist RC 2.00 5.00
174 Ryan Jones RC 2.00 5.00
175 Matthew Halischuk RC 1.25 3.00
176 Petr Vrana RC 1.25 3.00
177 Andreas Nodl RC 2.00 5.00
178 Luca Sbisa RC 1.25 3.00
179 Ben Bishop RC 3.00 8.00
180 T.J. Oshie RC 4.00 10.00
181 Patrik Berglund RC 1.50 4.00
182 Chris Porter RC 2.00 5.00
183 Jamie McGinn RC 2.00 5.00
184 Vladimir Mihalik RC 1.25 3.00
185 Luke Schenn RC 2.50 6.00
186 Nikolai Kulemin RC 2.00 5.00
187 Dwight Helminen RC 2.00 5.00
188 Patrick Dwyer RC 2.00 5.00
189 Alex Pietrangelo RC 3.00 8.00
190 Derek Dorsett RC 2.50 6.00
191 Steve MacIntyre RC 2.00 5.00
192 Darroll Powe RC 2.00 5.00
193 Chris Stewart RC 2.00 5.00
194 Dustin Jeffrey RC 2.00 5.00
195 Drew Doughty RC 5.00 12.00
196 Kevin Porter RC 1.50 4.00
197 Viktor Tikhonov RC 1.50 4.00
198 Mikkel Boedker RC 2.50 6.00
199 Fabian Brunnstrom RC 1.50 4.00
200 Steven Stamkos RC 10.00 25.00

2008-09 Upper Deck Champ's Fossils and Artifacts

FAAT Aterian Scraper 60.00 150.00
FAAU Auroch Femur 30.00 80.00
FANE Neolithic Stone Tools 200.00 300.00
FAPT Pterosaur Tooth 450.00 550.00
FAWM Woolly Mammoth Femur 25.00 60.00
FAWR Woolly Rhino Humerus 30.00 80.00

2008-09 Upper Deck Champ's Hall of Legends Sports Memorabilia

HOLAN Glenn Anderson 8.00 20.00
HOLBT Bryan Trottier 10.00 25.00
HOLCN Cam Neely 10.00 25.00
HOLDH Dale Hawerchuk 12.00 30.00
HOLDS Darryl Sittler 12.00 30.00
HOLFM Frank Mahovlich 10.00 25.00
HOLGF Grant Fuhr 15.00 40.00
HOLGH Gordie Howe 30.00 80.00
HOLGP Gilbert Perreault 10.00 25.00
HOLHK Dominik Hasek 15.00 40.00
HOLJB Johnny Bucyk 10.00 25.00
HOLJI Jarome Iginla 12.00 30.00
HOLJK Jari Kurri 10.00 25.00
HOLLY Larry Robinson 10.00 25.00
HOLML Mario Lemieux 40.00 100.00
HOLMM Mark Messier 20.00 50.00
HOLMW Mike Weir 15.00 40.00
HOLPE Phil Esposito 15.00 40.00
HOLPR Patrick Roy 25.00 60.00
HOLRB Ray Bourque 15.00 40.00
HOLTE Tony Esposito 10.00 25.00
HOLTW Tiger Woods 150.00 300.00
HOLWG Wayne Gretzky 60.00 150.00

2008-09 Upper Deck Champ's Mini

COMP BASE w/o SPs (200) 15.00 40.00
*BLUE BACK: 3X TO 8X BASIC CARDS
*BROWN BACK: 1X TO 2.5X BASIC CARDS
*PURPLE BACK: 5X TO 12X BASIC CARDS
*RED BACK: 3X TO 8X BASIC CARDS
C1 Ales Hemsky .50 1.25
C2 Alex Kovalev .50 1.25
C3 Alex Tanguay .40 1.00
C4 Alexander Frolov .40 1.00
C5 Alexander Ovechkin 2.50 6.00
C6 Anze Kopitar .60 1.50
C7 Andrei Kostitsyn .50 1.25
C8 Andrew Cogliano .40 1.00
C9 Anze Kopitar 1.00 2.50
C10 Bill Guerin .60 1.50
C11 Brad Boyes .40 1.00
C12 Brad Richards .60 1.50
C13 Brendan Morrison .40 1.00
C14 Aaron Voros .40 1.00
C15 Brenden Morrow .50 1.25
C16 Brian Campbell .50 1.25
C17 Brian Gionta .40 1.00
C18 Brian Rolston .40 1.00
C19 Cam Ward .60 1.50
C20 Carey Price 1.25 3.00
C21 Chris Drury .50 1.25
C22 Chris Higgins .40 1.00
C23 Chris Kunitz .60 1.50
C24 Chris Osgood .60 1.50
C25 Chris Pronger .60 1.50
C26 Colby Armstrong .40 1.00
C27 Corey Perry 1.00 2.50
C28 Cristobal Huet .50 1.25
C29 Dan Boyle .40 1.00
C30 Dan Cleary .50 1.25
C31 Dan Ellis .40 1.00
C32 Daniel Alfredsson .60 1.50
C33 Daniel Briere .60 1.50
C34 Daniel Carcillo .40 1.00
C35 Daniel Sedin .75 2.00
C36 Dany Heatley .50 1.25
C37 Darcy Tucker .50 1.25
C38 David Legwand .50 1.25
C39 Daymond Langkow .40 1.00
C40 Derek Roy .40 1.00
C41 Dion Phaneuf .50 1.25
C42 Doug Weight .60 1.50
C43 Drew Stafford .40 1.00
C44 Duncan Keith .50 1.25
C45 Dustin Brown .60 1.50
C46 Dustin Penner .50 1.25
C47 Dwayne Roloson .50 1.25
C48 Ed Jovanovski .50 1.25
C49 Eric Staal .75 2.00
C50 Erik Cole .40 1.00
C51 Erik Johnson .40 1.00
C52 Evgeni Malkin 1.25 3.00
C53 Evgeni Nabokov .50 1.25
C54 George Parros .40 1.00
C55 Sheldon Souray .40 1.00
C56 David Krejci .60 1.50
C57 Guillaume Latendresse .40 1.00
C58 Henrik Lundqvist 1.50 4.00
C59 Henrik Sedin .75 2.00
C60 Henrik Zetterberg .75 2.00
C61 Ilya Bryzgalov .50 1.25
C62 Ilya Kovalchuk .60 1.50
C63 J.P. Dumont .40 1.00
C64 Jack Johnson .40 1.00
C65 Jarome Iginla .75 2.00
C66 Jarret Stoll .50 1.25
C67 Jason Arnott .50 1.25
C68 Jason LaBarbera .50 1.25
C69 Jason Pominville .40 1.00
C70 Jason Spezza .60 1.50
C71 Jay Bouwmeester .60 1.50
C72 Jean-Sebastien Giguere .60 1.50
C73 Jeff Carter .50 1.25
C74 Jere Lehtinen .40 1.00
C75 Joe Sakic 1.25 3.00
C76 Joe Thornton 1.00 2.50
C77 Johan Franzen .50 1.25
C78 Johan Hedberg .50 1.25
C79 Loui Eriksson .50 1.25
C80 Jonathan Cheechoo .50 1.25
C81 Jonathan Toews 1.00 2.50
C82 Jordan Staal .50 1.25
C83 Josh Harding .60 1.50
C84 Jussi Jokinen .50 1.25
C85 Justin Williams .50 1.25
C86 Kari Lehtonen .75 2.00
C87 Keith Tkachuk .60 1.50
C88 Kristian Huselius .40 1.00
C89 Lee Stempniak .40 1.00
C90 Manny Legace .60 1.50
C91 Marc Savard .40 1.00
C92 Marc Staal .40 1.00
C93 Marc-Andre Fleury 1.25 3.00
C94 Marek Zidlicky .40 1.00
C95 Marian Gaborik .60 1.50
C96 Marian Hossa .60 1.50
C97 Markus Naslund .60 1.50
C98 Martin Biron .50 1.25
C99 Martin Brodeur 1.50 4.00
C100 Martin Erat .40 1.00
C101 Martin Gerber .50 1.25
C102 Martin Hanzal .50 1.25
C103 Martin Havlat .60 1.50
C104 Martin St. Louis .60 1.50
C105 Marty Turco .60 1.50
C106 Mats Sundin .60 1.50
C107 Matt Stajan .40 1.00
C108 Matthew Lombardi .40 1.00
C109 Michael Peca .50 1.25
C110 Michael Ryder .40 1.00
C111 Michal Rozsival .40 1.00
C112 Miikka Kiprusoff .60 1.50
C113 Mike Cammalleri .50 1.25
C114 Mike Comrie .50 1.25
C115 Mike Knuble .40 1.00
C116 Mike Modano 1.00 2.50
C117 Mike Ribeiro .40 1.00
C118 Mike Richards .60 1.50
C119 Mike Smith .60 1.50
C120 Mikko Koivu .60 1.50
C121 Milan Hejduk .50 1.25
C122 Milan Lucic 1.00 2.50
C123 Milan Michalek .40 1.00
C124 Miroslav Satan .60 1.50
C125 Nathan Horton .60 1.50
C126 Nicklas Backstrom .60 1.50
C127 Nicklas Lidstrom .60 1.50
C128 Niklas Backstrom .60 1.50
C129 Nik Antropov .50 1.25
C130 Nikolai Khabibulin .60 1.50
C131 Nikolai Zherdev .40 1.00
C132 Olli Jokinen .50 1.25
C133 Pascal Leclaire .50 1.25
C134 Patrice Bergeron .75 2.00
C135 Patrick Kane 1.25 3.00
C136 Patrick Marleau .60 1.50
C137 Patrick O'Sullivan .50 1.25
C138 Patrick Sharp .60 1.50
C139 Patrik Elias .60 1.50
C140 Paul Kariya .60 1.50
C141 Paul Stastny .50 1.25
C142 Pavel Datsyuk 1.00 2.50
C143 Peter Budaj .50 1.25
C144 John-Michael Liles .40 1.00
C145 Peter Mueller .50 1.25
C146 Phil Kessel .60 1.50
C147 Pierre-Marc Bouchard .60 1.50
C148 R.J. Umberger .40 1.00
C149 Mark Recchi .75 2.00
C150 Ray Whitney .50 1.25
C151 Rick DiPietro .50 1.25
C152 Rick Nash .60 1.50
C153 Robert Lang .40 1.00
C154 Roberto Luongo 1.00 2.50
C155 Rod Brind'Amour .60 1.50
C156 Ryan Getzlaf .60 1.50
C157 Ryan Kesler .60 1.50
C158 Ryan Malone .40 1.00
C159 Ryan Miller .60 1.50
C160 Ryan Smyth .50 1.25
C161 Ryan Suter .50 1.25
C162 Saku Koivu .60 1.50
C163 Sam Gagner .40 1.00
C164 Scott Gomez .50 1.25
C165 Scott Niedermayer .60 1.50
C166 Sergei Fedorov 1.00 2.50
C167 Sergei Zubov .50 1.25
C168 Shane Doan .50 1.25
C169 Shawn Horcoff .40 1.00
C170 Shea Weber .40 1.00
C171 Sidney Crosby 2.50 6.00
C172 Simon Gagne .60 1.50
C173 Slava Kozlov .40 1.00
C174 Steve Bernier .40 1.00
C175 Teemu Selanne 1.25 3.00
C176 Thomas Vanek .50 1.25
C177 Tim Thomas .60 1.50
C178 Tobias Enstrom .40 1.00
C179 Todd White .40 1.00
C180 Tomas Holmstrom .50 1.25
C181 Tomas Kaberle .40 1.00
C182 Tomas Vokoun .50 1.25
C183 Trent Hunter .40 1.00
C184 Ty Conklin .50 1.25
C185 Vaclav Prospal .40 1.00
C186 Valtteri Filppula .50 1.25
C187 Vesa Toskala .75 2.00
C188 Vincent Lecavalier .60 1.50
C189 Wade Redden .60 1.50
C190 Wojtek Wolski .50 1.25
C191 Zach Parise .60 1.50
C192 Zdeno Chara .60 1.50
C193 Adam Pardy .60 1.50
C194 Adam Pineault .50 1.25
C195 Simeon Varlamov 1.25 3.00
C196 Alex Goligoski .75 2.00
C197 Alex Pietrangelo 1.00 2.50
C198 Andreas Nodl .40 1.00
C199 Andrew Ebbett .40 1.00
C200 Andrew Murray .50 1.25
C201 Anssi Salmela 2.50 6.00
C202 Max Pacioretty 5.00 12.00
C203 Ben Bishop 4.00 10.00
C204 Blake Wheeler 6.00 15.00
C205 Boris Valabik 2.50 6.00
C206 Brad Staubitz 2.00 5.00
C207 Tim Kennedy 2.00 5.00
C208 Brandon Sutter 2.50 6.00
C209 Brett Skinner 2.00 5.00
C210 Brian Boyle 2.00 5.00
C211 Brian Lee 2.00 5.00
C212 Chris Porter 2.00 5.00
C213 Claude Giroux 5.00 12.00
C214 Colton Gillies 2.00 5.00
C215 Kenndal McArdle 2.00 5.00
C216 Darren Helm 2.50 6.00
C217 Cory Schneider 6.00 15.00
C218 David Brine 1.50 4.00
C219 Derek Dorsett 3.00 8.00
C220 Derick Brassard 2.50 6.00
C221 Drew Doughty 6.00 15.00
C222 Dwight Helminen 2.50 6.00
C223 Erik Ersberg 2.00 5.00
C224 Fabian Brunnstrom 2.00 5.00
C225 Ilya Zubov 2.00 5.00
C226 Jakub Voracek 5.00 12.00
C227 James Neal 5.00 12.00
C228 Jamie McGinn 2.50 6.00
C229 Janne Pesonen 2.00 5.00
C230 Ty Wishart 2.00 5.00
C231 Joe Jensen 2.50 6.00
C232 John Mitchell 2.00 5.00
C233 Justin Pogge 2.00 5.00
C234 Jonas Frogren 1.50 4.00
C235 Jonathan Ericsson 2.50 6.00
C236 Trevor Lewis 2.50 6.00
C237 Brendan Mikkelson 1.50 4.00
C238 Justin Abdelkader 4.00 10.00
C239 Kevin Porter 2.00 5.00
C240 Brett Sutter 2.50 6.00
C241 Kyle Okposo 3.00 8.00
C242 Kyle Turris 3.00 8.00
C243 Luca Sbisa 1.50 4.00
C244 Luke Schenn 3.00 8.00
C245 Mark Fistric 2.00 5.00
C246 Matt D'Agostini 2.00 5.00
C247 Matthew Halischuk 1.50 4.00
C248 Mattias Ritola 2.00 5.00
C249 Michael Frolik 2.50 6.00
C250 Mike Brown 2.50 6.00
C251 Mikkel Boedker 3.00 8.00
C252 Trevor Smith 2.00 5.00
C253 Josh Bailey 3.00 8.00
C254 Nathan Oystrick 2.50 6.00
C255 Nikita Filatov 2.50 6.00
C256 Niklas Hjalmarsson 2.50 6.00
C257 Nikolai Kulemin 2.50 6.00
C258 Oscar Moller 2.00 5.00
C259 Pascal Pelletier 1.50 4.00
C260 Patric Hornqvist 2.50 6.00
C261 Patrick Davis 2.00 5.00
C262 Patrick Dwyer 2.50 6.00
C263 Patrik Berglund 2.00 5.00
C264 Chris Stewart 2.50 6.00
C265 Petr Vrana 1.50 4.00
C266 Dustin Jeffrey 2.50 6.00
C267 Robbie Earl 1.50 4.00
C268 Ryan Jones 2.50 6.00
C269 Karl Alzner 1.50 4.00
C270 Sami Lepisto 2.00 5.00
C271 Shawn Matthias 2.50 6.00
C272 Steve MacIntyre 2.50 6.00
C273 Steve Mason 4.00 10.00
C274 Steven Stamkos 10.00 25.00
C275 T.J. Oshie 5.00 12.00
C276 Teddy Purcell 2.00 5.00
C277 Theo Peckham 2.00 5.00
C278 Michal Repik 2.50 6.00
C279 Ben Maxwell 2.50 6.00
C280 Tom Sestito 2.50 6.00
C281 Tyler Plante 2.00 5.00
C282 Tyler Sloan 3.00 8.00
C283 Viktor Tikhonov 2.00 5.00
C284 Vladimir Mihalik 1.50 4.00
C285 Wayne Simmonds 4.00 10.00
C286 Zach Bogosian 3.00 8.00
C287 Zach Boychuk 2.50 6.00
C288 Derek Joslin 2.00 5.00
C289 Great White Shark 1.25 3.00
C290 Tiger Shark 1.25 3.00
C291 Acrocanthosaurus 1.25 3.00
C292 African Elephant 1.25 3.00
C293 African Leopard 1.25 3.00
C294 African Lion 1.25 3.00
C295 African Wild Dog 1.25 3.00
C296 Hammerhead Shark 1.25 3.00
C297 Albertosaurus 1.25 3.00
C298 Alectrosaurus 1.25 3.00
C299 Allosaurus 1.25 3.00
C300 Amargasaurus 1.25 3.00
C301 American Alligator 1.25 3.00
C302 American Lion 1.25 3.00
C303 Bull Shark 1.25 3.00
C304 Shortfin Mako Shark 1.25 3.00
C305 Anchiceratops 1.25 3.00
C306 Ankylosaur 1.25 3.00
C307 Sand Tiger Shark 1.25 3.00
C308 Apatosaurus 1.25 3.00
C309 Archelon 1.25 3.00
C310 Archaeopteryx 1.25 3.00
C311 Arctic fox 1.25 3.00
C312 Auroch 1.25 3.00
C313 Baiji Dolphin 1.25 3.00
C314 Bald Eagle 1.25 3.00
C315 Baryonyx 1.25 3.00
C316 Oceanic Whitetip Shark 1.25 3.00
C317 Bird of Paradise 1.25 3.00
C318 Black Rhino 1.25 3.00
C319 Blue Whale 1.25 3.00
C320 Bowhead Whale 1.25 3.00
C321 Brachiosaurus 1.25 3.00
C322 Brontops 1.25 3.00
C323 Brontosaurus 1.25 3.00
C324 Brown Bear 1.25 3.00
C325 Brown Pelican 1.25 3.00
C326 Burgess Shale 1.25 3.00
C327 California Condor 1.25 3.00
C328 Cambrian Trilobite 1.25 3.00
C329 Cape Buffalo 1.25 3.00
C330 Carcharodontosaurus 1.25 3.00
C331 Carrier Pigeon 1.25 3.00
C332 Cave Bear 1.25 3.00
C333 Cheetah 1.25 3.00
C334 Chimpanzee 1.25 3.00
C335 Chinese Alligator 1.25 3.00
C336 Chinook Salmon 1.25 3.00
C337 Blue Shark 1.25 3.00
C338 Clouded Leopard 1.25 3.00
C339 Piranha 1.25 3.00
C340 Compsognathus 1.25 3.00
C341 Corythosaurus 1.25 3.00
C342 Barracuda 1.25 3.00
C343 Cro-Magnon Man 1.25 3.00
C344 Moray Eel 1.25 3.00
C345 Electric Eel 1.25 3.00
C346 Deinonychus 1.25 3.00
C347 Diatryma 1.25 3.00
C348 Dilong 1.25 3.00
C349 Dimetrodon 1.25 3.00
C350 Dimorphodon 1.25 3.00
C351 Australopithecus robustus 1.25 3.00
C352 Diplodocus 1.25 3.00
C353 Dire Wolf 1.25 3.00
C354 Dodo 1.25 3.00
C355 Dromaeosaurus 1.25 3.00
C356 Dunkleosteus 1.25 3.00
C357 Edmontosaurus 1.25 3.00
C358 Einiosaurus 1.25 3.00
C359 Elasmosaurus 1.25 3.00
C360 Emperor Penguin 1.25 3.00
C361 Euoplocephalus 1.25 3.00
C362 Fin Whale 1.25 3.00
C363 Fox 1.25 3.00
C364 Galapagos Hawk 1.25 3.00
C365 Galapagos Penguin 1.25 3.00
C366 Galapagos Tortoise 1.25 3.00
C367 Black Widow 1.25 3.00
C368 Giant Panda 1.25 3.00
C369 Giganotosaurus 1.25 3.00
C370 Portuguese Man O'War 1.25 3.00
C371 Glyptodon 1.25 3.00
C372 Gorgosaurus 1.25 3.00
C373 Gray Wolf 1.25 3.00
C374 Ground Sloth 1.25 3.00
C375 Hesperornis 1.25 3.00
C376 Hippopotamus 1.25 3.00
C377 Hominids 1.25 3.00
C378 Hoplophoneus 1.25 3.00
C379 Humpback Whale 1.25 3.00
C380 Hyaenodon 1.25 3.00
C381 Ichthyosaurus 1.25 3.00
C382 Coelacanth 1.25 3.00
C383 Iguanodon 1.25 3.00
C384 Jaguar 1.25 3.00
C385 Jobaria 1.25 3.00
C386 Kakapo 1.25 3.00
C387 Killer Whale 1.25 3.00
C388 Golden-Mantled Tree Kangaroo 1.25 3.00
C389 Komodo Dragon 1.25 3.00
C390 Lambeosaurus 1.25 3.00
C391 Lannacus Trilobite 1.25 3.00
C392 Box Jellyfish 1.25 3.00
C393 Leopard Seal 1.25 3.00
C394 Leptoceratops 1.25 3.00
C395 Lesothosaurus 1.25 3.00
C396 Maiasaura 1.25 3.00
C397 Mastodon 1.25 3.00
C398 Marbled Cone Snail 1.25 3.00
C399 Megalodon 1.25 3.00
C400 Megalosaurus 1.25 3.00
C401 Megatherium 1.25 3.00
C402 Australopithecus africanus 1.25 3.00
C403 Blue Ringed Octopus 1.25 3.00
C404 Microraptor 1.25 3.00
C405 Death Stalker Scorpion 1.25 3.00
C406 Moa 1.25 3.00
C407 Stonefish 1.25 3.00
C408 Moose 1.25 3.00
C409 Mountain Lion 1.25 3.00
C410 Muttaburrasaurus 1.25 3.00
C411 Sydney Funnel Web Spider 1.25 3.00
C412 Neanderthal Man 1.25 3.00
C413 Inland Taipan 1.25 3.00
C414 Ocelot 1.25 3.00
C415 Orangutan 1.25 3.00
C416 King Cobra 1.25 3.00
C417 Ornithomimus 1.25 3.00
C418 Ouranosaurus 1.25 3.00
C419 Oviraptor 1.25 3.00
C420 Brazilian Wandering Spider 1.25 3.00
C421 Panther 1.25 3.00
C422 Paradoxides trilobite 1.25 3.00
C423 Parasaurolophus 1.25 3.00
C424 Puffer Fish 1.25 3.00
C425 Homo habilis 1.25 3.00
C426 Plateosaurus 1.25 3.00
C427 Plesiosaurus 1.25 3.00
C428 Polacanthus 1.25 3.00
C429 Polar Bear 1.25 3.00
C430 Prairie Dog 1.25 3.00
C431 Pterodactyl 1.25 3.00
C432 Pterosaur 1.25 3.00
C433 Quetzalcoatlus 1.25 3.00
C434 Red Deer 1.25 3.00
C435 Red Wolf 1.25 3.00
C436 Rhoetosaurus 1.25 3.00
C437 Right Whale 1.25 3.00
C438 Royal Bengal Tiger 1.25 3.00
C439 Australopithecus afarensis 1.25 3.00
C440 Saber-Toothed Cat 1.25 3.00
C441 Salt Water Crocodile 1.25 3.00
C442 Saltasaurus 1.25 3.00
C443 Sarcosuchus 1.25 3.00
C444 Sea Otter 1.25 3.00
C445 Sea Turtle 1.25 3.00
C446 Seismosaurus 1.25 3.00
C447 Homo ergaster 1.25 3.00
C448 Poison Dart Frog 1.25 3.00
C449 Sinornithosaurus 1.25 3.00
C450 Sinosauropteryx 1.25 3.00
C451 Snow Leopard 1.25 3.00
C452 Sperm Whale 1.25 3.00
C453 Spider Monkey 1.25 3.00
C454 Spinosaurus 1.25 3.00
C455 Spotted Hyena 1.25 3.00
C456 Homo heidelbergensis 1.25 3.00
C457 Steelhead 1.25 3.00
C458 Stegosaurus 1.25 3.00
C459 Sturgeon 1.25 3.00
C460 Styracosaurus 1.25 3.00
C461 Sun Bear 1.25 3.00
C462 Tasmanian Devil 1.25 3.00
C463 Tasmanian Tiger 1.25 3.00
C464 Homo erectus 1.25 3.00
C465 Torosaurus 1.25 3.00
C466 Toxodon 1.25 3.00
C467 Triceratops 1.25 3.00
C468 Troodon 1.25 3.00
C469 Tropeognathus 1.25 3.00
C470 Tylosaurus 1.25 3.00
C471 Tyrannosaurus Rex 1.25 3.00
C472 Velociraptor 1.25 3.00
C473 Western Gorilla 1.25 3.00
C474 Whooping Crane 1.25 3.00
C475 Wolverine 1.25 3.00
C476 Woodpecker 1.25 3.00
C477 Woolly Mammoth 1.25 3.00
C478 Woolly Rhino 1.25 3.00
C479 Zebra 1.25 3.00
C480 Sahelanthropus tchadensis 1.25 3.00

2008-09 Upper Deck Champ's Mini Threads

CTAN Antero Niittymaki 4.00 10.00
CTAO Alexander Ovechkin 20.00 50.00
CTAP Alex Pietrangelo 8.00 20.00
CTBB Bob Bourne 3.00 8.00
CTBD Brandon Sutter 5.00 12.00
CTBG Brian Gionta 3.00 8.00
CTBK Mikkel Boedker 6.00 15.00
CTBN Bernie Nicholls 4.00 10.00
CTBO Ray Bourque 8.00 20.00
CTBS Billy Smith 5.00 12.00
CTBT Bryan Trottier 5.00 12.00
CTBW Blake Wheeler 12.00 30.00
CTCG Colton Gillies 4.00 10.00
CTCJ Curtis Joseph 6.00 15.00
CTDB Derick Brassard 5.00 12.00
CTDC Dino Ciccarelli 5.00 12.00
CTDD Drew Doughty 12.00 30.00
CTDG Doug Gilmour 6.00 15.00
CTDP Dion Phaneuf 4.00 10.00
CTEC Erik Cole 3.00 8.00
CTES Eric Staal 6.00 15.00
CTFB Fabian Brunnstrom 4.00 10.00
CTGA Glenn Anderson 4.00 10.00
CTHA Dale Hawerchuk 6.00 15.00
CTIK Ilya Kovalchuk 5.00 12.00
CTJL Jere Lehtinen 3.00 8.00
CTJS Joe Sakic 10.00 25.00
CTJV Jakub Voracek 10.00 25.00
CTKL Kari Lehtonen 6.00 15.00
CTLM Lanny McDonald 5.00 12.00
CTLR Luc Robitaille 5.00 12.00
CTMB Martin Brodeur 12.00 30.00
CTMF Manny Fernandez 3.00 8.00
CTMG Marian Gaborik 5.00 12.00
CTMH Marian Hossa 5.00 12.00
CTMK Mikko Koivu 4.00 10.00
CTML Mario Lemieux 20.00 50.00
CTMR Mike Ribeiro 3.00 8.00
CTMS Mats Sundin 5.00 12.00
CTMT Marty Turco 5.00 12.00
CTNZ Nikolai Zherdev 3.00 8.00
CTOA Adam Oates 5.00 12.00
CTOJ Olli Jokinen 4.00 10.00
CTOK Olaf Kolzig 5.00 12.00
CTPB Pierre-Marc Bouchard 5.00 12.00
CTPF Peter Forsberg 10.00 25.00
CTPS Peter Stastny 4.00 10.00
CTRB Rod Brind'Amour 5.00 12.00
CTRL Roberto Luongo 8.00 20.00
CTRM Ryan Malone 3.00 8.00
CTRN Rick Nash 5.00 12.00
CTRT Raffi Torres 3.00 8.00
CTRU Tuomo Ruutu 5.00 12.00
CTRY Michael Ryder 3.00 8.00
CTSB Steve Bernier 3.00 8.00
CTSC Sidney Crosby 15.00 40.00
CTSF Sergei Fedorov 8.00 20.00
CTSG Simon Gagne 5.00 12.00
CTSK Saku Koivu 5.00 12.00
CTSS Steve Shutt 5.00 12.00
CTST Steven Stamkos 15.00 40.00
CTSW Shea Weber 4.00 10.00
CTTF Theoren Fleury 6.00 15.00
CTTR Tuukka Rask 6.00 15.00
CTTW Tiger Williams 3.00 8.00
CTUM R.J. Umberger 3.00 8.00
CTVT Vesa Toskala 6.00 15.00
CTWR Wade Redden 3.00 8.00
CTWW Wojtek Wolski 4.00 10.00
CTZP Zach Parise 5.00 12.00

2009-10 Upper Deck Champ's Green

COMPLETE SET (100) 40.00 100.00
*SINGLES: 1.5X TO 4X BASIC CARDS

2009-10 Upper Deck Champ's Red

COMPLETE SET (100) 125.00 250.00
*SINGLES: 2.5X TO 6X BASIC CARDS

2009-10 Upper Deck Champ's Yellow

COMPLETE SET (100) 200.00 400.00
*SINGLES: 4X TO 10X BASIC CARDS

2009-10 Upper Deck Champ's Yellow Animal Icon

COMPLETE SET (100) 500.00 1000.00
*SINGLES: 8X TO 20X BASIC CARDS

2009-10 Upper Deck Champ's Mini Blue Backs

*ROOKIES: .8X TO 2X BASIC
*VETERANS: 4X TO 10X BASIC

2009-10 Upper Deck Champ's Mini Green Backs

*ROOKIES: 1.2X TO 3X BASIC
*VETERANS: 5X TO 12X BASIC

2009-10 Upper Deck Champ's Mini Parkhurst Backs

*VETERANS: 6X TO 15X BASIC

2009-10 Upper Deck Champ's Mini Red Backs

*ROOKIES: .5X TO 1.2X BASIC
*VETERANS: 2X TO 5X BASIC

2009-10 Upper Deck Champ's Threads

MTAO Alexander Ovechkin 12.00 30.00
MTAS Alexander Semin 3.00 8.00
MTBL Brian Leetch 2.50 6.00
MTCG Andrew Cogliano 2.00 5.00
MTCN Cam Neely 3.00 8.00
MTCO Chris Osgood 3.00 8.00
MTCP Carey Price 6.00 15.00
MTCW Cam Ward 3.00 8.00
MTDA Daniel Alfredsson 3.00 8.00
MTDB Derick Brassard 2.00 5.00
MTDG Doug Gilmour 4.00 10.00
MTDP Dion Phaneuf 2.50 6.00
MTEM Evgeni Malkin 6.00 15.00
MTGA Glenn Anderson 2.50 6.00
MTGB Marian Gaborik 3.00 8.00
MTGF Grant Fuhr 5.00 12.00
MTGH Gordie Howe 10.00 25.00
MTGP Gilbert Perreault 3.00 8.00
MTGR Sergei Gonchar 2.00 5.00
MTHL Henrik Lundqvist 8.00 20.00
MTHZ Henrik Zetterberg 4.00 10.00
MTIK Ilya Kovalchuk 3.00 8.00
MTJB Josh Bailey 2.50 6.00
MTJC Jeff Carter 2.50 6.00
MTJF Johan Franzen 2.50 6.00
MTJI Jarome Iginla 4.00 10.00
MTJM Joe Mullen 2.50 6.00
MTKI Miikka Kiprusoff 3.00 8.00
MTKL Kristopher Letang 4.00 10.00
MTLR Larry Robinson 3.00 8.00
MTMB Martin Brodeur 8.00 20.00
MTMF Marc-Andre Fleury 6.00 15.00
MTML Milan Lucic 3.00 8.00
MTMM Mike Modano 5.00 12.00
MTMR Mike Richards 2.50 6.00
MTMT Marty Turco 3.00 8.00
MTNA Nik Antropov 4.00 10.00
MTNH Nathan Horton 3.00 8.00
MTNL Nicklas Lidstrom 2.00 5.00
MTPD Pavel Datsyuk 5.00 12.00
MTPK Phil Kessel 3.00 8.00
MTPR Patrick Roy 8.00 20.00
MTPS Paul Stastny 2.50 6.00
MTRK Ryan Kesler 3.00 8.00
MTRL Roberto Luongo 5.00 12.00
MTRN Rick Nash 3.00 8.00
MTSB Steve Bernier 2.00 5.00
MTSC Sidney Crosby 8.00 20.00

MTSH Steve Shutt 3.00 8.00
MTSP Patrick Sharp 3.00 8.00
MTSS Steven Stamkos 6.00 15.00
MTST Jordan Staal 2.50 6.00
MTTK Tomas Kaberle 2.00 5.00
MTVO Tomas Vokoun 2.50 6.00
MTWW Wojtek Wolski 2.00 5.00

2015-16 Upper Deck Champ's

1 Dustin Brown .40 1.00
2 Nino Niederreiter .25 .60
3 Ryan Nugent-Hopkins .50 1.25
4 James Neal .25 .60
5 Vernon Fiddler .25 .60
6 Mats Zuccarello .40 1.00
7 Antti Niemi .30 .75
8 Brad Marchand .75 2.00
9 Artem Anisimov .25 .60
10 Andrew Cogliano .25 .60
11 Victor Rask .25 .60
12 Joel Ward .25 .60
13 Dion Phaneuf .30 .75
14 Mark Scheifele .60 1.50
15 Paul Stastny .30 .75
16 Brent Burns .40 1.00
17 Semyon Varlamov .40 1.00
18 Bo Horvat .50 1.25
19 Michael Cammalleri .30 .75
20 Cam Ward .40 1.00
21 P.A. Parenteau .25 .60
22 Ryan Kesler .40 1.00
23 Jonathan Huberdeau .50 1.25
24 Roman Josi .40 1.00
25 Kyle Okposo .25 .60
26 Justin Abdelkader .30 .75
27 Leon Draisaitl 1.25 3.00
28 Mika Zibanejad .50 1.25
29 Ryan Suter .30 .75
30 Tyler Bozak .25 .60
31 Michael Frolik .25 .60
32 Ondrej Palat .30 .75
33 Patrik Elias .40 1.00
34 Lars Eller .25 .60
35 Brian Elliott .30 .75
36 Tomas Plekanec .25 .60
37 Teuvo Teravainen .40 1.00
38 Troy Brouwer .25 .60
39 Nikita Kucherov .75 2.00
40 John Carlson .40 1.00
41 Jonas Hiller .30 .75
42 Steve Mason .30 .75
43 Justin Williams .30 .75
44 James Reimer .40 1.00
45 Chris Kunitz .40 1.00
46 Tyler Myers .25 .60
47 Chris Kreider .50 1.25
48 Evander Kane .40 1.00
49 Teddy Purcell .25 .60
50 Joe Thornton .60 1.50
51 Kevin Hayes .30 .75
52 Mikko Koivu .30 .75
53 Aleksander Barkov .60 1.50
54 Mike Hoffman .25 .60
55 Andrew Ladd .25 .60
56 Dougie Hamilton .30 .75
57 Chris Stewart .25 .60
58 Brandon Dubinsky .25 .60
59 Shane Doan .30 .75
60 Zdeno Chara .40 1.00
61 Carl Soderberg .25 .60
62 Jaden Schwartz .50 1.25
63 Blake Comeau .25 .60
64 Jason Zucker .40 1.00
65 Niklas Kronwall .30 .75
66 Kyle Turris .30 .75
67 Kris Letang .50 1.25
68 Nazem Kadri .50 1.25
69 Milan Lucic .30 .75
70 Kyle Palmieri .30 .75
71 Jeff Skinner .50 1.25
72 Alex Galchenyuk .25 .60
73 Patrick Sharp .40 1.00
74 Evgeny Kuznetsov .50 1.25
75 Lee Stempniak .25 .60
76 Nathan MacKinnon 1.50 4.00
77 Justin Faulk .30 .75
78 Torey Krug .30 .75
79 Vincent Trocheck .40 1.00
80 Derek Stepan .25 .60
81 David Jones .25 .60
82 Jim Howard .50 1.25
83 Victor Hedman .50 1.25
84 Matt Beleskey .25 .60
85 Brent Seabrook .25 .60
86 Seth Jones .40 1.00
87 Blake Wheeler .40 1.00
88 Marcus Johansson .30 .75
89 Andrew Shaw .25 .60
90 Brayden Schenn .40 1.00
91 David Pastrnak 1.00 2.50
92 Marian Gaborik .40 1.00
93 Kris Versteeg .25 .60
94 Mike Green .30 .75
95 John Klingberg .40 1.00
96 Colin Wilson .25 .60
97 Nick Leddy .25 .60
98 Martin Hanzal .25 .60
99 Jack Johnson .25 .60
100 Ryan O'Reilly .40 1.00
101 Radim Vrbata .25 .60
102 Jussi Jokinen .25 .60
103 Corey Crawford .50 1.25
104 Chris Neil .25 .60
105 Thomas Vanek .30 .75
106 Bryan Little .30 .75
107 Brad Richards .40 1.00
108 Mark Giordano .40 1.00
109 Jake Allen .40 1.00
110 Ryan McDonagh .25 .60
111 Ales Hemsky .25 .60
112 Mike Smith .40 1.00
113 Chad Johnson .30 .75
114 David Krejci .40 1.00
115 Anders Lee .40 1.00
116 Derick Brassard .25 .60
117 Brandon Saad .30 .75
118 Ryan Callahan .25 .60
119 Martin Jones .30 .75
120 Wayne Simmonds .50 1.25
121 Morgan Rielly .40 1.00
122 Alexander Steen .25 .60
123 Patric Hornqvist .25 .60
124 Jiri Sekac .25 .60
125 Loui Eriksson .25 .60
126 Scott Hartnell .25 .60
127 Riley Sheahan .25 .60
128 Cody Eakin .25 .60
129 Mikkel Boedker .25 .60
130 Tyler Toffoli .40 1.00
131 David Desharnais .25 .60
132 Mark Stone .50 1.25
133 Jaroslav Halak .40 1.00
134 Alex Pietrangelo .30 .75
135 Cam Talbot .40 1.00
136 David Perron .30 .75
137 Alexandre Burrows .25 .60
138 Frans Nielsen .25 .60
139 Marc-Edouard Vlasic .25 .60
140 Valtteri Filppula .25 .60
141 T.J. Oshie .40 1.00
142 Tyler Ennis .25 .60
143 Brendan Gallagher .40 1.00
144 Nail Yakupov .25 .60
145 Jeff Carter .30 .75
146 Mark Streit .25 .60
147 Jonathan Bernier .30 .75
148 Gustav Nyquist .25 .60
149 Jakob Silfverberg .25 .60
150 Curtis Lazar .25 .60
151 Frederik Andersen .50 1.25
152 Sam Gagner .25 .60
153 Keith Yandle .25 .60
154 Anthony Duclair .30 .75
155 Jonathan Drouin .30 .75
156 Ryan Hartman RC 2.00 5.00
157 Emile Poirier RC 1.25 3.00
158 Jacob de la Rose RC 1.50 4.00
159 Andreas Athanasiou RC 4.00 10.00
160 Andrew Copp RC 1.50 4.00
161 Chandler Stephenson RC 2.00 5.00
162 Mattias Janmark RC 1.50 4.00
163 Brendan Gaunce RC 2.00 5.00
164 Derek Forbort RC 1.25 3.00
165 Mike McCarron RC 2.00 5.00
166 Viktor Arvidsson RC 1.50 4.00
167 Brady Skjei RC 1.25 3.00
168 Devin Shore RC 1.50 4.00
169 Brock McGinn RC 1.50 4.00
170 Antoine Bibeau RC 1.50 4.00
171 Matt Puempel RC 1.25 3.00
172 Stanislav Galiev RC 1.50 4.00
173 Colton Parayko RC 2.50 6.00
174 Brett Pesce RC 1.25 3.00
175 Hunter Shinkaruk RC 1.50 4.00
176 Henrik Samuelsson RC 1.00 2.50
177 Radek Faksa RC 1.50 4.00
178 Linus Ullmark RC 3.00 8.00
179 Nick Ritchie RC 1.50 4.00
180 Shane Prince RC 1.00 2.50
181 Aaron Ekblad SP .75 2.00
182 Dustin Byfuglien SP .60 1.50
183 Daniel Sedin SP .75 2.00
184 Jiri Hudler SP .50 1.25
185 Jonathan Quick SP .75 2.00
186 Jakub Voracek SP .50 1.25
187 Cory Schneider SP .60 1.50
188 Logan Couture SP .75 2.00
189 Gabriel Landeskog SP .75 2.00
190 Matt Moulson SP .40 1.00
191 David Backes SP .40 1.00
192 Eric Staal SP .75 2.00
193 Ben Bishop SP .50 1.25
194 Sean Monahan SP .40 1.00
195 Nicklas Backstrom SP .60 1.50
196 Corey Perry SP 1.00 2.50
197 Oliver Ekman-Larsson SP .60 1.50
198 Zemgus Girgensons SP .50 1.25
199 Shea Weber SP .50 1.25
200 James van Riemsdyk SP .50 1.25
201 Ryan Strome SP .60 1.50
202 Tyler Seguin SP .75 2.00
203 Jason Pominville SP .40 1.00
204 Braden Holtby SP .75 2.00
205 Adam Henrique SP .50 1.25
206 Devan Dubnyk SP .50 1.25
207 Henrik Sedin SP .75 2.00
208 Jason Spezza SP .60 1.50
209 Matt Duchene SP .60 1.50
210 Roberto Luongo SP 1.00 2.50
211 Tyler Johnson SP .40 1.00
212 Jarome Iginla SP .75 2.00
213 Marc-Andre Fleury SP 1.25 3.00
214 Erik Karlsson SP .75 2.00
215 Ryan Johansen SP .50 1.25
216 Pavel Datsyuk SP 1.00 2.50
217 Tuukka Rask SP .75 2.00
218 Max Pacioretty SP .60 1.50
219 Andrew Hammond SP .75 2.00
220 Filip Forsberg SP 1.00 2.50
221 Joe Pavelski SP .75 2.00
222 Jordan Eberle SP .60 1.50
223 Duncan Keith SP .50 1.25
224 Marian Hossa SP .60 1.50
225 Patrick Marleau SP .60 1.50
226 Rick Nash SP .60 1.50
227 Taylor Hall SP .60 1.50
228 Ondrej Pavelec SP .60 1.50
229 Phil Kessel SP .60 1.50
230 Tomas Tatar SP .40 1.00
231 Bobby Ryan SP .50 1.25
232 Drew Doughty SP .75 2.00
233 Nick Foligno SP .50 1.25
234 Patrice Bergeron SP .75 2.00
235 Sergei Bobrovsky SP 1.00 2.50
236 Bobby Orr SP 2.50 6.00
237 Jari Kurri SP .60 1.50
238 Borje Salming SP .60 1.50
239 Guy Carbonneau SP .50 1.25
240 Lanny McDonald SP .60 1.50
241 Gilbert Perreault SP .60 1.50
242 Mike Richter SP .60 1.50
243 Steve Yzerman SP 1.50 4.00
244 Dominik Hasek SP 1.00 2.50
245 Doug Gilmour SP .75 2.00
246 Skookum Jim Mason SP .60 1.50
247 Pitikwahanapiwiyin SP .60 1.50
248 Kaylyn Kyle SP .60 1.50
249 Samuel de Champlain SP .60 1.50
250 Damian Warner SP .60 1.50
251 Louis Jolliet SP .60 1.50
252 Sir. Frederick Banting SP .60 1.50
253 John Moonlight SP .60 1.50
254 George Vancouver SP .60 1.50
255 Phil Mack SP .60 1.50
256 Malcolm Subban SP RC 3.00 8.00
257 Shea Theodore SP RC 3.00 8.00
258 Oscar Lindberg SP RC 2.00 5.00
259 Nicolas Petan SP RC 2.00 5.00
260 Kevin Fiala SP RC 2.50 6.00
261 Jared McCann SP RC 2.50 6.00
262 Noah Hanifin SP RC 3.00 8.00
263 Charles Hudon SP RC 2.00 5.00
264 Connor Hellebuyck SP RC 8.00 20.00
265 Daniel Sprong SP RC 2.50 6.00
266 Robby Fabbri SP RC 2.50 6.00
267 Mikko Rantanen SP RC 10.00 25.00
268 Jake Virtanen SP RC 2.50 6.00
269 Artemi Panarin SP RC 8.00 20.00
270 Sam Bennett SP RC 6.00 15.00
271 Evgeni Malkin SP 3.00 8.00
272 Jonathan Toews SP 2.50 6.00
273 P.K. Subban SP 2.00 5.00
274 Vladimir Tarasenko SP 2.00 5.00
275 Patrick Kane SP 3.00 8.00
276 Carey Price SP 3.00 8.00
277 Ryan Miller SP 1.50 4.00
278 Alexander Ovechkin SP 6.00 15.00
279 Zach Parise SP 1.50 4.00
280 Ryan Getzlaf SP 1.50 4.00
281 Johnny Gaudreau SP 2.50 6.00
282 Claude Giroux SP 1.50 4.00
283 John Tavares SP 2.50 6.00
284 Anze Kopitar SP 2.50 6.00
285 Steven Stamkos SP 3.00 8.00
286 Jamie Benn SP 1.50 4.00
287 Henrik Zetterberg SP 2.00 5.00
288 Jaromir Jagr SP 5.00 12.00
289 Sidney Crosby SP 6.00 15.00
290 Pekka Rinne SP 1.50 4.00
291 Henrik Lundqvist SP 4.00 10.00
292 Sir John A. Macdonald SP 1.50 4.00
293 Henry Hudson SP 1.50 4.00
294 Camille Leblanc-Bazinet SP 1.50 4.00
295 Jacques Cartier SP 1.50 4.00
296 Louis Riel SP 1.50 4.00
297 Sir Alexander MacKenzie SP 1.50 4.00
298 Alex McDonald SP 1.50 4.00
299 Jerry Potts SP 1.50 4.00
300 Jason Priestley SP 1.50 4.00
301 Bret Hart SP 1.50 4.00
302 Theoren Fleury SP 2.00 5.00
303 Denis Savard SP 1.50 4.00
304 Bob Bourne SP 1.00 2.50
305 Phil Esposito SP 2.50 6.00
306 Teemu Selanne SP 3.00 8.00
307 Peter Forsberg SP 3.00 8.00
308 Mark Messier SP 3.00 8.00
309 Patrick Roy SP 4.00 10.00
310 Wayne Gretzky SP 10.00 25.00
311 Nikolaj Ehlers SP RC 5.00 12.00
312 Max Domi SP RC 5.00 12.00
313 Dylan Larkin SP RC 8.00 20.00
314 Jack Eichel SP RC 10.00 25.00
315 Connor McDavid SP RC 20.00 50.00
316 Sam Bennett RR 25.00 60.00
317 Nikolaj Ehlers RR 15.00 40.00
318 Dylan Larkin RR 25.00 60.00
319 Max Domi RR 15.00 40.00
320 Jack Eichel RR 30.00 80.00
321 Connor McDavid RR 200.00 400.00
322 Carey Price RS 90.00 150.00
323 Alexander Ovechkin RS 15.00 40.00
324 Sidney Crosby RS 30.00 80.00
325 Patrick Roy RS 90.00 150.00
326 Mario Lemieux RS 30.00 80.00
327 Wayne Gretzky RS 40.00 100.00

2015-16 Upper Deck Champ's #1 Picks

1AE Aaron Ekblad 12.00 30.00
1AO Alexander Ovechkin 40.00 100.00
1CM Connor McDavid 150.00 400.00
1DH Dale Hawerchuk 12.00 30.00
1JT John Tavares 15.00 40.00
1ML Mario Lemieux 40.00 100.00
1MM Mike Modano 15.00 40.00
1RN Rick Nash 10.00 25.00
1SC Sidney Crosby 40.00 100.00
1TH Taylor Hall 10.00 25.00

2015-16 Upper Deck Champ's Autographs

7 Antti Niemi D 4.00 10.00
14 Mark Scheifele C 12.00 30.00
16 Brent Burns B 8.00 20.00
17 Semyon Varlamov B 8.00 20.00
18 Bo Horvat B 10.00 25.00
20 Cam Ward D 5.00 12.00
23 Jonathan Huberdeau E 6.00 15.00
39 Nikita Kucherov A 20.00 50.00
40 John Carlson D 5.00 12.00
42 Steve Mason C 6.00 15.00
51 Kevin Hayes B 6.00 15.00
54 Mike Hoffman D 3.00 8.00
64 Jason Zucker E 5.00 12.00
66 Kyle Turris C 6.00 15.00
77 Justin Faulk D 4.00 10.00
84 Matt Beleskey E 3.00 8.00
109 Jake Allen E 5.00 12.00
110 Ryan McDonagh C 5.00 12.00
117 Brandon Saad B 6.00 15.00
126 Scott Hartnell B 5.00 12.00
127 Riley Sheahan E 3.00 8.00
128 Cody Eakin D 3.00 8.00
130 Tyler Toffoli E 5.00 12.00
132 Mark Stone B 10.00 25.00
134 Alex Pietrangelo C 6.00 15.00
136 David Perron D 4.00 10.00
143 Brendan Gallagher C 8.00 20.00
148 Gustav Nyquist B 5.00 12.00
151 Frederik Andersen D 6.00 15.00
158 Jacob de la Rose D 5.00 12.00
159 Andreas Athanasiou E 12.00 30.00
160 Andrew Copp E 5.00 12.00
161 Chandler Stephenson E 6.00 15.00
162 Mattias Janmark D 5.00 12.00
163 Brendan Gaunce E 6.00 15.00
164 Derek Forbort E 4.00 10.00
165 Mike McCarron E 6.00 15.00
166 Viktor Arvidsson E 5.00 12.00
167 Brady Skjei D 4.00 10.00
168 Devin Shore E 5.00 12.00
169 Brock McGinn E 5.00 12.00
170 Antoine Bibeau E 5.00 12.00
171 Matt Puempel D 4.00 10.00
173 Colton Parayko A 15.00 40.00
174 Brett Pesce B 6.00 15.00
176 Henrik Samuelsson E 3.00 8.00
177 Radek Faksa E 5.00 12.00
178 Linus Ullmark E 10.00 25.00
180 Shane Prince D 3.00 8.00
181 Aaron Ekblad SP D 10.00 25.00
184 Jiri Hudler SP E 6.00 15.00
186 Jakub Voracek SP D 6.00 15.00
187 Cory Schneider SP C 10.00 25.00
189 Gabriel Landeskog SP D 10.00 25.00
190 Matt Moulson SP D 5.00 12.00
192 Eric Staal SP D 10.00 25.00
194 Sean Monahan SP D 5.00 12.00
201 Ryan Strome SP C 10.00 25.00
202 Tyler Seguin SP B 12.00 30.00
203 Jason Pominville SP D 5.00 12.00
205 Adam Henrique SP D 6.00 15.00
208 Jason Spezza SP D 8.00 20.00
212 Jarome Iginla SP B 12.00 30.00
213 Marc-Andre Fleury SP D 15.00 40.00
216 Pavel Datsyuk SP B 15.00 40.00
221 Joe Pavelski SP D 10.00 25.00
226 Rick Nash SP D 8.00 20.00
227 Taylor Hall SP C 10.00 25.00
230 Tomas Tatar SP D 5.00 12.00
231 Bobby Ryan SP D 6.00 15.00
233 Nick Foligno SP E 6.00 15.00
235 Sergei Bobrovsky SP C 15.00 40.00
236 Bobby Orr SP B 75.00 150.00
237 Jari Kurri SP D 8.00 20.00
240 Lanny McDonald SP D 15.00 40.00
241 Gilbert Perreault SP D 8.00 20.00
242 Mike Richter SP D 8.00 20.00
243 Steve Yzerman SP A 50.00 120.00
244 Dominik Hasek SP B 40.00 100.00
245 Doug Gilmour SP B 40.00 100.00
250 Damian Warner SP E 6.00 15.00
253 John Moonlight SP E 6.00 15.00
255 Phil Mack SP E 6.00 15.00
256 Malcolm Subban SP E 12.00 30.00
258 Oscar Lindberg SP E 8.00 20.00
263 Charles Hudon SP E 8.00 20.00
266 Robby Fabbri SP E 10.00 25.00
270 Sam Bennett SP E 25.00 60.00
271 Evgeni Malkin SP C 30.00 80.00
272 Jonathan Toews SP B 200.00 350.00
276 Carey Price SP B 60.00 150.00
278 Alexander Ovechkin SP B 40.00 100.00
279 Zach Parise SP B 15.00 40.00
283 John Tavares SP C 15.00 40.00
284 Anze Kopitar SP C 40.00 100.00
50 Jamie Benn SP C 20.00 50.00
288 Jaromir Jagr SP B 40.00 100.00
289 Sidney Crosby SP A 200.00 400.00
290 Pekka Rinne SP C 8.00 20.00
302 Theoren Fleury SP C 150.00 300.00
303 Denis Savard SP C 8.00 20.00
304 Bob Bourne SP D 6.00 15.00
306 Teemu Selanne SP B 40.00 100.00
307 Peter Forsberg SP A 30.00 80.00
308 Mark Messier SP B 40.00 100.00
309 Patrick Roy SP A 200.00 350.00
310 Wayne Gretzky SP A 250.00 600.00
313 Dylan Larkin SP D 40.00 100.00
315 Connor McDavid SP D 200.00 400.00

2015-16 Upper Deck Champ's Canadiana Relics

CRCPC 1906 Canadian Pacific Coast Map D 20.00 50.00
CRLWC 1856 Lower Canada Map C 25.00 60.00
CRMON 1895 City of Montreal Map B 30.0080.00
CRTOR 1914 City of Toronto Map B 30.00 80.00
CRUPC 1862 Upper Canada Map C 25.00 60.00
CRWCG 1907 Western Canada and Gold Fields Map D 20.00 50.00
CRWIN 1906 City of Winnipeg Map C 25.0060.00

2015-16 Upper Deck Champ's Canadiana Relics Oversized

RED Redemption Card 90.00 150.00
CRBG Bluegill B 90.00 150.00
CRBR Brook Trout C 90.00 150.00
CRBT Brown Trout A 90.00 150.00
CRCC Channel Catfish B 90.00 150.00
CRCO Coho Salmon B 90.00 150.00
CRLS Lake Sturgeon C 90.00 150.00
CRMU Muskellunge C 90.00 150.00
CRNP Northern Pike C 90.00 150.00
CRRT Rainbow Trout B 90.00 150.00
CRSM Smallmouth Bass C 90.00 150.00
CRSP Striper B 90.00 150.00
CRST Steelhead B 90.00 150.00
CRTM Tiger Musky B 90.00 150.00
CRWA Walleye C 90.00 150.00
CRACC Antique Crow Call A 90.00 150.00
CRACM Antique Casting Medal D 90.00 150.00
CRACW Antique N.A.A.C.C. Casting Weight C 90.00 150.00
CRADU Antique Duck Call D 90.00 150.00
CRAFF Antique Fishing Float D 90.00 150.00
CRAFR Antique Fly Reel D 90.00 150.00
CRAFS Antique Fish Scale A 90.00 150.00
CRAFW Antique Fishing Weight B 90.00 150.00
CRAGC Antique Goose Call A 90.00 150.00
CRAPC Antique Predator Call C 90.00 150.00
CRFDT Fly Line Dressing Tin C 90.00 150.00
CRFFS Antique Fishing Float Small A 90.00 150.00

2015-16 Upper Deck Champ's Conn Smythe Trophies

CSAM Al MacInnis 8.00 20.00
CSEM Evgeni Malkin 12.00 30.00
CSJT Jonathan Toews 10.00 25.00
CSLR Larry Robinson 6.00 15.00
CSNL Nicklas Lidstrom 6.00 15.00
CSPR Patrick Roy 15.00 40.00
CSSY Steve Yzerman 15.00 40.00
CSWG Wayne Gretzky 40.00 100.00

2015-16 Upper Deck Champ's Famous Foods

FF1 Coney Dog - Detroit 2.00 5.00
FF2 Smoked Meat Sandwich - Montreal 2.00 5.00
FF3 Peameal Bacon Sandwich - Toronto 2.00 5.00
FF4 Cheesesteak - Philadelphia 2.00 5.00
FF5 Pierogi - Pittsburgh 2.00 5.00
FF6 Deep-Dish Pizza - Chicago 2.00 5.00
FF7 Lobster Rolls - Boston 2.00 5.00
FF8 Reuben - New York 2.00 5.00
FF9 Poutine - Ottawa 2.00 5.00
FF10 Chicken Wings - Buffalo 2.00 5.00

2015-16 Upper Deck Champ's Fish

F1 Longnose Gar .75 2.00
F2 Black Crappie .75 2.00
F3 Steelhead .75 2.00
F4 Bowfin .75 2.00
F5 Brown Trout .75 2.00
F6 Flathead Catfish .75 2.00
F7 Chinook Salmon .75 2.00
F8 Coho Salmon .75 2.00
F9 Bull Trout .75 2.00
F10 Bluegill .75 2.00
F11 Cisco .75 2.00
F12 Brook Trout .75 2.00
F13 Common Carp .75 2.00
F14 Lake Trout .75 2.00
F15 Burbot .75 2.00
F16 Muskie .75 2.00
F17 Northern Pike .75 2.00
F18 Pink Salmon .75 2.00
F19 Pumpkinseed .75 2.00
F20 Rainbow Trout .75 2.00
F21 Rock Bass .75 2.00
F22 Green Sunfish .75 2.00
F23 Largemouth Bass .75 2.00
F24 Smallmouth Bass .75 2.00
F25 Sockeye Salmon .75 2.00
F26 Brook Stickleback .75 2.00
F27 Golden Shiner .75 2.00
F28 Walleye .75 2.00
F29 Yellow Perch .75 2.00
F30 Yellow Bullhead .75 2.00

2015-16 Upper Deck Champ's Framed Mini Autographs

MAHU Charles Hudon D 25.00 60.00
MAJI Jarome Iginla B 50.00 125.00
MAMG Markus Granlund D 20.00 50.00
MATT Tomas Tatar C 15.00 40.00
MAWG Wayne Gretzky A 250.00 600.00

2015-16 Upper Deck Champ's Framed Mini Jerseys

MJAO Alexander Ovechkin C 15.00 40.00
MJCM Connor McDavid C 60.00 150.00
MJCP Carey Price C 8.00 20.00
MJDG Doug Gilmour A 5.00 12.00
MJDL Dylan Larkin C 12.00 30.00
MJJE Jack Eichel C 15.00 40.00
MJJI Jarome Iginla C 5.00 12.00
MJJT Jonathan Toews C 6.00 15.00
MJMD Max Domi C 8.00 20.00
MJNE Nikolaj Ehlers C 8.00 20.00
MJPR Patrick Roy A 10.00 25.00
MJRF Robby Fabbri C 5.00 12.00
MJSC Sidney Crosby B 15.00 40.00
MJSS Steven Stamkos B 8.00 20.00
MJZP Zach Parise C 4.00 10.00

2015-16 Upper Deck Champ's Framed Tobacco Cards

NA Automobiles 20.00 50.00
NA Animals 20.00 50.00
NA Air Balloons 20.00 50.00
NA Fish 20.00 50.00
NA Canadian Scenes 20.00 50.00

2015-16 Upper Deck Champ's Jerseys

JAE Aaron Ekblad C 6.00 15.00
JAK Anze Kopitar C 8.00 20.00
JAO Alexander Ovechkin B 20.00 50.00
JBE Jonathan Bernier C 4.00 10.00
JCG Claude Giroux C 5.00 12.00
JCP Corey Perry C 8.00 20.00
JCW Cam Ward C 5.00 12.00
JDD Drew Doughty C 6.00 15.00
JDK Duncan Keith C 4.00 10.00
JDS Daniel Sedin C 6.00 15.00
JEK Erik Karlsson B 6.00 15.00
JHL Henrik Lundqvist B 12.00 30.00
JJI Jarome Iginla C 6.00 15.00
JJP Joe Pavelski C 6.00 15.00
JJS Jason Spezza C 5.00 12.00
JJT Jonathan Toews B 8.00 20.00
JKT Kyle Turris C 4.00 10.00
JMH Marian Hossa C 5.00 12.00
JMS Mark Scheifele C 8.00 20.00
JPE Carey Price B 10.00 25.00
JPK P.K. Subban B 6.00 15.00
JRL Roberto Luongo C 8.00 20.00
JRN Ryan Nugent-Hopkins C 6.00 15.00
JRO Patrick Roy A 12.00 30.00
JSC Sidney Crosby A 20.00 50.00
JSW Shea Weber C 4.00 10.00
JTH Taylor Hall C 5.00 12.00
JTR Tuukka Rask C 6.00 15.00
JTS Tyler Seguin B 6.00 15.00
JZP Zach Parise C 5.00 12.00

2015-16 Upper Deck Champ's Northern Wonders

NW1 Banff National Park 1.00 2.50
NW2 Gros Morne National Park 1.00 2.50
NW3 Haida Gwaii 1.00 2.50
NW4 Jasper National Park 1.00 2.50
NW5 Kootenay National Park 1.00 2.50
NW6 Nahanni National Park 1.00 2.50
NW7 Yoho National Park 1.00 2.50
NW8 Mingan Archipelago National Park 1.00 2.50
NW9 Cape Breton Highlands 1.00 2.50
NW10 Sleeping Giant 1.00 2.50
NW11 Bay of Fundy 1.00 2.50
NW12 Niagara Falls 1.00 2.50
NW13 Northern Lights 1.00 2.50
NW14 Perce Rock 1.00 2.50
NW15 Pacific Rim National Park 1.00 2.50

2015-16 Upper Deck Champ's Rookie Jerseys

JAP Artemi Panarin B 12.00 30.00
JBM Brock McGinn C 3.00 8.00
JCH Connor Hellebuyck C 12.00 30.00
JCM Connor McDavid A 25.00 50.00
JDF Derek Forbort C 2.50 6.00
JDL Dylan Larkin A 10.00 25.00
JEP Emile Poirier C 2.50 6.00
JHS Henrik Samuelsson C 2.00 5.00
JHU Charles Hudon C 3.00 8.00
JJD Jacob de la Rose B 3.00 8.00
JJE Jack Eichel A 12.00 30.00
JJM Jared McCann C 4.00 10.00
JKF Kevin Fiala B 4.00 10.00
JMD Max Domi A 6.00 15.00
JMP Matt Puempel C 2.50 6.00
JMR Mikko Rantanen B 15.00 40.00
JNE Nikolaj Ehlers A 6.00 15.00
JNG Nikolay Goldobin B 3.00 8.00
JNH Noah Hanifin B 5.00 12.00
JNP Nicolas Petan C 3.00 8.00
JNR Nick Ritchie B 3.00 8.00
JOL Oscar Lindberg B 3.00 8.00
JPR Shane Prince C 2.00 5.00
JRF Robby Fabbri A 4.00 10.00
JRH Ryan Hartman C 4.00 10.00
JSB Sam Bennett A 10.00 25.00
JSK Hunter Shinkaruk B 3.00 8.00
JSP Daniel Sprong C 4.00 10.00
JST Shea Theodore B 5.00 12.00
JVI Jake Virtanen B 4.00 10.00

2015-16 Upper Deck Champ's Traditions

T1 Don't Touch the Cup 1.00 2.50
T2 Playoff Beard 1.00 2.50
T3 Tapping the Goalie Pads 1.00 2.50
T4 Hat Trick Toss 1.00 2.50
T5 Playoff Handshake 1.00 2.50
T6 From Failing Hands 1.00 2.50
T7 Octopus Toss 1.00 2.50
T8 Fireman's Hat 1.00 2.50
T9 Victory Rats 1.00 2.50
T10 Winnipeg White Out 1.00 2.50
T11 Patrick Roy Talks to Goal Posts 1.00 2.50
T12 Chris Chelios Last to Put on Jersey 1.00 2.50
T13 Bill Ranford Puck Flip 1.00 2.50
T14 Ray Bourque Shoelaces 1.00 2.50
T15 Wayne Gretzky Drinks 1.00 2.50

1999-00 Upper Deck Century Legends

COMPLETE SET (89) 30.00 60.00
1 Wayne Gretzky 1.25 3.00
2 Bobby Orr 1.00 2.50
3 Gordie Howe .75 2.00
4 Mario Lemieux 1.00 2.50
5 Maurice Richard .50 1.25
6 Jean Beliveau .30 .75
7 Doug Harvey .20 .50
8 Bobby Hull .40 1.00
9 Jacques Plante .40 1.00
10 Eddie Shore .20 .50
11 Guy Lafleur .30 .75
12 Mark Messier .20 .50
13 Terry Sawchuk .40 1.00
14 Howie Morenz .15 .40
15 Denis Potvin .15 .40
16 Ray Bourque .30 .75
17 Glenn Hall .25 .60
18 Stan Mikita .30 .75
19 Phil Esposito .40 1.00
20 Mike Bossy .25 .60
21 Ted Lindsay .20 .50
22 Red Kelly .15 .40
24 Bobby Clarke .25 .60
25 Larry Robinson .20 .50
26 Milt Schmidt .15 .40
27 Frank Mahovlich .20 .50
28 Henri Richard .15 .40
29 Paul Coffey .20 .50
30 Bryan Trottier .15 .40
31 Dickie Moore .15 .40
32 Newsy Lalonde .15 .40
33 Syl Apps .15 .40
34 Bill Durnan .15 .40
35 Patrick Roy 1.00 2.50
36 Peter Stastny .20 .50
37 Jaromir Jagr .30 .75
38 Charlie Conacher .15 .40
39 Marcel Dionne .20 .50
40 Tim Horton .20 .50
41 Joe Malone .15 .40
42 Chris Chelios .20 .50
43 Bernie Geoffrion .30 .75
44 Dit Clapper .15 .40
45 Bill Cook .15 .40
46 Johnny Bucyk .15 .40
47 Serge Savard .20 .50
48 Jari Kurri .20 .50
49 Max Bentley .15 .40
50 Gilbert Perreault .15 .40
51 Dominik Hasek .40 1.00
52 Jaromir Jagr .30 .75
53 Peter Forsberg .50 1.25
54 Paul Kariya .30 .75
55 Patrick Roy 1.00 2.50
56 Steve Yzerman 1.00 2.50
57 Ray Bourque .30 .75
58 Pavel Bure .30 .75
59 Teemu Selanne .30 .75
60 Mike Modano .30 .75
61 Eric Lindros .20 .50
62 Brett Hull .25 .60
63 Martin Brodeur .60 1.50
64 Keith Tkachuk .20 .50
65 Joe Sakic .40 1.00
66 Mats Sundin .20 .50
67 John LeClair .20 .50
68 Alexei Yashin .02 .10
69 Peter Bondra .15 .40
70 Brendan Shanahan .20 .50
71 Sergei Samsonov .15 .40
72 Vincent Lecavalier .20 .50
73 Marian Hossa .20 .50
74 Chris Drury .15 .40
75 Milan Hejduk .20 .50
76 Paul Mara .02 .10
77 David Legwand .15 .40
78 Joe Thornton .30 .75
79 Pavel Rosa .02 .10
80 Patrik Elias .15 .40
81 Wayne Gretzky .75 2.00
82 Wayne Gretzky .75 2.00
83 Wayne Gretzky .75 2.00
84 Wayne Gretzky .75 2.00
85 Wayne Gretzky .75 2.00
86 Wayne Gretzky .75 2.00
87 Wayne Gretzky .75 2.00
88 Wayne Gretzky .75 2.00
89 Wayne Gretzky .75 2.00
90 Wayne Gretzky .75 2.00

1999-00 Upper Deck Century Legends All Century Team

COMPLETE SET (12) 40.00 80.00
AC1 Wayne Gretzky 6.00 15.00
AC2 Gordie Howe 4.00 10.00
AC3 Bobby Hull 2.50 6.00
AC4 Bobby Orr 5.00 12.00
AC5 Doug Harvey 2.00 5.00
AC6 Jacques Plante 2.00 5.00
AC7 Mario Lemieux 5.00 12.00
AC8 Maurice Richard 3.00 8.00
AC9 Ted Lindsay 2.00 5.00
AC10 Eddie Shore 2.00 5.00
AC11 Ray Bourque 4.00 10.00
AC12 Terry Sawchuk 2.50 6.00

1999-00 Upper Deck Century Legends Century Collection

*CENTURY COLL: 15X TO 40X BASIC CARDS

1999-00 Upper Deck Century Legends Epic Signatures

BC Bobby Clarke 10.00 25.00
BH Bobby Hull 20.00 50.00
BO Bobby Orr 75.00 150.00
BP Brad Park 6.00 15.00
FM Frank Mahovlich 12.00 30.00
GC Gerry Cheevers 8.00 20.00
GH Gordie Howe 75.00 150.00
JB John Bucyk 8.00 20.00
LR Larry Robinson 15.00 40.00
MB Mike Bossy 8.00 20.00
MD Marcel Dionne 10.00 25.00
ML Mario Lemieux 75.00 150.00
MR Maurice Richard 125.00 200.00
PB Pavel Bure 25.00 50.00
PE Phil Esposito 15.00 40.00
RB Ray Bourque 40.00 80.00
SM Stan Mikita 12.00 30.00
SS Sergei Samsonov 8.00 20.00
TE Tony Esposito 8.00 20.00
TL Ted Lindsay 10.00 25.00
BRH Brett Hull 12.00 30.00
JEB Jean Beliveau 25.00 50.00

1999-00 Upper Deck Century Legends Epic Signatures Gold 100

*GOLD/100: .8X TO 2X SILVER AU
BO Bobby Orr 100.00 250.00
GH Gordie Howe 125.00 250.00
ML Mario Lemieux 150.00 300.00
MR Maurice Richard 125.00 250.00
WG Wayne Gretzky 400.00 1000.00

1999-00 Upper Deck Century Legends Essence of the Game

COMPLETE SET (8) 25.00 50.00
E1 W.Gretzky/P.Kariya 5.00 12.00
E2 B.Orr/R.Bourque 5.00 12.00
E3 M.Lemieux/J.Jagr 4.00 10.00
E4 G.Howe/E.Lindros 2.50 6.00
E5 J. Plante/P. Roy 5.00 12.00
E6 M.Richard/P.Bure 2.50 6.00
E7 B.Hull/B.Hull 3.00 8.00
E8 T.Lindsay/K.Tkachuk 2.50 6.00

1999-00 Upper Deck Century Legends Greatest Moments

COMPLETE SET (10) 60.00 125.00
COMMON GRETZKY (GM1-GM10) 6.00 15.00

1999-00 Upper Deck Century Legends Jerseys of the Century

JC1 Bobby Clarke 12.00 30.00
JC2 Mike Bossy 15.00 40.00
JC3 Larry Robinson 12.00 30.00
JC4 Ray Bourque 15.00 40.00
JC5 Mario Lemieux 30.00 80.00
JC6 Wayne Gretzky 40.00 100.00
JCA1 Bobby Clarke AU/25 150.00 300.00
JCA2 Mario Lemieux AU/25 400.00 800.00

2002-03 Upper Deck Classic Portraits

COMPLETE SET (138) 125.00 250.00
COMP.SET w/o SP's (100) 25.00 50.00
1 Jean-Sebastien Giguere .40 1.00
2 Paul Kariya .40 1.00
3 Mike LeClerc .25 .60
4 Dany Heatley .30 .75
5 Ilya Kovalchuk .50 1.25
6 Milan Hnilicka .30 .75
7 Joe Thornton .60 1.50
8 Brian Rolston .30 .75
9 Sergei Samsonov .30 .75
10 Miroslav Satan .40 1.00
11 Martin Biron .30 .75
12 Tim Connolly .25 .60

13 Roman Turek .40 1.00
14 Jarome Iginla .50 1.25
15 Craig Conroy .25 .60
16 Arturs Irbe .30 .75
17 Ron Francis .50 1.25
18 Rod Brind'Amour .40 1.00
19 Jeff O'Neill .25 .60
20 Alexei Zhamnov .30 .75
21 Eric Daze .25 .60
22 Jocelyn Thibault .30 .75
23 Rob Blake .40 1.00
24 Patrick Roy 1.00 2.50
25 Joe Sakic .75 2.00
26 Peter Forsberg .75 2.00
27 Chris Drury .40 1.00
28 Marc Denis .30 .75
29 Espen Knutsen .25 .60
30 Rostislav Klesla .25 .60
31 Marty Turco .40 1.00
32 Brenden Morrow .30 .75
33 Mike Modano .60 1.50
34 Steve Yzerman 1.00 2.50
35 Nicklas Lidstrom .40 1.00
36 Sergei Fedorov .60 1.50
37 Brendan Shanahan .40 1.00
38 Curtis Joseph .50 1.25
39 Mike Comrie .40 1.00
40 Tommy Salo .30 .75
41 Ryan Smyth .30 .75
42 Roberto Luongo .60 1.50
43 Viktor Kozlov .25 .60
44 Kristian Huselius .25 .60
45 Zigmund Palffy .40 1.00
46 Felix Potvin .60 1.50
47 Jason Allison .30 .75
48 Manny Fernandez .25 .60
49 Andrew Brunette .25 .60
50 Marian Gaborik .40 1.00
51 Saku Koivu .40 1.00
52 Yanic Perreault .25 .60
53 Jose Theodore .40 1.00
54 Denis Arkhipov .25 .60
55 Scott Hartnell .25 .60
56 Mike Dunham .30 .75
57 Martin Brodeur 1.00 2.50
58 Patrik Elias .40 1.00
59 Joe Nieuwendyk .30 .75
60 Scott Niedermayer .40 1.00
61 Alexei Yashin .30 .75
62 Michael Peca .30 .75
63 Chris Osgood .40 1.00
64 Eric Lindros .60 1.50
65 Pavel Bure .40 1.00
66 Brian Leetch .30 .75
67 Dan Blackburn .30 .75
68 Martin Havlat .30 .75
69 Marian Hossa .40 1.00
70 Daniel Alfredsson .40 1.00
71 John LeClair .40 1.00
72 Jeremy Roenick .60 1.50
73 Keith Primeau .30 .75
74 Simon Gagne .40 1.00
75 Tony Amonte .30 .75
76 Sean Burke .25 .60
77 Daniel Briere .30 .75
78 Alexei Kovalev .30 .75
79 Johan Hedberg .40 1.00
80 Mario Lemieux 1.50 4.00
81 Patrick Marleau .40 1.00
82 Teemu Selanne .75 2.00
83 Evgeni Nabokov .30 .75
84 Owen Nolan .40 1.00
85 Chris Pronger .40 1.00
86 Doug Weight .40 1.00
87 Keith Tkachuk .40 1.00
88 Brad Richards .40 1.00
89 Nikolai Khabibulin .40 1.00
90 Vincent Lecavalier .40 1.00
91 Mats Sundin .40 1.00
92 Gary Roberts .25 .60
93 Ed Belfour .40 1.00
94 Alexander Mogilny .30 .75
95 Todd Bertuzzi .40 1.00
96 Brendan Morrison .30 .75
97 Markus Naslund .40 1.00
98 Jaromir Jagr 1.25 3.00
99 Peter Bondra .40 1.00
100 Olaf Kolzig .40 1.00
101 Alexei Smirnov RC 1.50 4.00
102 Stanislav Chistov RC 1.25 3.00
103 Martin Gerber RC 2.00 5.00
104 Kurt Sauer RC 1.25 3.00
105 Chuck Kobasew RC 1.50 4.00
106 Micki Dupont RC 1.25 3.00
107 Shawn Thornton RC 1.50 4.00
108 Jeff Paul RC 1.25 3.00
109 Rick Nash RC 6.00 15.00
110 Lasse Pirjeta RC 1.25 3.00
111 Henrik Zetterberg RC 6.00 15.00
112 Dmitri Bykov RC 1.25 3.00
113 Ales Hemsky RC 4.00 10.00
114 Mike Cammalleri RC 3.00 8.00
115 Ivan Majesky RC 1.25 3.00
116 Jay Bouwmeester RC 4.00 10.00
117 Alexander Frolov RC 4.00 10.00
118 Pierre-Marc Bouchard RC 4.00 10.00
119 Ron Hainsey RC 1.25 3.00
120 Adam Hall RC 1.25 3.00
121 Scottie Upshall RC 1.50 4.00
122 Anton Volchenkov RC 1.25 3.00
123 Dennis Seidenberg RC 2.00 5.00
124 Patrick Sharp RC 3.00 8.00
125 Jeff Taffe RC 1.25 3.00
126 Jason Spezza RC 6.00 15.00
127 Tom Koivisto RC 1.25 3.00
128 Alexander Svitov RC 1.25 3.00
129 Carlo Colaiacovo RC 2.00 5.00
130 Steve Eminger RC 1.25 3.00
131 Jared Aulin RC 1.25 3.00
132 Pascal LeClaire RC 1.50 4.00
133 Steve Ott RC 1.25 3.00
134 Brooks Orpik RC 1.25 3.00
135 Ari Ahonen RC 1.25 3.00
136 Mike Komisarek RC 2.00 5.00
137 Ryan Miller RC 5.00 12.00
138 Ray Emery RC 4.00 10.00

2002-03 Upper Deck Classic Portraits Etched in Time

COMPLETE SET (15) 15.00 30.00
ET1 Paul Kariya .50 1.25
ET2 Joe Sakic 1.00 2.50
ET3 Patrick Roy 2.00 5.00
ET4 Mike Modano .75 2.00
ET5 Steve Yzerman 2.50 6.00
ET6 Brendan Shanahan .75 2.00
ET7 Brett Hull .60 1.50
ET8 Mike Comrie .40 1.00
ET9 Jose Theodore .60 1.50
ET10 Martin Brodeur 1.50 4.00
ET11 Pavel Bure .60 1.50
ET12 Simon Gagne .60 1.50
ET13 Mario Lemieux 3.00 8.00
ET14 Teemu Selanne .50 1.25
ET15 Mats Sundin .50 1.25

2002-03 Upper Deck Classic Portraits Genuine Greatness

COMPLETE SET (7) 20.00 40.00
GG1 Paul Kariya 1.00 2.50
GG2 Peter Forsberg 1.50 4.00
GG3 Patrick Roy 3.00 8.00
GG4 Steve Yzerman 3.00 8.00
GG5 Wayne Gretzky 4.00 10.00
GG6 Pavel Bure 1.00 2.50
GG7 Jaromir Jagr 1.00 2.50

2002-03 Upper Deck Classic Portraits Headliners

*LTD: 1X TO 2.5X BASE HI
DZ E.Daze/A.Zhamnov 4.00 10.00
FS P.Forsberg/J.Sakic 12.50 30.00
JB J.Jagr/P.Bondra 4.00 10.00
KF P.Kariya/J.Friesen 4.00 10.00
LF N.Lidstrom/S.Fedorov 6.00 15.00
LK C.Lemieux/K.Kolanos 4.00 10.00
LM M.Lemieux/A.Morozov 12.50 30.00
RA P.Roy/D.Aebischer 8.00 20.00
RG J.Roenick/S.Gagne 6.00 15.00
ST S.Samsonov/J.Thornton 6.00 15.00
TK J.Theodore/S.Koivu 10.00 25.00
YH S.Yzerman/D.Hasek 12.50 30.00

2002-03 Upper Deck Classic Portraits Hockey Royalty

*LIMITED/25: .8X TO 2X BASIC JSY/90
BLB Burke/C.Lemieux/Briere 12.50 30.00
BPT Brodeur/Potvin/Thibault 25.00 60.00
DLH Dunham/Legwand/Hartnell 12.50 30.00
DPP Deadmarsh/Potvin/Palffy 15.00 40.00
DZT Daze/Zhamnov/Thibault 12.50 30.00
GLS Gretzky/M.Lemieux/Sakic 60.00 150.00
GTD Gagne/Tanguay/Daze 12.50 30.00
GTM Guerin/Thornton/Murray 20.00 50.00
GWA Weight/Amonte/Guerin 12.50 30.00
HBK Halpern/Bondra/Kolzig 12.50 30.00
JHL Jagr/Hejduk/Lang 12.50 30.00
KFB Fedorov/Bure/Kovalchuk 20.00 50.00
KFG Kariya/Friesen/Giguere 12.50 30.00
KGJ Konowalchuk/Gonchar/Jagr 12.50 30.00
KSI Kariya/Sakic/Iginla 30.00 80.00
KTK Knutsen/Tugnutt/Klesla 12.50 30.00
LBL Lindros/Bure/Leetch 12.50 30.00
LLN M.Lemieux/Lang/Nieminen 15.00 40.00
LLT M.Lemieux/Lindros/Thornton 30.00 80.00
LRR LeClair/Roenick/Recchi 20.00 50.00
MML Modano/Morrow/Lehtinen 20.00 50.00
PGF Primeau/Gagne/Fedotenko 12.50 30.00
RBT Brodeur/Roy/Theodore 40.00 100.00
RDF Reinprecht/Drury/Forsberg 15.00 40.00
SCA Satan/Connolly/Afinogenov 12.50 30.00
SIT Savard/Iginla/Turek 12.50 30.00
SLN Selanne/Lehtinen/Nieminen 12.50 30.00
SNL Naslund/Lidstrom/Sundin 15.00 40.00
SYL Shanahan/Yzerman/Lidstrom 30.00 80.00
TSH Tanguay/Sakic/Hinote 12.50 30.00

2002-03 Upper Deck Classic Portraits Mini-Busts

1 Brendan Shanahan A 8.00 20.00
2 Brendan Shanahan G 8.00 20.00
3 Brendan Shanahan H 6.00 15.00
4 Brendan Shanahan M 6.00 15.00
5 Curtis Joseph A 8.00 20.00
6 Curtis Joseph A AU/31 40.00 100.00
7 Curtis Joseph G 8.00 20.00
9 Curtis Joseph H 6.00 15.00
10 Curtis Joseph H AU 30.00 80.00
11 Curtis Joseph M 6.00 15.00
12 Curtis Joseph M AU/25 40.00 100.00
13 Dany Heatley A 8.00 20.00
15 Dany Heatley G 8.00 20.00
17 Dany Heatley H 6.00 15.00
18 Dany Heatley H AU 20.00 50.00
19 Dany Heatley M 6.00 15.00
20 Dany Heatley M AU/25 30.00 80.00
21 Dominik Hasek A 8.00 20.00
22 Dominik Hasek G 8.00 20.00
23 Dominik Hasek H 6.00 15.00
24 Dominik Hasek M 6.00 15.00
25 Dominik Hasek Third 6.00 15.00
26 Gordie Howe A 20.00 50.00
28 Gordie Howe G 20.00 50.00
30 Gordie Howe H 15.00 40.00
31 Gordie Howe H AU SP 50.00 125.00
32 Gordie Howe M 15.00 40.00
33 Gordie Howe M AU/25 100.00 250.00
34 Gordie Howe Third 15.00 40.00
35 Gordie Howe Third AU/50 60.00 150.00
36 Ilya Kovalchuk A 8.00 20.00
38 Ilya Kovalchuk G 8.00 20.00
40 Ilya Kovalchuk H 6.00 15.00
41 Ilya Kovalchuk H AU 20.00 50.00
42 Ilya Kovalchuk M 6.00 15.00
43 Ilya Kovalchuk M AU/25 30.00 80.00
44 Jarome Iginla A 8.00 20.00
46 Jarome Iginla G 8.00 20.00
48 Jarome Iginla H 6.00 15.00
49 Jarome Iginla H AU 12.50 30.00
50 Jarome Iginla M 6.00 15.00
51 Jarome Iginla M AU/25 20.00 50.00
52 Jaromir Jagr A 8.00 20.00
53 Jaromir Jagr G 8.00 20.00
54 Jaromir Jagr H 6.00 15.00
55 Jaromir Jagr M 12.50 30.00
56 Jason Spezza A 8.00 20.00
57 Jason Spezza A AU/39 50.00 125.00
58 Jason Spezza G 8.00 20.00
60 Jason Spezza H 6.00 15.00
61 Jason Spezza H AU 25.00 60.00
62 Jason Spezza M 10.00 25.00
63 Jason Spezza M AU/25 40.00 100.00
64 Jason Spezza Third 6.00 15.00
65 Jason Spezza Third AU/50 30.00 80.00
66 Joe Sakic A 20.00 50.00
67 Joe Sakic G 20.00 50.00
68 Joe Sakic H 12.50 30.00
69 Joe Sakic M 15.00 40.00
70 Joe Sakic Third 15.00 40.00
71 Joe Thornton A 8.00 20.00
73 Joe Thornton G 8.00 20.00
75 Joe Thornton H 6.00 15.00
76 Joe Thornton H AU 30.00 80.00
77 Joe Thornton M 6.00 15.00
78 Joe Thornton M AU/25 50.00 125.00
79 Joe Thornton Third 6.00 15.00
80 Joe Thornton Third AU/50 40.00 100.00
81 Mario Lemieux H 50.00 125.00
82 Mario Lemieux G 60.00 150.00
83 Martin Brodeur A 25.00 60.00
84 Martin Brodeur A AU/30 50.00 125.00
85 Martin Brodeur G 25.00 60.00
87 Martin Brodeur H 12.50 30.00
88 Martin Brodeur H AU 50.00 125.00
89 Martin Brodeur M 15.00 40.00
90 Martin Brodeur M AU/25 75.00 200.00
91 Patrick Roy A 30.00 80.00
92 Patrick Roy A AU/33 125.00 300.00
93 Patrick Roy G 30.00 80.00
95 Patrick Roy H 20.00 50.00
96 Patrick Roy H AU SP 75.00 150.00
97 Patrick Roy M 25.00 60.00
98 Patrick Roy M AU/25 125.00 300.00
99 Patrick Roy Third 25.00 60.00
100 Patrick Roy Third AU/50 100.00 250.00
101 Paul Kariya A 8.00 20.00
102 Paul Kariya G 8.00 20.00
103 Paul Kariya H 6.00 15.00
104 Paul Kariya M 6.00 15.00
105 Pavel Bure A 8.00 20.00
107 Pavel Bure G 8.00 20.00
109 Pavel Bure H 6.00 15.00
110 Pavel Bure H AU SP 30.00 80.00
111 Pavel Bure M 6.00 15.00
112 Pavel Bure M AU/25 60.00 150.00
113 Pavel Bure Third 6.00 15.00
114 Pavel Bure Third AU/50 40.00 100.00
115 Ray Bourque Bos.A 20.00 50.00
116 Ray Bourque Bos.A AU/77 50.00 125.00
117 Ray Bourque G 20.00 50.00
119 Ray Bourque Bos.H 12.50 30.00
120 Ray Bourque Bos.H AU SP 40.00 100.00
121 Ray Bourque M 15.00 40.00
122 Ray Bourque M AU/25 60.00 150.00
123 Ray Bourque Col.Third 15.00 40.00
124 Ray Bourque Col.Third AU/50 50.00 125.00

2002-03 Upper Deck Classic Portraits Pillars of Strength

COMPLETE SET (10) 10.00 20.00
PS1 Ilya Kovalchuk .75 2.00
PS2 Jarome Iginla .50 1.25
PS3 Joe Sakic 1.00 2.50
PS4 Mike Modano .75 2.00
PS5 Brendan Shanahan .75 2.00
PS6 Martin Brodeur 1.25 3.00
PS7 Eric Lindros .40 1.00
PS8 Mario Lemieux 3.00 8.00
PS9 Teemu Selanne .40 1.00
PS10 Olaf Kolzig .40 1.00

2002-03 Upper Deck Classic Portraits Portrait of a Legend

COMPLETE SET (10) 20.00 40.00
COMMON ORR (PL1-PL10) 2.00 5.00

2002-03 Upper Deck Classic Portraits Starring Cast

*LTD: .6X TO 1.5X BASE HI
CAT Alex Tanguay 4.00 10.00
CBG Bill Guerin 4.00 10.00
CBS Brendan Shanahan 5.00 12.00
CFP Felix Potvin 6.00 15.00
CJR Jeremy Roenick 5.00 12.00
CKT Keith Tkachuk 5.00 12.00
CMM Mike Modano 4.00 10.00
CMN Markus Naslund 4.00 10.00
CMS Mats Sundin 5.00 12.00
CPK Paul Kariya 5.00 12.00
CSA Miroslav Satan 4.00 10.00
CSB Sean Burke 4.00 10.00
CSG Simon Gagne 5.00 12.00
CSY Steve Yzerman 12.50 30.00
CZP Zigmund Palffy 4.00 10.00

2002-03 Upper Deck Classic Portraits Stitches

*LTD: .5X TO 1.25X BASE HI
CAD Adam Deadmarsh 3.00 8.00
CBO Peter Bondra 3.00 8.00
CCD Chris Drury 3.00 8.00
CJF Jeff Friesen 3.00 8.00
CJI Jarome Iginla 5.00 12.00
CJT Joe Thornton 6.00 15.00
CKK Krys Kolanos 3.00 8.00
CMD Mike Dunham 3.00 8.00
CPB Pavel Bure 4.00 10.00
CRS Rostislav Klesla 3.00 8.00
CSF Sergei Fedorov 5.00 12.00
CSG Simon Gagne 4.00 10.00
CSR Steven Reinprecht 3.00 8.00
CSS Sergei Samsonov 3.00 8.00
CTH Jose Theodore 5.00 12.00

2003-04 Upper Deck Classic Portraits

COMP.SET w/o SP's (100) 15.00 30.00
1 Sergei Fedorov .50 1.25
2 Stanislav Chistov .20 .50
3 Jean-Sebastien Giguere .30 .75
4 Dany Heatley .25 .60
5 Ilya Kovalchuk .30 .75
6 Joe Thornton .50 1.25
7 Glen Murray .25 .60
8 Sergei Samsonov .25 .60
9 Miroslav Satan .25 .60
10 Maxim Afinogenov .20 .50
11 Chris Drury .25 .60
12 Jarome Iginla .40 1.00
13 Steve Reinprecht .20 .50
14 Roman Turek .25 .60
15 Ron Francis .40 1.00
16 Jeff O'Neill .20 .50
17 Alexei Zhamnov .25 .60
18 Kyle Calder .20 .50
19 Jocelyn Thibault .25 .60
20 Teemu Selanne .60 1.50
21 Peter Forsberg .60 1.50
22 Paul Kariya .30 .75
23 Joe Sakic .60 1.50
24 David Aebischer .25 .60
25 Rick Nash .30 .75
26 Marc Denis .25 .60
27 Todd Marchant .20 .50
28 Mike Modano .50 1.25
29 Bill Guerin .30 .75
30 Marty Turco .30 .75
31 Brendan Shanahan .30 .75
32 Henrik Zetterberg .40 1.00
33 Steve Yzerman .75 2.00
34 Dominik Hasek .50 1.25
35 Ryan Smyth .25 .60
36 Mike Comrie .25 .60
37 Ales Hemsky .30 .75
38 Tommy Salo .25 .60
39 Olli Jokinen .30 .75
40 Stephen Weiss .20 .50
41 Jay Bouwmeester .20 .50
42 Roberto Luongo .50 1.25
43 Zigmund Palffy .30 .75
44 Alexander Frolov .25 .60
45 Roman Cechmanek .25 .60
46 Marian Gaborik .30 .75
47 P-M Bouchard .30 .75
48 Manny Fernandez .20 .50
49 Dwayne Roloson .25 .60
50 Saku Koivu .30 .75
51 Marcel Hossa .20 .50
52 Jose Theodore .30 .75
53 Michael Komisarek .20 .50
54 David Legwand .25 .60
55 Tomas Vokoun .25 .60
56 Patrik Elias .30 .75
57 Jamie Langenbrunner .25 .60
58 Scott Stevens .30 .75
59 Martin Brodeur .75 2.00
60 Alexei Yashin .25 .60
61 Rick DiPietro .25 .60
62 Alex Kovalev .25 .60
63 Eric Lindros .50 1.25
64 Pavel Bure .30 .75
65 Mike Dunham .25 .60
66 Marian Hossa .30 .75
67 Daniel Alfredsson .30 .75
68 Jason Spezza .30 .75
69 Patrick Lalime .25 .60
70 Jeremy Roenick .50 1.25
71 Tony Amonte .25 .60
72 John LeClair .30 .75
73 Simon Gagne .30 .75
74 Mike Johnson .20 .50
75 Chris Gratton .20 .50
76 Sean Burke .20 .50
77 Mario Lemieux 1.25 3.00
78 Martin Straka .20 .50
79 Sebastien Caron .25 .60
80 Mike Ricci .20 .50
81 Nicholas Dimitrakos .20 .50
82 Evgeni Nabokov .25 .60
83 Al MacInnis .40 1.00
84 Keith Tkachuk .30 .75
85 Chris Pronger .30 .75
86 Chris Osgood .30 .75
87 Vincent Lecavalier .30 .75
88 Martin St. Louis .30 .75
89 Nikolai Khabibulin .30 .75
90 Alexander Mogilny .25 .60
91 Mats Sundin .30 .75
92 Owen Nolan .30 .75
93 Ed Belfour .30 .75
94 Alexander Auld .20 .50
95 Markus Naslund .30 .75
96 Todd Bertuzzi .30 .75
97 Ed Jovanovski .25 .60
98 Jaromir Jagr 1.00 2.50
99 Peter Bondra .30 .75
100 Olaf Kolzig .30 .75
101 Jean-Sebastien Giguere ET 1.00 2.50
102 Joe Thornton ET 1.50 4.00
103 Mario Lemieux ET 4.00 10.00
104 Peter Forsberg ET 2.00 5.00
105 Steve Yzerman ET 2.50 6.00
106 Eric Lindros ET 1.50 4.00
107 Marian Gaborik ET 1.00 2.50
108 Paul Kariya ET 1.00 2.50
109 Joe Sakic ET 2.00 5.00
110 Martin Brodeur ET 2.50 6.00
111 Ed Belfour ET 1.00 2.50
112 Marian Hossa ET 1.00 2.50
113 Gordie Howe ET 3.00 8.00
114 Wayne Gretzky ET 6.00 15.00
115 Bobby Orr ET 3.00 8.00
116 Patrick Roy PL 4.00 10.00
117 Patrick Roy PL 4.00 10.00
118 Patrick Roy PL 4.00 10.00
119 Patrick Roy PL 4.00 10.00
120 Patrick Roy PL 4.00 10.00
121 Patrick Roy PL 4.00 10.00
122 Patrick Roy PL 4.00 10.00
123 Patrick Roy PL 4.00 10.00
124 Patrick Roy PL 4.00 10.00
125 Patrick Roy PL 4.00 10.00
126 Patrick Roy PL 4.00 10.00
127 Patrick Roy PL 4.00 10.00
128 Patrick Roy PL 4.00 10.00
129 Patrick Roy PL 4.00 10.00
130 Patrick Roy PL 4.00 10.00
131 Patrick Roy PL 4.00 10.00
132 Patrick Roy PL 4.00 10.00
133 Patrick Roy PL 4.00 10.00
134 Patrick Roy
Martin Brodeur PL 4.00 10.00
135 Patrick Roy/J-S Giguere PL 4.00 10.00
136 Mario Lemieux PS 6.00 15.00
137 Gordie Howe PS 5.00 12.00
138 Keith Tkachuk PS 1.50 4.00
139 Peter Forsberg PS 3.00 8.00
140 Jeremy Roenick PS 2.50 6.00
141 Eric Lindros PS 2.50 6.00
142 Jaromir Jagr PS 5.00 12.00
143 Zdeno Chara PS 1.50 4.00
144 Owen Nolan PS 1.50 4.00
145 Martin Brodeur PS 4.00 10.00
146 Ed Belfour PS 1.50 4.00
147 Marian Hossa PS 1.50 4.00
148 Jarome Iginla PS 2.00 5.00
149 Jocelyn Thibault PS 1.25 3.00
150 Marian Gaborik PS 1.50 4.00
151 Vincent Lecavalier PS 1.50 4.00
152 Joe Thornton PS 2.50 6.00
153 Rick Nash PS 1.50 4.00
154 Joe Sakic PS 3.00 8.00
155 Mike Modano PS 2.50 6.00
156 Jean-Sebastien Giguere PS 1.50 4.00
157 Olli Jokinen PS 1.50 4.00
158 Steve Yzerman PS 4.00 10.00
159 Jason Spezza PS 1.50 4.00
160 Chris Pronger PS 1.50 4.00
161 Joe DiPenta RC 1.50 4.00
162 Milan Bartovic RC 1.50 4.00
163 Rick Mrozik RC 1.25 3.00
164 Kent McDonell RC 1.50 4.00
165 Peter Sejna RC 1.50 4.00
166 Matt Stajan RC 2.00 5.00
167 Marc-Andre Fleury RC 8.00 20.00
168 Nathan Horton RC 3.00 8.00
169 Eric Staal RC 6.00 15.00
170 Joffrey Lupul RC 3.00 8.00
171 Dustin Brown RC 3.00 8.00
172 Jordin Tootoo RC 2.50 6.00
173 Joni Pitkanen RC 2.00 5.00
174 Milan Michalek RC 2.50 6.00
175 Pavel Vorobiev RC 1.50 4.00
176 Tuomo Ruutu RC 2.00 5.00
177 Patrice Bergeron RC 6.00 15.00
178 Antoine Vermette RC 4.00 10.00
179 Antti Miettinen RC 2.00 5.00
180 Dan Hamhuis RC 1.50 4.00
181 Sean Bergenheim RC 1.50 4.00
182 Maxim Kondratiev RC 1.25 3.00
183 Chris Higgins RC 2.50 6.00
184 John-Michael Liles RC 1.50 4.00
185 Brent Burns RC 4.00 10.00
186 Marek Svatos RC 2.50 6.00
187 Boyd Gordon RC 1.50 4.00
188 Cody McCormick RC 1.50 4.00
189 Alexander Semin RC 4.00 10.00
190 Timofei Shishkanov RC 1.25 3.00
191 Mikhail Yakubov RC 1.25 3.00
192 Ryan Kesler RC 5.00 12.00
193 Fredrik Sjostrom RC 2.00 5.00
194 Nikolai Zherdev RC 2.50 6.00
195 Derek Roy RC 2.00 5.00
196 Tomas Plekanec RC 4.00 10.00

2003-04 Upper Deck Classic Portraits Classic Colors

CCAM Al MacInnis 8.00 20.00
CCBH Brett Hull 20.00 50.00
CCBS Brendan Shanahan 12.50 30.00
CCCD Chris Drury 8.00 20.00
CCCJ Curtis Joseph 12.50 30.00
CCCO Chris Osgood 8.00 20.00
CCDW Doug Weight 8.00 20.00
CCEL Eric Lindros 12.50 30.00
CCJA Jason Allison 8.00 20.00
CCJB Jay Bouwmeester 8.00 20.00
CCJJ Jaromir Jagr 20.00 50.00
CCJS Jason Spezza 20.00 50.00
CCJS Joe Sakic 30.00 80.00
CCMD Mike Dunham 8.00 20.00
CCON Ed Belfour 12.50 30.00
CCPK Paul Kariya 12.50 30.00
CCRN Rick Nash 20.00 50.00
CCTA Tony Amonte 8.00 20.00
CCTS Teemu Selanne 12.50 30.00
CCWG Wayne Gretzky 75.00 150.00

2003-04 Upper Deck Classic Portraits Classic Stitches

CSAD Adam Deadmarsh 3.00 8.00
CSBB Brian Boucher 3.00 8.00
CSCP Chris Pronger 3.00 8.00
CSEB Ed Belfour 4.00 10.00
CSGM Glen Murray 3.00 8.00
CSJT Joe Thornton 6.00 15.00
CSMA Maxim Afinogenov 3.00 8.00
CSSK Saku Koivu 4.00 10.00
CSSY Steve Yzerman 10.00 25.00
CSTH Jocelyn Thibault 3.00 8.00

2003-04 Upper Deck Classic Portraits Genuine Greatness

GGDH Dany Heatley 10.00 25.00
GGGR Wayne Gretzky 50.00 125.00
GGJR Jeremy Roenick 10.00 25.00
GGJS Jason Spezza 12.50 30.00
GGJT Joe Thornton 12.50 30.00
GGMB Martin Brodeur 15.00 40.00
GGML Mario Lemieux 20.00 50.00
GGPR Patrick Roy 20.00 50.00
GGRN Rick Nash 12.50 30.00
GGSY Steve Yzerman 20.00 50.00
GGWG Wayne Gretzky 50.00 125.00

2003-04 Upper DeckClassic Portraits Headliners

HHEL Eric Lindros 8.00 20.00
HHHA Marcel Hossa 4.00 10.00
HHJJ Jaromir Jagr 10.00 25.00
HHJT Joe Thornton 8.00 20.00
HHMG Marian Gaborik 8.00 20.00
HHML Mario Lemieux 12.50 30.00
HHMN Markus Naslund 6.00 15.00
HHPK Paul Kariya 5.00 12.00
HHVB Valeri Bure 4.00 10.00

2003-04 Upper Deck Classic Portraits Hockey Royalty

BLC Bure/Lindros/Kovalev 10.00 25.00
BNM Bertuzzi/Naslund/Morrison 10.00 25.00
BSM Belfour/Sundin/Mogilny 15.00 40.00
DSB Domi/Stock/Brashear 15.00 40.00
FSK Forsberg/Sakic/Kariya 25.00 60.00
KTH Koivu/Theodore/Hossa 15.00 40.00
LYG Lemieux/Yzerman/Gilmour 30.00 80.00
PLB Pronger/Lidstrom/Bowmster 12.00 30.00
RLA Roenick/LeClair/Amonte 10.00 25.00
YHS Yzerman/Hull/Shanahan 30.00 80.00

2003-04 Upper Deck Classic Portraits Mini-Busts

*BRONZE: 1X TO 2.5X
1 Patrick Roy COL 15.00 40.00
2 Patrick Roy MON/50 25.00 60.00
3 Gordie Howe SC 15.00 40.00
4 Martin Brodeur SC 15.00 40.00
5 Mike Modano SC 15.00 40.00
6 Joe Sakic SC 15.00 40.00
7 Peter Forsberg SC 15.00 40.00
8 Brett Hull DET 15.00 40.00
9 Brett Hull DAL/50 20.00 50.00
10 Ray Bourque SC 15.00 40.00
11 Jaromir Jagr PITT 15.00 40.00
12 Mario Lemieux SC 25.00 60.00
13 Steve Yzerman SC 20.00 50.00
14 Mark Messier NYR SC 15.00 40.00
15 Mark Messier EDM SC/50 20.00 50.00
16 Phil Esposito SC 15.00 40.00
17 Terry Sawchuk DET 15.00 40.00
18 Terry Sawchuk TOR/50 20.00 50.00
19 Bryan Trottier NYI SC 15.00 40.00
20 Bryan Trottier PITT SC/50 15.00 40.00
21 Bobby Clarke SC 15.00 40.00
22 Guy Lafleur SC 15.00 40.00
23 Scotty Bowman DET 20.00 50.00
24 Scotty Bowman MON/50 20.00 50.00
25 Scotty Bowman PITT/50 20.00 50.00
26 Phil Esposito 500 15.00 40.00
27 Steve Yzerman 500 20.00 50.00
28 Guy Lafleur 500 25.00 60.00
29 Mario Lemieux 500 25.00 60.00
30 Brett Hull 500 20.00 50.00
31 Jaromir Jagr 500 15.00 40.00
32 Gordie Howe 500 15.00 40.00
33 Mark Messier 500 15.00 40.00
34 Bryan Trottier 500 15.00 40.00
35 Joe Sakic 500 15.00 40.00

2003-04 Upper Deck Classic Portraits Mini-Busts Signed

1 Patrick Roy COL 100.00 250.00
2 Patrick Roy MON/25 250.00 500.00
3 Gordie Howe SC 60.00 150.00
4 Martin Brodeur SC 60.00 150.00
10 Ray Bourque SC 40.00 100.00
11 Jaromir Jagr PITT 40.00 100.00
16 Phil Esposito SC 40.00 100.00
19 Bryan Trottier NYI SC 40.00 100.00
20 Bryan Trottier PITT SC/25 60.00 150.00
21 Bobby Clarke SC 25.00 60.00
22 Guy Lafleur SC 50.00 125.00
23 Scotty Bowman DET 40.00 100.00
25 Scotty Bowman PITT/25 50.00 125.00
26 Phil Esposito 500 30.00 80.00
28 Guy Lafleur 500 50.00 125.00
31 Jaromir Jagr 500 75.00 200.00
32 Gordie Howe 500 150.00 300.00
34 Bryan Trottier 500 75.00 200.00

2003-04 Upper Deck Classic Portraits Premium Portraits

PPJT Joe Thornton 25.00 60.00
PPMB Martin Brodeur 30.00 80.00
PPMH Gordie Howe 40.00 100.00
PPML Mario Lemieux 40.00 100.00
PPPF Peter Forsberg 25.00 60.00
PPPR Patrick Roy 40.00 100.00
PPSY Steve Yzerman 40.00 100.00
PPWG Wayne Gretzky 60.00 150.00

2003-04 Upper Deck Classic Portraits Starring Cast

SCCD Chris Drury 4.00 10.00
SCJG Jean-Sebastien Giguere 4.00 10.00
SCJH Johan Hedberg 4.00 10.00
SCMB Martin Brodeur 12.50 30.00
SCMM Mike Modano 8.00 20.00
SCPR Patrick Roy 12.50 30.00
SCRN Rick Nash 8.00 20.00
SCTA Tony Amonte 4.00 10.00
SCTB Todd Bertuzzi 4.00 10.00

2018-19 Upper Deck Clear Cut

CCAD Alex DeBrincat AU E 20.00 50.00
CCAI Arturs Irbe AU E 12.00 30.00
CCAL Anders Lee AU E 12.00 30.00
CCAV Andrei Vasilevskiy AU D 25.00 60.00
CCBB Brent Burns AU A 15.00 40.00
CCBM Brad Marchand AU C 30.00 80.00
CCBO Bobby Orr AU B 60.00 150.00
CCCA Cam Atkinson AU E 15.00 40.00
CCCM Connor McDavid AU B 250.00 350.00
CCDS Daniel Sedin AU C 20.00 50.00
CCEK Evgeny Kuznetsov AU D 20.00 50.00
CCES Eric Staal AU E 15.00 40.00
CCFP Felix Potvin AU D 25.00 60.00
CCJE Jack Eichel AU A 25.00 60.00
CCJG Jake Guentzel AU D 25.00 60.00
CCJJ Joe Thornton AU A 25.00 60.00
CCJT John Tavares AU C 25.00 60.00
CCLR Larry Robinson AU C 15.00 40.00
CCMB Martin Brodeur AU A 40.00 100.00
CCMS Mark Scheifele AU D 25.00 60.00
CCPR Patrick Roy AU A 40.00 100.00
CCPT Pierre Turgeon AU C 12.00 30.00
CCRH Ron Hextall AU D 15.00 40.00
CCST Dylan Strome AU E 20.00 50.00
CCTB Tyler Bertuzzi AU E 12.00 30.00
CCTM Timo Meier AU E 15.00 40.00
CCWG Wayne Gretzky AU B 250.00 600.00
CCWO Willie O'Ree AU E 20.00 50.00
CCRAC Anthony Cirelli AU E RC 25.00 60.00
CCRAG Adam Gaudette AU F RC 25.00 60.00
CCRAJ Andreas Johnsson AU C RC 20.00 50.00
CCRAN Joey Anderson AU F RC 15.00 40.00
CCRAS Andrei Svechnikov AU E RC 40.00 100.00
CCRAW Austin Wagner AU F RC 12.00 30.00
CCRBE Ethan Bear AU G RC 25.00 60.00
CCRBH Brett Howden AU F RC 20.00 50.00
CCRBS Brett Seney AU F RC 12.00 30.00
CCRBT Brady Tkachuk AU A RC 100.00 250.00
CCRCE Christoffer Ehn AU G RC 12.00 30.00
CCRCG Conor Garland AU F RC 15.00 40.00
CCRCH Carter Hart AU G RC 30.00 80.00
CCRCM Casey Mittelstadt AU G RC 30.00 80.00
CCRCP Cal Petersen AU G RC 12.00 30.00
CCRDC Dennis Cholowski AU G RC 15.00 40.00
CCRDG Dylan Gambrell AU G RC 15.00 40.00
CCRDK Dominik Kahun AU G RC 15.00 40.00
CCRDS Dylan Sikura AU G RC 20.00 50.00
CCRDT Dominic Turgeon AU G RC 15.00 40.00
CCRDV Dan Vladar AU F RC 20.00 50.00
CCREB Evan Bouchard AU C RC 40.00 100.00
CCREP Elias Pettersson AU D RC 150.00 300.00
CCRET Eeli Tolvanen AU G RC 30.00 80.00
CCRFH Filip Hronek AU G RC 15.00 40.00
CCRHB Henrik Borgstrom AU G RC 25.00 60.00
CCRHJ Henri Jokiharju AU G RC 12.00 30.00
CCRIL Isac Lundestrom AU G RC 12.00 30.00
CCRJA Jaret Anderson-Dolan AU F RC 12.00 30.00
CCRJB Jake Bean AU E RC 15.00 40.00
CCRJG Jordan Greenway AU F RC 15.00 40.00
CCRJK Jesperi Kotkaniemi AU F RC 30.00 80.00
CCRJL Jeremy Lauzon AU F RC 20.00 50.00
CCRJM Josh Mahura AU E RC 12.00 30.00
CCRJV Juuso Valimaki AU G RC 15.00 40.00
CCRKS Kiefer Sherwood AU G RC 12.00 30.00
CCRKV Kristian Vesalainen AU G RC 20.00 50.00
CCRLA Lias Andersson AU F RC 25.00 60.00
CCRMA Cooper Marody AU G RC 15.00 40.00
CCRMB Mackenzie Blackwood AU G RC 30.00 80.00
CCRMC Maxime Comtois AU F RC 15.00 40.00
CCRMD Michael Dal Colle AU G RC 15.00 40.00
CCRMH Miro Heiskanen AU G RC 40.00 100.00
CCRMJ Mathieu Joseph AU G RC 20.00 50.00
CCRMM Michael McLeod AU F RC 12.00 30.00
CCRMV Mikhail Vorobyev AU G RC 12.00 30.00
CCRNJ Noah Juulsen AU D RC 15.00 40.00
CCRNP Neal Pionk AU G RC 15.00 40.00
CCRNR Nicolas Roy AU G RC 10.00 25.00
CCRPL Par Lindholm AU G RC 15.00 40.00
CCRRT Robert Thomas AU B RC 30.00 80.00
CCRSF Spencer Foo AU G RC 12.00 30.00
CCRSS Sam Steel AU C RC 15.00 40.00
CCRSU Antti Suomela AU G RC 12.00 30.00
CCRUV Urho Vaakanainen AU F RC 30.00 80.00
CCRVE Victor Ejdsell AU G RC 12.00 30.00
CCRWF Warren Foegele AU E RC 15.00 40.00
CCRZA Zach Aston-Reese AU G RC 25.00 60.00
CCRZW Zach Whitecloud AU G RC 12.00 30.00

2018-19 Upper Deck Clear Cut Exclusives

*EXCLUSIVE/35-65: .75X TO 2X BASIC CARDS
CCCM Connor McDavid AU 250.00 400.00
CCJT John Tavares AU 80.00 200.00
CCMB Martin Brodeur AU 100.00 250.00
CCPR Patrick Roy AU 150.00 350.00
CCWG Wayne Gretzky AU 300.00 800.00
CCREP Elias Pettersson AU 200.00 350.00

2018-19 Upper Deck Clear Cut '90-91 UD Tribute Autographs

91TGL Guy Lafleur 80.00 200.00
91TRH Ron Hextall 40.00 100.00
91TSY Steve Yzerman 60.00 150.00
91TWG Wayne Gretzky 600.00 1500.00

2018-19 Upper Deck Clear Cut Canvas Rookies

RD1 Rasmus Dahlin 25.00 60.00
RD2 Elias Pettersson 30.00 80.00
RD3 Carter Hart 20.00 50.00
RD4 Brady Tkachuk 30.00 80.00
RD5 Jesperi Kotkaniemi 20.00 50.00
RD6 Casey Mittelstadt 20.00 50.00
RD7 Andrei Svechnikov 25.00 60.00
RD8 Andreas Johnsson 12.00 30.00
RD9 Miro Heiskanen 25.00 60.00
RD10 Robert Thomas 20.00 50.00

2018-19 Upper Deck Clear Cut Canvas Signatures

*RED/16-95: X TO X BASIC INSERTS
CSAM Auston Matthews 250.00 350.00
CSAS Andrei Svechnikov 60.00 150.00
CSBB Brent Burns 25.00 60.00
CSBH Brett Hull 50.00 125.00
CSBL Mackenzie Blackwood 50.00 125.00
CSBO Bobby Orr 100.00 250.00
CSBT Brady Tkachuk 80.00 200.00
CSCA Cam Atkinson 25.00 60.00
CSCH Carter Hart 50.00 125.00
CSCJ Curtis Joseph 30.00 80.00
CSCM Connor McDavid 250.00 350.00
CSDC Dennis Cholowski 25.00 60.00
CSEK Evgeny Kuznetsov 30.00 80.00
CSEP Elias Pettersson 80.00 200.00
CSET Eeli Tolvanen 50.00 125.00
CSGL Guy Lafleur 30.00 80.00
CSHB Henrik Borgstrom 40.00 100.00
CSHL Henrik Lundqvist 60.00 150.00
CSHO Brett Howden 30.00 80.00
CSJA Jaret Anderson-Dolan 20.00 50.00
CSJB Jake Bean 25.00 60.00
CSJG Jordan Greenway 25.00 60.00
CSJH Jayce Hawryluk 20.00 50.00
CSJK Jesperi Kotkaniemi 50.00 125.00
CSJT Joe Thornton 40.00 100.00
CSJV Juuso Valimaki 25.00 60.00
CSJZ Jakub Zboril 40.00 100.00
CSLA Lias Andersson 40.00 100.00
CSMB Martin Brodeur 60.00 150.00
CSMC Maxime Comtois 25.00 60.00
CSMD Michael Dal Colle 25.00 60.00
CSMF Marc-Andre Fleury 150.00 250.00
CSMH Miro Heiskanen 60.00 150.00
CSMI Casey Mittelstadt 50.00 125.00
CSMM Michael McLeod 20.00 50.00
CSMR Michael Rasmussen 30.00 80.00
CSMS Mark Scheifele 40.00 100.00
CSNH Nico Hischier 40.00 100.00

CSPM Patrick Marleau 25.00 60.00
CSPR Patrick Roy 60.00 150.00
CSRB Ray Bourque 40.00 100.00
CSRD Ryan Donato 40.00 100.00
CSRT Robert Thomas 50.00 125.00
CSSC Sidney Crosby 100.00 250.00
CSSS Steven Stamkos 50.00 125.00
CSSY Steve Yzerman 60.00 150.00
CSTT Teuvo Teravainen 25.00 60.00
CSTW Tom Wilson 25.00 60.00
CSUV Urho Vaakanainen 50.00 125.00
CSWG Wayne Gretzky 400.00 1000.00

2018-19 Upper Deck Clear Cut Embedded Endorsements

*GOLD/25: .6X TO 1.5X BASIC INSERTS
EEAL Anders Lee 12.00 30.00
EEAM Andy Moog 15.00 40.00
EEAT Alex Tuch 15.00 40.00
EEAV Andrei Vasilevskiy 25.00 60.00
EEBN Bernie Nicholls 12.00 30.00
EECA Cam Atkinson 15.00 40.00
EEDS Dylan Strome 20.00 50.00
EEJG Jake Guentzel 25.00 60.00
EEKM Kirk McLean 12.00 30.00
EELD Leon Draisaitl 50.00 125.00
EEML Mike Liut 10.00 25.00
EEMS Mark Scheifele 25.00 60.00
EEPL Pat LaFontaine 15.00 40.00
EETA Tony Amonte 12.00 30.00
EETM Timo Meier 15.00 40.00
EETT Teuvo Teravainen 15.00 40.00
EETW Tom Wilson 15.00 40.00
EERAG Adam Gaudette 25.00 60.00
EERAS Andrei Svechnikov 40.00 100.00
EERBH Brett Howden 20.00 50.00
EERBT Brady Tkachuk 50.00 125.00
EERCE Christoffer Ehn 12.00 30.00
EERCG Conor Garland 15.00 40.00
EERCH Carter Hart 30.00 80.00
EERCM Casey Mittelstadt 30.00 80.00
EERCP Cal Petersen 12.00 30.00
EERDC Dennis Cholowski 15.00 40.00
EERDK Dominik Kahun 15.00 40.00
EERDS Dylan Sikura 20.00 50.00
EERDV Dan Vladar 20.00 50.00
EEREB Ethan Bear 25.00 60.00
EERET Eeli Tolvanen 30.00 80.00
EERJA Jaret Anderson-Dolan 12.00 30.00
EERJG Jordan Greenway 15.00 40.00
EERJH Jayce Hawryluk 12.00 30.00
EERJK Jesperi Kotkaniemi 30.00 80.00
EERJV Juuso Valimaki 15.00 40.00
EERJZ Jakub Zboril 25.00 60.00
EERKS Kiefer Sherwood 12.00 30.00
EERLA Lias Andersson 25.00 60.00
EERMA Cooper Marody 15.00 40.00
EERMC Maxime Comtois 15.00 40.00
EERMD Michael Dal Colle 15.00 40.00
EERMH Miro Heiskanen 40.00 100.00
EERMM Michael McLeod 12.00 30.00
EERSU Antti Suomela 12.00 30.00
EERUV Urho Vaakanainen 30.00 80.00

2018-19 Upper Deck Clear Cut Hockey Heroes Headers Tribute Autographs

HHHBH Brett Hull 50.00 125.00
HHHMB Martin Brodeur 60.00 150.00
HHHMM Mark Messier 60.00 150.00
HHHSY Steve Yzerman 60.00 150.00
HHHWG Wayne Gretzky 200.00 500.00

2018-19 Upper Deck Clear Cut Hockey Heroes Tribute Autographs

HHBH Bobby Hull C 40.00 100.00
HHBO Mike Bossy B 20.00 50.00
HHDH Dale Hawerchuk C 25.00 60.00
HHG1 Wayne Gretzky B 250.00 600.00
HHG2 Wayne Gretzky B 250.00 600.00
HHGL Guy Lafleur B 25.00 60.00
HHJT John Tavares B 30.00 80.00
HHLR Larry Robinson C 20.00 50.00
HHMB Martin Brodeur A 50.00 125.00
HHMG Mike Gartner C 25.00 60.00
HHO1 Bobby Orr B 80.00 200.00
HHO2 Bobby Orr B 80.00 200.00
HHPC Paul Coffey C 20.00 50.00
HHPE Phil Esposito B 30.00 80.00
HHR1 Patrick Roy B 50.00 125.00
HHR2 Patrick Roy B 50.00 125.00
HHRB Ray Bourque B 30.00 80.00
HHSC Sidney Crosby A 80.00 200.00
HHSY Steve Yzerman A 50.00 120.00

2019-20 Upper Deck Clear Cut

CCAB Adam Boqvist AU E RC 15.00 40.00
CCAD Alex DeBrincat AU D 20.00 50.00
CCAF Adam Fox AU D RC 125.00 300.00
CCAL Anders Lee AU D 12.00 30.00
CCAP Artemi Panarin AU C 40.00 100.00
CCAT Alexandre Texier AU E RC 15.00 40.00
CCAV Andrei Vasilevskiy AU D 20.00 50.00
CCBA Aleksander Barkov AU D 25.00 60.00
CCBB Brent Burns AU C 15.00 40.00
CCBE Emil Bemstrom AU E RC 15.00 40.00
CCBL Blake Lizotte AU E RC 15.00 40.00
CCBM Brad Marchand AU C 30.00 80.00
CCBO Bobby Orr AU C 125.00 300.00
CCBR Brock Boeser AU C 20.00 50.00
CCBT Brady Tkachuk AU D 30.00 80.00
CCCG Cody Glass AU C RC 40.00 100.00
CCCH Carter Hart AU D 40.00 100.00
CCCP Carey Price AU B 30.00 80.00
CCDK Dominik Kubalik AU E RC 25.00 60.00
CCDS Darryl Sittler AU C 20.00 50.00
CCEB Erik Brannstrom AU E RC 15.00 40.00
CCEL Elvis Merzlikins AU D RC 25.00 60.00
CCFR Morgan Frost AU C RC 25.00 60.00
CCFZ Filip Zadina AU C RC 40.00 100.00
CCGR Carl Grundstrom AU E RC 15.00 40.00
CCHA Nicolas Hague AU E RC 15.00 40.00
CCHL Henrik Lundqvist AU B 40.00 100.00
CCIS Igor Shesterkin AU C RC 60.00 150.00
CCJD Joey Daccord AU E RC 30.00 80.00
CCJF Joel Farabee AU E RC 40.00 100.00
CCJH Jack Hughes AU A RC 125.00 300.00
CCJL John LeClair AU C 15.00 40.00
CCJS Jimmy Schuldt AU E RC 12.00 30.00
CCJW Jake Walman AU E RC 20.00 50.00
CCKC Kale Clague AU E RC 12.00 30.00
CCKT Keith Tkachuk AU C 15.00 40.00
CCMA Cale Makar AU B RC 125.00 300.00
CCMF Marc-Andre Fleury AU A 30.00 80.00
CCMH Miro Heiskanen AU D 20.00 50.00
CCMJ Max Jones AU E RC 15.00 40.00
CCML Mario Lemieux AU A 250.00 600.00
CCMS Mark Stone AU D 20.00 50.00
CCND Noah Dobson AU E RC 40.00 100.00
CCNH Nico Hischier AU C 25.00 60.00
CCNL Nicklas Lidstrom AU B 15.00 40.00
CCNS Nick Suzuki AU C RC 125.00 300.00
CCOL Victor Olofsson AU E RC 30.00 80.00
CCOW Oliver Wahlstrom AU E RC 30.00 80.00
CCPI Rem Pitlick AU E RC 15.00 40.00
CCPK Patrick Kane AU B 60.00 150.00
CCPM Philippe Myers AU E RC 12.00 30.00
CCPR Patrick Roy AU C 125.00 300.00
CCRA Rasmus Asplund AU E RC 12.00 30.00
CCRI Pekka Rinne AU D 15.00 40.00
CCRM Ryan MacInnis AU E RC 12.00 30.00
CCRO Ryan O'Reilly AU D 15.00 40.00
CCRP Ryan Poehling AU D RC 15.00 40.00
CCRS Rasmus Sandin AU D RC 25.00 60.00
CCSB Sergei Bobrovsky AU C 25.00 60.00
CCSC Mark Scheifele AU D 25.00 60.00
CCSL Sam Lafferty AU D RC 12.00 30.00
CCTA John Tavares AU A 25.00 60.00
CCTB Tyler Bertuzzi AU D 12.00 30.00
CCTH Taro Hirose AU E RC 15.00 40.00
CCTO Tobias Bjornfot AU E RC 15.00 40.00
CCTW Tom Wilson AU D 15.00 40.00
CCVH Ville Heinola AU E RC 20.00 50.00
CCVO Alexander Volkov AU E RC 12.00 30.00

2019-20 Upper Deck Clear Cut Exclusives

*EXCLUSIVES: .6X TO 1.5X BASIC

2019-20 Upper Deck Clear Cut Black Amber Autographs

HHAB Aleksander Barkov C 30.00 80.00
HHAD Alex DeBrincat C 25.00 60.00
HHBB Brock Boeser B 25.00 60.00
HHBM Brad Marchand B 40.00 100.00
HHBT Brady Tkachuk C 40.00 100.00
HHCH Carter Hart B 125.00 300.00
HHCM Connor McDavid B 1000.00 2500.00
HHJG John Gibson C 20.00 50.00
HHKY Keith Yandle C 12.00 30.00
HHMH Miro Heiskanen C 80.00 200.00
HHMS Mark Stone B 25.00 60.00
HHMT Matthew Tkachuk A 150.00 400.00
HHPK Patrick Kane B 150.00 400.00
HHRO Ryan O'Reilly C 30.00 80.00
HHSC Mark Scheifele C 60.00 150.00
HHSU Ryan Suter C 15.00 40.00

2019-20 Upper Deck Clear Cut Black Amber Rookie Autographs

HHHAB Adam Boqvist D 20.00 50.00
HHHAF Adam Fox C 80.00 200.00
HHHAT Alexandre Texier D 20.00 50.00
HHHBH Barrett Hayton B 40.00 100.00
HHHBR Erik Brannstrom D 20.00 50.00
HHHDF Dante Fabbro C 20.00 50.00
HHHDK Dominik Kubalik C 50.00 125.00
HHHEB Emil Bemstrom D 20.00 50.00
HHHFR Morgan Frost C 30.00 80.00
HHHFZ Filip Zadina B 30.00 80.00
HHHIS Igor Shesterkin A 80.00 200.00
HHHJF Joel Farabee C 60.00 150.00
HHHJH Jack Hughes B 150.00 400.00
HHHJS Jimmy Schuldt D 15.00 40.00
HHHJW Jake Walman D 25.00 60.00
HHHKC Kale Clague D 15.00 40.00
HHHKD Kirby Dach B 200.00 500.00
HHHMF Mario Ferraro D 15.00 40.00
HHHND Noah Dobson D 30.00 80.00
HHHNH Nicolas Hague D 20.00 50.00
HHHNS Nick Suzuki B 125.00 300.00
HHHOK Otto Koivula D 12.00 30.00
HHHOW Oliver Wahlstrom D 40.00 100.00
HHHRA Rasmus Asplund D 15.00 40.00
HHHRP Ryan Poehling C 30.00 80.00
HHHRS Rasmus Sandin D 30.00 80.00
HHHTB Tobias Bjornfot D 20.00 50.00
HHHTH Taro Hirose D 20.00 50.00
HHHVH Ville Heinola D 25.00 60.00
HHHVO Victor Olofsson B 40.00 100.00

2019-20 Upper Deck Clear Cut Canvas Rookie Debuts

CDCG Cody Glass 15.00 40.00
CDCM Cale Makar 50.00 125.00
CDFZ Filip Zadina 25.00 60.00
CDJH Jack Hughes 30.00 80.00
CDKD Kirby Dach 20.00 50.00
CDMF Morgan Frost 10.00 25.00
CDNS Nick Suzuki 40.00 100.00
CDQH Quinn Hughes 50.00 125.00
CDRP Ryan Poehling 6.00 15.00
CDVO Victor Olofsson 8.00 20.00

2019-20 Upper Deck Clear Cut Embedded Endorsements

EEAD Alex DeBrincat 15.00 40.00
EEAL Anders Lee 10.00 25.00
EEAM Auston Matthews 125.00 300.00
EEAP Artemi Panarin 40.00 100.00
EEAS Andrei Svechnikov 15.00 40.00
EEAV Andrei Vasilevskiy 20.00 50.00
EEBA Aleksander Barkov 20.00 50.00
EEBB Brock Boeser 15.00 40.00
EEBM Brad Marchand 25.00 60.00
EEBT Brady Tkachuk 20.00 50.00
EECA Cam Atkinson 12.00 30.00
EECH Carter Hart 40.00 100.00
EEDB Dustin Brown 12.00 30.00
EEDH Dougie Hamilton 10.00 25.00
EEES Eric Staal 12.00 30.00
EEGU Jake Guentzel 20.00 50.00
EEHO Bo Horvat 15.00 40.00
EEJG John Gibson 12.00 30.00
EEJK John Klingberg 12.00 30.00
EEJM Jonathan Marchessault 15.00 40.00
EEJP Joe Pavelski 15.00 40.00
EEJS Jaccob Slavin 10.00 25.00
EEJT Jacob Trouba 10.00 25.00
EEJV James van Riemsdyk 10.00 25.00
EEKK Kasperi Kapanen 10.00 25.00
EEKP Kyle Palmieri 10.00 25.00
EEKT Kyle Turris 10.00 25.00
EEKY Keith Yandle 8.00 20.00
EEMG Mark Giordano 12.00 30.00
EEMH Miro Heiskanen 15.00 40.00
EEMK Mikko Koivu 10.00 25.00
EEMS Mark Scheifele 20.00 50.00
EEMT Matthew Tkachuk 25.00 60.00
EEPA Colton Parayko 10.00 25.00
EEPG Philipp Grubauer 12.00 30.00
EERO Ryan O'Reilly 12.00 30.00
EESB Sergei Bobrovsky 20.00 50.00
EESM Sean Monahan 8.00 20.00
EESR Sam Reinhart 25.00 60.00
EEST Mark Stone 15.00 40.00
EESU Ryan Suter 10.00 25.00
EETB Tyler Bertuzzi 10.00 25.00
EETC Thomas Chabot 12.00 30.00
EETH Tomas Hertl 12.00 30.00
EETT Teuvo Teravainen 12.00 30.00
EETW Tom Wilson 12.00 30.00
EEYG Yanni Gourde 10.00 25.00

2019-20 Upper Deck Clear Cut Metal Universe Legend Palladium Autographs

TCC Chris Chelios C 30.00 80.00
TCJ Curtis Joseph D 30.00 80.00
TDD Dick Duff D 20.00 50.00
TDS Daniel Sedin B 30.00 80.00
TGR Wayne Gretzky A 1250.00 3000.00
THS Henrik Sedin B 30.00 80.00
TKT Keith Tkachuk D 25.00 60.00
TLM Lanny McDonald B 25.00 60.00
TLR Larry Robinson C 25.00 60.00
TMG Mike Gartner D 30.00 80.00
TML Mario Lemieux A 100.00 250.00
TMM Mike Modano C 100.00 250.00
TMR Mark Recchi D 30.00 80.00
TNL Nicklas Lidstrom A 25.00 60.00
TOR Bobby Orr C 125.00 300.00
TPA Patrick Roy C 125.00 300.00
TPL Pat LaFontaine D 25.00 60.00
TPT Pierre Turgeon C 20.00 50.00
TRH Ron Hextall D 40.00 100.00
TRO Patrick Roy C 125.00 300.00
TWC Wendel Clark C 30.00 80.00
TWG Wayne Gretzky A 1250.00 3000.00

2019-20 Upper Deck Clear Cut Metal Universe Palladium Autographs

TAB Aleksander Barkov C 30.00 80.00
TAD Alex DeBrincat D 25.00 60.00
TAP Artemi Panarin B 80.00 200.00
TBB Brock Boeser C 30.00 80.00
TBM Brad Marchand B 30.00 80.00
TBT Brady Tkachuk D 30.00 80.00
TCH Carter Hart C 40.00 100.00
TMA Mark Scheifele D 30.00 80.00
TMH Miro Heiskanen D 25.00 60.00
TMS Mark Stone C 25.00 60.00
TNH Nico Hischier B 40.00 100.00
TPR Pekka Rinne D 20.00 50.00
TRY Ryan O'Reilly D 25.00 60.00
TSU Ryan Suter D 15.00 40.00

2019-20 Upper Deck Clear Cut Metal Universe Rookie Palladium Autographs

TAF Adam Fox D 30.00 80.00
TAT Alexandre Texier E 20.00 50.00
TBE Emil Bemstrom E 20.00 50.00
TBO Adam Boqvist D 20.00 50.00
TDK Dominik Kubalik A 40.00 100.00
TEB Erik Brannstrom E 20.00 50.00
TFZ Filip Zadina E 30.00 80.00
THA Nicolas Hague E 20.00 50.00
TIS Igor Shesterkin C 80.00 200.00
TJF Joel Farabee D 30.00 80.00
TJH Jack Hughes C 80.00 200.00
TJW Jake Walman E 25.00 60.00
TMF Morgan Frost B 30.00 80.00
TND Noah Dobson E 50.00 125.00
TOW Oliver Wahlstrom E 30.00 80.00
TRP Ryan Poehling C 30.00 80.00
TRS Rasmus Sandin E 30.00 80.00

2019-20 Upper Deck Clear Cut Rookie Embedded Endorsements

EEAB Adam Boqvist 12.00 30.00
EEAF Adam Fox 40.00 100.00
EEAT Alexandre Texier 12.00 30.00
EEBE Emil Bemstrom 12.00 30.00
EEBH Barrett Hayton 25.00 60.00
EEBJ Tobias Bjornfot 12.00 30.00
EECG Cody Glass 20.00 50.00
EECP Cayden Primeau 30.00 80.00
EECV Carter Verhaeghe 20.00 50.00
EEDF Dante Fabbro 12.00 30.00
EEDK Dominik Kubalik 15.00 40.00
EEEB Erik Brannstrom 12.00 30.00
EEEM Elvis Merzlikins 25.00 60.00
EEFZ Filip Zadina 20.00 50.00
EEHI Taro Hirose 12.00 30.00
EEIS Igor Shesterkin 50.00 125.00
EEJF Joel Farabee 30.00 80.00
EEJH Jack Hughes 80.00 200.00
EEJW Jake Walman 15.00 40.00
EEKC Kale Clague 10.00 25.00
EEKD Kirby Dach 25.00 60.00
EEKU Karson Kuhlman 12.00 30.00
EEMA Cale Makar 80.00 200.00
EEMF Morgan Frost 15.00 40.00
EENH Nicolas Hague 12.00 30.00
EENS Nick Suzuki 60.00 150.00
EEOK Otto Koivula 8.00 20.00
EEOW Oliver Wahlstrom 30.00 80.00
EEQH Quinn Hughes 80.00 200.00
EERP Ryan Poehling 20.00 50.00
EERS Rasmus Sandin 20.00 50.00
EEVH Ville Heinola 15.00 40.00
EEVO Victor Olofsson 25.00 60.00

2020-21 Upper Deck Clear Cut

CCAA Alexander Alexeyev D RC 8.00 20.00
CCAB Alexander Barabanov D RC 10.00 25.00
CCAK Anze Kopitar B 12.00 30.00
CCAL Alexis Lafreniere A RC 30.00 80.00
CCAM Auston Matthews A 150.00 400.00
CCAR Alexander Romanov C RC 12.00 30.00
CCAT Cam Atkinson E 8.00 20.00
CCAV Andrei Vasilevskiy C 12.00 30.00
CCBB Brock Boeser C 10.00 25.00
CCBM Brad Marchand B 15.00 40.00
CCBO Bobby Orr B 80.00 200.00
CCBP Brayden Point D 10.00 25.00
CCBT Brady Tkachuk D 12.00 30.00
CCBU Brent Burns B 8.00 20.00
CCBY Bowen Byram B RC 20.00 50.00
CCCF Cal Foote D RC 12.00 30.00
CCCH Sasha Chmelevski D RC 8.00 20.00
CCCM Connor McDavid A 200.00 500.00
CCCN Cam Neely C 8.00 20.00
CCCP Carey Price A 50.00 125.00
CCDC Dylan Cozens C RC 15.00 40.00
CCEL Eric Lindros A 20.00 50.00
CCGI John Gibson D 8.00 20.00
CCHA Carter Hart C 8.00 20.00
CCIM Ian Mitchell D RC 8.00 20.00
CCIS Ilya Sorokin B RC 25.00 60.00
CCJB Josh Bailey E 6.00 15.00
CCJE Jake Evans D RC 10.00 25.00
CCJG Jake Guentzel D 12.00 30.00
CCJK Joel Kiviranta D RC 10.00 25.00
CCJN Josh Norris B RC 15.00 40.00
CCJR Jason Robertson C RC 25.00 60.00
CCJT John Tavares A 20.00 50.00
CCJV Jakub Vrana E 8.00 20.00
CCKA Arthur Kaliyev D RC 15.00 40.00
CCKB Kieffer Bellows D RC 8.00 20.00
CCKK Kirill Kaprizov C RC 300.00 800.00
CCKR Peyton Krebs C RC 15.00 40.00
CCKU Philipp Kurashev D RC 12.00 30.00
CCLD Leon Draisaitl A 25.00 60.00
CCLE Mario Lemieux A 50.00 125.00
CCLF Liam Foudy D RC 10.00 25.00
CCLM Lanny McDonald B 6.00 15.00
CCMA Cale Makar C 20.00 50.00
CCMG Morgan Geekie D RC 10.00 25.00
CCMH Miro Heiskanen C 10.00 25.00
CCML Maxim Letunov D RC 8.00 20.00
CCMM Mark Messier A 20.00 50.00
CCMS Mark Scheifele C 12.00 30.00
CCMT Matthew Tkachuk C 15.00 40.00
CCNF Nolan Foote D RC 10.00 25.00
CCNH Nils Hoglander C RC 10.00 25.00
CCNR Nick Robertson D RC 15.00 40.00
CCNS Nick Suzuki D 15.00 40.00
CCOJ Olli Juolevi C RC 10.00 25.00
CCPA Colton Parayko E 6.00 15.00
CCPJ Pierre-Olivier Joseph D RC 10.00 25.00
CCPK Patrick Kane A 20.00 50.00
CCPL Pat LaFontaine C 8.00 20.00
CCPR Patrick Roy B 20.00 50.00
CCPS Pius Suter D RC 12.00 30.00
CCQH Quinn Hughes B 20.00 50.00
CCRE Alec Regula D RC 6.00 15.00
CCRI Pekka Rinne D 8.00 20.00
CCRO Ryan O'Reilly E 8.00 20.00
CCSB Shane Bowers D RC 8.00 20.00
CCSC Sidney Crosby A 125.00 300.00
CCST Mark Stone C 10.00 25.00
CCSY Steve Yzerman A 30.00 80.00
CCTB Tyler Benson D RC 10.00 25.00
CCTD Ty Dellandrea D RC 10.00 25.00
CCTI Tim Stutzle A RC 150.00 400.00
CCTL Timothy Liljegren B RC 10.00 25.00
CCTS Ty Smith D RC 15.00 40.00
CCVS Victor Soderstrom D RC 8.00 20.00
CCVV Vitek Vanecek D RC 15.00 40.00
CCWG Wayne Gretzky A 200.00 500.00
CCYS Yegor Sharangovich D RC 15.00 40.00

2020-21 Upper Deck Clear Cut '90-91 UD Tribute Autographs

RTMM Mike Modano A 30.00 80.00
RTMR Mike Richter B 20.00 50.00
RTPB Peter Bondra B 20.00 50.00
RTRB Rod Brind'Amour B 20.00 50.00

2020-21 Upper Deck Clear Cut Canvas Rookie Debuts

CDAL Alexis Lafreniere 30.00 80.00
CDAR Alexander Romanov 12.00 30.00
CDBB Bowen Byram 20.00 50.00
CDCM Connor McMichael 15.00 40.00
CDDC Dylan Cozens 15.00 40.00
CDIS Ilya Sorokin 25.00 60.00
CDJR Jason Robertson 25.00 60.00
CDKK Kirill Kaprizov 40.00 100.00
CDNH Nils Hoglander 10.00 25.00
CDTS Tim Stutzle 20.00 50.00

2020-21 Upper Deck Clear Cut Canvas Signatures

CSAB Aleksander Barkov 30.00 80.00
CSAK Anze Kopitar 30.00 80.00
CSAL Alexis Lafreniere 300.00 800.00
CSAM Auston Matthews 200.00 500.00
CSAN Anthony Mantha 15.00 40.00
CSAR Alexander Romanov 30.00 80.00
CSAS Andrei Svechnikov 25.00 60.00
CSAV Andrei Vasilevskiy 30.00 80.00
CSBB Brent Burns 20.00 50.00
CSBE Tyler Benson 25.00 60.00
CSBO Brock Boeser 25.00 60.00
CSBP Brayden Point 25.00 60.00
CSBT Brady Tkachuk 30.00 80.00
CSBY Bowen Byram 50.00 125.00
CSCA Cam Atkinson 20.00 50.00
CSCH Carter Hart 20.00 50.00
CSCM Connor McDavid 300.00 800.00
CSCN Cam Neely 20.00 50.00
CSCO Connor Hellebuyck 40.00 100.00
CSCP Carey Price 80.00 200.00
CSDC Dylan Cozens 40.00 100.00
CSDG Doug Gilmour 25.00 60.00
CSDH Dominik Hasek 30.00 80.00
CSDW Doug Weight 15.00 40.00
CSEL Eric Lindros 30.00 80.00
CSFP Felix Potvin 30.00 80.00
CSGL Guy Lafleur 25.00 60.00
CSIM Ian Mitchell 20.00 50.00
CSJB Josh Bailey 15.00 40.00
CSJG Jake Guentzel 30.00 80.00
CSJK Joel Kiviranta 25.00 60.00
CSJL John LeClair 20.00 50.00
CSJN Josh Norris 80.00 200.00
CSJO Jake Oettinger 60.00 150.00
CSJR Jason Robertson 200.00 500.00
CSJS Joe Sakic 40.00 100.00
CSJV John Vanbiesbrouck 20.00 50.00
CSKA Arthur Kaliyev 40.00 100.00
CSKB Kieffer Bellows 20.00 50.00
CSKK Kirill Kaprizov 300.00 800.00
CSKM K'Andre Miller 50.00 125.00
CSKR Peyton Krebs 40.00 100.00
CSKT Keith Tkachuk 20.00 50.00
CSKU Philipp Kurashev 30.00 80.00
CSLD Leon Draisaitl 80.00 200.00
CSLF Liam Foudy 25.00 60.00
CSLI Trevor Linden 20.00 50.00
CSMA Cale Makar 50.00 125.00
CSMH Miro Heiskanen 25.00 60.00
CSMM Mike Modano 30.00 80.00
CSMP Max Pacioretty 20.00 50.00
CSMS Mark Stone 25.00 60.00
CSMT Matthew Tkachuk 40.00 100.00
CSNH Nils Hoglander 25.00 60.00
CSNR Nick Robertson 40.00 100.00
CSNS Nick Suzuki 40.00 100.00
CSOJ Olli Juolevi 25.00 60.00
CSPD Pierre-Luc Dubois 15.00 40.00
CSPK Patrick Kane 40.00 100.00
CSPR Patrick Roy 50.00 125.00
CSPS Pius Suter 30.00 80.00
CSQH Quinn Hughes 50.00 125.00
CSRI Pekka Rinne 20.00 50.00
CSRJ Roman Josi 20.00 50.00
CSRN Ryan Nugent-Hopkins 25.00 60.00
CSRO Ryan O'Reilly 20.00 50.00
CSSC Mark Scheifele 30.00 80.00
CSSM Ty Smith 40.00 100.00
CSSY Steve Yzerman 50.00 125.00
CSTD Ty Dellandrea 25.00 60.00
CSTL Timothy Liljegren 25.00 60.00
CSTS Tim Stutzle 150.00 400.00
CSTT Tyler Toffoli 20.00 50.00
CSVA James van Riemsdyk 15.00 40.00
CSVV Vitek Vanecek 40.00 100.00
CSWG Wayne Gretzky 300.00 800.00

2023-24 Upper Deck Clear Cut

CCAD Alex Delvecchio AU 20.00 50.00
CCAF Adam Fantilli SP AU RC 50.00 125.00
CCAG Adam Ginning AU RC 8.00 20.00
CCAH Akito Hirose AU RC 6.00 15.00
CCAK Andrei Kuzmenko AU 8.00 20.00
CCAL Alexis Lafreniere AU 20.00 50.00
CCAM Auston Matthews SP AU 80.00 200.00
CCAO Alex Ovechkin SP AU 150.00 400.00
CCAR Alexander Romanov AU 6.00 15.00
CCAS Andrei Svechnikov AU 10.00 25.00
CCAT Alex Tuch AU 8.00 20.00
CCAV Andrei Vasilevskiy SP AU 12.00 30.00
CCBA Mikael Backlund AU 6.00 15.00
CCBC Samuel Bolduc AU RC 8.00 20.00
CCBJ Boone Jenner AU 8.00 20.00
CCBK Owen Beck AU RC 12.00 30.00
CCBM Brad Marchand SP AU 15.00 40.00
CCBN Brock Nelson AU 8.00 20.00
CCBR Brandon Montour AU 10.00 25.00
CCBS Brayden Schenn AU 8.00 20.00
CCBT Brady Tkachuk AU 12.00 30.00
CCBY Bobby McMann AU RC 20.00 50.00
CCCB Connor Bedard SP AU RC 400.00 1000.00
CCCG Cole Guttman AU RC 8.00 20.00
CCCM Connor McDavid SP AU 150.00 400.00
CCCO Chris Osgood AU 20.00 50.00
CCCY Logan Cooley SP AU RC 80.00 200.00
CCDE Vincent Desharnais AU RC 10.00 25.00
CCDP David Perron AU 6.00 15.00
CCDR William Dufour AU RC 6.00 15.00
CCDT Devon Toews AU 6.00 15.00
CCDW Dustin Wolf AU RC 40.00 100.00
CCED Elliot Desnoyers AU RC 8.00 20.00
CCEN Simon Edvinsson SP AU RC 25.00 60.00
CCFM Fraser Minten AU RC 15.00 40.00
CCGN Jonathan Gruden AU RC 8.00 20.00
CCGR Jet Greaves AU RC 12.00 30.00
CCGU David Gust AU RC 8.00 20.00
CCGV Gabe Vilardi AU 8.00 20.00
CCHE Dany Heatley AU 6.00 15.00
CCHL Henrik Lundqvist SP AU 40.00 100.00
CCHM Hugh McGing AU RC 8.00 20.00
CCHT Henry Thrun AU RC 8.00 20.00
CCHU Jonathan Huberdeau AU 10.00 25.00
CCHZ Henrik Zetterberg AU 20.00 50.00
CCIM Ivan Miroshnichenko AU RC 12.00 30.00
CCIR Isak Rosen AU RC 8.00 20.00
CCJB John Beecher AU RC 15.00 40.00
CCJC Jalen Chatfield AU 5.00 12.00
CCJK Joona Koppanen AU RC 6.00 15.00
CCJM Jared McCann AU 6.00 15.00
CCJP Joe Pavelski AU 10.00 25.00
CCJT John Tavares SP AU 20.00 50.00
CCJV Kevin Hayes AU 6.00 15.00
CCJW Joseph Woll AU 20.00 50.00
CCKC Kyle Connor AU 12.00 30.00
CCKE Milos Kelemen AU RC 8.00 20.00
CCKH Jiri Kulich AU RC 40.00 100.00
CCKI Kevin Korchinski AU RC 12.00 30.00
CCKM Kirill Marchenko AU 10.00 25.00
CCKN Tyler Kleven AU RC 8.00 20.00
CCKO Samuel Knazko AU RC 8.00 20.00
CCLA Larry Robinson AU 20.00 50.00
CCLC Leo Carlsson AU RC 50.00 125.00
CCLD Leon Draisaitl SP AU 60.00 150.00
CCLF Alex Laferriere AU RC 12.00 30.00
CCLM Leevi Merilainen AU RC 8.00 20.00
CCLP Luke Philp AU RC 8.00 20.00
CCLV Devon Levi AU RC 20.00 50.00
CCMA Cale Makar SP AU 50.00 125.00
CCMC Matthew Coronato AU RC 12.00 30.00
CCME Mark Messier AU 40.00 100.00
CCMF Marc-Andre Fleury SP AU 50.00 125.00
CCMH Aidan McDonough AU RC 6.00 15.00
CCMI Mikey Anderson AU 6.00 15.00
CCMO Josh Morrissey AU 10.00 25.00
CCMP Matthew Poitras AU RC 15.00 40.00
CCMW Cole McWard AU RC 8.00 20.00
CCMY Matt Murray AU RC 8.00 20.00
CCNH Nico Hischier SP AU 12.00 30.00
CCNN Nikita Nesterenko AU RC 8.00 20.00
CCNS Nick Suzuki AU 25.00 60.00
CCOB Oliver Bjorkstrand AU 6.00 15.00
CCOP Owen Power SP AU 8.00 20.00
CCOR Bobby Orr SP AU 50.00 125.00
CCPA Jiri Patera AU RC 12.00 30.00
CCPB Patrice Bergeron AU 30.00 80.00
CCPM Pavel Mintyukov AU RC 12.00 30.00
CCPO Martin Pospisil AU RC 10.00 25.00
CCRC Ross Colton AU 6.00 15.00
CCRE Ryker Evans AU RC 10.00 25.00
CCRE Mark Recchi AU 15.00 40.00
CCRF Ron Francis SP AU 20.00 50.00
CCRG Ridly Greig AU RC 12.00 30.00
CCRK Lukas Rousek AU RC 6.00 15.00
CCRL Raphael Lavoie AU RC 8.00 20.00
CCRN Ryan Nugent-Hopkins SP AU 10.00 25.00
CCRO Ryan O'Reilly AU 8.00 20.00
CCRR Ryan Reaves AU 6.00 15.00
CCRV Rogie Vachon AU 8.00 20.00
CCSA Matt Savoie SP AU RC 15.00 40.00
CCSB Scotty Bowman AU 30.00 80.00
CCSF Sean Farrell AU RC 8.00 20.00
CCSK Spencer Knight AU 12.00 30.00
CCSM Mackie Samoskevich AU RC 12.00 30.00
CCSN Simon Nemec SP AU RC 15.00 40.00
CCSP Jared Spurgeon AU 8.00 20.00
CCST Jaxson Stauber AU RC 8.00 20.00
CCSV Stanislav Svozil AU RC 6.00 15.00
CCSY Nick Swaney AU RC 8.00 20.00
CCSZ Billy Sweezey AU RC 8.00 20.00
CCTF Tyson Foerster AU RC 15.00 40.00
CCTH Joe Thornton AU 20.00 50.00
CCTK Tye Kartye AU RC 12.00 30.00
CCTR Tristen Robins AU RC 8.00 20.00
CCTW Tiger Williams AU 60.00 150.00
CCVD Vince Dunn AU 6.00 15.00
CCVI Vincent Iorio AU RC 8.00 20.00
CCWC Will Cuylle AU RC 12.00 30.00
CCWD Walker Duehr AU RC 6.00 15.00
CCWG Wayne Gretzky SP AU 250.00 600.00
CCWJ Wyatt Johnston AU 40.00 100.00
CCWK Wyatt Kaiser AU RC 8.00 20.00
CCWR Shane Wright SP AU 10.00 25.00
CCYA Yaroslav Askarov AU RC 30.00 80.00

2023-24 Upper Deck Clear Cut Outburst

*OUTBURST/25: .8X TO 2X BASIC
CCAF Adam Fantilli AU 100.00 250.00
CCBY Bobby McMann AU 60.00 150.00
CCCB Connor Bedard AU 2500.00 6000.00
CCDW Dustin Wolf AU 100.00 250.00
CCLC Leo Carlsson AU 125.00 300.00
CCMP Matthew Poitras AU 50.00 125.00
CCNS Nick Suzuki AU 60.00 150.00
CCSM Mackie Samoskevich AU 60.00 150.00
CCTF Tyson Foerster AU 50.00 125.00
CCTH Joe Thornton AU 40.00 100.00
CCWC Will Cuylle AU 40.00 100.00
CCWG Wayne Gretzky AU 600.00 1500.00

2023-24 Upper Deck Clear Cut '03-04 UD Classic Portraits Autographs

UDPCB Connor Bedard SP 200.00 500.00
UDPCM Connor McDavid SP 125.00 300.00
UDPCO Logan Cooley SP 60.00 150.00
UDPDL Devon Levi 20.00 50.00
UDPDS Dave Schultz 6.00 15.00
UDPGC Guy Carbonneau 8.00 20.00
UDPIS Ilya Samsonov 8.00 20.00
UDPJP Joe Pavelski 10.00 25.00
UDPLC Leo Carlsson SP 25.00 60.00
UDPMP Matthew Poitras 15.00 40.00
UDPPB Peter Bondra 8.00 20.00
UDPTB Tom Barrasso 40.00 100.00

2023-24 Upper Deck Clear Cut '03-04 UD Classic Portraits Autographs Silver

*SILVER/35: .6X TO 1.5X BASIC
UDPCB Connor Bedard 600.00 1500.00
UDPCM Connor McDavid 250.00 600.00

2023-24 Upper Deck Clear Cut '06-07 UD Sweet Shot Autographs

SSCA Leo Carlsson 20.00 50.00
SSDL Devon Levi 15.00 40.00
SSDW Dustin Wolf 50.00 125.00
SSHL Henrik Lundqvist 30.00 80.00
SSKK Kevin Korchinski 10.00 25.00
SSLC Logan Cooley 30.00 80.00
SSMF Marc-Andre Fleury SP 40.00 100.00
SSMP Matthew Poitras 12.00 30.00
SSMS Matt Savoie 12.00 30.00
SSRB Ray Bourque 10.00 25.00
SSSN Simon Nemec 12.00 30.00
SSTF Tyson Foerster 12.00 30.00

2023-24 Upper Deck Clear Cut '06-07 UD Sweet Shot Autographs Blue

*BLUE/25: .6X TO 1.5X BASIC
SSCB Connor Bedard 400.00 1000.00
SSCM Connor McDavid 300.00 800.00
SSMF Marc-Andre Fleury 80.00 200.00

2023-24 Upper Deck Clear Cut '98-99 Black Diamond Myriad Autographs

BDMAL Alexis Lafreniere 10.00 25.00
BDMAT Alex Tuch 6.00 15.00
BDMDL Devon Levi 15.00 40.00
BDMEL Eric Lindros SP 10.00 25.00
BDMKM Kirill Marchenko 20.00 50.00
BDMKO Kevin Korchinski 10.00 25.00
BDMLA Alex Laferriere 10.00 25.00
BDMMC Matthew Coronato 10.00 25.00
BDMMM Mark Messier SP 30.00 80.00
BDMMP Matthew Poitras 12.00 30.00
BDMOB Owen Beck 10.00 25.00
BDMPM Pavel Mintyukov 10.00 25.00
BDMRE Ryker Evans 8.00 20.00
BDMRG Ridly Greig 10.00 25.00
BDMRO Ryan O'Reilly 6.00 15.00
BDMSN Simon Nemec 12.00 30.00
BDMSS Stanislav Svozil 5.00 12.00
BDMTF Tyson Foerster 12.00 30.00
BDMTK Tye Kartye 10.00 25.00
BDMWC Will Cuylle 10.00 25.00
BDMWD William Dufour 5.00 12.00
BDMWJ Wyatt Johnston 25.00 60.00

2023-24 Upper Deck Clear Cut '98-99 Black Diamond Myriad Autographs Blue

*BLUE/25: .8X TO 2X BASIC
BDMMM Mark Messier 100.00 250.00
BDMNL Nicklas Lidstrom 60.00 150.00

2023-24 Upper Deck Clear Cut '98-99 UD Ionix Authentics Autographs

UDIAM Auston Matthews SP 80.00 200.00
UDIAS Andrei Svechnikov 12.00 30.00
UDICB Connor Bedard SP 250.00 600.00
UDICM Connor McDavid SP 125.00 300.00
UDIDL Devon Levi 25.00 60.00
UDIHL Henrik Lundqvist 25.00 60.00
UDILC Logan Cooley 30.00 80.00
UDIMA Cale Makar SP 60.00 150.00
UDIMS Matt Savoie 20.00 50.00
UDIPC Paul Coffey 10.00 25.00
UDIPE Phil Esposito 15.00 40.00
UDIRG Ridly Greig 15.00 40.00
UDITF Tyson Foerster 20.00 50.00
UDITK Tye Kartye 15.00 40.00
UDIZH Zach Hyman 15.00 40.00

2023-24 Upper Deck Clear Cut Canvas Rookie Debuts

CDCB Connor Bedard 125.00 300.00

2023-24 Upper Deck Clear Cut Canvas Rookie Debuts Signatures

CDCO Logan Cooley 80.00 200.00
CDDL Devon Levi 50.00 125.00
CDKK Kevin Korchinski 30.00 80.00
CDLC Leo Carlsson 60.00 150.00
CDLH Luke Hughes 100.00 250.00
CDMK Matthew Knies 80.00 200.00
CDSN Simon Nemec 40.00 100.00

2023-24 Upper Deck Clear Cut Canvas Signatures

CSAL Alex Laferriere 12.00 30.00
CSAM Auston Matthews SP 60.00 150.00
CSAS Alexis Lafreniere 30.00 80.00
CSBN Brock Nelson 8.00 20.00
CSBT Bryan Trottier 8.00 20.00
CSCB Connor Bedard SP 500.00 1200.00
CSCC Chris Chelios SP 30.00 80.00
CSCO Logan Cooley SP 60.00 150.00
CSCP Colton Parayko 6.00 15.00
CSCZ Connor Zary 15.00 40.00
CSDL Devon Levi 20.00 50.00
CSDW Dustin Wolf 60.00 150.00
CSEL Eric Lindros SP 40.00 100.00
CSFG Filip Gustavsson 8.00 20.00
CSJB John Beecher 15.00 40.00
CSJP JJ Peterka 8.00 20.00
CSKK Kevin Korchinski 12.00 30.00
CSKN Matthew Knies 60.00 150.00
CSLC Leo Carlsson 40.00 100.00
CSLD Lukas Dostal 8.00 20.00
CSLE Luke Evangelista 12.00 30.00
CSLR Luc Robitaille SP 15.00 40.00
CSMB Martin Brodeur SP 60.00 150.00
CSMG Mike Gartner 10.00 25.00
CSMK Marco Kasper 20.00 50.00
CSMM Mark Messier SP 40.00 100.00
CSMP Matthew Poitras 15.00 40.00
CSMS Mackie Samoskevich 12.00 30.00
CSNH Nico Hischier 20.00 50.00
CSPM Pavel Mintyukov 12.00 30.00
CSRF Ron Francis SP 25.00 60.00
CSRN Ryan Nugent-Hopkins 10.00 25.00
CSSA Matt Savoie 15.00 40.00
CSSG Samuel Girard 5.00 12.00
CSSN Simon Nemec 15.00 40.00
CSTN Thomas Novak 5.00 12.00
CSTT Tage Thompson 10.00 25.00
CSTW Tom Wilson 8.00 20.00
CSYC Yvan Cournoyer 8.00 20.00

2023-24 Upper Deck Clear Cut Canvas Signatures Red Ink

CSAM Auston Matthews/34 125.00 300.00
CSCB Connor Bedard/98 2000.00 5000.00
CSCP Colton Parayko/55 25.00 60.00
CSDL Devon Levi/27 80.00 200.00
CSJB John Beecher/19 25.00 60.00
CSKK Kevin Korchinski/55 20.00 50.00
CSPM Pavel Mintyukov/34 30.00 80.00
CSSG Samuel Girard/49 12.00 30.00

2023-24 Upper Deck Clear Cut Champs Autographs

CAI Aidan McDonough 6.00 15.00
CAL Alex Laferriere 12.00 30.00
CBM Brandon Montour 10.00 25.00
CBO Bobby Orr SP 50.00 125.00
CBR Martin Brodeur SP 50.00 125.00
CCC Corey Crawford 15.00 40.00
CCO J.T. Compher 5.00 12.00
CCS Cole Sillinger 6.00 15.00
CCZ Connor Zary 15.00 40.00
CDH Dany Heatley 6.00 15.00
CDL Devon Levi 20.00 50.00
CDP David Perron 6.00 15.00
CDT Dave Taylor 6.00 15.00
CDU Walker Duehr SP 6.00 15.00
CDW Dustin Wolf 25.00 60.00
CFG Filip Gustavsson 8.00 20.00
CFM Fraser Minten SP 15.00 40.00
CFP Felix Potvin 40.00 100.00
CGR Jonathan Gruden 8.00 20.00
CIR Isak Rosen 8.00 20.00
CIS Ilya Samsonov 8.00 20.00
CJB John Beecher 15.00 40.00
CJG Jake Guentzel 12.00 30.00

CJH Jonathan Huberdeau 10.00 25.00
CJK Joonas Korpisalo 8.00 20.00
CJP JJ Peterka 8.00 20.00
CJS Jared Spurgeon 8.00 20.00
CJT John Tavares SP 12.00 30.00
CJV Joe Veleno 6.00 15.00
CKH Kevin Hayes 6.00 15.00
CKK Kevin Korchinski 12.00 30.00
CKS Kiefer Sherwood 5.00 12.00
CKT Keith Tkachuk 8.00 20.00
CLC Leo Carlsson SP 25.00 60.00
CLD Lukas Dostal 8.00 20.00
CLE Luke Evangelista 12.00 30.00
CLH Luke Hughes SP 25.00 60.00
CLM Leevi Merilainen 8.00 20.00
CLO Logan Cooley SP 30.00 80.00
CLR Lukas Reichel 8.00 20.00
CMA Marco Kasper 20.00 50.00
CMC Matthew Coronato 12.00 30.00
CMF Marc-Andre Fleury SP 40.00 100.00
CMI Casey Mittelstadt 8.00 20.00
CMK Matthew Knies 30.00 80.00
CML Mike Liut 12.00 30.00
CMO Andy Moog 8.00 20.00
CMP Pavel Mintyukov 12.00 30.00
CMW Matthew Poitras SP 15.00 40.00
CNC Noah Cates 5.00 12.00
CNS Nick Schmaltz 6.00 15.00
COB Owen Beck 12.00 30.00
CPA Joe Pavelski 10.00 25.00
CPC Pheonix Copley 5.00 12.00
CPM Petr Mrazek 6.00 15.00
CPO Martin Pospisil 10.00 25.00
CRC Ross Colton 6.00 15.00
CRG Ridly Greig 12.00 30.00
CRL Raphael Lavoie 8.00 20.00
CRN Rick Nash 8.00 20.00
CRR Ryan Reaves 6.00 15.00
CSA Mackie Samoskevich 12.00 30.00
CSB Samuel Bolduc 8.00 20.00
CSG Samuel Girard 5.00 12.00
CSK Samuel Knazko 8.00 20.00
CSN Simon Nemec 15.00 40.00
CSO Justin Sourdif 8.00 20.00
CSS Stuart Skinner 10.00 25.00
CSV Stanislav Svozil 6.00 15.00
CTF Tyson Foerster 15.00 40.00
CTK Tye Kartye SP 12.00 30.00
CTM Trevor Moore 5.00 12.00
CTN Thomas Novak 5.00 12.00
CTT Troy Terry 6.00 15.00
CVD Vince Dunn 6.00 15.00
CVI Vincent Iorio 8.00 20.00
CWC Will Cuylle 12.00 30.00
CWD William Dufour 6.00 15.00
CWK William Karlsson 10.00 25.00
CYA Yaroslav Askarov SP 25.00 60.00

2023-24 Upper Deck Clear Cut Champs Autographs Blue

*BLUE/50: .6X TO 1.5X BASIC
CAM Auston Matthews 150.00 400.00
CAO Alex Ovechkin 250.00 600.00
CCC Corey Crawford 30.00 80.00
CCM Connor McDavid 200.00 500.00
CDW Dustin Wolf 60.00 150.00
CFP Felix Potvin 80.00 200.00
CML Mike Liut 30.00 80.00
CMO Andy Moog 25.00 60.00

2023-24 Upper Deck Clear Cut Clearly Revered Autographs

*BLUE/25: .5X TO 1.2X BASIC
CRAG Adam Graves 20.00 50.00
CRAM Al MacInnis 30.00 80.00
CRBO Peter Bondra 25.00 60.00
CRBT Bryan Trottier 25.00 60.00
CRCC Chris Chelios 25.00 60.00
CRCN Cam Neely 25.00 60.00
CRGC Guy Carbonneau 25.00 60.00
CRGF Grant Fuhr 40.00 100.00
CRHZ Henrik Zetterberg 30.00 80.00
CRJI Jarome Iginla 30.00 80.00
CRJT Joe Thornton 40.00 100.00
CRLR Larry Robinson 25.00 60.00
CRMM Mike Modano 40.00 100.00
CRPB Patrice Bergeron 80.00 200.00
CRPE Phil Esposito 40.00 100.00
CRRB Ray Bourque 40.00 100.00
CRRF Ron Francis 30.00 80.00
CRTL Trevor Linden 25.00 60.00
CRTT Tim Thomas 25.00 60.00
CRWG Wayne Gretzky SP 150.00 400.00

2023-24 Upper Deck Clear Cut Supreme Skill

*BLUE/25: .8X TO 2X BASIC
SSKAB Aleksander Barkov 10.00 25.00
SSKAL Alexis Lafreniere 25.00 60.00
SSKAS Andrei Svechnikov 8.00 20.00
SSKBB Brock Boeser 8.00 20.00
SSKBF Brock Faber SP 15.00 40.00
SSKBM Brad Marchand 20.00 50.00
SSKBO Bobby Orr SP 50.00 125.00
SSKBT Brady Tkachuk 10.00 25.00
SSKCA Leo Carlsson SP 20.00 50.00
SSKDL Devon Levi 15.00 40.00
SSKDW Dustin Wolf SP 20.00 50.00
SSKIS Ilya Sorokin 10.00 25.00
SSKJB John Beecher 12.00 30.00
SSKJG Jake Guentzel 10.00 25.00
SSKJH Jonathan Huberdeau 8.00 20.00
SSKJP Joe Pavelski 8.00 20.00
SSKKK Kevin Korchinski 10.00 25.00
SSKKL Kris Letang 20.00 50.00
SSKLC Logan Cooley SP 20.00 50.00
SSKMC Matthew Coronato 10.00 25.00
SSKMP Matthew Poitras 12.00 30.00
SSKNS Nick Suzuki 20.00 50.00
SSKOB Owen Beck 10.00 25.00
SSKPM Pavel Mintyukov 10.00 25.00
SSKRE Ryker Evans 8.00 20.00
SSKRG Ridly Greig 10.00 25.00
SSKRL Raphael Lavoie 6.00 15.00
SSKSN Simon Nemec 12.00 30.00
SSKTF Tyson Foerster 12.00 30.00
SSKTK Tye Kartye 10.00 25.00

2023-24 Upper Deck Connor Bedard Collection

1 Connor Bedard HL 1.50 4.00
2 Connor Bedard HL 1.50 4.00
3 Connor Bedard HL 1.50 4.00
4 Connor Bedard HL 1.50 4.00
5 Connor Bedard HL 1.50 4.00
6 Connor Bedard HL 1.50 4.00
7 Connor Bedard HL 1.50 4.00
8 Connor Bedard HL 1.50 4.00
9 Connor Bedard HL 1.50 4.00
10 Connor Bedard HL 1.50 4.00
11 Connor Bedard HL 1.50 4.00
12 Connor Bedard HL 1.50 4.00
13 Connor Bedard HL 1.50 4.00
14 Connor Bedard HL 1.50 4.00
15 Connor Bedard HL 1.50 4.00
16 Connor Bedard HL 1.50 4.00
17 Connor Bedard HL 1.50 4.00
18 Connor Bedard HL 1.50 4.00
19 Connor Bedard HL 1.50 4.00
20 Connor Bedard HL 1.50 4.00
21 Connor Bedard HL 1.50 4.00
22 Connor Bedard HL 1.50 4.00
23 Connor Bedard HL 1.50 4.00
24 Connor Bedard HL 1.50 4.00
25 Connor Bedard HL 1.50 4.00
26 Connor Bedard AH SP 10.00 25.00
27 Connor Bedard AH SP 10.00 25.00
28 Connor Bedard AH SP 10.00 25.00
29 Connor Bedard AH SP 10.00 25.00
30 Connor Bedard AH SP 10.00 25.00

2015-16 Upper Deck Connor McDavid Collection

COMP.FACT.SET (26) 15.00 30.00
COMPLETE SET (25) 8.00 20.00
COMMON McDAVID .50 1.25

2015-16 Upper Deck Connor McDavid Collection Jumbos

C1 Connor McDavid 4.00 10.00

2015-16 Upper Deck Contours

1 Jonathan Toews 1.50 4.00
2 Steven Stamkos 2.00 5.00
3 Carey Price 2.00 5.00
4 Adam Henrique .75 2.00
5 Jarome Iginla 1.25 3.00
6 Phil Kessel 1.00 2.50
7 Anze Kopitar 1.50 4.00
8 Jamie Benn 1.00 2.50
9 Radim Vrbata .60 1.50
10 Corey Perry 1.50 4.00
11 Andrew Ladd .60 1.50
12 James van Riemsdyk .75 2.00
13 Alexander Ovechkin 4.00 10.00
14 Alexandre Burrows .60 1.50
15 Pekka Rinne 1.00 2.50
16 Zach Parise 1.00 2.50
17 Ryan Getzlaf 1.00 2.50
18 Jaden Schwartz 1.25 3.00
19 Kyle Turris .75 2.00
20 Pavel Datsyuk 1.50 4.00
21 John Tavares 1.50 4.00
22 Logan Couture 1.25 3.00
23 Eric Staal 1.25 3.00
24 Rick Nash 1.00 2.50
25 Patrice Bergeron 1.25 3.00
26 Evgeni Malkin 2.00 5.00
27 Oliver Ekman-Larsson 1.00 2.50
28 Jonathan Quick 1.25 3.00
29 Tyler Johnson .60 1.50
30 Patrick Kane 2.00 5.00
31 Jonathan Huberdeau .75 2.00
32 Ryan Johansen .75 2.00
33 Mark Stone 1.25 3.00
34 Jiri Hudler .75 2.00
35 P.K. Subban 1.25 3.00
36 T.J. Oshie 1.00 2.50
37 Blake Wheeler 1.00 2.50
38 Tyler Bozak .60 1.50
39 Thomas Vanek .75 2.00
40 Tyler Seguin 1.25 3.00
41 Henrik Zetterberg 1.25 3.00
42 Filip Forsberg 1.50 4.00
43 Henrik Lundqvist 2.50 6.00
44 Jordan Staal .75 2.00
45 Max Pacioretty 1.00 2.50
46 Michael Cammalleri .75 2.00
47 Taylor Hall 1.00 2.50
48 Nicklas Backstrom 1.00 2.50
49 Derick Brassard .60 1.50
50 Gabriel Landeskog 1.25 3.00
51 David Backes .60 1.50
52 Ben Bishop .75 2.00
53 Kyle Okposo .60 1.50
54 Jakub Voracek .75 2.00
55 Ryan Kesler 1.00 2.50
56 Nick Bjugstad .60 1.50
57 Daniel Sedin 1.25 3.00
58 Milan Lucic .75 2.00
59 Claude Giroux 1.00 2.50
60 Sean Monahan .60 1.50
61 Sergei Bobrovsky 1.50 4.00
62 Elias Lindholm 1.00 2.50
63 Loui Eriksson .60 1.50
64 Shea Weber .75 2.00
65 Joe Pavelski 1.25 3.00
66 Nikita Kucherov 2.00 5.00
67 John Gibson 1.00 2.50
68 Sam Gagner .60 1.50
69 Jason Spezza 1.25 3.00
70 Nazem Kadri 1.25 3.00
71 Johnny Gaudreau 1.50 4.00
72 Mikko Koivu .75 2.00
73 Colin Wilson .60 1.50
74 Erik Karlsson 1.25 3.00
75 Cory Schneider 1.00 2.50
76 Aaron Ekblad 1.25 3.00
77 Marcus Johansson .75 2.00
78 Chris Kreider 1.25 3.00
79 Brad Marchand 2.00 5.00
80 Marian Hossa 1.00 2.50
81 Shane Doan .75 2.00
82 Henrik Sedin 1.25 3.00
83 Anders Lee 1.00 2.50
84 Mark Scheifele 1.50 4.00
85 Jordan Eberle 1.00 2.50
86 Joe Thornton 1.50 4.00
87 Sidney Crosby 4.00 10.00
88 Nick Foligno .75 2.00
89 Vladimir Tarasenko 1.25 3.00
90 Corey Crawford 1.25 3.00
91 Curtis Joseph 1.25 3.00
92 Steve Yzerman 2.50 6.00
93 Jeremy Roenick 1.50 4.00
94 Glenn Hall 1.00 2.50
95 Paul Coffey 1.00 2.50
96 Doug Gilmour 1.25 3.00
97 Mark Messier 2.00 5.00
98 Borje Salming 1.00 2.50
99 Wayne Gretzky 6.00 15.00
100 Owen Nolan 1.00 2.50
101 Nick Ritchie AU RC 4.00 10.00
102 Zachary Fucale AU RC 3.00 8.00
103 Brady Skjei AU RC 3.00 8.00
104 Malcolm Subban AU RC 6.00 15.00
105 Andreas Athanasiou AU RC 10.00 25.00
106 Daniel Sprong AU RC 5.00 12.00
107 Hunter Shinkaruk AU RC 4.00 10.00
108 Dylan DeMelo AU RC 3.00 8.00
109 Sergei Plotnikov AU RC 2.50 6.00
110 Vincent Hinostroza AU RC 2.50 6.00
111 Charles Hudon AU RC 4.00 10.00
112 Andrew Copp AU RC 4.00 10.00
113 Colton Parayko AU RC 6.00 15.00
114 Chandler Stephenson AU RC 5.00 12.00
115 Anthony Stolarz AU RC 10.00 25.00
116 Brendan Ranford AU RC 3.00 8.00
117 Joel Edmundson AU RC 3.00 8.00
118 Tyler Randell AU RC 4.00 10.00
119 Mattias Janmark AU RC 4.00 10.00
120 Mike Condon AU RC 4.00 10.00
121 Anton Slepyshev AU RC 2.50 6.00
122 Ben Hutton AU RC 4.00 10.00
123 Joonas Donskoi AU RC 4.00 10.00
124 Radek Faksa AU RC 4.00 10.00
125 Nick Shore AU RC 2.50 6.00
126 Oscar Lindberg AU RC 4.00 10.00
127 Matt O'Connor AU RC 3.00 8.00
128 Jared McCann AU RC 5.00 12.00
129 Viktor Arvidsson AU RC 4.00 10.00
130 Shea Theodore AU RC 6.00 15.00
131 Connor McDavid JSY AU RC 200.00 300.00
132 Henrik Samuelsson JSY AU RC 2.50 6.00
133 Emile Poirier JSY AU RC 3.00 8.00
134 Slater Koekkoek JSY AU RC 2.50 6.00
135 Dylan Larkin JSY AU RC 60.00 120.00
136 Kyle Baun JSY AU RC 4.00 10.00
137 Antoine Bibeau JSY AU RC 4.00 10.00
138 Noah Hanifin JSY AU RC 6.00 15.00
139 Derek Forbort JSY AU RC 3.00 8.00
140 Matt Puempel JSY AU RC 3.00 8.00
141 Stefan Noesen JSY AU RC 2.50 6.00
142 Connor Hellebuyck JSY AU RC 15.00 40.00
143 Brock McGinn JSY AU RC 4.00 10.00
144 Sam Bennett JSY AU RC 12.00 30.00
145 Nikolaj Ehlers JSY AU RC 8.00 20.00
146 Jake Virtanen JSY AU RC 5.00 12.00
147 Shane Prince JSY AU RC 2.50 6.00
148 Mackenzie Skapski JSY AU RC 4.00 10.00
149 Robby Fabbri JSY AU RC 5.00 12.00
150 Kevin Fiala JSY AU RC 5.00 12.00
151 Nick Cousins JSY AU RC 4.00 10.00
152 Nikolay Goldobin JSY AU RC 4.00 10.00
153 Ryan Hartman JSY AU RC 5.00 12.00
154 Jacob de la Rose JSY AU RC 4.00 10.00
155 Nicolas Petan JSY AU RC 4.00 10.00
156 Max Domi JSY AU RC 20.00 50.00
157 Josh Anderson JSY AU RC 8.00 20.00
158 Artemi Panarin JSY AU RC 60.00 120.00
159 Mikko Rantanen JSY AU RC 20.00 50.00
160 Jack Eichel JSY RC 15.00 40.00

2015-16 Upper Deck Contours Blue

48 Nicklas Backstrom 1.25 3.00
90 Corey Crawford 1.50 4.00

2015-16 Upper Deck Contours Club Crest Jerseys

*PATCH/75: .6X TO 1.5X JSY
CC1 Jack Eichel A 12.00 30.00
CC2 Artemi Panarin B 12.00 30.00
CC3 Malcolm Subban C 5.00 12.00
CC4 Antoine Bibeau C 3.00 8.00
CC5 Sam Bennett B 10.00 25.00
CC6 Kevin Fiala C 4.00 10.00
CC7 Connor Hellebuyck C 12.00 30.00
CC8 Henrik Samuelsson C 2.00 5.00
CC9 Zachary Fucale B 2.50 6.00
CC10 Matt Puempel C 2.50 6.00
CC11 Nick Cousins C 3.00 8.00
CC12 Jake Virtanen C 4.00 10.00
CC13 Mackenzie Skapski C 3.00 8.00
CC14 Robby Fabbri C 4.00 10.00
CC15 Connor McDavid A 50.00 125.00
CC16 Nicolas Petan C 3.00 8.00
CC17 Dylan Larkin A 10.00 25.00
CC18 Noah Hanifin C 5.00 12.00
CC19 Nikolay Goldobin C 3.00 8.00
CC20 Daniel Sprong C 4.00 10.00
CC21 Slater Koekkoek C 2.00 5.00
CC22 Shea Theodore C 5.00 12.00
CC23 Shane Prince C 2.00 5.00
CC24 Mikko Rantanen B 15.00 40.00
CC25 Stefan Noesen C 2.00 5.00
CC26 Max Domi B 6.00 15.00
CC27 Jacob de la Rose C 3.00 8.00
CC28 Josh Anderson C 6.00 15.00
CC29 Nikolaj Ehlers C 6.00 15.00
CC30 Ryan Hartman C 4.00 10.00
CC31 Emile Poirier C 2.50 6.00
CC32 Brock McGinn C 3.00 8.00

2015-16 Upper Deck Contours High Profile Fans Jersey Autographs

HPAJJP Jason Priestley 5.00 12.00
HPAJKH Kevin Harvick 8.00 20.00
HPAJKS Kevin Smith 20.00 50.00
HPAJLK Larry King 8.00 20.00
HPAJRN Rachel Nichols 30.00 80.00

2015-16 Upper Deck Contours High Profile Fans Jerseys

*PATCHES: .75X TO 2X BASIC
HPJBH Bret Hart B 4.00 10.00
HPJCM CM Punk B 8.00 20.00
HPJJP Jason Priestley B 3.00 8.00
HPJKH Kevin Harvick B 2.50 6.00
HPJKS Kevin Smith B 5.00 12.00
HPJLK Larry King B 4.00 10.00
HPJRN Rachel Nichols A 12.00 30.00

2015-16 Upper Deck Contours Jumbo Fabrics

JJAB Aleksander Barkov B 4.00 10.00
JJCG Claude Giroux B 2.50 6.00
JJEK Erik Karlsson B 3.00 8.00
JJHZ Henrik Zetterberg A 3.00 8.00
JJJC Jeff Carter B 2.00 5.00
JJJP Joe Pavelski B 3.00 8.00
JJMH Marian Hossa A 2.50 6.00
JJMP Max Pacioretty B 2.50 6.00
JJNB Nicklas Backstrom A 2.50 6.00
JJNM Nathan MacKinnon B 10.00 25.00
JJOL Oliver Ekman-Larsson B 2.50 6.00
JJPB Patrice Bergeron A 3.00 8.00
JJRK Ryan Kesler B 2.50 6.00
JJTH Taylor Hall A 2.50 6.00
JJTS Tyler Seguin A 2.50 6.00
JJVH Victor Hedman B 3.00 8.00
JJVT Vladimir Tarasenko B 3.00 8.00
JJZP Zach Parise B 2.50 6.00

2015-16 Upper Deck Contours Rookie Jumbo Fabrics

RJJAB Antoine Bibeau C 3.00 8.00
RJJAP Artemi Panarin B 12.00 30.00
RJJBM Brock McGinn C 3.00 8.00
RJJCH Connor Hellebuyck C 12.00 30.00
RJJCM Connor McDavid A 50.00 125.00
RJJDF Derek Forbort C 2.50 6.00
RJJDL Dylan Larkin A 10.00 25.00
RJJEP Emile Poirier C 2.50 6.00
RJJHS Henrik Samuelsson C 2.00 5.00
RJJJA Josh Anderson C 6.00 15.00
RJJJD Jacob de la Rose C 3.00 8.00
RJJJE Jack Eichel B 12.00 30.00
RJJJV Jake Virtanen C 4.00 10.00
RJJKB Kyle Baun C 3.00 8.00
RJJKF Kevin Fiala C 4.00 10.00
RJJMD Max Domi B 6.00 15.00
RJJMP Matt Puempel C 2.50 6.00
RJJMR Mikko Rantanen C 15.00 40.00
RJJMS Mackenzie Skapski C 3.00 8.00
RJJNC Nick Cousins C 3.00 8.00
RJJNE Nikolaj Ehlers C 6.00 15.00
RJJNG Nikolay Goldobin C 3.00 8.00
RJJNH Noah Hanifin C 5.00 12.00
RJJNP Nicolas Petan C 3.00 8.00
RJJRF Robby Fabbri C 4.00 10.00
RJJRH Ryan Hartman C 4.00 10.00
RJJSB Sam Bennett B 10.00 25.00
RJJSK Slater Koekkoek C 2.00 5.00
RJJSN Stefan Noesen C 2.00 5.00
RJJSP Shane Prince C 2.00 5.00

2015-16 Upper Deck Contours Rookie Patch Autographs

131 Connor McDavid 400.00 650.00
133 Emile Poirier 6.00 15.00
134 Slater Koekkoek 5.00 12.00
135 Dylan Larkin 25.00 60.00
136 Kyle Baun 8.00 20.00
138 Noah Hanifin 12.00 30.00
139 Derek Forbort 6.00 15.00
140 Matt Puempel 6.00 15.00
141 Stefan Noesen 5.00 12.00
142 Connor Hellebuyck 30.00 80.00
143 Brock McGinn 8.00 20.00
144 Sam Bennett 25.00 60.00
145 Nikolaj Ehlers 15.00 40.00
146 Jake Virtanen 10.00 25.00
147 Shane Prince 5.00 12.00
148 Mackenzie Skapski 8.00 20.00
149 Robby Fabbri 10.00 25.00
150 Kevin Fiala 10.00 25.00
151 Nick Cousins 8.00 20.00
152 Nikolay Goldobin 8.00 20.00
153 Ryan Hartman 10.00 25.00
154 Jacob de la Rose 8.00 20.00
155 Nicolas Petan 8.00 20.00
156 Max Domi 15.00 40.00
157 Josh Anderson 15.00 40.00
158 Artemi Panarin 30.00 80.00
159 Mikko Rantanen 40.00 100.00
160 Jack Eichel No Auto 30.00 80.00

2015-16 Upper Deck Contours Rookie Resume

RR1 Jack Eichel 8.00 20.00
RR2 Oscar Lindberg 2.00 5.00
RR3 Matt Puempel 1.50 4.00
RR4 Emile Poirier 1.50 4.00
RR5 Dylan Larkin 6.00 15.00
RR6 Nikolaj Ehlers 4.00 10.00
RR7 Shane Prince 1.25 3.00
RR8 Colin Miller 1.50 4.00
RR9 Daniel Sprong 2.50 6.00
RR10 Antoine Bibeau 2.00 5.00
RR11 Phil Di Giuseppe 2.00 5.00
RR12 Vincent Hinostroza 1.25 3.00
RR13 Jake Virtanen 2.50 6.00
RR14 Ronalds Kenins 1.25 3.00
RR15 Connor McDavid 25.00 60.00
RR16 Stefan Noesen 1.25 3.00
RR17 Joseph Blandisi 2.00 5.00
RR18 Max Domi 4.00 10.00
RR19 Shea Theodore 3.00 8.00
RR20 Artemi Panarin 8.00 20.00
RR21 Viktor Arvidsson 2.00 5.00
RR22 Nick Ritchie 2.00 5.00
RR23 Colton Parayko 3.00 8.00
RR24 Connor Hellebuyck 8.00 20.00
RR25 Hunter Shinkaruk 2.00 5.00
RR26 Noah Hanifin 3.00 8.00
RR27 Garret Sparks 3.00 8.00
RR28 Andrew Copp 3.00 8.00
RR29 Juuse Saros 5.00 12.00
RR30 Mike McCarron 2.50 6.00
RR31 Andreas Athanasiou 5.00 12.00
RR32 Sergei Plotnikov 1.25 3.00
RR33 Mike Condon 2.00 5.00
RR34 Stanislav Galiev 2.00 5.00
RR35 Jared McCann 2.50 6.00
RR36 Malcolm Subban 3.00 8.00
RR37 Brock McGinn 2.00 5.00
RR38 Nikolay Goldobin 2.00 5.00
RR39 Nicolas Petan 2.00 5.00
RR40 Ryan Hartman 2.50 6.00
RR41 Jacob de la Rose 2.00 5.00
RR42 Mikko Rantanen 10.00 25.00
RR43 Kevin Fiala 2.50 6.00
RR44 Zachary Fucale 1.50 4.00
RR45 Mattias Janmark 2.00 5.00
RR46 Robby Fabbri 2.50 6.00
RR47 Chandler Stephenson 2.50 6.00
RR48 Nick Shore 1.25 3.00
RR49 Joonas Donskoi 2.00 5.00
RR50 Sam Bennett 6.00 15.00

2015-16 Upper Deck Contours Rookie Resume Gold Rainbow

*SINGLES: .6X TO 1.5X BASIC INSERTS
RR15 Connor McDavid 100.00 200.00
RR40 Ryan Hartman 4.00 10.00

2015-16 Upper Deck Contours Rookie Resume Gold Rainbow Autographs

RR2 Oscar Lindberg D 3.00 8.00
RR3 Matt Puempel C 2.50 6.00
RR4 Emile Poirier D 2.50 6.00
RR5 Dylan Larkin B 60.00 120.00
RR6 Nikolaj Ehlers C 6.00 15.00
RR7 Shane Prince D 2.00 5.00
RR8 Colin Miller D 2.50 6.00
RR9 Daniel Sprong C 8.00 20.00
RR10 Antoine Bibeau D 3.00 8.00
RR11 Phil Di Giuseppe D 3.00 8.00
RR12 Vincent Hinostroza D 2.00 5.00
RR13 Jake Virtanen B 4.00 10.00
RR14 Ronalds Kenins D 2.00 5.00
RR15 Connor McDavid A 200.00 350.00
RR16 Stefan Noesen D 2.00 5.00
RR19 Shea Theodore D 5.00 12.00
RR21 Viktor Arvidsson D 3.00 8.00
RR22 Nick Ritchie C 3.00 8.00
RR23 Colton Parayko C 5.00 12.00
RR25 Hunter Shinkaruk D 3.00 8.00
RR26 Noah Hanifin C 5.00 12.00
RR27 Garret Sparks D 3.00 8.00
RR28 Andrew Copp D 3.00 8.00
RR29 Juuse Saros D 8.00 20.00
RR30 Mike McCarron D 4.00 10.00
RR31 Andreas Athanasiou D 8.00 20.00
RR32 Sergei Plotnikov D 2.00 5.00
RR33 Mike Condon C 3.00 8.00
RR35 Jared McCann C 4.00 10.00
RR36 Malcolm Subban C 5.00 12.00
RR38 Nikolay Goldobin D 3.00 8.00
RR39 Nicolas Petan D 3.00 8.00
RR40 Ryan Hartman D 4.00 10.00
RR41 Jacob de la Rose D 3.00 8.00
RR43 Kevin Fiala D 4.00 10.00
RR44 Zachary Fucale C 2.50 6.00
RR45 Mattias Janmark D 3.00 8.00
RR46 Robby Fabbri B 4.00 10.00
RR47 Chandler Stephenson D 4.00 10.00
RR48 Nick Shore D 2.00 5.00
RR49 Joonas Donskoi D 3.00 8.00
RR50 Sam Bennett B 10.00 25.00

2015-16 Upper Deck Contours Rookie Resume Gold Rainbow Proofs

RR15 Connor McDavid 60.00 150.00
RR40 Ryan Hartman 5.00 12.00

2015-16 Upper Deck Contours Show Me Some Glove Jerseys

*PATCH/20: 1.5X TO 4X JSY
S1 Frederik Andersen C 4.00 10.00
S2 Tuukka Rask B 4.00 10.00
S4 Jonas Hiller C 2.50 6.00
S5 Cam Ward C 3.00 8.00
S6 Corey Crawford B 4.00 10.00
S7 Patrick Roy A 8.00 20.00
S8 Sergei Bobrovsky C 5.00 12.00
S9 Kari Lehtonen C 2.50 6.00
S11 Grant Fuhr A 5.00 12.00
S12 Roberto Luongo C 5.00 12.00
S13 Jonathan Quick C 4.00 10.00
S14 Devan Dubnyk C 2.50 6.00
S15 Carey Price B 6.00 15.00
S16 Pekka Rinne B 5.00 12.00
S17 Martin Brodeur A 8.00 20.00
S18 Jaroslav Halak C 3.00 8.00
S19 Henrik Lundqvist B 8.00 20.00
S20 Craig Anderson C 3.00 8.00
S21 Steve Mason C 2.50 6.00
S22 Mike Smith C 3.00 8.00
S23 Marc-Andre Fleury B 6.00 15.00
S24 Martin Jones C 2.50 6.00
S25 Jake Allen C 3.00 8.00
S27 Jonathan Bernier C 2.50 6.00
S28 Ryan Miller C 3.00 8.00
S29 Braden Holtby B 4.00 10.00
S30 Ondrej Pavelec C 3.00 8.00

2015-16 Upper Deck Contours Team Fanatics Jersey Autographs

TFAJLV Lindsey Vonn 15.00 40.00
TFAJTG Tom Glavine 8.00 20.00

2015-16 Upper Deck Contours Team Fanatics Jerseys

TFJLV Lindsey Vonn 8.00 20.00
TFJTG Tom Glavine 5.00 12.00

2015-16 Upper Deck Contours Youth Movement Autographs

YM1 Leon Draisaitl/399 15.00 40.00
YM3 Alexander Wennberg/399 3.00 8.00
YM4 Mark Scheifele/399 8.00 20.00
YM5 John Klingberg/399 5.00 12.00
YM6 Charlie Coyle/399 5.00 12.00
YM7 Nail Yakupov/399 3.00 8.00
YM8 Calle Jarnkrok/399 4.00 10.00
YM9 Curtis Lazar/399 3.00 8.00
YM10 Justin Faulk/399 4.00 10.00
YM11 Jake Allen/399 5.00 12.00
YM12 Morgan Rielly/399 5.00 12.00
YM13 Tomas Hertl/399 5.00 12.00
YM14 Dougie Hamilton/399 4.00 10.00
YM15 Kevin Hayes/399 4.00 10.00
YM16 Griffin Reinhart/399 3.00 8.00
YM17 Nikita Kucherov/399 10.00 25.00
YM18 Markus Granlund/399 4.00 10.00
YM19 Sean Couturier/399 4.00 10.00
YM20 Mike Hoffman/399 3.00 8.00
YM21 Aaron Ekblad/249 6.00 15.00
YM22 Sean Monahan/249 3.00 8.00
YM23 Taylor Hall/249 5.00 12.00
YM24 Johnny Gaudreau/249 8.00 20.00
YM25 Jonathan Drouin/249 4.00 10.00
YM26 Gabriel Landeskog/249 6.00 15.00
YM27 Alex Galchenyuk/249 3.00 8.00
YM28 Nathan MacKinnon/249 20.00 50.00
YM29 Ryan Johansen/249 4.00 10.00
YM30 Connor McDavid/49 175.00 300.00

2019-20 Upper Deck Credentials

1 Connor McDavid 2.00 5.00
2 Brad Marchand .75 2.00
3 Ryan Getzlaf .40 1.00
4 Jack Eichel .60 1.50
5 Steven Stamkos .75 2.00
6 Phil Kessel .40 1.00
7 Johnny Gaudreau .60 1.50
8 Seth Jones .40 1.00
9 Tyler Seguin .50 1.25
10 Alexander Ovechkin 1.50 4.00
11 Dylan Larkin .50 1.25
12 Sean Monahan .25 .60
13 Drew Doughty .50 1.25
14 Eric Staal .40 1.00
15 Leon Draisaitl 1.25 3.00
16 Sebastian Aho .60 1.50
17 Artemi Panarin .75 2.00
18 Aleksander Barkov .60 1.50
19 Carey Price .75 2.00
20 Erik Karlsson .50 1.25
21 Mathew Barzal .50 1.25
22 Carter Hart .40 1.00
23 Evgeni Malkin .75 2.00
24 Matt Duchene .40 1.00
25 Auston Matthews 1.50 4.00
26 Jordan Binnington .60 1.50
27 Elias Pettersson .60 1.50
28 Nathan MacKinnon 1.50 4.00
29 Jonathan Toews .60 1.50
30 John Tavares .60 1.50
31 Henrik Lundqvist 1.00 2.50
32 Ryan O'Reilly .40 1.00
33 Marc-Andre Fleury .75 2.00
34 Brent Burns .40 1.00
35 Taylor Hall .40 1.00
36 Mark Scheifele .60 1.50
37 Claude Giroux .50 1.25
38 Mark Stone .50 1.25
39 Jamie Benn .40 1.00
40 Nikita Kucherov .75 2.00
41 Blake Wheeler .40 1.00
42 Patrice Bergeron .50 1.25
43 Max Domi .40 1.00
44 Brady Tkachuk .50 1.25
45 P.K. Subban .50 1.25
46 Brock Boeser .50 1.25
47 Nicklas Backstrom .40 1.00
48 Mikko Rantanen 1.00 2.50
49 Patrick Kane .75 2.00
50 Sidney Crosby 1.50 4.00
51 Kaden Fulcher/999 RC 1.00 2.50
52 Klim Kostin/999 RC 1.00 2.50
53 Nick Caamano/999 RC .75 2.00
54 Matt Roy/999 RC 1.00 2.50
55 Brandon Gignac/999 RC .75 2.00
56 Josh Currie/999 RC .75 2.00
57 Jack Studnicka/999 RC 1.00 2.50
58 Dennis Gilbert/999 RC .75 2.00
59 Mackenzie MacEachern/999 RC 1.00 2.50
60 Cayden Primeau/999 RC 2.00 5.00
61 Carsen Twarynski/999 RC .75 2.00
62 Ryan Lindgren/999 RC 1.00 2.50
63 Kole Sherwood/999 RC 1.00 2.50
64 Nico Sturm/999 RC .75 2.00
65 Guillaume Brisebois/999 RC 1.00 2.50
66 Colton White/999 RC .75 2.00
67 Gaetan Haas/999 RC .75 2.00
68 John Marino/999 RC 1.50 4.00
69 Joel L'Esperance/999 RC .75 2.00
70 Jakob Lilja/999 RC .75 2.00
71 Scott Sabourin/999 RC .75 2.00
72 Vladislav Gavrikov/999 RC .75 2.00
73 Josh Teves/999 RC .75 2.00
74 David Gustafsson/999 RC .75 2.00
75 Josh Jacobs/999 RC .75 2.00
76 Riley Stillman/999 RC 1.00 2.50
77 Adam Boqvist/999 RC 1.00 2.50
78 Josh Brown/999 RC .75 2.00
79 Kevin Stenlund/999 RC .75 2.00
80 Mark Friedman/999 RC .75 2.00
81 Kevin Boyle/999 RC .75 2.00
82 Brogan Rafferty/999 RC 1.00 2.50
83 Otto Koivula/999 RC .60 1.50
84 Jacob Middleton/999 RC .75 2.00
85 Rudolfs Balcers/999 RC 1.00 2.50
86 Daniil Yurtaykin/999 RC .75 2.00
87 Collin Blackwell/999 RC 1.00 2.50
88 Adam Johnson/999 RC .75 2.00
89 Brady Keeper/999 RC .75 2.00
90 Max Veronneau/999 RC .75 2.00
91 Cale Fleury/699 RC 1.25 3.00
92 Libor Hajek/699 RC 1.00 2.50
93 Joey Daccord/699 RC 2.00 5.00
94 Julien Gauthier/699 RC 1.25 3.00
95 Nikolai Prokhorkin/699 RC .75 2.00
96 Mario Ferraro/699 RC .75 2.00
97 Carter Verhaeghe/699 RC 1.50 4.00
98 Conor Timmins/699 RC 1.00 2.50
99 Ryan Kuffner/699 RC .75 2.00
100 Trevor Moore/699 RC .75 2.00
101 Sam Lafferty/699 RC .75 2.00
102 Zack MacEwen/699 RC .75 2.00
103 Martin Fehervary/699 RC .75 2.00
104 Jimmy Schuldt/699 RC .75 2.00
105 Carl Grundstrom/699 RC 1.00 2.50
106 Joakim Nygard/699 RC .75 2.00
107 Rem Pitlick/699 RC 1.00 2.50
108 Rhett Gardner/699 RC .75 2.00
109 Elvis Merzlikins/699 RC 2.00 5.00
110 Joel Persson/699 RC .75 2.00
111 Zach Senyshyn/699 RC 1.00 2.50
112 Vitaly Abramov/699 RC 1.00 2.50
113 Nathan Bastian/699 RC 1.00 2.50
114 Joel Farabee/699 RC 1.50 4.00
115 Gerald Mayhew/699 RC .75 2.00
116 Connor Bunnaman/699 RC .75 2.00
117 Lean Bergmann/699 RC 1.00 2.50
118 Dmytro Timashov/699 RC 1.00 2.50
119 Ville Heinola/699 RC 1.25 3.00
120 Trent Frederic/699 RC 1.00 2.50
121 Blake Lizotte/699 RC 1.00 2.50
122 William Borgen/699 RC .75 2.00
123 Connor Clifton/699 RC 1.00 2.50
124 Max Jones/699 RC 1.00 2.50
125 Taro Hirose/699 RC 1.00 2.50
126 Oliver Wahlstrom/499 RC 1.50 4.00
127 Rasmus Sandin/499 RC 1.50 4.00
128 Erik Brannstrom/499 RC 1.00 2.50
129 Emil Bemstrom/499 RC 1.00 2.50
130 Jesper Boqvist/499 RC 1.00 2.50
131 Filip Zadina/499 RC 1.50 4.00
132 Nicolas Hague/499 RC 1.00 2.50
133 Dante Fabbro/499 RC 1.00 2.50
134 Morgan Frost/499 RC 1.50 4.00
135 Ryan Poehling/499 RC 1.50 4.00
136 Tobias Bjornfot/499 RC 1.00 2.50
137 Ilya Mikheyev/499 RC 1.50 4.00
138 Alexandre Texier/499 RC 1.00 2.50
139 Adam Fox/499 RC 2.50 6.00
140 Victor Olofsson/499 RC 2.00 5.00
141 Noah Dobson/299 RC 2.50 6.00
142 Barrett Hayton/299 RC 4.00 10.00
143 Cody Glass/299 RC 4.00 10.00
144 Cale Makar/299 RC 8.00 20.00
145 Kaapo Kakko/299 RC 8.00 20.00
146 Kirby Dach/299 RC 2.00 5.00
147 Nikita Gusev/299 RC 1.50 4.00
148 Nick Suzuki/299 RC 6.00 15.00
149 Quinn Hughes/299 RC 10.00 25.00
150 Jack Hughes/299 RC 5.00 12.00

2019-20 Upper Deck Credentials Green

*GREEN VET/99: .75X TO 2X BASIC
*GREEN RC/25: 1X TO 2.5X BASIC
1 Connor McDavid 6.00 15.00

2019-20 Upper Deck Credentials Purple

*PURPLE VET/25: 1.25X TO 3X BASIC
*PURPLE RC/10: NO PRICING
1 Connor McDavid 12.00 30.00

2019-20 Upper Deck Credentials Red

*RED: .6X TO 1.5X BASIC
1 Connor McDavid 10.00 12.00

2019-20 Upper Deck Credentials 1st Star of the Night

1S01 Connor McDavid 3.00 8.00
1S02 Auston Matthews 2.50 6.00
1S03 Sidney Crosby 2.50 6.00
1S04 John Tavares 1.00 2.50
1S05 Carey Price 1.25 3.00
1S06 Marc-Andre Fleury 1.25 3.00
1S07 Patrick Kane 1.25 3.00
1S08 Jack Hughes 3.00 8.00
1S09 Kaapo Kakko 1.00 2.50
1S10 Quinn Hughes 3.00 8.00
1S11 Cale Makar 3.00 8.00
1S12 Nick Suzuki 2.50 6.00

2019-20 Upper Deck Credentials 2nd Star of the Night

2S01 Mark Stone .75 2.00
2S02 Dylan Larkin .75 2.00
2S03 Ryan O'Reilly .60 1.50
2S04 Alex DeBrincat .75 2.00
2S05 John Gibson .60 1.50
2S06 Aleksander Barkov .75 2.00
2S07 Artemi Panarin 1.25 3.00
2S08 Filip Zadina 1.00 2.50
2S09 Ryan Poehling 1.00 2.50
2S10 Cody Glass 1.00 2.50
2S11 Nikita Gusev 1.00 2.50
2S12 Kirby Dach 1.25 3.00

2019-20 Upper Deck Credentials 2nd Star of the Night Autographs

2S01 Mark Stone/75 10.00 25.00
2S02 Dylan Larkin/25 10.00 25.00
2S05 John Gibson/75 8.00 20.00
2S07 Artemi Panarin/25 50.00 125.00
2S08 Filip Zadina/25 12.00 30.00
2S10 Cody Glass/25 12.00 30.00
2S11 Nikita Gusev/25 12.00 30.00
2S12 Kirby Dach/25 30.00 80.00

2019-20 Upper Deck Credentials 3rd Star of the Night

3S01 Zach Werenski 1.00 2.50
3S02 Jake Guentzel 1.00 2.50
3S03 Brayden Point .75 2.00
3S04 Matthew Tkachuk 1.25 3.00
3S05 Pierre-Luc Dubois .50 1.25
3S06 Thomas Chabot .60 1.50
3S07 Jonathan Drouin .50 1.25
3S08 Rasmus Sandin 1.00 2.50
3S09 Noah Dobson 1.50 4.00
3S10 Victor Olofsson 1.25 3.00
3S11 Erik Brannstrom .60 1.50
3S12 Barrett Hayton 1.25 3.00

2019-20 Upper Deck Credentials 3rd Star of the Night Autographs

3S02 Jake Guentzel/99 12.00 30.00
3S04 Matthew Tkachuk/99 15.00 40.00
3S06 Thomas Chabot/99 8.00 20.00
3S08 Rasmus Sandin/49 12.00 30.00
3S09 Noah Dobson/49 20.00 50.00
3S11 Erik Brannstrom/49 8.00 20.00
3S12 Barrett Hayton/49 15.00 40.00

2019-20 Upper Deck Credentials Debut Ticket Access Acetate
RTA1 Ryan Poehling/299 3.00 8.00
RTA2 Erik Brannstrom/299 2.00 5.00
RTA3 Alexandre Texier/299 4.00 10.00
RTA4 Dante Fabbro/299 2.00 5.00
RTA5 Taro Hirose/299 2.00 5.00
RTA6 Philippe Myers/299 1.50 4.00
RTA7 Max Jones/299 2.00 5.00
RTA8 Victor Olofsson/299 4.00 10.00
RTA9 Vitaly Abramov/299 2.00 5.00
RTA10 Noah Dobson/299 5.00 12.00
RTA11 Carl Grundstrom/299 2.00 5.00
RTA12 Jimmy Schuldt/299 1.50 4.00
RTA13 Karson Kuhlman/299 2.00 5.00
RTA14 Tobias Bjornfot/299 2.00 5.00
RTA15 Filip Zadina/299 3.00 8.00
RTA16 Rasmus Sandin/99 10.00 25.00
RTA17 Barrett Hayton/99 15.00 40.00
RTA18 Cody Glass/99 10.00 25.00
RTA19 Cale Makar/99 20.00 50.00
RTA20 Kaapo Kakko/99 15.00 40.00
RTA21 Kirby Dach/99 12.00 30.00
RTA22 Nick Suzuki/99 12.00 30.00
RTA23 Nikita Gusev/99 3.00 8.00
RTA24 Quinn Hughes/99 25.00 60.00
RTA25 Jack Hughes/99 10.00 25.00

2019-20 Upper Deck Credentials Debut Ticket Access Acetate Autographs
RTAAAF Adam Fox/99 30.00 80.00
RTAAAT Alexandre Texier/99 12.00 30.00
RTAACM Cale Makar/25 100.00 250.00
RTAACR Carl Grundstrom/99 12.00 30.00
RTAAEB Erik Brannstrom/99 12.00 30.00
RTAAFZ Filip Zadina/99 15.00 40.00
RTAAIM Ilya Mikheyev/99 20.00 50.00
RTAAJH Jack Hughes/25 80.00 200.00
RTAAKD Kirby Dach/25 25.00 60.00
RTAAKU Karson Kuhlman/99 12.00 30.00
RTAAMJ Max Jones/99 12.00 30.00
RTAANS Nick Suzuki/25 50.00 125.00
RTAAPM Philippe Myers/99 10.00 25.00
RTAAQH Quinn Hughes/25 200.00 500.00
RTAARP Ryan Poehling/99 15.00 40.00
RTAARS Rasmus Sandin/25 20.00 50.00
RTAATH Taro Hirose/99 12.00 30.00
RTAAVA Vitaly Abramov/99 12.00 30.00
RTAAVO Victor Olofsson/99 25.00 60.00

2019-20 Upper Deck Credentials Debut Ticket Access Autographs
*RED/65: .6X TO 1.5X BASIC
RTAAAT Alexandre Texier/299 6.00 15.00
RTAABE Emil Bemstrom/299 6.00 15.00
RTAABJ Tobias Bjornfot/299 6.00 15.00
RTAABK Brady Keeper/299 6.00 15.00
RTAABL Blake Lizotte/299 6.00 15.00
RTAACM Cale Makar/199 50.00 125.00
RTAADK Dominik Kubalik/299 20.00 50.00
RTAAEB Erik Brannstrom/299 6.00 15.00
RTAAEM Elvis Merzlikins/299 12.00 30.00
RTAAFZ Filip Zadina/299 10.00 25.00
RTAAGR Carl Grundstrom/299 6.00 15.00
RTAAIM Ilya Mikheyev/299 10.00 25.00
RTAAJD Joey Daccord/299 12.00 30.00
RTAAJH Jack Hughes/199 40.00 100.00
RTAAJL Joel L'Esperance/299 6.00 15.00
RTAAJS Jimmy Schuldt/299 5.00 12.00
RTAAKA Karson Kuhlman/299 6.00 15.00
RTAAKD Kirby Dach/199 12.00 30.00
RTAAKU Ryan Kuffner/299 5.00 12.00
RTAALH Libor Hajek/299 5.00 12.00
RTAAMJ Max Jones/299 6.00 15.00
RTAAMV Max Veronneau/299 5.00 12.00
RTAANB Nathan Bastian/299 6.00 15.00
RTAANS Nick Suzuki/199 30.00 80.00
RTAAOW Oliver Wahlstrom/299 10.00 25.00
RTAAPI Rem Pitlick/299 6.00 15.00
RTAAPM Philippe Myers/299 5.00 12.00
RTAAQH Quinn Hughes/199 40.00 100.00
RTAARP Ryan Poehling/299 10.00 25.00
RTAARS Rasmus Sandin/199 10.00 25.00
RTAAST Nico Sturm/299 5.00 12.00
RTAATB Teddy Blueger/299 6.00 15.00
RTAATF Trent Frederic/299 6.00 15.00
RTAATH Taro Hirose/299 6.00 15.00
RTAAVA Vitaly Abramov/299 6.00 15.00
RTAAVO Victor Olofsson/299 12.00 30.00

2019-20 Upper Deck Credentials Debut Ticket Access Autographs Green
*GREEN/25: .75X TO 2X BASIC
RTAAQH Quinn Hughes 150.00 400.00

2019-20 Upper Deck Credentials Debut Ticket Access Autographs Photo Variant
*RED/25: .75X TO 2X BASIC
RTAAVAF Adam Fox 20.00 50.00
RTAAVAT Alexandre Texier 8.00 20.00
RTAAVCM Cale Makar 50.00 125.00
RTAAVCR Carl Grundstrom 8.00 20.00
RTAAVEB Erik Brannstrom 8.00 20.00
RTAAVFZ Filip Zadina 30.00 80.00
RTAAVJH Jack Hughes 40.00 100.00
RTAAVJL Joel L'Esperance 8.00 20.00
RTAAVJS Jimmy Schuldt 6.00 15.00
RTAAVKD Kirby Dach 30.00 80.00
RTAAVKK Karson Kuhlman 8.00 20.00
RTAAVMJ Max Jones 8.00 20.00
RTAAVPM Philippe Myers 6.00 15.00
RTAAVQH Quinn Hughes 80.00 200.00
RTAAVRP Ryan Poehling 12.00 30.00
RTAAVRS Rasmus Sandin 20.00 50.00
RTAAVTH Taro Hirose 8.00 20.00
RTAAVVO Victor Olofsson 15.00 40.00

2019-20 Upper Deck Credentials Dual Ticket Access Autographs
RTAADMM M.Fleury/M.Stone 60.00 150.00

2019-20 Upper Deck Credentials Rookie Science
RS01 Jack Hughes 3.00 8.00
RS02 Ryan Poehling 1.00 2.50
RS03 Adam Fox 1.50 4.00
RS04 Erik Brannstrom .60 1.50
RS05 Filip Zadina 1.00 2.50
RS06 Noah Dobson 1.50 4.00
RS07 Rasmus Sandin 1.00 2.50
RS08 Taro Hirose .60 1.50
RS09 Victor Olofsson 1.25 3.00
RS10 Cody Glass 1.00 2.50
RS11 Alexandre Texier .60 1.50
RS12 Nikita Gusev 1.00 2.50
RS13 Emil Bemstrom .60 1.50
RS14 Ilya Mikheyev 1.00 2.50
RS15 Quinn Hughes 3.00 8.00
RS16 Carl Grundstrom .60 1.50
RS17 Dante Fabbro .60 1.50
RS18 Elvis Merzlikins 1.25 3.00
RS19 Jesper Boqvist .50 1.25
RS20 Nick Suzuki 2.50 6.00
RS21 Karson Kuhlman .60 1.50
RS22 Max Jones .60 1.50
RS23 Philippe Myers .50 1.25
RS24 Blake Lizotte .60 1.50
RS25 Cale Makar 3.00 8.00
RS26 Kirby Dach 1.25 3.00
RS27 Barrett Hayton 1.25 3.00
RS28 Mario Ferraro .50 1.25
RS29 Brady Keeper .60 1.50
RS30 Nico Sturm .50 1.25
RS31 Ryan Kuffner .50 1.25
RS32 Kaapo Kakko 1.00 2.50

2019-20 Upper Deck Credentials Rookie Science Autographs
RS01 Jack Hughes A 40.00 100.00
RS03 Adam Fox D 20.00 50.00
RS04 Erik Brannstrom A 8.00 20.00
RS05 Filip Zadina D 12.00 30.00
RS06 Noah Dobson D 20.00 50.00
RS07 Rasmus Sandin D 12.00 30.00
RS08 Taro Hirose C 8.00 20.00
RS10 Cody Glass D 12.00 30.00
RS11 Alexandre Texier D 8.00 20.00
RS12 Nikita Gusev B 12.00 30.00
RS13 Emil Bemstrom D 8.00 20.00
RS14 Ilya Mikheyev D 12.00 30.00
RS15 Quinn Hughes B 40.00 100.00
RS16 Carl Grundstrom D 8.00 20.00
RS17 Dante Fabbro D 8.00 20.00
RS18 Elvis Merzlikins D 15.00 40.00
RS19 Jesper Boqvist D 6.00 15.00
RS20 Nick Suzuki D 30.00 80.00
RS21 Karson Kuhlman D 8.00 20.00
RS22 Max Jones C 8.00 20.00
RS23 Philippe Myers D 6.00 15.00
RS24 Blake Lizotte D 8.00 20.00
RS25 Cale Makar B 40.00 100.00
RS26 Kirby Dach D 15.00 40.00
RS27 Barrett Hayton C 15.00 40.00
RS28 Mario Ferraro D 6.00 15.00
RS29 Brady Keeper D 8.00 20.00
RS30 Nico Sturm D 6.00 15.00
RS31 Ryan Kuffner D 6.00 15.00

2019-20 Upper Deck Credentials Steel Wheels
*GOLD/99: 1.25X TO 3X BASIC
SW1 Jack Hughes 8.00 20.00
SW2 Erik Brannstrom 1.50 4.00
SW3 Carl Grundstrom 1.50 4.00
SW4 Vitaly Abramov 1.50 4.00
SW5 Filip Zadina 2.50 6.00
SW6 Philippe Myers 1.25 3.00
SW7 Noah Dobson 4.00 10.00
SW8 Cody Glass 2.50 6.00
SW9 Alexandre Texier 1.50 4.00
SW10 Cale Makar 8.00 20.00
SW11 Kirby Dach 3.00 8.00
SW12 Rasmus Sandin 2.50 6.00
SW13 Brady Keeper 1.50 4.00
SW14 Barrett Hayton 3.00 8.00
SW15 Ryan Poehling 2.50 6.00
SW16 Taro Hirose 1.50 4.00
SW17 Nick Suzuki 6.00 15.00
SW18 Dominik Kubalik 3.00 8.00
SW19 Dante Fabbro 1.50 4.00
SW20 Quinn Hughes 8.00 20.00
SW21 Karson Kuhlman 1.50 4.00
SW22 Nikita Gusev 2.50 6.00
SW23 Victor Olofsson 3.00 8.00
SW24 Max Jones 1.50 4.00
SW25 Kaapo Kakko 2.50 6.00

2019-20 Upper Deck Credentials Through the Boards
TTB1 Connor McDavid 8.00 20.00
TTB2 Sidney Crosby 6.00 15.00
TTB3 Auston Matthews 6.00 15.00
TTB4 Patrick Kane 3.00 8.00
TTB5 Carey Price 3.00 8.00
TTB6 Nathan MacKinnon 6.00 15.00
TTB7 Marc-Andre Fleury 3.00 8.00
TTB8 Artemi Panarin 3.00 8.00
TTB9 Dylan Larkin 2.00 5.00
TTB10 David Pastrnak 4.00 10.00

2019-20 Upper Deck Credentials Through the Boards Young Bloods
TTBYB1 Jack Hughes 8.00 20.00
TTBYB2 Cale Makar 8.00 20.00
TTBYB3 Filip Zadina 2.50 6.00
TTBYB4 Kirby Dach 3.00 8.00
TTBYB5 Nikita Gusev 2.50 6.00
TTBYB6 Ryan Poehling 2.50 6.00
TTBYB7 Rasmus Sandin 2.50 6.00
TTBYB8 Nick Suzuki 6.00 15.00
TTBYB9 Quinn Hughes 8.00 20.00
TTBYB10 Kaapo Kakko 2.50 6.00

2019-20 Upper Deck Credentials Ticket Access Acetate
TAAD Alex DeBrincat 3.00 8.00
TAAM Auston Matthews 10.00 25.00
TABB Brock Boeser 3.00 8.00
TABM Brad Marchand 5.00 12.00
TACM Connor McDavid 12.00 30.00
TAJD Jonathan Drouin 2.00 5.00
TAJE Jack Eichel 4.00 10.00
TAJG Jake Guentzel 4.00 10.00
TAJT John Tavares 4.00 10.00
TALD Leon Draisaitl 8.00 20.00
TAMS Mark Stone 3.00 8.00
TAPK Patrick Kane 5.00 12.00
TARO Ryan O'Reilly 2.50 6.00
TASC Sidney Crosby 10.00 25.00
TASS Steven Stamkos 5.00 12.00

2019-20 Upper Deck Credentials Ticket Access Acetate Autographs
TAAAD Alex DeBrincat/99 12.00 30.00
TAAJG Jake Guentzel/99 15.00 40.00
TAAJT John Tavares/25 40.00 100.00
TAALD Leon Draisaitl/25 40.00 100.00
TAAMS Mark Stone/25 20.00 50.00

2019-20 Upper Deck Credentials Ticket Access Autographs
TAAAD Alex DeBrincat/99 15.00 40.00
TAAJG Jake Guentzel/99 20.00 50.00
TAAJT John Tavares/25 40.00 100.00
TAALD Leon Draisaitl/49 30.00 80.00
TAAMS Mark Stone/49 12.00 30.00

2020-21 Upper Deck Credentials
51 Jack Rathbone/999 XRC 1.25 3.00
52 Niko Mikkola/999 XRC 1.00 2.50
53 Cole Smith/999 XRC 1.00 2.50
54 William Lagesson/999 XRC 1.25 3.00
55 Mikko Lehtonen/999 XRC 1.00 2.50
56 Sasha Chmelevski/999 XRC 1.00 2.50
57 Gilles Senn/999 XRC 1.00 2.50
58 David Kase/999 XRC 1.00 2.50
59 Gustav Lindstrom/999 XRC 1.00 2.50
60 Joel Kellman/999 XRC .75 2.00
61 Gage Quinney/999 XRC .75 2.00
62 Brayden Burke/999 XRC 1.00 2.50
63 Fredrik Handemark/999 XRC 1.00 2.50
64 Reid Duke/999 XRC 1.25 3.00
65 MacKenzie Entwistle/999 XRC 1.00 2.50
66 Keegan Kolesar/999 XRC 1.00 2.50
67 Artem Zub/999 XRC 1.00 2.50
68 John Leonard/999 XRC 1.00 2.50
69 Artem Zagidulin/999 XRC 1.25 3.00
70 Steven Lorentz/999 XRC 1.00 2.50
71 Nikolai Knyzhov/999 XRC 1.00 2.50
72 Anthony Angello/999 XRC 1.00 2.50
73 Mikhail Maltsev/999 XRC 1.00 2.50
74 Maxim Letunov/999 XRC 1.00 2.50
75 Alex Belzile/999 XRC 1.00 2.50
76 Mathias Brome/999 XRC 1.00 2.50
77 Jansen Harkins/999 XRC 1.00 2.50
78 Emil Larmi/999 XRC 1.25 3.00
79 Jalen Chatfield/999 XRC 1.00 2.50
80 Lucas Carlsson/999 XRC 1.00 2.50
81 Alexander True/999 XRC 1.00 2.50
82 Drew O'Connor/999 XRC 1.25 3.00
83 Philippe Maillet/999 XRC 1.00 2.50
84 Stuart Skinner/999 XRC 2.50 6.00
85 Logan Stanley/999 XRC 1.25 3.00
86 Alexander Yelesin/999 XRC 1.00 2.50
87 Jani Hakanpaa/999 XRC .75 2.00
88 Jonas Johansson/999 XRC 1.25 3.00
89 Brandon Hagel/999 XRC 1.50 4.00
90 Nicolas Meloche/999 XRC 1.00 2.50
91 Mikey Anderson/799 XRC 1.25 3.00
92 Vitek Vanecek/799 XRC 2.00 5.00
93 Nicolas Beaudin/799 XRC 1.25 3.00
94 Kieffer Bellows/999 XRC 1.00 2.50
95 Tyler Benson/999 XRC 1.25 3.00
96 Kevin Lankinen/799 XRC 2.00 5.00
97 Joel Kiviranta/999 XRC 1.25 3.00
98 Kevin Bahl/999 XRC 1.00 2.50
99 Ryan McLeod/999 XRC 1.00 2.50
100 Morgan Geekie/999 XRC 1.25 3.00
101 Nolan Foote/799 XRC 1.25 3.00
102 Pavel Francouz/999 XRC 1.50 4.00
103 Alexander Barabanov/799 XRC 1.25 3.00
104 Connor Ingram/999 XRC 1.00 2.50
105 Martin Kaut/999 XRC 1.25 3.00
106 Cameron Hillis/999 XRC 1.00 2.50
107 Matiss Kivlenieks/799 XRC 1.50 4.00
108 Mikhail Berdin/999 XRC 1.25 3.00
109 Alexander Alexeyev/999 XRC 1.00 2.50
110 Egor Zamula/999 XRC 1.00 2.50
111 Timothy Liljegren/799 XRC 1.25 3.00
112 Callum Booth/999 XRC 1.00 2.50
113 Yegor Sharangovich/799 XRC 2.00 5.00
114 Joseph Woll/999 XRC 2.50 6.00
115 Olli Juolevi/999 XRC 1.25 3.00
116 Pierre-Olivier Joseph/999 XRC 1.25 3.00
117 Joel Hofer/999 XRC 1.25 3.00
118 Aleksi Heponiemi/799 XRC 1.50 4.00
119 Dylan Coghlan/999 XRC 1.25 3.00
120 Alec Regula/999 XRC .75 2.00
121 Cal Foote/799 XRC 1.50 4.00
122 Nils Hoglander/599 XRC 1.25 3.00
123 Josh Norris/599 XRC 2.00 5.00
124 Michael DiPietro/799 XRC 1.50 4.00
125 Ian Mitchell/799 XRC 1.00 2.50
126 Philip Broberg/799 XRC 1.25 3.00
127 Liam Foudy/799 XRC 1.25 3.00
128 Philipp Kurashev/799 XRC 1.50 4.00
129 Vitali Kravtsov/799 XRC 2.50 6.00
130 Thomas Harley/799 XRC 2.00 5.00
131 Victor Soderstrom/799 XRC 1.00 2.50
132 Arthur Kaliyev/599 XRC 2.00 5.00
133 K'Andre Miller/799 XRC 2.50 6.00
134 Ty Dellandrea/799 XRC 1.25 3.00
135 Shane Bowers/799 XRC 1.00 2.50
136 Gabe Vilardi/599 XRC 2.00 5.00
137 Jason Robertson/599 XRC 3.00 8.00
138 Pius Suter/799 XRC 1.50 4.00
139 Ty Smith/799 XRC 2.00 5.00
140 Jake Oettinger/799 XRC 3.00 8.00
141 Alexander Romanov/599 XRC 1.50 4.00
142 Ilya Sorokin/299 XRC 3.00 8.00
143 Peyton Krebs/599 XRC 2.00 5.00
144 Kirill Kaprizov/299 XRC 5.00 12.00
145 Tim Stutzle/299 XRC 2.50 6.00
146 Dylan Cozens/599 XRC 2.00 5.00
147 Bowen Byram/599 XRC 2.50 6.00
148 Nick Robertson/299 XRC 2.00 5.00
149 Connor McMichael/599 XRC 2.00 5.00
150 Alexis Lafreniere/299 XRC 4.00 10.00

2020-21 Upper Deck Credentials Blue
*BLUE/99: 1.2X TO 3X BASIC

2020-21 Upper Deck Credentials Green
*GREEN/25: 2X TO 5X BASIC

2020-21 Upper Deck Credentials Orange
*ORANGE/149: 1X TO 2.5X BASIC

2020-21 Upper Deck Credentials Pink
*PINK/49: 1.5X TO 4X BASIC

2020-21 Upper Deck Credentials Red
*RED/199: .75X TO 2X BASIC

2020-21 Upper Deck Credentials Yellow
*YELLOW/249: .6X TO 1.5X BASIC

2020-21 Upper Deck Credentials Debut Ticket Access Acetate
RTAAL Alexis Lafreniere 15.00 40.00
RTAAR Alexander Romanov 6.00 15.00
RTABB Bowen Byram 10.00 25.00
RTACM Connor McMichael 8.00 20.00
RTADC Dylan Cozens 8.00 20.00
RTAJN Josh Norris 8.00 20.00
RTAJO Jake Oettinger 12.00 30.00
RTAJR Jason Robertson 25.00 60.00
RTAKK Kirill Kaprizov 30.00 80.00
RTANH Nils Hoglander 5.00 12.00
RTAPK Peyton Krebs 8.00 20.00
RTAPS Pius Suter 6.00 15.00
RTATH Thomas Harley 8.00 20.00
RTATS Tim Stutzle 20.00 50.00
RTATY Ty Smith 8.00 20.00

2021-22 Upper Deck Credentials
1 Connor McDavid 2.00 5.00
2 Sidney Crosby 1.50 4.00
3 Alex Ovechkin 1.50 4.00
4 Nathan MacKinnon 1.50 4.00
5 Auston Matthews 1.50 4.00
6 Patrick Kane .75 2.00
7 Brayden Point .50 1.25
8 Johnny Gaudreau .60 1.50
9 John Tavares .60 1.50
10 Elias Pettersson .60 1.50
11 Max Pacioretty .40 1.00
12 Kirill Kaprizov 1.25 3.00
13 Cale Makar 1.00 2.50
14 Jason Robertson .60 1.50
15 Artemi Panarin .75 2.00
16 Steven Stamkos .75 2.00
17 Ryan O'Reilly .40 1.00
18 Leon Draisaitl 1.25 3.00
19 Matthew Tkachuk .75 2.00
20 Brad Marchand .75 2.00
21 Kyle Connor .60 1.50
22 Tyler Toffoli .40 1.00
23 Mathew Barzal .50 1.25
24 Shayne Gostisbehere .40 1.00
25 Carter Hart .40 1.00
26 Nick Suzuki .75 2.00
27 Philipp Grubauer .40 1.00
28 Tim Stutzle .50 1.25
29 Miro Heiskanen .50 1.25
30 Rasmus Dahlin .50 1.25
31 Mark Stone .50 1.25
32 Erik Karlsson .50 1.25
33 Ryan Getzlaf .40 1.00
34 Adam Fox .50 1.25
35 Anze Kopitar .60 1.50
36 Roman Josi .40 1.00
37 Evgeny Kuznetsov .50 1.25
38 Sebastian Aho .60 1.50
39 Dylan Larkin .50 1.25
40 Jack Hughes 1.00 2.50
41 Mitch Marner .60 1.50
42 Troy Terry .30 .75
43 Aleksander Barkov .60 1.50
44 Marc-Andre Fleury .75 2.00
45 Jordan Eberle .40 1.00
46 Brady Tkachuk .60 1.50
47 Patrik Laine .50 1.25
48 Quinn Hughes 1.00 2.50
49 David Pastrnak 1.00 2.50
50 Jordan Binnington .60 1.50
51 Parker Kelly/999 RC 1.00 2.50
52 Radim Zohorna/999 RC 1.00 2.50
53 Morgan Barron/999 RC .75 2.00
54 Jacob Peterson/999 RC 1.00 2.50
55 Tyce Thompson/999 RC 1.00 2.50
56 Tanner Laczynski/999 RC 1.00 2.50
57 Mattias Samuelsson/999 RC 1.00 2.50
58 Oskar Steen/999 RC 1.25 3.00
59 Boris Katchouk/999 RC .75 2.00
60 Matthew Phillips/999 RC 1.00 2.50
61 Jonah Gadjovich/999 RC 1.00 2.50
62 Jesse Ylonen/999 RC 1.00 2.50
63 Santeri Hatakka/999 RC 1.00 2.50
64 Brandon Duhaime/999 RC 1.00 2.50
65 Dysin Mayo/999 RC 1.00 2.50
66 Brett Leason/999 RC 1.00 2.50
67 Michael Pezzetta/999 RC 1.00 2.50
68 Garrett Pilon/999 RC 1.25 3.00
69 Vladimir Tkachev/999 RC 1.00 2.50
70 Gregory Hofmann/999 RC 1.00 2.50
71 Jake Leschyshyn/999 RC 1.00 2.50
72 Logan Thompson/999 RC 2.50 6.00
73 Aliaksei Protas/999 RC 1.00 2.50
74 Lassi Thomson/999 RC 1.00 2.50
75 Riley Tufte/999 RC 1.00 2.50
76 Karel Vejmelka/999 RC 1.25 3.00
77 Connor Dewar/999 RC 1.00 2.50
78 Jonas Rondbjerg/999 RC 1.00 2.50
79 William Lockwood/999 RC 1.00 2.50
80 Isaak Phillips/999 RC 1.00 2.50
81 Mason Geertsen/999 RC 1.00 2.50
82 Cam Dineen/999 RC 1.00 2.50
83 Tarmo Reunanen/999 RC 1.00 2.50
84 Brett Murray/999 RC 1.00 2.50
85 Ben McCartney/999 RC 1.00 2.50
86 Kirill Semyonov/999 RC 1.00 2.50
87 Kyle Burroughs/999 RC 1.00 2.50
88 Dakota Joshua/999 RC 1.00 2.50
89 Ivan Prosvetov/999 RC 1.00 2.50
90 Jack Ahcan/999 RC 1.00 2.50
91 Pavel Dorofeyev/999 RC 1.25 3.00
92 Arttu Ruotsalainen/999 RC 1.00 2.50
93 Wyatt Kalynuk/999 RC 1.00 2.50
94 Lane Pederson/999 RC 1.00 2.50
95 Joey Keane/999 RC .75 2.00
96 Zac Jones/999 RC 1.25 3.00
97 David Farrance/999 RC 1.00 2.50
98 Sampo Ranta/999 RC 1.00 2.50
99 Thomas Novak/999 RC 1.00 2.50
100 Taylor Raddysh/999 RC 1.50 4.00
101 Daniil Miromanov/999 RC 1.00 2.50
102 Mike Hardman/999 RC 1.00 2.50
103 Jan Jenik/999 RC 1.25 3.00
104 Egor Sokolov/999 RC 1.00 2.50
105 Nico Daws/999 RC 1.50 4.00
106 Jasper Weatherby/999 RC 1.00 2.50
107 Ross Colton/999 RC 1.25 3.00
108 Kole Lind/999 RC 1.25 3.00
109 Ryan Merkley/999 RC 1.25 3.00
110 Cam York/999 RC 1.00 2.50
111 Wade Allison/799 RC 1.00 2.50
112 Shane Pinto/799 RC 1.50 4.00
113 Alex Barre-Boulet/799 RC 1.00 2.50
114 Joe Veleno/799 RC 1.25 3.00
115 Jake Neighbours/799 RC 2.00 5.00
116 Rasmus Kupari/799 RC 1.00 2.50
117 Adam Beckman/799 RC 1.00 2.50
118 Tanner Jeannot/799 RC 1.00 2.50
119 Yegor Chinakhov/799 RC 1.50 4.00
120 Calen Addison/799 RC 1.00 2.50
121 Filip Gustavsson/799 RC 2.00 5.00
122 Ukko-Pekka Luukkonen/799 RC 1.50 4.00
123 Hendrix Lapierre/799 RC 1.00 2.50
124 Jonathan Dahlen/799 RC 1.00 2.50
125 Grigori Denisenko/799 RC 1.25 3.00
126 Jacob Bernard-Docker/799 RC 1.00 2.50
127 Benoit-Olivier Groulx/799 RC 1.00 2.50
128 Dawson Mercer/799 RC 2.50 6.00
129 Alex Turcotte/799 RC 1.25 3.00
130 J.J. Peterka/799 RC 2.00 5.00
131 Seth Jarvis/799 RC 2.50 6.00
132 Nils Lundkvist/799 RC 1.00 2.50
133 Philip Tomasino/799 RC 1.25 3.00
134 Scott Perunovich/799 RC 1.00 2.50
135 Cole Sillinger/799 RC 1.50 4.00
136 Alex Newhook/599 RC 1.50 4.00
137 Anton Lundell/599 RC 2.00 5.00
138 Jamie Drysdale/599 RC 1.50 4.00
139 Alexander Holtz/599 RC 1.50 4.00
140 Mason McTavish/599 RC 2.00 5.00
141 Cole Perfetti/599 RC 2.00 5.00
142 Vasily Podkolzin/599 RC 1.25 3.00
143 William Eklund/599 RC 2.50 6.00
144 Jeremy Swayman/599 RC 3.00 8.00
145 Quinton Byfield/599 RC 2.50 6.00
146 Spencer Knight/299 RC 2.00 5.00
147 Trevor Zegras/299 RC 8.00 20.00
148 Moritz Seider/299 RC 10.00 25.00
149 Cole Caufield/299 RC 20.00 50.00
150 Lucas Raymond/299 RC 3.00 8.00

2021-22 Upper Deck Credentials Blue
*BLUE/99: 1X TO 2.5X BASIC
*BLUE RC/99: 1.2X TO 3X BASIC
146 Spencer Knight 12.00 30.00
147 Trevor Zegras 25.00 60.00
148 Moritz Seider 25.00 60.00
149 Cole Caufield 40.00 100.00
150 Lucas Raymond 15.00 40.00

2021-22 Upper Deck Credentials Green
146 Spencer Knight 15.00 40.00
150 Lucas Raymond 20.00 50.00

2021-22 Upper Deck Credentials Indigo
*INDIGO/249: .6X TO 1.5X BASIC

2021-22 Upper Deck Credentials Neon Green
*NEON GREEN/75: 1.2X TO 3X BASIC

2021-22 Upper Deck Credentials Orange
*ORANGE/149: .75X TO 2X BASIC
*ORANGE RC/149: 1X TO 2.5X BASIC
146 Spencer Knight 10.00 25.00
147 Trevor Zegras 15.00 40.00
148 Moritz Seider 20.00 50.00
149 Cole Caufield 40.00 100.00
150 Lucas Raymond 12.00 30.00

2021-22 Upper Deck Credentials Pink
*PINK/49: 2X TO 5X BASIC
*PINK RC/49: 1.5X TO 4X BASIC
146 Spencer Knight 15.00 40.00
147 Trevor Zegras 15.00 80.00
148 Moritz Seider 30.00 80.00
149 Cole Caufield 50.00 125.00
150 Lucas Raymond 20.00 50.00

2021-22 Upper Deck Credentials Red
*RED/199: .6X TO 1.5X BASIC
*RED RC/199: .75X TO 2X BASIC
146 Spencer Knight 10.00 25.00
147 Trevor Zegras 15.00 40.00
148 Moritz Seider 15.00 40.00
149 Cole Caufield 30.00 80.00
150 Lucas Raymond 12.00 30.00

2021-22 Upper Deck Credentials Teal
*TEAL/399: .5X TO 1.2X BASIC

2021-22 Upper Deck Credentials Yellow
*YELLOW/299: .5X TO 1.2X BASIC
*YELLOW RC/249: .6X TO 1.5X BASIC
147 Trevor Zegras 10.00 25.00
148 Moritz Seider 12.00 30.00
149 Cole Caufield 25.00 60.00
150 Lucas Raymond 8.00 20.00

2021-22 Upper Deck Credentials 1st Star of the Night
1S1 Connor McDavid 4.00 10.00
1S2 Steven Stamkos 1.50 4.00
1S3 Sidney Crosby 3.00 8.00
1S4 Auston Matthews 3.00 8.00
1S5 Kris Letang 1.00 2.50
1S6 Patrick Kane 1.50 4.00
1S7 John Tavares 1.25 3.00
1S8 Quinn Hughes 2.00 5.00
1S9 Cale Makar 2.00 5.00
1S10 Taylor Hall .75 2.00

2021-22 Upper Deck Credentials 1st Star of the Night Rookies
1SR1 Lucas Raymond 2.50 6.00
1SR2 Cole Caufield 3.00 8.00
1SR3 Moritz Seider 2.00 5.00
1SR4 Trevor Zegras 1.50 4.00
1SR5 Jeremy Swayman 2.50 6.00
1SR6 Spencer Knight 1.50 4.00
1SR7 Quinton Byfield 2.00 5.00

2021-22 Upper Deck Credentials 2nd Star of the Night
2S1 Jonathan Marchessault 1.00 2.50
2S2 Connor Hellebuyck 1.50 4.00
2S3 Matthew Tkachuk 1.50 4.00
2S4 Alexis Lafreniere 1.25 3.00
2S5 Brad Marchand 1.50 4.00
2S6 Brady Tkachuk 1.25 3.00
2S7 Max Pacioretty .75 2.00
2S8 Brent Burns .75 2.00
2S9 Jason Robertson 1.25 3.00
2S10 Kevin Fiala .60 1.50

2021-22 Upper Deck Credentials 2nd Star of the Night Autographs
2S1 Jonathan Marchessault 12.00 30.00
2S2 Connor Hellebuyck 20.00 50.00
2S3 Matthew Tkachuk 20.00 50.00
2S4 Alexis Lafreniere 15.00 40.00
2S5 Brad Marchand 20.00 50.00
2S6 Brady Tkachuk 15.00 40.00
2S7 Max Pacioretty 10.00 25.00
2S8 Brent Burns 10.00 25.00
2S10 Kevin Fiala 8.00 20.00

2021-22 Upper Deck Credentials 2nd Star of the Night Rookie Autographs
2SR1 Alex Newhook 15.00 40.00
2SR2 Alexander Holtz 15.00 40.00
2SR3 William Eklund 25.00 60.00
2SR4 Mason McTavish 20.00 50.00
2SR5 Anton Lundell 20.00 50.00
2SR6 Vasily Podkolzin 12.00 30.00
2SR7 Dawson Mercer 25.00 60.00

2021-22 Upper Deck Credentials 2nd Star of the Night Rookies
2SR1 Alex Newhook 1.25 3.00
2SR2 Alexander Holtz 1.25 3.00
2SR3 William Eklund 2.00 5.00
2SR4 Mason McTavish 1.50 4.00
2SR5 Anton Lundell 1.50 4.00
2SR6 Vasily Podkolzin 1.00 2.50
2SR7 Dawson Mercer 2.00 5.00

2021-22 Upper Deck Credentials 3rd Star of the Night
3S1 Dylan Cozens .75 2.00
3S2 Thatcher Demko 1.00 2.50
3S3 Yanni Gourde .60 1.50
3S4 Conor Garland .60 1.50
3S5 Jack Roslovic .50 1.25
3S6 Drake Batherson .75 2.00
3S7 Eeli Tolvanen .75 2.00
3S8 Chris Kreider 1.00 2.50
3S9 Tyler Bertuzzi .60 1.50
3S10 Jordan Kyrou .75 2.00

2021-22 Upper Deck Credentials 3rd Star of the Night Autographs
3S1 Dylan Cozens 6.00 15.00
3S2 Thatcher Demko 8.00 20.00
3S4 Conor Garland 5.00 12.00
3S5 Jack Roslovic 4.00 10.00
3S6 Drake Batherson 6.00 15.00
3S7 Eeli Tolvanen 6.00 15.00

2021-22 Upper Deck Credentials 3rd Star of the Night Rookie Autographs
3SR1 Jamie Drysdale 10.00 25.00
3SR2 Cole Perfetti 12.00 30.00
3SR3 Scott Perunovich 6.00 15.00
3SR4 Philip Tomasino 8.00 20.00
3SR5 Joe Veleno 8.00 20.00
3SR6 Cole Sillinger 10.00 25.00

2021-22 Upper Deck Credentials 3rd Star of the Night Rookies
3SR1 Jamie Drysdale 1.25 3.00
3SR2 Cole Perfetti 1.50 4.00
3SR3 Scott Perunovich .75 2.00
3SR4 Philip Tomasino 1.00 2.50
3SR5 Joe Veleno 1.00 2.50
3SR6 Cole Sillinger 1.25 3.00

2021-22 Upper Deck Credentials Debut Ticket Access Acetate
DTAAB Adam Beckman 4.00 10.00
DTAAH Alexander Holtz 6.00 15.00
DTAAL Anton Lundell 8.00 20.00
DTAAN Alex Newhook 6.00 15.00
DTAAR Arttu Ruotsalainen 4.00 10.00
DTACC Cole Caufield 60.00 150.00
DTACP Cole Perfetti 8.00 20.00
DTACS Cole Sillinger 6.00 15.00
DTADM Dawson Mercer 10.00 25.00
DTAFG Filip Gustavsson 8.00 20.00
DTAJB Jacob Bernard-Docker 4.00 10.00
DTAJD Jamie Drysdale 6.00 15.00
DTAJJ Jan Jenik 5.00 12.00
DTAJK Joey Keane 3.00 8.00
DTAJN Jake Neighbours 8.00 20.00
DTAJS Jeremy Swayman 12.00 30.00
DTAJV Joe Veleno 5.00 12.00
DTAKL Kole Lind 5.00 12.00
DTALR Lucas Raymond 12.00 30.00
DTAMM Mason McTavish 8.00 20.00
DTAMS Moritz Seider 10.00 25.00
DTANL Nils Lundkvist 4.00 10.00
DTAOS Oskar Steen 5.00 12.00
DTAPD Pavel Dorofeyev 5.00 12.00
DTAPE Scott Perunovich 4.00 10.00
DTAPK Parker Kelly 4.00 10.00
DTAPT Philip Tomasino 5.00 12.00
DTAQB Quinton Byfield 10.00 25.00
DTARC Ross Colton 5.00 12.00
DTARK Rasmus Kupari 4.00 10.00
DTASJ Seth Jarvis 10.00 25.00
DTASK Spencer Knight 8.00 20.00
DTASP Shane Pinto 6.00 15.00
DTATJ Tanner Jeannot 4.00 10.00
DTATT Tyce Thompson 4.00 10.00
DTATZ Trevor Zegras 40.00 100.00
DTAUL Ukko-Pekka Luukkonen 6.00 15.00
DTAVP Vasily Podkolzin 5.00 12.00
DTAWE William Eklund 10.00 25.00
DTAZJ Zac Jones 5.00 12.00

2021-22 Upper Deck Credentials Debut Ticket Access Acetate Autographs
DTAAH Alexander Holtz 15.00 40.00
DTAAL Anton Lundell 20.00 50.00
DTAAN Alex Newhook 15.00 40.00
DTACP Cole Perfetti 20.00 50.00
DTADM Dawson Mercer 80.00 200.00
DTAFG Filip Gustavsson 20.00 50.00
DTAJB Jacob Bernard-Docker 10.00 25.00
DTAJD Jamie Drysdale 15.00 40.00
DTAJJ Jan Jenik 12.00 30.00
DTAJS Jeremy Swayman 125.00 300.00
DTAJV Joe Veleno 12.00 30.00
DTAKL Kole Lind 12.00 30.00
DTAMM Mason McTavish 80.00 200.00
DTANL Nils Lundkvist 10.00 25.00
DTAOS Oskar Steen 12.00 30.00
DTAPD Pavel Dorofeyev 12.00 30.00
DTAPK Parker Kelly 10.00 25.00
DTARC Ross Colton 12.00 30.00
DTARK Rasmus Kupari 10.00 25.00
DTASP Shane Pinto 30.00 80.00
DTATJ Tanner Jeannot 10.00 25.00
DTATT Tyce Thompson 10.00 25.00
DTAUL Ukko-Pekka Luukkonen 15.00 40.00
DTAVP Vasily Podkolzin 12.00 30.00
DTAWE William Eklund 25.00 60.00
DTAZJ Zac Jones 12.00 30.00

2021-22 Upper Deck Credentials Debut Ticket Access Autographs
*BLUE/35: .75X TO 2X BASIC
DTAAAH Alexander Holtz/199 10.00 25.00
DTAAAL Anton Lundell/199 12.00 30.00
DTAAAP Aliaksei Protas/299 6.00 15.00
DTAACA Calen Addison/299 6.00 15.00
DTAACP Cole Perfetti/199 12.00 30.00
DTAACS Cole Sillinger/299 10.00 25.00
DTAADM Dawson Mercer/199 15.00 40.00
DTAAGD Grigori Denisenko/299 8.00 20.00
DTAAGP Garrett Pilon/299 8.00 20.00
DTAAJA Jack Ahcan/299 6.00 15.00
DTAAJB Jacob Bernard-Docker/299 6.00 15.00
DTAAJD Jamie Drysdale/199 10.00 25.00
DTAAJJ Jan Jenik/299 8.00 20.00
DTAAJN Jake Neighbours/299 12.00 30.00
DTAAJS Jeremy Swayman/99 30.00 80.00
DTAAJV Joe Veleno/299 8.00 20.00
DTAAJY Jesse Ylonen/299 6.00 15.00
DTAAKL Kole Lind/299 8.00 20.00
DTAALP Lane Pederson/299 6.00 15.00
DTAALT Logan Thompson/299 15.00 40.00
DTAAMB Morgan Barron/299 5.00 12.00
DTAAMM Mason McTavish/199 12.00 30.00
DTAAMP Matthew Phillips/299 6.00 15.00
DTAAMS Moritz Seider/99 30.00 80.00
DTAANL Nils Lundkvist/299 6.00 15.00
DTAAOS Oskar Steen/299 8.00 20.00
DTAAPD Pavel Dorofeyev/299 8.00 20.00
DTAAPI Shane Pinto/299 10.00 25.00
DTAAPK Parker Kelly/299 6.00 15.00
DTAAPT Philip Tomasino/199 8.00 20.00
DTAARC Ross Colton/299 8.00 20.00
DTAARK Rasmus Kupari/299 6.00 15.00
DTAASJ Seth Jarvis/299 15.00 40.00
DTAASK Spencer Knight/99 25.00 60.00
DTAASP Scott Perunovich/199 6.00 15.00
DTAAUL Ukko-Pekka Luukkonen/299 10.00 25.00
DTAAVP Vasily Podkolzin/199 8.00 20.00
DTAAWE William Eklund/199 15.00 40.00
DTAAWK Wyatt Kalynuk/299 6.00 15.00
DTAAZJ Zac Jones/299 8.00 20.00

2021-22 Upper Deck Credentials Debut Ticket Access Autographs Green
*GREEN/25: 1X TO 2.5X BASIC
DTAADM Dawson Mercer 80.00 200.00
DTAAJD Jamie Drysdale 25.00 60.00
DTAAJS Jeremy Swayman 80.00 200.00
DTAAMS Moritz Seider 125.00 300.00

2021-22 Upper Deck Credentials Debut Ticket Access Autographs Orange
*ORANGE: .75X TO 2X BASIC
DTAADM Dawson Mercer/25 80.00 200.00
DTAAJS Jeremy Swayman/25 80.00 200.00
DTAAMS Moritz Seider/25 125.00 300.00
DTAASK Spencer Knight/25 30.00 80.00

2021-22 Upper Deck Credentials Debut Ticket Access Autographs Red
*RED: .6X TO 1.5X BASIC
DTAADM Dawson Mercer/49 30.00 80.00
DTAAJS Jeremy Swayman/25 80.00 200.00
DTAAMS Moritz Seider/25 125.00 300.00
DTAASK Spencer Knight/25 30.00 80.00

2021-22 Upper Deck Credentials Debut Ticket Access Autographs Yellow
*YELLOW: .5X TO 1.2X BASIC
DTAAJS Jeremy Swayman/25 80.00 200.00

DTAAMS Moritz Seider/25 125.00 300.00
DTAASK Spencer Knight/25 30.00 80.00

2021-22 Upper Deck Credentials Dual Ticket Access Autographs
DTAADKL S.Knight/A.Lundell 20.00 50.00
DTAADMG J.McCann/Y.Gourde 8.00 20.00

2021-22 Upper Deck Credentials Main Stage Signatures
*GOLD: .6X TO 1.5X BASIC
BTSAK Arthur Kaliyev E 8.00 20.00
BTSAN Mikey Anderson E 6.00 15.00
BTSBM Brad Marchand A 15.00 40.00
BTSCM Casey Mittelstadt D 8.00 20.00
BTSCT Cam Talbot D 8.00 20.00
BTSDC Dylan Cozens C 8.00 20.00
BTSDS Dylan Strome E 10.00 25.00
BTSDT Devon Toews E 6.00 15.00
BTSDV Dan Vladar E 6.00 15.00
BTSET Eeli Tolvanen B 8.00 20.00
BTSJE Jake Evans E 5.00 12.00
BTSJO Jake Oettinger B 12.00 30.00
BTSJP Jean-Gabriel Pageau E 5.00 12.00
BTSJR Jack Roslovic D 5.00 12.00
BTSJT John Tavares A 12.00 30.00
BTSJW Jake Walman E 5.00 12.00
BTSKB Kieffer Bellows E 5.00 12.00
BTSKF Kevin Fiala B 6.00 15.00
BTSKK Klim Kostin E 5.00 12.00
BTSKP Kyle Palmieri D 6.00 15.00
BTSMA Mason Appleton E 5.00 12.00
BTSMC Maxime Comtois D 6.00 15.00
BTSMN Martin Necas D 12.00 30.00
BTSMS Mike Smith E 5.00 12.00
BTSPF Pavel Francouz E 6.00 15.00
BTSPJ Pierre-Olivier Joseph E 5.00 12.00
BTSRL Robin Lehner E 6.00 15.00
BTSRS Ryan Suter E 6.00 15.00
BTSSG Samuel Girard E 5.00 12.00
BTSSR Sam Reinhart D 15.00 40.00
BTSSW Sean Walker E 5.00 12.00
BTSTB Tyler Benson E 5.00 12.00
BTSTH Taylor Hall A 8.00 20.00
BTSTS Travis Sanheim C 5.00 12.00
BTSVN Vladislav Namestnikov D 5.00 12.00
BTSVV Vitek Vanecek D 8.00 20.00
BTSZP Zach Parise C 8.00 20.00

2021-22 Upper Deck Credentials Rookie Arrivals
RA1 Lucas Raymond 1.50 4.00
RA2 Cole Caufield 2.00 5.00
RA3 Moritz Seider 1.25 3.00
RA4 Quinton Byfield 1.25 3.00
RA5 Jeremy Swayman 1.50 4.00
RA6 Spencer Knight 1.00 2.50
RA7 Trevor Zegras 1.00 2.50
RA8 Alexander Holtz .75 2.00
RA9 Alex Newhook .75 2.00
RA10 Vasily Podkolzin .60 1.50
RA11 Anton Lundell 1.00 2.50
RA12 William Eklund 1.25 3.00
RA13 Philip Tomasino .60 1.50
RA14 Scott Perunovich .50 1.25
RA15 Cole Perfetti 1.00 2.50
RA16 Seth Jarvis 1.25 3.00
RA18 Grigori Denisenko .60 1.50
RA19 Dawson Mercer 1.25 3.00
RA20 Cole Sillinger .75 2.00
RA21 Joey Keane .40 1.00
RA22 Jake Neighbours 1.00 2.50
RA23 Mason McTavish 1.00 2.50
RA24 Pavel Dorofeyev .60 1.50
RA25 Garrett Pilon .60 1.50
RA26 Zac Jones .60 1.50
RA27 Filip Gustavsson 1.00 2.50
RA28 Logan Thompson 1.25 3.00
RA29 Mattias Samuelsson .50 1.25
RA30 Wyatt Kalynuk .50 1.25
RA31 Wade Allison .50 1.25
RA32 David Farrance .50 1.25
RA33 Jacob Bernard-Docker .50 1.25
RA34 Tanner Laczynski .50 1.25
RA35 Aliaksei Protas .50 1.25
RA36 Ivan Prosvetov .50 1.25
RA37 Calen Addison .50 1.25
RA38 Adam Beckman .50 1.25
RA39 Joe Veleno .60 1.50
RA40 Oskar Steen .60 1.50
RA41 Arttu Ruotsalainen .50 1.25
RA42 Sampo Ranta .50 1.25
RA43 Jacob Bryson .50 1.25
RA44 Jesse Ylonen .50 1.25
RA45 Tyce Thompson .50 1.25
RA46 Ross Colton .60 1.50
RA47 Parker Kelly .50 1.25
RA48 Lane Pederson .50 1.25
RA49 Tanner Jeannot .50 1.25
RA50 Shane Pinto .75 2.00

2021-22 Upper Deck Credentials Rookie Arrivals Autographs
RA4 Quinton Byfield A 12.00 30.00
RA5 Jeremy Swayman C 15.00 40.00
RA6 Spencer Knight C 10.00 25.00
RA8 Alexander Holtz B 8.00 20.00
RA9 Alex Newhook D 8.00 20.00
RA10 Vasily Podkolzin D 6.00 15.00
RA11 Anton Lundell C 10.00 25.00
RA12 William Eklund D 12.00 30.00
RA13 Philip Tomasino D 6.00 15.00
RA14 Scott Perunovich B 5.00 12.00
RA15 Cole Perfetti E 10.00 25.00
RA17 Jamie Drysdale C 8.00 20.00
RA19 Dawson Mercer A 12.00 30.00
RA20 Cole Sillinger D 8.00 20.00
RA21 Joey Keane B 4.00 10.00
RA22 Jake Neighbours E 10.00 25.00
RA23 Mason McTavish B 10.00 25.00
RA24 Pavel Dorofeyev E 6.00 15.00
RA25 Garrett Pilon E 6.00 15.00
RA26 Zac Jones E 6.00 15.00
RA27 Filip Gustavsson E 10.00 25.00
RA28 Logan Thompson E 12.00 30.00
RA29 Mattias Samuelsson E 5.00 12.00
RA30 Wyatt Kalynuk E 5.00 12.00
RA31 Wade Allison C 5.00 12.00
RA34 Tanner Laczynski E 5.00 12.00
RA35 Aliaksei Protas E 5.00 12.00
RA36 Ivan Prosvetov E 5.00 12.00
RA37 Calen Addison E 5.00 12.00
RA38 Adam Beckman E 5.00 12.00
RA39 Joe Veleno B 6.00 15.00
RA40 Oskar Steen E 6.00 15.00
RA41 Arttu Ruotsalainen E 5.00 12.00
RA42 Sampo Ranta E 5.00 12.00
RA43 Jacob Bryson E 5.00 12.00
RA44 Jesse Ylonen E 5.00 12.00
RA45 Tyce Thompson E 5.00 12.00
RA47 Parker Kelly E 5.00 12.00
RA48 Lane Pederson E 5.00 12.00
RA49 Tanner Jeannot D 5.00 12.00
RA50 Shane Pinto C 8.00 20.00

2021-22 Upper Deck Credentials Speed of the Game
SG1 Connor McDavid 5.00 12.00
SG2 Anthony Duclair .75 2.00
SG3 Taylor Hall 1.00 2.50
SG4 Quinn Hughes 2.50 6.00
SG5 Cale Makar 2.50 6.00
SG6 Brayden Point 1.25 3.00
SG7 Evgeny Kuznetsov 1.25 3.00
SG8 Johnny Gaudreau 1.50 4.00
SG9 Nathan MacKinnon 4.00 10.00
SG10 Nikolaj Ehlers 1.00 2.50
SG11 Pierre-Luc Dubois .75 2.00
SG12 Patrick Kane 2.00 5.00
SG13 Kevin Fiala .75 2.00
SG14 Mark Scheifele 1.50 4.00
SG15 Robert Thomas 1.00 2.50
SG16 Troy Terry .75 2.00
SG17 Mark Stone 1.25 3.00
SG18 Sebastian Aho 1.50 4.00
SG19 Dylan Larkin 1.25 3.00
SG20 Brendan Gallagher 1.00 2.50
SG21 Auston Matthews 4.00 10.00
SG22 Mitch Marner 1.50 4.00
SG23 Alex DeBrincat 1.25 3.00
SG24 Jakub Vrana .75 2.00
SG25 Aleksander Barkov 1.50 4.00

2021-22 Upper Deck Credentials Speed of the Game Rookies
SGR1 Lucas Raymond 3.00 8.00
SGR2 Cole Caufield 4.00 10.00
SGR3 Moritz Seider 2.50 6.00
SGR4 Quinton Byfield 2.50 6.00
SGR5 Alex Newhook 1.50 4.00
SGR6 Anton Lundell 2.00 5.00
SGR7 Alexander Holtz 1.50 4.00
SGR8 Vasily Podkolzin 1.25 3.00
SGR9 Mason McTavish 2.00 5.00
SGR10 Dawson Mercer 2.50 6.00
SGR11 Seth Jarvis 2.50 6.00
SGR12 Benoit-Olivier Groulx 1.00 2.50
SGR13 Philip Tomasino 1.25 3.00
SGR14 William Eklund 2.50 6.00
SGR15 Oskar Steen 1.25 3.00
SGR16 Cole Perfetti 2.00 5.00
SGR17 Scott Perunovich 1.00 2.50
SGR18 Ross Colton 1.25 3.00
SGR19 Shane Pinto 1.50 4.00
SGR20 Joe Veleno 1.25 3.00
SGR21 Tyce Thompson 1.00 2.50
SGR22 Wade Allison 1.00 2.50
SGR23 Garrett Pilon 1.25 3.00
SGR24 Matthew Phillips 1.00 2.50
SGR25 Jake Neighbours 2.00 5.00

2021-22 Upper Deck Credentials Ticket Access Acetate
TAAL Alexis Lafreniere 3.00 8.00
TABB Brock Boeser 2.50 6.00
TABM Brad Marchand 4.00 10.00
TABT Brady Tkachuk 3.00 8.00
TABU Brent Burns 2.00 5.00
TACH Connor Hellebuyck 1.50 4.00
TACM Connor McDavid 10.00 25.00
TACP Colton Parayko 1.50 4.00
TADT Devon Toews 1.50 4.00
TAHE Tomas Hertl 2.00 5.00
TAJM Jonathan Marchessault 2.50 6.00
TAJR Jason Robertson 3.00 8.00
TAJT John Tavares 3.00 8.00
TAKF Kevin Fiala 1.50 4.00
TAKL Kris Letang 2.50 6.00
TAMG Mark Giordano 2.00 5.00
TAMP Max Pacioretty 2.00 5.00
TAMT Matthew Tkachuk 4.00 10.00
TAPG Philipp Grubauer 2.00 5.00
TAQH Quinn Hughes 5.00 12.00
TART Robert Thomas 2.00 5.00
TASR Sam Reinhart 4.00 10.00
TATH Taylor Hall 2.00 5.00
TAWK William Karlsson 2.50 6.00
TAZP Zach Parise 2.00 5.00

2021-22 Upper Deck Credentials Ticket Access Acetate Autographs
TAAL Alexis Lafreniere/25 20.00 50.00
TABM Brad Marchand/25 25.00 60.00
TABT Brady Tkachuk/25 20.00 50.00
TABU Brent Burns/25 12.00 30.00
TACH Connor Hellebuyck/25 25.00 60.00
TADT Devon Toews/99 10.00 25.00
TAKF Kevin Fiala/25 10.00 25.00
TAMT Matthew Tkachuk/25 25.00 60.00
TAPG Philipp Grubauer/99 12.00 30.00
TART Robert Thomas/99 12.00 30.00
TATH Taylor Hall/99 12.00 30.00
TAWK William Karlsson/25 15.00 40.00
TAZP Zach Parise/99 12.00 30.00

2021-22 Upper Deck Credentials Ticket Access Autographs
*YELLOW/25: .6X TO 1.5X BASIC
TAABB Brent Burns/25 10.00 25.00
TAABT Brady Tkachuk/25 15.00 40.00
TAACH Connor Hellebuyck/49 20.00 50.00
TAAET Eeli Tolvanen/25 10.00 25.00
TAAJP Jeff Petry/99 10.00 25.00
TAAJR Jack Roslovic/99 6.00 15.00
TAAKF Kevin Fiala/25 8.00 20.00
TAAKY Keith Yandle/99 6.00 15.00
TAAPG Philipp Grubauer/49 10.00 25.00
TAASG Samuel Girard/49 6.00 15.00
TAASW Sean Walker/99 6.00 15.00
TAATD Thatcher Demko/49 12.00 30.00

2021-22 Upper Deck Credentials View from the Glass
*GOLD/25: 1.2X TO 3X BASIC
VG1 Sidney Crosby 12.00 30.00
VG2 Connor McDavid 15.00 40.00
VG3 Patrick Kane 6.00 15.00
VG4 Auston Matthews 12.00 30.00
VG5 Alex Ovechkin 12.00 30.00
VG6 Mark Stone 4.00 10.00
VG7 Nathan MacKinnon 12.00 30.00
VG8 Brad Marchand 6.00 15.00
VG9 Kirill Kaprizov 10.00 25.00
VG10 Quinn Hughes 8.00 20.00
VG11 Lucas Raymond 10.00 25.00
VG12 Cole Caufield 12.00 30.00
VG13 Moritz Seider 8.00 20.00
VG14 Trevor Zegras 6.00 15.00
VG15 Anton Lundell 6.00 15.00
VG16 Vasily Podkolzin 4.00 10.00
VG17 Scott Perunovich 3.00 8.00
VG18 Alex Newhook 5.00 12.00
VG19 Alexander Holtz 5.00 12.00
VG20 Cole Perfetti 6.00 15.00

2022-23 Upper Deck Credentials
1 Trevor Zegras .40 1.00
2 Cam Fowler .40 1.00
3 John Gibson .40 1.00
4 Clayton Keller .50 1.25
5 Jakob Chychrun .40 1.00
6 Patrice Bergeron .50 1.25
7 Brad Marchand .75 2.00
8 David Pastrnak 1.00 2.50
9 Taylor Hall .40 1.00
10 Alex Tuch .40 1.00
11 Rasmus Dahlin .50 1.25
12 Jonathan Huberdeau .50 1.25
13 Jacob Markstrom .40 1.00
14 Nazem Kadri .50 1.25
15 Sebastian Aho .60 1.50
16 Andrei Svechnikov .50 1.25
17 Jonathan Toews .60 1.50
18 Patrick Kane .75 2.00
19 Seth Jones .40 1.00
20 Nathan MacKinnon 1.50 4.00
21 Gabriel Landeskog .50 1.25
22 Mikko Rantanen 1.00 2.50
23 Cale Makar 1.00 2.50
24 Johnny Gaudreau .60 1.50
25 Patrik Laine .50 1.25
26 Zach Werenski .60 1.50
27 Tyler Seguin .60 1.50
28 Miro Heiskanen .50 1.25
29 Jason Robertson .60 1.50
30 Dylan Larkin .50 1.25
31 Lucas Raymond .60 1.50
32 Moritz Seider .50 1.25
33 Connor McDavid 2.00 5.00
34 Leon Draisaitl 1.25 3.00
35 Darnell Nurse .30 .75
36 Aleksander Barkov .60 1.50
37 Matthew Tkachuk .75 2.00
38 Aaron Ekblad .50 1.25
39 Drew Doughty .50 1.25
40 Anze Kopitar .60 1.50
41 Jonathan Quick .50 1.25
42 Kirill Kaprizov 1.25 3.00
43 Marc-Andre Fleury .75 2.00
44 Cole Caufield .75 2.00
45 Nick Suzuki .75 2.00
46 Carey Price .75 2.00
47 Filip Forsberg .60 1.50
48 Roman Josi .40 1.00
49 Jack Hughes 1.00 2.50
50 Nico Hischier .60 1.50
51 Mathew Barzal .60 1.50
52 Anders Lee .30 .75
53 Mika Zibanejad .50 1.25
54 Artemi Panarin .75 2.00
55 Adam Fox .50 1.25
56 Igor Shesterkin .75 2.00
57 Josh Norris .40 1.00
58 Brady Tkachuk .60 1.50
59 Thomas Chabot .40 1.00
60 Kevin Hayes .30 .75
61 Travis Konecny .40 1.00
62 Cam Atkinson .40 1.00
63 Evgeni Malkin .75 2.00
64 Kris Letang .50 1.25
65 Jake Guentzel .60 1.50
66 Sidney Crosby 1.50 4.00
67 Tomas Hertl .40 1.00
68 Logan Couture .50 1.25
69 Erik Karlsson .50 1.25
70 Jordan Eberle .40 1.00
71 Yanni Gourde .30 .75
72 Jaden Schwartz .30 .75
73 Ryan O'Reilly .40 1.00
74 Vladimir Tarasenko .50 1.25
75 Torey Krug .30 .75
76 Brayden Point .50 1.25
77 Steven Stamkos .75 2.00
78 Nikita Kucherov .75 2.00
79 Victor Hedman .50 1.25
80 Andrei Vasilevskiy .60 1.50
81 Auston Matthews 1.50 4.00
82 John Tavares .60 1.50
83 Mitch Marner .60 1.50
84 Morgan Rielly .40 1.00
85 Quinn Hughes 1.00 2.50
86 Thatcher Demko .40 1.00
87 Brock Boeser .50 1.25
88 Jack Eichel .60 1.50
89 Mark Stone .50 1.25
90 Phil Kessel .40 1.00
91 Alex Pietrangelo .30 .75
92 Alex Ovechkin 1.50 4.00
93 Nicklas Backstrom .40 1.00
94 John Carlson .40 1.00
95 T.J. Oshie .40 1.00
96 Evgeny Kuznetsov .50 1.25
97 Mark Scheifele .60 1.50
98 Kyle Connor .60 1.50
99 Nikolaj Ehlers .40 1.00
100 Blake Wheeler .40 1.00
101 Nikita Okhotiuk/999 RC 1.00 2.50
102 Kaedan Korczak/999 RC 1.00 2.50
103 Vladislav Kolyachonok/999 RC 1.00 2.50
104 Chase Pearson/999 RC 1.00 2.50
105 Declan Chisholm/999 RC 1.25 3.00
106 Isaac Ratcliffe/999 RC 1.25 3.00
107 Fredrik Olofsson/999 RC 1.25 3.00
108 Nathan Smith/999 RC 1.00 2.50
109 Filip Roos/999 RC 1.00 2.50
110 Tyler Tucker/999 RC 1.25 3.00
111 Jakub Galvas/999 RC 1.25 3.00
112 Erik Kallgren/999 RC 1.25 3.00
113 Jack McBain/999 RC 1.25 3.00
114 Jake Christiansen/999 RC 1.25 3.00
115 William Bitten/999 RC 1.25 3.00
116 Hunter Drew/999 RC 1.00 2.50
117 Casey Fitzgerald/999 RC 1.00 2.50
118 Valtteri Puustinen/999 RC 1.00 2.50
119 Nick Blankenburg/999 RC 1.00 2.50
120 Matej Blumel/999 RC 1.50 4.00
121 Mac Hollowell/999 RC 1.25 3.00
122 Lucas Johansen/999 RC 1.00 2.50
123 Carson Meyer/999 RC 1.00 2.50
124 Filip Kral/999 RC 1.50 4.00
125 Marcus Bjork/999 RC 1.25 3.00
126 Hayden Hodgson/999 RC 1.00 2.50
127 Nick Perbix/999 RC 1.00 2.50
128 Pontus Holmberg/999 RC 1.25 3.00
129 Semyon Der-Arguchintsev/999 RC 1.25 3.00
130 Trey Fix-Wolansky/999 RC 1.25 3.00
131 Ronnie Attard/999 RC 1.25 3.00
132 Nick Cicek/999 RC 1.25 3.00
133 Olle Lycksell/999 RC 1.25 3.00
134 Michael Eyssimont/999 RC 1.25 3.00
135 Johnathan Kovacevic/999 RC 1.25 3.00
136 James Hamblin/999 RC 1.25 3.00
137 Viktor Lodin/999 RC 1.25 3.00
138 Adam Raska/999 RC 1.25 3.00
139 Zack Hayes/999 RC 1.00 2.50
140 Bokondji Imama/999 RC 1.00 2.50
141 Fredrik Karlstrom/999 RC 1.00 2.50
142 Cole Koepke/999 RC 1.25 3.00
143 Reilly Walsh/999 RC 1.25 3.00
144 Nick DeSimone/999 RC 1.25 3.00
145 Mark Kastelic/999 RC 1.00 2.50
146 Nick Abruzzese/999 RC 1.25 3.00
147 Nils Aman/999 RC 1.25 3.00
148 Ben Meyers/999 RC 1.25 3.00
149 Dylan Samberg/999 RC 1.25 3.00
150 Marc McLaughlin/999 RC 1.25 3.00
151 Jeff Malott/999 RC 1.25 3.00
152 Brayden Pachal/999 RC 1.00 2.50
153 Jayden Halbgewachs/999 RC 1.25 3.00
154 Ben Jones/999 RC 1.50 4.00
155 Jacob Moverare/999 RC 1.00 2.50
156 Arber Xhekaj/799 RC 2.50 6.00
157 David Jiricek/799 RC 2.50 6.00
158 Elmer Soderblom/799 RC 2.50 6.00
159 Aatu Raty/799 RC 1.25 3.00
160 Lukas Dostal/799 RC 2.50 6.00
161 Jordan Spence/799 RC 1.25 3.00
162 Bobby Brink/799 RC 1.25 3.00
163 Jordan Harris/799 RC 1.50 4.00
164 Brayden Tracey/799 RC 1.00 2.50
165 Noah Cates/799 RC 1.25 3.00
166 Braden Schneider/799 RC 2.00 5.00
167 Juuso Parssinen/799 RC 1.25 3.00
168 Mads Sogaard/799 RC 1.50 4.00
169 Thomas Bordeleau/799 RC 1.25 3.00
170 Samuel Poulin/799 RC 1.50 4.00
171 Jacob Perreault/799 RC 1.25 3.00
172 Simon Holmstrom/799 RC 1.25 3.00
173 Oskar Olausson/799 RC 1.25 3.00
174 Jakub Lauko/799 RC 1.50 4.00
175 Filip Hallander/799 RC 1.25 3.00
176 Pavol Regenda/799 RC 1.25 3.00
177 Samuel Ersson/799 RC 2.50 6.00
178 Jean-Luc Foudy/799 RC 1.25 3.00
179 Alex Vlasic/799 RC 1.00 2.50
180 Nikita Alexandrov/799 RC 1.25 3.00
181 Pyotr Kochetkov/599 RC 2.50 6.00
182 Lukas Reichel/599 RC 2.50 6.00
183 Jonatan Berggren/599 RC 2.00 5.00
184 Jack Quinn/599 RC 2.00 5.00
185 Dylan Holloway/599 RC 2.50 6.00
186 Marco Rossi/599 RC 3.00 8.00
187 Matias Maccelli/599 RC 2.00 5.00
188 Kirill Marchenko/599 RC 3.00 8.00
189 Brandt Clarke/599 RC 2.50 6.00
190 Kaiden Guhle/599 RC 2.50 6.00
191 Dylan Guenther/599 RC 3.00 8.00
192 Jake Sanderson/599 RC 3.00 8.00
193 Kent Johnson/599 RC 2.50 6.00
194 Andrei Kuzmenko/599 RC 2.50 6.00
195 Wyatt Johnston/599 RC 5.00 12.00
196 Juraj Slafkovsky/399 RC 6.00 15.00
197 Shane Wright/399 RC 4.00 10.00
198 Owen Power/399 RC 2.50 6.00
199 Matty Beniers/399 RC 3.00 8.00
200 Matt Boldy/399 RC 4.00 10.00

2022-23 Upper Deck Credentials Blue
*BLUE/99: 1X TO 2.5X BASIC

2022-23 Upper Deck Credentials Green
*GREEN/25: 3X TO 8X BASIC
*GREEN RC/25: 1.5X TO 4X BASIC

2022-23 Upper Deck Credentials Horizontal
*HORIZONTAL: .4X TO 1X BASIC

2022-23 Upper Deck Credentials Horizontal Blue
*HOR BLUE/99: 1X TO 2.5X BASIC

2022-23 Upper Deck Credentials Horizontal Green
*HOR GREEN/25: 1.5X TO 4X BASIC

2022-23 Upper Deck Credentials Horizontal Orange
*HOR ORNG/149: .75X TO 2X BASIC

2022-23 Upper Deck Credentials Horizontal Pink
*HOR PINK/49: 1.2X TO 3X BASIC

2022-23 Upper Deck Credentials Horizontal Red
*HOR RED/299: .6X TO 1.5X BASIC

2022-23 Upper Deck Credentials Horizontal Yellow
*HOR YLW: .6X TO 1.5X BASIC

2022-23 Upper Deck Credentials Neon Green
*NEON GRN/75: 1.2X TO 3X BASIC

2022-23 Upper Deck Credentials Orange
*ORANGE/149: X TO X BASIC

2022-23 Upper Deck Credentials Pink
*PINK/49: 2X TO 5X BASIC
*PINK RC/49: 1.2X TO 3X BASIC

2022-23 Upper Deck Credentials Red
*RED/299: .6X TO 1.5X BASIC

2022-23 Upper Deck Credentials Yellow
*YELLOW: 1X TO 2.5X BASIC
*YELLOW RC: .6X TO 1.5X BASIC

2022-23 Upper Deck Credentials 1st Star of the Night
1S1 Leon Draisaitl 2.50 6.00
1S2 Victor Hedman 1.00 2.50
1S3 Jack Eichel 1.25 3.00
1S4 Brent Burns .75 2.00
1S5 Alex DeBrincat 1.00 2.50
1S6 John Tavares 1.25 3.00
1S7 Connor McDavid 4.00 10.00
1S8 Brad Marchand 1.50 4.00
1S9 Alex Ovechkin 3.00 8.00
1S10 Sidney Crosby 3.00 8.00

2022-23 Upper Deck Credentials 1st Star of the Night Rookie Autographs
1SR1 Shane Wright 30.00 80.00
1SR2 Owen Power 25.00 60.00
1SR3 Juraj Slafkovsky 60.00 150.00
1SR6 Matt Boldy 40.00 100.00
1SR7 Jake Sanderson 30.00 80.00

2022-23 Upper Deck Credentials 1st Star of the Night Rookies
1SR1 Shane Wright 2.00 5.00
1SR2 Owen Power 1.50 4.00
1SR3 Juraj Slafkovsky 4.00 10.00
1SR4 Matty Beniers 2.00 5.00
1SR5 Kent Johnson 1.50 4.00
1SR6 Matt Boldy 2.50 6.00
1SR7 Jake Sanderson 2.00 5.00

2022-23 Upper Deck Credentials 2nd Star of the Night
2S1 Mark Stone 1.00 2.50
2S2 Alexis Lafreniere 1.25 3.00
2S3 Quinn Hughes 2.00 5.00
2S4 Joe Pavelski 1.00 2.50
2S5 Aleksander Barkov 1.25 3.00
2S6 Tim Stutzle 1.00 2.50
2S7 Jake Guentzel 1.25 3.00
2S8 Tyler Toffoli .75 2.00
2S9 Kirby Dach .75 2.00
2S10 Brayden Point 1.00 2.50

2022-23 Upper Deck Credentials 2nd Star of the Night Autographs
2S1 Mark Stone 12.00 30.00
2S2 Alexis Lafreniere 15.00 40.00
2S5 Aleksander Barkov 15.00 40.00
2S6 Tim Stutzle 12.00 30.00
2S8 Tyler Toffoli 10.00 25.00
2S9 Kirby Dach 10.00 25.00
2S10 Brayden Point 12.00 30.00

2022-23 Upper Deck Credentials 2nd Star of the Night Rookie Autographs
COMMON CARD 6.00 15.00
SEMISTARS 8.00 20.00
UNLISTED STARS 10.00 25.00
2SR1 Braden Schneider 15.00 40.00
2SR2 Kaiden Guhle 20.00 50.00
2SR3 Dylan Guenther 25.00 60.00
2SR4 Jack Quinn 15.00 40.00
2SR5 Marco Rossi 25.00 60.00
2SR6 Brandt Clarke 20.00 50.00
2SR7 Dylan Samberg 10.00 25.00

2022-23 Upper Deck Credentials 2nd Star of the Night Rookies
2SR1 Braden Schneider 1.25 3.00
2SR2 Kaiden Guhle 1.50 4.00
2SR3 Dylan Guenther 2.00 5.00
2SR4 Jack Quinn 1.25 3.00
2SR5 Marco Rossi 2.00 5.00
2SR6 Brandt Clarke 1.50 4.00
2SR7 Dylan Samberg .75 2.00

2022-23 Upper Deck Credentials 3rd Star of the Night
3S1 Kyle Connor 1.25 3.00
3S2 Brock Boeser 1.00 2.50
3S3 Mason McTavish .75 2.00
3S4 William Karlsson 1.00 2.50
3S5 Kevin Fiala .60 1.50
3S6 Lucas Raymond 1.25 3.00
3S7 Cam Atkinson .75 2.00
3S8 Teuvo Teravainen .75 2.00
3S9 Anthony Beauvillier .50 1.25
3S10 Roope Hintz 1.00 2.50

2022-23 Upper Deck Credentials 3rd Star of the Night Autographs
3S2 Brock Boeser 8.00 20.00
3S3 Mason McTavish 6.00 15.00
3S4 William Karlsson 8.00 20.00
3S5 Kevin Fiala 5.00 12.00
3S8 Teuvo Teravainen 6.00 15.00
3S9 Anthony Beauvillier 4.00 10.00
3S10 Roope Hintz 8.00 20.00

2022-23 Upper Deck Credentials 3rd Star of the Night Rookie Autographs
3SR1 Andrei Kuzmenko 12.00 30.00
3SR2 Elmer Soderblom 12.00 30.00
3SR4 Jack McBain 6.00 15.00
3SR6 Dylan Holloway 12.00 30.00

2022-23 Upper Deck Credentials 3rd Star of the Night Rookies
3SR1 Andrei Kuzmenko 1.50 4.00
3SR2 Elmer Soderblom 1.50 4.00
3SR3 Arber Xhekaj 1.50 4.00
3SR4 Jack McBain .75 2.00
3SR5 Wyatt Johnston 3.00 8.00
3SR6 Dylan Holloway 1.50 4.00

2022-23 Upper Deck Credentials Bubble Hockey
BHAM Auston Matthews 20.00 50.00
BHAO Alex Ovechkin 20.00 50.00
BHCM Connor McDavid 25.00 60.00
BHDP David Pastrnak 12.00 30.00
BHJE Jack Eichel 8.00 20.00
BHMA Cale Makar 12.00 30.00
BHMB Mathew Barzal 10.00 25.00
BHPK Patrick Kane 15.00 40.00
BHSC Sidney Crosby 20.00 50.00
BHSS Steven Stamkos 10.00 25.00

2022-23 Upper Deck Credentials Bubble Hockey Gold Spectrum
*GOLD/25: .75X TO 2X BASIC
BHPK Patrick Kane 25.00 60.00

2022-23 Upper Deck Credentials Bubble Hockey Rookies
*GOLD/25: 1X TO 2.5X BASIC
BHRBC Brandt Clarke 8.00 20.00
BHRBE Matty Beniers 10.00 25.00
BHRDH Dylan Holloway 8.00 20.00
BHRJS Jake Sanderson 10.00 25.00
BHRKJ Kent Johnson 8.00 20.00
BHRMB Matt Boldy 12.00 30.00
BHROP Owen Power 8.00 20.00
BHRSL Juraj Slafkovsky 20.00 50.00
BHRSW Shane Wright 10.00 25.00
BHRWJ Wyatt Johnston 15.00 40.00

2022-23 Upper Deck Credentials Debut Ticket Access Acetate
DTAAK Andrei Kuzmenko 8.00 20.00
DTAAV Alex Vlasic 3.00 8.00
DTABB Bobby Brink 4.00 10.00
DTABC Brandt Clarke 8.00 20.00
DTABE Matty Beniers 10.00 25.00
DTABL Fredrik Karlstrom 3.00 8.00
DTABS Braden Schneider 6.00 15.00
DTACK Cole Koepke 4.00 10.00
DTACM Carson Meyer 3.00 8.00
DTACZ Jakub Lauko 5.00 12.00
DTADG Dylan Guenther 10.00 25.00
DTADH Dylan Holloway 8.00 20.00
DTADJ David Jiricek 8.00 20.00
DTADS Dylan Samberg 4.00 10.00
DTAES Elmer Soderblom 8.00 20.00
DTAFK Lukas Dostal 8.00 20.00
DTAHD Hunter Drew 4.00 10.00
DTAHE Pyotr Kochetkov 8.00 20.00
DTAJP Jacob Perreault 4.00 10.00
DTAJQ Jack Quinn 6.00 15.00
DTAJS Juraj Slafkovsky 20.00 50.00
DTAKJ Kent Johnson 8.00 20.00
DTAKK Kaedan Korczak 3.00 8.00
DTALC Trey Fix-Wolansky 4.00 10.00
DTAMB Matt Boldy 12.00 30.00
DTAMC Brayden Tracey 3.00 8.00
DTAME Michael Eyssimont 4.00 10.00
DTAMK Mark Kastelic 3.00 8.00
DTAMO Kirill Marchenko 10.00 25.00
DTAMR Marco Rossi 10.00 25.00
DTAMS Mads Sogaard 5.00 12.00
DTANA Nick Abruzzese 4.00 10.00
DTANB Nick Blankenburg 3.00 8.00
DTANC Noah Cates 4.00 10.00
DTANS Nathan Smith 3.00 8.00
DTAOP Owen Power 8.00 20.00
DTAPO Samuel Poulin 5.00 12.00
DTARA Ronnie Attard 4.00 10.00
DTARS Chase Pearson 3.00 8.00
DTARW Reilly Walsh 4.00 10.00
DTASA Jake Sanderson 10.00 25.00
DTASE Filip Hallander 4.00 10.00
DTASN Zack Hayes 3.00 8.00
DTASP Jordan Spence 4.00 10.00
DTASW Shane Wright 10.00 25.00
DTATB Thomas Bordeleau 4.00 10.00
DTAWD Jack McBain 4.00 10.00
DTAWJ Wyatt Johnston 15.00 40.00
DTAYA Jordan Harris 5.00 12.00

2022-23 Upper Deck Credentials Debut Ticket Access Acetate Autographs
DTAAK Andrei Kuzmenko 20.00 50.00
DTABB Bobby Brink 10.00 25.00
DTABE Matty Beniers 100.00 250.00
DTABN Ben Meyers 6.00 15.00
DTABS Braden Schneider 15.00 40.00
DTACK Cole Koepke 10.00 25.00
DTACP Chase Pearson 8.00 20.00
DTADG Dylan Guenther 25.00 60.00
DTADJ David Jiricek 20.00 50.00
DTAFK Fredrik Karlstrom 8.00 20.00
DTAJH Jordan Harris 10.00 25.00
DTAJL Jakub Lauko 12.00 30.00
DTAJM Jack McBain 10.00 25.00
DTAJS Juraj Slafkovsky 125.00 300.00
DTAKJ Kent Johnson 20.00 50.00
DTAKK Kaedan Korczak 8.00 20.00
DTAMB Matt Boldy 30.00 80.00
DTAME Michael Eyssimont 10.00 25.00
DTAMK Mark Kastelic 8.00 20.00
DTAMO Kirill Marchenko 25.00 60.00
DTAMR Marco Rossi 25.00 60.00
DTANA Nick Abruzzese 10.00 25.00
DTANB Nick Blankenburg 8.00 20.00
DTANC Noah Cates 10.00 25.00
DTANS Nathan Smith 8.00 20.00
DTAOP Owen Power 80.00 80.00
DTARA Ronnie Attard 10.00 25.00
DTASW Shane Wright 25.00 60.00
DTAZH Zack Hayes 8.00 20.00

2022-23 Upper Deck Credentials Debut Ticket Access Autographs
*YELLOW: .5X TO 1.2X BASIC
*RED: .6X TO 1.5X BASIC
*BLUE: .75X TO 2X BASIC
DTAAAK Andrei Kuzmenko/299 12.00 30.00
DTAAAR Aatu Raty/299 6.00 15.00
DTAABB Bobby Brink/299 6.00 15.00
DTAABC Brandt Clarke/199 12.00 30.00
DTAABE Matty Beniers/99 30.00 80.00
DTAABK Marcus Bjork/299 6.00 15.00
DTAABS Braden Schneider/299 10.00 25.00
DTAADE Nick DeSimone/299 6.00 15.00
DTAADG Dylan Guenther/199 15.00 40.00
DTAADH Dylan Holloway/199 12.00 30.00
DTAADJ David Jiricek/199 12.00 30.00
DTAAJM Jack McBain/299 6.00 15.00
DTAAJS Juraj Slafkovsky/99 80.00 200.00
DTAAKJ Kent Johnson/99 20.00 50.00
DTAAKK Kaedan Korczak/299 5.00 12.00
DTAAMA Matej Blumel/299 8.00 20.00
DTAAMB Matt Boldy/99 20.00 50.00
DTAAME Michael Eyssimont/299 6.00 15.00
DTAAMK Mark Kastelic/299 5.00 12.00
DTAAMR Marco Rossi/199 15.00 40.00
DTAANA Nick Abruzzese/299 6.00 15.00
DTAANB Nick Blankenburg/299 5.00 12.00
DTAANC Noah Cates/299 6.00 15.00
DTAANS Nathan Smith/299 5.00 12.00
DTAANV Nikita Alexandrov/299 6.00 15.00
DTAAOP Owen Power/99 25.00 60.00
DTAAPN Juuso Parssinen/299 6.00 15.00
DTAARA Ronnie Attard/299 6.00 15.00
DTAASA Shane Wright/99 15.00 40.00
DTAASW Jake Sanderson/199 15.00 40.00
DTAAWJ Wyatt Johnston/199 25.00 60.00

2022-23 Upper Deck Credentials Debut Ticket Access Autographs Green
*GREEN/25: 1X TO 2.5X BASIC
DTAABE Matty Beniers 60.00 150.00
DTAAJS Juraj Slafkovsky 150.00 400.00
DTAAKJ Kent Johnson 40.00 100.00
DTAAWJ Wyatt Johnston 60.00 150.00

2022-23 Upper Deck Credentials Debut Ticket Access Autographs Horizontal
*YELLOW: .6X TO 1.5X BASIC
*RED: .75X TO 2X BASIC
DTAAHAK Andrei Kuzmenko/99 15.00 40.00
DTAAHBC Brandt Clarke/35 15.00 40.00
DTAAHBS Braden Schneider/99 12.00 30.00
DTAAHDH Dylan Holloway/35 15.00 40.00
DTAAHDJ David Jiricek/99 15.00 40.00
DTAAHJS Juraj Slafkovsky/35 125.00 300.00
DTAAHKG Kaiden Guhle/99 15.00 40.00
DTAAHKJ Kent Johnson/35 15.00 40.00
DTAAHMB Matt Boldy/35 40.00 100.00
DTAAHMK Mark Kastelic/99 6.00 15.00
DTAAHMR Marco Rossi/99 20.00 50.00
DTAAHOP Owen Power/35 40.00 100.00
DTAAHSA Shane Wright/35 40.00 100.00
DTAAHSW Jake Sanderson/35 30.00 80.00
DTAAHWJ Wyatt Johnston/99 30.00 80.00
DTAAHXJ Arber Xhekaj/99 15.00 40.00

2022-23 Upper Deck Credentials Debut Ticket Access Autographs Orange
*ORANGE: .75X TO 2X BASIC
DTAABE Matty Beniers/25 60.00 150.00
DTAAMB Matt Boldy/25 50.00 125.00
DTAAMR Marco Rossi/25 40.00 100.00
DTAAOP Owen Power/25 50.00 125.00
DTAASA Shane Wright/25 50.00 125.00
DTAASW Jake Sanderson/25 40.00 100.00
DTAAWJ Wyatt Johnston/25 60.00 150.00

2022-23 Upper Deck Credentials Highly Anticipated
HA1 Owen Power 1.25 3.00
HA2 Kent Johnson 1.25 3.00
HA3 Matt Boldy 2.00 5.00
HA4 Matty Beniers 1.50 4.00
HA5 Juraj Slafkovsky 3.00 8.00
HA6 Jake Sanderson 1.50 4.00
HA7 Jack Quinn 1.00 2.50
HA8 Dylan Holloway 1.25 3.00
HA9 Marco Rossi 1.50 4.00
HA10 Dylan Guenther 1.50 4.00
HA11 Elmer Soderblom 1.25 3.00
HA12 Brandt Clarke 1.25 3.00
HA13 Shane Wright 1.50 4.00
HA14 Wyatt Johnston 2.50 6.00
HA15 David Jiricek 1.25 3.00
HA16 Bobby Brink .60 1.50
HA17 Filip Kral .75 2.00
HA18 Cole Koepke .60 1.50
HA19 Nathan Smith .50 1.25
HA20 Nick Blankenburg .50 1.25
HA21 Noah Cates .60 1.50
HA22 Braden Schneider 1.00 2.50
HA23 Dylan Samberg .60 1.50
HA24 Ronnie Attard .60 1.50
HA25 Jordan Spence .60 1.50
HA26 Mark Kastelic .50 1.25
HA27 Nick Abruzzese .60 1.50
HA28 Kaedan Korczak .50 1.25
HA29 Andrei Kuzmenko 1.25 3.00
HA30 Lukas Dostal 1.25 3.00
HA31 Samuel Poulin .75 2.00
HA32 Nils Aman .60 1.50
HA33 Pavol Regenda .60 1.50
HA34 Filip Roos .50 1.25
HA35 Arber Xhekaj 1.25 3.00
HA36 Thomas Bordeleau .60 1.50
HA37 Carson Meyer .50 1.25
HA38 Mitchell Chaffee .50 1.25
HA39 Michael Eyssimont .60 1.50

HA40 Reilly Walsh .60 1.50
HA41 Jacob Perreault .60 1.50
HA42 Alex Vlasic .50 1.25
HA43 Mads Sogaard .75 2.00
HA44 Hunter Drew .60 1.50
HA45 Olle Lycksell .60 1.50
HA46 Kaiden Guhle 1.25 3.00
HA47 Nick Perbix .50 1.25
HA48 Jack McBain .60 1.50
HA49 Marc McLaughlin .60 1.50
HA50 Lukas Reichel 1.25 3.00

2022-23 Upper Deck Credentials Main Stage Signatures

*GOLD: .6X TO 1.5X BASIC
MSAL Anton Lundell SP 8.00 20.00
MSAN Alex Newhook SP 6.00 15.00
MSBC Blake Coleman 6.00 15.00
MSBD Brandon Duhaime 5.00 12.00
MSBH Brandon Hagel 6.00 15.00
MSBP Brayden Point SP 10.00 25.00
MSCJ Calle Jarnkrok 5.00 12.00
MSCO Charlie Coyle SP 8.00 20.00
MSDC Dylan Cozens SP 8.00 20.00
MSET Eeli Tolvanen 8.00 20.00
MSJB Josh Bailey SP 6.00 15.00
MSJK Jordan Kyrou SP 8.00 20.00
MSJM Jared McCann SP 6.00 15.00
MSJZ Jason Zucker 8.00 20.00
MSLE Anders Lee 6.00 15.00
MSLT Logan Thompson 10.00 25.00
MSMA Mason Appleton 5.00 12.00
MSMF Marcus Foligno 6.00 15.00
MSMI Mikey Anderson 6.00 15.00
MSNS Nick Schmaltz 6.00 15.00
MSPE Jeff Petry 8.00 20.00
MSRC Ross Colton 6.00 15.00
MSRH Roope Hintz SP 10.00 25.00
MSRR Ryan Reaves 6.00 15.00
MSSJ Seth Jarvis SP 10.00 25.00
MSST Shea Theodore SP 10.00 25.00
MSSW Sean Walker 5.00 12.00
MSTJ Tanner Jeannot 5.00 12.00
MSWK William Karlsson SP 10.00 25.00

2022-23 Upper Deck Credentials Pro Visions

1 Trevor Zegras 25.00 60.00
2 Shane Wright 20.00 50.00
3 Leon Draisaitl 25.00 60.00
4 Mathew Barzal 30.00 80.00
5 Kirill Kaprizov 25.00 60.00
6 Moritz Seider 40.00 100.00
7 Steven Stamkos 15.00 40.00
8 Cale Makar 20.00 50.00
9 Johnny Gaudreau 12.00 30.00
10 Owen Power 15.00 40.00

2022-23 Upper Deck Credentials Pro Visions Retro

NNO1 Steve Yzerman 40.00 100.00
NNO2 Brett Hull 30.00 80.00
NNO3 Wayne Gretzky 100.00 250.00
NNO4 Patrick Roy 50.00 125.00
NNO5 Mario Lemieux 50.00 125.00

2022-23 Upper Deck Credentials Retro Ticket Access Autographs

RTAABT Brady Tkachuk 8.00 20.00

2022-23 Upper Deck Credentials Speed of the Game Rookies

SGR1 Matt Boldy 3.00 8.00
SGR2 Matty Beniers 2.50 6.00
SGR3 Kent Johnson 2.00 5.00
SGR4 Jake Sanderson 2.50 6.00
SGR5 Dylan Guenther 2.50 6.00
SGR6 Jack Quinn 1.50 4.00
SGR7 Marco Rossi 2.50 6.00
SGR8 Jakub Lauko 1.25 3.00
SGR9 Brandt Clarke 2.00 5.00
SGR10 Kaiden Guhle 2.00 5.00
SGR11 Jordan Harris 1.25 3.00
SGR12 Cole Koepke 1.00 2.50
SGR13 Nick Blankenburg .75 2.00
SGR14 Matias Maccelli 1.50 4.00
SGR15 Noah Cates 1.00 2.50
SGR16 Andrei Kuzmenko 2.00 5.00
SGR17 Lukas Reichel 2.00 5.00
SGR18 Jacob Perreault 1.00 2.50
SGR19 Ben Meyers 1.00 2.50
SGR20 Dylan Holloway 2.00 5.00
SGR21 Jordan Spence 1.00 2.50
SGR22 Thomas Bordeleau 1.00 2.50
SGR23 Valtteri Puustinen .75 2.00
SGR24 Nick Abruzzese 1.00 2.50
SGR25 Shane Wright 2.50 6.00

2022-23 Upper Deck Credentials Speed of the Game Stars

SG1 Jack Eichel 1.50 4.00
SG2 Quinn Hughes 2.50 6.00
SG3 Mathew Barzal 1.25 3.00
SG4 Alex DeBrincat 1.25 3.00
SG5 Brendan Gallagher 1.00 2.50
SG6 Taylor Hall 1.00 2.50
SG7 Matt Duchene 1.00 2.50
SG8 Jake Guentzel 1.50 4.00
SG9 Zach Werenski 1.50 4.00
SG10 Brayden Point 1.25 3.00
SG11 Kyle Connor 1.50 4.00
SG12 Miro Heiskanen 1.25 3.00
SG13 Mats Zuccarello 1.00 2.50
SG14 Tomas Hertl 1.00 2.50
SG15 Jordan Eberle 1.00 2.50
SG16 Kevin Fiala .75 2.00
SG17 Cole Caufield 2.00 5.00
SG18 Jordan Kyrou 1.00 2.50
SG19 Clayton Keller 1.25 3.00
SG20 Anthony Beauvillier .60 1.50
SG21 Matt Grzelcyk .75 2.00
SG22 Noah Dobson 1.25 3.00
SG23 Jason Robertson 1.50 4.00
SG24 Torey Krug .75 2.00
SG25 K'Andre Miller .75 2.00

2022-23 Upper Deck Credentials Ticket Access Acetate

TAAC Andrew Copp 1.25 3.00
TAAK Anze Kopitar 3.00 8.00
TAAN Alex Nedeljkovic 1.50 4.00
TABB Brock Boeser 2.50 6.00
TABH Brandon Hagel 1.50 4.00
TABM Brad Marchand 4.00 10.00
TABP Brayden Point 2.50 6.00
TACC Charlie Coyle 2.00 5.00
TACP Colton Parayko 1.50 4.00
TACS Cole Sillinger 1.50 4.00
TAET Eeli Tolvanen 2.00 5.00
TAJA Josh Anderson 1.50 4.00
TAJE Joel Eriksson Ek 1.50 4.00
TAJK Jordan Kyrou 2.00 5.00
TAJM Jacob Markstrom 2.00 5.00
TAJP JJ Peterka 2.00 5.00
TAJT Jonathan Toews 3.00 8.00
TAJV James van Riemsdyk 1.50 4.00
TAMA Mason Appleton 1.25 3.00
TAMB Michael Bunting 2.00 5.00
TAMC Maxime Comtois 1.50 4.00
TAMM Mason McTavish 2.00 5.00
TAMN Martin Necas 3.00 8.00
TAOL Oskar Lindblom 1.50 4.00
TASD Sean Durzi 1.25 3.00
TASG Samuel Girard 1.25 3.00
TASJ Seth Jarvis 2.50 6.00
TATS Tim Stutzle 2.50 6.00
TATT Teuvo Teravainen 2.00 5.00
TAWK William Karlsson 2.50 6.00

2022-23 Upper Deck Credentials Ticket Access Acetate Autographs

TAAN Alex Nedeljkovic/99 10.00 25.00
TACC Charlie Coyle/25 12.00 30.00
TAJM Jacob Markstrom/25 12.00 30.00
TAMA Mason Appleton/99 8.00 20.00
TAMB Michael Bunting/25 12.00 30.00
TAMM Mason McTavish/25 12.00 30.00

2022-23 Upper Deck Credentials Ticket Access Autographs

TAAAS Andrei Svechnikov/49 20.00 50.00
TAALD Leon Draisaitl/25 50.00 125.00

2022-23 Upper Deck Credentials Ticket Access Autographs Yellow

*YELLOW/25: .5X TO 1.2X BASIC
TAAMF Marc-Andre Fleury 60.00 150.00

2023-24 Upper Deck Credentials

1 Trevor Zegras .40 1.00
2 Mason McTavish .40 1.00
3 Clayton Keller .50 1.25
4 Nick Schmaltz .30 .75
5 Linus Ullmark .40 1.00
6 Brad Marchand .75 2.00
7 David Pastrnak 1.00 2.50
8 Tage Thompson .50 1.25
9 Alex Tuch .40 1.00
10 Rasmus Dahlin .50 1.25
11 Jacob Markstrom .40 1.00
12 Nazem Kadri .50 1.25
13 Jonathan Huberdeau .50 1.25
14 Sebastian Aho .60 1.50
15 Brent Burns .40 1.00
16 Andrei Svechnikov .50 1.25
17 Seth Jones .40 1.00
18 Taylor Hall .40 1.00
19 Nathan MacKinnon 1.50 4.00
20 Cale Makar 1.00 2.50
21 Mikko Rantanen 1.00 2.50
22 Johnny Gaudreau .60 1.50
23 Patrik Laine .50 1.25
24 Jason Robertson .60 1.50
25 Jake Oettinger .60 1.50
26 Wyatt Johnston .75 2.00
27 Miro Heiskanen .50 1.25
28 Dylan Larkin .50 1.25
29 Alex DeBrincat .50 1.25
30 Moritz Seider .50 1.25
31 Lucas Raymond .60 1.50
32 Connor McDavid 2.00 5.00
33 Stuart Skinner .50 1.25
34 Mattias Ekholm .30 .75
35 Leon Draisaitl 1.25 3.00
36 Matthew Tkachuk .75 2.00
37 Aleksander Barkov .60 1.50
38 Sergei Bobrovsky .60 1.50
39 Pierre-Luc Dubois .30 .75
40 Quinton Byfield .50 1.25
41 Anze Kopitar .60 1.50
42 Kirill Kaprizov 1.25 3.00
43 Marc-Andre Fleury .75 2.00
44 Matt Boldy .60 1.50
45 Arber Xhekaj .40 1.00
46 Cole Caufield .75 2.00
47 Juraj Slafkovsky .75 2.00
48 Nick Suzuki .75 2.00
49 Juuse Saros .50 1.25
50 Roman Josi .40 1.00
51 Ryan O'Reilly .40 1.00
52 Nico Hischier .60 1.50
53 Timo Meier .40 1.00
54 Jack Hughes 1.00 2.50
55 Dawson Mercer .50 1.25
56 Bo Horvat .50 1.25
57 Ilya Sorokin .60 1.50
58 Mathew Barzal .50 1.25
59 Artemi Panarin .75 2.00
60 Mika Zibanejad .50 1.25
61 Adam Fox .50 1.25
62 Igor Shesterkin .75 2.00
63 Claude Giroux .40 1.00
64 Tim Stutzle .50 1.25
65 Drake Batherson .40 1.00
66 Brady Tkachuk .60 1.50
67 Morgan Frost .30 .75
68 Travis Konecny .40 1.00
69 Sidney Crosby 1.50 4.00
70 Evgeni Malkin .75 2.00
71 Erik Karlsson .50 1.25
72 Logan Couture .50 1.25
73 William Eklund .50 1.25
74 Matty Beniers .50 1.25
75 Shane Wright .50 1.25
76 Jared McCann .30 .75
77 Jordan Kyrou .40 1.00
78 Robert Thomas .40 1.00
79 Pavel Buchnevich .30 .75
80 Brayden Point .50 1.25
81 Andrei Vasilevskiy .60 1.50
82 Steven Stamkos .75 2.00
83 Nikita Kucherov .75 2.00
84 Tyler Bertuzzi .30 .75
85 Mitch Marner .60 1.50
86 William Nylander .75 2.00
87 John Tavares .60 1.50
88 Auston Matthews 1.50 4.00
89 J.T. Miller .50 1.25
90 Elias Pettersson .60 1.50
91 Quinn Hughes 1.00 2.50
92 Jack Eichel .60 1.50
93 Mark Stone .50 1.25
94 Logan Thompson .50 1.25
95 Alex Ovechkin 1.50 4.00
96 Nicklas Backstrom .40 1.00
97 Evgeny Kuznetsov .50 1.25
98 Mark Scheifele .60 1.50
99 Connor Hellebuyck .75 2.00
100 Kyle Connor .60 1.50
101 Matthew Kessel/999 RC 1.00 2.50
102 Jake Livingstone/999 RC 1.25 3.00
103 Luke Philp/999 RC 1.25 3.00
104 Tristen Robins/999 RC 1.25 3.00
105 Jaxson Stauber/999 RC 1.25 3.00
106 Henry Thrun/999 RC 1.25 3.00
107 Damien Giroux/999 RC 1.25 3.00
108 Billy Sweezey/999 RC 1.25 3.00
109 Arturs Silovs/999 RC 2.50 6.00
110 Mackie Samoskevich/999 RC 2.00 5.00
111 Drew Helleson/999 RC 1.25 3.00
112 Hugh McGing/999 RC 1.25 3.00
113 Adam Ginning/999 RC 1.25 3.00
114 Joel Teasdale/999 RC 1.25 3.00
115 David Gust/999 RC 1.25 3.00
116 Walker Duehr/999 RC 1.00 2.50
117 Jet Greaves/999 RC 2.00 5.00
118 Spencer Stastney/999 RC 1.25 3.00
119 Emil Andrae/999 RC 1.25 3.00
120 Ty Emberson/999 RC 1.25 3.00
121 Michael Kesselring/999 RC 1.25 3.00
122 Vincent Desharnais/999 RC 1.50 4.00
123 Hunter McKown/999 RC 1.25 3.00
124 Bobby McMann/999 RC 2.00 5.00
125 Tristan Luneau/999 RC 1.25 3.00
126 Arnaud Durandeau/999 RC 1.25 3.00
127 Cole Guttman/999 RC 1.25 3.00
128 Daemon Hunt/999 RC 1.25 3.00
129 Nick Swaney/999 RC 1.25 3.00
130 Olle Eriksson Ek/999 RC 1.25 3.00
131 Aidan McDonough/999 RC 1.00 2.50
132 Akito Hirose/999 RC 1.00 2.50
133 Lucas Condotta/999 RC 1.25 3.00
134 Tyler Angle/999 RC 1.25 3.00
135 Cole McWard/999 RC 1.25 3.00
136 Milos Kelemen/999 RC 1.25 3.00
137 Jiri Patera/999 RC 2.00 5.00
138 Jonathan Gruden/999 RC 1.25 3.00
139 Matt Murray/999 RC 1.25 3.00
140 Jiri Kulich/999 RC 2.50 6.00
141 Ilya Solovyov/999 RC 1.25 3.00
142 Joona Koppanen/999 RC 1.00 2.50
143 Uvis Balinskis/999 RC 1.25 3.00
144 Mason Lohrei/999 RC 2.00 5.00
145 Wyatt Kaiser/999 RC 1.25 3.00
146 Ondrej Pavel/999 RC 1.25 3.00
147 Mikael Pyyhtia/999 RC 1.25 3.00
148 Justin Sourdif/999 RC 1.25 3.00
149 Hardy Haman Aktell/999 RC 1.25 3.00
150 John Beecher/999 RC 2.50 6.00
151 Magnus Chrona/999 RC 1.25 3.00
152 Jayden Struble/999 RC 1.50 4.00
153 Isak Rosen/999 RC 1.25 3.00
154 Raphael Lavoie/999 RC 1.25 3.00
155 Martin Pospisil/999 RC 1.50 4.00
156 Brock Faber/799 RC 3.00 8.00
157 Jakob Pelletier/799 RC 1.50 4.00
158 Nikita Nesterenko/799 RC 1.25 3.00
159 Samuel Bolduc/799 RC 1.25 3.00
160 Pavel Mintyukov/799 RC 2.00 5.00
161 Elliot Desnoyers/799 RC 1.25 3.00
162 Tye Kartye/799 RC 2.00 5.00
163 Alex Laferriere/799 RC 2.00 5.00
164 Ivan Miroshnichenko/799 RC 2.00 5.00
165 Jackson LaCombe/799 RC 1.25 3.00
166 Ryker Evans/799 RC 1.50 4.00
167 Dmitri Voronkov/799 RC 1.50 4.00
168 Will Cuylle/799 RC 2.00 5.00
169 Danil Gushchin/799 RC 1.25 3.00
170 Sean Farrell/799 RC 1.25 3.00
171 Tyler Kleven/799 RC 1.25 3.00
172 William Dufour/799 RC 1.00 2.50
173 Vincent Iorio/799 RC 1.25 3.00
174 Stanislav Svozil/799 RC 1.00 2.50
175 Kevin Korchinski/799 RC 2.00 5.00
176 Lukas Rousek/799 RC 1.00 2.50
177 Samuel Knazko/799 RC 1.25 3.00
178 Leevi Merilainen/799 RC 1.25 3.00
179 Maxence Guenette/799 RC 1.25 3.00
180 Matt Savoie/799 RC 2.50 6.00
181 Simon Edvinsson/599 RC 2.50 6.00
182 Matthew Coronato/599 RC 2.00 5.00
183 Devon Levi/599 RC 3.00 8.00
184 Simon Nemec/599 RC 2.50 6.00
185 Connor Zary/599 RC 2.50 6.00
186 Owen Beck/599 RC 2.00 5.00
187 Luke Evangelista/599 RC 2.00 5.00
188 Zach Benson/599 RC 2.00 5.00
189 Yaroslav Askarov/599 RC 3.00 8.00
190 Dustin Wolf/599 RC 4.00 10.00
191 Matthew Knies/599 RC 5.00 12.00
192 Tyson Foerster/599 RC 2.50 6.00
193 Matthew Poitras/599 RC 2.50 6.00
194 Ridly Greig/599 RC 2.00 5.00
195 Marco Kasper/599 RC 3.00 8.00
196 Luke Hughes/399 RC 4.00 10.00
197 Leo Carlsson/399 RC 4.00 10.00
198 Connor Bedard/399 RC 40.00 100.00
199 Logan Cooley/399 RC 4.00 10.00
200 Adam Fantilli/399 RC 4.00 10.00

2023-24 Upper Deck Credentials Blue

*BLUE/149: .8X TO 2X BASIC

2023-24 Upper Deck Credentials Green

*GREEN/25: 3X TO 8X BASIC
*GREEN RC/25: 1.5X TO 4X BASIC

2023-24 Upper Deck Credentials Horizontal

*HORIZONTAL: .5X TO 1.2X BASIC

2023-24 Upper Deck Credentials Horizontal Blue

*HOR BLUE/49: 1.2X TO 3X BASIC

2023-24 Upper Deck Credentials Horizontal Orange

*HOR ORNG/99: 1X TO 2.5X BASIC

2023-24 Upper Deck Credentials Horizontal Pink

*HOR PINK/25: 1.5X TO 4X BASIC

2023-24 Upper Deck Credentials Horizontal Red

*HOR RED/125: .8X TO 2X BASIC

2023-24 Upper Deck Credentials Horizontal Yellow

*HOR YLW: .5X TO 1.2X BASIC

2023-24 Upper Deck Credentials Orange

*ORANGE/249: .6X TO 1.5X BASIC

2023-24 Upper Deck Credentials Pink

*PINK: 2X TO 5X BASIC
*PINK RC: 1.2X TO 3X BASIC

2023-24 Upper Deck Credentials Red

*RED/349: .5X TO 1.2X BASIC

2023-24 Upper Deck Credentials Yellow

*YELLOW: .5X TO 1.2X BASIC

2023-24 Upper Deck Credentials '91 Pro Vision

1 Cam Neely 12.00 30.00
2 Luc Robitaille 20.00 50.00
3 Jaromir Jagr 40.00 100.00
4 Eric Lindros 20.00 50.00

2023-24 Upper Deck Credentials '97 Season Ticket Acetate

1997AL Alexis Lafreniere 6.00 15.00
1997AS Andrei Svechnikov 5.00 12.00
1997CH Connor Hellebuyck 8.00 20.00
1997CM Connor McDavid 20.00 50.00
1997JT John Tavares 6.00 15.00
1997MS Moritz Seider 5.00 12.00
1997RJ Roman Josi 4.00 10.00
1997SC Sidney Crosby 15.00 40.00
1997ST Mark Stone 5.00 12.00
1997TW Tom Wilson 4.00 10.00

2023-24 Upper Deck Credentials '97 Season Ticket Acetate Autographs

1997CH Connor Hellebuyck 30.00 80.00
1997CM Connor McDavid 200.00 500.00
1997RJ Roman Josi 15.00 40.00
1997TW Tom Wilson 15.00 40.00

2023-24 Upper Deck Credentials '97 Season Ticket Acetate Rookie Autographs

1997AF Adam Fantilli 100.00 250.00
1997CA Leo Carlsson 100.00 250.00
1997CB Connor Bedard 1000.00 2500.00
1997KN Matthew Knies 125.00 300.00
1997LC Logan Cooley 100.00 250.00
1997MC Matthew Coronato 50.00 125.00

2023-24 Upper Deck Credentials '97 Season Ticket Acetate Rookies

1997AF Adam Fantilli 10.00 25.00
1997CA Leo Carlsson 10.00 25.00
1997CB Connor Bedard 40.00 100.00
1997KN Matthew Knies 12.00 30.00
1997LC Logan Cooley 10.00 25.00
1997MC Matthew Coronato 5.00 12.00
1997OB Owen Beck 5.00 12.00
1997RG Ridly Greig 5.00 12.00
1997SE Simon Edvinsson 6.00 15.00
1997TF Tyson Foerster 6.00 15.00

2023-24 Upper Deck Credentials Day with the Pup

DWTP1 Alex Ovechkin 20.00 50.00
DWTP2 David Pastrnak 12.00 30.00
DWTP3 Sebastian Aho 8.00 20.00
DWTP4 Brad Marchand 10.00 25.00
DWTP5 Gabriel Landeskog 6.00 15.00
DWTP6 Tyler Bertuzzi 4.00 10.00
DWTP7 Matt Grzelcyk 4.00 10.00
DWTP8 T.J. Oshie 5.00 12.00
DWTP9 Evgeny Kuznetsov 6.00 15.00
DWTP10 Linus Ullmark 5.00 12.00
DWTP11 Gordie Howe 15.00 40.00
DWTP12 Connor Clifton 3.00 8.00

2023-24 Upper Deck Credentials Debut Ticket Access Acetate

DTAAD Arnaud Durandeau 4.00 10.00
DTAAF Adam Fantilli 12.00 30.00
DTAAG Adam Ginning 4.00 10.00
DTAAH Akito Hirose 3.00 8.00
DTAAM Aidan McDonough 3.00 8.00
DTABF Brock Faber 10.00 25.00
DTABM Bobby McMann 6.00 15.00
DTACB Connor Bedard 100.00 250.00
DTACO Logan Cooley 12.00 30.00
DTACZ Connor Zary 8.00 20.00
DTADG Danil Gushchin 4.00 10.00
DTADU William Dufour 3.00 8.00
DTADW Dustin Wolf 12.00 30.00
DTAEA Egor Afanasyev 4.00 10.00
DTAHM Hunter McKown 4.00 10.00
DTAHT Henry Thrun 4.00 10.00
DTAJG Jonathan Gruden 4.00 10.00
DTAJP Jakob Pelletier 5.00 12.00
DTAKA Marco Kasper 10.00 25.00
DTAKE Matthew Kessel 3.00 8.00
DTAKN Matthew Knies 15.00 40.00
DTALC Leo Carlsson 12.00 30.00
DTALE Luke Evangelista 6.00 15.00
DTALH Luke Hughes 12.00 30.00
DTALM Leevi Merilainen 4.00 10.00
DTALP Luke Philp 4.00 10.00
DTALR Lukas Rousek 3.00 8.00
DTAMC Matthew Coronato 6.00 15.00
DTAMK Michael Kesselring 4.00 10.00
DTAMM Matt Murray 4.00 10.00
DTAMP Matthew Poitras 8.00 20.00
DTANN Nikita Nesterenko 4.00 10.00
DTAOB Owen Beck 6.00 15.00
DTAPA Jiri Patera 6.00 15.00
DTAPM Pavel Mintyukov 6.00 15.00
DTARG Ridly Greig 6.00 15.00
DTASB Samuel Bolduc 4.00 10.00
DTASE Simon Edvinsson 8.00 20.00
DTASF Sean Farrell 4.00 10.00
DTASK Samuel Knazko 4.00 10.00
DTASN Simon Nemec 8.00 20.00
DTASS Stanislav Svozil 3.00 8.00
DTATF Tyson Foerster 8.00 20.00
DTATK Tye Kartye 6.00 15.00
DTAVD Vincent Desharnais 5.00 12.00
DTAWC Will Cuylle 6.00 15.00
DTAWD Walker Duehr 3.00 8.00
DTAWK Wyatt Kaiser 4.00 10.00
DTAYA Yaroslav Askarov 10.00 25.00
DTAZB Zach Benson 6.00 15.00

2023-24 Upper Deck Credentials Debut Ticket Access Acetate Autographs

DTAAD Arnaud Durandeau 10.00 25.00
DTAAF Adam Fantilli 80.00 200.00
DTAAG Adam Ginning 10.00 25.00
DTAAH Akito Hirose 8.00 20.00
DTAAM Aidan McDonough 8.00 20.00
DTABF Brock Faber 100.00 250.00
DTABM Bobby McMann 15.00 40.00
DTACB Connor Bedard 600.00 1500.00
DTACO Logan Cooley 80.00 200.00
DTACZ Connor Zary 20.00 50.00
DTADU William Dufour 8.00 20.00
DTADW Dustin Wolf 50.00 125.00
DTAEA Egor Afanasyev 10.00 25.00
DTAHM Hunter McKown 10.00 25.00
DTAHT Henry Thrun 10.00 25.00
DTAJG Jonathan Gruden 10.00 25.00
DTAJP Jakob Pelletier 12.00 30.00
DTAKA Marco Kasper 25.00 60.00
DTAKE Matthew Kessel 8.00 20.00
DTAKN Matthew Knies 80.00 200.00
DTALC Leo Carlsson 80.00 200.00
DTALE Luke Evangelista 15.00 40.00
DTALH Luke Hughes 100.00 250.00
DTALM Leevi Merilainen 10.00 25.00
DTALP Luke Philp 10.00 25.00
DTALR Lukas Rousek 8.00 20.00
DTAMC Matthew Coronato 15.00 40.00
DTAMM Matt Murray 10.00 25.00
DTAMP Matthew Poitras 20.00 50.00
DTANN Nikita Nesterenko 10.00 25.00
DTAOB Owen Beck 15.00 40.00
DTAPA Jiri Patera 15.00 40.00
DTAPM Pavel Mintyukov 15.00 40.00
DTASE Simon Edvinsson 20.00 50.00
DTASF Sean Farrell 10.00 25.00
DTASK Samuel Knazko 10.00 25.00
DTASN Simon Nemec 60.00 150.00
DTASS Stanislav Svozil 8.00 20.00
DTATF Tyson Foerster 20.00 50.00
DTATK Tye Kartye 15.00 40.00
DTAVD Vincent Desharnais 12.00 30.00
DTAWC Will Cuylle 15.00 40.00
DTAWD Walker Duehr 8.00 20.00
DTAWK Wyatt Kaiser 10.00 25.00
DTAYA Yaroslav Askarov 40.00 100.00
DTAZB Zach Benson 15.00 40.00

2023-24 Upper Deck Credentials Debut Ticket Access Autographs

*YELLOW: .5X TO 1.2X BASIC
*RED: .6X TO 1.5X BASIC
*ORANGE: .8X TO 2X BASIC
*BLUE: .8X TO 2X BASIC
*GREEN/25: 1X TO 2.5X BASIC
DTAAAD Arnaud Durandeau/299 6.00 15.00
DTAAAF Adam Fantilli/99 60.00 150.00
DTAAAG Adam Ginning/299 6.00 15.00
DTAAAH Akito Hirose/299 5.00 12.00
DTAAAM Aidan McDonough/299 5.00 12.00
DTAABF Brock Faber/299 30.00 80.00
DTAABM Bobby McMann/299 10.00 25.00
DTAABS Billy Sweezey/299 6.00 15.00
DTAACA Leo Carlsson/99 50.00 125.00
DTAACB Connor Bedard/99 800.00 2000.00
DTAACZ Connor Zary/299 12.00 30.00
DTAADG David Gust/299 6.00 15.00
DTAADU William Dufour/299 5.00 12.00
DTAADW Dustin Wolf/199 20.00 50.00
DTAAEA Egor Afanasyev/299 6.00 15.00
DTAAGU Danil Gushchin/299 6.00 15.00
DTAAHM Hunter McKown/299 6.00 15.00
DTAAJG Jonathan Gruden/299 6.00 15.00
DTAAJP Jiri Patera/299 10.00 25.00
DTAAKE Michael Kesselring/299 6.00 15.00
DTAAKN Matthew Knies/199 40.00 100.00
DTAALC Logan Cooley/99 60.00 150.00
DTAALE Luke Evangelista/199 10.00 25.00
DTAALH Luke Hughes/99 60.00 150.00
DTAALM Leevi Merilainen/299 6.00 15.00
DTAALP Luke Philp/299 6.00 15.00
DTAALR Lukas Rousek/299 5.00 12.00
DTAAMA Matthew Kessel/299 5.00 12.00
DTAAMC Matthew Coronato/199 10.00 25.00
DTAAMK Marco Kasper/199 15.00 40.00
DTAAMM Matt Murray/299 6.00 15.00
DTAAMP Matthew Poitras/299 12.00 30.00
DTAANN Nikita Nesterenko/299 6.00 15.00
DTAAOB Owen Beck/199 10.00 25.00
DTAAPE Jakob Pelletier/299 8.00 20.00
DTAAPM Pavel Mintyukov/299 10.00 25.00
DTAARG Ridly Greig/299 10.00 25.00
DTAASB Samuel Bolduc/299 6.00 15.00
DTAASE Simon Edvinsson/199 12.00 30.00
DTAASF Sean Farrell/299 6.00 15.00
DTAASN Simon Nemec/99 40.00 100.00
DTAASS Stanislav Svozil/299 5.00 12.00
DTAATF Tyson Foerster/199 12.00 30.00
DTAATK Tye Kartye/299 10.00 25.00
DTAAVD Vincent Desharnais/299 8.00 20.00
DTAAWC Will Cuylle/299 10.00 25.00
DTAAWD Walker Duehr/299 5.00 12.00
DTAAWK Wyatt Kaiser/299 6.00 15.00
DTAAYA Yaroslav Askarov/199 30.00 80.00
DTAAZB Zach Benson/299 10.00 25.00

2023-24 Upper Deck Credentials Debut Ticket Access Autographs Horizontal

*YELLOW: .6X TO 1.5X BASIC
*RED: .8X TO 2X BASIC

2023-24 Upper Deck Credentials Fans at Heart

FH1 W.Gretzky/G.Howe 15.00 40.00
FH2 N.MacKinnon/B.Horvat 10.00 25.00
FH3 Kirill Kaprizov 8.00 20.00
FH4 S.Stamkos/L.Couture 5.00 12.00
FH5 J.Hughes/T.Zegras 6.00 15.00
FH6 A.Ovechkin/B.Marchand 10.00 25.00
FH7 Mitch Marner 4.00 10.00
FH8 C.Giroux/S.Stamkos 5.00 12.00

2023-24 Upper Deck Credentials Highly Anticipated

HA1 Connor Bedard 10.00 25.00
HA2 Leo Carlsson 2.00 5.00
HA3 Marco Kasper 1.50 4.00
HA4 Adam Fantilli 2.00 5.00
HA5 Danil Gushchin .60 1.50
HA6 Simon Nemec 1.25 3.00
HA7 Logan Cooley 2.00 5.00
HA8 Akito Hirose .50 1.25
HA9 Arnaud Durandeau .60 1.50
HA10 Fraser Minten 1.25 3.00
HA11 Brock Faber 1.50 4.00
HA12 Luke Philp .60 1.50
HA13 Joona Koppanen .50 1.25
HA14 Nikita Nesterenko .60 1.50
HA15 Matt Savoie 1.25 3.00
HA16 Egor Afanasyev .60 1.50
HA17 Pavel Mintyukov 1.00 2.50
HA18 William Dufour .50 1.25
HA19 Matt Murray .60 1.50
HA20 Adam Ginning .60 1.50
HA21 Stanislav Svozil .50 1.25
HA22 Michael Kesselring .60 1.50
HA23 Jiri Patera 1.00 2.50
HA24 Matthew Poitras 1.25 3.00
HA25 Walker Duehr .50 1.25
HA26 Samuel Bolduc .60 1.50
HA27 Aidan McDonough .50 1.25
HA28 Hunter McKown .60 1.50
HA29 Matthew Kessel .50 1.25
HA30 Jakob Pelletier .75 2.00
HA31 Wyatt Kaiser .60 1.50
HA32 Leevi Merilainen .60 1.50
HA33 Jonathan Gruden .60 1.50
HA34 Sean Farrell .60 1.50
HA35 Tye Kartye 1.00 2.50
HA36 Will Cuylle 1.00 2.50
HA37 Vincent Desharnais .75 2.00
HA38 Luke Evangelista 1.00 2.50
HA39 Matthew Coronato 1.00 2.50
HA40 Owen Beck 1.00 2.50
HA41 Henry Thrun .60 1.50
HA42 Ridly Greig 1.00 2.50
HA43 Dustin Wolf 2.00 5.00
HA44 Luke Hughes 2.00 5.00
HA45 Tyson Foerster 1.25 3.00
HA46 Yaroslav Askarov 1.50 4.00
HA47 Matthew Knies 2.50 6.00
HA48 Simon Edvinsson 1.25 3.00
HA49 Devon Levi 1.50 4.00
HA50 Zach Benson 1.00 2.50

2023-24 Upper Deck Credentials Highly Anticipated Autographs

HA1 Connor Bedard SP 500.00 1200.00
HA2 Leo Carlsson SP 40.00 100.00
HA3 Marco Kasper 12.00 30.00
HA5 Danil Gushchin 5.00 12.00
HA6 Simon Nemec SP 20.00 50.00
HA7 Logan Cooley SP 30.00 80.00
HA8 Akito Hirose 4.00 10.00
HA9 Arnaud Durandeau 5.00 12.00
HA10 Fraser Minten 10.00 25.00
HA12 Luke Philp 5.00 12.00
HA13 Joona Koppanen 4.00 10.00
HA14 Nikita Nesterenko SP 5.00 12.00
HA15 Matt Savoie SP 20.00 50.00
HA16 Egor Afanasyev 5.00 12.00
HA17 Pavel Mintyukov 8.00 20.00
HA18 William Dufour 4.00 10.00
HA19 Matt Murray 5.00 12.00
HA20 Adam Ginning 5.00 12.00
HA21 Stanislav Svozil 4.00 10.00
HA22 Michael Kesselring 5.00 12.00
HA23 Jiri Patera 8.00 20.00
HA25 Walker Duehr 4.00 10.00
HA26 Samuel Bolduc 5.00 12.00
HA27 Aidan McDonough 4.00 10.00
HA29 Matthew Kessel 4.00 10.00
HA31 Wyatt Kaiser 5.00 12.00
HA32 Leevi Merilainen 5.00 12.00
HA33 Jonathan Gruden 5.00 12.00
HA35 Tye Kartye 8.00 20.00
HA36 Will Cuylle 8.00 20.00
HA37 Vincent Desharnais SP 6.00 15.00
HA38 Luke Evangelista SP 8.00 20.00
HA39 Matthew Coronato 8.00 20.00
HA41 Henry Thrun 5.00 12.00
HA44 Luke Hughes SP 30.00 80.00
HA45 Tyson Foerster 10.00 25.00
HA46 Yaroslav Askarov SP 20.00 50.00
HA47 Matthew Knies 40.00 100.00
HA48 Simon Edvinsson SP 10.00 25.00
HA49 Devon Levi SP 30.00 80.00
HA50 Zach Benson 8.00 20.00

2023-24 Upper Deck Credentials Live Tonight

LT1 Connor McDavid 40.00 100.00
LT2 David Pastrnak 25.00 60.00
LT3 Adam Fantilli 30.00 80.00
LT4 Elias Pettersson 15.00 40.00
LT5 Mark Stone 12.00 30.00
LT6 Trevor Zegras 10.00 25.00
LT7 Sidney Crosby 40.00 100.00
LT8 Cale Makar 25.00 60.00
LT9 Mario Lemieux 40.00 100.00
LT10 Jason Robertson 15.00 40.00
LT11 Kirill Kaprizov 30.00 80.00
LT12 Matthew Tkachuk 20.00 50.00
LT13 Alex Ovechkin 40.00 100.00
LT14 Jack Hughes 25.00 60.00
LT15 Tim Stutzle 12.00 30.00
LT16 Logan Cooley 30.00 80.00
LT17 Auston Matthews 40.00 100.00
LT18 Connor Bedard 250.00 600.00
LT19 Cole Caufield 20.00 50.00
LT20 Wayne Gretzky 50.00 125.00

2023-24 Upper Deck Credentials Main Stage Signatures

MSAK Andrei Kuzmenko SP 8.00 20.00
MSAT Alex Tuch 8.00 20.00
MSAV Andrei Vasilevskiy SP 12.00 30.00
MSBH Bo Horvat SP 10.00 25.00
MSBO Matt Boldy SP 12.00 30.00
MSBR Bryan Rust 8.00 20.00
MSBU Michael Bunting 8.00 20.00
MSDV Dan Vladar SP 6.00 15.00
MSEB Evan Bouchard 10.00 25.00
MSGV Gabe Vilardi 8.00 20.00
MSJE Jack Eichel SP 12.00 30.00
MSJM Josh Morrissey SP 10.00 25.00
MSJN Jake Neighbours 8.00 20.00
MSJR Jason Robertson SP 12.00 30.00
MSJS Juraj Slafkovsky SP 15.00 40.00
MSJV James van Riemsdyk 6.00 15.00
MSKJ Kent Johnson 8.00 20.00
MSKM K'Andre Miller 6.00 15.00
MSLR Lukas Reichel 8.00 20.00
MSMA Cale Makar SP 20.00 50.00
MSMB Matty Beniers SP 10.00 25.00
MSMC Jared McCann 6.00 15.00
MSMF Morgan Frost 6.00 15.00
MSMS Mark Stone SP 10.00 25.00
MSNH Nico Hischier 12.00 30.00
MSPZ Pavel Zacha SP 6.00 15.00
MSRC Ross Colton 6.00 15.00
MSRO Ryan O'Reilly SP 8.00 20.00
MSSP Shane Pinto 6.00 15.00
MSTH Tomas Hertl 8.00 20.00
MSTS Tim Stutzle SP 10.00 25.00
MSTT Tyler Toffoli SP 8.00 20.00
MSTW Tom Wilson SP 8.00 20.00
MSWJ Wyatt Johnston SP 15.00 40.00
MSYS Yegor Sharangovich 8.00 20.00

2023-24 Upper Deck Credentials Main Stage Signatures Gold

*GOLD: .6X TO 1.5X BASIC
MSMS Mark Stone/25 40.00 100.00

2023-24 Upper Deck Credentials Pro Vision

1 Connor Bedard 150.00 400.00
2 Jason Robertson 12.00 30.00
3 David Pastrnak 20.00 50.00
4 Jack Eichel 12.00 30.00
5 Yaroslav Askarov 20.00 50.00
6 Luke Hughes 25.00 60.00
7 Elias Pettersson 12.00 30.00
8 Tim Stutzle 10.00 25.00
9 Sebastian Aho 12.00 30.00
10 Igor Shesterkin 15.00 40.00

2023-24 Upper Deck Credentials Rad Pads

RP1 Ilya Sorokin 8.00 20.00
RP2 Connor Hellebuyck 10.00 25.00
RP3 Linus Ullmark 5.00 12.00
RP4 Marc-Andre Fleury 12.00 30.00
RP5 Andrei Vasilevskiy 8.00 20.00
RP6 Tristan Jarry 5.00 12.00
RP7 Sergei Bobrovsky 8.00 20.00
RP8 Darcy Kuemper 5.00 12.00
RP9 Logan Thompson 6.00 15.00
RP10 Jake Allen 5.00 12.00
RP11 Stuart Skinner 10.00 25.00
RP12 Jacob Markstrom 5.00 12.00
RP13 Frederik Andersen 6.00 15.00
RP14 Thatcher Demko 6.00 15.00
RP15 Igor Shesterkin 10.00 25.00

2023-24 Upper Deck Credentials Retro Ticket Access Autographs

RTAAAM Auston Matthews 150.00 400.00
RTAACM Connor McDavid 200.00 500.00

2023-24 Upper Deck Credentials Speed of the Game Rookies

SGR1 Connor Bedard 6.00 15.00
SGR2 Logan Cooley 3.00 8.00
SGR3 Adam Fantilli 3.00 8.00
SGR4 Stanislav Svozil .75 2.00
SGR5 Zach Benson 1.50 4.00
SGR6 Matthew Coronato 1.50 4.00
SGR7 Jakob Pelletier 1.25 3.00
SGR8 Kevin Korchinski 1.50 4.00
SGR9 Marco Kasper 2.50 6.00
SGR10 Simon Edvinsson 2.00 5.00
SGR11 Brock Faber 2.50 6.00
SGR12 Owen Beck 1.50 4.00
SGR13 Fraser Minten 2.00 5.00
SGR14 Simon Nemec 2.00 5.00
SGR15 Luke Hughes 3.00 8.00
SGR16 Luke Evangelista 1.50 4.00
SGR17 Pavel Mintyukov 1.50 4.00
SGR18 Will Cuylle 1.50 4.00
SGR19 Ridly Greig 1.50 4.00
SGR20 Tyson Foerster 2.00 5.00
SGR21 Leo Carlsson 3.00 8.00
SGR22 Tye Kartye 1.50 4.00
SGR23 Matthew Knies 4.00 10.00

SGR24 Matthew Poitras 2.00 5.00
SGR25 Aidan McDonough .75 2.00

2023-24 Upper Deck Credentials Speed of the Game Stars

SG1 Connor McDavid 5.00 12.00
SG2 Cale Makar 2.50 6.00
SG3 Leon Draisaitl 3.00 8.00
SG4 Tim Stutzle 1.25 3.00
SG5 Dylan Cozens 1.00 2.50
SG6 Alexis Lafreniere 1.50 4.00
SG7 Auston Matthews 4.00 10.00
SG8 Nick Suzuki 2.00 5.00
SG9 Elias Pettersson 1.50 4.00
SG10 Clayton Keller 1.25 3.00
SG11 Pierre-Luc Dubois .75 2.00
SG12 Jonathan Marchessault 1.25 3.00
SG13 Jason Robertson 1.50 4.00
SG14 Alex DeBrincat 1.25 3.00
SG15 Jordan Kyrou 1.00 2.50
SG16 Brayden Point 1.25 3.00
SG17 Kyle Connor 1.50 4.00
SG18 Morgan Frost .75 2.00
SG19 Matthew Tkachuk 2.00 5.00
SG20 Sebastian Aho 1.50 4.00
SG21 Shane Wright 1.25 3.00
SG22 Tage Thompson 1.25 3.00
SG23 Jack Hughes 2.50 6.00
SG24 Roope Hintz 1.25 3.00
SG25 Mitch Marner 1.50 4.00

2023-24 Upper Deck Credentials Ticket Access Acetate

TAAM Auston Matthews 12.00 30.00
TAAO Alex Ovechkin 12.00 30.00
TAAV Andrei Vasilevskiy 5.00 12.00
TABH Bo Horvat 4.00 10.00
TABP Brayden Point 4.00 10.00
TABT Brady Tkachuk 5.00 12.00
TACM Connor McDavid 15.00 40.00
TACV Carter Verhaeghe 3.00 8.00
TADG Dylan Guenther 4.00 10.00
TADM Dawson Mercer 4.00 10.00
TAJD Jamie Drysdale 2.50 6.00
TAJH Jack Hughes 8.00 20.00
TAJM J.T. Miller 4.00 10.00
TAJO Jake Oettinger 5.00 12.00
TAJS Jeremy Swayman 5.00 12.00
TAKC Kyle Connor 5.00 12.00
TAKK Kirill Kaprizov 10.00 25.00
TALD Leon Draisaitl 10.00 25.00
TALR Lukas Reichel 3.00 8.00
TALT Logan Thompson 4.00 10.00
TAMA Jacob Markstrom 3.00 8.00
TAMB Matty Beniers 4.00 10.00
TAMM Mitch Marner 5.00 12.00
TAMO Josh Morrissey 4.00 10.00
TAMR Mikko Rantanen 8.00 20.00
TANS Nick Suzuki 6.00 15.00
TAOP Owen Power 3.00 8.00
TART Robert Thomas 3.00 8.00
TASC Sidney Crosby 12.00 30.00
TASL Juraj Slafkovsky 6.00 15.00

2023-24 Upper Deck Credentials Ticket Access Acetate Autographs

TABT Brady Tkachuk/25 15.00 40.00
TACV Carter Verhaeghe/99 10.00 25.00
TADG Dylan Guenther/99 25.00 60.00
TAJO Jake Oettinger/25 15.00 40.00
TAJS Jeremy Swayman/99 40.00 100.00
TAKC Kyle Connor/25 15.00 40.00
TALT Logan Thompson/99 12.00 30.00
TAMO Josh Morrissey/99 12.00 30.00
TAMR Mikko Rantanen/25 25.00 60.00

2023-24 Upper Deck Credentials Ticket Access Autographs

*YELLOW/25: .6X TO 1.5X BASIC
TAAAD Alex DeBrincat/49 12.00 30.00
TAAHU Jonathan Huberdeau/49 12.00 30.00
TAAMF Marc-Andre Fleury/25 40.00 100.00
TAAMH Miro Heiskanen/99 12.00 30.00
TAARO Ryan O'Reilly/49 10.00 25.00
TAATM Timo Meier/25 10.00 25.00

2023-24 Upper Deck Credentials Who's Best

WBAF Adam Fox 1.00 2.50
WBAM Auston Matthews 3.00 8.00
WBAO Alex Ovechkin 3.00 8.00
WBAV Andrei Vasilevskiy 1.25 3.00
WBBM Brandon Montour 1.00 2.50
WBCH Connor Hellebuyck 1.50 4.00
WBCM Connor McDavid 4.00 10.00
WBEK Erik Karlsson 1.00 2.50
WBEP Elias Pettersson 1.25 3.00
WBIS Ilya Sorokin 1.25 3.00
WBJH Jack Hughes 2.00 5.00
WBJM Jacob Markstrom .75 2.00
WBJM Josh Morrissey 1.00 2.50
WBJO Jake Oettinger 1.25 3.00
WBJR Jason Robertson 1.25 3.00
WBJS Juuse Saros 1.00 2.50
WBLD Leon Draisaitl 2.50 6.00
WBLT Logan Thompson 1.00 2.50
WBLU Linus Ullmark .75 2.00
WBMA Cale Makar 2.00 5.00
WBMC Charlie McAvoy 1.00 2.50
WBMF Marc-Andre Fleury 1.50 4.00
WBMT Matthew Tkachuk 1.50 4.00
WBQH Quinn Hughes 2.00 5.00
WBRD Rasmus Dahlin 1.00 2.50
WBRJ Roman Josi .75 2.00
WBSC Sidney Crosby 3.00 8.00
WBSH Igor Shesterkin 1.50 4.00
WBTT Tage Thompson 1.00 2.50
WBVH Victor Hedman 1.00 2.50

2023-24 Upper Deck Credentials Who's Best Autographs

WBAV Andrei Vasilevskiy/49 30.00 80.00
WBBM Brandon Montour/99 25.00 60.00
WBCH Connor Hellebuyck/49 10.00 25.00
WBIS Ilya Sorokin/49 30.00 80.00
WBJM Jacob Markstrom/49 20.00 50.00
WBJS Juuse Saros/49 25.00 60.00
WBLT Logan Thompson/49 25.00 60.00
WBMF Marc-Andre Fleury/49 40.00 100.00

2023-24 Upper Deck Credentials Who's Next

WNAF Adam Fantilli 3.00 8.00
WNBC Brandt Clarke 1.00 2.50
WNCB Connor Bedard 6.00 15.00
WNCP Cole Perfetti 1.00 2.50
WNDL Devon Levi 2.50 6.00
WNDW Dustin Wolf 3.00 8.00
WNER Samuel Ersson 1.00 2.50
WNFG Filip Gustavsson 1.00 2.50
WNJD Jamie Drysdale .75 2.00
WNJS Jeremy Swayman 1.50 4.00
WNJS Juraj Slafkovsky 2.00 5.00
WNLC Logan Cooley 3.00 8.00
WNLD Lukas Dostal 1.00 2.50
WNLH Luke Hughes 3.00 8.00
WNMB Matty Beniers 1.25 3.00
WNOP Owen Power 1.00 2.50
WNSA Jake Sanderson 1.25 3.00
WNSE Simon Edvinsson 2.00 5.00
WNWJ Wyatt Johnston 2.00 5.00
WNYA Yaroslav Askarov 2.50 6.00

2023-24 Upper Deck Credentials Who's Next Autographs

WNDL Devon Levi/49 25.00 60.00
WNFG Filip Gustavsson/49 10.00 25.00
WNJS Jeremy Swayman/49 15.00 40.00
WNLD Lukas Dostal/49 10.00 25.00
WNOP Owen Power/99 10.00 25.00
WNSE Simon Edvinsson/99 20.00 50.00
WNYA Yaroslav Askarov/49 25.00 60.00

2024-25 Upper Deck Credentials

1 Jeremy Swayman .60 1.50
2 Evan Bouchard .50 1.25
3 Mitch Marner .60 1.50
4 Miro Heiskanen .50 1.25
5 Josh Norris .40 1.00
6 Travis Sanheim .25 .60
7 Brock Faber .50 1.25
8 Alex Ovechkin 1.50 4.00
9 Filip Forsberg .60 1.50
10 Artemi Panarin .75 2.00
11 Adam Fantilli .60 1.50
12 Trevor Moore .25 .60
13 Kent Johnson .40 1.00
14 Jamie Benn .40 1.00
15 Elias Pettersson .60 1.50
16 Aleksander Barkov .60 1.50
17 Mario Ferraro .25 .60
18 Brayden Point .50 1.25
19 Matthew Tkachuk .75 2.00
20 Sebastian Aho .60 1.50
21 Jason Robertson .60 1.50
22 Cole Caufield .75 2.00
23 Lucas Raymond .60 1.50
24 Connor Hellebuyck .75 2.00
25 Zach Hyman .60 1.50
26 Rasmus Dahlin .50 1.25
27 John Tavares .60 1.50
28 Mathew Barzal .50 1.25
29 Nathan MacKinnon 1.50 4.00
30 Jack Eichel .60 1.50
31 Igor Shesterkin .75 2.00
32 Brady Tkachuk .60 1.50
33 Bo Horvat .50 1.25
34 Auston Matthews 1.50 4.00
35 Oliver Bjorkstrand .30 .75
36 John Gibson .40 1.00
37 Andrei Svechnikov .50 1.25
38 Andrei Vasilevskiy .60 1.50
39 Frank Vatrano .30 .75
40 Kris Letang .50 1.25
41 Tom Wilson .40 1.00
42 Cale Makar 1.00 2.60
43 Luke Hughes .60 1.50
44 Jared McCann .30 .75
45 Travis Konecny .40 1.00
46 Carter Verhaeghe .40 1.00
47 Leon Draisaitl 1.25 3.00
48 Quinn Hughes 1.00 2.50
49 Kirill Marchenko .50 1.25
50 Tim Stutzle .50 1.25
51 Seth Jarvis .50 1.25
52 William Eklund .50 1.25
53 Simon Nemec .50 1.25
54 Kirill Kaprizov 1.25 3.00
55 Mikko Rantanen 1.00 2.50
56 Wyatt Johnston .75 2.00
57 Matthew Knies .75 2.00
58 Alexis Lafreniere .60 1.50
59 Roman Josi .40 1.00
60 Leo Carlsson .60 1.50
61 Anze Kopitar .60 1.50
62 Juraj Slafkovsky .75 2.00
63 Brad Marchand .75 2.00
64 Trevor Zegras .40 1.00
65 Matty Beniers .50 1.25
66 Josh Morrissey .50 1.25
67 Matt Boldy .60 1.50
68 Nazem Kadri .50 1.25
69 Brock Nelson .40 1.00
70 Mark Stone .50 1.25
71 Dylan Larkin .50 1.25
72 Tage Thompson .50 1.25
73 Adam Fox .50 1.25
74 Jaccob Slavin .30 .75
75 Nick Suzuki .75 2.00
76 Brandon Saad .30 .75
77 Brock Boeser .50 1.25
78 Juuse Saros .50 1.25
79 Jack Quinn .30 .75
80 Nico Hischier .60 1.50
81 Jake Sanderson .50 1.25
82 Robert Thomas .40 1.00
83 Nick Foligno .25 .60
84 Evgeni Malkin .75 2.00
85 Samuel Montembeault .40 1.00
86 Jack Hughes 1.00 2.50
87 Sidney Crosby 1.50 4.00
88 David Pastrnak 1.00 2.50
89 Tomas Hertl .40 1.00
90 Jason Dickinson .25 .60
91 Tyson Foerster .40 1.00
92 John Carlson .40 1.00
93 Alex DeBrincat .50 1.25
94 Anders Lee .30 .75
95 Brandon Tanev .30 .75
96 Andrei Kuzmenko .40 1.00
97 Connor McDavid 2.00 5.00
98 Connor Bedard 1.25 3.00
99 Nikita Kucherov .75 2.00
100 Kyle Connor .60 1.50
101 Albert Johansson RC 1.25 3.00
102 Jett Luchanko RC 2.50 6.00
103 Joel Blomqvist RC 1.50 4.00
104 Maxim Tsyplakov RC 2.00 5.00
105 Oliver Kapanen RC 1.25 3.00
106 Samuel Honzek RC 1.25 3.00
107 Calum Ritchie RC 1.50 4.00
108 Victor Mancini RC 1.25 3.00
109 Nolan Allan RC 1.25 3.00
110 Seamus Casey RC 1.50 4.00
111 Macklin Celebrini RC 12.00 30.00
112 Rutger McGroarty RC 2.50 6.00
113 Will Smith RC 4.00 10.00
114 Conor Geekie RC 2.50 6.00
115 Matvei Michkov RC 10.00 25.00
116 Lukas Cormier RC 1.25 3.00
117 Brad Lambert RC 1.50 4.00
118 Zack Ostapchuk RC 1.25 3.00
119 Shakir Mukhamadullin RC 1.50 4.00
120 Scott Morrow RC 1.50 4.00
121 Brendan Brisson RC 1.50 4.00
122 Zachary Bolduc RC 2.50 6.00
123 Joshua Roy RC 2.00 5.00
124 Josh Doan RC 2.00 5.00
125 Marat Khusnutdinov RC 1.25 3.00
126 Lane Hutson RC 6.00 15.00
127 Cutter Gauthier RC 3.00 8.00
128 Matt Rempe RC 2.50 6.00
129 Frank Nazar RC 4.00 10.00
130 Mavrik Bourque RC 2.50 6.00
131 Jesper Wallstedt RC 3.00 8.00
132 Luca Del Bel Belluz RC 1.25 3.00
133 Zachary L'Heureux RC 1.50 4.00
134 Olen Zellweger RC 2.50 6.00
135 Ethan Del Mastro RC 1.25 3.00
136 Graeme Clarke RC 1.25 3.00
137 Logan Stankoven RC 3.00 8.00
138 Gavin Brindley RC 1.25 3.00
139 Zach Dean RC 1.25 3.00
140 Ivan Fedotov RC 2.50 6.00
141 Liam Ohgren RC 2.50 6.00
142 Logan Mailloux RC 2.00 5.00
143 Yan Kuznetsov RC 1.25 3.00
144 Akil Thomas RC 1.25 3.00
145 Collin Graf RC 1.25 3.00
146 Jason Polin RC 1.25 3.00
147 Sam Colangelo RC 1.25 3.00
148 Justin Brazeau RC 1.25 3.00
149 Brennan Othmann RC 2.00 5.00
150 Bradly Nadeau RC 2.00 5.00

2024-25 Upper Deck Credentials Blue

*BLUE/299: 1X TO 2.5X BASIC
*BLUE RC/399: .5X TO 1.2X BASIC
111 Macklin Celebrini/399 20.00 50.00
115 Matvei Michkov/399 15.00 40.00
126 Lane Hutson/399 15.00 40.00

2024-25 Upper Deck Credentials Green

*GREEN/25: 3X TO 8X BASIC
*GREEN RC/25: 1.5X TO 4X BASIC
111 Macklin Celebrini 100.00 250.00

2024-25 Upper Deck Credentials Horizontal

*HORIZONTAL: .4X TO 1X BASIC

2024-25 Upper Deck Credentials Horizontal Pink

*HOR PINK/25: X TO X BASIC
126 Lane Hutson 60.00 150.00
129 Frank Nazar 30.00 80.00

2024-25 Upper Deck Credentials Horizontal Red

*HOR RED/99: 1X TO 2.5X BASIC

2024-25 Upper Deck Credentials Orange

*ORANGE/199: .6X TO 1.5X BASIC
111 Macklin Celebrini 25.00 60.00
113 Will Smith 8.00 20.00
115 Matvei Michkov 25.00 60.00
126 Lane Hutson 20.00 50.00

2024-25 Upper Deck Credentials Pink

*PINK/99: 1.5X TO 4X BASIC
*PINK RC/50: 1.2X TO 3X BASIC
111 Macklin Celebrini/50 40.00 100.00
113 Will Smith/50 20.00 50.00
115 Matvei Michkov/50 40.00 100.00
126 Lane Hutson/50 40.00 100.00

2024-25 Upper Deck Credentials Arena Experience Autographs

AEAR Arlette Roxburgh 40.00 100.00
AEBR John Brancy 20.00 50.00
AECS Craig Simpson 4.00 10.00
AEDG Dave Goucher 10.00 25.00
AEDP Darren Pang 20.00 50.00
AEEO Eddie Olczyk 8.00 20.00
AEFO John Forslund 12.00 30.00
AEJB Joe Beninati 20.00 50.00
AEJF Jim Fox 8.00 20.00
AEJJ Jim Jackson 15.00 40.00
AEJR Jackie Redmond 60.00 150.00
AEKA Kenny Albert 12.00 30.00
AEKD Ken Daniels 20.00 50.00
AEKW Kevin Weekes 15.00 40.00
AERH Randy Hahn 15.00 40.00
AESG Steve Goldstein 15.00 40.00
AESL Steve Levy 15.00 40.00
AESL Steve Levy ESPN SP 25.00 60.00
AESM Sean McDonough 12.00 30.00
AESM Sean McDonough ESPN SP 15.00 40.00

2024-25 Upper Deck Credentials Arena Giveaways Bobbleheads

*BLUE/25: .6X TO 1.5X BASIC
BHAK Anze Kopitar/750 5.00 12.00
BHAM Auston Matthews/100 12.00 30.00
BHAO Alex Ovechkin/100 12.00 30.00
BHAS Andrei Svechnikov/750 4.00 10.00
BHBM Brad Marchand/250 6.00 15.00
BHCB Connor Bedard/100 10.00 25.00
BHCC Cole Caufield/750 6.00 15.00
BHCM Connor McDavid/100 15.00 40.00
BHDP David Pastrnak/100 8.00 20.00
BHEM Evgeni Malkin/750 6.00 15.00
BHEP Elias Pettersson/250 5.00 12.00
BHJE Jack Eichel/250 5.00 12.00
BHJH Jack Hughes/250 8.00 20.00
BHJR Jason Robertson/750 5.00 12.00
BHKK Kirill Kaprizov/250 10.00 25.00
BHLD Leon Draisaitl/100 10.00 25.00
BHLR Lucas Raymond/750 5.00 12.00
BHLS Logan Stankoven/750 8.00 20.00
BHMA Cale Makar/100 8.00 20.00
BHMB Mathew Barzal/750 4.00 10.00
BHMC Mason McTavish/750 3.00 8.00
BHMM Mitch Marner/750 5.00 12.00
BHMT Matthew Tkachuk/750 6.00 15.00
BHNK Nikita Kucherov/250 6.00 15.00
BHNM Nathan MacKinnon/100 12.00 30.00
BHNS Nick Suzuki/750 6.00 15.00
BHPK Patrick Kane/250 6.00 15.00
BHQB Quinton Byfield/750 4.00 10.00
BHQH Quinn Hughes/250 8.00 20.00
BHRD Rasmus Dahlin/750 4.00 10.00
BHSA Sebastian Aho/750 5.00 12.00
BHSC Sidney Crosby/100 12.00 30.00
BHSS Steven Stamkos/250 6.00 15.00
BHTS Tim Stutzle/750 4.00 10.00
BHWN William Nylander/750 6.00 15.00

2024-25 Upper Deck Credentials Arena Giveaways Championship Rings

*BLUE/25: .6X TO 1.5X BASIC
CRBB Boston Bruins 8.00 20.00
CRCA Colorado Avalanche 8.00 20.00
CRCB Chicago Blackhawks 8.00 20.00
CRFP Florida Panthers 8.00 20.00
CRLK Los Angeles Kings 8.00 20.00
CRPP Pittsburgh Penguins 8.00 20.00
CRSB St. Louis Blues 8.00 20.00
CRTL Tampa Bay Lightning 8.00 20.00
CRVG Vegas Golden Knights 8.00 20.00
CRWC Washington Capitals 8.00 20.00

2024-25 Upper Deck Credentials Arena Giveaways Hawai'ian Print Shirts

*BLUE/25: .6X TO 1.5X BASIC
HSAL Alexis Lafreniere 6.00 15.00
HSAM Auston Matthews 15.00 40.00
HSCB Connor Bedard 12.00 30.00
HSCC Cole Caufield 8.00 20.00
HSCM Connor McDavid 20.00 50.00
HSDP David Pastrnak 10.00 25.00
HSMT Matthew Tkachuk 8.00 20.00
HSPK Patrick Kane 8.00 20.00
HSQH Quinn Hughes 10.00 25.00
HSSC Sidney Crosby 15.00 40.00

2024-25 Upper Deck Credentials Arena Giveaways Jerseys

*BLUE/25: .6X TO 1.5X BASIC
JAF Adam Fantilli 3.00 8.00
JAM Auston Matthews 8.00 20.00
JAO Alex Ovechkin 8.00 20.00
JAP Artemi Panarin 4.00 10.00
JAV Andrei Vasilevskiy 3.00 8.00
JBH Bo Horvat 2.50 6.00
JBT Brady Tkachuk 3.00 8.00
JCB Connor Bedard 6.00 15.00
JCC Cole Caufield 4.00 10.00
JCG Cutter Gauthier 5.00 12.00
JCM Connor McDavid 10.00 25.00
JDP David Pastrnak 5.00 12.00
JEM Evgeni Malkin 4.00 10.00
JJE Jack Eichel 3.00 8.00
JJH Jack Hughes 5.00 12.00
JJR Jason Robertson 3.00 8.00
JJS Juraj Slafkovsky 4.00 10.00
JKA Nazem Kadri 2.50 6.00
JKK Kirill Kaprizov 6.00 15.00
JLC Leo Carlsson 3.00 8.00
JLD Leon Draisaitl 6.00 15.00
JLR Lucas Raymond 3.00 8.00
JMA Cale Makar 5.00 12.00
JMC Macklin Celebrini 10.00 25.00
JMT Matthew Tkachuk 4.00 10.00
JNK Nikita Kucherov 4.00 10.00
JNM Nathan MacKinnon 8.00 20.00
JQH Quinn Hughes 5.00 12.00
JRJ Roman Josi 2.00 5.00
JRT Robert Thomas 2.00 5.00
JSA Sebastian Aho 3.00 8.00
JSC Sidney Crosby 8.00 20.00
JSW Jeremy Swayman 3.00 8.00
JTK Travis Konecny 2.00 5.00
JWJ Wyatt Johnston 4.00 10.00

2024-25 Upper Deck Credentials Arena Giveaways Repetitive Head Shirts

RHAO Alex Ovechkin 10.00 25.00
RHAP Artemi Panarin 5.00 12.00
RHCC Cole Caufield 5.00 12.00
RHCM Connor McDavid 12.00 30.00
RHDP David Pastrnak 6.00 15.00
RHJH Jack Hughes 6.00 15.00
RHMA Cale Makar 6.00 15.00
RHMT Matthew Tkachuk 5.00 12.00
RHNM Nathan MacKinnon 10.00 25.00
RHSC Sidney Crosby 10.00 25.00

2024-25 Upper Deck Credentials Autographs

*HRZNTL/99: .5X TO 1.2X BASIC
4 Miro Heiskanen 10.00 25.00
6 Travis Sanheim 5.00 12.00
10 Artemi Panarin SP 15.00 40.00
11 Adam Fantilli 12.00 30.00
12 Trevor Moore 5.00 12.00
15 Elias Pettersson SP 12.00 30.00
16 Aleksander Barkov 12.00 30.00
24 Connor Hellebuyck 15.00 40.00
27 John Tavares 12.00 30.00
31 Igor Shesterkin 15.00 40.00
32 Brady Tkachuk 12.00 30.00
36 John Gibson 8.00 20.00
37 Andrei Svechnikov 10.00 25.00
38 Andrei Vasilevskiy 12.00 30.00
39 Frank Vatrano 6.00 15.00
41 Tom Wilson 8.00 20.00
43 Luke Hughes 12.00 30.00
44 Jared McCann 6.00 15.00
51 Seth Jarvis 10.00 25.00
52 William Eklund 10.00 25.00
53 Simon Nemec 10.00 25.00
56 Wyatt Johnston 15.00 40.00
63 Brad Marchand 15.00 40.00
66 Josh Morrissey 10.00 25.00
74 Jaccob Slavin 6.00 15.00
75 Nick Suzuki SP 15.00 40.00
76 Brandon Saad 6.00 15.00
78 Juuse Saros 10.00 25.00
80 Nico Hischier 12.00 30.00
81 Jake Sanderson 10.00 25.00
83 Nick Foligno 5.00 12.00
90 Jason Dickinson 5.00 12.00
91 Tyson Foerster 8.00 20.00
94 Anders Lee 6.00 15.00
95 Brandon Tanev 6.00 15.00
96 Andrei Kuzmenko 8.00 20.00
98 Connor Bedard SP 125.00 300.00
99 Nikita Kucherov SP 15.00 40.00
100 Kyle Connor 12.00 30.00
107 Calum Ritchie/199 10.00 25.00
111 Macklin Celebrini/99 250.00 600.00
112 Rutger McGroarty/99 15.00 40.00
113 Will Smith/99 80.00 200.00
115 Matvei Michkov/99 150.00 400.00
119 Shakir Mukhamadullin/199 10.00 25.00
121 Brendan Brisson/199 10.00 25.00
126 Lane Hutson/199 100.00 250.00
127 Cutter Gauthier/99 30.00 80.00
128 Matt Rempe/199 15.00 40.00
129 Frank Nazar/99 40.00 100.00
130 Mavrik Bourque/199 15.00 40.00
134 Olen Zellweger/199 15.00 40.00
136 Graeme Clarke/199 8.00 20.00
137 Logan Stankoven/99 30.00 80.00
139 Zach Dean/199 8.00 20.00
141 Liam Ohgren/99 15.00 40.00
145 Collin Graf/199 8.00 20.00
146 Jason Polin/199 8.00 20.00
147 Sam Colangelo/199 8.00 20.00
149 Brennan Othmann/199 12.00 30.00
150 Bradly Nadeau/199 12.00 30.00

2024-25 Upper Deck Credentials Autographs Green

*GREEN/25: .8X TO 2X BASIC
126 Lane Hutson 250.00 600.00

2024-25 Upper Deck Credentials Cheered to the Rafters

*RED/149: .6X TO 1.5X BASIC
*GREEN/49: 1.5X TO 4X BASIC
CRAL Alexis Lafreniere 1.00 2.50
CRAV Andrei Vasilevskiy 1.00 2.50
CRCB Connor Bedard 2.00 5.00
CRCH Connor Hellebuyck 1.25 3.00
CRDL Dylan Larkin .75 2.00
CRJE Jack Eichel 1.00 2.50
CRJS Jared Spurgeon .60 1.50
CRJT John Tavares 1.00 2.50
CRKC Kyle Connor 1.00 2.50
CRMH Miro Heiskanen .75 2.00
CRMR Mikko Rantanen 1.50 4.00
CRMT Matthew Tkachuk 1.25 3.00
CRNS Nick Suzuki 1.25 3.00
CRSA Juuse Saros .75 2.00
CRWJ Wyatt Johnston 1.25 3.00

2024-25 Upper Deck Credentials Cheered to the Rafters Autographs

CRAL Alexis Lafreniere 10.00 25.00
CRAV Andrei Vasilevskiy 10.00 25.00
CRCH Connor Hellebuyck 12.00 30.00
CRJS Jared Spurgeon 6.00 15.00
CRJT John Tavares SP 10.00 25.00
CRKC Kyle Connor 10.00 25.00
CRMH Miro Heiskanen 8.00 20.00
CRMR Mikko Rantanen SP 15.00 40.00
CRSA Juuse Saros 8.00 20.00
CRWJ Wyatt Johnston 12.00 30.00

2024-25 Upper Deck Credentials Debut Ticket Access Acetate

DTAAAT Akil Thomas 4.00 10.00
DTAABB Brendan Brisson 5.00 12.00
DTAABL Brad Lambert 5.00 12.00
DTAABN Bradly Nadeau 6.00 15.00
DTAABO Brennan Othmann 6.00 15.00
DTAABR Justin Brazeau 4.00 10.00
DTAACA Seamus Casey 5.00 12.00
DTAACG Cutter Gauthier 10.00 25.00
DTAACR Calum Ritchie 5.00 12.00
DTAADM Denton Mateychuk 8.00 20.00
DTAAED Ethan Del Mastro 4.00 10.00
DTAAFN Frank Nazar 12.00 30.00
DTAAGB Gavin Brindley 4.00 10.00
DTAAGC Graeme Clarke 4.00 10.00
DTAAGE Conor Geekie 8.00 20.00
DTAAGR Collin Graf 4.00 10.00
DTAAIF Ivan Fedotov 8.00 20.00
DTAAJB Joel Blomqvist 5.00 12.00
DTAAJD Josh Doan 6.00 15.00
DTAAJL Jett Luchanko 8.00 20.00
DTAAJP Jason Polin 4.00 10.00
DTAAJR Joshua Roy 6.00 15.00
DTAAJW Jesper Wallstedt 10.00 25.00
DTAALC Lukas Cormier 4.00 10.00
DTAALD Luca Del Bel Belluz 4.00 10.00
DTAALH Lane Hutson 40.00 100.00
DTAALM Logan Mailloux 6.00 15.00
DTAALO Liam Ohgren 8.00 20.00
DTAALS Logan Stankoven 10.00 25.00
DTAAMB Mavrik Bourque 8.00 20.00
DTAAMC Macklin Celebrini 40.00 100.00
DTAAMK Marat Khusnutdinov 4.00 10.00
DTAAMM Matvei Michkov 15.00 40.00
DTAAMO Scott Morrow 5.00 12.00
DTAAMR Matt Rempe 8.00 20.00
DTAAMT Maxim Tsyplakov 6.00 15.00
DTAANA Nolan Allan 4.00 10.00
DTAAOK Oliver Kapanen 4.00 10.00
DTAAOZ Olen Zellweger 8.00 20.00
DTAARM Rutger McGroarty 8.00 20.00
DTAASC Sam Colangelo 4.00 10.00
DTAASH Samuel Honzek 4.00 10.00
DTAASL Landon Slaggert 4.00 10.00
DTAASM Shakir Mukhamadullin 5.00 12.00
DTAAWS Will Smith 12.00 30.00
DTAAYK Yan Kuznetsov 4.00 10.00
DTAAZB Zachary Bolduc 8.00 20.00
DTAAZD Zach Dean 4.00 10.00
DTAAZO Zack Ostapchuk 4.00 10.00

2024-25 Upper Deck Credentials Debut Ticket Access Acetate Autographs

DTAABB Brendan Brisson 12.00 30.00
DTAABN Bradly Nadeau 15.00 40.00
DTAABO Brennan Othmann 15.00 40.00
DTAABR Justin Brazeau 10.00 25.00
DTAACG Cutter Gauthier 25.00 60.00
DTAACR Calum Ritchie 12.00 30.00
DTAADM Denton Mateychuk 20.00 50.00
DTAAFN Frank Nazar 40.00 100.00
DTAAGC Graeme Clarke 10.00 25.00
DTAAGE Conor Geekie 20.00 50.00
DTAAGR Collin Graf 10.00 25.00
DTAAJB Joel Blomqvist 12.00 30.00
DTAAJP Jason Polin 10.00 25.00
DTAALH Lane Hutson 150.00 400.00
DTAALM Logan Mailloux 15.00 40.00
DTAALO Liam Ohgren 20.00 50.00
DTAALS Logan Stankoven 25.00 60.00
DTAAMB Mavrik Bourque 20.00 50.00
DTAAMC Macklin Celebrini 200.00 500.00
DTAAMM Matvei Michkov 125.00 300.00
DTAAMR Matt Rempe 20.00 50.00
DTAANA Nolan Allan 10.00 25.00
DTAAOZ Olen Zellweger 20.00 50.00
DTAARM Rutger McGroarty 20.00 50.00
DTAASC Sam Colangelo 10.00 25.00
DTAASM Shakir Mukhamadullin 12.00 30.00
DTAAWS Will Smith 80.00 200.00
DTAAYK Yan Kuznetsov 10.00 25.00
DTAAZD Zach Dean 10.00 25.00
DTAAZO Zack Ostapchuk 10.00 25.00

2024-25 Upper Deck Credentials Fleer Pro Visions

1 Brad Marchand 30.00 80.00
2 Logan Stankoven 40.00 100.00
3 William Nylander 30.00 80.00
4 Aleksander Barkov 25.00 60.00
5 Patrick Kane 30.00 80.00
6 Evgeni Malkin 30.00 80.00
7 Evan Bouchard 20.00 50.00
8 Anze Kopitar 25.00 60.00
9 Quinn Hughes 40.00 100.00

2024-25 Upper Deck Credentials Fleer Pro Visions Legends

PV1 Dominik Hasek 30.00 80.00
PV2 Curtis Joseph 25.00 60.00
PV3 Al MacInnis 25.00 60.00
PV4 Martin Brodeur 50.00 125.00
PV5 Trevor Linden 20.00 50.00
PV6 Ron Hextall 20.00 50.00

2024-25 Upper Deck Credentials Front Row Talent

*RED/149: .8X TO 2X BASIC
*GREEN/49: 2X TO 5X BASIC
FRTAB Aleksander Barkov .75 2.00
FRTAD Alex DeBrincat .60 1.50
FRTAK Anze Kopitar .75 2.00
FRTAM Auston Matthews 2.00 5.00
FRTAO Alex Ovechkin 2.00 5.00
FRTAP Artemi Panarin 1.00 2.50
FRTBB Brent Burns .50 1.25
FRTBH Bo Horvat .60 1.50
FRTBO Brock Boeser .60 1.50
FRTCM Connor McDavid 2.50 6.00
FRTJF Justin Faulk .40 1.00
FRTJS Jeremy Swayman .75 2.00
FRTKJ Kent Johnson .50 1.25
FRTKL Kris Letang .60 1.50
FRTLD Leon Draisaitl 1.50 4.00
FRTMA Cale Makar 1.25 3.00
FRTMM Mitch Marner .75 2.00
FRTMS Mark Stone .60 1.50
FRTMW MacKenzie Weegar .30 .75
FRTMZ Mika Zibanejad .60 1.50
FRTNM Nathan MacKinnon 2.00 5.00
FRTRJ Roman Josi .50 1.25
FRTSC Sidney Crosby 2.00 5.00
FRTSS Steven Stamkos 1.00 2.50
FRTTH Tomas Hertl .50 1.25
FRTTK Travis Konecny .50 1.25
FRTTS Tyler Seguin .60 1.50
FRTTT Troy Terry .40 1.00
FRTVH Victor Hedman .60 1.50
FRTZH Zach Hyman .75 2.00

2024-25 Upper Deck Credentials Front Row Talent Autographs

FRTAB Aleksander Barkov 12.00 30.00
FRTAD Alex DeBrincat 10.00 25.00
FRTAK Anze Kopitar 12.00 30.00
FRTBB Brent Burns 8.00 20.00
FRTBH Bo Horvat SP 10.00 25.00
FRTBO Brock Boeser 10.00 25.00
FRTJF Justin Faulk 6.00 15.00
FRTJS Jeremy Swayman 12.00 30.00
FRTKJ Kent Johnson 8.00 20.00
FRTKL Kris Letang 10.00 25.00
FRTMW MacKenzie Weegar 5.00 12.00
FRTRJ Roman Josi 8.00 20.00
FRTTK Travis Konecny 8.00 20.00
FRTTS Tyler Seguin SP 10.00 25.00
FRTTT Troy Terry 6.00 15.00

2024-25 Upper Deck Credentials Frozen Fight

*RED/149: .8X TO 2X BASIC
FFBM C.Bedard/A.Matthews 3.00 8.00
FFBN J.Benn/W.Nylander 1.50 4.00
FFER J.Eichel/M.Rossi 1.25 3.00
FFFZ A.Fantilli/M.Zibanejad 1.25 3.00
FFHT J.Hughes/B.Tkachuk 2.00 5.00
FFJM W.Johnston/N.MacKinnon 3.00 8.00
FFKD A.Kopitar/L.Draisaitl 2.50 6.00
FFSF N.Suzuki/M.Frost 1.50 4.00
FFSP M.Scheifele/E.Pettersson 1.25 3.00
FFTM T.Thompson/J.Miller 1.00 2.50

2024-25 Upper Deck Credentials Frozen Fight Autographs

FFHT J.Hughes/B.Tkachuk 40.00 100.00
FFKD A.Kopitar/L.Draisaitl 50.00 125.00
FFSP M.Scheifele/E.Pettersson 25.00 60.00

2024-25 Upper Deck Credentials Jumping on the Ice

*RED/149: 1.2X TO 3X BASIC
*GREEN/49: 2X TO 5X BASIC
JIAF Adam Fantilli .75 2.00
JIBF Brock Faber .60 1.50
JIBM Bobby McMann .40 1.00
JICB Connor Bedard 1.50 4.00
JICG Cutter Gauthier 1.25 3.00
JICZ Connor Zary .50 1.25
JIFN Frank Nazar 1.50 4.00
JILC Leo Carlsson .75 2.00
JILE Luke Evangelista .40 1.00
JILH Luke Hughes .75 2.00
JILO Liam Ohgren 1.00 2.50
JILS Logan Stankoven 1.25 3.00
JIMC Macklin Celebrini 2.50 6.00
JIMK Matthew Knies 1.00 2.50
JIMM Matvei Michkov 2.00 5.00
JIPM Pavel Mintyukov .40 1.00
JISN Simon Nemec .60 1.50
JITF Tyson Foerster .50 1.25
JIWS Will Smith 1.50 4.00
JIZB Zach Benson .40 1.00

2024-25 Upper Deck Credentials Jumping on the Ice Autographs

JIBF Brock Faber 8.00 20.00
JIBM Bobby McMann 5.00 12.00
JICG Cutter Gauthier 20.00 50.00
JICZ Connor Zary 6.00 15.00
JIFN Frank Nazar 20.00 50.00
JILC Leo Carlsson 10.00 25.00
JILE Luke Evangelista 5.00 12.00
JILO Liam Ohgren 12.00 30.00
JILS Logan Stankoven 15.00 40.00
JIMC Macklin Celebrini SP 200.00 500.00
JIMK Matthew Knies 20.00 50.00
JIMM Matvei Michkov SP 80.00 200.00
JIPM Pavel Mintyukov 5.00 12.00
JISN Simon Nemec 8.00 20.00
JITF Tyson Foerster 6.00 15.00
JIWS Will Smith 50.00 125.00
JIZB Zach Benson 5.00 12.00

2024-25 Upper Deck Credentials Milestone Pucks

*RED/149: 1X TO 2.5X BASIC
*GREEN/49: 1.5X TO 4X BASIC
MPAO Alex Ovechkin 2.50 6.00
MPBF Brock Faber .75 2.00
MPBM Brad Marchand 1.25 3.00
MPCB Connor Bedard 2.00 5.00
MPCM Connor McDavid 3.00 8.00
MPJE Jack Eichel 1.00 2.50
MPLC Leo Carlsson 1.00 2.50
MPNM Nathan MacKinnon 2.50 6.00
MPTM Timo Meier .60 1.50
MPWE William Eklund .75 2.00

2024-25 Upper Deck Credentials Milestone Pucks Autographs

MPBF Brock Faber 20.00 50.00
MPLC Leo Carlsson 25.00 60.00
MPTM Timo Meier 15.00 40.00
MPWE William Eklund 20.00 50.00

2024-25 Upper Deck Credentials Retro Ticket Access Acetate

RTAO Alex Ovechkin 8.00 20.00
RTAP Artemi Panarin 4.00 10.00
RTBM Brad Marchand 4.00 10.00
RTCB Connor Bedard 6.00 15.00
RTKK Kirill Kaprizov 6.00 15.00
RTMA Auston Matthews 8.00 20.00
RTMD Connor McDavid 10.00 25.00
RTNM Nathan MacKinnon 8.00 20.00
RTSC Sidney Crosby 8.00 20.00
RTTT Tage Thompson 2.50 6.00

2024-25 Upper Deck Credentials Retro Ticket Access Acetate Autographs

RTBM Brad Marchand/25 30.00 80.00

2024-25 Upper Deck Credentials Retro Ticket Access Acetate Rookies

RTRCG Cutter Gauthier 5.00 12.00
RTRFN Frank Nazar 6.00 15.00
RTRGE Conor Geekie 4.00 10.00
RTRLH Lane Hutson 10.00 25.00
RTRLO Liam Ohgren 4.00 10.00
RTRLS Logan Stankoven 5.00 12.00
RTRMM Matvei Michkov 30.00 80.00
RTRRM Rutger McGroarty 4.00 10.00
RTRWS Will Smith 8.00 20.00

2024-25 Upper Deck Credentials Retro Ticket Access Autographs

RTAAB Aleksander Barkov 10.00 25.00
RTADG Dylan Guenther 8.00 20.00
RTAJB Jordan Binnington 10.00 25.00
RTAJD Jamie Drysdale 5.00 12.00
RTAJM Jared McCann 5.00 12.00
RTAJS Juuse Saros 8.00 20.00
RTAKC Kyle Connor 10.00 25.00
RTALC Logan Cooley 10.00 25.00
RTAMF Marc-Andre Fleury 12.00 30.00
RTAMM Mason McTavish 6.00 15.00
RTANK Nikita Kucherov 12.00 30.00
RTANS Nick Suzuki 12.00 30.00
RTASJ Seth Jarvis 8.00 20.00
RTAST Shea Theodore 8.00 20.00
RTATH Thomas Harley 6.00 15.00

RTATM Timo Meier 6.00 15.00
RTAWJ Wyatt Johnston 12.00 30.00

2024-25 Upper Deck Credentials Retro Ticket Access Rookie Autographs

RTARAB Arshdeep Bains 6.00 15.00
RTARAJ Albert Johansson 5.00 12.00
RTARAK Adam Klapka 5.00 12.00
RTARBB Brendan Brisson 6.00 15.00
RTARBN Bradly Nadeau 8.00 20.00
RTARBO Brennan Othmann 8.00 20.00
RTARBR Justin Brazeau 5.00 12.00
RTARCG Cutter Gauthier 20.00 50.00
RTARCR Calum Ritchie 6.00 15.00
RTARDC Declan Carlile 5.00 12.00
RTAREL Emil Lilleberg 5.00 12.00
RTARGC Graeme Clarke 5.00 12.00
RTARGE Conor Geekie 10.00 25.00
RTARGG Gage Goncalves 6.00 15.00
RTARJT Jack Thompson 5.00 12.00
RTARJW Jesper Wallstedt 12.00 30.00
RTARKM Kyle MacLean 5.00 12.00
RTARLH Lane Hutson 125.00 300.00
RTARLM Logan Mailloux 8.00 20.00
RTARLO Liam Ohgren 10.00 25.00
RTARMB Mavrik Bourque 10.00 25.00
RTARMR Matt Rempe 10.00 25.00
RTARMT Maxim Tsyplakov 8.00 20.00
RTARMU Shakir Mukhamadullin 6.00 15.00
RTARNA Nolan Allan 5.00 12.00
RTAROZ Olen Zellweger 10.00 25.00
RTARPK Phil Kemp 5.00 12.00
RTARRM Rutger McGroarty 12.00 30.00
RTARSC Sam Colangelo 5.00 12.00
RTARSH Samuel Honzek 5.00 12.00
RTARST Logan Stankoven 12.00 30.00
RTARYK Yan Kuznetsov 5.00 12.00
RTARZO Zack Ostapchuk 5.00 12.00

2024-25 Upper Deck Credentials Speed of the Game Rookies

SGRBB Brendan Brisson 1.25 3.00
SGRBN Bradly Nadeau 1.50 4.00
SGRBO Brennan Othmann 1.50 4.00
SGRCG Cutter Gauthier 2.50 6.00
SGRFN Frank Nazar 3.00 8.00
SGRGE Conor Geekie 2.00 5.00
SGRJD Josh Doan 1.50 4.00
SGRJL Jett Luchanko 2.00 5.00
SGRJW Jesper Wallstedt 2.50 6.00
SGRLH Lane Hutson 5.00 12.00
SGRLM Logan Mailloux 1.50 4.00
SGRLO Liam Ohgren 2.00 5.00
SGRLS Logan Stankoven 2.50 6.00
SGRMB Mavrik Bourque 2.00 5.00
SGRMC Macklin Celebrini 5.00 12.00
SGRMM Matvei Michkov 4.00 10.00
SGRMR Matt Rempe 2.00 5.00
SGROZ Olen Zellweger 2.00 5.00
SGRRM Rutger McGroarty 2.00 5.00
SGRSC Seamus Casey 1.25 3.00
SGRSH Samuel Honzek 1.00 2.50
SGRSM Shakir Mukhamadullin 1.25 3.00
SGRWS Will Smith 3.00 8.00
SGRZB Zachary Bolduc 2.00 5.00
SGRZD Zach Dean 1.00 2.50

2024-25 Upper Deck Credentials Speed of the Game Stars

SGAK Anze Kopitar 2.00 5.00
SGAM Auston Matthews 5.00 12.00
SGAO Alex Ovechkin 5.00 12.00
SGAP Artemi Panarin 2.50 6.00
SGBM Brad Marchand 2.50 6.00
SGBP Brayden Point 1.50 4.00
SGCB Connor Bedard 4.00 10.00
SGCC Cole Caufield 2.50 6.00
SGCM Connor McDavid 6.00 15.00
SGJE Jack Eichel 2.00 5.00
SGJH Jack Hughes 3.00 8.00
SGJR Jason Robertson 2.00 5.00
SGKK Kirill Kaprizov 4.00 10.00
SGLD Leon Draisaitl 4.00 10.00
SGMA Mitch Marner 2.00 5.00
SGMB Mathew Barzal 1.50 4.00
SGMM Mason McTavish 1.25 3.00
SGMT Matthew Tkachuk 2.50 6.00
SGNK Nikita Kucherov 2.50 6.00
SGNM Nathan MacKinnon 5.00 12.00
SGPK Patrick Kane 2.50 6.00
SGQH Quinn Hughes 3.00 8.00
SGRT Robert Thomas 1.25 3.00
SGSA Sebastian Aho 2.00 5.00
SGSC Sidney Crosby 5.00 12.00

2024-25 Upper Deck Credentials That's a Hatty

*RED/149: .6X TO 1.5X BASIC
*GREEN/49: 1.5X TO 4X BASIC
THAD Alex DeBrincat 1.00 2.50
THAL Alexis Lafreniere 1.25 3.00
THAM Auston Matthews 3.00 8.00
THBN Brock Nelson .75 2.00
THCM Cale Makar 2.00 5.00
THDP David Pastrnak 2.00 5.00
THJR Jason Robertson 1.25 3.00
THKK Kirill Kaprizov 2.50 6.00
THMB Matt Boldy 1.25 3.00
THMN Martin Necas 1.25 3.00
THNK Nikita Kucherov 1.50 4.00
THSA Sebastian Aho 1.25 3.00
THTK Travis Konecny .75 2.00
THTM Trevor Moore .50 1.25
THZH Zach Hyman 1.25 3.00

2024-25 Upper Deck Credentials That's a Hatty Autographs

THAD Alex DeBrincat 8.00 20.00
THAL Alexis Lafreniere 10.00 25.00
THBN Brock Nelson 6.00 15.00
THMB Matt Boldy 10.00 25.00
THMN Martin Necas 10.00 25.00
THNK Nikita Kucherov 12.00 30.00
THSA Sebastian Aho 10.00 25.00
THTK Travis Konecny 6.00 15.00
THTM Trevor Moore 4.00 10.00

2024-25 Upper Deck Credentials Ticket Access Acetate

TAAF Adam Fantilli 4.00 10.00
TAAK Anze Kopitar 4.00 10.00
TAAM Auston Matthews 10.00 25.00
TAAT Alex Tuch 2.50 6.00
TABA Mathew Barzal 3.00 8.00
TABF Brock Faber 3.00 8.00
TABT Brady Tkachuk 4.00 10.00
TACM Cale Makar 6.00 15.00
TADP David Pastrnak 6.00 15.00
TADT Devon Toews 2.00 5.00
TAEB Evan Bouchard 3.00 8.00
TAFF Filip Forsberg 4.00 10.00
TAGI John Gibson 2.50 6.00
TAIS Igor Shesterkin 5.00 12.00
TAJH Jack Hughes 6.00 15.00
TAJR Jason Robertson 4.00 10.00
TAJS Juraj Slafkovsky 5.00 12.00
TALD Leon Draisaitl 8.00 20.00
TAMB Matt Boldy 4.00 10.00
TAMC Connor McDavid 12.00 30.00
TAMN Martin Necas 4.00 10.00
TAMR Mikko Rantanen 6.00 15.00
TANK Nikita Kucherov 5.00 12.00
TANS Nick Suzuki 5.00 12.00
TAPK Patrick Kane 5.00 12.00
TARH Roope Hintz 3.00 8.00
TASA Sebastian Aho 4.00 10.00
TAVD Vince Dunn 2.00 5.00
TAWE William Eklund 3.00 8.00
TAWN William Nylander 5.00 12.00

2024-25 Upper Deck Credentials Ticket Access Acetate Autographs

TAAF Adam Fantilli/25 30.00 80.00
TAAT Alex Tuch/99 10.00 25.00
TADT Devon Toews/99 8.00 20.00
TAGI John Gibson/99 10.00 25.00
TAMN Martin Necas/99 15.00 40.00
TARH Roope Hintz/99 12.00 30.00
TAVD Vince Dunn/99 8.00 20.00
TAWE William Eklund/99 12.00 30.00

1997-98 Upper Deck Diamond Vision

COMPLETE SET (25) 40.00 100.00
1 Wayne Gretzky 10.00 25.00
2 Patrick Roy 8.00 20.00
3 Jaromir Jagr 3.00 8.00
4 Steve Yzerman 6.00 15.00
5 Martin Brodeur 5.00 12.00
6 Paul Kariya 2.00 5.00
7 John Vanbiesbrouck 1.25 3.00
8 Ray Bourque 2.00 5.00
9 Theo Fleury 1.25 3.00
10 Pavel Bure 1.50 4.00
11 Brendan Shanahan 2.00 5.00
12 Brian Leetch 1.25 3.00
13 Owen Nolan 1.25 3.00
14 Peter Forsberg 3.00 8.00
15 Doug Weight 1.25 3.00
16 Teemu Selanne 2.00 5.00
17 Mats Sundin 2.00 5.00
18 Keith Tkachuk 1.25 3.00
19 Tony Amonte 1.25 3.00
20 Joe Sakic 4.00 10.00
21 Zigmund Palffy 1.25 3.00
22 Eric Lindros 1.50 4.00
23 Sergei Fedorov 2.00 5.00
24 Dominik Hasek 4.00 10.00
25 Brett Hull 2.00 5.00
RT1 W.Gretzky REEL TIME 60.00 150.00

1997-98 Upper Deck Diamond Vision Defining Moments

DM1 Wayne Gretzky 20.00 50.00
DM2 Patrick Roy 15.00 40.00
DM3 Steve Yzerman 15.00 40.00
DM4 Jaromir Jagr 12.50 30.00
DM5 Joe Sakic 12.00 30.00
DM6 Brendan Shanahan 8.00 20.00

1997-98 Upper Deck Diamond Vision Signature Moves

*SIGN.MOVES: .8X TO 1.5X BASIC CARDS

2013-14 Upper Deck Edmonton Oilers

COMPLETE SET (90) 25.00 50.00
1 Wayne Gretzky 4.00 10.00
2 Al Hamilton .40 1.00
3 Dave Hunter .40 1.00
4 Mark Messier 1.25 3.00
5 Ronald Low .50 1.25
6 Eddie Mio .40 1.00
7 David Lumley .40 1.00
8 Dave Semenko .40 1.00
9 Lee Fogolin .40 1.00
10 Paul Coffey .60 1.50
11 Charlie Huddy .40 1.00
12 Matti Hagman .40 1.00
13 Andy Moog .60 1.50
14 Jari Kurri .60 1.50
15 Glenn Anderson .50 1.25
16 Don Jackson .40 1.00
17 Randy Gregg .40 1.00
18 Kevin McClelland .40 1.00
19 Grant Fuhr 1.00 2.50
20 Steve Smith .40 1.00
21 Mike Krushelnyski .40 1.00
22 Jeff Beukeboom .40 1.00
23 Craig MacTavish .50 1.25
24 Marty McSorley .50 1.25
25 Kent Nilsson .40 1.00
26 Craig Muni .40 1.00
27 Kelly Buchberger .40 1.00
28 Craig Simpson .40 1.00
29 Mark Lamb .40 1.00
30 Bill Ranford .60 1.50
31 Ken Linseman .40 1.00
32 Jimmy Carson .40 1.00
33 Joe Murphy .40 1.00
34 Bernie Nicholls .50 1.25
35 Vincent Damphousse .50 1.25
36 Louie Debrusk .40 1.00
37 Dave Manson .40 1.00
38 Doug Weight .60 1.50
39 Todd Marchant .40 1.00
40 Jason Arnott .50 1.25
41 Martin Gelinas .40 1.00
42 Curtis Joseph .75 2.00
43 Bob Essensa .60 1.50
44 Mike Grier .40 1.00
45 Janne Niinimaa .40 1.00
46 Georges Laraque .50 1.25
47 Sheldon Souray .40 1.00
48 Tommy Salo .50 1.25
49 Ethan Moreau .40 1.00
50 Jason Smith .40 1.00
51 Dan Cleary .60 1.50
52 Mike Comrie .40 1.00
53 Jason Chimera .40 1.00
54 Shawn Horcoff .40 1.00
55 Anson Carter .50 1.25
56 Marty Reasoner .40 1.00
57 Ty Conklin .50 1.25
58 Jussi Markkanen .40 1.00
59 Marc-Andre Bergeron .40 1.00
60 Bill Guerin .60 1.50
61 Scott Thornton .40 1.00
62 Jarret Stoll .50 1.25
63 Adam Oates .60 1.50
64 Raffi Torres .40 1.00
65 Matt Greene .40 1.00
66 Fernando Pisani .40 1.00
67 Chris Pronger .60 1.50
68 Dwayne Roloson .40 1.00
69 Robert Nilsson .40 1.00
70 Ladislav Smid .40 1.00
71 Dustin Penner .50 1.25
72 Sam Gagner .40 1.00
73 Andrew Cogliano .40 1.00
74 Mathieu Garon .50 1.25
75 Ryan Smyth .50 1.25
76 Ryan Jones .50 1.25
77 Devan Dubnyk .50 1.25
78 Nikolai Khabibulin .60 1.50
79 Ales Hemsky .40 1.00
80 Jordan Eberle .60 1.50
81 Taylor Hall .60 1.50
82 Magnus Paajarvi .50 1.25
83 Ryan Nugent-Hopkins .75 2.00
84 Darcy Hordichuk .40 1.00
85 Nick Schultz .40 1.00
86 Justin Schultz .60 1.50
87 Nail Yakupov 1.25 3.00
88 Boyd Gordon .40 1.00
89 David Perron .50 1.25
90 Andrew Ference .40 1.00

2013-14 Upper Deck Edmonton Oilers Rainbow

*RAINBOW: 1X TO 2.5X BASIC CARDS

2013-14 Upper Deck Edmonton Oilers Championship Banners

CBAM Andy Moog/99 15.00 40.00
CBAM Andy Moog/25 30.00 80.00
CBBR Bill Ranford/99 10.00 25.00
CBCH Charlie Huddy/99 10.00 25.00
CBCH Charlie Huddy/15 20.00 50.00
CBCH Charlie Huddy/25 20.00 50.00
CBCH Charlie Huddy/25 20.00 50.00
CBCM Craig MacTavish/99 8.00 20.00
CBCM Craig MacTavish/25 15.00 40.00
CBCS Craig Simpson/99 6.00 15.00
CBCS Craig Simpson/25 12.00 30.00
CBDH Dave Hunter/99 6.00 15.00
CBDH Dave Hunter/25 12.00 30.00
CBDJ Don Jackson/25 12.00 30.00
CBDL David Lumley/99 6.00 15.00
CBDS Dave Semenko/25 40.00 80.00
CBDS Dave Semenko/99 20.00 40.00
CBGA Glenn Anderson/15 20.00 50.00
CBGA Glenn Anderson/25 20.00 50.00
CBGA Glenn Anderson/99 10.00 25.00
CBGA Glenn Anderson/25 20.00 50.00
CBGA Glenn Anderson/99 10.00 25.00
CBGF Grant Fuhr/99 12.00 30.00
CBGF Grant Fuhr/25 25.00 60.00
CBGF Grant Fuhr/25 25.00 60.00
CBGF Grant Fuhr/99 15.00 40.00
CBJB Jeff Beukeboom/25 12.00 30.00
CBJB Jeff Beukeboom/99 6.00 15.00
CBJK Jari Kurri/25 20.00 50.00
CBJK Jari Kurri/99 10.00 25.00
CBJK Jari Kurri/25 20.00 50.00
CBJK Jari Kurri/99 10.00 25.00
CBJM Joe Murphy/99 6.00 15.00
CBKB Kelly Buchberger/99 6.00 15.00
CBKL Ken Linseman/25 12.00 30.00
CBKM Kevin McClelland/99 8.00 20.00
CBKM Kevin McClelland/25 15.00 40.00
CBKM Kevin McClelland/25 15.00 40.00
CBKN Kent Nilsson/99 6.00 15.00
CBLF Lee Fogolin/25 12.00 30.00
CBLF Lee Fogolin/99 6.00 15.00
CBMC Marty McSorley/25 15.00 40.00
CBMC Marty McSorley/99 8.00 20.00
CBMG Martin Gelinas/99 8.00 20.00
CBMK Mike Krushelnyski/99 6.00 15.00
CBMK Mike Krushelnyski/25 12.00 30.00
CBML Mark Lamb/25 12.00 30.00
CBMM Mark Messier/25 40.00 80.00
CBMM Mark Messier/25 40.00 80.00
CBMM Mark Messier/25 40.00 80.00
CBMM Mark Messier/99 15.00 40.00
CBMM Mark Messier/25 40.00 80.00
CBMU Craig Muni/25 15.00 40.00
CBMU Craig Muni/99 8.00 20.00
CBPC Paul Coffey/25 25.00 60.00
CBPC Paul Coffey/25 25.00 60.00
CBPC Paul Coffey/99 12.00 30.00
CBRG Randy Gregg/25 15.00 40.00
CBRG Randy Gregg/99 8.00 20.00
CBRG Randy Gregg/99 8.00 20.00
CBRG Randy Gregg/25 15.00 40.00
CBSS Steve Smith/99 6.00 15.00
CBSS Steve Smith/25 12.00 30.00
CBWG Wayne Gretzky/99 75.00 150.00
CBWG Wayne Gretzky/25 175.00 300.00
CBWG Wayne Gretzky/99 75.00 150.00

2013-14 Upper Deck Edmonton Oilers Championship Banners Autographs

CBAM Andy Moog/25 50.00 100.00
CBCM Craig MacTavish/25 30.00 60.00
CBCS Craig Simpson/25 20.00 40.00
CBDL David Lumley/25 40.00 100.00
CBJB Jeff Beukeboom/25 15.00 40.00
CBJK Jari Kurri/25 15.00 40.00
CBKM Kevin McClelland/25 20.00 50.00
CBMC Marty McSorley/25 30.00 60.00
CBMG Martin Gelinas/25 25.00 50.00
CBMK Mike Krushelnyski/25 25.00 50.00
CBMU Craig Muni/25 30.00 60.00

2013-14 Upper Deck Edmonton Oilers Franchise Ink

FIAC Anson Carter F 6.00 15.00
FIAH Al Hamilton G 5.00 12.00
FIAM Andy Moog D 8.00 20.00
FIAN Andrew Cogliano F 5.00 12.00
FIAO Adam Oates E 8.00 20.00
FIBE Bob Essensa G 8.00 20.00
FIBG Bill Guerin D 8.00 20.00
FIBN Bernie Nicholls E 6.00 15.00
FIBR Bill Ranford D 8.00 20.00
FICA Jimmy Carson G 5.00 12.00
FICH Charlie Huddy G 5.00 12.00
FICJ Curtis Joseph C 10.00 25.00
FICM Craig MacTavish D 6.00 15.00
FICP Chris Pronger B 8.00 20.00
FICS Craig Simpson F 5.00 12.00
FIDC Dan Cleary F 8.00 20.00
FIDD Devan Dubnyk G 6.00 15.00
FIDL David Lumley G 5.00 12.00
FIDM Dave Manson G 5.00 12.00
FIDP Dustin Penner D 6.00 15.00
FIDR Dwayne Roloson G 5.00 12.00
FIDW Doug Weight D 8.00 20.00
FIEM Eddie Mio G 5.00 12.00
FIFL Francois Leroux G 5.00 12.00
FIFP Fernando Pisani G 5.00 12.00
FIGA Glenn Anderson C 6.00 15.00
FIGF Grant Fuhr C 25.00 60.00
FIGL Georges Laraque G 6.00 15.00
FIGM Mathieu Garon F 6.00 15.00
FIGR Mike Grier G 5.00 12.00
FIHE Ales Hemsky D 5.00 12.00
FIHO Darcy Hordichuk F 5.00 12.00
FIJA Jason Arnott D 6.00 15.00
FIJB Jeff Beukeboom G 5.00 12.00
FIJC Jason Chimera G 5.00 12.00
FIJD Jeff Deslauriers G 5.00 12.00
FIJE Jordan Eberle C 8.00 20.00
FIJK Jari Kurri B 8.00 20.00
FIJM Joe Murphy G 5.00 12.00
FIJN Janne Niinimaa G 5.00 12.00
FIJS Jason Smith F 5.00 12.00
FIKB Kelly Buchberger F 5.00 12.00
FIKM Kevin McClelland G 5.00 12.00
FIKN Kent Nilsson F 5.00 12.00
FILD Louie Debrusk G 5.00 12.00
FILF Lee Fogolin G 5.00 12.00
FILI Ken Linseman G 5.00 12.00
FILS Ladislav Smid F 5.00 12.00
FIMA Marty McSorley D 6.00 15.00
FIMB Marc-Andre Bergeron F 5.00 12.00
FIMG Martin Gelinas G 5.00 12.00
FIMH Matti Hagman G 5.00 12.00
FIMK Mike Krushelnyski G 5.00 12.00
FIML Mark Lamb G 5.00 12.00
FIMM Mark Messier A 15.00 40.00
FIMO Ethan Moreau E 5.00 12.00
FIMP Magnus Paajarvi E 6.00 15.00
FIMR Marty Reasoner G 5.00 12.00
FIMU Craig Muni G 5.00 12.00
FINU Ryan Nugent-Hopkins C 10.00 25.00
FINY Nail Yakupov C 15.00 40.00
FIPC Paul Coffey A 8.00 20.00
FIPO Patrick O'Sullivan G 5.00 12.00
FIRG Randy Gregg G 5.00 12.00
FIRL Ronald Low G 6.00 15.00
FIRN Robert Nilsson F 5.00 12.00
FIRT Raffi Torres E 5.00 12.00
FISG Sam Gagner E 5.00 12.00
FISH Shawn Horcoff E 5.00 12.00
FISM Ryan Smyth C 6.00 15.00
FISO Sheldon Souray F 5.00 12.00
FISS Steve Smith F 5.00 12.00
FIST Jarret Stoll D 6.00 15.00
FISZ Justin Schultz E 8.00 20.00
FITC Ty Conklin F 6.00 15.00
FITH Taylor Hall C 8.00 20.00
FITM Todd Marchant G 5.00 12.00
FITN Scott Thornton F 5.00 12.00
FITS Tommy Salo F 6.00 15.00
FIVD Vincent Damphousse E 6.00 15.00
FIWG Wayne Gretzky B 250.00 600.00

2013-14 Upper Deck Edmonton Oilers Franchise Ink Duos

FI2CH P.Coffey/C.Huddy B 40.00 80.00
FI2CS T.Salo/T.Conklin E 20.00 50.00
FI2DS D.Dubnyk/J.Schultz D 15.00 40.00
FI2GB Buchberger/B.Guerin C 20.00 50.00
FI2GR D.Roloson/M.Garon E 15.00 40.00
FI2KM McSorley/Krushlnyski D 12.00 30.00
FI2KS J.Kurri/C.Simpson D 12.00 30.00
FI2LM D.Manson/G.Laraque E 12.00 30.00
FI2LS K.Linseman/S.Smith C 10.00 25.00
FI2MM McSorley/D.Manson D 15.00 40.00
FI2PC D.Penner/A.Cogliano C 12.00 30.00
FI2SB S.Smith/K.Buchberger E 10.00 25.00
FI2SG L.Smid/T.Gilbert E 10.00 25.00
FI2WA D.Weight/J.Arnott C 40.00 80.00

2013-14 Upper Deck Edmonton Oilers Franchise Ink Trios

FI3AMS Smpsn/Mssr/Andrsn B 60.00 120.00
FI3EHN Hall/RNH/Eberle A 15.00 40.00
FI3GFH Grgg/Fglin/Huddy C 25.00 50.00
FI3HPG Pnner/Ggner/Hmsky C 30.00 60.00
FI3LMM McSrly/McCln/Lrque D 25.00 50.00
FI3MRS Mreau/Rsner/Stoll C 15.00 40.00
FI3SHG Smyth/Ggner/Hmsky C 60.00 120.00
FI3SHO Oates/Stll/Hrcff B 12.00 30.00

2013-14 Upper Deck Edmonton Oilers Monumental Emblems

MEAH Ales Hemsky 8.00 20.00
MEAM Andy Moog 15.00 40.00
MEBR Bill Ranford 15.00 40.00
MECH Charlie Huddy 10.00 25.00
MECM Craig MacTavish 12.00 30.00
MECS Craig Simpson 12.00 30.00
MEDH Dave Hunter 8.00 20.00
MEDW Doug Weight 12.00 30.00
MEGA Glenn Anderson 12.00 30.00
MEGF Grant Fuhr 15.00 40.00
MEJE Jordan Eberle 12.00 30.00
MEJK Jari Kurri 15.00 40.00
MEJS Justin Schultz 12.00 30.00
MEMC Marty McSorley 10.00 25.00
MEMM Mark Messier 15.00 40.00
MENK Nikolai Khabibulin 12.00 30.00
MENY Nail Yakupov 25.00 50.00
MEPC Paul Coffey 12.00 30.00
MERN Ryan Nugent-Hopkins 15.00 40.00
MERS Ryan Smyth 15.00 40.00
MESG Sam Gagner 8.00 20.00
MESH Shawn Horcoff 8.00 20.00
METH Taylor Hall 12.00 30.00
MEWG Wayne Gretzky 100.00 175.00

2013-14 Upper Deck Edmonton Oilers Monumental Emblems Autographs

MEBR Bill Ranford 75.00 150.00
MECS Craig Simpson 40.00 80.00
MEGA Glenn Anderson 25.00 50.00
MEJE Jordan Eberle 30.00 60.00
MEMM Mark Messier 100.00 200.00
MERN Ryan Nugent-Hopkins 60.00 120.00
MERS Ryan Smyth 40.00 80.00

2013-14 Upper Deck Edmonton Oilers Retired Numbers

RNAH Al Hamilton 12.00 30.00
RNGA Glenn Anderson 15.00 40.00
RNGF Grant Fuhr 30.00 80.00
RNJK Jari Kurri 30.00 60.00
RNMM Mark Messier 30.00 60.00
RNPC Paul Coffey 25.00 50.00
RNWG Wayne Gretzky 100.00 175.00

2013-14 Upper Deck Edmonton Oilers Retired Numbers Autographs

RNAH Al Hamilton/25 30.00 60.00
RNJK Jari Kurri/25 40.00 80.00

2013-14 Upper Deck Edmonton Oilers Team Logo Patches

TL1 Dave Hunter 4.00 10.00
TL2 David Lumley 4.00 10.00
TL3 Jari Kurri 8.00 20.00
TL4 Glenn Anderson 5.00 12.00
TL5 Louie DeBrusk 4.00 10.00
TL6 Erik Cole 4.00 10.00
TL7 Curtis Glencross 4.00 10.00
TL8 Radek Dvorak 4.00 10.00
TL9 Scott Thornton 4.00 10.00
TL10 Craig Simpson 4.00 10.00
TL11 Martin Gelinas 5.00 12.00
TL12 Joe Murphy 4.00 10.00
TL13 Ryan Jones 6.00 15.00
TL14 Joffrey Lupul 4.00 10.00
TL15 Kent Nilsson 4.00 10.00
TL16 Todd Marchant 4.00 10.00
TL17 Ben Eager 5.00 12.00
TL18 Ryan Smyth 6.00 15.00
TL19 Fernando Pisani 4.00 10.00
TL20 Mike Grier 4.00 10.00
TL21 Ray Whitney 5.00 12.00
TL22 Ethan Moreau 4.00 10.00
TL23 Dan Cleary 6.00 15.00
TL24 Jason Chimera 4.00 10.00
TL25 Kevin McClelland 4.00 10.00
TL26 Anson Carter 5.00 12.00
TL27 David Perron 5.00 12.00
TL28 Ales Hemsky 4.00 10.00
TL29 Dean McAmmond 4.00 10.00
TL30 Raffi Torres 4.00 10.00
TL31 Dustin Penner 5.00 12.00
TL32 Jordan Eberle 6.00 15.00
TL33 Taylor Hall 6.00 15.00
TL34 Magnus Paajarvi 5.00 12.00
TL35 Nail Yakupov 8.00 20.00
TL36 Wayne Gretzky 30.00 60.00
TL37 Mark Messier 15.00 40.00
TL38 Boyd Gordon 5.00 12.00
TL39 Eric Belanger 5.00 12.00
TL40 Matti Hagman 5.00 12.00
TL41 Shawn Horcoff 5.00 12.00
TL42 Mike Krushelnyski 5.00 12.00
TL43 Kyle Brodziak 5.00 12.00
TL44 Craig MacTavish 6.00 15.00
TL45 Mark Lamb 5.00 12.00
TL46 Jimmy Carson 5.00 12.00
TL47 Vincent Damphousse 6.00 15.00
TL48 Bernie Nicholls 6.00 15.00
TL49 Doug Weight 8.00 20.00
TL50 Jason Arnott 6.00 15.00
TL51 Patrick O'Sullivan 5.00 12.00
TL52 Anton Lander 6.00 15.00
TL53 Mike Comrie 5.00 12.00
TL54 Marty Reasoner 5.00 12.00
TL55 Jarret Stoll 6.00 15.00
TL56 Adam Oates 8.00 20.00
TL57 Robert Nilsson 5.00 12.00
TL58 Sam Gagner 6.00 15.00
TL59 Andrew Cogliano 6.00 15.00
TL60 Ryan Nugent-Hopkins 10.00 25.00
TL61 Al Hamilton 8.00 20.00
TL62 Justin Schultz 12.00 30.00
TL63 Lee Fogolin 8.00 20.00
TL64 Charlie Huddy 8.00 20.00
TL65 Paul Coffey 12.00 30.00
TL66 Randy Gregg 8.00 20.00
TL67 Matt Greene 8.00 20.00
TL68 Steve Smith 8.00 20.00
TL69 Craig Muni 8.00 20.00
TL70 Janne Niinimaa 8.00 20.00
TL71 Sheldon Souray 8.00 20.00
TL72 Jason Smith 8.00 20.00
TL73 Marc-Andre Bergeron 8.00 20.00
TL74 Chris Pronger 15.00 40.00
TL75 Ladislav Smid 25.00 60.00
TL77 Ronald Low 12.00 30.00
TL85 Jussi Markkanen 20.00 50.00

2018-19 Upper Deck Engrained

1 Connor McDavid 8.00 20.00
2 Steven Stamkos 3.00 8.00
3 Carey Price 3.00 8.00
4 Patrick Kane 3.00 8.00
5 Sidney Crosby 6.00 15.00
6 P.K. Subban 2.00 5.00
7 David Pastrnak 4.00 10.00
8 Johnny Gaudreau 2.50 6.00
9 Matt Duchene 1.50 4.00
10 Auston Matthews 6.00 15.00
11 Brent Burns 1.50 4.00
12 Sean Couturier 1.25 3.00
13 Artemi Panarin 3.00 8.00
14 Jack Eichel 2.50 6.00
15 Marc-Andre Fleury 3.00 8.00
16 Mathew Barzal 2.00 5.00
17 Nathan MacKinnon 6.00 15.00
18 Mikael Granlund 1.25 3.00
19 Dylan Larkin 2.00 5.00
20 Alexander Ovechkin 6.00 15.00
21 Patrik Laine 2.00 5.00
22 Tyler Seguin 2.00 5.00
23 Brock Boeser 2.00 5.00
24 Nico Hischier 2.50 6.00
25 Jonathan Toews 2.50 6.00
26 Jonathan Quick 2.00 5.00
27 Nikita Kucherov 3.00 8.00
28 John Tavares 2.50 6.00
29 Clayton Keller 2.00 5.00
30 Henrik Lundqvist 4.00 10.00
31 Vladimir Tarasenko 2.00 5.00
32 Teemu Selanne 3.00 8.00
33 Bobby Orr 6.00 15.00
34 Dominik Hasek 2.50 6.00
35 Mark Messier 3.00 8.00
36 Mats Sundin 1.50 4.00
37 Guy Lafleur 2.00 5.00
38 Joe Sakic 3.00 8.00
39 Pat LaFontaine 1.50 4.00
40 Mario Lemieux 6.00 15.00
41 Rod Brind'Amour 1.50 4.00
42 Patrick Roy 4.00 10.00
43 Brett Hull 3.00 8.00
44 Mike Modano 3.00 8.00
45 Steve Yzerman 4.00 10.00
46 Peter Forsberg 3.00 8.00
47 Mike Bossy 1.50 4.00
48 Martin Brodeur 4.00 10.00
49 Pavel Bure 1.50 4.00
50 Wayne Gretzky 10.00 25.00
51 Elias Pettersson RC 25.00 60.00
52 Henrik Borgstrom RC 5.00 12.00
53 Robert Thomas RC 6.00 15.00
54 Michael Rasmussen RC 4.00 10.00
55 Ryan Donato RC 5.00 12.00
56 Kristian Vesalainen RC 4.00 10.00
57 Sam Steel RC 3.00 8.00
58 Andreas Johnsson RC 4.00 10.00
59 Brett Howden RC 4.00 10.00
60 Rasmus Dahlin RC 8.00 20.00
61 Dylan Sikura RC 4.00 10.00
62 Zach Aston-Reese RC 5.00 12.00
63 Ethan Bear RC 5.00 12.00
64 Dylan Gambrell RC 3.00 8.00
65 Jesperi Kotkaniemi RC 6.00 15.00
66 Nicolas Roy RC 2.00 5.00
67 Anthony Cirelli RC 5.00 12.00
68 Isac Lundestrom RC 2.50 6.00
69 Daniel Brickley RC 3.00 8.00
70 Brady Tkachuk RC 10.00 25.00
71 Zach Whitecloud RC 2.50 6.00
72 Filip Hronek RC 3.00 8.00
73 Maxime Comtois RC 3.00 8.00
74 Mathieu Joseph RC 4.00 10.00
75 Dillon Dube RC 4.00 10.00
76 Jordan Greenway RC 3.00 8.00
77 Victor Ejdsell RC 2.50 6.00
78 Travis Dermott RC 5.00 12.00
79 Jordan Kyrou RC 6.00 15.00
80 Andrei Svechnikov RC 8.00 20.00
81 Michael Dal Colle RC 3.00 8.00
82 Neal Pionk RC 3.00 8.00
83 Evan Bouchard RC 8.00 20.00
84 Drake Batherson RC 6.00 15.00
85 Miro Heiskanen RC 8.00 20.00
86 Dennis Cholowski RC 3.00 8.00
87 Antti Suomela RC 2.50 6.00
88 Jaret Anderson-Dolan RC 2.50 6.00
89 Noah Juulsen RC 3.00 8.00
90 Eeli Tolvanen RC 6.00 15.00
91 Troy Terry RC 5.00 12.00
92 Tomas Hyka RC 3.00 8.00
93 Lias Andersson RC 5.00 12.00
94 Max Lajoie RC 5.00 12.00
95 Casey Mittelstadt RC 6.00 15.00
96 Henri Jokiharju RC 2.50 6.00
97 Juuso Valimaki RC 3.00 8.00
98 Ilya Samsonov RC 6.00 15.00
99 Adam Gaudette RC 5.00 12.00
100 Warren Foegele RC 3.00 8.00

2018-19 Upper Deck Engrained Black

*VET/49: .5X TO 1.25X BASIC CARDS
*RC/49: .6X TO 1.5X BASIC CARDS
1 Connor McDavid 15.00 40.00
5 Sidney Crosby 12.00 30.00
15 Marc-Andre Fleury 15.00 40.00
23 Brock Boeser 12.00 30.00
25 Jonathan Toews 15.00 40.00
50 Wayne Gretzky 15.00 40.00
51 Elias Pettersson 40.00 100.00
65 Jesperi Kotkaniemi 10.00 25.00
72 Filip Hronek 20.00 50.00

2018-19 Upper Deck Engrained Autographs

1 Connor McDavid A 150.00 250.00
3 Carey Price A 15.00 40.00
10 Auston Matthews A 30.00 80.00
11 Brent Burns C 8.00 20.00
15 Marc-Andre Fleury B 15.00 40.00
18 Mikael Granlund C 6.00 15.00
20 Alexander Ovechkin A 30.00 80.00
25 Jonathan Toews A 12.00 30.00
28 John Tavares A 12.00 30.00
30 Henrik Lundqvist B 20.00 50.00
31 Vladimir Tarasenko B 10.00 25.00
33 Bobby Orr C 50.00 125.00
34 Dominik Hasek B 12.00 30.00
35 Mark Messier A 15.00 40.00
40 Mario Lemieux A 30.00 80.00
41 Rod Brind'Amour C 8.00 20.00
42 Patrick Roy A 20.00 50.00
43 Brett Hull B 15.00 40.00
44 Mike Modano C 15.00 40.00
45 Steve Yzerman A 20.00 50.00
47 Mike Bossy B 8.00 20.00
48 Martin Brodeur A 20.00 50.00
50 Wayne Gretzky A 200.00 500.00
51 Elias Pettersson A 150.00 250.00
53 Robert Thomas B 15.00 40.00
54 Michael Rasmussen B 10.00 25.00
56 Kristian Vesalainen B 10.00 25.00
57 Sam Steel B 8.00 20.00
59 Brett Howden B 10.00 25.00
62 Zach Aston-Reese C 12.00 30.00
63 Ethan Bear C 12.00 30.00
64 Dylan Gambrell C 8.00 20.00
65 Jesperi Kotkaniemi A 15.00 40.00
66 Nicolas Roy B 5.00 12.00
67 Anthony Cirelli B 12.00 30.00
69 Daniel Brickley C 8.00 20.00
70 Brady Tkachuk A 25.00 60.00
71 Zach Whitecloud C 6.00 15.00
72 Filip Hronek C 8.00 20.00
73 Maxime Comtois B 8.00 20.00
74 Mathieu Joseph B 10.00 25.00
75 Dillon Dube B 10.00 25.00
76 Jordan Greenway B 8.00 20.00
77 Victor Ejdsell C 6.00 15.00
78 Travis Dermott C 12.00 30.00
79 Jordan Kyrou B 15.00 40.00
80 Andrei Svechnikov A 20.00 50.00
81 Michael Dal Colle B 8.00 20.00
82 Neal Pionk C 8.00 20.00
83 Evan Bouchard C 20.00 50.00
84 Drake Batherson B 15.00 40.00
85 Miro Heiskanen B 20.00 50.00
86 Dennis Cholowski B 8.00 20.00
87 Antti Suomela C 6.00 15.00
88 Jaret Anderson-Dolan C 6.00 15.00
89 Noah Juulsen B 8.00 20.00
90 Eeli Tolvanen B 15.00 40.00
91 Troy Terry 20.00 50.00
92 Tomas Hyka C 8.00 20.00
94 Max Lajoie B 12.00 30.00
95 Casey Mittelstadt A 15.00 40.00
96 Henri Jokiharju C 6.00 15.00
98 Ilya Samsonov B 15.00 40.00
99 Adam Gaudette A 12.00 30.00
100 Warren Foegele B 8.00 20.00

2018-19 Upper Deck Engrained Carved in Time

CT1 Wayne Gretzky 125.00 300.00
CT2 Stan Mikita 20.00 50.00
CT3 Pavel Bure 20.00 50.00
CT4 Luc Robitaille 20.00 50.00
CT5 Jacques Plante 20.00 50.00
CT6 Mario Lemieux 80.00 200.00
CT7 Mike Bossy 20.00 50.00
CT8 Brett Hull 40.00 100.00
CT9 Mark Messier 40.00 100.00
CT10 Terry Sawchuk 20.00 50.00
CT11 Joe Sakic 40.00 100.00
CT12 Mats Sundin 20.00 50.00
CT13 Roberto Luongo 30.00 80.00
CT14 Tim Horton 30.00 80.00
CT15 Sidney Crosby 80.00 200.00
CT16 Marcel Dionne 25.00 60.00
CT17 Mike Modano 40.00 100.00
CT18 Bobby Orr 80.00 200.00
CT19 Dominik Hasek 30.00 80.00
CT20 Jean Beliveau 20.00 50.00
CT21 Peter Forsberg 40.00 100.00
CT22 Jarome Iginla 25.00 60.00
CT23 Steve Yzerman 50.00 120.00
CT24 Bobby Hull 40.00 100.00
CT25 Alexander Ovechkin 80.00 200.00
CT26 Martin Brodeur 50.00 125.00
CT27 Paul Coffey 20.00 50.00
CT28 Bobby Clarke 30.00 80.00
CT29 Willie O'Ree 25.00 60.00
CT30 Maurice Richard 40.00 100.00
CT31 Marc-Andre Fleury 40.00 100.00
CT32 Teemu Selanne 40.00 100.00
CT33 Ted Lindsay 20.00 50.00
CT34 Patrick Roy 50.00 125.00
CT35 Jonathan Toews 30.00 80.00
CT36 Martin St. Louis 20.00 50.00

2018-19 Upper Deck Engrained Complete Sticks

CSAB Andy Bathgate 15.00 40.00
CSAM Al MacInnis 25.00 60.00
CSBS Borje Salming 40.00 100.00
CSDG Doug Gilmour 25.00 60.00
CSGH Glenn Hall 20.00 50.00
CSIK Ilya Kovalchuk 15.00 40.00
CSIL Igor Larionov 20.00 50.00
CSJP Jacques Plante 50.00 125.00
CSMG Michel Goulet 20.00 50.00
CSMR Mark Recchi 25.00 60.00
CSPS Peter Stastny 15.00 40.00
CSRB Rob Blake 20.00 50.00
CSSL Steve Larmer 20.00 50.00
CSSS Steve Shutt 20.00 50.00
CSTD Tie Domi 15.00 40.00

2018-19 Upper Deck Engrained Complete Sticks Signatures

CSSAO Alexander Ovechkin 100.00 250.00
CSSBH Bobby Hull 50.00 125.00
CSSCC Chris Chelios 25.00 60.00
CSSCM Connor McDavid 125.00 300.00
CSSCP Carey Price 400.00 500.00
CSSDH Dominik Hasek 100.00 200.00
CSSDS Darryl Sittler 30.00 80.00
CSSLR Larry Robinson 25.00 60.00

CSSMB Martin Brodeur 60.00 150.00
CSSMD Marcel Dionne 30.00 80.00
CSSML Mario Lemieux 100.00 250.00
CSSMM Mark Messier 50.00 125.00
CSSNU Norm Ullman 25.00 60.00
CSSPR Patrick Roy 60.00 150.00
CSSSY Steve Yzerman 100.00 200.00

2018-19 Upper Deck Engrained Flexures

FBW Blake Wheeler A 8.00 20.00
FCP Corey Perry B 12.00 30.00
FDD Drew Doughty B 10.00 25.00
FDP David Pastrnak B 30.00 80.00
FMR Mark Recchi B 10.00 25.00
FWN William Nylander B 15.00 40.00

2018-19 Upper Deck Engrained Premium Memorabilia

7 David Pastrnak/35 15.00 40.00
8 Johnny Gaudreau/35 10.00 25.00
11 Brent Burns/35 6.00 15.00
12 Sean Couturier/35 5.00 12.00
13 Artemi Panarin/35 12.00 30.00
18 Mikael Granlund/35 5.00 12.00
19 Dylan Larkin/35 8.00 20.00
22 Tyler Seguin/35 8.00 20.00
29 Clayton Keller/35 8.00 20.00
52 Henrik Borgstrom/35 10.00 25.00
53 Robert Thomas/35 12.00 30.00
54 Michael Rasmussen/35 8.00 20.00
55 Ryan Donato/35 10.00 25.00
56 Kristian Vesalainen/35 8.00 20.00
57 Sam Steel/35 6.00 15.00
58 Andreas Johnsson/35 8.00 20.00
59 Brett Howden/35 8.00 20.00
61 Dylan Sikura/35 8.00 20.00
62 Zach Aston-Reese/35 10.00 25.00
63 Ethan Bear/35 8.00 20.00
64 Dylan Gambrell/35 6.00 15.00
66 Nicolas Roy/35 4.00 10.00
67 Anthony Cirelli/35 10.00 25.00
68 Isac Lundestrom/35 5.00 12.00
69 Daniel Brickley/35 6.00 15.00
71 Zach Whitecloud/35 5.00 12.00
72 Filip Hronek/35 6.00 15.00
73 Maxime Comtois/35 6.00 15.00
75 Dillon Dube/35 8.00 20.00
76 Jordan Greenway/35 6.00 15.00
77 Victor Ejdsell/35 5.00 12.00
78 Travis Dermott/35 10.00 25.00
79 Jordan Kyrou/35 12.00 30.00
81 Michael Dal Colle/35 6.00 15.00
82 Neal Pionk/35 6.00 15.00
83 Evan Bouchard/35 15.00 40.00
84 Drake Batherson/35 12.00 30.00
85 Miro Heiskanen/35 15.00 40.00
86 Dennis Cholowski/35 6.00 15.00
87 Antti Suomela/35 5.00 12.00
88 Jaret Anderson-Dolan/35 5.00 12.00
89 Noah Juulsen/35 6.00 15.00
90 Eeli Tolvanen/35 12.00 30.00
91 Troy Terry/35 25.00 60.00
92 Tomas Hyka/35 6.00 15.00
93 Lias Andersson/35 10.00 25.00
94 Max Lajoie/35 10.00 25.00
96 Henri Jokiharju/35 5.00 12.00
97 Juuso Valimaki/35 6.00 15.00
98 Ilya Samsonov/35 12.00 30.00
99 Adam Gaudette/35 10.00 25.00
100 Warren Foegele/35 6.00 15.00

2018-19 Upper Deck Engrained Premium Memorabilia Autographs

11 Brent Burns/25 12.00 30.00
15 Marc-Andre Fleury/25 50.00 125.00
18 Mikael Granlund/65 10.00 25.00
28 John Tavares/25 20.00 50.00
30 Henrik Lundqvist/25 30.00 80.00
31 Vladimir Tarasenko/25 40.00 100.00
51 Elias Pettersson/35 150.00 250.00
53 Robert Thomas/65 25.00 60.00
54 Michael Rasmussen/65 15.00 40.00
56 Kristian Vesalainen/65 15.00 40.00
57 Sam Steel/65 12.00 30.00
59 Brett Howden/65 15.00 40.00
62 Zach Aston-Reese/65 20.00 50.00
63 Ethan Bear/65 20.00 50.00
64 Dylan Gambrell/65 12.00 30.00
65 Jesperi Kotkaniemi/35 25.00 60.00
66 Nicolas Roy/65 8.00 20.00
67 Anthony Cirelli/65 20.00 50.00
69 Daniel Brickley/65 12.00 30.00
70 Brady Tkachuk/35 40.00 100.00
71 Zach Whitecloud/65 10.00 25.00
72 Filip Hronek/65 12.00 30.00
73 Maxime Comtois/65 12.00 30.00
75 Dillon Dube/65 15.00 40.00
76 Jordan Greenway/65 12.00 30.00
77 Victor Ejdsell/65 10.00 25.00
78 Travis Dermott/65 20.00 50.00
79 Jordan Kyrou/65 25.00 60.00
80 Andrei Svechnikov/35 30.00 80.00
81 Michael Dal Colle/65 12.00 30.00
82 Neal Pionk/65 12.00 30.00
83 Evan Bouchard/65 30.00 80.00
84 Drake Batherson/65 25.00 60.00
86 Dennis Cholowski/65 12.00 30.00
87 Antti Suomela/65 10.00 25.00
88 Jaret Anderson-Dolan/65 10.00 25.00
89 Noah Juulsen/65 12.00 30.00
90 Eeli Tolvanen/65 25.00 60.00
91 Troy Terry/65 25.00 60.00
92 Tomas Hyka/65 12.00 30.00
94 Max Lajoie/65 20.00 50.00
96 Henri Jokiharju/65 10.00 25.00
98 Ilya Samsonov/65 25.00 60.00
99 Adam Gaudette/65 20.00 50.00
100 Warren Foegele/65 12.00 30.00

2018-19 Upper Deck Engrained Remnants

RAB Andy Bathgate 6.00 15.00
RAL Al MacInnis 10.00 25.00
RAM Al MacInnis 10.00 25.00
RBB Bobby Smith 8.00 20.00
RBH Brett Hull 15.00 40.00
RBP Wendel Clark 12.00 30.00
RBS Billy Smith 8.00 20.00
RBT Bryan Trottier 8.00 20.00
RCC Chris Chelios 8.00 20.00
RCH Chris Pronger 8.00 20.00
RCL Claude Lemieux 8.00 20.00
RCM Connor McDavid 40.00 100.00
RCP Carey Price 15.00 40.00
RDD Drew Doughty 10.00 25.00
RDG Doug Gilmour 10.00 25.00
RDK Derek King 8.00 20.00
RDP Denis Potvin 6.00 15.00
RDS Darryl Sittler 10.00 25.00
REB Ed Belfour 8.00 20.00
REG Ed Giacomin 8.00 20.00
RGA Marian Gaborik 8.00 20.00
RGF Grant Fuhr 12.00 30.00
RGH Glenn Hall 8.00 20.00
RGI Doug Gilmour 10.00 25.00
RGN Glenn Resch 8.00 20.00
RGR Gary Roberts 8.00 20.00
RHE Guy Hebert 8.00 20.00
RIK Ilya Kovalchuk 6.00 15.00
RIL Igor Larionov 8.00 20.00
RJB Jean Beliveau 8.00 20.00
RJG Jean-Sebastien Giguere 8.00 20.00
RJM Joe Mullen 8.00 20.00
RJO Johnny Bucyk 8.00 20.00
RJP Jacques Plante 8.00 20.00
RJQ Jonathan Quick 10.00 25.00
RJS Jason Spezza 8.00 20.00
RKE Kevin Lowe 8.00 20.00
RKL Kevin Lowe 8.00 20.00
RKM Kirk Muller 6.00 15.00
RKP Keith Primeau 6.00 15.00
RLE Reggie Lemelin 5.00 12.00
RLR Larry Robinson 8.00 20.00
RLT John Tavares 8.00 20.00
RMD Marcel Dionne 10.00 25.00
RMG Michel Goulet 8.00 20.00
RMH Mark Howe 8.00 20.00
RMI Michael Peca 8.00 20.00
RML Milan Lucic 6.00 15.00
RMR Mark Recchi 10.00 25.00
RNL Nicklas Lidstrom 8.00 20.00
RNO Norm Ullman 8.00 20.00
RNU Norm Ullman 8.00 20.00
RPA David Pastrnak 20.00 50.00
RPB Pavel Bure 8.00 20.00
RPE Corey Perry 12.00 30.00
RPM Pete Mahovlich 8.00 20.00
RPR Bob Probert 8.00 20.00
RPS Peter Stastny 6.00 15.00
RRB Rob Blake 8.00 20.00
RRL Rod Langway 6.00 15.00
RRO Luc Robitaille 8.00 20.00
RSA Denis Savard 8.00 20.00
RSB Sergei Bobrovsky 12.00 30.00
RSC Clark Gillies 8.00 20.00
RSC Shayne Corson 6.00 15.00
RSH Steve Shutt 8.00 20.00
RSM Stan Mikita 8.00 20.00
RSS Serge Savard 8.00 20.00
RST Steve Thomas 6.00 15.00
RTD Tie Domi 6.00 15.00
RTE Tony Esposito 8.00 20.00
RTS Terry Sawchuk 8.00 20.00
RTT Tyler Toffoli 8.00 20.00
RTY Tyler Johnson 5.00 12.00
RWN William Nylander 15.00 40.00
RYC Yvan Cournoyer 8.00 20.00

2018-19 Upper Deck Engrained Rookie Signature Shots

RSSAC Anthony Cirelli/249 12.00 30.00
RSSAG Adam Gaudette/249 12.00 30.00
RSSAS Andrei Svechnikov/149 25.00 60.00
RSSBA Drake Batherson/249 15.00 40.00
RSSBH Brett Howden/249 10.00 25.00
RSSBO Evan Bouchard/249 20.00 50.00
RSSBT Brady Tkachuk/149 25.00 60.00
RSSCM Casey Mittelstadt/149 15.00 40.00
RSSDB Daniel Brickley/249 8.00 20.00
RSSDD Dillon Dube/249 10.00 25.00
RSSDG Dylan Gambrell/249 8.00 20.00
RSSEB Ethan Bear/249 12.00 30.00
RSSEP Elias Pettersson/149 100.00 200.00
RSSET Eeli Tolvanen/149 15.00 40.00
RSSFH Filip Hronek/249 8.00 20.00
RSSHJ Henri Jokiharju/249 6.00 15.00
RSSJA Joey Anderson/249 8.00 20.00
RSSJD Jaret Anderson-Dolan/249 6.00 15.00
RSSJG Jordan Greenway/249 8.00 20.00
RSSJK Jesperi Kotkaniemi/149 15.00 40.00
RSSJO Jordan Kyrou/249 12.00 30.00
RSSJV Juuso Valimaki/249 6.00 15.00
RSSKV Kristian Vesalainen/249 10.00 25.00
RSSMC Maxime Comtois/249 8.00 20.00
RSSMD Michael Dal Colle/249 8.00 20.00
RSSMH Miro Heiskanen/149 30.00 80.00
RSSMJ Mathieu Joseph/249 10.00 25.00
RSSMK Morgan Klimchuk/249 8.00 20.00
RSSML Max Lajoie/249 12.00 30.00
RSSMR Michael Rasmussen/149 10.00 25.00
RSSMV Mikhail Vorobyev/249 6.00 15.00
RSSNJ Noah Juulsen/249 6.00 15.00
RSSRH Roope Hintz/249 20.00 50.00
RSSRT Robert Thomas/149 15.00 40.00
RSSSF Spencer Foo/249 6.00 15.00
RSSSN Sami Niku/249 6.00 15.00
RSSSS Sam Steel/249 6.00 15.00
RSSSU Antti Suomela/249 6.00 15.00
RSSTD Travis Dermott/249 12.00 30.00
RSSTH Tomas Hyka/249 8.00 20.00
RSSTT Troy Terry/249 15.00 40.00
RSSVE Victor Ejdsell/249 6.00 15.00
RSSWF Warren Foegele/249 8.00 20.00
RSSZA Zach Aston-Reese/249 12.00 30.00
RSSZW Zach Whitecloud/249 6.00 15.00

2018-19 Upper Deck Engrained Rookie Signature Shots Blue Ink

*BLUE: .5X TO 1.25X BASIC INSERTS
RSSAS Andrei Svechnikov/25 200.00 300.00
RSSCM Casey Mittelstadt/25 40.00 100.00
RSSEP Elias Pettersson/25 250.00 400.00
RSSJK Jesperi Kotkaniemi/25 40.00 100.00

2018-19 Upper Deck Engrained Signature Flexures

SFAE Aaron Ekblad C 20.00 50.00
SFAK Anze Kopitar A 25.00 60.00
SFAO Alexander Ovechkin A 60.00 150.00
SFBH Brett Hull B 30.00 80.00
SFCC Chris Chelios B 15.00 40.00
SFCM Connor McDavid A 150.00 250.00
SFDS Darryl Sittler B 20.00 50.00
SFML Mario Lemieux A 60.00 150.00
SFMM Mark Messier A 50.00 120.00
SFRB Rod Brind'Amour C 15.00 40.00
SFSY Steve Yzerman A 40.00 100.00
SFWG Wayne Gretzky A 200.00 500.00

2018-19 Upper Deck Engrained Signature Remnants

SRBH Bobby Hull/35 40.00 100.00
SRBR Brett Hull/65 40.00 100.00
SRCJ Curtis Joseph/65 25.00 60.00
SRCP Carey Price/35 40.00 100.00
SRDH Dominik Hasek/35 30.00 80.00
SRHA Dale Hawerchuk/65 25.00 60.00
SRMM Mark Messier/35 40.00 100.00
SRRH Ron Hextall/65 20.00 50.00

2018-19 Upper Deck Engrained Signature Shots

*RED: .6X TO 1.5X BASIC INSERTS
SSAO Alexander Ovechkin/25 60.00 150.00
SSBO Bobby Orr/50 60.00 150.00
SSCJ Curtis Joseph/150 20.00 50.00
SSCM Connor McDavid/25 150.00 250.00
SSCP Carey Price/50 30.00 80.00
SSDH Dale Hawerchuk/150 20.00 50.00
SSDS Daniel Sedin/50 20.00 50.00
SSJT John Tavares/50 40.00 100.00
SSLR Larry Robinson/150 15.00 40.00
SSMA Marc-Andre Fleury/50 40.00 100.00
SSMM Mark Messier/25 30.00 80.00
SSPR Patrick Roy/25 60.00 150.00
SSRH Ron Hextall/150 15.00 40.00
SSSY Steve Yzerman/25 40.00 100.00
SSWG Wayne Gretzky/25 200.00 500.00
SSWO Willie O'Ree/150 20.00 50.00

2018-19 Upper Deck Engrained Synthesis

S1 Alexander Ovechkin 8.00 20.00
S2 Brock Boeser 2.50 6.00
S3 Jonathan Quick 2.50 6.00
S4 Jamie Benn 2.00 5.00
S5 Connor McDavid 10.00 25.00
S6 Cam Atkinson 2.00 5.00
S7 Patrick Kane 4.00 10.00
S8 Vladimir Tarasenko 2.50 6.00
S9 James Neal 1.25 3.00
S10 Sidney Crosby 8.00 20.00
S11 Pekka Rinne 2.00 5.00
S12 Steven Stamkos 4.00 10.00
S13 Brent Burns 2.00 5.00
S14 Nico Hischier 3.00 8.00
S15 Marc-Andre Fleury 4.00 10.00
S16 Matt Duchene 2.00 5.00
S17 Jonathan Drouin 1.50 4.00
S18 Clayton Keller 2.50 6.00
S19 Claude Giroux 2.00 5.00
S20 Auston Matthews 8.00 20.00
S21 Sebastian Aho 3.00 8.00
S22 Aleksander Barkov 3.00 8.00
S23 Patrik Laine 2.50 6.00
S24 Jack Eichel 3.00 8.00
S25 Henrik Lundqvist 5.00 12.00
S26 Zach Parise 2.00 5.00
S27 Erik Karlsson 2.50 6.00
S28 John Gibson 2.50 6.00
S29 Nathan MacKinnon 8.00 20.00
S30 John Tavares 3.00 8.00
S31 Brad Marchand 4.00 10.00
S32 Max Pacioretty 2.00 5.00
S33 Dylan Larkin 2.50 6.00
S34 Mathew Barzal 2.50 6.00
S35 Evgeni Malkin 4.00 10.00
S36 Andrei Vasilevskiy 3.00 8.00
S37 Jonathan Toews 3.00 8.00
S38 P.K. Subban 2.50 6.00
S39 Mitch Marner 3.00 8.00
S40 Carter Hart 4.00 10.00
S41 Rasmus Dahlin 5.00 12.00
S42 Elias Pettersson 12.00 30.00

2018-19 Upper Deck Engrained Synthesis Grip Parallel

*GRIP/50: .75X TO 2X BASIC INSERTS
S5 Connor McDavid 30.00 80.00
S15 Marc-Andre Fleury 20.00 50.00
S40 Carter Hart 50.00 125.00
S42 Elias Pettersson 25.00 60.00

2019-20 Upper Deck Engrained

1 Sidney Crosby 6.00 15.00
2 Matthew Tkachuk 3.00 8.00
3 Mitch Marner 3.00 8.00
4 Marc-Andre Fleury 3.00 8.00
5 Leon Draisaitl 5.00 12.00
6 Nathan MacKinnon 6.00 15.00
7 Patrick Kane 3.00 8.00
8 Steven Stamkos 3.00 8.00
9 Seth Jones 1.50 4.00
10 John Gibson 1.50 4.00
11 Jack Eichel 2.50 6.00
12 Ryan O'Reilly 1.50 4.00
13 Brady Tkachuk 2.50 6.00
14 Evgeni Malkin 3.00 8.00
15 Nikita Kucherov 3.00 8.00
16 Claude Giroux 1.50 4.00
17 Brad Marchand 3.00 8.00
18 Dylan Larkin 2.50 6.00
19 Sergei Bobrovsky 2.50 6.00
20 Henrik Lundqvist 4.00 10.00
21 Alex DeBrincat 2.00 5.00
22 Drew Doughty 2.00 5.00
23 Mark Scheifele 2.00 5.00
24 Auston Matthews 6.00 15.00
25 Aleksander Barkov 2.50 6.00
26 Brent Burns 1.50 4.00
27 Elias Pettersson 2.50 6.00
28 Mark Stone 2.00 5.00
29 Carey Price 3.00 8.00
30 Johnny Gaudreau 2.50 6.00
31 Connor McDavid 8.00 20.00
32 Billy Smith 1.50 4.00
33 Chris Chelios 1.50 4.00
34 Jaromir Jagr 5.00 12.00
35 Mark Messier 3.00 8.00
36 Jarome Iginla 2.00 5.00
37 Daniel Sedin 2.00 5.00
38 Curtis Joseph 2.00 5.00
39 Henrik Sedin 2.00 5.00
40 Patrick Roy 4.00 10.00
41 Martin Brodeur 4.00 10.00
42 Mario Lemieux 6.00 15.00
43 Teemu Selanne 3.00 8.00
44 Brett Hull 3.00 8.00
45 Wayne Gretzky 10.00 25.00
46 Bobby Orr 6.00 15.00
47 Ray Bourque 2.50 6.00
48 Keith Tkachuk 1.50 4.00
49 Gordie Howe 5.00 12.00
50 Jack Hughes RC 15.00 40.00
51 Kirby Dach RC 6.00 15.00
52 Joel Farabee RC 5.00 12.00
53 Noah Dobson RC 8.00 20.00
54 Barrett Hayton RC 6.00 15.00
55 Julien Gauthier RC 3.00 8.00
56 Vitaly Abramov RC 3.00 8.00
57 Jesper Boqvist RC 2.50 6.00
58 Emil Bemstrom RC 3.00 8.00
59 Elvis Merzlikins RC 6.00 15.00
60 Karson Kuhlman RC 3.00 8.00
61 Nikita Gusev RC 5.00 12.00
62 Blake Lizotte RC 3.00 8.00
63 Cale Makar RC 15.00 40.00
64 Adam Fox RC 8.00 20.00
65 Max Jones RC 3.00 8.00
66 Nicolas Hague RC 3.00 8.00
67 Taro Hirose RC 3.00 8.00
68 Joel L'Esperance RC 3.00 8.00
69 Rasmus Sandin RC 5.00 12.00
70 Brady Keeper RC 3.00 8.00
71 Adam Boqvist RC 3.00 8.00
72 Rudolfs Balcers RC 3.00 8.00
73 Ville Heinola RC 4.00 10.00
74 Klim Kostin RC 3.00 8.00
75 Morgan Frost RC 5.00 12.00
76 Jimmy Schuldt RC 2.50 6.00
77 Filip Zadina RC 5.00 12.00
78 Carl Grundstrom RC 3.00 8.00
79 Nick Suzuki RC 12.00 30.00
80 Zack MacEwen RC 2.50 6.00
81 Victor Olofsson RC 6.00 15.00
82 Connor Clifton RC 3.00 8.00
83 Trevor Moore RC 2.50 6.00
84 Zach Senyshyn RC 3.00 8.00
85 Nico Sturm RC 2.50 6.00
86 Quinn Hughes RC 15.00 40.00
87 Ilya Mikheyev RC 5.00 12.00
88 Dominik Kubalik RC 6.00 15.00
89 Oliver Wahlstrom RC 5.00 12.00
90 Teddy Blueger RC 3.00 8.00
91 Cody Glass RC 5.00 12.00
92 Erik Brannstrom RC 3.00 8.00
93 Philippe Myers RC 2.50 6.00
94 Trent Frederic RC 3.00 8.00
95 Alexandre Texier RC 3.00 8.00
96 Ryan Poehling RC 5.00 12.00
97 Dante Fabbro RC 3.00 8.00
98 Tobias Bjornfot RC 3.00 8.00
99 Kaapo Kakko RC 5.00 12.00

2019-20 Upper Deck Engrained Ebony

*EBONY VET: .5X TO 1.25X BASIC
*EBONY RC: .6X TO 1.5X BASIC RC

2019-20 Upper Deck Engrained Autographs Oak

4 Marc-Andre Fleury B 20.00 50.00
5 Leon Draisaitl C 20.00 50.00
19 Sergei Bobrovsky C 15.00 40.00
24 Auston Matthews A 120.00 300.00
29 Carey Price A 20.00 50.00
31 Connor McDavid B 80.00 200.00
33 Chris Chelios D 10.00 25.00
35 Mark Messier B 20.00 50.00
36 Jarome Iginla D 8.00 20.00
37 Daniel Sedin D 15.00 40.00
38 Curtis Joseph D 20.00 50.00
39 Henrik Sedin D 12.00 30.00
45 Wayne Gretzky C 400.00 1000.00
46 Bobby Orr C 80.00 200.00
48 Keith Tkachuk D 10.00 25.00
50 Jack Hughes A 40.00 100.00
53 Noah Dobson B 25.00 60.00
54 Barrett Hayton A 15.00 40.00
55 Julien Gauthier C 10.00 25.00
57 Jesper Boqvist C 8.00 20.00
58 Emil Bemstrom C 10.00 25.00
59 Elvis Merzlikins D 12.00 30.00
60 Karson Kuhlman D 10.00 25.00
61 Nikita Gusev A 15.00 40.00
63 Cale Makar A 60.00 150.00
64 Adam Fox C 25.00 60.00
70 Brady Keeper B 10.00 25.00
73 Ville Heinola C 8.00 20.00
74 Klim Kostin C 8.00 20.00
75 Morgan Frost B 15.00 40.00
76 Jimmy Schuldt D 8.00 20.00
78 Carl Grundstrom C 10.00 25.00
80 Zack MacEwen D 8.00 20.00
82 Connor Clifton D 10.00 25.00
83 Trevor Moore D 8.00 20.00
84 Zach Senyshyn D 10.00 25.00
85 Nico Sturm D 8.00 20.00
87 Ilya Mikheyev A 12.00 30.00
88 Dominik Kubalik D 20.00 50.00
89 Oliver Wahlstrom C 15.00 40.00
90 Teddy Blueger D 10.00 25.00
94 Trent Frederic B 10.00 25.00
98 Tobias Bjornfot C 10.00 25.00

2019-20 Upper Deck Engrained Carved in Time

CT1 Gordie Howe 30.00 80.00
CT2 Daniel Sedin 20.00 50.00
CT3 Henrik Sedin 15.00 40.00
CT4 Bobby Orr 30.00 80.00
CT5 Sidney Crosby 50.00 125.00
CT6 Henrik Lundqvist 30.00 80.00
CT7 Auston Matthews 50.00 125.00
CT8 Teemu Selanne 25.00 60.00
CT9 Evgeni Malkin 25.00 60.00
CT10 Doug Gilmour 15.00 40.00
CT11 Curtis Joseph 20.00 50.00
CT12 Jarome Iginla 25.00 60.00
CT13 Patrick Kane 25.00 60.00
CT14 Joe Thornton 15.00 40.00
CT15 Mario Lemieux 30.00 80.00
CT16 Mark Messier 25.00 60.00
CT17 Norm Ullman 15.00 40.00
CT18 Ray Bourque 25.00 60.00
CT19 Larry Robinson 15.00 40.00
CT20 Connor McDavid 60.00 150.00
CT21 Cam Neely 12.00 30.00
CT22 Jaromir Jagr 40.00 100.00
CT23 Steven Stamkos 25.00 60.00
CT24 Glenn Hall 12.00 30.00
CT25 Wayne Gretzky 60.00 150.00
CT26 Keith Tkachuk 12.00 30.00
CT27 Guy Lafleur 25.00 60.00
CT28 Ron Hextall 20.00 50.00
CT29 Chris Chelios 12.00 30.00
CT30 Patrick Roy 60.00 150.00

2019-20 Upper Deck Engrained Carved in Time Signatures

CTS1 Gordie Howe A 100.00 250.00
CTS2 Daniel Sedin C 40.00 100.00
CTS3 Henrik Sedin C 40.00 100.00
CTS4 Bobby Orr A 125.00 300.00
CTS5 Sidney Crosby A 125.00 300.00
CTS6 Henrik Lundqvist B 80.00 200.00
CTS7 Auston Matthews A 125.00 300.00
CTS10 Doug Gilmour B 40.00 100.00
CTS11 Curtis Joseph B 40.00 100.00
CTS12 Jarome Iginla C 40.00 100.00
CTS14 Joe Thornton C 50.00 125.00
CTS16 Mark Messier B 60.00 150.00
CTS19 Larry Robinson C 30.00 80.00
CTS20 Connor McDavid B 400.00 600.00
CTS21 Cam Neely C 30.00 80.00
CTS24 Glenn Hall C 30.00 80.00
CTS25 Wayne Gretzky A 400.00 1000.00
CTS26 Keith Tkachuk C 30.00 80.00
CTS28 Ron Hextall B 30.00 80.00
CTS29 Chris Chelios B 30.00 80.00

2019-20 Upper Deck Engrained Complete Sticks

CSAO Alexander Ovechkin 80.00 200.00
CSBB Brian Bellows 15.00 40.00
CSBP Bob Probert 20.00 50.00
CSDD Drew Doughty 25.00 60.00
CSDP Denis Potvin 20.00 50.00
CSET Esa Tikkanen 15.00 40.00
CSJK Jari Kurri 20.00 50.00
CSOA Adam Oates 20.00 50.00
CSRV Rogie Vachon 20.00 50.00
CSSG Sergei Gonchar 15.00 40.00
CSSM Stan Mikita 20.00 50.00
CSTL Ted Lindsay 30.00 80.00
CSVT Vladimir Tarasenko 25.00 60.00

2019-20 Upper Deck Engrained Complete Sticks Signatures

CSSAM Auston Matthews 200.00 500.00
CSSBN Bernie Nicholls 30.00 80.00
CSSCM Connor McDavid 250.00 600.00
CSSGF Grant Fuhr 60.00 150.00
CSSJT Joe Thornton 60.00 150.00
CSSLD Leon Draisaitl 125.00 300.00
CSSLI Mike Liut 25.00 60.00
CSSMF Marc-Andre Fleury 125.00 300.00
CSSPT Pierre Turgeon 25.00 60.00
CSSWG Wayne Gretzky 750.00 2000.00

2019-20 Upper Deck Engrained Honorary Engravings

HEAR03 Peter Forsberg 20.00 50.00
HEAR63 Gordie Howe 30.00 80.00
HEAR66 Bobby Hull 25.00 60.00
HEAR69 Phil Esposito 15.00 40.00
HEAR80 Marcel Dionne 12.00 30.00
HEAR85 Wayne Gretzky 60.00 150.00
HECM58 Frank Mahovlich 10.00 25.00
HECM66 Brit Selby 12.00 30.00
HECM76 Bryan Trottier 10.00 25.00
HECM81 Peter Stastny 8.00 20.00
HECM87 Luc Robitaille 10.00 25.00
HECM91 Ed Belfour 10.00 25.00
HECS03 Jean-Sebastien Giguere 10.00 25.00
HECS07 Scott Niedermayer 10.00 25.00
HECS74 Bernie Parent 12.00 30.00
HECS88 Wayne Gretzky 60.00 150.00
HECS92 Mario Lemieux 40.00 100.00
HECS95 Claude Lemieux 10.00 25.00

2019-20 Upper Deck Engrained Premium Material Autographs Ebony

2 Matthew Tkachuk/35 26.00 60.00
4 Marc-Andre Fleury/65 60.00 150.00
5 Leon Draisaitl/35 30.00 80.00
20 Henrik Lundqvist/35 40.00 100.00
26 Brent Burns/35 30.00 80.00
29 Carey Price/35 30.00 80.00
36 Jarome Iginla/35 20.00 50.00
37 Daniel Sedin/35 20.00 50.00
39 Henrik Sedin/35 20.00 50.00
48 Keith Tkachuk/35 15.00 40.00
50 Jack Hughes/35 80.00 200.00
53 Noah Dobson/35 40.00 100.00
54 Barrett Hayton/35 30.00 80.00
55 Julien Gauthier/65 12.00 30.00
57 Jesper Boqvist/65 12.00 30.00
58 Emil Bemstrom/65 15.00 40.00
59 Elvis Merzlikins/65 25.00 60.00
60 Karson Kuhlman/65 15.00 40.00
63 Cale Makar/35 80.00 200.00
68 Joel L'Esperance/65 15.00 40.00
70 Brady Keeper/65 15.00 40.00
72 Rudolfs Balcers/65 15.00 40.00
74 Klim Kostin/65 15.00 40.00
75 Morgan Frost/65 25.00 60.00
76 Jimmy Schuldt/65 12.00 30.00
78 Carl Grundstrom/65 10.00 25.00
79 Nick Suzuki/35 60.00 150.00
80 Zack MacEwen/65 12.00 30.00
83 Trevor Moore/65 12.00 30.00
84 Zach Senyshyn/65 15.00 40.00
85 Nico Sturm/65 12.00 30.00
86 Quinn Hughes/35 80.00 200.00
87 Ilya Mikheyev/65 25.00 60.00
88 Dominik Kubalik/65 30.00 80.00
89 Oliver Wahlstrom/65 25.00 60.00
90 Teddy Blueger/65 12.00 30.00
91 Cody Glass/35 25.00 60.00
93 Philippe Myers/65 12.00 30.00
94 Trent Frederic/65 12.00 30.00
95 Alexandre Texier/65 15.00 40.00
98 Tobias Bjornfot/65 10.00 25.00

2019-20 Upper Deck Engrained Premium Materials Mahogany

2 Matthew Tkachuk/35 12.00 30.00
3 Mitch Marner/35 10.00 25.00
4 Marc-Andre Fleury/65 20.00 50.00
5 Leon Draisaitl/35 20.00 50.00
10 John Gibson/65 6.00 15.00
11 Jack Eichel/35 10.00 25.00
12 Ryan O'Reilly/35 6.00 15.00
14 Evgeni Malkin/35 12.00 30.00
15 Nikita Kucherov/35 12.00 30.00
16 Claude Giroux/35 6.00 15.00
17 Brad Marchand/35 12.00 30.00
18 Dylan Larkin/35 8.00 20.00
20 Henrik Lundqvist/35 15.00 40.00
21 Alex DeBrincat/35 8.00 20.00
22 Drew Doughty/35 8.00 20.00
23 Mark Scheifele/35 10.00 25.00
25 Aleksander Barkov/35 10.00 25.00
26 Brent Burns/35 6.00 15.00
27 Elias Pettersson/35 10.00 25.00
28 Mark Stone/35 8.00 20.00
29 Carey Price/35 12.00 30.00
30 Johnny Gaudreau/35 10.00 25.00
50 Jack Hughes/35 30.00 80.00
51 Kirby Dach/35 12.00 30.00
52 Joel Farabee/35 10.00 25.00
53 Noah Dobson/35 15.00 40.00
54 Barrett Hayton/35 8.00 20.00
55 Julien Gauthier/35 6.00 15.00
56 Vitaly Abramov/35 6.00 15.00
57 Jesper Boqvist/35 5.00 12.00
58 Emil Bemstrom/35 6.00 15.00
59 Elvis Merzlikins/35 12.00 30.00
60 Karson Kuhlman/35 6.00 15.00
61 Nikita Gusev/35 10.00 25.00
62 Blake Lizotte/35 6.00 15.00
63 Cale Makar/35 30.00 80.00
64 Adam Fox/35 15.00 40.00
65 Max Jones/35 6.00 15.00
67 Taro Hirose/35 6.00 15.00
68 Joel L'Esperance/35 6.00 15.00
69 Rasmus Sandin/35 10.00 25.00
70 Brady Keeper/35 6.00 15.00
71 Adam Boqvist/35 10.00 25.00
72 Rudolfs Balcers/35 6.00 15.00
74 Klim Kostin/35 6.00 15.00
75 Morgan Frost/35 10.00 25.00
76 Jimmy Schuldt/35 5.00 12.00
77 Filip Zadina/35 10.00 25.00
78 Carl Grundstrom/35 6.00 15.00
79 Nick Suzuki/35 25.00 60.00
80 Zack MacEwen/35 6.00 15.00
81 Victor Olofsson/35 12.00 30.00
83 Trevor Moore/35 5.00 12.00
84 Zach Senyshyn/35 6.00 15.00
85 Nico Sturm/35 5.00 12.00
86 Quinn Hughes/35 30.00 80.00
87 Ilya Mikheyev/35 10.00 25.00
88 Dominik Kubalik/35 12.00 30.00
89 Oliver Wahlstrom/35 10.00 25.00
90 Teddy Blueger/35 6.00 15.00
91 Cody Glass/35 10.00 25.00
92 Erik Brannstrom/35 6.00 15.00
93 Philippe Myers/35 5.00 12.00
94 Trent Frederic/35 6.00 15.00
95 Alexandre Texier/35 6.00 15.00
96 Ryan Poehling/35 10.00 25.00
97 Dante Fabbro/35 6.00 15.00
98 Tobias Bjornfot/35 6.00 15.00

2019-20 Upper Deck Engrained Rare Remnants

RAA Andreas Athanasiou/65 8.00 20.00
RAC Andrew Cogliano/65 6.00 15.00
RAL Adam Larsson/65 6.00 15.00
RAW Alexander Wennberg/65 6.00 15.00
RBB Brian Bellows/35 6.00 15.00
RBD Brandon Dubinsky/65 6.00 15.00
RBE Brian Engblom/65 6.00 15.00
RBH Bo Horvat/65 12.00 30.00
RBO Bobby Smith/35 10.00 25.00
RBP Bob Probert/35 10.00 25.00
RBR Dustin Brown/65 10.00 25.00
RBT Bryan Trottier/35 10.00 25.00
RCG Clark Gillies/35 10.00 25.00
RDA Dave Andreychuk/35 10.00 25.00
RDB Daniel Briere/35 10.00 25.00
RDH Dale Hawerchuk/35 12.00 30.00
RDN Darnell Nurse/65 8.00 20.00
RDP Denis Potvin/35 10.00 25.00
REG Ed Giacomin/35 8.00 20.00
REJ Erik Johnson/65 6.00 15.00
REK Erik Karlsson/35 12.00 30.00
RFF Filip Forsberg/35 15.00 40.00
RFR Michael Frolik/65 8.00 20.00
RJE Jonathan Ericsson/65 6.00 15.00
RJM Joe Mullen/35 10.00 25.00
RJR Jeremy Roenick/35 15.00 40.00
RJS Jason Spezza/65 20.00 50.00
RJU Juuse Saros/65 12.00 30.00
RKL Kevin Lowe/35 10.00 25.00
RLA Lias Andersson/65 8.00 20.00
RLE Kris Letang/35 12.00 30.00
RLM Larry Murphy/35 20.00 50.00
RLU Luc Robitaille/35 10.00 25.00
RMD Mikkel Boedker/65 6.00 15.00
RMI Milan Lucic/65 8.00 20.00
RMO Andy Moog/65 15.00 40.00
RMP Michael Peca/35 8.00 20.00
RMR Mason Raymond/65 8.00 20.00
RMS Marc Staal/65 6.00 15.00
RMV Mike Vernon/35 8.00 20.00
RMZ Alec Martinez/65 6.00 15.00
RNF Nick Foligno/65 8.00 20.00
RNH Noah Hanifin/65 10.00 25.00
ROK Oscar Klefbom/65 10.00 25.00
RPB Patrice Brisebois/35 6.00 15.00
RPE David Perron/65 8.00 20.00
RPH Phil Housley/65 8.00 20.00
RRB Rod Brind'Amour/35 10.00 25.00
RRE Ryan Ellis/65 8.00 20.00
RRJ Ryan Johansen/65 8.00 20.00
RRM Ryan Miller/65 10.00 25.00
RSB Sean Burke/35 8.00 20.00
RSG Sergei Gonchar/35 8.00 20.00
RTD Tie Domi/35 12.00 30.00
RTJ Tyler Johnson/65 6.00 15.00
RVH Vic Hadfield/35 8.00 20.00
RVN Valeri Nichushkin/65 10.00 25.00
RVT Vladimir Tarasenko/35 12.00 30.00
RWN William Nylander/65 20.00 50.00
RWS Wayne Simmonds/65 10.00 25.00

2019-20 Upper Deck Engrained Rare Remnants Signatures

RBN Bernie Nicholls/65 15.00 40.00
RCC Chris Chelios/35 20.00 50.00
RCN Cam Neely/35 20.00 50.00
RCP Carey Price/35 50.00 125.00
RGF Grant Fuhr/35 30.00 80.00
RJT Joe Thornton/35 30.00 80.00
RLI Mike Liut/65 12.00 30.00
RLR Larry Robinson/35 20.00 50.00
RMF Marc-Andre Fleury/35 50.00 125.00
RSB Sergei Bobrovsky/35 30.00 80.00
RTB Tyler Bertuzzi/65 15.00 40.00

2019-20 Upper Deck Engrained Remnants

RAA Andreas Athanasiou 6.00 15.00
RAC Andrew Cogliano 5.00 12.00
RAL Adam Larsson 6.00 15.00
RAM Al MacInnis 10.00 25.00
RAO Alexander Ovechkin 25.00 60.00
RAS Al Secord 6.00 15.00
RAW Alexander Wennberg 5.00 12.00
RBB Brian Bellows 6.00 15.00
RBD Brandon Dubinsky 5.00 12.00
RBE Brian Engblom 5.00 12.00
RBG Bernie Geoffrion 6.00 15.00
RBH Bo Horvat 10.00 25.00
RBI Billy Smith 8.00 20.00
RBN Bernie Nicholls 6.00 15.00
RBO Bobby Smith 8.00 20.00
RBP Bob Probert 8.00 20.00
RBR Dustin Brown 8.00 20.00
RBS Brendan Shanahan 8.00 20.00
RBT Bryan Trottier 8.00 20.00
RCC Chris Chelios 8.00 20.00
RCM Connor McDavid 40.00 100.00
RCN Cam Neely 8.00 20.00
RDA Dave Andreychuk 8.00 20.00
RDB Daniel Briere 6.00 15.00
RDH Dale Hawerchuk 10.00 25.00
RDN Darnell Nurse 6.00 15.00
RDP Denis Potvin 8.00 20.00
REG Ed Giacomin 8.00 20.00
REJ Erik Johnson 5.00 12.00
REK Erik Karlsson 10.00 25.00
REM Evgeni Malkin 15.00 40.00
RFF Filip Forsberg 12.00 30.00
RGF Grant Fuhr 12.00 30.00
RGL Guy Lafleur 10.00 25.00
RHR Henri Richard 8.00 20.00
RJE Jonathan Ericsson 5.00 12.00
RJJ Jaromir Jagr 40.00 100.00
RJK Jari Kurri 8.00 20.00
RJM Joe Mullen 8.00 20.00
RJQ Jonathan Quick 10.00 25.00
RJR Jeremy Roenick 12.00 30.00
RJU Juuse Saros 10.00 25.00
RKL Kevin Lowe 6.00 15.00
RLA Lias Andersson 6.00 15.00
RLE Kris Letang 10.00 25.00
RLI Mike Liut 5.00 12.00
RLM Larry Murphy 6.00 15.00
RLR Larry Robinson 8.00 20.00
RLU Luc Robitaille 8.00 20.00
RMB Martin Brodeur 20.00 50.00
RMD Mikkel Boedker 5.00 12.00
RMF Marc-Andre Fleury 20.00 50.00
RMI Milan Lucic 6.00 15.00
RML Mario Lemieux 30.00 80.00
RMO Andy Moog 8.00 20.00
RMP Michael Peca 6.00 15.00
RMR Mason Raymond 5.00 12.00
RMV Mike Vernon 15.00 40.00
RNF Nick Foligno 6.00 15.00
ROA Adam Oates 6.00 15.00
RPB Patrice Brisebois 5.00 12.00
RPC Paul Coffey 8.00 20.00
RPE David Perron 6.00 15.00
RPH Phil Housley 6.00 15.00
RPM Pete Mahovlich 8.00 20.00
RPR Patrick Roy 20.00 50.00
RRB Rod Brind'Amour 8.00 20.00
RRE Ryan Ellis 6.00 15.00
RRJ Ryan Johansen 6.00 15.00
RSB Sean Burke 6.00 15.00
RSB Sergei Bobrovsky 12.00 30.00
RSG Sergei Gonchar 6.00 15.00
RTB Tyler Bertuzzi 6.00 15.00
RTD Tie Domi 6.00 15.00
RTJ Tyler Johnson 5.00 12.00
RVH Vic Hadfield 6.00 15.00
RVN Valeri Nichushkin 8.00 20.00
RVT Vladimir Tarasenko 20.00 50.00
RWG Wayne Gretzky 40.00 100.00
RWS Wayne Simmonds 8.00 20.00

2019-20 Upper Deck Engrained Rookie Signature Shots

RSSAF Adam Fox/249 20.00 50.00
RSSAS Aleksi Saarela/249 8.00 20.00
RSSAT Alexandre Texier/249 8.00 20.00
RSSAV Alexander Volkov/249 6.00 15.00
RSSBG Brandon Gignac/249 6.00 15.00
RSSBH Barrett Hayton/149 15.00 40.00
RSSBK Brady Keeper/249 8.00 20.00

RSSCG Cody Glass/149 12.00 30.00
RSSCM Cale Makar/149 60.00 150.00
RSSDK Dominik Kubalik/249 15.00 40.00
RSSEM Elvis Merzlikins/249 15.00 40.00
RSSGR Carl Grundstrom/249 8.00 20.00
RSSIM Ilya Mikheyev/249 20.00 50.00
RSSJB Jesper Boqvist/249 6.00 15.00
RSSJD Joey Daccord/249 10.00 25.00
RSSJG Julien Gauthier/249 8.00 20.00
RSSJH Jack Hughes/149 50.00 125.00
RSSJL Joel L'Esperance/249 8.00 20.00
RSSJS Jimmy Schuldt/249 6.00 15.00
RSSKD Kirby Dach/149 30.00 80.00
RSSKK Karson Kuhlman/249 8.00 20.00
RSSKL Klim Kostin/249 8.00 20.00
RSSLH Libor Hajek/249 6.00 15.00
RSSMF Morgan Frost/249 12.00 30.00
RSSMM Mackenzie MacEachern/249 8.00 20.00
RSSMV Max Veronneau/249 6.00 15.00
RSSNB Nathan Bastian/249 8.00 20.00
RSSND Noah Dobson/249 20.00 50.00
RSSNG Nikita Gusev/249 12.00 30.00
RSSNS Nico Sturm/249 6.00 15.00
RSSPM Philippe Myers/249 6.00 15.00
RSSQH Quinn Hughes/149 50.00 125.00
RSSRA Rasmus Asplund/249 6.00 15.00
RSSRB Rudolfs Balcers/249 8.00 20.00
RSSRK Ryan Kuffner/249 6.00 15.00
RSSRM Rem Pitlick/249 8.00 20.00
RSSRS Riley Stillman/249 8.00 20.00
RSSSL Sam Lafferty/249 6.00 15.00
RSSSU Nick Suzuki/249 40.00 100.00
RSSTB Teddy Blueger/249 8.00 20.00
RSSTF Trent Frederic/249 8.00 20.00
RSSTO Tobias Bjornfot/249 8.00 20.00
RSSVH Ville Heinola/249 10.00 25.00
RSSZM Zack MacEwen/249 6.00 15.00
RSSZS Zach Senyshyn/249 8.00 20.00

2019-20 Upper Deck Engrained Rookie Signature Shots Red Stick

*RED: .6X TO 1.5X BASIC
RSSAF Adam Fox/99 30.00 80.00
RSSAT Alexandre Texier/99 20.00 50.00
RSSCM Cale Makar/35 80.00 200.00
RSSEM Elvis Merzlikins/99 25.00 60.00
RSSJD Joey Daccord/99 15.00 40.00
RSSJH Jack Hughes/35 120.00 300.00
RSSKD Kirby Dach/35 60.00 150.00
RSSNG Nikita Gusev/99 12.00 30.00
RSSQH Quinn Hughes/35 120.00 300.00
RSSSU Nick Suzuki/99 60.00 150.00
RSSVH Ville Heinola/99 30.00 80.00

2019-20 Upper Deck Engrained Signature Flexures

SFCM Connor McDavid A 200.00 500.00
SFCN Cam Neely C 20.00 50.00
SFCP Carey Price B 40.00 100.00
SFDG Doug Gilmour C 25.00 60.00
SFJI Jarome Iginla B 50.00 125.00
SFJT Joe Thornton B 30.00 80.00
SFLD Leon Draisaitl B 40.00 100.00
SFLR Larry Robinson C 20.00 50.00
SFPL Pat LaFontaine C 20.00 50.00
SFSC Shayne Corson C 15.00 40.00
SFTS Tyler Seguin A 20.00 50.00
SFWC Wendel Clark C 30.00 80.00
SFWG Wayne Gretzky A 400.00 1000.00

2019-20 Upper Deck Engrained Signature Shots

SSJM Jonathan Marchessault/100 25.00 60.00
SSJP Joe Pavelski/50 25.00 60.00
SSJT John Tavares/25 30.00 80.00
SSLD Leon Draisaitl/25 40.00 100.00
SSNH Nico Hischier/50 40.00 80.00

2023-24 Upper Deck Engrained

1 Connor McDavid 8.00 20.00
2 Cale Makar 4.00 10.00
3 John Tavares 2.50 6.00
4 Patrik Laine 2.00 5.00
5 Bo Horvat 2.00 5.00
6 Tim Stutzle 2.00 5.00
7 Andrei Vasilevskiy 2.50 6.00
8 Jack Hughes 4.00 10.00
9 Ilya Sorokin 2.50 6.00
10 Anze Kopitar 2.50 6.00
11 Evan Bouchard 2.00 5.00
12 K'Andre Miller 1.25 3.00
13 Igor Shesterkin 3.00 8.00
14 Josh Morrissey 2.00 5.00
15 Jack Eichel 2.50 6.00
16 Anton Lundell 1.50 4.00
17 Elias Pettersson 2.50 6.00
18 William Eklund 2.00 5.00
19 Alex Ovechkin 6.00 15.00
20 Seth Jones 1.50 4.00
21 Mikko Rantanen 4.00 10.00
22 Philipp Grubauer 1.50 4.00
23 Trevor Zegras 1.50 4.00
24 Owen Power 1.50 4.00
25 Jonatan Berggren 1.25 3.00
26 Nikolaj Ehlers 1.50 4.00
27 Nathan MacKinnon 6.00 15.00
28 Jason Robertson 2.50 6.00
29 Kent Johnson 1.50 4.00
30 Roope Hintz 2.00 5.00
31 Matty Beniers 2.00 5.00
32 Victor Hedman 2.00 5.00
33 Mark Stone 2.00 5.00
34 Roman Josi 1.50 4.00
35 Nick Suzuki 3.00 8.00
36 Tage Thompson 2.00 5.00
37 Sidney Crosby 6.00 15.00
38 Brady Tkachuk 2.50 6.00
39 Evgeny Kuznetsov 2.00 5.00
40 Tomas Hertl 1.50 4.00
41 Brent Burns 1.50 4.00
42 David Pastrnak 4.00 10.00
43 Jonathan Huberdeau 2.00 5.00
44 Shane Pinto 1.25 3.00
45 Miro Heiskanen 2.00 5.00
46 Jared McCann 1.25 3.00
47 Nico Hischier 2.50 6.00
48 Aatu Raty 1.00 2.50
50 Jacob Markstrom 1.50 4.00
51 Sam Reinhart 3.00 8.00
52 Kirill Kaprizov 5.00 12.00
53 Brayden Point 2.00 5.00
54 Andrei Svechnikov 2.00 5.00
55 Juuse Saros 2.00 5.00
56 Clayton Keller 2.00 5.00
57 Juraj Slafkovsky 3.00 8.00
58 Robert Thomas 1.50 4.00
59 Leon Draisaitl 5.00 12.00
60 Filip Gustavsson 1.50 4.00
61 Matthew Tkachuk 3.00 8.00
62 Auston Matthews 6.00 15.00
63 Alexis Lafreniere 2.50 6.00
64 Brad Marchand 3.00 8.00
65 Jake Sanderson 2.00 5.00
66 Dominik Hasek 4.00 10.00
67 Steve Yzerman 6.00 15.00
68 Chris Chelios 2.50 6.00
69 Michel Goulet 2.50 6.00
70 Joe Nieuwendyk 2.00 5.00
71 Ryan Getzlaf 2.50 6.00
72 Mario Lemieux 10.00 25.00
73 Joe Sakic 5.00 12.00
74 Luc Robitaille 2.50 6.00
75 Mark Recchi 2.50 6.00
76 Dale Hawerchuk 3.00 8.00
77 Keith Primeau 2.00 5.00
78 Denis Potvin 2.50 6.00
79 Peter Forsberg 5.00 12.00
80 Teemu Selanne 5.00 12.00
81 Bob Probert 2.50 6.00
82 Rick Nash 2.50 6.00
83 Bernie Nicholls 2.00 5.00
84 Adam Oates 2.50 6.00
85 Doug Weight 2.50 6.00
86 Paul Coffey 2.50 6.00
87 John LeClair 2.50 6.00
88 Mark Messier 5.00 12.00
89 Mike Gartner 3.00 8.00
90 Shane Doan 2.00 5.00
91 Brett Hull 5.00 12.00
92 Doug Gilmour 3.00 8.00
93 Patrick Roy 6.00 15.00
94 Pat LaFontaine 2.50 6.00
95 Pekka Rinne 2.50 6.00
96 Larry Robinson 2.50 6.00
97 Ron Francis 3.00 8.00
98 Patrice Bergeron 3.00 8.00
99 Wayne Gretzky 15.00 40.00
100 Ray Bourque 4.00 10.00
101 Connor Bedard RC 40.00 100.00
102 Logan Cooley RC 10.00 25.00
103 Simon Edvinsson RC 5.00 12.00
104 Devon Levi RC 6.00 15.00
105 Luke Hughes RC 8.00 20.00
106 Matthew Knies RC 10.00 25.00
107 Akito Hirose RC 2.00 5.00
108 Luke Philp RC 2.50 6.00
109 Owen Beck RC 4.00 10.00
110 Wyatt Kaiser RC 2.50 6.00
111 Luke Evangelista RC 4.00 10.00
112 Samuel Bolduc RC 2.50 6.00
113 Joona Koppanen RC 2.00 5.00
114 Tyson Foerster RC 5.00 12.00
115 Stanislav Svozil RC 2.00 5.00
116 Nikita Nesterenko RC 2.50 6.00
117 Egor Afanasyev RC 2.50 6.00
118 Vincent Iorio RC 2.50 6.00
119 Marco Kasper RC 6.00 15.00
120 Hunter McKown RC 2.50 6.00
121 Jiri Patera RC 4.00 10.00
122 Vincent Desharnais RC 3.00 8.00
123 Zach Benson RC 4.00 10.00
124 William Dufour RC 2.00 5.00
125 Jet Greaves RC 4.00 10.00
126 Samuel Knazko RC 2.50 6.00
127 Matthew Coronato RC 4.00 10.00
128 Nick Swaney RC 2.50 6.00
129 Tristen Robins RC 2.50 6.00
130 Will Cuylle RC 4.00 10.00
131 Kevin Korchinski RC 4.00 10.00
132 Adam Ginning RC 2.50 6.00
133 Matthew Poitras RC 5.00 12.00
134 Ridly Greig RC 4.00 10.00
135 Matthew Kessel RC 2.00 5.00
136 Walker Duehr RC 2.00 5.00
137 Pavel Mintyukov RC 4.00 10.00
138 Brock Faber RC 6.00 15.00
139 Arnaud Durandeau RC 2.50 6.00
140 Cole McWard RC 2.50 6.00
141 Simon Nemec RC 5.00 12.00
142 Leevi Merilainen RC 2.50 6.00
143 Jonathan Gruden RC 2.50 6.00
144 Jakob Pelletier RC 3.00 8.00
145 Bobby McMann RC 4.00 10.00
146 Lukas Rousek RC 2.50 6.00
147 Aidan McDonough RC 2.00 5.00
148 Tye Kartye RC 4.00 10.00
149 Michael Kesselring RC 2.50 6.00
150 Henry Thrun RC 2.50 6.00
151 Sean Farrell RC 2.50 6.00
152 Matt Savoie RC 5.00 12.00
153 Matt Murray RC 2.50 6.00
154 Jake Livingstone RC 2.50 6.00
155 Jaxson Stauber RC 2.50 6.00
156 Hugh McGing RC 2.50 6.00
157 Dustin Wolf RC 8.00 20.00
158 Tyler Kleven RC 2.50 6.00
159 Connor Zary RC 5.00 12.00
160 Milos Kelemen RC 2.50 6.00
161 Elliot Desnoyers RC 2.50 6.00
162 Yaroslav Askarov RC 6.00 15.00
163 Tyler Angle RC 2.50 6.00
164 Adam Fantilli RC 8.00 20.00
165 Leo Carlsson RC 8.00 20.00
166 Juraj Slafkovsky '22 Rookie Update 6.00 15.00
167 Matty Beniers '22 Rookie Update 4.00 10.00
168 Dylan Guenther '22 Rookie Update 4.00 10.00
169 Kent Johnson '22 Rookie Update 3.00 8.00
170 Jack Quinn '22 Rookie Update 2.50 6.00
171 Owen Power '22 Rookie Update 3.00 8.00
172 Jonatan Berggren '22 Rookie Update 2.50 6.00
173 Jake Sanderson '22 Rookie Update 4.00 10.00
174 Pyotr Kochetkov '22 Rookie Update 3.00 8.00
175 Wyatt Johnston '22 Rookie Update 6.00 15.00
176 Dylan Holloway '22 Rookie Update 3.00 8.00
177 Shane Wright '22 Rookie Update 4.00 10.00
178 Brandt Clarke '22 Rookie Update 3.00 8.00
179 David Jiricek '22 Rookie Update 3.00 8.00
180 Matt Boldy '22 Rookie Update 5.00 12.00
181 Arber Xhekaj '22 Rookie Update 3.00 8.00
182 Andrei Kuzmenko '22 Rookie Update 3.00 8.00
183 Lukas Dostal '22 Rookie Update 3.00 8.00
184 Aatu Raty '22 Rookie Update 2.00 5.00
185 Elmer Soderblom '22 Rookie Update 3.00 8.00
186 Marco Rossi '22 Rookie Update 4.00 10.00
187 Kirill Marchenko '22 Rookie Update 4.00 10.00
188 Lukas Reichel '22 Rookie Update 3.00 8.00
189 Kaiden Guhle '22 Rookie Update 3.00 8.00
190 Matias Maccelli '22 Rookie Update 2.50 6.00
191 Cole Caufield '21 Rookie Update 6.00 15.00
192 Trevor Zegras '21 Rookie Update 3.00 8.00
193 Quinton Byfield '21 Rookie Update 4.00 10.00
194 Seth Jarvis '21 Rookie Update 4.00 10.00
195 Moritz Seider '21 Rookie Update 4.00 10.00
196 Jeremy Swayman '21 Rookie Update 5.00 12.00
197 Lucas Raymond '21 Rookie Update 5.00 12.00
198 Dawson Mercer '21 Rookie Update 4.00 10.00
199 Mason McTavish '21 Rookie Update 3.00 8.00
200 Logan Thompson '21 Rookie Update 4.00 10.00

2023-24 Upper Deck Engrained Ebony

*EBONY/49: .8X TO 2X BASIC
*EBONY LEG/RC: .6X TO 1.5X BASIC
*EBONY '21/'22 UPD: .6X TO 1.5X BASIC

2023-24 Upper Deck Engrained White Birch

*BIRCH/20: 1.5X TO 4X BASIC
*BIRCH LEG/20: 1.2X TO 3X BASIC

2023-24 Upper Deck Engrained Autographs

6 Tim Stutzle 10.00 25.00
7 Andrei Vasilevskiy SP 12.00 30.00
8 Jack Hughes SP 20.00 50.00
9 Ilya Sorokin SP 12.00 30.00
12 K'Andre Miller 6.00 15.00
13 Igor Shesterkin SP 15.00 40.00
14 Josh Morrissey 10.00 25.00
16 Anton Lundell 8.00 20.00
17 Elias Pettersson SP 12.00 30.00
18 William Eklund 10.00 25.00
19 Alex Ovechkin SP 60.00 150.00
22 Philipp Grubauer 8.00 20.00
24 Owen Power SP 8.00 20.00
25 Jonatan Berggren 6.00 15.00
27 Nathan MacKinnon SP 30.00 80.00
29 Kent Johnson 8.00 20.00
30 Roope Hintz 10.00 25.00
31 Matty Beniers SP 10.00 25.00
33 Mark Stone 10.00 25.00
36 Tage Thompson SP 10.00 25.00
38 Brady Tkachuk 12.00 30.00
40 Tomas Hertl 8.00 20.00
43 Jonathan Huberdeau 10.00 25.00
44 Shane Pinto 6.00 15.00
46 Jared McCann 6.00 15.00
47 Nico Hischier SP 12.00 30.00
50 Jacob Markstrom 8.00 20.00
51 Sam Reinhart 15.00 40.00
54 Andrei Svechnikov 10.00 25.00
55 Juuse Saros 10.00 25.00
57 Juraj Slafkovsky 15.00 40.00
58 Robert Thomas 8.00 20.00
60 Filip Gustavsson 8.00 20.00
61 Matthew Tkachuk SP 15.00 40.00
62 Auston Matthews SP 60.00 150.00
63 Alexis Lafreniere SP 12.00 30.00
64 Brad Marchand SP 15.00 40.00
65 Jake Sanderson 10.00 25.00
66 Dominik Hasek SP 12.00 30.00
67 Steve Yzerman SP 40.00 100.00
68 Chris Chelios SP 8.00 20.00
71 Ryan Getzlaf 8.00 20.00
74 Luc Robitaille SP 8.00 20.00
75 Mark Recchi 8.00 20.00
77 Keith Primeau 6.00 15.00
82 Rick Nash SP 8.00 20.00
87 John LeClair 8.00 20.00
88 Mark Messier SP 40.00 100.00
89 Mike Gartner 10.00 25.00
90 Shane Doan 6.00 15.00
92 Doug Gilmour SP 10.00 25.00
96 Larry Robinson SP 8.00 20.00
97 Ron Francis SP 10.00 25.00
98 Patrice Bergeron SP 40.00 100.00
100 Ray Bourque SP 12.00 30.00
101 Connor Bedard SP 400.00 1000.00
102 Logan Cooley SP 25.00 60.00
104 Devon Levi 15.00 40.00
105 Luke Hughes SP 20.00 50.00
106 Matthew Knies 40.00 100.00
107 Akito Hirose 5.00 12.00
108 Luke Philp 6.00 15.00
110 Wyatt Kaiser 6.00 15.00
111 Luke Evangelista 10.00 25.00
112 Samuel Bolduc 6.00 15.00
113 Joona Koppanen 5.00 12.00
114 Tyson Foerster 12.00 30.00
115 Stanislav Svozil 5.00 12.00
118 Vincent Iorio 6.00 15.00
119 Marco Kasper 15.00 40.00
121 Jiri Patera 10.00 25.00
122 Vincent Desharnais 8.00 20.00
123 Zach Benson 10.00 25.00
124 William Dufour 5.00 12.00
125 Jet Greaves 10.00 25.00
126 Samuel Knazko 6.00 15.00
127 Matthew Coronato 10.00 25.00
128 Nick Swaney 6.00 15.00
129 Tristen Robins 6.00 15.00
131 Kevin Korchinski 10.00 25.00
132 Adam Ginning 6.00 15.00
133 Matthew Poitras 25.00 60.00
134 Ridly Greig 10.00 25.00
135 Matthew Kessel 5.00 12.00
136 Walker Duehr 5.00 12.00
139 Arnaud Durandeau 6.00 15.00
140 Cole McWard 6.00 15.00
142 Leevi Merilainen 6.00 15.00
143 Jonathan Gruden 6.00 15.00
144 Jakob Pelletier 8.00 20.00
145 Bobby McMann 10.00 25.00
146 Lukas Rousek 6.00 15.00
147 Aidan McDonough 5.00 12.00
148 Tye Kartye 10.00 25.00
150 Henry Thrun 6.00 15.00
151 Sean Farrell 6.00 15.00
152 Matt Savoie 12.00 30.00
153 Matt Murray 6.00 15.00
154 Jake Livingstone 6.00 15.00
155 Jaxson Stauber 6.00 15.00
156 Hugh McGing 6.00 15.00
157 Dustin Wolf 20.00 50.00
158 Tyler Kleven 6.00 15.00
159 Connor Zary 12.00 30.00
160 Milos Kelemen 6.00 15.00
161 Elliot Desnoyers 6.00 15.00
164 Adam Fantilli SP 30.00 80.00
165 Leo Carlsson SP 40.00 100.00
166 Juraj Slafkovsky SP '22 Rookie Update 40.00 100.00
167 Matty Beniers SP '22 Rookie Update 12.00 30.00
168 Dylan Guenther '22 Rookie Update 12.00 30.00
169 Kent Johnson '22 Rookie Update 10.00 25.00
171 Owen Power SP '22 Rookie Update 10.00 25.00
172 Jonatan Berggren '22 Rookie Update 8.00 20.00
173 Jake Sanderson '22 Rookie Update 12.00 30.00
174 Pyotr Kochetkov '22 Rookie Update 15.00 40.00
175 Wyatt Johnston SP '22 Rookie Update 20.00 50.00
176 Dylan Holloway '22 Rookie Update 10.00 25.00
177 Shane Wright '22 Rookie Update 12.00 30.00
178 Brandt Clarke '22 Rookie Update 10.00 25.00
183 Lukas Dostal '22 Rookie Update 20.00 50.00
186 Marco Rossi '22 Rookie Update 12.00 30.00
188 Lukas Reichel '22 Rookie Update 10.00 25.00
189 Kaiden Guhle '22 Rookie Update 10.00 25.00
190 Matias Maccelli '22 Rookie Update 8.00 20.00
194 Seth Jarvis SP '21 Rookie Update 30.00 80.00
196 Jeremy Swayman '21 Rookie Update 15.00 40.00
198 Dawson Mercer SP '21 Rookie Update 20.00 50.00

2023-24 Upper Deck Engrained Autographs White Birch

*WHITE BIRCH: .6X TO 1.5X BASIC
66 Dominik Hasek/35 40.00 100.00
68 Chris Chelios/35 15.00 40.00
74 Luc Robitaille/35 40.00 100.00

2023-24 Upper Deck Engrained Carved in Time

CT1 Wayne Gretzky 50.00 125.00
CT2 Cale Makar 20.00 50.00
CT3 Eric Lindros 12.00 30.00
CT4 Joe Sakic 15.00 40.00
CT5 Frank Mahovlich 8.00 20.00
CT6 Ron Francis 10.00 25.00
CT7 Bernie Nicholls 6.00 15.00
CT8 Leon Draisaitl 25.00 60.00
CT9 Brendan Shanahan 8.00 20.00
CT10 Ray Bourque 12.00 30.00
CT11 Andy Bathgate 6.00 15.00
CT12 Paul Coffey 8.00 20.00
CT13 Chris Pronger 8.00 20.00
CT14 Dale Hawerchuk 10.00 25.00
CT15 Jaromir Jagr 25.00 60.00
CT16 Sid Abel 8.00 20.00
CT17 Jean Ratelle 6.00 15.00
CT18 Kirill Kaprizov 25.00 60.00
CT19 Teemu Selanne 15.00 40.00
CT20 Johnny Bower 8.00 20.00
CT21 Henrik Zetterberg 10.00 25.00
CT22 Bryan Trottier 8.00 20.00
CT23 Mike Gartner 10.00 25.00
CT24 Joe Nieuwendyk 6.00 15.00
CT25 Rogie Vachon 8.00 20.00
CT26 Borje Salming 8.00 20.00
CT27 Patrice Bergeron 10.00 25.00
CT28 Rod Brind'Amour 8.00 20.00
CT29 Jari Kurri 8.00 20.00
CT30 Henri Richard 8.00 20.00

2023-24 Upper Deck Engrained Carved in Time Signatures

CT6 Ron Francis 20.00 50.00
CT10 Ray Bourque 40.00 100.00
CT22 Bryan Trottier 15.00 40.00
CT23 Mike Gartner 20.00 50.00
CT25 Rogie Vachon 15.00 40.00
CT28 Rod Brind'Amour 15.00 40.00
CT29 Jari Kurri 15.00 40.00

2023-24 Upper Deck Engrained Clutch Components

CCEB Jordan Eberle/25 10.00 25.00
CCMS Mark Stone/25 12.00 30.00
CCPG Philipp Grubauer/25 10.00 25.00
CCZH Zach Hyman/25 15.00 40.00

2023-24 Upper Deck Engrained Complete Sticks

CSAO Alex Ovechkin 150.00 400.00
CSBT Brady Tkachuk 30.00 80.00
CSCM Cale Makar 100.00 250.00
CSDB Drake Batherson 20.00 50.00
CSDH Dany Heatley 15.00 40.00
CSDP Denis Potvin 20.00 50.00
CSDT Dave Taylor 15.00 40.00
CSEL Eric Lindros 100.00 250.00
CSHZ Henrik Zetterberg 25.00 60.00
CSJH Jack Hughes 100.00 250.00
CSJM Jared McCann 30.00 80.00
CSJT John Tavares 30.00 80.00
CSMA Jonathan Marchessault 25.00 60.00
CSPR Patrick Roy 150.00 400.00
CSRB Rod Brind'Amour 30.00 80.00
CSSC Sidney Crosby 150.00 400.00
CSTS Teemu Selanne 40.00 100.00

2023-24 Upper Deck Engrained Complete Sticks Signatures

CSSAO Alex Ovechkin 500.00 1200.00
CSSBT Brady Tkachuk 60.00 150.00
CSSDB Drake Batherson 40.00 100.00
CSSDH Dany Heatley 30.00 80.00
CSSDT Dave Taylor 40.00 100.00
CSSEL Eric Lindros 150.00 400.00
CSSJH Jack Hughes 150.00 400.00
CSSJM Jared McCann 60.00 150.00
CSSMA Jonathan Marchessault 50.00 125.00
CSSRB Rod Brind'Amour 60.00 150.00

2023-24 Upper Deck Engrained ElectroCast

EC1 Connor Bedard 20.00 50.00
EC2 Simon Edvinsson 5.00 12.00
EC3 Cole Sillinger 2.00 5.00
EC4 Quinn Hughes 6.00 15.00
EC5 Sam Bennett 4.00 10.00
EC6 Adrian Kempe 2.50 6.00
EC7 Mikael Backlund 2.00 5.00
EC8 Moritz Seider 3.00 8.00
EC9 Torey Krug 2.00 5.00
EC10 Brock Boeser 3.00 8.00
EC11 Jeff Petry 2.50 6.00
EC12 Anders Lee 2.00 5.00
EC13 Brandt Clarke 2.50 6.00
EC14 Jake Oettinger 4.00 10.00
EC15 Anton Lundell 2.50 6.00
EC16 Alexis Lafreniere 4.00 10.00
EC17 Drake Batherson 2.50 6.00
EC18 Matthew Knies 10.00 25.00
EC19 Jalen Chatfield 1.50 4.00
EC20 Zach Hyman 4.00 10.00
EC21 Seth Jarvis 3.00 8.00
EC22 Kirill Marchenko 3.00 8.00
EC23 Jacob Middleton 1.50 4.00
EC24 Jamie Drysdale 2.00 5.00
EC25 Carter Verhaeghe 2.50 6.00
EC26 David Perron 2.00 5.00
EC27 Ilya Samsonov 2.50 6.00
EC28 Pyotr Kochetkov 2.50 6.00
EC29 Vladimir Tarasenko 3.00 8.00
EC30 Alexandar Georgiev 2.50 6.00
EC31 Dylan Cozens 2.50 6.00
EC32 Marc-Andre Fleury 5.00 12.00
EC33 Josh Norris 2.50 6.00
EC34 J.T. Compher 1.50 4.00
EC35 Kevin Labanc 1.50 4.00
EC36 Nico Hischier 4.00 10.00
EC37 Alex DeBrincat 3.00 8.00
EC38 Owen Beck 4.00 10.00
EC39 Brendan Gallagher 2.50 6.00
EC40 Juuse Saros 3.00 8.00
EC41 Darnell Nurse 2.00 5.00
EC42 Alex Tuch 2.50 6.00
EC43 Gabe Vilardi 2.50 6.00
EC44 Nick Schmaltz 2.00 5.00
EC45 Bowen Byram 3.00 8.00
EC46 Jason Zucker 2.50 6.00
EC47 Stuart Skinner 3.00 8.00
EC48 Tom Wilson 2.50 6.00
EC49 Tyler Toffoli 2.50 6.00
EC50 Tyson Foerster 5.00 12.00

2023-24 Upper Deck Engrained ElectroCast Autographs

EC2 Simon Edvinsson 15.00 40.00
EC3 Cole Sillinger 6.00 15.00
EC7 Mikael Backlund 6.00 15.00
EC9 Torey Krug 6.00 15.00
EC10 Brock Boeser 15.00 40.00
EC11 Jeff Petry 8.00 20.00
EC12 Anders Lee 6.00 15.00
EC13 Brandt Clarke 8.00 20.00
EC14 Jake Oettinger 12.00 30.00
EC15 Anton Lundell 8.00 20.00
EC16 Alexis Lafreniere 12.00 30.00
EC18 Matthew Knies 30.00 80.00
EC21 Seth Jarvis 10.00 25.00
EC23 Jacob Middleton 5.00 12.00
EC26 David Perron 6.00 15.00
EC27 Ilya Samsonov 8.00 20.00
EC28 Pyotr Kochetkov 8.00 20.00
EC32 Marc-Andre Fleury 25.00 60.00
EC34 J.T. Compher 5.00 12.00
EC35 Kevin Labanc 5.00 12.00
EC36 Nico Hischier 12.00 30.00
EC40 Juuse Saros 10.00 25.00
EC42 Alex Tuch 8.00 20.00
EC43 Gabe Vilardi 8.00 20.00
EC44 Nick Schmaltz 6.00 15.00
EC45 Bowen Byram 10.00 25.00
EC46 Jason Zucker 8.00 20.00
EC47 Stuart Skinner 10.00 25.00
EC48 Tom Wilson SP 8.00 20.00
EC49 Tyler Toffoli 8.00 20.00
EC50 Tyson Foerster 15.00 40.00

2023-24 Upper Deck Engrained Flexures Autographs

FSFP Felix Potvin 25.00 60.00
FSJL John LeClair 15.00 40.00
FSJO Jordan Eberle 15.00 40.00
FSJS Jake Sanderson 20.00 50.00
FSLR Luc Robitaille 30.00 80.00
FSMA Martin St. Louis 15.00 40.00
FSMB Martin Brodeur SP 40.00 100.00
FSMF Marc-Andre Fleury 80.00 200.00
FSMM Mike Modano SP 25.00 60.00
FSSG Samuel Girard 10.00 25.00

2023-24 Upper Deck Engrained Honorary Engravings

HECA06 Alex Ovechkin 50.00 120.00
HECA19 Elias Pettersson 20.00 50.00
HECA20 Cale Makar 30.00 80.00
HECA21 Kirill Kaprizov 40.00 100.00
HECA22 Moritz Seider 15.00 40.00
HECA23 Matty Beniers 15.00 40.00
HECA87 Luc Robitaille 12.00 30.00
HECA93 Teemu Selanne 25.00 60.00
HENO02 Nicklas Lidstrom 12.00 30.00
HENO21 Adam Fox 15.00 40.00
HENO23 Erik Karlsson 15.00 40.00
HENO69 Bobby Orr 20.00 50.00
HENO83 Rod Langway 10.00 25.00
HEVE12 Henrik Lundqvist 30.00 80.00
HEVE15 Carey Price 25.00 60.00
HEVE22 Igor Shesterkin 25.00 60.00
HEVE23 Linus Ullmark 10.00 25.00
HEVE93 Ed Belfour 12.00 30.00
HEVE94 Dominik Hasek 20.00 50.00

2023-24 Upper Deck Engrained Legendary Signature Shots

LSSAM Andy Moog/99 20.00 50.00
LSSBG Bill Guerin/99 20.00 50.00
LSSBL Rob Blake/49 20.00 50.00
LSSBR Rod Brind'Amour/49 20.00 50.00
LSSCC Chris Chelios/49 20.00 50.00
LSSCN Cam Neely/49 20.00 50.00
LSSDH Dany Heatley/49 15.00 40.00
LSSEL Eric Lindros/25 30.00 80.00
LSSFP Felix Potvin/99 40.00 100.00
LSSGC Gerry Cheevers/49 20.00 50.00
LSSGF Grant Fuhr/25 30.00 80.00
LSSJB Johnny Bucyk/49 20.00 50.00
LSSJK Jari Kurri/49 20.00 50.00
LSSJT Joe Thornton/49 30.00 80.00
LSSKP Keith Primeau/49 20.00 50.00
LSSMA Al MacInnis/49 25.00 60.00
LSSMD Marcel Dionne/49 25.00 60.00
LSSML Mario Lemieux/25 200.00 500.00
LSSMM Mike Modano/25 30.00 80.00
LSSRA Bill Ranford/49 20.00 50.00
LSSRB Ray Bourque/25 30.00 80.00
LSSRH Ron Hextall/49 20.00 50.00
LSSRV Rogie Vachon/49 20.00 50.00
LSSSC Shayne Corson/99 15.00 40.00
LSSSD Shane Doan/99 15.00 40.00
LSSYC Yvan Cournoyer/49 20.00 50.00

2023-24 Upper Deck Engrained Premium Memorabilia Autographs Mahogany

12 K'Andre Miller/25 12.00 30.00
14 Josh Morrissey/25 20.00 50.00
16 Anton Lundell/25 15.00 40.00
18 William Eklund/25 20.00 50.00
22 Philipp Grubauer/25 15.00 40.00
29 Kent Johnson/25 15.00 40.00
30 Roope Hintz/25 20.00 50.00
33 Mark Stone/25 20.00 50.00
40 Tomas Hertl/25 15.00 40.00
43 Jonathan Huberdeau/25 20.00 50.00
46 Jared McCann/25 12.00 30.00
47 Nico Hischier/25 25.00 60.00
50 Jacob Markstrom/25 15.00 40.00
51 Sam Reinhart/25 30.00 80.00
54 Andrei Svechnikov/25 20.00 50.00
58 Robert Thomas/25 15.00 40.00
60 Filip Gustavsson/25 15.00 40.00
63 Alexis Lafreniere/25 25.00 60.00
65 Jake Sanderson/25 20.00 50.00
71 Ryan Getzlaf/25 15.00 40.00
82 Rick Nash/25 15.00 40.00
90 Shane Doan/25 12.00 30.00
104 Devon Levi/25 40.00 100.00
106 Matthew Knies/25 80.00 200.00
107 Akito Hirose/35 12.00 30.00
108 Luke Philp/49 15.00 40.00
110 Wyatt Kaiser/49 15.00 40.00
111 Luke Evangelista/25 25.00 60.00
112 Samuel Bolduc/49 15.00 40.00
113 Joona Koppanen/49 12.00 30.00
114 Tyson Foerster/25 30.00 80.00
115 Stanislav Svozil/35 12.00 30.00
118 Vincent Iorio/49 15.00 40.00
119 Marco Kasper/25 40.00 100.00
121 Jiri Patera/49 25.00 60.00
122 Vincent Desharnais/49 20.00 50.00
123 Zach Benson/25 25.00 60.00
124 William Dufour/49 12.00 30.00
125 Jet Greaves/49 25.00 60.00
126 Samuel Knazko/49 15.00 40.00
127 Matthew Coronato/25 25.00 60.00
128 Nick Swaney/49 15.00 40.00
129 Tristen Robins/49 15.00 40.00
131 Kevin Korchinski/25 25.00 60.00
132 Adam Ginning/49 15.00 40.00
133 Matthew Poitras/25 30.00 80.00
134 Ridly Greig/25 25.00 60.00
135 Matthew Kessel/49 12.00 30.00
136 Walker Duehr/49 12.00 30.00
137 Pavel Mintyukov/49 25.00 60.00
139 Arnaud Durandeau/49 15.00 40.00
140 Cole McWard/49 15.00 40.00
142 Leevi Merilainen/49 15.00 40.00
143 Jonathan Gruden/35 15.00 40.00
144 Jakob Pelletier/25 20.00 50.00
145 Bobby McMann/49 25.00 60.00
146 Lukas Rousek/49 15.00 40.00
147 Aidan McDonough/49 12.00 30.00
148 Tye Kartye/49 25.00 60.00
150 Henry Thrun/49 15.00 40.00
153 Matt Murray/49 15.00 40.00
154 Jake Livingstone/25 15.00 40.00
155 Jaxson Stauber/49 15.00 40.00
156 Hugh McGing/49 15.00 40.00
158 Tyler Kleven/49 15.00 40.00
159 Connor Zary/25 30.00 80.00
160 Milos Kelemen/49 15.00 40.00
161 Elliot Desnoyers/49 15.00 40.00
165 Leo Carlsson/25 60.00 150.00
166 Juraj Slafkovsky/25 '22 Rookie Update 60.00 150.00
168 Dylan Guenther/35 '22 Rookie Update 20.00 50.00
169 Kent Johnson/25 '22 Rookie Update 15.00 40.00
171 Owen Power/25 '22 Rookie Update 40.00 100.00
172 Jonatan Berggren/49 '22 Rookie Update 12.00 30.00
173 Jake Sanderson/35 '22 Rookie Update 20.00 50.00
174 Pyotr Kochetkov/25 '22 Rookie Update 15.00 40.00
176 Dylan Holloway/35 '22 Rookie Update 15.00 40.00
177 Shane Wright/25 '22 Rookie Update 20.00 50.00
178 Brandt Clarke/35 '22 Rookie Update 15.00 40.00
183 Lukas Dostal/25 '22 Rookie Update 15.00 40.00
186 Marco Rossi/35 '22 Rookie Update 20.00 50.00
188 Lukas Reichel/35 '22 Rookie Update 15.00 40.00
189 Kaiden Guhle/35 '22 Rookie Update 15.00 40.00
190 Matias Maccelli/35 '22 Rookie Update 12.00 30.00
194 Seth Jarvis/35 '21 Rookie Update 80.00 200.00
196 Jeremy Swayman/35 '21 Rookie Update 50.00 125.00
198 Dawson Mercer/35 '21 Rookie Update 30.00 80.00

2023-24 Upper Deck Engrained Premium Memorabilia Ebony

4 Patrik Laine/35 12.00 30.00
5 Bo Horvat/25 12.00 30.00
6 Tim Stutzle/35 12.00 30.00
9 Ilya Sorokin/35 15.00 40.00
14 Josh Morrissey/25 12.00 30.00
16 Anton Lundell/35 10.00 25.00
18 William Eklund/35 12.00 30.00
20 Seth Jones/25 10.00 25.00
33 Mark Stone/25 12.00 30.00
35 Nick Suzuki/25 20.00 50.00
39 Evgeny Kuznetsov/35 12.00 30.00
40 Tomas Hertl/35 10.00 25.00
43 Jonathan Huberdeau/35 12.00 30.00
47 Nico Hischier/25 15.00 40.00
54 Andrei Svechnikov/25 12.00 30.00
55 Juuse Saros/35 12.00 30.00
56 Clayton Keller/25 12.00 30.00
58 Robert Thomas/25 10.00 25.00
60 Filip Gustavsson/35 10.00 25.00
63 Alexis Lafreniere/25 15.00 40.00
65 Jake Sanderson/25 12.00 30.00
66 Dominik Hasek/25 15.00 40.00
68 Chris Chelios/25 10.00 25.00
69 Michel Goulet/25 10.00 25.00
70 Joe Nieuwendyk/25 8.00 20.00
71 Ryan Getzlaf/25 10.00 25.00
72 Mario Lemieux/25 40.00 100.00
73 Joe Sakic/25 20.00 50.00
74 Luc Robitaille/25 10.00 25.00
75 Mark Recchi/25 10.00 25.00
77 Keith Primeau/25 8.00 20.00
78 Denis Potvin/25 10.00 25.00
79 Peter Forsberg/25 20.00 50.00
80 Teemu Selanne/25 20.00 50.00
81 Bob Probert/25 10.00 25.00
82 Rick Nash/25 10.00 25.00
85 Doug Weight/25 10.00 25.00
86 Paul Coffey/25 10.00 25.00
87 John LeClair/25 10.00 25.00
88 Mark Messier/25 20.00 50.00
90 Shane Doan/25 8.00 20.00
92 Doug Gilmour/25 12.00 30.00
93 Patrick Roy/25 25.00 60.00
95 Pekka Rinne/25 10.00 25.00
97 Ron Francis/25 12.00 30.00
98 Patrice Bergeron/25 12.00 30.00
100 Ray Bourque/25 15.00 40.00
103 Simon Edvinsson/35 20.00 50.00
107 Akito Hirose/35 8.00 20.00
109 Owen Beck/35 15.00 40.00
110 Wyatt Kaiser/35 10.00 25.00
112 Samuel Bolduc/35 10.00 25.00
115 Stanislav Svozil/35 8.00 20.00
117 Egor Afanasyev/35 10.00 25.00
118 Vincent Iorio/35 10.00 25.00
120 Hunter McKown/35 10.00 25.00
122 Vincent Desharnais/35 12.00 30.00
126 Samuel Knazko/35 10.00 25.00
128 Nick Swaney/35 10.00 25.00
129 Tristen Robins/35 10.00 25.00
132 Adam Ginning/35 10.00 25.00
135 Matthew Kessel/35 8.00 20.00
136 Walker Duehr/35 8.00 20.00
139 Arnaud Durandeau/35 10.00 25.00
140 Cole McWard/35 10.00 25.00
142 Leevi Merilainen/35 10.00 25.00
143 Jonathan Gruden/35 10.00 25.00
145 Bobby McMann/35 15.00 40.00
146 Lukas Rousek/35 10.00 25.00
148 Tye Kartye/35 15.00 40.00

150 Henry Thrun/35 10.00 25.00
153 Matt Murray/35 10.00 25.00
154 Jake Livingstone/35 10.00 25.00
155 Jaxson Stauber/35 10.00 25.00
156 Hugh McGing/35 10.00 25.00
158 Tyler Kleven/35 10.00 25.00
160 Milos Kelemen/35 10.00 25.00
162 Yaroslav Askarov/35 25.00 60.00
179 David Jiricek/35
'22 Rookie Update 10.00 25.00
181 Arber Xhekaj/35
'22 Rookie Update 10.00 25.00
197 Lucas Raymond/35
'21 Rookie Update 15.00 40.00
200 Logan Thompson/35
'21 Rookie Update 12.00 30.00

2023-24 Upper Deck Engrained Remnants

*RARE/25: .6X TO 1.5X BASIC
RAD Alex DeBrincat 8.00 20.00
RAO Adam Oates 6.00 15.00
RAP Alex Pietrangelo 5.00 12.00
RAV Andrei Vasilevskiy 10.00 25.00
RBA Rod Brind'Amour 6.00 15.00
RBH Bobby Hull 12.00 30.00
RBL Rob Blake 6.00 15.00
RBM Brayden McNabb 4.00 10.00
RBN Bernie Nicholls 5.00 12.00
RBO Mike Bossy 6.00 15.00
RBR Bill Ranford 5.00 12.00
RBT Brady Tkachuk 10.00 25.00
RCC Chris Chelios 6.00 15.00
RCG Claude Giroux 6.00 15.00
RCH Connor Hellebuyck 12.00 30.00
RCJ Calle Jarnkrok 4.00 10.00
RCM Cale Makar SP 15.00 40.00
RCO Shayne Corson 5.00 12.00
RCP Carey Price 12.00 30.00
RCR Sidney Crosby SP 25.00 60.00
RCS Carson Soucy 4.00 10.00
RDB Drake Batherson 6.00 15.00
RDG Doug Gilmour 8.00 20.00
RDH Dany Heatley 5.00 12.00
RDP David Pastrnak 15.00 40.00
RDT Dave Taylor 5.00 12.00
REB Evan Bouchard 8.00 20.00
REJ Jordan Eberle 6.00 15.00
REL Eric Lindros SP 10.00 25.00
REM Evgeni Malkin 12.00 30.00
RFP Felix Potvin 10.00 25.00
RGA Mike Gartner 8.00 20.00
RGF Grant Fuhr 10.00 25.00
RHA Dominik Hasek 10.00 25.00
RHL Henrik Lundqvist 15.00 40.00
RHR Henri Richard SP 6.00 15.00
RHU Brett Hull 12.00 30.00
RHZ Henrik Zetterberg 8.00 20.00
RJC Jack Campbell 6.00 15.00
RJE Jack Eichel 10.00 25.00
RJH Jack Hughes 15.00 40.00
RJK Jari Kurri 6.00 15.00
RJL John LeClair 6.00 15.00
RJM Jared McCann 5.00 12.00
RJO Joe Sakic SP 12.00 30.00
RJQ Jonathan Quick 8.00 20.00
RJS Jaden Schwartz 5.00 12.00
RJT John Tavares 10.00 25.00
RJU Juuse Saros 8.00 20.00
RKP Keith Primeau 5.00 12.00
RLD Leon Draisaitl SP 20.00 50.00
RLR Larry Robinson 6.00 15.00
RLS Luke Schenn 6.00 15.00
RLU Milan Lucic 5.00 12.00
RMA Auston Matthews SP 25.00 60.00
RMB Martin Brodeur SP 15.00 40.00
RMC Connor McDavid SP 40.00 100.00
RMD Marcel Dionne 8.00 20.00
RMF Marc-Andre Fleury 12.00 30.00
RMG Mark Giordano 6.00 15.00
RMI Mike Modano 10.00 25.00
RMJ Jonathan Marchessault 8.00 20.00
RML Mario Lemieux SP 25.00 60.00
RMM Mark Messier 12.00 30.00
RMO Josh Morrissey 8.00 20.00
RMP Max Pacioretty 6.00 15.00
RMR Mark Recchi 6.00 15.00
RMS Mark Stone 8.00 20.00
RNH Noah Hanifin 6.00 15.00
RNL Nicklas Lidstrom 6.00 15.00
ROV Alex Ovechkin SP 40.00 100.00
RPC Paul Coffey 6.00 15.00
RPF Peter Forsberg 12.00 30.00
RPG Philipp Grubauer 6.00 15.00
RPK Patrick Kane 12.00 30.00
RPO Denis Potvin 6.00 15.00
RPR Patrick Roy SP 15.00 40.00
RRA Mikko Rantanen 15.00 40.00
RRB Ray Bourque 10.00 25.00
RRD Ryan Donato 5.00 12.00
RRH Ron Hextall 6.00 15.00
RRO Luc Robitaille 6.00 15.00
RSA Jake Sanderson 8.00 20.00
RSB Sergei Bobrovsky 10.00 25.00
RSC Justin Schultz 5.00 12.00
RSE Mikhail Sergachev 5.00 12.00
RSG Samuel Girard 4.00 10.00
RSP Shane Pinto 5.00 12.00
RST Martin St. Louis 6.00 15.00
RSY Steve Yzerman 15.00 40.00
RTH Shea Theodore 8.00 20.00
RTO Terry O'Reilly 5.00 12.00
RTS Teemu Selanne 12.00 30.00
RWG Wayne Gretzky SP 60.00 150.00
RYC Yvan Cournoyer 6.00 15.00

2023-24 Upper Deck Engrained Rookie Signature Shots

RSSAD Arnaud Durandeau/299 6.00 15.00
RSSAF Adam Fantilli/49 60.00 150.00
RSSAH Akito Hirose/299 5.00 12.00
RSSAM Aidan McDonough/299 5.00 12.00
RSSBM Bobby McMann/299 10.00 25.00
RSSCA Leo Carlsson/149 40.00 100.00
RSSCB Connor Bedard/99 600.00 1500.00
RSSCG Cole Guttman/299 6.00 15.00
RSSCM Cole McWard/299 6.00 15.00
RSSCO Matthew Coronato/149 10.00 25.00
RSSDU William Dufour/299 5.00 12.00
RSSDW Dustin Wolf/149 20.00 50.00
RSSED Elliot Desnoyers/299 6.00 15.00
RSSGD David Gust/299 6.00 15.00
RSSGR Jonathan Gruden/299 6.00 15.00
RSSHT Henry Thrun/299 6.00 15.00
RSSJG Jet Greaves/299 10.00 25.00
RSSJK Joona Koppanen/299 5.00 12.00
RSSJP Jiri Patera/299 10.00 25.00
RSSJS Jaxson Stauber/299 6.00 15.00
RSSKA Marco Kasper/149 15.00 40.00
RSSKK Kevin Korchinski/149 10.00 25.00
RSSKL Tyler Kleven/299 6.00 15.00
RSSLC Logan Cooley/99 40.00 100.00
RSSLE Luke Evangelista/149 10.00 25.00
RSSLH Luke Hughes/99 40.00 100.00
RSSLI Jake Livingstone/299 6.00 15.00
RSSLM Leevi Merilainen/299 6.00 15.00
RSSLP Luke Philp/299 6.00 15.00
RSSLR Lukas Rousek/299 6.00 15.00
RSSMC Hugh McGing/299 6.00 15.00
RSSMI Milos Kelemen/299 6.00 15.00
RSSMK Matthew Kessel/299 5.00 12.00
RSSMM Matt Murray/299 6.00 15.00
RSSMS Matt Savoie/149 12.00 30.00
RSSNS Nick Swaney/299 6.00 15.00
RSSOE Olle Eriksson Ek/299 6.00 15.00
RSSPE Jakob Pelletier/149 8.00 20.00
RSSRG Ridly Greig/99 10.00 25.00
RSSSB Samuel Bolduc/299 6.00 15.00
RSSSF Sean Farrell/149 6.00 15.00
RSSSK Samuel Knazko/299 6.00 15.00
RSSSS Stanislav Svozil/299 5.00 12.00
RSSTF Tyson Foerster/99 12.00 30.00
RSSTK Tye Kartye/299 10.00 25.00
RSSTR Tristen Robins/299 6.00 15.00
RSSVD Vincent Desharnais/299 8.00 20.00
RSSVI Vincent Iorio/299 6.00 15.00
RSSWD Walker Duehr/299 5.00 12.00
RSSWK Wyatt Kaiser/299 6.00 15.00

2023-24 Upper Deck Engrained Rookie Signature Shots Green Stick

*GREEN: .6X TO 1.5X BASIC
RSSCA Leo Carlsson/50 80.00 200.00
RSSDW Dustin Wolf/50 50.00 125.00
RSSLC Logan Cooley/35 100.00 250.00
RSSLH Luke Hughes/35 80.00 200.00
RSSTK Tye Kartye/75 25.00 60.00
RSSVD Vincent Desharnais/75 20.00 50.00

2023-24 Upper Deck Engrained Rookie Signature Shots Red Stick

*RED: .5X TO 1.2X BASIC
RSSCA Leo Carlsson/75 60.00 150.00
RSSDW Dustin Wolf/75 40.00 100.00
RSSLC Logan Cooley/45 80.00 200.00
RSSLH Luke Hughes/45 60.00 150.00
RSSTK Tye Kartye/99 20.00 50.00
RSSVD Vincent Desharnais/99 15.00 40.00

2023-24 Upper Deck Engrained Signature Remnants

RMJ Jonathan Marchessault 25.00 60.00
RSA Jake Sanderson 25.00 60.00
RSP Shane Pinto 15.00 40.00

2023-24 Upper Deck Engrained Signature Shots

SSAM Auston Matthews/25 125.00 300.00
SSAO Alex Ovechkin/25 150.00 400.00
SSAT Alex Tuch/49 12.00 30.00
SSAV Andrei Vasilevskiy/49 20.00 50.00
SSBM Brad Marchand/49 25.00 60.00
SSBN Brock Nelson/99 12.00 30.00
SSBS Brandon Saad/99 10.00 25.00
SSBY Bowen Byram/99 16.00 40.00
SSCH Connor Hellebuyck/49 25.00 60.00
SSCP Colton Parayko/99 10.00 25.00
SSCS Cole Sillinger/99 10.00 25.00
SSDB Drake Batherson/99 12.00 30.00
SSDP David Perron/99 10.00 25.00
SSEB Jordan Eberle/99 12.00 30.00
SSFG Filip Gustavsson/99 12.00 30.00
SSJB Jordan Binnington/99 20.00 50.00
SSJE Joel Eriksson Ek/99 10.00 25.00
SSJG Jake Guentzel/49 15.00 40.00
SSJH Jack Hughes/25 40.00 100.00
SSJM Jacob Markstrom/99 12.00 30.00
SSJO Jake Oettinger/49 20.00 50.00
SSKF Kevin Fiala/99 10.00 25.00
SSKM K'Andre Miller/99 10.00 25.00
SSKS Kiefer Sherwood/99 8.00 20.00
SSMA Mikey Anderson/99 10.00 25.00
SSMB Mikael Backlund/99 10.00 25.00
SSMF Mario Ferraro/99 8.00 20.00
SSMR Mikko Rantanen/49 30.00 80.00
SSMS Mark Stone/49 15.00 40.00
SSNE Jake Neighbours/99 12.00 30.00
SSNH Nico Hischier/99 20.00 50.00
SSON John Carlson/99 12.00 30.00
SSRO Ryan O'Reilly/99 12.00 30.00
SSSG Samuel Girard/99 8.00 20.00
SSSH Travis Sanheim/99 8.00 20.00
SSST Chandler Stephenson/99 10.00 25.00
SSSW Shane Wright/99 15.00 40.00
SSTS Tim Stutzle/49 15.00 40.00
SSTT Tage Thompson/49 15.00 40.00
SSTW Tom Wilson/49 12.00 30.00
SSVP Vasily Podkolzin/99 8.00 20.00

2023-24 Upper Deck Engrained Synthesis

*RED: .5X TO 1.2X BASIC
*BLUE: .6X TO 1.5X BASIC
S1 Auston Matthews 4.00 10.00
S2 David Pastrnak 2.50 6.00
S3 Juraj Slafkovsky 2.00 5.00
S4 Erik Karlsson 1.25 3.00
S5 Jake Oettinger 1.50 4.00
S6 Rasmus Dahlin 1.25 3.00
S7 Adam Fantilli 3.00 8.00
S8 Jack Hughes 2.50 6.00
S9 Cale Makar 2.50 6.00
S10 Igor Shesterkin 2.00 5.00
S11 Alex DeBrincat 1.25 3.00
S12 Brayden Point 1.25 3.00
S13 Kirill Kaprizov 3.00 8.00
S14 Andrei Vasilevskiy 1.50 4.00
S15 Trevor Zegras 1.00 2.50
S16 Martin Necas 1.25 3.00
S17 Mark Stone 1.25 3.00
S18 Alex Ovechkin 4.00 10.00
S19 Mitch Marner 1.50 4.00
S20 Nathan MacKinnon 4.00 10.00
S21 Moritz Seider 1.25 3.00
S22 Mika Zibanejad 1.25 3.00
S23 Pierre-Luc Dubois .75 2.00
S24 Quinn Hughes 2.50 6.00
S25 Connor McDavid 5.00 12.00
S26 Elias Pettersson 1.50 4.00
S27 Mackenzie Blackwood 1.00 2.50
S28 Patrik Laine 1.25 3.00
S29 Matthew Knies 4.00 10.00
S30 Clayton Keller 1.25 3.00
S31 Luke Hughes 3.00 8.00
S32 Jordan Kyrou 1.00 2.50
S33 Connor Hellebuyck 2.00 5.00
S34 Sidney Crosby 4.00 10.00
S35 Connor Bedard 12.00 30.00
S36 Charlie McAvoy 1.25 3.00
S37 Tim Stutzle 1.25 3.00
S38 Matthew Coronato 1.50 4.00
S39 Travis Konecny 1.00 2.50
S40 Brady Tkachuk 1.50 4.00
S41 Cole Caufield 2.00 5.00
S42 Ilya Sorokin 1.50 4.00
S43 Leo Carlsson 3.00 8.00
S44 Brent Burns 1.00 2.50
S45 Jason Robertson 1.50 4.00
S46 Leon Draisaitl 3.00 8.00
S47 Matty Beniers 1.25 3.00
S48 Logan Cooley 4.00 10.00
S49 Matthew Tkachuk 2.00 5.00
S50 Yaroslav Askarov 2.50 6.00

2023-24 Upper Deck Engrained Synthesis Signatures

SAM Auston Matthews SP 100.00 250.00
SAO Alex Ovechkin 100.00 250.00
SBT Brady Tkachuk 20.00 50.00
SCB Connor Bedard 300.00 800.00
SCH Connor Hellebuyck 25.00 60.00
SJH Jonathan Huberdeau 15.00 40.00
SLH Luke Hughes 40.00 100.00
SMH Miro Heiskanen 20.00 50.00
SMK Matthew Knies 50.00 125.00
SPB Patrice Bergeron 25.00 60.00
SRB Ray Bourque 20.00 50.00
SSE Simon Edvinsson 25.00 60.00
SST Tim Stutzle 15.00 40.00
SSY Steve Yzerman 30.00 80.00
STF Tyson Foerster 25.00 60.00
STT Tage Thompson 15.00 40.00

2002-03 Upper Deck Foundations

1 Andy Moog .20 .50
2 Bill Ranford .15 .40
3 Cam Neely .20 .50
4 Bobby Orr .75 2.00
5 Terry O'Reilly .20 .50
6 Ray Bourque .30 .75
7 Phil Esposito .30 .75
8 Clark Gillies .20 .50
9 Grant Fuhr .30 .75
10 Dale Hawerchuk .25 .60
11 Kent Nilsson .12 .30
12 Willi Plett .12 .30
13 Al Secord .12 .30
14 Denis Savard .20 .50
15 Bob Probert .20 .50
16 Steve Larmer .15 .40
17 Patrick Roy .50 1.25
18 Ray Bourque .30 .75
19 Andy Moog .20 .50
20 Alex Delvecchio .20 .50
21 Borje Salming .20 .50
22 Dino Ciccarelli .20 .50
23 Gordie Howe .60 1.50
24 John Ogrodnick .12 .30
25 Marcel Dionne .25 .60
26 Mark Howe .20 .50
27 Ron Duguay .15 .40
28 Steve Yzerman .50 1.25
29 Andy Moog .20 .50
30 Bill Ranford .15 .40
31 Grant Fuhr .30 .75
32 Mark Messier .40 1.00
33 Marty McSorley .15 .40
34 Wayne Gretzky 1.25 3.00
35 Glenn Anderson .15 .40
36 Gordie Howe .60 1.50
37 Mark Howe .20 .50
38 Gordie Howe .60 1.50
39 Butch Goring .12 .30
40 Charlie Simmer .12 .30
41 Ron Duguay .15 .40
42 Marcel Dionne .25 .60
43 Marty McSorley .15 .40
44 Wayne Gretzky 1.25 3.00
45 Wayne Gretzky 1.25 3.00
46 Brian Bellows .15 .40
47 Dino Ciccarelli .20 .50
48 Mike Modano .30 .75
49 Brian Bellows .15 .40
50 Denis Savard .20 .50
51 Guy Lafleur .25 .60
52 Mats Naslund .12 .30
53 Doug Gilmour .25 .60
54 Patrick Roy .50 1.25
55 Rod Langway .15 .40
56 Ryan Walter .12 .30
57 Yvan Cournoyer .20 .50
58 Martin Brodeur .50 1.25
59 Bob Nystrom .15 .40
60 Butch Goring .12 .30
61 Clark Gillies .20 .50
62 Mike Bossy .20 .50
63 Glenn Anderson .15 .40
64 Guy Lafleur .25 .60
65 Mark Messier .40 1.00
66 Marcel Dionne .25 .60
67 Phil Esposito .30 .75
68 Ron Duguay .15 .40
69 Steve Larmer .15 .40
70 Wayne Gretzky 1.25 3.00
71 Brian Propp .12 .30
72 Jeremy Roenick .30 .75
73 Mark Howe .20 .50
74 Ron Hextall .20 .50
75 Tim Kerr .12 .30
76 Anton Stastny .12 .30
77 Dale Hunter .15 .40
78 Guy Lafleur .25 .60
79 Ron Hextall .20 .50
80 Wendel Clark .30 .75
81 Wilf Paiement .12 .30
82 Brett Hull .40 1.00
83 Bernie Federko .15 .40
84 Dale Hawerchuk .25 .60
85 Grant Fuhr .30 .75
86 Tony Twist .15 .40
87 Wayne Gretzky 1.25 3.00
88 Borje Salming .20 .50
89 Mats Sundin .20 .50
90 Glenn Anderson .15 .40
91 Grant Fuhr .30 .75
92 Wendel Clark .30 .75
93 Wilf Paiement .12 .30
94 Harold Snepsts .12 .30
95 Pavel Bure .20 .50
96 Tony Tanti .12 .30
97 Dale Hunter .15 .40
98 Dino Ciccarelli .20 .50
99 Rod Langway .15 .40
100 Dale Hawerchuk .25 .60
101 Wayne Gretzky SE 5.00 12.00
102 Gordie Howe SE 2.50 6.00
103 Bobby Orr SE 3.00 8.00
104 Gordie Howe SE 2.50 6.00
105 Wayne Gretzky SE 5.00 12.00
106 Wayne Gretzky SE 5.00 12.00
107 Cam Neely SE .75 2.00
108 Ray Bourque SE 1.25 3.00
109 Phil Esposito SE 1.25 3.00
110 Grant Fuhr SE 1.25 3.00
111 Denis Savard SE .75 2.00
112 Patrick Roy SE 2.00 5.00
113 Steve Yzerman SE 2.00 5.00
114 Marcel Dionne SE 1.00 2.50
115 Guy Lafleur SE 1.00 2.50
116 Bernie Federko SE .60 1.50
117 Wayne Gretzky SE 5.00 12.00
118 Ray Bourque SE
Phil Esposito 1.25 3.00
119 Mike Bossy SE .75 2.00
120 Patrick Roy SE 2.00 5.00
121 Bob Nystrom SE .60 1.50
122 Pasi Nurminen NF .50 1.25
123 Mark Hartigan NF .50 1.25
124 Henrik Tallinder NF .50 1.25
125 Micki Dupont NF RC .50 1.25
126 Riku Hahl NF .50 1.25
127 Andrej Nedorost NF .50 1.25
128 Ales Pisa NF .50 1.25
129 Jani Rita NF .50 1.25
130 Stephen Weiss NF .75 2.00
131 Lukas Krajicek NF .60 1.50
132 Sylvain Blouin NF RC .50 1.25
133 Marcel Hossa NF .50 1.25
134 Adam Hall NF RC .50 1.25
135 Jan Lasak NF .60 1.50
136 Ray Schultz NF RC .50 1.25
137 Trent Hunter NF .50 1.25
138 Martin Prusek NF .50 1.25
139 Branko Radivojevic NF .50 1.25
140 Sebastien Centomo NF .50 1.25
141 Karel Pilar NF .50 1.25
142 Sebastien Charpentier NF .50 1.25
143 Stanislav Chistov NF RC .50 1.25
144 Alexei Smirnov NF RC .60 1.50
145 Joe Thornton SE 1.25 3.00
146 Chuck Kobasew NF RC .60 1.50
147 Patrick Roy SE 2.00 5.00
148 Mike Modano SE 1.25 3.00
149 Rick Nash NF RC 3.00 8.00
150 Mike Comrie SE .75 2.00
151 Henrik Zetterberg NF RC 5.00 12.00
152 Ales Hemsky NF RC 2.00 5.00
153 Jay Bouwmeester NF RC 1.50 4.00
154 Pavel Bure SE .75 2.00
155 Alexander Frolov NF RC 1.25 3.00
156 Pierre-Marc Bouchard NF RC .75 2.00
157 Ron Hainsey NF RC .50 1.25
158 Sean Burke SE .50 1.25
159 Mario Lemieux SE 3.00 8.00
160 Anton Volchenkov NF RC .50 1.25
161 Mats Sundin SE .75 2.00
162 Alexander Svitov NF RC .50 1.25
163 Steve Eminger NF RC .50 1.25
164 Jason Spezza NF RC 3.00 8.00
165 Pascal LeClaire NF RC .60 1.50
166 Ari Ahonen NF RC .50 1.25
167 Steve Ott NF RC .50 1.25

2002-03 Upper Deck Foundations 1000 Point Club

*SILVER JSY/85: .5X TO 1.2X BRONZE/110
*GOLD JSY/15: 1.2X TO 3X BRONZE/110
BT Bryan Trottier JSY 5.00 12.00
DC Dino Ciccarelli JSY 4.00 10.00
DE Denis Savard JSY 4.00 10.00
DP Denis Potvin JSY 4.00 10.00
GL Guy Lafleur JSY 6.00 15.00
JB Johnny Bucyk JSY 5.00 12.00
LA Guy Lafleur JSY 6.00 15.00
MB Mike Bossy JSY 6.00 15.00
MG Michel Goulet JSY 4.00 10.00
SY Steve Yzerman JSY 10.00 25.00
WG Wayne Gretzky JSY 20.00 50.00
YZ Steve Yzerman STK 10.00 25.00
AN Glenn Anderson STK 4.00 10.00
AN2 Glenn Anderson STK 4.00 10.00
BE Jean Beliveau STK 8.00 20.00
BO Mike Bossy STK 6.00 15.00
BO1 Ray Bourque STK 8.00 20.00
BO2 Ray Bourque STK 8.00 20.00
BU Johnny Bucyk STK 5.00 12.00
CI Dino Ciccarelli STK 4.00 10.00
DI Marcel Dionne STK 4.00 10.00
DI2 Marcel Dionne STK 4.00 10.00
ES Phil Esposito STK 6.00 15.00
ES2 Phil Esposito STK 6.00 15.00
GA Mike Gartner STK 5.00 12.00
GR Wayne Gretzky STK 20.00 50.00
HA Dale Hawerchuk STK 6.00 15.00
HA2 Dale Hawerchuk STK 6.00 15.00
HO Gordie Howe STK 15.00 40.00
KU Jari Kurri STK 6.00 15.00
KU2 Jari Kurri STK 6.00 15.00
LA1 Guy Lafleur STK 5.00 12.00
LA2 Guy Lafleur STK 5.00 12.00
LA3 Guy Lafleur STK 5.00 12.00
MC Lanny McDonald STK 4.00 10.00
MI Stan Mikita STK 6.00 15.00
PO Denis Potvin STK 5.00 12.00
SA Denis Savard STK 4.00 10.00
TR Bryan Trottier STK 5.00 12.00

2002-03 Upper Deck Foundations Calder Winners

*SILVER/85: .5X TO 1.2X BASIC JERSEY
*GOLD/15: 1.2X TO 3X BASIC JERSEY
TBT Bryan Trottier 6.00 15.00
TMB Mike Bossy 6.00 15.00
TPB Pavel Bure 6.00 15.00
TRB Ray Bourque 8.00 20.00
TWP Willi Plett 4.00 10.00

2002-03 Upper Deck Foundations Canadian Heroes

*SILVER/95: .5X TO 1.2X BASE JSY
*GOLD/50: .8X TO 2X BASE JSY
CBO Ray Bourque 6.00 15.00
CBT Bryan Trottier 6.00 15.00
CCN Cam Neely 6.00 15.00
CDC Dino Ciccarelli 5.00 12.00
CGF Grant Fuhr 8.00 20.00
CGL Guy Lafleur 5.00 12.00
CHS Harold Snepsts 5.00 12.00
CJB Johnny Bucyk 5.00 12.00
CMB Mike Bossy 5.00 12.00
CMG Michel Goulet 5.00 12.00
CMH Mark Howe 6.00 15.00
CMM Marty McSorley 5.00 12.00
CPR Patrick Roy 10.00 25.00
CRD Ron Duguay 5.00 12.00
CRO Patrick Roy 10.00 25.00
CRV Rick Vaive 4.00 10.00
CSA Denis Savard 5.00 12.00
CSY Steve Yzerman 8.00 20.00
CTT Tony Twist 5.00 12.00
CWC Wendel Clark 5.00 12.00
CWG Wayne Gretzky 20.00 50.00
CWP Willi Plett 4.00 10.00

2002-03 Upper Deck Foundations Classic Greats

*SILVER/95: .5X TO 1.2X BASE JSY
*GOLD/50: .8X TO 2X BASE JSY
GBN Bob Nystrom 5.00 12.00
GBO Ray Bourque 8.00 20.00
GBR Bill Ranford 5.00 12.00
GBS Borje Salming 6.00 15.00
GCN Cam Neely 6.00 15.00
GDC Dino Ciccarelli 5.00 12.00
GDP Denis Potvin 5.00 12.00
GDS Denis Savard 5.00 12.00
GGF Grant Fuhr 10.00 25.00
GGL Guy Lafleur 5.00 12.00
GMB Mike Bossy 5.00 12.00
GMG Michel Goulet 4.00 10.00
GMH Mark Howe 6.00 15.00
GRB Ray Bourque 8.00 20.00
GRD Ron Duguay 4.00 10.00
GWC Wendel Clark 6.00 15.00
GWG Wayne Gretzky 20.00 50.00

2002-03 Upper Deck Foundations Defense First

*SILVER/85: .5X TO 1.2X BASE JSY
*GOLD/15: 1.2X TO 3X BASE JSY
DBO Ray Bourque 8.00 20.00
DBS Borje Salming 6.00 15.00
DDP Denis Potvin 5.00 12.00
DGF Grant Fuhr 10.00 25.00
DHS Harold Snepsts 5.00 12.00
DMH Mark Howe 6.00 15.00
DMM Marty McSorley 5.00 12.00
DRB Ray Bourque 8.00 20.00

2002-03 Upper Deck Foundations Lasting Impressions Sticks

LBN Bob Nystrom 6.00 15.00
LBO Bobby Orr 40.00 100.00
LBR Bill Ranford 6.00 15.00
LCN Cam Neely 6.00 15.00
LJP Jacques Plante 12.50 30.00
LMN Mats Naslund 8.00 20.00
LWC Wendel Clark 8.00 20.00
LYC Yvan Cournoyer 6.00 15.00

2002-03 Upper Deck Foundations Milestones

*SILVER/95: .5X TO 1.25X BASE JSY
*GOLD/50: .8X TO 2X BASE JSY
NBO Ray Bourque 8.00 20.00
NBT Bryan Trottier 5.00 12.00
NCN Cam Neely 10.00 25.00
NDP Denis Potvin 5.00 12.00
NGF Grant Fuhr 10.00 25.00
NMB Mike Bossy 5.00 12.00
NPR Patrick Roy 12.50 30.00
NSY Steve Yzerman 12.50 30.00
NWG Wayne Gretzky 25.00 60.00

2002-03 Upper Deck Foundations Playoff Performers

*SILVER/95: .5X TO 1.2X BASE JSY
*GOLD/50: .8X TO 2X BASE JSY
PBN Bob Nystrom 5.00 12.00
PBS Borje Salming 6.00 15.00
PBT Bryan Trottier 5.00 12.00
PCN Cam Neely 6.00 15.00
PDC Dino Ciccarelli 5.00 12.00
PGF Grant Fuhr 8.00 20.00
PJB Johnny Bucyk 5.00 12.00
PMB Mike Bossy 5.00 12.00
PMG Michel Goulet 5.00 12.00
PMM Marty McSorley 5.00 12.00
PPB Pavel Bure 6.00 15.00
PPR Patrick Roy 12.50 30.00
PRB Ray Bourque 8.00 20.00
PRO Patrick Roy 12.50 30.00
PSY Steve Yzerman 12.50 30.00
PWG Wayne Gretzky 25.00 60.00

2002-03 Upper Deck Foundations Power Stations

*SILVER/85: .5X TO 1.2X BASE JSY
*GOLD/15: 1.2X TO 3X BASE JSY
SBN Bob Nystrom 5.00 12.00
SCN Cam Neely 6.00 15.00
SDC Dino Ciccarelli 5.00 12.00
SHS Harold Snepsts 5.00 12.00
SMB Mike Bossy 5.00 12.00
SMH Mark Howe 6.00 15.00
SMM Marty McSorley 5.00 12.00
SRV Rick Vaive 4.00 10.00
STT Tony Twist 5.00 12.00
SWC Wendel Clark 5.00 12.00
SWP Willi Plett 4.00 10.00

2002-03 Upper Deck Foundations Signs of Greatness

SGAS Al Secord/26* 40.00 80.00
SGBB Brian Bellows/26* 20.00 50.00
SGBC Bobby Clarke SP 10.00 25.00
SGBO Bobby Orr/48* 200.00 350.00
SGBP Brian Propp/87* 12.00 30.00
SGBS Billy Smith 10.00 25.00
SGCG Clark Gillies/26* 20.00 50.00
SGCN Cam Neely SP 15.00 40.00
SGCS Charlie Simmer/26* 30.00 80.00
SGDC Dino Ciccarelli SP 10.00 25.00
SGDH Dale Hawerchuk 10.00 25.00
SGDP Denis Potvin 10.00 25.00
SGDS Denis Savard SP 20.00 50.00
SGFM Frank Mahovlich SP 10.00 25.00
SGGA Glenn Anderson 10.00 25.00
SGGF Grant Fuhr SP 15.00 40.00
SGGH Gordie Howe/43* 75.00 150.00
SGGL Guy Lafleur SP 15.00 40.00
SGGP Gilbert Perreault SP 12.00 30.00
SGJB Jean Beliveau SP 25.00 50.00
SGJBU Johnny Bucyk 10.00 25.00
SGJK Jari Kurri 12.50 30.00
SGLM Lanny McDonald 10.00 25.00
SGMB Mike Bossy 10.00 25.00
SGMD Marcel Dionne SP 10.00 25.00
SGMG Mike Gartner 12.50 30.00
SGMGU Michel Goulet SP 12.00 30.00
SGMN Mats Naslund/87* 25.00 60.00
SGPS Peter Stastny 10.00 25.00
SGRA Ray Bourque/23* 40.00 100.00
SGRB Ray Bourque/23* 40.00 100.00
SGRH Ron Hextall/51* 20.00 50.00
SGSL Steve Larmer/26* 20.00 50.00
SGSM Stan Mikita SP 10.00 25.00
SGTL Ted Lindsay SP 10.00 25.00
SGWG Wayne Gretzky/46* 250.00 600.00

2015-16 Upper Deck Full Force

*1-100 VETS/25: 5X TO 12X BASIC CARDS
*ROOKIES: .8X TO 2X BASIC CARDS
1 Drew Doughty .30 .75
2 John Tavares .40 1.00
3 Anders Lee .25 .60
4 Sean Monahan .15 .40
5 Jakub Voracek .20 .50
6 John Carlson .25 .60
7 Tyler Bozak .15 .40
8 Nazem Kadri .30 .75
9 Nail Yakupov .15 .40
10 Tyler Johnson .15 .40
11 Loui Eriksson .15 .40
12 Jason Pominville .15 .40
13 Oliver Ekman-Larsson .25 .60
14 Jiri Hudler .20 .50
15 Kyle Turris .20 .50
16 Henrik Zetterberg .30 .75
17 Semyon Varlamov .25 .60
18 Sergei Bobrovsky .40 1.00
19 Patrick Kane .50 1.25
20 Logan Couture .30 .75
21 Jonathan Quick .30 .75
22 David Backes .15 .40
23 Steve Mason .20 .50
24 Nicklas Backstrom .25 .60
25 Ryan Strome .25 .60
26 Andrew Hammond .30 .75
27 Ryan Johansen .20 .50
28 Justin Faulk .20 .50
29 Nathan MacKinnon 1.00 2.50
30 Tuukka Rask .30 .75
31 Vladimir Tarasenko .30 .75
32 Henrik Lundqvist .60 1.50
33 Derek Stepan .15 .40
34 P.K. Subban .30 .75
35 Jonas Hiller .20 .50
36 Corey Crawford .30 .75
37 Tomas Plekanec .15 .40
38 Niklas Kronwall .20 .50
39 Cory Schneider .25 .60
40 Mikkel Boedker .15 .40
41 Devan Dubnyk .20 .50
42 Corey Perry .40 1.00
43 Elias Lindholm .25 .60
44 Jamie Benn .25 .60
45 Shea Weber .20 .50
46 Daniel Sedin .30 .75
47 Tobias Rieder .15 .40
48 Brad Marchand .50 1.25
49 Patrik Elias .25 .60
50 John Klingberg .25 .60
51 Taylor Hall .25 .60
52 Sidney Crosby 1.00 2.50
53 Rick Nash .25 .60
54 Carey Price .50 1.25
55 Roberto Luongo .40 1.00
56 Marc-Andre Fleury .50 1.25
57 Pavel Datsyuk .40 1.00
58 Brian Elliott .20 .50
59 Jonathan Toews .40 1.00
60 Nikita Kucherov .50 1.25
61 Ryan Miller .25 .60
62 Joe Pavelski .30 .75
63 Andrew Ladd .15 .40
64 Aaron Ekblad .30 .75
65 Gabriel Landeskog .30 .75
66 Steven Stamkos .50 1.25
67 Jonathan Huberdeau .30 .75
68 Matt Moulson .15 .40
69 Ryan Getzlaf .25 .60
70 Max Pacioretty .25 .60
71 Jordan Eberle .25 .60
72 Derick Brassard .15 .40
73 Blake Wheeler .25 .60
74 Cam Ward .25 .60
75 Tyler Seguin .30 .75
76 Alex Pietrangelo .20 .50
77 Evgeni Malkin .50 1.25
78 Claude Giroux .25 .60
79 Frederik Andersen .30 .75
80 Erik Karlsson .30 .75
81 Ryan Nugent-Hopkins .30 .75
82 Joe Thornton .40 1.00
83 Henrik Sedin .30 .75
84 Zemgus Girgensons .20 .50
85 Patric Hornqvist .15 .40
86 Patrice Bergeron .30 .75
87 Anze Kopitar .40 1.00
88 Ondrej Pavelec .25 .60
89 Alexander Ovechkin 1.00 2.50
90 Jonathan Bernier .20 .50
91 Pekka Rinne .25 .60
92 Evgeny Kuznetsov .30 .75
93 James van Riemsdyk .20 .50
94 Marian Hossa .25 .60
95 Filip Forsberg .40 1.00
96 Zach Parise .25 .60
97 Adam Henrique .20 .50
98 Nick Foligno .20 .50
99 Tomas Tatar .15 .40
100 Tyler Ennis .15 .40
101 Connor McDavid RC 125.00 300.00
102 Jacob de la Rose RC 3.00 8.00
103 Sam Bennett RC 10.00 25.00
104 Malcolm Subban RC 5.00 12.00
105 Matt Puempel RC 2.50 6.00
106 Emile Poirier RC 2.50 6.00
107 Ryan Hartman RC 4.00 10.00
108 Nick Cousins RC 3.00 8.00
109 Antoine Bibeau RC 3.00 8.00
110 Josh Anderson RC 6.00 15.00
111 Kevin Fiala RC 4.00 10.00
112 Jack Eichel RC 12.00 30.00
113 Max Domi RC 6.00 15.00
114 Noah Hanifin RC 5.00 12.00
115 Mikko Rantanen RC 15.00 40.00
116 Nikolaj Ehlers RC 6.00 15.00
117 Robby Fabbri RC 4.00 10.00
118 Jared McCann RC 4.00 10.00
119 Artemi Panarin RC 12.00 30.00
120 Dylan Larkin RC 10.00 25.00
121 Shane Prince RC 2.00 5.00
122 Connor Hellebuyck RC 12.00 30.00
123 Jake Virtanen RC 4.00 10.00

2015-16 Upper Deck Full Force Blueprint

BPAO Alexander Ovechkin 2.50 6.00
BPAS Andrew Shaw .40 1.00
BPBE Jonathan Bernier .50 1.25
BPBO Bobby Orr 2.50 6.00
BPBS Brayden Schenn .60 1.50
BPCM Connor McDavid SP 30.00 80.00
BPCP Carey Price 1.25 3.00
BPCS Cory Schneider .60 1.50
BPDD Devan Dubnyk .50 1.25
BPDL Dylan Larkin SP 2.00 5.00
BPDO Max Domi SP 1.25 3.00
BPDP Denis Potvin .60 1.50
BPDW Doug Weight .60 1.50
BPEM Evgeni Malkin 1.25 3.00
BPEP Emile Poirier .50 1.25
BPFA Frederik Andersen .75 2.00
BPHU Jonathan Huberdeau .75 2.00
BPJB Jamie Benn .60 1.50
BPJE Jack Eichel SP 2.50 6.00
BPJG Johnny Gaudreau 1.00 2.50
BPJH Jim Howard .75 2.00
BPJQ Jonathan Quick .75 2.00
BPJT John Tavares 1.00 2.50
BPJV Jakub Voracek .50 1.25
BPKF Kevin Fiala .75 2.00
BPMB Mike Bossy .60 1.50
BPMD Marcel Dionne .75 2.00
BPML Mario Lemieux 2.50 6.00
BPMM Mark Messier 1.25 3.00
BPMS Malcolm Subban 1.00 2.50
BPNE Nikolaj Ehlers SP 1.25 3.00
BPNH Noah Hanifin SP 1.00 2.50
BPNK Niklas Kronwall .50 1.25
BPNP Nicolas Petan SP .60 1.50
BPPE Phil Esposito 1.00 2.50
BPPR Pekka Rinne .60 1.50
BPRF Robby Fabbri SP .75 2.00
BPRH Ryan Hartman .75 2.00
BPRJ Ryan Johansen .50 1.25
BPRN Ryan Nugent-Hopkins .75 2.00
BPRO Patrick Roy 1.50 4.00
BPSB Sam Bennett 2.00 5.00
BPSC Sidney Crosby 2.50 6.00
BPSR Sean Couturier .50 1.25
BPSS Steven Stamkos 1.25 3.00
BPSW Shea Weber .50 1.25
BPTB Tyson Barrie .40 1.00
BPTH Taylor Hall .60 1.50
BPTO Jonathan Toews 1.00 2.50
BPTR Tuukka Rask .75 2.00
BPTT Tomas Tatar .40 1.00
BPVT Vladimir Tarasenko .75 2.00
BPWG Wayne Gretzky 4.00 10.00

2015-16 Upper Deck Full Force Blueprint Autographs

BPAO Alexander Ovechkin B 25.00 60.00
BPAS Andrew Shaw D 3.00 8.00
BPBE Jonathan Bernier C 4.00 10.00
BPBO Bobby Orr B 50.00 125.00
BPBS Brayden Schenn D 5.00 12.00
BPCH Connor Hellebuyck B 20.00 50.00
BPCM Connor McDavid A 600.00 1500.00
BPCP Carey Price C 10.00 25.00
BPCS Cory Schneider F 5.00 12.00
BPDD Devan Dubnyk C 4.00 10.00
BPDL Dylan Larkin B 15.00 40.00

BPDO Max Domi B 10.00 25.00
BPDP Denis Potvin B 5.00 12.00
BPDW Doug Weight B 5.00 12.00
BPEM Evgeni Malkin B 10.00 25.00
BPEP Emile Poirier G 4.00 10.00
BPFA Frederik Andersen G 6.00 15.00
BPHU Jonathan Huberdeau B 6.00 15.00
BPJB Jamie Benn C 5.00 12.00
BPJG Johnny Gaudreau E 8.00 20.00
BPJH Jim Howard C 6.00 15.00
BPJQ Jonathan Quick B 6.00 15.00
BPJT John Tavares D 8.00 20.00
BPKF Kevin Fiala E 6.00 15.00
BPMB Mike Bossy B 5.00 12.00
BPMD Marcel Dionne B 6.00 15.00
BPML Mario Lemieux A 40.00 100.00
BPMM Mark Messier A 30.00 80.00
BPMS Malcolm Subban G 8.00 20.00
BPNE Nikolaj Ehlers B 10.00 25.00
BPNH Noah Hanifin B 8.00 20.00
BPNK Niklas Kronwall E 4.00 10.00
BPNP Nicolas Petan B 5.00 12.00
BPPE Phil Esposito B 8.00 20.00
BPRF Robby Fabbri B 6.00 15.00
BPRH Ryan Hartman G 6.00 15.00
BPRJ Ryan Johansen C 4.00 10.00
BPRN Ryan Nugent-Hopkins C 6.00 15.00
BPRO Patrick Roy B 12.00 30.00
BPSB Sam Bennett F 15.00 40.00
BPSC Sidney Crosby A 60.00 150.00
BPSR Sean Couturier G 4.00 10.00
BPSW Shea Weber B 4.00 10.00
BPTB Tyson Barrie F 3.00 8.00
BPTO Jonathan Toews B 8.00 20.00
BPTT Tomas Tatar D 3.00 8.00
BPWG Wayne Gretzky B 150.00 400.00

2015-16 Upper Deck Full Force Calder Competitors

CCCM Connor McDavid 25.00 60.00
CCDL Dylan Larkin 5.00 12.00
CCJE Jack Eichel 6.00 15.00
CCJV Jake Virtanen 2.00 5.00
CCKF Kevin Fiala 2.00 5.00
CCMD Max Domi 3.00 8.00
CCNE Nikolaj Ehlers 3.00 8.00
CCSB Sam Bennett 5.00 12.00

2015-16 Upper Deck Full Force Draft Board

DBAE Aaron Ekblad 1.25 3.00
DBAO Alexander Ovechkin 4.00 10.00
DBCH Connor Hellebuyck SP 4.00 10.00
DBCM Connor McDavid SP 30.00 80.00
DBCP Carey Price 2.00 5.00
DBDD Drew Doughty 1.25 3.00
DBEI Jack Eichel SP 4.00 10.00
DBEM Evgeni Malkin 2.00 5.00
DBEP Emile Poirier SP .75 2.00
DBFF Filip Forsberg 1.50 4.00
DBHS Henrik Samuelsson SP .60 1.50
DBJD Jacob de la Rose 1.00 2.50
DBJE Jordan Eberle 1.00 2.50
DBJI Jarome Iginla 1.25 3.00
DBJJ Jaromir Jagr 3.00 8.00
DBJT Jonathan Toews 1.50 4.00
DBKF Kevin Fiala SP 1.25 3.00
DBMB Martin Brodeur 2.50 6.00
DBML Mario Lemieux 4.00 10.00
DBMS Mats Sundin 1.00 2.50
DBPF Peter Forsberg 2.00 5.00
DBPK Patrick Kane 2.00 5.00
DBRF Robby Fabbri SP 1.25 3.00
DBRG Ryan Getzlaf 1.00 2.50
DBRH Ryan Hartman SP 1.25 3.00
DBRN Rick Nash 1.00 2.50
DBSB Sam Bennett SP 3.00 8.00
DBSC Sidney Crosby 4.00 10.00
DBSS Steven Stamkos 2.00 5.00
DBSU Malcolm Subban SP 1.50 4.00
DBSY Steve Yzerman 2.50 6.00
DBTA John Tavares 1.50 4.00
DBVT Vladimir Tarasenko 1.25 3.00

2015-16 Upper Deck Full Force Dual Force

DF1 W.Gretzky/M.Messier 10.00 25.00
DF2 J.Toews/P.Kane 3.00 8.00
DF3 B.Orr/P.Esposito 6.00 15.00
DF4 E.Malkin/P.Hornqvist 3.00 8.00
DF5 S.Yzerman/N.Lidstrom 4.00 10.00
DF6 P.Datsyuk/H.Zetterberg 2.50 6.00
DF7 A.Oates/B.Hull 3.00 8.00
DF8 C.Price/P.Subban 3.00 8.00
DF9 J.Jagr/M.Lemieux 6.00 15.00
DF10 J.Gaudreau/S.Monahan 2.50 6.00
DF11 G.Anderson/G.Fuhr 2.50 6.00
DF12 C.Giroux/J.Voracek 1.50 4.00

2015-16 Upper Deck Full Force Goooal

GAE Aaron Ekblad 1.25 3.00
GAN Andrej Nestrasil .60 1.50
GAO Alexander Ovechkin 4.00 10.00
GBB Brent Burns 1.00 2.50
GCM Connor McDavid SP 30.00 80.00
GEK Evgeny Kuznetsov 1.25 3.00
GJD Jacob de la Rose 1.00 2.50
GJG Johnny Gaudreau 1.50 4.00
GJJ Josh Jooris .60 1.50
GJT John Tavares 1.50 4.00
GJV James van Riemsdyk .75 2.00
GNE Nikolaj Ehlers SP 2.00 5.00
GNY Nail Yakupov .60 1.50
GPK Patrick Kane 2.00 5.00
GPS P.K. Subban 1.25 3.00
GRJ Ryan Johansen .75 2.00
GRK Ronalds Kenins .60 1.50
GSB Jack Eichel SP 4.00 10.00
GSC Sidney Crosby 4.00 10.00
GTF Theoren Fleury 1.25 3.00
GTJ Tyler Johnson .60 1.50
GTS Teemu Selanne 2.00 5.00
GWG Wayne Gretzky 6.00 15.00

2015-16 Upper Deck Full Force Goooal Autographs

GAN Andrej Nestrasil E 4.00 10.00
GAO Alexander Ovechkin A 40.00 100.00
GBB Brent Burns E 6.00 15.00
GCM Connor McDavid A 600.00 1500.00
GEK Evgeny Kuznetsov E 8.00 20.00
GJD Jacob de la Rose E 6.00 15.00
GJG Johnny Gaudreau C 10.00 25.00
GJJ Josh Jooris E 4.00 10.00
GJT John Tavares D 10.00 25.00
GJV James van Riemsdyk D 5.00 12.00
GNE Nikolaj Ehlers C 12.00 30.00
GNY Nail Yakupov D 4.00 10.00
GPS P.K. Subban A 20.00 50.00
GRJ Ryan Johansen C 5.00 12.00
GRK Ronalds Kenins D EXCH 4.00 10.00
GSB Sam Bennett B 20.00 50.00
GSC Sidney Crosby A 60.00 150.00
GTF Theoren Fleury C 8.00 20.00
GTS Teemu Selanne B 20.00 50.00
GWG Wayne Gretzky B 150.00 400.00

2015-16 Upper Deck Full Force Ice Encounters

IEAR Antoine Roussel 1.50 4.00
IECM Cody McLeod 1.50 4.00
IECN Chris Neil 1.50 4.00
IEDB Dustin Byfuglien 2.50 6.00
IEDD Derek Dorsett 1.50 4.00
IEDP Dion Phaneuf 2.00 5.00
IEJT Jordin Tootoo 2.00 5.00
IEML Wayne Simmonds 3.00 8.00
IERR Ryan Reaves 1.50 4.00
IETW Tom Wilson 2.50 6.00

2015-16 Upper Deck Full Force Immediate Impacts

IIAB Antoine Bibeau 1.00 2.50
IIBR Brendan Ranford .75 2.00
IICM Connor McDavid SP 15.00 40.00
IIEP Emile Poirier .75 2.00
IIHS Henrik Samuelsson .60 1.50
IIJD Jacob de la Rose 1.00 2.50
IIJE Jack Eichel SP 4.00 10.00
IIKF Kevin Fiala 1.25 3.00
IIMD Max Domi SP 2.00 5.00
IIMP Matt Puempel .75 2.00
IIMS Malcolm Subban 1.50 4.00
IINE Nikolaj Ehlers SP 2.00 5.00
IINS Nick Shore .60 1.50
IIRH Ryan Hartman 1.25 3.00
IISB Sam Bennett 3.00 8.00
IISP Shane Prince .60 1.50

2015-16 Upper Deck Full Force Immediate Impacts Autographs

IIAB Antoine Bibeau B 6.00 15.00
IICM Connor McDavid A 150.00 250.00
IIEP Emile Poirier B 5.00 12.00
IIHS Henrik Samuelsson C 4.00 10.00
IIJD Jacob de la Rose C 6.00 15.00
IIKF Kevin Fiala A 8.00 20.00
IIMD Max Domi B 12.00 30.00
IIMP Matt Puempel B 5.00 12.00
IIMS Malcolm Subban B 10.00 25.00
IINE Nikolaj Ehlers B 12.00 30.00
IINP Nicolas Petan B 6.00 15.00
IIRH Ryan Hartman C 8.00 20.00
IISB Sam Bennett A 20.00 50.00
IISP Shane Prince C 4.00 10.00

2015-16 Upper Deck Full Force Rising Force

RFAB Aleksander Barkov 2.50 6.00
RFAE Aaron Ekblad 2.00 5.00
RFCM Connor McDavid 125.00 300.00
RFDE Jacob de la Rose 1.50 4.00
RFEK Evgeny Kuznetsov 2.00 5.00
RFEL Elias Lindholm 1.50 4.00
RFEP Emile Poirier 1.25 3.00
RFGI John Gibson 1.50 4.00
RFJD Jonathan Drouin 1.25 3.00
RFJE Jack Eichel 6.00 15.00
RFJG Johnny Gaudreau 2.50 6.00
RFJK John Klingberg 1.50 4.00
RFJV Jake Virtanen 2.00 5.00
RFKF Kevin Fiala 2.00 5.00
RFKH Kevin Hayes 1.25 3.00
RFMD Max Domi 3.00 8.00
RFMR Morgan Rielly 1.50 4.00
RFMS Mark Stone 1.50 4.00
RFNE Nikolaj Ehlers 3.00 8.00
RFNK Nikita Kucherov 3.00 8.00
RFNM Nathan MacKinnon 6.00 15.00
RFRH Ryan Hartman 2.00 5.00
RFRR Rasmus Ristolainen 1.00 2.50
RFRS Ryan Strome 1.50 4.00
RFSB Sam Bennett 5.00 12.00
RFSJ Seth Jones 1.50 4.00
RFSM Sean Monahan 1.00 2.50
RFTT Teuvo Teravainen 1.50 4.00
RFVT Vladimir Tarasenko 2.00 5.00
RFZG Zemgus Girgensons 1.25 3.00

2015-16 Upper Deck Full Force Rising Force Gold

*GOLD/99: .8X TO 2X BASIC INSERT/999
RFCM Connor McDavid 250.00 600.00

2015-16 Upper Deck Full Force Thermal Threats

TTAH Andrew Hammond 1.50 4.00
TTAO Alexander Ovechkin 5.00 12.00
TTCM Connor McDavid SP 30.00 80.00
TTGI Claude Giroux 1.25 3.00
TTHL Henrik Lundqvist 3.00 8.00
TTHZ Henrik Zetterberg 1.50 4.00
TTJB Jamie Benn 1.25 3.00
TTJE Jack Eichel SP 5.00 12.00
TTJV James van Riemsdyk 1.00 2.50
TTKF Kevin Fiala 1.50 4.00
TTMD Max Domi SP 2.50 6.00
TTMP Max Pacioretty 1.25 3.00
TTNE Nikolaj Ehlers SP 2.50 6.00
TTNK Nikita Kucherov 2.50 6.00
TTPD Pavel Datsyuk 2.00 5.00
TTPE Phil Esposito 2.00 5.00
TTPK P.K. Subban 1.50 4.00
TTPR Pekka Rinne 1.25 3.00
TTRG Ryan Getzlaf 1.25 3.00
TTSB Sam Bennett SP 4.00 10.00
TTSC Sidney Crosby 5.00 12.00
TTWG Wayne Gretzky 8.00 20.00

2015-16 Upper Deck Full Force Valuable Assets

VAB Andre Burakovsky .75 2.00
VAE Aaron Ekblad 1.50 4.00
VCM Connor McDavid SP 30.00 80.00
VJD Jonathan Drouin 1.00 2.50
VJE Jack Eichel SP 5.00 12.00
VJG Johnny Gaudreau 2.00 5.00
VJH Jonathan Huberdeau 1.50 4.00
VMD Max Domi SP 2.50 6.00
VPM Petr Mrazek 1.25 3.00
VSM Sean Monahan .75 2.00
VTB Tyson Barrie .75 2.00

2015-16 Upper Deck Full Force Valuable Assets Autographs

VAB Andre Burakovsky D 4.00 10.00
VCM Connor McDavid A 600.00 1500.00
VJD Jonathan Drouin C 5.00 12.00
VSB Sam Bennett B 20.00 50.00
VJG Johnny Gaudreau B 10.00 25.00
VJH Jonathan Huberdeau A 8.00 20.00
VMD Max Domi C 12.00 30.00
VPM Petr Mrazek D 6.00 15.00
VTB Tyson Barrie C 4.00 10.00

1998-99 Upper Deck Gold Reserve

COMPLETE SET (420) 100.00 200.00
COMP.SER.1 SET (210) 60.00 120.00
COMP.SER.2 SET (210) 40.00 80.00
*1-30 GOLD SR/RR: .6X TO 1.5X BASIC CARDS
*31-390 GOLD VETS: 1.2X TO 3X BASIC CARDS
*391-412 GOLD PE: .6X TO 1.5X UPPER DECK
*413-420 GOLD CC: .6X TO 1.5X UPPER DECK
SY S.Yzerman Stick/200 75.00 200.00
WG W.Gretzky Stick/200 60.00 150.00
WGA W.Gretzky Stick AU/99 400.00 1000.00
NNO1 W.Gretzky AU/200 400.00 1000.00
NNO2 S.Yzerman AU/200 60.00 150.00

1999-00 Upper Deck Gold Reserve

COMPLETE SET (350) 200.00 400.00
COMP.SERIES 1 (170) 75.00 150.00
COMP.SER.1 w/o SP's (135) 20.00 40.00
COMP.SERIES 2 (180) 100.00 250.00
COMP.SER.2 w/o SP's (150) 15.00 30.00
*GOLD RES VETS: .8X TO 2X BASIC UD
*GOLD RES SP: .8X TO 2X BASIC UD SP
*GOLD RES/2500: 1.5X TO 4X BASIC UD SP
199 Ron Francis .30 .75

1999-00 Upper Deck Gold Reserve Game-Used Souvenirs

GRBH Brett Hull 12.00 30.00
GREL Eric Lindros 12.00 30.00
GRPB Pavel Bure 10.00 25.00
GRPK Paul Kariya 10.00 25.00
GRPR Patrick Roy 15.00 40.00
GRSY Steve Yzerman 15.00 40.00
GRWG Wayne Gretzky 30.00 80.00

1999-00 Upper Deck Gold Reserve UD Authentics

BH Brett Hull 15.00 40.00
BL Brian Leetch UPD 8.00 20.00
BM Bill Muckalt 6.00 15.00
CD Chris Drury 8.00 20.00
CJ Curtis Joseph 8.00 20.00
DL David Legwand 8.00 20.00
PB Pavel Bure 8.00 20.00
PS Patrik Stefan UPD 6.00 15.00
SS Sergei Samsonov UPD 8.00 20.00
SY Steve Yzerman UPD 30.00 80.00

2009 Upper Deck Goodwin Champions Preview

GCP5 Gordie Howe 6.00 15.00

2014 Upper Deck Goodwin Champions Sport Royalty Autographs

SRAGL Guy Lafleur B 30.00 60.00
SRAWG Wayne Gretzky B 200.00 500.00

2015 Upper Deck Goodwin Champions Goudey Sport Royalty Autographs

SRAML Mario Lemieux B 40.00 100.00

2016 Upper Deck Goodwin Champions Goudey Sport Royalty Memorabilia

SRMWG Wayne Gretzky B 12.00 30.00

2016 Upper Deck Goodwin Champions Goudey Sport Royalty Memorabilia Dual Swatch

SRM2WG Wayne Gretzky A 20.00 50.00

2016 Upper Deck Goodwin Champions Goudey Sport Royalty Memorabilia Premium

SRMWG Wayne Gretzky 25.00 60.00

2016 Upper Deck Goodwin Champions Memorabilia Premium

MAI Aito Iguchi E 10.00 25.00

2016 Upper Deck Goodwin Champions Variations

SP3 Wayne Gretzky 20.00 50.00

2018 Upper Deck Goodwin Champions Goudey Sport Royalty Autographs

SRAWG Wayne Gretzky B 150.00 400.00

2009 Upper Deck Goudey Sport Royalty Autographs

MI Mike Bossy 12.50 30.00
NL Nicklas Lidstrom 30.00 60.00
OR Bobby Orr 100.00 200.00

1999-00 Upper Deck Gretzky Exclusives

COMPLETE SET (99) 100.00 250.00
COMMON GRETZKY (1-99) 1.00 3.00
*GOLD/99: 6X TO 15X BASIC INSERTS
NNO Gretzky Blues AU/99 250.00 600.00
NNO Gretzky Kings AU/99 250.00 600.00
NNO Gretzky Oilers AU/50 500.00 1200.00
NNO Gretzky Rangers AU/25 600.00 1500.00

1999-00 Upper Deck Gretzky Game Jersey Autographs

NNO Wayne Gretzky GJ AU/40 UD Century 600.00 1500.00
NNO Wayne Gretzky GJ AU/40 Upper Deck Retro 600.00 1500.00
NNO Wayne Gretzky GJ AU/40 Upper Deck MVP 600.00 1500.00

2000-01 Upper Deck Heroes

1 Steve Rucchin .12 .30
2 Marty McInnis .15 .40
3 Oleg Tverdovsky .12 .30
4 Guy Hebert .15 .40
5 Patrik Stefan .15 .40
6 Donald Audette .15 .40
7 Andrew Brunette .12 .30
8 Jason Allison .15 .40
9 Sergei Samsonov .15 .40
10 Joe Thornton .30 .75
11 Byron Dafoe .15 .40
12 Dominik Hasek .30 .75
13 Miroslav Satan .15 .40
14 Doug Gilmour .25 .60
15 J-P Dumont .12 .30
16 Fred Brathwaite .15 .40
17 Valeri Bure .15 .40
18 Marc Savard .12 .30
19 Cory Stillman .12 .30
20 Ron Francis .25 .60
21 Arturs Irbe .15 .40
22 Jeff O'Neill .15 .40
23 Sandis Ozolinsh .12 .30
24 Tony Amonte .15 .40
25 Jocelyn Thibault .15 .40
26 Alexei Zhamnov .15 .40
27 Steve Sullivan .12 .30
28 Chris Drury .15 .40
29 Milan Hejduk .15 .40
30 Alex Tanguay .15 .40
31 Peter Forsberg .40 1.00
32 Adam Deadmarsh .12 .30
33 Marc Denis .15 .40
34 Ron Tugnutt .15 .40
35 Tyler Wright .12 .30
36 David Vyborny .12 .30
37 Brett Hull .40 1.00
38 Ed Belfour .25 .60
39 Joe Nieuwendyk .15 .40
40 Sergei Zubov .15 .40
41 Jere Lehtinen .15 .40
42 Sergei Fedorov .30 .75
43 Martin Lapointe .15 .40
44 Chris Osgood .20 .50
45 Pat Verbeek .15 .40
46 Nicklas Lidstrom .20 .50
47 Doug Weight .20 .50
48 Tommy Salo .15 .40
49 Ryan Smyth .15 .40
50 Sean Brown .12 .30
51 Ray Whitney .15 .40
52 Trevor Kidd .15 .40
53 Viktor Kozlov .15 .40
54 Denis Shvidki .12 .30
55 Rob Blake .20 .50
56 Zigmund Palffy .20 .50
57 Luc Robitaille .20 .50
58 Glen Murray .15 .40
59 Manny Fernandez .12 .30
60 Scott Pellerin .12 .30
61 Maxim Sushinski .12 .30
62 Saku Koivu .20 .50
63 Jose Theodore .20 .50
64 Martin Rucinsky .12 .30
65 Darryl Shannon .12 .30
66 Cliff Ronning .12 .30
67 Randy Robitaille .12 .30
68 David Legwand .20 .50
69 Mike Dunham .12 .30
70 Alexander Mogilny .15 .40
71 Patrik Elias .20 .50
72 Bobby Holik .12 .30
73 Scott Stevens .15 .40
74 Mariusz Czerkawski .12 .30
75 Tim Connolly .12 .30
76 Aris Brimanis .12 .30
77 John Vanbiesbrouck .20 .50
78 Brian Leetch .15 .40
79 Mike York .15 .40
80 Theo Fleury .25 .60
81 Mike Richter .20 .50
82 Alexei Yashin .15 .40
83 Ricard Persson .12 .30
84 Radek Bonk .15 .40
85 Patrick Lalime .15 .40
86 Simon Gagne .20 .50
87 Brian Boucher .15 .40
88 Keith Primeau .15 .40
89 Mark Greig .12 .30
90 Teppo Numminen .12 .30
91 Shane Doan .15 .40
92 Keith Tkachuk .20 .50
93 Sean Burke .12 .30
94 Milan Kraft .12 .30
95 Alexei Kovalev .15 .40
96 Jean-Sebastien Aubin .15 .40
97 Martin Straka .15 .40
98 Vincent Damphousse .15 .40
99 Steve Shields .12 .30
100 Brad Stuart .15 .40
101 Owen Nolan .20 .50
102 Chris Pronger .20 .50
103 Pavol Demitra .25 .60
104 Roman Turek .15 .40
105 Pierre Turgeon .15 .40
106 Dan Cloutier .15 .40
107 Brad Richards .20 .50
108 Paul Mara .12 .30
109 Gary Roberts .12 .30
110 Sergei Berezin .12 .30
111 Mats Sundin .20 .50
112 Bryan McCabe .12 .30
113 Henrik Sedin .25 .60
114 Daniel Sedin .25 .60
115 Greg Hawgood .12 .30
116 Adam Oates .20 .50
117 Olaf Kolzig .20 .50
118 Sergei Gonchar .12 .30
119 Bobby Orr .75 2.00
120 Cam Neely .20 .50
121 Gilbert Perreault .20 .50
122 Bobby Hull .40 1.00
123 Stan Mikita .25 .60
124 Tony Esposito .20 .50
125 Gordie Howe .60 1.50
126 Wayne Gretzky 1.25 3.00
127 Marcel Dionne .25 .60
128 Maurice Richard .40 1.00
129 Guy Lafleur .25 .60
130 Jean Beliveau .25 .60
131 Bryan Trottier .20 .50
132 Denis Potvin .20 .50
133 Mike Bossy .20 .50
134 Bobby Clarke .30 .75
135 Bernie Parent .25 .60
136 Mario Lemieux .75 2.00
137 Michel Goulet .15 .40
138 Frank Mahovlich .20 .50
139 Paul Kariya .20 .50
140 Teemu Selanne .40 1.00
141 Patrick Roy .50 1.25
142 Joe Sakic .40 1.00
143 Peter Forsberg .40 1.00
144 Ray Bourque .30 .75
145 Mike Modano .30 .75
146 Steve Yzerman .50 1.25
147 Brendan Shanahan .20 .50
148 Pavel Bure .20 .50
149 Martin Brodeur .50 1.25
150 Scott Gomez .15 .40
151 Mark Messier .40 1.00
152 Marian Hossa .20 .50
153 John LeClair .20 .50
154 Jeremy Roenick .30 .75
155 Jaromir Jagr .60 1.50
156 Jeff Friesen .12 .30
157 Vincent Lecavalier .20 .50
158 Curtis Joseph .25 .60
159 Jonas Ronnqvist RC .20 .50
160 Jeff Cowan RC .20 .50
161 David Aebischer RC .40 1.00
162 Rostislav Klesla RC .50 1.25
163 Tyler Bouck RC .20 .50
164 Michel Riesen RC .25 .60
165 Steven Reinprecht RC .30 .75
166 Marian Gaborik RC 2.50 6.00
167 David Gosselin RC .25 .60
168 Scott Hartnell RC .50 1.25
169 Colin White RC .20 .50
170 Rick DiPietro RC .40 1.00
171 Johan Holmqvist RC .20 .50
172 Jani Hurme RC .20 .50
173 Martin Havlat RC 1.25 3.00
174 Justin Williams RC .50 1.25
175 Roman Cechmanek RC .25 .60
176 Roman Simicek RC .20 .50
177 Zdenek Blatny RC .20 .50
178 Jordan Krestanovich RC .20 .50
179 Mark Messier CL .30 .75
180 Wayne Gretzky CL .60 1.50

2000-01 Upper Deck Heroes Game Used Twigs

TBH Bobby Hull 12.00 30.00
TBO Bobby Orr 50.00 125.00
TBO Mike Bossy 5.00 12.00
TCJ Curtis Joseph 6.00 15.00
TDH Dominik Hasek 6.00 15.00
TGH Gordie Howe 20.00 50.00
TGP Gilbert Perreault 8.00 20.00
TJJ Jaromir Jagr 6.00 15.00
TJL John LeClair 5.00 12.00
TMB Martin Brodeur 10.00 25.00
TML Mario Lemieux 12.00 30.00
TMM Mark Messier 5.00 12.00
TMS Mats Sundin 5.00 12.00
TPK Paul Kariya 6.00 15.00
TPR Patrick Roy 8.00 20.00
TRB Ray Bourque 6.00 15.00
TSY Steve Yzerman 15.00 40.00
TTF Theo Fleury 8.00 20.00
TTS Teemu Selanne 5.00 12.00
TWG Wayne Gretzky 40.00 100.00

2000-01 Upper Deck Heroes Game Used Twigs Gold

CBO R.Bourque/B.Orr 150.00 400.00
CFL T.Fleury/J.LeClair 30.00 80.00
CGM W.Gretzky/M.Messier 100.00 200.00
CHB Bo.Hull/M.Bossy 60.00 150.00
CHP D.Hasek/G.Perreault 30.00 80.00
CHY G.Howe/S.Yzerman 150.00 350.00
CJS C.Joseph/M.Sundin 25.00 60.00
CKS P.Kariya/T.Selanne 30.00 80.00
CLJ M.Lemieux/J.Jagr 75.00 200.00
CRB P.Roy/M.Brodeur 60.00 150.00

2000-01 Upper Deck Heroes NHL Leaders

COMPLETE SET (10) 10.00 20.00
L1 Paul Kariya .50 1.25
L2 Ray Bourque 1.25 3.00
L3 Joe Sakic 1.25 3.00
L4 Steve Yzerman 3.00 8.00
L5 Mark Messier .75 2.00
L6 Alexei Yashin .50 1.25
L7 John LeClair .75 2.00
L8 Keith Tkachuk .60 1.50
L9 Jaromir Jagr 1.25 3.00
L10 Al MacInnis .50 1.25

2000-01 Upper Deck Heroes Player Idols

COMPLETE SET (6) 12.00 25.00
PI1 B.Shanahan/M.Messier 1.00 2.50
PI2 M.Brodeur/P.Roy 3.00 8.00
PI3 M.Alinogenov/P.Bure 1.00 2.50
PI4 P.Kariya/W.Gretzky 3.00 8.00
PI5 V.Lecavalier/M.Lemieux 4.00 10.00
PI6 R.Turek/D.Hasek 1.50 4.00

2000-01 Upper Deck Heroes Second Season Heroes

COMPLETE SET (10) 20.00 40.00
SS1 Patrick Roy 4.00 10.00
SS2 Peter Forsberg 2.00 5.00
SS3 Mike Modano 1.00 2.50
SS4 Ed Belfour 1.00 2.50
SS5 Steve Yzerman 4.00 10.00
SS6 Wayne Gretzky 5.00 12.00
SS7 Martin Brodeur 2.00 5.00
SS8 Mark Messier 1.00 2.50
SS9 John LeClair 1.00 2.50
SS10 Jaromir Jagr 1.25 3.00

2000-01 Upper Deck Heroes Signs of Greatness

BC Bobby Clarke 10.00 25.00
BH Bobby Hull SP 20.00 50.00
BO Bobby Orr SP 60.00 120.00
BP Bernie Parent 10.00 25.00
BT Bryan Trottier 10.00 25.00
CN Cam Neely 10.00 25.00
DP Denis Potvin 8.00 20.00
FM Frank Mahovlich 10.00 25.00
FP Felix Potvin 15.00 40.00
GH Gordie Howe SP 50.00 100.00
GL Guy Lafleur 15.00 40.00
GP Gilbert Perreault 6.00 15.00
JB Jean Beliveau 25.00 50.00
JL John LeClair 6.00 15.00
JR Jeremy Roenick SP 20.00 50.00
KJ Kenny Jonsson 4.00 10.00
MA Marc Denis 4.00 10.00
MD Marcel Dionne 10.00 25.00
MG Michel Goulet 10.00 25.00
ML Mario Lemieux SP 75.00 150.00
MM Mark Messier SP 50.00 100.00
MS Miroslav Satan 4.00 10.00
MY Mike York 4.00 10.00
PA Pavel Brendl 4.00 10.00
PB Pavel Bure SP 10.00 25.00
PB Peter Bondra 4.00 10.00
RL Roberto Luongo 8.00 20.00
RT Roman Turek 4.00 10.00
SG Scott Gomez 6.00 15.00
SM Stan Mikita 10.00 25.00
SY Steve Yzerman 30.00 80.00
TS Tommy Salo 4.00 10.00
WG Wayne Gretzky SP 150.00 400.00

2000-01 Upper Deck Heroes Timeless Moments

COMPLETE SET (10) 10.00 20.00
TM1 Teemu Selanne .60 1.50
TM2 Dominik Hasek 1.25 3.00
TM3 Patrick Roy 3.00 8.00
TM4 Brett Hull .75 2.00
TM5 Pavel Bure .75 2.00
TM6 Martin Brodeur 1.50 4.00
TM7 Mike York .50 1.25
TM8 Brian Boucher .60 1.50
TM9 Jaromir Jagr 1.00 2.50
TM10 Curtis Joseph .60 1.50

2000-01 Upper Deck Heroes Today's Snipers

COMPLETE SET (6) 5.00 10.00
TS1 Paul Kariya .60 1.50
TS2 Brendan Shanahan .75 2.00
TS3 Pavel Bure .75 2.00
TS4 John LeClair .75 2.00
TS5 Jaromir Jagr 1.00 2.50
TS6 Mats Sundin .60 1.50

2014-15 Upper Deck Heroic Inspirations Autographs

HEROJH Josh Harding/25 30.00 60.00

2005-06 Upper Deck Hockey Showcase

*BECKETT PROMOS: .4X TO 1X BASIC CARDS
HS1 Peter Forsberg 8.00 20.00
HS2 Chris Pronger 4.00 10.00
HS3 Adam Foote 2.50 6.00
HS4 Gary Roberts 2.50 6.00
HS5 Sergei Gonchar 2.50 6.00
HS6 Brian Leetch 3.00 8.00
HS7 Darren McCarty 2.50 6.00
HS8 Michael Peca 3.00 8.00
HS9 Bobby Holik 2.50 6.00
HS10 Eric Brewer 2.50 6.00
HS11 Paul Kariya 4.00 10.00
HS12 Jason Allison 3.00 8.00
HS13 Derian Hatcher 2.50 6.00
HS14 Sean Burke 3.00 8.00
HS15 Adrian Aucoin 2.50 6.00
HS16 Jeremy Roenick 6.00 15.00
HS17 Jocelyn Thibault 3.00 8.00
HS18 Alexander Mogilny 3.00 8.00
HS19 Pierre Turgeon 3.00 8.00
HS20 Anson Carter 3.00 8.00
HS21 Tony Amonte 3.00 8.00
HS22 Curtis Joseph 5.00 12.00
HS23 Miroslav Satan 3.00 8.00
HS24 Teemu Selanne 8.00 20.00
HS25 Mike York 2.50 6.00
HS26 Dany Heatley 3.00 8.00
HS27 Zigmund Palffy 3.00 8.00
HS28 Scott Niedermayer 4.00 10.00
HS29 Jeff O'Neill 2.50 6.00
HS30 Joe Nieuwendyk 3.00 8.00
HS31 Marian Hossa 4.00 10.00
HS32 Eric Lindros 6.00 15.00
HS33 Nikolai Khabibulin 4.00 10.00
HS34 Martin Straka 2.50 6.00
HS35 Chris Osgood 4.00 10.00
HS36 Pavol Demitra 5.00 12.00
HS37 Peter Bondra 4.00 10.00
HS38 John LeClair 4.00 10.00
HS39 Cory Stillman 3.00 8.00
HS40 Alexei Zhamnov 2.50 6.00

1999-00 Upper Deck HoloGrFx

COMPLETE SET (60) 15.00 30.00
1 Teemu Selanne .25 .60
2 Paul Kariya .25 .60
3 Patrik Stefan RC 1.50 4.00
4 Sergei Samsonov .20 .50
5 Ray Bourque .40 1.00
6 Dominik Hasek .50 1.25
7 Brian Campbell RC .07 .20
8 Marc Savard .07 .20
9 Oleg Saprykin RC 1.50 4.00
10 Sami Kapanen .07 .20
11 Keith Primeau .07 .20
12 Tony Amonte .07 .20
13 J-P Dumont .20 .50
14 Peter Forsberg .60 1.50
15 Joe Sakic .50 1.25
16 Chris Drury .20 .50
17 Patrick Roy 1.25 3.00
18 Brett Hull .30 .75
19 Mike Modano .40 1.00
20 Ed Belfour .25 .60
21 Steve Yzerman 1.25 3.00
22 Brendan Shanahan .25 .60
23 Sergei Fedorov .40 1.00
24 Doug Weight .20 .50
25 Bill Guerin .07 .20
26 Pavel Bure .25 .60
27 Mark Parrish .07 .20
28 Luc Robitaille .20 .50
29 Zigmund Palffy .20 .50
30 Mike Ribeiro .20 .50
31 David Legwand .20 .50
32 Scott Gomez .07 .20
33 Martin Brodeur .60 1.50
34 Vadim Sharifijanov .07 .20
35 Jorgen Jonsson RC .07 .20
36 Eric Brewer .20 .50
37 Tim Connolly .07 .20
38 Theo Fleury .07 .20
39 Brian Leetch .25 .60
40 Mike Richter .25 .60
41 Marian Hossa .25 .60
42 Simon Gagne .25 .60
43 Eric Lindros .25 .60
44 John LeClair .25 .60
45 Keith Tkachuk .25 .60
46 Jeremy Roenick .30 .75
47 Jaromir Jagr .40 1.00
48 Niklas Sundstrom .07 .20
49 Jeff Friesen .07 .20
50 Brad Stuart .20 .50
51 Pavol Demitra .20 .50
52 Al MacInnis .20 .50
53 Paul Mara .20 .50
54 Vincent Lecavalier .25 .60
55 Mats Sundin .25 .60
56 Sergei Berezin .20 .50
57 Curtis Joseph .25 .60
58 Steve Kariya RC 1.00 2.50
59 Peter Bondra .20 .50
60 Olaf Kolzig .20 .50

1999-00 Upper Deck HoloGrFx Ausome

*AUSOME: 5X TO 12X BASIC CARDS

1999-00 Upper Deck HoloGrFx Gretzky GrFx

COMPLETE SET (15) 15.00 30.00
COMMON GRETZKY (GG1-GG15) 1.25 3.00
*AUSOME: 3X TO 8X BASIC

1999-00 Upper Deck HoloGrFx Impact Zone

COMPLETE SET (6) 15.00 30.00
*AUSOME: 2.5X TO 6X BASIC INSERTS
IZ1 Dominik Hasek 2.50 6.00
IZ2 Jaromir Jagr 2.00 5.00
IZ3 Eric Lindros 2.50 6.00
IZ4 Patrick Roy 4.00 10.00
IZ5 Paul Kariya 2.50 6.00
IZ6 Peter Forsberg 3.00 8.00

1999-00 Upper Deck HoloGrFx Pure Skill

COMPLETE SET (9) 12.00 25.00
*AUSOME: 2.5X TO 6X BASIC INSERTS
PS1 Paul Kariya .75 2.00
PS2 Peter Forsberg 2.00 5.00
PS3 Dominik Hasek 1.50 4.00
PS4 Sergei Samsonov .75 2.00
PS5 Teemu Selanne .75 2.00
PS6 Patrick Roy 4.00 10.00
PS7 Brett Hull 1.00 2.50
PS8 Eric Lindros .75 2.00
PS9 Jaromir Jagr 1.25 3.00

1999-00 Upper Deck HoloGrFx UD Authentics

BH Brett Hull 15.00 40.00
BM Bill Muckalt 6.00 15.00
CD Chris Drury 10.00 25.00
DL David Legwand 6.00 15.00
PB Pavel Bure 15.00 40.00
PS Patrik Stefan 6.00 15.00
RB Ray Bourque 40.00 80.00
WG Wayne Gretzky 250.00 600.00
WG2 Wayne Gretzky Kings 250.00 600.00

2001-02 Upper Deck Honor Roll

1 Bobby Hull .30 .75
2 Wayne Gretzky 1.00 2.50
3 Gordie Howe .50 1.25
4 Bobby Orr .60 1.50
5 Ray Bourque .25 .60
6 Patrick Roy .40 1.00
7 Luc Robitaille .15 .40
8 Mario Lemieux .60 1.50
9 Jaromir Jagr .50 1.25
10 Chris Pronger .15 .40
11 Rob Blake .15 .40
12 Martin Brodeur .40 1.00
13 Paul Kariya .15 .40
14 Joe Sakic .30 .75
15 Pavel Bure .15 .40
16 Nicklas Lidstrom .15 .40
17 Brian Leetch .12 .30
18 Dominik Hasek .25 .60
19 Brendan Shanahan .15 .40
20 Steve Yzerman .40 1.00
21 Teemu Selanne .30 .75
22 Al MacInnis .15 .40
23 Scott Stevens .15 .40
24 Curtis Joseph .25 .60
25 Dany Heatley .12 .30
26 Joe Thornton .25 .60

27 Mark Parrish .10 .25
28 Rostislav Klesla .10 .25
29 Brad Stuart .10 .25
30 Rick DiPietro .12 .30
31 Bobby Hull .30 .75
32 Wayne Gretzky 1.00 2.50
33 Gordie Howe .50 1.25
34 Bobby Orr .60 1.50
35 Ray Bourque .25 .60
36 Patrick Roy .40 1.00
37 Luc Robitaille .15 .40
38 Mario Lemieux .60 1.50
39 Jaromir Jagr .50 1.25
40 Chris Pronger .15 .40
41 Rob Blake .15 .40
42 Martin Brodeur .40 1.00
43 Paul Kariya .15 .40
44 Joe Sakic .30 .75
45 Pavel Bure .15 .40
46 Nicklas Lidstrom .15 .40
47 Brian Leetch .12 .30
48 Dominik Hasek .25 .60
49 Brendan Shanahan .15 .40
50 Steve Yzerman .40 1.00
51 Teemu Selanne .30 .75
52 Al MacInnis .20 .50
53 Scott Stevens .15 .40
54 Curtis Joseph .20 .50
55 Dany Heatley .12 .30
56 Joe Thornton .25 .60
57 Mark Parrish .10 .25
58 Rostislav Klesla .10 .25
59 Brad Stuart .10 .25
60 Rick DiPietro .12 .30
61 Ilja Bryzgalov RC 3.00 8.00
62 Mike Weaver RC 1.25 3.00
63 Kamil Piros RC 1.25 3.00
64 Ben Simon RC 1.50 4.00
65 Ivan Huml RC 1.25 3.00
66 Ales Kotalik RC 2.50 6.00
67 Scott Nichol RC 1.25 3.00
68 Kelly Fairchild RC 1.25 3.00
69 Vaclav Nedorost RC 1.25 3.00
70 Niko Kapanen RC 2.00 5.00
71 Pavel Datsyuk RC 8.00 20.00
72 Sean Avery RC 1.25 3.00
73 Kristian Huselius RC 2.00 5.00
74 Nick Smith RC 1.25 3.00
75 Nick Schultz RC 1.25 3.00
76 Marcel Hossa RC 2.00 5.00
77 Olivier Michaud RC 2.00 5.00
78 Martin Erat RC 1.50 4.00
79 Christian Berglund RC 1.50 4.00
80 Andreas Salomonsson RC 1.25 3.00
81 Radek Martinek RC 1.25 3.00
82 Richard Scott RC 1.25 3.00
83 Ivan Ciernik RC 1.25 3.00
84 Bruno St. Jacques RC 1.25 3.00
85 Dan Focht RC 1.25 3.00
86 Jeff Jillson RC 1.25 3.00
87 Mark Rycroft RC 1.50 4.00
88 Nikita Alexeev RC 1.25 3.00
89 Justin Kurtz RC 2.00 5.00
90 Chris Corrinet RC 1.25 3.00
91 M.Spanhel RC/Amonte JSY 5.00 12.00
92 M.Davidson RC/C.Drury JSY 6.00 15.00
93 J.Bednar RC/Z.Palffy JSY 5.00 12.00
94 R.Torres RC/Shanahan JSY 8.00 20.00
95 Samuelsson RC/Fedorov JSY 6.00 15.00
96 Blackburn RC/Richter JSY 6.00 15.00
97 T.Divisek RC/J.LeClair JSY 6.00 15.00
98 J.Dopita RC/P.Demitra JSY 4.00 10.00
99 K.Kolanos RC/Modano JSY 6.00 15.00
100 I.Kovalchuk RC/J.Jagr JSY 12.50 30.00

2001-02 Upper Deck Honor Roll Defense First

COMPLETE SET (6) 10.00 20.00
DF1 Mike Modano 1.25 3.00
DF2 Jere Lehtinen .75 2.00
DF3 Steve Yzerman 4.00 10.00
DF4 Sergei Fedorov 1.25 3.00
DF5 John Madden .75 2.00
DF6 Michael Peca .75 2.00

2001-02 Upper Deck Honor Roll Honor Society

*GOLD/25: .8X TO 2X BASIC DUAL/100
HSBB P.Bure/V.Bure 20.00 50.00
HSCH R.Cechmanek/D.Hasek 20.00 50.00
HSHK M.Hejduk/P.Kariya 20.00 50.00
HSRB P.Roy/M.Brodeur 30.00 80.00

2001-02 Upper Deck Honor Roll Jerseys

*GOLD/50: 1.2X TO 3X BASIC JSY/225
BB Brian Boucher 4.00 10.00
BH Brett Hull 6.00 15.00
BL Brian Leetch 5.00 12.00
BS Brendan Shanahan 5.00 12.00
CD Chris Drury 4.00 10.00
DL David Legwand 4.00 10.00
DW Doug Weight 4.00 10.00
EB Ed Belfour 5.00 12.00
EL Eric Lindros 5.00 12.00
JH Jochen Hecht 4.00 10.00
JL John LeClair 4.00 10.00
JN Joe Nieuwendyk 4.00 10.00
JS Joe Sakic 8.00 20.00
JT Joe Thornton 6.00 15.00
LI Eric Lindros 5.00 12.00
LR Luc Robitaille 5.00 12.00
MB Martin Brodeur 8.00 20.00
ML Mario Lemieux 12.50 30.00
MM Mike Modano 6.00 15.00
MN Markus Naslund 4.00 10.00
MO Maxime Ouellet 4.00 10.00
MS Miroslav Satan 4.00 10.00
NL Nicklas Lidstrom 4.00 10.00
PB Peter Bondra 4.00 10.00
PD Pavol Demitra 4.00 10.00
PK Paul Kariya 5.00 12.00
RB Ray Bourque 8.00 20.00
RL Roberto Luongo 6.00 15.00
SF Sergei Fedorov 6.00 15.00
SS Sergei Samsonov 5.00 12.00
SU Mats Sundin 5.00 12.00
TC Tim Connolly 4.00 10.00

2001-02 Upper Deck Honor Roll Original Six

COMPLETE SET (6) 20.00 40.00
OS1 Bobby Orr 4.00 10.00
OS2 Bobby Hull 2.50 6.00
OS3 Gordie Howe 4.00 10.00
OS4 Patrick Roy 4.00 10.00
OS5 Wayne Gretzky 5.00 12.00
OS6 Curtis Joseph .75 2.00

2001-02 Upper Deck Honor Roll Playoff Matchups

*GOLD/25: .8X TO 2X BASIC DUAL/200
HSHT B.Hull/K.Tkachuk 12.50 30.00
HSLH M.Lemieux/D.Hasek 20.00 50.00
HSRB P.Roy/M.Brodeur 30.00 80.00
HSSR J.Sakic/L.Robitaille 20.00 50.00
HSSS M.Sundin/S.Stevens 12.50 30.00
HSTM A.Tanguay/A.MacInnis 12.50 30.00

2001-02 Upper Deck Honor Roll Pucks

GOLD/100: .8X TO 2X BASIC INSERT
PAK Alexei Kovalev 6.00 15.00
PBL Brian Leetch 6.00 15.00
PJI Jarome Iginla 12.00 30.00
PMH Marian Hossa 10.00 25.00
PMM Mark Messier 10.00 25.00
PMS Mats Sundin 10.00 25.00
PPB Pavel Bure 8.00 20.00
PPE Patrik Elias 6.00 15.00
PPO Peter Bondra 8.00 20.00
PSK Saku Koivu 10.00 25.00
PSS Scott Stevens 8.00 20.00
PVL Vincent Lecavalier 8.00 20.00

2001-02 Upper Deck Honor Roll Sharp Skaters

COMPLETE SET (6) 10.00 20.00
SS1 Paul Kariya .75 2.00
SS2 Mike Modano 1.25 3.00
SS3 Sergei Fedorov 1.50 4.00
SS4 Pavel Bure 1.00 2.50
SS5 Marian Hossa .75 2.00
SS6 Simon Gagne .75 2.00

2001-02 Upper Deck Honor Roll Student of the Game

COMPLETE SET (6) 10.00 20.00
SG1 Paul Kariya .75 2.00
SG2 Joe Sakic 1.50 4.00
SG3 Mike Modano 1.25 3.00
SG4 Steve Yzerman 4.00 10.00
SG5 Patrik Elias .75 2.00
SG6 Mats Sundin .75 2.00

2001-02 Upper Deck Honor Roll Tough Customers

COMPLETE SET (6) 4.00 8.00
TC1 Martin Lapointe .60 1.50
TC2 Rob Blake .60 1.50
TC3 Scott Stevens .60 1.50
TC4 Jeremy Roenick .75 2.00
TC5 Owen Nolan .60 1.50
TC6 Chris Pronger .60 1.50

2001-02 Upper Deck Honor Roll Tribute to 500

1 Patrick Roy Mon. 20.00 50.00
2 Patrick Roy Col. 20.00 50.00

2002-03 Upper Deck Honor Roll

1 Paul Kariya .15 .40
2 Jean-Sebastien Giguere .15 .40
3 Ilya Kovalchuk .20 .50
4 Dany Heatley .12 .30
5 Joe Thornton .25 .60
6 Sergei Samsonov .12 .30
7 Miroslav Satan .15 .40
8 Martin Biron .12 .30
9 Chris Drury .15 .40
10 Jarome Iginla .20 .50
11 Ron Francis .20 .50
12 Arturs Irbe .12 .30
13 Tylor Arnason .15 .40
14 Jocelyn Thibault .12 .30
15 Patrick Roy .40 1.00
16 Joe Sakic .30 .75
17 Peter Forsberg .30 .75
18 Rob Blake .15 .40
19 Ray Whitney .12 .30
20 Marc Denis .12 .30
21 Mike Modano .25 .60
22 Marty Turco .15 .40
23 Bill Guerin .15 .40
24 Steve Yzerman .40 1.00
25 Sergei Fedorov .25 .60
26 Nicklas Lidstrom .15 .40
27 Brett Hull .30 .75
28 Curtis Joseph .20 .50
29 Brendan Shanahan .15 .40
30 Mike Comrie .15 .40
31 Tommy Salo .12 .30
32 Roberto Luongo .25 .60
33 Kristian Huselius .10 .25
34 Felix Potvin .25 .60
35 Zigmund Palffy .15 .40
36 Marian Gaborik .15 .40
37 Manny Fernandez .10 .25
38 Jose Theodore .15 .40
39 Saku Koivu .15 .40
40 Patrik Elias .15 .40
41 Martin Brodeur .40 1.00
42 David Legwand .12 .30
43 Tomas Vokoun .12 .30
44 Alexei Yashin .12 .30
45 Chris Osgood .15 .40
46 Michael Peca .12 .30
47 Eric Lindros .25 .60
48 Mike Richter .15 .40
49 Pavel Bure .15 .40
50 Marian Hossa .15 .40
51 Daniel Alfredsson .15 .40
52 Jeremy Roenick .25 .60
53 John LeClair .15 .40
54 Roman Cechmanek .12 .30
55 Sean Burke .10 .25
56 Tony Amonte .12 .30
57 Alex Kovalev .12 .30
58 Mario Lemieux .60 1.50
59 Owen Nolan .15 .40
60 Evgeni Nabokov .12 .30
61 Keith Tkachuk .15 .40
62 Brent Johnson .12 .30
63 Nikolai Khabibulin .15 .40
64 Vincent Lecavalier .15 .40
65 Mats Sundin .15 .40
66 Ed Belfour .15 .40
67 Todd Bertuzzi .15 .40
68 Markus Naslund .15 .40
69 Olaf Kolzig .15 .40
70 Jaromir Jagr .50 1.25
71 Paul Kariya .15 .40
72 Shawn McEachern .10 .25
73 Joe Thornton .25 .60
74 Stu Barnes .10 .25
75 Craig Conroy .10 .25
76 Ron Francis .20 .50
77 Alexei Zhamnov .12 .30
78 Joe Sakic .30 .75
79 Ray Whitney .12 .30
80 Derian Hatcher .12 .30
81 Steve Yzerman .40 1.00
82 Jason Smith .10 .25
83 Valeri Bure .12 .30
84 Mattias Norstrom .10 .25
85 Andrew Brunette .10 .25
86 Saku Koivu .15 .40
87 Greg Johnson .10 .25
88 Scott Stevens .15 .40
89 Michael Peca .12 .30
90 Brian Leetch .12 .30
91 Daniel Alfredsson .15 .40
92 Keith Primeau .12 .30
93 Teppo Numminen .10 .25
94 Mario Lemieux .60 1.50
95 Owen Nolan .15 .40
96 Chris Pronger .15 .40
97 Vincent Lecavalier .15 .40
98 Mats Sundin .15 .40
99 Markus Naslund .15 .40
100 Steve Konowalchuk .10 .25
101 Alexei Smirnov RC 2.00 5.00
102 Martin Gerber RC 2.50 6.00
103 Kurt Sauer RC 1.50 4.00
104 Tim Thomas RC 6.00 15.00
105 Jordan Leopold RC 2.50 6.00
106 Dany Sabourin RC 1.50 4.00
107 Levente Szuper RC 2.50 6.00
108 Shawn Thornton RC 2.00 5.00
109 Matt Henderson RC 1.50 4.00
110 Lasse Pirjeta RC 1.50 4.00
111 Pascal LeClaire RC 2.00 5.00
112 Dmitri Bykov RC 1.50 4.00
113 Kari Haakana RC 1.50 4.00
114 Craig Andersson RC 5.00 12.00
115 Mike Cammalleri RC 5.00 12.00
116 Stephane Veilleux RC 1.50 4.00
117 Adam Hall RC 1.50 4.00
118 Greg Koehler RC 1.50 4.00
119 Vernon Fiddler RC 2.00 5.00
120 Ray Emery RC 5.00 12.00
121 Eric Godard RC 1.50 4.00
122 Dennis Seidenberg RC 2.50 6.00
123 Jeff Taffe RC 1.50 4.00
124 Dick Tarnstrom RC 1.50 4.00
125 Tom Koivisto RC 1.50 4.00
126 Curtis Sanford RC 2.50 6.00
127 Cody Rudkowsky RC 1.50 4.00
128 Carlo Colaiacovo RC 2.50 6.00
129 Paul Manning RC 1.50 4.00
130 Shaone Morrisonn RC 1.50 4.00
131 Ryan Miller RC 10.00 25.00
132 Jerred Smithson RC 1.50 4.00
133 Alexei Semenov RC 1.50 4.00
134 Michael Leighton RC 2.50 6.00
135 Ian MacNeil RC 1.50 4.00
136 Jared Aulin RC 1.50 4.00
137 Curtis Murphy RC 1.50 4.00
138 Jim Vandermeer RC 1.50 4.00
139 Steve Ott RC 1.50 4.00
140 Brooks Orpik RC 1.50 4.00
141 Jim Fahey RC 1.50 4.00
142 Matt Walker RC 1.50 4.00
143 Rickard Wallin RC 1.50 4.00
144 Tomas Malec RC 1.50 4.00
145 Jonathan Hedstrom RC 1.50 4.00
146 Stanislav Chistov JSY RC 2.00 5.00
147 Chuck Kobasew JSY RC 2.50 6.00
148 Micki Dupont JSY RC 2.00 5.00
149 Jeff Paul JSY RC 2.00 5.00
150 Rick Nash JSY RC 12.00 30.00
151 Henrik Zetterberg JSY RC 12.00 30.00
152 Ales Hemsky JSY RC 8.00 20.00
153 Jay Bouwmeester JSY RC 6.00 15.00
154 Alexander Frolov JSY RC 5.00 12.00
155 Pierre-Marc Bouchard JSY RC 3.00 8.00
156 Sylvain Blouin JSY RC 2.00 5.00
157 Ron Hainsey JSY RC 2.00 5.00
158 Scottie Upshall JSY RC 2.50 6.00
159 Tomi Pettinen JSY RC 2.00 5.00
160 Jason Spezza JSY RC 15.00 40.00
161 Anton Volchenkov JSY RC 2.00 5.00
162 Radovan Somik JSY RC 2.00 5.00
163 Lynn Loyns JSY RC 2.00 5.00
164 Alexander Svitov JSY RC 2.00 5.00
165 Mikael Tellqvist JSY RC 2.00 5.00
166 Steve Eminger JSY RC 2.00 5.00

2002-03 Upper Deck Honor Roll Grade A Jerseys

GAED Eric Daze 3.00 8.00
GAJJ Jaromir Jagr 5.00 12.00
GAMB Martin Brodeur 8.00 20.00
GAMD Mike Dunham 3.00 8.00
GAMM Mike Modano 4.00 10.00
GAMS Mats Sundin 3.00 8.00
GAOK Olaf Kolzig 3.00 8.00
GAPF Peter Forsberg 5.00 12.00
GAPK Paul Kariya 3.00 8.00
GAPR Patrick Roy 10.00 25.00
GARB Ray Bourque 5.00 12.00
GASA Miroslav Satan 3.00 8.00
GASG Simon Gagne 4.00 10.00
GASK Saku Koivu 3.00 8.00
TJKB Jagr/Kolzig/Bondra 12.50 30.00
TPRG Primeau/Roenick/Gagne 25.00 60.00
TRFS Roy/Forsberg/Sakic 40.00 100.00
TSTM Sams/Thornton/Murray 15.00 40.00
TYFS Yzerman/Fedorov/Shanny 30.00 80.00

2002-03 Upper Deck Honor Roll Signature Class

AS Alexander Svitov 10.00 25.00
BR Pavel Brendl 6.00 15.00
DH Dany Heatley 10.00 25.00
HZ Henrik Zetterberg 50.00 100.00
JB Jay Bouwmeester 8.00 20.00
JL John LeClair 8.00 20.00
JS Jason Spezza 200.00 350.00
MA Maxim Afinogenov 6.00 15.00
MB Martin Brodeur SP 150.00 300.00
MF Manny Fernandez 6.00 15.00
PB Pavel Bure 6.00 15.00
PR Patrick Roy 75.00 150.00
SC Stanislav Chistov 6.00 15.00
SY Steve Yzerman 40.00 100.00
TS Teemu Selanne SP 90.00 150.00

2002-03 Upper Deck Honor Roll Students of the Game

COMPLETE SET (30) 20.00 40.00
SG1 Paul Kariya .50 1.25
SG2 Dany Heatley .40 1.00
SG3 Joe Thornton .75 2.00
SG4 Jarome Iginla .60 1.50
SG5 Chris Drury .50 1.25
SG6 Joe Sakic 1.00 2.50
SG7 Patrick Roy 1.25 3.00
SG8 Peter Forsberg 1.00 2.50
SG9 Rick Nash 2.00 5.00
SG10 Mike Modano .75 2.00
SG11 Bill Guerin .50 1.25
SG12 Curtis Joseph .60 1.50
SG13 Steve Yzerman 1.25 3.00
SG14 Sergei Fedorov .75 2.00
SG15 Mike Comrie .50 1.25
SG16 Marian Gaborik .50 1.25
SG17 Saku Koivu .50 1.25
SG18 Martin Brodeur 1.25 3.00
SG19 Alexei Yashin .40 1.00
SG20 Pavel Bure .50 1.25
SG21 Eric Lindros .75 2.00
SG22 Jason Spezza 2.00 5.00
SG23 Jeremy Roenick .75 2.00
SG24 Tony Amonte .40 1.00
SG25 Mario Lemieux 2.00 5.00
SG26 Teemu Selanne 1.00 2.50
SG27 Keith Tkachuk .50 1.25
SG28 Vincent Lecavalier .50 1.25
SG29 Mats Sundin .50 1.25
SG30 Jaromir Jagr 1.50 4.00

2002-03 Upper Deck Honor Roll Team Warriors

COMPLETE SET (15) 10.00 20.00
TW1 Joe Thornton .60 1.50
TW2 Jarome Iginla .50 1.25
TW3 Jeff O'Neill .30 .75
TW4 Peter Forsberg 1.00 2.50
TW5 Mike Modano .60 1.50
TW6 Brendan Shanahan .60 1.50
TW7 Adam Deadmarsh .30 .75
TW8 Saku Koivu .40 1.00
TW9 Michael Peca .30 .75
TW10 Eric Lindros .40 1.00
TW11 John LeClair .40 1.00
TW12 Mario Lemieux 2.50 6.00
TW13 Owen Nolan .30 .75
TW14 Mats Sundin .40 1.00
TW15 Todd Bertuzzi .40 1.00

2003-04 Upper Deck Honor Roll

COMPLETE SET (191)
COMP. SET w/o SP's (90) 6.00 15.00
1 Jean-Sebastien Giguere .15 .40
2 Sergei Fedorov .25 .60
3 Dany Heatley .12 .30
4 Ilya Kovalchuk .15 .40
5 Felix Potvin .25 .60
6 Joe Thornton .25 .60
7 Sergei Samsonov .12 .30
8 Chris Drury .12 .30
9 Daniel Briere .15 .40
10 Jarome Iginla .20 .50
11 Roman Turek .12 .30
12 Jamie Storr .12 .30
13 Ron Francis .20 .50
14 Kyle Calder .10 .25
15 Jocelyn Thibault .12 .30
16 Tyler Arnason .10 .25
17 David Aebischer .12 .30
18 Joe Sakic .30 .75
19 Paul Kariya .15 .40
20 Peter Forsberg .30 .75
21 Marc Denis .12 .30
22 Rick Nash .15 .40
23 Todd Marchant .10 .25
24 Bill Guerin .15 .40
25 Marty Turco .15 .40
26 Mike Modano .25 .60
27 Dominik Hasek .25 .60
28 Henrik Zetterberg .20 .50
29 Steve Yzerman .40 1.00
30 Ales Hemsky .15 .40
31 Mike Comrie .12 .30
32 Tommy Salo .12 .30
33 Jay Bouwmeester .10 .25
34 Olli Jokinen .15 .40
35 Roberto Luongo .25 .60
36 Alexander Frolov .12 .30
37 Jason Allison .12 .30
38 Roman Cechmanek .12 .30
39 Zigmund Palffy .15 .40
40 Manny Fernandez .10 .25
41 Marian Gaborik .15 .40
42 Pierre-Marc Bouchard .15 .40
43 Jose Theodore .15 .40
44 Marcel Hossa .10 .25
45 Saku Koivu .15 .40
46 David Legwand .12 .30
47 Tomas Vokoun .12 .30
48 Martin Brodeur .40 1.00
48 Jeff Hackett .12 .30
49 Scott Gomez .12 .30
50 Scott Stevens .15 .40
51 Alexei Yashin .12 .30
52 Michael Peca .12 .30
53 Rick DiPietro .12 .30
54 Alex Kovalev .12 .30
55 Eric Lindros .25 .60
56 Mark Messier .30 .75
57 Mike Dunham .12 .30
58 Daniel Alfredsson .15 .40
59 Jason Spezza .15 .40
60 Marian Hossa .15 .40
61 Patrick Lalime .12 .30
62 John LeClair .15 .40
64 Jeremy Roenick .25 .60
65 Simon Gagne .15 .40
66 Mike Johnson .10 .25
67 Sean Burke .10 .25
68 Mario Lemieux .60 1.50
69 Martin Straka .10 .25
70 Evgeni Nabokov .12 .30
71 Patrick Marleau .15 .40
72 Vincent Damphousse .12 .30
73 Chris Pronger .15 .40
74 Chris Osgood .15 .40
75 Doug Weight .15 .40
76 Keith Tkachuk .15 .40
77 Pavol Demitra .20 .50
78 Nikolai Khabibulin .15 .40
79 Vincent Lecavalier .15 .40
80 Alexander Mogilny .12 .30
81 Ed Belfour .15 .40
82 Mats Sundin .15 .40
83 Owen Nolan .15 .40
84 Ed Jovanovski .12 .30
85 Johan Hedberg .12 .30
86 Markus Naslund .15 .40
87 Todd Bertuzzi .15 .40
88 Jaromir Jagr .50 1.25
89 Olaf Kolzig .15 .40
90 Peter Bondra .15 .40
91 Marian Gaborik SOG 1.00 2.50
92 Joe Thornton SOG 1.50 4.00
93 Jean-Sebastien Giguere SOG 1.00 2.50
94 Ilya Kovalchuk SOG 1.00 2.50
95 Ales Hemsky SOG 1.00 2.50
96 Mike Komisarek SOG .60 1.50
97 Rick Nash SOG 1.00 2.50
98 Marty Turco SOG 1.00 2.50
99 Alexander Frolov SOG .75 2.00
100 Jay Bouwmeester SOG .60 1.50
101 Henrik Zetterberg SOG 1.25 3.00
102 Marian Hossa SOG 1.00 2.50
103 Ales Kotalik SOG .60 1.50
104 Vincent Lecavalier SOG 1.00 2.50
105 Pavel Datsyuk SOG 1.50 4.00
106 Andrew Raycroft SOG .75 2.00
107 Philippe Sauve SOG .75 2.00
108 Marcel Hossa SOG .60 1.50
109 Rick DiPietro SOG .75 2.00
110 Jason Spezza SOG 1.00 2.50
111 Brendan Shanahan CR 1.50 4.00
112 Joe Sakic CR 3.00 8.00
113 Mike Modano CR 2.50 6.00
114 Jeremy Roenick CR 2.50 6.00
115 Teemu Selanne CR 3.00 8.00
116 Mats Sundin CR 1.50 4.00
117 Sergei Fedorov CR 2.50 6.00
118 Owen Nolan CR 1.50 4.00
119 Jaromir Jagr CR 5.00 12.00
120 Peter Forsberg CR 3.00 8.00
121 Markus Naslund CR 1.50 4.00
122 Alexei Yashin CR 1.25 3.00
123 Manny Fernandez CR 1.00 2.50
124 Paul Kariya CR 1.50 4.00
125 Saku Koivu CR 1.50 4.00
126 Peter Forsberg HOC 5.00 12.00
127 Steve Yzerman HOC 6.00 15.00
128 Joe Thornton HOC 4.00 10.00
129 Martin Brodeur HOC 6.00 15.00
130 Mario Lemieux HOC 10.00 25.00
131 Ed Belfour HOC 2.50 6.00
132 Mike Modano HOC 4.00 10.00
133 Darryl Bootland RC 1.50 4.00
134 Trevor Daley RC 2.00 5.00
135 John-Michael Liles RC 1.50 4.00
136 Paul Martin RC 1.50 4.00
137 Esa Pirnes RC 1.25 3.00
138 Seamus Kotyk RC 1.25 3.00
139 Pat Rissmiller RC 1.50 4.00
140 Marek Svatos RC 2.50 6.00
141 Maxim Kondratiev RC 1.25 3.00
142 Marek Zidlicky RC 1.25 3.00
143 Matthew Spiller RC 1.50 4.00
144 Nathan Smith RC 1.25 3.00
145 Brent Burns RC 4.00 10.00
146 Boyd Gordon RC 1.50 4.00
147 Andrew Hutchinson RC 1.25 3.00
148 Peter Sarno RC 1.25 3.00
149 Jed Ortmeyer RC 1.25 3.00
150 Cody McCormick RC 1.50 4.00
151 Christoph Brandner RC 1.50 4.00
152 Grant McNeill RC 1.25 3.00
153 Greg Campbell RC 1.25 3.00
154 Tony Salmelainen RC 1.25 3.00
155 Kent McDonell RC 1.50 4.00
156 Martin Strbak RC 1.50 4.00
157 Matt Murley RC 1.50 4.00
158 Rastislav Stana RC 2.00 5.00
159 Karl Stewart RC 1.25 3.00
160 Ryan Malone RC 2.50 6.00
161 Wade Brookbank RC 1.50 4.00
162 Mike Stuart RC 1.25 3.00
163 Sergei Zinovjev RC 1.25 3.00
164 Julien Vauclair RC 1.25 3.00
165 Alan Rourke RC 1.25 3.00
166 John Pohl RC 1.25 3.00
167 Dominic Moore RC 1.25 3.00
168 Peter Sejna JSY RC 2.50 6.00
169 Matt Stajan JSY RC 3.00 8.00
170 Milan Michalek JSY RC 4.00 10.00
171 Pavel Vorobiev JSY RC 2.50 6.00
172 Dan Hamhuis JSY RC 2.50 6.00
173 Chris Higgins JSY RC 4.00 10.00
174 Antti Miettinen JSY RC 3.00 8.00
175 Christian Ehrhoff JSY RC 2.50 6.00
176 Alexander Semin JSY RC 6.00 15.00
177 Antoine Vermette JSY RC 4.00 10.00
178 Travis Moen JSY RC 2.50 6.00
179 Joni Pitkanen JSY RC 3.00 8.00
180 Patrice Bergeron JSY RC 10.00 25.00
181 Jiri Hudler JSY RC 5.00 12.00
182 Marc-Andre Fleury JSY RC 15.00 40.00
183 Dustin Brown JSY RC 5.00 12.00
184 Joffrey Lupul JSY RC 5.00 12.00
185 Tuomo Ruutu JSY RC 3.00 8.00
186 Jordin Tootoo JSY RC 4.00 10.00
187 Eric Staal JSY RC 10.00 25.00
188 Nathan Horton JSY RC 5.00 12.00
189 Tim Gleason JSY RC 2.50 6.00
190 Sean Bergenheim JSY RC 2.50 6.00
191 Matthew Lombardi JSY RC 2.50 6.00

2003-04 Upper Deck Honor Roll Grade A Jerseys

GAAY Alexei Yashin 3.00 8.00
GAJI Jarome Iginla 4.00 10.00
GAJT Joe Thornton 4.00 10.00
GAMB Martin Brodeur 8.00 20.00
GAML Mario Lemieux 10.00 25.00
GAMM Mark Messier 6.00 15.00
GAMS Miroslav Satan 3.00 8.00
GASG Simon Gagne 4.00 10.00
GATM Marty Turco 3.00 8.00
GAVL Vincent Lecavalier 3.00 8.00
TBOS Thrntn/Smsnv/Mrray 12.00 30.00
TCOL Kariya/Sakic/Forsberg 20.00 50.00
TDET Hasek/Yzrmn/Zetter 25.00 60.00
TNYR Lindros/Bure/Kovalev 15.00 40.00
TTOR Sundin/Nolan/Belfour 12.00 30.00
TVAN Naslnd/Brtuzzi/Linden 15.00 40.00

2003-04 Upper Deck Honor Roll Signature Class

SC6 Marian Gaborik/24* 10.00 25.00
SC7 Jean-Sebastien Giguere/24* 15.00 40.00
SC14 Curtis Joseph/49* 20.00 50.00
SC17 John LeClair/49* 10.00 25.00
SC21 Ziggy Palffy/24* 15.00 40.00
SC22 Jeremy Roenick/24* 20.00 40.00
SC24 Sergei Samsonov/49* 10.00 25.00
SC25 Jose Theodore/49* 15.00 40.00
SC26 Joe Thornton/24* 15.00 40.00

1996-97 Upper Deck Ice

COMPLETE SET (150) 25.00 60.00
1 Kevin Todd .40 1.00
2 Adam Oates .60 1.50
3 Bill Ranford .50 1.25
4 Rick Tocchet .50 1.25
5 Dominik Hasek 1.00 2.50
6 Richard Smehlik .40 1.00
7 Derek Plante .40 1.00
8 Joel Bouchard .40 1.00
9 Theo Fleury 1.25 3.00
10 Chris Chelios .60 1.50
11 Ed Belfour .60 1.50
12 Eric Weinrich .40 1.00
13 Tony Amonte .50 1.25
14 Greg Adams .40 1.00
15 Jamie Langenbrunner .40 1.00
16 Sergei Zubov .50 1.25
17 Pat Verbeek .40 1.00
18 Chris Osgood .60 1.50
19 Rem Murray RC .60 1.50
20 Jason Arnott .50 1.25
21 Curtis Joseph .75 2.00
22 Bill Lindsay .40 1.00
23 Ray Sheppard .50 1.25
24 Martin Straka .40 1.00
25 Jean-Sebastien Giguere RC 3.00 8.00
26 Sean Burke .40 1.00
27 Keith Primeau .50 1.25
28 Geoff Sanderson .50 1.25
29 Rob Blake .60 1.50
30 Ian Laperriere .60 1.50
31 Byron Dafoe .50 1.25
32 Vincent Damphousse .50 1.25
33 Darcy Tucker .40 1.00
34 Brian Savage .40 1.00
35 Bill Guerin .60 1.50
36 Scott Niedermayer .60 1.50
37 Steve Thomas .40 1.00
38 Valeri Zelepukin .50 1.25
39 Bryan Smolinski .40 1.00
40 Derek King .40 1.00
41 Mike Richter .60 1.50
42 Daniel Goneau RC .60 1.50
43 Brian Leetch .50 1.25
44 Adam Graves .40 1.00
45 Damian Rhodes .50 1.25
46 Mikael Renberg .50 1.25
47 Eric Desjardins .50 1.25
48 Rod Brind'Amour .60 1.50
49 Janne Niinimaa .60 1.50
50 Dale Hawerchuk .75 2.00
51 Jeremy Roenick 1.00 2.50
52 Mike Gartner .75 2.00
53 Cliff Ronning .40 1.00
54 Patrick Lalime RC 2.00 5.00
55 Ron Francis .75 2.00
56 Petr Nedved .50 1.25
57 Bernie Nicholls .50 1.25
58 Jeff Friesen .40 1.00
59 Owen Nolan .60 1.50
60 Marty McSorley .50 1.25
61 Pierre Turgeon .50 1.25
62 Grant Fuhr 1.00 2.50
63 Chris Pronger .60 1.50
64 Jim Campbell .40 1.00
65 Chris Gratton .50 1.25
66 Dino Ciccarelli .60 1.50
67 Felix Potvin 1.00 2.50
68 Tie Domi .50 1.25
69 Doug Gilmour .75 2.00
70 Trevor Linden .60 1.50
71 Corey Hirsch .50 1.25
72 Jim Carey .60 1.50
73 Chris Simon .40 1.00
74 Mark Tinordi .40 1.00
75 Sergei Gonchar .40 1.00
76 Paul Kariya .60 1.50
77 Teemu Selanne 1.25 3.00
78 Jarome Iginla .75 2.00
79 Eric Daze .50 1.25
80 Sandis Ozolinsh .40 1.00
81 Peter Forsberg 1.25 3.00
82 Mike Modano 1.00 2.50
83 Anders Eriksson .40 1.00
84 Sergei Fedorov 1.00 2.50
85 Brendan Shanahan .60 1.50
86 Mike Grier RC .75 2.00
87 Doug Weight .60 1.50
88 Ed Jovanovski .50 1.25
89 Saku Koivu .60 1.50
90 Jose Theodore .75 2.00
91 Jocelyn Thibault .50 1.25
92 Martin Brodeur 1.50 4.00
93 Bryan Berard .60 1.50
94 Zigmund Palffy .60 1.50
95 Daniel Alfredsson .60 1.50
96 Alexei Yashin .50 1.25
97 Wade Redden .40 1.00
98 John LeClair .60 1.50
99 Oleg Tverdovsky .50 1.25
100 Keith Tkachuk .60 1.50
101 Jaromir Jagr 2.00 5.00
102 Roman Hamrlik .40 1.00
103 Sergei Berezin RC 1.00 2.50
104 Alexander Mogilny .50 1.25
105 Pavel Bure .60 1.50
106 Ray Bourque 1.00 2.50
107 Patrick Roy 1.50 4.00
108 Joe Sakic 1.25 3.00
109 Steve Yzerman 1.50 4.00
110 John Vanbiesbrouck .60 1.50
111 Mark Messier 1.25 3.00
112 Wayne Gretzky 4.00 10.00
113 Eric Lindros 1.00 2.50
114 Mario Lemieux 2.50 6.00
115 Brett Hull 1.25 3.00
116 Joe Thornton RC 3.00 8.00
117 Marc Denis .60 1.50
118 Martin Biron RC .75 2.00
119 Jason Doig .40 1.00
120 Daniel Briere RC 4.00 10.00
121 Trevor Letowski RC .50 1.25
122 Boyd Devereaux RC .60 1.50
123 Dwayne Hay RC .50 1.25
124 Hugh Hamilton RC .50 1.25
125 Brad Isbister RC .50 1.25
126 Shane Willis RC .60 1.50
127 Trent Whitfield RC .50 1.25
128 Jesse Wallin RC .50 1.25
129 Alyn McCauley .60 1.50
130 Cameron Mann RC .50 1.25
131 Jeff Ware .50 1.25
132 Corey Sarich .50 1.25
133 Richard Jackman RC .50 1.25
134 Brad Larsen .50 1.25
135 Peter Schaefer RC .50 1.25
136 Christian Dube .40 1.00
137 Chris Phillips .60 1.50
138 Sergei Samsonov .50 1.25
139 Alexei Morozov .50 1.25
140 Sergei Fedotov RC .50 1.25
141 Denis Khlopotnov RC .50 1.25
142 Andrei Markov RC 4.00 10.00
143 Andrei Petrunin .50 1.25
144 Roman Liachenko RC .50 1.25
145 Joe Corvo RC .50 1.25
146 Erik Rasmussen .50 1.25
147 Mike York RC .50 1.25
148 Brian Boucher .50 1.25
149 Paul Mara RC .50 1.25
150 Marty Reasoner .50 1.25

1996-97 Upper Deck Ice Acetate Parallel

*PERF.VETS: 3X TO 8X BASIC
*PERF.ROOKIES: 1.5X TO 4X
*PHENOM VETS: 6X TO 15X BASIC
*PHENOM ROOKIES: 2.5X TO 6X
*LEGENDS: 10X TO 25X BASIC

1996-97 Upper Deck Ice Stanley Cup Foundation

COMPLETE SET (10) 125.00 250.00
*DYNASTY: 1.5X TO 4X BASIC INSERTS
S1 W.Gretzky/M.Messier 12.00 30.00
S2 B.Shanahan/S.Yzerman 10.00 25.00
S3 J.Vanbies./E.Jovan. 6.00 15.00
S4 J.Thibault/S.Koivu 6.00 15.00
S5 J.Sakic/P.Roy 8.00 20.00
S6 P.Kariya/T.Selanne 5.00 12.00
S7 M.Lemieux/J.Jagr 12.50 30.00
S8 J.Roenick/K.Tkachuk 6.00 15.00
S9 D.Weight/J.Arnott 3.00 8.00
S10 J.LeClair/E.Lindros 10.00 25.00

1997-98 Upper Deck Ice

COMPLETE SET (90) 30.00 80.00
1 Nelson Emerson .40 1.00
2 Derian Hatcher .30 .75
3 Mike Richter .40 1.00
4 Sergei Berezin .30 .75
5 Nicklas Lidstrom .40 1.00
6 Ryan Smyth .30 .75
7 Martin Brodeur 1.00 2.50
8 Geoff Sanderson .30 .75
9 Doug Weight .40 1.00
10 Owen Nolan .40 1.00
11 Daniel Alfredsson .40 1.00
12 Peter Bondra .40 1.00
13 Jim Campbell .25 .60
14 Rob Niedermayer .25 .60
15 Daymond Langkow .25 .60
16 Zigmund Palffy .40 1.00
17 Adam Oates .40 1.00
18 Adam Deadmarsh .25 .60
19 Brian Holzinger .30 .75
20 Jarome Iginla .50 1.25
21 Janne Niinimaa .30 .75
22 Dino Ciccarelli .40 1.00
23 Mark Recchi .50 1.25
24 Sandis Ozolinsh .25 .60
25 Keith Primeau .30 .75
26 Ed Jovanovski .25 .60
27 Jeremy Roenick .60 1.50
28 Alexei Yashin .30 .75
29 Felix Potvin .60 1.50
30 Chris Osgood .40 1.00
31 Marc Denis .40 1.00
32 Tyler Moss RC .30 .75
33 Kevin Hodson .30 .75
34 Jamie Storr .30 .75
35 Roman Turek .30 .75
36 Jose Theodore .40 1.00

37 Magnus Arvedson .40 1.00
38 Daniel Cleary .30 .75
39 Mike Knuble .40 1.00
40 Jaroslav Svejkovsky .30 .75
41 Patrick Marleau .40 1.00
42 Mattias Ohlund .30 .75
43 Sergei Samsonov .30 .75
44 Espen Knutsen RC 1.00 2.50
45 Vaclav Prospal RC .30 .75
46 Joe Thornton .60 1.50
47 Chris Phillips .30 .75
48 Mike Johnson RC .30 .75
49 Dainius Zubrus .30 .75
50 Wade Redden .25 .60
51 Derek Morris RC .40 1.00
52 Marco Sturm RC .40 1.00
53 Don MacLean .40 1.00
54 Bryan Berard .25 .60
55 Richard Zednik .30 .75
56 Alexei Morozov .30 .75
57 Erik Rasmussen .30 .75
58 Olli Jokinen RC 1.00 2.50
59 Jan Bulis RC .40 1.00
60 Patrik Elias RC 3.00 8.00
61 Peter Forsberg .75 2.00
62 Mike Modano .60 1.50
63 Tony Amonte .30 .75
64 Theo Fleury .50 1.25
65 Ron Francis .50 1.25
66 Brett Hull .75 2.00
67 Chris Chelios .40 1.00
68 Jaromir Jagr 1.25 3.00
69 Sergei Fedorov .60 1.50
70 Keith Tkachuk .40 1.00
71 Mark Messier .75 2.00
72 Pat LaFontaine .40 1.00
73 Mats Sundin .40 1.00
74 John Vanbiesbrouck .40 1.00
75 John LeClair .40 1.00
76 Brian Leetch .30 .75
77 Ray Bourque .60 1.50
78 Saku Koivu .40 1.00
79 Joe Sakic .75 2.00
80 Teemu Selanne .75 2.00
81 Curtis Joseph .50 1.25
82 Doug Gilmour .50 1.25
83 Patrick Roy 1.00 2.50
84 Brendan Shanahan .40 1.00
85 Paul Kariya .40 1.00
86 Pavel Bure .40 1.00
87 Dominik Hasek .60 1.50
88 Eric Lindros .60 1.50
89 Steve Yzerman 1.00 2.50
90 Wayne Gretzky 2.50 6.00

1997-98 Upper Deck Ice Parallel

*VETS: .6X TO 1.5X BASIC CARDS
*PHENOMS: .8X TO 2X BASIC CARDS
*LEGENDS: 2X TO 5X BASIC CARDS

1997-98 Upper Deck Ice Champions

COMPLETE SET (20) 150.00 300.00
*DIE CUT/100: 2.5X TO 6X BASIC INSERTS
IC1 Wayne Gretzky 40.00 100.00
IC2 Patrick Roy 15.00 40.00
IC3 Eric Lindros 5.00 12.00
IC4 Saku Koivu 5.00 12.00
IC5 Dominik Hasek 10.00 25.00
IC6 Joe Thornton 8.00 20.00
IC7 Martin Brodeur 12.50 30.00
IC8 Teemu Selanne 5.00 12.00
IC9 Paul Kariya 5.00 12.00
IC10 Joe Sakic 10.00 25.00
IC11 Mark Messier 5.00 12.00
IC12 Peter Forsberg 12.50 30.00
IC13 Mats Sundin 5.00 12.00
IC14 Brendan Shanahan 5.00 12.00
IC15 Keith Tkachuk 5.00 12.00
IC16 Brett Hull 6.00 15.00
IC17 John Vanbiesbrouck 5.00 12.00
IC18 Jaromir Jagr 8.00 20.00
IC19 Steve Yzerman 12.00 30.00
IC20 Sergei Samsonov 5.00 12.00

1997-98 Upper Deck Ice Lethal Lines

COMPLETE SET (30) 60.00 150.00
*LETHAL LINES 2: 2X TO 5X BASIC INSERTS
L1A Paul Kariya 2.00 5.00
L1B Wayne Gretzky 10.00 25.00
L1C Joe Thornton 4.00 10.00
L2A Brendan Shanahan 2.00 5.00
L2B Eric Lindros 2.50 6.00
L2C Jaromir Jagr 3.00 8.00
L3A Keith Tkachuk 1.50 4.00
L3B Mark Messier 2.00 5.00
L3C Owen Nolan 1.50 4.00
L4A Daniel Alfredsson 1.50 4.00
L4B Peter Forsberg 3.00 8.00
L4C Mats Sundin 2.00 5.00
L5A Ryan Smyth 1.50 4.00
L5B Steve Yzerman 6.00 15.00
L5C Jarome Iginla 2.00 5.00
L6A Sergei Samsonov 1.50 4.00
L6B Igor Larionov 1.25 3.00
L6C Sergei Fedorov 3.00 8.00
L7A Patrik Elias 2.00 5.00
L7B Alexei Morozov 1.25 3.00
L7C Vaclav Prospal 1.25 3.00
L8A John LeClair 2.00 5.00
L8B Mike Modano 2.50 6.00
L8C Brett Hull 2.50 6.00
L9A Olli Jokinen 1.50 4.00
L9B Saku Koivu 2.00 5.00
L9C Teemu Selanne 2.50 6.00
L10A Brian Leetch 1.50 4.00
L10B Patrick Roy 8.00 20.00
L10C Nicklas Lidstrom 2.00 5.00

1997-98 Upper Deck Ice Power Shift

*VETS: 5X TO 12X BASIC CARDS
*ROOKIES: 2.5X TO 6X BASIC CARDS

2000-01 Upper Deck Ice

COMPLETE SET (123) 200.00 400.00
COMP.SER.1 w/o SP's (40) 6.00 15.00
1 Paul Kariya .30 .75
2 Teemu Selanne .60 1.50
3 Patrik Stefan .25 .60
4 Joe Thornton .50 1.25
5 Dominik Hasek .50 1.25
6 Michael Peca .25 .60
7 Valeri Bure .25 .60
8 Ron Francis .40 1.00
9 Tony Amonte .25 .60
10 Patrick Roy .75 2.00
11 Ray Bourque .60 1.50
12 Milan Hejduk .25 .60
13 Peter Forsberg .60 1.50
14 Brett Hull .60 1.50
15 Mike Modano .50 1.25
16 Brendan Shanahan .30 .75
17 Chris Osgood .30 .75
18 Steve Yzerman .75 2.00
19 Doug Weight .30 .75
20 Pavel Bure .30 .75
21 Luc Robitaille .30 .75
22 Jose Theodore .30 .75
23 David Legwand .30 .75
24 Martin Brodeur .75 2.00
25 Scott Gomez .25 .60
26 Tim Connolly .20 .50
27 Mike York .20 .50
28 Marian Hossa .30 .75
29 Brian Boucher .25 .60
30 John LeClair .30 .75
31 Jeremy Roenick .50 1.25
32 Jaromir Jagr 1.00 2.50
33 Steve Shields .20 .50
34 Chris Pronger .30 .75
35 Roman Turek .25 .60
36 Vincent Lecavalier .30 .75
37 Curtis Joseph .40 1.00
38 Mats Sundin .40 1.00
39 Mark Messier .60 1.50
40 Olaf Kolzig .30 .75
41 Matt Pettinger RC 1.50 4.00
42 Chris Nielsen RC 1.50 4.00
43 Dany Heatley RC 5.00 12.00
44 Matt Zultek RC 1.50 4.00
45 Dmitri Afanasenkov RC 1.50 4.00
46 Tyler Bouck RC 1.50 4.00
47 Jonas Andersson RC 1.50 4.00
48 Marc-Andre Thinel RC 1.50 4.00
49 Jaroslav Svoboda RC 1.50 4.00
50 Josef Vasicek RC 4.00 10.00
51 Andrew Raycroft RC 4.00 10.00
52 Juraj Kolnik RC 1.50 4.00
53 Zdenek Blatny RC 1.50 4.00
54 Sebastien Caron RC 2.00 5.00
55 Eric Nickulas RC 1.50 4.00
56 Serge Aubin RC 2.00 5.00
57 Steven Reinprecht RC 2.50 6.00
58 David Gosselin RC 2.00 5.00
59 Colin White RC 1.50 4.00
60 Steve Valiquette RC 2.00 5.00
61 Jeff Friesen .20 .50
62 Bill Guerin .20 .50
63 J-P Dumont .20 .50
64 Oleg Saprykin .20 .50
65 Shane Willis .20 .50
66 Josef Vasicek .50 1.25
67 Steve Reinprecht .50 1.25
68 Marc Denis .25 .60
69 Marty Turco RC 3.00 8.00
70 Sergei Fedorov .50 1.25
71 Adam Deadmarsh .20 .50
72 Keith Tkachuk .30 .75
73 Mark Messier .60 1.50
74 Alexei Yashin .25 .60
75 Mario Lemieux 1.25 3.00
76 Evgeni Nabokov .25 .60
77 Brad Richards .30 .75
78 Henrik Sedin .40 1.00
79 Daniel Sedin .40 1.00
80 Matt Pettinger .20 .50
81 Marc Chouinard RC 1.50 4.00
82 Bryan Adams RC 1.50 4.00
83 Martin Brochu RC 1.50 4.00
84 Craig Adams RC 1.50 4.00
85 David Aebischer RC 3.00 8.00
86 Rostislav Klesla RC 4.00 10.00
87 Shawn Horcoff RC 3.00 8.00
88 Mike Comrie RC 4.00 10.00
89 Eric Belanger RC 2.00 5.00
90 Marian Gaborik RC 5.00 12.00
91 Eric Landry RC 1.50 4.00
92 Scott Hartnell RC 5.00 12.00
93 Chris Mason RC 3.00 8.00
94 Rick DiPietro RC 3.00 8.00
95 Martin Havlat RC 5.00 12.00
96 Roman Cechmanek RC 2.00 5.00
97 Justin Williams RC 4.00 10.00
98 Ruslan Fedotenko RC 1.50 4.00
99 Jean-Guy Trudel RC 1.50 4.00
100 Reed Low RC 1.50 4.00
101 Alexei Ponikarovsky RC 2.50 6.00
102 Rob Blake .30 .75
103 Andy McDonald RC 3.00 8.00
104 Petr Tenkrat RC 1.50 4.00
105 Brad Tapper RC 1.50 4.00
106 Darcy Hordichuk RC 1.50 4.00
107 J.P. Vigier RC 1.50 4.00
108 Pavel Kolarik RC 1.50 4.00
109 Jarno Kultanen RC 1.50 4.00
110 Eric Manlow RC 1.50 4.00
111 Eric Boulton RC 1.50 4.00
112 Brian Swanson RC 1.50 4.00
113 Lubomir Sekeras RC 1.50 4.00
114 Greg Classen RC 1.50 4.00
115 Jiri Bicek RC 1.50 4.00
116 Jeff Ulmer RC 1.50 4.00
117 Johan Holmqvist RC 1.50 4.00
118 Shane Hnidy RC 1.50 4.00
119 Ossi Vaananen RC 1.50 4.00
120 Johan Hedberg RC 2.00 5.00
121 Mark Smith RC 1.50 4.00
122 Alexander Khavanov RC 1.50 4.00
123 Bryce Salvador RC 2.00 5.00

2000-01 Upper Deck Ice Champions

COMPLETE SET (6) 15.00 30.00
IC1 Patrick Roy 5.00 12.00
IC2 Mike Modano 2.00 5.00
IC3 Steve Yzerman 5.00 12.00
IC4 Martin Brodeur 2.50 6.00
IC5 John LeClair 1.50 4.00
IC6 Jaromir Jagr 1.50 4.00

2000-01 Upper Deck Ice Clear Cut Autographs

BH Brett Hull 15.00 40.00
BL Brian Leetch 8.00 20.00
CJ Curtis Joseph 10.00 25.00
MY Mike York 4.00 10.00
PB Pavel Bure 10.00 25.00
PS Patrik Stefan 4.00 10.00
RT Roman Turek 4.00 10.00
SG Scott Gomez 4.00 10.00
SY Steve Yzerman 30.00 80.00
TC Tim Connolly 4.00 10.00

2000-01 Upper Deck Ice Cool Competitors

CC1 Paul Kariya 2.50 6.00
CC2 Peter Forsberg 5.00 12.00
CC3 Pavel Bure 2.50 6.00
CC4 Scott Gomez 1.50 4.00
CC5 Jaromir Jagr 8.00 20.00
CC6 Curtis Joseph 3.00 8.00

2000-01 Upper Deck Ice Gallery

COMPLETE SET (9) 15.00 30.00
IG1 Teemu Selanne .75 2.00
IG2 Patrick Roy 4.00 10.00
IG3 Brendan Shanahan 1.25 3.00
IG4 Pavel Bure 1.00 2.50
IG5 Scott Gomez .75 2.00
IG6 John LeClair 1.00 2.50
IG7 Jaromir Jagr 1.25 3.00
IG8 Vincent Lecavalier .75 2.00
IG9 Curtis Joseph .75 2.00

2000-01 Upper Deck Ice Game Jerseys

JCAC Anson Carter 4.00 10.00
JCBH Brett Hull 5.00 12.00
JCBS Brendan Shanahan 5.00 12.00
JCCO Chris Osgood 5.00 12.00
JCDL David Legwand 4.00 10.00
JCJJ Jaromir Jagr 6.00 15.00
JCJL John LeClair 4.00 10.00
JCJN Joe Nieuwendyk 5.00 12.00
JCMB Martin Brodeur 12.50 30.00
JCMH Michal Handzus 4.00 10.00
JCMM Mike Modano 6.00 15.00
JCMS Miroslav Satan 4.00 10.00
JCPB Pavel Bure 5.00 12.00
JCPD Pavol Demitra 4.00 10.00
JCPK Paul Kariya 4.00 10.00
JCRB Ray Bourque 8.00 20.00
JCSF Sergei Fedorov 5.00 12.00
JCSS Sergei Samsonov 4.00 10.00
JCTC Tim Connolly 4.00 10.00
JCTS Teemu Selanne 5.00 12.00
IFO Peter Forsberg Upd 10.00 25.00
IJT Joe Thornton Upd 8.00 20.00
ILE John LeClair Upd 6.00 15.00
IMO Mike Modano Upd 6.00 15.00
IRO Patrick Roy Upd 15.00 40.00
ISA Joe Sakic Upd 10.00 25.00
ISH Brendan Shanahan Upd 6.00 15.00
ITH Jocelyn Thibault Upd 4.00 10.00
ITK Keith Tkachuk Upd 4.00 10.00

2000-01 Upper Deck Ice Immortals

*1-40 VETS: 20X TO 50X BASIC CARDS
*41-60 ROOKIES: 1.2X TO 3X SP/1500

2000-01 Upper Deck Ice Legends

*1-40 VETS: 3X TO 8X BASIC CARDS
*41-60 ROOKIES: .6X TO 1.5X SP/1500

2000-01 Upper Deck Ice Rink Favorites

COMPLETE SET (9) 15.00 30.00
FP1 Paul Kariya 1.00 2.50
FP2 Peter Forsberg 2.00 5.00
FP3 Ray Bourque 1.50 4.00
FP4 Mike Modano 1.25 3.00
FP5 Steve Yzerman 4.00 10.00
FP6 Pavel Bure 1.00 2.50
FP7 Martin Brodeur 2.00 5.00
FP8 John LeClair 1.00 2.50
FP9 Jaromir Jagr 1.25 3.00

2000-01 Upper Deck Ice Stars

*1-40 VETS/500: 2X TO 5X BASIC CARDS
*41-60 ROOK/500: .5X TO 1.2X RC/1500

2001-02 Upper Deck Ice

COMP.SET w/o RC's (84) 20.00 50.00
1 Paul Kariya .50 1.25
2 Joe Thornton .75 2.00
3 Sergei Samsonov .40 1.00
4 Martin Biron .40 1.00
5 Jarome Iginla .60 1.50
6 Arturs Irbe .40 1.00
7 Tony Amonte .40 1.00
8 Patrick Roy 1.25 3.00
9 Peter Forsberg 1.00 2.50
10 Ray Bourque .75 2.00
11 Ron Tugnutt .40 1.00
12 Mike Modano .75 2.00
13 Ed Belfour .50 1.25
14 Brett Hull 1.00 2.50
15 Steve Yzerman 1.25 3.00
16 Dominik Hasek .50 1.25
17 Sergei Fedorov .75 2.00
18 Tommy Salo .40 1.00
19 Mike Comrie .40 1.00
20 Pavel Bure .50 1.25
21 Adam Deadmarsh .30 .75
22 Zigmund Palffy .50 1.25
23 Marian Gaborik .50 1.25
24 Manny Fernandez .30 .75
25 Jose Theodore .50 1.25
26 Mike Dunham .40 1.00
27 Martin Brodeur 1.25 3.00
28 Patrik Elias .50 1.25
29 Rick DiPietro .40 1.00
30 Mark Messier 1.00 2.50
31 Martin Havlat .50 1.25
32 Marian Hossa .50 1.25
33 Jeremy Roenick .75 2.00
34 Sean Burke .30 .75
35 Johan Hedberg .40 1.00
36 Mario Lemieux 2.00 5.00
37 Evgeni Nabokov .40 1.00
38 Keith Tkachuk .50 1.25
39 Vincent Lecavalier .50 1.25
40 Curtis Joseph .60 1.50
41 Markus Naslund .50 1.25
42 Jaromir Jagr 1.50 4.00
43 Ilja Bryzgalov RC 4.00 10.00
44 Ilya Kovalchuk RC 12.00 30.00
45 Zdenek Kutlak RC 1.50 4.00
46 Ales Kotalik RC 3.00 8.00
47 Scott Nichol RC 1.50 4.00
48 Erik Cole RC 3.00 8.00
49 Casey Hankinson RC 1.50 4.00
50 Vaclav Nedorost RC 1.50 4.00
51 Martin Spanhel RC 1.50 4.00
52 Niko Kapanen RC 2.50 6.00
53 Pavel Datsyuk RC 15.00 30.00
54 Ty Conklin RC 2.50 6.00
55 Kristian Huselius RC 2.50 6.00
56 Jaroslav Bednar RC 1.50 4.00
57 Nick Schultz RC 1.50 4.00
58 Martti Jarventie 1.50 4.00
59 Martin Erat RC 2.00 5.00
60 Andreas Salomonsson RC 1.50 4.00
61 Radek Martinek RC 1.50 4.00
62 Dan Blackburn RC 2.00 5.00
63 Ivan Ciernik RC 1.50 4.00
64 Jiri Dopita RC 1.50 4.00
65 Krys Kolanos RC 1.50 4.00
66 Bill Tibbetts RC 1.50 4.00
67 Jeff Jillson RC 1.50 4.00
68 Mark Rycroft RC 2.00 5.00
69 Nikita Alexeev RC 1.50 4.00
70 Bob Wren RC 1.50 4.00
71 Pat Kavanagh RC 2.00 5.00
72 Brian Sutherby RC 1.50 4.00
73 Timo Parssinen RC 2.00 5.00
74 Kamil Piros RC 1.50 4.00
75 Jukka Hentunen RC 1.50 4.00
76 Niklas Hagman RC 2.00 5.00
77 Travis Roche RC 1.50 4.00
78 Pavel Skrbek RC 1.50 4.00
79 Scott Clemmensen RC 1.50 4.00
80 Chris Neil RC 2.00 5.00
81 Vaclav Pletka RC 1.50 4.00
82 Josef Boumedienne RC 1.50 4.00
83 Ryan Tobler RC 2.00 5.00
84 Chris Corrinet RC 1.50 4.00
85 Dany Heatley .40 1.00
86 Glen Murray .40 1.00
87 Jozef Stumpel .30 .75
88 Tim Connolly .30 .75
89 Roman Turek .40 1.00
90 Joe Sakic 1.00 2.50
91 Radim Vrbata .30 .75
92 Milan Hejduk .40 1.00
93 Brenden Morrow .40 1.00
94 Pierre Turgeon .40 1.00
95 Brett Hull 1.00 2.50
96 Luc Robitaille .50 1.25
97 Brendan Shanahan .50 1.25
98 Nicklas Lidstrom .50 1.25
99 Sandis Ozolinsh .30 .75
100 Jason Allison .40 1.00
101 Felix Potvin .75 2.00
102 Donald Audette .30 .75
103 Chris Osgood .50 1.25
104 Alexei Yashin .40 1.00
105 Mark Parrish .30 .75
106 Eric Lindros .75 2.00
107 Theo Fleury .60 1.50
108 Barrett Heisten .30 .75
109 Daniel Alfredsson .50 1.25
110 Donald Brashear .30 .75
111 Luke Richardson .30 .75
112 John LeClair .50 1.25
113 Brian Boucher .40 1.00
114 Alexei Kovalev .40 1.00
115 Teemu Selanne 1.00 2.50
116 Owen Nolan .40 1.00
117 Pavol Demitra .60 1.50
118 Chris Pronger .50 1.25
119 Doug Weight .50 1.25
120 Sheldon Keefe .30 .75
121 Nikolai Khabibulin .50 1.25
122 Mats Sundin .50 1.25
123 Jan Hlavac .30 .75
124 Trevor Linden .50 1.25
125 Peter Bondra .50 1.25
126 Olaf Kolzig .50 1.25
127 Pasi Nurminen RC 2.00 5.00
128 Ivan Huml RC 2.00 5.00
129 Tony Tuzzolino RC 2.00 5.00
130 Steve Montador RC 2.00 5.00
131 Mike Peluso RC 2.00 5.00
132 Steve Poapst RC 2.00 5.00
133 Riku Hahl RC 2.00 5.00
134 Blake Bellefeuille RC 2.00 5.00
135 David Ling RC 2.00 5.00
136 John Erskine RC 2.00 5.00
137 Brad Norton RC 2.00 5.00
138 Nick Smith RC 2.00 5.00
139 Ryan Flinn RC 2.00 5.00
140 Pascal Dupuis RC 3.00 8.00
141 Olivier Michaud RC 3.00 8.00
142 Marcel Hossa RC 3.00 8.00
143 Raffi Torres RC 3.00 8.00
144 Mikael Samuelsson RC 2.50 6.00
145 Christian Berglund RC 2.50 6.00
146 Shane Endicott RC 2.00 5.00
147 Eric Meloche RC 2.00 5.00
148 Steve Bancroft RC 3.00 8.00
149 Martin Cibak RC 2.00 5.00
150 Dean Melanson RC 2.00 5.00
151 Mike Farrell RC 2.00 5.00

2001-02 Upper Deck Ice Autographs

AI Arturs Irbe Upd 6.00 15.00
CJ Curtis Joseph Upd/31 20.00 50.00
DH Dany Heatley Upd 10.00 25.00
DS Daniel Sedin 8.00 20.00
HS Henrik Sedin 10.00 25.00
JI Jarome Iginla Upd 15.00 40.00
KH Kristian Huselius Upd 6.00 15.00
KK Krys Kolanos Upd 6.00 15.00
MB Martin Brodeur 30.00 80.00
MC Mike Comrie 8.00 20.00
MCU Mike Comrie Upd 8.00 20.00
MH Milan Hejduk Upd 8.00 20.00
MK Milan Kraft 6.00 15.00
MM Mike Modano 15.00 40.00
PB Peter Bondra Upd 8.00 20.00
PS Petr Sykora 6.00 15.00
RK Rostislav Klesla Upd 6.00 15.00
RL Roberto Luongo 10.00 25.00
SY Steve Yzerman 40.00 100.00
WG Wayne Gretzky 200.00 500.00

2001-02 Upper Deck Ice Jersey Combos

*GOLD/25: .8X TO 2X BASIC DUAL
JJ Jaromir Jagr 12.50 30.00
JL John LeClair 8.00 20.00
JR Jeremy Roenick 15.00 40.00
JS Joe Sakic 12.50 30.00
ML Mario Lemieux 30.00 80.00
MM Mike Modano 12.50 30.00
PK Paul Kariya 8.00 20.00
PR Patrick Roy 20.00 50.00
SF Sergei Fedorov 12.50 30.00
SY Steve Yzerman 20.00 50.00

2001-02 Upper Deck Ice First Rounders Jerseys

FJJ Jaromir Jagr 8.00 20.00
FJR Jeremy Roenick 5.00 12.00
FJS Joe Sakic 8.00 20.00
FMM Mike Modano 6.00 15.00
FPK Paul Kariya 5.00 12.00
FPS Patrik Stefan 5.00 12.00
FSY Steve Yzerman 6.00 15.00

2001-02 Upper Deck Ice Jerseys

JBH Brett Hull 5.00 12.00
JDW Doug Weight 6.00 15.00
JED Eric Daze 6.00 15.00
JJL John LeClair 4.00 10.00
JMS Marc Savard 4.00 10.00
JPR Patrick Roy 6.00 15.00
JSA Serge Aubin 4.00 10.00
JSF Sergei Fedorov 6.00 15.00

2003-04 Upper Deck Ice

COMP.SET w/o SP's (90) 12.50 25.00
1 Sergei Fedorov .40 1.00
2 Vaclav Prospal .15 .40
3 Jean-Sebastien Giguere .25 .60
4 Dany Heatley .20 .50
5 Ilya Kovalchuk .25 .60
6 Andrew Raycroft .20 .50
7 Joe Thornton .40 1.00
8 Sergei Samsonov .20 .50
9 Mika Noronen .15 .40
10 Chris Drury .20 .50
11 Daniel Briere .25 .60
12 Roman Turek .20 .50
13 Jarome Iginla .30 .75
14 Justin Williams .15 .40
15 Ron Francis .30 .75
16 Bryan Berard .20 .50
17 Alexei Zhamnov .20 .50
18 Jocelyn Thibault .20 .50
19 Joe Sakic .50 1.25
20 Paul Kariya .25 .60
21 Peter Forsberg .50 1.25
22 David Aebischer .20 .50
23 Todd Marchant .15 .40
24 Rick Nash .25 .60
25 Marc Denis .20 .50
26 Mike Modano .40 1.00
27 Marty Turco .20 .50
28 Bill Guerin .20 .50
29 Brett Hull .50 1.25
30 Pavel Datsyuk .40 1.00
31 Henrik Zetterberg .50 1.25
32 Steve Yzerman .60 1.50
33 Adam Oates .25 .60
34 Tommy Salo .20 .50
35 Raffi Torres .15 .40
36 Ales Hemsky .25 .60
37 Olli Jokinen .25 .60
38 Roberto Luongo .40 1.00
39 Jay Bouwmeester .15 .40
40 Martin Straka .15 .40
41 Roman Cechmanek .20 .50
42 Zigmund Palffy .20 .50
43 Marian Gaborik .25 .60
44 Alexandre Daigle .20 .50
45 Manny Fernandez .15 .40
46 Mike Ribeiro .15 .40
47 Saku Koivu .20 .50
48 Jose Theodore .20 .50
49 David Legwand .20 .50
50 Tomas Vokoun .20 .50
51 Patrik Elias .20 .50
52 Martin Brodeur .60 1.50
53 Scott Stevens .20 .50
54 Scott Gomez .20 .50
55 Rick DiPietro .20 .50
56 Alexei Yashin .20 .50
57 Trent Hunter .15 .40
58 Mark Messier .50 1.25
59 Eric Lindros .30 .75
60 Jaromir Jagr .75 2.00
61 Patrick Lalime .20 .50
62 Jason Spezza .25 .60
63 Marian Hossa .25 .60
64 Sean Burke .15 .40
65 Jeremy Roenick .40 1.00
66 Tony Amonte .20 .50
67 Ladislav Nagy .15 .40
68 Mike Comrie .20 .50
69 Mario Lemieux 1.00 2.50
70 Rico Fata .15 .40
71 Vincent Damphousse .20 .50
72 Patrick Marleau .25 .60
73 Evgeni Nabokov .20 .50
74 Keith Tkachuk .25 .60
75 Chris Osgood .20 .50
76 Doug Weight .20 .50
77 Pavol Demitra .30 .75
78 Vincent Lecavalier .25 .60
79 Nikolai Khabibulin .25 .60
80 Ed Belfour .25 .60
81 Mats Sundin .25 .60
82 Alexander Mogilny .20 .50
83 Owen Nolan .25 .60
84 Todd Bertuzzi .25 .60
85 Ed Jovanovski .20 .50
86 Jason King .15 .40
87 Markus Naslund .25 .60
88 Peter Bondra .25 .60
89 Anson Carter .20 .50
90 Olaf Kolzig .25 .60
91 Pavel Vorobiev RC 2.00 5.00
92 Antti Miettinen RC 2.50 6.00
93 Chris Higgins RC 4.00 10.00
94 Dan Hamhuis RC 2.00 5.00
95 Marek Zidlicky RC 1.50 4.00
96 Mikhail Yakubov RC 1.50 4.00
97 Antoine Vermette RC 3.00 8.00
98 Jiri Hudler RC 4.00 10.00
99 Milan Michalek RC 3.00 8.00
100 Peter Sejna RC 2.00 5.00
101 Matt Stajan RC 2.50 6.00
102 Maxim Kondratiev RC 1.50 4.00
103 Alexander Semin RC 8.00 20.00
104 Sergei Zinovjev RC 1.50 4.00
105 Julien Vauclair RC 1.50 4.00
106 Dominic Moore RC 1.50 4.00
107 Tony Salmelainen RC 1.50 4.00
108 Rastislav Stana RC 2.50 6.00
109 Peter Sarno RC 1.50 4.00
110 Jed Ortmeyer RC 1.50 4.00
111 Nathan Smith RC 1.50 4.00
112 Matthew Lombardi RC 2.00 5.00
113 Dustin Brown RC 6.00 15.00
114 John-Michael Liles RC 2.00 5.00
115 Tim Gleason RC 2.00 5.00
116 Boyd Gordon RC 2.00 5.00
117 Greg Campbell RC 1.50 4.00
118 Ryan Kesler RC 6.00 15.00
119 Trevor Daley RC 2.50 6.00
120 John Pohl RC 1.50 4.00
121 Joffrey Lupul RC 40.00 80.00
122 Patrice Bergeron RC 60.00 120.00
123 Eric Staal RC 75.00 150.00
124 Tuomo Ruutu RC 30.00 60.00
125 Nikolai Zherdev RC 25.00 50.00
126 Nathan Horton RC 40.00 100.00
127 Fredrik Sjostrom RC 12.00 30.00
128 Jordin Tootoo RC 15.00 40.00
129 Joni Pitkanen RC 15.00 40.00
130 Marc-Andre Fleury RC 100.00 200.00
90P M-A Fleury PROMO 4.00 10.00

2003-04 Upper Deck Ice Glass

*91-120 ROOK/25: 1.5X TO 4X RC/999
*121-130 ROOK/25: .4X TO 1X RC/99

2003-04 Upper Deck Ice Gold

*1-90 VETS/40: 5X TO 12X BASIC CARDS

2003-04 Upper Deck Ice Authentics

IAAC Anson Carter 8.00 20.00
IAAH Ales Hemsky 10.00 25.00
IACK Chuck Kobasew 6.00 15.00
IADA David Aebischer 10.00 25.00
IAHA Marcel Hossa 6.00 15.00
IAHZ Henrik Zetterberg 12.00 30.00
IAIK Ilya Kovalchuk 25.00 60.00
IAJI Jarome Iginla 25.00 60.00
IAJR Jeremy Roenick 15.00 40.00
IAJS Jason Spezza 15.00 40.00
IAJT Joe Thornton 25.00 60.00
IAMB Martin Brodeur 75.00 150.00
IAMH Marian Hossa 12.00 30.00
IAMH Gordie Howe 75.00 150.00
IAMN Markus Naslund 15.00 40.00
IAMT Marty Turco SP 40.00 100.00
IAON Owen Nolan 8.00 20.00
IAPR Patrick Roy SP 75.00 200.00
IARD Rick DiPietro 10.00 25.00
IARL Roberto Luongo 15.00 40.00
IARN Rick Nash 15.00 40.00
IASK Saku Koivu 10.00 25.00
IATB Todd Bertuzzi 10.00 25.00
IATH Jose Theodore 15.00 40.00
IAWG Wayne Gretzky 250.00 600.00
IAZP Zigmund Palffy 8.00 20.00

2003-04 Upper Deck Ice Breakers

*PATCH/25: 1.5X TO 4X BASIC JSY/75
IBAH Ales Hemsky 6.00 15.00
IBBG Bill Guerin 6.00 15.00
IBBH Brett Hull 8.00 20.00
IBBL Brian Leetch 6.00 15.00
IBBS Brendan Shanahan 6.00 15.00
IBDA David Aebischer 6.00 15.00
IBDH Dominik Hasek 10.00 25.00
IBEB Ed Belfour 10.00 25.00
IBHK Milan Hejduk 4.00 10.00
IBIK Ilya Kovalchuk 6.00 15.00
IBJJ Jaromir Jagr 10.00 25.00
IBJK Jason King 4.00 10.00
IBJR Jeremy Roenick 8.00 20.00
IBJS Joe Sakic 12.50 30.00
IBJT Joe Thornton 8.00 20.00
IBJSG Jean-Sebastien Giguere 6.00 15.00
IBKT Keith Tkachuk 6.00 15.00
IBMB Martin Brodeur 15.00 40.00
IBMH Marian Hossa 6.00 15.00
IBML Mario Lemieux 20.00 50.00
IBMM Mike Modano 8.00 20.00
IBMN Markus Naslund 6.00 15.00
IBMR Mark Messier 8.00 20.00
IBMS Mats Sundin 6.00 15.00
IBMT Marty Turco 6.00 15.00
IBNL Nicklas Lidstrom 6.00 15.00
IBPF Peter Forsberg 10.00 25.00
IBPK Paul Kariya 6.00 15.00
IBPR Patrick Roy 20.00 50.00
IBRB Rob Blake 4.00 10.00
IBRF Ron Francis 6.00 15.00
IBRN Rick Nash 10.00 25.00
IBRT Raffi Torres 4.00 10.00
IBSG Scott Gomez 4.00 10.00
IBSP Jason Spezza 8.00 20.00
IBSS Sergei Samsonov 6.00 15.00
IBST Scott Stevens 4.00 10.00
IBSY Steve Yzerman 15.00 40.00
IBTB Todd Bertuzzi 6.00 15.00
IBTH Jose Theodore 8.00 20.00
IBVL Vincent Lecavalier 6.00 15.00
IBZP Zigmund Palffy 6.00 15.00

2003-04 Upper Deck Ice Clear Cut Winners

*PATCH/25: 1.5X TO 4X BASIC JSY
CCBH Brett Hull 4.00 10.00
CCBL Brian Leetch 3.00 8.00
CCBS Brendan Shanahan 6.00 15.00
CCDH Dominik Hasek 6.00 15.00
CCEB Ed Belfour 6.00 15.00
CCJJ Jaromir Jagr 6.00 15.00
CCJS Joe Sakic 8.00 20.00
CCMB Martin Brodeur 8.00 20.00
CCMH Milan Hejduk 6.00 15.00
CCML Mario Lemieux 15.00 40.00
CCMM Mike Modano 6.00 15.00
CCMR Mark Messier 6.00 15.00
CCNL Nicklas Lidstrom 6.00 15.00
CCPF Peter Forsberg 8.00 20.00
CCPR Patrick Roy 12.50 30.00
CCRB Rob Blake 3.00 8.00
CCRF Ron Francis 3.00 8.00
CCSG Scott Gomez 3.00 8.00
CCSS Scott Stevens 3.00 8.00
CCSY Steve Yzerman 12.50 30.00

2003-04 Upper Deck Ice Frozen Fabrics

COMPLETE SET (20)
*PATCHES: 2X TO 5X
FFAH Ales Hemsky 4.00 10.00
FFBG Bill Guerin 4.00 10.00
FFDA David Aebischer 4.00 10.00
FFJK Jason King 4.00 10.00
FFJR Jeremy Roenick 5.00 12.00
FFJS Jason Spezza 5.00 12.00
FFJT Joe Thornton 6.00 15.00
FFJSG Jean-Sebastien Giguere 4.00 10.00
FFKT Keith Tkachuk 4.00 10.00
FFMH Marian Hossa 4.00 10.00
FFMN Markus Naslund 4.00 10.00
FFMS Mats Sundin 4.00 10.00
FFMT Marty Turco 4.00 10.00
FFPK Paul Kariya 4.00 10.00
FFRN Rick Nash 6.00 15.00
FFRT Raffi Torres 4.00 10.00
FFSS Sergei Samsonov 4.00 10.00
FFTB Todd Bertuzzi 4.00 10.00
FFTH Jose Theodore 5.00 12.00
FFZP Zigmund Palffy 4.00 10.00

2003-04 Upper Deck Ice Icons

COMPLETE SET (10) 20.00 50.00
IAM Al MacInnis 2.00 5.00
IBL Brian Leetch 2.00 5.00
IEB Ed Belfour 2.00 5.00
IJR Jeremy Roenick 2.50 6.00
IJS Joe Sakic 3.00 8.00
IMB Martin Brodeur 4.00 10.00
IML Mario Lemieux 5.00 12.00
IMM Mike Modano 2.50 6.00
ISY Steve Yzerman 5.00 12.00
ITD Tie Domi 2.00 5.00

2003-04 Upper Deck Ice Icons Jerseys

IAM Al MacInnis 4.00 10.00
IBL Brian Leetch 4.00 10.00
IEB Ed Belfour 6.00 15.00
IJR Jeremy Roenick 5.00 12.00
IMB Martin Brodeur 10.00 25.00
IML Mario Lemieux 12.50 30.00
IMM Mike Modano 5.00 12.00
ISY Steve Yzerman 12.50 30.00
ITD Tie Domi 4.00 10.00

2003-04 Upper Deck Ice Under Glass Autographs

UGAH Ales Hemsky 12.00 30.00
UGBO Bobby Orr 75.00 150.00
UGDC Don Cherry 25.00 60.00
UGEL Eric Lindros SP 50.00 100.00
UGHA Marian Hossa 12.00 30.00
UGHZ Henrik Zetterberg 20.00 50.00
UGIK Ilya Kovalchuk 15.00 40.00
UGJR Jeremy Roenick 20.00 50.00
UGJS Jason Spezza 40.00 100.00
UGJT Joe Thornton 15.00 40.00
UGMB Martin Brodeur 80.00 200.00
UGMG Marian Gaborik 25.00 60.00
UGMH Gordie Howe 75.00 150.00
UGON Owen Nolan 12.00 30.00
UGPR Patrick Roy SP 200.00 350.00
UGRD Rick DiPietro 20.00 50.00
UGRL Roberto Luongo 25.00 60.00
UGRN Rick Nash 15.00 40.00
UGTB Todd Bertuzzi 12.00 30.00
UGWG Wayne Gretzky 300.00 800.00

2005-06 Upper Deck Ice

COMP. SET w/o SPs (1-100) 10.00 25.00
1 Joffrey Lupul .25 .60
2 Scott Niedermayer .40 1.00
3 Jean-Sebastien Giguere .40 1.00
4 Teemu Selanne .75 2.00
5 Ilya Kovalchuk .40 1.00
6 Kari Lehtonen .30 .75
7 Marian Hossa .40 1.00
8 Andrew Raycroft .30 .75
9 Patrice Bergeron .50 1.25
10 Brian Leetch .30 .75
11 Glen Murray .30 .75
12 Ryan Miller .40 1.00
13 Chris Drury .30 .75
14 Jarome Iginla .50 1.25
15 Miikka Kiprusoff .40 1.00
16 Jordan Leopold .25 .60
17 Tony Amonte .25 .60
18 Erik Cole .25 .60
19 Eric Staal .50 1.25
20 Nikolai Khabibulin .40 1.00
21 Tuomo Ruutu .40 1.00
22 Joe Sakic .75 2.00
23 Milan Hejduk .30 .75
24 Alex Tanguay .40 1.00

25 David Aebischer .30 .75
26 Rick Nash .40 1.00
27 Sergei Fedorov .60 1.50
28 Mike Modano .60 1.50
29 Marty Turco .40 1.00
30 Bill Guerin .40 1.00
31 Steve Yzerman 1.00 2.50
32 Pavel Datsyuk .60 1.50
33 Brendan Shanahan .40 1.00
34 Nicklas Lidstrom .40 1.00
35 Henrik Zetterberg .50 1.25
36 Chris Pronger .40 1.00
37 Ty Conklin .30 .75
38 Ryan Smyth .30 .75
39 Michael Peca .30 .75
40 Roberto Luongo .60 1.50
41 Joe Nieuwendyk .30 .75
42 Jay Bouwmeester .25 .60
43 Stephen Weiss .25 .60
44 Jeremy Roenick .60 1.50
45 Luc Robitaille .40 1.00
46 Alexander Frolov .25 .60
47 Marian Gaborik .40 1.00
48 Dwayne Roloson .30 .75
49 Jose Theodore .40 1.00
50 Saku Koivu .40 1.00
51 Michael Ryder .30 .75
52 Mike Ribeiro .25 .60
53 Steve Sullivan .25 .60
54 Paul Kariya .40 1.00
55 Tomas Vokoun .30 .75
56 Martin Brodeur 1.00 2.50
57 Patrik Elias .40 1.00
58 Brian Gionta .25 .60
59 Alexei Yashin .30 .75
60 Miroslav Satan .30 .75
61 Rick DiPietro .30 .75
62 Jaromir Jagr 1.25 3.00
63 Kevin Weekes .30 .75
64 Tom Poti .25 .60
65 Dany Heatley .30 .75
66 Dominik Hasek .60 1.50
67 Martin Havlat .40 1.00
68 Jason Spezza .40 1.00
69 Daniel Alfredsson .40 1.00
70 Robert Esche .30 .75
71 Peter Forsberg .75 2.00
72 Keith Primeau .30 .75
73 Simon Gagne .40 1.00
74 Shane Doan .30 .75
75 Curtis Joseph .50 1.25
76 Mario Lemieux 1.50 4.00
77 Zigmund Palffy .40 1.00
78 Mark Recchi .50 1.25
79 Marc-Andre Fleury .75 2.00
80 Joe Thornton .60 1.50
81 Jonathan Cheechoo .30 .75
82 Evgeni Nabokov .30 .75
83 Patrick Marleau .40 1.00
84 Keith Tkachuk .40 1.00
85 Doug Weight .40 1.00
86 Martin St. Louis .40 1.00
87 Brad Richards .40 1.00
88 Sean Burke .25 .60
89 Vincent Lecavalier .40 1.00
90 Mats Sundin .40 1.00
91 Nik Antropov .30 .75
92 Eric Lindros .60 1.50
93 Ed Belfour .40 1.00
94 Jason Allison .30 .75
95 Markus Naslund .40 1.00
96 Todd Bertuzzi .40 1.00
97 Brendan Morrison .25 .60
98 Ed Jovanovski .30 .75
99 Jeff Friesen .25 .60
100 Olaf Kolzig .40 1.00
101 Gilbert Brule RC 60.00 120.00
102 Thomas Vanek RC 160.00 300.00
103 Alexander Ovechkin RC 1500.00 4000.00
104 Jeff Carter RC 40.00 100.00
105 Corey Perry RC 60.00 150.00
106 Sidney Crosby RC 2000.00 3500.00
107 Ryan Getzlaf RC 8.00 20.00
108 Hannu Toivonen RC 4.00 10.00
109 Dion Phaneuf RC 8.00 20.00
110 Cam Ward RC 6.00 15.00
111 Wojtek Wolski RC 3.00 8.00
112 Jim Howard RC 10.00 25.00
113 Rostislav Olesz RC 3.00 8.00
114 Alexander Perezhogin RC 3.00 8.00
115 Zach Parise RC 12.00 30.00
116 Mikko Koivu RC 5.00 12.00
117 Mike Richards RC 10.00 25.00
118 Alexander Steen RC 8.00 20.00
119 Braydon Coburn RC 3.00 8.00
120 Andrew Alberts RC 2.00 5.00
121 Eric Nystrom RC 2.50 6.00
122 Kevin Nastiuk RC 2.00 5.00
123 Brent Seabrook RC 6.00 15.00
124 R.J. Umberger RC 3.00 8.00
125 Cam Barker RC 2.50 6.00
126 Peter Budaj RC 4.00 10.00
127 Jussi Jokinen RC 3.00 8.00
128 Johan Franzen RC 6.00 15.00
129 Brad Winchester RC 3.00 8.00
130 Anthony Stewart RC 2.50 6.00
131 Matt Foy RC 2.00 5.00
132 Yann Danis RC 2.50 6.00
133 Ryan Suter RC 4.00 10.00
134 Petteri Nokelainen RC 2.00 5.00
135 Chris Campoli RC 2.00 5.00
136 Al Montoya RC 3.00 8.00
137 Henrik Lundqvist RC 12.00 30.00
138 Ryan Whitney RC 3.00 8.00
139 Andrej Meszaros RC 2.50 6.00
140 Keith Ballard RC 2.50 6.00
141 David Leneveu RC 2.50 6.00
142 Jeff Woywitka RC 2.00 5.00
143 Jim Slater RC 2.00 5.00
144 Adam Berkhoel RC 2.00 5.00
145 Kevin Dallman RC 2.00 5.00
146 Milan Jurcina RC 2.00 5.00
147 Niklas Nordgren RC 2.50 6.00
148 Duncan Keith RC 12.00 30.00
149 Jaroslav Balastik RC 1.50 4.00
150 Brett Lebda RC 1.50 4.00
151 Kyle Brodziak RC 1.50 4.00
152 George Parros RC 1.50 4.00
153 Derek Boogaard RC 4.00 10.00
154 Mark Streit RC 1.50 4.00
155 Raitis Ivanans RC 1.50 4.00
156 Ryan Hollweg RC 1.50 4.00
157 Chris Holt RC 1.50 4.00
158 Petr Prucha RC 2.50 6.00
159 Brian McGrattan RC 1.50 4.00
160 Patrick Eaves RC 2.50 6.00
161 Wade Skolney RC 1.50 4.00
162 Maxime Talbot RC 2.50 6.00
163 Ryane Clowe RC 3.00 8.00
164 Josh Gorges RC 2.00 5.00
165 Andy Roach RC 1.50 4.00
166 Jay McClement RC 1.50 4.00
167 Jeff Hoggan RC 1.50 4.00
168 Lee Stempniak RC 2.50 6.00
169 Colin Hemingway RC 1.50 4.00
170 Timo Helbling RC 1.50 4.00
171 Paul Ranger RC 1.50 4.00
172 Andrew Wozniewski RC 2.00 5.00
173 Robert Nilsson RC 2.50 6.00
174 Rene Bourque RC 2.50 6.00
175 Brandon Bochenski RC 2.50 6.00
176 Steve Bernier RC 2.50 6.00
177 Evgeny Artyukhin RC 2.00 5.00
178 Christoph Schubert RC 1.50 4.00
179 Jakub Klepis RC 1.50 4.00
180 Dimitri Patzold RC 1.50 4.00
181 Vojtech Polak RC 1.50 4.00
182 Rob McVicar RC 2.00 5.00
183 Staffan Kronwall RC 1.50 4.00
184 Jordan Sigalet RC 1.50 4.00
185 Dustin Penner RC 2.50 6.00
186 Michael Wall RC 2.00 5.00
187 Zenon Konopka RC 1.50 4.00
188 Jay Leach RC 2.00 5.00
189 Danny Richmond RC 1.50 4.00
190 Martin St. Pierre RC 1.50 4.00
191 Andrew Penner RC 2.00 5.00
192 Steve Goertzen RC 1.50 4.00
193 Ole-Kristian Tollefsen RC 2.00 5.00
194 Junior Lessard RC 1.50 4.00
195 Danny Syvret RC 1.50 4.00
196 Greg Jacina RC 1.50 4.00
197 Jeff Giuliano RC 2.00 5.00
198 Adam Hauser RC 2.00 5.00
199 Maxim Lapierre RC 2.50 6.00
200 Barry Tallackson RC 2.00 5.00
201 Cam Janssen RC 2.00 5.00
202 Kevin Colley RC 2.00 5.00
203 Jeremy Colliton RC 1.50 4.00
204 Yanick Lehoux RC 2.50 6.00
205 Erik Christensen RC 1.50 4.00
206 Dennis Wideman RC 1.50 4.00
207 Nick Tarnasky RC 1.50 4.00
208 Brian Eklund RC 2.00 5.00
209 Gerald Coleman RC 1.50 4.00
210 Tomas Fleischmann RC 2.50 6.00
211 Brad Richardson RC 2.50 6.00
212 Mark Cullen RC 2.00 5.00
213 Jean-Philippe Cote RC 1.50 4.00
214 Andrei Kostitsyn RC 4.00 10.00
215 Matt Jones RC 1.50 4.00
216 Ben Eager RC 2.00 5.00
217 Andrew Ladd RC 3.00 8.00
218 Bruno Gervais RC 1.50 4.00
219 Jeff Tambellini RC 1.50 4.00
220 Kevin Klein RC 1.50 4.00
221 Kyle Quincey RC 2.00 5.00
222 Chris Thorburn RC 2.00 5.00
223 Doug Murray RC 1.50 4.00
224 Eric Healey RC 2.00 5.00
225 Grant Stevenson RC 1.50 4.00
226 Ryan Ready RC 2.00 5.00
227 Vitaly Kolesnik RC 2.00 5.00
228 Geoff Platt RC 2.00 5.00
229 Chris Bourque RC 2.00 5.00
230 Jon DiSalvatore RC 2.00 5.00
231 Ben Walter RC 1.50 4.00
232 Jonathan Ferland RC 2.00 5.00
233 Kevin Bieksa RC 4.00 10.00
234 Rick Rypien RC 3.00 8.00
235 Alexandre Burrows RC 3.00 8.00
236 David Steckel RC 2.00 5.00
237 Mike Green RC 4.00 10.00
238 Richie Regehr RC 1.50 4.00
239 Josh Gratton RC 2.00 5.00
240 Chad Larose RC 1.50 4.00
241 Petr Kanko RC 2.00 5.00
242 Matt Ryan RC 2.00 5.00
243 Connor James RC 2.00 5.00
244 Richard Petiot RC 2.00 5.00
245 Darren Reid RC 1.50 4.00
246 Ryan Craig RC 1.50 4.00
247 Matt Greene RC 1.50 4.00
248 Rob Globke RC 1.50 4.00
249 Colby Armstrong RC 2.50 6.00
250 Greg Zanon RC 2.00 5.00
251 Pekka Rinne RC 8.00 20.00
252 Valtteri Filppula RC 3.00 8.00
253 Daniel Paille RC 2.50 6.00
254 Nathan Paetsch RC 2.00 5.00
255 Jiri Novotny RC 2.00 5.00
256 Petr Taticek RC 2.00 5.00
257 Alexandre Picard RC 1.50 4.00
258 Keith Aucoin RC 1.50 4.00
259 Alexandre Picard RC 1.50 4.00
260 Corey Crawford RC 8.00 20.00
261 Jason Ryznar RC 1.50 4.00
262 Doug O'Brien RC 1.50 4.00
263 Mike Glumac RC 2.00 5.00
264 Jay Harrison RC 2.00 5.00
265 Ben Guite RC 2.00 5.00
266 Mark Giordano RC 3.00 8.00
267 David Gove RC 2.00 5.00
268 J-F Jacques RC 1.50 4.00

2005-06 Upper Deck Ice Rainbow

*RAINBOW/100: 6X TO 15X BASIC CARDS

2005-06 Upper Deck Ice Cool Threads

*GLASS/100: .5X TO 1.25X BASIC JSY
*PATCH/50: 1.5X TO 4X BASIC JSY
CTAO Alexander Ovechkin 100.00 250.00
CTAP Alexander Perezhogin 1.50 4.00
CTAR Andrew Raycroft 1.50 4.00
CTAS Alexander Steen 3.00 8.00
CTBS Brent Seabrook 4.00 10.00
CTCP Corey Perry 6.00 15.00
CTCW Cam Ward 3.00 8.00
CTDP Dion Phaneuf 3.00 8.00
CTGB Gilbert Brule 2.00 5.00
CTHL Henrik Lundqvist 10.00 25.00
CTHT Hannu Toivonen 2.00 5.00
CTJB Jay Bouwmeester 1.25 3.00
CTJC Jeff Carter 3.00 8.00
CTJJ Jaromir Jagr 6.00 15.00
CTJK Jussi Jokinen 2.00 5.00
CTJO Jose Theodore 2.00 5.00
CTJT Joe Thornton 3.00 8.00
CTMB Martin Brodeur 5.00 12.00
CTMH Milan Hejduk 1.50 4.00
CTML Matthew Lombardi 1.25 3.00
CTMM Mike Modano 3.00 8.00
CTMN Markus Naslund 2.00 5.00
CTMP Michael Peca 1.50 4.00
CTMR Mike Richards 4.00 10.00
CTMV Martin Havlat 2.00 5.00
CTNH Nathan Horton 2.00 5.00
CTNI Robert Nilsson 2.00 5.00
CTPB Patrice Bergeron 2.50 6.00
CTPE Patrik Elias 2.00 5.00
CTRG Ryan Getzlaf 5.00 12.00
CTRL Roberto Luongo 3.00 8.00
CTRN Rick Nash 2.00 5.00
CTRS Ryan Suter 2.50 6.00
CTSC Sidney Crosby 12.00 30.00
CTSG Simon Gagne 2.00 5.00
CTTR Tuomo Ruutu 2.00 5.00
CTTV Thomas Vanek 4.00 10.00
CTVO Tomas Vokoun 1.50 4.00
CTZC Zdeno Chara 2.00 5.00
CTZP Zach Parise 5.00 12.00

2005-06 Upper Deck Ice Cool Threads Autographs

ACTAO Alexander Ovechkin 1000.00 2500.00
ACTAP Alexander Perezhogin 5.00 12.00
ACTAR Andrew Raycroft 5.00 12.00
ACTAS Alexander Steen 10.00 25.00
ACTBS Brent Seabrook 12.00 30.00
ACTCP Corey Perry 20.00 50.00
ACTCW Cam Ward 10.00 25.00
ACTDP Dion Phaneuf 10.00 25.00
ACTGB Gilbert Brule 6.00 15.00
ACTHL Henrik Lundqvist 30.00 80.00
ACTHT Hannu Toivonen 6.00 15.00
ACTJB Jay Bouwmeester 4.00 10.00
ACTJC Jeff Carter 25.00 60.00
ACTJK Jussi Jokinen 6.00 15.00
ACTJO Jose Theodore 6.00 15.00
ACTJT Joe Thornton 10.00 25.00
ACTMB Martin Brodeur 15.00 40.00
ACTMH Milan Hejduk 5.00 12.00
ACTMM Mike Modano 10.00 25.00
ACTMN Markus Naslund 6.00 15.00
ACTMP Michael Peca 5.00 12.00
ACTMR Mike Richards 12.00 30.00
ACTMV Martin Havlat 6.00 15.00
ACTNH Nathan Horton 6.00 15.00
ACTNI Robert Nilsson 6.00 15.00
ACTPB Patrice Bergeron 40.00 100.00
ACTRG Ryan Getzlaf 15.00 40.00
ACTRL Roberto Luongo 10.00 25.00
ACTRN Rick Nash 6.00 15.00
ACTRS Ryan Suter 8.00 20.00
ACTSC Sidney Crosby 300.00 500.00
ACTSD Shane Doan 5.00 12.00
ACTSG Simon Gagne 6.00 15.00
ACTTR Tuomo Ruutu 6.00 15.00
ACTTV Thomas Vanek 12.00 30.00
ACTZC Zdeno Chara 6.00 15.00
ACTZP Zach Parise 15.00 40.00

2005-06 Upper Deck Ice Fresh Ice

*GLASS: .8X TO 2X BASIC JSY
*GLSS PTCH/35-50: 1.5X TO 4X BASIC JSY
FIAF Alexander Frolov 2.00 5.00
FIAH Adam Hall 2.00 5.00
FIAS Anthony Stewart 2.50 6.00
FIBB Brandon Bochenski 3.00 8.00
FIBC Braydon Coburn 3.00 8.00
FIBS Brent Seabrook 6.00 15.00
FIBU Peter Budaj 4.00 10.00
FIBW Brad Winchester 3.00 8.00
FIDB Dustin Brown 3.00 8.00
FIEN Eric Nystrom 2.50 6.00
FIGP George Parros 2.00 5.00
FIHE Ales Hemsky 2.50 6.00
FIHV Martin Havlat 3.00 8.00
FIHZ Henrik Zetterberg 4.00 10.00
FIJB Jay Bouwmeester 2.00 5.00
FIJF Johan Franzen 5.00 12.00
FIJJ Jussi Jokinen 3.00 8.00
FIJL Jordan Leopold 2.00 5.00
FIJP Joni Pitkanen 2.00 5.00
FIKL Kari Lehtonen 2.50 6.00
FILU Joffrey Lupul 2.00 5.00
FIMC Jay McClement 2.00 5.00
FIMH Marcel Hossa 2.00 5.00
FIMJ Milan Jurcina 2.50 6.00
FIMM Milan Michalek 2.00 5.00
FIMR Mike Richards 6.00 15.00
FIMT Maxime Talbot 3.00 8.00
FIPB Patrice Bergeron 4.00 10.00
FIPN Petteri Nokelainen 2.00 5.00
FIPP Petr Prucha 3.00 8.00
FIPS Philippe Sauve 2.50 6.00
FIRC Ryane Clowe 4.00 10.00
FIRG Ryan Getzlaf 8.00 20.00
FIRI Mike Ribeiro 2.00 5.00
FIRK Ryan Kesler 3.00 8.00
FIRM Ryan Miller 3.00 8.00
FIRS Ryan Suter 4.00 10.00
FIRT Raffi Torres 2.00 5.00
FIYD Yann Danis 2.50 6.00
FIZP Zach Parise 8.00 20.00

2005-06 Upper Deck Ice Frozen Fabrics

*GLASS/100: .6X TO 1.5X BASIC JSY
*PATCH/50: 1X TO 2.5X BASIC JSY
FFAT Alex Tanguay 5.00 12.00
FFAY Alexei Yashin 4.00 10.00
FFBS Brendan Shanahan 5.00 12.00
FFCO Chris Osgood 5.00 12.00
FFCP Chris Pronger 5.00 12.00
FFDA Daniel Alfredsson 5.00 12.00
FFDH Dany Heatley 4.00 10.00
FFDW Doug Weight 5.00 12.00
FFEB Ed Belfour 5.00 12.00
FFGM Glen Murray 4.00 10.00
FFIK Ilya Kovalchuk 5.00 12.00
FFJI Jarome Iginla 6.00 15.00
FFJP Joni Pitkanen 3.00 8.00
FFJR Jeremy Roenick 8.00 20.00
FFJS Joe Sakic 6.00 15.00
FFJT Jocelyn Thibault 4.00 10.00
FFKP Keith Primeau 4.00 10.00
FFKT Keith Tkachuk 5.00 12.00
FFMB Martin Brodeur 8.00 20.00
FFMK Miikka Kiprusoff 5.00 12.00
FFML Mario Lemieux 8.00 20.00
FFMM Milan Michalek 3.00 8.00
FFMS Mats Sundin 5.00 12.00
FFMT Marty Turco 5.00 12.00
FFNK Nikolai Khabibulin 5.00 12.00
FFPD Pavel Datsyuk 8.00 20.00
FFPF Peter Forsberg 8.00 20.00
FFPK Paul Kariya 5.00 12.00
FFPM Patrick Marleau 5.00 12.00
FFPR Patrick Roy 8.00 20.00
FFRB Ray Bourque 6.00 15.00
FFRS Ryan Smyth 4.00 10.00
FFSC Sidney Crosby 15.00 40.00
FFSK Saku Koivu 5.00 12.00
FFSL Martin St. Louis 5.00 12.00
FFSP Jason Spezza 5.00 12.00
FFSY Steve Yzerman 8.00 20.00
FFSZ Sergei Zubov 4.00 10.00
FFTB Todd Bertuzzi 5.00 12.00
FFVL Vincent Lecavalier 5.00 12.00
FFZP Zigmund Palffy 5.00 12.00

2005-06 Upper Deck Ice Frozen Fabrics Autographs

AFFAT Alex Tanguay 15.00 40.00
AFFAY Alexei Yashin 12.00 30.00
AFFCO Chris Osgood 15.00 40.00
AFFCP Chris Pronger 15.00 40.00
AFFDH Dany Heatley 15.00 40.00
AFFDW Doug Weight 12.00 30.00
AFFEB Ed Belfour 30.00 80.00
AFFGM Glen Murray 15.00 40.00
AFFIK Ilya Kovalchuk 20.00 50.00
AFFJI Jarome Iginla 20.00 50.00
AFFJP Joni Pitkanen 12.00 30.00
AFFJR Jeremy Roenick 20.00 50.00
AFFJT Jocelyn Thibault 12.00 30.00
AFFKP Keith Primeau 15.00 40.00
AFFMB Martin Brodeur 60.00 125.00
AFFMM Milan Michalek 30.00 60.00
AFFPR Patrick Roy 100.00 200.00
AFFRB Ray Bourque 40.00 75.00
AFFRS Ryan Smyth 25.00 60.00
AFFSC Sidney Crosby 300.00 500.00
AFFSK Saku Koivu 20.00 50.00
AFFSL Martin St. Louis 12.50 30.00
AFFSP Jason Spezza 15.00 40.00
AFFTB Todd Bertuzzi 15.00 40.00
AFFVL Vincent Lecavalier 40.00 80.00
AFFZP Zigmund Palffy 12.00 30.00

2005-06 Upper Deck Ice Glacial Graphs

GGAF Alexander Frolov 4.00 10.00
GGAO Alexander Ovechkin 500.00 1200.00
GGAP Alex Perezhogin 6.00 15.00
GGAR Andrew Raycroft 5.00 12.00
GGCB Cam Barker 5.00 12.00
GGCP Corey Perry 8.00 20.00
GGCW Cam Ward 12.00 30.00
GGDP Dion Phaneuf 15.00 40.00
GGEN Eric Nystrom 4.00 10.00
GGGB Gilbert Brule 6.00 15.00
GGGH Gordie Howe SP 75.00 150.00
GGHO Marian Hossa 6.00 15.00
GGHT Hannu Toivonen 4.00 10.00
GGHV Martin Havlat 6.00 15.00
GGIK Ilya Kovalchuk 15.00 40.00
GGJB Jay Bouwmeester 4.00 10.00
GGJC Jeff Carter 12.00 30.00
GGJI Jarome Iginla 15.00 30.00
GGKB Keith Ballard 4.00 10.00
GGMB Martin Brodeur 40.00 80.00
GGMM Mike Modano SP 20.00 50.00
GGMP Michael Peca 6.00 15.00
GGMR Mike Ribeiro 4.00 10.00
GGMS Matt Stajan 4.00 10.00
GGMT Marty Turco 8.00 20.00
GGNA Rick Nash 12.00 30.00
GGRB Rob Blake SP 12.00 30.00
GGRI Mike Richards 10.00 25.00
GGRK Ryan Kesler 8.00 20.00
GGRL Roberto Luongo 15.00 40.00
GGRM Ryan Miller 15.00 30.00
GGRN Robert Nilsson 4.00 10.00
GGSC Sidney Crosby 175.00 350.00
GGSD Shane Doan 4.00 10.00
GGST Alexander Steen 8.00 20.00
GGTA Tyler Arnason 4.00 10.00
GGTH Trent Hunter 4.00 10.00
GGTL Trevor Linden 10.00 25.00
GGTV Thomas Vanek 10.00 25.00
GGWG Wayne Gretzky SP 1250.00 3000.00
GGWW Wojtek Wolski 8.00 20.00
GGZP Zach Parise 8.00 20.00

2005-06 Upper Deck Ice Glacial Graphs Labels

GGCB Cam Barker 8.00 20.00
GGCW Cam Ward 20.00 50.00
GGEN Eric Nystrom 8.00 20.00
GGHT Hannu Toivonen 12.50 30.00
GGJB Jay Bouwmeester 8.00 20.00
GGKB Keith Ballard 8.00 20.00
GGMS Matt Stajan 8.00 20.00
GGRK Ryan Kesler 8.00 20.00
GGRN Robert Nilsson 8.00 20.00
GGTA Tyler Arnason 8.00 20.00
GGTH Trent Hunter 8.00 20.00
GGTV Thomas Vanek 20.00 50.00
GGWW Wojtek Wolski 20.00 50.00
GGZP Zach Parise 12.50 30.00

2005-06 Upper Deck Ice Signature Swatches

SSAO Alexander Ovechkin 800.00 2000.00
SSAS Alexander Steen 15.00 40.00
SSAT Alex Tanguay 15.00 40.00
SSBL Brian Leetch 15.00 40.00
SSBO Mike Bossy SP 30.00 80.00
SSCP Chris Pronger 12.00 30.00
SSCW Cam Ward 15.00 40.00
SSDH Dominik Hasek SP 75.00 125.00
SSDW Doug Weight 15.00 40.00
SSEB Ed Belfour SP 20.00 50.00
SSGB Gilbert Brule 15.00 40.00
SSHE Dany Heatley SP 25.00 60.00
SSHZ Henrik Zetterberg 20.00 50.00
SSIK Ilya Kovalchuk/50 SP 30.00 80.00
SSJC Jeff Carter 6.00 15.00
SSJI Jarome Iginla 25.00 60.00
SSJK Jari Kurri/100 SP 25.00 60.00
SSJR Jeremy Roenick SP 15.00 40.00
SSJS Jason Spezza/25 SP 100.00 200.00
SSJT Joe Thornton SP 30.00 80.00
SSLC Luc Robitaille 10.00 25.00
SSMB Martin Brodeur SP 250.00 400.00
SSMH Milan Hejduk 15.00 40.00
SSMM Mike Modano/50 SP 25.00 60.00
SSMN Markus Naslund 15.00 40.00
SSMS Martin St. Louis SP 25.00 60.00
SSNZ Nikolai Zherdev 15.00 40.00
SSPB Patrice Bergeron 50.00 125.00
SSRB Ray Bourque SP 60.00 125.00
SSRN Rick Nash/25 SP 100.00 200.00
SSSC S.Crosby/100 SP 250.00 400.00
SSSG Simon Gagne 10.00 25.00
SSSK Saku Koivu SP 25.00 60.00
SSTB Todd Bertuzzi 15.00 40.00
SSTH Jose Theodore 12.00 30.00
SSVL Vincent Lecavalier SP 30.00 80.00
SSZP Z.Palffy/55 SP 25.00 60.00

2007-08 Upper Deck Ice

COMP.SET w/o SPs (100) 15.00 40.00
1 Martin Brodeur 1.25 3.00
2 Zach Parise .50 1.25
3 Patrik Elias .50 1.25
4 Rick DiPietro .40 1.00
5 Bill Guerin .50 1.25
6 Miroslav Satan .40 1.00
7 Jaromir Jagr 1.50 4.00
8 Henrik Lundqvist 1.25 3.00
9 Chris Drury .40 1.00
10 Brendan Shanahan .50 1.25
11 Simon Gagne .50 1.25
12 Daniel Briere .50 1.25
13 Jeff Carter .40 1.00
14 Sidney Crosby 2.00 5.00
15 Marc-Andre Fleury 1.00 2.50
16 Evgeni Malkin 1.00 2.50
17 Jordan Staal .40 1.00
18 Patrice Bergeron .60 1.50
19 Phil Kessel .50 1.25
20 Marc Savard .30 .75
21 Thomas Vanek .40 1.00
22 Ryan Miller .50 1.25
23 Jason Pominville .30 .75
24 Saku Koivu .50 1.25
25 Michael Ryder .30 .75
26 Guillaume Latendresse .40 1.00
27 Cristobal Huet .40 1.00
28 Jason Spezza .50 1.25
29 Daniel Alfredsson .50 1.25
30 Ray Emery .40 1.00
31 Dany Heatley .40 1.00
32 Mats Sundin .50 1.25
33 Darcy Tucker .40 1.00
34 Alexander Steen .30 .75
35 Vesa Toskala .40 1.00
36 Karl Lehtonen .40 1.00
37 Ilya Kovalchuk .50 1.25
38 Marian Hossa .50 1.25
39 Eric Staal .60 1.50
40 Cam Ward .50 1.25
41 Justin Williams .40 1.00
42 Tomas Vokoun .40 1.00
43 Nathan Horton .50 1.25
44 Olli Jokinen .40 1.00
45 Vincent Lecavalier .50 1.25
46 Martin St. Louis .50 1.25
47 Brad Richards .50 1.25
48 Alexander Ovechkin 2.00 5.00
49 Olaf Kolzig .50 1.25
50 Alexander Semin .50 1.25
51 Martin Havlat .50 1.25
52 Nikolai Khabibulin .50 1.25
53 Sergei Samsonov .40 1.00
54 Rick Nash .50 1.25
55 Sergei Fedorov .75 2.00
56 David Vyborny .30 .75
57 Gilbert Brule .40 1.00
58 Henrik Zetterberg .60 1.50
59 Nicklas Lidstrom .50 1.25
60 Dominik Hasek .75 2.00
61 Pavel Datsyuk .75 2.00
62 Alexander Radulov .50 1.25
63 Chris Mason .40 1.00
64 Jason Arnott .40 1.00
65 Paul Kariya .50 1.25
66 Doug Weight .50 1.25
67 Keith Tkachuk .50 1.25
68 Jarome Iginla .60 1.50
69 Miikka Kiprusoff .50 1.25
70 Alex Tanguay .40 1.00
71 Dion Phaneuf .40 1.00
72 Joe Sakic 1.00 2.50
73 Milan Hejduk .40 1.00
74 Paul Stastny .40 1.00
75 Ryan Smyth .40 1.00
76 Ales Hemsky .40 1.00
77 Dwayne Roloson .40 1.00
78 Joni Pitkanen .30 .75
79 Jarret Stoll .40 1.00
80 Marian Gaborik .50 1.25
81 Pavol Demitra .60 1.50
82 Mikko Koivu .40 1.00
83 Roberto Luongo .75 2.00
84 Markus Naslund .50 1.25
85 Daniel Sedin .60 1.50
86 Henrik Sedin .60 1.50
87 Ryan Getzlaf .50 1.25
88 Jean-Sebastien Giguere .50 1.25
89 Corey Perry .75 2.00
90 Mike Ribeiro .30 .75
91 Mike Modano .75 2.00
92 Marty Turco .50 1.25
93 Rob Blake .50 1.25
94 Anze Kopitar .75 2.00
95 Alexander Frolov .30 .75
96 David Aebischer .40 1.00
97 Shane Doan .40 1.00
98 Patrick Marleau .50 1.25
99 Jonathan Cheechoo .40 1.00
100 Joe Thornton .75 2.00
101 Tomi Maki/1999 RC 3.00 8.00
102 Tomas Plihal/1999 RC 3.00 8.00
103 Sheldon Brookbank/1999 RC 3.00 8.00
104 Shay Stephenson/1999 RC 3.00 8.00
105 Sebastien Bisaillon/1999 RC 3.00 8.00
106 Scott Munroe/1999 RC 3.00 8.00
107 Riley Cote/1999 RC 4.00 10.00
108 Rich Peverley/1999 RC 3.00 8.00
109 Pierre Parenteau/1999 RC 4.00 10.00
110 Olli Malmivaara/1999 RC 3.00 8.00
111 Nathan Guenin/1999 RC 4.00 10.00
112 Matt Ellis/1999 RC 4.00 10.00
113 Martin Lojek/1999 RC 3.00 8.00
114 Mark Mancari/1999 RC 3.00 8.00
115 Magnus Johansson/1999 RC 3.00 8.00
116 Krys Barch/1999 RC 4.00 10.00
117 Kent Huskins/1999 RC 3.00 8.00
118 Jonas Nordqvist/1999 RC 3.00 8.00
119 Joel Ward/1999 RC 5.00 12.00
120 Joel Lundqvist/1999 RC 3.00 8.00
121 Joe Piskula/1999 RC 3.00 8.00
122 Jamie Hunt/1999 RC 3.00 8.00
123 Gabe Gauthier/1999 RC 3.00 8.00
124 Duncan Milroy/1999 RC 3.00 8.00
125 Drew Fata/1999 RC 3.00 8.00
126 David Koci/1999 RC 3.00 8.00
127 Darcy Campbell/1999 RC 3.00 8.00
128 Danny Bois/1999 RC 3.00 8.00
129 Curtis Glencross/1999 RC 5.00 12.00
130 Colin Fraser/1999 RC 3.00 8.00
131 Bryan Young/1999 RC 3.00 8.00
132 Bryan Bickell/1999 RC 6.00 15.00
133 Bjorn Melin/1999 RC 3.00 8.00
134 Aaron Rome/1999 RC 4.00 10.00
135 Chris Bourque/1999 RC 4.00 10.00
136 Matt Hunwick/1999 RC 3.00 8.00
137 Tanner Glass/1999 RC 3.00 8.00
138 Aaron Voros/1999 RC 3.00 8.00
139 Alexander Nikulin/1999 RC 3.00 8.00
140 Vladimir Sobotka/1999 RC 4.00 10.00
141 Thomas Greiss/1999 RC 6.00 15.00
142 Ivan Baranka/1999 RC 4.00 10.00
143 Jonathan Sigalet/999 RC 4.00 10.00
144 Tom Gilbert/999 RC 5.00 12.00
145 Jeff Schultz/999 RC 5.00 12.00
146 Mark Fraser/999 RC 4.00 10.00
147 David Krejci/999 RC 12.00 30.00
148 David Moss/999 RC 6.00 15.00
149 Petteri Wirtanen/999 RC 4.00 10.00
150 Tomas Popperle/999 RC 4.00 10.00
151 Daniel Girardi/999 RC 5.00 12.00
152 Ryan Parent/999 RC 4.00 10.00
153 Tobias Stephan/999 RC 5.00 12.00
154 Marc Methot/999 RC 4.00 10.00
155 David Clarkson/999 RC 4.00 10.00
156 Tyler Weiman/999 RC 5.00 12.00
157 Mike Lundin/999 RC 4.00 10.00
158 Ryan Carter/999 RC 4.00 10.00
159 Mike Weber/999 RC 4.00 10.00
160 Daniel Winnik/999 RC 5.00 12.00
161 Tobias Enstrom/999 RC 6.00 15.00
162 Jared Boll/999 RC 5.00 12.00
163 Matt Keetley/999 RC 4.00 10.00
164 Stefan Meyer/999 RC 5.00 12.00
165 Patrick Kaleta/999 RC 4.00 10.00
166 Rod Pelley/999 RC 4.00 10.00
167 Jonas Hiller/999 RC 8.00 20.00
168 Brandon Dubinsky/999 RC 8.00 20.00
169 Jaroslav Hlinka/999 RC 5.00 12.00
170 Cory Murphy/999 RC 4.00 10.00
171 Denis Tolpeko/999 RC 4.00 10.00
172 Craig Weller/999 RC 4.00 10.00
173 Steve Wagner/999 RC 4.00 10.00
174 Jeff Finger/999 RC 4.00 10.00
175 Chris Conner/999 RC 4.00 10.00
176 Lukas Kaspar/999 RC 4.00 10.00
177 Ville Koistinen/999 RC 4.00 10.00
178 Zach Stortini/999 RC 4.00 10.00
179 Brady Murray/999 RC 4.00 10.00
180 Tyler Kennedy/999 RC 4.00 10.00
181 Matt Moulson/999 RC 6.00 15.00
182 John Zeiler/999 RC 4.00 10.00
183 Cal Clutterbuck/999 RC 8.00 20.00
184 Daniel Carcillo/999 RC 5.00 12.00
185 Kris Russell/499 RC 8.00 20.00
186 Matt Niskanen/499 RC 8.00 20.00
187 Nicklas Bergfors/499 RC 5.00 12.00
188 Brett Sterling/499 RC 5.00 12.00
189 Martin Hanzal/499 RC 6.00 15.00
190 Matt Smaby/499 RC 5.00 12.00
191 Petr Kalus/499 RC 5.00 12.00
192 Andy Greene/499 RC 6.00 15.00
193 Frans Nielsen/499 RC 8.00 20.00
194 Rob Schremp/499 RC 6.00 15.00
195 Kyle Chipchura/499 RC 8.00 20.00
196 Jonathan Bernier/499 RC 25.00 40.00
197 Tuukka Rask/499 RC 20.00 50.00
198 Lauri Tukonen/499 RC 5.00 12.00
199 Ondrej Pavelec/499 RC 10.00 25.00
200 Mason Raymond/499 RC 8.00 20.00
201 Ryan Callahan/499 RC 10.00 25.00
202 Curtis McElhinney/499 RC 8.00 20.00
203 Brian Elliott/499 RC 10.00 25.00
204 Drew Miller/499 RC 6.00 15.00
205 David Perron/499 RC 10.00 25.00
206 Anton Stralman/499 RC 5.00 12.00
207 Torrey Mitchell/499 RC 6.00 15.00
208 Jaroslav Halak/499 RC 15.00 40.00
209 Jannik Hansen/499 RC 6.00 15.00
210 Milan Lucic/499 RC 20.00 50.00
211 Bobby Ryan/99 RC 60.00 150.00
212 Jonathan Toews/99 RC 400.00 800.00
213 Sam Gagner/99 RC 125.00 200.00
214 Carey Price/99 RC 500.00 800.00
215 Jiri Tlusty/99 RC 40.00 100.00
216 Erik Johnson/99 RC 30.00 80.00
217 Nicklas Backstrom/99 RC 75.00 150.00
218 Jack Johnson/99 RC 25.00 60.00
219 Devin Setoguchi/99 RC 40.00 100.00
220 Bryan Little/99 RC 40.00 80.00
221 Patrick Kane/99 RC 600.00 1000.00
222 Andrew Cogliano/99 RC 40.00 100.00
223 Marc Staal/99 RC 40.00 100.00
224 Nick Foligno/99 RC 25.00 60.00
225 Peter Mueller/99 RC 30.00 80.00
226 James Sheppard/99 RC 25.00 60.00

2007-08 Upper Deck Ice Black Ice Jerseys

BIAO Alexander Ovechkin 15.00 40.00
BIAT Alex Tanguay 4.00 10.00
BIBC Bobby Clarke 10.00 25.00
BIBR Martin Brodeur 12.00 30.00
BIBS Borje Salming 5.00 12.00
BIDH Dany Heatley 4.00 10.00
BIEM Evgeni Malkin 10.00 25.00
BIES Eric Staal 6.00 15.00
BIGF Grant Fuhr 10.00 25.00
BIGP Gilbert Perreault 6.00 15.00
BIHA Dominik Hasek 8.00 20.00
BIIK Ilya Kovalchuk 5.00 12.00
BIJG Jean-Sebastien Giguere 5.00 12.00
BIJI Jarome Iginla 6.00 15.00
BIJS Jordan Staal 4.00 10.00
BIJT Joe Thornton 8.00 20.00
BILR Larry Robinson 6.00 15.00
BIMB Mike Bossy 5.00 12.00
BIMD Marcel Dionne 8.00 20.00
BIMG Marian Gaborik 5.00 12.00
BIML Mario Lemieux SP 15.00 40.00
BIMM Mark Messier SP 30.00 60.00
BIMN Markus Naslund 5.00 12.00
BIMO Mike Modano 8.00 20.00
BIMR Michael Ryder 3.00 8.00
BIMS Martin St. Louis 5.00 12.00
BINL Nicklas Lidstrom 5.00 12.00
BIPB Patrice Bergeron 6.00 15.00
BIPR Patrick Roy SP 25.00 60.00
BIRB Ray Bourque 10.00 25.00
BIRG Ryan Getzlaf 5.00 12.00
BIRM Ryan Miller 5.00 12.00
BIRN Rick Nash 5.00 12.00
BISC Sidney Crosby 20.00 50.00
BISD Shane Doan 4.00 10.00
BISG Simon Gagne 5.00 12.00
BISM Stan Mikita 8.00 20.00
BITV Thomas Vanek 4.00 10.00
BIVL Vincent Lecavalier 5.00 12.00
BIVO Tomas Vokoun 4.00 10.00
BIWG Wayne Gretzky SP 40.00 100.00
BIZP Zach Parise 5.00 12.00

2007-08 Upper Deck Ice Black Ice Jerseys Autographs

BIAO A. Ovechkin EXCH 300.00 450.00
BIEM Evgeni Malkin 60.00 120.00
BIES Eric Staal 25.00 60.00
BIHA D. Hasek EXCH 40.00 80.00
BIIK Ilya Kovalchuk 40.00 80.00
BIJI Jarome Iginla 40.00 80.00
BIJT Joe Thornton 30.00 80.00
BILR Larry Robinson 20.00 50.00
BIMG Marian Gaborik 20.00 50.00
BIML Mario Lemieux SP 250.00 350.00
BIMO Mike Modano 40.00 80.00
BIMS Martin St. Louis 20.00 50.00
BIPB Patrice Bergeron 25.00 60.00
BIPR P. Roy SP EXCH 300.00 450.00
BIRB R. Bourque EXCH 30.00 80.00
BIRG Ryan Getzlaf 20.00 50.00
BIRN Rick Nash 40.00 80.00
BISC S. Crosby EXCH 350.00 500.00
BISD Shane Doan 15.00 40.00
BISM Stan Mikita 20.00 50.00
BIVL Vincent Lecavalier 20.00 50.00
BIVO Tomas Vokoun 15.00 40.00
BIWG Wayne Gretzky SP 600.00 1500.00

2007-08 Upper Deck Ice Fresh Threads

*BLACK/25: 1X TO 2.5X BASIC JSY
*PARALLEL/100: .5X TO 1.2X BASIC JSY
*PATCH/25: 1.2X TO 3X BASIC JSY
FTAC Andrew Cogliano 2.50 6.00
FTAG Andy Greene 2.50 6.00
FTBA Nicklas Backstrom 6.00 15.00
FTBD Brandon Dubinsky 4.00 10.00
FTBE Brian Elliott 4.00 10.00
FTBL Bryan Little 2.50 6.00
FTBR Bobby Ryan 6.00 15.00
FTBS Brett Sterling 2.00 5.00
FTCA Ryan Callahan 4.00 10.00
FTCM Curtis McElhinney 3.00 8.00
FTCP Carey Price 12.00 30.00
FTDK David Krejci 6.00 15.00
FTDM Drew Miller 2.50 6.00
FTDP David Perron 4.00 10.00
FTEJ Erik Johnson 3.00 8.00
FTFN Frans Nielsen 3.00 8.00
FTHA Jaroslav Halak 6.00 15.00
FTJA Jannik Hansen 2.50 6.00
FTJB Jonathan Bernier 4.00 10.00
FTJH Jaroslav Hlinka 2.50 6.00
FTJJ Jack Johnson 2.50 6.00
FTJS James Sheppard 2.00 5.00
FTJT Jonathan Toews 12.00 30.00
FTKA Petr Kalus 2.00 5.00
FTKC Kyle Chipchura 3.00 8.00
FTKR Kris Russell 3.00 8.00
FTLT Lauri Tukonen 2.00 5.00
FTMH Martin Hanzal 2.50 6.00
FTML Milan Lucic 8.00 20.00
FTMN Matt Niskanen 3.00 8.00
FTMR Mason Raymond 3.00 8.00
FTMS Matt Smaby 2.00 5.00
FTNB Nicklas Bergfors 2.00 5.00

FTNF Nick Foligno 4.00 10.00
FTPK Patrick Kane 10.00 25.00
FTPM Peter Mueller 2.50 6.00
FTRC Ryan Carter 2.00 5.00
FTRP Ryan Parent 2.00 5.00
FTRS Rob Schremp 2.50 6.00
FTSG Sam Gagner 4.00 10.00
FTTG Tom Gilbert 2.50 6.00
FTTM Torrey Mitchell 2.50 6.00

2007-08 Upper Deck Ice Frozen Fabrics

*BLACK/25: .8X TO 2X BASIC JSY
*PATCH/25: 1X TO 2.5X BASIC JSY
FFAE David Aebischer 3.00 8.00
FFAH Ales Hemsky 3.00 8.00
FFAO Alexander Ovechkin 15.00 40.00
FFAT Alex Tanguay 3.00 8.00
FFBB Brad Boyes 2.50 6.00
FFBR Brad Richards 4.00 10.00
FFBS Brendan Shanahan 4.00 10.00
FFCD Chris Drury 3.00 8.00
FFDA Daniel Alfredsson 4.00 10.00
FFDB Daniel Briere 4.00 10.00
FFDH Dany Heatley 3.00 8.00
FFDR Dwayne Roloson 3.00 8.00
FFDW Doug Weight 4.00 10.00
FFES Eric Staal 5.00 12.00
FFHE Milan Hejduk 3.00 8.00
FFHZ Henrik Zetterberg 5.00 12.00
FFIK Ilya Kovalchuk 4.00 10.00
FFJB Jay Bouwmeester 2.50 6.00
FFJG Jean-Sebastien Giguere 4.00 10.00
FFJI Jarome Iginla 5.00 12.00
FFJJ Jaromir Jagr 12.00 30.00
FFJS Jason Spezza 4.00 10.00
FFJT Joe Thornton 6.00 15.00
FFKL Kari Lehtonen 3.00 8.00
FFKT Keith Tkachuk 4.00 10.00
FFMB Martin Brodeur 10.00 25.00
FFMG Marian Gaborik 4.00 10.00
FFMH Marian Hossa 4.00 10.00
FFMK Miikka Kiprusoff 4.00 10.00
FFMN Markus Naslund 4.00 10.00
FFMS Mats Sundin 4.00 10.00
FFPB Patrice Bergeron 5.00 12.00
FFPD Pavel Datsyuk 6.00 15.00
FFPF Peter Forsberg 8.00 20.00
FFPK Paul Kariya 4.00 10.00
FFPM Patrick Marleau 4.00 10.00
FFRL Roberto Luongo 6.00 15.00
FFRS Ryan Smyth 3.00 8.00
FFSA Joe Sakic 8.00 20.00
FFSC Sidney Crosby 15.00 40.00
FFSF Sergei Fedorov 6.00 15.00
FFZP Zach Parise 4.00 10.00

2007-08 Upper Deck Ice Glacial Graphs

GGAK Anze Kopitar 12.00 30.00
GGAO Adam Oates 8.00 20.00
GGAR Alexander Radulov 8.00 20.00
GGAT Alex Tanguay 6.00 15.00
GGBC Blake Comeau 5.00 12.00
GGBD Brandon Dubinsky 10.00 25.00
GGBH Bobby Hull SP 15.00 40.00
GGBO Dustin Boyd 5.00 12.00
GGCA Mike Cammalleri 6.00 15.00
GGCH Cristobal Huet 6.00 15.00
GGCM Clarke MacArthur 5.00 12.00
GGCP Chris Phillips 5.00 12.00
GGCW Cam Ward 8.00 20.00
GGDB Dustin Brown 8.00 20.00
GGDH Dany Heatley 6.00 15.00
GGDS Drew Stafford 5.00 12.00
GGDT Darcy Tucker 6.00 15.00
GGEM Evgeni Malkin 15.00 40.00
GGES Eric Staal 10.00 25.00
GGGA Simon Gagne 8.00 20.00
GGGH Gordie Howe SP 60.00 150.00
GGHA Dominik Hasek SP 12.00 30.00
GGHL Henrik Lundqvist 20.00 50.00
GGIK Ilya Kovalchuk 8.00 20.00
GGIW Ian White 5.00 12.00
GGJC Jonathan Cheechoo 6.00 15.00
GGJG Jean-Sebastien Giguere 8.00 20.00
GGJI Jarome Iginla 10.00 25.00
GGJJ Jack Johnson 6.00 15.00
GGJL John-Michael Liles 5.00 12.00
GGJS Jarret Stoll 6.00 15.00
GGJT Joe Thornton SP 12.00 30.00
GGJW Jeremy Williams 5.00 12.00
GGKB Kevin Bieksa 6.00 15.00
GGKD Kris Draper 5.00 12.00
GGKE Phil Kessel 8.00 20.00
GGLT Lauri Tukonen 5.00 12.00
GGMA Martin St. Louis 8.00 20.00
GGMB Martin Brodeur SP 25.00 60.00
GGMC Matt Carle 5.00 12.00
GGMF Marc-Andre Fleury 15.00 40.00
GGMG Marian Gaborik 8.00 20.00
GGMI Miroslav Satan 6.00 15.00
GGML Mario Lemieux SP 60.00 150.00
GGMM Mark Messier SP 15.00 40.00
GGMN Markus Naslund 8.00 20.00
GGMO Mike Modano 12.00 30.00
GGMP Marc-Antoine Pouliot 5.00 12.00
GGMR Michael Ryder 5.00 12.00
GGMS Marek Schwarz 8.00 20.00
GGMT Marty Turco 8.00 20.00
GGNL Nicklas Lidstrom 8.00 20.00
GGNW Noah Welch 5.00 12.00
GGOV Alexander Ovechkin SP 30.00 80.00
GGPB Patrice Bergeron 30.00 80.00
GGPE Corey Perry 12.00 30.00
GGPI Pierre-Marc Bouchard 8.00 20.00
GGPK Petr Kalus 5.00 12.00
GGPO Patrick O'Sullivan 6.00 15.00
GGPR Patrick Roy SP 60.00 150.00
GGRA Andrew Raycroft 6.00 15.00
GGRI Mike Richards 6.00 15.00
GGRM Ryan Miller 8.00 20.00
GGRN Rick Nash 8.00 20.00
GGRP Ryan Parent 5.00 12.00
GGRS Rob Schremp 6.00 15.00
GGRY Ryan Potulny 5.00 12.00
GGSA Marc Savard 5.00 12.00
GGSB Steve Bernier 5.00 12.00
GGSC Sidney Crosby SP 60.00 150.00
GGSD Shane Doan 6.00 15.00
GGSG Scott Gomez 6.00 15.00
GGSK Saku Koivu SP 8.00 20.00
GGST Jordan Staal 6.00 15.00
GGSW Shea Weber 6.00 15.00
GGTH Jose Theodore 8.00 20.00
GGTV Tomas Vokoun 6.00 15.00
GGVF Valtteri Filppula 5.00 12.00
GGVL Vincent Lecavalier 8.00 20.00
GGWG Wayne Gretzky SP 300.00 800.00
GGWI Justin Williams 6.00 15.00
GGWW Wojtek Wolski 6.00 15.00

2007-08 Upper Deck Ice Signature Swatches

SSAO Alexander Ovechkin 50.00 120.00
SSBB Brad Boyes 8.00 20.00
SSCW Cam Ward 12.00 30.00
SSDH Dany Heatley 10.00 25.00
SSDS Drew Stafford 8.00 20.00
SSES Eric Staal 15.00 40.00
SSGA Simon Gagne 12.00 30.00
SSIK Ilya Kovalchuk 12.00 30.00
SSJC Jonathan Cheechoo 10.00 25.00
SSJI Jarome Iginla 15.00 40.00
SSJL Joffrey Lupul 8.00 20.00
SSJP Joni Pitkanen 8.00 20.00
SSJT Joe Thornton 20.00 50.00
SSJW Justin Williams 10.00 25.00
SSMB Martin Brodeur 30.00 80.00
SSMC Mike Cammalleri 10.00 25.00
SSMG Marian Gaborik 12.00 30.00
SSML M. Lemieux EXCH 50.00 125.00
SSMM Mike Modano 20.00 50.00
SSMN Markus Naslund 12.00 30.00
SSMS Martin St. Louis 12.00 30.00
SSMT Marty Turco 12.00 30.00
SSNL Nicklas Lidstrom 12.00 30.00
SSPB Patrice Bergeron 15.00 40.00
SSPK Phil Kessel 12.00 30.00
SSPR Patrick Roy 30.00 80.00
SSRM Ryan Miller 12.00 30.00
SSRN Rick Nash 12.00 30.00
SSSC Sidney Crosby 80.00 200.00
SSSG Scott Gomez 10.00 25.00
SSTH Tomas Holmstrom 10.00 25.00
SSTV Tomas Vokoun 10.00 25.00
SSVL Vincent Lecavalier 12.00 30.00
SSWG Wayne Gretzky 400.00 1000.00

2008-09 Upper Deck Ice

COMP.SET w/o SPs (100) 12.00 30.00
1 Ales Hemsky .40 1.00
2 Alex Kovalev .40 1.00
3 Alex Tanguay .30 .75
4 Alexander Frolov .30 .75
5 Alexander Ovechkin 2.00 5.00
6 Anze Kopitar .75 2.00
7 Brad Boyes .30 .75
8 Brad Richards .50 1.25
9 Alexander Semin .50 1.25
10 Brenden Morrow .40 1.00
11 Cam Ward .50 1.25
12 Carey Price 1.00 2.50
13 Chris Drury .40 1.00
14 Chris Osgood .50 1.25
15 Chris Pronger .50 1.25
16 Corey Perry .75 2.00
17 Cristobal Huet .40 1.00
18 Dan Ellis .30 .75
19 Daniel Alfredsson .50 1.25
20 Daniel Briere .50 1.25
21 Daniel Carcillo .30 .75
22 Daniel Sedin .60 1.50
23 Dany Heatley .40 1.00
24 Derek Roy .30 .75
25 Dion Phaneuf .40 1.00
26 Eric Staal .60 1.50
27 Evgeni Malkin 1.00 2.50
28 Evgeni Nabokov .40 1.00
29 Henrik Lundqvist 1.25 3.00
30 Henrik Zetterberg .60 1.50
31 Ilya Kovalchuk .50 1.25
32 J.P. Dumont .30 .75
33 Jarome Iginla .60 1.50
34 Jason Arnott .40 1.00
35 Jason Pominville .30 .75
36 Jason Spezza .50 1.25
37 Jean-Sebastien Giguere .50 1.25
38 Joe Sakic 1.00 2.50
39 Joe Thornton .75 2.00
40 Jonathan Cheechoo .40 1.00
41 Jonathan Toews .75 2.00
42 Joni Pitkanen .30 .75
43 Jordan Staal .40 1.00
44 Kari Lehtonen .60 1.50
45 Manny Legace .50 1.25
46 Marc Savard .30 .75
47 Marc-Andre Fleury 1.00 2.50
48 Marek Svatos .30 .75
49 Marian Gaborik .50 1.25
50 Markus Naslund .50 1.25
51 Martin Biron .40 1.00
52 Martin Brodeur 1.25 3.00
53 Martin St. Louis .50 1.25
54 Marty Turco .50 1.25
55 Mikhail Grabovski .30 .75
56 Miikka Kiprusoff .50 1.25
57 Mike Comrie .40 1.00
58 Mike Green .40 1.00
59 Mike Modano .75 2.00
60 Mike Ribeiro .30 .75
61 Mike Richards .40 1.00
62 Milan Hejduk .40 1.00
63 Nathan Horton .40 1.00
64 Nicklas Backstrom .50 1.25
65 Nicklas Lidstrom .50 1.25
66 Nikolai Zherdev .30 .75
67 Olli Jokinen .40 1.00
68 Patrice Bergeron .60 1.50
69 Patrick Kane 1.00 2.50
70 Patrick Sharp .50 1.25
71 Patrik Elias .50 1.25
72 Paul Kariya .50 1.25
73 Paul Martin .30 .75
74 Paul Stastny .40 1.00
75 Pavel Datsyuk .75 2.00
76 Peter Mueller .40 1.00
77 Phil Kessel .50 1.25
78 Pierre-Marc Bouchard .50 1.25
79 Rick DiPietro .40 1.00
80 Rick Nash .50 1.25
81 Roberto Luongo .75 2.00
82 Ryan Getzlaf .50 1.25
83 Ryan Miller .50 1.25
84 Saku Koivu .50 1.25
85 Sam Gagner .30 .75
86 Sean Avery .30 .75
87 Shane Doan .40 1.00
88 Shawn Horcoff .30 .75
89 Sidney Crosby 2.00 5.00
90 Simon Gagne .50 1.25
91 Thomas Vanek .40 1.00
92 Tim Thomas .50 1.25
93 Tobias Enstrom .30 .75
94 Tomas Kaberle .30 .75
95 Tomas Vokoun .40 1.00
96 Vesa Toskala .60 1.50
97 Vincent Lecavalier .50 1.25
98 Wade Redden .30 .75
99 Zach Parise .50 1.25
100 Zdeno Chara .50 1.25
101 Jack Hillen RC 2.00 5.00
102 Mark Fistric RC 2.00 5.00
103 Tom Cavanagh RC 2.00 5.00
104 Dane Byers RC 2.00 5.00
105 Dwight Helminen RC 2.50 6.00
106 Jason Garrison RC 2.50 6.00
107 Pierre-Luc Letourneau-Leblond RC 1.50 4.00
108 Tyler Sloan RC 3.00 8.00
109 Simeon Varlamov RC 6.00 15.00
110 Janne Pesonen RC 2.00 5.00
111 Brad Staubitz RC 2.00 5.00
112 Patrick Davis RC 2.00 5.00
113 Cam Paddock RC 1.50 4.00
114 Karl Alzner RC 1.50 4.00
115 John Curry RC 2.50 6.00
116 Zack Smith RC 2.00 5.00
117 Jonathon Kalinski RC 2.50 6.00
118 Tim Sestito RC 2.00 5.00
119 Joey Crabb RC 2.00 5.00
120 Andre Deveaux RC 2.50 6.00
121 Alexandre Bolduc RC 2.00 5.00
122 Brian Boyle RC 2.50 6.00
123 Mike Brown RC 3.00 8.00
124 Ben Maxwell RC 3.00 8.00
125 Matt D'Agostini RC 2.50 6.00
126 Robbie Earl RC 2.00 5.00
127 Jonathan Ericsson RC 3.00 8.00
128 Erik Ersberg RC 2.50 6.00
129 Justin Pogge RC 2.50 6.00
130 Cory Schneider RC 8.00 20.00
131 Jonas Frogren RC 2.00 5.00
132 Alex Goligoski RC 4.00 10.00
133 Shawn Matthias RC 3.00 8.00
134 John Mitchell RC 2.50 6.00
135 Brian Lee RC 2.50 6.00
136 Adam Pardy RC 2.50 6.00
137 Theo Peckham RC 2.50 6.00
138 Teddy Purcell RC 2.50 6.00
139 Mattias Ritola RC 2.50 6.00
140 Tom Sestito RC 3.00 8.00
141 Ryan Stone RC 2.00 5.00
142 Ilya Zubov RC 2.50 6.00
143 T.J. Oshie RC 8.00 20.00
144 Andreas Nodl RC 2.50 6.00
145 Kyle Okposo RC 5.00 12.00
146 Vladimir Mihalik RC 2.50 6.00
147 Darroll Powe RC 4.00 10.00
148 Alex Pietrangelo RC 6.00 15.00
149 Patrik Berglund RC 3.00 8.00
150 Steve Mason RC 6.00 15.00
151 Wayne Simmonds RC 6.00 15.00
152 Drew Doughty RC 10.00 25.00
153 Kevin Porter RC 3.00 8.00
154 Ryan Jones RC 4.00 10.00
155 Matthew Halischuk RC 2.50 6.00
156 Luca Sbisa RC 2.50 6.00
157 Oscar Moller RC 3.00 8.00
158 Patric Hornqvist RC 4.00 10.00
159 Jamie McGinn RC 4.00 10.00
160 Petr Vrana RC 2.50 6.00
161 Claude Giroux RC 15.00 40.00
162 Derek Dorsett RC 5.00 12.00
163 Lauri Korpikoski RC 2.50 6.00
164 Steve MacIntyre RC 4.00 10.00
165 Nikolai Kulemin RC 4.00 10.00
166 Viktor Tikhonov RC 3.00 8.00
167 Justin Abdelkader RC 6.00 15.00
168 Ben Bishop RC 6.00 15.00
169 Jakub Voracek RC 50.00 100.00
170 Josh Bailey RC 25.00 60.00
171 Mikkel Boedker RC 25.00 60.00
172 James Neal RC 30.00 80.00
173 Derick Brassard RC 25.00 60.00
174 Zach Boychuk RC 15.00 40.00
175 Nikita Filatov RC 25.00 60.00
176 Colton Gillies RC 15.00 40.00
177 Luke Schenn RC 40.00 100.00
178 Blake Wheeler RC 40.00 100.00
179 Brandon Sutter RC 25.00 60.00
180 Kyle Turris RC 40.00 80.00
181 Michael Frolik RC 20.00 50.00
182 Fabian Brunnstrom RC 15.00 40.00
183 Zach Bogosian RC 25.00 60.00
184 Steven Stamkos RC 200.00 500.00

2008-09 Upper Deck Ice Fresh Threads

FTAG Alex Goligoski 4.00 10.00
FTAN Andreas Nodl 2.00 5.00
FTAP Alex Pietrangelo 5.00 12.00
FTBB Brian Boyle 2.50 6.00
FTBL Brian Lee 2.50 6.00
FTBO Zach Bogosian 4.00 10.00
FTBS Brandon Sutter 3.00 8.00
FTBW Blake Wheeler 8.00 20.00
FTCG Colton Gillies 2.50 6.00
FTDB Derick Brassard 3.00 8.00
FTDD Drew Doughty 8.00 20.00
FTFB Fabian Brunnstrom 2.50 6.00
FTFI Mark Fistric 2.50 6.00
FTGI Claude Giroux 6.00 15.00
FTIZ Ilya Zubov 2.50 6.00
FTJA Justin Abdelkader 5.00 12.00
FTJE Jonathan Ericsson 3.00 8.00
FTJF Jon Filewich 2.50 6.00
FTJN James Neal 6.00 15.00
FTJV Jakub Voracek 6.00 15.00
FTKO Kyle Okposo 4.00 10.00
FTKP Kevin Porter 2.50 6.00
FTKT Kyle Turris 5.00 12.00
FTLK Lauri Korpikoski 2.00 5.00
FTLS Luke Schenn 4.00 10.00
FTMA Steve Mason 5.00 12.00
FTMB Mikkel Boedker 4.00 10.00
FTMF Michael Frolik 3.00 8.00
FTMH Matthew Halischuk 2.00 5.00
FTNF Nikita Filatov 3.00 8.00
FTNK Nikolai Kulemin 3.00 8.00
FTOM Oscar Moller 2.50 6.00
FTPB Patrik Berglund 2.50 6.00
FTPH Patric Hornqvist 3.00 8.00
FTPV Petr Vrana 2.00 5.00
FTSB Luca Sbisa 2.00 5.00
FTSM Shawn Matthias 3.00 8.00
FTSS Steven Stamkos 12.00 30.00
FTTO T.J. Oshie 6.00 15.00
FTVM Vladimir Mihalik 2.00 5.00
FTVT Viktor Tikhonov 2.50 6.00
FTZB Zach Boychuk 3.00 8.00

2008-09 Upper Deck Ice Fresh Threads Black Parallel

*BLACK: .6X TO 1.5X BASE

2008-09 Upper Deck Ice Fresh Threads Parallel

*PARALLEL: .5X TO 1.2X BASE

2008-09 Upper Deck Ice Fresh Threads Patches

*PATCHES: .8X TO 2X BASE

2008-09 Upper Deck Ice Frozen Fabrics

FFAK Alex Kovalev 4.00 10.00
FFBD Brendan Shanahan 5.00 12.00
FFDG Doug Gilmour 6.00 15.00
FFDP Dion Phaneuf 4.00 10.00
FFEM Evgeni Malkin 8.00 20.00
FFES Eric Staal 6.00 15.00
FFFV Sergei Fedorov 8.00 20.00
FFGZ Scott Gomez 4.00 10.00
FFHW Dale Hawerchuk 6.00 15.00
FFIK Ilya Kovalchuk 5.00 12.00
FFJC Jonathan Cheechoo 4.00 10.00
FFJJ Joe Sakic 10.00 25.00
FFKL Kari Lehtonen 6.00 15.00
FFLR Larry Robinson 5.00 12.00
FFLW Rod Langway 4.00 10.00
FFMB Martin Brodeur 12.00 30.00
FFMH Marian Hossa 5.00 12.00
FFMK Mikko Koivu 4.00 10.00
FFMS Mats Sundin 5.00 12.00
FFNL Nicklas Lidstrom 5.00 12.00
FFOK Olaf Kolzig 5.00 12.00
FFOV Alexander Ovechkin 20.00 50.00
FFPE Patrik Elias 5.00 12.00
FFPF Peter Forsberg 10.00 25.00
FFPK Paul Kariya 5.00 12.00
FFPL Pascal Leclaire 4.00 10.00
FFPS Peter Stastny 4.00 10.00
FFRD Rod Brind`Amour 5.00 12.00
FFRN Rick Nash 5.00 12.00
FFSC Sidney Crosby 20.00 50.00
FFSD Shane Doan 4.00 10.00
FFSG Simon Gagne 5.00 12.00
FFSS Steve Shutt 5.00 12.00
FFST Jordan Staal 4.00 10.00
FFTB Todd Bertuzzi 5.00 12.00
FFTR Tuomo Ruutu 5.00 12.00
FFTS Teemu Selanne 10.00 25.00
FFVT Vesa Toskala 6.00 15.00
FFWB Shea Weber 4.00 10.00
FFWR Wade Redden 3.00 8.00
FFWW Wojtek Wolski 4.00 10.00
FFZP Zach Parise 5.00 12.00

2008-09 Upper Deck Ice Frozen Fabrics Black Parallel

*BLACK: .6X TO 1.5X BASE

2008-09 Upper Deck Ice Frozen Fabrics Parallel

*PARALLEL: .5X TO 1.2X BASE

2008-09 Upper Deck Ice Frozen Fabrics Patches

*PATCHES: 1X TO 2.5X BASE

2008-09 Upper Deck Ice Glacial Graphs

GGAE Alexander Edler 5.00 12.00
GGAP Alex Pietrangelo 12.00 30.00
GGAR Andrew Raycroft 6.00 15.00
GGCA Jeff Carter 6.00 15.00
GGCM Cory Murphy 5.00 12.00
GGDA Daniel Paille 5.00 12.00
GGDC Dan Cleary 6.00 15.00
GGDD Drew Doughty 20.00 50.00
GGDH Eddie Shack 8.00 20.00
GGDJ David Jones 5.00 12.00
GGDS Devin Setoguchi 6.00 15.00
GGEM Evgeni Malkin 15.00 40.00
GGES Eric Staal 10.00 25.00
GGHS Henrik Sedin 10.00 25.00
GGJH Jonas Hiller 6.00 15.00
GGJL Joffrey Lupul 5.00 12.00
GGJP Jason Pominville 5.00 12.00
GGJS Jordan Staal 6.00 15.00
GGJT Joe Thornton 12.00 30.00
GGJV Jakub Voracek 12.00 30.00
GGKC Kyle Chipchura 6.00 15.00
GGLS Luke Schenn 25.00 60.00
GGMB Mikkel Boedker 15.00 40.00
GGMC Marty McSorley 6.00 15.00
GGMF Marc-Andre Fleury 10.00 25.00
GGMH Milan Hejduk 6.00 15.00
GGMN Matt Niskanen 6.00 15.00
GGMT Maxime Talbot 5.00 12.00
GGND Nigel Dawes 5.00 12.00
GGNH Nathan Horton 6.00 15.00
GGNZ Nikolai Zherdev 5.00 12.00
GGOR Bobby Orr 75.00 135.00
GGPA Patrick Kane 15.00 40.00
GGPM Peter Mueller 6.00 15.00
GGPN Dustin Penner 6.00 15.00
GGPR Carey Price 20.00 50.00
GGRG Ryan Getzlaf 8.00 20.00
GGRL Rod Langway 6.00 15.00
GGRO Rob Schremp 6.00 15.00
GGRP Rod Pelley 5.00 12.00
GGSB Steve Bernier 5.00 12.00
GGSC Sidney Crosby 100.00 175.00
GGSE Daniel Sedin 6.00 15.00
GGSS Steven Stamkos 40.00 100.00
GGTH Tomas Holmstrom 6.00 15.00
GGTK Tyler Kennedy 6.00 15.00
GGTL Jiri Tlusty 5.00 12.00
GGTV Tomas Vokoun 6.00 15.00
GGTW Jonathan Toews 20.00 50.00
GGWG Wayne Gretzky 200.00 500.00
GGZB Zach Bogosian 10.00 25.00
GGZB2 Henrik Zetterberg 10.00 25.00

2008-09 Upper Deck Ice Pride of Canada

GOLD1 Bobby Clarke 12.00 30.00
GOLD2 Bobby Hull 15.00 40.00
GOLD3 Bobby Orr 30.00 80.00
GOLD4 Bryan Trottier 8.00 20.00
GOLD5 Darryl Sittler 10.00 25.00
GOLD6 Denis Potvin 8.00 20.00
GOLD7 Gilbert Perreault 8.00 20.00
GOLD8 Guy Lafleur 10.00 25.00
GOLD9 Jarome Iginla 10.00 25.00
GOLD10 Joe Sakic 15.00 40.00
GOLD11 Jonathan Toews 12.00 30.00
GOLD12 Marcel Dionne 10.00 25.00
GOLD13 Mario Lemieux 30.00 80.00
GOLD14 Martin Brodeur 20.00 50.00
GOLD15 Mike Bossy 8.00 20.00
GOLD16 Dany Heatley 6.00 15.00
GOLD17 Paul Coffey 10.00 25.00
GOLD18 Phil Esposito 12.00 30.00
GOLD19 Sidney Crosby 40.00 100.00
GOLD20 Steve Yzerman 20.00 50.00
GOLD21 Wayne Gretzky 75.00 150.00

2008-09 Upper Deck Ice Signature Swatches

SSJBN Bernie Nicholls 10.00 25.00
SSJCP Carey Price 25.00 60.00
SSJEM Evgeni Malkin 25.00 60.00
SSJGC Guy Carbonneau 12.00 30.00
SSJGH Gordie Howe 75.00 150.00
SSJGO Scott Gomez 10.00 25.00
SSJJF Jon Filewich 10.00 25.00
SSJJT Jonathan Toews 25.00 60.00
SSJKT Kyle Turris 20.00 50.00
SSJLR Luc Robitaille 12.00 30.00
SSJLX Mario Lemieux 60.00 120.00
SSJMA Shawn Matthias 12.00 30.00
SSJNZ Nikolai Zherdev 8.00 20.00
SSJPR Patrick Roy 30.00 80.00
SSJRE Robbie Earl 8.00 20.00
SSJRH Ron Hextall 12.00 30.00
SSJRL Rod Langway 10.00 25.00
SSJRS Ryan Stone 8.00 20.00
SSJSC Sidney Crosby 100.00 200.00
SSJSM Steve Mason 15.00 40.00
SSJTK Tuukka Rask 15.00 40.00
SSJZB Ilya Zubov 10.00 25.00

2008-09 Upper Deck Ice Stanley Cup Foundations

SCFAM Al MacInnis 10.00 25.00
SCFBH Bobby Hull 15.00 40.00
SCFBO Bobby Orr 30.00 80.00
SCFGH Gordie Howe 25.00 60.00
SCFGL Guy Lafleur 10.00 25.00
SCFHZ Henrik Zetterberg 10.00 25.00
SCFJB Jean Beliveau 8.00 20.00
SCFJK Jari Kurri 8.00 20.00
SCFJS Joe Sakic 15.00 40.00
SCFLM Lanny McDonald 8.00 20.00
SCFLR Larry Robinson 8.00 20.00
SCFMB Martin Brodeur 20.00 50.00
SCFMI Mike Bossy 8.00 20.00
SCFML Mario Lemieux 30.00 80.00
SCFMM Mark Messier 15.00 40.00
SCFMO Mike Modano 12.00 30.00
SCFNL Nicklas Lidstrom 8.00 20.00
SCFPF Peter Forsberg 15.00 40.00
SCFPR Patrick Roy 20.00 50.00
SCFSN Scott Niedermayer 6.00 15.00
SCFWG Wayne Gretzky 50.00 125.00

2009-10 Upper Deck Ice

COMP.SET w/o SPS (100) 15.00 40.00
1 Zdeno Chara .50 1.25
2 Patrice Bergeron .60 1.50
3 Tim Thomas .50 1.25
4 Marc Savard .30 .75
5 Alexander Ovechkin 2.00 5.00
6 Alexander Semin .50 1.25
7 Mike Green .40 1.00
8 Nicklas Backstrom .50 1.25
9 Martin Brodeur 1.25 3.00
10 Zach Parise .50 1.25
11 Patrik Elias .50 1.25
12 Sidney Crosby 2.00 5.00
13 Evgeni Malkin 1.00 2.50
14 Jordan Staal .40 1.00
15 Marc-Andre Fleury 1.00 2.50
16 Simon Gagne .50 1.25
17 Mike Richards .40 1.00
18 Jeff Carter .40 1.00
19 Daniel Briere .50 1.25
20 Eric Staal .60 1.50
21 Cam Ward .50 1.25
22 Jussi Jokinen .30 .75
23 Henrik Lundqvist 1.25 3.00
24 Marian Gaborik .50 1.25
25 Chris Drury .40 1.00
26 Sean Avery .40 1.00
27 Carey Price 1.00 2.50
28 Scott Gomez .40 1.00
29 Andrei Markov .50 1.25
30 Nathan Horton .50 1.25
31 Tomas Vokoun .40 1.00
32 David Booth .30 .75
33 Thomas Vanek .60 1.50
34 Ryan Miller .50 1.25
35 Jason Pominville .30 .75
36 Derek Roy .30 .75
37 Jason Spezza .50 1.25
38 Jonathan Cheechoo .40 1.00
39 Daniel Alfredsson .50 1.25
40 Luke Schenn .50 1.25
41 Mikhail Grabovski .30 .75
42 Vesa Toskala .50 1.25
43 Phil Kessel .50 1.25
44 Ilya Kovalchuk .50 1.25
45 Kari Lehtonen .40 1.00
46 Bryan Little .50 1.25
47 Vincent Lecavalier .50 1.25
48 Martin St. Louis .50 1.25
49 Steven Stamkos 1.00 2.50
50 Doug Weight .50 1.25
51 Rick DiPietro .40 1.00
52 Kyle Okposo .30 .75
53 Joe Thornton .75 2.00
54 Patrick Marleau .50 1.25
55 Evgeni Nabokov .40 1.00
56 Dany Heatley .40 1.00
57 Henrik Zetterberg .60 1.50
58 Nicklas Lidstrom .30 .75
59 Pavel Datsyuk .75 2.00
60 Chris Osgood .50 1.25
61 Roberto Luongo .75 2.00
62 Ryan Kesler .50 1.25
63 Daniel Sedin .60 1.50
64 Henrik Sedin .60 1.50
65 Patrick Kane 1.00 2.50
66 Jonathan Toews .75 2.00
67 Brian Campbell .40 1.00
68 Marian Hossa .50 1.25
69 Jarome Iginla .60 1.50
70 Dion Phaneuf .40 1.00
71 Olli Jokinen .40 1.00
72 Miikka Kiprusoff .50 1.25
73 David Perron .40 1.00
74 Paul Kariya .50 1.25
75 Patrik Berglund .30 .75
76 Rick Nash .50 1.25
77 Steve Mason .40 1.00
78 Derick Brassard .30 .75
79 Ryan Getzlaf .50 1.25
80 Bobby Ryan .40 1.00
81 Saku Koivu .50 1.25
82 Mikko Koivu .50 1.25
83 Niklas Backstrom .50 1.25
84 Owen Nolan .50 1.25
85 Jason Arnott .40 1.00
86 Pekka Rinne .50 1.25
87 Shea Weber .40 1.00
88 Sam Gagner .30 .75
89 Andrew Cogliano .30 .75
90 Nikolai Khabibulin .50 1.25
91 James Neal .30 .75
92 Mike Ribeiro .30 .75
93 Marty Turco .50 1.25
94 Shane Doan .40 1.00
95 Peter Mueller .40 1.00
96 Drew Doughty .60 1.50
97 Anze Kopitar .75 2.00
98 Paul Stastny .40 1.00
99 Wojtek Wolski .30 .75
100 Milan Hejduk .40 1.00
101 Scott Parse RC 2.50 6.00
102 Phil Oreskovic RC 2.50 6.00
103 Andreas Thuresson RC 2.00 5.00
104 Philippe Dupuis RC 2.50 6.00
105 Jaime Sifers RC 2.00 5.00
106 Matt Hendricks RC 2.00 5.00
107 Teemu Laakso RC 1.50 4.00
108 Ilkka Pikkarainen RC 2.50 6.00
109 Grant Lewis RC 2.00 5.00
110 Peter Olvecky RC 2.50 6.00
111 Byron Bitz RC 2.00 5.00
112 John Scott RC 2.50 6.00
113 Francis Wathier RC 2.00 5.00
114 James Reimer RC 10.00 25.00
115 Peter Regin RC 2.00 5.00
116 Matt Climie RC 2.00 5.00
117 Taylor Chorney RC 2.50 6.00
118 Davis Drewiske RC 2.50 6.00
119 Mika Pyorala RC 2.00 5.00
120 Victor Oreskovich RC 2.00 5.00
121 Tom Wandell RC 2.50 6.00
122 Michal Neuvirth RC 5.00 12.00
123 Mathieu Carle RC 3.00 8.00
124 Lars Eller RC 3.00 8.00
125 Alexander Salak RC 2.50 6.00
126 John Negrin RC 3.00 8.00
127 Aaron Gagnon RC 2.00 5.00
128 Mario Bliznak RC 3.00 8.00
129 Anton Khudobin RC 5.00 12.00
130 Jakub Kindl RC 3.00 8.00
131 Matthew Corrente RC 2.50 6.00
132 Steven Zalewski RC 2.50 6.00
133 David Laliberte RC 2.50 6.00
134 Bobby Sanguinetti RC 2.00 5.00
135 Devan Dubnyk RC 5.00 12.00
136 Matt Pelech RC 3.00 8.00
137 Alexander Sulzer RC 2.00 5.00
138 Frazer McLaren RC 2.50 6.00
139 Michael Sauer RC 2.50 6.00
140 Ryan Wilson RC 3.00 8.00
141 Danny Irmen RC 2.00 5.00
142 Braden Holtby RC 15.00 25.00
143 Brian Salcido RC 2.50 6.00
144 Luca Caputi RC 4.00 10.00
145 Spencer Machacek RC 4.00 10.00
146 T.J. Galiardi RC 4.00 10.00
147 Yannick Weber RC 4.00 10.00
148 Christian Hanson RC 4.00 10.00
149 Jhonas Enroth RC 5.00 12.00
150 Ivan Vishnevskiy RC 2.50 6.00
151 Riku Helenius RC 4.00 10.00
152 Kris Chucko RC 2.50 6.00
153 Perttu Lindgren RC 3.00 8.00
154 Ryan O'Reilly RC 8.00 20.00
155 Dmitry Kulikov RC 4.00 10.00
156 Matt Gilroy RC 4.00 10.00
157 Sergei Shirokov RC 2.50 6.00
158 Benn Ferriero RC 4.00 10.00
159 Alec Martinez RC 5.00 12.00
160 Erik Karlsson RC 25.00 50.00
161 Cal O'Reilly RC 3.00 8.00
162 Matt Beleskey RC 3.00 8.00
163 Ville Leino RC 3.00 8.00
164 Artem Anisimov RC 2.50 6.00
165 Antti Niemi RC 12.50 25.00
166 Jason Demers RC 6.00 15.00
167 Cody Franson RC 4.00 10.00
168 Ray Macias RC 3.00 8.00
169 Tyler Myers RC 30.00 80.00
170 Jamie Benn RC 150.00 225.00
171 Michael Del Zotto RC 25.00 60.00
172 Brad Marchand RC 40.00 80.00
173 Mikael Backlund RC 30.00 60.00
174 Tyler Bozak RC 30.00 60.00
175 Logan Couture RC 60.00 100.00
176 Michael Grabner RC 30.00 60.00
177 Viktor Stalberg RC 20.00 50.00
178 Jonas Gustavsson RC 25.00 50.00
179 Colin Wilson RC 20.00 50.00
180 James van Riemsdyk RC 125.00 200.00
181 Evander Kane RC 50.00 100.00
182 Victor Hedman RC 50.00 125.00
183 Matt Duchene RC 100.00 200.00
184 John Tavares RC 350.00 600.00

2009-10 Upper Deck Ice Fresh Threads

FTAA Artem Anisimov 3.00 8.00
FTAC Andrew Cogliano 3.00 8.00
FTAN Antti Niemi 8.00 20.00
FTBA Mikael Backlund 8.00 20.00
FTBF Benn Ferriero 5.00 12.00
FTBW Blake Wheeler 5.00 12.00
FTCB Chris Butler 5.00 12.00
FTCF Cody Franson 5.00 12.00
FTCG Claude Giroux 5.00 12.00
FTCW Colin Wilson 5.00 12.00
FTDD Drew Doughty 6.00 15.00
FTDK Dmitry Kulikov 5.00 12.00
FTDS Drew Stafford 3.00 8.00
FTDU Matt Duchene 12.00 30.00
FTEK Erik Karlsson 10.00 25.00
FTIV Ivan Vishnevskiy 3.00 8.00
FTJB Jamie Benn 15.00 40.00
FTJE Jhonas Enroth 6.00 15.00
FTJG Jonas Gustavsson 8.00 20.00
FTJT John Tavares 15.00 40.00
FTJV Jakub Voracek 4.00 10.00
FTKA Evander Kane 8.00 20.00
FTKC Kris Chucko 3.00 8.00
FTLC Luca Caputi 5.00 12.00
FTMD Michael Del Zotto 5.00 12.00
FTMG Michael Grabner 5.00 12.00
FTPL Perttu Lindgren 4.00 10.00
FTPO Patrick O'Sullivan 4.00 10.00
FTRH Riku Helenius 5.00 12.00
FTRO Ryan O'Reilly 10.00 25.00
FTSM Spencer Machacek 5.00 12.00
FTSS Sergei Shirokov 3.00 8.00
FTTB Tyler Bozak 8.00 20.00
FTTG T.J. Galiardi 5.00 12.00
FTTM Tyler Myers 12.00 30.00
FTVA James van Riemsdyk 10.00 25.00
FTVH Victor Hedman 8.00 20.00
FTVL Ville Leino 4.00 10.00
FTVS Viktor Stalberg 5.00 12.00
FTYW Yannick Weber 5.00 12.00

2009-10 Upper Deck Ice Fresh Threads Autographs

FTAC Andrew Cogliano 6.00 15.00
FTAN Antti Niemi 15.00 40.00
FTBA Mikael Backlund 15.00 40.00
FTBF Benn Ferriero 10.00 25.00
FTBW Blake Wheeler 10.00 25.00
FTCF Cody Franson 10.00 25.00
FTCG Claude Giroux 20.00 40.00
FTDB Derick Brassard 6.00 15.00
FTDD Drew Doughty 12.00 30.00
FTDS Drew Stafford 6.00 15.00
FTDU Matt Duchene 50.00 100.00
FTEK Erik Karlsson 40.00 80.00
FTIV Ivan Vishnevskiy 6.00 15.00
FTJB Jamie Benn 25.00 50.00
FTJE Jhonas Enroth 20.00 40.00
FTJG Jonas Gustavsson 12.00 30.00
FTJT John Tavares 40.00 100.00
FTJV Jakub Voracek 8.00 20.00
FTKC Kris Chucko 6.00 15.00
FTLC Luca Caputi 10.00 25.00
FTMR Mason Raymond 6.00 15.00
FTPK Patrick Kane 30.00 60.00
FTPO Patrick O'Sullivan 8.00 20.00
FTRH Riku Helenius 10.00 25.00
FTRO Ryan O'Reilly 20.00 50.00
FTSM Spencer Machacek 10.00 25.00
FTSS Sergei Shirokov 6.00 15.00
FTTB Tyler Bozak 15.00 40.00
FTTG T.J. Galiardi 10.00 25.00
FTTM Tyler Myers 50.00 100.00
FTTO Jonathan Toews 30.00 60.00
FTVA James van Riemsdyk 20.00 50.00
FTVH Victor Hedman 25.00 60.00
FTVL Ville Leino 8.00 20.00
FTYW Yannick Weber 10.00 25.00

2009-10 Upper Deck Ice Frozen Fabrics

*PATCH/15: 1.5X TO 4X BASIC JSY
FRAF Alexander Frolov 3.00 8.00
FRAK Anze Kopitar 6.00 15.00
FRBB Bob Bourne 2.50 6.00
FRBC Brian Campbell 3.00 8.00
FRBS Borje Salming 4.00 10.00
FRCH Cristobal Huet 4.00 10.00
FRCN Cam Neely 4.00 10.00
FRCP Carey Price 8.00 20.00
FRCW Cam Ward 4.00 10.00
FRDB Dustin Brown 4.00 10.00
FRDG Doug Gilmour 5.00 12.00
FRDH Dale Hawerchuk 5.00 12.00
FRDP Dion Phaneuf 3.00 8.00
FRDR Derek Roy 2.50 6.00
FRGA Glenn Anderson 3.00 8.00
FRHZ Henrik Zetterberg 5.00 12.00
FRIK Ilya Kovalchuk 4.00 10.00
FRJB Jay Bouwmeester 2.50 6.00

FRJC Jeff Carter 3.00 8.00
FRJI Jarome Iginla 5.00 12.00
FRJL Jordan Leopold 2.50 6.00
FRJP Jason Pominville 2.50 6.00
FRJT Joe Thornton 6.00 15.00
FRKT Kimmo Timonen 3.00 8.00
FRLM Lanny McDonald 4.00 10.00
FRMB Martin Brodeur 10.00 25.00
FRMR Mike Richards 3.00 8.00
FRNH Nathan Horton 4.00 10.00
FRPD Pavel Datsyuk 6.00 15.00
FRRD Rick DiPietro 3.00 8.00
FRRG Ryan Getzlaf 4.00 10.00
FRRM Ryan Miller 4.00 10.00
FRRN Rick Nash 4.00 10.00
FRSC Sidney Crosby 12.00 30.00
FRSK Saku Koivu 4.00 10.00
FRSP Jason Spezza 4.00 10.00
FRSS Steve Shutt 4.00 10.00
FRST Peter Stastny 3.00 8.00
FRSY Steve Yzerman 10.00 25.00
FRTV Thomas Vanek 3.00 8.00
FRVL Vincent Lecavalier 4.00 10.00
FRVO Tomas Vokoun 3.00 8.00

2009-10 Upper Deck Ice Frozen Fabrics Autographs

FRAK Anze Kopitar 20.00 50.00
FRBB Bob Bourne 8.00 20.00
FRBS Borje Salming 15.00 40.00
FRCN Cam Neely 12.00 30.00
FRCP Carey Price 25.00 60.00
FRCW Cam Ward 12.00 30.00
FRDG Doug Gilmour 15.00 40.00
FRDH Dale Hawerchuk 15.00 40.00
FRDP Dion Phaneuf 10.00 25.00
FREM Evgeni Malkin 25.00 60.00
FRHZ Henrik Zetterberg 15.00 40.00
FRIK Ilya Kovalchuk 12.00 30.00
FRJC Jeff Carter 10.00 25.00
FRJI Jarome Iginla 15.00 40.00
FRJP Jason Pominville 8.00 20.00
FRJT Joe Thornton 20.00 50.00
FRLM Lanny McDonald 12.00 30.00
FRMB Martin Brodeur 30.00 80.00
FRNH Nathan Horton 12.00 30.00
FRPB Patrice Bergeron 15.00 40.00
FRPD Pavel Datsyuk 15.00 40.00
FRRM Ryan Miller 12.00 30.00
FRRN Rick Nash 12.00 30.00
FRSC Sidney Crosby 125.00 200.00
FRSD Shane Doan 10.00 25.00
FRSS Steve Shutt 12.00 30.00
FRST Peter Stastny 15.00 40.00
FRSY Steve Yzerman 30.00 80.00
FRTV Thomas Vanek 10.00 25.00
FRVL Vincent Lecavalier 12.00 30.00
FRVO Tomas Vokoun 10.00 25.00

2009-10 Upper Deck Ice Glacial Graphs

GGAC Andrew Cogliano 4.00 10.00
GGAE Andrew Ebbett 4.00 10.00
GGBA Josh Bailey 5.00 12.00
GGBE Jamie Benn 20.00 50.00
GGBL Brian Lee 6.00 15.00
GGBO Bobby Orr 75.00 150.00
GGBR Bobby Ryan 5.00 12.00
GGBS Brian Sutter 6.00 15.00
GGCG Colton Gillies 6.00 15.00
GGCH Chris Stewart 5.00 12.00
GGCS Cory Schneider 6.00 15.00
GGDP Dustin Penner 4.00 10.00
GGDS Darryl Sutter 5.00 12.00
GGDU Matt Duchene 12.00 30.00
GGDZ Michael Del Zotto 6.00 15.00
GGEK Evander Kane 12.00 30.00
GGER Erik Karlsson 30.00 60.00
GGFB Fabian Brunnstrom 5.00 12.00
GGGC Guy Carbonneau 10.00 25.00
GGGH Gordie Howe 75.00 150.00
GGGI Claude Giroux 15.00 30.00
GGJA Justin Abdelkader 5.00 12.00
GGJC Jeff Carter 12.00 30.00
GGJE Jonathan Ericsson 4.00 10.00
GGJG Jonas Gustavsson 12.00 30.00
GGJJ Jack Johnson 4.00 10.00
GGJS Jordan Staal 5.00 12.00
GGJV Jakub Voracek 5.00 12.00
GGKA Karl Alzner 4.00 10.00
GGKM Kenndal McArdle 5.00 12.00
GGKR Niklas Kronwall 5.00 12.00
GGLS Luke Schenn 6.00 15.00
GGMF Mike Foligno 4.00 10.00
GGMK Mikael Backlund 10.00 25.00
GGML Mario Lemieux 50.00 100.00
GGMP Max Pacioretty 6.00 15.00
GGMR Mike Ribeiro 4.00 10.00
GGMT Maxime Talbot 4.00 10.00
GGMY Tyler Myers 15.00 40.00
GGNB Nicklas Backstrom 6.00 15.00
GGNG Nathan Gerbe 5.00 12.00
GGNK Nikolai Kulemin 4.00 10.00
GGPD Pavel Datsyuk 15.00 40.00
GGPE Phil Esposito 20.00 50.00
GGPR Patrick Roy 75.00 150.00
GGPS Peter Stastny 12.00 30.00
GGRI Mike Richards 6.00 15.00
GGRS Ron Sutter 8.00 20.00
GGSB Scotty Bowman 15.00 40.00
GGSC Sidney Crosby 75.00 150.00
GGSK Steven Stamkos 40.00 80.00
GGSM Steve Mason 8.00 20.00
GGSS Steve Shutt 6.00 15.00
GGST Paul Stastny 5.00 12.00
GGSU Brandon Sutter 4.00 10.00
GGSY Steve Yzerman 50.00 100.00
GGTA John Tavares 75.00 150.00
GGTJ T.J. Galiardi 6.00 15.00
GGTK Tim Kennedy 5.00 12.00
GGTL Ted Lindsay 12.00 30.00
GGTO T.J. Oshie 6.00 15.00
GGTV Thomas Vanek 5.00 12.00
GGVH Victor Hedman 15.00 40.00
GGVL Ville Leino 5.00 12.00
GGVR James van Riemsdyk 12.00 30.00
GGZA Zach Boychuk 5.00 12.00

2009-10 Upper Deck Ice Rinkside Signings

RSAK Anze Kopitar 15.00 40.00
RSDC Don Cherry 25.00 50.00
RSHL Henrik Lundqvist 30.00 60.00
RSHZ Henrik Zetterberg 15.00 40.00
RSMG Marian Gaborik 25.00 50.00
RSMM Mike Modano 25.00 50.00
RSNB Nicklas Backstrom 12.00 30.00
RSNL Nicklas Lidstrom 25.00 50.00
RSPK Patrick Kane 40.00 80.00
RSRM Ryan Miller 12.00 30.00
RSSD Shane Doan 10.00 25.00
RSTV Tomas Vokoun 12.00 30.00

2009-10 Upper Deck Ice Rinkside Signings Canadian

RSBO Bobby Orr 200.00 300.00
RSBR Bobby Ryan 12.00 30.00
RSCP Carey Price 25.00 60.00
RSCW Cam Ward 12.00 30.00
RSDD Drew Doughty EXCH 40.00 80.00
RSDH Dany Heatley 20.00 50.00
RSGH Gordie Howe 60.00 120.00
RSJC Jeff Carter 15.00 40.00
RSJI Jarome Iginla 20.00 50.00
RSJS Jordan Staal 15.00 40.00
RSJT Jonathan Toews 40.00 80.00
RSLS Luke Schenn 15.00 40.00
RSML Mario Lemieux 75.00 150.00
RSPS Paul Stastny 25.00 50.00
RSRN Rick Nash EXCH 25.00 50.00
RSSC Sidney Crosby 100.00 200.00
RSSM Steve Mason 15.00 40.00
RSSS Steven Stamkos 40.00 80.00
RSSY Steve Yzerman 200.00 300.00
RSTE Tony Esposito 30.00 80.00
RSTH Joe Thornton 25.00 50.00
RSVL Vincent Lecavalier EXCH 25.00 50.00
RSWG Wayne Gretzky 250.00 600.00

2009-10 Upper Deck Ice Signature Swatches

SSBL Brian Leetch 10.00 25.00
SSCN Cam Neely 12.00 30.00
SSCP Carey Price 25.00 60.00
SSEM Evgeni Malkin 25.00 60.00
SSGF Grant Fuhr 20.00 50.00
SSHZ Henrik Zetterberg 15.00 40.00
SSIK Ilya Kovalchuk 12.00 30.00
SSJI Jarome Iginla 15.00 40.00
SSJK Jari Kurri 12.00 30.00
SSJT Joe Thornton 20.00 50.00
SSLS Luke Schenn 12.00 30.00
SSMB Martin Brodeur 50.00 100.00
SSMF Marc-Andre Fleury 25.00 60.00
SSML Mario Lemieux 60.00 120.00
SSMR Mike Richards 10.00 25.00
SSMT Marty Turco 12.00 30.00
SSNB Nicklas Backstrom 12.00 30.00
SSPD Pavel Datsyuk 25.00 50.00
SSPK Patrick Kane 50.00 100.00
SSPR Patrick Roy 100.00 200.00
SSRM Ryan Miller 25.00 50.00
SSRN Rick Nash 12.00 30.00
SSSC Sidney Crosby 175.00 350.00
SSSS Steven Stamkos 25.00 60.00
SSTO Jonathan Toews 50.00 100.00
SSTV Thomas Vanek 10.00 25.00
SSVL Vincent Lecavalier 12.00 30.00

2010-11 Upper Deck Ice

COMP.SET w/o SPs (60) 20.00 50.00
1 Ilya Bryzgalov .40 1.00
2 Dustin Penner .30 .75
3 Henrik Lundqvist 1.25 3.00
4 Cam Ward .50 1.25
5 Andy McDonald .40 1.00
6 Tomas Plekanec .30 .75
7 Patrick Kane 1.00 2.50
8 Drew Doughty .60 1.50
9 Evgeni Malkin 1.00 2.50
10 Bobby Ryan .40 1.00
11 Patrick Marleau .50 1.25
12 Pavel Datsyuk .75 2.00
13 Mikko Koivu .50 1.25
14 Brad Richards .50 1.25
15 Steven Stamkos 1.00 2.50
16 John Tavares .75 2.00
17 Mike Richards .40 1.00
18 Nik Antropov .40 1.00
19 Zdeno Chara .50 1.25
20 Zach Parise .50 1.25
21 Henrik Sedin .60 1.50
22 Jarome Iginla .60 1.50
23 Ryan Miller .50 1.25
24 Phil Kessel .50 1.25
25 Daniel Alfredsson .50 1.25
26 Tomas Vokoun .40 1.00
27 Shea Weber .40 1.00
28 Alexander Ovechkin 2.00 5.00
29 Paul Stastny .40 1.00
30 Steve Mason .40 1.00
31 Ryan Getzlaf .50 1.25
32 Dustin Byfuglien .50 1.25
33 Patrice Bergeron .60 1.50
34 Thomas Vanek .40 1.00
35 Rene Bourque .30 .75
36 Eric Staal .60 1.50
37 Jonathan Toews .75 2.00
38 Matt Duchene .50 1.25
39 Rick Nash .50 1.25
40 Nicklas Lidstrom .50 1.25
41 Henrik Zetterberg .60 1.50
42 Ales Hemsky .40 1.00
43 Anze Kopitar .75 2.00
44 Guillaume Latendresse .40 1.00
45 Carey Price 1.00 2.50
46 Pekka Rinne .50 1.25
47 Ilya Kovalchuk .50 1.25
48 Martin Brodeur 1.25 3.00
49 Marian Gaborik .50 1.25
50 Jason Spezza .50 1.25
51 Jeff Carter .40 1.00
52 Shane Doan .40 1.00
53 Sidney Crosby 2.00 5.00
54 Dany Heatley .40 1.00
55 Jaroslav Halak .50 1.25
56 Martin St. Louis .50 1.25
57 Simon Gagne .50 1.25
58 Dion Phaneuf .40 1.00
59 Roberto Luongo .75 2.00
60 Nicklas Backstrom .50 1.25
61 Jake Muzzin/1999 B RC 5.00 12.00
62 Kyle Clifford/1999 B RC 2.50 6.00
63 Alexander Urbom/1999 B RC 2.00 5.00
64 Matt Taormina/1999 B RC 2.00 5.00
65 T.J. Brodie/1999 B RC 2.00 5.00
66 Jeremy Morin/1999 S RC 2.00 5.00
67 Evan Brophey/1999 S RC 2.00 5.00
68 Marco Scandella/1999 S RC 2.00 5.00
69 Jonas Holos/1999 S RC 2.00 5.00
70 Brandon Pirri/1999 S RC 2.00 5.00
71 Anders Lindback/999 B RC 2.50 6.00
72 Mark Olver/999 B RC 2.50 6.00
73 Nick Leddy/999 B RC 3.00 8.00
74 Justin Falk/999 B RC 2.00 5.00
75 Alex Plante/999 B RC 2.50 6.00
76 Brandon Yip/999 B RC 2.50 6.00
77 Dana Tyrell/999 B RC 2.50 6.00
78 Ian Cole/999 S RC 2.50 6.00
79 Philip Larsen/999 S RC 2.50 6.00
80 Eric Wellwood/999 S RC 3.00 8.00
81 Matt Kassian/999 S RC 2.50 6.00
82 Linus Klasen/999 S RC 2.50 6.00
83 Kyle Palmieri/999 S RC 5.00 12.00
84 Jared Cowen/999 S RC 2.50 6.00
85 Sergei Bobrovsky/499 B RC 12.00 30.00
86 Henrik Karlsson/499 B RC 3.00 8.00
87 Zach Hamill/499 B RC 3.00 8.00
88 Nino Niederreiter/499 B RC 6.00 15.00
89 Cam Fowler/499 B RC 8.00 20.00
90 Alexander Burmistrov/499 B RC 3.00 8.00
91 Oliver Ekman-Larsson/499 B RC 5.00 12.00
92 Jordan Caron/499 B RC 4.00 10.00
93 Luke Adam/499 S RC 3.00 8.00
94 Eric Tangradi/499 S RC 3.00 8.00
95 Jamie McBain/499 S RC 3.00 8.00
96 Evgeny Grachev/499 S RC 3.00 8.00
97 Zac Dalpe/499 S RC 4.00 10.00
98 Jacob Josefson/499 S RC 3.00 8.00
99 Marcus Johansson/499 S RC 5.00 12.00
100 Kevin Shattenkirk/499 S RC 6.00 15.00
101 Nazem Kadri/99 B RC 150.00 300.00
102 Derek Stepan/99 B RC 60.00 120.00
103 P.K. Subban/99 B RC 250.00 400.00
104A Tyler Seguin/99 B RC 250.00 450.00
105 Taylor Hall/99 B RC 400.00 700.00
106 Mattias Tedenby/99 S RC 15.00 40.00
107 Brayden Schenn/99 S RC 40.00 100.00
108 Jeff Skinner/99 S RC 200.00 400.00
109 Magnus Paajarvi/99 S RC 100.00 200.00
110 Jordan Eberle/99 S RC 300.00 450.00

2011-12 Upper Deck Ice

1 Corey Perry 1.00 2.50
2 Ryan Miller .60 1.50
3 Jarome Iginla .75 2.00
4 Eric Staal .75 2.00
5 Jonathan Toews 1.00 2.50
6 Matt Duchene .60 1.50
7 Rick Nash .60 1.50
8 Taylor Hall .60 1.50
9 Drew Doughty .75 2.00
10 Mikko Koivu .50 1.25
11 P.K. Subban .75 2.00
12 Shea Weber .50 1.25
13 Martin Brodeur 1.50 4.00
14 Michael Grabner .50 1.25
15 Henrik Lundqvist 1.50 4.00
16 Jason Spezza .60 1.50
17 Claude Giroux .60 1.50
18 Shane Doan .50 1.25
19 Sidney Crosby 2.50 6.00
20 Patrick Marleau .60 1.50
21 Steven Stamkos 1.25 3.00
22 Phil Kessel .60 1.50
23 Roberto Luongo 1.00 2.50
24 Nicklas Backstrom .60 1.50
25 Dustin Byfuglien .60 1.50
26 Ryan Getzlaf .60 1.50
27 Tim Thomas .60 1.50
28 Drew Stafford .40 1.00
29 Miikka Kiprusoff .60 1.50
30 Jeff Skinner .75 2.00
31 Patrick Kane 1.25 3.00
32 Paul Stastny .50 1.25
33 Steve Mason .50 1.25
34 Brenden Morrow .50 1.25
35 Henrik Zetterberg .75 2.00
36 Jordan Eberle .60 1.50
37 Anze Kopitar 1.00 2.50
38 Niklas Backstrom .60 1.50
39 Carey Price 1.25 3.00
40 Pekka Rinne .60 1.50
41 Ilya Kovalchuk .60 1.50
42 John Tavares 1.00 2.50
43 Daniel Alfredsson .60 1.50
44 Daniel Briere .60 1.50
45 Marc-Andre Fleury 1.25 3.00
46 Logan Couture .75 2.00
47 Dion Phaneuf .50 1.25
48 Ryan Kesler .60 1.50
49 Alexander Ovechkin 2.50 6.00
50 Evander Kane .60 1.50
51 Ben Scrivens RC 2.00 5.00
52 Joe Vitale RC 2.00 5.00
53 Erik Condra RC 2.00 5.00
54 Patrick Wiercioch RC 2.00 5.00
55 Ryan Ellis RC 2.00 5.00
56 Dmitry Orlov RC 5.00 12.00
57 Gustav Nyquist RC 8.00 12.00
58 Colin Greening RC 2.50 6.00
59 Alex Stalock 2.00 5.00
60 Jonathon Blum RC 2.50 6.00
61 Cam Atkinson RC 6.00 15.00
62 Brett Bulmer RC 2.50 6.00
63 Craig Smith RC 3.00 8.00
64 Erik Gustafsson RC 3.00 8.00
65 Raphael Diaz RC 2.50 6.00
66 Alexei Emelin RC 2.50 6.00
67 Colten Teubert RC 2.50 6.00
68 John Moore RC 2.50 6.00
69 Viatcheslav Voynov RC 2.50 6.00
70 Roman Horak RC 3.00 8.00
71 Stephane Da Costa RC 2.50 6.00
72 Keith Kinkaid RC 2.50 6.00
73 Peter Holland RC 2.50 6.00
74 Devante Smith-Pelly RC 4.00 10.00
75 Erik Gudbranson RC 4.00 10.00
76 Matt Frattin RC 3.00 8.00
77 Jake Gardiner RC 6.00 15.00
78 Aaron Palushaj RC 3.00 8.00
79 Adam Henrique RC 15.00 40.00
80 Marcus Kruger RC 5.00 12.00
81 Blake Geoffrion RC 8.00 20.00
82 Adam Larsson RC 12.50 25.00
83 Cody Eakin RC 5.00 12.00
84 David Rundblad RC 3.00 8.00
85 Teemu Hartikainen RC 3.00 8.00
86 Anton Lander RC 3.00 8.00
87 Brett Connolly RC 5.00 12.00
88 Joe Colborne RC 3.00 8.00
89 Justin Faulk RC 5.00 12.00
90 Brendan Smith RC 3.00 8.00
91 Andy Miele RC 3.00 8.00
92 Lennart Petrell RC 4.00 10.00
93 Andrew Shaw RC 10.00 25.00
94 Carl Klingberg RC 3.00 8.00
95 Zack Kassian RC 4.00 10.00
96 Mika Zibanejad RC 60.00 120.00
97 Ryan Johansen RC 90.00 150.00
98 Gabriel Landeskog RC 100.00 175.00
99 Cody Hodgson RC 75.00 150.00
100 Ryan Nugent-Hopkins RC 300.00 500.00
101 Matt Read/99 RC 50.00 120.00
102 Louis Leblanc/99 RC 30.00 80.00
103 Mark Scheifele/99 RC 50.00 120.00
104 Sean Couturier/99 RC 75.00 150.00

2012-13 Upper Deck Ice

1 Ryan Getzlaf .75 2.00
2 Patrice Bergeron 1.00 2.50
3 Ryan Miller .75 2.00
4 Jarome Iginla 1.00 2.50
5 Jonathan Toews 1.25 3.00
6 Jamie Benn .75 2.00
7 Taylor Hall .75 2.00
8 Kris Versteeg .50 1.25
9 Jonathan Quick 1.00 2.50
10 Dany Heatley .60 1.50
11 Carey Price 1.50 4.00
12 Shea Weber .60 1.50
13 Martin Brodeur 2.00 5.00
14 John Tavares 1.25 3.00
15 Ryan Callahan .50 1.25
16 Jason Spezza .75 2.00
17 Claude Giroux .75 2.00
18 Mike Smith .75 2.00
19 Evgeni Malkin 1.50 4.00
20 Antti Niemi .60 1.50
21 Steven Stamkos 1.50 4.00
22 Dion Phaneuf .60 1.50
23 Daniel Sedin 1.00 2.50
24 Alexander Ovechkin 3.00 8.00
25 Ondrej Pavelec .75 2.00
26 Reilly Smith/999 RC 6.00 15.00
27 Cody Goloubef/999 RC 2.00 5.00
28 Gabriel Dumont/999 RC 2.50 6.00
29 Tyler Cuma/999 RC 2.00 5.00
30 J.T. Brown/999 RC 2.50 6.00
31 Maxime Sauve/999 RC 2.00 5.00
32 Tyson Barrie/999 RC 6.00 15.00
33 Jason Zucker/999 RC 5.00 12.00
34 Jordan Nolan/999 RC 2.00 5.00
35 Mark Stone/999 RC 10.00 20.00
36 Scott Glennie/999 RC 2.50 6.00
37 Chet Pickard/499 RC 2.50 6.00
38 Riley Sheahan/499 RC 6.00 15.00
39 Jussi Rynnas/499 RC 10.00 25.00
40 Casey Cizikas/499 RC 5.00 12.00
41 Jakob Silfverberg/499 RC 8.00 20.00
42 Jake Allen/499 RC 8.00 20.00
43 Carter Ashton/499 RC 4.00 10.00
44 Jaden Schwartz/99 RC 80.00 200.00
45 Sven Baertschi/99 RC 40.00 80.00
46 Chris Kreider/99 RC 50.00 125.00

2013-14 Upper Deck Ice

COMP.SET w/o SP's (50) 10.00 25.00
1 Corey Perry 1.25 3.00
2 Brad Marchand 1.50 4.00
3 Tyler Ennis .50 1.25
4 Patrick Kane 1.50 4.00
5 Matt Duchene .75 2.00
6 Sergei Bobrovsky 1.25 3.00
7 Pavel Datsyuk 1.25 3.00
8 Jordan Eberle .75 2.00
9 Anze Kopitar 1.25 3.00
10 Ryan Suter .60 1.50
11 P.K. Subban 1.00 2.50
12 Pekka Rinne .75 2.00
13 Martin Brodeur 2.00 5.00
14 John Tavares 1.25 3.00
15 Derek Stepan .50 1.25
16 Erik Karlsson 1.00 2.50
17 Jakub Voracek .60 1.50
18 Shane Doan .60 1.50
19 Evgeni Malkin 1.50 4.00
20 Logan Couture 1.00 2.50
21 Alexander Steen .50 1.25
22 Martin St. Louis .75 2.00
23 Alexandre Burrows .50 1.25
24 Mike Green .60 1.50
25 Evander Kane .75 2.00
26 Ryan Getzlaf .75 2.00
27 Patrice Bergeron 1.00 2.50
28 Lee Stempniak .50 1.25
29 Eric Staal 1.00 2.50
30 Jonathan Toews 1.25 3.00
31 Marian Gaborik .75 2.00
32 Jamie Benn .75 2.00
33 Henrik Zetterberg 1.00 2.50
34 Taylor Hall .75 2.00
35 Tomas Fleischmann .50 1.25
36 Jonathan Quick 1.00 2.50
37 Zach Parise .75 2.00
38 Carey Price 1.50 4.00
39 Shea Weber .60 1.50
40 Patrik Elias .75 2.00
41 Ryan Callahan .50 1.25
42 Craig Anderson .75 2.00
43 Claude Giroux .75 2.00
44 Sidney Crosby 3.00 8.00
45 Joe Thornton 1.25 3.00
46 Steven Stamkos 1.50 4.00
47 Phil Kessel .75 2.00
48 Henrik Sedin 1.00 2.50
49 Alexander Ovechkin 3.00 8.00
50 Andrew Ladd .50 1.25
51 Chris Brown/999 RC 2.00 5.00
52 Danny DeKeyser/999 RC 4.00 10.00
53 Johan Larsson/999 RC 4.00 10.00
54 Connor Carrick/999 RC 2.50 6.00
55 Austin Watson/999 RC 2.50 6.00
56 Zach Redmond/999 RC 2.50 6.00
57 Anton Belov/999 RC 3.00 8.00
58 Justin Fontaine/999 RC 3.00 8.00
59 Jean-Gabriel Pageau/999 RC 3.00 8.00
60 Brock Nelson/999 RC 6.00 15.00
61 Joakim Nordstrom/999 RC 2.50 6.00
62 Drew LeBlanc/999 RC 2.00 5.00
63 Alex Petrovic/999 RC 2.50 6.00
64 Max Reinhart/999 RC 3.00 8.00
65 Jesper Fast/999 RC 3.00 8.00
66 Jason Akeson/999 RC 2.50 6.00
67 Eric Gryba/999 RC 2.50 6.00
68 Matthew Irwin/999 RC 2.50 6.00
69 Jeff Zatkoff/999 RC 3.00 8.00
70 Will Acton/999 RC 2.50 6.00
71 Ryan Stanton/999 RC 3.00 8.00
72 Spencer Abbott/999 RC 2.50 6.00
73 Carl Soderberg/499 RC 4.00 10.00
74 Matt Nieto/499 RC 3.00 8.00
75 Michael Latta/499 RC 3.00 8.00
76 Alex Chiasson/499 RC 4.00 10.00
77 Darcy Kuemper/499 RC 8.00 20.00
78 Tyler Johnson/499 RC 25.00 50.00
79 Anders Lee/499 RC 6.00 15.00
80 Nick Bjugstad/499 RC 5.00 12.00
81 Taylor Beck/499 RC 3.00 8.00
82 Edward Pasquale/499 RC 2.50 6.00
83 Mark Pysyk/499 RC 4.00 10.00
84 Radko Gudas/499 RC 4.00 10.00
85 Philipp Grubauer/499 RC 10.00 25.00
86 Sami Vatanen/499 RC 4.00 10.00
87 Damien Brunner/499 RC 3.00 8.00
88 Ryan Murphy/499 RC 4.00 10.00
89 Rickard Rakell/499 RC 4.00 10.00
90 Lucas Lessio/499 RC 2.50 6.00
91 Mathew Dumba/499 RC 2.50 6.00
92 Olli Maatta/499 RC 15.00 40.00
93 Tom Wilson/499 RC 8.00 20.00
94 Jarred Tinordi/499 RC 4.00 10.00
95 Viktor Fasth/499 RC 4.00 10.00
96 Zemgus Girgensons/499 RC 6.00 15.00
97 Jonas Brodin/499 RC 5.00 12.00
98 Nathan Beaulieu/499 RC 2.50 6.00
99 Charlie Coyle/249 RC 8.00 20.00
100 Jack Campbell/249 RC 8.00 20.00
101 Hampus Lindholm/249 RC 8.00 20.00
102 Ryan Spooner/249 RC 5.00 12.00
103 Scott Laughton/249 RC 6.00 15.00
104 Tanner Pearson/249 RC 10.00 25.00
105 J.T. Miller/249 RC 8.00 20.00
106 Petr Mrazek/249 RC 10.00 25.00
107 Morgan Rielly/249 RC 15.00 40.00
108 Emerson Etem/249 RC 5.00 12.00
109 Boone Jenner/249 RC 10.00 25.00
110 Mikael Granlund/249 RC 8.00 20.00
111 Tyler Toffoli/249 RC 12.00 30.00
112 Rasmus Ristolainen/249 RC 8.00 20.00
113 Cory Conacher/249 RC 3.00 8.00
114 Jacob Trouba/249 RC 8.00 20.00
115 Michael Bournival/249 RC 5.00 12.00
116 Nicklas Jensen/249 RC 4.00 10.00
117 Ryan Murray/249 RC 8.00 20.00
118 Beau Bennett/99 RC 40.00 100.00
119 Filip Forsberg/99 RC 125.00 250.00
120 Elias Lindholm/99 RC 60.00 120.00
121 Mikhail Grigorenko/99 RC 50.00 100.00
122 Justin Schultz/99 RC 40.00 100.00
123 Nathan MacKinnon/99 RC 300.00 700.00
124 Vladimir Tarasenko/99 RC 40.00 100.00
125 Sean Monahan/99 RC 150.00 250.00
126 Jonathan Huberdeau/99 RC 125.00 250.00
127 Brendan Gallagher/99 RC 150.00 300.00
128 Nail Yakupov/99 RC 150.00 300.00
129 Alex Galchenyuk/99 RC 350.00 500.00
130 Aleksander Barkov/99 RC 100.00 200.00
131 Tomas Hertl/99 RC 100.00 200.00
132 Dougie Hamilton/99 RC 75.00 150.00
133 Seth Jones/99 RC 75.00 150.00
134 Valeri Nichushkin/99 RC 100.00 200.00

2014-15 Upper Deck Ice

1 Claude Giroux .75 2.00
2 Shea Weber .60 1.50
3 Rick Nash .75 2.00
4 Phil Kessel .75 2.00
5 Duncan Keith .60 1.50
6 Jamie Benn .75 2.00
7 Anze Kopitar 1.25 3.00
8 Sean Monahan .50 1.25
9 Alexander Ovechkin 3.00 8.00
10 Jordan Eberle .75 2.00
11 Blake Wheeler .75 2.00
12 Ryan Getzlaf .75 2.00
13 Zdeno Chara .75 2.00
14 Jonathan Toews 1.25 3.00
15 Martin St. Louis .75 2.00
16 Henrik Zetterberg 1.00 2.50
17 John Tavares 1.25 3.00
18 Drew Doughty 1.00 2.50
19 Jonathan Huberdeau 1.00 2.50
20 Max Pacioretty .75 2.00
21 Steven Stamkos 1.50 4.00
22 P.K. Subban 1.00 2.50
23 Cody Hodgson .50 1.25
24 Nathan MacKinnon 3.00 8.00
25 T.J. Oshie .75 2.00
26 Henrik Sedin 1.00 2.50
27 Matt Duchene .75 2.00
28 Zach Parise .75 2.00
29 Joe Pavelski 1.00 2.50
30 Patrice Bergeron 1.00 2.50
31 Pavel Datsyuk 1.25 3.00
32 Erik Karlsson 1.00 2.50
33 Eric Staal 1.00 2.50
34 Ryan Johansen .60 1.50
35 Patrick Kane 1.50 4.00
36 Marian Gaborik .75 2.00
37 Jaromir Jagr 2.50 6.00
38 Evgeni Malkin 1.50 4.00
39 Shane Doan .60 1.50
40 Sidney Crosby 3.00 8.00
41 Taylor Hall .75 2.00
42 Tyler Seguin 1.00 2.50
43 Ben Bishop 1.50 4.00
44 Corey Crawford 2.50 6.00
45 Jonathan Bernier 1.50 4.00
46 Cam Ward 2.00 5.00
47 Antti Niemi 1.50 4.00
48 Cory Schneider 2.00 5.00
49 Craig Anderson 2.00 5.00
50 Martin Brodeur 5.00 12.00
52 Roberto Luongo 3.00 8.00
53 Karri Ramo 1.50 4.00
54 Tuukka Rask 2.50 6.00
55 Steve Mason 1.50 4.00
56 Carey Price 4.00 10.00
57 Ben Scrivens 1.50 4.00
58 Ryan Miller 2.00 5.00
59 Jhonas Enroth 2.00 5.00
60 Mike Smith 2.00 5.00
61 Ondrej Pavelec 2.00 5.00
62 Kari Lehtonen 1.50 4.00
63 Marc-Andre Fleury 4.00 10.00
64 Henrik Lundqvist 5.00 12.00
65 Jaroslav Halak 2.00 5.00
66 Darcy Kuemper 2.00 5.00
67 Jonathan Quick 2.50 6.00
68 Pekka Rinne 2.00 5.00
69 Semyon Varlamov 2.00 5.00
70 John Gibson 2.00 5.00
71 Jim Howard 2.50 6.00
72 Sergei Bobrovsky 3.00 8.00
73 Patrick Roy 5.00 12.00
74 Ray Bourque 3.00 8.00
75 Steve Yzerman 5.00 12.00
76 Wayne Gretzky 12.00 30.00
77 Peter Forsberg 4.00 10.00
78 Guy Lafleur 2.50 6.00
79 Bobby Hull 4.00 10.00
80 Mario Lemieux 8.00 20.00
81 Bobby Orr 8.00 20.00
82 Jean Beliveau 2.00 5.00
83 Joe Sakic 4.00 10.00
84 Mike Bossy 2.00 5.00
85 Brandon Defazio/999 RC 2.50 6.00
86 Micheal Ferland/999 RC 3.00 8.00
87 Mike Halmo/999 RC 2.00 5.00
88 Joe Morrow/999 RC 4.00 10.00
89 Joonas Nattinen/999 RC 3.00 8.00
90 Liam O'Brien/999 RC 3.00 8.00
91 Justin Hodgman/999 RC 2.50 6.00
92 Trevor van Riemsdyk/999 RC 5.00 12.00
93 Dennis Everberg/999 RC 3.00 8.00
94 Andrej Nestrasil/999 RC 3.00 8.00
95 Laurent Brossoit/999 RC 3.00 8.00
96 Andy Andreoff/999 RC 3.00 8.00
97 Christian Folin/999 RC 3.00 8.00
98 Nicolas Deslauriers/999 RC 3.00 8.00
99 Mark Visentin/999 RC 3.00 8.00
100 Patrik Nemeth/999 RC 3.00 8.00
101 Corban Knight/999 RC 3.00 8.00
102 Scott Mayfield/999 RC 2.50 6.00
103 Michael Zalewski/999 RC 2.50 6.00
104 Bogdan Yakimov/999 RC 3.00 8.00
105 P-E Bellemare/999 RC 3.00 8.00
106 Brandon Kozun/999 RC 2.50 6.00
107 Jake McCabe/999 RC 3.00 8.00
108 Scott Wilson/999 RC 2.50 6.00
109 Petter Granberg/999 RC 2.50 6.00
110 Andrew Agozzino/999 RC 2.50 6.00
111 Greg McKegg/999 RC 2.50 6.00
112 Curtis McKenzie/999 RC 2.50 6.00
113 Colton Sissons/999 RC 3.00 8.00
114 Oscar Klefbom/999 RC 6.00 15.00
115 Markus Granlund/799 RC 5.00 12.00
116 Scott Darling/799 RC 12.50 25.00
117 Rocco Grimaldi/799 RC 3.00 8.00
118 William Karlsson/799 RC 10.00 25.00
119 Barclay Goodrow/799 RC 3.00 8.00
120 Scott Harrington/799 RC 3.00 8.00
121 Jori Lehtera/799 RC 4.00 10.00
122 Brett Ritchie/799 RC 3.00 8.00
123 Jordan Binnington/799 RC 10.00 25.00
124 Teemu Pulkkinen/799 RC 4.00 10.00
125 Colin Smith/799 RC 3.00 8.00
126 Phillip Danault/799 RC 6.00 15.00
127 Ryan Sproul/499 RC 4.00 10.00
128 Mirco Mueller/499 RC 4.00 10.00
129 Adam Lowry/499 RC 6.00 15.00
130 Seth Helgeson/499 RC 3.00 8.00
131 John Klingberg/499 RC 8.00 20.00
132 Ty Rattie/499 RC 4.00 10.00
133 Brandon Gormley/499 RC 4.00 10.00
134 Marko Dano/499 RC 4.00 10.00
135 Vincent Trocheck/499 RC 8.00 20.00
136 Calle Jarnkrok/499 RC 4.00 10.00
137 Kerby Rychel/499 RC 3.00 8.00
138 Joey Hishon/499 RC 5.00 12.00
139 Josh Jooris/499 RC 4.00 10.00
140 Adam Clendening/499 RC 4.00 10.00
141 A.Khokhlachev/499 RC 4.00 10.00
142 V.Namestnikov/499 RC 6.00 15.00
143 Victor Rask/499 RC 4.00 10.00
144 Chris Tierney/499 RC 4.00 10.00
145 Damon Severson/499 RC 4.00 10.00
146 Stuart Percy/499 RC 4.00 10.00
147 Kevin Hayes/249 RC 12.00 30.00
148 Andrei Vasilevskiy/249 RC 50.00 125.00
149 Sven Andrighetto/249 RC 6.00 15.00
150 Jiri Sekac/249 RC 4.00 10.00
151 Derrick Pouliot/249 RC 6.00 15.00
152 Seth Griffith/249 RC 6.00 15.00
153 Darnell Nurse/249 RC 15.00 30.00
154 Griffin Reinhart/249 RC 5.00 12.00
155 Shayne Gostisbehere/249 RC 60.00 100.00
156 Alexander Wennberg/249 RC 8.00 20.00
157 Anthony Duclair/249 RC 8.00 20.00
158 Evgeny Kuznetsov/249 RC 12.00 30.00
159 David Pastrnak/99 RC 125.00 250.00
160 Sam Reinhart/99 RC 125.00 250.00
161 Leon Draisaitl/99 RC 200.00 500.00
162 Aaron Ekblad/99 RC 100.00 200.00
163 Curtis Lazar/99 RC 50.00 100.00
164 Bo Horvat/99 RC 75.00 150.00
165 Teuvo Teravainen/99 RC 100.00 200.00
166 Jonathan Drouin/99 RC 100.00 200.00
167 Johnny Gaudreau/99 RC 100.00 250.00
168 Andre Burakovsky/99 RC 60.00 120.00
51 Philipp Grubauer 2.00 5.00

2014-15 Upper Deck Ice Fresh Threads

*GOLD/20-30: .75X TO 2X BASIC JSY
FTAB Andre Burakovsky 3.00 8.00
FTAE Aaron Ekblad 5.00 12.00
FTAL Adam Lowry 3.00 8.00
FTAW Alexander Wennberg 3.00 8.00
FTCL Curtis Lazar 2.00 5.00
FTCT Chris Tierney 2.00 5.00
FTDN Darnell Nurse 4.00 10.00
FTDS Damon Severson 2.00 5.00
FTEK Evgeny Kuznetsov 5.00 12.00
FTGR Griffin Reinhart 2.00 5.00
FTJD Jonathan Drouin 4.00 10.00
FTJG Johnny Gaudreau 6.00 15.00
FTJS Jiri Sekac 1.50 4.00
FTKR Kerby Rychel 1.50 4.00
FTLD Leon Draisaitl 10.00 25.00
FTMD Marko Dano 2.00 5.00
FTSG Shayne Gostisbehere 4.00 10.00
FTSP Stuart Percy 2.00 5.00
FTSR Sam Reinhart 8.00 20.00
FTVR Victor Rask 2.00 5.00

2014-15 Upper Deck Ice Frozen Fabrics

*GOLD/20-30: .75X TO 2X BASIC JSY
FZFAO Alexander Ovechkin B 8.00 20.00
FZFAP Alex Pietrangelo C 1.50 4.00
FZFBD Brandon Dubinsky C 1.25 3.00
FZFBS Ben Scrivens C 1.50 4.00
FZFCP Corey Perry C 3.00 8.00
FZFGF Grant Fuhr A 3.00 8.00
FZFGL Gabriel Landeskog C 2.50 6.00
FZFHZ Henrik Zetterberg C 2.50 6.00
FZFLR Larry Robinson A 2.00 5.00
FZFMM Mark Messier A 4.00 10.00
FZFMO Sean Monahan C 1.25 3.00
FZFMR Morgan Rielly C 2.00 5.00
FZFPR Pekka Rinne C 2.00 5.00
FZFPS Patrick Sharp B 2.00 5.00
FZFRN Rick Nash C 2.00 5.00
FZFRO Patrick Roy A 5.00 12.00
FZFRS Ryan Strome C 2.00 5.00
FZFSB Sergei Bobrovsky C 3.00 8.00
FZFSM Steve Mason C 1.50 4.00
FZFSU P.K. Subban B 5.00 12.00

2014-15 Upper Deck Ice Frozen Foursomes

FFRC Ekbld/Lzr/Rnhrt/Drstl C 12.00 30.00
FFTC Stl/Ptrnglo/Bnn/Ctrr 3.00 8.00
FFAVS Ry/Frsbrg/Skc/Blke B 6.00 15.00
FFBEES Ots/Mrry/Brqe/Ptrs C 4.00 10.00
FFBOS Rsk/Khlchv/Chra/Lcc A 3.00 8.00
FFCAN1 Hmltn/Gllghr/Hbrdu/Hcky C 3.00 8.00
FFCAN2 Jnnr/Mrry/Strme/Hmltn C 2.50 6.00
FFCAPS Ovkn/Hlby/Kznsv/Brksky C 10.00 25.00
FFDAL Blfr/Hll/Lhtnn/Bnn C 5.00 12.00
FFKINGS Qck/Dghty/Vynv/Tffli C 3.00 8.00
FFLAK Kptr/Crtr/Tffli/Vynv B 4.00 10.00
FFMTL Prce/Sbbn/Glchn/Gllghr C 5.00 12.00
FFNJD Schndr/Hnrge/Brnnr/Jgr B 8.00 20.00
FFNYR Krdr/Zcrllo/Stpn/McDng C 3.00 8.00
FFRC2 Kzntsv/Trvnn/Gdru/Nmst C 8.00 20.00

2014-15 Upper Deck Ice Glacial Graphs

GGAB Aleksander Barkov D 10.00 25.00
GGAO Adam Oates C 6.00 15.00
GGBR Dustin Brown A 6.00 15.00
GGCH Carl Hagelin D 4.00 10.00
GGCO Colton Orr C 4.00 10.00
GGCP Carey Price B 12.00 30.00
GGDB Dustin Byfuglien 6.00 15.00
GGDD Danny DeKeyser D 4.00 10.00
GGDK Darcy Kuemper D 6.00 15.00
GGJB Jonathan Bernier C 5.00 12.00
GGJL John LeClair C 6.00 15.00
GGJP Joe Pavelski C 8.00 20.00
GGJT John Tavares A 10.00 25.00
GGKT Kyle Turris C 6.00 15.00
GGMK Mike Krushelnyski D 5.00 12.00
GGML Mike Liut C 4.00 10.00
GGMP Max Pacioretty D 6.00 15.00
GGNL Nicklas Lidstrom B 6.00 15.00
GGOM Olli Maatta D 4.00 10.00
GGPE Corey Perry B 10.00 25.00
GGPK Patrik Kane 12.00 30.00
GGPS Patrick Sharp B 6.00 15.00
GGRB Bobby Ryan A 5.00 12.00
GGSA Brandon Saad D 5.00 12.00
GGTE Tony Esposito B 6.00 15.00
GGTH Tomas Hertl D 6.00 15.00
GGTL Trevor Linden A 6.00 15.00
GGTT Tomas Tatar C 4.00 10.00

2014-15 Upper Deck Ice Glacial Graphs Gold

GGAB Aleksander Barkov B 12.00 30.00
GGAO Adam Oates
Go Bees D 8.00 20.00
GGBR Dustin Brown
Go Kings A 8.00 20.00
GGCH Carl Hagelin
Go Rangers D 5.00 12.00
GGCO Colton Orr
Go Leafs D 5.00 12.00
GGCP Carey Price B 15.00 40.00
GGDB Dustin Byfuglien 8.00 20.00
GGDD Danny DeKeyser
Go Wings D 5.00 12.00
GGDK Darcy Kuemper
Go Wild D 8.00 20.00
GGJB Jonathan Bernier D 6.00 15.00
GGJL John LeClair A 8.00 20.00
GGJP Joe Pavelski
Go Sharks D 10.00 25.00
GGJT John Tavares D 12.00 30.00
GGKT Kyle Turris C 8.00 20.00
GGMK Mike Krushelnyski
Go Oilers D 6.00 15.00
GGML Mike Liut

Go Whalers D	5.00	12.00
GGMP Max Pacioretty		
Go Habs B	8.00	20.00
GGNL Nicklas Lidstrom		
Go Wings C	8.00	20.00
GGOM Olli Maatta		
Go Pens D	5.00	12.00
GGPE Corey Perry C	12.00	30.00
GGPK Patrik Kane		
Go Hawks	15.00	40.00
GGRB Bobby Ryan A	6.00	15.00
GGSA Brandon Saad		
Go Hawks C	6.00	15.00
GGTE Tony Esposito B	8.00	20.00
GGTH Tomas Hertl		
Go Sharks D	8.00	20.00
GGTL Trevor Linden		
Go Canucks B	8.00	20.00
GGTT Tomas Tatar D	5.00	12.00

2014-15 Upper Deck Ice Ice Premieres Autographs

IPAAB Andre Burakovsky A	8.00	20.00
IPAAD Anthony Duclair B	8.00	20.00
IPAAE Aaron Ekblad B	12.00	30.00
IPAAK Alexander Khokhlachev B	5.00	12.00
IPAAL Adam Lowry A	8.00	20.00
IPAAW Alexander Wennberg B	8.00	20.00
IPABG Brandon Gormley C	5.00	12.00
IPACJ Calle Jarnkrok B	5.00	12.00
IPACL Curtis Lazar B	5.00	12.00
IPADN Darnell Nurse B	10.00	25.00
IPAEK Evgeny Kuznetsov C	12.00	30.00
IPAGO Shayne Gostisbehere C	10.00	25.00
IPAGR Griffin Reinhart B	5.00	12.00
IPAJD Jonathan Drouin B	10.00	25.00
IPAJG Johnny Gaudreau A	80.00	200.00
IPAJH Joey Hishon C	6.00	15.00
IPAJL Jori Lehtera A	6.00	15.00
IPAJM Jake McCabe A	5.00	12.00
IPAJS Jiri Sekac C	4.00	10.00
IPAKH Kevin Hayes C	12.00	30.00
IPALB Laurent Brossoit A	5.00	12.00
IPALD Leon Draisaitl B	60.00	150.00
IPAMD Marko Dano B	5.00	12.00
IPAMM Mirco Mueller C	5.00	12.00
IPAPN Patrik Nemeth B	5.00	12.00
IPASG Seth Griffith C	6.00	15.00
IPASP Stuart Percy C	5.00	12.00
IPASR Sam Reinhart B	20.00	50.00
IPATP Teemu Pulkkinen B	6.00	15.00
IPATR Ty Rattie B	5.00	12.00
IPATT Teuvo Teravainen C	8.00	20.00
IPAVR Victor Rask C	5.00	12.00
IPAVT Vincent Trocheck A	10.00	25.00

2014-15 Upper Deck Ice Rinkside Signings

RSAC Andrew Cogliano D	5.00	12.00
RSAG Alex Galchenyuk C	5.00	12.00
RSAI Arturs Irbe C	6.00	15.00
RSBD Brandon Dubinsky D	5.00	12.00
RSBH Brett Hull A	15.00	40.00
RSBS Brandon Saad D	6.00	15.00
RSCP Corey Perry B	12.00	30.00
RSDP Dion Phaneuf C	6.00	15.00
RSES Eric Staal B	10.00	25.00
RSFA Frederik Andersen D	10.00	25.00
RSFP Felix Potvin C	12.00	30.00
RSGN Gustav Nyquist D	5.00	12.00
RSJF Johan Franzen C	6.00	15.00
RSJR Jeremy Roenick B	12.00	30.00
RSJS Joe Sakic B	15.00	40.00
RSJT Jonathan Toews B	30.00	80.00
RSJV John Vanbiesbrouck B	8.00	20.00
RSLC Logan Couture B	10.00	25.00
RSMF Marc-Andre Fleury A	15.00	40.00
RSMR Morgan Rielly D	8.00	20.00
RSNY Nail Yakupov B	5.00	12.00
RSPD Pavel Datsyuk A	12.00	30.00
RSPG Philipp Grubauer D	8.00	20.00
RSPM Petr Mrazek C	8.00	20.00
RSRM Ryan McDonagh D	5.00	12.00
RSRO Ryan O'Reilly D	8.00	20.00
RSSH Andrew Shaw C	5.00	12.00
RSSW Shea Weber B	6.00	15.00
RSTB Tom Barrasso C	8.00	20.00
RSTH Taylor Hall B	8.00	20.00
RSTK Torey Krug D	6.00	15.00
RSTR Jacob Trouba D	6.00	15.00
RSVA James van Riemsdyk C	6.00	15.00
RSZP Zach Parise A	8.00	20.00

2014-15 Upper Deck Ice Signature Swatches

SSAK Anze Kopitar D	12.00	30.00
SSDH Dale Hawerchuk D	10.00	25.00
SSDS Denis Savard D	8.00	20.00
SSJP Joe Pavelski D	10.00	25.00
SSJR Jeremy Roenick D	12.00	30.00
SSMF Marc-Andre Fleury C	15.00	40.00
SSMG Mike Gartner D	10.00	25.00
SSPR Pekka Rinne D	8.00	20.00
SSSC Sidney Crosby A	60.00	150.00
SSWG Wayne Gretzky B	200.00	500.00

2015-16 Upper Deck Ice

1 Alexander Ovechkin	4.00	10.00
2 Tyler Seguin	1.25	3.00
3 Mats Zuccarello	1.00	2.50
4 Tyler Toffoli	1.00	2.50
5 Erik Karlsson	1.25	3.00
6 Alexander Steen	.60	1.50
7 Max Pacioretty	1.00	2.50
8 Pekka Rinne	1.00	2.50
9 Steven Stamkos	2.00	5.00
10 Joe Pavelski	1.25	3.00
11 Sidney Crosby	4.00	10.00
12 Ryan Suter	.75	2.00
13 Henrik Zetterberg	1.25	3.00
14 Mikkel Boedker	.60	1.50
15 Tuukka Rask	1.25	3.00
16 Jonathan Toews	1.50	4.00
17 Kyle Okposo	.60	1.50
18 Daniel Sedin	1.25	3.00
19 Reilly Smith	1.00	2.50
20 Blake Wheeler	1.00	2.50
21 Adam Henrique	.75	2.00
22 Ryan Getzlaf	1.00	2.50
23 Ryan O'Reilly	1.00	2.50
24 Nathan MacKinnon	4.00	10.00
25 Tyler Bozak	.60	1.50
26 Johnny Gaudreau	1.50	4.00
27 Eric Staal	1.25	3.00
28 Taylor Hall	1.00	2.50
29 Brandon Saad	.75	2.00
30 Claude Giroux	1.00	2.50
31 Frederik Andersen	1.25	3.00
32 John Klingberg	1.00	2.50
33 Brendan Gallagher	1.00	2.50
34 Loui Eriksson	.60	1.50
35 Tomas Plekanec	.60	1.50
36 Braden Holtby	1.25	3.00
37 Tyler Johnson	.60	1.50
38 Patrick Sharp	1.00	2.50
39 Sergei Bobrovsky	1.50	4.00
40 Nicklas Backstrom	1.00	2.50
41 Marc-Andre Fleury	2.00	5.00
42 Henrik Lundqvist	2.50	6.00
43 Jarome Iginla	1.25	3.00
44 Oliver Ekman-Larsson	1.00	2.50
45 Brandon Sutter	.60	1.50
46 Anze Kopitar	1.50	4.00
47 Patrick Kane	2.00	5.00
48 David Krejci	1.00	2.50
49 Corey Perry	1.50	4.00
50 P.K. Subban	1.25	3.00
51 Sean Monahan	.60	1.50
52 Evgeni Malkin	2.00	5.00
53 T.J. Oshie	1.00	2.50
54 Jakub Voracek	.75	2.00
55 Vladimir Tarasenko	1.25	3.00
56 Scott Hartnell	.60	1.50
57 Corey Crawford	1.25	3.00
58 Ryan Nugent-Hopkins	1.25	3.00
59 Jim Howard	1.25	3.00
60 Gabriel Landeskog	1.25	3.00
61 John Tavares	1.50	4.00
62 Milan Lucic	.75	2.00
63 Justin Faulk	.75	2.00
64 Mikko Koivu	.75	2.00
65 Martin Hanzal	.60	1.50
66 Evgeny Kuznetsov	1.25	3.00
67 Dion Phaneuf	.75	2.00
68 Jannik Hansen	.60	1.50
69 James Neal	.60	1.50
70 Michael Cammalleri	.75	2.00
71 Carey Price	2.00	5.00
72 Bryan Little	.75	2.00
73 Brent Burns	1.00	2.50
74 Phil Kessel	1.00	2.50
75 Derick Brassard	.60	1.50
76 Patrice Bergeron	1.25	3.00
77 Bobby Ryan	.75	2.00
78 Jaromir Jagr	3.00	8.00
79 Jamie Benn	1.00	2.50
80 Brent Seabrook	.60	1.50
81 Nikita Kucherov	2.00	5.00
82 Tyler Ennis	.60	1.50
83 Jonathan Quick	1.25	3.00
84 Gustav Nyquist	.60	1.50
85 Jiri Hudler	.75	2.00
86 Pavel Bure	1.00	2.50
87 Borje Salming	1.00	2.50
88 Phil Esposito	1.50	4.00
89 Marcel Dionne	1.25	3.00
90 Bobby Orr	4.00	10.00
91 Martin Brodeur	2.50	6.00
92 Teemu Selanne	2.00	5.00
93 Luc Robitaille	1.00	2.50
94 Jari Kurri	1.00	2.50
95 Mark Messier	2.00	5.00
96 Larry Robinson	1.00	2.50
97 Paul Coffey	1.00	2.50
98 Doug Gilmour	1.25	3.00
99 Wayne Gretzky	6.00	15.00
100 Terry Sawchuk	1.00	2.50
101 Dylan DeMelo/1999 RC	2.50	6.00
102 Slater Koekkoek/1999 RC	2.00	5.00
103 Joel Edmundson/1999 RC	2.50	6.00
104 Ronalds Kenins/1999 RC	2.00	5.00
105 Joel Vermin/1999 RC	2.50	6.00
106 Duncan Siemens/1999 RC	3.00	8.00
107 Chris Driedger/1999 RC	2.50	6.00
108 Tyler Randell/1999 RC	3.00	8.00
109 Jean-Francois Berube/1999 RC	2.50	6.00
110 Taylor Leier/1999 RC	3.00	8.00
111 Michael Keranen/1999 RC	2.50	6.00
112 Derek Forbort/1999 RC	2.50	6.00
113 Sam Brittain/1999 RC	3.00	8.00
114 Josh Anderson/1999 RC	6.00	15.00
115 Brendan Ranford/1999 RC	2.50	6.00
116 Laurent Dauphin/1999 RC	3.00	8.00
117 Markus Hannikainen/1999 RC	2.50	6.00
118 Keegan Lowe/1999 RC	3.00	8.00
119 Brett Kulak/1999 RC	2.50	6.00
120 Nick Shore/1999 RC	2.00	5.00
121 Stefan Noesen/1999 RC	2.00	5.00
122 Joonas Kemppainen/1999 RC	2.00	5.00
123 Frank Vatrano/1999 RC	4.00	10.00
124 Petr Straka/1999 RC	2.00	5.00
125 Ryan Hartman/1999 RC	4.00	10.00
126 Matt O'Connor/1999 RC	2.50	6.00
127 Mark Alt/1999 RC	2.00	5.00
128 Radek Faksa/1999 RC	3.00	8.00
129 Alexandre Grenier/1999 RC	2.50	6.00
130 Mackenzie Skapski/1999 RC	3.00	8.00
131 Jujhar Khaira/1999 RC	2.50	6.00
132 David Musil/1999 RC	2.50	6.00
133 Erik Gustafsson/1999 RC	4.00	10.00
134 Jaccob Slavin/1999 RC	5.00	12.00
135 Chris Wideman/1999 RC	3.00	8.00
136 Kyle Baun/1999 RC	3.00	8.00
137 Antoine Bibeau/1499 RC	4.00	10.00
138 Vincent Hinostroza/1499 RC	2.50	6.00
139 Brendan Gaunce/1499 RC	5.00	12.00
140 Andrew Copp/1499 RC	4.00	10.00
141 Henrik Samuelsson/1499 RC	2.50	6.00
142 Adam Pelech/1499 RC	3.00	8.00
143 Jacob de la Rose/1499 RC	4.00	10.00
144 Nick Cousins/1499 RC	4.00	10.00
145 Anton Slepyshev/1499 RC	2.50	6.00
146 Devin Shore/1499 RC	4.00	10.00
147 Christoph Bertschy/1499 RC	3.00	8.00
148 Matt Puempel/1499 RC	3.00	8.00
149 Connor Brickley/1499 RC	3.00	8.00
150 Stanislav Galiev/1499 RC	4.00	10.00
151 Jordan Weal/1499 RC	2.50	6.00
152 Brady Skjei/1499 RC	3.00	8.00
153 Viktor Arvidsson/1499 RC	4.00	10.00
154 Sergei Kalinin/1499 RC	2.50	6.00
155 Chandler Stephenson/1499 RC	5.00	12.00
156 Anthony Stolarz/1499 RC	10.00	25.00
157 Sergei Plotnikov/1499 RC	2.50	6.00
158 Daniel Carr/1499 RC	3.00	8.00
159 Brett Pesce/1499 RC	3.00	8.00
160 Shane Prince/1499 RC	2.50	6.00
161 Brock McGinn/999 RC	4.00	10.00
162 Andreas Athanasiou/999 RC	10.00	25.00
163 Gustav Olofsson/999 RC	4.00	10.00
164 Mattias Janmark/999 RC	4.00	10.00
165 Linus Ullmark/999 RC	8.00	20.00
166 Charles Hudon/999 RC	4.00	10.00
167 Mike McCarron/999 RC	4.00	10.00
168 Colton Parayko/999 RC	6.00	15.00
169 Daniel Sprong/999 RC	5.00	12.00
170 Matt Murray/999 RC	30.00	80.00
171 Hunter Shinkaruk/999 RC	4.00	10.00
172 Emile Poirier/999 RC	3.00	8.00
173 Colin Miller/999 RC	3.00	8.00
174 Joonas Donskoi/999 RC	4.00	10.00
175 Ben Hutton/999 RC	4.00	10.00
176 Juuse Saros/999 RC	10.00	25.00
177 Shea Theodore/999 RC	6.00	15.00
178 Louis Domingue/999 RC	4.00	10.00
179 Noah Hanifin/499 RC	10.00	25.00
180 Kevin Fiala/499 RC	8.00	20.00
181 Jared McCann/499 RC	8.00	20.00
182 Garret Sparks/499 RC	6.00	15.00
183 Nikolay Goldobin/499 RC	6.00	15.00
184 Zachary Fucale/499 RC	5.00	12.00
185 Nick Ritchie/499 RC	6.00	15.00
186 Mikko Rantanen/499 RC	30.00	80.00
187 Malcolm Subban/499 RC	10.00	25.00
188 Nicolas Petan/499 RC	6.00	15.00
189 Mike Condon/499 RC	6.00	15.00
190 Oscar Lindberg/499 RC	6.00	15.00
191 Robby Fabbri/99 RC	150.00	250.00
192 Nikolaj Ehlers/99 RC	100.00	200.00
193 Jake Virtanen/99 RC	75.00	150.00
194 Sam Bennett/99 RC	200.00	300.00
195 Connor Hellebuyck/99 RC	100.00	250.00
196 Max Domi/99 RC	150.00	250.00
197 Artemi Panarin/99 RC	80.00	200.00
198 Dylan Larkin/99 RC	350.00	450.00
199 Jack Eichel/99 RC	700.00	1000.00
200 Connor McDavid/99 RC	2500.00	3000.00

2015-16 Upper Deck Ice Frozen Fabrics

FFAO Alexander Ovechkin B	20.00	50.00
FFBR Bill Ranford B	5.00	12.00
FFBW Blake Wheeler C	4.00	10.00
FFDH Dominik Hasek B	8.00	20.00
FFDS Daniel Sedin C	5.00	12.00
FFHL Henrik Lundqvist C	10.00	25.00
FFJA Jake Allen C	4.00	10.00
FFJF Justin Faulk C	3.00	8.00
FFJI Jarome Iginla C	5.00	12.00
FFJR Jeremy Roenick B	8.00	20.00
FFKE Phil Kessel C	4.00	10.00
FFML Mario Lemieux A	25.00	60.00
FFMZ Mats Zuccarello C	4.00	10.00
FFPB Pavel Bure A	6.00	15.00
FFPK Patrick Kane B	10.00	25.00
FFPR Pekka Rinne C	4.00	10.00
FFPS P.K. Subban C	5.00	12.00
FFSC Sidney Crosby B	20.00	50.00
FFSS Steven Stamkos C	8.00	20.00
FFST Tyler Seguin C	5.00	12.00
FFTH Taylor Hall C	4.00	10.00
FFVT Vladimir Tarasenko C	5.00	12.00
FFWG Wayne Gretzky A	40.00	100.00

2015-16 Upper Deck Ice Glacial Graphs

COMMON CARD	4.00	10.00
SEMISTARS	5.00	12.00
UNLISTED STARS	6.00	15.00
GGAB Aleksander Barkov C	10.00	25.00
GGAH Andrew Hammond D	8.00	20.00
GGAL Anders Lee D	6.00	15.00
GGAM Andy Moog C	6.00	15.00
GGAN Antti Niemi C	5.00	12.00
GGAO Alexander Ovechkin A	40.00	80.00
GGAV Andrei Vasilevskiy	10.00	25.00
GGBC Bobby Clarke B	10.00	25.00
GGBR Bobby Ryan B	5.00	12.00
GGCC Charlie Coyle D	6.00	15.00
GGCH Carl Hagelin B	4.00	10.00
GGCM Connor McDavid A	300.00	400.00
GGCW Cam Ward B	6.00	15.00
GGDL Dylan Larkin D	20.00	50.00
GGDS Daniel Sprong C	8.00	20.00
GGEM Evgeni Malkin A	20.00	50.00
GGGA Glenn Anderson A	8.00	20.00
GGGL Guy Lafleur A	15.00	40.00
GGJC John Carlson C	6.00	15.00
GGJK John Klingberg D	6.00	15.00
GGJP Joe Pavelski B	8.00	20.00
GGJS Jason Spezza B	6.00	15.00
GGKY Keith Yandle	4.00	10.00
GGLA Andrew Ladd C	4.00	10.00
GGLC Logan Couture B	8.00	20.00
GGLE John LeClair C	6.00	15.00
GGMD Matt Duchene B	6.00	15.00
GGMF Marc-Andre Fleury A	20.00	50.00
GGMM Mike Modano A	15.00	40.00
GGMR Mike Richter B	6.00	15.00
GGMS Mark Stone C	8.00	20.00
GGNH Noah Hanifin	10.00	25.00
GGNK Nikita Kucherov C	12.00	30.00
GGOP Ondrej Palat D	5.00	12.00
GGPF Peter Forsberg A	30.00	60.00
GGPR Pekka Rinne	6.00	15.00
GGRF Robby Fabbri D	8.00	20.00
GGRM Ryan McDonagh C	4.00	10.00
GGSC Ben Scrivens C	5.00	12.00
GGSG Shayne Gostisbehere D	6.00	15.00
GGSP Stuart Percy D	6.00	15.00
GGSV Semyon Varlamov C	6.00	15.00
GGTB Tom Barrasso C	6.00	15.00
GGTH Taylor Hall B	6.00	15.00
GGTP Teemu Pulkkinen D	6.00	15.00
GGZP Zach Parise B	6.00	15.00

2015-16 Upper Deck Ice Glacial Graphs Black

*BLACK/75: .6X TO 1.5X BASIC INSERTS
*BLACK/49: .75X TO 2X BASIC INSERTS

GGAP Artemi Panarin/75		
Go Hawks	50.00	100.00
GGDL Dylan Larkin/75	40.00	100.00
GGSG Shayne Gostisbehere/75		
Flyer Hockey	30.00	80.00

2015-16 Upper Deck Ice Global Impact

GIAP Artemi Panarin	6.00	15.00
GICM Connor McDavid	25.00	60.00
GIDL Dylan Larkin	5.00	12.00
GIDS Daniel Sprong	2.00	5.00
GIEP Emile Poirier	1.25	3.00
GIJE Jack Eichel	6.00	15.00
GIJM Jared McCann	2.00	5.00
GIJS Juuse Saros	4.00	10.00
GIJV Jake Virtanen	2.00	5.00
GIKF Kevin Fiala	2.00	5.00
GIMC Mike Condon	1.50	4.00
GIMD Max Domi	3.00	8.00
GIMJ Mattias Janmark	1.50	4.00
GIMR Mikko Rantanen	8.00	20.00
GINE Nikolaj Ehlers	3.00	8.00
GING Nikolay Goldobin	1.50	4.00
GINH Noah Hanifin	2.50	6.00
GINP Nicolas Petan	1.50	4.00
GINR Nick Ritchie	1.50	4.00
GIOL Oscar Lindberg	1.50	4.00
GIRF Robby Fabbri	2.00	5.00
GISB Sam Bennett	5.00	12.00
GISG Stanislav Galiev	1.50	4.00
GIVA Viktor Arvidsson	1.50	4.00
GIZF Zachary Fucale	1.25	3.00

2015-16 Upper Deck Ice Ice Premieres Autographs

IPAAB Antoine Bibeau AU/499	5.00	12.00
IPAAS Anton Slepyshev AU/499	3.00	8.00
IPABG Brendan Gaunce AU/499	6.00	15.00
IPABH Ben Hutton AU/499	5.00	12.00
IPABR Brendan Ranford AU/499	4.00	10.00
IPACH Connor Hellebuyck AU/499	20.00	50.00
IPACM Connor McDavid AU/125	400.00	500.00
IPACP Colton Parayko AU/499	8.00	20.00
IPACS Chandler Stephenson AU/499	6.00	15.00
IPADF Derek Forbort AU/499	4.00	10.00
IPADL Dylan Larkin AU/199	60.00	120.00
IPADO Joonas Donskoi AU/499	5.00	12.00
IPADS Daniel Sprong AU/499	6.00	15.00
IPAEP Emile Poirier AU/499	4.00	10.00
IPAFA Robby Fabbri AU/199	12.00	30.00
IPAHS Henrik Samuelsson AU/499	3.00	8.00
IPAHU Hunter Shinkaruk AU/499	5.00	12.00
IPAJD Jacob de la Rose AU/499	5.00	12.00
IPAJM Jared McCann AU/499	6.00	15.00
IPAJV Jake Virtanen AU/199	12.00	30.00
IPAJW Jordan Weal AU/499	3.00	8.00
IPAKF Kevin Fiala AU/499	6.00	15.00
IPALU Linus Ullmark AU/499	10.00	25.00
IPAMD Max Domi AU/199	20.00	50.00
IPAMI Colin Miller AU/499	4.00	10.00
IPAMJ Mattias Janmark AU/499	5.00	12.00
IPAMR Mikko Rantanen AU/499	25.00	60.00
IPANC Nick Cousins AU/499	5.00	12.00
IPANE Nikolaj Ehlers AU/199	20.00	50.00
IPANG Nikolay Goldobin AU/199	10.00	25.00
IPANH Noah Hanifin AU/499	8.00	20.00
IPANP Nicolas Petan AU/499	5.00	12.00
IPANR Nick Ritchie AU/499	5.00	12.00
IPAOL Oscar Lindberg AU/499	5.00	12.00
IPAPS Shane Prince AU/499	3.00	8.00
IPARF Radek Faksa AU/499	5.00	12.00
IPARH Ryan Hartman AU/499	6.00	15.00
IPARK Ronalds Kenins AU/499	3.00	8.00
IPASB Sam Bennett AU/199	30.00	80.00
IPASP Sergei Plotnikov AU/499	3.00	8.00
IPAST Shea Theodore AU/499	8.00	20.00
IPAVA Viktor Arvidsson AU/499	5.00	12.00
IPAVH Vincent Hinostroza AU/199	6.00	15.00

2015-16 Upper Deck Ice '05-06 Retro Ice Premieres

R1 Zachary Fucale/799	3.00	8.00
R2 Nick Ritchie/799	4.00	10.00
R3 Malcolm Subban/799	6.00	15.00
R4 Jake Virtanen/799	5.00	12.00
R5 Oscar Lindberg/799	4.00	10.00
R6 Shane Prince/799	2.50	6.00
R7 Jared McCann/799	5.00	12.00
R8 Stanislav Galiev/799	4.00	10.00
R9 Mattias Janmark/799	4.00	10.00
R10 Garret Sparks/799	4.00	10.00
R11 Nicolas Petan/799	4.00	10.00
R12 Juuse Saros/799	10.00	25.00
R13 Kevin Fiala/799	5.00	12.00
R14 Linus Ullmark/799	8.00	20.00
R15 Robby Fabbri/799	5.00	12.00
R16 Andreas Athanasiou/799	10.00	25.00
R17 Noah Hanifin/799	6.00	15.00
R18 Nikolay Goldobin/799	4.00	10.00
R19 Mikko Rantanen/799	20.00	50.00
R20 Mike Condon/799	4.00	10.00
R21 Colton Parayko/799	6.00	15.00
R22 Gustav Olofsson/799	4.00	10.00
R23 Daniel Sprong/799	5.00	12.00
R24 Sam Bennett/149	50.00	125.00
R25 Artemi Panarin/149	30.00	80.00
R26 Dylan Larkin/149	100.00	200.00
R27 Nikolaj Ehlers/149	30.00	80.00
R28 Max Domi/149	30.00	80.00
R29 Jack Eichel/149	150.00	250.00
R30 Connor McDavid/149	500.00	900.00

2015-16 Upper Deck Ice Rinkside Signings

RSAB Andre Burakovsky D	5.00	12.00
RSAI Arturs Irbe D	6.00	15.00
RSAK Anze Kopitar A	20.00	50.00
RSBE Jonathan Bernier B	6.00	15.00
RSBG Bill Guerin B	8.00	20.00
RSCM Connor McDavid A	200.00	400.00
RSCO Chris Osgood	8.00	20.00
RSCP Carey Price A	60.00	150.00
RSDS Daniel Sprong D	10.00	25.00
RSES Eric Staal B	10.00	25.00
RSGL Gabriel Landeskog	10.00	25.00
RSJA Jake Allen D	8.00	20.00
RSJB Jamie Benn B	8.00	20.00
RSJH Jiri Hudler D	6.00	15.00
RSJP Joe Pavelski B	10.00	25.00
RSJS Jason Spezza B	8.00	20.00
RSJT Jonathan Toews A	30.00	80.00
RSJV Jakub Voracek	6.00	15.00
RSKY Keith Yandle	5.00	12.00
RSMB Martin Brodeur A	30.00	80.00
RSMK Mike Keane D	6.00	15.00
RSMM Mark Messier A	30.00	80.00
RSMO Matt Moulson C	5.00	12.00
RSMR Mikko Rantanen D	40.00	100.00
RSNL Nicklas Lidstrom A	8.00	20.00
RSON Owen Nolan B	8.00	20.00
RSRB Rod Brind'Amour D	6.00	15.00
RSSB Sergei Bobrovsky B	12.00	30.00
RSSD Scott Darling D	6.00	15.00
RSSG Shayne Gostisbehere D	8.00	20.00
RSSJ Seth Jones C	8.00	20.00
RSSM Sean Monahan	5.00	12.00
RSSR Sam Reinhart C	15.00	40.00
RSTH Tomas Hertl D	8.00	20.00
RSTO Tyler Toffoli C	8.00	20.00
RSTT Tomas Tatar C	5.00	12.00
RSZP Zach Parise A	8.00	20.00

2015-16 Upper Deck Ice Rookie Relic Jumbos

RRJAB Antoine Bibeau	2.00	5.00
RRJAP Artemi Panarin	8.00	20.00
RRJBH Ben Hutton	2.00	5.00
RRJBM Brock McGinn	2.00	5.00
RRJCH Connor Hellebuyck	8.00	20.00
RRJCM Connor McDavid	20.00	50.00
RRJDL Dylan Larkin	6.00	15.00
RRJEP Emile Poirier	1.50	4.00
RRJHS Henrik Samuelsson	1.25	3.00
RRJJD Jacob de la Rose	2.00	5.00
RRJJE Jack Eichel	15.00	40.00
RRJJM Jared McCann	2.50	6.00
RRJJV Jake Virtanen	2.50	6.00
RRJKF Kevin Fiala	2.50	6.00
RRJMC Mike Condon	2.00	5.00
RRJMD Max Domi	4.00	10.00
RRJMP Matt Puempel	1.50	4.00
RRJMR Mikko Rantanen	10.00	25.00
RRJMS Malcolm Subban	3.00	8.00
RRJNE Nikolaj Ehlers	4.00	10.00
RRJNG Nikolay Goldobin	2.00	5.00
RRJNH Noah Hanifin	3.00	8.00
RRJNP Nicolas Petan	2.00	5.00
RRJNR Nick Ritchie	2.00	5.00
RRJRF Robby Fabbri	2.50	6.00
RRJRH Ryan Hartman	2.50	6.00
RRJSB Sam Bennett	6.00	15.00
RRJSH Hunter Shinkaruk	2.00	5.00
RRJSP Shane Prince	1.25	3.00
RRJST Shea Theodore	3.00	8.00

2015-16 Upper Deck Ice Signature Swatches

SSAL Andrew Ladd E	4.00	10.00
SSAO Alexander Ovechkin A	40.00	80.00
SSCM Connor McDavid A	300.00	400.00
SSCP Corey Perry D	10.00	25.00
SSDG Doug Gilmour B	10.00	25.00
SSDL Dylan Larkin D	60.00	120.00
SSEM Evgeni Malkin B	15.00	40.00
SSEP Emile Poirier E	5.00	12.00
SSGF Grant Fuhr C	12.00	30.00
SSJB Jonathan Bernier E	5.00	12.00
SSJC John Carlson E	6.00	15.00
SSJH Jiri Hudler E	5.00	12.00
SSKT Kyle Turris E	5.00	12.00
SSLR Luc Robitaille A	12.00	30.00
SSMA Mark Scheifele E	10.00	25.00
SSMF Marc-Andre Fleury D	12.00	30.00
SSMG Mike Gartner C	8.00	20.00
SSMS Martin St. Louis C	12.00	30.00
SSNE Nikolaj Ehlers E	12.00	30.00
SSNG Nikolay Goldobin E	6.00	15.00
SSOP Ondrej Palat C	5.00	12.00
SSRB Rod Brind'Amour C	5.00	12.00
SSSB Sam Bennett D	20.00	50.00
SSSC Sidney Crosby A	75.00	150.00
SSSJ Seth Jones E	6.00	15.00
SSTH Tomas Hertl C	6.00	15.00

2015-16 Upper Deck Ice Superb Script

SSAB Antoine Bibeau	8.00	20.00
SSCH Connor Hellebuyck	30.00	80.00
SSCM Connor McDavid	300.00	600.00
SSDL Dylan Larkin	75.00	150.00
SSDS Daniel Sprong	10.00	25.00
SSFA Robby Fabbri	10.00	25.00
SSJD Jacob de la Rose	8.00	20.00
SSJM Jared McCann	10.00	25.00
SSJV Jake Virtanen	10.00	25.00
SSKF Kevin Fiala	10.00	25.00
SSMD Max Domi	15.00	40.00
SSMP Matt Puempel	6.00	15.00
SSMR Mikko Rantanen	40.00	100.00
SSMS Malcolm Subban	12.00	30.00
SSNE Nikolaj Ehlers	15.00	40.00
SSNG Nikolay Goldobin	8.00	20.00
SSNH Noah Hanifin	12.00	30.00
SSNP Nicolas Petan	8.00	20.00
SSOL Oscar Lindberg	8.00	20.00
SSRF Radek Faksa	8.00	20.00
SSSB Sam Bennett	25.00	60.00
SSSP Sergei Plotnikov	5.00	12.00
SSVA Viktor Arvidsson	8.00	20.00

2015-16 Upper Deck Ice World Juniors Championship

WJCM Connor McDavid/699	30.00	80.00
WJHS Hunter Shinkaruk/1299	3.00	8.00
WJJV Jake Virtanen/1299	4.00	10.00
WJMD Max Domi/699	6.00	15.00
WJMS Malcolm Subban/1299	5.00	12.00
WJNP Nicolas Petan/1299	3.00	8.00
WJNR Nick Ritchie/1299	3.00	8.00
WJRF Robby Fabbri/1299	4.00	10.00
WJSB Sam Bennett/1299	10.00	25.00
WJST Shea Theodore/1299	5.00	12.00
WJZF Zachary Fucale/1299	2.50	6.00

2016-17 Upper Deck Ice

1 Sidney Crosby	4.00	10.00
2 John Tavares	1.50	4.00
3 Jamie Benn	1.00	2.50
4 Vladimir Tarasenko	1.25	3.00
5 Johnny Gaudreau	1.50	4.00
6 Oliver Ekman-Larsson	1.00	2.50
7 Aaron Ekblad	1.25	3.00
8 Drew Doughty	1.25	3.00
9 Taylor Hall	1.00	2.50
10 Carey Price	2.00	5.00
11 Milan Lucic	.75	2.00
12 Teuvo Teravainen	1.00	2.50
13 Frans Nielsen	.60	1.50
14 Seth Jones	1.00	2.50
15 Eric Staal	1.25	3.00
16 Brad Marchand	2.00	5.00
17 Matt Duchene	1.00	2.50
18 P.K. Subban	1.25	3.00
19 Jonathan Toews	1.50	4.00
20 Mike Hoffman	.60	1.50
21 Nikita Kucherov	2.00	5.00
22 Mats Zuccarello	1.00	2.50
23 John Gibson	1.00	2.50
24 Kyle Okposo	.60	1.50
25 Alexander Ovechkin	4.00	10.00
26 Shayne Gostisbehere	1.00	2.50
27 Joe Thornton	1.50	4.00
28 Morgan Rielly	1.00	2.50
29 Matt Murray	1.50	4.00
30 Ryan Miller	1.00	2.50
31 Jonathan Drouin	.75	2.00
32 Tuukka Rask	1.25	3.00
33 Robby Fabbri	.60	1.50
34 Blake Wheeler	1.00	2.50
35 Torey Krug	.75	2.00
36 Jonathan Quick	1.25	3.00
37 Jaden Schwartz	1.25	3.00
38 Cory Schneider	1.00	2.50
39 Andrew Ladd	.60	1.50
40 Devan Dubnyk	.75	2.00
41 Ryan Johansen	.75	2.00
42 John Klingberg	1.00	2.50
43 Max Pacioretty	1.00	2.50
44 Steven Stamkos	2.00	5.00
45 Evgeny Kuznetsov	1.25	3.00
46 Mika Zibanejad	1.25	3.00
47 Sam Reinhart	2.00	5.00
48 Ryan Nugent-Hopkins	1.25	3.00
49 Frederik Andersen	1.25	3.00
50 Evgeni Malkin	2.00	5.00
51 Brayden Schenn	1.00	2.50
52 Bobby Ryan	.75	2.00
53 Brock Nelson	1.00	2.50
54 Logan Couture	1.25	3.00
55 Brandon Dubinsky	.60	1.50
56 Jeff Skinner	1.25	3.00
57 Patrick Kane	2.00	5.00
58 Vincent Trocheck	1.00	2.50
59 Petr Mrazek	1.00	2.50
60 Jarome Iginla	1.25	3.00
61 David Backes	.60	1.50
62 Mark Scheifele	1.50	4.00
63 Jason Spezza	1.00	2.50
64 Jeff Carter	.75	2.00
65 Mikko Koivu	.75	2.00
66 James Neal	.60	1.50
67 John Carlson	1.00	2.50
68 Derek Stepan	.60	1.50
69 Brendan Gallagher	1.00	2.50
70 Brian Elliott	.75	2.00
71 Dylan Larkin	1.25	3.00
72 Loui Eriksson	.60	1.50
73 Patrick Sharp	.75	2.00
74 Nikolaj Ehlers	1.00	2.50
75 Claude Giroux	1.00	2.50
76 Ryan O'Reilly	1.00	2.50
77 Tyler Johnson	.60	1.50
78 Artemi Panarin	2.00	5.00
79 Tyson Barrie	.60	1.50
80 Ryan McDonagh	.60	1.50
81 Victor Rask	.60	1.50
82 Kevin Shattenkirk	.60	1.50
83 Leon Draisaitl	3.00	8.00
84 Boone Jenner	1.00	2.50
85 Thomas Greiss	.75	2.00
86 Michael Cammalleri	.75	2.00
87 Ryan Getzlaf	1.00	2.50
88 Brent Burns	1.00	2.50
89 Anthony Duclair	.75	2.00
90 Alex Galchenyuk	.60	1.50
91 Mark Giordano	1.00	2.50
92 Pekka Rinne	1.00	2.50
93 Kris Letang	1.25	3.00
94 Corey Crawford	1.25	3.00
95 Nicklas Backstrom	1.00	2.50
96 Mark Stone	1.25	3.00
97 Ryan Kesler	1.00	2.50
98 Keith Yandle	.60	1.50
99 Bo Horvat	1.25	3.00
100 Connor McDavid	5.00	12.00
101 Anthony DeAngelo RC	3.00	8.00
102 Frederik Gauthier RC	3.00	8.00
103 Stephen Johns RC	3.00	8.00
104 Chase De Leo RC	4.00	10.00
105 Miles Wood RC	3.00	8.00
106 Joseph Cramarossa RC	4.00	10.00
107 Michal Kempny RC	4.00	10.00
108 Hudson Fasching RC	4.00	10.00
109 Markus Nutivaara RC	4.00	10.00
110 Jacob Larsson RC	6.00	15.00
111 Julius Honka RC	4.00	10.00
112 Mike Reilly RC	3.00	8.00
113 Denis Malgin RC	3.00	8.00
114 Alan Quine RC	4.00	10.00
115 Nikita Zaitsev RC	4.00	10.00
116 Yohann Auvitu RC	4.00	10.00
117 Jake Guentzel RC	15.00	40.00
118 Zane Mcintyre RC	5.00	12.00
119 Charlie Lindgren RC	6.00	15.00
120 Justin Bailey RC	4.00	10.00
121 Tom Kuhnhackl RC	3.00	8.00
122 Rob O'Gara RC	4.00	10.00
123 Chris Bigras RC	3.00	8.00
124 Roman Lyubimov RC	4.00	10.00
125 Nick Lappin RC	4.00	10.00
126 Cristoval Nieves RC	5.00	12.00
127 Nikita Tryamkin RC	3.00	8.00
128 John Quenneville RC	4.00	10.00
129 Aaron Dell RC	4.00	10.00
130 Gustav Forsling RC	8.00	20.00
131 Zack Mitchell RC	4.00	10.00
132 Gemel Smith RC	4.00	10.00
133 Lukas Sedlak RC	4.00	10.00
134 Kevin Gravel RC	5.00	12.00
135 Mark Jankowski RC	3.00	8.00
136 Kyle Rau RC	5.00	12.00
137 Drake Caggiula RC	4.00	10.00
138 Tristan Jarry RC	8.00	20.00
139 Thatcher Demko RC	10.00	25.00
140 Zach Hyman RC	12.00	30.00
141 Nikita Soshnikov RC	2.50	6.00
142 Trevor Carrick RC	4.00	10.00
143 Austin Czarnik RC	6.00	15.00
144 Jason Dickinson RC	3.00	8.00
145 Kevin Labanc RC	4.00	10.00
146 Nic Dowd RC	3.00	8.00
147 Zach Sanford RC	4.00	10.00
148 Jakob Chychrun RC	8.00	20.00
149 Dominik Simon RC	3.00	8.00
150 Ryan Pulock RC	4.00	10.00
151 Blake Speers RC	4.00	10.00
152 Pontus Aberg RC	5.00	12.00
153 Steven Santini RC	3.00	8.00
154 A.J. Greer RC	4.00	10.00
155 Michael Matheson RC	4.00	10.00
156 Matthew Benning RC	5.00	12.00
157 Oliver Kylington RC	3.00	8.00
158 Thomas Chabot RC	8.00	20.00
159 Brandon Tanev RC	5.00	12.00
160 Esa Lindell RC	4.00	10.00
161 Oliver Bjorkstrand RC	5.00	12.00
162 Nick Sorensen RC	4.00	10.00
163 Tyler Bertuzzi RC	6.00	15.00
164 Nick Baptiste RC	4.00	10.00
165 Nick Schmaltz RC	5.00	12.00
166 Brandon Carlo RC	8.00	20.00
167 Lawson Crouse RC	4.00	10.00
168 Timo Meier RC	10.00	25.00
169 Jakub Vrana RC	6.00	15.00
170 Tyler Motte RC	5.00	12.00
171 Sonny Milano RC	6.00	15.00
172 Danton Heinen RC	4.00	10.00
173 Josh Morrissey RC	12.00	30.00
174 Anthony Beauvillier RC	5.00	12.00
175 Mathew Barzal RC	15.00	40.00
176 Artturi Lehkonen RC	6.00	15.00
177 Brendan Leipsic RC	4.00	10.00
178 Troy Stecher RC	5.00	12.00
179 Kasperi Kapanen RC	8.00	20.00
180 Connor Brown RC	8.00	20.00
181 Ivan Provorov RC	12.00	30.00
182 Travis Konecny RC	15.00	40.00
183 Pavel Zacha RC	12.00	30.00
184 Brayden Point RC	30.00	80.00
185 Sebastian Aho RC	25.00	60.00
186 Kyle Connor RC	25.00	60.00
187 Joel Eriksson Ek RC	12.00	30.00
188 Christian Dvorak RC	10.00	25.00
189 Anthony Mantha RC	15.00	40.00
190 Pavel Buchnevich RC	12.00	30.00
191 William Nylander RC	200.00	500.00
192 Patrik Laine RC	600.00	1000.00
193 Jimmy Vesey RC	50.00	120.00
194 Matthew Tkachuk RC	40.00	100.00
195 Mitch Marner RC	300.00	600.00
196 Jesse Puljujarvi RC	60.00	150.00
197 Dylan Strome RC	80.00	200.00
198 Mikhail Sergachev RC	100.00	250.00
199 Zach Werenski RC	100.00	250.00
200 Auston Matthews RC	1500.00	2500.00

2016-17 Upper Deck Ice Fresh Threads

FTAB Anthony Beauvillier	2.00	5.00
FTAM Auston Matthews	25.00	60.00
FTBP Brayden Point	5.00	12.00
FTCD Christian Dvorak	2.50	6.00
FTCL Charlie Lindgren	3.00	8.00
FTDS Dylan Strome	5.00	12.00
FTIP Ivan Provorov	3.00	8.00
FTJC Jakob Chychrun	4.00	10.00
FTJE Joel Eriksson Ek	3.00	8.00
FTJP Jesse Puljujarvi	6.00	15.00
FTJV Jimmy Vesey	3.00	8.00
FTKC Kyle Connor	6.00	15.00
FTKK Kasperi Kapanen	3.00	8.00
FTMA Anthony Mantha	4.00	10.00
FTMB Mathew Barzal	6.00	15.00
FTMM Mitch Marner	6.00	15.00
FTMS Mikhail Sergachev	3.00	8.00
FTMT Matthew Tkachuk	8.00	20.00
FTNS Nick Schmaltz	2.50	6.00
FTPB Pavel Buchnevich	3.00	8.00
FTPL Patrik Laine	10.00	25.00
FTPZ Pavel Zacha	3.00	8.00
FTSA Sebastian Aho	6.00	15.00
FTSM Sonny Milano	2.50	6.00
FTSO Nikita Soshnikov	1.25	3.00
FTTC Thomas Chabot	4.00	10.00
FTTK Travis Konecny	4.00	10.00
FTTM Tyler Motte	2.00	5.00
FTWN William Nylander	8.00	20.00
FTZW Zach Werenski	6.00	15.00

2016-17 Upper Deck Ice Fresh Threads Red

*RED/25: 1X TO 2.5X BASIC INSERTS

FTAM Auston Matthews	50.00	125.00
FTPL Patrik Laine	40.00	100.00

2016-17 Upper Deck Ice Frozen Fabrics

FFAE Aaron Ekblad	4.00	10.00
FFCM Connor McDavid	25.00	60.00
FFCP Corey Perry	5.00	12.00
FFEK Erik Karlsson	4.00	10.00
FFEM Evgeni Malkin	6.00	15.00
FFFP Felix Potvin	5.00	12.00
FFHS Henrik Sedin	4.00	10.00
FFHZ Henrik Zetterberg	6.00	15.00
FFJB Jamie Benn	3.00	8.00

FFJG Johnny Gaudreau 5.00 12.00
FFJQ Jonathan Quick 4.00 10.00
FFJS Joe Sakic 8.00 20.00
FFJT John Tavares 5.00 12.00
FFMD Martin Brodeur 8.00 20.00
FFML Milan Lucic 2.50 6.00
FFMM Mark Messier 6.00 15.00
FFMP Max Pacioretty 3.00 8.00
FFMZ Mika Zibanejad 4.00 10.00
FFNH Noah Hanifin 3.00 8.00
FFPS P.K. Subban 4.00 10.00
FFSC Sidney Crosby 20.00 50.00
FFTO Jonathan Toews 15.00 40.00

2016-17 Upper Deck Ice Frozen Foursome

F4FW FW 20.00 50.00
F4DEF DEF 6.00 15.00
F4RC1 RC1 15.00 40.00
F4RC2 RC2 20.00 50.00
F4RC3 RC3 30.00 80.00
F4RC4 RC4 12.00 30.00
F4HABS HABS 10.00 25.00
F4NASH NASH 8.00 20.00
F4BLUES Blues 6.00 15.00
F4HAWKS HAWKS 10.00 25.00
F4WINGS WINGS 6.00 15.00
F4SHARKS SHARKS 8.00 20.00

2016-17 Upper Deck Ice Glacial Graphs

GGAA Andreas Athanasiou D 8.00 20.00
GGAE Aaron Ekblad 10.00 25.00
GGAM Al MacInnis 10.00 25.00
GGBB Bob Baun 8.00 20.00
GGBH Bo Horvat 10.00 25.00
GGBJ Boone Jenner 8.00 20.00
GGBS Borje Salming 8.00 20.00
GGBU Brent Burns 8.00 20.00
GGCH Carl Hagelin 5.00 12.00
GGCS Cory Schneider 8.00 20.00
GGDK David Krejci 8.00 20.00
GGDL Leon Draisaitl 25.00 60.00
GGDT Dave Taylor 8.00 20.00
GGGC Guy Carbonneau 8.00 20.00
GGHZ Henrik Zetterberg 10.00 25.00
GGJG John Gibson D 8.00 20.00
GGJO Ryan Johansen B 6.00 15.00
GGJZ Jason Zucker 8.00 20.00
GGKM Kirk McLean 8.00 20.00
GGKP Kyle Palmieri C 6.00 15.00
GGLD Louis Domingue 6.00 15.00
GGLM Larry Murphy A 6.00 15.00
GGMB Matt Beleskey 6.00 15.00
GGMM Matt Murray 12.00 30.00
GGMR Morgan Rielly 8.00 20.00
GGMS Mark Scheifele 12.00 30.00
GGNK Nikita Kucherov 15.00 40.00
GGNN Nino Niederreiter 5.00 12.00
GGRJ Roman Josi 8.00 20.00
GGRM Ryan Miller 8.00 20.00
GGRS Ryan Spooner 6.00 15.00
GGTB Tyson Barrie 5.00 12.00
GGTL Trevor Linden 8.00 20.00
GGTT Tyler Toffoli 8.00 20.00
GGTW Tom Wilson 8.00 20.00
GGVR Victor Rask 5.00 12.00

2016-17 Upper Deck Ice Champions

IC1 Sidney Crosby 15.00 40.00
IC2 Jonathan Quick 5.00 12.00
IC3 Zdeno Chara 4.00 10.00
IC4 Corey Perry 6.00 15.00
IC5 Patrick Kane 8.00 20.00
IC6 Cam Ward 4.00 10.00
IC7 Evgeni Malkin 8.00 20.00
IC8 Duncan Keith 3.00 8.00
IC9 Drew Doughty 5.00 12.00
IC10 Henrik Zetterberg 5.00 12.00
IC11 Matt Murray 6.00 15.00
IC12 Doug Harvey 12.00 30.00
IC13 Teemu Selanne 8.00 20.00
IC14 Bobby Orr 25.00 60.00
IC15 Ray Bourque 12.00 30.00
IC16 Red Kelly 4.00 10.00
IC17 Mark Messier 8.00 20.00
IC18 Al MacInnis 5.00 12.00
IC19 Mario Lemieux 15.00 40.00
IC20 Martin St. Louis 4.00 10.00
IC21 Steve Yzerman 12.00 30.00
IC22 Brian Leetch 3.00 8.00
IC23 Martin Brodeur 10.00 25.00
IC24 Wayne Gretzky 25.00 60.00

2016-17 Upper Deck Ice Premieres Autographs

IPAAB Anthony Beauvillier 10.00 25.00
IPAAL Artturi Lehkonen 12.00 30.00
IPAAM Auston Matthews 400.00 650.00
IPABC Brandon Carlo 15.00 40.00
IPABL Brendan Leipsic 8.00 20.00
IPACB Chris Bigras 8.00 20.00
IPACD Christian Dvorak 12.00 30.00
IPACL Charlie Lindgren 15.00 40.00
IPADA Daniel Altshuller 8.00 20.00
IPADH Danton Heinen 8.00 20.00
IPADS Dominik Simon 8.00 20.00
IPAHF Hudson Fasching 10.00 25.00
IPAIP Ivan Provorov 15.00 40.00
IPAJE Joel Eriksson Ek 15.00 40.00
IPAJP Jesse Puljujarvi 20.00 50.00
IPAJV Jakub Vrana 12.00 30.00
IPAKC Kyle Connor 30.00 80.00
IPAKK Kasperi Kapanen 15.00 40.00
IPALC Lawson Crouse 8.00 20.00
IPAMA Anthony Mantha 40.00 100.00
IPAMB Mathew Barzal 30.00 80.00
IPAMI Mitch Marner 250.00 600.00
IPAMM Michael Matheson 10.00 25.00
IPAMO Tyler Motte/299 5.00 12.00
IPAMS Mikhail Sergachev 15.00 40.00
IPAMT Matthew Tkachuk 50.00 125.00
IPAMW Miles Wood 8.00 20.00
IPANS Nick Schmaltz 12.00 30.00
IPAOK Oliver Kylington 8.00 20.00
IPAOS Oskar Sundqvist 10.00 25.00
IPAPB Pavel Buchnevich 15.00 40.00
IPAPL Patrik Laine 100.00 250.00
IPAPZ Pavel Zacha/99 8.00 20.00
IPARP Ryan Pulock 10.00 25.00
IPASA Sebastian Aho/299 30.00 80.00
IPASM Sonny Milano/299 4.00 10.00
IPASO Nikita Soshnikov 6.00 15.00
IPASS Steven Santini 8.00 20.00
IPAST Dylan Strome 25.00 60.00
IPATC Thomas Chabot 20.00 50.00
IPATK Travis Konecny 20.00 50.00
IPATM Timo Meier 20.00 50.00
IPATO Sergey Tolchinsky 8.00 20.00
IPAVE Jimmy Vesey 15.00 40.00
IPAWN William Nylander 100.00 250.00
IPAZW Zach Werenski 30.00 80.00

2016-17 Upper Deck Ice Rookie Relic Jumbos

RRJAB Anthony Beauvillier 5.00 12.00
RRJAD Anthony DeAngelo 4.00 10.00
RRJAM Auston Matthews 30.00 80.00
RRJBL Brendan Leipsic 4.00 10.00
RRJBP Brayden Point 12.00 30.00
RRJCB Connor Brown 8.00 20.00
RRJCD Christian Dvorak 6.00 15.00
RRJDS Dylan Strome 12.00 30.00
RRJHF Hudson Fasching 5.00 12.00
RRJIP Ivan Provorov 8.00 20.00
RRJJE Joel Eriksson Ek 8.00 20.00
RRJJM Josh Morrissey 12.00 30.00
RRJJP Jesse Puljujarvi 10.00 25.00
RRJJV Jimmy Vesey 8.00 20.00
RRJKC Kyle Connor 15.00 40.00
RRJKK Kasperi Kapanen 8.00 20.00
RRJKL Kevin Labanc 5.00 12.00
RRJMA Anthony Mantha 10.00 25.00
RRJMB Mathew Barzal 15.00 40.00
RRJMM Mitch Marner 15.00 40.00
RRJMS Mikhail Sergachev 8.00 20.00
RRJMT Matthew Tkachuk 20.00 50.00
RRJPB Pavel Buchnevich 8.00 20.00
RRJPL Patrik Laine 12.00 30.00
RRJPZ Pavel Zacha 8.00 20.00
RRJSA Sebastian Aho 15.00 40.00
RRJTK Travis Konecny 10.00 25.00
RRJTM Tyler Motte 5.00 12.00
RRJWN William Nylander 20.00 50.00
RRJZW Zach Werenski 15.00 40.00

2016-17 Upper Deck Ice Signature Swatches

SSAE Aaron Ekblad C 10.00 25.00
SSAG Alex Galchenyuk C 5.00 12.00
SSAH Adam Henrique C 6.00 15.00
SSAM Auston Matthews A 250.00 400.00
SSCP Carey Price A 40.00 100.00
SSHZ Henrik Zetterberg A 12.00 30.00
SSJJ Jaromir Jagr B 40.00 100.00
SSJP Joe Pavelski B 10.00 25.00
SSJT Jonathan Toews A 60.00 150.00
SSMA Anthony Mantha C 15.00 40.00
SSMB Matt Beleskey C 6.00 15.00
SSON Owen Nolan C 8.00 20.00
SSPL Patrik Laine B 50.00 120.00
SSRB Ray Bourque A 25.00 60.00
SSRJ Roman Josi C 8.00 20.00
SSRK Ryan Kesler C 8.00 20.00
SSRL Roberto Luongo B 12.00 30.00
SSTT Tyler Toffoli C 8.00 20.00
SSWN William Nylander C 30.00 80.00
SSZP Zach Parise C 8.00 20.00

2016-17 Upper Deck Ice Sub Zero

SZ1 Connor McDavid 5.00 12.00
SZ2 Henrik Zetterberg 1.25 3.00
SZ3 Braden Holtby 1.25 3.00
SZ4 Evgeni Malkin 2.00 5.00
SZ5 Jaromir Jagr 3.00 8.00
SZ6 Erik Karlsson 1.25 3.00
SZ7 Tyler Seguin 1.25 3.00
SZ8 Jordan Eberle 1.00 2.50
SZ9 Gustav Nyquist .60 1.50
SZ10 Patrick Kane 2.00 5.00
SZ11 Roberto Luongo 1.50 4.00
SZ12 Tyler Toffoli 1.00 2.50
SZ13 Joe Pavelski 1.25 3.00
SZ14 Filip Forsberg 1.50 4.00
SZ15 Daniel Sedin 1.25 3.00
SZ16 Dustin Byfuglien 1.00 2.50
SZ17 Jaroslav Halak 1.00 2.50
SZ18 Zach Parise 1.00 2.50
SZ19 Anze Kopitar 1.50 4.00
SZ20 Alexander Ovechkin 4.00 10.00
SZ21 Shea Weber .75 2.00
SZ22 Sam Bennett 1.50 4.00
SZ23 Ben Bishop .75 2.00
SZ24 Alexander Steen .60 1.50
SZ25 Jonathan Toews 1.50 4.00
SZ26 Alexander Wennberg .60 1.50
SZ27 Max Domi 1.00 2.50
SZ28 Henrik Lundqvist 2.50 6.00
SZ29 Adam Henrique .75 2.00
SZ30 John Tavares 1.50 4.00
SZ31 P.K. Subban 1.50 4.00
SZ32 Nino Niederreiter .60 1.50
SZ33 Mark Scheifele 1.25 3.00
SZ34 Nathan MacKinnon 4.00 10.00
SZ35 Sidney Crosby 4.00 10.00
SZ36 Jordan Staal .75 2.00
SZ37 James van Riemsdyk .75 2.00
SZ38 Sean Monahan .60 1.50
SZ39 Jack Eichel 1.50 4.00
SZ40 Carey Price 2.00 5.00
SZ41 David Krejci 1.00 2.50
SZ42 Kevin Hayes .75 2.00
SZ43 Corey Perry 1.50 4.00
SZ44 Jake Allen 1.00 2.50
SZ45 Jamie Benn 1.00 2.50
SZ46 Patrice Bergeron 1.25 3.00
SZ47 Henrik Sedin 1.25 3.00
SZ48 Martin Jones .75 2.00
SZ49 Gabriel Landeskog 1.25 3.00
SZ50 Steven Stamkos 2.00 5.00
SZ51 Jakub Voracek .75 2.00
SZ52 Brandon Saad .75 2.00
SZ53 Mario Lemieux 4.00 10.00
SZ54 Pat LaFontaine 1.00 2.50
SZ55 Mark Messier 2.00 5.00
SZ56 Stan Mikita 1.25 3.00
SZ57 Steve Yzerman 2.50 6.00
SZ58 Bobby Orr 4.00 10.00
SZ59 Patrick Roy 2.50 6.00
SZ60 Wayne Gretzky 6.00 15.00
SZ61 Auston Matthews 12.00 30.00
SZ62 Zach Werenski 3.00 8.00
SZ63 Patrik Laine 10.00 25.00
SZ64 Matthew Tkachuk 4.00 10.00
SZ65 William Nylander 4.00 10.00
SZ66 Jesse Puljujarvi 2.00 5.00
SZ67 Jimmy Vesey 1.50 4.00
SZ68 Anthony Mantha 2.00 5.00
SZ69 Tyler Motte 1.00 2.50
SZ70 Travis Konecny 2.00 5.00
SZ71 Pavel Zacha 1.50 4.00
SZ72 Pavel Buchnevich 1.50 4.00
SZ73 Dylan Strome 2.50 6.00
SZ74 Sebastian Aho 3.00 8.00
SZ75 Mitch Marner 3.00 8.00
SZ76 Brayden Point 2.50 6.00
SZ77 Connor Brown 1.50 4.00
SZ78 Mikhail Sergachev 1.50 4.00
SZ79 Anthony Beauvillier 1.00 2.50
SZ80 Kasperi Kapanen 1.50 4.00
SZ81 Ivan Provorov 1.50 4.00
SZ82 Christian Dvorak 1.25 3.00
SZ83 Kyle Connor 3.00 8.00
SZ84 Mathew Barzal 3.00 8.00
SZ85 Brandon Carlo 1.50 4.00
SZ86 Gustav Forsling 2.00 5.00
SZ87 Joel Eriksson Ek 1.50 4.00
SZ88 Frederik Gauthier .75 2.00
SZ89 Troy Stecher 1.00 2.50
SZ90 A.J. Greer 1.00 2.50
SZ91 Artturi Lehkonen 1.25 3.00
SZ92 Anthony DeAngelo .75 2.00
SZ93 Josh Morrissey 2.50 6.00
SZ94 Tyler Bertuzzi 1.50 4.00
SZ95 Nick Baptiste 1.00 2.50
SZ96 Mitch Marner 20.00 50.00
SZ97 Patrik Laine 60.00 150.00
SZ98 William Nylander 20.00 50.00
SZ99 Jesse Puljujarvi 10.00 25.00
SZ100 Auston Matthews 60.00 150.00

2016-17 Upper Deck Ice Superb Script

SSAM Auston Matthews 250.00 400.00
SSCB Connor Brown 15.00 40.00
SSCD Christian Dvorak 12.00 30.00
SSDH Danton Heinen 8.00 20.00
SSDS Dylan Strome 25.00 60.00
SSIP Ivan Provorov 40.00 100.00
SSJE Joel Eriksson Ek 20.00 50.00
SSJP Jesse Puljujarvi 20.00 50.00
SSJV Jimmy Vesey 15.00 40.00
SSKC Kyle Connor 30.00 80.00
SSKK Kasperi Kapanen 15.00 40.00
SSMA Anthony Mantha 20.00 50.00
SSMB Mathew Barzal 30.00 80.00
SSMM Mitch Marner 30.00 80.00
SSMS Mikhail Sergachev 40.00 100.00
SSMT Matthew Tkachuk 60.00 150.00
SSPL Patrik Laine 250.00 350.00
SSTC Thomas Chabot 20.00 50.00
SSWN William Nylander 40.00 100.00
SSZW Zach Werenski 30.00 80.00

2016-17 Upper Deck Ice World Juniors

WJBP Brayden Point 5.00 12.00
WJBS Blake Speers 2.00 5.00
WJDS Dylan Strome 5.00 12.00
WJJQ John Quenneville 2.00 5.00
WJLC Lawson Crouse 1.50 4.00
WJMB Mathew Barzal 6.00 15.00
WJMM Mitch Marner 6.00 15.00
WJTC Thomas Chabot 4.00 10.00
WJTK Travis Konecny 10.00 25.00

2017-18 Upper Deck Ice

1 Cory Schneider .75 2.00
2 Scott Hartnell .50 1.25
3 Justin Williams .60 1.50
4 Leon Draisaitl 2.50 6.00
5 Nathan MacKinnon 3.00 8.00
6 Niklas Hjalmarsson .50 1.25
7 Patrick Kane 1.50 4.00
8 Tuukka Rask 1.00 2.50
9 Artemi Panarin 1.50 4.00
10 Mark Giordano .75 2.00
11 Drew Doughty 1.00 2.50
12 Patrik Laine 2.00 5.00
13 Daniel Sedin 1.00 2.50
14 Calvin de Haan .50 1.25
15 Filip Forsberg 1.25 3.00
16 Erik Karlsson 1.00 2.50
17 Alexander Ovechkin 3.00 8.00
18 Aleksander Barkov 1.25 3.00
19 John Tavares 1.25 3.00
20 Brayden Schenn .75 2.00
21 David Krejci .75 2.00
22 Nail Yakupov .50 1.25
23 Kevin Labanc .50 1.25
24 Brayden Point 1.00 2.50
25 Wayne Simmonds 1.00 2.50
26 Shea Weber .60 1.50
27 Chris Kreider 1.00 2.50
28 Cam Talbot .75 2.00
29 Dustin Byfuglien .75 2.00
30 Patrick Marleau .75 2.00
31 Christopher Tanev .50 1.25
32 Darnell Nurse .50 1.25
33 Henrik Zetterberg 1.00 2.50
34 Josh Bailey .60 1.50
35 Brandon Saad .60 1.50
36 Steven Stamkos 1.50 4.00
37 Matt Duchene .75 2.00
38 Travis Hamonic .60 1.50
39 Kris Letang 1.00 2.50
40 Mark Scheifele 1.25 3.00
41 Nate Schmidt .60 1.50
42 Alex Pietrangelo .60 1.50
43 Brett Pesce .50 1.25
44 Andrew Cogliano .50 1.25
45 Mike Green .60 1.50
46 Nikita Kucherov 1.50 4.00
47 Matt Murray 1.25 3.00
48 Jordan Staal .60 1.50
49 Reilly Smith .75 2.00
50 Jake Gardiner .50 1.25
51 Marcus Johansson .60 1.50
52 Jonathan Marchessault 1.00 2.50
53 Mikael Backlund .60 1.50
54 Erik Johnson .50 1.25
55 Jonathan Toews 1.25 3.00
56 Mika Zibanejad 1.00 2.50
57 Oscar Klefbom .60 1.50
58 Ben Bishop .60 1.50
59 Nicklas Backstrom .75 2.00
60 Derick Brassard .50 1.25
61 Jakub Voracek .60 1.50
62 Evander Kane .75 2.00
63 Nick Bjugstad .50 1.25
64 Max Domi .75 2.00
65 Josh Manson .50 1.25
66 Anze Kopitar 1.25 3.00
67 Viktor Arvidsson .50 1.25
68 Jason Zucker .75 2.00
69 Patrice Bergeron 1.00 2.50
70 Jonathan Drouin .60 1.50
71 Corey Perry 1.25 3.00
72 Carey Price 1.50 4.00
73 Jared Spurgeon .75 2.00
74 Roberto Luongo 1.25 3.00
75 Thomas Vanek .60 1.50
76 Anthony Mantha .60 1.50
77 Brad Marchand 1.50 4.00
78 Henrik Lundqvist 2.00 5.00
79 Cam Atkinson .75 2.00
80 Sean Couturier .60 1.50
81 Ryan O'Reilly .75 2.00
82 Ryan Getzlaf .75 2.00
83 Mitch Marner 1.25 3.00
84 Kyle Okposo .50 1.25
85 Colton Parayko .60 1.50
86 Bryan Rust .60 1.50
87 Martin Jones .60 1.50
88 Jack Eichel 1.25 3.00
89 Tyler Seguin 1.00 2.50
90 Braden Holtby 1.00 2.50
91 Sami Vatanen .50 1.25
92 Alexander Radulov .75 2.00
93 Nino Niederreiter .50 1.25
94 Evgeni Malkin 1.50 4.00
95 Evgeny Kuznetsov 1.00 2.50
96 Joe Pavelski 1.00 2.50
97 Nick Foligno .60 1.50
98 William Nylander 1.50 4.00
99 Dustin Brown .75 2.00
100 Marc-Edouard Vlasic .50 1.25
101 Giovanni Fiore/1299 RC 4.00 10.00
102 David Rittich/1299 RC 10.00 25.00
103 Robbie Russo/1299 RC 4.00 10.00
104 Jaycob Megna/1299 RC 4.00 10.00
105 Joakim Ryan/1299 RC 4.00 10.00
106 Oscar Fantenberg/1299 RC 4.00 10.00
107 Griffen Molino/1299 RC 3.00 8.00
108 Vladislav Kamenev/1299 RC 4.00 10.00
109 Kalle Kossila/1299 RC 3.00 8.00
110 Tim Heed/1299 RC 3.00 8.00
111 Jan Rutta/1299 RC 4.00 10.00
112 Vadim Shipachyov/1299 RC 5.00 12.00
113 Michael Kapla/1299 RC 3.00 8.00
114 Alex Iafallo/1299 RC 4.00 10.00
115 Viktor Antipin/1299 RC 4.00 10.00
116 Andrew Poturalski/1299 RC 4.00 10.00
117 Marcus Sorensen/1299 RC 3.00 8.00
118 Michael Amadio/1299 RC 4.00 10.00
119 Ville Husso/1299 RC 5.00 12.00
120 Jonny Brodzinski/499 RC 5.00 12.00
121 Jake Dotchin/1299 RC 3.00 8.00
122 Jean-Sebastien Dea/1299 RC 4.00 10.00
123 Brendan Lemieux/1299 RC 4.00 10.00
124 Valentin Zykov/1299 RC 3.00 8.00
125 Carter Rowney/1299 RC 4.00 10.00
126 Tucker Poolman/999 RC 4.00 10.00
127 Kyle Capobianco/999 RC 4.00 10.00
128 Alex Nedeljkovic/999 RC 6.00 15.00
129 MacKenzie Weegar/999 RC 5.00 12.00
130 Lucas Wallmark/999 RC 4.00 10.00
131 Anton Lindholm/999 RC 4.00 10.00
132 Riley Barber/999 RC 4.00 10.00
133 Alexandre Carrier/999 RC 3.00 8.00
134 Ian McCoshen/999 RC 3.00 8.00
135 Mike Vecchione/999 RC 4.00 10.00
136 Remi Elie/999 RC 3.00 8.00
137 Henrik Haapala/999 RC 4.00 10.00
138 Jordan Schmaltz/999 RC 4.00 10.00
139 Maxime Lagace/999 RC 5.00 12.00
140 Rasmus Andersson/999 RC 4.00 10.00
141 Adin Hill/999 RC 8.00 20.00
142 Andreas Borgman/999 RC 4.00 10.00
143 Roland McKeown/999 RC 4.00 10.00
144 C.J. Smith/999 RC 3.00 8.00
145 Nicolas Kerdiles/999 RC 3.00 8.00
146 Peter Cehlarik/999 RC 4.00 10.00
147 Blake Coleman/999 RC 4.00 10.00
148 Gabriel Carlsson/999 RC 3.00 8.00
149 Robert Hagg/999 RC 3.00 8.00
150 John Hayden/999 RC 3.00 8.00
151 Samuel Blais/499 RC 8.00 20.00
152 Nick Merkley/1299 RC 4.00 10.00
153 Christian Jaros/499 RC 4.00 10.00
154 Samuel Morin/499 RC 4.00 10.00
155 Jesper Bratt/499 RC 10.00 25.00
156 Vince Dunn/499 RC 6.00 15.00
157 Alex Formenton/499 RC 4.00 10.00
158 Martin Necas/499 RC 15.00 40.00
159 Madison Bowey/499 RC 3.00 8.00
160 J.T. Compher/499 RC 4.00 10.00
161 Evgeny Svechnikov/499 RC 10.00 25.00
162 Jon Gillies/499 RC 5.00 12.00
163 Samuel Girard/499 RC 5.00 12.00
164 Nikita Scherbak/499 RC 6.00 15.00
165 Janne Kuokkanen/499 RC 4.00 10.00
166 Jakob Forsbacka-Karlsson/499 RC 5.00 12.00
167 Ivan Barbashev/499 RC 6.00 15.00
168 Filip Chlapik/499 RC 4.00 10.00
169 Eric Comrie/499 RC 4.00 10.00
170 Denis Gurianov/499 RC 12.00 30.00
171 Christian Fischer/499 RC 6.00 15.00
172 Christian Djoos/499 RC 4.00 10.00
173 Calle Rosen/499 RC 5.00 12.00
174 Haydn Fleury/499 RC 5.00 12.00
175 Jack Roslovic/499 RC 6.00 15.00
176 Will Butcher/249 RC 10.00 25.00
177 Alex Kerfoot/249 RC 15.00 40.00
178 Luke Kunin/249 RC 8.00 20.00
179 Tage Thompson/249 RC 20.00 50.00
180 Adrian Kempe/249 RC 15.00 40.00
181 Anders Bjork/249 RC 10.00 25.00
182 Colin White/249 RC 10.00 25.00
183 Victor Mete/249 RC 8.00 20.00
184 Jake DeBrusk/249 RC 20.00 50.00
185 Kailer Yamamoto/249 RC 20.00 50.00
186 Logan Brown/249 RC 8.00 20.00
187 Travis Sanheim/249 RC 8.00 20.00
188 Filip Chytil/249 RC 8.00 20.00
189 Alex Tuch/249 RC 20.00 50.00
190 Owen Tippett/249 RC 15.00 40.00
191 Charlie McAvoy/99 RC 350.00 700.00
192 Clayton Keller/99 RC 200.00 300.00
193 Brock Boeser/99 RC 350.00 600.00
194 Josh Ho-Sang/99 RC 250.00 350.00
195 Tyson Jost/99 RC 200.00 300.00
196 Pierre-Luc Dubois/99 RC 200.00 300.00
197 Alex DeBrincat/99 RC 200.00 300.00
199 Nolan Patrick/99 RC 350.00 450.00
200 Nico Hischier/99 RC 350.00 450.00

2017-18 Upper Deck Ice '07-08 Retro Ice Premieres

1 Nico Hischier 60.00 150.00
2 Clayton Keller 50.00 125.00
3 Brock Boeser 50.00 120.00
4 Charlie McAvoy 50.00 125.00
5 Pierre-Luc Dubois 30.00 80.00
6 Tyson Jost 40.00 100.00
7 Josh Ho-Sang 25.00 60.00
8 Alex DeBrincat 50.00 125.00
9 Filip Chytil 20.00 50.00
10 Nolan Patrick 40.00 100.00

2017-18 Upper Deck Ice Frozen Foursomes

F4BUF Eichel/O'Reilly/Pominville/Ristolainen C 5.00 12.00
F4DIV Pacioretty/Toews/Ovechkin/Getzlaf A 12.00 30.00
F4NOR Burns/Doughty/Karlsson/Keith B 4.00 10.00
F4OIL McDavid/Lucic/Larsson/Talbot A 15.00 40.00
F4RC1 McAvoy/Boeser/Keller/Ho-Sang D 8.00 20.00
F4RC2 Hischier/Patrick/DeBrincat/Dubois D 10.00 25.00
F4CBUS Wennberg/Jones/Werenski/Bobrovsky D 5.00 12.00
F4JETS Wheeler/Scheifele/Laine/Ehlers B 5.00 12.00
F4PENS Letang/Malkin/Kessel/Murray A 6.00 15.00
F4SENS Hoffman/Stone/Brassard/Anderson C 4.00 10.00
F4WILD Granlund/Niederreiter/Staal/Dubnyk C 4.00 10.00
F4BOLTS Stamkos/Kucherov/Hedman/Vasilevskiy B 6.00 15.00
F4BRUIN Marchand/Spooner/Pastrnak/Krug B 8.00 20.00
F4CANES Williams/Staal/Rask/Teravainen D 3.00 8.00
F4HAWKS Toews/Saad/Sharp/Crawford B 5.00 12.00
F4KINGS Carter/Toffoli/Pearson/Quick C 4.00 10.00
F4LEAFS Marner/Nylander/Rielly/Andersen C 6.00 15.00
F4SELKE Bergeron/Kopitar/Toews/Kesler A 5.00 12.00
F4YOTES Ekman-Larsson/Domi/Dvorak/Duclair D 3.00 8.00

2017-18 Upper Deck Ice Glacial Graphs

GGAB Aleksander Barkov B 12.00 30.00
GGAM Anthony Mantha C 6.00 15.00
GGAV Andrei Vasilevskiy C 12.00 30.00
GGBS Brayden Schenn 8.00 20.00
GGCA Cam Atkinson C 8.00 20.00
GGDS Dave Schultz C 8.00 20.00
GGJC John Carlson C 8.00 20.00
GGJD Jonathan Drouin 6.00 15.00
GGJE Joel Eriksson Ek C 6.00 15.00
GGJG Jake Guentzel A 12.00 30.00
GGJP Joe Pavelski A 10.00 25.00
GGJV John Vanbiesbrouck B 8.00 20.00
GGLR Larry Robinson A 8.00 20.00
GGMM Matt Murray C 12.00 30.00
GGMT Matthew Tkachuk C 15.00 40.00
GGNE Nikolaj Ehlers C 8.00 20.00
GGNN Nino Niederreiter B 5.00 12.00
GGPH Phil Housley B 6.00 15.00
GGPO Jason Pominville C 5.00 12.00
GGPZ Pavel Zacha C 6.00 15.00
GGRK Ryan Kesler C 8.00 20.00
GGRL Rod Langway C 8.00 20.00

2017-18 Upper Deck Ice Caps Autographs

ICAK Anze Kopitar/30 12.00 30.00
ICEK Erik Karlsson/30 12.00 30.00
ICMG Mark Giordano/65 6.00 15.00
ICMM Mark Messier/30 30.00 80.00
ICMP Max Pacioretty/65 6.00 15.00
ICRB Rod Brind'Amour/65 6.00 15.00
ICRL Rod Langway/65 6.00 15.00

2017-18 Upper Deck Ice Premieres Autographs

IPAAD Alex DeBrincat/299 25.00 60.00
IPAAF Alex Formenton/299 4.00 10.00
IPAAK Adrian Kempe/299 8.00 20.00
IPAAN Alexander Nylander/199 20.00 50.00
IPAAT Alex Tuch/299 15.00 40.00
IPABB Brock Boeser/199 100.00 200.00
IPACF Christian Fischer/299 5.00 12.00
IPACH Filip Chlapik/299 3.00 8.00
IPACK Clayton Keller/99 80.00 150.00
IPACM Charlie McAvoy/199 20.00 50.00
IPACW Colin White/299 5.00 12.00
IPADG Denis Gurianov/299 10.00 25.00
IPAES Evgeny Svechnikov/299 8.00 20.00
IPAFC Filip Chytil/299 4.00 10.00
IPAFK Jakob Forsbacka-Karlsson/299 4.00 10.00
IPAIB Ivan Barbashev/299 5.00 12.00
IPAJD Jake DeBrusk/299 10.00 25.00
IPAJG Jon Gillies/299 4.00 10.00
IPAJH Josh Ho-Sang/199 5.00 12.00
IPAJR Jack Roslovic/299 5.00 12.00
IPAJT J.T. Compher/299 4.00 10.00
IPAKY Kailer Yamamoto/299 15.00 40.00
IPALK Luke Kunin/299 4.00 10.00
IPAMB Madison Bowey/299 2.50 6.00
IPANS Nikita Scherbak/299 5.00 12.00
IPAOT Owen Tippett/199 8.00 20.00
IPAPL Pierre-Luc Dubois/199 6.00 15.00
IPARH Robert Hagg/299 4.00 10.00
IPATJ Tyson Jost/199 8.00 20.00
IPATT Tage Thompson/299 10.00 25.00
IPAVD Vince Dunn/299 5.00 12.00
IPAVH Ville Husso/299 5.00 12.00
IPAVK Vladislav Kamenev/299 4.00 10.00
IPAVM Victor Mete/299 4.00 10.00
IPAVZ Valentin Zykov/299 4.00 10.00

2017-18 Upper Deck Ice Premieres Jerseys

IPJAB Anders Bjork B 4.00 10.00
IPJAD Alex DeBrincat B 8.00 20.00
IPJAF Alex Formenton D 3.00 8.00
IPJAK Adrian Kempe C 6.00 15.00
IPJAN Alexander Nylander B 5.00 12.00
IPJAT Alex Tuch C 8.00 20.00
IPJBB Brock Boeser A 8.00 20.00
IPJCF Christian Fischer C 4.00 10.00
IPJCH Filip Chlapik C 2.50 6.00
IPJCK Clayton Keller A 8.00 20.00
IPJCM Charlie McAvoy A 8.00 20.00
IPJCW Colin White C 4.00 10.00
IPJDG Denis Gurianov D 8.00 20.00
IPJES Evgeny Svechnikov D 6.00 15.00
IPJFC Filip Chytil C 3.00 8.00
IPJFK Jakob Forsbacka-Karlsson D 3.00 8.00
IPJIB Ivan Barbashev D 4.00 10.00
IPJJD Jake DeBrusk B 8.00 20.00
IPJJG Jon Gillies D 3.00 8.00
IPJJH Josh Ho-Sang B 4.00 10.00
IPJJK Janne Kuokkanen D 3.00 8.00
IPJJR Jack Roslovic C 4.00 10.00
IPJJT J.T. Compher C 3.00 8.00
IPJKY Kailer Yamamoto C 8.00 20.00
IPJLB Logan Brown C 3.00 8.00
IPJLK Luke Kunin B 3.00 8.00
IPJMB Madison Bowey D 2.00 5.00
IPJNH Nico Hischier A 10.00 25.00
IPJNP Nolan Patrick A 6.00 15.00
IPJNS Nikita Scherbak C 4.00 10.00
IPJOT Owen Tippett B 6.00 15.00
IPJPL Pierre-Luc Dubois A 5.00 12.00
IPJRH Robert Hagg D 3.00 8.00
IPJTJ Tyson Jost B 6.00 15.00
IPJTT Tage Thompson C 8.00 20.00
IPJVD Vince Dunn D 4.00 10.00
IPJVK Vladislav Kamenev D 3.00 8.00
IPJVS Vadim Shipachyov B 4.00 10.00
IPJVZ Valentin Zykov D 3.00 8.00

2017-18 Upper Deck Ice Rinkside Signings

RSAA Artem Anisimov C 5.00 12.00
RSAD Alex DeBrincat C 20.00 50.00
RSAE Aaron Ekblad B 10.00 25.00
RSAW Alexander Wennberg C 5.00 12.00
RSBB Brock Boeser C 20.00 50.00
RSBC Bobby Clarke B 12.00 30.00
RSBP Brian Propp C 6.00 15.00
RSCK Clayton Keller C 20.00 50.00
RSDG Denis Gurianov C 20.00 50.00
RSDK David Krejci C 8.00 20.00
RSFC Filip Chytil C 8.00 20.00
RSFP Felix Potvin B 12.00 30.00
RSJH Josh Ho-Sang C 10.00 25.00
RSJR Jack Roslovic C 8.00 20.00
RSLC Logan Couture A 10.00 25.00
RSMD Marcel Dionne A 10.00 25.00
RSMG Mike Gartner A 10.00 25.00
RSMS Mark Scheifele B 12.00 30.00
RSNK Nikita Kucherov B 15.00 40.00
RSNS Nikita Scherbak C 10.00 25.00
RSPL Patrik Laine A 10.00 25.00
RSPM Patrick Marleau A 8.00 20.00
RSRL Roberto Luongo A 12.00 30.00
RSTJ Tyson Jost C 15.00 40.00
RSVH Victor Hedman B 10.00 25.00
RSWS Wayne Simmonds C 10.00 25.00

2017-18 Upper Deck Ice Rookie Relic Jumbos

RRJAB Anders Bjork 2.00 5.00
RRJAD Alex DeBrincat 4.00 10.00
RRJAN Alexander Nylander 2.50 6.00
RRJBB Brock Boeser 6.00 15.00
RRJCK Clayton Keller 4.00 10.00
RRJCM Charlie McAvoy 4.00 10.00
RRJCW Colin White 2.00 5.00
RRJES Evgeny Svechnikov 3.00 8.00
RRJHF Haydn Fleury 1.50 4.00
RRJHS Josh Ho-Sang 2.00 5.00
RRJIB Ivan Barbashev 2.00 5.00
RRJJG Jon Gillies 1.50 4.00
RRJNH Nico Hischier 5.00 12.00
RRJNP Nolan Patrick 3.00 8.00
RRJNS Nikita Scherbak 1.50 4.00
RRJPD Pierre-Luc Dubois 2.50 6.00
RRJSM Samuel Morin 1.00 2.50
RRJTJ Tyson Jost 3.00 8.00
RRJTS Travis Sanheim 1.50 4.00
RRJVS Vadim Shipachyov 2.00 5.00

2017-18 Upper Deck Ice Signature Swatches

SSCD Christian Dvorak/150 5.00 12.00
SSCP Carey Price/25 40.00 100.00
SSCW Colin White/150 8.00 20.00
SSDD Devan Dubnyk/150 5.00 12.00
SSEK Erik Karlsson/25 25.00 60.00
SSHL Henrik Lundqvist/75 40.00 100.00
SSHZ Henrik Zetterberg/75 20.00 50.00
SSIP Ivan Provorov/150 5.00 12.00
SSJP Joe Pavelski/75 20.00 50.00
SSJT Jonathan Toews/25 30.00 80.00
SSNH Noah Hanifin/150 6.00 15.00
SSNN Nino Niederreiter/150 4.00 10.00
SSSS Steven Stamkos/25 40.00 100.00
SSTA John Tavares/75 25.00 60.00
SSTF Theoren Fleury/75 15.00 40.00
SSTH Taylor Hall/75 15.00 40.00
SSTN Tage Thompson/150 6.00 15.00
SSTT Teuvo Teravainen/150 6.00 15.00

2017-18 Upper Deck Ice Sub Zero

SZ1 Wendel Clark 5.00 12.00
SZ2 Maurice Richard 6.00 15.00
SZ3 Ray Bourque 5.00 12.00
SZ4 Wayne Gretzky 20.00 50.00
SZ5 Pierre Pilote 3.00 8.00
SZ6 Alex Delvecchio 3.00 8.00
SZ7 Jarome Iginla 4.00 10.00
SZ8 Pelle Lindbergh 2.50 6.00
SZ9 Martin Brodeur 8.00 20.00
SZ10 Brett Hull 6.00 15.00
SZ11 Sergei Bobrovsky 5.00 12.00
SZ12 Marc-Andre Fleury 3.00 8.00
SZ13 Sidney Crosby 6.00 15.00
SZ14 Claude Giroux 1.50 4.00
SZ15 Henrik Lundqvist 4.00 10.00
SZ16 Derek Stepan 1.00 2.50
SZ17 William Nylander 3.00 8.00
SZ18 Taylor Hall 1.50 4.00
SZ19 Nikita Kucherov 3.00 8.00
SZ20 Corey Crawford 2.00 5.00
SZ21 James Neal 1.00 2.50
SZ22 Joe Thornton 2.50 6.00
SZ23 Erik Karlsson 2.00 5.00
SZ24 Evgeni Malkin 3.00 8.00
SZ25 Nathan MacKinnon 6.00 15.00
SZ26 Patrik Laine 2.00 5.00
SZ27 Ryan Getzlaf 1.50 4.00
SZ28 Alexander Ovechkin 6.00 15.00
SZ29 Jonathan Drouin 1.25 3.00
SZ30 Vincent Trocheck 1.50 4.00
SZ31 John Tavares 2.50 6.00
SZ32 Brent Burns 1.50 4.00
SZ33 Filip Forsberg 2.50 6.00
SZ34 Jeff Carter 1.25 3.00
SZ35 Jaromir Jagr 5.00 12.00
SZ36 Jack Eichel 2.50 6.00
SZ37 Connor McDavid 8.00 20.00
SZ38 Bo Horvat 2.00 5.00
SZ39 Johnny Gaudreau 2.50 6.00
SZ40 Auston Matthews 6.00 15.00
SZ41 Jeff Skinner 2.00 5.00
SZ42 Vladimir Tarasenko 2.00 5.00
SZ43 David Pastrnak 4.00 10.00
SZ44 Pekka Rinne 1.50 4.00
SZ45 Jamie Benn 1.50 4.00
SZ46 Patrick Kane 3.00 8.00
SZ47 Devan Dubnyk 1.25 3.00
SZ48 Matt Murray 2.50 6.00
SZ49 Steven Stamkos 3.00 8.00
SZ50 Dylan Larkin 2.00 5.00
SZ51 Christian Fischer 2.00 5.00
SZ52 Travis Sanheim 1.50 4.00
SZ53 Pierre-Luc Dubois 2.50 6.00
SZ54 Alex DeBrincat 4.00 10.00
SZ55 Adrian Kempe 3.00 8.00
SZ56 Alex Tuch 4.00 10.00
SZ57 Tyson Jost 3.00 8.00
SZ58 Colin White 2.00 5.00
SZ59 Jake DeBrusk 4.00 10.00
SZ60 Brock Boeser 2.50 6.00
SZ61 Owen Tippett 3.00 8.00
SZ62 Charlie McAvoy 4.00 10.00
SZ63 Nico Hischier 5.00 12.00
SZ64 Anders Bjork 2.00 5.00
SZ65 Clayton Keller 4.00 10.00
SZ66 Kailer Yamamoto 4.00 10.00
SZ67 Ivan Barbashev 2.00 5.00
SZ68 Alexander Nylander 2.50 6.00
SZ69 Evgeny Svechnikov 3.00 8.00
SZ70 Martin Necas 5.00 12.00
SZ71 Filip Chytil 1.50 4.00
SZ72 Luke Kunin 1.50 4.00
SZ73 Nolan Patrick 3.00 8.00
SZ74 Logan Brown 1.50 4.00
SZ75 Alex Kerfoot 3.00 8.00
SZ76 Haydn Fleury 1.50 4.00
SZ77 Victor Mete 1.50 4.00
SZ78 Tage Thompson 4.00 10.00
SZ79 Josh Ho-Sang 2.00 5.00
SZ80 Will Butcher 2.00 5.00

2017-18 Upper Deck Ice Sub Zero Rookie Variations

V1 Brock Boeser 12.00 30.00
V2 Charlie McAvoy 12.00 30.00
V3 Clayton Keller 12.00 30.00
V4 Nico Hischier 15.00 40.00
V5 Nolan Patrick 10.00 25.00
V6 Alex DeBrincat 12.00 30.00
V7 Josh Ho-Sang 6.00 15.00
V8 Pierre-Luc Dubois 8.00 20.00
V9 Tyson Jost 10.00 25.00
V10 Will Butcher 6.00 15.00

2018-19 Upper Deck Ice

1 Ryan Getzlaf .75 2.00
2 Oliver Ekman-Larsson .75 2.00
3 Jeff Skinner 1.00 2.50
4 Jonathan Huberdeau 1.00 2.50
5 Dougie Hamilton .60 1.50
6 Brad Marchand 1.50 4.00
7 Mats Zuccarello .75 2.00
8 Blake Wheeler .75 2.00
9 Eric Staal .75 2.00
10 Vladimir Tarasenko 1.00 2.50
11 Victor Hedman 1.00 2.50
12 Connor McDavid 4.00 10.00
13 Evander Kane .75 2.00
14 Ryan O'Reilly .75 2.00
15 William Karlsson 1.00 2.50
16 Sidney Crosby 3.00 8.00
17 Brent Burns .75 2.00
18 Max Domi .75 2.00
19 Henrik Lundqvist 2.00 5.00
20 Sebastian Aho 1.25 3.00
21 Tyler Seguin 1.00 2.50

22 Nico Hischier 1.25 3.00
23 Clayton Keller 1.00 2.50
24 Sergei Bobrovsky 1.25 3.00
25 Sean Couturier .60 1.50
26 Patrice Bergeron 1.00 2.50
27 P.K. Subban 1.00 2.50
28 Mitch Marner 1.25 3.00
29 Steven Stamkos 1.50 4.00
30 Aleksander Barkov 1.25 3.00
31 Evgeni Malkin 1.50 4.00
32 Jack Eichel 1.25 3.00
33 Jordan Eberle .75 2.00
34 John Gibson .75 2.00
35 Sean Monahan .50 1.25
36 Jonathan Toews 1.25 3.00
37 Jamie Benn .75 2.00
38 Mikko Rantanen 2.00 5.00
39 Bo Horvat 1.00 2.50
40 Seth Jones .75 2.00
41 Leon Draisaitl 2.50 6.00
42 Mikael Granlund .60 1.50
43 Patrik Laine 1.00 2.50
44 Alex DeBrincat 1.00 2.50
45 Thomas Chabot .75 2.00
46 Drew Doughty 1.00 2.50
47 Evgeny Kuznetsov 1.00 2.50
48 Auston Matthews 3.00 8.00
49 Nolan Patrick .75 2.00
50 Dylan Larkin 1.00 2.50
51 Mitch Reinke/1299 RC 2.50 6.00
52 Igor Ozhiganov/1299 RC 2.50 6.00
53 Gavin Bayreuther/1299 RC 2.50 6.00
54 Jonas Siegenthaler/1299 RC 3.00 8.00
55 Juho Lammikko/1299 RC 2.50 6.00
56 Collin Delia/1299 RC 3.00 8.00
57 Tim Gettinger/1299 RC 2.50 6.00
58 Dan Vladar/1299 RC 4.00 10.00
59 Zach Whitecloud/1299 RC 2.50 6.00
60 Eric Robinson/1299 RC 2.50 6.00
61 Mikhail Vorobyev/1299 RC 2.50 6.00
62 Nick Seeler/1299 RC 2.50 6.00
63 Samuel Montembeault/1299 RC 6.00 15.00
64 Daniel Brickley/1299 RC 3.00 8.00
65 Spencer Foo/1299 RC 2.50 6.00
66 Shane Gersich/1299 RC 2.50 6.00
67 Dylan Gambrell/999 RC 3.00 8.00
68 Jake Bean/999 RC 3.00 8.00
69 Devon Toews/999 RC 5.00 12.00
70 Josh Mahura/999 RC 2.50 6.00
71 Ethan Bear/999 RC 5.00 12.00
72 Par Lindholm/999 RC 3.00 8.00
73 Mason Appleton/999 RC 2.50 6.00
74 Michael Dal Colle/999 RC 3.00 8.00
75 Jayce Hawryluk/999 RC 2.50 6.00
76 Sheldon Dries/999 RC 2.50 6.00
77 Dominic Turgeon/999 RC 3.00 8.00
78 Matt Luff/999 RC 2.50 6.00
79 Rourke Chartier/999 RC 2.50 6.00
80 Sheldon Rempal/999 RC 2.50 6.00
81 Cooper Marody/999 RC 3.00 8.00
82 Roope Hintz/999 RC 8.00 20.00
83 Joey Anderson/999 RC 3.00 8.00
84 Alexandre Fortin/999 RC 2.50 6.00
85 Erik Cernak/999 RC 4.00 10.00
86 Brett Seney/999 RC 2.50 6.00
87 Louie Belpedio/999 RC 2.50 6.00
88 Oskar Lindblom/999 RC 5.00 12.00
89 Marcus Pettersson/999 RC 3.00 8.00
90 Sami Niku/999 RC 2.50 6.00
91 Nicolas Aube-Kubel/999 RC 2.50 6.00
92 Michael McLeod/999 RC 2.50 6.00
93 Christian Wolanin/999 RC 2.50 6.00
94 Joe Hicketts/999 RC 3.00 8.00
95 Austin Wagner/999 RC 2.50 6.00
96 Victor Ejdsell/999 RC 2.50 6.00
97 Nicolas Roy/999 RC 2.00 5.00
98 Antti Suomela/999 RC 2.50 6.00
99 Jakub Zboril/999 RC 5.00 12.00
100 Juuso Valimaki/499 RC 4.00 10.00
101 Anthony Cirelli/499 RC 8.00 20.00
102 Filip Hronek/499 RC 4.00 10.00
103 Dominik Kahun/499 RC 4.00 10.00
104 Adam Gaudette/499 RC 6.00 15.00
105 Conor Garland/499 RC 4.00 10.00
106 Kiefer Sherwood/499 RC 3.00 8.00
107 Kristian Vesalainen/499 RC 5.00 12.00
108 Cal Petersen/499 RC 3.00 8.00
109 Noah Juulsen/499 RC 4.00 10.00
110 Troy Terry/499 RC 6.00 15.00
111 Dillon Dube/499 RC 2.50 6.00
112 Warren Foegele/499 RC 8.00 20.00
113 Mackenzie Blackwood/499 RC 8.00 20.00
114 Urho Vaakanainen/499 RC 8.00 20.00
115 Dylan Sikura/499 RC 5.00 12.00
116 Maxime Comtois/499 RC 4.00 10.00
117 Christoffer Ehn/499 RC 3.00 8.00
118 Jaret Anderson-Dolan/499 RC 3.00 8.00
119 Isac Lundestrom/499 RC 3.00 8.00
120 Zach Aston-Reese/499 RC 6.00 15.00
121 Maxime Lajoie/499 RC 6.00 15.00
122 Neal Pionk/499 RC 4.00 10.00
123 Jeremy Lauzon/499 RC 5.00 12.00
124 Mathieu Joseph/499 RC 4.00 10.00
125 Brett Howden/249 RC 5.00 12.00
126 Henrik Borgstrom/249 RC 6.00 15.00
127 Travis Dermott/249 RC 6.00 15.00
128 Sam Steel/249 RC 4.00 10.00
129 Andreas Johnsson/249 RC 8.00 20.00
130 Ilya Samsonov/249 RC 8.00 20.00
131 Ryan Donato/249 RC 6.00 15.00
132 Robert Thomas/249 RC 8.00 20.00
133 Henri Jokiharju/249 RC 3.00 8.00
134 Evan Bouchard/249 RC 10.00 25.00
135 Jordan Greenway/249 RC 4.00 10.00
136 Drake Batherson/249 RC 8.00 20.00
137 Dennis Cholowski/249 RC 4.00 10.00
138 Jordan Kyrou/249 RC 8.00 20.00
139 Lias Andersson/249 RC 6.00 15.00
140 Elias Pettersson/99 RC 200.00 500.00
141 Rasmus Dahlin/99 RC 150.00 400.00
142 Andrei Svechnikov/99 RC 120.00 300.00
143 Casey Mittelstadt/99 RC 50.00 125.00
144 Carter Hart/99 RC 150.00 400.00
145 Michael Rasmussen/99 RC 60.00 150.00
146 Miro Heiskanen/99 RC 100.00 250.00
147 Eeli Tolvanen/99 RC 50.00 125.00
148 Jesperi Kotkaniemi/99 RC 20.00 50.00
149 Brady Tkachuk/99 RC 60.00 150.00

2018-19 Upper Deck Ice Clear Cut Champions

CCCAB Andre Burakovsky 6.00 15.00
CCCAO Alexander Ovechkin 40.00 100.00
CCCBH Braden Holtby 12.00 30.00
CCCDO Dmitry Orlov 10.00 25.00
CCCEK Evgeny Kuznetsov 12.00 30.00
CCCJC John Carlson 10.00 25.00
CCCLE Lars Eller 6.00 15.00
CCCMK Michal Kempny 10.00 25.00
CCCMN Matt Niskanen 8.00 20.00
CCCNB Nicklas Backstrom 10.00 25.00
CCCTO T.J. Oshie 10.00 25.00
CCCTW Tom Wilson 10.00 25.00

2018-19 Upper Deck Ice Frozen Foursomes Red

*RED/25: 2X TO 5X BASIC INSERTS
F4RC1 Andrei Svechnikov
Elias Pettersson
Jesperi Kotkaniemi
Brady Tkachuk/25 50.00 125.00
F4RC2 Andrei Svechnikov
Elias Pettersson
Adam Gaudette
Warren Foegele/25 150.00 250.00

2018-19 Upper Deck Ice Glacial Graphs

GGAK Anze Kopitar B 12.00 30.00
GGAR Alexander Radulov C 8.00 20.00
GGBO Bobby Orr A 80.00 200.00
GGCH Connor Hellebuyck C 15.00 40.00
GGCM Connor McDavid A 150.00 250.00
GGDS Dave Schultz C 6.00 15.00
GGKF Kevin Fiala C 6.00 15.00
GGKM Kirk Muller C 6.00 15.00
GGMD Marcel Dionne B 10.00 25.00
GGPB Pavel Buchnevich C 6.00 15.00
GGPH Patric Hornqvist C 5.00 12.00
GGRB Rod Brind'Amour C 8.00 20.00
GGTA Tony Amonte C 6.00 15.00
GGVT Vincent Trocheck C 8.00 20.00
GGWG Wayne Gretzky A 200.00 500.00
GGWK William Karlsson C 10.00 25.00
GGWO Willie O'Ree C 15.00 40.00

2018-19 Upper Deck Ice Ice Premieres Autographs

IPAAC Anthony Cirelli/299 15.00 40.00
IPAAG Adam Gaudette/299 12.00 30.00
IPAAS Andrei Svechnikov/99 25.00 60.00
IPABH Brett Howden/299 10.00 25.00
IPABT Brady Tkachuk/99 25.00 60.00
IPADD Dillon Dube/199 10.00 25.00
IPADT Dominic Turgeon/299 8.00 20.00
IPAEB Evan Bouchard/299 20.00 50.00
IPAEP Elias Pettersson/99 100.00 250.00
IPAET Eeli Tolvanen/199 15.00 40.00
IPAHB Henrik Borgstrom/199 12.00 30.00
IPAHJ Henri Jokiharju/299 6.00 15.00
IPAJA Jaret Anderson-Dolan/299 6.00 15.00
IPAJG Jordan Greenway/199 8.00 20.00
IPAJK Jesperi Kotkaniemi/99 15.00 40.00
IPAKV Kristian Vesalainen/199 10.00 25.00
IPAKY Jordan Kyrou/299 15.00 40.00
IPAMA Cooper Marody/299 8.00 20.00
IPAMC Maxime Comtois/199 8.00 20.00
IPAMJ Mathieu Joseph/299 10.00 25.00
IPAML Maxime Lajoie/299 12.00 30.00
IPAMP Marcus Pettersson/299 8.00 20.00
IPAMV Mikhail Vorobyev/299 6.00 15.00
IPANJ Noah Juulsen/299 8.00 20.00
IPART Robert Thomas/199 15.00 40.00
IPASF Spencer Foo/299 6.00 15.00
IPASS Sam Steel/299 8.00 20.00
IPASU Antti Suomela/299 6.00 15.00
IPATD Travis Dermott/299 12.00 30.00
IPATT Troy Terry/299 15.00 40.00
IPAVE Victor Ejdsell/299 6.00 15.00
IPAWF Warren Foegele/299 6.00 15.00
IPAZA Zach Aston-Reese/299 12.00 30.00

2018-19 Upper Deck Ice Ice Premieres Jerseys

IPJAC Anthony Cirelli C 5.00 12.00
IPJAG Adam Gaudette C 5.00 12.00
IPJAJ Andreas Johnsson C 4.00 10.00
IPJAN Joey Anderson D 3.00 8.00
IPJAS Andrei Svechnikov A 8.00 20.00
IPJBE Ethan Bear D 5.00 12.00
IPJBH Brett Howden B 4.00 10.00
IPJBT Brady Tkachuk A 10.00 25.00
IPJCM Casey Mittelstadt B 6.00 15.00
IPJDD Dillon Dube D 4.00 10.00
IPJDG Dylan Gambrell C 3.00 8.00
IPJDS Dylan Sikura C 4.00 10.00
IPJDT Dominic Turgeon D 3.00 8.00
IPJEB Evan Bouchard C 8.00 20.00
IPJEP Elias Pettersson A 10.00 25.00
IPJET Eeli Tolvanen B 6.00 15.00
IPJHB Henrik Borgstrom B 5.00 12.00
IPJHJ Henri Jokiharju B 2.50 6.00
IPJJA Jaret Anderson-Dolan C 2.50 6.00
IPJJG Jordan Greenway C 3.00 8.00
IPJJK Jesperi Kotkaniemi A 6.00 15.00
IPJJV Juuso Valimaki C 3.00 8.00
IPJKV Kristian Vesalainen C 4.00 10.00
IPJKY Jordan Kyrou D 6.00 15.00
IPJLA Lias Andersson B 5.00 12.00
IPJMA Cooper Marody D 3.00 8.00
IPJMC Maxime Comtois C 3.00 8.00
IPJMD Michael Dal Colle D 3.00 8.00
IPJMH Miro Heiskanen B 8.00 20.00
IPJMJ Mathieu Joseph C 4.00 10.00
IPJML Maxime Lajoie D 3.00 8.00
IPJMP Marcus Pettersson D 3.00 8.00
IPJNJ Noah Juulsen C 3.00 8.00
IPJRD Ryan Donato B 5.00 12.00
IPJRT Robert Thomas B 6.00 15.00
IPJSF Spencer Foo D 2.50 6.00
IPJSN Sami Niku D 2.50 6.00
IPJSS Sam Steel B 3.00 8.00
IPJSU Antti Suomela D 2.50 6.00
IPJTD Travis Dermott C 5.00 12.00
IPJTT Troy Terry C 5.00 12.00
IPJVE Victor Ejdsell D 2.50 6.00
IPJWF Warren Foegele D 3.00 8.00
IPJZA Zach Aston-Reese D 5.00 12.00

2018-19 Upper Deck Ice Premieres Retro

1 Rasmus Dahlin 20.00 50.00
2 Andrei Svechnikov 20.00 50.00
3 Michael Rasmussen 10.00 25.00
4 Ryan Donato 12.00 30.00
5 Eeli Tolvanen 15.00 40.00
6 Casey Mittelstadt 15.00 40.00
7 Brady Tkachuk 25.00 60.00
8 Miro Heiskanen 25.00 60.00
9 Jesperi Kotkaniemi 15.00 40.00
10 Elias Pettersson 40.00 100.00

2018-19 Upper Deck Ice Rinkside Signings

RSBO Bobby Orr A 80.00 200.00
RSBS Brayden Schenn B 10.00 25.00
RSCC Chris Chelios A 10.00 25.00
RSDN Darnell Nurse C 8.00 20.00
RSED Evgenii Dadonov C 6.00 15.00
RSJG Jake Gardiner C 6.00 15.00
RSJS Justin Schultz C 8.00 20.00
RSJV John Vanbiesbrouck B 10.00 25.00
RSKS Kevin Shattenkirk C 6.00 15.00
RSPT Pierre Turgeon A 8.00 20.00
RSRL Rod Langway C 8.00 20.00
RSWG Wayne Gretzky A 200.00 500.00
RSWK William Karlsson C 12.00 30.00
RSWP Wilf Paiement C 8.00 20.00

2018-19 Upper Deck Ice Rookie Relic Jumbos

RRJAS Andrei Svechnikov 5.00 12.00
RRJBH Brett Howden 2.50 6.00
RRJBT Brady Tkachuk 6.00 15.00
RRJCM Casey Mittelstadt 4.00 10.00
RRJDD Dillon Dube 2.50 6.00
RRJDG Dylan Gambrell 2.00 5.00
RRJDO Ryan Donato 3.00 8.00
RRJDS Dylan Sikura 2.50 6.00
RRJEB Evan Bouchard 5.00 12.00
RRJEP Elias Pettersson 12.00 30.00
RRJET Eeli Tolvanen 4.00 10.00
RRJHB Henrik Borgstrom 3.00 8.00
RRJJG Jordan Greenway 2.00 5.00
RRJJK Jesperi Kotkaniemi 4.00 10.00
RRJJL Jeremy Lauzon 2.50 6.00
RRJJV Juuso Valimaki 2.00 5.00
RRJKY Jordan Kyrou 4.00 10.00
RRJLA Lias Andersson 3.00 8.00
RRJMH Miro Heiskanen 5.00 12.00
RRJMR Michael Rasmussen 2.50 6.00
RRJOL Oskar Lindblom 3.00 8.00
RRJRD Rasmus Dahlin 5.00 12.00
RRJRT Robert Thomas 4.00 10.00
RRJSS Sam Steel 2.00 5.00
RRJTT Troy Terry 3.00 8.00

2018-19 Upper Deck Ice Rookie Rinkside Signings

RRSAS Andrei Svechnikov 12.00 30.00
RRSBT Brady Tkachuk 15.00 40.00
RRSEP Elias Pettersson 60.00 150.00
RRSHB Henrik Borgstrom 20.00 50.00
RRSJK Jesperi Kotkaniemi 15.00 40.00
RRSSS Sam Steel 8.00 20.00

2018-19 Upper Deck Ice Signature Swatches

SWAR Alexander Radulov/150 10.00 25.00
SWAS Andrei Svechnikov/150 25.00 60.00
SWAV Andrei Vasilevskiy/25 15.00 40.00
SWBS Brayden Schenn/99 10.00 25.00
SWCH Connor Hellebuyck/150 20.00 50.00
SWEK Evgeny Kuznetsov/99 12.00 30.00
SWEP Elias Pettersson/150 100.00 200.00
SWJG Jake Guentzel/150 15.00 40.00
SWJM Jonathan Marchessault/99 12.00 30.00
SWJT Jacob Trouba/150 8.00 20.00
SWPH Patric Hornqvist/150 6.00 15.00
SWTB Tom Barrasso/25 10.00 25.00
SWTH Tomas Hertl/150 10.00 25.00
SWTP Tanner Pearson/150 8.00 20.00
SWVT Vincent Trocheck/150 10.00 25.00

2018-19 Upper Deck Ice Sub Zero

*GOLD/24: 2.5X TO 6X BASIC INSERTS
SZ1 David Pastrnak 4.00 10.00
SZ2 Filip Forsberg 2.50 6.00
SZ3 Carey Price 3.00 8.00
SZ4 Alexander Ovechkin 6.00 15.00
SZ5 Sidney Crosby 6.00 15.00
SZ6 Anze Kopitar 2.50 6.00
SZ7 Brock Boeser 2.50 6.00
SZ8 Auston Matthews 6.00 15.00
SZ9 Claude Giroux 1.50 4.00
SZ10 Taylor Hall 1.50 4.00
SZ11 Nikita Kucherov 3.00 8.00
SZ12 Connor McDavid 8.00 20.00
SZ13 Patrick Kane 3.00 8.00
SZ14 Mathew Barzal 2.50 6.00
SZ15 John Tavares 3.00 8.00
SZ16 Marc-Andre Fleury 3.00 8.00
SZ17 Nathan MacKinnon 6.00 15.00
SZ18 Mark Scheifele 2.50 6.00
SZ19 Erik Karlsson 2.50 6.00
SZ20 Johnny Gaudreau 3.00 8.00
SZ21 Elias Pettersson 5.00 12.00
SZ22 Dillon Dube 2.00 5.00
SZ23 Noah Juulsen 1.50 4.00
SZ24 Brett Howden 2.00 5.00
SZ25 Dylan Sikura 2.00 5.00
SZ26 Jesperi Kotkaniemi 3.00 8.00
SZ27 Henrik Borgstrom 3.00 8.00
SZ28 Ryan Donato 2.50 6.00
SZ29 Eeli Tolvanen 3.00 8.00
SZ30 Henri Jokiharju 1.25 3.00
SZ31 Lias Andersson 2.50 6.00
SZ32 Andrei Svechnikov 4.00 10.00
SZ33 Anthony Cirelli 2.50 6.00
SZ34 Robert Thomas 3.00 8.00
SZ35 Kristian Vesalainen 2.00 5.00
SZ36 Jordan Greenway 1.50 4.00
SZ37 Miro Heiskanen 4.00 10.00
SZ38 Michael Rasmussen 2.00 5.00
SZ39 Maxime Comtois 1.50 4.00
SZ40 Casey Mittelstadt 3.00 8.00
SZ41 Dennis Cholowski 1.50 4.00
SZ42 Jordan Kyrou 3.00 8.00
SZ43 Evan Bouchard 4.00 10.00
SZ44 Travis Dermott 2.50 6.00
SZ45 Sam Steel 1.50 4.00
SZ46 Maxime Lajoie 2.50 6.00
SZ47 Warren Foegele 1.50 4.00
SZ48 Isac Lundestrom 1.25 3.00
SZ49 Brady Tkachuk 5.00 12.00
SZ50 Rasmus Dahlin 4.00 10.00

2018-19 Upper Deck Ice Sub Zero Autographs Blue

SZ3 Carey Price 30.00 80.00
SZ11 Nikita Kucherov 12.00 30.00
SZ12 Connor McDavid 30.00 80.00
SZ15 John Tavares 10.00 25.00
SZ16 Marc-Andre Fleury 12.00 30.00
SZ21 Elias Pettersson A 200.00 300.00
SZ22 Dillon Dube C 8.00 20.00
SZ23 Noah Juulsen C 6.00 15.00
SZ24 Brett Howden C 12.00 30.00
SZ26 Jesperi Kotkaniemi A 12.00 30.00
SZ27 Henrik Borgstrom C 10.00 25.00
SZ29 Eeli Tolvanen B 8.00 20.00
SZ30 Henri Jokiharju C 5.00 12.00
SZ32 Andrei Svechnikov A 15.00 40.00
SZ33 Anthony Cirelli 8.00 20.00
SZ34 Robert Thomas C 12.00 30.00
SZ35 Kristian Vesalainen C 8.00 20.00
SZ36 Jordan Greenway C 6.00 15.00
SZ38 Michael Rasmussen B 8.00 20.00
SZ39 Maxime Comtois C 6.00 15.00
SZ41 Dennis Cholowski C 6.00 15.00
SZ42 Jordan Kyrou C 20.00 50.00
SZ43 Evan Bouchard C 15.00 40.00
SZ44 Travis Dermott C 10.00 25.00
SZ45 Sam Steel C 6.00 15.00
SZ47 Warren Foegele C 6.00 15.00
SZ49 Brady Tkachuk A 20.00 50.00

2018-19 Upper Deck Ice Sub Zero Rookie Variations

SZVAS Andrei Svechnikov 12.00 30.00
SZVBT Brady Tkachuk 15.00 40.00
SZVEP Elias Pettersson 15.00 40.00
SZVJK Jesperi Kotkaniemi 10.00 25.00
SZVRD Rasmus Dahlin 12.00 30.00

2018-19 Upper Deck Ice Superb Script

SSAS Andrei Svechnikov/25 60.00 150.00
SSBH Brett Howden/49 12.00 30.00
SSBT Brady Tkachuk/25 60.00 150.00
SSDD Dillon Dube/49 12.00 30.00
SSEB Evan Bouchard/49 25.00 60.00
SSEP Elias Pettersson/25 300.00 400.00
SSET Eeli Tolvanen/49 20.00 50.00
SSFH Filip Hronek/49 20.00 50.00
SSHB Henrik Borgstrom/49 15.00 40.00
SSJG Jordan Greenway/49 10.00 25.00
SSJK Jesperi Kotkaniemi/25 20.00 50.00
SSKV Kristian Vesalainen/49 12.00 30.00
SSKY Jordan Kyrou/49 20.00 50.00
SSMC Maxime Comtois/49 10.00 25.00
SSMR Michael Rasmussen/49 12.00 30.00
SSPL Par Lindholm/49 10.00 25.00
SSRT Robert Thomas/49 20.00 50.00
SSSS Sam Steel/49 10.00 25.00
SSTT Troy Terry/49 25.00 60.00
SSWF Warren Foegele/49 10.00 25.00

2019-20 Upper Deck Ice

1 Sidney Crosby 3.00 8.00
2 Carey Price 1.50 4.00
3 Leon Draisaitl 2.50 6.00
4 Jonathan Toews 1.25 3.00
5 Jonathan Quick 1.00 2.50
6 Matthew Tkachuk 1.50 4.00
7 Patrick Kane 1.50 4.00
8 Alex Ovechkin 3.00 8.00
9 Miro Heiskanen 1.00 2.50
10 Pierre-Luc Dubois .60 1.50
11 Filip Forsberg 1.25 3.00
12 Logan Couture 1.00 2.50
13 Sebastian Aho 1.25 3.00
14 Elias Pettersson 1.25 3.00
15 Patrice Bergeron 1.00 2.50
16 Auston Matthews 2.50 6.00
17 Evgeni Malkin 1.50 4.00
18 Mark Scheifele 1.25 3.00
19 Mikko Rantanen 1.25 3.00
20 Marc-Andre Fleury 1.50 4.00
21 Seth Jones .75 2.00
22 Brock Boeser 1.00 2.50
23 Rasmus Dahlin 1.00 2.50
24 Jonathan Huberdeau 1.00 2.50
25 Nikita Kucherov 1.50 4.00
26 Jack Eichel 1.25 3.00
27 Alex Pietrangelo .60 1.50
28 Mathew Barzal 1.00 2.50
29 Brady Tkachuk 1.00 2.50
30 Aleksander Barkov 1.25 3.00
31 Taylor Hall .75 2.00
32 Henrik Lundqvist 2.00 5.00
33 Blake Wheeler .75 2.00
34 Ryan Getzlaf .75 2.00
35 Johnny Gaudreau .75 2.00
36 Anze Kopitar 1.25 3.00
37 Jacob Trouba .60 1.50
38 Steven Stamkos 1.50 4.00
39 Claude Giroux .75 2.00
40 Mitch Marner 1.25 3.00
41 Jesperi Kotkaniemi .75 2.00
42 Nathan MacKinnon 3.00 8.00
43 Tyler Seguin 1.00 2.50
44 Nico Hischier 1.25 3.00
45 Eric Staal .75 2.00
46 Carter Hart .75 2.00
47 Anthony Mantha .60 1.50
48 Connor McDavid 4.00 10.00
49 Phil Kessel .75 2.00
50 Jordan Binnington 1.25 3.00
51 Guillaume Brisebois/1299 RC 3.00 8.00
52 Brady Keeper/1299 RC 3.00 8.00
53 Mathieu Olivier/1299 RC 2.50 6.00
54 Scott Sabourin/1299 RC 2.50 6.00
55 Kevin Stenlund/1299 RC 2.50 6.00
56 Beck Malenstyn/1299 RC 3.00 8.00
57 Anton Wedin/1299 RC 2.50 6.00
58 Kasimir Kaskisuo/1299 RC 2.50 6.00
59 Adam Werner/1299 RC 2.50 6.00
60 Joona Luoto/1299 RC 2.50 6.00
61 Yakov Trenin/999 RC 2.50 6.00
62 J.C. Beaudin/999 RC 3.00 8.00
63 Otto Leskinen/999 RC 2.50 6.00
64 Gaetan Haas/999 RC 2.50 6.00
65 Givani Smith/999 RC 2.50 6.00
66 Rhett Gardner/999 RC 2.50 6.00
67 Lean Bergmann/999 RC 2.50 6.00
68 Joakim Nygard/999 RC 2.50 6.00
69 Nico Sturm/999 RC 2.50 6.00
70 Kole Sherwood/999 RC 3.00 8.00
71 Noah Gregor/999 RC 2.50 6.00
72 Pierre Engvall/999 RC 2.00 5.00
73 Nathan Bastian/999 RC 3.00 8.00
74 Nick Caamano/999 RC 2.50 6.00
75 Max Veronneau/999 RC 2.50 6.00
76 Ryan Lindgren/499 RC 4.00 10.00
77 Zack MacEwen/499 RC 3.00 8.00
78 Carter Verhaeghe/499 RC 6.00 15.00
79 Matt Roy/499 RC 4.00 10.00
80 Vladislav Gavrikov/499 RC 3.00 8.00
81 Joel Persson/499 RC 3.00 8.00
82 Kaapo Kahkonen/499 RC 15.00 40.00
83 Jake Walman/499 RC 5.00 12.00
84 Mackenzie MacEachern/499 RC 4.00 10.00
85 Rudolfs Balcers/499 RC 4.00 10.00
86 Eetu Luostarinen/499 RC 4.00 10.00
87 Jonathan Davidsson/499 RC 2.50 6.00
88 Aleksi Saarela/499 RC 4.00 10.00
89 German Rubtsov/499 RC 3.00 8.00
90 Vitaly Abramov/499 RC 4.00 10.00
91 Max Jones/499 RC 4.00 10.00
92 Alexander Volkov/499 RC 3.00 8.00
93 Trevor Moore/499 RC 3.00 8.00
94 Connor Clifton/499 RC 4.00 10.00
95 Julien Gauthier/499 RC 4.00 10.00
96 Joel L'Esperance/499 RC 4.00 10.00
97 Libor Hajek/499 RC 3.00 8.00
98 Karson Kuhlman/499 RC 4.00 10.00
99 John Marino/499 RC 6.00 15.00
100 Andrew Peeke/499 RC 2.50 6.00
101 Connor Timmins/499 RC 3.00 8.00
102 Rasmus Asplund/499 RC 4.00 10.00
103 Cale Fleury/499 RC 5.00 12.00
104 Nikolai Prokhorkin/499 RC 4.00 10.00
105 David Gustafsson/499 RC 3.00 8.00
106 Trent Frederic/499 RC 4.00 10.00
107 Carl Grundstrom/499 RC 4.00 10.00
108 Elvis Merzlikins/499 RC 8.00 20.00
109 Joey Daccord/499 RC 8.00 20.00
110 Martin Fehervary/499 RC 3.00 8.00
111 Sam Lafferty/499 RC 3.00 8.00
112 Dmytro Timashov/499 RC 4.00 10.00
113 Otto Koivula/499 RC 2.50 6.00
114 Jack Studnicka/499 RC 4.00 10.00
115 Emil Bemstrom/499 RC 4.00 10.00
116 Jesper Boqvist/249 RC 4.00 10.00
117 Tobias Bjornfot/249 RC 4.00 10.00
118 Alexandre Texier/249 RC 4.00 10.00
119 Philippe Myers/249 RC 4.00 10.00
120 Nikita Gusev/249 RC 6.00 15.00
121 Oliver Wahlstrom/249 RC 6.00 15.00
122 Klim Kostin/249 RC 4.00 10.00
123 Nicolas Hague/249 RC 4.00 10.00
124 Taro Hirose/249 RC 4.00 10.00
125 Mario Ferraro/249 RC 4.00 10.00
126 Dante Fabbro/249 RC 4.00 10.00
127 Dominik Kubalik/249 RC 8.00 20.00
128 Blake Lizotte/249 RC 4.00 10.00
129 Ville Heinola/249 RC 4.00 10.00
130 Cayden Primeau/249 RC 8.00 20.00
131 Morgan Frost/249 RC 8.00 20.00
132 Ryan Poehling/249 RC 5.00 12.00
133 Noah Dobson/249 RC 10.00 25.00
134 Adam Boqvist/249 RC 4.00 10.00
135 Ilya Mikheyev/249 RC 6.00 15.00
136 Igor Shesterkin/249 RC 30.00 80.00
137 Adam Fox/249 RC 10.00 25.00
138 Rasmus Sandin/249 RC 6.00 15.00
139 Erik Brannstrom/249 RC 6.00 15.00
140 Joel Farabee/249 RC 6.00 15.00
141 Kaapo Kakko/99 RC 100.00 250.00
142 Kirby Dach/99 RC 100.00 250.00
143 Victor Olofsson/99 RC 50.00 125.00
144 Nick Suzuki/99 RC 150.00 400.00
145 Filip Zadina/99 RC 100.00 250.00
146 Barrett Hayton/99 RC 80.00 200.00
147 Quinn Hughes/99 RC 120.00 300.00
148 Cody Glass/99 RC 80.00 200.00
149 Cale Makar/99 RC 200.00 500.00
150 Jack Hughes/99 RC 200.00 500.00

2019-20 Upper Deck Ice Fire and Ice Autographs

FIAD1 Alex DeBrincat FIRE C 15.00 40.00
FIAD2 Alex DeBrincat ICE B 15.00 40.00
FICM2 Connor McDavid ICE A 120.00 300.00
FICM1 Connor McDavid FIRE B 120.00 300.00
FILD1 Leon Draisaitl FIRE C 40.00 100.00
FILD2 Leon Draisaitl ICE B 40.00 100.00
FIMT2 Matthew Tkachuk ICE B 25.00 60.00

2019-20 Upper Deck Ice Glacial Graphs

GGAB Aleksander Barkov B 12.00 30.00
GGBB Ben Bishop B 6.00 15.00
GGBN Bernie Nicholls C 6.00 15.00
GGBR Bill Ranford C 6.00 15.00
GGCM Connor McDavid A 80.00 200.00
GGJG John Gibson A 8.00 20.00
GGJK Jesperi Kotkaniemi B 8.00 20.00
GGJP Joe Pavelski B 10.00 25.00
GGJT Joe Thornton A 12.00 30.00
GGKL Kevin Labanc C 5.00 12.00
GGKM Kirk McLean B 6.00 15.00
GGMG Mikael Granlund C 6.00 15.00
GGML Mike Liut C 5.00 12.00
GGMM Matt Murray C 8.00 20.00
GGPG Philipp Grubauer C 8.00 20.00
GGRL Roberto Luongo A 12.00 30.00
GGSB Sergei Bobrovsky B 12.00 30.00
GGTB Tyson Barrie C 5.00 12.00
GGTC Thomas Chabot C 8.00 20.00
GGWC Wendel Clark B 12.00 30.00

2019-20 Upper Deck Ice Glacial Graphs Black

GGKM Kirk McLean/50 25.00 60.00
GGPG Philipp Grubauer/50 25.00 60.00
GGTC Thomas Chabot/50 20.00 50.00

2019-20 Upper Deck Ice Ice Buckets Autographs

IBAB Aleksander Barkov/99 10.00 25.00
IBAD Alex DeBrincat/99 8.00 20.00
IBBB Brock Boeser/99 15.00 40.00
IBCN Cam Neely/99 12.00 30.00
IBJM Jonathan Marchessault/99 8.00 20.00
IBJP Joe Pavelski/99 8.00 20.00

2019-20 Upper Deck Ice Ice Premieres Autographs

IPAAF Adam Fox/299 20.00 50.00
IPAAT Alexandre Texier/299 8.00 20.00
IPABE Emil Bemstrom/399 8.00 20.00
IPABH Barrett Hayton/299 15.00 40.00
IPABK Brady Keeper/399 8.00 20.00
IPABL Blake Lizotte/399 8.00 20.00
IPACG Cody Glass/199 12.00 30.00
IPACM Cale Makar/99 120.00 300.00
IPADK Dominik Kubalik/399 10.00 25.00
IPAEM Elvis Merzlikins/399 15.00 40.00
IPAGR Carl Grundstrom/399 8.00 20.00
IPAIM Ilya Mikheyev/399 12.00 30.00
IPAJB Jesper Boqvist/399 6.00 15.00
IPAJH Jack Hughes/99 100.00 250.00
IPAJS Jimmy Schuldt/399 6.00 15.00
IPAMF Mario Ferraro/399 6.00 15.00
IPAMR Matt Roy/399 8.00 20.00
IPAMV Max Veronneau/399 6.00 15.00
IPAND Noah Dobson/299 20.00 50.00
IPANG Nikita Gusev/299 12.00 30.00
IPANS Nick Suzuki/199 30.00 80.00
IPAPI Rem Pitlick/399 8.00 20.00
IPAPM Philippe Myers/399 6.00 15.00
IPAQH Quinn Hughes/99 80.00 200.00
IPAST Nico Sturm/399 6.00 15.00
IPATE Teddy Blueger/399 8.00 20.00
IPAVH Ville Heinola/399 10.00 25.00

2019-20 Upper Deck Ice Ice Premieres Jerseys

IPJAF Adam Fox 4.00 10.00
IPJAT Alexandre Texier 1.50 4.00
IPJBE Emil Bemstrom 1.50 4.00
IPJBH Barrett Hayton 3.00 8.00
IPJBK Brady Keeper 1.50 4.00
IPJBL Blake Lizotte 1.50 4.00
IPJCG Cody Glass 2.50 6.00
IPJCM Cale Makar 8.00 20.00
IPJCT Conor Timmins 1.50 4.00
IPJDF Dante Fabbro 1.50 4.00
IPJDG David Gustafsson 1.25 3.00
IPJDK Dominik Kubalik 3.00 8.00
IPJEB Erik Brannstrom 1.50 4.00
IPJEM Elvis Merzlikins 3.00 8.00
IPJFE Martin Fehervary 1.25 3.00
IPJFZ Filip Zadina 2.50 6.00
IPJGB Guillaume Brisebois 1.50 4.00
IPJGR Carl Grundstrom 1.50 4.00
IPJIM Ilya Mikheyev 2.50 6.00
IPJJB Jesper Boqvist 1.50 4.00
IPJJF Joel Farabee 2.50 6.00
IPJJH Jack Hughes 8.00 20.00
IPJJS Jimmy Schuldt 1.25 3.00
IPJKD Kirby Dach 3.00 8.00
IPJKK Karson Kuhlman 1.50 4.00
IPJMF Mario Ferraro 1.25 3.00
IPJMJ Max Jones 1.25 3.00
IPJMR Matt Roy 1.50 4.00
IPJMV Max Veronneau 1.25 3.00
IPJND Noah Dobson 4.00 10.00
IPJNG Nikita Gusev 2.50 6.00
IPJNS Nick Suzuki 6.00 15.00
IPJPI Rem Pitlick 1.50 4.00
IPJPM Philippe Myers 1.25 3.00
IPJQH Quinn Hughes 8.00 20.00
IPJRP Ryan Poehling 2.50 6.00
IPJRS Rasmus Sandin 2.50 6.00
IPJST Nico Sturm 1.25 3.00
IPJTB Tobias Bjornfot 1.50 4.00
IPJTE Teddy Blueger 1.50 4.00
IPJTF Trent Frederic 1.50 4.00
IPJTH Taro Hirose 1.50 4.00
IPJVA Vitaly Abramov 1.50 4.00
IPJVO Victor Olofsson 3.00 8.00
IPJZM Zack MacEwen 1.50 4.00
IPJZS Zach Senyshyn 1.50 4.00

2019-20 Upper Deck Ice Ice Premieres Retro

1 Kaapo Kakko 8.00 20.00
2 Adam Boqvist 5.00 12.00
3 Barrett Hayton 10.00 25.00
4 Noah Dobson 12.00 30.00
5 Joel Farabee 8.00 20.00
6 Kirby Dach 10.00 25.00
7 Nikita Gusev 8.00 20.00
8 Filip Zadina 8.00 20.00
9 Tobias Bjornfot 5.00 12.00
10 Quinn Hughes 25.00 60.00
11 Karson Kuhlman 5.00 12.00
12 Carl Grundstrom 5.00 12.00
13 Teddy Blueger 5.00 12.00
14 Philippe Myers 4.00 10.00
15 Dominik Kubalik 10.00 25.00
16 Rasmus Sandin 8.00 20.00
17 Adam Fox 12.00 30.00
18 Ryan Poehling 8.00 20.00
19 Joakim Nygard 4.00 10.00
20 Cody Glass 8.00 20.00
21 Nicolas Hague 5.00 12.00
22 Conor Timmins 5.00 12.00
23 Victor Olofsson 10.00 25.00
24 Ville Heinola 6.00 15.00
25 Cale Makar 25.00 60.00
26 Elvis Merzlikins 10.00 25.00
27 Erik Brannstrom 5.00 12.00
28 Martin Fehervary 4.00 10.00
29 Emil Bemstrom 5.00 12.00
30 Nick Suzuki 20.00 50.00
31 Cale Fleury 6.00 15.00
32 Ilya Mikheyev 8.00 20.00
33 Max Jones 5.00 12.00
34 Blake Lizotte 5.00 12.00
35 Alexandre Texier 5.00 12.00
36 Jesper Boqvist 4.00 10.00
37 Dante Fabbro 5.00 12.00
38 Taro Hirose 5.00 12.00
39 Joel L'Esperance 5.00 12.00
40 Jack Hughes 25.00 60.00

2019-20 Upper Deck Ice Jerseys

1 Sidney Crosby 8.00 20.00
2 Carey Price 4.00 10.00
3 Leon Draisaitl 6.00 15.00
4 Jonathan Toews 3.00 8.00
5 Jonathan Quick 2.50 6.00
6 Matthew Tkachuk 4.00 10.00
7 Patrick Kane 4.00 10.00
8 Alex Ovechkin 8.00 20.00
9 Miro Heiskanen 2.50 6.00
10 Pierre-Luc Dubois 1.50 4.00
11 Filip Forsberg 3.00 8.00
12 Logan Couture 2.50 6.00
13 Sebastian Aho 3.00 8.00
14 Elias Pettersson 3.00 8.00
15 Patrice Bergeron 2.50 6.00
16 Auston Matthews 8.00 20.00
17 Evgeni Malkin 4.00 10.00
18 Mark Scheifele 3.00 8.00
19 Mikko Rantanen 5.00 12.00
20 Marc-Andre Fleury 4.00 10.00
21 Seth Jones 2.00 5.00
22 Brock Boeser 2.50 6.00
23 Rasmus Dahlin 2.50 6.00
24 Jonathan Huberdeau 2.50 6.00
25 Nikita Kucherov 4.00 10.00
26 Jack Eichel 3.00 8.00
27 Alex Pietrangelo 1.50 4.00
28 Mathew Barzal 2.50 6.00
29 Brady Tkachuk 3.00 8.00
30 Aleksander Barkov 3.00 8.00
32 Henrik Lundqvist 5.00 12.00
33 Blake Wheeler 2.00 5.00
34 Ryan Getzlaf 2.00 5.00
35 Johnny Gaudreau 3.00 8.00
36 Anze Kopitar 3.00 8.00
37 Jacob Trouba 1.50 4.00
38 Steven Stamkos 4.00 10.00
39 Claude Giroux 2.00 5.00
40 Mitch Marner 3.00 8.00
41 Jesperi Kotkaniemi 2.00 5.00
42 Nathan MacKinnon 8.00 20.00
43 Tyler Seguin 2.50 6.00
44 Nico Hischier 3.00 8.00
45 Eric Staal 2.00 5.00
46 Carter Hart 2.00 5.00
47 Anthony Mantha 1.50 4.00
48 Connor McDavid 10.00 25.00
49 Phil Kessel 2.00 5.00
50 Jordan Binnington 3.00 8.00

2019-20 Upper Deck Ice Rookie Ice Buckets Autographs

IBRAF Adam Fox/199 10.00 25.00
IBRAT Alexandre Texier/199 4.00 10.00
IBRCM Cale Makar/99 60.00 150.00
IBRDF Dante Fabbro/199 4.00 10.00
IBREB Erik Brannstrom/199 12.00 30.00
IBRJH Jack Hughes/99 50.00 125.00
IBRPM Philippe Myers/199 3.00 8.00
IBRQH Quinn Hughes/99 60.00 150.00

2019-20 Upper Deck Ice Rookie Ice Buckets Autographs Red

IBRAF Adam Fox/25 80.00 200.00
IBRAT Alexandre Texier/25 12.00 30.00
IBRDF Dante Fabbro/25 8.00 20.00

2019-20 Upper Deck Ice Rookie Relic Jumbos

RRJAB Adam Boqvist 2.00 5.00
RRJAF Adam Fox 5.00 12.00
RRJAT Alexandre Texier 2.00 5.00
RRJBH Barrett Hayton 4.00 10.00
RRJCG Carl Grundstrom 2.00 5.00
RRJCM Cale Makar 10.00 25.00
RRJDF Dante Fabbro 2.00 5.00
RRJEB Erik Brannstrom 2.00 5.00
RRJFZ Filip Zadina 3.00 8.00
RRJGL Cody Glass 3.00 8.00
RRJIM Ilya Mikheyev 3.00 8.00
RRJJF Joel Farabee 3.00 8.00
RRJJH Jack Hughes 10.00 25.00
RRJKD Kirby Dach 4.00 10.00
RRJMJ Max Jones 2.00 5.00
RRJND Noah Dobson 5.00 12.00
RRJNG Nikita Gusev 3.00 8.00
RRJNS Nick Suzuki 8.00 20.00
RRJOW Oliver Wahlstrom 3.00 8.00
RRJPM Philippe Myers 1.50 4.00
RRJQH Quinn Hughes 10.00 25.00
RRJRP Ryan Poehling 3.00 8.00
RRJTH Taro Hirose 2.00 5.00
RRJVA Vitaly Abramov 2.00 5.00
RRJVO Victor Olofsson 3.00 8.00

2019-20 Upper Deck Ice Signature Swatches

SWAD Alex DeBrincat/99 10.00 25.00
SWBB Brock Boeser/99 10.00 25.00
SWES Eric Staal/99 8.00 20.00
SWJH Jack Hughes/25 60.00 150.00
SWMA Cale Makar/150 60.00 150.00
SWPD Pierre-Luc Dubois/99 6.00 15.00

2019-20 Upper Deck Ice Sub Zero

*GOLD/24: 2.5X TO 6X BASIC
SZ1 Connor McDavid 8.00 20.00
SZ2 Sergei Bobrovsky 2.50 6.00
SZ3 Andrei Vasilevskiy 2.50 6.00
SZ4 Ryan O'Reilly 1.50 4.00
SZ5 Sidney Crosby 6.00 15.00
SZ6 Auston Matthews 6.00 15.00
SZ7 Alex DeBrincat 2.00 5.00
SZ8 Artemi Panarin 3.00 8.00
SZ9 Mark Stone 2.00 5.00
SZ10 John Gibson 1.50 4.00
SZ11 Nathan MacKinnon 6.00 15.00

SZ12 Dylan Larkin 2.00 5.00
SZ13 Jesper Boqvist 1.25 3.00
SZ14 Barrett Hayton 3.00 8.00
SZ15 Kirby Dach 3.00 8.00
SZ16 Noah Dobson 4.00 10.00
SZ17 Ville Heinola 2.00 5.00
SZ18 Oliver Wahlstrom 2.50 6.00
SZ19 Ilya Mikheyev 2.50 6.00
SZ20 Nikita Gusev 2.50 6.00
SZ21 Carl Grundstrom 1.50 4.00
SZ22 Morgan Frost 2.50 6.00
SZ23 Taro Hirose 1.50 4.00
SZ24 Teddy Blueger 1.50 4.00
SZ25 Victor Olofsson 3.00 8.00
SZ26 Filip Zadina 2.50 6.00
SZ27 Vitaly Abramov 1.50 4.00
SZ28 Philippe Myers 1.25 3.00
SZ29 Emil Bemstrom 1.50 4.00
SZ30 Nicolas Hague 1.50 4.00
SZ31 Adam Fox 4.00 10.00
SZ32 Karson Kuhlman 1.50 4.00
SZ33 Dominik Kubalik 3.00 8.00
SZ34 Alexandre Texier 1.50 4.00
SZ35 Mario Ferraro 1.25 3.00
SZ36 Dante Fabbro 1.50 4.00
SZ37 Max Jones 1.50 4.00
SZ38 Erik Brannstrom 1.50 4.00
SZ39 Blake Lizotte 1.50 4.00
SZ40 Rasmus Sandin 2.50 6.00
SZ41 Ryan Poehling 2.50 6.00
SZ42 Kaapo Kakko 2.50 6.00
SZ43 Quinn Hughes 8.00 20.00
SZ44 Cale Makar 8.00 20.00
SZ45 Cody Glass 2.50 6.00
SZ46 Nick Suzuki 6.00 15.00
SZ47 Jack Hughes 8.00 20.00

2019-20 Upper Deck Ice Sub Zero Autographs Blue

SZ1 Connor McDavid A 30.00 80.00
SZ2 Sergei Bobrovsky B 10.00 25.00
SZ5 Sidney Crosby A 25.00 60.00
SZ7 Alex DeBrincat A 8.00 20.00
SZ10 John Gibson B 6.00 15.00
SZ13 Jesper Boqvist C 5.00 12.00
SZ14 Barrett Hayton A 12.00 30.00
SZ15 Kirby Dach B 12.00 30.00
SZ16 Noah Dobson C 15.00 40.00
SZ17 Ville Heinola C 8.00 20.00
SZ18 Oliver Wahlstrom B 10.00 25.00
SZ19 Ilya Mikheyev B 10.00 25.00
SZ20 Nikita Gusev A 10.00 25.00
SZ21 Carl Grundstrom C 6.00 15.00
SZ22 Morgan Frost B 10.00 25.00
SZ24 Teddy Blueger C 6.00 15.00
SZ28 Philippe Myers C 5.00 12.00
SZ29 Emil Bemstrom C 6.00 15.00
SZ30 Nicolas Hague C 6.00 15.00
SZ31 Adam Fox C 15.00 40.00
SZ32 Karson Kuhlman C 6.00 15.00
SZ33 Dominik Kubalik C 50.00 125.00
SZ34 Alexandre Texier C 6.00 15.00
SZ36 Dante Fabbro B 6.00 15.00
SZ43 Quinn Hughes A 60.00 150.00
SZ44 Cale Makar A 30.00 80.00
SZ45 Cody Glass A 10.00 25.00
SZ46 Nick Suzuki C 25.00 60.00
SZ47 Jack Hughes A 60.00 150.00

2019-20 Upper Deck Ice Sub Zero Rookie Variants

SZ42V Kaapo Kakko 5.00 12.00
SZ43V Quinn Hughes 15.00 40.00
SZ44V Cale Makar 15.00 40.00
SZ45V Cody Glass 5.00 12.00
SZ46V Nick Suzuki 12.00 30.00
SZ47V Jack Hughes 15.00 40.00

2019-20 Upper Deck Ice Sub Zero Rookie Variants Autographs Green

SZ43V Quinn Hughes 100.00 250.00
SZ44V Cale Makar 80.00 200.00
SZ45V Cody Glass 30.00 80.00
SZ46V Nick Suzuki 60.00 150.00
SZ47V Jack Hughes 80.00 200.00

2019-20 Upper Deck Ice Superb Script

SSAF Adam Fox/49 25.00 60.00
SSAT Alexandre Texier/49 10.00 25.00
SSBE Emil Bemstrom/49 10.00 25.00
SSBH Barrett Hayton/49 20.00 50.00
SSCC Connor Clifton/49 10.00 25.00
SSCG Cody Glass/25 25.00 60.00
SSCM Cale Makar/25 100.00 250.00
SSDF Dante Fabbro/49 10.00 25.00
SSEB Erik Brannstrom/49 10.00 25.00
SSEM Elvis Merzlikins/49 20.00 50.00
SSGR Carl Grundstrom/49 10.00 25.00
SSIM Ilya Mikheyev/49 15.00 40.00
SSJB Jesper Boqvist/49 8.00 20.00
SSJH Jack Hughes/25 60.00 150.00
SSKK Karson Kuhlman/49 10.00 25.00
SSND Noah Dobson/49 25.00 60.00
SSNG Nikita Gusev/49 15.00 40.00
SSNS Nick Suzuki/25 80.00 200.00
SSOW Oliver Wahlstrom/49 15.00 40.00
SSPM Philippe Myers/49 8.00 20.00
SSQH Quinn Hughes/25 80.00 200.00
SSTB Tobias Bjornfot/49 15.00 40.00

2019-20 Upper Deck Ice Under Glass Rookie Signatures

GIM Ilya Mikheyev B 12.00 30.00
GNS Nick Suzuki B 25.00 60.00

2019-20 Upper Deck Ice Under Glass Signatures

GAB Aleksander Barkov C 12.00 30.00
GBB Ben Bishop C 6.00 15.00
GMF Marc-Andre Fleury B 30.00 80.00

2020-21 Upper Deck Ice

Nathan MacKinnon 3.00 8.00
Andrei Vasilevskiy 1.25 3.00
Adrian Kempe .75 2.00
Jordan Binnington 1.25 3.00
Joe Pavelski 1.00 2.50
Alex Ovechkin 3.00 8.00
7 Martin Jones .60 1.50
8 Patrick Kane 1.50 4.00
9 Jack Eichel 1.25 3.00
10 Ryan Suter .60 1.50
11 Nick Schmaltz .60 1.50
12 Alex DeBrincat 1.00 2.50
13 Auston Matthews 3.00 8.00
14 Brock Boeser 1.00 2.50
15 John Gibson .75 2.00
16 Aleksander Barkov 1.25 3.00
17 Zach Werenski 1.25 3.00
18 Mark Scheifele 1.25 3.00
19 Artemi Panarin 1.50 4.00
20 Rickard Rakell .60 1.50
21 Mark Stone 1.00 2.50
22 Quinn Hughes 2.00 5.00
23 Cale Makar 2.00 5.00
24 Jack Hughes 2.00 5.00
25 Anze Kopitar 1.25 3.00
26 Dylan Larkin 1.00 2.50
27 Mats Zuccarello .75 2.00
28 Anders Lee .60 1.50
29 David Pastrnak 2.00 5.00
30 Tyler Seguin 1.00 2.50
31 Tyler Bertuzzi .60 1.50
32 Sebastian Aho 1.25 3.00
33 Pekka Rinne .75 2.00
34 Steven Stamkos 1.50 4.00
35 Sean Monahan .50 1.25
36 Brendan Gallagher .75 2.00
37 Victor Olofsson .75 2.00
38 Teuvo Teravainen .75 2.00
39 Mathew Barzal 1.00 2.50
40 Brady Tkachuk 1.25 3.00
41 Seth Jones .75 2.00
42 Max Pacioretty .75 2.00
43 Elias Pettersson 1.25 3.00
44 Leon Draisaitl 2.50 6.00
45 John Tavares 1.25 3.00
46 Nick Suzuki 1.50 4.00
47 Igor Shesterkin 1.50 4.00
48 Brad Marchand 1.50 4.00
49 Thomas Chabot .75 2.00
50 Darcy Kuemper .75 2.00
51 Carter Hart .75 2.00
52 Roman Josi .75 2.00
53 Connor Hellebuyck 1.50 4.00
54 Ryan O'Reilly .75 2.00
55 Nikita Kucherov 1.50 4.00
56 Mitch Marner 1.25 3.00
57 Evgeni Malkin 1.50 4.00
58 John Carlson .75 2.00
59 Jonathan Huberdeau 1.00 2.50
60 Travis Konecny .75 2.00
61 Tomas Hertl .75 2.00
62 Matthew Tkachuk 1.50 4.00
63 Nico Hischier 1.25 3.00
64 Sidney Crosby 3.00 8.00
65 Connor McDavid 4.00 10.00
66 Steven Lorentz XRC 1.00 2.50
67 Pavel Francouz XRC 1.50 4.00
68 Jake Evans XRC 1.25 3.00
69 Nicolas Beaudin XRC 1.25 3.00
70 Kirill Kaprizov XRC 5.00 12.00
71 Tim Stutzle XRC 2.50 6.00
72 Olli Juolevi XRC 1.25 3.00
73 Martin Kaut XRC 1.25 3.00
74 Victor Soderstrom XRC 1.00 2.50
75 Gabe Vilardi XRC 2.00 5.00
76 Ty Dellandrea XRC 1.25 3.00
77 Tyler Benson XRC 1.25 3.00
78 Peyton Krebs XRC 2.00 5.00
79 Philipp Kurashev XRC 1.50 4.00
80 Michael DiPietro XRC 1.50 4.00
81 Vitali Kravtsov XRC 2.50 6.00
82 Dylan Cozens XRC 2.00 5.00
83 Thomas Harley XRC 2.00 5.00
84 Jake Oettinger XRC 3.00 8.00
85 Alexander Alexeyev XRC 1.00 2.50
86 Alexander Yelesin XRC 1.00 2.50
87 Alexander Romanov XRC 1.50 4.00
88 Jason Robertson XRC 3.00 8.00
89 Liam Foudy XRC 1.25 3.00
90 Pierre-Olivier Joseph XRC 1.25 3.00
91 Morgan Geekie XRC 1.25 3.00
92 Kieffer Bellows XRC 1.00 2.50
93 Shane Bowers XRC 1.00 2.50
94 Mikey Anderson XRC 1.25 3.00
95 Timothy Liljegren XRC 1.25 3.00
96 Connor McMichael XRC 2.00 5.00
97 Josh Norris XRC 2.00 5.00
98 Nick Robertson XRC 2.00 5.00
99 Bowen Byram XRC 2.50 6.00
100 Alexis Lafreniere XRC 4.00 10.00
101 Dylan Coghlan/1299 XRC 3.00 8.00
102 Gustav Lindstrom/1299 XRC 2.50 6.00
103 Steven Lorentz/1299 2.50 6.00
104 Jansen Harkins/1299 XRC 2.50 6.00
105 Callum Booth/1299 XRC 2.50 6.00
106 Alexander Yelesin/1299 2.50 6.00
107 Jonas Johansson/1299 XRC 3.00 8.00
108 Drew O'Connor/1299 XRC 3.00 8.00
109 Niko Mikkola/1299 XRC 2.50 6.00
110 Artem Zagidulin/1299 XRC 3.00 8.00
111 Brayden Burke/1299 XRC 2.50 6.00
112 Josef Korenar/1299 XRC 2.50 6.00
113 Patrick Khodorenko/1299 XRC 2.00 5.00
114 Jani Hakanpaa/1299 XRC 2.00 5.00
115 Maxim Letunov/1299 XRC 2.50 6.00
116 Nikolai Knyzhov/1299 XRC 2.50 6.00
117 Gage Quinney/1299 XRC 2.00 5.00
118 Austin Poganski/1299 XRC 2.50 6.00
119 Matiss Kivlenieks/1299 XRC 4.00 10.00
120 Nicolas Meloche/1299 XRC 2.50 6.00
121 Calvin Thurkauf/1299 XRC 2.50 6.00
122 Anthony Angello/1299 XRC 2.50 6.00
123 Reid Duke/1299 XRC 3.00 8.00
124 Cole Hults/1299 XRC 2.50 6.00
125 Alex Belzile/1299 XRC 2.50 6.00
126 Mikhail Maltsev/1299 XRC 2.50 6.00
127 Mikko Lehtonen/1299 XRC 2.50 6.00
128 Alexander Barabanov/1299 XRC 3.00 8.00
129 Gilles Senn/1299 XRC 2.50 6.00
130 Stuart Skinner/1299 XRC 6.00 15.00
131 Cameron Hillis/999 XRC 2.50 6.00
132 Glenn Gawdin/999 XRC 2.50 6.00
133 Michael Bunting/999 XRC 5.00 12.00
134 Timothy Liljegren/999 3.00 8.00
135 Keegan Kolesar/999 XRC 2.50 6.00
136 Logan Stanley/999 XRC 3.00 8.00
137 Egor Zamula/999 XRC 2.50 6.00
138 Alexander Alexeyev/999 2.50 6.00
139 Connor Ingram/999 XRC 2.50 6.00
140 Joel Kiviranta/999 XRC 3.00 8.00
141 Jake Evans/999 3.00 8.00
142 Tyler Benson/999 3.00 8.00
143 Mikey Anderson/999 3.00 8.00
144 Brandon Hagel/999 XRC 4.00 10.00
145 Lucas Carlsson/999 XRC 2.50 6.00
146 Pavel Francouz/999 4.00 10.00
147 Austin Strand/999 XRC 2.50 6.00
148 Alexander True/999 XRC 2.50 6.00
149 Ryan McLeod/999 XRC 2.50 6.00
150 Mikhail Berdin/999 XRC 3.00 8.00
151 MacKenzie Entwistle/999 XRC 2.50 6.00
152 John Leonard/999 XRC 2.50 6.00
153 Philip Broberg/999 XRC 3.00 8.00
154 Thomas Harley/999 5.00 12.00
155 Liam Foudy/999 3.00 8.00
156 Joseph Woll/999 XRC 6.00 15.00
157 Jack Rathbone/999 XRC 3.00 8.00
158 Aleksi Heponiemi/999 XRC 4.00 10.00
159 Mathias Brome/999 XRC 2.50 6.00
160 Morgan Geekie/999 3.00 8.00
161 Sasha Chmelevski/499 XRC 4.00 10.00
162 Artem Zub/499 XRC 4.00 10.00
163 Kieffer Bellows/499 4.00 10.00
164 Michael DiPietro/499 6.00 15.00
165 Jake Oettinger/499 12.00 30.00
166 Victor Soderstrom/499 4.00 10.00
167 Joel Hofer/499 XRC 5.00 12.00
168 Pierre-Olivier Joseph/499 5.00 12.00
169 Kevin Bahl/499 XRC 4.00 10.00
170 Nolan Foote/499 XRC 5.00 12.00
171 Shane Bowers/499 4.00 10.00
172 Olli Juolevi/499 5.00 12.00
173 Martin Kaut/499 5.00 12.00
174 Nicolas Beaudin/499 5.00 12.00
175 Ty Dellandrea/499 5.00 12.00
176 Yegor Sharangovich/499 XRC 8.00 20.00
177 Ian Mitchell/499 XRC 4.00 10.00
178 Cal Foote/499 XRC 6.00 15.00
179 Kevin Lankinen/499 XRC 8.00 20.00
180 Peyton Krebs/499 8.00 20.00
181 Nick Robertson/249 8.00 20.00
182 K'Andre Miller/249 XRC 10.00 25.00
183 Arthur Kaliyev/249 XRC 8.00 20.00
184 Ty Smith/249 XRC 8.00 20.00
185 Vitali Kravtsov/249 10.00 25.00
186 Vitek Vanecek/249 XRC 8.00 20.00
187 Josh Norris/249 8.00 20.00
188 Gabe Vilardi/249 8.00 20.00
189 Philipp Kurashev/249 6.00 15.00
190 Pius Suter/249 XRC 6.00 15.00
191 Connor McMichael/99 50.00 125.00
192 Jason Robertson/99 80.00 200.00
193 Nils Hoglander/99 XRC 30.00 80.00
194 Bowen Byram/99 60.00 150.00
195 Ilya Sorokin/99 XRC 80.00 200.00
196 Dylan Cozens/99 50.00 125.00
197 Alexander Romanov/99 40.00 100.00
198 Tim Stutzle/99 60.00 150.00
199 Kirill Kaprizov/99 125.00 300.00
200 Alexis Lafreniere/99 100.00 250.00

2020-21 Upper Deck Ice Green

*GREEN: .5X TO 1.2X BASIC

2020-21 Upper Deck Ice Ice Blue

*ICE BLUE: .75X TO 2X BASIC

2020-21 Upper Deck Ice Lavender

*LAVENDER: .6X TO 1.5X BASIC

2020-21 Upper Deck Ice Orange

*ORANGE: .5X TO 1.2X BASIC

2020-21 Upper Deck Ice Royal Blue

*ROYAL BLUE/99: 1X TO 2.5X BASIC

2021-22 Upper Deck Ice

1 Jacob Markstrom .75 2.00
2 Bryan Rust .75 2.00
3 Maxime Comtois .60 1.50
4 Pius Suter .60 1.50
5 Jake Guentzel 1.25 3.00
6 Cam Atkinson .75 2.00
7 Drake Batherson .75 2.00
8 Patrick Kane 1.50 4.00
9 Miro Heiskanen 1.00 2.50
10 Aleksander Barkov 1.25 3.00
11 Tyler Toffoli .75 2.00
12 Brock Boeser 1.00 2.50
13 Charlie McAvoy 1.00 2.50
14 Dominik Kubalik .75 2.00
15 Josh Bailey .60 1.50
16 Alex Ovechkin 3.00 8.00
17 Nick Schmaltz .60 1.50
18 Kirill Kaprizov 2.50 6.00
19 John Tavares 1.25 3.00
20 Connor McDavid 4.00 10.00
21 Carter Hart .75 2.00
22 Mark Giordano .75 2.00
23 Joe Pavelski 1.00 2.50
24 Max Pacioretty .75 2.00
25 Zach Werenski 1.25 3.00
26 Nikita Kucherov 1.50 4.00
27 Jesper Bratt .75 2.00
28 Mark Stone 1.00 2.50
29 Sam Reinhart 1.50 4.00
30 Ryan O'Reilly .75 2.00
31 Rasmus Dahlin 1.00 2.50
32 Dougie Hamilton .60 1.50
33 Viktor Arvidsson .50 1.25
34 Jakob Chychrun .75 2.00
35 Mikko Rantanen 2.00 5.00
36 Tomas Hertl .75 2.00
37 Anze Kopitar 1.25 3.00
38 Casey Mittelstadt .75 2.00
39 Teuvo Teravainen .75 2.00
40 Nick Suzuki 1.50 4.00
41 Elias Pettersson 1.25 3.00
42 Cale Makar 2.00 5.00
43 Jason Spezza .75 2.00
44 Robin Lehner .60 1.50
45 Brent Burns .75 2.00
46 Quinn Hughes 2.00 5.00
47 Sidney Crosby 3.00 8.00
48 Phillip Danault .75 2.00
49 Victor Olofsson .75 2.00
50 Zach Hyman 1.25 3.00
51 Cam Talbot .75 2.00
52 Artemi Panarin 1.50 4.00
53 Connor Hellebuyck 1.50 4.00
54 Dylan Larkin 1.00 2.50
55 Patrik Laine 1.00 2.50
56 Nathan MacKinnon 3.00 8.00
57 David Pastrnak 2.00 5.00
58 Marc-Andre Fleury 1.50 4.00
59 Joel Eriksson Ek .60 1.50
60 Anthony Mantha .60 1.50
61 Jean-Gabriel Pageau .50 1.25
62 Auston Matthews 3.00 8.00
63 Elias Lindholm .75 2.00
64 Jonathan Toews 1.25 3.00
65 Mario Ferraro .50 1.25
66 Mikael Granlund .60 1.50
67 Josh Norris .75 2.00
68 John Gibson .75 2.00
69 Jonathan Huberdeau 1.00 2.50
70 Anders Lee .60 1.50
71 Sebastian Aho 1.25 3.00
72 Jack Roslovic .50 1.25
73 Ivan Provorov .60 1.50
74 Juuse Saros 1.00 2.50
75 Steven Stamkos 1.50 4.00
76 Jaden Schwartz .60 1.50
77 Carey Price 1.50 4.00
78 Adam Fox 1.00 2.50
79 Vitek Vanecek .75 2.00
80 Philipp Grubauer .75 2.00
81 Alexis Lafreniere 1.25 3.00
82 Nico Hischier 1.25 3.00
83 Brad Marchand 1.50 4.00
84 Filip Forsberg 1.25 3.00
85 Jason Robertson 1.25 3.00
86 Andrei Vasilevskiy 1.25 3.00
87 Max Jones .50 1.25
88 Leon Draisaitl 2.50 6.00
89 Josh Morrissey 1.00 2.50
90 Jakub Vrana .60 1.50
91 Darnell Nurse .60 1.50
92 Pavel Buchnevich .60 1.50
93 Clayton Keller 1.00 2.50
94 Matthew Tkachuk 1.50 4.00
95 Colton Parayko .60 1.50
96 Brayden Point 1.00 2.50
97 Andrei Svechnikov 1.00 2.50
98 Nikolaj Ehlers .75 2.00
99 Brady Tkachuk 1.25 3.00
100 Mitch Marner 1.25 3.00
101 Anton Lundell RC 3.00 8.00
102 Ukko-Pekka Luukkonen RC 2.50 6.00
103 Alex Barre-Boulet RC 1.50 4.00
104 Cole Perfetti RC 3.00 8.00
105 Rasmus Kupari RC 1.50 4.00
106 Zac Jones RC 2.00 5.00
107 Philip Tomasino RC 2.00 5.00
108 Quinton Byfield RC 4.00 10.00
109 Lane Pederson RC 1.50 4.00
110 Ivan Prosvetov RC 1.50 4.00
111 Benoit-Olivier Groulx RC 1.50 4.00
112 Alex Newhook RC 2.50 6.00
113 Radim Zohorna RC 1.50 4.00
114 Jamie Drysdale RC 2.50 6.00
115 David Farrance RC 1.50 4.00
116 William Eklund RC 4.00 10.00
117 Jan Jenik RC 2.00 5.00
118 Scott Perunovich RC 1.50 4.00
119 Mattias Samuelsson RC 1.50 4.00
120 Joey Keane RC 1.25 3.00
121 Hendrix Lapierre RC 1.50 4.00
122 Cole Caufield RC 6.00 15.00
123 Trevor Zegras RC 3.00 8.00
124 Joe Veleno RC 2.00 5.00
125 Alexander Holtz RC 2.50 6.00
126 Spencer Knight RC 3.00 8.00
127 Wade Allison RC 1.50 4.00
128 Garrett Pilon RC 2.00 5.00
129 Mike Hardman RC 1.50 4.00
130 Dawson Mercer RC 4.00 10.00
131 Logan Thompson RC 4.00 10.00
132 Taylor Raddysh RC 2.50 6.00
133 Aliaksei Protas RC 1.50 4.00
134 Jake Neighbours RC 3.00 8.00
135 Jonathan Dahlen RC 1.50 4.00
136 Jack Ahcan RC 1.50 4.00
137 Calen Addison RC 1.50 4.00
138 Cole Sillinger RC 2.50 6.00
139 Adam Beckman RC 1.50 4.00
140 Jacob Bernard-Docker RC 1.50 4.00
141 Jeremy Swayman RC 5.00 12.00
142 Shane Pinto RC 2.50 6.00
143 Alex Turcotte RC 2.00 5.00
144 Lucas Raymond RC 5.00 12.00
145 Vasily Podkolzin RC 2.00 5.00
146 Grigori Denisenko RC 2.00 5.00
147 Ross Colton RC 2.00 5.00
148 Moritz Seider RC 4.00 10.00
149 Nils Lundkvist RC 1.50 4.00
150 Seth Jarvis RC 4.00 10.00
151 Adam Ruzicka/1299 RC 2.50 6.00
152 Daniil Miromanov/1299 RC 2.50 6.00
153 Marian Studenic/1299 RC 2.50 6.00
154 Jackson Cates/1299 RC 2.50 6.00
155 Jonah Gadjovich/1299 RC 2.50 6.00
156 Parker Kelly/1299 RC 2.50 6.00
157 Sean Durzi/1299 RC 2.50 6.00
158 Garrett Pilon 3.00 8.00
159 Mattias Samuelsson 2.50 6.00
160 Jack Drury/1299 RC 4.00 10.00
161 Kristian Reichel/1299 RC 1.50 4.00
162 Rafael Harvey-Pinard/1299 RC 2.50 6.00
163 Boris Katchouk/1299 RC 2.00 5.00
164 Tanner Laczynski/1299 RC 2.50 6.00
165 Sean Day/1299 RC 2.50 6.00
166 Veini Vehvilainen/1299 RC 2.50 6.00
167 Marc Michaelis/1299 RC 2.50 6.00
168 Olle Alsing/1299 RC 2.50 6.00
169 Gregory Hofmann/1299 RC 2.50 6.00
170 Ben Thomas/1299 RC 2.50 6.00
171 Maksim Sushko/1299 RC 2.50 6.00
172 Jeffrey Viel/1299 RC 2.50 6.00
173 Maxwell Willman/1299 RC 2.50 6.00
174 Simon Benoit/1299 RC 2.50 6.00
175 Frederic Allard/1299 RC 2.50 6.00
176 Brett Murray/1299 RC 2.50 6.00
177 Cam York/1299 RC 2.50 6.00
178 Tarmo Reunanen/1299 RC 2.50 6.00
179 Alex Turcotte 3.00 8.00
180 Jack Ahcan 2.50 6.00
181 Karel Vejmelka/999 RC 3.00 8.00
182 Taylor Raddysh 4.00 10.00
183 Radim Zohorna 2.50 6.00
184 Vladimir Tkachev/999 RC 2.50 6.00
185 Mason Geertsen/999 RC 2.50 6.00
186 Jan Jenik 3.00 8.00
187 Tyce Thompson/999 RC 2.50 6.00
188 Sampo Ranta/999 RC 2.50 6.00
189 Morgan Barron/999 RC 2.00 5.00
190 Joey Keane 2.00 5.00
191 Kole Lind/999 RC 3.00 8.00
192 Oskar Steen/999 RC 3.00 8.00
193 Pavel Dorofeyev/999 RC 3.00 8.00
194 Dysin Mayo/999 RC 2.50 6.00
195 David Farrance 2.50 6.00
196 Lane Pederson 2.50 6.00
197 Jacob Bernard-Docker 2.50 6.00
198 Hendrix Lapierre 2.50 6.00
199 Ross Colton 3.00 8.00
200 Matt Kiersted/999 RC 2.00 5.00
201 Mike Hardman 2.50 6.00
202 Brandon Duhaime/999 RC 2.50 6.00
203 Thomas Novak/999 RC 2.50 6.00
204 Jacob Peterson/999 RC 2.50 6.00
205 Filip Gustavsson/999 RC 5.00 12.00
206 Wade Allison 2.50 6.00
207 Nico Daws/999 RC 4.00 10.00
208 Matthew Phillips/999 RC 2.50 6.00
209 Jesse Ylonen/999 RC 2.50 6.00
210 Keaton Middleton/999 RC 2.50 6.00
211 J.J. Peterka/499 RC 8.00 20.00
212 Logan Thompson 10.00 25.00
213 Arttu Ruotsalainen/499 RC 4.00 10.00
214 Jake Leschyshyn/499 RC 4.00 10.00
215 Calen Addison 4.00 10.00
216 Rasmus Kupari 4.00 10.00
217 Benoit-Olivier Groulx 4.00 10.00
218 Wyatt Kalynuk/499 RC 4.00 10.00
219 Jasper Weatherby/499 RC 4.00 10.00
220 Joe Veleno 5.00 12.00
221 Jake Neighbours 8.00 20.00
222 Ivan Prosvetov 4.00 10.00
223 Zac Jones 5.00 12.00
224 Tanner Jeannot/499 RC 4.00 10.00
225 Adam Beckman 4.00 10.00
226 Ukko-Pekka Luukkonen 6.00 15.00
227 Grigori Denisenko 5.00 12.00
228 Shane Pinto 6.00 15.00
229 Jonathan Dahlen 4.00 10.00
230 Anton Lundell 8.00 20.00
231 Dawson Mercer 10.00 25.00
232 Jeremy Swayman 12.00 30.00
233 Scott Perunovich 4.00 10.00
234 Seth Jarvis 10.00 25.00
235 Cole Sillinger 6.00 15.00
236 William Eklund 10.00 25.00
237 Mason McTavish/249 RC 8.00 20.00
238 Nils Lundkvist 4.00 10.00
239 Alex Barre-Boulet 4.00 10.00
240 Alex Newhook 6.00 15.00
241 Vasily Podkolzin 40.00 100.00
242 Quinton Byfield 40.00 100.00
243 Philip Tomasino 30.00 80.00
244 Jamie Drysdale 40.00 100.00
245 Cole Perfetti 50.00 125.00
246 Spencer Knight 50.00 125.00
247 Trevor Zegras 125.00 300.00
248 Moritz Seider 60.00 150.00
249 Cole Caufield 250.00 600.00
250 Lucas Raymond 80.00 200.00

2021-22 Upper Deck Ice Blue

*BLUE/599: .5X TO 1.2X GREEN
249 Cole Caufield 30.00 80.00

2021-22 Upper Deck Ice Gold

*GOLD 1-150: .5X TO 1.2X BASIC
*GOLD/25: 1X TO 2.5X GREEN
232 Jeremy Swayman 60.00 150.00
234 Seth Jarvis 50.00 125.00
245 Cole Perfetti 30.00 80.00
246 Spencer Knight 30.00 80.00
247 Trevor Zegras 125.00 300.00
248 Moritz Seider 30.00 80.00
249 Cole Caufield 200.00 500.00
250 Lucas Raymond 30.00 80.00

2021-22 Upper Deck Ice Green

*GREEN 1-150: .5X TO 1.2X BASIC
151 Adam Ruzicka 2.50 6.00
152 Daniil Miromanov 2.50 6.00
153 Marian Studenic 2.50 6.00
154 Jackson Cates 2.50 6.00
155 Jonah Gadjovich 2.50 6.00
156 Parker Kelly 2.50 6.00
157 Sean Durzi 2.50 6.00
158 Garrett Pilon 3.00 8.00
159 Mattias Samuelsson 2.50 6.00
160 Jack Drury 4.00 10.00
161 Kristian Reichel 1.50 4.00
162 Rafael Harvey-Pinard 2.50 6.00
163 Boris Katchouk 2.00 5.00
164 Tanner Laczynski 2.50 6.00
165 Sean Day 2.50 6.00
166 Veini Vehvilainen 2.50 6.00
167 Marc Michaelis 2.50 6.00
168 Olle Alsing 2.50 6.00
169 Gregory Hofmann 2.50 6.00
170 Ben Thomas 2.50 6.00
171 Maksim Sushko 2.50 6.00
172 Jeffrey Viel 2.50 6.00
173 Maxwell Willman 2.50 6.00
174 Simon Benoit 2.50 6.00
175 Frederic Allard 2.50 6.00
176 Brett Murray 2.50 6.00
177 Cam York 2.50 6.00
178 Tarmo Reunanen 2.50 6.00
179 Alex Turcotte 3.00 8.00
180 Jack Ahcan 2.50 6.00
181 Karel Vejmelka 3.00 8.00
182 Taylor Raddysh 4.00 10.00
183 Radim Zohorna 2.50 6.00
184 Vladimir Tkachev 2.50 6.00
185 Mason Geertsen 2.50 6.00
186 Jan Jenik 3.00 8.00
187 Tyce Thompson 2.50 6.00
188 Sampo Ranta 2.50 6.00
189 Morgan Barron 2.00 5.00
190 Joey Keane 2.00 5.00
191 Kole Lind 3.00 8.00
192 Oskar Steen 3.00 8.00
193 Pavel Dorofeyev 3.00 8.00
194 Dysin Mayo 2.50 6.00
195 David Farrance 2.50 6.00
196 Lane Pederson 2.50 6.00
197 Jacob Bernard-Docker 2.50 6.00
198 Hendrix Lapierre 2.50 6.00
199 Ross Colton 3.00 8.00
200 Matt Kiersted 2.00 5.00
201 Mike Hardman 2.50 6.00
202 Brandon Duhaime 2.50 6.00
203 Thomas Novak 2.50 6.00
204 Jacob Peterson 2.50 6.00
205 Filip Gustavsson 5.00 12.00
206 Wade Allison 2.50 6.00
207 Nico Daws 4.00 10.00
208 Matthew Phillips 2.50 6.00
209 Jesse Ylonen 2.50 6.00
210 Keaton Middleton 2.50 6.00
211 J.J. Peterka 5.00 12.00
212 Logan Thompson 6.00 15.00
213 Arttu Ruotsalainen 2.50 6.00
214 Jake Leschyshyn 2.50 6.00
215 Calen Addison 2.50 6.00
216 Rasmus Kupari 2.50 6.00
217 Benoit-Olivier Groulx 2.50 6.00
218 Wyatt Kalynuk 2.50 6.00
219 Jasper Weatherby 2.50 6.00
220 Joe Veleno 3.00 8.00
221 Jake Neighbours 5.00 12.00
222 Ivan Prosvetov 2.50 6.00
223 Zac Jones 3.00 8.00
224 Tanner Jeannot 2.50 6.00
225 Adam Beckman 2.50 6.00
226 Ukko-Pekka Luukkonen 4.00 10.00
227 Grigori Denisenko 3.00 8.00
228 Shane Pinto 4.00 10.00
229 Jonathan Dahlen 2.50 6.00
230 Anton Lundell 5.00 12.00
231 Dawson Mercer 6.00 15.00
232 Jeremy Swayman 8.00 20.00
233 Scott Perunovich 2.50 6.00
234 Seth Jarvis 6.00 15.00
235 Cole Sillinger 4.00 10.00
236 William Eklund 6.00 15.00
237 Mason McTavish 5.00 12.00
238 Nils Lundkvist 2.50 6.00
239 Alex Barre-Boulet 2.50 6.00
240 Alex Newhook 4.00 10.00
241 Vasily Podkolzin 3.00 8.00
242 Quinton Byfield 6.00 15.00
243 Philip Tomasino 3.00 8.00
244 Jamie Drysdale 4.00 10.00
245 Cole Perfetti 5.00 12.00
246 Spencer Knight 5.00 12.00
247 Trevor Zegras 5.00 12.00
248 Moritz Seider 6.00 15.00
249 Cole Caufield 10.00 25.00
250 Lucas Raymond 8.00 20.00

2021-22 Upper Deck Ice Ice Blue

*ICE BLUE: 1X TO 2.5X BASIC
*ICE BLUE RC: .75X TO 2X BASIC
122 Cole Caufield 30.00 80.00

2021-22 Upper Deck Ice Lavender

*LAVENDER: .75X TO 2X BASIC
*LAVENDER RC: .6X TO 1.5X BASIC

2021-22 Upper Deck Ice Orange

*ORANGE: .6X TO 1.5X BASIC
*ORANGE RC: .5X TO 1.2X BASIC

2021-22 Upper Deck Ice Red

*RED/399: .6X TO 1.5X GREEN
249 Cole Caufield 40.00 100.00

2021-22 Upper Deck Ice Royal Blue

*ROYAL BLUE/99: .75X TO 2X BASIC
122 Cole Caufield 40.00 100.00
148 Moritz Seider 20.00 50.00

2021-22 Upper Deck Ice Autographs White Snowflake

1 Jacob Markstrom D 5.00 12.00
3 Maxime Comtois E 4.00 10.00
4 Pius Suter F 4.00 10.00
6 Cam Atkinson F 5.00 12.00
9 Miro Heiskanen D 6.00 15.00
10 Aleksander Barkov C 8.00 20.00
12 Brock Boeser C 6.00 15.00
15 Josh Bailey F 4.00 10.00
16 Alex Ovechkin B 150.00 400.00
17 Nick Schmaltz E 4.00 10.00
19 John Tavares C 8.00 20.00
20 Connor McDavid A 300.00 800.00
22 Mark Giordano E 5.00 12.00
23 Joe Pavelski E 6.00 15.00
27 Jesper Bratt E 5.00 12.00
29 Sam Reinhart E 10.00 25.00
30 Ryan O'Reilly D 5.00 12.00
36 Tomas Hertl D 5.00 12.00
37 Anze Kopitar B 8.00 20.00
40 Nick Suzuki C 10.00 25.00
45 Brent Burns C 5.00 12.00
53 Connor Hellebuyck C 10.00 25.00
58 Marc-Andre Fleury B 10.00 25.00
59 Joel Eriksson Ek F 4.00 10.00
61 Jean-Gabriel Pageau F 3.00 8.00
65 Mario Ferraro E 3.00 8.00
66 Mikael Granlund F 4.00 10.00
67 Josh Norris E 5.00 12.00
69 Jonathan Huberdeau C 6.00 15.00
72 Jack Roslovic F 3.00 8.00
74 Juuse Saros E 6.00 15.00
77 Carey Price D 10.00 25.00
78 Adam Fox C 6.00 15.00
79 Vitek Vanecek F 5.00 12.00
80 Philipp Grubauer D 5.00 12.00
81 Alexis Lafreniere C 8.00 20.00
83 Brad Marchand C 10.00 25.00
86 Andrei Vasilevskiy B 8.00 20.00
88 Leon Draisaitl B 15.00 40.00
93 Clayton Keller D 6.00 15.00
94 Matthew Tkachuk D 10.00 25.00
97 Andrei Svechnikov D 6.00 15.00
99 Brady Tkachuk D 8.00 20.00
101 Anton Lundell B 20.00 50.00
102 Ukko-Pekka Luukkonen B 15.00 40.00
103 Alex Barre-Boulet C 10.00 25.00
104 Cole Perfetti B 20.00 50.00
105 Rasmus Kupari B 10.00 25.00
106 Zac Jones C 12.00 30.00
107 Philip Tomasino B 12.00 30.00
112 Alex Newhook B 15.00 40.00
114 Jamie Drysdale B 15.00 40.00
116 William Eklund B 25.00 60.00
117 Jan Jenik C 12.00 30.00
118 Scott Perunovich C 10.00 25.00
121 Hendrix Lapierre C 10.00 25.00
122 Cole Caufield A 200.00 500.00
124 Joe Veleno C 12.00 30.00
125 Alexander Holtz B 15.00 40.00
126 Spencer Knight B 20.00 50.00
127 Wade Allison C 10.00 25.00
128 Garrett Pilon C 12.00 30.00
130 Dawson Mercer B 25.00 60.00
131 Logan Thompson C 25.00 60.00
133 Aliaksei Protas C 10.00 25.00
134 Jake Neighbours C 20.00 50.00
136 Jack Ahcan C 10.00 25.00
137 Calen Addison C 10.00 25.00
138 Cole Sillinger B 15.00 40.00
139 Adam Beckman C 10.00 25.00
140 Jacob Bernard-Docker C 10.00 25.00
141 Jeremy Swayman B 125.00 300.00
142 Shane Pinto C 15.00 40.00
143 Alex Turcotte B 12.00 30.00
145 Vasily Podkolzin B 12.00 30.00
146 Grigori Denisenko B 12.00 30.00
147 Ross Colton C 12.00 30.00
149 Nils Lundkvist C 10.00 25.00
150 Seth Jarvis B 25.00 60.00

2021-22 Upper Deck Ice Frozen In Ice

*GOLD/25: 1X TO 2.5X BASIC
FI1 Kirill Kaprizov 10.00 25.00
FI2 Mitch Marner 5.00 12.00
FI3 Dawson Mercer 8.00 20.00
FI4 Anze Kopitar 5.00 12.00
FI5 Sebastian Aho 5.00 12.00
FI6 Igor Shesterkin 6.00 15.00
FI7 Nathan MacKinnon 12.00 30.00
FI8 Brayden Point 4.00 10.00
FI9 Jake Guentzel 5.00 12.00
FI10 Moritz Seider 8.00 20.00
FI11 Mikko Rantanen 8.00 20.00
FI12 Sean Couturier 2.50 6.00
FI13 Kyle Connor 5.00 12.00
FI14 Andrei Svechnikov 4.00 10.00
FI15 Jacob Markstrom 3.00 8.00
FI16 Brad Marchand 6.00 15.00
FI17 Jonathan Dahlen 3.00 8.00
FI18 Gabriel Landeskog 4.00 10.00
FI19 Jack Campbell 3.00 8.00
FI20 Claude Giroux 3.00 8.00
FI21 Tyler Bertuzzi 2.50 6.00
FI22 Vladimir Tarasenko 4.00 10.00
FI23 Artemi Panarin 6.00 15.00
FI24 Johnny Gaudreau 5.00 12.00
FI25 Carter Hart 3.00 8.00
FI26 Elias Lindholm 3.00 8.00
FI27 Connor McDavid 15.00 40.00
FI28 Jamie Drysdale 5.00 12.00
FI29 Chris Kreider 4.00 10.00
FI30 Andrei Vasilevskiy 5.00 12.00
FI31 Patrick Kane 6.00 15.00
FI32 Nazem Kadri 4.00 10.00
FI33 Troy Terry 2.50 6.00
FI34 Sergei Bobrovsky 5.00 12.00
FI35 Evgeny Kuznetsov 4.00 10.00
FI36 Leon Draisaitl 10.00 25.00
FI37 Auston Matthews 12.00 30.00
FI38 Frederik Andersen 4.00 10.00
FI39 Cole Sillinger 5.00 12.00
FI40 David Pastrnak 8.00 20.00
FI41 Lucas Raymond 10.00 25.00
FI42 Adam Fox 4.00 10.00
FI43 Aleksander Barkov 5.00 12.00
FI44 Nikita Kucherov 6.00 15.00
FI45 Andrew Mangiapane 3.00 8.00
FI46 Sidney Crosby 12.00 30.00
FI47 Cam Talbot 3.00 8.00
FI48 Alex Ovechkin 12.00 30.00
FI49 Trevor Zegras 6.00 15.00
FI50 Steven Stamkos 6.00 15.00

2021-22 Upper Deck Ice Glacial Graphs

GGBB Brent Burns B 10.00 25.00
GGBM Brad Marchand B 20.00 50.00
GGBT Brady Tkachuk C 15.00 40.00
GGCH Connor Hellebuyck C 20.00 50.00
GGDS Darryl Sittler A 10.00 25.00
GGKF Kevin Fiala D 8.00 20.00
GGKL Kris Letang B 30.00 80.00
GGMG Mark Giordano D 10.00 25.00
GGML Mario Lemieux A 40.00 100.00
GGPG Philipp Grubauer C 10.00 25.00
GGPT Philip Tomasino D 12.00 30.00
GGSG Samuel Girard D 6.00 15.00
GGSP Shane Pinto D 15.00 40.00
GGTD Thatcher Demko C 12.00 30.00
GGVE Joe Veleno D 12.00 30.00

2021-22 Upper Deck Ice Glacial Graphs Black

*BLACK: .75X TO 2X BASIC
GGBB Brent Burns/25 20.00 50.00
GGBT Brady Tkachuk/25 60.00 150.00
GGCH Connor Hellebuyck/25 40.00 100.00
GGKF Kevin Fiala/25 15.00 40.00
GGMG Mark Giordano/50 20.00 50.00
GGPG Philipp Grubauer/25 30.00 80.00
GGPT Philip Tomasino/50 25.00 60.00

GGSG Samuel Girard/50 60.00 150.00
GGSP Shane Pinto/50 40.00 100.00
GGTD Thatcher Demko/25 50.00 125.00
GGVE Joe Veleno/50 25.00 60.00

2021-22 Upper Deck Ice Ice Crystals

IC1 Josh Anderson 1.00 2.50
IC2 Tage Thompson 1.50 4.00
IC3 Nicklas Backstrom 1.25 3.00
IC4 Andrew Mangiapane 1.25 3.00
IC5 Auston Matthews 5.00 12.00
IC6 Seth Jones 1.25 3.00
IC7 Ryan Suter 1.00 2.50
IC8 Blake Wheeler 1.25 3.00
IC9 Jamie Oleksiak 1.00 2.50
IC10 Kevin Fiala 1.00 2.50
IC11 Connor McDavid 6.00 15.00
IC12 Tim Stutzle 1.50 4.00
IC13 Rickard Rakell 1.00 2.50
IC14 Adam Pelech .75 2.00
IC15 Sean Couturier 1.00 2.50
IC16 Andrei Vasilevskiy 2.00 5.00
IC17 Jonathan Marchessault 1.50 4.00
IC18 Sidney Crosby 5.00 12.00
IC19 Frederik Andersen 1.50 4.00
IC20 Jack Hughes 3.00 8.00
IC21 Adam Fox 1.50 4.00
IC22 Jakub Voracek 1.00 2.50
IC23 Carter Verhaeghe 1.25 3.00
IC24 Dustin Brown 1.25 3.00
IC25 Jordan Binnington 2.00 5.00
IC26 Philipp Grubauer 1.25 3.00
IC27 Thatcher Demko 1.50 4.00
IC28 Timo Meier 1.25 3.00
IC29 Matt Duchene 1.25 3.00
IC30 Taylor Hall 1.25 3.00
IC31 Leon Draisaitl 4.00 10.00
IC32 Mikhail Sergachev 1.00 2.50
IC33 Tyler Bertuzzi 1.00 2.50
IC34 Mikko Rantanen 3.00 8.00
IC35 Clayton Keller 1.50 4.00
IC36 Spencer Knight 2.50 6.00
IC37 Philip Tomasino 1.50 4.00
IC38 Peyton Krebs 1.00 2.50
IC39 Brandon Duhaime 1.25 3.00
IC40 Joey Keane 1.00 2.50
IC41 William Eklund 3.00 8.00
IC42 Parker Kelly 1.25 3.00
IC43 Scott Perunovich 1.25 3.00
IC44 Jonathan Dahlen 1.25 3.00
IC45 Moritz Seider 3.00 8.00
IC46 Trevor Zegras 2.50 6.00
IC47 Wade Allison 1.25 3.00
IC48 Cole Sillinger 2.00 5.00
IC49 Lucas Raymond 4.00 10.00
IC50 Tanner Jeannot 1.25 3.00
IC51 Alex Newhook 2.00 5.00
IC52 Alex Barre-Boulet 1.25 3.00
IC53 Ukko-Pekka Luukkonen 2.00 5.00
IC54 Cole Caufield 5.00 12.00
IC55 Oskar Steen 1.50 4.00
IC56 Jamie Drysdale 2.00 5.00
IC57 Yegor Chinakhov 2.00 5.00
IC58 Cole Perfetti 2.50 6.00
IC59 Jeremy Swayman 4.00 10.00
IC60 Garrett Pilon 1.50 4.00
IC61 Vasily Podkolzin 1.50 4.00
IC62 Nils Lundkvist 1.25 3.00
IC63 Jake Leschyshyn 1.25 3.00
IC64 Dawson Mercer 3.00 8.00
IC65 Quinton Byfield 3.00 8.00

2021-22 Upper Deck Ice Ice Crystals Orange

*ORANGE/99: 1.2X TO 3X BASIC
IC45 Moritz Seider 25.00 60.00
IC49 Lucas Raymond 25.00 60.00
IC54 Cole Caufield 30.00 80.00
IC59 Jeremy Swayman 40.00 100.00

2021-22 Upper Deck Ice Ice Premieres Autographs

IPAAB Adam Beckman/199 6.00 15.00
IPAAH Alexander Holtz/49 20.00 50.00
IPAAN Alex Newhook/99 20.00 50.00
IPABA Morgan Barron/199 5.00 12.00
IPACA Calen Addison/99 6.00 15.00
IPACC Cole Caufield/49 200.00 500.00
IPACD Connor Dewar/199 6.00 15.00
IPACS Cole Sillinger/49 20.00 50.00
IPADM Dawson Mercer/99 60.00 150.00
IPAES Egor Sokolov/199 6.00 15.00
IPAFG Filip Gustavsson/199 12.00 30.00
IPAGD Grigori Denisenko/199 8.00 20.00
IPAGP Garrett Pilon/199 8.00 20.00
IPAHL Hendrix Lapierre/199 6.00 15.00
IPAJA Jack Ahcan/199 6.00 15.00
IPAJB Jacob Bernard-Docker/199 6.00 15.00
IPAJD Jamie Drysdale/49 20.00 50.00
IPAJJ Jan Jenik/199 8.00 20.00
IPAJN Jake Neighbours/199 12.00 30.00
IPAJP J.J. Peterka/199 15.00 40.00
IPAJS Jeremy Swayman/99 60.00 150.00
IPAJV Joe Veleno/99 8.00 20.00
IPAJW Jasper Weatherby/199 6.00 15.00
IPAJY Jesse Ylonen/199 6.00 15.00
IPAKL Kole Lind/199 8.00 20.00
IPAKV Karel Vejmelka/199 8.00 20.00
IPALT Logan Thompson/199 20.00 50.00
IPAMM Mason McTavish/49 80.00 200.00
IPAMZ Moritz Seider/49 80.00 200.00
IPANL Nils Lundkvist/99 6.00 15.00
IPAOS Oskar Steen/199 8.00 20.00
IPAPK Parker Kelly/199 6.00 15.00
IPAPO Shane Pinto/99 10.00 25.00
IPAPT Philip Tomasino/99 15.00 40.00
IPAQB Quinton Byfield/99 40.00 100.00
IPARC Ross Colton/199 8.00 20.00
IPARD Riley Damiani/199 6.00 15.00
IPARK Rasmus Kupari/199 6.00 15.00
IPASK Spencer Knight/49 12.00 30.00
IPASP Scott Perunovich/199 6.00 15.00
IPASR Sampo Ranta/199 6.00 15.00
IPATL Tanner Laczynski/199 6.00 15.00
IPATT Tyce Thompson/199 6.00 15.00
IPATZ Trevor Zegras/49 150.00 400.00
IPAUL Ukko-Pekka Luukkonen/199 10.00 25.00
IPAWA Wade Allison/199 6.00 15.00
IPAWE William Eklund/49 20.00 50.00
IPAWK Wyatt Kalynuk/199 6.00 15.00
IPAZJ Zac Jones/199 8.00 20.00

2021-22 Upper Deck Ice Ice Premieres Jerseys

IPAAB Adam Beckman 1.50 4.00
IPAAH Alexander Holtz 2.50 6.00
IPAAN Alex Newhook 2.50 6.00
IPAAR Arttu Ruotsalainen 1.50 4.00
IPABA Morgan Barron 1.25 3.00
IPACA Calen Addison 1.50 4.00
IPACC Cole Caufield 15.00 40.00
IPACD Connor Dewar 1.50 4.00
IPACS Cole Sillinger 2.50 6.00
IPACY Cam York 1.50 4.00
IPADF David Farrance 1.50 4.00
IPADM Dawson Mercer 4.00 10.00
IPAES Egor Sokolov 1.50 4.00
IPAFG Filip Gustavsson 3.00 8.00
IPAGD Grigori Denisenko 2.00 5.00
IPAGP Garrett Pilon 2.00 5.00
IPAHL Hendrix Lapierre 1.50 4.00
IPAIP Ivan Prosvetov 1.50 4.00
IPAJA Jack Ahcan 1.50 4.00
IPAJB Jacob Bernard-Docker 1.50 4.00
IPAJD Jamie Drysdale 2.50 6.00
IPAJJ Jan Jenik 2.00 5.00
IPAJK Joey Keane 1.25 3.00
IPAJN Jake Neighbours 3.00 8.00
IPAJP J.J. Peterka 3.00 8.00
IPAJS Jeremy Swayman 5.00 12.00
IPAJV Joe Veleno 2.00 5.00
IPAJW Jasper Weatherby 1.50 4.00
IPAJY Jesse Ylonen 1.50 4.00
IPAKL Kole Lind 2.00 5.00
IPAKV Karel Vejmelka 2.00 5.00
IPALP Lane Pederson 1.50 4.00
IPALR Lucas Raymond 5.00 12.00
IPALT Logan Thompson 4.00 10.00
IPAMH Mike Hardman 1.50 4.00
IPAMM Mason McTavish 3.00 8.00
IPAMS Mattias Samuelsson 1.50 4.00
IPAMZ Moritz Seider 4.00 10.00
IPAND Nico Daws 2.50 6.00
IPANL Nils Lundkvist 1.50 4.00
IPAOS Oskar Steen 2.00 5.00
IPAPK Parker Kelly 1.50 4.00
IPAPO Shane Pinto 2.50 6.00
IPAPT Philip Tomasino 2.00 5.00
IPAQB Quinton Byfield 4.00 10.00
IPARC Ross Colton 2.00 5.00
IPARD Riley Damiani 1.50 4.00
IPARK Rasmus Kupari 1.50 4.00
IPARZ Radim Zohorna 1.50 4.00
IPASK Spencer Knight 3.00 8.00
IPASP Scott Perunovich 1.50 4.00
IPASR Sampo Ranta 1.50 4.00
IPATL Tanner Laczynski 1.50 4.00
IPATT Tyce Thompson 1.50 4.00
IPATZ Trevor Zegras 3.00 8.00
IPAUL Ukko-Pekka Luukkonen 2.50 6.00
IPAWA Wade Allison 1.50 4.00
IPAWE William Eklund 4.00 10.00
IPAWK Wyatt Kalynuk 1.50 4.00
IPAZJ Zac Jones 2.00 5.00

2021-22 Upper Deck Ice Ice Premieres Mini

MI1 Trevor Zegras 3.00 8.00
MI2 Anton Lundell 3.00 8.00
MI3 Dawson Mercer 4.00 10.00
MI4 Hendrix Lapierre 1.50 4.00
MI5 Vasily Podkolzin 2.00 5.00
MI6 Filip Gustavsson 3.00 8.00
MI7 Cole Caufield 15.00 40.00
MI8 Jake Neighbours 3.00 8.00
MI9 Adam Beckman 1.50 4.00
MI10 Lucas Raymond 5.00 12.00
MI11 Philip Tomasino 2.00 5.00
MI12 Shane Pinto 2.50 6.00
MI13 Cam York 1.50 4.00
MI14 Wyatt Kalynuk 1.50 4.00
MI15 Ryan Merkley 2.00 5.00
MI16 Kole Lind 2.00 5.00
MI17 Ross Colton 2.00 5.00
MI18 Mason McTavish 3.00 8.00
MI19 Grigori Denisenko 2.00 5.00
MI20 Alex Turcotte 2.00 5.00
MI21 J.J. Peterka 3.00 8.00
MI22 Cole Sillinger 2.50 6.00
MI23 Scott Perunovich 1.50 4.00
MI24 Wade Allison 1.50 4.00
MI25 William Eklund 4.00 10.00
MI26 Alexander Holtz 2.50 6.00
MI27 Jacob Bernard-Docker 1.50 4.00
MI28 Cole Perfetti 3.00 8.00
MI29 Rasmus Kupari 1.50 4.00
MI30 Spencer Knight 3.00 8.00
MI31 Jack Ahcan 1.50 4.00
MI32 Logan Thompson 4.00 10.00
MI33 Calen Addison 1.50 4.00
MI34 Zac Jones 2.00 5.00
MI35 Quinton Byfield 4.00 10.00
MI36 Tanner Jeannot 1.50 4.00
MI37 Alex Newhook 2.50 6.00
MI38 Joe Veleno 2.00 5.00
MI39 Benoit-Olivier Groulx 1.50 4.00
MI40 Nils Lundkvist 1.50 4.00
MI41 Moritz Seider 4.00 10.00
MI42 Jonathan Dahlen 1.50 4.00
MI43 Joe Snively 1.00 2.50
MI44 Ukko-Pekka Luukkonen 2.50 6.00
MI45 Seth Jarvis 4.00 10.00
MI46 Jeremy Swayman 5.00 12.00
MI47 Arttu Ruotsalainen 1.50 4.00
MI48 Jamie Drysdale 2.50 6.00

2021-22 Upper Deck Ice Ice Premieres Mini Gold

*GOLD/99: 1.2X TO 3X BASIC
MI7 Cole Caufield 60.00 150.00

2021-22 Upper Deck Ice Ice Premieres Retro

1 Jeremy Swayman 20.00 50.00
2 Alex Newhook 6.00 15.00
3 Joe Veleno 5.00 12.00
4 Nils Lundkvist 4.00 10.00
5 Cole Perfetti 8.00 20.00
6 William Eklund 10.00 25.00
7 Jake Neighbours 8.00 20.00
8 Calen Addison 4.00 10.00
9 Philip Tomasino 5.00 12.00
10 Cam York 4.00 10.00
11 Cole Sillinger 6.00 15.00
12 Alex Barre-Boulet 4.00 10.00
13 J.J. Peterka 8.00 20.00
14 Jonathan Dahlen 4.00 10.00
15 Ross Colton 5.00 12.00
16 Tanner Jeannot 4.00 10.00
17 Benoit-Olivier Groulx 4.00 10.00
18 Jamie Drysdale 6.00 15.00
19 Shane Pinto 6.00 15.00
20 Karel Vejmelka 5.00 12.00
21 Spencer Knight 8.00 20.00
22 Alexander Holtz 6.00 15.00
23 Anton Lundell 8.00 20.00
24 Quinton Byfield 10.00 25.00
25 Vasily Podkolzin 5.00 12.00
26 Trevor Zegras 20.00 50.00
27 Dawson Mercer 10.00 25.00
28 Moritz Seider 25.00 60.00
29 Cole Caufield 80.00 200.00
30 Lucas Raymond 15.00 40.00

2021-22 Upper Deck Ice Jerseys

*GOLD/25: 1.5X TO 4X BASIC
1 Jacob Markstrom 2.50 6.00
2 Bryan Rust 2.50 6.00
3 Maxime Comtois 2.00 5.00
5 Jake Guentzel 4.00 10.00
6 Cam Atkinson 2.50 6.00
7 Drake Batherson 2.50 6.00
8 Patrick Kane 5.00 12.00
9 Miro Heiskanen 3.00 8.00
10 Aleksander Barkov 4.00 10.00
11 Tyler Toffoli 2.50 6.00
12 Brock Boeser 3.00 8.00
13 Charlie McAvoy 3.00 8.00
14 Dominik Kubalik 2.50 6.00
15 Josh Bailey 2.00 5.00
16 Alex Ovechkin 10.00 25.00
17 Nick Schmaltz 2.00 5.00
18 Kirill Kaprizov 8.00 20.00
19 John Tavares 4.00 10.00
20 Connor McDavid 12.00 30.00
21 Carter Hart 2.50 6.00
22 Mark Giordano 2.50 6.00
23 Joe Pavelski 3.00 8.00
24 Max Pacioretty 2.50 6.00
25 Zach Werenski 4.00 10.00
26 Nikita Kucherov 5.00 12.00
27 Jesper Bratt 2.50 6.00
28 Mark Stone 3.00 8.00
29 Sam Reinhart 5.00 12.00
30 Ryan O'Reilly 2.50 6.00
31 Rasmus Dahlin 3.00 8.00
32 Dougie Hamilton 2.00 5.00
33 Viktor Arvidsson 1.50 4.00
34 Jakob Chychrun 2.50 6.00
35 Mikko Rantanen 6.00 15.00
36 Tomas Hertl 2.50 6.00
37 Anze Kopitar 4.00 10.00
38 Casey Mittelstadt 2.50 6.00
39 Teuvo Teravainen 2.50 6.00
40 Nick Suzuki 5.00 12.00
41 Elias Pettersson 4.00 10.00
42 Cale Makar 6.00 15.00
43 Jason Spezza 2.50 6.00
44 Robin Lehner 2.00 5.00
45 Brent Burns 2.50 6.00
46 Quinn Hughes 6.00 15.00
47 Sidney Crosby 10.00 25.00
48 Phillip Danault 2.50 6.00
49 Victor Olofsson 2.50 6.00
50 Zach Hyman 4.00 10.00
51 Cam Talbot 2.50 6.00
52 Artemi Panarin 5.00 12.00
53 Connor Hellebuyck 5.00 12.00
54 Dylan Larkin 3.00 8.00
55 Patrik Laine 3.00 8.00
56 Nathan MacKinnon 10.00 25.00
57 David Pastrnak 6.00 15.00
58 Marc-Andre Fleury 5.00 12.00
59 Joel Eriksson Ek 2.00 5.00
60 Anthony Mantha 2.00 5.00
61 Jean-Gabriel Pageau 1.50 4.00
62 Auston Matthews 10.00 25.00
63 Elias Lindholm 2.50 6.00
64 Jonathan Toews 4.00 10.00
65 Mario Ferraro 1.50 4.00
66 Mikael Granlund 2.00 5.00
67 Josh Norris 2.50 6.00
68 John Gibson 2.50 6.00
69 Jonathan Huberdeau 3.00 8.00
70 Anders Lee 2.00 5.00
71 Sebastian Aho 4.00 10.00
72 Jack Roslovic 1.50 4.00
73 Ivan Provorov 2.00 5.00
74 Juuse Saros 3.00 8.00
75 Steven Stamkos 5.00 12.00
76 Jaden Schwartz 2.00 5.00
77 Carey Price 5.00 12.00
78 Adam Fox 3.00 8.00
79 Vitek Vanecek 2.50 6.00
80 Philipp Grubauer 2.50 6.00
81 Alexis Lafreniere 4.00 10.00
82 Nico Hischier 4.00 10.00
83 Brad Marchand 5.00 12.00
84 Filip Forsberg 4.00 10.00
85 Jason Robertson 4.00 10.00
86 Andrei Vasilevskiy 4.00 10.00
87 Max Jones 1.50 4.00
88 Leon Draisaitl 8.00 20.00
89 Josh Morrissey 3.00 8.00
90 Jakub Vrana 2.00 5.00
91 Darnell Nurse 2.00 5.00
92 Pavel Buchnevich 2.00 5.00
93 Clayton Keller 3.00 8.00
94 Matthew Tkachuk 5.00 12.00
95 Colton Parayko 2.00 5.00
96 Brayden Point 3.00 8.00
97 Andrei Svechnikov 3.00 8.00
98 Nikolaj Ehlers 2.50 6.00
99 Brady Tkachuk 4.00 10.00
100 Mitch Marner 4.00 10.00
101 Anton Lundell 5.00 12.00
102 Ukko-Pekka Luukkonen 4.00 10.00
103 Alex Barre-Boulet 2.50 6.00
104 Cole Perfetti 5.00 12.00
105 Rasmus Kupari 2.50 6.00
106 Zac Jones 3.00 8.00
107 Philip Tomasino 3.00 8.00
108 Quinton Byfield 6.00 15.00
109 Lane Pederson 2.50 6.00
110 Ivan Prosvetov 2.50 6.00
111 Benoit-Olivier Groulx 2.50 6.00
112 Alex Newhook 4.00 10.00
113 Radim Zohorna 2.50 6.00
114 Jamie Drysdale 4.00 10.00
115 David Farrance 2.50 6.00
116 William Eklund 6.00 15.00
117 Jan Jenik 3.00 8.00
118 Scott Perunovich 2.50 6.00
119 Mattias Samuelsson 2.50 6.00
120 Joey Keane 2.00 5.00
121 Hendrix Lapierre 2.50 6.00
122 Cole Caufield 10.00 25.00
123 Trevor Zegras 5.00 12.00
124 Joe Veleno 3.00 8.00
125 Alexander Holtz 4.00 10.00
126 Spencer Knight 5.00 12.00
127 Wade Allison 2.50 6.00
128 Garrett Pilon 3.00 8.00
129 Mike Hardman 2.50 6.00
130 Dawson Mercer 6.00 15.00
131 Logan Thompson 6.00 15.00
132 Taylor Raddysh 4.00 10.00
133 Aliaksei Protas 2.50 6.00
134 Jake Neighbours 5.00 12.00
135 Jonathan Dahlen 2.50 6.00
136 Jack Ahcan 2.50 6.00
137 Calen Addison 2.50 6.00
138 Cole Sillinger 4.00 10.00
139 Adam Beckman 2.50 6.00
140 Jacob Bernard-Docker 2.50 6.00
141 Jeremy Swayman 8.00 20.00
142 Shane Pinto 4.00 10.00
143 Alex Turcotte 3.00 8.00
144 Lucas Raymond 8.00 20.00
145 Vasily Podkolzin 3.00 8.00
146 Grigori Denisenko 3.00 8.00
147 Ross Colton 3.00 8.00
148 Moritz Seider 6.00 15.00
149 Nils Lundkvist 2.50 6.00
150 Seth Jarvis 6.00 15.00

2021-22 Upper Deck Ice Shrines

SH1 Connor McDavid 8.00 20.00
SH2 Nikita Kucherov 5.00 12.00
SH3 Sidney Crosby 8.00 20.00
SH4 Chris Kreider 3.00 8.00
SH5 Juuse Saros 3.00 8.00
SH6 Brock Nelson 2.50 6.00
SH7 Nick Suzuki 5.00 12.00
SH8 Patrick Kane 5.00 12.00
SH9 Miro Heiskanen 3.00 8.00
SH10 Quinn Hughes 6.00 15.00
SH11 Mark Scheifele 4.00 10.00
SH12 Auston Matthews 6.00 15.00
SH13 Kirill Kaprizov 8.00 20.00
SH14 Thomas Chabot 2.50 6.00
SH15 Patrice Bergeron 3.00 8.00
SH16 Jonathan Huberdeau 3.00 8.00
SH17 Ryan O'Reilly 2.50 6.00
SH18 Gabriel Landeskog 3.00 8.00
SH19 Leon Draisaitl 8.00 20.00
SH20 Max Pacioretty 2.50 6.00
SH21 Luc Robitaille 2.50 6.00
SH22 Scott Niedermayer 2.50 6.00
SH23 Mike Vernon 2.00 5.00
SH24 Bobby Orr 10.00 25.00
SH25 Chris Pronger 2.50 6.00
SH26 Al Iafrate 2.00 5.00
SH27 Adam Graves 2.00 5.00
SH28 Patrick Roy 6.00 15.00
SH29 Mario Lemieux 10.00 25.00
SH30 Jean Beliveau 2.50 6.00
SH31 Ed Belfour 2.50 6.00
SH32 Brian Propp 1.50 4.00
SH33 Wayne Gretzky 15.00 40.00
SH34 Doug Gilmour 3.00 8.00
SH35 Evgeni Nabokov 2.00 5.00
SH36 Mike Bossy 2.50 6.00
SH37 Steve Yzerman 6.00 15.00
SH38 Pierre Turgeon 2.00 5.00
SH39 Jeremy Roenick 4.00 10.00
SH40 Tony Esposito 2.50 6.00
SH41 Lucas Raymond 8.00 20.00
SH42 Mason McTavish 5.00 12.00
SH43 Cole Sillinger 4.00 10.00
SH44 Peyton Krebs 2.00 5.00
SH45 Cole Perfetti 5.00 12.00
SH46 J.J. Peterka 5.00 12.00
SH47 Spencer Knight 5.00 12.00
SH48 Tanner Jeannot 2.50 6.00
SH49 Alex Turcotte 3.00 8.00
SH50 Vasily Podkolzin 3.00 8.00
SH51 Anton Lundell 5.00 12.00
SH52 Ukko-Pekka Luukkonen 4.00 10.00
SH53 Alex Barre-Boulet 2.50 6.00
SH54 William Eklund 6.00 15.00
SH55 Moritz Seider 6.00 15.00
SH56 Alexander Holtz 4.00 10.00
SH57 Trevor Zegras 5.00 12.00
SH58 Seth Jarvis 6.00 15.00
SH59 Cam York 2.50 6.00
SH60 Alex Newhook 4.00 10.00

2021-22 Upper Deck Ice Signature Swatches

SSAL Alexis Lafreniere B 12.00 30.00
SSBB Brent Burns C 8.00 20.00
SSBH Brett Hull B 12.00 30.00
SSBT Brady Tkachuk C 12.00 30.00
SSCC Cole Caufield B 150.00 400.00
SSCM Cale Makar B 20.00 50.00
SSGF Grant Fuhr C 20.00 50.00
SSKL Kris Letang C 30.00 80.00
SSMT Matthew Tkachuk C 15.00 40.00
SSRB Ray Bourque B 12.00 30.00
SSRO Ryan O'Reilly C 8.00 20.00
SSSK Spencer Knight C 15.00 40.00
SSTB Tyler Bertuzzi C 6.00 15.00
SSTZ Trevor Zegras A 125.00 300.00

2021-22 Upper Deck Ice Sub Zero

SZ1 Joe Pavelski 1.25 3.00
SZ2 Mark Scheifele 1.50 4.00
SZ3 Mikko Rantanen 2.50 6.00
SZ4 Brock Boeser 1.25 3.00
SZ5 Sidney Crosby 4.00 10.00
SZ6 Connor McDavid 5.00 12.00
SZ7 Artemi Panarin 2.00 5.00
SZ8 Leon Draisaitl 3.00 8.00
SZ9 Sebastian Aho 1.50 4.00
SZ10 Kirill Kaprizov 3.00 8.00
SZ11 Auston Matthews 4.00 10.00
SZ12 Brad Marchand 2.00 5.00
SZ13 Alex DeBrincat 1.25 3.00
SZ14 Brayden Point 1.25 3.00
SZ15 Aleksander Barkov 1.50 4.00
SZ16 Johnny Gaudreau 1.50 4.00
SZ17 Mark Stone 1.25 3.00
SZ18 Kyle Connor 1.50 4.00
SZ19 Anze Kopitar 1.50 4.00
SZ20 David Perron .75 2.00
SZ21 Patrick Kane 2.00 5.00
SZ22 Andrei Vasilevskiy 1.50 4.00
SZ23 Mathew Barzal 1.25 3.00
SZ24 Alex Ovechkin 4.00 10.00
SZ25 Nathan MacKinnon 4.00 10.00
SZ26 Cole Sillinger/999 1.50 4.00
SZ27 Alex Barre-Boulet/999 1.00 2.50
SZ28 Jonathan Dahlen/999 1.00 2.50
SZ29 Cole Perfetti/999 2.00 5.00
SZ30 Jeremy Swayman/999 3.00 8.00
SZ31 Aliaksei Protas/999 1.00 2.50
SZ32 Shane Pinto/999 1.50 4.00
SZ33 Alexander Holtz/999 1.50 4.00
SZ34 Kole Lind/999 1.25 3.00
SZ35 Spencer Knight/999 2.00 5.00
SZ36 Anton Lundell/999 2.00 5.00
SZ37 Alex Newhook/999 1.50 4.00
SZ38 Grigori Denisenko/999 1.25 3.00
SZ39 Nils Lundkvist/999 1.00 2.50
SZ40 William Eklund/999 2.50 6.00
SZ41 Seth Jarvis/999 2.50 6.00
SZ42 Taylor Raddysh/999 1.50 4.00
SZ43 Riley Damiani/999 1.00 2.50
SZ44 Joe Veleno/999 1.25 3.00
SZ45 Scott Perunovich/999 1.00 2.50
SZ46 Hendrix Lapierre/999 1.00 2.50
SZ47 Wade Allison/999 1.00 2.50
SZ48 Jamie Drysdale/999 1.50 4.00
SZ49 Tyce Thompson/999 1.00 2.50
SZ50 Vasily Podkolzin/999 1.25 3.00
SZ51 Mason McTavish/999 2.00 5.00
SZ52 Philip Tomasino/999 1.25 3.00
SZ53 Tanner Jeannot/999 1.00 2.50
SZ54 Jake Neighbours/999 2.00 5.00
SZ55 Dawson Mercer/999 2.50 6.00
SZ56 Trevor Zegras/999 2.00 5.00
SZ57 Quinton Byfield/999 2.50 6.00
SZ58 Moritz Seider/999 6.00 15.00
SZ59 Cole Caufield/999 10.00 25.00
SZ60 Lucas Raymond/999 3.00 8.00

2021-22 Upper Deck Ice Sub Zero Gold

*GOLD/24: 3X TO 8X BASIC
SZ59 Cole Caufield/24 80.00 200.00

2021-22 Upper Deck Ice Sub Zero Autographs Blue

SZ26 Cole Sillinger C 10.00 25.00
SZ27 Alex Barre-Boulet E 6.00 15.00
SZ29 Cole Perfetti A 12.00 30.00
SZ30 Jeremy Swayman D 25.00 60.00
SZ31 Aliaksei Protas E 6.00 15.00
SZ32 Shane Pinto E 10.00 25.00
SZ33 Alexander Holtz D 10.00 25.00
SZ34 Kole Lind E 8.00 20.00
SZ35 Spencer Knight D 12.00 30.00
SZ36 Anton Lundell B 12.00 30.00
SZ37 Alex Newhook C 10.00 25.00
SZ38 Grigori Denisenko B 8.00 20.00
SZ39 Nils Lundkvist D 6.00 15.00
SZ40 William Eklund C 15.00 40.00
SZ44 Joe Veleno E 8.00 20.00
SZ45 Scott Perunovich E 6.00 15.00
SZ46 Hendrix Lapierre E 6.00 15.00
SZ47 Wade Allison E 6.00 15.00
SZ48 Jamie Drysdale B 10.00 25.00
SZ49 Tyce Thompson E 6.00 15.00
SZ50 Vasily Podkolzin A 8.00 20.00
SZ51 Mason McTavish D 25.00 60.00
SZ52 Philip Tomasino D 8.00 20.00
SZ53 Tanner Jeannot E 6.00 15.00
SZ54 Jake Neighbours E 12.00 30.00
SZ55 Dawson Mercer D 20.00 50.00
SZ56 Trevor Zegras A 80.00 200.00
SZ57 Quinton Byfield A 15.00 40.00
SZ58 Moritz Seider A 60.00 150.00
SZ59 Cole Caufield A 200.00 500.00

2021-22 Upper Deck Ice Sub Zero Rookie Variations

V56 Trevor Zegras 6.00 15.00
V58 Moritz Seider 12.00 30.00
V59 Cole Caufield 20.00 50.00
V60 Lucas Raymond 6.00 15.00

2021-22 Upper Deck Ice Sub Zero Rookies Variations Autographs Green

V56 Trevor Zegras 125.00 300.00
V59 Cole Caufield 200.00 500.00

2022-23 Upper Deck Ice

1 Johnny Gaudreau 1.25 3.00
2 Tim Stutzle 1.00 2.50
3 Kirill Kaprizov 2.50 6.00
4 Tony DeAngelo .50 1.25
5 Jeff Skinner .75 2.00
6 Robert Thomas .75 2.00
7 Connor McDavid 4.00 10.00
8 Mitch Marner 1.25 3.00
9 Clayton Keller 1.00 2.50
10 Brandon Saad .60 1.50
11 Joe Pavelski 1.00 2.50
12 Patrik Laine 1.00 2.50
13 Seth Jarvis 1.00 2.50
14 James van Riemsdyk .60 1.50
15 Yegor Sharangovich .75 2.00
16 Arthur Kaliyev .75 2.00
17 Brady Tkachuk 1.25 3.00
18 Tage Thompson 1.00 2.50
19 Nils Lundkvist .50 1.25
20 Kyle Connor 1.25 3.00
21 Jeremy Swayman 1.25 3.00
22 Cole Caufield 1.50 4.00
23 Lucas Raymond 1.25 3.00
24 Darcy Kuemper .75 2.00
25 Brayden Point 1.00 2.50
26 Mason McTavish .75 2.00
27 Jordan Kyrou .75 2.00
28 Brad Marchand 1.50 4.00
29 Tristan Jarry .75 2.00
30 Mark Scheifele 1.25 3.00
31 Jack Hughes 2.00 5.00
32 Marc-Andre Fleury 1.50 4.00
33 Sam Reinhart 1.50 4.00
34 Gabriel Landeskog 1.00 2.50
35 Andrei Vasilevskiy 1.25 3.00
36 Sebastian Aho 1.25 3.00
37 Nick Robertson .75 2.00
38 Vitek Vanecek .75 2.00
39 Matthew Tkachuk 1.50 4.00
40 Sidney Crosby 3.00 8.00
41 Jacob Markstrom .75 2.00
42 Auston Matthews 3.00 8.00
43 Alex Iafallo .50 1.25
44 Trevor Zegras .75 2.00
45 Charlie McAvoy 1.00 2.50
46 Dawson Mercer 1.00 2.50
47 Ukko-Pekka Luukkonen .60 1.50
48 Filip Forsberg 1.25 3.00
49 Bo Horvat 1.00 2.50
50 Timo Meier .75 2.00
51 Quinton Byfield 1.00 2.50
52 Brent Burns .75 2.00
53 Thomas Chabot .75 2.00
54 Kasperi Kapanen .60 1.50
55 Jonathan Huberdeau 1.00 2.50
56 Moritz Seider 1.00 2.50
57 Andrei Svechnikov 1.00 2.50
58 Anders Lee .60 1.50
59 Tanner Jeannot .50 1.25
60 Logan Thompson 1.00 2.50
61 Jake Oettinger 1.25 3.00
62 Neal Pionk .50 1.25
63 Jared McCann .60 1.50
64 Thatcher Demko 1.00 2.50
65 Jake Guentzel 1.25 3.00
66 Patrick Kane 1.50 4.00
67 Connor Hellebuyck 1.50 4.00
68 Tomas Hertl .75 2.00
69 Nathan MacKinnon 3.00 8.00
70 Oliver Bjorkstrand .60 1.50
71 Troy Terry .60 1.50
72 Elvis Merzlikins .75 2.00
73 Quinn Hughes 2.00 5.00
74 Josh Bailey .60 1.50
75 Karel Vejmelka .50 1.25
76 Marcus Foligno .60 1.50
77 Chris Kreider 1.00 2.50
78 Jack Campbell .75 2.00
79 Kirby Dach .75 2.00
80 Shea Theodore 1.00 2.50
81 Josh Norris .75 2.00
82 Igor Shesterkin 1.50 4.00
83 Cale Makar 2.00 5.00
84 Jack Eichel 1.25 3.00
85 David Pastrnak 2.00 5.00
86 Zach Werenski 1.25 3.00
87 Pavel Buchnevich .60 1.50
88 Noah Dobson 1.00 2.50
89 Alex Ovechkin 3.00 8.00
90 Spencer Knight .75 2.00
91 Nazem Kadri 1.00 2.50
92 Alexis Lafreniere 1.25 3.00
93 Sam Bennett 1.25 3.00
94 Victor Hedman 1.00 2.50
95 Kevin Fiala .60 1.50
96 Brock Boeser 1.00 2.50
97 Andrew Copp .50 1.25
98 Shayne Gostisbehere .75 2.00
99 Jonathan Toews 1.25 3.00
100 Juuse Saros 1.00 2.50
101 Dylan Holloway RC 3.00 8.00
102 Aatu Raty RC 1.50 4.00
103 Cole Koepke RC 1.50 4.00
104 Samuel Fagemo RC 1.25 3.00
105 Pyotr Kochetkov RC 3.00 8.00
106 Matt Boldy RC 5.00 12.00
107 Vladislav Kolyachonok RC 1.25 3.00
108 Jake Sanderson RC 4.00 10.00
109 Wyatt Johnston RC 6.00 15.00
110 Jacob Perreault RC 1.50 4.00
111 Jakub Lauko RC 2.00 5.00
112 David Jiricek RC 3.00 8.00
113 Marco Rossi RC 4.00 10.00
114 Dylan Guenther RC 4.00 10.00
115 Kaedan Korczak RC 1.25 3.00
116 Arber Xhekaj RC 3.00 8.00
117 Matty Beniers RC 4.00 10.00
118 Mark Kastelic RC 1.25 3.00
119 Braden Schneider RC 2.50 6.00
120 Matias Maccelli RC 2.50 6.00
121 Olle Lycksell RC 1.50 4.00
122 Owen Power RC 3.00 8.00
123 Jordan Spence RC 1.50 4.00
124 Elmer Soderblom RC 3.00 8.00
125 Shane Wright RC 4.00 10.00
126 Bobby Brink RC 1.50 4.00
127 Dylan Samberg RC 1.50 4.00
128 Isaac Ratcliffe RC 1.50 4.00
129 Filip Hallander RC 1.50 4.00
130 Chase Pearson RC 1.25 3.00
131 Jack Quinn RC 2.50 6.00
132 Ben Meyers RC 1.50 4.00
133 Brandt Clarke RC 3.00 8.00
134 Thomas Bordeleau RC 1.50 4.00
135 Andrei Kuzmenko RC 3.00 8.00
136 Nick Perbix RC 1.25 3.00
137 Mads Sogaard RC 2.00 5.00
138 Jake Christiansen RC 1.50 4.00
139 Jacob Moverare RC 1.25 3.00
140 Noah Cates RC 1.50 4.00
141 Kent Johnson RC 3.00 8.00
142 Michael Eyssimont RC 1.50 4.00
143 Juraj Slafkovsky RC 8.00 20.00
144 Lukas Reichel RC 3.00 8.00
145 Samuel Poulin RC 2.00 5.00
146 Marc McLaughlin RC 1.50 4.00
147 Jordan Harris RC 2.00 5.00
148 Nick Blankenburg RC 1.25 3.00
149 Lukas Dostal RC 3.00 8.00
150 Kaiden Guhle RC 3.00 8.00
151 Nils Aman/1299 RC 2.50 6.00
152 Ronnie Attard/1299 RC 2.50 6.00
153 Kaedan Korczak/1299 2.00 5.00
154 Jon Lizotte/1299 RC 2.00 5.00
155 Elmer Soderblom/1299 5.00 12.00
156 Casey Fitzgerald/1299 RC 2.00 5.00
157 Simon Holmstrom/1299 RC 2.50 6.00
158 Nikita Alexandrov/1299 RC 2.50 6.00
159 Jean-Luc Foudy/1299 RC 2.50 6.00
160 Pavol Regenda/1299 RC 2.50 6.00
161 Matej Blumel/1299 RC 3.00 8.00
162 Filip Roos/1299 RC 2.00 5.00
163 Marcus Bjork/1299 RC 2.50 6.00
164 Olle Lycksell/1299 2.50 6.00
165 Tyler Tucker/1299 RC 2.50 6.00
166 Zack Hayes/1299 RC 2.00 5.00
167 Brayden Tracey/1299 RC 2.00 5.00
168 James Hamblin/1299 RC 2.50 6.00
169 Keith Petruzzelli/1299 RC 2.00 5.00
170 Jakub Lauko/1299 3.00 8.00
171 Dylan Samberg/1299 2.50 6.00
172 Nick Cicek/1299 RC 2.50 6.00
173 Nikita Okhotiuk/1299 RC 2.00 5.00
174 Nick DeSimone/1299 RC 2.50 6.00
175 Mac Hollowell/1299 RC 2.50 6.00
176 Lucas Johansen/1299 RC 2.00 5.00
177 Bobby Brink/1299 2.50 6.00
178 Adam Raska/1299 RC 2.50 6.00
179 Michael Eyssimont/1299 2.50 6.00
180 Filip Kral/1299 RC 3.00 8.00
181 Jeff Malott/999 RC 2.50 6.00
182 Isaac Ratcliffe/999 2.50 6.00
183 Jakub Galvas/999 RC 2.50 6.00
184 Bokondji Imama/999 RC 2.00 5.00
185 Aatu Raty/999 2.50 6.00
186 Viktor Lodin/999 RC 2.50 6.00
187 Valtteri Puustinen/999 RC 2.00 5.00
188 Hunter Drew/999 RC 2.50 6.00
189 Jake Christiansen/999 2.50 6.00
190 Linus Hogberg/999 RC 2.00 5.00
191 Carson Meyer/999 RC 2.00 5.00
192 Chase Pearson/999 2.00 5.00
193 Nathan Smith/999 RC 2.00 5.00
194 Jacob Moverare/999 2.00 5.00
195 Cole Koepke/999 2.50 6.00
196 Cole Reinhardt/999 RC 2.50 6.00
197 Ben Meyers/999 2.50 6.00
198 Brayden Pachal/999 RC 2.00 5.00
199 Linus Sandin/999 RC 2.00 5.00
200 Reilly Walsh/999 RC 2.50 6.00
201 Jack McBain/999 RC 2.50 6.00
202 Mitchell Chaffee/999 RC 2.00 5.00
203 Alex Vlasic/999 RC 2.00 5.00
204 Filip Hallander/999 2.50 6.00
205 Brandon Biro/999 RC 4.00 10.00
206 Declan Chisholm/999 RC 2.50 6.00
207 Fredrik Karlstrom/999 RC 2.00 5.00
208 Hayden Hodgson/999 RC 2.00 5.00
209 Johnathan Kovacevic/999 RC 2.50 6.00
210 Thomas Bordeleau/999 2.50 6.00
211 Mark Kastelic/499 3.00 8.00
212 Nick Blankenburg/499 3.00 8.00
213 Jacob Perreault/499 4.00 10.00
214 Jordan Harris/499 5.00 12.00
215 Nick Abruzzese/499 RC 4.00 10.00
216 Jordan Spence/499 4.00 10.00
217 Mads Sogaard/499 5.00 12.00
218 Erik Kallgren/499 RC 4.00 10.00
219 Samuel Poulin/499 5.00 12.00
220 Lukas Dostal/499 8.00 20.00
221 David Jiricek/499 8.00 20.00
222 Marc McLaughlin/499 4.00 10.00
223 Pontus Holmberg/499 RC 4.00 10.00
224 Juuso Parssinen/499 RC 4.00 10.00
225 Samuel Fagemo/499 3.00 8.00
226 Vladislav Kolyachonok/499 3.00 8.00
227 Nick Perbix/499 3.00 8.00
228 Noah Cates/499 4.00 10.00
229 Trey Fix-Wolansky/499 RC 4.00 10.00
230 Jonatan Berggren/499 RC 6.00 15.00
231 Marco Rossi/249 10.00 25.00
232 Lukas Reichel/249 8.00 20.00
233 Jack Quinn/249 6.00 15.00
234 Arber Xhekaj/249 8.00 20.00
235 Dylan Holloway/249 8.00 20.00
236 Brandt Clarke/249 8.00 20.00
237 Braden Schneider/249 6.00 15.00
238 Kaiden Guhle/249 8.00 20.00
239 Dylan Guenther/249 10.00 25.00
240 Pyotr Kochetkov/249 8.00 20.00
241 Matty Beniers/99 20.00 50.00
242 Owen Power/99 15.00 40.00
243 Matias Maccelli/99 12.00 30.00
244 Kent Johnson/99 15.00 40.00
245 Wyatt Johnston/99 30.00 80.00
246 Matt Boldy/99 25.00 60.00
247 Andrei Kuzmenko/99 15.00 40.00
248 Juraj Slafkovsky/99 80.00 200.00
249 Jake Sanderson/99 20.00 50.00
250 Shane Wright/99 20.00 50.00

2022-23 Upper Deck Ice Blue

*BLUE/399: .6X TO 1.5X GREEN

2022-23 Upper Deck Ice Gold

*GOLD 1-150: .4X TO 1X GREEN
*GOLD/99: 1.2X TO 3X GREEN

2022-23 Upper Deck Ice Green

*GREEN 1-150: .5X TO 1.2X BASIC
151 Nils Aman 2.50 6.00
152 Ronnie Attard 2.50 6.00
153 Kaedan Korczak 2.00 5.00
154 Jon Lizotte 2.00 5.00
155 Elmer Soderblom 5.00 12.00
156 Casey Fitzgerald 2.00 5.00
157 Simon Holmstrom 2.50 6.00
158 Nikita Alexandrov 2.50 6.00

159 Jean-Luc Foudy 2.50 6.00
160 Pavol Regenda 2.50 6.00
161 Matej Blumel 3.00 8.00
162 Filip Roos 2.00 5.00
163 Marcus Bjork 2.50 6.00
164 Olle Lycksell 2.50 6.00
165 Tyler Tucker 2.50 6.00
166 Zack Hayes 2.00 5.00
167 Brayden Tracey 2.00 5.00
168 James Hamblin 2.50 6.00
169 Keith Petruzzelli 2.00 5.00
170 Jakub Lauko 3.00 8.00
171 Dylan Samberg 2.50 6.00
172 Nick Cicek 2.50 6.00
173 Nikita Okhotiuk 2.00 5.00
174 Nick DeSimone 2.50 6.00
175 Mac Hollowell 2.50 6.00
176 Lucas Johansen 2.00 5.00
177 Bobby Brink 2.50 6.00
178 Adam Raska 2.50 6.00
179 Michael Eyssimont 2.50 6.00
180 Filip Kral 3.00 8.00
181 Jeff Malott 2.50 6.00
182 Isaac Ratcliffe 2.50 6.00
183 Jakub Galvas 2.50 6.00
184 Bokondji Imama 2.00 5.00
185 Aatu Raty 2.50 6.00
186 Viktor Lodin 2.50 6.00
187 Valtteri Puustinen 2.00 5.00
188 Hunter Drew 2.50 6.00
189 Jake Christiansen 2.50 6.00
190 Linus Hogberg 2.00 5.00
191 Carson Meyer 2.00 5.00
192 Chase Pearson 2.00 5.00
193 Nathan Smith 2.00 5.00
194 Jacob Moverare 2.00 5.00
195 Cole Koepke 2.50 6.00
196 Cole Reinhardt 2.50 6.00
197 Ben Meyers 2.50 6.00
198 Brayden Pachal 2.00 5.00
199 Linus Sandin 2.00 5.00
200 Reilly Walsh 2.50 6.00
201 Jack McBain 2.50 6.00
202 Mitchell Chaffee 2.00 5.00
203 Alex Vlasic 2.00 5.00
204 Filip Hallander 2.50 6.00
205 Brandon Biro 4.00 10.00
206 Declan Chisholm 2.50 6.00
207 Fredrik Karlstrom 2.00 5.00
208 Hayden Hodgson 2.00 5.00
209 Johnathan Kovacevic 2.50 6.00
210 Thomas Bordeleau 2.50 6.00
211 Mark Kastelic 2.00 5.00
212 Nick Blankenburg 2.50 6.00
213 Jacob Perreault 2.50 6.00
214 Jordan Harris 3.00 8.00
215 Nick Abruzzese 2.50 6.00
216 Jordan Spence 2.50 6.00
217 Mads Sogaard 3.00 8.00
218 Erik Kallgren 2.50 6.00
219 Samuel Poulin 3.00 8.00
220 Lukas Dostal 5.00 12.00
221 David Jiricek 5.00 12.00
222 Marc McLaughlin 2.50 6.00
223 Pontus Holmberg 2.50 6.00
224 Juuso Parssinen 2.50 6.00
225 Samuel Fagemo 2.00 5.00
226 Vladislav Kolyachonok 2.00 5.00
227 Nick Perbix 2.00 5.00
228 Noah Cates 2.50 6.00
229 Trey Fix-Wolansky 2.50 6.00
230 Jonatan Berggren 4.00 10.00
231 Marco Rossi 6.00 15.00
232 Lukas Reichel 5.00 12.00
233 Jack Quinn 4.00 10.00
234 Arber Xhekaj 5.00 12.00
235 Dylan Holloway 5.00 12.00
236 Brandt Clarke 5.00 12.00
237 Braden Schneider 4.00 10.00
238 Kaiden Guhle 5.00 12.00
239 Dylan Guenther 6.00 15.00
240 Pyotr Kochetkov 5.00 12.00
241 Matty Beniers 6.00 15.00
242 Owen Power 5.00 12.00
243 Matias Maccelli 4.00 10.00
244 Kent Johnson 5.00 12.00
245 Wyatt Johnston 10.00 25.00
246 Matt Boldy 8.00 20.00
247 Andrei Kuzmenko 5.00 12.00
248 Juraj Slafkovsky 12.00 30.00
249 Jake Sanderson 6.00 15.00
250 Shane Wright 6.00 15.00

2022-23 Upper Deck Ice Greyscale

*GREYSCALE: .75X TO 2X BASIC

2022-23 Upper Deck Ice Ice Blue

*ICE BLUE: 1X TO 2.5X BASIC
*ICE BLUE RC: .75X TO 2X BASIC

2022-23 Upper Deck Ice Orange

*ORANGE: .6X TO 1.5X BASIC
*ORANGE RC: .5X TO 1.2X BASIC

2022-23 Upper Deck Ice Purple

*PURPLE: .75X TO 2X BASIC
*PURPLE RC: .6X TO 1.5X BASIC

2022-23 Upper Deck Ice Red

*RED/299: .6X TO 1.5X GREEN

2022-23 Upper Deck Ice Autographs White Snowflake

2 Tim Stutzle B 6.00 15.00
5 Robert Thomas D 5.00 12.00
7 Connor McDavid A 25.00 60.00
9 Clayton Keller B 6.00 15.00
10 Brandon Saad D 4.00 10.00
13 Seth Jarvis E 6.00 15.00
14 James van Riemsdyk D 4.00 10.00
15 Yegor Sharangovich E 5.00 12.00
16 Arthur Kaliyev E 5.00 12.00
17 Brady Tkachuk B 8.00 20.00
19 Nils Lundkvist E 3.00 8.00
21 Jeremy Swayman E 8.00 20.00
24 Darcy Kuemper C 5.00 12.00
26 Mason McTavish E 5.00 12.00
28 Brad Marchand A 10.00 25.00
29 Tristan Jarry D 5.00 12.00
33 Sam Reinhart B 10.00 25.00
35 Andrei Vasilevskiy C 8.00 20.00
38 Vitek Vanecek D 5.00 12.00
39 Matthew Tkachuk A 10.00 25.00
41 Jacob Markstrom C 5.00 12.00
42 Auston Matthews A 20.00 50.00
47 Ukko-Pekka Luukkonen E 4.00 10.00
49 Bo Horvat C 6.00 15.00
50 Timo Meier E 5.00 12.00
52 Brent Burns B 5.00 12.00
53 Thomas Chabot D 5.00 12.00
54 Kasperi Kapanen E 4.00 10.00
55 Jonathan Huberdeau C 6.00 15.00
57 Andrei Svechnikov C 6.00 15.00
58 Anders Lee C 4.00 10.00
59 Tanner Jeannot E 3.00 8.00
61 Jake Oettinger C 8.00 20.00
62 Neal Pionk D 3.00 8.00
63 Jared McCann D 4.00 10.00
74 Josh Bailey D 4.00 10.00
75 Karel Vejmelka E 3.00 8.00
76 Marcus Foligno D 4.00 10.00
79 Kirby Dach E 5.00 12.00
81 Josh Norris D 5.00 12.00
83 Cale Makar A 12.00 30.00
84 Jack Eichel B 8.00 20.00
86 Zach Werenski C 8.00 20.00
89 Alex Ovechkin A 20.00 50.00
90 Spencer Knight E 5.00 12.00
92 Alexis Lafreniere C 8.00 20.00
93 Sam Bennett B 8.00 20.00
97 Andrew Copp C 3.00 8.00
100 Juuse Saros D 6.00 15.00
101 Dylan Holloway B 20.00 50.00
106 Matt Boldy A 30.00 80.00
107 Vladislav Kolyachonok B 8.00 20.00
108 Jake Sanderson A 25.00 60.00
109 Wyatt Johnston A 40.00 100.00
110 Jacob Perreault B 10.00 25.00
111 Jakub Lauko B 12.00 30.00
112 David Jiricek B 20.00 50.00
113 Marco Rossi A 25.00 60.00
114 Dylan Guenther A 25.00 60.00
115 Kaedan Korczak B 8.00 20.00
116 Arber Xhekaj B 20.00 50.00
117 Matty Beniers A 25.00 60.00
118 Mark Kastelic B 8.00 20.00
119 Braden Schneider A 15.00 40.00
120 Matias Maccelli A 15.00 40.00
121 Olle Lycksell B 10.00 25.00
122 Owen Power A 20.00 50.00
123 Jordan Spence B 10.00 25.00
124 Elmer Soderblom B 20.00 50.00
125 Shane Wright A 25.00 60.00
127 Dylan Samberg B 10.00 25.00
128 Isaac Ratcliffe B 10.00 25.00
129 Filip Hallander B 10.00 25.00
130 Chase Pearson B 10.00 25.00
131 Jack Quinn A 15.00 40.00
132 Ben Meyers B 10.00 25.00
133 Brandt Clarke A 20.00 50.00
134 Thomas Bordeleau B 10.00 25.00
135 Andrei Kuzmenko A 20.00 50.00
136 Nick Perbix B 8.00 20.00
137 Mads Sogaard B 12.00 30.00
138 Jake Christiansen B 10.00 25.00
139 Jacob Moverare B 8.00 20.00
140 Noah Cates A 10.00 25.00
141 Kent Johnson A 20.00 50.00
142 Michael Eyssimont B 10.00 25.00
143 Juraj Slafkovsky A 50.00 125.00
144 Lukas Reichel A 20.00 50.00
145 Samuel Poulin B 12.00 30.00
146 Marc McLaughlin B 10.00 25.00
147 Jordan Harris A 12.00 30.00
148 Nick Blankenburg B 8.00 20.00
149 Lukas Dostal B 20.00 50.00
150 Kaiden Guhle A 20.00 50.00

2022-23 Upper Deck Ice Cool Cuts

CC1 David Pastrnak 4.00 10.00
CC2 Nikita Kucherov 3.00 8.00
CC3 Artemi Panarin 3.00 8.00
CC4 Tage Thompson 2.00 5.00
CC5 Elias Pettersson 2.50 6.00
CC6 Trevor Zegras 1.50 4.00
CC7 Matthew Tkachuk 3.00 8.00
CC8 Brady Tkachuk 2.50 6.00
CC9 Sidney Crosby 6.00 15.00
CC10 Mitch Marner 2.50 6.00
CC11 Kirill Kaprizov 5.00 12.00
CC12 Alex Ovechkin 6.00 15.00
CC13 Jason Robertson 2.50 6.00
CC14 Jeff Skinner 1.50 4.00
CC15 Mikko Rantanen 4.00 10.00
CC16 Leon Draisaitl 5.00 12.00
CC17 Auston Matthews 6.00 15.00
CC18 Cole Caufield 3.00 8.00
CC19 Jack Hughes 4.00 10.00
CC20 Connor McDavid 8.00 20.00
CC21 Shane Wright 4.00 10.00
CC22 Pyotr Kochetkov 3.00 8.00
CC23 Jack Quinn 2.50 6.00
CC24 Kaiden Guhle 3.00 8.00
CC25 Matias Maccelli 2.50 6.00
CC26 Noah Cates 1.50 4.00
CC27 Braden Schneider 2.50 6.00
CC28 Dylan Guenther 4.00 10.00
CC29 Matt Boldy 5.00 12.00
CC30 Andrei Kuzmenko 3.00 8.00
CC31 Arber Xhekaj 3.00 8.00
CC32 Brandt Clarke 3.00 8.00
CC33 Jonatan Berggren 2.50 6.00
CC34 Owen Power 3.00 8.00
CC35 Jordan Harris 2.00 5.00
CC36 Matty Beniers 4.00 10.00
CC37 Jake Sanderson 4.00 10.00
CC38 Kent Johnson 3.00 8.00
CC39 Juraj Slafkovsky 8.00 20.00
CC40 Wyatt Johnston 6.00 15.00
CC41 Mario Lemieux 6.00 15.00
CC42 Mark Messier 3.00 8.00
CC43 Joe Sakic 3.00 8.00
CC44 Maurice Richard 3.00 8.00
CC45 Tim Horton 2.50 6.00
CC46 Bobby Orr 6.00 15.00
CC47 Mike Bossy 1.50 4.00
CC48 Jaromir Jagr 5.00 12.00
CC49 Peter Forsberg 3.00 8.00
CC50 Mats Sundin 1.50 4.00
CC51 Wayne Gretzky 10.00 25.00
CC52 Steve Yzerman 4.00 10.00
CC53 Eric Lindros 2.50 6.00
CC54 Patrick Roy 4.00 10.00
CC55 Mike Modano 2.50 6.00
CC56 Brett Hull 3.00 8.00
CC57 Stan Mikita 1.50 4.00
CC58 Martin Brodeur 4.00 10.00
CC59 Jacques Plante 1.50 4.00
CC60 Gordie Howe 5.00 12.00

2022-23 Upper Deck Ice Frozen In Ice

*GOLD/25: 1X TO 2.5X BASIC
FI1 Alex Ovechkin 12.00 30.00
FI2 Kevin Fiala 2.50 6.00
FI3 Jack Hughes 8.00 20.00
FI4 Matthew Tkachuk 6.00 15.00
FI5 Matias Maccelli 5.00 12.00
FI6 Martin Necas 5.00 12.00
FI7 Steven Stamkos 6.00 15.00
FI8 Jason Robertson 5.00 12.00
FI9 Tage Thompson 4.00 10.00
FI10 Leon Draisaitl 10.00 25.00
FI11 Dylan Guenther 8.00 20.00
FI12 Mark Stone 4.00 10.00
FI13 Nikita Kucherov 6.00 15.00
FI14 Nick Suzuki 6.00 15.00
FI15 Matty Beniers 8.00 20.00
FI16 Mathew Barzal 4.00 10.00
FI17 Jake Sanderson 8.00 20.00
FI18 Timo Meier 3.00 8.00
FI19 Kirill Kaprizov 10.00 25.00
FI20 Connor McDavid 15.00 40.00
FI21 Mitch Marner 5.00 12.00
FI22 Sidney Crosby 12.00 30.00
FI23 Shane Wright 8.00 20.00
FI24 Jack Quinn 5.00 12.00
FI25 Patrick Kane 6.00 15.00
FI26 Wyatt Johnston 12.00 30.00
FI27 Trevor Zegras 3.00 8.00
FI28 Kaiden Guhle 6.00 15.00
FI29 Artemi Panarin 6.00 15.00
FI30 Jared McCann 2.50 6.00
FI31 Pyotr Kochetkov 6.00 15.00
FI32 Brady Tkachuk 5.00 12.00
FI33 Evgeni Malkin 6.00 15.00
FI34 Elias Pettersson 5.00 12.00
FI35 Carter Hart 3.00 8.00
FI36 Brayden Point 4.00 10.00
FI37 Johnny Gaudreau 5.00 12.00
FI38 Igor Shesterkin 6.00 15.00
FI39 Juraj Slafkovsky 15.00 40.00
FI40 Bo Horvat 4.00 10.00
FI41 Auston Matthews 12.00 30.00
FI42 David Pastrnak 8.00 20.00
FI43 Owen Power 6.00 15.00
FI44 Clayton Keller 4.00 10.00
FI45 Kyle Connor 5.00 12.00
FI46 Andrei Kuzmenko 6.00 15.00
FI47 Filip Forsberg 5.00 12.00
FI48 Cale Makar 8.00 20.00
FI49 Jordan Kyrou 3.00 8.00
FI50 Cole Caufield 6.00 15.00

2022-23 Upper Deck Ice Glacial Graphs

GGAE Aaron Ekblad B 12.00 30.00
GGAG Adam Graves C 8.00 20.00
GGAI Alex Iafallo 6.00 15.00
GGAL Anders Lee SP 8.00 20.00
GGAN Alex Nedeljkovic C 8.00 20.00
GGAV Andrei Vasilevskiy A 15.00 40.00
GGBC Blake Coleman B 8.00 20.00
GGDB Brandon Saad B 8.00 20.00
GGCC Charlie Coyle C 10.00 25.00
GGCD Connor Dewar C 6.00 15.00
GGDH Dany Heatley A 8.00 20.00
GGDK Darcy Kuemper B 10.00 25.00
GGDM Dawson Mercer 12.00 30.00
GGDP Denis Potvin A 10.00 25.00
GGFZ Fabian Zetterlund C 6.00 15.00
GGGE Morgan Geekie C 6.00 15.00
GGHL Hendrix Lapierre 6.00 15.00
GGJE Joel Eriksson Ek 8.00 20.00
GGJK Jari Kurri A 10.00 25.00
GGMC Maxime Comtois C 8.00 20.00
GGOL Oskar Lindblom 8.00 20.00
GGSK Spencer Knight B 10.00 25.00

2022-23 Upper Deck Ice Ice Crystals

*FRIGID/99: 1X TO 2.5X BASIC
IC1 Roope Hintz 1.50 4.00
IC2 Alex DeBrincat 1.50 4.00
IC3 Kevin Fiala 1.00 2.50
IC4 Matt Duchene 1.25 3.00
IC5 Nazem Kadri 1.50 4.00
IC6 Andre Burakovsky .75 2.00
IC7 Bo Horvat 1.50 4.00
IC8 Johnny Gaudreau 2.00 5.00
IC9 Connor McDavid 6.00 15.00
IC10 Cale Makar 3.00 8.00
IC11 Jack Eichel 2.00 5.00
IC12 Leon Draisaitl 4.00 10.00
IC13 Dominik Kubalik 1.25 3.00
IC14 Mitch Marner 2.00 5.00
IC15 Travis Konecny 1.25 3.00
IC16 Kirill Kaprizov 4.00 10.00
IC17 Mark Scheifele 2.00 5.00
IC18 Martin Necas 2.00 5.00
IC19 Brock Nelson 1.25 3.00
IC20 Jason Robertson 2.00 5.00
IC21 Jordan Kyrou 1.25 3.00
IC22 Nico Hischier 2.00 5.00
IC23 Auston Matthews 5.00 12.00
IC24 Max Domi 1.25 3.00
IC25 Erik Karlsson 1.50 4.00
IC26 David Pastrnak 3.00 8.00
IC27 Alex Ovechkin 5.00 12.00
IC28 Brayden Point 1.50 4.00
IC29 Troy Terry 1.00 2.50
IC30 Nick Suzuki 2.50 6.00
IC31 Shayne Gostisbehere 1.25 3.00
IC32 Tage Thompson 1.50 4.00
IC33 Carter Verhaeghe 1.25 3.00
IC34 Sidney Crosby 5.00 12.00
IC35 Igor Shesterkin 2.50 6.00
IC36 Pyotr Kochetkov 2.50 6.00
IC37 Kirill Marchenko 3.00 8.00
IC38 Nick Perbix 1.00 2.50
IC39 Matt Boldy 4.00 10.00
IC40 Wyatt Johnston 5.00 12.00
IC41 Matias Maccelli 2.00 5.00
IC42 Juuso Parssinen 1.25 3.00
IC43 Arber Xhekaj 2.50 6.00
IC44 Matty Beniers 3.00 8.00
IC45 Marcus Bjork 1.25 3.00
IC46 Dylan Holloway 2.50 6.00
IC47 Juraj Slafkovsky 6.00 15.00
IC48 Lukas Reichel 2.50 6.00
IC49 Noah Cates 1.25 3.00
IC50 Jake Sanderson 3.00 8.00
IC51 Aatu Raty 1.25 3.00
IC52 Jonatan Berggren 2.00 5.00
IC53 Brandt Clarke 2.50 6.00
IC54 Owen Power 2.50 6.00
IC55 David Jiricek 2.50 6.00
IC56 Dylan Guenther 3.00 8.00
IC57 Pontus Holmberg 1.25 3.00
IC58 Jordan Harris 1.50 4.00
IC59 Shane Wright 3.00 8.00
IC60 Andrei Kuzmenko 2.50 6.00
IC61 Mark Kastelic 1.00 2.50
IC62 Braden Schneider 2.00 5.00
IC63 Kaiden Guhle 2.50 6.00
IC64 Jack Quinn 2.00 5.00
IC65 Kent Johnson 2.50 6.00

2022-23 Upper Deck Ice Premieres '12-13 Retro

2012AK Andrei Kuzmenko 8.00 20.00
2012AR Aatu Raty 4.00 10.00
2012AX Arber Xhekaj 8.00 20.00
2012BC Brandt Clarke 8.00 20.00
2012BE Matty Beniers 10.00 25.00
2012BM Ben Meyers 4.00 10.00
2012BS Braden Schneider 6.00 15.00
2012DG Dylan Guenther 10.00 25.00
2012DH Dylan Holloway 8.00 20.00
2012DJ David Jiricek 8.00 20.00
2012ES Elmer Soderblom 8.00 20.00
2012JM Jack McBain 4.00 10.00
2012JQ Jack Quinn 6.00 15.00
2012JS Jake Sanderson 10.00 25.00
2012KJ Kent Johnson 8.00 20.00
2012LR Lukas Reichel 8.00 20.00
2012MA Matias Maccelli 6.00 15.00
2012MB Matt Boldy 12.00 30.00
2012MM Marc McLaughlin 4.00 10.00
2012MR Marco Rossi 10.00 25.00
2012NB Nick Blankenburg 3.00 8.00
2012NC Noah Cates 4.00 10.00
2012NO Nikita Okhotiuk 3.00 8.00
2012OP Owen Power 8.00 20.00
2012SL Juraj Slafkovsky 20.00 50.00
2012SP Samuel Poulin 5.00 12.00
2012SW Shane Wright 10.00 25.00
2012TB Thomas Bordeleau 4.00 10.00
2012WJ Wyatt Johnston 15.00 40.00

2022-23 Upper Deck Ice Ice Premieres Autographs

IPAAR Aatu Raty/99 25.00 60.00
IPAAX Arber Xhekaj/99 15.00 40.00
IPABC Brandt Clarke/199 15.00 40.00
IPABM Ben Meyers/199 8.00 20.00
IPACK Cole Koepke/199 8.00 20.00
IPADG Dylan Guenther/199 20.00 50.00
IPADJ David Jiricek/199 20.00 50.00
IPADS Dylan Samberg/199 8.00 20.00
IPAIR Isaac Ratcliffe/199 8.00 20.00
IPAJC Jake Christiansen/199 8.00 20.00
IPAJM Jack McBain/199 8.00 20.00
IPAKK Kaedan Korczak/199 6.00 15.00
IPAME Michael Eyssimont/199 8.00 20.00
IPAMJ Matej Blumel/199 15.00 40.00
IPAMK Mark Kastelic/199 6.00 15.00
IPAMS Mads Sogaard/99 10.00 25.00
IPANP Nick Perbix/199 6.00 15.00
IPANS Nathan Smith/199 6.00 15.00
IPAPK Pyotr Kochetkov/199 15.00 40.00
IPAPR Pavol Regenda/199 6.00 15.00
IPASA Jake Sanderson/199 20.00 50.00
IPASF Samuel Fagemo/199 6.00 15.00
IPASP Samuel Poulin/199 6.00 15.00
IPAVK Vladislav Kolyachonok/199 6.00 15.00
IPAVP Valtteri Puustinen/99 6.00 15.00
IPAWJ Wyatt Johnston/199 40.00 100.00

2022-23 Upper Deck Ice Ice Premieres Jerseys

IPAAK Andrei Kuzmenko 3.00 8.00
IPAAV Alex Vlasic 1.25 3.00
IPAAX Arber Xhekaj 3.00 8.00
IPABC Brandt Clarke 3.00 8.00
IPABE Matty Beniers 4.00 10.00
IPABM Ben Meyers 1.50 4.00
IPABO Matt Boldy 5.00 12.00
IPABS Braden Schneider 2.50 6.00
IPACK Cole Koepke 1.50 4.00
IPADG Dylan Guenther 4.00 10.00
IPADH Dylan Holloway 3.00 8.00
IPADJ David Jiricek 3.00 8.00
IPADS Dylan Samberg 1.50 4.00
IPAES Elmer Soderblom 3.00 8.00
IPAFH Filip Hallander 1.50 4.00
IPAJC Jake Christiansen 1.50 4.00
IPAJH Jordan Harris 2.00 5.00
IPAJL Jakub Lauko 2.00 5.00
IPAJM Jack McBain 1.25 3.00
IPAJQ Jack Quinn 2.50 6.00
IPAJS Juraj Slafkovsky 8.00 20.00
IPAKG Kaiden Guhle 3.00 8.00
IPAKJ Kent Johnson 3.00 8.00
IPAKK Kaedan Korczak 1.25 3.00
IPALD Lukas Dostal 3.00 8.00
IPALR Lukas Reichel 3.00 8.00
IPAMB Matej Blumel 2.00 5.00
IPAME Michael Eyssimont 1.50 4.00
IPAMK Mark Kastelic 1.25 3.00
IPAMM Matias Maccelli 2.50 6.00
IPAMR Marco Rossi 4.00 10.00
IPAMS Mads Sogaard 2.00 5.00
IPANB Nick Blankenburg 1.25 3.00
IPANC Noah Cates 1.50 4.00
IPANP Nick Perbix 1.25 3.00
IPANS Nathan Smith 1.25 3.00
IPAOP Owen Power 3.00 8.00
IPAPK Pyotr Kochetkov 3.00 8.00
IPAPR Pavol Regenda 1.50 4.00
IPASA Jake Sanderson 4.00 10.00
IPASE Jordan Spence 1.50 4.00
IPASF Samuel Fagemo 1.25 3.00
IPASH Simon Holmstrom 1.50 4.00
IPASP Samuel Poulin 2.00 5.00
IPASW Shane Wright 4.00 10.00
IPATB Thomas Bordeleau 1.50 4.00
IPATF Trey Fix-Wolansky 1.50 4.00
IPAVK Vladislav Kolyachonok 1.25 3.00
IPAWJ Wyatt Johnston 6.00 15.00

2022-23 Upper Deck Ice Ice Premieres Minis

*GOLD/99: 1X TO 2.5X BASIC
MI1 Andrei Kuzmenko 4.00 10.00
MI2 Marco Rossi 5.00 12.00
MI3 Kaiden Guhle 4.00 10.00
MI4 Ben Meyers 2.00 5.00
MI5 Olle Lycksell 2.00 5.00
MI6 Braden Schneider 3.00 8.00
MI7 Trey Fix-Wolansky 2.00 5.00
MI8 Brayden Pachal 1.50 4.00
MI9 Dylan Holloway 4.00 10.00
MI10 Wyatt Johnston 8.00 20.00
MI11 Jacob Perreault 2.00 5.00
MI12 Noah Cates 2.00 5.00
MI13 Matt Boldy 6.00 15.00
MI14 Nick DeSimone 2.00 5.00
MI15 Thomas Bordeleau 2.00 5.00
MI16 Lukas Reichel 4.00 10.00
MI17 Pontus Holmberg 2.00 5.00
MI18 Jeff Malott 2.00 5.00
MI19 Jordan Harris 2.50 6.00
MI20 Reilly Walsh 2.00 5.00
MI21 Jack McBain 2.00 5.00
MI22 Jack Quinn 2.50 6.00
MI23 Lucas Johansen 1.50 4.00
MI24 Carson Meyer 1.50 4.00
MI25 Marc McLaughlin 2.00 5.00
MI26 Brandt Clarke 4.00 10.00
MI27 Jonatan Berggren 3.00 8.00
MI28 Owen Power 4.00 10.00
MI29 Juraj Slafkovsky 10.00 25.00
MI30 Dylan Guenther 5.00 12.00
MI31 David Jiricek 4.00 10.00
MI32 Simon Holmstrom 2.00 5.00
MI33 Nikita Alexandrov 2.00 5.00
MI34 Shane Wright 5.00 12.00
MI35 Jake Sanderson 5.00 12.00
MI36 Aatu Raty 2.00 5.00
MI37 Matias Maccelli 3.00 8.00
MI38 Arber Xhekaj 4.00 10.00
MI39 Pyotr Kochetkov 4.00 10.00
MI40 Samuel Poulin 2.50 6.00
MI41 Mark Kastelic 1.50 4.00
MI42 Kent Johnson 4.00 10.00
MI43 Erik Kallgren 2.00 5.00
MI44 Juuso Parssinen 2.00 5.00
MI45 Matty Beniers 5.00 12.00
MI46 Nick Perbix 1.50 4.00
MI47 Dylan Samberg 2.00 5.00
MI48 Valtteri Puustinen 1.50 4.00

2022-23 Upper Deck Ice Jerseys

1 Johnny Gaudreau 4.00 10.00
2 Tim Stutzle 3.00 8.00
3 Kirill Kaprizov 8.00 20.00
4 Tony DeAngelo 1.50 4.00
5 Jeff Skinner 2.50 6.00
6 Robert Thomas 2.50 6.00
7 Connor McDavid 12.00 30.00
8 Mitch Marner 4.00 10.00
9 Clayton Keller 3.00 8.00
10 Brandon Saad 2.00 5.00
11 Joe Pavelski 3.00 8.00
12 Patrik Laine 3.00 8.00
13 Seth Jarvis 3.00 8.00
14 James van Riemsdyk 2.00 5.00
15 Yegor Sharangovich 2.50 6.00
16 Arthur Kaliyev 2.50 6.00
17 Brady Tkachuk 4.00 10.00
18 Tage Thompson 4.00 10.00
20 Kyle Connor 4.00 10.00
21 Jeremy Swayman 4.00 10.00
22 Cole Caufield 5.00 12.00
23 Lucas Raymond 4.00 10.00
24 Darcy Kuemper 2.50 6.00
25 Brayden Point 3.00 8.00
26 Mason McTavish 4.00 10.00
27 Jordan Kyrou 2.50 6.00
28 Brad Marchand 5.00 12.00
29 Tristan Jarry 2.50 6.00
30 Mark Scheifele 3.00 8.00
31 Jack Hughes 6.00 15.00
32 Marc-Andre Fleury 5.00 12.00
33 Sam Reinhart 5.00 12.00
34 Gabriel Landeskog 3.00 8.00
35 Andrei Vasilevskiy 5.00 12.00
36 Sebastian Aho 4.00 10.00
37 Nick Robertson 2.50 6.00
38 Vitek Vanecek 2.50 6.00
39 Matthew Tkachuk 5.00 12.00
40 Sidney Crosby 10.00 25.00
41 Jacob Markstrom 2.50 6.00
42 Auston Matthews 10.00 25.00
44 Trevor Zegras 2.50 6.00
45 Charlie McAvoy 3.00 8.00
46 Dawson Mercer 3.00 8.00
47 Ukko-Pekka Luukkonen 2.00 5.00
48 Filip Forsberg 4.00 10.00
49 Bo Horvat 3.00 8.00
50 Timo Meier 2.50 6.00
51 Quinton Byfield 3.00 8.00
52 Brent Burns 2.50 6.00
53 Thomas Chabot 2.50 6.00
55 Jonathan Huberdeau 3.00 8.00
56 Moritz Seider 3.00 8.00
57 Andrei Svechnikov 3.00 8.00
58 Anders Lee 2.00 5.00
59 Tanner Jeannot 1.50 4.00
61 Jake Oettinger 4.00 10.00
63 Jared McCann 2.00 5.00
64 Thatcher Demko 3.00 8.00
65 Jake Guentzel 4.00 10.00
66 Patrick Kane 5.00 12.00
67 Connor Hellebuyck 5.00 12.00
68 Tomas Hertl 2.50 6.00
69 Nathan MacKinnon 10.00 25.00
70 Oliver Bjorkstrand 2.00 5.00
71 Troy Terry 2.00 5.00
72 Elvis Merzlikins 2.50 6.00
73 Quinn Hughes 6.00 15.00
74 Josh Bailey 2.00 5.00
75 Karel Vejmelka 1.50 4.00
76 Marcus Foligno 2.00 5.00
77 Chris Kreider 3.00 8.00
78 Jack Campbell 2.50 6.00
79 Kirby Dach 2.50 6.00
80 Shea Theodore 3.00 8.00
81 Josh Norris 2.50 6.00
82 Igor Shesterkin 5.00 12.00
83 Cale Makar 6.00 15.00
84 Jack Eichel 4.00 10.00
85 David Pastrnak 6.00 15.00
86 Zach Werenski 4.00 10.00
87 Pavel Buchnevich 2.00 5.00
89 Alex Ovechkin 10.00 25.00
90 Spencer Knight 2.50 6.00
92 Alexis Lafreniere 4.00 10.00
93 Sam Bennett 4.00 10.00
94 Victor Hedman 3.00 8.00
95 Kevin Fiala 2.00 5.00
96 Brock Boeser 3.00 8.00
97 Andrew Copp 1.50 4.00
98 Shayne Gostisbehere 2.50 6.00
99 Jonathan Toews 4.00 10.00
100 Juuse Saros 3.00 8.00
101 Dylan Holloway 5.00 12.00
103 Cole Koepke 2.50 6.00
104 Samuel Fagemo 2.00 5.00
105 Pyotr Kochetkov 5.00 12.00
106 Matt Boldy 8.00 20.00
107 Vladislav Kolyachonok 2.00 5.00
108 Jake Sanderson 6.00 15.00
109 Wyatt Johnston 10.00 25.00
110 Jacob Perreault 2.50 6.00
111 Jakub Lauko 3.00 8.00
112 David Jiricek 5.00 12.00
113 Marco Rossi 6.00 15.00
114 Dylan Guenther 6.00 15.00
115 Kaedan Korczak 2.00 5.00
116 Arber Xhekaj 5.00 12.00
117 Matty Beniers 6.00 15.00
118 Mark Kastelic 2.00 5.00
119 Braden Schneider 4.00 10.00
120 Matias Maccelli 4.00 10.00
121 Olle Lycksell 2.50 6.00
122 Owen Power 5.00 12.00
123 Jordan Spence 2.50 6.00
124 Elmer Soderblom 5.00 12.00
125 Shane Wright 6.00 15.00
126 Bobby Brink 2.50 6.00
127 Dylan Samberg 2.50 6.00
128 Isaac Ratcliffe 2.50 6.00
129 Filip Hallander 2.50 6.00
130 Chase Pearson 2.00 5.00
131 Jack Quinn 4.00 10.00
132 Ben Meyers 2.50 6.00
133 Brandt Clarke 5.00 12.00
134 Thomas Bordeleau 2.50 6.00
135 Andrei Kuzmenko 5.00 12.00
136 Nick Perbix 2.00 5.00
137 Mads Sogaard 3.00 8.00
138 Jake Christiansen 2.50 6.00
139 Jacob Moverare 2.00 5.00
140 Noah Cates 2.50 6.00
141 Kent Johnson 5.00 12.00
142 Michael Eyssimont 2.50 6.00
143 Juraj Slafkovsky 12.00 30.00
144 Lukas Reichel 5.00 12.00
145 Samuel Poulin 3.00 8.00
146 Marc McLaughlin 2.50 6.00
147 Jordan Harris 3.00 8.00
148 Nick Blankenburg 2.00 5.00
149 Lukas Dostal 5.00 12.00
150 Kaiden Guhle 5.00 12.00

2022-23 Upper Deck Ice Patches Gold

1 Johnny Gaudreau/25 15.00 40.00
2 Tim Stutzle AU/25 20.00 50.00
3 Kirill Kaprizov/25 30.00 80.00
4 Tony DeAngelo/25 6.00 15.00
5 Jeff Skinner/25 10.00 25.00
6 Robert Thomas AU/25 15.00 40.00
9 Clayton Keller AU/49 20.00 50.00
10 Brandon Saad/25 8.00 20.00
11 Joe Pavelski AU/49 20.00 50.00
12 Patrik Laine/25 12.00 30.00
13 Seth Jarvis AU/25 20.00 50.00
14 James van Riemsdyk AU/49 12.00 30.00
15 Yegor Sharangovich/25 10.00 25.00
16 Arthur Kaliyev AU/49 15.00 40.00
17 Brady Tkachuk AU/25 25.00 60.00
20 Kyle Connor/25 15.00 40.00
21 Jeremy Swayman AU/49 25.00 60.00
24 Darcy Kuemper AU/49 15.00 40.00
25 Brayden Point AU/25 20.00 50.00
26 Mason McTavish AU/49 15.00 40.00
27 Jordan Kyrou AU/25 15.00 40.00
28 Brad Marchand AU/25 30.00 80.00
29 Tristan Jarry/25 8.00 20.00
31 Jack Hughes/25 25.00 60.00
32 Marc-Andre Fleury AU/25 30.00 80.00
33 Sam Reinhart AU/25 30.00 80.00
35 Andrei Vasilevskiy AU/25 25.00 60.00
37 Nick Robertson/25 8.00 20.00
38 Vitek Vanecek AU/49 15.00 40.00
39 Matthew Tkachuk AU/25 30.00 80.00
41 Jacob Markstrom AU/49 15.00 40.00
45 Charlie McAvoy/25 10.00 25.00
47 Ukko-Pekka Luukkonen/25 8.00 20.00
48 Filip Forsberg/25 15.00 40.00
49 Bo Horvat AU/25 20.00 50.00
50 Timo Meier AU/25 15.00 40.00
51 Quinton Byfield/25 12.00 30.00
52 Brent Burns AU/49 15.00 40.00
53 Thomas Chabot AU/25 15.00 40.00
55 Jonathan Huberdeau AU/25 20.00 50.00
56 Moritz Seider/25 12.00 30.00
57 Andrei Svechnikov/25 12.00 30.00
58 Anders Lee AU/49 12.00 30.00
59 Tanner Jeannot AU/49 10.00 25.00
61 Jake Oettinger AU/25 25.00 60.00
63 Jared McCann/25 8.00 20.00
64 Thatcher Demko/25 12.00 30.00
65 Jake Guentzel/25 15.00 40.00
68 Tomas Hertl AU/49 15.00 40.00
70 Oliver Bjorkstrand/25 8.00 20.00
71 Troy Terry/25 8.00 20.00
72 Elvis Merzlikins/25 10.00 25.00
73 Quinn Hughes/25 25.00 60.00
74 Josh Bailey AU/49 12.00 30.00
75 Karel Vejmelka AU/49 10.00 25.00
76 Marcus Foligno/25 8.00 20.00
77 Chris Kreider/25 12.00 30.00
78 Jack Campbell/25 10.00 25.00
79 Kirby Dach AU/49 15.00 40.00
80 Shea Theodore/25 12.00 30.00
81 Josh Norris/25 10.00 25.00
82 Igor Shesterkin/25 20.00 50.00
84 Jack Eichel AU/25 25.00 60.00
85 David Pastrnak/25 25.00 60.00
86 Zach Werenski AU/49 25.00 60.00
87 Pavel Buchnevich/25 8.00 20.00
90 Spencer Knight AU/49 15.00 40.00
92 Alexis Lafreniere AU/25 25.00 60.00
94 Victor Hedman AU/25 20.00 50.00
95 Kevin Fiala AU/49 12.00 30.00
96 Brock Boeser AU/25 20.00 50.00
97 Andrew Copp AU/49 10.00 25.00
98 Shayne Gostisbehere/25 10.00 25.00
99 Jonathan Toews/25 15.00 40.00
100 Juuse Saros AU/49 20.00 50.00
101 Dylan Holloway AU/99 25.00 60.00
106 Matt Boldy AU/99 50.00 125.00
107 Vladislav Kolyachonok AU/99 10.00 25.00
108 Jake Sanderson AU/99 30.00 80.00
109 Wyatt Johnston AU/99 50.00 125.00
110 Jacob Perreault AU/99 12.00 30.00
111 Jakub Lauko AU/99 40.00 100.00
112 David Jiricek AU/99 25.00 60.00
113 Marco Rossi AU/99 30.00 80.00
114 Dylan Guenther AU/99 25.00 60.00
115 Kaedan Korczak AU/99 12.00 30.00
116 Arber Xhekaj AU/99 50.00 125.00
117 Matty Beniers AU/99 30.00 80.00
118 Mark Kastelic AU/99 10.00 25.00
119 Braden Schneider AU/99 20.00 50.00
120 Matias Maccelli AU/99 20.00 50.00
121 Olle Lycksell AU/99 10.00 25.00
122 Owen Power AU/99 25.00 60.00
123 Jordan Spence AU/99 12.00 30.00
124 Elmer Soderblom AU/99 25.00 60.00
125 Shane Wright AU/99 30.00 80.00
127 Dylan Samberg AU/99 12.00 30.00
128 Isaac Ratcliffe AU/99 12.00 30.00
129 Filip Hallander AU/99 12.00 30.00
130 Chase Pearson AU/99 10.00 25.00
131 Jack Quinn AU/99 50.00 125.00
132 Ben Meyers AU/99 12.00 30.00
133 Brandt Clarke AU/99 25.00 60.00
134 Thomas Bordeleau AU/99 12.00 30.00
135 Andrei Kuzmenko AU/99 25.00 60.00
136 Nick Perbix AU/99 12.00 30.00
137 Mads Sogaard AU/99 15.00 40.00
138 Jake Christiansen AU/99 12.00 30.00
139 Jacob Moverare AU/99 10.00 25.00
140 Noah Cates AU/99 12.00 30.00
141 Kent Johnson AU/99 25.00 60.00
142 Michael Eyssimont AU/99 12.00 30.00
144 Lukas Reichel AU/99 30.00 80.00
145 Samuel Poulin AU/99 15.00 40.00
146 Marc McLaughlin AU/99 12.00 30.00
147 Jordan Harris AU/99 15.00 40.00
148 Nick Blankenburg AU/99 10.00 25.00
149 Lukas Dostal AU/99 25.00 60.00
150 Kaiden Guhle AU/99 60.00 150.00

2022-23 Upper Deck Ice Signature Swatches

SSAN Alex Nedeljkovic B 10.00 25.00
SSAV Andrei Vasilevskiy A 20.00 50.00
SSDP Denis Potvin B 12.00 30.00
SSHJ Henri Jokiharju B 8.00 20.00
SSJV James van Riemsdyk B 10.00 25.00
SSLA Alexis Lafreniere B 60.00 150.00
SSMC Maxime Comtois B 10.00 25.00
SSNS Nick Suzuki B 25.00 60.00
SSRB Rob Blake A 12.00 30.00
SSRG Ryan Getzlaf B 12.00 30.00
SSST Shea Theodore B 15.00 40.00
SSTK Torey Krug B 10.00 25.00
SSYS Yegor Sharangovich B 12.00 30.00

2022-23 Upper Deck Ice Sub Zero

SZAM Auston Matthews 4.00 10.00
SZAP Artemi Panarin 2.00 5.00
SZAS Andrei Svechnikov 1.25 3.00
SZBT Brady Tkachuk 1.50 4.00
SZCM Cale Makar 2.50 6.00
SZDP David Pastrnak 2.50 6.00
SZFF Filip Forsberg 1.50 4.00
SZHU Jack Hughes 2.50 6.00
SZJG Johnny Gaudreau 1.50 4.00
SZJH Jonathan Huberdeau 1.25 3.00
SZJK Jordan Kyrou 1.00 2.50
SZJO Jake Oettinger 1.50 4.00
SZKK Kirill Kaprizov 3.00 8.00
SZKU Nikita Kucherov 2.00 5.00
SZLD Leon Draisaitl 3.00 8.00
SZMC Connor McDavid 5.00 12.00
SZMM Mitch Marner 1.50 4.00
SZMS Mark Scheifele 1.50 4.00
SZNK Nazem Kadri 1.25 3.00
SZNM Nathan MacKinnon 4.00 10.00
SZPK Patrick Kane 2.00 5.00
SZQH Quinn Hughes 2.50 6.00
SZSC Sidney Crosby 4.00 10.00
SZTT Tage Thompson 1.25 3.00
SZTZ Trevor Zegras 1.00 2.50

2022-23 Upper Deck Ice Sub Zero Rookie Autographs Blue
SZAX Arber Xhekaj B 12.00 30.00
SZBC Brandt Clarke A 12.00 30.00
SZBE Matty Beniers A 15.00 40.00
SZDG Dylan Guenther A 15.00 40.00
SZDH Dylan Holloway B 12.00 30.00
SZDJ David Jiricek A 12.00 30.00
SZFK Fredrik Karlstrom B 5.00 12.00
SZJS Juraj Slafkovsky A 60.00 150.00
SZKO Kaedan Korczak B 5.00 12.00
SZMB Matt Boldy A 20.00 50.00
SZME Michael Eyssimont B 6.00 15.00
SZMR Marco Rossi A 15.00 40.00
SZNA Nick Abruzzese B 6.00 15.00
SZPL Samuel Poulin B 8.00 20.00
SZPY Pyotr Kochetkov A 25.00 60.00
SZSA Jake Sanderson A 15.00 40.00
SZSO Mads Sogaard B 8.00 20.00
SZSW Shane Wright A 15.00 40.00
SZWJ Wyatt Johnston A 25.00 60,00

2022-23 Upper Deck Ice Sub Zero Rookies
*GOLD/24: 3X TO 8X BASIC
SZAK Andrei Kuzmenko/599 2.00 5.00
SZAR Aatu Raty/999 1.00 2.50
SZAX Arber Xhekaj/999 2.00 5.00
SZBC Brandt Clarke/999 2.00 5.00
SZBE Matty Beniers/599 2.50 6.00
SZBS Braden Schneider/999 1.50 4.00
SZDG Dylan Guenther/599 2.50 6.00
SZDH Dylan Holloway/999 2.00 5.00
SZDJ David Jiricek/999 2.00 5.00
SZDO Lukas Dostal/999 2.00 5.00
SZES Elmer Soderblom/999 2.00 5.00
SZFH Filip Hallander/999 1.00 2.50
SZFK Fredrik Karlstrom/999 .75 2.00
SZHA Jordan Harris/999 1.25 3.00
SZJP Jacob Perreault/999 1.00 2.50
SZJQ Jack Quinn/999 1.50 4.00
SZJS Juraj Slafkovsky/599 5.00 12.00
SZKJ Kent Johnson/599 2.00 5.00
SZKO Kaedan Korczak/999 .75 2.00
SZLR Lukas Reichel/999 2.00 5.00
SZMA Matias Maccelli/999 1.50 4.00
SZMB Matt Boldy/599 3.00 8.00
SZME Michael Eyssimont/999 1.00 2.50
SZMR Marco Rossi/999 2.50 6.00
SZNA Nick Abruzzese/999 1.00 2.50
SZOP Owen Power/599 2.00 5.00
SZPL Samuel Poulin/999 1.25 3.00
SZPY Pyotr Kochetkov/999 2.00 5.00
SZSA Jake Sanderson/599 2.50 6.00
SZSO Mads Sogaard/999 1.25 3.00
SZSP Jordan Spence/999 1.00 2.50
SZSW Shane Wright/599 2.50 6.00
SZTB Thomas Bordeleau/999 1.00 2.50
SZTF Trey Fix-Wolansky/999 1.00 2.50
SZWJ Wyatt Johnston/599 4.00 10.00

2023-24 Upper Deck Ice
1 Erik Karlsson 1.00 2.50
2 Roope Hintz 1.00 2.50
3 Anders Lee .60 1.50
4 Jack Quinn .60 1.50
5 Timo Meier .75 2.00
6 Trevor Zegras .75 2.00
7 Brent Burns .75 2.00
8 Clayton Keller 1.00 2.50
9 Taylor Raddysh .60 1.50
10 Owen Power .75 2.00
11 Cale Makar 2.00 5.00
12 Bo Horvat 1.00 2.50
13 Joel Eriksson Ek .60 1.50
14 Brayden Point 1.00 2.50
15 Josh Morrissey 1.00 2.50
16 Pyotr Kochetkov .75 2.00
17 Mario Ferraro .50 1.25
18 Cam Atkinson .75 2.00
19 Matt Boldy 1.25 3.00
20 Jonathan Marchessault 1.00 2.50
21 Peyton Krebs .60 1.50
22 Travis Konecny .75 2.00
23 Lukas Reichel .75 2.00
24 Jordan Kyrou .75 2.00
25 Jared McCann .60 1.50
26 Andrei Vasilevskiy 1.25 3.00
27 Alex Ovechkin 3.00 8.00
28 Auston Matthews 3.00 8.00
29 Igor Shesterkin 1.50 4.00
30 Jack Eichel 1.25 3.00
31 Moritz Seider 1.00 2.50
32 Torey Krug .60 1.50
33 Jeff Petry .75 2.00
34 Artemi Panarin 1.50 4.00
35 Kent Johnson .75 2.00
36 James van Riemsdyk .60 1.50
37 Mitch Marner 1.25 3.00
38 Nikolaj Ehlers .75 2.00
39 Evgeny Kuznetsov 1.00 2.50
40 Jake Sanderson 1.00 2.50
41 Brandt Clarke .75 2.00
42 Connor McDavid 4.00 10.00
43 Blake Coleman .60 1.50
44 Charlie Coyle .75 2.00
45 Miro Heiskanen 1.00 2.50
46 Charlie McAvoy 1.00 2.50
47 Gabe Vilardi .75 2.00
48 Andrei Kuzmenko .75 2.00
49 Mikko Rantanen 2.00 5.00
50 Juuse Saros 1.00 2.50
51 Kirill Marchenko 1.00 2.50
52 Tanner Jeannot .50 1.25
53 Bryan Rust .75 2.00
54 Vitek Vanecek .75 2.00
55 Johnny Gaudreau 1.25 3.00
56 Seth Jarvis 1.00 2.50
57 Shane Pinto .60 1.50
58 Cole Perfetti .75 2.00
59 Calle Jarnkrok .50 1.25
60 Quinn Hughes 2.00 5.00
61 Aleksander Barkov 1.25 3.00
62 Sidney Crosby 3.00 8.00
63 Kirill Kaprizov 2.50 6.00
64 Matthew Tkachuk 1.50 4.00
65 Michael Bunting .75 2.00
66 Matias Maccelli .60 1.50
67 Brady Tkachuk 1.25 3.00
68 Noah Dobson 1.00 2.50
69 Jordan Eberle .75 2.00
70 Mason McTavish .75 2.00
71 Wyatt Johnston 1.50 4.00
72 Filip Gustavsson .75 2.00
73 Jason Robertson 1.25 3.00
74 Nick Suzuki 1.50 4.00
75 Sonny Milano .60 1.50
76 Zach Hyman 1.25 3.00
77 Tim Stutzle 1.00 2.50
78 Tage Thompson 1.00 2.50
79 Mark Stone 1.00 2.50
80 Jeremy Swayman 1.25 3.00
81 Jonatan Berggren .60 1.50
82 Adrian Kempe .75 2.00
83 David Pastrnak 2.00 5.00
84 Brandon Hagel .60 1.50
85 Robert Thomas .75 2.00
86 Anze Kopitar 1.25 3.00
87 Elias Pettersson 1.25 3.00
88 Jonathan Huberdeau 1.00 2.50
89 Ryan Nugent-Hopkins 1.00 2.50
90 Philipp Grubauer .75 2.00
91 Chandler Stephenson .60 1.50
92 Cole Caufield 1.50 4.00
93 Braden Schneider .60 1.50
94 Martin Necas 1.25 3.00
95 Jack Hughes 2.00 5.00
96 Ilya Sorokin 1.25 3.00
97 Matty Beniers 1.00 2.50
98 Dylan Larkin 1,00 2.50
99 Tyler Toffoli .75 2.00
100 Roman Josi .75 2.00
101 Dustin Wolf RC 5.00 12.00
102 Stanislav Svozil RC 1.25 3.00
103 Olle Eriksson Ek RC 1.50 4.00
104 Owen Beck RC 2.50 6.00
105 Matt Murray RC 1.50 4.00
106 Akito Hirose RC 1.25 3.00
107 Arnaud Durandeau RC 1.50 4.00
108 Tyson Foerster RC 3.00 8.00
109 Matthew Knies RC 6.00 15.00
110 Luke Evangelista RC 2.50 6.00
111 Jakob Pelletier RC 2.00 5.00
112 William Dufour RC 1.25 3.00
113 Marco Kasper RC 4.00 10.00
114 Vincent Iorio RC 1.50 4.00
115 Devon Levi RC 4.00 10.00
116 Bobby McMann RC 2.50 6.00
117 Tye Kartye RC 2.50 6.00
118 Jiri Patera RC 2.50 6.00
119 Lukas Rousek RC 1.25 3.00
120 Billy Sweezey RC 1.50 4.00
121 Tyler Kleven RC 1.50 4.00
122 Walker Duehr RC 1.25 3.00
123 Cole Guttman RC 1.50 4.00
124 Danil Gushchin RC 1.50 4.00
125 Will Cuylle RC 2.50 6.00
126 Egor Afanasyev RC 1.50 4.00
127 Luke Hughes RC 5.00 12.00
128 Hunter McKown RC 1.50 4.00
129 Hugh McGing RC 1.50 4.00
130 Wyatt Kaiser RC 1.50 4.00
131 Aidan McDonough RC 1.25 3.00
132 Vincent Desharnais RC 2.00 5.00
133 Leevi Merilainen RC 1.50 4.00
134 Jet Greaves RC 2.50 6.00
135 Jonathan Gruden RC 1.50 4.00
136 Samuel Bolduc RC 1.50 4.00
137 Ridly Greig RC 2.50 6.00
138 Luke Philp RC 1.50 4.00
139 Matthew Coronato RC 2.50 6.00
140 Arturs Silovs RC 3.00 8.00
141 Milos Kelemen RC 1.50 4.00
142 Henry Thrun RC 1.50 4.00
143 Simon Edvinsson RC 3.00 8.00
144 Brock Faber RC 4.00 10.00
145 Nikita Nesterenko RC 1.50 4.00
146 Yaroslav Askarov RC 4.00 10.00
147 Elliot Desnoyers RC 1.50 4.00
148 Michael Kesselring RC 1.50 4.00
149 Sean Farrell RC 1.50 4.00
150 Joona Koppanen RC 1.25 3.00
151 Michael Kesselring/999 2.50 6.00
152 Mikael Pyyhtia/999 RC 2.50 6.00
153 Waltteri Merela/999 RC 2.50 6.00
154 Tye Kartye/999 4.00 10.00
155 Zach Benson/999 RC 4.00 10.00
156 John Beecher/999 RC 5.00 12.00
157 Connor Zary/999 RC 5.00 12.00
158 Roby Jarventie/999 RC 2.50 6.00
159 David Gust/999 RC 2.50 6.00
160 Mackie Samoskevich/999 RC 4.00 10.00
161 Jakob Pelletier/999 3.00 8.00
162 Alex Laferriere/999 RC 4.00 10.00
163 Fraser Minten/999 RC 5.00 12.00
164 Raphael Lavoie/999 RC 2.50 6.00
165 Marc Del Gaizo/999 RC 2.50 6.00
166 Dmitri Voronkov/999 RC 3.00 8.00
167 Emil Andrae/999 RC 2.50 6.00
168 Ryan Shea/999 RC 2.50 6.00
169 Hardy Haman Aktell/999 RC 2.50 6.00
170 Uvis Balinskis/999 RC 2.50 6.00
171 Ty Emberson/999 RC 2.50 6.00
172 Tristan Luneau/999 RC 2.50 6.00
173 Ilya Solovyov/999 RC 2.50 6.00
174 Daemon Hunt/999 RC 2.50 6.00
175 Mason Lohrei/999 RC 4.00 10.00
176 Matt Tomkins/999 RC 2.50 6.00
177 Nikolas Matinpalo/999 RC 2.50 6.00
178 Ondrej Pavel/999 RC 2.50 6.00
179 Martin Pospisil/999 RC 3.00 8.00
180 Justin Sourdif/999 RC 2.50 6.00
181 Tyler Angle/799 RC 2.50 6.00
182 Tristen Robins/799 RC 2.50 6.00
183 Adam Ginning/799 RC 2.50 6.00
184 Milos Kelemen/799 2.50 6.00
185 Vincent Iorio/799 2.50 6.00
186 Lucas Condotta/799 RC 2.50 6.00
187 Egor Afanasyev/799 2.50 6.00
188 Hunter McKown/799 2.50 6.00
189 Arturs Silovs/799 5.00 12.00
190 Wyatt Kaiser/799 2.50 6.00
191 Joona Koppanen/799 2.00 5.00
192 Nick Swaney/799 RC 2.50 6.00
193 Spencer Stastney/799 RC 2.50 6.00
194 Jiri Patera/799 4.00 10.00
195 Olle Eriksson Ek/799 2.50 6.00
196 Jonathan Gruden/799 2.50 6.00
197 Jake Livingstone/799 RC 2.50 6.00
198 Jet Greaves/799 4.00 10.00
199 Henry Thrun/799 2.50 6.00
200 Damien Giroux/799 RC 2.50 6.00
201 Jaxson Stauber/799 RC 2.50 6.00
202 Vincent Desharnais/799 3.00 8.00
203 Matthew Kessel/799 RC 2.00 5.00
204 Owen Beck/799 4.00 10.00
205 Samuel Knazko/799 RC 2.50 6.00
206 Joel Teasdale/799 RC 2.50 6.00
207 Samuel Bolduc/799 2.50 6.00
208 Billy Sweezey/799 2.50 6.00
209 Drew Helleson/799 RC 2.50 6.00
210 Maxence Guenette/799 RC 2.50 6.00
211 Will Cuylle/499 6.00 15.00
212 Hugh McGing/499 4.00 10.00
213 Akito Hirose/499 3.00 8.00
214 Luke Philp/499 4.00 10.00
215 Danil Gushchin/499 4.00 10.00
216 Sean Farrell/499 4.00 10.00
217 Arnaud Durandeau/499 4.00 10.00
218 Simon Edvinsson/499 8.00 20.00
219 Matt Murray/499 4.00 10.00
220 Cole Guttman/499 4.00 10.00
221 Bobby McMann/499 6.00 15.00
222 Tyler Kleven/499 4.00 10.00
223 Nikita Nesterenko/499 4.00 10.00
224 Cole McWard/499 RC 4.00 10.00
225 Elliot Desnoyers/499 4.00 10.00
226 Lukas Rousek/499 3.00 8.00
227 Matthew Coronato/499 6.00 15.00
228 Stanislav Svozil/499 3.00 8.00
229 Aidan McDonough/499 3.00 8.00
230 William Dufour/499 3.00 8.00
231 Leevi Merilainen/249 4.00 10.00
232 Walker Duehr/249 3.00 8.00
233 Devon Levi/249 10.00 25.00
234 Marco Kasper/249 10.00 25.00
235 Jackson LaCombe/249 RC 4.00 10.00
236 Pavel Mintyukov/249 RC 6.00 15.00
237 Dustin Wolf/249 12.00 30.00
238 Brock Faber/249 10.00 25.00
239 Tyson Foerster/249 8.00 20.00
240 Yaroslav Askarov/249 10.00 25.00
241 Kevin Korchinski/99 RC 15.00 40.00
242 Ridly Greig/99 15.00 40.00
243 Adam Fantilli/99 RC 100.00 250.00
244 Luke Evangelista/99 15.00 40.00
246 Logan Cooley/99 RC 150.00 400.00
247 Matthew Knies/99 60.00 150.00
248 Matthew Poitras/99 RC 20.00 50.00
249 Leo Carlsson/99 RC 80.00 200.00
250 Connor Bedard/99 RC 1500.00 4000.00
251 Connor Bedard EXT 12.00 30.00
252 Logan Cooley EXT 5.00 12.00
253 Adam Fantilli EXT 5.00 12.00
254 Leo Carlsson EXT 5.00 12.00
255 Zach Benson EXT 2.50 6.00

2023-24 Upper Deck Ice Blue
*BLUE/799: .3X TO .75X GREEN

2023-24 Upper Deck Ice Gold
*GOLD/25: 1.2X TO 3X GREEN
245 Luke Hughes 50.00 125.00
246 Logan Cooley 100.00 250.00
250 Connor Bedard 150.00 400.00

2023-24 Upper Deck Ice Green
*GREEN 1-150: .5X TO 1.2X BASIC
151 Michael Kesselring 3.00 8.00
152 Mikael Pyyhtia 3.00 8.00
153 Waltteri Merela 3.00 8.00
154 Tye Kartye 5.00 12.00
155 Zach Benson 5.00 12.00
156 John Beecher 6.00 15.00
157 Connor Zary 6.00 15.00
158 Roby Jarventie 3.00 8.00
159 David Gust 3.00 8.00
160 Mackie Samoskevich 5.00 12.00
161 Jakob Pelletier 4.00 10.00
162 Alex Laferriere 5.00 12.00
163 Fraser Minten 6.00 15.00
164 Raphael Lavoie 3.00 8.00
165 Marc Del Gaizo 3.00 8.00
166 Dmitri Voronkov 4.00 10.00
167 Emil Andrae 3.00 8.00
168 Ryan Shea 3.00 8.00
169 Hardy Haman Aktell 3.00 8.00
170 Uvis Balinskis 3.00 8.00
171 Ty Emberson 3.00 8.00
172 Tristan Luneau 3.00 8.00
173 Ilya Solovyov 3.00 8.00
174 Daemon Hunt 3.00 8.00
175 Mason Lohrei 5.00 12.00
176 Matt Tomkins 3.00 8.00
177 Nikolas Matinpalo 3.00 8.00
178 Ondrej Pavel 3.00 8.00
179 Martin Pospisil 4.00 10.00
180 Justin Sourdif 3.00 8.00
181 Tyler Angle 3.00 8.00
182 Tristen Robins 3.00 8.00
183 Adam Ginning 3.00 8.00
184 Milos Kelemen 3.00 8.00
185 Vincent Iorio 3.00 8.00
186 Lucas Condotta 3.00 8.00
187 Egor Afanasyev 3.00 8.00
188 Hunter McKown 3.00 8.00
189 Arturs Silovs 6.00 15.00
190 Wyatt Kaiser 3.00 8.00
191 Joona Koppanen 2.50 6.00
192 Nick Swaney 3.00 8.00
193 Spencer Stastney 3.00 8.00
194 Jiri Patera 5.00 12.00
195 Olle Eriksson Ek 3.00 8.00
196 Jonathan Gruden 3.00 8.00
197 Jake Livingstone 3.00 8.00
198 Jet Greaves 5.00 12.00
199 Henry Thrun 3.00 8.00
200 Damien Giroux 3.00 8.00
201 Jaxson Stauber 3.00 8.00
202 Vincent Desharnais 4.00 10.00
203 Matthew Kessel 2.50 6.00
204 Owen Beck 5.00 12.00
205 Samuel Knazko 3.00 8.00
206 Joel Teasdale 3.00 8.00
207 Samuel Bolduc 3.00 8.00
208 Billy Sweezey 3.00 8.00
209 Drew Helleson 3.00 8.00
210 Maxence Guenette 3.00 8.00
211 Will Cuylle 5.00 12.00
212 Hugh McGing 3.00 8.00
213 Akito Hirose 2.50 6.00
214 Luke Philp 3.00 8.00
215 Danil Gushchin 3.00 8.00
216 Sean Farrell 3.00 8.00
217 Arnaud Durandeau 3.00 8.00
218 Simon Edvinsson 6.00 15.00
219 Matt Murray 3.00 8.00
220 Cole Guttman 3.00 8.00
221 Bobby McMann 5.00 12.00
222 Tyler Kleven 3.00 8.00
223 Nikita Nesterenko 3.00 8.00
224 Cole McWard 3.00 8.00
225 Elliot Desnoyers 3.00 8.00
226 Lukas Rousek 2.50 6.00
227 Matthew Coronato 5.00 12.00
228 Stanislav Svozil 2.50 6.00
229 Aidan McDonough 2.50 6.00
230 William Dufour 2.50 6.00
231 Leevi Merilainen 3.00 8.00
232 Walker Duehr 2.50 6.00
233 Devon Levi 8.00 20.00
234 Marco Kasper 8.00 20.00
235 Jackson LaCombe 3.00 8.00
236 Pavel Mintyukov 5.00 12.00
237 Dustin Wolf 10.00 25.00
238 Brock Faber 8.00 20.00
239 Tyson Foerster 6.00 15.00
240 Yaroslav Askarov 8.00 20.00
241 Kevin Korchinski 5.00 12.00
242 Ridly Greig 5.00 12.00
243 Adam Fantilli 10.00 25.00
244 Luke Evangelista 5.00 12.00
245 Luke Hughes 10.00 25.00
246 Logan Cooley 10.00 25.00
247 Matthew Knies 12.00 30.00
248 Matthew Poitras 6.00 15.00
249 Leo Carlsson 10.00 25.00
250 Connor Bedard 100.00 250.00

2023-24 Upper Deck Ice Greyscale
*GREY/99: .8X TO 2X BASIC
251 Connor Bedard EXT 125.00 300.00

2023-24 Upper Deck Ice Ice Blue
*ICE BLUE: 1X TO 2.5X BASIC
*ICE BLUE RC: .75X TO 2X BASIC

2023-24 Upper Deck Ice Purple
*PURPLE: .6X TO 1.5X BASIC
*PURPLE RC: .5X TO 1.2X BASIC

2023-24 Upper Deck Ice Autographs White Snowflake
2 Roope Hintz 8.00 20.00
3 Anders Lee SP 5.00 12.00
7 Brent Burns 6.00 15.00
15 Josh Morrissey SP 8.00 20.00
17 Mario Ferraro 4.00 10.00
23 Lukas Reichel 6.00 15.00
25 Jared McCann SP 5.00 12.00
28 Auston Matthews SP 25.00 60.00
32 Torey Krug SP 5.00 12.00
33 Jeff Petry 6.00 15.00
40 Jake Sanderson SP 8.00 20.00
41 Brandt Clarke 6.00 15.00
42 Connor McDavid SP 30.00 80.00
43 Blake Coleman 5.00 12.00
44 Charlie Coyle 6.00 15.00
45 Miro Heiskanen SP 8.00 20.00
47 Gabe Vilardi 6.00 15.00
49 Mikko Rantanen SP 15.00 40.00
50 Juuse Saros SP 8.00 20.00
52 Tanner Jeannot 4.00 10.00
54 Vitek Vanecek 6.00 15.00
57 Shane Pinto 5.00 12.00
58 Cole Perfetti 6.00 15.00
67 Brady Tkachuk SP 10.00 25.00
68 Noah Dobson 8.00 20.00
69 Jordan Eberle SP 6.00 15.00
71 Wyatt Johnston SP 12.00 30.00
78 Tage Thompson SP 8.00 20.00
80 Jeremy Swayman 10.00 25.00
81 Jonatan Berggren 5.00 12.00
88 Jonathan Huberdeau SP 8.00 20.00
96 Ilya Sorokin SP 10.00 25.00
100 Roman Josi SP 6.00 15.00
101 Dustin Wolf SP 30.00 80.00
102 Stanislav Svozil 8.00 20.00
103 Olle Eriksson Ek 10.00 25.00
104 Owen Beck 15.00 40.00
105 Matt Murray 10.00 25.00
106 Akito Hirose 8.00 20.00
107 Arnaud Durandeau 10.00 25.00
108 Tyson Foerster SP 40.00 100.00
109 Matthew Knies SP 40.00 100.00
110 Luke Evangelista 15.00 40.00
111 Jakob Pelletier 12.00 30.00
112 William Dufour 8.00 20.00
113 Marco Kasper 25.00 60.00
114 Vincent Iorio 10.00 25.00
115 Devon Levi 30.00 80.00
116 Bobby McMann 15.00 40.00
117 Tye Kartye 15.00 40.00
120 Billy Sweezey 10.00 25.00
121 Tyler Kleven 10.00 25.00
122 Walker Duehr 8.00 20.00
123 Cole Guttman 10.00 25.00
125 Will Cuylle 15.00 40.00
126 Egor Afanasyev 10.00 25.00
127 Luke Hughes SP 30.00 80.00
128 Hunter McKown 10.00 25.00
129 Hugh McGing 10.00 25.00
130 Wyatt Kaiser 10.00 25.00
131 Aidan McDonough 8.00 20.00
134 Jet Greaves 15.00 40.00
135 Jonathan Gruden 10.00 25.00
136 Samuel Bolduc 10.00 25.00
137 Ridly Greig 15.00 40.00
138 Luke Philp 10.00 25.00
139 Matthew Coronato SP 15.00 40.00
141 Milos Kelemen 10.00 25.00
142 Henry Thrun 10.00 25.00
143 Simon Edvinsson SP 20.00 50.00
144 Brock Faber SP 25.00 60.00
145 Nikita Nesterenko 10.00 25.00
146 Yaroslav Askarov SP 25.00 60.00
147 Elliot Desnoyers 10.00 25.00
149 Sean Farrell 10.00 25.00
150 Joona Koppanen 8.00 20.00
252 Logan Cooley EXT 60.00 150.00
253 Adam Fantilli EXT SP 60.00 150.00
254 Leo Carlsson EXT SP 50.00 125.00
255 Zach Benson EXT 15.00 40.00
256 Pavel Mintyukov EXT 15.00 40.00
257 Connor Zary EXT 20.00 50.00
258 Matthew Poitras EXT 20.00 50.00
259 Matt Savoie EXT 20.00 50.00
260 Dmitri Voronkov EXT 12.00 30.00
265 Nikita Okhotiuk 5.00 12.00

2023-24 Upper Deck Ice Depth of Winter
*BLUE/25: 2X TO 5X BASIC
DW1 Cole Caufield 2.00 5.00
DW2 Tyson Barrie .60 1.50
DW3 Timo Meier 1.00 2.50
DW4 Matt Boldy 1.50 4.00
DW5 Andrei Kuzmenko 1.00 2.50
DW6 Troy Terry .75 2.00
DW8 Claude Giroux 1.00 2.50
DW9 Owen Tippett .60 1.50
DW10 Jamie Benn 1.00 2.50
DW11 Alex Ovechkin 4.00 10.00
DW12 Mark Scheifele 1.50 4.00
DW13 Bo Horvat 1.25 3.00
DW14 Charlie McAvoy 1.25 3.00
DW15 Matthew Tkachuk 2.00 5.00
DW16 Connor McDavid 5.00 12.00
DW17 Andrei Svechnikov 1.25 3.00
DW18 Nathan MacKinnon 4.00 10.00
DW19 William Nylander 2.00 5.00
DW20 Chandler Stephenson .75 2.00
DW21 Lukas Reichel 1.00 2.50
DW22 Elias Lindholm 1.00 2.50
DW23 Pavel Buchnevich .75 2.00
DW24 Andre Burakovsky .60 1.50
DW25 Adrian Kempe 1.00 2.50
DW26 Sidney Crosby 4.00 10.00
DW27 Clayton Keller 1.25 3.00
DW28 Auston Matthews 4.00 10.00
DW29 Kirill Kaprizov 3.00 8.00
DW30 J.T. Miller 1.25 3.00
DW31 Alex DeBrincat 1.25 3.00
DW32 Patrik Laine 1.25 3.00
DW33 Tomas Hertl 1.00 2.50
DW34 Mikhail Sergachev .75 2.00
DW35 Victor Olofsson 1.00 2.50
DW36 Logan Cooley 3.00 8.00
DW37 Adam Fantilli 3.00 8.00
DW38 Tye Kartye 1.50 4.00
DW39 Adam Ginning 1.00 2.50
DW40 Jakob Pelletier 1.25 3.00
DW41 Marco Kasper 2.50 6.00
DW42 William Dufour .75 2.00
DW43 Leevi Merilainen 1.00 2.50
DW44 Brock Faber 2.50 6.00
DW45 Kevin Korchinski 1.50 4.00
DW46 Devon Levi 2.50 6.00
DW47 Luke Evangelista 1.50 4.00
DW48 Simon Edvinsson 2.00 5.00
DW49 Matthew Knies 4.00 10.00
DW50 Matthew Poitras 2.00 5.00
DW51 Vincent Desharnais 1.25 3.00
DW52 Cole McWard 1.00 2.50
DW53 Yaroslav Askarov 2.50 6.00
DW54 Leo Carlsson 3.00 8.00
DW55 Luke Hughes 3.00 8.00
DW56 Matthew Kessel .75 2.00
DW57 Sean Farrell 1.00 2.50
DW58 Luke Philp 1.00 2.50
DW59 Will Cuylle 1.50 4.00
DW60 Walker Duehr .75 2.00
DW61 Lukas Rousek .75 2.00
DW62 Tyson Foerster 2.00 5.00
DW63 Dustin Wolf 3.00 8.00
DW64 Stanislav Svozil .75 2.00
DW65 Connor Bedard 15.00 40.00

2023-24 Upper Deck Ice Depth of Winter White Frost
*WHITE/199: .6X TO 1.5X BASIC
DW65 Connor Bedard 50.00 125.00

2023-24 Upper Deck Ice Frozen In Ice
FI1 Cale Makar 10.00 25.00
FI2 Linus Ullmark 4.00 10.00
FI3 Alex Ovechkin 15.00 40.00
FI4 Jack Eichel 6.00 15.00
FI5 Igor Shesterkin 8.00 20.00
FI6 Yaroslav Askarov 10.00 25.00
FI7 Seth Jones 4.00 10.00
FI8 Sebastian Aho 6.00 15.00
FI9 Clayton Keller 5.00 12.00
FI10 Brock Faber 10.00 25.00
FI11 Auston Matthews 15.00 40.00
FI12 Travis Konecny 4.00 10.00
FI13 Leon Draisaitl 12.00 30.00
FI14 Adrian Kempe 4.00 10.00
FI15 Matthew Coronato 6.00 15.00
FI16 Elias Pettersson 6.00 15.00
FI17 Brock Nelson 4.00 10.00
FI18 David Pastrnak 10.00 25.00
FI19 Dustin Wolf 12.00 30.00
FI20 Ryan Nugent-Hopkins 5.00 12.00
FI21 Dylan Larkin 5.00 12.00
FI22 Matthew Knies 15.00 40.00
FI23 Sidney Crosby 15.00 40.00
FI24 Brady Tkachuk 6.00 15.00
FI25 Johnny Gaudreau 12.00 30.00
FI26 Kyle Connor 6.00 15.00
FI27 Jack Hughes 10.00 25.00
FI28 Connor Bedard 50.00 125.00
FI29 Trevor Zegras 4.00 10.00
FI30 Tim Stutzle 5.00 12.00
FI31 Cole Caufield 8.00 20.00
FI32 Mikko Rantanen 10.00 25.00
FI33 Matty Beniers 5.00 12.00
FI34 Mitch Marner 6.00 15.00
FI35 Simon Edvinsson 8.00 20.00
FI36 Luke Hughes 12.00 30.00
FI37 Chandler Stephenson 3.00 8.00
FI38 Luke Evangelista 6.00 15.00
FI39 Connor McDavid 20.00 50.00
FI40 Jake Oettinger 6.00 15.00
FI41 Nikita Kucherov 8.00 20.00
FI42 Kirill Kaprizov 12.00 30.00
FI43 Nathan MacKinnon 15.00 40.00
FI44 Tage Thompson 5.00 12.00
FI45 Tyson Foerster 8.00 20.00
FI46 Steven Stamkos 8.00 20.00
FI47 Jason Robertson 6.00 15.00
FI48 Matthew Tkachuk 8.00 20.00
FI49 Erik Karlsson 5.00 12.00
FI50 Jordan Kyrou 4.00 10.00

2023-24 Upper Deck Ice Frozen In Ice Gold
*GOLD/25: .8X TO 2X BASIC
FI28 Connor Bedard 200.00 500.00

2023-24 Upper Deck Ice Glacial Graphs
*BLACK: .6X TO 1.5X BASIC
GGAB Aleksander Barkov 15.00 40.00
GGAX Arber Xhekaj 10.00 25.00
GGBT Brady Tkachuk 15.00 40.00
GGBU Brent Burns SP 10.00 25.00
GGCM Connor McDavid SP 250.00 600.00
GGCP Cole Perfetti 10.00 25.00
GGCS Charlie Simmer 6.00 15.00
GGFP Felix Potvin SP 60.00 150.00
GGGV Gabe Vilardi 10.00 25.00
GGJB Jonatan Berggren 8.00 20.00
GGJS Juraj Slafkovsky 40.00 100.00
GGMC Jared McCann 8.00 20.00
GGMO Josh Morrissey 12.00 30.00
GGRH Roope Hintz 12.00 30.00
GGSA Jake Sanderson 12.00 30.00
GGSW Shane Wright 12.00 30.00
GGTT Tage Thompson SP 12.00 30.00
GGVV Vitek Vanecek 10.00 25.00
GGWJ Wyatt Johnston 20.00 50.00

2023-24 Upper Deck Ice Ice Premieres '13-14 Retro
2013AH Akito Hirose 3.00 8.00
2013AM Aidan McDonough 3.00 8.00
2013BF Brock Faber 10.00 25.00
2013BM Bobby McMann 6.00 15.00
2013CB Connor Bedard 200.00 500.00
2013CG Cole Guttman 4.00 10.00
2013DG Danil Gushchin 4.00 10.00
2013DL Devon Levi 10.00 25.00
2013DW Dustin Wolf 12.00 30.00
2013ED Elliot Desnoyers 4.00 10.00
2013HT Henry Thrun 4.00 10.00
2013JK Joona Koppanen 3.00 8.00
2013JP Jakob Pelletier 5.00 12.00
2013KA Marco Kasper 10.00 25.00
2013LE Luke Evangelista 6.00 15.00
2013LH Luke Hughes 20.00 50.00
2013LM Leevi Merilainen 4.00 10.00
2013LP Luke Philp 4.00 10.00
2013MK Matthew Knies 15.00 40.00
2013MP Mikael Pyyhtia 4.00 10.00
2013NN Nikita Nesterenko 4.00 10.00
2013NS Nick Swaney 4.00 10.00
2013SB Samuel Bolduc 4.00 10.00
2013SE Simon Edvinsson 8.00 20.00
2013SF Sean Farrell 4.00 10.00
2013SS Stanislav Svozil 3.00 8.00
2013TF Tyson Foerster 8.00 20.00
2013WC Will Cuylle 6.00 15.00
2013WD Walker Duehr 3.00 8.00
2013YA Yaroslav Askarov 20.00 50.00

2023-24 Upper Deck Ice Ice Premieres Autographs
IPAAD Arnaud Durandeau/199 8.00 20.00
IPAAF Adam Fantilli/199 80.00 200.00
IPAAH Akito Hirose/99 6.00 15.00
IPAAM Aidan McDonough/99 6.00 15.00
IPABF Brock Faber/49 60.00 150.00
IPABM Bobby McMann/99 12.00 30.00
IPABS Billy Sweezey/99 8.00 20.00
IPACB Connor Bedard/199 600.00 1500.00
IPACG Cole Guttman/99 8.00 20.00
IPACN Leo Carlsson/99 60.00 150.00
IPADL Devon Levi/49 40.00 100.00
IPADR Walker Duehr/99 6.00 15.00
IPADW Dustin Wolf/49 30.00 80.00
IPAEA Egor Afanasyev/199 8.00 20.00
IPAED Elliot Desnoyers/199 8.00 20.00
IPAHM Hunter McKown/199 8.00 20.00
IPAHT Henry Thrun/199 8.00 20.00
IPAJG Jet Greaves/199 12.00 30.00
IPAJK Joona Koppanen/199 6.00 15.00
IPAJP Jakob Pelletier/49 10.00 25.00
IPAKA Tye Kartye/199 12.00 30.00
IPAKR Marco Kasper/99 20.00 50.00
IPALC Logan Cooley/199 40.00 100.00
IPALE Luke Evangelista/49 40.00 100.00
IPALH Luke Hughes/25 100.00 250.00
IPALP Luke Philp/99 8.00 20.00
IPAMC Matthew Coronato/99 12.00 30.00
IPAMG Hugh McGing/199 8.00 20.00
IPAMK Matthew Knies/25 60.00 150.00
IPAMM Matt Murray/99 8.00 20.00
IPAOB Owen Beck/199 12.00 30.00
IPARG Ridly Greig/99 12.00 30.00
IPASE Simon Edvinsson/49 30.00 80.00
IPASF Sean Farrell/99 8.00 20.00
IPASS Stanislav Svozil/99 6.00 15.00
IPATF Tyson Foerster/25 40.00 100.00
IPATK Tyler Kleven/199 8.00 20.00
IPAWC Will Cuylle/199 12.00 30.00
IPAWD William Dufour/199 6.00 15.00
IPAWK Wyatt Kaiser/199 8.00 20.00
IPAYA Yaroslav Askarov/49 50.00 125.00

2023-24 Upper Deck Ice Ice Premieres Jerseys
IPJAD Arnaud Durandeau 1.50 4.00
IPJAF Adam Fantilli 5.00 12.00
IPJAH Akito Hirose 1.25 3.00
IPJAM Aidan McDonough 1.25 3.00
IPJBF Brock Faber 4.00 10.00
IPJBM Bobby McMann 2.50 6.00
IPJBS Billy Sweezey 1.50 4.00
IPJCB Connor Bedard 40.00 100.00
IPJCG Cole Guttman 1.50 4.00
IPJCN Leo Carlsson 5.00 12.00
IPJDG Danil Gushchin 1.50 4.00
IPJDR Walker Duehr 1.25 3.00
IPJDW Dustin Wolf 5.00 12.00
IPJEA Egor Afanasyev 1.50 4.00
IPJED Elliot Desnoyers 1.50 4.00
IPJHM Hunter McKown 1.50 4.00
IPJHT Henry Thrun 1.50 4.00
IPJJK Joona Koppanen 1.25 3.00
IPJJP Jakob Pelletier 2.00 5.00
IPJKA Tye Kartye 2.50 6.00
IPJKG Michael Kesselring 1.50 4.00
IPJKR Marco Kasper 4.00 10.00
IPJLC Logan Cooley 5.00 12.00
IPJLE Luke Evangelista 2.50 6.00
IPJLH Luke Hughes 5.00 12.00
IPJLM Leevi Merilainen 1.50 4.00
IPJLP Luke Philp 1.50 4.00
IPJLR Lukas Rousek 1.25 3.00
IPJMC Matthew Coronato 2.50 6.00
IPJMG Hugh McGing 1.50 4.00
IPJMK Matthew Knies 6.00 15.00
IPJMM Matt Murray 1.50 4.00
IPJNN Nikita Nesterenko 1.50 4.00
IPJOB Owen Beck 2.50 6.00
IPJPA Jiri Patera 2.50 6.00
IPJRG Ridly Greig 2.50 6.00
IPJSB Samuel Bolduc 1.50 4.00
IPJSE Simon Edvinsson 3.00 8.00
IPJSF Sean Farrell 1.50 4.00
IPJSS Stanislav Svozil 1.25 3.00
IPJTF Tyson Foerster 3.00 8.00
IPJTK Tyler Kleven 1.50 4.00
IPJVD Vincent Desharnais 2.00 5.00
IPJWC Will Cuylle 2.50 6.00
IPJWD William Dufour 1.25 3.00
IPJWK Wyatt Kaiser 1.50 4.00
IPJYA Yaroslav Askarov 4.00 10.00

2023-24 Upper Deck Ice Ice Premieres Minis
MI1 Ridly Greig 3.00 8.00
MI2 Akito Hirose 1.50 4.00
MI3 Jakob Pelletier 2.50 6.00
MI4 Yaroslav Askarov 5.00 12.00
MI5 Luke Hughes 6.00 15.00
MI6 Elliot Desnoyers 2.00 5.00
MI7 Hunter McKown 2.00 5.00
MI8 Vincent Iorio 2.00 5.00
MI9 Cole McWard 2.00 5.00
MI10 Henry Thrun 2.00 5.00
MI11 Sean Farrell 2.00 5.00
MI12 Nikita Nesterenko 2.00 5.00
MI13 Tyson Foerster 4.00 10.00
MI14 Dustin Wolf 6.00 15.00
MI15 Jiri Patera 3.00 8.00
MI16 Jackson LaCombe 2.00 5.00
MI17 Simon Edvinsson 4.00 10.00
MI18 Will Cuylle 3.00 8.00
MI19 Arnaud Durandeau 2.00 5.00
MI20 Matthew Knies 8.00 20.00
MI21 Joona Koppanen 1.50 4.00
MI22 David Gust 2.00 5.00
MI23 Samuel Bolduc 2.00 5.00
MI24 Nick Swaney 2.00 5.00
MI25 Matthew Coronato 3.00 8.00
MI26 Drew Helleson 2.00 5.00
MI27 Luke Philp 2.00 5.00
MI28 Jonathan Gruden 2.00 5.00
MI29 Bobby McMann 3.00 8.00
MI30 Adam Ginning 2.00 5.00
MI31 Aidan McDonough 1.50 4.00
MI32 Luke Evangelista 3.00 8.00
MI33 Danil Gushchin 2.00 5.00
MI34 Mikael Pyyhtia 2.00 5.00
MI35 Leevi Merilainen 2.00 5.00
MI36 Cole Guttman 2.00 5.00
MI37 Devon Levi 5.00 12.00
MI38 Walker Duehr 1.50 4.00
MI39 Stanislav Svozil 1.50 4.00
MI40 Marco Kasper 5.00 12.00
MI41 Brock Faber 5.00 12.00
MI42 Lukas Rousek 1.50 4.00
MI43 Matthew Poitras 4.00 10.00
MI44 Kevin Korchinski 3.00 8.00
MI45 Adam Fantilli 6.00 15.00
MI46 Leo Carlsson 6.00 15.00
MI47 Logan Cooley 6.00 15.00
MI48 Connor Bedard 40.00 100.00

2023-24 Upper Deck Ice Ice Premieres Minis Gold
*GOLD/99: 1X TO 2.5X BASIC
MI48 Connor Bedard 125.00 300.00

2023-24 Upper Deck Ice Jerseys
1 Erik Karlsson 3.00 8.00
2 Roope Hintz 3.00 8.00
3 Anders Lee 2.00 5.00
4 Jack Quinn 2.00 5.00
5 Timo Meier 2.50 6.00
6 Trevor Zegras 2.50 6.00
7 Brent Burns 2.50 6.00
8 Clayton Keller 3.00 8.00
9 Taylor Raddysh 2.00 5.00
10 Owen Power 2.50 6.00
11 Cale Makar 6.00 15.00
12 Bo Horvat 3.00 8.00
13 Joel Eriksson Ek 2.00 5.00
14 Brayden Point 3.00 8.00
15 Josh Morrissey 3.00 8.00
17 Mario Ferraro 1.50 4.00
18 Cam Atkinson 2.50 6.00
19 Matt Boldy 4.00 10.00
20 Jonathan Marchessault 3.00 8.00
21 Peyton Krebs 2.00 5.00
22 Travis Konecny 2.50 6.00
24 Jordan Kyrou 2.50 6.00
25 Jared McCann 2.00 5.00
26 Andrei Vasilevskiy 4.00 10.00
27 Alex Ovechkin 10.00 25.00
28 Auston Matthews 10.00 25.00
29 Igor Shesterkin 5.00 12.00
30 Jack Eichel 4.00 10.00
31 Moritz Seider 3.00 8.00
32 Torey Krug 2.00 5.00

33 Jeff Petry 2.50 6.00
34 Artemi Panarin 5.00 12.00
35 Kent Johnson 2.50 6.00
36 James van Riemsdyk 2.00 5.00
37 Mitch Marner 4.00 10.00
38 Nikolaj Ehlers 2.50 6.00
39 Evgeny Kuznetsov 3.00 8.00
40 Jake Sanderson 3.00 8.00
42 Connor McDavid 12.00 30.00
43 Blake Coleman 2.00 5.00
44 Charlie Coyle 2.50 6.00
45 Miro Heiskanen 3.00 8.00
46 Charlie McAvoy 3.00 8.00
47 Gabe Vilardi 2.50 6.00
48 Andrei Kuzmenko 2.50 6.00
49 Mikko Rantanen 6.00 15.00
50 Juuse Saros 3.00 8.00
51 Kirill Marchenko 3.00 8.00
52 Tanner Jeannot 1.50 4.00
53 Bryan Rust 2.50 6.00
54 Vitek Vanecek 2.50 6.00
55 Johnny Gaudreau 4.00 10.00
56 Seth Jarvis 3.00 8.00
58 Cole Perfetti 2.50 6.00
60 Quinn Hughes 6.00 15.00
61 Aleksander Barkov 4.00 10.00
62 Sidney Crosby 10.00 25.00
63 Kirill Kaprizov 8.00 20.00
64 Matthew Tkachuk 5.00 12.00
65 Michael Bunting 2.50 6.00
66 Matias Maccelli 2.00 5.00
67 Brady Tkachuk 4.00 10.00
68 Noah Dobson 3.00 8.00
69 Jordan Eberle 2.50 6.00
70 Mason McTavish 2.50 6.00
71 Wyatt Johnston 5.00 12.00
72 Filip Gustavsson 2.50 6.00
73 Jason Robertson 4.00 10.00
74 Nick Suzuki 5.00 12.00
75 Sonny Milano 2.00 5.00
76 Zach Hyman 4.00 10.00
77 Tim Stutzle 3.00 8.00
78 Tage Thompson 3.00 8.00
79 Mark Stone 3.00 8.00
80 Jeremy Swayman 4.00 10.00
82 Adrian Kempe 2.50 6.00
83 David Pastrnak 6.00 15.00
84 Brandon Hagel 2.00 5.00
85 Robert Thomas 2.50 6.00
86 Anze Kopitar 4.00 10.00
87 Elias Pettersson 4.00 10.00
88 Jonathan Huberdeau 3.00 8.00
89 Ryan Nugent-Hopkins 3.00 8.00
90 Philipp Grubauer 2.50 6.00
91 Chandler Stephenson 2.00 5.00
92 Cole Caufield 5.00 12.00
93 Braden Schneider 2.00 5.00
94 Martin Necas 4.00 10.00
95 Jack Hughes 6.00 15.00
96 Ilya Sorokin 4.00 10.00
97 Matty Beniers 3.00 8.00
98 Dylan Larkin 3.00 8.00
99 Tyler Toffoli 2.50 6.00
100 Roman Josi 2.50 6.00
101 Dustin Wolf 8.00 20.00
102 Stanislav Svozil 2.00 5.00
103 Olle Eriksson Ek 2.50 6.00
104 Owen Beck 4.00 10.00
105 Matt Murray 2.50 6.00
106 Akito Hirose 2.00 5.00
107 Arnaud Durandeau 2.50 6.00
108 Tyson Foerster 5.00 12.00
109 Matthew Knies 10.00 25.00
110 Luke Evangelista 4.00 10.00
111 Jakob Pelletier 3.00 8.00
112 William Dufour 2.00 5.00
113 Marco Kasper 6.00 15.00
114 Vincent Iorio 2.50 6.00
115 Devon Levi 6.00 15.00
116 Bobby McMann 4.00 10.00
117 Tye Kartye 4.00 10.00
118 Jiri Patera 4.00 10.00
119 Lukas Rousek 2.00 5.00
120 Billy Sweezey 2.50 6.00
121 Tyler Kleven 2.50 6.00
122 Walker Duehr 2.00 5.00
123 Cole Guttman 2.50 6.00
124 Danil Gushchin 2.50 6.00
125 Will Cuylle 4.00 10.00
126 Egor Afanasyev 2.50 6.00
127 Luke Hughes 8.00 20.00
128 Hunter McKown 2.50 6.00
129 Hugh McGing 2.50 6.00
130 Wyatt Kaiser 2.50 6.00
131 Aidan McDonough 2.00 5.00
132 Vincent Desharnais 3.00 8.00
133 Leevi Merilainen 2.50 6.00
135 Jonathan Gruden 2.50 6.00
136 Samuel Bolduc 2.50 6.00
137 Ridly Greig 4.00 10.00
138 Luke Philp 2.50 6.00
139 Matthew Coronato 4.00 10.00
141 Milos Kelemen 2.50 6.00
142 Henry Thrun 2.50 6.00
143 Simon Edvinsson 5.00 12.00
144 Brock Faber 6.00 15.00
145 Nikita Nesterenko 2.50 6.00
146 Yaroslav Askarov 6.00 15.00
147 Elliot Desnoyers 2.50 6.00
148 Michael Kesselring 2.50 6.00
149 Sean Farrell 2.50 6.00
150 Joona Koppanen 2.00 5.00

2023-24 Upper Deck Ice Patches Gold

1 Erik Karlsson/25 12.00 30.00
2 Roope Hintz AU/49 20.00 50.00
3 Anders Lee/25 8.00 20.00
5 Timo Meier/25 10.00 25.00
6 Trevor Zegras/25 10.00 25.00
7 Brent Burns AU/49 15.00 40.00
8 Clayton Keller/25 12.00 30.00
9 Taylor Raddysh/25 8.00 20.00
10 Owen Power AU/49 15.00 40.00
11 Cale Makar AU/49 60.00 150.00
12 Bo Horvat/25 12.00 30.00
14 Brayden Point/25 12.00 30.00
17 Mario Ferraro AU/49 10.00 25.00
21 Peyton Krebs/25 8.00 20.00
22 Travis Konecny/25 10.00 25.00
24 Jordan Kyrou/25 10.00 25.00
25 Jared McCann AU/49 12.00 30.00
29 Igor Shesterkin/25 20.00 50.00
31 Moritz Seider/25 12.00 30.00
32 Torey Krug/25 8.00 20.00
34 Artemi Panarin/25 20.00 50.00
37 Mitch Marner/25 15.00 40.00
40 Jake Sanderson AU/49 20.00 50.00
43 Blake Coleman/25 8.00 20.00
44 Charlie Coyle AU/25 15.00 40.00
46 Charlie McAvoy/25 12.00 30.00
47 Gabe Vilardi AU/49 15.00 40.00
49 Mikko Rantanen AU/49 40.00 100.00
50 Juuse Saros AU/49 20.00 50.00
53 Bryan Rust/25 10.00 25.00
54 Vitek Vanecek/25 10.00 25.00
55 Johnny Gaudreau/25 15.00 40.00
58 Cole Perfetti AU/49 15.00 40.00
60 Quinn Hughes/25 25.00 60.00
61 Aleksander Barkov AU/49 25.00 60.00
63 Kirill Kaprizov/25 30.00 80.00
67 Brady Tkachuk AU/49 25.00 60.00
72 Filip Gustavsson/25 10.00 25.00
73 Jason Robertson/25 15.00 40.00
74 Nick Suzuki AU/49 60.00 150.00
75 Sonny Milano/25 8.00 20.00
78 Tage Thompson AU/49 20.00 50.00
80 Jeremy Swayman AU/49 25.00 60.00
82 Adrian Kempe/25 10.00 25.00
83 David Pastrnak/25 25.00 60.00
84 Brandon Hagel/25 8.00 20.00
85 Robert Thomas/25 10.00 25.00
87 Elias Pettersson/25 15.00 40.00
88 Jonathan Huberdeau AU/49 20.00 50.00
92 Cole Caufield/25 20.00 50.00
93 Braden Schneider/25 8.00 20.00
95 Jack Hughes/25 25.00 60.00
96 Ilya Sorokin AU/49 25.00 60.00
97 Matty Beniers/25 12.00 30.00
98 Dylan Larkin/25 12.00 30.00
100 Roman Josi AU/49 15.00 40.00
101 Dustin Wolf AU/49 40.00 100.00
102 Stanislav Svozil AU/99 10.00 25.00
103 Olle Eriksson Ek AU/99 12.00 30.00
104 Owen Beck AU/49 20.00 50.00
105 Matt Murray AU/49 12.00 30.00
106 Akito Hirose AU/99 10.00 25.00
107 Arnaud Durandeau AU/99 12.00 30.00
108 Tyson Foerster AU/49 40.00 100.00
109 Matthew Knies AU/49 60.00 150.00
110 Luke Evangelista AU/49 40.00 100.00
111 Jakob Pelletier AU/99 15.00 40.00
112 William Dufour AU/99 10.00 25.00
113 Marco Kasper AU/49 40.00 100.00
114 Vincent Iorio AU/99 12.00 30.00
115 Devon Levi AU/99 50.00 125.00
116 Bobby McMann AU/99 20.00 50.00
117 Tye Kartye AU/49 20.00 50.00
120 Billy Sweezey AU/99 12.00 30.00
121 Tyler Kleven AU/99 12.00 30.00
122 Walker Duehr AU/99 10.00 25.00
123 Cole Guttman AU/99 12.00 30.00
125 Will Cuylle AU/49 20.00 50.00
126 Egor Afanasyev AU/99 12.00 30.00
128 Hunter McKown AU/99 12.00 30.00
129 Hugh McGing AU/99 12.00 30.00
130 Wyatt Kaiser AU/99 12.00 30.00
131 Aidan McDonough AU/99 10.00 25.00
134 Jet Greaves AU/99 20.00 50.00
135 Jonathan Gruden AU/99 12.00 30.00
136 Samuel Bolduc AU/99 12.00 30.00
137 Ridly Greig AU/49 20.00 50.00
138 Luke Philp AU/99 12.00 30.00
139 Matthew Coronato AU/99 20.00 50.00
141 Milos Kelemen AU/99 12.00 30.00
142 Henry Thrun AU/99 12.00 30.00
143 Simon Edvinsson AU/49 40.00 100.00
145 Nikita Nesterenko AU/99 12.00 30.00
146 Yaroslav Askarov AU/49 60.00 150.00
147 Elliot Desnoyers AU/99 12.00 30.00
149 Sean Farrell AU/49 12.00 30.00
150 Joona Koppanen AU/99 10.00 25.00

2023-24 Upper Deck Ice Signature Swatches

SSAB Aleksander Barkov 20.00 50.00
SSCP Cole Perfetti 12.00 30.00
SSIS Ilya Sorokin 30.00 80.00
SSJM Josh Morrissey SP 15.00 40.00
SSMC Jared McCann 10.00 25.00
SSMR Mikko Rantanen 30.00 80.00
SSNS Nick Suzuki SP 25.00 60.00
SSPR Brian Propp 10.00 25.00
SSRH Roope Hintz 15.00 40.00
SSRJ Roman Josi 12.00 30.00
SSTT Tage Thompson 15.00 40.00

2023-24 Upper Deck Ice Snow Men

SM1 Jared McCann 1.50 4.00
SM2 Trevor Zegras 2.00 5.00
SM3 Alex Ovechkin 8.00 20.00
SM4 Sidney Crosby 8.00 20.00
SM5 Jake Oettinger 3.00 8.00
SM6 Linus Ullmark 2.00 5.00
SM7 Connor McDavid 10.00 25.00
SM8 Kirill Kaprizov 6.00 15.00
SM9 Alexandar Georgiev 2.00 5.00
SM10 Jack Hughes 5.00 12.00
SM11 Elias Pettersson 3.00 8.00
SM12 Auston Matthews 8.00 20.00
SM13 Matthew Tkachuk 4.00 10.00
SM14 David Pastrnak 5.00 12.00
SM15 Jason Robertson 3.00 8.00
SM16 Cole Caufield 4.00 10.00
SM17 Mikko Rantanen 5.00 12.00
SM18 Tage Thompson 2.50 6.00
SM19 Mitch Marner 3.00 8.00
SM20 Leon Draisaitl 6.00 15.00
SM21 Leo Carlsson 6.00 15.00
SM22 Tyson Foerster 4.00 10.00
SM23 Yaroslav Askarov 5.00 12.00
SM24 Simon Edvinsson 4.00 10.00
SM25 Stanislav Svozil 1.50 4.00
SM26 Jakob Pelletier 2.50 6.00
SM27 Brock Faber 5.00 12.00
SM28 Marco Kasper 5.00 12.00
SM29 Cole Guttman 2.00 5.00
SM30 Matthew Knies 8.00 20.00
SM31 Walker Duehr 1.50 4.00
SM32 Tye Kartye 3.00 8.00
SM33 Devon Levi 5.00 12.00
SM34 Luke Hughes 6.00 15.00
SM35 Luke Evangelista 3.00 8.00
SM36 Dustin Wolf 6.00 15.00
SM37 Adam Fantilli 6.00 15.00
SM38 Logan Cooley 6.00 15.00
SM39 Ridly Greig 3.00 8.00
SM40 Connor Bedard 30.00 80.00
SM41 Wayne Gretzky 25.00 60.00
SM42 Martin Brodeur 12.00 30.00
SM43 Mario Lemieux 20.00 50.00
SM44 Maurice Richard 10.00 25.00
SM45 Gordie Howe 15.00 40.00
SM46 Bobby Orr 20.00 50.00
SM47 Patrick Roy 12.00 30.00
SM48 Chris Pronger 5.00 12.00
SM49 Mike Bossy 5.00 12.00
SM50 Johnny Bower 5.00 12.00
SM51 Teemu Selanne 10.00 25.00
SM52 Bobby Clarke 8.00 20.00
SM53 Mark Messier 10.00 25.00
SM54 Brett Hull 10.00 25.00
SM55 Mats Sundin 5.00 12.00
SM56 Steve Yzerman 12.00 30.00
SM57 Dominik Hasek 8.00 20.00
SM58 Jaromir Jagr 15.00 40.00
SM59 Peter Forsberg 10.00 25.00
SM60 Joe Sakic 10.00 25.00

2023-24 Upper Deck Ice Sub Zero

*GOLD/24: 3X TO 8X BASIC
SZ1 Alex Ovechkin 4.00 10.00
SZ2 Artemi Panarin 2.00 5.00
SZ3 Auston Matthews 4.00 10.00
SZ4 Brayden Point 1.25 3.00
SZ5 Cale Makar 2.50 6.00
SZ6 Clayton Keller 1.25 3.00
SZ7 Cole Caufield 2.00 5.00
SZ8 Connor McDavid 5.00 12.00
SZ9 David Pastrnak 2.50 6.00
SZ10 Elias Pettersson 1.50 4.00
SZ11 Erik Karlsson 1.25 3.00
SZ12 Jack Hughes 2.50 6.00
SZ13 Jason Robertson 1.50 4.00
SZ14 Kirill Kaprizov 3.00 8.00
SZ15 Leon Draisaitl 3.00 8.00
SZ16 Matthew Tkachuk 2.00 5.00
SZ17 Mikko Rantanen 2.50 6.00
SZ18 Mitch Marner 1.50 4.00
SZ19 Nathan MacKinnon 4.00 10.00
SZ20 Nikita Kucherov 2.00 5.00
SZ21 Ryan Nugent-Hopkins 1.25 3.00
SZ22 Sidney Crosby 4.00 10.00
SZ23 Tage Thompson 1.25 3.00
SZ24 Tim Stutzle 1.25 3.00
SZ25 William Nylander 2.00 5.00
SZ26 Marco Kasper/799 2.50 6.00
SZ27 Tyler Kleven/799 1.00 2.50
SZ28 Arturs Silovs/799 2.00 5.00
SZ29 Wyatt Kaiser/799 1.00 2.50
SZ30 Elliot Desnoyers/799 1.00 2.50
SZ31 Stanislav Svozil/799 .75 2.00
SZ32 Henry Thrun/799 1.00 2.50
SZ33 Lukas Rousek/799 .75 2.00
SZ34 Will Cuylle/799 1.50 4.00
SZ35 Jiri Patera/799 1.50 4.00
SZ36 Michael Kesselring/799 1.00 2.50
SZ37 Arnaud Durandeau/799 1.00 2.50
SZ38 Aidan McDonough/799 .75 2.00
SZ39 Egor Afanasyev/799 1.00 2.50
SZ40 Bobby McMann/799 1.50 4.00
SZ41 Ridly Greig/799 1.50 4.00
SZ42 Nikita Nesterenko/799 1.00 2.50
SZ43 Samuel Bolduc/799 1.00 2.50
SZ44 Matt Murray/799 1.00 2.50
SZ45 Cole Guttman/799 1.00 2.50
SZ46 William Dufour/799 .75 2.00
SZ47 Vincent Desharnais/799 1.25 3.00
SZ48 Hunter McKown/799 1.00 2.50
SZ49 Matthew Coronato/799 1.50 4.00
SZ50 Danil Gushchin/799 1.00 2.50
SZ51 Joona Koppanen/799 .75 2.00
SZ52 Leevi Merilainen/799 1.00 2.50
SZ53 Walker Duehr/799 .75 2.00
SZ54 Jakob Pelletier/799 1.25 3.00
SZ55 Luke Philp/799 1.00 2.50
SZ56 Jet Greaves/799 1.50 4.00
SZ57 Akito Hirose/799 .75 2.00
SZ58 Owen Beck/799 1.50 4.00
SZ59 Hugh McGing/799 1.00 2.50
SZ60 Sean Farrell/799 1.00 2.50
SZ61 Simon Edvinsson/599 2.00 5.00
SZ62 Dustin Wolf/599 3.00 8.00
SZ63 Brock Faber/599 2.50 6.00
SZ64 Devon Levi/599 2.50 6.00
SZ65 Yaroslav Askarov/599 2.50 6.00
SZ66 Matthew Knies/599 4.00 10.00
SZ67 Luke Hughes/599 3.00 8.00
SZ68 Tyson Foerster/599 2.00 5.00
SZ69 Luke Evangelista/599 1.50 4.00
SZ70 Connor Bedard/599 50.00 125.00

2023-24 Upper Deck Ice Sub Zero Autographs Blue

SZ61 Simon Edvinsson 20.00 50.00
SZ62 Dustin Wolf 30.00 80.00
SZ63 Brock Faber 25.00 60.00
SZ64 Devon Levi 25.00 60.00
SZ65 Yaroslav Askarov 25.00 60.00
SZ66 Matthew Knies 40.00 100.00
SZ67 Luke Hughes SP 30.00 80.00
SZ68 Tyson Foerster 20.00 50.00
SZ69 Luke Evangelista 15.00 40.00
SZ70 Connor Bedard SP 500.00 1200.00

2023-24 Upper Deck Ice Sub Zero Variant Autographs Green

SZ66V Matthew Knies 60.00 150.00
SZ67V Luke Hughes 50.00 125.00
SZ68V Tyson Foerster 30.00 80.00
SZ69V Luke Evangelista 25.00 60.00
SZ70V Connor Bedard 1200.00 3000.00

2023-24 Upper Deck Ice Sub Zero Variants

SZ66V Matthew Knies 6.00 15.00
SZ67V Luke Hughes 5.00 12.00
SZ68V Tyson Foerster 3.00 8.00
SZ69V Luke Evangelista 2.50 6.00
SZ70V Connor Bedard 40.00 100.00

2024-25 Upper Deck Ice

1 Jake Guentzel 1.25 3.00
2 Aaron Ekblad 1.00 2.50
3 K'Andre Miller .60 1.50
4 J.T. Miller 1.00 2.50
5 Andrei Svechnikov 1.00 2.50
6 Anze Kopitar 1.25 3.00
7 Vincent Trocheck .75 2.00
8 Jack Eichel 1.25 3.00
9 Rasmus Dahlin 1.00 2.50
10 Leon Draisaitl 2.50 6.00
11 Sidney Crosby 3.00 8.00
12 Quinn Hughes 2.00 5.00
13 Brady Tkachuk 1.25 3.00
14 Carter Verhaeghe .75 2.00
15 Seth Jarvis 1.00 2.50
16 Dylan Strome 1.00 2.50
17 Jared McCann .60 1.50
18 Mason Marchment .60 1.50
19 Troy Terry .60 1.50
20 Elias Pettersson 1.25 3.00
21 Tim Stutzle 1.00 2.50
22 Sam Reinhart 1.50 4.00
23 Sebastian Aho 1.25 3.00
24 Pavel Buchnevich .60 1.50
25 Mathew Barzal 1.00 2.50
26 Nick Suzuki 1.50 4.00
27 Cale Makar 2.00 5.00
28 Brayden Point 1.00 2.50
29 Timo Meier .75 2.00
30 Juraj Slafkovsky 1.50 4.00
31 Kirill Marchenko 1.00 2.50
32 William Nylander 1.50 4.00
33 Travis Konecny .75 2.00
34 Aleksander Barkov 1.25 3.00
35 Nazem Kadri 1.00 2.50
36 Connor Bedard 2.50 6.00
37 Adrian Kempe .75 2.00
38 Artemi Panarin 1.50 4.00
39 William Karlsson 1.00 2.50
40 Kevin Korchinski .60 1.50
41 Drew Doughty .75 2.00
42 Alexis Lafreniere 1.25 3.00
43 Jonathan Marchessault 1.00 2.50
44 Philipp Kurashev .60 1.50
45 Kirill Kaprizov 2.50 6.00
46 Igor Shesterkin 1.50 4.00
47 Tomas Hertl .75 2.00
48 Jason Robertson 1.25 3.00
49 Filip Forsberg 1.25 3.00
50 Ryan O'Reilly .75 2.00
51 Auston Matthews 3.00 8.00
52 Adam Fantilli 1.25 3.00
53 Roman Josi .75 2.00
54 Jack Hughes 2.00 5.00
55 Victor Hedman 1.00 2.50
56 Tage Thompson 1.00 2.50
57 Zach Hyman 1.25 3.00
58 Travis Sanheim .50 1.25
59 Yegor Sharangovich .75 2.00
60 Evan Bouchard 1.00 2.50
61 Owen Tippett .50 1.25
62 Leo Carlsson 1.25 3.00
63 Wyatt Johnston 1.50 4.00
64 Oliver Bjorkstrand .60 1.50
65 Alex Ovechkin 3.00 8.00
66 David Pastrnak 2.00 5.00
67 Dylan Larkin 1.00 2.50
68 Fabian Zetterlund .50 1.25
69 Kyle Connor 1.25 3.00
70 Andrei Kuzmenko .75 2.00
71 Matthew Tkachuk 1.50 4.00
72 Drake Batherson .75 2.00
73 Mitch Marner 1.25 3.00
74 Jeremy Swayman 1.25 3.00
75 Alex DeBrincat 1.00 2.50
76 William Eklund 1.00 2.50
77 Mark Scheifele 1.25 3.00
78 Alex Tuch .75 2.00
79 Connor McDavid 4.00 10.00
80 Erik Karlsson 1.00 2.50
81 Johnny Gaudreau 1.25 3.00
82 Cole Caufield 1.50 4.00
83 Nico Hischier 1.25 3.00
84 Nikita Kucherov 1.50 4.00
85 Frank Vatrano .60 1.50
86 Miro Heiskanen 1.00 2.50
87 Matty Beniers 1.00 2.50
88 John Carlson .75 2.00
89 Mikko Rantanen 2.00 5.00
90 Brock Faber 1.00 2.50
91 Noah Dobson 1.00 2.50
92 Jordan Kyrou .75 2.00
93 Brad Marchand 1.50 4.00
94 Lucas Raymond 1.25 3.00
95 Evgeni Malkin 1.50 4.00
96 Josh Morrissey 1.00 2.50
97 Nathan MacKinnon 3.00 8.00
98 Matt Boldy 1.25 3.00
99 Bo Horvat 1.00 2.50
100 Robert Thomas .75 2.00
101 Logan Stankoven RC 4.00 10.00
102 Arshdeep Bains RC 2.00 5.00
103 Olen Zellweger RC 3.00 8.00
104 Nikita Chibrikov RC 1.50 4.00
105 Justin Brazeau RC 1.50 4.00
106 Lukas Cormier RC 1.50 4.00
107 Luca Del Bel Belluz RC 1.50 4.00
108 Maxwell Crozier RC 1.50 4.00
109 Logan Mailloux RC 2.50 6.00
110 Brennan Othmann RC 2.50 6.00
111 Gavin Brindley RC 1.50 4.00
112 Gage Goncalves RC 2.00 5.00
113 Nikolai Kovalenko RC 1.25 3.00
114 Zach Dean RC 1.50 4.00
115 Ethan Del Mastro RC 1.50 4.00
116 Zachary Bolduc RC 3.00 8.00
117 Marat Khusnutdinov RC 1.50 4.00
118 Collin Graf RC 1.50 4.00
119 Landon Slaggert RC 1.50 4.00
120 Logan Morrison RC 1.50 4.00
121 Frank Nazar RC 5.00 12.00
122 Georgi Romanov RC 2.00 5.00
123 Scott Morrow RC 2.00 5.00
124 Devin Cooley RC 1.50 4.00
125 Cutter Gauthier RC 4.00 10.00
126 Sam Colangelo RC 1.50 4.00
127 Akil Thomas 1.50 4.00
128 Shakir Mukhamadullin RC 2.00 5.00
129 Mavrik Bourque RC 3.00 8.00
130 Jack Thompson RC 1.50 4.00
131 Kyle MacLean RC 1.50 4.00
132 Ruslan Iskhakov RC 1.50 4.00
133 Lane Hutson RC 8.00 20.00
134 Zack Ostapchuk RC 1.50 4.00
135 James Malatesta RC 1.50 4.00
136 Marshall Rifai RC 1.50 4.00
137 Joshua Roy RC 2.50 6.00
138 Ivan Fedotov RC 3.00 8.00
139 Liam Ohgren RC 3.00 8.00
140 Josh Doan RC 2.50 6.00
141 Brad Lambert RC 2.00 5.00
142 Graeme Clarke RC 1.50 4.00
143 Matt Rempe RC 3.00 8.00
144 Bradly Nadeau RC 2.50 6.00
145 Mason Morelli RC 1.50 4.00
146 Jesper Wallstedt RC 4.00 10.00
147 Jackson Blake RC 3.00 8.00
148 Brendan Brisson RC 2.00 5.00
149 Jack St. Ivany RC 1.50 4.00
150 Declan Carlile RC 1.50 4.00
151 Jason Polin/999 RC 2.50 6.00
152 Cameron Butler/999 RC 2.50 6.00
153 Brandon Scanlin/999 RC 2.50 6.00
154 Jackson Blake/999 5.00 12.00
155 Logan Morrison/999 2.50 6.00
156 Jack Thompson/999 2.50 6.00
157 Ivan Fedotov/999 5.00 12.00
158 Matt Villalta/999 RC 2.50 6.00
159 Georgi Romanov/999 3.00 8.00
160 Graeme Clarke/999 2.50 6.00
161 Patrik Koch/999 RC 2.50 6.00
162 Nikita Chibrikov/999 2.50 6.00
163 Gage Goncalves/999 3.00 8.00
164 Vasily Ponomarev/999 RC 2.50 6.00
165 Devin Cooley/999 2.50 6.00
166 Ruslan Iskhakov/999 2.50 6.00
167 Declan Carlile/999 2.50 6.00
168 Pierrick Dube/999 RC 2.50 6.00
169 Collin Graf/999 2.50 6.00
170 Cameron Crotty/999 RC 2.50 6.00
171 Nikolai Kovalenko/999 2.00 5.00
172 Phil Kemp/999 RC 2.50 6.00
173 Jack St. Ivany/999 2.50 6.00
174 Maksymilian Szuber/999 RC 2.50 6.00
175 James Malatesta/999 2.50 6.00
176 Marshall Rifai/999 2.50 6.00
177 Maxwell Crozier/999 2.50 6.00
178 Brian Halonen/999 RC 2.50 6.00
179 Landon Slaggert/999 2.50 6.00
180 Aku Raty/999 RC 2.50 6.00
181 Mason Morelli/999 2.50 6.00
182 Adam Klapka/999 RC 2.50 6.00
183 Helge Grans/999 RC 2.50 6.00
184 Sebastian Cossa/999 RC 6.00 15.00
185 Daniil Misyul/999 RC 2.50 6.00
186 Aleksei Kolosov/999 RC 2.50 6.00
187 Owen Pickering/999 RC 3.00 8.00
188 Nikita Prishchepov/999 RC 2.50 6.00
189 Samuel Helenius/999 RC 2.50 6.00
190 Trent Miner/999 RC 2.50 6.00
191 Luca Del Bel Belluz/799 2.50 6.00
192 Lukas Cormier/799 2.50 6.00
193 Marat Khusnutdinov/799 2.50 6.00
194 Scott Morrow/799 3.00 8.00
195 Akil Thomas/799 RC 2.50 6.00
196 Justin Brazeau/799 2.50 6.00
197 Matt Rempe/799 5.00 12.00
198 Shakir Mukhamadullin/799 3.00 8.00
199 Logan Mailloux/799 4.00 10.00
200 Zach Dean/799 2.50 6.00
201 Arshdeep Bains/799 3.00 8.00
202 Emil Lilleberg/799 RC 2.50 6.00
203 Kyle MacLean/799 2.50 6.00
204 Sam Colangelo/799 2.50 6.00
205 Yan Kuznetsov/799 RC 2.50 6.00
206 Zack Ostapchuk/799 2.50 6.00
207 Ethan Del Mastro/799 2.50 6.00
208 Nikita Grebenkin/799 RC 3.00 8.00
209 Patrick Giles/799 RC 2.50 6.00
210 Matt Stienburg/799 RC 2.50 6.00
211 Ethan Cardwell/799 RC 2.00 5.00
212 Maveric Lamoureux/799 RC 4.00 10.00
213 Noah Philp/799 RC 2.50 6.00
214 Isaiah George/799 RC 3.00 8.00
215 Jonathan Lekkerimaki/799 RC 6.00 15.00
216 Bradly Nadeau/499 6.00 15.00
217 Gavin Brindley/499 4.00 10.00
218 Jesper Wallstedt/499 10.00 25.00
219 Mavrik Bourque/499 8.00 20.00
220 Josh Doan/499 6.00 15.00
221 Joshua Roy/499 6.00 15.00
222 Zachary Bolduc/499 8.00 20.00
223 Brendan Brisson/499 5.00 12.00
224 Ivan Ivan/499 RC 4.00 10.00
225 Calum Ritchie/499 RC 5.00 12.00
226 Andre Lee/499 RC 4.00 10.00
227 Zachary L'Heureux/499 RC 5.00 12.00
228 Joel Blomqvist/499 RC 5.00 12.00
229 Oliver Kapanen/499 RC 4.00 10.00
230 Albert Johansson/499 RC 4.00 10.00
231 Brennan Othmann/249 6.00 15.00
232 Lane Hutson/249 20.00 50.00
233 Brad Lambert/249 5.00 12.00
234 Olen Zellweger/249 8.00 20.00
235 Rutger McGroarty/249 RC 8.00 20.00
236 Jett Luchanko/249 RC 8.00 20.00
237 Oskar Back/249 RC 4.00 10.00
238 Victor Mancini/249 RC 4.00 10.00
239 Samuel Honzek/249 RC 4.00 10.00
240 Nolan Allan/249 RC 4.00 10.00
241 Cutter Gauthier/99 30.00 80.00
242 Logan Stankoven/99 30.00 80.00
243 Frank Nazar/99 40.00 100.00
244 Liam Ohgren/99 25.00 60.00
245 Matvei Michkov/99 RC 100.00 250.00
246 Macklin Celebrini/99 RC 250.00 600.00
247 Maxim Tsyplakov/99 RC 20.00 50.00
248 Will Smith/99 RC 80.00 200.00
249 Conor Geekie/99 RC 25.00 60.00
250 Seamus Casey/99 RC 15.00 40.00

2024-25 Upper Deck Ice Blue

*BLUE/399: .3X TO .8X GREEN

2024-25 Upper Deck Ice Emerald Green

*GREEN 1-150: .5X TO 1.2X BASIC
151 Jason Polin/199 3.00 8.00
152 Cameron Butler/199 3.00 8.00
153 Brandon Scanlin/199 3.00 8.00
154 Jackson Blake/199 6.00 15.00
155 Logan Morrison/199 3.00 8.00
156 Jack Thompson/199 3.00 8.00
157 Ivan Fedotov/199 6.00 15.00
158 Matt Villalta/199 3.00 8.00
159 Georgi Romanov/199 4.00 10.00
160 Graeme Clarke/199 3.00 8.00
161 Patrik Koch/199 3.00 8.00
162 Nikita Chibrikov/199 3.00 8.00
163 Gage Goncalves/199 4.00 10.00
164 Vasily Ponomarev/199 3.00 8.00
165 Devin Cooley/199 3.00 8.00
166 Ruslan Iskhakov/199 3.00 8.00
167 Declan Carlile/199 3.00 8.00
168 Pierrick Dube/199 3.00 8.00
169 Collin Graf/199 3.00 8.00
170 Cameron Crotty/199 3.00 8.00
171 Nikolai Kovalenko/199 2.50 6.00
172 Phil Kemp/199 3.00 8.00
173 Jack St. Ivany/199 3.00 8.00
174 Maksymilian Szuber/199 3.00 8.00
175 James Malatesta/199 3.00 8.00
176 Marshall Rifai/199 3.00 8.00
177 Maxwell Crozier/199 3.00 8.00
178 Brian Halonen/199 3.00 8.00
179 Landon Slaggert/199 3.00 8.00
180 Aku Raty/199 3.00 8.00
181 Mason Morelli/199 3.00 8.00
182 Adam Klapka/199 3.00 8.00
183 Helge Grans/199 3.00 8.00
184 Sebastian Cossa/199 8.00 20.00
185 Daniil Misyul/199 3.00 8.00
186 Aleksei Kolosov/199 3.00 8.00
187 Owen Pickering/199 4.00 10.00
188 Nikita Prishchepov/199 3.00 8.00
189 Samuel Helenius/199 3.00 8.00
190 Trent Miner/199 3.00 8.00
191 Luca Del Bel Belluz/199 3.00 8.00
192 Lukas Cormier/199 3.00 8.00
193 Marat Khusnutdinov/199 3.00 8.00
194 Scott Morrow/199 4.00 10.00
195 Akil Thomas/199 3.00 8.00
196 Justin Brazeau/199 3.00 8.00
197 Matt Rempe/199 6.00 15.00
198 Shakir Mukhamadullin/199 4.00 10.00
199 Logan Mailloux/199 5.00 12.00
200 Zach Dean/199 3.00 8.00
201 Arshdeep Bains/199 4.00 10.00
202 Emil Lilleberg/199 3.00 8.00
203 Kyle MacLean/199 3.00 8.00
204 Sam Colangelo/199 3.00 8.00
205 Yan Kuznetsov/199 3.00 8.00
206 Zack Ostapchuk/199 3.00 8.00
207 Ethan Del Mastro/199 3.00 8.00
208 Nikita Grebenkin/199 4.00 10.00
209 Patrick Giles/199 3.00 8.00
210 Matt Stienburg/199 3.00 8.00
211 Ethan Cardwell/199 2.50 6.00
212 Maveric Lamoureux/199 5.00 12.00
213 Noah Philp/199 3.00 8.00
214 Isaiah George/199 4.00 10.00
215 Jonathan Lekkerimaki/199 8.00 20.00
216 Bradly Nadeau/199 5.00 12.00
217 Gavin Brindley/199 3.00 8.00
218 Jesper Wallstedt/199 8.00 20.00
219 Mavrik Bourque/199 6.00 15.00
220 Josh Doan/199 5.00 12.00
221 Joshua Roy/199 5.00 12.00
222 Zachary Bolduc/199 6.00 15.00
223 Brendan Brisson/199 4.00 10.00
224 Ivan Ivan/199 3.00 8.00
225 Calum Ritchie/199 4.00 10.00
226 Andre Lee/199 3.00 8.00
227 Zachary L'Heureux/199 4.00 10.00
228 Joel Blomqvist/199 4.00 10.00
229 Oliver Kapanen/199 3.00 8.00
230 Albert Johansson/199 3.00 8.00
231 Brennan Othmann/199 5.00 12.00
232 Lane Hutson/199 25.00 60.00
233 Brad Lambert/199 4.00 10.00
234 Olen Zellweger/199 6.00 15.00
235 Rutger McGroarty/199 6.00 15.00
236 Jett Luchanko/199 6.00 15.00
237 Oskar Back/199 3.00 8.00
238 Victor Mancini/199 3.00 8.00
239 Samuel Honzek/199 3.00 8.00
240 Nolan Allan/199 3.00 8.00
241 Cutter Gauthier/199 8.00 20.00
242 Logan Stankoven/199 8.00 20.00
243 Frank Nazar/199 10.00 25.00
244 Liam Ohgren/199 6.00 15.00
245 Matvei Michkov/199 20.00 50.00
246 Macklin Celebrini/199 30.00 80.00
247 Maxim Tsyplakov/199 5.00 12.00
248 Will Smith/199 10.00 25.00
249 Conor Geekie/199 6.00 15.00
250 Seamus Casey/199 4.00 10.00

2024-25 Upper Deck Ice Gold

*GOLD/25: 1.2X TO 3X GREEN
184 Sebastian Cossa 80.00 200.00
232 Lane Hutson 100.00 250.00
245 Matvei Michkov 125.00 300.00
246 Macklin Celebrini 200.00 500.00

2024-25 Upper Deck Ice Grayscale

*GRAY/99: .8X TO 2X BASIC
133 Lane Hutson 25.00 60.00

2024-25 Upper Deck Ice Purple

*PURPLE: .6X TO 1.5X BASIC
*PURPLE RC: .5X TO 1.2X BASIC

2024-25 Upper Deck Ice Articulates

AT1 Trevor Zegras 1.25 3.00
AT2 Clayton Keller 1.50 4.00
AT3 Charlie Coyle 1.25 3.00
AT4 Tage Thompson 1.50 4.00
AT5 Mikael Backlund 1.00 2.50
AT6 Brent Burns 1.25 3.00
AT7 Nathan MacKinnon 5.00 12.00
AT8 Zach Werenski 2.00 5.00
AT9 Connor Bedard 4.00 10.00
AT10 Tyler Seguin 1.50 4.00
AT11 Patrick Kane 2.50 6.00
AT12 Connor McDavid 6.00 15.00
AT13 Sam Bennett 2.00 5.00
AT14 Trevor Moore .75 2.00
AT15 Kevin Fiala 1.00 2.50
AT16 Matt Boldy 2.00 5.00
AT17 Cole Caufield 2.50 6.00
AT18 Luke Evangelista 1.00 2.50
AT19 Jesper Bratt 1.25 3.00
AT20 Brock Nelson 1.25 3.00
AT21 Chris Kreider 1.50 4.00
AT22 Claude Giroux 1.25 3.00
AT23 Joel Farabee 1.25 3.00
AT24 Kris Letang 1.50 4.00
AT25 Mikael Granlund 1.00 2.50
AT26 Jordan Eberle 1.25 3.00
AT27 Jake Neighbours 1.25 3.00
AT28 Andrei Vasilevskiy 2.00 5.00
AT29 John Tavares 2.00 5.00
AT30 Morgan Rielly 1.25 3.00
AT31 Brock Boeser 1.50 4.00
AT32 Jack Eichel 2.00 5.00
AT33 Tom Wilson 1.25 3.00
AT34 Nikolaj Ehlers 1.25 3.00
AT35 Thatcher Demko 1.50 4.00
AT36 Justin Brazeau 1.25 3.00
AT37 Logan Morrison 1.25 3.00
AT38 Zachary Bolduc 2.50 6.00
AT39 Brendan Brisson 1.50 4.00
AT40 Logan Stankoven 3.00 8.00
AT41 Akil Thomas 1.25 3.00
AT42 Zack Ostapchuk 1.25 3.00
AT43 Cutter Gauthier 3.00 8.00
AT44 Lane Hutson 6.00 15.00
AT45 Matt Rempe 2.50 6.00
AT46 Frank Nazar 4.00 10.00
AT47 Josh Doan 2.00 5.00
AT48 Gavin Brindley 1.25 3.00
AT49 Adam Klapka 1.25 3.00
AT50 Sam Colangelo 1.25 3.00
AT51 Landon Slaggert 1.25 3.00
AT52 Shakir Mukhamadullin 1.50 4.00
AT53 Marshall Rifai 1.25 3.00
AT54 Olen Zellweger 2.50 6.00
AT55 Kyle MacLean 1.25 3.00
AT56 Mason Morelli 1.25 3.00
AT57 Brad Lambert 1.50 4.00
AT58 Marat Khusnutdinov 1.25 3.00
AT59 Mavrik Bourque 2.50 6.00
AT60 Joshua Roy 2.00 5.00
AT61 Macklin Celebrini 6.00 15.00
AT62 Matvei Michkov 5.00 12.00
AT63 Nolan Allan 1.25 3.00
AT64 Will Smith 4.00 10.00
AT65 Seamus Casey 1.50 4.00

2024-25 Upper Deck Ice Articulates Gold

*GOLD/25: 1.2X TO 3X BASIC
AT43 Cutter Gauthier 20.00 50.00
AT44 Lane Hutson 60.00 150.00
AT01 Macklin Celebrini 00.00 150.00

2024-25 Upper Deck Ice Autographs White Snowflake

5 Andrei Svechnikov 10.00 25.00
13 Brady Tkachuk 12.00 30.00
14 Carter Verhaeghe 8.00 20.00
15 Seth Jarvis 10.00 25.00
17 Jared McCann 6.00 15.00
20 Elias Pettersson SP 12.00 30.00
21 Tim Stutzle 10.00 25.00
22 Sam Reinhart 15.00 40.00
23 Sebastian Aho 12.00 30.00
26 Nick Suzuki 15.00 40.00
27 Cale Makar SP 20.00 50.00
29 Timo Meier 8.00 20.00
31 Kirill Marchenko 10.00 25.00
33 Travis Konecny 8.00 20.00
38 Artemi Panarin SP 15.00 40.00
39 William Karlsson 10.00 25.00
43 Jonathan Marchessault 10.00 25.00
45 Kirill Kaprizov SP 25.00 60.00
46 Igor Shesterkin 15.00 40.00
50 Ryan O'Reilly 8.00 20.00
56 Tage Thompson 10.00 25.00
58 Travis Sanheim 5.00 12.00
59 Yegor Sharangovich 8.00 20.00
62 Leo Carlsson 12.00 30.00
63 Wyatt Johnston 15.00 40.00
69 Kyle Connor 12.00 30.00
72 Drake Batherson 8.00 20.00
76 William Eklund 10.00 25.00
78 Alex Tuch 8.00 20.00
83 Nico Hischier 12.00 30.00
84 Nikita Kucherov SP 15.00 40.00
85 Frank Vatrano 6.00 15.00
92 Jordan Kyrou 8.00 20.00
100 Robert Thomas 8.00 20.00
101 Logan Stankoven 20.00 50.00
102 Arshdeep Bains 10.00 25.00
103 Olen Zellweger 15.00 40.00
104 Nikita Chibrikov SP 8.00 20.00
105 Justin Brazeau 8.00 20.00
106 Lukas Cormier 8.00 20.00
109 Logan Mailloux 12.00 30.00
114 Zach Dean 8.00 20.00
117 Marat Khusnutdinov 8.00 20.00
118 Collin Graf 8.00 20.00
120 Logan Morrison 8.00 20.00
121 Frank Nazar 25.00 60.00
123 Scott Morrow 10.00 25.00

124 Devin Cooley 8.00 20.00
125 Cutter Gauthier 20.00 50.00
126 Sam Colangelo 8.00 20.00
127 Akil Thomas 8.00 20.00
128 Shakir Mukhamadullin 10.00 25.00
129 Mavrik Bourque 15.00 40.00
130 Jack Thompson 8.00 20.00
131 Kyle MacLean 8.00 20.00
133 Lane Hutson 100.00 250.00
136 Marshall Rifai 8.00 20.00
138 Ivan Fedotov 15.00 40.00
139 Liam Ohgren 15.00 40.00
142 Graeme Clarke 8.00 20.00
143 Matt Rempe 15.00 40.00
145 Mason Morelli 8.00 20.00
146 Jesper Wallstedt 20.00 50.00
150 Declan Carlile 8.00 20.00

2024-25 Upper Deck Ice Frozen In Ice

FI1 Mikko Rantanen 10.00 25.00
FI2 Auston Matthews 15.00 40.00
FI3 Jake Oettinger 6.00 15.00
FI4 Logan Couture 5.00 12.00
FI5 Patrick Kane 8.00 20.00
FI6 Sean Couturier 3.00 8.00
FI7 Sebastian Aho 6.00 15.00
FI8 Mitch Marner 6.00 15.00
FI9 Nico Hischier 6.00 15.00
FI10 Brennan Othmann 6.00 15.00
FI11 Andrew Mangiapane 4.00 10.00
FI12 J.T. Miller 5.00 12.00
FI13 Alex Tuch 4.00 10.00
FI14 William Karlsson 5.00 12.00
FI15 Charlie Coyle 4.00 10.00
FI16 Alex Ovechkin 15.00 40.00
FI17 Drew Doughty 4.00 10.00
FI18 David Pastrnak 10.00 25.00
FI19 Kyle Connor 6.00 15.00
FI20 Alex Kerfoot 3.00 8.00
FI21 Cutter Gauthier 10.00 25.00
FI22 Logan Stankoven 10.00 25.00
FI23 Kent Johnson 4.00 10.00
FI24 Jordan Kyrou 4.00 10.00
FI25 Mason McTavish 4.00 10.00
FI26 Jamie Benn 4.00 10.00
FI27 Jared McCann 3.00 8.00
FI28 Evan Rodrigues 3.00 8.00
FI29 Chris Kreider 5.00 12.00
FI30 Frank Nazar 12.00 30.00
FI31 Juuse Saros 5.00 12.00
FI32 Aleksander Barkov 6.00 15.00
FI33 Lane Hutson 25.00 60.00
FI34 Connor Bedard 12.00 30.00
FI35 Victor Hedman 5.00 12.00
FI36 Michael Matheson 2.50 6.00
FI37 Brad Lambert 5.00 12.00
FI38 Matt Boldy 6.00 15.00
FI39 Mavrik Bourque 8.00 20.00
FI40 Dylan Larkin 5.00 12.00
FI41 Reilly Smith 4.00 10.00
FI42 Bo Horvat 5.00 12.00
FI43 Liam Ohgren 8.00 20.00
FI44 Zach Hyman 6.00 15.00
FI45 Brady Tkachuk 6.00 15.00
FI46 Nick Suzuki 8.00 20.00
FI47 Olen Zellweger 8.00 20.00
FI48 Brendan Brisson 5.00 12.00
FI49 Leon Draisaitl 12.00 30.00
FI50 Claude Giroux 4.00 10.00

2024-25 Upper Deck Ice Frozen in Ice Gold

*GOLD/25: .8X TO 2X BASIC
FI33 Lane Hutson 80.00 200.00

2024-25 Upper Deck Ice Glacial Graphs

*BLACK: .5X TO 1.2X BASIC
GG1 Cole Sillinger 6.00 15.00
GG2 Mikael Granlund 6.00 15.00
GG3 Jake Sanderson 10.00 25.00
GG5 Kevin Korchinski 6.00 15.00
GG6 Kevin Hayes 6.00 15.00
GG7 J.T. Compher 5.00 12.00
GG9 Tanner Jeannot 5.00 12.00
GG10 Connor Zary 8.00 20.00
GG12 JJ Peterka 8.00 20.00
GG13 Brock Boeser SP 10.00 25.00
GG16 Pavel Zacha 6.00 15.00
GG17 Chandler Stephenson 6.00 15.00
GG18 Nick Schmaltz 6.00 15.00
GG19 Tom Wilson 8.00 20.00
GG20 Frank Vatrano 6.00 15.00
GG21 Cole Perfetti 8.00 20.00
GG23 Morgan Frost 6.00 15.00
GG25 Jeremy Roenick 12.00 30.00
GG27 Craig Janney 6.00 15.00
GG28 Wyatt Johnston 15.00 40.00
GG30 Casey Mittelstadt 8.00 20.00
GG31 Jared McCann 6.00 15.00
GG33 Trevor Moore 5.00 12.00
GG34 Brian Propp 6.00 15.00
GG38 Brandon Montour 10.00 25.00
GG39 Mattias Ohlund 5.00 12.00
GG40 Dawson Mercer 10.00 25.00

2024-25 Upper Deck Ice Go To Work

GTW1 Ryan Nugent-Hopkins 4.00 10.00
GTW2 Mark Stone 4.00 10.00
GTW3 Sebastian Aho 5.00 12.00
GTW4 Al MacInnis 4.00 10.00
GTW5 Mikko Rantanen 8.00 20.00
GTW6 Kirill Marchenko 4.00 10.00
GTW7 Matthew Tkachuk 6.00 15.00
GTW8 Ryan Getzlaf 3.00 8.00
GTW9 Kris Letang 4.00 10.00
GTW10 Larry Robinson 3.00 8.00
GTW11 Wyatt Johnston 6.00 15.00
GTW12 Timo Meier 3.00 8.00
GTW13 Michel Goulet 3.00 8.00
GTW14 John Tavares 5.00 12.00
GTW15 Collin Graf 3.00 8.00
GTW16 Tim Stutzle 3.00 8.00
GTW17 Jack Hughes 8.00 20.00
GTW18 Nikolaj Ehlers 3.00 8.00
GTW19 Denis Potvin 3.00 8.00
GTW20 Elias Pettersson 5.00 12.00

2024-25 Upper Deck Ice Ice Premieres Autographs

IPAAB Arshdeep Bains/199 10.00 25.00
IPAAK Adam Klapka/199 8.00 20.00
IPAAT Akil Thomas/99 8.00 20.00
IPABH Brian Halonen/199 8.00 20.00
IPABR Justin Brazeau/99 8.00 20.00
IPACG Collin Graf/199 8.00 20.00
IPADC Declan Carlile/199 8.00 20.00
IPAEC Easton Cowan/199 80.00 200.00
IPAFN Frank Nazar/99 50.00 125.00
IPAGC Graeme Clarke/199 8.00 20.00
IPAJW Jesper Wallstedt/99 20.00 50.00
IPAKM Kyle MacLean/199 8.00 20.00
IPALC Lukas Cormier/199 8.00 20.00
IPALH Lane Hutson/99 250.00 600.00
IPALM Logan Morrison/199 8.00 20.00
IPALO Liam Ohgren/99 15.00 40.00
IPALS Logan Stankoven/99 20.00 50.00
IPAMB Mavrik Bourque/99 15.00 40.00
IPAMC Macklin Celebrini/99 250.00 600.00
IPAMI Matvei Michkov/99 150.00 400.00
IPAMK Marat Khusnutdinov/99 8.00 20.00
IPAMM Mason Morelli/199 8.00 20.00
IPAMO Scott Morrow/99 10.00 25.00
IPAMR Marshall Rifai/199 8.00 20.00
IPANC Nikita Chibrikov/199 8.00 20.00
IPAOZ Olen Zellweger/99 15.00 40.00
IPAPD Pierrick Dube/199 8.00 20.00
IPARE Matt Rempe/199 15.00 40.00
IPASM Shakir Mukhamadullin/99 10.00 25.00
IPAWS Will Smith/99 125.00 300.00
IPAYK Yan Kuznetsov/199 8.00 20.00
IPAZD Zach Dean/99 8.00 20.00

2024-25 Upper Deck Ice Ice Premieres Jerseys

IPJ1 Bradly Nadeau 2.50 6.00
IPJ3 Olen Zellweger 3.00 8.00
IPJ4 Ethan Del Mastro 1.50 4.00
IPJ5 Will Smith 12.00 30.00
IPJ6 Justin Brazeau 1.50 4.00
IPJ7 Zack Ostapchuk 1.50 4.00
IPJ8 Joshua Roy 2.50 6.00
IPJ9 Scott Morrow 2.00 5.00
IPJ12 Brendan Brisson 2.00 5.00
IPJ13 Frank Nazar 5.00 12.00
IPJ14 Gage Goncalves 2.00 5.00
IPJ17 Gavin Brindley 1.50 4.00
IPJ18 Zach Dean 1.50 4.00
IPJ19 Sam Colangelo 1.50 4.00
IPJ22 Luca Del Bel Belluz 1.50 4.00
IPJ23 Zachary Bolduc 3.00 8.00
IPJ24 Logan Stankoven 4.00 10.00
IPJ26 Mavrik Bourque 3.00 8.00
IPJ27 Macklin Celebrini 12.00 30.00
IPJ28 Cutter Gauthier 4.00 10.00
IPJ29 Shakir Mukhamadullin 2.00 5.00
IPJ30 Akil Thomas 1.50 4.00
IPJ34 Lane Hutson 12.00 30.00
IPJ36 Jackson Blake 3.00 8.00
IPJ37 Rutger McGroarty 3.00 8.00
IPJ38 Lukas Cormier 1.50 4.00
IPJ39 Liam Ohgren 3.00 8.00
IPJ40 Nikita Chibrikov 1.50 4.00
IPJ41 Josh Doan 2.50 6.00
IPJ42 Matvei Michkov 12.00 30.00
IPJ44 Arshdeep Bains 2.00 5.00
IPJ46 Brennan Othmann 2.50 6.00
IPJ47 Jesper Wallstedt 4.00 10.00
IPJ49 Yan Kuznetsov 1.50 4.00
IPJ50 Matt Rempe 3.00 8.00

2024-25 Upper Deck Ice Ice Premieres Jerseys Patch

*PATCH/25: 1.5X TO 4X BASIC
IPP27 Macklin Celebrini 200.00 500.00
IPP34 Lane Hutson 60.00 150.00
IPP42 Matvei Michkov 60.00 150.00

2024-25 Upper Deck Ice Ice Premieres Minis

MPAB Arshdeep Bains 2.00 5.00
MPAL Artyom Levshunov 4.00 10.00
MPAT Akil Thomas 1.50 4.00
MPBB Brendan Brisson 2.00 5.00
MPBH Brian Halonen 1.50 4.00
MPBL Brad Lambert 2.00 5.00
MPBN Bradly Nadeau 2.50 6.00
MPBO Brennan Othmann 2.50 6.00
MPCG Conor Geekie 3.00 8.00
MPDR David Reinbacher 4.00 10.00
MPEC Easton Cowan 4.00 10.00
MPFN Frank Nazar 5.00 12.00
MPGA Cutter Gauthier 4.00 10.00
MPGB Gavin Brindley 1.50 4.00
MPIF Ivan Fedotov 3.00 8.00
MPJB Justin Brazeau 1.50 4.00
MPJD Josh Doan 2.50 6.00
MPJL Jonathan Lekkerimaki 4.00 10.00
MPJP Jason Polin 1.50 4.00
MPJR Joshua Roy 2.50 6.00
MPJS Jack St. Ivany 1.50 4.00
MPJW Jesper Wallstedt 4.00 10.00
MPLC Lukas Cormier 1.50 4.00
MPLD Luca Del Bel Belluz 1.50 4.00
MPLH Lane Hutson 8.00 20.00
MPLM Logan Mailloux 2.50 6.00
MPLO Liam Ohgren 3.00 8.00
MPLS Landon Slaggert 1.50 4.00
MPMB Mavrik Bourque 3.00 8.00
MPMC Macklin Celebrini 25.00 60.00
MPMK Marat Khusnutdinov 1.50 4.00
MPMR Marshall Rifai 1.50 4.00
MPMU Shakir Mukhamadullin 2.00 5.00
MPNC Nikita Chibrikov 1.50 4.00
MPND Nate Danielson 2.50 6.00
MPNK Nikolai Kovalenko 1.25 3.00
MPNO Noah Ostlund 3.00 8.00
MPOZ Olen Zellweger 3.00 8.00
MPRE Matt Rempe 3.00 8.00
MPRM Rutger McGroarty 3.00 8.00
MPSC Sam Colangelo 1.50 4.00
MPSM Scott Morrow 2.00 5.00
MPST Logan Stankoven 4.00 10.00
MPVP Vasily Ponomarev 1.50 4.00
MPWS Will Smith 5.00 12.00
MPZB Zachary Bolduc 3.00 8.00
MPZD Zach Dean 1.50 4.00
MPZO Zack Ostapchuk 1.50 4.00

2024-25 Upper Deck Ice Ice Premieres Minis Gold

*GOLD/99: 1X TO 2.5X BASIC
MPAL Artyom Levshunov 15.00 40.00
MPLH Lane Hutson 30.00 80.00

2024-25 Upper Deck Ice Ice Shelves

IS1 Dylan Larkin 3.00 8.00
IS2 Robert Thomas 2.50 6.00
IS3 Andrei Vasilevskiy 4.00 10.00
IS4 Vladimir Tarasenko 4.00 10.00
IS5 Jason Dickinson 1.50 4.00
IS6 Mats Zuccarello 2.50 6.00
IS7 Brendan Gallagher 2.50 6.00
IS8 Jamie Drysdale 2.00 5.00
IS9 Roman Josi 2.50 6.00
IS10 Anton Lundell 2.50 6.00
IS11 Anze Kopitar 4.00 10.00
IS12 Jared McCann 2.00 5.00
IS13 Matty Beniers 3.00 8.00
IS14 Brock Boeser 3.00 8.00
IS15 Alex DeBrincat 3.00 8.00
IS16 Jake Neighbours 2.50 6.00
IS17 Mathew Barzal 3.00 8.00
IS18 Owen Power 3.00 8.00
IS19 Alexis Lafreniere 4.00 10.00
IS20 Matt Duchene 2.50 6.00
IS21 Teuvo Teravainen 2.50 6.00
IS22 Zach Hyman 4.00 10.00
IS23 Tim Stutzle 3.00 8.00
IS24 Brady Tkachuk 4.00 10.00
IS25 Luke Hughes 4.00 10.00
IS26 Jonathan Huberdeau 3.00 8.00
IS27 Devon Toews 2.00 5.00
IS28 Kyle Connor 4.00 10.00
IS29 Mikey Anderson 2.00 5.00
IS30 Mitch Marner 4.00 10.00

2024-25 Upper Deck Ice Ice Shelves Autographs

IS8 Jamie Drysdale 10.00 25.00
IS23 Tim Stutzle 15.00 40.00
IS27 Devon Toews 10.00 25.00

2024-25 Upper Deck Ice Jerseys Blue

1 Jake Guentzel 4.00 10.00
2 Aaron Ekblad 3.00 8.00
3 K'Andre Miller 2.00 5.00
4 J.T. Miller 3.00 8.00
5 Andrei Svechnikov 3.00 8.00
6 Anze Kopitar 4.00 10.00
7 Vincent Trocheck 2.50 6.00
8 Jack Eichel 4.00 10.00
9 Rasmus Dahlin 3.00 8.00
10 Leon Draisaitl 8.00 20.00
11 Sidney Crosby 10.00 25.00
12 Quinn Hughes 6.00 15.00
13 Brady Tkachuk 4.00 10.00
14 Carter Verhaeghe 2.50 6.00
15 Seth Jarvis 3.00 8.00
16 Dylan Strome 3.00 8.00
17 Jared McCann 2.00 5.00
19 Troy Terry 2.00 5.00
20 Elias Pettersson 4.00 10.00
21 Tim Stutzle 3.00 8.00
22 Sam Reinhart 5.00 12.00
23 Sebastian Aho 4.00 10.00
24 Pavel Buchnevich 2.00 5.00
25 Mathew Barzal 3.00 8.00
26 Nick Suzuki 5.00 12.00
27 Cale Makar 6.00 15.00
28 Brayden Point 3.00 8.00
29 Timo Meier 2.50 6.00
30 Juraj Slafkovsky 5.00 12.00
31 Kirill Marchenko 3.00 8.00
32 William Nylander 5.00 12.00
33 Travis Konecny 2.50 6.00
34 Aleksander Barkov 4.00 10.00
35 Nazem Kadri 3.00 8.00
36 Connor Bedard 8.00 20.00
37 Adrian Kempe 2.50 6.00
38 Artemi Panarin 5.00 12.00
39 William Karlsson 3.00 8.00
40 Kevin Korchinski 2.00 5.00
41 Drew Doughty 2.50 6.00
42 Alexis Lafreniere 4.00 10.00
43 Jonathan Marchessault 3.00 8.00
44 Philipp Kurashev 2.00 5.00
45 Kirill Kaprizov 8.00 20.00
46 Igor Shesterkin 5.00 12.00
47 Tomas Hertl 2.50 6.00
48 Jason Robertson 4.00 10.00
49 Filip Forsberg 4.00 10.00
50 Ryan O'Reilly 2.50 6.00
51 Auston Matthews 10.00 25.00
52 Adam Fantilli 4.00 10.00
53 Roman Josi 2.50 6.00
54 Jack Hughes 6.00 15.00
55 Victor Hedman 3.00 8.00
56 Tage Thompson 3.00 8.00
57 Zach Hyman 4.00 10.00
58 Travis Sanheim 1.50 4.00
59 Yegor Sharangovich 2.50 6.00
60 Evan Bouchard 3.00 8.00
61 Owen Tippett 1.50 4.00
62 Leo Carlsson 4.00 10.00
63 Wyatt Johnston 5.00 12.00
64 Oliver Bjorkstrand 2.00 5.00
65 Alex Ovechkin 10.00 25.00
66 David Pastrnak 6.00 15.00
67 Dylan Larkin 3.00 8.00
68 Fabian Zetterlund 1.50 4.00
69 Kyle Connor 4.00 10.00
70 Andrei Kuzmenko 2.50 6.00
71 Matthew Tkachuk 5.00 12.00
72 Drake Batherson 2.50 6.00
73 Mitch Marner 4.00 10.00
74 Jeremy Swayman 4.00 10.00
75 Alex DeBrincat 3.00 8.00
76 William Eklund 3.00 8.00
77 Mark Scheifele 4.00 10.00
78 Alex Tuch 2.50 6.00
79 Connor McDavid 12.00 30.00
80 Erik Karlsson 3.00 8.00
82 Cole Caufield 5.00 12.00
83 Nico Hischier 4.00 10.00
84 Nikita Kucherov 5.00 12.00
85 Frank Vatrano 2.00 5.00
86 Miro Heiskanen 3.00 8.00
87 Matty Beniers 3.00 8.00
88 John Carlson 2.50 6.00
89 Mikko Rantanen 6.00 15.00
90 Brock Faber 3.00 8.00
91 Noah Dobson 3.00 8.00
92 Jordan Kyrou 2.50 6.00
93 Brad Marchand 5.00 12.00
94 Lucas Raymond 4.00 10.00
95 Evgeni Malkin 5.00 12.00
96 Josh Morrissey 3.00 8.00
97 Nathan MacKinnon 10.00 25.00
98 Matt Boldy 4.00 10.00
99 Bo Horvat 3.00 8.00
100 Robert Thomas 2.50 6.00
101 Logan Stankoven 6.00 15.00
102 Arshdeep Bains 3.00 8.00
103 Olen Zellweger 5.00 12.00
104 Nikita Chibrikov 2.50 6.00
107 Luca Del Bel Belluz 2.50 6.00
109 Logan Mailloux 4.00 10.00
110 Brennan Othmann 4.00 10.00
111 Gavin Brindley 2.50 6.00
112 Gage Goncalves 3.00 8.00
113 Nikolai Kovalenko 2.00 5.00
114 Zach Dean 2.50 6.00
115 Ethan Del Mastro 2.50 6.00
116 Zachary Bolduc 5.00 12.00
118 Collin Graf 2.50 6.00
121 Frank Nazar 8.00 20.00
123 Scott Morrow 3.00 8.00
125 Cutter Gauthier 6.00 15.00
126 Sam Colangelo 2.50 6.00
127 Akil Thomas 2.50 6.00
128 Shakir Mukhamadullin 3.00 8.00
129 Mavrik Bourque 5.00 12.00
130 Jack Thompson 2.50 6.00
133 Lane Hutson 12.00 30.00
134 Zack Ostapchuk 2.50 6.00
137 Joshua Roy 4.00 10.00
138 Ivan Fedotov 5.00 12.00
139 Liam Ohgren 5.00 12.00
140 Josh Doan 4.00 10.00
143 Matt Rempe 5.00 12.00
144 Bradly Nadeau 4.00 10.00
146 Jesper Wallstedt 6.00 15.00
147 Jackson Blake 5.00 12.00
148 Brendan Brisson 3.00 8.00

2024-25 Upper Deck Ice Jerseys Patch Gold

*PATCH: 1.5X TO 4X BASIC
133 Lane Hutson/35 60.00 150.00

2024-25 Upper Deck Ice Patch Autographs Gold

5 Andrei Svechnikov/49 15.00 40.00
10 Leon Draisaitl/25 40.00 100.00
13 Brady Tkachuk/25 20.00 50.00
14 Carter Verhaeghe/49 12.00 30.00
17 Jared McCann/49 10.00 25.00
20 Elias Pettersson/25 20.00 50.00
21 Tim Stutzle/25 15.00 40.00
23 Sebastian Aho/25 20.00 50.00
26 Nick Suzuki/25 50.00 125.00
27 Cale Makar/25 30.00 80.00
29 Timo Meier/49 12.00 30.00
31 Kirill Marchenko/49 15.00 40.00
33 Travis Konecny/49 12.00 30.00
39 William Karlsson/49 15.00 40.00
46 Igor Shesterkin/25 25.00 60.00
50 Ryan O'Reilly/49 12.00 30.00
56 Tage Thompson/49 15.00 40.00
58 Travis Sanheim/49 8.00 20.00
62 Leo Carlsson/49 20.00 50.00
69 Kyle Connor/25 20.00 50.00
78 Alex Tuch/49 12.00 30.00
83 Nico Hischier/49 12.00 30.00
101 Logan Stankoven/49 30.00 80.00
102 Arshdeep Bains/49 15.00 40.00
103 Olen Zellweger/49 25.00 60.00
104 Nikita Chibrikov/49 12.00 30.00
105 Justin Brazeau/49 12.00 30.00
106 Lukas Cormier/49 12.00 30.00
114 Zach Dean/49 12.00 30.00
118 Collin Graf/49 12.00 30.00
120 Logan Morrison/49 12.00 30.00
121 Frank Nazar/49 60.00 150.00
123 Scott Morrow/49 15.00 40.00
125 Cutter Gauthier/49 30.00 80.00
126 Sam Colangelo/49 12.00 30.00
127 Akil Thomas/49 12.00 30.00
128 Shakir Mukhamadullin/49 15.00 40.00
129 Mavrik Bourque/49 25.00 60.00
130 Jack Thompson/49 12.00 30.00
131 Kyle MacLean/49 12.00 30.00
133 Lane Hutson/49 300.00 800.00
136 Marshall Rifai/49 12.00 30.00
138 Ivan Fedotov/49 25.00 60.00
139 Liam Ohgren/49 25.00 60.00
142 Graeme Clarke/49 12.00 30.00
143 Matt Rempe/49 25.00 60.00
145 Mason Morelli/49 12.00 30.00
146 Jesper Wallstedt/49 30.00 80.00
150 Declan Carlile/49 12.00 30.00

2024-25 Upper Deck Ice SP Ice Level 1 Mild

*MEDIUM: .6X TO 1.5X BASIC
*HOT: .8X TO 2X BASIC
*FIRE: 1X TO 2.5X BASIC
SP1 Connor McDavid 5.00 12.00
SP2 David Pastrnak 2.50 6.00
SP3 Connor Bedard 3.00 8.00
SP4 Zach Hyman 1.50 4.00
SP5 Jack Eichel 1.50 4.00
SP6 Matthew Tkachuk 2.00 5.00
SP7 Kirill Kaprizov 2.50 6.00
SP8 Filip Forsberg 1.50 4.00
SP9 Nikita Kucherov 2.50 6.00
SP10 Jack Hughes 2.50 6.00
SP11 Mathew Barzal 1.25 3.00
SP12 Artemi Panarin 2.00 5.00
SP13 Logan Stankoven 2.50 6.00
SP14 Sidney Crosby 4.00 10.00
SP15 Brady Tkachuk 1.50 4.00
SP16 Josh Doan 1.50 4.00
SP17 Quinn Hughes 2.50 6.00
SP18 Leon Draisaitl 3.00 8.00
SP19 Elias Pettersson 1.50 4.00
SP20 Auston Matthews 4.00 10.00
SP21 Jake Guentzel 1.50 4.00
SP22 Alex Ovechkin 4.00 10.00
SP23 Nathan MacKinnon 4.00 10.00
SP24 William Nylander 2.00 5.00
SP25 Cale Makar 2.50 6.00

2024-25 Upper Deck Ice Sub Zero Rookie Autographs Blue

SZCT Cutter Gauthier 25.00 60.00
SZMI Matvei Michkov 40.00 100.00
SZOZ Olen Zellweger 20.00 50.00
SZRE Matt Rempe 20.00 50.00
SZST Logan Stankoven 25.00 60.00
SZWS Will Smith 30.00 80.00

2024-25 Upper Deck Ice Sub Zero Rookie Variant Autographs Green

SV66V Justin Brazeau 12.00 30.00
SV68V Logan Stankoven 30.00 80.00
SV69V Will Smith 40.00 100.00
SV70V Macklin Celebrini 300.00 800.00

2024-25 Upper Deck Ice Sub Zero Rookie Variants

SV66V Justin Brazeau 1.50 4.00
SV67V Zachary Bolduc 3.00 8.00
SV68V Logan Stankoven 4.00 10.00
SV69V Will Smith 5.00 12.00
SV70V Macklin Celebrini 12.00 30.00

2024-25 Upper Deck Ice Sub Zero Rookies

SZAB Arshdeep Bains/699 1.25 3.00
SZAK Adam Klapka/699 1.00 2.50
SZAL Artyom Levshunov/499 2.50 6.00
SZAR Aku Raty/699 1.00 2.50
SZAT Akil Thomas/699 1.00 2.50
SZBB Brendan Brisson/699 1.25 3.00
SZBL Brad Lambert/699 1.25 3.00
SZBN Bradly Nadeau/699 1.50 4.00
SZBR Justin Brazeau/699 1.00 2.50
SZCE Macklin Celebrini/499 8.00 20.00
SZCG Collin Graf/699 1.00 2.50
SZCT Cutter Gauthier/499 2.50 6.00
SZED Ethan Del Mastro/699 1.00 2.50
SZFN Frank Nazar/699 3.00 8.00
SZGB Gavin Brindley/699 1.00 2.50
SZGC Graeme Clarke/699 1.00 2.50
SZGG Gage Goncalves/699 1.25 3.00
SZJB Jackson Blake/699 1.00 2.50
SZJD Josh Doan/699 1.50 4.00
SZJR Joshua Roy/699 1.50 4.00
SZKM Kyle MacLean/699 1.00 2.50
SZLC Lukas Cormier/699 1.00 2.50
SZLD Luca Del Bel Belluz/699 1.00 2.50
SZLH Lane Hutson/699 5.00 12.00
SZLM Logan Morrison/699 1.00 2.50
SZLO Liam Ohgren/699 2.00 5.00
SZLS Landon Slaggert/699 1.00 2.50
SZMB Mavrik Bourque/699 2.00 5.00
SZMC Maxwell Crozier/699 1.00 2.50
SZMI Matvei Michkov/499 12.00 30.00
SZMK Marat Khusnutdinov/699 1.00 2.50
SZMM Mason Morelli/699 1.00 2.50
SZMO Scott Morrow/699 1.25 3.00
SZMR Marshall Rifai/699 1.00 2.50
SZNC Nikita Chibrikov/699 1.00 2.50
SZOZ Olen Zellweger/499 2.00 5.00
SZRE Matt Rempe/499 2.00 5.00
SZRM Rutger McGroarty/499 2.00 5.00
SZSC Sam Colangelo/699 1.00 2.50
SZSM Shakir Mukhamadullin/699 1.25 3.00
SZST Logan Stankoven/499 2.50 6.00
SZWS Will Smith/499 3.00 8.00
SZZB Zachary Bolduc/499 2.00 5.00
SZZD Zach Dean/699 1.00 2.50
SZZO Zack Ostapchuk/699 1.00 2.50

2024-25 Upper Deck Ice Sub Zero Rookies Gold

*GOLD/24: 2X TO 5X BASIC
SZFN Frank Nazar 100.00 250.00
SZLH Lane Hutson 30.00 80.00

2024-25 Upper Deck Ice Sub Zero Stars

1 William Nylander 2.00 5.00
2 Alex Ovechkin 4.00 10.00
3 J.T. Miller 1.25 3.00
4 Nikita Kucherov 2.00 5.00
5 Connor Bedard 3.00 8.00
6 Sidney Crosby 4.00 10.00
7 Artemi Panarin 2.00 5.00
8 Jack Hughes 2.50 6.00
9 Leon Draisaitl 3.00 8.00
10 Filip Forsberg 1.50 4.00
11 Kirill Kaprizov 3.00 8.00
12 Matthew Tkachuk 2.00 5.00
13 Connor Hellebuyck 2.00 5.00
14 Connor McDavid 5.00 12.00
15 Sam Reinhart 2.00 5.00
16 David Pastrnak 2.50 6.00
17 Cale Makar 2.50 6.00
18 Steven Stamkos 2.00 5.00
19 Nathan MacKinnon 4.00 10.00
20 Thomas Harley 1.25 3.00
21 Jack Eichel 1.50 4.00
22 Sebastian Aho 1.50 4.00
23 Quinn Hughes 2.50 6.00
24 Mikko Rantanen 2.50 6.00
25 Auston Matthews 4.00 10.00

2024-25 Upper Deck Ice World Junior Championship

WJC1 Logan Stankoven 4.00 10.00
WJC2 Dylan Guenther 2.00 5.00
WJC3 Shane Wright 2.00 5.00
WJC4 Connor Bedard 5.00 12.00
WJC5 Adam Fantilli 2.50 6.00
WJC6 Zack Ostapchuk 1.25 3.00
WJC7 Olen Zellweger 3.00 8.00
WJC8 Brandt Clarke 1.50 4.00
WJC9 Ethan Del Mastro 1.50 4.00
WJC10 Kevin Korchinski 1.25 3.00
WJC11 Zach Dean 1.50 4.00
WJC12 Owen Beck 1.25 3.00
WJC13 Matthew Poitras 1.50 4.00
WJC14 Joshua Roy 2.50 6.00
WJC15 Fraser Minten 1.50 4.00
WJC16 Matt Savoie 1.50 4.00
WJC17 Tyson Foerster 1.50 4.00
WJC18 Will Cuylle 1.25 3.00
WJC19 Ridly Greig 1.25 3.00
WJC20 Mason McTavish 1.50 4.00

2001-02 Upper Deck Legends

COMPLETE SET (100) 25.00 50.00
1 Bobby Orr 1.25 3.00
2 Eddie Shore .40 1.00
3 Phil Esposito .60 1.50
4 Johnny Bucyk .30 .75
5 Cam Neely .40 1.00
6 Gerry Cheevers .40 1.00
7 Gilbert Perreault .30 .75
8 Rene Robert .10 .25
9 Lanny McDonald .30 .75
10 Al Secord .10 .25
11 Bobby Hull .75 2.00
12 Glenn Hall .40 1.00
13 Stan Mikita .40 1.00
14 Tony Esposito .40 1.00
15 Gordie Howe 1.25 3.00
16 Terry Sawchuk .60 1.50
17 Ted Lindsay .40 1.00
18 Sid Abel .10 .25
19 Red Kelly .40 1.00
20 Alex Delvecchio .40 1.00
21 Glenn Anderson .10 .25
22 Wayne Gretzky 1.50 4.00
23 Jari Kurri .30 .75
24 Grant Fuhr .30 .75
25 Bill Ranford .30 .75
26 Gordie Howe 1.25 3.00
27 Marcel Dionne .30 .75
28 Butch Goring .15 .40
29 Rogie Vachon .15 .40
30 Maurice Richard .75 2.00
31 Jean Beliveau .40 1.00
32 Serge Savard .40 1.00
33 Jacques Plante .60 1.50
34 Guy Lafleur .40 1.00
35 Yvan Cournoyer .40 1.00
36 Steve Shutt .10 .25
37 Rick Green .10 .25
38 Henri Richard .40 1.00
39 Bernie Geoffrion .40 1.00
40 Guy Lapointe .10 .25
41 Denis Potvin .30 .75
42 Mike Bossy .30 .75
43 Bryan Trottier .30 .75
44 Clark Gillies .10 .25
45 Billy Smith .30 .75
46 Ed Giacomin .40 1.00
47 Jean Ratelle .10 .25
48 Lester Patrick .10 .25
49 William Jennings .10 .25
50 Ray Bourque .75 2.00
51 Frank Calder .10 .25
52 Andy van Hellemond .10 .25
53 Bobby Clarke .30 .75
54 Bernie Parent .40 1.00
55 Bill Barber .10 .25
56 Syl Apps .10 .25
57 Bernie Federko .10 .25
58 Frank Mahovlich .40 1.00
59 Darryl Sittler .40 1.00
60 Tim Horton .40 1.00
61 Rick Vaive .10 .25
62 Frank Selke .10 .25
63 Conn Smythe .10 .25
64 King Clancy .10 .25
65 Tony Tanti .10 .25
66 Mike Ridley .10 .25
67 Rod Langway .10 .25
68 Mike Gartner .30 .75
69 Kent Nilsson .10 .25
70 Reggie Leach .10 .25
71 Dennis Maruk .10 .25
72 Wilf Paiement .10 .25
73 Barry Beck .10 .25
74 Simon Nolet .10 .25
75 Don Beaupre .10 .25
76 Peter Stastny .30 .75
77 Michel Goulet .30 .75
78 Dale Hawerchuk .30 .75
79 Gerry Cheevers .40 1.00
80 Glenn Hall .40 1.00
81 Terry Sawchuk .60 1.50
82 Grant Fuhr .30 .75
83 Bernie Parent .40 1.00
84 Jacques Plante .60 1.50
85 Ed Giacomin .40 1.00
86 Bill Ranford .30 .75
87 Billy Smith .30 .75
88 Tony Esposito .40 1.00
89 Bobby Orr 1.25 3.00
90 Bobby Hull .75 2.00
91 Gordie Howe 1.25 3.00
92 Wayne Gretzky 1.50 4.00
93 Marcel Dionne .30 .75
94 Maurice Richard .75 2.00
95 Guy Lafleur .50 1.25
96 Mike Bossy .30 .75
97 Jari Kurri .30 .75
98 Mike Gartner .40 1.00
99 Gordie Howe CL .60 1.50
100 Wayne Gretzky CL .75 2.00

2001-02 Upper Deck Legends Epic Signatures

AD Alex Delvecchio 12.50 30.00
BC Bobby Clarke 12.50 30.00
BH Bobby Hull 10.00 25.00
BO Bobby Orr 100.00 200.00
BT Bryan Trottier 10.00 25.00
CN Cam Neely 12.00 30.00
FM Frank Mahovlich 12.50 30.00
GH Gordie Howe 60.00 150.00
GL Guy Lafleur 15.00 40.00
GP Gilbert Perreault 12.50 30.00
JB Jean Beliveau 25.00 50.00
MB Mike Bossy 12.50 30.00
MD Marcel Dionne 10.00 25.00
PE Phil Esposito 12.50 30.00
SM Stan Mikita 10.00 25.00
TE Tony Esposito 15.00 40.00
TL Ted Lindsay 12.50 30.00
WG Wayne Gretzky 250.00 600.00

2001-02 Upper Deck Legends Fiorentino Collection

COMPLETE SET (15) 40.00 80.00
FCBC Bobby Clarke 1.50 4.00
FCBH Bobby Hull 2.50 6.00
FCBO Bobby Orr 6.00 15.00
FCBT Bryan Trottier 1.50 4.00
FCGH Gordie Howe 3.00 8.00
FCGL Guy Lafleur 1.50 4.00
FCJP Jacques Plante 1.50 4.00
FCMB Mike Bossy 1.50 4.00
FCMD Marcel Dionne 1.50 4.00
FCMR Maurice Richard 3.00 8.00
FCPE Phil Esposito 1.50 4.00
FCSM Stan Mikita 1.50 4.00
FCTE Tony Esposito 1.50 4.00
FCTS Terry Sawchuk 1.50 4.00
FCWG Wayne Gretzky 6.00 15.00

2001-02 Upper Deck Legends Timeless Tributes Jerseys

*PLATINUM/100: .5X TO 1.2X BASIC JSY
TTBB Bill Barber 5.00 12.00
TTBH Bobby Hull 10.00 25.00
TTBR Bill Ranford 5.00 12.00
TTBS Billy Smith 5.00 12.00
TTBT Bryan Trottier 5.00 12.00
TTCG Clark Gillies 5.00 12.00
TTCN Cam Neely 12.50 30.00
TTDP Denis Potvin 5.00 12.00
TTFL Guy Lafleur Que. 5.00 12.00
TTGC Gerry Cheevers 5.00 12.00
TTGH Gordie Howe 12.50 30.00
TTGL Guy Lafleur AS 5.00 12.00
TTGP Gilbert Perreault 5.00 12.00
TTGU Guy Lafleur Mon/Que 10.00 25.00
TTGY Guy Lafleur NY/AS 12.50 30.00
TTHM B.Hull/S.Mikita 12.50 30.00
TTLA Guy Lafleur Mon. 5.00 12.00
TTLF Guy Lafleur NY 5.00 12.00
TTMG Mike Gartner 5.00 12.00
TTPE Phil Esposito 6.00 15.00
TTSL S.Shutt/G.Lafleur 10.00 25.00
TTSM Stan Mikita 5.00 12.00
TTSS Steve Shutt 5.00 12.00
TTST B.Smith/B.Trottier 12.50 30.00
TTVH Andy van Hellemond 5.00 12.00
TTWG Wayne Gretzky 15.00 40.00

2001-02 Upper Deck Legends Milestones Jerseys

MBB Bill Barber 6.00 15.00
MBC Bobby Clarke 8.00 20.00
MBS Brent Sutter 6.00 15.00
MBT Bryan Trottier 6.00 15.00
MCN Cam Neely 6.00 15.00
MDP Denis Potvin 6.00 15.00
MGP Gilbert Perreault 6.00 15.00
MLM Lanny McDonald 6.00 15.00
MMB Mike Bossy 6.00 15.00
MMG Mike Gartner 6.00 15.00
MNB Neal Broten 6.00 15.00
MSS Steve Shutt 6.00 15.00
MSY Steve Yzerman 8.00 20.00
MWG Wayne Gretzky 20.00 40.00

2001-02 Upper Deck Legends Pieces of History Sticks

PHBC Bobby Clarke 12.50 30.00
PHBH Bobby Hull 12.50 30.00
PHBO Bobby Orr 25.00 60.00
PHBS Billy Smith 8.00 20.00
PHBT Bryan Trottier 10.00 25.00
PHDP Denis Potvin 8.00 20.00
PHDS Darryl Sittler 8.00 20.00
PHES Phil Esposito 10.00 25.00
PHFM Frank Mahovlich 8.00 20.00
PHGC Gerry Cheevers 10.00 25.00
PHGH Gordie Howe Det. 15.00 40.00
PHGL Guy Lafleur 8.00 20.00
PHGR Wayne Gretzky LA 40.00 100.00
PHHU Bobby Hull 10.00 25.00
PHJB Jean Beliveau 15.00 40.00
PHJK Jari Kurri 15.00 40.00
PHJP Jacques Plante 15.00 40.00
PHJR Jean Ratelle 8.00 20.00
PHMB Mike Bossy 10.00 25.00
PHMD Marcel Dionne 8.00 20.00
PHMG Mike Gartner 8.00 20.00
PHMH Gordie Howe NE 15.00 40.00
PHMR Maurice Richard 30.00 80.00
PHPE Phil Esposito 10.00 25.00
PHRA Ray Bourque Col. 15.00 40.00
PHRB Ray Bourque Bos. 12.50 30.00
PHSM Stan Mikita 10.00 25.00
PHTE Tony Esposito 10.00 25.00
PHWG Wayne Gretzky Edm. 50.00 100.00

2000-01 Upper Deck Legends

1 Paul Kariya .20 .50
2 Teemu Selanne .40 1.00
3 P.Kariya/T.Selanne .40 1.00
4 Patrik Stefan .15 .40
5 P.Stefan/D.Rhodes .15 .40
6 Bobby Orr .75 2.00
7 Phil Esposito .30 .75
8 Johnny Bucyk .20 .50
9 Cam Neely .20 .50
10 Eddie Shore .20 .50
11 Joe Thornton .30 .75
12 Sergei Samsonov .15 .40
13 C.Neely/J.Thornton .30 .75
14 Gilbert Perreault .20 .50
15 Pat LaFontaine .20 .50
16 Dominik Hasek .30 .75
17 Doug Gilmour .25 .60
18 G.Perreault/D.Hasek .30 .75
19 Lanny McDonald .15 .40
20 Valeri Bure .15 .40
21 T.Fleury/V.Bure .25 .60

22 Ron Francis .25 .60
23 Arturs Irbe .15 .40
24 R.Francis/A.Irbe .25 .60
25 Bobby Hull .40 1.00
26 Stan Mikita .25 .60
27 Tony Esposito .20 .50
28 Glenn Hall .20 .50
29 Tony Amonte .15 .40
30 B.Hull/T.Amonte .40 1.00
31 Patrick Roy .50 1.25
32 Ray Bourque .30 .75
33 Chris Drury .15 .40
34 Peter Forsberg .40 1.00
35 Milan Hejduk .15 .40
36 P.Roy/P.Forsberg .50 1.25
37 Brett Hull .40 1.00
38 Ed Belfour .20 .50
39 Mike Modano .30 .75
40 M.Modano/E.Belfour .30 .75
41 Gordie Howe .60 1.50
42 Ted Lindsay .20 .50
43 Terry Sawchuk .30 .75
44 Brendan Shanahan .20 .50
45 Chris Osgood .20 .50
46 Steve Yzerman .50 1.25
47 G.Howe/S.Yzerman .60 1.50
48 Grant Fuhr .30 .75
49 Wayne Gretzky 1.25 3.00
50 Jari Kurri .20 .50
51 Mark Messier .40 1.00
52 Paul Coffey .20 .50
53 Doug Weight .20 .50
54 W.Gretzky/D.Weight 1.25 3.00
55 Pavel Bure .20 .50
56 Viktor Kozlov .15 .40
57 Vanbiesbrouck/Bure .20 .50
58 Marcel Dionne .25 .60
59 Zigmund Palffy .20 .50
60 Luc Robitaille .20 .50
61 Gretzky/L.Robitaille 1.25 3.00
62 Dino Ciccarelli .20 .50
63 Saku Koivu .20 .50
64 Jean Beliveau .25 .60
65 Doug Harvey .20 .50
66 Jacques Plante .20 .50
67 Guy Lafleur .25 .60
68 Serge Savard .20 .50
69 Larry Robinson .20 .50
70 Eric Weinrich .12 .30
71 Bernie Geoffrion .20 .50
72 Jose Theodore .20 .50
73 G.Lafleur/P.Roy .50 1.25
74 David Legwand .20 .50
75 D.Legwand/M.Dunham .20 .50
76 Martin Brodeur .50 1.25
77 Scott Gomez .15 .40
78 Scott Stevens .20 .50
79 S.Stevens/M.Brodeur .50 1.25
80 Denis Potvin .20 .50
81 Mike Bossy .20 .50
82 Bryan Trottier .20 .50
83 Butch Goring .12 .30
84 Bob Nystrom .15 .40
85 Chico Resch .12 .30
86 Clark Gilles .20 .50
87 Tim Connolly .12 .30
88 B.Trottier/T.Connolly .20 .50
89 Ed Giacomin .15 .40
90 Rod Gilbert .20 .50
91 Theo Fleury .25 .60
92 M.Messier/B.Leetch .40 1.00
93 Marian Hossa .20 .50
94 Radek Bonk .15 .40
95 R.Bonk/M.Hossa .20 .50
96 Bobby Clarke .30 .75
97 Bernie Parent .25 .60
98 Eric Lindros .30 .75
99 Brian Boucher .15 .40
100 John LeClair .20 .50
101 B.Clarke/J.LeClair .30 .75
102 Jeremy Roenick .30 .75
103 Keith Tkachuk .20 .50
104 J.Roenick/K.Tkachuk .30 .75
105 Mario Lemieux .75 2.00
106 Joe Mullen .15 .40
107 Jaromir Jagr .60 1.50
108 M.Lemieux/J.Jagr .75 2.00
109 Peter Stastny .15 .40
110 Michel Goulet .15 .40
111 Steve Shields .12 .30
112 Jeff Friesen .12 .30
113 O.Nolan/J.Friesen .20 .50
114 Bernie Federko .15 .40
115 Chris Pronger .20 .50
116 Roman Turek .15 .40
117 B.Hull/P.Demitra .40 1.00
118 Vincent Lecavalier .20 .50
119 V.Lecavalier/P.Mara .20 .50
120 Frank Mahovlich .20 .50
121 Syl Apps .15 .40
122 Tim Horton .20 .50
123 Eddie Shack .20 .50
124 Curtis Joseph .25 .60
125 Mats Sundin .20 .50
126 F.Mahovlich/C.Joseph .25 .60
127 Richard Brodeur .15 .40
128 R.Brodeur/M.Naslund .20 .50
129 Mike Gartner .25 .60
130 Adam Oates .20 .50
131 Olaf Kolzig .20 .50
132 M.Gartner/O.Kolzig .25 .60
133 Dale Hawerchuk .25 .60
134 Wayne Gretzky CL 1.25 3.00
135 Steve Yzerman CL .50 1.25

2000-01 Upper Deck Legends Enshrined Stars

COMPLETE SET (15) 30.00 60.00
ES1 Wayne Gretzky 6.00 15.00
ES2 Gordie Howe 4.00 10.00
ES3 Mario Lemieux 5.00 12.00
ES4 Bobby Hull 2.50 6.00
ES5 Marcel Dionne 1.50 4.00
ES6 Denis Potvin 1.50 4.00
ES7 Guy Lafleur 2.00 5.00
ES8 Mike Bossy 1.50 4.00
ES9 Bobby Clarke 1.50 4.00
ES10 Frank Mahovlich 1.50 4.00
ES11 Gilbert Perreault 1.50 4.00
ES12 Phil Esposito 2.50 6.00
ES13 Tony Esposito 2.00 5.00
ES14 Stan Mikita 2.00 5.00
ES15 Ted Lindsay 1.50 4.00

2000-01 Upper Deck Legends Epic Signatures

BC Bobby Clarke 10.00 25.00
BG Bernie Geoffrion 20.00 50.00
BH Brett Hull 15.00 40.00
BO Bobby Orr 60.00 150.00
BT Bryan Trottier 10.00 25.00
CJ Curtis Joseph 8.00 20.00
CN Cam Neely 12.00 30.00
DH Dale Hawerchuk 8.00 20.00
DP Denis Potvin 6.00 15.00
FM Frank Mahovlich 12.00 30.00
GH Gordie Howe 80.00 200.00
GL Guy Lafleur 15.00 40.00
GP Gilbert Perreault 8.00 20.00
JB John Bucyk 6.00 15.00
JK Jari Kurri 8.00 20.00
JL John LeClair 5.00 12.00
JM Joe Mullen 8.00 20.00
JN Joe Nieuwendyk 12.00 30.00
JT Joe Thornton 8.00 20.00
KT Keith Tkachuk 6.00 15.00
LM Lanny McDonald 8.00 20.00
LR Larry Robinson 6.00 15.00
MB Mike Bossy 8.00 20.00
MD Marcel Dionne 6.00 15.00
MG Mike Gartner 8.00 20.00
ML Mario Lemieux 50.00 120.00
MM Mark Messier 30.00 80.00
PB Pavel Bure 15.00 40.00
PE Phil Esposito 15.00 40.00
PL Pat LaFontaine 8.00 20.00
PS Patrik Stefan 6.00 15.00
PV Pat Verbeek 8.00 20.00
SF Sergei Fedorov 40.00 100.00
SM Stan Mikita 15.00 40.00
SS Sergei Samsonov 5.00 12.00
SY Steve Yzerman 40.00 100.00
TE Tony Esposito 8.00 20.00
TL Ted Lindsay 8.00 20.00
WG Wayne Gretzky 150.00 400.00
BHU Bobby Hull 20.00 50.00
JBE Jean Beliveau 20.00 50.00
MBR Martin Brodeur 25.00 60.00
MGO Michel Goulet 6.00 15.00
PBO Peter Bondra 8.00 20.00

2000-01 Upper Deck Legends Essence of the Game

COMPLETE SET (8) 30.00 60.00
EG1 G.Lafleur/P.Kariya 1.50 4.00
EG2 J.Jagr/W.Gretzky 4.00 10.00
EG3 P.Bure/M.Bossy 1.50 4.00
EG4 P.Roy/T.Sawchuk 5.00 12.00
EG5 M.Brodeur/B.Parent 2.50 6.00
EG6 C.Neely/B.Shanahan 1.50 4.00
EG7 R.Bourque/B.Orr 5.00 12.00
EG8 S.Yzerman/G.Howe 5.00 12.00

2000-01 Upper Deck Legends Legendary Collection Bronze

*BRONZE/25: 20X TO 50X BASIC CARDS

2000-01 Upper Deck Legends Legendary Collection Gold

*GOLD/375: 4X TO 10X BASIC CARDS

2000-01 Upper Deck Legends Legendary Collection Silver

*SILVER/100: 6X TO 15X BASIC CARDS

2000-01 Upper Deck Legends Legendary Game Jerseys

JAM Al MacInnis 5.00 12.00
JBG Butch Goring 2.50 6.00
JBH Brett Hull 8.00 20.00
JBN Bob Nystrom 3.00 8.00
JBO Bobby Orr SP 25.00 60.00
JBT Bryan Trottier 4.00 10.00
JCG Clark Gillies 4.00 10.00
JCR Chico Resch 2.50 6.00
JDG Doug Gilmour 5.00 12.00
JDH Dominik Hasek 6.00 15.00
JDP Denis Potvin 4.00 10.00
JGF Grant Fuhr SP 6.00 15.00
JGH Gordie Howe 12.00 30.00
JJJ Jaromir Jagr 12.00 30.00
JJK Jari Kurri SP 4.00 10.00
JJL John LeClair 4.00 10.00
JJS Joe Sakic 8.00 20.00
JKT Keith Tkachuk 4.00 10.00
JLR Larry Robinson SP 4.00 10.00
JMB Mike Bossy 4.00 10.00
JMD Marcel Dionne SP 5.00 12.00
JMG Mike Gartner 5.00 12.00
JML Mario Lemieux 15.00 40.00
JMM Mike Modano 6.00 15.00
JMS Mats Sundin 4.00 10.00
JPB Pavel Bure 4.00 10.00
JPF Peter Forsberg 8.00 20.00
JPK Paul Kariya 4.00 10.00
JPL Pat LaFontaine 4.00 10.00
JPR Patrick Roy 10.00 25.00
JRB Ray Bourque 6.00 15.00
JSF Sergei Fedorov 4.00 10.00
JSY Steve Yzerman 10.00 25.00
JTS Teemu Selanne 8.00 20.00
JWG Wayne Gretzky 25.00 60.00
JMBR Martin Brodeur 12.00 30.00

2000-01 Upper Deck Legends of the Cage

COMPLETE SET (10) 20.00 40.00
LC1 Patrick Roy 5.00 12.00
LC2 Martin Brodeur 3.00 8.00
LC3 Dominik Hasek 2.50 6.00
LC4 Curtis Joseph 1.25 3.00
LC5 Ed Belfour 1.50 4.00
LC6 Grant Fuhr 1.25 3.00
LC7 Mike Richter 1.25 3.00
LC8 Jacques Plante 1.50 4.00
LC9 Terry Sawchuk 2.50 6.00
LC10 Tony Esposito 2.00 5.00

2000-01 Upper Deck Legends Playoff Heroes

COMPLETE SET (12) 30.00 60.00
PH1 Patrick Roy 5.00 12.00
PH2 Steve Yzerman 5.00 12.00
PH3 Jaromir Jagr 1.50 4.00
PH4 Mike Modano 2.00 5.00
PH5 Peter Forsberg 2.50 6.00
PH6 Mark Messier 1.50 4.00
PH7 Wayne Gretzky 6.00 15.00
PH8 Brett Hull 1.50 4.00
PH9 Gordie Howe 4.00 10.00
PH10 Bobby Hull 2.50 6.00
PH11 Bryan Trottier 1.50 4.00
PH12 Phil Esposito 2.50 6.00

2000-01 Upper Deck Legends Supreme Milestones

COMPLETE SET (15) 25.00 50.00
SM1 Wayne Gretzky 4.00 10.00
SM2 Gordie Howe 2.50 6.00
SM3 Bobby Hull 1.50 4.00
SM4 Wayne Gretzky 4.00 10.00
SM5 Steve Yzerman 2.00 5.00
SM6 Brett Hull .75 2.00
SM7 Joe Sakic 1.25 3.00
SM8 Mark Messier .75 2.00
SM9 Patrick Roy 3.00 8.00
SM10 Luc Robitaille .75 2.00
SM11 Mario Lemieux 3.00 8.00
SM12 Mike Bossy 1.00 2.50
SM13 Phil Esposito 1.50 4.00
SM14 Tony Esposito 1.25 3.00
SM15 Ray Bourque 2.00 5.00

2014-15 Upper Deck Memorable Moments Spring Expo

MMCM1 Connor McDavid 15.00 25.00

2008-09 Upper Deck Montreal Canadiens Centennial

COMPLETE SET (300) 125.00 250.00
COMP.SET w/o SPs (200) 30.00 80.00
1 Toe Blake .20 .50
2 Jean Beliveau .30 .75
3 Donnie Marshall .20 .50
4 Bill Nyrop .20 .50
5 Mickey Redmond .20 .50
6 Yvan Cournoyer .30 .75
7 Dick Duff .25 .60
8 Ken Dryden .60 1.50
9 Bill Durnan .30 .75
10 Bob Gainey .30 .75
11 Herb Gardiner .20 .50
12 Bernard Geoffrion .20 .50
13 George Hainsworth .40 1.00
14 Doug Harvey .20 .50
15 Tom Johnson .25 .60
16 Aurele Joliat .30 .75
17 Elmer Lach .25 .60
18 Guy Lafleur .40 1.00
19 Newsy Lalonde .25 .60
20 Rod Langway .25 .60
21 Jacques Laperriere .20 .50
22 Guy Lapointe .20 .50
23 Jack Laviolette .25 .60
24 Jacques Lemaire .25 .60
25 Frank Mahovlich .30 .75
26 Joe Malone .25 .60
27 Sylvio Mantha .25 .60
28 Dickie Moore .25 .60
29 Howie Morenz .20 .50
30 Buddy O'Connor .20 .50
31 Bert Olmstead .25 .60
32 Didier Pitre .20 .50
33 Jacques Plante .50 1.25
34 Ken Reardon .20 .50
35 Henri Richard .40 1.00
36 Larry Robinson .20 .50
37 Maurice Richard .60 1.50
38 Mark Recchi .40 1.00
39 Patrick Roy .75 2.00
40 Denis Savard .30 .75
41 Serge Savard .20 .50
42 Albert Siebert .25 .60
43 Steve Shutt .30 .75
44 Georges Vezina .50 1.25
45 Butch Bouchard .40 1.00
46 Chris Nilan .20 .50
47 Doug Jarvis .20 .50
48 Pete Mahovlich .40 1.00
49 Mats Naslund .20 .50
50 Claude Provost .20 .50
51 Pierre Mondou .20 .50
52 Craig Ludwig .20 .50
53 Karl Dykhuis .20 .50
54 Ken Mosdell .20 .50
55 Georges Mantha .20 .50
56 Mark Napier .30 .75
57 Peter Popovic .20 .50
58 Vladimir Malakhov .20 .50
59 Cliff Goupille .20 .50
60 Lyle Odelein .20 .50
61 Ted Harris .20 .50
62 Gerry McNeil .20 .50
63 Murph Chamberlain .20 .50
64 Mike McPhee .20 .50
65 Andre Pronovost .20 .50
66 Kirk Muller .25 .60
67 Scott Thornton .20 .50
68 Keith Acton .20 .50
69 Brian Engblom .20 .50
70 Ralph Backstrom .20 .50
71 John Ambrose O'Brien .25 .60
72 Marcel Bonin .30 .75
73 Pierre Bouchard .30 .75
74 Armand Mondou .20 .50
75 Benoit Brunet .20 .50
76 Valeri Bure .20 .50
77 Walter Buswell .20 .50
78 Guy Carbonneau .30 .75
79 Albert LeDuc .25 .60
80 Chris Chelios .30 .75
81 Sprague Cleghorn .50 1.25
82 Bob Fillion .20 .50
83 Shayne Corson .25 .60
84 Russ Courtnall .20 .50
85 Billy Coutu .25 .60
86 Wilf Cude .40 1.00
87 Floyd Curry .20 .50
88 Leo Lamoureux .25 .60
89 Jean-Jacques Daigneault .25 .60
90 Vincent Damphousse .25 .60
91 Lorne Worsley .25 .60
92 Dave Balon .20 .50
93 Eric Desjardins .25 .60
94 Patrick Poulin .20 .50
95 John Ferguson .20 .50
96 Johnny Gagnon .20 .50
97 James Gardner .20 .50
98 Ray Getliffe .20 .50
99 Brent Gilchrist .25 .60
100 Gaston Gingras .20 .50
101 Phil Goyette .20 .50
102 Rick Green .20 .50
103 Howard McNamara .20 .50
104 Glen Harmon .20 .50
105 Terry Harper .20 .50
106 Bill Hicke .20 .50
107 Charlie Hodge .20 .50
108 Rejean Houle .30 .75
109 Marty Burke .20 .50
110 Joe Juneau .20 .50
111 Mike Keane .25 .60
112 Ab McDonald .25 .60
113 Patrice Brisebois .25 .60
114 Marc Tardif .25 .60
115 Yvon Lambert .30 .75
116 Wildor Larochelle .20 .50
117 Michel Larocque .25 .60
118 Claude Larose .20 .50
119 Pierre Larouche .20 .50
120 Stephan Lebeau .20 .50
121 John LeClair .30 .75
122 Roman Hamrlik .20 .50
123 Claude Lemieux .25 .60
124 Pit Lepine .40 1.00
125 Francis Bouillon .25 .60
126 Billy Reay .20 .50
127 Stephane Richer .25 .60
128 Doug Risebrough .25 .60
129 Craig Rivet .20 .50
130 Jim Roberts .20 .50
131 Bud MacPherson .20 .50
132 Bobby Rousseau .25 .60
133 Martin Rucinsky .20 .50
134 Brian Savage .20 .50
135 Mathieu Schneider .20 .50
136 Brian Skrudland .20 .50
137 Bobby Smith .20 .50
138 Turner Stevenson .20 .50
139 Petr Svoboda .20 .50
140 Jean-Guy Talbot .25 .60
141 Jose Theodore .30 .75
142 Gilles Tremblay .50 1.25
143 Jean-Claude Tremblay .20 .50
144 Mario Tremblay .40 1.00
145 Pierre Turgeon .25 .60
146 Rogie Vachon .40 1.00
147 Ryan Walter .20 .50
148 Paul Meger .20 .50
149 Dick Irvin .20 .50
150 Murray Wilson .30 .75
151 Joe Hall .20 .50
152 William Northey .20 .50
153 Senator Donat Raymond .20 .50
154 Leo Dandurand
Jos Cattarinich
Louis Letourneau .20 .50
155 Hartland De Montarville Molson .20 .50
156 Sam Pollock .20 .50
157 Frank J. Selke .20 .50
158 Tom P. Gorman .20 .50
159 Bob Turner .20 .50
160 Scotty Bowman .30 .75
161 Calum MacKay .20 .50
162 Paul Haynes .20 .50
163 Youppi MASCOT .20 .50
164 Toe Blake .20 .50
165 Oleg Petrov .20 .50
166 Stephane Quintal .20 .50
167 Saku Koivu .30 .75
168 Carey Price .60 1.50
169 Alex Kovalev .20 .50
170 Tomas Plekanec .20 .50
171 Andrei Markov .30 .75
172 Andrei Kostitsyn .25 .60
173 Christopher Higgins .20 .50
174 Rick Chartraw .20 .50
175 Dollard St. Laurent .20 .50
176 Mike Komisarek .20 .50
177 Coupe Stanley Cup .20 .50
178 Coupe Stanley Cup .20 .50
179 Coupe Stanley Cup .20 .50
180 Coupe Stanley Cup .20 .50
181 Coupe Stanley Cup .20 .50
182 Coupe Stanley Cup .20 .50
183 Coupe Stanley Cup .20 .50
184 Coupe Stanley Cup .20 .50
185 Coupe Stanley Cup .20 .50
186 Coupe Stanley Cup .20 .50
187 Coupe Stanley Cup .20 .50
188 Coupe Stanley Cup .20 .50
189 Coupe Stanley Cup .20 .50
190 Coupe Stanley Cup .20 .50
191 Coupe Stanley Cup .20 .50
192 Coupe Stanley Cup .20 .50
193 Coupe Stanley Cup .20 .50
194 Coupe Stanley Cup .20 .50
195 Coupe Stanley Cup .20 .50
196 Coupe Stanley Cup .20 .50
197 Coupe Stanley Cup .20 .50
198 Coupe Stanley Cup .20 .50
199 Coupe Stanley Cup .20 .50
200 Coupe Stanley Cup .20 .50
201 Jack Laviolette 1.50 4.00
202 Newsy Lalonde 1.50 4.00
203 James Gardner 1.25 3.00
204 Howard McNamara 1.25 3.00
205 Sprague Cleghorn 3.00 8.00
206 Billy Coutu 1.25 3.00
207 Sylvio Mantha 1.50 4.00
208 George Hainsworth 2.50 6.00
209 Albert Siebert 1.50 4.00
210 Walter Buswell 1.25 3.00
211 Toe Blake 1.25 3.00
212 Bill Durnan 2.00 5.00
213 Butch Bouchard 2.50 6.00
214 Maurice Richard 4.00 10.00
215 Doug Harvey 2.00 5.00
216 Jean Beliveau 2.00 5.00
217 Henri Richard 2.50 6.00
218 Yvan Cournoyer 2.00 5.00
219 Serge Savard 3.00 8.00
220 Bob Gainey 2.00 5.00
221 Chris Chelios 2.00 5.00
222 Guy Carbonneau 2.00 5.00
223 Kirk Muller 1.50 4.00
224 Mike Keane 1.50 4.00
225 Pierre Turgeon 1.50 4.00
226 Vincent Damphousse 1.50 4.00
227 Saku Koivu 2.00 5.00
228 Arena Jubilee Arena 1.25 3.00
229 Arena Westmount Arena 1.25 3.00
230 Arena Mont-Royal Arena 1.25 3.00
231 Forum - 1924 1.25 3.00
232 Forum - 1949 1.25 3.00
233 Forum - 1949 1.25 3.00
234 Centre Bell Centre 1.25 3.00
235 Henri Richard 2.50 6.00
236 Maurice Richard 4.00 10.00
237 Guy Lafleur 2.50 6.00
238 Guy Lafleur 2.50 6.00
239 Chris Nilan 1.25 3.00
240 Maurice Richard 4.00 10.00
241 Jacques Plante 3.00 8.00
242 George Hainsworth 2.50 6.00
243 Larry Robinson 2.00 5.00
244 Henri Richard 2.50 6.00
245 Jean Beliveau 2.00 5.00
246 Jacques Plante 3.00 8.00
247 George Hainsworth 2.50 6.00
248 Henri Richard 2.50 6.00
249 Maurice Richard 4.00 10.00
250 Guy Lafleur 2.50 6.00
251 Newsy Lalonde 1.50 4.00
252 Howie Morenz 2.00 5.00
253 Toe Blake 1.25 3.00
254 Elmer Lach 1.50 4.00
255 Bernard Geoffrion 1.25 3.00
256 Guy Lafleur 2.50 6.00
257 Ken Dryden 4.00 10.00
258 Doug Harvey 2.00 5.00
259 Guy Carbonneau 2.00 5.00
260 Jacques Plante 3.00 8.00
261 Jean Beliveau 2.00 5.00
262 Bob Gainey 2.00 5.00
263 Bill Durnan 2.00 5.00
264 George Hainsworth 2.50 6.00
265 Dickie Moore 1.50 4.00
266 Jacques Laperriere 1.50 4.00
267 Michel Larocque 1.50 4.00
268 Serge Savard 3.00 8.00
269 Charlie Hodge 1.50 4.00
270 Lorne Worsley 1.50 4.00
271 Patrick Roy 5.00 12.00
272 Larry Robinson 2.00 5.00
273 Jacques Plante 3.00 8.00
274 Doug Harvey 2.00 5.00
275 Jean Beliveau 2.00 5.00
276 Bernard Geoffrion 1.25 3.00
277 Howie Morenz 2.00 5.00
278 Maurice Richard 4.00 10.00
279 Guy Lafleur 2.50 6.00
280 Dickie Moore 1.50 4.00
281 Yvan Cournoyer 2.00 5.00
282 Henri Richard 2.50 6.00
283 Serge Savard 3.00 8.00
284 Larry Robinson 2.00 5.00
285 Ken Dryden 4.00 10.00
286 Bob Gainey 2.00 5.00
287 Georges Vezina 3.00 8.00
288 Howie Morenz 1.25 3.00
289 Jean Beliveau 2.00 5.00
290 Maurice Richard 4.00 10.00
291 Elmer Lach 1.50 4.00
292 Jacques Plante 3.00 8.00
293 Bernard Geoffrion 1.25 3.00
294 Henri Richard 2.50 6.00
295 Guy Lafleur 2.50 6.00
296 Bob Gainey 2.00 5.00
297 Patrick Roy 5.00 12.00
298 Guy Carbonneau 2.00 5.00
299 Maurice Richard 4.00 10.00
300 Saku Koivu 2.00 5.00

2008-09 Upper Deck Montreal Canadiens Centennial Parallel 100

*PARALLEL (1-200): 10X TO 25X BASIC CARDS
*PARALLEL (201-300): .8X TO 2X BASIC CARDS

2008-09 Upper Deck Montreal Canadiens Centennial AKA Signings

AKAAK Alex Kovalev 100.00 175.00
AKABG Bob Gainey 125.00 200.00
AKACN Chris Nilan 200.00 350.00
AKADD Dick Duff 125.00 200.00
AKADM Dickie Moore 100.00 175.00
AKAGC Guy Carbonneau 175.00 300.00
AKAGL Guy Lafleur 125.00 250.00
AKAHR Henri Richard 150.00 250.00
AKAJB Jean Beliveau 175.00 300.00
AKAJL Jacques Laperriere 150.00 250.00
AKALA Guy Lapointe 150.00 250.00
AKALE Jacques Lemaire 350.00 500.00
AKALR Larry Robinson 125.00 400.00
AKAMT Mario Tremblay 150.00 250.00
AKAPB Patrice Brisebois 175.00 300.00
AKAPR Patrick Roy 350.00 600.00
AKARH Rejean Houle 175.00 400.00
AKASS Serge Savard 350.00 500.00
AKAYC Yvan Cournoyer 150.00 300.00

2008-09 Upper Deck Montreal Canadiens Centennial Habs INKS

HABSAK Alex Kovalev 10.00 25.00
HABSAM Andrei Markov 12.00 30.00
HABSBB Benoit Brunet 15.00 40.00
HABSBG Bob Gainey 40.00 100.00
HABSCH Chris Chelios SP 150.00 300.00
HABSCL Claude Larose 60.00 120.00
HABSCN Chris Nilan SP 100.00 200.00
HABSCP Carey Price 50.00 100.00
HABSDD Dick Duff 75.00 125.00
HABSDJ Doug Jarvis 12.00 30.00
HABSDM Dickie Moore 125.00 200.00
HABSDR Doug Risebrough 25.00 50.00
HABSDS Denis Savard SP 150.00 250.00
HABSED Eric Desjardins 25.00 50.00
HABSFB Francis Bouillon 10.00 25.00
HABSGC Guy Carbonneau 15.00 40.00
HABSGG Gaston Gingras 10.00 25.00
HABSGL Guy Lafleur 60.00 100.00
HABSGT Gilles Tremblay SP 60.00 120.00
HABSHA Roman Hamrlik 10.00 25.00
HABSHI Christopher Higgins 10.00 25.00
HABSHR Henri Richard 40.00 80.00
HABSJB Jean Beliveau SP 200.00 350.00
HABSJD Jean-Jacques Daigneault 20.00 50.00
HABSJL Jacques Laperriere 60.00 120.00
HABSJO John LeClair 25.00 50.00
HABSJT Jean-Guy Talbot SP 50.00 100.00
HABSKA Keith Acton 20.00 40.00
HABSKM Kirk Muller 10.00 25.00
HABSKO Andrei Kostitsyn 10.00 25.00
HABSKS Saku Koivu 12.00 30.00
HABSLA Guy Lapointe SP 100.00 200.00
HABSLE Claude Lemieux 25.00 60.00
HABSLO Lyle Odelein 60.00 120.00
HABSLR Larry Robinson SP 200.00 350.00
HABSMB Marcel Bonin 30.00 60.00
HABSMI Mike Komisarek 8.00 20.00
HABSMN Mark Napier 15.00 40.00
HABSMO Pierre Mondou 15.00 40.00
HABSMT Mario Tremblay 30.00 80.00
HABSMW Murray Wilson 15.00 40.00
HABSPB Patrice Brisebois 10.00 25.00
HABSPG Phil Goyette 50.00 100.00
HABSPI Pierre Bouchard 30.00 60.00
HABSPL Pierre Larouche SP 60.00 120.00
HABSPM Pete Mahovlich 20.00 50.00
HABSPR Patrick Roy 150.00 250.00
HABSPT Pierre Turgeon SP 75.00 150.00
HABSRH Rejean Houle 12.00 30.00
HABSRL Rod Langway SP 250.00 400.00
HABSRV Rogie Vachon 40.00 100.00
HABSSA Brian Savage 12.00 30.00
HABSSB Scotty Bowman SP 400.00 600.00
HABSSH Steve Shutt 10.00 25.00
HABSSK Brian Skrudland 15.00 40.00
HABSSQ Stephane Quintal 8.00 20.00
HABSSR Stephane Richer 25.00 60.00
HABSSS Serge Savard SP 100.00 175.00
HABSTP Tomas Plekanec 10.00 25.00
HABSVD Vincent Damphousse 15.00 40.00
HABSY Youppi MASCOT 12.00 30.00
HABSYC Yvan Cournoyer 25.00 60.00
HABSYI Youppi MASCOT 12.00 30.00
HABSYL Yvon Lambert 15.00 40.00

2008-09 Upper Deck Montreal Canadiens Centennial HOF Induction INKS

HOFBB Butch Bouchard/66 125.00 200.00
HOFBG Bob Gainey/92 90.00 150.00
HOFBO Bert Olmstead/85 90.00 150.00
HOFDD Dick Duff/106 90.00 150.00
HOFDS Denis Savard/100 90.00 150.00
HOFEL Elmer Lach/66 150.00 250.00
HOFGL Guy Lapointe/93 125.00 225.00
HOFGU Guy Lafleur/88 150.00 250.00
HOFHR Henri Richard/79 125.00 250.00
HOFJB Jean Beliveau/72 250.00 450.00
HOFJL Jacques Lemaire/84 100.00 175.00
HOFLA Jacques Laperriere/87 100.00 175.00
HOFLR Larry Robinson/95 100.00 175.00
HOFPR Patrick Roy/106 200.00 350.00
HOFRL Rod Langway/102 100.00 175.00
HOFSA Serge Savard/86 90.00 150.00
HOFSB Scotty Bowman/91 125.00 200.00
HOFSS Steve Shutt/93 100.00 150.00
HOFYC Yvan Cournoyer/82 125.00 200.00

2008-09 Upper Deck Montreal Canadiens Centennial Le Bleu Blanc Rouge Jerseys

LBBRAK Alex Kovalev 6.00 15.00
LBBRAL Alex Kovalev 6.00 15.00
LBBRAM Andrei Markov 8.00 20.00
LBBRBO Francis Bouillon 6.00 15.00
LBBRCH Christopher Higgins 6.00 15.00
LBBRCP Carey Price 15.00 40.00
LBBRFB Francis Bouillon 6.00 15.00
LBBRFR Francis Bouillon 6.00 15.00
LBBRGL Guy Lapointe 8.00 20.00
LBBRHA Roman Hamrlik 5.00 12.00
LBBRKO Andrei Kostitsyn 6.00 15.00
LBBRKV Saku Koivu 8.00 20.00
LBBRMA Andrei Markov 8.00 20.00
LBBRMI Mike Komisarek 8.00 20.00
LBBRMK Mike Komisarek 5.00 12.00
LBBRPB Patrice Brisebois 5.00 12.00
LBBRPL Tomas Plekanec 5.00 12.00
LBBRRH Roman Hamrlik 5.00 12.00
LBBRSK Saku Koivu 8.00 20.00
LBBRTP Tomas Plekanec 5.00 12.00

2008-09 Upper Deck Montreal Canadiens Centennial Mini Banners

COMPLETE SET (24) 350.00 500.00
1 Stanley Cup 1915-16 10.00 25.00
2 Stanley Cup 1923-24 10.00 25.00
3 Stanley Cup 1929-30 10.00 25.00
4 Stanley Cup 1930-31 10.00 25.00
5 Stanley Cup 1943-44 10.00 25.00
6 Stanley Cup 1945-46 10.00 25.00
7 Stanley Cup 1952-53 10.00 25.00
8 Stanley Cup 1955-56 10.00 25.00
9 Stanley Cup 1956-57 10.00 25.00
10 Stanley Cup 1957-58 10.00 25.00
11 Stanley Cup 1958-59 10.00 25.00
12 Stanley Cup 1959-60 10.00 25.00
13 Stanley Cup 1964-65 10.00 25.00
14 Stanley Cup 1965-66 10.00 25.00
15 Stanley Cup 1967-68 10.00 25.00
16 Stanley Cup 1968-69 10.00 25.00
17 Stanley Cup 1970-71 10.00 25.00
18 Stanley Cup 1972-73 10.00 25.00
19 Stanley Cup 1975-76 10.00 25.00
20 Stanley Cup 1976-77 10.00 25.00
21 Stanley Cup 1977-78 10.00 25.00
22 Stanley Cup 1978-79 10.00 25.00
23 Stanley Cup 1985-86 10.00 25.00
24 Stanley Cup 1992-93 10.00 25.00

2008-09 Upper Deck Montreal Canadiens Centennial Signatures Dual

AA A.Kostitsyn/A.Kovalev 75.00 150.00
BB B.Bouchard/P.Bouchard 100.00 200.00
BH F.Bouillon/R.Hamrlik 100.00 200.00
BL J.Laperriere/P.Brisebois 60.00 120.00
BS S.Bowman/S.Savard 75.00 150.00
CC Carbonneau/C.Chelios 90.00 150.00
CG B.Gainey/Carbonneau 100.00 175.00
CN C.Lemieux/C.Nilan 60.00 120.00
DL D.Duff/J.Lemaire 15.00 40.00
GA G.Lapointe/A.Markov 25.00 60.00
HL R.Houle/Y.Lambert 75.00 150.00
HM K.Muller/C.Higgins 15.00 40.00
HR R.Houle/D.Risebrough 20.00 50.00
JG B.Gainey/D.Jarvis 75.00 150.00
JR D.Jarvis/D.Risebrough 60.00 120.00
KB J.Beliveau/S.Koivu 40.00 80.00
KD Damphousse/S.Koivu 20.00 50.00
KP M.Komisarek/C.Price 100.00 175.00
KS S.Savard/M.Komisarek 30.00 80.00
LK G.Lafleur/A.Kovalev 75.00 150.00
LN P.Larouche/M.Napier 20.00 50.00
LR G.Lafleur/S.Richer 25.00 60.00
MC Y.Cournoyer/D.Moore 20.00 50.00
MD K.Muller/Damphousse 150.00 250.00
MH D.Moore/C.Higgins 20.00 50.00
MP A.Markov/C.Price 125.00 250.00
MT P.Mondou/M.Tremblay 100.00 200.00
ON C.Nilan/L.Odelein 50.00 100.00
PC Cournoyer/Plekanec 150.00 250.00
QB S.Quintal/P.Brisebois 12.00 30.00
RB J.Beliveau/H.Richard 200.00 350.00
RH L.Robinson/R.Hamrlik 20.00 50.00
RL H.Richard/E.Lach 50.00 100.00
TL M.Tremblay/J.Lemaire 40.00 80.00

1998-99 Upper Deck MVP

*SILVER: 1X TO 2.5X BASIC CARDS
*GOLD: 8X TO 20X BASIC CARDS
1 Paul Kariya .12 .30
2 Teemu Selanne .25 .60
3 Tomas Sandstrom .07 .20
4 Johan Davidsson .07 .20
5 Mike Crowley RC .10 .25
6 Guy Hebert .10 .25
7 Marty McInnis .07 .20
8 Steve Rucchin .07 .20
9 Ray Bourque .20 .50
10 Sergei Samsonov .10 .25
11 Cameron Mann .07 .20
12 Joe Thornton .20 .50
13 Jason Allison .10 .25
14 Byron Dafoe .10 .25
15 Kyle McLaren .07 .20
16 Dimitri Khristich .07 .20
17 Hal Gill .07 .20
18 Anson Carter .10 .25
19 Miroslav Satan .10 .25
20 Brian Holzinger .07 .20
21 Dominik Hasek .20 .50
22 Matthew Barnaby .07 .20
23 Erik Rasmussen .07 .20
24 Geoff Sanderson .07 .20
25 Michal Grosek .07 .20
26 Michael Peca .07 .20
27 Rico Fata .10 .25
28 Derek Morris .07 .20
29 Phil Housley .10 .25
30 Valeri Bure .07 .20
31 Ed Ward .07 .20
32 Jean-Sebastien Giguere .10 .25
33 Jeff Shantz .07 .20
34 Jarome Iginla .15 .40
35 Ron Francis .15 .40
36 Trevor Kidd .07 .20
37 Keith Primeau .10 .25
38 Sami Kapanen .07 .20
39 Martin Gelinas .07 .20
40 Jeff O'Neill .07 .20
41 Gary Roberts .07 .20
42 Jocelyn Thibault .10 .25
43 Doug Gilmour .15 .40
44 Chris Chelios .12 .30
45 Tony Amonte .10 .25
46 Bob Probert .12 .30
47 Daniel Cleary .07 .20
48 Eric Daze .10 .25
49 Mike Maneluk RC .10 .25
50 Remi Royer RC .07 .20
51 Peter Forsberg .25 .60
52 Patrick Roy .30 .75
53 Joe Sakic .25 .60
54 Chris Drury .10 .25
55 Milan Hejduk RC .20 .50
56 Greg DeVries .07 .20
57 Theo Fleury .15 .40
58 Adam Deadmarsh .07 .20
59 Brett Hull .25 .60
60 Ed Belfour .12 .30
61 Mike Modano .20 .50
62 Darryl Sydor .07 .20
63 Joe Nieuwendyk .10 .25
64 Grant Marshall .07 .20
65 Sergei Zubov .10 .25
66 Derian Hatcher .07 .20
67 Jere Lehtinen .10 .25
68 Sergei Fedorov .20 .50
69 Steve Yzerman .30 .75
70 Nicklas Lidstrom .15 .40
71 Chris Osgood .10 .25
72 Brendan Shanahan .12 .30
73 Darren McCarty .07 .20
74 Tomas Holmstrom .07 .20
75 Norm Maracle RC .10 .25
76 Doug Brown .07 .20
77 Doug Weight .12 .30
78 Janne Niinimaa .07 .20
79 Tom Poti .07 .20
80 Bill Guerin .12 .30

81 Mike Grier .07 .20
82 Ryan Smyth .10 .25
83 Roman Hamrlik .07 .20
84 Kevin Brown .07 .20
85 Pavel Bure .12 .30
86 Jaroslav Spacek .07 .20
87 Rob Niedermayer .07 .20
88 Robert Svehla .07 .20
89 Ray Whitney .07 .20
90 Peter Worrell RC .10 .25
91 Mark Parrish RC .20 .50
92 Oleg Kvasha RC .12 .30
93 Steve Duchesne .10 .25
94 Rob Blake .12 .30
95 Olli Jokinen .10 .25
96 Donald Audette .07 .20
97 Luc Robitaille .12 .30
98 Josh Green .12 .30
99 Philippe Boucher .07 .20
100 Matt Johnson .07 .20
101 Vincent Damphousse .10 .25
102 Dainius Zubrus .07 .20
103 Terry Ryan .07 .20
104 Saku Koivu .12 .30
105 Brett Clark RC .07 .20
106 Dave Morissette RC .10 .25
107 Eric Weinrich .07 .20
108 Brian Savage .07 .20
109 Shayne Corson .10 .25
110 Mike Dunham .10 .25
111 Greg Johnson .07 .20
112 Cliff Ronning .07 .20
113 Andrew Brunette .10 .25
114 Sergei Krivokrasov .07 .20
115 Sebastien Bordeleau .07 .20
116 Scott Stevens .12 .30
117 Martin Brodeur .30 .75
118 Brendan Morrison .07 .20
119 Patrik Elias .12 .30
120 Scott Niedermayer .12 .30
121 Bobby Holik .07 .20
122 Jason Arnott .10 .25
123 Jay Pandolfo .07 .20
124 Eric Brewer .12 .30
125 Zigmund Palffy .12 .30
126 Felix Potvin .20 .50
127 Robert Reichel .07 .20
128 Mike Watt .07 .20
129 Tommy Salo .10 .25
130 Kenny Jonsson .07 .20
131 Trevor Linden .12 .30
132 Wayne Gretzky .75 2.00
133 Brian Leetch .10 .25
134 Manny Malhotra .12 .30
135 Mike Richter .12 .30
136 Mike Knuble .07 .20
137 Niklas Sundstrom .07 .20
138 Todd Harvey .07 .20
139 Alexei Yashin .10 .25
140 Damian Rhodes .12 .30
141 Daniel Alfredsson .12 .30
142 Magnus Arvedson .07 .20
143 Shawn McEachern .07 .20
144 Chris Phillips .07 .20
145 Vaclav Prospal .07 .20
146 Wade Redden .07 .20
147 Eric Lindros .20 .50
148 John LeClair .12 .30
149 John Vanbiesbrouck .12 .30
150 Keith Jones .07 .20
151 Colin Forbes .07 .20
152 Mark Recchi .15 .40
153 Dan McGillis .07 .20
154 Eric Desjardins .10 .25
155 Rod Brind'Amour .12 .30
156 Keith Tkachuk .12 .30
157 Daniel Briere .10 .25
158 Nikolai Khabibulin .12 .30
159 Brad Isbister .07 .20
160 Jeremy Roenick .20 .50
161 Oleg Tverdovsky .12 .30
162 Rick Tocchet .10 .25
163 Jaromir Jagr .40 1.00
164 Tom Barrasso .10 .25
165 Alexei Morozov .07 .20
166 Robert Dome .07 .20
167 Stu Barnes .07 .20
168 Martin Straka .07 .20
169 German Titov .07 .20
170 Patrick Marleau .12 .30
171 Andrei Zyuzin .07 .20
172 Marco Sturm .07 .20
173 Owen Nolan .12 .30
174 Jeff Friesen .07 .20
175 Bob Rouse .07 .20
176 Mike Vernon .10 .25
177 Mike Ricci .07 .20
178 Marty Reasoner .12 .30
179 Al MacInnis .15 .40
180 Chris Pronger .12 .30
181 Pierre Turgeon .10 .25
182 Michal Handzus RC .15 .40
183 Jim Campbell .07 .20
184 Tony Twist .07 .20
185 Pavol Demitra .15 .40
186 Daren Puppa .10 .25
187 Vincent Lecavalier .25 .60
188 Bill Ranford .10 .25
189 Alexandre Daigle .07 .20
190 Wendel Clark .20 .50
191 Rob Zamuner .07 .20
192 Chris Gratton .10 .25
193 Fredrik Modin .07 .20
194 Curtis Joseph .15 .40
195 Mats Sundin .12 .30
196 Steve Thomas .07 .20
197 Tomas Kaberle RC .15 .40
198 Alyn McCauley .07 .20
199 Mike Johnson .07 .20
200 Bryan Berard .10 .25
201 Mark Messier .25 .60
202 Jason Strudwick RC .12 .30
203 Mattias Ohlund .07 .20
204 Alexander Mogilny .10 .25
205 Bill Muckalt RC .07 .20
206 Ed Jovanovski .10 .25
207 Josh Holden .07 .20
208 Peter Schaefer .07 .20
209 Peter Bondra .12 .30
210 Olaf Kolzig .12 .30
211 Sergei Gonchar .07 .20
212 Adam Oates .12 .30
213 Brian Bellows .10 .25
214 Matt Herr RC .07 .20
215 Richard Zednik .07 .20
216 Joe Juneau .07 .20
217 Jaroslav Svejkovski .07 .20
218 Wayne Gretzky CL .75 2.00
219 Wayne Gretzky CL .75 2.00
220 Wayne Gretzky CL .75 2.00
132A Wayne Gretzky 99 Retires/99 100.00 200.00

1998-99 Upper Deck MVP Super Script

*VETS: 40X TO 100X BASIC CARDS
*ROOKIES: 12X TO 30X BASIC CARDS

1998-99 Upper Deck MVP Dynamics

COMMON GRETZKY (D1-D15) 3.00 8.00

1998-99 Upper Deck MVP Game Souvenirs

BH Brett Hull 12.00 30.00
BS Brendan Shanahan 6.00 15.00
EL Eric Lindros 10.00 25.00
JL John LeClair 6.00 15.00
MM Mike Modano 10.00 25.00
PR Patrick Roy 15.00 40.00
RB Ray Bourque 10.00 25.00
SF Sergei Fedorov 10.00 25.00
SS Sergei Samsonov 5.00 12.00
SY Steve Yzerman 15.00 40.00
VL Vincent Lecavalier 12.00 30.00
WG Wayne Gretzky 40.00 100.00
SYA S.Yzerman AU/19 250.00 500.00
VLA V.Lecavalier AU/14 250.00 500.00

1998-99 Upper Deck MVP OT Heroes

COMPLETE SET (15) 20.00 40.00
OT1 Steve Yzerman 4.00 10.00
OT2 Patrick Roy 4.00 10.00
OT3 Jaromir Jagr 1.25 3.00
OT4 Ray Bourque 1.25 3.00
OT5 Wayne Gretzky 5.00 12.00
OT6 Sergei Samsonov .60 1.50
OT7 Dominik Hasek 1.50 4.00
OT8 Peter Forsberg 2.00 5.00
OT9 Paul Kariya .75 2.00
OT10 Eric Lindros .75 2.00
OT11 Pavel Bure .75 2.00
OT12 Keith Tkachuk .75 2.00
OT13 Brendan Shanahan .75 2.00
OT14 John LeClair .75 2.00
OT15 Joe Sakic 1.50 4.00

1998-99 Upper Deck MVP Power Game

COMPLETE SET (15) 12.00 25.00
PG1 Brendan Shanahan .75 2.00
PG2 Keith Tkachuk .75 2.00
PG3 Eric Lindros .75 2.00
PG4 Mike Modano 1.25 3.00
PG5 Vincent Lecavalier 2.00 5.00
PG6 John LeClair .75 2.00
PG7 Mark Messier .75 2.00
PG8 Mats Sundin .75 2.00
PG9 Peter Forsberg 2.00 5.00
PG10 Jaromir Jagr 1.25 3.00
PG11 Keith Primeau .40 1.00
PG12 Mark Parrish .60 1.50
PG13 Patrick Marleau .40 1.00
PG14 Bill Guerin .60 1.50
PG15 Jeremy Roenick 1.00 2.50

1998-99 Upper Deck MVP ProSign

AM Alyn McCauley 4.00 10.00
BB Brian Bellows 4.00 10.00
BM Brendan Morrison 4.00 10.00
CD Chris Drury 5.00 12.00
DN Dmitri Nabokov 4.00 10.00
DW Doug Weight 5.00 12.00
EB Eric Brewer 4.00 10.00
ER Erik Rasmussen 4.00 10.00
JA Jason Allison 4.00 10.00
JI Jarome Iginla 12.50 30.00
JT Jose Theodore 12.50 30.00
MD Mike Dunham 4.00 10.00
MJ Mike Johnson 4.00 10.00
MM Manny Malhotra 4.00 10.00
MP Mark Parrish 4.00 10.00
OT Oleg Tverdovsky 4.00 10.00
RF Rico Fata 4.00 10.00
RN Rob Niedermayer 4.00 10.00
SY Steve Yzerman 40.00 100.00
VL Vincent Lecavalier 10.00 25.00
WG Wayne Gretzky 250.00 600.00
WR Wade Redden 4.00 10.00
JAR Jason Arnott 4.00 10.00

1998-99 Upper Deck MVP Snipers

COMPLETE SET (12) 10.00 20.00
S1 Vincent Lecavalier 1.00 2.50
S2 Wayne Gretzky 2.50 6.00
S3 Sergei Samsonov .30 .75
S4 Teemu Selanne .40 1.00
S5 Peter Forsberg 1.00 2.50
S6 Paul Kariya .40 1.00
S7 Eric Lindros .40 1.00
S8 Pavel Bure .40 1.00
S9 Peter Bondra .30 .75
S10 Joe Sakic .75 2.00
S11 Steve Yzerman 2.00 5.00
S12 Sergei Fedorov .60 1.50

1998-99 Upper Deck MVP Special Forces

COMPLETE SET (15) 30.00 60.00
F01 Brett Hull 1.25 3.00
F02 Sergei Samsonov .75 2.00
F03 Vincent Lecavalier 2.50 6.00
F04 Dominik Hasek 2.00 5.00
F05 Eric Lindros 1.00 2.50
F06 Paul Kariya 1.00 2.50
F07 Steve Yzerman 5.00 12.00
F08 Brendan Shanahan 1.00 2.50
F09 Martin Brodeur 2.50 6.00
F10 Teemu Selanne 1.00 2.50
F11 Jaromir Jagr 1.50 4.00
F12 Wayne Gretzky 6.00 15.00
F13 Patrick Roy 5.00 12.00
F14 Peter Forsberg 2.50 6.00
F15 Joe Sakic 2.00 5.00

1999-00 Upper Deck MVP

COMPLETE SET (220) 15.00 30.00
1 Wayne Gretzky .75 2.00
2 Damian Rhodes .08 .25
3 Jody Hull .02 .10
4 Paul Kariya .10 .30
5 Teemu Selanne .10 .30
6 Guy Hebert .08 .25
7 Matt Cullen .02 .10
8 Steve Rucchin .08 .25
9 Oleg Tverdovsky .02 .10
10 Johan Davidsson .02 .10
11 Ray Bourque .20 .50
12 Sergei Samsonov .08 .25
13 Joe Thornton .20 .50
14 Anson Carter .08 .25
15 Jason Allison .02 .10
16 Kyle McLaren .02 .10
17 Byron Dafoe .08 .25
18 Shawn Bates .08 .25
19 Jonathan Girard .02 .10
20 Hal Gill .02 .10
21 Dominik Hasek .25 .60
22 Joe Juneau .08 .25
23 Michael Peca .08 .25
24 Cory Sarich .02 .10
25 Martin Biron .08 .25
26 Miroslav Satan .08 .25
27 Dixon Ward .02 .10
28 Michal Grosek .02 .10
29 Valeri Bure .02 .10
30 Phil Housley .08 .25
31 Derek Morris .02 .10
32 Jarome Iginla .15 .40
33 Wade Belak .02 .10
34 Rico Fata .02 .10
35 Jean-Sebastien Giguere .08 .25
36 Rene Corbet .02 .10
37 Arturs Irbe .08 .25
38 Keith Primeau .02 .10
39 Sami Kapanen .02 .10
40 Ron Francis .08 .25
41 Shane Willis .08 .25
42 Gary Roberts .02 .10
43 Bates Battaglia .08 .25
44 J-P Dumont .08 .25
45 Ty Jones .02 .10
46 Tony Amonte .08 .25
47 Jocelyn Thibault .08 .25
48 Doug Gilmour .08 .25
49 Remi Royer .02 .10
50 Alexei Zhamnov .02 .10
51 Joe Sakic .30 .75
52 Peter Forsberg .30 .75
53 Theo Fleury .02 .10
54 Chris Drury .08 .25
55 Patrick Roy .60 1.50
56 Sandis Ozolinsh .02 .10
57 Adam Deadmarsh .02 .10
58 Milan Hejduk .10 .30
59 Mike Modano .20 .50
60 Brett Hull .15 .40
61 Darryl Sydor .02 .10
62 Ed Belfour .10 .30
63 Jere Lehtinen .08 .25
64 Jamie Langenbrunner .02 .10
65 Derian Hatcher .02 .10
66 Jon Sim RC .08 .25
67 Joe Nieuwendyk .08 .25
68 Sergei Fedorov .20 .50
69 Steve Yzerman .60 1.50
70 Brendan Shanahan .10 .30
71 Chris Osgood .08 .25
72 Nicklas Lidstrom .10 .30
73 Chris Chelios .10 .30
74 Igor Larionov .02 .10
75 Tomas Holmstrom .02 .10
76 Vyacheslav Kozlov .08 .25
77 Josef Beranek .02 .10
78 Bill Guerin .02 .10
79 Doug Weight .08 .25
80 Tommy Salo .08 .25
81 Mike Grier .08 .25
82 Tom Poti .02 .10
83 Fredrik Lindquist .02 .10
84 Mark Parrish .02 .10
85 Pavel Bure .10 .30
86 Viktor Kozlov .02 .10
87 Ray Whitney .08 .25
88 Rob Niedermayer .08 .25
89 Oleg Kvasha .08 .25
90 Scott Mellanby .02 .10
91 Chris Allen RC .08 .25
92 Rob Blake .08 .25
93 Pavel Rosa .02 .10
94 Jamie Storr .08 .25
95 Donald Audette .02 .10
96 Luc Robitaille .08 .25
97 Jozef Stumpel .08 .25
98 Vladimir Tsyplakov .02 .10
99 Manny Legace .15 .40
100 Saku Koivu .10 .30
101 Martin Rucinsky .02 .10
102 Vladimir Malakhov .02 .10
103 Eric Weinrich .02 .10
104 Jeff Hackett .08 .25
105 Arron Asham .02 .10
106 Trevor Linden .08 .25
107 Brian Savage .02 .10
108 Cliff Ronning .08 .25
109 Sergei Krivokrasov .02 .10
110 David Legwand .08 .25
111 Kimmo Timonen .02 .10
112 Mark Mowers RC .02 .10
113 Mike Dunham .08 .25
114 Scott Stevens .08 .25
115 Martin Brodeur .30 .75
116 Patrik Elias .08 .25
117 Brendan Morrison .08 .25
118 Scott Niedermayer .02 .10
119 Petr Sykora .02 .10
120 Jason Arnott .02 .10
121 Vadim Sharifijanov .02 .10
122 John Madden RC .25 .60
123 Mariusz Czerkawski .02 .10
124 Felix Potvin .10 .30
125 Mike Watt .02 .10
126 Eric Brewer .08 .25
127 Dmitri Nabokov .02 .10
128 Claude Lapointe .02 .10
129 Kenny Jonsson .02 .10
130 Zdeno Chara .10 .25
131 Wayne Gretzky .75 2.00
132 Brian Leetch .10 .30
133 Mike Richter .10 .30
134 Petr Nedved .08 .25
135 Adam Graves .02 .10
136 Manny Malhotra .08 .25
137 John MacLean .02 .10
138 Alexei Yashin .02 .10
139 Magnus Arvedson .02 .10
140 Daniel Alfredsson .08 .25
141 Wade Redden .02 .10
142 Ron Tugnutt .08 .25
143 Sami Salo .08 .25
144 Marian Hossa .10 .30
145 Shawn McEachern .02 .10
146 Eric Lindros .10 .30
147 Jean-Marc Pelletier .08 .25
148 John LeClair .10 .30
149 Rod Brind'Amour .08 .25
150 Mark Recchi .08 .25
151 Keith Jones .02 .10
152 Eric Desjardins .08 .25
153 Ryan Bast RC .02 .10
154 Brian Wesenberg RC .02 .10
155 John Vanbiesbrouck .08 .25
156 Jeremy Roenick .15 .40
157 Robert Reichel .02 .10
158 Keith Tkachuk .10 .30
159 Rick Tocchet .08 .25
160 Robert Esche RC .10 .30
161 Nikolai Khabibulin .08 .25
162 Daniel Briere .02 .10
163 Greg Adams .02 .10
164 Trevor Letowski .02 .10
165 Jaromir Jagr .20 .50
166 Martin Straka .02 .10
167 German Titov .02 .10
168 Tom Barrasso .08 .25
169 Jan Hrdina .02 .10
170 Alexei Kovalev .02 .10
171 Matthew Barnaby .08 .25
172 Jean-Sebastien Aubin .08 .25
173 Vincent Damphousse .02 .10
174 Owen Nolan .08 .25
175 Jeff Friesen .02 .10
176 Patrick Marleau .08 .25
177 Marco Sturm .08 .25
178 Mike Ricci .08 .25
179 Gary Suter .02 .10
180 Scott Hannan .02 .10
181 Andy Sutton .02 .10
182 Pavol Demitra .08 .25
183 Al MacInnis .08 .25
184 Pierre Turgeon .08 .25
185 Grant Fuhr .08 .25
186 Chris Pronger .08 .25
187 Lubos Bartecko .02 .10
188 Jochen Hecht RC .30 .75
189 Michal Handzus .08 .25
190 Vincent Lecavalier .10 .30
191 Paul Mara .08 .25
192 Darcy Tucker .02 .10
193 Chris Gratton .02 .10
194 Pavel Kubina .02 .10
195 Kevin Hodson .08 .25
196 Mats Sundin .10 .30
197 Daniil Markov .02 .10
198 Curtis Joseph .10 .30
199 Sergei Berezin .08 .25
200 Steve Thomas .02 .10
201 Bryan Berard .08 .25
202 Mike Johnson .08 .25
203 Tomas Kaberle .02 .10
204 Mark Messier .10 .30
205 Bill Muckalt .08 .25
206 Markus Naslund .10 .30
207 Mattias Ohlund .08 .25
208 Kevin Weekes .08 .25
209 Ed Jovanovski .02 .10
210 Alexander Mogilny .08 .25
211 Josh Holden .08 .25
212 Richard Zednik .02 .10
213 Jaroslav Svejkovsky .02 .10
214 Adam Oates .08 .25
215 Peter Bondra .08 .25
216 Sergei Gonchar .02 .10
217 Olaf Kolzig .08 .25
218 Jan Bulis .02 .10
219 Wayne Gretzky CL .40 1.00
220 Wayne Gretzky CL .40 1.00

1999-00 Upper Deck MVP Gold Script

*GOLD SCRIPT: 30X TO 80X BASIC CARDS
1 Wayne Gretzky 30.00 80.00
55 Patrick Roy 25.00 60.00
69 Steve Yzerman 25.00 60.00
131 Wayne Gretzky 30.00 80.00
219 Wayne Gretzky CL 30.00 80.00
220 Wayne Gretzky CL 30.00 80.00

1999-00 Upper Deck MVP Silver Script

COMPLETE SET (220) 75.00 150.00
*SILVER SCRIPT: 1.2X TO 3X BASIC CARDS

1999-00 Upper Deck MVP Super Script

*SUPER SCRIPT: 50X TO 120X BASIC CARDS

1999-00 Upper Deck MVP 21st Century NHL

COMPLETE SET (10) 5.00 10.00
1 David Legwand .30 .75
2 Sergei Samsonov .30 .75
3 Paul Kariya .40 1.00
4 Peter Forsberg 1.00 2.50
5 Vincent Lecavalier .40 1.00
6 Jaromir Jagr .60 1.50
7 Paul Mara .30 .75
8 Marian Hossa .40 1.00
9 Pavel Bure .50 1.25
10 Chris Drury .30 .75

1999-00 Upper Deck MVP 90's Snapshots

COMPLETE SET (10) 15.00 40.00
S1 Wayne Gretzky 6.00 15.00
S2 Jaromir Jagr 1.50 4.00
S3 Patrick Roy 4.00 10.00
S4 Eric Lindros 1.50 4.00
S5 Brendan Shanahan 1.50 4.00
S6 Peter Forsberg 2.00 5.00
S7 Steve Yzerman 3.00 8.00
S8 Teemu Selanne 1.50 4.00
S9 Dominik Hasek 2.00 5.00
S10 Pavel Bure 1.25 3.00

1999-00 Upper Deck MVP Draft Report

COMPLETE SET (10) 2.50 6.00
DR1 Damian Rhodes (Patrick Stefan named on back) .20 .50
DR2 Bill Muckalt (Daniel Sedin named on back) .20 .50
DR3 Wayne Gretzky (Pavel Brendl named on back) 2.00 5.00
DR4 Eric Brewer (Tim Connolly named on back) .20 .50
DR5 David Legwand (Brian Finley named on back) .20 .50
DR6 Peter Bondra (Kris Beech named on back) .30 .75
DR7 Rico Fata (Oleg Saprykin named on back) .20 .50
DR8 Mark Parrish (Denis Shvidki named on back) .20 .50
DR9 Tom Poti (Jani Rita named on back) .20 .50
DR10 Jeff Friesen (Jeff Jillison named on back) .25 .60

1999-00 Upper Deck MVP Draw Your Own Trading Card

COMPLETE SET (45) 15.00 30.00
W1 Joey Kocur .08 .25
W2 Mike Richter .10 .30
W3 Wayne Gretzky 1.25 3.00
W4 Dominik Hasek .40 1.00
W5 Steve Yzerman 1.00 2.50
W6 Ray Bourque .30 .75
W7 Arturs Irbe .08 .25
W8 Wayne Gretzky 1.25 3.00
W9 Martin Brodeur .50 1.25
W10 Patrick Roy 1.00 2.50
W11 Wayne Gretzky 1.25 3.00
W12 Paul Kariya .20 .50
W13 Wayne Gretzky 1.25 3.00
W14 Jaromir Jagr .30 .75
W15 Wayne Gretzky 1.25 3.00
W16 Felix Potvin .10 .30
W17 Marc Denis .08 .25
W18 Dominik Hasek .40 1.00
W19 Patrick Roy .75 2.00
W20 Robert Svehla .08 .25
W21 Joe Juneau .08 .25
W22 Mattias Ohlund .08 .25
W23 Kirk Muller .08 .25
W24 Peter Forsberg .50 1.25
W25 Stu Barnes .08 .25
W26 Nikolai Khabibulin .08 .25
W27 Sergei Samsonov .08 .25
W28 Jeremy Roenick .15 .40
W29 Wayne Gretzky 1.25 3.00
W30 Sergei Fedorov .40 1.00
W31 Wayne Gretzky .75 2.00
W32 Wayne Gretzky .75 2.00
W33 Wayne Gretzky .75 2.00
W34 Wayne Gretzky .75 2.00
W35 Wayne Gretzky .75 2.00
W36 Wayne Gretzky .75 2.00
W37 Wayne Gretzky .75 2.00
W38 Wayne Gretzky .75 2.00
W39 Wayne Gretzky .75 2.00
W40 Wayne Gretzky .75 2.00
W41 Wayne Gretzky .75 2.00
W42 Wayne Gretzky .75 2.00
W43 Wayne Gretzky .75 2.00
W44 Wayne Gretzky .75 2.00
W45 Wayne Gretzky .75 2.00

1999-00 Upper Deck MVP Game-Used Souvenirs

GU1 Paul Kariya P 6.00 15.00
GU2 Teemu Selanne P 6.00 15.00
GU3 Brett Hull P 8.00 20.00
GU4 Pavel Bure P 6.00 15.00
GU5 Marian Hossa P 6.00 15.00
GU6 Wayne Gretzky P 15.00 40.00
GU7 Brendan Shanahan P 6.00 15.00
GU8 Sergei Samsonov P 6.00 15.00
GU9 Eric Lindros P 6.00 15.00
GU10 Keith Tkachuk P 6.00 15.00
GU11 Steve Yzerman P 20.00 50.00
GU12 Jaromir Jagr P 10.00 25.00
GU13 Alexei Yashin P 6.00 15.00
GU14 Curtis Joseph P 6.00 15.00
GU15 Paul Kariya S 8.00 20.00
GU16 Teemu Selanne S 8.00 20.00
GU17 Dominik Hasek S 15.00 40.00
GU18 Pavel Bure S 10.00 25.00
GU19 Peter Forsberg S 12.50 30.00
GU20 Wayne Gretzky S 30.00 80.00
GU21 Brendan Shanahan S 8.00 20.00
GU22 Joe Sakic S 15.00 40.00
GU23 Eric Lindros S 8.00 20.00
GU24 Keith Tkachuk S 8.00 20.00
GU25 Jeremy Roenick S 10.00 25.00
GU26 Alexei Yashin S 8.00 20.00
GU27 Curtis Joseph S 8.00 20.00
GU28 Steve Yzerman S 15.00 40.00
GUS1 W.Gretzky AU/25 400.00 1000.00
GUS2 P.Bure AU/25 125.00 250.00

1999-00 Upper Deck MVP Hands of Gold

COMPLETE SET (10) 12.00 25.00
H1 Wayne Gretzky 2.50 6.00
H2 Brett Hull .50 1.25
H3 Pavel Bure .60 1.50
H4 Teemu Selanne .60 1.50
H5 Sergei Samsonov .30 .75
H6 Peter Forsberg 1.00 2.50
H7 Eric Lindros .60 1.50
H8 Paul Kariya .60 1.50
H9 Jaromir Jagr .60 1.50
H10 Steve Yzerman 2.00 5.00
H11 Mike Modano .60 1.50

1999-00 Upper Deck MVP Last Line

COMPLETE SET (10) 5.00 10.00
LL1 Dominik Hasek .75 2.00
LL2 Martin Brodeur 1.00 2.50
LL3 Patrick Roy 2.00 5.00
LL4 Byron Dafoe .30 .75
LL5 Ed Belfour .40 1.00
LL6 Curtis Joseph .30 .75
LL7 John Vanbiesbrouck .30 .75
LL8 Tom Barrasso .30 .75
LL9 Chris Osgood .30 .75
LL10 Nikolai Khabibulin .30 .75

1999-00 Upper Deck MVP Legendary One

COMPLETE SET (10) 25.00 60.00
COMMON GRETZKY (LO1-LO10) 3.00 8.00

1999-00 Upper Deck MVP ProSign

BH Brett Hull 12.00 30.00
BM Bill Muckalt 2.00 5.00
CD Chris Drury 5.00 12.00
DA Donald Audette 2.00 5.00
DM Derek Morris 2.00 5.00
GM Glen Murray 4.00 10.00
IL Igor Larionov 4.00 10.00
JF Jeff Friesen 4.00 10.00
JH Jeff Hackett 5.00 12.00
JR Jeremy Roenick 12.00 30.00
JT Joe Thornton 12.00 30.00
LR Luc Robitaille 8.00 20.00
MC Matt Cullen 2.00 5.00
PB Pavel Bure 8.00 20.00
PD Pavol Demitra 6.00 15.00
RB Ray Bourque 30.00 80.00
RT Ron Tugnutt 5.00 12.00
SG Sergei Gonchar 2.00 5.00
SK Sami Kapanen 2.00 5.00
SY Steve Yzerman 40.00 80.00
TF Theo Fleury 4.00 10.00
TK Tomas Kaberle 2.00 5.00
TL Trevor Linden 4.00 10.00
TP Tom Poti 2.00 5.00
WC Wendel Clark 4.00 10.00
WG Wayne Gretzky 200.00 500.00
JHR Jan Hrdina 2.00 5.00
RBR Rod Brind'Amour 5.00 12.00

1999-00 Upper Deck MVP Talent

COMPLETE SET (10) 10.00 20.00
MVP1 Wayne Gretzky 2.50 6.00
MVP2 Paul Kariya .75 2.00
MVP3 Dominik Hasek .75 2.00
MVP4 Eric Lindros .60 1.50
MVP5 Ray Bourque .60 1.50
MVP6 Steve Yzerman 2.00 5.00
MVP7 Patrick Roy 2.00 5.00
MVP8 Jaromir Jagr .75 2.00
MVP9 Martin Brodeur 1.25 3.00
MVP10 Mike Modano .60 1.50

1999-00 Upper Deck MVP SC Edition

COMPLETE SET (220) 20.00 40.00
1 Teemu Selanne .10 .30
2 Paul Kariya .10 .30
3 Guy Hebert .08 .25
4 Oleg Tverdovsky .05 .15
5 Tony Hrkac .05 .15
6 Mike Leclerc .05 .15
7 Ladislav Kohn .05 .15
8 Ray Ferraro .05 .15
9 Ed Ward .05 .15
10 Norm Maracle .08 .25
11 Dean Sylvester RC .08 .25
12 Yannick Tremblay .05 .15
13 Patrik Stefan RC .40 1.00
14 Johan Garpenlov .05 .15
15 Per-Johan Axelsson .05 .15
16 Joe Thornton .20 .50
17 Sergei Samsonov .08 .25
18 Jay Henderson RC .05 .15
19 Byron Dafoe .08 .25
20 Steve Heinze .05 .15
21 Marty McSorley .05 .15
22 Dominik Hasek .25 .60
23 Miroslav Satan .08 .25
24 Curtis Brown .05 .15
25 Martin Biron .08 .25
26 Jason Woolley .05 .15
27 Michael Peca .08 .25
28 Wayne Primeau .05 .15
29 Valeri Bure .05 .15
30 Derek Morris .08 .25
31 Cory Stillman .05 .15
32 Fred Brathwaite .08 .25
33 Jarome Iginla .15 .40
34 Andre Nazarov .05 .15
35 Jeff Shantz .05 .15
36 Ron Francis .05 .15
37 Jeff O'Neill .05 .15
38 Arturs Irbe .08 .25
39 Sami Kapanen .05 .15
40 Sean Hill .05 .15
41 Byron Ritchie RC .08 .25
42 Tommy Westlund RC .05 .15
43 Tony Amonte .08 .25
44 Doug Gilmour .08 .25
45 Blair Atcheynum .05 .15
46 Alexei Zhamnov .05 .15
47 Dean Mcammond .05 .15
48 Michael Nylander .05 .15
49 Aaron Miller .05 .15
50 Milan Hejduk .10 .30
51 Patrick Roy .60 1.50
52 Joe Sakic .30 .75
53 Chris Drury .08 .25
54 Peter Forsberg .30 .75
55 Ray Bourque .20 .50
56 Marc Denis .08 .25
57 Brett Hull .15 .40
58 Mike Modano .20 .50
59 Ed Belfour .10 .30
60 Kirk Muller .05 .15
61 Brenden Morrow .10 .30
62 Mike Keane .05 .15
63 Brad Lukowich RC .05 .15
64 Sergei Fedorov .20 .50
65 Steve Yzerman .60 1.50
66 Chris Osgood .08 .25
67 Brendan Shanahan .10 .30
68 Martin Lapointe .08 .25
69 Pat Verbeek .05 .15
70 Stacy Roest .05 .15
71 Tommy Salo .08 .25
72 Doug Weight .08 .25
73 Alexander Selivanov .05 .15
74 Ryan Smyth .05 .15
75 Boyd Devereaux .05 .15
76 Ethan Moreau .05 .15
77 Pavel Bure .10 .30
78 Viktor Kozlov .05 .15
79 Mike Vernon .08 .25
80 Ivan Novoseltsev RC .25 .60
81 Ray Whitney .08 .25
82 Filip Kuba RC .05 .15
83 Ray Sheppard .05 .15
84 Zigmund Palffy .08 .25
85 Luc Robitaille .08 .25
86 Bryan Smolinski .08 .25
87 Rob Blake .08 .25
88 Jere Karalahti RC .05 .15
89 Marko Tuomainen .05 .15
90 Garry Galley .05 .15
91 Saku Koivu .10 .30
92 Dainius Zubrus .05 .15
93 Jose Theodore .15 .40
94 Karl Dykhuis .05 .15
95 Sergei Zholtok .05 .15
96 Francis Bouillon RC .05 .15
97 David Legwand .08 .25
98 Mike Dunham .08 .25
99 Rob Valicevic RC .05 .15
100 Cliff Ronning .08 .25
101 Drake Berehowsky .05 .15
102 Greg Johnson .05 .15
103 Patric Kjellberg .05 .15
104 Martin Brodeur .30 .75
105 Scott Stevens .08 .25
106 Claude Lemieux .05 .15
107 Scott Gomez .05 .15
108 Partik Elias .08 .25
109 Randy McKay .05 .15
110 Sergei Brylin .05 .15
111 Tim Connolly .05 .15
112 Roberto Luongo .15 .40
113 Dave Scatchard .05 .15
114 Kenny Jonsson .05 .15
115 Vladimir Orszagh RC .05 .15
116 Ted Drury .05 .15
117 Theo Fleury .05 .15
118 Mike Richter .10 .30
119 Mike York .05 .15
120 Brian Leetch .10 .30
121 Petr Nedved .05 .15
122 Radek Dvorak .05 .15
123 Jan Hlavac .05 .15
124 Marian Hossa .10 .30
125 Radek Bonk .05 .15
126 Daniel Alfredsson .08 .25
127 Ron Tugnutt .08 .25
128 Rob Zamuner .05 .15
129 Jason York .05 .15
130 Shaun Van Allen .05 .15
131 Eric Lindros .10 .30
132 John LeClair .10 .30
133 Simon Gagne .10 .30
134 Mark Recchi .08 .25
135 Keith Primeau .05 .15
136 Daymond Langkow .08 .25
137 Brian Boucher .10 .30
138 Luke Richardson .05 .15
139 Keith Tkachuk .10 .30
140 Jeremy Roenick .15 .40
141 Travis Green .05 .15
142 Dallas Drake .05 .15
143 Jyrki Lumme .05 .15
144 Shane Doan .05 .15
145 Sean Burke .08 .25
146 Jaromir Jagr .20 .50
147 Alexei Kovalev .05 .15
148 Tom Barrasso .08 .25
149 Martin Sonnenberg RC .05 .15
150 Robert Lang .05 .15
151 Robert Dome .05 .15
152 Darius Kasparaitis .05 .15
153 Owen Nolan .08 .25
154 Jeff Friesen .05 .15
155 Steve Shields .08 .25
156 Vincent Damphousse .05 .15
157 Mike Rathje .05 .15
158 Alexander Korolyuk .05 .15
159 Todd Harvey .08 .25
160 Pavol Demitra .08 .25
161 Pierre Turgeon .08 .25
162 Roman Turek .08 .25
163 Chris Pronger .08 .25
164 Jochen Hecht RC .50 1.25
165 Todd Reirden RC .05 .15
166 Scott Young .05 .15
167 Vincent Lecavalier .10 .30
168 Dan Cloutier .05 .15
169 Chris Gratton .05 .15
170 Todd Warriner .05 .15
171 Mike Sillinger .05 .15
172 Petr Svoboda .05 .15
173 Mats Sundin .10 .30
174 Curtis Joseph .10 .30
175 Jonas Hoglund .05 .15

176 Sergei Berezin .05 .15
177 Nathan Dempsey RC .05 .15
178 Nikolai Antropov RC .50 1.25
179 Alyn McCauley .05 .15
180 Alexander Karpovtsev .05 .15
181 Steve Kariya RC .30 .75
182 Mark Messier .10 .30
183 Markus Naslund .10 .30
184 Adrian Aucoin .05 .15
185 Andrew Cassels .05 .15
186 Artem Chubarov .05 .15
187 Brad May .08 .25
188 Peter Bondra .10 .30
189 Olaf Kolzig .08 .25
190 Dmitri Mironov .05 .15
191 Jeff Halpern RC .30 .75
192 Andrei Nikolishin .05 .15
193 Terry Yake .08 .25
194 Pavel Brendl RC .50 1.25
195 Sheldon Keefe RC .40 1.00
196 Branislav Mezei RC .08 .25
197 Milan Kraft RC .50 1.25
198 Ryan Jardine RC .30 .75
199 Kristian Kudroc RC .08 .25
200 Alexander Buturlin RC .15 .40
201 Jaroslav Kristek RC .10 .30
202 Andrei Shefer RC .10 .30
203 Brad Moran RC .15 .40
204 Brett Lysak RC .08 .25
205 Michal Sivek RC .15 .40
206 Luke Sellars RC .08 .25
207 Brad Ralph RC .08 .25
208 Bryan Kazarian RC .08 .25
209 Barret Jackman .08 .25
210 Brian Finley .08 .25
211 Jamie Lundmark .08 .25
212 Denis Shvidki .08 .25
213 Taylor Pyatt .08 .25
214 Kris Beech .05 .15
215 Michael Zigomanis .08 .25
216 Justin Papineau .08 .25
217 Daniel Sedin .05 .15
218 Henrik Sedin .05 .15
219 Checklist .05 .15
220 Checklist .05 .15

1999-00 Upper Deck MVP SC Edition Gold Script
*GOLD SCRIPT: 30X TO 80X BASIC CARDS

1999-00 Upper Deck MVP SC Edition Silver Script
*SILVER SCRIPT: 1.2X TO 3X BASIC CARDS

1999-00 Upper Deck MVP SC Edition Super Script
*SUPER SCRIPT: 50X TO 120X BASIC CARDS

1999-00 Upper Deck MVP SC Edition Clutch Performers
COMPLETE SET (10) 15.00 30.00
CP1 Paul Kariya 1.00 2.50
CP2 Ray Bourque 1.50 4.00
CP3 Joe Sakic 2.00 5.00
CP4 Steve Yzerman 5.00 12.00
CP5 Luc Robitaille .75 2.00
CP6 Martin Brodeur 2.50 6.00
CP7 Theo Fleury .75 2.00
CP8 John LeClair 1.25 3.00
CP9 Jaromir Jagr 1.50 4.00
CP10 Curtis Joseph 1.00 2.50

1999-00 Upper Deck MVP SC Edition Cup Contenders
COMPLETE SET (10) 5.00 10.00
CC1 Patrik Stefan .75 2.00
CC2 Sergei Samsonov .60 1.50
CC3 Milan Hejduk .75 2.00
CC4 Chris Drury .60 1.50
CC5 David Legwand .40 1.00
CC6 Scott Gomez .50 1.25
CC7 Marian Hossa .60 1.50
CC8 Jeff Friesen .50 1.25
CC9 Vincent Lecavalier .50 1.25
CC10 Steve Kariya .50 1.25

1999-00 Upper Deck MVP SC Edition Game-Used Souvenirs
GUBH Brett Hull 6.00 15.00
GUBJ Barret Jackman 3.00 8.00
GUCJ Curtis Joseph 5.00 12.00
GUDS Denis Shvidki 3.00 8.00
GUEL Eric Lindros 6.00 15.00
GUJL John LeClair 5.00 12.00
GUJS Joe Sakic 10.00 25.00
GUKB Kris Beech 3.00 8.00
GUMK Milan Kraft 3.00 8.00
GUMO Maxime Ouellet 3.00 8.00
GUPB Pavel Brendl 3.00 8.00
GUPF Peter Forsberg 10.00 25.00
GUPV Pavel Bure 6.00 15.00
GURB Ray Bourque 10.00 25.00
GUSK Scott Kelman 3.00 8.00
GUSY Steve Yzerman 10.00 25.00
GUTP Taylor Pyatt 3.00 8.00
GUTS Teemu Selanne 5.00 12.00
SGDS Denis Shvidki Super 4.00 10.00
SGKB Kris Beech Super 4.00 10.00
SGMK Milan Kraft Super 4.00 10.00
SGPB Pavel Brendl Super 4.00 10.00

1999-00 Upper Deck MVP SC Edition Golden Memories
COMPLETE SET (10) 12.00 25.00
GM1 Paul Kariya .50 1.25
GM2 Patrick Roy 2.50 6.00
GM3 Peter Forsberg 1.25 3.00
GM4 Mike Modano .75 2.00
GM5 Steve Yzerman 2.50 6.00
GM6 Martin Brodeur 1.25 3.00
GM7 Theo Fleury .50 1.25
GM8 Eric Lindros .75 2.00
GM9 Jaromir Jagr .75 2.00
GM10 Curtis Joseph .50 1.25

1999-00 Upper Deck MVP SC Edition Great Combinations
GOLD/25: 1.2X TO 3X SILVER
GCBK P.Bure/V.Kozlov 10.00 25.00
GCGL W.Gretzky/B.Leetch 15.00 40.00
GCGR W.Gretzky/M.Richter 15.00 40.00
GCHM B.Hull/M.Modano 12.50 30.00
GCHP D.Hasek/M.Peca 8.00 20.00
GCJS J.Jagr/M.Straka 10.00 25.00
GCKS P.Kariya/T.Selanne 10.00 25.00
GCLL E.Lindros/J.LeClair 10.00 25.00
GCLS V.Lecavalier/P.Svoboda 8.00 20.00
GCRF P.Roy/P.Forsberg 15.00 40.00
GCSF B.Shanahan/S.Fedorov 10.00 25.00
GCSJ M.Sundin/C.Joseph 8.00 20.00
GCSR P.Stefan/D.Rhodes 8.00 20.00
GCTR K.Tkachuk/J.Roenick 8.00 20.00
GCTS J.Thornton/S.Samsonov 10.00 25.00
GCYO S.Yzerman/C.Osgood 12.50 30.00

1999-00 Upper Deck MVP SC Edition Great Combinations Gold
*GOLD/25: 1.2X TO 3X SILVER

1999-00 Upper Deck MVP SC Edition Playoff Heroes
COMPLETE SET (10) 40.00 80.00
PH1 Paul Kariya 3.00 8.00
PH2 Dominik Hasek 5.00 12.00
PH3 Patrick Roy 12.50 30.00
PH4 Mike Modano 4.00 10.00
PH5 Sergei Fedorov 5.00 12.00
PH6 Pavel Bure 3.00 8.00
PH7 Martin Brodeur 6.00 15.00
PH8 Eric Lindros 4.00 10.00
PH9 Jaromir Jagr 4.00 10.00
PH10 Mark Messier 3.00 8.00

1999-00 Upper Deck MVP SC Edition ProSign
AM Al MacInnis 6.00 15.00
AT Alex Tanguay 6.00 15.00
BF Brian Finley 4.00 10.00
BH Brett Hull 15.00 40.00
BJ Barret Jackman 6.00 15.00
BL Brian Leetch 8.00 20.00
CJ Curtis Joseph 20.00 50.00
DA Dave Andreychuk 4.00 10.00
DL David Legwand 4.00 10.00
DS Denis Shvidki 2.00 5.00
JH Jochen Hecht 4.00 10.00
JS Jozef Stumpel 2.00 5.00
KB Kris Beech 2.00 5.00
MB Martin Biron 4.00 10.00
MK Milan Kraft 2.00 5.00
MO Maxime Ouellet 4.00 10.00
PB Pavel Bure 6.00 15.00
PS Patrik Stefan 2.00 5.00
SG Simon Gagne 6.00 15.00
SK Scott Kelman 2.00 5.00
SS Sergei Samsonov 2.00 5.00
SY Steve Yzerman 100.00 175.00
TP Taylor Pyatt 2.00 5.00
PBR Pavel Brendl 4.00 10.00

1999-00 Upper Deck MVP SC Edition Second Season Snipers
COMPLETE SET (12) 12.00 25.00
SS1 Teemu Selanne 1.00 2.50
SS2 Joe Thornton 1.00 2.50
SS3 Peter Forsberg 2.50 6.00
SS4 Brendan Shanahan 1.00 2.50
SS5 Pavel Bure 1.00 2.50
SS6 Claude Lemieux .75 2.00
SS7 Eric Lindros 1.00 2.50
SS8 John LeClair 1.00 2.50
SS9 Keith Tkachuk 1.00 2.50
SS10 Jaromir Jagr 1.50 4.00
SS11 Mats Sundin 1.00 2.50
SS12 Mark Messier 1.00 2.50

1999-00 Upper Deck MVP SC Edition Stanley Cup Talent
COMPLETE SET (20) 8.00 15.00
SC1 Paul Kariya .30 .75
SC2 Teemu Selanne .30 .75
SC3 Ray Bourque .50 1.25
SC4 Joe Sakic .60 1.50
SC5 Patrick Roy 1.50 4.00
SC6 Brett Hull .40 1.00
SC7 Sergei Fedorov .50 1.25
SC8 Pavel Bure .30 .75
SC9 Zigmund Palffy .25 .60
SC10 Martin Brodeur .75 2.00
SC11 Theo Fleury .20 .50
SC12 Eric Lindros .30 .75
SC13 John LeClair .30 .75
SC14 Jaromir Jagr .50 1.25
SC15 Jeremy Roenick .40 1.00
SC16 Keith Tkachuk .30 .75
SC17 Steve Shields .20 .50
SC18 Mats Sundin .30 .75
SC19 Mark Messier .30 .75
SC20 Peter Bondra .20 .50

2000-01 Upper Deck MVP
COMPLETE SET (220) 12.00 30.00
1 Antti Aalto .12 .30
2 Matt Cullen .12 .30
3 Oleg Tverdovsky .12 .30
4 Paul Kariya .20 .50
5 Steve Rucchin .12 .30
6 Teemu Selanne .40 1.00
7 Maxim Balmochnykh .12 .30
8 Andrew Brunette .12 .30
9 Damian Rhodes .12 .30
10 Dean Sylvester .12 .30
11 Donald Audette .15 .40
12 Patrik Stefan .15 .40
13 Ray Ferraro .12 .30
14 Brian Rolston .12 .30
15 Sergei Samsonov .15 .40
16 Jason Allison .12 .30
17 Joe Thornton .30 .75
18 Kyle McLaren .12 .30
19 Byron Dafoe .15 .40
20 Hal Gill .12 .30
21 Curtis Brown .12 .30
22 Stu Barnes .15 .40
23 Dominik Hasek .30 .75
24 Doug Gilmour .25 .60
25 Maxim Afinogenov .12 .30
26 Michael Peca .15 .40
27 Miroslav Satan .12 .30
28 Chris Gratton .12 .30
29 Derek Morris .12 .30
30 Fred Brathwaite .15 .40
31 Jarome Iginla .25 .60
32 Marc Savard .12 .30
33 Phil Housley .15 .40
34 Valeri Bure .15 .40
35 Arturs Irbe .15 .40
36 Dave Tanabe .12 .30
37 Jeff O'Neill .15 .40
38 Rod Brind'Amour .20 .50
39 Ron Francis .25 .60
40 Sami Kapanen .12 .30
41 Alexei Zhamnov .15 .40
42 Eric Daze .15 .40
43 Jocelyn Thibault .15 .40
44 Michael Nylander .12 .30
45 Steve Sullivan .12 .30
46 Tony Amonte .15 .40
47 Chris Drury .15 .40
48 Joe Sakic .40 1.00
49 Milan Hejduk .15 .40
50 Patrick Roy .50 1.25
51 Peter Forsberg .40 1.00
52 Ray Bourque .30 .75
53 Adam Deadmarsh .12 .30
54 Alex Tanguay .15 .40
55 Marc Denis .15 .40
56 Brenden Morrow .15 .40
57 Brett Hull .40 1.00
58 Darian Hatcher .15 .40
59 Ed Belfour .20 .50
60 Jamie Langenbrunner .15 .40
61 Mike Modano .30 .75
62 Sergei Zubov .15 .40
63 Joe Nieuwendyk .15 .40
64 Brendan Shanahan .20 .50
65 Chris Chelios .20 .50
66 Chris Osgood .20 .50
67 Nicklas Lidstrom .20 .50
68 Pat Verbeek .15 .40
69 Sergei Fedorov .30 .75
70 Steve Yzerman .50 1.25
71 Darren McCarty .12 .30
72 Tom Poti .12 .30
73 Bill Guerin .20 .50
74 Doug Weight .20 .50
75 Mike Grier .12 .30
76 Ryan Smyth .15 .40
77 Tommy Salo .15 .40
78 Bret Hedican .12 .30
79 Pavel Bure .20 .50
80 Ray Whitney .15 .40
81 Scott Mellanby .15 .40
82 Trevor Kidd .12 .30
83 Viktor Kozlov .15 .40
84 Bryan Smolinski .15 .40
85 Stephane Fiset .12 .30
86 Jozef Stumpel .12 .30
87 Luc Robitaille .20 .50
88 Rob Blake .20 .50
89 Zigmund Palffy .20 .50
90 Brian Savage .12 .30
91 Dainius Zubrus .12 .30
92 Jose Theodore .20 .50
93 Martin Rucinsky .12 .30
94 Saku Koivu .20 .50
95 Sergei Zholtok .12 .30
96 Manny Fernandez .12 .30
97 Cliff Ronning .12 .30
98 David Legwand .20 .50
99 Drake Berehowsky .12 .30
100 Vitali Yachmenev .12 .30
101 Mike Dunham .12 .30
102 Patric Kjellberg .12 .30
103 Alexander Mogilny .15 .40
104 Claude Lemieux .15 .40
105 John Madden .15 .40
106 Martin Brodeur .50 1.25
107 Patrik Elias .20 .50
108 Scott Gomez .15 .40
109 Scott Stevens .20 .50
110 Dave Scatchard .12 .30
111 Kenny Jonsson .12 .30
112 Mariusz Czerkawski .12 .30
113 Mathieu Biron .12 .30
114 Tim Connolly .12 .30
115 Claude Lapointe .12 .30
116 Adam Graves .15 .40
117 Brian Leetch .15 .40
118 Mike York .15 .40
119 Mike Richter .20 .50
120 Petr Nedved .15 .40
121 Theo Fleury .25 .60
122 Daniel Alfredsson .20 .50
123 Patrick Lalime .15 .40
124 John LeClair .20 .50
125 Marian Hossa .15 .40
126 Keith Primeau .15 .40
127 Radek Bonk .15 .40
128 Shawn McEachern .12 .30
129 Andreas Dackell .12 .30
130 Brian Boucher .15 .40
131 Mark Recchi .25 .60
132 Simon Gagne .20 .50
133 Eric Desjardins .15 .40
134 Jeremy Roenick .30 .75
135 Keith Tkachuk .12 .30
136 Teppo Numminen .12 .30
137 Eric Lindros .30 .75
138 Shane Doan .15 .40
139 Travis Green .12 .30
140 Trevor Letowski .12 .30
141 Alexei Kovalev .12 .30
142 Jan Hrdina .12 .30
143 Jaromir Jagr .60 1.50
144 Jean-Sebastien Aubin .15 .40
145 Martin Straka .15 .40
146 Matthew Barnaby .12 .30
147 Brad Stuart .15 .40
148 Jeff Friesen .12 .30
149 Mike Ricci .12 .30
150 Owen Nolan .20 .50
151 Steve Shields .15 .40
152 Vincent Damphousse .15 .40
153 Al MacInnis .25 .60
154 Chris Pronger .20 .50
155 Jochen Hecht .12 .30
156 Pavol Demitra .25 .60
157 Pierre Turgeon .15 .40
158 Roman Turek .15 .40
159 Dan Cloutier .15 .40
160 Fredrik Modin .12 .30
161 Mike Johnson .12 .30
162 Paul Mara .12 .30
163 Vincent Lecavalier .20 .50
164 Petr Svoboda .12 .30
165 Curtis Joseph .25 .60
166 Darcy Tucker .20 .50
167 Mats Sundin .20 .50
168 Nikolai Antropov .15 .40
169 Sergei Berezin .12 .30
170 Steve Thomas .12 .30
171 Dimitri Yushkevich .12 .30
172 Brendan Morrison .20 .50
173 Ed Jovanovski .12 .30
174 Felix Potvin .30 .75
175 Harold Druken .12 .30
176 Todd Bertuzzi .15 .40
177 Markus Naslund .20 .50
178 Adam Oates .20 .50
179 Chris Simon .12 .30
180 Jeff Halpern .12 .30
181 Olaf Kolzig .20 .50
182 Peter Bondra .20 .50
183 Sergei Gonchar .20 .50
184 Vitali Vishnevsky .12 .30
185 Andreas Karlsson .12 .30
186 Eric Nickulas RC .20 .50
187 Brandon Smith RC .20 .50
188 Dmitri Kalinin .20 .50
189 Chris Herperger .20 .50
190 Serge Aubin RC .25 .60
191 Alan Letang .20 .50
192 Keith Aldridge RC .20 .50
193 Steven Reinprecht RC .30 .75
194 Brad Chartrand .20 .50
195 David Gosselin RC .25 .60
196 Colin White RC .30 .75
197 Willie Mitchell RC .30 .75
198 Jason Krog .20 .50
199 Steve Valiquette RC .25 .60
200 Petr Schastlivy .20 .50
201 Andy Delmore .20 .50
202 Mark Eaton .20 .50
203 Evgeni Nabokov .25 .60
204 Ladislav Nagy .25 .60
205 Kyle Freadrich RC .25 .60
206 Greg Andrusak RC .25 .60
207 Alfie Michaud .30 .75
208 Brent Sopel RC .30 .75
209 Matt Pettinger RC .20 .50
210 Chris Nielsen RC .20 .50
211 Dany Heatley RC 2.00 5.00
212 Josef Vasicek RC .50 1.25
213 Matt Zultek RC .20 .50
214 Dmitri Afanasenkov RC .20 .50
215 Tyler Bouck RC .20 .50
216 Jonas Andersson RC .20 .50
217 Juraj Kolnik RC .20 .50
218 Andrew Raycroft RC 1.00 2.50
219 Pavel Bure CL .20 .50
220 Steve Yzerman CL .50 1.25

2000-01 Upper Deck MVP Excellence
COMPLETE SET (10) 15.00 30.00
ME1 C.Joseph/R.Luongo 1.25 3.00
ME2 P.Bure/P.Brendl 1.25 3.00
ME3 S.Samsonov/O.Saprykin 1.25 3.00
ME4 M.Hejduk/I.Novoseltsev 1.25 3.00
ME5 S.Yzerman/P.Verbeek 4.00 10.00
ME6 R.Turek/M.Biron 1.25 3.00
ME7 H.Sedin/D.Sedin 2.00 5.00
ME8 P.Stefan/L.Nagy 1.25 3.00
ME9 M.Malhotra/M.York 1.25 3.00
ME10 W.Gretzky/R.Bourque 6.00 15.00

2000-01 Upper Deck MVP First Stars
*VETS/25: 20X TO 50X BASIC CARDS
*ROOKIES/25: 12X TO 30X BASIC RC

2000-01 Upper Deck MVP Game-Used Souvenirs
CGCJ Curtis Joseph 6.00 15.00
CGCO Chris Osgood 6.00 15.00
CGEB Ed Belfour 6.00 15.00
CGFP Felix Potvin 10.00 25.00
CGMB Martin Brodeur 10.00 25.00
CGMS Mats Sundin 6.00 15.00
CGWG Wayne Gretzky 25.00 60.00
GSAI Arturs Irbe 6.00 15.00
GSBS Brendan Shanahan 6.00 15.00
GSCC Chris Chelios 6.00 15.00
GSDH Dominik Hasek 10.00 25.00
GSEL Eric Lindros 6.00 15.00
GSJA Jason Allison 6.00 15.00
GSJJ Jaromir Jagr 10.00 25.00
GSJL John LeClair 6.00 15.00
GSKT Keith Tkachuk 6.00 15.00
GSMM Mark Messier 6.00 15.00
GSMR Mike Richter 10.00 25.00
GSPB Pavel Bure 6.00 15.00
GSPF Peter Forsberg 12.50 30.00
GSPK Paul Kariya 6.00 15.00
GSPR Patrick Roy 15.00 40.00
GSRB Ray Bourque 8.00 20.00
GSRL Roberto Luongo 10.00 25.00
GSSF Sergei Fedorov 10.00 25.00
GSSY Steve Yzerman 15.00 40.00
GSTS Teemu Selanne 6.00 15.00
GSWG Wayne Gretzky 25.00 60.00
GSZP Zigmund Palffy 6.00 15.00

2000-01 Upper Deck MVP Mark of Excellence
SGBB P.Bure/P.Brendl 20.00 50.00
SGHN M.Hejduk/I.Novoseltsev 15.00 40.00
SGJL C.Joseph/R.Luongo 40.00 100.00
SGMY M.Malhotra/M.York 12.00 30.00
SGSE H.Sedin/D.Sedin 125.00 300.00
SGSL P.Stefan/L.Nagy 15.00 40.00
SGSS S.Samsonov/O.Saprykin 15.00 40.00
SGTB R.Turek/M.Biron 15.00 40.00
SGYV S.Yzerman/P.Verbeek 75.00 150.00

2000-01 Upper Deck MVP Masked Men
COMPLETE SET (10) 15.00 30.00
MM1 Dominik Hasek 2.00 5.00
MM2 Patrick Roy 5.00 12.00
MM3 Ed Belfour 1.00 2.50
MM4 Chris Osgood .75 2.00
MM5 Martin Brodeur 2.50 6.00
MM6 Brian Boucher 1.00 2.50
MM7 Steve Shields .75 2.00
MM8 Roman Turek .75 2.00
MM9 Curtis Joseph 1.00 2.50
MM10 Olaf Kolzig .75 2.00

2000-01 Upper Deck MVP ProSign
AM Al MacInnis 8.00 20.00
BM Brenden Morrow 8.00 20.00
CB Curtis Brown 6.00 15.00
CJ Curtis Joseph 12.50 30.00
DL David Legwand 8.00 20.00
IV Ivan Novoseltsev 6.00 15.00
LN Ladislav Nagy 6.00 15.00
MJ Mike Johnson 6.00 15.00
MM Manny Malhotra 6.00 15.00
MR Mike Ribeiro 6.00 15.00
MY Mike York 6.00 15.00
OS Oleg Saprykin 6.00 15.00
PB Pavel Bure 10.00 25.00
PS Patrik Stefan 6.00 15.00
RL Roberto Luongo 12.50 30.00
RT Roman Turek 6.00 15.00
SM Steven McCarthy 6.00 15.00
SS Sergei Samsonov 8.00 20.00

2000-01 Upper Deck MVP Second Stars
*VETS/100: 12X TO 30X BASIC CARDS
*ROOKIES/100: 6X TO 15X BASIC RC

2000-01 Upper Deck MVP Talent
COMPLETE SET (15) 10.00 20.00
M1 Paul Kariya .30 .75
M2 Teemu Selanne .30 .75
M3 Ray Bourque .60 1.50
M4 Joe Sakic .60 1.50
M5 Patrick Roy 1.50 4.00
M6 Brett Hull .40 1.00
M7 Sergei Fedorov .60 1.50
M8 Pavel Bure .40 1.00
M9 Zigmund Palffy .30 .75
M10 Martin Brodeur .75 2.00
M11 Theo Fleury .30 .75
M12 Eric Lindros .50 1.25
M13 John LeClair .40 1.00
M14 Jaromir Jagr .50 1.25
M15 Jeremy Roenick .40 1.00

2000-01 Upper Deck MVP Third Stars
COMPLETE SET (218) 75.00 150.00
*VETS: 1.5X TO 4X BASIC CARDS
*ROOKIES: .8X TO 2X BASIC CARDS

2000-01 Upper Deck MVP Top Draws
COMPLETE SET (10) 5.00 10.00
TD1 Teemu Selanne .30 .75
TD2 Dominik Hasek .60 1.50
TD3 Peter Forsberg .75 2.00
TD4 Brendan Shanahan .50 1.25
TD5 Pavel Bure .40 1.00
TD6 Scott Gomez .30 .75
TD7 Eric Lindros .50 1.25
TD8 John LeClair .40 1.00
TD9 Keith Tkachuk .30 .75
TD10 Jaromir Jagr .50 1.25

2000-01 Upper Deck MVP Top Playmakers
COMPLETE SET (10) 15.00 30.00
TP1 Paul Kariya .75 2.00
TP2 Dominik Hasek 1.50 4.00
TP3 Peter Forsberg 2.00 5.00
TP4 Mike Modano 1.25 3.00
TP5 Steve Yzerman 4.00 10.00
TP6 Pavel Bure 1.00 2.50
TP7 Scott Gomez .75 2.00
TP8 Eric Lindros 1.25 3.00
TP9 Jaromir Jagr 1.25 3.00
TP10 Jeremy Roenick 1.00 2.50

2000-01 Upper Deck MVP Valuable Commodities
COMPLETE SET (10) 20.00 40.00
VC1 Paul Kariya .75 2.00
VC2 Patrick Roy 4.00 10.00
VC3 Peter Forsberg 2.00 5.00
VC4 Mike Modano 1.25 3.00
VC5 Steve Yzerman 4.00 10.00
VC6 Martin Brodeur 2.00 5.00
VC7 Theo Fleury .75 2.00
VC8 Eric Lindros 1.25 3.00
VC9 Jaromir Jagr 1.25 3.00
VC10 Curtis Joseph .75 2.00

2001-02 Upper Deck MVP
COMPLETE SET (233) 40.00 80.00
COMP.SERIES I (220) 15.00 30.00
1 Jean-Sebastien Giguere .15 .40
2 Paul Kariya .15 .40
3 Jeff Friesen .10 .25
4 Oleg Tverdovsky .10 .25
5 Mike Leclerc .10 .25
6 Milan Hnilicka .12 .30
7 Patrik Stefan .10 .25
8 Ray Ferraro .10 .25
9 Jiri Slegr .10 .25
10 Hnat Domenichelli .10 .25
11 Jason Allison .12 .30
12 Joe Thornton .25 .60
13 Bill Guerin .15 .40
14 Sergei Samsonov .12 .30
15 Kyle McLaren .10 .25
16 Jonathan Girard .10 .25
17 Maxim Afinogenov .10 .25
18 Stu Barnes .12 .30
19 Doug Gilmour .20 .50
20 Chris Gratton .10 .25
21 Martin Biron .12 .30
22 J-P Dumont .10 .25
23 Miroslav Satan .12 .30
24 Craig Conroy .10 .25
25 Jarome Iginla .20 .50
26 Rico Fata .10 .25
27 Derek Morris .10 .25
28 Marc Savard .10 .25
29 Oleg Saprykin .10 .25
30 Arturs Irbe .12 .30
31 Shane Willis .10 .25
32 Rod Brind'Amour .15 .40
33 Jeff O'Neill .10 .25
34 Sami Kapanen .10 .25
35 Ron Francis .20 .50
36 Dave Tanabe .10 .25
37 Steve Sullivan .10 .25
38 Tony Amonte .12 .30
39 Jaroslav Spacek .10 .25
40 Eric Daze .12 .30
41 Michael Nylander .10 .25
42 Alexei Zhamnov .12 .30
43 Joe Sakic .30 .75
44 Peter Forsberg .30 .75
45 Milan Hejduk .12 .30
46 Chris Drury .12 .30
47 Rob Blake .15 .40
48 Ray Bourque .25 .60
49 Patrick Roy .40 1.00
50 Alex Tanguay .12 .30
51 Geoff Sanderson .10 .25
52 Espen Knutsen .10 .25
53 Ray Whitney .10 .25
54 Rostislav Klesla .10 .25
55 Ron Tugnutt .12 .30
56 Tyler Wright .10 .25
57 Mike Modano .25 .60
58 Jere Lehtinen .12 .30
59 Sergei Zubov .10 .25
60 Brenden Morrow .12 .30
61 Ed Belfour .15 .40
62 Joe Nieuwendyk .12 .30
63 Pierre Turgeon .12 .30
64 Steve Yzerman .40 1.00
65 Brendan Shanahan .15 .40
66 Brett Hull .30 .75
67 Luc Robitaille .15 .40
68 Sergei Fedorov .25 .60
69 Dominik Hasek .25 .60
70 Darren McCarty .10 .25
71 Mike Grier .10 .25
72 Ryan Smyth .12 .30
73 Anson Carter .10 .25
74 Tom Poti .12 .30
75 Tommy Salo .12 .30
76 Mike Comrie .12 .30
77 Todd Marchant .10 .25
78 Pavel Bure .15 .40
79 Viktor Kozlov .10 .25
80 Marcus Nilson .10 .25
81 Kevyn Adams .10 .25
82 Roberto Luongo .25 .60
83 Denis Shvidki .10 .25
84 Zigmund Palffy .15 .40
85 Jozef Stumpel .10 .25
86 Adam Deadmarsh .10 .25
87 Mathieu Schneider .10 .25
88 Bryan Smolinski .10 .25
89 Eric Belanger .10 .25
90 Lubomir Visnovsky .10 .25
91 Marian Gaborik .15 .40
92 Lubomir Sekeras .10 .25
93 Wes Walz .10 .25
94 Manny Fernandez .10 .25
95 Roman Simicek .10 .25
96 Stacy Roest .10 .25
97 Saku Koivu .15 .40
98 Oleg Petrov .10 .25
99 Patrice Brisebois .10 .25
100 Jose Theodore .15 .40
101 Richard Zednik .12 .30
102 Martin Rucinsky .12 .30
103 Andrei Markov .15 .40
104 David Legwand .12 .30
105 Cliff Ronning .12 .30
106 Mike Dunham .12 .30
107 Kimmo Timonen .10 .25
108 Scott Walker .10 .25
109 Patric Kjellberg .10 .25
110 Martin Brodeur .40 1.00
111 Scott Stevens .15 .40
112 Patrik Elias .15 .40
113 Scott Niedermayer .15 .40
114 Petr Sykora .10 .25
115 Jason Arnott .12 .30
116 Scott Gomez .12 .30
117 Rick DiPietro .12 .30
118 Mark Parrish .10 .25
119 Roman Hamrlik .10 .25
120 Mariusz Czerkawski .10 .25
121 Kenny Jonsson .10 .25
122 Dave Scatchard .10 .25
123 Mark Messier .30 .75
124 Brian Leetch .15 .40
125 Jan Hlavac .12 .30
126 Theo Fleury .20 .50
127 Eric Lindros .25 .60
128 Petr Nedved .12 .30
129 Daniel Alfredsson .15 .40
130 Radek Bonk .10 .25
131 Marian Hossa .15 .40
132 Shawn McEachern .10 .25
133 Patrick Lalime .12 .30
134 Wade Redden .10 .25
135 Magnus Arvedson .10 .25
136 Martin Havlat .12 .30
137 Simon Gagne .15 .40
138 Roman Cechmanek .12 .30
139 Justin Williams .12 .30
140 John LeClair .15 .40
141 Mark Recchi .20 .50
142 Eric Desjardins .10 .25
143 Jeremy Roenick .25 .60
144 Paul Mara .10 .25
145 Shane Doan .12 .30
146 Landon Wilson .10 .25
147 Sean Burke .12 .30
148 Michal Handzus .10 .25
149 Ladislav Nagy .10 .25
150 Mario Lemieux .60 1.50
151 Jan Hrdina .10 .25
152 Johan Hedberg .12 .30
153 Robert Lang .10 .25
154 Alexei Kovalev .12 .30
155 Martin Straka .10 .25
156 Owen Nolan .15 .40
157 Vincent Damphousse .12 .30
158 Brad Stuart .10 .25
159 Teemu Selanne .30 .75
160 Evgeni Nabokov .12 .30
161 Mike Ricci .10 .25
162 Chris Pronger .15 .40
163 Keith Tkachuk .15 .40
164 Scott Young .10 .25
165 Pavol Demitra .20 .50
166 Doug Weight .15 .40
167 Al MacInnis .20 .50
168 Cory Stillman .10 .25
169 Vincent Lecavalier .15 .40
170 Brad Richards .15 .40
171 Nikolai Khabibulin .15 .40
172 Fredrik Modin .10 .25
173 Mats Sundin .15 .40
174 Gary Roberts .10 .25
175 Curtis Joseph .20 .50
176 Nikolai Antropov .10 .25
177 Darcy Tucker .10 .25
178 Jonas Hoglund .10 .25
179 Markus Naslund .15 .40
180 Brendan Morrison .12 .30
181 Todd Bertuzzi .15 .40
182 Daniel Sedin .20 .50
183 Ed Jovanovski .12 .30
184 Peter Bondra .15 .40
185 Sergei Gonchar .10 .25
186 Jeff Halpern .10 .25
187 Olaf Kolzig .15 .40
188 Jaromir Jagr .50 1.25
189 Gregg Naumenko .30 .75
190 Dan Snyder RC .40 1.00
191 Zdenek Kutlak RC .30 .75
192 Niclas Wallin .30 .75
193 Michel Larocque RC .30 .75
194 Casey Hankinson RC .30 .75
195 Chris Nielsen .30 .75
196 Martin Spanhel RC .30 .75
197 Mathieu Darche RC .50 1.25
198 Matt Davidson RC .30 .75
199 Brad Larsen .30 .75
200 Steve Gainey .30 .75
201 Jason Chimera RC .30 .75
202 Andrej Podkonicky RC .30 .75
203 Mike Matteucci RC .30 .75
204 Pascal Dupuis RC .50 1.25
205 Francis Belanger RC .40 1.00
206 Mike Jefferson RC .30 .75
207 Stanislav Gron RC .30 .75
208 Peter Smrek RC .30 .75
209 Joel Kwiatkowski RC .30 .75
210 Kirby Law RC .30 .75
211 Tomas Divisek RC .40 1.00
212 David Cullen RC .30 .75
213 Billy Tibbetts RC .30 .75
214 Dan Lacouture .30 .75
215 Jaroslav Obsut RC .30 .75
216 Dale Clarke RC .30 .75
217 Thomas Ziegler RC .40 1.00
218 Mike Brown .40 1.00
219 Steve Yzerman CL .25 .60
220 Curtis Joseph CL .12 .30
221 Ilya Kovalchuk RC 5.00 12.00
222 Erik Cole RC 2.00 5.00
223 Pavel Datsyuk RC 5.00 12.00
224 Kristian Huselius RC 1.50 4.00
225 Marcel Hossa RC 1.50 4.00
226 Martin Erat RC 1.25 3.00
227 Christian Berglund RC 1.25 3.00
228 Raffi Torres RC 1.50 4.00
229 Dan Blackburn RC 1.25 3.00
230 Jiri Dopita RC 1.00 2.50
231 Krys Kolanos RC 1.00 2.50
232 Brian Sutherby RC 1.00 2.50
233 Olivier Michaud RC 1.50 4.00

2001-02 Upper Deck MVP Goalie Sticks
GAI Arturs Irbe 12.50 30.00
GBD Byron Dafoe 12.50 30.00
GCJ Curtis Joseph 20.00 50.00
GCO Chris Osgood 12.50 30.00
GDH Dominik Hasek 25.00 60.00
GEB Ed Belfour 20.00 50.00
GJT Jose Theodore 25.00 60.00
GMB Martin Brodeur 30.00 80.00
GMR Mike Richter 15.00 40.00
GNK Nikolai Khabibulin 20.00 50.00
GOK Olaf Kolzig 12.50 30.00
GPR Patrick Roy 40.00 100.00
GRC Roman Cechmanek 12.50 30.00
GRD Rick DiPietro 12.50 30.00
GTS Tommy Salo 12.50 30.00

2001-02 Upper Deck MVP Masked Men
COMPLETE SET (14) 10.00 20.00
MM1 Martin Brodeur 1.50 4.00
MM2 Ed Belfour .60 1.50
MM3 Patrick Roy 3.00 8.00
MM4 Jocelyn Thibault .50 1.25
MM5 Tommy Salo .50 1.25
MM6 Olaf Kolzig .50 1.25
MM7 Johan Hedberg .50 1.25
MM8 Evgeni Nabokov .50 1.25
MM9 Patrick Lalime .50 1.25
MM10 Sean Burke .50 1.25
MM11 Curtis Joseph .60 1.50
MM12 Arturs Irbe .50 1.25
MM13 Roman Cechmanek .50 1.25
MM14 Felix Potvin .60 1.50

2001-02 Upper Deck MVP Morning Skate Jersey Autographs
SJBB Brian Boucher 12.50 30.00
SJJA Jarome Iginla 25.00 60.00
SJJI Jarome Iginla 25.00 60.00

SJJL John LeClair 15.00 40.00
SJKP Keith Primeau 15.00 40.00
SJMH Milan Hejduk 10.00 25.00
SJMM Mike Modano 20.00 50.00
SJMR Mark Recchi 15.00 40.00
SJRB Rod Brind'Amour 15.00 40.00
SJSG Simon Gagne 15.00 40.00

2001-02 Upper Deck MVP Morning Skate Jerseys

JBB Brian Boucher 4.00 10.00
JEL Eric Lindros 4.00 10.00
JJA Jarome Iginla 6.00 15.00
JJI Jarome Iginla 6.00 15.00
JJJ Jaromir Jagr 8.00 20.00
JJL John LeClair 4.00 10.00
JJO John LeClair 4.00 10.00
JJS Joe Sakic 8.00 20.00
JKP Keith Primeau 4.00 10.00
JMH Milan Hejduk 4.00 10.00
JMM Mike Modano 6.00 15.00
JMR Mark Recchi 4.00 10.00
JPF Peter Forsberg 8.00 20.00
JRB Rod Brind'Amour 4.00 10.00
JSG Simon Gagne 4.00 10.00

2001-02 Upper Deck MVP Souvenirs

*GOLD/50: 1X TO 2.5X BASIC INSERT
CAM Al MacInnis 10.00 25.00
CDA Daniel Alfredsson 10.00 25.00
CJR Jeremy Roenick 12.50 30.00
CJS Joe Sakic 15.00 40.00
CMM Mike Modano 15.00 40.00
CPB Pavel Bure 10.00 25.00
CSS Sergei Samsonov 10.00 25.00
CVL Vincent Lecavalier 10.00 25.00
CWG Wayne Gretzky 50.00 100.00
CZP Zigmund Palffy 10.00 25.00
SAM Alexander Mogilny 6.00 15.00
SBH Brett Hull 12.50 30.00
SBS Brendan Shanahan 8.00 20.00
SJA Jason Allison 6.00 15.00
SJJ Jaromir Jagr 12.50 30.00
SJL John LeClair 8.00 20.00
SKT Keith Tkachuk 8.00 20.00
SLR Luc Robitaille 6.00 15.00
SML Mario Lemieux 30.00 60.00
SMM Mark Messier 8.00 20.00
SMR Mark Recchi 6.00 15.00
SMS Mats Sundin 8.00 20.00
SPB Peter Bondra 8.00 20.00
SPF Peter Forsberg 6.00 15.00
SPS Patrik Stefan 6.00 15.00
SRB Ray Bourque 12.50 30.00
SSH Scott Hartnell 6.00 15.00
SSY Steve Yzerman 20.00 40.00
STA Tony Amonte 6.00 15.00
STS Teemu Selanne 8.00 20.00

2001-02 Upper Deck MVP Talent

COMPLETE SET (14) 12.00 30.00
MT1 Peter Forsberg 1.25 3.00
MT2 Joe Sakic 1.00 2.50
MT3 Mike Modano .75 2.00
MT4 Mario Lemieux 3.00 8.00
MT5 Sergei Fedorov 1.00 2.50
MT6 Steve Yzerman 2.50 6.00
MT7 Pavel Bure .60 1.50
MT8 Paul Kariya .40 1.00
MT9 Teemu Selanne .40 1.00
MT10 Patrik Elias .30 .75
MT11 Zigmund Palffy .30 .75
MT12 John LeClair .60 1.50
MT13 Chris Pronger .30 .75
MT14 Martin Brodeur 1.25 3.00

2001-02 Upper Deck MVP Valuable Commodities

COMPLETE SET (7) 10.00 25.00
VC1 Steve Yzerman 3.00 8.00
VC2 Pavel Bure .75 2.00
VC3 Joe Sakic 1.25 3.00
VC4 Martin Brodeur 1.50 4.00
VC5 Mario Lemieux 4.00 10.00
VC6 Peter Forsberg 1.50 4.00
VC7 Mike Modano 1.00 2.50

2001-02 Upper Deck MVP Watch

COMPLETE SET (7) 10.00 20.00
MW1 Mario Lemieux 4.00 10.00
MW2 Joe Sakic 1.25 3.00
MW3 Jaromir Jagr 1.00 2.50
MW4 Brett Hull .75 2.00
MW5 Sergei Fedorov 1.25 3.00
MW6 Mark Messier .75 2.00
MW7 Chris Pronger .40 1.00

2002-03 Upper Deck MVP

COMPLETE SET (220) 15.00 40.00
1 Mike LeClerc .10 .25
2 Jean-Sebastien Giguere .15 .40
3 Matt Cullen .10 .25
4 Andy McDonald .15 .40
5 Jason York .10 .25
6 Paul Kariya .15 .40
7 Frantisek Kaberle .10 .25
8 Dany Heatley .12 .30
9 Pasi Nurminen .10 .25
10 Ilya Kovalchuk .20 .50
11 Patrik Stefan .12 .30
12 Pascal Rheaume .10 .25
13 Sergei Samsonov .12 .30
14 Joe Thornton .25 .60
15 Brian Rolston .12 .30
16 Martin Lapointe .12 .30
17 Nick Boynton .10 .25
18 Jozef Stumpel .10 .25
19 Stu Barnes .10 .25
20 J-P Dumont .10 .25
21 Miroslav Satan .15 .40
22 Tim Connolly .10 .25
23 Maxim Afinogenov .10 .25
24 Martin Biron .12 .30
25 Craig Conroy .10 .25
26 Roman Turek .15 .40
27 Derek Morris .10 .25
28 Marc Savard .10 .25
29 Jarome Iginla .20 .50
30 Igor Kravchuk .10 .25
31 Sami Kapanen .10 .25
32 Bates Battaglia .10 .25
33 Ron Francis .20 .50
34 Erik Cole .10 .25
35 Jeff O'Neill .10 .25
36 Arturs Irbe .12 .30
37 Rod Brind'Amour .15 .40
38 Alexei Zhamnov .12 .30
39 Michael Nylander .10 .25
40 Steve Sullivan .10 .25
41 Jocelyn Thibault .12 .30
42 Kyle Calder .10 .25
43 Eric Daze .10 .25
44 Patrick Roy .40 1.00
45 Milan Hejduk .12 .30
46 Peter Forsberg .30 .75
47 Rob Blake .15 .40
48 Chris Drury .15 .40
49 Joe Sakic .30 .75
50 Steven Reinprecht .10 .25
51 Brad Moran .10 .25
52 Jaroslav Spacek .10 .25
53 Marc Denis .12 .30
54 Ray Whitney .12 .30
55 Rostislav Klesla .10 .25
56 Espen Knutsen .10 .25
57 Marty Turco .15 .40
58 Jere Lehtinen .15 .40
59 Mike Modano .25 .60
60 Derian Hatcher .12 .30
61 Brenden Morrow .12 .30
62 Jason Arnott .12 .30
63 Dominik Hasek .25 .60
64 Brendan Shanahan .15 .40
65 Curtis Joseph .20 .50
66 Brett Hull .30 .75
67 Steve Yzerman .40 1.00
68 Nicklas Lidstrom .15 .40
69 Pavel Datsyuk .25 .60
70 Ryan Smyth .12 .30
71 Anson Carter .12 .30
72 Mike Comrie .15 .40
73 Tommy Salo .12 .30
74 Eric Brewer .10 .25
75 Todd Marchant .10 .25
76 Roberto Luongo .25 .60
77 Kristian Huselius .10 .25
78 Marcus Nilsson .10 .25
79 Viktor Kozlov .10 .25
80 Sandis Ozolinsh .10 .25
81 Valeri Bure .12 .30
82 Jason Allison .12 .30
83 Zigmund Palffy .15 .40
84 Adam Deadmarsh .10 .25
85 Felix Potvin .25 .60
86 Mathieu Schneider .10 .25
87 Bryan Smolinski .12 .30
88 Jim Dowd .10 .25
89 Marian Gaborik .15 .40
90 Manny Fernandez .10 .25
91 Andrew Brunette .10 .25
92 Wes Walz .10 .25
93 Antti Laaksonen .10 .25
94 Yanic Perreault .10 .25
95 Richard Zednik .10 .25
96 Jose Theodore .15 .40
97 Oleg Petrov .10 .25
98 Donald Audette .10 .25
99 Saku Koivu .15 .40
100 Kimmo Timonen .10 .25
101 Stu Grimson .10 .25
102 Denis Arkhipov .10 .25
103 Scott Hartnell .10 .25
104 Mike Dunham .12 .30
105 Andy Delmore .10 .25
106 Brian Rafalski .10 .25
107 John Madden .10 .25
108 Martin Brodeur .40 1.00
109 Scott Stevens .15 .40
110 Patrik Elias .15 .40
111 Scott Niedermayer .15 .40
112 Joe Nieuwendyk .12 .30
113 Mark Parrish .10 .25
114 Michael Peca .12 .30
115 Alexei Yashin .12 .30
116 Adrian Aucoin .10 .25
117 Chris Osgood .15 .40
118 Stephen Webb .10 .25
119 Eric Lindros .25 .60
120 Brian Leetch .12 .30
121 Tom Poti .10 .25
122 Pavel Bure .15 .40
123 Petr Nedved .10 .25
124 Dan Blackburn .12 .30
125 Daniel Alfredsson .15 .40
126 Patrick Lalime .12 .30
127 Marian Hossa .15 .40
128 Martin Havlat .12 .30
129 Zdeno Chara .15 .40
130 Radek Bonk .12 .30
131 Wade Redden .10 .25
132 Keith Primeau .12 .30
133 John LeClair .15 .40
134 Mark Recchi .20 .50
135 Eric Desjardins .10 .25
136 Jeremy Roenick .25 .60
137 Justin Williams .12 .30
138 Simon Gagne .15 .40
139 Tony Amonte .12 .30
140 Daniel Briere .12 .30
141 Sean Burke .10 .25
142 Ladislav Nagy .10 .25
143 Shane Doan .12 .30
144 Teppo Numminen .10 .25
145 Alexei Kovalev .12 .30
146 Johan Hedberg .15 .40
147 Jan Hrdina .10 .25
148 Mario Lemieux .60 1.50
149 Martin Straka .12 .30
150 Hans Jonsson .10 .25
151 Vincent Damphousse .12 .30
152 Owen Nolan .15 .40
153 Adam Graves .12 .30
154 Evgeni Nabokov .12 .30
155 Mike Ricci .10 .25
156 Patrick Marleau .15 .40
157 Teemu Selanne .30 .75
158 Brent Johnson .12 .30
159 Doug Weight .15 .40
160 Keith Tkachuk .15 .40
161 Al MacInnis .20 .50
162 Chris Pronger .15 .40
163 Pavol Demitra .20 .50
164 Tyson Nash .10 .25
165 Nikolai Khabibulin .15 .40
166 Vincent Lecavalier .15 .40
167 Martin St. Louis .15 .40
168 Fredrik Modin .10 .25
169 Brad Richards .15 .40
170 Shane Willis .10 .25
171 Alyn McCauley .10 .25
172 Gary Roberts .10 .25
173 Darcy Tucker .10 .25
174 Ed Belfour .15 .40
175 Mats Sundin .15 .40
176 Alexander Mogilny .12 .30
177 Todd Bertuzzi .15 .40
178 Brendan Morrison .12 .30
179 Markus Naslund .15 .40
180 Dan Cloutier .12 .30
181 Daniel Sedin .20 .50
182 Henrik Sedin .20 .50
183 Sergei Gonchar .12 .30
184 Jaromir Jagr .50 1.25
185 Peter Bondra .15 .40
186 Olaf Kolzig .15 .40
187 Robert Lang .10 .25
188 Steve Konowalchuk .10 .25
189 Patrick Roy .40 1.00
190 Steve Yzerman .40 1.00
191 Mark Hartigan .10 .25
192 Mike Weaver .10 .25
193 Frederic Cassivi .10 .25
194 Andy Hilbert .10 .25
195 Chris Kelleher .10 .25
196 Henrik Tallinder .10 .25
197 Micki Dupont RC .10 .25
198 Tyler Arnason .15 .40
199 Riku Hahl .10 .25
200 Andrej Nedorost .10 .25
201 Sean Avery .12 .30
202 Stephen Weiss .15 .40
203 Lukas Krajicek .12 .30
204 Kyle Rossiter .10 .25
205 Eric Beaudoin .10 .25
206 Tony Virta .10 .25
207 Marcel Hossa .10 .25
208 Jan Lasak .12 .30
209 Trent Hunter .10 .25
210 Ray Schultz RC .10 .25
211 Martin Prusek .10 .25
212 Chris Bala .10 .25
213 Neil Little .10 .25
214 Guillaume Lefebvre .10 .25
215 Hannes Hyvonen .10 .25
216 Gaetan Royer .10 .25
217 Martin Cibak .10 .25
218 Sebastien Centomo .10 .25
219 Karel Pilar .10 .25
220 Sebastien Charpentier .10 .25

2002-03 Upper Deck MVP Classics

*CLASSICS: .75X TO 1.5X BASE HI

2002-03 Upper Deck MVP Gold

*GOLD: 6X TO 15X BASIC CARDS

2002-03 Upper Deck MVP Golden Classics

*GLDN CLASSICS: 12.5X TO 30X BASE HI

2002-03 Upper Deck MVP Highlight Nights

COMPLETE SET (7) 8.00 15.00
HN1 Ilya Kovalchuk .75 2.00
HN2 Joe Thornton 1.00 2.50
HN3 Jarome Iginla .50 1.25
HN4 Brendan Shanahan .60 1.50
HN5 Eric Lindros .40 1.00
HN6 Mario Lemieux 3.00 8.00
HN7 Markus Naslund .40 1.00

2002-03 Upper Deck MVP Masked Men

COMPLETE SET (7) 10.00 20.00
MM1 Patrick Roy 2.50 6.00
MM2 Dominik Hasek 1.50 4.00
MM3 Jose Theodore .75 2.00
MM4 Martin Brodeur 2.00 5.00
MM5 Mike Richter .50 1.25
MM6 Sean Burke .50 1.25
MM7 Olaf Kolzig .50 1.25

2002-03 Upper Deck MVP Overdrive

COMPLETE SET (14) 6.00 12.00
SO1 Paul Kariya .50 1.25
SO2 Ilya Kovalchuk .60 1.50
SO3 Jarome Iginla .60 1.50
SO4 Sami Kapanen .40 1.00
SO5 Chris Drury .40 1.00
SO6 Peter Forsberg 1.00 2.50
SO7 Mike Modano .60 1.50
SO8 Sergei Fedorov .60 1.50
SO9 Sandis Ozolinsh .40 1.00
SO10 Marian Hossa .50 1.25
SO11 Simon Gagne .50 1.25
SO12 Alexei Kovalev .40 1.00
SO13 Markus Naslund .50 1.25
SO14 Peter Bondra .50 1.25

2002-03 Upper Deck MVP Prosign

BO Bobby Orr 125.00 250.00
CJ Curtis Joseph 15.00 40.00
DH Dany Heatley 10.00 25.00
DS Daniel Sedin 8.00 20.00
GH Gordie Howe 75.00 150.00
HS Henrik Sedin/33 10.00 25.00
KH Kristian Huselius 6.00 15.00
MF Manny Fernandez 6.00 15.00
MO Maxime Ouellet 6.00 15.00
PB Pavel Bure/145 10.00 25.00
PR Patrick Roy/48 100.00 200.00
RB Ray Bourque 30.00 80.00
SE Teemu Selanne 12.00 30.00
TS Tommy Salo 10.00 25.00
WG Wayne Gretzky 150.00 400.00

2002-03 Upper Deck MVP Skate Around Jerseys

SAAD Adam Deadmarsh 4.00 10.00
SACD Chris Drury 4.00 10.00
SAEK Espen Knutsen 4.00 10.00
SAEL Eric Lindros 5.00 12.00
SAFP Felix Potvin 5.00 12.00
SAJI Jarome Iginla 6.00 15.00
SAJL John LeClair 4.00 10.00
SAJS Joe Sakic 10.00 25.00
SAJT Joe Thornton 8.00 20.00
SAKP Keith Primeau 4.00 10.00
SAMM Mike Modano 8.00 20.00
SAOK Olaf Kolzig 5.00 12.00
SAPF Peter Forsberg 10.00 25.00
SAPK Paul Kariya 5.00 12.00
SAPR Patrick Roy 12.50 30.00
SDBK R.Blake/R.Klesla 8.00 20.00
SDBN R.Brind'Amour/J.Nieuwendyk 8.00 20.00
SDBP E.Belfour/F.Potvin 10.00 25.00
SDCB R.Cechmanek/B.Boucher 8.00 20.00
SDDB J.Dumont/M.Biron 8.00 20.00
SDDG C.Drury/S.Gagne 10.00 25.00
SDDH C.Drury/M.Hejduk 10.00 25.00
SDDL A.Deadmarsh/J.LeClair 8.00 20.00
SDFL P.Forsberg/E.Lindros 15.00 40.00
SDHP M.Hejduk/Z.Palffy 10.00 25.00
SDHR D.Hinote/S.Reinprecht 8.00 20.00
SDJM J.Jagr/M.Messier 12.00 30.00
SDKC O.Kolzig/R.Cechmanek 10.00 25.00
SDKR A.Kovalev/M.Recchi 8.00 20.00
SDLC J.LeClair/R.Cechmanek 8.00 20.00
SDLF E.Lindros/T.Fleury 10.00 25.00
SDLP J.LeClair/K.Primeau 8.00 20.00
SDMS M.Modano/T.Selanne 10.00 25.00
SDMT M.Modano/M.Turco 10.00 25.00
SDNL J.Nieuwendyk/E.Lindros 8.00 20.00
SDPO F.Potvin/C.Osgood 15.00 40.00
SDPP Z.Palffy/F.Potvin 12.00 30.00
SDRA P.Roy/D.Aebischer 40.00 100.00
SDRG M.Recchi/S.Gagne 8.00 20.00
SDSD J.Sakic/C.Drury 20.00 50.00
SDTBE M.Turco/E.Belfour 10.00 25.00
SDTBL A.Tanguay/R.Blake 8.00 20.00
SDTD R.Tugnutt/M.Denis 8.00 20.00
SDWF J.Williams/R.Fedotenko 8.00 20.00
SDWG J.Williams/S.Gagne 8.00 20.00
STDAP Deadmarsh/Allison/Palffy 8.00 20.00
STDSB Dumont/Satan/Biron 10.00 25.00
STKFS Kovalev/Fleury/Satan 12.50 30.00
STLNT Lindros/Nieuwdyk/Thrnton 15.00 40.00
STLPR LeClair/Primeau/Recchi 12.50 30.00
STMMT Mess./Mdno/Thornton 25.00 60.00
STSFR Sakic/Forsberg/Roy 25.00 60.00
STSHP Selanne/Hejduk/Palffy 12.50 30.00
STSMJ Selanne/Modano/Jagr 20.00 50.00
STTDG Thornton/Drury/Gagne 12.50 30.00
STTDH Tanguay/Drury/Hejduk 12.50 30.00
STWKT Whitney/Klesla/Tugnutt 10.00 25.00

2002-03 Upper Deck MVP Souvenirs Jerseys

SAK Alexei Kovalev 3.00 8.00
SAT Alex Tanguay 4.00 10.00
SBB Brian Boucher 3.00 8.00
SBR Rod Brind'Amour 3.00 8.00
SCO Chris Osgood 6.00 15.00
SDH Dan Hinote 3.00 8.00
SDU Mike Dunham 3.00 8.00
SEB Ed Belfour 4.00 10.00
SJJ Jaromir Jagr 8.00 20.00
SJN Joe Nieuwendyk 3.00 8.00
SJW Justin Williams 3.00 8.00
SMB Martin Biron 3.00 8.00
SMD Marc Denis 3.00 8.00
SMM Mark Messier 8.00 20.00
SMO Mike Modano 8.00 20.00
SMR Mark Recchi 3.00 8.00
SMS Miroslav Satan 3.00 8.00
SMT Marty Turco 4.00 10.00
SRB Rob Blake 3.00 8.00
SRC Roman Cechmanek 3.00 8.00
SRK Rostislav Klesla 3.00 8.00
SRT Ron Tugnutt 3.00 8.00
SSG Simon Gagne 6.00 15.00
STF0 Theo Fleury 3.00 8.00
STS Teemu Selanne 6.00 15.00
SVN Ville Nieminen 3.00 8.00
SZP Zigmund Palffy 3.00 8.00

2002-03 Upper Deck MVP Vital Forces

COMPLETE SET (14) 15.00 30.00
VF1 Paul Kariya .40 1.00
VF2 Ilya Kovalchuk .60 1.50
VF3 Joe Thornton .60 1.50
VF4 Jarome Iginla .60 1.50
VF5 Patrick Roy 2.00 5.00
VF6 Joe Sakic .75 2.00
VF7 Mike Modano .60 1.50
VF8 Dominik Hasek .75 2.00
VF9 Steve Yzerman 2.00 5.00
VF10 Eric Lindros .40 1.00
VF11 Jeremy Roenick .50 1.25
VF12 Mario Lemieux 2.50 6.00
VF13 Teemu Selanne .40 1.00
VF14 Jaromir Jagr .60 1.50

2003-04 Upper Deck MVP

COMPLETE SET (470) 30.00 60.00
COMP.SET w/o SP's (440) 20.00 40.00
1 Jason Krog .12 .30
2 Petr Sykora .15 .40
3 Steve Rucchin .12 .30
4 Cam Severson .12 .30
5 Sandis Ozolinsh .12 .30
6 Steve Thomas .12 .30
7 Stanislav Chistov .12 .30
8 Sergei Fedorov .30 .75
9 Rob Niedermayer .15 .40
10 Keith Carney .12 .30
11 Alexei Smirnov .12 .30
12 Kurt Sauer .12 .30
13 Martin Gerber .12 .30
14 Jean-Sebastien Giguere .20 .50
15 Dany Heatley .15 .40
16 Slava Kozlov .12 .30
17 Ilya Kovalchuk .20 .50
18 Marc Savard .12 .30
19 Patrik Stefan .12 .30
20 Yannick Tremblay .12 .30
21 Shawn McEachern .12 .30
22 Frantisek Kaberle .12 .30
23 Andy Sutton .12 .30
24 Lubos Bartecko .12 .30
25 Jeff Odgers .12 .30
26 Pasi Nurminen .15 .40
27 Simon Gamache .12 .30
28 Byron Dafoe .15 .40
29 Garnet Exelby .12 .30
30 Joe DiPenta RC .15 .40
31 Joe Thornton .30 .75
32 Glen Murray .15 .40
33 Mike Knuble .12 .30
34 Brian Rolston .15 .40
35 Ivan Huml .12 .30
36 Bryan Berard .15 .40
37 P-J Axelsson .12 .30
38 Nick Boynton .12 .30
39 Jonathan Girard .12 .30
40 Dan McGillis .12 .30
41 Michal Grosek .12 .30
42 Hal Gill .12 .30
43 Sergei Samsonov .15 .40
44 P.J. Stock .12 .30
45 Martin Lapointe .15 .40
46 Jeff Jillson .12 .30
47 Andrew Raycroft .15 .40
48 Martin Samuelsson .15 .40
49 Krzysztof Oliwa .12 .30
50 Steve Shields .15 .40
51 Miroslav Satan .15 .40
52 Daniel Briere .20 .50
53 Ales Kotalik .12 .30
54 J-P Dumont .12 .30
55 Curtis Brown .12 .30
56 Taylor Pyatt .12 .30
57 Jochen Hecht .12 .30
58 Chris Drury .15 .40
59 Alexei Zhitnik .15 .40
60 Maxim Afinogenov .12 .30
61 Martin Biron .15 .40
62 Mika Noronen .12 .30
63 Ryan Miller .20 .50
64 Milan Bartovic RC .15 .40
65 Jarome Iginla .25 .60
66 Craig Conroy .12 .30
67 Steve Reinprecht .12 .30
68 Martin Gelinas .12 .30
69 Oleg Saprykin .12 .30
70 Dave Lowry .12 .30
71 Dean McAmmond .12 .30
72 Jordan Leopold .12 .30
73 Chuck Kobasew .12 .30
74 Roman Turek .15 .40
75 Jamie McLennan .12 .30
76 Rick Mrozik RC .12 .30
77 Jeff O'Neill .12 .30
78 Ron Francis .25 .60
79 Rod Brind'Amour .20 .50
80 Radim Vrbata .12 .30
81 Sean Hill .12 .30
82 Erik Cole .12 .30
83 Jan Hlavac .12 .30
84 Ryan Bayda .12 .30
85 Jaroslav Svoboda .12 .30
86 Pavel Brendl .12 .30
87 Aaron Ward .12 .30
88 Patrick DesRochers .12 .30
89 Kevin Weekes .15 .40
90 Steve Sullivan .12 .30
91 Alexei Zhamnov .15 .40
92 Eric Daze .15 .40
93 Kyle Calder .12 .30
94 Tyler Arnason .12 .30
95 Mark Bell .12 .30
96 Chris Simon .12 .30
97 Alexander Karpovtsev .12 .30
98 Igor Radulov .12 .30
99 Michael Leighton .12 .30
100 Jocelyn Thibault .15 .40
101 Peter Forsberg .40 1.00
102 Milan Hejduk .15 .40
103 Alex Tanguay .15 .40
104 Joe Sakic .40 1.00
105 Paul Kariya .20 .50
106 Derek Morris .12 .30
107 Rob Blake .20 .50
108 Adam Foote .12 .30
109 Eric Messier .12 .30
110 Teemu Selanne .40 1.00
111 Dan Hinote .12 .30
112 David Aebischer .15 .40
113 Patrick Roy .50 1.25
114 Ray Whitney .15 .40
115 Andrew Cassels .12 .30
116 Geoff Sanderson .12 .30
117 David Vyborny .12 .30
118 Jaroslav Spacek .12 .30
119 Mike Sillinger .12 .30
120 Rick Nash .20 .50
121 Tyler Wright .12 .30
122 Todd Marchant .12 .30
123 Rostislav Klesla .12 .30
124 Jody Shelley .12 .30
125 Marc Denis .15 .40
126 Kent McDonell RC .15 .40
127 Mike Modano .30 .75
128 Sergei Zubov .15 .40
129 Bill Guerin .20 .50
130 Jere Lehtinen .15 .40
131 Jason Arnott .15 .40
132 Brenden Morrow .15 .40
133 Scott Young .12 .30
134 Darryl Sydor .12 .30
135 Niko Kapanen .12 .30
136 Don Sweeney .12 .30
137 Steve Ott .12 .30
138 Jason Bacashihua .12 .30
139 Marty Turco .20 .50
140 Stephane Robidas .15 .40
141 Ron Tugnutt .15 .40
142 Sergei Fedorov .30 .75
143 Brett Hull .40 1.00
144 Brendan Shanahan .20 .50
145 Nicklas Lidstrom .20 .50
146 Pavel Datsyuk .30 .75
147 Mathieu Schneider .12 .30
148 Henrik Zetterberg .25 .60
149 Igor Larionov .20 .50
150 Tomas Holmstrom .15 .40
151 Jason Woolley .12 .30
152 Darren McCarty .12 .30
153 Derian Hatcher .12 .30
154 Chris Chelios .20 .50
155 Dominik Hasek .30 .75
156 Steve Yzerman .50 1.25
157 Jiri Fischer .12 .30
158 Manny Legace .12 .30
159 Curtis Joseph .25 .60
160 Ryan Smyth .15 .40
161 Marty Reasoner .12 .30
162 Mike York .12 .30
163 Mike Comrie .15 .40
164 Radek Dvorak .15 .40
165 Ales Hemsky .20 .50
166 Eric Brewer .12 .30
167 Brad Isbister .12 .30
168 Fernando Pisani .12 .30
169 Georges Laraque .15 .40
170 Alexei Semenov .12 .30
171 Raffi Torres .12 .30
172 Jani Rita .12 .30
173 Jarret Stoll .12 .30
174 Cory Cross .12 .30
175 Jason Chimera .12 .30
176 Tommy Salo .15 .40
177 Olli Jokinen .20 .50
178 Viktor Kozlov .12 .30
179 Kristian Huselius .12 .30
180 Marcus Nilson .12 .30
181 Ivan Novoseltsev .12 .30
182 Stephen Weiss .12 .30
183 Jay Bouwmeester .12 .30
184 Valeri Bure .12 .30
185 Denis Shvidki .12 .30
186 Jaroslav Bednar .12 .30
187 Peter Worrell .12 .30
188 Roberto Luongo .30 .75
189 Jani Hurme .12 .30
190 Zigmund Palffy .20 .50
191 Jaroslav Modry .12 .30
192 Eric Belanger .12 .30
193 Alexander Frolov .15 .40
194 Jason Allison .15 .40
195 Lubomir Visnovsky .12 .30
196 Ian Laperriere .12 .30
197 Adam Deadmarsh .12 .30
198 Maxim Kuznetsov .12 .30
199 Joe Corvo .12 .30
200 Mike Cammalleri .20 .50
201 Aaron Miller .12 .30
202 Mattias Norstrom .12 .30
203 Jared Aulin .12 .30
204 Jozef Stumpel .12 .30
205 Roman Cechmanek .15 .40
206 Cristobal Huet .15 .40
207 Marian Gaborik .20 .50
208 Pascal Dupuis .12 .30
209 Cliff Ronning .12 .30
210 Andrew Brunette .12 .30
211 Sergei Zholtok .12 .30
212 Wes Walz .12 .30
213 Filip Kuba .12 .30
214 P-M Bouchard .20 .50
215 Willie Mitchell .12 .30
216 Matt Johnson .12 .30
217 Darby Hendrickson .12 .30
218 Andrei Zyuzin .12 .30
219 Manny Fernandez .12 .30
220 Dwayne Roloson .15 .40
221 Saku Koivu .20 .50
222 Richard Zednik .12 .30
223 Yanic Perreault .12 .30
224 Jan Bulis .12 .30
225 Andrei Markov .20 .50
226 Niklas Sundstrom .12 .30
227 Joe Juneau .12 .30
228 Mike Ribeiro .12 .30
229 Marcel Hossa .12 .30
230 Stephane Quintal .12 .30
231 Jose Theodore .20 .50
232 Michael Komisarek .12 .30
233 Mathieu Garon .12 .30
234 Ron Hainsey .12 .30
235 David Legwand .15 .40
236 Kimmo Timonen .12 .30
237 Andreas Johansson .12 .30
238 Denis Arkhipov .12 .30
239 Darren Haydar .12 .30
240 Scott Hartnell .12 .30
241 Scott Walker .12 .30
242 Adam Hall .12 .30
243 Greg Johnson .12 .30
244 Scottie Upshall .15 .40
245 Tomas Vokoun .15 .40
246 Brian Finley .12 .30
247 Patrik Elias .20 .50
248 Jamie Langenbrunner .15 .40
249 Scott Gomez .15 .40
250 Jeff Friesen .12 .30
251 Joe Nieuwendyk .15 .40
252 John Madden .12 .30
253 Brian Rafalski .15 .40
254 Scott Niedermayer .20 .50
255 Grant Marshall .12 .30
256 Brian Gionta .12 .30
257 Scott Stevens .20 .50
258 Colin White .12 .30
259 Michael Rupp .12 .30
260 Martin Brodeur .50 1.25
261 Corey Schwab .15 .40
262 Ken Daneyko .12 .30
263 Alexei Yashin .15 .40
264 Jason Blake .12 .30
265 Mark Parrish .12 .30
266 Dave Scatchard .12 .30
267 Michael Peca .15 .40
268 Roman Hamrlik .12 .30
269 Adrian Aucoin .12 .30
270 Arron Asham .12 .30
271 Janne Niinimaa .12 .30
272 Mattias Weinhandl .12 .30
273 Rick DiPietro .15 .40
274 Garth Snow .15 .40
275 Eric Godard .12 .30
276 Alex Kovalev .15 .40
277 Anson Carter .15 .40
278 Petr Nedved .12 .30
279 Eric Lindros .30 .75
280 Tom Poti .12 .30
281 Bobby Holik .12 .30
282 Matthew Barnaby .12 .30
283 Pavel Bure .20 .50
284 Vladimir Malakhov .12 .30
285 Jamie Lundmark .12 .30
286 Mike Dunham .15 .40
287 Dan Blackburn .15 .40
288 Marian Hossa .20 .50
289 Daniel Alfredsson .20 .50
290 Todd White .12 .30
291 Martin Havlat .20 .50
292 Radek Bonk .15 .40
293 Wade Redden .12 .30
294 Zdeno Chara .20 .50
295 Magnus Arvedson .12 .30
296 Shaun Van Allen .12 .30
297 Karel Rachunek .12 .30
298 Peter Schaefer .12 .30
299 Jason Spezza .20 .50
300 Vaclav Varada .12 .30
301 Anton Volchenkov .12 .30
302 Patrick Lalime .15 .40
303 Ray Emery .15 .40
304 Jody Hull .12 .30
305 Jeremy Roenick .30 .75
306 Mark Recchi .25 .60
307 Tony Amonte .15 .40
308 Keith Primeau .15 .40
309 Michal Handzus .15 .40
310 Kim Johnsson .12 .30
311 Eric Desjardins .15 .40
312 Sami Kapanen .12 .30
313 John LeClair .20 .50
314 Simon Gagne .20 .50
315 Donald Brashear .12 .30
316 Justin Williams .15 .40
317 Eric Weinrich .12 .30
318 Jeff Hackett .15 .40
319 Robert Esche .12 .30
320 Mike Johnson .12 .30
321 Shane Doan .15 .40
322 Ladislav Nagy .12 .30
323 Daymond Langkow .12 .30
324 Chris Gratton .12 .30
325 Jan Hrdina .12 .30
326 Teppo Numminen .12 .30
327 Branko Radivojevic .12 .30
328 Paul Mara .12 .30
329 Tyson Nash .12 .30
330 Jeff Taffe .12 .30
331 Brian Boucher .15 .40
332 Sean Burke .12 .30
333 Mario Lemieux .75 2.00
334 Martin Straka .12 .30
335 Dick Tarnstrom .12 .30
336 Aleksey Morozov .12 .30
337 Mikael Samuelsson .12 .30
338 Ville Nieminen .12 .30
339 Rico Fata .12 .30
340 Dan Focht .12 .30
341 Johan Hedberg .15 .40
342 Sebastien Caron .15 .40
343 Brooks Orpik .12 .30
344 Vincent Damphousse .15 .40
345 Patrick Marleau .20 .50
346 Marco Sturm .12 .30
347 Mike Ricci .12 .30
348 Scott Hannan .12 .30
349 Jim Fahey .12 .30
350 Todd Harvey .12 .30
351 Adam Graves .15 .40
352 Jonathan Cheechoo .15 .40
353 Brad Stuart .12 .30
354 Niko Dimitrakos .12 .30
355 Kyle McLaren .12 .30
356 Miikka Kiprusoff .20 .50
357 Evgeni Nabokov .15 .40
358 Pavol Demitra .25 .60
359 Al MacInnis .25 .60
360 Eric Boguniecki .12 .30
361 Doug Weight .20 .50
362 Scott Mellanby .12 .30
363 Keith Tkachuk .20 .50
364 Petr Cajanek .12 .30
365 Alexander Khavanov .12 .30
366 Barret Jackman .12 .30
367 Steve Martins .12 .30
368 Bryce Salvador .12 .30
369 Dallas Drake .12 .30
370 Ryan Johnson .12 .30
371 Reed Low .12 .30
372 Chris Pronger .20 .50
373 Brent Johnson .15 .40
374 Chris Osgood .20 .50
375 Peter Sejna RC .15 .40
376 Vaclav Prospal .12 .30
377 Vincent Lecavalier .20 .50
378 Brad Richards .20 .50
379 Martin St. Louis .20 .50
380 Dan Boyle .12 .30
381 Fredrik Modin .12 .30
382 Dave Andreychuk .20 .50
383 Pavel Kubina .12 .30
384 Alexander Svitov .12 .30
385 Nikita Alexeev .12 .30
386 Nikolai Khabibulin .20 .50
387 John Grahame .12 .30
388 Chris Dingman .12 .30
389 Tim Taylor .12 .30
390 Alexander Mogilny .15 .40
391 Mats Sundin .20 .50
392 Owen Nolan .20 .50
393 Tomas Kaberle .12 .30
394 Nik Antropov .15 .40
395 Ed Belfour .20 .50
396 Darcy Tucker .15 .40

397 Doug Gilmour .25 .60
398 Tie Domi .15 .40
399 Phil Housley .15 .40
400 Aki Berg .12 .30
401 Bryan McCabe .12 .30
402 Gary Roberts .12 .30
403 Carlo Colaiacovo .12 .30
404 Jyrki Lumme .12 .30
405 Mikael Tellqvist .15 .40
406 Trevor Kidd .12 .30
407 Matt Stajan RC .20 .50
408 Markus Naslund .20 .50
409 Todd Bertuzzi .20 .50
410 Brendan Morrison .15 .40
411 Ed Jovanovski .15 .40
412 Matt Cooke .12 .30
413 Trevor Linden .20 .50
414 Henrik Sedin .25 .60
415 Brent Sopel .12 .30
416 Daniel Sedin .25 .60
417 Mattias Ohlund .12 .30
418 Brandon Reid .12 .30
419 Marek Malik .12 .30
420 Bryan Allen .12 .30
421 Jarkko Ruutu .12 .30
422 Alexander Auld .12 .30
423 Dan Cloutier .15 .40
424 Jaromir Jagr .60 1.50
425 Robert Lang .12 .30
426 Sergei Gonchar .12 .30
427 Michael Nylander .12 .30
428 Peter Bondra .20 .50
429 Sergei Berezin .12 .30
430 Jeff Halpern .12 .30
431 Mike Grier .12 .30
432 Steve Konowalchuk .12 .30
433 Ivan Ciernik .12 .30
434 Steve Eminger .12 .30
435 Olaf Kolzig .20 .50
436 Sebastien Charpentier .12 .30
437 Joe Thornton CL .30 .75
438 Martin Brodeur CL .50 1.25
439 Dany Heatley CL .15 .40
440 Jean-Sebastien Giguere CL .20 .50
441 Eric Staal RC 5.00 12.00
442 Boyd Gordon RC .75 2.00
443 Joni Pitkanen RC 1.00 2.50
444 Christopher Brandner RC .75 2.00
445 Joffrey Lupul RC 1.50 4.00
446 Matthew Lombardi RC .75 2.00
447 Cody McCormick RC .75 2.00
448 Tim Gleason RC .75 2.00
449 Jiri Hudler RC 1.50 4.00
450 Antoine Vermette RC 1.25 3.00
451 Alexander Semin RC 2.00 5.00
452 Tuomo Ruutu RC 1.00 2.50
453 Dan Hamhuis RC .75 2.00
454 Sean Bergenheim RC .75 2.00
455 Brent Burns RC 2.00 5.00
456 Dan Fritsche RC .60 1.50
457 Antti Miettinen RC 1.00 2.50
458 Nathan Horton RC 1.50 4.00
459 Maxim Kondratiev RC .60 1.50
460 Matthew Spiller RC .75 2.00
461 Marc-Andre Fleury RC 10.00 25.00
462 David Hale RC .60 1.50
463 Marek Svatos RC 1.25 3.00
464 Milan Michalek RC 1.25 3.00
465 John-Michael Liles RC .75 2.00
466 Dustin Brown RC 1.50 4.00
467 Chris Higgins RC 1.25 3.00
468 Patrice Bergeron RC 12.00 30.00
469 Pavel Vorobiev RC .75 2.00
470 Jordin Tootoo RC 3.00 8.00
188J Roberto Luongo JUM/299 1.50 4.00

2003-04 Upper Deck MVP Gold Script

*1-440 VETS/25: 15X TO 40X BASIC CARDS
*1-440 ROOKIES/25: 10X TO 25X RC

2003-04 Upper Deck MVP Silver Script

*1-440 VETS/150: 5X TO 12X BASIC CARDS
*1-440 ROOKIE/150: 3X TO 8X RC

2003-04 Upper Deck MVP Canadian Exclusives

1-440 VETS/25: 15X TO 40X BASIC CARDS
*1-440 ROOKIES/25: 10X TO 25X RC

2003-04 Upper Deck MVP Clutch Performers

COMPLETE SET (7) 8.00 15.00
CP1 Patrick Roy 2.50 6.00
CP2 Markus Naslund .60 1.50
CP3 Martin Brodeur 2.00 5.00
CP4 Joe Thornton .75 2.00
CP5 Jean-Sebastien Giguere .60 1.50
CP6 Marian Gaborik .75 2.00
CP7 Steve Yzerman 2.00 5.00

2003-04 Upper Deck MVP Lethal Lineups

LL1 Hejduk/Sakic/Forsberg 60.00 150.00
LL2 Amonte/Roenick/LeClair 20.00 50.00
LL3 Thornton/Samsonov/Murray 30.00 80.00
LL4 Naslund/Bertuzzi/Linden 30.00 80.00
LL5 Gilmour/Sundin/Nolan 30.00 80.00
LL6 Shanahan/Hull/Yzerman 60.00 150.00

2003-04 Upper Deck MVP Masked Men

MM1 Martin Brodeur 2.00 5.00
MM2 Patrick Roy 2.50 6.00
MM3 Nikolai Khabibulin .50 1.25
MM4 Jocelyn Thibault .50 1.25
MM5 Jean-Sebastien Giguere .50 1.25
MM6 Patrick Lalime .50 1.25
MM7 Roberto Luongo .60 1.50
MM8 Ed Belfour .50 1.25
MM9 David Aebischer .50 1.25
MM10 Marty Turco .50 1.25

2003-04 Upper Deck MVP ProSign

PSBO Bobby Orr 100.00 200.00
PSDH Dany Heatley 15.00 40.00
PSEC Erik Cole 6.00 15.00
PSGH Gordie Howe 100.00 200.00
PSHZ Henrik Zetterberg 15.00 40.00
PSJT Joe Thornton 30.00 80.00
PSMA Maxim Afinogenov 6.00 15.00
PSMB Martin Brodeur 100.00 200.00
PSMC Mike Comrie 10.00 25.00
PSMH Martin Havlat 10.00 25.00
PSMN Markus Naslund 15.00 40.00
PSRB Ray Bourque 30.00 80.00
PSRD Rick DiPietro 10.00 25.00
PSRM Adam Hall 6.00 15.00
PSSC Stanislav Chistov 6.00 15.00
PSSG Simon Gagne 12.50 30.00
PSSH Scott Hartnell 10.00 25.00
PSWG Wayne Gretzky 300.00 800.00

2003-04 Upper Deck MVP Souvenirs

S1 Chris Drury 5.00 12.00
S2 Joe Sakic 10.00 25.00
S3 Patrick Roy 12.00 30.00
S4 Rob Blake 5.00 12.00
S5 Ray Whitney 5.00 12.00
S6 Jaromir Jagr 8.00 20.00
S7 Olaf Kolzig 5.00 12.00
S8 Peter Bondra 5.00 12.00
S9 Paul Kariya 5.00 12.00
S10 John LeClair 5.00 12.00
S11 Keith Primeau 5.00 12.00
S12 Mark Recchi 5.00 12.00
S13 Roman Cechmanek 5.00 12.00
S14 Felix Potvin 5.00 12.00
S15 Jason Allison 5.00 12.00
S16 Zigmund Palffy 5.00 12.00
S17 Peter Forsberg 8.00 20.00
S18 Alex Kovalev 5.00 12.00
S19 J-P Dumont 5.00 12.00
S20 Maxim Afinogenov 5.00 12.00
S21 Brett Hull 6.00 15.00
S22 Simon Gagne 5.00 12.00
S23 Brian Boucher 5.00 12.00
S24 Ville Nieminen 5.00 12.00
S25 Eric Lindros 5.00 12.00
S26 Jarome Iginla 6.00 15.00

2003-04 Upper Deck MVP SportsNut

SN1 Jean-Sebastien Giguere .40 1.00
SN2 Paul Kariya .40 1.00
SN3 Petr Sykora .40 1.00
SN4 Pasi Nurminen .40 1.00
SN5 Ilya Kovalchuk 1.00 2.50
SN6 Dany Heatley 1.00 2.50
SN7 Jeff Hackett .40 1.00
SN8 Joe Thornton 1.25 3.00
SN9 Glen Murray .20 .50
SN10 Sergei Samsonov .40 1.00
SN11 Martin Biron .40 1.00
SN12 Miroslav Satan .40 1.00
SN13 Maxim Afinogenov .20 .50
SN14 Roman Turek .40 1.00
SN15 Jarome Iginla .75 2.00
SN16 Chris Drury .40 1.00
SN17 Pavel Brendl .20 .50
SN18 Jeff O'Neill .20 .50
SN19 Jocelyn Thibault .40 1.00
SN20 Eric Daze .20 .50
SN21 David Aebischer .40 1.00
SN22 Peter Forsberg 1.50 4.00
SN23 Joe Sakic 2.00 5.00
SN24 Milan Hejduk .40 1.00
SN25 Marc Denis .40 1.00
SN26 Rick Nash .75 2.00
SN27 Marty Turco .40 1.00
SN28 Mike Modano 1.25 3.00
SN29 Bill Guerin .40 1.00
SN30 Dominik Hasek 2.00 5.00
SN31 Steve Yzerman 4.00 10.00
SN32 Sergei Fedorov 1.00 2.50
SN33 Brett Hull 1.00 2.50
SN34 Tommy Salo .40 1.00
SN35 Mike Comrie .40 1.00
SN36 Ryan Smyth .20 .50
SN37 Ales Hemsky .40 1.00
SN38 Roberto Luongo .75 2.00
SN39 Olli Jokinen .40 1.00
SN40 Stephen Weiss .20 .50
SN41 Roman Cechmanek .40 1.00
SN42 Zigmund Palffy .40 1.00
SN43 Dwayne Roloson .40 1.00
SN44 Manny Fernandez .40 1.00
SN45 Marian Gaborik 1.25 3.00
SN46 Jose Theodore .75 2.00
SN47 Saku Koivu .40 1.00
SN48 Marcel Hossa .20 .50
SN49 Tomas Vokoun .40 1.00
SN50 Martin Brodeur 2.00 5.00
SN51 Jamie Langenbrunner .20 .50
SN52 Patrik Elias .40 1.00
SN53 Garth Snow .40 1.00
SN54 Alexei Yashin .20 .50
SN55 Mike Dunham .40 1.00
SN56 Dan Blackburn .40 1.00
SN57 Eric Lindros .50 1.25
SN58 Pavel Bure .50 1.25
SN59 Alex Kovalev .40 1.00
SN60 Patrick Lalime .40 1.00
SN61 Marian Hossa .50 1.25
SN62 Daniel Alfredsson .40 1.00
SN63 Jason Spezza .60 1.50
SN64 Robert Esche .40 1.00
SN65 Jeremy Roenick 1.00 2.50
SN66 John LeClair .40 1.00
SN67 Tony Amonte .40 1.00
SN68 Sean Burke .40 1.00
SN69 Mike Johnson .20 .50
SN70 Johan Hedberg .40 1.00
SN71 Mario Lemieux 4.00 10.00
SN72 Martin Straka .20 .50
SN73 Evgeni Nabokov .40 1.00
SN74 Vincent Damphousse .20 .50
SN75 Chris Osgood .40 1.00
SN76 Keith Tkachuk .40 1.00
SN77 Al MacInnis .40 1.00
SN78 Nikolai Khabibulin .40 1.00
SN79 Vincent Lecavalier .50 1.25
SN80 Martin St. Louis .40 1.00
SN81 Ed Belfour .50 1.25
SN82 Mats Sundin .40 1.00
SN83 Owen Nolan .40 1.00
SN84 Alexander Mogilny .40 1.00
SN85 Alexander Auld .20 .50
SN86 Todd Bertuzzi .40 1.00
SN87 Markus Naslund .40 1.00
SN88 Ed Jovanovski .40 1.00
SN89 Olaf Kolzig .40 1.00
SN90 Jaromir Jagr 1.25 3.00
SN91 Peter Bondra .40 1.00

2003-04 Upper Deck MVP Talent

COMPLETE SET (15) 15.00 30.00
MT1 Mario Lemieux 3.00 8.00
MT2 Martin Brodeur 2.00 5.00
MT3 Markus Naslund .40 1.00
MT4 Marian Gaborik 1.50 4.00
MT5 Dany Heatley 1.00 2.50
MT6 Joe Thornton 1.25 3.00
MT7 Steve Yzerman 2.50 6.00
MT8 Marian Hossa .40 1.00
MT9 Ed Belfour .40 1.00
MT10 Pavel Bure .40 1.00
MT11 Peter Forsberg 1.50 4.00
MT12 Ilya Kovalchuk 1.00 2.50
MT13 Jaromir Jagr 1.25 3.00
MT14 Zigmund Palffy .40 1.00
MT15 Mike Modano 1.25 3.00

2003-04 Upper Deck MVP Threads

TC1 Al MacInnis 12.50 30.00
TC2 Bill Guerin 12.50 30.00
TC3 Brendan Shanahan 15.00 40.00
TC4 Brett Hull 20.00 50.00
TC5 Chris Osgood 12.50 30.00
TC6 Ed Belfour 15.00 40.00
TC7 Jaromir Jagr 20.00 50.00
TC8 Keith Primeau 12.50 30.00
TC9 Patrick Roy 30.00 80.00
TC10 Ray Bourque 25.00 60.00

2003-04 Upper Deck MVP Wal-Mart Jumbos

*VETS: 3X TO 8X BASIC CARDS
*ROOKIES: .6X TO 1.5X BASIC CARDS

2003-04 Upper Deck MVP Winning Formula

COMPLETE SET (10) 10.00 20.00
WF1 Rick Nash .75 2.00
WF2 Todd Bertuzzi .75 2.00
WF3 Jeremy Roenick 1.25 3.00
WF4 Steve Yzerman 2.00 5.00
WF5 Jason Spezza .75 2.00
WF6 Brett Hull 1.50 4.00
WF7 Jean-Sebastien Giguere .75 2.00
WF8 Mike Modano 1.25 3.00
WF9 Paul Kariya .75 2.00
WF10 Henrik Zetterberg 1.00 2.50

2005-06 Upper Deck MVP

COMPLETE SET (445) 75.00 150.00
1 Sergei Fedorov .30 .75
2 Sandis Ozolinsh .12 .30
3 Scott Niedermayer .20 .50
4 Rob Niedermayer .15 .40
5 Teemu Selanne .40 1.00
6 Jean-Sebastien Giguere .20 .50
7 Ruslan Salei .12 .30
8 Joffrey Lupul .12 .30
9 Andy McDonald .15 .40
10 Keith Carney .12 .30
11 Vitali Vishnevsky .12 .30
12 Petr Sykora .15 .40
13 Marian Hossa .20 .50
14 Patrik Stefan .12 .30
15 Kari Lehtonen .15 .40
16 Bobby Holik .12 .30
17 Andy Sutton .12 .30
18 Serge Aubin .12 .30
19 Marc Savard .12 .30
20 Peter Bondra .20 .50
21 Jaroslav Modry .12 .30
22 Niclas Havelid .12 .30
23 Mike Dunham .12 .30
24 Slava Kozlov .12 .30
25 Scott Mellanby .12 .30
26 Ilya Kovalchuk .20 .50
27 Glen Murray .15 .40
28 Joe Thornton .30 .75
29 Andrew Raycroft .15 .40
30 Patrice Bergeron .25 .60
31 Hal Gill .12 .30
32 P.J. Axelsson .12 .30
33 Shawn McEachern .12 .30
34 Brian Leetch .15 .40
35 Alexei Zhamnov .12 .30
36 Nick Boynton .12 .30
37 Brad Isbister .12 .30
38 Jiri Slegr .12 .30
39 Brad Boyes .15 .40
40 Travis Green .12 .30
41 Tom Fitzgerald .12 .30
42 Dave Scatchard .12 .30
43 Chris Drury .15 .40
44 Martin Biron .15 .40
45 Maxim Afinogenov .12 .30
46 Daniel Briere .20 .50
47 Mika Noronen .15 .40
48 Jean-Pierre Dumont .12 .30
49 Derek Roy .12 .30
50 Mike Grier .12 .30
51 Jochen Hecht .12 .30
52 Jeff Jillson .12 .30
53 Teppo Numminen .12 .30
54 Ryan Miller .20 .50
55 Tim Connolly .12 .30
56 Jarome Iginla .25 .60
57 Jordan Leopold .12 .30
58 Tony Amonte .15 .40
59 Chris Simon .12 .30
60 Shean Donovan .12 .30
61 Roman Hamrlik .12 .30
62 Chuck Kobasew .12 .30
63 Darren McCarty .12 .30
64 Robyn Regehr .12 .30
65 Phillippe Sauve .15 .40
66 Stephane Yelle .12 .30
67 Daymond Langkow .12 .30
68 Matthew Lombardi .12 .30
69 Marcus Nilson .12 .30
70 Jason Wiemer .12 .30
71 Erik Cole .12 .30
72 Glen Wesley .12 .30
73 Josef Vasicek .12 .30
74 Radim Vrbata .12 .30
75 Niclas Wallin .12 .30
76 Martin Gerber .15 .40
77 Rod Brind'Amour .20 .50
78 Eric Staal .25 .60
79 Justin Williams .15 .40
80 Ray Whitney .15 .40
81 Oleg Tverdovsky .12 .30
82 Bret Hedican .12 .30
83 Jesse Boulerice .12 .30
84 Cory Stillman .15 .40
85 Nikolai Khabibulin .20 .50
86 Tuomo Ruutu .20 .50
87 Eric Daze .15 .40
88 Kyle Calder .12 .30
89 Matthew Barnaby .12 .30
90 Adrian Aucoin .12 .30
91 Tyler Arnason .12 .30
92 Martin Lapointe .12 .30
93 Jaroslav Spacek .12 .30
94 Curtis Brown .12 .30
95 Mark Bell .12 .30
96 Pavel Vorobiev .12 .30
97 Joe Sakic .40 1.00
98 Rob Blake .20 .50
99 Alex Tanguay .20 .50
100 Milan Hejduk .15 .40
101 John-Michael Liles .12 .30
102 Steve Konowalchuk .12 .30
103 David Aebischer .15 .40
104 Brad May .12 .30
105 Patrice Brisebois .12 .30
106 Pierre Turgeon .15 .40
107 Andrew Brunette .12 .30
108 Antti Laaksonen .12 .30
109 Riku Hahl .12 .30
110 Dan Hinote .12 .30
111 Karlis Skrastins .12 .30
112 Rick Nash .20 .50
113 Marc Denis .15 .40
114 Todd Marchant .12 .30
115 David Vyborny .12 .30
116 Manny Malhotra .15 .40
117 Tyler Wright .12 .30
118 Jan Hrdina .12 .30
119 Nikolai Zherdev .12 .30
120 Bryan Berard .12 .30
121 Adam Foote .12 .30
122 Luke Richardson .12 .30
123 Trevor Letowski .12 .30
124 Jody Shelley .12 .30
125 Mike Modano .30 .75
126 Brenden Morrow .15 .40
127 Sergei Zubov .15 .40
128 Marty Turco .20 .50
129 Steve Ott .12 .30
130 Jason Arnott .15 .40
131 Bill Guerin .20 .50
132 Stu Barnes .12 .30
133 Jere Lehtinen .15 .40
134 Jaroslav Svoboda .12 .30
135 Phillippe Boucher .12 .30
136 Johan Hedberg .15 .40
137 Trevor Daley .12 .30
138 Martin Skoula .12 .30
139 Steve Yzerman .50 1.25
140 Chris Chelios .20 .50
141 Robert Lang .12 .30
142 Chris Osgood .20 .50
143 Tomas Holmstrom .15 .40
144 Kris Draper .25 .60
145 Jiri Fischer .12 .30
146 Brendan Shanahan .20 .50
147 Nicklas Lidstrom .20 .50
148 Manny Legace .20 .50
149 Henrik Zetterberg .25 .60
150 Mathieu Schneider .12 .30
151 Pavel Datsyuk .30 .75
152 Ty Conklin .15 .40
153 Ryan Smyth .15 .40
154 Jason Smith .12 .30
155 Ales Hemsky .15 .40
156 Michael Peca .15 .40
157 Chris Pronger .20 .50
158 Radek Dvorak .12 .30
159 Georges Laraque .15 .40
160 Raffi Torres .12 .30
161 Alexei Semenov .12 .30
162 Todd Harvey .12 .30
163 Igor Ulanov .12 .30
164 Jani Rita .12 .30
165 Roberto Luongo .30 .75
166 Jay Bouwmeester .12 .30
167 Olli Jokinen .20 .50
168 Sean Hill .12 .30
169 Nathan Horton .20 .50
170 Stephen Weiss .12 .30
171 Chris Gratton .12 .30
172 Joe Nieuwendyk .15 .40
173 Gary Roberts .12 .30
174 Jamie McLennan .12 .30
175 Mike Van Ryn .12 .30
176 Martin Gelinas .12 .30
177 Jozef Stumpel .12 .30
178 Luc Robitaille .20 .50
179 Mathieu Garon .15 .40
180 Lubomir Visnovsky .12 .30
181 Jeremy Roenick .30 .75
182 Mattias Norstrom .12 .30
183 Dustin Brown .20 .50
184 Alexander Frolov .12 .30
185 Valeri Bure .12 .30
186 Pavol Demitra .25 .60
187 Mike Cammalleri .20 .50
188 Aaron Miller .12 .30
189 Manny Fernandez .12 .30
190 Marian Gaborik .20 .50
191 Brian Rolston .15 .40
192 Filip Kuba .12 .30
193 P-M Bouchard .20 .50
194 Andrei Zyuzin .12 .30
195 Pascal Dupuis .12 .30
196 Alexandre Daigle .12 .30
197 Dwayne Roloson .15 .40
198 Marc Chouinard .12 .30
199 Nick Schultz .12 .30
200 Saku Koivu .20 .50
201 Richard Zednik .12 .30
202 Michael Ryder .15 .40
203 Radek Bonk .12 .30
204 Alexei Kovalev .15 .40
205 Jan Bulis .12 .30
206 Pierre Dagenais .12 .30
207 Mike Ribeiro .12 .30
208 Jose Theodore .20 .50
209 Mike Komisarek .12 .30
210 Sheldon Souray .12 .30
211 Niklas Sundstrom .12 .30
212 Mathieu Dandenault .12 .30
213 Andrei Markov .20 .50
214 Craig Rivet .12 .30
215 Tomas Vokoun .15 .40
216 David Legwand .15 .40
217 Steve Sullivan .12 .30
218 Adam Hall .12 .30
219 Scott Walker .12 .30
220 Martin Erat .12 .30
221 Paul Kariya .20 .50
222 Scott Hartnell .12 .30
223 Scott Nichol .12 .30
224 Randy Robitaille .12 .30
225 Kimmo Timonen .12 .30
226 Danny Markov .12 .30
227 Jordin Tootoo .20 .50
228 Scott Gomez .15 .40
229 Patrik Elias .20 .50
230 Martin Brodeur .40 1.00
231 Sergei Brylin .12 .30
232 John Madden .12 .30
233 Dan McGillis .12 .30
234 Paul Martin .12 .30
235 Alexander Mogilny .15 .40
236 Brian Rafalski .15 .40
237 Brian Gionta .12 .30
238 Viktor Kozlov .12 .30
239 Jamie Langenbrunner .12 .30
240 Jay Pandolfo .12 .30
241 Erik Rasmussen .12 .30
242 Alexei Yashin .15 .40
243 Rick DiPietro .15 .40
244 Alexei Zhitnik .12 .30
245 Brent Sopel .12 .30
246 Jason Blake .12 .30
247 Janne Niinimaa .12 .30
248 Mark Parrish .12 .30
249 Miroslav Satan .15 .40
250 Trent Hunter .12 .30
251 Garth Snow .15 .40
252 Mike York .12 .30
253 Shawn Bates .12 .30
254 Tom Poti .12 .30
255 Martin Straka .12 .30
256 Jaromir Jagr .60 1.50
257 Darius Kasparaitis .12 .30
258 Michael Nylander .12 .30
259 Kevin Weekes .15 .40
260 Steve Rucchin .12 .30
261 Fedor Tyutin .12 .30
262 Martin Rucinsky .12 .30
263 Ville Nieminen .12 .30
264 Jason Ward .12 .30
265 Marcel Hossa .12 .30
266 Dany Heatley .15 .40
267 Dominik Hasek .30 .75
268 Wade Redden .12 .30
269 Jason Spezza .20 .50
270 Chris Phillips .12 .30
271 Bryan Smolinski .12 .30
272 Zdeno Chara .20 .50
273 Daniel Alfredsson .20 .50
274 Martin Havlat .20 .50
275 Vaclav Varada .12 .30
276 Peter Schaefer .12 .30
277 Antoine Vermette .15 .40
278 Mike Fisher .12 .30
279 Simon Gagne .20 .50
280 Peter Forsberg .40 1.00
281 Keith Primeau .15 .40
282 Derian Hatcher .12 .30
283 Kim Johnsson .12 .30
284 Sami Kapanen .12 .30
285 Mike Knuble .12 .30
286 Eric Desjardins .15 .40
287 Robert Esche .15 .40
288 Donald Brashear .12 .30
289 Joni Pitkanen .12 .30
290 Mike Rathje .12 .30
291 Chris Therien .12 .30
292 Michal Handzus .15 .40
293 Geoff Sanderson .12 .30
294 Curtis Joseph .25 .60
295 Mike Ricci .12 .30
296 Derek Morris .12 .30
297 Mike Johnson .12 .30
298 Petr Nedved .12 .30
299 Oleg Saprykin .12 .30
300 Shane Doan .15 .40
301 Ladislav Nagy .12 .30
302 Tyson Nash .12 .30
303 Mike Comrie .15 .40
304 Brad Ference .12 .30
305 Paul Mara .12 .30
306 Mario Lemieux .75 2.00
307 Zigmund Palffy .20 .50
308 Ryan Malone .12 .30
309 Rico Fata .12 .30
310 John LeClair .20 .50
311 Lasse Pirjeta .12 .30
312 Konstantin Koltsov .12 .30
313 Mark Recchi .25 .60
314 Jocelyn Thibault .15 .40
315 Sergei Gonchar .12 .30
316 Lyle Odelein .12 .30
317 Dick Tarnstrom .12 .30
318 Jonathan Cheechoo .15 .40
319 Marco Sturm .12 .30
320 Evgeni Nabokov .15 .40
321 Alyn McCauley .12 .30
322 Milan Michalek .12 .30
323 Brad Stuart .12 .30
324 Wayne Primeau .12 .30
325 Patrick Marleau .20 .50
326 Scott Thornton .12 .30
327 Vesa Toskala .15 .40
328 Marcel Goc .15 .40
329 Kyle McLaren .12 .30
330 Christian Ehrhoff .12 .30
331 Keith Tkachuk .20 .50
332 Barret Jackman .12 .30
333 Patrick Lalime .15 .40
334 Doug Weight .20 .50
335 Mark Rycroft .12 .30
336 Christian Backman .12 .30
337 Dallas Drake .12 .30
338 Mike Sillinger .12 .30
339 Jamal Mayers .12 .30
340 Eric Brewer .12 .30
341 Scott Young .12 .30
342 Dean McAmmond .12 .30
343 Brad Richards .20 .50
344 Fredrik Modin .12 .30
345 Martin St. Louis .20 .50
346 Ruslan Fedotenko .12 .30
347 Dave Andreychuk .20 .50
348 Pavel Kubina .12 .30
349 Tim Taylor .12 .30
350 Vincent Lecavalier .20 .50
351 Sean Burke .12 .30
352 Darryl Sydor .12 .30
353 Vaclav Prospal .12 .30
354 Mats Sundin .20 .50
355 Tie Domi .15 .40
356 Bryan McCabe .12 .30
357 Darcy Tucker .15 .40
358 Tomas Kaberle .12 .30
359 Kyle Wellwood .15 .40
360 Nikolai Antropov .15 .40
361 Ken Klee .12 .30
362 Ed Belfour .20 .50
363 Matt Stajan .12 .30
364 Eric Lindros .30 .75
365 Jason Allison .15 .40
366 Jeff O'Neill .12 .30
367 Mariusz Czerkawski .12 .30
368 J-S Aubin .12 .30
369 Markus Naslund .20 .50
370 Dan Cloutier .15 .40
371 Trevor Linden .20 .50
372 Anson Carter .15 .40
373 Todd Bertuzzi .20 .50
374 Daniel Sedin .25 .60
375 Sami Salo .12 .30
376 Mattias Ohlund .12 .30
377 Henrik Sedin .25 .60
378 Jarkko Ruutu .12 .30
379 Brendan Morrison .12 .30
380 Ed Jovanovski .15 .40
381 Jason King .12 .30
382 Alex Auld .12 .30
383 Matt Cooke .12 .30
384 Olaf Kolzig .20 .50
385 Brendan Witt .12 .30
386 Jeff Halpern .12 .30
387 Dainius Zubrus .12 .30
388 Alexander Semin .20 .50
389 Jeff Friesen .12 .30
390 Andrew Cassels .12 .30
391 Brian Willsie .12 .30
392 Boyd Gordon .12 .30
393 Sidney Crosby RC 30.00 80.00
394 Alexander Ovechkin RC 30.00 80.00
395 Gilbert Brule RC 2.50 6.00
396 Woitek Wolski RC 2.00 5.00
397 Rene Bourque RC 2.50 6.00
398 Jeff Woywitka RC 1.50 4.00
399 Hannu Toivonen RC 2.50 6.00
400 Yann Danis RC 2.00 5.00
401 Alexander Perezhogin RC 2.00 5.00
402 David Leneveu RC 2.00 5.00
403 Zach Parise RC 6.00 15.00
404 Dion Phaneuf RC 4.00 10.00
405 Eric Nystrom RC 2.00 5.00
406 Mike Richards RC 5.00 12.00
407 Jeff Carter RC 4.00 10.00
408 Cam Ward RC 4.00 10.00
409 Kevin Nastiuk RC 1.50 4.00
410 Petteri Nokelainen RC 1.50 4.00
411 Robert Nilsson RC 2.50 6.00
412 Andy Wozniewski RC 2.00 5.00
413 Alexander Steen RC 4.00 10.00
414 Ryan Getzlaf RC 6.00 15.00
415 Corey Perry RC 8.00 20.00
416 Rostislav Olesz RC 2.00 5.00
417 Ryan Suter RC 3.00 8.00
418 Henrik Lundqvist RC 4.00 10.00
419 Petr Prucha RC 2.50 6.00
420 Jimmy Howard RC 6.00 15.00
421 Johan Franzen RC 4.00 10.00
422 Thomas Vanek RC 5.00 12.00
423 Brandon Bochenski RC 2.50 6.00
424 Andrej Meszaros RC 2.00 5.00
425 Ryane Clowe RC 3.00 8.00
426 Jussi Jokinen RC 2.50 6.00
427 Braydon Coburn RC 2.50 6.00
428 Jim Slater RC 2.00 5.00
429 Matthew Foy RC 1.50 4.00
430 Peter Budaj RC 3.00 8.00
431 Brent Seabrook RC 5.00 12.00
432 Lee Stempniak RC 2.50 6.00
433 Andrew Alberts RC 1.50 4.00
434 Keith Ballard RC 2.00 5.00
435 Duncan Keith RC 5.00 12.00
436 Milan Jurcina RC 2.00 5.00
437 Chris Campoli RC 1.50 4.00
438 Joe Sakic CL .30 .75
439 Joe Thornton CL .25 .60
440 Jarome Iginla CL .20 .50
441 Steve Yzerman CL .40 1.00
442 Martin Brodeur CL .50 1.25
443 Peter Forsberg CL .30 .75
444 Mario Lemieux CL .60 1.50
445 Martin St. Louis CL .15 .40

2005-06 Upper Deck MVP Gold

*VETS/100: 10X TO 25X BASIC CARDS
*ROOKIES/100: 1.2X TO 3X BASE RC
393 Sidney Crosby 120.00 300.00
394 Alexander Ovechkin 80.00 200.00

2005-06 Upper Deck MVP Materials

MAA Aaron Asham 3.00 8.00
MAF Adam Foote 3.00 8.00
MAH Adam Hall 3.00 8.00
MBB Brian Boucher 3.00 8.00
MBO Brooks Orpik 3.00 8.00
MCO Chris Osgood 3.00 8.00
MCS Chris Simon 3.00 8.00
MDC Dan Cloutier 3.00 8.00
MDH Derian Hatcher 3.00 8.00
MDR Derek Roy 3.00 8.00
MED Eric Daze 3.00 8.00
MGM Glen Murray 3.00 8.00
MJA Jason Arnott 3.00 8.00
MJB Jason Blake 3.00 8.00
MJJ Jaromir Jagr 5.00 12.00
MJL John LeClair 3.00 8.00
MJR Jarkko Ruutu 3.00 8.00
MKJ Kenny Jonsson 3.00 8.00
MLO Lyle Odelein 3.00 8.00
MMD Marc Denis 3.00 8.00
MMF Manny Fernandez 3.00 8.00
MMP Mark Parrish 3.00 8.00
MMR Mark Recchi 3.00 8.00
MMS Martin Straka 3.00 8.00
MPD Pavol Demitra 3.00 8.00
MPE Patrik Elias 3.00 8.00
MPL Patrick Lalime 3.00 8.00
MRB Rob Blake 3.00 8.00
MRF Ruslan Fedotenko 3.00 8.00
MRK Ryan Kesler 3.00 8.00
MRL Robert Lang 3.00 8.00
MSK Steve Konowalchuk 3.00 8.00
MSN Scott Niedermayer 3.00 8.00
MSS Scott Stevens 3.00 8.00
MSW Stephen Weiss 3.00 8.00
MSY Steve Yzerman SP 30.00 80.00
MTA Tony Amonte 3.00 8.00
MTB Todd Bertuzzi 3.00 8.00
MTP Tom Poti 3.00 8.00
MVD Vincent Damphousse 3.00 8.00
MVK Viktor Kozlov 3.00 8.00
MZC Zdeno Chara 3.00 8.00

2005-06 Upper Deck MVP Materials Duals

DCO Z.Chara/L.Odelein 8.00 20.00
DDR P.Demitra/M.Recchi 8.00 20.00
DHH M.Havlat/M.Hejduk 12.00 30.00
DJF E.Jovanovski/A.Foote 8.00 20.00
DLC T.Linden/D.Cloutier 20.00 50.00
DLJ M.Lemieux/J.Jagr 30.00 80.00
DPB M.Peca/R.Blake 8.00 20.00
DPD K.Primeau/E.Daze 8.00 20.00
DRN W.Redden/S.Niedermayer 8.00 20.00
DSH J.Sakic/D.Hinote 20.00 50.00

2005-06 Upper Deck MVP Materials Triples

TTFD Theo/Fernan/Denis 40.00 100.00
TGST Gretzky/Sakic/Thorn 100.00 250.00
TVAN Naslund/Linden/Jovo 40.00 100.00
TGPD Gaborik/Palffy/Demitra 40.00 100.00
TSKF Sakic/Kariya/Forsberg 50.00 125.00
TLKF St. Louis/Khabi/Fedot 30.00 80.00

2005-06 Upper Deck MVP Monumental Moments

COMPLETE SET (7) 8.00 20.00
MM1 Wayne Gretzky 5.00 12.00
MM2 Gordie Howe 2.50 6.00
MM3 Brett Hull 1.50 4.00
MM4 Steve Yzerman 2.00 5.00
MM5 Mario Lemieux 3.00 8.00
MM6 Jaromir Jagr 2.50 6.00
MM7 Dominik Hasek 1.25 3.00

2005-06 Upper Deck MVP Platinum

*VETS/25: 30X TO 80X BASIC CARDS
*ROOKIES/25: 3X TO 8X BASIC RC
393 Sidney Crosby 200.00 500.00
394 Alexander Ovechkin 300.00 800.00

2005-06 Upper Deck MVP ProSign

PAL Daniel Alfredsson SP 20.00 50.00
PBG Boyd Gordon 6.00 15.00
PBM Bryan McCabe 10.00 25.00
PDA David Aebischer 15.00 40.00
PDH Dany Heatley SP 15.00 40.00
PDM Darren McCarty 15.00 40.00
PDW Doug Weight 10.00 25.00
PEC Erik Cole 10.00 25.00
PED Eric Daze 6.00 15.00
PJI Jarome Iginla SP 12.00 30.00
PJL John-Michael Liles 10.00 25.00
PJR Jeremy Roenick 20.00 50.00
PJT Joe Thornton SP 30.00 80.00
PMB Martin Biron 10.00 25.00
PMC Mike Cammalleri 10.00 25.00
PMH Milan Hejduk SP 15.00 40.00
PMO Brendan Morrison 12.00 30.00
PMP Michael Peca 10.00 25.00
PMW Brenden Morrow 10.00 25.00
PNA Nikolai Antropov 6.00 15.00
POK Olaf Kolzig 10.00 25.00
PON Owen Nolan 20.00 50.00
PPO Mark Popovic 6.00 15.00
PRB Rob Blake 15.00 40.00
PRE Robert Esche 10.00 25.00
PRK Ryan Kesler 6.00 15.00
PRN Rick Nash SP 40.00 80.00
PRS Ryan Smyth 10.00 25.00
PSD Shane Doan 10.00 25.00
PSG Simon Gagne 15.00 40.00
PSL Martin St. Louis 20.00 50.00
PSS Sheldon Souray 6.00 15.00
PSU Steve Sullivan 6.00 15.00
PTA Tyler Arnason 6.00 15.00
PTH Trent Hunter 6.00 15.00
PTL Trevor Linden 20.00 50.00

PTP Tom Poti 6.00 15.00
PTS Tony Salmelainen 6.00 15.00
PZC Zdeno Chara 10.00 25.00
TMR Mike Ribeiro 6.00 15.00

2005-06 Upper Deck MVP Rising to the Occasion

COMPLETE SET (14) 8.00 20.00
RO1 Joe Sakic 1.25 3.00
RO2 Mario Lemieux 2.50 6.00
RO3 Martin St. Louis .60 1.50
RO4 Jarome Iginla .75 2.00
RO5 Martin Brodeur 1.50 4.00
RO6 Steve Yzerman 1.50 4.00
RO7 Dominik Hasek 1.00 2.50
RO8 Peter Forsberg 1.25 3.00
RO9 Mike Modano 1.00 2.50
RO10 Jose Theodore .60 1.50
RO11 Jaromir Jagr 2.00 5.00
RO12 Ed Belfour .60 1.50
RO13 Wayne Gretzky 4.00 10.00
RO14 Ilya Kovalchuk .60 1.50

2005-06 Upper Deck MVP Rookie Breakthrough

COMPLETE SET (14) 25.00 60.00
RB1 Sidney Crosby 12.00 30.00
RB2 Alexander Ovechkin 25.00 60.00
RB3 Jeff Carter 1.50 4.00
RB4 Gilbert Brule 1.00 2.50
RB5 Wojtek Wolski .75 2.00
RB6 Alexander Perezhogin .75 2.00
RB7 Zach Parise 2.50 6.00
RB8 Dion Phaneuf 1.50 4.00
RB9 Corey Perry 3.00 8.00
RB10 Alexander Steen 1.50 4.00
RB11 Thomas Vanek 2.00 5.00
RB12 Hannu Toivonen 1.00 2.50
RB13 Mike Richards 2.00 5.00
RB14 Robert Nilsson 1.00 2.50

2005-06 Upper Deck MVP Tribute to Greatness

COMPLETE SET (7) 10.00 25.00
COMMON GRETZKY (TG1-TG7) 2.00 5.00
TG1 Wayne Gretzky 2.00 5.00
TG2 Wayne Gretzky 2.00 5.00
TG3 Wayne Gretzky 2.00 5.00
TG4 Wayne Gretzky 2.00 5.00
TG5 Wayne Gretzky 2.00 5.00
TG6 Wayne Gretzky 2.00 5.00
TG7 Wayne Gretzky 2.00 5.00

2006-07 Upper Deck MVP

COMPLETE SET (360) 75.00 150.00
1 Chris Pronger .20 .50
2 Ilya Bryzgalov .20 .50
3 Andy McDonald .15 .40
4 Teemu Selanne .40 1.00
5 Francois Beauchemin .12 .30
6 Chris Kunitz .20 .50
7 Corey Perry .30 .75
8 Scott Niedermayer .20 .50
9 Ryan Getzlaf .20 .50
10 Jean-Sebastien Giguere .20 .50
11 Ilya Kovalchuk .20 .50
12 Jim Slater .12 .30
13 Slava Kozlov .12 .30
14 Kari Lehtonen .15 .40
15 Bobby Holik .12 .30
16 Marian Hossa .20 .50
17 Niko Kapanen .12 .30
18 Steve Rucchin .12 .30
19 Johan Hedberg .15 .40
20 Brad Boyes .12 .30
21 Hannu Toivonen .15 .40
22 Zdeno Chara .20 .50
23 Tim Thomas .20 .50
24 Marco Sturm .12 .30
25 Patrice Bergeron .25 .60
26 Brad Stuart .12 .30
27 Marc Savard .12 .30
28 Glen Murray .15 .40
29 Paul Mara .12 .30
30 Daniel Briere .20 .50
31 Chris Drury .15 .40
32 Ryan Miller .20 .50
33 Ales Kotalik .12 .30
34 Thomas Vanek .15 .40
35 Jaroslav Spacek .12 .30
36 Maxim Afinogenov .12 .30
37 Jason Pominville .12 .30
38 Derek Roy .12 .30
39 Jochen Hecht .12 .30
40 Martin Biron .15 .40
41 Miikka Kiprusoff .20 .50
42 Alex Tanguay .12 .30
43 Jamie Lundmark .12 .30
44 Jeff Friesen .12 .30
45 Jarome Iginla .25 .60
46 Dion Phaneuf .15 .40
47 Tony Amonte .15 .40
48 Chuck Kobasew .12 .30
49 Kristian Huselius .20 .50
50 Daymond Langkow .12 .30
51 Cam Ward .20 .50
52 Rod Brind'Amour .20 .50
53 Erik Cole .12 .30
54 Mike Commodore .12 .30
55 Andrew Ladd .12 .30
56 Eric Staal .25 .60
57 Cory Stillman .12 .30
58 Justin Williams .15 .40
59 Ray Whitney .15 .40
60 Frantisek Kaberle .12 .30
61 Nikolai Khabibulin .20 .50
62 Michal Handzus .15 .40
63 Pavel Vorobiev .12 .30
64 Rene Bourque .12 .30
65 Martin Havlat .12 .30
66 Duncan Keith .15 .40
67 Bryan Smolinski .12 .30
68 Tuomo Ruutu .20 .50
69 Brandon Bochenski .12 .30
70 Joe Sakic .40 1.00
71 Jose Theodore .20 .50
72 John-Michael Liles .12 .30
73 Marek Svatos .12 .30
74 Brad Richardson .12 .30
75 Wojtek Wolski .15 .40
76 Milan Hejduk .15 .40
77 Pierre Turgeon .15 .40
78 Andrew Brunette .12 .30
79 Peter Budaj .15 .40
80 Patrice Brisebois .12 .30
81 Rick Nash .20 .50
82 Rostislav Klesla .12 .30
83 Gilbert Brule .15 .40
84 Pascal Leclaire .15 .40
85 Bryan Berard .12 .30
86 Fredrik Modin .12 .30
87 David Vyborny .12 .30
88 Sergei Fedorov .30 .75
89 Nikolai Zherdev .12 .30
90 Adam Foote .12 .30
91 Jody Shelley .12 .30
92 Marty Turco .20 .50
93 Brenden Morrow .15 .40
94 Sergei Zubov .15 .40
95 Eric Lindros .30 .75
96 Jussi Jokinen .15 .40
97 Mike Modano .30 .75
98 Jere Lehtinen .12 .30
99 Steve Ott .12 .30
100 Jeff Halpern .12 .30
101 Pavel Datsyuk .30 .75
102 Tomas Holmstrom .15 .40
103 Kris Draper .12 .30
104 Dominik Hasek .30 .75
105 Nicklas Lidstrom .20 .50
106 Henrik Zetterberg .25 .60
107 Robert Lang .12 .30
108 Mikael Samuelsson .12 .30
109 Chris Chelios .20 .50
110 Mathieu Schneider .12 .30
111 Jason Williams .12 .30
112 Dwayne Roloson .15 .40
113 Ales Hemsky .15 .40
114 Fernando Pisani .12 .30
115 Shawn Horcoff .12 .30
116 Jarret Stoll .15 .40
117 Jason Smith .12 .30
118 Ryan Smyth .15 .40
119 Raffi Torres .12 .30
120 Jussi Markkanen .12 .30
121 Joffrey Lupul .12 .30
122 Marc-Andre Bergeron .12 .30
123 Nathan Horton .20 .50
124 Stephen Weiss .12 .30
125 Alex Auld .12 .30
126 Olli Jokinen .20 .50
127 Todd Bertuzzi .20 .50
128 Joe Nieuwendyk .15 .40
129 Ed Belfour .20 .50
130 Jay Bouwmeester .12 .30
131 Rostislav Olesz .12 .30
132 Alexander Frolov .12 .30
133 Dan Cloutier .15 .40
134 Mike Cammalleri .12 .30
135 Rob Blake .20 .50
136 Craig Conroy .12 .30
137 Lubomir Visnovsky .12 .30
138 Mathieu Garon .15 .40
139 Sean Avery .12 .30
140 Dustin Brown .20 .50
141 Marian Gaborik .20 .50
142 Mark Parrish .12 .30
143 Pierre-Marc Bouchard .20 .50
144 Mikko Koivu .15 .40
145 Wes Walz .12 .30
146 Brian Rolston .15 .40
147 Manny Fernandez .12 .30
148 Pavol Demitra .25 .60
149 Kim Johnsson .12 .30
150 Todd White .12 .30
151 Cristobal Huet .15 .40
152 Saku Koivu .20 .50
153 Chris Higgins .12 .30
154 Andrei Markov .20 .50
155 Mike Ribeiro .12 .30
156 David Aebischer .15 .40
157 Alex Kovalev .15 .40
158 Sergei Samsonov .15 .40
159 Michael Ryder .12 .30
160 Sheldon Souray .12 .30
161 Alexander Perezhogin .12 .30
162 Paul Kariya .20 .50
163 Jason Arnott .15 .40
164 Jordin Tootoo .20 .50
165 J.P. Dumont .12 .30
166 Steve Sullivan .12 .30
167 Tomas Vokoun .15 .40
168 Marek Zidlicky .12 .30
169 Martin Erat .12 .30
170 Scott Hartnell .12 .30
171 Martin Brodeur .50 1.25
172 Brian Gionta .12 .30
173 John Madden .12 .30
174 Zach Parise .20 .50
175 Brian Rafalski .15 .40
176 Patrik Elias .20 .50
177 Sergei Brylin .12 .30
178 Scott Gomez .15 .40
179 Jamie Langenbrunner .12 .30
180 Paul Martin .12 .30
181 Miroslav Satan .15 .40
182 Mike Sillinger .12 .30
183 Tom Poti .12 .30
184 Jason Blake .12 .30
185 Trent Hunter .12 .30
186 Alexei Yashin .15 .40
187 Rick DiPietro .15 .40
188 Alexei Zhitnik .12 .30
189 Shawn Bates .12 .30
190 Jeff Tambellini .12 .30
191 Jaromir Jagr .60 1.50
192 Brendan Shanahan .20 .50
193 Martin Straka .12 .30
194 Marek Malik .12 .30
195 Petr Prucha .15 .40
196 Henrik Lundqvist .50 1.25
197 Sandis Ozolinsh .12 .30
198 Matt Cullen .12 .30
199 Michael Nylander .12 .30
200 Fedor Tyutin .12 .30
201 Jason Spezza .20 .50
202 Ray Emery .15 .40
203 Wade Redden .12 .30
204 Patrick Eaves .12 .30
205 Daniel Alfredsson .20 .50
206 Martin Gerber .15 .40
207 Dany Heatley .15 .40
208 Andrej Meszaros .12 .30
209 Mike Fisher .12 .30
210 Peter Schaefer .12 .30
211 Simon Gagne .20 .50
212 Joni Pitkanen .12 .30
213 Jeff Carter .15 .40
214 R.J. Umberger .12 .30
215 Peter Forsberg .40 1.00
216 Antero Niittymaki .15 .40
217 Mike Richards .15 .40
218 Mike Knuble .12 .30
219 Robert Esche .15 .40
220 Kyle Calder .12 .30
221 Geoff Sanderson .12 .30
222 Shane Doan .15 .40
223 Ed Jovanovski .15 .40
224 Ladislav Nagy .12 .30
225 Curtis Joseph .25 .60
226 Jeremy Roenick .30 .75
227 Keith Ballard .12 .30
228 Mike Comrie .15 .40
229 David Leneveu .15 .40
230 Owen Nolan .20 .50
231 Sidney Crosby .75 2.00
232 Mark Recchi .25 .60
233 Nils Ekman .12 .30
234 Ryan Whitney .15 .40
235 Colby Armstrong .15 .40
236 John LeClair .20 .50
237 Marc-Andre Fleury .40 1.00
238 Sergei Gonchar .12 .30
239 Ryan Malone .12 .30
240 Joe Thornton .30 .75
241 Vesa Toskala .15 .40
242 Mark Bell .12 .30
243 Steve Bernier .12 .30
244 Christian Ehrhoff .12 .30
245 Jonathan Cheechoo .15 .40
246 Patrick Marleau .20 .50
247 Mike Grier .12 .30
248 Milan Michalek .12 .30
249 Evgeni Nabokov .15 .40
250 Keith Tkachuk .20 .50
251 Manny Legace .15 .40
252 Martin Rucinsky .12 .30
253 Bill Guerin .20 .50
254 Lee Stempniak .12 .30
255 Petr Cajanek .12 .30
256 Doug Weight .20 .50
257 Jay McKee .12 .30
258 Martin St. Louis .20 .50
259 Marc Denis .15 .40
260 Vaclav Prospal .12 .30
261 Brad Richards .20 .50
262 Paul Ranger .12 .30
263 Ruslan Fedotenko .12 .30
264 Vincent Lecavalier .20 .50
265 Filip Kuba .12 .30
266 Ryan Craig .12 .30
267 Dan Boyle .12 .30
268 Mats Sundin .20 .50
269 Michael Peca .15 .40
270 Alexander Steen .15 .40
271 Bryan McCabe .12 .30
272 Tomas Kaberle .12 .30
273 Andrew Raycroft .15 .40
274 Nikolai Antropov .15 .40
275 Kyle Wellwood .15 .40
276 Mikael Tellqvist .20 .50
277 Darcy Tucker .15 .40
278 Matt Stajan .12 .30
279 Jeff O'Neill .12 .30
280 Matt Cooke .12 .30
281 Sami Salo .12 .30
282 Roberto Luongo .30 .75
283 Markus Naslund .20 .50
284 Daniel Sedin .25 .60
285 Mattias Ohlund .12 .30
286 Ryan Kesler .20 .50
287 Henrik Sedin .25 .60
288 Brendan Morrison .12 .30
289 Mika Noronen .15 .40
290 Brian Sutherby .12 .30
291 Steve Eminger .12 .30
292 Alexander Ovechkin .75 2.00
293 Olaf Kolzig .20 .50
294 Richard Zednik .12 .30
295 Dainius Zubrus .12 .30
296 Brent Johnson .15 .40
297 Chris Clark .12 .30
298 Patrick O'Sullivan RC 2.00 5.00
299 Phil Kessel RC 6.00 15.00
300 G. Latendresse RC 2.00 5.00
301 Jordan Staal RC 3.00 8.00
302 Paul Stastny RC 3.00 8.00
303 Evgeni Malkin RC 8.00 20.00
304 Luc Bourdon RC 2.00 5.00
305 Alexei Kaigorodov RC 1.25 3.00
306 Anze Kopitar RC 6.00 15.00
307 Travis Zajac RC 2.50 6.00
308 Nigel Dawes RC 1.25 3.00
309 Kristopher Letang RC 5.00 12.00
310 Marc-Edouard Vlasic RC 2.00 5.00
311 Patrick Thoresen RC 1.25 3.00
312 Ladislav Smid RC 1.25 3.00
313 Loui Eriksson RC 2.50 6.00
314 Shane O'Brien RC 1.25 3.00
315 Ryan Shannon RC 1.25 3.00
316 John Oduya RC 2.00 5.00
317 Fredrik Norrena RC 1.25 3.00
318 Niklas Backstrom RC 2.50 6.00
319 D.J. King RC 1.25 3.00
320 Patrick Fischer RC 1.25 3.00
321 Mikko Lehtonen RC 1.50 4.00
322 Roman Polak RC 1.50 4.00
323 Ben Ondrus RC 1.25 3.00
324 Bill Thomas RC 1.25 3.00
325 Billy Thompson RC 1.25 3.00
326 Brendan Bell RC 1.25 3.00
327 Carsen Germyn RC 1.25 3.00
328 Keith Yandle RC 3.00 8.00
329 Dan Jancevski RC 1.25 3.00
330 David Liffiton RC 1.25 3.00
331 David Printz RC 1.25 3.00
332 Dustin Byfuglien RC 3.00 8.00
333 Eric Fehr RC 2.50 6.00
334 Erik Reitz RC 1.25 3.00
335 Filip Novak RC 1.25 3.00
336 Frank Doyle RC 1.50 4.00
337 Ian White RC 1.50 4.00
338 Jarkko Immonen RC 1.50 4.00
339 Jeremy Williams RC 1.25 3.00
340 Joel Perrault RC 1.25 3.00
341 Jonas Johansson RC 1.25 3.00
342 Konstantin Pushkarev RC 1.50 4.00
343 Marc-Antoine Pouliot RC 1.25 3.00
344 Mark Stuart RC 1.25 3.00
345 Masi Marjamaki RC 1.25 3.00
346 Matt Carle RC 1.25 3.00
347 Matt Koalska RC 1.25 3.00
348 Michel Ouellet RC 1.50 4.00
349 Miroslav Kopriva RC 1.25 3.00
350 Noah Welch RC 1.25 3.00
351 Rob Collins RC 1.25 3.00
352 Ryan Caldwell RC 1.25 3.00
353 Ryan Potulny RC 1.25 3.00
354 Shea Weber RC 3.00 8.00
355 Enver Lisin RC 1.25 3.00
356 Tomas Kopecky RC 1.50 4.00
357 Yan Stastny RC 1.25 3.00
358 Joe Thornton CL .25 .60
359 Martin St. Louis CL .15 .40
360 Peter Forsberg CL .30 .75

2006-07 Upper Deck MVP Gold Script

*VETS/100: 10X TO 25X BASIC CARDS
*ROOKIES/100 1.2X TO 3X BASIC RC

2006-07 Upper Deck MVP Super Script

*VETS/25: 25X TO 60X BASIC CARDS
*ROOKIES: 2.5X TO 6X BASE HI
231 Sidney Crosby 125.00 250.00
303 Evgeni Malkin 100.00 200.00

2006-07 Upper Deck MVP Autographs

OAAT Antropov/Tellqvist 12.00 30.00
OABK Bourque/Keith 8.00 20.00
OABM Bernier/Michalek 12.00 30.00
OABP Bouchard/Parrish 12.00 30.00
OABS Boyes/Stastny EXCH 12.00 30.00
OACL Cole/Ladd 8.00 20.00
OACR Carter/Richards 30.00 80.00
OACS Chara/Stuart 12.00 30.00
OADA Drury/Afinogenov 12.00 30.00
OADO Draper/Osgood 15.00 40.00
OAEE Esche/Eager 8.00 20.00
OAEG Elias/Gionta 12.00 30.00
OAFC Frolov/Cammalleri 12.00 30.00
OAFQ Filppula/Quincey 12.00 30.00
OAGA Gerber/Aebischer SP 25.00 60.00
OAHC Heatley/Cheechoo SP 25.00 60.00
OAHH Havlat/Handzus 12.00 30.00
OAHT Hejduk/Theodore 15.00 40.00
OAKL Kipper/Luongo SP 40.00 80.00
OALH Lupul/Horcoff 8.00 20.00
OALS Leneveu/Sauve 8.00 20.00
OALW Legace/Woywitka 8.00 20.00
OAMC Malone/Christensen 12.00 30.00
OAMK McDonald/Kunitz 8.00 20.00
OANI Nash/Iginla SP 60.00 100.00
OANM Naslund/Morrison 12.00 30.00
OAPK Phaneuf/Kobasew SP 12.00 30.00
OAPT Peca/Tucker SP 20.00 50.00
OARK Ribeiro/Kostitsyn SP 15.00 40.00
OARL Richardson/Liles 8.00 20.00
OARS Ryder/Samsonov SP 12.00 30.00
OASC Satan/Colliton 8.00 20.00
OATM Thornton/Marleau 25.00 60.00
OAVV Vokoun/Vasicek SP 15.00 40.00

2006-07 Upper Deck MVP Clutch Performers

COMPLETE SET (25) 10.00 25.00
CP1 Cam Ward .60 1.50
CP2 Peter Forsberg 1.25 3.00
CP3 Joe Sakic 1.25 3.00
CP4 Martin Brodeur 1.50 4.00
CP5 Jarome Iginla .75 2.00
CP6 Jaromir Jagr 2.00 5.00
CP7 Mats Sundin .60 1.50
CP8 Dany Heatley .50 1.25
CP9 Ryan Miller .60 1.50
CP10 Alexander Ovechkin 1.50 4.00
CP11 Eric Staal .75 2.00
CP12 Mike Modano 1.00 2.50
CP13 Martin St. Louis .60 1.50
CP14 Ryan Smyth .50 1.25
CP15 Chris Pronger .60 1.50
CP16 Henrik Zetterberg .75 2.00
CP17 Jonathan Cheechoo .50 1.25
CP18 Ilya Kovalchuk .60 1.50
CP19 Marian Gaborik .60 1.50
CP20 Shane Doan .75 2.00
CP21 Rick Nash .60 1.50
CP22 Sidney Crosby 2.50 6.00
CP23 Markus Naslund .60 1.50
CP24 Dominik Hasek 1.00 2.50
CP25 Mario Lemieux 2.50 6.00

2006-07 Upper Deck MVP Gotta Have Hart

COMPLETE SET (25) 10.00 25.00
HH1 Joe Thornton 1.00 2.50
HH2 Peter Forsberg 1.25 3.00
HH3 Martin St. Louis .60 1.50
HH4 Jose Theodore .60 1.50
HH5 Joe Sakic 1.25 3.00
HH6 Chris Pronger .60 1.50
HH7 Jaromir Jagr 2.00 5.00
HH8 Mario Lemieux 2.50 6.00
HH9 Wayne Gretzky 3.00 8.00
HH10 Eric Lindros 1.00 2.50
HH11 Sergei Fedorov 1.00 2.50
HH12 Alexander Ovechkin 1.50 4.00
HH13 Sidney Crosby 2.50 6.00
HH14 Jarome Iginla .75 2.00
HH15 Eric Staal .75 2.00
HH16 Martin Brodeur 1.50 4.00
HH17 Miikka Kiprusoff .60 1.50
HH18 Rick Nash .60 1.50
HH19 Ilya Kovalchuk .60 1.50
HH20 Dominik Hasek 1.00 2.50
HH21 Marian Gaborik .60 1.50
HH22 Patrice Bergeron .75 2.00
HH23 Mats Sundin .60 1.50
HH24 Markus Naslund .60 1.50
HH25 Dany Heatley .50 1.25

2006-07 Upper Deck MVP International Icons

COMPLETE SET (25) 15.00 40.00
II1 Teemu Selanne 1.25 3.00
II2 Ilya Kovalchuk .60 1.50
II3 Marian Hossa .60 1.50
II4 Marco Sturm .40 1.00
II5 Milan Hejduk .50 1.25
II6 Sergei Fedorov 1.00 2.50
II7 Mike Modano 1.00 2.50
II8 Nicklas Lidstrom .60 1.50
II9 Dominik Hasek 1.00 2.50
II10 Olli Jokinen .60 1.50
II11 Marian Gaborik .60 1.50
II12 Saku Koivu .60 1.50
II13 Tomas Vokoun .50 1.25
II14 Martin Brodeur 1.50 4.00
II15 Miroslav Satan .50 1.25
II16 Rick DiPietro .50 1.25
II17 Jaromir Jagr 2.00 5.00
II18 Martin Gerber .50 1.25
II19 Peter Forsberg 1.25 3.00
II20 Sidney Crosby 2.50 6.00
II21 Vincent Lecavalier .60 1.50
II22 Mats Sundin .60 1.50
II23 Nikolai Antropov .50 1.25
II24 Alexander Ovechkin 2.50 6.00
II25 Olaf Kolzig .60 1.50

2006-07 Upper Deck MVP Jerseys

OJAB A.Picard/B.Bochenski 4.00 10.00
OJAR Aebischer/Raycroft 6.00 15.00
OJBJ J.Bouwmeester/O.Jokinen 4.00 10.00
OJBK P.Bouchard/R.Kesler 4.00 10.00
OJBL M.Brodeur/H.Lundqvist 15.00 40.00
OJBN Brodeur/Niittymaki 12.00 30.00
OJBR P.Bergeron/M.Ryder 6.00 15.00
OJCF Crosby/Forsberg SP 40.00 80.00
OJCG J.Carter/S.Gomez 6.00 15.00
OJCJ C.Kobasew/J.Stoll 4.00 10.00
OJCO Crosby/Ovechkin SP 75.00 150.00
OJCR Z.Chara/W.Redden 4.00 10.00
OJCS J.Cheechoo/T.Selanne 8.00 20.00
OJDH P.Demitra/A.Hemsky 4.00 10.00
OJDK C.Drury/A.Kovalev 4.00 10.00
OJDM S.Doan/B.Morrow 6.00 15.00
OJDP K.Draper/M.Peca 4.00 10.00
OJDR Brodeur/Jagr 15.00 40.00
OJEP P.Elias/P.Prucha 4.00 10.00
OJER E.Staal/R.Smyth 6.00 15.00
OJES P.Elias/M.Satan 4.00 10.00
OJEV Staal/Lecavalier 8.00 20.00
OJFA S.Fedorov/J.Arnott 6.00 15.00
OJFD Fedorov/Datsyuk 8.00 20.00
OJFM F.Pisani/M.Lombardi 4.00 10.00
OJFN A.Frolov/L.Nagy 6.00 15.00
OJFR M.Fernandez/D.Roloson 6.00 15.00
OJGC R.Getzlaf/M.Cammalleri 5.00 12.00
OJGH Gaborik/Havlat 10.00 25.00
OJGL Gretzky/Lemieux SP 150.00 300.00
OJHB Heatley/Briere SP 15.00 40.00
OJHF M.Hossa/R.Fedotenko 4.00 10.00
OJHH M.Hejduk/A.Hemsky 4.00 10.00
OJHL N.Horton/A.Ladd 4.00 10.00
OJHM T.Hunter/R.Malone 4.00 10.00
OJHS Heatley/Steen 8.00 20.00
OJHV Hasek/Vokoun 10.00 25.00
OJIS Iginla/Smyth 8.00 20.00
OJJC C.Joseph/D.Cloutier 6.00 15.00
OJJF Jagr/Forsberg 10.00 25.00
OJJJ J.Stoll/J.Friesen 4.00 10.00
OJJL E.Jovanovski/J.Leopold 4.00 10.00
OJJM J.Stoll/M.Svatos 4.00 10.00
OJJS Jagr/Satan 10.00 25.00
OJKD O.Kolzig/M.Denis 6.00 15.00
OJKL Kiprusoff/Luongo 15.00 40.00
OJKR M.Koivu/T.Ruutu 6.00 15.00
OJKS J.Spezza/S.Koivu 6.00 15.00
OJKW P.Kariya/D.Weight 6.00 15.00
OJKZ Kariya/Zetterberg 8.00 20.00
OJLD Lundqvist/DiPietro 10.00 25.00
OJLF A.Ladd/T.Fleischmann 4.00 10.00
OJLJ V.Lecavalier/O.Jokinen 6.00 15.00
OJLK K.Lehtonen/O.Kolzig 6.00 15.00
OJLM Lidstrom/McCabe 10.00 25.00
OJLS R.Lang/S.Sullivan 4.00 10.00
OJLZ N.Lidstrom/S.Zubov 6.00 15.00
OJMJ A.Meszaros/M.Jurcina 4.00 10.00
OJMS M.St.Louis/S.Gagne 6.00 15.00
OJMT M.Modano/P.Turgeon 6.00 15.00
OJNJ S.Niedermayer/E.Jovanovski 4.00 10.00
OJNT R.Nash/K.Tkachuk 6.00 15.00
OJOC C.Osgood/T.Conklin 6.00 15.00
OJOK Ovechkin/Kovalchuk 20.00 50.00
OJOT Spezza/Sundin 10.00 25.00
OJPB C.Pronger/R.Blake 6.00 15.00
OJPJ C.Perry/J.Jokinen 4.00 10.00
OJPL D.Phaneuf/J.Liles 10.00 25.00
OJPN D.Phaneuf/S.Niedermayer 6.00 15.00
OJPO J.Pitkanen/S.Ozolinsh 4.00 10.00
OJPR J.Pitkanen/B.Rafalski 4.00 10.00
OJRB B.Richards/R.Brind'Amour 6.00 15.00
OJRL J.Roenick/E.Lindros 8.00 20.00
OJRM R.Luongo/M.Fernandez 6.00 15.00
OJRW B.Rafalski/B.Witt 4.00 10.00
OJSA S.Samsonov/M.Afinogenov 4.00 10.00
OJSC S.Sullivan/K.Calder 4.00 10.00
OJSD M.Savard/C.Drury 4.00 10.00
OJSF T.Selanne/A.Frolov 6.00 15.00
OJSG Shanahan/Gagne 8.00 20.00
OJSH M.St.Louis/N.Horton 6.00 15.00
OJSK M.Sundin/S.Koivu 6.00 15.00
OJSL Shanahan/LeClair SP 15.00 40.00
OJSM Sakic/Modano 10.00 25.00
OJSN S.Samsonov/N.Antropov 4.00 10.00
OJSS M.Satan/M.Straka 4.00 10.00
OJST Sakic/Thornton 12.00 30.00
OJSV M.Svatos/J.Lupul 4.00 10.00
OJTG Turco/Giguere 8.00 20.00
OJTH K.Tkachuk/M.Havlat 4.00 10.00
OJTN A.Tanguay/M.Naslund 6.00 15.00
OJWA D.Weight/J.Arnott 4.00 10.00
OJWC D.Weight/K.Calder 4.00 10.00
OJWD Ward/Denis 8.00 20.00
OJWL Ward/Lehtonen 8.00 20.00
OJWW J.Williams/S.Weiss 4.00 10.00
OJZN Zetterberg/Nash 8.00 20.00

2006-07 Upper Deck MVP Last Line of Defense

COMPLETE SET (25) 10.00 25.00
LL1 Martin Brodeur 2.00 5.00
LL2 Miikka Kiprusoff 1.00 2.50
LL3 Henrik Lundqvist 2.50 6.00
LL4 Marty Turco 1.00 2.50
LL5 Cristobal Huet .75 2.00
LL6 Marc-Andre Fleury 2.00 5.00
LL7 Roberto Luongo 1.50 4.00
LL8 Cam Ward 1.00 2.50
LL9 Ryan Miller 1.00 2.50
LL10 Nikolai Khabibulin 1.00 2.50
LL11 Kari Lehtonen .75 2.00
LL12 Tomas Vokoun .75 2.00
LL13 Dwayne Roloson .75 2.00
LL14 Olaf Kolzig 1.00 2.50
LL15 Ed Belfour 1.00 2.50
LL16 Vesa Toskala .75 2.00
LL17 Jose Theodore 1.00 2.50
LL18 Curtis Joseph 1.25 3.00
LL19 Manny Fernandez .60 1.50
LL20 Dominik Hasek 1.50 4.00
LL21 Martin Gerber .75 2.00
LL22 Andrew Raycroft .75 2.00
LL23 Rick DiPietro .75 2.00
LL24 Hannu Toivonen .75 2.00
LL25 Manny Legace .75 2.00

2007-08 Upper Deck MVP

COMPLETE SET (380) 75.00 150.00
COMP.SET w/o RCs (300) 15.00 40.00
1 Joe Sakic .40 1.00
2 Brett Clark .12 .30
3 Peter Budaj .15 .40
4 Marek Svatos .12 .30
5 Andrew Brunette .12 .30
6 Paul Stastny .15 .40
7 Milan Hejduk .15 .40
8 Wojtek Wolski .15 .40
9 John-Michael Liles .12 .30
10 Tyler Arnason .12 .30
11 Jose Theodore .20 .50
12 Martin Havlat .20 .50
13 Patrick Sharp .20 .50
14 Nikolai Khabibulin .20 .50
15 Duncan Keith .15 .40
16 Jason Williams .12 .30
17 Radim Vrbata .12 .30
18 Brent Seabrook .12 .30
19 Patrick Lalime .15 .40
20 Jeff Hamilton .12 .30
21 Tuomo Ruutu .20 .50
22 Rick Nash .20 .50
23 Fredrik Norrena .12 .30
24 Fredrik Modin .12 .30
25 Gilbert Brule .15 .40
26 Jody Shelley .12 .30
27 David Vyborny .12 .30
28 Pascal Leclaire .15 .40
29 Sergei Fedorov .30 .75
30 Nikolai Zherdev .12 .30
31 Rostislav Klesla .12 .30
32 Doug Weight .20 .50
33 Jay McClement .12 .30
34 Manny Legace .15 .40
35 Barret Jackman .12 .30
36 David Backes .12 .30
37 Lee Stempniak .12 .30
38 Brad Boyes .12 .30
39 Eric Brewer .12 .30
40 Jason Bacashihua .15 .40
41 Patrice Bergeron .25 .60
42 Zdeno Chara .20 .50
43 Tim Thomas .20 .50
44 Marco Sturm .12 .30
45 Chuck Kobasew .12 .30
46 Glen Murray .15 .40
47 Phil Kessel .20 .50
48 Hannu Toivonen .15 .40
49 Marc Savard .12 .30
50 Dennis Wideman .12 .30
51 Saku Koivu .20 .50
52 Chris Higgins .12 .30
53 Andrei Markov .20 .50
54 Cristobal Huet .15 .40
55 Guillaume Latendresse .15 .40
56 Sheldon Souray .12 .30
57 Tomas Plekanec .12 .30
58 Alex Kovalev .15 .40
59 Michael Ryder .12 .30
60 Maxim Lapierre .12 .30
61 Andrei Kostitsyn .15 .40
62 Roberto Luongo .30 .75
63 Markus Naslund .20 .50
64 Sami Salo .12 .30
65 Taylor Pyatt .12 .30
66 Daniel Sedin .25 .60
67 Henrik Sedin .25 .60
68 Kevin Bieksa .15 .40
69 Brendan Morrison .12 .30
70 Ryan Kesler .20 .50
71 Mattias Ohlund .12 .30
72 Trevor Linden .20 .50
73 Alexander Ovechkin .75 2.00
74 Mike Green .15 .40
75 Brent Johnson .15 .40
76 Jiri Novotny .12 .30
77 Chris Clark .12 .30
78 Matt Pettinger .12 .30
79 Brian Pothier .12 .30
80 Alexander Semin .20 .50
81 Olaf Kolzig .20 .50
82 Shane Doan .15 .40
83 Mikael Tellqvist .15 .40
84 Zbynek Michalek .12 .30
85 Keith Ballard .12 .30
86 Owen Nolan .20 .50
87 Steven Reinprecht .12 .30
88 Derek Morris .12 .30
89 Ed Jovanovski .15 .40
90 Curtis Joseph .25 .60
91 Martin Brodeur .50 1.25
92 Scott Gomez .15 .40
93 Travis Zajac .12 .30
94 Brian Rafalski .15 .40
95 Patrik Elias .20 .50
96 Jamie Langenbrunner .12 .30
97 Brian Gionta .12 .30
98 Johnny Oduya .15 .40
99 Jay Pandolfo .12 .30
100 John Madden .12 .30
101 Teemu Selanne .40 1.00
102 Chris Pronger .20 .50
103 Ilya Bryzgalov .20 .50
104 Dustin Penner .15 .40
105 Ryan Getzlaf .20 .50
106 Scott Niedermayer .20 .50
107 Chris Kunitz .20 .50
108 Corey Perry .30 .75
109 Andy McDonald .15 .40
110 Jean-Sebastien Giguere .20 .50
111 Jarome Iginla .25 .60
112 Matthew Lombardi .12 .30
113 Daymond Langkow .12 .30
114 Miikka Kiprusoff .20 .50
115 Robyn Regehr .12 .30
116 Dion Phaneuf .15 .40
117 Kristian Huselius .12 .30
118 Stephane Yelle .12 .30
119 Alex Tanguay .15 .40
120 Roman Hamrlik .12 .30
121 Tony Amonte .15 .40
122 Simon Gagne .20 .50
123 Martin Biron .15 .40
124 Joni Pitkanen .12 .30
125 R.J. Umberger .12 .30
126 Jeff Carter .15 .40
127 Mike Knuble .12 .30
128 Ben Eager .12 .30
129 Mike Richards .15 .40
130 Antero Niittymaki .15 .40
131 Eric Staal .25 .60
132 Ray Whitney .15 .40
133 Mike Commodore .12 .30
134 Cory Stillman .12 .30
135 John Grahame .12 .30
136 Rod Brind'Amour .20 .50
137 Erik Cole .12 .30
138 Cam Ward .20 .50
139 Glen Wesley .12 .30
140 Justin Williams .15 .40
141 Alexei Yashin .15 .40
142 Rick DiPietro .15 .40
143 Ryan Smyth .15 .40
144 Brendan Witt .12 .30
145 Jason Blake .12 .30
146 Chris Simon .12 .30
147 Viktor Kozlov .12 .30
148 Mike Sillinger .12 .30
149 Miroslav Satan .15 .40
150 Alexander Frolov .12 .30
151 Dan Cloutier .15 .40
152 Rob Blake .20 .50
153 Dustin Brown .20 .50
154 Patrick O'Sullivan .15 .40
155 Lubomir Visnovsky .12 .30
156 Anze Kopitar .30 .75
157 Mike Cammalleri .15 .40
158 Derek Armstrong .12 .30
159 Vincent Lecavalier .20 .50
160 Marc Denis .15 .40
161 Dan Boyle .12 .30
162 Eric Perrin .12 .30
163 Filip Kuba .12 .30
164 Brad Richards .20 .50
165 Ruslan Fedotenko .12 .30
166 Vaclav Prospal .12 .30
167 Martin St. Louis .20 .50
168 Johan Holmqvist .15 .40
169 Mats Sundin .20 .50
170 Ian White .12 .30
171 Matt Stajan .12 .30
172 Darcy Tucker .15 .40
173 Bryan McCabe .12 .30
174 Andrew Raycroft .15 .40
175 Kyle Wellwood .15 .40
176 Alexei Ponikarovsky .12 .30
177 Alexander Steen .12 .30
178 Tomas Kaberle .12 .30
179 Vesa Toskala .15 .40
180 Dwayne Roloson .15 .40
181 Petr Sykora .15 .40
182 Marc-Antoine Pouliot .12 .30
183 Raffi Torres .12 .30
184 Joffrey Lupul .12 .30
185 Steve Staios .12 .30
186 Jussi Markkanen .15 .40
187 Shawn Horcoff .12 .30
188 Jarret Stoll .15 .40
189 Ladislav Smid .12 .30
190 Ales Hemsky .15 .40
191 Olli Jokinen .15 .40
192 Rostislav Olesz .12 .30
193 Jay Bouwmeester .12 .30
194 Alex Auld .12 .30
195 Nathan Horton .20 .50
196 Mike Van Ryn .12 .30
197 Jozef Stumpel .12 .30
198 Stephen Weiss .12 .30
199 Tomas Vokoun .15 .40
200 Sidney Crosby .75 2.00
201 Evgeni Malkin .40 1.00
202 Ryan Whitney .15 .40
203 Mark Recchi .25 .60
204 Marc-Andre Fleury .40 1.00
205 Sergei Gonchar .12 .30
206 Michel Ouellet .12 .30
207 Jordan Staal .15 .40
208 Colby Armstrong .12 .30
209 Erik Christensen .12 .30
210 Peter Forsberg .40 1.00
211 Paul Kariya .20 .50

212 Chris Mason .15 .40
213 Shea Weber .15 .40
214 Jason Arnott .15 .40
215 Alexander Radulov .20 .50
216 J.P. Dumont .12 .30
217 Steve Sullivan .12 .30
218 Kimmo Timonen .12 .30
219 David Legwand .15 .40
220 Jaromir Jagr .60 1.50
221 Sean Avery .12 .30
222 Petr Prucha .12 .30
223 Henrik Lundqvist .50 1.25
224 Martin Straka .12 .30
225 Michael Nylander .12 .30
226 Michal Rozsival .12 .30
227 Marek Malik .12 .30
228 Matt Cullen .12 .30
229 Brendan Shanahan .20 .50
230 Dominik Hasek .30 .75
231 Pavel Datsyuk .30 .75
232 Robert Lang .12 .30
233 Dan Cleary .15 .40
234 Nicklas Lidstrom .20 .50
235 Johan Franzen .15 .40
236 Tomas Holmstrom .15 .40
237 Kris Draper .12 .30
238 Mathieu Schneider .12 .30
239 Jiri Hudler .15 .40
240 Henrik Zetterberg .25 .60
241 Daniel Briere .20 .50
242 Thomas Vanek .15 .40
243 Ryan Miller .20 .50
244 Brian Campbell .15 .40
245 Chris Drury .15 .40
246 Andrew Peters .12 .30
247 Maxim Afinogenov .12 .30
248 Derek Roy .12 .30
249 Jason Pominville .12 .30
250 Drew Stafford .12 .30
251 Dany Heatley .15 .40
252 Ray Emery .15 .40
253 Wade Redden .12 .30
254 Chris Neil .12 .30
255 Mike Fisher .12 .30
256 Patrick Eaves .12 .30
257 Jason Spezza .20 .50
258 Daniel Alfredsson .20 .50
259 Martin Gerber .15 .40
260 Antoine Vermette .12 .30
261 Chris Phillips .12 .30
262 Joe Thornton .30 .75
263 Evgeni Nabokov .15 .40
264 Patrick Marleau .20 .50
265 Bill Guerin .20 .50
266 Milan Michalek .12 .30
267 Steve Bernier .12 .30
268 Matt Carle .12 .30
269 Jonathan Cheechoo .15 .40
270 Marc-Edouard Vlasic .12 .30
271 Joe Pavelski .25 .60
272 Mike Modano .30 .75
273 Jere Lehtinen .12 .30
274 Marty Turco .20 .50
275 Mike Ribeiro .12 .30
276 Sergei Zubov .15 .40
277 Brenden Morrow .15 .40
278 Jussi Jokinen .12 .30
279 Philippe Boucher .12 .30
280 Eric Lindros .30 .75
281 Kari Lehtonen .15 .40
282 Marian Hossa .20 .50
283 Keith Tkachuk .20 .50
284 Alexei Zhitnik .12 .30
285 Bobby Holik .12 .30
286 Slava Kozlov .12 .30
287 Ilya Kovalchuk .20 .50
288 Eric Belanger .12 .30
289 Mark Parrish .12 .30
290 Marian Gaborik .20 .50
291 Pavol Demitra .25 .60
292 Manny Fernandez .12 .30
293 Brian Rolston .15 .40
294 Mikko Koivu .15 .40
295 Pierre-Marc Bouchard .20 .50
296 Derek Boogaard .12 .30
297 Niklas Backstrom .20 .50
298 Roberto Luongo CL .30 .75
299 Vincent Lecavalier CL .20 .50
300 Sidney Crosby CL .75 2.00
301 Jeff Finger RC .75 2.00
302 Colin Fraser RC .75 2.00
303 Pierre Parenteau RC 1.00 2.50
304 Bryan Bickell RC 1.50 4.00
305 Tomas Popperle RC .75 2.00
306 Curtis Glencross RC 1.25 3.00
307 Marc Methot RC .75 2.00
308 David Krejci RC 2.50 6.00
309 Jonathan Sigalet RC .75 2.00
310 Petr Kalus RC .75 2.00
311 Jaroslav Halak RC 2.50 6.00
312 Duncan Milroy RC .75 2.00
313 Jannik Hansen RC 1.00 2.50
314 Jeff Schultz RC 1.00 2.50
315 Jamie Hunt RC .75 2.00
316 Daniel Carcillo RC 1.00 2.50
317 Andy Greene RC 1.00 2.50
318 Mark Fraser RC .75 2.00
319 Rod Pelley RC .75 2.00
320 David Clarkson RC .75 2.00
321 Aaron Rome RC 1.00 2.50
322 Drew Miller RC 1.00 2.50
323 David Moss RC 1.25 3.00
324 Tomi Maki RC .75 2.00
325 Scott Munroe RC .75 2.00
326 Ryan Parent RC .75 2.00
327 Frans Nielsen RC 1.25 3.00
328 Lauri Tukonen RC .75 2.00
329 Yutaka Fukufuji RC 1.00 2.50
330 John Zeiler RC .75 2.00
331 Joe Piskula RC .75 2.00
332 Jack Johnson RC 1.00 2.50
333 Tom Gilbert RC 1.00 2.50
334 Mathieu Roy RC .75 2.00
335 Zack Stortini RC .75 2.00
336 Bryan Young RC .75 2.00
337 Sebastien Bisaillon RC .75 2.00
338 Rob Schremp RC 1.00 2.50
339 Martin Lojek RC .75 2.00
340 Rich Peverley RC .75 2.00
341 Ryan Callahan RC 1.50 4.00
342 Daniel Girardi RC 1.00 2.50
343 Brandon Dubinsky RC 1.50 4.00
344 Matt Ellis RC 1.00 2.50
345 Patrick Kaleta RC .75 2.00
346 Mark Mancari RC .75 2.00
347 Danny Bois RC .75 2.00
348 Thomas Plihal RC .75 2.00
349 Tobias Stephan RC 1.00 2.50
350 Krys Barch RC 1.00 2.50
351 Jonathan Toews RC 8.00 20.00
352 Carey Price RC 6.00 15.00
353 Bobby Ryan RC 2.50 6.00
354 Sam Gagner RC 2.00 5.00
355 Patrick Kane RC 12.00 30.00
356 Nicklas Bergfors RC 1.00 2.50
357 Erik Johnson RC 1.50 4.00
358 Nicklas Backstrom RC 3.00 8.00
359 Anton Stralman RC 1.00 2.50
360 Jonathan Bernier RC 2.00 5.00
361 Bryan Little RC 1.50 4.00
362 Kris Russell RC 1.50 4.00
363 Andrew Cogliano RC 1.25 3.00
364 Marc Staal RC 1.50 4.00
365 Nick Foligno RC 2.00 5.00
366 Peter Mueller RC 1.25 3.00
367 Ondrej Pavelec RC 2.00 5.00
368 Martin Hanzal RC 1.25 3.00
369 Matt Smaby RC 1.00 2.50
370 Brian Elliott RC 2.00 5.00
371 Brett Sterling RC 1.00 2.50
372 Matt Niskanen RC 1.50 4.00
373 Devin Setoguchi RC 1.50 4.00
374 James Sheppard RC 1.00 2.50
375 Kyle Chipchura RC 1.50 4.00
376 Tyler Kennedy RC 1.00 2.50
377 Jiri Tlusty RC 1.50 4.00
378 Mason Raymond RC 1.50 4.00
379 David Perron RC 2.00 5.00
380 Milan Lucic RC 4.00 10.00

2007-08 Upper Deck MVP Gold Script

*VETS/100: 10X TO 25X BASIC CARDS
*301-350 ROOK/100: 1.2X TO 3X RC
*351-380 ROOK/25: 1.2X TO 3X RC

2007-08 Upper Deck MVP Super Script

*VETS/25: 20X TO 50X BASIC CARDS
*301-350 ROOK/25: 4X TO 10X RC
*351-380 ROOK/25: 4X TO 10X RC

2007-08 Upper Deck MVP Game Faces

COMPLETE SET (7) 6.00 15.00
GF1 Sidney Crosby 2.00 5.00
GF2 Jaromir Jagr 1.50 4.00
GF3 Jarome Iginla .60 1.50
GF4 Ilya Kovalchuk .50 1.25
GF5 Peter Forsberg 1.00 2.50
GF6 Joe Thornton .75 2.00
GF7 Alexander Ovechkin 2.00 5.00

2007-08 Upper Deck MVP Hart Candidates

COMPLETE SET (7) 6.00 15.00
HC1 Roberto Luongo .75 2.00
HC2 Sidney Crosby 2.00 5.00
HC3 Martin Brodeur 1.25 3.00
HC4 Joe Thornton .75 2.00
HC5 Vincent Lecavalier .50 1.25
HC6 Miikka Kiprusoff .50 1.25
HC7 Dany Heatley .40 1.00

2007-08 Upper Deck MVP Monumental Moments

COMPLETE SET (14) 0.00 20.00
MM1 Joe Sakic 1.00 2.50
MM2 Mats Sundin .50 1.25
MM3 Sidney Crosby 2.00 5.00
MM4 Martin Brodeur 1.25 3.00
MM5 Evgeni Malkin 1.00 2.50
MM6 Mark Recchi .60 1.50
MM7 Mike Modano .75 2.00
MM8 Joe Thornton .75 2.00
MM9 Brendan Shanahan .50 1.25
MM10 Daniel Briere .50 1.25
MM11 Roberto Luongo .75 2.00
MM12 Vincent Lecavalier .50 1.25
MM13 Daniel Alfredsson .50 1.25
MM14 Scott Niedermayer .50 1.25

2007-08 Upper Deck MVP New World Order

COMPLETE SET (14) 8.00 20.00
NW1 Sidney Crosby 2.00 5.00
NW2 Alexander Ovechkin 2.00 5.00
NW3 Milan Michalek .30 .75
NW4 Ryan Miller .50 1.25
NW5 Marian Gaborik .50 1.25
NW6 Anze Kopitar .75 2.00
NW7 Mikko Koivu .40 1.00
NW8 Henrik Zetterberg .60 1.50
NW9 Evgeni Malkin 1.00 2.50
NW10 Thomas Vanek .40 1.00
NW11 Marc-Andre Fleury 1.00 2.50
NW12 Henrik Lundqvist 1.25 3.00
NW13 Kari Lehtonen .40 1.00
NW14 Zach Parise .50 1.25

2007-08 Upper Deck MVP One on One Autographs

OABS Briere/Stafford 12.00 30.00
OABW Budaj/Wolski SP 40.00 80.00
OACA Higgins/Kostitsyn 10.00 25.00
OACK Kessel/Chara 12.00 30.00
OACS Cole/Staal 10.00 25.00
OAEM Edler/McIver 8.00 20.00
OAFK Frolov/Kopitar 20.00 50.00
OAGP Gomez/Parise SP 40.00 80.00
OAHH Hemsky/Horcoff 10.00 25.00
OAHK Kovalchuk/Hossa SP 40.00 80.00
OAHL Hejduk/Liles 10.00 25.00
OAHS Hejduk/Stastny 10.00 25.00
OAHZ Hasek/Zetterberg 40.00 80.00
OAIK Kovalchuk/Lehtonen 12.00 30.00
OAIP Iginla/Phaneuf SP 25.00 60.00
OAJF Stoll/Pisani 10.00 25.00
OAJS Jurcina/Stuart 8.00 20.00
OAJW Jokinen/Weiss 10.00 25.00
OAKK Khabibulin/Keith 12.00 30.00
OALM Lemieux/Malkin SP 100.00 200.00
OALP Prucha/Lundqvist 30.00 80.00
OAMR McCabe/Raycroft 10.00 25.00
OAMV Michalek/Vlasic 8.00 20.00
OAOM Ovechkin/Malkin SP 150.00 250.00
OAPB Bouchard/Parrish 12.00 30.00
OAPD Dawes/Prucha 8.00 20.00
OAPG Perry/Getzlaf 20.00 50.00
OARG Redden/Gerber 10.00 25.00
OARL Latendresse/Ryder 40.00 80.00
OARS Raycroft/Steen 10.00 25.00
OAST Schremp/Thoresen 10.00 25.00
OASZ Sullivan/Zidlicky 8.00 20.00
OATC Thornton/Cheechoo SP 40.00 100.00
OATK Tanguay/Kiprusoff 12.00 30.00
OATW Tucker/Williams 10.00 25.00
OAVM Vanek/MacArthur 10.00 25.00
OAZB Brule/Zherdev 10.00 25.00

2007-08 Upper Deck MVP One on One Jerseys

OOAJ Tanguay/Lupul 4.00 10.00
OOAK Antropov/Kostitsyn 4.00 10.00
OOBL Brodeur/Lundqvist 12.00 30.00
OOBP Boyes/Picard 4.00 10.00
OOBS Briere/Savard 5.00 12.00
OOBW Belfour/Ward 5.00 12.00
OOCB Crosby/Brodeur SP 40.00 100.00
OOCK Cola/Komisarek 3.00 8.00
OOCM Chara/Meszaros 5.00 12.00
OOCP Carter/Parise 5.00 12.00
OOCV Lombardi/Kesler 5.00 12.00
OODE DiPietro/Esche 4.00 10.00
OODI Rafalski/Witt 4.00 10.00
OODL Datsyuk/Lehtinen 8.00 20.00
OODM Doan/Morrow 4.00 10.00
OOFL Forsberg/Lidstrom 10.00 25.00
OOFT Fernan/Theodore 5.00 12.00
OOGC Giguere/Cloutier 5.00 12.00
OOGG Gagne/Gionta 5.00 12.00
OOGH Gaborik/Hejduk 5.00 12.00
OOHG Huet/Gerber 4.00 10.00
OOHK Heatley/Kovalchuk 5.00 12.00
OOHM Horcoff/Morrison 3.00 8.00
OOHR Heatley/Ryder 4.00 10.00
OOHT Heatley/Tanguay 4.00 10.00
OOHV Hasek/Vokoun 8.00 20.00
OOIN Iginla/Naslund 6.00 15.00
OOJD Bouw/Hamhuis 4.00 10.00
OOJE Jagr/Elias 15.00 40.00
OOJT Joseph/Turco 6.00 15.00
OOKD Kolzig/Denis 5.00 12.00
OOKN Kariya/Nash 5.00 12.00
OOLC Ladd/Craig 3.00 8.00
OOLJ Lecavalier/Jokinen 5.00 12.00
OOLK Luongo/Kiprusoff 8.00 20.00
OOLL Leclaire/Legace 4.00 10.00
OOLN Lehtonen/Niittymaki 4.00 10.00
OOLR Luongo/Roloson 8.00 20.00
OOLW Lang/Williams 3.00 8.00
OOMH Morrison/Hall 3.00 8.00
OOMK Murray/Kovalev 4.00 10.00
OOMM Marleau/Modano 8.00 20.00
OOMR McCabe/Redden 3.00 8.00
OONM Nagy/Michalek 3.00 8.00
OONY Straka/Satan 4.00 10.00
OOOH Ondrus/Hoggan 3.00 8.00
OOOL Osgood/Lalime 5.00 12.00
OOOM Ovechkin/Malkin 20.00 50.00
OOPJ Pronger/Jovo 5.00 12.00
OORH Havlat/Rolston 5.00 12.00
OORS Brind/Weiss 5.00 12.00
OORT Raycroft/Thomas 5.00 12.00
OOSA Sundin/Alfredsson 5.00 12.00
OOSC Selanne/Cheech 10.00 25.00
OOSF Sakic/Forsberg 10.00 25.00
OOSS Shanahan/Smyth 5.00 12.00
OOTL Thornton/Lindros 8.00 20.00
OOTM Torres/McCarty 3.00 8.00
OOVS Vanek/Steen 4.00 10.00
OOWH Weight/Handzus 5.00 12.00

2008-09 Upper Deck MVP

COMPLETE SET (392) 150.00 300.00
COMP.SET w/o RCs (300) 15.00 40.00
1 Ryan Getzlaf .30 .75
2 Corey Perry .50 1.25
3 Teemu Selanne .60 1.50
4 Jean-Sebastien Giguere .30 .75
5 Chris Pronger .30 .75
6 Mathieu Schneider .20 .50
7 George Parros .20 .50
8 Scott Niedermayer .30 .75
9 Chris Kunitz .30 .75
10 Brendan Morrison .20 .50
11 Ilya Kovalchuk .30 .75
12 Eric Perrin .20 .50
13 Tobias Enstrom .20 .50
14 Eric Boulton .20 .50
15 Colby Armstrong .20 .50
16 Bryan Little .25 .60
17 Erik Christensen .20 .50
18 Kari Lehtonen .40 1.00
19 Johan Hedberg .25 .60
20 Jason Williams .20 .50
21 Patrice Bergeron .40 1.00
22 Marc Savard .20 .50
23 Zdeno Chara .30 .75
24 Chuck Kobasew .20 .50
25 Phil Kessel .30 .75
26 Tim Thomas .30 .75
27 Marco Sturm .20 .50
28 Milan Lucic .50 1.25
29 Tuukka Rask .40 1.00
30 Derek Roy .20 .50
31 Jason Pominville .20 .50
32 Thomas Vanek .25 .60
33 Maxim Afinogenov .20 .50
34 Jochen Hecht .20 .50
35 Ales Kotalik .20 .50
36 Ryan Miller .30 .75
37 Drew Stafford .20 .50
38 Andrew Peters .20 .50
39 Daniel Paille .20 .50
40 Craig Rivet .20 .50
41 Patrick Lalime .25 .60
42 Todd Bertuzzi .30 .75
43 Robyn Regehr .20 .50
44 Jarome Iginla .40 1.00
45 Dion Phaneuf .25 .60
46 Daymond Langkow .20 .50
47 Miikka Kiprusoff .30 .75
48 Matthew Lombardi .20 .50
49 Adrian Aucoin .20 .50
50 Mike Cammalleri .25 .60
51 Eric Staal .40 1.00
52 Ray Whitney .25 .60
53 Rod Brind'Amour .30 .75
54 Matt Cullen .20 .50
55 Justin Williams .25 .60
56 Cam Ward .30 .75
57 Scott Walker .20 .50
58 Sergei Samsonov .25 .60
59 Joni Pitkanen .20 .50
60 Patrick Kane .60 1.50
61 Jonathan Toews .50 1.25
62 Patrick Sharp .30 .75
63 Dustin Byfuglien .30 .75
64 Adam Burish .25 .60
65 Nikolai Khabibulin .30 .75
66 Duncan Keith .25 .60
67 Martin Havlat .30 .75
68 James Wisniewski .20 .50
69 Brian Campbell .25 .60
70 Cristobal Huet .25 .60
71 Paul Stastny .25 .60
72 Joe Sakic .60 1.50
73 Peter Forsberg .60 1.50
74 Ryan Smyth .25 .60
75 Wojtek Wolski .25 .60
76 Milan Hejduk .25 .60
77 Marek Svatos .20 .50
78 Ian Laperriere .20 .50
79 Peter Budaj .25 .60
80 T.J. Hensick .25 .60
81 Darcy Tucker .25 .60
82 Kristian Huselius .20 .50
83 Rick Nash .30 .75
84 Michael Peca .25 .60
85 Pascal Leclaire .25 .60
86 Fredrik Norrena .20 .50
87 Jared Boll .20 .50
88 Kris Russell .20 .50
89 R.J. Umberger .20 .50
90 Mike Ribeiro .20 .50
91 Mike Modano .50 1.25
92 Brad Richards .30 .75
93 Marty Turco .30 .75
94 Sergei Zubov .25 .60
95 Jere Lehtinen .20 .50
96 Steve Ott .20 .50
97 Brenden Morrow .25 .60
98 Sean Avery .20 .50
99 Philippe Boucher .20 .50
100 Ty Conklin .25 .60
101 Niklas Kronwall .25 .60
102 Jiri Hudler .25 .60
103 Valtteri Filppula .20 .50
104 Mikael Samuelsson .20 .50
105 Chris Osgood .30 .75
106 Henrik Zetterberg .40 1.00
107 Pavel Datsyuk .50 1.25
108 Nicklas Lidstrom .30 .75
109 Brian Rafalski .25 .60
110 Dan Cleary .25 .60
111 Tomas Holmstrom .25 .60
112 Johan Franzen .25 .60
113 Marian Hossa .30 .75
114 Erik Cole .20 .50
115 Gilbert Brule .20 .50
116 Ales Hemsky .25 .60
117 Shawn Horcoff .20 .50
118 Sam Gagner .20 .50
119 Dustin Penner .25 .60
120 Andrew Cogliano .20 .50
121 Zach Stortini .20 .50
122 Robert Nilsson .20 .50
123 Mathieu Garon .25 .60
124 Dwayne Roloson .25 .60
125 Lubomir Visnovsky .20 .50
126 Nathan Horton .25 .60
127 Stephen Weiss .20 .50
128 Jay Bouwmeester .20 .50
129 Tomas Vokoun .25 .60
130 David Booth .20 .50
131 Brett McLean .20 .50
132 Rostislav Olesz .20 .50
133 Cory Stillman .20 .50
134 Jarret Stoll .25 .60
135 Anze Kopitar .50 1.25
136 Alexander Frolov .20 .50
137 Dustin Brown .30 .75
138 Patrick O'Sullivan .25 .60
139 Jason LaBarbera .25 .60
140 Jack Johnson .20 .50
141 Andrew Brunette .20 .50
142 Marian Gaborik .30 .75
143 Pierre-Marc Bouchard .30 .75
144 Brent Burns .30 .75
145 James Sheppard .20 .50
146 Mikko Koivu .25 .60
147 Niklas Backstrom .30 .75
148 Josh Harding .30 .75
149 Derek Boogaard .20 .50
150 Marek Zidlicky .20 .50
151 Alex Tanguay .20 .50
152 Alex Kovalev .25 .60
153 Tomas Plekanec .20 .50
154 Andrei Markov .30 .75
155 Saku Koivu .30 .75
156 Andrei Kostitsyn .25 .60
157 Sergei Kostitsyn .20 .50
158 Chris Higgins .20 .50
159 Carey Price .60 1.50
160 Kyle Chipchura .25 .60
161 Guillaume Latendresse .20 .50
162 Georges Laraque .25 .60
163 Jason Arnott .25 .60
164 J.P. Dumont .20 .50
165 Shea Weber .25 .60
166 Martin Erat .20 .50
167 David Legwand .25 .60
168 Dan Ellis .20 .50
169 Jordin Tootoo .30 .75
170 Ryan Suter .25 .60
171 Brian Rolston .25 .60
172 Zach Parise .30 .75
173 Patrik Elias .30 .75
174 Brian Gionta .20 .50
175 Martin Brodeur .75 2.00
176 David Clarkson .25 .60
177 John Madden .20 .50
178 Jamie Langenbrunner .20 .50
179 Dainius Zubrus .20 .50
180 Travis Zajac .20 .50
181 Mark Streit .20 .50
182 Mike Comrie .25 .60
183 Bill Guerin .30 .75
184 Trent Hunter .20 .50
185 Rick DiPietro .25 .60
186 Chris Campoli .20 .50
187 Sean Bergenheim .20 .50
188 Jeff Tambellini .20 .50
189 Blake Comeau .20 .50
190 Doug Weight .30 .75
191 Nikolai Zherdev .20 .50
192 Scott Gomez .25 .60
193 Brendan Shanahan .30 .75
194 Chris Drury .25 .60
195 Brandon Dubinsky .20 .50
196 Henrik Lundqvist .75 2.00
197 Colton Orr .20 .50
198 Stephen Valiquette .25 .60
199 Marc Staal .20 .50
200 Wade Redden .20 .50
201 Markus Naslund .30 .75
202 Jason Spezza .30 .75
203 Daniel Alfredsson .30 .75
204 Dany Heatley .25 .60
205 Antoine Vermette .20 .50
206 Mike Fisher .20 .50
207 Filip Kuba .20 .50
208 Chris Neil .20 .50
209 Chris Phillips .20 .50
210 Martin Gerber .25 .60
211 Mike Richards .25 .60
212 Daniel Briere .30 .75
213 Mike Knuble .20 .50
214 Jeff Carter .25 .60
215 Martin Biron .25 .60
216 Joffrey Lupul .20 .50
217 Kimmo Timonen .20 .50
218 Riley Cote .20 .50
219 Scott Hartnell .20 .50
220 Olli Jokinen .25 .60
221 Ilya Bryzgalov .25 .60
222 Shane Doan .25 .60
223 Peter Mueller .25 .60
224 Ed Jovanovski .25 .60
225 Martin Hanzal .25 .60
226 Daniel Winnik .20 .50
227 Daniel Carcillo .20 .50
228 Mikael Tellqvist .25 .60
229 Eric Godard .20 .50
230 Miroslav Satan .30 .75
231 Sidney Crosby 1.25 3.00
232 Evgeni Malkin .60 1.50
233 Jordan Staal .25 .60
234 Sergei Gonchar .20 .50
235 Ryan Whitney .30 .75
236 Petr Sykora .25 .60
237 Marc-Andre Fleury .60 1.50
238 Tyler Kennedy .25 .60
239 Rob Blake .30 .75
240 Doug Murray .20 .50
241 Joe Thornton .50 1.25
242 Milan Michalek .20 .50
243 Patrick Marleau .30 .75
244 Joe Pavelski .40 1.00
245 Jonathan Cheechoo .25 .60
246 Jeremy Roenick .50 1.25
247 Evgeni Nabokov .25 .60
248 Devin Setoguchi .25 .60
249 Dan Boyle .20 .50
250 Chris Mason .25 .60
251 Brad Boyes .20 .50
252 Paul Kariya .30 .75
253 Manny Legace .30 .75
254 David Backes .20 .50
255 Erik Johnson .20 .50
256 David Perron .25 .60
257 Keith Tkachuk .30 .75
258 Andy McDonald .25 .60
259 Lee Stempniak .20 .50
260 Radim Vrbata .20 .50
261 Ryan Malone .20 .50
262 Vincent Lecavalier .30 .75
263 Martin St. Louis .30 .75
264 Mike Smith .30 .75
265 Michel Ouellet .20 .50
266 Paul Ranger .20 .50
267 Shane O'Brien .20 .50
268 Jussi Jokinen .20 .50
269 Andrej Meszaros .20 .50
270 Mats Sundin .30 .75
271 Nikolai Antropov .25 .60
272 Tomas Kaberle .20 .50
273 Pavel Kubina .20 .50
274 Jason Blake .20 .50
275 Alexander Steen .20 .50
276 Jiri Tlusty .20 .50
277 Vesa Toskala .40 1.00
278 Matt Stajan .20 .50
279 Steve Bernier .20 .50
280 Pavol Demitra .40 1.00
281 Daniel Sedin .40 1.00
282 Henrik Sedin .40 1.00
283 Ryan Kesler .30 .75
284 Alexander Edler .20 .50
285 Kevin Bieksa .25 .60
286 Roberto Luongo .50 1.25
287 Taylor Pyatt .20 .50
288 Alexandre Burrows .20 .50
289 Jason Blake .20 .50
290 Jose Theodore .30 .75
291 Alexander Ovechkin 1.25 3.00
292 Nicklas Backstrom .30 .75
293 Mike Green .25 .60
294 Viktor Kozlov .20 .50
295 Alexander Semin .30 .75
296 Donald Brashear .20 .50
297 Sergei Fedorov .50 1.25
298 Jarome Iginla CL .40 1.00
299 Evgeni Malkin CL .60 1.50
300 Alexander Ovechkin CL 1.25 3.00
301 Tyler Plante RC 1.00 2.50
302 Tom Sestito RC 1.25 3.00
303 Tom Cavanagh RC 1.00 2.50
304 Tim Ramholt RC 1.00 2.50
305 Tim Conboy RC 1.00 2.50
306 Theo Peckham RC 1.00 2.50
307 Teddy Purcell RC 1.00 2.50
308 Steve Mason RC 2.00 5.00
309 Shawn Matthias RC 1.25 3.00
310 Sami Lepisto RC 1.00 2.50
311 Ryan Stone RC .75 2.00
312 Robbie Earl RC .75 2.00
313 Zach Bogosian RC 1.50 4.00
314 Pascal Pelletier RC .75 2.00
315 Niklas Hjalmarsson RC 1.25 3.00
316 Mike Mole RC 1.00 2.50
317 Mike Iggulden RC 1.00 2.50
318 Mike Brown RC 1.25 3.00
319 Mattias Ritola RC 1.00 2.50
320 Matt D'Agostini RC 1.00 2.50
321 Mark Fistric RC 1.00 2.50
322 Marc-Andre Gragnani RC 1.00 2.50
323 Lauri Korpikoski RC .75 2.00
324 Kyle Turris RC 2.00 5.00
325 Kyle Okposo RC 1.50 4.00
326 Kyle Greentree RC 1.25 3.00
327 Blake Wheeler RC 3.00 8.00
328 Justin Abdelkader RC 2.00 5.00
329 Jordan LaVallee RC 1.25 3.00
330 Jordan Hendry RC 1.00 2.50
331 Jonathan Ericsson RC 1.25 3.00
332 Jon Filewich RC 1.00 2.50
333 Joey Mormina RC 1.00 2.50
334 Joe Jensen RC 1.25 3.00
335 Jesse Winchester RC .75 2.00
336 Jack Hillen RC 1.00 2.50
337 Ilya Zubov RC 1.00 2.50
338 Garrett Stafford RC 1.25 3.00
339 Erik Ersberg RC 1.00 2.50
340 Derick Brassard RC 1.25 3.00
341 David Brine RC .75 2.00
342 Darryl Boyce RC 1.00 2.50
343 Darren Helm RC 1.25 3.00
344 Danny Taylor RC 1.00 2.50
345 Dan LaCosta RC 1.25 3.00
346 Corey Locke RC 1.00 2.50
347 Colin Stuart RC 1.00 2.50
348 Cody McLeod RC 1.00 2.50
349 Clay Wilson RC .75 2.00
350 Claude Giroux RC 2.50 6.00
351 Chris Minard RC 1.25 3.00
352 Brian Lee RC 1.00 2.50
353 Brian Boyle RC 1.00 2.50
354 Brandon Nolan RC 1.00 2.50
355 Boris Valabik RC 1.25 3.00
356 B.J. Crombeen RC .75 2.00
357 Andrew Murray RC 1.00 2.50
358 Andrew Ebbett RC .75 2.00
359 Alex Goligoski RC 1.50 4.00
360 Alex Foster RC 1.00 2.50
361 Adam Pineault RC 1.00 2.50
362 Adam Pardy RC 1.00 2.50
363 Brandon Sutter RC 1.25 3.00
364 Jakub Voracek RC 2.50 6.00
365 Michael Frolik RC 1.25 3.00
366 James Neal RC 2.50 6.00
367 Drew Doughty RC 3.00 8.00
368 Wayne Simmonds RC 2.00 5.00
369 Oscar Moller RC 1.00 2.50
370 Colton Gillies RC 1.00 2.50
371 Ryan Jones RC 1.25 3.00
372 Patric Hornqvist RC 1.25 3.00
373 Anssi Salmela RC 1.25 3.00
374 Luca Sbisa RC .75 2.00
375 Jared Ross RC 1.25 3.00
376 Mikkel Boedker RC 1.50 4.00
377 Patrik Berglund RC 1.00 2.50
378 Chris Porter RC 1.25 3.00
379 T.J. Oshie RC 2.50 6.00
380 Alex Pietrangelo RC 2.00 5.00
381 Steven Stamkos RC 6.00 15.00
382 Vladimir Mihalik RC .75 2.00
383 Janne Niskala RC 1.25 3.00
384 Nikolai Kulemin RC 1.25 3.00
385 Luke Schenn RC 1.50 4.00
386 John Mitchell RC 1.00 2.50
387 Jonas Frogren RC .75 2.00
388 Derek Dorsett RC 1.50 4.00
389 Viktor Tikhonov RC 1.00 2.50
390 Kevin Porter RC 1.00 2.50
391 Paul Bissonnette RC 1.50 4.00
392 Zach Fitzgerald RC 1.25 3.00

2008-09 Upper Deck MVP Gold Script

*1-300 VETS: 2.5X TO 6X BASIC CARDS
*301-392 ROOKIES: .8X TO 2X BASIC RC
292 Nicklas Backstrom 2.00 5.00
381 Steven Stamkos 15.00 40.00

2008-09 Upper Deck MVP Super Script

*1-300 VETS: 6X TO 15X BASIC CARDS
*301-392 ROOKIES: 2X TO 5X BASIC RC
292 Nicklas Backstrom 5.00 12.00
381 Steven Stamkos 30.00 80.00

2008-09 Upper Deck MVP Alexander the Gr8

COMPLETE SET (8) 6.00 15.00
COMMON OVECHKIN (A01-A08) 1.25 3.00

2008-09 Upper Deck MVP First Line Phenoms

COMPLETE SET (15) 8.00 20.00
FL1 Alexander Ovechkin 2.00 5.00
FL2 Marian Gaborik .50 1.25
FL3 Andrei Kostitsyn .40 1.00
FL4 Evgeni Malkin 1.00 2.50
FL5 Jonathan Toews .75 2.00
FL6 Mike Richards .40 1.00
FL7 Nicklas Backstrom .50 1.25
FL8 Patrick Kane 1.00 2.50
FL9 Paul Stastny .40 1.00
FL10 Peter Mueller .40 1.00
FL11 Ryan Getzlaf .50 1.25
FL12 Sam Gagner .30 .75
FL13 Sidney Crosby 2.00 5.00
FL14 Thomas Vanek .40 1.00
FL15 Zach Parise .50 1.25

2008-09 Upper Deck MVP Magnificent Sevens

COMPLETE SET (7) 8.00 20.00
M7CP Carey Price 1.50 4.00
M7CW Cam Ward .75 2.00
M7GL Guy Lafleur 1.00 2.50
M7MB Martin Brodeur 2.00 5.00
M7PL Pat LaFontaine .75 2.00
M7TB Turk Broda .75 2.00
M7WG Wayne Gretzky 5.00 12.00

2008-09 Upper Deck MVP Marked by Valor

COMPLETE SET (15) 10.00 25.00

2008-09 Upper Deck MVP One on One Autographs

ABC D.Cleary/B.Boyes 12.00 30.00
ABD Dubinsky/Clarkson 15.00 40.00
ABW D.Boyle/N.Welch 6.00 15.00
ACB N.Backstrom/J.Carter 25.00 60.00
ACF N.Foligno/K.Chipchura 10.00 25.00
ADC J.Carter/C.Drury 15.00 40.00
ADD S.Downie/B.Dubinsky 15.00 40.00
ADH Harding/Drouin-Deslauriers 8.00 20.00
ADJ D.Setoguchi/J.Pavelski 12.00 30.00
AED E.Johnson/D.Byfuglien 8.00 20.00
AES P.Elias/M.Satan 15.00 40.00
AFG D.Girardi/M.Fraser 10.00 25.00
AFM E.Malkin/M.Fleury 60.00 100.00
AFT J.Tlusty/N.Foligno 15.00 40.00
AGR G.Moore/R.Pelley 15.00 40.00
AHB P.Budaj/M.Hejduk 15.00 40.00
AHM R.Malone/N.Horton 12.00 30.00
AHR M.Raymond/J.Hansen 15.00 40.00
AHS J.Sheppard/T.Hensick 12.00 30.00
AJB J.Bernier/J.Johnson 12.00 30.00
AKK A.Kostitsyn/S.Kostitsyn 20.00 50.00
AKL G.Latendresse/P.Kessel 15.00 40.00
AKP P.Kane/D.Perron 20.00 50.00
AKT D.Krejci/J.Tlusty 15.00 40.00
AMG R.Getzlaf/B.Morrow 15.00 40.00
AMK M.Michalek/L.Kaspar 8.00 20.00
ANY M.Staal/R.Callahan 10.00 25.00
APA P.Mueller/A.Kopitar 25.00 60.00
APK C.Perry/A.Kopitar 15.00 40.00
APM C.Phillips/B.McCabe 8.00 20.00
APP D.Penner/M.Pouliot 10.00 25.00
APR C.Price/T.Rask 25.00 60.00
APT C.Price/J.Tlusty 25.00 60.00
ARM M.Ribeiro/B.Morrow 10.00 25.00
ASD D.Sedin/H.Sedin 12.00 30.00
ASH M.Stajan/C.Higgins 10.00 25.00
ASS M.Staal/J.Staal 12.00 30.00
ATK P.Kane/J.Toews 50.00 100.00
AZC T.Zajac/D.Clarkson 12.00 30.00

2008-09 Upper Deck MVP Two on Two Jerseys

J2AWLS Arnt/Webr/Lgwnd/Sullvn 6.00 15.00
J2BDLP Brod/Prise/Lndqvst/Drury 20.00 50.00
J2BEGP Brod/Parise/Elias/Gnta 20.00 50.00
J2BGRC Gagne/Rchrds/Crtr/Biron 8.00 20.00
J2BNLE Enstrm/Niska/Bksa/Lund 6.00 15.00
J2BTTL Tosk/Blake/Thms/Lucic 12.50 30.00
J2CHSN Crsby/Htly/Spza/Nash 12.00 30.00
J2DCKM Doan/Mller/Kopitr/Clder 12.00 30.00
J2DSTC Drury/Shan/Tamb/Cmrie 8.00 20.00
J2DZSK Zettr/Datsyk/Kane/Shrp 10.00 25.00
J2FCMS Crsby/Malkin/Flry/Staal 30.00 80.00
J2FGOB Ovech/Back/Grn/Fedor 30.00 80.00
J2GBSC Crsby/Satn/Bre/Ggne 30.00 80.00
J2GBSO Ggne/Brie/Ovch/Flsch 12.00 30.00
J2GCDA Gmez/Drury/Conly/Afing 6.00 15.00
J2GCOM Crsby/Mlkin/Ovch/Gren 60.00 120.00
J2HDSK Hasek/Drapr/Shrp/Khab 12.00 30.00
J2HHSB Osgd/Hlmst/Svtos/Budaj 8.00 20.00
J2HLDZ Zett/Lids/Hasek/Dtsyk 10.00 25.00
J2JSDL Lndq/Zhrdv/DiPiet/Hntr 20.00 50.00
J2KGBK Gabrik/Koiv/Brnr/Ksler 8.00 20.00
J2KKSJ Koivu/Kovl/Snd/Jseph 10.00 25.00
J2KPKL Koivu/Plkn/Latnd/Kov 8.00 20.00
J2KSLW Staal/Ward/Kvlck/Leht 10.00 25.00
J2KTAW Kriya/Tkch/Arnt/Webr 8.00 20.00
J2KTBP Kriya/Boyes/Tkch/Pron 8.00 20.00
J2LBSD Lngo/Bern/Sdin/Demit 12.00 30.00
J2LJLT Lngo/Josph/Lclre/Thms 12.00 30.00
J2LNCP Phnf/Ldstrm/Niedr/Chra 8.00 20.00
J2LOHG Lngo/Ohlnd/Ggnr/Hrcf 12.00 30.00
J2LSBS Staal/Brnd/Lecv/St.Lu 10.00 25.00
J2MMNI Nabv/Mrlu/Irco/Mdno 12.00 30.00
J2MTNC Thrn/Chch/Marlu/Nabkv 12.00 30.00
J2MZLT Mdno/Trco/Leht/Zbov 12.00 30.00
J2NGKJ Getz/Niedr/Kpitr/Jhnsn 12.00 30.00
J2PDGB Gabrk/Bch/Brnr/Dmtra 10.00 25.00
J2PRRC Phanf/Rghr/Rolsn/Cole 6.00 15.00
J2RDTG Brod/DiPiet/Tosk/Grbr 12.00 30.00
J2SBHR St.L/Rngr/Hortn/Bouw 8.00 20.00
J2SCBK Brgrn/Kessl/Svrd/Chara 10.00 25.00
J2SDRC Rchrds/Crtr/Drury/Shan 8.00 20.00
J2SHSW Skic/Hjdk/Wlski/Smyth 15.00 40.00
J2SHVS Spez/Htley/Vanek/Staf 8.00 20.00
J2SHZS Zett/Hlms/Sund/Steen 10.00 25.00
J2SJGL Prise/Rlstn/Shan/Gomz 8.00 20.00
J2SKHG Gabrik/Kvu/Skic/Hjduk 10.00 25.00
J2SMRG Getz/Sene/Mdno/Ribro 15.00 40.00
J2SNGG Selne/Gtz/Nieder/Gig 15.00 40.00
J2SSHA Sndin/Antv/Htley/Spez 8.00 20.00
J2SSTS Sund/Steen/Tsk/Stjan 10.00 25.00
J2STMA Sund/Tskla/Millr/Afing 10.00 25.00
J2TCPG Thrnt/Chch/Getz/Perry 12.00 30.00
J2THGS Htley/Grbr/Stn/Tosk 10.00 25.00
J2TLLN Tkch/Lgce/Nsh/Leclre 8.00 20.00
J2TRBK Berg/Kssl/Thms/Ryder 10.00 25.00
J2VWKL Kovl/Leht/Vokn/Weiss 10.00 25.00
J2WBSW Staal/Brind/Wrd/Willi 10.00 25.00

2008-09 Upper Deck MVP Winter Classic

Card	Low	High
COMPLETE SET (20)	8.00	20.00
WC1 Sidney Crosby	2.00	5.00
WC2 Chris Chelios	.50	1.25
WC3 Pavel Datsyuk	.75	2.00
WC4 Johan Franzen	.40	1.00
WC5 Tomas Holmstrom	.40	1.00
WC6 Marian Hossa	.50	1.25
WC7 Nicklas Lidstrom	.50	1.25
WC8 Chris Osgood	.50	1.25
WC9 Brian Rafalski	.40	1.00
WC10 Henrik Zetterberg	.60	1.50
WC11 Brian Campbell	.40	1.00
WC12 Martin Havlat	.50	1.25
WC13 Cristobal Huet	.40	1.00
WC14 Duncan Keith	.40	1.00
WC15 Patrick Kane	1.00	2.50
WC16 Dustin Byfuglien	.50	1.25
WC17 Brent Seabrook	.30	.75
WC18 Patrick Sharp	.50	1.25
WC19 Jonathan Toews	.75	2.00
WC20 Wrigley Field	.30	.75

2009-10 Upper Deck MVP

Card	Low	High
COMPLETE SET (394)	250.00	400.00
COMP.SET w/o SPS (300)	12.00	30.00
1 Alexander Ovechkin	1.25	3.00
2 Nicklas Backstrom	.30	.75
3 Alexander Semin	.30	.75
4 Mike Green	.25	.60
5 Brooks Laich	.20	.50
6 Tomas Fleischmann	.20	.50
7 Jose Theodore	.30	.75
8 Michael Nylander	.20	.50
9 Eric Fehr	.20	.50
10 Karl Alzner	.20	.50
11 Roberto Luongo	.50	1.25
12 Ryan Kesler	.30	.75
13 Pavol Demitra	.40	1.00
14 Henrik Sedin	.40	1.00
15 Kevin Bieksa	.25	.60
16 Alexander Edler	.20	.50
17 Steve Bernier	.20	.50
18 Daniel Sedin	.40	1.00
19 Willie Mitchell	.20	.50
20 Mason Raymond	.20	.50
21 Jason Blake	.20	.50
22 Alexei Ponikarovsky	.20	.50
23 Francois Beauchemin	.20	.50
24 Mikhail Grabovski	.20	.50
25 Lee Stempniak	.20	.50
26 Tomas Kaberle	.20	.50
27 Nikolai Kulemin	.20	.50
28 Luke Schenn	.30	.75
29 Vesa Toskala	.30	.75
30 Mike Komisarek	.25	.60
31 Martin St. Louis	.30	.75
32 Vincent Lecavalier	.30	.75
33 Steven Stamkos	.60	1.50
34 Steve Downie	.20	.50
35 Ryan Malone	.20	.50
36 Mike Smith	.30	.75
37 Alex Tanguay	.20	.50
38 Lukas Krajicek	.20	.50
39 Paul Ranger	.20	.50
40 Brad Boyes	.20	.50
41 David Backes	.20	.50
42 David Perron	.25	.60
43 Patrik Berglund	.20	.50
44 T.J. Oshie	.30	.75
45 Paul Kariya	.30	.75
46 Chris Mason	.25	.60
47 Andy McDonald	.25	.60
48 Keith Tkachuk	.30	.75
49 Ty Conklin	.25	.60
50 Joe Thornton	.50	1.25
51 Patrick Marleau	.30	.75
52 Devin Setoguchi	.25	.60
53 Joe Pavelski	.40	1.00
54 Rob Blake	.30	.75
55 Evgeni Nabokov	.25	.60
56 Dan Boyle	.20	.50
57 Ryane Clowe	.20	.50
58 Jonathan Cheechoo	.25	.60
59 Marc-Edouard Vlasic	.20	.50
60 Evgeni Malkin	.60	1.50
61 Sidney Crosby	1.25	3.00
62 Chris Kunitz	.30	.75
63 Jordan Staal	.25	.60
64 Tyler Kennedy	.25	.60
65 Marc-Andre Fleury	.60	1.50
66 Maxime Talbot	.20	.50
67 Pascal Dupuis	.20	.50
68 Kristopher Letang	.40	1.00
69 Brooks Orpik	.20	.50
70 Shane Doan	.25	.60
71 Matthew Lombardi	.20	.50
72 Ed Jovanovski	.20	.50
73 Peter Mueller	.25	.60
74 Scottie Upshall	.20	.50
75 Martin Hanzal	.25	.60
76 Mikkel Boedker	.20	.50
77 Kyle Turris	.30	.75
78 Ilya Bryzgalov	.25	.60
79 Viktor Tikhonov	.25	.60
80 Jeff Carter	.25	.60
81 Mike Richards	.25	.60
82 Simon Gagne	.30	.75
83 Scott Hartnell	.20	.50
84 Chris Pronger	.30	.75
85 Claude Giroux	.30	.75
86 Daniel Briere	.30	.75
87 Kimmo Timonen	.25	.60
88 Braydon Coburn	.20	.50
89 Daniel Carcillo	.20	.50
90 Daniel Alfredsson	.30	.75
91 Jason Spezza	.30	.75
92 Dany Heatley	.25	.60
93 Nick Foligno	.25	.60
94 Brian Elliott	.25	.60
95 Pascal Leclaire	.30	.75
96 Jarkko Ruutu	.20	.50
97 Filip Kuba	.20	.50
98 Mike Fisher	.20	.50
99 Alex Kovalev	.25	.60
100 Marian Gaborik	.30	.75
101 Sean Avery	.25	.60
102 Chris Drury	.25	.60
103 Chris Higgins	.20	.50
104 Brandon Dubinsky	.20	.50
105 Ryan Callahan	.20	.50
106 Michal Rozsival	.20	.50
107 Henrik Lundqvist	.75	2.00
108 Wade Redden	.20	.50
109 Marc Staal	.20	.50
110 Mark Streit	.20	.50
111 Kyle Okposo	.20	.50
112 Doug Weight	.30	.75
113 Frans Nielsen	.20	.50
114 Trent Hunter	.20	.50
115 Josh Bailey	.25	.60
116 Rick DiPietro	.25	.60
117 Blake Comeau	.20	.50
118 Richard Park	.20	.50
119 Martin Brodeur	.75	2.00
120 Zach Parise	.30	.75
121 Patrik Elias	.30	.75
122 Jamie Langenbrunner	.20	.50
123 Travis Zajac	.20	.50
124 Dainius Zubrus	.20	.50
125 David Clarkson	.25	.60
126 Paul Martin	.20	.50
127 Brian Rolston	.25	.60
128 Colin White	.20	.50
129 Pekka Rinne	.30	.75
130 J.P. Dumont	.20	.50
131 Jason Arnott	.25	.60
132 Shea Weber	.25	.60
133 Martin Erat	.20	.50
134 Ryan Suter	.25	.60
135 David Legwand	.25	.60
136 Jordin Tootoo	.30	.75
137 Dan Hamhuis	.25	.60
138 Dan Ellis	.20	.50
139 Andrei Markov	.30	.75
140 Andrei Kostitsyn	.25	.60
141 Carey Price	.60	1.50
142 Tomas Plekanec	.20	.50
143 Maxim Lapierre	.20	.50
144 Guillaume Latendresse	.25	.60
145 Scott Gomez	.25	.60
146 Max Pacioretty	.30	.75
147 Roman Hamrlik	.20	.50
148 Brian Gionta	.20	.50
149 Mikko Koivu	.30	.75
150 Andrew Brunette	.20	.50
151 Pierre-Marc Bouchard	.30	.75
152 Niklas Backstrom	.30	.75
153 Colton Gillies	.30	.75
154 Owen Nolan	.30	.75
155 James Sheppard	.20	.50
156 Marek Zidlicky	.20	.50
157 Antti Miettinen	.20	.50
158 Cal Clutterbuck	.20	.50
159 Anze Kopitar	.50	1.25
160 Alexander Frolov	.25	.60
161 Dustin Brown	.30	.75
162 Jarret Stoll	.25	.60
163 Drew Doughty	.40	1.00
164 Jack Johnson	.20	.50
165 Jonathan Quick	.40	1.00
166 Erik Ersberg	.25	.60
167 Justin Williams	.25	.60
168 Ryan Smyth	.25	.60
169 Tomas Vokoun	.25	.60
170 Stephen Weiss	.20	.50
171 David Booth	.20	.50
172 Cory Stillman	.20	.50
173 Nathan Horton	.30	.75
174 Michael Frolik	.25	.60
175 Bryan McCabe	.25	.60
176 Keith Ballard	.20	.50
177 Gregory Campbell	.20	.50
178 Brett McLean	.20	.50
179 Ales Hemsky	.25	.60
180 Sheldon Souray	.20	.50
181 Shawn Horcoff	.20	.50
182 Tom Gilbert	.20	.50
183 Patrick O'Sullivan	.25	.60
184 Sam Gagner	.20	.50
185 Andrew Cogliano	.20	.50
186 Ethan Moreau	.20	.50
187 Lubomir Visnovsky	.20	.50
188 Nikolai Khabibulin	.30	.75
189 Pavel Datsyuk	.50	1.25
190 Henrik Zetterberg	.40	1.00
191 Nicklas Lidstrom	.20	.50
192 Brian Rafalski	.20	.50
193 Valtteri Filppula	.20	.50
194 Tomas Holmstrom	.25	.60
195 Kris Draper	.20	.50
196 Chris Osgood	.30	.75
197 Niklas Kronwall	.25	.60
198 Johan Franzen	.25	.60
199 Mike Ribeiro	.20	.50
200 Loui Eriksson	.20	.50
201 Brad Richards	.30	.75
202 Mike Modano	.50	1.25
203 Steve Ott	.20	.50
204 James Neal	.20	.50
205 Matt Niskanen	.25	.60
206 Krys Barch	.20	.50
207 Brenden Morrow	.25	.60
208 Marty Turco	.30	.75
209 Steve Mason	.25	.60
210 Rick Nash	.30	.75
211 Kristian Huselius	.20	.50
212 R.J. Umberger	.25	.60
213 Jakub Voracek	.25	.60
214 Antoine Vermette	.20	.50
215 Derick Brassard	.20	.50
216 Mike Commodore	.20	.50
217 Marc Methot	.20	.50
218 Fedor Tyutin	.20	.50
219 David Jones	.20	.50
220 Milan Hejduk	.25	.60
221 Wojtek Wolski	.20	.50
222 Paul Stastny	.25	.60
223 John-Michael Liles	.20	.50
224 Chris Stewart	.25	.60
225 T.J. Hensick	.20	.50
226 Cody McLeod	.20	.50
227 Peter Budaj	.25	.60
228 Patrick Kane	.60	1.50
229 Jonathan Toews	.50	1.25
230 Kris Versteeg	.20	.50
231 Cristobal Huet	.30	.75
232 Brian Campbell	.25	.60
233 Patrick Sharp	.30	.75
234 Duncan Keith	.25	.60
235 Dustin Byfuglien	.30	.75
236 Marian Hossa	.30	.75
237 Cam Barker	.20	.50
238 Ray Whitney	.25	.60
239 Eric Staal	.40	1.00
240 Tuomo Ruutu	.20	.50
241 Rod Brind`Amour	.30	.75
242 Sergei Samsonov	.25	.60
243 Jussi Jokinen	.20	.50
244 Cam Ward	.30	.75
245 Joe Corvo	.20	.50
246 Brandon Sutter	.20	.50
247 Anton Babchuk	.25	.60
248 Jarome Iginla	.40	1.00
249 Olli Jokinen	.25	.60
250 Daymond Langkow	.20	.50
251 Miikka Kiprusoff	.30	.75
252 Craig Conroy	.20	.50
253 Dion Phaneuf	.25	.60
254 Rene Bourque	.20	.50
255 Dustin Boyd	.20	.50
256 Jay Bouwmeester	.20	.50
257 Cory Sarich	.20	.50
258 Derek Roy	.20	.50
259 Jason Pominville	.20	.50
260 Thomas Vanek	.25	.60
261 Tim Connolly	.20	.50
262 Ryan Miller	.30	.75
263 Drew Stafford	.20	.50
264 Clarke MacArthur	.20	.50
265 Daniel Paille	.25	.60
266 Paul Gaustad	.25	.60
267 Jochen Hecht	.20	.50
268 Marc Savard	.20	.50
269 Tim Thomas	.30	.75
270 David Krejci	.30	.75
271 Phil Kessel	.30	.75
272 Michael Ryder	.20	.50
273 Zdeno Chara	.30	.75
274 Blake Wheeler	.30	.75
275 Patrice Bergeron	.40	1.00
276 Milan Lucic	.25	.60
277 Dennis Wideman	.20	.50
278 Ilya Kovalchuk	.30	.75
279 Slava Kozlov	.20	.50
280 Todd White	.20	.50
281 Bryan Little	.30	.75
282 Rich Peverley	.25	.60
283 Colby Armstrong	.20	.50
284 Kari Lehtonen	.25	.60
285 Zach Bogosian	.25	.60
286 Nik Antropov	.25	.60
287 Tobias Enstrom	.30	.75
288 Ryan Getzlaf	.30	.75
289 Corey Perry	.50	1.25
290 Bobby Ryan	.25	.60
291 Teemu Selanne	.60	1.50
292 Saku Koivu	.30	.75
293 George Parros	.20	.50
294 Jonas Hiller	.25	.60
295 Jean-Sebastien Giguere	.30	.75
296 Andrew Ebbett	.20	.50
297 Scott Niedermayer	.30	.75
298 Alexander Ovechkin CL	.75	2.00
299 Carey Price CL	.40	1.00
300 Sidney Crosby CL	.75	2.00
301 Brian Salcido RC	.75	2.00
302 Luca Caputi RC	1.25	3.00
303 Spencer Machacek RC	1.25	3.00
304 Matt Beleskey RC	1.00	2.50
305 T.J. Galiardi RC	1.25	3.00
306 Michael Sauer RC	1.00	2.50
307 Yannick Weber RC	1.25	3.00
308 Jesse Joensuu RC	1.00	2.50
309 Cal O'Reilly RC	1.00	2.50
310 Grant Lewis RC	1.00	2.50
311 Tim Stapleton RC	1.25	3.00
312 Christian Hanson RC	1.25	3.00
313 Mikael Backlund RC	2.00	5.00
314 Artem Anisimov RC	.75	2.00
315 Jhonas Enroth RC	1.50	4.00
316 Ivan Vishnevskiy RC	.75	2.00
317 Riku Helenius RC	1.25	3.00
318 Kris Chucko RC	.75	2.00
319 Matt Pelech RC	1.25	3.00
320 Michal Neuvirth RC	2.00	5.00
321 Ray Macias RC	1.00	2.50
322 Ville Leino RC	1.00	2.50
323 Taylor Chorney RC	1.25	3.00
324 John Negrin RC	1.25	3.00
325 Alexander Sulzer RC	.75	2.00
326 Mike Santorelli RC	1.25	3.00
327 Tom Wandell RC	1.25	3.00
328 Andrew MacDonald RC	.75	2.00
329 Kevin Quick RC	.75	2.00
330 David Van Der Gulik RC	1.00	2.50
331 Jakub Petruzalek RC	1.25	3.00
332 Chris Durno RC	1.00	2.50
333 Peter Regin RC	1.00	2.50
334 Kurtis McLean RC	1.00	2.50
335 John Scott RC	1.25	3.00
336 Bryan Rodney RC	1.00	2.50
337 Riley Armstrong RC	1.00	2.50
338 Ryan Vesce RC	1.00	2.50
339 Brandon Segal RC	1.00	2.50
340 Antti Niemi RC	2.00	5.00
341 Derek Peltier RC	.75	2.00
342 Matt Hendricks RC	1.00	2.50
343 Mike McKenna RC	1.00	2.50
344 Aaron MacKenzie RC	1.25	3.00
345 David Sloane RC	1.25	3.00
346 Jamie Fritsch RC	1.25	3.00
347 Geoff Kinrade RC	1.25	3.00
348 Tyson Strachan RC	.75	2.00
349 Troy Bodie RC	1.00	2.50
350 Kevin Westgarth RC	1.00	2.50
351 Byron Bitz RC	1.00	2.50
352 Tim Wallace RC	.75	2.00
353 Ben Lovejoy RC	1.25	3.00
354 Jaime Sifers RC	1.00	2.50
355 Sean Collins RC	1.00	2.50
356 Davis Drewiske RC	1.25	3.00
357 David Schlemko RC	1.00	2.50
358 Jay Beagle RC	1.50	4.00
359 Phil Oreskovic RC	1.25	3.00
360 Joel Rechlicz RC	.75	2.00
361 Michael Vernace RC	1.00	2.50
362 Scott Lehman RC	.75	2.00
363 Dan Turple RC	1.25	3.00
364 Matt Climie RC	1.00	2.50
365 Jamie Fraser RC	1.00	2.50
366 Per Ledin RC	1.25	3.00
367 Wes O'Neill RC	1.25	3.00
368 Sean Bentivoglio RC	1.00	2.50
369 Evander Kane RC	2.50	6.00
370 Tyler Myers RC	2.00	5.00
371 Matt Duchene RC	2.50	6.00
372 Ryan O'Reilly RC	2.50	6.00
373 Jamie Benn RC	4.00	10.00
374 Dmitri Kulikov RC	1.25	3.00
375 Alec Martinez RC	1.50	4.00
376 Teemu Laakso RC	.75	2.00
377 John Tavares RC	10.00	25.00
378 Matt Gilroy RC	1.25	3.00
379 Michael Del Zotto RC	1.25	3.00
380 Erik Karlsson RC	3.00	8.00
381 James van Riemsdyk RC	2.50	6.00
382 Johan Backlund RC	1.25	3.00
383 Mika Pyorala RC	1.00	2.50
384 Jason Demers RC	2.00	5.00
385 Benn Ferriero RC	1.25	3.00
386 Frazer McLaren RC	1.00	2.50
387 Victor Hedman RC	3.00	8.00
388 Viktor Stalberg RC	1.25	3.00
389 Jay Rosehill RC	1.25	3.00
390 Jonas Gustavsson RC	3.00	8.00
391 Sergei Shirokov RC	.75	2.00
392 Ilkka Pikkarainen RC	1.25	3.00
393 Colin Wilson RC	1.25	3.00
394 Tyler Bozak RC	2.00	5.00

2009-10 Upper Deck MVP Gold Script

*1-300 VETS/100: 3X TO 8X BASIC CARDS
*301-394 ROOKIES: 1.2X TO 3X BASIC CARDS

Card	Low	High
302 Luca Caputi	4.00	10.00
377 John Tavares	30.00	80.00
390 Jonas Gustavsson	5.00	12.00

2009-10 Upper Deck MVP Super Script

*VETS: 6X TO 15X BASIC CARDS
*ROOKIES: 2.5X TO 6X BASIC CARDS

Card	Low	High
2 Nicklas Backstrom	5.00	12.00
36 Mike Smith	5.00	12.00
68 Kristopher Letang	6.00	15.00
85 Claude Giroux	5.00	12.00
120 Zach Parise	5.00	12.00
302 Luca Caputi	8.00	20.00
307 Yannick Weber	8.00	20.00
377 John Tavares	100.00	200.00
390 Jonas Gustavsson	40.00	100.00

2009-10 Upper Deck MVP Hart Candidates

Card	Low	High
COMPLETE SET (30)	12.00	30.00
HC1 Tim Thomas	.75	2.00
HC2 Nicklas Backstrom	.75	2.00
HC3 Zach Parise	.75	2.00
HC4 Evgeni Malkin	1.50	4.00
HC5 Jeff Carter	.60	1.50
HC6 Eric Staal	1.00	2.50
HC7 Henrik Lundqvist	2.00	5.00
HC8 Carey Price	1.50	4.00
HC9 Tomas Vokoun	.60	1.50
HC10 Thomas Vanek	.60	1.50
HC11 Jason Spezza	.75	2.00
HC12 Luke Schenn	.75	2.00
HC13 Ilya Kovalchuk	.75	2.00
HC14 Steven Stamkos	1.50	4.00
HC15 Rick DiPietro	.60	1.50
HC16 Evgeni Nabokov	.60	1.50
HC17 Henrik Zetterberg	1.00	2.50
HC18 Roberto Luongo	1.25	3.00
HC19 Jonathan Toews	1.25	3.00
HC20 Jarome Iginla	1.00	2.50
HC21 David Perron	.60	1.50
HC22 Rick Nash	.75	2.00
HC23 Ryan Getzlaf	.75	2.00
HC24 Niklas Backstrom	.75	2.00
HC25 Pekka Rinne	.75	2.00
HC26 Sam Gagner	.50	1.25
HC27 Mike Ribeiro	.50	1.25
HC28 Peter Mueller	.60	1.50
HC29 Anze Kopitar	1.25	3.00
HC30 Paul Stastny	.60	1.50

2009-10 Upper Deck MVP Hart Winners

Card	Low	High
COMPLETE SET (10)	20.00	50.00
HW1 Alexander Ovechkin	4.00	10.00
HW2 Sidney Crosby	4.00	10.00
HW3 Joe Thornton	1.50	4.00
HW4 Martin St. Louis	1.00	2.50
HW5 Mark Messier	2.00	5.00
HW6 Bobby Hull	2.00	5.00
HW7 Gordie Howe	3.00	8.00
HW8 Mario Lemieux	4.00	10.00
HW9 Bobby Orr	4.00	10.00
HW10 Wayne Gretzky	6.00	15.00

2009-10 Upper Deck MVP One on One Autographs

Card	Low	High
AAB Bogosian/Alzner	8.00	20.00
ABB Brunnstrom/Boedker	8.00	20.00
ACH Conklin/Huet	10.00	25.00
ACR Cleary/Ryder	10.00	25.00
AES Ebbett/Simmonds	12.00	30.00
AFD Doughty/Fistric	12.00	30.00
AFS Frolik/Stamkos	20.00	50.00
AGR Gomez/Ryder	8.00	20.00
AGS Gillies/Stewart	10.00	25.00
AGV Vanek/Gaborik	10.00	25.00
AHB Hornqvist/Berglund	15.00	40.00
AHE Ersberg/Hiller	8.00	20.00
AKG Kunitz/Giroux	10.00	25.00
AKO Kane/Oshie	30.00	60.00
ALP Price/Lundqvist	30.00	80.00
ALS Schenn/Lee	15.00	30.00
AMD Mikkelson/Doughty	12.00	30.00
AOM Malkin/Ovechkin	60.00	120.00
APA Hemsky/Stastny	8.00	20.00
APC Clowe/Perry	12.00	30.00
APL Price/Leclaire	25.00	60.00
APW Wheeler/Pominville	10.00	25.00
ARG Redden/Green	8.00	20.00
ARP Parise/Richards	30.00	60.00
ARS Setoguchi/Ryan	8.00	20.00
ASO Ovechkin/Staal	40.00	100.00
AST Setoguchi/Turris	15.00	30.00
AVM Vokoun/Mason	8.00	20.00
AWB Bogosian/Weber	8.00	20.00
AWP Wheeler/Pacioretty	10.00	25.00

2009-10 Upper Deck MVP Two on Two Jerseys

Card	Low	High
JBDLP Lundq/Drury/Parse/Brod	8.00	20.00
JBFCP Parse/Brodr/Sid/Fleur	15.00	40.00
JBKMB Bodkr/Muellr/Kopitr/Brwn	10.00	25.00
JBOCR Bernir/Rymd/O'Sull/Coglino	5.00	12.00
JBSHS Spez/Heatly/Blak/Stmpnk	6.00	15.00
JBSOF Fleisch/Ovie/Stal/Brind	12.00	30.00
JCHRW Weber/Rin/Cmpbll/Huet	6.00	15.00
JCMZH Zettr/Holms/Sid/Malkn	20.00	50.00
JCOMB Malk/Sid/Ovie/Backs	20.00	50.00
JCTHS Schen/Tskla/Campb/Huet	6.00	15.00
JDGCM Dubn/Gabrik/Sid/Malkn	15.00	40.00
JDLSB Svats/Budaj/Lngo/Dmtr	10.00	25.00
JDZTK Datsk/Zettr/Toews/Kan	12.00	30.00
JEGAC Asham/Gagn/Eli/Clrksn	6.00	15.00
JHBKS Koiv/Bchrd/Hejdk/Ststny	6.00	15.00
JHDSB Holms/Drapr/Bollnd/Sharp	6.00	15.00
JJICG Igin/Jokn/Cogln/Gagnr	8.00	20.00
JKCVB Brglnd/Clco/Klsla/Vorck	6.00	15.00
JKLHV Horton/Vokn/Koval/Lehtn	6.00	15.00
JLDHS Sharp/Huet/Lngo/Dmtra	10.00	25.00
JLJKD Demt/Lngo/Kiprsf/Jokn	10.00	25.00
JMCFB Brwn/Frol/Chch/Marlu	6.00	15.00
JMDTS Setog/Thrntn/Doan/Muelr	10.00	25.00
JMFBS Frolk/Booth/Stamk/Malon	12.00	30.00
JMSKS Markv/Kostit/Stajn/Schen	6.00	15.00
JNDLW Dubin/Naslnd/Lucic/Wheel	6.00	15.00
JNMKB Bouchrd/Koiv/Neal/Mdno	10.00	25.00
JNSPK Sharp/Kane/Peca/Nash	12.00	30.00
JPLWE Pitknn/Ward/Leht/Enstrm	6.00	15.00
JRCMS Rich/Cartr/Malkn/Staal	12.00	30.00
JRRDM Richrds/Ribir/Doan/Muelr	6.00	15.00
JRTCS Carle/Timon/Staal/Redden	5.00	12.00
JSBHJ Stillmn/Hortn/Jokin/Brind	6.00	15.00
JSDGB Getzlf/Selan/Boedkr/Doan	12.00	30.00
JSKLS Little/Koval/St.L/Stamk	12.00	30.00
JSORW Osgd/Webr/Rinne/Sturt	6.00	15.00
JSRBV Savard/Bergern/Roy/Vank	20.00	50.00
JTCRM Richs/Mod/Chch/Thrntn	10.00	25.00
JTJLS Jurcn/Theo/Lund/Staal	15.00	40.00
JTMSH Tskla/Hollwg/Staffrd/Millr	6.00	15.00
JTWCG Wolski/Tuckr/Gagnr/Cogl	5.00	12.00
JWNDL Wght/DiPit/Naslnd/Lund	8.00	20.00
JWNJD Dgty/Jhsn/Whtny/Nied	8.00	20.00

2009-10 Upper Deck MVP Winter Classic

Card	Low	High
WC1 Jeff Carter	.75	2.00
WC2 Daniel Briere	1.00	2.50
WC3 Chris Pronger	1.00	2.50
WC4 Ray Emery	.75	2.00
WC5 Mike Richards	.75	2.00
WC6 Simon Gagne	1.00	2.50
WC7 Claude Giroux	1.00	2.50
WC8 Daniel Carcillo	.60	1.50
WC9 Scott Hartnell	.60	1.50
WC10 Michael Ryder	.60	1.50
WC11 Tim Thomas	1.00	2.50
WC12 Blake Wheeler	1.00	2.50
WC13 Zdeno Chara	1.00	2.50
WC14 Milan Lucic	.75	2.00
WC15 Marc Savard	.60	1.50
WC16 David Krejci	1.00	2.50
WC17 Mark Recchi	1.25	3.00
WC18 Patrice Bergeron	1.25	3.00
WC19 City of Boston	.60	1.50
WC20 Wrigley Field	.60	1.50

2011-12 Upper Deck MVP

Card	Low	High
COMPLETE SET (100)	40.00	100.00
COMP.SET w/o SPs (88)	12.00	30.00
1 Ryan Getzlaf	.40	1.00
2 Corey Perry	.60	1.50
3 Bobby Ryan	.30	.75
4 Evander Kane	.40	1.00
5 Dustin Byfuglien	.40	1.00
6 Ondrej Pavelec	.40	1.00
7 Zdeno Chara	.40	1.00
8 Nathan Horton	.40	1.00
9 Tim Thomas	.40	1.00
10 Milan Lucic	.40	1.00
11 Derek Roy	.25	.60
12 Ryan Miller	.40	1.00
13 Jarome Iginla	.50	1.25
14 Miikka Kiprusoff	.40	1.00
15 Cam Ward	.40	1.00
16 Eric Staal	.50	1.25
17 Jeff Skinner	.50	1.25
18 Duncan Keith	.30	.75
19 Patrick Kane	.75	2.00
20 Patrick Sharp	.40	1.00
21 Jonathan Toews	.60	1.50
22 Matt Duchene	.40	1.00
23 Paul Stastny	.30	.75
24 Erik Johnson	.25	.60
25 Derick Brassard	.25	.60
26 Rick Nash	.40	1.00
27 Loui Eriksson	.25	.60
28 Mike Ribeiro	.25	.60
29 Brad Richards	.40	1.00
30 Henrik Zetterberg	.50	1.25
31 Nicklas Lidstrom	.25	.60
32 Pavel Datsyuk	.60	1.50
33 Taylor Hall	.40	1.00
34 Jordan Eberle	.40	1.00
35 Stephen Weiss	.30	.75
36 Jacob Markstrom	.40	1.00
37 Drew Doughty	.50	1.25
38 Jonathan Quick	.50	1.25
39 Anze Kopitar	.60	1.50
40 Martin Havlat	.30	.75
41 Niklas Backstrom	.40	1.00
42 Mikko Koivu	.30	.75
43 Tomas Plekanec	.25	.60
44 Michael Cammalleri	.30	.75
45 Carey Price	.75	2.00
46 P.K. Subban	.50	1.25
47 Patric Hornqvist	.25	.60
48 Shea Weber	.30	.75
49 Ilya Kovalchuk	.40	1.00
50 Martin Brodeur	1.00	2.50
51 Zach Parise	.40	1.00
52 Matt Moulson	.25	.60
53 John Tavares	.60	1.50
54 Brandon Dubinsky	.25	.60
55 Henrik Lundqvist	1.00	2.50
56 Marian Gaborik	.40	1.00
57 Daniel Alfredsson	.40	1.00
58 Jason Spezza	.40	1.00
59 Jeff Carter	.30	.75
60 Claude Giroux	.40	1.00
61 Sergei Bobrovsky	.60	1.50
62 Mike Richards	.30	.75
63 Ilya Bryzgalov	.40	1.00
64 Shane Doan	.30	.75
65 Evgeni Malkin	.75	2.00
66 Kristopher Letang	.50	1.25
67 Marc-Andre Fleury	.75	2.00
68 Sidney Crosby	1.50	4.00
69 Joe Thornton	.60	1.50
70 Patrick Marleau	.40	1.00
71 Dany Heatley	.30	.75
72 Chris Stewart	.30	.75
73 David Backes	.25	.60
74 Jaroslav Halak	.40	1.00
75 Steven Stamkos	.75	2.00
76 Martin St. Louis	.40	1.00
77 Vincent Lecavalier	.40	1.00
78 Phil Kessel	.40	1.00
79 Nikolai Kulemin	.25	.60
80 Dion Phaneuf	.30	.75
81 Daniel Sedin	.50	1.25
82 Henrik Sedin	.50	1.25
83 Ryan Kesler	.40	1.00
84 Roberto Luongo	.60	1.50
85 Alexander Ovechkin	1.50	4.00
86 Alexander Semin	.40	1.00
87 Nicklas Backstrom	.40	1.00
88 Mike Green	.30	.75
89 Carl Klingberg RC	1.00	2.50
90 Greg Nemisz RC	1.00	2.50
91 Marcus Kruger RC	1.50	4.00
92 John Moore RC	1.00	2.50
93 Aaron Palushaj RC	1.00	2.50
94 Jonathon Blum RC	1.00	2.50
95 Blake Geoffrion RC	1.00	2.50
96 Adam Henrique RC	2.50	6.00
97 Alex Stalock	.75	2.00
98 Joe Colborne RC	1.00	2.50
99 Matt Frattin RC	1.00	2.50
100 Cody Hodgson RC	6.00	15.00
101 Ville Leino	.30	.75
102 Christian Ehrhoff	.25	.60
103 Semyon Varlamov	.40	1.00
104 Jean-Sebastien Giguere	.40	1.00
105 Jeff Carter	.30	.75
106 Tomas Fleischmann	.25	.60
107 Kris Versteeg	.25	.60
108 Jose Theodore	.40	1.00
109 Mike Richards	.30	.75
110 Dany Heatley	.30	.75
111 Devin Setoguchi	.30	.75
112 Evgeni Nabokov	.30	.75
113 Brad Richards	.40	1.00
114 Ilya Bryzgalov	.40	1.00
115 Jaromir Jagr	1.25	3.00
116 Maxime Talbot	.25	.60
117 Brent Burns	.40	1.00
118 Martin Havlat	.30	.75
119 John-Michael Liles	.25	.60
120 David Booth	.25	.60
121 Tomas Vokoun	.30	.75
122 Ondrej Pavelec	.40	1.00
123 Evander Kane	.40	1.00
124 Alexander Burmistrov	.30	.75
125 Gabriel Landeskog RC	3.00	8.00
126 Ryan Johansen RC	3.00	8.00
127 Ryan Nugent-Hopkins RC	8.00	20.00
128 Zack Kassian RC	1.25	3.00
129 Craig Smith RC	1.25	3.00
130 Adam Larsson RC	1.25	3.00
131 Mika Zibanejad RC	3.00	8.00
132 Sean Couturier RC	2.00	5.00
133 Matt Read RC	1.25	3.00
134 Brett Connolly RC	1.00	2.50
135 Louis Leblanc RC	2.50	6.00
136 Mark Scheifele RC	4.00	10.00

2011-12 Upper Deck MVP One on One Autographs

Card	Low	High
MVP12 N-Hopkins/Landeskog B	125.00	250.00
MVPCH J.Colborne/C.Hodgson C	25.00	60.00
MVPDT P.Datsyuk/J.Toews A	40.00	80.00
MVPHO B.Hull/A.Oates A	60.00	120.00
MVPOS A.Ovechkin/S.Stamkos B	100.00	200.00
MVPPE M.Paajarvi/J.Eberle C	30.00	60.00

2012-13 Upper Deck MVP

Card	Low	High
1 Corey Perry	1.00	2.50
2 Teemu Selanne	1.25	3.00
3 Zdeno Chara	.60	1.50
4 Patrice Bergeron	.75	2.00
5 Brad Marchand	1.25	3.00
6 Thomas Vanek	.50	1.25
7 Ryan Miller	.60	1.50
8 Jarome Iginla	.75	2.00
9 Miikka Kiprusoff	.60	1.50
10 Jonathan Toews	1.00	2.50
11 Patrick Kane	1.25	3.00
12 Patrick Sharp	.60	1.50
13 Matt Duchene	.60	1.50
14 Jack Johnson	.40	1.00
15 Ryan Nugent-Hopkins	.75	2.00
16 Taylor Hall	.60	1.50
17 Jordan Eberle	.60	1.50
18 Tomas Fleischmann	.40	1.00
19 Mike Richards	.50	1.25
20 Jonathan Quick	.75	2.00
21 Dany Heatley	.50	1.25
22 Mikko Koivu	.50	1.25
23 Josh Gorges	.50	1.25
24 P.K. Subban	.75	2.00
25 Carey Price	1.25	3.00
26 Pekka Rinne	.60	1.50
27 Ilya Kovalchuk	.60	1.50
28 Martin Brodeur	1.50	4.00
29 John Tavares	1.00	2.50
30 Brad Richards	.60	1.50
31 Marian Gaborik	.60	1.50
32 Henrik Lundqvist	1.50	4.00
33 Claude Giroux	.60	1.50
34 Scott Hartnell	.40	1.00
35 Brayden Schenn	.60	1.50
36 Keith Yandle	.40	1.00
37 Sidney Crosby	2.50	6.00
38 James Neal	.40	1.00
39 Evgeni Malkin	1.25	3.00
40 Logan Couture	.75	2.00
41 Joe Pavelski	.75	2.00
42 Brian Elliott	.50	1.25
43 Steven Stamkos	1.25	3.00
44 Joffrey Lupul	.40	1.00
45 Phil Kessel	.60	1.50
46 Braden Holtby	.75	2.00
47 Alexander Ovechkin	2.50	6.00
48 Ondrej Pavelec	.60	1.50
49 Evander Kane	.60	1.50
50 Alexander Burmistrov	.50	1.25
51 Sven Baertschi RC	1.25	3.00
52 Brandon Bollig RC	.75	2.00
53 Tyson Barrie RC	2.50	6.00
54 Reilly Smith RC	2.50	6.00
55 Scott Glennie RC	1.00	2.50
56 Riley Sheahan RC	1.25	3.00
57 Jordan Nolan RC	.75	2.00
58 Jason Zucker RC	2.00	5.00
59 Gabriel Dumont RC	1.00	2.50
60 Chet Pickard RC	1.00	2.50
61 Casey Cizikas RC	1.00	2.50
62 Chris Kreider RC	3.00	8.00
63 Jakob Silfverberg RC	1.50	4.00
64 Mark Stone RC	3.00	8.00
65 Michael Stone RC	1.00	2.50
66 Jake Allen RC	2.50	6.00
67 Jaden Schwartz RC	2.50	6.00
68 J.T. Brown RC	1.00	2.50
69 Carter Ashton RC	.75	2.00
70 Jussi Rynnas RC	.75	2.00

2013-14 Upper Deck MVP

Card	Low	High
COMP.SERIES 1 w/o SP's (30)	10.00	25.00
COMP.SERIES 1 (70)	40.00	80.00
COMMON CARD (71-75)	.75	2.00
UNLISTED STARS 71-75	1.00	2.50
1 Tomas Fleischmann	.40	1.00
2 Adam Henrique	.50	1.25
3 Logan Couture	.75	2.00
4 Taylor Hall	.60	1.50
5 John Tavares	1.00	2.50
6 Jim Howard	.75	2.00
7 Steven Stamkos	1.25	3.00
8 Jack Johnson	.40	1.00
9 Alexander Ovechkin	2.50	6.00
10 Thomas Vanek	.50	1.25
11 Jonathan Toews	1.00	2.50
12 Jason Spezza	.60	1.50
13 Zdeno Chara	.60	1.50
14 Matt Duchene	.60	1.50
15 Nazem Kadri	.75	2.00
16 Ondrej Pavelec	.60	1.50
17 Kari Lehtonen	.50	1.25
18 Mikko Koivu	.50	1.25
19 Sidney Crosby	2.50	6.00
20 Mike Smith	.60	1.50
21 Jeff Skinner	.75	2.00
22 Pekka Rinne	.60	1.50
23 P.K. Subban	.75	2.00
24 Corey Perry	1.00	2.50
25 Alex Pietrangelo	.50	1.25
26 Jakub Voracek	.50	1.25
27 Matt Stajan	.40	1.00
28 Roberto Luongo	1.00	2.50
29 Henrik Lundqvist	1.50	4.00
30 Jonathan Quick	.75	2.00
31 Bobby Orr	6.00	15.00
32 Ray Bourque	2.50	6.00
33 Chris Pronger	1.50	4.00
34 Paul Coffey	1.50	4.00
35 Mario Lemieux	6.00	15.00
36 Patrick Roy	4.00	10.00
37 Dominik Hasek	2.50	6.00
38 Ed Belfour	1.50	4.00
39 Andy Moog	1.50	4.00
40 Mats Sundin	1.50	4.00
41 Bobby Hull	3.00	8.00
42 Wayne Gretzky	4.00	10.00
43 Brett Hull	3.00	8.00
44 Theoren Fleury	2.00	5.00
45 Mark Messier	3.00	8.00
46 Curtis Joseph	2.00	5.00
47 Pavel Bure	1.50	4.00
48 Joe Sakic	3.00	8.00
49 Ron Francis	2.00	5.00
50 Luc Robitaille	1.50	4.00
51 Justin Schultz RC	.60	1.50
52 Nail Yakupov RC	1.25	3.00
53 J.T. Miller RC	1.50	4.00
54 Alex Galchenyuk RC	1.50	4.00
55 Mikael Granlund RC	1.00	2.50
56 Emerson Etem RC	1.00	2.50
57 Jonathan Huberdeau RC	1.50	4.00
58 Cory Conacher RC	.40	1.00
59 Beau Bennett RC	.75	2.00
60 Vladimir Tarasenko RC	1.50	4.00
61 Jonas Brodin RC	.75	2.00
62 Charlie Coyle RC	1.00	2.50
63 Tyler Toffoli RC	1.25	3.00
64 Petr Mrazek RC	1.25	3.00
65 Nathan Beaulieu RC	.40	1.00
66 Filip Forsberg RC	2.00	5.00
67 Dougie Hamilton RC	1.00	2.50
68 Brendan Gallagher RC	1.50	4.00
69 Mikhail Grigorenko RC	.40	1.00
70 Damien Brunner RC	.50	1.25
71 Ryan Getzlaf	1.00	2.50
72 Phil Kessel	1.00	2.50
73 Martin St. Louis	1.00	2.50
74 Tuukka Rask	1.25	3.00
75 Evgeni Malkin	2.00	5.00

76 Morgan Rielly RC 2.00 5.00
77 Martin Jones RC 1.25 3.00
78 Rasmus Ristolainen RC 1.25 3.00
79 Valeri Nichushkin RC 1.50 4.00
80 Nathan MacKinnon RC 6.00 15.00
81 Tomas Hertl RC 1.50 4.00
82 Elias Lindholm RC 2.00 5.00
83 Antti Raanta RC 1.50 4.00
84 Jacob Trouba RC 1.25 3.00
85 Tomas Jurco RC 1.00 2.50
86 Seth Jones RC 1.50 4.00
87 Sean Monahan RC 1.25 3.00
88 Mark Arcobello RC .75 2.00
89 Ryan Strome RC 1.25 3.00
90 Aleksander Barkov RC 2.50 6.00

2013-14 Upper Deck MVP Gold Script

*1-30 VETS/100: 2X TO 5X BASIC CARDS
*31-50 RET/100: 1.2X TO 3X BASIC CARD
*51-70 ROOK/100: 2X TO 5X BASIC RC
*71-75 VETS/100: 1.2X TO 3X BASIC CARDS
*75-90 ROOK/100: 1.2X TO 3X BASIC RC
42 Wayne Gretzky 25.00 60.00
80 Nathan MacKinnon 25.00 50.00

2013-14 Upper Deck MVP Oversized

4 Taylor Hall 1.25 3.00
5 John Tavares 2.00 5.00
7 Steven Stamkos 2.50 6.00
9 Alexander Ovechkin 5.00 12.00
11 Jonathan Toews 2.00 5.00
19 Sidney Crosby 5.00 12.00
23 P.K. Subban 1.50 4.00
29 Henrik Lundqvist 3.00 8.00
30 Jonathan Quick 1.50 4.00
31 Bobby Orr 5.00 12.00
35 Mario Lemieux 5.00 12.00
36 Patrick Roy 3.00 8.00
42 Wayne Gretzky 8.00 20.00
47 Pavel Bure 1.25 3.00

2013-14 Upper Deck MVP Rookie Jumbos

*ROOKIE JUMBO: .4X TO 1X MVP RC

2013-14 Upper Deck MVP Super Script

*1-30 VETS/25: 4X TO 10X BASIC CARDS
*31-50 RET/25: 2.5X TO 6X BASIC CARD
*51-70 ROOKIE/25: 3X TO 8X BASIC RC
*71-75 VETS/25: 2.5X TO 6X BASIC CARDS
*75-90 ROOK/25: 2.5X TO 6X BASIC RC
42 Wayne Gretzky 50.00 100.00
80 Nathan MacKinnon 150.00 250.00

2014-15 Upper Deck MVP

COMP.SET w/o SP's (200) 12.00 30.00
1 Ben Scrivens .20 .50
2 Ondrej Palat .20 .50
3 John Carlson .25 .60
4 Dion Phaneuf .20 .50
5 Seth Jones .25 .60
6 Colton Orr .15 .40
7 Tyler Myers .15 .40
8 Tanner Pearson .15 .40
9 David Clarkson .15 .40
10 Brayden Schenn .25 .60
11 Calle Jarnkrok RC .50 1.25
12 Paul Stastny .20 .50
13 Wayne Simmonds .30 .75
14 Brent Burns .25 .60
15 Oliver Ekman-Larsson .25 .60
16 Nathan MacKinnon 1.00 2.50
17 Mika Zibanejad .30 .75
18 Nick Bjugstad .15 .40
19 Cody Hodgson .15 .40
20 Brendan Gallagher .25 .60
21 Joe Pavelski .30 .75
22 Cody Eakin .15 .40
23 Braden Holtby .30 .75
24 T.J. Oshie .25 .60
25 Alexander Semin .25 .60
26 Jaden Schwartz .30 .75
27 Michael Grabner .20 .50
28 Cam Ward .25 .60
29 Niklas Hjalmarsson .15 .40
30 Olli Jokinen .20 .50
31 Reilly Smith .25 .60
32 Antti Raanta .25 .60
33 Jussi Jokinen .15 .40
34 Thomas Vanek .20 .50
35 Mike Fisher .15 .40
36 Brian Campbell .15 .40
37 Dustin Penner .20 .50
38 Valtteri Filppula .15 .40
39 Saku Koivu .25 .60
40 Jay Bouwmeester .15 .40
41 Morgan Rielly .25 .60
42 Justin Williams .20 .50
43 Scottie Upshall .15 .40
44 Tomas Hertl .25 .60
45 David Desharnais .15 .40
46 Kyle Turris .25 .60
47 Justin Abdelkader .20 .50
48 Andrej Sekera .15 .40
49 Tom Wilson .25 .60
50 Jason Chimera .15 .40
51 Vladislav Namestnikov RC .75 2.00
52 Mike Richards .20 .50
53 Brandon Bollig .20 .50
54 Olli Maatta .15 .40
55 Matt Stajan .15 .40
56 Justin Faulk .20 .50
57 Brian Elliott .20 .50
58 Matt Cooke .15 .40
59 Nail Yakupov .15 .40
60 Blake Wheeler .25 .60
61 Alex Chiasson .20 .50
62 Dougie Hamilton .20 .50
63 Hampus Lindholm .15 .40
64 Erik Johnson .15 .40
65 Josh Bailey .20 .50
66 Semyon Varlamov .25 .60
67 Marcus Foligno .20 .50
68 Robin Lehner .20 .50
69 Patrik Berglund .15 .40
70 Bryan Little .25 .60
71 Daniel Paille .15 .40
72 Brandon Saad .20 .50
73 Alex Goligoski .15 .40
74 Jacob Markstrom .25 .60
75 Cam Fowler .25 .60
76 Ryan O'Reilly .25 .60
77 Joel Ward .15 .40
78 Mark Giordano .25 .60
79 Darcy Kuemper .25 .60
80 Jhonas Enroth .25 .60
81 Mike Ribeiro .15 .40
82 Jakub Voracek .20 .50
83 Tomas Fleischmann .15 .40
84 Lars Eller .15 .40
85 Ben Bishop .20 .50
86 Mike Smith .25 .60
87 Chris Kreider .30 .75
88 Mikael Granlund .20 .50
89 Kyle Okposo .15 .40
90 Alexander Edler .15 .40
91 Mikkel Boedker .15 .40
92 Ondrej Pavelec .25 .60
93 Alex Galchenyuk .15 .40
94 Dan Boyle .15 .40
95 Frans Nielsen .15 .40
96 Carl Soderberg .15 .40
97 Victor Hedman .30 .75
98 Joffrey Lupul .15 .40
99 Brian Gionta .15 .40
100 Jean-Sebastien Giguere .25 .60
101 Keith Yandle .15 .40
102 Slava Voynov .25 .60
103 Steve Mason .20 .50
104 Cory Schneider .25 .60
105 David Krejci .25 .60
106 Paul Martin .15 .40
107 Martin Hanzal .15 .40
108 Sean Monahan .15 .40
109 Ryan Murray .15 .40
110 Ilya Bryzgalov .25 .60
111 Brent Seabrook .15 .40
112 Radim Vrbata .15 .40
113 Derek Roy .15 .40
114 Pascal Dupuis .15 .40
115 James Reimer .25 .60
116 Brad Boyes .15 .40
117 Zac Rinaldo .20 .50
118 Dennis Wideman .15 .40
119 Petr Mrazek .25 .60
120 Marc-Edouard Vlasic .15 .40
121 Andrew Ference .15 .40
122 Brandon Gormley RC .50 1.25
123 Tyler Bozak .15 .40
124 Kevin Shattenkirk .15 .40
125 Tyler Johnson .15 .40
126 Patrick Marleau .25 .60
127 Brock Nelson .25 .60
128 Vladimir Tarasenko .30 .75
129 Zack Kassian .15 .40
130 Andy Greene .15 .40
131 Greg McKegg RC .40 1.00
132 Vladimir Sobotka .15 .40
133 Travis Zajac .15 .40
134 Kari Lehtonen .20 .50
135 Brandon Dubinsky .15 .40
136 Andrew Shaw .15 .40
137 David Perron .20 .50
138 Gustav Nyquist .15 .40
139 Jonathan Ericsson .15 .40
140 Ryan Johansen .20 .50
141 Ales Hemsky .15 .40
142 Clarke MacArthur .15 .40
143 Nick Bonino .15 .40
144 Nathan Gerbe .15 .40
145 Michael Ryder .15 .40
146 P.A. Parenteau .15 .40
147 Ryan McDonagh .15 .40
148 Loui Eriksson .15 .40
149 Marcus Johansson .20 .50
150 Valeri Nichushkin .25 .60
151 Dustin Brown .25 .60
152 Rich Peverley .25 .60
153 Matt Niskanen .20 .50
154 Marek Zidlicky .15 .40
155 Danny DeKeyser .15 .40
156 Zdeno Chara .25 .60
157 Nick Foligno .20 .50
158 Chris Higgins .15 .40
159 Lee Stempniak .15 .40
160 Jake Gardiner .15 .40
161 Patric Hornqvist .15 .40
162 Tomas Plekanec .15 .40
163 Jack Johnson .15 .40
164 Jacob Trouba .20 .50
165 Aleksander Barkov .40 1.00
166 Daniel Girardi .15 .40
167 Antoine Vermette .15 .40
168 Scott Hartnell .15 .40
169 Marc Staal .15 .40
170 Brad Marchand .50 1.25
171 Carl Hagelin .15 .40
172 Tommy Wingels .15 .40
173 Jiri Hudler .20 .50
174 Torey Krug .20 .50
175 Tyler Toffoli .25 .60
176 Dave Bolland .15 .40
177 Jonas Hiller .20 .50
178 Michael Cammalleri .20 .50
179 Mason Raymond .15 .40
180 Alexandre Burrows .15 .40
181 Jeff Skinner .30 .75
182 Mats Zuccarello-Aasen .25 .60
183 Tomas Tatar .15 .40
184 Sam Gagner .15 .40
185 Teddy Purcell .15 .40
186 Mark Scheifele .40 1.00
187 Andrei Markov .15 .40
188 Jason Garrison .15 .40
189 Milan Lucic .25 .60
190 Evander Kane .25 .60
191 Oscar Klefbom RC 1.00 2.50
192 Derek Stepan .15 .40
193 Eddie Lack .20 .50
194 Andrew Cogliano .15 .40
195 Sean Couturier .20 .50
196 Matt Moulson .15 .40
197 Ryan Smyth .20 .50
198 Jonathan Huberdeau .30 .75
199 Alexander Ovechkin CL .60 1.50
200 Sidney Crosby CL .60 1.50
201 Patrick Kane SP 2.00 5.00
202 Jim Howard SP 1.25 3.00
203 Jaromir Jagr SP 3.00 8.00
204 Sergei Bobrovsky SP 1.50 4.00
205 Eric Staal SP 1.25 3.00
206 Rick Nash SP 1.00 2.50
207 Evgeni Malkin SP 2.00 5.00
208 Ryan Getzlaf SP 1.00 2.50
209 Henrik Lundqvist SP 2.50 6.00
210 Patrice Bergeron SP 1.25 3.00
211 Bobby Ryan SP .75 2.00
212 Alexander Steen SP .60 1.50
213 Taylor Hall SP 1.00 2.50
214 Brad Richards SP 1.00 2.50
215 James van Riemsdyk SP .75 2.00
216 Marian Gaborik SP 1.00 2.50
217 Joe Thornton SP 1.50 4.00
218 Jason Pominville SP .60 1.50
219 Chris Kunitz SP 1.00 2.50
220 Daniel Sedin SP 1.25 3.00
221 Martin St. Louis SP 1.00 2.50
222 Niklas Kronwall SP .75 2.00
223 Jonathan Quick SP 1.25 3.00
224 Mike Green SP .75 2.00
225 Patrik Elias SP 1.00 2.50
226 Evgeny Kuznetsov SP RC 2.50 6.00
227 Corey Perry SP 1.50 4.00
228 Jordan Eberle SP 1.00 2.50
229 Claude Giroux SP 1.00 2.50
230 Nazem Kadri SP 1.25 3.00
231 Drew Doughty SP 1.25 3.00
232 Henrik Sedin SP 1.25 3.00
233 P.K. Subban SP 1.25 3.00
234 Jarome Iginla SP 1.25 3.00
235 Nicklas Backstrom SP 1.00 2.50
236 Zach Parise SP 1.00 2.50
237 Logan Couture SP 1.25 3.00
238 Duncan Keith SP .75 2.00
239 John Tavares SP 1.50 4.00
240 Jason Spezza SP 1.00 2.50
241 Henrik Zetterberg SP 1.25 3.00
242 Shea Weber SP .75 2.00
243 Marc-Andre Fleury SP 2.00 5.00
244 Steven Stamkos SP 2.00 5.00
245 Craig Anderson SP 1.00 2.50
246 Matt Duchene SP 1.00 2.50
247 Carey Price SP 2.00 5.00
248 Phil Kessel SP 1.00 2.50
249 Mikko Koivu SP .75 2.00
250 Ryan Kesler SP 1.00 2.50
251 Tyler Seguin SP 1.25 3.00
252 Adam Henrique SP .75 2.00
253 Vincent Lecavalier SP 1.00 2.50
254 Antti Niemi SP .75 2.00
255 Anze Kopitar SP 1.50 4.00
256 Erik Karlsson SP 1.25 3.00
257 Marian Hossa SP 1.00 2.50
258 Tuukka Rask SP 1.25 3.00
259 Corey Crawford SP 1.25 3.00
260 Teemu Selanne SP 2.00 5.00
261 David Backes SP .60 1.50
262 Teuvo Teravainen SP RC 1.50 4.00
263 James Neal SP .60 1.50
264 Andrew Ladd SP .60 1.50
265 Ryan Suter SP .75 2.00
266 Ryan Nugent-Hopkins SP 1.25 3.00
267 Jamie Benn SP 1.00 2.50
268 Pekka Rinne SP 1.00 2.50
269 Patrick Sharp SP 1.00 2.50
270 Jonathan Bernier SP .75 2.00
271 Martin Brodeur SP 2.50 6.00
272 Johan Franzen SP .75 2.00
273 Alexander Ovechkin SP 4.00 10.00
274 Max Pacioretty SP 1.00 2.50
275 Kric Lotang SP 1.25 3.00
276 Dustin Byfuglien SP 1.00 2.50
277 Daniel Alfredsson SP 1.00 2.50
278 Shane Doan SP .75 2.00
279 Ryan Callahan SP .60 1.50
280 Alex Pietrangelo SP .75 2.00
281 Roberto Luongo SP 1.50 4.00
282 Dany Heatley SP .75 2.00
283 Jonathan Toews SP 1.50 4.00
284 Tyler Ennis SP .60 1.50
285 Ryan Miller SP 1.00 2.50
286 Jeff Carter SP .75 2.00
287 Sidney Crosby SP 4.00 10.00
288 Gabriel Landeskog SP 1.25 3.00
289 Pavel Datsyuk SP 1.50 4.00
290 Theoren Fleury SP 1.25 3.00
291 Joe Sakic SP 2.00 5.00
292 Peter Forsberg SP 2.00 5.00
293 Steve Yzerman SP 2.50 6.00
294 Mario Lemieux SP 4.00 10.00
295 Felix Potvin SP 1.50 4.00
296 Bobby Orr SP 4.00 10.00
297 Mark Messier SP 2.00 5.00
298 Patrick Roy SP 2.50 6.00
299 Wayne Gretzky SP 6.00 15.00
300 Wayne Gretzky CL SP 4.00 10.00
301 Seth Griffith RC 2.00 5.00
302 Sam Reinhart RC 6.00 15.00
303 Teemu Pulkkinen RC 2.00 5.00
304 Aaron Ekblad RC 4.00 10.00
305 Jiri Sekac RC 1.25 3.00
306 Curtis Lazar RC 1.50 4.00
307 Jonathan Drouin RC 3.00 8.00
308 Stuart Percy RC 1.50 4.00
309 David Pastrnak RC 8.00 20.00
310 Victor Rask RC 1.50 4.00
311 Alexander Wennberg RC 2.50 6.00
312 Marko Dano RC 1.50 4.00
313 Damon Severson RC 1.50 4.00
314 Griffin Reinhart RC 1.50 4.00
315 Anthony Duclair RC 2.50 6.00
316 Shayne Gostisbehere RC 3.00 8.00
317 Adam Payerl RC 1.25 3.00
318 Andre Burakovsky RC 2.50 6.00
319 Dennis Everberg RC 1.50 4.00
320 Adam Clendening RC 1.50 4.00
321 Phillip Danault RC 3.00 8.00
322 Curtis McKenzie RC 1.25 3.00
323 Christian Folin RC 1.50 4.00
324 Colton Sissons RC 1.50 4.00
325 Ty Rattie RC 1.50 4.00
326 Jori Lehtera RC 2.00 5.00
327 Adam Lowry RC 2.50 6.00
328 Johnny Gaudreau RC 5.00 12.00
329 Leon Draisaitl RC 8.00 20.00
330 Darnell Nurse RC 3.00 8.00
331 Chris Tierney RC 1.50 4.00
332 Mirco Mueller RC 1.50 4.00
333 Tobias Rieder RC 1.50 4.00
334 William Karlsson RC 5.00 12.00
335 Bo Horvat RC 4.00 10.00
336 Andy Andreoff RC 1.50 4.00

2014-15 Upper Deck MVP Colors and Contours

*1-200 T3 VET: 3X TO 8X BASIC CARDS
*1-200 T3 ROOK: 1.5X TO 4X BASIC RC
*201-300 T3: .8X TO 2X BASIC SP
*1-200 G2/T1 VET: 4X TO 10X BASIC CARDS
*201-300 G2/T1: 1X TO 2.5X BASIC SP
*1-200 G1/P1/T2 VET: 5X TO 12X BASIC CARDS
*201-300 G1/P1/T2: 1.2X TO 3X BASIC SP
*1-200 G3/P2: 6X TO 15X BASIC CARDS
*201-300 G3/P2: 1.5X TO 4X BASIC SP
*1-200 P3: 10X TO 25X BASIC CARDS
*201-300 P3: 2.5X TO 6X BASIC SP
235 Nicklas Backstrom T2 3.00 8.00
259 Corey Crawford P3 8.00 20.00

2014-15 Upper Deck MVP Gold Script

*1-200 VETS/100: 5X TO 12X BASIC CARDS
*1-200 ROOKIES/100: 2.5X TO 6X BASIC RC
*201-300 VETS/100: 1.2X TO 3X BASIC SP
*201-300 ROOK/100: .8X TO 2X BASIC SP RC
235 Nicklas Backstrom 3.00 8.00
259 Corey Crawford 4.00 10.00

2014-15 Upper Deck MVP Silver Script

*1-200 VETS: 1.5X TO 4X BASIC CARDS
*1-200 ROOKIES: .8X TO 2X BASIC RC
*201-300 VETS: .5X TO 1.2X BASIC SP
*201-300 ROOKIES: .5X TO 1.2X BASIC SP RC
235 Nicklas Backstrom 1.25 3.00
259 Corey Crawford 1.50 4.00

2014-15 Upper Deck MVP NHL Three Stars Player of the Month

3SM0114 Khdbn/Kssl/Pvlski 1.50 4.00
3SM0314 Ignla/Nyqst/Grx 1.50 4.00
3SM1013 Stn/Crsby/Nmi 5.00 12.00
3SM1113 Kne/Mlkn/Hrdng 2.50 6.00
3SM1213 Kne/Crsby/Hllr 5.00 12.00

2014-15 Upper Deck MVP NHL Three Stars Player of the Week

3SW010614 Sknnr/Elltt/Ster 1.25 3.00
3SW011314 Tvrs/Hllr/Lndqvst 2.50 6.00
3SW012014 St.Ls/Qck/Crwfrd 1.25 3.00
3SW012714 Lhtnn/Nyqst/Skra .75 2.00
3SW020314 Prse/Kssl/Bcklnd 1.00 2.50
3SW021014 Prce/Lhtnn/Ignla 2.00 5.00
3SW030314 Frnzn/Hnrqe/Kmpr 1.00 2.50
3SW031014 Sgn/Ansmv/Hnrqe 1.25 3.00
3SW031714 Bbrvsky/Okpso/Nmi 1.50 4.00
3SW032414 Nyqst/Lndqvst/Ignla 2.50 6.00
3SW033114 Trrs/Brgrn/Oshie 1.25 3.00
3SW040714 Hll/Vrlmv/Pcrtty 1.00 2.50
3SW041414 Lndbck/Gbsn/Jhnsn 1.00 2.50
3SW100713 Ovchkn/Ellr/Flry 4.00 10.00
3SW101413 Hrtl/Vrlmv/Ggre/Crsby 4.00 10.00
3SW102113 Gstvsn/Crsby/Mrlau 4.00 10.00
3SW102813 Stmks/Kssl/Kslr 2.00 5.00
3SW110413 Pmnvlle/Flry/Chmra 2.00 5.00
3SW111113 Lhnr/Andrsn/Shrp 1.25 3.00
3SW111813 Scrvns/Sgn/Hrdng 1.25 3.00
3SW112513 Mlkn/Pcrtty/Dbnyk 2.00 5.00
3SW120213 Mlkn/Krnwll/Kth 2.00 5.00
3SW120913 Sknnr/Hll/Lngo 1.50 4.00
3SW121613 Ovchkn/Jnes/Httn 4.00 10.00
3SW122313 Stwrt/Crsby/Dchne 4.00 10.00
3SW123013 Shrp/Mllr/Neal 1.00 2.50

2014-15 Upper Deck MVP Ono on One Autographs

1ON1DM M.Duchene
N.MacKinnon 125.00 200.00
1ON1SP R.Suter/Z.Parise 20.00 40.00
1ON1TK J.Toews/P.Kane 90.00 150.00

2014-15 Upper Deck MVP Pro Sign

PROAL Adam Larsson B 5.00 12.00
PROBB Bill Barber B 6.00 15.00
PROBR Bobby Ryan C 4.00 10.00
PROBY Dustin Byfuglien C 5.00 12.00
PRODB David Backes C 3.00 8.00
PRODM Dylan McIlrath C 4.00 10.00
PRODR Derek Roy C 3.00 8.00
PRODW Doug Wilson B 6.00 15.00
PROJK Jari Kurri B 5.00 12.00
PROKU Chris Kunitz C 5.00 12.00
PROMB Mike Brown C 5.00 12.00
PROMS Mike Smith C 5.00 12.00
PRONK Niklas Kronwall C 4.00 10.00
PROPH Peter Holland C 5.00 12.00
PROPU Teddy Purcell C 3.00 8.00
PRORF Ron Francis A 15.00 40.00
PRORS Ryan Strome C 5.00 12.00
PROSB Sergei Bobrovsky C 5.00 12.00
PROTM Todd Marchant B 6.00 15.00
PROTP Tanner Pearson C 3.00 8.00
PROTT Tomas Tatar C 6.00 15.00
PROTW Tom Wilson C 5.00 12.00
PROWG Wayne Gretzky A 250.00 600.00
PROZR Zach Redmond C 3.00 8.00

2014-15 Upper Deck MVP Rookie MVP Redemptions

RR1 Atlantic Conference 25.00 50.00
RR2 Metropolitan Conference 12.00 30.00
RR3 Central Conference 12.00 30.00
RR4 Pacific Conference 15.00 40.00

2014-15 Upper Deck MVP Rookie of the Month

ROM0114 Ondrej Palat 1.50 4.00
ROM0314 Ondrej Palat 1.50 4.00
ROM1013 Tomas Hertl 2.00 5.00
ROM1113 Marek Mazanec 1.50 4.00
ROM1213A Martin Jones 1.50 4.00
ROM1213B Antti Raanta 2.00 5.00

2014-15 Upper Deck MVP Souvenirs

SJAH Adam Henrique B 2.50 6.00
SJAK Anze Kopitar B 5.00 12.00
SJAN Antti Niemi B 2.50 6.00
SJBE Brian Elliott B 2.50 6.00
SJCP Carey Price B 6.00 15.00
SJCS Cory Schneider B 3.00 8.00
SJDB Dustin Brown B 3.00 8.00
SJDK Duncan Keith B 2.50 6.00
SJDS Drew Stafford B 2.00 5.00
SJEM Evgeni Malkin B 6.00 15.00
SJGL Gabriel Landeskog B 4.00 10.00
SJMG Mike Green B 2.50 6.00
SJMR Matt Read B 2.00 5.00
SJPB Patrice Bergeron B 4.00 10.00
SJPK Phil Kessel B 3.00 8.00
SJRN Rick Nash B 3.00 8.00
SJSC Sean Couturier B 2.50 6.00
SJSE Tyler Seguin B 4.00 10.00
SJTR Tuukka Rask B 4.00 10.00
SJTS Teemu Selanne B 6.00 15.00

2014-15 Upper Deck MVP Souvenirs Combos

SJSAO Alexander Ovechkin 15.00 40.00
SJSBR Brad Richards 4.00 10.00
SJSHZ Henrik Zetterberg 3.00 8.00
SJSJC Jeff Carter 3.00 8.00
SJSJV Jakub Voracek 3.00 8.00
SJSML Mario Lemieux 15.00 40.00
SJSMM Mark Messier 8.00 20.00
SJSPE Phil Esposito 6.00 15.00
SJSPK Phil Kessel 4.00 10.00
SJSPS P.K. Subban 5.00 12.00
SJSRN Rick Nash 4.00 10.00
SJSSC Sidney Crosby 15.00 40.00
SJSSE Tyler Seguin 3.00 8.00
SJSSV Semyon Varlamov 4.00 10.00
SJSTS Teemu Selanne 8.00 20.00

2014-15 Upper Deck MVP Super Script

*1-200 VETS/25: 10X TO 25X BASIC CARDS
*1-200 ROOKIES/25: 5X TO 12X BASIC RC
*201-300 VETS/25: 2.5X TO 6X BASIC SP
*201-300 ROOK/25: 1.2X TO 3X BASIC SP RC
235 Nicklas Backstrom 6.00 15.00
259 Corey Crawford 8.00 20.00
299 Wayne Gretzky 30.00 80.00
300 Wayne Gretzky CL 25.00 60.00

2014-15 Upper Deck MVP Two on Two Jerseys

2JANALAK Gtzlf/Prry/Kptr/Crtr 8.00 20.00
2JBOSMON Mrchnd/Lcc/Sbbn/Pcrtty 12.0030.00
2JBOSNYR Brgrn/Krjci/Nsh/Krder 8.00 20.00
2JCHIDRW Sbrk/Saad/Zttrbrg/Hwrd 8.00 20.00
2JCHISTL Crwfrd/Kth/Elltt/Brglnd 8.00 20.00
2JCOLCHI Dchne/Lndskg/Kth/Crwfrd 8.00 20.00
2JNJDNYI Brdr/Hnrque/Tvrs/Okpso 15.00 40.00
2JOTTTOR Krlssn/Trrs/Kdri/Frnsn 8.00 20.00
2JPHIPIT Hrtnll/Read/Mlkn/Orpk 8.00 20.00
2JTORDET Brnr/Kssl/Hwrd/Zttrbrg 8.00 20.00

2015-16 Upper Deck MVP

COMP.SET w/o SP's (100) 12.00 30.00
1 Sean Monahan .15 .40
2 Milan Lucic .20 .50
3 Zemgus Girgensons .20 .50
4 Carl Soderberg .15 .40
5 Jonas Hiller .20 .50
6 Sergei Bobrovsky .40 1.00
7 Drew Doughty .30 .75
8 Jason Pominville .15 .40
9 P.A. Parenteau .15 .40
10 Shea Weber .20 .50
11 Cory Schneider .25 .60
12 Ryan Strome .25 .60
13 Derick Brassard .15 .40
14 Brendan Gallagher .25 .60
15 Bobby Ryan .20 .50
16 Frederik Andersen .30 .75
17 Justin Faulk .20 .50
18 Curtis Lazar .15 .40
19 Roberto Luongo .40 1.00
20 Brayden Schenn .25 .60
21 Keith Yandle .15 .40
22 Marian Hossa .25 .60
23 Bryan Little .20 .50
24 Chris Kunitz .25 .60
25 Zdeno Chara .25 .60
26 Braden Holtby .30 .75
27 Tomas Hertl .25 .60
28 Joe Thornton .40 1.00
29 Clarke MacArthur .15 .40
30 Cam Ward .25 .60
31 Kyle Turris .20 .50
32 David Desharnais .15 .40
33 Mark Schelfele .40 1.00
34 Nazem Kadri .30 .75
35 Jeff Carter .20 .50
36 Mikkel Boedker .15 .40
37 Jason Spezza .25 .60
38 Brandon Sutter .15 .40
39 Peter Holland .15 .40
40 Jori Lehtera .15 .40
41 Ryan Callahan .15 .40
42 Joffrey Lupul .15 .40
43 Matt Moulson .15 .40
44 Patrick Marleau .25 .60
45 Radim Vrbata .15 .40
46 Bo Horvat .30 .75
47 Ben Scrivens .20 .50
48 Marcus Johansson .20 .50
49 T.J. Oshie .25 .60
50 Mike Green .20 .50
51 Matt Nieto .15 .40
52 Dustin Byfuglien .25 .60
53 T.J. Brodie .15 .40
54 Justin Abdelkader .20 .50
55 Blake Wheeler .25 .60
56 Kris Letang .30 .75
57 Henrik Sedin .30 .75
58 Nail Yakupov .15 .40
59 James Neal .15 .40
60 Mats Zuccarello .25 .60
61 Jonathan Drouin .20 .50
62 Alexander Steen .15 .40
63 Blake Comeau .15 .40
64 Alex Tanguay .15 .40
65 Steve Mason .20 .50
66 Andrew Shaw .15 .40
67 Johnny Boychuk .20 .50
68 Matt Duchene .25 .60
69 Vincent Lecavalier .25 .60
70 Sami Vatanen .15 .40
71 Marian Gaborik .25 .60
72 Jordan Eberle .25 .60
73 Sean Couturier .20 .50
74 Nathan MacKinnon 1.00 2.50
75 Loui Eriksson .15 .40
76 Duncan Keith .20 .50
77 Jarome Iginla .30 .75
78 Brock Nelson .25 .60
79 Gustav Nyquist .15 .40
80 Wayne Simmonds .30 .75
81 Kevin Hayes .20 .50
82 Mikko Koivu .20 .50
83 Jonathan Huberdeau .30 .75
84 Chris Kreider .30 .75
85 Ben Bishop .20 .50
86 Nick Foligno .20 .50
87 Derek Stepan .15 .40
88 Jaroslav Halak .25 .60
89 Patrik Elias .25 .60
90 Seth Jones .25 .60
91 Tomas Tatar .15 .40
92 Roman Josi .25 .60
93 Tomas Plekanec .15 .40
94 Ryan Suter .20 .50
95 Tyler Toffoli .25 .60
96 Andrew Cogliano .15 .40
97 Nick Bjugstad .15 .40
98 Jim Howard .30 .75
99 Jamie Benn .25 .60
100 Jonathan Drouin CL .15 .40
101 Ryan Getzlaf SP .60 1.50
102 Brandon Saad SP .50 1.25
103 Evgeni Malkin SP 1.25 3.00
104 Tuukka Rask SP .75 2.00
105 Tyler Ennis SP .40 1.00
106 Eric Staal SP .75 2.00
107 Jonathan Quick SP .75 2.00
108 Carey Price SP 1.25 3.00
109 Filip Forsberg SP 1.00 2.50
110 Tyler Seguin SP .75 2.00
111 Jaromir Jagr SP 2.00 5.00
112 John Tavares SP 1.00 2.50
113 Corey Perry SP 1.00 2.50
114 Rick Nash SP .60 1.50
115 Henrik Zetterberg SP .75 2.00
116 Erik Karlsson SP .75 2.00
117 Claude Giroux SP .60 1.50
118 Johnny Gaudreau SP 1.00 2.50
119 Marc-Andre Fleury SP 1.25 3.00
120 Vladimir Tarasenko SP .75 2.00
121 Steven Stamkos SP 1.25 3.00
122 Aaron Ekblad SP .75 2.00
123 Antti Niemi SP .50 1.25
124 Brian Elliott SP .50 1.25
125 Phil Kessel SP .60 1.50
126 Ryan Miller SP .60 1.50
127 Ryan Kesler SP .60 1.50
128 Jonathan Toews SP 1.00 2.50
129 Jaden Schwartz SP .75 2.00
130 Alexander Ovechkin SP 2.50 6.00
131 Patric Hornqvist SP .40 1.00
132 John Carlson SP .60 1.50
133 Daniel Sedin SP .75 2.00
134 Andrew Ladd SP .40 1.00
135 Pekka Rinne SP .60 1.50
136 Alex Galchenyuk SP .40 1.00
137 James van Riemsdyk SP .50 1.25
138 Tyler Bozak SP .40 1.00
139 Henrik Lundqvist SP 1.50 4.00
140 Max Pacioretty SP .60 1.50
141 Jiri Hudler SP .50 1.25
142 Michael Hutchinson SP .40 1.00
143 Patrick Kane SP 1.25 3.00
144 Evgeny Kuznetsov SP .75 2.00
145 Joe Pavelski SP .75 2.00
146 Tyler Johnson SP .40 1.00
147 Jonathan Bernier SP .50 1.25
148 Ryan Nugent-Hopkins SP .75 2.00
149 David Backes SP .40 1.00
150 Patrice Bergeron SP .75 2.00
151 Logan Couture SP .75 2.00
152 Niklas Backstrom SP .50 1.25
153 Sidney Crosby SP 2.50 6.00
154 Jakub Voracek SP .50 1.25
155 Andrew Hammond SP .75 2.00
156 Martin St. Louis SP .60 1.50
157 Kyle Okposo SP .40 1.00
158 Adam Henrique SP .50 1.25
159 P.K. Subban SP .75 2.00
160 Zach Parise SP .60 1.50
161 Corey Crawford SP .75 2.00
162 Anze Kopitar SP 1.00 2.50
163 Taylor Hall SP .60 1.50
164 Pavel Datsyuk SP 1.00 2.50
165 Ryan Johansen SP .50 1.25
166 Pelle Lindbergh SP .50 1.25
167 Wayne Gretzky SP 4.00 10.00
168 Arturs Irbe SP .50 1.25
169 Grant Fuhr SP 1.00 2.50
170 Bobby Orr SP 2.50 6.00
171 Mark Messier SP 1.25 3.00
172 Mario Lemieux SP 2.50 6.00
173 Mike Bossy SP .60 1.50
174 Terry Sawchuk SP .60 1.50
175 Brett Hull SP 1.25 3.00
176 Slater Koekkoek SP RC .60 1.50
177 Luke Witkowski SP RC .60 1.50
178 David Wolf SP RC .75 2.00
179 Antoine Bibeau SP RC 1.00 2.50
180 Malcolm Subban SP RC 1.50 4.00
181 Ronalds Kenins SP RC .60 1.50
182 Ryan Hartman SP RC 1.25 3.00
183 Josh Anderson SP RC 2.00 5.00
184 Shane Prince SP RC .60 1.50
185 Brendan Ranford SP RC .75 2.00
186 Viktor Arvidsson SP RC 1.00 2.50
187 Andrew Copp SP RC 1.00 2.50
188 Sam Bennett SP RC 3.00 8.00
189 Kevin Fiala SP RC 1.25 3.00
190 Nick Shore SP RC .60 1.50
191 Jacob de la Rose SP RC 1.00 2.50
192 Nick Cousins SP RC 1.00 2.50
193 Oscar Dansk SP RC 1.25 3.00
194 Petr Straka SP RC .60 1.50
195 Stefan Noesen SP RC .60 1.50
196 Matt Puempel SP RC .75 2.00
197 Kyle Baun SP RC 1.00 2.50
198 Mackenzie Skapski SP RC 1.00 2.50
199 Emile Poirier SP RC .75 2.00
200 Alexander Ovechkin CL SP 1.50 4.00
201 Sidney Crosby NT 5.00 12.00
202 Evgeni Malkin NT 2.50 6.00
203 Tyler Toffoli NT 1.25 3.00
204 Wayne Gretzky NT 8.00 20.00
205 Bobby Orr NT 5.00 12.00
206 Jamie Benn NT 1.25 3.00
207 Tomas Hertl NT 1.25 3.00
208 Ryan Kesler NT 1.25 3.00
209 Torey Krug NT 1.00 2.50
210 Jonathan Toews NT 2.00 5.00
211 Brett Hull NT 2.50 6.00
212 Gustav Nyquist NT .75 2.00
213 Taylor Hall NT 1.25 3.00
214 Patrick Roy NT 3.00 8.00
215 Charlie Coyle NT 1.25 3.00
216 Johnny Gaudreau NT 2.00 5.00
217 Max Pacioretty NT 1.25 3.00
218 Seth Jones NT 1.25 3.00
219 Cory Schneider NT 1.25 3.00
220 Kyle Okposo NT .75 2.00
221 David Backes NT .75 2.00
222 Ben Bishop NT 1.00 2.50
223 Jonathan Bernier NT 1.00 2.50
224 Daniel Sedin NT 1.50 4.00
225 Matt Moulson NT .75 2.00
226 Linden Vey NT .75 2.00
227 Tobias Rieder NT .75 2.00
228 Evgeny Kuznetsov NT 1.50 4.00
229 Eric Staal NT 1.50 4.00
230 Aaron Ekblad NT 1.50 4.00
231 Alexander Ovechkin NT 5.00 12.00
232 Matt Duchene NT 1.25 3.00
233 Grant Fuhr NT 2.00 5.00
234 Mats Zuccarello NT 1.25 3.00
235 Brandon Dubinsky NT .75 2.00
236 Claude Giroux NT 1.25 3.00
237 Blake Wheeler NT 1.25 3.00
238 Markus Granlund NT 1.00 2.50
239 Shea Weber NT 1.00 2.50
240 Vincent Damphousse NT 1.00 2.50
241 Arturs Irbe NT 1.00 2.50
242 Carey Price NT 2.50 6.00
243 Jakub Voracek NT 1.00 2.50
244 Ondrej Palat NT 1.00 2.50
245 Leon Draisaitl NT 4.00 10.00
246 Carl Hagelin NT .75 2.00
247 Kyle Quincey NT .75 2.00
248 Marc-Andre Fleury NT 2.50 6.00
249 Kyle Turris NT 1.00 2.50
250 Mats Sundin NT 1.25 3.00
251 Colin Miller RC 3.00 8.00
252 Jack Eichel RC 15.00 40.00
253 Dylan Larkin RC 12.00 30.00
254 Connor Brickley RC 3.00 8.00
255 Charles Hudon RC 4.00 10.00
256 Matt Oâ€™Connor RC 3.00 8.00
257 Joel Vermin RC 3.00 8.00
258 Garret Sparks RC 4.00 10.00
259 Artemi Panarin RC 15.00 40.00
260 Mikko Rantanen RC 20.00 50.00
261 Mattias Janmark RC 4.00 10.00
262 Gustav Olofsson RC 4.00 10.00
263 Anthony Bitetto RC 2.50 6.00
264 Robby Fabbri RC 5.00 12.00
265 Nicolas Petan RC 4.00 10.00
266 Nikolaj Ehlers RC 8.00 20.00
267 Noah Hanifin RC 6.00 15.00
268 Markus Hannikainen RC 3.00 8.00
269 Sergei Kalinin RC 2.50 6.00
270 Adam Pelech RC 3.00 8.00
271 Oscar Lindberg RC 4.00 10.00
272 Taylor Leier RC 4.00 10.00
273 Daniel Sprong RC 5.00 12.00
274 Chandler Stephenson RC 5.00 12.00
275 Nick Ritchie RC 4.00 10.00
276 Max Domi RC 8.00 20.00
277 Brett Kulak RC 3.00 8.00
278 Connor McDavid RC 80.00 200.00
279 Jordan Weal RC 2.50 6.00
280 Nikolay Goldobin RC 4.00 10.00
281 Jake Virtanen RC 5.00 12.00
282 Jared McCann RC 5.00 12.00
DP1 Draft Pick McDavid EXCH 150.00 250.00
DP1A Draft Pick McDavid AU EXCH 500.00900.00

2015-16 Upper Deck MVP Colors and Contours

*1-100 LT1/L2G/L3T: 2.5X TO 6X BASIC CARDS
*101-200 L1T/L2G/L3T: 1X TO 2.5X BASIC SP
*176-199 L1T/L2G/L3T: .6X TO 1.5X BASIC RC
*1-100 L1G/L1P/L2T: 3X TO 8X BASIC CARDS
*101-200 L1G/L1P/L2T: 1.2X TO 3X BASIC SP
*176-199 L1G/L1P/L2T: .8X TO 2X BASIC RC
*101-200 L3G: 1.5X TO 4X BASIC SP
*101-200 L2P: 2X TO 5X BASIC SP
*101-200 L3P: 3X TO 8X BASIC SP
61 Jonathan Drouin L1P 1.50 4.00
100 Jonathan Drouin CL L1T .75 2.00
144 Evgeny Kuznetsov L2P 4.00 10.00
161 Corey Crawford L3G 3.00 8.00
167 Wayne Gretzky L3P 40.00 80.00
170 Bobby Orr L3P 25.00 50.00
182 Ryan Hartman L3T 2.00 5.00

2015-16 Upper Deck MVP Gold Script

*1-100 VETS/100: 5X TO 12X BASIC CARDS
*101-200 VETS/100: 2X TO 5X BASIC SP
*176-199 ROOKIE/100: 1.2X TO 3X BASIC RC
61 Jonathan Drouin 2.50 6.00
100 Jonathan Drouin CL 2.00 5.00
144 Evgeny Kuznetsov 4.00 10.00

161 Corey Crawford 4.00 10.00
182 Ryan Hartman 4.00 10.00

2015-16 Upper Deck MVP Silver Script

*1-100 VETS: 1.5X TO 4X BASIC CARDS
*101-200 VETS: .8X TO 2X BASIC SP
*176-199 ROOKIES: .6X TO 1.5X BASIC RC
61 Jonathan Drouin .75 2.00
100 Jonathan Drouin CL .60 1.50
144 Evgeny Kuznetsov 1.50 4.00
161 Corey Crawford 1.50 4.00
182 Ryan Hartman 2.00 5.00

2015-16 Upper Deck MVP NHL Territory Autographs

NTAE Aaron Ekblad E 8.00 20.00
NTAI Arturs Irbe C 25.00 60.00
NTAO Alexander Ovechkin A 30.00 80.00
NTBB Ben Bishop B 8.00 20.00
NTBD Brandon Dubinsky C 5.00 12.00
NTBE Jonathan Bernier B 8.00 20.00
NTBO Bobby Orr A 150.00 300.00
NTCC Charlie Coyle E 6.00 15.00
NTCG Claude Giroux B 10.00 25.00
NTCH Carl Hagelin B 6.00 15.00
NTCP Carey Price B 20.00 50.00
NTCS Cory Schneider B 10.00 25.00
NTDB David Backes B 6.00 15.00
NTEK Evgeny Kuznetsov D 8.00 20.00
NTES Eric Staal B 12.00 30.00
NTGN Gustav Nyquist C 5.00 12.00
NTHE Tomas Hertl E 8.00 20.00
NTJB Jamie Benn B 10.00 25.00
NTJG Johnny Gaudreau D 15.00 30.00
NTJT Jonathan Toews A 15.00 40.00
NTKO Kyle Okposo B 6.00 15.00
NTKQ Kyle Quincey E 4.00 10.00
NTKT Kyle Turris C 6.00 15.00
NTLD Leon Draisaitl B 30.00 80.00
NTLV Linden Vey E 4.00 10.00
NTMD Matt Duchene B 10.00 25.00
NTMF Marc-Andre Fleury B 20.00 50.00
NTMG Markus Granlund D 5.00 12.00
NTMM Matt Moulson B 6.00 15.00
NTMP Max Pacioretty A 10.00 25.00
NTMS Mats Sundin B 10.00 25.00
NTMZ Mats Zuccarello A 10.00 25.00
NTOP Ondrej Palat B 8.00 20.00
NTPR Patrick Roy A 25.00 60.00
NTRK Ryan Kesler C 12.00 30.00
NTSJ Seth Jones C 8.00 20.00
NTSW Shea Weber B 8.00 20.00
NTTH Taylor Hall B 10.00 25.00
NTTK Torey Krug D 5.00 12.00
NTTR Tobias Rieder E 4.00 10.00
NTTT Tyler Toffoli C 10.00 25.00
NTVD Vincent Damphousse B 8.00 20.00

2015-16 Upper Deck MVP NHL Territory Jerseys

TMAE Aaron Ekblad B 6.00 15.00
TMAO Alexander Ovechkin B 20.00 50.00
TMBB Ben Bishop B 4.00 10.00
TMBD Brandon Dubinsky B 3.00 8.00
TMBE Jonathan Bernier B 4.00 10.00
TMBH Brett Hull B 10.00 25.00
TMBW Blake Wheeler B 5.00 12.00
TMCC Charlie Coyle B 5.00 12.00
TMCG Claude Giroux B 5.00 12.00
TMCP Carey Price B 10.00 25.00
TMDB David Backes B 3.00 8.00
TMDS Daniel Sedin B 6.00 15.00
TMEK Evgeny Kuznetsov B 6.00 15.00
TMEM Evgeni Malkin B 6.00 15.00
TMES Eric Staal B 6.00 15.00
TMGF Grant Fuhr B 8.00 20.00
TMGN Gustav Nyquist B 3.00 8.00
TMHA Taylor Hall B 5.00 12.00
TMJB Jamie Benn B 5.00 12.00
TMJG Johnny Gaudreau B 8.00 20.00
TMJT Jonathan Toews B 8.00 20.00
TMJV Jakub Voracek B 4.00 10.00
TMKO Kyle Okposo B 3.00 8.00
TMKT Kyle Turris B 4.00 10.00
TMLD Leon Draisaitl B 15.00 40.00
TMMD Matt Duchene B 5.00 12.00
TMMF Marc-Andre Fleury B 10.00 25.00
TMMM Matt Moulson B 3.00 8.00
TMMP Max Pacioretty B 5.00 12.00
TMMZ Mats Zuccarello B 5.00 12.00
TMOP Ondrej Palat B 4.00 10.00
TMPR Patrick Roy A 20.00 50.00
TMRK Ryan Kesler B 5.00 12.00
TMSC Sidney Crosby A 20.00 50.00
TMSJ Seth Jones B 5.00 12.00
TMSW Shea Weber B 4.00 10.00
TMTH Tomas Hertl B 5.00 12.00
TMTK Torey Krug B 4.00 10.00
TMTT Tyler Toffoli B 5.00 12.00
TMVD Vincent Damphousse A 20.00 50.00
TMWG Wayne Gretzky A 40.00 100.00

2015-16 Upper Deck MVP One on One Autographs

1ON1BL J.Boychuk/Leddy D 10.00 25.00
1ON1JH Johansen/Hartnell C 10.00 25.00
1ON1NA Nyquist/Abdelkader C 10.00 25.00
1ON1NH R.N-Hopkins/T.Hall A 15.00 40.00
1ON1NL R.Nash/E.Lindholm D 12.00 30.00
1ON1TK T.Toffoli/A.Kopitar B 20.00 50.00

2015-16 Upper Deck MVP Post Season

PS1 Duncan Keith 5.00 12.00
PS2 Tyler Johnson 4.00 10.00
PS3 Jonathan Toews 10.00 25.00
PS4 Nikita Kucherov 12.00 30.00
PS5 Patrick Kane 12.00 30.00
PS6 Steven Stamkos 12.00 30.00
PS7 Brandon Saad 5.00 12.00
PS8 Ben Bishop 5.00 12.00
PS9 Antoine Vermette 4.00 10.00
PS10 Victor Hedman 8.00 20.00
PS11 Teuvo Teravainen 6.00 15.00
PS12 Anton Stralman 4.00 10.00
PS13 Corey Crawford 8.00 20.00
PS14 Ondrej Palat 5.00 12.00
PS15 Marian Hossa 6.00 15.00
PS16 Alex Killorn 4.00 10.00
PS17 Niklas Hjalmarsson 4.00 10.00
PS18 Andrei Vasilevskiy 10.00 25.00

2015-16 Upper Deck MVP Pro Sign

PSAH Andrew Hammond A 20.00 50.00
PSAI Arturs Irbe C 15.00 40.00
PSAO Adam Oates D 6.00 15.00
PSAV Andrei Vasilevskiy G 10.00 25.00
PSBB Ben Bishop C 5.00 12.00
PSBM Brad Marchand D 12.00 30.00
PSBO Bobby Orr B 100.00 250.00
PSBR Brett Ritchie G 4.00 10.00
PSCS Cory Schneider D 6.00 15.00
PSDC David Clarkson F 4.00 10.00
PSDD Danny DeKeyser C 4.00 10.00
PSDP Derrick Pouliot G 4.00 10.00
PSFA Frederik Andersen E 8.00 20.00
PSJG Johnny Gaudreau E 12.00 30.00
PSJT Jacob Trouba E 5.00 12.00
PSLS Luke Schenn D 6.00 15.00
PSMJ Martin Jones F 5.00 12.00
PSMS Michael Stone F 4.00 10.00
PSNM Nathan MacKinnon A 25.00 60.00
PSNY Nail Yakupov B 4.00 10.00
PSOP Ondrej Palat E 5.00 12.00
PSPS P.K. Subban A 8.00 20.00
PSRJ Ryan Johansen C 5.00 12.00
PSRM Ryan McDonagh C 4.00 10.00
PSRR Rasmus Ristolainen G 4.00 10.00
PSSC Sean Couturier C 5.00 12.00
PSTR Tuukka Rask D 8.00 20.00
PSTR Tobias Rieder F 4.00 10.00
PSVN Valeri Nichushkin B 6.00 15.00
PSWG Wayne Gretzky A 250.00 600.00

2015-16 Upper Deck MVP Rookie MVP Redemptions

RR1 Atlantic Div/Eichel/Larkin 50.00 80.00
RR2 Metropolitan Division 25.00 50.00
RR3 Central Division/Panarin 25.00 50.00
RR4 Pacific Division/McDavid 100.00 175.00

2015-16 Upper Deck MVP Super Script

*1-100 VETS/25: X TO X BASIC CARDS
*101-200 VETS/25: X TO X BASIC SP
*176-199 ROOKIE/25: 3X TO 8X BASIC RC
61 Jonathan Drouin 5.00 12.00
100 Jonathan Drouin CL 3.00 8.00
144 Evgeny Kuznetsov 8.00 20.00
161 Corey Crawford 8.00 20.00
167 Wayne Gretzky 30.00 80.00
182 Ryan Hartman 10.00 25.00

2016-17 Upper Deck MVP

1 Patrick Sharp .20 .50
2 Roman Josi .25 .60
3 Ben Bishop .20 .50
4 Cam Fowler .25 .60
5 Cody Eakin .15 .40
6 Bo Horvat .30 .75
7 Jussi Jokinen .25 .60
8 Ryan Strome .25 .60
9 Mark Streit .20 .50
10 John Klingberg .25 .60
11 Sam Reinhart .50 1.25
12 Jiri Hudler .20 .50
13 Anton Stralman .20 .50
14 David Desharnais .15 .40
15 Patrik Elias .25 .60
16 Martin Jones .20 .50
17 Marian Hossa .25 .60
18 Jason Spezza .25 .60
19 Nazem Kadri .30 .75
20 Cody Ceci .15 .40
21 Tomas Tatar .15 .40
22 Noah Hanifin .25 .60
23 Niklas Hjalmarsson .15 .40
24 Tyler Bozak .15 .40
25 Jaroslav Halak .25 .60
26 Evgeny Kuznetsov .30 .75
27 David Pastrnak .60 1.50
28 Torey Krug .20 .50
29 Jake Muzzin .25 .60
30 Teuvo Teravainen .25 .60
31 Shayne Gostisbehere .25 .60
32 Riley Sheahan .15 .40
33 Mike Green .20 .50
34 Vincent Trocheck .25 .60
35 Jason Pominville .15 .40
36 Gustav Nyquist .15 .40
37 Elias Lindholm .25 .60
38 Mike Smith .25 .60
39 Mark Stone .30 .75
40 Ryan McDonagh .15 .40
41 Bryan Little .20 .50
42 Kyle Palmieri .20 .50
43 Antti Niemi .20 .50
44 Hampus Lindholm .15 .40
45 Phil Kessel .25 .60
46 Sean Monahan .15 .40
47 Antoine Vermette .25 .60
48 Mike Hoffman .15 .40
49 Aaron Ekblad .30 .75
50 Charlie Coyle .25 .60
51 Jakob Silfverberg .15 .40
52 Zdeno Chara .25 .60
53 Darnell Nurse .20 .50
54 Jake Allen .25 .60
55 James Neal .15 .40
56 Max Domi .25 .60
57 Mats Zuccarello .25 .60
58 Alex Pietrangelo .20 .50
59 David Krejci .25 .60
60 Nathan MacKinnon 1.00 2.50
61 Nikita Kucherov .50 1.25
62 Thomas Vanek .20 .50
63 Frans Nielsen .15 .40
64 Brent Seabrook .15 .40
65 Aleksander Barkov .40 1.00
66 Victor Rask .15 .40
67 Michael Cammalleri .20 .50
68 Braden Holtby .30 .75
69 Mikko Rantanen .60 1.50
70 Ryan Miller .25 .60
71 David Perron .20 .50
72 Nail Yakupov .15 .40
73 Jaden Schwartz .30 .75
74 Michael Frolik .20 .50
75 Tyson Barrie .15 .40
76 Dion Phaneuf .20 .50
77 Colton Parayko .20 .50
78 Brandon Saad .20 .50
79 T.J. Brodie .20 .50
80 Justin Schultz .20 .50
81 Nicklas Backstrom .25 .60
82 Shane Doan .20 .50
83 Jack Johnson .15 .40
84 Leon Draisaitl .75 2.00
85 Lee Stempniak .15 .40
86 Travis Zajac .15 .40
87 Olli Maatta .15 .40
88 Anthony Duclair .20 .50
89 Martin Hanzal .20 .50
90 Jonathan Quick .30 .75
91 Marcus Johansson .25 .60
92 Scott Hartnell .15 .40
93 Jori Lehtera .15 .40
94 Colin Wilson .25 .60
95 Tyler Myers .15 .40
96 Andrew Ladd .15 .40
97 Anders Lee .25 .60
98 Mikael Backlund .20 .50
99 Carl Hagelin .15 .40
100 Alexander Ovechkin CL 1.00 2.50
101 Cam Talbot .25 .60
102 Alex Galchenyuk .15 .40
103 Craig Anderson .25 .60
104 Mikko Koivu .20 .50
105 Ryan Callahan .15 .40
106 Johnny Oduya .20 .50
107 Adam Larsson .25 .60
108 Robby Fabbri .15 .40
109 Jeff Skinner .30 .75
110 Cam Ward .25 .60
111 Steve Mason .20 .50
112 Alexander Steen .15 .40
113 J.T. Miller .30 .75
114 Mikael Granlund .20 .50
115 Milan Lucic .20 .50
116 Bobby Ryan .20 .50
117 Evander Kane .25 .60
118 Nino Niederreiter .15 .40
119 Brad Marchand .50 1.25
120 Valeri Nichushkin .25 .60
121 Tanner Pearson .20 .50
122 Johnny Boychuk .20 .50
123 Zemgus Girgensons .20 .50
124 Jake Virtanen .30 .75
125 Dylan Larkin .30 .75
126 Tyler Johnson .15 .40
127 Patrick Marleau .25 .60
128 Reilly Smith .25 .60
129 Rasmus Ristolainen .15 .40
130 Dan Hamhuis .20 .50
131 Brendan Gallagher .25 .60
132 Michael Del Zotto .20 .50
133 Ondrej Palat .20 .50
134 Corey Crawford .30 .75
135 Keith Yandle .15 .40
136 Valtteri Filppula .15 .40
137 Matt Beleskey .20 .50
138 Derick Brassard .15 .40
139 John Gibson .25 .60
140 Joel Ward .20 .50
141 Brayden Schenn .25 .60
142 Nick Bjugstad .15 .40
143 Mike Fisher .15 .40
144 Jeff Carter .20 .50
145 Ondrej Pavelec .25 .60
146 Sean Couturier .20 .50
147 Sami Vatanen .20 .50
148 Jim Howard .30 .75
149 Patric Hornqvist .15 .40
150 Justin Abdelkader .20 .50
151 Mathieu Perreault .15 .40
152 Boone Jenner .25 .60
153 Jonas Hiller .20 .50
154 Radim Vrbata .15 .40
155 Brian Gionta .15 .40
156 Cam Atkinson .25 .60
157 Peter Holland .15 .40
158 Brian Elliott .20 .50
159 Marian Gaborik .25 .60
160 Brent Burns .25 .60
161 Andrei Markov .15 .40
162 T.J. Oshie .25 .60
163 Wayne Simmonds .30 .75
164 Andrew Hammond .20 .50
165 Brandon Dubinsky .15 .40
166 Devan Dubnyk .20 .50
167 Artemi Panarin .50 1.25
168 Tyler Toffoli .25 .60
169 Nick Foligno .20 .50
170 Ryan Kesler .25 .60
171 Lars Eller .15 .40
172 Benoit Pouliot .20 .50
173 Jordan Staal .20 .50
174 Dougie Hamilton .20 .50
175 Brock Nelson .25 .60
176 Mike Ribeiro .15 .40
177 Jonathan Huberdeau .30 .75
178 Chris Kunitz .25 .60
179 Tomas Hertl .25 .60
180 Derek Stepan .15 .40
181 Mark Scheifele .40 1.00
182 Robin Lehner .20 .50
183 Mika Zibanejad .30 .75
184 Seth Jones .25 .60
185 Joe Pavelski .30 .75
186 Brett Connolly .15 .40
187 Justin Williams .20 .50
188 Jonathan Bernier .20 .50
189 Mikkel Boedker .15 .40
190 Alex Tanguay .15 .40
191 Tyler Ennis .15 .40
192 Nikolaj Ehlers .25 .60
193 Marc-Andre Fleury .50 1.25
194 Tomas Plekanec .15 .40
195 Semyon Varlamov .25 .60
196 Chris Kreider .30 .75
197 Jarome Iginla .30 .75
198 Tuukka Rask .30 .75
199 Alexander Edler .15 .40
200 Patrick Kane CL .50 1.25
201 Steven Stamkos 1.25 3.00
202 Erik Karlsson .75 2.00
203 Anze Kopitar 1.00 2.50
204 Carey Price 1.25 3.00
205 Cory Schneider .60 1.50
206 Logan Couture .75 2.00
207 John Tavares 1.00 2.50
208 Jordan Eberle .60 1.50
209 Ryan Suter .50 1.25
210 Rick Nash .60 1.50
211 Henrik Lundqvist 1.50 4.00
212 Dustin Byfuglien .60 1.50
213 Henrik Zetterberg .75 2.00
214 Joe Thornton 1.00 2.50
215 Jack Eichel 1.00 2.50
216 Eric Staal .75 2.00
217 Duncan Keith .50 1.25
218 Jonathan Toews 1.00 2.50
219 Oliver Ekman-Larsson .60 1.50
220 Claude Giroux .60 1.50
221 Henrik Sedin .75 2.00
222 Jamie Benn .60 1.50
223 Ryan Nugent-Hopkins .75 2.00
224 Gabriel Landeskog .75 2.00
225 Matt Duchene .60 1.50
226 Ryan Getzlaf .60 1.50
227 Roberto Luongo 1.00 2.50
228 Ryan Johansen .50 1.25
229 Blake Wheeler .60 1.50
230 Pavel Datsyuk 1.00 2.50
231 Pekka Rinne .60 1.50
232 Adam Henrique .50 1.25
233 Tyler Seguin .75 2.00
234 Max Pacioretty .60 1.50
235 Evgeni Malkin 1.25 3.00
236 Sam Bennett 1.00 2.50
237 Jaromir Jagr 2.00 5.00
238 James van Riemsdyk .50 1.25
239 Alexander Ovechkin 2.50 6.00
240 Jakub Voracek .50 1.25
241 Kyle Turris .50 1.25
242 Connor McDavid 3.00 8.00
243 Kevin Shattenkirk .40 1.00
244 Kyle Okposo .40 1.00
245 Victor Hedman .75 2.00
246 Ryan O'Reilly .60 1.50
247 Patrice Bergeron .75 2.00
248 Kris Letang .75 2.00
249 Sergei Bobrovsky 1.00 2.50
250 Filip Forsberg 1.00 2.50
251 Taylor Hall .60 1.50
252 Vladimir Tarasenko .75 2.00
253 Morgan Rielly .60 1.50
254 Drew Doughty .75 2.00
255 Sidney Crosby 2.50 6.00
256 Daniel Sedin .75 2.00
257 Mark Giordano .60 1.50
258 Shea Weber .50 1.25
259 Johnny Gaudreau 1.00 2.50
260 Zach Parise .60 1.50
261 John Carlson .60 1.50
262 P.K. Subban .75 2.00
263 Corey Perry 1.00 2.50
264 Justin Faulk .50 1.25
265 Patrick Kane 1.25 3.00
266 Guy Lafleur .75 2.00
267 Peter Forsberg 1.25 3.00
268 Bobby Hull 1.25 3.00
269 Al MacInnis .75 2.00
270 Borje Salming .60 1.50
271 Mark Messier 1.25 3.00
272 Gerry Cheevers .60 1.50
273 Glenn Anderson .50 1.25
274 Larry Robinson .60 1.50
275 Wayne Gretzky 4.00 10.00
276 Mike Reilly RC .75 2.00
277 Kevin Gravel RC 1.25 3.00
278 Tom Kuhnhackl RC .75 2.00
279 Ryan Pulock RC 1.00 2.50
280 Mark McNeill RC 1.00 2.50
281 Charlie Lindgren RC 1.50 4.00
282 Josh Morrissey RC 2.50 6.00
283 Hudson Fasching RC 1.00 2.50
284 William Nylander RC 4.00 10.00
285 Oskar Sundqvist RC 1.00 2.50
286 Michael Matheson RC 1.00 2.50
287 Brendan Leipsic RC .75 2.00
288 Steven Santini RC .75 2.00
289 Justin Bailey RC 1.00 2.50
290 Kasperi Kapanen RC 1.50 4.00
291 Chris Bigras RC .75 2.00
292 Esa Lindell RC 1.00 2.50
293 Oliver Kylington RC .75 2.00
294 Connor Brown RC 1.50 4.00
295 Pavel Zacha RC 1.50 4.00
296 Anthony Mantha RC 2.00 5.00
297 Jason Dickinson RC .75 2.00
298 Sonny Milano RC 1.25 3.00
299 Nick Paul RC 1.25 3.00
300 Connor McDavid CL 3.00 8.00
301 John Gibson NHLT 1.25 3.00
302 Oliver Ekman-Larsson NHLT 1.25 3.00
303 Patrice Bergeron NHLT 1.50 4.00
304 Jack Eichel NHLT 2.00 5.00
305 Sean Monahan NHLT .75 2.00
306 Justin Faulk NHLT 1.00 2.50
307 Patrick Kane NHLT 2.50 6.00
308 Gabriel Landeskog NHLT 1.50 4.00
309 Nick Foligno NHLT 1.00 2.50
310 Tyler Seguin NHLT 1.50 4.00
311 Tomas Tatar NHLT .75 2.00
312 Connor McDavid NHLT 6.00 15.00
313 Aleksander Barkov NHLT 2.00 5.00
314 Anze Kopitar NHLT 2.00 5.00
315 Jason Zucker NHLT 1.25 3.00
316 P.K. Subban NHLT 1.50 4.00
317 Ryan Johansen NHLT 1.00 2.50
318 Adam Henrique NHLT 1.00 2.50
319 Ryan Strome NHLT 1.25 3.00
320 Derek Stepan NHLT .75 2.00
321 Mika Zibanejad NHLT 1.50 4.00
322 Shayne Gostisbehere NHLT 1.25 3.00
323 Marc-Andre Fleury NHLT 2.50 6.00
324 Joe Pavelski NHLT 1.50 4.00
325 Vladimir Tarasenko NHLT 1.50 4.00
326 Steven Stamkos NHLT 2.50 6.00
327 James van Riemsdyk NHLT 1.00 2.50
328 Bo Horvat NHLT 1.50 4.00
329 Braden Holtby NHLT 1.50 4.00
330 Jacob Trouba NHLT 1.00 2.50
331 Corey Perry LL 3.00 8.00
332 Tobias Rieder LL 1.25 3.00
333 David Krejci LL 2.00 5.00
334 Ryan O'Reilly LL 2.00 5.00
335 Johnny Gaudreau LL 3.00 8.00
336 Noah Hanifin LL 2.00 5.00
337 Jonathan Toews LL 3.00 8.00
338 Joe Sakic LL 4.00 10.00
339 Jack Johnson LL 1.25 3.00
340 John Klingberg LL 2.00 5.00
341 Dylan Larkin LL 2.50 6.00
342 Leon Draisaitl LL 6.00 15.00
343 Jonathan Huberdeau LL 2.50 6.00
344 Jeff Carter LL 1.50 4.00
345 Mikael Granlund LL 1.50 4.00
346 Carey Price LL 4.00 10.00
347 Shea Weber LL 1.50 4.00
348 Cory Schneider LL 2.00 5.00
349 John Tavares LL 3.00 8.00
350 Ryan McDonagh LL 1.25 3.00
351 Kyle Turris LL 1.50 4.00
352 Jakub Voracek LL 1.50 4.00
353 Evgeni Malkin LL 4.00 10.00
354 Owen Nolan LL 2.00 5.00
355 Jake Allen LL 2.00 5.00
356 Victor Hedman LL 2.50 6.00
357 Morgan Rielly LL 2.00 5.00
358 Daniel Sedin LL 2.50 6.00
359 John Carlson LL 2.00 5.00
360 Mark Scheifele LL 3.00 8.00
361 Brandon Carlo RC 3.00 8.00
362 Nick Baptiste RC 2.00 5.00
363 Tyler Bertuzzi RC 3.00 8.00
364 Mitch Marner RC 12.00 30.00
365 Mikhail Sergachev RC 3.00 8.00
366 Thomas Chabot RC 4.00 10.00
366 Brayden Point RC 5.00 12.00
368 Auston Matthews RC 30.00 80.00
369 Sebastian Aho RC 6.00 15.00
370 Zach Werenski RC 6.00 15.00
371 Nick Lappin RC 2.00 5.00
372 Anthony Beauvillier RC 2.00 5.00
373 Jimmy Vesey RC 3.00 8.00
374 Travis Konecny RC 4.00 10.00
375 Jake Guentzel RC 20.00 50.00
376 Jakub Vrana RC 2.50 6.00
377 Nick Schmaltz RC 2.50 6.00
378 A.J. Greer RC 2.00 5.00
379 Julius Honka RC 2.00 5.00
380 Joel Eriksson Ek RC 3.00 8.00
381 Pontus Aberg RC 2.50 6.00
382 Tyler Motte RC 2.00 5.00
383 Patrik Laine RC 15.00 40.00
384 Kyle Connor RC 6.00 15.00
385 Jacob Larsson RC 3.00 8.00
386 Dylan Strome RC 5.00 12.00
387 Matthew Tkachuk RC 8.00 20.00
388 Jesse Puljujarvi RC 4.00 10.00
389 Nic Dowd RC 1.50 4.00
390 Timo Meier RC 4.00 10.00
391 Thatcher Demko RC 5.00 12.00
392 Christian Dvorak RC 2.50 6.00

2016-17 Upper Deck MVP '16 NHL Draft Pick #1

DP1 Draft Pick Redemption SP
Exchanged for Auston Matthews 80.00 150.00

2016-17 Upper Deck MVP All Star Variations

AS1 Drew Doughty 8.00 20.00
AS2 John Tavares 10.00 25.00
AS3 Patrick Kane 12.00 30.00
AS4 John Gibson 6.00 15.00
AS5 Steven Stamkos 12.00 30.00
AS6 Dylan Larkin 8.00 20.00
AS7 Erik Karlsson 8.00 20.00
AS8 Braden Holtby 8.00 20.00
AS9 Vladimir Tarasenko 8.00 20.00
AS10 Shea Weber 5.00 12.00

2016-17 Upper Deck MVP Leading Lights Autographs Gold

351 Kyle Turris D 8.00 20.00
357 Morgan Rielly E 8.00 20.00
360 Mark Scheifele D 8.00 20.00

2016-17 Upper Deck MVP Leading Lights Jerseys Gold

334 Ryan O'Reilly B 8.00 20.00
336 Noah Hanifin C 8.00 20.00
337 Jonathan Toews A 12.00 30.00
339 Jack Johnson C 5.00 12.00
342 Leon Draisaitl B 25.00 60.00
344 Jeff Carter B 6.00 15.00
346 Carey Price A 15.00 40.00
349 John Tavares A 12.00 30.00
352 Jakub Voracek C 6.00 15.00
353 Evgeni Malkin A 15.00 40.00
354 Owen Nolan A 8.00 20.00
355 Jake Allen C 8.00 20.00
356 Victor Hedman B 10.00 25.00
358 Daniel Sedin B 10.00 25.00
359 John Carlson C 8.00 20.00

2016-17 Upper Deck MVP NHL Territory Autographs

NTCM Connor McDavid D 100.00 250.00
NTJF Justin Faulk E 5.00 12.00
NTJZ Jason Zucker E 5.00 12.00
NTNF Nick Foligno D 8.00 20.00
NTRS Ryan Strome E 5.00 12.00
NTSM Sean Monahan B 5.00 12.00
NTTA Tomas Tatar E 6.00 15.00

2016-17 Upper Deck MVP NHL Territory Materials

TMAB Aleksander Barkov B 8.00 20.00
TMAH Adam Henrique B 4.00 10.00
TMAK Anze Kopitar B 8.00 20.00
TMBH Braden Holtby B 6.00 15.00
TMBO Bo Horvat C 5.00 12.00
TMCM Connor McDavid A 40.00 100.00
TMDS Derek Stepan C 2.50 6.00
TMGL Gabriel Landeskog C 5.00 12.00
TMJE Jack Eichel A 8.00 20.00
TMJF Justin Faulk C 3.00 8.00
TMJG John Gibson C 4.00 10.00
TMJP Joe Pavelski B 6.00 15.00
TMJT Jacob Trouba C 3.00 8.00
TMJV James van Riemsdyk C 3.00 8.00
TMJZ Jason Zucker C 4.00 10.00
TMMF Marc-Andre Fleury B 10.00 25.00
TMMZ Mika Zibanejad C 5.00 12.00
TMNF Nick Foligno C 3.00 8.00
TMOE Oliver Ekman-Larsson B 5.00 12.00
TMPB Patrice Bergeron B 6.00 15.00
TMPK Patrick Kane A 10.00 25.00
TMPS P.K. Subban A 5.00 12.00
TMRS Ryan Strome C 4.00 10.00
TMSM Sean Monahan B 3.00 8.00
TMSS Steven Stamkos A 6.00 15.00
TMTA Tomas Tatar C 2.50 6.00
TMTS Tyler Seguin B 6.00 15.00
TMVT Vladimir Tarasenko B 6.00 15.00

2016-17 Upper Deck MVP Pro Sign

PROAA Andy Andreoff E 5.00 12.00
PROAB Aleksander Barkov C 8.00 20.00
PROAS Andrew Shaw D 12.00 30.00
PROBD Brandon Dubinsky B 8.00 20.00
PROBH Bo Horvat D 12.00 30.00
PROCC Charlie Coyle C 15.00 30.00
PROCF Cody Franson C 5.00 12.00
PROCT Chris Tierney E 5.00 12.00
PROJC John Carlson D 10.00 25.00
PROKT Kyle Turris D 10.00 25.00
PROMB Matt Beleskey D 10.00 25.00
PROOK Oscar Klefbom E 6.00 15.00
PRORS Reilly Smith D 5.00 12.00
PROTH Thomas Hickey E 6.00 15.00
PROTV Trevor van Riemsdyk C 8.00 20.00
PROVR Victor Rask E 5.00 12.00

2016-17 Upper Deck MVP Rookie Redemption Cards

RR1 Atlantic Division 60.00 150.00
RR2 Central Division 40.00 100.00
RR3 Metropolitan Division 25.00 60.00
RR4 Pacific Division 30.00 80.00

2017-18 Upper Deck MVP

1 Evgeni Malkin .50 1.25
2 Patrice Bergeron .30 .75
3 Max Domi .25 .60
4 Corey Perry .40 1.00
5 Sean Monahan .15 .40
6 Alexander Wennberg .15 .40
7 Milan Lucic .25 .60
8 Mikko Koivu .20 .50
9 Filip Forsberg .40 1.00
10 Jonathan Toews .40 1.00
11 Mike Hoffman .15 .40
12 Jack Eichel .40 1.00
13 Bo Horvat .30 .75
14 Mark Scheifele .40 1.00
15 Joe Thornton .40 1.00
16 Jaden Schwartz .30 .75
17 Victor Hedman .30 .75
18 Rick Nash .25 .60
19 Nazem Kadri .30 .75
20 Evgeny Kuznetsov .30 .75
21 Anders Lee .25 .60
22 Cory Schneider .25 .60
23 Alex Galchenyuk .15 .40
24 Aleksander Barkov .40 1.00
25 Dylan Larkin .30 .75
26 Jeff Carter .20 .50
27 Tyler Seguin .30 .75
28 Matt Duchene .25 .60
29 Jordan Staal .20 .50
30 Wayne Simmonds .30 .75
31 Ryan Getzlaf .25 .60
32 Leon Draisaitl .75 2.00
33 Martin Hanzal .20 .50
34 Martin Jones .20 .50
35 Phil Kessel .25 .60
36 Ryan Spooner .20 .50
37 Nick Foligno .20 .50
38 Kevin Shattenkirk .15 .40
39 Calle Jarnkrok .20 .50
40 Corey Crawford .30 .75
41 Nikolaj Ehlers .25 .60
42 Patrik Berglund .15 .40
43 Travis Konecny .25 .60
44 Loui Eriksson .15 .40
45 Max Pacioretty .25 .60
46 Matthew Tkachuk .50 1.25
47 Patrick Marleau .25 .60
48 Kris Versteeg .15 .40
49 Mika Zibanejad .30 .75
50 William Nylander .50 1.25
51 Damon Severson .15 .40
52 Bobby Ryan .20 .50
53 Justin Abdelkader .20 .50
54 Rickard Rakell .20 .50
55 Mitch Marner .40 1.00
56 Drew Doughty .30 .75
57 Jordan Eberle .25 .60
58 Kris Letang .30 .75
59 David Backes .15 .40
60 Nicklas Backstrom .25 .60
61 Alex Killorn .15 .40
62 Sam Gagner .15 .40
63 Richard Panik .15 .40
64 Mikko Rantanen .60 1.50
65 Shea Weber .20 .50
66 Brandon Sutter .15 .40
67 Teuvo Teravainen .25 .60
68 Matt Moulson .15 .40
69 Vincent Trocheck .25 .60
70 Mikkel Boedker .15 .40
71 Alexander Steen .15 .40
72 James van Riemsdyk .20 .50
73 Jason Spezza .25 .60
74 Ryan Nugent-Hopkins .30 .75
75 Tuukka Rask .30 .75
76 Mark Giordano .25 .60
77 Anthony Mantha .20 .50
78 J.T. Miller .30 .75
79 Zack Smith .15 .40
80 Zach Werenski .40 1.00
81 Devan Dubnyk .20 .50
82 Tanner Pearson .20 .50
83 Adam Henrique .20 .50
84 Jakub Voracek .20 .50
85 James Neal .15 .40
86 Blake Wheeler .25 .60
87 Andrei Vasilevskiy .40 1.00
88 T.J. Oshie .25 .60
89 Ryan Strome .25 .60
90 Markus Granlund .20 .50
91 Andrew Cogliano .15 .40
92 Marc-Edouard Vlasic .15 .40
93 Sebastian Aho .40 1.00
94 Rasmus Ristolainen .15 .40
95 Matt Murray .40 1.00
96 Mike Smith .25 .60
97 Alexander Radulov .25 .60
98 Jonathan Marchessault .30 .75
99 Duncan Keith .20 .50
100 Connor McDavid 1.25 3.00
101 Tyson Barrie .15 .40
102 Patrick Eaves .20 .50
103 Pekka Rinne .25 .60
104 Michael Cammalleri .20 .50
105 Tyler Johnson .15 .40
106 Chris Kreider .30 .75
107 Paul Stastny .20 .50
108 Tomas Tatar .15 .40
109 Alec Martinez .15 .40
110 Dustin Byfuglien .25 .60
111 Andrew Ladd .15 .40
112 Cam Talbot .25 .60
113 Ryan O'Reilly .25 .60
114 Victor Rask .15 .40
115 Brayden Schenn .25 .60
116 Derick Brassard .15 .40
117 Artem Anisimov .15 .40
118 Thomas Vanek .20 .50
119 Andrew Shaw .15 .40
120 Morgan Rielly .25 .60
121 Patric Hornqvist .15 .40
122 Nino Niederreiter .15 .40
123 Radim Vrbata .15 .40
124 Gabriel Landeskog .30 .75
125 Brock Nelson .25 .60
126 Marcus Johansson .20 .50
127 Alex Pietrangelo .20 .50
128 Ryan Hartman .15 .40
129 Roberto Luongo .40 1.00
130 Seth Jones .25 .60
131 Logan Couture .30 .75
132 Sam Bennett .40 1.00
133 John Klingberg .25 .60
134 Tyler Toffoli .25 .60
135 Kevin Hayes .20 .50
136 Jonathan Drouin .20 .50
137 Roman Josi .25 .60
138 Mike Green .20 .50
139 Derek Stepan .15 .40
140 Phillip Danault .25 .60
141 Tobias Rieder .15 .40
142 Torey Krug .20 .50
143 Carl Soderberg .15 .40
144 Travis Zajac .15 .40
145 Kyle Turris .25 .60
146 Bryan Little .20 .50
147 John Gibson .25 .60
148 Charlie Coyle .25 .60
149 Sam Reinhart .50 1.25
150 Adam Larsson .25 .60
151 Brett Ritchie .15 .40
152 Viktor Arvidsson .15 .40
153 Sergei Bobrovsky .40 1.00
154 Shayne Gostisbehere .25 .60
155 Tyler Bozak .15 .40
156 Daniel Sedin .30 .75
157 Ben Bishop .20 .50
158 Aaron Ekblad .30 .75
159 Tomas Plekanec .15 .40
160 Nick Leddy .15 .40
161 Bryan Rust .25 .60
162 Conor Sheary .25 .60
163 Dougie Hamilton .20 .50
164 Marian Hossa .25 .60
165 Justin Faulk .20 .50
166 Gustav Nyquist .15 .40
167 Cam Fowler .25 .60
168 Shane Doan .20 .50
169 Braden Holtby .30 .75
170 David Krejci .25 .60
171 Kyle Palmieri .20 .50
172 Adam Lowry .20 .50
173 Mark Stone .30 .75
174 Brent Burns .25 .60
175 Sean Couturier .20 .50
176 Jarome Iginla .30 .75
177 Evander Kane .25 .60
178 Ryan Johansen .20 .50
179 Cam Ward .25 .60
180 Reilly Smith .25 .60
181 Calvin Pickard .25 .60
182 Josh Bailey .20 .50
183 Kari Lehtonen .20 .50
184 Artemi Panarin .50 1.25
185 Nikita Kucherov .50 1.25
186 Frederik Andersen .30 .75
187 Jake Guentzel .40 1.00
188 Mats Zuccarello .25 .60
189 Frans Nielsen .15 .40
190 David Pastrnak .60 1.50
191 John Carlson .25 .60
192 Mikael Backlund .20 .50
193 Jakob Silfverberg .15 .40
194 Brandon Saad .20 .50
195 Jimmy Vesey .20 .50
196 Brendan Gallagher .25 .60
197 Christian Dvorak .20 .50
198 Mikael Granlund .20 .50
199 Jake Allen .25 .60
200 Sidney Crosby 1.00 2.50
201 Connor McDavid 3.00 8.00
202 Taylor Hall .60 1.50
203 Claude Giroux .60 1.50
204 Joe Pavelski .75 2.00
205 Carey Price 1.25 3.00
206 Jeff Skinner .75 2.00
207 Alexander Ovechkin 2.50 6.00
208 Anze Kopitar 1.00 2.50
209 Jaromir Jagr 2.00 5.00

210 Auston Matthews 2.50 6.00
211 Jamie Benn .60 1.50
212 Johnny Gaudreau 1.00 2.50
213 Nathan MacKinnon 2.50 6.00
214 Oliver Ekman-Larsson .60 1.50
215 Patrick Kane 1.25 3.00
216 Cam Atkinson .60 1.50
217 Henrik Zetterberg .75 2.00
218 Brad Marchand 1.25 3.00
219 Henrik Lundqvist 1.50 4.00
220 Sidney Crosby 2.50 6.00
221 Eric Staal .75 2.00
222 Vladimir Tarasenko .75 2.00
223 Patrik Laine .75 2.00
224 John Tavares 1.00 2.50
225 P.K. Subban .75 2.00
226 Ryan Kesler .60 1.50
227 Henrik Sedin .75 2.00
228 Erik Karlsson .75 2.00
229 Steven Stamkos 1.25 3.00
230 Alexander Ovechkin 2.50 6.00
231 Ivan Barbashev RC 2.50 6.00
232 Charlie McAvoy RC 5.00 12.00
233 Nikita Scherbak RC 2.50 6.00
234 Evgeny Svechnikov RC 4.00 10.00
235 Riley Barber RC 2.00 5.00
236 Nicolas Kerdiles RC 2.00 5.00
237 Vladislav Kamenev RC 2.00 5.00
238 Denis Gurianov RC 5.00 12.00
239 Christian Fischer RC 2.50 6.00
240 Adrian Kempe RC 4.00 10.00
241 Brock Boeser RC 5.00 12.00
242 Jack Roslovic RC 2.50 6.00
243 J.T. Compher RC 2.00 5.00
244 Jordan Schmaltz RC 2.50 6.00
245 Josh Ho-Sang RC 2.50 6.00
246 Colin White RC 2.50 6.00
247 Alex Tuch RC 5.00 12.00
248 Clayton Keller RC 5.00 12.00
249 Alexander Nylander RC 3.00 8.00
250 Tyson Jost RC 4.00 10.00
251 Anders Bjork RC 2.50 6.00
252 Viktor Antipin RC 2.00 5.00
253 Robbie Russo RC 2.00 5.00
254 Owen Tippett RC 4.00 10.00
255 Victor Mete RC 2.00 5.00
256 Logan Brown RC 2.00 5.00
257 Jake Dotchin RC 1.50 4.00
258 Calle Rosen RC 2.00 5.00
259 Haydn Fleury RC 2.00 5.00
260 Nolan Patrick RC 4.00 10.00
261 Connor Jones RC 1.50 4.00
262 Pierre-Luc Dubois RC 3.00 8.00
263 Filip Chytil RC 2.00 5.00
264 Casey DeSmith RC 3.00 8.00
265 Nico Hischier RC 6.00 15.00
266 Christian Djoos RC 2.00 5.00
267 Alex DeBrincat RC 5.00 12.00
268 Remi Elie RC 1.50 4.00
269 Luke Kunin RC 2.00 5.00
270 Alex Kerfoot RC 4.00 10.00
271 Alexandre Carrier RC 1.50 4.00
272 Tage Thompson RC 5.00 12.00
273 Brendan Lemieux RC 2.00 5.00
274 Samuel Girard RC 2.00 5.00
275 Kailer Yamamoto RC 5.00 12.00
276 Mario Kempe RC 1.25 3.00
277 Jon Gillies RC 2.00 5.00
278 Giovanni Fiore RC 2.00 5.00
279 Michael Amadio RC 2.00 5.00
280 Griffen Molino RC 1.50 4.00
281 Joakim Ryan RC 2.00 5.00
282 Alex Tuch RC 5.00 12.00

2017-18 Upper Deck MVP Super Script

*SUPER/25: 5X TO 12X BASIC CARDS
*SUPER.SP/25: 2X TO 5X BASIC CARDS
*SUPER.RC/25: 2X TO 5X BASIC CARDS
40 Corey Crawford 2.50 6.00
60 Nicklas Backstrom 2.00 5.00
141 Tobias Rieder 10.00 25.00
200 Sidney Crosby 12.00 30.00
201 Connor McDavid 25.00 60.00
210 Auston Matthews 80.00 200.00
215 Patrick Kane 15.00 40.00
223 Patrik Laine 12.00 30.00
246 Colin White 25.00 60.00
249 Alexander Nylander 15.00 40.00

2017-18 Upper Deck MVP Colors and Contours

*G1,G2,B1,B2: 2.5X TO 6X BASIC CARDS
*G3,B3: 3X TO 8X BASIC CARDS
*VETS P1,P2: 2X TO 5X BASIC CARDS
*RC P1,P2: .6X TO 1.5X BASIC CARDS
*P3: 3X TO 8X BASIC CARDS

2017-18 Upper Deck MVP NHL Player Credentials Level 1 Access

NHLAG Alex Galchenyuk .75 2.00
NHLAL Anders Lee 1.25 3.00
NHLAS Andrew Shaw .75 2.00
NHLAW Alexander Wennberg .75 2.00
NHLBB Brent Burns 1.25 3.00
NHLBH Braden Holtby 1.50 4.00
NHLCC Corey Crawford 1.50 4.00
NHLDD Jonathan Quick 1.50 4.00
NHLDP David Pastrnak 3.00 8.00
NHLHS Henrik Sedin 1.50 4.00
NHLHZ Henrik Zetterberg 1.50 4.00
NHLJE Jack Eichel 2.00 5.00
NHLJP Jason Pominville .75 2.00
NHLJS Jaden Schwartz 1.50 4.00
NHLMD Matt Duchene 1.25 3.00
NHLMH Mike Hoffman .75 2.00
NHLMM Matt Murray 2.00 5.00
NHLMS Mark Scheifele 2.00 5.00
NHLNB Nicklas Backstrom 1.25 3.00
NHLNK Nikita Kucherov 2.50 6.00
NHLOE Oliver Ekman-Larsson 1.25 3.00
NHLPS P.K. Subban 1.50 4.00
NHLRK Ryan Kesler 1.25 3.00
NHLSE Tyler Seguin 1.50 4.00
NHLSM Sean Monahan .75 2.00
NHLST Derek Stepan .75 2.00
NHLTH Taylor Hall 1.25 3.00
NHLTR Tuukka Rask 1.50 4.00
NHLTT Teuvo Teravainen 1.25 3.00
NHLWS Wayne Simmonds 1.50 4.00

2017-18 Upper Deck MVP NHL Player Credentials Level 1 VIP Access

NHLAM Auston Matthews 6.00 15.00
NHLCM Connor McDavid 8.00 20.00
NHLDS Darryl Sittler 2.00 5.00
NHLJJ Jaromir Jagr 5.00 12.00
NHLMB Martin Brodeur 4.00 10.00
NHLPK Patrick Kane 3.00 8.00
NHLSC Sidney Crosby 6.00 15.00
NHLSY Steve Yzerman 4.00 10.00
NHLTS Teemu Selanne 3.00 8.00
NHLWG Wayne Gretzky 10.00 25.00

2017-18 Upper Deck MVP NHL Player Credentials Level 4 Access

NHLAL Anders Lee AU C 8.00 20.00
NHLAW Alexander Wennberg AU C 8.00 20.00
NHLMM Matt Murray AU B 40.00 100.00
NHLMS Mark Scheifele AU B 25.00 60.00
NHLTT Teuvo Teravainen AU C 8.00 20.00

2018-19 Upper Deck MVP

1 John Tavares .40 1.00
2 Ryan Getzlaf .25 .60
3 Brad Marchand .50 1.25
4 Sean Monahan .15 .40
5 Jonathan Quick .30 .75
6 Sean Couturier .20 .50
7 Duncan Keith .20 .50
8 Mitch Marner .40 1.00
9 Evgeny Kuznetsov .30 .75
10 Oliver Ekman-Larsson .25 .60
11 James Neal .15 .40
12 Ryan O'Reilly .25 .60
13 Teuvo Teravainen .25 .60
14 Seth Jones .25 .60
15 Jamie Benn .25 .60
16 Dylan Larkin .30 .75
17 Aleksander Barkov .40 1.00
18 Mikael Granlund .20 .50
19 Max Pacioretty .25 .60
20 P.K. Subban .30 .75
21 Gabriel Landeskog .30 .75
22 Nico Hischier .40 1.00
23 Mark Stone .30 .75
24 Joe Pavelski .30 .75
25 Evgeni Malkin .50 1.25
26 Leon Draisaitl .75 2.00
27 Brayden Schenn .25 .60
28 Mats Zuccarello .25 .60
29 Brayden Point .30 .75
30 Daniel Sedin .30 .75
31 Patrik Laine .30 .75
32 Evander Kane .25 .60
33 John Klingberg .25 .60
34 Mike Smith .20 .50
35 Artemi Panarin .50 1.25
36 John Carlson .25 .60
37 Clayton Keller .30 .75
38 Nick Schmaltz .25 .60
39 Jonathan Huberdeau .30 .75
40 Henrik Zetterberg .30 .75
41 Shayne Gostisbehere .25 .60
42 Jonathan Marchessault .30 .75
43 David Pastrnak .60 1.50
44 Sebastian Aho .40 1.00
45 William Nylander .50 1.25
46 Jason Zucker .25 .60
47 Dustin Brown .25 .60
48 Filip Forsberg .40 1.00
49 Mikko Rantanen .60 1.50
50 Taylor Hall .25 .60
51 Mike Hoffman .15 .40
52 Milan Lucic .20 .50
53 Logan Couture .30 .75
54 Jakob Silfverberg .15 .40
55 Alex Galchenyuk .15 .40
56 Josh Bailey .20 .50
57 Kris Letang .30 .75
58 Kyle Okposo .15 .40
59 Jaden Schwartz .30 .75
60 Kevin Shattenkirk .15 .40
61 Dougie Hamilton .20 .50
62 Max Domi .25 .60
63 T.J. Oshie .25 .60
64 Oliver Bjorkstrand .20 .50
65 Blake Wheeler .25 .60
66 Thomas Vanek .20 .50
67 Brandon Saad .20 .50
68 Alexander Radulov .25 .60
69 Vincent Trocheck .25 .60
70 Henrik Sedin .30 .75
71 Nazem Kadri .30 .75
72 Mika Zibanejad .30 .75
73 Alex Tuch .25 .60
74 Rickard Rakell .25 .60
75 Mark Scheifele .40 1.00
76 Victor Hedman .30 .75
77 Viktor Arvidsson .15 .40
78 Justin Williams .20 .50
79 Rick Nash .25 .60
80 Eric Staal .25 .60
81 Tyson Barrie .15 .40
82 Nick Foligno .20 .50
83 Dion Phaneuf .20 .50
84 David Perron .20 .50
85 Ryan Nugent-Hopkins .50 1.25
86 Derick Brassard .15 .40
87 Justin Abdelkader .20 .50
88 Jakub Voracek .20 .50
89 Cory Schneider .25 .60
90 Ben Bishop .20 .50
91 Anders Lee .20 .50
92 Micheal Ferland .15 .40
93 Sam Reinhart .50 1.25
94 Tomas Hertl .50 1.25
95 Roberto Luongo .40 1.00
96 Alex DeBrincat .30 .75
97 Jake Gardiner .15 .40
98 Tom Wilson .20 .50
99 Jonathan Drouin .20 .50
100 Auston Matthews CL 1.00 2.50
101 Steven Stamkos .50 1.25
102 Alex Pietrangelo .20 .50
103 Ryan Suter .20 .50
104 Reilly Smith .25 .60
105 Joe Thornton .40 1.00
106 Kevin Hayes .20 .50
107 Jordan Staal .20 .50
108 Alexander Wennberg .15 .40
109 Drew Doughty .30 .75
110 Patrick Marleau .25 .60
111 Phil Kessel .50 1.25
112 Ryan McDonagh .15 .40
113 Wayne Simmonds .25 .60
114 Ryan Johansen .20 .50
115 Matt Duchene .25 .60
116 Tomas Tatar .15 .40
117 Ondrej Kase .15 .40
118 Alex Kerfoot .20 .50
119 Tyler Johnson .15 .40
120 Kyle Palmieri .25 .60
121 Rasmus Ristolainen .15 .40
122 Bo Horvat .30 .75
123 T.J. Brodie .20 .50
124 Oscar Klefbom .20 .50
125 Aaron Ekblad .30 .75
126 Andrew Shaw .15 .40
127 Nikolaj Ehlers .25 .60
128 Jake Muzzin .25 .60
129 Roman Josi .25 .60
130 Patrick Kane .50 1.25
131 Tuukka Rask .30 .75
132 Cody Eakin .15 .40
133 Ryan Spooner .20 .50
134 Christian Dvorak .20 .50
135 Jake Guentzel .40 1.00
136 Cam Atkinson .25 .60
137 Andrei Vasilevskiy .40 1.00
138 Jordan Eberle .25 .60
139 Claude Giroux .25 .60
140 Chris Kreider .30 .75
141 Justin Faulk AS .20 .50
142 Alexander Steen .15 .40
143 Zach Hyman .40 1.00
144 Anze Kopitar .40 1.00
145 Braden Holtby .30 .75
146 Anthony Mantha .20 .50
147 Jason Spezza .30 .75
148 Corey Perry .40 1.00
149 Carl Soderberg .15 .40
150 Matt Murray .25 .60
151 David Krejci .25 .60
152 Dustin Byfuglien .25 .60
153 William Karlsson .30 .75
154 Ryan Strome .20 .50
155 Conor Sheary .25 .60
156 Martin Jones .20 .50
157 Andrew Ladd .15 .40
158 Colton Parayko .20 .50
159 Anthony Duclair .20 .50
160 Tomas Plekanec .15 .40
161 Pekka Rinne .25 .60
162 Connor Hellebuyck .50 1.25
163 Alex Killorn .15 .40
164 Olli Maatta .15 .40
165 J.T. Miller .30 .75
166 Tyler Toffoli .25 .60
167 Jake Allen .25 .60
168 Connor Brown .20 .50
169 Ondrej Palat .20 .50
170 Loui Eriksson .15 .40
171 Shea Weber .25 .60
172 Nick Leddy .15 .40
173 Gustav Nyquist .15 .40
174 Jake DeBrusk .25 .60
175 Jesper Bratt .25 .60
176 Carl Hagelin .15 .40
177 Mikkel Boedker .15 .40
178 Kyle Turris .20 .50
179 Bobby Ryan .20 .50
180 Cam Talbot .25 .60
181 Keith Yandle .25 .60
182 Jason Pominville .15 .40
183 Danton Heinen .20 .50
184 Pierre-Luc Dubois .25 .60
185 Jim Howard .30 .75
186 Nicklas Backstrom .25 .60
187 Brendan Gallagher .25 .60
188 Erik Johnson .15 .40
189 Adam Henrique .20 .50
190 Victor Rask .15 .40
191 Radek Faksa .20 .50
192 Derek Stepan .20 .50
193 Matthew Tkachuk .50 1.25
194 Jeff Skinner .30 .75
195 Ryan Hartman .20 .50
196 Nolan Patrick .25 .60
197 Frederik Andersen .30 .75
198 Erik Haula .15 .40
199 Devan Dubnyk .20 .50
200 Connor McDavid CL 1.25 3.00
201 Sidney Crosby 2.00 5.00
202 Marc-Andre Fleury 1.00 2.50
203 Tyler Seguin .60 1.50
204 Vladimir Tarasenko .60 1.50
205 Auston Matthews 2.00 5.00
206 Carey Price 1.00 2.50
207 Mathew Barzal .60 1.50
208 Johnny Gaudreau .75 2.00
209 Patrice Bergeron .60 1.50
210 Alexander Ovechkin 2.00 5.00
211 Brock Boeser .60 1.50
212 Erik Karlsson .60 1.50
213 Nathan MacKinnon 2.00 5.00
214 Jack Eichel .75 2.00
215 Jonathan Toews .75 2.00
216 Nikita Kucherov 1.00 2.50
217 Brent Burns .50 1.25
218 Henrik Lundqvist 1.25 3.00
219 Connor McDavid 2.50 6.00
220 Alexander Ovechkin CL 2.00 5.00
221 Michael Dal Colle RC 1.50 4.00
222 Dillon Heatherington RC 1.50 4.00
223 Dominic Turgeon RC 1.50 4.00
224 Daniel Brickley RC 1.50 4.00
225 Morgan Klimchuk RC 1.50 4.00
226 Justin Holl RC 1.50 4.00
227 Neal Pionk RC 1.50 4.00
228 Dylan Sikura RC 2.00 5.00
229 Ethan Bear RC 2.50 6.00
230 Oskar Lindblom RC 2.50 6.00
231 Maxim Mamin RC 1.50 4.00
232 Ryan Donato RC 2.50 6.00
233 Casey Mittelstadt RC 3.00 8.00
234 Adam Gaudette RC 2.50 6.00
235 Travis Dermott RC 2.50 6.00
236 Zach Aston-Reese RC 2.50 6.00
237 Jordan Greenway RC 1.50 4.00
238 Troy Terry RC 2.50 6.00
239 Anthony Cirelli RC 2.50 6.00
240 Joe Hicketts RC 1.50 4.00
241 Eeli Tolvanen RC 3.00 8.00
242 Matthew Highmore RC 1.50 4.00
243 Henrik Borgstrom RC 2.50 6.00
244 Samuel Montembeault RC 3.00 8.00
245 Tomas Hyka RC 1.50 4.00
246 Lias Andersson RC 2.50 6.00
247 Warren Foegele RC 1.50 4.00
248 Ryan Lomberg RC 1.50 4.00
249 Andreas Johnsson RC 2.00 5.00
250 Noah Juulsen RC 1.50 4.00
251 Rasmus Dahlin 4.00 10.00
252 Brady Tkachuk 5.00 12.00
253 Jesperi Kotkaniemi 3.00 8.00
254 Michael Rasmussen 2.00 5.00
255 Par Lindholm 1.50 4.00
256 Jeremy Lauzon 2.00 5.00
257 Juho Lammikko 1.25 3.00
258 Mathieu Joseph 2.00 5.00
259 Juuso Riikola 1.25 3.00
260 Andrei Svechnikov 4.00 10.00
261 Shane Gersich 1.25 3.00
262 Mikhail Vorobyev 1.25 3.00
263 Brett Howden 2.00 5.00
264 Michael Dal Colle 1.50 4.00
265 Joey Anderson 1.50 4.00
266 Eric Robinson 1.25 3.00
267 Dominik Kahun 1.50 4.00
268 Kristian Vesalainen 2.00 5.00
269 Robert Thomas 3.00 8.00
270 Miro Heiskanen 4.00 10.00
271 Nick Seeler 1.25 3.00
272 Sheldon Dries 1.25 3.00
273 Eeli Tolvanen 3.00 8.00
274 Henri Jokiharju 1.25 3.00
275 Elias Pettersson 5.00 12.00
276 Zach Whitecloud 1.25 3.00
277 Antti Suomela 1.25 3.00
278 Evan Bouchard 4.00 10.00
279 Maxime Comtois 1.50 4.00
280 Dillon Dube 2.00 5.00
281 Ilya Lyubushkin 1.25 3.00
282 Austin Wagner 1.25 3.00

2018-19 Upper Deck MVP 20th Anniversary Colors and Contours

1 Sidney Crosby 8.00 20.00
2 Ryan Getzlaf 2.00 5.00
3 Steven Stamkos 4.00 10.00
4 Evgeny Kuznetsov 2.50 6.00
5 Connor McDavid 10.00 25.00
6 Ryan O'Reilly 2.00 5.00
7 Dylan Larkin 2.50 6.00
8 Mikael Granlund 1.50 4.00
9 Nico Hischier 3.00 8.00
10 Auston Matthews 8.00 20.00
11 Leon Draisaitl 6.00 15.00
12 Brayden Schenn 2.00 5.00
13 Patrik Laine 2.50 6.00
14 Roberto Luongo 3.00 8.00
15 Brock Boeser 2.50 6.00
16 William Nylander 4.00 10.00
17 Taylor Hall 2.00 5.00
18 Alex Galchenyuk 1.25 3.00
19 Erik Karlsson 2.50 6.00
20 Johnny Gaudreau 3.00 8.00
21 Mark Scheifele 3.00 8.00
22 Eric Staal 2.00 5.00
23 Clayton Keller 2.50 6.00
24 Drew Doughty 2.50 6.00
25 Patrick Kane 4.00 10.00
26 Wayne Simmonds 2.00 5.00
27 Matt Duchene 2.00 5.00
28 Tomas Tatar 1.25 3.00
29 Aaron Ekblad 2.50 6.00
30 Carey Price 4.00 10.00
31 Blake Wheeler 2.00 5.00
32 Roman Josi 2.00 5.00
33 Matt Murray 2.00 5.00
34 Pierre-Luc Dubois 1.50 4.00
35 Vladimir Tarasenko 2.50 6.00
36 Nolan Patrick 2.00 5.00
37 Mathew Barzal 2.50 6.00
38 Tuukka Rask 2.50 6.00
39 Nikita Kucherov 4.00 10.00
40 Tyler Seguin 2.50 6.00
41 Jeff Skinner 2.50 6.00
42 Jonathan Quick 2.50 6.00
43 James Neal 1.25 3.00
44 Teuvo Teravainen 2.00 5.00
45 Marc-Andre Fleury 4.00 10.00
46 Joe Pavelski 2.50 6.00
47 Mats Zuccarello 1.50 4.00
48 Petr Mrazek 2.00 5.00
49 Mikko Rantanen 5.00 12.00
50 Alexander Ovechkin 8.00 20.00
51 Jaden Schwartz 2.50 6.00
52 Henrik Sedin 2.50 6.00
53 Joe Thornton 3.00 8.00
54 Jake Guentzel 3.00 8.00
55 John Tavares 3.00 8.00
56 Andrei Vasilevskiy 3.00 8.00
57 Corey Perry 2.00 5.00
58 William Karlsson 2.50 6.00
59 Pekka Rinne 2.50 6.00
60 Brad Marchand 4.00 10.00
61 Cam Talbot 2.00 5.00
62 Jack Eichel 3.00 8.00
63 Brent Burns 2.50 6.00
64 Mark Stone 2.50 6.00
65 Mitch Marner 3.00 8.00
66 Sean Couturier 1.50 4.00
67 Jonathan Marchessault 2.00 5.00
68 Anze Kopitar 2.50 6.00
69 Patrice Bergeron 2.50 6.00
70 Jamie Benn 2.00 5.00
71 Duncan Keith 1.50 4.00
72 Max Pacioretty 2.00 5.00
73 Artemi Panarin 4.00 10.00
74 Logan Couture 2.50 6.00
75 Henrik Lundqvist 5.00 12.00
76 Oliver Ekman-Larsson 2.00 5.00
77 Phil Kessel 2.00 5.00
78 Jonathan Drouin 1.50 4.00
79 Connor Hellebuyck 4.00 10.00
80 Jonathan Toews 3.00 8.00
81 David Pastrnak 5.00 12.00
82 Braden Holtby 2.50 6.00
83 Sean Monahan 1.25 3.00
84 Patrick Marleau 2.00 5.00
85 P.K. Subban 2.50 6.00
86 Nikolaj Ehlers 2.00 5.00
87 Frederik Andersen 2.50 6.00
88 Henrik Zetterberg 2.50 6.00
89 Daniel Sedin 2.50 6.00
90 Nathan MacKinnon 8.00 20.00
91 Evgeni Malkin 4.00 10.00
92 Lias Andersson 3.00 8.00
93 Oskar Lindblom 3.00 8.00
94 Travis Dermott 3.00 8.00
95 Eeli Tolvanen 4.00 10.00
96 Noah Juulsen 3.00 8.00
97 Zach Aston-Reese 3.00 8.00
98 Adam Gaudette 3.00 8.00
99 Ryan Donato 3.00 8.00
100 Casey Mittelstadt 4.00 10.00

2018-19 Upper Deck MVP 20th Anniversary Tribute Silver Script

1 Sidney Crosby 4.00 10.00
2 Ryan Getzlaf 1.00 2.50
3 Steven Stamkos 2.00 5.00
4 Evgeny Kuznetsov 1.25 3.00
5 Connor McDavid 5.00 12.00
6 Ryan O'Reilly 1.00 2.50
7 Dylan Larkin 1.25 3.00
8 Mikael Granlund .75 2.00
9 Nico Hischier 1.50 4.00
10 Auston Matthews 4.00 10.00
11 Leon Draisaitl 3.00 8.00
12 Brayden Schenn 1.00 2.50
13 Patrik Laine 1.25 3.00
14 Roberto Luongo 1.50 4.00
15 Brock Boeser 1.25 3.00
16 William Nylander 2.00 5.00
17 Taylor Hall 1.00 2.50
18 Alex Galchenyuk .60 1.50
19 Erik Karlsson 1.25 3.00
20 Johnny Gaudreau 1.50 4.00
21 Mark Scheifele 1.50 4.00
22 Eric Staal 1.00 2.50
23 Clayton Keller 1.25 3.00
24 Drew Doughty 1.25 3.00
25 Patrick Kane 2.00 5.00
26 Wayne Simmonds 1.00 2.50
27 Matt Duchene 1.00 2.50
28 Tomas Tatar .60 1.50
29 Aaron Ekblad 1.25 3.00
30 Carey Price 2.00 5.00
31 Blake Wheeler 1.00 2.50
32 Roman Josi 1.00 2.50
33 Matt Murray 1.00 2.50
34 Pierre-Luc Dubois .75 2.00
35 Vladimir Tarasenko 1.25 3.00
36 Nolan Patrick 1.00 2.50
37 Mathew Barzal 1.25 3.00
38 Tuukka Rask 1.25 3.00
39 Nikita Kucherov 2.00 5.00
40 Tyler Seguin 1.25 3.00
41 Jeff Skinner 1.25 3.00
42 Jonathan Quick 1.25 3.00
43 James Neal .60 1.50
44 Teuvo Teravainen 1.00 2.50
45 Marc-Andre Fleury 2.00 5.00
46 Joe Pavelski 1.25 3.00
47 Mats Zuccarello .75 2.00
48 Petr Mrazek 1.00 2.50
49 Mikko Rantanen 2.50 6.00
50 Alexander Ovechkin 4.00 10.00
51 Jaden Schwartz 1.25 3.00
52 Henrik Sedin 1.25 3.00
53 Joe Thornton 1.50 4.00
54 Jake Guentzel 1.50 4.00
55 John Tavares 1.50 4.00
56 Andrei Vasilevskiy 1.50 4.00
57 Corey Perry 1.00 2.50
58 William Karlsson 1.25 3.00
59 Pekka Rinne 1.25 3.00
60 Brad Marchand 2.00 5.00
61 Cam Talbot 1.00 2.50
62 Jack Eichel 1.50 4.00
63 Brent Burns 1.25 3.00
64 Mark Stone 1.25 3.00
65 Mitch Marner 1.50 4.00
66 Sean Couturier .75 2.00
67 Jonathan Marchessault 1.00 2.50
68 Anze Kopitar 1.25 3.00
69 Patrice Bergeron 1.25 3.00
70 Jamie Benn 1.00 2.50
71 Duncan Keith .75 2.00
72 Max Pacioretty 1.00 2.50
73 Artemi Panarin 2.00 5.00
74 Logan Couture 1.25 3.00
75 Henrik Lundqvist 2.50 6.00
76 Oliver Ekman-Larsson 1.00 2.50
77 Phil Kessel 1.00 2.50
78 Jonathan Drouin .75 2.00
79 Connor Hellebuyck 2.00 5.00
80 Jonathan Toews 1.50 4.00
81 David Pastrnak 2.50 6.00
82 Braden Holtby 1.25 3.00
83 Sean Monahan .60 1.50
84 Patrick Marleau 1.00 2.50
85 P.K. Subban 1.25 3.00
86 Nikolaj Ehlers 1.00 2.50
87 Frederik Andersen 1.25 3.00
88 Henrik Zetterberg 1.25 3.00
89 Daniel Sedin 1.25 3.00
90 Nathan MacKinnon 4.00 10.00
91 Evgeni Malkin 2.00 5.00
92 Lias Andersson 1.50 4.00
93 Oskar Lindblom 1.50 4.00
94 Travis Dermott 1.50 4.00
95 Eeli Tolvanen 2.00 5.00
96 Noah Juulsen 1.00 2.50
97 Zach Aston-Reese 1.50 4.00
98 Adam Gaudette 1.50 4.00
99 Ryan Donato 1.50 4.00
100 Casey Mittelstadt 2.00 5.00

2018-19 Upper Deck MVP NHL Player Credentials Entry Level Access

NHLET Eeli Tolvanen 2.50 6.00
NHLHB Henrik Borgstrom 2.00 5.00
NHLLA Lias Andersson 2.00 5.00
NHLMD Michael Dal Colle 1.25 3.00
NHLMI Casey Mittelstadt 2.50 6.00
NHLNJ Noah Juulsen 1.25 3.00
NHLOL Oskar Lindblom 2.00 5.00
NHLRD Ryan Donato 2.00 5.00
NHLTD Travis Dermott 2.00 5.00
NHLZA Zach Aston-Reese 2.00 5.00

2018-19 Upper Deck MVP NHL Player Credentials Level 1 Access

NHLAM Anthony Mantha .75 2.00
NHLAV Andrei Vasilevskiy 1.50 4.00
NHLBG Brendan Gallagher 1.00 2.50
NHLBM Brad Marchand 2.00 5.00
NHLDK Duncan Keith .75 2.00
NHLEM Evgeni Malkin 2.00 5.00
NHLGU Jake Guentzel 1.50 4.00
NHLJB Jamie Benn 1.00 2.50
NHLJC Jeff Carter .75 2.00
NHLJG Johnny Gaudreau 1.50 4.00
NHLJN James Neal .60 1.50
NHLJP Joe Pavelski 1.25 3.00
NHLKS Kevin Shattenkirk .60 1.50
NHLKU Evgeny Kuznetsov 1.25 3.00
NHLMB Mathew Barzal 1.25 3.00
NHLMM Mitch Marner 1.50 4.00
NHLMR Mikko Rantanen 2.50 6.00
NHLPL Patrik Laine 1.25 3.00
NHLRI Pekka Rinne 1.00 2.50
NHLTR Vincent Trocheck 1.00 2.50

2018-19 Upper Deck MVP NHL Player Credentials Level 1 Access Autographs

NHLAV Andrei Vasilevskiy C 15.00 40.00
NHLBG Brendan Gallagher B 10.00 25.00
NHLGU Jake Guentzel C 15.00 40.00
NHLJB Jamie Benn B 10.00 25.00
NHLJC Jeff Carter B 8.00 20.00
NHLJG Johnny Gaudreau B 15.00 40.00
NHLJP Joe Pavelski B 12.00 30.00
NHLKS Kevin Shattenkirk C 6.00 15.00
NHLKU Evgeny Kuznetsov A 12.00 30.00
NHLMB Mathew Barzal C 12.00 30.00
NHLMM Mitch Marner B 15.00 40.00
NHLMR Mikko Rantanen C 25.00 60.00
NHLPL Patrik Laine C 12.00 30.00
NHLRI Pekka Rinne C 10.00 25.00
NHLTR Vincent Trocheck C 10.00 25.00

2018-19 Upper Deck MVP NHL Player Credentials VIP Access

NHLAO Alexander Ovechkin 5.00 12.00
NHLBB Brock Boeser 1.50 4.00
NHLBO Bobby Orr 5.00 12.00
NHLCM Connor McDavid 6.00 15.00
NHLEK Erik Karlsson 1.50 4.00
NHLHL Henrik Lundqvist 3.00 8.00
NHLJT Jonathan Toews 2.00 5.00
NHLPD Pavel Datsyuk 2.00 5.00
NHLPR Patrick Roy 3.00 8.00
NHLVT Vladimir Tarasenko 1.50 4.00

2018-19 Upper Deck MVP NHL Player Credentials VIP Access Autographs

NHLAO Alexander Ovechkin A 40.00 100.00
NHLBB Brock Boeser B 12.00 30.00
NHLBO Bobby Orr B 40.00 100.00
NHLCM Connor McDavid A 50.00 125.00
NHLEK Erik Karlsson A 12.00 30.00
NHLHL Henrik Lundqvist B 25.00 60.00
NHLJT Jonathan Toews A 15.00 40.00
NHLPD Pavel Datsyuk B 15.00 40.00
NHLPR Patrick Roy A 25.00 60.00
NHLVT Vladimir Tarasenko A 12.00 30.00

2019-20 Upper Deck MVP

1 Ryan Murray .20 .50
2 Jeff Carter .20 .50
3 Travis Zajac .15 .40
4 Ty Rattie .15 .40
5 David Pastrnak .60 1.50
6 Derek Stepan .15 .40
7 Brent Burns .25 .60
8 Marcus Johansson .20 .50
9 Brad Marchand .50 1.25
10 Andrei Vasilevskiy .40 1.00
11 Blake Wheeler .25 .60
12 Nathan MacKinnon 1.00 2.50
13 Mikko Rantanen .60 1.50
14 Jack Eichel .50 1.25
15 Brady Tkachuk .40 1.00
16 Brayden Point .30 .75
17 Mark Scheifele .40 1.00
18 Charlie McAvoy .30 .75
19 Patrice Bergeron .30 .75
20 Charlie Coyle .20 .50
21 Damon Severson .15 .40
22 Tyler Seguin .30 .75
23 Mikael Backlund .20 .50
24 Artemi Panarin .50 1.25
25 Vladimir Tarasenko .30 .75
26 Joe Morrow .20 .50
27 Frederik Andersen .30 .75
28 Tuukka Rask .30 .75
29 Ryan McDonagh .15 .40
30 Morgan Rielly .25 .60
31 Reilly Smith .25 .60
32 Elias Lindholm .25 .60
33 Sebastian Aho .40 1.00
34 Jeff Skinner .25 .60
35 John Carlson .25 .60
36 Filip Forsberg .40 1.00
37 Evgeny Kuznetsov .30 .75
38 Kris Letang .30 .75
39 Mark Giordano .25 .60
40 Lars Eller .15 .40
41 Gabriel Landeskog .30 .75
42 Evgeni Malkin .50 1.25
43 Evander Kane .25 .60
44 Phil Kessel .25 .60
45 Matt Murray .25 .60
46 Cam Atkinson .25 .60
47 Joe Pavelski .30 .75
48 Matt Niskanen .20 .50
49 Mark Stone .30 .75
50 Matt Duchene .25 .60
51 Victor Hedman .30 .75
52 Matthew Tkachuk .50 1.25
53 Nicklas Backstrom .25 .60
54 Seth Jones .25 .60
55 Dustin Byfuglien .25 .60
56 Tomas Hertl .25 .60
57 Dylan Larkin .30 .75
58 Roman Josi .25 .60
59 Nick Ritchie .15 .40
60 Ben Bishop .20 .50
61 Viktor Arvidsson .15 .40
62 Martin Jones .20 .50
63 Alexander Wennberg .15 .40
64 Pierre-Luc Dubois .20 .50
65 Brock Boeser .30 .75
66 Jake Guentzel .40 1.00
67 Alex DeBrincat .30 .75
68 Jonathan Toews .40 1.00
69 Ryan O'Reilly .25 .60
70 Ryan Johansen .20 .50
71 John Klingberg .25 .60
72 Mathew Barzal .30 .75
73 Timo Meier .25 .60
74 Connor Hellebuyck .50 1.25
75 Jamie Benn .25 .60
76 Thomas Chabot .25 .60
77 Shea Weber .25 .60
78 Jacob Trouba .20 .50
79 Ryan Nugent-Hopkins .30 .75
80 Nick Leddy .15 .40
81 Alexander Radulov .25 .60
82 Mika Zibanejad .30 .75
83 Jonathan Drouin .20 .50
84 Mattias Ekholm .20 .50
85 Teuvo Teravainen .25 .60
86 Devan Dubnyk .20 .50
87 Aleksander Barkov .40 1.00
88 Logan Couture .30 .75
89 Braden Holtby .30 .75
90 Jonathan Marchessault .30 .75
91 Andrew Shaw .15 .40
92 John Gibson .25 .60
93 Zach Parise .25 .60
94 Keith Yandle .15 .40
95 Robin Lehner .20 .50
96 Sergei Bobrovsky .40 1.00
97 Tyson Barrie .15 .40
98 Mike Hoffman .15 .40
99 Jordan Binnington .40 1.00
100 Alexander Ovechkin CL 1.00 2.50
101 Sean Couturier .20 .50
102 Jakub Voracek .20 .50
103 T.J. Oshie .25 .60
104 Nino Niederreiter .15 .40
105 Ryan Suter .20 .50
106 Jake Muzzin .25 .60
107 Alex Tuch .20 .50
108 Kyle Connor .40 1.00
109 Drew Doughty .30 .75
110 Corey Crawford .25 .60
111 Sam Reinhart .50 1.25
112 Chris Kreider .30 .75
113 Chris Tierney .20 .50
114 Anze Kopitar .40 1.00
115 Andreas Johnsson .25 .60
116 Anders Lee .20 .50
117 Claude Giroux .25 .60
118 Mats Zuccarello .25 .60
119 Brendan Gallagher .25 .60
120 Tom Wilson .20 .50
121 Thomas Greiss .20 .50
122 David Rittich .20 .50
123 Vincent Trocheck .25 .60
124 Bo Horvat .30 .75
125 Ryan Ellis .20 .50
126 Oliver Ekman-Larsson .25 .60
127 Jonathan Huberdeau .30 .75
128 Antoine Roussel .15 .40
129 Mikael Granlund .20 .50
130 William Karlsson .30 .75
131 Dylan Strome .30 .75
132 Zach Werenski .40 1.00
133 Elias Pettersson .40 1.00
134 Jimmy Vesey .20 .50
135 Darcy Kuemper .25 .60
136 Jonathan Quick .30 .75
137 Aaron Ekblad .30 .75
138 Paul Stastny .20 .50
139 Tyler Johnson .15 .40
140 Kyle Palmieri .20 .50
141 Patric Hornqvist .15 .40
142 Shayne Gostisbehere .25 .60
143 Miro Heiskanen .30 .75
144 Anthony Mantha .20 .50
145 Ryan Dzingel .20 .50
146 Evgenii Dadonov .15 .40
147 Jared Spurgeon .20 .50
148 Oscar Klefbom .25 .60
149 Dougie Hamilton .20 .50
150 Jake Gardiner .15 .40
151 Travis Konecny .25 .60
152 Nico Hischier .40 1.00
153 Taylor Hall .25 .60
154 Josh Anderson .20 .50
155 Danton Heinen .20 .50
156 Micheal Ferland .15 .40
157 William Nylander .50 1.25
158 Ryan Pulock .20 .50
159 Josh Morrissey .30 .75
160 Jim Howard .30 .75
161 Josh Bailey .20 .50
162 Tomas Tatar .15 .40
163 Rickard Rakell .25 .60
164 Clayton Keller .30 .75
165 P.K. Subban .30 .75

166 Yanni Gourde .20 .50
167 Ryan Getzlaf .25 .60
168 Andreas Athanasiou .20 .50
169 Justin Schultz .25 .60
170 Jakub Vrana .25 .60
171 Petr Mrazek .25 .60
172 Linus Ullmark .25 .60
173 T.J. Brodie .20 .50
174 Dominik Kahun .15 .40
175 Dustin Brown .25 .60
176 Bobby Ryan .20 .50
177 Wayne Simmonds .25 .60
178 Rasmus Dahlin .30 .75
179 Darnell Nurse .20 .50
180 Alex Pietrangelo .20 .50
181 Kasperi Kapanen .20 .50
182 Carter Hart .25 .60
183 Nazem Kadri .30 .75
184 Kevin Hayes .20 .50
185 Patrick Marleau .25 .60
186 Andre Burakovsky .15 .40
187 Jaden Schwartz .30 .75
188 David Krejci .25 .60
189 Alex Galchenyuk .15 .40
190 Tyler Toffoli .25 .60
191 J.T. Miller .30 .75
192 Zach Hyman .40 1.00
193 Colton Parayko .20 .50
194 Adam Henrique .20 .50
195 Tyler Bertuzzi .20 .50
196 Kevin Labanc .15 .40
197 Bryan Rust .25 .60
198 Brooks Orpik .15 .40
199 Johnny Boychuk .20 .50
200 Sidney Crosby CL 1.00 2.50
201 Henrik Lundqvist SP 1.25 3.00
202 Joe Thornton SP .75 2.00
203 Steven Stamkos SP 1.00 2.50
204 Patrick Kane SP 1.00 2.50
205 Marc-Andre Fleury SP 1.00 2.50
206 Sean Monahan SP .30 .75
207 Johnny Gaudreau SP .75 2.00
208 Mitch Marner SP .75 2.00
209 Connor McDavid SP 2.50 6.00
210 Leon Draisaitl SP 1.50 4.00
211 Max Pacioretty SP .50 1.25
212 Sidney Crosby SP 2.00 5.00
213 Carey Price SP 1.00 2.50
214 John Tavares SP .75 2.00
215 Nikita Kucherov SP 1.00 2.50
216 Patrik Laine SP .60 1.50
217 Auston Matthews SP 2.00 5.00
218 Alexander Ovechkin SP 2.00 5.00
219 Max Domi SP .50 1.25
220 Brandon Gignac SP RC 1.25 3.00
221 Carl Grundstrom SP RC 1.50 4.00
222 Colin Blackwell SP RC 1.50 4.00
223 Filip Zadina SP RC 2.50 6.00
224 Guillaume Brisebois SP RC 1.50 4.00
225 Jacob Middleton SP RC 1.25 3.00
226 Joel L'Esperance SP RC 1.50 4.00
227 Erik Brannstrom SP RC 1.50 4.00
228 Taro Hirose SP RC 1.50 4.00
229 Karson Kuhlman SP RC 1.50 4.00
230 Kevin Boyle SP RC 1.50 4.00
231 Alexandre Texier SP RC 1.50 4.00
232 Kole Sherwood SP RC 1.50 4.00
233 Libor Hajek SP RC 1.25 3.00
234 Mackenzie MacEachern SP RC 1.50 4.00
235 Matt Roy SP RC 1.50 4.00
236 Max Jones SP RC 1.50 4.00
237 Dante Fabbro SP RC 1.50 4.00
238 Nathan Bastian SP RC 1.50 4.00
239 Philippe Myers SP RC 1.25 3.00
240 Riley Stillman SP RC 1.50 4.00
241 Rudolfs Balcers SP RC 1.50 4.00
242 Ryan Lindgren SP RC 1.50 4.00
243 Teddy Blueger SP RC 1.50 4.00
244 Trent Frederic SP RC 1.50 4.00
245 Vitaly Abramov SP RC 1.50 4.00
246 Zack MacEwen SP RC 1.25 3.00
247 Cale Makar SP RC 8.00 20.00
248 Quinn Hughes SP RC 8.00 20.00
249 Ryan Poehling SP RC 2.50 6.00
250 Cale Makar CL SP RC 8.00 20.00

2019-20 Upper Deck MVP Autographs

201 Henrik Lundqvist B 40.00 100.00
202 Joe Thornton C 25.00 60.00
203 Steven Stamkos A 100.00 200.00
205 Marc-Andre Fleury C 30.00 80.00
206 Sean Monahan D 10.00 25.00
207 Johnny Gaudreau B 25.00 60.00
208 Mitch Marner D 25.00 60.00
209 Connor McDavid C 80.00 200.00
210 Leon Draisaitl C 50.00 125.00
211 Max Pacioretty D 15.00 40.00
213 Carey Price B 30.00 80.00
214 John Tavares B 25.00 60.00
215 Nikita Kucherov A 30.00 80.00
216 Patrik Laine C 20.00 50.00
217 Auston Matthews A 60.00 150.00
218 Alexander Ovechkin A 60.00 150.00
219 Max Domi D 15.00 40.00
220 Brandon Gignac F 12.00 30.00
223 Filip Zadina E 25.00 60.00
227 Erik Brannstrom E 15.00 40.00
228 Taro Hirose D 15.00 40.00
231 Alexandre Texier D 15.00 40.00
233 Libor Hajek F 12.00 30.00
236 Max Jones F 15.00 40.00
238 Nathan Bastian F 15.00 40.00
239 Philippe Myers F 12.00 30.00
241 Rudolfs Balcers F 15.00 40.00
245 Vitaly Abramov E 15.00 40.00
246 Zack MacEwen E 12.00 30.00
248 Quinn Hughes E 80.00 200.00
249 Ryan Poehling E 25.00 60.00

2019-20 Upper Deck MVP Laser Shots

S1 Alexander Ovechkin 2.00 5.00
S2 Steven Stamkos 1.00 2.50
S3 Evgeni Malkin 1.00 2.50
S4 Patrick Kane 1.00 2.50
S5 Connor McDavid 2.50 6.00
S6 Sidney Crosby 2.00 5.00
S7 Drew Doughty .60 1.50
S8 Nikita Kucherov 1.00 2.50
S9 Victor Hedman .60 1.50
S10 Erik Karlsson .60 1.50

2019-20 Upper Deck MVP Net Crashers

NC1 Johnny Gaudreau .75 2.00
NC2 John Tavares .75 2.00
NC3 Patrice Bergeron .60 1.50
NC4 Vladimir Tarasenko .60 1.50
NC5 Taylor Hall .50 1.25
NC6 Anze Kopitar .75 2.00
NC7 Patrick Kane 1.00 2.50
NC8 Nathan MacKinnon 2.00 5.00
NC9 Sidney Crosby 2.00 5.00
NC10 Jonathan Toews .75 2.00

2019-20 Upper Deck MVP Stanley Cup Edition 20th Anniversary Colors and Contours

1 Nikita Kucherov/249 4.00 10.00
2 Patrick Kane/249 4.00 10.00
3 Travis Zajac/249 1.25 3.00
4 Alexander Ovechkin/249 8.00 20.00
5 David Pastrnak/249 5.00 12.00
6 Sidney Crosby/249 8.00 20.00
7 Brent Burns/249 2.00 5.00
8 Marcus Johansson/249 1.50 4.00
9 Brad Marchand/249 4.00 10.00
10 Andrei Vasilevskiy/249/249 3.00 8.00
11 Blake Wheeler/249 2.00 5.00
12 Nathan MacKinnon/249 8.00 20.00
13 Mikko Rantanen/249 5.00 12.00
14 Jack Eichel/249 3.00 8.00
15 Brady Tkachuk/249 3.00 8.00
16 Brayden Point/249 2.50 6.00
17 Mark Scheifele/249 3.00 8.00
18 Charlie McAvoy/249 2.50 6.00
19 Patrice Bergeron/249 2.50 6.00
20 Charlie Coyle/249 2.00 5.00
21 Damon Severson/249 1.25 3.00
22 Tyler Seguin/249 2.50 6.00
23 Mikael Backlund/249 1.50 4.00
24 Artemi Panarin/249 4.00 10.00
25 Vladimir Tarasenko/249 2.50 6.00
26 Auston Matthews/249 8.00 20.00
27 Frederik Andersen/249 2.50 6.00
28 Tuukka Rask/249 2.50 6.00
29 Ryan McDonagh/249 1.25 3.00
30 Morgan Rielly/249 2.00 5.00
31 Marc-Andre Fleury/249 4.00 10.00
32 Elias Lindholm/249 2.00 5.00
33 Sebastian Aho/249 3.00 8.00
34 Jeff Skinner/249 2.00 5.00
35 John Carlson/249 2.00 5.00
36 Filip Forsberg/249 3.00 8.00
37 Evgeny Kuznetsov/249 2.50 6.00
38 Kris Letang/249 2.50 6.00
39 Mark Giordano/249 2.00 5.00
40 Lars Eller/249 1.25 3.00
41 Gabriel Landeskog/249 2.50 6.00
42 Evgeni Malkin/249 4.00 10.00
43 Evander Kane/249 2.00 5.00
44 Phil Kessel/249 2.00 5.00
45 Matt Murray/249 2.00 5.00
46 Cam Atkinson/249 2.00 5.00
47 Joe Pavelski/249 2.50 6.00
48 Matt Niskanen/249 1.50 4.00
49 Mark Stone/249 2.50 6.00
50 Matt Duchene/249 2.00 5.00
51 Victor Hedman/249 2.50 6.00
52 Matthew Tkachuk/249 4.00 10.00
53 Nicklas Backstrom/249 2.00 5.00
54 Seth Jones/249 2.00 5.00
55 Dustin Byfuglien/249 2.00 5.00
56 Tomas Hertl/249 2.00 5.00
57 Dylan Larkin/249 2.50 6.00
58 Roman Josi/249 2.00 5.00
59 Nick Ritchie/249 1.25 3.00
60 Ben Bishop/249 1.50 4.00
61 Viktor Arvidsson/249 1.25 3.00
62 Martin Jones/249 1.50 4.00
63 Alexander Wennberg/249 1.25 3.00
64 Pierre-Luc Dubois/249 1.50 4.00
65 Brock Boeser/249 2.50 6.00
66 Jake Guentzel/249 3.00 8.00
67 Alex DeBrincat/249 2.50 6.00
68 Jonathan Toews/249 3.00 8.00
69 Ryan O'Reilly/249 2.00 5.00
70 Ryan Johansen/249 1.50 4.00
71 John Klingberg/249 2.00 5.00
72 Mathew Barzal/249 2.50 6.00
73 Timo Meier/249 2.00 5.00
74 Connor Hellebuyck/249 4.00 10.00
75 Jamie Benn/249 2.00 5.00
76 Thomas Chabot/249 2.00 5.00
77 Shea Weber/249 2.00 5.00
78 Patrik Laine/249 2.50 6.00
79 Ryan Nugent-Hopkins/249 2.50 6.00
80 Nick Leddy/249 1.25 3.00
81 Alexander Radulov/249 2.00 5.00
82 Mika Zibanejad/249 2.50 6.00
83 Jonathan Drouin/249 1.50 4.00
84 Mattias Ekholm/249 1.50 4.00
85 Elias Pettersson/249 3.00 8.00
86 Rasmus Dahlin/249 2.50 6.00
87 Carter Hart/249 2.00 5.00
88 Steven Stamkos/249 4.00 10.00
89 Connor McDavid/249 10.00 25.00
90 Leon Draisaitl/249 6.00 15.00
91 Max Pacioretty/249 2.00 5.00
92 Carey Price/249 4.00 10.00
93 John Tavares/249 3.00 8.00
94 Carl Grundstrom/249 2.00 5.00
95 Colin Blackwell/249 2.00 5.00
96 Filip Zadina/249 3.00 8.00
97 Quinn Hughes/249 10.00 25.00
98 Ryan Poehling/249 3.00 8.00
99 Mackenzie MacEachern/249 2.00 5.00
100 Cale Makar/249 10.00 25.00
101 Jack Hughes/99 15.00 40.00
102 Morgan Frost/99 5.00 12.00
103 Kirby Dach/99 6.00 15.00
104 Julien Gauthier/99 3.00 8.00
105 Noah Dobson/99 8.00 20.00
106 Alexander Volkov/99 2.50 6.00
107 Joel Farabee/99 5.00 12.00
108 Ilya Mikheyev/99 5.00 12.00
109 Elvis Merzlikins/99 6.00 15.00
110 Tobias Bjornfot/99 3.00 8.00
111 Oliver Wahlstrom/99 5.00 12.00
112 Ville Heinola/99 4.00 10.00
113 Cale Fleury/99 4.00 10.00
114 Barrett Hayton/99 6.00 15.00
115 Victor Olofsson/99 6.00 15.00
116 Adam Fox/99 8.00 20.00
117 Cody Glass/99 5.00 12.00
118 Nick Suzuki/99 12.00 30.00
119 Nikita Gusev/99 5.00 12.00
120 Rasmus Sandin/99 5.00 12.00
121 Teddy Blueger/99 3.00 8.00
122 Max Jones/99 3.00 8.00
123 Nico Sturm/99 2.50 6.00
124 Rem Pitlick/99 3.00 8.00
125 Sam Lafferty/99 2.50 6.00
126 Joel L'Esperance/99 3.00 8.00
127 Joel Persson/99 2.50 6.00
128 Joey Daccord/99 6.00 15.00
129 Karson Kuhlman/99 3.00 8.00
130 Mario Ferraro/99 2.50 6.00
131 Martin Fehervary/99 2.50 6.00
132 Adam Boqvist/99 3.00 8.00
133 Alexandre Texier/99 3.00 8.00
134 Dante Fabbro/99 3.00 8.00
135 Dominik Kubalik/99 6.00 15.00
136 Emil Bemstrom/99 3.00 8.00
137 Erik Brannstrom/99 3.00 8.00
138 Jesper Boqvist/99 2.50 6.00
139 Nicolas Hague/99 3.00 8.00
140 Nikolai Prokhorkin/99 2.50 6.00
141 Philippe Myers/99 2.50 6.00
142 Taro Hirose/99 3.00 8.00
143 Trevor Moore/99 2.50 6.00
144 Blake Lizotte/99 3.00 8.00
145 Carter Verhaeghe/99 5.00 12.00
146 Connor Clifton/99 3.00 8.00
147 Conor Timmins/99 3.00 8.00
148 David Gustafsson/99 2.50 6.00
149 Dmytro Timashov/99 3.00 8.00
150 Kaapo Kakko/99 5.00 12.00

2019-20 Upper Deck MVP Stanley Cup Edition 20th Anniversary Silver Script

1 Nikita Kucherov 2.00 5.00
2 Patrick Kane 2.00 5.00
3 Travis Zajac .60 1.50
4 Alexander Ovechkin 4.00 10.00
5 David Pastrnak 2.50 6.00
6 Sidney Crosby 4.00 10.00
7 Brent Burns 1.00 2.50
8 Marcus Johansson .75 2.00
9 Brad Marchand 2.00 5.00
10 Andrei Vasilevskiy 1.50 4.00
11 Blake Wheeler 1.00 2.50
12 Nathan MacKinnon 4.00 10.00
13 Mikko Rantanen 2.50 6.00
14 Jack Eichel 1.50 4.00
15 Brady Tkachuk 1.50 4.00
16 Brayden Point 1.25 3.00
17 Mark Scheifele 1.50 4.00
18 Charlie McAvoy 1.25 3.00
19 Patrice Bergeron 1.25 3.00
20 Charlie Coyle 1.00 2.50
21 Damon Severson .60 1.50
22 Tyler Seguin 1.25 3.00
23 Mikael Backlund .75 2.00
24 Artemi Panarin 2.00 5.00
25 Vladimir Tarasenko 1.25 3.00
26 Auston Matthews 4.00 10.00
27 Frederik Andersen 1.25 3.00
28 Tuukka Rask 1.25 3.00
29 Ryan McDonagh .60 1.50
30 Morgan Rielly 1.00 2.50
31 Marc-Andre Fleury 2.00 5.00
32 Elias Lindholm 1.00 2.50
33 Sebastian Aho 1.50 4.00
34 Jeff Skinner 1.00 2.50
35 John Carlson 1.00 2.50
36 Filip Forsberg 1.50 4.00
37 Evgeny Kuznetsov 1.25 3.00
38 Kris Letang 1.25 3.00
39 Mark Giordano 1.00 2.50
40 Lars Eller .60 1.50
41 Gabriel Landeskog 1.25 3.00
42 Evgeni Malkin 2.00 5.00
43 Evander Kane 1.00 2.50
44 Phil Kessel 1.00 2.50
45 Matt Murray 1.00 2.50
46 Cam Atkinson 1.00 2.50
47 Joe Pavelski 1.25 3.00
48 Matt Niskanen .75 2.00
49 Mark Stone 1.25 3.00
50 Matt Duchene 1.00 2.50
51 Victor Hedman 1.25 3.00
52 Matthew Tkachuk 2.00 5.00
53 Nicklas Backstrom 1.00 2.50
54 Seth Jones 1.00 2.50
55 Dustin Byfuglien 1.00 2.50
56 Tomas Hertl 1.00 2.50
57 Dylan Larkin 1.25 3.00
58 Roman Josi 1.00 2.50
59 Nick Ritchie .60 1.50
60 Ben Bishop .75 2.00
61 Viktor Arvidsson .60 1.50
62 Martin Jones .75 2.00
63 Alexander Wennberg .60 1.50
64 Pierre-Luc Dubois .75 2.00
65 Brock Boeser 1.25 3.00
66 Jake Guentzel 1.50 4.00
67 Alex DeBrincat 1.25 3.00
68 Jonathan Toews 1.50 4.00
69 Ryan O'Reilly 1.00 2.50
70 Ryan Johansen .75 2.00
71 John Klingberg 1.00 2.50
72 Mathew Barzal 1.25 3.00
73 Timo Meier 1.00 2.50
74 Connor Hellebuyck 2.00 5.00
75 Jamie Benn 1.00 2.50
76 Thomas Chabot 1.00 2.50
77 Shea Weber 1.00 2.50
78 Patrik Laine 1.25 3.00
79 Ryan Nugent-Hopkins 1.25 3.00
80 Nick Leddy .60 1.50
81 Alexander Radulov 1.00 2.50
82 Mika Zibanejad 1.25 3.00
83 Jonathan Drouin .75 2.00
84 Mattias Ekholm .75 2.00
85 Elias Pettersson 1.50 4.00
86 Rasmus Dahlin 1.25 3.00
87 Carter Hart 1.00 2.50
88 Steven Stamkos 2.00 5.00
89 Connor McDavid 5.00 12.00
90 Leon Draisaitl 3.00 8.00
91 Max Pacioretty 1.00 2.50
92 Carey Price 2.00 5.00
93 John Tavares 1.50 4.00
94 Carl Grundstrom 1.00 2.50
95 Colin Blackwell 1.00 2.50
96 Filip Zadina 1.50 4.00
97 Quinn Hughes 5.00 12.00
98 Ryan Poehling 1.50 4.00
99 Mackenzie MacEachern 1.00 2.50
100 Cale Makar 5.00 12.00

2020-21 Upper Deck MVP

1 Jeff Skinner .25 .60
2 Corey Crawford .25 .60
3 Clayton Keller .30 .75
4 Alec Martinez .15 .40
5 Dylan Larkin .30 .75
6 Gabriel Landeskog .30 .75
7 Alex DeBrincat .30 .75
8 Nick Foligno .20 .50
9 Jeff Petry .25 .60
10 Oliver Ekman-Larsson .25 .60
11 Filip Forsberg .40 1.00
12 Brandon Saad .20 .50
13 Darnell Nurse .20 .50
14 Sam Reinhart .50 1.25
15 Matt Murray .25 .60
16 Colin White .15 .40
17 Ryan Suter .20 .50
18 Miro Heiskanen .30 .75
19 Zack Kassian .15 .40
20 Anthony Mantha .20 .50
21 Kaapo Kakko .20 .50
22 Shea Weber .25 .60
23 Brock Nelson .25 .60
24 Andrew Shaw .15 .40
25 Alexander Radulov .25 .60
26 Mikko Rantanen .60 1.50
27 Mark Scheifele .40 1.00
28 Nicklas Backstrom .25 .60
29 Viktor Arvidsson .15 .40
30 Charlie McAvoy .30 .75
31 Patric Hornqvist .15 .40
32 Josh Bailey .20 .50
33 Dougie Hamilton .20 .50
34 Morgan Rielly .25 .60
35 Artem Anisimov .15 .40
36 Ryan Getzlaf .25 .60
37 Drew Doughty .30 .75
38 Danny DeKeyser .15 .40
39 Ryan Nugent-Hopkins .30 .75
40 Bo Horvat .30 .75
41 Anders Lee .20 .50
42 J.T. Miller .30 .75
43 Marcus Johansson .20 .50
44 Anthony Beauvillier .15 .40
45 Anze Kopitar .40 1.00
46 Sean Couturier .20 .50
47 Erik Gustafsson .15 .40
48 Brady Tkachuk .40 1.00
49 Eric Staal .25 .60
50 Teuvo Teravainen .25 .60
51 Matt Duchene .25 .60
52 William Karlsson .30 .75
53 Dustin Brown .25 .60
54 Vladimir Tarasenko .30 .75
55 David Pastrnak .60 1.50
56 Jakub Vrana .25 .60
57 Filip Zadina .20 .50
58 Tyler Bertuzzi .20 .50
59 Brent Burns .25 .60
60 Bryan Rust .25 .60
61 Semyon Varlamov .25 .60
62 Carter Hart .25 .60
63 Tuukka Rask .30 .75
64 Mika Zibanejad .30 .75
65 Evander Kane .25 .60
66 Jonathan Quick .30 .75
67 Ryan Johansen .20 .50
68 Darcy Kuemper .25 .60
69 Nikita Kucherov .50 1.25
70 Henrik Lundqvist .60 1.50
71 Cam Atkinson .25 .60
72 Wayne Simmonds .25 .60
73 Cam Fowler .25 .60
74 Philipp Grubauer .25 .60
75 Tom Wilson .25 .60
76 Jamie Benn .25 .60
77 Jared Spurgeon .25 .60
78 Patrik Laine .30 .75
79 Pierre-Luc Dubois .20 .50
80 Marcus Sorensen .20 .50
81 Kailer Yamamoto .25 .60
82 Craig Anderson .20 .50
83 Jacob Trouba .20 .50
84 Jonathan Drouin .20 .50
85 Adam Henrique .20 .50
86 Joonas Korpisalo .25 .60
87 Jack Hughes .60 1.50
88 Nate Schmidt .20 .50
89 Ben Bishop .20 .50
90 Johnny Gaudreau .40 1.00
91 Brayden Point .30 .75
92 Josh Morrissey .30 .75
93 David Perron .20 .50
94 Anthony Duclair .20 .50
95 Zach Werenski .40 1.00
96 Alex Tuch .25 .60
97 Brady Skjei .20 .50
98 Shea Theodore .30 .75
99 Rickard Rakell .20 .50
100 Nathan MacKinnon CL 1.00 2.50
101 Kasperi Kapanen .20 .50
102 Andrei Vasilevskiy .40 1.00
103 Christian Dvorak .20 .50
104 Elias Lindholm .25 .60
105 Blake Wheeler .25 .60
106 Alex Ovechkin 1.00 2.50
107 Jordan Binnington .40 1.00
108 Ivan Provorov .20 .50
109 Charlie Coyle .25 .60
110 Alex Pietrangelo .20 .50
111 Tyler Johnson .15 .40
112 Tyler Seguin .30 .75
113 Jakub Voracek .20 .50
114 Timo Meier .25 .60
115 Brandon Sutter .15 .40
116 Alexander Steen .15 .40
117 Mark Giordano .25 .60
118 Torey Krug .20 .50
119 Oscar Klefbom .25 .60
120 Andreas Johnsson .25 .60
121 Max Pacioretty .25 .60
122 Kyle Connor .40 1.00
123 Jason Zucker .25 .60
124 William Nylander .50 1.25
125 Patrick Marleau .25 .60
126 Matthew Tkachuk .50 1.25
127 Jakob Silfverberg .15 .40
128 Mike Smith .15 .40
129 Nico Hischier .40 1.00
130 James van Riemsdyk .20 .50
131 Travis Zajac .15 .40
132 Nathan MacKinnon 1.00 2.50
133 Jonathan Marchessault .30 .75
134 Sergei Bobrovsky .40 1.00
135 Connor Hellebuyck .50 1.25
136 Victor Hedman .30 .75
137 Evgenii Dadonov .15 .40
138 Frederik Andersen .30 .75
139 Alex Killorn .15 .40
140 Logan Couture .30 .75
141 Jake Muzzin .25 .60
142 Thomas Chabot .25 .60
143 Zach Parise .25 .60
144 Braden Holtby .30 .75
145 Patrice Bergeron .30 .75
146 Mark Stone .30 .75
147 Brendan Gallagher .25 .60
148 Jean-Gabriel Pageau .15 .40
149 Pekka Rinne .25 .60
150 P.K. Subban .30 .75
151 Linus Ullmark .25 .60
152 Chris Kreider .30 .75
153 Jeff Carter .20 .50
154 Mitch Marner .40 1.00
155 Jesper Bratt .25 .60
156 Kyle Palmieri .20 .50
157 Jaccob Slavin .20 .50
158 Taylor Hall .25 .60
159 Oliver Bjorkstrand .20 .50
160 Hampus Lindholm .15 .40
161 Sebastian Aho .40 1.00
162 Andreas Athanasiou .20 .50
163 Colton Parayko .20 .50
164 Phillip Danault .25 .60
165 Keith Yandle .15 .40
166 Nick Leddy .15 .40
167 David Rittich .20 .50
168 Rocco Grimaldi .15 .40
169 Andrei Svechnikov .30 .75
170 Jacob Markstrom .25 .60
171 T.J. Oshie .25 .60
172 Alexander Edler .15 .40
173 Mathew Barzal .30 .75
174 Aleksander Barkov .40 1.00
175 Nazem Kadri .30 .75
176 Ryan Strome .25 .60
177 Jonathan Huberdeau .30 .75
178 Bryan Little .20 .50
179 Tristan Jarry .25 .60
180 Victor Olofsson .25 .60
181 Nino Niederreiter .15 .40
182 John Klingberg .25 .60
183 John Carlson .25 .60
184 Sean Monahan .15 .40
185 Nick Suzuki .50 1.25
186 Rasmus Dahlin .30 .75
187 Kevin Labanc .15 .40
188 Jim Howard .30 .75
189 Devan Dubnyk .20 .50
190 Travis Konecny .25 .60
191 Kris Letang .30 .75
192 Seth Jones .25 .60
193 Jake Guentzel .40 1.00
194 Brayden Schenn .25 .60
195 Ryan Ellis .20 .50
196 Zach Hyman .40 1.00
197 Roman Josi .25 .60
198 Phil Kessel .25 .60
199 Dylan Strome .30 .75
200 Alex Ovechkin CL 1.00 2.50
201 Connor McDavid SP 2.50 6.00
202 Leon Draisaitl SP 1.50 4.00
203 Sidney Crosby SP 2.00 5.00
204 Auston Matthews SP 2.00 5.00
205 Jonathan Toews SP .75 2.00
206 Patrick Kane SP 1.00 2.50
207 Carey Price SP 1.00 2.50
208 Ryan O'Reilly SP .50 1.25
209 John Tavares SP .75 2.00
210 Evgeni Malkin SP 1.00 2.50
211 Elias Pettersson SP .75 2.00
212 Marc-Andre Fleury SP 1.00 2.50
213 Brad Marchand SP 1.00 2.50
214 Jack Eichel SP .75 2.00
215 Quinn Hughes SP 1.25 3.00
216 Cale Makar SP 1.25 3.00
217 Artemi Panarin SP 1.00 2.50
218 Claude Giroux SP .50 1.25
219 Steven Stamkos SP 1.00 2.50
220 Jansen Harkins SP RC 1.50 4.00
221 Michael DiPietro SP RC 2.50 6.00
222 Nicolas Beaudin SP RC 2.00 5.00
223 Brandon Hagel SP RC 2.50 6.00
224 Nikolai Knyzhov SP RC 1.50 4.00
225 Morgan Geekie SP RC 2.00 5.00
226 Jani Hakanpaa SP RC 1.25 3.00
227 Mikey Anderson SP RC 2.00 5.00
228 Martin Kaut SP RC 2.00 5.00
229 Keegan Kolesar SP RC 1.50 4.00
230 Gage Quinney SP RC 1.25 3.00
231 Egor Korshkov SP RC 1.25 3.00
232 Alexander True SP RC 1.50 4.00
233 Anthony Angello SP RC 1.50 4.00
234 Josh Norris SP RC 3.00 8.00
235 Gabe Vilardi SP RC 3.00 8.00
236 Gustav Lindstrom SP RC 1.50 4.00
237 Alexander Yelesin SP RC 1.50 4.00
238 Jonas Johansson SP RC 2.00 5.00
239 Calvin Thurkauf SP RC 1.50 4.00
240 Lucas Carlsson SP RC 1.50 4.00
241 Andrei Chibisov SP RC 1.25 3.00
242 Matiss Kivlenieks SP RC 2.50 6.00
243 Timothy Liljegren SP RC 2.00 5.00
244 Kieffer Bellows SP RC 1.50 4.00
245 Maxim Letunov SP RC 1.50 4.00
246 Jake Evans SP RC 2.00 5.00
247 Tyler Benson SP RC 2.00 5.00
248 Liam Foudy SP RC 2.00 5.00
249 Jason Robertson SP RC 5.00 12.00
250 Connor McDavid SP CL 2.50 6.00

2020-21 Upper Deck MVP Gold Script

*GOLD: 1.5X TO 4X BASIC
*SP.GOLD: 2X TO 5X BASIC
*RC.GOLD: .75X TO 2X BASIC

2020-21 Upper Deck MVP Puzzle Back

*PUZZLE: 1X TO 2.5X BASIC

2020-21 Upper Deck MVP Silver Script

*SLVR: .75X TO 2X BASIC
*SP.SLVR: .75X TO 2X BASIC
*RC.SLVR: .6X TO 1.5X BASIC

2020-21 Upper Deck MVP Super Script

*SUPER: 4X TO 10X BASIC
*SP.SUPER: 3X TO 8X BASIC
*RC.SUPER: 1.25X TO 3X BASIC
23 Brock Nelson 5.00 12.00
33 Dougie Hamilton 4.00 10.00
36 Ryan Getzlaf 6.00 15.00
38 Danny DeKeyser 5.00 12.00
57 Filip Zadina 6.00 15.00
62 Carter Hart 12.00 30.00
74 Philipp Grubauer 6.00 15.00
87 Jack Hughes 12.00 30.00
110 Alex Pietrangelo 8.00 20.00
113 Jakub Voracek 4.00 10.00
118 Torey Krug 4.00 10.00
128 Mike Smith 12.00 30.00
143 Zach Parise 5.00 12.00
149 Pekka Rinne 6.00 15.00
158 Taylor Hall 10.00 25.00
161 Sebastian Aho 6.00 15.00
179 Tristan Jarry 8.00 20.00
180 Victor Olofsson 12.00 30.00
185 Nick Suzuki 12.00 30.00
193 Jake Guentzel 6.00 15.00
208 Ryan O'Reilly 8.00 20.00
216 Cale Makar 30.00 80.00
229 Keegan Kolesar 12.00 30.00
234 Josh Norris 12.00 30.00
236 Gustav Lindstrom 8.00 20.00

2020-21 Upper Deck MVP '20 NHL Draft Pick #1

*GOLD: 1.5X TO 4X BASIC
DP1 Alexis Lafreniere 100.00 250.00

2020-21 Upper Deck MVP 20th Anniversary Third Star

*2ND/100: 2X TO 5X BASIC
*1ST/25: 4X TO 10X BASIC
1 Connor McDavid 2.50 6.00
2 Sidney Crosby 2.00 5.00
3 Nathan MacKinnon 2.00 5.00
4 Jack Eichel .75 2.00
5 Mark Scheifele .75 2.00
6 Leon Draisaitl 1.50 4.00
7 Jonathan Toews .75 2.00
8 Auston Matthews 2.00 5.00
9 Brad Marchand 1.00 2.50
10 Henrik Lundqvist 1.25 3.00
11 Brent Burns .50 1.25
12 Artemi Panarin 1.00 2.50
13 Victor Hedman .60 1.50
14 Elias Pettersson .75 2.00
15 Mitch Marner .75 2.00
16 Carey Price 1.00 2.50
17 Shea Weber .50 1.25
18 Rasmus Dahlin .60 1.50
19 Steven Stamkos 1.00 2.50
20 Evgeni Malkin 1.00 2.50
21 Johnny Gaudreau .75 2.00
22 Marc-Andre Fleury 1.00 2.50
23 Mikko Rantanen 1.25 3.00
24 Carter Hart .50 1.25
25 P.K. Subban .60 1.50
26 Dylan Larkin .60 1.50
27 Tyler Seguin .60 1.50
28 Ryan Getzlaf .50 1.25
29 Claude Giroux .50 1.25
30 David Pastrnak 1.25 3.00
31 Sebastian Aho .75 2.00
32 Sergei Bobrovsky .75 2.00
33 Mark Stone .60 1.50
34 John Carlson .50 1.25
35 Morgan Rielly .50 1.25
36 Brayden Point .60 1.50
37 Quinn Hughes 1.25 3.00
38 Logan Couture .60 1.50
39 Blake Wheeler .50 1.25
40 John Tavares .75 2.00
41 Taylor Hall .50 1.25
42 Sean Monahan .30 .75
43 Vladimir Tarasenko .60 1.50
44 Torey Krug .40 1.00
45 Mark Giordano .50 1.25
46 Nico Hischier .75 2.00
47 Drew Doughty .60 1.50
48 Tyler Bertuzzi .40 1.00
49 Tristan Jarry .50 1.25
50 Jordan Binnington .75 2.00
51 Anthony Duclair .40 1.00
52 Mathew Barzal .60 1.50
53 Zack Kassian .30 .75
54 Ben Bishop .40 1.00
55 Tuukka Rask .60 1.50
56 Viktor Arvidsson .30 .75
57 Seth Jones .50 1.25
58 Anze Kopitar .75 2.00
59 Jaccob Slavin .40 1.00
60 Travis Konecny .50 1.25
61 Braden Holtby .60 1.50
62 Zach Parise .50 1.25
63 Sam Reinhart 1.00 2.50
64 Brayden Schenn .50 1.25
65 Tyler Benson .60 1.50
66 Liam Foudy .60 1.50
67 Nick Suzuki 1.00 2.50
68 Mika Zibanejad .60 1.50
69 Martin Kaut .60 1.50
70 Josh Norris 1.00 2.50
71 Jonathan Huberdeau .60 1.50
72 Jason Robertson 1.50 4.00
73 Patrice Bergeron .60 1.50
74 Matthew Tkachuk 1.00 2.50
75 Jamie Benn .50 1.25
76 Andreas Athanasiou .40 1.00
77 Keith Yandle .30 .75
78 Matt Duchene .50 1.25
79 Andrei Vasilevskiy .75 2.00
80 Timothy Liljegren .60 1.50
81 Chris Kreider .60 1.50
82 Ryan Nugent-Hopkins .60 1.50
83 Max Pacioretty .50 1.25
84 Cale Makar 1.25 3.00
85 Roman Josi .50 1.25
86 Alex DeBrincat .60 1.50
87 T.J. Oshie .50 1.25
88 Kris Letang .60 1.50
89 Alex Pietrangelo .40 1.00
90 Erik Gustafsson .30 .75
91 Nicklas Backstrom .50 1.25
92 Jake Guentzel .75 2.00
93 Jacob Markstrom .50 1.25
94 Oliver Ekman-Larsson .50 1.25
95 Aleksander Barkov .75 2.00
96 Patrick Kane 1.00 2.50
97 Gabe Vilardi 1.00 2.50
98 Nikita Kucherov 1.00 2.50
99 Ryan O'Reilly .50 1.25
100 Alex Ovechkin 2.00 5.00

2020-21 Upper Deck MVP All Star

AS1 Jack Eichel 5.00 12.00
AS2 David Pastrnak 8.00 20.00
AS3 Jordan Binnington 5.00 12.00
AS4 John Carlson 3.00 8.00
AS5 Travis Konecny 3.00 8.00
AS6 Nico Hischier 5.00 12.00
AS7 Kris Letang 4.00 10.00
AS8 Patrick Kane 6.00 15.00

2020-21 Upper Deck MVP Autographs

223 Brandon Hagel 12.00 30.00
225 Morgan Geekie 10.00 25.00
227 Mikey Anderson 10.00 25.00
230 Gage Quinney 6.00 15.00
231 Egor Korshkov 6.00 15.00
235 Gabe Vilardi 15.00 40.00
240 Lucas Carlsson 8.00 20.00
243 Timothy Liljegren 10.00 25.00
244 Kieffer Bellows 8.00 20.00
245 Maxim Letunov 8.00 20.00
246 Jake Evans 10.00 25.00
247 Tyler Benson 10.00 25.00
248 Liam Foudy 10.00 25.00
249 Jason Robertson 25.00 60.00

2020-21 Upper Deck MVP Colors and Contours

1 Connor McDavid 10.00 25.00
2 Sidney Crosby 8.00 20.00
3 Nathan MacKinnon 8.00 20.00
4 Jack Eichel 3.00 8.00
5 Mark Scheifele 3.00 8.00
6 Leon Draisaitl 6.00 15.00
7 Jonathan Toews 3.00 8.00
8 Auston Matthews 8.00 20.00
9 Brad Marchand 4.00 10.00
10 Henrik Lundqvist 5.00 12.00
11 Brent Burns 2.00 5.00
12 Artemi Panarin 4.00 10.00
13 Victor Hedman 2.50 6.00
14 Elias Pettersson 3.00 8.00
15 Mitch Marner 3.00 8.00
16 Carey Price 4.00 10.00
17 Shea Weber 2.00 5.00
18 Rasmus Dahlin 2.50 6.00
19 Steven Stamkos 4.00 10.00
20 Evgeni Malkin 4.00 10.00
21 Johnny Gaudreau 3.00 8.00
22 Marc-Andre Fleury 4.00 10.00
23 Mikko Rantanen 5.00 12.00
24 Carter Hart 2.00 5.00
25 P.K. Subban 2.50 6.00
26 Dylan Larkin 2.50 6.00
27 Tyler Seguin 2.50 6.00
28 Ryan Getzlaf 2.00 5.00
29 Claude Giroux 2.00 5.00
30 David Pastrnak 5.00 12.00
31 Sebastian Aho 3.00 8.00
32 Sergei Bobrovsky 3.00 8.00
33 Mark Stone 2.50 6.00
34 John Carlson 2.00 5.00
35 Morgan Rielly 2.00 5.00
36 Brayden Point 2.50 6.00
37 Quinn Hughes 5.00 12.00
38 Logan Couture 2.50 6.00
39 Blake Wheeler 2.00 5.00
40 John Tavares 3.00 8.00
41 Taylor Hall 2.00 5.00

42 Sean Monahan 1.25 3.00
43 Vladimir Tarasenko 2.50 6.00
44 Torey Krug 1.50 4.00
45 Mark Giordano 2.00 5.00
46 Nico Hischier 3.00 8.00
47 Drew Doughty 2.50 6.00
48 Tyler Bertuzzi 1.50 4.00
49 Tristan Jarry 2.00 5.00
50 Jordan Binnington 3.00 8.00
51 Anthony Duclair 1.50 4.00
52 Mathew Barzal 2.50 6.00
53 Zack Kassian 1.25 3.00
54 Ben Bishop 1.50 4.00
55 Tuukka Rask 2.50 6.00
56 Viktor Arvidsson 1.25 3.00
57 Seth Jones 2.00 5.00
58 Anze Kopitar 3.00 8.00
59 Jaccob Slavin 1.50 4.00
60 Travis Konecny 2.00 5.00
61 Braden Holtby 2.50 6.00
62 Zach Parise 2.00 5.00
63 Sam Reinhart 4.00 10.00
64 Brayden Schenn 2.00 5.00
65 Tyler Benson 2.50 6.00
66 Liam Foudy 2.50 6.00
67 Nick Suzuki 4.00 10.00
68 Mika Zibanejad 2.50 6.00
69 Martin Kaut 3.00 8.00
70 Josh Norris 4.00 10.00
71 Jonathan Huberdeau 2.50 6.00
72 Jason Robertson 6.00 15.00
73 Patrice Bergeron 2.50 6.00
74 Matthew Tkachuk 4.00 10.00
75 Jamie Benn 2.00 5.00
76 Andreas Athanasiou 1.50 4.00
77 Keith Yandle 1.25 3.00
78 Matt Duchene 2.00 5.00
79 Andrei Vasilevskiy 3.00 8.00
80 Timothy Liljegren 2.50 6.00
81 Chris Kreider 2.50 6.00
82 Ryan Nugent-Hopkins 2.50 6.00
83 Max Pacioretty 2.00 5.00
84 Cale Makar 5.00 12.00
85 Roman Josi 2.00 5.00
86 Alex DeBrincat 2.50 6.00
87 T.J. Oshie 2.00 5.00
88 Kris Letang 2.50 6.00
89 Alex Pietrangelo 1.50 4.00
90 Erik Gustafsson 1.25 3.00
91 Nicklas Backstrom 2.00 5.00
92 Jake Guentzel 3.00 8.00
93 Jacob Markstrom 2.00 5.00
94 Oliver Ekman-Larsson 2.00 5.00
95 Aleksander Barkov 3.00 8.00
96 Patrick Kane 4.00 10.00
97 Gabe Vilardi 4.00 10.00
98 Nikita Kucherov 4.00 10.00
99 Ryan O'Reilly 2.00 5.00
100 Alex Ovechkin 8.00 20.00

2020-21 Upper Deck MVP Global Series Czech Republic

GSC1 Patrick Kane 10.00 25.00
GSC2 Jonathan Toews 8.00 20.00
GSC4 Travis Konecny 5.00 12.00
GSC5 Sean Couturier 4.00 10.00
GSC6 Claude Giroux 10.00 25.00

2020-21 Upper Deck MVP Global Series Sweden

GSS1 Nikita Kucherov 4.00 10.00
GSS2 Victor Hedman 4.00 10.00
GSS3 Steven Stamkos 4.00 10.00
GSS4 Victor Olofsson 10.00 25.00
GSS5 Jack Eichel 10.00 25.00

2020-21 Upper Deck MVP Heritage Classic

HC1 Patrik Laine 4.00 10.00
HC2 Mark Scheifele 5.00 12.00
HC3 Blake Wheeler 3.00 8.00
HC4 Johnny Gaudreau 8.00 20.00
HC5 Sean Monahan 6.00 15.00
HC6 Mark Giordano 6.00 15.00

2020-21 Upper Deck MVP High Speed

HS1 Connor McDavid 2.00 5.00
HS2 Brayden Point .50 1.25
HS3 Mathew Barzal .50 1.25
HS4 Elias Pettersson .60 1.50
HS5 Jack Eichel .60 1.50
HS6 Chris Kreider .50 1.25
HS7 Nathan MacKinnon 1.50 4.00
HS8 Quinn Hughes 1.00 2.50
HS9 Anthony Duclair .30 .75
HS10 Travis Konecny .40 1.00
HS11 Andreas Athanasiou .30 .75
HS12 Taylor Hall .40 1.00
HS13 Dylan Larkin .50 1.25
HS14 Jonathan Drouin .30 .75
HS15 Jake Virtanen .40 1.00
HS16 Miro Heiskanen .50 1.25
HS17 Clayton Keller .50 1.25
HS18 Cam Atkinson .40 1.00
HS19 Kasperi Kapanen .30 .75
HS20 Phil Kessel .40 1.00

2020-21 Upper Deck MVP Mirror Mirror

*VAR: .75X TO 2X BASIC
MM1 Connor McDavid 1.50 4.00
MM2 Nathan MacKinnon 1.25 3.00
MM3 Brent Burns .30 .75
MM4 Sidney Crosby 1.25 3.00
MM5 Patrick Kane .60 1.50
MM6 Nikita Kucherov .60 1.50
MM7 Aleksander Barkov .50 1.25
MM8 Alex Ovechkin 1.25 3.00
MM9 Brad Marchand .60 1.50
MM10 Johnny Gaudreau .50 1.25

2020-21 Upper Deck MVP Net Crashers

NC1 John Tavares .75 2.00
NC2 Nathan MacKinnon 2.00 5.00
NC3 Patrice Bergeron .60 1.50
NC4 Patrick Kane 1.00 2.50
NC5 Johnny Gaudreau .75 2.00
NC6 Sidney Crosby 2.00 5.00
NC7 Jonathan Toews .75 2.00
NC8 Taylor Hall .50 1.25
NC9 Jonathan Drouin .40 1.00
NC10 Elias Pettersson .75 2.00

2020-21 Upper Deck MVP Postseason

PS1 Eric Staal 4.00 10.00
PS2 Ryan Getzlaf 4.00 10.00
PS3 Sidney Crosby 30.00 80.00
PS4 Evgeni Malkin 8.00 20.00
PS5 Jonathan Toews 6.00 15.00
PS6 Zdeno Chara 4.00 10.00
PS7 Jonathan Quick 8.00 20.00
PS8 Patrick Kane 8.00 20.00

2020-21 Upper Deck MVP Rookie Redemption

R1 Atlantic Divison 30.00 80.00
R2 Metropolitan Division 50.00 125.00
R3 Central Division 20.00 50.00
R4 Pacific Division 50.00 125.00

2020-21 Upper Deck MVP Winter Classic

WC1 Tyler Seguin 10.00 25.00
WC2 Alexander Radulov 10.00 25.00
WC3 Ben Bishop 6.00 15.00
WC4 Roman Josi 8.00 20.00
WC5 Filip Forsberg 12.00 30.00
WC6 Pekka Rinne 8.00 20.00

2021-22 Upper Deck MVP

1 Alexis Lafreniere .40 1.00
2 Mitch Marner .40 1.00
3 Seth Jones .25 .60
4 Miro Heiskanen .30 .75
5 Mark Giordano .25 .60
6 Brock Boeser .30 .75
7 Alex Pietrangelo .20 .50
8 Alex Ovechkin 1.00 2.50
9 Clayton Keller .30 .75
10 Brayden Schenn .25 .60
11 Anze Kopitar .40 1.00
12 Josh Bailey .20 .50
13 Mathew Barzal .30 .75
14 Sean Couturier .20 .50
15 Ryan Getzlaf .25 .60
16 Ryan Strome .25 .60
17 Bryan Rust .25 .60
18 Tim Stutzle .30 .75
19 Matthew Tkachuk .50 1.25
20 Chris Kreider .30 .75
21 Gabriel Landeskog .30 .75
22 Rasmus Dahlin .30 .75
23 Jakob Chychrun .25 .60
24 Dylan Cozens .25 .60
25 James van Riemsdyk .20 .50
26 Blake Wheeler .25 .60
27 Alexander Romanov .20 .50
28 Dylan Larkin .30 .75
29 Mackenzie Blackwood .25 .60
30 Ilya Sorokin .40 1.00
31 Igor Shesterkin .50 1.25
32 Kevin Lankinen .25 .60
33 Viktor Arvidsson .15 .40
34 Denis Gurianov .30 .75
35 Gabe Vilardi .25 .60
36 Mats Zuccarello .25 .60
37 Patrice Bergeron .30 .75
38 Maxime Comtois .20 .50
39 Logan Couture .30 .75
40 John Gibson .25 .60
41 Kevin Fiala .20 .50
42 Jeff Petry .25 .60
43 Quinn Hughes .60 1.50
44 Sebastian Aho .40 1.00
45 Tyson Barrie .15 .40
46 John Klingberg .25 .60
47 Torey Krug .20 .50
48 Tomas Hertl .25 .60
49 Samuel Girard .15 .40
50 Jordan Binnington .40 1.00
51 Joel Eriksson Ek .20 .50
52 Jeff Carter .20 .50
53 Bo Horvat .30 .75
54 Elias Lindholm .25 .60
55 Jack Eichel .40 1.00
56 Marc-Andre Fleury .50 1.25
57 David Perron .20 .50
58 Kris Letang .30 .75
59 Ondrej Palat .20 .50
60 Nick Ritchie .15 .40
61 Mark Stone .30 .75
62 Kevin Labanc .15 .40
63 Brad Marchand .50 1.25
64 Oliver Bjorkstrand .20 .50
65 Erik Karlsson .30 .75
66 David Krejci .25 .60
67 Max Pacioretty .25 .60
68 Victor Olofsson .25 .60
69 Travis Konecny .25 .60
70 Patric Hornqvist .15 .40
71 William Karlsson .30 .75
72 Thomas Chabot .25 .60
73 Tyler Toffoli .25 .60
74 John Carlson .25 .60
75 Sergei Bobrovsky .40 1.00
76 P.K. Subban .30 .75
77 Victor Hedman .30 .75
78 Evander Kane .25 .60
79 Carter Hart .25 .60
80 Alex Killorn .15 .40
81 Kyle Connor .40 1.00
82 Evgeny Kuznetsov .30 .75
83 Pavel Buchnevich .20 .50
84 Joel Farabee .25 .60
85 Aaron Ekblad .30 .75
86 Teuvo Teravainen .25 .60
87 Nick Suzuki .50 1.25
88 Brent Burns .25 .60
89 Nazem Kadri .30 .75
90 Drew Doughty .30 .75
91 Philipp Grubauer .25 .60
92 Ryan Johansen .20 .50
93 Mika Zibanejad .30 .75
94 Cam Fowler .25 .60
95 Juuse Saros .30 .75
96 Mikko Rantanen .60 1.50
97 Elias Pettersson .40 1.00
98 Jack Roslovic .15 .40
99 Adrian Kempe .25 .60
100 Alex Ovechkin CL 1.00 2.50
101 Jordan Staal .20 .50
102 Max Domi .25 .60
103 Cam Atkinson .25 .60
104 MacKenzie Weegar .20 .50
105 Devon Toews .20 .50
106 Shea Weber .25 .60
107 Brady Tkachuk .40 1.00
108 Joe Pavelski .30 .75
109 Ivan Provorov .20 .50
110 Yanni Gourde .20 .50
111 Zach Parise .25 .60
112 Filip Zadina .20 .50
113 Nico Hischier .40 1.00
114 Jamie Benn .25 .60
115 Rasmus Andersson .20 .50
116 Vincent Trocheck .25 .60
117 Marcus Foligno .20 .50
118 Pierre-Luc Dubois .20 .50
119 Nicklas Backstrom .25 .60
120 Taylor Hall .25 .60
121 Nino Niederreiter .15 .40
122 Roope Hintz .30 .75
123 Sean Monahan .15 .40
124 Matt Dumba .20 .50
125 Darnell Nurse .20 .50
126 Drake Batherson .25 .60
127 Shea Theodore .30 .75
128 Claude Giroux .25 .60
129 Conor Garland .20 .50
130 Connor Brown .20 .50
131 Brock Nelson .25 .60
132 Sam Reinhart .50 1.25
133 Jakob Silfverberg .15 .40
134 Dustin Brown .25 .60
135 Carter Verhaeghe .25 .60
136 Artemi Panarin .50 1.25
137 Andrei Svechnikov .30 .75
138 Mike Hoffman .15 .40
139 Timo Meier .25 .60
140 Josh Anderson .20 .50
141 Christian Dvorak .20 .50
142 Phillip Danault .25 .60
143 Tom Wilson .25 .60
144 Nikolaj Ehlers .25 .60
145 Jordan Eberle .25 .60
146 Yegor Sharangovich .25 .60
147 Nick Schmaltz .20 .50
148 Nils Hoglander .20 .50
149 Anthony Cirelli .20 .50
150 Mikhail Sergachev .20 .50
151 Robby Fabbri .15 .40
152 Alex Tuch .25 .60
153 Tristan Jarry .25 .60
154 Miles Wood .15 .40
155 Connor Hellebuyck .50 1.25
156 Jacob Markstrom .25 .60
157 Thatcher Demko .30 .75
158 Pius Suter .20 .50
159 Roman Josi .25 .60
160 Evgeni Malkin .50 1.25
161 Jonathan Marchessault .30 .75
162 Pavel Zacha .20 .50
163 Evgenii Dadonov .15 .40
164 Adam Henrique .20 .50
165 Filip Hronek .15 .40
166 Dougie Hamilton .20 .50
167 Rickard Rakell .20 .50
168 Zach Hyman .40 1.00
169 J.T. Miller .30 .75
170 Kevin Hayes .20 .50
171 Jakub Voracek .20 .50
172 Justin Faulk .20 .50
173 Charlie McAvoy .30 .75
174 Martin Necas .40 1.00
175 Anders Lee .20 .50
176 Ty Smith .25 .60
177 Kirby Dach .25 .60
178 T.J. Oshie .25 .60
179 Vitek Vanecek .25 .60
180 Josh Norris .25 .60
181 Phil Kessel .25 .60
182 Tuukka Rask .30 .75
183 Johnny Gaudreau .40 1.00
184 Filip Forsberg .40 1.00
185 Anthony Mantha .20 .50
186 Brayden Point .30 .75
187 Jonathan Huberdeau .30 .75
188 William Nylander .50 1.25
189 Jean-Gabriel Pageau .15 .40
190 Adam Fox .30 .75
191 Vladimir Tarasenko .30 .75
192 Patrik Laine .30 .75
193 Ryan Nugent-Hopkins .30 .75
194 Morgan Rielly .25 .60
195 Andre Burakovsky .15 .40
196 David Pastrnak .60 1.50
197 Dominik Kubalik .25 .60
198 Zach Werenski .40 1.00
199 John Tavares .40 1.00
200 Artemi Panarin CL .50 1.25
201 Mark Scheifele SP .75 2.00
202 Carey Price SP 1.00 2.50
203 Jake Guentzel SP .75 2.00
204 Aleksander Barkov SP .75 2.00
205 Andrei Vasilevskiy SP .75 2.00
206 John Gibson SP .50 1.25
207 Jack Hughes SP 1.25 3.00
208 Cale Makar SP 1.25 3.00
209 Jason Robertson SP .75 2.00
210 Leon Draisaitl SP 1.50 4.00
211 Alex DeBrincat SP .60 1.50
212 Ryan O'Reilly SP .50 1.25
213 Miro Heiskanen SP .60 1.50
214 Steven Stamkos SP 1.00 2.50
215 Auston Matthews SP 2.00 5.00
216 Nathan MacKinnon SP 2.00 5.00
217 Patrick Kane SP 1.00 2.50
218 Kirill Kaprizov SP 1.50 4.00
219 Sidney Crosby SP 2.00 5.00
220 Connor McDavid SP 2.50 6.00
221 Calen Addison SP RC 1.50 4.00
222 Wyatt Kalynuk SP RC 1.50 4.00
223 Jeremy Davies SP RC 1.50 4.00
224 Jacob Bryson SP RC 1.50 4.00
225 Zac Jones SP RC 2.00 5.00
226 Kole Lind SP RC 2.00 5.00
227 Ross Colton SP RC 2.00 5.00
228 Garrett Pilon SP RC 2.00 5.00
229 Veini Vehvilainen SP RC 1.50 4.00
230 David Farrance SP RC 1.50 4.00
231 Wade Allison SP RC 1.50 4.00
232 Jacob Bernard-Docker SP RC 1.50 4.00
233 Cameron York SP RC 1.50 4.00
234 Alex Newhook SP RC 2.50 6.00
235 Jeremy Swayman SP RC 6.00 15.00
236 Shane Pinto SP RC 2.50 6.00
237 Radim Zohorna SP RC 1.50 4.00
238 Jan Jenik SP RC 2.00 5.00
239 Tyce Thompson SP RC 1.50 4.00
240 Joseph Veleno SP RC 1.50 4.00
241 Ukko-Pekka Luukkonen SP RC 2.50 6.00
242 Spencer Knight SP RC 3.00 8.00
243 Cole Caufield SP RC 8.00 20.00
244 Quinton Byfield SP RC 4.00 10.00
245 Jamie Drysdale SP RC 2.50 6.00
246 Alex Barre-Boulet SP RC 1.50 4.00
247 Rasmus Kupari SP RC 1.50 4.00
248 Grigori Denisenko SP RC 2.00 5.00
249 Trevor Zegras SP RC 3.00 8.00
250 Trevor Zegras SP CL 3.00 8.00
251 Moritz Seider RC 8.00 20.00
252 Lucas Raymond RC 8.00 20.00
253 Anton Lundell RC 3.00 8.00
254 Boris Katchouk RC 1.25 3.00
255 Taylor Raddysh RC 2.50 6.00
256 Michael Pezzetta RC 1.50 4.00
257 Kirill Semyonov RC 1.50 4.00
258 Lassi Thomson RC 1.50 4.00
259 Alexander Holtz RC 2.50 6.00
260 Cole Sillinger RC 2.50 6.00
261 Nico Daws RC 2.50 6.00
262 Nils Lundkvist RC 1.50 4.00
263 Dawson Mercer RC 4.00 10.00
264 Yegor Chinakhov RC 2.50 6.00
265 Hendrix Lapierre RC 1.50 4.00
266 Seth Jarvis RC 4.00 10.00
267 Adam Beckman RC 1.50 4.00
268 Riley Tufte RC 1.50 4.00
269 Karel Vejmelka RC 2.00 5.00
270 Philip Tomasino RC 2.00 5.00
271 Cole Perfetti RC 3.00 8.00
272 Jake Neighbours RC 3.00 8.00
273 Brandon Duhaime RC 1.50 4.00
274 Scott Perunovich RC 1.50 4.00
275 Mason McTavish RC 3.00 8.00
276 William Eklund RC 4.00 10.00
277 Vladimir Tkachev RC 1.50 4.00
278 Jake Leschyshyn RC 1.50 4.00
279 Benoit-Olivier Groulx RC 1.50 4.00
280 Jonathan Dahlen RC 1.50 4.00
281 Ryan Merkley RC 2.00 5.00
282 Vasily Podkolzin RC 2.00 5.00

2021-22 Upper Deck MVP Factory Set

1 Alexis Lafreniere .40 1.00
2 Mitch Marner .40 1.00
3 Seth Jones .25 .60
4 Miro Heiskanen .30 .75
5 Mark Giordano .25 .60
6 Brock Boeser .30 .75
7 Alex Pietrangelo .20 .50
8 Alex Ovechkin 1.00 2.50
9 Clayton Keller .30 .75
10 Brayden Schenn .25 .60
11 Anze Kopitar .40 1.00
12 Josh Bailey .20 .50
13 Mathew Barzal .30 .75
14 Sean Couturier .20 .50
15 Ryan Getzlaf .25 .60
16 Ryan Strome .25 .60
17 Bryan Rust .25 .60
18 Tim Stutzle .30 .75
19 Matthew Tkachuk .50 1.25
20 Chris Kreider .30 .75
21 Gabriel Landeskog .30 .75
22 Rasmus Dahlin .30 .75
23 Jakob Chychrun .25 .60
24 Dylan Cozens .25 .60
25 James van Riemsdyk .20 .50
26 Blake Wheeler .25 .60
27 Alexander Romanov .20 .50
28 Dylan Larkin .30 .75
29 Mackenzie Blackwood .25 .60
30 Ilya Sorokin .40 1.00
31 Igor Shesterkin .50 1.25
32 Kevin Lankinen .25 .60
33 Viktor Arvidsson .15 .40
34 Denis Gurianov .30 .75
35 Gabe Vilardi .25 .60
36 Mats Zuccarello .25 .60
37 Patrice Bergeron .30 .75
38 Maxime Comtois .20 .50
39 Logan Couture .30 .75
40 John Gibson .25 .60
41 Kevin Fiala .20 .50
42 Jeff Petry .25 .60
43 Quinn Hughes .60 1.50
44 Sebastian Aho .40 1.00
45 Tyson Barrie .15 .40
46 John Klingberg .25 .60
47 Torey Krug .20 .50
48 Tomas Hertl .25 .60
49 Samuel Girard .15 .40
50 Jordan Binnington .40 1.00
51 Joel Eriksson Ek .20 .50
52 Jeff Carter .20 .50
53 Bo Horvat .30 .75
54 Elias Lindholm .25 .60
55 Jack Eichel .40 1.00
56 Marc-Andre Fleury .50 1.25
57 David Perron .20 .50
58 Kris Letang .30 .75
59 Ondrej Palat .20 .50
60 Nick Ritchie .15 .40
61 Mark Stone .30 .75
62 Kevin Labanc .15 .40
63 Brad Marchand .50 1.25
64 Oliver Bjorkstrand .20 .50
65 Erik Karlsson .30 .75
66 David Krejci .25 .60
67 Max Pacioretty .25 .60
68 Victor Olofsson .25 .60
69 Travis Konecny .25 .60
70 Patric Hornqvist .15 .40
71 William Karlsson .30 .75
72 Thomas Chabot .25 .60
73 Tyler Toffoli .25 .60
74 John Carlson .25 .60
75 Sergei Bobrovsky .40 1.00
76 P.K. Subban .30 .75
77 Victor Hedman .30 .75
78 Evander Kane .25 .60
79 Carter Hart .25 .60
80 Alex Killorn .15 .40
81 Kyle Connor .40 1.00
82 Evgeny Kuznetsov .30 .75
83 Pavel Buchnevich .20 .50
84 Joel Farabee .25 .60
85 Aaron Ekblad .30 .75
86 Teuvo Teravainen .25 .60
87 Nick Suzuki .50 1.25
88 Brent Burns .25 .60
89 Nazem Kadri .30 .75
90 Drew Doughty .30 .75
91 Philipp Grubauer .25 .60
92 Ryan Johansen .20 .50
93 Mika Zibanejad .30 .75
94 Cam Fowler .25 .60
95 Juuse Saros .30 .75
96 Mikko Rantanen .60 1.50
97 Elias Pettersson .40 1.00
98 Jack Roslovic .15 .40
99 Adrian Kempe .25 .60
100 Alex Ovechkin CL 1.00 2.50
101 Jordan Staal .20 .50
102 Max Domi .25 .60
103 Cam Atkinson .25 .60
104 MacKenzie Weegar .20 .50
105 Devon Toews .20 .50
106 Shea Weber .25 .60
107 Brady Tkachuk .40 1.00
108 Joe Pavelski .30 .75
109 Ivan Provorov .20 .50
110 Yanni Gourde .20 .50
111 Zach Parise .25 .60
112 Filip Zadina .20 .50
113 Nico Hischier .40 1.00
114 Jamie Benn .25 .60
115 Rasmus Andersson .20 .50
116 Vincent Trocheck .25 .60
117 Marcus Foligno .20 .50
118 Pierre-Luc Dubois .20 .50
119 Nicklas Backstrom .25 .60
120 Taylor Hall .25 .60
121 Nino Niederreiter .15 .40
122 Roope Hintz .30 .75
123 Sean Monahan .15 .40
124 Matt Dumba .20 .50
125 Darnell Nurse .20 .50
126 Drake Batherson .25 .60
127 Shea Theodore .30 .75
128 Claude Giroux .25 .60
129 Conor Garland .20 .50
130 Connor Brown .20 .50
131 Brock Nelson .25 .60
132 Sam Reinhart .50 1.25
133 Jakob Silfverberg .15 .40
134 Dustin Brown .25 .60
135 Carter Verhaeghe .25 .60
136 Artemi Panarin .50 1.25
137 Andrei Svechnikov .30 .75
138 Mike Hoffman .15 .40
139 Timo Meier .25 .60
140 Josh Anderson .20 .50
141 Christian Dvorak .20 .50
142 Phillip Danault .25 .60
143 Tom Wilson .25 .60
144 Nikolaj Ehlers .25 .60
145 Jordan Eberle .25 .60
146 Yegor Sharangovich .25 .60
147 Nick Schmaltz .20 .50
148 Nils Hoglander .20 .50
149 Anthony Cirelli .20 .50
150 Mikhail Sergachev .20 .50
151 Robby Fabbri .15 .40
152 Alex Tuch .25 .60
153 Tristan Jarry .25 .60
154 Miles Wood .15 .40
155 Connor Hellebuyck .50 1.25
156 Jacob Markstrom .25 .60
157 Thatcher Demko .30 .75
158 Pius Suter .20 .50
159 Roman Josi .25 .60
160 Evgeni Malkin .50 1.25
161 Jonathan Marchessault .30 .75
162 Pavel Zacha .20 .50
163 Evgenii Dadonov .15 .40
164 Adam Henrique .20 .50
165 Filip Hronek .15 .40
166 Dougie Hamilton .20 .50
167 Rickard Rakell .20 .50
168 Zach Hyman .40 1.00
169 J.T. Miller .30 .75
170 Kevin Hayes .20 .50
171 Jakub Voracek .20 .50
172 Justin Faulk .20 .50
173 Charlie McAvoy .30 .75
174 Martin Necas .40 1.00
175 Anders Lee .20 .50
176 Ty Smith .25 .60
177 Kirby Dach .25 .60
178 T.J. Oshie .25 .60
179 Vitek Vanecek .25 .60
180 Josh Norris .25 .60
181 Phil Kessel .25 .60
182 Tuukka Rask .30 .75
183 Johnny Gaudreau .40 1.00
184 Filip Forsberg .40 1.00
185 Anthony Mantha .20 .50
186 Brayden Point .30 .75
187 Jonathan Huberdeau .30 .75
188 William Nylander .50 1.25
189 Jean-Gabriel Pageau .15 .40
190 Adam Fox .30 .75
191 Vladimir Tarasenko .30 .75
192 Patrik Laine .30 .75
193 Ryan Nugent-Hopkins .30 .75
194 Morgan Rielly .25 .60
195 Andre Burakovsky .15 .40
196 David Pastrnak .60 1.50
197 Dominik Kubalik .25 .60
198 Zach Werenski .40 1.00
199 John Tavares .40 1.00
200 Artemi Panarin CL .50 1.25
201 Mark Scheifele SP 2.50 6.00
202 Carey Price SP 3.00 8.00
203 Jake Guentzel SP 2.50 6.00
204 Aleksander Barkov SP 2.50 6.00
205 Andrei Vasilevskiy SP 2.50 6.00
206 John Gibson SP 1.50 4.00
207 Jack Hughes SP 4.00 10.00
208 Cale Makar SP 4.00 10.00
209 Jason Robertson SP 2.50 6.00
210 Leon Draisaitl SP 5.00 12.00
211 Alex DeBrincat SP 2.00 5.00
212 Ryan O'Reilly SP 1.50 4.00
213 Miro Heiskanen SP 2.00 5.00
214 Steven Stamkos SP 3.00 8.00
215 Auston Matthews SP 6.00 15.00
216 Nathan MacKinnon SP 6.00 15.00
217 Patrick Kane SP 3.00 8.00
218 Kirill Kaprizov SP 5.00 12.00
219 Sidney Crosby SP 6.00 15.00
220 Connor McDavid SP 8.00 20.00
221 Calen Addison SP 1.50 4.00
222 Wyatt Kalynuk SP 1.50 4.00
223 Jeremy Davies SP 1.50 4.00
224 Jacob Bryson SP 1.50 4.00
225 Zac Jones SP 2.00 5.00
226 Kole Lind SP 2.00 5.00
227 Ross Colton SP 2.00 5.00
228 Garrett Pilon SP 2.00 5.00
229 Veini Vehvilainen SP 1.50 4.00
230 David Farrance SP 1.50 4.00
231 Wade Allison SP 1.50 4.00
232 Jacob Bernard-Docker SP 1.50 4.00
233 Cameron York SP 1.50 4.00
234 Alex Newhook SP 2.50 6.00
235 Jeremy Swayman SP 5.00 12.00
236 Shane Pinto SP 2.50 6.00
237 Radim Zohorna SP 1.50 4.00
238 Jan Jenik SP 2.00 5.00
239 Tyce Thompson SP 1.50 4.00
240 Joseph Veleno SP 1.50 4.00
241 Ukko-Pekka Luukkonen SP 2.50 6.00
242 Spencer Knight SP 3.00 8.00
243 Cole Caufield SP 6.00 15.00
244 Quinton Byfield SP 4.00 10.00
245 Jamie Drysdale SP 2.50 6.00
246 Alex Barre-Boulet SP 1.50 4.00
247 Rasmus Kupari SP 1.50 4.00
248 Grigori Denisenko SP 2.00 5.00
249 Trevor Zegras SP 3.00 8.00
250 Trevor Zegras SP CL 3.00 8.00

2021-22 Upper Deck MVP Gold Script

*GOLD.SCRIPT: 2.5X TO 6X BASIC
*GOLD.SCRIPT.SP: 2.5X TO 6X BASIC
*GOLD.SCRIPT.RC: 1X TO 2.5X BASIC
243 Cole Caufield SP 30.00 80.00
244 Quinton Byfield SP 25.00 60.00
249 Trevor Zegras SP 40.00 100.00
250 Trevor Zegras SP CL 40.00 100.00

2021-22 Upper Deck MVP Silver Script

*SILVER: .75X TO 2X BASIC
*SILVER.SP: .75X TO 2X BASIC
*SILVER.RC: .6X TO 1.5X BASIC

2021-22 Upper Deck MVP Super Script

*SUPER: 4X TO 10X BASIC
*SUPER.SP: 4X TO 10X BASIC
*SUPER.RC: 1.5X TO 4X BASIC
243 Cole Caufield 80.00 200.00
244 Quinton Byfield 40.00 100.00
249 Trevor Zegras 80.00 200.00
250 Trevor Zegras CL 80.00 200.00

2021-22 Upper Deck MVP 20th Anniversary

COMMON CARD .60 1.50
SEMISTARS .75 2.00
UNLISTED STARS 1.00 2.50
1 Connor McDavid 5.00 12.00
2 Alex Ovechkin 4.00 10.00
3 Sidney Crosby 4.00 10.00
4 Nikita Kucherov 2.00 5.00
5 Auston Matthews 4.00 10.00
6 Patrick Kane 2.00 5.00
7 Nathan MacKinnon 4.00 10.00
8 Evgeni Malkin 2.00 5.00
9 Elias Pettersson 1.50 4.00
10 David Pastrnak 2.50 6.00
11 Leon Draisaitl 3.00 8.00
12 Steven Stamkos 2.00 5.00
13 Patrice Bergeron 1.25 3.00
14 Jack Hughes 2.50 6.00
15 Artemi Panarin 2.00 5.00
16 Erik Karlsson 1.25 3.00
17 Carter Hart 1.00 2.50
18 Carey Price 2.00 5.00
19 Sebastian Aho 1.50 4.00
20 Jason Robertson 1.50 4.00
21 Tuukka Rask 1.25 3.00
22 Mark Scheifele 1.50 4.00
23 John Gibson 1.00 2.50
24 Anze Kopitar 1.50 4.00
25 Tim Stutzle 1.25 3.00
26 Mark Stone 1.25 3.00
27 Andrei Vasilevskiy 1.50 4.00
28 Ryan O'Reilly 1.00 2.50
29 Brady Tkachuk 1.50 4.00
30 Kirill Kaprizov 3.00 8.00
31 Mathew Barzal 1.25 3.00
32 Brad Marchand 2.00 5.00
33 Mitch Marner 1.50 4.00
34 Brayden Point 1.25 3.00
35 Johnny Gaudreau 1.50 4.00
36 Dylan Larkin 1.25 3.00
37 Brent Burns 1.00 2.50
38 Vladimir Tarasenko 1.25 3.00
39 Alex DeBrincat 1.25 3.00
40 Devon Toews .75 2.00
41 Roman Josi 1.00 2.50
42 Jack Eichel 1.50 4.00
43 Brayden Schenn 1.00 2.50
44 Ryan Nugent-Hopkins 1.25 3.00
45 Mika Zibanejad 1.25 3.00
46 Max Domi 1.00 2.50
47 John Tavares 1.50 4.00
48 Sean Monahan .60 1.50
49 Tyler Toffoli 1.00 2.50
50 Jordan Binnington 1.50 4.00
51 Blake Wheeler 1.00 2.50
52 David Perron .75 2.00
53 Travis Konecny 1.00 2.50
54 Brock Boeser 1.25 3.00
55 Victor Olofsson 1.00 2.50
56 Bryan Rust 1.00 2.50
57 Kyle Connor 1.50 4.00
58 Max Pacioretty 1.00 2.50
59 Matthew Tkachuk 2.00 5.00
60 Jonathan Huberdeau 1.25 3.00
61 Andre Burakovsky .60 1.50
62 Teuvo Teravainen 1.00 2.50
63 Tristan Jarry 1.00 2.50
64 Dominik Kubalik 1.00 2.50
65 Andrei Svechnikov 1.25 3.00
66 Dougie Hamilton .75 2.00
67 Cale Makar 2.50 6.00
68 Aleksander Barkov 1.50 4.00
69 Keith Yandle .60 1.50
70 John Carlson 1.00 2.50
71 Quinn Hughes 2.50 6.00
72 Drew Doughty 1.25 3.00
73 Alex Pietrangelo .75 2.00
74 J.T. Miller 1.25 3.00
75 Cam Atkinson 1.00 2.50
76 Joe Pavelski 1.25 3.00
77 Phil Kessel 1.00 2.50
78 Zach Werenski 1.50 4.00
79 William Nylander 2.00 5.00
80 Seth Jones 1.00 2.50
81 Filip Forsberg 1.50 4.00
82 Thomas Chabot 1.00 2.50
83 Pierre-Luc Dubois .75 2.00
84 Alexander Romanov .75 2.00
85 T.J. Oshie 1.00 2.50
86 Marc-Andre Fleury 2.00 5.00
87 Connor Hellebuyck 2.00 5.00
88 Sergei Bobrovsky 1.50 4.00
89 Mikko Rantanen 2.50 6.00
90 Nick Suzuki 2.00 5.00
91 Alexis Lafreniere 1.50 4.00
92 Zach Parise 1.00 2.50
93 Claude Giroux 1.00 2.50
94 Bo Horvat 1.25 3.00
95 Jeremy Swayman 6.00 15.00
96 Spencer Knight 5.00 12.00
97 Alex Newhook 3.00 8.00
98 Quinton Byfield 4.00 10.00
99 Cole Caufield 8.00 20.00
100 Trevor Zegras 15.00 40.00

2021-22 Upper Deck MVP 20th Anniversary Gold

*GOLD: .75X TO 2X BASIC
95 Jeremy Swayman 30.00 80.00
98 Quinton Byfield 12.00 30.00
99 Cole Caufield 20.00 50.00
100 Trevor Zegras 50.00 125.00

2021-22 Upper Deck MVP Before and After

COMMON CARD .30 .75
SEMISTARS .40 1.00
UNLISTED STARS .50 1.25
*GOLD: .6X TO 1.5X BASIC
BA1 Auston Matthews 2.00 5.00
BA2 Connor McDavid 2.50 6.00
BA3 Tyler Seguin .60 1.50
BA4 Carey Price 1.00 2.50
BA5 P.K. Subban .60 1.50
BA6 Erik Karlsson .60 1.50
BA7 Evander Kane .50 1.25
BA8 Artemi Panarin 1.00 2.50
BA9 Andrei Vasilevskiy .75 2.00
BA10 Patrice Bergeron .60 1.50
BA11 Brent Burns .50 1.25
BA12 Elias Pettersson .75 2.00
BA13 Patrick Kane 1.00 2.50
BA14 Mark Stone .60 1.50
BA15 Jack Hughes 1.25 3.00
BA16 Matthew Tkachuk 1.00 2.50
BA17 Claude Giroux .50 1.25
BA18 David Pastrnak 1.25 3.00
BA19 William Karlsson .60 1.50
BA20 Aaron Ekblad .60 1.50

2021-22 Upper Deck MVP Colors and Contours

COMMON CARD 1.50 4.00
SEMISTARS 2.00 5.00
UNLISTED STARS 2.50 6.00
1 Connor McDavid 12.00 30.00
2 Alex Ovechkin 10.00 25.00
3 Sidney Crosby 10.00 25.00
4 Nikita Kucherov 5.00 12.00
5 Auston Matthews 10.00 25.00
6 Patrick Kane 5.00 12.00
7 Nathan MacKinnon 10.00 25.00
8 Evgeni Malkin 5.00 12.00
9 Elias Pettersson 4.00 10.00
10 David Pastrnak 6.00 15.00
11 Leon Draisaitl 8.00 20.00
12 Steven Stamkos 5.00 12.00
13 Patrice Bergeron 3.00 8.00
14 Jack Hughes 6.00 15.00
15 Artemi Panarin 5.00 12.00
16 Erik Karlsson 3.00 8.00
17 Carter Hart 2.50 6.00
18 Carey Price 5.00 12.00
19 Sebastian Aho 4.00 10.00
20 Tyler Seguin 3.00 8.00

21 Tuukka Rask 3.00 8.00
22 Mark Scheifele 4.00 10.00
23 John Gibson 2.50 6.00
24 Anze Kopitar 4.00 10.00
25 Tim Stutzle 3.00 8.00
26 Mark Stone 3.00 8.00
27 Andrei Vasilevskiy 4.00 10.00
28 Ryan O'Reilly 2.50 6.00
29 Brady Tkachuk 4.00 10.00
30 Kirill Kaprizov 8.00 20.00
31 Mathew Barzal 3.00 8.00
32 Brad Marchand 5.00 12.00
33 Mitch Marner 4.00 10.00
34 Brayden Point 3.00 8.00
35 Johnny Gaudreau 4.00 10.00
36 Dylan Larkin 3.00 8.00
37 Brent Burns 2.50 6.00
38 Vladimir Tarasenko 3.00 8.00
39 Alex DeBrincat 3.00 8.00
40 Devon Toews 2.00 5.00
41 Roman Josi 2.50 6.00
42 Jack Eichel 4.00 10.00
43 Brayden Schenn 2.50 6.00
44 Ryan Nugent-Hopkins 3.00 8.00
45 Mika Zibanejad 3.00 8.00
46 Max Domi 2.50 6.00
47 John Tavares 4.00 10.00
48 Sean Monahan 1.50 4.00
49 Tyler Toffoli 2.50 6.00
50 Jordan Binnington 4.00 10.00
51 Blake Wheeler 2.50 6.00
52 David Perron 2.00 5.00
53 Travis Konecny 2.50 6.00
54 Brock Boeser 3.00 8.00
55 Victor Olofsson 2.50 6.00
56 Bryan Rust 2.50 6.00
57 Kyle Connor 4.00 10.00
58 Max Pacioretty 2.50 6.00
59 Matthew Tkachuk 5.00 12.00
60 Jonathan Huberdeau 3.00 8.00
61 Andre Burakovsky 1.50 4.00
62 Teuvo Teravainen 2.50 6.00
63 Jonathan Drouin 2.00 5.00
64 Dominik Kubalik 2.50 6.00
65 Andrei Svechnikov 3.00 8.00
66 Dougie Hamilton 2.00 5.00
67 Cale Makar 6.00 15.00
68 Aleksander Barkov 4.00 10.00
69 Keith Yandle 1.50 4.00
70 John Carlson 2.50 6.00
71 Quinn Hughes 6.00 15.00
72 Drew Doughty 3.00 8.00
73 Alex Pietrangelo 2.00 5.00
74 J.T. Miller 3.00 8.00
75 Cam Atkinson 2.50 6.00
76 Joe Pavelski 3.00 8.00
77 Phil Kessel 2.50 6.00
78 Zach Werenski 4.00 10.00
79 Braden Holtby 3.00 8.00
80 Seth Jones 2.50 6.00
81 Filip Forsberg 4.00 10.00
82 Thomas Chabot 2.50 6.00
83 Pierre-Luc Dubois 2.00 5.00
84 Alexander Romanov 2.00 5.00
85 T.J. Oshie 2.50 6.00
86 Marc-Andre Fleury 5.00 12.00
87 Connor Hellebuyck 5.00 12.00
88 Sergei Bobrovsky 4.00 10.00
89 Mikko Rantanen 6.00 15.00
90 Nick Suzuki 5.00 12.00
91 Alexis Lafreniere 4.00 10.00
92 Zach Parise 2.50 6.00
93 Claude Giroux 2.50 6.00
94 Bo Horvat 3.00 8.00
95 Jeremy Swayman 30.00 80.00
96 Spencer Knight 20.00 50.00
97 Alex Newhook 4.00 10.00
98 Quinton Byfield 15.00 40.00
99 Cole Caufield 40.00 100.00
100 Trevor Zegras 80.00 200.00

2021-22 Upper Deck MVP Hart Attack

COMMON CARD .30 .75
SEMISTARS .40 1.00
UNLISTED STARS .50 1.25
*GOLD: 1.25X TO 3X BASIC
HA1 Connor McDavid 2.50 6.00
HA2 Leon Draisaitl 1.50 4.00
HA3 Auston Matthews 2.00 5.00
HA4 Nathan MacKinnon 2.00 5.00
HA5 Jonathan Huberdeau .60 1.50
HA6 Patrick Kane 1.00 2.50
HA7 Mark Scheifele .75 2.00
HA8 Artemi Panarin 1.00 2.50
HA9 Alex Ovechkin 2.00 5.00
HA10 Jack Hughes 1.25 3.00
HA11 Brayden Point .60 1.50
HA12 Anze Kopitar .75 2.00
HA13 David Pastrnak 1.25 3.00
HA14 Travis Konecny .50 1.25
HA15 Evgeni Malkin 1.00 2.50
HA16 Elias Pettersson .75 2.00
HA17 Sebastian Aho .75 2.00
HA18 Ryan O'Reilly .50 1.25
HA19 Mark Stone .60 1.50
HA20 Carey Price 1.00 2.50

2021-22 Upper Deck MVP Ice Battles

IB1 Alexis Lafreniere .75 2.00
IB2 Mitch Marner .75 2.00
IB3 Seth Jones .50 1.25
IB4 Miro Heiskanen .60 1.50
IB5 Mark Giordano .50 1.25
IB6 Brock Boeser .60 1.50
IB7 Alex Pietrangelo .40 1.00
IB8 Alex Ovechkin 2.00 5.00
IB9 Clayton Keller .60 1.50
IB10 Brayden Schenn .50 1.25
IB11 Anze Kopitar .75 2.00
IB12 Josh Bailey .40 1.00
IB13 Mathew Barzal .60 1.50
IB14 Sean Couturier .40 1.00
IB15 Ryan Getzlaf .50 1.25
IB16 Ryan Strome .50 1.25
IB17 Bryan Rust .50 1.25
IB18 Tim Stutzle .60 1.50
IB19 Matthew Tkachuk 1.00 2.50
IB20 Chris Kreider .60 1.50
IB21 Gabriel Landeskog .60 1.50
IB22 Rasmus Dahlin .60 1.50
IB23 Jakob Chychrun .50 1.25
IB24 Dylan Cozens .50 1.25
IB25 James van Riemsdyk .40 1.00
IB26 Blake Wheeler .50 1.25
IB27 Alexander Romanov .40 1.00
IB28 Dylan Larkin .60 1.50
IB29 Mackenzie Blackwood .50 1.25
IB30 Ilya Sorokin .75 2.00
IB31 Igor Shesterkin 1.00 2.50
IB32 Kevin Lankinen .50 1.25
IB33 Viktor Arvidsson .30 .75
IB34 Denis Gurianov .60 1.50
IB35 Gabe Vilardi .50 1.25
IB36 Mats Zuccarello .50 1.25
IB37 Patrice Bergeron .60 1.50
IB38 Maxime Comtois .40 1.00
IB39 Logan Couture .60 1.50
IB40 John Gibson .50 1.25
IB41 Kevin Fiala .40 1.00
IB42 Jeff Petry .50 1.25
IB43 Quinn Hughes 1.25 3.00
IB44 Sebastian Aho .75 2.00
IB45 Tyson Barrie .30 .75
IB46 John Klingberg .50 1.25
IB47 Torey Krug .40 1.00
IB48 Tomas Hertl .50 1.25
IB49 Samuel Girard .30 .75
IB50 Jordan Binnington .75 2.00
IB51 Joel Eriksson Ek .40 1.00
IB52 Jeff Carter .40 1.00
IB53 Bo Horvat .60 1.50
IB54 Elias Lindholm .50 1.25
IB55 Jack Eichel .75 2.00
IB56 Marc-Andre Fleury 1.00 2.50
IB57 David Perron .40 1.00
IB58 Kris Letang .60 1.50
IB59 Ondrej Palat .40 1.00
IB60 Nick Ritchie .30 .75
IB61 Mark Stone .60 1.50
IB62 Kevin Labanc .30 .75
IB63 Brad Marchand 1.00 2.50
IB64 Oliver Bjorkstrand .40 1.00
IB65 Erik Karlsson .60 1.50
IB66 David Krejci .50 1.25
IB67 Max Pacioretty .50 1.25
IB68 Victor Olofsson .50 1.25
IB69 Travis Konecny .50 1.25
IB70 Patric Hornqvist .30 .75
IB71 William Karlsson .60 1.50
IB72 Thomas Chabot .50 1.25
IB73 Tyler Toffoli .50 1.25
IB74 John Carlson .50 1.25
IB75 Sergei Bobrovsky .75 2.00
IB76 P.K. Subban .60 1.50
IB77 Victor Hedman .60 1.50
IB78 Evander Kane .50 1.25
IB79 Carter Hart .50 1.25
IB80 Alex Killorn .30 .75
IB81 Kyle Connor .75 2.00
IB82 Evgeny Kuznetsov .60 1.50
IB83 Pavel Buchnevich .40 1.00
IB84 Joel Farabee .50 1.25
IB85 Aaron Ekblad .60 1.50
IB86 Teuvo Teravainen .50 1.25
IB87 Nick Suzuki 1.00 2.50
IB88 Brent Burns .50 1.25
IB89 Nazem Kadri .60 1.50
IB90 Drew Doughty .60 1.50
IB91 Philipp Grubauer .50 1.25
IB92 Ryan Johansen .40 1.00
IB93 Mika Zibanejad .60 1.50
IB94 Cam Fowler .50 1.25
IB95 Juuse Saros .60 1.50
IB96 Mikko Rantanen 1.25 3.00
IB97 Elias Pettersson .75 2.00
IB98 Jack Roslovic .30 .75
IB99 Adrian Kempe .50 1.25
IB250 Trevor Zegras SP CL 2.00 5.00
IB100 Alex Ovechkin CL 2.00 5.00
IB101 Jordan Staal .40 1.00
IB102 Max Domi .50 1.25
IB103 Cam Atkinson .50 1.25
IB104 MacKenzie Weegar .40 1.00
IB105 Devon Toews .40 1.00
IB106 Shea Weber .50 1.25
IB107 Brady Tkachuk .75 2.00
IB108 Joe Pavelski .60 1.50
IB109 Ivan Provorov .40 1.00
IB110 Yanni Gourde .40 1.00
IB111 Zach Parise .50 1.25
IB112 Filip Zadina .40 1.00
IB113 Nico Hischier .75 2.00
IB114 Jamie Benn .50 1.25
IB115 Rasmus Andersson .40 1.00
IB116 Vincent Trocheck .50 1.25
IB117 Marcus Foligno .40 1.00
IB118 Pierre-Luc Dubois .40 1.00
IB119 Nicklas Backstrom .50 1.25
IB120 Taylor Hall .50 1.25
IB121 Nino Niederreiter .30 .75
IB122 Roope Hintz .60 1.50
IB123 Sean Monahan .30 .75
IB124 Matt Dumba .40 1.00
IB125 Darnell Nurse .40 1.00
IB126 Drake Batherson .50 1.25
IB127 Shea Theodore .60 1.50
IB128 Claude Giroux .50 1.25
IB129 Conor Garland .40 1.00
IB130 Connor Brown .40 1.00
IB131 Brock Nelson .50 1.25
IB132 Sam Reinhart 1.00 2.50
IB133 Jakob Silfverberg .30 .75
IB134 Dustin Brown .50 1.25
IB135 Carter Verhaeghe .50 1.25
IB136 Artemi Panarin 1.00 2.50
IB137 Andrei Svechnikov .60 1.50
IB138 Mike Hoffman .30 .75
IB139 Timo Meier .50 1.25
IB140 Josh Anderson .40 1.00
IB141 Christian Dvorak .40 1.00
IB142 Phillip Danault .50 1.25
IB143 Tom Wilson .50 1.25
IB144 Nikolaj Ehlers .50 1.25
IB145 Jordan Eberle .50 1.25
IB146 Yegor Sharangovich .50 1.25
IB147 Nick Schmaltz .40 1.00
IB148 Nils Hoglander .40 1.00
IB149 Anthony Cirelli .40 1.00
IB150 Mikhail Sergachev .40 1.00
IB151 Robby Fabbri .30 .75
IB152 Alex Tuch .50 1.25
IB153 Tristan Jarry .50 1.25
IB154 Miles Wood .30 .75
IB155 Connor Hellebuyck 1.00 2.50
IB156 Jacob Markstrom .50 1.25
IB157 Thatcher Demko .60 1.50
IB158 Pius Suter .40 1.00
IB159 Roman Josi .50 1.25
IB160 Evgeni Malkin 1.00 2.50
IB161 Jonathan Marchessault .60 1.50
IB162 Pavel Zacha .40 1.00
IB163 Evgenii Dadonov .30 .75
IB164 Adam Henrique .40 1.00
IB165 Filip Hronek .30 .75
IB166 Dougie Hamilton .40 1.00
IB167 Rickard Rakell .40 1.00
IB168 Zach Hyman .75 2.00
IB169 J.T. Miller .60 1.50
IB170 Kevin Hayes .40 1.00
IB171 Jakub Voracek .40 1.00
IB172 Justin Faulk .40 1.00
IB173 Charlie McAvoy .60 1.50
IB174 Martin Necas .75 2.00
IB175 Anders Lee .40 1.00
IB176 Ty Smith .50 1.25
IB177 Kirby Dach .50 1.25
IB178 T.J. Oshie .50 1.25
IB179 Vitek Vanecek .50 1.25
IB180 Josh Norris .50 1.25
IB181 Phil Kessel .50 1.25
IB182 Tuukka Rask .60 1.50
IB183 Johnny Gaudreau .75 2.00
IB184 Filip Forsberg .75 2.00
IB185 Anthony Mantha .40 1.00
IB186 Brayden Point .60 1.50
IB187 Jonathan Huberdeau .60 1.50
IB188 William Nylander 1.00 2.50
IB189 Jean-Gabriel Pageau .30 .75
IB190 Adam Fox .60 1.50
IB191 Vladimir Tarasenko .60 1.50
IB192 Patrik Laine .60 1.50
IB193 Ryan Nugent-Hopkins .60 1.50
IB194 Morgan Rielly .50 1.25
IB195 Andre Burakovsky .30 .75
IB196 David Pastrnak 1.25 3.00
IB197 Dominik Kubalik .50 1.25
IB198 Zach Werenski .75 2.00
IB199 John Tavares .75 2.00
IB200 Artemi Panarin CL 1.00 2.50
IB201 Mark Scheifele SP 1.00 2.50
IB202 Carey Price SP 1.25 3.00
IB203 Jake Guentzel SP 1.00 2.50
IB204 Aleksander Barkov SP 1.00 2.50
IB205 Andrei Vasilevskiy SP 1.00 2.50
IB206 John Gibson SP .60 1.50
IB207 Jack Hughes SP 1.50 4.00
IB208 Cale Makar SP 1.50 4.00
IB209 Jason Robertson SP 1.00 2.50
IB210 Leon Draisaitl SP 2.00 5.00
IB211 Alex DeBrincat SP .75 2.00
IB212 Ryan O'Reilly SP .60 1.50
IB213 Miro Heiskanen SP .75 2.00
IB214 Steven Stamkos SP 1.25 3.00
IB215 Auston Matthews SP 2.50 6.00
IB216 Nathan MacKinnon SP 2.50 6.00
IB217 Patrick Kane SP 1.25 3.00
IB218 Kirill Kaprizov SP 2.00 5.00
IB219 Sidney Crosby SP 2.50 6.00
IB220 Connor McDavid SP 3.00 8.00
IB221 Calen Addison SP 1.00 2.50
IB222 Wyatt Kalynuk SP 1.00 2.50
IB223 Jeremy Davies SP 1.00 2.50
IB224 Jacob Bryson SP 1.00 2.50
IB225 Zac Jones SP 1.25 3.00
IB226 Kole Lind SP 1.25 3.00
IB227 Ross Colton SP 1.25 3.00
IB228 Garrett Pilon SP 1.25 3.00
IB229 Veini Vehvilainen SP 1.00 2.50
IB230 David Farrance SP 1.00 2.50
IB231 Wade Allison SP 1.00 2.50
IB232 Jacob Bernard-Docker SP 1.00 2.50
IB233 Cameron York SP 1.00 2.50
IB234 Alex Newhook SP 1.50 4.00
IB235 Jeremy Swayman SP 3.00 8.00
IB236 Shane Pinto SP 1.50 4.00
IB237 Radim Zohorna SP 1.00 2.50
IB238 Jan Jenik SP 1.25 3.00
IB239 Tyce Thompson SP 1.00 2.50
IB240 Joseph Veleno SP 1.00 2.50
IB241 Ukko-Pekka Luukkonen SP 1.50 4.00
IB242 Spencer Knight SP 2.00 5.00
IB243 Cole Caufield SP 8.00 20.00
IB244 Quinton Byfield SP 2.50 6.00
IB245 Jamie Drysdale SP 1.50 4.00
IB246 Alex Barre-Boulet SP 1.00 2.50
IB247 Rasmus Kupari SP 1.00 2.50
IB248 Grigori Denisenko SP 1.25 3.00
IB249 Trevor Zegras SP 8.00 20.00

2021-22 Upper Deck MVP Mascot Gaming Cards

M1 Wild Wing 1.50 4.00
M2 Howler the Coyote 1.50 4.00
M3 Blades The Bruin 1.50 4.00
M4 Sabretooth 1.50 4.00
M5 Harvey The Hound 1.50 4.00
M6 Stormy 1.50 4.00
M7 Tommy Hawk 1.50 4.00
M8 Bernie the St. Bernard 1.50 4.00
M9 Stinger 1.50 4.00
M10 Victor E. Green 1.50 4.00
M11 Al The Octopus 1.50 4.00
M12 Hunter 1.50 4.00
M13 Stanley C. Panther 1.50 4.00
M14 Bailey 1.50 4.00
M15 Nordy 1.50 4.00
M16 Youppi 1.50 4.00
M17 Gnash 1.50 4.00
M18 N.J. Devil 1.50 4.00
M19 Sparky The Dragon 1.50 4.00
M20 Spartacat 1.50 4.00
M21 Gritty 4.00 10.00
M22 Iceburgh 1.50 4.00
M23 S.J. Sharkie 1.50 4.00
M24 Louie 1.50 4.00
M25 Thunderbug 1.50 4.00
M26 Carlton the Bear 1.50 4.00
M27 Fin The Whale 1.50 4.00
M28 Chance 1.50 4.00
M29 Slapshot 1.50 4.00
M30 Mick E Moose 1.50 4.00

2021-22 Upper Deck MVP Mascot Gaming Cards Sparkle

*SPARKLE: .5X TO 1.25X BASIC
M21 Gritty 10.00 25.00

2021-22 Upper Deck MVP Postseason

PS1 Connor McDavid 12.00 30.00
PS2 Auston Matthews 10.00 25.00
PS3 Sidney Crosby 10.00 25.00
PS4 Alex Ovechkin 10.00 25.00
PS5 Mathew Barzal 3.00 8.00
PS6 David Pastrnak 6.00 15.00
PS7 Mark Scheifele 4.00 10.00
PS8 Carey Price 5.00 12.00
PS9 Sebastian Aho 4.00 10.00
PS10 Roman Josi 2.50 6.00
PS11 Jonathan Huberdeau 3.00 8.00
PS12 Steven Stamkos 5.00 12.00
PS13 Nathan MacKinnon 10.00 25.00
PS14 Ryan O'Reilly 2.50 6.00
PS15 Marc-Andre Fluery 5.00 12.00
PS16 Kirill Kaprizov 8.00 20.00
PS17 Tyler Toffoli 2.50 6.00
PS18 Mitch Marner 4.00 10.00

2022-23 Upper Deck MVP

1 Lucas Raymond .40 1.00
2 Steven Stamkos .50 1.25
3 Carey Price .50 1.25
4 Elias Pettersson .40 1.00
5 David Pastrnak .60 1.50
6 Jonathan Toews .40 1.00
7 Morgan Rielly .25 .60
8 Cale Makar .60 1.50
9 Jack Hughes .60 1.50
10 Artemi Panarin .50 1.25
11 Nikita Kucherov .50 1.25
12 Mitch Marner .40 1.00
13 Kyle Connor .40 1.00
14 Rasmus Dahlin .30 .75
15 Andrei Svechnikov .30 .75
16 Mikko Rantanen .60 1.50
17 Tyler Seguin .30 .75
18 Dylan Larkin .30 .75
19 Anze Kopitar .40 1.00
20 Brent Burns .25 .60
21 Ryan O'Reilly .25 .60
22 Mark Scheifele .40 1.00
23 Miro Heiskanen .30 .75
24 Igor Shesterkin .50 1.25
25 Jake Guentzel .40 1.00
26 Max Pacioretty .25 .60
27 Andrei Vasilevskiy .40 1.00
28 Jonathan Huberdeau .30 .75
29 Brayden Point .30 .75
30 Drew Doughty .30 .75
31 Carter Hart .25 .60
32 Mathew Barzal .30 .75
33 Adam Fox .30 .75
34 William Nylander .50 1.25
35 Jordan Binnington .40 1.00
36 Erik Karlsson .30 .75
37 Sean Couturier .20 .50
38 John Carlson .25 .60
39 Alex DeBrincat .30 .75
40 Troy Terry .20 .50
41 Nicklas Backstrom .25 .60
42 Sebastian Aho .40 1.00
43 Nico Hischier .40 1.00
44 Seth Jones .25 .60
45 Alex Pietrangelo .20 .50
46 Ryan Nugent-Hopkins .30 .75
47 Dylan Cozens .25 .60
48 Martin Necas .40 1.00
49 Samuel Girard .15 .40
50 Jason Robertson .40 1.00
51 Tyler Toffoli .25 .60
52 Ryan Reaves .20 .50
53 Jordan Eberle .25 .60
54 William Karlsson .30 .75
55 Jonathan Marchessault .30 .75
56 Roman Josi .25 .60
57 Kirill Kaprizov .75 2.00
58 Nick Suzuki .50 1.25
59 Gabriel Landeskog .30 .75
60 Pavel Buchnevich .20 .50
61 Jordan Kyrou .25 .60
62 Brock Boeser .30 .75
63 Evgeny Kuznetsov .30 .75
64 Alex Nedeljkovic .20 .50
65 Moritz Seider .30 .75
66 Spencer Knight .25 .60
67 Jeremy Swayman .40 1.00
68 Tristan Jarry .25 .60
69 Robin Lehner .20 .50
70 Anthony Cirelli .20 .50
71 Patrik Laine .30 .75
72 Tim Stutzle .30 .75
73 David Perron .20 .50
74 Elias Lindholm .25 .60
75 Sonny Milano .20 .50
76 Taylor Hall .25 .60
77 Noah Hanifin .25 .60
78 Teuvo Teravainen .25 .60
79 Marc-Andre Fleury .50 1.25
80 Charlie McAvoy .30 .75
81 Devon Toews .20 .50
82 Jakub Voracek .20 .50
83 Ryan Hartman .15 .40
84 Clayton Keller .30 .75
85 Cole Caufield .50 1.25
86 Sean Monahan .15 .40
87 Jack Campbell .25 .60
88 Mikael Granlund .20 .50
89 Dougie Hamilton .20 .50
90 Elvis Merzlikins .25 .60
91 Rickard Rakell .20 .50
92 Anders Lee .20 .50
93 James van Riemsdyk .20 .50
94 Alex Iafallo .15 .40
95 Joel Farabee .25 .60
96 Roope Hintz .30 .75
97 Adam Henrique .20 .50
98 Cam Talbot .25 .60
99 Anton Lundell .25 .60
100 Lucas Raymond CL .40 1.00
101 Jaccob Slavin .20 .50
102 John Marino .25 .60
103 Boone Jenner .25 .60
104 Jesper Bratt .25 .60
105 Nick Schmaltz .20 .50
106 Christian Dvorak .20 .50
107 Zach Hyman .40 1.00
108 Timo Meier .25 .60
109 Patrice Bergeron .30 .75
110 Alex Tuch .25 .60
111 Jaden Schwartz .20 .50
112 Victor Hedman .30 .75
113 Eeli Tolvanen .25 .60
114 Jeff Skinner .25 .60
115 Jacob Markstrom .25 .60
116 Chris Kreider .30 .75
117 Jakob Chychrun .25 .60
118 Ilya Sorokin .40 1.00
119 Juuse Saros .30 .75
120 Aaron Ekblad .30 .75
121 Jamie Drysdale .20 .50
122 Alex Killorn .15 .40
123 Filip Hronek .15 .40
124 Travis Konecny .25 .60
125 John Tavares .40 1.00
126 Marc-Edouard Vlasic .15 .40
127 Josh Norris .25 .60
128 Oliver Bjorkstrand .20 .50
129 Drake Batherson .25 .60
130 Casey Mittelstadt .25 .60
131 Adrian Kempe .25 .60
132 Michael Bunting .25 .60
133 Torey Krug .20 .50
134 Jonathan Drouin .20 .50
135 J.T. Miller .30 .75
136 Jordan Staal .20 .50
137 Matt Dumba .15 .40
138 Mark Stone .30 .75
139 Ryan Suter .20 .50
140 Craig Smith .15 .40
141 Dawson Mercer .30 .75
142 Oliver Wahlstrom .15 .40
143 Sam Bennett .40 1.00
144 Connor Brown .20 .50
145 Jamie Oleksiak .20 .50
146 Zach Werenski .40 1.00
147 Nazem Kadri .30 .75
148 Ryan Johansen .20 .50
149 Jacob Trouba .20 .50
150 Brandon Saad .20 .50
151 T.J. Oshie .25 .60
152 Joe Pavelski .30 .75
153 Josh Morrissey .30 .75
154 Yanni Gourde .20 .50
155 Henri Jokiharju .15 .40
156 Pierre-Luc Dubois .20 .50
157 Dan Vladar .20 .50
158 Adam Pelech .15 .40
159 Phillip Danault .25 .60
160 Cam Atkinson .25 .60
161 Robby Fabbri .15 .40
162 Mats Zuccarello .25 .60
163 Thomas Chabot .25 .60
164 Johnny Gaudreau .40 1.00
165 Josh Anderson .20 .50
166 Darcy Kuemper .25 .60
167 Tomas Tatar .15 .40
168 Matt Duchene .25 .60
169 Carter Verhaeghe .25 .60
170 Kevin Labanc .15 .40
171 Thatcher Demko .30 .75
172 Brock Nelson .25 .60
173 Chandler Stephenson .20 .50
174 Dmitry Orlov .25 .60
175 Jean-Gabriel Pageau .15 .40
176 Andrew Mangiapane .25 .60
177 Bo Horvat .30 .75
178 Ivan Provorov .20 .50
179 Josh Bailey .20 .50
180 Jesse Puljujarvi .25 .60
181 Shayne Gostisbehere .25 .60
182 Aleksander Barkov .40 1.00
183 Filip Forsberg .40 1.00
184 Kevin Fiala .20 .50
185 Mika Zibanejad .30 .75
186 Blake Wheeler .25 .60
187 Anthony Duclair .20 .50
188 Tom Wilson .25 .60
189 Nikolaj Ehlers .25 .60
190 Alex Kerfoot .20 .50
191 Ryan Strome .25 .60
192 Alexis Lafreniere .40 1.00
193 Logan Couture .30 .75
194 Reilly Smith .25 .60
195 Marcus Foligno .20 .50
196 Tomas Hertl .25 .60
197 Kevin Shattenkirk .15 .40
198 Quinton Byfield .30 .75
199 Trevor Zegras .25 .60
200 John Tavares CL .40 1.00
201 Philipp Grubauer SP .50 1.25
202 Patrick Kane SP 1.00 2.50
203 Brady Tkachuk SP .75 2.00
204 Conor Garland SP .40 1.00
205 Connor Hellebuyck SP 1.00 2.50
206 Matthew Tkachuk SP 1.00 2.50
207 Kris Letang SP .60 1.50
208 Quinn Hughes SP 1.25 3.00
209 Jared McCann SP .40 1.00
210 Jason Zucker SP .50 1.25
211 Sam Reinhart SP 1.00 2.50
212 Jack Roslovic SP .30 .75
213 Tyler Bertuzzi SP .40 1.00
214 Brad Marchand SP 1.00 2.50
215 Auston Matthews SP 2.00 5.00
216 Nathan MacKinnon SP 2.00 5.00
217 Alex Ovechkin SP 2.00 5.00
218 Sidney Crosby SP 2.00 5.00
219 Leon Draisaitl SP 1.50 4.00
220 Connor McDavid SP 2.50 6.00
221 Marco Rossi SP RC 4.00 10.00
222 Matt Boldy SP RC 5.00 12.00
223 Isaac Ratcliffe SP RC 1.50 4.00
224 Jacob Moverare SP RC 1.25 3.00
225 Jacob Perreault SP RC 1.50 4.00
226 Brayden Tracey SP RC 1.25 3.00
227 Lukas Dostal SP RC 3.00 8.00
228 Jack Quinn SP RC 2.50 6.00
229 Jakub Galvas SP RC 1.50 4.00
230 Adam Raska SP RC 1.50 4.00
231 Vladislav Kolyachonok SP RC 1.25 3.00
232 Braden Schneider SP RC 2.50 6.00
233 Dylan Samberg SP RC 1.50 4.00
234 Lukas Reichel SP RC 3.00 8.00
235 Samuel Fagemo SP RC 1.25 3.00
236 Declan Chisholm SP RC 1.50 4.00
237 Jack LaFontaine SP RC 1.50 4.00
238 Michael McNiven SP RC 1.50 4.00
239 Trey Fix-Wolansky SP RC 1.50 4.00
240 Johnny Kovacevic SP RC 1.50 4.00
241 Mark Kastelic SP RC 1.25 3.00
242 Kent Johnson SP RC 3.00 8.00
243 Owen Power SP RC 3.00 8.00
244 Matty Beniers SP RC 4.00 10.00
245 Erik Kallgren SP RC 1.50 4.00
246 Bobby Brink SP RC 1.50 4.00
247 Valtteri Puustinen SP RC 1.25 3.00
248 Matias Maccelli SP RC 2.50 6.00
249 Jordan Spence SP RC 1.50 4.00
250 Matt Boldy CL SP RC 5.00 12.00
251 Jakub Lauko RC 2.00 5.00
252 Pontus Holmberg RC 1.50 4.00
253 Jonatan Berggren RC 2.50 6.00
254 Nick Perbix RC 1.25 3.00
255 Kaiden Guhle RC 3.00 8.00
256 Juraj Slafkovsky RC 15.00 40.00
257 Elmer Soderblom RC 3.00 8.00
258 Jake Sanderson RC 4.00 10.00
259 Reilly Walsh RC 1.50 4.00
260 Nikita Okhotiuk RC 1.25 3.00
261 Pyotr Kochetkov RC 3.00 8.00
262 Samuel Poulin RC 2.00 5.00
263 Simon Holmstrom RC 1.50 4.00
264 Filip Hallander RC 1.50 4.00
265 Ronnie Attard RC 1.50 4.00
266 David Jiricek RC 3.00 8.00
267 Wyatt Johnston RC 10.00 20.00
268 Michael Eyssimont RC 1.50 4.00
269 Oskar Olausson RC 1.50 4.00
270 Nikita Alexandrov RC 1.50 4.00
271 Mitchell Chaffee RC 1.25 3.00
272 Juuso Parssinen RC 1.50 4.00
273 Dylan Guenther RC 4.00 10.00
274 Filip Roos RC 1.25 3.00
275 Zack Hayes RC 1.25 3.00
276 Shane Wright RC 15.00 40.00
277 Brandt Clarke RC 3.00 8.00
278 Dylan Holloway RC 3.00 8.00
279 Nick DeSimone RC 1.50 4.00
280 Andrei Kuzmenko RC 3.00 8.00
281 Thomas Bordeleau RC 1.50 4.00
282 Pavol Regenda RC 1.50 4.00

2022-23 Upper Deck MVP Gold Script

*GOLD.SCRIPT: 2.5X TO 6X BASIC
*GOLD.SCRIPT.SP: 2.5X TO 6X BASIC
*GOLD.SCRIPT.RC: 1X TO 2.5X BASIC

2022-23 Upper Deck MVP Silver Script

*SILVER.SCRIPT: .75X TO 2X BASIC
*SILVER.SCRIPT.SP: .75X TO 2X BASIC
*SILVER.SCRIPT.RC: .6X TO 1.5X BASIC

2022-23 Upper Deck MVP Super Script

*SUPER.SCRIPT: 4X TO 10X BASIC
*SUPER.SCRIPT.SP: 4X TO 10X BASIC
*SUPER.SCRIPT.RC: 1.5X TO 4X BASIC

2022-23 Upper Deck MVP 20th Anniversary

*GOLD.SCRIPT: .75X TO 2X BASIC
1 Connor McDavid 5.00 12.00
2 Sidney Crosby 4.00 10.00
3 Alex Ovechkin 4.00 10.00
4 Patrick Kane 2.00 5.00
5 Auston Matthews 4.00 10.00
6 Leon Draisaitl 3.00 8.00
7 Mark Stone 1.25 3.00
8 Kyle Connor 1.50 4.00
9 Troy Terry .75 2.00
10 Brad Marchand 2.00 5.00
11 Steven Stamkos 2.00 5.00
12 Adam Fox 1.25 3.00
13 Matthew Tkachuk 2.00 5.00
14 Sebastian Aho 1.50 4.00
15 Brady Tkachuk 1.50 4.00
16 Elias Pettersson 1.50 4.00
17 Mitch Marner 1.50 4.00
18 Brayden Point 1.25 3.00
19 Kirill Kaprizov 3.00 8.00
20 Jordan Kyrou 1.00 2.50
21 Mathew Barzal 1.25 3.00
22 Lucas Raymond 1.50 4.00
23 Quinn Hughes 2.50 6.00
24 Jordan Eberle 1.00 2.50
25 Andrei Vasilevskiy 1.50 4.00
26 Drake Batherson 1.00 2.50
27 Artemi Panarin 2.00 5.00
28 Ryan Nugent-Hopkins 1.25 3.00
29 Matt Duchene 1.00 2.50
30 Igor Shesterkin 2.00 5.00
31 Jonathan Huberdeau 1.25 3.00
32 Evgeny Kuznetsov 1.25 3.00
33 Tyler Bertuzzi .75 2.00
34 Jonathan Marchessault 1.25 3.00
35 Victor Hedman 1.25 3.00
36 Aleksander Barkov 1.50 4.00
37 Brock Boeser 1.25 3.00
38 Nicklas Backstrom 1.00 2.50
39 Philipp Grubauer 1.00 2.50
40 Mark Scheifele 1.50 4.00
41 Brent Burns 1.00 2.50
42 Nazem Kadri 1.25 3.00
43 John Tavares 1.50 4.00
44 Frederik Andersen 1.25 3.00
45 Tyler Seguin 1.25 3.00
46 John Carlson 1.00 2.50
47 Patrik Laine 1.25 3.00
48 Mikko Rantanen 2.50 6.00
49 Cam Talbot 1.00 2.50
50 Dylan Larkin 1.25 3.00
51 Miro Heiskanen 1.25 3.00
52 Roman Josi 1.00 2.50
53 Nico Hischier 1.50 4.00
54 Tim Stutzle 1.25 3.00
55 Jake Guentzel 1.50 4.00
56 Seth Jones 1.00 2.50
57 Sean Couturier .75 2.00
58 David Perron .75 2.00
59 Joe Pavelski 1.25 3.00
60 Erik Karlsson 1.25 3.00
61 Johnny Gaudreau 1.50 4.00
62 Alex DeBrincat 1.25 3.00
63 Jordan Binnington 1.50 4.00
64 Jack Campbell 1.00 2.50
65 Anze Kopitar 1.50 4.00
66 Nick Suzuki 2.00 5.00
67 Jason Robertson 1.50 4.00
68 Cole Caufield 2.00 5.00
69 Moritz Seider 1.25 3.00
70 Oliver Bjorkstrand .75 2.00
71 Trevor Zegras 1.00 2.50
72 Brock Nelson 1.00 2.50
73 Claude Giroux 1.00 2.50
74 Dylan Cozens 1.00 2.50
75 Jeremy Swayman 1.50 4.00
76 Marc-Andre Fleury 2.00 5.00
77 Carter Hart 1.00 2.50
78 Kevin Fiala .75 2.00
79 Andrei Svechnikov 1.25 3.00
80 Ryan O'Reilly 1.00 2.50
81 Elias Lindholm 1.00 2.50
82 Rasmus Dahlin 1.25 3.00
83 Jack Eichel 1.50 4.00
84 Jack Hughes 2.50 6.00
85 Cale Makar 2.50 6.00
86 Alexis Lafreniere 1.50 4.00
87 Patrice Bergeron 1.25 3.00
88 Kris Letang 1.25 3.00
89 David Pastrnak 2.50 6.00
90 Nathan MacKinnon 4.00 10.00
91 Spencer Knight 1.00 2.50
92 Gabriel Landeskog 1.25 3.00
93 J.T. Miller 1.25 3.00
94 William Nylander 2.00 5.00
95 Chris Kreider 1.25 3.00
97 Matt Boldy 3.00 8.00
98 Lukas Reichel 3.00 8.00
99 Jacob Perreault 2.00 5.00
100 Jack Quinn 2.00 5.00

2022-23 Upper Deck MVP Colors and Contours

1 Connor McDavid 12.00 30.00
2 Sidney Crosby 10.00 25.00
3 Alex Ovechkin 10.00 25.00
4 Patrick Kane 5.00 12.00
5 Auston Matthews 10.00 25.00
6 Leon Draisaitl 8.00 20.00
7 Mark Stone 3.00 8.00
8 Kyle Connor 4.00 10.00
9 Troy Terry 2.00 5.00
10 Brad Marchand 5.00 12.00
11 Steven Stamkos 5.00 12.00
12 Adam Fox 3.00 8.00
13 Matthew Tkachuk 5.00 12.00
14 Sebastian Aho 4.00 10.00
15 Brady Tkachuk 4.00 10.00
16 Elias Pettersson 4.00 10.00
17 Mitch Marner 4.00 10.00
18 Brayden Point 3.00 8.00
19 Kirill Kaprizov 8.00 20.00
20 Jordan Kyrou 2.50 6.00
21 Mathew Barzal 3.00 8.00
22 Lucas Raymond 4.00 10.00
23 Quinn Hughes 6.00 15.00
24 Jordan Eberle 2.50 6.00
25 Andrei Vasilevskiy 4.00 10.00
26 Drake Batherson 2.50 6.00
27 Artemi Panarin 5.00 12.00
28 Ryan Nugent-Hopkins 3.00 8.00
29 Matt Duchene 2.50 6.00
30 Igor Shesterkin 5.00 12.00
31 Jonathan Huberdeau 3.00 8.00
32 Evgeny Kuznetsov 3.00 8.00
33 Tyler Bertuzzi 2.00 5.00
34 Jonathan Marchessault 3.00 8.00
35 Victor Hedman 3.00 8.00
36 Aleksander Barkov 4.00 10.00
37 Brock Boeser 3.00 8.00
38 Nicklas Backstrom 2.50 6.00
39 Philipp Grubauer 2.50 6.00
40 Mark Scheifele 4.00 10.00
41 Brent Burns 2.50 6.00
42 Nazem Kadri 3.00 8.00
43 John Tavares 4.00 10.00
44 Frederik Andersen 3.00 8.00
45 Tyler Seguin 3.00 8.00
46 John Carlson 2.50 6.00
47 Patrik Laine 3.00 8.00
48 Mikko Rantanen 6.00 15.00
49 Cam Talbot 2.50 6.00
50 Dylan Larkin 3.00 8.00
51 Miro Heiskanen 3.00 8.00
52 Roman Josi 2.50 6.00
53 Nico Hischier 4.00 10.00
54 Tim Stutzle 3.00 8.00
55 Jake Guentzel 4.00 10.00
56 Seth Jones 2.50 6.00
57 Sean Couturier 2.00 5.00
58 David Perron 2.00 5.00
59 Joe Pavelski 3.00 8.00

60 Erik Karlsson 3.00 8.00
61 Johnny Gaudreau 4.00 10.00
62 Alex DeBrincat 3.00 8.00
63 Jordan Binnington 4.00 10.00
64 Jack Campbell 2.50 6.00
65 Anze Kopitar 4.00 10.00
66 Nick Suzuki 5.00 12.00
67 Jason Robertson 4.00 10.00
68 Cole Caufield 5.00 12.00
69 Moritz Seider 3.00 8.00
70 Oliver Bjorkstrand 2.00 5.00
71 Trevor Zegras 2.50 6.00
72 Brock Nelson 2.50 6.00
73 Claude Giroux 2.50 6.00
74 Dylan Cozens 2.50 6.00
75 Jeremy Swayman 4.00 10.00
76 Marc-Andre Fleury 5.00 12.00
77 Carter Hart 2.50 6.00
78 Kevin Fiala 2.00 5.00
79 Andrei Svechnikov 3.00 8.00
80 Ryan O'Reilly 2.50 6.00
81 Elias Lindholm 2.50 6.00
82 Rasmus Dahlin 3.00 8.00
83 Jack Eichel 4.00 10.00
84 Jack Hughes 6.00 15.00
85 Cale Makar 6.00 15.00
86 Alexis Lafreniere 4.00 10.00
87 Patrice Bergeron 3.00 8.00
88 Kris Letang 3.00 8.00
89 David Pastrnak 6.00 15.00
90 Nathan MacKinnon 10.00 25.00
91 Spencer Knight 2.50 6.00
92 Gabriel Landeskog 3.00 8.00
93 J.T. Miller 3.00 8.00
94 William Nylander 5.00 12.00
95 Chris Kreider 3.00 8.00

2022-23 Upper Deck MVP Domains

*GOLD: .5X TO 1.25X BASIC
NA1 Connor McDavid 4.00 10.00
NA2 Auston Matthews 3.00 8.00
NA3 Sidney Crosby 3.00 8.00
NA4 Elias Pettersson 1.25 3.00
NA5 Cole Caufield 1.50 4.00
NA6 Cale Makar 2.00 5.00
NA7 Lucas Raymond 1.25 3.00
NA8 Alex Ovechkin 3.00 8.00
NA9 Jack Hughes 2.00 5.00
NA10 David Pastrnak 2.00 5.00
NA11 Brady Tkachuk 1.25 3.00
NA12 Nikita Kucherov 1.50 4.00
NA13 Kevin Fiala .60 1.50
NA14 Artemi Panarin 1.50 4.00
NA15 Nico Hischier 1.25 3.00
NA16 Roman Josi .75 2.00
NA17 Patrick Kane 1.50 4.00
NA18 Alexis Lafreniere 1.25 3.00
NA19 Andrei Svechnikov 1.00 2.50
NA20 Kirill Kaprizov 2.50 6.00
NA21 Moritz Seider 1.00 2.50
NA22 Jack Eichel 1.25 3.00
NA23 Tim Stutzle 1.00 2.50
NA24 Andrei Vasilevskiy 1.25 3.00
NA25 Steven Stamkos 1.50 4.00
NA26 Trevor Zegras .75 2.00
NA27 Igor Shesterkin 1.50 4.00
NA28 Quinn Hughes 2.00 5.00
NA29 Nathan MacKinnon 3.00 8.00
NA30 Leon Draisaitl 2.50 6.00

2022-23 Upper Deck MVP Encounters on Ice

*GOLD: .5X TO 1.2X BASIC
EI1 Matthew Tkachuk
Zack Kassian 2.00 5.00
EI2 Patrick Kane
Ryan O'Reilly 2.00 5.00
EI3 Artemi Panarin
Brad Marchand 2.00 5.00
EI4 Auston Matthews
Lucas Raymond 4.00 10.00
EI5 John Tavares
Nick Suzuki 2.00 5.00
EI6 Jean-Gabriel Pageau
Jacob Trouba .75 2.00
EI7 David Pastrnak
Brendan Gallagher 2.50 6.00
EI8 Wayne Simmonds
Charlie McAvoy 1.25 3.00
EI9 Brady Tkachuk
William Nylander 2.00 5.00
EI10 Victor Hedman
Aleksander Barkov 1.50 4.00
EI11 Trevor Zegras
Quinton Byfield 1.25 3.00
EI12 Jeff Skinner
Morgan Rielly 1.00 2.50
EI13 Sean Couturier
Jake Guentzel 1.50 4.00
EI14 P.K. Subban
Chris Kreider 1.25 3.00
EI15 Kevin Hayes
Nico Hischier 1.50 4.00
EI16 Anze Kopitar
Logan Couture 1.50 4.00
EI17 Alex DeBrincat
Kevin Fiala 1.25 3.00
EI18 Torey Krug
Jamie Benn 1.00 2.50
EI19 Kyle Palmieri
Kris Letang 1.25 3.00
EI20 Mark Scheifele
Leon Draisaitl 3.00 8.00

2022-23 Upper Deck MVP Ice Battles

*ICE BATTLES: .75X TO 2X BASIC
*ICE BATTLES SP: .5X TO 1.2X BASIC
*ICE BATTLES RC: .3X TO .75X BASIC

2022-23 Upper Deck MVP Ice Battles Gold

*ICE BATT GOLD: 1X TO 2.5X BASIC
*ICE BATT GOLD SP: .6X TO 1.5X BASIC
*ICE BATT GOLD RC: .4X TO 1X BASIC

2022-23 Upper Deck MVP Pinpoints

*GOLD: .5X TO 1.2X BASIC
PP1 Patrick Kane 1.50 4.00
PP2 Sidney Crosby 3.00 8.00
PP3 Nikita Kucherov 1.50 4.00
PP4 Mark Scheifele 1.25 3.00
PP5 Auston Matthews 3.00 8.00
PP6 Artemi Panarin 1.50 4.00
PP7 Leon Draisaitl 2.50 6.00
PP8 Alex Ovechkin 3.00 8.00
PP9 Kyle Connor 1.25 3.00
PP10 Troy Terry .60 1.50
PP11 Alex DeBrincat 1.00 2.50
PP12 Chris Kreider 1.00 2.50
PP13 Tyler Bertuzzi .60 1.50
PP14 Max Pacioretty .75 2.00
PP15 Pierre-Luc Dubois .60 1.50
PP16 Johnny Gaudreau 1.25 3.00
PP17 Brayden Point 1.00 2.50
PP18 Brad Marchand 1.50 4.00
PP19 Steven Stamkos 1.50 4.00
PP20 Sebastian Aho 1.25 3.00
PP21 Jake Guentzel 1.25 3.00
PP22 Jordan Eberle .75 2.00
PP23 Andrei Svechnikov 1.00 2.50
PP24 John Tavares 1.25 3.00
PP25 Connor McDavid 4.00 10.00

2023-24 Upper Deck MVP

1 Jonathan Marchessault .30 .75
2 Andrei Vasilevskiy .40 1.00
3 John Tavares .40 1.00
4 Darnell Nurse .20 .50
5 Mika Zibanejad .30 .75
6 Bo Horvat .30 .75
7 Jesse Puljujarvi .25 .60
8 Semyon Varlamov .25 .60
9 Rasmus Ristolainen .15 .40
10 John Gibson .25 .60
11 Ryan O'Reilly .25 .60
12 Ryan Nugent-Hopkins .30 .75
13 Tage Thompson .30 .75
14 Jacob Markstrom .25 .60
15 Cole Caufield .50 1.25
16 Sergei Bobrovsky .40 1.00
17 Kasperi Kapanen .20 .50
18 Tom Wilson .25 .60
19 Tyler Johnson .15 .40
20 Joel Farabee .25 .60
21 Alexander Wennberg .15 .40
22 Carter Hart .25 .60
23 Kirill Kaprizov .75 2.00
24 Morgan Rielly .25 .60
25 T.J. Oshie .25 .60
26 Trevor Zegras .25 .60
27 Leon Draisaitl .75 2.00
28 Gabriel Landeskog .30 .75
29 Jack Roslovic .15 .40
30 Adrian Kempe .25 .60
31 Sidney Crosby 1.00 2.50
32 Jakub Voracek .20 .50
33 Sean Couturier .20 .50
34 Adam Fox .30 .75
35 Connor McDavid 1.25 3.00
36 Mikko Rantanen .60 1.50
37 John Klingberg .25 .60
38 Mitch Marner .40 1.00
39 Rasmus Dahlin .30 .75
40 Barrett Hayton .25 .60
41 Jeff Carter .20 .50
42 Robby Fabbri .15 .40
43 Ryan Johansen .20 .50
44 Max Domi .25 .60
45 Kevin Fiala .20 .50
46 Kevin Hayes .20 .50
47 Nazem Kadri .30 .75
48 Martin Jones .20 .50
49 Pierre-Luc Dubois .20 .50
50 Matthew Tkachuk .50 1.25
51 Boone Jenner .25 .60
52 Tim Stutzle .30 .75
53 Auston Matthews 1.00 2.50
54 Miro Heiskanen .30 .75
55 Jaden Schwartz .20 .50
56 Filip Forsberg .40 1.00
57 Johnny Gaudreau .40 1.00
58 Mathew Barzal .30 .75
59 Alex Killorn .15 .40
60 Patrick Kane .50 1.25
61 Jake Oettinger .40 1.00
62 Nikolaj Ehlers .25 .60
63 J.T. Miller .30 .75
64 Jonathan Quick .30 .75
65 Max Jones .15 .40
66 Alexis Lafreniere .40 1.00
67 Mark Scheifele .40 1.00
68 Dylan Cozens .25 .60
69 Philipp Grubauer .25 .60
70 Kevin Labanc .15 .40
71 Sean Durzi .15 .40
72 Vitek Vanecek .25 .60
73 Dylan Larkin .30 .75
74 Dougie Hamilton .20 .50
75 Nathan MacKinnon 1.00 2.50
76 Brad Marchand .50 1.25
77 Moritz Seider .30 .75
78 Tyler Toffoli .25 .60
79 Patrik Laine .30 .75
80 Andrew Copp .15 .40
81 Robert Thomas .25 .60
82 Kirby Dach .25 .60
83 Elias Lindholm .25 .60
84 Clayton Keller .30 .75
85 Christian Fischer .15 .40
86 Josh Anderson .20 .50
87 Alex Ovechkin 1.00 2.50
88 Charlie McAvoy .30 .75
89 Jaccob Slavin .20 .50
90 Alex Pietrangelo .20 .50
91 Sam Bennett .40 1.00
92 Jordan Binnington .40 1.00
93 Jacob Trouba .20 .50
94 Bryan Rust .25 .60
95 Chris Kreider .30 .75
96 Jason Robertson .40 1.00
97 Tomas Hertl .25 .60
98 Jakob Chychrun .25 .60
99 Evgeny Kuznetsov .30 .75
100 Igor Shesterkin .50 1.25
101 Tyler Seguin .30 .75
102 Phil Kessel .25 .60
103 William Nylander .50 1.25
104 Victor Hedman .30 .75
105 Seth Jones .25 .60
106 Viktor Arvidsson .15 .40
107 Mats Zuccarello .20 .50
108 Claude Giroux .25 .60
109 Rickard Rakell .20 .50
110 Ryan McDonagh .15 .40
111 Sean Monahan .15 .40
112 Thomas Chabot .25 .60
113 Joel Eriksson Ek .20 .50
114 Lucas Raymond .40 1.00
115 Brock Boeser .30 .75
116 Cam Fowler .25 .60
117 Elias Pettersson .40 1.00
118 Travis Konecny .25 .60
119 Mikhail Sergachev .20 .50
120 Vladimir Tarasenko .30 .75
121 Sebastian Aho .40 1.00
122 Andrei Svechnikov .30 .75
123 Nikita Kucherov .50 1.25
124 Jake Muzzin .25 .60
125 Nico Hischier .40 1.00
126 Brent Burns .25 .60
127 Brady Tkachuk .40 1.00
128 Oliver Ekman-Larsson .15 .40
129 Quinn Hughes .60 1.50
130 Marc-Edouard Vlasic .15 .40
131 Blake Wheeler .25 .60
132 Robin Lehner .20 .50
133 Brady Skjei .15 .40
134 Josh Norris .25 .60
135 David Pastrnak .60 1.50
136 Artemi Panarin .50 1.25
137 Kris Letang .30 .75
138 David Perron .20 .50
139 Kyle Palmieri .20 .50
140 Jeff Skinner .20 .50
141 Zach Werenski .40 1.00
142 Evander Kane .25 .60
143 Steven Stamkos .50 1.25
144 Martin Necas .40 1.00
145 Vincent Trocheck .25 .60
146 Adam Henrique .25 .60
147 Spencer Knight .25 .60
148 Aleksander Barkov .40 1.00
149 Mathieu Joseph .15 .40
150 Milan Lucic .20 .50
151 Miles Wood .15 .40
152 Reilly Smith .25 .60
153 Andreas Athanasiou .20 .50
154 Jake Guentzel .40 1.00
155 Jonathan Toews .40 1.00
156 Jakub Vrana .20 .50
157 Ryan Suter .20 .50
158 Alex Tuch .25 .60
159 Jordan Eberle .25 .60
160 Yanni Gourde .20 .50
161 Nick Suzuki .50 1.25
162 Erik Karlsson .30 .75
163 Nicklas Backstrom .30 .75
164 Drew Doughty .25 .60
165 Torey Krug .25 .60
166 Roman Josi .25 .60
167 Mark Stone .30 .75
168 Evgeni Malkin .50 1.25
169 Thatcher Demko .30 .75
170 Noah Hanifin .25 .60
171 Devon Toews .20 .50
172 Brayden Schenn .25 .60
173 Kyle Connor .40 1.00
174 Eeli Tolvanen .25 .60
175 Taylor Hall .25 .60
176 Jack Hughes .60 1.50
177 Roope Hintz .30 .75
178 Brandon Saad .20 .50
179 David Krejci .25 .60
180 Jared Spurgeon .25 .60
181 Juuse Saros .30 .75
182 Jonathan Huberdeau .30 .75
183 John Carlson .25 .60
184 Shayne Gostisbehere .25 .60
185 Joonas Donskoi .15 .40
186 Marc-Andre Fleury .50 1.25
187 James Reimer .15 .40
188 Logan Couture .30 .75
189 Matt Duchene .25 .60
190 Shea Theodore .30 .75
191 Cale Makar .60 1.50
192 Anze Kopitar .40 1.00
193 Jordan Kyrou .25 .60
194 Matt Dumba .15 .40
195 Patrice Bergeron .30 .75
196 Brock Nelson .25 .60
197 Jamie Benn .25 .60
198 Corey Perry .40 1.00
199 Alex DeBrincat .30 .75
200 Brayden Point CL .30 .75
201 Jack Eichel SP .75 2.00
202 Aaron Ekblad SP .50 1.25
203 Joe Pavelski SP .60 1.50
204 Zach Parise SP .50 1.25
205 Colton Parayko SP .40 1.00
206 Tyler Bertuzzi SP .40 1.00
207 Drake Batherson SP .50 1.25
208 Tristan Jarry SP .50 1.25
209 Troy Terry SP .40 1.00
210 Victor Olofsson SP .50 1.25
211 Seth Jarvis SP .60 1.50
212 Jared McCann SP .40 1.00
213 Tanner Jeannot SP .30 .75
214 Mikey Anderson SP .40 1.00
215 Ross Colton SP .40 1.00
216 Michael Bunting SP .50 1.25
217 Oskar Lindblom SP .40 1.00
218 Dawson Mercer SP .60 1.50
219 Cole Sillinger SP .40 1.00
220 Jeremy Swayman SP .75 2.00
221 Vincent Desharnais SP RC 2.00 5.00
222 Bobby McMann SP RC 2.50 6.00
223 Yaroslav Askarov SP RC 4.00 10.00
224 Joona Koppanen SP RC 1.25 3.00
225 Jonathan Gruden SP RC 1.50 4.00
226 William Dufour SP RC 1.25 3.00
227 Jaxson Stauber SP RC 1.50 4.00
228 Jakob Pelletier SP RC 2.00 5.00
229 Samuel Bolduc SP RC 1.50 4.00
230 Milos Kelemen SP RC 1.50 4.00
231 Luke Philp SP RC 1.50 4.00
232 Will Cuylle SP RC 2.50 6.00
233 Ridly Greig SP RC 2.50 6.00
234 Owen Beck SP RC 2.50 6.00
235 Arturs Silovs SP RC 3.00 8.00
236 Cole Guttman SP RC 1.50 4.00
237 Arnaud Durandeau SP RC 1.50 4.00
238 Billy Sweezey SP RC 1.50 4.00
239 Luke Evangelista SP RC 2.50 6.00
240 Matt Murray SP RC 1.50 4.00
241 Vincent Iorio SP RC 1.50 4.00
242 Luke Hughes SP RC 5.00 12.00
243 Leevi Merilainen SP RC 1.50 4.00
244 Matthew Knies SP RC 6.00 15.00
245 Egor Afanasyev SP RC 1.50 4.00
246 Tyson Foerster SP RC 3.00 8.00
247 Simon Edvinsson SP RC 3.00 8.00
248 Jiri Patera SP RC 1.50 4.00
249 Devon Levi SP RC 4.00 10.00
250 Yaroslav Askarov SP CL 4.00 10.00
251 Connor Bedard RC 100.00 250.00
252 Hugh McGing RC 1.50 4.00
253 Michael Kesselring RC 1.50 4.00
254 Kevin Korchinski RC 2.50 6.00
255 Nick Swaney RC 1.50 4.00
256 Matthew Kessel RC 1.25 3.00
257 Brock Faber RC 4.00 10.00
258 Logan Cooley RC 5.00 12.00
259 Alex Laferriere RC 2.50 6.00
260 Jackson LaCombe RC 1.50 4.00
261 Dustin Wolf RC 5.00 12.00
262 Pavel Mintyukov RC 2.50 6.00
263 Matthew Coronato RC 2.50 6.00
264 Tye Kartye RC 2.50 6.00
265 Leo Carlsson RC 5.00 12.00
266 Henry Thrun RC 1.50 4.00
267 Stanislav Svozil RC 1.25 3.00
268 Elliot Desnoyers RC 1.50 4.00
269 Dmitri Voronkov RC 2.00 5.00
270 Adam Fantilli RC 5.00 12.00
271 Emil Andrae RC 1.50 4.00
272 Hunter McKown RC 1.50 4.00
273 Adam Ginning RC 1.50 4.00
274 Hardy Haman Aktell RC 1.50 4.00
275 Zach Benson RC 2.50 6.00
276 Mackie Samoskevich RC 2.50 6.00
277 Fraser Minten RC 3.00 8.00
278 Matthew Poitras RC 3.00 8.00
279 Marco Kasper RC 4.00 10.00
280 Justin Sourdif RC 1.50 4.00
281 Sean Farrell RC 1.50 4.00
282 John Beecher RC 3.00 8.00

2023-24 Upper Deck MVP Gold Script

*GOLD SCRIPT: 2.5X TO 6X BASIC
*GOLD SCRIPT SP: 2.5X TO 6X BASIC
*GOLD SCRIPT RC: 1X TO 2.5X BASIC

2023-24 Upper Deck MVP Ice Battles

*ICE BATTLES: .75X TO 2X BASIC
*ICE BATTLES SP: .5X TO 1.2X BASIC
*ICE BATTLES RC: .3X TO .75X BASIC

2023-24 Upper Deck MVP Silver Script

*SILVER SCRIPT: .75X TO 2X BASIC
*SILVER SCRIPT SP: .75X TO 2X BASIC
*SILVER SCRIPT RC: .5X TO 1.2X BASIC

2023-24 Upper Deck MVP Super Script

*SUPER SCRIPT: 4X TO 10X BASIC
*SUPER SCRIPT SP: 4X TO 10X BASIC
*SUPER SCRIPT RC: 1.5X TO 4X BASIC

2023-24 Upper Deck MVP '23 NHL Draft #1 Pick

*GOLD: 1.2X TO 3X BASIC
DP1 Redemption Card
Connor Bedard 250.00 600.00

2023-24 Upper Deck MVP Alternate Threads

*GOLD: .6X TO 1.5X BASIC
AT1 MacKinnon/Makar/Georgiev 5.00 12.00
AT2 Seguin/Suter/Oettinger 2.00 5.00
AT3 Huberdeau/Weegar/Markstrom 1.50 4.00
AT4 Stamkos/Hedman/Vasilevskiy 2.50 6.00
AT6 Konecny/Sanheim/Hart 1.25 3.00
AT7 Guentzel/Letang/Jarry 2.00 5.00
AT8 Kopitar/Doughty/Quick 2.00 5.00
AT9 Hughes/Hamilton/Vanecek 3.00 8.00
AT10 Zibanejad/Fox/Shesterkin 2.50 6.00
AT11 Forsberg/Josi/Saros 2.00 5.00
AT12 Kaprizov/Spurgeon/Fleury 4.00 10.00
AT13 Svechnikov/Slavin/Andersen 1.50 4.00
AT14 Barzal/Pelech/Sorokin 2.00 5.00
AT15 McDavid/Nurse/Skinner 6.00 15.00
AT16 Larkin/Seider/Husso 1.50 4.00
AT17 Pastrnak/McAvoy/Swayman 3.00 8.00
AT18 Ovechkin/Carlson/Kuemper 5.00 12.00
AT19 Chabot/Forsberg/Tkachuk 2.00 5.00
AT20 Matthews/Rielly/Samsonov 5.00 12.00

2023-24 Upper Deck MVP Colors and Contours

*GREEN/20: 1.2X TO 3X BASIC
MT1 Max Domi 2.50 6.00
MT2 Zach Werenski 4.00 10.00
MT3 Kirby Dach 2.50 6.00
MT4 Mikko Rantanen 6.00 15.00
MT5 Moritz Seider 3.00 8.00
MT6 Jaden Schwartz 2.00 5.00
MT7 Auston Matthews 10.00 25.00
MT8 Josh Anderson 2.00 5.00
MT9 Nathan MacKinnon 10.00 25.00
MT10 John Gibson 2.50 6.00
MT11 Aleksander Barkov 4.00 10.00
MT12 Elias Pettersson 4.00 10.00
MT13 Victor Hedman 3.00 8.00
MT14 Matt Dumba 1.50 4.00
MT15 John Carlson 2.50 6.00
MT16 Gabriel Landeskog 3.00 8.00
MT17 Tomas Hertl 2.50 6.00
MT18 Troy Terry 2.00 5.00
MT19 Andrei Vasilevskiy 4.00 10.00
MT20 Rasmus Dahlin 3.00 8.00
MT21 Aaron Ekblad 3.00 8.00
MT22 Patrik Laine 3.00 8.00
MT23 Matt Duchene 2.50 6.00
MT24 Morgan Rielly 2.50 6.00
MT25 Jakob Chychrun 2.50 6.00
MT26 Kyle Okposo 1.50 4.00
MT27 Sidney Crosby 10.00 25.00
MT28 Elias Lindholm 2.50 6.00
MT29 Anze Kopitar 4.00 10.00
MT30 Clayton Keller 3.00 8.00
MT31 Matthew Tkachuk 5.00 12.00
MT32 Jonathan Toews 4.00 10.00
MT33 Noah Hanifin 2.50 6.00
MT34 Roman Josi 2.50 6.00
MT35 Mitch Marner 4.00 10.00
MT36 Yaroslav Askarov 6.00 15.00
MT37 Brady Skjei 1.50 4.00
MT38 Charlie Coyle 2.50 6.00
MT39 Cam Atkinson 2.50 6.00
MT40 Jakob Pelletier 3.00 8.00
MT41 Mika Zibanejad 3.00 8.00
MT42 Adrian Kempe 2.50 6.00
MT43 Brayden Schenn 2.50 6.00
MT44 Yanni Gourde 2.00 5.00
MT45 Seth Jones 2.50 6.00
MT46 Nico Hischier 4.00 10.00
MT47 Samuel Bolduc 2.50 6.00
MT48 Tim Stutzle 3.00 8.00
MT49 Will Cuylle 4.00 10.00
MT50 Artemi Panarin 5.00 12.00
MT51 Jason Robertson 4.00 10.00
MT52 Ridly Greig 4.00 10.00
MT53 Connor McDavid 12.00 30.00
MT54 Trevor Zegras 2.50 6.00
MT55 Cale Makar 6.00 15.00
MT56 Adam Fox 3.00 8.00
MT57 Erik Karlsson 3.00 8.00
MT58 Vladimir Tarasenko 3.00 8.00
MT59 Ryan Nugent-Hopkins 3.00 8.00
MT60 Oliver Wahlstrom 1.50 4.00
MT61 Nikita Kucherov 5.00 12.00
MT62 Tyler Seguin 3.00 8.00
MT63 Steven Stamkos 5.00 12.00
MT64 James van Riemsdyk 2.00 5.00
MT65 Marc-Andre Fleury 5.00 12.00
MT66 Andrei Svechnikov 3.00 8.00
MT67 Roope Hintz 3.00 8.00
MT68 Owen Beck 4.00 10.00
MT69 Kris Letang 3.00 8.00
MT70 Jack Hughes 6.00 15.00
MT71 Dylan Larkin 3.00 8.00
MT72 Brady Tkachuk 4.00 10.00
MT73 Miro Heiskanen 3.00 8.00
MT74 Igor Shesterkin 5.00 12.00
MT75 Patrice Bergeron 3.00 8.00
MT76 Jordan Staal 2.00 5.00
MT77 Ryan O'Reilly 2.50 6.00
MT78 Jack Eichel 4.00 10.00
MT79 Luke Evangelista 4.00 10.00
MT80 Kevin Hayes 2.00 5.00
MT81 Blake Wheeler 2.50 6.00
MT82 Alex Ovechkin 10.00 25.00
MT83 Kirill Kaprizov 8.00 20.00
MT84 Mathew Barzal 3.00 8.00
MT85 Evgeni Malkin 5.00 12.00
MT86 Johnny Gaudreau 4.00 10.00
MT87 Cole Caufield 5.00 12.00
MT88 Tage Thompson 3.00 8.00
MT89 Leon Draisaitl 8.00 20.00
MT90 Kyle Connor 4.00 10.00
MT91 Vincent Iorio 2.50 6.00
MT92 Quinn Hughes 6.00 15.00
MT93 Patrick Kane 5.00 12.00
MT94 Mikael Backlund 2.00 5.00
MT95 Drew Doughty 2.50 6.00
MT96 Lucas Raymond 4.00 10.00
MT97 Tyson Foerster 5.00 12.00
MT98 Evander Kane 2.50 6.00
MT99 Jacob Markstrom 2.50 6.00
MT100 Simon Edvinsson 5.00 12.00

2023-24 Upper Deck MVP Ice Reps

*GOLD: .5X TO 1.2X BASIC
IR1 A.Kopitar/Bailey 1.50 4.00
IR2 J.Toews/Tommy Hawk 1.50 4.00
IR3 C.McDavid/Hunter 5.00 12.00
IR4 J.Staal/Stormy .75 2.00
IR5 R.O'Reilly/Louie 1.00 2.50
IR6 S.Crosby/Iceburgh 4.00 10.00
IR7 A.Ovechkin/Slapshot 4.00 10.00
IR8 S.Stamkos/Thunderbug 2.00 5.00
IR9 N.Hischier/N.J. Devil 1.50 4.00
IR10 N.Suzuki/Youppi! 2.00 5.00
IR11 J.Spurgeon/Nordy 1.00 2.50
IR12 A.Lee/Sparky The Dragon .75 2.00
IR13 J.Benn/Victor E. Green 1.00 2.50
IR14 A.Barkov/Stanley C. Panther 1.50 4.00
IR15 M.Beniers/Buoy 1.25 3.00
IR16 G.Landeskog/Bernie
the St. Bernard 1.25 3.00
IR17 L.Couture/S.J. Sharkie 1.25 3.00
IR18 K.Okposo/Sabretooth .60 1.50
IR19 J.Tavares/Carlton the Bear 1.50 4.00
IR20 R.Josi/Gnash 1.00 2.50
IR21 P.Bergeron/Blades The Bruin 1.25 3.00
IR22 B.Tkachuk/Spartacat 1.25 3.00
IR23 B.Horvat/Fin The Whale 1.25 3.00
IR24 B.Jenner/Stinger 1.00 2.50
IR25 D.Larkin/Al The Octopus 1.25 3.00

2023-24 Upper Deck MVP Magenta Autographs

203 Joe Pavelski A 10.00 25.00
204 Zach Parise E 8.00 20.00
205 Colton Parayko B 6.00 15.00
206 Tyler Bertuzzi D 6.00 15.00
212 Jared McCann C 6.00 15.00
213 Tanner Jeannot C 5.00 12.00
215 Ross Colton D 6.00 15.00
216 Michael Bunting A 8.00 20.00
218 Dawson Mercer B 10.00 25.00
220 Jeremy Swayman A 12.00 30.00
223 Yaroslav Askarov B 20.00 50.00
226 William Dufour E 6.00 15.00
228 Jakob Pelletier C 10.00 25.00
229 Samuel Bolduc E 8.00 20.00
233 Ridly Greig C 12.00 30.00
234 Owen Beck D 12.00 30.00
235 Arturs Silovs C 60.00 150.00
237 Arnaud Durandeau E 8.00 20.00
239 Luke Evangelista B 12.00 30.00
245 Egor Afanasyev B 8.00 20.00
247 Simon Edvinsson B 15.00 40.00

2023-24 Upper Deck MVP Rookie Redemptions

RR1 Central Division 150.00 400.00
RR2 Pacific Division 25.00 60.00
RR3 Metropolitan Division 25.00 60.00
RR4 Atlantic Division 25.00 60.00

2023-24 Upper Deck MVP Stars of the Rink

*GOLD: .5X TO 1.2X BASIC
SS1 Andrei Svechnikov 1.00 2.50
SS2 Mathew Barzal 1.00 2.50
SS3 Mark Stone 1.00 2.50
SS4 Connor McDavid 4.00 10.00
SS5 Erik Karlsson 1.00 2.50
SS6 Rasmus Dahlin 1.00 2.50
SS7 Jonathan Huberdeau 1.00 2.50
SS8 Kirill Kaprizov 2.50 6.00
SS9 Auston Matthews 3.00 8.00
SS10 Patrik Laine 1.00 2.50
SS11 Aleksander Barkov 1.25 3.00
SS13 Artemi Panarin 1.50 4.00
SS14 Kevin Hayes .60 1.50
SS15 Matt Duchene .75 2.00
SS16 Ryan O'Reilly .75 2.00
SS17 Kyle Connor 1.25 3.00
SS18 Dylan Larkin 1.00 2.50
SS19 Trevor Zegras .75 2.00
SS20 Cole Caufield 1.50 4.00
SS21 Jack Hughes 2.00 5.00
SS22 Alex Ovechkin 3.00 8.00
SS23 Sidney Crosby 3.00 8.00
SS24 Anze Kopitar 1.25 3.00
SS25 Patrice Bergeron 1.00 2.50
SS26 Brady Tkachuk 1.25 3.00
SS27 Quinn Hughes 2.00 5.00
SS28 Patrick Kane 1.50 4.00
SS29 Joe Pavelski 1.00 2.50
SS30 Steven Stamkos 1.50 4.00

2023-24 Upper Deck MVP Talent

*GOLD SCRIPT: .6X TO 1.5X BASIC
*DIE CUT/250: 1X TO 2.5X BASIC
*SUPER SCRIPT/25: 2X TO 5X BASIC
MT1 Max Domi .75 2.00
MT2 Zach Werenski 1.25 3.00
MT3 Kirby Dach .75 2.00
MT4 Mikko Rantanen 2.00 5.00
MT5 Moritz Seider 1.00 2.50
MT6 Jaden Schwartz .60 1.50
MT7 Auston Matthews 3.00 8.00
MT8 Josh Anderson .60 1.50
MT9 Nathan MacKinnon 3.00 8.00
MT10 John Gibson .75 2.00
MT11 Aleksander Barkov 1.25 3.00
MT12 Elias Pettersson 1.25 3.00
MT13 Victor Hedman 1.00 2.50
MT14 Matt Dumba .50 1.25
MT15 John Carlson .75 2.00
MT16 Gabriel Landeskog 1.00 2.50
MT17 Tomas Hertl .75 2.00
MT18 Troy Terry .60 1.50
MT19 Andrei Vasilevskiy 1.25 3.00
MT20 Rasmus Dahlin 1.00 2.50
MT21 Aaron Ekblad 1.00 2.50
MT22 Patrik Laine 1.00 2.50
MT23 Matt Duchene .75 2.00
MT24 Morgan Rielly .75 2.00
MT25 Jakob Chychrun .75 2.00
MT26 Kyle Okposo .50 1.25
MT27 Sidney Crosby 3.00 8.00
MT28 Elias Lindholm .75 2.00
MT29 Anze Kopitar 1.25 3.00
MT30 Clayton Keller 1.00 2.50
MT31 Matthew Tkachuk 1.50 4.00
MT32 Jonathan Toews 1.25 3.00
MT33 Noah Hanifin .75 2.00
MT34 Roman Josi .75 2.00
MT35 Mitch Marner 1.25 3.00
MT36 Yaroslav Askarov 2.00 5.00
MT37 Brady Skjei .50 1.25
MT38 Charlie Coyle .75 2.00
MT39 Cam Atkinson .75 2.00
MT40 Jakob Pelletier 1.00 2.50
MT41 Mika Zibanejad 1.00 2.50
MT42 Adrian Kempe .75 2.00
MT43 Brayden Schenn .75 2.00
MT44 Yanni Gourde .60 1.50
MT45 Seth Jones .75 2.00
MT46 Nico Hischier 1.25 3.00
MT47 Samuel Bolduc .75 2.00
MT48 Tim Stutzle 1.00 2.50
MT49 Will Cuylle 1.25 3.00
MT50 Artemi Panarin 1.50 4.00
MT51 Jason Robertson 1.25 3.00
MT52 Ridly Greig 1.25 3.00
MT53 Connor McDavid 4.00 10.00
MT54 Trevor Zegras .75 2.00
MT55 Cale Makar 2.00 5.00
MT56 Adam Fox 1.00 2.50
MT57 Erik Karlsson 1.00 2.50
MT58 Vladimir Tarasenko 1.00 2.50
MT59 Ryan Nugent-Hopkins 1.00 2.50
MT60 Oliver Wahlstrom .50 1.25
MT61 Nikita Kucherov 1.50 4.00
MT62 Tyler Seguin 1.00 2.50
MT63 Steven Stamkos 1.50 4.00
MT64 James van Riemsdyk .60 1.50
MT65 Marc-Andre Fleury 1.50 4.00
MT66 Andrei Svechnikov 1.00 2.50
MT67 Roope Hintz 1.00 2.50
MT68 Owen Beck 1.25 3.00
MT69 Kris Letang 1.00 2.50
MT70 Jack Hughes 2.00 5.00
MT71 Dylan Larkin 1.00 2.50
MT72 Brady Tkachuk 1.25 3.00
MT73 Miro Heiskanen 1.00 2.50
MT74 Igor Shesterkin 1.50 4.00
MT75 Patrice Bergeron 1.00 2.50
MT76 Jordan Staal .60 1.50
MT77 Ryan O'Reilly .75 2.00
MT78 Jack Eichel 1.25 3.00
MT79 Luke Evangelista 1.25 3.00
MT80 Kevin Hayes .60 1.50
MT81 Blake Wheeler .75 2.00
MT82 Alex Ovechkin 3.00 8.00
MT83 Kirill Kaprizov 2.50 6.00
MT84 Mathew Barzal 1.00 2.50
MT85 Evgeni Malkin 1.50 4.00
MT86 Johnny Gaudreau 1.25 3.00
MT87 Cole Caufield 1.50 4.00
MT88 Tage Thompson 1.00 2.50
MT89 Leon Draisaitl 2.50 6.00
MT90 Kyle Connor 1.25 3.00
MT91 Vincent Iorio .75 2.00
MT92 Quinn Hughes 2.00 5.00
MT93 Patrick Kane 1.50 4.00
MT94 Mikael Backlund .60 1.50
MT95 Drew Doughty .75 2.00
MT96 Lucas Raymond 1.25 3.00
MT97 Tyson Foerster 1.50 4.00
MT98 Evander Kane .75 2.00
MT99 Jacob Markstrom .75 2.00
MT100 Simon Edvinsson 1.50 4.00

2024-25 Upper Deck MVP

1 Kirill Kaprizov .75 2.00
2 Artemi Panarin .50 1.25
3 Filip Forsberg .40 1.00
4 Erik Karlsson .30 .75
5 Leon Draisaitl .75 2.00
6 Brayden Point .30 .75
7 J.T. Miller .30 .75
8 Cale Makar .60 1.50
9 Kyle Connor .40 1.00
10 Jared McCann .20 .50
11 Jack Eichel .40 1.00
12 Nikita Kucherov .50 1.25
13 Travis Konecny .25 .60
14 Michael Bunting .25 .60
15 Darcy Kuemper .25 .60
16 Joe Pavelski .30 .75
17 Josh Morrissey .30 .75
18 Brady Tkachuk .40 1.00
19 Kevin Hayes .20 .50
20 Martin Necas .40 1.00
21 Jason Robertson .40 1.00
22 Auston Matthews 1.00 2.50
23 Thomas Chabot .25 .60
24 Anze Kopitar .40 1.00
25 Ukko-Pekka Luukkonen .20 .50
26 Mika Zibanejad .30 .75
27 Mason McTavish .25 .60
28 Jesperi Kotkaniemi .25 .60
29 Nathan MacKinnon 1.00 2.50
30 Ilya Sorokin .40 1.00
31 Mark Stone .30 .75
32 Ryan Nugent-Hopkins .30 .75
33 Ryan Strome .25 .60
34 Ryan O'Reilly .25 .60
35 Mark Scheifele .40 1.00
36 Josh Norris .25 .60
37 Elvis Merzlikins .25 .60
38 Logan Cooley .40 1.00
39 Alex Ovechkin 1.00 2.50
40 Drew Doughty .25 .60
41 Brock Boeser .30 .75
42 Roope Hintz .30 .75
43 Pierre Engvall .15 .40
44 Joonas Korpisalo .25 .60
45 Charlie Coyle .25 .60
46 Jonathan Marchessault .30 .75
47 Jack Hughes .60 1.50
48 Phillip Danault .25 .60
49 Jeff Skinner .25 .60
50 Cam Atkinson .25 .60
51 Justin Faulk .20 .50
52 Brandon Hagel .25 .60
53 Moritz Seider .30 .75
54 Troy Terry .20 .50
55 Jaccob Slavin .20 .50
56 Michael Matheson .15 .40
57 Ryan Graves .15 .40
58 Jacob Markstrom .25 .60
59 Kyle Palmieri .20 .50
60 Aaron Ekblad .30 .75
61 Igor Shesterkin .50 1.25
62 Tim Stutzle .30 .75
63 Zach Werenski .40 1.00
64 John Carlson .25 .60
65 Chris Kreider .30 .75
66 Evander Kane .25 .60
67 Tristan Jarry .25 .60
68 Seth Jarvis .25 .60
69 Logan Thompson .30 .75
70 Roman Josi .25 .60
71 Johnny Gaudreau .40 1.00
72 Jordan Binnington .40 1.00
73 Adrian Kempe .25 .60
74 Mario Ferraro .15 .40
75 David Pastrnak .60 1.50
76 Alex Iafallo .15 .40
77 Mats Zuccarello .25 .60
78 Elias Pettersson .40 1.00
79 Alexandar Georgiev .25 .60
80 Cole Caufield .50 1.25
81 Jacob Middleton .15 .40
82 Sergei Bobrovsky .40 1.00
83 Mitch Marner .40 1.00
84 Dylan Cozens .25 .60
85 Jesper Bratt .25 .60
86 Shea Theodore .30 .75
87 Brent Burns .25 .60
88 Sidney Crosby 1.00 2.50
89 Steven Stamkos .50 1.25
90 Jaden Schwartz .20 .50
91 Leo Carlsson .40 1.00
92 Brendan Gallagher .25 .60

93 Filip Hronek .15 .40
94 Jamie Benn .25 .60
95 Sean Couturier .20 .50
96 Quinton Byfield .30 .75
97 Connor McDavid 1.25 3.00
98 Connor Bedard 1.50 4.00
99 Alexander Barabanov .15 .40
100 Linus Ullmark CL .25 .60
101 Ryan Hartman .15 .40
102 Ville Husso .15 .40
103 Adam Fantilli .40 1.00
104 John Tavares .40 1.00
105 Dougie Hamilton .20 .50
106 MacKenzie Weegar .20 .50
107 Connor Hellebuyck .50 1.25
108 Matthew Tkachuk .50 1.25
109 Jordan Kyrou .25 .60
110 Vince Dunn .20 .50
111 Devon Toews .20 .50
112 J.T. Compher .15 .40
113 Brock Nelson .25 .60
114 Thatcher Demko .30 .75
115 Andrei Svechnikov .30 .75
116 Brad Marchand .50 1.25
117 Vincent Trocheck .25 .60
118 Jesperi Kotkaniemi .25 .60
119 Stuart Skinner .30 .75
120 Alex Pietrangelo .20 .50
121 Kevin Fiala .20 .50
122 Claude Giroux .25 .60
123 Owen Power .25 .60
124 Lucas Raymond .40 1.00
125 Andrei Kuzmenko .25 .60
126 Adam Fox .30 .75
127 Miro Heiskanen .30 .75
128 T.J. Oshie .25 .60
129 Joel Eriksson Ek .20 .50
130 Kris Letang .30 .75
131 Clayton Keller .30 .75
132 Logan Couture .30 .75
133 Nick Suzuki .50 1.25
134 Andrei Vasilevskiy .40 1.00
135 Matty Beniers .30 .75
136 Aleksander Barkov .40 1.00
137 Jake Guentzel .40 1.00
138 Luke Hughes .40 1.00
139 Nazem Kadri .30 .75
140 Dylan Larkin .30 .75
141 Andre Burakovsky .15 .40
142 Patrik Laine .30 .75
143 Jacob Trouba .20 .50
144 Nino Niederreiter .15 .40
145 Sebastian Aho .40 1.00
146 Jake Sanderson .30 .75
147 Pierre-Luc Dubois .20 .50
148 William Nylander .50 1.25
149 Nico Hischier .40 1.00
150 Karel Vejmelka .15 .40
151 Sam Bennett .40 1.00
152 Marco Rossi .30 .75
153 Joel Farabee .25 .60
154 Seth Jones .25 .60
155 Mathew Barzal .30 .75
156 Brayden Schenn .25 .60
157 Alex DeBrincat .30 .75
158 Rasmus Dahlin .30 .75
159 Adin Hill .25 .60
160 Tyler Seguin .30 .75
161 Alexis Lafreniere .40 1.00
162 Evgeny Kuznetsov .30 .75
163 Andrew Mangiapane .25 .60
164 Tyler Toffoli .25 .60
165 Travis Sanheim .15 .40
166 Trevor Zegras .25 .60
167 Sam Reinhart .50 1.25
168 Mackenzie Blackwood .25 .60
169 Mikko Rantanen .60 1.50
170 Victor Hedman .30 .75
171 Vitek Vanecek .25 .60
172 Jakob Chychrun .25 .60
173 Charlie McAvoy .30 .75
174 Philipp Kurashev .20 .50
175 Filip Gustavsson .25 .60
176 Reilly Smith .25 .60
177 Gabriel Landeskog .30 .75
178 Drake Batherson .25 .60
179 Morgan Rielly .25 .60
180 Nick Schmaltz .20 .50
181 Frank Vatrano .20 .50
182 Bo Horvat .30 .75
183 Adam Lowry .20 .50
184 Taylor Hall .25 .60
185 William Eklund .30 .75
186 Evan Rodrigues .20 .50
187 Philipp Grubauer .25 .60
188 Jonathan Huberdeau .30 .75
189 Ilya Samsonov .25 .60
190 Owen Tippett .15 .40
191 John Gibson .25 .60
192 Alex Newhook .20 .50
193 Pavel Buchnevich .20 .50
194 Boone Jenner .25 .60
195 Evgeni Malkin .50 1.25
196 K'Andre Miller .20 .50
197 Alex Tuch .25 .60
198 Oliver Bjorkstrand .20 .50
199 Jake Oettinger .40 1.00
200 Mikhail Sergachev .20 .50
201 Matt Boldy SP .75 2.00
202 Tomas Hertl SP .50 1.25
203 Luke Evangelista SP .40 1.00
204 Ryan Reaves SP .40 1.00
205 Wyatt Johnston SP 1.00 2.50
206 William Karlsson SP .60 1.50
207 Timo Meier SP .50 1.25
208 Bryan Rust SP .50 1.25
209 Anton Lundell SP .50 1.25
210 Tom Wilson SP .50 1.25
211 Robert Thomas SP .50 1.25
212 Juuse Saros SP .60 1.50
213 Matthew Knies SP 1.00 2.50
214 Nikolaj Ehlers SP .50 1.25
215 Tage Thompson SP .60 1.50
216 Noah Dobson SP .60 1.50
217 Artturi Lehkonen SP .60 1.50
218 Arber Xhekaj SP .50 1.25
219 Quinn Hughes SP 1.25 3.00
220 Zach Hyman SP .75 2.00
221 Olen Zellweger SP RC 3.00 8.00
222 Adam Klapka SP RC 1.50 4.00
223 Brendan Brisson SP RC 2.00 5.00
224 Declan Carlile SP RC 1.50 4.00
225 Graeme Clarke SP RC 1.50 4.00
226 Justin Brazeau SP RC 1.50 4.00
227 Kyle MacLean SP RC 1.50 4.00
228 Mason Morelli SP RC 1.50 4.00
229 Shakir Mukhamadullin SP RC 2.00 5.00
230 Zachary Bolduc SP RC 3.00 8.00
231 Matt Villalta SP RC 1.50 4.00
232 Phil Kemp SP RC 1.50 4.00
233 Brennan Othmann SP RC 2.50 6.00
234 Emil Lilleberg SP RC 1.50 4.00
235 Gage Goncalves SP RC 2.00 5.00
236 Jack Thompson SP RC 1.50 4.00
237 Jesper Wallstedt SP RC 4.00 10.00
238 Lukas Cormier SP RC 1.50 4.00
239 Marshall Rifai SP RC 1.50 4.00
240 Matt Rempe SP RC 3.00 8.00
241 Vasily Ponomarev SP RC 1.50 4.00
242 Arshdeep Bains SP RC 2.00 5.00
243 Joshua Roy SP RC 2.50 6.00
244 Jason Polin SP RC 1.50 4.00
245 Yan Kuznetsov SP RC 1.50 4.00
246 Maxwell Crozier SP RC 1.50 4.00
247 Logan Stankoven SP RC 4.00 10.00
248 Zack Ostapchuk SP RC 1.50 4.00
249 Pierrick Dube SP RC 1.50 4.00
250 Olen Zellweger SP CL 3.00 8.00

2024-25 Upper Deck MVP Gold Script

*GOLD SCRIPT: 2.5X TO 6X BASIC
*GOLD SCRIPT SP: 2.5X TO 6X BASIC
*GOLD SCRIPT RC: 1X TO 2.5X BASIC
98 Connor Bedard 12.00 30.00
240 Matt Rempe SP 15.00 40.00

2024-25 Upper Deck MVP Silver Script

*SLVR SCRIPT: .75X TO 2X BASIC
*SLVR SCRIPT SP: .75X TO 2X BASIC
*SLVR SCRIPT RC: .5X TO 1.2X BASIC
98 Connor Bedard 6.00 15.00

2024-25 Upper Deck MVP Super Script

*SUPER SCRIPT: 4X TO 10X BASIC
*SUPER SCRIPT SP: 4X TO 10X BASIC
*SUPER SCRIPT RC: 1.5X TO 4X BASIC
98 Connor Bedard 60.00 150.00
233 Brennan Othmann 25.00 60.00
240 Matt Rempe 40.00 100.00
247 Logan Stankoven 60.00 150.00

2024-25 Upper Deck MVP '24 NHL Draft #1 Pick

DP1 Macklin Celebrini 40.00 100.00

2024-25 Upper Deck MVP 10th Anniversary

*GOLD SCRIPT: .6X TO 1.5X BASIC
*SUPER SCRIPT/25: 2X TO 5X BASIC
MR1 Kyle Connor 1.25 3.00
MR2 Kirill Kaprizov 2.50 6.00
MR3 Sidney Crosby 3.00 8.00
MR4 Jack Hughes 2.00 5.00
MR5 Logan Stankoven 2.00 5.00
MR6 Jack Eichel 1.25 3.00
MR7 Alex Ovechkin 3.00 8.00
MR8 Cale Makar 2.00 5.00
MR9 David Pastrnak 2.00 5.00
MR10 Brady Tkachuk 1.25 3.00
MR11 Brendan Brisson 1.00 2.50
MR12 Connor Bedard 2.50 6.00
MR13 Elias Pettersson 1.25 3.00
MR14 Josh Doan 1.25 3.00
MR15 Sebastian Aho 1.25 3.00
MR16 Mitch Marner 1.25 3.00
MR17 Leon Draisaitl 2.50 6.00
MR18 Zachary Bolduc 1.50 4.00
MR19 Matthew Tkachuk 1.50 4.00
MR20 Brennan Othmann 1.25 3.00
MR21 Jason Robertson 1.25 3.00
MR22 Cole Caufield 1.50 4.00
MR23 Filip Forsberg 1.25 3.00
MR24 Olen Zellweger 1.50 4.00
MR25 Artemi Panarin 1.50 4.00
MR26 Rasmus Dahlin 1.00 2.50
MR27 Zach Dean .75 2.00
MR28 Brayden Point 1.00 2.50
MR29 Nathan MacKinnon 3.00 8.00
MR30 Connor McDavid 4.00 10.00
MR31 Shakir Mukhamadullin 1.00 2.50
MR32 Anze Kopitar 1.25 3.00
MR33 Dylan Larkin 1.00 2.50
MR34 Auston Matthews 3.00 8.00

2024-25 Upper Deck MVP Above the Crease

*GOLD: 1X TO 2.5X BASIC
AC1 Alexandar Georgiev 1.00 2.50
AC2 Ilya Sorokin 1.50 4.00
AC3 Filip Gustavsson 1.00 2.50
AC4 Tristan Jarry 1.00 2.50
AC5 Linus Ullmark 1.00 2.50
AC6 Ilya Samsonov 1.00 2.50
AC7 Philipp Grubauer 1.00 2.50
AC8 Sergei Bobrovsky 1.50 4.00
AC9 Darcy Kuemper 1.00 2.50
AC10 Joonas Korpisalo 1.00 2.50
AC11 Logan Thompson 1.25 3.00
AC12 John Gibson 1.00 2.50
AC13 Andrei Vasilevskiy 1.50 4.00
AC14 Thatcher Demko 1.25 3.00
AC15 Jake Oettinger 1.50 4.00
AC16 Connor Hellebuyck 2.00 5.00
AC17 Jordan Binnington 1.50 4.00
AC18 Jacob Markstrom 1.00 2.50
AC19 Juuse Saros 1.25 3.00
AC20 Igor Shesterkin 2.00 5.00

2024-25 Upper Deck MVP Colors and Contours Gold

*TEAL/20: 1.2X TO 3X BASIC
MR1 Kyle Connor 4.00 10.00
MR2 Kirill Kaprizov 8.00 20.00
MR3 Sidney Crosby 10.00 25.00
MR4 Jack Hughes 6.00 15.00
MR5 Logan Stankoven 12.00 30.00
MR6 Jack Eichel 4.00 10.00
MR7 Alex Ovechkin 10.00 25.00
MR8 Cale Makar 6.00 15.00
MR9 David Pastrnak 6.00 15.00
MR10 Brady Tkachuk 4.00 10.00
MR11 Brendan Brisson 3.00 8.00
MR12 Connor Bedard 25.00 60.00
MR13 Elias Pettersson 4.00 10.00
MR14 Josh Doan 4.00 10.00
MR15 Sebastian Aho 4.00 10.00
MR16 Mitch Marner 4.00 10.00
MR17 Leon Draisaitl 8.00 20.00
MR18 Zachary Bolduc 5.00 12.00
MR19 Matthew Tkachuk 5.00 12.00
MR20 Brennan Othmann 4.00 10.00
MR21 Jason Robertson 4.00 10.00
MR22 Cole Caufield 5.00 12.00
MR23 Filip Forsberg 4.00 10.00
MR24 Olen Zellweger 5.00 12.00
MR25 Artemi Panarin 5.00 12.00
MR26 Rasmus Dahlin 3.00 8.00
MR27 Zach Dean 2.50 6.00
MR28 Brayden Point 3.00 8.00
MR29 Nathan MacKinnon 10.00 25.00
MR30 Connor McDavid 12.00 30.00
MR31 Shakir Mukhamadullin 3.00 8.00
MR32 Anze Kopitar 4.00 10.00
MR33 Dylan Larkin 3.00 8.00
MR34 Auston Matthews 10.00 25.00

2024-25 Upper Deck MVP It's Their Time

IT1 Connor Bedard 5.00 12.00
IT2 Moritz Seider 1.00 2.50
IT3 William Eklund 1.00 2.50
IT4 Mason McTavish .75 2.00
IT5 Cole Caufield 1.50 4.00
IT6 Quinton Byfield 1.00 2.50
IT7 Alexis Lafreniere 1.25 3.00
IT8 Seth Jarvis 1.00 2.50
IT9 Jack Hughes 2.00 5.00
IT10 Wyatt Johnston 1.50 4.00
IT11 Lucas Raymond 1.25 3.00
IT12 Matthew Knies 1.50 4.00
IT13 Logan Cooley 1.25 3.00
IT14 Jake Sanderson 1.00 2.50
IT15 Pavel Mintyukov .60 1.50
IT16 Adam Fantilli 1.25 3.00
IT17 Matty Beniers 1.00 2.50
IT18 Luke Hughes 1.25 3.00
IT19 Owen Power .75 2.00
IT20 Jason Robertson 1.25 3.00
IT21 Matt Boldy 1.25 3.00
IT22 Elias Pettersson 1.25 3.00
IT23 Leo Carlsson 1.25 3.00
IT24 Dylan Cozens .75 2.00
IT25 Luke Evangelista .60 1.50

2024-25 Upper Deck MVP It's Their Time Gold

*GOLD: 1X TO 2.5X BASIC

2024-25 Upper Deck MVP Magenta Autographs

201 Matt Boldy 15.00 40.00
206 William Karlsson 12.00 30.00
207 Timo Meier 10.00 25.00
208 Bryan Rust 10.00 25.00
210 Tom Wilson 10.00 25.00
213 Matthew Knies 20.00 50.00
214 Nikolaj Ehlers 10.00 25.00
215 Tage Thompson SP 12.00 30.00
217 Artturi Lehkonen 8.00 20.00
218 Arber Xhekaj 10.00 25.00
221 Olen Zellweger SP 20.00 50.00
223 Brendan Brisson SP 12.00 30.00
225 Graeme Clarke 10.00 25.00
228 Mason Morelli 10.00 25.00
233 Brennan Othmann 15.00 40.00
235 Gage Goncalves 12.00 30.00
237 Jesper Wallstedt 25.00 60.00
243 Joshua Roy 15.00 40.00
247 Logan Stankoven SP 25.00 60.00

2024-25 Upper Deck MVP Mascot Talent

*GOLD: .6X TO 1.5X BASIC
*SPECTRUM/99: 2X TO 5X BASIC
*RED/50: 2.5X TO 6X BASIC
MT1 Gnash 1.25 3.00
MT2 Slapshot 1.25 3.00
MT3 SJ Sharkie 1.25 3.00
MT4 Youppi 1.25 3.00
MT5 Blades The Bruin 1.25 3.00
MT6 Sparky The Dragon 1.25 3.00
MT7 Wild Wing 1.25 3.00
MT8 Iceburgh 1.25 3.00
MT9 N.J. Devil 1.25 3.00
MT10 Fin The Whale 1.25 3.00
MT11 Bailey 1.25 3.00
MT12 Thunderbug 1.25 3.00
MT13 Sabretooth 1.25 3.00
MT14 Gritty 2.50 6.00
MT15 Stanley C. Panther 1.25 3.00
MT16 Al The Octopus 1.25 3.00
MT17 Mick E Moose 1.25 3.00
MT18 Howler 1.25 3.00
MT19 Nordy 1.25 3.00
MT20 Chance 1.25 3.00
MT21 Victor E. Green 1.25 3.00
MT22 Hunter 1.25 3.00
MT23 Carlton the Bear 1.25 3.00
MT24 Stormy 1.25 3.00
MT25 Harvey The Hound 1.25 3.00
MT26 Stinger 1.25 3.00
MT27 Louie 1.25 3.00
MT28 Spartacat 1.25 3.00
MT29 Buoy 1.25 3.00
MT30 Tommy Hawk 1.25 3.00
MT31 Bernie the St. Bernard 1.25 3.00
MT32 Metal 1.25 3.00

2024-25 Upper Deck MVP Photo Variations

BSR1 Quinn Hughes 12.00 30.00
BSR2 Robert Thomas 5.00 12.00
BSR3 Logan Stankoven 20.00 50.00
BSR4 Tomas Hertl 5.00 12.00
BSR5 Nikolaj Ehlers 5.00 12.00
BSR6 Tom Wilson 5.00 12.00
BSR7 Shakir Mukhamadullin 6.00 15.00
BSR8 Wyatt Johnston 10.00 25.00
BSR9 Matthew Knies 10.00 25.00
BSR10 Zach Hyman 8.00 20.00
BSR11 Zachary Bolduc 10.00 25.00
BSR12 Noah Dobson 6.00 15.00
BSR13 Timo Meier 5.00 12.00
BSR14 Artturi Lehkonen 4.00 10.00
BSR15 Brendan Brisson 6.00 15.00
BSR16 Bryan Rust 5.00 12.00
BSR17 Juuse Saros 6.00 15.00
BSR18 Matt Rempe 10.00 25.00
BSR19 William Karlsson 6.00 15.00
BSR20 Tage Thompson 6.00 15.00

2024-25 Upper Deck MVP Rookie Redemptions

RR1 Pacific Division 30.00 80.00
RR2 Atlantic Division 25.00 60.00
RR3 Metropolitan Division 25.00 60.00
RR4 Central Division 30.00 80.00

2024-25 Upper Deck MVP Under the Scope

*GOLD: .6X TO 1.5X BASIC
US1 Alex DeBrincat 1.00 2.50
US2 Tim Stutzle 1.00 2.50
US3 Roman Josi .75 2.00
US4 Andrei Svechnikov 1.00 2.50
US5 John Tavares 1.25 3.00
US6 Nick Suzuki 1.50 4.00
US7 Nikita Kucherov 1.50 4.00
US8 Quinn Hughes 2.00 5.00
US9 Brad Marchand 1.50 4.00
US10 Alex Ovechkin 3.00 8.00
US11 Mika Zibanejad 1.00 2.50
US12 Erik Karlsson 1.00 2.50
US13 Nathan MacKinnon 3.00 8.00
US14 Mark Scheifele 1.25 3.00
US15 Bo Horvat 1.00 2.50
US16 Jack Hughes 2.00 5.00
US17 Roope Hintz 1.00 2.50
US18 Chandler Stephenson .60 1.50
US19 Jordan Kyrou .75 2.00
US20 Nazem Kadri 1.00 2.50
US21 Cale Makar 2.00 5.00
US22 Jesper Bratt .75 2.00
US23 Logan Couture 1.00 2.50
US24 Victor Hedman 1.00 2.50
US25 Johnny Gaudreau 1.25 3.00
US26 Sidney Crosby 3.00 8.00
US27 Auston Matthews 3.00 8.00
US28 Aleksander Barkov 1.25 3.00
US29 Chris Kreider 1.00 2.50
US30 Travis Konecny .75 2.00

2025-26 Upper Deck MVP

1 Connor McDavid 1.25 3.00
2 Morgan Geekie .15 .40
3 Kaiden Guhle .25 .60
4 Brock Boeser .30 .75
5 Robert Thomas .25 .60
6 William Eklund .30 .75
7 Claude Giroux .25 .60
8 Aleksander Barkov .40 1.00
9 Clayton Keller .30 .75
10 Jake DeBrusk .25 .60
11 Joseph Woll .30 .75
12 Brayden Point .30 .75
13 Carter Verhaeghe .25 .60
14 Martin Necas .40 1.00
15 Mika Zibanejad .30 .75
16 Pyotr Kochetkov .25 .60
17 Macklin Celebrini .75 2.00
18 Jack Hughes .60 1.50
19 Kyle Connor .40 1.00
20 Jacob Markstrom .25 .60
21 JJ Peterka .25 .60
22 William Nylander .50 1.25
23 Noah Dobson .30 .75
24 Matt Boldy .40 1.00
25 Steven Stamkos .50 1.25
26 Roope Hintz .30 .75
27 David Pastrnak .60 1.50
28 Cole Perfetti .25 .60
29 Igor Shesterkin .50 1.25
30 Kris Letang .30 .75
31 Jason Zucker .25 .60
32 Max Domi .25 .60
33 Joey Daccord .25 .60
34 Conor Geekie .25 .60
35 Anton Lundell .25 .60
36 Simon Edvinsson .25 .60
37 Nazem Kadri .30 .75
38 Nick Foligno .15 .40
39 Zach Werenski .40 1.00
40 Nick Suzuki .50 1.25
41 Ryan O'Reilly .25 .60
42 Elias Lindholm .25 .60
43 Tyler Toffoli .25 .60
44 Travis Konecny .25 .60
45 Dylan Guenther .30 .75
46 Artemi Panarin .50 1.25
47 Dylan Larkin .30 .75
48 Jake Walman .15 .40
49 Bryan Rust .25 .60
50 Nathan MacKinnon 1.00 2.50
51 Pavel Zacha .20 .50
52 Juraj Slafkovsky .50 1.25
53 Juuse Saros .30 .75
54 Ilya Sorokin .40 1.00
55 Gustav Forsling .25 .60
56 Anthony Cirelli .20 .50
57 Jonathan Huberdeau .30 .75
58 Marco Rossi .30 .75
59 Roman Josi .25 .60
60 Sebastian Cossa .30 .75
61 Will Smith .40 1.00
62 Nick Schmaltz .20 .50
63 Alex Ovechkin 1.00 2.50
64 Linus Ullmark .25 .60
65 Tomas Hertl .25 .60
66 Devon Toews .20 .50
67 Mason McTavish .25 .60
68 Seth Jones .25 .60
69 Samuel Montembeault .25 .60
70 Elias Pettersson .40 1.00
71 Dougie Hamilton .20 .50
72 Yaroslav Askarov .30 .75
73 Kevin Fiala .20 .50
74 Gabe Vilardi .25 .60
75 Ryan Nugent-Hopkins .30 .75
76 Alex DeBrincat .30 .75
77 Shea Theodore .30 .75
78 Mikael Granlund .20 .50
79 Tyler Bertuzzi .20 .50
80 Bowen Byram .30 .75
81 Kent Johnson .25 .60
82 Michael Bunting .25 .60
83 Brandt Clarke .25 .60
84 Lane Hutson .75 2.00
85 Dmitri Voronkov .15 .40
86 Nikita Kucherov .50 1.25
87 Stefan Noesen .15 .40
88 Colton Parayko .20 .50
89 John Carlson .25 .60
90 Brad Marchand .50 1.25
91 Rasmus Dahlin .30 .75
92 Adam Fox .30 .75
93 Dylan Strome .30 .75
94 Zach Hyman .40 1.00
95 Connor Bedard .75 2.00
96 Wyatt Johnston .50 1.25
97 Jaden Schwartz .20 .50
98 Mathew Barzal .30 .75
99 Connor McMichael .25 .60
100 Filip Forsberg CL .40 1.00
101 Charlie McAvoy .30 .75
102 Artturi Lehkonen .20 .50
103 Drew Doughty .25 .60
104 Patrik Laine .30 .75
105 Logan Cooley .40 1.00
106 Noah Hanifin .25 .60
107 Sergei Bobrovsky .40 1.00
108 Fabian Zetterlund .15 .40
109 Stuart Skinner .30 .75
110 Vincent Trocheck .25 .60
111 Jake Guentzel .40 1.00
112 Morgan Rielly .25 .60
113 Trevor Zegras .25 .60
114 Alex Tuch .25 .60
115 Sean Couturier .20 .50
116 Mikhail Sergachev .20 .50
117 Connor Hellebuyck .50 1.25
118 Sam Reinhart .50 1.25
119 Kirill Marchenko .30 .75
120 Jake Oettinger .40 1.00
121 Anze Kopitar .40 1.00
122 Darnell Nurse .20 .50
123 Lucas Raymond .40 1.00
124 Jaccob Slavin .20 .50
125 Brady Tkachuk .40 1.00
126 Mark Scheifele .40 1.00
127 Pierre-Luc Dubois .20 .50
128 Andrei Svechnikov .30 .75
129 Mitch Marner .40 1.00
130 Cale Makar .60 1.50
131 Jeremy Swayman .40 1.00
132 Teuvo Teravainen .25 .60
133 Cutter Gauthier .30 .75
134 Adrian Kempe .25 .60
135 Matt Coronato .20 .50
136 Josh Norris .25 .60
137 Owen Tippett .15 .40
138 Barrett Hayton .25 .60
139 Evgeni Malkin .50 1.25
140 Dustin Wolf .40 1.00
141 Auston Matthews 1.00 2.50
142 Jared McCann .20 .50
143 Jonathan Marchessault .30 .75
144 Dylan Holloway .25 .60
145 Adin Hill .25 .60
146 Leon Draisaitl .75 2.00
147 Pavel Buchnevich .20 .50
148 Matvei Michkov .60 1.50
149 Aliaksei Protas .15 .40
150 Nico Hischier .40 1.00
151 Miro Heiskanen .30 .75
152 Conor Garland .20 .50
153 Tage Thompson .30 .75
154 Mackenzie Blackwood .25 .60
155 Rickard Rakell .20 .50
156 Jonathan Lekkerimaki .30 .75
157 Tim Stutzle .30 .75
158 Yegor Sharangovich .25 .60
159 Mats Zuccarello .25 .60
160 Matthew Tkachuk .50 1.25
161 Andrei Vasilevskiy .40 1.00
162 Chandler Stephenson .20 .50
163 Tom Wilson .25 .60
164 Darcy Kuemper .25 .60
165 Moritz Seider .30 .75
166 Alexis Lafreniere .40 1.00
167 Kirill Kaprizov .75 2.00
168 Victor Hedman .30 .75
169 Frank Nazar .40 1.00
170 Josh Morrissey .30 .75
171 Anders Lee .20 .50
172 J.T. Miller .30 .75
173 Erik Karlsson .30 .75
174 Owen Power .25 .60
175 Brandon Hagel .20 .50
176 Jake Sanderson .30 .75
177 Jason Robertson .40 1.00
178 Joel Farabee .25 .60
179 Brock Faber .30 .75
180 Jordan Binnington .40 1.00
181 Mikko Rantanen .60 1.50
182 Filip Gustavsson .25 .60
183 Adam Fantilli .40 1.00
184 Jack Eichel .40 1.00
185 Sidney Crosby 1.00 2.50
186 Jordan Kyrou .25 .60
187 Nolan Allan .15 .40
188 Jordan Eberle .25 .60
189 Bo Horvat .30 .75
190 Jesper Bratt .25 .60
191 John Tavares .40 1.00
192 Mark Stone .30 .75
193 Cole Caufield .50 1.25
194 Travis Sanheim .15 .40
195 Leo Carlsson .40 1.00
196 Matty Beniers .30 .75
197 Sean Monahan .15 .40
198 Sebastian Aho .40 1.00
199 Troy Terry .20 .50
200 Quinn Hughes .60 1.50
201 Joel Eriksson Ek SP .40 1.00
202 Yanni Gourde SP .40 1.00
203 Drake Batherson SP .50 1.25
204 Olen Zellweger SP .50 1.25
205 Dawson Mercer SP .60 1.50
206 MacKenzie Weegar SP .40 1.00
207 Matthew Knies SP 1.00 2.50
208 Nikolaj Ehlers SP .50 1.25
209 Casey Mittelstadt SP .50 1.25
210 Thatcher Demko SP .60 1.50
211 Timo Meier SP .50 1.25
212 Ivan Barbashev SP .40 1.00
213 Seth Jarvis SP .60 1.50
214 Mason Marchment SP .40 1.00
215 Jacob Trouba SP .40 1.00
216 Brock Nelson SP .50 1.25
217 Evan Bouchard SP .60 1.50
218 Mike Matheson SP .30 .75
219 Samuel Girard SP .30 .75
220 Pavel Dorofeyev SP .30 .75
221 Ozzy Wiesblatt SP RC 1.50 4.00
222 Colton Dach SP RC 2.00 5.00
223 Owen Sillinger SP RC 1.50 4.00
224 Ethen Frank SP RC 1.50 4.00
225 Rory Kerins SP RC 1.50 4.00
226 Jack Finley SP RC 2.00 5.00
227 Michael Callahan SP RC 1.50 4.00
228 Marc Gatcomb SP RC 1.50 4.00
229 Donovan Sebrango SP RC 1.50 4.00
230 Rodrigo Abols SP RC 1.50 4.00
231 Jacob Quillan SP RC 1.50 4.00
232 Elias Pettersson SP RC 2.50 6.00
233 Ivan Demidov SP RC 20.00 50.00
234 Ryan Suzuki SP RC 1.50 4.00
235 Parker Ford SP RC 1.50 4.00
236 Jacob Gaucher SP RC 1.50 4.00
237 Jakub Skarek SP RC 1.50 4.00
238 Joakim Kemell SP RC 1.50 4.00
239 Dylan Duke SP RC 1.50 4.00
240 Niklas Kokko SP RC 2.00 5.00
241 Jacob Melanson SP RC 1.50 4.00
242 Carter Mazur SP RC 1.50 4.00
243 Artyom Levshunov SP RC 3.00 8.00
244 Jani Nyman SP RC 2.00 5.00
245 Luca Cagnoni SP RC 1.50 4.00
246 Dalibor Dvorsky SP RC 3.00 8.00
247 Olivier Rodrigue SP RC 3.00 8.00
248 Cam Lund SP RC 1.50 4.00
249 Ryan Leonard SP RC 2.50 6.00
250 Gabe Perreault SP RC CL 2.00 5.00

2025-26 Upper Deck MVP Gold Script

*GOLD SCRIPT: 2.5X TO 6X BASIC
*GOLD SCRIPT RC: 1X TO 2.5X BASIC

2025-26 Upper Deck MVP Silver Script

*SILVER SCRIPT: .8X TO 2X BASIC
*SLVR SCRIPT RC: .5X TO 1.2X BASIC
233 Ivan Demidov SP 40.00 100.00

2025-26 Upper Deck MVP Super Script

*SUPER SCRIPT/25: 4X TO 10X BASIC
*SUPER SCRIPT RC/25: 1.5X TO 4X BASIC

2025-26 Upper Deck MVP '25 NHL Draft #1 Pick

DP1 Redemption Card 60.00 150.00

2025-26 Upper Deck MVP Coming to Your Rink

CR1 M.McTavish/C.Gauthier 1.25 3.00
CR2 D.Pastrnak/J.Swayman 2.50 6.00
CR3 T.Thompson/R.Dahlin 1.25 3.00
CR4 D.Wolf/J.Huberdeau 1.50 4.00
CR5 S.Aho/A.Svechnikov 1.50 4.00
CR6 C.Bedard/T.Bertuzzi 3.00 8.00
CR7 N.MacKinnon/C.Makar 4.00 10.00
CR8 K.Marchenko/Z.Werenski 1.50 4.00
CR9 J.Robertson/J.Oettinger 1.50 4.00
CR10 M.Seider/L.Raymond 1.50 4.00
CR11 C.McDavid/L.Draisaitl 5.00 12.00
CR12 A.Barkov/M.Tkachuk 2.00 5.00
CR13 A.Kopitar/A.Kempe 1.50 4.00
CR14 K.Kaprizov/M.Boldy 3.00 8.00
CR15 C.Caufield/L.Hutson 3.00 8.00
CR16 F.Forsberg/S.Stamkos 2.00 5.00
CR17 J.Hughes/N.Hischier 2.50 6.00
CR18 M.Barzal/B.Horvat 1.25 3.00
CR19 A.Panarin/I.Shesterkin 2.00 5.00
CR20 B.Tkachuk/T.Stutzle 1.50 4.00
CR21 T.Konecny/M.Michkov 2.50 6.00
CR22 S.Crosby/E.Malkin 4.00 10.00
CR23 M.Celebrini/W.Smith 3.00 8.00
CR24 J.McCann/M.Beniers 1.25 3.00
CR25 J.Kyrou/R.Thomas 1.00 2.50
CR26 J.Guentzel/B.Point 1.50 4.00
CR27 A.Matthews/M.Marner 4.00 10.00
CR28 C.Keller/L.Cooley 1.50 4.00
CR29 Q.Hughes/E.Pettersson 2.50 6.00
CR30 J.Eichel/M.Stone 1.50 4.00
CR31 A.Ovechkin/D.Strome 4.00 10.00
CR32 K.Connor/M.Scheifele 1.50 4.00

2025-26 Upper Deck MVP Hello My Name Is Stickers

HNI1 Ozzy Wiesblatt 1.25 3.00
HNI2 Colton Dach 1.50 4.00
HNI3 Owen Sillinger 1.25 3.00
HNI4 Ethen Frank 1.25 3.00
HNI5 Rory Kerins 1.25 3.00
HNI6 Jack Finley 1.50 4.00
HNI7 Michael Callahan 1.25 3.00
HNI8 Marc Gatcomb 1.25 3.00
HNI9 Donovan Sebrango 1.25 3.00
HNI10 Rodrigo Abols 1.25 3.00
HNI11 Jacob Quillan 1.25 3.00
HNI12 Elias Pettersson 2.00 5.00
HNI13 Dominik Shine .75 2.00
HNI14 Ryan Suzuki 1.25 3.00
HNI15 Parker Ford 1.25 3.00
HNI16 Jacob Gaucher 1.25 3.00
HNI17 Jakub Skarek 1.25 3.00
HNI18 Joakim Kemell 1.25 3.00
HNI19 Dylan Duke 1.25 3.00
HNI20 Carter Mazur 1.25 3.00
HNI21 Artyom Levshunov 2.50 6.00

2025-26 Upper Deck MVP Laser Focused

*BLUE/249: .5X TO 1.2X BASIC
LF1 Igor Shesterkin 5.00 12.00
LF2 Dustin Wolf 4.00 10.00
LF3 Jeremy Swayman 4.00 10.00
LF4 Mackenzie Blackwood 2.50 6.00
LF5 Joseph Woll 3.00 8.00
LF6 Thatcher Demko 3.00 8.00
LF7 Jake Oettinger 4.00 10.00
LF8 Samuel Montembeault 2.50 6.00
LF9 Logan Thompson 3.00 8.00
LF10 Stuart Skinner 3.00 8.00
LF11 Filip Gustavsson 2.50 6.00
LF12 Adin Hill 2.50 6.00
LF13 Connor Ingram 1.50 4.00
LF14 Darcy Kuemper 2.50 6.00
LF15 Joey Daccord 2.50 6.00
LF16 Connor Hellebuyck 5.00 12.00
LF17 John Gibson 2.50 6.00
LF18 Andrei Vasilevskiy 4.00 10.00
LF19 Linus Ullmark 2.50 6.00
LF20 Sergei Bobrovsky 4.00 10.00
LF21 Ilya Sorokin 4.00 10.00
LF22 Jacob Markstrom 2.50 6.00
LF23 Sebastian Cossa 3.00 8.00
LF24 Pyotr Kochetkov 2.50 6.00
LF25 Ukko-Pekka Luukkonen 2.00 5.00
LF26 Juuse Saros 3.00 8.00
LF27 Yaroslav Askarov 3.00 8.00
LF28 Anthony Stolarz 3.00 8.00
LF29 Kevin Lankinen 2.50 6.00
LF30 Jordan Binnington 4.00 10.00

2025-26 Upper Deck MVP Mascot Battle

MB1 Hunter
Harvey The Hound 1.25 3.00
MB2 Bailey
Wild Wing 1.25 3.00
MB3 Iceburgh
Gritty 1.25 3.00
MB4 Bernie the St. Bernard
Fin The Whale 1.25 3.00
MB5 Thunderbug
Stanley C. Panther 1.25 3.00
MB6 Youppi
Blades The Bruin 1.25 3.00
MB7 Tommy Hawk
Louie 1.25 3.00
MB8 Nordy
Victor E. Green 1.25 3.00
MB9 Spartacat
Carlton the Bear 1.25 3.00
MB10 Chance
S.J. Sharkie 1.25 3.00
MB11 Sparky The Dragon
N.J. Devil 1.25 3.00
MB12 Slapshot
Stormy 1.25 3.00
MB13 Mick E Moose
Stinger 1.25 3.00

2025-26 Upper Deck MVP Mascot Stickers

MS1 Wild Wing 1.25 3.00
MS2 Blades The Bruin 1.25 3.00
MS3 Sabretooth 1.25 3.00
MS4 Harvey The Hound 1.25 3.00
MS5 Stormy 1.25 3.00
MS6 Tommy Hawk 1.25 3.00
MS7 Bernie the St. Bernard 1.25 3.00
MS8 Stinger 1.25 3.00
MS9 Victor E. Green 1.25 3.00
MS10 Hunter 1.25 3.00
MS11 Stanley C. Panther 1.25 3.00
MS12 Bailey 1.25 3.00
MS13 Nordy 1.25 3.00
MS14 Youppi 1.25 3.00
MS15 Gnash 1.25 3.00
MS16 N.J. Devil 1.25 3.00
MS17 Sparky The Dragon 1.25 3.00
MS18 Spartacat 1.25 3.00
MS19 Gritty 1.25 3.00
MS20 Iceburgh 1.25 3.00
MS21 S.J. Sharkie 1.25 3.00
MS22 Buoy 1.25 3.00
MS23 Louie 1.25 3.00
MS24 Thunderbug 1.25 3.00
MS25 Carlton the Bear 1.25 3.00
MS26 Fin The Whale 1.25 3.00
MS27 Chance 1.25 3.00
MS28 Slapshot 1.25 3.00
MS29 Mick E Moose 1.25 3.00

2025-26 Upper Deck MVP Net Presence

NP1 Adrian Kempe .50 1.25
NP2 Connor McDavid 2.50 6.00
NP3 Brayden Point .60 1.50
NP4 Sam Reinhart 1.00 2.50
NP5 Jack Hughes 1.25 3.00
NP6 William Nylander 1.00 2.50
NP7 Mikko Rantanen 1.25 3.00
NP8 Mark Scheifele .75 2.00
NP9 Brady Tkachuk .75 2.00
NP10 Macklin Celebrini 1.50 4.00
NP11 David Pastrnak 1.25 3.00
NP12 Matthew Tkachuk 1.00 2.50
NP13 Kirill Kaprizov 1.50 4.00
NP14 Cole Caufield 1.00 2.50
NP15 Leon Draisaitl 1.50 4.00
NP16 Nathan MacKinnon 2.00 5.00
NP17 Connor Bedard 1.50 4.00
NP18 Jake Guentzel .75 2.00

NP19 Sidney Crosby 2.00 5.00
NP20 Chris Kreider .60 1.50

2025-26 Upper Deck MVP Rising to the Occasion

RO1 Cale Makar 1.50 4.00
RO2 Jack Hughes 1.50 4.00
RO3 Mark Scheifele 1.00 2.50
RO4 Lane Hutson 2.00 5.00
RO5 Sam Reinhart 1.25 3.00
RO6 Artyom Levshunov 1.25 3.00
RO7 Brayden Point .75 2.00
RO8 Zach Werenski 1.00 2.50
RO9 David Pastrnak 1.50 4.00
RO10 William Nylander 1.25 3.00
RO11 Kirill Kaprizov 2.00 5.00
RO12 Connor McDavid 3.00 8.00
RO13 Jani Nyman .75 2.00
RO14 Jordan Kyrou .60 1.50
RO15 Mikko Rantanen 1.50 4.00
RO16 Cole Caufield 1.25 3.00
RO17 Matthew Tkachuk 1.25 3.00
RO18 Travis Konecny .60 1.50
RO19 Auston Matthews 2.50 6.00
RO20 Connor Bedard 2.00 5.00
RO21 Joakim Kemell .60 1.50
RO22 Nikita Kucherov 1.25 3.00
RO23 Alex Ovechkin 2.50 6.00
RO24 Macklin Celebrini 2.00 5.00
RO25 Quinn Hughes 1.50 4.00
RO26 Jack Eichel 1.00 2.50
RO27 Leon Draisaitl 2.00 5.00
RO28 Ryan Suzuki .60 1.50
RO29 Nathan MacKinnon 2.50 6.00
RO30 Sidney Crosby 2.50 6.00
RO31 Mitch Marner 1.00 2.50
RO32 Adrian Kempe .60 1.50
RO33 Kyle Connor 1.00 2.50
RO34 Dylan Larkin .75 2.00
RO35 Niklas Kokko .75 2.00

2025-26 Upper Deck MVP Rookie Redemptions

RR1 Pacific Division 30.00 80.00
RR2 Atlantic Division 30.00 80.00
RR3 Metropolitan Division 30.00 80.00
RR4 Central Division 30.00 80.00

2018-19 Upper Deck MVP Factory Set

1 John Tavares .40 1.00
2 Ryan Getzlaf .25 .60
3 Brad Marchand .50 1.25
4 Sean Monahan .15 .40
5 Jonathan Quick .30 .75
6 Sean Couturier .20 .50
7 Duncan Keith .20 .50
8 Mitch Marner .40 1.00
9 Evgeny Kuznetsov .30 .75
10 Oliver Ekman-Larsson .25 .60
11 James Neal .15 .40
12 Ryan O'Reilly .25 .60
13 Teuvo Teravainen .25 .60
14 Seth Jones .25 .60
15 Jamie Benn .25 .60
16 Dylan Larkin .30 .75
17 Aleksander Barkov .40 1.00
18 Mikael Granlund .20 .50
19 Max Pacioretty .25 .60
20 P.K. Subban .30 .75
21 Gabriel Landeskog .30 .75
22 Nico Hischier .40 1.00
23 Mark Stone .30 .75
24 Joe Pavelski .30 .75
25 Evgeni Malkin .50 1.25
26 Leon Draisaitl .75 2.00
27 Brayden Schenn .25 .60
28 Mats Zuccarello .25 .60
29 Brayden Point .30 .75
30 Daniel Sedin .30 .75
31 Patrik Laine .30 .75
32 Evander Kane .25 .60
33 John Klingberg .25 .60
34 Mike Smith .20 .50
35 Artemi Panarin .50 1.25
36 John Carlson .25 .60
37 Clayton Keller .30 .75
38 Nick Schmaltz .20 .50
39 Jonathan Huberdeau .30 .75
40 Henrik Zetterberg .30 .75
41 Shayne Gostisbehere .25 .60
42 Jonathan Marchessault .30 .75
43 David Pastrnak .60 1.50
44 Sebastian Aho .40 1.00
45 William Nylander .50 1.25
46 Jason Zucker .25 .60
47 Dustin Brown .25 .60
48 Filip Forsberg .40 1.00
49 Mikko Rantanen .60 1.50
50 Taylor Hall .25 .60
51 Mike Hoffman .15 .40
52 Milan Lucic .20 .50
53 Logan Couture .30 .75
54 Jakob Silfverberg .15 .40
55 Alex Galchenyuk .15 .40
56 Josh Bailey .20 .50
57 Kris Letang .30 .75
58 Kyle Okposo .15 .40
59 Jaden Schwartz .30 .75
60 Kevin Shattenkirk .15 .40
61 Dougie Hamilton .20 .50
62 Max Domi .25 .60
63 T.J. Oshie .25 .60
64 Oliver Bjorkstrand .20 .50
65 Blake Wheeler .25 .60
66 Thomas Vanek .20 .50
67 Brandon Saad .20 .50
68 Alexander Radulov .25 .60
69 Vincent Trocheck .25 .60
70 Henrik Sedin .30 .75
71 Nazem Kadri .30 .75
72 Mika Zibanejad .30 .75
73 Alex Tuch .25 .60
74 Rickard Rakell .20 .50
75 Mark Scheifele .40 1.00
76 Victor Hedman .30 .75
77 Viktor Arvidsson .15 .40
78 Justin Williams .20 .50
79 Rick Nash .25 .60
80 Eric Staal .25 .60
81 Tyson Barrie .15 .40
82 Nick Foligno .20 .50
83 Dion Phaneuf .20 .50
84 David Perron .20 .50
85 Ryan Nugent-Hopkins .30 .75
86 Derick Brassard .15 .40
87 Justin Abdelkader .20 .50
88 Jakub Voracek .20 .50
89 Cory Schneider .25 .60
90 Ben Bishop .20 .50
91 Anders Lee .20 .50
92 Micheal Ferland .15 .40
93 Sam Reinhart .50 1.25
94 Tomas Hertl .25 .60
95 Roberto Luongo .40 1.00
96 Alex DeBrincat .30 .75
97 Jake Gardiner .15 .40
98 Tom Wilson .25 .60
99 Jonathan Drouin .20 .50
100 Auston Matthews CL 1.00 2.50
101 Steven Stamkos .50 1.25
102 Alex Pietrangelo .20 .50
103 Ryan Suter .20 .50
104 Reilly Smith .25 .60
105 Joe Thornton .40 1.00
106 Kevin Hayes .20 .50
107 Jordan Staal .20 .50
108 Alexander Wennberg .15 .40
109 Drew Doughty .30 .75
110 Patrick Marleau .25 .60
111 Phil Kessel .25 .60
112 Ryan McDonagh .15 .40
113 Wayne Simmonds .25 .60
114 Ryan Johansen .20 .50
115 Matt Duchene .25 .60
116 Tomas Tatar .15 .40
117 Ondrej Kase .15 .40
118 Alex Kerfoot .20 .50
119 Tyler Johnson .15 .40
120 Kyle Palmieri .20 .50
121 Rasmus Ristolainen .15 .40
122 Bo Horvat .30 .75
123 T.J. Brodie .20 .50
124 Oscar Klefbom .20 .50
125 Aaron Ekblad .30 .75
126 Andrew Shaw .15 .40
127 Nikolaj Ehlers .25 .60
128 Jake Muzzin .25 .60
129 Roman Josi .25 .60
130 Patrick Kane .50 1.25
131 Tuukka Rask .30 .75
132 Cody Eakin .15 .40
133 Ryan Spooner .20 .50
134 Christian Dvorak .20 .50
135 Jake Guentzel .40 1.00
136 Cam Atkinson .25 .60
137 Andrei Vasilevskiy .40 1.00
138 Jordan Eberle .25 .60
139 Claude Giroux .25 .60
140 Chris Kreider .30 .75
141 Justin Faulk AS .20 .50
142 Alexander Steen .15 .40
143 Zach Hyman .40 1.00
144 Anze Kopitar .40 1.00
145 Braden Holtby .30 .75
146 Anthony Mantha .20 .50
147 Jason Spezza .25 .60
148 Corey Perry .40 1.00
149 Carl Soderberg .15 .40
150 Matt Murray .25 .60
151 David Krejci .25 .60
152 Dustin Byfuglien .25 .60
153 William Karlsson .30 .75
154 Ryan Strome .25 .60
155 Conor Sheary .25 .60
156 Martin Jones .20 .50
157 Andrew Ladd .15 .40
158 Colton Parayko .20 .50
159 Anthony Duclair .20 .50
160 Tomas Plekanec .15 .40
161 Pekka Rinne .25 .60
162 Connor Hellebuyck .50 1.25
163 Alex Killorn .15 .40
164 Olli Maatta .15 .40
165 J.T. Miller .30 .75
166 Tyler Toffoli .25 .60
167 Jake Allen .25 .60
168 Connor Brown .20 .50
169 Ondrej Palat .20 .50
170 Loui Eriksson .15 .40
171 Shea Weber .25 .60
172 Nick Leddy .15 .40
173 Gustav Nyquist .15 .40
174 Jake DeBrusk .25 .60
175 Jesper Bratt .25 .60
176 Carl Hagelin .15 .40
177 Mikkel Boedker .15 .40
178 Kyle Turris .20 .50
179 Bobby Ryan .20 .50
180 Cam Talbot .25 .60
181 Keith Yandle .15 .40
182 Jason Pominville .15 .40
183 Danton Heinen .20 .50
184 Pierre-Luc Dubois .20 .50
185 Jim Howard .30 .75
186 Nicklas Backstrom .25 .60
187 Brendan Gallagher .25 .60
188 Erik Johnson .15 .40
189 Adam Henrique .20 .50
190 Victor Rask .15 .40
191 Radek Faksa .20 .50
192 Derek Stepan .15 .40
193 Matthew Tkachuk .50 1.25
194 Jeff Skinner .30 .75
195 Ryan Hartman .15 .40
196 Nolan Patrick .25 .60
197 Frederik Andersen .30 .75
198 Erik Haula .15 .40
199 Devan Dubnyk .20 .50
200 Connor McDavid CL 1.25 3.00
201 Sidney Crosby 1.00 2.50
202 Marc-Andre Fleury .50 1.25
203 Tyler Seguin .30 .75
204 Vladimir Tarasenko .30 .75
205 Auston Matthews 1.00 2.50
206 Carey Price .50 1.25
207 Mathew Barzal .30 .75
208 Johnny Gaudreau .40 1.00
209 Patrice Bergeron .30 .75
210 Alexander Ovechkin 1.00 2.50
211 Brock Boeser .30 .75
212 Erik Karlsson .30 .75
213 Nathan MacKinnon 1.00 2.50
214 Jack Eichel .40 1.00
215 Jonathan Toews .40 1.00
216 Nikita Kucherov .50 1.25
217 Brent Burns .25 .60
218 Henrik Lundqvist .60 1.50
219 Connor McDavid 1.25 3.00
220 Alexander Ovechkin CL 1.00 2.50
221 Michael Dal Colle .25 .60
222 Dillon Heatherington 1.50 4.00
223 Dominic Turgeon 1.50 4.00
224 Daniel Brickley 1.50 4.00
225 Morgan Klimchuk 1.50 4.00
226 Justin Holl 1.50 4.00
227 Neal Pionk 1.50 4.00
228 Dylan Sikura 2.00 5.00
229 Ethan Bear 2.50 6.00
230 Oskar Lindblom 2.50 6.00
231 Maxim Mamin 1.50 4.00
232 Ryan Donato 2.50 6.00
233 Casey Mittelstadt 3.00 8.00
234 Adam Gaudette 2.50 6.00
235 Travis Dermott 2.50 6.00
236 Zach Aston-Reese 2.50 6.00
237 Jordan Greenway 1.50 4.00
238 Marcus Pettersson 1.50 4.00
239 Anthony Cirelli 2.50 6.00
240 Joe Hicketts 1.50 4.00
241 Eeli Tolvanen 3.00 8.00
242 Matthew Highmore 1.50 4.00
243 Henrik Borgstrom 2.50 6.00
244 Samuel Montembeault 3.00 8.00
245 Tomas Hyka 1.50 4.00
246 Lias Andersson 2.50 6.00
247 Warren Foegele 1.50 4.00
248 Ryan Lomberg 1.50 4.00
249 Andreas Johnsson 2.00 5.00
250 Noah Juulsen 1.50 4.00

2018-19 Upper Deck MVP Factory Set Eastern Stars

ES1 Sidney Crosby 1.50 4.00
ES2 Alexander Ovechkin 1.50 4.00
ES3 Auston Matthews 1.50 4.00
ES4 Steven Stamkos .75 2.00
ES5 Carey Price .75 2.00

2018-19 Upper Deck MVP Factory Set Star Formations

SF1 Rasmus Dahlin 1.00 2.50
SF2 Elias Pettersson 1.25 3.00
SF3 Ryan Donato .60 1.50
SF4 Eeli Tolvanen .75 2.00
SF5 Casey Mittelstadt .75 2.00

2022-23 Upper Deck MVP Factory Set Blue Script

*BLUE SCRIPT: .5X TO 1.2X BASIC

2022-23 Upper Deck MVP Factory Set Silver Script

*SILVER SCRIPT: .6X TO 1.5X BASIC

2022-23 Upper Deck MVP Factory Set Eastern Stars

ES1 Alex Ovechkin 1.50 4.00
ES2 Sebastian Aho .60 1.50
ES3 Artemi Panarin .75 2.00
ES4 Steven Stamkos .75 2.00
ES5 Auston Matthews 1.50 4.00

2022-23 Upper Deck MVP Factory Set Rookie Formations

RF1 Marco Rossi 2.50 6.00
RF2 Lukas Dostal 2.00 5.00
RF3 Jacob Perreault 1.00 2.50
RF4 Matt Boldy 3.00 8.00
RF5 Jack Quinn 1.50 4.00

2022-23 Upper Deck MVP Factory Set Western Stars

WS1 Connor McDavid 2.00 5.00
WS2 Kirill Kaprizov 1.25 3.00
WS3 Kyle Connor .60 1.50
WS4 Leon Draisaitl 1.25 3.00
WS5 Troy Terry .30 .75

2004 Upper Deck National Convention VIP

VIP5 Wayne Gretzky 4.00 10.00

2006 Upper Deck National NHL

COMPLETE SET (3) 25.00 50.00
NHL1 Sidney Crosby 15.00 40.00
NHL2 Wayne Gretzky 6.00 15.00
NHL3 Alexander Ovechkin 6.00 15.00

2006 Upper Deck National NHL Autographs

COMPLETE SET (2)

2006 Upper Deck National NHL VIP

COMPLETE SET (6) 30.00 60.00
1 Alexander Ovechkin 6.00 15.00
2 Wayne Gretzky 6.00 15.00
3 Sidney Crosby 15.00 40.00
4 Martin Brodeur 4.00 10.00
5 Steve Yzerman 4.00 10.00
6 Jean-Sebastien Giguere .75 2.00

2011 Upper Deck National Convention VIP

2 Wayne Gretzky 1.50 4.00
3 Sidney Crosby 1.00 2.50
5 Bobby Orr 1.00 2.50

2012 Upper Deck National Convention VIP

4 Sidney Crosby 2.00 5.00
6 Wayne Gretzky 2.50 6.00

2013 Upper Deck National Convention

COMPLETE SET (20) 15.00 40.00
4 Jonathan Toews .40 1.00
8 Wayne Gretzky .75 2.00
10 Brandon Saad .30 .75
12 Bobby Hull .50 1.25
18 Patrick Kane .30 .75

2013 Upper Deck National Convention Autographs

3 Patrick Kane 50.00 100.00

2013 Upper Deck National Convention VIP

COMPLETE SET (6) 3.00 8.00
2 Wayne Gretzky 1.00 2.50
4 Jonathan Toews .50 1.25

2008-09 Upper Deck National Hockey Card Day

COMPLETE SET (15) 8.00 20.00
HCD1 Steven Stamkos 2.50 6.00
HCD2 Kyle Turris 1.00 2.50
HCD3 Josh Bailey .75 2.00
HCD4 Colton Gillies .50 1.25
HCD5 Derick Brassard .60 1.50
HCD6 Sidney Crosby 2.50 6.00
HCD7 Vincent Lecavalier .60 1.50
HCD8 Jarome Iginla .75 2.00
HCD9 Joe Sakic 1.25 3.00
HCD10 Martin Brodeur 1.50 4.00
HCD11 Wayne Gretzky 4.00 10.00
HCD12 Mario Lemieux 2.50 6.00
HCD13 Gordie Howe 2.00 5.00
HCD14 Bobby Orr 2.50 6.00
HCD15 Don Cherry 1.50 4.00

2009-10 Upper Deck National Hockey Card Day

COMPLETE SET (15) 10.00 25.00
HCD1 John Tavares 1.50 4.00
HCD2 Matt Duchene .75 2.00
HCD3 Jamie Benn 1.25 3.00
HCD4 Evander Kane .75 2.00
HCD5 Logan Couture .75 2.00
HCD6 Sidney Crosby 1.50 4.00
HCD7 Vincent Lecavalier .40 1.00
HCD8 Martin Brodeur 1.00 2.50
HCD9 Mike Richards .30 .75
HCD10 Rick Nash .40 1.00
HCD11 Jarome Iginla .50 1.25
HCD12 Jonathan Toews .60 1.50
HCD13 Roberto Luongo .60 1.50
HCD14 Wayne Gretzky 2.50 6.00
HCD15 Steve Yzerman 1.00 2.50

2010-11 Upper Deck National Hockey Card Day

NHCD1 Taylor Hall .60 1.50
NHCD2 Tyler Seguin .75 2.00
NHCD3 Jeff Skinner .60 1.50
NHCD4 Jordan Eberle .60 1.50
NHCD5 P.K. Subban .75 2.00
NHCD6 Jason Spezza .50 1.25
NHCD7 Dion Phaneuf .40 1.00
NHCD8 Jarome Iginla .60 1.50
NHCD9 Roberto Luongo .75 2.00
NHCD10 Sidney Crosby 2.00 5.00
NHCD11 Patrick Roy 1.25 3.00
NHCD12 Mario Lemieux 2.00 5.00
NHCD13 Gordie Howe 1.50 4.00
NHCD14 Bobby Orr 2.00 5.00
NHCD15 Wayne Gretzky 3.00 8.00
NNO Cover Card CL .30 .75
PROMO Jonathan Toews Promo .75 2.00
HCDSC Sidney Crosby AU/87 60.00 120.00

2011-12 Upper Deck National Hockey Card Day Canada

COMPLETE SET (17) 6.00 15.00
1 Cody Hodgson .40 1.00
2 Ryan Nugent-Hopkins 3.00 8.00
3 Brett Connolly .25 .60
4 Mark Scheifele 1.00 2.50
5 Sean Couturier .50 1.25
6 Taylor Hall .30 .75
7 P.K. Subban .40 1.00
8 Roberto Luongo .50 1.25
9 Steven Stamkos .60 1.50
10 Jonathan Toews .50 1.25
11 Wayne Gretzky 2.00 5.00
12 Bobby Orr 1.25 3.00
13 Mario Lemieux 1.25 3.00
14 Mark Messier .60 1.50
15 Martin Brodeur .75 2.00
16 Sidney Crosby SP 2.50 6.00
NNO Checklist .20 .50

2011-12 Upper Deck National Hockey Card Day Canada Jumbos

COMPLETE SET (5)
OS1 Ryan Nugent-Hopkins 2.00 5.00
OS2 Roberto Luongo 1.00 2.50
OS3 Jonathan Toews 1.00 2.50
OS4 Mario Lemieux 2.50 6.00
OS5 Wayne Gretzky 4.00 10.00

2011-12 Upper Deck National Hockey Card Day USA

COMPLETE SET (17) 5.00 12.00
1 Gabriel Landeskog .75 2.00
2 Alexander Ovechkin 1.25 3.00
3 Henrik Lundqvist .75 2.00
4 Pekka Rinne .30 .75
5 Jaromir Jagr 1.00 2.50
6 Zdeno Chara .30 .75
7 Ryan Kesler .30 .75
8 Patrick Kane .60 1.50
9 Ryan Miller .30 .75
10 Zach Parise .30 .75
11 Andy Miele .25 .60
12 Willie O'Ree .40 1.00
13 Mike Modano .50 1.25
14 Brett Hull .60 1.50
15 Brian Leetch .25 .60
16 Tim Thomas SP .60 1.50
NNO Checklist .20 .50

2012-13 Upper Deck National Hockey Card Day Canada

COMPLETE SET (17) 5.00 12.00
NHCD1 Jaden Schwartz CR .50 1.25
NHCD2 Tyson Barrie CR .50 1.25
NHCD3 Carter Ashton CR .15 .40
NHCD4 Mark Stone CR .60 1.50
NHCD5 Casey Cizikas CR .20 .50
NHCD6 Sidney Crosby PC 1.00 2.50
NHCD7 Jarome Iginla PC .30 .75
NHCD8 Jordan Eberle PC .25 .60
NHCD9 John Tavares PC .40 1.00
NHCD10 Martin Brodeur PC .60 1.50
NHCD11 Bobby Orr HH 1.00 2.50
NHCD12 Joe Sakic HH .50 1.25
NHCD13 Eric Lindros HH .40 1.00
NHCD14 Mario Lemieux HH 1.00 2.50
NHCD15 Wayne Gretzky HH 1.50 4.00
NHCD16 Gretzky/Lemieux MM SP 2.50 6.00
NNO Checklist .15 .40

2012-13 Upper Deck National Hockey Card Day USA

COMPLETE SET (17) 5.00 12.00
NHCD1 Evgeni Malkin AF .60 1.50
NHCD2 Alexander Ovechkin AF 1.25 3.00
NHCD3 Ilya Kovalchuk AF .30 .75
NHCD4 Henrik Lundqvist AF .75 2.00
NHCD5 Anze Kopitar AF .50 1.25
NHCD6 Zach Parise SS .30 .75
NHCD7 Jonathan Quick SS .40 1.00
NHCD8 Patrick Kane SS .60 1.50
NHCD9 Dustin Brown SS .30 .75
NHCD10 Ryan Miller SS .30 .75
NHCD11 Mike Modano AI .50 1.25
NHCD12 Brett Hull AI .60 1.50
NHCD13 Brian Leetch AI .25 .60
NHCD14 Tim Thomas AI .30 .75
NHCD15 Neal Broten AI .25 .60
NHCD16 Jonathan Quick MM SP .75 2.00
NNO Checklist .20 .50

2013-14 Upper Deck National Hockey Card Day Canada

COMPLETE SET (22) 5.00 12.00
NHCD1 Nathan MacKinnon CR .60 1.50
NHCD2 Jonathan Huberdeau CR .30 .75
NHCD3 Alex Galchenyuk CR .30 .75
NHCD4 Dougie Hamilton CR .20 .50
NHCD5 Morgan Rielly CR .30 .75
NHCD6 Nail Yakupov CR .25 .60
NHCD7 Justin Schultz CR .12 .30
NHCD8 Sean Monahan CR .20 .50
NHCD9 Brendan Gallagher CR .30 .75
NHCD10 Cory Conacher CR .20 .50
NHCD11 Steven Stamkos PC .40 1.00
NHCD12 Sidney Crosby PC .75 2.00
NHCD13 Martin St. Louis PC .20 .50
NHCD14 Taylor Hall PC .20 .50
NHCD15 Claude Giroux PC .20 .50
NHCD16 Mario Lemieux
Wayne Gretzky HH 1.25 3.00
NHCD17 Mario Lemieux HH .75 2.00
NHCD18 Bobby Orr HH .75 2.00
NHCD19 Steve Yzerman HH .50 1.25
NHCD20 Dale Hawerchuk HH .25 .60
NHCD21 Jonathan Huberdeau
Nathan MacKinnon MM SP .60 1.50

2013-14 Upper Deck National Hockey Card Day USA

COMPLETE SET (22)
NHCD1 Aleksander Barkov AM .40 1.00
NHCD2 Alex Galchenyuk AM .30 .75
NHCD3 Beau Bennett AM .15 .40
NHCD4 Charlie Coyle AM .20 .50
NHCD5 Brock Nelson AM .20 .50
NHCD6 Filip Forsberg AM .20 .50
NHCD7 Petr Mrazek AM .25 .60
NHCD8 Seth Jones AM .25 .60
NHCD9 Tomas Hertl AM .25 .60
NHCD10 Valeri Nichushkin AM .25 .60
NHCD11 David Backes SS .12 .30
NHCD12 Jonathan Quick SS .25 .60
NHCD13 Patrick Kane SS .40 1.00
NHCD14 Phil Kessel SS .20 .50
NHCD15 Zach Parise SS .20 .50
NHCD16 Bill Guerin AI .20 .50
NHCD17 Brett Hull AI .40 1.00
NHCD18 Doug Weight AI .20 .50
NHCD19 Mike Modano AI .30 .75
NHCD20 Tony Esposito AI .20 .50
NHCD21 Alex Galchenyuk
Seth Jones MM .50 1.25
NNO Checklist .10 .25

2014-15 Upper Deck National Hockey Card Day Canada

COMPLETE SET (17) 4.00 10.00
NHCD1 Sidney Crosby .75 2.00
NHCD2 Steven Stamkos .40 1.00
NHCD3 Ryan Getzlaf .20 .50
NHCD4 Evander Kane .20 .50
NHCD5 P.K. Subban .25 .60
NHCD6 Bo Horvat .30 .75
NHCD7 Sam Reinhart .50 1.25
NHCD8 Aaron Ekblad .30 .75
NHCD9 Jonathan Drouin .25 .60
NHCD10 Curtis Lazar .12 .30
NHCD11 Joe Sakic .40 1.00
NHCD12 Patrick Roy .50 1.25
NHCD13 Terry Sawchuk .20 .50
NHCD14 Bobby Orr .75 2.00
NHCD15 Wayne Gretzky 1.25 3.00
NHCD16 Jonathan Toews .30 .75
NNO Checklist .10 .25

2014-15 Upper Deck National Hockey Card Day USA

COMPLETE SET (17) 4.00 10.00
NHCD1 Ryan Miller .20 .50
NHCD2 Joe Pavelski .25 .60
NHCD3 Bobby Ryan .15 .40
NHCD4 Phil Kessel .20 .50
NHCD5 Patrick Kane .40 1.00
NHCD6 Johnny Gaudreau .40 1.00
NHCD7 Kevin Hayes .30 .75
NHCD8 Rocco Grimaldi .12 .30
NHCD9 Jori Lehtera .15 .40
NHCD10 Andre Burakovsky .20 .50
NHCD11 Mike Richter .20 .50
NHCD12 John Leclair .20 .50
NHCD13 Brian Leetch .15 .40
NHCD14 Chris Chelios .20 .50
NHCD15 Jeremy Roenick .30 .75
NHCD16 Wayne Gretzky 1.25 3.00
NNO Checklist .10 .25

2015-16 Upper Deck National Hockey Card Day Canada

COMPLETE SET (17)
CAN1 John Tavares .50 1.25
CAN2 Carey Price .60 1.50
CAN3 Taylor Hall .30 .75
CAN4 Andrew Ladd .20 .50
CAN5 Sean Monahan .20 .50
CAN6 Connor McDavid 5.00 12.00
CAN7 Sam Bennett 1.00 2.50
CAN8 Robby Fabbri .40 1.00
CAN9 Max Domi .60 1.50
CAN10 Nicolas Petan .30 .75
CAN11 Wayne Gretzky 2.00 5.00
CAN12 Bobby Orr 1.25 3.00
CAN13 Lanny McDonald .30 .75
CAN14 Glenn Anderson .25 .60
CAN15 Doug Gilmour .40 1.00
CAN16 Connor McDavid MM 5.00 12.00

2015-16 Upper Deck National Hockey Card Day USA

COMPLETE SET (17)
USA1 John Carlson .75 2.00
USA2 Phil Kessel .75 2.00
USA3 Zach Parise .75 2.00
USA4 Kevin Shattenkirk .50 1.25
USA5 Cory Schneider .75 2.00
USA6 Jack Eichel 3.00 8.00
USA7 Dylan Larkin 2.50 6.00
USA8 Noah Hanifin 1.25 3.00
USA9 Artemi Panarin 3.00 8.00
USA10 Oscar Lindberg .75 2.00
USA11 John Vanbiesbrouck .75 2.00
USA12 Doug Weight .75 2.00
USA13 Chris Chelios .75 2.00
USA14 Brett Hull 1.50 4.00
USA15 John LeClair .75 2.00
USA16 Jack Eichel MM 3.00 8.00

2016-17 Upper Deck National Hockey Card Day Canada

CAN1 Auston Matthews 1.25 3.00
CAN2 Patrik Laine .50 1.25
CAN3 Matthew Tkachuk .75 2.00
CAN4 Mikhail Sergachev .30 .75
CAN5 Mitch Marner .60 1.50
CAN6 Jonathan Toews .30 .75
CAN7 Steven Stamkos .40 1.00
CAN8 John Tavares .30 .75
CAN9 Connor McDavid 1.00 2.50
CAN10 Sidney Crosby .75 2.00
CAN11 Bobby Orr .75 2.00
CAN12 Patrick Roy .50 1.25
CAN13 Mike Bossy .20 .50
CAN14 Joe Sakic .40 1.00
CAN15 Wayne Gretzky 1.25 3.00
CAN16 Auston Matthews 1.25 3.00

2016-17 Upper Deck National Hockey Card Day USA

USA1 Auston Matthews 1.25 3.00
USA2 Tyler Motte .20 .50
USA3 Zach Werenski .60 1.50
USA4 Ivan Provorov .30 .75
USA5 Jimmy Vesey .30 .75
USA6 Dylan Larkin .25 .60
USA7 Jack Eichel .30 .75
USA8 Joe Pavelski .25 .60
USA9 Jonathan Quick .25 .60
USA10 Patrick Kane .40 1.00
USA11 Jeremy Roenick .30 .75
USA12 Bill Guerin .20 .50
USA13 Brian Leetch .15 .40
USA14 Ed Olczyk .15 .40
USA15 Mike Modano .30 .75
USA16 Auston Matthews 1.25 3.00

2017-18 Upper Deck National Hockey Card Day Canada

CAN1 Nolan Patrick 1.00 2.50
CAN2 Josh Ho-Sang .60 1.50
CAN3 Tyson Jost 1.00 2.50
CAN4 Pierre-Luc Dubois .75 2.00
CAN5 Owen Tippett 1.00 2.50
CAN6 Erik Karlsson .60 1.50
CAN7 Carey Price 1.00 2.50
CAN8 Mark Scheifele .75 2.00
CAN9 Connor McDavid 2.50 6.00
CAN10 Auston Matthews 2.00 5.00
CAN11 Steve Yzerman 1.25 3.00
CAN12 Guy Lafleur .60 1.50
CAN13 Darryl Sittler .60 1.50
CAN14 Mark Messier 1.00 2.50
CAN15 Mario Lemieux 2.00 5.00
CAN16 P.K. Subban MM .60 1.50

2018-19 Upper Deck National Hockey Card Day Canada

CAN1 Elias Pettersson 1.50 4.00
CAN2 Evan Bouchard 1.25 3.00
CAN3 Kristian Vesalainen .60 1.50
CAN4 Jesperi Kotkaniemi 1.00 2.50
CAN5 Brady Tkachuk 1.50 4.00
CAN6 Brock Boeser .60 1.50
CAN7 John Tavares .75 2.00
CAN8 Max Domi .50 1.25
CAN9 Drew Doughty .60 1.50
CAN10 Connor McDavid 2.50 6.00
CAN11 Darryl Sittler .60 1.50
CAN12 Jarome Iginla .60 1.50
CAN13 Mark Messier 1.00 2.50
CAN14 Maurice Richard 1.00 2.50
CAN15 Johnny Bower .50 1.25
CAN16 John Tavares MM .75 2.00
PROMO Checklist .10 .25

2017-18 Upper Deck National Hockey Card Day Canada 10th Anniversary Tribute

10THCM Connor McDavid 1.00 2.50
10THJT John Tavares .30 .75
10THNM Nathan MacKinnon .75 2.00
10THPS P.K. Subban .25 .60
10THSS Steven Stamkos .40 1.00

2018-19 Upper Deck National Hockey Card Day Canada NHL Global Series Canada vs USA

GS6 Connor McDavid 10.00 25.00
GS7 Milan Lucic 1.50 4.00
GS8 Oscar Klefbom 1.50 4.00
GS9 Patrik Laine 2.50 6.00
GS10 Blake Wheeler 2.00 5.00

2019-20 Upper Deck National Hockey Card Day Canada

CAN1 Nick Suzuki 2.00 5.00
CAN2 Ville Heinola .60 1.50
CAN3 Ryan Poehling .75 2.00
CAN4 Rasmus Sandin .75 2.00
CAN5 Erik Brannstrom .50 1.25
CAN6 Nathan MacKinnon 2.00 5.00
CAN7 Mark Scheifele .75 2.00
CAN8 Connor McDavid 2.50 6.00
CAN9 Sean Monahan .30 .75
CAN10 Marc-Andre Fleury 1.00 2.50
CAN11 Grant Fuhr .75 2.00
CAN12 Lanny McDonald .50 1.25
CAN13 Steve Yzerman 1.25 3.00
CAN14 Phil Esposito .75 2.00
CAN15 Joe Sakic 1.00 2.50
CAN16 Quinn Hughes 2.50 6.00

2019-20 Upper Deck National Hockey Card Day Mascots

M1 Gritty 4.00 10.00
M2 SJ Sharkie 2.50 6.00
M3 Bernie the St. Bernard 2.50 6.00
M4 Tommy Hawk 2.50 6.00
M5 Bailey 2.50 6.00
M6 Carlton the Bear 2.50 6.00
M7 Harvey the Hound 2.50 6.00
M8 Fin the Whale 2.50 6.00
M9 Youppi! 2.50 6.00
M10 Spartacat 2.50 6.00

2022-23 Upper Deck National Hockey Card Day

NHCD1 Juraj Slafkovsky 1.50 4.00
NHCD2 Shane Wright .75 2.00
NHCD3 Owen Power .60 1.50
NHCD4 Kent Johnson .60 1.50
NHCD5 Jake Sanderson .75 2.00
NHCD6 Matty Beniers .75 2.00
NHCD7 Andrei Kuzmenko .60 1.50
NHCD8 Matt Boldy 1.00 2.50
NHCD9 Dylan Guenther .75 2.00
NHCD10 Dylan Holloway .60 1.50
NHCD11 Connor McDavid 1.50 4.00
NHCD12 Sidney Crosby 1.25 3.00
NHCD13 Alex Ovechkin 1.25 3.00
NHCD14 Cale Makar .75 2.00
NHCD15 Auston Matthews 1.25 3.00
NHCD16 Kirill Kaprizov 1.00 2.50
NHCD17 Nick Suzuki .60 1.50
NHCD18 Igor Shesterkin .60 1.50
NHCD19 Jonathan Huberdeau .40 1.00
NHCD20 Patrick Kane .60 1.50
NHCD21 Patrick Roy .75 2.00
NHCD22 Teemu Selanne .60 1.50
NHCD23 Mark Messier .60 1.50
NHCD24 Jarome Iginla .40 1.00
NHCD25 Ray Bourque .50 1.25
NHCD26 Mario Lemieux 1.25 3.00
NHCD27 Steve Yzerman .75 2.00
NHCD28 Doug Gilmour .40 1.00
NHCD29 Joe Sakic .60 1.50
NHCD30 Wayne Gretzky 2.00 5.00
NHCD31 Checklist 4.00 1.00

2022-23 Upper Deck National Hockey Card Day Mascot

M1 Slapshot 3.00 8.00
M2 Stormy 3.00 8.00
M3 Buoy 8.00 20.00
M4 Spartacat 3.00 8.00
M5 Harvey The Hound 3.00 8.00
M6 Bernie the St. Bernard 3.00 8.00
M7 Al The Octopus 3.00 8.00
M8 Blades The Bruin 3.00 8.00
M9 Tommy Hawk 3.00 8.00
M10 Howler 3.00 8.00

2022-23 Upper Deck National Hockey Card Day Rookie Moments

NHCDBE Matty Beniers 1.00 2.50

2022-23 Upper Deck National Hockey Card Day Victory Black Rookies

V1 Shane Wright 4.00 10.00
V2 Juraj Slafkovsky 8.00 20.00
V3 Jake Sanderson 4.00 10.00
V4 Andrei Kuzmenko 3.00 8.00
V5 Wyatt Johnston 6.00 15.00
V6 Kent Johnson 3.00 8.00
V7 Dylan Guenther 4.00 10.00
V8 Owen Power 3.00 8.00
V9 Kaiden Guhle 3.00 8.00
V10 Matty Beniers 4.00 10.00

2012-13 Upper Deck NHL Draft

COMPLETE SET (6) 5.00 12.00
D1 Sidney Crosby 1.50 4.00
D2 Evgeni Malkin .75 2.00
D3 Marc-Andre Fleury .60 1.50
D4 Alex Ovechkin 1.00 2.50
D5 Steven Stamkos .75 2.00
D6 Jaromir Jagr .75 2.00

2013-14 Upper Deck NHL Draft

COMPLETE SET (6) 5.00 10.00
D1 Martin Brodeur 1.50 4.00
D2 Ilya Kovalchuk .60 1.50

D3 Patrik Elias .60 1.50
D4 Sidney Crosby 2.50 6.00
D5 Steven Stamkos 1.25 3.00
D6 Ryan Nugent-Hopkins .75 2.00

2014-15 Upper Deck NHL Draft

COMPLETE SET (6) 5.00 10.00
D1 Claude Giroux .60 1.50
D2 Sean Couturier .50 1.25
D3 Scott Laughton .40 1.00
D4 Alexander Ovechkin 2.50 6.00
D5 Sidney Crosby 2.50 6.00
D6 Nathan MacKinnon 2.50 6.00

1999-00 Upper Deck Ovation

COMPLETE SET (90) 30.00 80.00
1 Paul Kariya .30 .75
2 Teemu Selanne .30 .75
3 Patrik Stefan RC .75 2.00
4 Sergei Samsonov .25 .60
5 Ray Bourque .50 1.25
6 Dominik Hasek .60 1.50
7 Michael Peca .25 .60
8 Miroslav Satan .25 .60
9 Oleg Saprykin RC .60 1.50
10 Valeri Bure .20 .50
11 Ron Francis .25 .60
12 Dave Tanabe .20 .50
13 Tony Amonte .25 .60
14 J-P Dumont .25 .60
15 Patrick Roy 1.50 4.00
16 Alex Tanguay .25 .60
17 Joe Sakic .60 1.50
18 Peter Forsberg .60 1.50
19 Mike Modano .50 1.25
20 Ed Belfour .30 .75
21 Brett Hull .40 1.00
22 Sergei Fedorov .50 1.25
23 Chris Osgood .25 .60
24 Steve Yzerman 1.50 4.00
25 Doug Weight .25 .60
26 Tom Poti .20 .50
27 Pavel Bure .30 .75
28 Ivan Novoseltsev RC .50 1.25
29 Luc Robitaille .25 .60
30 Zigmund Palffy .25 .60
31 Mike Ribeiro .25 .60
32 David Legwand .20 .50
33 Martin Brodeur .75 2.00
34 Scott Gomez .25 .60
35 Tim Connolly .20 .50
36 Theo Fleury .30 .75
37 Mike Richter .30 .75
38 Brian Leetch .30 .75
39 Marian Hossa .30 .75
40 Daniel Alfredsson .25 .60
41 Eric Lindros .30 .75
42 John LeClair .30 .75
43 Simon Gagne .30 .75
44 Keith Tkachuk .40 1.00
45 Jeremy Roenick .40 1.00
46 Jaromir Jagr .50 1.25
47 Alexei Kovalev .25 .60
48 Pavol Demitra .25 .60
49 Al MacInnis .25 .60
50 Owen Nolan .25 .60
51 Brad Stuart .25 .60
52 Steve Shields .20 .50
53 Vincent Lecavalier .30 .75
54 Paul Mara .20 .50
55 Curtis Joseph .30 .75
56 Mats Sundin .30 .75
57 Steve Kariya RC .60 1.50
58 Mark Messier .30 .75
59 Peter Bondra .25 .60
60 Olaf Kolzig .25 .60
61 Pavel Brendl PP SP RC 1.25 3.00
62 Daniel Sedin PP SP 1.25 3.00
63 Henrik Sedin PP SP 1.25 3.00
64 Sheldon Keefe PP SP RC 1.25 3.00
65 Jeff Heerema PP SP .75 2.00
66 Norm Milley PP SP .75 2.00
67 Branislav Mezei PP SP RC .75 2.00
68 Denis Shvidki PP SP .75 2.00
69 Brian Finley PP SP .75 2.00
70 Taylor Pyatt PP SP .75 2.00
71 Jamie Lundmark PP SP .75 2.00
72 Milan Kraft PP SP RC 1.25 3.00
73 Kris Beech PP SP .75 2.00
74 Alexei Volkov PP SP 1.00 2.50
75 Mathieu Chouinard PP SP .75 2.00
76 Justin Papineau PP SP .75 2.00
77 Brad Moran PP SP RC .75 2.00
78 Jonathan Cheechoo PP SP 1.25 3.00
79 Mark Bell PP SP .75 2.00
80 Mattias Weinhandl PP SP .75 2.00
81 Jaromir Jagr SS SP 1.50 4.00
82 Steve Kariya SS SP 1.00 2.50
83 Dominik Hasek SS SP 2.00 5.00
84 Paul Kariya SS SP 1.25 3.00
85 Eric Lindros SS SP 1.00 2.50
86 Patrick Roy SS SP 5.00 12.00
87 Steve Yzerman SS SP 5.00 12.00
88 Pavel Bure SS SP 1.00 2.50
89 Theo Fleury SS SP 1.00 2.50
90 Patrik Stefan SS SP 1.25 3.00

1999-00 Upper Deck Ovation A Piece Of History

BH Brett Hull 12.50 30.00
CJ Curtis Joseph 8.00 20.00
JJ Jaromir Jagr 12.50 30.00
MB Martin Brodeur 15.00 40.00
MR Mike Ribeiro 8.00 20.00
PB Pavel Bure 8.00 20.00
PK Paul Kariya 8.00 20.00
PR Patrick Roy 12.00 30.00
PS Patrik Stefan 8.00 20.00
SK Steve Kariya 8.00 20.00
SS Sergei Samsonov 8.00 20.00
TC Tim Connolly 8.00 20.00
WG Wayne Gretzky 15.00 40.00
BHS Brett Hull AU/25 150.00 300.00
CJS Curtis Joseph AU/25 125.00 250.00
PBS Pavel Bure AU/25 200.00 400.00
PSS Patrik Stefan AU/25 30.00 75.00

1999-00 Upper Deck Ovation Center Stage

COMMON GRETZKY (CS1-CS5) 2.00 5.00
COMMON HOWE (CS6-CS10) 1.25 3.00
COMMON GRETZY (CS11-CS20) 6.00 15.00
COMMON HOWE (CS16-CS19) 4.00 10.00
COMMON GRETZKY (CS22-CS25) 20.00 50.00
COMMON HOWE (CS26-CS27) 12.50 30.00
COMMON DUAL (CS21/CS28-CS30) 25.0060.00

1999-00 Upper Deck Ovation Lead Performers

COMPLETE SET (20) 15.00 30.00
LP1 Mike Modano .75 2.00
LP2 Theo Fleury .25 .60
LP3 Paul Kariya .50 1.25
LP4 Peter Forsberg 1.25 3.00
LP5 Pavel Bure .60 1.50
LP6 John LeClair .60 1.50
LP7 Keith Tkachuk .50 1.25
LP8 Jaromir Jagr .75 2.00
LP9 Patrik Stefan .25 .60
LP10 Steve Kariya .25 .60
LP11 Ray Bourque .75 2.00
LP12 Teemu Selanne .50 1.25
LP13 Zigmund Palffy .50 1.25
LP14 Steve Yzerman 2.50 6.00
LP15 Eric Lindros .75 2.00
LP16 Dominik Hasek 1.00 2.50
LP17 Martin Brodeur 1.25 3.00
LP18 Brendan Shanahan .75 2.00
LP19 Ed Belfour .50 1.25
LP20 Patrick Roy 2.50 6.00

1999-00 Upper Deck Ovation Standing Ovation

*1-60 VET: 15X TO 40X BASIC CARDS
*1-60 ROOKIE/50: 5X TO 12X BASIC RC
*61-80 PP/50: 3X TO 8X BASIC SP
*81-90 SS/50: 4X TO 10X BASIC SP

1999-00 Upper Deck Ovation Super Signatures

SS1 Wayne Gretzky/99 200.00 500.00
SS2 Gordie Howe/99 60.00 150.00
SSG1 Wayne Gretzky GOLD/50 300.00 800.00
SSG2 Gordie Howe GOLD/50 125.00 250.00
SSR1 W.Gretzky RNBW/25 600.00 1500.00
SSR2 G.Howe RNBW/25 300.00 500.00

1999-00 Upper Deck Ovation Superstar Theater

COMPLETE SET (10) 10.00 20.00
ST1 Paul Kariya .60 1.50
ST2 Sergei Fedorov 1.00 2.50
ST3 Brett Hull .60 1.50
ST4 Patrick Roy 2.50 6.00
ST5 Dominik Hasek 1.00 2.50
ST6 Eric Lindros .75 2.00
ST7 Jaromir Jagr .75 2.00
ST8 Martin Brodeur 1.25 3.00
ST9 Pavel Bure .60 1.50
ST10 Teemu Selanne .60 1.50

2006-07 Upper Deck Ovation

1 Jean-Sebastien Giguere .40 1.00
2 Teemu Selanne .75 2.00
3 Slava Kozlov .20 .50
4 Brad Boyes .20 .50
5 Hannu Toivonen .30 .75
6 Thomas Vanek .30 .75
7 Ales Kotalik .20 .50
8 Miikka Kiprusoff .40 1.00
9 Erik Cole .20 .50
10 Nikolai Khabibulin .40 1.00
11 Tuomo Ruutu .40 1.00
12 Alex Tanguay .20 .50
13 Jose Theodore .40 1.00
14 David Vyborny .20 .50
15 Jason Arnott .30 .75
16 Brendan Shanahan .40 1.00
17 Pavel Datsyuk .60 1.50
18 Nicklas Lidstrom .40 1.00
19 Chris Pronger .40 1.00
20 Jarret Stoll .30 .75
21 M-A Pouliot RC .75 2.00
22 Joe Nieuwendyk .30 .75
23 Lubomir Visnovsky .20 .50
24 Manny Fernandez .20 .50
25 Erik Reitz RC .75 2.00
26 Mike Ribeiro .20 .50
27 Chris Higgins .20 .50
28 Martin Brodeur .75 2.00
29 Brian Gionta .20 .50
30 Miroslav Satan .30 .75
31 Jason Blake .20 .50
32 Petr Prucha .30 .75
33 Jason Spezza .40 1.00
34 Filip Novak RC .75 2.00
35 Simon Gagne .40 1.00
36 Robert Esche .30 .75
37 Ryan Potulny RC .75 2.00
38 Mike Comrie .30 .75
39 Bill Thomas RC .75 2.00
40 Marc-Andre Fleury .75 2.00
41 Sergei Gonchar .20 .50
42 Evgeni Nabokov .30 .75
43 Keith Tkachuk .40 1.00
44 Martin St. Louis .40 1.00
45 Mike Commodore .20 .50
46 Bryan McCabe .20 .50
47 Alexander Steen .20 .50
48 Markus Naslund .40 1.00
49 Ed Jovanovski .30 .75
50 Dainius Zubrus .20 .50
51 Scott Niedermayer .40 1.00
52 Joffrey Lupul .20 .50
53 Ilya Kovalchuk .40 1.00
54 Brian Leetch .30 .75
55 Marco Sturm .20 .50
56 Martin Biron .30 .75
57 Dion Phaneuf .30 .75
58 Daymond Langkow .20 .50
59 Cam Ward .40 1.00
60 Kyle Calder .20 .50
61 Dustin Byfuglien RC 2.00 5.00
62 Milan Hejduk .30 .75
63 Rick Nash .40 1.00
64 Sergei Fedorov .60 1.50
65 Nikolai Zherdev .20 .50
66 Sergei Zubov .30 .75
67 Henrik Zetterberg .40 1.00
68 Kris Draper .20 .50
69 Tomas Kopecky RC 1.00 2.50
70 Dwayne Roloson .30 .75
71 Roberto Luongo .60 1.50
72 Jay Bouwmeester .20 .50
73 Nathan Horton .40 1.00
74 Mathieu Garon .30 .75
75 Pierre-Marc Bouchard .40 1.00
76 Cristobal Huet .30 .75
77 Steve Sullivan .20 .50
78 Scott Gomez .30 .75
79 Alexei Yashin .30 .75
80 Mike York .20 .50
81 Ryan Caldwell RC .75 2.00
82 Jaromir Jagr 1.25 3.00
83 Jason Spezza .40 1.00
84 Ray Emery .30 .75
85 Jeff Carter .30 .75
86 Mike Knuble .20 .50
87 Keith Ballard .20 .50
88 Joel Perrault RC .75 2.00
89 John LeClair .40 1.00
90 Joe Thornton .60 1.50
91 Matt Carle RC .75 2.00
92 Scott Young .20 .50
93 Vincent Lecavalier .40 1.00
94 Brad Richards .40 1.00
95 Vaclav Prospal .20 .50
96 Darcy Tucker .30 .75
97 Ian White RC 1.00 2.50
98 Brendan Morrison .20 .50
99 Alexander Ovechkin 1.50 4.00
100 Jeff Halpern .20 .50
101 Corey Perry .60 1.50
102 Ryan Getzlaf .40 1.00
103 Kari Lehtonen .30 .75
104 Marian Hossa .40 1.00
105 Tim Thomas .40 1.00
106 Mark Stuart RC .75 2.00
107 Ryan Miller .40 1.00
108 Maxim Afinogenov .20 .50
109 Chuck Kobasew .20 .50
110 Carsen Germyn RC .75 2.00
111 Eric Staal .40 1.00
112 Rod Brind`Amour .40 1.00
113 Mark Bell .20 .50
114 Rob Blake .40 1.00
115 Pascal Leclaire .30 .75
116 Mike Modano .60 1.50
117 Brenden Morrow .30 .75
118 Jussi Jokinen .30 .75
119 Tomas Holmstrom .30 .75
120 Ryan Smyth .30 .75
121 Raffi Torres .20 .50
122 Alexander Frolov .20 .50
123 Mike Cammalleri .20 .50
124 Konstantin Pushkarev RC 1.00 2.50
125 Marian Gaborik .40 1.00
126 Brian Rolston .30 .75
127 Alex Kovalev .30 .75
128 Tomas Vokoun .30 .75
129 Scott Hartnell .20 .50
130 Brian Rafalski .30 .75
131 Henrik Lundqvist .75 2.00
132 Michael Nylander .20 .50
133 David Liffiton RC .75 2.00
134 Daniel Alfredsson .40 1.00
135 Wade Redden .20 .50
136 Billy Thompson RC .75 2.00
137 Peter Forsberg .75 2.00
138 Keith Primeau .30 .75
139 Ladislav Nagy .20 .50
140 Sidney Crosby 1.50 4.00
141 Jonathan Cheechoo .30 .75
142 Vesa Toskala .30 .75
143 Petr Cajanek .20 .50
144 Fredrik Modin .20 .50
145 Mats Sundin .40 1.00
146 Kyle Wellwood .30 .75
147 Alexander Steen .20 .50
148 Brendan Bell .20 .50
149 Daniel Sedin .40 1.00
150 Eric Fehr RC 1.25 3.00
151 Marc Savard .20 .50
152 Patrice Bergeron .40 1.00
153 Glen Murray .30 .75
154 Phil Kessel RC 2.50 6.00
155 Chris Drury .30 .75
156 Daniel Briere .40 1.00
157 Jarome Iginla .40 1.00
158 Doug Weight .40 1.00
159 Justin Williams .30 .75
160 Brent Seabrook .20 .50
161 Joe Sakic .75 2.00
162 Marek Svatos .20 .50
163 Paul Stastny RC 2.00 5.00
164 Marty Turco .40 1.00
165 Jere Lehtinen .20 .50
166 Fernando Pisani .20 .50
167 Ales Hemsky .30 .75
168 Shawn Horcoff .20 .50
169 Olli Jokinen .40 1.00
170 Pavol Demitra .40 1.00
171 Mikko Koivu .30 .75
172 Guillaume Latendresse RC 1.25 3.00
173 Saku Koivu .40 1.00
174 Michael Ryder .20 .50
175 David Aebischer .30 .75
176 Paul Kariya .40 1.00
177 Mike Sillinger .20 .50
178 Shea Weber RC 2.00 5.00
179 Patrik Elias .40 1.00
180 Rick DiPietro .30 .75
181 Steve Regier RC .75 2.00
182 Masi Marjamaki RC .75 2.00
183 Martin Straka .20 .50
184 Jarkko Immonen XRC 1.00 2.50
185 Patrick O'Sullivan RC 1.25 3.00
186 Martin Havlat .20 .50
187 Antero Niittymaki .30 .75
188 Shane Doan .30 .75
189 Curtis Joseph .40 1.00
190 Colby Armstrong .30 .75
191 Jordan Staal RC 2.00 5.00
192 Evgeni Malkin RC 6.00 15.00
193 Patrick Marleau .40 1.00
194 Steve Bernier .20 .50
195 Curtis Sanford .30 .75
196 Ruslan Fedotenko .20 .50
197 Andrew Raycroft .30 .75
198 Henrik Sedin .40 1.00
199 Luc Bourdon RC 1.25 3.00
200 Alexander Ovechkin 1.50 4.00

2007-08 Upper Deck Ovation

COMPLETE SET (225) 60.00 120.00
1 Olaf Kolzig .40 1.00
2 Daniel Sedin .50 1.25
3 Henrik Sedin .50 1.25
4 Alexander Steen .25 .60
5 Bryan McCabe .25 .60
6 Brad Richards .40 1.00
7 Manny Legace .30 .75
8 Jonathan Cheechoo .30 .75
9 Joe Pavelski .50 1.25
10 Mark Recchi .50 1.25
11 Sidney Crosby 1.50 4.00
12 Shane Doan .30 .75
13 Jeff Carter .30 .75
14 Jason Spezza .40 1.00
15 Martin Straka .25 .60
16 Brendan Shanahan .40 1.00
17 Rick DiPietro .30 .75
18 Martin Brodeur 1.00 2.50
19 Travis Zajac .25 .60
20 Kimmo Timonen .25 .60
21 Peter Forsberg .75 2.00
22 Cristobal Huet .30 .75
23 Guillaume Latendresse .30 .75
24 Manny Fernandez .25 .60
25 Pavol Demitra .50 1.25
26 Anze Kopitar .60 1.50
27 Jay Bouwmeester .25 .60
28 Ales Hemsky .30 .75
29 Rob Schremp RC .50 1.25
30 Tomas Holmstrom .30 .75
31 Nicklas Lidstrom .40 1.00
32 Mike Ribeiro .25 .60
33 Brenden Morrow .30 .75
34 David Vyborny .25 .60
35 Pascal Leclaire .30 .75
36 Paul Stastny .30 .75
37 Marek Svatos .25 .60
38 Tuomo Ruutu .40 1.00
39 Duncan Keith .30 .75
40 Justin Williams .30 .75
41 Erik Cole .25 .60
42 Daymond Langkow .25 .60
43 Jarome Iginla .50 1.25
44 Thomas Vanek .30 .75
45 Daniel Briere .40 1.00
46 Marc Savard .25 .60
47 Petr Kalus RC .40 1.00
48 Marian Hossa .40 1.00
49 Andy McDonald .30 .75
50 Ryan Getzlaf .40 1.00
51 Alexander Ovechkin 1.50 4.00
52 Brendan Morrison .25 .60
53 Trevor Linden .40 1.00
54 Owen Nolan .40 1.00
55 Andrew Raycroft .30 .75
56 Yanic Perreault .25 .60
57 Vincent Lecavalier .40 1.00
58 Brad Boyes .25 .60
59 Barret Jackman .25 .60
60 Vesa Toskala .30 .75
61 Bill Guerin .40 1.00
62 Marc-Andre Fleury .75 2.00
63 Jordan Staal .30 .75
64 Zbynek Michalek .25 .60
65 Simon Gagne .40 1.00
66 Daniel Alfredsson .40 1.00
67 Ray Emery .30 .75
68 Michael Nylander .25 .60
69 Michal Rozsival .25 .60
70 Jason Blake .25 .60
71 Alexei Yashin .30 .75
72 Zach Parise .40 1.00
73 Scott Gomez .30 .75
74 Paul Kariya .40 1.00
75 Jason Arnott .30 .75
76 Alex Kovalev .30 .75
77 Jaroslav Halak RC 1.25 3.00
78 Mikko Koivu .30 .75
79 Mike Cammalleri .30 .75
80 Jack Johnson RC .50 1.25
81 Nathan Horton .40 1.00
82 Olli Jokinen .30 .75
83 Shawn Horcoff .25 .60
84 Joffrey Lupul .25 .60
85 Dominik Hasek .60 1.50
86 Kris Draper .25 .60
87 Mike Modano .60 1.50
88 Rick Nash .40 1.00
89 Peter Budaj .30 .75
90 Wojtek Wolski .30 .75
91 Nikolai Khabibulin .40 1.00
92 Eric Staal .50 1.25
93 Dion Phaneuf .30 .75
94 Matthew Lombardi .25 .60
95 Ryan Miller .40 1.00
96 Jason Pominville .25 .60
97 Patrice Bergeron .50 1.25
98 Kari Lehtonen .30 .75
99 Scott Niedermayer .40 1.00
100 Corey Perry .60 1.50
101 Chris Clark .25 .60
102 Eric Fehr .25 .60
103 Markus Naslund .40 1.00
104 Tomas Kaberle .25 .60
105 Jeff O'Neill .25 .60
106 Johan Holmqvist .30 .75
107 Vaclav Prospal .25 .60
108 Lee Stempniak .25 .60
109 Jay McClement .25 .60
110 Patrick Marleau .40 1.00
111 Evgeni Nabokov .30 .75
112 Evgeni Malkin .75 2.00
113 Sergei Gonchar .25 .60
114 Curtis Joseph .50 1.25
115 Ryan Parent .25 .60
116 Mike Richards .30 .75
117 Mike Fisher .25 .60
118 Wade Redden .25 .60
119 Henrik Lundqvist 1.00 2.50
120 Ryan Smyth .30 .75
121 Brian Rafalski .30 .75
122 Brian Gionta .25 .60
123 Steve Sullivan .25 .60
124 Chris Mason .30 .75
125 Saku Koivu .40 1.00
126 Brian Rolston .30 .75
127 P-M Bouchard .40 1.00
128 Lauri Tukonen RC .40 1.00
129 Alexander Frolov .25 .60
130 Stephen Weiss .25 .60
131 Jozef Stumpel .25 .60
132 Jarret Stoll .30 .75
133 Pavel Datsyuk .60 1.50
134 Philippe Boucher .25 .60
135 Eric Lindros .60 1.50
136 Gilbert Brule .30 .75
137 Fredrik Modin .25 .60
138 Andrew Brunette .25 .60
139 Joe Sakic .75 2.00
140 Martin Havlat .40 1.00
141 Cam Ward .40 1.00
142 Miikka Kiprusoff .40 1.00
143 Maxim Afinogenov .25 .60
144 Brian Campbell .30 .75
145 Glen Murray .30 .75
146 Phil Kessel .40 1.00
147 Slava Kozlov .25 .60
148 Ilya Kovalchuk .40 1.00
149 Jean-Sebastien Giguere .40 1.00
150 Chris Pronger .40 1.00
151 Alexander Semin .40 1.00
152 Nicklas Backstrom RC 1.25 3.00
153 Roberto Luongo .60 1.50
154 Darcy Tucker .30 .75
155 Mats Sundin .40 1.00
156 Martin St. Louis .40 1.00
157 Doug Weight .40 1.00
158 Erik Johnson RC .60 1.50
159 Joe Thornton .60 1.50
160 Ryan Whitney .30 .75
161 Peter Mueller RC .50 1.25
162 Martin Biron .30 .75
163 Dany Heatley .30 .75
164 Nick Foligno RC .75 2.00
165 Jaromir Jagr 1.25 3.00
166 Marc Staal RC .60 1.50
167 Miroslav Satan .30 .75
168 Patrik Elias .40 1.00
169 Nicklas Bergfors RC .40 1.00
170 Carey Price RC 2.50 6.00
171 Chris Higgins .25 .60
172 Michael Ryder .25 .60
173 Mark Parrish .25 .60
174 Marian Gaborik .40 1.00
175 Jack Johnson RC .50 1.25
176 Jonathan Bernier RC .75 2.00
177 Rob Blake .40 1.00
178 Sam Gagner RC .75 2.00
179 Dwayne Roloson .30 .75
180 Andrew Cogliano RC .50 1.25
181 Henrik Zetterberg .50 1.25
182 Marty Turco .40 1.00
183 Sergei Fedorov .60 1.50
184 Fredrik Norrena .25 .60
185 Milan Hejduk .30 .75
186 John-Michael Liles .25 .60
187 Patrick Kane RC 8.00 20.00
188 Jason Williams .25 .60
189 Ray Whitney .30 .75
190 Rod Brind'Amour .40 1.00
191 Kristian Huselius .25 .60
192 Alex Tanguay .30 .75
193 Derek Roy .25 .60
194 Zdeno Chara .40 1.00
195 Tim Thomas .40 1.00
196 Bryan Little RC .60 1.50
197 Bobby Holik .25 .60
198 Brett Sterling RC .40 1.00
199 Bobby Ryan RC 1.50 4.00
200 Chris Kunitz .40 1.00
201 Vincent Lecavalier .40 1.00
202 Daniel Alfredsson .40 1.00
203 Evgeni Malkin .75 2.00
204 Ilya Kovalchuk .40 1.00
205 Alexander Ovechkin 1.50 4.00
206 Eric Staal .50 1.25
207 Jason Spezza .40 1.00
208 Martin St. Louis .40 1.00
209 Andrei Markov .40 1.00
210 Tomas Kaberle .25 .60
211 Dion Phaneuf .30 .75
212 Nicklas Lidstrom .40 1.00
213 Scott Niedermayer .40 1.00
214 Jarome Iginla .50 1.25
215 Joe Thornton .60 1.50
216 Rick Nash .40 1.00
217 Tuukka Rask RC 1.50 4.00
218 T.J. Hensick RC .50 1.25
219 Jonathan Toews RC 3.00 8.00
220 Steve Downie RC .50 1.25
221 Devin Setoguchi RC .60 1.50
222 David Perron RC .75 2.00
223 Jiri Tlusty RC .60 1.50
224 James Sheppard RC .40 1.00
225 Sergei Kostitsyn .30 .75

2007-08 Upper Deck Ovation 3x5s

XL1 Alexander Ovechkin 8.00 20.00
XL3 Roberto Luongo 3.00 8.00
XL4 Andrew Raycroft 1.50 4.00
XL6 Vincent Lecavalier 2.00 5.00
XL7 Patrick Marleau 2.00 5.00
XL8 Sidney Crosby 8.00 20.00
XL10 Jason Spezza 2.00 5.00
XL11 Dany Heatley 1.50 4.00
XL12 Martin Brodeur 5.00 12.00
XL13 Guillaume Latendresse 1.50 4.00
XL18 Rick Nash 2.00 5.00
XL20 Eric Staal 2.50 6.00
XL21 Jarome Iginla 2.50 6.00
XL22 Dion Phaneuf 1.50 4.00
XL24 Thomas Vanek 1.50 4.00

2008-09 Upper Deck Ovation

COMPLETE SET (200) 75.00 150.00
COMP.FACT.SER.1 (50) 15.00 40.00
COMP.FACT.SER.2 (50) 15.00 40.00
COMP.FACT.SER.3 (50) 15.00 40.00
COMP.FACT.SER.4 (50) 20.00 50.00
1 Teemu Selanne .75 2.00
2 Jean-Sebastien Giguere .40 1.00
3 Tobias Enstrom .25 .60
4 Phil Kessel .40 1.00
5 Zdeno Chara .40 1.00
6 Marc-Andre Gragnani .30 .75
7 Jason Pominville .25 .60
8 Alex Tanguay .25 .60
9 Kristian Huselius .25 .60
10 Erik Cole .25 .60
11 Patrick Kane .75 2.00
12 Duncan Keith .30 .75
13 Ryan Smyth .30 .75
14 Wojtek Wolski .30 .75
15 Steve Mason RC 3.00 8.00
16 Rick Nash .40 1.00
17 Mike Modano .60 1.50
18 Brenden Morrow .30 .75
19 Dominik Hasek .60 1.50
20 Valtteri Filppula .25 .60
21 Dwayne Roloson .30 .75
22 Shawn Matthias RC .40 1.00
23 Tomas Vokoun .30 .75
24 Jay Bouwmeester .25 .60
25 Pierre-Marc Bouchard .40 1.00
26 Carey Price .75 2.00
27 Saku Koivu .40 1.00
28 Alex Kovalev .30 .75
29 Andrei Markov .40 1.00
30 Martin Erat .25 .60
31 Martin Brodeur 1.00 2.50
32 Travis Zajac .25 .60
33 Bill Guerin .40 1.00
34 Henrik Lundqvist 1.00 2.50
35 Chris Drury .30 .75
36 Ray Emery .30 .75
37 Simon Gagne .40 1.00
38 Daniel Briere .40 1.00
39 Ilya Bryzgalov .30 .75
40 Jon Filewich RC .30 .75
41 Evgeni Malkin .75 2.00
42 Jordan Staal .30 .75
43 Evgeni Nabokov .30 .75
44 Lee Stempniak .25 .60
45 Martin St. Louis .40 1.00
46 Johan Holmqvist .30 .75
47 Robbie Earl RC .25 .60
48 Nikolai Antropov .30 .75
49 Darcy Tucker .30 .75
50 Alexander Edler .25 .60
51 Corey Perry .60 1.50
52 Bryan Little .30 .75
53 Ilya Kovalchuk .40 1.00
54 Derek Roy .25 .60
55 Thomas Vanek .30 .75
56 Dion Phaneuf .30 .75
57 Justin Williams .30 .75
58 Martin Havlat .40 1.00
59 Joe Sakic .75 2.00
60 Paul Stastny .30 .75
61 Nikolai Zherdev .25 .60
62 Mark Fistric RC .30 .75
63 Marty Turco .40 1.00
64 Sergei Zubov .30 .75
65 Henrik Zetterberg .50 1.25
66 Ales Hemsky .30 .75
67 Dustin Penner .30 .75
68 Nathan Horton .30 .75
69 Anze Kopitar .60 1.50
70 Brian Boyle RC .30 .75
71 Mikko Koivu .30 .75
72 Andrei Kostitsyn .30 .75
73 Michael Ryder .25 .60
74 David Legwand .30 .75
75 Jason Arnott .30 .75
76 John Madden .25 .60
77 Mike Comrie .30 .75
78 Miroslav Satan .40 1.00
79 Jaromir Jagr 1.25 3.00
80 Scott Gomez .30 .75
81 Daniel Alfredsson .40 1.00
82 Ilya Zubov RC .30 .75
83 Nick Foligno .40 1.00
84 Claude Giroux RC .75 2.00
85 Mike Knuble .25 .60
86 R.J. Umberger .25 .60
87 Ed Jovanovski .30 .75
88 Shane Doan .30 .75
89 Marian Hossa .40 1.00
90 Ryan Stone RC .25 .60
91 Joe Thornton .60 1.50
92 Jonathan Cheechoo .30 .75
93 Milan Michalek .25 .60
94 Erik Johnson .25 .60
95 Dan Boyle .25 .60
96 Tomas Kaberle .25 .60
97 Daniel Sedin .50 1.25
98 Markus Naslund .40 1.00
99 Alexander Ovechkin 1.50 4.00
100 Mike Green .30 .75
101 Chris Pronger .40 1.00
102 Ryan Getzlaf .40 1.00
103 Kari Lehtonen .50 1.25
104 Johan Hedberg .30 .75
105 Marco Sturm .25 .60
106 Ryan Miller .40 1.00
107 Jarome Iginla .50 1.25
108 Daymond Langkow .25 .60
109 Eric Staal .50 1.25
110 Rod Brind`Amour .40 1.00
111 Jonathan Toews .60 1.50
112 Nikolai Khabibulin .40 1.00
113 Milan Hejduk .30 .75
114 Peter Budaj .30 .75
115 Derick Brassard RC .40 1.00
116 Pascal Leclaire .30 .75
117 Jonathan Ericsson RC .40 1.00
118 Nicklas Lidstrom .40 1.00
119 Dan Cleary .30 .75
120 Sam Gagner .25 .60
121 Shawn Horcoff .25 .60
122 Olli Jokinen .30 .75
123 Teddy Purcell RC .30 .75
124 Alexander Frolov .25 .60
125 Jack Johnson .25 .60
126 Marian Gaborik .40 1.00
127 Brian Rolston .30 .75
128 Chris Higgins .25 .60
129 Alexander Radulov .40 1.00
130 J.P. Dumont .25 .60
131 Patrik Elias .40 1.00
132 Trent Hunter .25 .60
133 Brendan Shanahan .40 1.00
134 Brandon Dubinsky .25 .60
135 Dany Heatley .30 .75
136 Patrick Sharp .40 1.00
137 Jeff Carter .30 .75
138 Peter Mueller .30 .75
139 Kyle Turris RC .60 1.50
140 Alex Goligoski RC .50 1.25
141 Mike Iggulden .30 .75
142 Brad Boyes .25 .60
143 David Perron .30 .75
144 Vincent Lecavalier .40 1.00
145 Paul Ranger .25 .60
146 Vesa Toskala .50 1.25
147 Henrik Sedin .50 1.25
148 Nicklas Backstrom .40 1.00
149 Alexander Semin .40 1.00
150 Viktor Kozlov .25 .60
151 Scott Niedermayer .40 1.00
152 Zach Bogosian RC .50 1.25
153 Tim Thomas .40 1.00
154 Patrice Bergeron .50 1.25
155 Marc Savard .25 .60
156 Chuck Kobasew .25 .60
157 Drew Stafford .25 .60
158 Miikka Kiprusoff .40 1.00
159 Matthew Lombardi .25 .60
160 Cam Ward .40 1.00
161 Brandon Sutter RC .40 1.00
162 Robert Lang .25 .60
163 Peter Forsberg .75 2.00
164 Marek Svatos .25 .60
165 James Neal RC .75 2.00
166 Brad Richards .40 1.00
167 Pavel Datsyuk .60 1.50
168 Tomas Holmstrom .30 .75
169 Andrew Cogliano .25 .60
170 Michael Frolik RC .40 1.00
171 Stephen Weiss .25 .60
172 Dustin Brown .40 1.00
173 Drew Doughty RC 1.00 2.50
174 Josh Harding .40 1.00
175 Colton Gillies RC .30 .75
176 Guillaume Latendresse .25 .60
177 Chris Mason .30 .75
178 Zach Parise .40 1.00
179 Brian Gionta .25 .60
180 Rick DiPietro .30 .75
181 Ruslan Fedotenko .25 .60
182 Michal Rozsival .25 .60
183 Martin Gerber .30 .75
184 Jason Spezza .40 1.00
185 Mike Richards .30 .75
186 Mikkel Boedker RC .50 1.25
187 Sidney Crosby 1.50 4.00
188 Marc-Andre Fleury .75 2.00
189 Ryan Whitney .40 1.00
190 Patrick Marleau .40 1.00
191 T.J. Oshie RC .75 2.00
192 Alex Pietrangelo RC .60 1.50
193 Steven Stamkos RC 4.00 10.00
194 Nikolai Kulemin RC .40 1.00
195 Matt Stajan .25 .60
196 Luke Schenn RC 4.00 10.00
197 Roberto Luongo .60 1.50
198 Brendan Morrison .25 .60
199 Sergei Fedorov .60 1.50
200 Cristobal Huet .30 .75

2008-09 Upper Deck Ovation Jumbo

XL1 Teemu Selanne 2.00 5.00
XL2 Patrick Kane 2.00 5.00
XL3 Dominik Hasek 1.50 4.00
XL4 Carey Price 2.00 5.00
XL5 Martin Brodeur 2.50 6.00
XL6 Evgeni Malkin 2.00 5.00
XL7 Joe Sakic 2.00 5.00
XL8 Henrik Zetterberg 1.25 3.00
XL9 Jaromir Jagr 3.00 8.00
XL10 Daniel Alfredsson 1.00 2.50
XL11 Joe Thornton 1.50 4.00
XL12 Alexander Ovechkin 4.00 10.00
XL13 Jarome Iginla 1.25 3.00
XL14 Eric Staal 1.25 3.00
XL15 Sam Gagner .60 1.50
XL16 Marian Gaborik 1.00 2.50
XL17 Dany Heatley .75 2.00
XL18 Vincent Lecavalier 1.00 2.50
XL19 Patrice Bergeron 1.25 3.00
XL20 Miikka Kiprusoff 1.00 2.50
XL21 Peter Forsberg 2.00 5.00
XL22 Sidney Crosby 4.00 10.00
XL23 Steven Stamkos 4.00 10.00
XL24 Roberto Luongo 1.50 4.00

2008-09 Upper Deck Ovation Jumbo Autographs

XLANB Nicklas Backstrom 15.00 40.00

2009-10 Upper Deck Ovation

COMPLETE SET (150) 25.00 60.00
1 Corey Perry .50 1.25
2 Ryan Getzlaf .30 .75
3 Brian Salcido RC .20 .50
4 Matt Beleskey RC .25 .60
5 Ilya Kovalchuk .30 .75
6 Bryan Little .30 .75
7 Spencer Machacek RC .30 .75
8 Tim Thomas .30 .75
9 Phil Kessel .30 .75

10 Zdeno Chara .30 .75
11 Marc Savard .20 .50
12 David Krejci .30 .75
13 Byron Bitz RC .25 .60
14 Blake Wheeler .30 .75
15 Thomas Vanek .25 .60
16 Ryan Miller .30 .75
17 Jason Pominville .20 .50
18 Jhonas Enroth RC .40 1.00
19 Derek Roy .20 .50
20 Dion Phaneuf .25 .60
21 Jarome Iginla .40 1.00
22 Miikka Kiprusoff .30 .75
23 Olli Jokinen .25 .60
24 Daymond Langkow .20 .50
25 Kris Chucko RC .20 .50
26 Mikael Backlund RC .50 1.25
27 Eric Staal .40 1.00
28 Cam Ward .30 .75
29 Erik Cole .20 .50
30 Jonathan Toews .50 1.25
31 Patrick Sharp .30 .75
32 Patrick Kane .60 1.50
33 Dustin Byfuglien .30 .75
34 Brian Campbell .25 .60
35 Kris Versteeg .20 .50
36 Paul Stastny .25 .60
37 Milan Hejduk .25 .60
38 T.J. Galiardi RC .30 .75
39 Steve Mason .25 .60
40 Rick Nash .30 .75
41 Derick Brassard .20 .50
42 Brenden Morrow .25 .60
43 Evander Kane RC .60 1.50
44 Marty Turco .30 .75
45 Henrik Zetterberg .40 1.00
46 Pavel Datsyuk .50 1.25
47 Johan Franzen .25 .60
48 Nicklas Lidstrom .20 .50
49 Tomas Holmstrom .25 .60
50 Chris Osgood .30 .75
51 Ville Leino RC .25 .60
52 Sheldon Souray .20 .50
53 Ales Hemsky .25 .60
54 Sam Gagner .20 .50
55 Andrew Cogliano .20 .50
56 Dustin Penner .20 .50
57 Dwayne Roloson .25 .60
58 Shawn Horcoff .20 .50
59 Tomas Vokoun .25 .60
60 Nathan Horton .30 .75
61 David Booth .20 .50
62 Anze Kopitar .50 1.25
63 Drew Doughty .40 1.00
64 Alexander Frolov .25 .60
65 Brent Burns .30 .75
66 Niklas Backstrom .30 .75
67 Mikko Koivu .30 .75
68 Andrei Markov .30 .75
69 Carey Price .60 1.50
70 John Tavares RC 4.00 10.00
71 Saku Koivu .30 .75
72 Tomas Plekanec .20 .50
73 James van Riemsdyk RC .60 1.50
74 Yannick Weber RC .30 .75
75 J.P. Dumont .20 .50
76 Pekka Rinne .30 .75
77 Jason Arnott .25 .60
78 Cal O'Reilly RC .25 .60
79 Mike Santorelli RC .30 .75
80 Martin Brodeur .75 2.00
81 Zach Parise .30 .75
82 Brian Gionta .20 .50
83 Jamie Langenbrunner .20 .50
84 Travis Zajac .20 .50
85 Kyle Okposo .20 .50
86 Rick DiPietro .25 .60
87 Jesse Joensuu RC .25 .60
88 Henrik Lundqvist .75 2.00
89 Nik Antropov .25 .60
90 Matt Duchene RC .60 1.50
91 Scott Gomez .25 .60
92 Artem Anisimov RC .20 .50
93 Victor Hedman RC .75 2.00
94 Ryan Stoa .25 .60
95 Dany Heatley .25 .60
96 Jason Spezza .30 .75
97 Brian Elliott .25 .60
98 Filip Kuba .20 .50
99 Daniel Alfredsson .30 .75
100 Mike Fisher .20 .50
101 Ryan Shannon .25 .60
102 Mike Richards .25 .60
103 Jeff Carter .25 .60
104 Martin Biron .25 .60
105 Daniel Briere .30 .75
106 Scott Hartnell .20 .50
107 Daniel Carcillo .20 .50
108 Sergei Shirokov RC .20 .50
109 Peter Mueller .25 .60
110 Shane Doan .25 .60
111 Jonas Gustavsson RC .40 1.00
112 Ilya Bryzgalov .25 .60
113 Sidney Crosby 1.25 3.00
114 Evgeni Malkin .60 1.50
115 Jordan Staal .25 .60
116 Marc-Andre Fleury .60 1.50
117 Chris Kunitz .30 .75
118 Luca Caputi RC .30 .75
119 Joe Thornton .50 1.25
120 Evgeni Nabokov .25 .60
121 Patrick Marleau .30 .75
122 Rob Blake .30 .75
123 Dan Boyle .20 .50
124 Devin Setoguchi .25 .60
125 Joe Pavelski .40 1.00
126 Brad Boyes .20 .50
127 Patrik Berglund .20 .50
128 David Backes .20 .50
129 Chris Mason .25 .60
130 Riku Helenius RC .30 .75
131 Steven Stamkos .60 1.50
132 Martin St. Louis .30 .75
133 Vincent Lecavalier .30 .75
134 Luke Schenn .30 .75
135 Matt Stajan .20 .50
136 Alexei Ponikarovsky .20 .50
137 Tomas Kaberle .20 .50
138 Nikolai Kulemin .20 .50
139 Niklas Hagman .20 .50
140 Matt Corrente .25 .60
141 Willie Mitchell .20 .50
142 Ryan Kesler .30 .75
143 Alexandre Burrows .20 .50
144 Kyle Wellwood .25 .60
145 Roberto Luongo .50 1.25
146 Michal Neuvirth RC .50 1.25
147 Alexander Ovechkin 1.25 3.00
148 Alexander Semin .30 .75
149 Nicklas Backstrom .30 .75
150 Mike Green .25 .60

2009-10 Upper Deck Ovation Spotlight

COMPLETE SET (30) 15.00 40.00
OS1 Saku Koivu 1.00 2.50
OS2 Alexander Ovechkin 4.00 10.00
OS3 Marc-Andre Fleury 2.00 5.00
OS4 Steven Stamkos 2.00 5.00
OS5 Thomas Vanek .75 2.00
OS6 Carey Price 2.00 5.00
OS7 Jeff Carter .75 2.00
OS8 Jason Spezza 1.00 2.50
OS9 Evgeni Malkin 2.00 5.00
OS10 Miikka Kiprusoff 1.00 2.50
OS11 Martin Brodeur 2.50 6.00
OS12 Jonathan Toews 1.50 4.00
OS13 Dany Heatley .75 2.00
OS14 Henrik Lundqvist 2.50 6.00
OS15 Jarome Iginla 1.25 3.00
OS16 Mike Green .75 2.00
OS17 Joe Thornton 1.50 4.00
OS18 Henrik Zetterberg 1.25 3.00
OS19 Dion Phaneuf .75 2.00
OS20 Sidney Crosby 4.00 10.00
OS21 Ales Hemsky .75 2.00
OS22 Alexandre Burrows .60 1.50
OS23 Pavel Datsyuk 1.50 4.00
OS24 Luke Schenn 1.00 2.50
OS25 Patrick Kane 2.00 5.00
OS26 Mike Richards .75 2.00
OS27 Justin Pogge 1.00 2.50
OS28 Ilya Kovalchuk 1.00 2.50
OS29 Roberto Luongo 1.50 4.00
OS30 Rick Nash 1.00 2.50

2021-22 Upper Deck Ovation

1 Carey Price 1.00 2.50
2 Seth Jones .50 1.25
3 Connor Hellebuyck 1.00 2.50
4 Jordan Eberle .50 1.25
5 Brock Nelson .50 1.25
6 Quinn Hughes 1.25 3.00
7 Ivan Barbashev .40 1.00
8 Chandler Stephenson .40 1.00
9 Claude Giroux .50 1.25
10 Troy Terry .40 1.00
11 Ryan Nugent-Hopkins .60 1.50
12 Sebastian Aho .75 2.00
13 Jakob Chychrun .50 1.25
14 Carter Hart .50 1.25
15 Sonny Milano .40 1.00
16 David Pastrnak 1.25 3.00
17 Shayne Gostisbehere .50 1.25
18 Cale Makar 1.25 3.00
19 Cam Talbot .50 1.25
20 Jake Guentzel .75 2.00
21 John Gibson .50 1.25
22 Nazem Kadri .60 1.50
23 Alex Ovechkin 2.00 5.00
24 Tristan Jarry .50 1.25
25 William Nylander 1.00 2.50
26 Clayton Keller .60 1.50
27 Jeff Skinner .50 1.25
28 Mikko Rantanen 1.25 3.00
29 Vladimir Tarasenko .60 1.50
30 Jake Oettinger .75 2.00
31 Morgan Rielly .50 1.25
32 Brady Tkachuk .75 2.00
33 Matthew Tkachuk 1.00 2.50
34 Aleksander Barkov .75 2.00
35 Juuse Saros .60 1.50
36 Charlie McAvoy .60 1.50
37 Steven Stamkos 1.00 2.50
38 Tom Wilson .50 1.25
39 Tage Thompson .60 1.50
40 Adam Fox .60 1.50
41 Sidney Crosby 2.00 5.00
42 Alex DeBrincat .60 1.50
43 Anze Kopitar .75 2.00
44 Kyle Connor .75 2.00
45 Patrick Kane 1.00 2.50
46 Artemi Panarin 1.00 2.50
47 Tomas Hertl .50 1.25
48 John Carlson .50 1.25
49 Zach Werenski .75 2.00
50 Jesper Bratt .50 1.25
51 Evgeny Kuznetsov .60 1.50
52 Jaden Schwartz .40 1.00
53 Jacob Markstrom .50 1.25
54 Connor McDavid 2.50 6.00
55 Chris Kreider .60 1.50
56 Frederik Andersen .60 1.50
57 Dougie Hamilton .40 1.00
58 Mikael Granlund .40 1.00
59 Kirill Kaprizov 1.50 4.00
60 Alex Nedeljkovic .40 1.00
61 Aaron Ekblad .60 1.50
62 Robin Lehner .40 1.00
63 Tyler Bertuzzi .40 1.00
64 J.T. Miller .60 1.50
65 Marcus Foligno .40 1.00
66 Jack Campbell .50 1.25
67 Jason Robertson .75 2.00
68 Jonathan Huberdeau .60 1.50
69 Drew Doughty .60 1.50
70 Johnny Gaudreau .75 2.00
71 Pierre-Luc Dubois .40 1.00
72 Auston Matthews 2.00 5.00
73 Taylor Hall .50 1.25
74 Jonathan Quick .60 1.50
75 Pavel Buchnevich .40 1.00
76 Brad Marchand 1.00 2.50
77 Roope Hintz .60 1.50
78 Nikolaj Ehlers .50 1.25
79 Leon Draisaitl 1.50 4.00
80 Evan Rodrigues .40 1.00
81 John Tavares .75 2.00
82 Nick Suzuki 1.00 2.50
83 Roman Josi .50 1.25
84 Timo Meier .50 1.25
85 Andrei Vasilevskiy .75 2.00
86 Elias Lindholm .50 1.25
87 Andrei Svechnikov .60 1.50
88 Igor Shesterkin 1.00 2.50
89 Brayden Point .60 1.50
90 Nathan MacKinnon 2.00 5.00
91 Conor Garland .40 1.00
92 Ilya Sorokin .75 2.00
93 Teuvo Teravainen .50 1.25
94 Drake Batherson .50 1.25
95 Victor Hedman .60 1.50
96 Jack Eichel .75 2.00
97 Moritz Seider 1.25 3.00
98 Jonathan Marchessault .60 1.50
99 Jack Hughes 1.25 3.00
100 Boone Jenner .50 1.25
101 Moritz Seider RC 2.50 6.00
102 Taylor Raddysh RC 1.50 4.00
103 Wade Allison RC 1.00 2.50
104 Spencer Knight RC 2.00 5.00
105 Brett Leason RC 1.00 2.50
106 Trevor Zegras RC 2.00 5.00
107 Cole Perfetti RC 2.00 5.00
108 Grigori Denisenko RC 1.25 3.00
109 Calen Addison RC 1.00 2.50
110 Mike Hardman RC 1.00 2.50
111 Zac Jones RC 1.25 3.00
112 Jan Jenik RC 1.25 3.00
113 Alex Newhook RC 1.50 4.00
114 Anton Lundell RC 2.00 5.00
115 Jonathan Dahlen RC 1.00 2.50
116 Cole Sillinger RC 1.50 4.00
117 Tyce Thompson RC 1.00 2.50
118 Alex Barre-Boulet RC 1.00 2.50
119 Seth Jarvis RC 2.50 6.00
120 Jacob Bernard-Docker RC 1.00 2.50
121 Markus Niemelainen RC 1.00 2.50
122 Ukko-Pekka Luukkonen RC 1.50 4.00
123 Jacob Peterson RC 1.00 2.50
124 Tanner Jeannot RC 1.00 2.50
125 Lucas Raymond RC 3.00 8.00
126 Radim Zohorna RC 1.00 2.50
127 Alex Turcotte RC 1.25 3.00
128 Jamie Drysdale RC 1.50 4.00
129 J.J. Peterka RC 2.00 5.00
130 Aliaksei Protas RC 1.00 2.50
131 Brandon Duhaime RC 1.00 2.50
132 Shane Pinto RC 1.50 4.00
133 Quinton Byfield RC 2.50 6.00
134 Sampo Ranta RC 1.00 2.50
135 Dawson Mercer RC 2.50 6.00
136 Jesse Ylonen RC 1.00 2.50
137 Jeremy Swayman RC 3.00 8.00
138 Robin Salo RC 1.00 2.50
139 Karel Vejmelka RC 1.25 3.00
140 Rasmus Kupari RC 1.00 2.50
141 Logan Thompson RC 2.50 6.00
142 Kole Lind RC 1.25 3.00
143 Philip Tomasino RC 1.25 3.00
144 Scott Perunovich RC 1.00 2.50
145 Vasily Podkolzin RC 1.25 3.00
146 Joey Keane RC .75 2.00
147 Alexander Holtz RC 1.50 4.00
148 Riley Damiani RC 1.00 2.50
149 Cam York RC 1.00 2.50
150 Cole Caufield RC 4.00 10.00

2021-22 Upper Deck Ovation Gold Foil

*GOLD FOIL: .4X TO 1X BASIC

2021-22 Upper Deck Ovation Silver Foil

*SILVER: .5X TO 1.2X BASIC

2021-22 Upper Deck Ovation Standing Ovation

*STAND/500: .75X TO 2X BASIC
*STAND RC/500: .5X TO 1.2X BASIC

2021-22 Upper Deck Ovation Standing Ovation Gold Spectrum

*STAND GOLD/250: 1.2X TO 3X BASIC
*STAND GOLD RC/250: .75X TO 2X BASIC

2021-22 Upper Deck Ovation Standing Ovation Red

*STAND RED/100: 1.5X TO 4X BASIC
*STAND RED RC/100: 1X TO 2.5X BASIC

2021-22 Upper Deck Ovation Big Hand

BH1 Juuse Saros 12.00 30.00
BH2 Jonathan Quick 12.00 30.00
BH3 Carter Hart 10.00 25.00
BH4 Marc-Andre Fleury 20.00 50.00
BH5 John Gibson 10.00 25.00
BH6 Darcy Kuemper 10.00 25.00
BH7 Ilya Samsonov 10.00 25.00
BH8 Jacob Markstrom 10.00 25.00
BH9 Evgeni Nabokov 8.00 20.00
BH10 Thatcher Demko 12.00 30.00
BH11 Tristan Jarry 10.00 25.00
BH12 Cam Talbot 10.00 25.00
BH13 Alex Nedeljkovic 8.00 20.00
BH14 Ed Belfour 10.00 25.00
BH15 Robin Lehner 8.00 20.00
BH16 Carey Price 20.00 50.00
BH17 James Reimer 6.00 15.00
BH18 Frederik Andersen 12.00 30.00
BH19 Mike Vernon 8.00 20.00
BH20 Connor Hellebuyck 20.00 50.00
BH21 Mikko Koskinen 6.00 15.00
BH22 Jeremy Swayman 30.00 80.00
BH23 Charlie Lindgren 8.00 20.00
BH24 Jean-Sebastien Giguere 10.00 25.00
BH25 Igor Shesterkin 20.00 50.00
BH26 Sergei Bobrovsky 15.00 40.00
BH27 Andrei Vasilevskiy 15.00 40.00
BH28 Patrick Roy 25.00 60.00
BH29 Jake Oettinger 15.00 40.00
BH30 Jordan Binnington 15.00 40.00
BH31 Jack Campbell 10.00 25.00
BH32 Dan Vladar 8.00 20.00
BH33 Terry Sawchuk 10.00 25.00

2021-22 Upper Deck Ovation Bravo

B1 Mark Messier 15.00 40.00
B2 Brayden Point 10.00 25.00
B3 Mitch Marner 12.00 30.00
B4 Alex Newhook 12.00 30.00
B5 Trevor Zegras 15.00 40.00
B6 Jonathan Huberdeau 10.00 25.00
B7 Moritz Seider 20.00 50.00
B8 Scott Niedermayer 8.00 20.00
B9 Jake Guentzel 12.00 30.00
B10 Nazem Kadri 10.00 25.00
B11 Carey Price 15.00 40.00
B12 Victor Hedman 10.00 25.00
B13 Frank Mahovlich 8.00 20.00
B14 Lucas Raymond 25.00 60.00
B15 Patrick Kane 15.00 40.00
B16 Philip Tomasino 10.00 25.00
B17 Andrei Svechnikov 10.00 25.00
B18 Sidney Crosby 30.00 80.00
B19 Leon Draisaitl 25.00 60.00
B20 Artemi Panarin 15.00 40.00
B21 John Tavares 12.00 30.00
B22 Stan Mikita 8.00 20.00
B23 Jamie Drysdale 12.00 30.00
B24 Alex Ovechkin 30.00 80.00
B25 Nathan MacKinnon 30.00 80.00
B26 Quinn Hughes 20.00 50.00
B27 Wayne Gretzky 50.00 120.00
B28 Roman Josi 8.00 20.00
B29 Nick Suzuki 15.00 40.00
B30 Anze Kopitar 12.00 30.00
B31 Auston Matthews 30.00 80.00
B32 Gordie Howe 25.00 60.00
B33 Connor McDavid 40.00 100.00

2021-22 Upper Deck Ovation Captivating

C1 Kyle Connor 3.00 8.00
C2 Dominik Kubalik 2.00 5.00
C3 Brock Boeser 2.50 6.00
C4 Jesper Bratt 2.00 5.00
C5 Alex Newhook 3.00 8.00
C6 Arttu Ruotsalainen 2.00 5.00
C7 Jean-Gabriel Pageau 1.25 3.00
C8 Tyler Bertuzzi 1.50 4.00
C9 Alex Barre-Boulet 2.00 5.00
C10 Mark Stone 2.50 6.00
C11 Drake Batherson 2.00 5.00
C12 Johnny Gaudreau 3.00 8.00
C13 Yegor Sharangovich 2.00 5.00
C14 Carter Verhaeghe 2.00 5.00
C15 Victor Olofsson 2.00 5.00
C16 Alex Turcotte 2.50 6.00
C17 Martin Necas 3.00 8.00
C18 Jason Robertson 3.00 8.00
C19 Joel Eriksson Ek 1.50 4.00
C20 Troy Terry 1.50 4.00
C21 Nazem Kadri 2.50 6.00
C22 Teuvo Teravainen 2.00 5.00
C23 Ilya Mikheyev 1.50 4.00
C24 Alexis Lafreniere 3.00 8.00
C25 Trevor Zegras 4.00 10.00
C26 Taylor Hall 2.00 5.00
C27 Tim Stutzle 2.50 6.00
C28 Dylan Cozens 2.00 5.00
C29 Tyler Toffoli 2.00 5.00
C30 Nils Hoglander 1.50 4.00

2021-22 Upper Deck Ovation High Regard Rookies

HRR1 Trevor Zegras 2.00 5.00
HRR2 Nils Lundkvist 1.00 2.50
HRR3 Alex Turcotte 1.25 3.00
HRR4 Seth Jarvis 2.50 6.00
HRR5 Spencer Knight 2.00 5.00
HRR6 J.J. Peterka 2.00 5.00
HRR7 Alex Barre-Boulet 1.00 2.50
HRR8 Jonathan Dahlen 1.00 2.50
HRR9 Moritz Seider 2.50 6.00
HRR10 Taylor Raddysh 1.50 4.00
HRR11 Quinton Byfield 2.50 6.00
HRR12 Philip Tomasino 1.25 3.00
HRR13 Ukko-Pekka Luukkonen 1.50 4.00
HRR14 Vasily Podkolzin 1.25 3.00
HRR15 Logan Thompson 2.50 6.00
HRR16 Cole Sillinger 1.50 4.00
HRR17 Anton Lundell 2.00 5.00
HRR18 Scott Perunovich 1.00 2.50
HRR19 Brett Leason 1.00 2.50
HRR20 Jamie Drysdale 1.50 4.00
HRR21 Lucas Raymond 3.00 8.00
HRR22 Jasper Weatherby 1.00 2.50
HRR23 Jeremy Swayman 3.00 8.00
HRR24 Tanner Jeannot 1.00 2.50
HRR25 Alex Newhook 1.50 4.00
HRR26 Dawson Mercer 2.50 6.00
HRR27 Brandon Duhaime 1.00 2.50
HRR28 Cole Caufield 4.00 10.00
HRR29 Aliaksei Protas 1.00 2.50
HRR30 Cole Perfetti 2.00 5.00

2021-22 Upper Deck Ovation High Regard Rookies Autographs

HRR1 Trevor Zegras 20.00 50.00
HRR2 Nils Lundkvist 10.00 25.00
HRR3 Alex Turcotte 12.00 30.00
HRR5 Spencer Knight 20.00 50.00
HRR6 J.J. Peterka 20.00 50.00
HRR8 Jonathan Dahlen 10.00 25.00
HRR9 Moritz Seider 25.00 60.00
HRR10 Taylor Raddysh 15.00 40.00
HRR11 Quinton Byfield 25.00 60.00
HRR12 Philip Tomasino 12.00 30.00
HRR13 Ukko-Pekka Luukkonen 15.00 40.00
HRR16 Cole Sillinger 15.00 40.00
HRR17 Anton Lundell 20.00 50.00
HRR18 Scott Perunovich 10.00 25.00
HRR19 Brett Leason 10.00 25.00
HRR20 Jamie Drysdale 15.00 40.00
HRR21 Lucas Raymond 30.00 80.00
HRR22 Jasper Weatherby 10.00 25.00
HRR23 Jeremy Swayman 30.00 80.00
HRR24 Tanner Jeannot 10.00 25.00
HRR25 Alex Newhook 15.00 40.00
HRR26 Dawson Mercer 25.00 60.00
HRR27 Brandon Duhaime 10.00 25.00
HRR28 Cole Caufield 40.00 100.00
HRR29 Aliaksei Protas 10.00 25.00
HRR30 Cole Perfetti 20.00 50.00

2021-22 Upper Deck Ovation Lauded Signatures

LSAC Anthony Cirelli 5.00 12.00
LSAO Andrew Copp 4.00 10.00
LSBB Bob Bourne 6.00 15.00
LSBS Brandon Saad 5.00 12.00
LSCK Clayton Keller 8.00 20.00
LSDG Dirk Graham 5.00 12.00
LSDV Dan Vladar 5.00 12.00
LSDW Doug Weight 6.00 15.00
LSEM Elvis Merzlikins 6.00 15.00
LSFG Filip Gustavsson 12.00 30.00
LSHL Hendrix Lapierre 6.00 15.00
LSIP Ivan Prosvetov 6.00 15.00
LSJP J.J. Peterka 12.00 30.00
LSJV Joe Veleno 8.00 20.00
LSJW Jasper Weatherby 6.00 15.00
LSJY Jesse Ylonen 6.00 15.00
LSKK Keegan Kolesar 4.00 10.00
LSMA Mikey Anderson 5.00 12.00
LSMN Martin Necas 10.00 25.00
LSMP Matthew Phillips 6.00 15.00
LSMS Malcolm Subban 5.00 12.00
LSPA Jean-Gabriel Pageau 4.00 10.00
LSPC Paul Cotter 6.00 15.00
LSPK Philipp Kurashev 5.00 12.00
LSRG Ryan Getzlaf 6.00 15.00
LSSB Sam Bennett 10.00 25.00
LSSL Steven Lorentz 4.00 10.00
LSSM Sean Monahan 4.00 10.00
LSSR Sam Reinhart 12.00 30.00
LSSW Sean Walker 4.00 10.00
LSTL Tanner Laczynski 6.00 15.00
LSTS Tim Stutzle 8.00 20.00
LSVV Vitek Vanecek 6.00 15.00
LSZP Zach Parise 6.00 15.00

2021-22 Upper Deck Ovation Lead Performers

LP1 Alex Ovechkin 4.00 10.00
LP2 Mikey Anderson .75 2.00
LP3 Nick Suzuki 2.00 5.00
LP4 Joe Pavelski 1.25 3.00
LP5 Mark Giordano 1.00 2.50
LP6 Anthony Beauvillier .60 1.50
LP7 Martin Necas 1.50 4.00
LP8 Sean Monahan .60 1.50
LP9 Alex Tuch 1.00 2.50
LP10 Leon Draisaitl 3.00 8.00
LP11 Mark Stone 1.25 3.00
LP12 Jeff Petry 1.00 2.50
LP13 Alexander Barabanov .60 1.50
LP15 John Tavares 1.50 4.00
LP16 Anze Kopitar 1.50 4.00
LP17 Brock Boeser 1.25 3.00
LP18 Anders Lee .75 2.00
LP19 Ryan O'Reilly 1.00 2.50
LP20 Brent Burns 1.00 2.50
LP21 Jordan Eberle 1.00 2.50
LP22 Connor Hellebuyck 2.00 5.00
LP23 Josh Anderson .75 2.00
LP24 Conor Garland .75 2.00
LP25 Marc-Andre Fleury 2.00 5.00
LP26 Max Pacioretty 1.00 2.50
LP27 Dougie Hamilton .75 2.00
LP28 Aleksander Barkov 1.50 4.00
LP29 Devon Toews .75 2.00
LP30 Matthew Tkachuk 2.00 5.00
LP31 Kris Letang 1.25 3.00
LP32 Kyle Palmieri .75 2.00
LP33 Josh Morrissey 1.25 3.00
LP34 Brad Marchand 2.00 5.00
LP35 Jonathan Huberdeau 1.25 3.00
LP36 Cam Atkinson 1.00 2.50
LP37 Boone Jenner 1.00 2.50
LP38 Brendan Gallagher 1.00 2.50
LP39 Jake Guentzel 1.50 4.00
LP40 Auston Matthews 4.00 10.00

2021-22 Upper Deck Ovation Lead Performers Autographs

LP1 Alex Ovechkin 40.00 100.00
LP3 Nick Suzuki 20.00 50.00
LP4 Joe Pavelski 12.00 30.00
LP6 Anthony Beauvillier 6.00 15.00
LP7 Martin Necas 30.00 80.00
LP8 Sean Monahan 6.00 15.00
LP9 Alex Tuch 10.00 25.00
LP10 Leon Draisaitl 30.00 80.00
LP11 Mark Stone 12.00 30.00
LP12 Jeff Petry 10.00 25.00
LP15 John Tavares 15.00 40.00
LP16 Anze Kopitar 25.00 60.00
LP17 Brock Boeser 12.00 30.00
LP18 Anders Lee 8.00 20.00
LP19 Ryan O'Reilly 10.00 25.00
LP20 Brent Burns 10.00 25.00
LP21 Jordan Eberle 10.00 25.00
LP22 Connor Hellebuyck 20.00 50.00
LP24 Conor Garland 8.00 20.00
LP25 Marc-Andre Fleury 20.00 50.00
LP28 Aleksander Barkov 15.00 40.00
LP29 Devon Toews 8.00 20.00
LP30 Matthew Tkachuk 20.00 50.00
LP31 Kris Letang 25.00 60.00
LP32 Kyle Palmieri 8.00 20.00
LP33 Josh Morrissey 12.00 30.00
LP34 Brad Marchand 20.00 50.00
LP35 Jonathan Huberdeau 12.00 30.00
LP36 Cam Atkinson 10.00 25.00
LP37 Boone Jenner 10.00 25.00
LP38 Brendan Gallagher 10.00 25.00
LP39 Jake Guentzel 15.00 40.00
LP40 Auston Matthews 80.00 200.00

2021-22 Upper Deck Ovation Praised Penmanship Autographs

PPAD Adam Deadmarsh 6.00 15.00
PPAN Alex Nedeljkovic 8.00 20.00
PPAT Alex Tuch 15.00 40.00
PPBB Brock Boeser 12.00 30.00
PPBM Brenden Morrow 8.00 20.00
PPCA Cam Atkinson 10.00 25.00
PPCJ Calle Jarnkrok 6.00 15.00
PPCM Casey Mittelstadt 10.00 25.00
PPDB Drake Batherson 10.00 25.00
PPDS Dylan Strome 12.00 30.00
PPDT Dave Taylor 8.00 20.00
PPET Eeli Tolvanen 10.00 25.00
PPIM Ilya Mikheyev 8.00 20.00
PPJM Josh Morrissey 12.00 30.00
PPJR Jack Roslovic 6.00 15.00
PPJZ Jason Zucker 10.00 25.00
PPKL Kris Letang 50.00 125.00
PPKM K'Andre Miller 8.00 20.00
PPMA Mason Appleton 6.00 15.00
PPMC Maxime Comtois 8.00 20.00
PPMS Mike Smith 6.00 15.00
PPNH Nils Hoglander 8.00 20.00
PPRC Ross Colton 12.00 30.00
PPRS Ryan Suter 8.00 20.00
PPSB Sam Bennett 15.00 40.00
PPSM Sean Monahan 6.00 15.00
PPTF Theoren Fleury 10.00 25.00
PPVN Vladislav Namestnikov 6.00 15.00
PPWC Wendel Clark 15.00 40.00
PPYS Yegor Sharangovich 10.00 25.00
PPZP Zach Parise 10.00 25.00

2021-22 Upper Deck Ovation Praised Rookie Penmanship Autographs

PRPAL Anton Lundell 20.00 50.00
PRPAN Alex Newhook 15.00 40.00
PRPAP Aliaksei Protas 10.00 25.00
PRPAT Alex Turcotte 12.00 30.00
PRPBD Brandon Duhaime 10.00 25.00
PRPCP Cole Perfetti 20.00 50.00
PRPCS Cole Sillinger 15.00 40.00
PRPDA Jonathan Dahlen 10.00 25.00
PRPDM Dawson Mercer 25.00 60.00
PRPJB Jacob Bernard-Docker 10.00 25.00
PRPJD Jamie Drysdale 15.00 40.00
PRPJP J.J. Peterka 20.00 50.00
PRPJS Jeremy Swayman 30.00 80.00
PRPLR Lucas Raymond 30.00 80.00
PRPLT Logan Thompson 25.00 60.00
PRPMS Moritz Seider 25.00 60.00
PRPPT Philip Tomasino 12.00 30.00
PRPQB Quinton Byfield 25.00 60.00
PRPSK Spencer Knight 20.00 50.00
PRPSP Scott Perunovich 10.00 25.00
PRPTZ Trevor Zegras 20.00 50.00
PRPUL Ukko-Pekka Luukkonen 15.00 40.00
PRPVP Vasily Podkolzin 12.00 30.00
PRPZJ Zac Jones 12.00 30.00

2021-22 Upper Deck Ovation Round of Applause

RA1 Moritz Seider 8.00 20.00
RA2 Brady Tkachuk 5.00 12.00
RA3 Nathan MacKinnon 12.00 30.00
RA4 Aaron Ekblad 4.00 10.00
RA5 Cole Caufield 20.00 50.00
RA6 Matthew Tkachuk 6.00 15.00
RA7 Elias Pettersson 5.00 12.00
RA8 William Nylander 6.00 15.00
RA9 Trevor Zegras 6.00 15.00
RA10 Auston Matthews 12.00 30.00
RA11 Leon Draisaitl 10.00 25.00
RA12 Andrei Vasilevskiy 5.00 12.00
RA13 Lucas Raymond 10.00 25.00
RA14 Alexis Lafreniere 5.00 12.00
RA15 Charlie McAvoy 4.00 10.00
RA16 Nick Suzuki 6.00 15.00
RA17 Seth Jarvis 8.00 20.00
RA18 Cale Makar 8.00 20.00
RA19 Quinn Hughes 8.00 20.00
RA20 Kyle Connor 5.00 12.00
RA21 Jack Hughes 8.00 20.00
RA22 Tim Stutzle 4.00 10.00
RA23 Andrei Svechnikov 4.00 10.00
RA24 Jamie Drysdale 5.00 12.00
RA25 Dylan Larkin 4.00 10.00
RA26 Alex Newhook 5.00 12.00
RA27 Miro Heiskanen 4.00 10.00
RA28 Mitch Marner 5.00 12.00
RA29 Dawson Mercer 8.00 20.00
RA30 Jack Eichel 5.00 12.00
RA31 Aleksander Barkov 5.00 12.00
RA32 Quinton Byfield 8.00 20.00
RA33 Connor McDavid 15.00 40.00

2021-22 Upper Deck Ovation Standing Ovation Signatures

SOSAB Anthony Beauvillier 8.00 20.00
SOSAC Anthony Cirelli 10.00 25.00
SOSAN Alex Nedeljkovic 10.00 25.00
SOSBB Brent Burns 12.00 30.00
SOSBC Blake Coleman 10.00 25.00
SOSBO Brock Boeser 15.00 40.00
SOSBU Michael Bunting 12.00 30.00
SOSBY Sergei Bobrovsky 20.00 50.00
SOSCG Conor Garland 10.00 25.00
SOSCH Connor Hellebuyck 25.00 60.00
SOSCJ Calle Jarnkrok 8.00 20.00
SOSDB Drake Batherson 12.00 30.00
SOSDC Dylan Cozens 12.00 30.00
SOSET Eeli Tolvanen 12.00 30.00
SOSGA Simon Gagne 12.00 30.00
SOSGC Gerry Cheevers 12.00 30.00
SOSGF Grant Fuhr 20.00 50.00
SOSJB Jesper Bratt 12.00 30.00
SOSJM Jared McCann 10.00 25.00
SOSJP Jeff Petry 12.00 30.00
SOSJR Jason Robertson 20.00 50.00
SOSKC Kyle Connor 20.00 50.00
SOSMI Casey Mittelstadt 12.00 30.00
SOSMN Martin Necas 20.00 50.00
SOSMS Mike Smith 8.00 20.00
SOSPA Joe Pavelski 15.00 40.00
SOSRB Rod Brind'Amour 12.00 30.00
SOSRH Ron Hextall 12.00 30.00
SOSRO Jack Roslovic 8.00 20.00
SOSSB Sam Bennett 20.00 50.00
SOSSC Shayne Corson 10.00 25.00
SOSSG Samuel Girard 8.00 20.00
SOSSW Sean Walker 8.00 20.00
SOSTB Tyler Bertuzzi 10.00 25.00
SOSTS Tim Stutzle 30.00 80.00
SOSTW Tony Twist 8.00 20.00
SOSVL Vincent Lecavalier 12.00 30.00
SOSVO Victor Olofsson 12.00 30.00
SOSWK William Karlsson 15.00 40.00
SOSYC Yvan Cournoyer 12.00 30.00
SOSYG Yanni Gourde 10.00 25.00

2021-22 Upper Deck Ovation Superstar Theater

ST1 Mario Lemieux 20.00 50.00
ST2 Steven Stamkos 10.00 25.00
ST3 Aleksander Barkov 8.00 20.00
ST4 Sebastian Aho 8.00 20.00
ST5 Jonathan Dahlen 5.00 12.00
ST6 Dawson Mercer 12.00 30.00
ST7 Kirill Kaprizov 15.00 40.00
ST8 Trevor Zegras 10.00 25.00
ST9 Wayne Gretzky 30.00 80.00
ST10 Cale Makar 12.00 30.00
ST11 Lucas Raymond 15.00 40.00
ST13 Peter Stastny 4.00 10.00
ST14 Johnny Gaudreau 8.00 20.00
ST15 Brad Marchand 10.00 25.00
ST16 Connor McDavid 25.00 60.00
ST17 Artemi Panarin 20.00 50.00
ST18 Jonathan Huberdeau 6.00 15.00
ST19 Peter Forsberg 10.00 25.00
ST20 Brayden Point 6.00 15.00
ST21 Leon Draisaitl 15.00 40.00
ST22 Troy Terry 4.00 10.00
ST23 Alex Ovechkin 40.00 100.00
ST24 Nicklas Lidstrom 5.00 12.00
ST25 Adam Fox 6.00 15.00
ST26 William Nylander 10.00 25.00
ST27 Tanner Jeannot 5.00 12.00
ST28 Kyle Connor 8.00 20.00
ST29 Jack Eichel 8.00 20.00
ST30 Mike Modano 8.00 20.00
ST31 Moritz Seider 12.00 30.00
ST32 Nathan MacKinnon 20.00 50.00
ST33 Sidney Crosby 20.00 50.00

2021-22 Upper Deck Ovation UD Glass Magnifying Marks Autographs

MMAB Alex Barre-Boulet 10.00 25.00
MMAH Alexander Holtz 15.00 40.00
MMAK Anze Kopitar 15.00 40.00
MMAL Alex Nedeljkovic 8.00 20.00
MMAN Alex Newhook 15.00 40.00
MMAP Aliaksei Protas 10.00 25.00
MMAT Alex Tuch 10.00 25.00
MMBD Brandon Duhaime 10.00 25.00
MMBL Brett Leason 10.00 25.00
MMBU Michael Bunting 10.00 25.00
MMBY Bowen Byram 12.00 30.00
MMCA Cal Petersen 6.00 15.00
MMCF Cal Foote 8.00 20.00
MMCM Connor McDavid 250.00 600.00
MMCP Cole Perfetti 20.00 50.00
MMCS Cole Sillinger 15.00 40.00
MMCT Cam Talbot 10.00 25.00
MMDA Riley Damiani 10.00 25.00
MMDB Drake Batherson 10.00 25.00
MMDC Dylan Cozens 10.00 25.00
MMDM Dawson Mercer 25.00 60.00
MMDR Jamie Drysdale 15.00 40.00
MMDV Dan Vladar 8.00 20.00
MMFH Filip Hronek 6.00 15.00
MMIM Ilya Mikheyev 8.00 20.00
MMJB Jesper Bratt 10.00 25.00
MMJG Jake Guentzel 15.00 40.00
MMJH Jonathan Huberdeau 12.00 30.00
MMJL John LeClair 10.00 25.00
MMJM Jared McCann 8.00 20.00
MMJP Joe Pavelski 12.00 30.00
MMJR Jack Roslovic 6.00 15.00
MMJS Joe Sakic 20.00 50.00
MMJW Jasper Weatherby 10.00 25.00
MMJY Jesse Ylonen 10.00 25.00
MMJZ Jason Zucker 10.00 25.00
MMKC Kyle Connor 15.00 40.00
MMKK Keegan Kolesar 6.00 15.00
MMLR Lucas Raymond 30.00 80.00
MMLT Logan Thompson 25.00 60.00
MMLU Anton Lundell 20.00 50.00
MMMB Martin Brodeur 25.00 60.00
MMMC Maxime Comtois 8.00 20.00
MMMH Mike Hardman 10.00 25.00
MMMI Casey Mittelstadt 10.00 25.00
MMMJ Josh Morrissey 12.00 30.00
MMML Mario Lemieux 40.00 100.00
MMMO Moritz Seider 25.00 60.00
MMNE Nikolaj Ehlers 10.00 25.00
MMNL Nils Lundkvist 10.00 25.00
MMPE J.J. Peterka 20.00 50.00
MMPK Philipp Kurashev 8.00 20.00
MMPS Pius Suter 8.00 20.00
MMPT Philip Tomasino 12.00 30.00
MMQB Quinton Byfield 25.00 60.00
MMQH Quinn Hughes 25.00 60.00
MMRD Ryan Dzingel 8.00 20.00
MMRH Ron Hextall 10.00 25.00
MMRK Rasmus Kupari 10.00 25.00
MMRR Ryan Reaves 8.00 20.00
MMRS Ryan Suter 8.00 20.00
MMSB Sergei Bobrovsky 15.00 40.00
MMSC Scott Perunovich 10.00 25.00
MMSE Teemu Selanne 20.00 50.00
MMSG Samuel Girard 6.00 15.00
MMSK Spencer Knight 20.00 50.00
MMSM Mike Smith 6.00 15.00
MMSP Shane Pinto 15.00 40.00
MMSW Jeremy Swayman 30.00 80.00
MMTD Thatcher Demko 12.00 30.00
MMTJ Tanner Jeannot 10.00 25.00
MMTR Taylor Raddysh 15.00 40.00
MMTS Tim Stutzle 12.00 30.00
MMTU Alex Turcotte 12.00 30.00
MMVL Vincent Lecavalier 10.00 25.00
MMVP Vasily Podkolzin 12.00 30.00
MMWC Wendel Clark 15.00 40.00

MMWO Willie O'Ree 12.00 30.00
MMYS Yegor Sharangovich 10.00 25.00
MMZP Zach Parise 10.00 25.00

2021-22 Upper Deck Ovation UD Glass Rookies

*RED/25: .6X TO 1.5X BASIC
GR1 Lucas Raymond 15.00 40.00
GR2 Rasmus Kupari 5.00 12.00
GR3 Vasily Podkolzin 6.00 15.00
GR4 Tanner Jeannot 5.00 12.00
GR5 Logan Thompson 12.00 30.00
GR6 Anton Lundell 10.00 25.00
GR7 Cole Sillinger 8.00 20.00
GR8 Brett Leason 5.00 12.00
GR9 Jeremy Swayman 15.00 40.00
GR10 Alex Newhook 8.00 20.00
GR11 Spencer Knight 10.00 25.00
GR12 Jasper Weatherby 5.00 12.00
GR13 Philip Tomasino 6.00 15.00
GR14 Cole Caufield 20.00 50.00
GR15 Moritz Seider 12.00 30.00
GR16 Quinton Byfield 12.00 30.00
GR17 Aliaksei Protas 5.00 12.00
GR18 Trevor Zegras 10.00 25.00
GR19 Ukko-Pekka Luukkonen 8.00 20.00
GR20 Seth Jarvis 12.00 30.00
GR21 Taylor Raddysh 8.00 20.00
GR22 Scott Perunovich 5.00 12.00
GR23 Brandon Duhaime 5.00 12.00
GR24 Jamie Drysdale 8.00 20.00
GR25 J.J. Peterka 10.00 25.00
GR26 Dawson Mercer 12.00 30.00
GR27 Jonathan Dahlen 5.00 12.00
GR28 Nils Lundkvist 5.00 12.00
GR29 Alex Barre-Boulet 5.00 12.00

2021-22 Upper Deck Ovation UD Glass Rookies Gold

*GOLD/99: .5X TO 1.2X BASIC
GR14 Cole Caufield 50.00 125.00

2021-22 Upper Deck Ovation UD Glass Stars

GS1 Connor McDavid 15.00 40.00
GS2 Kirill Kaprizov 10.00 25.00
GS3 Sidney Crosby 12.00 30.00
GS4 Aleksander Barkov 5.00 12.00
GS5 Nathan MacKinnon 12.00 30.00
GS6 Brayden Point 4.00 10.00
GS7 Johnny Gaudreau 5.00 12.00
GS8 Auston Matthews 12.00 30.00
GS9 Artemi Panarin 6.00 15.00
GS10 Sebastian Aho 5.00 12.00
GS11 Anze Kopitar 5.00 12.00
GS12 Brad Marchand 6.00 15.00
GS13 Leon Draisaitl 10.00 25.00
GS14 Nazem Kadri 4.00 10.00
GS15 Andrei Vasilevskiy 5.00 12.00
GS16 Adam Fox 4.00 10.00
GS17 William Nylander 6.00 15.00
GS18 Nick Suzuki 6.00 15.00
GS19 Alex Ovechkin 12.00 30.00
GS20 Jonathan Huberdeau 4.00 10.00
GS21 Steven Stamkos 6.00 15.00
GS22 Kyle Connor 5.00 12.00
GS23 John Tavares 5.00 12.00
GS24 Troy Terry 2.50 6.00
GS25 Igor Shesterkin 6.00 15.00
GS26 Mikko Rantanen 8.00 20.00
GS27 J.T. Miller 4.00 10.00
GS28 Victor Hedman 4.00 10.00
GS29 Cale Makar 8.00 20.00
GS30 Connor McDavid Achievement 15.00 40.00

2021-22 Upper Deck Ovation UD Glass Stars Gold

*GOLD/99: .5X TO 1.2X BASIC
GS2 Kirill Kaprizov 30.00 80.00
GS10 Sebastian Aho 20.00 50.00
GS14 Nazem Kadri 12.00 30.00
GS19 Alex Ovechkin 25.00 60.00
GS22 Kyle Connor 8.00 20.00

2021-22 Upper Deck Ovation UD Glass Stars Red

*RED/25: X TO X BASIC
GS1 Connor McDavid 80.00 200.00
GS5 Nathan MacKinnon 25.00 60.00
GS11 Anze Kopitar 15.00 40.00
GS19 Alex Ovechkin 50.00 125.00

2021-22 Upper Deck Ovation World Premiere

*GOLD/299: .5X TO 1.2X BASIC
*RED/199: .6X TO 1.5X BASIC
*BLUE/99: .75X TO 2X BASIC
*PURPLE/65: 1X TO 2.5X BASIC
*PINK/49: 1.2X TO 3X BASIC
*GREEN/25: 1.5X TO 4X BASIC
WP1 Scott Perunovich 1.00 2.50
WP2 Jacob Peterson 1.00 2.50
WP3 Ukko-Pekka Luukkonen 1.50 4.00
WP4 Sean Durzi 1.00 2.50
WP5 Robin Salo 1.00 2.50
WP6 Rafael Harvey-Pinard 1.00 2.50
WP7 J.J. Peterka 2.00 5.00
WP8 Jacob Bernard-Docker 1.00 2.50
WP9 Cam York 1.00 2.50
WP10 Cole Caufield 4.00 10.00
WP11 Rasmus Kupari 1.00 2.50
WP12 Mike Hardman 1.00 2.50
WP13 Zac Jones 1.25 3.00
WP14 Alexander Holtz 1.50 4.00
WP15 Brandon Duhaime 1.00 2.50
WP16 Sampo Ranta 1.00 2.50
WP17 Anton Lundell 2.00 5.00
WP18 Cole Sillinger 1.50 4.00
WP19 Lucas Raymond 3.00 8.00
WP20 Alex Barre-Boulet 1.00 2.50
WP21 Riley Damiani 1.00 2.50
WP22 Spencer Knight 2.00 5.00
WP23 Shane Pinto 1.50 4.00
WP24 Radim Zohorna 1.00 2.50
WP25 Tanner Jeannot 1.00 2.50
WP26 Jeremy Swayman 3.00 8.00
WP28 Kole Lind 1.25 3.00
WP29 Alex Turcotte 1.25 3.00
WP30 Jesse Ylonen 1.00 2.50
WP31 Trevor Zegras 2.00 5.00
WP32 Alex Newhook 1.50 4.00
WP33 Grigori Denisenko 1.25 3.00
WP34 Vasily Podkolzin 1.25 3.00
WP35 Seth Jarvis 2.50 6.00
WP36 Quinton Byfield 2.50 6.00
WP37 Tyce Thompson 1.00 2.50
WP38 Moritz Seider 2.50 6.00
WP39 Cole Perfetti 2.00 5.00
WP40 Logan Thompson 2.50 6.00
WP41 Dawson Mercer 2.50 6.00
WP42 Aliaksei Protas 1.00 2.50
WP43 Thomas Novak 1.00 2.50
WP44 Taylor Raddysh 1.50 4.00
WP45 Joey Keane .75 2.00
WP46 Wade Allison 1.00 2.50
WP47 Brett Leason 1.00 2.50
WP48 Philip Tomasino 1.25 3.00
WP49 Jan Jenik 1.25 3.00
WP50 Jonathan Dahlen 1.00 2.50

2013-14 Upper Deck Overtime

COMPLETE SET (92) 30.00 80.00
COMP.SERIES 1 (50) 12.00 30.00
COMP.SERIES 2 (42) 20.00 50.00
*GOLD/99: 2X TO 5X BASIC CARDS
1 Alex Chiasson .50 1.25
2 Alex Galchenyuk 1.25 3.00
3 Austin Watson .40 1.00
4 Beau Bennett .60 1.50
5 Brendan Gallagher 1.25 3.00
6 Calvin Pickard .60 1.50
7 Charlie Coyle .75 2.00
8 Chris Brown .30 .75
9 Christian Thomas .40 1.00
10 Cory Conacher .30 .75
11 Cristopher Nilstorp .40 1.00
12 Damien Brunner .40 1.00
13 Dougie Hamilton .75 2.00
14 Drew Shore .40 1.00
15 Emerson Etem .50 1.25
16 Filip Forsberg 1.50 4.00
17 Jack Campbell 1.25 3.00
18 Jamie Oleksiak .40 1.00
19 Jared Staal .40 1.00
20 Jarred Tinordi .50 1.25
21 Johan Larsson .60 1.50
22 Jonas Brodin .60 1.50
23 Jonathan Huberdeau 1.25 3.00
24 Jordan Schroeder .50 1.25
25 Justin Schultz .50 1.25
26 Leo Komarov .50 1.25
27 Mark Pysyk .50 1.25
28 Max Reinhart .50 1.25
29 Mikael Granlund .75 2.00
30 Mikhail Grigorenko .30 .75
31 Nail Yakupov 1.00 2.50
32 Nathan Beaulieu .30 .75
33 Nick Bjugstad .60 1.50
34 Nick Petrecki .30 .75
35 Nicklas Jensen .40 1.00
36 Petr Mrazek 1.00 2.50
37 Quinton Howden .40 1.00
38 Richard Panik .50 1.25
39 Rickard Rakell .50 1.25
40 Roman Cervenka .40 1.00
41 Ryan Murphy .50 1.25
42 Ryan Spooner .50 1.25
43 Scott Laughton .60 1.50
44 Stefan Matteau .40 1.00
45 Thomas Hickey .40 1.00
46 Tye McGinn .50 1.25
47 Tyler Toffoli 1.00 2.50
48 Viktor Fasth .50 1.25
49 Vladimir Tarasenko 1.25 3.00
50 Zach Redmond .40 1.00
51 Aleksander Barkov 1.50 4.00
52 Alex Killorn .75 2.00
53 Antoine Roussel .50 1.25
54 Anton Belov .50 1.25
55 Boone Jenner 1.00 2.50
56 Brock Nelson 1.00 2.50
57 Cameron Schilling .30 .75
58 Connor Carrick .40 1.00
59 Danny DeKeyser .60 1.50
60 Elias Lindholm 1.25 3.00
61 Hampus Lindholm .75 2.00
62 Jacob Trouba .75 2.00
63 Jamie Devane .40 1.00
64 Jean-Gabriel Pageau .50 1.25
65 Jeff Zatkoff .50 1.25
66 Jesper Fast .50 1.25
67 Joakim Nordstrom .40 1.00
68 Justin Fontaine .50 1.25
69 Lucas Lessio .30 .75
70 Luke Gazdic .40 1.00
71 Mark Barberio .30 .75
72 Mathew Dumba .30 .75
73 Matthew Irwin .40 1.00
74 Matt Nieto .40 1.00
75 Michael Bournival .50 1.25
76 Michael Latta .40 1.00
77 Mike Kostka .40 1.00
78 Morgan Rielly 1.25 3.00
79 Nathan MacKinnon 4.00 10.00
80 Olli Maatta 2.00 5.00
81 Radko Gudas .50 1.25
82 Rasmus Ristolainen .75 2.00
83 Ryan Murray .75 2.00
84 Sami Vatanen .50 1.25
85 Sean Monahan .75 2.00
86 Seth Jones 1.00 2.50
87 Spencer Abbott .40 1.00
88 Tomas Hertl 1.00 2.50
89 Tyler Johnson 1.00 2.50
90 Valeri Nichushkin 1.25 3.00
91 Will Acton .40 1.00
92 Zemgus Girgensons .75 2.00

2013-14 Upper Deck Overtime Autographs

3 Austin Watson 4.00 10.00
4 Beau Bennett 8.00 20.00
5 Brendan Gallagher 15.00 40.00
6 Calvin Pickard 6.00 15.00
7 Charlie Coyle 8.00 20.00
8 Chris Brown 3.00 8.00
9 Christian Thomas 4.00 10.00
10 Cory Conacher 3.00 8.00
13 Dougie Hamilton 10.00 25.00
15 Emerson Etem 6.00 15.00
17 Jack Campbell 12.00 30.00
19 Jared Staal 4.00 10.00
20 Jarred Tinordi 5.00 12.00
23 Jonathan Huberdeau 12.00 30.00
25 Justin Schultz 5.00 12.00
27 Mark Pysyk 5.00 12.00
30 Mikhail Grigorenko 3.00 8.00
31 Nail Yakupov 20.00 40.00
32 Nathan Beaulieu 3.00 8.00
37 Quinton Howden 4.00 10.00
41 Ryan Murphy 5.00 12.00
42 Ryan Spooner 8.00 20.00
43 Scott Laughton 10.00 25.00
45 Thomas Hickey 4.00 10.00
47 Tyler Toffoli 10.00 25.00
51 Aleksander Barkov 15.00 40.00
56 Brock Nelson 10.00 25.00
57 Cameron Schilling 5.00 12.00
59 Danny DeKeyser 6.00 15.00
60 Elias Lindholm 12.00 30.00
61 Hampus Lindholm 6.00 15.00
62 Jacob Trouba 8.00 20.00
63 Jamie Devane 4.00 10.00
64 Jean-Gabriel Pageau 5.00 12.00
66 Jesper Fast 5.00 12.00
67 Joakim Nordstrom 6.00 15.00
69 Lucas Lessio 3.00 8.00
72 Mathew Dumba 3.00 8.00
77 Mike Kostka 4.00 10.00
78 Morgan Rielly 15.00 40.00
79 Nathan MacKinnon 30.00 80.00
85 Sean Monahan 15.00 40.00
86 Seth Jones 10.00 25.00
88 Tomas Hertl 12.00 30.00
91 Will Acton 4.00 10.00

2013-14 Upper Deck Overtime Rookie Profiles

COMPLETE SET (51) 40.00 80.00
COMP.SERIES 1 (30) 20.00 40.00
COMP.SERIES 2 (21) 20.00 40.00
RP1 Nail Yakupov 1.50 4.00
RP2 Jonathan Huberdeau 2.00 5.00
RP3 Alex Galchenyuk 2.00 5.00
RP4 Brendan Gallagher 2.00 5.00
RP5 Vladimir Tarasenko 2.00 5.00
RP6 Mikhail Grigorenko .50 1.25
RP7 Mikael Granlund 1.25 3.00
RP8 Nathan Beaulieu .50 1.25
RP9 Justin Schultz .75 2.00
RP10 Charlie Coyle 1.50 4.00
RP11 Cory Conacher .50 1.25
RP12 Damien Brunner .60 1.50
RP13 Dougie Hamilton 1.25 3.00
RP14 Emerson Etem .75 2.00
RP15 Jonas Brodin 1.00 2.50
RP16 Jordan Schroeder .75 2.00
RP17 Petr Mrazek 1.50 4.00
RP18 Quinton Howden .60 1.50
RP19 Ryan Spooner .75 2.00
RP20 Scott Laughton 1.00 2.50
RP21 Stefan Matteau .60 1.50
RP22 Viktor Fasth .75 2.00
RP23 Jarred Tinordi .75 2.00
RP24 Tyler Toffoli 1.50 4.00
RP25 Beau Bennett 1.00 2.50
RP26 Jack Campbell 2.00 5.00
RP27 Ryan Murphy .75 2.00
RP28 Rickard Rakell .75 2.00
RP29 Thomas Hickey .60 1.50
RP30 Jamie Oleksiak .60 1.50
RP31 Nathan MacKinnon 4.00 10.00
RP32 Seth Jones 1.50 4.00
RP33 Morgan Rielly 2.00 5.00
RP34 Sean Monahan 1.25 3.00
RP35 Boone Jenner 1.50 4.00
RP36 Elias Lindholm 2.50 6.00
RP37 Hampus Lindholm 1.25 3.00
RP38 Rasmus Ristolainen 1.25 3.00
RP39 Ryan Murray 1.25 3.00
RP40 Jacob Trouba 1.25 3.00
RP41 Olli Maatta 3.00 8.00
RP42 Lucas Lessio .50 1.25
RP43 Valeri Nichushkin 1.50 4.00
RP44 Mathew Dumba .50 1.25
RP45 Jesper Fast .75 2.00
RP46 Tomas Hertl 1.50 4.00
RP47 Michael Latta .60 1.50
RP48 Zemgus Girgensons 1.25 3.00
RP49 Joakim Nordstrom .60 1.50
RP50 Sami Vatanen .75 2.00
RP51 Justin Fontaine .75 2.00

2014-15 Upper Deck Overtime

*BLUE VETS: .8X TO 2X BASIC CARDS
*BLUE LEG: .6X TO 1.5X BASIC CARDS
*BLUE ROOKIE: .5X TO 1.2X BASIC CARDS
*GREEN VETS/99: 3X TO 8X BASIC CARDS
*GREEN LEG/99: 2.5X TO 6X BASIC CARDS
*GREEN ROOKIE/99: 1X TO 2.5X BASIC CARDS
1 Jim Howard .50 1.25
2 Tuukka Rask .50 1.25
3 Steve Mason .30 .75
4 Carey Price .75 2.00
5 Joe Pavelski .50 1.25
6 James van Riemsdyk .30 .75
7 Gabriel Landeskog .50 1.25
8 Jonathan Quick .50 1.25
9 Patrick Kane .75 2.00
10 Sidney Crosby 1.50 4.00
11 Claude Giroux .40 1.00
12 Ryan Getzlaf .40 1.00
13 Patrice Bergeron .50 1.25
14 Cody Hodgson .25 .60
15 Sean Monahan .25 .60
16 Eric Staal .50 1.25
17 Jonathan Toews .60 1.50
18 Matt Duchene .40 1.00
19 Sergei Bobrovsky .60 1.50
20 Tyler Seguin .50 1.25
21 Pavel Datsyuk .60 1.50
22 Taylor Hall .40 1.00
23 Roberto Luongo .60 1.50
24 Anze Kopitar .60 1.50
25 Zach Parise .40 1.00
26 P.K. Subban .50 1.25
27 Shea Weber .30 .75
28 Adam Henrique .30 .75
29 John Tavares .60 1.50
30 Martin St. Louis .40 1.00
31 Bobby Ryan .30 .75
32 Keith Yandle .25 .60
33 Logan Couture .50 1.25
34 T.J. Oshie .40 1.00
35 Steven Stamkos .75 2.00
36 Phil Kessel .40 1.00
37 Jonathan Bernier .30 .75
38 Alexander Ovechkin 1.50 4.00
39 Blake Wheeler .40 1.00
40 Corey Perry .60 1.50
41 Theoren Fleury LEG 1.25 3.00
42 Mike Modano LEG 1.50 4.00
43 Dominik Hasek LEG 1.50 4.00
44 Stan Mikita LEG 1.25 3.00
45 Larry Robinson LEG 1.00 2.50
46 Guy Lafleur LEG 1.25 3.00
47 Mats Sundin LEG 1.00 2.50
48 Teemu Selanne LEG 2.00 5.00
49 Bobby Orr LEG 4.00 10.00
50 Wayne Gretzky LEG 6.00 15.00
51 Brandon Gormley RC 1.00 2.50
52 Mark Visentin RC 1.00 2.50
53 Teuvo Teravainen RC 1.50 4.00
54 Joey Hishon RC 1.25 3.00
55 Greg McKegg RC .75 2.00
56 Calle Jarnkrok RC 1.00 2.50
57 Ty Rattie RC 1.00 2.50
58 Vladislav Namestnikov RC 1.50 4.00
59 Evgeny Kuznetsov RC 2.50 6.00
60 Oscar Klefbom RC 2.00 5.00
61 Erik Karlsson .50 1.25
62 Duncan Keith .30 .75
63 Patrick Marleau .40 1.00
64 Dany Heatley .30 .75
65 Drew Doughty .50 1.25
66 Chris Kunitz .40 1.00
67 Sam Gagner .25 .60
68 James Neal .25 .60
69 Brandon Dubinsky .25 .60
70 Vincent Lecavalier .40 1.00
71 John Gibson .40 1.00
72 Gustav Nyquist .25 .60
73 Jason Pominville .25 .60
74 Shane Doan .30 .75
75 Alex Galchenyuk .25 .60
76 Jarome Iginla .50 1.25
77 Zdeno Chara .40 1.00
78 Ben Bishop .30 .75
79 Dustin Byfuglien .40 1.00
80 Marc-Andre Fleury .75 2.00
81 Nail Yakupov .25 .60
82 Ryan Miller .40 1.00
83 Jonas Hiller .30 .75
84 Craig Anderson .40 1.00
85 Nicklas Backstrom .40 1.00
86 Valeri Nichushkin .40 1.00
87 Matt Moulson .25 .60
88 Kyle Okposo .25 .60
89 Alexandre Burrows .25 .60
90 Dion Phaneuf .30 .75
91 Jonathan Huberdeau .50 1.25
92 Patrick Sharp .40 1.00
93 Henrik Lundqvist 1.00 2.50
94 Kari Lehtonen .30 .75
95 Alexander Steen .25 .60
96 Jaromir Jagr 1.25 3.00
97 Viktor Fasth .30 .75
98 Tomas Plekanec .25 .60
99 Patrik Berglund .25 .60
100 Joe Thornton .60 1.50
101 Leon Draisaitl RC 5.00 12.00
102 Dennis Everberg RC 1.00 2.50
103 Johnny Gaudreau RC 6.00 15.00
104 Andre Burakovsky RC 1.50 4.00
105 Colton Sissons RC 1.00 2.50
106 Alexander Khokhlachev RC 1.00 2.50
107 Teemu Pulkkinen RC 1.25 3.00
108 Curtis Lazar RC 1.00 2.50
109 Patrik Nemeth RC 1.00 2.50
110 Sam Reinhart RC 4.00 10.00
111 Anthony Duclair RC 1.50 4.00
112 Christian Folin RC 1.00 2.50
113 Alexander Wennberg RC 1.50 4.00
114 Damon Severson RC 1.00 2.50
115 Pierre-Edouard Bellemare RC 1.00 2.50
116 Corban Knight RC 1.00 2.50
117 Stuart Percy RC 1.00 2.50
118 Markus Granlund RC 1.50 4.00
119 Chris Tierney RC 1.00 2.50
120 Aaron Ekblad RC 2.50 6.00
121 Antti Niemi .30 .75
122 Marian Gaborik .40 1.00
123 Nathan MacKinnon 1.50 4.00
124 Rick Nash .40 1.00
125 Evander Kane .40 1.00
126 Niklas Kronwall .30 .75
127 Ryan Kesler .40 1.00
128 Mark Giordano .40 1.00
129 Seth Jones .40 1.00
130 Jakub Voracek .30 .75
131 Mike Smith .40 1.00
132 Niklas Backstrom .30 .75
133 Kris Letang .50 1.25
134 Scott Hartnell .25 .60
135 Milan Lucic .40 1.00
136 Ryan McDonagh .25 .60
137 Braden Holtby .50 1.25
138 Aleksander Barkov .60 1.50
139 Jiri Hudler .30 .75
140 Henrik Sedin .50 1.25
141 Ryan Nugent-Hopkins .50 1.25
142 Brad Marchand .75 2.00
143 Tyler Ennis .25 .60
144 Valtteri Filppula .25 .60
145 Mikko Koivu .30 .75
146 Daniel Sedin .50 1.25
147 Marian Hossa .40 1.00
148 Corey Crawford .50 1.25
149 Evgeni Malkin .75 2.00
150 Henrik Zetterberg .50 1.25
151 Kyle Turris .40 1.00
152 David Backes .25 .60
153 Jamie Benn .40 1.00
154 Wayne Simmonds .50 1.25
155 Max Pacioretty .40 1.00
156 David Perron .30 .75
157 Jaroslav Halak .40 1.00
158 Pekka Rinne .40 1.00
159 Jeff Carter .30 .75
160 Cory Schneider .40 1.00
161 Jonathan Drouin RC 2.00 5.00
162 Jiri Sekac RC .75 2.00
163 Tobias Rieder RC 1.00 2.50
164 Adam Clendening RC 1.00 2.50
165 Darnell Nurse RC 2.00 5.00
166 Trevor van Riemsdyk RC 1.50 4.00
167 Sven Andrighetto RC 1.25 3.00
168 Victor Rask RC 1.00 2.50
169 Bo Horvat RC 2.50 6.00
170 Jori Lehtera RC 1.25 3.00
171 Kerby Rychel RC .75 2.00
172 Griffin Reinhart RC 1.00 2.50
173 Mirco Mueller RC 1.00 2.50
174 William Karlsson RC 3.00 8.00
175 Adam Lowry RC 1.50 4.00
176 Andy Andreoff RC 1.00 2.50
177 Seth Helgeson RC .75 2.00
178 Kevin Hayes RC 2.50 6.00
179 David Pastrnak RC 5.00 12.00
180 Marko Dano RC 1.00 2.50

2014-15 Upper Deck Overtime Autographs

1 Jim Howard 6.00 15.00
2 Tuukka Rask 6.00 15.00
3 Steve Mason 8.00 20.00
5 Joe Pavelski 6.00 15.00
6 James van Riemsdyk 4.00 10.00
7 Gabriel Landeskog 6.00 15.00
8 Jonathan Quick 6.00 15.00
9 Patrick Kane 25.00 50.00
11 Claude Giroux 20.00 40.00
12 Ryan Getzlaf 5.00 12.00
13 Patrice Bergeron 15.00 40.00
14 Cody Hodgson 8.00 20.00
15 Sean Monahan 3.00 8.00
16 Eric Staal 6.00 15.00
18 Matt Duchene 5.00 12.00
19 Sergei Bobrovsky 8.00 20.00
20 Tyler Seguin 20.00 40.00
21 Pavel Datsyuk 8.00 20.00
22 Taylor Hall 15.00 40.00
24 Anze Kopitar 8.00 20.00
25 Zach Parise 5.00 12.00
27 Shea Weber 4.00 10.00
28 Adam Henrique 4.00 10.00
29 John Tavares 8.00 20.00
30 Martin St. Louis 60.00
31 Bobby Ryan 8.00 20.00
32 Keith Yandle 3.00 8.00
33 Logan Couture 8.00 20.00
34 T.J. Oshie 10.00 25.00
36 Phil Kessel 8.00 20.00
37 Jonathan Bernier 8.00 20.00
38 Alexander Ovechkin 30.00 80.00
39 Blake Wheeler 5.00 12.00
40 Corey Perry 12.00 30.00
41 Theoren Fleury 15.00 40.00
45 Larry Robinson 5.00 12.00
46 Guy Lafleur 20.00 50.00
47 Mats Sundin 5.00 12.00
48 Teemu Selanne 10.00 25.00
49 Bobby Orr 90.00 150.00
50 Wayne Gretzky 150.00 400.00
51 Brandon Gormley 5.00 12.00
52 Mark Visentin 10.00 25.00
53 Teuvo Teravainen 25.00 50.00
54 Joey Hishon 6.00 15.00
55 Greg McKegg 8.00 20.00
56 Calle Jarnkrok 5.00 12.00
57 Ty Rattie 5.00 12.00
58 Vladislav Namestnikov 8.00 20.00
59 Evgeny Kuznetsov 12.00 30.00
60 Oscar Klefbom 8.00 20.00
61 Erik Karlsson 6.00 15.00
63 Patrick Marleau 5.00 12.00
64 Dany Heatley 4.00 10.00
65 Drew Doughty 6.00 15.00
66 Chris Kunitz 5.00 12.00
67 Sam Gagner 3.00 8.00
68 James Neal 3.00 8.00
69 Brandon Dubinsky 3.00 8.00
72 Gustav Nyquist 3.00 8.00
73 Jason Pominville 3.00 8.00
74 Shane Doan 4.00 10.00
76 Jarome Iginla 8.00 20.00
79 Dustin Byfuglien 5.00 12.00
80 Marc-Andre Fleury 10.00 25.00
81 Nail Yakupov 3.00 8.00
82 Ryan Miller 5.00 12.00
83 Jonas Hiller 4.00 10.00
84 Craig Anderson 5.00 12.00
85 Nicklas Backstrom 5.00 12.00
86 Valeri Nichushkin 5.00 12.00
87 Matt Moulson 3.00 8.00
88 Kyle Okposo 8.00 20.00
89 Alexandre Burrows 3.00 8.00
90 Dion Phaneuf 4.00 10.00
91 Jonathan Huberdeau 6.00 15.00
92 Patrick Sharp 5.00 12.00
93 Henrik Lundqvist 12.00 30.00
94 Kari Lehtonen 8.00 20.00
95 Alexander Steen 3.00 8.00
97 Viktor Fasth 4.00 10.00
98 Tomas Plekanec 3.00 8.00
99 Patrik Berglund 3.00 8.00
101 Leon Draisaitl 50.00 125.00
102 Dennis Everberg 5.00 12.00
103 Johnny Gaudreau 20.00 50.00
104 Andre Burakovsky 8.00 20.00
105 Colton Sissons 5.00 12.00
106 Alexander Khokhlachev 5.00 12.00
107 Teemu Pulkkinen 6.00 15.00
109 Patrik Nemeth 5.00 12.00
110 Sam Reinhart 20.00 50.00
111 Anthony Duclair 8.00 20.00
112 Christian Folin 5.00 12.00
113 Alexander Wennberg 8.00 20.00
114 Damon Severson 5.00 12.00
115 Pierre-Edouard Bellemare 5.00 12.00
116 Corban Knight 5.00 12.00
117 Stuart Percy 5.00 12.00
118 Markus Granlund 8.00 20.00
119 Chris Tierney 5.00 12.00
120 Aaron Ekblad 15.00 40.00
121 Antti Niemi 4.00 10.00
122 Marian Gaborik 5.00 12.00
124 Rick Nash 5.00 12.00
125 Evander Kane 5.00 12.00
126 Niklas Kronwall 4.00 10.00
127 Ryan Kesler 5.00 12.00
128 Mark Giordano 5.00 12.00
130 Jakub Voracek 4.00 10.00
131 Mike Smith 5.00 12.00
132 Niklas Backstrom 4.00 10.00
133 Kris Letang 6.00 15.00
134 Scott Hartnell 3.00 8.00
135 Milan Lucic 5.00 12.00
136 Ryan McDonagh 10.00 25.00
137 Braden Holtby 8.00 20.00
138 Aleksander Barkov 8.00 20.00
139 Jiri Hudler 4.00 10.00
140 Henrik Sedin 6.00 15.00
141 Ryan Nugent-Hopkins 6.00 15.00
142 Brad Marchand 10.00 25.00
143 Tyler Ennis 3.00 8.00
145 Mikko Koivu 8.00 20.00
146 Daniel Sedin 6.00 15.00
147 Marian Hossa 5.00 12.00
149 Evgeni Malkin 10.00 25.00
150 Henrik Zetterberg 6.00 15.00
151 Kyle Turris 5.00 12.00
152 David Backes 3.00 8.00
154 Wayne Simmonds 6.00 15.00
155 Max Pacioretty 5.00 12.00
156 David Perron 4.00 10.00
157 Jaroslav Halak 25.00 60.00
158 Pekka Rinne 5.00 12.00
159 Jeff Carter 4.00 10.00
160 Cory Schneider 5.00 12.00
161 Jonathan Drouin 10.00 25.00
162 Jiri Sekac 4.00 10.00
163 Tobias Rieder 5.00 12.00
164 Adam Clendening 5.00 12.00
166 Trevor van Riemsdyk 8.00 20.00
167 Sven Andrighetto 12.00 30.00
168 Victor Rask 5.00 12.00
171 Kerby Rychel 4.00 10.00
173 Mirco Mueller 5.00 12.00
174 William Karlsson 15.00 40.00
175 Adam Lowry 8.00 20.00
176 Andy Andreoff 5.00 12.00
177 Seth Helgeson 4.00 10.00
180 Marko Dano 5.00 12.00

2014-15 Upper Deck Overtime Flash of Excellence

COMPLETE SET (30) 15.00 40.00
*ORANGE/25: 4X TO 10X BASIC INSERTS
FOE1 Pavel Datsyuk 1.00 2.50
FOE2 Matt Duchene .60 1.50
FOE3 Dion Phaneuf .50 1.25
FOE4 Alex Galchenyuk .40 1.00
FOE5 Pekka Rinne .60 1.50
FOE6 Nail Yakupov .40 1.00
FOE7 Ryan Johansen .50 1.25
FOE8 Evander Kane .60 1.50
FOE9 Jonathan Toews 1.00 2.50
FOE10 Anze Kopitar 1.00 2.50
FOE11 Bobby Ryan .50 1.25
FOE12 Ryan Nugent-Hopkins .75 2.00
FOE13 David Backes .40 1.00
FOE14 Joe Thornton 1.00 2.50
FOE15 Tuukka Rask .75 2.00
FOE16 Dustin Byfuglien .60 1.50
FOE17 Jaromir Jagr 2.00 5.00
FOE18 Patrick Kane 1.25 3.00
FOE19 John Tavares 1.00 2.50
FOE20 Zach Parise .60 1.50
FOE21 Lars Eller .40 1.00
FOE22 Evgeni Malkin 1.25 3.00
FOE23 Martin St. Louis .60 1.50
FOE24 Steve Mason .50 1.25
FOE25 Doug Gilmour 1.00 2.50
FOE26 Wayne Gretzky 5.00 12.00
FOE27 Jean Beliveau .75 2.00
FOE28 Teuvo Teravainen .75 2.00
FOE29 Ty Rattie .50 1.25
FOE30 Evgeny Kuznetsov 1.25 3.00

2014-15 Upper Deck Overtime Lords of the Rink

*BLUE/25: 1.2X TO 3X BASIC INSERTS
LR1 Wayne Gretzky 15.00 40.00
LR2 Bobby Clarke 4.00 10.00
LR3 Jarome Iginla 2.50 6.00
LR4 Matt Duchene 2.00 5.00
LR5 Adam Oates 2.00 5.00
LR6 Tuukka Rask 2.50 6.00
LR7 Zach Parise 2.00 5.00
LR8 Dominik Hasek 3.00 8.00
LR9 Alexander Ovechkin 8.00 20.00
LR10 Joe Pavelski 2.50 6.00
LR11 Teemu Selanne 4.00 10.00
LR12 Ryan McDonagh 1.25 3.00
LR13 Anze Kopitar 3.00 8.00
LR14 David Backes 1.25 3.00
LR15 John Tavares 3.00 8.00
LR16 Corey Perry 3.00 8.00
LR17 Steve Mason 1.50 4.00
LR18 Jonathan Bernier 1.50 4.00
LR19 Mats Sundin 2.00 5.00
LR20 Jamie Benn 2.00 5.00
LR21 Doug Gilmour 3.00 8.00
LR22 Pavel Datsyuk 3.00 8.00
LR23 Evgeni Malkin 4.00 10.00
LR24 Nicklas Lidstrom 2.00 5.00
LR25 Nail Yakupov 1.25 3.00
LR26 Carey Price 4.00 10.00
LR27 Ryan Miller 2.00 5.00
LR28 Martin St. Louis 2.00 5.00
LR29 Phil Kessel 2.00 5.00
LR30 Nathan MacKinnon 8.00 20.00

2014-15 Upper Deck Overtime Rookie Review

*BLUE/25: 1.5X TO 4X BASIC INSERTS
RRC1 Aaron Ekblad 3.00 8.00
RRC2 Griffin Reinhart 1.25 3.00
RRC3 Johnny Gaudreau 8.00 20.00
RRC4 Adam Lowry 2.00 5.00
RRC5 Anthony Duclair 2.00 5.00
RRC6 Ty Rattie 1.25 3.00
RRC7 Brandon Gormley 1.25 3.00
RRC8 Jiri Sekac 1.00 2.50
RRC9 Vladislav Namestnikov 2.00 5.00
RRC10 Bo Horvat 3.00 8.00
RRC11 Joey Hishon 1.50 4.00
RRC12 Evgeny Kuznetsov 3.00 8.00
RRC13 Alexander Khokhlachev 1.25 3.00
RRC14 Jonathan Drouin 2.50 6.00
RRC15 Andre Burakovsky 2.00 5.00
RRC16 Teemu Pulkkinen 1.50 4.00
RRC17 Teuvo Teravainen 2.00 5.00
RRC18 Marko Dano 1.25 3.00
RRC19 Jori Lehtera 1.50 4.00
RRC20 Sam Reinhart 5.00 12.00
RRC21 Curtis Lazar 1.25 3.00
RRC22 Mirco Mueller 1.25 3.00
RRC23 Markus Granlund 2.00 5.00
RRC24 Alexander Wennberg 2.00 5.00
RRC25 Damon Severson 1.25 3.00
RRC26 Chris Tierney 1.25 3.00
RRC27 Leon Draisaitl 6.00 15.00
RRC28 Calle Jarnkrok 1.25 3.00
RRC29 Oscar Klefbom 2.50 6.00
RRC30 Vincent Trocheck 2.50 6.00

2015-16 Upper Deck Overtime

COMP.SERIES 1 (60) 25.00 50.00
COMP.SERIES 2 (60) 25.00 50.00
*BLUE VETS: 1X TO 2.5X BASIC CARDS
*BLUE LEG: .6X TO 1.5X BASIC CARDS
*BLUE ROOKIE: .5X TO 1.2X BASIC CARDS
*RED VETS/99: 3X TO 8X BASIC CARDS
*RED LEG/99: 2X TO 5X BASIC CARDS
*RED ROOKIE/99: 1.5X TO 4X BASIC RC
1 Steven Stamkos .75 2.00
2 Pekka Rinne .40 1.00
3 Jamie Benn .40 1.00
4 Brad Marchand .75 2.00
5 Max Pacioretty .40 1.00
6 Mikko Koivu .30 .75
7 Drew Doughty .50 1.25
8 Kyle Okposo .25 .60
9 Joe Pavelski .50 1.25
10 Matt Duchene .40 1.00
11 David Backes .25 .60
12 Tyler Ennis .25 .60
13 Alexander Ovechkin 1.50 4.00
14 Oliver Ekman-Larsson .40 1.00
15 Jonas Hiller .30 .75
16 Henrik Lundqvist 1.00 2.50
17 Erik Karlsson .50 1.25
18 Steve Mason .30 .75
19 Marc-Andre Fleury .75 2.00
20 James van Riemsdyk .30 .75
21 Patrick Kane .75 2.00
22 Vladimir Tarasenko .50 1.25
23 Ryan Johansen .30 .75
24 Andrew Ladd .25 .60
25 Daniel Sedin .50 1.25
26 Jordan Eberle .40 1.00
27 Nathan MacKinnon 1.50 4.00
28 Patrice Bergeron .50 1.25
29 Carey Price .75 2.00
30 Adam Henrique .30 .75
31 Rick Nash .40 1.00
32 Kris Letang .50 1.25
33 Ben Bishop .30 .75
34 Pavel Datsyuk .60 1.50
35 Marian Hossa .40 1.00
36 Logan Couture .50 1.25
37 Ryan Kesler .40 1.00
38 Roberto Luongo .60 1.50
39 Marian Gaborik .40 1.00
40 Eric Staal .50 1.25
41 Wayne Gretzky LEG 4.00 10.00
42 Patrick Roy LEG 1.50 4.00
43 Phil Esposito LEG 1.00 2.50
44 Mario Lemieux LEG 2.50 6.00
45 Mark Messier LEG 1.25 3.00
46 Glenn Anderson LEG .50 1.25
47 Ray Bourque LEG 1.00 2.50
48 Bobby Clarke LEG 1.00 2.50
49 Mike Bossy LEG .60 1.50
50 Guy Lafleur LEG .75 2.00
51 Malcolm Subban RC 1.25 3.00
52 Sam Bennett RC 2.50 6.00
53 Kevin Fiala RC 1.00 2.50
54 Ryan Hartman RC 1.00 2.50
55 Henrik Samuelsson RC .50 1.25
56 Nick Cousins RC .75 2.00
57 Josh Anderson RC 1.50 4.00
58 Jacob de la Rose RC .75 2.00
59 Emile Poirier RC .60 1.50
60 Matt Puempel RC .60 1.50
61 Sidney Crosby 1.50 4.00
62 Bobby Ryan .30 .75
63 Patrick Marleau .40 1.00
64 Filip Forsberg .60 1.50
65 P.K. Subban .50 1.25
66 Ryan Miller .40 1.00
67 Ryan Suter .30 .75
68 Derick Brassard .25 .60
69 Dustin Brown .40 1.00
70 John Tavares .60 1.50
71 Claude Giroux .40 1.00
72 Jonathan Toews .60 1.50
73 Gabriel Landeskog .50 1.25
74 Jeff Skinner .50 1.25
75 Nikita Kucherov .75 2.00
76 John Carlson .40 1.00
77 Keith Yandle .25 .60
78 Ryan Getzlaf .40 1.00
79 Ryan Nugent-Hopkins .50 1.25
80 Nick Foligno .30 .75
81 Jake Allen .40 1.00

82 David Perron .30 .75
83 Darcy Kuemper .40 1.00
84 Michael Hutchinson .25 .60
85 Gustav Nyquist .25 .60
86 Kari Lehtonen .30 .75
87 Shane Doan .30 .75
88 Tomas Plekanec .25 .60
89 Jonathan Bernier .30 .75
90 Sean Monahan .25 .60
91 Zemgus Girgensons .30 .75
92 Anze Kopitar .60 1.50
93 Corey Crawford .50 1.25
94 Ondrej Palat .30 .75
95 Jiri Hudler .30 .75
96 Cory Schneider .40 1.00
97 Jaromir Jagr 1.25 3.00
98 Joe Thornton .60 1.50
99 Jaroslav Halak .40 1.00
100 Sergei Bobrovsky .60 1.50
101 Artemi Panarin RC 3.00 8.00
102 Brian O'Neill RC .60 1.50
103 Connor Hellebuyck RC 3.00 8.00
104 Raman Hrabarenka RC .60 1.50
105 Shane Prince RC .50 1.25
106 Joel Edmundson RC .60 1.50
107 Nicolas Petan RC .75 2.00
108 Andrew Copp RC .75 2.00
109 Jared McCann RC 1.00 2.50
110 Anton Slepyshev RC .50 1.25
111 Noah Hanifin RC 1.25 3.00
112 Colin Miller RC .60 1.50
113 Sergei Plotnikov RC .50 1.25
114 Mike Condon RC .75 2.00
115 Robby Fabbri RC 1.00 2.50
116 Stefan Noesen RC .50 1.25
117 Sergei Kalinin RC .50 1.25
118 Slater Koekkoek RC .50 1.25
119 Joonas Donskoi RC .75 2.00
120 Jack Eichel RC 4.00 10.00
121 Taylor Hall .75 2.00
122 Jarome Iginla 1.00 2.50
123 Evgeni Malkin 1.50 4.00
124 Shea Weber .60 1.50
125 Tyler Seguin 1.00 2.50
126 Cody Franson .50 1.25
127 Dustin Byfuglien .75 2.00
128 Justin Abdelkader .60 1.50
129 Brendan Gallagher .75 2.00
130 Alex Pietrangelo .60 1.50
131 Jonathan Quick 1.00 2.50
132 Johnny Gaudreau 1.25 3.00
133 Patrik Elias .75 2.00
134 Matt Moulson .50 1.25
135 Corey Perry 1.25 3.00
136 Mike Hoffman .50 1.25
137 Tuukka Rask 1.00 2.50
138 Jonathan Huberdeau 1.00 2.50
139 Cam Atkinson .75 2.00
140 Zach Parise .75 2.00
141 Mike Ribeiro .50 1.25
142 Jakub Voracek .60 1.50
143 Henrik Zetterberg 1.00 2.50
144 Justin Faulk .60 1.50
145 Jeff Carter .60 1.50
146 Ondrej Pavelec .75 2.00
147 Mark Giordano .75 2.00
148 Henrik Sedin 1.00 2.50
149 Ryan Callahan .50 1.25
150 Kyle Turris .60 1.50
151 Patrick Sharp .75 2.00
152 Patric Hornqvist .50 1.25
153 Craig Anderson .75 2.00
154 Mikkel Boedker .50 1.25
155 Tyler Johnson .50 1.25
156 John Carlson .75 2.00
157 Brent Burns .75 2.00
158 Anders Lee .75 2.00
159 Nazem Kadri 1.00 2.50
160 Devan Dubnyk .60 1.50
161 Charles Hudon RC .75 2.00
162 Max Domi RC 1.50 4.00
163 Stanislav Galiev RC .75 2.00
164 Antoine Bibeau RC .75 2.00
165 Ben Hutton RC .75 2.00
166 Andreas Athanasiou RC 2.00 5.00
167 Colton Parayko RC 1.25 3.00
168 Mattias Janmark RC .75 2.00
169 Jordan Weal RC .50 1.25
170 Devin Shore RC .75 2.00
171 Mikko Rantanen RC 4.00 10.00
172 Daniel Sprong RC 1.00 2.50
173 Nikolay Goldobin RC .75 2.00
174 Dylan Larkin RC 2.50 6.00
175 Connor Brickley RC .60 1.50
176 Jake Virtanen RC .60 1.50
177 Viktor Svedberg RC .60 1.50
178 Matt O'Connor RC .60 1.50
179 Zachary Fucale RC .60 1.50
180 Connor McDavid RC 60.00 150.00

2015-16 Upper Deck Overtime Autographs

1 Steven Stamkos 15.00 40.00
2 Pekka Rinne 8.00 20.00
3 Jamie Benn 8.00 20.00
4 Brad Marchand 15.00 40.00
5 Max Pacioretty 8.00 20.00
6 Mikko Koivu 6.00 15.00
7 Drew Doughty 10.00 25.00
8 Kyle Okposo 5.00 12.00
9 Joe Pavelski 10.00 25.00
10 Matt Duchene 8.00 20.00
11 David Backes 5.00 12.00
12 Tyler Ennis 5.00 12.00
13 Alexander Ovechkin 75.00 125.00
14 Oliver Ekman-Larsson 8.00 20.00
15 Jonas Hiller 6.00 15.00
16 Henrik Lundqvist 20.00 50.00
17 Erik Karlsson 10.00 25.00
18 Steve Mason 6.00 15.00
19 Marc-Andre Fleury 15.00 40.00
20 James van Riemsdyk 6.00 15.00
21 Patrick Kane 15.00 40.00
22 Vladimir Tarasenko 10.00 25.00
23 Ryan Johansen 6.00 15.00
24 Andrew Ladd 5.00 12.00
25 Daniel Sedin 10.00 25.00
26 Jordan Eberle 8.00 20.00
27 Nathan MacKinnon 30.00 80.00
28 Patrice Bergeron 10.00 25.00
29 Carey Price 15.00 40.00
30 Adam Henrique 6.00 15.00
31 Rick Nash 8.00 20.00
32 Kris Letang 10.00 25.00
33 Ben Bishop 6.00 15.00
34 Pavel Datsyuk 12.00 30.00
35 Marian Hossa 8.00 20.00
36 Logan Couture 10.00 25.00
37 Ryan Kesler 8.00 20.00
38 Roberto Luongo 12.00 30.00
39 Marian Gaborik 8.00 20.00
40 Eric Staal 10.00 25.00
41 Wayne Gretzky LEG 250.00 600.00
42 Patrick Roy LEG 40.00 80.00
43 Phil Esposito LEG 12.50 25.00
44 Mario Lemieux LEG 40.00 100.00
45 Mark Messier LEG 20.00 50.00
46 Glenn Anderson LEG 8.00 20.00
47 Ray Bourque LEG 15.00 40.00
48 Bobby Clarke LEG 15.00 40.00
49 Mike Bossy LEG 15.00 30.00
50 Guy Lafleur LEG 12.00 30.00
51 Malcolm Subban 15.00 30.00
52 Sam Bennett 15.00 40.00
53 Kevin Fiala 6.00 15.00
54 Ryan Hartman 6.00 15.00
55 Henrik Samuelsson 3.00 8.00
56 Nick Cousins 5.00 12.00
57 Josh Anderson 10.00 25.00
58 Jacob de la Rose 5.00 12.00
59 Emile Poirier 4.00 10.00
60 Matt Puempel 4.00 10.00
62 Bobby Ryan 6.00 15.00
63 Patrick Marleau 8.00 20.00
64 Filip Forsberg 12.00 30.00
65 P.K. Subban 10.00 25.00
67 Ryan Suter 6.00 15.00
69 Dustin Brown 8.00 20.00
70 John Tavares 12.00 30.00
71 Claude Giroux 8.00 20.00
72 Jonathan Toews 12.00 30.00
73 Gabriel Landeskog 10.00 25.00
74 Jeff Skinner 10.00 25.00
75 Nikita Kucherov 12.50 25.00
76 John Carlson 8.00 20.00
77 Keith Yandle 5.00 12.00
78 Ryan Getzlaf 8.00 20.00
79 Ryan Nugent-Hopkins 10.00 25.00
80 Nick Foligno 6.00 15.00
81 Jake Allen 8.00 20.00
82 David Perron 6.00 15.00
83 Darcy Kuemper 8.00 20.00
84 Michael Hutchinson 5.00 12.00
85 Gustav Nyquist 5.00 12.00
86 Kari Lehtonen 6.00 15.00
88 Tomas Plekanec 5.00 12.00
89 Jonathan Bernier 6.00 15.00
91 Zemgus Girgensons 6.00 15.00
92 Anze Kopitar 12.00 30.00
94 Ondrej Palat 6.00 15.00
96 Cory Schneider 8.00 20.00
97 Jaromir Jagr 25.00 60.00
98 Joe Thornton 12.00 30.00
99 Jaroslav Halak 8.00 20.00
100 Sergei Bobrovsky 12.00 30.00
103 Connor Hellebuyck 30.00 80.00
105 Shane Prince 5.00 12.00
107 Nicolas Petan 8.00 20.00
111 Noah Hanifin 12.00 30.00
115 Robby Fabbri 10.00 25.00
116 Stefan Noesen 5.00 12.00
118 Slater Koekkoek 5.00 12.00
122 Jarome Iginla 10.00 25.00
123 Evgeni Malkin 15.00 40.00
124 Shea Weber 6.00 15.00
125 Tyler Seguin 10.00 25.00
126 Cody Franson 5.00 12.00
128 Justin Abdelkader 6.00 15.00
129 Brendan Gallagher 8.00 20.00
130 Alex Pietrangelo 6.00 15.00
131 Jonathan Quick 10.00 25.00
133 Patrik Elias 8.00 20.00
134 Matt Moulson 5.00 12.00
135 Corey Perry 12.00 30.00
137 Tuukka Rask 10.00 25.00
138 Jonathan Huberdeau 10.00 25.00
139 Cam Atkinson 8.00 20.00
140 Zach Parise 8.00 20.00
141 Mike Ribeiro 5.00 12.00
142 Jakub Voracek 6.00 15.00
144 Justin Faulk 6.00 15.00
145 Jeff Carter 6.00 15.00
149 Ryan Callahan 5.00 12.00
150 Kyle Turris 6.00 15.00
151 Patrick Sharp 8.00 20.00
155 Tyler Johnson 5.00 12.00
156 John Carlson 8.00 20.00
157 Brent Burns 8.00 20.00
158 Anders Lee 8.00 20.00
161 Charles Hudon 8.00 20.00
164 Antoine Bibeau 8.00 20.00
166 Andreas Athanasiou 20.00 50.00
167 Colton Parayko 12.00 30.00
168 Mattias Janmark 8.00 20.00
169 Jordan Weal 5.00 12.00
170 Devin Shore 8.00 20.00
173 Nikolay Goldobin 8.00 20.00
174 Dylan Larkin 60.00 100.00
177 Viktor Svedberg 6.00 15.00
178 Matt O'Connor 6.00 15.00
179 Zachary Fucale 6.00 15.00
180 Connor McDavid 200.00 500.00

2015-16 Upper Deck Overtime Flash of Excellence

*BLUE/25: 3X TO 8X BASIC INSERTS
FOE1 Alexander Ovechkin 2.50 6.00
FOE2 Rick Nash .60 1.50
FOE3 Steven Stamkos 1.25 3.00
FOE4 Joe Pavelski .75 2.00
FOE5 Max Pacioretty .60 1.50
FOE6 Patrick Kane 1.25 3.00
FOE7 Patrice Bergeron .75 2.00
FOE8 Jamie Benn .60 1.50
FOE9 Pavel Datsyuk 1.00 2.50
FOE10 Andrew Ladd .40 1.00
FOE11 Carey Price 1.25 3.00
FOE12 Pekka Rinne .60 1.50
FOE13 Henrik Lundqvist 1.50 4.00
FOE14 Wayne Gretzky 4.00 10.00
FOE15 Bobby Clarke 1.00 2.50
FOE16 Bobby Hull 1.25 3.00
FOE17 Mario Lemieux 2.50 6.00
FOE18 Mark Messier 1.25 3.00
FOE19 Malcolm Subban 1.00 2.50
FOE20 Sam Bennett 2.00 5.00

2015-16 Upper Deck Overtime Luminary Legends

LL1 Sidney Crosby 6.00 15.00
LL2 Joe Pavelski 2.00 5.00
LL3 Jamie Benn 1.50 4.00
LL4 Nathan MacKinnon 6.00 15.00
LL5 Alexander Ovechkin 6.00 15.00
LL6 Pekka Rinne 1.50 4.00
LL7 Anze Kopitar 2.50 6.00
LL8 P.K. Subban 2.00 5.00
LL9 Henrik Zetterberg 2.00 5.00
LL10 Steven Stamkos 3.00 8.00
LL11 Evgeni Malkin 3.00 8.00
LL12 Tyler Seguin 2.00 5.00
LL13 Claude Giroux 1.50 4.00
LL14 Taylor Hall 1.50 4.00
LL15 Rick Nash 1.50 4.00
LL16 Corey Perry 2.50 6.00
LL17 John Tavares 2.50 6.00
LL18 Jonathan Toews 2.50 6.00
LL19 Vladimir Tarasenko 2.00 5.00
LL20 Carey Price 3.00 8.00
LL21 Wayne Gretzky 10.00 25.00
LL22 Mark Messier 3.00 8.00
LL23 Glenn Anderson 1.25 3.00
LL24 Mike Bossy 1.50 4.00
LL25 Curtis Joseph 2.00 5.00
LL26 Cam Neely 1.50 4.00
LL27 Mike Modano 2.50 6.00
LL28 Teemu Selanne 3.00 8.00
LL29 Bobby Clarke 2.50 6.00
LL30 Jeremy Roenick 2.50 6.00

2015-16 Upper Deck Overtime Next in Line

COMPLETE SET (30) 50.00 100.00
NL1 Jack Eichel 6.00 15.00
NL2 Joonas Donskoi 1.00 2.50
NL3 Artemi Panarin 4.00 10.00
NL4 Nikolaj Ehlers 2.00 5.00
NL5 Mattias Janmark 1.00 2.50
NL6 Connor Hellebuyck 4.00 10.00
NL7 Dylan Larkin 6.00 15.00
NL8 Anton Slepyshev .60 1.50
NL9 Jared McCann 1.25 3.00
NL10 Max Domi 2.00 5.00
NL11 Daniel Sprong 1.25 3.00
NL12 Oscar Lindberg 1.00 2.50
NL13 Jake Virtanen 1.25 3.00
NL14 Nikolay Goldobin 1.00 2.50
NL15 Viktor Arvidsson 1.00 2.50
NL16 Nick Shore .60 1.50
NL17 Stanislav Galiev 1.00 2.50
NL18 Malcolm Subban 1.50 4.00
NL19 Stefan Noesen .60 1.50
NL20 Slater Koekkoek .60 1.50
NL21 Colton Parayko 1.50 4.00
NL22 Mikko Rantanen 5.00 12.00
NL23 Sergei Plotnikov .60 1.50
NL24 Sam Bennett 3.00 8.00
NL25 Robby Fabbri 1.25 3.00
NL26 Matt O'Connor .75 2.00
NL27 Nicolas Petan 1.00 2.50
NL28 Brock McGinn 1.00 2.50
NL29 Noah Hanifin 1.50 4.00
NL30 Connor McDavid 30.00 80.00

2015-16 Upper Deck Overtime Next in Line Blue Rainbow

*BLUE/25: 2.5X TO 6X BASIC INSERTS

2016-17 Upper Deck Overtime

1 Connor McDavid 5.00 12.00
2 Aaron Ekblad 1.25 3.00
3 Ryan McDonagh .60 1.50
4 Ondrej Palat .75 2.00
5 John Gibson 1.00 2.50
6 Brayden Schenn 1.00 2.50
7 Claude Giroux 1.00 2.50
8 James van Riemsdyk .75 2.00
9 Ryan Nugent-Hopkins 1.25 3.00
10 Semyon Varlamov 1.00 2.50
11 Sam Reinhart 2.00 5.00
12 Dion Phaneuf .75 2.00
13 Michal Neuvirth .75 2.00
14 Rick Nash 1.00 2.50
15 Artemi Panarin 2.00 5.00
16 Ryan Miller 1.00 2.50
17 Brian Boyle .60 1.50
18 Riley Sheahan .60 1.50
19 Oscar Klefbom 1.50 4.00
20 Gabriel Landeskog 1.25 3.00
21 Alex Galchenyuk .60 1.50
22 Aleksander Barkov 1.50 4.00
23 Jamie Benn 1.00 2.50
24 Noah Hanifin 1.00 2.50
25 Jesper Fast .60 1.50
26 Dylan Larkin 1.25 3.00
27 Jacob Trouba .75 2.00
28 Robby Fabbri .60 1.50
29 Kevin Shattenkirk .60 1.50
30 Matt Beleskey .75 2.00
31 Seth Jones 1.00 2.50
32 Mark Giordano 1.00 2.50
33 John Tavares 1.50 4.00
34 Cory Schneider 1.00 2.50
35 Jonathan Quick 1.25 3.00
36 Joe Pavelski 1.25 3.00
37 Marian Gaborik 1.00 2.50
38 Olli Maatta .60 1.50
39 Sidney Crosby 4.00 10.00
40 Jaromir Jagr 3.00 8.00
41 Luc Robitaille LEG 2.00 5.00
42 Teemu Selanne LEG 4.00 10.00
43 Steve Yzerman LEG 5.00 12.00
44 Larry Robinson LEG 2.00 5.00
45 Rob Blake LEG 2.00 5.00
46 Glenn Hall LEG 2.00 5.00
47 Trevor Linden LEG 2.00 5.00
48 Wendel Clark LEG 3.00 8.00
49 Ron Hextall LEG 2.00 5.00
50 Wayne Gretzky LEG 12.00 30.00
51 Pavel Zacha RC 3.00 8.00
52 Jason Dickinson RC 1.50 4.00
53 Trevor Carrick RC 2.00 5.00
54 Chase De Leo RC 2.00 5.00
55 Connor Brown RC 3.00 8.00
56 Josh Morrissey RC 5.00 12.00
57 Sonny Milano RC 2.50 6.00
58 Kasperi Kapanen RC 3.00 8.00
59 Anthony Mantha RC 4.00 10.00
60 William Nylander RC 8.00 20.00
61 Braden Holtby 1.25 3.00
62 Evander Kane 1.00 2.50
63 Aaron Ekblad 1.25 3.00
64 Brock Nelson 1.00 2.50
65 Morgan Rielly 1.00 2.50
66 Martin Jones .75 2.00
67 Corey Crawford 1.25 3.00
68 Carl Hagelin .60 1.50
69 Matt Duchene 1.00 2.50
70 Nick Bjugstad .60 1.50
71 Ryan Johansen .75 2.00
72 Tyler Toffoli 1.00 2.50
73 Elias Lindholm 1.00 2.50
74 Jason Pominville .60 1.50
75 Richard Panik .60 1.50
76 Tyler Seguin 1.25 3.00
77 Patrick Marleau 1.00 2.50
78A Henrik Zetterberg 1.25 3.00
78B Henrik Zetterberg VAR 2.00 5.00
79 Brent Seabrook .60 1.50
80 Sam Reinhart 2.00 5.00
81 Ryan Spooner .75 2.00
82 Robby Fabbri .60 1.50
83 Jakub Voracek .75 2.00
84A Ryan Getzlaf 1.00 2.50
84B Ryan Getzlaf VAR 1.50 4.00
85 Leon Draisaitl 3.00 8.00
86 Sean Couturier .75 2.00
87 Tyler Johnson .60 1.50
88 Bobby Ryan .75 2.00
89 Andy Greene .60 1.50
90 Brad Marchand 2.00 5.00
91 Boone Jenner 1.00 2.50
92 Ondrej Pavelec 1.00 2.50
93 Kyle Palmieri .75 2.00
94 Johnny Boychuk .75 2.00
95 Alexander Wennberg .60 1.50
96 Kyle Turris .75 2.00
97 Derek Stepan .60 1.50
98A Carey Price 2.00 5.00
98B Carey Price VAR 3.00 8.00
99 Bo Horvat 1.25 3.00
100 Ben Bishop .75 2.00
101 Michael Matheson RC 2.00 5.00
102A Brendan Leipsic RC 1.50 4.00
102B Brendan Leipsic VAR 2.00 5.00
103 Nikita Soshnikov RC 1.25 3.00
104 Justin Bailey RC 2.00 5.00
105 Esa Lindell RC 2.00 5.00
106 Dominik Simon RC 1.50 4.00
107 Pontus Aberg RC 2.50 6.00
108 Chris Bigras RC 1.50 4.00
109 Oliver Kylington RC 1.50 4.00
110 Mike Reilly RC 1.50 4.00
111 JC Lipon RC 2.00 5.00
112 Daniel Altshuller RC 1.50 4.00
113 Miles Wood RC 1.50 4.00
114 Ryan Pulock RC 2.00 5.00
115 Oliver Bjorkstrand RC 2.50 6.00
116 Sergey Tolchinsky RC 1.50 4.00
117 Oskar Sundqvist RC 2.00 5.00
118 Pavel Zacha RC 3.00 8.00
119A Hudson Fasching RC 2.00 5.00
119B Hudson Fasching VAR 2.50 6.00
120A Charlie Lindgren RC 3.00 8.00
120B Charlie Lindgren VAR 2.50 6.00
121 Keith Yandle .60 1.50
122 Oscar Lindberg .60 1.50
123 Jason Zucker 1.00 2.50
124A Taylor Hall 1.00 2.50
124B Taylor Hall VAR 1.00 2.50
125 Jason Demers .60 1.50
126 Thomas Vanek .75 2.00
127 Vladislav Namestnikov .60 1.50
128 Radko Gudas .60 1.50
129 Tomas Tatar .60 1.50
130 Jiri Hudler .75 2.00
131A P.K. Subban 1.25 3.00
131B P.K. Subban VAR 1.25 3.00
132 Zemgus Girgensons .75 2.00
133 Alexander Radulov 1.00 2.50
134 Anders Lee 1.00 2.50
135 Adam Henrique .75 2.00
136 Nino Niederreiter .60 1.50
137 Nikita Kucherov 2.00 5.00
138 Cam Ward 1.00 2.50
139 Andrei Vasilevskiy 1.50 4.00
140 Andrew Ladd .60 1.50
141 Shayne Gostisbehere 1.00 2.50
142 Nick Ritchie .60 1.50
143 Kyle Okposo .60 1.50
144 Anthony Duclair .75 2.00
145 Mats Zuccarello 1.00 2.50
146 Viktor Arvidsson .60 1.50
147 Jean-Gabriel Pageau .60 1.50
148 Frank Vatrano 1.00 2.50
149 Eric Staal 1.25 3.00
150 Victor Rask .60 1.50
151 Marc-Andre Fleury 2.00 5.00
152 Casey Cizikas .60 1.50
153 Jake Allen 1.00 2.50
154 Zach Parise 1.00 2.50
155 Connor Hellebuyck 2.00 5.00
156 Loui Eriksson .60 1.50
157 Jake Muzzin 1.00 2.50
158 Teuvo Teravainen 1.00 2.50
159 Artem Anisimov .60 1.50
160A Brent Burns 1.00 2.50
160B Brent Burns VAR 2.50 6.00
161A Patrik Laine RC 5.00 12.00
161B Patrik Laine VAR 6.00 15.00
162 Jakob Chychrun RC 4.00 10.00
163 Christian Dvorak RC 2.50 6.00
164 Thomas Chabot RC 4.00 10.00
165 Tyler Motte RC 2.00 5.00
166 Ivan Provorov RC 3.00 8.00
167 Zach Werenski RC 6.00 15.00
168 Kyle Connor RC 6.00 15.00
169 Jimmy Vesey RC 3.00 8.00
170 Mathew Barzal RC 6.00 15.00
171 Pavel Buchnevich RC 3.00 8.00
172 Lawson Crouse RC 1.50 4.00
173 Dylan Strome RC 5.00 12.00
174 Matthew Tkachuk RC 8.00 20.00
175A Mitch Marner RC 6.00 15.00
175B Mitch Marner VAR 8.00 20.00
176 Mikhail Sergachev RC 3.00 8.00
177 Julius Honka RC 2.00 5.00
178 Jesse Puljujarvi RC 4.00 10.00
179 Nick Schmaltz RC 2.50 6.00
180A Auston Matthews RC 12.00 30.00
180B Auston Matthews VAR 15.00 40.00

2016-17 Upper Deck Overtime Autographs

1 Connor McDavid A 50.00 125.00
2 Aaron Ekblad C 8.00 20.00
3 Ryan McDonagh A 6.00 15.00
4 Ondrej Palat C 5.00 12.00
5 John Gibson C 6.00 15.00
6 Brayden Schenn B 8.00 20.00
7 Claude Giroux A 10.00 25.00
8 James van Riemsdyk C 5.00 12.00
9 Ryan Nugent-Hopkins B 10.00 25.00
10 Semyon Varlamov C 6.00 15.00
11 Sam Reinhart C 12.00 30.00
12 Dion Phaneuf B 6.00 15.00
13 Michal Neuvirth B 6.00 15.00
14 Rick Nash B 8.00 20.00
16 Ryan Miller C 6.00 15.00
17 Brian Boyle C 4.00 10.00
18 Riley Sheahan C 4.00 10.00
19 Oscar Klefbom C 10.00 25.00
20 Gabriel Landeskog B 10.00 25.00
21 Alex Galchenyuk B 5.00 12.00
22 Aleksander Barkov B 12.00 30.00
23 Jamie Benn A 10.00 25.00
24 Noah Hanifin C 6.00 15.00
25 Jesper Fast C 4.00 10.00
26 Dylan Larkin C 8.00 20.00
27 Jacob Trouba A 8.00 20.00
28 Robby Fabbri C 4.00 10.00
29 Kevin Shattenkirk C 4.00 10.00
30 Matt Beleskey C 5.00 12.00
31 Seth Jones C 6.00 15.00
33 John Tavares B 12.00 30.00
34 Cory Schneider C 6.00 15.00
35 Jonathan Quick B 10.00 25.00
36 Joe Pavelski B 10.00 25.00
37 Marian Gaborik A 10.00 25.00
41 Luc Robitaille LEG A 15.00 40.00
42 Teemu Selanne LEG B 30.00 80.00
43 Steve Yzerman LEG A 40.00 100.00
44 Larry Robinson LEG C 10.00 25.00
45 Rob Blake LEG B 15.00 40.00
46 Glenn Hall LEG C 10.00 25.00
47 Trevor Linden LEG C 10.00 25.00
48 Wendel Clark LEG C 15.00 40.00
50 Wayne Gretzky LEG A 200.00 500.00
51 Pavel Zacha A 12.00 30.00
52 Jason Dickinson A 6.00 15.00
53 Trevor Carrick B 8.00 20.00
54 Chase De Leo B 8.00 20.00
55 Connor Brown B 12.00 30.00
56 Josh Morrissey B 20.00 50.00
57 Sonny Milano A 10.00 25.00
58 Kasperi Kapanen B 12.00 30.00
59 Anthony Mantha A 15.00 40.00
60 William Nylander A 30.00 80.00
62 Evander Kane 5.00 12.00
63 Aaron Ekblad 6.00 15.00
64 Brock Nelson 5.00 12.00
65 Morgan Rielly 5.00 12.00
68 Carl Hagelin 3.00 8.00
69 Matt Duchene 5.00 12.00
70 Nick Bjugstad 3.00 8.00
72 Tyler Toffoli 5.00 12.00
74 Jason Pominville 3.00 8.00
75 Richard Panik 3.00 8.00
76 Tyler Seguin 6.00 15.00
77 Patrick Marleau 5.00 12.00
78 Henrik Zetterberg 6.00 15.00
80 Sam Reinhart 10.00 25.00
81 Ryan Spooner 4.00 10.00
82 Robby Fabbri 3.00 8.00
83 Jakub Voracek 4.00 10.00
85 Leon Draisaitl 15.00 40.00
86 Sean Couturier 4.00 10.00
87 Tyler Johnson 3.00 8.00
88 Bobby Ryan 4.00 10.00
90 Brad Marchand 10.00 25.00
91 Boone Jenner 5.00 12.00
93 Kyle Palmieri 4.00 10.00
94 Johnny Boychuk 4.00 10.00
95 Alexander Wennberg 3.00 8.00
96 Kyle Turris 4.00 10.00
97 Derek Stepan 3.00 8.00
98 Carey Price 10.00 25.00
99 Bo Horvat 6.00 15.00
100 Ben Bishop 4.00 10.00
101 Michael Matheson 5.00 12.00
102 Brendan Leipsic 4.00 10.00
103 Nikita Soshnikov 3.00 8.00
104 Justin Bailey 5.00 12.00
105 Esa Lindell 5.00 12.00
106 Dominik Simon 4.00 10.00
107 Pontus Aberg 6.00 15.00
108 Chris Bigras 4.00 10.00
110 Mike Reilly 4.00 10.00
111 JC Lipon 5.00 12.00
112 Daniel Altshuller 4.00 10.00
113 Miles Wood 4.00 10.00
114 Ryan Pulock 5.00 12.00
115 Oliver Bjorkstrand 6.00 15.00
116 Sergey Tolchinsky 4.00 10.00
117 Oskar Sundqvist 5.00 12.00
118 Pavel Zacha 8.00 20.00
119 Hudson Fasching 5.00 12.00
120 Charlie Lindgren 8.00 20.00
121 Keith Yandle 3.00 8.00
122 Oscar Lindberg 3.00 8.00
123 Jason Zucker 5.00 12.00
124 Taylor Hall 5.00 12.00
125 Jason Demers 3.00 8.00
126 Thomas Vanek 4.00 10.00
127 Vladislav Namestnikov 3.00 8.00
128 Radko Gudas 3.00 8.00
129 Tomas Tatar 3.00 8.00
130 Jiri Hudler 4.00 10.00
131 P.K. Subban 6.00 15.00
132 Zemgus Girgensons 4.00 10.00
133 Alexander Radulov 5.00 12.00
134 Anders Lee 5.00 12.00
135 Adam Henrique 4.00 10.00
138 Cam Ward 5.00 12.00
139 Andrei Vasilevskiy 8.00 20.00
140 Andrew Ladd 3.00 8.00
142 Nick Ritchie 3.00 8.00
144 Anthony Duclair 4.00 10.00
145 Mats Zuccarello 5.00 12.00
146 Viktor Arvidsson 3.00 8.00
147 Jean-Gabriel Pageau 3.00 8.00
148 Frank Vatrano 5.00 12.00
149 Eric Staal 6.00 15.00
150 Victor Rask 3.00 8.00
151 Marc-Andre Fleury 10.00 25.00
152 Casey Cizikas 3.00 8.00
153 Jake Allen 5.00 12.00
154 Zach Parise 5.00 12.00
155 Connor Hellebuyck 10.00 25.00
156 Loui Eriksson 3.00 8.00
157 Jake Muzzin 5.00 12.00
158 Teuvo Teravainen 5.00 12.00
159 Artem Anisimov 3.00 8.00
160 Brent Burns 5.00 12.00
161 Patrik Laine 80.00 150.00
162 Jakob Chychrun 15.00 40.00
163 Christian Dvorak 10.00 25.00
164 Thomas Chabot 15.00 40.00
166 Ivan Provorov 12.00 30.00
167 Zach Werenski 25.00 60.00
168 Kyle Connor 25.00 60.00
169 Jimmy Vesey 12.00 30.00
170 Mathew Barzal 25.00 60.00
171 Pavel Buchnevich 12.00 30.00
172 Lawson Crouse 6.00 15.00
173 Dylan Strome 20.00 50.00
174 Matthew Tkachuk 30.00 80.00
176 Mikhail Sergachev 12.00 30.00
177 Julius Honka 8.00 20.00
178 Jesse Puljujarvi 15.00 40.00
179 Nick Schmaltz 10.00 25.00
180 Auston Matthews 200.00 500.00

2016-17 Upper Deck Overtime Next in Line

NL1 Auston Matthews 8.00 20.00
NL2 Mikhail Sergachev 2.00 5.00
NL3 Dylan Strome 3.00 8.00
NL4 Jimmy Vesey 2.00 5.00
NL5 Kasperi Kapanen 2.00 5.00
NL6 Sebastian Aho 4.00 10.00
NL7 Ivan Provorov 2.00 5.00
NL8 Christian Dvorak 1.50 4.00
NL9 Sonny Milano 1.50 4.00
NL10 Kyle Connor 4.00 10.00
NL11 Nick Schmaltz 1.50 4.00
NL12 Zach Werenski 4.00 10.00
NL13 Anthony Mantha 2.50 6.00
NL14 Mathew Barzal 4.00 10.00
NL15 Pavel Buchnevich 2.00 5.00
NL16 Brayden Point 3.00 8.00
NL17 Thomas Chabot 2.50 6.00
NL18 William Nylander 5.00 12.00
NL19 Jakob Chychrun 2.50 6.00
NL20 Travis Konecny 2.50 6.00
NL21 Josh Morrissey 3.00 8.00
NL22 Jesse Puljujarvi 2.50 6.00
NL23 Danton Heinen 1.00 2.50
NL24 Anthony Beauvillier 1.25 3.00
NL25 Lawson Crouse 1.00 2.50
NL26 Artturi Lehkonen 1.50 4.00
NL27 Tyler Motte 1.25 3.00
NL28 Matthew Tkachuk 5.00 12.00
NL29 Mitch Marner 4.00 10.00
NL30 Patrik Laine 3.00 8.00

2016-17 Upper Deck Overtime Optimum Performance

OP1 Jonathan Toews 2.00 5.00
OP2 Henrik Lundqvist 3.00 8.00
OP3 Connor McDavid 6.00 15.00
OP4 Anthony Mantha 2.50 6.00
OP5 Jamie Benn 1.25 3.00
OP6 Pavel Zacha 2.00 5.00
OP7 Aaron Ekblad 1.50 4.00
OP8 Carey Price 2.50 6.00
OP9 Brent Burns 1.25 3.00
OP10 Bobby Hull 2.50 6.00
OP11 John Tavares 2.00 5.00
OP12 Oliver Ekman-Larsson 1.25 3.00
OP13 Steven Stamkos 2.50 6.00
OP14 Kyle Palmieri 1.00 2.50
OP15 Mark Messier 2.50 6.00
OP16 Kyle Okposo .75 2.00
OP17 Teemu Selanne 2.50 6.00
OP18 P.K. Subban 1.50 4.00
OP19 Steve Yzerman 3.00 8.00
OP20 Wayne Gretzky 8.00 20.00

2016-17 Upper Deck Overtime Top Rated

TR1 Connor McDavid 8.00 20.00
TR2 Marc-Andre Fleury 3.00 8.00
TR3 Luc Robitaille 1.50 4.00
TR4 Anze Kopitar 2.50 6.00
TR5 Pekka Rinne 1.50 4.00
TR6 Joe Pavelski 2.00 5.00
TR7 Rick Nash 1.50 4.00
TR8 William Nylander 6.00 15.00
TR9 Anthony Mantha 3.00 8.00
TR10 Corey Perry 2.50 6.00
TR11 Max Pacioretty 1.50 4.00
TR12 Rob Blake 2.00 5.00
TR13 John Tavares 2.50 6.00
TR14 Sean Monahan 1.00 2.50
TR15 Kyle Turris 1.25 3.00
TR16 Mark Scheifele 2.50 6.00
TR17 Ryan Strome 1.50 4.00
TR18 Pavel Zacha 2.50 6.00
TR19 James van Riemsdyk 1.25 3.00
TR20 Wayne Gretzky 10.00 25.00

2017-18 Upper Deck Overtime

1 Mats Zuccarello 1.00 2.50
2 Bobby Ryan .75 2.00
3 Radek Faksa .75 2.00
4 Brady Skjei .75 2.00
5A Max Pacioretty 1.00 2.50
5B Max Pacioretty VAR 1.50 4.00
6 Evander Kane 1.00 2.50
7 Keith Yandle .60 1.50
8 Martin Jones .75 2.00
9 Mikael Granlund .75 2.00
10 Sebastian Aho 1.50 4.00
11 David Krejci 1.00 2.50
12 Seth Jones 1.00 2.50
13 Tyler Johnson .60 1.50
14 Zach Parise 1.00 2.50
15 Henrik Zetterberg 1.25 3.00
16 Brendan Gallagher 1.00 2.50
17 Aleksander Barkov 1.50 4.00
18 Jakub Voracek .75 2.00
19 Rick Nash 1.00 2.50
20 Marian Gaborik 1.00 2.50
21 Max Domi 1.00 2.50
22 Ryan Nugent-Hopkins 1.25 3.00
23 David Backes .60 1.50
24 John Tavares 1.50 4.00
25 Kyle Turris 1.00 2.50
26 Jonathan Quick 1.25 3.00
27 Nikolaj Ehlers 1.00 2.50
28 Viktor Arvidsson .60 1.50
29 Jake Muzzin 1.00 2.50
30 Timo Meier 1.00 2.50
31 Carl Hagelin .60 1.50
32 Jason Spezza 1.00 2.50
33 Joe Pavelski 1.25 3.00
34 Loui Eriksson .60 1.50
35 Anthony Mantha .75 2.00
36A Mitch Marner 1.50 4.00
36B Mitch Marner VAR 2.50 6.00
37 Pavel Buchnevich .75 2.00
38 Jonathan Huberdeau 1.25 3.00
39 Dion Phaneuf .75 2.00
40 Nathan MacKinnon 4.00 10.00
41 Bobby Orr 4.00 10.00
42 Mike Bossy 1.00 2.50
43 Larry Murphy .75 2.00
44 Pavel Bure 1.00 2.50
45A Steve Yzerman 2.50 6.00
45B Steve Yzerman VAR 4.00 10.00
46 Vladislav Kamenev RC 2.00 5.00
47A Alexander Nylander RC 3.00 8.00
47B Alexander Nylander VAR 4.00 10.00
48 Jack Roslovic RC 2.50 6.00
49 Jon Gillies RC 2.00 5.00
50 Evgeny Svechnikov RC 4.00 10.00
51 Ivan Barbashev RC 2.50 6.00
52A Adrian Kempe RC 4.00 10.00
52B Adrian Kempe VAR 5.00 12.00
53 Riley Barber RC 2.00 5.00
54 Samuel Morin RC 1.25 3.00
55 Nikita Scherbak RC 2.50 6.00
56 Christian Fischer RC 2.50 6.00
57 Gabriel Carlsson RC 1.50 4.00
58 J.T. Compher RC 2.00 5.00
59 Jonny Brodzinski RC 2.00 5.00
60A Brock Boeser RC 5.00 12.00
60B Brock Boeser VAR 6.00 15.00
61 Nikita Kucherov 2.00 5.00
62 Antti Raanta 1.00 2.50
63 Jason Zucker 1.00 2.50
64 Anders Lee 1.00 2.50
65 Brayden Point 1.25 3.00
66 Oscar Lindberg .75 2.00
67 Brandon Carlo .75 2.00
68 Evgeny Dadonov .60 1.50
69 Ryan Spooner .75 2.00
70 Cam Atkinson 1.00 2.50
71 Mark Stone 1.25 3.00
72 Alex Galchenyuk .60 1.50
73 Ivan Provorov .75 2.00
74 Sam Gagner .60 1.50
75 Luke Glendening .60 1.50
76 Anthony DeAngelo .60 1.50
77 Vladislav Namestnikov .60 1.50
78 Brandon Montour 1.25 3.00
79 Mark Scheifele 1.50 4.00
80 John Carlson 1.00 2.50
81 Victor Hedman 1.25 3.00
82 Artem Anisimov .60 1.50
83 Mark Giordano 1.00 2.50
84 Jonathan Drouin .75 2.00
85 Leon Draisaitl 3.00 8.00
86 Teuvo Teravainen 1.00 2.50
87 Reilly Smith 1.00 2.50
88 Brian Boyle .60 1.50
89 Sam Bennett 1.50 4.00
90 David Desharnais .60 1.50
91 Josh Anderson .75 2.00
92 Jim Howard 1.25 3.00
93 Joe Colborne .75 2.00
94 Connor Brown .75 2.00
95 Colin Miller .60 1.50
96 Phillip Danault 1.00 2.50
97 Matt Moulson .60 1.50
98 Devan Dubnyk .75 2.00
99 Tanner Pearson .75 2.00
100 Jake Guentzel 1.50 4.00
101 Jakob Forsbacka-Karlsson RC 2.00 5.00
102 Alex Tuch RC 5.00 12.00
103 Jordan Schmaltz RC 2.50 6.00
104 Mike Vecchione RC 1.50 4.00
105 Tyson Jost RC 4.00 10.00
106 Remi Elie RC 1.50 4.00
107 Valentin Zykov RC 2.00 5.00

108 Alex Nedeljkovic RC 3.00 8.00
109 Denis Gurianov RC 5.00 12.00
110 Charlie McAvoy RC 5.00 12.00
111 Peter Cehlarik RC 2.00 5.00
112 Colin White RC 2.50 6.00
113 Lucas Wallmark RC 2.00 5.00
114 John Hayden RC 1.50 4.00
115 Josh Ho-Sang RC 2.50 6.00
116 Nicolas Kerdiles RC 2.00 5.00
117 Robbie Russo RC 2.00 5.00
118 Andrew Poturalski RC 2.00 5.00
119 Eric Comrie RC 1.50 4.00
120 Clayton Keller RC 5.00 12.00
121 Ben Bishop .75 2.00
122 Andrew Shaw .60 1.50
123 Alexander Wennberg .60 1.50
124 Andreas Athanasiou 1.00 2.50
125 Matthew Tkachuk 2.00 5.00
126 Jason Pominville .60 1.50
127 Marc-Andre Fleury 2.00 5.00
128 Chris Kreider 1.25 3.00
129 Charlie Coyle 1.00 2.50
130 Adam Henrique .75 2.00
131 Alexander Radulov 1.00 2.50
132 Petr Mrazek 1.00 2.50
133 Kevin Fiala .75 2.00
134 Bo Horvat 1.25 3.00
135 Joel Eriksson Ek .75 2.00
136 Matt Murray 1.50 4.00
137 Cam Ward 1.00 2.50
138 Brayden Schenn 1.00 2.50
139 Mikhail Sergachev .75 2.00
140 Ryan Miller 1.00 2.50
141 Slater Koekkoek .60 1.50
142 Miles Wood .60 1.50
143 Aaron Ekblad 1.25 3.00
144 Frederik Andersen 1.25 3.00
145 Andrei Vasilevskiy 1.50 4.00
146 Jonathan Bernier .75 2.00
147 Riley Sheahan .60 1.50
148 Nick Foligno .75 2.00
149 Michael Grabner .60 1.50
150 Nick Schmaltz .75 2.00
151 Jacob de la Rose .60 1.50
152 Ryan Pulock .75 2.00
153 Casey Cizikas .60 1.50
154 Ryan Hartman .60 1.50
155 Olli Maatta .60 1.50
156 Robin Lehner .75 2.00
157 Tobias Rieder .60 1.50
158 Nail Yakupov .60 1.50
159 Sonny Milano .75 2.00
160 Matt Duchene 1.00 2.50
161 Nolan Patrick RC 5.00 12.00
162 Alex DeBrincat RC 6.00 15.00
163 Filip Chytil RC 2.50 6.00
164 Jake DeBrusk RC 6.00 15.00
165 Logan Brown RC 2.50 6.00
166 Owen Tippett RC 5.00 12.00
167 Jesper Bratt RC 5.00 12.00
168 Luke Kunin RC 2.50 6.00
169 Anders Bjork RC 3.00 8.00
170 Martin Necas RC 8.00 20.00
171 Pierre-Luc Dubois RC 4.00 10.00
172 Alex Kerfoot RC 5.00 12.00
173 Kailer Yamamoto RC 6.00 15.00
174 Calle Rosen RC 2.50 6.00
175 Will Butcher RC 3.00 8.00
176 Chris DiDomenico RC 2.00 5.00
177 Victor Mete RC 2.50 6.00
178 Tage Thompson RC 6.00 15.00
179 Haydn Fleury RC 2.50 6.00
180 Nico Hischier RC 8.00 20.00

2017-18 Upper Deck Overtime Gold

1 Mats Zuccarello AU 6.00 15.00
2 Bobby Ryan AU 5.00 12.00
3 Radek Faksa AU 5.00 12.00
4 Brady Skjei AU 5.00 12.00
5 Max Pacioretty AU 6.00 15.00
6 Evander Kane AU 6.00 15.00
7 Keith Yandle AU 4.00 10.00
8 Martin Jones AU 5.00 12.00
9 Mikael Granlund AU 5.00 12.00
10 Sebastian Aho AU 10.00 25.00
11 David Krejci AU 6.00 15.00
12 Seth Jones AU 6.00 15.00
13 Tyler Johnson AU 4.00 10.00
14 Zach Parise AU 6.00 15.00
15 Henrik Zetterberg AU 8.00 20.00
16 Brendan Gallagher AU 6.00 15.00
17 Aleksander Barkov AU 10.00 25.00
18 Jakub Voracek AU 5.00 12.00
19 Rick Nash AU 6.00 15.00
20 Marian Gaborik AU 6.00 15.00
21 Max Domi AU 6.00 15.00
22 Ryan Nugent-Hopkins AU 8.00 20.00
23 David Backes AU 4.00 10.00
24 John Tavares AU 10.00 25.00
25 Kyle Turris AU 6.00 15.00
26 Jonathan Quick AU 8.00 20.00
27 Nikolaj Ehlers AU 6.00 15.00
28 Viktor Arvidsson AU 4.00 10.00
29 Jake Muzzin AU 6.00 15.00
30 Timo Meier AU 6.00 15.00
31 Carl Hagelin AU 4.00 10.00
32 Jason Spezza AU 6.00 15.00
33 Joe Pavelski AU 8.00 20.00
34 Loui Eriksson AU 4.00 10.00
35 Anthony Mantha AU 5.00 12.00
36 Mitch Marner AU 10.00 25.00
37 Pavel Buchnevich AU 5.00 12.00
38 Jonathan Huberdeau AU 8.00 20.00
39 Dion Phaneuf AU 5.00 12.00
40 Nathan MacKinnon AU 25.00 60.00
41 Bobby Orr AU 25.00 60.00
42 Mike Bossy AU 6.00 15.00
43 Larry Murphy AU 5.00 12.00
44 Pavel Bure AU 6.00 15.00
45 Steve Yzerman AU 15.00 40.00
46 Vladislav Kamenev AU 6.00 15.00
47 Alexander Nylander AU 10.00 25.00
48 Jack Roslovic AU 8.00 20.00
49 Jon Gillies AU 6.00 15.00
50 Evgeny Svechnikov AU 12.00 30.00
51 Ivan Barbashev AU 8.00 20.00
52 Adrian Kempe AU 12.00 30.00
53 Riley Barber AU 6.00 15.00
54 Samuel Morin AU 4.00 10.00
61 Nikita Kucherov AU A 12.00 30.00
62 Antti Raanta AU A 6.00 15.00
63 Jason Zucker AU A 6.00 15.00
64 Anders Lee AU B 6.00 15.00
65 Brayden Point AU A 8.00 20.00
66 Oscar Lindberg AU B 5.00 12.00
67 Brandon Carlo AU B 5.00 12.00
68 Evgeny Dadonov AU B 4.00 10.00
70 Cam Atkinson AU B 6.00 15.00
71 Mark Stone AU A 8.00 20.00
72 Alex Galchenyuk AU A 4.00 10.00
73 Ivan Provorov AU B 5.00 12.00
74 Sam Gagner AU B 4.00 10.00
75 Luke Glendening AU B 4.00 10.00
76 Anthony DeAngelo AU B 4.00 10.00
77 Vladislav Namestnikov AU C 4.00 10.00
78 Brandon Montour AU B 8.00 20.00
79 Mark Scheifele AU B 10.00 25.00
80 John Carlson AU B 6.00 15.00
81 Victor Hedman AU A 8.00 20.00
82 Artem Anisimov AU B 4.00 10.00
83 Mark Giordano AU A 6.00 15.00
85 Leon Draisaitl AU A 20.00 50.00
86 Teuvo Teravainen AU A 6.00 15.00
87 Reilly Smith AU B 6.00 15.00
88 Brian Boyle AU B 4.00 10.00
89 Sam Bennett AU B 10.00 25.00
90 David Desharnais AU C 4.00 10.00
91 Josh Anderson AU C 5.00 12.00
92 Jim Howard AU A 8.00 20.00
93 Joe Colborne AU C 5.00 12.00
94 Connor Brown AU C 5.00 12.00
95 Colin Miller AU B 4.00 10.00
96 Phillip Danault AU C 6.00 15.00
97 Matt Moulson AU A 4.00 10.00
98 Devan Dubnyk AU A 5.00 12.00
99 Tanner Pearson AU B 5.00 12.00
100 Jake Guentzel AU B 10.00 25.00
102 Alex Tuch AU C 15.00 40.00
103 Jordan Schmaltz AU B 8.00 20.00
104 Mike Vecchione AU C 5.00 12.00
105 Tyson Jost AU C 12.00 30.00
107 Valentin Zykov AU C 6.00 15.00
109 Denis Gurianov AU D 15.00 40.00
110 Charlie McAvoy AU A 15.00 40.00
113 Lucas Wallmark AU C 6.00 15.00
115 Josh Ho-Sang AU C 8.00 20.00
118 Andrew Poturalski AU C 6.00 15.00
120 Clayton Keller AU C 15.00 40.00
121 Ben Bishop AU C 5.00 12.00
122 Andrew Shaw AU C 4.00 10.00
123 Alexander Wennberg AU C 4.00 10.00
124 Andreas Athanasiou AU D 6.00 15.00
125 Matthew Tkachuk AU C 12.00 30.00
126 Jason Pominville AU C 4.00 10.00
127 Marc-Andre Fleury AU B 12.00 30.00
128 Chris Kreider AU C 8.00 20.00
129 Charlie Coyle AU D 6.00 15.00
130 Adam Henrique AU C 5.00 12.00
131 Alexander Radulov AU C 6.00 15.00
132 Petr Mrazek AU C 6.00 15.00
133 Kevin Fiala AU D 5.00 12.00
134 Bo Horvat AU C 8.00 20.00
135 Joel Eriksson Ek AU D 5.00 12.00
136 Matt Murray AU C 10.00 25.00
137 Cam Ward AU B 6.00 15.00
138 Brayden Schenn AU B 6.00 15.00
139 Mikhail Sergachev AU C 5.00 12.00
140 Ryan Miller AU B 6.00 15.00
141 Slater Koekkoek AU E 4.00 10.00
142 Miles Wood AU A 4.00 10.00
143 Aaron Ekblad AU B 8.00 20.00
144 Frederik Andersen AU C 8.00 20.00
145 Andrei Vasilevskiy AU C 10.00 25.00
146 Jonathan Bernier AU C 5.00 12.00
147 Riley Sheahan AU D 4.00 10.00
149 Michael Grabner AU C 4.00 10.00
150 Nick Schmaltz AU D 5.00 12.00
151 Jacob de la Rose AU D 4.00 10.00
152 Ryan Pulock AU E 5.00 12.00
153 Casey Cizikas AU E 4.00 10.00
154 Ryan Hartman AU E 4.00 10.00
155 Olli Maatta AU C 4.00 10.00
156 Robin Lehner AU D 5.00 12.00
157 Tobias Rieder AU C 4.00 10.00
158 Nail Yakupov AU B 4.00 10.00
159 Sonny Milano AU C 5.00 12.00
160 Matt Duchene AU C 6.00 15.00
162 Alex DeBrincat AU 15.00 40.00
166 Owen Tippett AU 12.00 30.00
167 Jesper Bratt AU 12.00 30.00
168 Luke Kunin AU 6.00 15.00
169 Anders Bjork AU 8.00 20.00
171 Pierre-Luc Dubois AU 10.00 25.00
175 Will Butcher AU 8.00 20.00
176 Chris DiDomenico AU 5.00 12.00
177 Victor Mete AU 6.00 15.00
178 Tage Thompson AU 15.00 40.00

2017-18 Upper Deck Overtime Red

36 Mitch Marner 12.00 30.00
45 Steve Yzerman 25.00 60.00
47 Alexander Nylander 12.00 30.00
60 Brock Boeser 12.00 30.00

2017-18 Upper Deck Overtime A-1

A11 Mark Messier 1.00 2.50
A12 Henrik Lundqvist 1.25 3.00
A13 Leon Draisaitl 1.50 4.00
A14 Luc Robitaille .50 1.25
A15 Nicklas Lidstrom .50 1.25
A16 Mark Stone .60 1.50
A17 Jonathan Quick .60 1.50
A18 Alexander Ovechkin 2.00 5.00
A19 Brock Boeser 1.25 3.00
A110 Nikita Kucherov 1.00 2.50
A111 Carey Price 1.00 2.50
A112 Pat LaFontaine .50 1.25
A113 Tyler Seguin .60 1.50
A114 Vladimir Tarasenko .60 1.50
A115 Bobby Orr 2.00 5.00
A116 John Tavares .75 2.00
A117 Steven Stamkos 1.00 2.50
A118 Martin Brodeur 1.25 3.00
A119 Joe Thornton .75 2.00
A120 Clayton Keller 1.25 3.00

2017-18 Upper Deck Overtime A-1 Red

*RED/25: 1.5X TO 4X BASIC INSERTS
A111 Carey Price 12.00 30.00

2017-18 Upper Deck Overtime Ice Cold

IC1 Connor McDavid 8.00 20.00
IC2 Anze Kopitar 2.50 6.00
IC3 Ryan McDonagh 1.00 2.50
IC4 Jamie Benn 1.50 4.00
IC5 Jonathan Quick 2.00 5.00
IC6 Max Pacioretty 1.50 4.00
IC7 Frank Mahovlich 1.50 4.00
IC8 Zach Parise 1.50 4.00
IC9 Mitch Marner 2.50 6.00
IC10 Pat LaFontaine 1.50 4.00
IC11 Henrik Zetterberg 2.00 5.00
IC12 Roman Josi 1.50 4.00
IC13 Taylor Hall 1.50 4.00
IC14 Nikita Kucherov 3.00 8.00
IC15 Guy Lafleur 2.00 5.00
IC16 Patrick Kane 3.00 8.00
IC17 Ryan Kesler 1.50 4.00
IC18 Vladimir Tarasenko 2.00 5.00
IC19 John Tavares 2.50 6.00
IC20 Joe Pavelski 2.00 5.00

2017-18 Upper Deck Overtime Next In Line

NL1 Nico Hischier 1.50 4.00
NL2 Vadim Shipachyov .60 1.50
NL3 Brock Boeser 1.25 3.00
NL4 Pierre-Luc Dubois .75 2.00
NL5 Alex DeBrincat 1.25 3.00
NL6 Owen Tippett 1.00 2.50
NL7 Kailer Yamamoto 1.25 3.00
NL8 Logan Brown .50 1.25
NL9 Victor Mete .50 1.25
NL10 Filip Chytil .50 1.25
NL11 Josh Ho-Sang .60 1.50
NL12 Anders Bjork .60 1.50
NL13 Tucker Poolman .40 1.00
NL14 Tyson Jost 1.00 2.50
NL15 Jake DeBrusk 1.25 3.00
NL16 Martin Necas 1.50 4.00
NL17 Tage Thompson 1.25 3.00
NL18 Charlie McAvoy 1.25 3.00
NL19 Clayton Keller 1.25 3.00
NL20 Nolan Patrick 1.00 2.50

2017-18 Upper Deck Overtime Next In Line Red

NL1 Nico Hischier 10.00 25.00
NL3 Brock Boeser 30.00 80.00
NL7 Kailer Yamamoto 8.00 20.00

2018-19 Upper Deck Overtime

1 Mark Scheifele 1.00 2.50
2 Kyle Palmieri .50 1.25
3 Patrick Marleau .60 1.50
4 Adam Henrique .50 1.25
5 Anders Lee .50 1.25
6 David Krejci .60 1.50
7 Jonathan Huberdeau .75 2.00
8 Nikolaj Ehlers .60 1.50
9 Brayden Point .75 2.00
10 Malcolm Subban .50 1.25
11 Brady Skjei .50 1.25
12 Timo Meier .60 1.50
13 Jake Guentzel 1.00 2.50
14 Matt Murray .60 1.50
15 Andrew Ladd .40 1.00
16 Carl Hagelin .40 1.00
17 Evander Kane .60 1.50
18 Pavel Buchnevich .50 1.25
19 Jake Muzzin .60 1.50
20 Derek Stepan .40 1.00
21 Tanner Pearson .50 1.25
22 Jesse Puljujarvi .60 1.50
23 David Backes .40 1.00
24 Ben Bishop .50 1.25
25 Tyler Johnson .40 1.00
26 Charlie Coyle .60 1.50
27 Oscar Klefbom .50 1.25
28 Olli Maatta .40 1.00
29 Kevin Fiala .50 1.25
30 Mark Giordano .60 1.50
31 Martin Jones .50 1.25
32 Matthew Tkachuk 1.25 3.00
33 Seth Jones .60 1.50
34 Andrew Shaw .40 1.00
35 Oscar Lindberg .50 1.25
36 Jason Spezza .60 1.50
37 Jake Allen .60 1.50
38 Andreas Athanasiou .50 1.25
39 Clayton Keller .75 2.00
40 Cam Atkinson .60 1.50
41 Paul Coffey .60 1.50
42 Darryl Sittler .75 2.00
43 Bobby Orr 2.50 6.00
44 Mike Bossy .60 1.50
45 Patrick Roy 1.50 4.00
46 Eeli Tolvanen RC 1.25 3.00
47 Jordan Greenway RC 1.00 2.50
48 Dylan Gambrell RC 1.00 2.50
49 Michael Dal Colle RC 1.00 2.50
50 Morgan Klimchuk RC 1.00 2.50
51 Noah Juulsen RC 1.00 2.50
52 Oskar Lindblom RC 1.50 4.00
53 Travis Dermott RC 1.50 4.00
54 Sami Niku RC .75 2.00
55 Adam Gaudette RC 1.50 4.00
56 Joe Hicketts RC 1.00 2.50
57 Henrik Borgstrom RC 1.50 4.00
58 Dylan Sikura RC 1.25 3.00
59 Lias Andersson RC 1.50 4.00
60 Casey Mittelstadt RC 2.00 5.00
61 Anthony Mantha .50 1.25
62 Shea Theodore .75 2.00
63 John Carlson .60 1.50
64 Joe Pavelski .75 2.00
65 Zach Werenski 1.00 2.50
66 Ryan Spooner .50 1.25
67 Kailer Yamamoto .60 1.50
68 Noah Hanifin .60 1.50
69 Mikko Rantanen 1.50 4.00
70 Jakub Vrana .60 1.50
71 Chris Kreider .75 2.00
72 Jonathan Drouin .50 1.25
73 Jake Virtanen .50 1.25
74 Vincent Trocheck .60 1.50
75 Reilly Smith .60 1.50
76 Erik Haula .40 1.00
77 Cory Schneider .60 1.50
78A Mitch Marner 1.00 2.50
78B Mitch Marner VAR 3.00 8.00
79 Andrew Copp .40 1.00
80 Kevin Hayes .50 1.25
81 Radek Faksa .50 1.25
82 Jonathan Bernier .50 1.25
83A Patrik Laine VAR 2.50 6.00
83B Patrik Laine .75 2.00
84 Cam Ward .60 1.50
85 Joe Morrow .50 1.25
86 Ivan Provorov .50 1.25
87 Tobias Rieder .40 1.00
88 Miles Wood .40 1.00
89 Chandler Stephenson .50 1.25
90 Sam Bennett 1.00 2.50
91 Pavel Zacha .50 1.25
92 Pontus Aberg .40 1.00
93 Kevin Labanc .40 1.00
94 Mikael Granlund .50 1.25
95 Anders Bjork .50 1.25
96 Adrian Kempe .60 1.50
97 Aaron Ekblad .75 2.00
98 Tyler Toffoli .60 1.50
99 Filip Chytil .50 1.25
100A Evgeny Kuznetsov .75 2.00
100B Evgeny Kuznetsov VAR 2.50 6.00
101 Brady Tkachuk RC 3.00 8.00
102 Michael Rasmussen RC 1.25 3.00
103 Kristian Vesalainen RC 1.25 3.00
104 Dillon Dube RC 1.25 3.00
105 Henri Jokiharju RC .75 2.00
106 Maxime Comtois RC 1.00 2.50
107 Ryan Donato RC 1.50 4.00
108 Brett Howden RC 1.25 3.00
109 Evan Bouchard RC 2.50 6.00
110A Andrei Svechnikov RC 2.50 6.00
110B Andrei Svechnikov VAR RC 6.00 15.00
111 Roope Hintz RC 2.50 6.00
112 Juuso Valimaki RC 1.00 2.50
113 Jordan Kyrou RC 2.00 5.00
114 Miro Heiskanen RC 2.50 6.00
115A Rasmus Dahlin RC 2.50 6.00
115B Rasmus Dahlin VAR RC 6.00 15.00
116 Mathieu Joseph RC 1.25 3.00
117 Sam Steel RC 1.00 2.50
118 Robert Thomas RC 2.00 5.00
119 Jesperi Kotkaniemi RC 2.00 5.00
120A Elias Pettersson RC 3.00 8.00
120B Elias Pettersson VAR RC 8.00 20.00
121 Jimmy Vesey .50 1.25
122 Zach Hyman 1.00 2.50
123 Colin Miller .40 1.00
124 Luke Kunin .40 1.00
125 Artemi Panarin 1.25 3.00
126 Alexander Wennberg .40 1.00
127 Mats Zuccarello .60 1.50
128 Slater Koekkoek .40 1.00
129 Erik Gudbranson .40 1.00
130 Sean Monahan .40 1.00
131 Joonas Donskoi .40 1.00
132 Jack Campbell .60 1.50
133 Travis Hamonic .50 1.25
134 Alexander Radulov .60 1.50
135 Ondrej Palat .50 1.25
136 Robby Fabbri .40 1.00
137 Victor Rask .40 1.00
138 Ryan Johansen .50 1.25
139 Travis Sanheim .40 1.00
140 Artturi Lehkonen .50 1.25
141 Vladislav Namestnikov .40 1.00
142 Juuse Saros .75 2.00
143 Jason Dickinson .40 1.00
144 Tyler Motte .40 1.00
145 Pierre-Edouard Bellemare .40 1.00
146 Gustav Nyquist .40 1.00
147 Connor Brown .50 1.25
148 Will Butcher .50 1.25
149 Andrew Cogliano .40 1.00
150 Devan Dubnyk .50 1.25
151 James Neal .40 1.00
152 Jesper Bratt .60 1.50
153 Vladimir Tarasenko .75 2.00
154 Conor Sheary .60 1.50
155 Alex Kerfoot .50 1.25
156 Ryan Miller .60 1.50
157 Evgenii Dadonov .40 1.00
158 Boone Jenner .60 1.50
159 Ryan Ellis .50 1.25
160 William Karlsson .75 2.00
161 Isac Lundestrom RC .75 2.00
162 Kiefer Sherwood RC .75 2.00
163 Maxime Lajoie RC 1.50 4.00
164 Sam Steel RC 1.00 2.50
165 Troy Terry RC 1.50 4.00
166 Warren Foegele RC 1.00 2.50
167 Ethan Bear RC 1.50 4.00
168 Jaret Anderson-Dolan RC .75 2.00
169 Antti Suomela RC .75 2.00
170 Ilya Samsonov RC 2.00 5.00
171 Daniel Brickley RC 1.00 2.50
172 Filip Hronek RC 1.00 2.50
173 Spencer Foo RC .75 2.00
174 Victor Ejdsell RC .75 2.00
175 Mikhail Vorobyev RC .75 2.00
176 Cooper Marody RC 1.00 2.50
177 Andreas Johnsson RC 1.25 3.00
178 Par Lindholm RC 1.00 2.50
179 Jake Bean RC 1.00 2.50
180 Carter Hart RC 2.00 5.00

2018-19 Upper Deck Overtime Gold

1 Mark Scheifele AU A 10.00 25.00
2 Kyle Palmieri AU A 5.00 12.00
3 Patrick Marleau AU A 6.00 15.00
4 Adam Henrique AU A 5.00 12.00
5 Anders Lee AU A 5.00 12.00
6 David Krejci AU A 6.00 15.00
7 Jonathan Huberdeau AU A 8.00 20.00
8 Nikolaj Ehlers AU A 6.00 15.00
9 Brayden Point AU A 8.00 20.00
10 Malcolm Subban AU A 5.00 12.00
11 Brady Skjei AU A 5.00 12.00
12 Timo Meier AU A 6.00 15.00
13 Jake Guentzel AU A 10.00 25.00
14 Matt Murray AU A 6.00 15.00
15 Andrew Ladd AU A 4.00 10.00
16 Carl Hagelin AU A 4.00 10.00
17 Evander Kane AU A 6.00 15.00
18 Pavel Buchnevich AU A 5.00 12.00
19 Jake Muzzin AU A 6.00 15.00
20 Derek Stepan AU A 4.00 10.00
21 Tanner Pearson AU A 5.00 12.00
22 Jesse Puljujarvi AU A 6.00 15.00
23 David Backes AU A 4.00 10.00
24 Ben Bishop AU A 5.00 12.00
25 Tyler Johnson AU A 4.00 10.00
26 Charlie Coyle AU A 6.00 15.00
27 Oscar Klefbom AU A 5.00 12.00
28 Olli Maatta AU A 4.00 10.00
29 Kevin Fiala AU A 5.00 12.00
30 Mark Giordano AU A 6.00 15.00
31 Martin Jones AU A 5.00 12.00
32 Matthew Tkachuk AU A 12.00 30.00
33 Seth Jones AU A 6.00 15.00
34 Andrew Shaw AU A 4.00 10.00
35 Oscar Lindberg AU A 5.00 12.00
36 Jason Spezza AU A 6.00 15.00
37 Jake Allen AU A 6.00 15.00
38 Andreas Athanasiou AU B 5.00 12.00
40 Cam Atkinson AU A 6.00 15.00
41 Paul Coffey AU A 6.00 15.00
42 Darryl Sittler AU A 8.00 20.00
43 Bobby Orr AU A 25.00 60.00
44 Mike Bossy AU A 6.00 15.00
45 Patrick Roy AU A 15.00 40.00
46 Eeli Tolvanen AU B 12.00 30.00
47 Jordan Greenway AU C 6.00 15.00
48 Dylan Gambrell AU C 6.00 15.00
49 Michael Dal Colle AU C 6.00 15.00
50 Morgan Klimchuk AU C 6.00 15.00
51 Noah Juulsen AU B 6.00 15.00
52 Oskar Lindblom AU C 10.00 25.00
53 Travis Dermott AU C 10.00 25.00
54 Sami Niku AU C 5.00 12.00
55 Adam Gaudette AU C 10.00 25.00
57 Henrik Borgstrom AU C 10.00 25.00
58 Dylan Sikura AU C 8.00 20.00
60 Casey Mittelstadt AU B 12.00 30.00
61 Anthony Mantha AU 5.00 12.00
62 Shea Theodore AU 8.00 20.00
63 John Carlson AU 6.00 15.00
64 Joe Pavelski AU 8.00 20.00
65 Zach Werenski AU 10.00 25.00
66 Ryan Spooner AU 5.00 12.00
67 Kailer Yamamoto AU 6.00 15.00
68 Noah Hanifin AU 6.00 15.00
69 Mikko Rantanen AU 15.00 40.00
70 Jakub Vrana AU 6.00 15.00
71 Chris Kreider AU 8.00 20.00
72 Jonathan Drouin AU 5.00 12.00
73 Jake Virtanen AU 5.00 12.00
74 Vincent Trocheck AU 6.00 15.00
75 Reilly Smith AU 6.00 15.00
76 Erik Haula AU 4.00 10.00
77 Cory Schneider AU 6.00 15.00
78 Mitch Marner AU 10.00 25.00
79 Andrew Copp AU 4.00 10.00
80 Kevin Hayes AU 5.00 12.00
81 Radek Faksa AU 5.00 12.00
82 Jonathan Bernier AU 5.00 12.00
83 Patrik Laine AU 8.00 20.00
84 Cam Ward AU 6.00 15.00
85 Joe Morrow AU 5.00 12.00
86 Ivan Provorov AU 5.00 12.00
87 Tobias Rieder AU 4.00 10.00
88 Miles Wood AU 4.00 10.00
89 Chandler Stephenson AU 5.00 12.00
90 Sam Bennett AU 10.00 25.00
91 Pavel Zacha AU 5.00 12.00
92 Pontus Aberg AU 4.00 10.00
93 Kevin Labanc AU 4.00 10.00
94 Mikael Granlund AU 5.00 12.00
95 Anders Bjork AU 5.00 12.00
96 Adrian Kempe AU 6.00 15.00
97 Aaron Ekblad AU 8.00 20.00
98 Tyler Toffoli AU 6.00 15.00
99 Filip Chytil AU 5.00 12.00
100 Evgeny Kuznetsov AU 8.00 20.00
101 Brady Tkachuk AU 20.00 50.00
102 Michael Rasmussen AU 8.00 20.00
103 Kristian Vesalainen AU 8.00 20.00
104 Dillon Dube AU 8.00 20.00
105 Henri Jokiharju AU 5.00 12.00
106 Maxime Comtois AU 6.00 15.00
107 Ryan Donato AU 10.00 25.00
108 Brett Howden AU 8.00 20.00
109 Evan Bouchard AU 15.00 40.00
110 Andrei Svechnikov AU 15.00 40.00
111 Roope Hintz AU 15.00 40.00
112 Juuso Valimaki AU 6.00 15.00
113 Jordan Kyrou AU 20.00 50.00
114 Miro Heiskanen AU 15.00 40.00
115 Rasmus Dahlin AU 15.00 40.00
116 Mathieu Joseph AU 8.00 20.00
117 Sam Steel AU 6.00 15.00
118 Robert Thomas AU 12.00 30.00
119 Jesperi Kotkaniemi AU 12.00 30.00
120 Elias Pettersson AU 200.00 300.00
121 Jimmy Vesey AU B 5.00 12.00
122 Zach Hyman AU C 10.00 25.00
123 Colin Miller AU B 4.00 10.00
124 Luke Kunin AU C 4.00 10.00
125 Artemi Panarin AU A 12.00 30.00
126 Alexander Wennberg AU B 4.00 10.00
127 Mats Zuccarello AU B 6.00 15.00
128 Slater Koekkoek AU B 4.00 10.00
129 Erik Gudbranson AU C 4.00 10.00
130 Sean Monahan AU A 4.00 10.00
131 Joonas Donskoi AU B 4.00 10.00
132 Jack Campbell AU C 6.00 15.00
133 Travis Hamonic AU C 5.00 12.00
134 Alexander Radulov AU A 6.00 15.00
135 Ondrej Palat AU A 5.00 12.00
136 Robby Fabbri AU B 4.00 10.00
137 Victor Rask AU A 4.00 10.00
138 Ryan Johansen AU B 5.00 12.00
139 Travis Sanheim AU C 4.00 10.00
140 Artturi Lehkonen AU C 5.00 12.00
141 Vladislav Namestnikov AU B 4.00 10.00
142 Juuse Saros AU C 8.00 20.00
143 Jason Dickinson AU C 4.00 10.00
145 Pierre-Edouard Bellemare AU B 4.00 10.00
146 Gustav Nyquist AU A 4.00 10.00
147 Connor Brown AU C 5.00 12.00
148 Will Butcher AU C 5.00 12.00
149 Andrew Cogliano AU C 4.00 10.00
150 Devan Dubnyk AU A 5.00 12.00
151 James Neal AU A 4.00 10.00
152 Jesper Bratt AU C 6.00 15.00
153 Vladimir Tarasenko AU A 8.00 20.00
154 Conor Sheary AU B 6.00 15.00
155 Alex Kerfoot AU C 5.00 12.00
156 Ryan Miller AU A 6.00 15.00
157 Evgenii Dadonov AU B 4.00 10.00
158 Boone Jenner AU B 6.00 15.00
159 Ryan Ellis AU B 5.00 12.00
160 William Karlsson AU B 8.00 20.00
161 Isac Lundestrom AU B 5.00 12.00
162 Kiefer Sherwood AU B 5.00 12.00
163 Maxime Lajoie AU B 10.00 25.00
164 Sam Steel AU B 6.00 15.00
165 Troy Terry AU B 10.00 25.00
166 Warren Foegele AU B 6.00 15.00
167 Ethan Bear AU B 10.00 25.00
168 Jaret Anderson-Dolan AU B 5.00 12.00
169 Antti Suomela AU B 5.00 12.00
171 Daniel Brickley AU B 6.00 15.00
172 Filip Hronek AU B 6.00 15.00
173 Spencer Foo AU B 5.00 12.00
174 Victor Ejdsell AU B 5.00 12.00
175 Mikhail Vorobyev AU B 5.00 12.00
176 Cooper Marody AU B 6.00 15.00
177 Andreas Johnsson AU A 8.00 20.00
178 Par Lindholm AU B 6.00 15.00
179 Jake Bean AU B 6.00 15.00

2018-19 Upper Deck Overtime Lights Out

LO1 Patrik Laine 1.00 2.50
LO2 Brent Burns .75 2.00
LO3 Patrick Marleau .75 2.00
LO4 Mikko Rantanen 2.00 5.00
LO5 Andrei Svechnikov 2.00 5.00
LO6 Artemi Panarin 1.50 4.00
LO7 Pavel Datsyuk 1.25 3.00
LO8 Nikita Kucherov 1.50 4.00
LO9 Jamie Benn .75 2.00
LO10 Bobby Orr 3.00 8.00
LO11 Mitch Marner 1.25 3.00
LO12 Carey Price 1.50 4.00
LO13 Sean Monahan .50 1.25
LO14 Mike Bossy .75 2.00
LO15 Patrick Roy 2.00 5.00
LO16 Joe Thornton 1.25 3.00
LO17 Henrik Lundqvist 2.00 5.00
LO18 Joe Pavelski 1.00 2.50
LO19 Pekka Rinne .75 2.00
LO20 Elias Pettersson 2.50 6.00

2018-19 Upper Deck Overtime Next In Line

NL1 Elias Pettersson 3.00 8.00
NL2 Kristian Vesalainen 1.25 3.00
NL3 Ryan Donato 1.50 4.00
NL4 Michael Rasmussen 1.25 3.00
NL5 Brady Tkachuk 3.00 8.00
NL6 Jordan Kyrou 2.00 5.00
NL7 Dillon Dube 1.25 3.00
NL8 Brett Howden 1.25 3.00
NL9 Evan Bouchard 2.50 6.00
NL10 Andrei Svechnikov 2.50 6.00
NL11 Henri Jokiharju .75 2.00
NL12 Sam Steel 1.00 2.50
NL13 Maxime Comtois 1.00 2.50
NL14 Jordan Greenway 1.00 2.50
NL15 Jaret Anderson-Dolan .75 2.00
NL16 Eeli Tolvanen 2.00 5.00
NL17 Robert Thomas 2.00 5.00
NL18 Miro Heiskanen 2.50 6.00
NL19 Jesperi Kotkaniemi 2.00 5.00
NL20 Casey Mittelstadt 2.00 5.00

2018-19 Upper Deck Overtime Shootout

SO1 Jonathan Toews 2.00 5.00
SO2 Nikita Kucherov 2.50 6.00
SO3 Mikko Rantanen 3.00 8.00
SO4 Brayden Schenn 1.25 3.00
SO5 Mark Scheifele 2.00 5.00
SO6 Mats Zuccarello 1.25 3.00
SO7 Kevin Labanc .75 2.00
SO8 Evgenii Dadonov .75 2.00
SO9 Aleksander Barkov 2.00 5.00
SO10 Anze Kopitar 2.00 5.00
SO11 William Nylander 2.50 6.00
SO12 Evgeni Malkin 2.50 6.00
SO13 Brayden Point 1.50 4.00
SO14 Alexander Radulov 1.25 3.00
SO15 Patrick Marleau 1.25 3.00
SO16 Mika Zibanejad 1.50 4.00
SO17 Mikael Granlund 1.00 2.50
SO18 Sam Gagner .75 2.00
SO19 Mitch Marner 2.00 5.00
SO20 Alexander Ovechkin 5.00 12.00

2019-20 Upper Deck Overtime

*BLUE.VETS: .6X TO 1.5X BASIC CARDS
*BLUE.RC: .5X TO 1.25X BASIC CARDS
*RED.VET/99: 1.25X TO 3X BASIC CARDS
1 Teuvo Teravainen .60 1.50
2 Robby Fabbri .40 1.00
3 David Krejci .60 1.50
4 Victor Rask .40 1.00
5 Lias Andersson .50 1.25
6 Anders Bjork .40 1.00
7 Reilly Smith .60 1.50
8 Anders Lee .50 1.25
9 Colton Parayko .50 1.25
10 Jake DeBrusk .60 1.50
11 Matt Dumba .40 1.00
12 Tyson Jost .50 1.25
13 Shea Theodore .75 2.00
14 Jimmy Vesey .50 1.25
15 Filip Chytil .50 1.25
16 Kyle Turris .50 1.25
17 Timo Meier .60 1.50
18 Travis Hamonic .40 1.00
19 Seth Jones .60 1.50
20 Jason Spezza .60 1.50
21 Chris Kreider .75 2.00
22 Alexander Wennberg .40 1.00
23 Ryan Hartman .40 1.00
24 Joonas Donskoi .40 1.00
25 Olli Maatta .40 1.00
26 Ryan Johansen .50 1.25
27 Tyler Toffoli .60 1.50
28 Casey Mittelstadt .60 1.50
29 Max Pacioretty .60 1.50
30 Petr Mrazek .60 1.50
31 Carl Hagelin .40 1.00
32 Colin Miller .40 1.00
33 Aaron Ekblad .75 2.00
34 Ryan Ellis .50 1.25
35 David Backes .40 1.00
36 Adrian Kempe .60 1.50
37 John Carlson .60 1.50
38 Andrew Shaw .40 1.00
39 Evander Kane 1.00 2.50
40 Anthony DeAngelo RC .60 1.50
41 Alexandre Texier RC 1.00 2.50
42 Dante Fabbro RC 1.00 2.50
43 Erik Brannstrom RC 1.00 2.50
44 Zack MacEwen RC .75 2.00
45 Taro Hirose RC 1.00 2.50
46 Ryan Poehling RC 1.50 4.00
47 Trent Frederic RC 1.00 2.50
48 Rem Pitlick RC 1.00 2.50
49 Zach Senyshyn RC 1.00 2.50
50 Quinn Hughes RC 5.00 12.00
51 Max Jones RC 1.00 2.50
52 Rudolfs Balcers RC 1.00 2.50
53 Philippe Myers RC .75 2.00
54 Brady Keeper RC 1.00 2.50
55 Filip Zadina RC 1.50 4.00
56 Carl Grundstrom RC 1.00 2.50
57 Joey Daccord RC 2.00 5.00
58 Kaden Fulcher RC 1.00 2.50
59 Libor Hajek RC .75 2.00
60 Cale Makar RC 5.00 12.00
61 Anthony Cirelli .50 1.25
62 Brian Dumoulin .40 1.00
63 Nick Foligno .50 1.25
64 Malcolm Subban .50 1.25
65 Conor Sheary .60 1.50
66 Pavel Buchnevich .50 1.25
67 Viktor Arvidsson .40 1.00
68 Zach Hyman 1.00 2.50
69 Christian Dvorak .50 1.25
70 Devan Dubnyk .50 1.25
71 Tyler Johnson .40 1.00
72 Ryan Murray .50 1.25
73 Ivan Provorov .50 1.25
74 Jacob Trouba .50 1.25
75 Jakob Chychrun .60 1.50
76 Kevin Hayes .50 1.25
77 Brandon Montour .75 2.00
78 Dmitry Orlov .60 1.50
79 Martin Jones .50 1.25
80 Ryan Dzingel .50 1.25
81 Kyle Palmieri .50 1.25
82 Mikhail Sergachev .50 1.25
83 Will Butcher .50 1.25
84 Keith Yandle .40 1.00
85 Gustav Nyquist .40 1.00
86 Philipp Grubauer .60 1.50
87 Danton Heinen .50 1.25
88 Anze Kopitar 1.00 2.50
89 Zach Werenski 1.00 2.50
90 Boone Jenner .60 1.50
91 Vincent Trocheck .60 1.50
92 Micheal Ferland .40 1.00
93 Luke Kunin .40 1.00
94 Vladislav Namestnikov .40 1.00
95 Jaccob Slavin .50 1.25
96 Kasperi Kapanen .50 1.25
97 Sean Monahan .40 1.00
98 Andrew Copp .40 1.00
99 Jeff Carter .50 1.25
100 Kevin Labanc .40 1.00
101 Kirby Dach RC 2.00 5.00
102 Dominik Kubalik RC 2.00 5.00
103 Rasmus Sandin RC 1.50 4.00
104 Elvis Merzlikins RC 2.00 5.00
105 Conor Timmins RC 1.00 2.50
106 Adam Fox RC 2.50 6.00
107 Jesper Boqvist RC .75 2.00
108 Barrett Hayton RC 2.00 5.00
109 Mario Ferraro RC .75 2.00
110 Kaapo Kakko RC 1.50 4.00
111 Nicolas Hague RC 1.00 2.50
112 Oliver Wahlstrom RC 1.50 4.00
113 Tobias Bjornfot RC 1.00 2.50
114 Emil Bemstrom RC 1.00 2.50
115 Nikita Gusev RC 1.50 4.00
116 Cale Fleury RC 1.25 3.00
117 Ville Heinola RC 1.25 3.00
118 Noah Dobson RC 2.50 6.00
119 Cody Glass RC 1.50 4.00
120 Jack Hughes RC 5.00 12.00

2019-20 Upper Deck Overtime Autographs Gold

1 Teuvo Teravainen 6.00 15.00
2 Robby Fabbri 4.00 10.00
3 David Krejci 6.00 15.00
4 Victor Rask 4.00 10.00
5 Lias Andersson 5.00 12.00
6 Anders Bjork 4.00 10.00
7 Reilly Smith 6.00 15.00
8 Anders Lee 5.00 12.00
9 Colton Parayko 5.00 12.00
10 Jake DeBrusk 6.00 15.00

11 Matt Dumba 4.00 10.00
12 Tyson Jost 5.00 12.00
13 Shea Theodore 8.00 20.00
14 Jimmy Vesey 5.00 12.00
15 Filip Chytil 5.00 12.00
16 Kyle Turris 5.00 12.00
17 Timo Meier 6.00 15.00
18 Travis Hamonic 4.00 10.00
19 Seth Jones 6.00 15.00
20 Jason Spezza 6.00 15.00
21 Chris Kreider 8.00 20.00
22 Alexander Wennberg 4.00 10.00
23 Ryan Hartman 4.00 10.00
24 Joonas Donskoi 4.00 10.00
25 Olli Maatta 4.00 10.00
26 Ryan Johansen 5.00 12.00
27 Tyler Toffoli 6.00 15.00
28 Casey Mittelstadt 6.00 15.00
29 Max Pacioretty 6.00 15.00
30 Petr Mrazek 6.00 15.00
31 Carl Hagelin 4.00 10.00
32 Colin Miller 4.00 10.00
33 Aaron Ekblad 8.00 20.00
34 Ryan Ellis 5.00 12.00
35 David Backes 4.00 10.00
36 Adrian Kempe 6.00 15.00
37 John Carlson 6.00 15.00
38 Andrew Shaw 4.00 10.00
39 Evander Kane 6.00 15.00
40 Anthony DeAngelo 4.00 10.00
41 Alexandre Texier 6.00 15.00
42 Dante Fabbro 6.00 15.00
43 Erik Brannstrom 6.00 15.00
44 Zack MacEwen 5.00 12.00
45 Taro Hirose 6.00 15.00
46 Ryan Poehling 10.00 25.00
47 Trent Frederic 6.00 15.00
48 Rem Pitlick 6.00 15.00
49 Zach Senyshyn 6.00 15.00
50 Quinn Hughes 50.00 125.00
51 Max Jones 6.00 15.00
52 Rudolfs Balcers 6.00 15.00
53 Philippe Myers 5.00 12.00
54 Brady Keeper 6.00 15.00
55 Filip Zadina 10.00 25.00
56 Carl Grundstrom 6.00 15.00
57 Joey Daccord 12.00 30.00
58 Kaden Fulcher 6.00 15.00
59 Libor Hajek 5.00 12.00
60 Cale Makar 60.00 150.00
61 Anthony Cirelli C 5.00 12.00
62 Brian Dumoulin C 4.00 10.00
63 Nick Foligno A 5.00 12.00
64 Malcolm Subban C 5.00 12.00
65 Conor Sheary A 6.00 15.00
66 Pavel Buchnevich B 5.00 12.00
68 Zach Hyman C 10.00 25.00
69 Christian Dvorak C 5.00 12.00
70 Devan Dubnyk A 5.00 12.00
71 Tyler Johnson A 4.00 10.00
72 Ryan Murray C 5.00 12.00
73 Ivan Provorov B 5.00 12.00
74 Jacob Trouba A 5.00 12.00
75 Jakob Chychrun B 6.00 15.00
76 Kevin Hayes C 5.00 12.00
77 Brandon Montour B 8.00 20.00
78 Dmitry Orlov B 6.00 15.00
79 Martin Jones A 5.00 12.00
80 Ryan Dzingel A 5.00 12.00
81 Kyle Palmieri A 5.00 12.00
82 Mikhail Sergachev A 5.00 12.00
83 Will Butcher B 5.00 12.00
84 Keith Yandle A 4.00 10.00
85 Gustav Nyquist C 4.00 10.00
86 Philipp Grubauer B 6.00 15.00
87 Danton Heinen B 5.00 12.00
88 Anze Kopitar A 10.00 25.00
89 Zach Werenski A 10.00 25.00
90 Boone Jenner A 6.00 15.00
91 Vincent Trocheck A 6.00 15.00
92 Micheal Ferland A 4.00 10.00
93 Luke Kunin C 4.00 10.00
94 Vladislav Namestnikov B 4.00 10.00
95 Jaccob Slavin A 5.00 12.00
96 Kasperi Kapanen B 5.00 12.00
98 Andrew Copp C 4.00 10.00
99 Jeff Carter A 5.00 12.00
100 Kevin Labanc B 4.00 10.00
101 Kirby Dach C 12.00 30.00
102 Dominik Kubalik C 12.00 30.00
103 Rasmus Sandin C 10.00 25.00
104 Elvis Merzlikins C 12.00 30.00
109 Mario Ferraro C 5.00 12.00
111 Nicolas Hague C 6.00 15.00
112 Oliver Wahlstrom C 10.00 25.00
113 Tobias Bjornfot C 6.00 15.00
114 Emil Bemstrom C 6.00 15.00
118 Noah Dobson A 15.00 40.00
119 Cody Glass C 10.00 25.00
120 Jack Hughes A 50.00 125.00
121 Johan Larsson C 5.00 12.00
123 Sam Bennett B 10.00 25.00
124 Rocco Grimaldi C 4.00 10.00
125 Radek Faksa C 5.00 12.00
126 Mike Reilly B 4.00 10.00
127 Jordan Weal C 4.00 10.00
128 Ryan Miller A 6.00 15.00
130 Alexander Nylander B 5.00 12.00
131 Adam Gaudette C 5.00 12.00
133 Brett Howden B 4.00 10.00
134 Pierre-Edouard Bellemare B 4.00 10.00
135 Ryan Ellis B 5.00 12.00
136 Jamie Benn A 6.00 15.00
137 Jaroslav Halak B 6.00 15.00
138 Leon Draisaitl A 20.00 50.00
139 Carl Soderberg B 4.00 10.00
140 Jonathan Marchessault B 8.00 20.00
141 Oliver Bjorkstrand B 5.00 12.00
142 Dominik Kahun B 4.00 10.00
143 Radko Gudas C 5.00 12.00
144 Mikael Granlund A 5.00 12.00
145 Laurent Brossoit C 4.00 10.00
146 Andrei Svechnikov A 8.00 20.00
147 Nicolas Deslauriers B 4.00 10.00
148 Eric Staal A 6.00 15.00
149 Jakub Voracek A 5.00 12.00
151 Thatcher Demko A 8.00 20.00
154 Bo Horvat A 8.00 20.00
155 Derek Stepan B 4.00 10.00
157 Yanni Gourde C 5.00 12.00
158 Slater Koekkoek C 4.00 10.00
159 Jack Campbell C 6.00 15.00
160 Maxime Comtois A 4.00 10.00
162 Danil Yurtaykin B 5.00 12.00
163 Riley Stillman C 6.00 15.00
164 Victor Olofsson B 12.00 30.00
165 Alexander Volkov B 5.00 12.00
166 Vitaly Abramov B 6.00 15.00
167 Mackenzie MacEachern B 6.00 15.00
168 Julien Gauthier A 6.00 15.00
169 Ilya Mikheyev B 10.00 25.00
171 Klim Kostin B 6.00 15.00
172 Carter Verhaeghe B 10.00 25.00
173 Nico Sturm C 5.00 12.00
174 Connor Clifton B 6.00 15.00
175 Martin Fehervary C 5.00 12.00
176 Karson Kuhlman C 6.00 15.00
177 Jimmy Schuldt B 5.00 12.00
178 Guillaume Brisebois B 6.00 15.00
179 Sam Lafferty C 5.00 12.00
180 Adam Boqvist A 6.00 15.00

2019-20 Upper Deck Overtime Next In Line

*RED/25: 2X TO 5X BASIC INSERTS
NL1 Jack Hughes 4.00 10.00
NL2 Adam Fox 2.00 5.00
NL3 Erik Brannstrom .75 2.00
NL4 Nick Suzuki 3.00 8.00
NL5 Cale Makar 4.00 10.00
NL6 Nicolas Hague .75 2.00
NL7 Jesper Boqvist .60 1.50
NL8 Barrett Hayton 1.50 4.00
NL9 Oliver Wahlstrom 1.25 3.00
NL10 Filip Zadina 1.25 3.00
NL11 Rasmus Sandin 1.25 3.00
NL12 Ryan Poehling 1.25 3.00
NL13 Ville Heinola 1.00 2.50
NL14 Quinn Hughes 4.00 10.00
NL15 Victor Olofsson 1.50 4.00
NL16 Nikita Gusev 1.25 3.00
NL17 Noah Dobson 2.00 5.00
NL18 Dominik Kubalik 1.50 4.00
NL19 Kaapo Kakko 1.25 3.00
NL20 Cody Glass 1.25 3.00

2019-20 Upper Deck Overtime OT Winners

*RED/25: 2X TO 5X BASIC INSERTS
OW1 Danny DeKeyser .50 1.25
OW2 Derek Stepan .50 1.25
OW3 Timo Meier .75 2.00
OW4 Kevin Hayes .60 1.50
OW5 Alex DeBrincat 1.00 2.50
OW6 Tyler Seguin 1.00 2.50
OW7 Bo Horvat 1.00 2.50
OW8 Craig Smith .50 1.25
OW9 Gabriel Landeskog 1.00 2.50
OW10 Tomas Hertl .75 2.00
OW11 Jason Dickinson .50 1.25
OW12 Tyler Toffoli .75 2.00
OW13 Max Pacioretty .75 2.00
OW14 Kyle Turris .60 1.50
OW15 Brayden Schenn .75 2.00
OW16 Brock McGinn .50 1.25
OW17 Shea Theodore 1.00 2.50
OW18 Ryan Pulock .60 1.50
OW19 Michael Grabner .60 1.50
OW20 John Tavares 1.25 3.00

2020-21 Upper Deck Overtime

1 Mark Stone .75 2.00
2 Alexander Radulov .60 1.50
3 Noah Hanifin .60 1.50
4 Tanner Pearson .60 1.50
5 William Karlsson .75 2.00
6 Austin Wagner .40 1.00
7 Robert Thomas .60 1.50
8 Calle Jarnkrok .40 1.00
9 Brayden Point .75 2.00
10 Anthony Cirelli .50 1.25
11 Henri Jokiharju .40 1.00
12 Max Jones .40 1.00
13 Ethan Bear .40 1.00
14 Alex Kerfoot .50 1.25
15 Neal Pionk .40 1.00
16 Ryan Dzingel .50 1.25
17 Adam Gaudette .50 1.25
18 Ivan Provorov .50 1.25
19 Olli Maatta .40 1.00
20 Filip Hronek .40 1.00
21 Yanni Gourde .50 1.25
22 Ondrej Kase .40 1.00
23 Nick Foligno .50 1.25
24 Joel Eriksson Ek .50 1.25
25 Philipp Grubauer .60 1.50
26 Jean-Gabriel Pageau .40 1.00
27 Marcus Pettersson .40 1.00
28 Dylan Gambrell .40 1.00
29 Alex Tuch .60 1.50
30 Jamie Oleksiak .50 1.25
31 Oskar Sundqvist .40 1.00
32 Alex DeBrincat .75 2.00
33 Nick Suzuki 1.25 3.00
34 Alex Stalock .40 1.00
35 Nikita Gusev .50 1.25
36 Jonathan Bernier .50 1.25
37 Mario Ferraro .40 1.00
38 Chris Driedger .40 1.00
39 Ryan Lindgren .40 1.00
40 Elias Lindholm .60 1.50
41 Alexander True RC 1.00 2.50
42 Anthony Angello RC 1.00 2.50
43 Gabe Vilardi RC 2.00 5.00
44 Gage Quinney RC .75 2.00
45 Gustav Lindstrom RC 1.00 2.50
46 Jake Evans RC 1.25 3.00
47 Jani Hakanpaa RC .75 2.00
48 Jason Robertson RC 3.00 8.00
49 Josh Norris RC 2.00 5.00
50 Kieffer Bellows RC 1.00 2.50
51 Liam Foudy RC 1.25 3.00
52 Lucas Carlsson RC 1.00 2.50
53 Martin Kaut RC 1.25 3.00
54 Matiss Kivlenieks RC 1.50 4.00
55 Maxim Letunov RC 1.00 2.50
56 Mikey Anderson RC 1.25 3.00
57 Morgan Geekie RC 1.25 3.00
58 Nicolas Beaudin RC 1.25 3.00
59 Timothy Liljegren RC 1.25 3.00
60 Tyler Benson RC 1.25 3.00
61 Kirby Dach .60 1.50
62 Matt Dumba .40 1.00
63 Tyler Johnson .40 1.00
64 Oliver Bjorkstrand .50 1.25
65 Semyon Varlamov .60 1.50
66 Ilya Mikheyev .50 1.25
67 Anthony Beauvillier .40 1.00
68 Dillon Dube .40 1.00
69 Michael Amadio .40 1.00
70 Jordan Staal .50 1.25
71 Zach Whitecloud .50 1.25
72 Richard Panik .40 1.00
73 Pekka Rinne .60 1.50
74 Mirco Mueller .40 1.00
75 Artem Anisimov .40 1.00
76 Jake Walman .40 1.00
77 J.T. Compher .40 1.00
78 Robert Hagg .40 1.00
79 John Marino .60 1.50
80 Warren Foegele .50 1.25
81 Dan Vladar .50 1.25
82 Josh Bailey .50 1.25
83 Alexander Volkov .40 1.00
84 Sami Niku .40 1.00
85 Jonathan Huberdeau .75 2.00
86 Martin Jones .50 1.25
87 Sonny Milano .50 1.25
88 Dustin Brown .60 1.50
89 Tyler Motte .40 1.00
90 Philippe Myers .40 1.00
91 Victor Rask .40 1.00
92 Kailer Yamamoto .60 1.50
93 Adam Fox .75 2.00
94 Kyle Palmieri .50 1.25
95 Connor Clifton .40 1.00
96 Jesperi Kotkaniemi .60 1.50
97 Seth Jones .60 1.50
98 Jake Gardiner .40 1.00
99 Trevor Moore .40 1.00
100 Ryan Poehling .60 1.50
101 Nick Robertson RC 2.00 5.00
102 Alexander Alexeyev RC 1.00 2.50
103 Nikolai Knyzhov RC 1.00 2.50
104 Shane Bowers RC 1.00 2.50
105 Calvin Thurkauf RC 1.00 2.50
106 Ty Dellandrea RC 1.25 3.00
107 Dylan Coghlan RC 1.25 3.00
108 Olli Juolevi RC 1.25 3.00
109 Connor Ingram RC 1.00 2.50
110 Pierre-Olivier Joseph RC 1.25 3.00
111 Alexander Yelesin RC 1.00 2.50
112 Vitek Vanecek RC 2.00 5.00
113 Peyton Krebs RC 2.00 5.00
114 Brandon Hagel RC 1.50 4.00
115 Victor Soderstrom RC 1.00 2.50
116 Gage Quinney RC .75 2.00
117 Steven Lorentz RC 1.00 2.50
118 Bowen Byram RC 2.50 6.00
119 Philipp Kurashev RC 1.50 4.00
120 Alexis Lafreniere RC 4.00 10.00
121 Aleksander Barkov 1.00 2.50
122 Joe Thornton 1.00 2.50
123 Jordan Kyrou .60 1.50
124 David Rittich .50 1.25
125 Petr Mrazek .60 1.50
126 Owen Tippett .50 1.25
127 Roope Hintz .75 2.00
128 Zach Hyman 1.00 2.50
129 Timo Meier .60 1.50
130 Bo Horvat .75 2.00
131 Colton Parayko .50 1.25
132 Joel Farabee .60 1.50
133 Dmitry Orlov .60 1.50
134 Michael Rasmussen .40 1.00
135 Jake DeBrusk .60 1.50
136 Victor Olofsson .60 1.50
137 Adam Larsson .50 1.25
138 Oskar Lindblom .50 1.25
139 Cody Glass .50 1.25
140 Elvis Merzlikins .60 1.50
141 Jared McCann .50 1.25
142 Sam Reinhart 1.25 3.00
143 Slater Koekkoek .40 1.00
144 Matt Murray .60 1.50
145 Andre Burakovsky .40 1.00
146 Kevin Fiala .50 1.25
147 Miles Wood .40 1.00
148 Travis Sanheim .40 1.00
149 Kevin Shattenkirk .40 1.00
150 Adam Boqvist .50 1.25
151 Jamie Benn .60 1.50
152 Kyle Turris .50 1.25
153 Barrett Hayton .60 1.50
154 Josh Anderson .50 1.25
155 Mackenzie Blackwood .60 1.50
156 Sam Steel .50 1.25
157 Derek Stepan .50 1.25
158 Maxime Comtois .50 1.25
159 Evgeny Kuznetsov .75 2.00
160 Connor McDavid 3.00 8.00
161 Kirill Kaprizov RC 5.00 12.00
162 K'Andre Miller RC 2.50 6.00
163 Alexander Barabanov RC 1.25 3.00
164 Ian Mitchell RC 1.00 2.50
165 Ilya Sorokin RC 3.00 8.00
166 Jalen Chatfield RC 1.00 2.50
167 Cal Foote RC 1.50 4.00
168 Alexander Romanov RC 1.50 4.00
169 Mathias Bromé RC 1.00 2.50
170 Yegor Sharangovich RC 2.00 5.00
171 Kevin Lankinen RC 2.00 5.00
172 Nils Hoglander RC 1.25 3.00
173 Logan Stanley RC 1.25 3.00
174 Pius Suter RC 1.50 4.00
175 John Leonard RC 1.00 2.50
176 Ty Smith RC 2.00 5.00
177 Mikko Lehtonen RC 1.00 2.50
178 Dylan Cozens RC 2.00 5.00
179 Nicolas Meloche RC 1.00 2.50
180 Tim Stutzle RC 2.50 6.00

2020-21 Upper Deck Overtime Blue

*BLUE: .75X TO 2X BASIC
*BLUE RC: .5X TO 1.25X BASIC

2020-21 Upper Deck Overtime Red

*RED: 1.5X TO 4X BASIC
*RED RC: 1X TO 2.5X BASIC

2020-21 Upper Deck Overtime Autographs Gold

1 Mark Stone A 8.00 20.00
2 Alexander Radulov A 6.00 15.00
3 Noah Hanifin B 6.00 15.00
4 Tanner Pearson A 6.00 15.00
5 William Karlsson A 8.00 20.00
6 Austin Wagner A 4.00 10.00
7 Robert Thomas B 6.00 15.00
8 Calle Jarnkrok B 4.00 10.00
10 Anthony Cirelli B 5.00 12.00
11 Henri Jokiharju B 4.00 10.00
12 Max Jones A 4.00 10.00
13 Ethan Bear C 4.00 10.00
14 Alex Kerfoot A 5.00 12.00
15 Neal Pionk B 4.00 10.00
16 Ryan Dzingel A 5.00 12.00
17 Adam Gaudette B 5.00 12.00
18 Ivan Provorov A 5.00 12.00
19 Olli Maatta B 4.00 10.00
20 Filip Hronek B 4.00 10.00
21 Yanni Gourde A 5.00 12.00
22 Ondrej Kase B 4.00 10.00
23 Nick Foligno A 5.00 12.00
24 Joel Eriksson Ek A 5.00 12.00
25 Philipp Grubauer A 6.00 15.00
26 Jean-Gabriel Pageau A 4.00 10.00
27 Marcus Pettersson B 4.00 10.00
28 Dylan Gambrell A 4.00 10.00
29 Alex Tuch C 6.00 15.00
30 Jamie Oleksiak C 5.00 12.00
31 Oskar Sundqvist A 4.00 10.00
32 Alex DeBrincat A 8.00 20.00
33 Nick Suzuki A 12.00 30.00
34 Alex Stalock C 4.00 10.00
35 Nikita Gusev B 5.00 12.00
36 Jonathan Bernier A 5.00 12.00
37 Mario Ferraro B 4.00 10.00
38 Chris Driedger C 4.00 10.00
39 Ryan Lindgren C 4.00 10.00
40 Elias Lindholm A 6.00 15.00
41 Alexander True A 4.00 10.00
42 Anthony Angello C 6.00 15.00
43 Gabe Vilardi C 12.00 30.00
44 Gage Quinney C 5.00 12.00
46 Jake Evans C 8.00 20.00
48 Jason Robertson C 30.00 80.00
49 Josh Norris A 12.00 30.00
50 Kieffer Bellows B 6.00 15.00
51 Liam Foudy B 6.00 15.00
52 Lucas Carlsson C 6.00 15.00
54 Matiss Kivlenieks C 10.00 25.00
55 Maxim Letunov C 6.00 15.00
56 Mikey Anderson C 8.00 20.00
57 Morgan Geekie C 8.00 20.00
58 Nicolas Beaudin C 8.00 20.00
59 Timothy Liljegren C 8.00 20.00
60 Tyler Benson C 8.00 20.00
61 Kirby Dach 6.00 15.00
62 Matt Dumba 4.00 10.00
63 Tyler Johnson 4.00 10.00
64 Oliver Bjorkstrand 5.00 12.00
65 Semyon Varlamov 6.00 15.00
66 Ilya Mikheyev 5.00 12.00
67 Anthony Beauvillier 4.00 10.00
68 Dillon Dube 4.00 10.00
69 Michael Amadio 4.00 10.00
70 Jordan Staal 5.00 12.00
71 Zach Whitecloud 5.00 12.00
72 Richard Panik 4.00 10.00
73 Pekka Rinne 6.00 15.00
74 Mirco Mueller 4.00 10.00
75 Artem Anisimov 4.00 10.00
76 Jake Walman 4.00 10.00
77 J.T. Compher 4.00 10.00
78 Robert Hagg 4.00 10.00
79 John Marino 6.00 15.00
80 Warren Foegele 5.00 12.00
81 Dan Vladar 5.00 12.00
82 Josh Bailey 5.00 12.00
83 Alexander Volkov 4.00 10.00
84 Sami Niku 4.00 10.00
85 Jonathan Huberdeau 8.00 20.00
87 Sonny Milano 5.00 12.00
88 Dustin Brown 6.00 15.00
90 Philippe Myers 4.00 10.00
91 Victor Rask 4.00 10.00
92 Kailer Yamamoto 6.00 15.00
93 Adam Fox 8.00 20.00
94 Kyle Palmieri 5.00 12.00
95 Connor Clifton 4.00 10.00
96 Jesperi Kotkaniemi 6.00 15.00
97 Seth Jones 6.00 15.00
98 Jake Gardiner 4.00 10.00
99 Trevor Moore 4.00 10.00
100 Ryan Poehling 6.00 15.00
101 Nick Robertson C 12.00 30.00
102 Alexander Alexeyev C 5.00 12.00
103 Nikolai Knyzhov D 6.00 15.00
104 Shane Bowers C 6.00 15.00
105 Calvin Thurkauf D 6.00 15.00
107 Dylan Coghlan D 8.00 20.00
108 Olli Juolevi D 8.00 20.00
109 Connor Ingram B 6.00 15.00
110 Pierre-Olivier Joseph D 8.00 20.00
112 Vitek Vanecek D 12.00 30.00
113 Peyton Krebs C 12.00 30.00
115 Victor Soderstrom C 5.00 12.00
116 Gage Quinney D 5.00 12.00
117 Steven Lorentz D 6.00 15.00
118 Bowen Byram C 15.00 40.00
119 Philipp Kurashev D 10.00 25.00

2020-21 Upper Deck Overtime Center of Excellence

*RED/25: 1.5X TO 4X BASIC
CE1 Connor McDavid 4.00 10.00
CE2 Bo Horvat 1.00 2.50
CE3 Sean Monahan .50 1.25
CE4 John Tavares 1.25 3.00
CE5 Sebastian Aho 1.25 3.00
CE6 Pierre-Luc Dubois .60 1.50
CE7 Tyler Seguin 1.00 2.50
CE8 Dylan Strome 1.00 2.50
CE9 Evgeny Kuznetsov 1.00 2.50
CE10 Nick Suzuki 1.50 4.00
CE11 William Karlsson 1.00 2.50
CE12 Evgeni Malkin 1.50 4.00
CE13 Anze Kopitar 1.25 3.00
CE14 Jonathan Toews 1.25 3.00
CE15 Tomas Hertl .75 2.00
CE16 Steven Stamkos 1.50 4.00
CE17 Leon Draisaitl 2.50 6.00
CE18 Joe Pavelski 1.00 2.50
CE19 Brayden Point 1.00 2.50
CE20 Auston Matthews 3.00 8.00

2020-21 Upper Deck Overtime Next In Line

*RED/25: 1.5X TO 4X BASIC
NL1 Alexis Lafreniere 3.00 8.00
NL2 Ty Dellandrea 1.00 2.50
NL3 Victor Soderstrom .75 2.00
NL4 Tyler Benson 1.00 2.50
NL5 Shane Bowers .75 2.00
NL6 Josh Norris 1.50 4.00
NL7 Kieffer Bellows .75 2.00
NL8 Olli Juolevi 1.00 2.50
NL9 Liam Foudy 1.00 2.50
NL10 Nick Robertson 1.50 4.00
NL11 Philipp Kurashev 1.25 3.00
NL12 Jason Robertson 2.50 6.00
NL13 Pierre-Olivier Joseph 1.00 2.50
NL14 Connor Ingram .75 2.00
NL15 Gabe Vilardi 1.50 4.00
NL16 Vitali Kravtsov 2.00 5.00
NL17 Alexander Alexeyev .75 2.00
NL18 Alexander True .75 2.00
NL19 Peyton Krebs 1.50 4.00
NL20 Bowen Byram 2.00 5.00

2024-25 Upper Deck Overtime

1 Sebastian Aho 1.00 2.50
2 Alexis Lafreniere 1.25 3.00
3 Auston Matthews 2.50 6.00
4 Lucas Raymond 1.00 2.50
5 Mika Zibanejad .75 2.00
6 Dylan Larkin .75 2.00
7 Tim Stutzle .75 2.00
8 Kyle Connor .75 2.00
9 Connor Bedard 2.00 5.00
10 Noah Dobson .75 2.00
11 Mitch Marner 1.00 2.50
12 David Pastrnak 1.50 4.00
13 Matt Boldy 1.00 2.50
14 William Eklund .75 2.00
15 Philipp Kurashev .50 1.25
16 Mathew Barzal .75 2.00
17 Elias Pettersson 1.00 2.50
18 Nathan MacKinnon 2.50 6.00
19 Nico Hischier 1.00 2.50
20 Quinn Hughes 1.50 4.00
21 Mikko Rantanen 1.50 4.00
22 Jack Hughes 1.50 4.00
23 Thatcher Demko .75 2.00
24 Yegor Sharangovich .60 1.50
25 Matthew Tkachuk 1.25 3.00
26 Jordan Kyrou .60 1.50
27 Cale Makar 1.50 4.00
28 Roman Josi .60 1.50
29 Jack Eichel 1.50 4.00
30 Kent Johnson .60 1.50
31 Filip Forsberg 1.00 2.50
32 William Karlsson .75 2.00
33 Zach Werenski 1.00 2.50
34 Juraj Slafkovsky 1.25 3.00
35 Alex Ovechkin 2.50 6.00
36 Leon Draisaitl 2.00 5.00
37 Igor Shesterkin 1.25 3.00
38 Connor McDavid 3.00 8.00
39 K'Andre Miller .50 1.25
40 Nazem Kadri .75 2.00
41 Aleksander Barkov 1.00 2.50
42 Nikita Kucherov 1.25 3.00
43 Jake Guentzel 1.00 2.50
44 Zach Hyman 1.00 2.50
45 Brayden Point .75 2.00
46 Leo Carlsson 1.00 2.50
47 Cole Caufield 1.25 3.00
48 Sidney Crosby 2.50 6.00
49 Brad Marchand 1.25 3.00
50 Kirill Kaprizov 2.00 5.00
51 Fabian Zetterlund .40 1.00
52 Seth Jarvis .50 1.25
53 Artemi Panarin 1.25 3.00
54 William Nylander 1.25 3.00
55 Charlie McAvoy .75 2.00
56 Kevin Fiala .50 1.25
57 Jared McCann .50 1.25
58 Rasmus Dahlin .75 2.00
59 Carter Verhaeghe .60 1.50
60 Robert Thomas .60 1.50
61 Alex DeBrincat .75 2.00
62 Brady Tkachuk 1.00 2.50
63 Josh Morrissey .75 2.00
64 Mason McTavish .60 1.50
65 Nick Suzuki 1.25 3.00
66 Evgeni Malkin 1.25 3.00
67 Jason Robertson 1.00 2.50
68 Travis Konecny .60 1.50
69 Connor Hellebuyck 1.25 3.00
70 Alex Tuch .60 1.50
71 Anze Kopitar 1.00 2.50
72 Oliver Bjorkstrand .50 1.25
73 Wyatt Johnston 1.25 3.00
74 Travis Sanheim .40 1.00
75 Dylan Strome .75 2.00
76 Brendan Brisson RC .75 2.00
77 Justin Brazeau RC .75 2.00
78 Lane Hutson RC 6.00 15.00
79 Olen Zellweger RC 1.25 3.00
80 Marat Khusnutdinov RC .60 1.50
81 Frank Nazar RC 2.00 5.00
82 Josh Doan RC 1.00 2.50
83 Yan Kuznetsov RC .60 1.50
84 Scott Morrow RC .75 2.00
85 Shakir Mukhamadullin RC .75 2.00
86 Gavin Brindley RC .60 1.50
87 Zach Dean RC .60 1.50
88 Logan Stankoven RC 1.50 4.00
89 Gage Goncalves RC .75 2.00
90 Zachary Bolduc RC 1.25 3.00
91 Luca Del Bel Belluz RC .60 1.50
92 Cutter Gauthier RC 1.50 4.00
93 Mavrik Bourque RC 1.25 3.00
94 Sam Colangelo RC .60 1.50
95 Liam Ohgren RC 1.25 3.00
96 Brennan Othmann RC 1.00 2.50
97 Zack Ostapchuk RC .60 1.50
98 Bradly Nadeau RC 1.00 2.50
99 Jesper Wallstedt RC 1.50 4.00
100 Akil Thomas RC .60 1.50

2024-25 Upper Deck Overtime Blue Foil

*BLUE/99: 1.2X TO 3X BASIC

2024-25 Upper Deck Overtime '21-22 Overtime Rookie Update

2021AL Anton Lundell 4.00 10.00
2021LR Lucas Raymond 6.00 15.00
2021MB Matt Boldy 6.00 15.00
2021MS Moritz Seider 5.00 12.00
2021QB Quinton Byfield 5.00 12.00
2021SJ Seth Jarvis 5.00 12.00

2024-25 Upper Deck Overtime '22-23 Overtime Rookie Update

2022AK Andrei Kuzmenko 4.00 10.00
2022JS Jake Sanderson 5.00 12.00
2022MB Matty Beniers 5.00 12.00
2022SL Juraj Slafkovsky 8.00 20.00
2022SW Shane Wright 5.00 12.00
2022WJ Wyatt Johnston 8.00 20.00

2024-25 Upper Deck Overtime '23-24 Overtime Rookie Update

2023AF Adam Fantilli 6.00 15.00
2023BF Brock Faber 5.00 12.00
2023CB Connor Bedard 12.00 30.00
2023CO Logan Cooley 6.00 15.00
2023LC Leo Carlsson 6.00 15.00
2023LH Luke Hughes 6.00 15.00

2024-25 Upper Deck Overtime Autographs Gold Foil

2 Alexis Lafreniere 12.00 30.00
13 Matt Boldy 25.00 60.00
14 William Eklund 10.00 25.00
15 Philipp Kurashev 6.00 15.00
17 Elias Pettersson 20.00 50.00
20 Quinn Hughes SP 20.00 50.00
21 Mikko Rantanen 20.00 50.00
22 Jack Hughes SP 20.00 50.00
23 Thatcher Demko 10.00 25.00
25 Matthew Tkachuk 15.00 40.00
27 Cale Makar SP 20.00 50.00
28 Roman Josi 8.00 20.00
29 Jack Eichel SP 12.00 30.00
30 Kent Johnson 8.00 20.00
34 Juraj Slafkovsky 20.00 50.00
37 Igor Shesterkin 15.00 40.00
39 K'Andre Miller 6.00 15.00
41 Aleksander Barkov 12.00 30.00
42 Nikita Kucherov SP 15.00 40.00
43 Jake Guentzel 12.00 30.00
47 Cole Caufield 25.00 60.00
50 Kirill Kaprizov SP 80.00 200.00
51 Fabian Zetterlund 5.00 12.00
52 Seth Jarvis 10.00 25.00
57 Jared McCann 6.00 15.00
60 Robert Thomas SP 8.00 20.00
61 Alex DeBrincat 10.00 25.00
62 Brady Tkachuk 12.00 30.00
63 Josh Morrissey 10.00 25.00
64 Mason McTavish 8.00 20.00
65 Nick Suzuki 15.00 40.00
69 Connor Hellebuyck 15.00 40.00
70 Alex Tuch 8.00 20.00
71 Anze Kopitar 12.00 30.00
72 Oliver Bjorkstrand 6.00 15.00
73 Wyatt Johnston 15.00 40.00
74 Travis Sanheim 5.00 12.00
76 Brendan Brisson 10.00 25.00
77 Justin Brazeau 8.00 20.00
78 Lane Hutson 150.00 400.00
79 Olen Zellweger 15.00 40.00
80 Marat Khusnutdinov 8.00 20.00
81 Frank Nazar 25.00 60.00
82 Josh Doan 12.00 30.00
83 Yan Kuznetsov 8.00 20.00
84 Scott Morrow 10.00 25.00
85 Shakir Mukhamadullin 10.00 25.00
87 Zach Dean 8.00 20.00
88 Logan Stankoven 20.00 50.00
89 Gage Goncalves 10.00 25.00
90 Zachary Bolduc 15.00 40.00
93 Mavrik Bourque 15.00 40.00
94 Sam Colangelo 8.00 20.00
95 Liam Ohgren 15.00 40.00
96 Brennan Othmann 12.00 30.00
98 Bradly Nadeau 12.00 30.00
99 Jesper Wallstedt 20.00 50.00
100 Akil Thomas 8.00 20.00

2024-25 Upper Deck Overtime Determination

*RED/25: 2.5X TO 6X BASIC
DT1 Connor Bedard 1.50 4.00
DT2 Jack Hughes 1.25 3.00
DT3 Matthew Tkachuk 1.00 2.50
DT4 Artemi Panarin 1.00 2.50
DT5 Zach Hyman .75 2.00
DT6 Kirill Kaprizov 1.50 4.00
DT7 Nikita Kucherov 1.00 2.50
DT8 Mitch Marner .75 2.00
DT9 Jake Guentzel .75 2.00
DT10 J.T. Miller .60 1.50
DT11 Cutter Gauthier 1.25 3.00
DT12 Robert Thomas .50 1.25
DT13 David Pastrnak 1.25 3.00
DT14 Sam Reinhart 1.00 2.50
DT15 Roman Josi .50 1.25
DT16 Nathan MacKinnon 2.00 5.00
DT17 Sidney Crosby 2.00 5.00
DT18 Auston Matthews 2.00 5.00
DT19 Aleksander Barkov .75 2.00
DT20 Connor McDavid 2.50 6.00
DT21 Cale Makar 1.25 3.00
DT22 Mathew Barzal .60 1.50
DT23 Leon Draisaitl 1.50 4.00
DT24 Quinn Hughes 1.25 3.00
DT25 Mikko Rantanen 1.25 3.00
DT26 William Nylander 1.00 2.50
DT27 Filip Forsberg .75 2.00
DT28 Elias Pettersson .75 2.00
DT29 Jason Robertson .75 2.00
DT30 Logan Stankoven 1.25 3.00

2024-25 Upper Deck Overtime Imminent Impact

II1 Brendan Brisson 1.50 4.00
II2 Lane Hutson 6.00 15.00
II3 Vasily Ponomarev 1.25 3.00
II4 Olen Zellweger 2.50 6.00
II5 Shakir Mukhamadullin 1.50 4.00
II6 Lukas Cormier 1.25 3.00
II7 Josh Doan 2.00 5.00
II8 Yan Kuznetsov 1.25 3.00
II9 Scott Morrow 1.50 4.00
II10 Mason Morelli 1.25 3.00
II11 Frank Nazar 4.00 10.00
II12 Matvei Michkov 5.00 12.00
II13 Gavin Brindley 1.25 3.00
II14 Arshdeep Bains 1.50 4.00
II15 Luca Del Bel Belluz 1.25 3.00
II16 Marshall Rifai 1.25 3.00
II17 Logan Stankoven 3.00 8.00
II18 Justin Brazeau 1.25 3.00
II19 Akil Thomas 1.25 3.00
II20 Marat Khusnutdinov 1.25 3.00
II21 Bradly Nadeau 2.00 5.00
II22 Emil Lilleberg 1.25 3.00
II23 Cutter Gauthier 3.00 8.00
II24 Maxwell Crozier 1.25 3.00
II25 Zach Dean 1.25 3.00
II26 Macklin Celebrini 6.00 15.00
II27 Brennan Othmann 2.00 5.00
II28 Jackson Blake 2.50 6.00
II29 Sam Colangelo 1.25 3.00
II30 Jesper Wallstedt 3.00 8.00
II31 Phil Kemp 1.25 3.00
II32 Mavrik Bourque 2.50 6.00
II33 Matt Rempe 2.50 6.00
II34 Zack Ostapchuk 1.25 3.00
II35 Zachary Bolduc 2.50 6.00
II36 Jack Thompson 1.25 3.00
II37 Gage Goncalves 1.50 4.00
II38 Liam Ohgren 2.50 6.00
II39 Joshua Roy 2.00 5.00
II40 Nikita Chibrikov 1.25 3.00

2024-25 Upper Deck Overtime Top Dogs

*RED/25: 2.5X TO 6X BASIC
TD1 Jeremy Swayman .75 2.00
TD2 Igor Shesterkin 1.00 2.50
TD3 Thatcher Demko .60 1.50
TD4 Connor Hellebuyck 1.00 2.50
TD5 Sergei Bobrovsky .75 2.00
TD6 Nikita Kucherov 1.00 2.50
TD7 Nathan MacKinnon 2.00 5.00
TD8 Connor McDavid 2.50 6.00
TD9 Artemi Panarin 1.00 2.50
TD10 David Pastrnak 1.25 3.00
TD11 Auston Matthews 2.00 5.00
TD12 Leon Draisaitl 1.50 4.00
TD13 Mikko Rantanen 1.25 3.00
TD14 J.T. Miller .60 1.50
TD15 William Nylander 1.00 2.50
TD16 Kirill Kaprizov 1.50 4.00
TD17 Sam Reinhart 1.00 2.50
TD18 Filip Forsberg .75 2.00
TD19 Sidney Crosby 2.00 5.00
TD20 Quinn Hughes 1.25 3.00
TD21 Brayden Point .60 1.50
TD22 Cale Makar 1.25 3.00
TD23 Sebastian Aho .75 2.00
TD24 Elias Pettersson .75 2.00
TD25 Matthew Tkachuk 1.00 2.50
TD26 Robert Thomas .50 1.25
TD27 Mitch Marner .75 2.00
TD28 Roman Josi .50 1.25
TD29 Jason Robertson .75 2.00
TD30 Mathew Barzal .60 1.50

2018-19 Upper Deck Pittsburgh Penguins '09 Stanley Cup 10th Anniversary Giveaway

PIT1 Sidney Crosby 5.00 12.00
PIT2 Evgeni Malkin 3.00 8.00
PIT3 Kris Letang 3.00 8.00
PIT4 Marc-Andre Fleury 3.00 8.00
PIT5 Jordan Staal 3.00 8.00
PIT6 Chris Kunitz 3.00 8.00
PIT7 Sergei Gonchar 3.00 8.00
PIT8 Max Talbot 3.00 8.00
PIT9 Bill Guerin 3.00 8.00

2015-16 Upper Deck Portfolio

1 Jeff Carter .30 .75
2 Brent Seabrook .20 .50
3 Leo Komarov .20 .50
4 David Krejci .40 1.00
5 Tyler Ennis .20 .50
6 Tuukka Rask .40 1.00
7 Victor Hedman .40 1.00
8 Justin Faulk .30 .75
9 Bobby Ryan .30 .75
10 Ryan Strome .40 1.00
11 Dustin Byfuglien .40 1.00
12 Antti Niemi .30 .75
13 Nick Foligno .30 .75
14 Tomas Hertl .40 1.00
15 Aaron Ekblad .40 1.00
16 Ryan Nugent-Hopkins .40 1.00
17 Marc-Andre Fleury .75 2.00

18 Kris Versteeg .20 .50
19 Mikko Koivu .30 .75
20 Jonathan Huberdeau .40 1.00
21 Boone Jenner .40 1.00
22 Mark Scheifele .60 1.50
23 Jack Johnson .20 .50
24 Duncan Keith .30 .75
25 Mike Smith .40 1.00
26 Tyler Bozak .20 .50
27 James Neal .20 .50
28 Jake Allen .40 1.00
29 Bo Horvat .40 1.00
30 Bryan Little .30 .75
31 Mathieu Perreault .20 .50
32 Alexander Ovechkin 1.50 4.00
33 Dougie Hamilton .30 .75
34 Anthony Duclair .30 .75
35 Matt Duchene .40 1.00
36 Ben Bishop .30 .75
37 Pavel Datsyuk .60 1.50
38 Nathan MacKinnon 1.50 4.00
39 Sergei Bobrovsky .60 1.50
40 Patrice Bergeron .40 1.00
41 Mats Zuccarello .40 1.00
42 Nick Bjugstad .20 .50
43 Brent Burns .40 1.00
44 Kyle Palmieri .30 .75
45 Patrick Sharp .40 1.00
46 Jamie Benn .40 1.00
47 Tobias Rieder .20 .50
48 Filip Forsberg .60 1.50
49 Claude Giroux .40 1.00
50 Wayne Simmonds .40 1.00
51 Ryan Getzlaf .40 1.00
52 Brayden Schenn .40 1.00
53 P.K. Subban .40 1.00
54 Kyle Okposo .20 .50
55 Dion Phaneuf .30 .75
56 Kris Letang .40 1.00
57 Shayne Gostisbehere .40 1.00
58 Corey Perry .60 1.50
59 Mike Green .30 .75
60 Mark Giordano .40 1.00
61 Johnny Gaudreau .60 1.50
62 Jarome Iginla .40 1.00
63 Jussi Jokinen .20 .50
64 John Klingberg .40 1.00
65 Shea Weber .30 .75
66 Anze Kopitar .60 1.50
67 Brandon Saad .30 .75
68 Brendan Gallagher .40 1.00
69 Mikkel Boedker .20 .50
70 Devan Dubnyk .30 .75
71 Phil Kessel .40 1.00
72 Jaden Schwartz .40 1.00
73 Cory Schneider .40 1.00
74 Carey Price .75 2.00
75 Tomas Plekanec .20 .50
76 Pekka Rinne .40 1.00
77 Tyler Seguin .40 1.00
78 Victor Rask .20 .50
79 Jakub Voracek .30 .75
80 Brock Nelson .20 .50
81 Martin Hanzal .20 .50
82 Evgeny Kuznetsov .40 1.00
83 T.J. Brodie .20 .50
84 Blake Wheeler .40 1.00
85 Gabriel Landeskog .40 1.00
86 Nikita Kucherov .75 2.00
87 Matt Moulson .20 .50
88 Mark Stone .40 1.00
89 Steven Stamkos .75 2.00
90 John Tavares .60 1.50
91 Erik Johnson .20 .50
92 Kari Lehtonen .30 .75
93 Scott Hartnell .20 .50
94 Mike Hoffman .20 .50
95 Joe Thornton .60 1.50
96 Henrik Lundqvist .75 2.00
97 Andrew Ladd .40 1.00
98 Martin Jones .30 .75
99 Corey Crawford .40 1.00
100 Vladimir Tarasenko .40 1.00
101 Cam Fowler .20 .50
102 David Pastrnak .75 2.00
103 Mike Ribeiro .20 .50
104 Nino Niederreiter .20 .50
105 Henrik Zetterberg .40 1.00
106 Patrick Marleau .40 1.00
107 T.J. Oshie .40 1.00
108 Nicklas Backstrom .40 1.00
109 Teuvo Teravainen .40 1.00
110 Torey Krug .30 .75
111 Petr Mrazek .30 .75
112 Johnny Boychuk .30 .75
113 Zach Parise .40 1.00
114 Ryan Oâ•™Reilly .40 1.00
115 Loui Eriksson .20 .50
116 Kevin Shattenkirk .20 .50
117 Jason Spezza .40 1.00
118 Jordan Staal .30 .75
119 Drew Doughty .40 1.00
120 Taylor Hall .40 1.00
121 Jonathan Quick .40 1.00
122 Joe Pavelski .40 1.00
123 Patrick Kane .75 2.00
124 Rasmus Ristolainen .20 .50
125 Charlie Coyle .40 1.00
126 John Carlson .40 1.00
127 Sidney Crosby 1.50 4.00
128 Semyon Varlamov .40 1.00
129 Alexander Steen .20 .50
130 Ryan Kesler .40 1.00
131 Ryan Johansen .30 .75
132 Adam Henrique .30 .75
133 Michael Cammalleri .30 .75
134 Evgeni Malkin .75 2.00
135 Jiri Hudler .30 .75
136 Roman Josi .40 1.00
137 Marian Gaborik .40 1.00
138 Jordan Eberle .40 1.00
139 Eric Staal .40 1.00
140 Erik Karlsson .40 1.00
141 Sami Vatanen .20 .50
142 Kevin Hayes .30 .75
143 Kyle Turris .30 .75
144 Tomas Tatar .20 .50
145 Morgan Rielly .40 1.00
146 Oscar Klefbom .60 1.50
147 Rick Nash .40 1.00
148 Oliver Ekman-Larsson .40 1.00
149 Evander Kane .40 1.00
150 Jonathan Toews .60 1.50
151 Craig Anderson .40 1.00
152 Mika Zibanejad .40 1.00
153 Ryan Miller .40 1.00
154 Justin Williams .30 .75
155 Alex Pietrangelo .30 .75
156 Jeff Skinner .40 1.00
157 Nail Yakupov .20 .50
158 Tyler Johnson .20 .50
159 Gustav Nyquist .20 .50
160 James van Riemsdyk .30 .75
161 Sam Reinhart .75 2.00
162 Alex Galchenyuk .20 .50
163 John Gibson .40 1.00
164 Leon Draisaitl 1.00 3.00
165 Jaromir Jagr 1.25 3.00
166 Tyler Toffoli .40 1.00
167 Henrik Sedin .40 1.00
168 Travis Hamonic .20 .50
169 James Reimer .40 1.00
170 Nazem Kadri .40 1.00
171 Max Pacioretty .40 1.00
172 Derick Brassard .20 .50
173 Braden Holtby .40 1.00
174 Radim Vrbata .20 .50
175 Roberto Luongo .60 1.50
176 Sean Monahan .20 .50
177 Thomas Vanek .30 .75
178 Daniel Sedin .40 1.00
179 Ryan Suter .30 .75
180 Aleksander Barkov .60 1.50
181 Brian Leetch .30 .75
182 Lanny McDonald .40 1.00
183 Clark Gillies .40 1.00
184 Rod Brind' Amour .30 .75
185 Doug Gilmour .40 1.00
186 Pavel Bure .40 1.00
187 Bobby Orr 1.50 4.00
188 Glenn Hall .40 1.00
189 Joe Sakic .75 2.00
190 Doug Harvey .40 1.00
191 Nicklas Lidstrom .40 1.00
192 Jari Kurri .40 1.00
193 Guy Lafleur .40 1.00
194 Martin Brodeur .75 2.00
195 Mark Messier .75 2.00
196 Bobby Clarke .60 1.50
197 Mario Lemieux 1.50 4.00
198 Al MacInnis .40 1.00
199 Borje Salming .40 1.00
200 Wayne Gretzky 2.00 5.00
201 Jack Eichel RC 3.00 8.00
202 Jake Virtanen RC 1.00 2.50
203 Brett Pesce RC .60 1.50
204 Jujhar Khaira RC .60 1.50
205 Brady Skjei RC .60 1.50
206 Nikolaj Ehlers RC 1.50 4.00
207 Shane Prince RC .50 1.25
208 Joonas Donskoi RC .75 2.00
209 Nick Ritchie RC .75 2.00
210 Andreas Athanasiou RC 2.00 5.00
211 Colton Parayko RC 1.25 3.00
212 Christoph Bertschy RC .60 1.50
213 Garret Sparks RC .75 2.00
214 Joonas Korpisalo RC 3.00 8.00
215 Artemi Panarin RC 3.00 8.00
216 Mikko Rantanen RC 4.00 10.00
217 Robby Fabbri RC 1.00 2.50
218 Joseph Blandisi RC .75 2.00
219 Nikolay Goldobin RC .75 2.00
220 Oscar Lindberg RC .75 2.00
221 Taylor Leier RC .75 2.00
222 Viktor Arvidsson RC .75 2.00
223 Matt Murray RC 3.00 8.00
224 Mike McCarron RC 1.00 2.50
225 Brock McGinn RC .75 2.00
226 Dylan Larkin RC 2.50 6.00
227 Ben Hutton RC .75 2.00
228 Charles Hudon RC .75 2.00
229 Sergei Plotnikov RC .50 1.25
230 Malcolm Subban RC 1.25 3.00
231 Juuse Saros RC 2.00 5.00
232 Linus Ullmark RC 1.50 4.00
233 Nicolas Petan RC .75 2.00
234 Sam Bennett RC 2.50 6.00
235 Jean-Francois Berube RC .60 1.50
236 Louis Domingue RC .75 2.00
237 Laurent Dauphin RC .75 2.00
238 Connor Hellebuyck RC 3.00 8.00
239 Hunter Shinkaruk RC .75 2.00
240 Mike Condon RC .75 2.00
241 Jared McCann RC .75 2.00
242 Colin Miller RC .60 1.50
243 Antoine Bibeau RC .75 2.00
244 Shea Theodore RC 1.25 3.00
245 Zachary Fucale RC .60 1.50
246 Daniel Carr RC .60 1.50
247 Frank Vatrano RC 1.00 2.50
248 Max Domi RC 1.50 4.00
249 Noah Hanifin RC 1.25 3.00
250 Connor McDavid RC 12.00 30.00
251 Alexander Ovechkin 5.00 12.00
252 Borje Salming 1.25 3.00
253 Jamie Benn 1.25 3.00
254 Bobby Clarke 2.00 5.00
255 Brian Leetch 1.00 2.50
256 Filip Forsberg 2.00 5.00
257 Jari Kurri 1.25 3.00
258 Vladimir Tarasenko 1.50 4.00
259 Cory Schneider 1.25 3.00
260 Clark Gillies 1.25 3.00
261 Max Pacioretty 1.25 3.00
262 Mario Lemieux 5.00 12.00
263 Guy Lafleur 1.50 4.00
264 Aaron Ekblad 1.50 4.00
265 Rod Brind' Amour 1.00 2.50
266 John Tavares 2.00 5.00
267 Taylor Hall 1.50 4.00
268 Shayne Gostisbehere 1.25 3.00
269 Lanny McDonald 1.25 3.00
270 Wayne Gretzky 8.00 20.00
271 Carey Price 3.00 8.00
272 Nicklas Lidstrom 1.50 4.00
273 Tyler Seguin 2.00 5.00
274 Bobby Ryan 1.25 3.00
275 Joe Pavelski 2.00 5.00
276 Henrik Lundqvist 4.00 10.00
277 Guy Lafleur 2.00 5.00
278 Jonathan Toews 2.50 6.00
279 Mark Scheifele 2.50 6.00
280 Nicklas Backstrom 1.50 4.00
281 Ryan Oâ•™Reilly 1.50 4.00
282 Morgan Rielly 1.50 4.00
283 Johnny Gaudreau 2.50 6.00
284 Vladimir Tarasenko 2.00 5.00
285 Wayne Gretzky 10.00 25.00
286 Vladimir Tarasenko 4.00 10.00
287 Taylor Hall 3.00 8.00
288 Alexander Ovechkin 12.00 30.00
289 Wayne Gretzky 20.00 50.00
290 John Tavares 5.00 12.00
291 Mario Lemieux 12.00 30.00
292 Bobby Clarke 5.00 12.00
293 Carey Price 12.00 30.00
294 Jari Kurri 3.00 8.00
295 Bobby Orr 12.00 30.00
296 Max Domi 2.50 6.00
297 Robby Fabbri 1.50 4.00
298 Shea Theodore 2.00 5.00
299 Nikolaj Ehlers 2.50 6.00
300 Charles Hudon 1.25 3.00
301 Mike McCarron 1.50 4.00
302 Noah Hanifin 2.00 5.00
303 Dylan Larkin 4.00 10.00
304 Oscar Lindberg 1.25 3.00
305 Matt Murray 5.00 12.00
306 Andreas Athanasiou 3.00 8.00
307 Jake Virtanen 1.50 4.00
308 Jack Eichel 5.00 12.00
309 Jared McCann 1.50 4.00
310 Mattias Janmark 1.25 3.00
311 Artemi Panarin 5.00 12.00
312 Colton Parayko 2.00 5.00
313 Nick Shore .75 2.00
314 Sam Bennett 4.00 10.00
315 Connor McDavid 20.00 50.00
316 Colton Parayko 3.00 8.00
317 Max Domi 4.00 10.00
318 Noah Hanifin 2.00 5.00
319 Jake Virtanen 2.50 6.00
320 Oscar Lindberg 2.00 5.00
321 Artemi Panarin 8.00 20.00
322 Nikolaj Ehlers 4.00 10.00
323 Jack Eichel 8.00 20.00
324 Robby Fabbri 2.50 6.00
325 Mike McCarron 2.50 6.00
326 Sam Bennett 6.00 15.00
327 Mattias Janmark 2.50 6.00
328 Dylan Larkin 6.00 15.00
329 Charles Hudon 2.00 5.00
330 Connor McDavid 30.00 80.00
331 Sam Bennett 10.00 25.00
332 Noah Hanifin 5.00 12.00
333 Zachary Fucale 2.50 6.00
334 Robby Fabbri 4.00 10.00
335 Jack Eichel 12.00 30.00
336 Dylan Larkin 10.00 25.00
337 Nikolaj Ehlers 6.00 15.00
338 Artemi Panarin 12.00 30.00
339 Max Domi 6.00 15.00
340 Connor McDavid 50.00 125.00
343 Jesse Puljujarvi 6.00 15.00

2015-16 Upper Deck Portfolio Autographs

3 Leo Komarov G 4.00 10.00
8 Justin Faulk F 6.00 15.00
9 Bobby Ryan E 8.00 20.00
10 Ryan Strome G 6.00 15.00
12 Antti Niemi E 8.00 20.00
13 Nick Foligno G 5.00 12.00
15 Aaron Ekblad E 12.00 30.00
17 Marc-Andre Fleury D 30.00 80.00
22 Mark Scheifele G 10.00 25.00
28 Jake Allen G 6.00 15.00
32 Alexander Ovechkin B 50.00 125.00
35 Matt Duchene E 10.00 25.00
37 Pavel Datsyuk D 25.00 60.00
39 Sergei Bobrovsky F 12.00 30.00
41 Mats Zuccarello A 30.00 80.00
42 Nick Bjugstad G 4.00 10.00
45 Patrick Sharp C 15.00 40.00
46 Jamie Benn D 15.00 40.00
48 Filip Forsberg C 25.00 60.00
49 Claude Giroux C 15.00 40.00
53 P.K. Subban C 20.00 50.00
57 Shayne Gostisbehere F 8.00 20.00
58 Corey Perry E 15.00 40.00
62 Jarome Iginla D 20.00 50.00
66 Anze Kopitar E 15.00 40.00
68 Brendan Gallagher D 15.00 40.00
73 Cory Schneider E 10.00 25.00
74 Carey Price D 30.00 80.00
76 Pekka Rinne F 8.00 20.00
77 Tyler Seguin A 40.00 100.00
79 Jakub Voracek F 6.00 15.00
82 Evgeny Kuznetsov F 10.00 25.00
85 Gabriel Landeskog E 12.00 30.00
86 Nikita Kucherov E 20.00 50.00
87 Matt Moulson G 4.00 10.00
88 Mark Stone G 8.00 20.00
90 John Tavares E 15.00 40.00
93 Scott Hartnell E 6.00 15.00
94 Mike Hoffman G 8.00 20.00
101 Cam Fowler E 10.00 25.00
114 Ryan Oâ•™Reilly G 6.00 15.00
120 Taylor Hall E 10.00 25.00
121 Jonathan Quick C 20.00 50.00
122 Joe Pavelski E 12.00 30.00
125 Charlie Coyle G 6.00 15.00
126 John Carlson E 10.00 25.00
128 Semyon Varlamov F 8.00 20.00
130 Ryan Kesler E 10.00 25.00
134 Evgeni Malkin A 60.00 150.00
143 Kyle Turris G 5.00 12.00
144 Tomas Tatar F 5.00 12.00
145 Morgan Rielly E 10.00 25.00
146 Oscar Klefbom G 10.00 25.00
150 Jonathan Toews D 25.00 60.00
153 Ryan Miller D 15.00 40.00
157 Nail Yakupov E 6.00 15.00
158 Tyler Johnson F 5.00 12.00
161 Sam Reinhart F 15.00 40.00
162 Alex Galchenyuk B 25.00 60.00
164 Leon Draisaitl D 50.00 125.00
165 Jaromir Jagr B 40.00 100.00
166 Tyler Toffoli G 6.00 15.00
171 Max Pacioretty E 10.00 25.00
173 Braden Holtby A 40.00 100.00
180 Aleksander Barkov F 12.00 30.00
181 Brian Leetch D 12.00 30.00
182 Lanny McDonald D 15.00 40.00
183 Clark Gillies D 15.00 40.00
184 Rod Brind' Amour G 5.00 12.00
185 Doug Gilmour D 20.00 50.00
186 Pavel Bure B 12.00 30.00
187 Bobby Orr A 120.00 300.00
188 Glenn Hall E 10.00 25.00
189 Joe Sakic B 25.00 60.00
191 Nicklas Lidstrom D 15.00 40.00
192 Jari Kurri F 8.00 20.00
193 Guy Lafleur A 40.00 100.00
194 Martin Brodeur B 30.00 80.00
195 Mark Messier B 25.00 60.00
196 Bobby Clarke F 12.00 30.00
197 Mario Lemieux A 125.00 300.00
198 Al MacInnis D 20.00 50.00
200 Wayne Gretzky A 400.00 1000.00
202 Jake Virtanen C 20.00 50.00
203 Brett Pesce E 8.00 20.00
204 Jujhar Khaira E 8.00 20.00
205 Brady Skjei E 8.00 20.00
206 Nikolaj Ehlers C 30.00 80.00
207 Shane Prince E 6.00 15.00
208 Joonas Donskoi D 12.00 30.00
209 Nick Ritchie D 12.00 30.00
210 Andreas Athanasiou B 30.00 80.00
211 Colton Parayko C 20.00 50.00
212 Christoph Bertschy E 8.00 20.00
213 Garret Sparks E 10.00 25.00
214 Joonas Korpisalo D 25.00 60.00
215 Artemi Panarin A 125.00 300.00
216 Mikko Rantanen B 60.00 150.00
217 Robby Fabbri C 12.00 30.00
219 Nikolay Goldobin D 12.00 30.00
220 Oscar Lindberg B 12.00 30.00
221 Taylor Leier D 12.00 30.00
222 Viktor Arvidsson E 10.00 25.00
223 Matt Murray D 50.00 120.00
224 Mike McCarron E 12.00 30.00
226 Dylan Larkin C 50.00 125.00
227 Ben Hutton D 12.00 30.00
228 Charles Hudon E 12.00 30.00
229 Sergei Plotnikov E 6.00 15.00
230 Malcolm Subban C 25.00 60.00
231 Juuse Saros C 25.00 60.00
232 Linus Ullmark E 20.00 50.00
233 Nicolas Petan E 10.00 25.00
234 Sam Bennett C 50.00 125.00
235 Jean-Francois Berube E 8.00 20.00
236 Louis Domingue E 10.00 25.00
238 Connor Hellebuyck C 60.00 150.00
240 Mike Condon D 12.00 30.00
241 Jared McCann D 15.00 40.00
242 Colin Miller E 8.00 20.00
243 Antoine Bibeau D 12.00 30.00
244 Shea Theodore E 15.00 40.00
245 Zachary Fucale D 10.00 25.00
246 Daniel Carr D 10.00 25.00
247 Frank Vatrano E 12.00 30.00
249 Noah Hanifin C 25.00 60.00
250 Connor McDavid C 200.00 500.00
251 Alexander Ovechkin B 30.00 80.00
253 Jamie Benn B 25.00 60.00
254 Bobby Clarke C 25.00 60.00
255 Brian Leetch B 15.00 40.00
256 Filip Forsberg A 50.00 125.00
257 Jari Kurri E 10.00 25.00
259 Cory Schneider E 10.00 25.00
260 Clark Gillies C 12.00 30.00
261 Max Pacioretty D 12.00 30.00
262 Mario Lemieux A 125.00 300.00
264 Aaron Ekblad D 15.00 40.00
265 Rod Brind' Amour E 8.00 20.00
266 John Tavares C 25.00 60.00
267 Taylor Hall D 12.00 30.00
268 Shayne Gostisbehere D 15.00 40.00
269 Lanny McDonald B 12.00 30.00
270 Wayne Gretzky A 400.00 1000.00
271 Carey Price A 60.00 150.00
272 Nicklas Lidstrom A 20.00 50.00
273 Tyler Seguin A 40.00 100.00
274 Bobby Ryan B 10.00 25.00
275 Joe Pavelski B 15.00 40.00
278 Jonathan Toews A 50.00 125.00
279 Mark Scheifele C 25.00 60.00
280 Nicklas Backstrom B 20.00 50.00
281 Ryan O'Reilly C 12.00 30.00
282 Morgan Rielly B 12.00 30.00
285 Wayne Gretzky A 400.00 1000.00
287 Taylor Hall C 15.00 40.00
288 Alexander Ovechkin A 120.00 300.00
289 Wayne Gretzky A 400.00 1000.00
290 John Tavares B 20.00 50.00
291 Mario Lemieux A 125.00 300.00
293 Carey Price B 100.00 200.00
294 Jari Kurri C 15.00 40.00
297 Robby Fabbri C 20.00 50.00
298 Shea Theodore C 20.00 50.00
299 Nikolaj Ehlers D 20.00 50.00
300 Charles Hudon C 12.00 30.00
301 Mike McCarron C 12.00 30.00
302 Noah Hanifin C 25.00 60.00
303 Dylan Larkin B 60.00 150.00
304 Oscar Lindberg C 12.00 30.00
305 Matt Murray B 200.00 300.00
306 Andreas Athanasiou D 30.00 80.00
307 Jake Virtanen D 15.00 40.00
309 Jared McCann D 15.00 40.00
310 Mattias Janmark D 12.00 30.00
312 Colton Parayko B 20.00 50.00
313 Nick Shore D 8.00 20.00
314 Sam Bennett B 40.00 100.00
315 Connor McDavid A 500.00 1200.00
316 Colton Parayko A 50.00 125.00
318 Noah Hanifin B 20.00 50.00
319 Jake Virtanen C 20.00 50.00
320 Oscar Lindberg A 30.00 80.00
322 Nikolaj Ehlers C 30.00 80.00
324 Robby Fabbri B 15.00 40.00
325 Mike McCarron C 20.00 50.00
326 Sam Bennett B 40.00 100.00
327 Mattias Janmark C 15.00 40.00
328 Dylan Larkin A 100.00 250.00
329 Charles Hudon C 15.00 40.00
330 Connor McDavid A 500.00 1200.00
331 Sam Bennett B 40.00 100.00
333 Zachary Fucale C 12.00 30.00
334 Robby Fabbri C 20.00 50.00
337 Nikolaj Ehlers C 30.00 80.00
340 Connor McDavid A 500.00 1200.00

2015-16 Upper Deck Portfolio Profiles Material

PMAK Anze Kopitar D 3.00 8.00
PMAO Alexander Ovechkin B 8.00 20.00
PMAP Artemi Panarin B 8.00 20.00
PMBH Brett Hull A 8.00 20.00
PMCG Claude Giroux D 2.00 5.00
PMCM Connor McDavid B 30.00 80.00
PMCP Carey Price B 4.00 10.00
PMDH Dale Hawerchuk C 2.50 6.00
PMDL Dylan Larkin B 6.00 15.00
PMEK Erik Karlsson C 2.50 6.00
PMGL Gabriel Landeskog D 2.50 6.00
PMHL Henrik Lundqvist C 5.00 12.00
PMHO Braden Holtby C 2.50 6.00
PMJC Jeff Carter D 1.50 4.00
PMJE Jack Eichel B 8.00 20.00
PMJI Jarome Iginla C 2.50 6.00
PMJK Jari Kurri A 2.00 5.00
PMJL John LeClair C 2.00 5.00
PMJO Joe Thornton C 3.00 8.00
PMJQ Jonathan Quick C 2.50 6.00
PMJR Jeremy Roenick B 3.00 8.00
PMJS Joe Sakic A 8.00 20.00
PMJT Jonathan Toews B 3.00 8.00
PMLR Larry Robinson A 2.00 5.00
PMMD Max Domi B 4.00 10.00
PMMR Morgan Rielly D 2.00 5.00
PMMS Mark Scheifele D 3.00 8.00
PMMZ Mats Zuccarello D 2.00 5.00
PMNE Nikolaj Ehlers D 4.00 10.00
PMNH Noah Hanifin D 3.00 8.00
PMNK Nazem Kadri D 2.50 6.00
PMOE Oliver Ekman-Larsson C 2.00 5.00
PMRB Ray Bourque A 6.00 15.00
PMRF Robby Fabbri C 2.50 6.00
PMRK Ryan Kesler D 2.00 5.00
PMRL Roberto Luongo D 3.00 8.00
PMRN Ryan Nugent-Hopkins D 2.50 6.00
PMSC Sidney Crosby B 8.00 20.00
PMSP Jason Spezza D 2.00 5.00
PMTH Taylor Hall D 2.00 5.00

2015-16 Upper Deck Portfolio Profiles Material Dual

PM2AP Artemi Panarin A 12.00 30.00
PM2BH Braden Holtby C 4.00 10.00
PM2BR Bill Ranford A 3.00 8.00
PM2CA John Carlson C 3.00 8.00
PM2CM Connor McDavid A 50.00 125.00
PM2CP Corey Perry C 5.00 12.00
PM2DD Drew Doughty B 4.00 10.00
PM2DH Dominik Hasek A 5.00 12.00
PM2DK Duncan Keith B 2.50 6.00
PM2DL Dylan Larkin A 10.00 25.00
PM2DS Daniel Sedin C 4.00 10.00
PM2EM Evgeni Malkin B 6.00 15.00
PM2FF Filip Forsberg C 5.00 12.00
PM2GL Guy Lafleur A 4.00 10.00
PM2HA Dale Hawerchuk A 4.00 10.00
PM2HL Henrik Lundqvist B 8.00 20.00
PM2JC Jeff Carter C 2.50 6.00
PM2JE Jack Eichel A 12.00 30.00
PM2JI Jarome Iginla B 4.00 10.00
PM2JJ Jaromir Jagr B 10.00 25.00
PM2JP Joe Pavelski C 4.00 10.00
PM2JS Joe Sakic A 6.00 15.00
PM2JT Jonathan Toews B 5.00 12.00
PM2JV Jakub Voracek C 2.50 6.00
PM2MD Max Domi B 6.00 15.00
PM2NH Noah Hanifin B 5.00 12.00
PM2RB Ray Bourque A 6.00 15.00
PM2RG Ryan Getzlaf B 3.00 8.00
PM2RN Ryan Nugent-Hopkins C 3.00 8.00
PM2SK Jeff Skinner C 4.00 10.00

2015-16 Upper Deck Portfolio Profiles Material Quad

PM4AP Artemi Panarin B 15.00 40.00
PM4BH Brett Hull A 8.00 20.00
PM4CG Claude Giroux C 4.00 10.00
PM4CM Connor McDavid A 40.00 100.00
PM4DL Dylan Larkin B 12.00 30.00
PM4JE Jack Eichel B 15.00 40.00
PM4JJ Joe Thornton C 6.00 15.00
PM4JQ Jonathan Quick B 5.00 12.00
PM4JS Joe Sakic A 8.00 20.00
PM4JT Jonathan Toews B 6.00 15.00
PM4MD Max Domi B 6.00 15.00
PM4MR Morgan Rielly C 4.00 10.00
PM4MS Mark Scheifele C 6.00 15.00
PM4OE Oliver Ekman-Larsson C 2.50 6.00
PM4PK P.K. Subban B 5.00 12.00
PM4RB Ray Bourque A 6.00 15.00
PM4RF Robby Fabbri C 5.00 12.00
PM4RL Roberto Luongo C 6.00 15.00
PM4TH Taylor Hall C 4.00 10.00
PM4WG Wayne Gretzky A 25.00 60.00

2015-16 Upper Deck Portfolio Profiles Material Six

PM6CM Connor McDavid A 80.00 200.00
PM6CP Carey Price A 10.00 25.00
PM6DL Dylan Larkin C 15.00 40.00
PM6EK Erik Karlsson B 6.00 15.00
PM6JE Jack Eichel B 20.00 50.00
PM6PB Patrice Bergeron C 6.00 15.00
PM6PK P.K. Subban B 6.00 15.00
PM6SC Sidney Crosby B 20.00 50.00
PM6TH Taylor Hall C 5.00 12.00
PM6WG Wayne Gretzky A 30.00 80.00

1999-00 Upper Deck PowerDeck

COMPLETE SET (20) 25.00 60.00
1 Paul Kariya 1.25 3.00
2 Teemu Selanne 1.25 3.00
3 Patrik Stefan 1.00 2.50
4 Ray Bourque 2.00 5.00
5 Sergei Samsonov 1.25 3.00
6 Dominik Hasek 2.00 5.00
7 Peter Forsberg 2.00 5.00
8 Patrick Roy 4.00 10.00
9 Brett Hull 1.50 4.00
10 Mike Modano 2.00 5.00
11 Steve Yzerman 4.00 10.00
12 Pavel Bure 1.25 3.00
13 David Legwand 1.00 2.50
14 Martin Brodeur 2.50 6.00
15 Theo Fleury 1.25 3.00
16 Eric Lindros 1.25 3.00
17 Jaromir Jagr 1.50 4.00
18 Bobby Orr 6.00 15.00
19 Gordie Howe 4.00 10.00
20 Wayne Gretzky 6.00 15.00

1999-00 Upper Deck PowerDeck Auxiliary

COMPLETE SET (20) 30.00 60.00
*AUXILIARY: .2X TO .5X BASIC CARDS

1999-00 Upper Deck PowerDeck Powerful Moments

COMPLETE SET (4) 20.00 40.00
COMMON GRETZKY (PM1-PM4) 6.00 15.00
*AUXILIARY: .4X TO 1X BASIC INSERTS

1999-00 Upper Deck PowerDeck Time Capsule

COMPLETE SET (8) 20.00 50.00
*AUXILIARY: .4X TO 1X
T1 Jaromir Jagr 2.00 5.00
T2 Paul Kariya 2.00 5.00
T3 Patrick Roy 6.00 15.00
T4 Bobby Orr 8.00 20.00
T5 Dominik Hasek 3.00 8.00
T6 Gordie Howe 4.00 10.00
T7 Brett Hull 2.00 5.00
T8 Steve Yzerman 5.00 12.00

2005-06 Upper Deck Power Play

COMP.SET w/o SP's (90) 8.00 15.00
1 Jean-Sebastien Giguere .20 .50
2 Joffrey Lupul .12 .30
3 Sergei Fedorov .30 .75
4 Dany Heatley .15 .40
5 Ilya Kovalchuk .20 .50
6 Kari Lehtonen .15 .40
7 Sergei Samsonov .15 .40
8 Joe Thornton .30 .75
9 Andrew Raycroft .15 .40
10 Glen Murray .15 .40
11 Ryan Miller .20 .50
12 Daniel Briere .20 .50
13 Miroslav Satan .15 .40
14 Jarome Iginla .25 .60
15 Jordan Leopold .12 .30
16 Miikka Kiprusoff .20 .50
17 Eric Staal .25 .60
18 Josef Vasicek .12 .30
19 Eric Daze .15 .40
20 Tuomo Ruutu .20 .50
21 Jocelyn Thibault .15 .40
22 Joe Sakic .40 1.00
23 Alex Tanguay .20 .50
24 Milan Hejduk .15 .40
25 Peter Forsberg .40 1.00
26 Rick Nash .20 .50
27 Nikolai Zherdev .12 .30
28 Marc Denis .15 .40
29 Mike Modano .30 .75
30 Bill Guerin .20 .50
31 Marty Turco .20 .50
32 Pavel Datsyuk .30 .75
33 Brendan Shanahan .20 .50
34 Steve Yzerman .50 1.25
35 Nicklas Lidstrom .20 .50
36 Ales Hemsky .15 .40
37 Ryan Smyth .15 .40
38 Patrice Bergeron .25 .60
39 Roberto Luongo .30 .75
40 Olli Jokinen .20 .50
41 Luc Robitaille .20 .50
42 Zigmund Palffy .15 .40
43 Lubomir Visnovsky .12 .30
44 Marian Gaborik .20 .50
45 Dwayne Roloson .15 .40
46 Michael Ryder .15 .40
47 Jose Theodore .20 .50
48 Mike Ribeiro .12 .30
49 Steve Sullivan .12 .30
50 Nathan Horton .20 .50
51 Tomas Vokoun .15 .40
52 Martin Brodeur .50 1.25
53 Patrik Elias .20 .50
54 Scott Niedermayer .20 .50
55 Michael Peca .15 .40
56 Mark Messier .40 1.00
57 Jaromir Jagr .60 1.50
58 Mark Parrish .12 .30
59 Rick DiPietro .20 .50
60 Daniel Alfredsson .20 .50
61 Marian Hossa .20 .50
62 Jason Spezza .20 .50
63 Dominik Hasek .30 .75
64 Jeremy Roenick .30 .75
65 Keith Primeau .15 .40
66 John LeClair .20 .50
67 Brett Hull .40 1.00
68 Ladislav Nagy .12 .30
69 Shane Doan .15 .40
70 Marc-Andre Fleury .40 1.00
71 Mario Lemieux .75 2.00
72 Mark Recchi .25 .60
73 Jonathan Cheechoo .20 .50
74 Evgeni Nabokov .15 .40
75 Patrick Marleau .20 .50
76 Chris Pronger .20 .50
77 Doug Weight .20 .50
78 Keith Tkachuk .20 .50
79 Brad Richards .20 .50
80 Nikolai Khabibulin .20 .50
81 Martin St. Louis .20 .50
82 Dave Andreychuk .20 .50
83 Joe Nieuwendyk .15 .40
84 Ed Belfour .20 .50
85 Mats Sundin .20 .50
86 Brian Leetch .15 .40
87 Brendan Morrison .12 .30
88 Markus Naslund .20 .50
89 Todd Bertuzzi .20 .50
90 Olaf Kolzig .20 .50
91 Sergei Fedorov IP .60 1.50
92 Dany Heatley IP .30 .75
93 Joe Thornton IP .60 1.50
94 Daniel Briere IP .40 1.00
95 Jarome Iginla IP .50 1.25
96 Joe Sakic IP .75 2.00
97 Steve Yzerman IP 1.00 2.50
98 Martin Havlat IP .40 1.00
99 Jeremy Roenick IP .60 1.50
100 Mario Lemieux IP 1.50 4.00
101 Chris Pronger IP .40 1.00
102 Dave Andreychuk IP .40 1.00
103 Martin St. Louis IP .40 1.00
104 Mats Sundin IP .40 1.00
105 Ilya Kovalchuk IA .40 1.00
106 Andrew Raycroft IA .30 .75
107 Peter Forsberg IA .75 2.00
108 Rick Nash IA .40 1.00
109 Jose Theodore IA .40 1.00
110 Tomas Vokoun IA .30 .75
111 Jaromir Jagr IA 1.25 3.00
112 Mark Messier IA .75 2.00
113 Jason Spezza IA .40 1.00
114 Marc-Andre Fleury IA .75 2.00
115 Jonathan Cheechoo IA .30 .75
116 Patrick Marleau IA .40 1.00
117 Nikolai Khabibulin IA .40 1.00
118 Markus Naslund IA .40 1.00
119 Dave Andreychuk CC .40 1.00
120 Martin Brodeur CC 5.00 12.00
121 Joe Sakic CC 4.00 10.00
122 Patrick Roy CC 5.00 12.00
123 Wayne Gretzky CC 12.00 30.00
124 Mark Messier CC 4.00 10.00
125 Steve Yzerman CC 5.00 12.00
126 Andrew Raycroft GR 1.00 2.50
127 Martin Brodeur GR 3.00 8.00
128 Patrick Roy GR 3.00 8.00
129 Jose Theodore GR 1.25 3.00
130 Marc-Andre Fleury GR 2.50 6.00
131 Marty Turco GR 1.25 3.00
132 Nikolai Khabibulin GR 1.25 3.00
133 Sidney Crosby RC 10.00 25.00
134 Wojtek Wolski RC 1.00 2.50
135 Hannu Toivonen RC 1.25 3.00
136 Alexander Steen RC 2.00 5.00
137 Jeff Woywitka RC .75 2.00
138 Jussi Jokinen RC 1.25 3.00
139 Kevin Nastiuk RC .75 2.00
140 Brent Seabrook RC 2.50 6.00
141 Brad Winchester RC 1.25 3.00
142 Brandon Bochenski RC 1.25 3.00
143 Alexander Ovechkin RC 40.00 100.00
144 Thomas Vanek RC 2.50 6.00
145 Yann Danis RC 1.00 2.50
146 Ryan Getzlaf RC 3.00 8.00
147 Ryan Suter RC 1.25 3.00
148 Henrik Lundqvist RC 6.00 15.00
149 Johan Franzen RC 2.00 5.00
150 Rene Bourque RC 1.25 3.00
151 Eric Nystrom RC 1.00 2.50
152 Patrick Eaves RC 1.25 3.00
153 Corey Perry RC 4.00 10.00
154 Alexander Perezhogin RC 1.00 2.50
155 Zach Parise RC 3.00 8.00
156 Mike Richards RC 2.50 6.00
157 Braydon Coburn RC 1.25 3.00
158 Cam Ward RC 2.00 5.00
159 David Leneveu RC 1.00 2.50
160 Andrew Alberts RC .75 2.00
161 Petteri Nokelainen RC .75 2.00
162 Lee Stempniak RC 1.25 3.00
163 Jeff Carter RC 2.00 5.00
164 Gilbert Brule RC 1.25 3.00
165 Dion Phaneuf RC 2.00 5.00
166 Jim Howard RC 3.00 8.00
167 Rostislav Olesz RC 1.00 2.50
168 Robert Nilsson RC 1.25 3.00
169 Peter Budaj RC 1.50 4.00
170 Andrej Meszaros RC 1.00 2.50
171 Petr Prucha RC 1.25 3.00
172 Matt Foy RC .75 2.00

2008-09 Upper Deck Power Play

COMPLETE SET (400) 30.00 80.00
COMP.FACT.SET (300) 25.00 50.00
COMP.FACT.UPDATE (100) 12.00 30.00
1 Francois Beauchemin .10 .25
2 George Parros .10 .25
3 Bobby Ryan .12 .30
4 Ryan Getzlaf .15 .40
5 Jean-Sebastien Giguere .10 .25
6 Corey Perry .25 .60
7 Teemu Selanne .30 .75
8 Chris Pronger .15 .40
9 Chris Kunitz .15 .40
10 Scott Niedermayer .15 .40
11 Brendan Morrison .10 .25
12 Slava Kozlov .10 .25
13 Todd White .10 .25
14 Ilya Kovalchuk .15 .40
15 Eric Perrin .10 .25
16 Colby Armstrong .10 .25
17 Kari Lehtonen .10 .25
18 Bryan Little .12 .30
19 Tobias Enstrom .10 .25
20 Jason Williams .10 .25
21 David Krejci .15 .40
22 Milan Lucic .25 .60
23 Peter Schaefer .10 .25
24 Patrice Bergeron .20 .50

25 Marc Savard .10 .25
26 Tim Thomas .15 .40
27 Zdeno Chara .15 .40
28 Marco Sturm .10 .25
29 Phil Kessel .15 .40
30 Aaron Ward .10 .25
31 Michael Ryder .10 .25
32 Jochen Hecht .10 .25
33 Ales Kotalik .10 .25
34 Tim Connolly .10 .25
35 Thomas Vanek .12 .30
36 Ryan Miller .15 .40
37 Derek Roy .10 .25
38 Jason Pominville .10 .25
39 Drew Stafford .10 .25
40 Eric Nystrom .10 .25
41 Cory Sarich .10 .25
42 Adrian Aucoin .10 .25
43 Todd Bertuzzi .15 .40
44 Miikka Kiprusoff .15 .40
45 Jarome Iginla .20 .50
46 Daymond Langkow .10 .25
47 Dion Phaneuf .12 .30
48 Matthew Lombardi .10 .25
49 Robyn Regehr .10 .25
50 Mike Cammalleri .12 .30
51 Sergei Samsonov .12 .30
52 Matt Cullen .10 .25
53 Eric Staal .20 .50
54 Rod Brind'Amour .15 .40
55 Cam Ward .15 .40
56 Justin Williams .12 .30
57 Ray Whitney .12 .30
58 Joni Pitkanen .10 .25
59 Adam Burish .12 .30
60 Dustin Byfuglien .15 .40
61 Patrick Kane .30 .75
62 Nikolai Khabibulin .15 .40
63 Patrick Sharp .15 .40
64 Brent Seabrook .10 .25
65 Jonathan Toews .25 .60
66 Martin Havlat .15 .40
67 Duncan Keith .12 .30
68 Brian Campbell .12 .30
69 Cristobal Huet .12 .30
70 John-Michael Liles .10 .25
71 T.J. Hensick .12 .30
72 David Jones .10 .25
73 Joe Sakic .30 .75
74 Ryan Smyth .12 .30
75 Milan Hejduk .12 .30
76 Marek Svatos .10 .25
77 Paul Stastny .12 .30
78 Wojtek Wolski .12 .30
79 Andrew Raycroft .12 .30
80 Darcy Tucker .12 .30
81 Kristian Huselius .10 .25
82 Derick Brassard RC .15 .40
83 Steve Mason RC 3.00 8.00
84 Jason Chimera .10 .25
85 Fredrik Norrena .10 .25
86 Rick Nash .15 .40
87 Kris Russell .10 .25
88 Pascal Leclaire .12 .30
89 Rostislav Klesla .10 .25
90 Jared Boll .10 .25
91 R.J. Umberger .10 .25
92 Loui Eriksson .10 .25
93 Sergei Zubov .12 .30
94 Stephane Robidas .10 .25
95 Mike Modano .25 .60
96 Brad Richards .15 .40
97 Marty Turco .15 .40
98 Mike Ribeiro .10 .25
99 Brenden Morrow .12 .30
100 Jere Lehtinen .10 .25
101 Sean Avery .10 .25
102 Johan Franzen .12 .30
103 Jiri Hudler .12 .30
104 Mikael Samuelsson .10 .25
105 Kris Draper .10 .25
106 Andreas Lilja .10 .25
107 Nicklas Lidstrom .15 .40
108 Pavel Datsyuk .25 .60
109 Chris Osgood .15 .40
110 Henrik Zetterberg .20 .50
111 Dan Cleary .12 .30
112 Tomas Holmstrom .12 .30
113 Valtteri Filppula .10 .25
114 Ty Conklin .12 .30
115 Marian Hossa .12 .30
116 Erik Cole .10 .25
117 Sheldon Souray .10 .25
118 Sam Gagner .10 .25
119 Ales Hemsky .12 .30
120 Mathieu Garon .12 .30
121 Shawn Horcoff .10 .25
122 Dustin Penner .10 .25
123 Andrew Cogliano .12 .30
124 Dwayne Roloson .12 .30
125 Shawn Matthias RC .12 .30
126 Craig Anderson .15 .40
127 Brett McLean .10 .25
128 Rostislav Olesz .10 .25
129 Tomas Vokoun .12 .30
130 Nathan Horton .12 .30
131 David Booth .10 .25
132 Stephen Weiss .10 .25
133 Jay Bouwmeester .10 .25
134 Jarret Stoll .12 .30
135 Jack Johnson .10 .25
136 Jason LaBarbera .12 .30
137 Anze Kopitar .25 .60
138 Alexander Frolov .10 .25
139 Dustin Brown .15 .40
140 Patrick O'Sullivan .12 .30
141 Andrew Brunette .10 .25
142 Brent Burns .15 .40
143 James Sheppard .10 .25
144 Derek Boogaard .10 .25
145 Marian Gaborik .15 .40
146 Niklas Backstrom .15 .40
147 Pierre-Marc Bouchard .10 .25
148 Josh Harding .15 .40
149 Mikko Koivu .12 .30
150 Marek Zidlicky .10 .25
151 Alex Tanguay .10 .25
152 Andrei Kostitsyn .12 .30
153 Sergei Kostitsyn .10 .25
154 Maxim Lapierre .10 .25
155 Saku Koivu .15 .40
156 Carey Price .30 .75
157 Tomas Plekanec .10 .25
158 Alex Kovalev .12 .30
159 Chris Higgins .10 .25
160 Andrei Markov .15 .40
161 Guillaume Latendresse .12 .30
162 Dan Ellis .10 .25
163 Shea Weber .12 .30
164 Ryan Suter .12 .30
165 Jason Arnott .12 .30
166 Martin Erat .10 .25
167 J.P. Dumont .10 .25
168 David Legwand .12 .30
169 Bobby Holik .10 .25
170 Brian Rolston .12 .30
171 Paul Martin .10 .25
172 Jamie Langenbrunner .10 .25
173 Johnny Oduya .12 .30
174 Martin Brodeur .40 1.00
175 Zach Parise .15 .40
176 Patrik Elias .15 .40
177 Brian Gionta .12 .30
178 John Madden .10 .25
179 Travis Zajac .10 .25
180 Kyle Okposo RC .20 .50
181 Mike Sillinger .10 .25
182 Blake Comeau .10 .25
183 Rick DiPietro .12 .30
184 Mike Comrie .12 .30
185 Bill Guerin .15 .40
186 Trent Hunter .10 .25
187 Nikolai Zherdev .10 .25
188 Stephen Valiquette .12 .30
189 Nigel Dawes .10 .25
190 Lauri Korpikoski RC .10 .25
191 Henrik Lundqvist .40 1.00
192 Chris Drury .12 .30
193 Scott Gomez .12 .30
194 Brendan Shanahan .15 .40
195 Marc Staal .12 .30
196 Brandon Dubinsky .10 .25
197 Wade Redden .12 .30
198 Markus Naslund .15 .40
199 Chris Phillips .10 .25
200 Chris Neil .10 .25
201 Filip Kuba .10 .25
202 Anton Volchenkov .10 .25
203 Jason Spezza .12 .30
204 Dany Heatley .12 .30
205 Nick Foligno .10 .25
206 Antoine Vermette .10 .25
207 Mike Fisher .10 .25
208 Daniel Alfredsson .15 .40
209 Martin Gerber .12 .30
210 Kimmo Timonen .10 .25
211 Scottie Upshall .10 .25
212 Claude Giroux RC .30 .75
213 Mike Richards .12 .30
214 Martin Biron .12 .30
215 Daniel Briere .15 .40
216 Simon Gagne .15 .40
217 Mike Knuble .10 .25
218 Jeff Carter .12 .30
219 Olli Jokinen .10 .25
220 Kyle Turris RC .25 .60
221 Steven Reinprecht .10 .25
222 Daniel Carcillo .10 .25
223 Daniel Winnik .10 .25
224 Peter Mueller .12 .30
225 Shane Doan .12 .30
226 Ilya Bryzgalov .12 .30
227 Ed Jovanovski .10 .25
228 Martin Hanzal .12 .30
229 Miroslav Satan .15 .40
230 Ruslan Fedotenko .10 .25
231 Tyler Kennedy .10 .25
232 Brooks Orpik .10 .25
233 Maxime Talbot .10 .25
234 Sidney Crosby .60 1.50
235 Marc-Andre Fleury .30 .75
236 Evgeni Malkin .30 .75
237 Sergei Gonchar .10 .25
238 Jordan Staal .12 .30
239 Ryan Whitney .15 .40
240 Rob Blake .15 .40
241 Ryane Clowe .10 .25
242 Joe Pavelski .20 .50
243 Torrey Mitchell .10 .25
244 Joe Thornton .25 .60
245 Evgeni Nabokov .12 .30
246 Jonathan Cheechoo .12 .30
247 Milan Michalek .10 .25
248 Patrick Marleau .15 .40
249 Dan Boyle .10 .25
250 Chris Mason .12 .30
251 Andy McDonald .12 .30
252 David Backes .10 .25
253 David Perron .10 .25
254 Paul Kariya .15 .40
255 Manny Legace .15 .40
256 Erik Johnson .10 .25
257 Brad Boyes .10 .25
258 Lee Stempniak .10 .25
259 Keith Tkachuk .15 .40
260 Radim Vrbata .10 .25
261 Ryan Malone .10 .25
262 Mark Recchi .20 .50
263 Vaclav Prospal .10 .25
264 Jussi Jokinen .10 .25
265 Michel Ouellet .10 .25
266 Vincent Lecavalier .15 .40
267 Mike Smith .15 .40
268 Matt Carle .10 .25
269 Martin St. Louis .15 .40
270 Paul Ranger .10 .25
271 Andrej Meszaros .10 .25
272 Olaf Kolzig .15 .40
273 Ian White .10 .25
274 Pavel Kubina .10 .25
275 Jason Blake .10 .25
276 Robbie Earl RC .10 .25
277 Mats Sundin .15 .40
278 Vesa Toskala .20 .50
279 Alexander Steen .10 .25
280 Tomas Kaberle .10 .25
281 Nikolai Antropov .12 .30
282 Matt Stajan .10 .25
283 Jiri Tlusty .10 .25
284 Steve Bernier .10 .25
285 Pavol Demitra .20 .50
286 Taylor Pyatt .12 .30
287 Kevin Bieksa .12 .30
288 Roberto Luongo .25 .60
289 Daniel Sedin .20 .50
290 Ryan Kesler .15 .40
291 Alexander Edler .10 .25
292 Henrik Sedin .20 .50
293 Jose Theodore .15 .40
294 Brooks Laich .10 .25
295 Tomas Fleischmann .10 .25
296 Alexander Ovechkin .60 1.50
297 Nicklas Backstrom .15 .40
298 Sergei Fedorov .25 .60
299 Mike Green .12 .30
300 Alexander Semin .15 .40
301 Brett Festerling RC .20 .50
302 Andrew Ebbett RC .15 .40
303 Zach Bogosian RC .30 .75
304 Boris Valabik RC .25 .60
305 Nathan Oystrick RC .25 .60
306 Blake Wheeler RC .60 1.50
307 Nathan Gerbe RC .25 .60
308 Adam Pardy RC .20 .50
309 Brandon Sutter RC .25 .60
310 Zach Boychuk RC .25 .60
311 Cristobal Huet .20 .50
312 Kris Versteeg .15 .40
313 Brian Campbell .20 .50
314 Chris Stewart RC .25 .60
315 Nikita Filatov RC .25 .60
316 Jakub Voracek RC .50 1.25
317 Adam Pineault RC .20 .50
318 Dan LaCosta RC .20 .50
319 Tom Sestito RC .25 .60
320 Derek Dorsett RC .30 .75
321 Mike Commodore .20 .50
322 Fabian Brunnstrom RC .20 .50
323 Mark Fistric RC .20 .50
324 James Neal RC .50 1.25
325 Mark Parrish .15 .40
326 Marian Hossa .15 .40
327 Justin Abdelkader RC .40 1.00
328 Jonathan Ericsson RC .25 .60
329 Darren Helm RC .25 .60
330 Jeff Drouin-Deslauriers .15 .40
331 Steve MacIntyre RC .25 .60
332 Theo Peckham RC .20 .50
333 Michael Frolik RC .25 .60
334 Kenndal McArdle RC .25 .60
335 Michal Repik RC .25 .60
336 Drew Doughty RC .60 1.50
337 Brian Boyle RC .20 .50
338 Oscar Moller RC .25 .60
339 Trevor Lewis RC .25 .60
340 Erik Ersberg RC .20 .50
341 Wayne Simmonds RC .40 1.00
342 Colton Gillies RC .20 .50
343 Antti Miettinen .15 .40
344 Alex Tanguay .15 .40
345 Matt D'Agostini RC .25 .60
346 Ben Maxwell RC .25 .60
347 Patric Hornqvist RC .25 .60
348 Ryan Jones RC .25 .60
349 Petr Vrana RC .15 .40
350 Scott Clemmensen .15 .40
351 Matthew Halischuk RC .15 .40
352 Patrick Davis RC .20 .50
353 Josh Bailey RC .30 .75
354 Mark Streit .15 .40
355 Peter Manning RC .15 .40
356 Mitch Fritz RC .20 .50
357 Markus Naslund .25 .60
358 Brian Lee RC .25 .60
359 Ilya Zubov RC .20 .50
360 Alex Auld .15 .40
361 Jared Ross RC .25 .60
362 Luca Sbisa RC .25 .60
363 Nate Raduns RC .15 .40
364 Andreas Nodl RC .15 .40
365 Jonathon Kalinski RC .25 .60
366 Olli Jokinen .20 .50
367 Mikkel Boedker RC .30 .75
368 Viktor Tikhonov RC .25 .60
369 Kevin Porter RC .25 .60
370 Janne Pesonen RC .20 .50
371 Paul Bissonnette RC .30 .75
372 Alex Goligoski RC .30 .75
373 Jon Filewich RC .20 .50
374 Ryan Stone RC .15 .40
375 Miroslav Satan .20 .50
376 Brad Staubitz RC .20 .50
377 Rob Blake .20 .50
378 Devin Setoguchi .20 .50
379 Jamie McGinn RC .25 .60
380 Alex Pietrangelo RC .40 1.00
381 Patrik Berglund RC .20 .50
382 T.J. Oshie RC .50 1.25
383 Ben Bishop RC .40 1.00
384 Chris Porter RC .25 .60
385 Cam Paddock RC .15 .40
386 Radek Smolenak RC .30 .75
387 Steven Stamkos RC 3.00 8.00
388 Vladimir Mihalik RC .15 .40
389 Luke Schenn RC .30 .75
390 Nikolai Kulemin RC .25 .60
391 Niklas Hagman .15 .40
392 Mikhail Grabovski .15 .40
393 Andre Deveaux RC .25 .60
394 Jonas Frogren RC .25 .60
395 John Mitchell RC .20 .50
396 Justin Pogge RC .40 1.00
397 Cory Schneider RC .60 1.50
398 Mats Sundin .25 .60
399 Tyler Sloan RC .30 .75
400 Karl Alzner RC .15 .40

2008-09 Upper Deck Power Play Jerseys

PPAO Alexander Ovechkin 20.00 50.00
PPEM Evgeni Malkin 10.00 25.00
PPHL Henrik Lundqvist 12.00 30.00
PPHZ Henrik Zetterberg 6.00 15.00
PPIK Ilya Kovalchuk 5.00 12.00
PPJC Jonathan Cheechoo 4.00 10.00
PPJG Jean-Sebastien Giguere 5.00 12.00
PPJI Jarome Iginla 6.00 15.00
PPJS Jason Spezza 5.00 12.00
PPJT Joe Thornton 8.00 20.00
PPKL Kari Lehtonen 6.00 15.00
PPKT Keith Tkachuk 5.00 12.00
PPMA Marc-Andre Fleury 10.00 25.00
PPMB Martin Brodeur 12.00 30.00
PPMG Marian Gaborik 5.00 12.00
PPMM Mike Modano 8.00 20.00
PPMN Markus Naslund 5.00 12.00
PPMR Mike Richards 4.00 10.00
PPMS Mats Sundin 5.00 12.00
PPMT Marty Turco 5.00 12.00
PPNL Nicklas Lidstrom 5.00 12.00
PPPB Patrice Bergeron 6.00 15.00
PPPD Pavel Datsyuk 8.00 20.00
PPPK Paul Kariya 5.00 12.00
PPRL Roberto Luongo 8.00 20.00
PPRM Ryan Miller 5.00 12.00
PPRN Rick Nash 5.00 12.00
PPSC Sidney Crosby 20.00 50.00
PPSK Saku Koivu 5.00 12.00
PPVL Vincent Lecavalier 5.00 12.00

2005-06 Upper Deck Power Play Power Marks

PMAC Anson Carter 10.00 25.00
PMBB Brad Boyes 8.00 20.00
PMCK Chuck Kobasew 6.00 15.00
PMDA Daniel Alfredsson SP 20.00 50.00
PMDB Dustin Brown 4.00 10.00
PMEJ Ed Jovanovski 6.00 15.00
PMEN Evgeni Nabokov SP 12.00 30.00
PMFS Fredrik Sjostrom 4.00 10.00
PMGH Gordie Howe SP 125.00 250.00
PMHA Martin Havlat 10.00 25.00
PMHE Milan Hejduk 10.00 25.00
PMHZ Henrik Zetterberg SP 20.00 50.00
PMIK Ilya Kovalchuk SP 50.00 100.00
PMJC Jonathan Cheechoo 12.00 30.00
PMJP Jarome Iginla SP 30.00 60.00
PMJP Joni Pitkanen 4.00 10.00
PMJT Joe Thornton 25.00 60.00
PMJW Justin Williams 10.00 25.00
PMKD Kris Draper 8.00 20.00
PMKP Keith Primeau 4.00 10.00
PMLR Luc Robitaille 30.00 80.00
PMMB Milan Bartovic 4.00 10.00
PMMC Mike Comrie SP 30.00 60.00
PMMG Marian Gaborik SP 20.00 50.00
PMMH Marian Hossa 20.00 50.00
PMMN Markus Naslund 10.00 25.00
PMMP Mark Popovic 4.00 10.00
PMMR Mike Ribeiro 8.00 20.00
PMMS Martin St. Louis SP 25.00 60.00
PMNK Nikolai Khabibulin SP 40.00 80.00
PMNO Mika Noronen 4.00 10.00
PMNS Nathan Smith 4.00 10.00
PMPS Peter Sejna 4.00 10.00
PMRK Ryan Kesler 12.00 30.00
PMRN Rick Nash 20.00 50.00
PMRY Michael Ryder 15.00 40.00
PMSS Sheldon Souray SP 15.00 40.00
PMWG Wayne Gretzky SP 400.00 1000.00
PMZP Zigmund Palffy 10.00 25.00
PMZP Roman Turek 6.00 15.00

2005-06 Upper Deck Power Play Specialists Jerseys

*MULT.COLOR: 1.25X TO 3X HI
TSAB David Aebischer 3.00 8.00
TSAH Ales Hemsky 3.00 8.00
TSAK Alex Kovalev 3.00 8.00
TSAS Alexei Semenov 2.50 6.00
TSAY Alexei Yashin 3.00 8.00
TSBH Brett Hull 8.00 20.00
TSBK Radek Bonk 2.50 6.00
TSBO Peter Bondra 4.00 10.00
TSBS Brendan Shanahan 4.00 10.00
TSCC Chris Chelios 4.00 10.00
TSCD Chris Drury 3.00 8.00
TSCE Christian Ehrhoff 2.50 6.00
TSDA Daniel Alfredsson 4.00 10.00
TSDH Dany Heatley 3.00 8.00
TSDO Dominik Hasek 6.00 15.00
TSDW Doug Weight 4.00 10.00
TSEB Eric Brewer 2.50 6.00
TSEJ Ed Jovanovski 3.00 8.00
TSGM Glen Murray 3.00 8.00
TSHA Derian Hatcher 2.50 6.00
TSJD J-P Dumont 2.50 6.00
TSJI Jarome Iginla 5.00 12.00
TSJJ Jaromir Jagr 12.00 30.00
TSJL Joffrey Lupul 2.50 6.00
TSJL John LeClair 4.00 10.00
TSJN Joe Nieuwendyk 3.00 8.00
TSJS Jean-Sebastien Giguere 4.00 10.00
TSJT Joe Thornton 6.00 15.00
TSKP Keith Primeau 3.00 8.00
TSLC Pascal Leclaire 3.00 8.00
TSLE Jordan Leopold 2.50 6.00
TSMB Martin Brodeur 10.00 25.00
TSMC Mike Comrie 3.00 8.00
TSMH Milan Hejduk 3.00 8.00
TSML Mario Lemieux 12.00 30.00
TSMM Mike Modano 6.00 15.00
TSMR Mark Recchi 3.00 8.00
TSMT Marty Turco SP 5.00 12.00
TSNA Nikolai Antropov 2.50 6.00
TSOJ Olli Jokinen 4.00 10.00
TSOK Olaf Kolzig 4.00 10.00
TSPB P-M Bouchard 4.00 10.00
TSPB Pavel Bure 4.00 10.00
TSPD Pavol Demitra 2.50 6.00
TSPK Paul Kariya SP 25.00 60.00
TSPL Patrick Lalime 3.00 8.00
TSRB Rob Blake 4.00 10.00
TSRE Robert Esche 3.00 8.00
TSRL Robert Lang 2.50 6.00
TSRT Roman Turek 3.00 8.00
TSSB Sean Burke 2.50 6.00
TSSG Scott Gomez 3.00 8.00
TSSP Jason Spezza 4.00 10.00
TSTA Tony Amonte SP 4.00 10.00
TSTJ Jocelyn Thibault 3.00 8.00
TSTL Trevor Linden 8.00 20.00
TSTS Teemu Selanne 8.00 20.00
TSVL Vincent Lecavalier SP 25.00 60.00
TSVN Ville Nieminen 2.50 6.00
TSWG Wayne Gretzky SP 40.00 100.00

2014-15 Upper Deck Premier

*GOLD/25: 1X TO 2.5X BASIC CARDS
1 Jaromir Jagr 5.00 12.00
2 Alexander Ovechkin 6.00 15.00
3 Kyle Okposo 1.00 2.50
4 Craig Anderson 1.50 4.00
5 Patrick Sharp 1.50 4.00
6 Steven Stamkos 3.00 8.00
7 Jonathan Quick 2.00 5.00
8 Dustin Brown 1.50 4.00
9 Marc-Andre Fleury 3.00 8.00
10 Tyler Seguin 2.00 5.00
11 Daniel Sedin 2.00 5.00
12 Ryan Suter 1.25 3.00
13 Tomas Hertl 1.50 4.00
14 Aleksander Barkov 2.50 6.00
15 P.K. Subban 2.00 5.00
16 Steve Mason 1.25 3.00
17 James van Riemsdyk 1.25 3.00
18 Ryan Getzlaf 1.50 4.00
19 Pekka Rinne 1.50 4.00
20 David Backes 1.00 2.50
21 Jonathan Bernier 1.25 3.00
22 Dustin Byfuglien 1.50 4.00
23 Claude Giroux 1.50 4.00
24 Eric Staal 2.00 5.00
25 Carey Price 3.00 8.00
26 Sean Monahan 1.00 2.50
27 Henrik Lundqvist 4.00 10.00
28 Chris Kunitz 1.50 4.00
29 Paul Stastny 1.25 3.00
30 Max Pacioretty 1.50 4.00
31 Jason Spezza 1.50 4.00
32 Phil Kessel 1.50 4.00
33 Rick Nash 1.50 4.00
34 Zdeno Chara 1.50 4.00
35 Jonathan Toews 2.50 6.00
36 Joe Pavelski 2.00 5.00
37 Antti Niemi 1.25 3.00
38 Taylor Hall 1.50 4.00
39 Anze Kopitar 2.50 6.00
40 Sergei Bobrovsky 2.50 6.00
41 Cory Schneider 1.50 4.00
42 Victor Hedman 2.00 5.00
43 Ryan Kesler 1.50 4.00
44 Alex Galchenyuk 1.00 2.50
45 Erik Karlsson 2.00 5.00
46 Sidney Crosby 6.00 15.00
47 Patrice Bergeron 2.00 5.00
48 Evgeni Malkin 3.00 8.00
49 John Tavares 2.50 6.00
50 Zach Parise 1.50 4.00
51 Ryan Miller 1.50 4.00
52 Chris Chelios 1.50 4.00
53 Doug Gilmour 2.00 5.00
54 Zemgus Girgensons 1.25 3.00
55 Brett Hull 3.00 8.00
56 Gabriel Landeskog 2.00 5.00
57 Ed Belfour 1.50 4.00
58 Pavel Datsyuk 2.50 6.00
59 Corey Perry 2.50 6.00
60 Jordan Eberle 1.50 4.00
61 Andy Andreoff AU/299 RC 5.00 12.00
62 Patrick Brown AU/299 RC 5.00 12.00
63 Greg McKegg AU/299 RC 4.00 10.00
64 P.E. Bellemare AU/299 RC 5.00 12.00
65 Nicolas Deslauriers AU/299 RC 5.00 12.00
66 Josh Jooris AU/299 RC 5.00 12.00
67 John Klingberg AU/299 RC 10.00 25.00
68 Brandon Kozun AU/299 RC 4.00 10.00
69 Joni Ortio AU/299 RC 6.00 15.00
70 Andrej Nestrasil AU/299 RC 5.00 12.00
71 Justin Hodgman AU/299 RC 4.00 10.00
72 Mark Visentin AU/299 RC 5.00 12.00
73 Teemu Pulkkinen AU/299 RC 6.00 15.00
74 Christian Folin AU/299 RC 5.00 12.00
75 Seth Helgeson AU/299 RC 4.00 10.00
76 Patrik Nemeth AU/299 RC 6.00 15.00
77 Liam O'Brien AU/299 RC 5.00 12.00
78 A.Hammond AU/299 RC EXCH 8.00 20.00
79 Barclay Goodrow AU/299 RC 5.00 12.00
80 Joonas Nattinen AU/299 RC 5.00 12.00
81 A.Vasilevskiy JSY AU/299 RC 100.00 250.00
82 C.McKenzie JSY AU/299 RC 8.00 20.00
83 Derrick Pouliot JSY AU/299 RC 12.00 30.00
84 Griffin Reinhart JSY AU/299 RC 10.00 25.00
85 A.Clendening JSY AU/299 RC 10.00 25.00
86 Gaudreau JSY AU/199 RC EXCH 100.00250.00
87 Stuart Percy JSY AU/299 RC 10.00 25.00
88 V.Trocheck JSY AU/299 RC 20.00 50.00
89 Pastrnak JSY AU/199 RC EXCH 300.00800.00
90 Mirco Mueller JSY AU/299 RC 10.00 25.00
91 Adam Lowry JSY AU/299 RC 15.00 40.00
92 C.Jarnkrok JSY AU/299 RC 10.00 25.00
93 A.Khokhlachev JSY AU/299 RC 10.00 25.00
94 Phillip Danault JSY AU/299 RC 20.00 50.00
95 D.Severson JSY AU/299 RC 10.00 25.00
96 Tobias Rieder JSY AU/299 RC 10.00 25.00
97 Marko Dano JSY AU/299 RC 10.00 25.00
98 Victor Rask JSY AU/299 RC 10.00 25.00
99 D.Nurse JSY AU/299 RC 20.00 50.00
100 Jori Lehtera JSY AU/299 RC 12.00 30.00
101 Kevin Hayes JSY AU/299 RC 25.00 60.00
102 Bo Horvat JSY AU/199 RC 25.00 60.00
103 Namestnikov JSY AU/299 RC 15.00 40.00
104 Gostisbehere JSY AU/299 RC 20.00 50.00
105 R.Sproul JSY AU/299 RC 10.00 25.00
106 Seth Griffith JSY AU/299 RC 12.00 30.00
107 E.Kuznetsov JSY AU/299 RC 25.00 60.00
108 K.Rychel JSY AU/299 RC 8.00 20.00
109 Chris Tierney JSY AU/299 RC 10.00 25.00
110 R.Grimaldi JSY AU/299 RC 10.00 25.00
111 Jiri Sekac JSY AU/299 RC 8.00 20.00
112 T.Teravainen JSY AU/299 RC 15.00 40.00
113 L.Brossoit JSY AU/299 RC 10.00 25.00
114 Burakovsky JSY AU/299 RC 15.00 40.00
115 W.Karlsson JSY AU/299 RC 30.00 80.00
116 Curtis Lazar JSY AU/299 RC 10.00 25.00
117 A.Duclair JSY AU/299 RC EX 15.00 40.00
118 A.Wennberg JSY AU/299 RC 15.00 40.00
119 L.Draisaitl JSY AU/299 RC 150.00 400.00
120 S.Reinhart JSY AU/199 RC 40.00 100.00
121 A.Ekblad JSY AU/199 RC 25.00 60.00
122 J.Drouin JSY AU/199 RC 20.00 50.00
123 Theoren Fleury JSY AU/49 20.00 50.00
124 Cory Schneider JSY AU/49 15.00 40.00
125 Chris Chelios JSY AU/49 15.00 40.00
126 Max Pacioretty JSY AU/49 15.00 40.00
127 Patrick Sharp JSY AU/49 15.00 40.00
128 Teemu Selanne JSY AU/49 30.00 80.00
129 Joe Sakic JSY AU/49 30.00 80.00
130 Taylor Hall JSY AU/49 15.00 40.00
131 Jamie Benn JSY AU/49 15.00 40.00
132 van Riemsdyk JSY AU/49 12.00 30.00
133 Carey Price JSY AU/49 30.00 80.00
134 Sergei Bobrovsky JSY AU/49 25.00 60.00
135 Tyler Seguin JSY AU/49 20.00 50.00
136 Evgeni Malkin JSY AU/49 30.00 80.00
137 Torey Krug JSY AU/49 12.00 30.00
139 Brett Hull JSY AU/25 30.00 80.00
140 Wayne Gretzky JSY AU/25 250.00 600.00
141 Sidney Crosby JSY AU/25 150.00 250.00
142 Mats Sundin JSY AU/25 15.00 40.00
143 Mark Messier JSY AU/25 30.00 80.00

2014-15 Upper Deck Premier Gold Spectrum

*GOLD JSY/25: 1.2X TO 3X SILVER JSY/125

2006-07 Upper Deck Power Play

1 Jean-Sebastien Giguere .15 .40
2 Teemu Selanne .30 .75
3 Chris Pronger .15 .40
4 Ilya Kovalchuk .15 .40
5 Marian Hossa .15 .40
6 Kari Lehtonen .12 .30
7 Patrice Bergeron .20 .50
8 Brad Boyes .10 .25
9 Hannu Toivonen .10 .25
10 Zdeno Chara .15 .40
11 Chris Drury .12 .30
12 Ryan Miller .15 .40
13 Maxim Afinogenov .10 .25
14 Miikka Kiprusoff .15 .40
15 Jarome Iginla .20 .50
16 Dion Phaneuf .12 .30
17 Alex Tanguay .10 .25
18 Eric Staal .20 .50
19 Cam Ward .15 .40
20 Rod Brind'Amour .15 .40
21 Erik Cole .10 .25
22 Tuomo Ruutu .15 .40
23 Nikolai Khabibulin .15 .40
24 Michal Handzus .12 .30
25 Martin Havlat .10 .25
26 Marek Svatos .10 .25
27 Milan Hejduk .12 .30
28 Joe Sakic .30 .75
29 Rick Nash .15 .40
30 Sergei Fedorov .25 .60
31 Pascal Leclaire .12 .30
32 Mike Modano .25 .60
33 Brenden Morrow .12 .30
34 Marty Turco .15 .40
35 Eric Lindros .25 .60
36 Henrik Zetterberg .20 .50
37 Nicklas Lidstrom .15 .40
38 Pavel Datsyuk .25 .60
39 Dominik Hasek .25 .60
40 Joffrey Lupul .10 .25
41 Ales Hemsky .12 .30
42 Ryan Smyth .12 .30
43 Olli Jokinen .15 .40
44 Todd Bertuzzi .15 .40
45 Jay Bouwmeester .10 .25
46 Alexander Frolov .10 .25
47 Rob Blake .10 .25
48 Mike Cammalleri .10 .25
49 Marian Gaborik .15 .40
50 Manny Fernandez .15 .40
51 Pavol Demitra .20 .50
52 Saku Koivu .15 .40
53 Cristobal Huet .12 .30
54 Alex Kovalev .12 .30
55 Michael Ryder .10 .25
56 Steve Sullivan .10 .25
57 Paul Kariya .15 .40
58 Tomas Vokoun .12 .30
59 Martin Brodeur .40 1.00
60 Patrik Elias .10 .25
61 Brian Gionta .10 .25
62 Miroslav Satan .12 .30
63 Alexei Yashin .12 .30
64 Rick DiPietro .12 .30
65 Jaromir Jagr .50 1.25
66 Henrik Lundqvist .40 1.00
67 Brendan Shanahan .15 .40
68 Martin Gerber .12 .30
69 Jason Spezza .12 .30
70 Dany Heatley .12 .30
71 Daniel Alfredsson .15 .40
72 Peter Forsberg .30 .75
73 Simon Gagne .15 .40
74 Robert Esche .12 .30
75 Jeff Carter .12 .30
76 Shane Doan .12 .30
77 Curtis Joseph .12 .30
78 Jeremy Roenick .25 .60
79 Sergei Gonchar .10 .25
80 Sidney Crosby .60 1.50
81 Marc-Andre Fleury .30 .75
82 Joe Thornton .25 .60
83 Jonathan Cheechoo .12 .30
84 Patrick Marleau .15 .40
85 Doug Weight .15 .40
86 Keith Tkachuk .15 .40
87 Manny Legace .12 .30
88 Brad Richards .15 .40
89 Martin St. Louis .15 .40
90 Vincent Lecavalier .15 .40
91 Mats Sundin .15 .40
92 Alexander Steen .10 .25
93 Bryan McCabe .10 .25
94 Andrew Raycroft .12 .30
95 Markus Naslund .15 .40
96 Roberto Luongo .25 .60
97 Brendan Morrison .10 .25
98 Henrik Sedin .20 .50
99 Alexander Ovechkin .60 1.50
100 Olaf Kolzig .15 .40
101 Yan Stastny RC .75 2.00
102 Mark Stuart RC .75 2.00
103 Carsen Germyn RC .75 2.00
104 Dustin Byfuglien RC 2.00 5.00
105 Tomas Kopecky RC 1.00 2.50
106 Marc-Antoine Pouliot RC .75 2.00
107 Konstantin Pushkarev RC 1.00 2.50
108 Erik Reitz RC .75 2.00
109 Miroslav Kopriva RC .75 2.00
110 Shea Weber RC 2.00 5.00
111 David Printz RC .75 2.00
112 Steve Regier RC .75 2.00
113 Ryan Caldwell RC .75 2.00
114 Masi Marjamaki RC .75 2.00
115 Matt Koalska RC .75 2.00
116 Jarkko Immonen RC 1.00 2.50
117 Cole Jarrett RC .75 2.00
118 Rob Collins RC .75 2.00
119 Filip Novak RC .75 2.00
120 Ryan Potulny RC .75 2.00
121 Bill Thomas RC .75 2.00
122 Joel Perrault RC .75 2.00
123 Noah Welch RC .75 2.00
124 Michel Ouellet RC 1.00 2.50
125 Matt Carle RC .75 2.00
126 Ben Ondrus RC .75 2.00
127 Brendan Bell RC .75 2.00
128 Ian White RC 1.00 2.50
129 Jeremy Williams RC .75 2.00
130 Eric Fehr RC 1.25 3.00

2014-15 Upper Deck Premier Silver Spectrum

*SILVER/125: .5X TO 1.25X BASIC CARDS
*SILVER/25-49: X TO X BASIC CARDS
86 Johnny Gaudreau JSY AU 150.00 400.00
89 David Pastrnak JSY AU 400.00 500.00
119 Leon Draisaitl JSY AU 250.00 600.00
122 Jonathan Drouin JSY AU 100.00 250.00

2006-07 Upper Deck Power Play Impact Rainbow

*VETS/25: 20X TO 50X BASIC CARDS
*ROOKIES/25: 3X TO 8X BASIC RC

2006-07 Upper Deck Power Play Cup Celebrations

COMPLETE SET (7) 10.00 25.00
CC1 Eric Staal 1.25 3.00
CC2 Cam Ward 1.25 3.00
CC3 Dominik Hasek 1.50 4.00
CC4 Mike Modano 1.25 3.00
CC5 Martin St. Louis 1.00 2.50
CC6 Mario Lemieux 4.00 10.00
CC7 Patrick Roy 3.00 8.00

2014-15 Upper Deck Premier 02-03 Tribute Rookies Autographs Patches

SRRAB Andre Burakovsky 20.00 50.00
SRRAE Aaron Ekblad 30.00 80.00
SRRAW Alexander Wennberg 20.00 50.00
SRRBH Bo Horvat 30.00 80.00
SRRCL Curtis Lazar 12.00 30.00
SRRDN Darnell Nurse 25.00 60.00
SRRDP David Pastrnak 60.00 150.00
SRRDS Damon Severson 12.00 30.00
SRREK Evgeny Kuznetsov 30.00 80.00
SRRGR Griffin Reinhart 12.00 30.00
SRRJD Jonathan Drouin 25.00 60.00
SRRJG Johnny Gaudreau 100.00 250.00
SRRJS Jiri Sekac 10.00 25.00
SRRLD Leon Draisaitl 250.00 600.00
SRRMD Marko Dano 12.00 30.00
SRRPD Phillip Danault 25.00 60.00
SRRRS Ryan Sproul 12.00 30.00
SRRSG Seth Griffith 15.00 40.00
SRRSH Shayne Gostisbehere 25.00 60.00
SRRSP Stuart Percy 12.00 30.00
SRRSR Sam Reinhart 50.00 125.00
SRRTT Teuvo Teravainen 20.00 50.00
SRRVN Vladislav Namestnikov 20.00 50.00

2006-07 Upper Deck Power Play Goal Robbers

COMPLETE SET (14) 12.00 30.00
GR1 Jean-Sebastien Giguere 1.25 3.00
GR2 Kari Lehtonen 1.00 2.50
GR3 Ryan Miller 1.25 3.00
GR4 Miikka Kiprusoff 1.25 3.00
GR5 Cam Ward 1.25 3.00
GR6 Jose Theodore 1.25 3.00
GR7 Marty Turco 1.25 3.00
GR8 Marc-Andre Fleury 2.50 6.00
GR9 Roberto Luongo 2.00 5.00
GR10 Manny Fernandez .75 2.00
GR11 Tomas Vokoun 1.00 2.50
GR12 Martin Brodeur 3.00 8.00
GR13 Henrik Lundqvist 3.00 8.00
GR14 Cristobal Huet 1.00 2.50

2006-07 Upper Deck Power Play In Action

COMPLETE SET (14) 10.00 25.00
IA1 Jarome Iginla 1.00 2.50
IA2 Joe Sakic 1.50 4.00
IA3 Rick Nash .75 2.00
IA4 Henrik Zetterberg 1.00 2.50
IA5 Saku Koivu .75 2.00
IA6 Martin Brodeur 2.00 5.00
IA7 Jaromir Jagr 2.50 6.00
IA8 Dany Heatley .60 1.50
IA9 Peter Forsberg 1.50 4.00
IA10 Sidney Crosby 3.00 8.00
IA11 Joe Thornton 1.25 3.00
IA12 Mats Sundin .75 2.00
IA13 Markus Naslund .75 2.00
IA14 Alexander Ovechkin 2.00 5.00

2014-15 Upper Deck Premier 02-03 Tribute Stars Autographs Patches

SRVAG Alex Galchenyuk 12.00 30.00
SRVCC Chris Chelios 20.00 50.00
SRVCK Chris Kunitz 20.00 50.00
SRVES Eric Staal 25.00 60.00
SRVJB Jonathan Bernier 15.00 40.00
SRVJR Jeremy Roenick EXCH 30.00 80.00
SRVJT Jonathan Toews EXCH 30.00 80.00
SRVKL Kari Lehtonen 15.00 40.00
SRVLR Larry Robinson 20.00 50.00
SRVMF Marc-Andre Fleury 40.00 100.00
SRVMG Mike Gartner 25.00 60.00
SRVMO Sean Monahan 12.00 30.00
SRVMP Max Pacioretty 20.00 50.00
SRVOM Olli Maatta 12.00 30.00
SRVPR Patrick Roy EXCH 50.00 125.00
SRVRM Ryan McDonagh 12.00 30.00
SRVSB Sergei Bobrovsky 30.00 80.00
SRVSC Sidney Crosby EXCH 80.00 200.00
SRVSE Teemu Selanne 40.00 100.00
SRVSJ Seth Jones 20.00 50.00
SRVSM Steve Mason 15.00 40.00
SRVSW Shea Weber 15.00 40.00
SRVTA John Tavares EXCH 30.00 80.00
SRVTH Taylor Hall EXCH 20.00 50.00
SRVVD Vincent Damphousse 15.00 40.00

2006-07 Upper Deck Power Play Last Man Standing

COMPLETE SET (7) 6.00 15.00
LM1 Jody Shelley 1.25 3.00
LM2 Derek Boogaard 1.25 3.00
LM3 George Parros 1.25 3.00
LM4 Donald Brashear 1.25 3.00
LM5 Georges Laraque 1.50 4.00
LM6 Chris Simon 1.25 3.00
LM7 Todd Fedoruk 1.25 3.00

2006-07 Upper Deck Power Play Power Marks Autographs

PMAA Andrew Alberts 8.00 20.00
PMAM Andrej Meszaros 12.00 30.00
PMAS Anthony Stewart 8.00 20.00
PMAY Alexei Yashin 8.00 20.00
PMBB Brad Boyes 8.00 20.00
PMBE Ben Eager 8.00 20.00
PMCD Chris Drury SP 8.00 20.00
PMCK Chris Kunitz 8.00 20.00
PMDW Doug Weight 8.00 20.00
PMHZ Henrik Zetterberg 20.00 40.00
PMJH Jeff Hoggan 8.00 20.00
PMJI Jarome Iginla SP 40.00 80.00
PMMH Marian Hossa SP 25.00 50.00
PMMT Maxime Talbot 10.00 25.00
PMMV Mike Van Ryn 8.00 20.00
PMPR Paul Ranger 8.00 20.00
PMRS Ryan Smyth 12.00 30.00
PMSC Sidney Crosby 100.00 200.00
PMSG Scott Gomez 8.00 20.00
PMSH Scott Hartnell 10.00 25.00
PMTH Jose Theodore SP 30.00 60.00
PMZP Zach Parise 12.00 30.00

2014-15 Upper Deck Premier Duals

PQ2BC D.Brown/J.Carter 4.00 10.00
PQ2BH E.Belfour/B.Hull 8.00 20.00
PQ2BS J.Spezza/J.Benn 4.00 10.00
PQ2DJ B.Dubinsky/R.Johansen 3.00 8.00
PQ2DL M.Duchene/G.Landeskog 5.00 12.00
PQ2EH T.Hall/J.Eberle 4.00 10.00
PQ2EK E.Malkin/C.Kunitz 8.00 20.00
PQ2ES E.Staal/A.Semin 5.00 12.00
PQ2GA J.Gibson/F.Andersen 5.00 12.00
PQ2GK A.Kopitar/M.Gaborik 6.00 15.00
PQ2GP J.Pominville/M.Granlund 3.00 8.00
PQ2HB A.Barkov/J.Huberdeau 6.00 15.00
PQ2HN R.Nugent-Hopkins/T.Hall 5.00 12.00
PQ2HO D.Hasek/C.Osgood 6.00 15.00
PQ2KK T.Rask/P.Rinne 5.00 12.00
PQ2KS D.Keith/B.Seabrook 3.00 8.00
PQ2KT E.Kane/J.Trouba 4.00 10.00
PQ2LM B.Marchand/M.Lucic 8.00 20.00
PQ2LR L.Robinson/G.Lafleur 5.00 12.00
PQ2LW B.Wheeler/A.Ladd 4.00 10.00
PQ2MA M.Pacioretty/A.Galchenyuk 4.00 10.00
PQ2MB M.Pacioretty/B.Gallagher 4.00 10.00
PQ2ML R.Miller/E.Lack 4.00 10.00
PQ2NS T.Seguin/V.Nichushkin 5.00 12.00
PQ2OB A.Ovechkin/N.Backstrom 15.00 40.00
PQ2OC K.Okposo/C.Conacher 2.50 6.00
PQ2PC Z.Parise/C.Coyle 4.00 10.00
PQ2PG R.Getzlaf/C.Perry 6.00 15.00
PQ2PH J.Pavelski/T.Hertl 5.00 12.00
PQ2PR D.Phaneuf/M.Rielly 4.00 10.00
PQ2PS C.Price/P.Subban 8.00 20.00
PQ2RD P.Roy/V.Damphousse 10.00 25.00
PQ2RL J.Roenick/J.LeClair 6.00 15.00
PQ2RR R.Getzlaf/R.Kesler 4.00 10.00
PQ2SE D.Sedin/H.Sedin 5.00 12.00
PQ2SN R.Nash/M.St. Louis 4.00 10.00
PQ2SS S.Stamkos/M.St. Louis 8.00 20.00
PQ2TK P.Kane/J.Toews 8.00 20.00
PQ2TP T.Toffoli/T.Pearson 4.00 10.00
PQ2TR K.Turris/B.Ryan 4.00 10.00
PQ2TS J.Tavares/R.Strome 6.00 15.00
PQ2VB V.Hedman/B.Bishop 5.00 12.00
PQ2VK J.van Riemsdyk/N.Kadri 5.00 12.00
PQ2WJ S.Weber/S.Jones 4.00 10.00
PQ2ZL H.Lundqvist/H.Zetterberg 10.00 25.00

2006-07 Upper Deck Power Play Specialists Jerseys

SAF Alexander Frolov 3.00 8.00
SAH Ales Hemsky 3.00 8.00
SAK Alex Kovalev 3.00 8.00
SAL Jason Allison 3.00 8.00
SAO Alexander Ovechkin 20.00 50.00
SAT Alex Tanguay 4.00 10.00
SBG Bill Guerin 3.00 8.00
SBL Brian Leetch 5.00 12.00
SBM Bryan McCabe 3.00 8.00
SBR Brian Rolston 3.00 8.00
SBS Brendan Shanahan 5.00 12.00
SCP Chris Pronger 4.00 10.00
SDB Donald Brashear 3.00 8.00
SDH Dominik Hasek 8.00 20.00
SDP Dion Phaneuf 8.00 20.00
SDW Doug Weight 3.00 8.00
SEB Ed Belfour 5.00 12.00
SEJ Ed Jovanovski 3.00 8.00
SES Eric Staal 5.00 12.00
SGA Simon Gagne 5.00 12.00
SGM Glen Murray 3.00 8.00
SIK Ilya Kovalchuk 8.00 20.00
SJA Jason Arnott 3.00 8.00
SJG Jean-Sebastien Giguere 4.00 10.00
SJI Jarome Iginla 8.00 20.00
SJJ Jaromir Jagr 8.00 20.00
SJL Jere Lehtinen 3.00 8.00
SJS Joe Sakic SP 15.00 40.00
SJT Joe Thornton 8.00 20.00
SKL Kari Lehtonen 5.00 12.00
SKP Keith Primeau 3.00 8.00
SMB Martin Brodeur 8.00 20.00
SMF Manny Fernandez 4.00 10.00
SMG Marian Gaborik 8.00 20.00
SMH Marian Hossa 4.00 10.00
SMK Miikka Kiprusoff 5.00 12.00
SMM Mike Modano 8.00 20.00
SMN Markus Naslund 5.00 12.00
SMO Brendan Morrison 3.00 8.00
SMP Michael Peca 3.00 8.00
SMS Marc Savard 3.00 8.00
SMT Marty Turco 4.00 10.00
SOK Olaf Kolzig 10.00 25.00
SPB Patrice Bergeron 5.00 12.00
SPD Pavel Datsyuk 4.00 10.00
SPF Peter Forsberg 8.00 20.00
SPK Paul Kariya 5.00 12.00
SPM Patrick Marleau 4.00 10.00
SRB Rob Blake 4.00 10.00
SRE Robert Esche 4.00 10.00
SRI Brad Richards 4.00 10.00
SRM Ryan Miller 5.00 12.00
SSC Sidney Crosby SP 30.00 80.00
SSF Sergei Fedorov 5.00 12.00
SSG Scott Gomez 3.00 8.00
SSN Scott Niedermayer 3.00 8.00
SSP Jason Spezza 5.00 12.00
STR Tuomo Ruutu 3.00 8.00
STS Teemu Selanne 5.00 12.00
SZC Zdeno Chara 3.00 8.00

2014-15 Upper Deck Premier Emblems

PEAB Alexandre Burrows 5.00 12.00
PEAG Alex Galchenyuk 5.00 12.00
PEBG Bill Guerin 8.00 20.00
PEBH Brett Hull 15.00 40.00
PECC Chris Chelios 8.00 20.00
PECJ Curtis Joseph 10.00 25.00
PECR Corey Crawford 10.00 25.00
PECW Cam Ward 8.00 20.00
PEDB Dustin Brown 8.00 20.00
PEDE Derek Stepan 5.00 12.00
PEDS Daniel Sedin 10.00 25.00
PEEB Ed Belfour 8.00 20.00
PEEL Eddie Lack 6.00 15.00
PEES Eric Staal 10.00 25.00
PEGA Marian Gaborik 8.00 20.00
PEGM Glen Murray 6.00 15.00
PEHL Henrik Lundqvist 20.00 50.00
PEHZ Henrik Zetterberg 10.00 25.00
PEJB Jamie Benn 8.00 20.00
PEJE Jordan Eberle 8.00 20.00
PEJL John LeClair 8.00 20.00
PEJQ Jonathan Quick 10.00 25.00
PEJR Jeremy Roenick 12.00 30.00
PEJT Joe Thornton 12.00 30.00
PEMB Martin Biron 6.00 15.00
PEMD Marcel Dionne 10.00 25.00
PEMF Marc-Andre Fleury 15.00 40.00
PEMG Mike Green 6.00 15.00
PEMI Mike Gartner 10.00 25.00
PEMM Matt Moulson 5.00 12.00
PEMS Mats Sundin 8.00 20.00
PEPB Patrice Bergeron 10.00 25.00
PEPS P.K. Subban 10.00 25.00
PERG Ryan Getzlaf 8.00 20.00
PESC Sidney Crosby 30.00 80.00
PESS Steven Stamkos 15.00 40.00
PEST Drew Stafford 5.00 12.00
PETR Tuukka Rask 10.00 25.00

2014-15 Upper Deck Premier Inked Inscriptions

IIAE Aaron Ekblad/99 25.00 60.00
IIAI Arturs Irbe/50 8.00 20.00
IIAO Alexander Ovechkin/25 40.00 100.00
IIBH Bo Horvat/99 25.00 60.00
IICL Curtis Lazar/99 10.00 25.00
IICP Carey Price/25 20.00 50.00
IIES Eric Staal/50 12.00 30.00
IIJB Jonathan Bernier/25 8.00 20.00
IIJD Jonathan Drouin/99 20.00 50.00
IIJI Jarome Iginla/50 12.00 30.00
IIJT John Tavares/50 15.00 40.00
IILD Leon Draisaitl/99 200.00 500.00
IILI Mike Liut/99 6.00 15.00
IIMG Mikael Granlund/50 8.00 20.00
IIML Mario Lemieux/25 40.00 100.00
IIMM Mark Messier/25 40.00 100.00
IIMP Max Pacioretty/25 10.00 25.00
IIPF Peter Forsberg/25 40.00 100.00
IIRS Ryan Suter/50 8.00 20.00
IISM Sean Monahan/99 6.00 15.00
IISR Sam Reinhart/99 40.00 100.00
IISW Shea Weber/50 8.00 20.00
IITH Tomas Hertl/50 10.00 25.00
IITK Torey Krug/99 8.00 20.00
IITS Teemu Selanne/50 20.00 50.00

2014-15 Upper Deck Premier Legendary Premier Signatures

LPSBH Bobby Hull B 25.00 60.00
LPSBP Brad Park C 10.00 25.00
LPSCN Cam Neely C 12.00 30.00
LPSJS Joe Sakic B 25.00 60.00
LPSMB Mike Bossy B 12.00 30.00
LPSML Mario Lemieux A 50.00 125.00
LPSMS Mats Sundin B 12.00 30.00
LPSPR Patrick Roy A 30.00 80.00
LPSRB Ray Bourque B 20.00 50.00
LPSWG Wayne Gretzky A 250.00 600.00

2014-15 Upper Deck Premier Mega Patch Chest Logos

PMPAB Aleksander Barkov/28 30.00 80.00
PMPAE Aaron Ekblad/27 50.00 120.00
PMPAN Antti Niemi/24 15.00 40.00
PMPAS Alexander Semin/20 20.00 50.00
PMPBB Ben Bishop/20 15.00 40.00
PMPBS Brayden Schenn/19 20.00 50.00
PMPBU Alexandre Burrows/20 12.00 30.00
PMPBW Blake Wheeler/24 20.00 50.00
PMPCA Craig Anderson/24 20.00 50.00
PMPCC Charlie Coyle/20 20.00 50.00
PMPCH Cody Hodgson/20 12.00 30.00
PMPCJ Calle Jarnkrok/21 20.00 50.00
PMPDD Drew Doughty/18 25.00 60.00
PMPDK Darcy Kuemper/20 20.00 50.00
PMPDS Daniel Sedin/20 25.00 60.00
PMPEK Evgeny Kuznetsov/22 50.00 125.00
PMPGA Johnny Gaudreau/28 60.00 150.00
PMPHL Henrik Lundqvist/21 50.00 120.00
PMPHO Braden Holtby/20 25.00 60.00
PMPHS Henrik Sedin/20 25.00 60.00
PMPHZ Henrik Zetterberg/22 25.00 60.00
PMPJA Jack Johnson/24 12.00 30.00
PMPJB Jamie Benn/20 20.00 50.00
PMPJC Jeff Carter/18 15.00 40.00
PMPJD Jonathan Drouin/19 40.00 100.00
PMPJE Jordan Eberle/24 20.00 50.00
PMPJN James Neal/21 12.00 30.00
PMPJO John Carlson/19 20.00 50.00
PMPJQ Jonathan Quick/18 25.00 60.00
PMPJR Jeremy Roenick/25 30.00 80.00
PMPJS Jason Spezza/20 20.00 50.00
PMPJT John Tavares/22 30.00 80.00
PMPJU Tomas Jurco/21 12.00 30.00
PMPJV James van Riemsdyk/18 15.00 40.00
PMPKA Erik Karlsson/25 25.00 60.00
PMPKE Duncan Keith/24 15.00 40.00
PMPKT Kyle Turris/23 20.00 50.00
PMPLC Logan Couture/23 25.00 60.00
PMPLD Leon Draisaitl/24 100.00 250.00
PMPLL Morgan Rielly/16 20.00 50.00
PMPMG Mike Gartner/18 25.00 60.00
PMPML Milan Lucic/24 20.00 50.00
PMPMO Sean Monahan/28 12.00 30.00
PMPMR Mike Richards/18 15.00 40.00
PMPMS Mike Smith/26 20.00 50.00
PMPMZ Mats Zuccarello/17 20.00 50.00
PMPNB Nicklas Backstrom/23 20.00 50.00
PMPNK Nazem Kadri/18 25.00 60.00
PMPNM Nathan MacKinnon/16 80.00 200.00
PMPNU Ryan Nugent-Hopkins/24 25.00 60.00
PMPOM Olli Maatta/31 12.00 30.00
PMPOP Ondrej Palat/19 15.00 40.00
PMPPB Patrice Bergeron/24 25.00 60.00
PMPPC Carey Price/19 40.00 100.00
PMPPK Phil Kessel/18 20.00 50.00
PMPPM Patrick Marleau/23 20.00 50.00
PMPPR Patrick Roy/30 50.00 125.00
PMPRF Ron Francis/29 25.00 60.00
PMPRG Ryan Getzlaf/21 20.00 50.00
PMPRI Pekka Rinne/22 20.00 50.00
PMPRJ Ryan Johansen/24 15.00 40.00
PMPRK Ryan Kesler/20 20.00 50.00
PMPRL Roberto Luongo/27 30.00 80.00
PMPRY Ryan Strome/23 20.00 50.00
PMPSJ Seth Jones/21 20.00 50.00
PMPSK Jeff Skinner/20 25.00 60.00
PMPSM Steve Mason/19 15.00 40.00
PMPSR Sam Reinhart/18 80.00 200.00
PMPSU P.K. Subban/21 25.00 60.00
PMPTF Theoren Fleury/18 25.00 60.00
PMPTH Tomas Hertl/24 20.00 50.00
PMPTJ Jacob Trouba/24 15.00 40.00
PMPTL Trevor Linden/27 20.00 50.00
PMPTR Tuukka Rask/24 25.00 60.00
PMPVA Semyon Varlamov/30 20.00 50.00
PMPVO Jakub Voracek/19 15.00 40.00
PMPVT Vladimir Tarasenko/19 25.00 60.00
PMPZC Zdeno Chara/24 20.00 50.00
PMPZG Zemgus Girgensons/20 15.00 40.00
PMPZK Zack Kassian/20 12.00 30.00

2014-15 Upper Deck Premier Quads

PQ4ANALAK Gtzlf/Kslr/Kptr/Gbrk 6.00 15.00
PQ4BOSMON Rsk/Chra/Prce/Sbbn 8.00 20.00
PQ4BUFF Hdgsn/Mlsn/Grg/Enr 4.00 10.00
PQ4CAL Mnhn/Rmo/Hllr/Hdlr 3.00 8.00
PQ4CAR Stl/Sknr/Smn/Lndh 5.00 12.00
PQ4DETCBH Dtsyk/Zttr/Kne/Tws 8.00 20.00
PQ4FIN Rnne/Rsk/Nmi/Lht 5.00 12.00
PQ4FLO Bjgs/Lng/Brkv/Hbr 6.00 15.00
PQ4LAKANA Prry/Gbsn/Qck/Crtr 6.00 15.00
PQ4MON Sbbn/Pcrt/Glg/Glch 5.00 12.00
PQ4NET Gbsn/Grbr/Kmp/Jns 4.00 10.00
PQ4NYINYR Tvrs/Okps/Nsh/Stpn 6.00 15.00
PQ4NYR Zcrllo/St.L/Nsh/Krdr 5.00 12.00
PQ4OFFENSE McKn/Hrtl/Brk/Mnh 15.00 40.00
PQ4OTT Trrs/Krlsn/Ryn/Zbn 5.00 12.00
PQ4PHI Grx/Ctrr/Vrck/Msn 4.00 10.00
PQ4PREDS Wbr/Nl/Jns/Rnne 4.00 10.00
PQ4SJS Thrntn/Ctre/Pvl/Mrl 6.00 15.00
PQ4TBL Stmks/Plt/Hdm/Bsh 8.00 20.00
PQ4USA Kssl/Kne/Qck/Oshe 8.00 20.00
PQ4VAN Sdn/Mllr/Kssn/Brrws 5.00 12.00
PQ4WAS Ovch/Bckm/Crlsn/Hlt 15.00 40.00
PQ4WIN Whlr/Trba/Kne/Sch 6.00 15.00

2014-15 Upper Deck Premier Rinks of Honor Autographs Booklet

RHAO Alexander Ovechkin B 50.00 120.00
RHBH Bobby Hull B 25.00 60.00
RHBO Bo Horvat F 30.00 80.00
RHCC Charlie Coyle E 12.00 30.00
RHCJ Curtis Joseph E 15.00 40.00
RHCN Cam Neely D 12.00 30.00
RHDH Dominik Hasek C 20.00 50.00
RHEM Evgeni Malkin C 25.00 60.00
RHES Eric Staal E 15.00 40.00
RHFP Felix Potvin E 20.00 50.00
RHGF Grant Fuhr C 20.00 50.00
RHHU Brett Hull C 25.00 60.00
RHJB Jonathan Bernier D 10.00 25.00
RHJD Jonathan Drouin F 25.00 60.00
RHJG Johnny Gaudreau F 100.00 250.00
RHJP Joe Pavelski E 15.00 40.00
RHJR James van Riemsdyk D 10.00 25.00
RHJT John Tavares E 20.00 50.00
RHJV John Vanbiesbrouck F 12.00 30.00
RHLA Gabriel Landeskog A 15.00 40.00
RHLI Mike Liut F 8.00 20.00
RHMI Mike Modano A 20.00 50.00
RHML Mario Lemieux C 50.00 125.00
RHMM Marty McSorley E 10.00 25.00
RHMP Max Pacioretty E 12.00 30.00
RHPD Pavel Datsyuk D 20.00 50.00
RHPR Patrick Roy C 30.00 80.00
RHRK Ryan Kesler E 12.00 30.00
RHRN Rick Nash D 12.00 30.00
RHSB Sergei Bobrovsky C 20.00 50.00
RHSJ Seth Jones F 12.00 30.00
RHSL Steve Larmer F 10.00 25.00
RHSR Sam Reinhart F 50.00 125.00
RHTB Tom Barrasso F 12.00 30.00
RHVO Jakub Voracek B 10.00 25.00
RHZP Zach Parise B 12.00 30.00

2014-15 Upper Deck Premier Rookie Premier Signatures

RPSAB Andre Burakovsky A 8.00 20.00
RPSAE Aaron Ekblad A 12.00 30.00
RPSBH Bo Horvat C 12.00 30.00
RPSCL Curtis Lazar B 5.00 12.00
RPSDN Darnell Nurse B 10.00 25.00
RPSDP Derrick Pouliot C 6.00 15.00
RPSDS Damon Severson C 5.00 12.00
RPSEK Evgeny Kuznetsov B 12.00 30.00
RPSJD Jonathan Drouin A 10.00 25.00
RPSJG Johnny Gaudreau B 20.00 50.00
RPSKR Kerby Rychel C 4.00 10.00
RPSLD Leon Draisaitl A 40.00 100.00
RPSSG Shayne Gostisbehere C 10.00 25.00
RPSSR Sam Reinhart A 20.00 50.00
RPSTT Teuvo Teravainen B EXCH 8.00 20.00

2014-15 Upper Deck Premier Rookies

R1 Victor Rask 2.00 5.00
R2 Leon Draisaitl 15.00 40.00
R3 Mirco Mueller 2.00 5.00
R4 Oscar Klefbom 4.00 10.00
R5 Joey Hishon 2.50 6.00
R6 Tobias Rieder 2.00 5.00
R7 Curtis Lazar 2.00 5.00
R8 Rocco Grimaldi 2.00 5.00
R9 Teemu Pulkkinen 2.50 6.00
R10 Ryan Sproul 2.00 5.00
R11 Andy Andreoff 2.00 5.00
R12 Damon Severson 2.00 5.00
R13 Seth Griffith 2.50 6.00
R14 Bogdan Yakimov 2.00 5.00
R15 Curtis McKenzie 1.50 4.00
R16 Adam Lowry 3.00 8.00
R17 Kevin Hayes 5.00 12.00
R18 Barclay Goodrow 2.00 5.00
R19 Griffin Reinhart 2.00 5.00
R20 Teuvo Teravainen 3.00 8.00
R21 Seth Helgeson 1.50 4.00
R22 Sam Reinhart 8.00 20.00
R23 Colton Sissons 2.00 5.00
R24 Mark Visentin 2.00 5.00
R25 Darnell Nurse 4.00 10.00
R26 Calle Jarnkrok 2.00 5.00
R27 Marko Dano 2.00 5.00
R28 Corban Knight 2.00 5.00
R29 Dennis Everberg 2.00 5.00
R30 Adam Clendening 2.00 5.00
R31 Jori Lehtera 2.50 6.00
R32 Vincent Trocheck 4.00 10.00
R33 John Klingberg 4.00 10.00
R34 Bo Horvat 5.00 12.00
R35 Evgeny Kuznetsov 5.00 12.00
R36 Vladislav Namestnikov 3.00 8.00
R37 David Pastrnak 10.00 25.00
R38 Greg McKegg 1.50 4.00
R39 Josh Jooris 2.00 5.00
R40 Ty Rattie 2.00 5.00
R41 William Karlsson 6.00 15.00
R42 Laurent Brossoit 2.00 5.00
R43 Jiri Sekac 1.50 4.00
R44 Shayne Gostisbehere 4.00 10.00
R45 P.E. Bellemare 2.00 5.00
R46 Chris Tierney 2.00 5.00
R47 Kerby Rychel 1.50 4.00
R48 Aaron Ekblad 5.00 12.00
R49 Alexander Wennberg 3.00 8.00
R50 Brandon Gormley 2.00 5.00
R51 Markus Granlund 3.00 8.00
R52 Anthony Duclair 3.00 8.00
R53 Johnny Gaudreau 6.00 15.00
R54 Alexander Khokhlachev 2.00 5.00
R55 Stuart Percy 2.00 5.00
R56 Joonas Nattinen 2.00 5.00
R57 Phillip Danault 4.00 10.00
R58 Trevor van Riemsdyk 3.00 8.00
R59 Andre Burakovsky 3.00 8.00
R60 Jonathan Drouin 4.00 10.00

2014-15 Upper Deck Premier Rookies Jerseys Silver Spectrum

*GOLD JSY/25: 1X TO 2.5X SILVER JSY/125
R1 Victor Rask 2.50 6.00
R2 Leon Draisaitl 12.00 30.00
R3 Mirco Mueller 2.50 6.00
R4 Oscar Klefbom 5.00 12.00
R5 Joey Hishon 3.00 8.00
R6 Tobias Rieder 2.50 6.00
R7 Curtis Lazar 2.50 6.00
R8 Rocco Grimaldi 2.50 6.00
R9 Teemu Pulkkinen 3.00 8.00
R10 Ryan Sproul 2.50 6.00
R11 Andy Andreoff 2.50 6.00
R12 Damon Severson 2.50 6.00
R13 Seth Griffith 3.00 8.00
R14 Bogdan Yakimov 2.50 6.00
R15 Curtis McKenzie 2.00 5.00
R16 Adam Lowry 4.00 10.00
R18 Barclay Goodrow 2.50 6.00
R19 Griffin Reinhart 2.50 6.00
R20 Teuvo Teravainen 4.00 10.00
R21 Seth Helgeson 2.00 5.00
R22 Sam Reinhart 10.00 25.00
R23 Colton Sissons 2.50 6.00
R24 Mark Visentin 2.50 6.00
R25 Darnell Nurse 5.00 12.00
R27 Marko Dano 2.50 6.00
R28 Corban Knight 2.50 6.00
R29 Dennis Everberg 2.50 6.00
R30 Adam Clendening 2.50 6.00
R31 Jori Lehtera 3.00 8.00
R32 Vincent Trocheck 5.00 12.00
R33 John Klingberg 5.00 12.00
R34 Bo Horvat 6.00 15.00
R35 Evgeny Kuznetsov 6.00 15.00
R36 Vladislav Namestnikov 4.00 10.00
R37 David Pastrnak 12.00 30.00
R38 Greg McKegg 2.00 5.00
R39 Josh Jooris 2.50 6.00
R40 Ty Rattie 2.50 6.00
R41 William Karlsson 8.00 20.00
R42 Laurent Brossoit 2.50 6.00
R43 Jiri Sekac 2.00 5.00
R44 Shayne Gostisbehere 5.00 12.00
R45 P.E. Bellemare 2.50 6.00
R46 Chris Tierney 2.50 6.00
R47 Kerby Rychel 2.00 5.00
R48 Aaron Ekblad 6.00 15.00
R49 Alexander Wennberg 4.00 10.00
R50 Brandon Gormley 2.50 6.00
R53 Johnny Gaudreau 8.00 20.00
R54 Alexander Khokhlachev 2.50 6.00
R55 Stuart Percy 2.50 6.00
R56 Joonas Nattinen 2.50 6.00
R57 Phillip Danault 5.00 12.00
R58 Trevor van Riemsdyk 4.00 10.00
R59 Andre Burakovsky 4.00 10.00
R60 Jonathan Drouin 5.00 12.00

2014-15 Upper Deck Premier Signature Champions

SCAK Anze Kopitar/50 20.00 50.00
SCCC Chris Chelios/99 12.00 30.00
SCCP Corey Perry/50 20.00 50.00
SCDB Dustin Brown/50 12.00 30.00
SCEM Evgeni Malkin/25 25.00 60.00
SCES Eric Staal/99 15.00 40.00
SCGF Grant Fuhr/50 20.00 50.00
SCGL Guy Lafleur/99 15.00 40.00
SCHU Brett Hull/25 25.00 60.00
SCJJ Jaromir Jagr/25 40.00 100.00
SCJS Joe Sakic/25 25.00 60.00
SCJT Jonathan Toews/50 20.00 50.00
SCMB Martin Brodeur/99 30.00 80.00
SCMF Marc-Andre Fleury/99 25.00 60.00
SCMK Mike Krushelnyski/99 10.00 25.00
SCMM Mark Messier/25 25.00 60.00
SCMS Martin St. Louis/99 12.00 30.00
SCPD Pavel Datsyuk/50 20.00 50.00
SCRB Rob Blake/99 12.00 30.00
SCTB Tom Barrasso/99 12.00 30.00

2014-15 Upper Deck Premier Signatures

PSAG Alex Galchenyuk 6.00 15.00
PSGL Gabriel Landeskog 12.00 30.00
PSGN Gustav Nyquist C 6.00 15.00
PSJT Jonathan Toews A 15.00 40.00
PSNM Nathan MacKinnon C 40.00 100.00
PSPD Pavel Datsyuk A 15.00 40.00
PSPK Patrick Kane 20.00 50.00
PSRN Rick Nash B 10.00 25.00
PSSC Sidney Crosby A 40.00 100.00
PSVN Valeri Nichushkin 10.00 25.00
PSZP Zach Parise A 10.00 25.00

2014-15 Upper Deck Premier Sixes

PQ6ANASJS Gz/Py/Ks/Pv/Ct/Mr 6.00 15.00
PQ6AVS Dch/Ld/Mc/Ig/Vr/Hs 15.00 40.00
PQ6BOSMON Lc/Mn/Rk/Pcy/Gk/Pr 8.00 20.00
PQ6CALVAN Mn/Hd/Rm/Mlr/Sn/Sd 5.00 12.00
PQ6CAPS Ov/Bck/Gr/Kz/Grn/Brk 15.00 40.00
PQ6DAL Sg/Bn/Spz/Lt/Nch/Rt 5.00 12.00
PQ6HAWKS Tw/Kn/Shp/Cr/Sb/Kh 8.00 20.00
PQ6KINGS Qk/Kp/Dgh/Cr/Tf/Bw 6.00 15.00
PQ6MON Pr/Sb/Pc/Glg/Gln/Plk 8.00 20.00
PQ6NYR Ns/St.L/Lnd/St/Zc/Kr 10.00 25.00
PQ6RC1 Dr/Dst/Rn/Lz/Wnb/Hr 20.00 50.00
PQ6RC2 Ek/Nr/Sv/Rn/Gb/Mlr 10.00 25.00
PQ6SJS Hrt/Pv/Ctr/Nm/Thr/Mlr 6.00 15.00
PQ6TOR Ksl/Kd/Rms/Brn/Rly/Or 5.00 12.00

2015-16 Upper Deck Premier

1 Ryan Kesler 2.50 6.00
2 Vladimir Tarasenko 3.00 8.00
3 Jonathan Toews 4.00 10.00
4 Alex Galchenyuk 1.50 4.00
5 Alexander Ovechkin 10.00 25.00
6 Oliver Ekman-Larsson 2.50 6.00
7 Henrik Lundqvist 6.00 15.00
8 Jiri Hudler 2.00 5.00
9 Scott Hartnell 1.50 4.00
10 Jamie Benn 2.50 6.00
11 Johnny Gaudreau 4.00 10.00
12 Claude Giroux 2.50 6.00
13 Adam Henrique 2.00 5.00
14 Carey Price 5.00 12.00
15 Steven Stamkos 5.00 12.00
16 Pavel Datsyuk 4.00 10.00
17 James van Riemsdyk 2.00 5.00
18 Anze Kopitar 4.00 10.00
19 David Krejci 2.50 6.00
20 Sidney Crosby 10.00 25.00
21 Nathan MacKinnon 10.00 25.00
22 Blake Wheeler 2.50 6.00
23 Joe Pavelski 3.00 8.00
24 Mike Hoffman 1.50 4.00
25 John Tavares 4.00 10.00
26 Mikael Granlund 2.00 5.00
27 Aaron Ekblad 3.00 8.00
28 Henrik Sedin 3.00 8.00
29 Pekka Rinne 2.50 6.00
30 Jakub Voracek 2.00 5.00
31 Drew Doughty 3.00 8.00
32 Shea Weber 2.00 5.00
33 Taylor Hall 2.50 6.00
34 Jake Allen 2.50 6.00
35 P.K. Subban 3.00 8.00
36 Jeff Skinner 3.00 8.00
37 Ryan Miller 2.50 6.00
38 Marc-Andre Fleury 5.00 12.00
39 Jason Spezza 2.50 6.00
40 Jonathan Quick 3.00 8.00
41 Ryan O'Reilly 2.50 6.00
42 Erik Karlsson 3.00 8.00
43 Evgeny Kuznetsov 3.00 8.00
44 Mario Lemieux 20.00 50.00
45 Joe Sakic 10.00 25.00
46 Mark Messier 10.00 25.00
47 Steve Yzerman 12.00 30.00
48 Patrick Roy 12.00 30.00
49 Pavel Bure 5.00 12.00
50 Wayne Gretzky 30.00 80.00
51 Frank Vafrano AU RC 10.00 25.00
52 Josh Anderson AU RC 15.00 40.00
53 Jaccob Slavin AU RC 12.00 30.00
54 Devin Shore AU RC 8.00 20.00
55 Juuse Saros AU RC 20.00 50.00
56 Anton Slepyshev AU RC 5.00 12.00
57 Garret Sparks AU RC 8.00 20.00
58 Connor Brickley AU RC 6.00 15.00
59 Matt Murray AU RC 30.00 80.00
60 Christoph Bertschy AU RC 6.00 15.00
61 Stanislav Galiev AU RC 8.00 20.00
62 Matt O'Connor AU RC 6.00 15.00
63 Louis Domingue AU RC 8.00 20.00
64 Anthony Stolarz AU RC 20.00 50.00
65 Tyler Randell AU RC 8.00 20.00
66 Viktor Svedberg AU RC 6.00 15.00
67 Daniel Carr AU RC 6.00 15.00
68 Brendan Ranford AU RC 6.00 15.00
69 Kyle Baun AU RC 8.00 20.00
70 Sam Brittain AU RC 8.00 20.00
71 Jake Virtanen JSY AU/375 RC 12.00 30.00
72 Kevin Fiala JSY AU/375 RC 12.00 30.00
73 Shane Prince JSY AU/375 RC 6.00 15.00
74 Derek Forbort JSY AU/375 RC 8.00 20.00
75 Ryan Hartman JSY AU/375 RC 12.00 30.00
76 Stefan Noesen JSY AU/375 RC 6.00 15.00
77 Nicolas Petan JSY AU/375 RC 10.00 25.00
78 Brock McGinn JSY AU/375 RC 10.00 25.00
79 Jacob de la Rose JSY AU/375 RC 10.00 25.00
80 Emile Poirier JSY AU/375 RC 8.00 20.00
81 Jared McCann JSY AU/375 RC 12.00 30.00
82 Zachary Fucale JSY AU/375 RC 8.00 20.00
83 Ronalds Kenins JSY AU/375 RC 6.00 15.00
84 Matt Puempel JSY AU/375 RC 8.00 20.00
85 Daniel Sprong JSY AU/375 RC 12.00 30.00
86 Nikolay Goldobin JSY AU/375 RC 10.00 25.00
87 Mike McCarron JSY AU/375 RC 12.00 30.00
88 Chandler Stephenson JSY AU/375 RC 12.00 30.00
89 Vincent Hinostroza JSY AU/375 RC 6.00 15.00
90 Shea Theodore JSY AU/375 RC 15.00 40.00
91 Joonas Donskoi JSY AU/375 RC 10.00 25.00
92 Slater Koekkoek JSY AU/375 RC 6.00 15.00
93 Nick Ritchie JSY AU/375 RC 10.00 25.00
94 Charles Hudon JSY AU/375 RC 10.00 25.00
95 Henrik Samuelsson JSY AU/375 RC 6.00 15.00
96 Radek Faksa JSY AU/375 RC 10.00 25.00
97 Nick Cousins JSY AU/375 RC 10.00 25.00
98 Mackenzie Skapski JSY AU/375 RC 10.00 25.00
99 Hunter Shinkaruk JSY AU/375 RC 10.00 25.00
100 Noah Hanifin JSY AU/375 RC 15.00 40.00
101 Mikko Rantanen JSY AU/375 RC 60.00 150.00
102 Oscar Lindberg JSY AU/375 RC 10.00 25.00
103 Brendan Gaunce JSY AU/375 RC 12.00 30.00
104 Antoine Bibeau JSY AU/375 RC 10.00 25.00
105 Andreas Athanasiou JSY AU/375 RC 25.00 60.00
106 Connor Hellebuyck JSY AU/375 RC 40.00 100.00
107 Brady Skjei JSY AU/375 RC 8.00 20.00
108 Colton Parayko JSY AU/375 RC 15.00 40.00
109 Mike Condon JSY AU/375 RC 10.00 25.00
110 Nikolaj Ehlers JSY AU/375 RC 20.00 50.00
111 Gustav Olofsson JSY AU/375 RC 10.00 25.00
112 Robby Fabbri JSY AU/375 RC 12.00 30.00
113 Artemi Panarin JSY AU/375 RC 30.00 80.00
114 Max Domi JSY AU/199 RC 25.00 60.00
115 Connor McDavid JSY AU/199 RC 3000.00 8000.00
116 Sam Bennett JSY AU/199 RC 20.00 50.00
117 Dylan Larkin JSY AU/199 RC 40.00 100.00
118 Jack Eichel JSY RC 40.00 100.00

2015-16 Upper Deck Premier Silver Spectrum

*VETS: 1.5X TO 4X BASIC CARDS
*ROOKIES: .5X TO 1.25X BASIC CARDS
50 Wayne Gretzky AU 250.00 600.00
55 Juuse Saros AU 30.00 80.00
113 Artemi Panarin JSY AU/65 60.00 150.00
115 Connor McDavid JSY AU/35 5000.00 12000.00
116 Sam Bennett JSY AU/35 20.00 50.00
117 Dylan Larkin JSY AU/35 60.00 150.00

2015-16 Upper Deck Premier '03-04 Tribute Rookies Autograph Patches

SRRAP Artemi Panarin/49 60.00 150.00
SRRBG Brendan Gaunce/99 20.00 50.00
SRRBH Ben Hutton/99 15.00 40.00
SRRCM Connor McDavid/49 1000.00 1500.00
SRRCP Colton Parayko/99 30.00 80.00
SRRDL Dylan Larkin/49 50.00 125.00
SRRDS Daniel Sprong/99 20.00 50.00
SRRHS Hunter Shinkaruk/99 15.00 40.00
SRRJD Joonas Donskoi/99 15.00 40.00
SRRJE Jack Eichel/49 (No Auto) 60.00 150.00
SRRJM Jared McCann/99 20.00 50.00
SRRJV Jake Virtanen/49 20.00 50.00
SRRLU Linus Ullmark/99 30.00 80.00
SRRMC Mike Condon/99 15.00 40.00
SRRMD Max Domi/49 30.00 80.00
SRRMI Colin Miller/99 12.00 30.00
SRRMJ Mattias Janmark/99 15.00 40.00
SRRNE Nikolaj Ehlers/49 30.00 80.00
SRRNG Nikolay Goldobin/99 15.00 40.00
SRRNH Noah Hanifin/49 25.00 60.00
SRRNR Nick Ritchie/99 15.00 40.00
SRROL Oscar Lindberg/99 15.00 40.00
SRRRF Robby Fabbri/99 20.00 50.00
SRRSB Sam Bennett/49 50.00 125.00
SRRSP Shane Prince/99 10.00 25.00
SRRST Shea Theodore/99 25.00 60.00
SRRZF Zachary Fucale/49 12.00 30.00

2015-16 Upper Deck Premier Inked Script

INAH Anze Kopitar 25.00 60.00
INAO Alexander Ovechkin 60.00 150.00
INBO Bobby Hull 30.00 80.00
INBR Brett Hull 30.00 80.00
INBS Borje Salming 15.00 40.00
INCJ Curtis Joseph 20.00 50.00
INDH Dominik Hasek 25.00 60.00
INGH Glenn Hall 15.00 40.00
INJS Joe Sakic 30.00 80.00
INMM Mark Messier 30.00 80.00
INMP Max Pacioretty 15.00 40.00
INPB Pavel Bure 15.00 40.00
INSC Sidney Crosby 100.00 250.00
INTS Teemu Selanne 30.00 80.00
INWG Wayne Gretzky 300.00 800.00

2015-16 Upper Deck Premier Jerseys

*PRIME/25: 1X TO 2.5X BASIC INSERTS
1 Ryan Kesler 2.50 6.00
2 Vladimir Tarasenko 3.00 8.00
3 Jonathan Toews 4.00 10.00
4 Alex Galchenyuk 1.50 4.00
5 Alexander Ovechkin 10.00 25.00
6 Oliver Ekman-Larsson 2.50 6.00
7 Henrik Lundqvist 6.00 15.00
8 Jiri Hudler 2.00 5.00
10 Jamie Benn 2.50 6.00
11 Johnny Gaudreau 4.00 10.00
12 Claude Giroux 2.50 6.00
13 Adam Henrique 2.00 5.00
14 Carey Price 5.00 12.00
15 Steven Stamkos 5.00 12.00
16 Pavel Datsyuk 4.00 10.00
17 James van Riemsdyk 2.00 5.00
18 Anze Kopitar 4.00 10.00
19 David Krejci 2.50 6.00
20 Sidney Crosby 10.00 25.00
22 Blake Wheeler 2.50 6.00
23 Joe Pavelski 3.00 8.00
24 Mike Hoffman 1.50 4.00
25 John Tavares 4.00 10.00
26 Mikael Granlund 2.00 5.00
27 Aaron Ekblad 3.00 8.00
28 Henrik Sedin 3.00 8.00
29 Pekka Rinne 2.50 6.00
30 Jakub Voracek 2.00 5.00
31 Drew Doughty 3.00 8.00
32 Shea Weber 2.00 5.00
33 Taylor Hall 2.50 6.00
34 Jake Allen 2.50 6.00
35 P.K. Subban 3.00 8.00
36 Jeff Skinner 3.00 8.00
37 Ryan Miller 2.50 6.00
38 Marc-Andre Fleury 5.00 12.00
39 Jason Spezza 2.50 6.00
40 Jonathan Quick 3.00 8.00
41 Ryan O'Reilly 2.50 6.00
43 Evgeny Kuznetsov 3.00 8.00
44 Mario Lemieux 10.00 25.00
45 Joe Sakic 5.00 12.00
48 Patrick Roy 6.00 15.00
49 Pavel Bure 2.50 6.00

2015-16 Upper Deck Premier Mega Patch Chest Logos

PMPAB Aleksander Barkov/31 40.00 100.00
PMPAD Anthony Duclair/25 20.00 50.00
PMPAE Aaron Ekblad/25 30.00 80.00
PMPAG Alex Galchenyuk/20 15.00 40.00
PMPAH Adam Henrique/26 20.00 50.00
PMPAL Anders Lee/20 25.00 60.00
PMPAN Andrew Hammond/23 30.00 80.00
PMPAS Alexander Steen/18 15.00 40.00
PMPBB Bob Bourne/20 15.00 40.00
PMPBB Brent Burns/22 25.00 60.00
PMPBG Brendan Gallagher/19 25.00 60.00
PMPBO Sergei Bobrovsky/21 40.00 100.00
PMPBS Brandon Saad/21 20.00 50.00
PMPBW Blake Wheeler/24 25.00 60.00
PMPCC Corey Crawford/24 30.00 80.00
PMPCG Claude Giroux/18 25.00 60.00
PMPCK Chris Kreider/18 30.00 80.00
PMPCM Connor McDavid/20 600.00 900.00
PMPCP Corey Perry/22 40.00 100.00
PMPCS Cory Schneider/25 25.00 60.00
PMPCW Cam Ward/18 25.00 60.00
PMPDB Dustin Byfuglien/24 25.00 60.00
PMPDD Drew Doughty/18 30.00 80.00
PMPDD David Desharnais/20 15.00 40.00
PMPDE Devan Dubnyk/20 20.00 50.00
PMPDH Dougie Hamilton/20 20.00 50.00
PMPDK Duncan Keith/22 20.00 50.00
PMPDP David Pastrnak/24 60.00 150.00
PMPDS Derek Stepan/17 15.00 40.00
PMPDS Daniel Sedin/20 30.00 80.00
PMPDU Matt Duchene/26 25.00 60.00
PMPEB Jordan Eberle/22 25.00 60.00
PMPEK Evander Kane/24 25.00 60.00
PMPEM Evgeni Malkin/30 50.00 125.00
PMPES Eric Staal/20 30.00 80.00
PMPFA Frederik Andersen/21 30.00 80.00
PMPFF Filip Forsberg/20 40.00 100.00
PMPGL Gabriel Landeskog/27 30.00 80.00
PMPGN Gustav Nyquist/16 15.00 40.00
PMPGR Mikael Granlund/18 20.00 50.00
PMPHA Jaroslav Halak/22 25.00 60.00
PMPHL Henrik Lundqvist/18 60.00 150.00
PMPHO Marian Hossa/23 25.00 60.00
PMPHO Braden Holtby/18 30.00 80.00
PMPHS Henrik Sedin/20 30.00 80.00
PMPHU Jonathan Huberdeau/24 30.00 80.00
PMPHZ Henrik Zetterberg/17 30.00 80.00
PMPJA Jake Allen/19 25.00 60.00
PMPJC John Carlson/21 25.00 60.00
PMPJE Jack Eichel/22 80.00 200.00
PMPJF Justin Faulk/19 20.00 50.00

PMPJG Johnny Gaudreau/20 40.00 100.00
PMPJH Jiri Hudler/20 20.00 50.00
PMPJI Jarome Iginla/24 30.00 80.00
PMPJJ Jaromir Jagr/22 80.00 200.00
PMPJK John Klingberg/19 25.00 60.00
PMPJO Jack Johnson/21 15.00 40.00
PMPJP Joe Pavelski/25 30.00 80.00
PMPJQ Jonathan Quick/16 30.00 80.00
PMPJR James van Riemsdyk/16 20.00 50.00
PMPJS Jakob Silfverberg/21 15.00 40.00
PMPJT Jacob Trouba/19 20.00 50.00
PMPJV Jakub Voracek/19 20.00 50.00
PMPJZ Jason Zucker/18 25.00 60.00
PMPKA Erik Karlsson/22 30.00 80.00
PMPKA Nazem Kadri/16 30.00 80.00
PMPKE Phil Kessel/29 25.00 60.00
PMPKH Kevin Hayes/19 20.00 50.00
PMPKL Kris Letang/30 30.00 80.00
PMPKS Kevin Shattenkirk/20 15.00 40.00
PMPKT Kyle Turris/23 20.00 50.00
PMPKU Evgeny Kuznetsov/20 30.00 80.00
PMPLE Loui Eriksson/24 15.00 40.00
PMPMB Matt Beleskey/20 15.00 40.00
PMPMC Michael Cammalleri/26 20.00 50.00
PMPMC Mike Condon/20 25.00 60.00
PMPMD Max Domi/26 50.00 125.00
PMPMF Marc-Andre Fleury/30 50.00 125.00
PMPMG Marian Gaborik/16 25.00 60.00
PMPMH Martin Hanzal/24 15.00 40.00
PMPMI Mike Hoffman/23 15.00 40.00
PMPMJ Martin Jones/21 20.00 50.00
PMPMP Max Pacioretty/19 25.00 60.00
PMPMR Michael Raffl/18 15.00 40.00
PMPMS Mike Smith/24 25.00 60.00
PMPMS Mark Scheifele/22 40.00 100.00
PMPNE Nikolaj Ehlers/20 50.00 125.00
PMPNF Nick Foligno/20 20.00 50.00
PMPNH Noah Hanifin/20 40.00 100.00
PMPNK Nikita Kucherov/20 50.00 125.00
PMPNL Nick Leddy/22 15.00 40.00
PMPNN Nino Niederreiter/18 15.00 40.00
PMPOE Oliver Ekman-Larsson/22 25.00 60.00
PMPON Owen Nolan/27 25.00 60.00
PMPOP Ondrej Palat/20 20.00 50.00
PMPPB Patrice Bergeron/20 30.00 80.00
PMPPE Patrik Elias/23 25.00 60.00
PMPPK Patrick Kane/24 50.00 125.00
PMPPM Petr Mrazek/17 25.00 60.00
PMPPM Patrick Marleau/22 25.00 60.00
PMPPR Pekka Rinne/19 25.00 60.00
PMPPS Patrick Sharp/18 25.00 60.00
PMPPT Pierre Turgeon/24 20.00 50.00
PMPRG Ryan Getzlaf/21 25.00 60.00
PMPRJ Roman Josi/20 25.00 60.00
PMPRK Ryan Kesler/26 25.00 60.00
PMPRL Roberto Luongo/29 40.00 100.00
PMPRM Ryan Miller/19 25.00 60.00
PMPRN Ryan Nugent-Hopkins/24 30.00 80.00
PMPRO Ryan O'Reilly/24 25.00 60.00
PMPRR Rasmus Ristolainen/24 15.00 40.00
PMPRS Ryan Strome/24 25.00 60.00
PMPSB Sam Bennett/18 80.00 200.00
PMPSK Jeff Skinner/20 30.00 80.00
PMPSM Steve Mason/18 20.00 50.00
PMPSM Sean Monahan/22 15.00 40.00
PMPSP Jason Spezza/21 25.00 60.00
PMPSR Sam Reinhart/22 50.00 125.00
PMPSS Steven Stamkos/22 50.00 125.00
PMPST Mark Stone/22 30.00 80.00
PMPSU P.K. Subban/18 30.00 80.00
PMPSV Semyon Varlamov/26 25.00 60.00
PMPSW Shea Weber/20 20.00 50.00
PMPTH Taylor Hall/22 25.00 60.00
PMPTJ Tyler Johnson/22 15.00 40.00
PMPTO Tyler Toffoli/18 25.00 60.00
PMPTO T.J. Oshie/20 25.00 60.00
PMPTR Tuukka Rask/24 30.00 80.00
PMPTR Tuukka Rask/22 30.00 80.00
PMPTS Tyler Seguin/18 30.00 80.00
PMPTT Tomas Tatar/19 15.00 40.00
PMPVH Victor Hedman/21 30.00 80.00
PMPVI Jake Virtanen/19 30.00 80.00
PMPVT Vladimir Tarasenko/19 30.00 80.00
PMPWS Wayne Simmonds/18 30.00 80.00
PMPZP Zach Parise/20 25.00 60.00

2015-16 Upper Deck Premier Mega Patch Duos

MP2BE P.Bergeron/L.Eriksson 15.00 40.00
MP2BJ P.Bure/J.Jagr 40.00 100.00
MP2BS B.Saad/S.Hartnell 10.00 25.00
MP2BT B.Bourne/J.Tavares 20.00 50.00
MP2CM E.Malkin/P.Coffey 25.00 60.00
MP2DZ H.Zetterberg/P.Datsyuk 20.00 50.00
MP2GS C.Giroux/W.Simmonds 15.00 40.00
MP2HB J.Huberdeau/A.Barkov 20.00 50.00
MP2HC M.Cammalleri/A.Henrique 10.00 25.00
MP2HD T.Hall/L.Draisaitl 40.00 100.00
MP2ID M.Duchene/J.Iginla 15.00 40.00
MP2KH E.Karlsson/M.Hoffman 15.00 40.00
MP2KP C.Perry/R.Kesler 20.00 50.00
MP2KT A.Kopitar/T.Toffoli 20.00 50.00
MP2LD A.Duclair/O.Ekman-Larsson 12.0030.00
MP2LS B.Wheeler/M.Scheifele 20.00 50.00
MP2MG J.Gaudreau/S.Monahan 20.00 50.00
MP2MK E.Malkin/P.Kessel 25.00 60.00
MP2MP J.Pavelski/P.Marleau 15.00 40.00
MP2NT O.Nolan/J.Thornton 20.00 50.00
MP2NZ M.Zuccarello/R.Nash 12.00 30.00
MP2OB A.Ovechkin/N.Backstrom 50.00 120.00
MP2OR R.O'Reilly/S.Reinhart 25.00 60.00
MP2PS M.Pacioretty/P.Subban 15.00 40.00
MP2SB J.Benn/P.Sharp 12.00 30.00
MP2SK N.Kucherov/S.Stamkos 25.00 60.00
MP2SS D.Sedin/H.Sedin 15.00 40.00
MP2ST V.Tarasenko/A.Steen 15.00 40.00
MP2TK P.Kane/J.Toews 25.00 60.00
MP2TL J.Tavares/A.Lee 20.00 50.00
MP2VK J.van Riemsdyk/N.Kadri 15.00 40.00
MP2WJ R.Josi/S.Weber 12.00 30.00

2015-16 Upper Deck Premier Mega Patch Trios

MP3BRE Bergeron/Rask/Eriksson/25 30.0080.00
MP3DML Duchene/MacKinnon
Landeskog/25 100.00 250.00
MP3HGM Hamilton/Gaudreau
Monahan/25 40.00 100.00
PMP3KLS Karlsson/Ekman-
Larsson/Subban/25 30.00 80.00
PMP3KQT Kopitar/Quick/Toffoli/25 40.00 100.00
PMP3MZT Mrazek/Zetterberg
Tatar/25 30.00 80.00
PMP3NLK Nash/Lundqvist
Kreider/25 60.00 150.00
PMP3PGK Perry/Getzlaf/Kesler/25 40.00 100.00
PMP3PTM Pavelski/Thornton
Marleau/25 40.00 100.00
PMP3SSB Sharp/Seguin/Benn/25 30.00 80.00
PMP3ZYD Zetterberg/Yzerman
Datsyuk/25 60.00 150.00

2015-16 Upper Deck Premier Mega Stick Duos

PMS2BB R.Bourque/P.Bergeron 25.00 60.00
PMS2CH B.Clarke/R.Hextall 25.00 60.00
PMS2CS G.Carbonneau/D.Savard 15.00 40.00
PMS2DZ P.Datsyuk/H.Zetterberg 25.00 60.00
PMS2EH T.Esposito/B.Hull 30.00 80.00
PMS2GM W.Gretzky/M.Messier 100.00 250.00
PMS2HH D.Hawerchuk/D.Hasek 25.00 60.00
PMS2MG L.McDonald/D.Gilmour 20.00 50.00
PMS2OC A.Ovechkin/J.Carlson 60.00 150.00
PMS2RB L.Robinson/R.Blake 15.00 40.00
PMS2RH L.Robitaille/B.Hull 30.00 80.00
PMS2SF J.Sakic/P.Forsberg 30.00 80.00
PMS2YC S.Yzerman/C.Chelios 40.00 100.00

2015-16 Upper Deck Premier Mega Stick Trios

PMS3GOC Gartner
Ovechkin/Carlson/30 50.00 125.00

2015-16 Upper Deck Premier Premier Duals Jerseys

PD2BE P.Bergeron/L.Eriksson/149 6.00 15.00
PD2BS P.Bure/H.Sedin/49 6.00 15.00
PD2CH B.Holtby/C.Crawford/149 6.00 15.00
PD2DB M.Domi/S.Bennett/149 15.00 40.00
PD2DL M.Duchene/G.Landeskog/149 6.00 15.00
PD2EP J.Eichel/A.Panarin/149 20.00 50.00
PD2GH J.Gaudreau/D.Hamilton/149 8.00 20.00
PD2GL W.Gretzky/M.Lemieux/49 30.00 80.00
PD2HB B.Hull/D.Backes/149 10.00 25.00
PD2HC C.Hellebuyck/M.Condon/149 20.0050.00
PD2HJ J.Huberdeau/J.Jagr/149 15.00 40.00
PD2KK P.Kane/D.Keith/149 10.00 25.00
PD2MK E.Malkin/P.Kessel/149 10.00 25.00
PD2ML C.McDavid/D.Larkin/49 80.00 200.00
PD2NM O.Nolan/P.Marleau/49 5.00 12.00
PD2OK A.Ovechkin/E.Kuznetsov/149 20.00 50.00
PD2PK C.Perry/R.Kesler/149 8.00 20.00
PD2PR C.Price/T.Rask/149 10.00 25.00
PD2PS M.Pacioretty/P.Subban/149 6.00 15.00
PD2RE N.Ritchie/N.Ehlers/149 10.00 25.00
PD2RK J.van Riemsdyk/N.Kadri/149 6.00 15.00
PD2SB T.Seguin/J.Benn/149 6.00 15.00
PD2SK S.Stamkos/N.Kucherov/149 10.00 25.00
PD2SM D.Sedin/R.Miller/149 6.00 15.00
PD2TS V.Tarasenko/A.Steen/149 6.00 15.00
PD2ZD H.Zetterberg/P.Datsyuk/149 8.00 20.00

2015-16 Upper Deck Premier Premier Quads Jerseys

PQ4BSKS Benn/Seguin
Klingberg/Sharp/65 6.00 15.00
PQ4GMBH Gaudreau/Monahan
Bennett/Hamilton/65 15.00 40.00
PQ4JHBL Jagr/Huberdeau
Barkov/Luongo/65 15.00 40.00
PQ4KTCD Kopitar/Toffoli
Carter/Doughty/65 8.00 20.00
PQ4MKLF Malkin/Kessel
Letang/Fleury/65 10.00 25.00
PQ4MRRZ McCann/Rantanen
Ritchie/Fucale/65 25.00 60.00
PQ4OBKH Ovechkin/Backstrom
Kuznetsov/Holtby/65 20.00 50.00
PQ4PBVE Panarin/Bennett
Virtanen/Ehlers/65 20.00 50.00
PQ4PSGG Pacioretty/Subban
Galchenyuk/Gallagher/65 6.00 15.00
PQ4TKSK Toews/Kane
Seabrook/Keith/65 10.00 25.00
PQ4TSLH Tavares/Strome
Lee/Halak/65 8.00 20.00
PQ4TSSB Tarasenko/Steen
Shattenkirk/Backes/65 6.00 15.00
PQ4ZDTN Zetterberg/Datsyuk
Tatar/Nyquist/65 8.00 20.00

2015-16 Upper Deck Premier Premier Rookie Materials

PRMAA Andreas Athanasiou 25.00 60.00
PRMAP Artemi Panarin 40.00 100.00
PRMBG Brendan Gaunce 12.00 30.00
PRMBH Ben Hutton 10.00 25.00
PRMBM Brock McGinn 10.00 25.00
PRMCH Connor Hellebuyck 40.00 100.00
PRMCM Connor McDavid 150.00 400.00
PRMCP Colton Parayko 15.00 40.00
PRMDL Dylan Larkin 30.00 80.00
PRMDS Daniel Sprong 12.00 30.00
PRMHS Hunter Shinkaruk 10.00 25.00
PRMJE Jack Eichel 40.00 100.00
PRMJM Jared McCann 12.00 30.00
PRMJV Jake Virtanen 12.00 30.00
PRMLU Linus Ullmark 20.00 50.00
PRMMD Max Domi 20.00 50.00
PRMMI Colin Miller 8.00 20.00
PRMMJ Mattias Janmark 10.00 25.00
PRMMR Mikko Rantanen 50.00 125.00
PRMNE Nikolaj Ehlers 20.00 50.00
PRMNG Nikolay Goldobin 10.00 25.00
PRMNH Noah Hanifin 15.00 40.00
PRMNP Nicolas Petan 10.00 25.00
PRMNR Nick Ritchie 10.00 25.00
PRMNS Nick Shore 6.00 15.00
PRMOL Oscar Lindberg 10.00 25.00
PRMRF Robby Fabbri 12.00 30.00
PRMSB Sam Bennett 30.00 80.00
PRMST Shea Theodore 15.00 40.00
PRMZF Zachary Fucale 8.00 20.00

2015-16 Upper Deck Premier Premier Signatures

PSAE Aaron Ekblad A 12.00 30.00
PSEM Evgeni Malkin A 20.00 50.00
PSJA Jake Allen B 10.00 25.00
PSJD Jonathan Drouin B 8.00 20.00
PSJG Johnny Gaudreau B 15.00 40.00
PSJP Joe Pavelski B 12.00 30.00
PSJT Jonathan Toews A 15.00 40.00
PSKH Kevin Hayes B 8.00 20.00
PSMS Mark Stone B 12.00 30.00
PSPD Pavel Datsyuk A 15.00 40.00
PSTT Tyler Toffoli B 10.00 25.00
PSZP Zach Parise A 10.00 25.00

2015-16 Upper Deck Premier Premier Signatures Legends

LPSBO Bobby Orr C 40.00 100.00
LPSBS Borje Salming 10.00 25.00
LPSGH Glenn Hall C 10.00 25.00
LPSGL Guy Lafleur A 12.00 30.00
LPSJK Jari Kurri C 10.00 25.00
LPSJS Joe Sakic A 20.00 50.00
LPSLR Larry Robinson C 10.00 25.00
LPSMB Mike Bossy B 10.00 25.00
LPSMM Mike Modano B 15.00 40.00
LPSNL Nicklas Lidstrom B 10.00 25.00
LPSPC Paul Coffey B 10.00 25.00
LPSPE Phil Esposito A 15.00 40.00
LPSRO Luc Robitaille B 10.00 25.00
LPSTL Mario Lemieux A 60.00 150.00
LPSWG Wayne Gretzky C 200.00 500.00

2015-16 Upper Deck Premier Premier Signatures Rookies

RPSCM Connor McDavid A 200.00 500.00
RPSCP Colton Parayko C 12.00 30.00
RPSDL Dylan Larkin 25.00 60.00
RPSJM Jared McCann C 10.00 25.00
RPSJV Jake Virtanen B 10.00 25.00
RPSLU Linus Ullmark C 15.00 40.00
RPSMC Mike Condon C 8.00 20.00
RPSNE Nikolaj Ehlers C 15.00 40.00
RPSNR Nick Ritchie C 8.00 20.00
RPSOL Oscar Lindberg C 8.00 20.00
RPSRF Robby Fabbri C 10.00 25.00
RPSSB Sam Bennett B 25.00 60.00
RPSZF Zachary Fucale C 6.00 15.00

2015-16 Upper Deck Premier Premier Swatches

PSAS Alexander Steen 2.00 5.00
PSBB Brent Burns 3.00 8.00
PSBH Braden Holtby 4.00 10.00
PSBS Brandon Saad 2.50 6.00
PSCC Corey Crawford 4.00 10.00
PSCH Chris Chelios 3.00 8.00
PSCP Corey Perry 5.00 12.00
PSDH Dougie Hamilton 2.50 6.00
PSDS Daniel Sedin 4.00 10.00
PSEM Evgeni Malkin 6.00 15.00
PSJF Justin Faulk 2.50 6.00
PSJJ Jaromir Jagr 10.00 25.00
PSKU Nikita Kucherov 6.00 15.00
PSMC Michael Cammalleri 2.50 6.00
PSMD Matt Duchene 3.00 8.00
PSMP Max Pacioretty 3.00 8.00
PSMS Mark Scheifele 5.00 12.00
PSMZ Mats Zuccarello 3.00 8.00
PSNB Nicklas Backstrom 3.00 8.00
PSNK Nazem Kadri 4.00 10.00
PSON Owen Nolan 3.00 8.00
PSPB Patrice Bergeron 4.00 10.00
PSPC Paul Coffey 3.00 8.00
PSPK Patrick Kane 6.00 15.00
PSPS Patrick Sharp 3.00 8.00
PSRJ Roman Josi 3.00 8.00
PSRN Ryan Nugent-Hopkins 4.00 10.00
PSTS Tyler Seguin 4.00 10.00
PSTT Tyler Toffoli 3.00 8.00
PSZP Zach Parise 3.00 8.00

2015-16 Upper Deck Premier Premier Teammates Jerseys

PT3BJE Barkov/Jagr/Ekblad/25 20.00 50.00
PT3BRE Bergeron/Rask/Eriksson/99 8.00 20.00
PT3BSS Benn/Seguin/Spezza/25 8.00 20.00
PT3BWS Byfuglien/Wheeler
Scheifele/99 10.00 25.00
PT3CHS Cammalleri/Henrique
Schneider/99 6.00 15.00
PT3HSF Hartnell/Saad/Foligno/99 5.00 12.00
PT3JFW Josi/Forsberg/Weber/99 10.00 25.00
PT3KHT Karlsson/Hoffman/Turris/99 8.00 20.00
PT3KQG Kopitar/Quick/Gaborik/25 10.00 25.00
PT3KSH Kucherov/Stamkos
Hedman/99 12.00 30.00
PT3NLK Nash/Lundqvist/Kreider/99 15.00 40.00
PT3OOC Oshie/Ovechkin/Carlson/25 25.0060.00
PT3ORR O'Reilly/Ristolainen
Reinhart/99 12.00 30.00
PT3PGK Perry/Getzlaf/Kesler/99 10.00 25.00
PT3PMB Pavelski/Marleau/Burns/99 8.00 20.00
PT3SFS Staal/Faulk/Skinner/99 8.00 20.00
PT3SLH Smith/Ekman-Larsson
Hanzal/99 6.00 15.00
PT3TCH Toews/Crawford/Hossa/25 10.00 25.00
PT3VGS Voracek/Giroux
Simmonds/99 8.00 20.00

2015-16 Upper Deck Premier Rookies

R1 Nick Ritchie 2.50 6.00
R2 Andreas Athanasiou 6.00 15.00
R3 Jared McCann 3.00 8.00
R4 Andrew Copp 2.50 6.00
R5 Kevin Fiala 3.00 8.00
R6 Matt Puempel 2.00 5.00
R7 Colin Miller 2.00 5.00
R8 Daniel Sprong 3.00 8.00
R9 Nikolay Goldobin 2.50 6.00
R10 Mikko Rantanen 12.00 30.00
R11 Antoine Bibeau 2.50 6.00
R12 Mike McCarron 3.00 8.00
R13 Chandler Stephenson 3.00 8.00
R14 Connor Hellebuyck 10.00 25.00
R15 Oscar Lindberg 2.50 6.00
R16 Vincent Hinostroza 1.50 4.00
R17 Linus Ullmark 5.00 12.00
R18 Shea Theodore 4.00 10.00
R19 Charles Hudon 2.50 6.00
R20 Malcolm Subban 4.00 10.00
R21 Slater Koekkoek 1.50 4.00
R22 Emile Poirier 2.00 5.00
R23 Brendan Gaunce 3.00 8.00
R24 Henrik Samuelsson 1.50 4.00
R25 Colton Parayko 4.00 10.00
R26 Brady Skjei 2.00 5.00
R27 Nick Cousins 2.50 6.00
R28 Mackenzie Skapski 2.50 6.00
R29 Shane Prince 1.50 4.00
R30 Noah Hanifin 4.00 10.00
R31 Nicolas Petan 2.50 6.00
R32 Brock McGinn 2.50 6.00
R33 Jacob de la Rose 2.50 6.00
R34 Ronalds Kenins 1.50 4.00
R35 Hunter Shinkaruk 2.50 6.00
R36 Derek Forbort 2.00 5.00
R37 Ryan Hartman 3.00 8.00
R38 Gustav Olofsson 2.50 6.00
R39 Stefan Noesen 1.50 4.00
R40 Mike Condon 2.50 6.00
R41 Jack Eichel 10.00 25.00
R42 Artemi Panarin 10.00 25.00
R43 Jake Virtanen 3.00 8.00
R44 Max Domi 5.00 12.00
R45 Sam Bennett 8.00 20.00
R46 Robby Fabbri 3.00 8.00
R47 Connor McDavid 30.00 80.00
R48 Nikolaj Ehlers 5.00 12.00
R49 Zachary Fucale 2.00 5.00
R50 Dylan Larkin 8.00 20.00

2015-16 Upper Deck Premier Rookies Jerseys

R1 Nick Ritchie C 3.00 8.00
R2 Andreas Athanasiou C 8.00 20.00
R3 Jared McCann C 4.00 10.00
R4 Andrew Copp C 3.00 8.00
R5 Kevin Fiala C 4.00 10.00
R6 Matt Puempel C 2.50 6.00
R7 Colin Miller C 2.50 6.00
R8 Daniel Sprong C 4.00 10.00
R9 Nikolay Goldobin C 3.00 8.00
R10 Mikko Rantanen C 15.00 40.00
R11 Antoine Bibeau C 3.00 8.00
R12 Mike McCarron C 4.00 10.00
R13 Chandler Stephenson C 4.00 10.00
R14 Connor Hellebuyck C 12.00 30.00
R15 Oscar Lindberg C 3.00 8.00
R16 Vincent Hinostroza C 2.00 5.00
R17 Linus Ullmark C 6.00 15.00
R18 Shea Theodore C 5.00 12.00
R19 Charles Hudon C 3.00 8.00
R20 Malcolm Subban C 5.00 12.00
R21 Slater Koekkoek C 2.00 5.00
R22 Emile Poirier C 2.50 6.00
R23 Brendan Gaunce C 4.00 10.00
R24 Henrik Samuelsson C 2.00 5.00
R25 Colton Parayko C 5.00 12.00
R26 Brady Skjei C 2.50 6.00
R27 Nick Cousins C 3.00 8.00
R28 Mackenzie Skapski C 3.00 8.00
R29 Shane Prince C 2.00 5.00
R30 Noah Hanifin C 5.00 12.00
R31 Nicolas Petan C 3.00 8.00
R32 Brock McGinn A 3.00 8.00
R33 Jacob de la Rose C 3.00 8.00
R34 Ronalds Kenins C 2.00 5.00
R35 Hunter Shinkaruk C 3.00 8.00
R36 Derek Forbort C 2.50 6.00
R37 Ryan Hartman C 4.00 10.00
R38 Gustav Olofsson C 3.00 8.00
R39 Stefan Noesen C 2.00 5.00
R40 Mike Condon C 3.00 8.00
R41 Jack Eichel B 12.00 30.00
R42 Artemi Panarin B 12.00 30.00
R43 Jake Virtanen B 4.00 10.00
R44 Max Domi B 6.00 15.00
R45 Sam Bennett B 10.00 25.00
R46 Robby Fabbri C 4.00 10.00
R47 Connor McDavid B 30.00 80.00
R48 Nikolaj Ehlers B 6.00 15.00
R49 Zachary Fucale C 2.50 6.00
R50 Dylan Larkin B 10.00 25.00

2015-16 Upper Deck Premier Rookies Silver Spectrum

R1 Nick Ritchie AU 8.00 20.00
R2 Andreas Athanasiou AU 20.00 50.00
R3 Jared McCann AU 10.00 25.00
R4 Andrew Copp AU 8.00 20.00
R5 Kevin Fiala AU 10.00 25.00
R6 Matt Puempel AU 6.00 15.00
R7 Colin Miller AU 6.00 15.00
R8 Daniel Sprong AU 10.00 25.00
R9 Nikolay Goldobin AU 8.00 20.00
R10 Mikko Rantanen AU 40.00 100.00
R11 Antoine Bibeau AU 8.00 20.00
R12 Mike McCarron AU 10.00 25.00
R13 Chandler Stephenson AU 10.00 25.00
R14 Connor Hellebuyck AU 30.00 80.00
R15 Oscar Lindberg AU 8.00 20.00
R16 Vincent Hinostroza AU 5.00 12.00
R17 Linus Ullmark AU 15.00 40.00
R18 Shea Theodore AU 12.00 30.00
R19 Charles Hudon AU 8.00 20.00
R21 Slater Koekkoek AU 5.00 12.00
R22 Emile Poirier AU 6.00 15.00
R23 Brendan Gaunce AU 10.00 25.00
R24 Henrik Samuelsson AU 5.00 12.00
R25 Colton Parayko AU 12.00 30.00
R26 Brady Skjei AU 6.00 15.00
R27 Nick Cousins AU 8.00 20.00
R28 Mackenzie Skapski AU 8.00 20.00
R29 Shane Prince AU 5.00 12.00
R30 Noah Hanifin AU 12.00 30.00
R31 Nicolas Petan AU 8.00 20.00
R32 Brock McGinn AU 8.00 20.00
R33 Jacob de la Rose AU 8.00 20.00
R34 Ronalds Kenins AU 5.00 12.00
R35 Hunter Shinkaruk AU 8.00 20.00
R36 Derek Forbort AU 6.00 15.00
R37 Ryan Hartman AU 10.00 25.00
R38 Gustav Olofsson AU 8.00 20.00
R39 Stefan Noesen AU 5.00 12.00
R40 Mike Condon AU 8.00 20.00
R43 Jake Virtanen AU 10.00 25.00
R45 Sam Bennett AU 25.00 60.00
R46 Robby Fabbri AU 10.00 25.00
R47 Connor McDavid AU 200.00 500.00
R48 Nikolaj Ehlers AU 15.00 40.00
R49 Zachary Fucale AU 6.00 15.00
R50 Dylan Larkin AU 25.00 60.00

2015-16 Upper Deck Premier Signature Award Winners

SAAE Aaron Ekblad 10.00 25.00
SAAO Alexander Ovechkin 30.00 80.00
SABL Brian Leetch 6.00 15.00
SABO Bobby Orr 60.00 150.00
SACP Carey Price 15.00 40.00
SAJB Jamie Benn 8.00 20.00
SAJH Jiri Hudler 6.00 15.00
SAJI Jarome Iginla 10.00 25.00
SAJJ Jaromir Jagr 50.00 125.00
SAMB Martin Brodeur 20.00 50.00
SAMS Martin St. Louis 8.00 20.00
SANM Nathan MacKinnon 30.00 80.00
SAPE Corey Perry 12.00 30.00
SARB Rod Brind'Amour 6.00 15.00
SARO Ryan O'Reilly 8.00 20.00
SASC Sidney Crosby 60.00 150.00
SASY Steve Yzerman 20.00 50.00
SAWG Wayne Gretzky 200.00 500.00

2015-16 Upper Deck Premier Signature Champions

SCAK Anze Kopitar 12.00 30.00
SCBL Brian Leetch 6.00 15.00
SCBO Bobby Orr 60.00 150.00
SCCP Corey Perry 12.00 30.00
SCEM Evgeni Malkin 15.00 40.00
SCES Eric Staal 10.00 25.00
SCGL Guy Lafleur 10.00 25.00
SCJS Joe Sakic 15.00 40.00
SCJT Jonathan Toews 12.00 30.00
SCLM Lanny McDonald 8.00 20.00
SCMB Martin Brodeur 20.00 50.00
SCML Mario Lemieux 60.00 150.00
SCMM Mike Modano 12.00 30.00
SCPD Pavel Datsyuk 12.00 30.00
SCPK Patrick Kane 15.00 40.00
SCSC Sidney Crosby 100.00 250.00
SCSY Steve Yzerman 20.00 50.00
SCTS Teemu Selanne 15.00 40.00
SCWG Wayne Gretzky 200.00 500.00

2015-16 Upper Deck Premier Stars Autograph Patches

SAG Alex Galchenyuk/99 10.00 25.00
SAK Anze Kopitar/49 25.00 60.00
SAO Alexander Ovechkin/25 60.00 150.00
SBH Brett Hull/49 30.00 80.00
SCP Carey Price/49 60.00 150.00
SEM Evgeni Malkin/49 40.00 100.00
SJG Johnny Gaudreau/99 25.00 60.00
SJR Jeremy Roenick/99 25.00 60.00
SJS Joe Sakic/49 30.00 80.00
SJT Jonathan Toews/49 40.00 100.00
SNM Nathan MacKinnon/99 60.00 150.00
SPO Patrick Roy/25 150.00 250.00
SSC Sidney Crosby/25 150.00 300.00
SSY Steve Yzerman/25 60.00 150.00
STS Tyler Seguin/99 20.00 50.00
SWG Wayne Gretzky/25 500.00 1200.00

2016-17 Upper Deck Premier

1 Sidney Crosby 4.00 10.00
2 Carey Price 2.00 5.00
3 Mika Zibanejad 1.25 3.00
4 Steven Stamkos 2.00 5.00
5 John Tavares 1.50 4.00
6 P.K. Subban 1.25 3.00
7 Mark Stone 1.25 3.00
8 Jamie Benn 1.00 2.50
9 Anze Kopitar 1.50 4.00
10 Jonathan Toews 1.50 4.00
11 Connor McDavid 5.00 12.00
12 Zach Parise 1.00 2.50
13 Loui Eriksson .60 1.50
14 Max Domi 1.00 2.50
15 Alexander Ovechkin 4.00 10.00
16 Joe Thornton 1.50 4.00
17 David Backes .60 1.50
18 Rasmus Ristolainen .60 1.50
19 Henrik Zetterberg 1.25 3.00
20 Roberto Luongo 1.50 4.00
21 Johnny Gaudreau 1.50 4.00
22 Corey Perry 1.50 4.00
23 Matt Duchene 1.00 2.50
24 Patrick Kane 2.00 5.00
25 Teuvo Teravainen 1.00 2.50
26 Andrew Shaw .60 1.50
27 Evgeni Malkin 2.00 5.00
28 Vladimir Tarasenko 1.25 3.00
29 Mark Scheifele 1.50 4.00
30 Henrik Lundqvist 2.50 6.00
31 Jakub Voracek .75 2.00
32 Boone Jenner 1.00 2.50
33 Roman Josi 1.00 2.50
34 Taylor Hall 1.00 2.50
35 Marcus Johansson 1.00 2.50
36 Frederik Andersen 1.25 3.00
37 Alex Galchenyuk .60 1.50
38 Jaromir Jagr 3.00 8.00
39 Jonathan Drouin .75 2.00
40 Matt Murray 1.50 4.00
41 Bobby Orr 4.00 10.00
42 Pat LaFontaine 1.00 2.50
43 Paul Coffey 1.00 2.50
44 Igor Larionov 1.00 2.50
45 Mario Lemieux 4.00 10.00
46 Darryl Sittler 1.25 3.00
47 Trevor Linden 1.00 2.50
48 Steve Yzerman 2.50 6.00
49 Martin Brodeur 2.50 6.00
50 Wayne Gretzky 6.00 15.00
51 Joel Eriksson Ek 12.00 30.00
52 Sergey Tolchinsky AU/399 RC 6.00 15.00
53 Chris Bigras 6.00 15.00
54 Daniel Altshuller AU/399 RC 6.00 15.00
55 Danton Heinen AU/399 RC 6.00 15.00
56 Miles Wood 6.00 15.00
57 Brandon Montour AU/399 RC 20.00 50.00
58 Mark Jankowski AU/399 RC 6.00 15.00
59 Timo Meier AU/399 RC 15.00 40.00
60 Jake Guentzel AU/399 RC 25.00 60.00
61 J.C. Lipon AU/399 RC 8.00 20.00
62 Justin Bailey AU/399 RC 8.00 20.00
63 Brandon Carlo AU/399 RC 12.00 30.00
64 Mike Reilly AU/399 RC 6.00 15.00
65 Artturi Lehkonen 10.00 25.00
66 Sebastian Aho JSY AU/299 RC 100.00 250.00
67 Christian Dvorak JSY AU/299 RC 10.00 25.00
68 Oskar Sundqvist JSY AU/299 RC 8.00 20.00
69 Brayden Point JSY AU/299 RC 100.00 250.00
70 Matthew Tkachuk
JSY AU/299 RC 100.00 250.00
71 Jakub Vrana JSY AU/299 RC 30.00 80.00
73 Thomas Chabot JSY AU/299 RC 30.00 80.00
74 Brendan Leipsic JSY AU/299 RC 6.00 15.00
75 Kyle Connor JSY AU/299 RC 25.00 60.00
76 Hudson Fasching JSY AU/299 RC 8.00 20.00
77 Jakob Chychrun JSY AU/299 RC 15.00 40.00
78 Anthony DeAngelo JSY AU/299 RC 6.00 15.00
79 Oliver Bjorkstrand JSY AU/299 RC 10.0025.00
80 Dylan Strome JSY AU/299 RC 25.00 60.00
81 Sonny Milano JSY AU/299 RC 10.00 25.00
82 Kasperi Kapanen JSY AU/299 RC 12.00 30.00
83 Tyler Motte JSY AU/299 RC 8.00 20.00
84 Oliver Kylington JSY AU/299 RC 6.00 15.00
85 Pavel Zacha JSY AU/299 RC 12.00 30.00
86 Charlie Lindgren JSY AU/299 RC 8.00 20.00
87 Lawson Crouse JSY AU/299 RC 6.00 15.00
88 Zach Werenski JSY AU/299 RC 25.00 60.00
89 Michael Matheson JSY AU/299 RC 8.00 20.00
90 Anthony Beauvillier
JSY AU/299 RC 8.00 20.00
91 Mikhail Sergachev JSY AU/299 RC 12.0030.00
92 Travis Konecny JSY AU/299 RC 15.00 40.00
93 Nikita Soshnikov JSY AU/299 RC 5.00 12.00
95 Anthony Mantha JSY AU/299 RC 15.00 40.00
96 Ryan Pulock JSY AU/299 RC 8.00 20.00
97 Nick Schmaltz JSY AU/299 RC 10.00 25.00
98 Esa Lindell JSY AU/299 RC 8.00 20.00
99 Mathew Barzal JSY AU/299 RC 60.00 150.00
100 Josh Morrissey JSY AU/299 RC 25.00 60.00
101 Julius Honka JSY AU/299 RC 8.00 20.00
102 Connor Brown JSY AU/299 RC 12.00 30.00
103 Jesse Puljujarvi JSY AU/299 RC 40.00100.00
104 Mitch Marner JSY AU/199 RC 500.001200.00
105 Jimmy Vesey JSY AU/199 RC 20.00 50.00
106 William Nylander
JSY AU/199 RC 80.00 200.00
107 Patrik Laine JSY AU/199 RC 100.00 250.00
108 Auston Matthews
JSY AU/199 RC 800.00 2000.00

2016-17 Upper Deck Premier Gold Spectrum

51 Joel Eriksson Ek AU 30.00 80.00
52 Sergey Tolchinsky AU 15.00 40.00
54 Daniel Altshuller AU 15.00 40.00
55 Danton Heinen AU 15.00 40.00
57 Brandon Montour AU 50.00 125.00
58 Mark Jankowski AU 15.00 40.00
59 Timo Meier AU 40.00 100.00
60 Jake Guentzel AU 60.00 150.00
61 J.C. Lipon AU 20.00 50.00
62 Justin Bailey AU 20.00 50.00
63 Brandon Carlo AU 30.00 80.00
64 Mike Reilly AU 15.00 40.00
66 Sebastian Aho JSY AU 100.00 250.00
67 Christian Dvorak JSY AU 25.00 60.00
68 Oskar Sundqvist JSY AU 20.00 50.00
70 Matthew Tkachuk JSY AU 150.00 400.00
73 Thomas Chabot JSY AU 40.00 100.00
75 Kyle Connor JSY AU 60.00 150.00
76 Hudson Fasching JSY AU 20.00 50.00
77 Jakob Chychrun JSY AU 40.00 100.00
78 Anthony DeAngelo JSY AU 15.00 40.00
79 Oliver Bjorkstrand JSY AU 25.00 60.00
80 Dylan Strome JSY AU 50.00 125.00
81 Sonny Milano JSY AU 25.00 60.00
83 Tyler Motte JSY AU 20.00 50.00
84 Oliver Kylington JSY AU 15.00 40.00
85 Pavel Zacha JSY AU 30.00 80.00
87 Lawson Crouse JSY AU 15.00 40.00
89 Michael Matheson JSY AU 20.00 50.00
90 Anthony Beauvillier JSY AU 20.00 50.00
91 Mikhail Sergachev JSY AU 30.00 80.00
92 Travis Konecny JSY AU 40.00 100.00
93 Nikita Soshnikov JSY AU 12.00 30.00
95 Anthony Mantha JSY AU 40.00 100.00
96 Ryan Pulock JSY AU 20.00 50.00
97 Nick Schmaltz JSY AU 25.00 60.00
99 Mathew Barzal JSY AU 60.00 150.00
100 Josh Morrissey JSY AU 50.00 125.00
102 Connor Brown JSY AU 30.00 80.00
103 Jesse Puljujarvi JSY AU 60.00 150.00
104 Mitch Marner JSY AU 200.00 350.00
105 Jimmy Vesey JSY AU 30.00 80.00
106 William Nylander JSY AU 250.00 600.00
107 Patrik Laine JSY AU 200.00 350.00
108 Auston Matthews AU 800.00 1000.00

2016-17 Upper Deck Premier '02-03 Tribute Rookies Autograph Patches

SRVAE Aaron Ekblad/25 30.00 80.00
SRVAK Anze Kopitar/25 40.00 100.00
SRVEM Evgeni Malkin/25 50.00 125.00
SRVHZ Henrik Zetterberg/25 30.00 80.00
SRVJT Joe Thornton/25 40.00 100.00
SRVLD Leon Draisaitl/25 80.00 200.00
SRVMM Matt Murray/25 40.00 100.00
SRVRB Ray Bourque/25 40.00 100.00
SRVSM Sean Monahan/25 15.00 40.00

2016-17 Upper Deck Premier '03-04 Tribute Rookies Autograph Patches

SSRAD Anthony DeAngelo 10.00 25.00
SSRAM Auston Matthews 350.00 500.00
SSRCB Connor Brown 20.00 50.00
SSRCD Christian Dvorak 15.00 40.00
SSRDS Dylan Strome 30.00 80.00
SSRIP Ivan Provorov 20.00 50.00
SSRJC Jakob Chychrun 25.00 60.00
SSRJE Joel Eriksson Ek 20.00 50.00
SSRJP Jesse Puljujarvi 25.00 60.00
SSRJR Jakub Vrana 15.00 40.00
SSRJV Jimmy Vesey 20.00 50.00
SSRKC Kyle Connor 50.00 125.00
SSRKK Kasperi Kapanen 20.00 50.00
SSRLC Lawson Crouse 10.00 25.00
SSRMA Anthony Mantha 25.00 60.00
SSRMB Mathew Barzal 80.00 200.00
SSRME Timo Meier 25.00 60.00
SSRMM Mitch Marner 200.00 500.00
SSRMS Mikhail Sergachev 20.00 50.00
SSRMT Matthew Tkachuk 50.00 125.00
SSRPB Pavel Buchnevich 20.00 50.00
SSRPL Patrik Laine 100.00 250.00
SSRPZ Pavel Zacha 20.00 50.00
SSRSA Sebastian Aho 60.00 150.00
SSRTC Thomas Chabot 25.00 60.00
SSRTK Travis Konecny 25.00 60.00
SSRTM Tyler Motte 12.00 30.00
SSRWN William Nylander 50.00 125.00
SSRZW Zach Werenski 40.00 100.00

2016-17 Upper Deck Premier Acetate Stars Autograph Patches

ASCM Connor McDavid/25 250.00 400.00
ASGL Guy Lafleur/49 50.00 125.00
ASHL Henrik Lundqvist/49 40.00 100.00
ASHZ Henrik Zetterberg/49 30.00 80.00
ASJJ Jaromir Jagr/49 150.00 300.00
ASPK Patrick Kane/49 60.00 150.00
ASSC Sidney Crosby/25 300.00 450.00
ASSY Steve Yzerman/25 150.00 300.00
ASWG Wayne Gretzky/25 300.00 800.00

2016-17 Upper Deck Premier Inked Script

INFP Felix Potvin/99 25.00 60.00
INGL Guy Lafleur/25 20.00 50.00
INHL Henrik Lundqvist/25 40.00 100.00
INIL Igor Larionov/99 15.00 40.00
INJP Jesse Puljujarvi/99 30.00 80.00
INJT Joe Thornton/25 25.00 60.00
INLD Leon Draisaitl/99 50.00 125.00
INLM Lanny McDonald/25 15.00 40.00
INMD Marcel Dionne/25 20.00 50.00
INPA Joe Pavelski/99 20.00 50.00
INPK Patrick Kane/25 30.00 80.00
INPL Patrik Laine/25 40.00 100.00
INTL Trevor Linden/25 15.00 40.00
INWC Wendel Clark/25 25.00 60.00

2016-17 Upper Deck Premier Jerseys

*PREMIUM/25: 1.25X TO 3X BASIC INSERTS
1 Sidney Crosby/199 10.00 25.00
2 Carey Price/199 5.00 12.00
3 Mika Zibanejad/199 3.00 8.00
4 Steven Stamkos/199 5.00 12.00
5 John Tavares/199 4.00 10.00
6 P.K. Subban/199 3.00 8.00
7 Mark Stone/199 3.00 8.00
8 Jamie Benn/199 2.50 6.00
9 Anze Kopitar/199 4.00 10.00
10 Jonathan Toews/199 4.00 10.00
11 Connor McDavid/199 20.00 50.00
12 Zach Parise/199 2.50 6.00
13 Loui Eriksson/199 1.50 4.00
14 Max Domi/199 2.50 6.00
15 Alexander Ovechkin/199 10.00 25.00
16 Joe Thornton/199 4.00 10.00
17 David Backes/199 1.50 4.00
18 Rasmus Ristolainen/199 1.50 4.00
19 Henrik Zetterberg/199 3.00 8.00
20 Roberto Luongo/199 4.00 10.00
21 Johnny Gaudreau/199 4.00 10.00
22 Corey Perry/199 4.00 10.00
23 Matt Duchene/199 2.50 6.00
24 Patrick Kane/199 5.00 12.00
25 Teuvo Teravainen/199 2.50 6.00
26 Andrew Shaw/199 1.50 4.00
27 Evgeni Malkin/199 5.00 12.00
28 Vladimir Tarasenko/199 3.00 8.00
29 Mark Scheifele/199 4.00 10.00
30 Henrik Lundqvist/199 6.00 15.00
31 Jakub Voracek/199 2.00 5.00
32 Boone Jenner/199 2.50 6.00
33 Roman Josi/199 2.50 6.00
34 Taylor Hall/199 2.50 6.00
36 Frederik Andersen/199 3.00 8.00
37 Alex Galchenyuk/199 1.50 4.00
38 Jaromir Jagr/199 8.00 20.00
39 Jonathan Drouin/199 2.00 5.00
40 Matt Murray/199 4.00 10.00
44 Igor Larionov/99 2.50 6.00
45 Mario Lemieux/25 10.00 25.00
48 Steve Yzerman/25 6.00 15.00
49 Martin Brodeur/49 6.00 15.00
50 Wayne Gretzky/25 15.00 40.00

2016-17 Upper Deck Premier Mega Patch Chest Logos

PMPAB Justin Abdelkader/18 30.00 80.00
PMPAE Aaron Ekblad/22 30.00 80.00
PMPAG Alex Galchenyuk/19 15.00 40.00
PMPAH Adam Henrique/26 20.00 50.00
PMPAK Anze Kopitar/18 40.00 100.00
PMPAL Andrew Ladd/24 15.00 40.00
PMPAM Auston Matthews/25 250.00 600.00
PMPAP Artemi Panarin/23 50.00 125.00
PMPAS Andrew Shaw/19 15.00 40.00
PMPAW Alexander Wennberg/21 15.00 40.00
PMPBB Brent Burns/23 25.00 60.00
PMPBE Brian Elliott/28 20.00 50.00
PMPBH Bo Horvat/32 30.00 80.00
PMPBI Ben Bishop/24 20.00 50.00
PMPBJ Boone Jenner/21 25.00 60.00
PMPBM Brad Marchand/24 50.00 125.00
PMPBN Brock Nelson/23 25.00 60.00
PMPBR Derick Brassard/18 15.00 40.00
PMPBU Andre Burakovsky/21 15.00 40.00
PMPCA Craig Anderson/18 25.00 60.00
PMPCG Claude Giroux/24 25.00 60.00
PMPCP Corey Perry/21 40.00 100.00
PMPDB David Backes/24 15.00 40.00
PMPDD Drew Doughty/18 30.00 80.00
PMPDL Dylan Larkin/18 30.00 80.00

PMPDP David Pastrnak/24 60.00 150.00
PMPDS Derek Stepan/19 15.00 40.00
PMPDU Matt Duchene/24 25.00 60.00
PMPEK Evgeny Kuznetsov/22 30.00 80.00
PMPES Eric Staal/19 30.00 80.00
PMPFN Frans Nielsen/19 15.00 40.00
PMPGA Brendan Gallagher/20 25.00 60.00
PMPHS Henrik Sedin/20 30.00 80.00
PMPHZ Henrik Zetterberg/18 30.00 80.00
PMPJA Jake Allen/20 25.00 60.00
PMPJB Jamie Benn/19 25.00 60.00
PMPJD Jonathan Drouin/25 20.00 50.00
PMPJG Johnny Gaudreau/26 40.00 100.00
PMPJJ Jaromir Jagr/22 80.00 200.00
PMPJN James Neal/21 15.00 40.00
PMPJP Jesse Puljujarvi/24 50.00 125.00
PMPJS Jason Spezza/19 25.00 60.00
PMPJT Jonathan Toews/23 40.00 100.00
PMPJV Jimmy Vesey/20 40.00 100.00
PMPKE Phil Kessel/28 25.00 60.00
PMPKL Kris Letang/28 30.00 80.00
PMPKO Kyle Okposo/24 15.00 40.00
PMPKP Kyle Palmieri/26 20.00 50.00
PMPLD Leon Draisaitl/24 80.00 200.00
PMPLE Loui Eriksson/31 15.00 40.00
PMPMD Max Domi/22 25.00 60.00
PMPMJ Martin Jones/23 20.00 50.00
PMPMK Mikko Koivu/21 20.00 50.00
PMPML Milan Lucic/24 20.00 50.00
PMPMM Mitch Marner/19 80.00 200.00
PMPMS Mark Stone/16 30.00 80.00
PMPMU Matt Murray/28 40.00 100.00
PMPMZ Mats Zuccarello/20 25.00 60.00
PMPNB Nicklas Backstrom/21 25.00 60.00
PMPNK Nikita Kucherov/24 50.00 125.00
PMPNM Nathan MacKinnon/27 100.00 250.00
PMPNN Nino Niederreiter/20 15.00 40.00
PMPOE Oliver Ekman-Larsson/23 25.00 60.00
PMPPA Joe Pavelski/23 30.00 80.00
PMPPE Tanner Pearson/18 20.00 50.00
PMPPK Patrick Kane/23 50.00 125.00
PMPPL Patrik Laine/24 100.00 250.00
PMPPS P.K. Subban/19 30.00 80.00
PMPRF Robby Fabbri/20 15.00 40.00
PMPRJ Ryan Johansen/19 20.00 50.00
PMPRK Ryan Kesler/21 25.00 60.00
PMPRO Ryan O'Reilly/20 25.00 60.00
PMPRR Rickard Rakell/21 20.00 50.00
PMPSC Mark Scheifele/24 40.00 100.00
PMPSG Shayne Gostisbehere/21 25.00 60.00
PMPSM Sean Monahan/26 15.00 40.00
PMPSR Sam Reinhart/24 50.00 125.00
PMPSS Steven Stamkos/24 50.00 125.00
PMPST Jordan Staal/21 20.00 50.00
PMPSW Shea Weber/19 20.00 50.00
PMPTA John Tavares/23 40.00 100.00
PMPTB Tyson Barrie/26 15.00 40.00
PMPTH Taylor Hall/26 25.00 60.00
PMPTK Torey Krug/28 20.00 50.00
PMPTR Vincent Trocheck/20 25.00 60.00
PMPTS Tyler Seguin/21 30.00 80.00
PMPTT Teuvo Teravainen/19 25.00 60.00
PMPVH Victor Hedman/23 30.00 80.00
PMPVR Victor Rask/19 15.00 40.00
PMPVT Vladimir Tarasenko/23 30.00 80.00
PMPWN William Nylander/20 100.00 250.00
PMPWS Wayne Simmonds/21 30.00 80.00
PMPZW Zach Werenski/21 80.00 200.00

2016-17 Upper Deck Premier Mega Patch Duos

PMP2BS P.Bure/H.Sedin 15.00 40.00
PMP2CD J.Carter/D.Doughty 15.00 40.00
PMP2DE M.Domi/O.Ekman-Larsson 12.00 30.00
PMP2EO J.Eichel/K.Okposo 20.00 50.00
PMP2ES L.Eriksson/D.Sedin 15.00 40.00
PMP2GB J.Gaudreau/S.Bennett 20.00 50.00
PMP2HP T.Hall/K.Palmieri 20.00 50.00
PMP2JT J.Benn/T.Seguin 15.00 40.00
PMP2KG R.Kesler/R.Getzlaf 12.00 30.00
PMP2KP P.Kane/A.Panarin 25.00 60.00
PMP2KT P.Kane/V.Tarasenko 25.00 60.00
PMP2LL H.Lundqvist/R.Luongo 30.00 80.00
PMP2MB B.Marchand/D.Backes 25.00 60.00
PMP2MD C.McDavid/L.Draisaitl 200.00 350.00
PMP2MK E.Malkin/P.Kessel 25.00 60.00
PMP2ML N.MacKinnon G.Landeskog 50.00 120.00
PMP2NL F.Nielsen/D.Larkin 15.00 40.00
PMP2OM A.Ovechkin/E.Malkin 50.00 120.00
PMP2PC J.Pavelski/L.Couture 15.00 40.00
PMP2RK M.Rielly/N.Kadri 15.00 40.00
PMP2RS P.Roy/J.Sakic 30.00 80.00
PMP2SB P.Subban/B.Burns 15.00 40.00
PMP2SE M.Scheifele/N.Ehlers 20.00 50.00
PMP2SH S.Stamkos/V.Hedman 25.00 60.00
PMP2SJ P.Subban/R.Johansen 15.00 40.00
PMP2TF V.Tarasenko/R.Fabbri 15.00 40.00
PMP2TT J.Tavares/J.Toews 20.00 50.00
PMP2VS J.Voracek/W.Simmonds 15.00 40.00
PMP2WB A.Wennberg/S.Bobrovsky 20.00 50.00
PMP2WP M.Pacioretty/S.Weber 12.00 30.00

2016-17 Upper Deck Premier Mega Stick Duos

PMS2BH J.Benn/T.Hall 8.00 20.00
PMS2BL J.Beliveau/G.Lafleur 10.00 25.00
PMS2BQ M.Brodeur/J.Quick 20.00 50.00
PMS2DK B.Dubinsky/W.Karlsson 10.00 25.00
PMS2GJ W.Gretzky/J.Jagr 50.00 125.00
PMS2JT J.Spezza/T.Seguin 10.00 25.00
PMS2KC A.Kopitar/J.Carter 12.00 30.00
PMS2KH P.Kessel/C.Hagelin 8.00 20.00
PMS2LN M.Lucic/R.Nugent-Hopkins 10.00 25.00
PMS2SB J.Sakic/R.Bourque 15.00 40.00
PMS2SH T.Selanne/D.Hawerchuk 15.00 40.00
PMS2SZ M.Zuccarello/M.Staal 8.00 20.00
PMS2TD J.Thornton/V.Damphousse 12.00 30.00
PMS2WH C.Ward/N.Hanifin 8.00 20.00
PMS2YP S.Yzerman/B.Probert 20.00 50.00

2016-17 Upper Deck Premier Premier Duals Jersey

PD2BD B.Burns/D.Doughty 5.00 12.00
PD2BM P.Bure/K.McLean 4.00 10.00
PD2BS J.Benn/J.Spezza 4.00 10.00
PD2BT A.Barkov/V.Trocheck 6.00 15.00
PD2DL L.Draisaitl/M.Lucic 12.00 30.00
PD2ED O.Ekman-Larsson/M.Domi 4.00 10.00
PD2GM J.Gaudreau/S.Monahan 6.00 15.00
PD2KH E.Karlsson/M.Hoffman 5.00 12.00
PD2LC P.Laine/K.Connor 12.00 30.00
PD2LD I.Larionov/P.Datsyuk 6.00 15.00
PD2LG K.Letang/S.Gostisbehere 5.00 12.00
PD2LY M.Lemieux/S.Yzerman 15.00 40.00
PD2MM A.Matthews/M.Marner 25.00 60.00
PD2MO C.McDavid/A.Ovechkin 20.00 50.00
PD2NB W.Nylander/C.Brown 15.00 40.00
PD2OE R.O'Reilly/J.Eichel 6.00 15.00
PD2PK I.Provorov/T.Konecny 8.00 20.00
PD2PR C.Perry/R.Rakell 6.00 15.00
PD2RK N.Kadri/M.Rielly 5.00 12.00
PD2SD E.Staal/D.Dubnyk 5.00 12.00
PD2SF P.Subban/F.Forsberg 6.00 15.00
PD2SR J.Skinner/V.Rask 5.00 12.00
PD2SW M.Scheifele/B.Wheeler 6.00 15.00
PD2TL J.Tavares/A.Ladd 6.00 15.00
PD2TP V.Tarasenko/A.Panarin 8.00 20.00
PD2TS J.Tavares/D.Stepan 6.00 15.00
PD2VB J.Vesey/P.Buchnevich 6.00 15.00
PD2VS J.Voracek/W.Simmonds 5.00 12.00
PD2WP Z.Werenski/J.Puljujarvi 12.00 30.00

2016-17 Upper Deck Premier Premier Quads Jersey

PQ4CBJ Wennberg/Saad Foligno/Bobrovsky/49 15.00 40.00
PQ4DRW Yzerman/Larionov Chelios/Datsyuk/25 25.00 60.00
PQ4NYR Stepan/Hayes Kreider/Zuccarello/49 12.00 30.00
PQ4BEES Pastrnak/Marchand Backes/Rask/49 25.00 60.00
PQ4CAPS Backstrom/Kuznetsov Carlson/Oshie/49 12.00 30.00
PQ4DMEN Burns/Subban Hedman/Karlsson/49 12.00 30.00
PQ4GLTR Price/Lundqvist Holtby/Crawford/49 25.00 60.00
PQ4HABS Pacioretty/Weber/Galchenyuk Gallagher/49 10.00 25.00
PQ4HAWK Kane/Panarin Toews/Hossa/49 20.00 50.00
PQ4LMWP Laine/Marner Werenski/Puljujarvi/49 30.00 80.00
PQ4NYNY Tavares/Ladd Stepan/Nash/49 15.00 40.00
PQ4PCKT Point/Connor Konecny/Tkachuk/49 40.00 100.00
PQ4PENS Malkin/Kessel Letang/Murray/49 20.00 50.00
PQ4RUSS Ovechkin/Malkin Tarasenko/Panarin/49 40.00 100.00
PQ4VNSM Vesey/Nylander Sergachev/Mantha/49 40.00 100.00
PQ4STARS Tavares/Ovechkin Kane/Malkin/25 40.00 100.00

2016-17 Upper Deck Premier Premier Signature Booklets

PSAB Anthony Beauvillier 12.00 30.00
PSBO Mike Bossy 12.00 30.00
PSDA Daniel Altshuller 10.00 25.00
PSDI Marcel Dionne 15.00 40.00
PSDS Dylan Strome 30.00 80.00
PSHL Henrik Lundqvist 30.00 80.00
PSIL Igor Larionov 12.00 30.00
PSIP Ivan Provorov 20.00 50.00
PSJE Joel Eriksson Ek 20.00 50.00
PSJG John Gibson 12.00 30.00
PSJS Joe Sakic 25.00 60.00
PSJT Joe Thornton 20.00 50.00
PSKM Kirk McLean 12.00 30.00
PSMB Martin Brodeur 30.00 80.00
PSMM Matt Murray 20.00 50.00
PSMS Mark Stone 15.00 40.00
PSPK Patrick Kane 25.00 60.00
PSPL Patrik Laine 30.00 80.00
PSRJ Roman Josi 12.00 30.00
PSRK Red Kelly 12.00 30.00
PSRL Roberto Luongo 20.00 50.00
PSRS Ryan Spooner 10.00 25.00
PSSE Tyler Seguin 15.00 40.00
PSTL Trevor Linden 12.00 30.00
PSZW Zach Werenski 40.00 100.00

2016-17 Upper Deck Premier Premier Signatures

PSAL Andrew Ladd 5.00 12.00
PSBE Brian Elliott 6.00 15.00
PSCM Connor McDavid 200.00 300.00
PSCS Cory Schneider 8.00 20.00
PSDB David Backes 5.00 12.00
PSEM Evgeni Malkin 40.00 100.00
PSGN Gustav Nyquist 5.00 12.00
PSHL Henrik Lundqvist 40.00 100.00
PSHZ Henrik Zetterberg 10.00 25.00
PSJJ Jaromir Jagr 50.00 125.00
PSJO Roman Josi 8.00 20.00
PSJT Joe Thornton 12.00 30.00
PSLD Leon Draisaitl 20.00 50.00
PSLE Loui Eriksson 5.00 12.00
PSMG Marian Gaborik 8.00 20.00
PSPK Patrick Kane 25.00 60.00
PSPR Carey Price 80.00 150.00
PSRJ Ryan Johansen 6.00 15.00
PSRL Roberto Luongo 12.00 30.00
PSRO Ryan O'Reilly 8.00 20.00

2016-17 Upper Deck Premier Premier Signatures Legends

LPSBO Bobby Orr 60.00 150.00
LPSCN Cam Neely 15.00 40.00
LPSGL Guy Lafleur 25.00 60.00
LPSML Mario Lemieux 50.00 125.00
LPSPH Phil Housley 20.00 50.00
LPSPL Pat LaFontaine 20.00 50.00
LPSSY Steve Yzerman 60.00 150.00

2016-17 Upper Deck Premier Premier Swatches

PSAB Aleksander Barkov/99 8.00 20.00
PSAK Anze Kopitar/49 8.00 20.00
PSBN Brock Nelson/99 5.00 12.00
PSCM Connor McDavid/25 60.00 150.00
PSDD Devan Dubnyk/99 4.00 10.00
PSDG Doug Gilmour/49 6.00 15.00
PSDP David Pastrnak/99 12.00 30.00
PSDS Derek Stepan/99 3.00 8.00
PSEK Erik Karlsson/49 6.00 15.00
PSGL Gabriel Landeskog/99 6.00 15.00
PSHS Henrik Sedin/49 6.00 15.00
PSHZ Henrik Zetterberg/49 6.00 15.00
PSJG Johnny Gaudreau/99 8.00 20.00
PSJP Joe Pavelski/99 6.00 15.00
PSJS Joe Sakic/25 10.00 25.00
PSJT Jonathan Toews/25 15.00 40.00
PSKO Kyle Okposo/99 3.00 8.00
PSKU Evgeny Kuznetsov/99 6.00 15.00
PSMD Max Domi/99 5.00 12.00
PSPK Phil Kessel/49 5.00 12.00
PSPS P.K. Subban/49 6.00 15.00
PSRR Rickard Rakell/99 4.00 10.00
PSSB Sergei Bobrovsky/99 8.00 20.00
PSSP Jason Spezza/99 5.00 12.00
PSSW Shea Weber/99 4.00 10.00
PSTH Taylor Hall/49 5.00 12.00
PSVH Victor Hedman/99 6.00 15.00
PSVT Vladimir Tarasenko/49 6.00 15.00
PSWS Wayne Simmonds/99 6.00 15.00

2016-17 Upper Deck Premier Premier Trios Jersey

PT3ARZ Strome/Dvorak/Crouse 10.00 25.00
PT3AVS MacKinnon Duchene/Landeskog 15.00 40.00
PT3CGY Jankowski Tkachuk/Kylington 15.00 40.00
PT3DEF Keith/Ekman-Larsson/Weber 4.00 10.00
PT3DET Zetterberg/Larkin/Nielsen 5.00 12.00
PT3GYR Dubnyk/Bobrovsky/Rask 6.00 15.00
PT3LAK Kopitar/Carter/Toffoli 6.00 15.00
PT3NJD Hall/Henrique/Schneider 4.00 10.00
PT3PTS Gretzky/Jagr/Messier 20.00 50.00
PT3STL Tarasenko/Fabbri/Schwartz 5.00 12.00
PT3TBL Stamkos/Hedman/Kucherov 8.00 20.00
PT3TOR Matthews/Marner/Nylander 30.00 80.00
PT3VAN Sedin/Horvat/Sedin 5.00 12.00
PT3MTLR Sergachev Lehkonen/Lindgren 6.00 15.00
PT3SJCPT Nolan/Thornton/Marleau 6.00 15.00

2016-17 Upper Deck Premier Rookies

R1 Mikhail Sergachev/299 4.00 10.00
R2 Christian Dvorak/299 3.00 8.00
R3 Kevin Labanc/299 2.50 6.00
R4 Nick Baptiste/299 2.50 6.00
R5 Joel Eriksson Ek/299 4.00 10.00
R6 Oskar Sundqvist/299 2.50 6.00
R7 Tyler Motte/299 2.50 6.00
R8 Kasperi Kapanen/299 4.00 10.00
R9 Anthony Beauvillier/299 2.50 6.00
R10 Pavel Zacha/299 4.00 10.00
R11 Timo Meier/299 5.00 12.00
R12 Thomas Chabot/299 5.00 12.00
R13 Chris Bigras/299 2.00 5.00
R14 Anthony DeAngelo/299 2.00 5.00
R15 Anthony Mantha/299 5.00 12.00
R16 Jacob Larsson/299 4.00 10.00
R17 Nikita Soshnikov/299 1.50 4.00
R18 Mathew Barzal/299 8.00 20.00
R19 Oliver Kylington/299 2.00 5.00
R20 A.J. Greer/299 2.50 6.00
R21 Artturi Lehkonen/299 3.00 8.00
R22 John Quenneville/299 2.50 6.00
R23 Zach Werenski/299 8.00 20.00
R24 Julius Honka/299 2.50 6.00
R25 Jakob Chychrun/299 5.00 12.00
R26 Drake Caggiula/299 2.50 6.00
R27 Pavel Buchnevich/299 4.00 10.00
R28 Mark Jankowski/299 2.00 5.00
R29 Brayden Point/299 6.00 15.00
R30 Connor Brown/299 4.00 10.00
R31 Troy Stecher/299 2.50 6.00
R32 Nic Dowd/299 2.00 5.00
R33 Sebastian Aho/299 8.00 20.00
R34 Tyler Bertuzzi/299 4.00 10.00
R35 Nick Schmaltz/299 3.00 8.00
R36 Jakub Vrana/299 3.00 8.00
R37 Brandon Carlo/299 4.00 10.00
R38 Travis Konecny/299 5.00 12.00
R39 Oliver Bjorkstrand/299 3.00 8.00
R40 Lawson Crouse/299 2.00 5.00
R41 Jesse Puljujarvi/199 5.00 12.00
R42 Matthew Tkachuk/199 10.00 25.00
R43 Mitch Marner/199 20.00 50.00
R44 Dylan Strome/199 6.00 15.00
R45 Kyle Connor/199 8.00 20.00
R46 William Nylander/199 15.00 40.00
R47 Patrik Laine/199 20.00 50.00
R48 Ivan Provorov/199 4.00 10.00
R49 Jimmy Vesey/199 4.00 10.00
R50 Auston Matthews/199 60.00 150.00

2016-17 Upper Deck Premier Rookies Jerseys

R1 Mikhail Sergachev 5.00 12.00
R2 Christian Dvorak 4.00 10.00
R3 Kevin Labanc 3.00 8.00
R4 Nick Baptiste 3.00 8.00
R5 Joel Eriksson Ek 5.00 12.00
R6 Oskar Sundqvist 3.00 8.00
R7 Tyler Motte 3.00 8.00
R8 Kasperi Kapanen 5.00 12.00
R9 Anthony Beauvillier 3.00 8.00
R10 Pavel Zacha 5.00 12.00
R11 Timo Meier 6.00 15.00
R12 Thomas Chabot 6.00 15.00
R13 Chris Bigras 2.50 6.00
R14 Anthony DeAngelo 2.50 6.00
R15 Anthony Mantha 6.00 15.00
R17 Nikita Soshnikov 2.00 5.00
R18 Mathew Barzal 10.00 25.00
R19 Oliver Kylington 2.50 6.00
R20 A.J. Greer 3.00 8.00
R21 Artturi Lehkonen 4.00 10.00
R22 John Quenneville 3.00 8.00
R23 Zach Werenski 10.00 25.00
R24 Julius Honka 3.00 8.00
R25 Jakob Chychrun 6.00 15.00
R27 Pavel Buchnevich 5.00 12.00
R28 Mark Jankowski 2.50 6.00
R29 Brayden Point 8.00 20.00
R30 Connor Brown 5.00 12.00
R32 Nic Dowd 2.50 6.00
R33 Sebastian Aho 10.00 25.00
R34 Tyler Bertuzzi 5.00 12.00
R35 Nick Schmaltz 4.00 10.00
R36 Jakub Vrana 4.00 10.00
R37 Brandon Carlo 5.00 12.00
R38 Travis Konecny 6.00 15.00
R39 Oliver Bjorkstrand 4.00 10.00
R40 Lawson Crouse 2.50 6.00
R41 Jesse Puljujarvi 6.00 15.00
R42 Matthew Tkachuk 12.00 30.00
R43 Mitch Marner 10.00 25.00
R44 Dylan Strome 8.00 20.00
R45 Kyle Connor 10.00 25.00
R46 William Nylander 12.00 30.00
R47 Patrik Laine 8.00 20.00
R48 Ivan Provorov 5.00 12.00
R49 Jimmy Vesey 5.00 12.00
R50 Auston Matthews 30.00 80.00

2016-17 Upper Deck Premier Rookies Jerseys Patch

*PATCH/25: 1X TO 2.5X BASIC INSERTS
R47 Patrik Laine 80.00 150.00
R50 Auston Matthews 100.00 250.00

2016-17 Upper Deck Premier Signature Award Winners

SAAK Anze Kopitar/25 40.00 100.00
SAAM Al MacInnis/99 8.00 20.00
SACN Cam Neely/49 15.00 40.00
SADG Doug Gilmour/49 25.00 60.00
SADT Dave Taylor/99 6.00 15.00
SAHL Henrik Lundqvist/25 40.00 100.00
SAJJ Jaromir Jagr/25 80.00 150.00
SAJT Jonathan Toews/25 30.00 80.00
SAMG Mark Giordano/99 8.00 20.00
SAPK Patrick Kane/25 30.00 80.00
SARB Ray Bourque/25 12.00 30.00
SARK Ryan Kesler/99 6.00 15.00

2016-17 Upper Deck Premier Signature Champions

SCBG Bill Guerin/99 10.00 25.00
SCCW Cam Ward/99 5.00 12.00
SCEM Evgeni Malkin/25 40.00 100.00
SCGC Guy Carbonneau/99 6.00 15.00
SCHZ Henrik Zetterberg/25 15.00 40.00
SCJK Jari Kurri/25 15.00 40.00
SCJT Jonathan Toews/25 40.00 100.00
SCMO Mike Modano/99 20.00 50.00
SCMU Matt Murray/99 60.00 150.00
SCPK Patrick Kane/25 40.00 100.00
SCRB Ray Bourque/25 30.00 80.00

2017-18 Upper Deck Premier

1 Patrice Bergeron 1.25 3.00
2 Alexander Ovechkin 4.00 10.00
3 Filip Forsberg 1.50 4.00
4 Nikita Kucherov 2.00 5.00
5 Mikael Granlund .75 2.00
6 Auston Matthews 4.00 10.00
7 Vincent Trocheck 1.00 2.50
8 Patrik Laine 1.25 3.00
9 Jack Eichel 1.50 4.00
10 Claude Giroux 1.00 2.50
11 James Neal .60 1.50
12 Artemi Panarin 2.00 5.00
13 Jeff Skinner 1.25 3.00
14 Blake Wheeler 1.00 2.50
15 Bo Horvat 1.25 3.00
16 Jordan Eberle 1.00 2.50
17 Devan Dubnyk .75 2.00
18 Steven Stamkos 2.00 5.00
19 John Tavares 1.50 4.00
20 John Gibson 1.00 2.50
21 Nathan MacKinnon 4.00 10.00
22 Sidney Crosby 4.00 10.00
23 Vladimir Tarasenko 1.25 3.00
24 Taylor Hall 1.00 2.50
25 Jonathan Huberdeau 1.25 3.00
26 Kevin Shattenkirk .60 1.50
27 Anthony Mantha .75 2.00
28 Jonathan Quick 1.25 3.00
29 Mark Giordano 1.00 2.50
30 Erik Karlsson 1.25 3.00
31 Connor McDavid 5.00 12.00
32 Carey Price 2.00 5.00
33 Duncan Keith .75 2.00
34 Marc-Andre Fleury 2.00 5.00
35 Tyler Seguin 1.25 3.00
36 Logan Couture 1.25 3.00
37 Kris Letang 1.25 3.00
38 Jonathan Drouin .75 2.00
39 Derek Stepan .60 1.50
40 Nazem Kadri 1.25 3.00
41 Wayne Gretzky 6.00 15.00
42 Bobby Orr 4.00 10.00
43 Brett Hull 2.00 5.00
44 Dale Hawerchuk 1.25 3.00
45 Pavel Bure 1.00 2.50
46 Patrick Roy 2.50 6.00
47 Joe Sakic 2.00 5.00
48 Rod Langway 1.00 2.50
49 Ray Bourque 1.50 4.00
50 Mario Lemieux 6.00 15.00
51 Janne Kuokkanen RC 2.50 6.00
52 Filip Chlapik RC 2.00 5.00
53 Calle Rosen RC 2.50 6.00
54 Alex Kerfoot RC 5.00 12.00
55 Jesper Bratt RC 5.00 12.00
56 Victor Mete RC 2.50 6.00
57 Tage Thompson RC 6.00 15.00
58 Lucas Wallmark RC 2.50 6.00
59 Nick Merkley RC 2.50 6.00
60 Ville Husso RC 3.00 8.00
61 Martin Necas RC 8.00 20.00
62 Adrian Kempe RC 5.00 12.00
63 Logan Brown RC 2.50 6.00
64 Madison Bowey RC 1.50 4.00
65 Jake DeBrusk RC 6.00 15.00
66 Ivan Barbashev RC 3.00 8.00
67 Denis Gurianov RC 6.00 15.00
68 Alex Nedeljkovic RC 4.00 10.00
69 Samuel Morin RC 1.50 4.00
70 Alex Formenton RC 2.50 6.00
71 Evgeny Svechnikov RC 5.00 12.00
72 Jon Gillies RC 2.50 6.00
73 Filip Chytil RC 2.50 6.00
74 Vladislav Kamenev RC 2.50 6.00
75 Will Butcher RC 3.00 8.00
76 Travis Sanheim RC 2.50 6.00
77 Haydn Fleury RC 2.50 6.00
78 Nikita Scherbak RC 3.00 8.00
79 Vince Dunn RC 3.00 8.00
80 Christian Fischer RC 3.00 8.00
81 Colin White RC 3.00 8.00
82 Jack Roslovic RC 3.00 8.00
83 J.T. Compher RC 2.50 6.00
84 Luke Kunin RC 2.50 6.00
85 Jakob Forsbacka-Karlsson RC 2.50 6.00
86 Alex Tuch RC 6.00 15.00
87 Robert Hagg RC 2.50 6.00
88 Anders Bjork RC 3.00 8.00
89 Kailer Yamamoto RC 6.00 15.00
90 Owen Tippett RC 5.00 12.00
91 Brock Boeser RC 15.00 40.00
92 Clayton Keller RC 6.00 15.00
93 Charlie McAvoy RC 6.00 15.00
94 Tyson Jost RC 5.00 12.00
95 Alexander Nylander RC 4.00 10.00
96 Josh Ho-Sang RC 3.00 8.00
97 Alex DeBrincat RC 6.00 15.00
98 Pierre-Luc Dubois RC 4.00 10.00
99 Nolan Patrick RC 12.00 30.00
100 Nico Hischier RC 12.00 30.00

2017-18 Upper Deck Premier '02-03 Tribute Autograph Patches

SRVCP Carey Price/49 40.00 100.00
SRVDH Dale Hawerchuk/49 25.00 60.00
SRVDK Duncan Keith/49 15.00 40.00
SRVHL Henrik Lundqvist/49 50.00 125.00
SRVJC John Carlson/49 20.00 50.00
SRVJI Jarome Iginla/49 25.00 60.00
SRVLC Logan Couture/49 25.00 60.00
SRVMP Max Pacioretty/49 20.00 50.00
SRVNE Nikolaj Ehlers/49 20.00 50.00
SRVNK Nikita Kucherov/49 40.00 100.00
SRVPL Patrik Laine/49 25.00 60.00
SRVVL Vladimir Tarasenko/49 25.00 60.00
SRVVT Vincent Trocheck/49 20.00 50.00

2017-18 Upper Deck Premier '03-04 Tribute Rookie Autograph Patches

SSRAB Anders Bjork 25.00 60.00
SSRAD Alex DeBrincat 50.00 125.00
SSRAN Alexander Nylander 30.00 80.00
SSRAT Alex Tuch 50.00 120.00
SSRBB Brock Boeser 150.00 300.00
SSRCF Christian Fischer 25.00 60.00
SSRCK Clayton Keller 50.00 125.00
SSRCM Charlie McAvoy 50.00 125.00
SSRCW Colin White 25.00 60.00
SSRHF Haydn Fleury 20.00 50.00
SSRIB Ivan Barbashev 25.00 60.00
SSRJB Jesper Bratt 40.00 100.00
SSRJH Josh Ho-Sang 25.00 60.00
SSRJR Jack Roslovic 25.00 60.00
SSRKY Kailer Yamamoto 50.00 125.00
SSRLK Luke Kunin 20.00 50.00
SSRMB Madison Bowey 12.00 30.00
SSRNH Nico Hischier (No Auto) 40.00 100.00
SSRNP Nolan Patrick (No Auto) 25.00 60.00
SSRNS Nikita Scherbak 25.00 60.00
SSROT Owen Tippett 40.00 100.00
SSRPD Pierre-Luc Dubois 30.00 80.00
SSRTJ Tyson Jost 40.00 100.00
SSRTT Tage Thompson 50.00 125.00
SSRVM Victor Mete 20.00 50.00
SSRWB Will Butcher 25.00 60.00

2017-18 Upper Deck Premier Acetate Rookies Autograph Patches

*PLATINUM: 1X TO 2.5X BASIC INSERTS
ARAB Anders Bjork/299 10.00 25.00
ARAD Alex DeBrincat/199 30.00 80.00
ARAK Adrian Kempe/299 15.00 40.00
ARAN Alexander Nylander/199 25.00 60.00
ARAT Alex Tuch/299 20.00 50.00
ARBB Brock Boeser/199 80.00 200.00
ARCF Christian Fischer/299 10.00 25.00
ARCH Filip Chlapik/299 6.00 15.00
ARCK Clayton Keller/199 30.00 80.00
ARCM Charlie McAvoy/199 50.00 125.00
ARCW Colin White/299 10.00 25.00
ARDG Denis Gurianov/299 20.00 50.00
ARHF Haydn Fleury/299 8.00 20.00
ARIB Ivan Barbashev/299 10.00 25.00
ARJB Jesper Bratt/299 30.00 80.00
ARJC J.T. Compher/299 8.00 20.00
ARJF Jakob Forsbacka-Karlsson/299 8.00 20.00
ARJG Jon Gillies/299 8.00 20.00
ARJH Josh Ho-Sang/299 10.00 25.00
ARJK Janne Kuokkanen/299 8.00 20.00
ARJR Jack Roslovic/299 10.00 25.00
ARKY Kailer Yamamoto/199 20.00 50.00
ARLK Luke Kunin/299 8.00 20.00
ARLW Lucas Wallmark/299 8.00 20.00
ARMB Madison Bowey/299 5.00 12.00
ARNH Nico Hischier/99 (No Auto) 25.00 60.00
ARNM Nick Merkley/299 8.00 20.00
ARNP Nolan Patrick/99 (No Auto) 20.00 50.00
ARNS Nikita Scherbak/299 10.00 25.00
AROT Owen Tippett/299 15.00 40.00
ARPD Pierre-Luc Dubois/199 30.00 80.00
ARRH Robert Hagg/299 8.00 20.00
ARSM Samuel Morin/299 5.00 12.00
ARTJ Tyson Jost/199 15.00 40.00
ARTS Travis Sanheim/299 8.00 20.00
ARTT Tage Thompson/299 20.00 50.00
ARVD Vince Dunn/299 10.00 25.00
ARVH Ville Husso/299 10.00 25.00
ARVK Vladislav Kamenev/299 8.00 20.00
ARVM Victor Mete/299 8.00 20.00
ARWB Will Butcher/299 10.00 25.00

2017-18 Upper Deck Premier Inked Script

ISAD Alex Delvecchio/49 12.00 30.00
ISBH Brett Hull/99 25.00 60.00
ISBP Brian Propp/99 8.00 20.00
ISCN Cam Neely/99 15.00 40.00
ISJV John Vanbiesbrouck/99 12.00 30.00
ISNE Nikolaj Ehlers/49 15.00 40.00
ISPM Patrick Marleau/99 12.00 30.00
ISRL Rod Langway/25 15.00 40.00
ISTF Theoren Fleury/49 25.00 60.00

2017-18 Upper Deck Premier Jerseys

*PATCH/25-36: 1X TO 2.5X BASIC INSERTS
1 Patrice Bergeron 2.50 6.00
2 Alexander Ovechkin 8.00 20.00
3 Filip Forsberg 3.00 8.00
4 Nikita Kucherov 4.00 10.00
5 Mikael Granlund 1.50 4.00
6 Auston Matthews 8.00 20.00
7 Vincent Trocheck 2.00 5.00
8 Patrik Laine 2.50 6.00
9 Jack Eichel 3.00 8.00
10 Claude Giroux 2.00 5.00
11 James Neal 1.25 3.00
12 Artemi Panarin 4.00 10.00
13 Jeff Skinner 2.50 6.00
14 Blake Wheeler 2.00 5.00
15 Bo Horvat 2.50 6.00
16 Jordan Eberle 2.00 5.00
17 Devan Dubnyk 1.50 4.00
18 Steven Stamkos 4.00 10.00
19 John Tavares 3.00 8.00
20 John Gibson 2.00 5.00
21 Nathan MacKinnon 8.00 20.00
22 Sidney Crosby 8.00 20.00
23 Vladimir Tarasenko 2.50 6.00
24 Taylor Hall 2.00 5.00
25 Jonathan Huberdeau 2.50 6.00
26 Kevin Shattenkirk 1.25 3.00
27 Anthony Mantha 1.50 4.00
28 Jonathan Quick 2.50 6.00
29 Mark Giordano 2.00 5.00
30 Erik Karlsson 2.50 6.00
31 Connor McDavid 10.00 25.00
32 Carey Price 4.00 10.00
33 Duncan Keith 1.50 4.00
34 Marc-Andre Fleury 4.00 10.00
35 Tyler Seguin 2.50 6.00
36 Logan Couture 2.50 6.00
37 Kris Letang 2.50 6.00
38 Jonathan Drouin 1.50 4.00
39 Derek Stepan 1.25 3.00
40 Nazem Kadri 2.50 6.00
41 Wayne Gretzky 12.00 30.00
43 Brett Hull 4.00 10.00
44 Dale Hawerchuk 2.50 6.00
45 Pavel Bure 2.00 5.00
46 Patrick Roy 5.00 12.00
47 Joe Sakic 4.00 10.00
48 Rod Langway 2.00 5.00
49 Ray Bourque 3.00 8.00
50 Mario Lemieux 8.00 20.00
51 Janne Kuokkanen 2.00 5.00
52 Filip Chlapik 1.50 4.00
55 Jesper Bratt 4.00 10.00
56 Victor Mete 2.00 5.00
57 Tage Thompson 5.00 12.00
58 Lucas Wallmark 2.00 5.00
59 Nick Merkley 2.00 5.00
60 Ville Husso 2.50 6.00
61 Martin Necas 6.00 15.00
62 Adrian Kempe 4.00 10.00
63 Logan Brown 2.00 5.00
64 Madison Bowey 1.25 3.00
66 Ivan Barbashev 2.50 6.00
67 Denis Gurianov 5.00 12.00
68 Alex Nedeljkovic 3.00 8.00
69 Samuel Morin 1.25 3.00
70 Alex Formenton 2.00 5.00
71 Evgeny Svechnikov 4.00 10.00
72 Jon Gillies 2.00 5.00
74 Vladislav Kamenev 2.00 5.00
75 Will Butcher 2.50 6.00
76 Travis Sanheim 2.00 5.00
77 Haydn Fleury 2.00 5.00
78 Nikita Scherbak 2.50 6.00
79 Vince Dunn 2.50 6.00
80 Christian Fischer 2.50 6.00
81 Colin White 2.50 6.00
82 Jack Roslovic 2.50 6.00
83 J.T. Compher 2.00 5.00
84 Luke Kunin 2.00 5.00
85 Jakob Forsbacka-Karlsson 2.00 5.00
86 Alex Tuch 5.00 12.00
87 Robert Hagg 2.00 5.00
88 Anders Bjork 2.50 6.00
89 Kailer Yamamoto 5.00 12.00
90 Owen Tippett 4.00 10.00
91 Brock Boeser 5.00 12.00
92 Clayton Keller 5.00 12.00
93 Charlie McAvoy 5.00 12.00
94 Tyson Jost 4.00 10.00
95 Alexander Nylander 3.00 8.00
96 Josh Ho-Sang 2.50 6.00
97 Alex DeBrincat 5.00 12.00
98 Pierre-Luc Dubois 3.00 8.00
99 Nolan Patrick 4.00 10.00
100 Nico Hischier 6.00 15.00

2017-18 Upper Deck Premier Magnificent Marks

MMAB Aleksander Barkov 8.00 20.00
MMAE Aaron Ekblad 6.00 15.00
MMAM Anthony Mantha 4.00 10.00
MMAW Alexander Wennberg 3.00 8.00
MMBB Brock Boeser 12.00 30.00
MMBE Brian Elliott 4.00 10.00
MMBO Bobby Orr 100.00 200.00
MMBS Borje Salming 5.00 12.00
MMCA Cam Atkinson 5.00 12.00
MMCK Clayton Keller 12.00 30.00
MMCM Connor McDavid 150.00 300.00
MMCP Carey Price 10.00 25.00
MMCS Charlie Simmer 3.00 8.00
MMDD Devan Dubnyk 4.00 10.00
MMDT Dave Taylor 4.00 10.00
MMFC Filip Chlapik 4.00 10.00
MMHF Haydn Fleury 5.00 12.00
MMJC John Carlson 5.00 12.00
MMJD Jonathan Drouin 4.00 10.00
MMJI Jarome Iginla 6.00 15.00
MMKM Kirk Muller 4.00 10.00
MMKS Kevin Shattenkirk 3.00 8.00
MMLC Logan Couture 6.00 15.00
MMLD Leon Draisaitl 15.00 40.00
MMMG Mark Giordano 5.00 12.00
MMMH Mike Hoffman 3.00 8.00
MMMK Mike Krushelnyski 4.00 10.00
MMMM Mark Messier 10.00 25.00
MMMS Mark Scheifele 8.00 20.00
MMNK Nikita Kucherov 10.00 25.00
MMON Owen Nolan 5.00 12.00
MMPR Patrick Roy 40.00 100.00
MMPT Pierre Turgeon 4.00 10.00
MMPZ Pavel Zacha 4.00 10.00
MMRE Ryan Ellis 4.00 10.00
MMSH Conor Sheary 5.00 12.00
MMSS Steven Stamkos 10.00 25.00
MMTA Tony Amonte 4.00 10.00
MMTH Taylor Hall 5.00 12.00
MMTR Tobias Rieder 3.00 8.00
MMVH Ville Husso 6.00 15.00
MMVL Vladimir Tarasenko 6.00 15.00
MMVT Vincent Trocheck 5.00 12.00
MMWG Wayne Gretzky 250.00 600.00
MMWO Willie O'Ree 6.00 15.00

2017-18 Upper Deck Premier Mega Patch Chest Logos

PMPAA Artem Anisimov 12.00 30.00
PMPAE Aaron Ekblad 25.00 60.00
PMPAK Anze Kopitar 30.00 80.00
PMPAL Anders Lee 20.00 50.00
PMPAM Auston Matthews 80.00 200.00
PMPAO Alexander Ovechkin 80.00 200.00
PMPAP Artemi Panarin 40.00 100.00
PMPAV Andrei Vasilevskiy 30.00 80.00
PMPBB Ben Bishop 15.00 40.00
PMPBH Bo Horvat 25.00 60.00
PMPBM Brandon Montour 25.00 60.00
PMPBO Brock Boeser 50.00 120.00
PMPBR Brayden Schenn 20.00 50.00
PMPBS Brandon Saad 15.00 40.00
PMPBU Brent Burns 20.00 50.00
PMPCG Claude Giroux 20.00 50.00
PMPCK Clayton Keller 50.00 125.00
PMPCM Connor McDavid 100.00 250.00
PMPCP Carey Price 40.00 100.00
PMPCT Cam Talbot 20.00 50.00
PMPDE Derek Stepan 12.00 30.00
PMPDK David Krejci 20.00 50.00
PMPDL Dylan Larkin 25.00 60.00
PMPDS Daniel Sedin 25.00 60.00
PMPEB Jordan Eberle 20.00 50.00
PMPEE Joel Eriksson Ek 15.00 40.00
PMPEK Erik Karlsson 25.00 60.00
PMPEM Evgeni Malkin 40.00 100.00
PMPGL Gabriel Landeskog 25.00 60.00
PMPGU Jake Guentzel 30.00 80.00
PMPHL Henrik Lundqvist 50.00 120.00
PMPHZ Henrik Zetterberg 25.00 60.00
PMPJA Jake Allen 20.00 50.00
PMPJB Jamie Benn 20.00 50.00
PMPJD Jonathan Drouin 15.00 40.00
PMPJE Jack Eichel 30.00 80.00
PMPJG Johnny Gaudreau 30.00 80.00
PMPJH Jonathan Huberdeau 25.00 60.00
PMPJM Jonathan Marchessault 25.00 60.00
PMPJN James Neal 12.00 30.00
PMPJO Marcus Johansson 15.00 40.00
PMPJP Joe Pavelski 25.00 60.00
PMPJQ Jonathan Quick 25.00 60.00
PMPJS Jaden Schwartz 25.00 60.00
PMPJT John Tavares 30.00 80.00
PMPKA Nazem Kadri 25.00 60.00
PMPKP Kyle Palmieri 15.00 40.00
PMPKS Kevin Shattenkirk 12.00 30.00
PMPKU Evgeny Kuznetsov 25.00 60.00
PMPLD Leon Draisaitl 60.00 150.00
PMPMA Anthony Mantha 15.00 40.00
PMPMC Charlie McAvoy 50.00 125.00
PMPMD Max Domi 20.00 50.00
PMPMF Marc-Andre Fleury 40.00 100.00
PMPMG Mikael Granlund 15.00 40.00
PMPMI J.T. Miller 25.00 60.00
PMPMJ Martin Jones 15.00 40.00
PMPMM Matt Murray 30.00 80.00
PMPMO Sean Monahan 12.00 30.00
PMPMR Mikko Rantanen 50.00 125.00
PMPMS Mark Scheifele 30.00 80.00
PMPMT Matthew Tkachuk 40.00 100.00
PMPMZ Alec Martinez 12.00 30.00
PMPNB Nicklas Backstrom 20.00 50.00
PMPNE Nikolaj Ehlers 20.00 50.00
PMPNK Nikita Kucherov 40.00 100.00
PMPPB Patrice Bergeron 25.00 60.00
PMPPD Pierre-Luc Dubois 30.00 80.00
PMPPE Corey Perry 30.00 80.00
PMPPK Patrick Kane 40.00 100.00
PMPPL Patrik Laine 25.00 60.00
PMPPM Patrick Marleau 20.00 50.00
PMPPO Jason Pominville 12.00 30.00
PMPPR Pekka Rinne 20.00 50.00
PMPPS P.K. Subban 25.00 60.00
PMPRG Ryan Getzlaf 20.00 50.00
PMPRJ Roman Josi 20.00 50.00
PMPRO Ryan O'Reilly 20.00 50.00
PMPRY Ryan Johansen 15.00 40.00
PMPSA Sebastian Aho 30.00 80.00
PMPSB Sergei Bobrovsky 30.00 80.00
PMPSC Sidney Crosby 80.00 200.00
PMPSG Shayne Gostisbehere 20.00 50.00
PMPSK Jeff Skinner 25.00 60.00
PMPSM Mike Smith 20.00 50.00
PMPSS Steven Stamkos 40.00 100.00
PMPST Mark Stone 25.00 60.00
PMPSW Shea Weber 15.00 40.00
PMPTH Taylor Hall 20.00 50.00
PMPTJ Tyson Jost 40.00 100.00
PMPTO Jonathan Toews 30.00 80.00
PMPTR Vincent Trocheck 20.00 50.00

PMPTS Tyler Seguin 25.00 60.00
PMPVH Victor Hedman 25.00 60.00
PMPVT Vladimir Tarasenko 25.00 60.00
PMPWN William Nylander 40.00 100.00
PMPZU Mats Zuccarello 20.00 50.00
PMPZW Zach Werenski 30.00 80.00

2017-18 Upper Deck Premier Mega Patch Duos

PMP2BH A.Barkov/J.Huberdeau/25 30.00 80.00
PMP2BT B.Burns/J.Thornton/25 30.00 80.00
PMP2DL L.Draisaitl/M.Lucic/25 60.00 150.00
PMP2EO J.Eichel/R.O'Reilly/25 30.00 80.00
PMP2FN M.Fleury/J.Neal/25 40.00 100.00
PMP2GF R.Getzlaf/C.Fowler/25 20.00 50.00
PMP2GK C.Giroux/T.Konecny/25 20.00 50.00
PMP2GM J.Guentzel/M.Murray/25 30.00 80.00
PMP2GN M.Granlund
N.Niederreiter/25 15.00 40.00
PMP2GT J.Gaudreau/M.Tkachuk/25 40.00100.00
PMP2HJ T.Hall/M.Johansson/25 20.00 50.00
PMP2HV V.Hedman/A.Vasilevskiy/25 30.0080.00
PMP2KB A.Kopitar/D.Brown/25 30.00 80.00
PMP2KH E.Karlsson/M.Hoffman/25 25.00 60.00
PMP2KS C.Kreider/K.Shattenkirk/25 25.00 60.00
PMP2LE P.Laine/N.Ehlers/25 25.00 60.00
PMP2MB B.Marchand
P.Bergeron/25 40.00 100.00
PMP2MK P.Marleau/N.Kadri/25 25.00 60.00
PMP2ML A.Mantha/D.Larkin/25 25.00 60.00
PMP2MN A.Matthews
W.Nylander/25 80.00 200.00
PMP2MR N.MacKinnon
M.Rantanen/25 80.00 200.00
PMP2OK A.Ovechkin
E.Kuznetsov/25 80.00 200.00
PMP2PB A.Panarin/S.Bobrovsky/25 40.00100.00
PMP2PD C.Price/J.Drouin/25 40.00 100.00
PMP2SA J.Skinner/S.Aho/25 30.00 80.00
PMP2SE D.Stepan
O.Ekman-Larsson/25 20.00 50.00
PMP2SJ P.Subban/R.Josi/25 25.00 60.00
PMP2SK S.Stamkos/N.Kucherov/25 40.00100.00
PMP2ST B.Saad/J.Toews/25 30.00 80.00
PMP2SW M.Scheifele/B.Wheeler/25 30.00 80.00
PMP2TL J.Tavares/A.Lee/25 30.00 80.00
PMP2TS V.Tarasenko/J.Schwartz/25 25.00 60.00

2017-18 Upper Deck Premier Mega Stick Duos

PMS2AO A.Larsson/O.Klefbom/25 20.00 50.00
PMS2BS J.Benn/T.Seguin/25 25.00 60.00
PMS2DJ B.Dubinsky/J.Johnson/25 12.00 30.00
PMS2DK D.Doughty/E.Karlsson/25 25.00 60.00
PMS2DS D.Dubnyk/R.Suter/25 15.00 40.00
PMS2KB A.Kopitar/D.Brown/25 30.00 80.00
PMS2LK A.Ladd/N.Kulemin/25 12.00 30.00
PMS2NP J.Neal/D.Perron/25 15.00 40.00
PMS2SG D.Sedin/S.Gagner/25 25.00 60.00
PMS2SH J.Staal/N.Hanifin/25 20.00 50.00
PMS2TP T.Toffoli/T.Pearson/25 20.00 50.00

2017-18 Upper Deck Premier NHL Legendary Sticks

LSDH Doug Harvey 25.00 60.00
LSEB Ed Belfour 30.00 80.00
LSFM Frank Mahovlich 25.00 60.00
LSGF Grant Fuhr 40.00 100.00
LSJB Johnny Bower 25.00 60.00
LSJS Joe Sakic 50.00 125.00
LSMM Mark Messier 50.00 125.00
LSMR Maurice Richard 50.00 125.00
LSRB Ray Bourque 40.00 100.00
LSSM Stan Mikita 30.00 80.00

2017-18 Upper Deck Premier Premier Duals Jerseys

PD2AP J.Allen/A.Pietrangelo/99 5.00 12.00
PD2BB W.Butcher/J.Bratt/99 10.00 25.00
PD2BV B.Burns/M.Vlasic/99 5.00 12.00
PD2DC P.Dubois/G.Carlsson/99 8.00 20.00
PD2EL N.Ehlers/P.Laine/99 6.00 15.00
PD2EO J.Eichel/R.O'Reilly/99 8.00 20.00
PD2GB W.Gretzky/R.Blake/25 30.00 80.00
PD2HB B.Horvat/B.Boeser/99 12.00 30.00
PD2HP N.Hischier/N.Patrick/99 15.00 40.00
PD2HV V.Hedman/A.Vasilevskiy/99 8.00 20.00
PD2JC T.Jost/J.Compher/99 10.00 25.00
PD2JF R.Johansen/F.Forsberg/99 8.00 20.00
PD2JW S.Jones/Z.Werenski/99 8.00 20.00
PD2KB A.Kempe/J.Brodzinski/99 10.00 25.00
PD2KF C.Keller/C.Fischer/99 12.00 30.00
PD2LN M.Lucic/R.Nugent-Hopkins/99 6.0015.00
PD2MA A.Mantha/A.Athanasiou/99 5.00 12.00
PD2MD C.McDavid/L.Draisaitl/99 25.00 60.00
PD2MF J.Marchessault/M.Fleury/99 10.00 25.00
PD2MG B.Montour/J.Gibson/99 6.00 15.00
PD2ML E.Malkin/K.Letang/99 10.00 25.00
PD2MN A.Matthews/W.Nylander/99 20.00 50.00
PD2MS V.Mete/N.Scherbak/99 6.00 15.00
PD2ND N.Niederreiter/D.Dubnyk/99 4.00 10.00
PD2PG I.Provorov/S.Gostisbehere/99 5.00 12.00
PD2RB A.Radulov/B.Bishop/99 5.00 12.00
PD2RP P.Roy/C.Price/99 12.00 30.00
PD2SF J.Staal/J.Faulk/99 4.00 10.00
PD2SJ P.Subban/R.Josi/99 6.00 15.00
PD2TA J.Toews/A.Anisimov/99 8.00 20.00

2017-18 Upper Deck Premier Premier Quads Jerseys

PQ4ANA Getzlaf/Perry/Kesler/49 6.00 15.00
PQ4AST Lafleur/Yzerman/Jagr/25 8.00 20.00
PQ4BUF Eichel/Pominville
O'Reilly/49 10.00 25.00
PQ4CAL Gaudreau/Monahan
Tkachuk/49 10.00 25.00
PQ4CAR Fleury/Necas/Kuokkanen/49 6.00 15.00
PQ4CHI Toews/Saad/Kane/49 10.00 25.00
PQ4COL Panarin/Werenski
Atkinson/49 12.00 30.00
PQ4FLO Barkov/Ekblad/Huberdeau/49 10.0025.00
PQ4LAK Kopitar/Brown/Doughty/25 10.00 25.00
PQ4MIN Staal/Spurgeon/Zucker/49 8.00 20.00
PQ4OTT Karlsson/Brassard/Stone/49 8.00 20.00
PQ4PHI Giroux/Konecny/Couturier/49 6.00 15.00
PQ4RC4 Boeser/DeBrincat/Keller/49 15.00 40.00
PQ4SJS Thornton/Burns/Pavelski/49 10.00 25.00
PQ4TBL Stamkos/Hedman
Kucherov/25 12.00 30.00
PQ4TML Marleau/Kadri/van/49 6.00 15.00
PQ4VAN Bure/Larionov/Sedin/25 6.00 15.00
PQ4VEZ Bobrovsky/Holtby/Price/49 10.00 25.00
PQ4WAS Ovechkin/Kuznetsov
Backstrom/49 25.00 60.00
PQ4WIN Scheifele/Ehlers/Laine/25 10.00 25.00

2017-18 Upper Deck Premier Premier Signature Booklets

PSBAE Aaron Ekblad 12.00 30.00
PSBAK Anze Kopitar 15.00 40.00
PSBAN Alexander Nylander 15.00 40.00
PSBBB Brock Boeser 25.00 60.00
PSBBO Bobby Orr 40.00 100.00
PSBCK Clayton Keller 25.00 60.00
PSBCM Connor McDavid 200.00 300.00
PSBDK Duncan Keith 8.00 20.00
PSBJT Jonathan Toews 15.00 40.00
PSBLD Leon Draisaitl 30.00 80.00
PSBLK Luke Kunin 10.00 25.00
PSBMP Max Pacioretty 10.00 25.00
PSBMS Mark Scheifele 15.00 40.00
PSBNK Nikita Kucherov 20.00 50.00
PSBOT Owen Tippett 20.00 50.00
PSBPC Paul Coffey 10.00 25.00
PSBPE Phil Esposito 15.00 40.00
PSBPH Phil Housley 8.00 20.00
PSBTS Tyler Seguin 12.00 30.00
PSBWG Wayne Gretzky 125.00 300.00

2017-18 Upper Deck Premier Premier Signature Booklets Dual

DSBBP M.Bossy/D.Potvin/40 80.00 150.00
DSBDY A.Delvecchio/S.Yzerman/40 80.00150.00
DSBOE B.Orr/P.Esposito/20 150.00 250.00

2017-18 Upper Deck Premier Premier Swatches

PSAA Artem Anisimov/99 3.00 8.00
PSAL Anders Lee/99 5.00 12.00
PSAM Auston Matthews/25 20.00 50.00
PSBB Ben Bishop/50 4.00 10.00
PSBH Bo Horvat/99 6.00 15.00
PSBM Brandon Montour/99 6.00 15.00
PSBS Brayden Schenn/50 5.00 12.00
PSBW Blake Wheeler/50 5.00 12.00
PSCK Chris Kreider/99 6.00 15.00
PSCS Conor Sheary/99 5.00 12.00
PSDS Derek Stepan/99 3.00 8.00
PSJD Jonathan Drouin/50 4.00 10.00
PSJE Jack Eichel/50 8.00 20.00
PSJH Jonathan Huberdeau/99 6.00 15.00
PSJN James Neal/50 3.00 8.00
PSLD Leon Draisaitl/25 15.00 40.00
PSMA Anthony Mantha/99 4.00 10.00
PSMF Marc-Andre Fleury/25 10.00 25.00
PSMG Mikael Granlund/99 4.00 10.00
PSMH Mike Hoffman/50 3.00 8.00
PSMJ Martin Jones/50 4.00 10.00
PSMR Mikko Rantanen/99 12.00 30.00
PSMS Mark Scheifele/50 8.00 20.00
PSNB Nicklas Backstrom/50 5.00 12.00
PSNK Nikita Kucherov/25 10.00 25.00
PSPB Patrice Bergeron/25 6.00 15.00
PSRJ Roman Josi/99 5.00 12.00
PSSA Sebastian Aho/99 8.00 20.00
PSTK Travis Konecny/99 5.00 12.00
PSZW Zach Werenski/99 8.00 20.00

2017-18 Upper Deck Premier Premier Trios Jerseys

PT3BBR Bjork/McAvoy/DeBrusk 12.00 30.00
PT3BOS Marchand/Bergeron/Pastrnak 12.0030.00
PT3CAL Tkachuk/Gaudreau/Monahan 10.0025.00
PT3COL Landeskog
MacKinnon/Rantanen 20.00 50.00
PT3DAL Benn/Seguin/Radulov 6.00 15.00
PT3DET Mantha/Larkin/Athanasiou 6.00 15.00
PT3FLO Huberdeau/Barkov/Bjugstad 8.00 20.00
PT3ISL Ladd/Barzal/Eberle 6.00 15.00
PT3NJD Johansson/Hall/Palmieri 5.00 12.00
PT3NJR Bratt/Hischier/Butcher 15.00 40.00
PT3NYI Lee/Tavares/Bailey 8.00 20.00
PT3NYR Zibanejad/Kreider/Zuccarello 6.00 15.00
PT3OTT Brown/White/Chlapik 6.00 15.00
PT3PEN Guentzel/Malkin/Kessel 10.00 25.00
PT3PHI Giroux/Couturier/Simmonds 6.00 15.00
PT3STL Schwartz/Schenn/Tarasenko 6.00 15.00
PT3TCL Simmer/Dionne/Taylor 6.00 15.00
PT3WAS Carlson/Ovechkin/Holtby 20.00 50.00
PT3WIN Ehlers/Scheifele/Wheeler 8.00 20.00

2017-18 Upper Deck Premier Signature Award Winners

SABB Bruce Boudreau/99 8.00 20.00
SACA Craig Anderson/49 10.00 25.00
SADH Dale Hawerchuk/99 12.00 30.00
SAJB Jason Blake/99 6.00 15.00
SAJV John Vanbiesbrouck/99 10.00 25.00
SAPC Paul Coffey/49 10.00 25.00
SARB Rod Brind`Amour/99 10.00 25.00
SARL Rod Langway/99 10.00 25.00
SASS Steven Stamkos/49 20.00 50.00

2017-18 Upper Deck Premier Signature Champions

SCBC Bobby Clarke/49 25.00 60.00
SCDK Duncan Keith/49 12.00 30.00
SCDP Denis Potvin/49 15.00 40.00
SCGF Grant Fuhr/49 25.00 60.00
SCJC Jeff Carter/99 12.00 30.00
SCKM Kirk Muller/99 12.00 30.00
SCSB Scotty Bowman/49 20.00 50.00
SCTB Tom Barrasso/99 12.00 30.00

2018-19 Upper Deck Premier

SILVER: 4X TO 10X BASIC CARDS
*SILVER.RC: 1.5X TO 4X BASIC CARDS
1 Carey Price 2.00 5.00
2 Tyler Seguin 1.25 3.00
3 Steven Stamkos 2.00 5.00
4 Auston Matthews 4.00 10.00
5 Taylor Hall 1.00 2.50
6 Alexander Ovechkin 4.00 10.00
7 Evgenii Dadonov .60 1.50
8 Blake Wheeler 1.00 2.50
9 Mark Stone 1.25 3.00
10 Max Domi 1.00 2.50
11 Matthew Tkachuk 2.00 5.00
12 Ryan O'Reilly 1.00 2.50
13 Filip Forsberg 1.50 4.00
14 Brent Burns 1.00 2.50
15 Mikko Rantanen 2.50 6.00
16 Jack Eichel 1.50 4.00
17 John Tavares 1.50 4.00
18 Henrik Lundqvist 2.50 6.00
19 Mark Scheifele 1.50 4.00
20 Brock Boeser 1.25 3.00
21 Patrice Bergeron 1.25 3.00
22 Nathan MacKinnon 4.00 10.00
23 John Gibson 1.00 2.50
24 Evgeni Malkin 2.00 5.00
25 Antti Raanta 1.00 2.50
26 Dylan Larkin 1.25 3.00
27 Patrick Kane 2.00 5.00
28 Evgeny Kuznetsov 1.25 3.00
29 Nico Hischier 1.50 4.00
30 Anders Lee .75 2.00
31 Connor McDavid 5.00 12.00
32 Jonathan Marchessault 1.25 3.00
33 Mikael Granlund .75 2.00
34 Seth Jones 1.00 2.50
35 Sebastian Aho 1.50 4.00
36 Drew Doughty 1.25 3.00
37 Mathew Barzal 1.25 3.00
38 Ilya Kovalchuk .75 2.00
39 Claude Giroux 1.00 2.50
40 Sidney Crosby 4.00 10.00
41 Chris Chelios 1.00 2.50
42 Daniel Sedin 1.25 3.00
43 Henrik Sedin 1.25 3.00
44 Guy Lafleur 1.25 3.00
45 Curtis Joseph 1.25 3.00
46 Wayne Gretzky 6.00 15.00
47 Mario Lemieux 4.00 10.00
48 Steve Yzerman 2.50 6.00
49 Bobby Orr 4.00 10.00
50 Patrick Roy 2.50 6.00
51 Jake Bean RC 2.50 6.00
52 Drake Batherson RC 5.00 12.00
53 Robert Thomas RC 5.00 12.00
54 Henri Jokiharju RC 2.00 5.00
55 Dennis Cholowski RC 2.50 6.00
56 Maxime Comtois RC 2.50 6.00
57 Jeremy Lauzon RC 3.00 8.00
58 Mathieu Joseph RC 3.00 8.00
59 Sami Niku RC 2.00 5.00
60 Max Lajoie RC 4.00 10.00
61 Ryan Donato RC 4.00 10.00
62 Par Lindholm RC 2.50 6.00
63 Kristian Vesalainen RC 3.00 8.00
64 Sam Steel RC 2.50 6.00
65 Michael McLeod RC 2.00 5.00
66 Jayce Hawryluk RC 2.00 5.00
67 Joey Anderson RC 2.50 6.00
68 Jordan Kyrou RC 5.00 12.00
69 Travis Dermott RC 4.00 10.00
70 Brett Howden RC 3.00 8.00
71 Dominik Kahun RC 2.50 6.00
72 Isac Lundestrom RC 2.00 5.00
73 Henrik Borgstrom RC 4.00 10.00
74 Dylan Sikura RC 3.00 8.00
75 Jordan Greenway RC 2.50 6.00
76 Dillon Dube RC 3.00 8.00
77 Jaret Anderson-Dolan RC 2.00 5.00
78 Kiefer Sherwood RC 2.00 5.00
79 Michael Dal Colle RC 2.50 6.00
80 Antti Suomela RC 2.00 5.00
81 Adam Gaudette RC 4.00 10.00
82 Lias Andersson RC 4.00 10.00
83 Andreas Johnsson RC 3.00 8.00
84 Anthony Cirelli RC 4.00 10.00
85 Oskar Lindblom RC 4.00 10.00
86 Troy Terry RC 4.00 10.00
87 Juuso Valimaki RC 2.50 6.00
88 Evan Bouchard RC 6.00 15.00
89 Tomas Hyka RC 2.50 6.00
90 Noah Juulsen RC 2.50 6.00
91 Casey Mittelstadt RC 5.00 12.00
92 Carter Hart RC 5.00 12.00
93 Michael Rasmussen RC 3.00 8.00
94 Miro Heiskanen RC 6.00 15.00
95 Eeli Tolvanen RC 5.00 12.00
96 Brady Tkachuk RC 8.00 20.00
97 Andrei Svechnikov RC 6.00 15.00
98 Jesperi Kotkaniemi RC 5.00 12.00
99 Elias Pettersson RC 8.00 20.00
100 Rasmus Dahlin RC 6.00 15.00

2018-19 Upper Deck Premier '03-04 Retro Rookie Signatures

03AS Andrei Svechnikov 30.00 80.00
03BT Brady Tkachuk 40.00 100.00
03CM Casey Mittelstadt 25.00 60.00
03DB Drake Batherson 25.00 60.00
03EP Elias Pettersson 150.00 250.00
03JK Jesperi Kotkaniemi 25.00 60.00
03MH Miro Heiskanen 30.00 80.00

2018-19 Upper Deck Premier Acetate Rookie Autograph Patches

ARAG Adam Gaudette/249 12.00 30.00
ARAJ Andreas Johnsson/249 10.00 25.00
ARAS Andrei Svechnikov/99 100.00 200.00
ARBA Drake Batherson/249 25.00 60.00
ARBE Ethan Bear/249 12.00 30.00
ARBH Brett Howden/249 10.00 25.00
ARBT Brady Tkachuk/99 200.00 300.00
ARCH Carter Hart/99 100.00 250.00
ARCM Casey Mittelstadt/99 30.00 80.00
ARDD Dillon Dube/249 10.00 25.00
ARDG Dylan Gambrell/249 8.00 20.00
ARDS Dylan Sikura/249 10.00 25.00
ARDT Dominic Turgeon/249 8.00 20.00
AREB Evan Bouchard/249 20.00 50.00
AREP Elias Pettersson/99 400.00 600.00
ARFH Filip Hronek/249 8.00 20.00
ARHB Henrik Borgstrom/249 12.00 30.00
ARHI Blake Hillman/249 8.00 20.00
ARHJ Henri Jokiharju/249 6.00 15.00
ARIL Isac Lundestrom/249 6.00 15.00
ARJA Jaret Anderson-Dolan/249 6.00 15.00
ARJB Jake Bean/249 8.00 20.00
ARJG Jordan Greenway/249 8.00 20.00
ARJK Jesperi Kotkaniemi/99 15.00 40.00
ARKV Kristian Vesalainen/249 10.00 25.00
ARKY Jordan Kyrou/249 50.00 125.00
ARLA Lias Andersson/249 12.00 30.00
ARMA Cooper Marody/249 8.00 20.00
ARMC Maxime Comtois/249 8.00 20.00
ARMD Michael Dal Colle/249 8.00 20.00
ARMH Miro Heiskanen/99 60.00 150.00
ARML Max Lajoie/249 12.00 30.00
ARMM Michael McLeod/249 6.00 15.00
ARNJ Noah Juulsen/249 8.00 20.00
ARRD Rasmus Dahlin/49 (No Auto) 40.00 100.00
ARRT Robert Thomas/249 15.00 40.00
ARSS Sam Steel/249 8.00 20.00
ARTT Troy Terry/249 60.00 150.00
ARVE Victor Ejdsell/249 6.00 15.00
ARWF Warren Foegele/249 8.00 20.00
ARZA Zach Aston-Reese/249 12.00 30.00

2018-19 Upper Deck Premier Acetate Rookie Autograph Patches Gold Spectrum

*GOLD: .6X TO 1.5X BASIC INSERTS
ARAS Andrei Svechnikov/25 125.00 225.00
ARBT Brady Tkachuk/25 250.00 350.00
ARCH Carter Hart/25 200.00 500.00
ARCM Casey Mittelstadt/25 50.00 125.00
AREP Elias Pettersson/25 600.00 1200.00
ARJK Jesperi Kotkaniemi/25 30.00 80.00
ARKY Jordan Kyrou/99 80.00 200.00
ARMH Miro Heiskanen/25 250.00 350.00

2018-19 Upper Deck Premier Inked Script

ISBT Brady Tkachuk/99 20.00 50.00
ISEP Elias Pettersson/99 50.00 125.00
ISES Eric Staal/50 6.00 15.00
ISJK Jesperi Kotkaniemi/99 12.00 30.00
ISNH Nico Hischier/50 10.00 25.00
ISTH Tomas Hertl/99 6.00 15.00
ISTT Teuvo Teravainen/99 6.00 15.00
ISVA Viktor Arvidsson/99 4.00 10.00

2018-19 Upper Deck Premier Jerseys

*PATCH/25-49: 1.3X TO 3X BASIC INSERTS
1 Carey Price 4.00 10.00
2 Tyler Seguin 2.50 6.00
3 Steven Stamkos 4.00 10.00
4 Auston Matthews 8.00 20.00
5 Taylor Hall 2.00 5.00
6 Alexander Ovechkin 8.00 20.00
7 Evgenii Dadonov 1.25 3.00
8 Blake Wheeler 2.00 5.00
9 Mark Stone 2.50 6.00
10 Max Domi 2.00 5.00
11 Matthew Tkachuk 4.00 10.00
12 Ryan O'Reilly 2.00 5.00
13 Filip Forsberg 3.00 8.00
14 Brent Burns 2.00 5.00
15 Mikko Rantanen 5.00 12.00
16 Jack Eichel 3.00 8.00
17 John Tavares 3.00 8.00
18 Henrik Lundqvist 5.00 12.00
19 Mark Scheifele 3.00 8.00
20 Brock Boeser 2.50 6.00
21 Patrice Bergeron 2.50 6.00
22 Nathan MacKinnon 8.00 20.00
23 John Gibson 2.00 5.00
24 Evgeni Malkin 4.00 10.00
26 Dylan Larkin 2.50 6.00
27 Patrick Kane 4.00 10.00
28 Evgeny Kuznetsov 2.50 6.00
29 Nico Hischier 3.00 8.00
30 Anders Lee 1.50 4.00
31 Connor McDavid 10.00 25.00
32 Jonathan Marchessault 2.50 6.00
33 Mikael Granlund 1.50 4.00
34 Seth Jones 2.00 5.00
35 Sebastian Aho 3.00 8.00
36 Drew Doughty 2.50 6.00
37 Mathew Barzal 2.50 6.00
38 Ilya Kovalchuk 1.50 4.00
39 Claude Giroux 2.00 5.00
40 Sidney Crosby 8.00 20.00
42 Daniel Sedin 2.50 6.00
43 Henrik Sedin 2.50 6.00
46 Wayne Gretzky 12.00 30.00
47 Mario Lemieux 8.00 20.00
50 Patrick Roy 5.00 12.00
51 Jake Bean 2.00 5.00
52 Drake Batherson 4.00 10.00
53 Robert Thomas 4.00 10.00
54 Henri Jokiharju 1.50 4.00
55 Dennis Cholowski 2.00 5.00
56 Maxime Comtois 2.00 5.00
57 Jeremy Lauzon 2.50 6.00
58 Mathieu Joseph 2.50 6.00
59 Sami Niku 1.50 4.00
61 Ryan Donato 3.00 8.00
62 Par Lindholm 2.00 5.00
63 Kristian Vesalainen 2.50 6.00
64 Sam Steel 2.00 5.00
65 Michael McLeod 1.50 4.00
66 Jayce Hawryluk 1.50 4.00
67 Joey Anderson 2.00 5.00
68 Jordan Kyrou 4.00 10.00
69 Travis Dermott 3.00 8.00
70 Brett Howden 2.50 6.00
71 Dominik Kahun 2.00 5.00
72 Isac Lundestrom 1.50 4.00
73 Henrik Borgstrom 3.00 8.00
74 Dylan Sikura 2.50 6.00
75 Jordan Greenway 2.00 5.00
76 Dillon Dube 2.50 6.00
77 Jaret Anderson-Dolan 1.50 4.00
78 Kiefer Sherwood 1.50 4.00
79 Michael Dal Colle 2.00 5.00
80 Antti Suomela 1.50 4.00
81 Adam Gaudette 3.00 8.00
82 Lias Andersson 3.00 8.00
83 Andreas Johnsson 2.50 6.00
84 Anthony Cirelli 3.00 8.00
85 Oskar Lindblom 3.00 8.00
86 Troy Terry 3.00 8.00
87 Juuso Valimaki 2.00 5.00
88 Evan Bouchard 5.00 12.00
89 Tomas Hyka 2.00 5.00
90 Noah Juulsen 2.00 5.00
91 Casey Mittelstadt 4.00 10.00
92 Carter Hart 4.00 10.00
93 Michael Rasmussen 2.50 6.00
94 Miro Heiskanen 5.00 12.00
95 Eeli Tolvanen 4.00 10.00
96 Brady Tkachuk 6.00 15.00
97 Andrei Svechnikov 5.00 12.00
98 Jesperi Kotkaniemi 4.00 10.00
99 Elias Pettersson 6.00 15.00
100 Rasmus Dahlin 5.00 12.00

2018-19 Upper Deck Premier Mega Patch Chest Logos

PMPAA Andreas Athanasiou/21 40.00 100.00
PMPAD Alex DeBrincat/24 60.00 150.00
PMPAE Aaron Ekblad/22 60.00 150.00
PMPAG Alex Galchenyuk/24 30.00 80.00
PMPAH Adam Henrique/21 40.00 100.00
PMPAL Anders Lee/22 40.00 100.00
PMPAM Auston Matthews/24 200.00 500.00
PMPAO Alexander Ovechkin/23 200.00 500.00
PMPAP Alex Pietrangelo/18 40.00 100.00
PMPAS Andrei Svechnikov/21 125.00 300.00
PMPAV Andrei Vasilevskiy/25 80.00 200.00
PMPBA Josh Bailey/22 40.00 100.00
PMPBB Brent Burns/24 50.00 125.00
PMPBM Brad Marchand/22 100.00 250.00
PMPBO Bo Horvat/31 60.00 150.00
PMPBP Brayden Point/24 60.00 150.00
PMPBR Brock Boeser/27 60.00 150.00
PMPBT Brady Tkachuk/21 150.00 400.00
PMPCC Charlie Coyle/18 50.00 125.00
PMPCG Claude Giroux/20 50.00 125.00
PMPCK Clayton Keller/23 60.00 150.00
PMPCM Connor McDavid/22 250.00 600.00
PMPCO Sean Couturier/20 40.00 100.00
PMPCP Carey Price/20 100.00 250.00
PMPCS Conor Sheary/22 50.00 125.00
PMPCW Colin White/21 30.00 80.00
PMPDL Dylan Larkin/21 60.00 150.00
PMPDP David Pastrnak/22 125.00 300.00
PMPDS Dylan Strome/24 60.00 150.00
PMPED Evgenii Dadonov/22 30.00 80.00
PMPEK Evander Kane/25 50.00 125.00
PMPEL Elias Lindholm/26 50.00 125.00
PMPEM Evgeni Malkin/29 100.00 250.00
PMPEP Elias Pettersson/27 150.00 400.00
PMPES Eric Staal/18 50.00 125.00
PMPFF Filip Forsberg/18 80.00 200.00
PMPGU Jake Guentzel/29 80.00 200.00
PMPHA Noah Hanifin/26 50.00 125.00
PMPHE Miro Heiskanen/18 125.00 300.00
PMPHJ Niklas Hjalmarsson/24 30.00 80.00
PMPHT Tomas Hertl/24 50.00 125.00
PMPJB Jamie Benn/20 50.00 125.00
PMPJC John Carlson/22 50.00 125.00
PMPJD Jonathan Drouin/20 40.00 100.00
PMPJE Jack Eichel/22 80.00 200.00
PMPJG Johnny Gaudreau/26 80.00 200.00
PMPJM Jonathan Marchessault/21 60.00 150.00
PMPJN James Neal/26 30.00 80.00
PMPJT John Tavares/24 80.00 200.00
PMPJV James van Riemsdyk/20 40.00 100.00
PMPJZ Jason Zucker/18 50.00 125.00
PMPKC Kyle Connor/22 80.00 200.00
PMPKP Kyle Palmieri/26 40.00 100.00
PMPKT Kyle Turris/18 40.00 100.00
PMPKU Evgeny Kuznetsov/22 60.00 150.00
PMPLD Leon Draisaitl/22 150.00 400.00
PMPMA Anthony Mantha/21 40.00 100.00
PMPMB Mathew Barzal/22 60.00 150.00
PMPMC Charlie McAvoy/22 60.00 150.00
PMPMD Max Domi/20 50.00 125.00
PMPMF Marc-Andre Fleury/21 100.00 250.00
PMPMH Mike Hoffman/22 30.00 80.00
PMPMI Casey Mittelstadt/22 100.00 250.00
PMPMM Mitch Marner/24 80.00 200.00
PMPMR Mikko Rantanen/27 125.00 300.00
PMPMS Mark Scheifele/22 80.00 200.00
PMPMT Matthew Tkachuk/26 100.00 250.00
PMPNE Nikolaj Ehlers/22 50.00 125.00
PMPNH Nico Hischier/25 80.00 200.00
PMPNK Nikita Kucherov/25 100.00 250.00
PMPNM Nathan MacKinnon/27 200.00 500.00
PMPNP Nolan Patrick/19 50.00 125.00
PMPOB Oliver Bjorkstrand/20 40.00 100.00
PMPPD Pierre-Luc Dubois/19 40.00 100.00
PMPPK Patrick Kane/24 100.00 250.00
PMPPL Patrik Laine/22 60.00 150.00
PMPPM Patrick Marleau/24 50.00 125.00
PMPPS P.K. Subban/18 60.00 150.00
PMPRD Rasmus Dahlin/22 125.00 300.00
PMPRK Ryan Kesler/21 50.00 125.00
PMPRN Ryan Nugent-Hopkins/22 60.00 150.00
PMPRO Ryan O'Reilly/18 50.00 125.00
PMPRR Rickard Rakell/21 40.00 100.00
PMPSA Sebastian Aho/21 80.00 200.00
PMPSC Sidney Crosby/29 200.00 500.00
PMPSS Steven Stamkos/22 100.00 250.00
PMPST Paul Stastny/21 40.00 100.00
PMPTB Tyson Barrie/27 30.00 80.00
PMPTC Thomas Chabot/21 50.00 125.00
PMPTH Taylor Hall/23 50.00 125.00
PMPTO Jonathan Toews/23 80.00 200.00
PMPTS Tyler Seguin/17 60.00 150.00
PMPTT Teuvo Teravainen/21 50.00 125.00
PMPVT Vladimir Tarasenko/18 60.00 150.00
PMPWK William Karlsson/21 60.00 150.00
PMPZW Zach Werenski/20 80.00 200.00

2018-19 Upper Deck Premier Premier Attractions Autograph Patches

PACM Connor McDavid/25 200.00 300.00

2018-19 Upper Deck Premier Premier Attractions Rookie Autograph Patches

PARDB Drake Batherson 25.00 60.00
PARDC Dennis Cholowski 10.00 25.00
PAREP Elias Pettersson 80.00 200.00
PARML Max Lajoie 15.00 40.00

2018-19 Upper Deck Premier Premier Duals Jerseys

PDSD E.Staal/M.Dumba 5.00 12.00

2018-19 Upper Deck Premier Premier Quads Jerseys

PQCB Jok/Khn/Skr/Ejd/49 8.00 20.00
PQCF Gdr/Mnhn/Grdn/Tkck/25 12.00 30.00
PQDS Ben/Sgn/Rdlv/Klbg/49 8.00 20.00
PQFP Brkv/Hub/Ekb/Luo/49 10.00 25.00
PQLA Kptr/Crtr/Dou/Qck/49 10.00 25.00
PQMC Drn/Dom/Glgr/Prc/49 12.00 30.00
PQML Mrnr/Tvrs/Mrl/Rlly/25 10.00 25.00
PQMW Stl/Prs/Str/Dbnk/49 6.00 15.00
PQNJ Hll/Hsch/Plmr/Zjc/49 10.00 25.00
PQNP Fsbg/Jnsn/Sbn/Jos/49 10.00 25.00
PQNY Brzl/Lee/Nlsn/Bly/49 8.00 20.00
PQPF Grx/Ptrk/Gost/Prov/49 6.00 15.00
PQPP Mlkn/Ksl/Ltng/Mry/49 12.00 30.00
PQRC Ptrsn/Dhln/Tkck/Ktkm/49 20.00 50.00
PQRW Rmsn/Chlwk/Trgn/Hrnk/49 8.00 20.00
PQST O'Rly/Ptrgl/Schn/Trsnk/49 8.00 20.00
PQTB Stmks/Pnt/Kchrv/Vslvk/25 12.00 30.00
PQWC Ovch/Hltb/Bkstm/Crlsn/25 25.00 60.00
PQWJ Schfl/Whlr/Lne/Hlbyck/25 12.00 30.00

2018-19 Upper Deck Premier Premier Signatures

PSBO Bobby Orr A 40.00 100.00
PSBT Brady Tkachuk B 30.00 80.00
PSCJ Curtis Joseph B 12.00 30.00
PSCM Connor McDavid A 50.00 125.00
PSEK Evgeny Kuznetsov C 12.00 30.00
PSJK Jesperi Kotkaniemi C 20.00 50.00
PSKT Kyle Turris C 8.00 20.00
PSMB Martin Brodeur A 25.00 60.00
PSMI Casey Mittelstadt C 20.00 50.00
PSMR Mikko Rantanen C 25.00 60.00
PSMS Mark Stone C 12.00 30.00
PSPR Patrick Roy A 25.00 60.00

2018-19 Upper Deck Premier Premier Swatches

PSAM Auston Matthews 12.00 30.00
PSAO Alexander Ovechkin 8.00 20.00
PSCM Connor McDavid 15.00 40.00
PSCP Carey Price 8.00 20.00
PSDD Drew Doughty 4.00 10.00
PSJT John Tavares 8.00 20.00
PSMM Mitch Marner 8.00 20.00
PSPK Patrick Kane 8.00 20.00
PSSC Sidney Crosby 12.00 30.00
PSTC Thomas Chabot 3.00 8.00

2018-19 Upper Deck Premier Signature Award Winners

SAJT Joe Thornton/25 15.00 40.00

2018-19 Upper Deck Premier Signature Champions

SCPD Pavel Datsyuk/25 15.00 40.00

2019-20 Upper Deck Premier

1 Sidney Crosby/199 4.00 10.00
2 John Tavares/299 1.50 4.00
3 Taylor Hall/299 1.00 2.50
4 Steven Stamkos/299 2.00 5.00
5 Nathan MacKinnon/199 4.00 10.00
6 Ryan O'Reilly/299 1.00 2.50
7 Aleksander Barkov/299 1.50 4.00
8 Henrik Lundqvist/299 2.50 6.00
9 Claude Giroux/299 1.00 2.50
10 Patrick Kane/199 2.00 5.00
11 Marc-Andre Fleury/299 2.00 5.00
12 Drew Doughty/299 1.25 3.00
13 Auston Matthews/199 4.00 10.00
14 Roman Josi/299 1.00 2.50
15 John Gibson/299 1.00 2.50
16 David Pastrnak/199 2.50 6.00
17 Seth Jones/299 1.00 2.50
18 Jonathan Drouin/299 .75 2.00
19 Leon Draisaitl/299 3.00 8.00
20 Brent Burns/299 1.00 2.50
21 Jack Eichel/299 1.50 4.00
22 Andrei Vasilevskiy/299 1.50 4.00
23 Tyler Seguin/299 1.25 3.00
24 Artemi Panarin/199 2.00 5.00
25 Alex Ovechkin/199 4.00 10.00
26 Jordan Binnington/299 1.50 4.00
27 Alex DeBrincat/299 1.25 3.00
28 Brad Marchand/199 2.00 5.00
29 Dylan Larkin/299 1.25 3.00
30 Elias Pettersson/199 1.50 4.00
31 Eric Staal/299 1.00 2.50
32 Mikko Rantanen/299 2.50 6.00
33 Mitch Marner/299 1.50 4.00
34 Sergei Bobrovsky/299 1.50 4.00
35 Blake Wheeler/299 1.00 2.50
36 Oliver Ekman-Larsson/299 1.00 2.50
37 Evgeni Malkin/299 2.00 5.00
38 Joe Pavelski/299 1.25 3.00
39 Nikita Kucherov/299 2.00 5.00
40 Zach Werenski/299 1.50 4.00
41 Thomas Chabot/199 1.00 2.50
42 Carey Price/299 2.00 5.00
43 Johnny Gaudreau/299 1.50 4.00
44 Mark Scheifele/299 1.50 4.00
45 Anthony Mantha/299 .75 2.00
46 John Carlson/299 1.00 2.50
47 Sebastian Aho/299 1.50 4.00
48 Tomas Hertl/299 1.00 2.50
49 Anders Lee/299 .75 2.00
50 Connor McDavid/199 5.00 12.00
51 Nikita Gusev/299 RC 4.00 10.00
52 Sam Lafferty/299 RC 2.00 5.00
53 Erik Brannstrom/299 RC 2.50 6.00
54 Tobias Bjornfot/299 RC 2.50 6.00
55 Nico Sturm/299 RC 2.00 5.00
56 Dominik Kubalik/299 RC 5.00 12.00
57 Elvis Merzlikins/299 RC 5.00 12.00
58 Oliver Wahlstrom/299 RC 4.00 10.00
59 Alexandre Texier/299 RC 2.50 6.00
60 Julien Gauthier/299 RC 2.50 6.00
61 Carl Grundstrom/299 RC 2.50 6.00
62 Trent Frederic/299 RC 2.50 6.00
63 Rasmus Sandin/299 RC 4.00 10.00
64 Igor Shesterkin/299 RC 10.00 25.00
65 Ilya Mikheyev/299 RC 4.00 10.00
66 Joey Daccord/299 RC 5.00 12.00
67 Brandon Gignac/299 RC 2.00 5.00
68 Noah Dobson/299 RC 6.00 15.00
69 Ville Heinola/299 RC 3.00 8.00
70 Connor Clifton/299 RC 2.50 6.00
71 Emil Bemstrom/299 RC 2.50 6.00
72 Brady Keeper/299 RC 2.50 6.00
73 Nicolas Hague/299 RC 2.50 6.00
74 Philippe Myers/299 RC 2.00 5.00
75 Victor Olofsson/299 RC 5.00 12.00
76 Martin Fehervary/299 RC 2.00 5.00
77 Joel L'Esperance/299 RC 2.50 6.00
78 Blake Lizotte/299 RC 2.50 6.00
79 Dante Fabbro/299 RC 2.50 6.00
80 Adam Boqvist/299 RC 2.50 6.00
81 Morgan Frost/299 RC 4.00 10.00
82 Taro Hirose/299 RC 2.50 6.00
83 Carter Verhaeghe/299 RC 4.00 10.00
84 Adam Fox/299 RC 6.00 15.00
85 Mario Ferraro/299 RC 2.00 5.00
86 Vitaly Abramov/299 RC 2.50 6.00
87 Jesper Boqvist/299 RC 2.00 5.00
88 Trevor Moore/299 RC 2.00 5.00
89 Joel Persson/299 RC 2.00 5.00
90 Max Jones/299 RC 2.50 6.00
91 Kaapo Kakko/199 RC 4.00 10.00
92 Cale Makar/199 RC 12.00 30.00
93 Quinn Hughes/199 RC 12.00 30.00
94 Kirby Dach/199 RC 5.00 12.00
95 Filip Zadina/199 RC 4.00 10.00
96 Nick Suzuki/199 RC 10.00 25.00
97 Barrett Hayton/199 RC 5.00 12.00
98 Joel Farabee/199 RC 4.00 10.00
99 Ryan Poehling/199 RC 4.00 10.00
100 Jack Hughes/199 RC 12.00 30.00

2019-20 Upper Deck Premier '02-03 Premier Collection Retro Dual Jerseys

02DAM M.Marner/F.Andersen 5.00 12.00
02DBB A.Barkov/S.Bobrovsky 12.00 30.00
02DBS T.Seguin/B.Bishop 4.00 10.00
02DCH J.Carlson/B.Holtby 4.00 10.00
02DCK P.Kane/C.Crawford 6.00 15.00
02DKJ E.Karlsson/M.Jones 4.00 10.00
02DKQ A.Kopitar/J.Quick 5.00 12.00
02DPD J.Drouin/C.Price 6.00 15.00
02DRD M.Duchene/P.Rinne 3.00 8.00
02DRP D.Pastrnak/T.Rask 8.00 20.00
02DSD E.Staal/D.Dubnyk 6.00 15.00
02DSF M.Stone/M.Fleury 10.00 25.00
02DSV S.Stamkos/A.Vasilevskiy 6.00 15.00
02DTB V.Tarasenko/J.Binnington 5.00 12.00

2019-20 Upper Deck Premier '02-03 Premier Collection Retro Jerseys

02AF Adam Fox 6.00 15.00
02AM Auston Matthews 10.00 25.00
02BM Brad Marchand 5.00 12.00
02CG Cody Glass 4.00 10.00
02CM Connor McDavid 12.00 30.00
02DP David Pastrnak 12.00 30.00
02EP Elias Pettersson 4.00 10.00
02JG Johnny Gaudreau 4.00 10.00
02JH Jack Hughes 12.00 30.00
02KD Kirby Dach 12.00 30.00
02KK Kaapo Kakko 4.00 10.00
02LD Leon Draisaitl 8.00 20.00
02MA Cale Makar 15.00 40.00
02MF Morgan Frost 4.00 10.00
02NK Nikita Kucherov 5.00 12.00
02NM Nathan MacKinnon 10.00 25.00
02NS Nick Suzuki 15.00 40.00
02PK Patrick Kane 5.00 12.00
02VO Victor Olofsson 5.00 12.00

2019-20 Upper Deck Premier '02-03 Premier Collection Retro Super Rookie Patch Autographs

02BH Barrett Hayton/99 30.00 80.00
02CG Cody Glass/99 25.00 60.00
02CM Cale Makar/99 120.00 300.00
02FZ Filip Zadina/99 40.00 100.00
02JH Jack Hughes/99 150.00 400.00
02NG Nikita Gusev/99 25.00 60.00
02NS Nick Suzuki/99 60.00 150.00
02QH Quinn Hughes/99 150.00 400.00
02RP Ryan Poehling/99 25.00 60.00
02VO Victor Olofsson/99 40.00 100.00

2019-20 Upper Deck Premier '03-04 Premier Collection Retro Plexi Autographs

03PAB Aleksander Barkov B 40.00 100.00
03PAM Auston Matthews A 150.00 400.00
03PAP Artemi Panarin B 60.00 150.00
03PAV Andrei Vasilevskiy C 40.00 100.00
03PBH Barrett Hayton B 50.00 125.00
03PCG Cody Glass B 40.00 100.00
03PCM Cale Makar B 125.00 300.00
03PCP Carey Price B 100.00 250.00
03PHU Bobby Hull B 60.00 150.00
03PJH Jack Hughes A 150.00 400.00
03PJP Joe Pavelski C 30.00 80.00
03PKD Kirby Dach B 50.00 125.00
03PNS Nick Suzuki B 100.00 250.00
03PPK Patrick Kane B 50.00 125.00
03PSY Steve Yzerman B 80.00 200.00
03PWG Wayne Gretzky A 300.00 800.00

2019-20 Upper Deck Premier Acetate Rookie Autographs

ARAAB Adam Brooks 10.00 25.00
ARAAP Andrew Peeke 3.00 8.00
ARAAV Alexander Volkov 8.00 20.00
ARACC Connor Clifton 8.00 20.00
ARADG David Gustafsson 4.00 10.00
ARAGS Givani Smith 4.00 10.00
ARAJD Jonathan Davidsson 3.00 8.00
ARAOK Otto Koivula 3.00 8.00
ARARG Rhett Gardner 4.00 10.00

2019-20 Upper Deck Premier Acetate Rookie Autographs Gold Spectrum

*GOLD: .75X TO 2X BASIC
ARAAP Andrew Peeke 10.00 25.00

2019-20 Upper Deck Premier Acetate Rookie Horizontal Autographs

ARAT Alexandre Texier 8.00 20.00
ARBH Barrett Hayton 15.00 40.00
ARBJ Tobias Bjornfot 8.00 20.00
ARBL Blake Lizotte 8.00 20.00
ARBR Erik Brannstrom 8.00 20.00
ARCC Connor Clifton 8.00 20.00
ARCG Carl Grundstrom 8.00 20.00
ARCM Cale Makar 125.00 300.00
ARCP Cayden Primeau 15.00 40.00
ARCV Carter Verhaeghe 12.00 30.00
ARDK Dominik Kubalik 15.00 40.00
AREB Emil Bemstrom 8.00 20.00
AREM Elvis Merzlikins 25.00 60.00
ARFE Mario Ferraro 6.00 15.00
ARFZ Filip Zadina 12.00 30.00
ARGB Guillaume Brisebois 8.00 20.00
ARGL Cody Glass 30.00 80.00
ARIM Ilya Mikheyev 12.00 30.00
ARJB Jesper Boqvist 6.00 15.00
ARJG Julien Gauthier 8.00 20.00
ARJH Jack Hughes 60.00 150.00
ARKK Kaapo Kakko (No Auto) 12.00 30.00
ARKO Klim Kostin 8.00 20.00
ARKS Kole Sherwood 8.00 20.00
ARKU Karson Kuhlman 8.00 20.00
ARMF Morgan Frost 12.00 30.00
ARMJ Max Jones 8.00 20.00
ARMR Matt Roy 8.00 20.00
ARMV Max Veronneau 6.00 15.00
ARNH Nicolas Hague 8.00 20.00
ARNS Nick Suzuki 60.00 150.00
AROW Oliver Wahlstrom 12.00 30.00
ARPO Ryan Poehling 12.00 30.00
ARQH Quinn Hughes 100.00 250.00
ARRI Riley Stillman 8.00 20.00
ARRP Rem Pitlick 8.00 20.00
ARRS Rasmus Sandin 12.00 30.00
ARSL Sam Lafferty 6.00 15.00
ARTH Taro Hirose 8.00 20.00
ARTM Trevor Moore 6.00 15.00
ARVO Victor Olofsson 15.00 40.00

2019-20 Upper Deck Premier Acetate Rookie Patch Autographs

*GOLD: .75X TO 2X BASIC
ARAB Adam Boqvist/149 15.00 40.00
ARAF Adam Fox/149 30.00 80.00
ARAT Alexandre Texier/149 12.00 30.00
ARBG Brandon Gignac/249 10.00 25.00
ARBH Barrett Hayton/149 60.00 150.00
ARBJ Tobias Bjornfot/149 12.00 30.00
ARBK Brady Keeper/249 20.00 50.00
ARBR Erik Brannstrom/149 12.00 30.00
ARCG Carl Grundstrom/149 12.00 30.00
ARCM Cale Makar/99 300.00 800.00
ARCP Cayden Primeau/149 40.00 100.00
ARCV Carter Verhaeghe/149 20.00 50.00
ARDK Dominik Kubalik/149 40.00 100.00
AREB Emil Bemstrom/149 12.00 30.00
AREM Elvis Merzlikins/149 80.00 200.00
ARES Eetu Luostarinen/249 12.00 30.00
ARFE Mario Ferraro/149 10.00 25.00
ARFZ Filip Zadina/99 80.00 200.00
ARGB Guillaume Brisebois/249 12.00 30.00
ARGL Cody Glass/99 40.00 100.00
ARGR German Rubtsov/249 10.00 25.00
ARIM Ilya Mikheyev/149 25.00 60.00
ARIS Igor Shesterkin/149 120.00 300.00
ARJB Jesper Boqvist/149 10.00 25.00
ARJD Joey Daccord/249 25.00 60.00
ARJG Julien Gauthier/249 12.00 30.00
ARJH Jack Hughes/99 150.00 400.00
ARJS Jimmy Schuldt/249 10.00 25.00
ARKC Kale Clague/149 10.00 25.00
ARKD Kirby Dach/99 150.00 400.00
ARKO Klim Kostin/149 12.00 30.00
ARKS Kole Sherwood/249 12.00 30.00
ARKU Karson Kuhlman/249 12.00 30.00
ARLB Lean Bergmann/249 10.00 25.00
ARMA Martin Fehervary/249 10.00 25.00
ARMF Morgan Frost/149 20.00 50.00
ARMJ Max Jones/149 12.00 30.00
ARMM Mackenzie MacEachern/149 12.00 30.00
ARMR Matt Roy/249 12.00 30.00
ARMV Max Veronneau/249 10.00 25.00
ARNG Nikita Gusev/149 20.00 50.00
ARNH Nicolas Hague/149 12.00 30.00
ARNS Nick Suzuki/99 200.00 500.00
AROW Oliver Wahlstrom/149 20.00 50.00
ARPO Ryan Poehling/99 20.00 50.00
ARQH Quinn Hughes/99 200.00 500.00
ARRA Rasmus Asplund/149 10.00 25.00
ARRB Rudolfs Balcers/249 12.00 30.00
ARRI Riley Stillman/249 12.00 30.00
ARRK Ryan Kuffner/249 10.00 25.00
ARRP Rem Pitlick/149 12.00 30.00
ARRS Rasmus Sandin/149 30.00 80.00
ARSL Sam Lafferty/149 10.00 25.00
ARST Nico Sturm/249 10.00 25.00
ARTF Trent Frederic/149 12.00 30.00
ARTH Taro Hirose/149 12.00 30.00
ARTM Trevor Moore/149 10.00 25.00
ARVO Victor Olofsson/99 80.00 200.00

2019-20 Upper Deck Premier Acetate Stars Patch Autographs

ASAB Aleksander Barkov/49 50.00 120.00
ASAP Artemi Panarin/25 60.00 150.00
ASBP Brayden Point/49 40.00 100.00
ASCH Carter Hart/25 30.00 80.00
ASNH Nico Hischier/49 50.00 120.00

2019-20 Upper Deck Premier Autographs Silver Spectrum

2 John Tavares B 20.00 50.00
6 Ryan O'Reilly B 6.00 15.00
7 Aleksander Barkov C 10.00 25.00
8 Henrik Lundqvist B 25.00 60.00
10 Patrick Kane B 12.00 30.00
13 Auston Matthews A 150.00 400.00
20 Brent Burns C 6.00 15.00
22 Andrei Vasilevskiy C 10.00 25.00
24 Artemi Panarin C 25.00 60.00
31 Eric Staal C 6.00 15.00
34 Sergei Bobrovsky C 10.00 25.00
38 Joe Pavelski C 8.00 20.00
42 Carey Price B 12.00 30.00
46 John Carlson C 6.00 15.00
48 Tomas Hertl C 6.00 15.00
49 Anders Lee C 5.00 12.00
51 Nikita Gusev 10.00 25.00
52 Sam Lafferty 5.00 12.00
53 Erik Brannstrom 6.00 15.00
54 Tobias Bjornfot 6.00 15.00
55 Nico Sturm 5.00 12.00
56 Dominik Kubalik 12.00 30.00
57 Elvis Merzlikins 12.00 30.00
58 Oliver Wahlstrom 10.00 25.00
59 Alexandre Texier 6.00 15.00
60 Julien Gauthier 6.00 15.00
61 Carl Grundstrom 6.00 15.00
62 Trent Frederic 6.00 15.00
63 Rasmus Sandin 10.00 25.00
64 Igor Shesterkin 40.00 100.00
65 Ilya Mikheyev 10.00 25.00
66 Joey Daccord 12.00 30.00
67 Brandon Gignac 5.00 12.00
71 Emil Bemstrom 6.00 15.00
72 Brady Keeper 6.00 15.00
73 Nicolas Hague 6.00 15.00
75 Victor Olofsson 12.00 30.00
76 Martin Fehervary 5.00 12.00
78 Blake Lizotte 6.00 15.00
81 Morgan Frost 10.00 25.00
82 Taro Hirose 6.00 15.00
83 Carter Verhaeghe 10.00 25.00
85 Mario Ferraro 5.00 12.00
87 Jesper Boqvist 5.00 12.00
88 Trevor Moore 5.00 12.00
90 Max Jones 6.00 15.00
91 Kaapo Kakko (No Auto) 10.00 25.00
95 Filip Zadina 25.00 60.00
96 Nick Suzuki 25.00 60.00
97 Barrett Hayton 20.00 50.00
99 Ryan Poehling 10.00 25.00
100 Jack Hughes 60.00 150.00

2019-20 Upper Deck Premier Jerseys

1 Sidney Crosby 8.00 20.00
2 John Tavares 3.00 8.00
3 Taylor Hall 2.00 5.00
4 Steven Stamkos 4.00 10.00
5 Nathan MacKinnon 8.00 20.00
6 Ryan O'Reilly 2.00 5.00
7 Aleksander Barkov 3.00 8.00
8 Henrik Lundqvist 5.00 12.00
9 Claude Giroux 2.00 5.00
10 Patrick Kane 4.00 10.00
11 Marc-Andre Fleury 4.00 10.00
12 Drew Doughty 2.50 6.00
13 Auston Matthews 8.00 20.00
14 Roman Josi 2.00 5.00
15 John Gibson 2.00 5.00
16 David Pastrnak 5.00 12.00
17 Seth Jones 2.00 5.00
18 Jonathan Drouin 1.50 4.00
19 Leon Draisaitl 6.00 15.00
20 Brent Burns 2.00 5.00
21 Jack Eichel 3.00 8.00
22 Andrei Vasilevskiy 3.00 8.00
23 Tyler Seguin 2.50 6.00
24 Artemi Panarin 4.00 10.00
25 Alex Ovechkin 8.00 20.00
26 Jordan Binnington 3.00 8.00
27 Alex DeBrincat 2.50 6.00
28 Brad Marchand 4.00 10.00
29 Dylan Larkin 2.50 6.00
30 Elias Pettersson 3.00 8.00
31 Eric Staal 2.00 5.00
32 Mikko Rantanen 5.00 12.00
33 Mitch Marner 3.00 8.00
34 Sergei Bobrovsky 3.00 8.00
35 Blake Wheeler 2.00 5.00
36 Oliver Ekman-Larsson 2.00 5.00
37 Evgeni Malkin 4.00 10.00
38 Joe Pavelski 2.50 6.00
39 Nikita Kucherov 4.00 10.00
40 Zach Werenski 3.00 8.00
41 Thomas Chabot 2.00 5.00
42 Carey Price 4.00 10.00
43 Johnny Gaudreau 3.00 8.00
44 Mark Scheifele 3.00 8.00
45 Anthony Mantha 1.50 4.00
46 John Carlson 2.00 5.00
47 Sebastian Aho 3.00 8.00
48 Tomas Hertl 2.00 5.00
49 Anders Lee 1.50 4.00
50 Connor McDavid 10.00 25.00
51 Nikita Gusev B 3.00 8.00
52 Sam Lafferty B 1.50 4.00
53 Erik Brannstrom B 2.00 5.00
54 Tobias Bjornfot B 2.00 5.00
55 Nico Sturm B 1.50 4.00
56 Dominik Kubalik B 4.00 10.00
57 Elvis Merzlikins B 4.00 10.00
58 Oliver Wahlstrom B 3.00 8.00
59 Alexandre Texier B 2.00 5.00
60 Julien Gauthier B 2.00 5.00
61 Carl Grundstrom B 2.00 5.00
62 Trent Frederic B 2.00 5.00
63 Rasmus Sandin B 3.00 8.00
64 Igor Shesterkin B 10.00 25.00
65 Ilya Mikheyev B 3.00 8.00
66 Joey Daccord B 4.00 10.00
67 Brandon Gignac B 1.50 4.00
68 Noah Dobson B 5.00 12.00
69 Ville Heinola B 3.00 8.00
70 Connor Clifton B 2.00 5.00
71 Emil Bemstrom B 2.00 5.00
72 Brady Keeper B 2.00 5.00
73 Nicolas Hague B 2.00 5.00
74 Philippe Myers B 1.50 4.00
75 Victor Olofsson B 4.00 10.00
76 Martin Fehervary B 1.50 4.00
77 Joel L'Esperance B 2.00 5.00
78 Blake Lizotte B 2.00 5.00
79 Dante Fabbro B 2.00 5.00
80 Adam Boqvist B 2.00 5.00
81 Morgan Frost B 3.00 8.00
82 Taro Hirose B 2.00 5.00
83 Carter Verhaeghe B 3.00 8.00
84 Adam Fox B 5.00 12.00
85 Mario Ferraro B 1.50 4.00
86 Vitaly Abramov B 2.00 5.00
87 Jesper Boqvist B 1.50 4.00
88 Trevor Moore B 1.50 4.00
89 Joel Persson B 1.50 4.00
90 Max Jones B 2.00 5.00
91 Kaapo Kakko A 3.00 8.00
92 Cale Makar A 10.00 25.00
93 Quinn Hughes A 10.00 25.00
94 Kirby Dach A 4.00 10.00
95 Filip Zadina A 3.00 8.00
96 Nick Suzuki A 8.00 20.00
97 Barrett Hayton A 4.00 10.00
98 Joel Farabee A 3.00 8.00
99 Ryan Poehling A 3.00 8.00
100 Jack Hughes A 10.00 25.00

2019-20 Upper Deck Premier Jerseys Premium Materials

*PREMIUM: 1X TO 2.5X BASIC
24 Artemi Panarin/25 15.00 40.00
64 Igor Shesterkin/49 30.00 80.00
96 Nick Suzuki/49 30.00 80.00

2019-20 Upper Deck Premier Mega Patch Chest Logos

PMPAA Andreas Athanasiou/21 25.00 60.00
PMPAK Anze Kopitar/18 50.00 120.00
PMPAM Anthony Mantha/21 25.00 60.00
PMPAP Alex Pietrangelo/18 25.00 60.00
PMPAV Andrei Vasilevskiy/22 50.00 125.00
PMPBB Brent Burns/25 30.00 80.00
PMPBG Brendan Gallagher/20 30.00 80.00
PMPBH Bo Horvat/27 40.00 100.00
PMPBM Brad Marchand/23 60.00 150.00
PMPBP Brayden Point/22 40.00 100.00
PMPBS Brent Seabrook/24 20.00 50.00
PMPBT Brady Tkachuk/21 50.00 125.00
PMPCG Claude Giroux/23 30.00 80.00
PMPCH Carter Hart/23 30.00 80.00
PMPCM Charlie McAvoy/23 40.00 100.00
PMPCP Colton Parayko/18 25.00 60.00
PMPDD Drew Doughty/18 40.00 100.00
PMPDL Dylan Larkin/21 40.00 100.00
PMPDO Max Domi/20 30.00 80.00
PMPDP David Pastrnak/23 80.00 200.00
PMPDS Derek Stepan/25 20.00 50.00
PMPDU Matt Duchene/19 30.00 80.00
PMPEK Erik Karlsson/25 40.00 100.00
PMPEL Elias Lindholm/26 30.00 80.00
PMPEM Evgeni Malkin/34 60.00 150.00
PMPES Eric Staal/18 30.00 80.00
PMPEV Evgeny Kuznetsov/20 40.00 100.00
PMPFA Frederik Andersen/24 40.00 100.00
PMPFF Filip Forsberg/19 50.00 125.00
PMPGA Johnny Gaudreau/26 50.00 125.00
PMPGL Gabriel Landeskog/23 40.00 100.00
PMPGN Gustav Nyquist/22 20.00 50.00
PMPGU Jake Guentzel/34 50.00 120.00
PMPHL Henrik Lundqvist/16 80.00 200.00
PMPJC John Carlson/20 30.00 80.00
PMPJD Jonathan Drouin/20 25.00 60.00
PMPJE Jack Eichel/22 50.00 120.00
PMPJG John Gibson/22 30.00 80.00
PMPJH Jonathan Huberdeau/24 40.00 100.00
PMPJO Ryan Johansen/19 25.00 60.00
PMPJP Joe Pavelski/21 40.00 100.00
PMPJQ Jonathan Quick/18 40.00 100.00
PMPJV Jakub Vrana/20 30.00 80.00
PMPKA Evander Kane/25 30.00 80.00
PMPKI Alex Killorn/22 20.00 50.00
PMPKL Kris Letang/34 40.00 100.00
PMPKP Kyle Palmieri/28 25.00 60.00
PMPKU Nikita Kucherov/22 60.00 150.00
PMPKY Keith Yandle/24 20.00 50.00
PMPLD Leon Draisaitl/22 100.00 250.00
PMPMA Mitch Marner/24 50.00 125.00
PMPMB Mathew Barzal/22 40.00 100.00
PMPMC Connor McDavid/22 150.00 400.00
PMPMD Matt Dumba/18 20.00 50.00
PMPMG Mark Giordano/24 30.00 80.00
PMPMK Mikko Koskinen/22 20.00 50.00
PMPMM Matt Murray/34 30.00 80.00
PMPMR Mikko Rantanen/31 80.00 200.00
PMPMS Mark Scheifele/22 50.00 125.00
PMPMT Matthew Tkachuk/26 60.00 150.00
PMPMZ Mats Zuccarello/18 30.00 80.00
PMPNE Nikolaj Ehlers/22 30.00 80.00
PMPNH Nico Hischier/28 50.00 120.00
PMPNK Nazem Kadri/31 40.00 100.00
PMPNM Nathan MacKinnon/31 125.00 300.00
PMPNN Nino Niederreiter/22 20.00 50.00
PMPOK Ondrej Kase/22 20.00 50.00
PMPPB Pavel Buchnevich/15 25.00 60.00
PMPPL Patrik Laine/22 40.00 100.00
PMPPS P.K. Subban/28 40.00 100.00
PMPRD Rasmus Dahlin/22 40.00 100.00
PMPRI Morgan Rielly/24 30.00 80.00
PMPRJ Roman Josi/19 30.00 80.00
PMPRO Ryan O'Reilly/18 30.00 80.00
PMPRT Robert Thomas/18 30.00 80.00
PMPSA Sebastian Aho/22 50.00 125.00
PMPSC Sean Couturier/23 25.00 60.00
PMPSJ Seth Jones/22 30.00 80.00
PMPSM Sean Monahan/26 20.00 50.00
PMPSS Steven Stamkos/22 60.00 150.00
PMPST Mark Stone/23 40.00 100.00
PMPSV Semyon Varlamov/22 30.00 80.00
PMPSW Shea Weber/20 30.00 80.00
PMPTA Vladimir Tarasenko/18 40.00 100.00
PMPTB Tyler Bertuzzi/21 25.00 60.00
PMPTD Thatcher Demko/25 40.00 100.00
PMPTH Tomas Hertl/25 30.00 80.00
PMPTJ John Tavares/24 50.00 125.00
PMPTK Travis Konecny/23 30.00 80.00
PMPTM Timo Meier/25 30.00 80.00
PMPTR Jacob Trouba/16 25.00 60.00
PMPTS Tyler Seguin/21 40.00 100.00
PMPTT Teuvo Teravainen/21 30.00 80.00
PMPVA Viktor Arvidsson/19 20.00 50.00
PMPVH Victor Hedman/22 40.00 100.00
PMPVT Vincent Trocheck/24 30.00 80.00
PMPZI Mika Zibanejad/16 40.00 100.00
PMPZP Zach Parise/18 30.00 80.00

2019-20 Upper Deck Premier Memorable Premieres Jerseys

MPAB Aleksander Barkov C 3.00 8.00
MPAK Anze Kopitar C 3.00 8.00
MPAM Auston Matthews A 8.00 20.00
MPAO Alex Ovechkin A 8.00 20.00
MPAP Artemi Panarin C 4.00 10.00
MPAV Andrei Vasilevskiy C 3.00 8.00
MPBB Brock Boeser B 2.50 6.00
MPCG Cody Glass C 3.00 8.00
MPCH Carter Hart B 2.00 5.00
MPCM Cale Makar B 10.00 25.00
MPCP Carey Price A 4.00 10.00
MPDL Dylan Larkin C 2.50 6.00
MPDS Derek Stepan C 1.25 3.00
MPEP Elias Pettersson A 3.00 8.00
MPGU Jake Guentzel C 3.00 8.00
MPIS Igor Shesterkin B 8.00 20.00
MPJE Jack Eichel B 3.00 8.00
MPJG John Gibson C 2.00 5.00
MPJH Jonathan Huberdeau C 2.50 6.00
MPJT Jonathan Toews A 3.00 8.00
MPMC Connor McDavid A 10.00 25.00
MPMF Morgan Frost C 3.00 8.00
MPMM Matt Murray B 2.00 5.00
MPNK Nikita Kucherov B 4.00 10.00
MPNM Nathan MacKinnon A 8.00 20.00
MPPK Patrick Kane A 4.00 10.00
MPRP Ryan Poehling C 3.00 8.00
MPSC Sidney Crosby A 15.00 40.00
MPTA John Tavares A 3.00 8.00
MPVT Vladimir Tarasenko C 2.50 6.00

2019-20 Upper Deck Premier Premier Attractions Patch Autographs

PAAL Anders Lee/99 8.00 20.00
PAAS Andrei Svechnikov/99 30.00 80.00
PACH Connor Hellebuyck/99 20.00 50.00
PACP Carey Price/25 20.00 50.00
PAJT Joe Thornton/25 15.00 40.00
PAPR Pekka Rinne/99 12.00 30.00

2019-20 Upper Deck Premier Premier Attractions Rookie Patch Autographs

PAAT Alexandre Texier/99 20.00 50.00
PABE Emil Bemstrom/99 8.00 20.00
PABH Barrett Hayton/99 15.00 40.00
PABL Blake Lizotte/99 8.00 20.00
PACG Cody Glass/49 40.00 100.00
PACM Cale Makar/49 120.00 300.00
PADK Dominik Kubalik/99 40.00 100.00
PAEB Erik Brannstrom/99 20.00 50.00
PAFR Morgan Frost/49 30.00 80.00
PAIM Ilya Mikheyev/99 12.00 30.00
PAJB Jesper Boqvist/99 6.00 15.00
PAJH Jack Hughes/49 100.00 250.00
PAKK Kaapo Kakko/25 (No Auto) 12.00 30.00
PAMJ Max Jones/49 8.00 20.00
PANG Nikita Gusev/99 12.00 30.00
PANS Nick Suzuki/49 80.00 200.00
PAOW Oliver Wahlstrom/99 15.00 40.00
PAQH Quinn Hughes/49 150.00 400.00
PARP Ryan Poehling/49 12.00 30.00
PARS Rasmus Sandin/99 20.00 50.00
PATB Tobias Bjornfot/99 8.00 20.00
PATH Taro Hirose/99 8.00 20.00
PATM Trevor Moore/99 6.00 15.00
PAVO Victor Olofsson/99 25.00 60.00

2019-20 Upper Deck Premier Premier Duals Jerseys

PDAD P.Dubois/C.Atkinson 5.00 12.00
PDBB B.Bishop/J.Benn 5.00 12.00
PDBP B.Boeser/E.Pettersson 8.00 20.00
PDCM B.Marchand/Z.Chara 10.00 25.00
PDDB A.Boqvist/K.Dach 8.00 20.00
PDDW O.Wahlstrom/N.Dobson 6.00 15.00
PDFF M.Frost/J.Farabee 8.00 20.00
PDGB J.Boqvist/N.Gusev 6.00 15.00
PDGM S.Monahan/M.Giordano 5.00 12.00
PDGS R.Getzlaf/J.Silfverberg 5.00 12.00
PDHC C.Hellebuyck/K.Connor 8.00 20.00
PDHE J.Huberdeau/A.Ekblad 6.00 15.00
PDHG N.Hague/C.Glass 8.00 20.00
PDHH Q.Hughes/J.Hughes 25.00 60.00
PDHK V.Hedman/N.Kucherov 6.00 15.00
PDLN L.Draisaitl/D.Nurse 8.00 20.00
PDLZ H.Lundqvist/M.Zibanejad 6.00 15.00
PDMF A.Fox/C.Makar 20.00 50.00
PDMG J.Guentzel/M.Murray 8.00 20.00
PDML D.Larkin/A.Mantha 6.00 15.00
PDOH A.Ovechkin/B.Holtby 10.00 25.00
PDPB A.Pietrangelo/J.Binnington 12.00 30.00
PDPK Z.Parise/M.Koivu 5.00 12.00
PDRE J.Eichel/S.Reinhart 4.00 10.00
PDRJ R.Josi/P.Rinne 5.00 12.00
PDTA S.Aho/T.Teravainen 8.00 20.00
PDTB B.Burns/J.Thornton 8.00 20.00
PDTM A.Matthews/J.Tavares 12.00 30.00
PDTT M.Tkachuk/B.Tkachuk 8.00 20.00
PDWP S.Weber/C.Price 10.00 25.00

2019-20 Upper Deck Premier Premier Quads Jerseys

PQAVS Sakic/Forsberg MacKinnon/Makar 25.00 60.00
PQBOS Marchand/McAvoy Bergeron/Pastrnak 20.00 50.00
PQCAL Gilmour/Iginla Gaudreau/Giordano 12.00 30.00
PQCHI Keith/Crawford/Shaw/Seabrook 8.0020.00
PQGOL Gibson/Fleury Lundqvist/Rask 20.00 50.00
PQNOR Giordano/Hedman Burns/Doughty 10.00 25.00
PQNYR Messier/Gretzky Jagr/Lundqvist 40.00 100.00
PQRCS Farabee/Dach/Glass/Suzuki 15.00 40.00
PQROO Hayton/Farabee Dobson/Olofsson 20.00 50.00
PQSJS Nolan/Nabokov Marleau/Thornton 12.00 30.00
PQTOR Nylander/Marner Rielly/Tavares 15.00 40.00
PQVAN Pettersson/Boeser Horvat/Hughes 15.00 40.00
PQVEZ Vasilevskiy/Rinne Holtby/Price 15.00 40.00
PQVGS Tuch/Marchessault Stastny/Theodore 20.00 50.00

2019-20 Upper Deck Premier Premier Rookie Backdrop Swatches

SSAB Adam Boqvist 2.50 6.00
SSAF Adam Fox 6.00 15.00
SSAT Alexandre Texier 2.50 6.00
SSBH Barrett Hayton 5.00 12.00
SSBR Erik Brannstrom 2.50 6.00
SSCG Cody Glass 4.00 10.00
SSCM Cale Makar 12.00 30.00
SSDF Dante Fabbro 2.50 6.00
SSDK Dominik Kubalik 5.00 12.00
SSEB Emil Bemstrom 2.50 6.00
SSFZ Filip Zadina 4.00 10.00
SSIM Ilya Mikheyev 4.00 10.00
SSIS Igor Shesterkin 10.00 25.00
SSJF Joel Farabee 4.00 10.00
SSJH Jack Hughes 12.00 30.00
SSKD Kirby Dach 5.00 12.00
SSKK Klim Kostin 2.50 6.00
SSMF Morgan Frost 4.00 10.00
SSMJ Max Jones 2.50 6.00
SSND Noah Dobson 6.00 15.00
SSNG Nikita Gusev 4.00 10.00
SSNH Nicolas Hague 2.50 6.00
SSNS Nick Suzuki 15.00 40.00
SSOW Oliver Wahlstrom 4.00 10.00
SSPM Philippe Myers 2.00 5.00
SSQH Quinn Hughes 12.00 30.00
SSRP Ryan Poehling 4.00 10.00
SSRS Rasmus Sandin 4.00 10.00
SSTB Tobias Bjornfot 2.50 6.00
SSTH Taro Hirose 2.50 6.00
SSTM Trevor Moore 2.00 5.00
SSVH Ville Heinola 6.00 15.00
SSVO Victor Olofsson 5.00 12.00

2019-20 Upper Deck Premier Premier Swatches

PSAB Aleksander Barkov 4.00 10.00
PSAK Anze Kopitar 4.00 10.00
PSAM Auston Matthews 10.00 25.00
PSAO Alex Ovechkin 10.00 25.00
PSAS Andrei Svechnikov 3.00 8.00
PSAV Andrei Vasilevskiy 4.00 10.00
PSBM Brad Marchand 5.00 12.00
PSBW Blake Wheeler 2.50 6.00
PSCH Connor Hellebuyck 5.00 12.00
PSCM Connor McDavid 12.00 30.00
PSDP David Pastrnak 6.00 15.00
PSEM Evgeni Malkin 5.00 12.00
PSEP Elias Pettersson 4.00 10.00
PSHL Henrik Lundqvist 6.00 15.00
PSJB Jordan Binnington 5.00 12.00
PSJC John Carlson 2.50 6.00
PSJE Jack Eichel 4.00 10.00
PSJT John Tavares 6.00 15.00
PSLC Logan Couture 3.00 8.00
PSLD Leon Draisaitl 6.00 15.00
PSMB Mathew Barzal 3.00 8.00
PSMF Marc-Andre Fleury 8.00 20.00
PSMM Mitch Marner 4.00 10.00
PSMT Matthew Tkachuk 5.00 12.00
PSNH Nico Hischier 4.00 10.00
PSNK Nikita Kucherov 5.00 12.00
PSNM Nathan MacKinnon 10.00 25.00
PSPB Patrice Bergeron 3.00 8.00
PSPK Patrick Kane 5.00 12.00
PSRD Rasmus Dahlin 3.00 8.00
PSRJ Roman Josi 2.50 6.00
PSSC Sidney Crosby 10.00 25.00
PSSS Steven Stamkos 5.00 12.00
PSTS Tyler Seguin 3.00 8.00
PSWN William Nylander 5.00 12.00

2019-20 Upper Deck Premier Premier Swatches Premium

*PREMIUM: 1X TO 2.5X BASIC
PSAK Anze Kopitar/25 12.00 30.00
PSHL Henrik Lundqvist/25 20.00 50.00
PSPB Patrice Bergeron/25 12.00 30.00
PSRD Rasmus Dahlin/25 20.00 50.00
PSWN William Nylander/25 15.00 40.00

2019-20 Upper Deck Premier Premier Trios Jerseys

PTANA Gibson/Getzlaf/Silfverberg 8.00 20.00
PTBLK Kane/Strome/DeBrincat 10.00 25.00
PTBLU Binnington Pietrangelo/O'Reilly 12.00 30.00
PTBRU Rask/Marchand/Chara 8.00 20.00
PTBUF Dahlin/Eichel/Reinhart 8.00 20.00
PTCBR Dach/Kubalik/Boqvist 40.00 100.00
PTDAL Seguin/Radulov/Benn 10.00 25.00
PTDEV Hughes/Hischier/Gusev 20.00 50.00
PTFLY Hart/Voracek/Konecny 8.00 20.00
PTHUR Svechnikov/Aho/Hamilton 8.00 20.00
PTISL Barzal/Lee/Nelson 10.00 25.00
PTMTL Domi/Weber/Gallagher 8.00 20.00
PTNSH Rinne/Josi/Ellis 8.00 20.00
PTNYR Lundqvist Buchnevich/Zibanejad 20.00 50.00
PTOHM Olofsson/Hughes/Makar 20.00 50.00
PTPEN Murray/Letang/Hornqvist 10.00 25.00
PTSJS Burns/Couture/Thornton 12.00 30.00
PTTOR Matthews/Rielly/Andersen 30.00 80.00
PTVAN Pettersson/Horvat/Boeser 10.00 25.00

2019-20 Upper Deck Premier Pursuing Greatness Signatures

PGAB Aleksander Barkov/49 25.00 60.00
PGCG Cody Glass/25 50.00 125.00
PGNH Nico Hischier/25 25.00 60.00
PGVO Victor Olofsson/49 15.00 40.00

2019-20 Upper Deck Premier Signature Award Winners

SAAP Artemi Panarin/25 25.00 60.00
SAAV Andrei Vasilevskiy/25 25.00 60.00
SABR Bill Ranford/49 20.00 50.00
SACJ Curtis Joseph/25 30.00 80.00
SACN Cam Neely/25 25.00 60.00
SADG Dirk Graham/49 20.00 50.00
SAGF Grant Fuhr/49 20.00 50.00
SARO Ryan O'Reilly/25 25.00 60.00
SASB Sergei Bobrovsky/25 40.00 100.00

2019-20 Upper Deck Premier Signature Champions

SCBB Bill Barber/49 10.00 25.00
SCDG Doug Gilmour/25 25.00 60.00
SCES Eric Staal/49 15.00 40.00
SCMR Mark Recchi/49 20.00 50.00
SCTW Tom Wilson/49 20.00 50.00
SCYC Yvan Cournoyer/49 20.00 50.00

2020-21 Upper Deck Premier

*GOLD VET/65: X TO X BASIC CARDS
*GOLD RC/65: X TO X BASIC CARDS
1 Connor McDavid 5.00 12.00
2 Carter Hart 1.00 2.50
3 Quinn Hughes 2.50 6.00
4 Matthew Tkachuk 2.00 5.00
5 Andrei Vasilevskiy 1.50 4.00
6 Clayton Keller 1.25 3.00
7 Logan Couture 1.25 3.00
8 Mikko Rantanen 2.50 6.00
9 J.T. Miller 1.25 3.00
10 Auston Matthews 4.00 10.00
11 Alex DeBrincat 1.25 3.00
12 David Pastrnak 2.50 6.00
13 Aleksander Barkov 1.50 4.00
14 Evgeni Malkin 2.00 5.00
15 David Perron .75 2.00
16 Victor Olofsson 1.00 2.50
17 Mark Scheifele 1.50 4.00
18 Elias Lindholm 1.00 2.50
19 Steven Stamkos 2.00 5.00
20 Jonathan Drouin .75 2.00
21 Patrick Kane 2.00 5.00
22 Artemi Panarin 2.00 5.00
23 Anthony Mantha .75 2.00
24 Cam Atkinson 1.00 2.50
25 Miro Heiskanen 1.25 3.00
26 Leon Draisaitl 3.00 8.00
27 Dougie Hamilton .75 2.00
28 Nikolaj Ehlers 1.00 2.50
29 John Gibson 1.00 2.50
30 Pavel Buchnevich .75 2.00
31 Maxime Comtois .75 2.00
32 Tomas Hertl 1.00 2.50
33 Mitch Marner 1.50 4.00
34 Mathew Barzal 1.25 3.00
35 Anze Kopitar 1.50 4.00
36 Mackenzie Blackwood 1.00 2.50
37 Jack Eichel 1.50 4.00
38 Dylan Larkin 1.25 3.00
39 Brad Marchand 2.00 5.00
40 Brayden Schenn 1.00 2.50
41 Jonathan Huberdeau 1.25 3.00
42 Roman Josi 1.00 2.50
43 Ryan Suter .75 2.00
44 Brady Tkachuk 1.50 4.00
45 Nathan MacKinnon 4.00 10.00
46 Anders Lee .75 2.00
47 Mark Stone 1.25 3.00
48 Tyler Toffoli 1.00 2.50
49 Alex Ovechkin 4.00 10.00
50 Sidney Crosby 4.00 10.00
51 Kirill Kaprizov RC 12.00 30.00
52 Connor McMichael RC 5.00 12.00
53 Josh Norris RC 5.00 12.00
54 Kevin Lankinen RC 5.00 12.00
55 Nick Robertson RC 5.00 12.00
56 Joel Kiviranta RC 3.00 8.00
57 Gabe Vilardi RC 5.00 12.00
58 Philipp Kurashev RC 4.00 10.00
59 Thomas Harley RC 5.00 12.00
60 Bowen Byram RC 6.00 15.00
61 Philip Broberg RC 3.00 8.00
62 K'Andre Miller RC 6.00 15.00
63 Vitek Vanecek RC 5.00 12.00
64 Pius Suter RC 4.00 10.00
65 Vitali Kravtsov RC 6.00 15.00
66 Nicolas Beaudin RC 3.00 8.00
67 Ian Mitchell RC 2.50 6.00
68 Liam Foudy RC 3.00 8.00
69 Jason Robertson RC 8.00 20.00
70 Dylan Cozens RC 5.00 12.00
71 Alec Regula RC 2.00 5.00
72 Michael DiPietro RC 4.00 10.00
73 Pavel Francouz RC 4.00 10.00
74 Ty Dellandrea RC 3.00 8.00
75 Tim Stutzle RC 6.00 15.00
76 Jake Oettinger RC 8.00 20.00
77 Cal Foote RC 4.00 10.00
78 Martin Kaut RC 3.00 8.00
79 Mathias Brome RC 2.50 6.00
80 Alexander Romanov RC 4.00 10.00
81 Tyler Benson RC 3.00 8.00
82 Yegor Sharangovich RC 5.00 12.00
83 Olli Juolevi RC 3.00 8.00
84 Aleksi Heponiemi RC 4.00 10.00
85 Ilya Sorokin RC 8.00 20.00
86 Egor Zamula RC 2.50 6.00
87 Victor Soderstrom RC 2.50 6.00
88 Logan Stanley RC 3.00 8.00
89 Jake Evans RC 3.00 8.00
90 Nils Hoglander RC 3.00 8.00
91 Kieffer Bellows RC 2.50 6.00
92 Pierre-Olivier Joseph RC 3.00 8.00
93 Morgan Geekie RC 3.00 8.00
94 Timothy Liljegren RC 3.00 8.00
95 Sasha Chmelevski RC 2.50 6.00
96 Peyton Krebs RC 5.00 12.00
97 Ty Smith RC 5.00 12.00
98 Arthur Kaliyev RC 5.00 12.00
99 Alexander Alexeyev RC 2.50 6.00
100 Alexis Lafreniere RC 10.00 25.00

2020-21 Upper Deck Premier Acetate Rookie Horizontal Autographs

*GOLD/25: .75X TO 1.5X BASIC INSERTS
AHRAK Arthur Kaliyev 15.00 40.00
AHRAL Alexis Lafreniere 30.00 80.00
AHRAR Alexander Romanov 12.00 30.00
AHRBB Bowen Byram 20.00 50.00
AHRCM Connor McMichael 15.00 40.00
AHRDC Dylan Cozens 15.00 40.00
AHRIM Ian Mitchell 8.00 20.00
AHRIS Ilya Sorokin 25.00 60.00
AHRJO Jake Oettinger 25.00 60.00
AHRKK Kirill Kaprizov 40.00 100.00
AHRKM K'Andre Miller 20.00 50.00
AHRLF Liam Foudy 10.00 25.00
AHRNH Nils Hoglander 10.00 25.00
AHRNR Nick Robertson 15.00 40.00
AHROJ Olli Juolevi 10.00 25.00
AHRPK Peyton Krebs 15.00 40.00
AHRPS Pius Suter 12.00 30.00
AHRSC Sasha Chmelevski 8.00 20.00
AHRTS Tim Stutzle 20.00 50.00
AHRTY Ty Smith 15.00 40.00
AHRVV Vitek Vanecek 15.00 40.00
AHRYS Yegor Sharangovich 15.00 40.00

2020-21 Upper Deck Premier Acetate Rookie Patch Autographs

*GOLD/35-65: .5X TO 1.2X BASIC
ARAA Alexander Alexeyev 12.00 30.00
ARAB Alex Belzile 12.00 30.00
ARAK Arthur Kaliyev 25.00 60.00
ARAL Alexis Lafreniere 50.00 125.00
ARAN Anthony Angello 12.00 30.00
ARAR Alexander Romanov 20.00 50.00
ARAT Alexander True 12.00 30.00
ARBA Alexander Barabanov 15.00 40.00
ARBB Bowen Byram 30.00 80.00
ARCF Cal Foote 20.00 50.00
ARCM Connor McMichael 25.00 60.00
ARCP Chase Priskie 12.00 30.00
ARCT Calvin Thurkauf 12.00 30.00
ARDC Dylan Cozens 25.00 60.00
ARGL Gustav Lindstrom 12.00 30.00
ARGQ Gage Quinney 10.00 25.00
ARGS Gilles Senn 12.00 30.00
ARHO Joel Hofer 15.00 40.00
ARIS Ilya Sorokin 40.00 100.00
ARJE Jake Evans 15.00 40.00
ARJH Jani Hakanpaa 10.00 25.00
ARJJ Jonas Johansson 15.00 40.00
ARJL John Leonard 12.00 30.00
ARJN Josh Norris 25.00 60.00
ARJO Jake Oettinger 40.00 100.00
ARJR Jack Rathbone 15.00 40.00
ARKB Kieffer Bellows 12.00 30.00
ARKK Kirill Kaprizov 60.00 150.00
ARKM K'Andre Miller 30.00 80.00
ARKU Philipp Kurashev 20.00 50.00
ARLC Lucas Carlsson 12.00 30.00
ARLF Liam Foudy 15.00 40.00
ARMA Mikey Anderson 15.00 40.00
ARMI Ian Mitchell 12.00 30.00
ARMK Martin Kaut 15.00 40.00
ARML Maxim Letunov 12.00 30.00
ARNF Nolan Foote 15.00 40.00
ARNH Nils Hoglander 15.00 40.00
ARNK Nikolai Knyzhov 12.00 30.00
ARNR Nick Robertson 25.00 60.00
AROC Drew O'Connor 15.00 40.00
AROJ Olli Juolevi 15.00 40.00
ARPF Pavel Francouz 20.00 50.00
ARPJ Pierre-Olivier Joseph 15.00 40.00
ARPK Peyton Krebs 25.00 60.00
ARPS Pius Suter 20.00 50.00
ARRD Reid Duke 15.00 40.00
ARRE Alec Regula 10.00 25.00
ARRO Jason Robertson 400.00 1000.00
ARSC Sasha Chmelevski 12.00 30.00
ARSL Steven Lorentz 12.00 30.00
ARTD Ty Dellandrea 15.00 40.00
ARTS Tim Stutzle 30.00 80.00
ARTY Ty Smith 25.00 60.00
ARVV Vitek Vanecek 25.00 60.00
ARYS Yegor Sharangovich 25.00 60.00

2020-21 Upper Deck Premier Acetate Stars Patch Autographs

AVAL Anders Lee 15.00 40.00
AVBB Brent Burns 20.00 50.00
AVBO Brock Boeser 25.00 60.00
AVBS Brayden Schenn 20.00 50.00
AVBT Brady Tkachuk 30.00 80.00
AVCA Cam Atkinson 20.00 50.00
AVCH Connor Hellebuyck 40.00 100.00
AVCM Cale Makar 50.00 125.00
AVDP David Perron 15.00 40.00
AVDS Dylan Strome 25.00 60.00
AVJA Jacob Markstrom 20.00 50.00
AVJG John Gibson 20.00 50.00
AVJH Jonathan Huberdeau 25.00 60.00
AVJM J.T. Miller 25.00 60.00
AVJP Joe Pavelski 25.00 60.00
AVMP Max Pacioretty 20.00 50.00
AVMS Mark Scheifele 30.00 80.00
AVMT Matthew Tkachuk 40.00 100.00
AVNE Nikolaj Ehlers 20.00 50.00
AVRS Ryan Suter 15.00 40.00
AVRT Robert Thomas 20.00 50.00
AVSB Sergei Bobrovsky 30.00 80.00
AVSR Sam Reinhart 40.00 100.00

2020-21 Upper Deck Premier Autographs Silver Spectrum

*GOLD/10-35: .75X TO 2X BASIC INSERTS
1 Connor McDavid 40.00 100.00
4 Matthew Tkachuk 15.00 40.00
9 J.T. Miller 10.00 25.00
10 Auston Matthews 30.00 80.00
15 David Perron 6.00 15.00
17 Mark Scheifele 12.00 30.00
18 Elias Lindholm 8.00 20.00
24 Cam Atkinson 8.00 20.00
25 Miro Heiskanen 10.00 25.00
26 Leon Draisaitl 25.00 60.00
27 Dougie Hamilton 6.00 15.00
28 Nikolaj Ehlers 8.00 20.00
29 John Gibson 8.00 20.00
30 Pavel Buchnevich 6.00 15.00
31 Maxime Comtois 6.00 15.00
32 Tomas Hertl 8.00 20.00

39 Brad Marchand 15.00 40.00
40 Brayden Schenn 8.00 20.00
41 Jonathan Huberdeau 10.00 25.00
43 Ryan Suter 6.00 15.00
44 Brady Tkachuk 12.00 30.00
46 Anders Lee 6.00 15.00
51 Kirill Kaprizov 40.00 100.00
55 Nick Robertson 15.00 40.00
58 Philipp Kurashev 12.00 30.00
60 Bowen Byram 20.00 50.00
62 K'Andre Miller 20.00 50.00
63 Vitek Vanecek 15.00 40.00
64 Pius Suter 12.00 30.00
67 Ian Mitchell 8.00 20.00
68 Liam Foudy 10.00 25.00
69 Jason Robertson 25.00 60.00
71 Alec Regula 6.00 15.00
73 Pavel Francouz 12.00 30.00
74 Ty Dellandrea 10.00 25.00
75 Tim Stutzle 60.00 150.00
76 Jake Oettinger 25.00 60.00
77 Cal Foote 12.00 30.00
78 Martin Kaut 10.00 25.00
82 Yegor Sharangovich 15.00 40.00
83 Olli Juolevi 10.00 25.00
85 Ilya Sorokin 25.00 60.00
89 Jake Evans 10.00 25.00
90 Nils Hoglander 10.00 25.00
91 Kieffer Bellows 8.00 20.00
92 Pierre-Olivier Joseph 10.00 25.00
95 Sasha Chmelevski 8.00 20.00
97 Ty Smith 15.00 40.00
98 Arthur Kaliyev 15.00 40.00
99 Alexander Alexeyev 8.00 20.00
100 Alexis Lafreniere 30.00 80.00

2020-21 Upper Deck Premier Jerseys

*PREMIUM/25-49: .75X TO 2X BASIC INSERTS
1 Connor McDavid 8.00 20.00
2 Carter Hart 1.50 4.00
3 Quinn Hughes 4.00 10.00
4 Matthew Tkachuk 3.00 8.00
5 Andrei Vasilevskiy 2.50 6.00
6 Clayton Keller 2.00 5.00
7 Logan Couture 2.00 5.00
8 Mikko Rantanen 4.00 10.00
9 J.T. Miller 2.00 5.00
10 Auston Matthews 6.00 15.00
11 Alex DeBrincat 2.00 5.00
12 David Pastrnak 4.00 10.00
13 Aleksander Barkov 2.50 6.00
14 Evgeni Malkin 3.00 8.00
15 David Perron 1.25 3.00
16 Victor Olofsson 1.50 4.00
17 Mark Scheifele 2.50 6.00
18 Elias Lindholm 1.50 4.00
19 Steven Stamkos 3.00 8.00
20 Jonathan Drouin 1.25 3.00
21 Patrick Kane 3.00 8.00
22 Artemi Panarin 3.00 8.00
23 Anthony Mantha 1.25 3.00
24 Cam Atkinson 1.50 4.00
25 Miro Heiskanen 2.00 5.00
26 Leon Draisaitl 5.00 12.00
27 Dougie Hamilton 1.25 3.00
28 Nikolaj Ehlers 1.50 4.00
29 John Gibson 1.50 4.00
30 Pavel Buchnevich 1.25 3.00
31 Maxime Comtois 1.25 3.00
32 Tomas Hertl 1.50 4.00
33 Mitch Marner 2.50 6.00
34 Mathew Barzal 2.00 5.00
35 Anze Kopitar 2.50 6.00
36 Mackenzie Blackwood 1.50 4.00
37 Jack Eichel 2.50 6.00
38 Dylan Larkin 2.00 5.00
39 Brad Marchand 3.00 8.00
40 Brayden Schenn 1.50 4.00
41 Jonathan Huberdeau 2.00 5.00
42 Roman Josi 1.50 4.00
43 Ryan Suter 1.25 3.00
44 Brady Tkachuk 2.50 6.00
45 Nathan MacKinnon 6.00 15.00
46 Anders Lee 1.25 3.00
47 Mark Stone 2.00 5.00
48 Tyler Toffoli 1.50 4.00
49 Alex Ovechkin 6.00 15.00
50 Sidney Crosby 6.00 15.00
51 Kirill Kaprizov 8.00 20.00
52 Connor McMichael 3.00 8.00
53 Josh Norris 3.00 8.00
54 Kevin Lankinen 3.00 8.00
55 Nick Robertson 3.00 8.00
56 Joel Kiviranta 2.00 5.00
57 Gabe Vilardi 3.00 8.00
58 Philipp Kurashev 2.50 6.00
59 Thomas Harley 3.00 8.00
60 Bowen Byram 4.00 10.00
61 Philip Broberg 2.00 5.00
62 K'Andre Miller 4.00 10.00
63 Vitek Vanecek 3.00 8.00
64 Pius Suter 2.50 6.00
65 Vitali Kravtsov 4.00 10.00
66 Nicolas Beaudin 2.00 5.00
67 Ian Mitchell 1.50 4.00
68 Liam Foudy 2.00 5.00
69 Jason Robertson 5.00 12.00
70 Dylan Cozens 3.00 8.00
71 Alec Regula 1.25 3.00
72 Michael DiPietro 2.50 6.00
73 Pavel Francouz 2.50 6.00
74 Ty Dellandrea 2.00 5.00
75 Tim Stutzle 4.00 10.00
76 Jake Oettinger 5.00 12.00
77 Cal Foote 2.50 6.00
78 Martin Kaut 2.00 5.00
79 Mathias Brome 1.50 4.00
80 Alexander Romanov 2.50 6.00
81 Tyler Benson 2.00 5.00
82 Yegor Sharangovich 3.00 8.00
83 Olli Juolevi 2.00 5.00
84 Aleksi Heponiemi 2.50 6.00
85 Ilya Sorokin 5.00 12.00
86 Egor Zamula 1.50 4.00
87 Victor Soderstrom 1.50 4.00
88 Logan Stanley 2.00 5.00
89 Jake Evans 2.00 5.00
90 Nils Hoglander 2.00 5.00
91 Kieffer Bellows 1.50 4.00
92 Pierre-Olivier Joseph 2.00 5.00
93 Morgan Geekie 2.00 5.00
94 Timothy Liljegren 2.00 5.00
95 Sasha Chmelevski 1.50 4.00
96 Peyton Krebs 3.00 8.00
97 Ty Smith 3.00 8.00
98 Arthur Kaliyev 3.00 8.00
99 Alexander Alexeyev 1.50 4.00
100 Alexis Lafreniere 6.00 15.00

2020-21 Upper Deck Premier Mega Jersey Duos

*PATCH/25: .6X TO 1.5X BASIC INSERTS
PM2AB Cam Atkinson
Oliver Bjorkstrand 5.00 12.00
PM2BB Brock Boeser
Bo Horvat 6.00 15.00
PM2BT Brady Tkachuk
Connor Brown 8.00 20.00
PM2CH Logan Couture
Tomas Hertl 6.00 15.00
PM2CO Alex Ovechkin
John Carlson 20.00 50.00
PM2DF Filip Forsberg
Matt Duchene 8.00 20.00
PM2EO Jack Eichel
Victor Olofsson 8.00 20.00
PM2GL Elias Lindholm
Mark Giordano 5.00 12.00
PM2HB Jonathan Huberdeau
Aleksander Barkov 8.00 20.00
PM2ML Evgeni Malkin
Kris Letang 10.00 25.00
PM2ND Leon Draisaitl
Darnell Nurse 15.00 40.00
PM2PB Joe Pavelski
Jamie Benn 6.00 15.00
PM2SS Jordan Staal
Andrei Svechnikov 6.00 15.00
PM2TM John Tavares
Auston Matthews 20.00 50.00
PM2WP Shea Weber
Carey Price 10.00 25.00

2020-21 Upper Deck Premier Mega Jersey Trios

PM3ELB Jordan Eberle
Mathew Barzal
Anders Lee 8.00 20.00
PM3GDK Jesperi Kotkaniemi
Jonathan Drouin
Brendan Gallagher 6.00 15.00
PM3KSD Patrick Kane
Alex DeBrincat
Dylan Strome 12.00 30.00
PM3LMR Mikko Rantanen
Nathan MacKinnon
Gabriel Landeskog 25.00 60.00
PM3OBP Ryan O'Reilly
Colton Parayko
Jordan Binnington 10.00 25.00
PM3VGC Claude Giroux
Sean Couturier
Jakub Voracek 6.00 15.00
PM3WSE Blake Wheeler
Mark Scheifele
Nikolaj Ehlers 10.00 25.00

2020-21 Upper Deck Premier Premier Attractions Jerseys

*PATCH/35: .75X TO 2X BASIC INSERTS
PAAK Anze Kopitar 3.00 8.00
PAAM Auston Matthews 8.00 20.00
PAAO Alex Ovechkin 8.00 20.00
PAAP Artemi Panarin 4.00 10.00
PACH Connor Hellebuyck 4.00 10.00
PACM Connor McDavid 10.00 25.00
PACO Sean Couturier 1.50 4.00
PACP Carey Price 4.00 10.00
PADL Dylan Larkin 2.50 6.00
PAEK Evander Kane 2.00 5.00
PAEP Elias Pettersson 3.00 8.00
PAFF Filip Forsberg 3.00 8.00
PAGA Johnny Gaudreau 3.00 8.00
PAHU Jonathan Huberdeau 2.50 6.00
PAJB Jordan Binnington 3.00 8.00
PAJE Jack Eichel 3.00 8.00
PAJG Jordan Greenway 1.50 4.00
PAJH Jack Hughes 5.00 12.00
PAJK John Klingberg 2.00 5.00
PAMB Mathew Barzal 2.50 6.00
PANM Nathan MacKinnon 8.00 20.00
PAPB Patrice Bergeron 2.50 6.00
PAPK Patrick Kane 4.00 10.00
PARG Ryan Getzlaf 2.00 5.00
PASA Sebastian Aho 3.00 8.00
PASC Sidney Crosby 8.00 20.00
PASJ Seth Jones 2.00 5.00
PASS Steven Stamkos 4.00 10.00
PATC Thomas Chabot 2.00 5.00

2020-21 Upper Deck Premier Premier Dual Jerseys

PDAJ Seth Jones
Cam Atkinson 4.00 10.00
PDBO Alex Ovechkin
Nicklas Backstrom 15.00 40.00
PDBP David Pastrnak
Patrice Bergeron 10.00 25.00
PDCK Anze Kopitar
Jeff Carter 6.00 15.00
PDCT Brady Tkachuk
Thomas Chabot 6.00 15.00
PDDK Jonathan Drouin
Jesperi Kotkaniemi 4.00 10.00
PDEB Mathew Barzal
Jordan Eberle 5.00 12.00
PDEG Jordan Greenway
Joel Eriksson Ek 3.00 8.00
PDGH Claude Giroux
Carter Hart 4.00 10.00
PDGT Matthew Tkachuk
Johnny Gaudreau 8.00 20.00
PDHH Nico Hischier
Jack Hughes 10.00 25.00
PDJF Filip Forsberg
Roman Josi 6.00 15.00
PDKH John Klingberg
Miro Heiskanen 5.00 12.00
PDKK Patrick Kane
Duncan Keith 8.00 20.00
PDML Evgeni Malkin
Kris Letang 8.00 20.00
PDMM Auston Matthews
Mitch Marner 15.00 40.00
PDMR Nathan MacKinnon
Mikko Rantanen 15.00 40.00
PDND Leon Draisaitl
Ryan Nugent-Hopkins 12.00 30.00
PDPB Artemi Panarin
Pavel Buchnevich 8.00 20.00
PDPH Elias Pettersson
Quinn Hughes 10.00 25.00
PDSK Clayton Keller
Nick Schmaltz 5.00 12.00
PDWS Mark Scheifele
Blake Wheeler 6.00 15.00

2020-21 Upper Deck Premier Premier Quad Jerseys

PQ1ST Auston Matthews
Nico Hischier
Rasmus Dahlin
Jack Hughes 25.00 60.00
PQCAL Auston Matthews
Mathew Barzal
Elias Pettersson
Cale Makar 25.00 60.00
PQCOL Nathan MacKinnon
Gabriel Landeskog
Mikko Rantanen
Cale Makar 25.00 60.00
PQFLA Matthew Tkachuk
Sean Monahan
Johnny Gaudreau
Elias Lindholm 12.00 30.00
PQMTL Jonathan Drouin
Brendan Gallagher
Shea Weber
Carey Price 12.00 30.00
PQNOR Brent Burns
Victor Hedman
Mark Giordano
Roman Josi 8.00 20.00
PQSEL Patrice Bergeron
Anze Kopitar
Ryan O'Reilly
Sean Couturier 10.00 25.00
PQTML John Tavares
William Nylander
Morgan Rielly
Frederik Andersen 12.00 30.00
PQVAN Bo Horvat
Brock Boeser
Elias Pettersson
Quinn Hughes 15.00 40.00

2020-21 Upper Deck Premier Premier Trio Jerseys

PTBEP Jack Eichel
Mathew Barzal
Artemi Panarin 10.00 25.00
PTCKH Tomas Hertl
Evander Kane
Logan Couture 6.00 15.00
PTGGL Ryan Getzlaf
Hampus Lindholm
John Gibson 5.00 12.00
PTGKC Logan Couture
Anze Kopitar
Ryan Getzlaf 8.00 20.00
PTHFR Aleksander Barkov
Jonathan Huberdeau
Aaron Ekblad 8.00 20.00
PTMLB Dylan Larkin
Anthony Mantha
Tyler Bertuzzi 6.00 15.00
PTMMH Zach Hyman
Auston Matthews
Mitch Marner 20.00 50.00
PTPSO Brayden Schenn
Ryan O'Reilly
David Perron 5.00 12.00
PTREO Jack Eichel
Victor Olofsson
Sam Reinhart 10.00 25.00
PTSHP Steven Stamkos
Brayden Point
Victor Hedman 10.00 25.00
PTSMK Mark Stone
William Karlsson
Jonathan Marchessault 6.00 15.00
PTSTS Andrei Svechnikov
Jordan Staal
Teuvo Teravainen 6.00 15.00

2020-21 Upper Deck Premier Rookie Expose

EAA Anthony Angello 20.00 50.00
EAB Alexander Barabanov 25.00 60.00
EAK Arthur Kaliyev 40.00 100.00
EAL Alexis Lafreniere 300.00 500.00
EAR Alec Regula 15.00 40.00
EAT Alexander True 20.00 50.00
EBB Bowen Byram 50.00 125.00
EIS Ilya Sorokin 60.00 150.00
EJE Jake Evans 25.00 60.00
EJR Jack Rathbone 25.00 60.00
EKM K'Andre Miller 50.00 125.00
ELF Liam Foudy 25.00 60.00
ENF Nolan Foote 25.00 60.00
ENH Nils Hoglander 25.00 60.00
EOJ Olli Juolevi 25.00 60.00
EPS Pius Suter 30.00 80.00
ESC Sasha Chmelevski 20.00 50.00
ETS Tim Stutzle 100.00 250.00
EVV Vitek Vanecek 40.00 100.00
EYS Yegor Sharangovich 40.00 100.00

2020-21 Upper Deck Premier Rookie Jersey Autographs

PRAAA Alexander Alexeyev 12.00 30.00
PRAAB Alex Belzile 12.00 30.00
PRAAK Arthur Kaliyev 25.00 60.00
PRAAL Alexis Lafreniere 50.00 125.00
PRAAN Anthony Angello 12.00 30.00
PRAAR Alec Regula 10.00 25.00
PRAAT Alexander True 12.00 30.00
PRABA Alexander Barabanov 15.00 40.00
PRABB Bowen Byram 30.00 80.00
PRACF Cal Foote 20.00 50.00
PRACO Dylan Cozens 30.00 80.00
PRACP Chase Priskie 12.00 30.00
PRACT Calvin Thurkauf 12.00 30.00
PRAGL Gustav Lindstrom 12.00 30.00
PRAGQ Gage Quinney 10.00 25.00
PRAGS Gilles Senn 12.00 30.00
PRAIM Ian Mitchell 12.00 30.00
PRAIS Ilya Sorokin 40.00 100.00
PRAJA Jason Robertson 150.00 400.00
PRAJE Jake Evans 15.00 40.00
PRAJH Jani Hakanpaa 10.00 25.00
PRAJK Joel Kiviranta 15.00 40.00
PRAJN Josh Norris 25.00 60.00
PRAJO Jake Oettinger 40.00 100.00
PRAJR Jack Rathbone 15.00 40.00
PRAKB Kieffer Bellows 12.00 30.00
PRAKM K'Andre Miller 30.00 80.00
PRAKU Philipp Kurashev 20.00 50.00
PRALC Lucas Carlsson 12.00 30.00
PRALF Liam Foudy 15.00 40.00
PRALS Logan Stanley 15.00 40.00
PRAMA Mikey Anderson 15.00 40.00
PRAMK Martin Kaut 15.00 40.00
PRAML Maxim Letunov 12.00 30.00
PRANB Nicolas Beaudin 15.00 40.00
PRANF Nolan Foote 15.00 40.00
PRANH Nils Hoglander 15.00 40.00
PRANK Nikolai Knyzhov 12.00 30.00
PRANR Nick Robertson 25.00 60.00
PRAOC Drew O'Connor 15.00 40.00
PRAOJ Olli Juolevi 15.00 40.00
PRAPF Pavel Francouz 20.00 50.00
PRAPK Peyton Krebs 25.00 60.00
PRAPS Pius Suter 20.00 50.00
PRASB Shane Bowers 12.00 30.00
PRASC Sasha Chmelevski 12.00 30.00
PRASL Steven Lorentz 12.00 30.00
PRASM Ty Smith 25.00 60.00
PRATD Ty Dellandrea 15.00 40.00
PRATS Tim Stutzle 30.00 80.00
PRAVV Vitek Vanecek 25.00 60.00
PRAYS Yegor Sharangovich 25.00 60.00

2020-21 Upper Deck Premier Rookie Paramount Patch Autographs

PAL Alexis Lafreniere 80.00 200.00
PBB Bowen Byram 50.00 125.00
PIM Ian Mitchell 20.00 50.00
PIS Ilya Sorokin 60.00 150.00
PJN Josh Norris 40.00 100.00
PJO Jake Oettinger 60.00 150.00
PKK Kirill Kaprizov 100.00 250.00
PKM K'Andre Miller 50.00 125.00
PKU Philipp Kurashev 30.00 80.00
PLF Liam Foudy 25.00 60.00
PMK Martin Kaut 25.00 60.00
PNH Nils Hoglander 25.00 60.00
PNR Nick Robertson 40.00 100.00
POJ Olli Juolevi 25.00 60.00
PPS Pius Suter 30.00 80.00
PSC Sasha Chmelevski 20.00 50.00
PSM Ty Smith 40.00 100.00
PTD Ty Dellandrea 25.00 60.00
PTS Tim Stutzle 125.00 300.00
PVV Vitek Vanecek 40.00 100.00

2020-21 Upper Deck Premier Rookie Paramount Jerseys

*PATCH/35: 1.25X TO 3X BASIC INSERTS
PAK Arthur Kaliyev 5.00 12.00
PAL Alexis Lafreniere 10.00 25.00
PAR Alexander Romanov 4.00 10.00
PBB Bowen Byram 6.00 15.00
PCM Connor McMichael 5.00 12.00
PDC Dylan Cozens 5.00 12.00
PGV Gabe Vilardi 5.00 12.00
PIM Ian Mitchell 2.50 6.00
PIS Ilya Sorokin 8.00 20.00
PJK Joel Kiviranta 3.00 8.00
PJN Josh Norris 5.00 12.00
PJO Jake Oettinger 8.00 20.00
PKK Kirill Kaprizov 12.00 30.00
PKM K'Andre Miller 6.00 15.00
PKU Philipp Kurashev 4.00 10.00
PLF Liam Foudy 3.00 8.00
PMG Morgan Geekie 3.00 8.00
PMK Martin Kaut 3.00 8.00
PNH Nils Hoglander 3.00 8.00
PNR Nick Robertson 5.00 12.00
POJ Olli Juolevi 3.00 8.00
PPK Peyton Krebs 5.00 12.00
PPS Pius Suter 4.00 10.00
PSC Sasha Chmelevski 2.50 6.00
PSM Ty Smith 5.00 12.00
PTD Ty Dellandrea 3.00 8.00
PTL Timothy Liljegren 3.00 8.00
PTS Tim Stutzle 6.00 15.00
PVV Vitek Vanecek 5.00 12.00

2020-21 Upper Deck Premier Signature Pursuit Autographs

SPAL Anders Lee 25.00 60.00
SPAM Anthony Mantha 25.00 60.00
SPBB Brent Burns 30.00 80.00
SPBM Brad Marchand 60.00 150.00
SPBO Brock Boeser 40.00 100.00
SPBS Brayden Schenn 30.00 80.00
SPBT Brady Tkachuk 50.00 125.00
SPCA Cam Atkinson 30.00 80.00
SPCM Cale Makar 80.00 200.00
SPCO Maxime Comtois 25.00 60.00
SPDP David Perron 25.00 60.00
SPDT Devon Toews 25.00 60.00
SPEL Elias Lindholm 30.00 80.00
SPEP Elias Pettersson 50.00 125.00
SPHA Dougie Hamilton 25.00 60.00
SPIM Ilya Mikheyev 25.00 60.00
SPJG John Gibson 30.00 80.00
SPJH Jonathan Huberdeau 40.00 100.00
SPJM J.T. Miller 40.00 100.00
SPJS Jason Spezza 30.00 80.00
SPJT John Tavares 50.00 125.00
SPJV Jakub Vrana 30.00 80.00
SPKP Kyle Palmieri 25.00 60.00
SPLD Leon Draisaitl 100.00 250.00
SPMA Auston Matthews 125.00 300.00
SPMC Connor McDavid 150.00 400.00
SPMH Miro Heiskanen 40.00 100.00
SPMP Max Pacioretty 30.00 80.00
SPMS Mark Scheifele 50.00 125.00
SPMT Matthew Tkachuk 60.00 150.00
SPNE Nikolaj Ehlers 30.00 80.00
SPPB Pavel Buchnevich 25.00 60.00
SPPR Carey Price 60.00 150.00
SPRI Pekka Rinne 30.00 80.00
SPRS Ryan Suter 25.00 60.00
SPSB Sergei Bobrovsky 50.00 125.00
SPSR Sam Reinhart 60.00 150.00
SPST Jordan Staal 25.00 60.00
SPTJ Tristan Jarry 30.00 80.00

2021-22 Upper Deck Premier

1 Auston Matthews 4.00 10.00
2 Quinn Hughes 2.50 6.00
3 Mathew Barzal 1.25 3.00
4 Jonathan Huberdeau 1.25 3.00
5 Andrei Svechnikov 1.25 3.00
6 Matthew Tkachuk 2.00 5.00
7 Brady Tkachuk 1.50 4.00
8 Alex Ovechkin 4.00 10.00
9 Andrei Vasilevskiy 1.50 4.00
10 Taylor Hall 1.00 2.50
11 Tim Stutzle 1.25 3.00
12 Brent Burns 1.00 2.50
13 Brock Boeser 1.25 3.00
14 Cale Makar 2.50 6.00
15 Alexis Lafreniere 1.50 4.00
16 Kirill Kaprizov 3.00 8.00
17 Dylan Cozens 1.00 2.50
18 Kris Letang 1.25 3.00
19 John Tavares 1.50 4.00
20 Charlie Coyle 1.00 2.50
21 Seth Jones 1.00 2.50
22 Vladimir Tarasenko 1.25 3.00
23 Connor Hellebuyck 2.00 5.00
24 Patrick Kane 2.00 5.00
25 Aleksander Barkov 1.50 4.00
26 Troy Terry .75 2.00
27 Igor Shesterkin 2.00 5.00
28 Brad Marchand 2.00 5.00
29 Steven Stamkos 2.00 5.00
30 Clayton Keller 1.25 3.00
31 Tyler Bertuzzi .75 2.00
32 Joe Pavelski 1.25 3.00
33 Brock Nelson 1.00 2.50
34 Kyle Connor 1.50 4.00
35 Sebastian Aho 1.50 4.00
36 Nathan MacKinnon 4.00 10.00
37 David Pastrnak 2.50 6.00
38 Jeff Petry 1.00 2.50
39 Jack Eichel 1.50 4.00
40 Rasmus Dahlin 1.25 3.00
41 Mitch Marner 1.50 4.00
42 Martin Necas 1.50 4.00
43 Roman Josi 1.00 2.50
44 Jason Robertson 1.50 4.00
45 Anze Kopitar 1.50 4.00
46 Jordan Eberle 1.00 2.50
47 Leon Draisaitl 3.00 8.00
48 Adam Fox 1.25 3.00
49 Jake Guentzel 1.50 4.00
50 Marc-Andre Fleury 2.00 5.00
51 Conor Garland .75 2.00
52 Alex Nedeljkovic .75 2.00
53 Nikolaj Ehlers 1.00 2.50
54 Sean Monahan .60 1.50
55 Jack Roslovic .60 1.50
56 Elias Pettersson 1.50 4.00
57 Anthony Beauvillier .60 1.50
58 Ryan O'Reilly 1.00 2.50
59 Philipp Grubauer 1.00 2.50
60 Roope Hintz 1.25 3.00
61 Jack Hughes 2.50 6.00
62 Dylan Larkin 1.25 3.00
63 Jesse Puljujarvi 1.00 2.50
64 Carey Price 2.00 5.00
65 Sam Bennett 1.50 4.00
66 Josh Anderson .75 2.00
67 William Karlsson 1.25 3.00
68 Filip Hronek .60 1.50
69 Artemi Panarin 2.00 5.00
70 Eeli Tolvanen 1.00 2.50
71 Mikko Rantanen 2.50 6.00
72 Brendan Gallagher 1.00 2.50
73 Kevin Fiala .75 2.00
74 John Gibson 1.00 2.50
75 Colton Parayko .75 2.00
76 Nicklas Backstrom 1.00 2.50
77 Josh Morrissey 1.25 3.00
78 Miro Heiskanen 1.25 3.00
79 Sam Reinhart 2.00 5.00
80 Casey Mittelstadt 1.00 2.50
81 Boone Jenner 1.00 2.50
82 Nick Schmaltz .75 2.00
83 Zach Parise 1.00 2.50
84 Nazem Kadri 1.25 3.00
85 Evgeni Malkin 2.00 5.00
86 Johnny Gaudreau 1.50 4.00
87 Sidney Crosby 4.00 10.00
88 Nikita Kucherov 2.00 5.00
89 Alex DeBrincat 1.25 3.00
90 Connor McDavid 5.00 12.00
91 Sergei Zubov 3.00 8.00
92 Henrik Zetterberg 5.00 12.00
93 Martin Brodeur 10.00 25.00
94 Vincent Lecavalier 4.00 10.00
95 Teemu Selanne 8.00 20.00
96 Martin St. Louis 4.00 10.00
97 Joe Sakic 8.00 20.00
98 Wendel Clark 6.00 15.00
99 Mario Lemieux 15.00 40.00
100 Wayne Gretzky 25.00 60.00
101 Trevor Zegras RC 5.00 12.00
102 Moritz Seider RC 6.00 15.00
103 Lucas Raymond RC 8.00 20.00
104 Michael Bunting RC 2.50 6.00
105 Tanner Jeannot RC 2.50 6.00
106 Cole Caufield RC 10.00 25.00
107 Jeremy Swayman RC 8.00 20.00
108 Spencer Knight RC 5.00 12.00
109 Quinton Byfield RC 6.00 15.00
110 Dawson Mercer RC 6.00 15.00
111 Alex Newhook RC 4.00 10.00
112 Alex Turcotte RC 3.00 8.00
113 Philip Tomasino RC 3.00 8.00
114 Jamie Drysdale RC 4.00 10.00
115 Cole Perfetti RC 5.00 12.00
116 Cole Sillinger RC 4.00 10.00
117 Lassi Thomson RC 2.50 6.00
118 Seth Jarvis RC 6.00 15.00
119 Shane Pinto RC 4.00 10.00
120 Nils Lundkvist RC 2.50 6.00
121 Scott Perunovich RC 2.50 6.00
122 JJ Peterka RC 5.00 12.00
123 Vasily Podkolzin RC 3.00 8.00
124 Jonathan Dahlen RC 2.50 6.00
125 Mason McTavish RC 5.00 12.00
126 Grigori Denisenko RC 3.00 8.00
127 Riley Damiani RC 2.50 6.00
128 Jake Neighbours RC 5.00 12.00
129 Robin Salo RC 2.50 6.00
130 Gabriel Fortier RC 2.50 6.00
131 Wade Allison RC 2.50 6.00
132 Calen Addison RC 2.50 6.00
133 Joe Veleno RC 3.00 8.00
134 Riley Tufte RC 2.50 6.00
135 Benoit-Olivier Groulx RC 2.50 6.00
136 Rasmus Kupari RC 2.50 6.00
137 Ryan Merkley RC 3.00 8.00
138 J.J. Moser RC 2.50 6.00
139 Cam York RC 2.50 6.00
140 Karel Vejmelka RC 3.00 8.00
141 Adam Beckman RC 2.50 6.00
142 Brandon Duhaime RC 2.50 6.00
143 Egor Sokolov RC 2.50 6.00
144 Ross Colton RC 3.00 8.00
145 Zac Jones RC 3.00 8.00
146 Kasper Bjorkqvist RC 2.50 6.00
147 Anton Lundell RC 5.00 12.00
148 Kole Lind RC 3.00 8.00
149 Ukko-Pekka Luukkonen RC 4.00 10.00
150 Alexander Holtz RC 4.00 10.00

2021-22 Upper Deck Premier Bronze

*BRONZE RC/65: .75X TO 2X BASIC

2021-22 Upper Deck Premier Gold

*GOLD VET/65: .6X TO 1.5X BASIC
*GOLD LEG/25: 1X TO 2.5X BASIC
*GOLD RC/199: .6X TO 1.5X BASIC
93 Martin Brodeur 20.00 50.00

2021-22 Upper Deck Premier '02-03 Super Rookie Patch Autographs

SRRAL Anton Lundell/49 30.00 80.00
SRRAN Alex Newhook/49 25.00 60.00
SRRAT Alex Turcotte/49 30.00 80.00
SRRCP Cole Perfetti/49 30.00 80.00
SRRCS Cole Sillinger/49 40.00 100.00
SRRDM Dawson Mercer/49 80.00 200.00
SRRJD Jamie Drysdale/49 25.00 60.00
SRRJP JJ Peterka/49 60.00 150.00
SRRJS Jeremy Swayman/49 150.00 400.00
SRRLT Lassi Thomson/49 15.00 40.00
SRRMB Michael Bunting/49 15.00 40.00
SRRPT Philip Tomasino/49 20.00 50.00
SRRSJ Seth Jarvis/49 40.00 100.00
SRRSK Spencer Knight/49 100.00 250.00
SRRSP Scott Perunovich/49 15.00 40.00
SRRTJ Tanner Jeannot/49 15.00 40.00

2021-22 Upper Deck Premier '21 Premier Rookie Jersey Autographs

PRAAB Adam Beckman/99 10.00 25.00
PRAAH Alexander Holtz/25 15.00 40.00
PRAAL Anton Lundell/25 40.00 100.00
PRAAN Justus Annunen/99 12.00 30.00
PRAAR Arttu Ruotsalainen/99 10.00 25.00
PRABD Brandon Duhaime/99 10.00 25.00
PRABG Benoit-Olivier Groulx/99 10.00 25.00
PRABK Boris Katchouk/99 8.00 20.00
PRACA Calen Addison/99 10.00 25.00
PRACD Connor Dewar/99 10.00 25.00
PRACP Cole Perfetti/99 20.00 50.00
PRACS Cole Sillinger/99 15.00 40.00
PRADF David Farrance/99 10.00 25.00
PRADM Daniil Miromanov/99 10.00 25.00
PRADR Jamie Drysdale/25 40.00 100.00
PRAFZ Fabian Zetterlund/99 10.00 25.00
PRAGF Gabriel Fortier/99 10.00 25.00
PRAJA Jack Ahcan/99 10.00 25.00
PRAJB Jacob Bryson/99 10.00 25.00
PRAJM J.J. Moser/99 10.00 25.00
PRAJP JJ Peterka/99 40.00 100.00
PRAJS Jeremy Swayman/25 60.00 150.00
PRAJV Joe Veleno/99 12.00 30.00
PRAJW Jasper Weatherby/99 10.00 25.00
PRAJY Jesse Ylonen/99 10.00 25.00
PRAKB Kasper Bjorkqvist/99 10.00 25.00
PRAKL Kole Lind/99 12.00 30.00
PRALR Lucas Raymond/25 80.00 200.00
PRALT Lassi Thomson/99 10.00 25.00
PRAMB Michael Bunting/25 10.00 25.00
PRAMM Mason McTavish/99 40.00 100.00
PRAMP Matthew Phillips/99 10.00 25.00
PRAND Nico Daws/99 15.00 40.00
PRANL Nils Lundkvist/99 10.00 25.00
PRAOS Oskar Steen/99 12.00 30.00
PRAPD Pavel Dorofeyev/99 12.00 30.00
PRAPE Scott Perunovich/99 10.00 25.00
PRAPT Philip Tomasino/99 12.00 30.00
PRAQB Quinton Byfield/25 40.00 100.00
PRARC Ross Colton/99 12.00 30.00
PRARK Rasmus Kupari/99 10.00 25.00
PRARM Ryan Merkley/99 12.00 30.00
PRART Riley Tufte/99 10.00 25.00
PRASB Simon Benoit/99 10.00 25.00
PRASD Sean Durzi/99 10.00 25.00
PRASJ Seth Jarvis/25 100.00 250.00
PRASK Spencer Knight/25 60.00 150.00
PRASP Shane Pinto/99 15.00 40.00
PRASR Sampo Ranta/99 10.00 25.00
PRATH Logan Thompson/99 40.00 100.00
PRATJ Tanner Jeannot/25 10.00 25.00
PRATL Tanner Laczynski/99 10.00 25.00
PRATT Tyce Thompson/99 10.00 25.00
PRAUL Ukko-Pekka Luukkonen/99 15.00 40.00
PRAVP Vasily Podkolzin/25 12.00 30.00
PRAWE William Eklund/99 40.00 100.00
PRAWK Wyatt Kalynuk/99 10.00 25.00

2021-22 Upper Deck Premier 20th Anniversary Autographs

AAAM Auston Matthews/35 40.00 100.00
AABB Brock Boeser/100 12.00 30.00
AABH Brett Hull/35 15.00 40.00
AACN Cam Neely/35 8.00 20.00
AADH Dominik Hasek/35 15.00 40.00
AADS Darryl Sittler/35 10.00 25.00
AAJI Jarome Iginla/35 12.00 30.00
AAJM Jared McCann/100 8.00 20.00
AAKL Kris Letang/100 12.00 30.00
AANL Nicklas Lidstrom/35 10.00 25.00
AANR Nick Robertson/100 10.00 25.00
AAPG Philipp Grubauer/100 10.00 25.00
AARB Ray Bourque/35 15.00 40.00
AARH Roope Hintz/100 12.00 30.00
AATB Tyler Bertuzzi/100 8.00 20.00
AATS Teemu Selanne/35 20.00 50.00
AATT Troy Terry/100 8.00 20.00
AAWK William Karlsson/100 12.00 30.00

2021-22 Upper Deck Premier 20th Anniversary Jerseys

*BLACK/25: 1.5X TO 4X BASIC
AJAK Anze Kopitar 2.50 6.00
AJAL Anton Lundell 3.00 8.00
AJAM Auston Matthews 6.00 15.00
AJAN Alex Newhook 2.50 6.00
AJAO Alex Ovechkin 6.00 15.00
AJAT Alex Turcotte 2.00 5.00
AJAV Andrei Vasilevskiy 2.50 6.00
AJCA Calen Addison 1.50 4.00
AJCC Cole Caufield 6.00 15.00
AJCM Connor McDavid 8.00 20.00
AJCP Cole Perfetti 3.00 8.00
AJCS Cole Sillinger 2.50 6.00
AJCY Cam York 1.50 4.00
AJDM Dawson Mercer 4.00 10.00
AJDP David Pastrnak 4.00 10.00
AJDR Jamie Drysdale 2.50 6.00
AJEP Elias Pettersson 2.50 6.00
AJHL Hendrix Lapierre 1.50 4.00
AJHU Jack Hughes 4.00 10.00
AJJD Jonathan Dahlen 1.50 4.00
AJJH Jonathan Huberdeau 2.00 5.00
AJJJ JJ Peterka 3.00 8.00
AJJP Joe Pavelski 2.00 5.00
AJJS Jeremy Swayman 5.00 12.00
AJJV Joe Veleno 2.00 5.00
AJLD Leon Draisaitl 5.00 12.00
AJLR Lucas Raymond 5.00 12.00
AJMF Marc-Andre Fleury 3.00 8.00
AJMM Mason McTavish 3.00 8.00
AJMS Moritz Seider 4.00 10.00
AJNM Nathan MacKinnon 6.00 15.00
AJNS Nick Suzuki 3.00 8.00
AJPB Patrice Bergeron 2.00 5.00
AJPI Shane Pinto 2.50 6.00
AJPL Patrik Laine 2.00 5.00
AJPT Philip Tomasino 2.00 5.00
AJQB Quinton Byfield 4.00 10.00
AJRD Rasmus Dahlin 2.00 5.00
AJSC Sidney Crosby 6.00 15.00
AJSJ Seth Jarvis 4.00 10.00
AJSK Spencer Knight 3.00 8.00
AJSP Scott Perunovich 1.50 4.00
AJSS Steven Stamkos 3.00 8.00
AJTJ Tanner Jeannot 1.50 4.00
AJTZ Trevor Zegras 3.00 8.00
AJUL Ukko-Pekka Luukkonen 2.50 6.00
AJVH Victor Hedman 2.00 5.00
AJVP Vasily Podkolzin 2.00 5.00
AJWE William Eklund 4.00 10.00

2021-22 Upper Deck Premier 20th Anniversary Rookie Autographs

AARAH Alexander Holtz/99 12.00 30.00
AARAL Anton Lundell/99 15.00 40.00
AARAN Alex Newhook/99 12.00 30.00
AARAT Alex Turcotte/99 10.00 25.00
AARCC Cole Caufield/35 200.00 500.00
AARCP Cole Perfetti/99 15.00 40.00
AARCS Cole Sillinger/99 12.00 30.00
AARJD Jamie Drysdale/99 12.00 30.00
AARJP JJ Peterka/99 15.00 40.00
AARJS Jeremy Swayman/99 25.00 60.00
AARLR Lucas Raymond/35 25.00 60.00
AARPI Shane Pinto/99 12.00 30.00
AARPT Philip Tomasino/99 10.00 25.00
AARQB Quinton Byfield/35 20.00 50.00
AARSK Spencer Knight/99 15.00 40.00
AARSP Scott Perunovich/99 8.00 20.00
AARVP Vasily Podkolzin/99 10.00 25.00
AARWE William Eklund/99 20.00 50.00

2021-22 Upper Deck Premier Acetate Horizontal Rookie Patch Autographs

AHRAH Alexander Holtz/99 25.00 60.00
AHRAL Anton Lundell/49 40.00 100.00
AHRAN Alex Newhook/99 40.00 100.00
AHRCC Cole Caufield/49 800.00 2000.00
AHRCP Cole Perfetti/99 30.00 80.00
AHRDM Dawson Mercer/99 40.00 100.00
AHRJD Jamie Drysdale/99 25.00 60.00
AHRJP JJ Peterka/99 60.00 150.00
AHRJS Jeremy Swayman/99 60.00 150.00
AHRLR Lucas Raymond/49 150.00 400.00
AHRLT Lassi Thomson/99 15.00 40.00
AHRMB Michael Bunting/99 15.00 40.00
AHRMM Mason McTavish/99 30.00 80.00
AHRPT Philip Tomasino/99 20.00 50.00

AHRQB Quinton Byfield/99 60.00 150.00
AHRRD Riley Damiani/99 15.00 40.00
AHRSJ Seth Jarvis/99 40.00 100.00
AHRSK Spencer Knight/99 30.00 80.00
AHRSP Scott Perunovich/99 15.00 40.00
AHRTJ Tanner Jeannot/99 15.00 40.00
AHRVP Vasily Podkolzin/99 20.00 50.00
AHRWE William Eklund/99 40.00 100.00

2021-22 Upper Deck Premier Acetate Horizontal Rookie Patch Autographs Gold

*GOLD/25: .5X TO 1.2X BASIC
AHRAH Alexander Holtz/25 50.00 125.00
AHRAN Alex Newhook/25 50.00 125.00
AHRJP JJ Peterka/25 80.00 200.00
AHRJS Jeremy Swayman/25 80.00 200.00
AHRSJ Seth Jarvis/25 100.00 250.00
AHRWE William Eklund/25 125.00 300.00

2021-22 Upper Deck Premier Acetate Rookie Patch Autographs

ARAH Alexander Holtz/249 20.00 50.00
ARAL Anton Lundell/99 30.00 80.00
ARAN Alex Newhook/249 20.00 50.00
ARAR Arttu Ruotsalainen/249 12.00 30.00
ARAT Alex Turcotte/249 15.00 40.00
ARBD Brandon Duhaime/249 12.00 30.00
ARBE Jacob Bernard-Docker/249 12.00 30.00
ARBG Benoit-Olivier Groulx/249 12.00 30.00
ARBK Boris Katchouk/249 10.00 25.00
ARBR Jacob Bryson/249 12.00 30.00
ARCA Calen Addison/249 12.00 30.00
ARCC Cole Caufield/99 600.00 1500.00
ARCP Cole Perfetti/99 40.00 100.00
ARCS Cole Sillinger/249 20.00 50.00
ARDF David Farrance/249 12.00 30.00
ARDM Dawson Mercer/249 40.00 100.00
ARDR Jamie Drysdale/99 30.00 80.00
ARES Egor Sokolov/249 12.00 30.00
ARGD Grigori Denisenko/249 15.00 40.00
ARGF Gabriel Fortier/249 12.00 30.00
ARHL Hendrix Lapierre/249 12.00 30.00
ARJA Jack Ahcan/249 12.00 30.00
ARJB Justin Barron/249 20.00 50.00
ARJL Jake Leschyshyn/249 12.00 30.00
ARJM J.J. Moser/249 12.00 30.00
ARJN Jake Neighbours/249 25.00 60.00
ARJP JJ Peterka/249 60.00 150.00
ARJS Jeremy Swayman/99 100.00 250.00
ARJU Justus Annunen/249 15.00 40.00
ARJV Joe Veleno/249 15.00 40.00
ARJW Jasper Weatherby/249 12.00 30.00
ARJY Jesse Ylonen/249 12.00 30.00
ARKB Kasper Bjorkqvist/249 12.00 30.00
ARLP Lane Pederson/249 12.00 30.00
ARLR Lucas Raymond/99 80.00 200.00
ARLT Lassi Thomson/249 12.00 30.00
ARMB Michael Bunting/99 12.00 30.00
ARMI Daniil Miromanov/249 12.00 30.00
ARMM Mason McTavish/249 80.00 200.00
ARMP Matthew Phillips/249 12.00 30.00
ARND Nico Daws/249 20.00 50.00
ARNL Nils Lundkvist/249 12.00 30.00
ARPE Scott Perunovich/249 12.00 30.00
ARPK Parker Kelly/249 12.00 30.00
ARPT Philip Tomasino/249 15.00 40.00
ARRC Ross Colton/249 15.00 40.00
ARRD Riley Damiani/249 12.00 30.00
ARRK Rasmus Kupari/249 12.00 30.00
ARRM Ryan Merkley/249 15.00 40.00
ARRT Riley Tufte/249 12.00 30.00
ARSC Cole Schwindt/249 12.00 30.00
ARSD Sean Durzi/249 12.00 30.00
ARSJ Seth Jarvis/249 30.00 80.00
ARSP Shane Pinto/249 20.00 50.00
ARSR Sampo Ranta/249 12.00 30.00
ARTJ Tanner Jeannot/249 12.00 30.00
ARTT Tyce Thompson/249 12.00 30.00
ARTZ Trevor Zegras/99 400.00 1000.00
ARUL Ukko-Pekka Luukkonen/249 20.00 50.00
ARVP Vasily Podkolzin/99 40.00 100.00
ARWA Wade Allison/249 12.00 30.00
ARWE William Eklund/249 40.00 100.00
ARWK Wyatt Kalynuk/249 12.00 30.00
ARZJ Zac Jones/249 15.00 40.00

2021-22 Upper Deck Premier Acetate Rookie Patch Autographs Gold

*GOLD: .6X TO 1.5X BASIC
ARAL Anton Lundell/35 80.00 200.00
ARCA Calen Addison/65 30.00 80.00
ARCP Cole Perfetti/35 80.00 200.00
ARDM Dawson Mercer/65 80.00 200.00
ARDR Jamie Drysdale/35 80.00 200.00
ARJP JJ Peterka/65 80.00 200.00
ARJS Jeremy Swayman/35 150.00 400.00
ARLR Lucas Raymond/35 125.00 150.00
ARMM Mason McTavish/65 150.00 400.00
ARSJ Seth Jarvis/65 80.00 200.00
ARVP Vasily Podkolzin/35 80.00 200.00
ARWE William Eklund/65 80.00 200.00

2021-22 Upper Deck Premier Autographs

1 Auston Matthews 30.00 80.00
2 Quinn Hughes 20.00 50.00
4 Jonathan Huberdeau 10.00 25.00
5 Andrei Svechnikov 10.00 25.00
6 Matthew Tkachuk 15.00 40.00
7 Brady Tkachuk 12.00 30.00
8 Alex Ovechkin 30.00 80.00
11 Tim Stutzle 10.00 25.00
12 Brent Burns 8.00 20.00
13 Brock Boeser 10.00 25.00
14 Cale Makar 20.00 50.00
15 Alexis Lafreniere 12.00 30.00
17 Dylan Cozens 8.00 20.00
18 Kris Letang 10.00 25.00
20 Charlie Coyle 8.00 20.00
25 Aleksander Barkov 12.00 30.00
26 Troy Terry 6.00 15.00
27 Igor Shesterkin 15.00 40.00
28 Brad Marchand 15.00 40.00
30 Clayton Keller 10.00 25.00
31 Tyler Bertuzzi 6.00 15.00
32 Joe Pavelski 10.00 25.00
33 Brock Nelson 8.00 20.00
35 Sebastian Aho 12.00 30.00
45 Anze Kopitar 12.00 30.00
46 Jordan Eberle 8.00 20.00
49 Jake Guentzel 12.00 30.00
50 Marc-Andre Fleury 15.00 40.00
52 Alex Nedeljkovic 6.00 15.00
54 Sean Monahan 5.00 12.00
55 Jack Roslovic 5.00 12.00
57 Anthony Beauvillier 5.00 12.00
58 Ryan O'Reilly 8.00 20.00
59 Philipp Grubauer 8.00 20.00
60 Roope Hintz 10.00 25.00
63 Jesse Puljujarvi 8.00 20.00
64 Carey Price 15.00 40.00
65 Sam Bennett 12.00 30.00
66 Josh Anderson 6.00 15.00
67 William Karlsson 10.00 25.00
70 Eeli Tolvanen 8.00 20.00
74 John Gibson 8.00 20.00
75 Colton Parayko 6.00 15.00
79 Sam Reinhart 15.00 40.00
80 Casey Mittelstadt 8.00 20.00
81 Boone Jenner 8.00 20.00
82 Nick Schmaltz 6.00 15.00
87 Sidney Crosby 30.00 80.00
89 Alex DeBrincat 10.00 25.00
90 Connor McDavid 40.00 100.00
91 Sergei Zubov 12.00 30.00
93 Martin Brodeur 40.00 100.00
95 Teemu Selanne 30.00 80.00
96 Martin St. Louis 15.00 40.00
98 Wendel Clark 25.00 60.00
99 Mario Lemieux 60.00 150.00
100 Wayne Gretzky 100.00 250.00
103 Lucas Raymond 25.00 60.00
104 Michael Bunting 8.00 20.00
105 Tanner Jeannot 8.00 20.00
107 Jeremy Swayman 25.00 60.00
108 Spencer Knight 15.00 40.00
109 Quinton Byfield 20.00 50.00
110 Dawson Mercer 20.00 50.00
111 Alex Newhook 12.00 30.00
112 Alex Turcotte 10.00 25.00
113 Philip Tomasino 10.00 25.00
114 Jamie Drysdale 12.00 30.00
115 Cole Perfetti 15.00 40.00
116 Cole Sillinger 12.00 30.00
117 Lassi Thomson 8.00 20.00
118 Seth Jarvis 20.00 50.00
119 Shane Pinto 12.00 30.00
120 Nils Lundkvist 8.00 20.00
121 Scott Perunovich 8.00 20.00
122 JJ Peterka 15.00 40.00
123 Vasily Podkolzin 10.00 25.00
125 Mason McTavish 15.00 40.00
126 Grigori Denisenko 10.00 25.00
127 Riley Damiani 8.00 20.00
128 Jake Neighbours 15.00 40.00
130 Gabriel Fortier 8.00 20.00
131 Wade Allison 8.00 20.00
132 Calen Addison 8.00 20.00
133 Joe Veleno 10.00 25.00
134 Riley Tufte 8.00 20.00
135 Benoit-Olivier Groulx 8.00 20.00
136 Rasmus Kupari 8.00 20.00
137 Ryan Merkley 10.00 25.00
138 J.J. Moser 8.00 20.00
140 Karel Vejmelka 10.00 25.00
141 Adam Beckman 8.00 20.00
142 Brandon Duhaime 8.00 20.00
143 Egor Sokolov 8.00 20.00
144 Ross Colton 10.00 25.00
145 Zac Jones 10.00 25.00
146 Kasper Bjorkqvist 8.00 20.00
147 Anton Lundell 15.00 40.00
148 Kole Lind 10.00 25.00
149 Ukko-Pekka Luukkonen 12.00 30.00
150 Alexander Holtz 12.00 30.00

2021-22 Upper Deck Premier Autographs Gold

*GOLD: .75X TO 2X BASIC
1 Auston Matthews/25 100.00 250.00
8 Alex Ovechkin/25 150.00 400.00
27 Igor Shesterkin/25 60.00 150.00
87 Sidney Crosby/25 150.00 400.00
90 Connor McDavid/25 250.00 600.00
100 Wayne Gretzky/25 150.00 400.00

2021-22 Upper Deck Premier Jerseys

1 Auston Matthews 6.00 15.00
2 Quinn Hughes 4.00 10.00
3 Mathew Barzal 2.00 5.00
4 Jonathan Huberdeau 2.00 5.00
5 Andrei Svechnikov 2.00 5.00
6 Matthew Tkachuk 3.00 8.00
7 Brady Tkachuk 2.50 6.00
8 Alex Ovechkin 6.00 15.00
9 Andrei Vasilevskiy 2.50 6.00
10 Taylor Hall 1.50 4.00
11 Tim Stutzle 2.00 5.00
12 Brent Burns 1.50 4.00
13 Brock Boeser 2.00 5.00
14 Cale Makar 4.00 10.00
15 Alexis Lafreniere 2.50 6.00
16 Kirill Kaprizov 5.00 12.00
17 Dylan Cozens 1.50 4.00
18 Kris Letang 2.00 5.00
19 John Tavares 2.50 6.00
20 Charlie Coyle 1.50 4.00
21 Seth Jones 1.50 4.00
22 Vladimir Tarasenko 2.00 5.00
23 Connor Hellebuyck 3.00 8.00
24 Patrick Kane 3.00 8.00
25 Aleksander Barkov 2.50 6.00
26 Troy Terry 1.25 3.00
27 Igor Shesterkin 3.00 8.00
28 Brad Marchand 3.00 8.00
29 Steven Stamkos 3.00 8.00
30 Clayton Keller 2.00 5.00
31 Tyler Bertuzzi 1.25 3.00
32 Joe Pavelski 2.00 5.00
33 Brock Nelson 1.50 4.00
34 Kyle Connor 2.50 6.00
35 Sebastian Aho 2.50 6.00
36 Nathan MacKinnon 6.00 15.00
37 David Pastrnak 4.00 10.00
38 Jeff Petry 1.50 4.00
39 Jack Eichel 2.50 6.00
40 Rasmus Dahlin 2.00 5.00
41 Mitch Marner 2.50 6.00
42 Martin Necas 2.50 6.00
43 Roman Josi 1.50 4.00
44 Jason Robertson 2.50 6.00
45 Anze Kopitar 2.50 6.00
46 Jordan Eberle 1.50 4.00
47 Leon Draisaitl 5.00 12.00
48 Adam Fox 2.00 5.00
49 Jake Guentzel 2.50 6.00
50 Marc-Andre Fleury 3.00 8.00
51 Conor Garland 1.25 3.00
52 Alex Nedeljkovic 1.25 3.00
53 Nikolaj Ehlers 1.50 4.00
54 Sean Monahan 1.00 2.50
55 Jack Roslovic 1.00 2.50
56 Elias Pettersson 2.50 6.00
57 Anthony Beauvillier 1.00 2.50
58 Ryan O'Reilly 1.50 4.00
59 Philipp Grubauer 1.50 4.00
60 Roope Hintz 2.00 5.00
61 Jack Hughes 4.00 10.00
62 Dylan Larkin 2.00 5.00
63 Jesse Puljujarvi 1.50 4.00
64 Carey Price 3.00 8.00
65 Sam Bennett 2.50 6.00
66 Josh Anderson 1.25 3.00
67 William Karlsson 2.00 5.00
69 Artemi Panarin 3.00 8.00
70 Eeli Tolvanen 1.50 4.00
71 Mikko Rantanen 4.00 10.00
72 Brendan Gallagher 1.50 4.00
73 Kevin Fiala 1.25 3.00
74 John Gibson 1.50 4.00
75 Colton Parayko 1.25 3.00
76 Nicklas Backstrom 1.50 4.00
77 Josh Morrissey 2.00 5.00
78 Miro Heiskanen 2.00 5.00
79 Sam Reinhart 3.00 8.00
80 Casey Mittelstadt 1.50 4.00
81 Boone Jenner 1.50 4.00
82 Nick Schmaltz 1.25 3.00
83 Zach Parise 1.50 4.00
84 Nazem Kadri 2.00 5.00
85 Evgeni Malkin 3.00 8.00
86 Johnny Gaudreau 2.50 6.00
87 Sidney Crosby 6.00 15.00
88 Nikita Kucherov 3.00 8.00
89 Alex DeBrincat 2.00 5.00
90 Connor McDavid 8.00 20.00
92 Henrik Zetterberg 6.00 15.00
93 Martin Brodeur 12.00 30.00
94 Vincent Lecavalier 5.00 12.00
95 Teemu Selanne 10.00 25.00
96 Martin St. Louis 5.00 12.00
99 Mario Lemieux 20.00 50.00
101 Trevor Zegras 3.00 8.00
102 Moritz Seider 4.00 10.00
103 Lucas Raymond 5.00 12.00
104 Michael Bunting 1.50 4.00
105 Tanner Jeannot 1.50 4.00
106 Cole Caufield 6.00 15.00
107 Jeremy Swayman 5.00 12.00
108 Spencer Knight 3.00 8.00
109 Quinton Byfield 4.00 10.00
110 Dawson Mercer 4.00 10.00
111 Alex Newhook 2.50 6.00
112 Alex Turcotte 2.00 5.00
113 Philip Tomasino 2.00 5.00
114 Jamie Drysdale 2.50 6.00
115 Cole Perfetti 3.00 8.00
116 Cole Sillinger 2.50 6.00
117 Lassi Thomson 1.50 4.00
118 Seth Jarvis 4.00 10.00
119 Shane Pinto 2.50 6.00
120 Nils Lundkvist 1.50 4.00
121 Scott Perunovich 1.50 4.00
122 JJ Peterka 3.00 8.00
123 Vasily Podkolzin 2.00 5.00
124 Jonathan Dahlen 1.50 4.00
125 Mason McTavish 3.00 8.00
126 Grigori Denisenko 2.00 5.00
127 Riley Damiani 1.50 4.00
128 Jake Neighbours 3.00 8.00
129 Robin Salo 1.50 4.00
130 Gabriel Fortier 1.50 4.00
131 Wade Allison 1.50 4.00
132 Calen Addison 1.50 4.00
133 Joe Veleno 2.00 5.00
134 Riley Tufte 1.50 4.00
135 Benoit-Olivier Groulx 1.50 4.00
136 Rasmus Kupari 1.50 4.00
137 Ryan Merkley 2.00 5.00
138 J.J. Moser 1.50 4.00
139 Cam York 1.50 4.00
140 Karel Vejmelka 2.00 5.00
141 Adam Beckman 1.50 4.00
142 Brandon Duhaime 1.50 4.00
143 Egor Sokolov 1.50 4.00
144 Ross Colton 2.00 5.00
145 Zac Jones 2.00 5.00
146 Kasper Bjorkqvist 1.50 4.00
147 Anton Lundell 3.00 8.00
148 Kole Lind 2.00 5.00
149 Ukko-Pekka Luukkonen 2.50 6.00
150 Alexander Holtz 2.50 6.00

2021-22 Upper Deck Premier Jerseys Premium Memorabilia

*PREMIUM/25: .75X TO 2X BASIC
*PREMIUM RC: 2.5X TO 6X BASIC
106 Cole Caufield/25 60.00 150.00

2021-22 Upper Deck Premier Premier Attractions Jerseys

*PATCH: 1X TO 2.5X BASIC
PAAM Auston Matthews/49 8.00 20.00
PAAO Alex Ovechkin/49 8.00 20.00
PABT Brady Tkachuk/99 3.00 8.00
PACK Clayton Keller/99 2.50 6.00
PACM Connor McDavid/49 10.00 25.00
PACO Sean Couturier/99 1.50 4.00
PADL Dylan Larkin/99 2.50 6.00
PAEK Erik Karlsson/99 2.50 6.00
PAEP Elias Pettersson/99 3.00 8.00
PAJG Johnny Gaudreau/99 3.00 8.00
PAJH Jack Hughes/99 5.00 12.00
PAJQ Jonathan Quick/99 2.50 6.00
PAJT Jonathan Toews/99 3.00 8.00
PAKK Kirill Kaprizov/99 6.00 15.00
PALD Leon Draisaitl/99 6.00 15.00
PAMF Marc-Andre Fleury/99 4.00 10.00
PAMG Mark Giordano/99 2.00 5.00
PAMR Mikko Rantanen/99 5.00 12.00
PAMS Mark Stone/99 2.50 6.00
PANK Nikita Kucherov/99 4.00 10.00
PAOB Oliver Bjorkstrand/99 1.50 4.00
PARD Rasmus Dahlin/99 2.50 6.00
PARG Ryan Getzlaf/99 2.00 5.00
PARJ Roman Josi/99 2.00 5.00
PASA Sebastian Aho/99 3.00 8.00
PASC Sidney Crosby/49 8.00 20.00
PATA John Tavares/99 3.00 8.00
PATS Tyler Seguin/99 2.50 6.00
PAVH Victor Hedman/99 2.50 6.00
PAVT Vladimir Tarasenko/99 2.50 6.00

2021-22 Upper Deck Premier Premier Dual Jerseys

PDAS S.Aho/A.Svechnikov 6.00 15.00
PDBK B.Burns/E.Karlsson 5.00 12.00
PDBL O.Bjorkstrand/P.Laine 5.00 12.00
PDCN T.Chabot/J.Norris 4.00 10.00
PDCT T.Chabot/B.Tkachuk 6.00 15.00
PDDN L.Draisaitl/R.Nugent-Hopkins 12.00 30.00
PDDO V.Olofsson/R.Dahlin 5.00 12.00
PDFC J.Farabee/S.Couturier 4.00 10.00
PDFK M.Fleury/P.Kane 8.00 20.00
PDGE M.Giordano/J.Eberle 4.00 10.00
PDJF R.Josi/F.Forsberg 6.00 15.00
PDJG T.Jarry/J.Guentzel 6.00 15.00
PDLB D.Larkin/T.Bertuzzi 5.00 12.00
PDMM A.Matthews/M.Marner 15.00 40.00
PDNC N.MacKinnon/C.Makar 15.00 40.00
PDPK A.Panarin/C.Kreider 8.00 20.00
PDRR N.Robertson/J.Robertson 6.00 15.00
PDSE J.Eriksson Ek/J.Spurgeon 4.00 10.00
PDSO R.O'Reilly/B.Schenn 4.00 10.00
PDSP M.Stone/M.Pacioretty 5.00 12.00
PDVH A.Vasilevskiy/V.Hedman 6.00 15.00

2021-22 Upper Deck Premier Premier Gear Jerseys

PGAM Auston Matthews 10.00 25.00
PGAO Alex Ovechkin 10.00 25.00
PGAP Artemi Panarin 5.00 12.00
PGAV Andrei Vasilevskiy 4.00 10.00
PGCM Connor McDavid 12.00 30.00
PGKK Kirill Kaprizov 8.00 20.00
PGNM Nathan MacKinnon 10.00 25.00
PGPK Patrick Kane 5.00 12.00
PGRJ Roman Josi 2.50 6.00
PGSC Sidney Crosby 10.00 25.00

2021-22 Upper Deck Premier Premier Gear Rookie Jerseys

*PATCH/25: 1.5X TO 4X BASIC
PGRAH Alexander Holtz 4.00 10.00
PGRAL Anton Lundell 5.00 12.00
PGRAT Alex Turcotte 3.00 8.00
PGRCC Cole Caufield 10.00 25.00
PGRCP Cole Perfetti 5.00 12.00
PGRCS Cole Sillinger 4.00 10.00
PGRGD Grigori Denisenko 3.00 8.00
PGRJD Jamie Drysdale 4.00 10.00
PGRJS Jeremy Swayman 8.00 20.00
PGRLR Lucas Raymond 8.00 20.00
PGRMS Moritz Seider 6.00 15.00
PGRNL Nils Lundkvist 2.50 6.00
PGRPT Philip Tomasino 3.00 8.00
PGRQB Quinton Byfield 6.00 15.00
PGRSK Spencer Knight 5.00 12.00
PGRSP Scott Perunovich 2.50 6.00
PGRTJ Tanner Jeannot 2.50 6.00
PGRTZ Trevor Zegras 5.00 12.00
PGRVP Vasily Podkolzin 3.00 8.00
PGRWE William Eklund 6.00 15.00

2021-22 Upper Deck Premier Premier Mega Jersey Duos

*PATCH/25: .75X TO 2X BASIC
PM2BL P.Laine/O.Bjorkstrand 6.00 15.00
PM2BN D.Nurse/T.Barrie 4.00 10.00
PM2BP E.Pettersson/B.Boeser 8.00 20.00
PM2CF M.Ferraro/L.Couture 6.00 15.00
PM2CO A.Ovechkin/J.Carlson 20.00 50.00
PM2DO R.Dahlin/V.Olofsson 6.00 15.00
PM2ES J.Eberle/J.Schwartz 5.00 12.00
PM2GG M.Giordano/Y.Gourde 5.00 12.00
PM2GT T.Toffoli/B.Gallagher 5.00 12.00
PM2HH M.Heiskanen/R.Hintz 6.00 15.00
PM2KP A.Panarin/C.Kreider 10.00 25.00
PM2KS P.Kessel/N.Schmaltz 5.00 12.00
PM2LB D.Larkin/T.Bertuzzi 6.00 15.00
PM2MN P.Mrazek/W.Nylander 10.00 25.00
PM2SS B.Schenn/B.Saad 5.00 12.00

2021-22 Upper Deck Premier Premier Mega Jersey Trios

PM3BMP Pastrnak Bergeron/Marchand 25.00 60.00
PM3FTK Kane/Fleury/Toews 20.00 50.00
PM3KPL Panarin/Kreider/Lafreniere 20.00 50.00
PM3KQD Quick/Kopitar/Doughty 15.00 40.00
PM3MLT Tkachuk/Lindholm Monahan 20.00 50.00
PM3NND Draisaitl/Nurse Nugent-Hopkins 30.00 80.00
PM3PDS Stone/Pacioretty/Dadonov 12.00 30.00
PM3TAS Aho/Svechnikov/Teravainen 15.0040.00

2021-22 Upper Deck Premier Premier Mega Patch Chest Logos

PMPAB Aleksander Barkov/24 50.00 120.00
PMPAD Alex DeBrincat/24 40.00 100.00
PMPAE Aaron Ekblad/24 40.00 100.00
PMPAF Adam Fox/20 40.00 100.00
PMPAK Anze Kopitar/18 50.00 120.00
PMPAM Auston Matthews/24 125.00 300.00
PMPAN Alex Nedeljkovic/21 25.00 60.00
PMPAO Alex Ovechkin/20 120.00 300.00
PMPAP Artemi Panarin/20 60.00 150.00
PMPAS Andrei Svechnikov/22 40.00 100.00
PMPAV Andrei Vasilevskiy/23 50.00 125.00
PMPBC Blake Coleman/26 25.00 60.00
PMPBG Brendan Gallagher/20 30.00 80.00
PMPBM Brad Marchand/22 60.00 150.00
PMPBO Brock Boeser/27 40.00 100.00
PMPBS Brandon Saad/18 25.00 60.00
PMPBT Brady Tkachuk/29 50.00 125.00
PMPBU Pavel Buchnevich/18 25.00 60.00
PMPBW Blake Wheeler/22 30.00 80.00
PMPCA Cam Atkinson/23 30.00 80.00
PMPCF Cam Fowler/22 30.00 80.00
PMPCG Conor Garland/27 25.00 60.00
PMPCH Connor Hellebuyck/22 60.00 150.00
PMPCK Chris Kreider/20 40.00 100.00
PMPCM Connor McDavid/22 150.00 400.00
PMPDL Dylan Larkin/21 40.00 100.00
PMPDN Darnell Nurse/22 25.00 60.00
PMPDP David Pastrnak/22 80.00 200.00
PMPEK Erik Karlsson/25 40.00 100.00
PMPEL Elias Lindholm/25 30.00 80.00
PMPEP Elias Pettersson/27 50.00 125.00
PMPFA Frederik Andersen/24 40.00 100.00
PMPGL Gabriel Landeskog/31 40.00 100.00
PMPGU Jake Guentzel/32 50.00 120.00
PMPHU Jack Hughes/30 80.00 200.00
PMPIS Igor Shesterkin/20 60.00 150.00
PMPJB Jordan Binnington/18 50.00 125.00
PMPJC Jakob Chychrun/23 30.00 80.00
PMPJE Jordan Eberle/28 30.00 80.00
PMPJG John Gibson/22 30.00 80.00
PMPJH Jonathan Huberdeau/24 40.00 100.00
PMPJM Jacob Markstrom/26 30.00 80.00
PMPJN Josh Norris/29 30.00 80.00
PMPJO John Carlson/20 30.00 80.00
PMPJP Joe Pavelski/21 40.00 100.00
PMPJS Jaden Schwartz/28 25.00 60.00
PMPJT John Tavares/24 50.00 125.00
PMPJU Juuse Saros/19 40.00 100.00
PMPJV Jakub Voracek/24 25.00 60.00
PMPKE Clayton Keller/23 40.00 100.00
PMPKK Kirill Kaprizov/19 100.00 250.00
PMPLC Logan Couture/25 40.00 100.00
PMPLD Leon Draisaitl/22 100.00 250.00
PMPMA Cale Makar/31 80.00 200.00
PMPMB Mathew Barzal/22 40.00 100.00
PMPMC Maxime Comtois/22 25.00 60.00
PMPMF Marc-Andre Fleury/24 60.00 150.00
PMPMG Mark Giordano/28 30.00 80.00
PMPMH Miro Heiskanen/21 40.00 100.00
PMPMM Mitch Marner/24 50.00 125.00
PMPMP Max Pacioretty/23 30.00 80.00
PMPMR Mikko Rantanen/30 80.00 200.00
PMPMS Mark Scheifele/22 50.00 125.00
PMPMT Matthew Tkachuk/26 60.00 150.00
PMPNE Nikolaj Ehlers/22 30.00 80.00
PMPNH Nico Hischier/30 50.00 125.00
PMPNI Nick Schmaltz/23 25.00 60.00
PMPNK Nikita Kucherov/24 60.00 150.00
PMPNM Nathan MacKinnon/31 125.00 300.00
PMPNS Nick Suzuki/20 60.00 150.00
PMPOB Oliver Bjorkstrand/24 25.00 60.00
PMPPB Patrice Bergeron/22 40.00 100.00
PMPPD Phillip Danault/18 30.00 80.00
PMPPH Phil Kessel/23 30.00 80.00
PMPPK Patrick Kane/25 60.00 150.00
PMPPL Patrik Laine/24 40.00 100.00
PMPQH Quinn Hughes/26 80.00 200.00
PMPRD Rasmus Dahlin/27 40.00 100.00
PMPRE Ryan Ellis/23 20.00 50.00
PMPRH Roope Hintz/21 40.00 100.00
PMPRJ Roman Josi/19 30.00 80.00
PMPRN Ryan Nugent-Hopkins/22 40.00 100.00
PMPRO Ryan O'Reilly/18 30.00 80.00
PMPSC Sidney Crosby/33 125.00 300.00
PMPSM Mark Stone/23 40.00 100.00
PMPSO Ilya Sorokin/22 50.00 125.00
PMPSR Sam Reinhart/24 60.00 150.00
PMPSS Steven Stamkos/23 60.00 150.00
PMPST Shea Theodore/23 40.00 100.00
PMPSV Semyon Varlamov/22 30.00 80.00
PMPTB Tyson Barrie/22 20.00 50.00
PMPTH Tomas Hertl/25 30.00 80.00
PMPTJ Tristan Jarry/33 30.00 80.00
PMPTS Tim Stutzle/29 40.00 100.00
PMPVH Victor Hedman/23 40.00 100.00
PMPVO Victor Olofsson/27 30.00 80.00
PMPVV Vitek Vanecek/20 30.00 80.00
PMPWN William Nylander/24 60.00 150.00

2021-22 Upper Deck Premier Premier Quad Jerseys

PQBOS Pastrnak/Marchand Bergeron/McAvoy 15.00 40.00
PQCGY Tkachuk/Monahan Lindholm/Gaudreau 12.00 30.00
PQCOL MacKinnon/Makar Rantanen/Landeskog 25.00 60.00
PQHAB Toffoli/Suzuki/Gallagher/Price 12.0030.00
PQNYR Panarin/Lafreniere Kreider/Fox 12.00 30.00
PQRCS Zegras/Lundell Seider/Raymond 20.00 50.00
PQTBL Vasilevskiy/Stamkos Kucherov/Hedman 12.00 30.00
PQTOR Matthews/Marner Nylander/Tavares 25.00 60.00
PQWAS Ovechkin/Carlson Kuznetsov/Oshie 25.00 60.00

2021-22 Upper Deck Premier Premier Signature Seats

PSSAB Anthony Beauvillier 5.00 12.00
PSSAH Alexander Holtz 12.00 30.00
PSSAL Alexis Lafreniere 15.00 40.00
PSSAO Alex Ovechkin 30.00 80.00
PSSAP Aliaksei Protas 8.00 20.00
PSSAS Andrei Svechnikov 10.00 25.00
PSSAT Alex Turcotte 10.00 25.00
PSSBB Brock Boeser 10.00 25.00
PSSBD Brandon Duhaime 8.00 20.00
PSSBH Brett Hull 25.00 60.00
PSSBJ Boone Jenner 8.00 20.00
PSSBM Brad Marchand 15.00 40.00
PSSBN Bernie Nicholls 6.00 15.00
PSSBO Bobby Orr 100.00 250.00
PSSBR Martin Brodeur 20.00 50.00
PSSBT Brady Tkachuk 12.00 30.00
PSSBY Bowen Byram 10.00 25.00
PSSCH Connor Hellebuyck 15.00 40.00
PSSCJ Calle Jarnkrok 5.00 12.00
PSSCM Casey Mittelstadt 8.00 20.00
PSSCS Cole Sillinger 12.00 30.00
PSSCY Charlie Coyle 8.00 20.00
PSSDC Dylan Cozens 8.00 20.00
PSSDH Dominik Hasek 12.00 30.00
PSSDM Dawson Mercer 20.00 50.00
PSSDS Dylan Strome 10.00 25.00
PSSDW Doug Weight 8.00 20.00
PSSET Eeli Tolvanen 8.00 20.00
PSSGP Garrett Pilon 10.00 25.00
PSSHJ Henri Jokiharju 5.00 12.00
PSSHL Hendrix Lapierre 8.00 20.00
PSSJA Josh Anderson 6.00 15.00
PSSJB Justin Barron 12.00 30.00
PSSJC Jack Campbell 8.00 20.00
PSSJG Jake Guentzel 12.00 30.00
PSSJH Jonathan Huberdeau 10.00 25.00
PSSJL John LeClair 8.00 20.00
PSSJM J.J. Moser 8.00 20.00
PSSJP Jesse Puljujarvi 8.00 20.00
PSSJR Jack Roslovic 5.00 12.00
PSSJV Joe Veleno 10.00 25.00
PSSLR Lucas Raymond 25.00 60.00
PSSLT Lassi Thomson 8.00 20.00
PSSLU Anton Lundell 15.00 40.00
PSSMA Mason McTavish 25.00 60.00
PSSMB Michael Bunting 8.00 20.00
PSSMD Marcel Dionne 10.00 25.00
PSSMF Marc-Andre Fleury 15.00 40.00
PSSMG Mike Gartner 10.00 25.00
PSSML Mario Lemieux 30.00 80.00
PSSMM Mark Messier 15.00 40.00
PSSMT Matthew Tkachuk 15.00 40.00
PSSND Nico Daws 12.00 30.00
PSSNE Brock Nelson 8.00 20.00
PSSNL Nils Lundkvist 8.00 20.00
PSSNR Nick Robertson 8.00 20.00
PSSPA Joe Pavelski 10.00 25.00
PSSPD Pavel Dorofeyev 10.00 25.00
PSSPK Peyton Krebs 6.00 15.00
PSSPT Philip Tomasino 10.00 25.00
PSSRH Ron Hextall 8.00 20.00
PSSRM Ryan Merkley 10.00 25.00
PSSSH Shayne Corson 6.00 15.00
PSSSJ Seth Jarvis 30.00 80.00
PSSSK Saku Koivu 8.00 20.00
PSSST Martin St. Louis 8.00 20.00
PSSSZ Sergei Zubov 6.00 15.00
PSSTB Tyler Bertuzzi 6.00 15.00
PSSTF Theoren Fleury 8.00 20.00
PSSTI Tim Stutzle 15.00 40.00
PSSTJ Tanner Jeannot 8.00 20.00
PSSTS Teemu Selanne 15.00 40.00
PSSTT Tony Twist 5.00 12.00
PSSWE William Eklund 20.00 50.00
PSSWG Wayne Gretzky 250.00 600.00
PSSWK William Karlsson 10.00 25.00

2021-22 Upper Deck Premier Premier Triple Jerseys

PTBPS Pastrnak/Swayman/Bergeron 15.00 40.00
PTBSO Binnington/Schenn/O'Reilly 8.00 20.00
PTCTS Stutzle/Tkachuk/Chabot 8.00 20.00
PTDJF Josi/Duchene/Forsberg 8.00 20.00
PTEBR Barkov/Ekblad/Reinhart 10.00 25.00
PTFKT Fleury/Kane/Toews 10.00 25.00
PTGFG Fowler/Gibson/Getzlaf 5.00 12.00
PTHBP Boeser/Pettersson/Horvat 8.00 20.00
PTKGC Chychrun/Gostisbehere/Kessel 5.0012.00
PTLDT Lehner/Dadonov/Theodore 6.00 15.00
PTMRN Muzzin/Rielly/Nylander 10.00 25.00
PTPSC Suzuki/Price/Caufield 20.00 50.00

2021-22 Upper Deck Premier Rookie Patch-Taculars Chest Logos

RPTAB Adam Beckman 10.00 25.00
RPTAH Alexander Holtz 20.00 50.00
RPTAN Alex Newhook 30.00 80.00
RPTAR Arttu Ruotsalainen 10.00 25.00
RPTBD Brandon Duhaime 10.00 25.00
RPTBE Jacob Bernard-Docker 10.00 25.00
RPTBG Benoit-Olivier Groulx 10.00 25.00
RPTBK Boris Katchouk 8.00 20.00
RPTBL Brett Leason 10.00 25.00
RPTCA Calen Addison 10.00 25.00
RPTCP Cole Perfetti 20.00 50.00
RPTCS Cole Sillinger 15.00 40.00
RPTCY Cam York 10.00 25.00
RPTDA Jonathan Dahlen 10.00 25.00
RPTDF David Farrance 10.00 25.00
RPTFG Filip Gustavsson 20.00 50.00
RPTGD Grigori Denisenko 15.00 40.00
RPTGF Gabriel Fortier 12.00 30.00
RPTHL Hendrix Lapierre 10.00 25.00
RPTIP Ivan Prosvetov 10.00 25.00
RPTJA Jack Ahcan 10.00 25.00
RPTJB Jacob Bryson 10.00 25.00
RPTJD Jamie Drysdale 15.00 40.00
RPTJK Joey Keane 8.00 20.00
RPTJL Jake Leschyshyn 10.00 25.00
RPTJN Jake Neighbours 20.00 50.00
RPTJP JJ Peterka 40.00 100.00
RPTJS Jeremy Swayman 30.00 80.00
RPTJV Joe Veleno 12.00 30.00
RPTJW Jasper Weatherby 10.00 25.00
RPTKB Kasper Bjorkqvist 10.00 25.00
RPTKL Kole Lind 20.00 50.00
RPTKV Karel Vejmelka 12.00 30.00
RPTLP Lane Pederson 10.00 25.00
RPTLR Lucas Raymond 30.00 80.00
RPTLT Lassi Thomson 10.00 25.00
RPTMH Mike Hardman 10.00 25.00
RPTMI Daniil Miromanov 10.00 25.00
RPTMM Mason McTavish 20.00 50.00
RPTMS Moritz Seider 50.00 125.00
RPTOS Oskar Steen 12.00 30.00
RPTPD Pavel Dorofeyev 12.00 30.00
RPTPI Shane Pinto 15.00 40.00
RPTPK Parker Kelly 10.00 25.00
RPTPT Philip Tomasino 40.00 100.00
RPTRC Ross Colton 12.00 30.00
RPTRD Riley Damiani 10.00 25.00
RPTRK Rasmus Kupari 10.00 25.00
RPTRM Ryan Merkley 12.00 30.00
RPTRZ Radim Zohorna 10.00 25.00
RPTSK Spencer Knight 30.00 80.00
RPTSP Scott Perunovich 10.00 25.00
RPTSR Sampo Ranta 10.00 25.00
RPTTH Logan Thompson 60.00 150.00
RPTTJ Tanner Jeannot 10.00 25.00
RPTTL Tanner Laczynski 10.00 25.00
RPTTR Taylor Raddysh 15.00 40.00
RPTTT Tyce Thompson 15.00 40.00
RPTTZ Trevor Zegras 150.00 400.00
RPTUL Ukko-Pekka Luukkonen 15.00 40.00
RPTVP Vasily Podkolzin 12.00 30.00
RPTWE William Eklund 50.00 125.00
RPTWK Wyatt Kalynuk 10.00 25.00
RPTZJ Zac Jones 12.00 30.00

2021-22 Upper Deck Premier Star Systems Autographs

SSBY Bowen Byram/49 25.00 60.00
SSDC Dylan Cozens/49 12.00 30.00
SSKR Peyton Krebs/49 10.00 25.00
SSSR Sam Reinhart/49 25.00 60.00
SSTS Teemu Selanne/25 25.00 60.00

2021-22 Upper Deck Premier Star Systems Patch Autographs

*GOLD: .5X TO 1.2X BASIC
SSAS Andrei Svechnikov/49 20.00 50.00
SSBJ Boone Jenner/49 15.00 40.00
SSBM Brad Marchand/49 30.00 80.00
SSBT Brady Tkachuk/49 25.00 60.00
SSJH Jonathan Huberdeau/49 20.00 50.00
SSMF Marc-Andre Fleury/49 30.00 80.00
SSST Tim Stutzle/49 20.00 50.00
SSTT Troy Terry/49 12.00 30.00

2021-22 Upper Deck Premier Star Systems Rookie Patch Autographs

SSRAB Adam Beckman/149 10.00 25.00
SSRAL Anton Lundell/75 25.00 60.00
SSRAR Arttu Ruotsalainen/149 10.00 25.00
SSRAT Alex Turcotte/149 12.00 30.00
SSRBD Brandon Duhaime/149 10.00 25.00
SSRBG Benoit-Olivier Groulx/149 10.00 25.00
SSRBK Boris Katchouk/149 8.00 20.00
SSRCC Cole Caufield/25 300.00 800.00
SSRCP Cole Perfetti/149 20.00 50.00
SSRCS Cole Sillinger/149 15.00 40.00
SSRDF David Farrance/149 10.00 25.00
SSRDM Dawson Mercer/149 30.00 80.00
SSRDR Jamie Drysdale/75 15.00 40.00
SSRGF Gabriel Fortier/149 10.00 25.00
SSRHL Hendrix Lapierre/149 10.00 25.00
SSRJB Jacob Bryson/149 10.00 25.00
SSRJM J.J. Moser/149 10.00 25.00
SSRJN Jake Neighbours/149 20.00 50.00
SSRJP JJ Peterka/149 30.00 80.00
SSRJV Joe Veleno/149 12.00 30.00
SSRJW Jasper Weatherby/149 10.00 25.00
SSRKB Kasper Bjorkqvist/149 10.00 25.00
SSRMB Morgan Barron/149 8.00 20.00
SSRMI Daniil Miromanov/149 10.00 25.00
SSRMM Mason McTavish/149 20.00 50.00
SSRPD Pavel Dorofeyev/149 12.00 30.00
SSRPE Scott Perunovich/149 10.00 25.00
SSRPK Parker Kelly/149 10.00 25.00
SSRPT Philip Tomasino/149 12.00 30.00
SSRRC Ross Colton/149 12.00 30.00
SSRRD Riley Damiani/149 10.00 25.00
SSRRK Rasmus Kupari/149 10.00 25.00
SSRRM Ryan Merkley/149 12.00 30.00
SSRRT Riley Tufte/149 10.00 25.00
SSRSD Sean Durzi/149 10.00 25.00
SSRSJ Seth Jarvis/75 25.00 60.00
SSRSK Spencer Knight/75 20.00 50.00
SSRSR Sampo Ranta/149 10.00 25.00
SSRTJ Tanner Jeannot/149 10.00 25.00
SSRWE William Eklund/149 25.00 60.00
SSRZJ Zac Jones/149 12.00 30.00

2021-22 Upper Deck Premier Star Systems Rookie Patch Autographs Gold

*GOLD/25: .6X TO 1.5X BASIC
SSRJN Jake Neighbours/25 40.00 100.00

2022-23 Upper Deck Premier

1 Alex Ovechkin 4.00 10.00
2 Ryan Nugent-Hopkins 1.25 3.00
3 Adam Fox 1.25 3.00
4 Nico Hischier 1.50 4.00
5 Yanni Gourde .75 2.00
6 Artemi Panarin 2.00 5.00
7 Sebastian Aho 1.50 4.00
8 Dawson Mercer 1.25 3.00
9 Trevor Zegras 1.00 2.50
10 Matt Duchene 1.00 2.50
11 Brad Marchand 2.00 5.00
12 Jason Robertson 1.50 4.00
13 David Pastrnak 2.50 6.00
14 Roope Hintz 1.25 3.00
15 Roman Josi 1.00 2.50
16 Gabriel Landeskog 1.25 3.00
17 Jonathan Huberdeau 1.25 3.00
18 Nikolaj Ehlers 1.00 2.50
19 Victor Hedman 1.25 3.00
20 Josh Norris 1.00 2.50
21 Miro Heiskanen 1.25 3.00
22 Lucas Raymond 1.50 4.00
24 Johnny Gaudreau 1.50 4.00
25 Kris Letang 1.25 3.00
26 Jake Oettinger 1.50 4.00
27 Auston Matthews 4.00 10.00
28 Jack Hughes 2.50 6.00
29 Joe Pavelski 1.25 3.00
30 John Tavares 1.50 4.00
31 Jacob Markstrom 1.00 2.50
32 Zach Werenski 1.50 4.00
33 Thatcher Demko 1.25 3.00
34 Clayton Keller 1.25 3.00
35 Tim Stutzle 1.25 3.00

36 Brady Tkachuk 1.50 4.00
37 Leon Draisaitl 3.00 8.00
38 Evgeni Malkin 2.00 5.00
39 Mats Zuccarello 1.00 2.50
40 Logan Couture 1.25 3.00
41 Patrice Bergeron 1.25 3.00
42 Nick Schmaltz .75 2.00
43 Elias Pettersson 1.50 4.00
44 Sidney Crosby 4.00 10.00
45 Tage Thompson 1.25 3.00
46 Nick Suzuki 2.00 5.00
47 Alex DeBrincat 1.25 3.00
48 Quinn Hughes 2.50 6.00
49 Kirill Kaprizov 3.00 8.00
50 Aleksander Barkov 1.50 4.00
51 Ryan Strome 1.00 2.50
52 Cole Caufield 2.00 5.00
53 Evgeny Kuznetsov 1.25 3.00
54 Jordan Eberle 1.00 2.50
55 Juuse Saros 1.25 3.00
56 Mikko Rantanen 2.50 6.00
57 Igor Shesterkin 2.00 5.00
58 Kyle Connor 1.50 4.00
59 John Carlson 1.00 2.50
60 Filip Forsberg 1.50 4.00
61 Marc-Andre Fleury 2.00 5.00
62 Erik Karlsson 1.25 3.00
63 Andrei Svechnikov 1.25 3.00
64 Jordan Kyrou 1.00 2.50
65 Connor McDavid .5.00 12.00
66 Kirby Dach 1.00 2.50
67 Mitch Marner 1.50 4.00
68 Robert Thomas 1.00 2.50
69 Aaron Ekblad 1.25 3.00
70 Ilya Sorokin 1.50 4.00
71 Anders Lee .75 2.00
72 Jaccob Slavin .75 2.00
73 Brock Nelson 1.00 2.50
74 Anze Kopitar 1.50 4.00
75 Cam Atkinson 1.00 2.50
76 Dylan Larkin 1.25 3.00
77 Tyler Toffoli 1.00 2.50
78 Alexis Lafreniere 1.50 4.00
79 Andrei Vasilevskiy 1.50 4.00
80 Cale Makar 2.50 6.00
81 Nathan MacKinnon 4.00 10.00
82 Moritz Seider 1.25 3.00
83 Steven Stamkos 2.00 5.00
84 Kevin Fiala .75 2.00
85 Thomas Chabot 1.00 2.50
86 Jack Eichel 1.50 4.00
87 Matthew Tkachuk 2.00 5.00
88 Colton Parayko .75 2.00
89 Rasmus Dahlin 1.25 3.00
90 Mark Stone 1.25 3.00
91 Dominik Hasek 6.00 15.00
92 Joe Sakic 8.00 20.00
93 Wayne Gretzky 25.00 60.00
94 Patrick Roy 10.00 25.00
95 Mario Lemieux 15.00 40.00
96 Martin Brodeur 10.00 25.00
97 Henrik Zetterberg 5.00 12.00
98 Mark Messier 8.00 20.00
99 Peter Forsberg 8.00 20.00
100 Eric Lindros 6.00 15.00
101 Jonatan Berggren RC 3.00 8.00
102 Matty Beniers RC 5.00 12.00
103 Kaiden Guhle RC 4.00 10.00
104 Jordan Spence RC 2.00 5.00
105 Elmer Soderblom RC 4.00 10.00
106 Wyatt Johnston RC 8.00 20.00
107 Pyotr Kochetkov RC 4.00 10.00
108 Dylan Holloway RC 4.00 10.00
109 Filip Roos RC 1.50 4.00
110 Cole Koepke RC 2.00 5.00
111 Owen Power RC 4.00 10.00
112 Jean-Luc Foudy RC 2.00 5.00
113 Bobby Brink RC 2.00 5.00
114 Lukas Dostal RC 4.00 10.00
115 Juraj Slafkovsky RC 10.00 25.00
116 Juuso Parssinen RC 2.00 5.00
117 Thomas Bordeleau RC 2.00 5.00
118 Pavol Regenda RC 2.00 5.00
119 Noah Cates RC 2.00 5.00
120 Zack Hayes RC 1.50 4.00
121 Braden Schneider RC 3.00 8.00
122 Brayden Tracey RC 1.50 4.00
123 Johnathan Kovacevic RC 2.00 5.00
124 Jack Quinn RC 3.00 8.00
125 Lukas Reichel RC 4.00 10.00
126 Matias Maccelli RC 3.00 8.00
127 Kirill Marchenko RC 5.00 12.00
128 Matt Boldy RC 6.00 15.00
129 Dylan Guenther RC 5.00 12.00
130 Reilly Walsh RC 2.00 5.00
131 Kent Johnson RC 4.00 10.00
132 Shane Wright RC 5.00 12.00
133 Pontus Holmberg RC 2.00 5.00
134 Mads Sogaard RC 2.50 6.00
135 David Jiricek RC 4.00 10.00
136 Aatu Raty RC 2.00 5.00
137 Brandt Clarke RC 4.00 10.00
138 Samuel Poulin RC 2.50 6.00
139 Dylan Samberg RC 2.00 5.00
140 Marc McLaughlin RC 2.00 5.00
141 Andrei Kuzmenko RC 4.00 10.00
142 Marco Rossi RC 5.00 12.00
143 Arber Xhekaj RC 4.00 10.00
144 Simon Holmstrom RC 2.00 5.00
145 Oskar Olausson RC 2.00 5.00
146 Nick Perbix RC 1.50 4.00
147 Jake Sanderson RC 5.00 12.00
148 Nick Abruzzese RC 2.00 5.00
149 Samuel Fagemo RC 1.50 4.00
150 Jakub Lauko RC 2.50 6.00

2022-23 Upper Deck Premier Bronze

BRONZE RC/199: .5X TO 1.2X BASIC

2022-23 Upper Deck Premier Gold

GOLD/65: .6X TO 1.5X BASIC
GOLD LEG/25: .8X TO 2X BASIC
GOLD RC/65: .8X TO 2X BASIC

2022-23 Upper Deck Premier '03-04 Rookie Patch Autographs

SRRBC Brandt Clarke/99 25.00 60.00
SRRBO Matt Boldy/49 80.00 200.00
SRRDG Dylan Guenther/99 30.00 80.00
SRRDH Dylan Holloway/99 25.00 60.00
SRRDJ David Jiricek/99 25.00 60.00
SRRES Elmer Soderblom/99 25.00 60.00
SRRHG Kaiden Guhle/99 40.00 100.00
SRRHJ Kent Johnson/99 25.00 60.00
SRRHM Kirill Marchenko/99 30.00 80.00
SRRJS Juraj Slafkovsky/49 100.00 250.00
SRRLD Lukas Dostal/99 50.00 125.00
SRRLR Lukas Reichel/99 25.00 60.00
SRRMB Matty Beniers/49 60.00 150.00
SRRMR Marco Rossi/99 30.00 80.00
SRROP Owen Power/49 25.00 60.00
SRRSA Jake Sanderson/99 30.00 80.00
SRRSF Samuel Fagemo/99 10.00 25.00
SRRSW Shane Wright/49 500.00 125.00
SRRTB Thomas Bordeleau/99 12.00 30.00
SRRWJ Wyatt Johnston/99 100.00 250.00

2022-23 Upper Deck Premier '22 Premier Rookie Jersey Autographs

PRAAM Nils Aman/99 10.00 25.00
PRAAX Arber Xhekaj/99 30.00 80.00
PRABC Brandt Clarke/25 20.00 50.00
PRABL Matej Blumel/99 12.00 30.00
PRABM Ben Meyers/99 10.00 25.00
PRABO Matt Boldy/25 30.00 80.00
PRABR Bobby Brink/99 10.00 25.00
PRACK Cole Koepke/99 10.00 25.00
PRADG Dylan Guenther/99 25.00 60.00
PRADJ David Jiricek/25 20.00 50.00
PRADS Dylan Samberg/25 10.00 25.00
PRAES Elmer Soderblom/99 20.00 50.00
PRAFH Filip Hallander/99 10.00 25.00
PRAFK Fredrik Karlstrom/99 8.00 20.00
PRAFR Filip Roos/99 8.00 20.00
PRAHH Hayden Hodgson/99 8.00 20.00
PRAJB Jonatan Berggren/99 15.00 40.00
PRAJK Johnathan Kovacevic/99 10.00 25.00
PRAJM Jack McBain/99 10.00 25.00
PRAJP Jacob Perreault/99 10.00 25.00
PRAJS Juraj Slafkovsky/25 80.00 200.00
PRAKG Kaiden Guhle/99 20.00 50.00
PRAKJ Kent Johnson/25 20.00 50.00
PRAKK Kaedan Korczak/99 8.00 20.00
PRALD Lukas Dostal/99 30.00 80.00
PRALR Lukas Reichel/25 20.00 50.00
PRAMB Matty Beniers/25 25.00 60.00
PRAMC Marc McLaughlin/99 10.00 25.00
PRAMM Matias Maccelli/99 15.00 40.00
PRAMR Marco Rossi/25 25.00 60.00
PRANA Nick Abruzzese/99 10.00 25.00
PRANB Nick Blankenburg/99 8.00 20.00
PRANC Noah Cates/99 10.00 25.00
PRAND Nick DeSimone/99 10.00 25.00
PRANP Nick Perbix/99 8.00 20.00
PRANS Nathan Smith/99 8.00 20.00
PRAOL Olle Lycksell/99 10.00 25.00
PRAOO Oskar Olausson/99 10.00 25.00
PRAOP Owen Power/25 20.00 50.00
PRAPA Juuso Parssinen/99 10.00 25.00
PRAPH Pontus Holmberg/99 10.00 25.00
PRAPK Pyotr Kochetkov/25 20.00 50.00
PRAPR Pavol Regenda/99 10.00 25.00
PRARA Ronnie Attard/99 10.00 25.00
PRARW Reilly Walsh/99 10.00 25.00
PRASA Jake Sanderson/25 25.00 60.00
PRASF Samuel Fagemo/99 8.00 20.00
PRASW Shane Wright/25 25.00 60.00
PRATB Thomas Bordeleau/99 10.00 25.00
PRAVK Vladislav Kolyachonok/99 8.00 20.00
PRAVP Valtteri Puustinen/99 8.00 20.00
PRAWB William Bitten/99 10.00 25.00
PRAWJ Wyatt Johnston/99 60.00 150.00
PRAZH Zack Hayes/99 8.00 20.00

2022-23 Upper Deck Premier Acetate Horizontal Rookie Patch Autographs

*GOLD: .5X TO 1.2X BASIC
AHRBC Brandt Clarke/99 30.00 80.00
AHRBO Matt Boldy/49 50.00 125.00
AHRDG Dylan Guenther/99 60.00 150.00
AHRDH Dylan Holloway/99 30.00 80.00
AHRDJ David Jiricek/99 30.00 80.00
AHRDS Dylan Samberg/99 15.00 40.00
AHRJP Jacob Perreault/99 15.00 40.00
AHRJS Juraj Slafkovsky/49 125.00 300.00
AHRKG Kaiden Guhle/99 30.00 80.00
AHRKJ Kent Johnson/99 30.00 80.00
AHRLD Lukas Dostal/99 60.00 150.00
AHRLR Lukas Reichel/99 30.00 80.00
AHRMB Matty Beniers/49 60.00 150.00
AHRMR Marco Rossi/99 40.00 100.00
AHROP Owen Power/49 30.00 80.00
AHRSA Jake Sanderson/99 40.00 100.00
AHRSW Shane Wright/49 40.00 100.00
AHRTB Thomas Bordeleau/99 15.00 40.00
AHRWJ Wyatt Johnston/99 60.00 150.00

2022-23 Upper Deck Premier Acetate Patch Autographs

AVAC Andrew Copp/49 10.00 25.00
AVAL Alexis Lafreniere/35 40.00 100.00
AVAN Anton Lundell/49 15.00 40.00
AVAS Andrei Svechnikov/35 30.00 80.00
AVBC Blake Coleman/49 12.00 30.00
AVBJ Boone Jenner/49 15.00 40.00
AVBN Brock Nelson/49 15.00 40.00
AVBT Brady Tkachuk/35 25.00 60.00
AVCC Charlie Coyle/49 15.00 40.00
AVCP Cole Perfetti/35 15.00 40.00
AVDM Dawson Mercer/49 20.00 50.00
AVEB Jordan Eberle/35 15.00 40.00
AVEK Joel Eriksson Ek/49 12.00 30.00
AVGL Gabriel Landeskog/49 20.00 50.00
AVJG Jake Guentzel/35 25.00 60.00
AVJH Jonathan Huberdeau/35 20.00 50.00
AVJK Jordan Kyrou/49 15.00 40.00
AVJM Jacob Markstrom/49 15.00 40.00
AVJO Jake Oettinger/35 25.00 60.00
AVJS Jeremy Swayman/35 25.00 60.00
AVKM K'Andre Miller/49 12.00 30.00
AVLE Anders Lee/49 12.00 30.00
AVMB Michael Bunting/35 15.00 40.00
AVMC Jared McCann/49 12.00 30.00
AVMH Miro Heiskanen/35 20.00 50.00
AVMN Martin Necas/49 25.00 60.00
AVMR Mikko Rantanen/35 40.00 100.00
AVMS Mark Stone/35 40.00 100.00
AVMT Matthew Tkachuk/35 50.00 125.00
AVPK Peyton Krebs/49 12.00 30.00
AVQH Quinn Hughes/49 40.00 100.00
AVRH Roope Hintz/49 20.00 50.00
AVRS Ryan Strome/49 15.00 40.00
AVRT Robert Thomas/49 15.00 40.00
AVRY Ryan O'Reilly/49 15.00 40.00
AVSK Spencer Knight/49 15.00 40.00
AVSL Jaccob Slavin/49 12.00 30.00
AVSO Ilya Sorokin/49 60.00 150.00
AVST Shea Theodore/35 20.00 50.00
AVTH Tomas Hertl/35 15.00 40.00
AVTO Tyler Toffoli/35 15.00 40.00
AVTS Tim Stutzle/35 40.00 100.00
AVTT Tage Thompson/35 30.00 80.00

2022-23 Upper Deck Premier Acetate Rookie Patch Autographs

ARAB Nick Abruzzese/249 10.00 25.00
ARAX Arber Xhekaj/249 20.00 50.00
ARBB Bobby Brink/249 10.00 25.00
ARBC Brandt Clarke/249 40.00 100.00
ARBL Matej Blumel/249 12.00 30.00
ARBO Matt Boldy/99 50.00 125.00
ARCK Cole Koepke/249 10.00 25.00
ARDG Dylan Guenther/249 40.00 100.00
ARDH Dylan Holloway/249 20.00 50.00
ARDJ David Jiricek/249 20.00 50.00
ARDS Dylan Samberg/249 10.00 25.00
ARES Elmer Soderblom/249 20.00 50.00
ARFH Filip Hallander/249 10.00 25.00
ARFK Fredrik Karlstrom/249 8.00 20.00
ARFR Filip Roos/249 8.00 20.00
ARJB Jonatan Berggren/249 15.00 40.00
ARJF Jean-Luc Foudy/249 10.00 25.00
ARJH Jordan Harris/249 12.00 30.00
ARJK Johnathan Kovacevic/249 10.00 25.00
ARJP Jacob Perreault/249 10.00 25.00
ARJS Juraj Slafkovsky/99 80.00 200.00
ARJU Juuso Parssinen/249 10.00 25.00
ARKG Kaiden Guhle/249 20.00 50.00
ARKJ Kent Johnson/99 60.00 150.00
ARKK Kaedan Korczak/249 8.00 20.00
ARKM Kirill Marchenko/249 25.00 60.00
ARLD Lukas Dostal/249 20.00 50.00
ARLR Lukas Reichel/249 20.00 50.00
ARMA Matias Maccelli/249 15.00 40.00
ARMB Matty Beniers/99 60.00 150.00
ARMC Jack McBain/249 10.00 25.00
ARMM Marc McLaughlin/249 10.00 25.00
ARMR Marco Rossi/249 40.00 100.00
ARMS Mads Sogaard/249 12.00 30.00
ARNA Nils Aman/249 10.00 25.00
ARNB Nick Blankenburg/249 8.00 20.00
ARNC Noah Cates/249 10.00 25.00
ARND Nick DeSimone/249 10.00 25.00
ARNI Nikita Alexandrov/249 10.00 25.00
ARNP Nick Perbix/249 8.00 20.00
ARNS Nathan Smith/249 8.00 20.00
AROL Olle Lycksell/249 10.00 25.00
AROO Oskar Olausson/249 10.00 25.00
AROP Owen Power/99 40.00 100.00
ARPH Pontus Holmberg/249 10.00 25.00
ARPR Pavol Regenda/249 10.00 25.00
ARRA Ronnie Attard/249 10.00 25.00
ARRW Reilly Walsh/249 10.00 25.00
ARSA Jake Sanderson/99 25.00 60.00
ARSF Samuel Fagemo/249 8.00 20.00
ARSW Shane Wright/99 50.00 125.00
ARTB Thomas Bordeleau/249 10.00 25.00
ARVK Vladislav Kolyachonok/249 8.00 20.00
ARVP Valtteri Puustinen/249 8.00 20.00
ARWB William Bitton/249 10.00 25.00
ARWJ Wyatt Johnston/99 80.00 200.00
ARZH Zack Hayes/249 8.00 20.00

2022-23 Upper Deck Premier Acetate Rookie Patch Autographs Gold

*GOLD: .8X TO 2X BASIC
ARDG Dylan Guenther/65 100.00 250.00
ARLD Lukas Dostal/65 80.00 200.00
ARPK Pyotr Kochetkov/65 125.00 300.00

2022-23 Upper Deck Premier Autographs

*GOLD: .6X TO 1.5X BASIC
1 Alex Ovechkin SP 125.00 300.00
2 Ryan Nugent-Hopkins 10.00 25.00
4 Nico Hischier SP 12.00 30.00
8 Dawson Mercer 10.00 25.00
11 Brad Marchand SP 15.00 40.00
14 Roope Hintz 10.00 25.00
15 Roman Josi 8.00 20.00
16 Gabriel Landeskog 10.00 25.00
17 Jonathan Huberdeau 10.00 25.00
21 Miro Heiskanen 10.00 25.00
26 Jake Oettinger 12.00 30.00
29 Joe Pavelski 10.00 25.00
31 Jacob Markstrom 8.00 20.00
35 Tim Stutzle 10.00 25.00
36 Brady Tkachuk 12.00 30.00
41 Patrice Bergeron 10.00 25.00
42 Nick Schmaltz 6.00 15.00
43 Elias Pettersson 12.00 30.00
45 Tage Thompson 10.00 25.00
47 Alex DeBrincat 10.00 25.00
48 Quinn Hughes SP 20.00 50.00
51 Ryan Strome 8.00 20.00
54 Jordan Eberle 8.00 20.00
55 Juuse Saros 10.00 25.00
56 Mikko Rantanen SP 20.00 50.00
57 Igor Shesterkin SP 40.00 100.00
58 Kyle Connor 12.00 30.00
59 John Carlson SP 20.00 50.00
61 Marc-Andre Fleury SP 40.00 100.00
63 Andrei Svechnikov 10.00 25.00
64 Jordan Kyrou 8.00 20.00
65 Connor McDavid SP 150.00 400.00
67 Mitch Marner SP 12.00 30.00
68 Robert Thomas 8.00 20.00
70 Ilya Sorokin SP 12.00 30.00
71 Anders Lee 6.00 15.00
72 Jaccob Slavin 6.00 15.00
73 Brock Nelson 8.00 20.00
75 Cam Atkinson 8.00 20.00
77 Tyler Toffoli 8.00 20.00
78 Alexis Lafreniere SP 12.00 30.00
79 Andrei Vasilevskiy SP 12.00 30.00
80 Cale Makar SP 60.00 150.00
84 Kevin Fiala 6.00 15.00
87 Matthew Tkachuk 15.00 40.00
88 Colton Parayko 6.00 15.00
90 Mark Stone 10.00 25.00
91 Dominik Hasek SP 25.00 60.00
93 Wayne Gretzky SP 125.00 300.00
94 Patrick Roy SP 50.00 125.00
95 Mario Lemieux SP 60.00 150.00
96 Martin Brodeur SP 40.00 100.00
97 Henrik Zetterberg SP 20.00 50.00
98 Mark Messier SP 30.00 80.00
100 Eric Lindros SP 40.00 100.00
101 Jonatan Berggren 12.00 30.00
102 Matty Beniers SP 20.00 50.00
103 Kaiden Guhle 15.00 40.00
105 Elmer Soderblom 15.00 40.00
106 Wyatt Johnston 30.00 80.00
107 Pyotr Kochetkov 15.00 40.00
108 Dylan Holloway 15.00 40.00
110 Cole Koepke 8.00 20.00
111 Owen Power SP 15.00 40.00
112 Jean-Luc Foudy 8.00 20.00
113 Bobby Brink 8.00 20.00
114 Lukas Dostal 15.00 40.00
115 Juraj Slafkovsky SP 80.00 200.00
116 Juuso Parssinen 8.00 20.00
117 Thomas Bordeleau 8.00 20.00
118 Pavol Regenda 8.00 20.00
119 Noah Cates 8.00 20.00
120 Zack Hayes 6.00 15.00
123 Johnathan Kovacevic 8.00 20.00
125 Lukas Reichel 15.00 40.00
126 Matias Maccelli 12.00 30.00
127 Kirill Marchenko 20.00 50.00
128 Matt Boldy SP 50.00 125.00
129 Dylan Guenther 20.00 50.00
130 Reilly Walsh 8.00 20.00
131 Kent Johnson 15.00 40.00
132 Shane Wright SP 20.00 50.00
133 Pontus Holmberg 8.00 20.00
134 Mads Sogaard 10.00 25.00
135 David Jiricek 15.00 40.00
136 Aatu Raty 8.00 20.00
137 Brandt Clarke 15.00 40.00
139 Dylan Samberg 8.00 20.00
140 Marc McLaughlin 8.00 20.00
142 Marco Rossi 20.00 50.00
143 Arber Xhekaj 15.00 40.00
145 Oskar Olausson 8.00 20.00
146 Nick Perbix 6.00 15.00
147 Jake Sanderson 20.00 50.00
148 Nick Abruzzese 8.00 20.00
149 Samuel Fagemo 6.00 15.00

2022-23 Upper Deck Premier Dual Rookie Patch-Taculars Chest Logos

DRPTBA W.Bitten/N.Alexandrov 10.00 25.00
DRPTBM K.Marchenko N.Blankenburg 25.00 60.00
DRPTBR B.Brink/I.Ratcliffe 10.00 25.00
DRPTCF B.Clarke/S.Fagemo 20.00 50.00
DRPTDK S.Der-Arguchintsev E.Kallgren 10.00 25.00
DRPTFC T.Fix-Wolansky J.Christiansen 10.00 25.00
DRPTFO O.Olausson/J.Foudy 10.00 25.00
DRPTGM D.Guenther/M.Maccelli 25.00 60.00
DRPTHX J.Harris/A.Xhekaj 20.00 50.00
DRPTJB W.Johnston/M.Blumel 40.00 100.00
DRPTJJ K.Johnson/D.Jiricek 20.00 50.00
DRPTKD L.Dostal/P.Kochetkov 20.00 50.00
DRPTKH K.Korczak/Z.Hayes 8.00 20.00
DRPTKP N.Perbix/C.Koepke 10.00 25.00
DRPTLM J.Lauko/M.McLaughlin 12.00 30.00
DRPTMS J.Moverare/J.Spence 10.00 25.00
DRPTOW N.Okhotiuk/R.Walsh 10.00 25.00
DRPTPH S.Poulin/F.Hallander 12.00 30.00
DRPTPT J.Perreault/B.Tracey 10.00 25.00
DRPTQP J.Quinn/O.Power 20.00 50.00
DRPTRB M.Boldy/M.Rossi 30.00 80.00
DRPTRC N.Cates/I.Ratcliffe 10.00 25.00
DRPTRV L.Reichel/A.Vlasic 20.00 50.00
DRPTSM N.Smith/J.McBain 10.00 25.00
DRPTSS J.Sanderson/M.Sogaard 25.00 60.00
DRPTWB S.Wright/M.Beniers 25.00 60.00

2022-23 Upper Deck Premier Jerseys

*PREMIUM/25: .8X TO 2X BASIC
*PREMIUM RC: 2X TO 5X BASIC
1 Alex Ovechkin 6.00 15.00
2 Ryan Nugent-Hopkins 2.00 5.00
3 Adam Fox 2.00 5.00
4 Nico Hischier 2.50 6.00
5 Yanni Gourde 1.25 3.00
6 Artemi Panarin 3.00 8.00
7 Sebastian Aho 2.50 6.00
8 Dawson Mercer 2.00 5.00
9 Trevor Zegras 1.50 4.00
10 Matt Duchene 1.50 4.00
11 Brad Marchand 3.00 8.00
12 Jason Robertson 2.50 6.00
13 David Pastrnak 4.00 10.00
14 Roope Hintz 2.00 5.00
15 Roman Josi 1.50 4.00
16 Gabriel Landeskog 2.00 5.00
17 Jonathan Huberdeau 2.00 5.00
18 Nikolaj Ehlers 1.50 4.00
19 Victor Hedman 2.00 5.00
20 Josh Norris 1.50 4.00
21 Miro Heiskanen 2.00 5.00
22 Lucas Raymond 2.50 6.00
24 Johnny Gaudreau 2.50 6.00
25 Kris Letang 2.00 5.00
26 Jake Oettinger 2.50 6.00
27 Auston Matthews 6.00 15.00
28 Jack Hughes 4.00 10.00
29 Joe Pavelski 2.00 5.00
30 John Tavares 2.50 6.00
31 Jacob Markstrom 1.50 4.00
32 Zach Werenski 2.50 6.00
33 Thatcher Demko 2.00 5.00
34 Clayton Keller 2.00 5.00
35 Tim Stutzle 2.00 5.00
36 Brady Tkachuk 2.50 6.00
37 Leon Draisaitl 5.00 12.00
38 Evgeni Malkin 3.00 8.00
39 Mats Zuccarello 1.50 4.00
40 Logan Couture 2.00 5.00
41 Patrice Bergeron 2.00 5.00
42 Nick Schmaltz 1.25 3.00
43 Elias Pettersson 2.50 6.00
44 Sidney Crosby 6.00 15.00
45 Tage Thompson 2.00 5.00
46 Nick Suzuki 3.00 8.00
47 Alex DeBrincat 2.00 5.00
48 Quinn Hughes 4.00 10.00
49 Kirill Kaprizov 5.00 12.00
50 Aleksander Barkov 2.50 6.00
51 Ryan Strome 1.50 4.00
52 Cole Caufield 3.00 8.00
53 Evgeny Kuznetsov 2.00 5.00
54 Jordan Eberle 1.50 4.00
55 Juuse Saros 2.00 5.00
56 Mikko Rantanen 4.00 10.00
57 Igor Shesterkin 3.00 8.00
58 Kyle Connor 2.50 6.00
59 John Carlson 1.50 4.00
60 Filip Forsberg 2.50 6.00
61 Marc-Andre Fleury 3.00 8.00
62 Erik Karlsson 2.00 5.00
63 Andrei Svechnikov 2.00 5.00
64 Jordan Kyrou 1.50 4.00
65 Connor McDavid 8.00 20.00
66 Kirby Dach 1.50 4.00
67 Mitch Marner 2.50 6.00
68 Robert Thomas 1.50 4.00
69 Aaron Ekblad 2.00 5.00
70 Ilya Sorokin 2.50 6.00
71 Anders Lee 1.25 3.00
72 Jaccob Slavin 1.25 3.00
73 Brock Nelson 1.50 4.00
74 Anze Kopitar 2.50 6.00
75 Cam Atkinson 1.50 4.00
76 Dylan Larkin 2.00 5.00
77 Tyler Toffoli 1.50 4.00
78 Alexis Lafreniere 2.50 6.00
79 Andrei Vasilevskiy 2.50 6.00
80 Cale Makar 4.00 10.00
81 Nathan MacKinnon 6.00 15.00
82 Moritz Seider 2.00 5.00
83 Steven Stamkos 3.00 8.00
84 Kevin Fiala 1.25 3.00
85 Thomas Chabot 1.50 4.00
86 Jack Eichel 2.50 6.00
87 Matthew Tkachuk 3.00 8.00
88 Colton Parayko 1.25 3.00
89 Rasmus Dahlin 2.00 5.00
90 Mark Stone 2.00 5.00
92 Joe Sakic 8.00 20.00
93 Wayne Gretzky 25.00 60.00
94 Patrick Roy 10.00 25.00
95 Mario Lemieux 15.00 40.00
96 Martin Brodeur 10.00 25.00
97 Henrik Zetterberg 5.00 12.00
98 Mark Messier 8.00 20.00
99 Peter Forsberg 8.00 20.00
100 Eric Lindros 6.00 15.00
101 Jonatan Berggren 2.50 6.00
102 Matty Beniers 4.00 10.00
103 Kaiden Guhle 3.00 8.00
104 Jordan Spence 1.50 4.00
105 Elmer Soderblom 3.00 8.00
106 Wyatt Johnston 6.00 15.00
107 Pyotr Kochetkov 3.00 8.00
108 Dylan Holloway 3.00 8.00
109 Filip Roos 1.25 3.00
110 Cole Koepke 1.50 4.00
111 Owen Power 3.00 8.00
112 Jean-Luc Foudy 1.50 4.00
113 Bobby Brink 1.50 4.00
114 Lukas Dostal 3.00 8.00
115 Juraj Slafkovsky 8.00 20.00
116 Juuso Parssinen 1.50 4.00
117 Thomas Bordeleau 1.50 4.00
118 Pavol Regenda 1.50 4.00
119 Noah Cates 1.50 4.00
120 Zack Hayes 1.25 3.00
121 Braden Schneider 2.50 6.00
122 Brayden Tracey 1.25 3.00
123 Johnathan Kovacevic 1.50 4.00
124 Jack Quinn 2.50 6.00
125 Lukas Reichel 3.00 8.00
126 Matias Maccelli 2.50 6.00
127 Kirill Marchenko 4.00 10.00
128 Matt Boldy 5.00 12.00
129 Dylan Guenther 4.00 10.00
130 Reilly Walsh 1.50 4.00
132 Shane Wright 4.00 10.00
133 Pontus Holmberg 1.50 4.00
134 Mads Sogaard 2.00 5.00
135 David Jiricek 3.00 8.00
137 Brandt Clarke 3.00 8.00
138 Samuel Poulin 2.00 5.00
139 Dylan Samberg 1.50 4.00
140 Marc McLaughlin 1.50 4.00
141 Andrei Kuzmenko 3.00 8.00
142 Marco Rossi 4.00 10.00
143 Arber Xhekaj 3.00 8.00
144 Simon Holmstrom 1.50 4.00
145 Oskar Olausson 1.50 4.00
146 Nick Perbix 1.25 3.00
147 Jake Sanderson 4.00 10.00
148 Nick Abruzzese 1.50 4.00
149 Samuel Fagemo 1.25 3.00
150 Jakub Lauko 2.00 5.00

2022-23 Upper Deck Premier Premier Attractions Jerseys

*PATCH: 1X TO 2.5X BASIC
PAAB Aleksander Barkov/99 3.00 8.00
PAAK Anze Kopitar/99 3.00 8.00
PAAL Alexis Lafreniere/99 3.00 8.00
PAAM Auston Matthews/49 8.00 20.00
PAAO Alex Ovechkin/49 8.00 20.00
PAAS Andrei Svechnikov/99 2.50 6.00
PABT Brady Tkachuk/99 3.00 8.00
PACC Cole Caufield/99 4.00 10.00
PACK Clayton Keller/99 2.50 6.00
PACM Connor McDavid/49 10.00 25.00
PADP David Pastrnak/99 5.00 12.00
PAEK Erik Karlsson/99 2.50 6.00
PAEP Elias Pettersson/99 3.00 8.00
PAFF Filip Forsberg/99 3.00 8.00
PAHU Jack Hughes/99 5.00 12.00
PAJE Jack Eichel/99 3.00 8.00
PAJH Jonathan Huberdeau/99 2.50 6.00
PAJK Jordan Kyrou/99 2.00 5.00
PAJO Jake Oettinger/99 3.00 8.00
PAJT Jonathan Toews/99 3.00 8.00
PAKC Kyle Connor/99 3.00 8.00
PAKK Kirill Kaprizov/99 6.00 15.00
PAMB Mathew Barzal/99 2.50 6.00
PAMS Moritz Seider/99 2.50 6.00
PANM Nathan MacKinnon/49 8.00 20.00
PAPL Patrik Laine/99 2.50 6.00
PARD Rasmus Dahlin/99 2.50 6.00
PASC Sidney Crosby/49 8.00 20.00
PASS Steven Stamkos/99 4.00 10.00
PATZ Trevor Zegras/99 2.00 5.00

2022-23 Upper Deck Premier Premier Dual Jerseys

PDABAE A.Barkov/A.Ekblad 6.00 15.00
PDAMMM A.Matthews/M.Marner 15.00 40.00
PDAOKK A.Ovechkin/K.Kaprizov 15.00 40.00
PDAZAK A.Kopitar/A.Kempe 6.00 15.00
PDCCNS C.Caufield/N.Suzuki 8.00 20.00
PDCKNS C.Keller/N.Schmaltz 5.00 12.00
PDCMLD C.McDavid/L.Draisaitl 20.00 50.00
PDCMNM C.Makar/N.MacKinnon 15.00 40.00
PDDPPB D.Pastrnak/P.Bergeron 10.00 25.00
PDEKTM E.Karlsson/T.Meier 5.00 12.00
PDJHNH J.Hughes/N.Hischier 10.00 25.00
PDKCCP K.Connor/C.Perfetti 6.00 15.00
PDKLJG K.Letang/J.Guentzel 6.00 15.00
PDLRMS L.Raymond/M.Seider 6.00 15.00
PDMBOW M.Barzal/O.Wahlstrom 5.00 12.00
PDMTAB M.Tkachuk/A.Barkov 8.00 20.00
PDSCEM S.Crosby/E.Malkin 15.00 40.00
PDSHSO I.Shesterkin/I.Sorokin 8.00 20.00
PDSSNK S.Stamkos/N.Kucherov 8.00 20.00
PDTSJB J.Pavelski/R.Hintz 5.00 12.00
PDTTRD T.Thompson/R.Dahlin 5.00 12.00
PDTZMM T.Zegras/M.McTavish 4.00 10.00

2022-23 Upper Deck Premier Premier Dynamic Imagery Autographs

PDIAAL Alexis Lafreniere 12.00 30.00
PDIAAS Andrei Svechnikov 10.00 25.00
PDIABB Brock Boeser 10.00 25.00
PDIACP Colton Parayko 6.00 15.00
PDIAGL Gabriel Landeskog 20.00 50.00
PDIAMS Mark Stone 10.00 25.00
PDIAQH Quinn Hughes 20.00 50.00
PDIARJ Roman Josi 8.00 20.00

2022-23 Upper Deck Premier Premier Dynamic Imagery Jerseys

*BLACK/25: 1.5X TO 4X BASIC
PDJAM Auston Matthews 10.00 25.00
PDJAO Alex Ovechkin 10.00 25.00
PDJAS Andrei Svechnikov 3.00 8.00
PDJCC Cole Caufield 5.00 12.00
PDJCM Connor McDavid 12.00 30.00
PDJDP David Pastrnak 6.00 15.00
PDJEP Elias Pettersson 4.00 10.00
PDJFF Filip Forsberg 4.00 10.00
PDJJG Johnny Gaudreau 4.00 10.00
PDJJH Jack Hughes 6.00 15.00
PDJKK Kirill Kaprizov 8.00 20.00
PDJLD Leon Draisaitl 8.00 20.00
PDJMM Mitch Marner 4.00 10.00
PDJMS Moritz Seider 3.00 8.00
PDJMT Matthew Tkachuk 5.00 12.00
PDJNK Nikita Kucherov 5.00 12.00
PDJNM Nathan MacKinnon 10.00 25.00
PDJRD Rasmus Dahlin 3.00 8.00
PDJSC Sidney Crosby 10.00 25.00
PDJTZ Trevor Zegras 2.50 6.00

2022-23 Upper Deck Premier Premier Dynamic Imagery Rookie Autographs

PDARBC Brandt Clarke/99 20.00 50.00
PDARBO Matt Boldy/49 30.00 80.00
PDARDG Dylan Guenther/99 25.00 60.00
PDARDH Dylan Holloway/99 20.00 50.00
PDARDJ David Jiricek/99 20.00 50.00
PDARDO Lukas Dostal/99 20.00 50.00
PDARJP Jacob Perreault/99 10.00 25.00
PDARJS Juraj Slafkovsky/49 50.00 125.00
PDARKG Kaiden Guhle/99 20.00 50.00
PDARKJ Kent Johnson/99 20.00 50.00
PDARLR Lukas Reichel/99 20.00 50.00
PDARMB Matty Beniers/49 25.00 60.00
PDARMR Marco Rossi/99 25.00 60.00
PDAROP Owen Power/49 20.00 50.00
PDARSW Shane Wright/49 25.00 60.00
PDARWJ Wyatt Johnston/99 40.00 100.00

2022-23 Upper Deck Premier Premier Dynamic Imagery Rookie Jerseys

*BLACK/75: 1X TO 2.5X BASIC
PDJRAK Andrei Kuzmenko 4.00 10.00
PDJRBB Bobby Brink 2.00 5.00
PDJRBC Brandt Clarke 4.00 10.00
PDJRBO Matt Boldy 6.00 15.00
PDJRBS Braden Schneider 3.00 8.00
PDJRDG Dylan Guenther 5.00 12.00
PDJRDH Dylan Holloway 4.00 10.00
PDJRDJ David Jiricek 4.00 10.00
PDJRDS Dylan Samberg 2.00 5.00
PDJRES Elmer Soderblom 4.00 10.00
PDJRJL Jakub Lauko 2.50 6.00
PDJRJQ Jack Quinn 3.00 8.00
PDJRJS Jake Sanderson 5.00 12.00
PDJRKG Kaiden Guhle 4.00 10.00
PDJRKJ Kent Johnson 4.00 10.00
PDJRKK Kaedan Korczak 1.50 4.00
PDJRLD Lukas Dostal 4.00 10.00
PDJRLR Lukas Reichel 4.00 10.00
PDJRMB Matty Beniers 5.00 12.00
PDJRMR Marco Rossi 5.00 12.00
PDJROO Oskar Olausson 2.00 5.00
PDJROP Owen Power 4.00 10.00
PDJRPK Pyotr Kochetkov 4.00 10.00
PDJRRW Juuso Parssinen 2.00 5.00
PDJRSF Samuel Fagemo 1.50 4.00
PDJRSL Juraj Slafkovsky 10.00 25.00
PDJRSP Samuel Poulin 2.50 6.00
PDJRSW Shane Wright 5.00 12.00
PDJRTB Thomas Bordeleau 2.00 5.00
PDJRWJ Wyatt Johnston 8.00 20.00

2022-23 Upper Deck Premier Premier Dynamic Imagery Star Autographs

PDLSAG Adam Graves 12.00 30.00
PDLSAM Auston Matthews 60.00 150.00
PDLSJI Jarome Iginla 20.00 50.00
PDLSLM Lanny McDonald 15.00 40.00
PDLSMB Martin Brodeur 60.00 150.00
PDLSMR Mark Messier 50.00 125.00
PDLSNL Nicklas Lidstrom 15.00 40.00
PDLSOK Wayne Gretzky 150.00 400.00
PDLSPR Patrick Roy 60.00 150.00
PDLSRB Ray Bourque 40.00 100.00
PDLSRF Ron Francis 20.00 50.00

2022-23 Upper Deck Premier Premier Focus Autographs

PFAAL Alexis Lafreniere/49 40.00 100.00
PFAAS Andrei Svechnikov/25 30.00 80.00
PFABO Bobby Orr/49 100.00 250.00
PFAEL Eric Lindros/25 60.00 150.00
PFAIS Igor Shesterkin/49 50.00 125.00
PFAMM Mark Messier/25 60.00 150.00
PFASY Steve Yzerman/25 60.00 150.00
PFATS Tim Stutzle/99 30.00 80.00

2022-23 Upper Deck Premier Premier Focus Patch Autographs

PFAPAC Andrew Copp/99 8.00 20.00
PFAPAD Alex DeBrincat/25 15.00 40.00
PFAPAH Alexander Holtz/99 12.00 30.00
PFAPBS Brandon Saad/49 10.00 25.00
PFAPCP Cole Perfetti/49 12.00 30.00
PFAPDM Dawson Mercer/49 20.00 50.00
PFAPHE Connor Hellebuyck/25 25.00 60.00
PFAPIS Ilya Sorokin/25 40.00 100.00
PFAPJK Jordan Kyrou/49 12.00 30.00
PFAPJM Jacob Markstrom/25 12.00 30.00
PFAPJP Joe Pavelski/25 25.00 60.00
PFAPJS Jeremy Swayman/49 20.00 50.00
PFAPKF Kevin Fiala/49 10.00 25.00
PFAPRJ Roman Josi/25 30.00 80.00
PFAPSA Juuse Saros/49 15.00 40.00
PFAPST Shea Theodore/49 15.00 40.00
PFAPTO Tyler Toffoli/49 12.00 30.00
PFAPTT Teuvo Teravainen/49 12.00 30.00
PFAPTW Tom Wilson/49 12.00 30.00

2022-23 Upper Deck Premier Premier Focus Rookie Patch Autographs

PFPRAB Nick Abruzzese/125 12.00 30.00
PFPRAX Arber Xhekaj/125 25.00 60.00
PFPRBB Bobby Brink/125 12.00 30.00
PFPRBC Brandt Clarke/75 40.00 100.00
PFPRBO Matt Boldy/50 100.00 250.00
PFPRCK Cole Koepke/125 12.00 30.00
PFPRDG Dylan Guenther/125 30.00 80.00
PFPRDH Dylan Holloway/125 25.00 60.00
PFPRDJ David Jiricek/75 25.00 60.00
PFPRES Elmer Soderblom/125 25.00 60.00
PFPRFR Filip Roos/125 10.00 25.00
PFPRHH Hayden Hodgson/125 10.00 25.00
PFPRJB Jonatan Berggren/125 20.00 50.00
PFPRJK Johnathan Kovacevic/125 12.00 30.00
PFPRJM Jack McBain/125 12.00 30.00
PFPRJP Jacob Perreault/125 12.00 30.00
PFPRJS Juraj Slafkovsky/50 100.00 250.00
PFPRKG Kaiden Guhle/125 25.00 60.00
PFPRKJ Kent Johnson/75 30.00 80.00
PFPRKK Kaedan Korczak/125 10.00 25.00
PFPRKM Kirill Marchenko/125 30.00 80.00
PFPRLD Lukas Dostal/125 60.00 150.00
PFPRLR Lukas Reichel/125 25.00 60.00
PFPRMB Matty Beniers/50 50.00 125.00
PFPRMM Matias Maccelli/125 20.00 50.00
PFPRMR Marco Rossi/75 30.00 80.00
PFPRNA Nils Aman/125 12.00 30.00
PFPRNB Nick Blankenburg/125 10.00 25.00
PFPRND Nick DeSimone/125 12.00 30.00
PFPROL Olle Lycksell/125 12.00 30.00
PFPROP Owen Power/50 25.00 60.00
PFPRPH Pontus Holmberg/125 12.00 30.00
PFPRPR Pavol Regenda/125 12.00 30.00
PFPRRA Ronnie Attard/125 12.00 30.00
PFPRRW Reilly Walsh/125 12.00 30.00
PFPRSA Jake Sanderson/75 40.00 100.00
PFPRSF Samuel Fagemo/125 10.00 25.00
PFPRSW Shane Wright/50 50.00 125.00
PFPRTB Thomas Bordeleau/125 12.00 30.00
PFPRVK Vladislav Kolyachonok/125 10.00 25.00
PFPRWJ Wyatt Johnston/125 80.00 200.00

2022-23 Upper Deck Premier Premier Focus Rookie Patch Autographs Gold

*GOLD: .6X TO 1.5X BASIC
PFPRJS Juraj Slafkovsky/25 200.00 500.00
PFPRMB Matty Beniers/25 100.00 250.00

2022-23 Upper Deck Premier Premier Gear Jerseys

PGAB Aleksander Barkov 8.00 20.00
PGAM Auston Matthews 20.00 50.00

PGAO Alex Ovechkin 20.00 50.00
PGCM Connor McDavid 25.00 60.00
PGKK Kirill Kaprizov 15.00 40.00
PGLD Leon Draisaitl 15.00 40.00
PGMA Cale Makar 12.00 30.00
PGNM Nathan MacKinnon 20.00 50.00
PGSC Sidney Crosby 20.00 50.00
PGVH Victor Hedman 6.00 15.00

2022-23 Upper Deck Premier Premier Gear Rookie Jerseys

PGRAK Andrei Kuzmenko 6.00 15.00
PGRBC Brandt Clarke 6.00 15.00
PGRBE Matty Beniers 8.00 20.00
PGRBS Braden Schneider 5.00 12.00
PGRDG Dylan Guenther 8.00 20.00
PGRDH Dylan Holloway 6.00 15.00
PGRDS Dylan Samberg 3.00 8.00
PGRJQ Jack Quinn 5.00 12.00
PGRJS Juraj Slafkovsky 15.00 40.00
PGRKJ Kent Johnson 6.00 15.00
PGRLD Lukas Dostal 6.00 15.00
PGRLR Lukas Reichel 6.00 15.00
PGRMB Matt Boldy 10.00 25.00
PGRMR Marco Rossi 8.00 20.00
PGROP Owen Power 6.00 15.00
PGRPK Pyotr Kochetkov 6.00 15.00
PGRSA Jake Sanderson 8.00 20.00
PGRSP Samuel Poulin 4.00 10.00
PGRSW Shane Wright 8.00 20.00
PGRTB Thomas Bordeleau 3.00 8.00

2022-23 Upper Deck Premier Premier Gear Rookie Jerseys Patch

*PATCH/25: 1.2X TO 3X BASIC
PGRAK Andrei Kuzmenko 30.00 80.00
PGRDH Dylan Holloway 30.00 80.00
PGRLD Lukas Dostal 30.00 80.00
PGRLR Lukas Reichel 50.00 125.00

2022-23 Upper Deck Premier Premier Mega Jersey Duos

*PATCH/25: .8X TO 2X BASIC
PM2BO A.Ovechkin/N.Backstrom 20.00 50.00
PM2GL J.Gaudreau/P.Laine 8.00 20.00
PM2HH J.Hughes/Q.Hughes 12.00 30.00
PM2KQ A.Kopitar/J.Quick 8.00 20.00
PM2MD C.McDavid/L.Draisaitl 25.00 60.00
PM2MM A.Matthews/M.Marner 20.00 50.00
PM2MP B.Marchand/D.Pastrnak 12.00 30.00
PM2MR N.MacKinnon/M.Rantanen 20.00 50.00
PM2SC C.Caufield/N.Suzuki 10.00 25.00
PM2SE J.Eichel/M.Stone 8.00 20.00
PM2SK S.Stamkos/N.Kucherov 10.00 25.00
PM2SR M.Seider/L.Raymond 8.00 20.00
PM2TD R.Dahlin/T.Thompson 6.00 15.00
PM2TT B.Tkachuk/M.Tkachuk 10.00 25.00
PM2ZM T.Zegras/M.McTavish 5.00 12.00

2022-23 Upper Deck Premier Premier Mega Patch Chest Logos

PMPAB Aleksander Barkov/30 50.00 125.00
PMPAD Alex DeBrincat/28 40.00 100.00
PMPAE Aaron Ekblad/28 40.00 100.00
PMPAF Adam Fox/21 40.00 100.00
PMPAK Adrian Kempe/26 50.00 125.00
PMPAL Alexis Lafreniere/21 50.00 125.00
PMPAM Auston Matthews/26 150.00 400.00
PMPAO Alex Ovechkin/22 150.00 400.00
PMPAP Artemi Panarin/21 100.00 250.00
PMPAS Andrei Svechnikov/23 40.00 100.00
PMPAV Andrei Vasilevskiy/24 50.00 125.00
PMPBA Mathew Barzal/26 100.00 250.00
PMPBB Brock Boeser/27 40.00 100.00
PMPBE Jamie Benn/21 30.00 80.00
PMPBM Brad Marchand/22 60.00 150.00
PMPBO Matt Boldy/20 100.00 250.00
PMPBT Brady Tkachuk/28 50.00 125.00
PMPCC Cole Caufield/22 100.00 250.00
PMPCH Connor Hellebuyck/26 60.00 150.00
PMPCK Clayton Keller/26 40.00 100.00
PMPCM Connor McDavid/26 200.00 500.00
PMPCP Cole Perfetti/26 30.00 80.00
PMPDL Dylan Larkin/21 80.00 200.00
PMPDM Dawson Mercer/28 40.00 100.00
PMPDP David Pastrnak/22 80.00 200.00
PMPEB Jordan Eberle/28 30.00 80.00
PMPEK Erik Karlsson/26 40.00 100.00
PMPEM Evgeni Malkin/35 60.00 150.00
PMPEP Elias Pettersson/27 50.00 125.00
PMPFF Filip Forsberg/22 50.00 125.00
PMPIP Ivan Provorov/27 25.00 60.00
PMPIS Igor Shesterkin/21 80.00 200.00
PMPJB Jordan Binnington/23 50.00 125.00
PMPJC John Carlson/22 30.00 80.00
PMPJE Jack Eichel/23 50.00 125.00
PMPJG Johnny Gaudreau/24 50.00 125.00
PMPJH Jack Hughes/28 80.00 200.00
PMPJO Jake Oettinger/21 60.00 150.00
PMPJS Juraj Slafkovsky/30 200.00 500.00
PMPJT John Tavares/22 50.00 125.00
PMPKC Kyle Connor/26 50.00 120.00
PMPKJ Kent Johnson/26 60.00 150.00
PMPKK Kirill Kaprizov/24 100.00 250.00
PMPKL Kris Letang/20 40.00 100.00
PMPKO Anze Kopitar/35 50.00 120.00
PMPKU Evgeny Kuznetsov/26 40.00 100.00
PMPKV Karel Vejmelka/22 20.00 50.00
PMPLC Logan Couture/26 40.00 100.00
PMPLD Leon Draisaitl/26 100.00 250.00
PMPLI Tyler Toffoli/26 30.00 80.00
PMPLR Lucas Raymond/21 50.00 125.00
PMPMA Cale Makar/31 80.00 200.00
PMPMB Matty Beniers/28 60.00 150.00
PMPMC Mason McTavish/25 30.00 80.00
PMPMH Miro Heiskanen/23 40.00 100.00
PMPMM Mitch Marner/26 50.00 125.00
PMPMR Mikko Rantanen/31 80.00 200.00
PMPMS Mark Stone/23 100.00 250.00
PMPMT Matthew Tkachuk/28 60.00 150.00
PMPNH Nico Hischier/28 50.00 125.00
PMPNI Nick Schmaltz/26 25.00 60.00
PMPNK Nikita Kucherov/24 60.00 150.00
PMPNM Nathan MacKinnon/31 125.00 300.00
PMPNS Nick Suzuki/22 80.00 200.00
PMPOB Oliver Bjorkstrand/28 25.00 60.00
PMPOP Owen Power/27 60.00 150.00
PMPPA Colton Parayko/23 25.00 60.00
PMPPK Patrick Kane/27 60.00 150.00
PMPPL Patrik Laine/24 40.00 100.00
PMPQB Quinton Byfield/21 40.00 100.00
PMPQH Quinn Hughes/27 60.00 150.00
PMPRD Rasmus Dahlin/27 40.00 100.00
PMPRJ Roman Josi/23 40.00 100.00
PMPRN Ryan Nugent-Hopkins/26 40.00 100.00
PMPRT Robert Thomas/23 30.00 80.00
PMPSA Sebastian Aho/23 60.00 150.00
PMPSC Sidney Crosby/34 150.00 400.00
PMPSE Moritz Seider/21 40.00 100.00
PMPSJ Seth Jones/27 30.00 80.00
PMPSO Ilya Sorokin/26 50.00 125.00
PMPSP Jared Spurgeon/20 30.00 80.00
PMPSS Steven Stamkos/24 60.00 150.00
PMPST Shea Theodore/23 80.00 200.00
PMPTC Thomas Chabot/28 30.00 80.00
PMPTE Teuvo Teravainen/23 30.00 80.00
PMPTH Taylor Hall/22 30.00 80.00
PMPTJ Tanner Jeannot/22 20.00 50.00
PMPTK Travis Konecny/27 30.00 80.00
PMPTM Timo Meier/26 30.00 80.00
PMPTO Jonathan Toews/27 50.00 125.00
PMPTR Troy Terry/26 25.00 60.00
PMPTS Tim Stutzle/27 40.00 100.00
PMPTT Tage Thompson/27 40.00 100.00
PMPTY Tyler Seguin/23 40.00 100.00
PMPTZ Trevor Zegras/25 30.00 80.00
PMPWN William Nylander/26 60.00 150.00

2022-23 Upper Deck Premier Premier Quad Jerseys

PQCDSW Connor/Dubois Scheifele/Wheeler 10.00 25.00
PQCSDS Caufield/Suzuki Dach/Slafkovsky 30.00 80.00
PQESMS Eichel/Stone Marchessault/Stephenson 10.00 25.00
PQFZPS Fox/Zibanejad Panarin/Shesterkin 12.00 30.00
PQKFDQ Kopitar/Fiala/Doughty/Quick 10.00 25.00
PQMMRL MacKinnon/Makar Rantanen/Landeskog 25.00 60.00
PQMMTN Matthews/Marner Tavares/Nylander 25.00 60.00
PQRHOP Hintz/Heiskanen Oettinger/Pavelski 10.00 25.00
PQSANB Svechnikov Aho/Necas/Burns 10.00 25.00

2022-23 Upper Deck Premier Premier Slapshots Autographs

PSAAL Anders Lee 5.00 12.00
PSABB Brent Burns 6.00 15.00
PSABM Brad Marchand SP 12.00 30.00
PSABT Brady Tkachuk 10.00 25.00
PSAHE Tomas Hertl 6.00 15.00
PSAJG Jake Guentzel 10.00 25.00
PSAKC Kyle Connor 10.00 25.00
PSAMT Matthew Tkachuk 15.00 40.00
PSATA Tage Thompson 8.00 20.00
PSATS Tim Stutzle SP 20.00 50.00
PSATT Troy Terry 5.00 12.00
PSAWK William Karlsson 8.00 20.00

2022-23 Upper Deck Premier Premier Slapshots Legend Autographs

PSALBL Rob Blake 10.00 25.00
PSALCC Chris Chelios 10.00 25.00
PSALDG Doug Gilmour 25.00 60.00
PSALDH Dany Heatley 8.00 20.00
PSALEL Eric Lindros SP 15.00 40.00
PSALHZ Henrik Zetterberg 12.00 30.00
PSALJI Jarome Iginla SP 12.00 30.00
PSALKT Keith Tkachuk 10.00 25.00
PSALLR Luc Robitaille SP 10.00 25.00
PSALMM Mark Messier SP 40.00 100.00
PSALMO Mike Modano SP 15.00 40.00
PSALNL Nicklas Lidstrom SP 10.00 25.00
PSALPR Patrick Roy SP 80.00 200.00
PSALRB Rod Brind'Amour 10.00 25.00
PSALRG Ryan Getzlaf 10.00 25.00
PSALSZ Sergei Zubov 8.00 20.00
PSALTL Trevor Linden 10.00 25.00

2022-23 Upper Deck Premier Premier Slapshots Rookie Autographs

PSARAX Arber Xhekaj 12.00 30.00
PSARBB Bobby Brink 6.00 15.00
PSARBC Brandt Clarke 12.00 30.00
PSARBO Matt Boldy SP 20.00 50.00
PSARDG Dylan Guenther 15.00 40.00
PSARDH Dylan Holloway 12.00 30.00
PSARDJ David Jiricek 12.00 30.00
PSARDS Dylan Samberg 6.00 15.00
PSARES Elmer Soderblom 12.00 30.00
PSARJB Jonatan Berggren 10.00 25.00
PSARJS Jake Sanderson 15.00 40.00
PSARKG Kaiden Guhle 12.00 30.00
PSARKJ Kent Johnson SP 12.00 30.00
PSARKM Kirill Marchenko 15.00 40.00
PSARLR Lukas Reichel 12.00 30.00
PSARMB Matty Beniers SP 15.00 40.00
PSARMM Matias Maccelli 10.00 25.00
PSARMR Marco Rossi SP 15.00 40.00
PSAROP Owen Power SP 12.00 30.00
PSARRA Ronnie Attard 6.00 15.00
PSARSF Samuel Fagemo 5.00 12.00
PSARSL Juraj Slafkovsky SP 40.00 100.00
PSARSW Shane Wright SP 25.00 60.00
PSARTB Thomas Bordeleau 6.00 15.00
PSARWJ Wyatt Johnston 25.00 60.00

2022-23 Upper Deck Premier Premier Triple Jerseys

PTCSD Caufield/Suzuki/Dach 10.00 25.00
PTDJF Duchene/Josi/Forsberg 8.00 20.00
PTHHH Hughes/Hischier/Hamilton 12.00 30.00
PTJMR Oettinger/Heiskanen/Hintz 8.00 20.00
PTKAZ Kaprizov/Fleury/Boldy 15.00 40.00
PTKTP Kyrou/Thomas/Parayko 5.00 12.00
PTLSR Larkin/Seider/Raymond 8.00 20.00
PTMMM Mitch MacKinnon
Makar/Landeskog 20.00 50.00
PTPHH Pettersson/Hughes/Horvat 12.00 30.00
PTSKH Stamkos/Kucherov/Hedman 10.00 25.00
PTTSC Tkachuk/Stutzle/Chabot 8.00 20.00
PTZFT Power/Beniers/Johnson 12.00 30.00

2022-23 Upper Deck Premier Rookie Patch-Taculars Chest Logos

RPTAM Nils Aman 10.00 25.00
RPTAV Alex Vlasic 8.00 20.00
RPTBB Bobby Brink 10.00 25.00
RPTBC Brandt Clarke 20.00 50.00
RPTBE Matty Beniers 25.00 60.00
RPTBO Matt Boldy 30.00 80.00
RPTBS Braden Schneider 25.00 60.00
RPTBT Brayden Tracey 8.00 20.00
RPTCK Cole Koepke 10.00 25.00
RPTDG Dylan Guenther 25.00 60.00
RPTDH Dylan Holloway 20.00 50.00
RPTDJ David Jiricek 20.00 50.00
RPTDS Dylan Samberg 10.00 25.00
RPTEK Erik Kallgren 10.00 25.00
RPTES Elmer Soderblom 20.00 50.00
RPTFH Filip Hallander 10.00 25.00
RPTFR Filip Roos 8.00 20.00
RPTHH Hayden Hodgson 8.00 20.00
RPTJH Jordan Harris 12.00 30.00
RPTJK Johnathan Kovacevic 10.00 25.00
RPTJL Jakub Lauko 12.00 30.00
RPTJM Jack McBain 10.00 25.00
RPTJP Jacob Perreault 10.00 25.00
RPTJQ Jack Quinn 15.00 40.00
RPTJS Jordan Spence 10.00 25.00
RPTKG Kaiden Guhle 20.00 50.00
RPTKJ Kent Johnson 25.00 60.00
RPTKK Kaedan Korczak 8.00 20.00
RPTKM Kirill Marchenko 25.00 60.00
RPTLD Lukas Dostal 20.00 50.00
RPTLR Lukas Reichel 20.00 50.00
RPTMB Matej Blumel 12.00 30.00
RPTMC Marc McLaughlin 10.00 25.00
RPTME Michael Eyssimont 10.00 25.00
RPTMM Matias Maccelli 15.00 40.00
RPTMO Jacob Moverare 8.00 20.00
RPTMR Marco Rossi 25.00 60.00
RPTMS Mads Sogaard 12.00 30.00
RPTNA Nick Abruzzese 10.00 25.00
RPTNB Nick Blankenburg 8.00 20.00
RPTNC Noah Cates 10.00 25.00
RPTND Nick DeSimone 10.00 25.00
RPTNO Nikita Okhotiuk 8.00 20.00
RPTNP Nick Perbix 8.00 20.00
RPTNS Nathan Smith 8.00 20.00
RPTOL Olle Lycksell 10.00 25.00
RPTOP Owen Power 20.00 50.00
RPTPA Juuso Parssinen 10.00 25.00
RPTPH Pontus Holmberg 10.00 25.00
RPTPK Pyotr Kochetkov 30.00 80.00
RPTPR Pavol Regenda 10.00 25.00
RPTRA Ronnie Attard 10.00 25.00
RPTRW Reilly Walsh 10.00 25.00
RPTSD Semyon Der-Arguchintsev 10.00 25.00
RPTSF Samuel Fagemo 8.00 20.00
RPTSP Samuel Poulin 12.00 30.00
RPTSW Shane Wright 25.00 60.00
RPTTB Thomas Bordeleau 10.00 25.00
RPTVK Vladislav Kolyachonok 8.00 20.00
RPTVP Valtteri Puustinen 8.00 20.00
RPTWJ Wyatt Johnston 40.00 100.00
RPTZH Zack Hayes 8.00 20.00

2023-24 Upper Deck Premier

1 Connor McDavid/299 5.00 12.00
2 Matt Boldy/299 1.50 4.00
3 Leon Draisaitl/299 3.00 8.00
4 Mason McTavish/299 1.00 2.50
5 Tomas Hertl/299 1.00 2.50
6 Nikita Kucherov/299 2.00 5.00
7 Miro Heiskanen/299 1.25 3.00
8 Johnny Gaudreau/299 1.50 4.00
9 Josh Morrissey/299 1.25 3.00
10 Anze Kopitar/299 1.50 4.00
11 Joel Eriksson Ek/299 .75 2.00
12 Mark Stone/299 1.25 3.00
13 Nathan MacKinnon/299 4.00 10.00
14 Andrei Vasilevskiy/299 1.50 4.00
15 Matty Beniers/299 1.25 3.00
16 Martin Necas/299 1.25 3.00
17 Travis Konecny/299 1.00 2.50
18 Elias Pettersson/299 1.50 4.00
19 Andrei Kuzmenko/299 1.00 2.50
20 Juuse Saros/299 1.25 3.00
21 Logan Couture/299 1.25 3.00
22 Roope Hintz/299 1.25 3.00
23 Ryan Nugent-Hopkins/299 1.25 3.00
24 John Tavares/299 1.50 4.00
25 Nick Suzuki/299 2.00 5.00
26 Jack Eichel/299 1.50 4.00
27 Brady Tkachuk/299 1.50 4.00
28 Ilya Sorokin/299 1.25 3.00
29 Brad Marchand/299 2.00 5.00
30 Dylan Cozens/299 1.00 2.50
31 Boone Jenner/299 1.00 2.50
32 Jake Guentzel/299 1.50 4.00
33 Timo Meier/299 1.25 3.00
34 Clayton Keller/299 1.25 3.00
35 Lucas Raymond/299 1.50 4.00
36 Cale Makar/299 2.50 6.00
37 Nico Hischier/299 1.50 4.00
38 Jared McCann/299 .75 2.00
39 Aleksander Barkov/299 1.50 4.00
40 Seth Jones/299 1.00 2.50
41 Jordan Kyrou/299 1.00 2.50
42 Jonathan Huberdeau/299 1.25 3.00
43 Chris Kreider/299 1.25 3.00
44 Alex Tuch/299 1.00 2.50
45 Steven Stamkos/299 2.00 5.00
46 Moritz Seider/299 1.25 3.00
47 Roman Josi/299 1.00 2.50
48 Jason Robertson/299 1.50 4.00
49 Jack Hughes/299 2.50 6.00
50 Matias Maccelli/299 .75 2.00
51 Ryan O'Reilly/299 1.00 2.50
52 Kevin Fiala/299 .75 2.00
53 Blake Coleman/299 .75 2.00
54 Sidney Crosby/299 4.00 10.00
55 Matthew Tkachuk/299 2.00 5.00
56 Trevor Zegras/299 1.00 2.50
57 Auston Matthews/299 4.00 10.00
58 Alex Ovechkin/299 4.00 10.00
59 Evgeni Malkin/299 2.00 5.00
60 Jeremy Swayman/299 1.50 4.00
61 Artemi Panarin/299 2.00 5.00
62 Kyle Connor/299 1.50 4.00
63 Taylor Raddysh/299 .75 2.00
64 Brock Nelson/299 1.00 2.50
65 Jake Sanderson/299 1.25 3.00
66 Mitch Marner/299 1.50 4.00
67 Cam Atkinson/299 1.00 2.50
68 Andrei Svechnikov/299 1.25 3.00
69 Troy Terry/299 .75 2.00
70 Robert Thomas/299 1.00 2.50
71 John Carlson/299 1.00 2.50
72 Cole Caufield/299 2.00 5.00
73 Kent Johnson/299 1.00 2.50
74 Alex Newhook/299 .75 2.00
75 Kirill Kaprizov/299 3.00 8.00
76 Mathew Barzal/299 1.25 3.00
77 Tim Stutzle/299 1.25 3.00
78 Tage Thompson/299 1.25 3.00
79 David Pastrnak/299 2.50 6.00
80 Quinn Hughes/299 2.50 6.00
81 Mikael Backlund/299 .75 2.00
82 Brent Burns/299 1.00 2.50
83 Marc-Andre Fleury/299 2.00 5.00
84 Jason Zucker/299 1.00 2.50
85 Rasmus Dahlin/299 1.25 3.00
86 Juraj Slafkovsky/299 2.00 5.00
87 Devon Toews/299 .75 2.00
88 Zach Werenski/299 1.50 4.00
89 Dylan Larkin/299 1.25 3.00
90 Wyatt Johnston/299 2.00 5.00
91 Patrice Bergeron/99 5.00 12.00
92 Dominik Hasek/99 6.00 15.00
93 Steve Yzerman/99 10.00 25.00
94 Wayne Gretzky/99 25.00 60.00
95 Mario Lemieux/99 15.00 40.00
96 Mark Messier/99 8.00 20.00
97 Jaromir Jagr/99 12.00 30.00
98 Gordie Howe/99 12.00 30.00
99 Joe Sakic/99 8.00 20.00
100 Phil Esposito/99 6.00 15.00
101 Connor Bedard/399 RC 25.00 60.00
102 Vincent Iorio/399 RC 2.00 5.00
103 Tye Kartye/399 RC 3.00 8.00
104 Brock Faber/399 RC 5.00 12.00
105 William Dufour/399 RC 1.50 4.00
106 Daniil Gushchin/399 RC 2.00 5.00
107 Matthew Poitras/399 RC 4.00 10.00
108 Joona Koppanen/399 RC 1.50 4.00
109 Simon Nemec/399 RC 4.00 10.00
110 Matt Savoie/399 RC 4.00 10.00
111 Matthew Coronato/399 RC 3.00 8.00
112 Luke Evangelista/399 RC 3.00 8.00
113 Matt Murray/399 RC 2.00 5.00
114 Connor Zary/399 RC 4.00 10.00
115 Henry Thrun/399 RC 2.00 5.00
116 Aidan McDonough/399 RC 1.50 4.00
117 Dustin Wolf/399 RC 6.00 15.00
118 Tyson Foerster/399 RC 15.00 40.00
119 Devon Levi/399 RC 5.00 12.00
120 Will Cuyille/399 RC 3.00 8.00
121 Hunter McKown/399 RC 2.00 5.00
122 Owen Beck/399 RC 3.00 8.00
123 Simon Edvinsson/399 RC 4.00 10.00
124 Tristan Luneau/399 RC 2.00 5.00
125 Leevi Merilainen/399 RC 2.00 5.00
126 Hugh McGing/399 RC 2.00 5.00
127 Ridly Greig/399 RC 3.00 8.00
128 Jonathan Gruden/399 RC 3.00 8.00
129 Luke Hughes/399 RC 6.00 15.00
130 Luke Philp/399 RC 2.00 5.00
131 Sean Farrell/399 RC 2.00 5.00
132 Milos Kelemen/399 RC 2.00 5.00
133 Nikita Nesterenko/399 RC 2.00 5.00
134 Adam Fantilli/399 RC 6.00 15.00
135 Yaroslav Askarov/399 RC 5.00 12.00
136 Jiri Patera/399 RC 3.00 8.00
137 Jakob Pelletier/399 RC 2.50 6.00
138 Matthew Knies/399 RC 8.00 20.00
139 Stanislav Svozil/399 RC 1.50 4.00
140 Logan Cooley/399 RC 6.00 15.00
141 Pavel Mintyukov/399 RC 3.00 8.00
142 Mackie Samoskevich/399 RC 3.00 8.00
143 Justin Sourdif/399 RC 2.00 5.00
144 John Beecher/399 RC 4.00 10.00
145 Marco Kasper/399 RC 5.00 12.00
146 Kevin Korchinski/399 RC 3.00 8.00
147 Alex Laferriere/399 RC 3.00 8.00
148 Zach Benson/399 RC 3.00 8.00
149 Fraser Minten/399 RC 4.00 10.00
150 Leo Carlsson/399 RC 6.00 15.00

2023-24 Upper Deck Premier Bronze

*BRONZE RC/199: .5X TO 1.2X BASIC

2023-24 Upper Deck Premier Gold

*GOLD/65: .6X TO 1.5X BASIC
*GOLD LEG/25: .8X TO 2X BASIC
*GOLD RC/65: .8X TO 2X BASIC
101 Connor Bedard/65 60.00 150.00

2023-24 Upper Deck Premier Rose Gold

*ROSE GOLD/25: 1X TO 2.5X BASIC
101 Connor Bedard 100.00 250.00

2023-24 Upper Deck Premier Ruby

*RUBY/35: 1X TO 2.5X BASIC
*RUBY RC/49: .8X TO 2X BASIC
101 Connor Bedard/49 80.00 200.00

2023-24 Upper Deck Premier '03-04 Rookie Patch Autographs

SRRAF Adam Fantilli/49 125.00 300.00
SRRCB Connor Bedard/49 1200.00 3000.00
SRRDW Dustin Wolf/99 80.00 200.00
SRREV Luke Evangelista/99 25.00 60.00
SRRJP Jakob Pelletier/99 20.00 50.00
SRRKK Kevin Korchinski/99 25.00 60.00
SRRLC Logan Cooley/49 125.00 300.00
SRRLE Leo Carlsson/49 100.00 250.00
SRRLH Luke Hughes/49 125.00 300.00
SRRMC Matthew Coronato/99 40.00 100.00
SRRMS Mackie Samoskevich/99 25.00 60.00
SRROB Owen Beck/99 25.00 60.00
SRRPM Pavel Mintyukov/99 25.00 60.00
SRRRG Ridly Greig/99 25.00 60.00
SRRSE Simon Edvinsson/99 80.00 200.00
SRRSF Sean Farrell/99 15.00 40.00
SRRSS Stanislav Svozil/99 12.00 30.00
SRRTF Tyson Foerster/99 30.00 80.00
SRRWC Will Cuylle/99 25.00 60.00
SRRWD William Dufour/99 12.00 30.00
SRRYA Yaroslav Askarov/99 60.00 150.00
SRRZB Zach Benson/99 25.00 60.00

2023-24 Upper Deck Premier '23 Premier Rookie Jersey Autographs

PRAAG Adam Ginning/99 10.00 25.00
PRAAH Akito Hirose/99 8.00 20.00
PRAAL Alex Laferriere/99 15.00 40.00
PRAAM Aidan McDonough/99 8.00 20.00
PRABM Bobby McMann/99 15.00 40.00
PRABS Billy Sweezey/99 10.00 25.00
PRACG Cole Guttman/99 10.00 25.00
PRACM Cole McWard/99 10.00 25.00
PRACO Matthew Coronato/25 40.00 100.00
PRADG Danil Gushchin/99 10.00 25.00
PRADU William Dufour/99 8.00 20.00
PRAED Elliot Desnoyers/99 10.00 25.00
PRAFM Fraser Minten/99 20.00 50.00
PRAGU David Gust/99 10.00 25.00
PRAHM Hugh McGing/99 10.00 25.00
PRAHT Henry Thrun/99 10.00 25.00
PRAJB John Beecher/99 20.00 50.00
PRAJG Jet Greaves/99 15.00 40.00
PRAJK Joona Koppanen/99 8.00 20.00
PRAJL Jake Livingstone/99 10.00 25.00
PRAKE Michael Kesselring/99 10.00 25.00
PRAKK Kevin Korchinski/25 30.00 80.00
PRAKL Tyler Kleven/99 10.00 25.00
PRAKS Marco Kasper/25 40.00 100.00
PRALC Logan Cooley/25 60.00 150.00
PRALM Leevi Merilainen/99 10.00 25.00
PRALP Luke Philp/99 10.00 25.00
PRALR Lukas Rousek/99 8.00 20.00
PRAMI Milos Kelemen/99 10.00 25.00
PRAMP Matthew Poitras/99 20.00 50.00
PRAMS Matt Savoie/99 20.00 50.00
PRANN Nikita Nesterenko/99 10.00 25.00
PRANS Nick Swaney/99 10.00 25.00
PRAOB Owen Beck/25 25.00 60.00
PRAOE Olle Eriksson Ek/99 10.00 25.00
PRAPA Jiri Patera/99 15.00 40.00
PRAPM Pavel Mintyukov/25 30.00 80.00
PRARG Ridly Greig/99 15.00 40.00
PRASB Samuel Bolduc/99 10.00 25.00
PRASE Simon Edvinsson/25 40.00 100.00
PRASF Sean Farrell/99 10.00 25.00
PRASK Samuel Knazko/99 10.00 25.00
PRASM Simon Nemec/99 20.00 50.00
PRASS Stanislav Svozil/99 8.00 20.00
PRATF Tyson Foerster/25 40.00 100.00
PRATK Tye Kartye/99 10.00 25.00
PRATR Tristen Robins/99 10.00 25.00
PRAVD Vincent Desharnais/99 10.00 25.00
PRAVI Vincent Iorio/99 12.00 30.00
PRAWC Will Cuylle/99 15.00 40.00
PRAWD Walker Duehr/99 8.00 20.00
PRAWK Wyatt Kaiser/99 10.00 25.00
PRAYA Yaroslav Askarov/25 40.00 100.00

2023-24 Upper Deck Premier Acetate Rookie Patch Autographs

ARAF Adam Fantilli/99 125.00 300.00
ARAG Adam Ginning/249 12.00 30.00
ARAH Akito Hirose/249 10.00 25.00
ARAM Aidan McDonough/249 10.00 25.00
ARBF Brock Faber/249 80.00 200.00
ARBM Bobby McMann/249 20.00 50.00
ARBS Billy Sweezey/249 12.00 30.00
ARCB Connor Bedard/99 800.00 2000.00
ARCG Cole Guttman/249 12.00 30.00
ARCM Cole McWard/249 12.00 30.00
ARCO Logan Cooley/99 150.00 400.00
ARDG Danil Gushchin/249 12.00 30.00
ARDL Devon Levi/249 60.00 150.00
ARDU Walker Duehr/249 8.00 20.00
ARDW Dustin Wolf/249 80.00 200.00
ARED Elliot Desnoyers/249 12.00 30.00
ARFM Fraser Minten/249 25.00 60.00
ARGU David Gust/249 8.00 20.00
ARHT Henry Thrun/249 12.00 30.00
ARJB John Beecher/249 25.00 60.00
ARJK Joona Koppanen/249 10.00 25.00
ARJL Jake Livingstone/249 10.00 25.00
ARJP Jiri Patera/249 20.00 50.00
ARJS Justin Sourdif/249 10.00 25.00
ARKA Tye Kartye/249 20.00 50.00
ARKE Michael Kesselring/249 10.00 25.00
ARKK Kevin Korchinski/99 20.00 50.00
ARKN Matthew Knies/99 125.00 300.00
ARKU Jiri Kulich/249 50.00 125.00
ARLC Leo Carlsson/99 125.00 300.00
ARLH Luke Hughes/99 125.00 300.00
ARLR Lukas Rousek/249 10.00 25.00
ARMC Hugh McGing/249 12.00 30.00
ARMI Milos Kelemen/249 12.00 30.00
ARMK Marco Kasper/99 60.00 150.00
ARMM Matt Murray/249 12.00 30.00
ARMP Matthew Poitras/249 50.00 125.00
ARNN Nikita Nesterenko/249 12.00 30.00
AROB Owen Beck/249 20.00 50.00
AROE Olle Eriksson Ek/249 12.00 30.00
ARPM Pavel Mintyukov/249 25.00 60.00
ARRE Ryker Evans/249 15.00 40.00
ARSA Matt Savoie/249 25.00 60.00
ARSB Samuel Bolduc/249 12.00 30.00
ARSF Sean Farrell/249 12.00 30.00
ARSK Samuel Knazko/249 12.00 30.00
ARSN Simon Nemec/249 40.00 100.00
ARSS Stanislav Svozil/249 10.00 25.00
ARTF Tyson Foerster/249 30.00 80.00
ARTK Tyler Kleven/249 12.00 30.00
ARTR Tristen Robins/249 12.00 30.00
ARVD Vincent Desharnais/249 15.00 40.00
ARVI Vincent Iorio/249 12.00 30.00
ARWC Will Cuylle/249 40.00 100.00
ARWD William Dufour/249 10.00 25.00
ARWK Wyatt Kaiser/249 12.00 30.00
ARYA Yaroslav Askarov/99 60.00 150.00

2023-24 Upper Deck Premier Acetate Rookie Patch Autographs Gold

*GOLD: .6X TO 1.5X BASIC
ARKK Kevin Korchinski/35 40.00 100.00
AROB Owen Beck/65 60.00 150.00

2023-24 Upper Deck Premier Acetate Star Patch Autographs

AVAB Aleksander Barkov/35 25.00 60.00
AVAD Alex DeBrincat/35 50.00 125.00
AVAL Alexis Lafreniere/35 25.00 60.00
AVAS Andrei Svechnikov/49 20.00 50.00
AVBA Mikael Backlund/49 12.00 30.00
AVBO Matt Boldy/49 25.00 60.00
AVBS Brayden Schenn/49 15.00 40.00
AVBT Brady Tkachuk/49 25.00 60.00
AVCH Connor Hellebuyck/49 60.00 150.00
AVCP Colton Parayko/49 12.00 30.00
AVCS Chandler Stephenson/49 12.00 30.00
AVDT Devon Toews/49 12.00 30.00
AVHU Jonathan Huberdeau/35 20.00 50.00
AVJK Jordan Kyrou/49 15.00 40.00
AVJM Jonathan Marchessault/49 20.00 50.00
AVJO Jake Oettinger/35 25.00 60.00
AVJS Juuse Saros/49 20.00 50.00
AVJT John Tavares/35 40.00 100.00
AVKL Kris Letang/49 20.00 50.00
AVKU Andrei Kuzmenko/35 15.00 40.00
AVLU Anton Lundell/49 15.00 40.00
AVMA Cale Makar/35 150.00 400.00
AVMC Matias Maccelli/49 12.00 30.00
AVMH Miro Heiskanen/49 20.00 50.00
AVMI Casey Mittelstadt/49 15.00 40.00
AVMN Martin Necas/49 20.00 50.00
AVMS Mark Stone/49 20.00 50.00
AVMT Matthew Tkachuk/35 50.00 125.00
AVMV Mason McTavish/35 15.00 40.00
AVND Noah Dobson/49 20.00 50.00
AVNH Nico Hischier/49 25.00 60.00
AVOB Oliver Bjorkstrand/49 12.00 30.00
AVOP Owen Power/35 15.00 40.00
AVRJ Roman Josi/35 15.00 40.00
AVRN Ryan Nugent-Hopkins/35 20.00 50.00
AVRO Marco Rossi/49 20.00 50.00
AVSI Cole Sillinger/49 12.00 30.00
AVSJ Seth Jarvis/49 20.00 50.00
AVSO Ilya Sorokin/35 25.00 60.00
AVSR Sam Reinhart/49 30.00 80.00
AVTH Tomas Hertl/49 15.00 40.00
AVTR Taylor Raddysh/49 12.00 30.00
AVWK William Karlsson/49 20.00 50.00

2023-24 Upper Deck Premier Autographs

1 Connor McDavid SP 150.00 400.00
2 Matt Boldy SP 12.00 30.00
3 Leon Draisaitl SP 50.00 125.00
4 Mason McTavish 8.00 20.00
5 Tomas Hertl 8.00 20.00
9 Josh Morrissey 10.00 25.00
12 Mark Stone 10.00 25.00
14 Andrei Vasilevskiy 12.00 30.00
16 Martin Necas 10.00 25.00
19 Andrei Kuzmenko 8.00 20.00
20 Juuse Saros 10.00 25.00
22 Roope Hintz 10.00 25.00
23 Ryan Nugent-Hopkins 10.00 25.00
24 John Tavares SP 12.00 30.00
25 Nick Suzuki 15.00 40.00
27 Brady Tkachuk SP 12.00 30.00
28 Ilya Sorokin 10.00 25.00
29 Brad Marchand SP 15.00 40.00
31 Boone Jenner 8.00 20.00
33 Timo Meier 8.00 20.00
36 Cale Makar SP 60.00 150.00
37 Nico Hischier 12.00 30.00
38 Jared McCann 6.00 15.00
39 Aleksander Barkov 12.00 30.00
41 Jordan Kyrou 8.00 20.00
42 Jonathan Huberdeau SP 10.00 25.00
44 Alex Tuch 8.00 20.00
47 Roman Josi 8.00 20.00
50 Matias Maccelli 6.00 15.00
51 Ryan O'Reilly 8.00 20.00
52 Kevin Fiala 8.00 20.00
53 Blake Coleman 6.00 15.00
55 Matthew Tkachuk SP 15.00 40.00
57 Auston Matthews SP 60.00 150.00
58 Alex Ovechkin SP 125.00 300.00
63 Taylor Raddysh 6.00 15.00
65 Jake Sanderson 12.00 30.00
66 Mitch Marner SP 20.00 50.00
67 Cam Atkinson 8.00 20.00
68 Andrei Svechnikov 8.00 20.00
69 Troy Terry 6.00 15.00
70 Robert Thomas SP 8.00 20.00
71 John Carlson 8.00 20.00
73 Kent Johnson 8.00 20.00
81 Mikael Backlund 6.00 15.00
83 Marc-Andre Fleury SP 40.00 100.00
84 Jason Zucker 6.00 15.00
87 Devon Toews 6.00 15.00
90 Wyatt Johnston 15.00 40.00
91 Patrice Bergeron 20.00 50.00
92 Dominik Hasek 25.00 60.00
93 Steve Yzerman 50.00 120.00
94 Wayne Gretzky SP 125.00 300.00
95 Mario Lemieux SP 60.00 150.00
96 Mark Messier SP 30.00 80.00
99 Joe Sakic 30.00 80.00
100 Phil Esposito 25.00 60.00
101 Connor Bedard SP 200.00 500.00
103 Tye Kartye 12.00 30.00
105 William Dufour 6.00 15.00
107 Matthew Poitras SP 25.00 60.00
108 Joona Koppanen 6.00 15.00
109 Simon Nemec 15.00 40.00
110 Matt Savoie SP 15.00 40.00
111 Matthew Coronato 12.00 30.00
113 Matt Murray 8.00 20.00
115 Henry Thrun 8.00 20.00
116 Aidan McDonough 6.00 15.00
117 Dustin Wolf SP 25.00 60.00
118 Tyson Foerster 15.00 40.00
119 Devon Levi 20.00 50.00
120 Will Cuylle 12.00 30.00
122 Owen Beck 12.00 30.00
123 Simon Edvinsson 15.00 40.00
125 Leevi Merilainen 8.00 20.00
126 Hugh McGing 8.00 20.00
127 Ridly Greig 12.00 30.00
130 Luke Philp 8.00 20.00
131 Sean Farrell 8.00 20.00
132 Milos Kelemen 8.00 20.00
133 Nikita Nesterenko 8.00 20.00
134 Adam Fantilli SP 25.00 60.00
135 Yaroslav Askarov 20.00 50.00
136 Jiri Patera 12.00 30.00
138 Matthew Knies SP 30.00 80.00
139 Stanislav Svozil 6.00 15.00
140 Logan Cooley SP 25.00 60.00
141 Pavel Mintyukov SP 12.00 30.00
144 John Beecher 15.00 40.00
145 Marco Kasper SP 20.00 50.00
146 Kevin Korchinski 12.00 30.00
147 Alex Laferriere 12.00 30.00
150 Leo Carlsson SP 25.00 60.00

2023-24 Upper Deck Premier Autographs Gold

*GOLD: .6X TO 1.5X BASIC
83 Marc-Andre Fleury/25 80.00 200.00
150 Leo Carlsson/25 80.00 200.00

2023-24 Upper Deck Premier Dual Rookie Patch-Taculars Chest Logos

DRPTAE Y.Askarov/L.Evangelista 40.00 100.00
DRPTBF O.Beck/S.Farrell 25.00 60.00
DRPTBP J.Beecher/M.Poitras 30.00 80.00
DRPTBS Z.Benson/M.Savoie 30.00 80.00
DRPTCP M.Coronato/J.Pelletier 25.00 60.00
DRPTDB W.Dufour/S.Bolduc 15.00 40.00
DRPTDC A.Durandeau/W.Cuylle 40.00 100.00
DRPTDW D.Levi/W.Kaiser 15.00 40.00
DRPTFC A.Fantilli/L.Cooley 50.00 125.00
DRPTFG T.Foerster/A.Ginning 30.00 80.00
DRPTGD J.Gruden/E.Desnoyers 15.00 40.00
DRPTGK R.Greig/T.Kleven 25.00 60.00
DRPTGT D.Gushchin/H.Thrun 15.00 40.00
DRPTHM A.Hirose/A.McDonough 15.00 40.00
DRPTHN L.Hughes/S.Nemec 50.00 125.00
DRPTKE M.Kasper/S.Edvinsson 100.00 250.00
DRPTKF M.Knies/F.Minten 60.00 150.00
DRPTKK M.Kesselring/M.Kelemen 15.00 40.00
DRPTKM M.Kessel/H.McGing 15.00 40.00
DRPTLA J.Livingstone/E.Afanasyev 15.00 40.00
DRPTLD R.Levi/V.Desharnais 20.00 50.00
DRPTLR D.Levi/I.Rosen 40.00 100.00
DRPTMC P.Mintyukov/L.Carlsson 50.00 125.00
DRPTMI I.Miroshnichenko/V.Iorio 25.00 60.00
DRPTPG L.Philp/C.Guttman 15.00 40.00
DRPTSK S.Svozil/S.Knazko 15.00 40.00
DRPTSS M.Samoskevich/J.Sourdif 25.00 60.00
DRPTTR T.Kartye/R.Evans 25.00 60.00
DRPTWZ D.Wolf/C.Zary 50.00 125.00

2023-24 Upper Deck Premier Flourishing Talent Patch Autographs

FTAB Aleksander Barkov/50 40.00 100.00
FTAF Adam Fantilli/25 100.00 250.00
FTBF Brock Faber/99 80.00 200.00
FTCP Cole Perfetti/99 15.00 40.00
FTCS Chandler Stephenson/99 12.00 30.00
FTDL Devon Levi/50 60.00 150.00
FTJD Jamie Drysdale/99 12.00 30.00
FTJP JJ Peterka/99 15.00 40.00
FTKM Kirill Marchenko/99 20.00 50.00
FTKO Kevin Korchinski/99 25.00 60.00
FTLD Leon Draisaitl/50 150.00 400.00
FTLH Luke Hughes/50 80.00 200.00
FTMK Matthew Knies/50 125.00 300.00
FTMR Marco Rossi/99 20.00 50.00
FTNC Nick Schmaltz/99 12.00 30.00
FTND Noah Dobson/99 20.00 50.00
FTNH Nico Hischier/50 25.00 60.00
FTNS Nick Suzuki/50 30.00 80.00
FTRT Robert Thomas/50 25.00 60.00
FTTS Travis Sanheim/50 10.00 25.00
FTWC Will Cuylle/99 25.00 60.00
FTZB Zach Benson/99 25.00 60.00

2023-24 Upper Deck Premier Global Notability Jersey Autographs

GNAAB Aleksander Barkov 20.00 50.00
GNABT Brady Tkachuk 20.00 50.00
GNACC Chris Chelios 12.00 30.00
GNAEP Elias Pettersson 30.00 80.00
GNAHL Henrik Lundqvist 30.00 80.00
GNAJP Joe Pavelski 15.00 40.00
GNALD Leon Draisaitl 50.00 125.00
GNANS Nick Suzuki 25.00 60.00
GNAPB Patrice Bergeron 80.00 200.00
GNARF Ron Francis 15.00 40.00
GNARJ Roman Josi 12.00 30.00

2023-24 Upper Deck Premier Global Notability Jerseys

*BLACK/25: 1X TO 2.5X BASIC
GNCA Cole Caufield 4.00 10.00
GNCC Corey Crawford 2.00 5.00
GNCM Connor McDavid 10.00 25.00
GNDP David Pastrnak 5.00 12.00
GNJS Joe Sakic 4.00 10.00
GNMS Moritz Seider 2.50 6.00
GNMT Matthew Tkachuk 4.00 10.00
GNMZ Mats Zuccarello 2.00 5.00
GNNM Nathan MacKinnon 8.00 20.00
GNPL Patrik Laine 2.50 6.00
GNRD Rasmus Dahlin 2.50 6.00
GNRG Ryan Getzlaf 2.00 5.00
GNTH Tomas Hertl 2.00 5.00
GNWN William Nylander 4.00 10.00
GNZC Zdeno Chara 2.00 5.00

2023-24 Upper Deck Premier Horizontal Acetate Rookie Patch Autographs

AHRAF Adam Fantilli/49 125.00 300.00
AHRBF Brock Faber/99 80.00 200.00
AHRCO Logan Cooley/49 125.00 300.00
AHRKK Kevin Korchinski/99 25.00 60.00
AHRLC Leo Carlsson/49 125.00 300.00
AHRMK Matthew Knies/99 125.00 300.00
AHRMP Matthew Poitras/99 60.00 150.00
AHRMS Matt Savoie/99 30.00 80.00
AHROB Owen Beck/99 25.00 60.00
AHRSF Sean Farrell/99 15.00 40.00
AHRSN Simon Nemec/99 30.00 80.00
AHRSS Stanislav Svozil/99 12.00 30.00
AHRTF Tyson Foerster/99 30.00 80.00
AHRWC Will Cuylle/99 25.00 60.00
AHRWD William Dufour/99 12.00 30.00
AHRYA Yaroslav Askarov/99 40.00 100.00

2023-24 Upper Deck Premier Jerseys

*PREMIUM: .8X TO 2X BASIC
*PREMIUM RC: 2X TO 5X BASIC
1 Connor McDavid 8.00 20.00
2 Matt Boldy 2.50 6.00
3 Leon Draisaitl 5.00 12.00
4 Mason McTavish 1.50 4.00
5 Tomas Hertl 1.50 4.00
6 Nikita Kucherov 3.00 8.00
7 Miro Heiskanen 2.00 5.00
8 Johnny Gaudreau 2.50 6.00
9 Josh Morrissey 2.00 5.00
10 Anze Kopitar 2.50 6.00
11 Joel Eriksson Ek 1.25 3.00
12 Mark Stone 2.00 5.00
13 Nathan MacKinnon 6.00 15.00
14 Andrei Vasilevskiy 2.50 6.00
15 Matty Beniers 2.00 5.00
16 Martin Necas 2.00 5.00
17 Travis Konecny 1.50 4.00
18 Elias Pettersson 2.50 6.00
19 Andrei Kuzmenko 1.50 4.00
20 Juuse Saros 2.00 5.00
21 Logan Couture 2.00 5.00
22 Roope Hintz 2.00 5.00
23 Ryan Nugent-Hopkins 2.00 5.00
24 John Tavares 2.50 6.00
25 Nick Suzuki 3.00 8.00
26 Jack Eichel 2.50 6.00
27 Brady Tkachuk 2.50 6.00
28 Ilya Sorokin 2.50 6.00
29 Brad Marchand 3.00 8.00
30 Dylan Cozens 1.50 4.00
31 Boone Jenner 1.50 4.00
32 Jake Guentzel 2.50 6.00
33 Timo Meier 1.50 4.00
34 Clayton Keller 2.00 5.00
35 Lucas Raymond 2.50 6.00
36 Cale Makar 4.00 10.00
37 Nico Hischier 2.50 6.00
38 Jared McCann 1.25 3.00
39 Aleksander Barkov 2.50 6.00
40 Seth Jones 1.50 4.00
41 Jordan Kyrou 1.50 4.00
42 Jonathan Huberdeau 2.00 5.00
43 Chris Kreider 2.00 5.00
44 Alex Tuch 1.50 4.00
45 Steven Stamkos 3.00 8.00
46 Moritz Seider 2.00 5.00
47 Roman Josi 1.50 4.00
48 Jason Robertson 2.50 6.00
49 Jack Hughes 4.00 10.00
50 Matias Maccelli 1.25 3.00
51 Ryan O'Reilly 1.50 4.00
52 Kevin Fiala 1.25 3.00
53 Blake Coleman 1.25 3.00
54 Sidney Crosby 6.00 15.00
55 Matthew Tkachuk 3.00 8.00
56 Trevor Zegras 1.50 4.00
57 Auston Matthews 6.00 15.00
58 Alex Ovechkin 6.00 15.00
59 Evgeni Malkin 3.00 8.00
60 Jeremy Swayman 2.50 6.00
61 Artemi Panarin 3.00 8.00
62 Kyle Connor 2.50 6.00
63 Taylor Raddysh 1.25 3.00
64 Brock Nelson 1.50 4.00
65 Jake Sanderson 2.00 5.00
66 Mitch Marner 2.50 6.00
67 Cam Atkinson 1.50 4.00
68 Andrei Svechnikov 2.00 5.00
69 Troy Terry 1.25 3.00
70 Robert Thomas 1.50 4.00
71 John Carlson 1.50 4.00
72 Cole Caufield 3.00 8.00
73 Kent Johnson 1.50 4.00
74 Alex Newhook 1.25 3.00
75 Kirill Kaprizov 5.00 12.00
76 Mathew Barzal 2.00 5.00
77 Tim Stutzle 2.00 5.00
78 Tage Thompson 2.00 5.00
79 David Pastrnak 4.00 10.00
80 Quinn Hughes 4.00 10.00
81 Mikael Backlund 1.25 3.00
82 Brent Burns 1.50 4.00
83 Marc-Andre Fleury 3.00 8.00
84 Jason Zucker 1.50 4.00
85 Rasmus Dahlin 2.00 5.00
86 Juraj Slafkovsky 3.00 8.00
87 Devon Toews 1.25 3.00
88 Zach Werenski 2.50 6.00
89 Dylan Larkin 2.00 5.00
90 Wyatt Johnston 3.00 8.00
91 Patrice Bergeron 5.00 12.00
92 Dominik Hasek 6.00 15.00
93 Steve Yzerman 10.00 25.00
95 Mario Lemieux 15.00 40.00
96 Mark Messier 8.00 20.00
97 Jaromir Jagr 12.00 30.00
99 Joe Sakic 8.00 20.00
100 Phil Esposito 6.00 15.00
101 Connor Bedard 25.00 60.00
102 Vincent Iorio 1.50 4.00
103 Tye Kartye 2.50 6.00
104 Brock Faber 4.00 10.00
105 William Dufour 1.25 3.00
106 Danil Gushchin 1.50 4.00
107 Matthew Poitras 3.00 8.00
108 Joona Koppanen 1.25 3.00
109 Simon Nemec 3.00 8.00
110 Matt Savoie 3.00 8.00
111 Matthew Coronato 2.50 6.00
112 Luke Evangelista 2.50 6.00
113 Matt Murray 1.50 4.00
114 Connor Zary 3.00 8.00
115 Henry Thrun 1.50 4.00
116 Aidan McDonough 1.25 3.00
117 Dustin Wolf 5.00 12.00
118 Tyson Foerster 3.00 8.00
119 Devon Levi 4.00 10.00
120 Will Cuylle 2.50 6.00
121 Hunter McKown 1.50 4.00
122 Owen Beck 2.50 6.00
123 Simon Edvinsson 3.00 8.00
124 Tristan Luneau 1.50 4.00
125 Leevi Merilainen 1.50 4.00
126 Hugh McGing 1.50 4.00
127 Ridly Greig 2.50 6.00
128 Jonathan Gruden 1.50 4.00
129 Luke Hughes 5.00 12.00
130 Luke Philp 1.50 4.00
131 Sean Farrell 1.50 4.00
132 Milos Kelemen 1.50 4.00
133 Nikita Nesterenko 1.50 4.00
134 Adam Fantilli 5.00 12.00
135 Yaroslav Askarov 4.00 10.00
136 Jiri Patera 2.50 6.00
137 Jakob Pelletier 2.00 5.00
138 Matthew Knies 6.00 15.00
139 Stanislav Svozil 1.25 3.00
140 Logan Cooley 5.00 12.00
141 Pavel Mintyukov 2.50 6.00
142 Mackie Samoskevich 2.50 6.00
143 Justin Sourdif 1.50 4.00
144 John Beecher 3.00 8.00
145 Marco Kasper 4.00 10.00
146 Kevin Korchinski 2.50 6.00
147 Alex Laferriere 2.50 6.00
148 Zach Benson 2.50 6.00
149 Fraser Minten 3.00 8.00
150 Leo Carlsson 5.00 12.00

2023-24 Upper Deck Premier On the Forefront Autographs

OFABU Michael Bunting 6.00 15.00
OFACM Casey Mittelstadt 6.00 15.00
OFAJC J.T. Compher 4.00 10.00
OFAJP JJ Peterka 6.00 15.00
OFAMA Mason Marchment 5.00 12.00
OFAMB Matt Boldy 10.00 25.00
OFAMM Mason McTavish 6.00 15.00
OFAMN Martin Necas 8.00 20.00
OFAMR Marco Rossi 8.00 20.00
OFAPZ Pavel Zacha 5.00 12.00
OFAVD Vince Dunn 5.00 12.00
OFAWJ Wyatt Johnston 15.00 40.00

2023-24 Upper Deck Premier On the Forefront Jerseys

OFAB Aleksander Barkov 3.00 8.00
OFAM Auston Matthews 8.00 20.00
OFAP Artemi Panarin 4.00 10.00
OFBB Brock Boeser 2.50 6.00
OFCC Cole Caufield 4.00 10.00
OFCK Chris Kreider 2.50 6.00
OFCM Connor McDavid 10.00 25.00
OFDP David Pastrnak 5.00 12.00
OFEM Evgeni Malkin 4.00 10.00
OFEP Elias Pettersson 3.00 8.00
OFFF Filip Forsberg 3.00 8.00
OFJB Jesper Bratt 2.00 5.00
OFLD Leon Draisaitl 6.00 15.00
OFMB Mathew Barzal 2.50 6.00
OFMM Mitch Marner 3.00 8.00
OFNK Nikita Kucherov 4.00 10.00
OFNM Nathan MacKinnon 8.00 20.00
OFSC Sidney Crosby 8.00 20.00
OFSS Steven Stamkos 4.00 10.00
OFTS Tim Stutzle 2.50 6.00

2023-24 Upper Deck Premier On the Forefront Jerseys Black

*BLACK/50: 1.2X TO 3X BASIC
OFSC Sidney Crosby 40.00 100.00

2023-24 Upper Deck Premier On the Forefront Legends and Superstars Autographs

OFSAM Auston Matthews 80.00 200.00
OFSCM Cale Makar 80.00 200.00
OFSCO Chris Osgood 10.00 25.00
OFSFP Felix Potvin 15.00 40.00
OFSKC Kyle Connor 15.00 40.00
OFSRB Rob Blake 10.00 25.00
OFSTA Tony Amonte 8.00 20.00

2023-24 Upper Deck Premier On the Forefront Rookies Jerseys

*BLACK/75: .8X TO 2X BASIC
OFRAF Adam Fantilli 5.00 12.00
OFRAL Alex Laferriere 2.50 6.00
OFRBF Brock Faber 4.00 10.00
OFRCB Connor Bedard 25.00 60.00
OFRCO Logan Cooley 5.00 12.00
OFRCZ Connor Zary 3.00 8.00
OFRDL Devon Levi 4.00 10.00
OFRDW Dustin Wolf 5.00 12.00
OFRHT Henry Thrun 1.50 4.00
OFRJP Jiri Patera 2.50 6.00
OFRKK Kevin Korchinski 2.50 6.00
OFRLC Leo Carlsson 5.00 12.00
OFRLE Luke Evangelista 2.50 6.00
OFRLH Luke Hughes 5.00 12.00
OFRMK Matthew Knies 6.00 15.00
OFRMP Matthew Poitras 3.00 8.00
OFRMS Matt Savoie 3.00 8.00
OFROB Owen Beck 2.50 6.00
OFRPM Pavel Mintyukov 2.50 6.00
OFRSB Samuel Bolduc 1.50 4.00
OFRSE Simon Edvinsson 3.00 8.00
OFRTF Tyson Foerster 3.00 8.00
OFRTK Tye Kartye 2.50 6.00
OFRWC Will Cuylle 2.50 6.00
OFRZB Zach Benson 2.50 6.00

2023-24 Upper Deck Premier Premier Attractions Jerseys

PAAD Alex DeBrincat/99 2.50 6.00
PAAK Anze Kopitar/99 3.00 8.00
PAAM Auston Matthews/49 8.00 20.00
PAAO Alex Ovechkin/49 8.00 20.00
PAAP Artemi Panarin/99 4.00 10.00
PACC Cole Caufield/99 4.00 10.00
PACM Connor McDavid/49 10.00 25.00
PADP David Pastrnak/99 5.00 12.00
PAEM Evgeni Malkin/99 4.00 10.00
PAEP Elias Pettersson/99 3.00 8.00
PAHU Jack Hughes/99 5.00 12.00
PAJE Jack Eichel/99 3.00 8.00
PAJH Jonathan Huberdeau/99 2.50 6.00
PAJK Jordan Kyrou/99 2.00 5.00
PAJR Jason Robertson/49 3.00 8.00
PAKK Kirill Kaprizov/99 6.00 15.00
PAKU Andrei Kuzmenko/99 2.00 5.00
PALD Leon Draisaitl/99 6.00 15.00
PAMB Matty Beniers/99 2.50 6.00
PAMM Mitch Marner/99 3.00 8.00
PAMT Matthew Tkachuk/99 4.00 10.00
PAMZ Mika Zibanejad/99 2.50 6.00
PANK Nikita Kucherov/99 4.00 10.00
PARD Rasmus Dahlin/99 2.50 6.00
PARO Ryan O'Reilly/99 2.00 5.00
PASC Sidney Crosby/49 8.00 20.00
PATS Tim Stutzle/99 2.50 6.00
PATT Tage Thompson/99 2.50 6.00
PATZ Trevor Zegras/99 2.00 5.00
PAWN William Nylander/99 4.00 10.00

2023-24 Upper Deck Premier Premier Attractions Jerseys Patch

*PATCH: 1.2X TO 3X BASIC
PADP David Pastrnak/20 20.00 50.00
PAMB Matty Beniers/35 10.00 25.00

2023-24 Upper Deck Premier Premier Dual Jerseys

PDAMMM A.Matthews/M.Marner 15.00 40.00
PDAOJC A.Ovechkin/J.Carlson 15.00 40.00
PDAPIS A.Panarin/I.Shesterkin 8.00 20.00
PDBMDP B.Marchand/D.Pastrnak 10.00 25.00
PDCCNS C.Caufield/N.Suzuki 8.00 20.00
PDCMLD C.McDavid/L.Draisaitl 20.00 50.00
PDJEMS J.Eichel/M.Stone 6.00 15.00
PDJHLH J.Hughes/L.Hughes 12.00 30.00
PDJPJR J.Pavelski/J.Robertson 6.00 15.00
PDKCJM K.Connor/J.Morrissey 6.00 15.00
PDKKMF K.Kaprizov/M.Fleury 12.00 30.00
PDMBJM M.Beniers/J.McCann 5.00 12.00
PDMBND M.Barzal/N.Dobson 5.00 12.00
PDMRCM M.Rantanen/C.Makar 10.00 25.00
PDMSLR M.Seider/L.Raymond 6.00 15.00
PDMTAB M.Tkachuk/A.Barkov 8.00 20.00
PDNKSS N.Kucherov/S.Stamkos 8.00 20.00
PDQHEP Q.Hughes/E.Pettersson 10.00 25.00
PDRDOP R.Dahlin/O.Power 5.00 12.00
PDSAAS S.Aho/A.Svechnikov 6.00 15.00
PDTSBT T.Stutzle/B.Tkachuk 6.00 15.00
PDTZTT T.Zegras/T.Terry 4.00 10.00

2023-24 Upper Deck Premier Premier Focus Autographs

PFAAM Auston Matthews/25 150.00 400.00
PFAJT Joe Thornton/50 25.00 60.00
PFALD Leon Draisaitl/35 100.00 250.00

2023-24 Upper Deck Premier Premier Focus Patch Autographs

PFPBT Brady Tkachuk/25 20.00 50.00
PFPJK Jordan Kyrou/50 12.00 30.00
PFPJM Jared McCann/50 10.00 25.00
PFPJP Joe Pavelski/50 15.00 40.00
PFPMA Jonathan Marchessault/50 20.00 50.00
PFPMB Matt Boldy/50 20.00 50.00
PFPNH Nico Hischier/50 30.00 80.00
PFPNS Nick Suzuki/50 25.00 60.00
PFPSR Sam Reinhart/50 25.00 60.00
PFPTH Tomas Hertl/75 12.00 30.00
PFPWJ Wyatt Johnston/50 40.00 100.00
PFPZH Zach Hyman/50 40.00 100.00

2023-24 Upper Deck Premier Premier Focus Rookie Patch Autographs

PFRAF Adam Fantilli/50 125.00 300.00
PFRAG Adam Ginning/175 8.00 20.00
PFRAM Aidan McDonough/175 6.00 15.00
PFRBF Brock Faber/175 80.00 200.00
PFRBM Bobby McMann/175 12.00 30.00
PFRCB Connor Bedard/50 600.00 1500.00
PFRCG Cole Guttman/175 8.00 20.00
PFRCO Logan Cooley/50 100.00 250.00
PFRDG Danil Gushchin/175 8.00 20.00
PFRDL Devon Levi/99 25.00 60.00
PFRDW Dustin Wolf/175 60.00 150.00
PFRHT Henry Thrun/175 8.00 20.00
PFRHU Hugh McGing/175 8.00 20.00
PFRJB John Beecher/175 15.00 40.00
PFRJK Joona Koppanen/175 6.00 15.00
PFRJS Justin Sourdif/175 8.00 20.00
PFRKA Marco Kasper/175 40.00 100.00
PFRKE Michael Kesselring/175 8.00 20.00
PFRKK Kevin Korchinski/175 12.00 30.00
PFRKN Matthew Knies/99 80.00 200.00
PFRLC Leo Carlsson/50 80.00 200.00
PFRLH Luke Hughes/50 80.00 200.00
PFRLR Lukas Rousek/175 6.00 15.00
PFRMK Milos Kelemen/175 8.00 20.00
PFRMM Matt Murray/175 8.00 20.00
PFRMP Matthew Poitras/99 50.00 125.00
PFRNN Nikita Nesterenko/175 8.00 20.00
PFRNS Nick Swaney/175 8.00 20.00
PFROB Owen Beck/175 12.00 30.00
PFRPA Jiri Patera/175 12.00 30.00
PFRPM Pavel Mintyukov/175 12.00 30.00
PFRSB Samuel Bolduc/175 8.00 20.00
PFRSF Sean Farrell/175 8.00 20.00
PFRSN Simon Nemec/175 15.00 40.00
PFRTF Tyson Foerster/175 15.00 40.00
PFRTK Tye Kartye/175 12.00 30.00
PFRVD Vincent Desharnais/175 10.00 25.00
PFRVI Vincent Iorio/175 8.00 20.00
PFRWC Will Cuylle/175 12.00 30.00
PFRWD Walker Duehr/175 6.00 15.00
PFRWK Wyatt Kaiser/175 8.00 20.00
PFRYA Yaroslav Askarov/175 40.00 100.00

2023-24 Upper Deck Premier Premier Focus Rookie Patch Autographs Gold

*GOLD: .6X TO 1.5X BASIC
PFRBM Bobby McMann/49 30.00 80.00
PFRDL Devon Levi/49 50.00 125.00

2023-24 Upper Deck Premier Premier Gear Jerseys

PGAK Anze Kopitar 8.00 20.00
PGAM Auston Matthews 20.00 50.00
PGAO Alex Ovechkin 20.00 50.00
PGAP Artemi Panarin 10.00 25.00
PGCM Connor McDavid 25.00 60.00
PGDP David Pastrnak 12.00 30.00
PGJH Jack Hughes 12.00 30.00
PGLD Leon Draisaitl 15.00 40.00
PGNM Nathan MacKinnon 20.00 50.00
PGSC Sidney Crosby 20.00 50.00

2023-24 Upper Deck Premier Premier Gear Rookie Jerseys

PGRAF Adam Fantilli 12.00 30.00
PGRCB Connor Bedard 80.00 200.00
PGRCO Logan Cooley 12.00 30.00
PGRDW Dustin Wolf 12.00 30.00
PGRJP Jakob Pelletier 5.00 12.00
PGRKA Marco Kasper 10.00 25.00
PGRKK Kevin Korchinski 6.00 15.00
PGRLC Leo Carlsson 12.00 30.00
PGRLE Luke Evangelista 6.00 15.00
PGRLH Luke Hughes 12.00 30.00
PGRMC Matthew Coronato 6.00 15.00
PGRMK Matthew Knies 15.00 40.00
PGROB Owen Beck 6.00 15.00
PGRPM Pavel Mintyukov 6.00 15.00
PGRRG Ridly Greig 6.00 15.00
PGRSE Simon Edvinsson 8.00 20.00
PGRSF Sean Farrell 4.00 10.00
PGRTF Tyson Foerster 8.00 20.00
PGRYA Yaroslav Askarov 10.00 25.00
PGRZB Zach Benson 6.00 15.00

2023-24 Upper Deck Premier Premier Gear Rookie Jerseys Patch

*PATCH/25: 1.2X TO 3X BASIC
PGRAF Adam Fantilli 125.00 300.00
PGRDW Dustin Wolf 60.00 150.00
PGRTF Tyson Foerster 30.00 80.00
PGRYA Yaroslav Askarov 60.00 150.00

2023-24 Upper Deck Premier Premier Mega Jersey Duos

PM2AS S.Aho/A.Svechnikov 12.00 30.00
PM2BN M.Barzal/B.Nelson 6.00 15.00
PM2BR C.Bedard/T.Raddysh 30.00 80.00
PM2DS A.DeBrincat/M.Seider 6.00 15.00
PM2HH J.Hughes/L.Hughes 15.00 40.00
PM2KB K.Kaprizov/M.Boldy 15.00 40.00
PM2KH A.Kuzmenko/Q.Hughes 12.00 30.00
PM2MC E.Malkin/S.Crosby 20.00 50.00
PM2MD C.McDavid/L.Draisaitl 25.00 60.00
PM2MM A.Matthews/M.Marner 20.00 50.00
PM2OK A.Ovechkin/E.Kuznetsov 20.00 50.00
PM2PM D.Pastrnak/B.Marchand 12.00 30.00
PM2RM M.Rantanen/N.MacKinnon 20.00 50.00
PM2TB M.Tkachuk/A.Barkov 15.00 40.00
PM2TT A.Tuch/T.Thompson 6.00 15.00

2023-24 Upper Deck Premier Premier Mega Jersey Duos Patch

*PATCH/25: .8X TO 2X BASIC
PM2AS S.Aho/A.Svechnikov 30.00 80.00
PM2BR C.Bedard/T.Raddysh 125.00 300.00
PM2KB K.Kaprizov/M.Boldy 40.00 100.00
PM2MC E.Malkin/S.Crosby 80.00 200.00
PM2TB M.Tkachuk/A.Barkov 40.00 100.00
PM2TT A.Tuch/T.Thompson 40.00 100.00

2023-24 Upper Deck Premier Premier Mega Jersey Trios

PM3DHN Draisaitl/McDavid
Nugent-Hopkins 50.00 125.00
PM3DTT Dahlin/Thompson/Tuch 12.00 30.00
PM3GFL Gaudreau/Fantilli/Laine 30.00 80.00
PM3HHM Hughes/Hischier/Mercer 25.00 60.00
PM3MMN Marner
Matthews/Nylander 40.00 100.00
PM3MMR MacKinnon
Makar/Rantanen 40.00 100.00
PM3PZF Panarin/Zibanejad/Fox 20.00 50.00
PM3SDR Seider/DeBrincat/Raymond 15.00 40.00

2023-24 Upper Deck Premier Premier Mega Patch Chest Logos

PMPAB Aleksander Barkov/24 50.00 125.00
PMPAD Alex DeBrincat/21 40.00 100.00
PMPAF Adam Fantilli/24 100.00 250.00
PMPAK Anze Kopitar/18 50.00 120.00
PMPAL Alexis Lafreniere/20 50.00 125.00
PMPAM Auston Matthews/24 125.00 300.00
PMPAO Alex Ovechkin/20 120.00 300.00
PMPAP Artemi Panarin/20 60.00 150.00
PMPAS Andrei Svechnikov/22 40.00 100.00
PMPAV Andrei Vasilevskiy/24 50.00 125.00
PMPBA Alexander Barabanov/24 20.00 50.00
PMPBB Brock Boeser/27 40.00 100.00
PMPBE Matty Beniers/28 40.00 100.00
PMPBG Brendan Gallagher/20 30.00 80.00
PMPBM Brad Marchand/22 60.00 150.00
PMPBP Brayden Point/23 40.00 100.00
PMPBT Brady Tkachuk/29 50.00 125.00
PMPCB Connor Bedard/24 200.00 500.00
PMPCC Cole Caufield/20 60.00 150.00
PMPCF Cam Fowler/22 30.00 80.00
PMPCG Claude Giroux/29 30.00 80.00
PMPCK Clayton Keller/23 40.00 100.00
PMPCM Cale Makar/30 80.00 200.00
PMPCO Logan Cooley/23 100.00 250.00
PMPCS Chandler Stephenson/22 25.00 60.00
PMPDC Dylan Cozens/27 30.00 80.00
PMPDL Devon Levi/27 80.00 200.00
PMPDP David Pastrnak/22 80.00 200.00
PMPDT Devon Toews/30 25.00 60.00
PMPEL Elias Lindholm/26 30.00 80.00
PMPEM Evgeni Malkin/33 60.00 150.00
PMPEP Elias Pettersson/27 50.00 125.00
PMPFF Filip Forsberg/20 50.00 125.00
PMPGA Johnny Gaudreau/24 50.00 125.00
PMPGU Jake Guentzel/33 50.00 125.00
PMPHU Jack Hughes/28 80.00 200.00
PMPIS Ilya Sorokin/22 50.00 125.00
PMPJC John Carlson/20 30.00 80.00
PMPJD Jamie Drysdale/22 25.00 60.00
PMPJE Jack Eichel/22 50.00 125.00
PMPJG John Gibson/22 30.00 80.00
PMPJH Jonathan Huberdeau/26 40.00 100.00
PMPJK Jordan Kyrou/18 30.00 80.00
PMPJM Jared McCann/28 25.00 60.00
PMPJN Josh Norris/29 30.00 80.00
PMPJO Jake Oettinger/21 50.00 125.00
PMPJP Joe Pavelski/21 40.00 100.00
PMPJS Jeremy Swayman/22 50.00 125.00
PMPJT John Tavares/24 50.00 125.00
PMPJU Juuse Saros/20 40.00 100.00
PMPKC Kyle Connor/22 50.00 125.00
PMPKF Kevin Fiala/26 25.00 60.00
PMPKK Kirill Kaprizov/18 100.00 250.00
PMPKR Chris Kreider/21 40.00 100.00
PMPLC Leo Carlsson/21 100.00 250.00
PMPLD Leon Draisaitl/26 100.00 250.00
PMPLH Luke Hughes/28 100.00 250.00
PMPLR Lucas Raymond/21 50.00 125.00
PMPMA Mitch Marner/24 50.00 125.00
PMPMB Mathew Barzal/22 40.00 100.00
PMPMC Connor McDavid/26 150.00 400.00
PMPMF Marc-Andre Fleury/18 60.00 150.00
PMPMJ Jonathan Marchessault/22 40.00 100.00
PMPMK Matthew Knies/24 125.00 300.00
PMPMM Mason McTavish/22 30.00 80.00
PMPMR Mikko Rantanen/30 80.00 200.00
PMPMS Moritz Seider/21 40.00 100.00
PMPMT Matthew Tkachuk/24 60.00 150.00
PMPMZ Mats Zuccarello/18 30.00 80.00
PMPNK Nikita Kucherov/24 60.00 150.00
PMPNM Nathan MacKinnon/30 125.00 300.00
PMPNS Nick Schmaltz/23 25.00 60.00
PMPOP Owen Power/27 30.00 80.00
PMPPK Philipp Kurashev/24 25.00 60.00
PMPQH Quinn Hughes/27 80.00 200.00
PMPRD Rasmus Dahlin/27 40.00 100.00
PMPRH Roope Hintz/21 40.00 100.00
PMPRI Morgan Rielly/24 30.00 80.00
PMPRJ Roman Josi/20 30.00 80.00
PMPRO Marco Rossi/18 40.00 100.00
PMPRT Robert Thomas/17 30.00 80.00
PMPSA Sebastian Aho/22 50.00 125.00
PMPSC Sidney Crosby/33 125.00 300.00
PMPSH Igor Shesterkin/20 60.00 150.00
PMPSJ Seth Jarvis/20 40.00 100.00
PMPSM Mark Scheifele/22 50.00 125.00
PMPSR Sam Reinhart/24 60.00 150.00
PMPSS Steven Stamkos/24 60.00 150.00
PMPSU Nick Suzuki/20 60.00 150.00
PMPTD Thatcher Demko/27 40.00 100.00
PMPTF Tyson Foerster/23 60.00 150.00
PMPTH Tomas Hertl/24 30.00 80.00
PMPTK Travis Konecny/23 30.00 80.00
PMPTR Taylor Raddysh/24 25.00 60.00
PMPTT Tage Thompson/27 40.00 100.00
PMPTZ Trevor Zegras/22 30.00 80.00
PMPWJ Wyatt Johnston/21 60.00 150.00
PMPZH Zach Hyman/26 50.00 125.00

2023-24 Upper Deck Premier Premier Precipice Autographs

PPAB Aleksander Barkov 8.00 20.00
PPAK Andrei Kuzmenko 5.00 12.00
PPAT Alex Tuch 5.00 12.00
PPAV Andrei Vasilevskiy 8.00 20.00
PPBJ Boone Jenner 5.00 12.00
PPBM Brad Marchand 20.00 50.00
PPBT Brady Tkachuk SP 8.00 20.00
PPDP David Perron 4.00 10.00
PPEP Elias Pettersson SP 8.00 20.00
PPJM Jared McCann 4.00 10.00
PPJZ Jason Zucker 5.00 12.00
PPKC Kyle Connor 8.00 20.00
PPKH Kevin Hayes 4.00 10.00
PPKL Kris Letang 15.00 40.00
PPMB Mikael Backlund 4.00 10.00
PPMO Brandon Montour 6.00 15.00
PPNS Nick Suzuki 15.00 40.00
PPRO Ryan O'Reilly 5.00 12.00
PPSA Juuse Saros 6.00 15.00
PPSR Sam Reinhart 10.00 25.00
PPTH Tomas Hertl 5.00 12.00
PPTT Tyler Toffoli 5.00 12.00
PPZH Zach Hyman 8.00 20.00

2023-24 Upper Deck Premier Premier Precipice Legend Autographs

PPLAD Alex Delvecchio 10.00 25.00
PPLAG Adam Graves 8.00 20.00
PPLBT Bryan Trottier 10.00 25.00
PPLDH Dany Heatley 8.00 20.00
PPLDS Dave Schultz 8.00 20.00
PPLHZ Henrik Zetterberg 12.00 30.00
PPLJK Jari Kurri 10.00 25.00
PPLJS Joe Sakic SP 60.00 150.00
PPLMG Mike Gartner SP 12.00 30.00
PPLML Mike Liut 6.00 15.00
PPLMO Mike Modano 20.00 50.00
PPLPB Peter Bondra 10.00 25.00
PPLRB Rod Brind'Amour 10.00 25.00
PPLRM Rick Middleton 12.00 30.00
PPLRN Rick Nash 10.00 25.00
PPLRV Rogie Vachon 10.00 25.00
PPLSD Shane Doan 8.00 20.00
PPLSI Darryl Sittler 10.00 25.00
PPLTB Tom Barrasso 20.00 50.00
PPLTT Tony Twist 6.00 15.00
PPLWO Willie O'Ree SP 12.00 30.00
PPLYC Yvan Cournoyer 10.00 25.00

2023-24 Upper Deck Premier Premier Precipice Rookie Autographs

PPRBM Bobby McMann 8.00 20.00
PPRCB Connor Bedard SP 250.00 600.00
PPRCO Logan Cooley SP 30.00 80.00
PPRCZ Connor Zary 10.00 25.00
PPRDL Devon Levi 12.00 30.00
PPRJB John Beecher 10.00 25.00
PPRJP Jakob Pelletier 6.00 15.00
PPRLE Luke Evangelista SP 8.00 20.00
PPRLR Lukas Rousek 4.00 10.00
PPRMK Marco Kasper 12.00 30.00
PPRMP Matthew Poitras 10.00 25.00
PPRMS Matt Savoie 10.00 25.00
PPRPA Jiri Patera 8.00 20.00
PPRPM Pavel Mintyukov 8.00 20.00
PPRSN Simon Nemec SP 10.00 25.00
PPRTF Tyson Foerster 10.00 25.00
PPRTK Tye Kartye 8.00 20.00
PPRWC Will Cuylle 8.00 20.00
PPRZB Zach Benson 8.00 20.00

2023-24 Upper Deck Premier Premier Quad Jerseys

PQBRHH Benn/Robertson
Heiskanen/Hintz 10.00 25.00
PQDNNH Draisaitl/Nugent-Hopkins
Nurse/Hyman 20.00 50.00
PQEMSH Eichel/Marchessault
Stone/Hill 10.00 25.00
PQHHMB Hughes/Hischier
Mercer/Bratt 15.00 40.00
PQNDBS Nelson/Dobson
Barzal/Sorokin 10.00 25.00
PQNMMT Nylander/Marner
Matthews/Tavares 25.00 60.00
PQPZFL Panarin/Zibanejad
Fox/Lafreniere 12.00 30.00
PQSPKV Stamkos/Point
Kucherov/Vasilevskiy 12.00 30.00
PQTCDP Thompson/Cozens
Dahlin/Power 8.00 20.00

2023-24 Upper Deck Premier Premier Triple Jerseys

PTDNH Draisaitl/Nugent-
Hopkins/Hyman 15.00 40.00
PTGML Guentzel/Malkin/Letang 10.00 25.00
PTHHH Hughes/Hughes/Hughes 15.00 40.00
PTHRH Hintz/Robertson/Heiskanen 8.00 20.00
PTKVS Kucherov/Vasilevskiy/Stamkos 10.0025.00
PTMMT Marner/Matthews/Tavares 20.00 50.00
PTPSM Pastrnak/Swayman/Marchand 12.0030.00
PTPZF Panarin/Zibanejad/Fox 10.00 25.00
PTRMM Rantanen/Makar/MacKinnon 20.0050.00
PTSDR Seider/DeBrincat/Raymond 8.00 20.00
PTSVS Shesterkin
Vasilevskiy/Sorokin 10.00 25.00
PTTTD Tuch/Thompson/Dahlin 6.00 15.00

2023-24 Upper Deck Premier Rookie Patch-Taculars Chest Logos

RPTAD Arnaud Durandeau 10.00 25.00
RPTAG Adam Ginning 10.00 25.00
RPTAH Akito Hirose 8.00 20.00
RPTAL Alex Laferriere 15.00 40.00
RPTAM Aidan McDonough 8.00 20.00
RPTBF Brock Faber 25.00 60.00
RPTBM Bobby McMann 15.00 40.00
RPTCB Connor Bedard 200.00 500.00
RPTCG Cole Guttman 10.00 25.00
RPTCM Cole McWard 10.00 25.00
RPTCO Logan Cooley 60.00 150.00
RPTCZ Connor Zary 20.00 50.00
RPTDG David Gust 10.00 25.00
RPTDL Devon Levi 25.00 60.00
RPTDU William Dufour 8.00 20.00
RPTDW Dustin Wolf 30.00 80.00
RPTEA Egor Afanasyev 10.00 25.00
RPTED Elliot Desnoyers 10.00 25.00
RPTFM Fraser Minten 20.00 50.00
RPTGR Jonathan Gruden 10.00 25.00
RPTGU Danil Gushchin 10.00 25.00
RPTHM Hugh McGing 10.00 25.00
RPTHT Henry Thrun 10.00 25.00
RPTIM Ivan Miroshnichenko 15.00 40.00
RPTJB John Beecher 20.00 50.00
RPTJG Jet Greaves 15.00 40.00
RPTJK Joona Koppanen 8.00 20.00
RPTJP Jakob Pelletier 12.00 30.00
RPTJS Jaxson Stauber 10.00 25.00
RPTKA Marco Kasper 25.00 60.00
RPTKE Michael Kesselring 10.00 25.00
RPTKK Kevin Korchinski 15.00 40.00
RPTKN Matthew Knies 80.00 200.00
RPTLE Luke Evangelista 15.00 40.00
RPTLI Jake Livingstone 10.00 25.00
RPTLM Leevi Merilainen 10.00 25.00
RPTLP Luke Philp 10.00 25.00
RPTLR Lukas Rousek 8.00 20.00
RPTMA Matthew Kessel 8.00 20.00
RPTMC Matthew Coronato 15.00 40.00
RPTMK Milos Kelemen 10.00 25.00
RPTMM Matt Murray 10.00 25.00
RPTMP Matthew Poitras 20.00 50.00
RPTMS Matt Savoie 20.00 50.00
RPTNN Nikita Nesterenko 10.00 25.00
RPTOB Owen Beck 50.00 125.00
RPTOE Olle Eriksson Ek 10.00 25.00
RPTPA Jiri Patera 15.00 40.00
RPTPM Pavel Mintyukov 15.00 40.00
RPTRE Ryker Evans 12.00 30.00
RPTRG Ridly Greig 15.00 40.00
RPTSB Samuel Bolduc 10.00 25.00
RPTSE Simon Edvinsson 20.00 50.00
RPTSF Sean Farrell 10.00 25.00
RPTSN Simon Nemec 20.00 50.00
RPTTF Tyson Foerster 20.00 50.00
RPTTK Tyler Kleven 10.00 25.00
RPTTL Tristan Luneau 10.00 25.00
RPTTR Tristen Robins 10.00 25.00
RPTTY Tye Kartye 15.00 40.00
RPTVD Vincent Desharnais 12.00 30.00
RPTVI Vincent Iorio 10.00 25.00
RPTWC Will Cuylle 15.00 40.00
RPTWD Walker Duehr 8.00 20.00
RPTWK Wyatt Kaiser 10.00 25.00
RPTYA Yaroslav Askarov 40.00 100.00
RPTZB Zach Benson 15.00 40.00

2000-01 Upper Deck Pros and Prospects

1 Paul Kariya .25 .60
2 Teemu Selanne .50 1.25
3 Guy Hebert .20 .50
4 Donald Audette .20 .50
5 Adam Burt .15 .40
6 Patrik Stefan .20 .50
7 Joe Thornton .40 1.00
8 Jason Allison .20 .50
9 Sergei Samsonov .20 .50
10 Dominik Hasek .40 1.00
11 Doug Gilmour .30 .75
12 Maxim Afinogenov .15 .40
13 Oleg Saprykin .15 .40
14 Valeri Bure .20 .50
15 Mike Vernon .20 .50
16 Ron Francis .30 .75
17 Jeff O'Neill .20 .50
18 Arturs Irbe .20 .50
19 Steve Sullivan .15 .40
20 Alexei Zhamnov .20 .50
21 Tony Amonte .20 .50
22 Ray Bourque .40 1.00
23 Patrick Roy .60 1.50
24 Peter Forsberg .50 1.25
25 Marc Denis .20 .50
26 Tyler Wright .15 .40
27 Mike Modano .40 1.00
28 Brett Hull .50 1.25
29 Ed Belfour .25 .60
30 Brendan Shanahan .25 .60
31 Sergei Fedorov .40 1.00
32 Steve Yzerman .60 1.50
33 Ryan Smyth .20 .50
34 Tommy Salo .20 .50
35 Doug Weight .25 .60
36 Pavel Bure .25 .60
37 Ray Whitney .20 .50
38 Viktor Kozlov .20 .50
39 Luc Robitaille .25 .60
40 Rob Blake .25 .60
41 Zigmund Palffy .25 .60
42 Manny Fernandez .15 .40
43 Scott Pellerin .15 .40
44 Jose Theodore .25 .60
45 Brian Savage .15 .40
46 Martin Rucinsky .15 .40
47 David Legwand .25 .60
48 Mike Dunham .15 .40
49 Cliff Ronning .15 .40
50 Scott Gomez .20 .50
51 Scott Stevens .25 .60
52 Martin Brodeur .60 1.50
53 Tim Connolly .15 .40
54 Brad Isbister .15 .40
55 Roman Hamrlik .15 .40
56 Theo Fleury .30 .75
57 Mike Richter .25 .60
58 Mark Messier .50 1.25
59 Marian Hossa .25 .60
60 Alexei Yashin .20 .50
61 Radek Bonk .20 .50
62 John LeClair .25 .60
63 Mark Recchi .30 .75
64 Simon Gagne .25 .60
65 Jeremy Roenick .40 1.00
66 Shane Doan .20 .50
67 Keith Tkachuk .25 .60
68 Jaromir Jagr .75 2.00
69 Mario Lemieux 1.00 2.50
70 Alexei Kovalev .20 .50
71 Owen Nolan .25 .60
72 Jeff Friesen .15 .40
73 Patrick Marleau .25 .60
74 Chris Pronger .25 .60
75 Roman Turek .20 .50
76 Pierre Turgeon .20 .50
77 Kevin Weekes .15 .40
78 Fredrik Modin .15 .40
79 Vincent Lecavalier .25 .60
80 Curtis Joseph .30 .75
81 Mats Sundin .25 .60
82 Gary Roberts .15 .40
83 Markus Naslund .25 .60
84 Daniel Sedin .30 .75
85 Henrik Sedin .30 .75
86 Adam Oates .25 .60
87 Peter Bondra .25 .60
88 Olaf Kolzig .25 .60
89 Mark Messier .50 1.25
90 Steve Yzerman .60 1.50
91 Jonas Ronnqvist RC 1.50 4.00
92 Andy McDonald RC 3.00 8.00
93 Eric Nickulas RC 1.50 4.00
94 Andrew Raycroft RC 4.00 10.00
95 Jarno Kultanen RC 1.50 4.00
96 Jeff Cowan RC 1.50 4.00
97 Josef Vasicek RC 4.00 10.00
98 Reto Von Arx RC 2.00 5.00
99 David Aebischer RC 3.00 8.00
100 Serge Aubin RC 2.00 5.00
101 Rostislav Klesla RC 4.00 10.00
102 Marty Turco RC 3.00 8.00
103 Tyler Bouck RC 1.50 4.00
104 Brian Swanson RC 1.50 4.00
105 Michel Riesen RC 2.00 5.00
106 Eric Belanger RC 2.00 5.00
107 Steven Reinprecht RC 2.50 6.00
108 Marian Gaborik RC 5.00 12.00
109 Scott Hartnell RC 4.00 10.00
110 Greg Classen RC 1.50 4.00
111 Willie Mitchell RC 2.50 6.00
112 Colin White RC 1.50 4.00
113 Petr Mika RC 1.50 4.00
114 Rick DiPietro RC 3.00 8.00
115 Jason Labarbera RC 2.00 5.00
116 Martin Havlat RC 5.00 12.00
117 Jani Hurme RC 1.50 4.00
118 Petr Hubacek RC 1.50 4.00
119 Justin Williams RC 4.00 10.00

120 Roman Cechmanek RC 2.00 5.00
121 Roman Simicek RC 1.50 4.00
122 Mark Smith RC 1.50 4.00
123 Alexander Kharitonov RC 1.50 4.00
124 Matt Elich RC 2.00 5.00
125 Jakub Cutta RC 1.50 4.00
126 Fedor Fedorov RC 2.00 5.00
127 Marc-Andre Thinel RC 1.50 4.00
128 Zdenek Blatny RC 1.50 4.00
129 Jeff Bateman RC 1.50 4.00
130 Jason Jaspers RC 1.50 4.00
131 Jordan Krestanovich RC 1.50 4.00
132 Damian Surma RC 1.50 4.00

2000-01 Upper Deck Pros and Prospects Championship Rings

COMPLETE SET (8) 12.00 25.00
CR1 Patrick Roy 3.00 8.00
CR2 Brendan Shanahan 1.00 2.50
CR3 Steve Yzerman 3.00 8.00
CR4 Wayne Gretzky 4.00 10.00
CR5 Scott Stevens .60 1.50
CR6 Martin Brodeur 1.50 4.00
CR7 Mark Messier .75 2.00
CR8 Jaromir Jagr 1.00 2.50

2000-01 Upper Deck Pros and Prospects Game Jerseys

*EXCLUSIVE/50: .8X TO 2X BASIC JSY
BS Brendan Shanahan 3.00 8.00
CP Chris Pronger 3.00 8.00
JJ Jaromir Jagr 5.00 12.00
MM Mike Modano 4.00 10.00
PF Peter Forsberg 6.00 15.00
PK Paul Kariya 3.00 8.00
PR Patrick Roy 8.00 20.00
RB Ray Bourque 8.00 20.00
SF Sergei Fedorov 4.00 10.00
TS Teemu Selanne 3.00 8.00

2000-01 Upper Deck Pros and Prospects Game Jersey Autographs

*EXCLUSIVE/50: .8X TO 2X BASIC JSY AU
SJL John LeClair 10.00 25.00
SJR Jeremy Roenick 15.00 40.00
SKT Keith Tkachuk 12.50 30.00
SLB Lubos Bartecko 10.00 25.00
SMM Mark Messier 40.00 80.00
SPB Pavel Bure 12.50 30.00
SSG Scott Gomez 10.00 25.00
SSS Sergei Samsonov 12.50 30.00
SSY Steve Yzerman 40.00 100.00
SWG Wayne Gretzky 250.00 600.00

2000-01 Upper Deck Pros and Prospects Great Skates

COMPLETE SET (8) 10.00 20.00
GS1 Paul Kariya .60 1.50
GS2 Mario Lemieux 4.00 10.00
GS3 Patrick Roy 3.00 8.00
GS4 Brendan Shanahan 1.00 2.50
GS5 Pavel Bure .75 2.00
GS6 Alexei Yashin .60 1.50
GS7 John LeClair .75 2.00
GS8 Jaromir Jagr 1.00 2.50

2000-01 Upper Deck Pros and Prospects NHL Passion

COMPLETE SET (9) 10.00 20.00
NP1 Ray Bourque 1.00 3.00
NP2 Brett Hull .75 2.00
NP3 Steve Yzerman 3.00 8.00
NP4 Mark Messier .75 2.00
NP5 John LeClair .75 2.00
NP6 Jeremy Roenick .75 2.00
NP7 Jaromir Jagr 1.00 2.50
NP8 Mario Lemieux 4.00 10.00
NP9 Curtis Joseph .60 1.50

2000-01 Upper Deck Pros and Prospects Now Appearing

COMPLETE SET (8) 10.00 20.00
NA1 Maxim Afinogenov .60 1.50
NA2 Marian Gaborik 3.00 8.00
NA3 Scott Hartnell 1.00 2.50
NA4 Scott Gomez .60 1.50
NA5 Rick DiPietro 3.00 8.00
NA6 Justin Williams 1.25 3.00
NA7 Daniel Sedin .60 1.50
NA8 Henrik Sedin .60 1.50

2000-01 Upper Deck Pros and Prospects ProMotion

COMPLETE SET (9) 10.00 20.00
PM1 Teemu Selanne .75 2.00
PM2 Dominik Hasek 1.50 4.00
PM3 Peter Forsberg 1.50 4.00
PM4 Sergei Fedorov 1.25 3.00
PM5 Mike Modano 1.00 2.50
PM6 Pavel Bure 1.00 2.50
PM7 Martin Brodeur 1.50 4.00
PM8 John LeClair .75 2.00
PM9 Jaromir Jagr 1.00 2.50

2024-25 Upper Deck PWHL First Edition

1 Abbey Levy 1.25 3.00
2 Corinne Schroeder 1.25 3.00
3 Elaine Chuli 1.25 3.00
4 Hannah Miller 1.25 3.00
5 Jade Downie-Landry 1.25 3.00
6 Kelly Pannek 1.25 3.00
7 Maddie Rooney 1.25 3.00
8 Nicole Hensley 1.25 3.00
9 Rebecca Leslie 1.25 3.00
10 Susanna Tapani 1.25 3.00
11 Kelly Babstock 1.25 3.00
12 Tereza Vanisova 1.25 3.00
13 Abby Roque 1.25 3.00
14 Aerin Frankel 2.50 6.00
15 Akane Shiga 1.25 3.00
16 Elizabeth Giguere 1.25 3.00
17 Chloe Aurard 1.25 3.00
18 Hannah Brandt 1.25 3.00
19 Emerance Maschmeyer 1.50 4.00
20 Jill Saulnier 1.50 4.00
21 Kaleigh Fratkin 1.25 3.00
22 Jincy Roese 1.25 3.00
23 Mellissa Channell 1.25 3.00
24 Katerina Mrazova 1.25 3.00
25 Kristen Campbell 2.00 5.00
26 Laura Stacey 2.50 6.00
27 Lee Stecklein 1.25 3.00
28 Lexie Adzija 1.25 3.00
29 Jamie Lee Rattray 1.50 4.00
30 Loren Gabel 1.25 3.00
31 Samantha Cogan 1.25 3.00
32 Victoria Bach 1.25 3.00
33 Renata Fast 1.25 3.00
34 Sayannah Harmon 1.25 3.00
35 Michela Cava 1.25 3.00
36 Micah Zandee-Hart 1.50 4.00
37 Natalie Buchbinder 1.25 3.00
38 Sandra Abstreiter 1.25 3.00
39 Aneta Tejralova 1.25 3.00
40 Daryl Watts 1.25 3.00
41 Theresa Schafzahl 1.25 3.00
42 Madison Packer 1.25 3.00
43 Kennedy Marchment 1.25 3.00
44 Sophia Kunin 1.25 3.00
45 Claire Dalton 1.25 3.00
46 Liz Schepers 1.25 3.00
47 Jocelyne Larocque 1.25 3.00
48 Jaime Bourbonnais 1.25 3.00
49 Kali Flanagan 1.25 3.00
50 Ashton Bell 1.25 3.00
51 Sarah Nurse YG RC 25.00 60.00
52 Grace Zumwinkle YG RC 6.00 15.00
53 Kendall Coyne YG RC 10.00 25.00
54 Alex Carpenter YG RC 8.00 20.00
55 Brianne Jenner YG RC 8.00 20.00
56 Alina Muller YG RC 8.00 20.00
57 Maureen Murphy YG RC 8.00 20.00
58 Sophie Jaques YG RC 10.00 25.00
59 Emma Maltais YG RC 12.00 30.00
60 Ann-Renee Desbiens YG RC 25.00 60.00
61 Taylor Heise YG RC 60.00 150.00
62 Hilary Knight YG RC 25.00 60.00
63 Natalie Spooner YG RC 40.00 100.00
64 Ella Shelton YG RC 6.00 15.00
65 Marie-Philip Poulin YG RC 100.00 250.00
66 Jessie Eldridge YG RC 6.00 15.00
67 Gabbie Hughes YG RC 8.00 20.00
68 Megan Keller YG RC 8.00 20.00
69 Erin Ambrose YG RC 10.00 25.00
70 Emily Clark YG RC 20.00 50.00

2024-25 Upper Deck PWHL First Edition Deluxe

*DELUXE/250: 1.5X TO 4X BASIC
*DELUXE RC/250: .8X TO 2X BASIC
62 Hilary Knight YG 40.00 100.00

2024-25 Upper Deck PWHL First Edition Exclusives

*EXCLUSIVES/100: 4X TO 10X BASIC
*EXCL RC/100: 2X TO 5X BASIC

2024-25 Upper Deck PWHL First Edition Outburst

*OUTBURST: .5X TO 1.2X BASIC
52 Grace Zumwinkle YG 15.00 40.00
57 Maureen Murphy YG 15.00 40.00
59 Emma Maltais YG 25.00 60.00
61 Taylor Heise YG 80.00 200.00
62 Hilary Knight YG 30.00 80.00
64 Ella Shelton YG 12.00 30.00

2024-25 Upper Deck PWHL First Edition Dazzlers Blue

DZ1 Laura Stacey 8.00 20.00
DZ2 Marie-Philip Poulin 40.00 100.00
DZ3 Hannah Miller 4.00 10.00
DZ4 Kelly Pannek 4.00 10.00
DZ5 Jaime Bourbonnais 4.00 10.00
DZ6 Kali Flanagan 4.00 10.00
DZ7 Kendall Coyne 10.00 25.00
DZ8 Loren Gabel 4.00 10.00
DZ9 Daryl Watts 4.00 10.00
DZ10 Emily Clark 12.00 30.00
DZ11 Jocelyne Larocque 4.00 10.00
DZ12 Rebecca Leslie 4.00 10.00
DZ13 Jamie Lee Rattray 5.00 12.00
DZ14 Savannah Harmon 4.00 10.00
DZ15 Chloe Aurard 4.00 10.00
DZ16 Lexie Adzija 4.00 10.00
DZ17 Gabbie Hughes 8.00 20.00
DZ18 Kristen Campbell 6.00 15.00
DZ19 Aerin Frankel 8.00 20.00
DZ20 Maddie Rooney 4.00 10.00

2024-25 Upper Deck PWHL First Edition UD Portraits

*GOLD/299: .8X TO 2X BASIC
UDP1 Laura Stacey 12.00 40.00
UDP2 Marie-Philip Poulin 40.00 100.00
UDP3 Hannah Miller 3.00 8.00
UDP4 Kelly Pannek 3.00 8.00
UDP5 Alex Carpenter 6.00 15.00
UDP6 Brianne Jenner 6.00 15.00
UDP7 Natalie Spooner 12.00 30.00
UDP8 Sarah Nurse 10.00 25.00
UDP9 Alina Muller 6.00 15.00
UDP10 Ella Shelton 5.00 12.00
UDP11 Jaime Bourbonnais 3.00 8.00
UDP12 Jamie Lee Rattray 4.00 10.00
UDP13 Nicole Hensley 3.00 8.00
UDP14 Claire Dalton 3.00 8.00
UDP15 Jade Downie-Landry 3.00 8.00
UDP16 Abby Roque 3.00 8.00
UDP17 Renata Fast 3.00 8.00
UDP18 Ashton Bell 3.00 8.00
UDP19 Lee Stecklein 3.00 8.00
UDP20 Katerina Mrazova 3.00 8.00

2024-25 Upper Deck PWHL First Edition UD Portraits Red

*RED/99: 1.2X TO 3X BASIC
UDP4 Kelly Pannek 15.00 40.00
UDP8 Sarah Nurse 50.00 125.00
UDP18 Ashton Bell 20.00 50.00
UDP19 Lee Stecklein 15.00 40.00

1999-00 Upper Deck Retro

COMPLETE SET (109) 20.00 40.00
1 Paul Kariya .20 .50
2 Teemu Selanne .20 .50
3 Jim McKenzie .02 .10
4 Ray Bourque .20 .50
5 Sergei Samsonov .15 .40
6 Joe Thornton .20 .50
7 Dominik Hasek .40 1.00
8 Miroslav Satan .15 .40
9 Michael Peca .15 .40
10 Todd Simpson .02 .10
11 Valeri Bure .02 .10
12 Jarome Iginla .25 .60
13 Kent Manderville .25 .60
14 Keith Primeau .02 .10
15 Sami Kapanen .02 .10
16 Mark Janssens .02 .10
17 Tony Amonte .15 .40
18 Doug Gilmour .15 .40
19 Peter Forsberg .50 1.25
20 Patrick Roy .50 1.25
21 Joe Sakic .40 1.00
22 Theo Fleury .15 .40
23 Chris Drury .15 .40
24 Mike Modano .20 .50
25 Brett Hull .20 .50
26 Ed Belfour .20 .50
27 Steve Yzerman 1.00 2.50
28 Sergei Fedorov .30 .75
29 Brendan Shanahan .20 .50
30 Chris Chelios .20 .50
31 Doug Weight .15 .40
32 Bill Guerin .15 .40
33 Tom Poti .02 .10
34 Gord Murphy .02 .10
35 Pavel Bure .20 .50
36 Mark Parrish .02 .10
37 Rob Blake .15 .40
38 Pavel Rosa .02 .10
39 Luc Robitaille .15 .40
40 Stephane Quintal .02 .10
41 Saku Koivu .20 .50
42 Bob Boughner .02 .10
43 David Legwand .15 .40
44 Mike Dunham .15 .40
45 Martin Brodeur .60 1.50
46 Scott Stevens .15 .40
47 John Madden RC .20 .50
48 Vadim Sharifijanov .02 .10
49 Wayne Gretzky 1.25 3.00
50 Manny Malhotra .02 .10
51 Brian Leetch .15 .40
52 Mike Richter .20 .50
53 Eric Brewer .02 .10
54 Alexei Yashin .02 .10
55 Marian Hossa .20 .50
56 Chris Phillips .02 .10
57 Eric Lindros .20 .50
58 John LeClair .20 .50
59 Mark Recchi .15 .40
60 Jeremy Roenick .30 .75
61 Keith Tkachuk .20 .50
62 Nikolia Khabibulin .15 .40
63 Robert Esche RC .15 .40
64 Jaromir Jagr .30 .75
65 Martin Straka .02 .10
66 Jeff Friesen .02 .10
67 Vincent Damphousse .02 .10
68 Chris Pronger .15 .40
69 Pavol Demitra .15 .40
70 Al MacInnis .15 .40
71 Paul Mara .02 .10
72 Vincent Lecavalier .20 .50
73 Sergei Berezin .02 .10
74 Mats Sundin .20 .50
75 Curtis Joseph .20 .50
76 Markus Naslund .20 .50
77 Mark Messier .20 .50
78 Bill Muckalt .02 .10
79 Peter Bondra .20 .50
80 Adam Oates .15 .40
81 Bobby Orr 1.00 2.50
83 Mario Lemieux 1.00 2.50
84 Maurice Richard .50 1.25
85 Jean Beliveau .20 .50
86 Bobby Hull .40 1.00
87 Terry Sawchuk .40 1.00
88 Eddie Shore .25 .60
89 Alex Delvecchio .25 .60
90 Jacques Plante .25 .60
91 Stan Mikita .20 .50
92 Gerry Cheevers .40 1.00
93 Glenn Hall .25 .60
94 Phil Esposito .40 1.00
95 Lanny McDonald .25 .60
96 Mike Bossy .25 .60
97 Ted Lindsay .25 .60
98 Red Kelly .25 .60
99 Bobby Clarke .25 .60
100 Larry Robinson .25 .60
101 Ken Dryden 1.00 2.50
102 Vladislav Tretiak RC .50 1.25
103 Marcel Dionne .25 .60
104 Bernie Geoffrion .20 .50
105 Johnny Bucyk .25 .60
106 Brad Park .25 .60
107 Tony Esposito .20 .50
108 Jari Kurri .25 .60
109 Henri Richard .25 .60
110 Mike Gartner .25 .60

1999-00 Upper Deck Retro Distant Replay

COMPLETE SET (14) 30.00 60.00
*LEVEL 2/100: 6X TO 15X BASIC INSERTS
DR1 Ray Bourque 1.50 4.00
DR2 Martin Brodeur 2.50 6.00
DR3 Jaromir Jagr 1.50 4.00
DR4 Paul Kariya 1.00 2.50
DR5 Steve Yzerman 5.00 12.00
DR6 Mark Messier 1.00 2.50
DR7 Patrick Roy 5.00 12.00
DR8 Dominik Hasek 2.50 5.00
DR9 Wayne Gretzky 6.00 15.00
DR10 Bobby Orr 5.00 12.00
DR12 Mario Lemieux 5.00 12.00
DR13 Lanny McDonald 1.00 2.50
DR14 Maurice Richard 3.00 8.00
DR15 Vladislav Tretiak 2.00 5.00

1999-00 Upper Deck Retro Epic Gretzky

COMPLETE SET (10) 75.00 150.00
COMMON GRETZKY (EG1-EG10) 6.00 15.00
*LEVEL 2/50: 3X TO 8X BASIC INSERTS

1999-00 Upper Deck Retro Generation

COMPLETE SET (29) 20.00 40.00
*LEVEL 2/500: 1.5X TO 4X BASIC INSERTS
G1A Bobby Orr 2.50 6.00
G1B Brian Leetch .40 1.00
G1C Bryan Berard .40 1.00
G2B Bobby Clarke .75 2.00
G2C Keith Tkachuk .75 2.00
G3A Glenn Hall .75 2.00
G3B Patrick Roy 2.50 6.00
G3C Jean-Marc Pelletier .40 1.00
G4A Eddie Shore .75 2.00
G4B Bobby Orr 2.50 6.00
G4C Ray Bourque .75 2.00
G5A Jean Beliveau 1.00 2.50
G5B Mario Lemieux 2.50 6.00
G5C Vincent Lecavalier .75 2.00
G6A Maurice Richard 1.50 4.00
G6B Pavel Bure .75 2.00
G6C Sergei Samsonov .40 1.00
G7A Stan Mikita 1.00 2.50
G7B Theo Fleury .40 1.00
G7C Paul Kariya .75 2.00
G8A Jari Kurri .75 2.00
G8B Teemu Selanne .75 2.00
G8C Olli Jokinen .40 1.00
G9A Phil Esposito 1.25 3.00
G9B Brendan Shanahan .75 2.00
G9C Mark Parrish .40 1.00
G10A Terry Sawchuk 1.25 3.00
G10B Dominik Hasek 1.00 2.50
G10C Jean-Sebastien Giguere .40 1.00

1999-00 Upper Deck Retro Gold

*GOLD: 12X TO 30X BASIC CARDS

1999-00 Upper Deck Retro Inkredible

AD Alex Delvecchio 12.00 30.00
BC Bobby Clarke 10.00 25.00
BG Bernie Geoffrion 25.00 60.00
BO Bobby Orr 250.00 400.00
BOH Bobby Hull 15.00 40.00
BP Brad Park 8.00 20.00
BRH Brett Hull 15.00 40.00
DW Doug Weight 6.00 15.00
GC Gerry Cheevers 10.00 25.00
JEB Jean Beliveau 30.00 80.00
JOB John Bucyk 8.00 20.00
KP Keith Primeau 6.00 15.00
LM Lanny McDonald 10.00 25.00
MAR Maurice Richard 100.00 200.00
MB Mike Bossy 12.00 30.00
MD Marcel Dionne 10.00 25.00
ML Mario Lemieux 100.00 200.00
PAB Pavel Bure 15.00 40.00
PE Phil Esposito 20.00 50.00
RB Ray Bourque 25.00 60.00
SM Stan Mikita 15.00 40.00
SS Sergei Samsonov 6.00 15.00
SY Steve Yzerman 30.00 80.00
TA Tony Amonte 10.00 25.00
TE Tony Esposito 15.00 40.00
TL Ted Lindsay 8.00 20.00
VL Vincent Lecavalier 15.00 40.00
VT Vladislav Tretiak 25.00 60.00
WG Wayne Gretzky 300.00 800.00

1999-00 Upper Deck Retro Inkredible Level 2

*LEVEL 2/25: 1.2X TO 3X BASIC INSERTS

1999-00 Upper Deck Retro Lunchboxes

COMPLETE SET (4) 35.00 70.00
1 Wayne Gretzky Kings 7.50 15.00
2 Wayne Gretzky Oilers 7.50 15.00
3 Wayne Gretzky Rangers 7.50 15.00
4 Wayne Gretzky Tribute 15.00 40.00

1999-00 Upper Deck Retro Memento

RM1 Wayne Gretzky 75.00 150.00
RM2 Marcel Dionne 12.00 30.00
RM3 Mario Lemieux 40.00 100.00
RM4 Phil Esposito 20.00 50.00
RM5 Ken Dryden 75.00 150.00

1999-00 Upper Deck Retro Turn of the Century

COMPLETE SET (14) 40.00 80.00
TC1 Vincent Lecavalier 2.00 5.00
TC2 Martin Brodeur 5.00 12.00
TC3 Jaromir Jagr 6.00 15.00
TC4 Paul Kariya 2.00 5.00
TC5 Steve Yzerman 5.00 12.00
TC6 Ray Bourque 3.00 8.00
TC7 Patrick Roy 5.00 12.00
TC8 Dominik Hasek 3.00 8.00
TC9 Wayne Gretzky 12.00 30.00
TC10 Bobby Clarke 3.00 8.00
TC11 Larry Robinson 2.00 5.00
TC13 Mario Lemieux 8.00 20.00
TC14 Maurice Richard 4.00 10.00
TC15 Bobby Orr 8.00 20.00

2006-07 Upper Deck Rookie Class

COMPLETE SET (50) 8.00 20.00
1 Shea Weber .60 1.50
2 Matt Carle .25 .60
3 Patrick O'Sullivan .40 1.00
4 Phil Kessel .75 2.00
5 Guillaume Latendresse .40 1.00
6 Loui Eriksson .50 1.25
7 Luc Bourdon .40 1.00
8 Enver Lisin .25 .60
9 Evgeni Malkin 1.50 4.00
10 Dustin Boyd .25 .60
11 Mark Stuart .25 .60
12 Eric Fehr .40 1.00
13 Noah Welch .25 .60
14 Anze Kopitar 1.25 3.00
15 Travis Zajac .50 1.25
16 Jordan Staal .60 1.50
17 Ladislav Smid .25 .60
18 Alexander Radulov .50 1.25
19 Ryan Potulny .25 .60
20 Marc-Antoine Pouliot .25 .60
21 Jarkko Immonen .30 .75
22 Paul Stastny .60 1.50
23 Alexei Kaigorodov .25 .60
24 Dave Bolland .40 1.00
25 Nigel Dawes .25 .60
26 Jeremy Williams .25 .60
27 Marc-Edouard Vlasic .40 1.00
28 Keith Yandle .60 1.50
29 Matt Lashoff .25 .60
30 Ian White .30 .75
31 Alexei Mikhnov .25 .60
32 Tomas Kopecky .30 .75
33 Konstantin Pushkarev .30 .75
34 Kristopher Letang 1.00 2.50
35 Michael Blunden .25 .60
36 Brandon Prust .25 .60
37 Dustin Byfuglien .60 1.50
38 Ben Ondrus .25 .60
39 Brendan Bell .25 .60
40 Janis Sprukts .25 .60
41 Ryan Shannon .25 .60
42 Shane O'Brien .25 .60
43 Patrick Thoresen .25 .60
44 Nathan McIver .25 .60
45 Drew Stafford .40 1.00
46 Alexander Edler .40 1.00
47 Yan Stastny .25 .60
48 Kelly Guard .30 .75
49 Nate Thompson .25 .60
50 Adam Burish .40 1.00

2007-08 Upper Deck Rookie Class

COMPLETE SET (50) 8.00 20.00
COMP.FACT.SET (51) 10.00 25.00
1 Bobby Ryan .40 1.00
2 Ondrej Pavelec .30 .75
3 Patrick Kane 15.00 40.00
4 Kris Russell .25 .60
5 Matt Niskanen .25 .60
6 Andrew Cogliano .20 .50
7 Jonathan Bernier .30 .75
8 Marc Staal .25 .60
9 Nick Foligno .30 .75
10 Peter Mueller .20 .50
11 Jiri Tlusty .25 .60
12 Brett Sterling .15 .40
13 Petr Kalus .15 .40
14 Rob Schremp .20 .50
15 Andy Greene .20 .50
16 Frans Nielsen .25 .60
17 Martin Hanzal .20 .50
18 Devin Setoguchi .25 .60
19 Matt Smaby .15 .40
20 James Sheppard .15 .40
21 Kyle Chipchura .25 .60
22 Ryan Parent .15 .40
23 David Krejci .50 1.25
24 Lauri Tukonen .15 .40
25 Anton Stralman .15 .40
26 Tobias Enstrom .25 .60
27 Tyler Kennedy .15 .40
28 Mason Raymond .25 .60
29 Thomas Greiss .30 .75
30 Drew Miller .20 .50
31 Curtis McElhinney .25 .60
32 Ryan Callahan .30 .75
33 Brian Elliott .30 .75
34 Vladimir Sobotka .20 .50
35 Jonathan Sigalet .15 .40
36 Ville Koistinen .15 .40
37 Torrey Mitchell .20 .50
38 David Perron .30 .75
39 Jannik Hansen .20 .50
40 Chris Bourque .20 .50
41 Milan Lucic .60 1.50
42 Tuukka Rask .60 1.50
43 Jonathan Toews 1.00 2.50
44 Sam Gagner .30 .75
45 Jack Johnson .20 .50
46 Carey Price 1.00 2.50
47 Nicklas Bergfors .15 .40
48 Erik Johnson .25 .60
49 Bryan Little .20 .50
50 Nicklas Backstrom .50 1.25

2007-08 Upper Deck Rookie Class C-Card Insert

CC1 Jonathan Toews 2.50 6.00
CC2 Patrick Kane 6.00 15.00
CC3 Carey Price 2.50 6.00
CC4 Jack Johnson .50 1.25
CC5 Nicklas Backstrom 1.25 3.00
CC6 Sam Gagner .75 2.00

2008-09 Upper Deck Rookie Class

COMP.FACT.SET (51) 10.00 25.00
COMPLETE SET (50) 8.00 20.00
1 Steven Stamkos 1.00 2.50
2 Michael Frolik .25 .60
3 Drew Doughty .60 1.50
4 Claude Giroux .50 1.25
5 Zach Bogosian .30 .75
6 Mark Fistric .20 .50
7 Alex Pietrangelo .40 1.00
8 Vladimir Mihalik .15 .40
9 Luke Schenn .30 .75
10 Nikita Filatov .25 .60
11 Patrik Berglund .20 .50
12 Karl Alzner .15 .40
13 Mikkel Boedker .30 .75
14 Justin Abdelkader .40 1.00
15 Brian Boyle .20 .50
16 Adam Pineault .20 .50
17 Jonathan Ericsson .25 .60
18 Shawn Matthias .25 .60
19 Zach Boychuk .25 .60
20 Cory Schneider .60 1.50
21 Josh Bailey .30 .75
22 Oscar Moller .20 .50
23 Colton Gillies .20 .50
24 Matt D'Agostini .20 .50
25 Luca Sbisa .15 .40
26 Lauri Korpikoski .15 .40
27 Robbie Earl .15 .40
28 Andreas Nodl .15 .40
29 Blake Wheeler .60 1.50
30 Dan LaCosta .25 .60
31 Steve Mason .40 1.00
32 Viktor Tikhonov .20 .50
33 Tom Sestito .25 .60
34 Fabian Brunnstrom .20 .50
35 Teddy Purcell .20 .50
36 Kyle Okposo .30 .75
37 Brian Lee .20 .50
38 Kyle Turris .40 1.00
39 Alex Goligoski .30 .75
40 Patric Hornqvist .25 .60
41 Petr Vrana .15 .40
42 T.J. Oshie .50 1.25
43 Nikolai Kulemin .25 .60
44 Boris Valabik .25 .60
45 Brandon Sutter .25 .60
46 Derick Brassard .25 .60
47 Jakub Voracek .50 1.25
48 James Neal .50 1.25
49 Darren Helm .25 .60
50 Ilya Zubov .20 .50

2008-09 Upper Deck Rookie Class Autographs

1 Steven Stamkos 60.00 120.00
3 Drew Doughty 50.00 100.00
11 Patrik Berglund 8.00 20.00
23 Colton Gillies 8.00 20.00
31 Steve Mason 15.00 40.00
32 Viktor Tikhonov 8.00 20.00
43 Nikolai Kulemin 10.00 25.00
49 Darren Helm 10.00 25.00

2008-09 Upper Deck Rookie Class C-Card Insert

C1 Steven Stamkos 2.50 6.00
C2 Kyle Turris 1.00 2.50
C3 Drew Doughty 1.50 4.00
C4 Luke Schenn .75 2.00
C5 Blake Wheeler 1.50 4.00
C6 Derick Brassard .60 1.50
C7 Cory Schneider 1.50 4.00
C8 Colton Gillies .50 1.25
C9 Fabian Brunnstrom .50 1.25
C10 Kyle Okposo .75 2.00
C11 Nikita Filatov .60 1.50
C12 Nikolai Kulemin .60 1.50
C13 Jakub Voracek 1.25 3.00
C14 Brandon Sutter .60 1.50

2024-25 Upper Deck Rookie Debut

1 Cutter Gauthier 2.50 6.00
2 Josh Doan 1.50 4.00
3 Liam Ohgren 2.00 5.00
4 Brennan Othmann 1.50 4.00
5 Logan Stankoven 2.50 6.00
6 Frank Nazar 3.00 8.00
7 Jesper Wallstedt 2.50 6.00
8 Gavin Brindley 1.00 2.50
9 Lane Hutson 10.00 25.00
10 Bradly Nadeau 1.50 4.00
11 Olen Zellweger 2.00 5.00
12 Matt Rempe 2.00 5.00
13 Mavrik Bourque 2.00 5.00
14 Akil Thomas 1.00 2.50
15 Zach Dean 1.00 2.50
16 Zachary Bolduc 2.00 5.00
17 Brendan Brisson 1.25 3.00
18 Brad Lambert 1.25 3.00
19 Macklin Celebrini 15.00 40.00
20 Will Smith 3.00 8.00
21 Matvei Michkov 15.00 40.00
22 Jett Luchanko 2.00 5.00
23 Rutger McGroarty 2.00 5.00
24 Seamus Casey 1.25 3.00
25 Conor Geekie 2.00 5.00
26 Calum Ritchie 1.25 3.00
27 Maxim Tsyplakov 1.50 4.00

2024-25 Upper Deck Rookie Debut Blue

*BLUE/249: 1X TO 2.5X BASIC
9 Lane Hutson 20.00 50.00
19 Macklin Celebrini 30.00 80.00
21 Matvei Michkov 25.00 60.00

2024-25 Upper Deck Rookie Debut Red

*RED/99: 2X TO 5X BASIC
9 Lane Hutson 50.00 125.00
19 Macklin Celebrini 80.00 200.00
21 Matvei Michkov 60.00 150.00

2024-25 Upper Deck Rookie Debut Image Variant

*BLUE: 1X TO 2.5X BASIC
*RED: 1.5X TO 4X BASIC
19 Macklin Celebrini 25.00 60.00

2024-25 Upper Deck Rookie Debut Image Variant Autographs

19 Macklin Celebrini 400.00 1000.00

2024-25 Upper Deck Rookie Debut Smashing Debuts

SD1 Cutter Gauthier 6.00 15.00
SD2 Josh Doan 5.00 12.00
SD3 Liam Ohgren 5.00 12.00
SD4 Brennan Othmann 5.00 12.00
SD5 Logan Stankoven 6.00 15.00
SD6 Frank Nazar 8.00 20.00
SD7 Jesper Wallstedt 6.00 15.00
SD8 Gavin Brindley 2.50 6.00
SD9 Lane Hutson 15.00 40.00
SD10 Bradly Nadeau 3.00 8.00
SD11 Olen Zellweger 6.00 15.00
SD12 Matt Rempe 5.00 12.00
SD13 Mavrik Bourque 5.00 12.00
SD14 Akil Thomas 2.50 6.00
SD15 Zach Dean 2.50 6.00
SD16 Zachary Bolduc 4.00 10.00
SD17 Brendan Brisson 3.00 8.00
SD18 Brad Lambert 3.00 8.00
SD19 Macklin Celebrini 20.00 50.00
SD20 Will Smith 8.00 20.00
SD21 Matvei Michkov 20.00 50.00
SD22 Jett Luchanko 5.00 12.00
SD23 Rutger McGroarty 5.00 12.00
SD24 Seamus Casey 3.00 8.00
SD25 Conor Geekie 4.00 10.00
SD26 Calum Ritchie 3.00 8.00
SD27 Maxim Tsyplakov 4.00 10.00

2024-25 Upper Deck Rookie Debut Smashing Debuts Image Variant

SD19 Macklin Celebrini 30.00 80.00

2002-03 Upper Deck Rookie Update

1 Paul Kariya .25 .60
2 Adam Oates .25 .60
3 Jean-Sebastien Giguere .25 .60
4 Sandis Ozolinsh .15 .40
5 Dany Heatley .20 .50
6 Ilya Kovalchuk .30 .75
7 Patrik Stefan .20 .50
8 Dan McGillis .15 .40
9 Joe Thornton .40 1.00
10 Sergei Samsonov .20 .50
11 Jeff Hackett .20 .50
12 Glen Murray .20 .50
13 Miroslav Satan .25 .60
14 Martin Biron .20 .50
15 Daniel Briere .20 .50
16 Chris Drury .25 .60
17 Jarome Iginla .30 .75
18 Roman Turek .25 .60
19 Pavel Brendl .15 .40
20 Rod Brind'Amour .25 .60
21 Ron Francis .30 .75
22 Tyler Arnason .25 .60
23 Jocelyn Thibault .20 .50
24 Bryan Marchment .20 .50
25 Joe Sakic .50 1.25
26 Peter Forsberg .50 1.25
27 Patrick Roy .60 1.50
28 Rob Blake .25 .60
29 Geoff Sanderson .20 .50
30 Marc Denis .20 .50
31 Mike Modano .40 1.00
32 Bill Guerin .25 .60
33 Marty Turco .25 .60
34 Steve Yzerman .60 1.50
35 Brendan Shanahan .25 .60
36 Brett Hull .50 1.25
37 Curtis Joseph .30 .75
38 Nicklas Lidstrom .25 .60
39 Sergei Fedorov .40 1.00
40 Mathieu Schneider .15 .40
41 Mike Comrie .25 .60
42 Tommy Salo .20 .50
43 Olli Jokinen .25 .60
44 Kristian Huselius .15 .40
45 Roberto Luongo .40 1.00
46 Adam Deadmarsh .15 .40
47 Zigmund Palffy .25 .60
48 Felix Potvin .40 1.00
49 Marian Gaborik .25 .60
50 Gordie Howe .75 2.00
51 Pascal Dupuis .15 .40
52 Saku Koivu .25 .60
53 Marcel Hossa .15 .40
54 Jose Theodore .25 .60
55 David Legwand .20 .50
56 Scott Hartnell .15 .40
57 Tomas Vokoun .20 .50
58 John Madden .15 .40
59 Scott Gomez .20 .50
60 Martin Brodeur .60 1.50
61 Alexei Yashin .20 .50
62 Mark Parrish .15 .40
63 Janne Niinimaa .15 .40
64 Alex Kovalev .20 .50
65 Pavel Bure .25 .60
66 Mike Dunham .20 .50
67 Mark Messier .50 1.25
68 Brian Leetch .20 .50
69 Daniel Alfredsson .25 .60
70 Marian Hossa .25 .60
71 Patrick Lalime .20 .50
72 Jeremy Roenick .40 1.00
73 John LeClair .25 .60
74 Tony Amonte .20 .50
75 Gordie Howe .75 2.00
76 Roman Cechmanek .20 .50
77 Brian Boucher .20 .50
78 Shane Doan .20 .50
79 Mario Lemieux 1.00 2.50
80 Martin Straka .20 .50
81 Sebastien Caron .20 .50
82 Alexei Morozov .15 .40
83 Doug Weight .25 .60
84 Keith Tkachuk .25 .60
85 Chris Osgood .25 .60
86 Teemu Selanne .50 1.25
87 Kyle McLaren .15 .40
88 Evgeni Nabokov .20 .50
89 Martin St. Louis .25 .60
90 Nikolai Khabibulin .25 .60
91 Doug Gilmour .30 .75
92 Mats Sundin .25 .60
93 Owen Nolan .25 .60
94 Ed Belfour .25 .60
95 Todd Bertuzzi .25 .60
96 Markus Naslund .25 .60
97 Dan Cloutier .20 .50
98 Jaromir Jagr .75 2.00
99 Olaf Kolzig .25 .60
100 Michael Nylander .15 .40
101 Gordie Howe RRM 2.50 6.00
102 Wayne Gretzky RRM 5.00 12.00
103 Bobby Orr RRM 3.00 8.00
104 Patrick Roy RRM 2.00 5.00
105 Mario Lemieux RRM 3.00 8.00
106 Joe Thornton RRM 1.25 3.00
107 Martin Brodeur RRM 2.00 5.00

108 Steve Yzerman RRM 2.00 5.00
109 Jaromir Jagr RRM 2.50 6.00
110 Paul Kariya RRM .75 2.00
111 Jarome Iginla RRM 1.00 2.50
112 Joe Sakic RRM 1.50 4.00
113 Mats Sundin RRM .75 2.00
114 Ilya Kovalchuk RRM 1.00 2.50
115 Marian Gaborik RRM .75 2.00
116 Mike Modano RRM 1.25 3.00
117 Carlo Colaiacovo RC 2.00 5.00
118 Jay Bouwmeester RC 4.00 10.00
119 Ari Ahonen RC 1.25 3.00
120 Patrick Boileau RC 1.25 3.00
121 Mike Komisarek RC 2.00 5.00
122 Cristobal Huet RC 2.50 6.00
123 Josh Harding RC 5.00 12.00
124 Chris Schmidt RC 1.25 3.00
125 Niko Dimitrakos RC 1.25 3.00
126 Ryan Bayda RC 1.25 3.00
127 Radoslav Hecl RC 1.25 3.00
128 Burke Henry RC 1.25 3.00
129 Frederic Cloutier RC 1.25 3.00
130 Tomas Kurka RC 1.25 3.00
131 John Tripp RC 1.25 3.00
132 Francois Beauchemin RC 2.00 5.00
133 Brandon Reid RC 1.25 3.00
134 Tomas Surovy RC 1.25 3.00
135 Chad Wiseman RC 1.25 3.00
136 Jason Bacashihua RC 1.50 4.00
137 Jesse Fibiger RC 1.25 3.00
138 Marc-Andre Bergeron RC 1.50 4.00
139 Ryan Miller RC 8.00 20.00
140 Ryan Kraft RC 1.25 3.00
141 Simon Gamache RC 1.25 3.00
142 Rob Davison RC 1.25 3.00
143 Jason King RC 2.00 5.00
144 Brad Defauw RC 1.25 3.00
145 Miroslav Zalesak RC 1.25 3.00
146 Sean McMorrow RC 1.25 3.00
147 Mike Siklenka RC 3.00 8.00
148 Doug Janik RC 1.25 3.00
149A A.Svitov RC/Shanahan 4.00 10.00
149B A.Svitov RC/T.Bertuzzi 4.00 10.00
149C A.Svitov RC/J.LeClair 4.00 10.00
150A A.Smirnov RC/A.Yashin 3.00 8.00
150B A.Smirnov RC/T.Bertuzzi 4.00 10.00
150C A.Smirnov RC/J.LeClair 4.00 10.00
151A B.Orpik RC/R.Blake 4.00 10.00
151B B.Orpik RC/E.Jovanoski 3.00 8.00
151C B.Orpik RC/S.Stevens 4.00 10.00
152A A.Hall RC/J.LeClair 4.00 10.00
152B A.Hall RC/A.Deadmarsh 2.50 6.00
152C A.Hall RC/J.Iginla 5.00 12.00
153A J.Taffe RC/C.Drury 4.00 10.00
153B J.Taffe RC/M.York 2.50 6.00
153C J.Taffe RC/J.Roenick 6.00 15.00
154A S.Eminger RC/N.Lidstrom 4.00 10.00
154B S.Eminger RC/S.Gonchar 3.00 8.00
154C S.Eminger RC/B.Leetch 3.00 8.00
155A J.Leopold RC/A.MacInnis 5.00 12.00
155B J.Leopold RC/B.Leetch 4.00 10.00
155C Leopold RC/S.Niedermayer 4.00 10.00
156A P.Sharp RC/S.Reinprecht 6.00 15.00
156B P.Sharp RC/M.Peca 6.00 15.00
156C P.Sharp RC/J.Roenick 6.00 15.00
157A S.Ott RC/P.Kariya 4.00 10.00
157B S.Ott RC/S.Samsonov 3.00 8.00
157C S.Ott RC/T.Fleury 5.00 12.00
158A A.Hemsky RC/J.Jagr 10.00 25.00
158B A.Hemsky RC/M.Hejduk 8.00 20.00
158C A.Hemsky RC/P.Elias 6.00 15.00
159A A.Frolov RC/J.LeClair 6.00 15.00
159B A.Frolov RC/A.Yashin 6.00 15.00
159C A.Frolov RC/J.Jagr 12.00 30.00
160A J.Stoll RC/J.LeClair 8.00 20.00
160B J.Stoll RC/K.Tkachuk 8.00 20.00
160C J.Stoll RC/B.Guerin 8.00 20.00
161A Volchenkov RC/R.Blake 4.00 10.00
161B Volchenkov RC/S.Stevens 4.00 10.00
161C Volchenkov RC/Jovanoski 3.00 8.00
162A D.Bykov RC/B.Leetch 3.00 8.00
162B D.Bykov RC/N.Lidstrom 4.00 10.00
162C D.Bykov RC/S.Gonchar 3.00 8.00
163 J.Spezza RC/W.Gretzky 250.00 600.00
164 P.Bouchard RC/S.Samsonov 15.00 40.00
165 R.Hainsey RC/R.Bourque 20.00 50.00
166 S.Chistov RC/P.Bure 12.00 30.00
167 C.Kobasew RC/J.Iginla 15.00 40.00
168 H.Zetterberg RC/G.Howe 75.00 150.00
169 S.Upshall RC/M.Comrie 12.00 30.00
170 P.LeClaire RC/P.Roy 30.00 80.00
171 M.Tellqvist RC/E.Belfour 20.00 50.00
172 R.Nash RC/J.Thornton 30.00 80.00
173 Igor Radulov RC 1.25 3.00
174 Paul Gaustad RC 1.25 3.00
175 Christian Backman RC 1.25 3.00
176 Cam Severson RC 1.25 3.00

2002-03 Upper Deck Rookie Update Autographs

BR Pavel Brendl 10.00 25.00
CJ Curtis Joseph 15.00 40.00
CK Chuck Kobasew/24* 10.00 25.00
DH Dany Heatley 15.00 40.00
EC Erik Cole 10.00 25.00
GH Gordie Howe/24* 100.00 175.00
HZ Henrik Zetterberg/24* 50.00 100.00
K Ilya Kovalchuk 15.00 40.00
JA Jason Spezza/24* 30.00 80.00
JB Jay Bouwmeester/24* 15.00 40.00
JI Jarome Iginla 15.00 40.00
L John LeClair 10.00 25.00
MA Maxim Afinogenov 10.00 25.00
MC Mike Comrie 10.00 25.00
MH Martin Havlat 12.50 30.00
MN Markus Naslund 10.00 25.00
MT Mikael Tellqvist/24* 25.00 60.00
B Pavel Bure 10.00 25.00
M Pierre-Marc Bouchard/24* 12.50 30.00
R Patrick Roy/24* 100.00 150.00
B Ray Bourque/24* 30.00 80.00
H Ron Hainsey/24* 20.00 40.00
C Stanislav Chistov/24* 10.00 25.00
G Simon Gagne 10.00 25.00
O Steve Ott 10.00 25.00
S Sergei Samsonov 10.00 25.00

SY Steve Yzerman 30.00 80.00
WG Wayne Gretzky 200.00 500.00

2002-03 Upper Deck Rookie Update Jerseys

*SINGLE GOLD/125: .6X TO 1.5X BASIC
DAY Alexei Yashin 4.00 10.00
DBG Bill Guerin 4.00 10.00
DBS Brendan Shanahan 5.00 12.00
DCO Chris Osgood 4.00 10.00
DDH Dany Heatley 5.00 12.00
DEL Eric Lindros 6.00 15.00
DFP Felix Potvin 6.00 15.00
DHO Marian Hossa 4.00 10.00
DIK Ilya Kovalchuk 5.00 12.00
DJG Jean-Sebastien Giguere 10.00 25.00
DJI Jarome Iginla 6.00 15.00
DJJ Jaromir Jagr 8.00 20.00
DJR Jeremy Roenick 6.00 15.00
DJS Joe Sakic 8.00 20.00
DJT Joe Thornton 5.00 12.00
DKP Keith Primeau 4.00 10.00
DMD Mike Dunham 3.00 8.00
DMH Milan Hejduk 4.00 10.00
DML Mario Lemieux 12.50 30.00
DMM Mike Modano 6.00 15.00
DMS Mats Sundin 5.00 12.00
DOK Olaf Kolzig 4.00 10.00
DPB Pavel Bure 5.00 12.00
DPD Pavol Demitra 4.00 10.00
DPK Paul Kariya 5.00 12.00
DPR Patrick Roy 12.50 30.00
DRC Roman Cechmanek 4.00 10.00
DRL Roberto Luongo 6.00 15.00
DRT Roman Turek 4.00 10.00
DSK Saku Koivu 4.00 10.00
DSS Sergei Samsonov 4.00 10.00
DSY Steve Yzerman 12.50 30.00
DTB Todd Bertuzzi 4.00 10.00
DTH Jose Theodore 5.00 12.00
DTS Tommy Salo 4.00 10.00
DZP Zigmund Palffy 4.00 10.00
SJK J.Jagr/O.Kolzig 12.50 30.00
SKH I.Kovalchuk/D.Heatley 12.50 20.00
SLB E.Lindros/P.Bure 12.50 30.00
SRS P.Roy/J.Sakic 15.00 40.00
STS J.Thornton/S.Samsonov 12.50 30.00
SYS S.Yzerman/B.Shanahan 20.00 50.00

2003-04 Upper Deck Rookie Update

COMP.SET w/o SP's (90) 25.00 50.00
1 Petr Sykora .25 .60
2 Jean-Sebastien Giguere .30 .75
3 Sergei Fedorov .50 1.25
4 Dany Heatley .25 .60
5 Ilya Kovalchuk .30 .75
6 Sergei Samsonov .25 .60
7 Joe Thornton .50 1.25
8 Andrew Raycroft .25 .60
9 Chris Drury .25 .60
10 Daniel Briere .30 .75
11 Mika Noronen .20 .50
12 Jarome Iginla .40 1.00
13 Miikka Kiprusoff .30 .75
14 Justin Williams .25 .60
15 Ron Francis .40 1.00
16 Jocelyn Thibault .25 .60
17 Bryan Berard .25 .60
18 Mark Bell .20 .50
19 Joe Sakic .60 1.50
20 Paul Kariya .30 .75
21 Peter Forsberg .60 1.50
22 David Aebischer .25 .60
23 Todd Marchant .20 .50
24 Rick Nash .30 .75
25 Marc Denis .25 .60
26 Bill Guerin .30 .75
27 Marty Turco .30 .75
28 Mike Modano .50 1.25
29 Pavel Datsyuk .50 1.25
30 Henrik Zetterberg .40 1.00
31 Brett Hull .60 1.50
32 Steve Yzerman .75 2.00
33 Adam Oates .30 .75
34 Tommy Salo .25 .60
35 Raffi Torres .20 .50
36 Ales Hemsky .30 .75
37 Roberto Luongo .50 1.25
38 Jay Bouwmeester .20 .50
39 Olli Jokinen .30 .75
40 Martin Straka .20 .50
41 Roman Cechmanek .25 .60
42 Zigmund Palffy .30 .75
43 Marian Gaborik .30 .75
44 Alexandre Daigle .25 .60
45 Manny Fernandez .20 .50
46 Jose Theodore .30 .75
47 Saku Koivu .30 .75
48 Mike Ribeiro .20 .50
49 Steve Sullivan .20 .50
50 Tomas Vokoun .25 .60
51 Patrik Elias .30 .75
52 Scott Gomez .25 .60
53 Martin Brodeur .75 2.00
54 Scott Stevens .30 .75
55 Alexei Yashin .25 .60
56 Trent Hunter .20 .50
57 Rick DiPietro .25 .60
58 Jaromir Jagr 1.00 2.50
59 Mark Messier .60 1.50
60 Peter Bondra .30 .75
61 Jason Spezza .30 .75
62 Marian Hossa .30 .75
63 Patrick Lalime .25 .60
64 Sean Burke .20 .50
65 Jeremy Roenick .50 1.25
66 Alexei Zhamnov .25 .60
67 Brian Boucher .25 .60
68 Mike Comrie .25 .60
69 Mario Lemieux 1.25 3.00
70 Sebastien Caron .25 .60
71 Vincent Damphousse .25 .60
72 Evgeni Nabokov .25 .60
73 Patrick Marleau .30 .75
74 Chris Osgood .30 .75
75 Doug Weight .30 .75
76 Pavol Demitra .40 1.00
77 Keith Tkachuk .30 .75
78 Nikolai Khabibulin .30 .75
79 Vincent Lecavalier .30 .75
80 Mats Sundin .30 .75
81 Alexander Mogilny .25 .60
82 Owen Nolan .30 .75
83 Ed Belfour .30 .75
84 Todd Bertuzzi .30 .75
85 Ed Jovanovski .25 .60
86 Markus Naslund .30 .75
87 Jason King .20 .50
88 Dan Cloutier .25 .60
89 Anson Carter .25 .60
90 Olaf Kolzig .30 .75
91 Niklas Kronwall RC 4.00 10.00
92 Doug Doull RC 1.50 4.00
93 Fedor Tyutin RC 1.50 4.00
94 Dwayne Zinger RC 1.50 4.00
95 Jason MacDonald RC 1.50 4.00
96 Ryan Malone RC 3.00 8.00
97 Rob Skrlac RC 1.50 4.00
98 Jame Pollock RC 1.50 4.00
99 Grant McNeill RC 1.50 4.00
100 Noah Clarke RC 1.50 4.00
101 Joey MacDonald RC 3.00 8.00
102 John Pohl RC 1.50 4.00
103 Tony Martensson RC 1.50 4.00
104 Antti Miettinen RC 2.50 6.00
105 Ryan Barnes RC 1.50 4.00
106 Graham Mink RC 1.50 4.00
107 Patrick Leahy RC 2.00 5.00
108 Sergei Zinovjev RC 1.50 4.00
109 Steve McLaren RC 1.50 4.00
110 Seamus Kotyk RC 1.50 4.00
111 Tim Jackman RC 2.00 5.00
112 Andrew Hutchinson RC 1.50 4.00
113 Andy Chiodo RC 1.50 4.00
114 Timofei Shishkanov RC 1.50 4.00
115 Milan Michalek RC 3.00 8.00
116 Trevor Daley RC 2.50 6.00
117 Jeff MacMillan RC 2.00 5.00
118 Jason Pominville RC 4.00 10.00
119 Mikko Luoma RC 1.50 4.00
120 Brad Boyes RC 2.50 6.00
121 Michael Morrison RC 2.00 5.00
122 Tomas Plekanec RC 5.00 12.00
123 Mike Stuart RC 1.50 4.00
124 Tuomas Pihlman RC 2.00 5.00
125 Darcy Verot RC 1.50 4.00
126 Mark Popovic RC 2.00 5.00
127 Erik Westrum RC 1.50 4.00
128 Aaron Johnson RC 1.50 4.00
129 Doug Lynch RC 1.50 4.00
130 Randy Jones RC 1.50 4.00
131 Nathan Smith RC 1.50 4.00
132 Aleksander Suglobov RC 1.50 4.00
133 Kyle Wellwood RC 2.50 6.00
134 Chris Kunitz RC 3.00 8.00
135 Jeff Hamilton RC 1.50 4.00
136 Garth Murray RC 2.00 5.00
137 Peter Sejna RC 2.00 5.00
138 Mike Smith RC 5.00 12.00
139 Antero Niittymaki RC 4.00 10.00
140 Carl Corazzini RC 1.50 4.00
141 Anton Babchuk RC 1.50 4.00
142 Julien Vauclair RC 1.50 4.00
143 Nathan Robinson RC 1.50 4.00
144 Dan Ellis RC 2.00 5.00
145 Colton Orr RC 2.00 5.00
146 Rastislav Stana RC 2.50 6.00
147 Gavin Morgan RC 2.00 5.00
148 Dan Hamhuis RC 2.00 5.00
149 Nolan Schaefer RC 1.50 4.00
150 Pat Rissmiller RC 2.00 5.00
151 Bergeron J RC/Thornton J 8.00 20.00
152 Hudler J RC/Yzerman J 10.00 25.00
153 R.Kesler J RC/T.Bertuzzi J 6.00 15.00
154 Semin J RC/Bure J 8.00 20.00
155 Higgins J RC/Koivu J 6.00 15.00
156 J.Lupul J RC/S.Fedorov J 6.00 15.00
157 D.Brown J RC/Z.Palffy J 6.00 15.00
158 J.Pitkanen J RC/J. Roenick J 5.00 12.00
159 Fleury AU RC/Roy AU 125.00 300.00
160 Ruutu AU RC/Koivu AU 20.00 50.00
161 Staal AU RC/Gretzky AU 200.00 500.00
162 Horton AU RC/Howe AU 40.00 100.00
163 Zherdev AU RC/Nash AU 25.00 60.00
164 Sjostrom AU RC/Naslund AU 15.00 40.00
165 Tootoo AU RC/Nolan AU 20.00 50.00
166 Zbynek Michalek RC 1.50 4.00
167 Lawrence Nycholat RC 2.00 5.00
168 Fred Meyer RC 1.50 4.00
169 Mike Bishai RC 1.50 4.00
170 Mike Green RC 2.00 5.00
171 Matt Ellison RC 1.50 4.00
172 Joe Motzko RC 1.50 4.00
173 D.Roy J RC/C. Drury J 4.00 10.00
174 D.Fritsche J RC/Nash J 5.00 12.00
175 Stajan AU RC/Nolan AU 20.00 50.00
176 Kari Lehtonen RC 15.00 40.00
177 Goran Bezina RC 4.00 10.00
178 Owen Fussey RC 4.00 10.00
179 Josh Olson RC 4.00 10.00
180 Michal Barinka RC 4.00 10.00
181 Bryce Lampman RC 5.00 12.00
182 Matt Hussey RC 4.00 10.00
183 Mike Stutzel RC 4.00 10.00
184 Roman Tvrdon RC 4.00 10.00
185 Matthew Yeats RC 4.00 10.00
186 Thomas Pock RC 5.00 12.00
187 Wade Dubielewicz RC 4.00 10.00
188 Greg Mauldin RC 5.00 12.00
189 Mike Pandolfo RC 4.00 10.00
190 Eric Perrin RC 4.00 10.00
191 Christoph Brandner RC 5.00 12.00
192 Matthew Lombardi RC 5.00 12.00
193 John-Michael Liles RC 5.00 12.00
194 Marek Svatos RC 8.00 20.00
195 Tony Salmelainen RC 4.00 10.00
196 Dominic Moore RC 4.00 10.00
197 Brooks Laich RC 6.00 15.00
198 Cory Larose RC 4.00 10.00
199 Adam Munro RC 4.00 10.00
200 Mikhail Kuleshov RC 4.00 10.00
201 Matt Keith RC 4.00 10.00
202 Denis Grebeshkov RC 4.00 10.00
203 Quintin Laing RC 4.00 10.00
204 Benoit Dusablon RC 4.00 10.00
205 Matt Underhill RC 4.00 10.00
206 Jozef Balej RC 4.00 10.00
207 Robert Scuderi RC 5.00 12.00
208 Libor Pivko RC 4.00 10.00
209 Mikhail Yakubov RC 4.00 10.00
210 Tom Preissing RC 5.00 12.00
211 Cody McCormick RC 5.00 12.00
212 Pavel Vorobiev RC 5.00 12.00
213 Matt Murley RC 5.00 12.00
214 Matthew Spiller RC 5.00 12.00
215 Marek Zidlicky RC 4.00 10.00
216 Christian Ehrhoff RC 5.00 12.00
217 Brent Burns RC 12.00 30.00
RR1 Rookie EXCH expired .20 .50

2003-04 Upper Deck Rookie Update All-Star Lineup

AS1 Martin Brodeur 20.00 50.00
AS2 Ilya Kovalchuk 15.00 40.00
AS3 Joe Thornton 20.00 50.00
AS4 Marian Hossa 10.00 25.00
AS5 Scott Niedermayer 8.00 20.00
AS7 Marty Turco 8.00 20.00
AS8 Markus Naslund 8.00 20.00
AS9 Joe Sakic 12.50 30.00
AS10 Brett Hull 20.00 50.00
AS11 Rob Blake 12.50 30.00
AS12 Nicklas Lidstrom 10.00 25.00

2003-04 Upper Deck Rookie Update Skills

SKJSG Jean-Sebastien Giguere 3.00 8.00
SKAH Ales Hemsky 3.00 8.00
SKAY Alexei Yashin 3.00 8.00
SKBG Bill Guerin 3.00 8.00
SKBH Brett Hull 5.00 12.00
SKCD Chris Drury 3.00 8.00
SKDA David Aebischer 3.00 8.00
SKDH Dany Heatley 5.00 12.00
SKDW Doug Weight 3.00 8.00
SKEB Ed Belfour 4.00 10.00
SKEL Eric Lindros 4.00 10.00
SKGM Glen Murray 3.00 8.00
SKJJ Jaromir Jagr 6.00 15.00
SKJR Jeremy Roenick 5.00 12.00
SKJS Jason Spezza 5.00 12.00
SKJT Jose Theodore 5.00 12.00
SKMB Martin Brodeur 12.50 30.00
SKMF Manny Fernandez 3.00 8.00
SKMG Marian Gaborik 6.00 15.00
SKMH Marian Hossa 4.00 10.00
SKMK Mark Messier 5.00 12.00
SKML Mario Lemieux 12.50 30.00
SKMM Mike Modano 6.00 15.00
SKMN Markus Naslund 4.00 10.00
SKMS Mats Sundin 4.00 10.00
SKMT Marty Turco 3.00 8.00
SKNK Nikolai Khabibulin 4.00 10.00
SKON Owen Nolan 3.00 8.00
SKPF Peter Forsberg 8.00 20.00
SKPK Paul Kariya 4.00 10.00
SKPL Patrick Lalime 3.00 8.00
SKRN Rick Nash 5.00 12.00
SKSA Joe Sakic 8.00 20.00
SKSB Sean Burke 3.00 8.00
SKSF Sergei Fedorov 6.00 15.00
SKSK Saku Koivu 4.00 10.00
SKSY Steve Yzerman 12.50 30.00
SKTA Tony Amonte 4.00 10.00
SKTB Todd Bertuzzi 4.00 10.00
SKTH Joe Thornton 6.00 15.00
SKVL Vincent Lecavalier 4.00 10.00
SKZP Zigmund Palffy 3.00 8.00

2003-04 Upper Deck Rookie Update Super Stars

SSMSL Martin St. Louis 3.00 8.00
SSHJK Milan Hejduk 4.00 10.00
SSAF Alexander Frolov 3.00 8.00
SSAM Alexander Mogilny 3.00 8.00
SSBH Brett Hull 5.00 12.00
SSBM Brendan Morrison 3.00 8.00
SSDA David Aebischer 3.00 8.00
SSDH Dany Heatley 5.00 12.00
SSDW Doug Weight 3.00 8.00
SSEB Ed Belfour 4.00 10.00
SSGM Glen Murray 3.00 8.00
SSHZ Henrik Zetterberg 5.00 12.00
SSJB Jay Bouwmeester 4.00 10.00
SSJI Jarome Iginla 5.00 12.00
SSJL John LeClair 4.00 10.00
SSJO Joe Sakic 8.00 20.00
SSJR Jeremy Roenick 6.00 15.00
SSJS Jason Spezza 5.00 12.00
SSJT Joe Thornton 6.00 15.00
SSKT Keith Tkachuk 4.00 10.00
SSLR Luc Robitaille 3.00 8.00
SSMB Martin Brodeur 12.50 30.00
SSMF Manny Fernandez 3.00 8.00
SSMG Marian Gaborik 8.00 20.00
SSMH Marian Hossa 4.00 10.00
SSMK Mark Messier 4.00 10.00
SSML Mario Lemieux 12.50 30.00
SSMM Mike Modano 6.00 15.00
SSMS Mats Sundin 4.00 10.00
SSMT Marty Turco 3.00 8.00
SSON Owen Nolan 3.00 8.00
SSPD Pavol Demitra 3.00 8.00
SSPF Peter Forsberg 8.00 20.00
SSPL Patrick Lalime 3.00 8.00
SSRC Roman Cechmanek 3.00 8.00
SSSD Shane Doan 3.00 8.00
SSSF Sergei Fedorov 6.00 15.00
SSSK Saku Koivu 4.00 10.00
SSSS Sergei Samsonov 3.00 8.00
SSSY Steve Yzerman 12.50 30.00
SSVL Vincent Lecavalier 4.00 10.00
SSZP Zigmund Palffy 3.00 8.00

2003-04 Upper Deck Rookie Update Top Draws

TD1 Evgeni Nabokov 6.00 15.00
TD2 Teemu Selanne 8.00 20.00
TD3 Todd Bertuzzi SP 20.00 50.00
TD6 Jason Spezza SP 75.00 150.00
TD7 Rick DiPietro 6.00 15.00
TD8 Jean-Sebastien Giguere 50.00 100.00
TD9 Nikolai Zherdev 6.00 15.00
TD10 Ales Hemsky 6.00 15.00
TD11 Ilya Kovalchuk SP 12.50 30.00
TD12 Pascal Leclaire 6.00 15.00
TD13 Rick Nash 8.00 20.00
TD14 Nikolai Khabibulin SP 25.00 60.00
TD15 Steve Yzerman 25.00 60.00
TD16 John LeClair 8.00 15.00
TD17 Patrick Roy 60.00 150.00
TD18 Jay Bouwmeester 6.00 15.00
TD19 Alexander Svitov 6.00 15.00
TD20 Fredrik Sjostrom 6.00 15.00

2003-04 Upper Deck Rookie Update YoungStars

YS1 Michael Ryder 8.00 20.00
YS2 Eric Staal 12.00 30.00
YS2A Eric Staal 12.00 30.00
YS3 Patrice Bergeron 10.00 25.00
YS3A Patrice Bergeron 12.00 30.00
YS4 Trent Hunter 4.00 10.00
YS5 Ryan Malone 5.00 12.00
YS6 Derek Roy 4.00 10.00
YS6A Derek Roy 4.00 10.00
YS7 Matt Stajan 4.00 10.00
YS7A Matt Stajan 4.00 10.00
YS8 Joni Pitkanen 4.00 10.00
YS8A Joni Pitkanen 4.00 10.00
YS9 Paul Martin 4.00 10.00
YS10 Brooks Orpik 4.00 10.00
YS11 Andrew Raycroft 8.00 20.00
YS11A Andrew Raycroft 8.00 20.00
YS12 Pierre-Marc Bouchard 4.00 10.00
YS13 Joffrey Lupul 6.00 15.00
YS14 Matthew Lombardi 4.00 10.00
YS15 Tuomo Ruutu 8.00 20.00
YS15A Tuomo Ruutu 8.00 20.00
YS16 Raffi Torres 4.00 10.00
YS17 Nikolai Zherdev 8.00 20.00
YS17A Nikolai Zherdev 8.00 20.00
YS18 Jonathan Cheechoo 12.00 30.00
YS19 Christian Ehrhoff 4.00 10.00
YS20 Dan Hamhuis 5.00 12.00
YS21 Alexei Semenov 4.00 10.00
YS22 Philippe Sauve 4.00 10.00

2005-06 Upper Deck Rookie Update

COMPLETE SET w/o SPs (100) 8.00 20.00
1 Jean-Sebastien Giguere .40 1.00
2 Teemu Selanne .75 2.00
3 Joffrey Lupul .25 .60
4 Ilya Kovalchuk .40 1.00
5 Marian Hossa .40 1.00
6 Kari Lehtonen .30 .75
7 Andrew Raycroft .30 .75
8 Brian Leetch .30 .75
9 Patrice Bergeron .50 1.25
10 Glen Murray .30 .75
11 Chris Drury .30 .75
12 Ryan Miller .40 1.00
13 Jarome Iginla .50 1.25
14 Miikka Kiprusoff .40 1.00
15 Daymond Langkow .25 .60
16 Eric Staal .50 1.25
17 Martin Gerber .30 .75
18 Doug Weight .40 1.00
19 Erik Cole .25 .60
20 Nikolai Khabibulin .40 1.00
21 Tuomo Ruutu .40 1.00
22 Jose Theodore .40 1.00
23 Alex Tanguay .40 1.00
24 Joe Sakic .75 2.00
25 Marek Svatos .30 .75
26 Milan Hejduk .30 .75
27 Rob Blake .40 1.00
28 Rick Nash .40 1.00
29 Sergei Fedorov .60 1.50
30 Mike Modano .60 1.50
31 Brenden Morrow .30 .75
32 Marty Turco .40 1.00
33 Steve Yzerman 1.00 2.50
34 Pavel Datsyuk .60 1.50
35 Henrik Zetterberg .50 1.25
36 Brendan Shanahan .40 1.00
37 Nicklas Lidstrom .40 1.00
38 Ryan Smyth .30 .75
39 Chris Pronger .40 1.00
40 Ales Hemsky .30 .75
41 Roberto Luongo .60 1.50
42 Nathan Horton .40 1.00
43 Olli Jokinen .40 1.00
44 Alexander Frolov .25 .60
45 Jeremy Roenick .60 1.50
46 Pavol Demitra .50 1.25
47 Luc Robitaille .40 1.00
48 Marian Gaborik .40 1.00
49 Manny Fernandez .25 .60
50 Saku Koivu .40 1.00
51 David Aebischer .30 .75
52 Michael Ryder .30 .75
53 Mike Ribeiro .25 .60
54 Paul Kariya .40 1.00
55 Tomas Vokoun .30 .75
56 Martin Brodeur 1.00 2.50
57 Patrik Elias .40 1.00
58 Brian Gionta .25 .60
59 Scott Gomez .30 .75
60 Alexei Yashin .30 .75
61 Miroslav Satan .30 .75
62 Rick DiPietro .30 .75
63 Jaromir Jagr 1.25 3.00
64 Martin Straka .25 .60
65 Dominik Hasek .60 1.50
66 Dany Heatley .30 .75
67 Daniel Alfredsson .40 1.00
68 Jason Spezza .40 1.00
69 Wade Redden .25 .60
70 Peter Forsberg .75 2.00
71 Simon Gagne .40 1.00
72 Antero Niittymaki .30 .75
73 Keith Primeau .30 .75
74 Joni Pitkanen .25 .60
75 Curtis Joseph .50 1.25
76 Shane Doan .30 .75
77 Ladislav Nagy .25 .60
78 Mario Lemieux 1.50 4.00
79 Ryan Malone .25 .60
80 Marc-Andre Fleury .75 2.00
81 Joe Thornton .60 1.50
82 Patrick Marleau .40 1.00
83 Evgeni Nabokov .30 .75
84 Jonathan Cheechoo .30 .75
85 Keith Tkachuk .40 1.00
86 Barret Jackman .25 .60
87 Vincent Lecavalier .40 1.00
88 Martin St. Louis .40 1.00
89 Brad Richards .40 1.00
90 Vaclav Prospal .25 .60
91 Mats Sundin .40 1.00
92 Ed Belfour .40 1.00
93 Jason Allison .30 .75
94 Bryan McCabe .25 .60
95 Eric Lindros .60 1.50
96 Markus Naslund .40 1.00
97 Alex Auld .25 .60
98 Todd Bertuzzi .40 1.00
99 Brendan Morrison .25 .60
100 Olaf Kolzig .40 1.00
101 Dustin Penner RC 3.00 8.00
102 Michael Wall RC 2.50 6.00
103 Zenon Konopka RC 2.00 5.00
104 Adam Berkhoel RC 2.50 6.00
105 Jay Leach RC 2.50 6.00
106 Eric Healey RC 2.50 6.00
107 Ben Guite RC 2.50 6.00
108 Ben Walter RC 2.00 5.00
109 Brian Eklund RC 2.50 6.00
110 Nathan Paetsch RC 2.50 6.00
111 Jiri Novotny RC 2.50 6.00
112 Mark Giordano RC 4.00 10.00
113 Richie Regehr RC 2.00 5.00
114 Chad Larose RC 2.00 5.00
115 Keith Aucoin RC 2.00 5.00
116 David Gove RC 2.50 6.00
117 Mark Cullen RC 2.50 6.00
118 Rene Bourque RC 3.00 8.00
119 Martin St. Pierre RC 2.00 5.00
120 Corey Crawford RC 12.00 30.00
121 James Wisniewski RC 2.50 6.00
122 Vitaly Kolesnik RC 2.50 6.00
123 Andrew Penner RC 2.50 6.00
124 Steven Goertzen RC 2.00 5.00
125 Geoff Platt RC 2.50 6.00
126 Joakim Lindstrom RC 2.00 5.00
127 Junior Lessard RC 2.00 5.00
128 Vojtech Polak RC 2.00 5.00
129 Brett Lebda RC 2.00 5.00
130 Kyle Brodziak RC 2.00 5.00
131 Danny Syvret RC 2.00 5.00
132 Matt Greene RC 2.00 5.00
133 J-F Jacques RC 2.00 5.00
134 Mathieu Roy RC 3.00 8.00
135 Greg Jacina RC 2.00 5.00
136 Rob Globke RC 2.00 5.00
137 Petr Taticek RC 2.50 6.00
138 Adam Hauser RC 2.50 6.00
139 George Parros RC 2.00 5.00
140 Yanick Lehoux RC 3.00 8.00
141 Petr Kanko RC 2.50 6.00
142 Jeff Giuliano RC 2.50 6.00
143 Matt Ryan RC 2.50 6.00
144 Connor James RC 2.50 6.00
145 Richard Petiot RC 2.50 6.00
146 Derek Boogaard RC 5.00 12.00
147 Matt Foy RC 2.00 5.00
148 Raitis Ivanans RC 2.00 5.00
149 Mark Streit RC 2.00 5.00
150 Jonathan Ferland RC 2.50 6.00
151 J-P Cote RC 2.00 5.00
152 Kevin Klein RC 2.00 5.00
153 Pekka Rinne RC 8.00 20.00
154 Greg Zanon RC 2.50 6.00
155 Cam Janssen RC 2.50 6.00
156 Jason Ryznar RC 2.00 5.00
157 Bruno Gervais RC 2.00 5.00
158 Kevin Colley RC 2.50 6.00
159 Ryan Hollweg RC 2.00 5.00
160 Chris Holt RC 2.00 5.00
161 Brian McGrattan RC 2.00 5.00
162 Wade Skolney RC 2.00 5.00
163 Josh Gratton RC 2.50 6.00
164 Ryan Ready RC 2.50 6.00
165 Alexandre Picard RC 2.00 5.00
166 Stefan Ruzicka RC 2.00 5.00
167 Matt Jones RC 2.00 5.00
168 Colby Armstrong RC 3.00 8.00
169 Doug Murray RC 2.00 5.00
170 Grant Stevenson RC 2.00 5.00
171 Kevin Dallman RC 2.50 6.00
172 Andy Roach RC 2.00 5.00
173 Jon DiSalvatore RC 2.50 6.00
174 Dennis Wideman RC 2.00 5.00
175 Jeff Hoggan RC 2.00 5.00
176 Colin Hemingway RC 2.00 5.00
177 Chris Beckford-Tseu RC 2.50 6.00
178 Mike Glumac RC 2.50 6.00
179 Timo Helbling RC 2.00 5.00
180 Nick Tarnasky RC 2.00 5.00
181 Gerald Coleman RC 2.00 5.00
182 Paul Ranger RC 2.00 5.00
183 Darren Reid RC 2.00 5.00
184 Doug O'Brien RC 2.00 5.00
185 Staffan Kronwall RC 2.00 5.00
186 Jay Harrison RC 2.50 6.00
187 Rick Rypien RC 4.00 10.00
188 Rob McVicar RC 2.50 6.00
189 Alexandre Burrows RC 4.00 10.00
190 Tomas Mojzis RC 2.00 5.00
191 Prestin Ryan RC 1.50 4.00
192 David Steckel RC 2.50 6.00
193 Mike Green RC 4.00 10.00
194 Joey Tenute RC 2.50 6.00
195 Louis Robitaille RC 2.00 5.00
196 Coburn JSY RC
Bouwmeester JSY 5.00 12.00
197 Slater JSY RC/Draper JSY 6.00 15.00
198 Jurcina JSY RC/Chara JSY 5.00 12.00
199 Sigalet JSY RC/Raycroft JSY 4.00 10.00
200 Nystrom JSY RC/Amonte JSY 4.00 10.00
201 Nastiuk JSY RC/Biron JSY 4.00 10.00
202 Richmond JSY RC/Rafalski JSY 4.00 10.00
203 Seabrook JSY RC/Jovn JSY 10.00 25.00
204 Barker JSY RC/Blake JSY 5.00 12.00
205 Budaj JSY RC/Vokoun JSY 6.00 15.00
206 Richrdsn JSY RC/Sakic JSY 10.00 25.00
207 Jokinen JSY RC/Lehtinen JSY 5.00 12.00
208 Howard JSY RC/Conklin JSY 8.00 20.00
209 Franzen JSY RC/Zetter JSY 8.00 20.00
210 Winchester JSY RC/Tkachuk JSY 5.00 12.00
211 Stewart JSY RC/Doan JSY 4.00 10.00
212 Tambellini JSY RC/St.Louis JSY 5.00 12.00
213 Danis JSY RC/Theodore JSY 5.00 12.00
214 Lapierre JSY RC/Turgeon JSY 5.00 12.00
215 Suter JSY RC/Chelios JSY 6.00 15.00
216 Parise JSY RC/Rnick JSY 8.00 20.00
217 Tallackson JSY RC/Guerin JSY 5.00 12.00
218 Nokelainen JSY RC/Jokinen JSY 5.00 12.00
219 Nilsson JSY RC/Naslund JSY 5.00 12.00
220 Campoli JSY RC/McCabe JSY 3.00 8.00
221 Montoya JSY RC/Esche JSY 5.00 12.00
222 Schubert JSY RC/Pitkanen JSY 3.00 8.00
223 Bochenski JSY RC/Parrish JSY 5.00 12.00
224 Eaves JSY RC/Peca JSY 5.00 12.00
225 Umberger JSY RC/Primeau JSY 5.00 12.00
226 Ballard JSY RC/Niedermayer JSY 5.00 12.00
227 Leneveu JSY RC/Joseph JSY 6.00 15.00
228 Talbot JSY RC/Morrison JSY 5.00 12.00
229 Whitney JSY RC/Leetch JSY 5.00 12.00
230 Bernier JSY RC/Heatley JSY 5.00 12.00
231 Clowe JSY RC/Cheech JSY 6.00 15.00
232 Woywitka JSY RC/Foote JSY 3.00 8.00
233 Stemp JSY RC/Bergeron JSY 6.00 15.00
234 Artyukin JSY RC/Jagr JSY 15.00 40.00
235 Woznw JSY RC/Hatcher JSY 4.00 10.00
236 Klepis JSY RC/Hemsky JSY 4.00 10.00
237 Fleischm JSY RC/Hejduk JSY 5.00 12.00
238 Alberts JSY RC/Boynton JSY 3.00 8.00
239 Eager JSY RC/Daze JSY 4.00 10.00
240 Picard JSY RC/Robitaille JSY 8.00 20.00
241 Tollefsen JSY RC/Klesla JSY 4.00 10.00
242 Paille JSY RC/Stillman JSY 5.00 12.00
243 Christensen JSY RC/Staal JSY 6.00 15.00
244 Patzold JSY RC/Nabokov JSY 4.00 10.00
245 Craig JSY RC/Lecavalier JSY 5.00 12.00
246 Bieksa JSY RC/Jackman JSY 5.00 12.00
247 Colliton JSY RC/Hunter JSY 3.00 8.00
248 McClement JSY RC/Arnott JSY 4.00 10.00
249 Gorges JSY RC/Hamhuis JSY 4.00 10.00
250 Quincey JSY RC/Regehr JSY 4.00 10.00
251 Thorburn JSY RC/Brind'A JSY 5.00 12.00
252 Nordgren JSY RC/Holms JSY 5.00 12.00
253 Keith JSY RC/Stuart JSY 6.00 15.00
254 Balastik JSY RC/Prospal JSY 3.00 8.00
255 Prucha JSY RC/Straka JSY 5.00 12.00
256 Getzlaf AU RC/Spezza AU 20.00 50.00
257 Perry AU RC/Tanguay AU 15.00 30.00
258 Toivonen AU RC/Lehtn AU 15.00 40.00
259 Vanek AU RC/Iginla AU 20.00 50.00
260 Steen AU RC/Gilmour AU 15.00 40.00
261 Ladd AU RC/Bertuzzi AU 12.00 30.00
262 Ward AU RC/Turco AU 8.00 20.00
263 Wolski AU RC/Smyth AU 10.00 25.00
264 Brule AU RC/Gagne AU 10.00 25.00
265 Filppula AU RC/Rtu AU 12.00 30.00
266 Olesz AU RC/Havlat AU 10.00 25.00
267 Koivu AU RC/Koivu AU 10.00 25.00
268 Perezhogin AU RC/Yashin AU 10.00 25.00
269 Kostitsyn AU RC/Frolov AU 15.00 40.00
270 Lundqvist AU RC/Hask AU 25.00 60.00
271 Meszaros AU RC/Redden AU 12.00 30.00
272 Carter AU RC/Thrntn AU 15.00 40.00
273 Richards AU RC/Mdno AU 12.00 30.00
274 Phanf AU RC/Prngr AU/199 30.00 80.00
275 Ovch AU RC/Kovl AU/199 800.00 2000.00
276 Sidney Crosby/199 RC 800.00 1200.00
276B Sidney Crosby SP/23 1400.00 1800.00

2005-06 Upper Deck Rookie Update Inspirations Patch Rookies

*PATCH/25: 1X TO 2.5X BASIC DUAL JSY

2020-21 Upper Deck Rookies Box Set

1 Alexis Lafreniere 1.50 4.00
2 Connor McMichael .75 2.00
3 Olli Juolevi .50 1.25
4 Nick Robertson .75 2.00
5 Liam Foudy .50 1.25
6 Timothy Liljegren .50 1.25
7 Ty Dellandrea .50 1.25
8 Gabe Vilardi .75 2.00
9 Josh Norris .75 2.00
10 Philipp Kurashev .60 1.50
11 Arthur Kaliyev .75 2.00
13 Ty Smith .75 2.00
14 Dylan Cozens .75 2.00
15 K'Andre Miller 1.00 2.50
16 Peyton Krebs .75 2.00
17 Victor Soderstrom .40 1.00
18 Nils Hoglander .50 1.25
19 Ian Mitchell .40 1.00
20 Cal Foote .60 1.50
21 Bowen Byram 1.00 2.50
22 Alexander Romanov .60 1.50
23 Tim Stutzle 1.00 2.50
24 Ilya Sorokin 1.25 3.00
25 Kirill Kaprizov 2.00 5.00

2007 Upper Deck Sportsfest

SF10 Evgeni Malkin 2.00 5.00
SF11 Alex Ovechkin 2.00 5.00
SF12 Sidney Crosby 3.00 6.00

2017-18 Upper Deck Splendor

BDAO Alexander Ovechkin STK AU 80.00 150.00
BDBB Brock Boeser PATCH AU RC 300.00600.00
BDBH Bobby Hull STK AU 30.00 80.00
BDCK Clayton Keller PATCH AU RC 80.00150.00
BDCM Connor McDavid
PATCH AU 300.00 600.00
BDCP Carey Price PAD AU 60.00 150.00
BDDG Doug Gilmour STK AU 40.00 100.00
BDDH Dominik Hasek PAD AU 60.00 150.00
BDDK Duncan Keith PATCH AU 25.00 60.00
BDDU Pierre-Luc Dubois
PATCH AU RC 40.00 100.00
BDEK Erik Karlsson GLV AU 50.00 120.00

BDFM Frank Mahovlich STK AU 30.00 80.00
BDGF Grant Fuhr PAD AU 40.00 100.00
BDGL Guy Lafleur PATCH AU 30.00 80.00
BDHA Dale Hawerchuk STK AU 25.00 60.00
BDHL Henrik Lundqvist PATCH AU 60.00 150.00
BDHU Brett Hull PATCH AU 60.00 150.00
BDJI Jarome Iginla PATCH AU 25.00 60.00
BDJS Joe Sakic PATCH AU 30.00 80.00
BDJT Jonathan Toews PATCH AU 60.00 150.00
BDLD Leon Draisaitl PATCH AU 50.00 120.00
BDMA Anthony Mantha PATCH AU 30.00 80.00
BDMB Martin Brodeur GLV AU 80.00 150.00
BDMC Charlie McAvoy
PATCH AU RC 50.00 120.00
BDML Mario Lemieux JSY AU 150.00 250.00
BDMM Mark Messier STK AU 50.00 120.00
BDMU Matt Murray PATCH AU 50.00 120.00
BDNH Nico Hischier PATCH RC 30.00 80.00
BDNL Nicklas Lidstrom STK AU 100.00 200.00
BDNP Nolan Patrick PATCH RC 30.00 80.00
BDPK Patrick Kane PATCH AU 60.00 150.00
BDPL Patrik Laine PATCH AU 80.00 150.00
BDPR Patrick Roy PAD AU 100.00 200.00
BDRB Ray Bourque STK AU 30.00 80.00
BDRL Roberto Luongo BLKR AU 25.00 60.00
BDSC Sidney Crosby PATCH AU 250.00 350.00
BDSE Tyler Seguin GLV AU 30.00 80.00
BDSS Steven Stamkos PATCH AU 50.00 120.00
BDSY Steve Yzerman STK AU 50.00 120.00
BDTA John Tavares PATCH AU 80.00 150.00
BDTH Joe Thornton PATCH AU 30.00 80.00
BDTS Teemu Selanne STK AU 50.00 120.00
BDVT Vladimir Tarasenko GLV AU 30.00 80.00
BDWG Wayne Gretzky JSY AU 300.00 800.00

2017-18 Upper Deck Splendor Borderless

BLAO Alexander Ovechkin STK AU 80.00 150.00
BLBB Brock Boeser PATCH AU 350.00 450.00
BLBH Bobby Hull STK AU 30.00 80.00
BLCK Clayton Keller PATCH AU 80.00 150.00
BLCM Connor McDavid PATCH AU 250.00350.00
BLCP Carey Price PAD AU 60.00 150.00
BLDG Doug Gilmour STK AU 40.00 100.00
BLDH Dominik Hasek PAD AU 60.00 150.00
BLDK Duncan Keith PATCH AU 25.00 60.00
BLDU Pierre-Luc Dubois PATCH AU 40.00100.00
BLEK Erik Karlsson GLV AU 50.00 120.00
BLFM Frank Mahovlich STK AU 30.00 80.00
BLGF Grant Fuhr PAD AU 40.00 100.00
BLGL Guy Lafleur PATCH AU 30.00 80.00
BLHA Dale Hawerchuk STK AU 25.00 60.00
BLHL Henrik Lundqvist PATCH AU 60.00 150.00
BLHU Brett Hull GLV AU 60.00 150.00
BLJI Jarome Iginla PATCH AU 25.00 60.00
BLJS Joe Sakic PATCH AU 30.00 80.00
BLJT Jonathan Toews PATCH AU 60.00 150.00
BLLD Leon Draisaitl PATCH AU 50.00 120.00
BLMA Anthony Mantha PATCH AU 30.00 80.00
BLMB Martin Brodeur GLV AU 80.00 150.00
BLMC Charlie McAvoy PATCH AU 50.00 120.00
BLML Mario Lemieux JSY AU 100.00 200.00
BLMM Mark Messier STK AU 50.00 120.00
BLMU Matt Murray PATCH AU 50.00 120.00
BLNH Nico Hischier PATCH 30.00 80.00
BLNL Nicklas Lidstrom STK AU 60.00 150.00
BLNP Nolan Patrick PATCH 30.00 80.00
BLPK Patrick Kane PATCH AU 60.00 150.00
BLPL Patrik Laine PATCH AU 80.00 150.00
BLPR Patrick Roy PAD AU 100.00 200.00
BLRB Ray Bourque STK AU 30.00 80.00
BLRL Roberto Luongo BLKR AU 25.00 60.00
BLSC Sidney Crosby PATCH AU 200.00 300.00
BLSE Tyler Seguin GLV AU 30.00 80.00
BLSS Steven Stamkos PATCH AU 50.00 120.00
BLSY Steve Yzerman STK AU 50.00 120.00
BLTA John Tavares PATCH AU 80.00 150.00
BLTH Joe Thornton PATCH AU 30.00 80.00
BLTS Teemu Selanne STK AU 50.00 120.00
BLVT Vladimir Tarasenko GLV AU 30.00 80.00
BLWG Wayne Gretzky JSY AU 300.00 800.00

2017-18 Upper Deck Splendor Showpieces

SPAD Alex Delvecchio STK AU 30.00 80.00
SPAO Alexander Ovechkin TAPE AU 60.00150.00
SPBB Bob Baun SKT AU 60.00 150.00
SPBO Brock Boeser STK AU 100.00 250.00
SPBO Johnny Bower STK AU 80.00 150.00
SPCC Chris Chelios STK AU 50.00 120.00
SPCN Cam Neely STK AU 50.00 120.00
SPDA Dave Andreychuk STK AU 40.00 100.00
SPDH Dominik Hasek TAPE AU 60.00 150.00
SPDS Darryl Sittler STK AU 40.00 100.00
SPEK Erik Karlsson STK AU 50.00 120.00
SPFM Frank Mahovlich TAPE AU 40.00 100.00
SPFP Felix Potvin STK AU 60.00 150.00
SPGL Guy Lafleur TAPE AU 50.00 120.00
SPJB Jean Beliveau STK 40.00 100.00
SPJK Jari Kurri STK AU 25.00 60.00
SPJS Joe Sakic TAPE AU 50.00 120.00
SPJV John Vanbiesbrouck STK AU 40.00 100.00
SPLI Pelle Lindbergh STK 60.00 150.00
SPLR Larry Robinson STK AU 40.00 100.00
SPMB Martin Brodeur STK AU 100.00 200.00
SPMC Charlie McAvoy STK AU 80.00 150.00
SPMD Marcel Dionne STK AU 25.00 60.00
SPML Mario Lemieux TAPE AU 150.00 250.00
SPPC Paul Coffey STK AU 100.00 200.00
SPPP Pierre Pilote STK 20.00 50.00
SPPR Patrick Roy TAPE AU 100.00 200.00
SPRB Ray Bourque STK AU 40.00 100.00
SPRL Roberto Luongo GLV AU 40.00 100.00
SPSM Stan Mikita STK 20.00 50.00
SPSY Steve Yzerman TAPE AU 50.00 120.00
SPTB Tom Barrasso BLKR AU 25.00 60.00
SPTS Teemu Selanne TAPE AU 80.00 150.00
SPWG Wayne Gretzky STK AU 300.00 800.00

2017-18 Upper Deck Splendor Splendid Signatures

SAAO Alexander Ovechkin 100.00 250.00
SABB Bobby Orr 150.00 250.00
SABO Bobby Orr 150.00 250.00
SABS Borje Salming 40.00 100.00
SACM Connor McDavid 350.00 450.00
SACP Carey Price 50.00 125.00
SADG Doug Gilmour 30.00 80.00
SADH Dale Hawerchuk 30.00 80.00
SADP Denis Potvin 25.00 60.00
SAEB Ed Belfour 30.00 80.00
SAEK Erik Karlsson 30.00 80.00
SAHL Henrik Lundqvist 60.00 150.00
SAJT Jonathan Toews 40.00 100.00
SALM Lanny McDonald 25.00 60.00
SAMB Mike Bossy 25.00 60.00
SAML Mario Lemieux 100.00 250.00
SAMM Mark Messier 50.00 125.00
SANL Nicklas Lidstrom 25.00 60.00
SANU Norm Ullman 25.00 60.00
SAOR Bobby Orr 100.00 250.00
SAPE Phil Esposito 40.00 100.00
SAPH Phil Housley 20.00 50.00
SAPK Patrick Kane 50.00 125.00
SAPM Patrick Marleau 25.00 60.00
SAPR Patrick Roy 60.00 150.00
SASC Sidney Crosby 100.00 250.00
SASS Steven Stamkos 50.00 125.00
SASY Steve Yzerman 60.00 150.00
SAWC Wendel Clark 30.00 80.00
SAWG Wayne Gretzky 250.00 600.00

2017-18 Upper Deck Splendor Splendid Starts

SSTAT Alex Tuch 30.00 80.00
SSTBB Brock Boeser 30.00 80.00
SSTCK Clayton Keller 30.00 80.00
SSTCM Charlie McAvoy 30.00 80.00
SSTNH Nico Hischier 40.00 100.00
SSTNP Nolan Patrick 25.00 60.00
SSTPD Pierre-Luc Dubois 20.00 50.00

2019-20 Upper Deck Splendor

SPAB Aleksander Barkov PATCH AU 60.00150.00
SPAM Auston Matthews PATCH AU 200.00500.00
SPAO Alex Ovechkin PATCH 60.00 150.00
SPAP Artemi Panarin PATCH AU 150.00 400.00
SPBH Bobby Hull AU 40.00 100.00
SPBO Bobby Orr AU 60.00 150.00
SPCG Claude Giroux PATCH 40.00 100.00
SPCH Connor Hellebuyck PATCH AU 30.0080.00
SPCM Connor McDavid PATCH AU 200.00500.00
SPCP Carey Price PATCH AU 80.00 200.00
SPDK Dominik Kubalik
PATCH AU RC 80.00 200.00
SPDP David Pastrnak PATCH AU 100.00 250.00
SPDS Daniel Sedin PATCH AU 50.00 125.00
SPGI John Gibson PATCH AU 40.00 100.00
SPGL Cody Glass PATCH AU RC 60.00 150.00
SPHS Henrik Sedin PATCH AU 50.00 125.00
SPIM Ilya Mikheyev PATCH AU RC 40.00 100.00
SPJC John Carlson PATCH 25.00 60.00
SPJG Jake Guentzel PATCH AU 60.00 150.00
SPJH Jack Hughes PATCH AU RC 250.00 600.00
SPJT John Tavares PATCH AU 60.00 150.00
SPKD Kirby Dach PATCH AU RC 80.00 200.00
SPMB Martin Brodeur PATCH AU 150.00 400.00
SPMF Morgan Frost PATCH AU RC 60.00 150.00
SPMH Miro Heiskanen PATCH AU 50.00 120.00
SPNM Nathan MacKinnon PATCH 60.00 150.00
SPNS Nick Suzuki PATCH AU RC 300.00 800.00
SPPR Patrick Roy GLV AU 100.00 250.00
SPQH Quinn Hughes
PATCH AU RC 200.00 500.00
SPRL Roberto Luongo PATCH AU 60.00 150.00
SPRP Ryan Poehling PATCH AU RC 30.00 80.00
SPTC Thomas Chabot PATCH AU 25.00 60.00
SPVO Victor Olofsson
PATCH AU RC 80.00 200.00
SPWG Wayne Gretzky AU 500.00 1200.00

2015-16 Upper Deck Star Rookies

1 Connor McDavid 15.00 40.00
2 Mike Condon .75 2.00
3 Sam Bennett 2.50 6.00
4 Colton Parayko 1.25 3.00
5 Artemi Panarin 3.00 8.00
6 Joonas Donskoi .75 2.00
7 Max Domi 1.50 4.00
8 Nikolaj Ehlers 1.50 4.00
9 Colin Miller .60 1.50
10 Noah Hanifin 1.25 3.00
11 Robby Fabbri 1.00 2.50
12 Dylan Larkin 2.50 6.00
13 Nicolas Petan .75 2.00
14 Mikko Rantanen 4.00 10.00
15 Daniel Sprong 1.00 2.50
16 Devin Shore .75 2.00
17 Jake Virtanen 1.00 2.50
18 Mattias Janmark .75 2.00
19 Matt O'Connor .60 1.50
20 Andreas Athanasiou 2.00 5.00
21 Jared McCann 1.00 2.50
22 Viktor Svedberg .60 1.50
23 Tyler Randell .75 2.00
24 Jordan Weal .50 1.25
25 Jack Eichel 3.00 8.00

2015-16 Upper Deck Star Rookies Autographs

COMPLETE SET (24)

2021-22 Upper Deck Star Rookies

1 Cole Caufield 3.00 8.00
2 Trevor Zegras 1.50 4.00
3 Jeremy Swayman 2.50 6.00
4 Alex Newhook 1.25 3.00
5 Spencer Knight 1.50 4.00
6 Grigori Denisenko 1.00 2.50
7 Jamie Drysdale 1.25 3.00
8 Quinton Byfield 2.00 5.00
9 Calen Addison .75 2.00
10 Ross Colton 1.00 2.50
11 Shane Pinto 1.25 3.00
12 Alex Barre-Boulet .75 2.00
13 Jesse Ylonen .75 2.00
14 Zac Jones 1.00 2.50
15 Alexander Holtz 1.25 3.00
16 Nils Lundkvist .60 1.50
17 Cole Perfetti 1.50 4.00
18 Moritz Seider 2.00 5.00
19 Vasily Podkolzin 1.00 2.50
20 Lucas Raymond 2.50 6.00
21 Philip Tomasino 1.00 2.50
22 Anton Lundell 1.50 4.00
23 Mason McTavish 1.50 4.00
24 William Eklund 2.00 5.00
25 Jake Neighbours 1.50 4.00

2021-22 Upper Deck Star Rookies Autographs

1 Cole Caufield 30.00 80.00
2 Trevor Zegras 15.00 40.00
3 Jeremy Swayman 25.00 60.00
4 Alex Newhook 12.00 30.00
5 Spencer Knight 15.00 40.00
6 Grigori Denisenko 10.00 25.00
7 Jamie Drysdale 12.00 30.00
8 Quinton Byfield 20.00 50.00
9 Calen Addison 8.00 20.00
10 Ross Colton 10.00 25.00
11 Shane Pinto 12.00 30.00
12 Alex Barre-Boulet 8.00 20.00
13 Jesse Ylonen 8.00 20.00
14 Zac Jones 10.00 25.00
15 Alexander Holtz 12.00 30.00
16 Nils Lundkvist 6.00 15.00
17 Cole Perfetti 15.00 40.00
18 Moritz Seider 20.00 50.00
19 Vasily Podkolzin 10.00 25.00
20 Lucas Raymond 25.00 60.00
21 Philip Tomasino 10.00 25.00
22 Anton Lundell 15.00 40.00
23 Mason McTavish 15.00 40.00
24 William Eklund 20.00 50.00
25 Jake Neighbours 15.00 40.00

2022-23 Upper Deck Star Rookies

1 Shane Wright RC 2.00 5.00
2 Juraj Slafkovsky RC 4.00 10.00
3 Matt Boldy RC 2.50 6.00
4 Owen Power RC 1.50 4.00
5 Matty Beniers RC 2.00 5.00
6 Kent Johnson RC 1.50 4.00
7 Jake Sanderson RC 2.00 5.00
8 Jack Quinn RC 1.25 3.00
9 Lukas Reichel RC 1.50 4.00
10 Elmer Soderblom RC 1.50 4.00
11 Braden Schneider RC 1.25 3.00
12 Brandt Clarke RC 1.50 4.00
13 Dylan Guenther RC 2.00 5.00
14 Trey Fix-Wolansky RC .75 2.00
15 Jacob Perreault RC .75 2.00
16 Nick Abruzzese RC .75 2.00
17 Mads Sogaard RC 1.00 2.50
18 Matias Maccelli RC 1.25 3.00
19 Lukas Dostal RC 1.50 4.00
20 Dylan Samberg RC .75 2.00
21 Isaac Ratcliffe RC .75 2.00
22 Dylan Holloway RC 1.50 4.00
23 Kaedan Korczak RC .60 1.50
24 Andrei Kuzmenko RC 1.50 4.00
25 Pyotr Kochetkov RC 1.50 4.00

2022-23 Upper Deck Star Rookies Blue

*BLUE: .5X TO 1.2X BASIC

2022-23 Upper Deck Star Rookies Gold

*GOLD: 1X TO 2.5X BASIC

2022-23 Upper Deck Star Rookies Red

*RED: 2X TO 5X BASIC

2022-23 Upper Deck Star Rookies Autographs

1 Shane Wright A 25.00 60.00
3 Matt Boldy B 30.00 80.00
4 Owen Power C 80.00 200.00
6 Kent Johnson C 20.00 50.00
7 Jake Sanderson C 25.00 60.00
8 Jack Quinn C 15.00 40.00
9 Lukas Reichel C 20.00 50.00
12 Brandt Clarke C 20.00 50.00
13 Dylan Guenther C 25.00 60.00
14 Trey Fix-Wolansky D 10.00 25.00
15 Jacob Perreault C 10.00 25.00
17 Mads Sogaard D 12.00 30.00
19 Lukas Dostal C 20.00 50.00
20 Dylan Samberg D 10.00 25.00
21 Isaac Ratcliffe D 10.00 25.00
22 Dylan Holloway C 20.00 50.00
23 Kaedan Korczak D 8.00 20.00
24 Andrei Kuzmenko C 20.00 50.00
25 Pyotr Kochetkov D 20.00 50.00

2023-24 Upper Deck Star Rookies

1 Connor Bedard RC 15.00 40.00
2 Adam Fantilli RC 3.00 8.00
3 Logan Cooley RC 3.00 8.00
4 Matthew Knies RC 4.00 10.00
5 Luke Evangelista RC 1.50 4.00
6 Brock Faber RC 2.50 6.00
7 Leo Carlsson RC 3.00 8.00
8 Ridly Greig RC 1.50 4.00
9 Owen Beck RC 1.50 4.00
10 Yaroslav Askarov RC 2.50 6.00
11 Matthew Coronato RC 1.50 4.00
12 Matthew Poitras RC 2.00 5.00
13 Tyson Foerster RC 2.00 5.00
14 Devon Levi RC 2.50 6.00
15 Simon Edvinsson RC 2.00 5.00
16 Kevin Korchinski RC 1.50 4.00
17 Vincent Desharnais RC 1.25 3.00
18 Samuel Bolduc RC 1.00 2.50
19 Akito Hirose RC .75 2.00
20 Will Cuylle RC 1.50 4.00
21 Pavel Mintyukov RC 1.50 4.00
22 Tye Kartye RC 1.50 4.00
23 Fraser Minten RC 2.00 5.00
24 Marco Kasper RC 2.50 6.00
25 Zach Benson RC 1.50 4.00

2023-24 Upper Deck Star Rookies Blue

1 Connor Bedard 60.00 150.00

2023-24 Upper Deck Star Rookies Gold

1 Connor Bedard 250.00 600.00

2023-24 Upper Deck Star Rookies Red

1 Connor Bedard 400.00 1000.00

2023-24 Upper Deck Star Rookies Autographs

1 Connor Bedard SP 1200.00 3000.00
3 Logan Cooley SP 40.00 100.00
4 Matthew Knies 50.00 125.00
5 Luke Evangelista 20.00 50.00
6 Brock Faber 60.00 150.00
7 Leo Carlsson SP 60.00 150.00
8 Ridly Greig 20.00 50.00
9 Owen Beck 20.00 50.00
10 Yaroslav Askarov 30.00 80.00
11 Matthew Coronato 20.00 50.00
12 Matthew Poitras 40.00 100.00
13 Tyson Foerster 25.00 60.00
15 Simon Edvinsson 25.00 60.00
16 Kevin Korchinski 20.00 50.00
20 Will Cuylle 20.00 50.00
21 Pavel Mintyukov 20.00 50.00
22 Tye Kartye 20.00 50.00
23 Fraser Minten 25.00 60.00
24 Marco Kasper 30.00 80.00
25 Zach Benson 30.00 80.00

2024-25 Upper Deck Star Rookies

1 Cutter Gauthier RC 1.50 4.00
2 Logan Stankoven RC 1.50 4.00
3 Frank Nazar RC 2.00 5.00
4 Bradly Nadeau RC 1.00 2.50
5 Brennan Othmann RC 1.00 2.50
6 Gavin Brindley RC .60 1.50
7 Jesper Wallstedt RC 1.50 4.00
8 Lane Hutson RC 3.00 8.00
9 Liam Ohgren RC 1.25 3.00
10 Olen Zellweger RC 1.25 3.00
11 Josh Doan RC 1.00 2.50
12 Matt Rempe RC 1.25 3.00
13 Macklin Celebrini RC 3.00 8.00
14 Will Smith RC 2.00 5.00
15 Matvei Michkov RC 2.50 6.00
16 Jett Luchanko RC 1.25 3.00
17 Seamus Casey RC .75 2.00
18 Rutger McGroarty RC 1.25 3.00
19 Conor Geekie RC 1.25 3.00
20 Calum Ritchie RC .75 2.00
21 Maxim Tsyplakov RC 1.00 2.50
22 Jonathan Lekkerimaki RC 1.50 4.00
23 Samuel Honzek RC .60 1.50
24 Joel Blomqvist RC .75 2.00
25 Zachary L'Heureux RC .75 2.00

2024-25 Upper Deck Star Rookies Blue

*BLUE: .6X TO 1.5X BASIC

2024-25 Upper Deck Star Rookies Gold

*GOLD/249: 3X TO 8X BASIC
13 Macklin Celebrini 30.00 80.00

2024-25 Upper Deck Star Rookies Red

*RED/75: 5X TO 12X BASIC
13 Macklin Celebrini 60.00 150.00

2024-25 Upper Deck Star Rookies Autographs

1 Cutter Gauthier 25.00 60.00
2 Logan Stankoven 25.00 60.00
3 Frank Nazar 30.00 80.00
4 Bradly Nadeau 15.00 40.00
5 Brennan Othmann 15.00 40.00
7 Jesper Wallstedt 25.00 60.00
9 Liam Ohgren 20.00 50.00
10 Olen Zellweger 20.00 50.00
11 Josh Doan 15.00 40.00
12 Matt Rempe 20.00 50.00
16 Jett Luchanko 20.00 50.00
17 Seamus Casey 12.00 30.00
18 Rutger McGroarty 20.00 50.00
19 Conor Geekie 20.00 50.00
20 Calum Ritchie 12.00 30.00
21 Maxim Tsyplakov 15.00 40.00
22 Jonathan Lekkerimaki 25.00 60.00
24 Joel Blomqvist 12.00 30.00
25 Zachary L'Heureux 12.00 30.00

2019-20 Upper Deck Stature

1 Auston Matthews 4.00 10.00
2 Alex Ovechkin 4.00 10.00
3 Blake Wheeler 1.00 2.50
4 Connor McDavid 5.00 12.00
5 Anders Lee .75 2.00
6 Elias Pettersson 1.50 4.00
7 Mikko Rantanen 2.50 6.00
8 Jonathan Drouin .75 2.00
9 Vladimir Tarasenko 1.25 3.00
10 Thomas Chabot 1.00 2.50
11 Mark Scheifele 1.50 4.00
12 Jack Eichel 1.50 4.00
13 Artemi Panarin 2.00 5.00
14 John Carlson 1.00 2.50
15 Eric Staal 1.00 2.50
16 Brent Burns 1.00 2.50
17 Alex DeBrincat 1.25 3.00
18 Jesperi Kotkaniemi 1.00 2.50
19 Sebastian Aho 1.50 4.00
20 Patrice Bergeron 1.25 3.00
21 Steven Stamkos 2.00 5.00
22 Mathew Barzal 1.25 3.00
23 Carter Hart 1.00 2.50
24 William Karlsson 1.25 3.00
25 Mitch Marner 1.50 4.00
26 Matthew Tkachuk 2.00 5.00
27 Jonathan Toews 1.50 4.00
28 Ryan O'Reilly 1.00 2.50
29 Anthony Mantha .75 2.00
30 Patrick Kane 2.00 5.00
31 Jake Guentzel 1.50 4.00
32 Drew Doughty 1.25 3.00
33 Phil Kessel 1.00 2.50
34 Jonathan Quick 1.25 3.00
35 Mark Stone 1.25 3.00
36 Brad Marchand 2.00 5.00
37 Henrik Lundqvist 2.50 6.00
38 Joe Thornton 1.50 4.00
39 Nathan MacKinnon 4.00 10.00
40 Evgeni Malkin 2.00 5.00
41 Tyler Seguin 1.25 3.00
42 Cam Atkinson 1.00 2.50
43 John Gibson 1.00 2.50
44 David Pastrnak 2.50 6.00
45 Matt Dumba .60 1.50
46 Tuukka Rask 1.25 3.00
47 Sergei Bobrovsky 1.50 4.00
48 Rasmus Dahlin 1.25 3.00
49 Johnny Gaudreau 1.50 4.00
50 Sidney Crosby 4.00 10.00
51 Andrei Vasilevskiy 1.50 4.00
52 Oliver Ekman-Larsson 1.00 2.50
53 Zach Werenski 1.50 4.00
54 Brock Boeser 1.25 3.00
55 Roman Josi 1.00 2.50
56 Seth Jones 1.00 2.50
57 Dylan Larkin 1.25 3.00
58 John Tavares 1.50 4.00
59 Marc-Andre Fleury 2.00 5.00
60 Taylor Hall 1.00 2.50
61 Brady Tkachuk 1.50 4.00
62 Ben Bishop .75 2.00
63 Jordan Binnington 1.50 4.00
64 Carey Price 2.00 5.00
65 Joe Pavelski 1.25 3.00
66 Nico Hischier 1.50 4.00
67 Erik Karlsson 1.25 3.00
68 Rickard Rakell .75 2.00
69 Matt Murray 1.00 2.50
70 Claude Giroux 1.00 2.50
71 Leon Draisaitl 3.00 8.00
72 Jonathan Marchessault 1.25 3.00
73 Brayden Point 1.25 3.00
74 Teuvo Teravainen 1.00 2.50
75 Aleksander Barkov 1.50 4.00
76 Patrick Roy 5.00 12.00
77 Jarome Iginla 1.25 3.00
78 Glenn Hall 1.00 2.50
79 Willie O'Ree 1.25 3.00
80 Jaromir Jagr 3.00 8.00
81 Larry Robinson 1.00 2.50
82 Martin Brodeur 2.50 6.00
83 Bobby Hull 2.50 6.00
84 Jean Beliveau 1.00 2.50
85 Mark Messier 2.00 5.00
86 Steve Yzerman 2.50 6.00
87 Phil Esposito 1.50 4.00
88 Joe Sakic 2.00 5.00
89 Ray Bourque 1.50 4.00
90 Bobby Orr 4.00 10.00
91 Guy Lafleur 1.25 3.00
92 Teemu Selanne 2.00 5.00
93 Mike Modano 1.50 4.00
94 Grant Fuhr 1.50 4.00
95 Chris Chelios 1.00 2.50
96 Keith Tkachuk 1.00 2.50
97 Cam Neely 1.00 2.50
98 Peter Forsberg 2.00 5.00
99 Wayne Gretzky 8.00 20.00
100 Doug Gilmour 1.25 3.00
101 Kaapo Kakko RC 2.50 6.00
102 Adam Boqvist RC 1.50 4.00
103 Otto Koivula RC 1.00 2.50
104 Jack Studnicka RC 1.50 4.00
105 Cayden Primeau RC 3.00 8.00
106 Morgan Frost RC 2.50 6.00
107 Klim Kostin RC 1.50 4.00
108 Jonathan Davidsson RC 1.00 2.50
109 Eetu Luostarinen RC 1.50 4.00
110 Kaapo Kahkonen RC 10.00 25.00
111 Alexander Volkov RC 1.25 3.00
112 Julien Gauthier RC 1.50 4.00
113 Adam Fox RC 4.00 10.00
114 Joel Farabee RC 2.50 6.00
115 Kaden Fulcher RC 1.50 4.00
116 Nick Caamano RC 1.25 3.00
117 Trevor Moore RC 1.25 3.00
118 Quinn Hughes RC 8.00 20.00
119 Joakim Nygard RC 1.25 3.00
120 Gerald Mayhew RC 1.25 3.00
121 Mackenzie MacEachern RC 1.50 4.00
122 Tobias Bjornfot RC 1.50 4.00
123 Rem Pitlick RC 1.50 4.00
124 Cale Makar RC 8.00 20.00
125 Kirby Dach RC 3.00 8.00
126 Lean Bergmann RC 1.25 3.00
127 Aleksi Saarela RC 1.50 4.00
128 Dominik Kubalik RC 3.00 8.00
129 Sam Lafferty RC 1.25 3.00
130 Ryan Kuffner RC 1.25 3.00
131 Elvis Merzlikins RC 3.00 8.00
132 Carter Verhaeghe RC 2.50 6.00
133 John Marino RC 2.50 6.00
134 Kole Sherwood RC 1.50 4.00
135 Kevin Boyle RC 1.50 4.00
136 Dmytro Timashov RC 1.50 4.00
137 Gaetan Haas RC 1.25 3.00
138 Nicolas Hague RC 1.50 4.00
139 Connor Clifton RC 1.50 4.00
140 Colin Blackwell RC 1.50 4.00
141 Scott Sabourin RC 1.25 3.00
142 Ryan Lindgren RC 1.50 4.00
143 Jacob Middleton RC 1.25 3.00
144 Rhett Gardner RC 1.25 3.00
145 Mario Ferraro RC 1.25 3.00
146 Joey Daccord RC 3.00 8.00
147 Martin Fehervary RC 1.25 3.00
148 Carl Grundstrom RC 1.50 4.00
149 Igor Shesterkin RC 12.00 30.00
150 Jack Hughes RC 8.00 20.00
151 Taro Hirose RC 1.50 4.00
152 Joel Persson RC 1.25 3.00
153 Danil Yurtaykin RC 1.25 3.00
154 Alexandre Texier RC 1.50 4.00
155 David Gustafsson RC 1.25 3.00
156 Ilya Mikheyev RC 2.50 6.00
157 Filip Zadina RC 2.50 6.00
158 Karson Kuhlman RC 1.50 4.00
159 Ryan Poehling RC 2.50 6.00
160 Matt Roy RC 1.50 4.00
161 Zack MacEwen RC 1.25 3.00
162 Ville Heinola RC 2.00 5.00
163 Conor Timmins RC 1.50 4.00
164 Erik Brannstrom RC 1.50 4.00
165 Nick Suzuki RC 6.00 15.00
166 Jesper Boqvist RC 1.25 3.00
167 Libor Hajek RC 1.25 3.00
168 Jimmy Schuldt RC 1.25 3.00
169 Josh Brown RC 1.25 3.00
170 Trent Frederic RC 1.50 4.00
171 Blake Lizotte RC 1.50 4.00
172 Emil Bemstrom RC 1.50 4.00
173 Victor Olofsson RC 3.00 8.00
174 Max Veronneau RC 1.25 3.00
175 Barrett Hayton RC 3.00 8.00
176 Jakob Lilja RC 1.25 3.00
177 Carsen Twarynski RC 1.25 3.00
178 Oliver Wahlstrom RC 2.50 6.00
179 Zach Senyshyn RC 1.50 4.00
180 Brady Keeper RC 1.50 4.00
181 Cale Fleury RC 2.00 5.00
182 Dennis Gilbert RC 1.25 3.00
183 Brandon Gignac RC 1.25 3.00
184 Givani Smith RC 1.25 3.00
185 Joel L'Esperance RC 1.50 4.00
186 Connor Bunnaman RC 1.25 3.00
187 Teddy Blueger RC 1.50 4.00
188 Vitaly Abramov RC 1.50 4.00
189 Riley Stillman RC 1.50 4.00
190 Dante Fabbro RC 1.50 4.00
191 Rudolfs Balcers RC 1.50 4.00
192 Nikita Gusev RC 2.50 6.00
193 William Borgen RC 1.25 3.00
194 Guillaume Brisebois RC 1.50 4.00
195 Rasmus Sandin RC 2.50 6.00
196 Max Jones RC 1.50 4.00
197 Nikolai Prokhorkin RC 1.25 3.00
198 Nico Sturm RC 1.25 3.00
199 Noah Dobson RC 4.00 10.00
200 Cody Glass RC 2.50 6.00

2019-20 Upper Deck Stature Blue

*BLUE: 1.5X TO 4X BASIC
50 Sidney Crosby 30.00 80.00
76 Patrick Roy 25.00 60.00
80 Jaromir Jagr 25.00 60.00
99 Wayne Gretzky 20.00 50.00
149 Igor Shesterkin 50.00 125.00
165 Nick Suzuki 30.00 80.00

2019-20 Upper Deck Stature Green

*GREEN: .6X TO 1.5X BASIC
76 Patrick Roy 12.00 30.00

2019-20 Upper Deck Stature Portrait

*PORTRAIT: 1X TO 2.5X BASIC
*PORT RC: 1.25X TO 3X BASIC RC
6 Elias Pettersson 6.00 15.00
120 Gerald Mayhew 8.00 20.00

2019-20 Upper Deck Stature Red

*RED: .75X TO 2X BASIC
50 Sidney Crosby 25.00 60.00
76 Patrick Roy 15.00 40.00
80 Jaromir Jagr 20.00 50.00
149 Igor Shesterkin 30.00 80.00
165 Nick Suzuki 25.00 60.00

2019-20 Upper Deck Stature Autographs

1 Auston Matthews A 80.00 200.00
4 Connor McDavid A 120.00 300.00
5 Anders Lee B 4.00 10.00
10 Thomas Chabot E 5.00 12.00
13 Artemi Panarin C 40.00 100.00
15 Eric Staal D 5.00 12.00
16 Brent Burns C 5.00 12.00
18 Jesperi Kotkaniemi C 5.00 12.00
23 Carter Hart D 20.00 50.00
36 Brad Marchand C 10.00 25.00
38 Joe Thornton B 8.00 20.00
41 Tyler Seguin D 6.00 15.00
42 Cam Atkinson E 5.00 12.00
43 John Gibson E 5.00 12.00
47 Sergei Bobrovsky E 8.00 20.00
51 Andrei Vasilevskiy D 12.00 30.00
54 Brock Boeser C 6.00 15.00
58 John Tavares B 15.00 40.00
59 Marc-Andre Fleury C 30.00 80.00
62 Ben Bishop E 4.00 10.00
64 Carey Price A 60.00 150.00
65 Joe Pavelski D 6.00 15.00
76 Patrick Roy A 80.00 200.00
77 Jarome Iginla B 12.00 30.00
78 Glenn Hall A 5.00 12.00
79 Willie O'Ree C 10.00 25.00
80 Jaromir Jagr A 80.00 200.00
81 Larry Robinson B 5.00 12.00
82 Martin Brodeur A 30.00 80.00
83 Bobby Hull B 12.00 30.00
85 Mark Messier A 30.00 80.00
86 Steve Yzerman A 80.00 200.00
88 Joe Sakic A 40.00 100.00
90 Bobby Orr A 60.00 150.00
92 Teemu Selanne B 40.00 100.00
94 Grant Fuhr B 25.00 60.00
95 Chris Chelios B 25.00 60.00
96 Keith Tkachuk C 5.00 12.00
98 Peter Forsberg B 60.00 150.00
99 Wayne Gretzky A 300.00 800.00
100 Doug Gilmour B 20.00 50.00
102 Adam Boqvist 5.00 12.00
103 Otto Koivula 3.00 8.00
105 Cayden Primeau 20.00 50.00
106 Morgan Frost 8.00 20.00
107 Klim Kostin 5.00 12.00
108 Jonathan Davidsson 3.00 8.00
109 Eetu Luostarinen 5.00 12.00
112 Julien Gauthier 5.00 12.00
113 Adam Fox 60.00 150.00
114 Joel Farabee 20.00 50.00
115 Kaden Fulcher 5.00 12.00
117 Trevor Moore 4.00 10.00
118 Quinn Hughes 30.00 80.00
121 Mackenzie MacEachern 5.00 12.00
123 Rem Pitlick 5.00 12.00
124 Cale Makar 80.00 200.00
125 Kirby Dach 25.00 60.00
126 Lean Bergmann 4.00 10.00
127 Aleksi Saarela 5.00 12.00
128 Dominik Kubalik 20.00 50.00
129 Sam Lafferty 4.00 10.00
130 Ryan Kuffner 4.00 10.00
131 Elvis Merzlikins 15.00 40.00
132 Carter Verhaeghe 8.00 20.00
134 Kole Sherwood 5.00 12.00
138 Nicolas Hague 5.00 12.00
139 Connor Clifton 5.00 12.00
144 Rhett Gardner 4.00 10.00
145 Mario Ferraro 4.00 10.00
146 Joey Daccord 10.00 25.00
148 Carl Grundstrom 5.00 12.00
149 Igor Shesterkin 60.00 150.00
150 Jack Hughes 30.00 80.00
151 Taro Hirose 5.00 12.00
154 Alexandre Texier 5.00 12.00
156 Ilya Mikheyev 8.00 20.00
157 Filip Zadina 8.00 20.00
158 Karson Kuhlman 5.00 12.00
159 Ryan Poehling 8.00 20.00
160 Matt Roy 5.00 12.00
161 Zack MacEwen 4.00 10.00
164 Erik Brannstrom 5.00 12.00
165 Nick Suzuki 60.00 150.00
166 Jesper Boqvist 4.00 10.00
167 Libor Hajek 4.00 10.00
168 Jimmy Schuldt 4.00 10.00
170 Trent Frederic 5.00 12.00
171 Blake Lizotte 5.00 12.00
174 Max Veronneau 4.00 10.00
178 Oliver Wahlstrom 15.00 40.00
179 Zach Senyshyn 5.00 12.00
180 Brady Keeper 5.00 12.00
183 Brandon Gignac 4.00 10.00
184 Givani Smith 4.00 10.00
185 Joel L'Esperance 5.00 12.00
187 Teddy Blueger 5.00 12.00
189 Riley Stillman 5.00 12.00
190 Dante Fabbro 5.00 12.00
191 Rudolfs Balcers 5.00 12.00
192 Nikita Gusev 8.00 20.00
194 Guillaume Brisebois 5.00 12.00
196 Max Jones 5.00 12.00
198 Nico Sturm 4.00 10.00
199 Noah Dobson 12.00 30.00
200 Cody Glass 10.00 25.00

2019-20 Upper Deck Stature Autographs Green

*GREEN: .5X TO 1.25X BASIC
1 Auston Matthews/25 100.00 250.00
13 Artemi Panarin/65 40.00 100.00
23 Carter Hart/65 30.00 80.00
36 Brad Marchand/25 15.00 40.00
47 Sergei Bobrovsky/65 15.00 40.00
51 Andrei Vasilevskiy/65 15.00 40.00
58 John Tavares/25 30.00 80.00
59 Marc-Andre Fleury/65 40.00 100.00
65 Joe Pavelski/65 8.00 20.00
76 Patrick Roy/25 100.00 250.00
78 Glenn Hall/65 8.00 20.00
79 Willie O'Ree/65 20.00 50.00
95 Chris Chelios/65 10.00 25.00
100 Doug Gilmour/65 25.00 60.00
105 Cayden Primeau/85 30.00 80.00
106 Morgan Frost/85 15.00 40.00
114 Joel Farabee/85 30.00 80.00
125 Kirby Dach/85 30.00 80.00
131 Elvis Merzlikins/85 20.00 50.00
149 Igor Shesterkin/85 120.00 300.00
150 Jack Hughes/85 40.00 100.00
156 Ilya Mikheyev/85 15.00 40.00
165 Nick Suzuki/85 80.00 200.00
178 Oliver Wahlstrom/85 25.00 60.00
200 Cody Glass/85 15.00 40.00

2019-20 Upper Deck Stature Century Momentous

*GREEN: .5X TO 1.25X BASIC
*RED: .75X TO 2X BASIC
CM1 Wayne Gretzky 12.00 30.00
CM2 Glenn Hall 3.00 8.00
CM3 Phil Esposito 3.00 8.00
CM4 Patrick Kane 4.00 10.00
CM5 Chris Chelios 3.00 8.00
CM6 Teemu Selanne 4.00 10.00
CM7 Joe Sakic 4.00 10.00
CM8 Guy Lafleur 3.00 8.00
CM9 Jaromir Jagr 6.00 15.00
CM10 Doug Gilmour 2.50 6.00
CM11 Peter Forsberg 4.00 10.00
CM12 Larry Robinson 3.00 8.00
CM13 Grant Fuhr 3.00 8.00
CM14 Alex Ovechkin 8.00 20.00
CM15 Patrick Roy 5.00 12.00
CM16 Mario Lemieux 8.00 20.00
CM17 Mike Modano 3.00 8.00
CM18 Bobby Hull 5.00 12.00
CM19 Martin Brodeur 5.00 12.00
CM20 Steve Yzerman 5.00 12.00
CM21 Ray Bourque 3.00 8.00
CM22 Mark Messier 4.00 10.00
CM23 Jean Beliveau 3.00 8.00
CM24 Sidney Crosby 8.00 20.00
CM25 Bobby Orr 8.00 20.00

2019-20 Upper Deck Stature Esteemed

*GREEN: .75X TO 2X BASIC
E1 Connor McDavid 6.00 15.00
E2 Blake Wheeler 1.25 3.00
E3 Marc-Andre Fleury 2.50 6.00
E4 Brad Marchand 2.50 6.00
E5 Joe Thornton 2.00 5.00
E6 Carey Price 2.50 6.00
E7 Jack Eichel 2.00 5.00
E8 Joe Pavelski 1.50 4.00
E9 Nathan MacKinnon 5.00 12.00
E10 Alex Ovechkin 5.00 12.00
E11 Jonathan Quick 1.50 4.00
E12 Steven Stamkos 2.50 6.00

E13 Jonathan Toews 2.00 5.00
E14 Henrik Lundqvist 3.00 8.00
E15 John Tavares 2.00 5.00
E16 Dylan Larkin 1.50 4.00
E17 Patrice Bergeron 1.50 4.00
E18 Claude Giroux 1.25 3.00
E19 Eric Staal 1.25 3.00
E20 Ryan O'Reilly 1.25 3.00
E21 Erik Karlsson 1.50 4.00
E22 Phil Kessel 1.25 3.00
E23 David Pastrnak 3.00 8.00
E24 Patrick Kane 2.50 6.00
E25 Sidney Crosby 5.00 12.00

2019-20 Upper Deck Stature Esteemed Red

*RED: 1X TO 2.5X BASIC INSERTS
E23 David Pastrnak 6.00 15.00

2019-20 Upper Deck Stature Esteemed Autographs

E1 Connor McDavid A 120.00 300.00
E3 Marc-Andre Fleury B 30.00 80.00
E4 Brad Marchand C 12.00 30.00
E5 Joe Thornton B 8.00 20.00
E8 Joe Pavelski C 10.00 25.00
E15 John Tavares B 20.00 50.00
E19 Eric Staal D 4.00 10.00

2019-20 Upper Deck Stature Esteemed Autographs Green

E4 Brad Marchand 15.00 40.00
E8 Joe Pavelski 15.00 40.00
E15 John Tavares 25.00 60.00
E19 Eric Staal 8.00 20.00

2019-20 Upper Deck Stature Rookie Reliance

*GREEN: .75X TO 2X BASIC
*RED: .75X TO 2X BASIC
RR1 Jack Hughes 6.00 15.00
RR2 Klim Kostin 1.25 3.00
RR3 Morgan Frost 2.00 5.00
RR4 Alexander Volkov 1.00 2.50
RR5 Nikolai Prokhorkin 1.00 2.50
RR6 Cody Glass 2.00 5.00
RR7 Filip Zadina 2.00 5.00
RR8 Max Jones 1.25 3.00
RR9 Tobias Bjornfot 1.25 3.00
RR10 Ilya Mikheyev 2.00 5.00
RR11 Julien Gauthier 1.25 3.00
RR12 Cale Makar 6.00 15.00
RR13 Ville Heinola 1.50 4.00
RR14 Oliver Wahlstrom 2.00 5.00
RR15 Trevor Moore 1.00 2.50
RR16 Dominik Kubalik 2.50 6.00
RR17 Nikita Gusev 2.00 5.00
RR18 Max Veronneau 1.00 2.50
RR19 Carter Verhaeghe 2.00 5.00
RR20 Erik Brannstrom 1.25 3.00
RR21 Adam Boqvist 1.25 3.00
RR22 Joel Farabee 2.00 5.00
RR23 Carl Grundstrom 1.25 3.00
RR24 Taro Hirose 1.25 3.00
RR25 Kaapo Kakko 2.00 5.00
RR26 Mackenzie MacEachern 1.25 3.00
RR27 Brandon Gignac 1.00 2.50
RR28 Elvis Merzlikins 2.50 6.00
RR29 Rudolfs Balcers 1.25 3.00
RR30 Dante Fabbro 1.25 3.00
RR31 Jesper Boqvist 1.00 2.50
RR32 Quinn Hughes 6.00 15.00
RR33 Rasmus Sandin 2.00 5.00
RR34 Dmytro Timashov 1.25 3.00
RR35 Ryan Poehling 2.00 5.00
RR36 Mario Ferraro 1.00 2.50
RR37 Nicolas Hague 1.50 4.00
RR38 Adam Fox 3.00 8.00
RR39 Kirby Dach 2.50 6.00
RR40 Conor Timmins 1.25 3.00
RR41 Sam Lafferty 1.00 2.50
RR42 Gerald Mayhew 1.00 2.50
RR43 Noah Dobson 3.00 8.00
RR44 Cale Fleury 1.50 4.00
RR45 Alexandre Texier 1.25 3.00
RR46 Nick Suzuki 5.00 12.00
RR47 Barrett Hayton 2.50 6.00
RR48 Connor Bunnaman 1.00 2.50
RR49 Connor Clifton 1.25 3.00
RR50 Victor Olofsson 2.50 6.00

2019-20 Upper Deck Stature Rookie Reliance Blue

*BLUE: 1X TO 2.5X BASIC
RR7 Filip Zadina 15.00 40.00
RR32 Quinn Hughes 25.00 60.00

2019-20 Upper Deck Stature Rookie Reliance Autographs

RR1 Jack Hughes A 25.00 60.00
RR2 Klim Kostin C 5.00 12.00
RR3 Morgan Frost C 8.00 20.00
RR6 Cody Glass C 8.00 20.00
RR7 Filip Zadina C 8.00 20.00
RR8 Max Jones C 5.00 12.00
RR10 Ilya Mikheyev C 8.00 20.00
RR11 Julien Gauthier C 5.00 12.00
RR12 Cale Makar B 40.00 100.00
RR14 Oliver Wahlstrom C 8.00 20.00
RR15 Trevor Moore C 4.00 10.00
RR16 Dominik Kubalik C 25.00 60.00
RR17 Nikita Gusev C 8.00 20.00
RR18 Max Veronneau C 4.00 10.00
RR19 Carter Verhaeghe C 8.00 20.00
RR20 Erik Brannstrom C 5.00 12.00
RR21 Adam Boqvist C 5.00 12.00
RR22 Joel Farabee C 8.00 20.00
RR23 Carl Grundstrom C 5.00 12.00
RR24 Taro Hirose C 5.00 12.00
RR26 Mackenzie MacEachern C 5.00 12.00
RR27 Brandon Gignac C 4.00 10.00
RR28 Elvis Merzlikins C 15.00 40.00
RR30 Dante Fabbro C 5.00 12.00
RR31 Jesper Boqvist C 4.00 10.00
RR32 Quinn Hughes B 30.00 80.00
RR35 Ryan Poehling C 8.00 20.00
RR36 Mario Ferraro C 4.00 10.00
RR37 Nicolas Hague C 5.00 12.00
RR38 Adam Fox C 40.00 100.00
RR39 Kirby Dach B 30.00 80.00
RR43 Noah Dobson C 12.00 30.00
RR45 Alexandre Texier C 5.00 12.00
RR46 Nick Suzuki B 20.00 50.00
RR49 Connor Clifton C 5.00 12.00

2019-20 Upper Deck Stature Rookie Reliance Autographs Green

*GREEN: .6X TO 1.5X BASIC
RR12 Cale Makar 80.00 200.00
RR32 Quinn Hughes 50.00 125.00

2020-21 Upper Deck Stature

1 Alex Ovechkin 4.00 10.00
2 Mathew Barzal 1.25 3.00
3 Eric Staal 1.00 2.50
4 Sidney Crosby 4.00 10.00
5 Nathan MacKinnon 4.00 10.00
6 Zach Parise 1.00 2.50
7 Elias Lindholm 1.00 2.50
8 Tomas Hertl 1.00 2.50
9 John Klingberg 1.00 2.50
10 Teuvo Teravainen 1.00 2.50
11 Brady Tkachuk 1.50 4.00
12 Mark Scheifele 1.50 4.00
13 Mackenzie Blackwood 1.00 2.50
14 Jack Eichel 1.50 4.00
15 Evgeni Malkin 2.00 5.00
16 Aleksander Barkov 1.50 4.00
17 Cale Makar 2.50 6.00
18 Ryan Suter .75 2.00
19 Dylan Larkin 1.25 3.00
20 Andrei Vasilevskiy 1.50 4.00
21 Pierre-Luc Dubois .75 2.00
22 Josh Bailey .75 2.00
23 Anze Kopitar 1.50 4.00
24 Brad Marchand 2.00 5.00
25 Brock Boeser 1.25 3.00
26 Auston Matthews 4.00 10.00
27 David Pastrnak 2.50 6.00
28 Oliver Ekman-Larsson 1.00 2.50
29 Ryan O'Reilly 1.00 2.50
30 Nikita Gusev .75 2.00
31 Steven Stamkos 2.00 5.00
32 Carter Hart 1.50 4.00
33 Matthew Tkachuk 2.00 5.00
34 Nikita Kucherov 2.00 5.00
35 John Gibson 1.00 2.50
36 Ilya Samsonov 1.00 2.50
37 Nick Schmaltz .75 2.00
38 Connor Hellebuyck 2.00 5.00
39 Tom Wilson 1.00 2.50
40 Tuukka Rask 1.25 3.00
41 Roman Josi 1.00 2.50
42 Ryan Nugent-Hopkins 1.25 3.00
43 Brent Burns 1.00 2.50
44 Anthony Mantha .75 2.00
45 John Tavares 1.50 4.00
46 Thomas Chabot 1.00 2.50
47 Jonathan Huberdeau 1.25 3.00
48 Jonathan Drouin .75 2.00
49 Travis Konecny 1.00 2.50
50 Connor McDavid 5.00 12.00
51 Igor Shesterkin 2.00 5.00
52 Sebastian Aho 1.50 4.00
53 Jonathan Marchessault 1.25 3.00
54 Dominik Kubalik 1.25 3.00
55 Artemi Panarin 2.00 5.00
56 Leon Draisaitl 3.00 8.00
57 Miro Heiskanen 1.25 3.00
58 Quinn Hughes 2.50 6.00
59 Brayden Schenn 1.00 2.50
60 Patrik Laine 1.50 4.00
61 Brendan Gallagher 1.00 2.50
62 Nico Hischier 1.50 4.00
63 Mark Stone 1.25 3.00
64 Cam Fowler 1.00 2.50
65 Mitch Marner 1.50 4.00
66 Sergei Bobrovsky 1.50 4.00
67 Drew Doughty 1.25 3.00
68 David Perron .75 2.00
69 Andrei Svechnikov 1.25 3.00
70 Jake Guentzel 1.25 3.00
71 Patrick Kane 2.00 5.00
72 Pekka Rinne 1.00 2.50
73 Elias Pettersson 1.50 4.00
74 Elvis Merzlikins 1.00 2.50
75 Carey Price 2.00 5.00
76 Wayne Gretzky 6.00 15.00
77 Pat LaFontaine 1.00 2.50
78 John Vanbiesbrouck 1.00 2.50
79 Dominik Hasek 1.50 4.00
80 Phil Esposito 1.50 4.00
81 Nicklas Lidstrom 1.00 2.50
82 Martin Brodeur 2.50 6.00
83 Billy Smith 1.00 2.50
84 Bobby Orr 4.00 10.00
85 Henrik Sedin 1.25 3.00
86 Gordie Howe 3.00 8.00
87 Martin St. Louis 1.00 2.50
88 Lanny McDonald .75 2.00
89 Guy Lafleur 1.25 3.00
90 Mario Lemieux 4.00 10.00
91 John LeClair 1.00 2.50
92 Patrick Roy 2.50 6.00
93 Daniel Sedin 1.25 3.00
94 Henrik Zetterberg 1.25 3.00
95 Mike Gartner 1.00 2.50
96 Brett Hull 2.00 5.00
97 Peter Bondra 1.00 2.50
98 Steve Yzerman 2.50 6.00
99 Mike Richter 1.00 2.50
100 Gerry Cheevers 1.00 2.50
101 Alexis Lafreniere RC 20.00 50.00
102 Kirill Kaprizov RC 50.00 125.00
103 Jordan Gross RC 1.50 4.00
104 Ty Smith RC 3.00 8.00
105 Callum Booth RC 1.50 4.00
106 Alexander Yelesin RC 1.50 4.00
107 Austin Strand RC 1.50 4.00
108 Sasha Chmelevski RC 1.50 4.00
109 Aleksi Heponiemi RC 2.50 6.00
110 Arthur Kaliyev RC 3.00 8.00
111 Kevin Bahl RC 1.50 4.00
112 Cole Smith RC 1.50 4.00
113 Nicolas Beaudin RC 2.00 5.00
114 Cameron Hillis RC 1.50 4.00
115 Philippe Maillet RC 1.50 4.00
116 Artem Zub RC 1.50 4.00
117 Jack Rathbone RC 2.00 5.00
118 Reese Johnson RC 1.50 4.00
119 Mikhail Maltsev RC 1.50 4.00
120 Stuart Skinner RC 4.00 10.00
121 Drew O'Connor RC 2.00 5.00
122 Kevin Lankinen RC 3.00 8.00
123 Nolan Foote RC 2.00 5.00
124 Joel Hofer RC 2.00 5.00
125 Fredrik Handemark RC 1.50 4.00
126 Alexander Barabanov RC 2.00 5.00
127 Yegor Sharangovich RC 3.00 8.00
128 John Leonard RC 1.50 4.00
129 K'Andre Miller RC 4.00 10.00
130 Mathias Brome RC 1.50 4.00
131 Ilya Sorokin RC 5.00 12.00
132 Tim Stutzle RC 15.00 40.00
133 Logan Stanley RC 2.00 5.00
134 Mikko Lehtonen RC 1.50 4.00
135 Dylan Cozens RC 3.00 8.00
136 Ian Mitchell RC 1.50 4.00
137 Nicolas Meloche RC 1.50 4.00
138 Cal Foote RC 2.50 6.00
139 Nils Hoglander RC 2.00 5.00
140 Alexander Romanov RC 2.50 6.00
141 Pius Suter RC 2.50 6.00
142 Michael DiPietro RC 2.50 6.00
143 Peyton Krebs RC 3.00 8.00
144 Joseph Woll RC 4.00 10.00
145 Alexander True RC 1.50 4.00
146 Matiss Kivlenieks RC 2.50 6.00
147 Gustav Lindstrom RC 1.50 4.00
148 Keegan Kolesar RC 1.50 4.00
149 Mikhail Berdin RC 2.00 5.00
150 Jason Robertson RC 5.00 12.00
151 Artem Zagidulin RC 2.00 5.00
152 Egor Zamula RC 1.50 4.00
153 Martin Kaut RC 2.00 5.00
154 Nikolai Knyzhov RC 1.50 4.00
155 Liam Foudy RC 2.00 5.00
156 Dylan Coghlan RC 2.00 5.00
157 Connor McMichael RC 3.00 8.00
158 Olli Juolevi RC 2.00 5.00
159 Morgan Geekie RC 2.00 5.00
160 Alexander Alexeyev RC 1.50 4.00
161 Alec Regula RC 1.25 3.00
162 Jake Oettinger RC 5.00 12.00
163 Shane Bowers RC 1.50 4.00
164 Jonas Johansson RC 2.00 5.00
165 Victor Soderstrom RC 1.50 4.00
166 Mikey Anderson RC 2.00 5.00
167 Egor Korshkov RC 1.25 3.00
168 MacKenzie Entwistle RC 1.50 4.00
169 Jansen Harkins RC 1.50 4.00
170 Reid Duke RC 2.00 5.00
171 Kieffer Bellows RC 1.50 4.00
172 Alex Belzile RC 1.50 4.00
173 Philip Broberg RC 2.00 5.00
174 Pavel Francouz RC 2.50 6.00
175 Calvin Thurkauf RC 1.50 4.00
176 Maxim Letunov RC 1.50 4.00
177 Kirill Ustimenko RC 1.50 4.00
178 Vitali Kravtsov RC 4.00 10.00
179 Bowen Byram RC 4.00 10.00
180 Ty Dellandrea RC 1.50 4.00
181 Ryan McLeod RC 1.50 4.00
182 Brandon Hagel RC 2.50 6.00
183 Jani Hakanpaa RC 1.25 3.00
184 Gage Quinney RC 1.25 3.00
185 Tyler Benson RC 2.00 5.00
186 Anthony Angello RC 1.50 4.00
187 Gabe Vilardi RC 3.00 8.00
188 Connor Ingram RC 1.50 4.00
189 Joel Kiviranta RC 2.00 5.00
190 Lucas Carlsson RC 1.50 4.00
191 Michael McNiven RC 1.50 4.00
192 Thomas Harley RC 3.00 8.00
193 Timothy Liljegren RC 2.00 5.00
194 Nick Robertson RC 3.00 8.00
195 Josh Norris RC 3.00 8.00
196 Vitek Vanecek RC 3.00 8.00
197 Philipp Kurashev RC 2.50 6.00
198 Jake Evans RC 2.00 5.00
199 Pierre-Olivier Joseph RC 2.00 5.00
200 Hayden Verbeek RC 1.50 4.00

2020-21 Upper Deck Stature Blue

1 Alex Ovechkin 25.00 60.00
26 Auston Matthews 25.00 60.00
92 Patrick Roy 30.00 80.00
102 Kirill Kaprizov 150.00 400.00
131 Ilya Sorokin 30.00 80.00
132 Tim Stutzle 80.00 200.00

2020-21 Upper Deck Stature Green

1 Alex Ovechkin 20.00 50.00
4 Sidney Crosby 20.00 50.00
50 Connor McDavid 40.00 100.00
51 Igor Shesterkin 25.00 60.00
84 Bobby Orr 25.00 60.00
92 Patrick Roy 25.00 60.00
101 Alexis Lafreniere 25.00 60.00
102 Kirill Kaprizov 100.00 250.00
132 Tim Stutzle 25.00 60.00
150 Jason Robertson 40.00 100.00

2020-21 Upper Deck Stature Red

1 Alex Ovechkin 30.00 80.00
17 Cale Makar 40.00 100.00
26 Auston Matthews 30.00 80.00
51 Igor Shesterkin 30.00 80.00
76 Wayne Gretzky 40.00 100.00
101 Alexis Lafreniere 40.00 100.00
102 Kirill Kaprizov 150.00 400.00
132 Tim Stutzle 30.00 80.00
150 Jason Robertson 80.00 200.00

2020-21 Upper Deck Stature Autographs Green

17 Cale Makar 150.00 400.00
50 Connor McDavid 200.00 500.00
132 Tim Stutzle 60.00 150.00

2020-21 Upper Deck Stature Autographs Red

*RED/10-45: X TO X BASIC INSERTS
20 Andrei Vasilevskiy 80.00 200.00
132 Tim Stutzle 80.00 200.00

2020-21 Upper Deck Stature Century Momentous

*GREEN/149: .6X TO 1.5X BASIC INSERTS
*RED/75: .75X TO 2X BASIC INSERTS
*BLUE/25: 1X TO 2.5X BASIC INSERTS
CM1 Mario Lemieux 10.00 25.00
CM2 Steve Yzerman 6.00 15.00
CM3 Mark Messier 5.00 12.00
CM4 Lanny McDonald 2.00 5.00
CM5 Bobby Orr 10.00 25.00
CM6 Dominik Hasek 4.00 10.00
CM7 Mike Gartner 3.00 8.00
CM8 Darryl Sittler 3.00 8.00
CM9 Glenn Hall 2.50 6.00
CM10 Gerry Cheevers 2.50 6.00
CM11 Mike Richter 2.50 6.00
CM12 Henrik Zetterberg 3.00 8.00
CM13 Patrick Roy 6.00 15.00
CM14 Henrik Sedin 3.00 8.00
CM15 Daniel Sedin 3.00 8.00
CM16 Brett Hull 5.00 12.00
CM17 Billy Smith 2.50 6.00
CM18 Jarome Iginla 3.00 8.00
CM19 Jaromir Jagr 8.00 20.00
CM20 Gordie Howe 8.00 20.00
CM21 Grant Fuhr 4.00 10.00
CM22 Phil Esposito 4.00 10.00
CM23 Martin Brodeur 6.00 15.00
CM24 Joe Sakic 5.00 12.00
CM25 Wayne Gretzky 15.00 40.00

2020-21 Upper Deck Stature Gravitas Autographs

G1 Connor McDavid 125.00 300.00
G5 Andrei Vasilevskiy 15.00 40.00
G6 Matthew Tkachuk 20.00 50.00
G7 Mark Stone 12.00 30.00
G10 Miro Heiskanen 12.00 30.00
G16 Carey Price 20.00 50.00
G21 Brad Marchand 20.00 50.00
G23 Elias Pettersson 15.00 40.00
G25 Auston Matthews 80.00 200.00

2020-21 Upper Deck Stature Gravitas Autographs Green

*GREEN/25: .75X TO 2X BASIC INSERTS
G1 Connor McDavid 250.00 600.00
G25 Auston Matthews 125.00 300.00

2020-21 Upper Deck Stature Portrait Red

*RED: .75X TO 2X BASIC INSERTS
102 Kirill Kaprizov 200.00 500.00

2020-21 Upper Deck Stature Portrait Patch Autographs

6 Zach Parise 20.00 50.00
7 Elias Lindholm 20.00 50.00
8 Tomas Hertl 20.00 50.00
11 Brady Tkachuk 30.00 80.00
12 Mark Scheifele 30.00 80.00
18 Ryan Suter 15.00 40.00
35 John Gibson 20.00 50.00
36 Ilya Samsonov 20.00 50.00
44 Anthony Mantha 15.00 40.00
47 Jonathan Huberdeau 25.00 60.00
53 Jonathan Marchessault 25.00 60.00
59 Brayden Schenn 20.00 50.00
66 Sergei Bobrovsky 30.00 80.00
68 David Perron 15.00 40.00
78 John Vanbiesbrouck 20.00 50.00
87 Martin St. Louis 20.00 50.00
91 John LeClair 20.00 50.00
95 Mike Gartner 25.00 60.00
97 Peter Bondra 80.00 200.00
101 Alexis Lafreniere 80.00 200.00
102 Kirill Kaprizov 100.00 250.00
104 Ty Smith 40.00 100.00
108 Sasha Chmelevski 40.00 100.00
110 Arthur Kaliyev 40.00 100.00
117 Jack Rathbone 25.00 60.00
121 Drew O'Connor 25.00 60.00
123 Nolan Foote 25.00 60.00
124 Joel Hofer 25.00 60.00
126 Alexander Barabanov 25.00 60.00
127 Yegor Sharangovich 40.00 100.00
128 John Leonard 20.00 50.00
129 K'Andre Miller 80.00 200.00
131 Ilya Sorokin 60.00 150.00
132 Tim Stutzle 200.00 500.00
133 Logan Stanley 25.00 60.00
134 Mikko Lehtonen 20.00 50.00
135 Dylan Cozens 40.00 100.00
136 Ian Mitchell 20.00 50.00
138 Cal Foote 20.00 50.00
139 Nils Hoglander 25.00 60.00
141 Pius Suter 30.00 80.00
145 Alexander True 20.00 50.00
147 Gustav Lindstrom 20.00 50.00
148 Keegan Kolesar 20.00 50.00
150 Jason Robertson 60.00 150.00
153 Martin Kaut 25.00 60.00
154 Nikolai Knyzhov 20.00 50.00
155 Liam Foudy 25.00 60.00
158 Olli Juolevi 25.00 60.00
159 Morgan Geekie 20.00 50.00
160 Alexander Alexeyev 20.00 50.00
161 Alec Regula 15.00 40.00
162 Jake Oettinger 60.00 150.00
163 Shane Bowers 20.00 50.00
164 Jonas Johansson 25.00 60.00
166 Mikey Anderson 25.00 60.00
170 Reid Duke 25.00 60.00
171 Kieffer Bellows 20.00 50.00
172 Alex Belzile 20.00 50.00
174 Pavel Francouz 30.00 80.00
176 Maxim Letunov 20.00 50.00
179 Bowen Byram 50.00 125.00
180 Ty Dellandrea 25.00 60.00
183 Jani Hakanpaa 15.00 40.00
184 Gage Quinney 15.00 40.00
185 Tyler Benson 25.00 60.00
186 Anthony Angello 20.00 50.00
189 Joel Kiviranta 25.00 60.00
190 Lucas Carlsson 20.00 50.00
194 Nick Robertson 40.00 100.00
195 Josh Norris 40.00 100.00
196 Vitek Vanecek 40.00 100.00
197 Philipp Kurashev 30.00 80.00
198 Jake Evans 25.00 60.00
199 Pierre-Olivier Joseph 25.00 60.00

2020-21 Upper Deck Stature Proteges Blue

*BLUE/25: 1.25X TO 3X BASIC INSERTS
P7 Kirill Kaprizov 80.00 200.00
P9 Tim Stutzle 40.00 100.00

2020-21 Upper Deck Stature Proteges Green

*GREEN/149: .5X TO 1.25X BASIC INSERTS
P7 Kirill Kaprizov 50.00 125.00

2020-21 Upper Deck Stature Proteges Red

*RED/75: .6X TO 1.5X BASIC INSERTS
P7 Kirill Kaprizov 60.00 150.00
P9 Tim Stutzle 25.00 60.00

2020-21 Upper Deck Stature Proteges Autographs

*GREEN/49: .6X TO 1.5X BASIC INSERTS
P1 Alexis Lafreniere 40.00 100.00
P3 Vitek Vanecek 20.00 50.00
P5 Arthur Kaliyev 20.00 50.00
P8 Ilya Sorokin 30.00 80.00
P9 Tim Stutzle 25.00 60.00
P10 Pius Suter 15.00 40.00
P11 Nils Hoglander 12.00 30.00
P12 Dylan Cozens 20.00 50.00
P13 K'Andre Miller 25.00 60.00
P14 Ty Smith 20.00 50.00
P16 Ian Mitchell 10.00 25.00
P20 Jason Robertson 30.00 80.00
P21 Kieffer Bellows 10.00 25.00
P22 Olli Juolevi 12.00 30.00
P23 Liam Foudy 12.00 30.00
P24 Pierre-Olivier Joseph 12.00 30.00
P26 Yegor Sharangovich 20.00 50.00
P29 Martin Kaut 12.00 30.00
P33 Bowen Byram 25.00 60.00
P34 Morgan Geekie 12.00 30.00
P35 Mikey Anderson 12.00 30.00
P40 Nick Robertson 20.00 50.00
P41 Alexander Alexeyev 10.00 25.00
P45 Philipp Kurashev 15.00 40.00
P47 Alexander True 10.00 25.00
P48 Shane Bowers 10.00 25.00
P50 Nolan Foote 12.00 30.00

2021-22 Upper Deck Stature

1 Bobby Hull 1.50 4.00
2 Nick Suzuki 2.00 5.00
3 Anthony Beauvillier .60 1.50
4 Brady Tkachuk 1.50 4.00
5 Dominik Hasek 1.50 4.00
6 Taylor Hall 1.00 2.50
7 John Tavares 1.50 4.00
8 Kirill Kaprizov 3.00 8.00
9 Theoren Fleury 1.00 2.50
10 Andrei Vasilevskiy 1.50 4.00
11 Leon Draisaitl 3.00 8.00
12 Jason Zucker 1.00 2.50
13 Brett Hull 1.50 4.00
14 Joel Eriksson Ek .75 2.00
15 Brad Marchand 2.00 5.00
16 Adam Fox 1.25 3.00
17 Patrick Roy 2.50 6.00
18 Dylan Cozens 1.00 2.50
19 Cam Atkinson 1.00 2.50
20 Bernie Nicholls .75 2.00
21 Brayden Point 1.25 3.00
22 Sam Reinhart 2.00 5.00
23 Henrik Zetterberg 1.25 3.00
24 Nikolaj Ehlers 1.00 2.50
25 Cam Talbot 1.00 2.50
26 Alex Ovechkin 4.00 10.00
27 Pekka Rinne 1.00 2.50
28 Roope Hintz 1.25 3.00
29 Arthur Kaliyev 1.00 2.50
30 Connor McDavid 5.00 12.00
31 Conor Garland .75 2.00
32 Vincent Lecavalier 1.00 2.50
33 Phil Kessel 1.00 2.50
34 Carter Hart 1.00 2.50
35 Sean Monahan .60 1.50
36 Tim Stutzle 1.25 3.00
37 Joe Sakic 2.00 5.00
38 Mark Stone 1.00 2.50
39 Victor Olofsson 1.00 2.50
40 Sidney Crosby 4.00 10.00
41 Ryan O'Reilly 1.00 2.50
42 Gerry Cheevers 1.00 2.50
43 Jack Hughes 2.50 6.00
44 Artemi Panarin 2.00 5.00
45 Jason Robertson 1.50 4.00
46 William Karlsson 1.00 2.50
47 Filip Hronek .60 1.50
48 Mike Bossy 1.00 2.50
49 Joe Pavelski 1.25 3.00
50 Kyle Connor 1.50 4.00
51 Jordan Eberle 1.00 2.50
52 Jaromir Jagr 3.00 8.00
53 Yegor Sharangovich 1.00 2.50
54 Mathew Barzal 1.25 3.00
55 Thatcher Demko 1.25 3.00
56 Troy Terry .75 2.00
57 Kris Letang 1.25 3.00
58 Olaf Kolzig 1.00 2.50
59 Nathan MacKinnon 4.00 10.00
60 Marc-Andre Fleury 2.00 5.00
61 Jake Guentzel 1.50 4.00
62 Anthony Cirelli .75 2.00
63 Billy Smith 1.00 2.50
64 Jesper Bratt 1.00 2.50
65 Auston Matthews 4.00 10.00
66 Eeli Tolvanen 1.00 2.50
67 Brock Nelson 1.00 2.50
68 Mike Gartner 1.25 3.00
69 Maxime Comtois .75 2.00
70 Teuvo Teravainen 1.00 2.50
71 Mario Lemieux 4.00 10.00
72 Matthew Tkachuk 2.00 5.00
73 Jakub Voracek .75 2.00
74 Nicklas Lidstrom 1.00 2.50
75 Josh Anderson .75 2.00
76 Seth Jones 1.00 2.50
77 Roman Josi 1.00 2.50
78 John Vanbiesbrouck 1.00 2.50
79 Connor McMichael 1.00 2.50
80 Cale Makar 2.50 6.00
81 Jeff Petry 1.00 2.50
82 Martin St. Louis 1.00 2.50
83 Anze Kopitar 1.50 4.00
84 Brock Boeser 1.25 3.00
85 Tomas Hertl 1.00 2.50
86 Paul Coffey 1.25 3.00
87 Connor Hellebuyck 2.00 5.00
88 Jonathan Huberdeau 1.25 3.00
89 Jarome Iginla 1.25 3.00
90 Brent Burns 1.00 2.50
91 Philipp Grubauer 1.00 2.50
92 Pavel Buchnevich .75 2.00
93 Tyler Bertuzzi .75 2.00
94 Pat LaFontaine 1.00 2.50
95 Drake Batherson 1.00 2.50
96 Martin Necas 1.50 4.00
97 Teemu Selanne 2.00 5.00
98 Jack Roslovic .60 1.50
99 Alex Nedeljkovic .75 2.00
100 Bobby Orr 4.00 10.00
101 Trevor Zegras RC 8.00 20.00
102 Jesse Ylonen RC 1.50 4.00
103 Jonathan Dahlen RC 1.50 4.00
104 Alex Turcotte RC 2.00 5.00
105 Seth Jarvis RC 4.00 10.00
106 Yegor Chinakhov RC 2.50 6.00
107 Brett Murray RC 1.50 4.00
108 Dawson Mercer RC 4.00 10.00
109 Mike Hardman RC 1.50 4.00
110 Kasper Bjorkqvist RC 1.50 4.00
111 Spencer Knight RC 3.00 8.00
112 Simon Benoit RC 1.50 4.00
113 Calen Addison RC 1.50 4.00
114 Matthew Phillips RC 1.50 4.00
115 Sampo Ranta RC 1.50 4.00
116 Wyatt Kalynuk RC 1.50 4.00
117 Ross Colton RC 2.00 5.00
118 Wade Allison RC 1.50 4.00
119 Grigori Denisenko RC 2.00 5.00
120 Mattias Samuelsson RC 1.50 4.00
121 Alexander Holtz RC 2.50 6.00
122 Sean Durzi RC 1.50 4.00
123 Ivan Prosvetov RC 1.50 4.00
124 Lassi Thomson RC 1.50 4.00
125 Alex Barre-Boulet RC 1.50 4.00
126 David Farrance RC 1.50 4.00
127 Connor Dewar RC 1.50 4.00
128 Egor Sokolov RC 1.50 4.00
129 Taylor Raddysh RC 2.50 6.00
130 Karel Vejmelka RC 2.00 5.00
131 Jacob Bryson RC 1.50 4.00
132 Cam York RC 1.50 4.00
133 Jack Ahcan RC 1.50 4.00
134 Alex Newhook RC 2.50 6.00
135 Joey Keane RC 1.25 3.00
136 Riley Damiani RC 1.50 4.00
137 Shane Pinto RC 2.50 6.00
138 Jasper Weatherby RC 1.50 4.00
139 Vasily Podkolzin RC 2.00 5.00
140 Cam Dineen RC 1.50 4.00
141 Arttu Ruotsalainen RC 1.50 4.00
142 Nico Daws RC 2.50 6.00
143 Daniil Tarasov RC 1.50 4.00
144 Nils Lundkvist RC 1.50 4.00
145 Anton Lundell RC 3.00 8.00
146 Tyce Thompson RC 1.50 4.00
147 Jamie Drysdale RC 2.50 6.00
148 Daniil Miromanov RC 1.50 4.00
149 Ukko-Pekka Luukkonen RC 2.50 6.00
150 Moritz Seider RC 8.00 20.00
151 Cole Perfetti RC 3.00 8.00
152 Kole Lind RC 2.00 5.00
153 Jake Neighbours RC 3.00 8.00
154 Aliaksei Protas RC 1.50 4.00
155 Lane Pederson RC 1.50 4.00
156 J.J. Peterka RC 3.00 8.00
157 Pavel Dorofeyev RC 2.00 5.00
158 Morgan Barron RC 1.25 3.00
159 Thomas Novak RC 1.50 4.00
160 Tanner Laczynski RC 1.50 4.00
161 Benoit-Olivier Groulx RC 1.50 4.00
162 Jeremy Swayman RC 5.00 12.00
163 Ryan Merkley RC 2.00 5.00
164 Zac Jones RC 2.00 5.00
165 Cole Caufield RC 20.00 50.00
166 Paul Cotter RC 1.50 4.00
167 Brandon Duhaime RC 1.50 4.00
168 Filip Gustavsson RC 3.00 8.00
169 Riley Tufte RC 1.50 4.00
170 Philip Tomasino RC 2.00 5.00
171 Hendrix Lapierre RC 2.50 6.00
172 Gabriel Fortier RC 1.50 4.00
173 Gregory Hofmann RC 1.50 4.00
174 Rasmus Kupari RC 1.50 4.00
175 William Eklund RC 4.00 10.00
176 Oskar Steen RC 2.00 5.00
177 Joe Veleno RC 2.50 6.00
178 Justin Barron RC 2.50 6.00
179 Jan Jenik RC 2.00 5.00
180 Scott Perunovich RC 1.50 4.00
181 Garrett Pilon RC 2.00 5.00
182 Jacob Bernard-Docker RC 1.50 4.00
183 Dakota Joshua RC 1.50 4.00
184 Scott Reedy RC 1.25 3.00
185 J.J. Moser RC 1.50 4.00
186 Brett Leason RC 1.50 4.00
187 Quinton Byfield RC 4.00 10.00
188 Tanner Jeannot RC 1.50 4.00
189 Mason McTavish RC 3.00 8.00
190 Jack Drury RC 2.50 6.00
191 Parker Kelly RC 1.50 4.00
192 Adam Ruzicka RC 1.50 4.00
193 Robin Salo RC 1.50 4.00
194 Logan Thompson RC 4.00 10.00
195 Michael Bunting RC 1.50 4.00
196 Kyle Burroughs RC 1.50 4.00
197 Radim Zohorna RC 1.50 4.00
198 Cole Sillinger RC 2.50 6.00
199 Adam Beckman RC 1.50 4.00
200 Lucas Raymond RC 5.00 12.00

2021-22 Upper Deck Stature Blue

*BLUE/35: 2.5X TO 6X BASIC
*BLUE RC/35: 2X TO 5X BASIC
101 Trevor Zegras 60.00 150.00
150 Moritz Seider 40.00 100.00
165 Cole Caufield 80.00 200.00
200 Lucas Raymond 30.00 80.00

2021-22 Upper Deck Stature Green

*GREEN/149: .6X TO 1.5X BASIC
*GREEN RC/149: .5X TO 1.2X BASIC
101 Trevor Zegras 15.00 40.00
150 Moritz Seider 10.00 25.00
165 Cole Caufield 40.00 100.00
200 Lucas Raymond 10.00 25.00

2021-22 Upper Deck Stature Red

*RED/75: .75X TO 2X BASIC
101 Trevor Zegras 25.00 60.00
150 Moritz Seider 25.00 60.00
165 Cole Caufield 60.00 150.00
200 Lucas Raymond 20.00 50.00

2021-22 Upper Deck Stature Autographs

2 Nick Suzuki 12.00 30.00
3 Anthony Beauvillier 4.00 10.00
4 Brady Tkachuk 10.00 25.00
5 Dominik Hasek 10.00 25.00
7 John Tavares 10.00 25.00
9 Theoren Fleury 6.00 15.00
10 Andrei Vasilevskiy 10.00 25.00
11 Leon Draisaitl 20.00 50.00
12 Jason Zucker 6.00 15.00
13 Brett Hull 10.00 25.00
14 Joel Eriksson Ek 5.00 12.00
15 Brad Marchand 12.00 30.00
17 Patrick Roy 15.00 40.00
19 Cam Atkinson 6.00 15.00
20 Bernie Nicholls 5.00 12.00
24 Nikolaj Ehlers 6.00 15.00
26 Alex Ovechkin 25.00 60.00
28 Roope Hintz 8.00 20.00
29 Arthur Kaliyev 6.00 15.00
36 Tim Stutzle 8.00 20.00
37 Joe Sakic 12.00 30.00
40 Sidney Crosby 25.00 60.00
42 Gerry Cheevers 6.00 15.00
46 William Karlsson 6.00 15.00
49 Joe Pavelski 8.00 20.00
51 Jordan Eberle 6.00 15.00
53 Yegor Sharangovich 6.00 15.00
56 Troy Terry 5.00 12.00
57 Kris Letang 8.00 20.00
60 Marc-Andre Fleury 12.00 30.00
61 Jake Guentzel 10.00 25.00
63 Billy Smith 6.00 15.00
64 Jesper Bratt 6.00 15.00
66 Eeli Tolvanen 6.00 15.00
67 Brock Nelson 6.00 15.00
68 Mike Gartner 6.00 15.00
69 Maxime Comtois 5.00 12.00
70 Teuvo Teravainen 6.00 15.00
71 Mario Lemieux 25.00 60.00
72 Matthew Tkachuk 12.00 30.00
74 Nicklas Lidstrom 6.00 15.00
75 Josh Anderson 5.00 12.00
78 John Vanbiesbrouck 6.00 15.00
80 Cale Makar 15.00 40.00
81 Jeff Petry 6.00 15.00
82 Martin St. Louis 6.00 15.00
83 Anze Kopitar 10.00 25.00
84 Brock Boeser 8.00 20.00
86 Paul Coffey 8.00 20.00
88 Jonathan Huberdeau 8.00 20.00
89 Jarome Iginla 8.00 20.00
90 Brent Burns 6.00 15.00
93 Tyler Bertuzzi 5.00 12.00
94 Pat LaFontaine 6.00 15.00
95 Drake Batherson 6.00 15.00
96 Martin Necas 10.00 25.00
98 Jack Roslovic 4.00 10.00
99 Alex Nedeljkovic 5.00 12.00
101 Trevor Zegras/99 80.00 200.00
104 Alex Turcotte/199 8.00 20.00
107 Brett Murray/199 6.00 15.00
108 Dawson Mercer/99 15.00 40.00
109 Mike Hardman/199 6.00 15.00
110 Kasper Bjorkqvist/199 6.00 15.00
112 Simon Benoit/199 6.00 15.00
113 Calen Addison/199 6.00 15.00
114 Matthew Phillips/199 6.00 15.00
115 Sampo Ranta/199 6.00 15.00
116 Wyatt Kalynuk/199 6.00 15.00
117 Ross Colton/199 8.00 20.00
118 Wade Allison/199 6.00 15.00
119 Grigori Denisenko/199 8.00 20.00
120 Mattias Samuelsson/199 6.00 15.00
121 Alexander Holtz/199 10.00 25.00
122 Sean Durzi/199 6.00 15.00
124 Lassi Thomson/199 6.00 15.00
125 Alex Barre-Boulet/199 6.00 15.00
128 Egor Sokolov/199 6.00 15.00
129 Taylor Raddysh/199 10.00 25.00
130 Karel Vejmelka/199 8.00 20.00
131 Jacob Bryson/199 6.00 15.00
133 Jack Ahcan/199 6.00 15.00
134 Alex Newhook/99 10.00 25.00
137 Shane Pinto/199 10.00 25.00
138 Jasper Weatherby/199 6.00 15.00
139 Vasily Podkolzin/199 8.00 20.00
144 Nils Lundkvist/199 6.00 15.00
145 Anton Lundell/99 12.00 30.00
146 Tyce Thompson/199 6.00 15.00
147 Jamie Drysdale/99 10.00 25.00
148 Daniil Miromanov/199 6.00 15.00
149 Ukko-Pekka Luukkonen/199 10.00 25.00
151 Cole Perfetti/199 12.00 30.00
152 Kole Lind/199 8.00 20.00
154 Aliaksei Protas/199 6.00 15.00

155 Lane Pederson/199 6.00 15.00
156 J.J. Peterka/199 12.00 30.00
158 Morgan Barron/199 5.00 12.00
160 Tanner Laczynski/199 6.00 15.00
162 Jeremy Swayman/199 20.00 50.00
164 Zac Jones/199 8.00 20.00
166 Paul Cotter/199 6.00 15.00
167 Brandon Duhaime/199 6.00 15.00
168 Filip Gustavsson/199 12.00 30.00
169 Riley Tufte/199 6.00 15.00
170 Philip Tomasino/99 8.00 20.00
171 Hendrix Lapierre/199 6.00 15.00
172 Gabriel Fortier/199 6.00 15.00
174 Rasmus Kupari/199 6.00 15.00
175 William Eklund/199 15.00 40.00
176 Oskar Steen/199 8.00 20.00
178 Justin Barron/199 10.00 25.00
179 Jan Jenik/199 8.00 20.00
181 Garrett Pilon/199 8.00 20.00
182 Jacob Bernard-Docker/199 6.00 15.00
185 J.J. Moser/199 6.00 15.00
188 Tanner Jeannot/99 6.00 15.00
189 Mason McTavish/199 12.00 30.00
190 Jack Drury/199 10.00 25.00
191 Parker Kelly/199 6.00 15.00
193 Robin Salo/199 6.00 15.00
194 Logan Thompson/199 15.00 40.00
195 Michael Bunting/199 6.00 15.00
196 Kyle Burroughs/199 6.00 15.00
197 Radim Zohorna/199 6.00 15.00
199 Adam Beckman/199 6.00 15.00

2021-22 Upper Deck Stature Autographs Green

*GREEN: 1X TO 2.5X BASIC
28 Roope Hintz/50 25.00 60.00
30 Connor McDavid/25 250.00 600.00
40 Sidney Crosby/25 150.00 400.00
80 Cale Makar/50 60.00 150.00
100 Bobby Orr/25 125.00 300.00
200 Lucas Raymond/25 80.00 200.00

2021-22 Upper Deck Stature Design Photo Variant

1 Bobby Hull 10.00 25.00
2 Nick Suzuki 12.00 30.00
3 Anthony Beauvillier 4.00 10.00
4 Brady Tkachuk 10.00 25.00
5 Dominik Hasek 10.00 25.00
6 Taylor Hall 6.00 15.00
7 John Tavares 10.00 25.00
8 Kirill Kaprizov 20.00 50.00
9 Theoren Fleury 6.00 15.00
10 Andrei Vasilevskiy 10.00 25.00
11 Leon Draisaitl 20.00 50.00
12 Jason Zucker 6.00 15.00
13 Brett Hull 10.00 25.00
14 Joel Eriksson Ek 5.00 12.00
15 Brad Marchand 12.00 30.00
16 Adam Fox 8.00 20.00
17 Patrick Roy 15.00 40.00
18 Dylan Cozens 6.00 15.00
19 Cam Atkinson 6.00 15.00
20 Bernie Nicholls 5.00 12.00
21 Brayden Point 8.00 20.00
22 Sam Reinhart 12.00 30.00
23 Henrik Zetterberg 8.00 20.00
24 Nikolaj Ehlers 6.00 15.00
25 Cam Talbot 6.00 15.00
26 Alex Ovechkin 25.00 60.00
27 Pekka Rinne 6.00 15.00
28 Roope Hintz 8.00 20.00
29 Arthur Kaliyev 6.00 15.00
30 Connor McDavid 30.00 80.00
31 Conor Garland 5.00 12.00
32 Vincent Lecavalier 6.00 15.00
33 Phil Kessel 6.00 15.00
34 Carter Hart 6.00 15.00
35 Sean Monahan 4.00 10.00
36 Tim Stutzle 8.00 20.00
37 Joe Sakic 12.00 30.00
38 Mark Stone 8.00 20.00
39 Victor Olofsson 6.00 15.00
40 Sidney Crosby 25.00 60.00
41 Ryan O'Reilly 6.00 15.00
42 Gerry Cheevers 6.00 15.00
43 Jack Hughes 15.00 40.00
44 Artemi Panarin 12.00 30.00
45 Jason Robertson 10.00 25.00
46 William Karlsson 8.00 20.00
47 Filip Hronek 4.00 10.00
48 Mike Bossy 6.00 15.00
49 Joe Pavelski 8.00 20.00
50 Kyle Connor 10.00 25.00
51 Jordan Eberle 6.00 15.00
52 Jaromir Jagr 20.00 50.00
53 Yegor Sharangovich 6.00 15.00
54 Mathew Barzal 8.00 20.00
55 Thatcher Demko 8.00 20.00
56 Troy Terry 5.00 12.00
57 Kris Letang 8.00 20.00
58 Olaf Kolzig 6.00 15.00
59 Nathan MacKinnon 25.00 60.00
60 Marc-Andre Fleury 12.00 30.00
61 Jake Guentzel 10.00 25.00
62 Anthony Cirelli 5.00 12.00
63 Billy Smith 6.00 15.00
64 Jesper Bratt 6.00 15.00
65 Auston Matthews 25.00 60.00
66 Eeli Tolvanen 6.00 15.00
67 Brock Nelson 6.00 15.00
68 Mike Gartner 8.00 20.00
69 Maxime Comtois 6.00 15.00
70 Teuvo Teravainen 6.00 15.00
71 Mario Lemieux 25.00 60.00
72 Matthew Tkachuk 12.00 30.00
73 Jakub Voracek 5.00 12.00
74 Nicklas Lidstrom 6.00 15.00
75 Josh Anderson 5.00 12.00
76 Seth Jones 6.00 15.00
77 Roman Josi 6.00 15.00
78 John Vanbiesbrouck 6.00 15.00
79 Connor McMichael 6.00 15.00
80 Cale Makar 15.00 40.00
81 Jeff Petry 6.00 15.00
82 Martin St. Louis 6.00 15.00
83 Anze Kopitar 6.00 15.00
84 Brock Boeser 8.00 20.00
85 Tomas Hertl 6.00 15.00
86 Paul Coffey 8.00 20.00
87 Connor Hellebuyck 12.00 30.00
88 Jonathan Huberdeau 8.00 20.00
89 Jarome Iginla 8.00 20.00
90 Brent Burns 6.00 15.00
91 Philipp Grubauer 6.00 15.00
92 Pavel Buchnevich 5.00 12.00
93 Tyler Bertuzzi 5.00 12.00
94 Pat LaFontaine 6.00 15.00
95 Drake Batherson 6.00 15.00
96 Martin Necas 10.00 25.00
97 Teemu Selanne 12.00 30.00
98 Jack Roslovic 4.00 10.00
99 Alex Nedeljkovic 5.00 12.00
100 Bobby Orr 25.00 60.00
102 Jesse Ylonen 8.00 20.00
103 Jonathan Dahlen 8.00 20.00
104 Alex Turcotte 10.00 25.00
105 Seth Jarvis 20.00 50.00
106 Yegor Chinakhov 12.00 30.00
107 Brett Murray 8.00 20.00
108 Dawson Mercer 20.00 50.00
109 Mike Hardman 8.00 20.00
110 Kasper Bjorkqvist 8.00 20.00
111 Spencer Knight 15.00 40.00
112 Simon Benoit 8.00 20.00
113 Calen Addison 8.00 20.00
114 Matthew Phillips 8.00 20.00
115 Sampo Ranta 8.00 20.00
116 Wyatt Kalynuk 8.00 20.00
117 Ross Colton 10.00 25.00
118 Wade Allison 8.00 20.00
119 Grigori Denisenko 10.00 25.00
120 Mattias Samuelsson 8.00 20.00
121 Alexander Holtz 12.00 30.00
122 Sean Durzi 8.00 20.00
123 Ivan Prosvetov 8.00 20.00
124 Lassi Thomson 8.00 20.00
125 Alex Barre-Boulet 8.00 20.00
126 David Farrance 8.00 20.00
127 Connor Dewar 8.00 20.00
128 Egor Sokolov 8.00 20.00
129 Taylor Raddysh 12.00 30.00
130 Karel Vejmelka 10.00 25.00
131 Jacob Bryson 8.00 20.00
132 Cam York 8.00 20.00
133 Jack Ahcan 8.00 20.00
134 Alex Newhook 12.00 30.00
135 Joey Keane 6.00 15.00
136 Riley Damiani 8.00 20.00
137 Shane Pinto 12.00 30.00
138 Jasper Weatherby 8.00 20.00
139 Vasily Podkolzin 10.00 25.00
140 Cam Dineen 8.00 20.00
141 Arttu Ruotsalainen 8.00 20.00
142 Nico Daws 12.00 30.00
143 Daniil Tarasov 10.00 25.00
144 Nils Lundkvist 8.00 20.00
145 Anton Lundell 15.00 40.00
146 Tyce Thompson 8.00 20.00
147 Jamie Drysdale 12.00 30.00
148 Daniil Miromanov 8.00 20.00
149 Ukko-Pekka Luukkonen 8.00 20.00
150 Moritz Seider 20.00 50.00
151 Cole Perfetti 15.00 40.00
152 Kole Lind 10.00 25.00
153 Jake Neighbours 15.00 40.00
154 Aliaksei Protas 8.00 20.00
155 Lane Pederson 8.00 20.00
156 J.J. Peterka 15.00 40.00
157 Pavel Dorofeyev 10.00 25.00
158 Morgan Barron 6.00 15.00
159 Thomas Novak 8.00 20.00
160 Tanner Laczynski 8.00 20.00
161 Benoit-Olivier Groulx 8.00 20.00
162 Jeremy Swayman 25.00 60.00
163 Ryan Merkley 10.00 25.00
164 Zac Jones 10.00 25.00
166 Paul Cotter 8.00 20.00
167 Brandon Duhaime 8.00 20.00
168 Filip Gustavsson 15.00 40.00
169 Riley Tufte 8.00 20.00
170 Philip Tomasino 10.00 25.00
171 Hendrix Lapierre 8.00 20.00
172 Gabriel Fortier 8.00 20.00
173 Gregory Hofmann 8.00 20.00
174 Rasmus Kupari 8.00 20.00
175 William Eklund 20.00 50.00
176 Oskar Steen 10.00 25.00
177 Joe Veleno 10.00 25.00
178 Justin Barron 12.00 30.00
179 Jan Jenik 10.00 25.00
180 Scott Perunovich 8.00 20.00
181 Garrett Pilon 10.00 25.00
182 Jacob Bernard-Docker 8.00 20.00
183 Dakota Joshua 8.00 20.00
184 Scott Reedy 6.00 15.00
185 J.J. Moser 8.00 20.00
186 Brett Leason 8.00 20.00
187 Quinton Byfield 20.00 50.00
188 Tanner Jeannot 8.00 20.00
189 Mason McTavish 15.00 40.00
190 Jack Drury 12.00 30.00
191 Parker Kelly 8.00 20.00
192 Adam Ruzicka 8.00 20.00
193 Robin Salo 8.00 20.00
194 Logan Thompson 20.00 50.00
195 Michael Bunting 8.00 20.00
196 Kyle Burroughs 8.00 20.00
197 Radim Zohorna 8.00 20.00
198 Cole Sillinger 12.00 30.00
199 Adam Beckman 8.00 20.00
200 Lucas Raymond 25.00 60.00

2021-22 Upper Deck Stature Design Variant

1 Bobby Hull 5.00 12.00
2 Nick Suzuki 6.00 15.00
3 Anthony Beauvillier 2.00 5.00
4 Brady Tkachuk 5.00 12.00
5 Dominik Hasek 5.00 12.00
6 Taylor Hall 3.00 8.00
7 John Tavares 5.00 12.00
8 Kirill Kaprizov 10.00 25.00
9 Theoren Fleury 3.00 8.00
10 Andrei Vasilevskiy 5.00 12.00
11 Leon Draisaitl 10.00 25.00
12 Jason Zucker 3.00 8.00
13 Brett Hull 5.00 12.00
14 Joel Eriksson Ek 2.50 6.00
15 Brad Marchand 6.00 15.00
16 Adam Fox 4.00 10.00
17 Patrick Roy 8.00 20.00
18 Dylan Cozens 3.00 8.00
19 Cam Atkinson 3.00 8.00
20 Bernie Nicholls 2.50 6.00
21 Brayden Point 4.00 10.00
22 Sam Reinhart 6.00 15.00
23 Henrik Zetterberg 4.00 10.00
24 Nikolaj Ehlers 3.00 8.00
25 Cam Talbot 3.00 8.00
26 Alex Ovechkin 12.00 30.00
27 Pekka Rinne 3.00 8.00
28 Roope Hintz 4.00 10.00
29 Arthur Kaliyev 3.00 8.00
30 Connor McDavid 15.00 40.00
31 Conor Garland 2.50 6.00
32 Vincent Lecavalier 3.00 8.00
33 Phil Kessel 3.00 8.00
34 Carter Hart 3.00 8.00
35 Sean Monahan 2.00 5.00
36 Tim Stutzle 4.00 10.00
37 Joe Sakic 6.00 15.00
38 Mark Stone 4.00 10.00
39 Victor Olofsson 3.00 8.00
40 Sidney Crosby 12.00 30.00
41 Ryan O'Reilly 3.00 8.00
42 Gerry Cheevers 3.00 8.00
43 Jack Hughes 8.00 20.00
44 Artemi Panarin 6.00 15.00
45 Jason Robertson 5.00 12.00
46 William Karlsson 4.00 10.00
47 Filip Hronek 2.00 5.00
48 Mike Bossy 3.00 8.00
49 Joe Pavelski 4.00 10.00
50 Kyle Connor 5.00 12.00
51 Jordan Eberle 3.00 8.00
52 Jaromir Jagr 10.00 25.00
53 Yegor Sharangovich 3.00 8.00
54 Mathew Barzal 4.00 10.00
55 Thatcher Demko 4.00 10.00
56 Troy Terry 2.50 6.00
57 Kris Letang 4.00 10.00
58 Olaf Kolzig 3.00 8.00
59 Nathan MacKinnon 12.00 30.00
60 Marc-Andre Fleury 6.00 15.00
61 Jake Guentzel 5.00 12.00
62 Anthony Cirelli 2.50 6.00
63 Billy Smith 3.00 8.00
64 Jesper Bratt 3.00 8.00
65 Auston Matthews 12.00 30.00
66 Eeli Tolvanen 3.00 8.00
67 Brock Nelson 3.00 8.00
68 Mike Gartner 4.00 10.00
69 Maxime Comtois 2.50 6.00
70 Teuvo Teravainen 3.00 8.00
71 Mario Lemieux 12.00 30.00
72 Matthew Tkachuk 6.00 15.00
73 Jakub Voracek 2.50 6.00
74 Nicklas Lidstrom 3.00 8.00
75 Josh Anderson 2.50 6.00
76 Seth Jones 3.00 8.00
77 Roman Josi 3.00 8.00
78 John Vanbiesbrouck 3.00 8.00
79 Connor McMichael 3.00 8.00
80 Cale Makar 8.00 20.00
81 Jeff Petry 3.00 8.00
82 Martin St. Louis 3.00 8.00
83 Anze Kopitar 5.00 12.00
84 Brock Boeser 4.00 10.00
85 Tomas Hertl 3.00 8.00
86 Paul Coffey 4.00 10.00
87 Connor Hellebuyck 6.00 15.00
88 Jonathan Huberdeau 4.00 10.00
89 Jarome Iginla 4.00 10.00
90 Brent Burns 3.00 8.00
91 Philipp Grubauer 3.00 8.00
92 Pavel Buchnevich 2.50 6.00
93 Tyler Bertuzzi 2.50 6.00
94 Pat LaFontaine 3.00 8.00
95 Drake Batherson 3.00 8.00
96 Martin Necas 5.00 12.00
97 Teemu Selanne 6.00 15.00
98 Jack Roslovic 2.00 5.00
99 Alex Nedeljkovic 2.50 6.00
100 Bobby Orr 12.00 30.00
102 Jesse Ylonen 5.00 12.00
103 Jonathan Dahlen 5.00 12.00
104 Alex Turcotte 5.00 12.00
105 Seth Jarvis 12.00 30.00
106 Yegor Chinakhov 8.00 20.00
107 Brett Murray 5.00 12.00
108 Dawson Mercer 12.00 30.00
109 Mike Hardman 5.00 12.00
110 Kasper Bjorkqvist 5.00 12.00
111 Spencer Knight 10.00 25.00
112 Simon Benoit 5.00 12.00
113 Calen Addison 5.00 12.00
114 Matthew Phillips 5.00 12.00
115 Sampo Ranta 5.00 12.00
116 Wyatt Kalynuk 5.00 12.00
117 Ross Colton 6.00 15.00
118 Wade Allison 5.00 12.00
119 Grigori Denisenko 6.00 15.00
120 Mattias Samuelsson 5.00 12.00
121 Alexander Holtz 8.00 20.00
122 Sean Durzi 5.00 12.00
123 Ivan Prosvetov 5.00 12.00
124 Lassi Thomson 5.00 12.00
125 Alex Barre-Boulet 5.00 12.00
126 David Farrance 5.00 12.00
127 Connor Dewar 5.00 12.00
128 Egor Sokolov 5.00 12.00
129 Taylor Raddysh 8.00 20.00
130 Karel Vejmelka 6.00 15.00
131 Jacob Bryson 5.00 12.00
132 Cam York 5.00 12.00
133 Jack Ahcan 5.00 12.00
134 Alex Newhook 8.00 20.00
135 Joey Keane 4.00 10.00
136 Riley Damiani 5.00 12.00
137 Shane Pinto 8.00 20.00
138 Jasper Weatherby 5.00 12.00
139 Vasily Podkolzin 6.00 15.00
140 Cam Dineen 5.00 12.00
141 Arttu Ruotsalainen 5.00 12.00
142 Nico Daws 8.00 20.00
143 Daniil Tarasov 5.00 12.00
144 Nils Lundkvist 5.00 12.00
145 Anton Lundell 10.00 25.00
146 Tyce Thompson 5.00 12.00
147 Jamie Drysdale 8.00 20.00
148 Daniil Miromanov 5.00 12.00
149 Ukko-Pekka Luukkonen 8.00 20.00
150 Moritz Seider 12.00 30.00
151 Cole Perfetti 10.00 25.00
152 Kole Lind 6.00 15.00
153 Jake Neighbours 10.00 25.00
154 Aliaksei Protas 5.00 12.00
155 Lane Pederson 5.00 12.00
156 J.J. Peterka 10.00 25.00
157 Pavel Dorofeyev 6.00 15.00
158 Morgan Barron 4.00 10.00
159 Thomas Novak 5.00 12.00
160 Tanner Laczynski 5.00 12.00
161 Benoit-Olivier Groulx 5.00 12.00
162 Jeremy Swayman 15.00 40.00
163 Ryan Merkley 6.00 15.00
164 Zac Jones 6.00 15.00
166 Paul Cotter 5.00 12.00
167 Brandon Duhaime 5.00 12.00
168 Filip Gustavsson 10.00 25.00
169 Riley Tufte 5.00 12.00
170 Philip Tomasino 6.00 15.00
171 Hendrix Lapierre 5.00 12.00
172 Gabriel Fortier 5.00 12.00
173 Gregory Hofmann 5.00 12.00
174 Rasmus Kupari 5.00 12.00
175 William Eklund 12.00 30.00
176 Oskar Steen 6.00 15.00
177 Joe Veleno 6.00 15.00
178 Justin Barron 8.00 20.00
179 Jan Jenik 6.00 15.00
180 Scott Perunovich 5.00 12.00
181 Garrett Pilon 6.00 15.00
182 Jacob Bernard-Docker 5.00 12.00
183 Dakota Joshua 5.00 12.00
184 Scott Reedy 4.00 10.00
185 J.J. Moser 5.00 12.00
186 Brett Leason 5.00 12.00
187 Quinton Byfield 12.00 30.00
188 Tanner Jeannot 5.00 12.00
189 Mason McTavish 10.00 25.00
190 Jack Drury 8.00 20.00
191 Parker Kelly 5.00 12.00
192 Adam Ruzicka 5.00 12.00
193 Robin Salo 5.00 12.00
194 Logan Thompson 12.00 30.00
195 Michael Bunting 5.00 12.00
196 Kyle Burroughs 5.00 12.00
197 Radim Zohorna 5.00 12.00
198 Cole Sillinger 8.00 20.00
199 Adam Beckman 5.00 12.00
200 Lucas Raymond 15.00 40.00

2021-22 Upper Deck Stature Design Variant Red

*RED/25: .75X TO 2X BASIC
*RED RC/25: .6X TO 1.5X BASIC

2021-22 Upper Deck Stature Gravitas

*GREEN/125: .6X TO 1.5X BASIC
*RED/75: .75X TO 2X BASIC
G2 Mark Stone 2.00 5.00
G3 Connor Hellebuyck 3.00 8.00
G4 Jake Guentzel 2.50 6.00
G5 Thatcher Demko 2.00 5.00
G6 Connor McDavid 8.00 20.00
G7 Joe Pavelski 2.00 5.00
G8 Brent Burns 1.50 4.00
G9 Nikita Kucherov 3.00 8.00
G10 Ryan O'Reilly 1.50 4.00
G11 Roman Josi 1.50 4.00
G12 Drake Batherson 1.50 4.00
G13 Dylan Larkin 2.00 5.00
G14 Jonathan Huberdeau 2.00 5.00
G15 Matthew Tkachuk 3.00 8.00
G16 Leon Draisaitl 5.00 12.00
G17 Jesper Bratt 1.50 4.00
G18 Sidney Crosby 6.00 15.00
G19 Jean-Gabriel Pageau 1.00 2.50
G20 Taylor Hall 1.50 4.00
G21 Troy Terry 1.25 3.00
G22 Kirill Kaprizov 5.00 12.00
G23 Samuel Girard 1.00 2.50
G24 Jack Campbell 1.50 4.00
G25 Anze Kopitar 2.50 6.00

2021-22 Upper Deck Stature Gravitas Autographs

G4 Jake Guentzel 15.00 40.00
G7 Joe Pavelski 12.00 30.00
G8 Brent Burns 10.00 25.00
G12 Drake Batherson 10.00 25.00
G15 Matthew Tkachuk 20.00 50.00
G16 Leon Draisaitl 30.00 80.00
G17 Jesper Bratt 12.00 30.00
G19 Jean-Gabriel Pageau 6.00 15.00
G21 Troy Terry 8.00 20.00
G23 Samuel Girard 6.00 15.00
G24 Jack Campbell 10.00 25.00

2021-22 Upper Deck Stature Legendary Heights

*GREEN/125: .6X TO 1.5X BASIC
LH1 Cam Neely 1.25 3.00
LH2 Mike Richter 1.50 4.00
LH3 Bernie Nicholls 1.25 3.00
LH4 Darryl Sittler 1.50 4.00
LH5 Ron Hextall 1.50 4.00
LH6 Vincent Lecavalier 1.50 4.00
LH7 Doug Wilson 1.25 3.00
LH8 Bob Bourne 1.50 4.00
LH9 Alex Ovechkin 6.00 15.00
LH10 Martin St. Louis 1.50 4.00
LH11 Ken Morrow 1.00 2.50
LH12 Mike Modano 2.50 6.00
LH13 John LeClair 1.50 4.00
LH14 Martin Brodeur 4.00 10.00
LH15 Ray Bourque 2.50 6.00
LH16 Nicklas Lidstrom 1.50 4.00
LH17 Wayne Gretzky 10.00 25.00
LH18 Guy Lafleur 2.00 5.00
LH19 Patrick Roy 4.00 10.00
LH20 Marcel Dionne 2.00 5.00
LH21 Mark Messier 3.00 8.00
LH22 Doug Gilmour 2.00 5.00
LH23 Lanny McDonald 1.50 4.00
LH24 Peter Bondra 1.50 4.00
LH25 Peter Forsberg 3.00 8.00

2021-22 Upper Deck Stature Legendary Heights Red

*RED/75: 1X TO 2.5X BASIC
LH17 Wayne Gretzky 30.00 80.00
LH18 Guy Lafleur 12.00 30.00

2021-22 Upper Deck Stature Legendary Heights Autographs

LH1 Cam Neely 15.00 40.00
LH3 Bernie Nicholls 10.00 25.00
LH4 Darryl Sittler 12.00 30.00
LH5 Ron Hextall 12.00 30.00
LH8 Bob Bourne 4.00 10.00
LH10 Martin St. Louis 12.00 30.00
LH11 Ken Morrow 8.00 20.00
LH12 Mike Modano 20.00 50.00
LH13 John LeClair 15.00 40.00
LH14 Martin Brodeur 30.00 80.00
LH16 Nicklas Lidstrom 30.00 80.00
LH17 Wayne Gretzky 200.00 500.00
LH19 Patrick Roy 30.00 80.00
LH20 Marcel Dionne 15.00 40.00
LH21 Mark Messier 25.00 60.00
LH22 Doug Gilmour 20.00 50.00
LH23 Lanny McDonald 12.00 30.00
LH25 Peter Forsberg 25.00 60.00

2021-22 Upper Deck Stature Photo Variant

1 Bobby Hull 2.50 6.00
2 Nick Suzuki 3.00 8.00
3 Anthony Beauvillier 1.00 2.50
4 Brady Tkachuk 2.50 6.00
5 Dominik Hasek 2.50 6.00
6 Taylor Hall 1.50 4.00
7 John Tavares 2.50 6.00
8 Kirill Kaprizov 5.00 12.00
9 Theoren Fleury 1.50 4.00
10 Andrei Vasilevskiy 2.50 6.00
11 Leon Draisaitl 5.00 12.00
12 Jason Zucker 1.50 4.00
13 Brett Hull 2.50 6.00
14 Joel Eriksson Ek 1.25 3.00
15 Brad Marchand 3.00 8.00
16 Adam Fox 2.00 5.00
17 Patrick Roy 4.00 10.00
18 Dylan Cozens 1.50 4.00
19 Cam Atkinson 1.50 4.00
20 Bernie Nicholls 1.25 3.00
21 Brayden Point 2.00 5.00
22 Sam Reinhart 3.00 8.00
23 Henrik Zetterberg 2.00 5.00
24 Nikolaj Ehlers 1.50 4.00
25 Cam Talbot 1.50 4.00
26 Alex Ovechkin 6.00 15.00
27 Pekka Rinne 1.50 4.00
28 Roope Hintz 2.00 5.00
29 Arthur Kaliyev 1.50 4.00
30 Connor McDavid 8.00 20.00
31 Conor Garland 1.25 3.00
32 Vincent Lecavalier 1.50 4.00
33 Phil Kessel 1.50 4.00
34 Carter Hart 1.50 4.00
35 Sean Monahan 1.00 2.50
36 Tim Stutzle 2.00 5.00
37 Joe Sakic 3.00 8.00
38 Mark Stone 2.00 5.00
39 Victor Olofsson 1.50 4.00
40 Sidney Crosby 6.00 15.00
41 Ryan O'Reilly 1.50 4.00
42 Gerry Cheevers 1.50 4.00
43 Jack Hughes 4.00 10.00
44 Artemi Panarin 3.00 8.00
45 Jason Robertson 2.50 6.00
46 William Karlsson 2.00 5.00
47 Filip Hronek 1.00 2.50
48 Mike Bossy 1.50 4.00
49 Joe Pavelski 2.00 5.00
50 Kyle Connor 2.50 6.00
51 Jordan Eberle 1.50 4.00
52 Jaromir Jagr 5.00 12.00
53 Yegor Sharangovich 1.50 4.00
54 Mathew Barzal 2.00 5.00
55 Thatcher Demko 2.00 5.00
56 Troy Terry 1.25 3.00
57 Kris Letang 2.00 5.00
58 Olaf Kolzig 1.50 4.00
59 Nathan MacKinnon 6.00 15.00
60 Marc-Andre Fleury 3.00 8.00
61 Jake Guentzel 2.50 6.00
62 Anthony Cirelli 1.25 3.00
63 Billy Smith 1.50 4.00
64 Jesper Bratt 1.50 4.00
65 Auston Matthews 6.00 15.00
66 Eeli Tolvanen 1.50 4.00
67 Brock Nelson 1.50 4.00
68 Mike Gartner 2.00 5.00
69 Maxime Comtois 1.25 3.00
70 Teuvo Teravainen 1.50 4.00
71 Mario Lemieux 6.00 15.00
72 Matthew Tkachuk 3.00 8.00
73 Jakub Voracek 1.25 3.00
74 Nicklas Lidstrom 1.50 4.00
75 Josh Anderson 1.25 3.00
76 Seth Jones 1.50 4.00
77 Roman Josi 1.50 4.00
78 John Vanbiesbrouck 1.50 4.00
79 Connor McMichael 1.50 4.00
80 Cale Makar 4.00 10.00
81 Jeff Petry 1.50 4.00
82 Martin St. Louis 1.50 4.00
83 Anze Kopitar 2.50 6.00
84 Brock Boeser 2.00 5.00
85 Tomas Hertl 1.50 4.00
86 Paul Coffey 2.00 5.00
87 Connor Hellebuyck 3.00 8.00
88 Jonathan Huberdeau 2.00 5.00
89 Jarome Iginla 2.00 5.00
90 Brent Burns 1.50 4.00
91 Philipp Grubauer 1.50 4.00
92 Pavel Buchnevich 1.25 3.00
93 Tyler Bertuzzi 1.25 3.00
94 Pat LaFontaine 1.50 4.00
95 Drake Batherson 1.50 4.00
96 Martin Necas 2.50 6.00
97 Teemu Selanne 3.00 8.00
98 Jack Roslovic 1.00 2.50
99 Alex Nedeljkovic 1.25 3.00
100 Bobby Orr 6.00 15.00
101 Trevor Zegras 15.00 40.00
102 Jesse Ylonen 2.50 6.00
103 Jonathan Dahlen 2.50 6.00
104 Alex Turcotte 3.00 8.00
105 Seth Jarvis 6.00 15.00
106 Yegor Chinakhov 4.00 10.00
107 Brett Murray 2.50 6.00
108 Dawson Mercer 6.00 15.00
109 Mike Hardman 2.50 6.00
110 Kasper Bjorkqvist 2.50 6.00
111 Spencer Knight 5.00 12.00
112 Simon Benoit 2.50 6.00
113 Calen Addison 2.50 6.00
114 Matthew Phillips 2.50 6.00
115 Sampo Ranta 2.50 6.00
116 Wyatt Kalynuk 2.50 6.00
117 Ross Colton 3.00 8.00
118 Wade Allison 2.50 6.00
119 Grigori Denisenko 3.00 8.00
120 Mattias Samuelsson 2.50 6.00
121 Alexander Holtz 4.00 10.00
122 Sean Durzi 2.50 6.00
123 Ivan Prosvetov 2.50 6.00
124 Lassi Thomson 2.50 6.00
125 Alex Barre-Boulet 2.50 6.00
126 David Farrance 2.50 6.00
127 Connor Dewar 2.50 6.00
128 Egor Sokolov 2.50 6.00
129 Taylor Raddysh 4.00 10.00
130 Karel Vejmelka 3.00 8.00
131 Jacob Bryson 2.50 6.00
132 Cam York 2.50 6.00
133 Jack Ahcan 2.50 6.00
134 Alex Newhook 4.00 10.00
135 Joey Keane 2.00 5.00
136 Riley Damiani 2.50 6.00
137 Shane Pinto 4.00 10.00
138 Jasper Weatherby 2.50 6.00
139 Vasily Podkolzin 3.00 8.00
140 Cam Dineen 2.50 6.00
141 Arttu Ruotsalainen 2.50 6.00
142 Nico Daws 4.00 10.00
143 Daniil Tarasov 2.50 6.00
144 Nils Lundkvist 2.50 6.00
145 Anton Lundell 5.00 12.00
146 Tyce Thompson 2.50 6.00
147 Jamie Drysdale 4.00 10.00
148 Daniil Miromanov 2.50 6.00
149 Ukko-Pekka Luukkonen 2.50 6.00
150 Moritz Seider 6.00 15.00
151 Cole Perfetti 5.00 12.00
152 Kole Lind 3.00 8.00
153 Jake Neighbours 5.00 12.00
154 Aliaksei Protas 2.50 6.00
155 Lane Pederson 2.50 6.00
156 J.J. Peterka 5.00 12.00
157 Pavel Dorofeyev 3.00 8.00
158 Morgan Barron 2.00 5.00
159 Thomas Novak 2.50 6.00
160 Tanner Laczynski 2.50 6.00
161 Benoit-Olivier Groulx 2.50 6.00
162 Jeremy Swayman 8.00 20.00
163 Ryan Merkley 3.00 8.00
164 Zac Jones 3.00 8.00
165 Cole Caufield 30.00 80.00
166 Paul Cotter 2.50 6.00
167 Brandon Duhaime 2.50 6.00
168 Filip Gustavsson 5.00 12.00
169 Riley Tufte 2.50 6.00
170 Philip Tomasino 3.00 8.00
171 Hendrix Lapierre 2.50 6.00
172 Gabriel Fortier 2.50 6.00
173 Gregory Hofmann 2.50 6.00
174 Rasmus Kupari 2.50 6.00
175 William Eklund 6.00 15.00
176 Oskar Steen 3.00 8.00
177 Joe Veleno 3.00 8.00
178 Justin Barron 4.00 10.00
179 Jan Jenik 3.00 8.00
180 Scott Perunovich 2.50 6.00
181 Garrett Pilon 3.00 8.00
182 Jacob Bernard-Docker 2.50 6.00
183 Dakota Joshua 2.50 6.00
184 Scott Reedy 2.00 5.00
185 J.J. Moser 2.50 6.00
186 Brett Leason 2.50 6.00
187 Quinton Byfield 6.00 15.00
188 Tanner Jeannot 2.50 6.00
189 Mason McTavish 5.00 12.00
190 Jack Drury 4.00 10.00
191 Parker Kelly 2.50 6.00
192 Adam Ruzicka 2.50 6.00
193 Robin Salo 2.50 6.00
194 Logan Thompson 6.00 15.00
195 Michael Bunting 2.50 6.00
196 Kyle Burroughs 2.50 6.00
197 Radim Zohorna 2.50 6.00
198 Cole Sillinger 4.00 10.00
199 Adam Beckman 2.50 6.00
200 Lucas Raymond 8.00 20.00

2021-22 Upper Deck Stature Photo Variant Green

*GREEN/66: .75X TO 2X BASIC
101 Trevor Zegras 25.00 60.00
165 Cole Caufield 50.00 125.00

2021-22 Upper Deck Stature Photo Variant Red

*RED/33: 1.5X TO 4X BASIC
*RED RC/33: 1.2X TO 3X BASIC
17 Patrick Roy 25.00 60.00

2021-22 Upper Deck Stature Photo Variant Autographs

2 Nick Suzuki 20.00 50.00
3 Anthony Beauvillier 8.00 20.00
4 Brady Tkachuk 20.00 50.00
5 Dominik Hasek 20.00 50.00
7 John Tavares 20.00 50.00
9 Theoren Fleury 12.00 30.00
10 Andrei Vasilevskiy 20.00 50.00
11 Leon Draisaitl 40.00 100.00
12 Jason Zucker 12.00 30.00
13 Brett Hull 20.00 50.00
14 Joel Eriksson Ek 10.00 25.00
15 Brad Marchand 25.00 60.00
17 Patrick Roy 30.00 80.00
20 Bernie Nicholls 10.00 25.00
24 Nikolaj Ehlers 12.00 30.00
28 Roope Hintz 15.00 40.00
29 Arthur Kaliyev 12.00 30.00
34 Carter Hart 12.00 30.00
36 Tim Stutzle 15.00 40.00
37 Joe Sakic 25.00 60.00
42 Gerry Cheevers 12.00 30.00
46 William Karlsson 15.00 40.00
47 Filip Hronek 8.00 20.00
49 Joe Pavelski 15.00 40.00
51 Jordan Eberle 12.00 30.00
53 Yegor Sharangovich 12.00 30.00
57 Kris Letang 15.00 40.00
60 Marc-Andre Fleury 25.00 60.00
61 Jake Guentzel 20.00 50.00
63 Billy Smith 12.00 30.00
64 Jesper Bratt 12.00 30.00
66 Eeli Tolvanen 12.00 30.00
67 Brock Nelson 12.00 30.00
68 Mike Gartner 15.00 40.00
69 Maxime Comtois 10.00 25.00
70 Teuvo Teravainen 12.00 30.00
71 Mario Lemieux 50.00 125.00
72 Matthew Tkachuk 25.00 60.00
74 Nicklas Lidstrom 15.00 40.00
75 Josh Anderson 10.00 25.00
78 John Vanbiesbrouck 12.00 30.00
80 Cale Makar 30.00 80.00
81 Jeff Petry 12.00 30.00
82 Martin St. Louis 12.00 30.00
84 Brock Boeser 15.00 40.00
85 Tomas Hertl 12.00 30.00
87 Connor Hellebuyck 25.00 60.00
89 Jarome Iginla 15.00 40.00
90 Brent Burns 12.00 30.00
91 Philipp Grubauer 12.00 30.00
94 Pat LaFontaine 12.00 30.00
95 Drake Batherson 12.00 30.00
96 Martin Necas 20.00 50.00
97 Teemu Selanne 25.00 60.00
99 Alex Nedeljkovic 10.00 25.00
100 Bobby Orr 50.00 125.00
101 Trevor Zegras 125.00 300.00
104 Alex Turcotte 15.00 40.00
107 Brett Murray 12.00 30.00
108 Dawson Mercer 30.00 80.00
109 Mike Hardman 12.00 30.00
110 Kasper Bjorkqvist 12.00 30.00
112 Simon Benoit 12.00 30.00
113 Calen Addison 12.00 30.00
114 Matthew Phillips 12.00 30.00
115 Sampo Ranta 12.00 30.00
116 Wyatt Kalynuk 12.00 30.00
117 Ross Colton 15.00 40.00
118 Wade Allison 12.00 30.00
119 Grigori Denisenko 15.00 40.00
120 Mattias Samuelsson 12.00 30.00
121 Alexander Holtz 20.00 50.00
122 Sean Durzi 12.00 30.00
124 Lassi Thomson 12.00 30.00
125 Alex Barre-Boulet 12.00 30.00
128 Egor Sokolov 12.00 30.00
129 Taylor Raddysh 20.00 50.00
130 Karel Vejmelka 15.00 40.00
131 Jacob Bryson 12.00 30.00
133 Jack Ahcan 12.00 30.00
134 Alex Newhook 20.00 50.00
137 Shane Pinto 20.00 50.00
138 Jasper Weatherby 12.00 30.00
139 Vasily Podkolzin 15.00 40.00
144 Nils Lundkvist 12.00 30.00
145 Anton Lundell 25.00 60.00
146 Tyce Thompson 12.00 30.00
147 Jamie Drysdale 20.00 50.00
148 Daniil Miromanov 12.00 30.00
149 Ukko-Pekka Luukkonen 20.00 50.00
150 Moritz Seider 30.00 80.00
151 Cole Perfetti 25.00 60.00
152 Kole Lind 15.00 40.00
154 Aliaksei Protas 12.00 30.00
155 Lane Pederson 12.00 30.00
156 J.J. Peterka 25.00 60.00
158 Morgan Barron 10.00 25.00
160 Tanner Laczynski 12.00 30.00
162 Jeremy Swayman 40.00 100.00
164 Zac Jones 12.00 30.00
166 Paul Cotter 12.00 30.00
167 Brandon Duhaime 12.00 30.00
168 Filip Gustavsson 25.00 60.00
169 Riley Tufte 12.00 30.00
170 Philip Tomasino 15.00 40.00
171 Hendrix Lapierre 12.00 30.00
172 Gabriel Fortier 12.00 30.00
174 Rasmus Kupari 12.00 30.00
175 William Eklund 30.00 80.00
176 Oskar Steen 15.00 40.00
178 Justin Barron 20.00 50.00
179 Jan Jenik 15.00 40.00
181 Garrett Pilon 15.00 40.00
182 Jacob Bernard-Docker 12.00 30.00
185 J.J. Moser 12.00 30.00
188 Tanner Jeannot 12.00 30.00
189 Mason McTavish 25.00 60.00
190 Jack Drury 20.00 50.00

191 Parker Kelly 12.00 30.00
193 Robin Salo 12.00 30.00
194 Logan Thompson 30.00 80.00
195 Michael Bunting 12.00 30.00
196 Kyle Burroughs 12.00 30.00
197 Radim Zohorna 12.00 30.00
199 Adam Beckman 12.00 30.00
200 Lucas Raymond 60.00 150.00

2021-22 Upper Deck Stature Rookie Excellence

RE1 Trevor Zegras 2.00 5.00
RE2 Adam Beckman 1.00 2.50
RE3 Joe Veleno 1.25 3.00
RE4 Jake Neighbours 2.00 5.00
RE5 Logan Thompson 2.50 6.00
RE6 Shane Pinto 1.50 4.00
RE7 Matthew Phillips 1.00 2.50
RE8 Sampo Ranta 1.00 2.50
RE9 Philip Tomasino 1.25 3.00
RE10 Parker Kelly 1.00 2.50
RE11 Moritz Seider 2.50 6.00
RE12 Jamie Drysdale 1.50 4.00
RE13 Ivan Prosvetov 1.00 2.50
RE14 Riley Damiani 1.00 2.50
RE15 Grigori Denisenko 1.25 3.00
RE16 Tanner Jeannot 1.00 2.50
RE17 Dawson Mercer 2.50 6.00
RE18 David Farrance 1.00 2.50
RE19 Alexander Holtz 1.50 4.00
RE20 Scott Perunovich 1.00 2.50
RE21 Cole Caufield 8.00 20.00
RE22 Lucas Raymond 3.00 8.00
RE23 Alex Newhook 1.50 4.00
RE24 Riley Tufte 1.00 2.50
RE25 Jan Jenik 1.25 3.00
RE26 Joey Keane .75 2.00
RE27 Mattias Samuelsson 1.00 2.50
RE28 Jasper Weatherby 1.00 2.50
RE29 Benoit-Olivier Groulx 1.00 2.50
RE30 Mike Hardman 1.00 2.50
RE31 Cam York 1.00 2.50
RE32 Seth Jarvis 2.50 6.00
RE33 Nils Lundkvist 1.00 2.50
RE34 Pavel Dorofeyev 1.25 3.00
RE35 Calen Addison 1.00 2.50
RE36 Cole Perfetti 2.00 5.00
RE37 Brandon Duhaime 1.00 2.50
RE38 Lane Pederson 1.00 2.50
RE39 Jesse Ylonen 1.00 2.50
RE40 Jeremy Swayman 3.00 8.00
RE41 Quinton Byfield 2.50 6.00
RE42 Robin Salo 1.00 2.50
RE43 Jacob Bryson 1.00 2.50
RE44 Morgan Barron .75 2.00
RE45 Ross Colton 1.25 3.00
RE46 Filip Gustavsson 2.00 5.00
RE47 Spencer Knight 2.00 5.00
RE48 Jack Ahcan 1.00 2.50
RE50 Anton Lundell 2.00 5.00

2021-22 Upper Deck Stature Rookie Excellence Green

*GREEN/125: .6X TO 1.5X BASIC
RE21 Cole Caufield 20.00 50.00

2021-22 Upper Deck Stature Rookie Excellence Red

*RED/75: .75X TO 2X BASIC
RE1 Trevor Zegras 20.00 50.00
RE11 Moritz Seider 15.00 40.00
RE21 Cole Caufield 30.00 80.00
RE22 Lucas Raymond 10.00 25.00
RE40 Jeremy Swayman 10.00 25.00
RE47 Spencer Knight 8.00 20.00

2021-22 Upper Deck Stature Rookie Excellence Autographs

RE5 Logan Thompson 15.00 40.00
RE6 Shane Pinto 10.00 25.00
RE7 Matthew Phillips 6.00 15.00
RE8 Sampo Ranta 6.00 15.00
RE9 Philip Tomasino 8.00 20.00
RE10 Parker Kelly 6.00 15.00
RE11 Moritz Seider 15.00 40.00
RE12 Jamie Drysdale 10.00 25.00
RE15 Grigori Denisenko 8.00 20.00
RE16 Tanner Jeannot 6.00 15.00
RE17 Dawson Mercer 15.00 40.00
RE19 Alexander Holtz 10.00 25.00
RE22 Lucas Raymond 20.00 50.00
RE23 Alex Newhook 10.00 25.00
RE24 Riley Tufte 6.00 15.00
RE25 Jan Jenik 8.00 20.00
RE27 Mattias Samuelsson 6.00 15.00
RE28 Jasper Weatherby 6.00 15.00
RE33 Nils Lundkvist 6.00 15.00
RE34 Pavel Dorofeyev 8.00 20.00
RE35 Calen Addison 6.00 15.00
RE36 Cole Perfetti 12.00 30.00
RE37 Brandon Duhaime 6.00 15.00
RE38 Lane Pederson 6.00 15.00
RE40 Jeremy Swayman 30.00 80.00
RE42 Robin Salo 6.00 15.00
RE43 Jacob Bryson 6.00 15.00
RE44 Morgan Barron 5.00 12.00
RE45 Ross Colton 8.00 20.00
RE46 Filip Gustavsson 12.00 30.00
RE48 Jack Ahcan 6.00 15.00
RE50 Anton Lundell 12.00 30.00

2021-22 Upper Deck Stature Rookie Excellence Autographs Green

*GREEN/25: .6X TO 1.5X BASIC
RE11 Moritz Seider 80.00 200.00
RE17 Dawson Mercer 60.00 150.00
RE22 Lucas Raymond 60.00 150.00

2022-23 Upper Deck Stature

1 Wayne Gretzky 6.00 15.00
2 Mario Lemieux 4.00 10.00
3 Teemu Selanne 2.00 5.00
4 Brett Hull 2.00 5.00
5 Bobby Hull 2.00 5.00
6 Ray Bourque 1.50 4.00
7 Steve Yzerman 2.50 6.00
8 Peter Forsberg 2.00 5.00
9 Luc Robitaille 1.00 2.50
10 Martin Brodeur 2.50 6.00
11 Henrik Lundqvist 2.50 6.00
12 Eric Lindros 1.50 4.00
13 Jaromir Jagr 3.00 8.00
14 Rob Blake 1.00 2.50
15 Ron Francis 1.25 3.00
16 Billy Smith 1.00 2.50
17 Grant Fuhr 1.50 4.00
18 Gerry Cheevers 1.00 2.50
19 Marcel Dionne 1.25 3.00
20 Pat LaFontaine 1.00 2.50
21 Vincent Lecavalier 1.00 2.50
22 Keith Tkachuk 1.00 2.50
23 Jarome Iginla 1.25 3.00
24 Ryan Getzlaf 1.00 2.50
25 Pekka Rinne 1.00 2.50
26 Nick Suzuki 2.00 5.00
27 Zach Werenski 1.50 4.00
28 Brad Marchand 2.00 5.00
29 John Tavares 1.50 4.00
30 Jake Oettinger 1.50 4.00
31 Tim Stutzle 1.25 3.00
32 Sebastian Aho 1.50 4.00
33 Josh Norris 1.00 2.50
34 Teuvo Teravainen 1.00 2.50
35 Drake Batherson 1.00 2.50
36 Cole Caufield 2.00 5.00
37 Spencer Knight 1.00 2.50
38 Brendan Gallagher 1.00 2.50
39 Tyler Bertuzzi .75 2.00
40 Mark Stone 1.25 3.00
41 Lucas Raymond 1.50 4.00
42 James van Riemsdyk .75 2.00
43 Cam Atkinson 1.00 2.50
44 Patrick Kane 2.00 5.00
45 Dougie Hamilton .75 2.00
46 John Gibson 1.00 2.50
47 Nick Schmaltz .75 2.00
48 Jonathan Toews 1.50 4.00
49 Leon Draisaitl 3.00 8.00
50 Joel Eriksson Ek .75 2.00
51 Gabriel Landeskog 1.25 3.00
52 Timo Meier 1.00 2.50
53 Connor Hellebuyck 2.00 5.00
54 Brady Tkachuk 1.50 4.00
55 Sidney Crosby 4.00 10.00
56 Connor McDavid 5.00 12.00
57 Elias Lindholm 1.00 2.50
58 Tom Wilson 1.00 2.50
59 Jason Robertson 1.50 4.00
60 Tomas Hertl 1.00 2.50
61 Jonathan Marchessault 1.25 3.00
62 Ilya Sorokin 1.50 4.00
63 Robert Thomas 1.00 2.50
64 Miro Heiskanen 1.25 3.00
65 Moritz Seider 1.25 3.00
66 Taylor Hall 1.00 2.50
67 Andrei Svechnikov 1.25 3.00
68 Kyle Connor 1.50 4.00
69 Jacob Markstrom 1.00 2.50
70 Cole Sillinger .75 2.00
71 Jesper Bratt 1.00 2.50
72 Dylan Cozens 1.00 2.50
73 Aaron Ekblad 1.25 3.00
74 Trevor Zegras 1.00 2.50
75 Aleksander Barkov 1.50 4.00
76 Quinton Byfield 1.25 3.00
77 Cale Makar 2.50 6.00
78 Alexis Lafreniere 1.50 4.00
79 Andrei Vasilevskiy 1.50 4.00
80 Casey Mittelstadt 1.00 2.50
81 Quinn Hughes 2.50 6.00
82 Mikael Granlund .75 2.00
83 Auston Matthews 4.00 10.00
84 Mathew Barzal 1.25 3.00
85 Philipp Grubauer 1.00 2.50
86 Steven Stamkos 2.00 5.00
87 Jake Guentzel 1.50 4.00
88 Anze Kopitar 1.50 4.00
89 Alex Newhook .75 2.00
90 Brock Boeser 1.25 3.00
91 Kris Letang 1.25 3.00
92 Ryan O'Reilly 1.00 2.50
93 Alex Ovechkin 4.00 10.00
94 Adam Fox 1.25 3.00
95 Bowen Byram 1.25 3.00
96 Jeremy Swayman 1.50 4.00
97 Yanni Gourde .75 2.00
98 Kirill Kaprizov 3.00 8.00
99 Roman Josi 1.00 2.50
100 Clayton Keller 1.25 3.00
101 Matt Boldy RC 5.00 12.00
102 Matty Beniers RC 4.00 10.00
103 Kent Johnson RC 3.00 8.00
104 Owen Power RC 3.00 8.00
105 Juraj Slafkovsky RC 8.00 20.00
106 Shane Wright RC 4.00 10.00
107 Nick Cicek RC 1.50 4.00
108 Kaedan Korczak RC 1.25 3.00
109 Jacob Perreault RC 1.50 4.00
110 Marcus Bjork RC 1.50 4.00
111 Dylan Guenther RC 4.00 10.00
112 Reilly Walsh RC 1.50 4.00
113 Matej Blumel RC 2.00 5.00
114 Matias Maccelli RC 2.50 6.00
115 Jack Quinn RC 2.50 6.00
116 Samuel Poulin RC 2.00 5.00
117 Michael Eyssimont RC 1.50 4.00
118 Jonatan Berggren RC 2.50 6.00
119 Alex Vlasic RC 1.25 3.00
120 Zack Hayes RC 1.25 3.00
121 Filip Hallander RC 1.50 4.00
122 Pyotr Kochetkov RC 3.00 8.00
123 Fredrik Karlstrom RC 1.25 3.00
124 Nick DeSimone RC 1.50 4.00
125 Jack McBain RC 1.50 4.00
126 Dylan Wells RC 1.50 4.00
127 Jordan Spence RC 1.50 4.00
128 Marco Rossi RC 4.00 10.00
129 Oskar Olausson RC 1.50 4.00
130 Chase Pearson RC 1.25 3.00
131 David Jiricek RC 3.00 8.00
132 Filip Kral RC 2.00 5.00
133 Ronnie Attard RC 1.50 4.00
134 Mark Kastelic RC 1.25 3.00
135 Nikita Alexandrov RC 1.50 4.00
136 Nick Perbix RC 1.25 3.00
137 Olle Lycksell RC 1.50 4.00
138 Linus Hogberg RC 1.25 3.00
139 Kaiden Guhle RC 3.00 8.00
140 Dylan Holloway RC 3.00 8.00
141 Brandt Clarke RC 3.00 8.00
142 William Bitten RC 1.50 4.00
143 Ben Meyers RC 1.50 4.00
144 Jacob Moverare RC 1.25 3.00
145 Samuel Fagemo RC 1.25 3.00
146 Tyler Tucker RC 1.50 4.00
147 Erik Kallgren RC 1.50 4.00
148 Hunter Drew RC 1.50 4.00
149 Semyon Der-Arguchintsev RC 1.50 4.00
150 Vladislav Kolyachonok RC 1.25 3.00
151 Linus Sandin RC 1.25 3.00
152 Nick Abruzzese RC 1.50 4.00
153 Lukas Reichel RC 3.00 8.00
154 Bobby Brink RC 1.50 4.00
155 Juuso Parssinen RC 1.50 4.00
156 Jeff Malott RC 1.50 4.00
157 Jordan Harris RC 2.00 5.00
158 Mac Hollowell RC 1.50 4.00
159 Dylan Samberg RC 1.50 4.00
160 Valtteri Puustinen RC 1.25 3.00
161 Pontus Holmberg RC 1.50 4.00
162 Simon Holmstrom RC 1.50 4.00
163 Braden Schneider RC 2.50 6.00
164 Lukas Dostal RC 3.00 8.00
165 James Hamblin RC 1.50 4.00
166 Noah Cates RC 1.50 4.00
167 Nathan Smith RC 1.25 3.00
168 Trey Fix-Wolansky RC 1.50 4.00
169 Mads Sogaard RC 2.00 5.00
170 Lucas Johansen RC 1.25 3.00
171 Jean-Luc Foudy RC 1.50 4.00
172 Jakub Galvas RC 1.50 4.00
173 Thomas Bordeleau RC 1.50 4.00
174 Jake Sanderson RC 4.00 10.00
175 Elmer Soderblom RC 3.00 8.00
176 Wyatt Johnston RC 6.00 15.00
177 Marc McLaughlin RC 1.50 4.00
178 Nils Aman RC 1.50 4.00
179 Jakub Lauko RC 2.00 5.00
180 Filip Roos RC 1.25 3.00
181 Cole Koepke RC 1.50 4.00
182 Pavol Regenda RC 1.50 4.00
183 Jack LaFontaine RC 1.50 4.00
184 Brayden Tracey RC 1.25 3.00
185 Isaac Ratcliffe RC 1.50 4.00
186 Andrei Kuzmenko RC 3.00 8.00
187 Arber Xhekaj RC 3.00 8.00
188 Johnathan Kovacevic RC 1.50 4.00
189 Declan Chisholm RC 1.50 4.00
190 Brayden Pachal RC 1.25 3.00
191 Adam Raska RC 1.50 4.00
192 Hayden Hodgson RC 1.25 3.00
193 Viktor Lodin RC 1.50 4.00
194 Cole Reinhardt RC 1.50 4.00
195 Nikita Okhotiuk RC 1.25 3.00
196 Mitchell Chaffee RC 1.25 3.00
197 Jake Christiansen RC 1.50 4.00
198 Nick Blankenburg RC 1.25 3.00
199 Brandon Biro RC 2.50 6.00
200 Bokondji Imama RC 1.25 3.00

2022-23 Upper Deck Stature Blue

*BLUE/35: 2.5X TO 6X BASIC
*BLUE RC/35: 2X TO 5X BASIC

2022-23 Upper Deck Stature Green

*GREEN/99: .6X TO 1.5X BASIC
*GREEN RC/99: .5X TO 1.2X BASIC

2022-23 Upper Deck Stature Orange

*ORANGE/55: 1.5X TO 4X BASIC
*ORANGE RC/45: 1.2X TO 3X BASIC

2022-23 Upper Deck Stature Red

*RED/75: .75X TO 2X BASIC

2022-23 Upper Deck Stature Autographs

3 Teemu Selanne B 12.00 30.00
4 Brett Hull B 25.00 60.00
6 Ray Bourque B 10.00 25.00
7 Steve Yzerman B 80.00 200.00
8 Peter Forsberg A 12.00 30.00
9 Luc Robitaille B 6.00 15.00
10 Martin Brodeur A 15.00 40.00
11 Henrik Lundqvist B 15.00 40.00
12 Eric Lindros C 10.00 25.00
14 Rob Blake B 6.00 15.00
15 Ron Francis C 8.00 20.00
17 Grant Fuhr B 10.00 25.00
18 Gerry Cheevers D 6.00 15.00
19 Marcel Dionne B 8.00 20.00
20 Pat LaFontaine C 6.00 15.00
22 Keith Tkachuk C 6.00 15.00
23 Jarome Iginla B 8.00 20.00
24 Ryan Getzlaf B 6.00 15.00
26 Nick Suzuki D 12.00 30.00
27 Zach Werenski D 10.00 25.00
28 Brad Marchand C 12.00 30.00
30 Jake Oettinger E 10.00 25.00
31 Tim Stutzle C 8.00 20.00
33 Josh Norris E 6.00 15.00
34 Teuvo Teravainen E 6.00 15.00
38 Brendan Gallagher E 6.00 15.00
40 Mark Stone D 8.00 20.00
41 Lucas Raymond E 10.00 25.00
42 James van Riemsdyk D 5.00 12.00
43 Cam Atkinson E 6.00 15.00
46 John Gibson D 6.00 15.00
47 Nick Schmaltz F 5.00 12.00
50 Joel Eriksson Ek F 5.00 12.00
52 Timo Meier E 6.00 15.00
54 Brady Tkachuk D 10.00 25.00
60 Tomas Hertl E 6.00 15.00
61 Jonathan Marchessault E 8.00 20.00
63 Robert Thomas E 6.00 15.00
67 Andrei Svechnikov C 8.00 20.00
69 Jacob Markstrom D 6.00 15.00
73 Aaron Ekblad C 8.00 20.00
75 Aleksander Barkov D 10.00 25.00
77 Cale Makar B 15.00 40.00
78 Alexis Lafreniere C 10.00 25.00
81 Quinn Hughes B 15.00 40.00
83 Auston Matthews A 50.00 125.00
85 Philipp Grubauer F 6.00 15.00
87 Jake Guentzel D 10.00 25.00
93 Alex Ovechkin A 50.00 125.00
101 Matt Boldy/199 25.00 60.00
102 Matty Beniers/199 50.00 125.00
103 Kent Johnson/199 12.00 30.00
104 Owen Power/199 25.00 60.00
105 Juraj Slafkovsky/199 50.00 125.00
106 Shane Wright/199 15.00 40.00
108 Kaedan Korczak/199 5.00 12.00
110 Marcus Bjork/199 6.00 15.00
111 Dylan Guenther/199 15.00 40.00
114 Matias Maccelli/199 10.00 25.00
116 Samuel Poulin/199 8.00 20.00
117 Michael Eyssimont/199 6.00 15.00
120 Zack Hayes/199 5.00 12.00
121 Filip Hallander/199 6.00 15.00
122 Pyotr Kochetkov/199 12.00 30.00
123 Fredrik Karlstrom/199 5.00 12.00
124 Nick DeSimone/199 6.00 15.00
125 Jack McBain/199 6.00 15.00
128 Marco Rossi/199 15.00 40.00
130 Chase Pearson/199 5.00 12.00
133 Ronnie Attard/199 6.00 15.00
134 Mark Kastelic/199 5.00 12.00
135 Nikita Alexandrov/199 6.00 15.00
137 Olle Lycksell/199 6.00 15.00
140 Dylan Holloway/199 12.00 30.00
142 William Bitten/199 6.00 15.00
143 Ben Meyers/199 6.00 15.00
144 Jacob Moverare/199 5.00 12.00
148 Hunter Drew/199 6.00 15.00
150 Vladislav Kolyachonok/199 5.00 12.00
152 Nick Abruzzese/199 6.00 15.00
153 Lukas Reichel/199 12.00 30.00
155 Juuso Parssinen/199 6.00 15.00
157 Jordan Harris/199 8.00 20.00
159 Dylan Samberg/199 6.00 15.00
160 Valtteri Puustinen/199 5.00 12.00
164 Lukas Dostal/199 12.00 30.00
166 Noah Cates/199 6.00 15.00
167 Nathan Smith/199 5.00 12.00
168 Trey Fix-Wolansky/199 6.00 15.00
169 Mads Sogaard/199 8.00 20.00
173 Thomas Bordeleau/199 6.00 15.00
174 Jake Sanderson/199 15.00 40.00
176 Wyatt Johnston/199 25.00 60.00
180 Filip Roos/199 5.00 12.00
182 Pavol Regenda/199 6.00 15.00
185 Isaac Ratcliffe/199 6.00 15.00
186 Andrei Kuzmenko/199 12.00 30.00
187 Arber Xhekaj/199 12.00 30.00
192 Hayden Hodgson/99 5.00 12.00
195 Nikita Okhotiuk/99 5.00 12.00
197 Jake Christiansen/99 6.00 15.00
198 Nick Blankenburg/99 5.00 12.00

2022-23 Upper Deck Stature Autographs Green

*GREEN: 1X TO 2.5X BASIC
*GREEN RC: .75X TO 2X BASIC
3 Teemu Selanne/25 40.00 100.00
4 Brett Hull/25 80.00 200.00
6 Ray Bourque/25 40.00 100.00
7 Steve Yzerman/25 100.00 250.00
9 Luc Robitaille/25 20.00 50.00
10 Martin Brodeur/25 80.00 200.00
11 Henrik Lundqvist/25 60.00 150.00
12 Eric Lindros/25 60.00 150.00
55 Sidney Crosby/50 80.00 200.00
56 Connor McDavid/50 150.00 400.00
77 Cale Makar/50 60.00 150.00
83 Auston Matthews/50 125.00 300.00
93 Alex Ovechkin/50 125.00 300.00
105 Juraj Slafkovsky/65 60.00 150.00

2022-23 Upper Deck Stature Autographs Red

*RED: 1.2X TO 3X BASIC
*RED RC: 1X TO 2.5X BASIC
55 Sidney Crosby/25 100.00 250.00
56 Connor McDavid/25 200.00 500.00
77 Cale Makar/25 80.00 200.00
83 Auston Matthews/25 150.00 400.00
93 Alex Ovechkin/25 150.00 400.00
105 Juraj Slafkovsky/35 80.00 200.00

2022-23 Upper Deck Stature Design Photo Variant

1 Wayne Gretzky 40.00 100.00
2 Mario Lemieux 25.00 60.00
3 Teemu Selanne 12.00 30.00
4 Brett Hull 12.00 30.00
5 Bobby Hull 12.00 30.00
6 Ray Bourque 10.00 25.00
7 Steve Yzerman 15.00 40.00
8 Peter Forsberg 12.00 30.00
9 Luc Robitaille 6.00 15.00
10 Martin Brodeur 15.00 40.00
11 Henrik Lundqvist 15.00 40.00
12 Eric Lindros 10.00 25.00
13 Jaromir Jagr 20.00 50.00
14 Rob Blake 6.00 15.00
15 Ron Francis 8.00 20.00
16 Billy Smith 6.00 15.00
17 Grant Fuhr 10.00 25.00
18 Gerry Cheevers 6.00 15.00
19 Marcel Dionne 8.00 20.00
20 Pat LaFontaine 6.00 15.00
21 Vincent Lecavalier 6.00 15.00
22 Keith Tkachuk 6.00 15.00
23 Jarome Iginla 8.00 20.00
24 Ryan Getzlaf 6.00 15.00
25 Pekka Rinne 6.00 15.00
26 Nick Suzuki 12.00 30.00
27 Zach Werenski 10.00 25.00
28 Brad Marchand 12.00 30.00
29 John Tavares 10.00 25.00
30 Jake Oettinger 10.00 25.00
31 Tim Stutzle 8.00 20.00
32 Sebastian Aho 10.00 25.00
33 Josh Norris 6.00 15.00
34 Teuvo Teravainen 6.00 15.00
35 Drake Batherson 6.00 15.00
36 Cole Caufield 12.00 30.00
37 Spencer Knight 6.00 15.00
38 Brendan Gallagher 6.00 15.00
39 Tyler Bertuzzi 5.00 12.00
40 Mark Stone 8.00 20.00
41 Lucas Raymond 10.00 25.00
42 James van Riemsdyk 5.00 12.00
43 Cam Atkinson 6.00 15.00
44 Patrick Kane 12.00 30.00
45 Dougie Hamilton 5.00 12.00
46 John Gibson 6.00 15.00
47 Nick Schmaltz 5.00 12.00
48 Jonathan Toews 10.00 25.00
49 Leon Draisaitl 20.00 50.00
50 Joel Eriksson Ek 5.00 12.00
51 Gabriel Landeskog 8.00 20.00
52 Timo Meier 6.00 15.00
53 Connor Hellebuyck 12.00 30.00
54 Brady Tkachuk 10.00 25.00
55 Sidney Crosby 25.00 60.00
56 Connor McDavid 30.00 80.00
57 Elias Lindholm 6.00 15.00
58 Tom Wilson 6.00 15.00
59 Jason Robertson 10.00 25.00
60 Tomas Hertl 6.00 15.00
61 Jonathan Marchessault 8.00 20.00
62 Ilya Sorokin 10.00 25.00
63 Robert Thomas 6.00 15.00
64 Miro Heiskanen 8.00 20.00
65 Moritz Seider 8.00 20.00
66 Taylor Hall 6.00 15.00
67 Andrei Svechnikov 8.00 20.00
68 Kyle Connor 10.00 25.00
69 Jacob Markstrom 6.00 15.00
70 Cole Sillinger 5.00 12.00
71 Jesper Bratt 6.00 15.00
72 Dylan Cozens 6.00 15.00
73 Aaron Ekblad 8.00 20.00
74 Trevor Zegras 6.00 15.00
75 Aleksander Barkov 10.00 25.00
76 Quinton Byfield 8.00 20.00
77 Cale Makar 15.00 40.00
78 Alexis Lafreniere 10.00 25.00
79 Andrei Vasilevskiy 10.00 25.00
80 Casey Mittelstadt 6.00 15.00
81 Quinn Hughes 15.00 40.00
82 Mikael Granlund 5.00 12.00
83 Auston Matthews 25.00 60.00
84 Mathew Barzal 8.00 20.00
85 Philipp Grubauer 6.00 15.00
86 Steven Stamkos 12.00 30.00
87 Jake Guentzel 10.00 25.00
88 Anze Kopitar 10.00 25.00
89 Alex Newhook 5.00 12.00
90 Brock Boeser 8.00 20.00
91 Kris Letang 8.00 20.00
92 Ryan O'Reilly 6.00 15.00
93 Alex Ovechkin 25.00 60.00
94 Adam Fox 8.00 20.00
95 Bowen Byram 8.00 20.00
96 Jeremy Swayman 10.00 25.00
97 Yanni Gourde 5.00 12.00
98 Kirill Kaprizov 20.00 50.00
99 Roman Josi 6.00 15.00
100 Clayton Keller 8.00 20.00
101 Matt Boldy 25.00 60.00
102 Matty Beniers 20.00 50.00
103 Kent Johnson 15.00 40.00
104 Owen Power 15.00 40.00
105 Juraj Slafkovsky 40.00 100.00
106 Shane Wright 20.00 50.00
107 Nick Cicek 8.00 20.00
108 Kaedan Korczak 6.00 15.00
109 Jacob Perreault 8.00 20.00
110 Marcus Bjork 8.00 20.00
111 Dylan Guenther 20.00 50.00
112 Reilly Walsh 8.00 20.00
113 Matej Blumel 10.00 25.00
114 Matias Maccelli 12.00 30.00
115 Jack Quinn 12.00 30.00
116 Samuel Poulin 10.00 25.00
117 Michael Eyssimont 8.00 20.00
118 Jonatan Berggren 12.00 30.00
119 Alex Vlasic 6.00 15.00
120 Zack Hayes 6.00 15.00
121 Filip Hallander 8.00 20.00
122 Pyotr Kochetkov 15.00 40.00
123 Fredrik Karlstrom 6.00 15.00
124 Nick DeSimone 8.00 20.00
125 Jack McBain 8.00 20.00
126 Dylan Wells 8.00 20.00
127 Jordan Spence 8.00 20.00
128 Marco Rossi 20.00 50.00
129 Oskar Olausson 8.00 20.00
130 Chase Pearson 6.00 15.00
131 David Jiricek 15.00 40.00
132 Filip Kral 10.00 25.00
133 Ronnie Attard 8.00 20.00
134 Mark Kastelic 6.00 15.00
135 Nikita Alexandrov 8.00 20.00
136 Nick Perbix 6.00 15.00
137 Olle Lycksell 8.00 20.00
138 Linus Hogberg 6.00 15.00
139 Kaiden Guhle 15.00 40.00
140 Dylan Holloway 15.00 40.00
141 Brandt Clarke 15.00 40.00
142 William Bitten 8.00 20.00
143 Ben Meyers 8.00 20.00
144 Jacob Moverare 6.00 15.00
145 Samuel Fagemo 6.00 15.00
146 Tyler Tucker 8.00 20.00
147 Erik Kallgren 8.00 20.00
148 Hunter Drew 8.00 20.00
149 Semyon Der-Arguchintsev 8.00 20.00
150 Vladislav Kolyachonok 6.00 15.00
151 Linus Sandin 6.00 15.00
152 Nick Abruzzese 8.00 20.00
153 Lukas Reichel 15.00 40.00
154 Bobby Brink 8.00 20.00
155 Juuso Parssinen 8.00 20.00
156 Jeff Malott 8.00 20.00
157 Jordan Harris 10.00 25.00
158 Mac Hollowell 8.00 20.00
159 Dylan Samberg 8.00 20.00
160 Valtteri Puustinen 6.00 15.00
161 Pontus Holmberg 8.00 20.00
162 Simon Holmstrom 8.00 20.00
163 Braden Schneider 12.00 30.00
164 Lukas Dostal 15.00 40.00
165 James Hamblin 8.00 20.00
166 Noah Cates 8.00 20.00
167 Nathan Smith 6.00 15.00
168 Trey Fix-Wolansky 8.00 20.00
169 Mads Sogaard 10.00 25.00
170 Lucas Johansen 6.00 15.00
171 Jean-Luc Foudy 8.00 20.00
172 Jakub Galvas 8.00 20.00
173 Thomas Bordeleau 8.00 20.00
174 Jake Sanderson 20.00 50.00
175 Elmer Soderblom 15.00 40.00
176 Wyatt Johnston 30.00 80.00
177 Marc McLaughlin 8.00 20.00
178 Nils Aman 8.00 20.00
179 Jakub Lauko 10.00 25.00
180 Filip Roos 6.00 15.00
181 Cole Koepke 8.00 20.00
182 Pavol Regenda 8.00 20.00
183 Jack LaFontaine 8.00 20.00
184 Brayden Tracey 6.00 15.00
185 Isaac Ratcliffe 8.00 20.00
186 Andrei Kuzmenko 15.00 40.00
187 Arber Xhekaj 15.00 40.00
188 Johnathan Kovacevic 8.00 20.00
189 Declan Chisholm 8.00 20.00
190 Brayden Pachal 6.00 15.00
191 Adam Raska 8.00 20.00
192 Hayden Hodgson 6.00 15.00
193 Viktor Lodin 8.00 20.00
194 Cole Reinhardt 8.00 20.00
195 Nikita Okhotiuk 6.00 15.00
196 Mitchell Chaffee 6.00 15.00
197 Jake Christiansen 8.00 20.00
198 Nick Blankenburg 6.00 15.00
199 Brandon Biro 12.00 30.00
200 Bokondji Imama 6.00 15.00

2022-23 Upper Deck Stature Design Variant

*RED/25: .75X TO 2X BASIC
*RED RC/25: .6X TO 1.5X BASIC
1 Wayne Gretzky 20.00 50.00
2 Mario Lemieux 12.00 30.00
3 Teemu Selanne 6.00 15.00
4 Brett Hull 6.00 15.00
5 Bobby Hull 6.00 15.00
6 Ray Bourque 5.00 12.00
7 Steve Yzerman 8.00 20.00
8 Peter Forsberg 6.00 15.00
9 Luc Robitaille 3.00 8.00
10 Martin Brodeur 8.00 20.00
11 Henrik Lundqvist 8.00 20.00
12 Eric Lindros 5.00 12.00
13 Jaromir Jagr 10.00 25.00
14 Rob Blake 3.00 8.00
15 Ron Francis 4.00 10.00
16 Billy Smith 3.00 8.00
17 Grant Fuhr 5.00 12.00
18 Gerry Cheevers 3.00 8.00
19 Marcel Dionne 4.00 10.00
20 Pat LaFontaine 3.00 8.00
21 Vincent Lecavalier 3.00 8.00
22 Keith Tkachuk 3.00 8.00
23 Jarome Iginla 4.00 10.00
24 Ryan Getzlaf 3.00 8.00
25 Pekka Rinne 3.00 8.00
26 Nick Suzuki 6.00 15.00
27 Zach Werenski 5.00 12.00
28 Brad Marchand 6.00 15.00
29 John Tavares 5.00 12.00
30 Jake Oettinger 5.00 12.00
31 Tim Stutzle 4.00 10.00
32 Sebastian Aho 5.00 12.00
33 Josh Norris 3.00 8.00
34 Teuvo Teravainen 3.00 8.00
35 Drake Batherson 3.00 8.00
36 Cole Caufield 6.00 15.00
37 Spencer Knight 3.00 8.00
38 Brendan Gallagher 3.00 8.00
39 Tyler Bertuzzi 2.50 6.00
40 Mark Stone 4.00 10.00
41 Lucas Raymond 5.00 12.00
42 James van Riemsdyk 2.50 6.00
43 Cam Atkinson 3.00 8.00
44 Patrick Kane 6.00 15.00
45 Dougie Hamilton 2.50 6.00
46 John Gibson 3.00 8.00
47 Nick Schmaltz 2.50 6.00
48 Jonathan Toews 5.00 12.00
49 Leon Draisaitl 10.00 25.00
50 Joel Eriksson Ek 2.50 6.00
51 Gabriel Landeskog 4.00 10.00
52 Timo Meier 3.00 8.00
53 Connor Hellebuyck 6.00 15.00
54 Brady Tkachuk 5.00 12.00
55 Sidney Crosby 12.00 30.00
56 Connor McDavid 15.00 40.00
57 Elias Lindholm 3.00 8.00
58 Tom Wilson 3.00 8.00
59 Jason Robertson 5.00 12.00
60 Tomas Hertl 3.00 8.00
61 Jonathan Marchessault 4.00 10.00
62 Ilya Sorokin 5.00 12.00
63 Robert Thomas 3.00 8.00
64 Miro Heiskanen 4.00 10.00
65 Moritz Seider 4.00 10.00
66 Taylor Hall 3.00 8.00
67 Andrei Svechnikov 4.00 10.00
68 Kyle Connor 5.00 12.00
69 Jacob Markstrom 3.00 8.00
70 Cole Sillinger 2.50 6.00
71 Jesper Bratt 3.00 8.00
72 Dylan Cozens 3.00 8.00
73 Aaron Ekblad 4.00 10.00
74 Trevor Zegras 3.00 8.00
75 Aleksander Barkov 5.00 12.00
76 Quinton Byfield 4.00 10.00
77 Cale Makar 8.00 20.00
78 Alexis Lafreniere 5.00 12.00
79 Andrei Vasilevskiy 5.00 12.00
80 Casey Mittelstadt 3.00 8.00
81 Quinn Hughes 8.00 20.00
82 Mikael Granlund 2.50 6.00
83 Auston Matthews 12.00 30.00
84 Mathew Barzal 4.00 10.00
85 Philipp Grubauer 3.00 8.00
86 Steven Stamkos 6.00 15.00
87 Jake Guentzel 5.00 12.00
88 Anze Kopitar 5.00 12.00
89 Alex Newhook 2.50 6.00
90 Brock Boeser 4.00 10.00
91 Kris Letang 4.00 10.00
92 Ryan O'Reilly 3.00 8.00
93 Alex Ovechkin 12.00 30.00
94 Adam Fox 4.00 10.00
95 Bowen Byram 4.00 10.00
96 Jeremy Swayman 5.00 12.00
97 Yanni Gourde 2.50 6.00
98 Kirill Kaprizov 10.00 25.00
99 Roman Josi 3.00 8.00
100 Clayton Keller 4.00 10.00
101 Matt Boldy 15.00 40.00
102 Matty Beniers 12.00 30.00
103 Kent Johnson 10.00 25.00
104 Owen Power 10.00 25.00
105 Juraj Slafkovsky 25.00 60.00
106 Shane Wright 12.00 30.00
107 Nick Cicek 5.00 12.00
108 Kaedan Korczak 4.00 10.00
109 Jacob Perreault 5.00 12.00
110 Marcus Bjork 5.00 12.00
111 Dylan Guenther 12.00 30.00
112 Reilly Walsh 5.00 12.00
113 Matej Blumel 6.00 15.00
114 Matias Maccelli 8.00 20.00
115 Jack Quinn 8.00 20.00
116 Samuel Poulin 6.00 15.00
117 Michael Eyssimont 5.00 12.00
118 Jonatan Berggren 8.00 20.00
119 Alex Vlasic 4.00 10.00
120 Zack Hayes 4.00 10.00
121 Filip Hallander 5.00 12.00
122 Pyotr Kochetkov 10.00 25.00
123 Fredrik Karlstrom 4.00 10.00
124 Nick DeSimone 5.00 12.00
125 Jack McBain 5.00 12.00
126 Dylan Wells 5.00 12.00
127 Jordan Spence 5.00 12.00
128 Marco Rossi 12.00 30.00
129 Oskar Olausson 5.00 12.00
130 Chase Pearson 4.00 10.00
131 David Jiricek 10.00 25.00
132 Filip Kral 6.00 15.00
133 Ronnie Attard 5.00 12.00
134 Mark Kastelic 4.00 10.00
135 Nikita Alexandrov 5.00 12.00
136 Nick Perbix 4.00 10.00
137 Olle Lycksell 5.00 12.00
138 Linus Hogberg 4.00 10.00
139 Kaiden Guhle 10.00 25.00
140 Dylan Holloway 10.00 25.00
141 Brandt Clarke 10.00 25.00
142 William Bitten 5.00 12.00
143 Ben Meyers 5.00 12.00
144 Jacob Moverare 4.00 10.00
145 Samuel Fagemo 4.00 10.00
146 Tyler Tucker 5.00 12.00
147 Erik Kallgren 5.00 12.00
148 Hunter Drew 5.00 12.00
149 Semyon Der-Arguchintsev 5.00 12.00
150 Vladislav Kolyachonok 4.00 10.00
151 Linus Sandin 4.00 10.00
152 Nick Abruzzese 5.00 12.00
153 Lukas Reichel 10.00 25.00
154 Bobby Brink 5.00 12.00
155 Juuso Parssinen 5.00 12.00
156 Jeff Malott 5.00 12.00
157 Jordan Harris 6.00 15.00
158 Mac Hollowell 5.00 12.00
159 Dylan Samberg 5.00 12.00
160 Valtteri Puustinen 4.00 10.00
161 Pontus Holmberg 5.00 12.00
162 Simon Holmstrom 5.00 12.00
163 Braden Schneider 8.00 20.00
164 Lukas Dostal 10.00 25.00
165 James Hamblin 5.00 12.00
166 Noah Cates 5.00 12.00
167 Nathan Smith 4.00 10.00
168 Trey Fix-Wolansky 5.00 12.00
169 Mads Sogaard 6.00 15.00
170 Lucas Johansen 4.00 10.00
171 Jean-Luc Foudy 5.00 12.00
172 Jakub Galvas 5.00 12.00
173 Thomas Bordeleau 5.00 12.00
174 Jake Sanderson 12.00 30.00
175 Elmer Soderblom 10.00 25.00
176 Wyatt Johnston 20.00 50.00
177 Marc McLaughlin 5.00 12.00
178 Nils Aman 5.00 12.00
179 Jakub Lauko 6.00 15.00
180 Filip Roos 4.00 10.00
181 Cole Koepke 5.00 12.00
182 Pavol Regenda 5.00 12.00
183 Jack LaFontaine 5.00 12.00
184 Brayden Tracey 4.00 10.00
185 Isaac Ratcliffe 5.00 12.00
186 Andrei Kuzmenko 10.00 25.00
187 Arber Xhekaj 10.00 25.00
188 Johnathan Kovacevic 5.00 12.00
189 Declan Chisholm 5.00 12.00
190 Brayden Pachal 4.00 10.00
191 Adam Raska 5.00 12.00
192 Hayden Hodgson 4.00 10.00
193 Viktor Lodin 5.00 12.00
194 Cole Reinhardt 5.00 12.00
195 Nikita Okhotiuk 4.00 10.00
196 Mitchell Chaffee 4.00 10.00
197 Jake Christiansen 5.00 12.00
198 Nick Blankenburg 4.00 10.00
199 Brandon Biro 8.00 20.00
200 Bokondji Imama 4.00 10.00

2022-23 Upper Deck Stature Dignified

*GREEN/150: .5X TO 1.2X BASIC
*RED/75: 1X TO 2.5X BASIC
*ORANGE/35: 1.5X TO 4X BASIC
D1 Wayne Gretzky 8.00 20.00

D2 Mario Lemieux	5.00	12.00
D3 Teemu Selanne	2.50	6.00
D4 Brett Hull	2.50	6.00
D5 Bobby Hull	2.50	6.00
D6 Ray Bourque	2.00	5.00
D7 Steve Yzerman	3.00	8.00
D8 Peter Forsberg	2.50	6.00
D9 Luc Robitaille	1.25	3.00
D10 Martin Brodeur	3.00	8.00
D11 Henrik Lundqvist	3.00	8.00
D13 Jaromir Jagr	4.00	10.00
D14 Rob Blake	1.25	3.00
D15 Ron Francis	1.50	4.00
D16 Billy Smith	1.25	3.00
D17 Grant Fuhr	2.00	5.00
D18 Gerry Cheevers	1.25	3.00
D19 Marcel Dionne	1.50	4.00
D20 Pat LaFontaine	1.25	3.00
D21 Vincent Lecavalier	1.25	3.00
D22 Keith Tkachuk	1.25	3.00
D23 Jarome Iginla	1.50	4.00
D24 Ryan Getzlaf	1.25	3.00
D25 Pekka Rinne	1.25	3.00

2022-23 Upper Deck Stature Dignified Autographs

D6 Ray Bourque B	15.00	40.00
D8 Peter Forsberg B	20.00	50.00
D9 Luc Robitaille C	15.00	40.00
D10 Martin Brodeur B	25.00	60.00
D11 Henrik Lundqvist B	25.00	60.00
D12 Eric Lindros C	30.00	80.00
D14 Rob Blake C	10.00	25.00
D15 Ron Francis B	12.00	30.00
D17 Grant Fuhr C	15.00	40.00
D19 Marcel Dionne C	12.00	30.00
D20 Pat LaFontaine C	10.00	25.00
D22 Keith Tkachuk C	10.00	25.00
D23 Jarome Iginla C	12.00	30.00
D24 Ryan Getzlaf C	10.00	25.00

2022-23 Upper Deck Stature Photo Variant

*GREEN/66: .75X TO 2X BASIC
*RED/33: 1.5X TO 4X BASIC
*RED RC/33: 1.2X TO 3X BASIC
*ORANGE/25: 2X TO 5X BASIC

1 Wayne Gretzky	10.00	25.00
2 Mario Lemieux	6.00	15.00
3 Teemu Selanne	3.00	8.00
4 Brett Hull	3.00	8.00
5 Bobby Hull	3.00	8.00
6 Ray Bourque	2.50	6.00
7 Steve Yzerman	4.00	10.00
8 Peter Forsberg	3.00	8.00
9 Luc Robitaille	1.50	4.00
10 Martin Brodeur	4.00	10.00
11 Henrik Lundqvist	4.00	10.00
12 Eric Lindros	2.50	6.00
13 Jaromir Jagr	5.00	12.00
14 Rob Blake	1.50	4.00
15 Ron Francis	2.00	5.00
16 Billy Smith	1.50	4.00
17 Grant Fuhr	2.50	6.00
18 Gerry Cheevers	1.50	4.00
19 Marcel Dionne	2.00	5.00
20 Pat LaFontaine	1.50	4.00
21 Vincent Lecavalier	1.50	4.00
22 Keith Tkachuk	1.50	4.00
23 Jarome Iginla	2.00	5.00
24 Ryan Getzlaf	1.50	4.00
25 Pekka Rinne	1.50	4.00
26 Nick Suzuki	3.00	8.00
27 Zach Werenski	2.50	6.00
28 Brad Marchand	3.00	8.00
29 John Tavares	2.50	6.00
30 Jake Oettinger	2.50	6.00
31 Tim Stutzle	2.00	5.00
32 Sebastian Aho	2.50	6.00
33 Josh Norris	1.50	4.00
34 Teuvo Teravainen	1.50	4.00
35 Drake Batherson	1.50	4.00
36 Cole Caufield	3.00	8.00
37 Spencer Knight	1.50	4.00
38 Brendan Gallagher	1.50	4.00
39 Tyler Bertuzzi	1.25	3.00
40 Mark Stone	2.00	5.00
41 Lucas Raymond	2.50	6.00
42 James van Riemsdyk	1.25	3.00
43 Cam Atkinson	1.50	4.00
44 Patrick Kane	3.00	8.00
45 Dougie Hamilton	1.25	3.00
46 John Gibson	1.50	4.00
47 Nick Schmaltz	1.25	3.00
48 Jonathan Toews	2.50	6.00
49 Leon Draisaitl	5.00	12.00
50 Joel Eriksson Ek	1.25	3.00
51 Gabriel Landeskog	2.00	5.00
52 Timo Meier	1.50	4.00
53 Connor Hellebuyck	3.00	8.00
54 Brady Tkachuk	2.50	6.00
55 Sidney Crosby	6.00	15.00
56 Connor McDavid	8.00	20.00
57 Elias Lindholm	1.50	4.00
58 Tom Wilson	1.50	4.00
59 Jason Robertson	2.50	6.00
60 Tomas Hertl	1.50	4.00
61 Jonathan Marchessault	2.00	5.00
62 Ilya Sorokin	2.50	6.00
63 Robert Thomas	1.50	4.00
64 Miro Heiskanen	2.00	5.00
65 Moritz Seider	2.00	5.00
66 Taylor Hall	1.50	4.00
67 Andrei Svechnikov	2.00	5.00
68 Kyle Connor	2.50	6.00
69 Jacob Markstrom	1.50	4.00
70 Cole Sillinger	1.25	3.00
71 Jesper Bratt	1.50	4.00
72 Dylan Cozens	1.50	4.00
73 Aaron Ekblad	2.00	5.00
74 Trevor Zegras	1.50	4.00
75 Aleksander Barkov	2.50	6.00
76 Quinton Byfield	2.00	5.00
77 Cale Makar	4.00	10.00
78 Alexis Lafreniere	2.50	6.00
79 Andrei Vasilevskiy	2.50	6.00
80 Casey Mittelstadt	1.50	4.00
81 Quinn Hughes	4.00	10.00
82 Mikael Granlund	1.25	3.00
83 Auston Matthews	6.00	15.00
84 Mathew Barzal	2.00	5.00
85 Philipp Grubauer	1.50	4.00
86 Steven Stamkos	3.00	8.00
87 Jake Guentzel	2.50	6.00
88 Anze Kopitar	2.50	6.00
89 Alex Newhook	1.25	3.00
90 Brock Boeser	2.00	5.00
91 Kris Letang	2.00	5.00
92 Ryan O'Reilly	1.50	4.00
93 Alex Ovechkin	6.00	15.00
94 Adam Fox	2.00	5.00
95 Bowen Byram	2.00	5.00
96 Jeremy Swayman	2.50	6.00
97 Yanni Gourde	1.25	3.00
98 Kirill Kaprizov	5.00	12.00
99 Roman Josi	1.50	4.00
100 Clayton Keller	2.00	5.00
101 Matt Boldy	8.00	20.00
102 Matty Beniers	6.00	15.00
103 Kent Johnson	5.00	12.00
104 Owen Power	5.00	12.00
105 Juraj Slafkovsky	12.00	30.00
106 Shane Wright	6.00	15.00
107 Nick Cicek	2.50	6.00
108 Kaedan Korczak	2.00	5.00
109 Jacob Perreault	2.50	6.00
110 Marcus Bjork	2.50	6.00
111 Dylan Guenther	6.00	15.00
112 Reilly Walsh	2.50	6.00
113 Matej Blumel	3.00	8.00
114 Matias Maccelli	4.00	10.00
115 Jack Quinn	4.00	10.00
116 Samuel Poulin	3.00	8.00
117 Michael Eyssimont	2.50	6.00
118 Jonatan Berggren	4.00	10.00
119 Alex Vlasic	2.00	5.00
120 Zack Hayes	2.00	5.00
121 Filip Hallander	2.50	6.00
122 Pyotr Kochetkov	5.00	12.00
123 Fredrik Karlstrom	2.00	5.00
124 Nick DeSimone	2.50	6.00
125 Jack McBain	2.50	6.00
126 Dylan Wells	2.50	6.00
127 Jordan Spence	2.50	6.00
128 Marco Rossi	6.00	15.00
129 Oskar Olausson	2.50	6.00
130 Chase Pearson	2.00	5.00
131 David Jiricek	5.00	12.00
132 Filip Kral	3.00	8.00
133 Ronnie Attard	2.50	6.00
134 Mark Kastelic	2.00	5.00
135 Nikita Alexandrov	2.50	6.00
136 Nick Perbix	2.00	5.00
137 Olle Lycksell	2.50	6.00
138 Linus Hogberg	2.00	5.00
139 Kaiden Guhle	5.00	12.00
140 Dylan Holloway	5.00	12.00
141 Brandt Clarke	5.00	12.00
142 William Bitten	2.50	6.00
143 Ben Meyers	2.50	6.00
144 Jacob Moverare	2.00	5.00
145 Samuel Fagemo	2.00	5.00
146 Tyler Tucker	2.50	6.00
147 Erik Kallgren	2.50	6.00
148 Hunter Drew	2.50	6.00
149 Semyon Der-Arguchintsev	2.50	6.00
150 Vladislav Kolyachonok	2.00	5.00
151 Linus Sandin	2.00	5.00
152 Nick Abruzzese	2.50	6.00
153 Lukas Reichel	5.00	12.00
154 Bobby Brink	2.50	6.00
155 Juuso Parssinen	2.50	6.00
156 Jeff Malott	2.50	6.00
157 Jordan Harris	3.00	8.00
158 Mac Hollowell	2.50	6.00
159 Dylan Samberg	2.50	6.00
160 Valtteri Puustinen	2.00	5.00
161 Pontus Holmberg	2.50	6.00
162 Simon Holmstrom	2.50	6.00
163 Braden Schneider	4.00	10.00
164 Lukas Dostal	5.00	12.00
165 James Hamblin	2.50	6.00
166 Noah Cates	2.50	6.00
167 Nathan Smith	2.00	5.00
168 Trey Fix-Wolansky	2.50	6.00
169 Mads Sogaard	3.00	8.00
170 Lucas Johansen	2.00	5.00
171 Jean-Luc Foudy	2.50	6.00
172 Jakub Galvas	2.50	6.00
173 Thomas Bordeleau	2.50	6.00
174 Jake Sanderson	6.00	15.00
175 Elmer Soderblom	5.00	12.00
176 Wyatt Johnston	10.00	25.00
177 Marc McLaughlin	2.50	6.00
178 Nils Aman	2.50	6.00
179 Jakub Lauko	3.00	8.00
180 Filip Roos	2.00	5.00
181 Cole Koepke	2.50	6.00
182 Pavol Regenda	2.50	6.00
183 Jack LaFontaine	2.50	6.00
184 Brayden Tracey	2.00	5.00
185 Isaac Ratcliffe	2.50	6.00
186 Andrei Kuzmenko	5.00	12.00
187 Arber Xhekaj	5.00	12.00
188 Johnathan Kovacevic	2.50	6.00
189 Declan Chisholm	2.50	6.00
190 Brayden Pachal	2.00	5.00
191 Adam Raska	2.50	6.00
192 Hayden Hodgson	2.00	5.00
193 Viktor Lodin	2.50	6.00
194 Cole Reinhardt	2.50	6.00
195 Nikita Okhotiuk	2.00	5.00
196 Mitchell Chaffee	2.00	5.00
197 Jake Christiansen	2.50	6.00
198 Nick Blankenburg	2.00	5.00
199 Brandon Biro	4.00	10.00
200 Bokondji Imama	2.00	5.00

2022-23 Upper Deck Stature Photo Variant Autographs

3 Teemu Selanne B	20.00	50.00
4 Brett Hull B	20.00	50.00
6 Ray Bourque B	15.00	40.00
7 Steve Yzerman A	25.00	60.00
8 Peter Forsberg A	20.00	50.00
9 Luc Robitaille B	10.00	25.00
10 Martin Brodeur A	25.00	60.00
11 Henrik Lundqvist B	25.00	60.00
12 Eric Lindros B	15.00	40.00
14 Rob Blake B	10.00	25.00
15 Ron Francis B	12.00	30.00
17 Grant Fuhr B	15.00	40.00
18 Gerry Cheevers C	10.00	25.00
19 Marcel Dionne C	12.00	30.00
20 Pat LaFontaine C	10.00	25.00
22 Keith Tkachuk C	10.00	25.00
23 Jarome Iginla B	12.00	30.00
24 Ryan Getzlaf B	10.00	25.00
26 Nick Suzuki D	20.00	50.00
27 Zach Werenski D	15.00	40.00
28 Brad Marchand D	20.00	50.00
30 Jake Oettinger E	15.00	40.00
31 Tim Stutzle C	12.00	30.00
33 Josh Norris D	10.00	25.00
34 Teuvo Teravainen E	10.00	25.00
40 Mark Stone D	12.00	30.00
41 Lucas Raymond D	15.00	40.00
42 James van Riemsdyk D	8.00	20.00
43 Cam Atkinson D	10.00	25.00
46 John Gibson D	10.00	25.00
47 Nick Schmaltz F	8.00	20.00
50 Joel Eriksson Ek F	8.00	20.00
52 Timo Meier E	10.00	25.00
54 Brady Tkachuk C	15.00	40.00
60 Tomas Hertl D	10.00	25.00
61 Jonathan Marchessault E	12.00	30.00
63 Robert Thomas E	10.00	25.00
67 Andrei Svechnikov C	12.00	30.00
69 Jacob Markstrom D	10.00	25.00
70 Cole Sillinger F	8.00	20.00
73 Aaron Ekblad D	12.00	30.00
75 Aleksander Barkov C	15.00	40.00
77 Cale Makar B	25.00	60.00
78 Alexis Lafreniere C	15.00	40.00
81 Quinn Hughes C	25.00	60.00
85 Philipp Grubauer F	10.00	25.00
87 Jake Guentzel D	15.00	40.00
101 Matt Boldy	30.00	80.00
102 Matty Beniers	25.00	60.00
103 Kent Johnson	20.00	50.00
104 Owen Power	20.00	50.00
105 Juraj Slafkovsky	60.00	150.00
106 Shane Wright	25.00	60.00
108 Kaedan Korczak	8.00	20.00
109 Jacob Perreault	10.00	25.00
111 Dylan Guenther	25.00	60.00
114 Matias Maccelli	15.00	40.00
116 Samuel Poulin	12.00	30.00
117 Michael Eyssimont	10.00	25.00
120 Zack Hayes	8.00	20.00
121 Filip Hallander	10.00	25.00
122 Pyotr Kochetkov	20.00	50.00
123 Fredrik Karlstrom	8.00	20.00
124 Nick DeSimone	10.00	25.00
125 Jack McBain	10.00	25.00
128 Marco Rossi	25.00	60.00
130 Chase Pearson	8.00	20.00
133 Ronnie Attard	10.00	25.00
134 Mark Kastelic	8.00	20.00
135 Nikita Alexandrov	10.00	25.00
136 Nick Perbix	8.00	20.00
137 Olle Lycksell	10.00	25.00
140 Dylan Holloway	20.00	50.00
141 Brandt Clarke	20.00	50.00
142 William Bitten	10.00	25.00
143 Ben Meyers	10.00	25.00
144 Jacob Moverare	8.00	20.00
148 Hunter Drew	10.00	25.00
150 Vladislav Kolyachonok	8.00	20.00
152 Nick Abruzzese	10.00	25.00
153 Lukas Reichel	20.00	50.00
154 Bobby Brink	10.00	25.00
155 Juuso Parssinen	10.00	25.00
157 Jordan Harris	12.00	30.00
159 Dylan Samberg	10.00	25.00
160 Valtteri Puustinen	8.00	20.00
161 Pontus Holmberg	10.00	25.00
164 Lukas Dostal	20.00	50.00
166 Noah Cates	10.00	25.00
167 Nathan Smith	8.00	20.00
168 Trey Fix-Wolansky	10.00	25.00
169 Mads Sogaard	12.00	30.00
173 Thomas Bordeleau	10.00	25.00
174 Jake Sanderson	25.00	60.00
176 Wyatt Johnston	40.00	100.00
178 Nils Aman	10.00	25.00
180 Filip Roos	8.00	20.00
182 Pavol Regenda	10.00	25.00
184 Brayden Tracey	8.00	20.00
185 Isaac Ratcliffe	10.00	25.00
186 Andrei Kuzmenko	20.00	50.00
187 Arber Xhekaj	20.00	50.00
188 Johnathan Kovacevic	10.00	25.00
192 Hayden Hodgson	8.00	20.00
195 Nikita Okhotiuk	8.00	20.00
197 Jake Christiansen	10.00	25.00
198 Nick Blankenburg	8.00	20.00

2022-23 Upper Deck Stature Splendid Skaters

*GREEN/150: .6X TO 1.5X BASIC
*RED/75: .75X TO 2X BASIC
*ORANGE/35: 1.2X TO 3X BASIC

SS1 Carey Price	2.00	5.00
SS2 Anders Lee	.75	2.00
SS3 Brock Nelson	1.00	2.50
SS4 Yegor Sharangovich	1.00	2.50
SS5 Sam Reinhart	2.00	5.00
SS6 Alexander Holtz	1.00	2.50
SS7 Thomas Chabot	1.00	2.50
SS8 Jared McCann	.75	2.00
SS9 Jordan Eberle	1.00	2.50
SS10 Colton Parayko	.75	2.00
SS11 Pavel Buchnevich	.75	2.00
SS12 Thatcher Demko	1.25	3.00
SS13 Robin Lehner	.75	2.00
SS14 Nikolaj Ehlers	1.00	2.50
SS15 Josh Norris	1.00	2.50
SS16 Tom Wilson	1.00	2.50
SS17 Arthur Kaliyev	1.00	2.50
SS18 Moritz Seider	1.25	3.00
SS19 Spencer Knight	1.00	2.50
SS20 Connor McDavid	5.00	12.00
SS21 Auston Matthews	4.00	10.00
SS22 Alex Ovechkin	4.00	10.00
SS23 Cale Makar	2.50	6.00
SS24 Andrei Vasilevskiy	1.50	4.00
SS25 Brad Marchand	2.00	5.00

2022-23 Upper Deck Stature Splendid Skaters Autographs

SS2 Anders Lee C	8.00	20.00
SS5 Sam Reinhart B	20.00	50.00
SS6 Alexander Holtz D	10.00	25.00
SS8 Jared McCann D	8.00	20.00
SS9 Jordan Eberle B	10.00	25.00
SS10 Colton Parayko B.	8.00	20.00
SS13 Robin Lehner C	8.00	20.00
SS14 Nikolaj Ehlers B	10.00	25.00
SS15 Josh Norris B	10.00	25.00
SS17 Arthur Kaliyev D	10.00	25.00
SS21 Auston Matthews A	125.00	300.00
SS22 Alex Ovechkin A	125.00	300.00
SS23 Cale Makar A	25.00	60.00

2022-23 Upper Deck Stature Splendid Skaters Patch Autographs

SS2 Anders Lee/24	12.00	30.00
SS8 Jared McCann/24	12.00	30.00

2022-23 Upper Deck Stature Wunderkind

*GREEN/150: .6X TO 1.5X BASIC
*RED/75: 1X TO 2.5X BASIC
*ORANGE/35: 1.5X TO 4X BASIC

W1 Jacob Perreault	.75	2.00
W2 Brayden Tracey	.60	1.50
W3 Lukas Dostal	1.50	4.00
W4 Matias Maccelli	1.25	3.00
W5 Owen Power	1.50	4.00
W6 Jack Quinn	1.25	3.00
W7 Pyotr Kochetkov	1.50	4.00
W8 Lukas Reichel	1.50	4.00
W9 Alex Vlasic	.60	1.50
W10 Kent Johnson	1.50	4.00
W11 Trey Fix-Wolansky	.75	2.00
W12 Chase Pearson	.60	1.50
W13 Dylan Holloway	1.50	4.00
W14 Jordan Spence	.75	2.00
W15 Jacob Moverare	.60	1.50
W16 Marco Rossi	2.00	5.00
W17 Matt Boldy	2.50	6.00
W18 Jordan Harris	1.00	2.50
W19 Braden Schneider	1.25	3.00
W20 Mark Kastelic	.60	1.50
W21 Mads Sogaard	1.00	2.50
W22 Isaac Ratcliffe	.75	2.00
W23 Thomas Bordeleau	.75	2.00
W24 Matty Beniers	2.00	5.00
W25 Nick Abruzzese	.75	2.00
W26 Michael Eyssimont	.75	2.00
W27 Dylan Samberg	.75	2.00
W28 Hunter Drew	.75	2.00
W29 Nathan Smith	.60	1.50
W30 Jack McBain	.75	2.00
W31 Marc McLaughlin	.75	2.00
W32 Jack LaFontaine	.75	2.00
W33 Fredrik Karlstrom	.60	1.50
W34 Samuel Fagemo	.60	1.50
W35 Reilly Walsh	.75	2.00
W36 Noah Cates	.75	2.00
W37 Bobby Brink	.75	2.00
W38 Ronnie Attard	.75	2.00
W39 Dylan Guenther	2.00	5.00
W40 Andrei Kuzmenko	1.50	4.00
W41 David Jiricek	1.50	4.00
W42 Samuel Poulin	1.00	2.50
W43 Lucas Johansen	.60	1.50
W44 Juraj Slafkovsky	4.00	10.00
W45 Simon Holmstrom	.75	2.00
W46 Oskar Olausson	.75	2.00
W47 Jake Sanderson	2.00	5.00
W48 Shane Wright	2.00	5.00
W49 Brandt Clarke	1.50	4.00
W50 Wyatt Johnston	3.00	8.00

2022-23 Upper Deck Stature Wunderkind Autographs

W2 Brayden Tracey B	5.00	12.00
W3 Lukas Dostal C	12.00	30.00
W4 Matias Maccelli D	10.00	25.00
W5 Owen Power A	12.00	30.00
W7 Pyotr Kochetkov D	12.00	30.00
W8 Lukas Reichel C	12.00	30.00
W10 Kent Johnson B	12.00	30.00
W11 Trey Fix-Wolansky E	6.00	15.00
W12 Chase Pearson E	5.00	12.00
W13 Dylan Holloway C	12.00	30.00
W15 Jacob Moverare E	5.00	12.00
W16 Marco Rossi B	15.00	40.00
W17 Matt Boldy B	20.00	50.00
W18 Jordan Harris E	8.00	20.00
W20 Mark Kastelic E	5.00	12.00
W21 Mads Sogaard D	8.00	20.00
W22 Isaac Ratcliffe D	6.00	15.00
W23 Thomas Bordeleau D	6.00	15.00
W24 Matty Beniers A	15.00	40.00
W25 Nick Abruzzese E	6.00	15.00
W26 Michael Eyssimont E	6.00	15.00
W27 Dylan Samberg C	6.00	15.00
W28 Hunter Drew E	6.00	15.00
W29 Nathan Smith E	5.00	12.00
W30 Jack McBain E	6.00	15.00
W33 Fredrik Karlstrom E	5.00	12.00
W36 Noah Cates E	6.00	15.00
W37 Bobby Brink D	6.00	15.00
W38 Ronnie Attard E	6.00	15.00
W39 Dylan Guenther C	15.00	40.00
W40 Andrei Kuzmenko C	12.00	30.00
W42 Samuel Poulin C	8.00	20.00
W44 Juraj Slafkovsky A	30.00	80.00
W47 Jake Sanderson C	15.00	40.00
W48 Shane Wright A	15.00	40.00
W49 Brandt Clarke C	12.00	30.00

2022-23 Upper Deck Stature Wunderkind Autographs Green

*GREEN/25: .6X TO 1.5X BASIC

W5 Owen Power	40.00	100.00
W17 Matt Boldy	60.00	150.00
W24 Matty Beniers	80.00	200.00
W44 Juraj Slafkovsky	80.00	200.00
W48 Shane Wright	50.00	125.00
W49 Brandt Clarke	30.00	80.00

2022-23 Upper Deck Stature Wunderkind Patch Autographs

W4 Matias Maccelli/24	25.00	60.00
W12 Chase Pearson/24	12.00	30.00
W15 Jacob Moverare/24	12.00	30.00
W20 Mark Kastelic/24	12.00	30.00
W21 Mads Sogaard/24	20.00	50.00
W22 Isaac Ratcliffe/24	15.00	40.00
W25 Nick Abruzzese/24	15.00	40.00
W26 Michael Eyssimont/24	15.00	40.00
W29 Nathan Smith/24	12.00	30.00
W36 Noah Cates/24	15.00	40.00
W37 Bobby Brink/24	15.00	40.00

2005-06 Upper Deck Sunkist

COMPLETE SET (6)	6.00	15.00
1 Richard Brodeur	1.00	2.50
2 Wendel Clark	1.00	2.50
3 Yvan Cournoyer	1.00	2.50
4 Doug Gilmour	1.25	3.00
5 Dale Hawerchuk	1.00	2.50
6 Lanny McDonald	1.25	3.00

2006-07 Upper Deck Sunkist

COMPLETE SET (10)	10.00	20.00
1 Alex Kovalev	.40	1.00
2 Jason Spezza	.75	2.00
3 Mats Sundin	1.25	3.00
4 Jarome Iginla	1.25	3.00
5 Ryan Smyth	.75	2.00
6 Markus Naslund	.75	2.00
7 Alexander Ovechkin	2.00	5.00
8 Vincent Lecavalier	1.25	3.00
9 Joe Thornton	1.50	4.00
10 Miikka Kiprusoff	1.25	3.00

2007-08 Upper Deck Sunkist

COMPLET SET (10)	10.00	25.00
1 Saku Koivu	1.25	3.00
2 Mats Sundin	1.25	3.00
3 Dany Heatley	1.25	3.00
4 Alex Hemsky	1.25	3.00
5 Jarome Iginla	1.25	3.00
6 Roberto Luongo	1.50	4.00
7 Joe Thornton	1.50	4.00
8 Vincent LeCavalier	1.25	3.00
9 Chris Pronger	1.25	3.00
10 Eric Staal	1.25	3.00

2008-09 Upper Deck Sunkist

COMPLETE SET (10)	10.00	20.00
1 Sidney Crosby	3.00	8.00
2 Alexander Ovechkin	2.00	5.00
3 Carey Price	1.50	4.00
4 Mike Cammalleri	.75	2.00
5 Matt Stajan	1.00	2.50
6 Dany Heatley	1.25	3.00
7 Jarome Iginla	1.25	3.00
8 Daniel Sedin	1.00	2.50
9 Sam Gagner	.75	2.00
10 Sergei Kostitsyn	.75	2.00

2008-09 Upper Deck Sunkist Autographs

1 Sidney Crosby	60.00	100.00
2 Alexander Ovechkin	40.00	80.00
5 Matt Stajan	8.00	20.00
10 Sergei Kostitsyn	8.00	20.00

2009-10 Upper Deck Sunkist

COMPLETE SET (10)	10.00	20.00
1 Sidney Crosby	3.00	8.00
2 Martin Brodeur	1.50	4.00
3 Jarome Iginla	1.25	3.00
4 Rick Nash	1.25	3.00
5 Mike Richards	1.00	2.50
6 Vincent LeCavalier	1.25	3.00
7 Roberto Luongo	1.50	4.00
8 Ryan Getzlaf	1.00	2.50
9 Scott Niedermayer	1.00	2.50
10 Jay Bouwmeester	1.00	2.50

2013-14 Upper Deck Team Canada

COMP.SET w/o SP's (100)	8.00	20.00
1 Cam Ward	.40	1.00
2 Adam Henrique	.30	.75
3 Milan Lucic	.40	1.00
4 Alex Pietrangelo	.30	.75
5 Alex Tanguay	.25	.60
6 Andrew Cogliano	.25	.60
7 Andrew Ladd	.25	.60
8 Bill Ranford	.50	1.25
9 Blake Comeau	.25	.60
10 Bobby Orr	.75	2.00
11 Brad Boyes	.25	.60
12 Brad Marchand	.75	2.00
13 Jason Spezza	.40	1.00
14 Braden Holtby	.50	1.25
15 Brandon McMillan	.25	.60
16 Brayden McNabb	.25	.60
17 Brayden Schenn	.40	1.00
18 Brendan Mikkelson	.25	.60
19 Brenden Morrow	.30	.75
20 Brent Seabrook	.25	.60
21 Brett Connolly	.25	.60
22 Bryan Little	.40	1.00
23 Calvin de Haan	.25	.60
24 Steve Yzerman	1.00	2.50
25 Carter Ashton	.25	.60
26 Chet Pickard	.25	.60
27 Chris Phillips	.25	.60
28 Chris Stewart	.30	.75
29 Ryan Spooner	.40	1.00
30 Clarke MacArthur	.25	.60
31 Cody Eakin	.25	.60
32 Cody Hodgson	.25	.60
33 Colby Armstrong	.25	.60
34 Colten Teubert	.25	.60
35 Dana Tyrell	.25	.60
36 Daniel Carcillo	.25	.60
37 Derek Roy	.25	.60
38 Devante Smith-Pelly	.30	.75
39 Dustin Tokarski	.40	1.00
40 Dylan Olsen	.25	.60
41 Shane Doan	.30	.75
42 Erik Gudbranson	.25	.60
43 Glen Murray	.30	.75
44 Greg Nemisz	.25	.60
45 Jaden Schwartz	.50	1.25
46 Jake Allen	.40	1.00
47 James Neal	.25	.60
48 Jamie Benn	.50	1.00
49 Jamie Oleksiak	.30	.75
50 Chris Pronger	.40	1.00
51 Jay Bouwmeester	.25	.60
52 Jay McClement	.25	.60
53 Jeremy Colliton	.25	.60
54 John Negrin	.25	.60
55 Jordan Eberle	.40	1.00
56 Justin Pogge	.25	.60
57 Karl Alzner	.25	.60
58 Keaton Ellerby	.25	.60
59 Keith Aulie	.25	.60
60 Kyle Clifford	.25	.60
61 Luke Adam	.30	.75
62 Luke Schenn	.40	1.00
63 Devan Dubnyk	.30	.75
64 Marc-Andre Gragnani	.25	.60
65 Marco Scandella	.25	.60
66 Mark Stone	.50	1.25
67 Matt Beleskey	.25	.60
68 Matthew Halischuk	.25	.60
69 Michael Cammalleri	.30	.75
70 Justin Schultz	.75	2.00
71 Michael Ryder	.25	.60
72 Patrice Cormier	.25	.60
73 Pierre-Marc Bouchard	.40	1.00
74 Quinton Howden	.30	.75
75 Ryan Ellis	.30	.75
76 Ryan Getzlaf	.40	1.00
77 Ryan Johansen	.30	.75
78 Ryan Smyth	.30	.75
79 Sam Gagner	.25	.60
80 Scott Laughton	.60	1.50
81 Sean Couturier	.30	.75
82 Sheldon Souray	.25	.60
83 Simon Despres	.30	.75
84 Simon Gagne	.40	1.00
85 Stefan Della Rovere	.25	.60
86 Stefan Elliott	.30	.75
87 Stephen Weiss	.30	.75
88 Steve Bernier	.25	.60
89 Steve Sullivan	.25	.60
90 Thomas Hickey	.30	.75
91 Tim Brent	.25	.60
92 Travis Hamonic	.25	.60
93 Tyler Ennis	.25	.60
94 Tyler Myers	.25	.60
95 Zach Boychuk	.25	.60
96 Tyson Barrie	.25	.60
97 Wade Redden	.25	.60
98 Yann Sauve	.25	.60
99 Wayne Gretzky	2.50	6.00
100 Zack Kassian	.25	.60
101 Alexandre Burrows	.50	1.25
102 Bill Barber	.75	2.00
103 Mike Green	.60	1.50
104 Bobby Clarke	1.25	3.00
105 Bobby Hull	1.50	4.00
106 Bobby Orr	3.00	8.00
107 Paul Coffey	.75	2.00
108 Jared Cowen	.50	1.25
109 Casey Cizikas	.50	1.25
110 Corey Perry	1.25	3.00
111 Curtis Joseph	1.00	2.50
112 Dale Hawerchuk	1.00	2.50
113 Dan Boyle	.50	1.25
114 Dany Heatley	.60	1.50
115 Darryl Sittler	1.00	2.50
116 Dion Phaneuf	.60	1.50
117 Dougie Hamilton	1.25	3.00
118 Drew Doughty	1.00	2.50
119 Ed Belfour	.75	2.00
120 Brayden Schenn	.75	2.00
121 Eric Lindros	1.25	3.00
122 Eric Staal	1.00	2.50
123 Evander Kane	.75	2.00
124 Vincent Damphousse	.60	1.50
125 Felix Potvin	1.25	3.00
126 Tanner Pearson	.75	2.00
127 Gilbert Perreault	.75	2.00
128 Guillaume Latendresse	.60	1.50
129 Guy Lafleur	1.00	2.50
130 Jarome Iginla	1.00	2.50
131 Jean-Sebastien Giguere	.75	2.00
132 Jeff Skinner	1.00	2.50
133 Joe Sakic	1.50	4.00
134 Joe Thornton	1.25	3.00
135 John Tavares	1.25	3.00
136 Jonathan Bernier	.60	1.50
137 Carey Price	1.50	4.00
138 Jonathan Huberdeau	1.50	4.00
139 Jonathan Toews	1.25	3.00
140 Jordan Eberle	.75	2.00
141 Theoren Fleury	1.00	2.50
142 Jordan Staal	.60	1.50
143 Jose Theodore	.75	2.00
144 Josh Gorges	.60	1.50
145 Kris Draper	.60	1.50
146 Kyle Turris	.50	1.25
147 Nathan Beaulieu	.50	1.25
148 Larry Robinson	.75	2.00
149 Logan Couture	1.00	2.50
150 Louis Leblanc	.50	1.25
151 Luc Robitaille	.75	2.00
152 Marc-Andre Fleury	1.50	4.00
153 Marcel Dionne	1.00	2.50
154 Shea Weber	.60	1.50
155 Mario Lemieux	3.00	8.00
156 Mark Messier	1.50	4.00
157 Mark Scheifele	1.00	2.50
158 Martin Brodeur	2.00	5.00
159 Roberto Luongo	1.25	3.00
160 Martin St. Louis	.75	2.00
161 Marty Turco	.75	2.00
162 Matt Duchene	.75	2.00
163 Maxime Talbot	.50	1.25
164 Mike Bossy	.75	2.00
165 Mike Ribeiro	.50	1.25
166 Mike Richards	.60	1.50
167 Marc Staal	.50	1.25
168 P.K. Subban	1.00	2.50
169 Patrice Bergeron	1.00	2.50
170 Patrick Marleau	.75	2.00
171 Patrick Roy	2.00	5.00
172 Phil Esposito	1.25	3.00
173 Ray Bourque	1.25	3.00
174 Claude Giroux	.75	2.00
175 Rick Nash	1.00	2.50
176 Kris Letang	1.00	2.50
177 Rogie Vachon	1.00	2.50
178 Ron Francis	1.00	2.50
179 Ron Hextall	.75	2.00
180 Ryan Nugent-Hopkins	1.00	2.50
181 Nazem Kadri	1.00	2.50
182 Patrick Sharp	.75	2.00
183 Scott Hartnell	.50	1.25
184 Steve Mason	.60	1.50
185 Steve Shutt	.60	1.50
186 Sidney Crosby	3.00	8.00
187 Steven Stamkos	1.50	4.00
188 Taylor Hall	.75	2.00
189 Michael Del Zotto	.50	1.25
190 Tyler Seguin	1.00	2.50
191 Vincent Lecavalier	.75	2.00
192 Wayne Gretzky	5.00	12.00
193 Wayne Simmonds	1.00	2.50
194 Wendel Clark	1.25	3.00
195 Josh Harding	.75	2.00
196 Brendan Gallagher	1.50	4.00
197 Jamie Tardif	.50	1.25
198 Michael Sgarbossa	1.00	2.50
199 Jaden Schwartz	1.00	2.50
200 Ryan Murphy	.75	2.00
201 Stefan Elliott PEA	1.00	2.50
202 Cody Hodgson PEA	.75	2.00
203 Jamie Oleksiak PEA	1.00	2.50
204 Scott Glennie PEA	1.25	3.00
205 Dougie Hamilton PEA	2.50	6.00
206 Jaden Schwartz PEA	1.50	4.00
207 Mark Scheifele PEA	1.50	4.00
208 Scott Laughton PEA	1.50	4.00
209 Thomas Hickey PEA	1.00	2.50
210 Ryan Murphy PEA	1.25	3.00
211 Quinton Howden PEA	1.00	2.50
212 Erik Gudbranson PEA	.75	2.00
213 Dylan Olsen PEA	.75	2.00
214 Carter Ashton PEA	.75	2.00
215 Brendan Gallagher PEA	2.00	5.00
216 Jamie Tardif PEA	.75	2.00
217 Michael Sgarbossa PEA	1.25	3.00
218 Ryan Spooner PEA	1.25	3.00
219 Jake Allen PEA	1.25	3.00
220 Casey Cizikas PEA	.75	2.00
221 Tyson Barrie PEA	1.25	3.00
222 Cody Goloubef PEA	1.50	4.00
223 Mark Stone PEA	1.50	4.00
224 Chet Pickard PEA	1.50	4.00
225 Jeff Skinner PEA	1.50	4.00
226 Taylor Hall PEA	1.25	3.00
227 Jordan Eberle PEA	2.00	5.00
228 Ryan Nugent-Hopkins PEA	1.50	4.00
229 John Tavares PEA	2.00	5.00
230 Jonathan Huberdeau PEA	1.50	4.00
SP1 Nathan MacKinnon PEA	10.00	25.00
SP2 Sean Monahan PEA	6.00	15.00

2013-14 Upper Deck Team Canada Special Edition

SE1 Wayne Gretzky	10.00	25.00
SE2 Tyson Barrie	2.00	5.00
SE3 Thomas Hickey	1.25	3.00
SE4 Theoren Fleury	2.00	5.00
SE5 Taylor Hall	1.50	4.00
SE6 Steve Mason	1.25	3.00
SE7 Stefan Elliott	1.25	3.00
SE8 Sidney Crosby	5.00	12.00
SE9 Shea Weber	1.25	3.00
SE10 Scott Laughton	2.00	5.00
SE11 Scott Hartnell	1.00	2.50
SE12 Scott Glennie	1.25	3.00
SE13 Ryan Spooner	.75	2.00
SE14 Ryan Smyth	1.50	4.00
SE15 Ryan Nugent-Hopkins	2.00	5.00
SE16 Ryan Murphy	1.50	4.00
SE17 Ryan Getzlaf	2.00	5.00
SE18 Roberto Luongo	2.50	6.00
SE19 Rick Nash	1.50	4.00
SE20 Quinton Howden	1.50	4.00
SE21 Patrice Bergeron	2.00	5.00
SE22 P.K. Subban	2.00	5.00
SE23 Mike Richards	1.25	3.00
SE24 Michael Sgarbossa	1.50	4.00
SE25 Martin Brodeur	4.00	10.00
SE26 Mark Stone	2.00	5.00
SE27 Mark Scheifele	2.50	6.00
SE28 Mark Messier	3.00	8.00
SE29 Mario Lemieux	6.00	15.00
SE30 Marc-Andre Fleury	3.00	8.00
SE31 Kris Letang	2.00	5.00
SE32 Jordan Eberle	1.50	4.00
SE33 Jonathan Toews	2.50	6.00
SE34 Jonathan Huberdeau	2.00	5.00
SE35 John Tavares	2.50	6.00
SE36 Joe Sakic	3.00	8.00
SE37 Jeff Skinner	2.00	5.00
SE38 Jeff Carter	1.25	3.00
SE39 Jarome Iginla	2.00	5.00
SE40 Jamie Oleksiak	1.25	3.00
SE41 Jake Allen	1.50	4.00
SE42 Jaden Schwartz	2.00	5.00
SE43 Erik Gudbranson	1.00	2.50
SE44 Eric Lindros	2.50	6.00
SE45 Ed Belfour	2.00	5.00
SE46 Drew Doughty	2.00	5.00
SE47 Dougie Hamilton	1.25	3.00
SE48 Curtis Joseph	2.00	5.00
SE49 Corey Perry	2.50	6.00
SE50 Cody Hodgson	1.00	2.50
SE51 Cody Goloubef	1.00	2.50
SE52 Claude Giroux	1.50	4.00

SE53 Chet Pickard 1.00 2.50
SE54 Casey Cizikas 1.25 3.00
SE55 Carey Price 3.00 8.00
SE56 Brendan Gallagher 2.00 5.00
SE57 Brayden Schenn 1.50 4.00
SE58 Brad Marchand 2.50 6.00
SE59 Bobby Orr 3.00 8.00
SE60 Adam Henrique 1.25 3.00

2013-14 Upper Deck Team Canada Special Edition Gold Die Cut

SE1 Wayne Gretzky 40.00 80.00

2013-14 Upper Deck Team Canada Red

*1-100 VETS/100: 4X TO 10X BASIC CARDS
*101-200 VETS/100: 2X TO 5X BASIC CARDS
*201-230 PEA/100: 1.2X TO 3X BASIC PEA

2013-14 Upper Deck Team Canada Autographs

1 Cam Ward C 8.00 20.00
2 Adam Henrique G 6.00 15.00
4 Alex Pietrangelo G 6.00 15.00
5 Alex Tanguay C 5.00 12.00
6 Andrew Cogliano I 5.00 12.00
7 Andrew Ladd G 5.00 12.00
8 Bill Ranford E 8.00 20.00
9 Blake Comeau C 5.00 12.00
10 Bobby Orr E 60.00 150.00
11 Brad Boyes D 5.00 12.00
12 Brad Marchand E 15.00 40.00
14 Braden Holtby E 10.00 25.00
15 Brandon McMillan D 5.00 12.00
16 Brayden McNabb H 5.00 12.00
17 Brayden Schenn F 8.00 20.00
18 Brendan Mikkelson H 5.00 12.00
19 Brenden Morrow A 6.00 15.00
20 Brent Seabrook E 5.00 12.00
21 Brett Connolly H 5.00 12.00
22 Bryan Little C 8.00 20.00
23 Calvin de Haan D 5.00 12.00
24 Steve Yzerman A 20.00 50.00
25 Carter Ashton D 5.00 12.00
26 Chet Pickard D 5.00 12.00
27 Chris Phillips I 5.00 12.00
28 Chris Stewart C 6.00 15.00
29 Ryan Spooner H 8.00 20.00
30 Clarke MacArthur F 5.00 12.00
31 Cody Eakin G 5.00 12.00
32 Cody Hodgson E 5.00 12.00
33 Colby Armstrong C 5.00 12.00
34 Colten Teubert H 5.00 12.00
35 Dana Tyrell C 5.00 12.00
36 Daniel Carcillo H 5.00 12.00
37 Derek Roy G 5.00 12.00
38 Devante Smith-Pelly C 6.00 15.00
39 Dustin Tokarski E 8.00 20.00
40 Dylan Olsen E 5.00 12.00
41 Shane Doan C 6.00 15.00
42 Erik Gudbranson F 5.00 12.00
43 Glen Murray E 6.00 15.00
45 Jaden Schwartz B 10.00 25.00
46 Jake Allen E 8.00 20.00
47 James Neal A 5.00 12.00
48 Jamie Benn E 8.00 20.00
49 Jamie Oleksiak E 6.00 15.00
50 Chris Pronger C 8.00 20.00
52 Jay McClement D 5.00 12.00
53 Jeremy Colliton G 5.00 12.00
54 John Negrin F 5.00 12.00
56 Justin Pogge E 5.00 12.00
57 Karl Alzner F 5.00 12.00
58 Keaton Ellerby I 5.00 12.00
59 Keith Aulie F 5.00 12.00
60 Kyle Clifford F 5.00 12.00
61 Luke Adam C 6.00 15.00
62 Luke Schenn H 8.00 20.00
63 Devan Dubnyk E 6.00 15.00
64 Marc-Andre Gragnani B 5.00 12.00
65 Marco Scandella G 5.00 12.00
66 Mark Stone I 10.00 25.00
67 Matt Beleskey G 5.00 12.00
68 Matthew Halischuk G 5.00 12.00
69 Michael Cammalleri A 6.00 15.00
70 Justin Schultz E 8.00 20.00
71 Michael Ryder E 5.00 12.00
72 Patrice Cormier A 5.00 12.00
73 Pierre-Marc Bouchard B 8.00 20.00
74 Quinton Howden I 6.00 15.00
75 Ryan Ellis H 6.00 15.00
77 Ryan Johansen G 6.00 15.00
78 Ryan Smyth D 6.00 15.00
79 Sam Gagner F 5.00 12.00
80 Scott Laughton F 10.00 25.00
83 Simon Despres D 6.00 15.00
84 Simon Gagne C 8.00 20.00
85 Stefan Della Rovere H 5.00 12.00
87 Stephen Weiss H 6.00 15.00
88 Steve Bernier C 5.00 12.00
89 Steve Sullivan D 5.00 12.00
90 Thomas Hickey I 6.00 15.00
91 Tim Brent H 5.00 12.00
92 Travis Hamonic G 5.00 12.00
93 Tyler Ennis F 5.00 12.00
94 Tyler Myers D 5.00 12.00
95 Zach Boychuk G 5.00 12.00
96 Tyson Barrie G 5.00 12.00
97 Wade Redden F 5.00 12.00
98 Yann Sauve H 5.00 12.00
99 Wayne Gretzky E 200.00 500.00
100 Zack Kassian F 5.00 12.00
101 Alexandre Burrows H 5.00 12.00
102 Bill Barber F 8.00 20.00
104 Bobby Clarke E 12.00 30.00
105 Bobby Hull B 15.00 40.00
106 Bobby Orr F 60.00 150.00
107 Paul Coffey C 8.00 20.00
108 Jared Cowen F 5.00 12.00
109 Casey Cizikas I 5.00 12.00
110 Corey Perry F 12.00 30.00
111 Curtis Joseph C 10.00 25.00
113 Dan Boyle E 5.00 12.00
114 Dany Heatley B 6.00 15.00
115 Darryl Sittler B 10.00 25.00
116 Dion Phaneuf E 6.00 15.00
117 Dougie Hamilton G 12.00 30.00
119 Ed Belfour B 8.00 20.00
120 Brayden Schenn D 8.00 20.00
121 Eric Lindros A 12.00 30.00
122 Eric Staal E 10.00 25.00
123 Evander Kane D 8.00 20.00
124 Vincent Damphousse E 6.00 15.00
125 Felix Potvin E 12.00 30.00
126 Tanner Pearson G 8.00 20.00
127 Gilbert Perreault C 8.00 20.00
128 Guillaume Latendresse I 6.00 15.00
129 Guy Lafleur B 10.00 25.00
130 Jarome Iginla B 10.00 25.00
131 Jean-Sebastien Giguere E 8.00 20.00
132 Jeff Skinner D 10.00 25.00
133 Joe Sakic A 25.00 60.00
134 Joe Thornton B 12.00 30.00
135 John Tavares E 12.00 30.00
136 Jonathan Bernier G 6.00 15.00
137 Carey Price B 15.00 40.00
138 Jonathan Huberdeau D 20.00 50.00
139 Jonathan Toews B 12.00 30.00
141 Theoren Fleury A 10.00 25.00
142 Jordan Staal D 6.00 15.00
143 Jose Theodore A 8.00 20.00
144 Josh Gorges D 6.00 15.00
145 Kris Draper F 6.00 15.00
146 Kyle Turris G 5.00 12.00
147 Nathan Beaulieu I 5.00 12.00
148 Larry Robinson E 8.00 20.00
149 Logan Couture B 10.00 25.00
150 Louis Leblanc I 5.00 12.00
151 Luc Robitaille C 8.00 20.00
152 Marc-Andre Fleury C 15.00 40.00
153 Marcel Dionne E 10.00 25.00
155 Mario Lemieux A 30.00 80.00
156 Mark Messier B 15.00 40.00
157 Mark Scheifele H 12.00 30.00
158 Martin Brodeur B 20.00 50.00
160 Martin St. Louis C 8.00 20.00
161 Marty Turco E 8.00 20.00
162 Matt Duchene C 8.00 20.00
163 Maxime Talbot G 5.00 12.00
164 Mike Bossy C 8.00 20.00
165 Mike Ribeiro E 5.00 12.00
166 Mike Richards B 6.00 15.00
167 Marc Staal D 5.00 12.00
168 P.K. Subban C 10.00 25.00
170 Patrick Marleau C 8.00 20.00
171 Patrick Roy A 20.00 50.00
172 Phil Esposito A 12.00 30.00
173 Ray Bourque B 12.00 30.00
174 Claude Giroux B 8.00 20.00
175 Rick Nash C 8.00 20.00
177 Rogie Vachon B 10.00 25.00
178 Ron Francis C 10.00 25.00
179 Ron Hextall D 8.00 20.00
183 Scott Hartnell E 5.00 12.00
184 Steve Mason F 6.00 15.00
185 Steve Shutt C 6.00 15.00
186 Sidney Crosby D 80.00 200.00
187 Steven Stamkos E 15.00 40.00
188 Taylor Hall D 8.00 20.00
189 Michael Del Zotto F 5.00 12.00
190 Tyler Seguin B 10.00 25.00
191 Vincent Lecavalier A 8.00 20.00
192 Wayne Gretzky D 250.00 600.00
193 Wayne Simmonds C 10.00 25.00
194 Wendel Clark E 12.00 30.00
195 Josh Harding D 8.00 20.00
196 Brendan Gallagher H 20.00 50.00
198 Michael Sgarbossa I 8.00 20.00
199 Jaden Schwartz A 10.00 25.00
200 Ryan Murphy I 8.00 20.00
201S Stefan Elliott PEA 6.00 15.00
202S Cody Hodgson PEA 5.00 12.00
203S Jamie Oleksiak PEA 6.00 15.00
204S Scott Glennie PEA 5.00 12.00
205S Dougie Hamilton PEA 12.00 30.00
206S Jaden Schwartz PEA 10.00 25.00
207S Mark Scheifele PEA 12.00 30.00
208S Scott Laughton PEA 10.00 25.00
209S Thomas Hickey PEA 6.00 15.00
210S Ryan Murphy PEA 8.00 20.00
211S Quinton Howden PEA 6.00 15.00
212S Erik Gudbranson PEA 5.00 12.00
213S Dylan Olsen PEA 5.00 12.00
214S Carter Ashton PEA 5.00 12.00
215S Brendan Gallagher PEA 20.00 50.00
217S Michael Sgarbossa PEA 8.00 20.00
218S Ryan Spooner PEA 8.00 20.00
219S Jake Allen PEA 8.00 20.00
220S Casey Cizikas PEA 5.00 12.00
221S Tyson Barrie PEA 5.00 12.00
222S Cody Goloubef PEA 5.00 12.00
223S Mark Stone PEA 10.00 25.00
224S Chet Pickard PEA 5.00 12.00
225S Jeff Skinner PEA 10.00 25.00
226S Taylor Hall PEA 8.00 20.00
228S Ryan Nugent-Hopkins PEA 10.00 25.00
229S John Tavares PEA 12.00 30.00
230S Jonathan Huberdeau PEA 20.00 50.00
SP1 Nathan MacKinnon/99 40.00 100.00
SP2 Sean Monahan/99 12.00 30.00

2013-14 Upper Deck Team Canada Captains

C1 Phil Esposito 2.50 6.00
C2 Marcel Dionne 2.00 5.00
C3 Bobby Clarke 2.50 6.00
C4 Darryl Sittler 2.00 5.00
C5 Theoren Fleury 2.00 5.00
C6 Paul Coffey 2.00 5.00
C7 Eric Lindros 2.50 6.00
C8 Luc Robitaille 1.50 4.00
C9 Mario Lemieux 6.00 15.00
C10 Jarret Stoll 2.00 5.00
C11 Ryan Smyth SP 6.00 15.00
C12 Joe Sakic SP 12.00 30.00
C13 Shane Doan SP 5.00 12.00
C14 Kris Letang SP 10.00 25.00
C15 Karl Alzner SP 5.00 12.00
C16 Thomas Hickey SP 6.00 15.00
C17 Patrice Cormier SP 8.00 20.00
C18 Rick Nash SP 8.00 20.00
C19 Ryan Ellis SP 6.00 15.00
C20 Ryan Getzlaf SP 8.00 20.00
C21 Jaden Schwartz SP 15.00 40.00
C22 Ryan Nugent-Hopkins SP 25.00 50.00
C23 Thomas Hickey AU C 30.00 60.00
C24 Steve Yzerman AU A 150.00 300.00
C25 Ryan Nugent-Hopkins AU A 150.00 250.00
C26 Mario Lemieux AU A 250.00 450.00
C28 Jaden Schwartz AU C 15.00 40.00
C29 Joe Sakic AU B 100.00 175.00
C30 Theoren Fleury AU B 60.00 120.00
C31 Phil Esposito AU B 90.00 150.00
C32 Ryan Ellis AU C 25.00 60.00

2013-14 Upper Deck Team Canada Clear Cut Program of Excellence

CCPOE1 Wayne Gretzky 30.00 60.00
CCPOE2 Theoren Fleury 12.00 30.00
CCPOE3 Taylor Hall 10.00 25.00
CCPOE4 Sidney Crosby 25.00 50.00
CCPOE5 Scott Laughton 8.00 20.00
CCPOE6 Ryan Spooner 8.00 20.00
CCPOE7 Ryan Smyth 10.00 25.00
CCPOE8 Ryan Nugent-Hopkins 15.00 30.00
CCPOE9 Ryan Murphy 10.00 25.00
CCPOE10 Ryan Getzlaf 10.00 25.00
CCPOE11 Roberto Luongo 15.00 40.00
CCPOE12 Rick Nash 10.00 25.00
CCPOE13 Quinton Howden 8.00 20.00
CCPOE14 Patrice Bergeron 12.00 30.00
CCPOE15 P.K. Subban 12.00 30.00
CCPOE16 Mike Richards 8.00 20.00
CCPOE17 Martin Brodeur 25.00 60.00
CCPOE18 Mark Messier 20.00 50.00
CCPOE19 Mario Lemieux 40.00 100.00
CCPOE20 Marc-Andre Fleury 20.00 50.00
CCPOE21 Kris Letang 10.00 25.00
CCPOE22 Jordan Eberle 10.00 25.00
CCPOE23 Jonathan Toews 15.00 40.00
CCPOE24 Jonathan Huberdeau 8.00 20.00
CCPOE25 John Tavares 15.00 40.00
CCPOE26 Joe Sakic 20.00 50.00
CCPOE27 Jarome Iginla 12.00 30.00
CCPOE28 Jamie Oleksiak 8.00 20.00
CCPOE29 Jake Allen 8.00 20.00
CCPOE30 Jaden Schwartz 12.00 30.00
CCPOE31 Eric Lindros 10.00 25.00
CCPOE32 Ed Belfour 12.00 30.00
CCPOE33 Drew Doughty 12.00 30.00
CCPOE34 Dougie Hamilton 5.00 12.00
CCPOE35 Curtis Joseph 12.00 30.00
CCPOE36 Corey Perry 15.00 40.00
CCPOE37 Cody Hodgson 6.00 15.00
CCPOE38 Carey Price 25.00 50.00
CCPOE39 Brendan Gallagher 8.00 20.00
CCPOE40 Brayden Schenn 10.00 25.00
CCPOE41 Brad Marchand 20.00 50.00
CCPOE42 Bobby Orr 40.00 80.00

2017-18 Upper Deck Team Canada

*SILVER/100: 1.25X TO 3X BASE
*SP/100: .6X TO 1.5X SP
*HEIR/100: .6X TO 1.5X HEIR
1 Connor McDavid 1.50 4.00
2 Robby Fabbri .20 .50
3 Brendan Gallagher .30 .75
4 Matt Beleskey .20 .50
5 Matt Murray .50 1.25
6 Tyler Ennis .20 .50
7 Jeff Carter .25 .60
8 Sean Monahan .20 .50
9 Sean Couturier .25 .60
10 Jonathan Toews .50 1.25
11 Tyler Toffoli .30 .75
12 Andrew Ladd .20 .50
13 Jason Spezza .30 .75
14 Martin Jones .25 .60
15 Bo Horvat .40 1.00
16 Ryan Ellis .25 .60
17 Josh Morrissey .40 1.00
18 Derick Brassard .20 .50
19 Ryan Nugent-Hopkins .40 1.00
20 Sidney Crosby 1.25 3.00
21 Mark Giordano .30 .75
22 Jaden Schwartz .40 1.00
23 Brett Ritchie .20 .50
24 Claude Giroux .30 .75
25 Cam Talbot .30 .75
26 Morgan Rielly .30 .75
27 Jarome Iginla .40 1.00
28 David Savard .20 .50
29 Ryan Murray .30 .75
30 Marc-Andre Fleury .60 1.50
31 Eric Staal .40 1.00
32 Calvin Pickard .30 .75
33 Jordan Staal .25 .60
34 Brayden Schenn .30 .75
35 Matt Dumba .20 .50
36 Chris Kunitz .30 .75
37 Braden Holtby .40 1.00
38 Justin Williams .25 .60
39 Logan Couture .40 1.00
40 Evander Kane .30 .75
41 Mark Stone .40 1.00
42 Jeff Skinner .40 1.00
43 Jake Muzzin .30 .75
44 Sam Reinhart .60 1.50
45 Brent Seabrook .20 .50
46 Ryan O'Reilly .30 .75
47 Dan Hamhuis .20 .50
48 Ryan Spooner .25 .60
49 Marc Staal .20 .50
50 Mitch Marner .50 1.25
51 Jonathan Huberdeau .40 1.00
52 Boone Jenner .30 .75
53 Jay Bouwmeester .20 .50
54 Ryan Johansen .25 .60
55 Griffin Reinhart .20 .50
56 Duncan Keith .25 .60
57 Devan Dubnyk .25 .60
58 Shane Doan .25 .60
59 Mike Smith .30 .75
60 Adam Henrique .25 .60
61 Patrick Sharp .25 .60
62 Kris Letang .40 1.00
63 Tyson Barrie .20 .50
64 Nazem Kadri .40 1.00
65 James Neal .20 .50
66 Alexandre Burrows .20 .50
67 Meaghan Mikkelson .25 .60
68 Marie-Philip Poulin 1.00 2.50
69 Haily Wickenheiser .25 .60
70 Kirk Muller .25 .60
71 Ed Belfour .40 1.00
72 Lanny McDonald .30 .75
73 Dale Hawerchuk .40 1.00
74 Felix Potvin .50 1.25
75 Larry Robinson .30 .75
76 Shayne Corson .25 .60
77 Larry Murphy .25 .60
78 Ray Bourque .50 1.25
79 Theoren Fleury .30 .75
80 Marcel Dionne .40 1.00
81 Charlie Simmer .20 .50
82 Mike Gartner .40 1.00
83 Owen Nolan .30 .75
84 Bobby Clarke .50 1.25
85 Grant Fuhr .50 1.25
86 Joe Sakic .60 1.50
87 Darryl Sittler .40 1.00
88 Denis Potvin .30 .75
89 Mark Recchi .40 1.00
90 Doug Gilmour .40 1.00
91 Rod Brind`Amour .30 .75
92 Rogie Vachon .40 1.00
93 Bobby Orr 1.25 3.00
94 Wendel Clark .50 1.25
95 Phil Esposito .50 1.25
96 Bobby Hull .60 1.50
97 Vincent Damphousse .25 .60
98 Glenn Anderson .25 .60
99 Trevor Linden .30 .75
100 Paul Coffey .30 .75
101 Sidney Crosby SP 5.00 12.00
102 Brad Marchand SP 2.50 6.00
103 P.K. Subban SP 1.50 4.00
104 Jonathan Toews SP 2.00 5.00
105 Jordan Eberle SP 1.25 3.00
106 Jamie Benn SP 1.25 3.00
107 Tyler Seguin SP 1.50 4.00
108 Aaron Ekblad SP 1.50 4.00
109 Taylor Hall SP 1.25 3.00
110 Nathan MacKinnon SP 5.00 12.00
111 Alex Pietrangelo SP 1.00 2.50
112 Shea Weber SP 1.00 2.50
113 Mark Scheifele SP 2.00 5.00
114 Wayne Simmonds SP 1.50 4.00
115 Carey Price SP 2.50 6.00
116 Jonathan Drouin SP 1.00 2.50
117 Brent Burns SP 1.25 3.00
118 Rick Nash SP 1.25 3.00
119 Matt Duchene SP 1.25 3.00
120 Steven Stamkos SP 2.50 6.00
121 Patrick Marleau SP 1.25 3.00
122 Drew Doughty SP 1.50 4.00
123 Roberto Luongo SP 2.00 5.00
124 Patrice Bergeron SP 1.50 4.00
125 John Tavares SP 2.00 5.00
126 Corey Perry SP 2.00 5.00
127 Joe Thornton SP 2.00 5.00
128 Connor McDavid SP 6.00 15.00
129 Ryan Getzlaf SP 1.25 3.00
130 Mitch Marner SP 2.00 5.00
131 Steve Yzerman SP 3.00 8.00
132 Mike Bossy SP 1.25 3.00
133 Mario Lemieux SP 5.00 12.00
134 Patrick Roy SP 3.00 8.00
135 Mark Messier SP 2.50 6.00
136 Guy Lafleur SP 1.50 4.00
137 Frank Mahovlich SP 1.25 3.00
138 Bobby Orr SP 5.00 12.00
139 Martin Brodeur SP 3.00 8.00
140 Wayne Gretzky SP 8.00 20.00
141 Connor McDavid HEIR 10.00 25.00
142 Brayden Point HEIR 2.50 6.00
143 Anthony Mantha HEIR 1.50 4.00
144 Dylan Strome HEIR 2.50 6.00
145 Alexandre Carrier HEIR 1.50 4.00
146 Matt Murray HEIR 3.00 8.00
147 Lawson Crouse HEIR 1.25 3.00
148 Mathew Barzal HEIR 2.50 6.00
149 Max Domi HEIR 2.00 5.00
150 Samuel Morin HEIR 1.25 3.00
151 Mitch Marner HEIR 3.00 8.00
152 Eric Comrie HEIR 1.50 4.00
153 Tyson Jost HEIR 4.00 10.00
154 Travis Konecny HEIR 2.00 5.00
155 Thomas Chabot HEIR 2.00 5.00
156 Anthony Beauvillier HEIR 1.25 3.00
157 Blake Speers HEIR 2.00 5.00
158 John Quenneville HEIR 1.50 4.00
159 Shea Theodore HEIR 2.50 6.00
160 Sam Bennett HEIR 3.00 8.00
SP1 Nolan Patrick 50.00 120.00

2017-18 Upper Deck Team Canada Canvas

TCC1 Sidney Crosby 8.00 20.00
TCC2 Brent Burns 2.00 5.00
TCC3 Jamie Benn 2.00 5.00
TCC4 Taylor Hall 2.00 5.00
TCC5 Connor McDavid 10.00 25.00
TCC6 Nathan MacKinnon 8.00 20.00
TCC7 Jeff Carter 1.50 4.00
TCC8 Ryan O'Reilly 2.00 5.00
TCC9 Mitch Marner 3.00 8.00
TCC10 Joe Thornton 3.00 8.00
TCC11 Corey Perry 3.00 8.00
TCC12 Matt Duchene 2.00 5.00
TCC13 Jonathan Toews 3.00 8.00
TCC14 Shea Weber 1.50 4.00
TCC15 P.K. Subban 2.50 6.00
TCC16 Patrice Bergeron 2.50 6.00
TCC17 Carey Price 4.00 10.00
TCC18 Duncan Keith 1.50 4.00
TCC19 Morgan Rielly 2.00 5.00
TCC20 Rick Nash 2.00 5.00
TCC21 Matt Murray 3.00 8.00
TCC22 Tyler Seguin 2.50 6.00
TCC23 Steven Stamkos 4.00 10.00
TCC24 Brad Marchand 4.00 10.00
TCC25 John Tavares 3.00 8.00
TCC26 Drew Doughty 2.50 6.00
TCC27 Jeff Skinner 2.50 6.00
TCC28 Ryan Getzlaf 2.00 5.00
TCC29 Claude Giroux 2.00 5.00
TCC30 Darryl Sittler 2.50 6.00
TCC31 Guy Lafleur 2.50 6.00
TCC32 Mike Bossy 2.00 5.00
TCC33 Bobby Hull 4.00 10.00
TCC34 Bobby Clarke 3.00 8.00
TCC35 Ed Belfour 2.50 6.00
TCC36 Bobby Orr 8.00 20.00
TCC37 Lanny McDonald 2.00 5.00
TCC38 Steve Yzerman 5.00 12.00
TCC39 Denis Potvin 2.00 5.00
TCC40 Theoren Fleury 2.00 5.00
TCC41 Phil Esposito 3.00 8.00
TCC42 Shayne Corson 1.50 4.00
TCC43 Larry Robinson 2.00 5.00
TCC44 Mike Gartner 2.50 6.00
TCC45 Marcel Dionne 2.50 6.00
TCC46 Mario Lemieux SP 15.00 40.00
TCC47 Ray Bourque SP 6.00 15.00
TCC48 Grant Fuhr SP 6.00 15.00
TCC49 Larry Murphy SP 3.00 8.00
TCC50 Doug Gilmour SP 5.00 12.00
TCC51 Mark Messier SP 8.00 20.00
TCC52 Paul Coffey SP 4.00 10.00
TCC53 Glenn Anderson SP 3.00 8.00
TCC54 Dale Hawerchuk SP 5.00 12.00
TCC55 Wayne Gretzky SP 25.00 60.00

2017-18 Upper Deck Team Canada Clear Cut Program of Excellence

POE1 Carey Price 20.00 50.00
POE2 Mitch Marner 15.00 40.00
POE3 Jonathan Toews 15.00 40.00
POE4 Taylor Hall 10.00 25.00
POE5 Sidney Crosby 40.00 100.00
POE6 Brent Burns 10.00 25.00
POE7 Ryan Getzlaf 10.00 25.00
POE8 Nathan MacKinnon 40.00 100.00
POE9 Shea Weber 8.00 20.00
POE10 Matt Murray 15.00 40.00
POE11 Brad Marchand 20.00 50.00
POE12 Corey Perry 15.00 40.00
POE13 Steven Stamkos 20.00 50.00
POE14 P.K. Subban 12.00 30.00
POE15 John Tavares 15.00 40.00
POE16 Claude Giroux 10.00 25.00
POE17 Mark Scheifele 15.00 40.00
POE18 Jamie Benn 10.00 25.00
POE19 Matt Duchene 10.00 25.00
POE20 Connor McDavid 50.00 125.00
POE21 Mario Lemieux 40.00 100.00
POE22 Martin Brodeur 25.00 60.00
POE23 Bobby Orr 40.00 100.00
POE24 Joe Sakic 20.00 50.00
POE25 Mark Messier 20.00 50.00
POE26 Steve Yzerman 25.00 60.00
POE27 Paul Coffey 10.00 25.00
POE28 Mike Bossy 10.00 25.00
POE29 Frank Mahovlich 10.00 25.00
POE30 Wayne Gretzky 60.00 150.00

2017-18 Upper Deck Team Canada Clear Cut World Juniors

WJC1 Connor McDavid 60.00 150.00
WJC2 Matt Murray 20.00 50.00
WJC3 Mitch Marner 20.00 50.00
WJC4 Anthony Mantha 10.00 25.00
WJC5 Dylan Strome 15.00 40.00
WJC6 Mathew Barzal 15.00 40.00
WJC7 Brayden Point 15.00 40.00
WJC8 Thomas Chabot 12.00 30.00
WJC9 Travis Konecny 12.00 30.00
WJC10 Tyson Jost 25.00 60.00

2017-18 Upper Deck Team Canada Retro

R1 Connor McDavid 10.00 25.00
R2 Mitch Marner 3.00 8.00
R3 Jonathan Toews 3.00 8.00
R4 John Tavares 3.00 8.00
R5 Sidney Crosby 8.00 20.00
R6 P.K. Subban 2.50 6.00
R7 Carey Price 4.00 10.00
R8 Steven Stamkos 4.00 10.00
R9 Patrick Roy 5.00 12.00
R10 Mario Lemieux 8.00 20.00
R11 Mark Messier 4.00 10.00
R12 Wayne Gretzky 12.00 30.00

2017-18 Upper Deck Team Canada VS

VS1 Auston Matthews 5.00 12.00
VS2 Alexander Ovechkin 5.00 12.00
VS3 Artemi Panarin 2.50 6.00
VS4 Anze Kopitar 2.00 5.00
VS5 Patrik Laine 1.50 4.00
VS6 Johnny Gaudreau 2.00 5.00
VS7 Jaromir Jagr 4.00 10.00
VS8 William Nylander 2.50 6.00
VS9 Evgeni Malkin 2.50 6.00
VS10 Patrick Kane 2.50 6.00
VS11 Roman Josi 1.25 3.00
VS12 Henrik Zetterberg 1.50 4.00
VS13 Leon Draisaitl 4.00 10.00
VS14 Vladimir Tarasenko 1.50 4.00
VS15 Erik Karlsson 1.50 4.00
VS16 Max Pacioretty 1.25 3.00
VS17 Henrik Sedin 1.50 4.00
VS18 Joe Pavelski 1.50 4.00
VS19 Marian Hossa 1.25 3.00
VS20 Mats Zuccarello 1.25 3.00
VS21 Gabriel Landeskog 1.50 4.00
VS22 Pavel Bure 1.25 3.00
VS23 Brett Hull 2.50 6.00
VS24 Teemu Selanne 2.50 6.00

2017-18 Upper Deck Team Canada VS Black

VSBAM Auston Matthews 6.00 15.00
VSBHL Henrik Lundqvist 4.00 10.00
VSBLD Leon Draisaitl 3.00 8.00
VSBNH Nico Hischier 30.00 80.00
VSBWN William Nylander 4.00 10.00

2014-15 Upper Deck Team Canada Juniors

COMP.SET w/o SP's (100) 15.00 40.00
1 Rourke Chartier .25 .60
2 Michael Dal Colle .50 1.25
3 Robby Fabbri .30 .75
4 Brendan Lemieux .40 1.00
5 Carl Neill .25 .60
6 Alexis Pepin .30 .75
7 Spencer Watson .40 1.00
8 Nick Baptiste .25 .60
9 Sam Bennett 1.00 2.50
10 Madison Bowey .25 .60
11 Philippe Desrosiers .30 .75
12 Jason Dickinson .30 .75
13 Hunter Garlent .25 .60
14 Dillon Heatherington .25 .60
15 Austin Lotz .30 .75
16 Spencer Martin .50 1.25
17 Samuel Morin .25 .60
18 Nick Ritchie .40 1.00
19 Shea Theodore .50 1.25
20 Carter Verhaeghe .50 1.25
21 Kerby Rychel .30 .75
22 Daniel Audette .40 1.00
23 Mathew Barzal .75 2.00
24 Julio Billia .30 .75
25 Clark Bishop .25 .60
26 Conner Bleackley .40 1.00
27 Alexandre Carrier .30 .75
28 Lawson Crouse .40 1.00
29 Haydn Fleury .40 1.00
30 Ryan Gropp .40 1.00
31 Jayce Hawryluk .25 .60
32 Joe Hicketts .25 .60
33 Travis Konecny .75 2.00
34 Jared McCann .50 1.25
35 Mason McDonald .40 1.00
36 Roland McKeown .40 1.00
37 Brent Moran .30 .75
38 Brendan Perlini .60 1.50
39 Ryan Pilon .25 .60
40 Brayden Point .50 1.25
41 John Quenneville .30 .75
42 Travis Sanheim .40 1.00
43 Ben Thomas .40 1.00
44 Jake Virtanen .50 1.25
45 Josh Anderson .40 1.00
46 Chris Bigras .30 .75
47 Jonathan Drouin .75 2.00
48 Aaron Ekblad .75 2.00
49 Zach Fucale .50 1.25
50 Frederik Gauthier .40 1.00
51 Bo Horvat 1.00 2.50
52 Charles Hudon .40 1.00
53 Curtis Lazar .40 1.00
54 Taylor Leier .40 1.00
55 Anthony Mantha .60 1.50
56 Connor McDavid 2.00 5.00
57 Jake Paterson .30 .75
58 Adam Pelech .30 .75
59 Nic Petan .40 1.00
60 Derrick Pouliot .50 1.25
61 Griffin Reinhart .40 1.00
62 Sam Reinhart 1.50 4.00
63 Hayley Wickenheiser .75 2.00
64 Courtney Birchard .40 1.00
65 Tessa Bonhomme .50 1.25
66 Bailey Bram .40 1.00
67 Sarah Vaillancourt .50 1.25
68 Meghan Agosta-Marciano .60 1.50
69 Gillian Apps .60 1.50
70 Melodie Daoust .60 1.50
71 Laura Fortino .40 1.00
72 Jayna Hefford .60 1.50
73 Haley Irwin .40 1.00
74 Brianne Jenner 1.00 2.50
75 Rebecca Johnston .40 1.00
76 Charline Labonte .60 1.50
77 Genevieve Lacasse .50 1.25
78 Jocelyne Larocque .60 1.50
79 Meaghan Mikkelson .60 1.50
80 Caroline Ouellette .60 1.50
81 Marie-Philip Poulin 2.00 5.00
82 Lauriane Rougeau .40 1.00
83 Natalie Spooner 1.50 4.00
84 Shannon Szabados .75 2.00
85 Jennifer Wakefield .40 1.00
86 Catherine Ward .50 1.25
87 Tara Watchorn .40 1.00
88 Kerby Rychel .30 .75
89 Nick Ritchie .40 1.00
90 Curtis Lazar .40 1.00
91 Anthony Mantha .60 1.50
92 Bo Horvat 1.00 2.50
93 Samuel Morin .25 .60
94 Griffin Reinhart .40 1.00
95 Michael Dal Colle .50 1.25
96 Sam Bennett 1.00 2.50
97 Sam Reinhart 1.50 4.00
98 Aaron Ekblad .75 2.00
99 Connor McDavid 2.00 5.00
100 Jonathan Drouin .75 2.00
101 Aaron Ekblad SP 1.50 4.00
102 Adam Pelech SP .60 1.50
103 Samuel Morin SP .50 1.25
104 Anthony Mantha SP 1.25 3.00
105 Bo Horvat SP 2.00 5.00
106 Brayden Point SP 1.00 2.50
107 Mason McDonald SP .75 2.00
108 Charles Hudon SP .75 2.00
109 Chris Bigras SP .60 1.50
110 Connor McDavid SP 4.00 10.00
111 Curtis Lazar SP .75 2.00
112 Derrick Pouliot SP 1.00 2.50
113 Frederik Gauthier SP .75 2.00
114 Griffin Reinhart SP .75 2.00
115 Haydn Fleury SP .75 2.00
116 Jake Paterson SP .60 1.50
117 Jake Virtanen SP 1.00 2.50
118 Jared McCann SP 1.00 2.50
119 Daniel Audette SP .75 2.00
120 Jonathan Drouin SP 1.50 4.00
121 Mathew Barzal SP 1.50 4.00
122 Josh Anderson SP .75 2.00
123 Nick Baptiste SP .50 1.25
124 Kerby Rychel SP .60 1.50
125 Nick Ritchie SP .75 2.00
126 Travis Sanheim SP .75 2.00
127 Michael Dal Colle SP 1.00 2.50
128 Julio Billia SP .60 1.50
129 Nic Petan SP .75 2.00
130 Travis Konecny SP 1.50 4.00
131 Conner Bleackley SP .75 2.00
132 Brendan Perlini SP 1.25 3.00
133 Robby Fabbri SP .60 1.50
134 Roland McKeown SP .75 2.00
135 Sam Bennett SP 2.00 5.00
136 Sam Reinhart SP 3.00 8.00
137 Lawson Crouse SP .75 2.00
138 Spencer Watson SP .75 2.00
139 Zach Fucale SP 1.00 2.50
140 Brianne Jenner SP 2.00 5.00
141 Charline Labonte SP 1.25 3.00
142 Caroline Ouellette SP 1.25 3.00
143 Catherine Ward SP 1.00 2.50
144 Hayley Wickenheiser SP 1.50 4.00
145 Jayna Hefford SP 1.25 3.00
146 Gillian Apps SP 1.25 3.00
147 Meghan Agosta-Marciano SP 1.25 3.00
148 Natalie Spooner SP 3.00 8.00
149 Rebecca Johnston SP .75 2.00
150 Shannon Szabados SP 1.50 4.00
151 Adam Pelech JSY 2.50 6.00
152 Alexandre Carrier JSY 2.50 6.00
153 Brayden Point JSY 4.00 10.00
154 Taylor Leier JSY 3.00 8.00
155 Chris Bigras JSY 2.50 6.00
156 Curtis Lazar JSY 3.00 8.00
157 Derrick Pouliot JSY 4.00 10.00
158 Frederik Gauthier JSY 3.00 8.00
159 Griffin Reinhart JSY 3.00 8.00
160 Haydn Fleury JSY 3.00 8.00
161 Jake Paterson JSY 2.50 6.00
162 Mason McDonald JSY 3.00 8.00
163 Lawson Crouse JSY 3.00 8.00
164 Josh Anderson JSY 3.00 8.00
165 Travis Konecny JSY 6.00 15.00
166 Julio Billia JSY 2.50 6.00
167 Kerby Rychel JSY 2.50 6.00
168 Mathew Barzal JSY 6.00 15.00
169 Travis Sanheim JSY 3.00 8.00
170 Brendan Perlini JSY 5.00 12.00
171 Nic Petan JSY 3.00 8.00
172 Jayce Hawryluk JSY 2.00 5.00
173 Clark Bishop JSY 2.00 5.00
174 Ryan Gropp JSY 3.00 8.00
175 Conner Bleackley JSY 3.00 8.00
176 Roland McKeown JSY 3.00 8.00
177 Daniel Audette JSY 3.00 8.00
178 John Quenneville JSY 2.50 6.00
179 Jared McCann JSY 4.00 10.00
180 Zach Fucale JSY 4.00 10.00
181 Aaron Ekblad JSY 5.00 12.00
182 Bo Horvat JSY 4.00 10.00
183 Connor McDavid JSY 15.00 40.00
184 Jonathan Drouin JSY 6.00 15.00
185 Anthony Mantha JSY 5.00 12.00
186 Sam Reinhart JSY 5.00 12.00
187 Brianne Jenner JSY 10.00 25.00
188 Caroline Ouellette JSY 6.00 15.00
189 Catherine Ward JSY 5.00 12.00
190 Charline Labonte JSY 6.00 15.00
191 Genevieve Lacasse JSY 5.00 12.00
192 Gillian Apps JSY 6.00 15.00
193 Haley Irwin JSY 4.00 10.00
194 Hayley Wickenheiser JSY 8.00 20.00
195 Jayna Hefford JSY 6.00 15.00
196 Jennifer Wakefield JSY 4.00 10.00
197 Jocelyne Larocque JSY 6.00 15.00
198 Laura Fortino JSY 4.00 10.00
199 Lauriane Rougeau JSY 4.00 10.00
200 Marie-Philip Poulin JSY 20.00 50.00
201 Meaghan Mikkelson JSY 6.00 15.00
202 Meghan Agosta-Marciano JSY 6.00 15.00
203 Melodie Daoust JSY 6.00 15.00
204 Natalie Spooner JSY 15.00 40.00
205 Rebecca Johnston JSY 4.00 10.00
206 Shannon Szabados JSY 8.00 20.00
207 Tara Watchorn JSY 4.00 10.00

2014-15 Upper Deck Team Canada Juniors Gold

*1-100 GOLD: .8X TO 2X BASIC CARDS
*101-150 GOLD: .6X TO 1.5X BASIC CARDS
*151-186 JSY/20-31: 1X TO 2.5X BASIC JSY
*151-186 JSY/14-19: 1.2X TO 3X BASIC JSY

2014-15 Upper Deck Team Canada Juniors Glossy

*1-100 GLOSSY/25: 3X TO 8X BASIC CARDS
*101-150 GLOSS/10: 2X TO 5X BASIC SP
56 Connor McDavid 60.00 120.00
99 Connor McDavid 60.00 120.00
110 Connor McDavid 125.00 200.00

2014-15 Upper Deck Team Canada Juniors Autographs Gold

21 Kerby Rychel A 5.00 12.00
22 Daniel Audette C 6.00 15.00
23 Mathew Barzal C 12.00 30.00
24 Julio Billia C 5.00 12.00
25 Clark Bishop C 4.00 10.00
26 Conner Bleackley C 6.00 15.00
27 Alexandre Carrier C 5.00 12.00
28 Lawson Crouse C 6.00 15.00
29 Haydn Fleury C 6.00 15.00
30 Ryan Gropp C 6.00 15.00
31 Jayce Hawryluk C 4.00 10.00
32 Joe Hicketts E 4.00 10.00
33 Travis Konecny C 12.00 30.00
34 Jared McCann C 8.00 20.00
35 Mason McDonald C 6.00 15.00
36 Roland McKeown C 6.00 15.00
37 Brent Moran E 5.00 12.00
38 Brendan Perlini C 10.00 25.00
39 Ryan Pilon E 4.00 10.00
40 Brayden Point C 8.00 20.00
41 John Quenneville C 5.00 12.00
42 Travis Sanheim C 6.00 15.00
43 Ben Thomas E 6.00 15.00
44 Jake Virtanen E 8.00 20.00
45 Josh Anderson C 6.00 15.00

46 Chris Bigras C 5.00 12.00
47 Jonathan Drouin D 12.00 30.00
48 Aaron Ekblad D 15.00 40.00
49 Zach Fucale C 8.00 20.00
51 Bo Horvat D 15.00 40.00
52 Charles Hudon E 6.00 15.00
53 Curtis Lazar D 6.00 15.00
54 Taylor Leier C 6.00 15.00
55 Anthony Mantha D 10.00 25.00
56 Connor McDavid D 200.00 350.00
57 Jake Paterson C 5.00 12.00
58 Adam Pelech C 5.00 12.00
59 Nic Petan C 6.00 15.00
60 Derrick Pouliot C 8.00 20.00
61 Griffin Reinhart D 6.00 15.00
62 Sam Reinhart D 25.00 60.00
63 Hayley Wickenheiser C 8.00 20.00
68 Meghan Agosta-Marciano C 6.00 15.00
69 Gillian Apps C 6.00 15.00
70 Melodie Daoust C 6.00 15.00
71 Laura Fortino C 4.00 10.00
72 Jayna Hefford C 6.00 15.00
74 Brianne Jenner C 10.00 25.00
75 Rebecca Johnston C 4.00 10.00
76 Charline Labonte C 6.00 15.00
77 Genevieve Lacasse C 5.00 12.00
78 Jocelyne Larocque C 6.00 15.00
79 Meaghan Mikkelson C 6.00 15.00
80 Caroline Ouellette C 6.00 15.00
81 Marie-Philip Poulin C 30.00 80.00
82 Lauriane Rougeau C 4.00 10.00
83 Natalie Spooner C 15.00 40.00
84 Shannon Szabados C 8.00 20.00
85 Jennifer Wakefield C 4.00 10.00
86 Catherine Ward C 5.00 12.00
87 Tara Watchorn C 4.00 10.00
88 Kerby Rychel A 5.00 12.00
90 Curtis Lazar B 6.00 15.00
91 Anthony Mantha B 10.00 25.00
93 Samuel Morin B 4.00 10.00
94 Griffin Reinhart B 6.00 15.00
97 Sam Reinhart B 25.00 60.00
98 Aaron Ekblad B 15.00 40.00
99 Connor McDavid B 30.00 80.00
100 Jonathan Drouin B 12.00 30.00

2014-15 Upper Deck Team Canada Juniors Clear Cut Playing for a Nation Combos

PFNC1 A.Pelech/A.Ekblad 10.00 25.00
PFNC2 J.Drouin/A.Mantha 12.00 30.00
PFNC3 S.Reinhart/C.McDavid 40.00 80.00
PFNC4 S.Bennett/M.DalColle 15.00 40.00
PFNC5 J.Paterson/M.McDonald 6.00 15.00
PFNC6 B.Horvat/K.Rychel 15.00 40.00

2014-15 Upper Deck Team Canada Juniors Clear Cut Playing for a Nation

PFN1 Aaron Ekblad 8.00 20.00
PFN2 Adam Pelech 4.00 10.00
PFN3 Anthony Mantha 8.00 20.00
PFN4 Bo Horvat 10.00 25.00
PFN5 Brayden Point 6.00 15.00
PFN6 Josh Anderson 5.00 12.00
PFN7 Chris Bigras 4.00 10.00
PFN8 Connor McDavid 40.00 80.00
PFN9 Curtis Lazar 8.00 20.00
PFN10 Derrick Pouliot 6.00 15.00
PFN11 Frederik Gauthier 5.00 12.00
PFN12 Griffin Reinhart 6.00 15.00
PFN13 Haydn Fleury 5.00 12.00
PFN14 Jake Paterson 4.00 10.00
PFN15 Jake Virtanen 6.00 15.00
PFN16 Jared McCann 6.00 15.00
PFN17 Brendan Perlini 8.00 20.00
PFN18 Jonathan Drouin 10.00 25.00
PFN19 Taylor Leier 5.00 12.00
PFN20 Michael Dal Colle 5.00 12.00
PFN21 Kerby Rychel 4.00 10.00
PFN22 Nick Ritchie 5.00 12.00
PFN23 Travis Sanheim 5.00 12.00
PFN24 Mathew Barzal 10.00 25.00
PFN25 Travis Konecny 10.00 25.00
PFN26 Nic Petan 4.00 10.00
PFN27 Julio Billia 4.00 10.00
PFN28 Sam Bennett 12.00 30.00
PFN29 Jayce Hawryluk 3.00 8.00
PFN30 Roland McKeown 5.00 12.00
PFN31 Lawson Crouse 5.00 12.00
PFN32 Sam Reinhart 8.00 20.00
PFN33 Daniel Audette 5.00 12.00
PFN34 Nick Baptiste 3.00 8.00
PFN35 Mason McDonald 5.00 12.00
PFN36 Samuel Morin 6.00 15.00

2014-15 Upper Deck Team Canada Juniors Dual Jerseys

*GOLD/99: .5X TO 1.2X BASIC DUAL
TCDBA C.Bishop/D.Audette 3.00 8.00
TCDBG B.Horvat/G.Reinhart 4.00 10.00
TCDBM M.McDonald/J.Billia 3.00 8.00
TCDDM J.Drouin/A.Mantha 6.00 15.00
TCDER S.Reinhart/A.Ekblad 6.00 15.00
TCDHR B.Horvat/K.Rychel 8.00 20.00
TCDLP N.Petan/C.Lazar 5.00 12.00
TCDMD C.McDavid/J.Drouin 15.00 40.00
TCDMR C.McDavid/S.Reinhart 15.00 40.00
TCDRG K.Rychel/F.Gauthier 3.00 8.00
TCDSP J.Paterson/Z.Fucale 4.00 10.00
TCDVP J.Virtanen/B.Perlini 5.00 12.00

2014-15 Upper Deck Team Canada Juniors Jumbo Swatch

JS1 Aaron Ekblad 6.00 15.00
JS2 Anthony Mantha 8.00 20.00
JS3 Bo Horvat 12.00 30.00
JS4 Connor McDavid 30.00 60.00
JS5 Curtis Lazar 6.00 15.00
JS6 Frederik Gauthier 5.00 12.00
JS7 Jake Virtanen 6.00 15.00
JS8 Jonathan Drouin 8.00 20.00
JS9 Kerby Rychel 4.00 10.00
JS10 Mathew Barzal 10.00 25.00
JS11 Jake Paterson 4.00 10.00
JS12 Travis Konecny 6.00 15.00
JS13 Brendan Perlini 6.00 15.00
JS14 Mason McDonald 5.00 12.00
JS15 Sam Reinhart 8.00 20.00

2014-15 Upper Deck Team Canada Juniors Patch Autographs

151 Adam Pelech 6.00 15.00
152 Alexandre Carrier 6.00 15.00
153 Brayden Point 10.00 25.00
154 Taylor Leier 8.00 20.00
155 Chris Bigras 6.00 15.00
156 Curtis Lazar 8.00 20.00
157 Derrick Pouliot 10.00 25.00
158 Frederik Gauthier 8.00 20.00
159 Griffin Reinhart 8.00 20.00
160 Haydn Fleury 8.00 20.00
161 Jake Paterson 6.00 15.00
162 Mason McDonald 8.00 20.00
163 Lawson Crouse 8.00 20.00
164 Josh Anderson 8.00 20.00
165 Travis Konecny 15.00 40.00
166 Julio Billia 6.00 15.00
167 Kerby Rychel 6.00 15.00
168 Mathew Barzal 15.00 40.00
169 Travis Sanheim 8.00 20.00
170 Brendan Perlini 12.00 30.00
171 Nic Petan 8.00 20.00
172 Jayce Hawryluk 5.00 12.00
173 Clark Bishop 5.00 12.00
174 Ryan Gropp 8.00 20.00
175 Conner Bleackley 8.00 20.00
176 Roland McKeown 8.00 20.00
177 Daniel Audette 8.00 20.00
178 John Quenneville 6.00 15.00
179 Jared McCann 10.00 25.00
180 Zach Fucale 10.00 25.00
181 Aaron Ekblad/125 20.00 50.00
182 Bo Horvat/125 20.00 50.00
183 Connor McDavid/125 250.00 400.00
184 Jonathan Drouin/125 15.00 40.00
185 Anthony Mantha/125 12.00 30.00
186 Sam Reinhart/125 30.00 80.00
187 Brianne Jenner 12.00 30.00
188 Caroline Ouellette 8.00 20.00
189 Catherine Ward 6.00 15.00
190 Charline Labonte 8.00 20.00
191 Genevieve Lacasse 6.00 15.00
192 Gillian Apps 8.00 20.00
194 Hayley Wickenheiser 10.00 25.00
195 Jayna Hefford 8.00 20.00
196 Jennifer Wakefield 5.00 12.00
197 Jocelyne Larocque 8.00 20.00
198 Laura Fortino 5.00 12.00
199 Lauriane Rougeau 5.00 12.00
200 Marie-Philip Poulin 40.00 100.00
201 Meaghan Mikkelson 8.00 20.00
202 Meghan Agosta-Marciano 8.00 20.00
203 Melodie Daoust 8.00 20.00
204 Natalie Spooner 20.00 50.00
205 Rebecca Johnston 5.00 12.00
206 Shannon Szabados 10.00 25.00
207 Tara Watchorn 5.00 12.00

2014-15 Upper Deck Team Canada Juniors Quad Jerseys

*GOLD/25: .6X TO 1.5X BASIC QUAD
EMDM Mnt/McD/Drn/Ekb 25.00 60.00
MDHR McD/Drn/Hrv/Rnh 25.00 60.00
PFMB Fcle/Ptr/McD/Bla 6.00 15.00
PKVB Prl/Kncy/Blcy/Vrt 6.00 15.00
PPLG Rnh/Gthr/Ryc/Lzr 8.00 20.00

2014-15 Upper Deck Team Canada Juniors Special Edition

*GOLD: .8X TO 2X BASIC INSERTS
SE1 Aaron Ekblad 3.00 8.00
SE2 Adam Pelech 1.00 2.50
SE3 Jayce Hawryluk .75 2.00
SE4 Lawson Crouse 1.25 3.00
SE5 Anthony Mantha 2.00 5.00
SE6 Bo Horvat 3.00 8.00
SE7 Brayden Point 1.50 4.00
SE8 Ryan Gropp 1.25 3.00
SE9 Charles Hudon 1.25 3.00
SE10 Chris Bigras 1.00 2.50
SE11 Connor McDavid 6.00 15.00
SE12 Curtis Lazar 1.25 3.00
SE13 Daniel Audette 1.25 3.00
SE14 Derrick Pouliot 1.50 4.00
SE15 Frederik Gauthier 1.25 3.00
SE16 Griffin Reinhart 1.25 3.00
SE17 Haydn Fleury 1.25 3.00
SE18 Travis Sanheim 1.25 3.00
SE19 Jake Paterson 1.00 2.50
SE20 Jake Virtanen 1.50 4.00
SE21 Jared McCann 1.50 4.00
SE22 Brendan Perlini 2.00 5.00
SE23 Jonathan Drouin 2.50 6.00
SE24 Alexandre Carrier 1.00 2.50
SE25 Josh Anderson 1.25 3.00
SE26 Spencer Martin 1.25 3.00
SE27 Julio Billia 1.25 3.00
SE28 Kerby Rychel 1.00 2.50
SE29 Conner Bleackley 1.25 3.00
SE30 Ben Thomas 1.25 3.00
SE31 Carter Verhaeghe 1.50 4.00
SE32 Sam Reinhart 5.00 12.00
SE33 Clark Bishop .75 2.00
SE34 Nic Petan 1.25 3.00
SE35 Mason McDonald 1.25 3.00
SE36 Joe Hicketts .75 2.00
SE37 John Quenneville 1.00 2.50
SE38 Mathew Barzal 2.50 6.00
SE39 Ryan Pilon .75 2.00
SE40 Roland McKeown 1.25 3.00
SE41 Travis Konecny 2.50 6.00
SE42 Zach Fucale 1.50 4.00
SE43 Taylor Leier 1.25 3.00
SE44 Michael Dal Colle 1.50 4.00
SE45 Nick Baptiste .75 2.00
SE46 Nick Ritchie 1.25 3.00
SE47 Robby Fabbri 1.00 2.50
SE48 Sam Bennett 3.00 8.00
SE49 Samuel Morin .75 2.00
SE50 Catherine Ward 1.25 3.00
SE51 Haley Irwin 1.00 2.50
SE52 Caroline Ouellette 1.50 4.00
SE53 Gillian Apps 1.50 4.00
SE54 Jayna Hefford 1.50 4.00
SE55 Meaghan Mikkelson 1.50 4.00
SE56 Meghan Agosta-Marciano 1.50 4.00
SE57 Hayley Wickenheiser 2.00 5.00
SE58 Natalie Spooner 4.00 10.00
SE59 Rebecca Johnston 1.00 2.50
SE60 Shannon Szabados 2.00 5.00

2014-15 Upper Deck Team Canada Juniors Triple Jerseys

*GOLD/49: .6X TO 1.5X BASIC TRIPLE
TCTDLP Pelan/Lazr/Drouin 6.00 15.00
TCTEPR Plch/Ekbld/Rnhrt 8.00 20.00
TCTKPA Kncny/Adtte/Prlni 6.00 15.00
TCTMDR Drn/McDvd/Rnhrt 15.00 40.00
TCTMGR Rychl/Gthr/Mntha 5.00 12.00
TCTMHR Rnhrt/McDvd/Hrvt 15.00 40.00
TCTPMF Fcle/Ptrsn/McDnld 6.00 15.00

2015-16 Upper Deck Team Canada Juniors

1 Callum Booth .25 .60
2 Mitchell Vande Sompel .25 .60
3 Mitch Marner 1.25 3.00
4 Adam Musil .30 .75
5 Nick Merkley .50 1.25
6 Nicolas Meloche .30 .75
7 Dylan Strome .75 2.00
8 Connor Hobbs .25 .60
9 Tyler Soy .25 .60
10 Travis Konecny .75 2.00
11 Graham Knott .25 .60
12 Nicolas Roy .25 .60
13 Jeremy Roy .25 .60
14 Jansen Harkins .40 1.00
15 Ethan Bear .25 .60
16 Anthony Beauvillier .30 .75
17 Matthew Spencer .25 .60
18 Zachary Sawchenko .25 .60
19 Mitchell Stephens .25 .60
20 Mathew Barzal 1.00 2.50
21 Guillaume Brisebois .30 .75
22 Evan Cormier .30 .75
23 Kyle Capobianco .25 .60
24 Thomas Chabot .40 1.00
25 Parker Wotherspoon .25 .60
26 Glenn Gawdin .30 .75
27 Nathan Noel .25 .60
28 Deven Sideroff .25 .60
29 Brett Howden .25 .60
30 Tyler Benson .50 1.25
31 Pierre-Luc Dubois .60 1.50
32 Joe Hicketts .25 .60
33 Max Domi .60 1.50
34 Nicolas Petan .40 1.00
35 Shea Theodore .60 1.50
36 Madison Bowey .25 .60
37 Nick Paul .30 .75
38 Lawson Crouse .30 .75
39 Zach Fucale .30 .75
40 Josh Morrissey .40 1.00
41 Brayden Point .60 1.50
42 Frederik Gauthier .40 1.00
43 Samuel Morin .25 .60
44 Robby Fabbri .50 1.25
45 Nick Ritchie .40 1.00
46 Dillon Heatherington .25 .60
47 Eric Comrie .40 1.00
48 Jake Virtanen .50 1.25
49 Connor McDavid 6.00 15.00
50 Jennifer Wakefield .25 .60
51 Tara Watchorn .30 .75
52 Brianne Jenner .60 1.50
53 Bailey Bram .25 .60
54 Jessica Campbell .75 2.00
55 Laura Fortino .25 .60
56 Caroline Ouellette .40 1.00
57 Sarah Davis .25 .60
58 Halli Krzyzaniak .30 .75
59 Brigette Lacquette .30 .75
60 Jamie Lee Rattray .50 1.25
61 Jillian Saulnier .50 1.25
62 Emily Clark .75 2.00
63 Marie-Philip Poulin 1.25 3.00
64 Ann-Renee Desbiens 1.00 2.50
65 Jocelyne Larocque .50 1.25
66 Emerance Maschmeyer .50 1.25
67 Kelly Terry .25 .60
68 Natalie Spooner 1.00 2.50
69 Rebecca Johnston .30 .75
70 Lauriane Rougeau .30 .75
71 Genevieve Lacasse .30 .75
72 Courtney Birchard .25 .60
73 Thomas Chabot .40 1.00
74 Anthony Beauvillier .30 .75
75 Jansen Harkins .40 1.00
76 Mitch Marner 1.25 3.00
77 Dylan Strome .75 2.00
78 Travis Konecny .75 2.00
79 Nick Merkley .50 1.25
80 Mathew Barzal 1.00 2.50
81 Lawson Crouse .30 .75
82 Josh Morrissey .40 1.00
83 Zach Fucale .30 .75
84 Jake Virtanen .50 1.25
85 Frederik Gauthier .40 1.00
86 Nick Ritchie .40 1.00
87 Nicolas Petan .40 1.00
88 Robby Fabbri .50 1.25
89 Max Domi .60 1.50
90 Connor McDavid 6.00 15.00
91 Dylan Strome .75 2.00
92 Mitch Marner 1.25 3.00
93 Mathew Barzal 1.00 2.50
94 Mitchell Stephens .25 .60
95 Zach Fucale .30 .75
96 Max Domi .60 1.50
97 Nicolas Petan .40 1.00
98 Connor McDavid 6.00 15.00
99 Ann-Renee Desbiens 1.00 2.50
100 Natalie Spooner 1.00 2.50
101 Connor McDavid JSY 20.00 40.00
102 Zach Fucale JSY 3.00 8.00
103 Max Domi JSY 6.00 15.00
104 Jake Virtanen JSY 5.00 12.00
105 Nick Ritchie JSY 4.00 10.00
106 Lawson Crouse JSY 4.00 10.00
107 Nicolas Petan JSY 4.00 10.00
108 Eric Comrie JSY 4.00 10.00
109 Samuel Morin JSY 2.50 6.00
110 Nick Paul JSY 3.00 8.00
111 Brayden Point JSY 6.00 15.00
112 Dillon Heatherington JSY 2.50 6.00
113 Josh Morrissey JSY 4.00 10.00
114 Robby Fabbri JSY 5.00 12.00
115 Frederik Gauthier JSY 4.00 10.00
116 Shea Theodore JSY 6.00 15.00
117 Joe Hicketts JSY 2.50 6.00
118 Madison Bowey JSY 2.50 6.00
119 Evan Cormier JSY 3.00 8.00
120 Mitchell Stephens JSY 2.50 6.00
121 Ethan Bear JSY 2.50 6.00
122 Mathew Barzal JSY 10.00 25.00
123 Kyle Capobianco JSY 2.50 6.00
124 Parker Wotherspoon JSY 2.50 6.00
125 Anthony Beauvillier JSY 3.00 8.00
126 Jansen Harkins JSY 4.00 10.00
127 Nathan Noel JSY 2.50 6.00
128 Thomas Chabot JSY 4.00 10.00
129 Jeremy Roy JSY 2.50 6.00
130 Deven Sideroff JSY 2.50 6.00
131 Zachary Sawchenko JSY 2.50 6.00
132 Guillaume Brisebois JSY 3.00 8.00
133 Glenn Gawdin JSY 3.00 8.00
134 Matthew Spencer JSY 2.50 6.00
135 Nicolas Roy JSY 2.50 6.00
136 Tyler Benson JSY 5.00 12.00
137 Brett Howden JSY 2.50 6.00
138 Tyler Soy JSY 2.50 6.00
139 Graham Knott JSY 2.50 6.00
140 Pierre-Luc Dubois JSY 6.00 15.00
141 Sarah Davis JSY 2.50 6.00
142 Bailey Bram JSY 2.50 6.00
143 Jessica Campbell JSY 8.00 20.00
144 Halli Krzyzaniak JSY 2.50 6.00
145 Genevieve Lacasse JSY 3.00 8.00
146 Ann-Renee Desbiens JSY 10.00 25.00
147 Rebecca Johnston JSY 3.00 8.00
148 Marie-Philip Poulin JSY 12.00 30.00
149 Jillian Saulnier JSY 5.00 12.00
150 Natalie Spooner JSY 10.00 25.00
151 Caroline Ouellette JSY 4.00 10.00
152 Lauriane Rougeau JSY 2.50 6.00
153 Courtney Birchard JSY 2.50 6.00
154 Brigette Lacquette JSY 3.00 8.00
155 Laura Fortino JSY 2.50 6.00
156 Jennifer Wakefield JSY 2.50 6.00
157 Jamie Lee Rattray JSY 5.00 12.00
158 Tara Watchorn JSY 3.00 8.00
159 Emily Clark JSY 8.00 20.00
160 Brianne Jenner JSY 6.00 15.00

2015-16 Upper Deck Team Canada Juniors Exclusives Red

*EXCLUSIVE/199: 1.5X TO 4X BASIC CARDS

2015-16 Upper Deck Team Canada Juniors Glossy

*GLOSSY/25: 3X TO 8X BASIC CARDS
49 Connor McDavid 40.00 80.00
90 Connor McDavid 40.00 80.00
98 Connor McDavid 40.00 80.00

2015-16 Upper Deck Team Canada Juniors Gold

*1-100 GOLD: .8X TO 2X BASIC CARDS
*101-140 JSY/20-31: .8X TO 2X BASIC JSY
*101-140 JSY/14-19: 1X TO 2.5X BASIC JSY
*141-160 JSY/24-38: .8X TO 2X BASIC JSY
*141-160 JSY/14-19: 1X TO 2.5X BASIC JSY
101 Connor McDavid JSY/17 150.00 400.00

2015-16 Upper Deck Team Canada Juniors Patch Autographs

101 Connor McDavid JSY AU/125 200.00 350.00
102 Zach Fucale JSY AU/125 8.00 20.00
103 Max Domi JSY AU/125 40.00 80.00
104 Jake Virtanen JSY AU/125 20.00 40.00
105 Nick Ritchie JSY AU/125 10.00 25.00
106 Lawson Crouse JSY AU/125 10.00 25.00
107 Nicolas Petan JSY AU/199 8.00 20.00
109 Samuel Morin JSY AU/199 5.00 12.00
110 Nick Paul JSY AU/199 6.00 15.00
111 Brayden Point JSY AU/199 12.00 30.00
112 Dillon Heatherington JSY AU/199 5.00 12.00
113 Josh Morrissey JSY AU/199 8.00 20.00
114 Robby Fabbri JSY AU/199 10.00 25.00
115 Frederik Gauthier JSY AU/199 8.00 20.00
116 Shea Theodore JSY AU/199 12.00 30.00
117 Joe Hicketts JSY AU/199 5.00 12.00
118 Madison Bowey JSY AU/199 5.00 12.00
119 Evan Cormier JSY AU/199 6.00 15.00
120 Mitchell Stephens JSY AU/199 5.00 12.00
121 Ethan Bear JSY AU/199 5.00 12.00
122 Mathew Barzal JSY AU/199 20.00 50.00
123 Kyle Capobianco JSY AU/199 5.00 12.00
124 Parker Wotherspoon JSY AU/199 5.00 12.00
125 Anthony Beauvillier JSY AU/199 6.00 15.00
127 Nathan Noel JSY AU/199 5.00 12.00
128 Thomas Chabot JSY AU/199 8.00 20.00
129 Jeremy Roy JSY AU/199 5.00 12.00
130 Deven Sideroff JSY AU/199 5.00 12.00
131 Zachary Sawchenko JSY AU/199 5.00 12.00
132 Guillaume Brisebois JSY AU/199 6.00 15.00
133 Glenn Gawdin JSY AU/199 6.00 15.00
134 Matthew Spencer JSY AU/199 5.00 12.00
135 Nicolas Roy JSY AU/199 5.00 12.00
136 Tyler Benson JSY AU/199 10.00 25.00
137 Brett Howden JSY AU/199 5.00 12.00
138 Tyler Soy JSY AU/199 5.00 12.00
140 Pierre-Luc Dubois JSY AU/199 12.00 30.00
141 Sarah Davis JSY AU/199 5.00 12.00
142 Bailey Bram JSY AU/199 5.00 12.00
144 Halli Krzyzaniak JSY AU/199 5.00 12.00
146 Ann-Renee Desbiens JSY AU/199 20.00 50.00
147 Rebecca Johnston JSY AU/199 6.00 15.00
148 Marie-Philip Poulin JSY AU/199 40.00 100.00
149 Jillian Saulnier JSY AU/199 10.00 25.00
150 Natalie Spooner JSY AU/199 20.00 50.00
151 Caroline Ouellette JSY AU/199 8.00 20.00
152 Lauriane Rougeau JSY AU/199 5.00 12.00
153 Courtney Birchard JSY AU/199 5.00 12.00
154 Brigette Lacquette JSY AU/199 6.00 15.00
155 Laura Fortino JSY AU/199 5.00 12.00
157 Jamie Lee Rattray JSY AU/199 10.00 25.00
159 Emily Clark JSY AU/199 15.00 40.00
160 Brianne Jenner JSY AU/199 12.00 30.00

2015-16 Upper Deck Team Canada Juniors '90-91 Retros U20

R201 Nick Ritchie 6.00 15.00
R202 Zach Fucale 5.00 12.00
R203 Max Domi 10.00 25.00
R204 Connor McDavid 40.00 100.00
R205 Samuel Morin 4.00 10.00
R206 Lawson Crouse 6.00 15.00
R207 Robby Fabbri 8.00 20.00
R208 Frederik Gauthier 6.00 15.00
R209 Madison Bowey 4.00 10.00
R2010 Nick Paul 5.00 12.00
R2011 Brayden Point 10.00 25.00
R2012 Eric Comrie 6.00 15.00
R2013 Jake Virtanen 10.00 25.00
R2014 Nicolas Petan 6.00 15.00
R2015 Josh Morrissey 6.00 15.00

2015-16 Upper Deck Team Canada Juniors '91-92 Retros U18

R181 Dylan Strome 10.00 25.00
R182 Mitch Marner 15.00 40.00
R183 Travis Konecny 10.00 25.00
R184 Nick Merkley 6.00 15.00
R185 Jeremy Roy 3.00 8.00
R186 Nicolas Roy 3.00 8.00
R187 Zachary Sawchenko 3.00 8.00
R188 Mathew Barzal 12.00 30.00
R189 Jansen Harkins 5.00 12.00
R1810 Mitchell Stephens 3.00 8.00
R1811 Thomas Chabot 5.00 12.00
R1812 Ethan Bear 3.00 8.00
R1813 Evan Cormier 4.00 10.00
R1814 Anthony Beauvillier 4.00 10.00
R1815 Matthew Spencer 3.00 8.00

2015-16 Upper Deck Team Canada Juniors '97-98 Retros Women

RW1 Jennifer Wakefield 3.00 8.00
RW2 Genevieve Lacasse 4.00 10.00
RW3 Marie-Philip Poulin 15.00 40.00
RW4 Natalie Spooner 12.00 30.00
RW5 Laura Fortino 3.00 8.00
RW6 Caroline Ouellette 5.00 12.00

2015-16 Upper Deck Team Canada Juniors Dual Jerseys

TCDBB M.Barzal/A.Beauvillier 10.00 25.00
TCDDF R.Fabbri/M.Domi 5.00 12.00
TCDFC Z.Fucale/E.Comrie 5.00 12.00
TCDGP F.Gauthier/N.Petan 4.00 10.00
TCDJL B.Jenner/G.Lacasse 5.00 12.00
TCDMC C.McDavid/L.Crouse 12.00 30.00
TCDMD C.McDavid/M.Domi 12.00 30.00
TCDRV J.Virtanen/N.Ritchie 5.00 12.00
TCDSC Z.Sawchenko/E.Cormier 2.50 6.00
TCDSP N.Spooner/M.Poulin 12.00 30.00

2015-16 Upper Deck Team Canada Juniors Hydro

*RED: .8X TO 2X BASIC INSERTS
H1 Nick Merkley 2.50 6.00
H2 Dylan Strome 2.50 6.00
H3 Travis Konecny 2.50 6.00
H4 Mitch Marner 6.00 15.00
H5 Adam Musil 1.50 4.00
H6 Jansen Harkins 2.00 5.00
H7 Anthony Beauvillier 1.50 4.00
H8 Tyler Soy 1.25 3.00
H9 Brett Howden 1.25 3.00
H10 Tyler Benson 2.50 6.00
H11 Kyle Capobianco 1.25 3.00
H12 Matthew Spencer 1.25 3.00
H13 Graham Knott 1.25 3.00
H14 Deven Sideroff 1.25 3.00
H15 Thomas Chabot 2.00 5.00
H16 Parker Wotherspoon 1.25 3.00
H17 Glenn Gawdin 1.50 4.00
H18 Nathan Noel 1.25 3.00
H19 Zachary Sawchenko 1.25 3.00
H20 Guillaume Brisebois 1.50 4.00
H21 Nicolas Roy 1.25 3.00
H22 Mitchell Stephens 1.25 3.00
H23 Jeremy Roy 1.25 3.00
H24 Pierre-Luc Dubois 3.00 8.00
H25 Mathew Barzal 5.00 12.00
H26 Ethan Bear 1.25 3.00
H27 Evan Cormier 1.50 4.00
H28 Josh Morrissey 2.00 5.00
H29 Brayden Point 3.00 8.00
H30 Nicolas Petan 2.00 5.00
H31 Samuel Morin 1.25 3.00
H32 Lawson Crouse 2.00 5.00
H33 Madison Bowey 1.25 3.00
H34 Max Domi 6.00 15.00
H35 Shea Theodore 3.00 8.00
H36 Robby Fabbri 2.50 6.00
H37 Connor McDavid 12.00 30.00
H38 Zach Fucale 1.50 4.00
H39 Jake Virtanen 2.50 6.00
H40 Frederik Gauthier 2.00 5.00
H41 Dillon Heatherington 1.25 3.00
H42 Nick Paul 1.50 4.00
H43 Joe Hicketts 1.25 3.00
H44 Nick Ritchie 2.00 5.00
H45 Eric Comrie 2.00 5.00
H46 Caroline Ouellette 2.00 5.00
H47 Ann-Renee Desbiens 5.00 12.00
H48 Brigette Lacquette 1.50 4.00
H49 Genevieve Lacasse 1.50 4.00
H50 Jennifer Wakefield 1.25 3.00
H51 Laura Fortino 1.25 3.00
H52 Rebecca Johnston 1.50 4.00
H53 Halli Krzyzaniak 1.25 3.00
H54 Jamie Lee Rattray 2.50 6.00
H55 Jessica Campbell 4.00 10.00
H56 Courtney Birchard 1.25 3.00
H57 Marie-Philip Poulin 6.00 15.00
H58 Brianne Jenner 3.00 8.00
H59 Emily Clark 4.00 10.00
H60 Natalie Spooner 5.00 12.00

2015-16 Upper Deck Team Canada Juniors Jumbo Jerseys

JSAB Anthony Beauvillier 3.00 8.00
JSCM Connor McDavid 20.00 40.00
JSFG Frederik Gauthier 4.00 10.00
JSJH Jansen Harkins 4.00 10.00
JSJV Jake Virtanen 5.00 12.00
JSLC Lawson Crouse 4.00 10.00
JSMB Mathew Barzal 10.00 25.00
JSMD Max Domi 12.00 30.00
JSMS Mitchell Stephens 2.50 6.00
JSNP Nicolas Petan 4.00 10.00
JSNR Nick Ritchie 4.00 10.00
JSPA Nick Paul 3.00 8.00
JSRF Robby Fabbri 5.00 12.00
JSSM Samuel Morin 2.50 6.00
JSZF Zach Fucale 3.00 8.00
JSZS Zachary Sawchenko 2.50 6.00

2015-16 Upper Deck Team Canada Juniors Local Legends Jerseys

*GOLD/25: .6X TO 1.5X BASIC JSY
LLBJ Brianne Jenner 6.00 15.00
LLBP Brayden Point 6.00 15.00
LLCM Connor McDavid 20.00 40.00
LLEC Emily Clark 8.00 20.00
LLGL Genevieve Lacasse 3.00 8.00
LLJV Jake Virtanen 5.00 12.00
LLLC Lawson Crouse 4.00 10.00
LLMB Madison Bowey 2.50 6.00
LLMD Max Domi 12.00 30.00
LLNP Nicolas Petan 4.00 10.00
LLNR Nick Ritchie 4.00 10.00
LLRF Robby Fabbri 5.00 12.00
LLSM Samuel Morin 2.50 6.00
LLTB Tyler Benson 5.00 12.00
LLZF Zach Fucale 3.00 8.00

2015-16 Upper Deck Team Canada Juniors Maple Leaf Forever Autographs

MLAB Anthony Beauvillier M2 5.00 12.00
MLAD Ann-Renee Desbiens W 10.00 25.00
MLBB Bailey Bram W 6.00 15.00
MLBH Brett Howden M2 4.00 10.00
MLBJ Brianne Jenner W 8.00 20.00
MLBL Brigette Lacquette W 8.00 20.00
MLBP Brayden Point M2 10.00 25.00
MLCL Emily Clark W 20.00 50.00
MLCM Connor McDavid M1 100.00 250.00
MLDH Dillon Heatherington M2 4.00 10.00
MLDS Deven Sideroff M2 4.00 10.00
MLEB Ethan Bear M2 4.00 10.00
MLEC Evan Cormier M2 5.00 12.00
MLEM Emerance Maschmeyer W 10.00 25.00
MLFG Frederik Gauthier M2 6.00 15.00
MLGB Guillaume Brisebois M2 5.00 12.00
MLGG Glenn Gawdin M2 5.00 12.00
MLHI Joe Hicketts M2 4.00 10.00
MLHK Halli Krzyzaniak W 10.00 25.00
MLJM Josh Morrissey M2 6.00 15.00
MLJR Jeremy Roy M2 4.00 10.00
MLJS Jillian Saulnier W 12.00 30.00
MLJV Jake Virtanen M1 12.00 30.00
MLKC Kyle Capobianco M2 4.00 10.00
MLLC Lawson Crouse M1 6.00 15.00
MLLF Laura Fortino W 6.00 15.00
MLLR Lauriane Rougeau W 6.00 15.00
MLMB Mathew Barzal M2 15.00 40.00
MLMD Max Domi M1 20.00 50.00
MLMP Marie-Philip Poulin W 30.00 80.00
MLMS Matthew Spencer M2 4.00 10.00
MLNN Nathan Noel M2 4.00 10.00
MLNP Nick Paul M2 5.00 12.00
MLNS Natalie Spooner W 25.00 60.00
MLOU Caroline Ouellette W 10.00 25.00
MLPD Pierre-Luc Dubois M2 10.00 25.00
MLPE Nicolas Petan M2 6.00 15.00
MLPW Parker Wotherspoon M2 4.00 10.00
MLRA Jamie Lee Rattray W 12.00 30.00
MLRF Robby Fabbri M2 8.00 20.00
MLRJ Rebecca Johnston W 8.00 20.00
MLRO Nicolas Roy M2 4.00 10.00
MLSM Samuel Morin M2 4.00 10.00
MLST Mitchell Stephens M2 4.00 10.00
MLTB Tyler Benson M2 12.00 30.00
MLTC Thomas Chabot M2 6.00 15.00
MLTH Shea Theodore M2 10.00 25.00
MLTS Tyler Soy M2 4.00 10.00
MLTW Tara Watchorn W 10.00 25.00
MLZF Zach Fucale M1 10.00 25.00
MLZS Zachary Sawchenko M2 10.00 25.00

2015-16 Upper Deck Team Canada Juniors Quad Jerseys

TCQBBHC Brzl/Bvlr/Hrkns/Crse 10.00 25.00
TCQMPGF McDav/Fbr/Ghr/Pnt 25.00 50.00
TCQMRVP Mrn/Rtch/Vrtn/Ptan 10.00 25.00
TCQPJLS Jnr/Pln/Spnr/Lacse 25.00 60.00

2015-16 Upper Deck Team Canada Juniors Triple Jerseys

TCTBHB Barzal/Harkins/Beauv 8.00 20.00
TCTMFD McDavid/Fabbri/Domi 20.00 40.00
TCTMPC Morin/Petan/Crouse 6.00 15.00
TCTVGR Virtanen/Gauth/Ritchie 8.00 20.00
TCTWPS Wakefd/Poulin/Spooner 8.00 20.00

2015-16 Upper Deck Team Canada Juniors True North Jerseys

*GOLD/49: .5X TO 1.2X BASIC JSY
TNAB Anthony Beauvillier 3.00 8.00
TNBH Brett Howden 2.50 6.00
TNCM Connor McDavid 20.00 40.00
TNEC Evan Cormier 3.00 8.00
TNFG Frederik Gauthier 4.00 10.00
TNGL Genevieve Lacasse 3.00 8.00
TNJH Jansen Harkins 4.00 10.00
TNJM Josh Morrissey 4.00 10.00
TNJV Jake Virtanen 5.00 12.00
TNJW Jennifer Wakefield 2.50 6.00
TNLF Laura Fortino 2.50 6.00
TNMB Mathew Barzal 10.00 25.00
TNMD Max Domi 12.00 30.00
TNMP Marie-Philip Poulin 12.00 30.00
TNMS Mitchell Stephens 2.50 6.00
TNNN Nathan Noel 2.50 6.00
TNNP Nicolas Petan 4.00 10.00
TNNR Nick Ritchie 4.00 10.00
TNNS Natalie Spooner 10.00 25.00
TNRF Robby Fabbri 5.00 12.00
TNSM Samuel Morin 2.50 6.00
TNTB Tyler Benson 5.00 12.00
TNTC Thomas Chabot 4.00 10.00
TNZF Zach Fucale 3.00 8.00
TNZS Zachary Sawchenko 2.50 6.00

2015-16 Upper Deck Team Canada Master Collection

1 Wayne Gretzky 15.00 40.00
2 Corey Perry 4.00 10.00
3 Glenn Anderson 2.00 5.00
4 Ed Belfour 2.50 6.00
5 Paul Coffey 2.50 6.00
6 Mark Messier 5.00 12.00
7 Eric Lindros 3.00 8.00
8 Bill Ranford 3.00 8.00
9 Rick Nash 2.50 6.00
10 Jarome Iginla 3.00 8.00
11 Steven Stamkos 5.00 12.00
12 Luc Robitaille 2.50 6.00
13 Joe Sakic 5.00 12.00
14 Felix Potvin 4.00 10.00
15 Bobby Clarke 4.00 10.00
16 Vincent Lecavalier 2.50 6.00
17 Doug Gilmour 3.00 8.00
18 John Tavares 4.00 10.00
19 Theoren Fleury 3.00 8.00
20 Bobby Orr 10.00 25.00
21 Dale Hawerchuk 3.00 8.00
22 Marcel Dionne 3.00 8.00
23 Jordan Eberle 2.50 6.00
24 Sidney Crosby 6.00 15.00
25 Ryan Smyth 2.00 5.00
26 Bobby Hull 5.00 12.00
27 Marc-Andre Fleury 5.00 12.00
28 Larry Robinson 2.50 6.00
29 Grant Fuhr 4.00 10.00
30 Dany Heatley 2.00 5.00
31 Ryan Nugent-Hopkins 3.00 8.00
32 Shea Weber 2.00 5.00
33 Patrick Roy 6.00 15.00
34 Ron Hextall 2.50 6.00
35 Taylor Hall 3.00 8.00
36 Eric Staal 3.00 8.00
37 P.K. Subban 3.00 8.00
38 Mike Gartner 3.00 8.00
39 Jonathan Toews 4.00 10.00
40 Jeff Skinner 3.00 8.00
41 Mario Lemieux 10.00 25.00
42 Martin St. Louis 2.50 6.00
43 Mike Bossy 2.50 6.00
44 Chris Pronger 2.50 6.00
45 Ray Bourque 4.00 10.00
46 James Neal 1.50 4.00
47 Ryan Getzlaf 2.50 6.00
48 Martin Brodeur 6.00 15.00
49 Steve Yzerman 6.00 15.00
50 Carey Price 5.00 12.00

2015-16 Upper Deck Team Canada Master Collection Inscriptions

IMB Mike Bossy/25 15.00 40.00
IRN Rick Nash/25 30.00 60.00

2015-16 Upper Deck Team Canada Master Collection Luminaries Autographs

LSBC Bobby Clarke/25 40.00 80.00
LSBO Bobby Orr/99 100.00 200.00
LSMG Mike Gartner/25 20.00 50.00
LSWG Wayne Gretzky/99 250.00 600.00

2015-16 Upper Deck Team Canada Master Collection Program of Excellence Dual Autographs

POES2KH Evander Kane
Cody Hodgson 20.00 50.00
POES2SS Jaden Schwartz
Devante Smith-Pelly 25.00 60.00

2015-16 Upper Deck Team Canada Master Collection Program of Excellence Quad Jersey Autographs

*PATCH/25: .6X TO 1.5X BASIC JSY AU/99
POEDH Dougie Hamilton 10.00 25.00
POEQH Quinton Howden 8.00 20.00

2015-16 Upper Deck Team Canada Master Collection Signature Moments Booklets

SMBR Bill Ranford 30.00 60.00
SMJS Jeff Skinner 25.00 60.00
SMJT John Tavares 40.00 80.00
SMRNH Ryan Nugent-Hopkins 25.00 60.00
SMTF Theoren Fleury 40.00 80.00

2015-16 Upper Deck Team Canada Master Collection Silver Spectrum Autographs

12 Luc Robitaille/15 20.00 50.00
18 John Tavares/25 30.00 60.00
46 James Neal/25 20.00 50.00
47 Ryan Getzlaf/20 15.00 40.00

2015-16 Upper Deck Team Canada Master Collection Team Canada Autographs

TCSAB Alexandre Burrows/25 20.00 40.00
TCSBO Bobby Orr/25 125.00 200.00
TCSBR Brett Connolly/25 10.00 25.00
TCSCW Cam Ward/15 15.00 40.00
TCSHD Dougie Hamilton/25 25.00 50.00
TCSJN James Neal/25 25.00 50.00
TCSJT John Tavares/15 40.00 80.00
TCSMD Matt Duchene/25 15.00 40.00
TCSOB Bobby Orr/25 125.00 200.00
TCSRW Ray Whitney/25 10.00 25.00
TCSSJ Jaden Schwartz/25 20.00 50.00
TCSSK Jeff Skinner/15 20.00 50.00

TCSSS Sheldon Souray/25 10.00 25.00
TCSTS Tyler Seguin/15 20.00 40.00
TCSORR Bobby Orr/25 125.00 200.00

2015-16 Upper Deck Team Canada Master Collection Team Canada Autographs Dual

TCS2SC J.Schwartz/B.Connolly 20.00 50.00

2015-16 Upper Deck Team Canada Master Collection Team Canada Autographs Triple

TCS3STG Stl/Thrntn/Gtzlf 40.00 80.00

2015-16 Upper Deck Team Canada Master Collection Winning Standard Autographed Jumbo Jersey

WSSJSC Sidney Crosby 200.00 350.00
WSSJSW Shea Weber 40.00 80.00

2015-16 Upper Deck Team Canada Master Collection Winning Standard Autographs

WSSDH Dany Heatley 12.00 30.00
WSSJI Jarome Iginla 40.00 80.00
WSSPB Patrice Bergeron 25.00 50.00
WSSRN Rick Nash 15.00 40.00
WSSSW Shea Weber 12.00 30.00

2015-16 Upper Deck Team Canada Master Collection Winning Standard Autographs Dual

WSS2PG R.Getzlaf/C.Perry 30.00 80.00

2015-16 Upper Deck Team Canada Master Collection Winning Standard Jerseys

*JUM.PATCH/10: 1X TO 2.5X BASIC JSY
*PATCH/35: .6X TO 1.5X BASIC JSY
WSBM Brenden Morrow 5.00 12.00
WSBS Brent Seabrook 4.00 10.00
WSCP Chris Pronger 6.00 15.00
WSDB Dan Boyle 4.00 10.00
WSDD Drew Doughty 8.00 20.00
WSDH Dany Heatley 5.00 12.00
WSDK Duncan Keith 5.00 12.00
WSES Eric Staal 8.00 20.00
WSJI Jarome Iginla 8.00 20.00
WSJT Joe Thornton 10.00 25.00
WSMB Martin Brodeur 12.00 30.00
WSMF Marc-Andre Fleury 12.00 30.00
WSMR Mike Richards 5.00 12.00
WSPB Patrice Bergeron 8.00 20.00
WSPE Corey Perry 10.00 25.00
WSPM Patrick Marleau 6.00 15.00
WSRG Ryan Getzlaf 6.00 15.00
WSRL Roberto Luongo 10.00 25.00
WSRN Rick Nash 6.00 15.00
WSSC Sidney Crosby 15.00 40.00
WSSW Shea Weber 5.00 12.00
WSTO Jonathan Toews 10.00 25.00

2015-16 Upper Deck Team Canada Master Collection Winning Standard Jerseys and Patch Dual

*DUAL JSY/15: .4X TO 1X PATCH/25
WS2BD Dan Boyle Drew Doughty 12.00 30.00
WS2BI Patrice Bergeron Jarome Iginla 12.00 30.00
WS2BP Dan Boyle Chris Pronger 10.00 25.00
WS2IN Jarome Iginla Rick Nash 15.00 40.00
WS2MM Patrick Marleau Brenden Morrow 10.00 25.00
WS2TB Jonathan Toews Patrice Bergeron 15.00 40.00

2016-17 Upper Deck Team Canada Juniors

1 Hayley Wickenheiser .40 1.00
2 Tara Watchorn .40 1.00
3 Meghan Agosta-Marciano .40 1.00
4 Brigette Lacquette .30 .75
5 Jamie Lee Rattray .50 1.25
6 Jillian Saulnier .50 1.25
7 Jennifer Wakefield .25 .60
8 Marie-Philip Poulin 1.25 3.00
9 Halli Krzyzaniak .25 .60
10 Lauriane Rougeau .30 .75
11 Natalie Spooner 1.00 2.50
12 Brianne Jenner .60 1.50
13 Charline Labonte .40 1.00
14 Sarah Davis .30 .75
15 Blayre Turnbull .30 .75
16 Meaghan Mikkelson .30 .75
17 Emerance Maschmeyer .50 1.25
18 Rebecca Johnston .30 .75
19 Emily Clark .75 2.00
20 Jocelyne Larocque .40 1.00
21 Bailey Bram .30 .75
22 Laura Fortino .40 1.00
23 Dylan Strome 1.00 2.50
24 Mitch Marner 1.25 3.00
25 Brandon Hickey .30 .75
26 Mackenzie Blackwood .50 1.25
27 Mason McDonald .40 1.00
28 Samuel Montembeault .60 1.50
29 Thomas Chabot .75 2.00
30 Travis Dermott .60 1.50
31 Joe Hicketts .25 .60
32 Roland McKeown .30 .75
33 Mathew Barzal 1.25 3.00
34 Anthony Beauvillier .40 1.00
35 Rourke Chartier .40 1.00
36 Lawson Crouse .30 .75
37 Julien Gauthier .40 1.00
38 Travis Konecny .75 2.00
39 Brayden Point 1.00 2.50
40 Mitchell Stephens .25 .60
41 Haydn Fleury .40 1.00
42 Travis Sanheim .40 1.00
43 Brendan Perlini .40 1.00
44 John Quenneville .40 1.00
45 Sam Steel .40 1.00
46 Carter Hart .60 1.50
47 Dylan Wells .40 1.00
48 Jake Bean .40 1.00
49 Kale Clague .40 1.00
50 Dante Fabbro .30 .75
51 Josh Mahura .30 .75
52 Samuel Girard .30 .75
53 Victor Mete .30 .75
54 David Quenneville .40 1.00
55 Tyler Benson .30 .75
56 William Bitten .30 .75
57 Dillon Dube .40 1.00
58 Pierre-Luc Dubois .30 .75
59 Brett Howden .25 .60
60 Tyson Jost .40 1.00
61 Tanner Kaspick .40 1.00
62 Jordan Kyrou .40 1.00
63 Beck Malenstyn .40 1.00
64 Michael McLeod .40 1.00
65 Nolan Patrick 2.50 6.00
66 Zach Poirier .30 .75
67 Pascal Laberge .30 .75
68 Evan Fitzpatrick .40 1.00
69 Connor Hall .40 1.00
70 Maxime Comtois .50 1.25
71 Stuart Skinner .50 1.25
72 Jakob Chychrun .75 2.00
73 Cameron Morrison .30 .75
74 Nicolas Hague .30 .75
75 Markus Phillips .30 .75
76 Logan Stanley .40 1.00
77 Boris Katchouk .75 2.00
78 Mason Shaw .40 1.00
79 Noah Gregor .40 1.00
80 Owen Tippett .40 1.00
81 Mitch Marner 1.25 3.00
82 Lawson Crouse .30 .75
83 Dylan Strome 1.00 2.50
84 Haydn Fleury .40 1.00
85 John Quenneville .40 1.00
86 Pierre-Luc Dubois .30 .75
87 Tyson Jost .40 1.00
88 Jakob Chychrun .75 2.00
89 Nolan Patrick 2.50 6.00
90 Michael McLeod .40 1.00
91 Doug Gilmour .50 1.25
92 Martin Brodeur 1.00 2.50
93 Grant Fuhr .60 1.50
94 Mark Messier .75 2.00
95 Rod Brind'Amour .40 1.00
96 Martin St. Louis .40 1.00
97 Joe Sakic .75 2.00
98 Steve Yzerman 1.00 2.50
99 Mario Lemieux 1.50 4.00
100 Wayne Gretzky 2.50 6.00
101 Mitch Marner JSY 12.00 30.00
102 Dylan Strome JSY 10.00 25.00
103 Lawson Crouse JSY 3.00 8.00
104 Mason McDonald JSY 4.00 10.00
105 Anthony Beauvillier JSY 4.00 10.00
106 Brayden Point JSY 10.00 25.00
107 Travis Dermott JSY 6.00 15.00
108 Joe Hicketts JSY 2.50 6.00
109 Roland McKeown JSY 3.00 8.00
110 Mathew Barzal JSY 12.00 30.00
111 Brandon Hickey JSY 3.00 8.00
112 Rourke Chartier JSY 4.00 10.00
113 Thomas Chabot JSY 8.00 20.00
114 Julien Gauthier JSY 4.00 10.00
115 Travis Konecny JSY 8.00 20.00
116 Samuel Montembeault JSY 6.00 15.00
117 Mitchell Stephens JSY 2.50 6.00
118 Haydn Fleury JSY 4.00 10.00
119 Travis Sanheim JSY 4.00 10.00
120 Brendan Perlini JSY 4.00 10.00
121 John Quenneville JSY 4.00 10.00
122 Mackenzie Blackwood JSY 5.00 12.00
123 Evan Fitzpatrick JSY 4.00 10.00
124 Dante Fabbro JSY 3.00 8.00
125 Jakob Chychrun JSY 8.00 20.00
126 David Quenneville JSY 4.00 10.00
127 Logan Stanley JSY 4.00 10.00
128 William Bitten JSY 3.00 8.00
129 Pascal Laberge JSY 3.00 8.00
130 Michael McLeod JSY 4.00 10.00
131 Tyson Jost JSY 4.00 10.00
132 Connor Hall JSY 3.00 8.00
133 Maxime Comtois JSY 5.00 12.00
134 Jordan Kyrou JSY 4.00 10.00
135 Cameron Morrison JSY 3.00 8.00
136 Boris Katchouk JSY 8.00 20.00
137 Mason Shaw JSY 4.00 10.00
138 Brett Howden JSY 2.50 6.00
139 Stuart Skinner JSY 5.00 12.00
140 Nicolas Hague JSY 3.00 8.00
141 Owen Tippett JSY 4.00 10.00
142 Noah Gregor JSY 4.00 10.00
143 Meaghan Mikkelson JSY 3.00 8.00
144 Meghan Agosta-Marciano JSY 4.00 10.00
145 Halli Krzyzaniak JSY 2.50 6.00
146 Jillian Saulnier JSY 4.00 10.00
147 Sarah Davis JSY 3.00 8.00
148 Jamie Lee Rattray JSY 5.00 12.00
149 Emerance Maschmeyer JSY 5.00 12.00
150 Tara Watchorn JSY 4.00 10.00
151 Emily Clark JSY 8.00 20.00
152 Bailey Bram JSY 3.00 8.00
153 Brianne Jenner JSY 6.00 15.00
154 Charline Labonte JSY 4.00 10.00
155 Rebecca Johnston JSY 3.00 8.00
156 Lauriane Rougeau JSY 3.00 8.00
157 Laura Fortino JSY 4.00 10.00
158 Jennifer Wakefield JSY 2.50 6.00
159 Jocelyne Larocque JSY 4.00 10.00
160 Natalie Spooner JSY 10.00 25.00
161 Hayley Wickenheiser JSY 4.00 10.00
162 Marie-Philip Poulin JSY 12.00 30.00

2016-17 Upper Deck Team Canada Juniors Jumbo Material Autographs

JSAB Anthony Beauvillier 6.00 15.00
JSBL Mackenzie Blackwood 8.00 20.00
JSBP Brayden Point 15.00 40.00
JSDS Dylan Strome 15.00 40.00
JSHF Haydn Fleury 6.00 15.00
JSJG Julien Gauthier 6.00 15.00
JSJH Joe Hicketts 4.00 10.00
JSJQ John Quenneville 6.00 15.00
JSLC Lawson Crouse 5.00 12.00
JSMB Mathew Barzal 20.00 50.00
JSMC Mason McDonald 6.00 15.00
JSMM Mitch Marner 20.00 50.00
JSMS Mitchell Stephens 4.00 10.00
JSRC Rourke Chartier 6.00 15.00
JSTC Thomas Chabot 12.00 30.00
JSTD Travis Dermott 10.00 25.00
JSTK Travis Konecny 12.00 30.00
JSTS Travis Sanheim 6.00 15.00

2016-17 Upper Deck Team Canada Juniors Jumbo Materials

JSAB Anthony Beauvillier 4.00 10.00
JSBL Mackenzie Blackwood 5.00 12.00
JSBP Brayden Point 10.00 25.00
JSDS Dylan Strome 10.00 25.00
JSHF Haydn Fleury 4.00 10.00
JSJG Julien Gauthier 4.00 10.00
JSJH Joe Hicketts 2.50 6.00
JSJQ John Quenneville 4.00 10.00
JSLC Lawson Crouse 3.00 8.00
JSMB Mathew Barzal 12.00 30.00
JSMC Mason McDonald 4.00 10.00
JSMM Mitch Marner 12.00 30.00
JSMS Mitchell Stephens 2.50 6.00
JSRC Rourke Chartier 4.00 10.00
JSTC Thomas Chabot 8.00 20.00
JSTD Travis Dermott 6.00 15.00
JSTK Travis Konecny 8.00 20.00
JSTS Travis Sanheim 4.00 10.00

2016-17 Upper Deck Team Canada Juniors Local Legends Relics

LLBA Mathew Barzal 10.00 25.00
LLBP Brendan Perlini 3.00 8.00
LLDS Dylan Strome 8.00 20.00
LLHW Hayley Wickenheiser 3.00 8.00
LLJH Joe Hicketts 2.00 5.00
LLJQ John Quenneville 3.00 8.00
LLLF Laura Fortino 3.00 8.00
LLMB Mackenzie Blackwood 4.00 10.00
LLMC Mason McDonald 3.00 8.00
LLMM Mitch Marner 10.00 25.00
LLMS Mitchell Stephens 2.00 5.00
LLNS Natalie Spooner 8.00 20.00
LLRC Rourke Chartier 3.00 8.00
LLTJ Tyson Jost 3.00 8.00
LLTK Travis Konecny 6.00 15.00

2016-17 Upper Deck Team Canada Juniors Manufactured Logo Patches 100 Years

LPAB Anthony Beauvillier 8.00 20.00
LPBP Brayden Point 20.00 50.00
LPBR Martin Brodeur 20.00 50.00
LPDG Doug Gilmour 10.00 25.00
LPDS Dylan Strome 20.00 50.00
LPEF Evan Fitzpatrick 8.00 20.00
LPGL Guy Lafleur 10.00 25.00
LPHF Haydn Fleury 8.00 20.00
LPJC Jakob Chychrun 15.00 40.00
LPJG Julien Gauthier 8.00 20.00
LPJQ John Quenneville 8.00 20.00
LPJS Joe Sakic 15.00 40.00
LPLC Lawson Crouse 6.00 15.00
LPMB Mathew Barzal 25.00 60.00
LPMC Mason McDonald 8.00 20.00
LPME Mark Messier 15.00 40.00
LPMI Michael McLeod 8.00 20.00
LPML Mario Lemieux 30.00 80.00
LPMM Mitch Marner 30.00 80.00
LPMS Mitchell Stephens 5.00 12.00
LPRB Rod Brind'Amour 8.00 20.00
LPRC Rourke Chartier 8.00 20.00
LPST Martin St. Louis 8.00 20.00
LPSY Steve Yzerman 20.00 50.00
LPTD Travis Dermott 12.00 30.00
LPTK Travis Konecny 15.00 40.00
LPTS Travis Sanheim 8.00 20.00
LPWG Wayne Gretzky 90.00 150.00

2017-18 Upper Deck Team Canada Juniors

1 Connor Ingram .40 1.00
2 Jake Bean .40 1.00
3 Noah Juulsen .40 1.00
4 Mitchell Stephens .25 .60
5 Michael McLeod 1.00 2.50
6 Taylor Raddysh .40 1.00
7 Carter Hart .60 1.50
8 Pierre-Luc Dubois 2.50 6.00
9 Dillon Dube .40 1.00
10 Kale Clague .30 .75
11 Mathieu Joseph .30 .75
12 Julien Gauthier .40 1.00
13 Nicolas Roy .25 .60
14 Anthony Cirelli .30 .75
15 Jeremy Lauzon .30 .75
16 Philippe Myers .30 .75
17 Dante Fabbro .40 1.00
18 Jennifer Wakefield .25 .60
19 Jocelyne Larocque .40 1.00
20 Lauriane Rougeau .25 .60
21 Sarah Potomak .30 .75
22 Laura Stacey .50 1.25
23 Erin Ambrose .60 1.50
24 Natalie Spooner 1.00 2.50
25 Brianne Jenner .60 1.50
26 Emily Clark .75 2.00
27 Halli Krzyzaniak .25 .60
28 Rebecca Johnston .40 1.00
29 Marie-Philip Poulin 1.25 3.00
30 Emerance Maschmeyer .50 1.25
31 Genevieve Lacasse .30 .75
32 Meghan Mikkelson .30 .75
33 Meghan Agosta .30 .75
34 Shannon Szabados .30 .75
35 Bailey Bram .30 .75
36 Renata Fast .40 1.00
37 Sarah Davis .30 .75
38 Haley Irwin .30 .75
39 Laura Fortino .30 .75
40 Blayre Turnbull .30 .75
41 Jaret Anderson-Dolan .40 1.00
42 Jett Woo .30 .75
43 Isaac Ratcliffe .30 .75
44 Nate Schnarr .30 .75
45 Kyle Olson .30 .75
46 Josh Brook .30 .75
47 Jared McIsaac .30 .75
48 Ian Mitchell .30 .75
49 Cody Glass .60 1.50
50 Maxime Comtois .40 1.00
51 Ty Smith .40 1.00
52 MacKenzie Entwistle .30 .75
53 Akil Thomas .30 .75
54 Alexis Gravel .30 .75
55 Matthew Strome .30 .75
56 Ty Dellandrea .30 .75
57 Jocktan Chainey .30 .75
58 Ian Scott .30 .75
59 Jacob McGrath .30 .75
60 Stelio Mattheos .30 .75
61 David Noel .30 .75
62 Liam Hawel .30 .75
63 Jack Studnicka .40 1.00
64 Owen Tippett .75 2.00
65 Michael Rasmussen .25 .60
66 Michael DiPietro .25 .60
67 Markus Phillips .25 .60
68 Shane Bowers .25 .60
69 Evan Bouchard .75 2.00
70 Joseph Veleno .30 .75
71 Greg Meireles .30 .75
72 Jonathan Smart .30 .75
73 Ryan McLeod .30 .75
74 Antoine Crete-Belzile .30 .75
75 Nick Suzuki .75 2.00
76 Jordy Bellerive .30 .75
77 Elijah Roberts .30 .75
78 Sam Steel .30 .75
79 Matthew Spencer .25 .60
80 Nolan Patrick .75 2.00
81 Jordan Kyrou .40 1.00
82 Guillaume Brisebois .40 1.00
83 Mitchell Vande Sompel .30 .75
84 Brett Howden .25 .60
85 Nicholas Merkley .30 .75
86 Bobby Orr 1.50 4.00
87 Theoren Fleury .40 1.00
88 Mike Gartner .50 1.25
89 Glenn Anderson .30 .75
90 Darryl Sittler .50 1.25
91 Doug Gilmour .50 1.25
92 Marcel Dionne .50 1.25
93 Grant Fuhr .60 1.50
94 Larry Murphy .30 .75
95 Joe Sakic .75 2.00
96 Steve Yzerman 1.00 2.50
97 Mike Bossy .40 1.00
98 Martin Brodeur 1.00 2.50
99 Mario Lemieux 1.50 4.00
100 Wayne Gretzky 2.50 6.00

2017-18 Upper Deck Team Canada Juniors Jerseys

1 Connor Ingram 1.50 4.00
2 Jake Bean 1.50 4.00
3 Noah Juulsen 1.50 4.00
4 Mitchell Stephens 1.00 2.50
5 Michael McLeod 4.00 10.00
6 Taylor Raddysh 1.50 4.00
7 Carter Hart 2.50 6.00
8 Pierre-Luc Dubois 2.50 6.00
9 Dillon Dube 1.50 4.00
10 Kale Clague 1.25 3.00
11 Mathieu Joseph 1.25 3.00
12 Julien Gauthier 1.50 4.00
13 Nicolas Roy 1.00 2.50
14 Anthony Cirelli 1.25 3.00
15 Jeremy Lauzon 1.25 3.00
16 Philippe Myers 1.25 3.00
17 Dante Fabbro 1.50 4.00
18 Jennifer Wakefield 1.00 2.50
19 Jocelyne Larocque 1.50 4.00
20 Lauriane Rougeau 1.00 2.50
21 Sarah Potomak 1.25 3.00
22 Laura Stacey 2.00 5.00
23 Erin Ambrose 2.50 6.00
24 Natalie Spooner 4.00 10.00
25 Brianne Jenner 2.50 6.00
26 Emily Clark 3.00 8.00
27 Halli Krzyzaniak 1.00 2.50
28 Rebecca Johnston 1.50 4.00
29 Marie-Philip Poulin 5.00 12.00
30 Emerance Maschmeyer 2.00 5.00
31 Genevieve Lacasse 1.25 3.00
32 Meghan Mikkelson 1.25 3.00
33 Meghan Agosta 1.25 3.00
34 Shannon Szabados 1.25 3.00
35 Bailey Bram 1.25 3.00
36 Renata Fast 1.50 4.00
37 Sarah Davis 1.25 3.00
38 Haley Irwin 1.25 3.00
39 Laura Fortino 1.25 3.00
40 Blayre Turnbull 1.25 3.00
41 Jaret Anderson-Dolan 1.50 4.00
42 Jett Woo 1.25 3.00
43 Isaac Ratcliffe 1.25 3.00
44 Nate Schnarr 1.25 3.00
45 Kyle Olson 1.25 3.00
46 Josh Brook 1.25 3.00
47 Jared McIsaac 1.25 3.00
48 Ian Mitchell 1.25 3.00
49 Cody Glass 2.50 6.00
50 Maxime Comtois 1.50 4.00
51 Ty Smith 1.50 4.00
52 MacKenzie Entwistle 1.25 3.00
53 Akil Thomas 1.25 3.00
54 Alexis Gravel 1.25 3.00
55 Matthew Strome 1.25 3.00
56 Ty Dellandrea 1.25 3.00
57 Jocktan Chainey 1.25 3.00
58 Ian Scott 1.25 3.00
59 Jacob McGrath 1.25 3.00
60 Stelio Mattheos 1.25 3.00

2017-18 Upper Deck Team Canada Juniors Local Legends

LLCH Carter Hart 1.50 4.00
LLDF Dante Fabbro 1.00 2.50
LLJA Jaret Anderson-Dolan 1.00 2.50
LLJG Julien Gauthier 1.00 2.50
LLJV Joseph Veleno .75 2.00
LLNP Nolan Patrick 2.00 5.00
LLNS Nick Suzuki 2.00 5.00
LLPD Pierre-Luc Dubois 1.50 4.00
LLSS Shannon Szabados .75 2.00
LLTR Taylor Raddysh 1.00 2.50

2017-18 Upper Deck Team Canada Juniors Local Legends Retired

LLRJS Joe Sakic 3.00 8.00
LLRMB Martin Brodeur 4.00 10.00
LLRMD Marcel Dionne 2.00 5.00
LLRSY Steve Yzerman 4.00 10.00
LLRWG Wayne Gretzky 10.00 25.00

2017-18 Upper Deck Team Canada Juniors Premium Material Autographs

1 Connor Ingram/199 8.00 20.00
2 Jake Bean/199 8.00 20.00
3 Noah Juulsen/199 8.00 20.00
4 Mitchell Stephens/199 5.00 12.00
5 Michael McLeod/125 20.00 50.00
6 Taylor Raddysh/125 8.00 20.00
7 Carter Hart/125 20.00 50.00
8 Pierre-Luc Dubois/125 20.00 50.00
9 Dillon Dube/199 8.00 20.00
10 Kale Clague/199 6.00 15.00
11 Mathieu Joseph/199 6.00 15.00
12 Julien Gauthier/199 8.00 20.00
13 Nicolas Roy/199 5.00 12.00
14 Anthony Cirelli/199 6.00 15.00
15 Jeremy Lauzon/199 6.00 15.00
16 Philippe Myers/199 6.00 15.00
17 Dante Fabbro/125 8.00 20.00
18 Jennifer Wakefield/199 5.00 12.00
19 Jocelyne Larocque/199 8.00 20.00
21 Sarah Potomak/199 6.00 15.00
23 Erin Ambrose/199 12.00 30.00
24 Natalie Spooner/199 20.00 50.00
25 Brianne Jenner/199 12.00 30.00
26 Emily Clark/199 15.00 40.00
28 Rebecca Johnston/199 8.00 20.00
29 Marie-Philip Poulin/199 40.00 100.00
33 Meghan Agosta/199 6.00 15.00
34 Shannon Szabados/199 6.00 15.00
38 Haley Irwin/199 6.00 15.00
40 Blayre Turnbull/199 6.00 15.00
41 Jaret Anderson-Dolan/125 12.00 30.00
42 Jett Woo/199 6.00 15.00
43 Isaac Ratcliffe/199 6.00 15.00
44 Nate Schnarr/199 6.00 15.00
45 Kyle Olson/199 6.00 15.00
46 Josh Brook/199 6.00 15.00
47 Jared McIsaac/199 6.00 15.00
48 Ian Mitchell/199 6.00 15.00
49 Cody Glass/125 12.00 30.00
50 Maxime Comtois/125 8.00 20.00
51 Ty Smith/199 8.00 20.00
52 MacKenzie Entwistle/199 6.00 15.00
53 Akil Thomas/199 6.00 15.00
54 Alexis Gravel/199 6.00 15.00
55 Matthew Strome/199 6.00 15.00
56 Ty Dellandrea/199 6.00 15.00
57 Jocktan Chainey/199 6.00 15.00
58 Ian Scott/199 6.00 15.00
59 Jacob McGrath/199 6.00 15.00
60 Stelio Mattheos/199 6.00 15.00

2017-18 Upper Deck Team Canada Juniors Program of Excellence

POE1 Pierre-Luc Dubois 1.25 3.00
POE2 Michael McLeod 2.00 5.00
POE3 Jake Bean .75 2.00
POE4 Mitchell Stephens .50 1.25
POE5 Taylor Raddysh .75 2.00
POE6 Noah Juulsen .75 2.00
POE7 Julien Gauthier .75 2.00
POE8 Kale Clague .60 1.50
POE9 Carter Hart 1.25 3.00
POE10 Dante Fabbro .75 2.00
POE11 Philippe Myers .60 1.50
POE12 Maxime Comtois .75 2.00
POE13 Ty Dellandrea .60 1.50
POE14 Jared McIsaac .60 1.50
POE15 Akil Thomas .60 1.50
POE16 Jaret Anderson-Dolan .75 2.00
POE17 MacKenzie Entwistle .60 1.50
POE18 Cody Glass 1.25 3.00
POE19 Stelio Mattheos .60 1.50
POE20 Matthew Strome .60 1.50
POE21 Sam Steel .60 1.50
POE22 Michael Rasmussen .50 1.25
POE23 Owen Tippett 1.50 4.00
POE24 Joseph Veleno .60 1.50
POE25 Wayne Gretzky 5.00 12.00
POE26 Nick Suzuki 1.50 4.00
POE27 Mario Lemieux 3.00 8.00
POE28 Martin Brodeur 2.00 5.00
POE29 Mike Bossy .75 2.00
POE30 Nolan Patrick 1.50 4.00

2017-18 Upper Deck Team Canada Juniors Program of Excellence Retro

POE971 Pierre-Luc Dubois 2.50 6.00
POE972 Taylor Raddysh 1.50 4.00
POE973 Noah Juulsen 1.50 4.00
POE974 Carter Hart 2.50 6.00
POE975 Joseph Veleno 1.25 3.00
POE976 Wayne Gretzky 10.00 25.00
POE977 Nick Suzuki 3.00 8.00
POE978 Mario Lemieux 6.00 15.00
POE979 Martin Brodeur 4.00 10.00
POE9710 Nolan Patrick 3.00 8.00

2017-18 Upper Deck Team Canada Juniors Team Canada Manufactured Patches

LPCH Carter Hart 5.00 12.00
LPDF Dante Fabbro 3.00 8.00
LPJG Julien Gauthier 3.00 8.00
LPML Mario Lemieux 20.00 50.00
LPMM Michael McLeod 8.00 20.00
LPNJ Noah Juulsen 3.00 8.00
LPPD Pierre-Luc Dubois 5.00 12.00
LPSY Steve Yzerman 15.00 40.00
LPTR Taylor Raddysh 3.00 8.00
LPWG Wayne Gretzky 30.00 80.00

2018-19 Upper Deck Team Canada Juniors

1 Jordan Kyrou .75 2.00
2 Jake Bean .40 1.00
3 Conor Timmins .30 .75
4 Robert Thomas .75 2.00
5 Carter Hart .75 2.00
6 Cal Foote .30 .75
7 Cale Makar 5.00 12.00
8 Dante Fabbro .40 1.00
9 Dillon Dube .50 1.25
10 Kale Clague .30 .75
11 Jonah Gadjovich .30 .75
12 Boris Katchouk .30 .75
13 Sam Steel .40 1.00
14 Maxime Comtois .40 1.00
15 Colton Point .30 .75
16 Taylor Raddysh .30 .75
17 Tyler Steenbergen .30 .75
18 Brett Howden .50 1.25
19 Drake Batherson .75 2.00
20 Michael McLeod .30 .75
21 Colten Ellis .30 .75
22 Chase Wouters .30 .75
23 Matthew Robertson .30 .75
24 Jared McIsaac .30 .75
25 Alexis Lafreniere 1.50 4.00
26 Serron Noel .30 .75
27 Ryan Merkley .30 .75
28 Ty Dellandrea .30 .75
29 Olivier Rodrigue .30 .75
30 Kevin Mandolese .30 .75
31 Bowen Byram .50 1.25
32 Kevin Bahl .30 .75
33 Ty Smith .40 1.00
34 Cole Fonstad .30 .75
35 Raphael Lavoie .30 .75
36 Allan McShane .30 .75
37 Liam Foudy .40 1.00
38 Jack McBain .30 .75
39 Joseph Veleno .30 .75
40 Akil Thomas .30 .75
41 Jonathan Tychonick .30 .75
42 Aidan Dudas .30 .75
43 Cameron Hillis .30 .75
44 Jett Woo .30 .75
45 Benoit-Olivier Groulx .40 1.00
46 Anderson MacDonald .30 .75
47 Gabriel Fortier .40 1.00
48 Jackson Shepard .30 .75
49 Luka Burzan .30 .75
50 Nolan Foote .30 .75
51 Alexis Gravel .30 .75
52 Calen Addison .40 1.00
53 Barrett Hayton .40 1.00
54 Noah Dobson .50 1.25
55 Lauriane Rougeau .30 .75
56 Jillian Saulnier .50 1.25
57 Meaghan Mikkelson .30 .75
58 Laura Fortino .30 .75
59 Renata Fast .40 1.00
60 Meghan Agosta .30 .75
61 Shannon Szabados .30 .75
62 Halli Krzyzaniak .25 .60
63 Jennifer Wakefield .25 .60
64 Natalie Spooner 1.00 2.50
65 Ann-Renee Desbiens 1.00 2.50
66 Rebecca Johnston .30 .75
67 Laura Stacey .50 1.25
68 Jocelyne Larocque .40 1.00
69 Marie-Philip Poulin 1.25 3.00
70 Blayre Turnbull .30 .75
71 Genevieve Lacasse .30 .75
72 Sarah Potomak .30 .75
73 Micah Zandee-Hart .50 1.25
74 Brigette Lacquette .30 .75
75 Melodie Daoust .30 .75
76 Amy Potomak .30 .75
77 Bailey Bram .30 .75
78 Emily Clark .75 2.00
79 Sarah Nurse 1.00 2.50
80 Haley Irwin .30 .75
81 Brianne Jenner .60 1.50
82 Erin Ambrose .60 1.50
83 Bobby Orr 1.50 4.00
84 Ed Belfour .40 1.00
85 Bobby Clarke .60 1.50
86 Larry Robinson .40 1.00
87 Jarome Iginla .50 1.25
88 Dale Hawerchuk .50 1.25
89 Paul Coffey .40 1.00
90 Guy Lafleur .50 1.25
91 Mark Messier .75 2.00
92 Denis Potvin .30 .75
93 Shayne Corson .30 .75
94 Owen Nolan .30 .75
95 Joe Sakic .75 2.00
96 Felix Potvin .60 1.50
97 Steve Yzerman 1.00 2.50
98 Wendel Clark .60 1.50
99 Wayne Gretzky 2.50 6.00
100 Mario Lemieux 1.50 4.00

2018-19 Upper Deck Team Canada Juniors Golden Futures

GF1 Drake Batherson 4.00 10.00
GF2 Jake Bean 2.00 5.00
GF3 Jordan Kyrou 4.00 10.00
GF4 Dante Fabbro 2.00 5.00
GF5 Sam Steel 2.00 5.00
GF6 Cal Foote 1.50 4.00
GF7 Robert Thomas 4.00 10.00
GF8 Cale Makar 25.00 60.00
GF9 Michael McLeod 1.50 4.00
GF10 Carter Hart 4.00 10.00

2018-19 Upper Deck Team Canada Juniors Jerseys

1 Jordan Kyrou 3.00 8.00
2 Jake Bean 1.50 4.00
3 Conor Timmins 1.25 3.00
4 Robert Thomas 3.00 8.00
5 Carter Hart 3.00 8.00
6 Cal Foote 1.25 3.00
7 Cale Makar 20.00 50.00
8 Dante Fabbro 1.50 4.00
9 Dillon Dube 2.00 5.00
10 Kale Clague 1.25 3.00
11 Jonah Gadjovich 1.25 3.00
12 Boris Katchouk 1.25 3.00
13 Sam Steel 1.50 4.00
14 Maxime Comtois 1.50 4.00
15 Colton Point 1.25 3.00
16 Taylor Raddysh 1.25 3.00
17 Tyler Steenbergen 1.25 3.00
18 Brett Howden 2.00 5.00
19 Drake Batherson 3.00 8.00
20 Michael McLeod 1.25 3.00
21 Colten Ellis 1.25 3.00
22 Chase Wouters 1.25 3.00
23 Matthew Robertson 1.25 3.00
24 Jared McIsaac 1.25 3.00
25 Alexis Lafreniere 6.00 15.00
26 Serron Noel 1.25 3.00
27 Ryan Merkley 1.25 3.00
28 Ty Dellandrea 1.25 3.00
29 Olivier Rodrigue 1.25 3.00
30 Kevin Mandolese 1.25 3.00
31 Bowen Byram 2.00 5.00
32 Kevin Bahl 1.25 3.00
33 Ty Smith 1.50 4.00
34 Cole Fonstad 1.25 3.00
35 Raphael Lavoie 1.25 3.00
36 Allan McShane 1.25 3.00
37 Liam Foudy 1.50 4.00
38 Jack McBain 1.25 3.00
39 Joseph Veleno 1.25 3.00
40 Akil Thomas 1.25 3.00
41 Jonathan Tychonick 1.25 3.00
42 Aidan Dudas 1.25 3.00
43 Cameron Hillis 1.25 3.00
56 Jillian Saulnier 2.00 5.00
58 Laura Fortino 1.25 3.00
60 Meghan Agosta 1.25 3.00
61 Shannon Szabados 1.25 3.00
62 Halli Krzyzaniak 1.00 2.50
63 Jennifer Wakefield 1.00 2.50
64 Natalie Spooner 4.00 10.00
66 Rebecca Johnston 1.25 3.00
68 Jocelyne Larocque 1.50 4.00
69 Marie-Philip Poulin 5.00 12.00
70 Blayre Turnbull 1.25 3.00
72 Sarah Potomak 1.25 3.00
73 Micah Zandee-Hart 2.00 5.00
75 Melodie Daoust 1.25 3.00
76 Amy Potomak 1.25 3.00
79 Sarah Nurse 4.00 10.00
81 Brianne Jenner 2.50 6.00

2018-19 Upper Deck Team Canada Juniors Premium Swatch Autographs

1 Jordan Kyrou/199 15.00 40.00
2 Jake Bean/199 8.00 20.00
3 Conor Timmins/199 6.00 15.00
4 Robert Thomas/199 15.00 40.00
5 Carter Hart/125 15.00 40.00
6 Cal Foote/199 6.00 15.00
8 Dante Fabbro/199 8.00 20.00
9 Dillon Dube/199 10.00 25.00
10 Kale Clague/199 6.00 15.00
11 Jonah Gadjovich/199 6.00 15.00
12 Boris Katchouk/199 6.00 15.00
13 Sam Steel/125 8.00 20.00
14 Maxime Comtois/199 8.00 20.00
15 Colton Point/199 6.00 15.00
16 Taylor Raddysh/199 6.00 15.00
17 Tyler Steenbergen/199 6.00 15.00
18 Brett Howden/199 10.00 25.00
19 Drake Batherson/199 15.00 40.00
20 Michael McLeod/125 6.00 15.00
21 Colten Ellis/199 6.00 15.00
22 Chase Wouters/199 6.00 15.00
23 Matthew Robertson/199 6.00 15.00
24 Jared McIsaac/199 6.00 15.00
25 Alexis Lafreniere/125 150.00 400.00
26 Serron Noel/125 6.00 15.00
27 Ryan Merkley/199 6.00 15.00
28 Ty Dellandrea/199 6.00 15.00
29 Olivier Rodrigue/199 6.00 15.00
30 Kevin Mandolese/199 6.00 15.00
31 Bowen Byram/199 10.00 25.00
32 Kevin Bahl/199 6.00 15.00
33 Ty Smith/125 8.00 20.00
34 Cole Fonstad/199 6.00 15.00
35 Raphael Lavoie/199 6.00 15.00
36 Allan McShane/199 6.00 15.00
37 Liam Foudy/199 8.00 20.00
38 Jack McBain/199 6.00 15.00
40 Akil Thomas/199 6.00 15.00
41 Jonathan Tychonick/199 6.00 15.00
42 Aidan Dudas/199 6.00 15.00
43 Cameron Hillis/199 6.00 15.00
55 Lauriane Rougeau/199 6.00 15.00
56 Jillian Saulnier/199 10.00 25.00
57 Meaghan Mikkelson/199 6.00 15.00
58 Laura Fortino/199 6.00 15.00
59 Renata Fast/199 8.00 20.00
60 Meghan Agosta/199 6.00 15.00
61 Shannon Szabados/199 6.00 15.00
62 Halli Krzyzaniak/199 5.00 12.00
63 Jennifer Wakefield/199 5.00 12.00
64 Natalie Spooner/199 20.00 50.00
66 Rebecca Johnston/199 6.00 15.00
67 Laura Stacey/199 10.00 25.00
68 Jocelyne Larocque/199 8.00 20.00
69 Marie-Philip Poulin/199 40.00 100.00
70 Blayre Turnbull/199 6.00 15.00
72 Sarah Potomak/199 6.00 15.00
75 Melodie Daoust/199 6.00 15.00
76 Amy Potomak/199 6.00 15.00
77 Bailey Bram/199 6.00 15.00
79 Sarah Nurse/199 20.00 50.00
81 Brianne Jenner/199 12.00 30.00

2018-19 Upper Deck Team Canada Juniors Program of Excellence

POE1 Alexis Lafreniere 3.00 8.00
POE2 Sam Steel .75 2.00
POE3 Serron Noel .60 1.50
POE4 Michael McLeod .60 1.50
POE5 Dante Fabbro .75 2.00
POE6 Joseph Veleno .60 1.50

POE7 Jonathan Tychonick .60 1.50
POE8 Jordan Kyrou 1.50 4.00
POE9 Ryan Merkley .60 1.50
POE10 Conor Timmins .60 1.50
POE11 Jett Woo .60 1.50
POE12 Taylor Raddysh .60 1.50
POE13 Ty Smith .75 2.00
POE14 Robert Thomas 1.50 4.00
POE15 Barrett Hayton .75 2.00
POE16 Cale Makar 10.00 25.00
POE17 Akil Thomas .60 1.50
POE18 Jake Bean .75 2.00
POE19 Kale Clague .60 1.50
POE20 Noah Dobson 1.00 2.50
POE21 Carter Hart 1.50 4.00
POE22 Jared McIsaac .60 1.50
POE23 Joe Sakic 1.50 4.00
POE24 Mark Messier 1.50 4.00
POE25 Jarome Iginla 1.00 2.50
POE26 Felix Potvin 1.25 3.00
POE27 Shayne Corson .60 1.50
POE28 Steve Yzerman 2.00 5.00
POE29 Mario Lemieux 3.00 8.00
POE30 Wayne Gretzky 5.00 12.00

2018-19 Upper Deck Team Canada Juniors Provincial Prowess

PP1 Noah Dobson 1.25 3.00
PP2 Carter Hart 2.00 5.00
PP3 Cal Foote .75 2.00
PP4 Jared McIsaac .75 2.00
PP5 Brett Howden 1.25 3.00
PP6 Serron Noel .75 2.00
PP7 Drake Batherson 2.00 5.00
PP8 Joseph Veleno .75 2.00
PP9 Boris Katchouk .75 2.00
PP10 Jett Woo .75 2.00
PP11 Theoren Fleury 1.00 2.50
PP12 Ed Belfour 1.00 2.50
PP13 Mike Bossy 1.00 2.50
PP14 Glenn Anderson .75 2.00
PP15 Wayne Gretzky 6.00 15.00

2019-20 Upper Deck Team Canada Juniors

1 Graeme Clarke .30 .75
2 Jamieson Rees .30 .75
3 Jakob Pelletier .30 .75
4 Sasha Mutala .30 .75
5 Josh Williams .30 .75
6 Ryan Suzuki .40 1.00
7 Kirby Dach .75 2.00
8 Peyton Krebs .50 1.25
9 Samuel Poulin .40 1.00
10 Dylan Holloway .75 2.00
11 Dylan Cozens .60 1.50
12 Xavier Parent .25 .60
13 Justin Barron .50 1.25
14 Matthew Robertson .40 1.00
15 Bowen Byram .50 1.25
16 Michael Vukojevic .30 .75
17 Kaedan Korczak .30 .75
18 Maxence Guenette .25 .60
19 Alexis Lafreniere 1.50 4.00
20 Taylor Gauthier .40 1.00
21 Nolan Maier .30 .75
22 Cody Glass .60 1.50
23 Joseph Veleno .30 .75
24 Shane Bowers .40 1.00
25 MacKenzie Entwistle .40 1.00
26 Nick Suzuki 1.50 4.00
27 Brett Leason .40 1.00
28 Ty Smith .40 1.00
29 Jack Studnicka .40 1.00
30 Morgan Frost .60 1.50
31 Barrett Hayton .75 2.00
32 Josh Brook .40 1.00
33 Jared McIsaac .30 .75
34 Ian Mitchell .40 1.00
35 Noah Dobson 1.00 2.50
36 Markus Phillips .40 1.00
37 Alexis Lafreniere 1.50 4.00
38 Michael DiPietro .40 1.00
39 Ian Scott .40 1.00
40 Rebecca Johnston .30 .75
41 Laura Stacey .50 1.25
42 Jillian Saulnier .50 1.25
43 Melodie Daoust .30 .75
44 Brianne Jenner .60 1.50
45 Sarah Nurse 1.00 2.50
46 Natalie Spooner 1.00 2.50
47 Emily Clark .75 2.00
48 Marie-Philip Poulin 1.25 3.00
49 Loren Gabel .40 1.00
50 Ann-Sophie Bettez .30 .75
51 Blayre Turnbull .30 .75
52 Jamie Lee Rattray .50 1.25
53 Jocelyne Larocque .40 1.00
54 Brigette Lacquette .30 .75
55 Laura Fortino .25 .60
56 Renata Fast .40 1.00
57 Erin Ambrose .60 1.50
58 Jaime Bourbonnais .40 1.00
59 Micah Zandee-Hart .50 1.25
60 Shannon Szabados .30 .75
61 Genevieve Lacasse .30 .75
62 Emerance Maschmeyer .50 1.25
63 Brayden Tracey .30 .75
64 Keean Washkurak .30 .75
65 Nathan Legare .30 .75
66 Dylan Holloway .75 2.00
67 Jakob Pelletier .30 .75
68 Jamieson Rees .30 .75
69 Alex Newhook .40 1.00
70 Ryan Suzuki .40 1.00
71 Dylan Cozens .60 1.50
72 Connor Zary .50 1.25
73 Peyton Krebs .50 1.25
74 Philip Tomasino .40 1.00
75 Samuel Poulin .40 1.00
76 Braden Schneider .50 1.25
77 Kaedan Korczak .30 .75
78 Thomas Harley .50 1.25
79 Michael Vukojevic .30 .75
80 Jamie Drysdale 1.00 2.50
81 Jordan Spence .30 .75
82 Daemon Hunt .30 .75
83 Taylor Gauthier .40 1.00
84 Nolan Maier .30 .75
85 Jonathan Lemieux .30 .75
86 Bill Ranford .30 .75
87 Ray Bourque .60 1.50
88 Mark Recchi .50 1.25
89 Phil Esposito .60 1.50
90 Bill Barber .40 1.00
91 Shayne Corson .30 .75
92 Bobby Orr 1.50 4.00
93 Guy Lafleur .50 1.25
94 Curtis Joseph .50 1.25
95 Martin Brodeur 1.00 2.50
96 Joe Sakic .75 2.00
97 Steve Yzerman 1.00 2.50
98 Mario Lemieux 1.50 4.00
99 Wayne Gretzky 2.50 6.00
100 Dirk Graham .30 .75
101 Michael DiPietro POE .40 1.00
102 Ian Mitchell POE .40 1.00
103 Jameison Rees POE .30 .75
104 Daemon Hunt POE .30 .75
105 Kaedan Korczak POE .30 .75
106 Taylor Gauthier POE .40 1.00
107 Sasha Mutala POE .30 .75
108 Josh Williams POE .30 .75
109 Josh Brook POE .40 1.00
110 Brett Leason POE .40 1.00
111 Jared McIsaac POE .30 .75
112 Kirby Dach POE .75 2.00
113 Shane Bowers POE .40 1.00
114 Ryan Suzuki POE .40 1.00
115 Alexis Lafreniere POE 1.50 4.00
116 Alex Newhook POE .40 1.00
117 Thomas Harley POE .50 1.25
118 Jack Studnicka POE .40 1.00
119 Cody Glass POE .60 1.50
120 Connor Zary POE .50 1.25
121 Noah Dobson POE 1.00 2.50
122 Barrett Hayton POE .75 2.00
123 Markus Phillips POE .40 1.00
124 Ian Scott POE .40 1.00
125 Dylan Holloway POE .75 2.00
126 Ty Smith POE .40 1.00
127 Morgan Frost POE .60 1.50
128 Jakob Pelletier POE .30 .75
129 Joseph Veleno POE .30 .75
130 Dylan Cozens POE .60 1.50
131 Brayden Tracey POE .30 .75
132 Michael Vukojevic POE .30 .75
133 Justin Barron POE .50 1.25
134 Jamie Drysdale POE 1.00 2.50
135 Matthew Robertson POE .40 1.00
136 Bowen Byram POE .50 1.25
137 MacKenzie Entwistle POE .40 1.00
138 Nick Suzuki POE 1.50 4.00
139 Peyton Krebs POE .50 1.25
140 Samuel Poulin POE .40 1.00

2019-20 Upper Deck Team Canada Juniors Exclusives

*EXCLUSIVES/150-250: 1.25X TO 3X BASIC INSERTS
19 Alexis Lafreniere 15.00 40.00
37 Alexis Lafreniere 15.00 40.00
115 Alexis Lafreniere POE 15.00 40.00

2019-20 Upper Deck Team Canada Juniors High Gloss

*HIGHGLOSS/25: 2X TO 5X BASIC CARDS

2019-20 Upper Deck Team Canada Juniors Jerseys

1 Graeme Clarke 1.25 3.00
2 Jamieson Rees 1.25 3.00
3 Jakob Pelletier 1.25 3.00
6 Ryan Suzuki 1.50 4.00
7 Kirby Dach 3.00 8.00
8 Peyton Krebs 2.00 5.00
9 Samuel Poulin 1.50 4.00
10 Dylan Holloway 3.00 8.00
11 Dylan Cozens 2.50 6.00
14 Matthew Robertson 1.50 4.00
15 Bowen Byram 2.00 5.00
16 Michael Vukojevic 1.25 3.00
17 Kaedan Korczak 1.25 3.00
19 Alexis Lafreniere 40.00 100.00
20 Taylor Gauthier 1.50 4.00
21 Nolan Maier 1.25 3.00
22 Cody Glass 2.50 6.00
23 Joseph Veleno 1.25 3.00
24 Shane Bowers 1.50 4.00
25 MacKenzie Entwistle 1.50 4.00
26 Nick Suzuki 6.00 15.00
27 Brett Leason 1.50 4.00
28 Ty Smith 1.50 4.00
29 Jack Studnicka 1.50 4.00
30 Morgan Frost 2.50 6.00
31 Barrett Hayton 3.00 8.00
32 Josh Brook 1.50 4.00
33 Jared McIsaac 1.25 3.00
34 Ian Mitchell 1.50 4.00
35 Noah Dobson 4.00 10.00
36 Markus Phillips 1.50 4.00
37 Alexis Lafreniere 40.00 100.00
38 Michael DiPietro 1.50 4.00
39 Ian Scott 1.50 4.00
40 Rebecca Johnston 1.25 3.00
41 Laura Stacey 2.00 5.00
42 Jillian Saulnier 2.00 5.00
43 Melodie Daoust 1.25 3.00
44 Brianne Jenner 2.50 6.00
45 Sarah Nurse 4.00 10.00
46 Natalie Spooner 4.00 10.00
47 Emily Clark 3.00 8.00
48 Marie-Philip Poulin 5.00 12.00
49 Loren Gabel 1.50 4.00
50 Ann-Sophie Bettez 1.25 3.00
51 Blayre Turnbull 1.25 3.00
52 Jamie Lee Rattray 2.00 5.00
53 Jocelyne Larocque 1.50 4.00
54 Brigette Lacquette 1.25 3.00
55 Laura Fortino 1.00 2.50
56 Renata Fast 1.50 4.00
57 Erin Ambrose 2.50 6.00
58 Jaime Bourbonnais 1.50 4.00
59 Micah Zandee-Hart 2.00 5.00
60 Shannon Szabados 1.25 3.00
61 Genevieve Lacasse 1.25 3.00
62 Emerance Maschmeyer 2.00 5.00
63 Brayden Tracey 1.25 3.00
64 Keean Washkurak 1.25 3.00
65 Nathan Legare 1.25 3.00
66 Dylan Holloway 3.00 8.00
67 Jakob Pelletier 1.25 3.00
68 Jamieson Rees 1.25 3.00
69 Alex Newhook 1.50 4.00
70 Ryan Suzuki 1.50 4.00
71 Dylan Cozens 2.50 6.00
72 Connor Zary 2.00 5.00
73 Peyton Krebs 2.00 5.00
74 Philip Tomasino 1.50 4.00
75 Samuel Poulin 1.50 4.00
76 Braden Schneider 2.00 5.00
77 Kaedan Korczak 1.25 3.00
78 Thomas Harley 2.00 5.00
79 Michael Vukojevic 1.25 3.00
80 Jamie Drysdale 4.00 10.00
81 Jordan Spence 1.25 3.00
82 Daemon Hunt 1.25 3.00
83 Taylor Gauthier 1.50 4.00
84 Nolan Maier 1.25 3.00
85 Jonathan Lemieux 1.25 3.00

2019-20 Upper Deck Team Canada Juniors Golden Futures

GF1 Bowen Byram 2.50 6.00
GF2 Ty Smith 2.00 5.00
GF3 Cody Glass 3.00 8.00
GF4 Nick Suzuki 8.00 20.00
GF5 Barrett Hayton 4.00 10.00
GF6 Ryan Suzuki 2.00 5.00
GF7 Dylan Cozens 3.00 8.00
GF8 Justin Barron 2.50 6.00
GF9 Kirby Dach 4.00 10.00
GF10 Noah Dobson 5.00 12.00
GF11 Joseph Veleno 1.50 4.00
GF12 Alexis Lafreniere 15.00 40.00
GF13 Morgan Frost 3.00 8.00
GF14 Jack Studnicka 2.00 5.00
GF15 Jakob Pelletier 1.50 4.00
GF16 Jared McIsaac 1.50 4.00
GF17 Matthew Robertson 2.00 5.00
GF18 Peyton Krebs 2.50 6.00
GF19 MacKenzie Entwistle 2.00 5.00
GF20 Shane Bowers 2.00 5.00

2019-20 Upper Deck Team Canada Juniors Golden Futures Autographs

GF1 Bowen Byram 10.00 25.00
GF2 Ty Smith 8.00 20.00
GF3 Cody Glass 12.00 30.00
GF4 Nick Suzuki 30.00 80.00
GF5 Barrett Hayton 15.00 40.00
GF6 Ryan Suzuki 8.00 20.00
GF7 Dylan Cozens 12.00 30.00
GF8 Justin Barron 10.00 25.00
GF9 Kirby Dach 15.00 40.00
GF10 Noah Dobson 20.00 50.00
GF11 Joseph Veleno 6.00 15.00
GF12 Alexis Lafreniere 150.00 250.00
GF13 Morgan Frost 12.00 30.00
GF14 Jack Studnicka 8.00 20.00
GF15 Jakob Pelletier 6.00 15.00
GF16 Jared McIsaac 6.00 15.00
GF17 Matthew Robertson 8.00 20.00
GF18 Peyton Krebs 10.00 25.00
GF19 MacKenzie Entwistle 8.00 20.00
GF20 Shane Bowers 8.00 20.00

2019-20 Upper Deck Team Canada Juniors Premium Swatch Autographs

1 Graeme Clarke 6.00 15.00
6 Ryan Suzuki 8.00 20.00
7 Kirby Dach 15.00 40.00
9 Samuel Poulin 8.00 20.00
10 Dylan Holloway 15.00 40.00
11 Dylan Cozens 12.00 30.00
14 Matthew Robertson 8.00 20.00
15 Bowen Byram 10.00 25.00
16 Michael Vukojevic 6.00 15.00
17 Kaedan Korczak 6.00 15.00
19 Alexis Lafreniere 250.00 350.00
21 Nolan Maier 6.00 15.00
22 Cody Glass 12.00 30.00
24 Shane Bowers 8.00 20.00
25 MacKenzie Entwistle 8.00 20.00
26 Nick Suzuki 30.00 80.00
27 Brett Leason 8.00 20.00
28 Ty Smith 8.00 20.00
29 Jack Studnicka 8.00 20.00
30 Morgan Frost 12.00 30.00
31 Barrett Hayton 15.00 40.00
32 Josh Brook 8.00 20.00
33 Jared McIsaac 6.00 15.00
34 Ian Mitchell 8.00 20.00
35 Noah Dobson 20.00 50.00
36 Markus Phillips 8.00 20.00
37 Alexis Lafreniere 150.00 250.00
38 Michael DiPietro 8.00 20.00
39 Ian Scott 8.00 20.00
40 Rebecca Johnston 6.00 15.00
41 Laura Stacey 10.00 25.00
42 Jillian Saulnier 10.00 25.00
43 Melodie Daoust 6.00 15.00
44 Brianne Jenner 12.00 30.00
45 Sarah Nurse 20.00 50.00
46 Natalie Spooner 20.00 50.00
47 Emily Clark 15.00 40.00
48 Marie-Philip Poulin 25.00 60.00
49 Loren Gabel 8.00 20.00
50 Ann-Sophie Bettez 6.00 15.00
51 Blayre Turnbull 6.00 15.00
52 Jamie Lee Rattray 10.00 25.00
53 Jocelyne Larocque 8.00 20.00
54 Brigette Lacquette 6.00 15.00
55 Laura Fortino 5.00 12.00
56 Renata Fast 8.00 20.00
57 Erin Ambrose 12.00 30.00
58 Jaime Bourbonnais 8.00 20.00
59 Micah Zandee-Hart 10.00 25.00
60 Shannon Szabados 6.00 15.00
61 Genevieve Lacasse 6.00 15.00
62 Emerance Maschmeyer 10.00 25.00
63 Brayden Tracey 6.00 15.00
64 Keean Washkurak 6.00 15.00
65 Nathan Legare 6.00 15.00
66 Dylan Holloway 15.00 40.00
67 Jakob Pelletier 6.00 15.00
68 Jamieson Rees 6.00 15.00
69 Alex Newhook 8.00 20.00
70 Ryan Suzuki 8.00 20.00
71 Dylan Cozens 12.00 30.00
72 Connor Zary 10.00 25.00
73 Peyton Krebs 10.00 25.00
74 Philip Tomasino 8.00 20.00
75 Samuel Poulin 8.00 20.00
76 Braden Schneider 10.00 25.00
77 Kaedan Korczak 6.00 15.00
78 Thomas Harley 10.00 25.00
79 Michael Vukojevic 6.00 15.00
80 Jamie Drysdale 20.00 50.00
81 Jordan Spence 6.00 15.00
82 Daemon Hunt 6.00 15.00
83 Taylor Gauthier 8.00 20.00
84 Nolan Maier 6.00 15.00
85 Jonathan Lemieux 6.00 15.00

2020-21 Upper Deck Team Canada Juniors

1 Cole Perfetti H .75 2.00
2 Theo Rochette H .30 .75
3 Ozzy Wiesblatt H .40 1.00
4 Justin Sourdif H .30 .75
5 Jean-Luc Foudy H .30 .75
6 Ridly Greig H .30 .75
7 Connor McClennon H .30 .75
8 Will Cuylle H .50 1.25
9 Hendrix Lapierre H .40 1.00
10 Quinton Byfield H 1.00 2.50
11 Jake Neighbours H .50 1.25
12 Mavrik Bourque H .40 1.00
13 Seth Jarvis H .75 2.00
14 Daemon Hunt H .30 .75
15 Lukas Cormier H .30 .75
16 Jamie Drysdale H 1.00 2.50
17 Jeremie Poirier H .30 .75
18 Kaiden Guhle H .50 1.25
19 Donovan Sebrango H .30 .75
20 Ryan O'Rourke H .30 .75
21 Tristan Lennox H .30 .75
22 Dylan Garand H .30 .75
23 Nicolas Daws U20 .40 1.00
24 Kevin Bahl U20 .40 1.00
25 Calen Addison U20 .40 1.00
26 Bowen Byram U20 1.00 2.50
27 Jacob Bernard-Docker U20 .25 .60
28 Jamie Drysdale U20 1.00 2.50
29 Olivier Rodrigue U20 .25 .60
30 Joseph Veleno U20 .25 .60
31 Raphael Lavoie U20 .25 .60
32 Alexis Lafreniere U20 1.50 4.00
33 Jared McIsaac U20 .25 .60
34 Akil Thomas U20 .30 .75
35 Connor McMichael U20 .75 2.00
36 Ty Dellandrea U20 .50 1.25
37 Quinton Byfield U20 1.00 2.50
38 Dawson Mercer U20 .60 1.50
39 Dylan Cozens U20 .75 2.00
40 Ty Smith U20 .75 2.00
41 Aidan Dudas U20 .30 .75
42 Joel Hofer U20 .50 1.25
43 Nolan Foote U20 .50 1.25
44 Victoria Bach WWC .40 1.00
45 Jessie Eldridge WWC .50 1.25
46 Genevieve Lacasse WWC .30 .75
47 Jocelyne Larocque WWC .40 1.00
48 Marie-Philip Poulin WWC 1.25 3.00
49 Brianne Jenner WWC .60 1.50
50 Emerance Maschmeyer WWC .50 1.25
51 Meaghan Mikkelson WWC .25 .60
52 Blayre Turnbull WWC .30 .75
53 Jaime Bourbonnais WWC .40 1.00
54 Jillian Saulnier WWC .50 1.25
55 Ann-Renee Desbiens WWC 1.00 2.50
56 Jamie Lee Rattray WWC .50 1.25
57 Renata Fast WWC .40 1.00
58 Loren Gabel WWC .40 1.00
59 Brigette Lacquette WWC .30 .75
60 Erin Ambrose WWC .60 1.50
61 Sarah Nurse WWC 1.00 2.50
62 Micah Zandee-Hart WWC .50 1.25
63 Melodie Daoust WWC .30 .75
64 Lauriane Rougeau WWC .30 .75
65 Emily Clark WWC .75 2.00
66 Natalie Spooner WWC 1.00 2.50
67 Laura Stacey WWC .50 1.25
68 Ann-Sophie Bettez WWC .30 .75
69 Meghan Agosta WWC .30 .75
70 Rebecca Johnston WWC .25 .60
71 Theo Rochette .30 .75
72 Natalie Spooner 1.00 2.50
73 Alexis Lafreniere 1.50 4.00
74 Marie-Philip Poulin 1.25 3.00
75 Cole Perfetti .75 2.00
76 Meghan Agosta .30 .75
77 Kaiden Guhle .50 1.25
78 Jamie Drysdale 1.00 2.50
79 Mavrik Bourque .40 1.00
80 Emerance Maschmeyer .50 1.25
81 Hendrix Lapierre .40 1.00
82 Quinton Byfield 1.00 2.50
83 Jean-Luc Foudy .30 .75
84 Manon Rheaume 1.00 2.50
85 Calen Addison D .40 1.00
86 Kevin Bahl D .40 1.00
87 Jacob Bernard-Docker D .25 .60
88 Jared McIsaac D .25 .60
89 Ty Smith D .75 2.00
90 Ty Dellandrea D .50 1.25
91 Aidan Dudas D .30 .75
92 Olivier Rodrigue D .25 .60
93 Joel Hofer D .50 1.25
94 Akil Thomas D .30 .75
95 Joseph Veleno D .25 .60
96 Bowen Byram D 1.00 2.50
97 Nolan Foote D .50 1.25
98 Raphael Lavoie D .25 .60
99 Connor McMichael D .75 2.00
100 Dylan Cozens D .75 2.00
101 Alexis Lafreniere POE 1.50 4.00
102 Joseph Veleno POE .25 .60
103 Calen Addison POE .40 1.00
104 Jared McIsaac POE .25 .60
105 Ty Smith POE .75 2.00
106 Jamie Drysdale POE 1.00 2.50
107 Olivier Rodrigue POE .25 .60
108 Bowen Byram POE 1.00 2.50
109 Dawson Mercer POE .60 1.50
110 Jacob Bernard-Docker POE .25 .60
111 Nolan Foote POE .50 1.25
112 Cole Perfetti POE .75 2.00
113 Kevin Bahl POE .40 1.00
114 Aidan Dudas POE .30 .75
115 Akil Thomas POE .30 .75
116 Alexis Lafreniere POE 1.50 4.00
117 Raphael Lavoie POE .25 .60
118 Quinton Byfield POE 1.00 2.50
119 Ty Dellandrea POE .50 1.25
120 Joel Hofer POE .50 1.25
121 Connor McMichael POE .75 2.00
122 Dylan Cozens POE .75 2.00
123 Nicolas Daws POE .40 1.00
124 Dylan Garand POE .30 .75
125 Tristan Lennox POE .30 .75
126 Lukas Cormier POE .30 .75
127 Jamie Drysdale POE 1.00 2.50
128 Kaiden Guhle POE .50 1.25
129 Daemon Hunt POE .30 .75
130 Ryan O'Rourke POE .30 .75
131 Jeremie Poirier POE .30 .75
132 Donovan Sebrango POE .30 .75
133 Mavrik Bourque POE .40 1.00
134 Quinton Byfield POE 1.00 2.50
135 Will Cuylle POE .50 1.25
136 Jean-Luc Foudy POE .30 .75
137 Ridly Greig POE .30 .75
138 Seth Jarvis POE .75 2.00
139 Hendrix Lapierre POE .40 1.00
140 Connor McClennon POE .30 .75
141 Jake Neighbours POE .50 1.25
142 Cole Perfetti POE .75 2.00
143 Theo Rochette POE .30 .75
144 Justin Sourdif POE .30 .75
145 Ozzy Wiesblatt POE .40 1.00

2020-21 Upper Deck Team Canada Juniors Exclusives

*EXCLUSIVES/165-250: 1.25X TO 3X BASIC INSERTS
32 Alexis Lafreniere U20 12.00 30.00
73 Alexis Lafreniere 12.00 30.00
101 Alexis Lafreniere POE 15.00 40.00
116 Alexis Lafreniere POE 15.00 40.00

2020-21 Upper Deck Team Canada Juniors High Gloss

*HIGH GLOSS/15-25: 4X TO 10X BASIC INSERTS

2020-21 Upper Deck Team Canada Juniors Autographs

101 Alexis Lafreniere POE A 40.00 100.00
103 Calen Addison POE B 10.00 25.00
104 Jared McIsaac POE D 6.00 15.00
105 Ty Smith POE D 20.00 50.00
106 Jamie Drysdale POE C 25.00 60.00
107 Olivier Rodrigue POE C 6.00 15.00
108 Bowen Byram POE C 25.00 60.00
109 Dawson Mercer POE C 15.00 40.00
110 Jacob Bernard-Docker POE B 6.00 15.00
111 Nolan Foote POE A 12.00 30.00
112 Cole Perfetti POE B 20.00 50.00
114 Aidan Dudas POE D 8.00 20.00
115 Akil Thomas POE C 8.00 20.00
117 Raphael Lavoie POE D 6.00 15.00
119 Ty Dellandrea POE D 12.00 30.00
120 Joel Hofer POE B 12.00 30.00
121 Connor McMichael POE D 20.00 50.00
122 Dylan Cozens POE B 20.00 50.00
123 Nicolas Daws POE B 10.00 25.00
124 Dylan Garand POE D 8.00 20.00
125 Tristan Lennox POE D 8.00 20.00
126 Lukas Cormier POE D 8.00 20.00
128 Kaiden Guhle POE C 12.00 30.00
129 Daemon Hunt POE D 8.00 20.00
130 Ryan O'Rourke POE D 8.00 20.00
131 Jeremie Poirier POE B 8.00 20.00
133 Mavrik Bourque POE C 10.00 25.00
134 Quinton Byfield POE A 25.00 60.00
135 Will Cuylle POE B 12.00 30.00
136 Jean-Luc Foudy POE C 8.00 20.00
137 Ridly Greig POE D 8.00 20.00
138 Seth Jarvis POE D 20.00 50.00
139 Hendrix Lapierre POE A 10.00 25.00
140 Connor McClennon POE B 8.00 20.00
141 Jake Neighbours POE C 12.00 30.00
143 Theo Rochette POE C 8.00 20.00
144 Justin Sourdif POE D 8.00 20.00
145 Ozzy Wiesblatt POE B 10.00 25.00

2020-21 Upper Deck Team Canada Juniors Autographs Purple

44 Victoria Bach A 10.00 25.00
46 Genevieve Lacasse C 8.00 20.00
47 Jocelyne Larocque C 10.00 25.00
48 Marie-Philip Poulin B 30.00 80.00
49 Brianne Jenner B 15.00 40.00
50 Emerance Maschmeyer B 12.00 30.00
52 Blayre Turnbull B 8.00 20.00
53 Jaime Bourbonnais B 10.00 25.00
54 Jillian Saulnier C 12.00 30.00
55 Ann-Renee Desbiens B 25.00 60.00
56 Jamie Lee Rattray B 12.00 30.00
57 Renata Fast B 10.00 25.00
58 Loren Gabel B 10.00 25.00
59 Brigette Lacquette C 8.00 20.00
60 Erin Ambrose C 15.00 40.00
61 Sarah Nurse B 25.00 60.00
62 Micah Zandee-Hart C 12.00 30.00
63 Melodie Daoust B 8.00 20.00
64 Lauriane Rougeau A 8.00 20.00
65 Emily Clark B 20.00 50.00
66 Natalie Spooner B 25.00 60.00
67 Laura Stacey C 12.00 30.00
68 Ann-Sophie Bettez A 8.00 20.00
70 Rebecca Johnston C 6.00 15.00

2020-21 Upper Deck Team Canada Juniors Golden Futures

*ROSE GOLD: .6X TO 1.25X BASIC INSERTS
GF1 Alexis Lafreniere 5.00 12.00
GF2 Nicolas Daws 1.25 3.00
GF3 Kaiden Guhle 1.50 4.00
GF4 Bowen Byram 3.00 8.00
GF5 Kevin Bahl 1.25 3.00
GF6 Jamie Drysdale 3.00 8.00
GF7 Ozzy Wiesblatt 1.25 3.00
GF8 Cole Perfetti 2.50 6.00
GF9 Akil Thomas 1.00 2.50
GF10 Jake Neighbours 1.50 4.00
GF11 Jean-Luc Foudy 1.00 2.50
GF12 Olivier Rodrigue .75 2.00
GF13 Ty Smith 2.50 6.00
GF14 Seth Jarvis 2.50 6.00
GF15 Connor McMichael 2.50 6.00
GF16 Hendrix Lapierre 1.25 3.00
GF17 Joseph Veleno .75 2.00
GF18 Quinton Byfield 3.00 8.00
GF19 Dylan Cozens 2.50 6.00
GF20 Nolan Foote 1.50 4.00
GF21 Will Cuylle 1.50 4.00
GF22 Dawson Mercer 2.00 5.00
GF23 Jeremie Poirier 1.00 2.50
GF24 Mavrik Bourque 1.25 3.00
GF25 Connor McClennon 1.00 2.50

2020-21 Upper Deck Team Canada Juniors Golden Futures Autographs

GF1 Alexis Lafreniere A 40.00 100.00
GF2 Nicolas Daws B 10.00 25.00
GF4 Bowen Byram C 25.00 60.00
GF6 Jamie Drysdale B 25.00 60.00
GF7 Ozzy Wiesblatt C 10.00 25.00
GF8 Cole Perfetti B 20.00 50.00
GF9 Akil Thomas C 8.00 20.00
GF10 Jake Neighbours C 12.00 30.00
GF12 Olivier Rodrigue B 6.00 15.00
GF13 Ty Smith C 20.00 50.00
GF15 Connor McMichael C 20.00 50.00
GF16 Hendrix Lapierre A 10.00 25.00
GF18 Quinton Byfield A 25.00 60.00
GF19 Dylan Cozens C 20.00 50.00
GF20 Nolan Foote A 12.00 30.00
GF21 Will Cuylle C 12.00 30.00
GF23 Jeremie Poirier C 8.00 20.00
GF24 Mavrik Bourque C 10.00 25.00
GF25 Connor McClennon C 8.00 20.00

2020-21 Upper Deck Team Canada Juniors Jerseys

1 Cole Perfetti H 3.00 8.00
2 Theo Rochette H 1.25 3.00
3 Ozzy Wiesblatt H 1.50 4.00
4 Justin Sourdif H 1.25 3.00
5 Jean-Luc Foudy H 1.25 3.00
6 Ridly Greig H 1.25 3.00
7 Connor McClennon H 1.25 3.00
8 Will Cuylle H 2.00 5.00
9 Hendrix Lapierre H 1.50 4.00
11 Jake Neighbours H 2.00 5.00
12 Mavrik Bourque H 1.50 4.00
13 Seth Jarvis H 3.00 8.00
14 Daemon Hunt H 1.25 3.00
15 Lukas Cormier H 1.25 3.00
17 Jeremie Poirier H 1.25 3.00
18 Kaiden Guhle H 2.00 5.00
19 Donovan Sebrango H 1.25 3.00
20 Ryan O'Rourke H 1.25 3.00
21 Tristan Lennox H 1.25 3.00
22 Dylan Garand H 1.25 3.00
23 Nicolas Daws U20 1.50 4.00
24 Kevin Bahl U20 1.50 4.00
25 Calen Addison U20 1.50 4.00
26 Bowen Byram U20 4.00 10.00
27 Jacob Bernard-Docker U20 1.00 2.50
28 Jamie Drysdale U20 4.00 10.00
29 Olivier Rodrigue U20 1.00 2.50
30 Joseph Veleno U20 1.00 2.50
31 Raphael Lavoie U20 1.00 2.50
32 Alexis Lafreniere U20 6.00 15.00
33 Jared McIsaac U20 1.00 2.50
34 Akil Thomas U20 1.25 3.00
35 Connor McMichael U20 3.00 8.00
36 Ty Dellandrea U20 2.00 5.00
37 Quinton Byfield U20 4.00 10.00
38 Dawson Mercer U20 2.50 6.00
39 Dylan Cozens U20 3.00 8.00
40 Ty Smith U20 3.00 8.00
41 Aidan Dudas U20 1.25 3.00
42 Joel Hofer U20 2.00 5.00
43 Nolan Foote U20 2.00 5.00
44 Victoria Bach WWC 1.50 4.00
46 Genevieve Lacasse WWC 1.25 3.00
47 Jocelyne Larocque WWC 1.50 4.00
48 Marie-Philip Poulin WWC 5.00 12.00
49 Brianne Jenner WWC 2.50 6.00
50 Emerance Maschmeyer WWC 2.00 5.00
51 Meaghan Mikkelson WWC 1.00 2.50
52 Blayre Turnbull WWC 1.25 3.00
53 Jaime Bourbonnais WWC 1.50 4.00
54 Jillian Saulnier WWC 2.00 5.00
55 Ann-Renee Desbiens WWC 4.00 10.00
56 Jamie Lee Rattray WWC 2.00 5.00
57 Renata Fast WWC 1.50 4.00
58 Loren Gabel WWC 1.50 4.00
59 Brigette Lacquette WWC 1.25 3.00
60 Erin Ambrose WWC 2.50 6.00
61 Sarah Nurse WWC 4.00 10.00
62 Micah Zandee-Hart WWC 2.00 5.00
63 Melodie Daoust WWC 1.25 3.00
64 Lauriane Rougeau WWC 1.25 3.00
65 Emily Clark WWC 3.00 8.00
66 Natalie Spooner WWC 4.00 10.00
67 Laura Stacey WWC 2.00 5.00
68 Ann-Sophie Bettez WWC 1.25 3.00
69 Meghan Agosta WWC 1.25 3.00
70 Rebecca Johnston WWC 1.00 2.50
71 Theo Rochette SP 1.25 3.00
72 Natalie Spooner SP 4.00 10.00
73 Alexis Lafreniere SP 6.00 15.00
74 Marie-Philip Poulin SP 5.00 12.00
75 Cole Perfetti SP 3.00 8.00
76 Meghan Agosta SP 1.25 3.00
77 Kaiden Guhle SP 2.00 5.00
78 Jamie Drysdale SP 4.00 10.00
79 Mavrik Bourque SP 1.50 4.00
80 Emerance Maschmeyer SP 2.00 5.00
81 Hendrix Lapierre SP 1.50 4.00
82 Quinton Byfield SP 4.00 10.00
83 Jean-Luc Foudy SP 1.25 3.00
85 Calen Addison D 1.50 4.00
86 Kevin Bahl D 1.50 4.00
87 Jacob Bernard-Docker D 1.00 2.50
88 Jared McIsaac D 1.00 2.50
89 Ty Smith D 3.00 8.00
90 Ty Dellandrea D 2.00 5.00
91 Aidan Dudas D 1.25 3.00
92 Olivier Rodrigue D 1.00 2.50
93 Joel Hofer D 2.00 5.00
94 Akil Thomas D 1.25 3.00
95 Joseph Veleno D 1.00 2.50
96 Bowen Byram D 4.00 10.00
97 Nolan Foote D 2.00 5.00
98 Raphael Lavoie D 1.00 2.50
99 Connor McMichael D 3.00 8.00
100 Dylan Cozens D 3.00 8.00

2020-21 Upper Deck Team Canada Juniors Patch Autographs

1 Cole Perfetti H/125 25.00 60.00
2 Theo Rochette H/199 10.00 25.00
3 Ozzy Wiesblatt H/199 12.00 30.00
4 Justin Sourdif H/199 10.00 25.00
5 Jean-Luc Foudy H/199 10.00 25.00
6 Ridly Greig H/199 10.00 25.00
7 Connor McClennon H/199 10.00 25.00
8 Will Cuylle H/199 15.00 40.00
9 Hendrix Lapierre H/199 12.00 30.00
11 Jake Neighbours H/199 15.00 40.00
12 Mavrik Bourque H/125 12.00 30.00
13 Seth Jarvis H/125 25.00 60.00
14 Daemon Hunt H/199 10.00 25.00
15 Lukas Cormier H/199 10.00 25.00
17 Jeremie Poirier H/199 10.00 25.00
18 Kaiden Guhle H/199 15.00 40.00
19 Donovan Sebrango H/199 10.00 25.00
20 Ryan O'Rourke H/199 10.00 25.00
21 Tristan Lennox H/199 10.00 25.00
22 Dylan Garand H/199 10.00 25.00
23 Nicolas Daws U20/199 12.00 30.00
25 Calen Addison U20/199 12.00 30.00
26 Bowen Byram U20/125 30.00 80.00
27 Jacob Bernard-Docker U20/199 8.00 20.00
28 Jamie Drysdale U20/125 30.00 80.00
29 Olivier Rodrigue U20/199 8.00 20.00
31 Raphael Lavoie U20/199 8.00 20.00
32 Alexis Lafreniere U20/125 150.00 400.00
33 Jared McIsaac U20/199 8.00 20.00
34 Akil Thomas U20/199 10.00 25.00
35 Connor McMichael U20/125 25.00 60.00
36 Ty Dellandrea U20/199 15.00 40.00
37 Quinton Byfield U20/125 30.00 80.00
38 Dawson Mercer U20/199 20.00 50.00
39 Dylan Cozens U20/199 25.00 60.00
40 Ty Smith U20/199 25.00 60.00
41 Aidan Dudas U20/199 10.00 25.00
42 Joel Hofer U20/199 15.00 40.00
43 Nolan Foote U20/199 15.00 40.00
44 Victoria Bach WWC/199 12.00 30.00
46 Genevieve Lacasse WWC/199 10.00 25.00
47 Jocelyne Larocque WWC/199 12.00 30.00
48 Marie-Philip Poulin WWC/199 40.00 100.00
49 Brianne Jenner WWC/199 20.00 50.00
50 Emerance Maschmeyer WWC/199 15.00 40.00
52 Blayre Turnbull WWC/199 10.00 25.00
53 Jaime Bourbonnais WWC/199 12.00 30.00
54 Jillian Saulnier WWC/199 15.00 40.00
55 Ann-Renee Desbiens WWC/199 30.00 80.00
56 Jamie Lee Rattray WWC/199 15.00 40.00
57 Renata Fast WWC/199 12.00 30.00
58 Loren Gabel WWC/199 12.00 30.00
60 Erin Ambrose WWC/199 20.00 50.00
61 Sarah Nurse WWC/199 30.00 80.00
62 Micah Zandee-Hart WWC/199 15.00 40.00
63 Melodie Daoust WWC/199 10.00 25.00
64 Lauriane Rougeau WWC/199 10.00 25.00
65 Emily Clark WWC/199 25.00 60.00
66 Natalie Spooner WWC/199 30.00 80.00
67 Laura Stacey WWC/199 15.00 40.00
74 Marie-Philip Poulin/25 80.00 200.00

2021-22 Upper Deck Team Canada Juniors

*EXCLUSIVES/165-250: 1.25X TO 3X BASIC CARDS
*MIDNIGHT/50: 3X TO 8X BASIC CARDS
*HG/15-25: 4X TO 10X BASIC INSERTS
1 Devon Levi U20 .30 .75
2 Braden Schneider U20 .50 1.25
3 Dylan Holloway U20 .60 1.50
4 Kaedan Korczak U20 .30 .75
5 Jordan Spence U20 .30 .75
6 Connor Zary U20 .30 .75
7 Cole Perfetti U20 .75 2.00
8 Jakob Pelletier U20 .30 .75
9 Ryan Suzuki U20 .40 1.00
10 Dawson Mercer U20 1.00 2.50
11 Kaiden Guhle U20 .50 1.25
12 Philip Tomasino U20 .50 1.25
13 Justin Barron U20 .60 1.50
14 Jack Quinn U20 .60 1.50
15 Taylor Gauthier U20 .30 .75
16 Dylan Garand U20 .40 1.00
17 Thomas Milic U18 .30 .75
18 Nolan Allan U18 .50 1.25
19 Olen Zellweger U18 .50 1.25
20 Corson Ceulemans U18 .40 1.00
21 Brandt Clarke U18 .50 1.25
22 Chase Stillman U18 .50 1.25
23 Brennan Othmann U18 .50 1.25
24 Brett Harrison U18 .40 1.00
25 Francesco Pinelli U18 .40 1.00
26 Danny Zhilkin U18 .50 1.25
27 Logan Stankoven U18 1.00 2.50
28 Conner Roulette U18 .50 1.25
29 Ethan Del Mastro U18 .40 1.00

30 Shane Wright U18 1.00 2.50
31 Denton Mateychuk U18 .40 1.00
32 Connor Bedard U18 30.00 80.00
33 Wyatt Johnston U18 1.25 3.00
34 Ryan Winterton U18 .30 .75
35 Dylan Guenther U18 .60 1.50
36 Mason McTavish U18 .75 2.00
37 Guillaume Richard U18 .30 .75
38 Jack Matier U18 .40 1.00
39 Benjamin Gaudreau U18 .50 1.25
40 Shane Wright U18 1.00 2.50
41 Connor Bedard U18 30.00 80.00
42 Mason McTavish U18 .75 2.00
43 Meaghan Mikkelson WWC .30 .75
44 Jamie Lee Rattray WWC .50 1.25
45 Ann-Renee Desbiens WWC 1.00 2.50
46 Erin Ambrose WWC .60 1.50
47 Sarah Nurse WWC 1.00 2.50
48 Marie-Philip Poulin WWC 1.25 3.00
49 Sarah Fillier WWC .30 .75
50 Brianne Jenner WWC .60 1.50
51 Rebecca Johnston WWC .40 1.00
52 Victoria Bach WWC .40 1.00
53 Renata Fast WWC .40 1.00
54 Melodie Daoust WWC .40 1.00
55 Emily Clark WWC .75 2.00
56 Micah Zandee-Hart WWC .50 1.25
57 Jillian Saulnier WWC .50 1.25
58 Blayre Turnbull WWC .40 1.00
59 Julia Gosling WWC .30 .75
60 Laura Stacey WWC .50 1.25
61 Emerance Maschmeyer WWC .50 1.25
62 Jocelyne Larocque WWC .40 1.00
63 Natalie Spooner WWC 1.00 2.50
64 Kristen Campbell WWC .60 1.50
65 Ashton Bell WWC .40 1.00
66 Jaime Bourbonnais WWC .40 1.00
67 Jessie Eldridge WWC .50 1.25
68 Emma Maltais WWC .75 2.00
69 Kristen O'Neill WWC .30 .75
70 Logan Stankoven U18 1.00 2.50
71 Mason McTavish U18 .75 2.00
72 Connor Zary U20 .30 .75
73 Shane Wright U18 1.00 2.50
74 Jack Quinn U20 .60 1.50
75 Philip Tomasino U20 .50 1.25
76 Connor Bedard U18 30.00 80.00
77 Ryan Suzuki U20 .40 1.00
78 Chase Stillman U18 .50 1.25
79 Cole Perfetti U20 .75 2.00
80 Brandt Clarke U18 .50 1.25
81 Brennan Othmann U18 .50 1.25
82 Corson Ceulemans U18 .40 1.00
83 Jakob Pelletier U20 .30 .75
84 Wyatt Johnston U18 1.25 3.00
85 Dylan Guenther U18 .60 1.50
86 Devon Levi U20 .30 .75
87 Dawson Mercer U20 1.00 2.50
88 Conner Roulette U18 .50 1.25
89 Kaiden Guhle U20 .50 1.25
90 Benjamin Gaudreau U20 .50 1.25
91 Justin Barron U20 .60 1.50
92 Francesco Pinelli U18 .40 1.00
93 Jack Matier U18 .40 1.00
94 Braden Schneider U20 .50 1.25
95 Olen Zellweger U18 .50 1.25
96 Thomas Milic U18 .30 .75
97 Jordan Spence U20 .30 .75
98 Guillaume Richard U18 .30 .75
99 Kaedan Korczak U18 .30 .75
100 Danny Zhilkin U18 .50 1.25
101 Cole Perfetti POE .75 2.00
102 Philip Tomasino POE .50 1.25
103 Mason McTavish POE .75 2.00
104 Ryan Suzuki POE .40 1.00
105 Shane Wright POE 1.00 2.50
106 Jack Quinn POE .60 1.50
107 Logan Stankoven POE 1.00 2.50
108 Kaiden Guhle POE .50 1.25
109 Brandt Clarke POE .50 1.25
110 Brennan Othmann POE .50 1.25
111 Justin Barron POE .60 1.50
112 Francesco Pinelli POE .40 1.00
113 Dawson Mercer POE 1.00 2.50
114 Danny Zhilkin POE .50 1.25
115 Jordan Spence POE .30 .75
116 Chase Stillman POE .50 1.25
117 Connor Bedard POE 30.00 80.00
118 Brett Harrison POE .40 1.00
119 Jack Matier POE .40 1.00
120 Conner Roulette POE .50 1.25
121 Kaedan Korczak POE .30 .75
122 Dylan Holloway POE .60 1.50
123 Devon Levi POE .30 .75
124 Olen Zellweger POE .50 1.25
125 Connor Zary POE .30 .75
126 Benjamin Gaudreau POE .50 1.25
127 Ethan Del Mastro POE .40 1.00
128 Denton Mateychuk POE .40 1.00
129 Braden Schneider POE .50 1.25
130 Dylan Guenther POE .60 1.50
131 Corson Ceulemans POE .40 1.00
132 Dylan Garand POE .40 1.00
133 Thomas Milic POE .30 .75
134 Nolan Allan POE .50 1.25
135 Jakob Pelletier POE .30 .75
136 Wyatt Johnston POE 1.25 3.00
137 Guillaume Richard POE .30 .75
138 Ryan Winterton POE .30 .75
139 Shane Wright Triggers Celebration POE 1.00 2.50
140 Team Canada Celebrates POE 1.00 2.50

2021-22 Upper Deck Team Canada Juniors Autographs Gold Spectrum

01 Cole Perfetti POE D 20.00 50.00
02 Philip Tomasino POE E 12.00 30.00
03 Mason McTavish POE B 20.00 50.00
04 Ryan Suzuki POE E 10.00 25.00
05 Shane Wright POE B 25.00 60.00
06 Jack Quinn POE D 15.00 40.00
07 Logan Stankoven POE D 25.00 60.00
08 Kaiden Guhle POE E 12.00 30.00
09 Brandt Clarke POE D 12.00 30.00
10 Brennan Othmann POE E 12.00 30.00
111 Justin Barron POE C 15.00 40.00
112 Francesco Pinelli POE B 10.00 25.00
113 Dawson Mercer POE E 25.00 60.00
114 Danny Zhilkin POE C 12.00 30.00
115 Jordan Spence POE D 8.00 20.00
116 Chase Stillman POE E 12.00 30.00
118 Brett Harrison POE D 10.00 25.00
119 Jack Matier POE E 10.00 25.00
120 Conner Roulette POE C 12.00 30.00
121 Kaedan Korczak POE E 8.00 20.00
122 Dylan Holloway POE C 15.00 40.00
123 Devon Levi POE B 8.00 20.00
124 Olen Zellweger POE B 12.00 30.00
125 Connor Zary POE E 8.00 20.00
126 Benjamin Gaudreau POE B 12.00 30.00
127 Ethan Del Mastro POE D 10.00 25.00
128 Denton Mateychuk POE D 10.00 25.00
129 Braden Schneider POE C 12.00 30.00
132 Dylan Garand POE D 10.00 25.00
133 Thomas Milic POE C 8.00 20.00
134 Nolan Allan POE C 12.00 30.00
135 Jakob Pelletier POE D 8.00 20.00
137 Guillaume Richard POE C 8.00 20.00
138 Ryan Winterton POE E 8.00 20.00
139 Shane Wright Triggers Celebration POE B 25.00 60.00

2021-22 Upper Deck Team Canada Juniors Jerseys

1 Devon Levi U20 1.25 3.00
2 Braden Schneider U20 2.00 5.00
3 Dylan Holloway U20 2.50 6.00
4 Kaedan Korczak U20 1.25 3.00
5 Jordan Spence U20 1.25 3.00
6 Connor Zary U20 1.25 3.00
7 Cole Perfetti U20 3.00 8.00
8 Jakob Pelletier U20 1.25 3.00
9 Ryan Suzuki U20 1.50 4.00
10 Dawson Mercer U20 4.00 10.00
11 Kaiden Guhle U20 2.00 5.00
12 Philip Tomasino U20 2.00 5.00
13 Justin Barron U20 2.50 6.00
14 Jack Quinn U20 2.50 6.00
15 Taylor Gauthier U20 1.25 3.00
16 Dylan Garand U20 1.50 4.00
17 Thomas Milic U18 1.25 3.00
18 Nolan Allan U18 2.00 5.00
19 Olen Zellweger U18 2.00 5.00
20 Corson Ceulemans U18 1.50 4.00
21 Brandt Clarke U18 2.00 5.00
22 Chase Stillman U18 2.00 5.00
23 Brennan Othmann U18 2.00 5.00
24 Brett Harrison U18 1.50 4.00
25 Francesco Pinelli U18 1.50 4.00
26 Danny Zhilkin U18 2.00 5.00
27 Logan Stankoven U18 4.00 10.00
28 Conner Roulette U18 2.00 5.00
29 Ethan Del Mastro U18 1.50 4.00
30 Shane Wright U18 4.00 10.00
31 Denton Mateychuk U18 1.50 4.00
32 Connor Bedard U18 60.00 150.00
33 Wyatt Johnston U18 5.00 12.00
34 Ryan Winterton U18 1.25 3.00
35 Dylan Guenther U18 2.50 6.00
36 Mason McTavish U18 3.00 8.00
37 Guillaume Richard U18 1.25 3.00
38 Jack Matier U18 1.50 4.00
39 Benjamin Gaudreau U18 2.00 5.00
43 Meaghan Mikkelson WWC 1.25 3.00
44 Jamie Lee Rattray WWC 2.00 5.00
45 Ann-Renee Desbiens WWC 4.00 10.00
46 Erin Ambrose WWC 2.50 6.00
47 Sarah Nurse WWC 4.00 10.00
48 Marie-Philip Poulin WWC 5.00 12.00
49 Sarah Fillier WWC 1.25 3.00
50 Brianne Jenner WWC 2.50 6.00
51 Rebecca Johnston WWC 1.50 4.00
52 Victoria Bach WWC 1.50 4.00
53 Renata Fast WWC 1.50 4.00
54 Melodie Daoust WWC 1.50 4.00
55 Emily Clark WWC 3.00 8.00
56 Micah Zandee-Hart WWC 2.00 5.00
57 Jillian Saulnier WWC 2.00 5.00
58 Blayre Turnbull WWC 1.50 4.00
60 Laura Stacey WWC 2.00 5.00
61 Emerance Maschmeyer WWC 2.00 5.00
62 Jocelyne Larocque WWC 1.50 4.00
63 Natalie Spooner WWC 4.00 10.00
66 Jaime Bourbonnais WWC 1.50 4.00
70 Logan Stankoven U18 SP 4.00 10.00
71 Mason McTavish U18 SP 3.00 8.00
72 Connor Zary U20 SP 1.25 3.00
73 Shane Wright U18 SP 4.00 10.00
74 Jack Quinn U20 SP 2.50 6.00
75 Philip Tomasino U20 SP 2.00 5.00
76 Connor Bedard U18 SP 80.00 200.00
77 Ryan Suzuki U20 SP 1.50 4.00
78 Chase Stillman U18 SP 2.00 5.00
79 Cole Perfetti U20 SP 3.00 8.00
80 Brandt Clarke U18 SP 2.00 5.00
81 Brennan Othmann U18 SP 2.00 5.00
82 Corson Ceulemans U18 SP 1.50 4.00
83 Jakob Pelletier U20 SP 1.25 3.00
84 Wyatt Johnston U18 SP 5.00 12.00
85 Dylan Guenther U18 SP 2.50 6.00
86 Devon Levi U20 SP 1.25 3.00
87 Dawson Mercer U20 SP 4.00 10.00
88 Conner Roulette U18 SP 2.00 5.00
89 Kaiden Guhle U20 SP 2.00 5.00
90 Benjamin Gaudreau U20 SP 2.00 5.00
91 Justin Barron U20 SP 2.50 6.00
92 Francesco Pinelli U18 SP 1.50 4.00
93 Jack Matier U18 SP 1.50 4.00
94 Braden Schneider U20 SP 2.00 5.00
95 Olen Zellweger U18 SP 2.00 5.00
96 Thomas Milic U18 SP 1.25 3.00
97 Jordan Spence U20 SP 1.25 3.00
98 Guillaume Richard U18 SP 1.25 3.00
99 Kaedan Korczak U18 SP 1.25 3.00
100 Danny Zhilkin U18 SP 2.00 5.00

2021-22 Upper Deck Team Canada Juniors Prospectus Momentous

*RED/275: .6X TO 1.5X BASIC INSERTS
*BLUE/49: 1X TO 2.5X BASIC INSERTS
PM1 Cole Perfetti 1.50 4.00
PM2 Philip Tomasino 1.00 2.50
PM3 Francesco Pinelli .75 2.00
PM4 Dawson Mercer 2.00 5.00
PM5 Logan Stankoven 2.00 5.00
PM6 Braden Schneider 1.00 2.50
PM7 Devon Levi .60 1.50
PM8 Dylan Holloway 1.25 3.00
PM9 Kaiden Guhle 1.00 2.50
PM10 Benjamin Gaudreau 1.00 2.50
PM11 Jack Quinn 1.25 3.00
PM12 Ryan Suzuki .75 2.00
PM13 Dylan Guenther 1.25 3.00
PM14 Seth Jarvis 2.00 5.00
PM15 Shane Wright 2.00 5.00
PM16 Brennan Othmann 1.00 2.50
PM17 Connor Bedard 30.00 80.00
PM18 Olen Zellweger 1.00 2.50
PM19 Connor Zary .60 1.50
PM20 Jordan Spence .60 1.50
PM21 Nolan Allan 1.00 2.50
PM22 Chase Stillman 1.00 2.50
PM23 Kaedan Korczak .60 1.50
PM24 Corson Ceulemans .75 2.00
PM25 Wyatt Johnston 2.50 6.00

2021-22 Upper Deck Team Canada Juniors Prospectus Momentous Autographs

PM1 Cole Perfetti C 15.00 40.00
PM2 Philip Tomasino D 10.00 25.00
PM3 Francesco Pinelli B 8.00 20.00
PM4 Dawson Mercer D 20.00 50.00
PM5 Logan Stankoven D 20.00 50.00
PM6 Braden Schneider C 10.00 25.00
PM7 Devon Levi B 6.00 15.00
PM8 Dylan Holloway C 12.00 30.00
PM9 Kaiden Guhle D 10.00 25.00
PM10 Benjamin Gaudreau B 10.00 25.00
PM11 Jack Quinn D 12.00 30.00
PM12 Ryan Suzuki D 8.00 20.00
PM14 Seth Jarvis C 20.00 50.00
PM15 Shane Wright B 20.00 50.00
PM16 Brennan Othmann C 10.00 25.00
PM18 Olen Zellweger A 10.00 25.00
PM19 Connor Zary D 6.00 15.00
PM20 Jordan Spence C 6.00 15.00
PM21 Nolan Allan C 10.00 25.00
PM22 Chase Stillman C 10.00 25.00
PM23 Kaedan Korczak D 6.00 15.00

2022-23 Upper Deck Team Canada Juniors

1 Shane Wright U20 1.25 3.00
2 Connor Bedard U20 12.00 30.00
3 Xavier Bourgault U20 .50 1.25
4 Mavrik Bourque U20 .50 1.25
5 Will Cuylle U20 .60 1.50
6 Olen Zellweger U20 .60 1.50
7 Ridly Greig U20 .50 1.25
8 Dylan Guenther U20 1.25 3.00
9 Sebastian Cossa U20 1.00 2.50
10 Donovan Sebrango U20 .50 1.25
11 Logan Stankoven U20 1.25 3.00
12 Lukas Cormier U20 .50 1.25
13 Kaiden Guhle U20 1.00 2.50
14 Carson Lambos U20 .60 1.50
15 Ryan O'Rourke U20 .50 1.25
16 Justin Sourdif U20 .50 1.25
17 Dylan Garand U20 .50 1.25
18 Elliot Desnoyers U20 .50 1.25
19 Ronan Seeley U20 .50 1.25
20 Josh Filmon U18 .50 1.25
21 Kocha Delic U18 .75 2.00
22 Mathew Ward U18 .50 1.25
23 Connor Bedard U18 12.00 30.00
24 Pano Fimis U18 .60 1.50
25 David Goyette U18 .60 1.50
26 Brayden Schuurman U18 .50 1.25
27 Adam Fantilli U18 6.00 15.00
28 Connor Hvidston U18 .50 1.25
29 Rieger Lorenz U10 .50 1.25
30 Matthew Wood U18 .50 1.25
31 Nolan Collins U18 .50 1.25
32 Lukas Dragicevic U18 .75 2.00
33 Michael Mastrodomenico U18 .50 1.25
34 Kalem Parker U18 .50 1.25
35 Grayden Siepmann U18 .75 2.00
36 Spencer Sova U18 .60 1.50
37 Owen Pickering U18 .60 1.50
38 Matthew Morden U18 .50 1.25
39 Nolan Lalonde U18 .50 1.25
40 Brett Brochu U18 .50 1.25
41 Reid Dyck U18 .60 1.50
42 Tanner Howe U18 .60 1.50
43 Nick Moldenhauer U18 .50 1.25
44 Josh Davies U18 .60 1.50
45 Sarah Fillier WWC .50 1.25
46 Jillian Saulnier WWC .60 1.50
47 Rebecca Johnston WWC .50 1.25
48 Melodie Daoust WWC .50 1.25
49 Ella Shelton WWC .60 1.50
50 Brianne Jenner WWC .75 2.00
51 Sarah Nurse WWC 1.25 3.00
52 Ashton Bell WWC .50 1.25
53 Erin Ambrose WWC .75 2.00
54 Natalie Spooner WWC 1.25 3.00
55 Jaime Bourbonnais WWC .50 1.25
56 Emily Clark WWC 1.00 2.50
57 Emma Maltais WWC 1.00 2.50
58 Marie-Philip Poulin WWC 1.50 4.00
59 Ann-Renee Desbiens WWC 1.25 3.00
60 Emerance Maschmeyer WWC .60 1.50
61 Blayre Turnbull WWC .50 1.25
62 Claire Thompson WWC .50 1.25
63 Kristin O'Neill WWC .50 1.25
64 Jamie Lee Rattray WWC .60 1.50
65 Kristen Campbell WWC .75 2.00
66 Victoria Bach WWC .50 1.25
67 Jocelyne Larocque WWC .50 1.25
68 Renata Fast WWC .50 1.25
69 Laura Stacey WWC .60 1.50
70 Sebastian Cossa POP 1.00 2.50
71 Kaiden Guhle POP 1.00 2.50
72 Carson Lambos POP .60 1.50
73 Olen Zellweger POP .60 1.50
74 Shane Wright POP 1.25 3.00
75 Will Cuylle POP .60 1.50
76 Ridly Greig POP .50 1.25
77 Logan Stankoven POP 1.25 3.00
78 Connor Bedard POP 12.00 30.00
79 Dylan Guenther POP 1.25 3.00
80 Xavier Bourgault POP .50 1.25
81 Mavrik Bourque POP .50 1.25
82 Ryan O'Rourke POP .50 1.25
83 Lukas Dragicevic POP .75 2.00
84 Tanner Howe POP .60 1.50
85 Kocha Delic POP .75 2.00
86 Reid Dyck POP .60 1.50
87 Spencer Sova POP .60 1.50
88 Josh Filmon POP .50 1.25
89 Rieger Lorenz POP .50 1.25
90 Grayden Siepmann POP .75 2.00
91 Nolan Lalonde POP .50 1.25
92 Owen Pickering POP .60 1.50
93 Mathew Ward POP .50 1.25
94 David Goyette POP .60 1.50
95 Michael Mastrodomenico POP .50 1.25
96 Adam Fantilli POP 6.00 15.00
97 Pano Fimis POP .60 1.50
98 Matthew Wood POP .50 1.25
99 Brayden Schuurman POP .50 1.25
100 Matthew Morden POP .50 1.25
101 Ryan O'Rourke POE .50 1.25
102 Dylan Garand POE .50 1.25
103 Lukas Cormier POE .50 1.25
104 Mavrik Bourque POE .50 1.25
105 Elliot Desnoyers POE .50 1.25
106 Ronan Seeley POE .50 1.25
107 Connor Bedard POE 12.00 30.00
108 Brett Brochu POE .50 1.25
109 Donovan Sebrango POE .50 1.25
110 Justin Sourdif POE .50 1.25
111 Will Cuylle POE .60 1.50
112 Dylan Guenther POE 1.25 3.00
113 Carson Lambos POE .60 1.50
114 Ridly Greig POE .50 1.25
115 Shane Wright POE 1.25 3.00
116 Sebastian Cossa POE 1.00 2.50
117 Xavier Bourgault POE .50 1.25
118 Logan Stankoven POE 1.25 3.00
119 Kaiden Guhle POE 1.00 2.50
120 Olen Zellweger POE .60 1.50
121 Nick Moldenhauer POE .50 1.25
122 Brayden Schuurman POE .50 1.25
123 Matthew Wood POE .50 1.25
124 Tanner Howe POE .60 1.50
125 Adam Fantilli POE 6.00 15.00
126 Josh Filmon POE .50 1.25
127 Owen Pickering POE .60 1.50
128 Michael Mastrodomenico POE .50 1.25
129 Lukas Dragicevic POE .75 2.00
130 Josh Davies POE .60 1.50
131 Rieger Lorenz POE .50 1.25
132 Reid Dyck POE .60 1.50
133 Kalem Parker POE .50 1.25
134 Connor Hvidston POE .50 1.25
135 Connor Bedard POE 12.00 30.00
136 Matthew Wood POE .50 1.25
137 Spencer Sova POE .60 1.50
138 Grayden Siepmann POE .75 2.00
139 Kocha Delic POE .75 2.00
140 Mathew Ward POE .50 1.25
141 Matthew Morden POE .50 1.25
142 Nolan Lalonde POE .50 1.25
143 David Goyette POE .60 1.50
144 Nolan Collins POE .50 1.25
145 Pano Fimis POE .60 1.50
146 Connor Bedard POE 12.00 30.00
147 Shane Wright POE 1.25 3.00
148 Dylan Guenther POE 1.25 3.00
149 Adam Fantilli POE 6.00 15.00
150 Sebastian Cossa POE 1.00 2.50

2022-23 Upper Deck Team Canada Juniors Clear Cut

*CLEAR.CUT: 2.5X TO 6X BASIC
2 Connor Bedard U20 50.00 125.00
23 Connor Bedard U18 50.00 125.00
27 Adam Fantilli U18 25.00 60.00
78 Connor Bedard POP 50.00 125.00
96 Adam Fantilli POP 25.00 60.00
107 Connor Bedard POE 50.00 125.00
125 Adam Fantilli POE 25.00 60.00
135 Connor Bedard POE 50.00 125.00
146 Connor Bedard POE 50.00 125.00
149 Adam Fantilli POE 25.00 60.00

2022-23 Upper Deck Team Canada Juniors Exclusives

*EXCLUSIVES: 3X TO 8X BASIC
2 Connor Bedard U20 150.00 400.00
23 Connor Bedard U18 150.00 400.00
27 Adam Fantilli U18 50.00 125.00
78 Connor Bedard POP 150.00 400.00
96 Adam Fantilli POP 50.00 125.00
107 Connor Bedard POE 150.00 400.00
125 Adam Fantilli POE 50.00 125.00
135 Connor Bedard POE 150.00 400.00
146 Connor Bedard POE 150.00 400.00
149 Adam Fantilli POE 50.00 125.00

2022-23 Upper Deck Team Canada Juniors Gold Dots

*VETS: 5X TO 12X BASIC
2 Connor Bedard U20 300.00 800.00
23 Connor Bedard U18 300.00 800.00
27 Adam Fantilli U18 125.00 300.00
78 Connor Bedard POP 300.00 800.00
96 Adam Fantilli POP 125.00 300.00

2022-23 Upper Deck Team Canada Juniors Green Frenzy

*GREEN: 3X TO 8X BASIC

2022-23 Upper Deck Team Canada Juniors Pillars of Light

*PILLARS: .75X TO 2X BASIC

2022-23 Upper Deck Team Canada Juniors Red

*RED: .5X TO 1.2X BASIC

2022-23 Upper Deck Team Canada Juniors Red Champagne

*RED.CHAMP: 1X TO 2.5X BASIC
2 Connor Bedard U20 60.00 150.00
23 Connor Bedard U18 60.00 150.00
78 Connor Bedard POP 60.00 150.00

2022-23 Upper Deck Team Canada Juniors Rose Gold

*ROSE.GOLD: .6X TO 1.5X BASIC

2022-23 Upper Deck Team Canada Juniors Jerseys

1 Shane Wright U20 4.00 10.00
2 Connor Bedard U20 60.00 150.00
3 Xavier Bourgault U20 1.50 4.00
4 Mavrik Bourque U20 1.50 4.00
5 Will Cuylle U20 2.00 5.00
6 Olen Zellweger U20 2.00 5.00
7 Ridly Greig U20 1.50 4.00
8 Dylan Guenther U20 4.00 10.00
9 Sebastian Cossa U20 3.00 8.00
10 Donovan Sebrango U20 1.50 4.00
11 Logan Stankoven U20 4.00 10.00
12 Lukas Cormier U20 1.50 4.00
13 Kaiden Guhle U20 3.00 8.00
14 Carson Lambos U20 2.00 5.00
15 Ryan O'Rourke U20 1.50 4.00
16 Justin Sourdif U20 1.50 4.00
17 Dylan Garand U20 1.50 4.00
18 Elliot Desnoyers U20 1.50 4.00
19 Ronan Seeley U20 1.50 4.00
20 Josh Filmon U18 1.50 4.00
21 Kocha Delic U18 2.50 6.00
22 Mathew Ward U18 1.50 4.00
23 Connor Bedard U18 60.00 150.00
24 Pano Fimis U18 2.00 5.00
25 David Goyette U18 2.00 5.00
26 Brayden Schuurman U18 1.50 4.00
27 Adam Fantilli U18 12.00 30.00
28 Connor Hvidston U18 1.50 4.00
29 Rieger Lorenz U18 1.50 4.00
30 Matthew Wood U18 1.50 4.00
31 Nolan Collins U18 1.50 4.00
32 Lukas Dragicevic U18 2.50 6.00
33 Michael Mastrodomenico U18 1.50 4.00
34 Kalem Parker U18 1.50 4.00
35 Grayden Siepmann U18 2.50 6.00
36 Spencer Sova U18 2.00 5.00
37 Owen Pickering U18 2.00 5.00
38 Matthew Morden U18 1.50 4.00
39 Nolan Lalonde U18 1.50 4.00
40 Brett Brochu U18 1.50 4.00
41 Reid Dyck U18 2.00 5.00
42 Tanner Howe U18 2.00 5.00
43 Nick Moldenhauer U18 1.50 4.00
44 Josh Davies U18 2.00 5.00
45 Sarah Fillier WWC 1.50 4.00
46 Jillian Saulnier WWC 2.00 5.00
47 Rebecca Johnston WWC 1.50 4.00
48 Melodie Daoust WWC 1.50 4.00
49 Ella Shelton WWC 2.00 5.00
50 Brianne Jenner WWC 2.50 6.00
51 Sarah Nurse WWC 4.00 10.00
52 Ashton Bell WWC 1.50 4.00
53 Erin Ambrose WWC 2.50 6.00
54 Natalie Spooner WWC 4.00 10.00
55 Jaime Bourbonnais WWC 1.50 4.00
56 Emily Clark WWC 3.00 8.00
57 Emma Maltais WWC 3.00 8.00
58 Marie-Philip Poulin WWC 5.00 12.00
59 Ann-Renee Desbiens WWC 4.00 10.00
60 Emerance Maschmeyer WWC 2.00 5.00
61 Blayre Turnbull WWC 1.50 4.00
62 Claire Thompson WWC 1.50 4.00
63 Kristin O'Neill WWC 1.50 4.00
64 Jamie Lee Rattray WWC 2.00 5.00
65 Kristen Campbell WWC 2.50 6.00
66 Victoria Bach WWC 1.50 4.00
67 Jocelyne Larocque WWC 1.50 4.00
68 Renata Fast WWC 1.50 4.00
69 Laura Stacey WWC 2.00 5.00
70 Sebastian Cossa POP 3.00 8.00
71 Kaiden Guhle POP 3.00 8.00
72 Carson Lambos POP 2.00 5.00
73 Olen Zellweger POP 2.00 5.00
74 Shane Wright POP 4.00 10.00
75 Will Cuylle POP 2.00 5.00
76 Ridly Greig POP 1.50 4.00
77 Logan Stankoven POP 4.00 10.00
78 Connor Bedard POP 60.00 150.00
79 Dylan Guenther POP 4.00 10.00
80 Xavier Bourgault POP 1.50 4.00
81 Mavrik Bourque POP 1.50 4.00
82 Ryan O'Rourke POP 1.50 4.00
83 Lukas Dragicevic POP 2.50 6.00
84 Tanner Howe POP 2.00 5.00
85 Kocha Delic POP 2.50 6.00
86 Reid Dyck POP 2.00 5.00
87 Spencer Sova POP 2.00 5.00
88 Josh Filmon POP 1.50 4.00
89 Rieger Lorenz POP 1.50 4.00
90 Grayden Siepmann POP 2.50 6.00
91 Nolan Lalonde POP 1.50 4.00
92 Owen Pickering POP 2.00 5.00
93 Mathew Ward POP 1.50 4.00
94 David Goyette POP 2.00 5.00
95 Michael Mastrodomenico POP 1.50 4.00
96 Adam Fantilli POP 12.00 30.00
97 Pano Fimis POP 2.00 5.00
98 Matthew Wood POP 1.50 4.00
99 Brayden Schuurman POP 1.50 4.00
100 Matthew Morden POP 1.50 4.00

2022-23 Upper Deck Team Canada Juniors Medal Hopefuls

MH1 Ridly Greig 8.00 20.00
MH2 Kaiden Guhle 15.00 40.00
MH3 Olen Zellweger 10.00 25.00
MH4 Sebastian Cossa 15.00 40.00
MH5 Carson Lambos 10.00 25.00
MH6 Xavier Bourgault 8.00 20.00
MH7 Shane Wright 20.00 50.00
MH8 Mavrik Bourque 8.00 20.00
MH9 Connor Bedard 200.00 500.00
MH10 Dylan Guenther 20.00 50.00
MH11 Lukas Dragicevic 12.00 30.00
MH12 Matthew Wood 8.00 20.00
MH13 Connor Bedard 200.00 500.00
MH14 Mathew Ward 8.00 20.00
MH15 Reid Dyck 10.00 25.00
MH16 Owen Pickering 10.00 25.00
MH17 Nick Moldenhauer 8.00 20.00
MH18 Pano Fimis 10.00 25.00
MH19 Adam Fantilli 60.00 150.00
MH20 Kocha Delic 12.00 30.00
MH21 Spencer Sova 10.00 25.00
MH22 David Goyette 10.00 25.00
MH23 Brayden Schuurman 8.00 20.00
MH24 Rieger Lorenz 8.00 20.00
MH25 Nolan Lalonde 8.00 20.00
MH26 Claire Thompson 8.00 20.00
MH27 Jillian Saulnier 10.00 25.00
MH28 Marie-Philip Poulin 25.00 60.00
MH29 Erin Ambrose 12.00 30.00
MH30 Sarah Fillier 8.00 20.00

2022-23 Upper Deck Team Canada Juniors Medal Hopefuls Red

MH9 Connor Bedard 250.00 600.00
MH13 Connor Bedard 250.00 600.00
MH19 Adam Fantilli 100.00 250.00

2022-23 Upper Deck Team Canada Juniors Patch Autographs

1 Shane Wright U20 30.00 80.00
3 Xavier Bourgault U20 12.00 30.00
4 Mavrik Bourque U20 12.00 30.00
5 Will Cuylle U20 15.00 40.00
6 Olen Zellweger U20 15.00 40.00
7 Ridly Greig U20 12.00 30.00
9 Sebastian Cossa U20 25.00 60.00
10 Donovan Sebrango U20 12.00 30.00
11 Logan Stankoven U20 30.00 80.00
12 Lukas Cormier U20 12.00 30.00
13 Kaiden Guhle U20 25.00 60.00
14 Carson Lambos U20 15.00 40.00
15 Ryan O'Rourke U20 12.00 30.00
16 Justin Sourdif U20 12.00 30.00
17 Dylan Garand U20 12.00 30.00
18 Elliot Desnoyers U20 12.00 30.00
19 Ronan Seeley U20 12.00 30.00
21 Kocha Delic U18 20.00 50.00
22 Mathew Ward U18 12.00 30.00
24 Pano Fimis U18 15.00 40.00
25 David Goyette U18 15.00 40.00
26 Brayden Schuurman U18 12.00 30.00
28 Connor Hvidston U18 12.00 30.00
31 Nolan Collins U18 12.00 30.00
32 Lukas Dragicevic U18 20.00 50.00
34 Kalem Parker U18 12.00 30.00
35 Grayden Siepmann U18 20.00 50.00
36 Spencer Sova U18 15.00 40.00
40 Brett Brochu U18 12.00 30.00
41 Reid Dyck U18 15.00 40.00
44 Josh Davies U18 15.00 40.00
45 Sarah Fillier WWC 12.00 30.00
46 Jillian Saulnier WWC 15.00 40.00
47 Rebecca Johnston WWC 12.00 30.00
49 Ella Shelton WWC 15.00 40.00
50 Brianne Jenner WWC 20.00 50.00
52 Ashton Bell WWC 12.00 30.00
53 Erin Ambrose WWC 20.00 50.00
54 Natalie Spooner WWC 30.00 80.00
56 Emily Clark WWC 25.00 60.00
57 Emma Maltais WWC 25.00 60.00
58 Marie-Philip Poulin WWC 40.00 100.00
60 Emerance Maschmeyer WWC 15.00 40.00
61 Blayre Turnbull WWC 12.00 30.00
62 Claire Thompson WWC 12.00 30.00
63 Kristin O'Neill WWC 12.00 30.00
65 Kristen Campbell WWC 20.00 50.00
66 Victoria Bach WWC 12.00 30.00
68 Renata Fast WWC 12.00 30.00
69 Laura Stacey WWC 15.00 40.00
70 Sebastian Cossa POP 40.00 100.00
71 Kaiden Guhle POP 40.00 100.00
72 Carson Lambos POP 25.00 60.00
73 Olen Zellweger POP 25.00 60.00
74 Shane Wright POP 50.00 125.00
75 Will Cuylle POP 25.00 60.00
76 Ridly Greig POP 20.00 50.00
77 Logan Stankoven POP 50.00 125.00
78 Connor Bedard POP 1500.00 4000.00
79 Dylan Guenther POP 50.00 125.00
80 Xavier Bourgault POP 20.00 50.00
81 Mavrik Bourque POP 20.00 50.00
82 Ryan O'Rourke POP 20.00 50.00
83 Lukas Dragicevic POP 30.00 80.00
84 Tanner Howe POP 25.00 60.00
85 Kocha Delic POP 30.00 80.00
86 Reid Dyck POP 25.00 60.00
87 Spencer Sova POP 25.00 60.00
88 Josh Filmon POP 20.00 50.00
90 Grayden Siepmann POP 30.00 80.00
91 Nolan Lalonde POP 20.00 50.00
92 Owen Pickering POP 25.00 60.00
93 Mathew Ward POP 20.00 50.00
94 David Goyette POP 25.00 60.00
95 Michael Mastrodomenico POP 20.00 50.00
97 Pano Fimis POP 25.00 60.00
99 Brayden Schuurman POP 20.00 50.00
100 Matthew Morden POP 20.00 50.00

2022-23 Upper Deck Team Canada Juniors Prospectus Momentous

PM1 Sebastian Cossa 2.00 5.00
PM2 Donovan Sebrango 1.00 2.50
PM3 David Goyette 1.25 3.00
PM4 Connor Hvidston 1.00 2.50
PM5 Olen Zellweger 1.25 3.00
PM6 Justin Sourdif 1.00 2.50
PM7 Kaiden Guhle 2.00 5.00
PM8 Adam Fantilli 8.00 20.00
PM9 Josh Davies 1.25 3.00
PM10 Elliot Desnoyers 1.00 2.50
PM11 Adam Fantilli 8.00 20.00
PM12 Connor Bedard 20.00 50.00
PM13 Ronan Seeley 1.00 2.50
PM14 Matthew Morden 1.00 2.50
PM15 Kalem Parker 1.00 2.50
PM16 Nick Moldenhauer 1.00 2.50
PM17 Dylan Garand 1.00 2.50
PM18 Mathew Ward 1.00 2.50
PM19 Nolan Collins 1.00 2.50
PM20 Lukas Dragicevic 1.50 4.00
PM21 Carson Lambos 1.25 3.00
PM22 Tanner Howe 1.25 3.00
PM23 Shane Wright 2.50 6.00
PM24 Will Cuylle 1.25 3.00
PM25 Kocha Delic 1.50 4.00
PM26 Grayden Siepmann 1.50 4.00
PM27 Michael Mastrodomenico 1.00 2.50
PM28 Brett Brochu 1.00 2.50
PM29 Xavier Bourgault 1.00 2.50
PM30 Pano Fimis 1.25 3.00
PM31 Spencer Sova 1.25 3.00
PM32 Matthew Wood 1.00 2.50
PM33 Nolan Lalonde 1.00 2.50
PM34 Lukas Cormier 1.00 2.50
PM35 Owen Pickering 1.25 3.00
PM36 Reid Dyck 1.25 3.00
PM37 Mavrik Bourque 1.00 2.50
PM38 Ridly Greig 1.00 2.50
PM39 Rieger Lorenz 1.00 2.50
PM40 Dylan Guenther 2.50 6.00
PM41 Ryan O'Rourke 1.00 2.50
PM42 Logan Stankoven 2.50 6.00
PM43 Josh Filmon 1.00 2.50
PM44 Brayden Schuurman 1.00 2.50
PM45 Marie-Philip Poulin 3.00 8.00
PM46 Natalie Spooner 2.50 6.00
PM47 Rebecca Johnston 1.00 2.50
PM48 Melodie Daoust 1.00 2.50
PM49 Sarah Fillier 1.00 2.50
PM50 Ann-Renee Desbiens 2.50 6.00

2022-23 Upper Deck Team Canada Juniors Prospectus Momentous Electric Blue

*BLUE: .6X TO 1.5X BASIC
PM8 Adam Fantilli 20.00 50.00
PM11 Adam Fantilli 20.00 50.00
PM12 Connor Bedard 80.00 200.00

2022-23 Upper Deck Team Canada Juniors Prospectus Momentous Electric Gold

*GOLD: 1X TO 2.5X BASIC
PM8 Adam Fantilli 30.00 80.00
PM11 Adam Fantilli 30.00 80.00
PM12 Connor Bedard 150.00 400.00

2022-23 Upper Deck Team Canada Juniors Prospectus Momentous Electric Orange

*ORANGE: 1.2X TO 3X BASIC
PM8 Adam Fantilli 40.00 100.00
PM11 Adam Fantilli 40.00 100.00
PM12 Connor Bedard 200.00 500.00

2022-23 Upper Deck Team Canada Juniors Prospectus Momentous Electric Red

*RED: .5X TO 1.2X BASIC
PM8 Adam Fantilli 15.00 40.00
PM11 Adam Fantilli 15.00 40.00
PM12 Connor Bedard 30.00 80.00

2022-23 Upper Deck Team Canada Juniors Prospectus Momentous Electric Yellow

*YELLOW: .75X TO 2X BASIC
PM8 Adam Fantilli 30.00 80.00
PM11 Adam Fantilli 30.00 80.00
PM12 Connor Bedard 125.00 300.00

2022-23 Upper Deck Team Canada Juniors Prospectus Momentous Autographs

PM1 Sebastian Cossa B 15.00 40.00
PM2 Donovan Sebrango A 8.00 20.00
PM3 David Goyette C 10.00 25.00
PM4 Connor Hvidston A 8.00 20.00
PM5 Olen Zellweger D 10.00 25.00
PM6 Justin Sourdif E 8.00 20.00
PM7 Kaiden Guhle E 15.00 40.00
PM9 Josh Davies A 10.00 25.00
PM10 Elliot Desnoyers A 8.00 20.00
PM13 Ronan Seeley A 8.00 20.00
PM14 Matthew Morden B 8.00 20.00
PM15 Kalem Parker A 8.00 20.00
PM17 Dylan Garand A 8.00 20.00
PM18 Mathew Ward B 8.00 20.00
PM19 Nolan Collins A 8.00 20.00
PM20 Lukas Dragicevic C 12.00 30.00
PM21 Carson Lambos A 10.00 25.00
PM22 Tanner Howe B 10.00 25.00
PM23 Shane Wright C 20.00 50.00
PM24 Will Cuylle E 10.00 25.00
PM25 Kocha Delic A 12.00 30.00
PM27 Michael Mastrodomenico C 8.00 20.00
PM28 Brett Brochu A 8.00 20.00
PM29 Xavier Bourgault D 8.00 20.00
PM30 Pano Fimis D 10.00 25.00
PM31 Spencer Sova D 10.00 25.00
PM33 Nolan Lalonde C 8.00 20.00
PM34 Lukas Cormier E 8.00 20.00
PM35 Owen Pickering B 10.00 25.00
PM36 Reid Dyck A 10.00 25.00
PM37 Mavrik Bourque E 8.00 20.00
PM38 Ridly Greig E 8.00 20.00
PM40 Dylan Guenther D 20.00 50.00
PM41 Ryan O'Rourke D 8.00 20.00
PM42 Logan Stankoven C 20.00 50.00
PM43 Josh Filmon B 8.00 20.00
PM44 Brayden Schuurman A 8.00 20.00
PM45 Marie-Philip Poulin C 25.00 60.00
PM46 Natalie Spooner B 20.00 50.00
PM47 Rebecca Johnston D 8.00 20.00
PM48 Melodie Daoust C 8.00 20.00
PM49 Sarah Fillier C 8.00 20.00
PM50 Ann-Renee Desbiens B 20.00 50.00

2022-23 Upper Deck Team Canada Juniors Signatures

1 Shane Wright U20 B 25.00 60.00
2 Connor Bedard U20 A 400.00 1000.00
3 Xavier Bourgault U20 C 10.00 25.00
4 Mavrik Bourque U20 E 10.00 25.00
5 Will Cuylle U20 D 12.00 30.00
6 Olen Zellweger U20 D 12.00 30.00
7 Ridly Greig U20 E 10.00 25.00

8 Dylan Guenther U20 E 25.00 60.00
10 Donovan Sebrango U20 B 10.00 25.00
11 Logan Stankoven U20 C 25.00 60.00
12 Lukas Cormier U20 C 10.00 25.00
13 Kaiden Guhle U20 E 20.00 50.00
14 Carson Lambos U20 B 12.00 30.00
15 Ryan O'Rourke U20 D 10.00 25.00
16 Justin Sourdif U20 D 10.00 25.00
17 Dylan Garand U20 C 10.00 25.00
18 Elliot Desnoyers U20 B 10.00 25.00
19 Ronan Seeley U20 B 10.00 25.00
20 Josh Filmon U18 C 10.00 25.00
21 Kocha Delic U18 A 15.00 40.00
23 Connor Bedard U18 A 400.00 1000.00
24 Pano Fimis U18 C 12.00 30.00
25 David Goyette U18 C 12.00 30.00
26 Brayden Schuurman U18 A 10.00 25.00
28 Connor Hvidston U18 B 10.00 25.00
31 Nolan Collins U18 B 10.00 25.00
32 Lukas Dragicevic U18 D 15.00 40.00
33 Michael Mastrodomenico U18 C 10.00 25.00
34 Kalem Parker U18 B 10.00 25.00
36 Spencer Sova U18 D 12.00 30.00
37 Owen Pickering U18 C 12.00 30.00
38 Matthew Morden U18 C 10.00 25.00
39 Nolan Lalonde U18 C 10.00 25.00
40 Brett Brochu U18 B 10.00 25.00
41 Reid Dyck U18 A 12.00 30.00
42 Tanner Howe U18 C 12.00 30.00
44 Josh Davies U18 B 12.00 30.00
45 Sarah Fillier WWC C 12.00 30.00
46 Jillian Saulnier WWC D 12.00 30.00
47 Rebecca Johnston WWC D 10.00 25.00
48 Melodie Daoust WWC D 10.00 25.00
49 Ella Shelton WWC C 12.00 30.00
50 Brianne Jenner WWC D 15.00 40.00
51 Sarah Nurse WWC D 25.00 60.00
52 Ashton Bell WWC C 10.00 25.00
53 Erin Ambrose WWC E 15.00 40.00
54 Natalie Spooner WWC C 25.00 60.00
55 Jaime Bourbonnais WWC D 10.00 25.00
56 Emily Clark WWC E 20.00 50.00
57 Emma Maltais WWC C 20.00 50.00
58 Marie-Philip Poulin WWC C 30.00 80.00
59 Ann-Renee Desbiens WWC E 25.00 60.00
60 Emerance Maschmeyer WWC E 12.00 30.00
61 Blayre Turnbull WWC D 10.00 25.00
62 Claire Thompson WWC E 10.00 25.00
63 Kristin O'Neill WWC B 10.00 25.00
64 Jamie Lee Rattray WWC E 12.00 30.00
65 Kristen Campbell WWC C 15.00 40.00
66 Victoria Bach WWC D 10.00 25.00
67 Jocelyne Larocque WWC E 10.00 25.00
68 Renata Fast WWC E 10.00 25.00
69 Laura Stacey WWC E 12.00 30.00
71 Kaiden Guhle POP E 20.00 50.00
72 Carson Lambos POP B 12.00 30.00
73 Olen Zellweger POP C 12.00 30.00
74 Shane Wright POP B 25.00 60.00
75 Will Cuylle POP D 12.00 30.00
76 Ridly Greig POP E 10.00 25.00
77 Logan Stankoven POP D 25.00 60.00
78 Connor Bedard POP A 400.00 1000.00
79 Dylan Guenther POP E 25.00 60.00
80 Xavier Bourgault POP D 10.00 25.00
81 Mavrik Bourque POP E 10.00 25.00
82 Ryan O'Rourke POP D 10.00 25.00
83 Lukas Dragicevic POP D 15.00 40.00
84 Tanner Howe POP C 12.00 30.00
85 Kocha Delic POP A 15.00 40.00
86 Reid Dyck POP A 12.00 30.00
87 Spencer Sova POP D 12.00 30.00
88 Josh Filmon POP C 10.00 25.00
91 Nolan Lalonde POP D 10.00 25.00
92 Owen Pickering POP C 12.00 30.00
94 David Goyette POP C 12.00 30.00
95 Michael Mastrodomenico POP C 10.00 25.00
97 Pano Fimis POP C 12.00 30.00
99 Brayden Schuurman POP A 10.00 25.00
100 Matthew Morden POP D 10.00 25.00
101 Ryan O'Rourke POE D 10.00 25.00
102 Dylan Garand POE C 10.00 25.00
103 Lukas Cormier POE E 10.00 25.00
104 Mavrik Bourque POE E 10.00 25.00
105 Elliot Desnoyers POE E 10.00 25.00
106 Ronan Seeley POE B 10.00 25.00
107 Connor Bedard POE B 400.00 1000.00
108 Brett Brochu POE B 10.00 25.00
109 Donovan Sebrango POE B 10.00 25.00
110 Justin Sourdif POE E 10.00 25.00
111 Will Cuylle POE E 12.00 30.00
112 Dylan Guenther POE D 25.00 60.00
113 Carson Lambos POE C 12.00 30.00
114 Ridly Greig POE E 10.00 25.00
115 Shane Wright POE C 25.00 60.00
116 Sebastian Cossa POE C 20.00 50.00
117 Xavier Bourgault POE D 10.00 25.00
118 Logan Stankoven POE D 25.00 60.00
119 Kaiden Guhle POE D 20.00 50.00
120 Olen Zellweger POE C 12.00 30.00
122 Brayden Schuurman POE A 10.00 25.00
124 Tanner Howe POE C 12.00 30.00
126 Josh Filmon POE C 10.00 25.00
127 Owen Pickering POE C 12.00 30.00
128 Michael Mastrodomenico POE C 10.00 25.00
129 Lukas Dragicevic POE D 15.00 40.00
130 Josh Davies POE B 12.00 30.00
132 Reid Dyck POE A 12.00 30.00
133 Kalem Parker POE B 10.00 25.00
134 Connor Hvidston POE B 10.00 25.00
135 Connor Bedard POE A 400.00 1000.00
137 Spencer Sova POE D 12.00 30.00
139 Kocha Delic POE A 15.00 40.00
141 Matthew Morden POE C 10.00 25.00
142 Nolan Lalonde POE C 10.00 25.00
143 David Goyette POE C 12.00 30.00
144 Nolan Collins POE B 10.00 25.00
145 Pano Fimis POE D 12.00 30.00
147 Shane Wright POE C 25.00 60.00
148 Dylan Guenther POE D 25.00 60.00
150 Sebastian Cossa POE D 20.00 50.00

2022-23 Upper Deck Team Canada Juniors Sparkling Standouts

SS1 Shane Wright 4.00 10.00
SS2 Lukas Cormier 1.50 4.00
SS3 Logan Stankoven 4.00 10.00
SS4 Will Cuylle 2.00 5.00
SS5 Xavier Bourgault 1.50 4.00
SS6 Olen Zellweger 2.00 5.00
SS7 Mavrik Bourque 1.50 4.00
SS8 Kaiden Guhle 3.00 8.00
SS9 Sebastian Cossa 3.00 8.00
SS10 Dylan Guenther 4.00 10.00
SS11 Ryan O'Rourke 1.50 4.00
SS12 Connor Bedard 60.00 150.00
SS13 Carson Lambos 2.00 5.00
SS14 Donovan Sebrango 1.50 4.00
SS15 Ridly Greig 1.50 4.00
SS16 Josh Filmon 1.50 4.00
SS17 Owen Pickering 2.00 5.00
SS18 David Goyette 2.00 5.00
SS19 Adam Fantilli 15.00 40.00
SS20 Rieger Lorenz 1.50 4.00
SS21 Matthew Wood 1.50 4.00
SS22 Lukas Dragicevic 2.50 6.00
SS23 Mathew Ward 1.50 4.00
SS24 Pano Fimis 2.00 5.00
SS25 Spencer Sova 2.00 5.00
SS26 Michael Mastrodomenico 1.50 4.00
SS27 Reid Dyck 2.00 5.00
SS28 Tanner Howe 2.00 5.00
SS29 Kocha Delic 2.50 6.00
SS30 Brayden Schuurman 1.50 4.00
SS31 Grayden Siepmann 2.50 6.00
SS32 Connor Hvidston 1.50 4.00
SS33 Nick Moldenhauer 1.50 4.00
SS34 Connor Bedard 60.00 150.00
SS35 Josh Davies 2.00 5.00
SS36 Natalie Spooner 4.00 10.00
SS37 Marie-Philip Poulin 5.00 12.00
SS38 Rebecca Johnston 1.50 4.00
SS39 Sarah Nurse 4.00 10.00
SS40 Brianne Jenner 2.50 6.00

2022-23 Upper Deck Team Canada Juniors Team Canada Acetates

CA1 Justin Sourdif 5.00 12.00
CA2 Brett Brochu 5.00 12.00
CA3 Kaiden Guhle 10.00 25.00
CA4 Ryan O'Rourke 5.00 12.00
CA5 Mavrik Bourque 5.00 12.00
CA6 Logan Stankoven 12.00 30.00
CA7 Donovan Sebrango 5.00 12.00
CA8 Carson Lambos 6.00 15.00
CA9 Connor Bedard 250.00 600.00
CA10 Sebastian Cossa 10.00 25.00
CA11 Dylan Guenther 12.00 30.00
CA12 Shane Wright 12.00 30.00
CA13 Ridly Greig 5.00 12.00
CA14 Olen Zellweger 6.00 15.00
CA15 Xavier Bourgault 5.00 12.00
CA16 Owen Pickering 6.00 15.00
CA17 Adam Fantilli 40.00 100.00
CA18 Shane Wright 12.00 30.00
CA19 David Goyette 6.00 15.00
CA20 Connor Bedard 250.00 600.00
CA21 Mathew Ward 5.00 12.00
CA22 Kocha Delic 8.00 20.00
CA23 Grayden Siepmann 8.00 20.00
CA24 Lukas Dragicevic 8.00 20.00
CA25 Matthew Morden 5.00 12.00
CA26 Josh Filmon 5.00 12.00
CA27 Nick Moldenhauer 5.00 12.00
CA28 Reid Dyck 6.00 15.00
CA29 Nolan Lalonde 5.00 12.00
CA30 Matthew Wood 5.00 12.00
CA31 Connor Hvidston 5.00 12.00
CA32 Brayden Schuurman 5.00 12.00
CA33 Rieger Lorenz 5.00 12.00
CA34 Pano Fimis 6.00 15.00
CA35 Spencer Sova 6.00 15.00
CA36 Ann-Renee Desbiens 12.00 30.00
CA37 Brianne Jenner 8.00 20.00
CA38 Natalie Spooner 12.00 30.00
CA39 Melodie Daoust 5.00 12.00
CA40 Jamie Lee Rattray 6.00 15.00

2022-23 Upper Deck Team Canada Juniors Team Canada Breakouts

TCB1 Carson Lambos 8.00 20.00
TCB2 Mavrik Bourque 6.00 15.00
TCB3 Shane Wright 15.00 40.00
TCB4 Connor Bedard 200.00 500.00
TCB5 Kaiden Guhle 12.00 30.00
TCB6 Xavier Bourgault 6.00 15.00
TCB8 Rieger Lorenz 6.00 15.00
TCB9 Adam Fantilli 40.00 100.00
TCB10 Owen Pickering 8.00 20.00
TCB11 Lukas Dragicevic 10.00 25.00
TCB12 Mathew Ward 6.00 15.00
TCB13 David Goyette 8.00 20.00
TCB14 Pano Fimis 8.00 20.00
TCB15 Matthew Wood 6.00 15.00
TCB16 Spencer Sova 8.00 20.00
TCB17 Connor Bedard 200.00 500.00
TCB18 Blayre Turnbull 6.00 15.00
TCB19 Brianne Jenner 10.00 25.00
TCB20 Sarah Fillier 6.00 15.00

2022-23 Upper Deck Team Canada Juniors Team Canada FX

FX1 Kaiden Guhle 8.00 20.00
FX2 Xavier Bourgault 4.00 10.00
FX3 Connor Bedard 60.00 150.00
FX4 Olen Zellweger 5.00 12.00
FX5 Carson Lambos 5.00 12.00
FX6 Dylan Guenther 10.00 25.00
FX7 Shane Wright 10.00 25.00
FX8 Sebastian Cossa 8.00 20.00
FX9 Ridly Greig 4.00 10.00
FX10 Mavrik Bourque 4.00 10.00
FX11 Rieger Lorenz 4.00 10.00
FX12 Lukas Dragicevic 6.00 15.00
FX13 Matthew Wood 4.00 10.00
FX14 Adam Fantilli 25.00 60.00
FX15 David Goyette 5.00 12.00
FX16 Connor Bedard 60.00 150.00
FX17 Owen Pickering 5.00 12.00
FX18 Renata Fast 4.00 10.00
FX19 Claire Thompson 4.00 10.00
FX20 Ann-Renee Desbiens 10.00 25.00

2023-24 Upper Deck Team Canada Juniors

1 Thomas Milic U20 .40 1.00
2 Nolan Allan U20 .60 1.50
3 Olen Zellweger U20 .60 1.50
4 Brennan Othmann U20 .60 1.50
5 Joshua Roy U20 .60 1.50
6 Logan Stankoven U20 1.25 3.00
7 Zach Dean U20 .50 1.25
8 Connor Bedard U20 10.00 25.00
9 Adam Fantilli U20 1.50 4.00
10 Nathan Gaucher U20 .60 1.50
11 Ethan Del Mastro U20 .50 1.25
12 Jack Matier U20 .50 1.25
13 Benjamin Gaudreau U20 .60 1.50
14 Tyson Hinds U20 .50 1.25
15 Reid Schaefer U20 .60 1.50
16 Caedan Bankier U20 .50 1.25
17 Zack Ostapchuk U20 .60 1.50
18 Kevin Korchinski U20 .75 2.00
19 Tanner Howe U18 .60 1.50
20 Matthew Wood U18 .50 1.25
21 Ty Halaburda U18 .50 1.25
22 Colby Barlow U18 .60 1.50
23 Berkly Catton U18 1.25 3.00
24 Andrew Cristall U18 .60 1.50
25 Nick Lardis U18 .50 1.25
26 Macklin Celebrini U18 5.00 12.00
27 Angus MacDonell U18 .50 1.25
28 Calum Ritchie U18 .60 1.50
29 Porter Martone U18 1.25 3.00
30 Alex Pharand U18 .50 1.25
31 Lukas Dragicevic U18 .75 2.00
32 Caden Price U18 .50 1.25
33 Andrew Gibson U18 .60 1.50
34 Cameron Allen U18 .60 1.50
35 Quinton Burns U18 .50 1.25
36 Carter Yakemchuk U18 .50 1.25
37 Tristan Bertucci U18 .50 1.25
38 Gabriel D'Aigle U18 1.25 3.00
39 Carson Bjarnason U18 .50 1.25
40 Riley Heidt U18 .75 2.00
41 Emerance Maschmeyer WWC .60 1.50
42 Ann-Renee Desbiens WWC 1.25 3.00
43 Kristen Campbell WWC .75 2.00
44 Jocelyne Larocque WWC .50 1.25
45 Renata Fast WWC .50 1.25
46 Micah Zandee-Hart WWC .60 1.50
47 Ella Shelton WWC .60 1.50
48 Erin Ambrose WWC .75 2.00
49 Jaime Bourbonnais WWC .50 1.25
50 Claire Thompson WWC .50 1.25
51 Rebecca Johnston WWC .60 1.50
52 Laura Stacey WWC .60 1.50
53 Sarah Fillier WWC .50 1.25
54 Brianne Jenner WWC .75 2.00
55 Sarah Nurse WWC 1.25 3.00
56 Natalie Spooner WWC 1.25 3.00
57 Emily Clark WWC 1.00 2.50
58 Emma Maltais WWC 1.00 2.50
59 Marie-Philip Poulin WWC 1.50 4.00
60 Blayre Turnbull WWC .50 1.25
61 Kristin O'Neill WWC .50 1.25
62 Jamie Lee Rattray WWC .60 1.50
63 Danielle Serdachny WWC .50 1.25
64 Tyson Hinds POP .50 1.25
65 Connor Bedard POP 10.00 25.00
66 Brennan Othmann POP .60 1.50
67 Caedan Bankier POP .50 1.25
68 Nathan Gaucher POP .60 1.50
69 Olen Zellweger POP .60 1.50
70 Ethan Del Mastro POP .50 1.25
71 Zach Dean POP .50 1.25
72 Kevin Korchinski POP .75 2.00
73 Reid Schaefer POP .60 1.50
74 Zack Ostapchuk POP .60 1.50
75 Adam Fantilli POP 1.50 4.00
76 Nolan Allan POP .60 1.50
77 Jack Matier POP .50 1.25
78 Logan Stankoven POP 1.25 3.00
79 Benjamin Gaudreau POP .60 1.50
80 Joshua Roy POP .60 1.50
81 Thomas Milic POP .40 1.00
82 Colby Barlow POP .60 1.50
83 Tristan Bertucci POP .50 1.25
84 Angus MacDonell POP .50 1.25
85 Alex Pharand POP .50 1.25
86 Tanner Howe POP .60 1.50
87 Caden Price POP .50 1.25
88 Andrew Gibson POP .60 1.50
89 Andrew Cristall POP .60 1.50
90 Porter Martone POP 1.25 3.00
91 Cameron Allen POP .60 1.50
92 Berkly Catton POP 1.25 3.00
93 Carter Yakemchuk POP .50 1.25
94 Nick Lardis POP .50 1.25
95 Calum Ritchie POP .60 1.50
96 Lukas Dragicevic POP .75 2.00
97 Macklin Celebrini POP 5.00 12.00
98 Quinton Burns POP .50 1.25
99 Matthew Wood POP .50 1.25
100 Ty Halaburda POP .50 1.25
101 Andrew Cristall POE .60 1.50
102 Ethan Del Mastro POE .50 1.25
103 Ty Halaburda POE .50 1.25
104 Tanner Howe POE .60 1.50
105 Andrew Gibson POE .60 1.50
106 Carter Yakemchuk POE .50 1.25
107 Jack Matier POE .50 1.25
108 Connor Bedard POE 10.00 25.00
109 Gabriel D'Aigle POE 1.25 3.00
110 Benjamin Gaudreau POE .60 1.50
111 Quinton Burns POE .50 1.25
112 Caden Price POE .50 1.25
113 Riley Heidt POE .75 2.00
114 Logan Stankoven POE 1.25 3.00
115 Thomas Milic POE .40 1.00
116 Tristan Bertucci POE .50 1.25
117 Macklin Celebrini POE 5.00 12.00
118 Berkly Catton POE 1.25 3.00
119 Caedan Bankier POE .50 1.25
120 Calum Ritchie POE .60 1.50
121 Kevin Korchinski POE .75 2.00
122 Alex Pharand POE .50 1.25
123 Lukas Dragicevic POE .75 2.00
124 Olen Zellweger POE .60 1.50
125 Reid Schaefer POE .60 1.50
126 Zack Ostapchuk POE .60 1.50
127 Joshua Roy POE .60 1.50
128 Porter Martone POE 1.25 3.00
129 Adam Fantilli POE 1.50 4.00
130 Colby Barlow POE .60 1.50
131 Tyson Hinds POE .50 1.25
132 Carson Bjarnason POE .50 1.25
133 Zach Dean POE .50 1.25
134 Nathan Gaucher POE .60 1.50
135 Nick Lardis POE .50 1.25
136 Cameron Allen POE .60 1.50
137 Brennan Othmann POE .60 1.50
138 Angus MacDonell POE .50 1.25
139 Nolan Allan POE .60 1.50
140 Matthew Wood POE .50 1.25
141 Connor Bedard POE 10.00 25.00
142 Ty Halaburda POE .50 1.25
143 Nolan Allan POE .60 1.50
144 Porter Martone POE 1.25 3.00
145 Reid Schaefer POE .60 1.50
146 Matthew Wood POE .50 1.25
147 Nathan Gaucher POE .60 1.50
148 Andrew Cristall POE .60 1.50
149 Thomas Milic POE .40 1.00
150 Logan Stankoven POE 1.25 3.00

2023-24 Upper Deck Team Canada Juniors Clear Cut

*CLEAR CUT: 2.5X TO 6X BASIC
8 Connor Bedard U20 125.00 300.00
26 Macklin Celebrini U18 60.00 150.00
65 Connor Bedard POP 125.00 300.00
97 Macklin Celebrini POP 60.00 150.00
108 Connor Bedard POE 125.00 300.00
117 Macklin Celebrini POE 60.00 150.00
141 Connor Bedard POE 125.00 300.00

2023-24 Upper Deck Team Canada Juniors Exclusives

*EXCL/100: 3X TO 8X BASIC

2023-24 Upper Deck Team Canada Juniors Patterned Foilboard

*PAT FOIL: .75X TO 2X BASIC
8 Connor Bedard U20 12.00 30.00
26 Macklin Celebrini U18 6.00 15.00
65 Connor Bedard POP 12.00 30.00
97 Macklin Celebrini POP 6.00 15.00

2023-24 Upper Deck Team Canada Juniors Patterned Foilboard Blue

*PAT FOIL BLUE: 2X TO 5X BASIC
8 Connor Bedard U20 30.00 80.00
26 Macklin Celebrini U18 15.00 40.00
65 Connor Bedard POP 30.00 80.00
97 Macklin Celebrini POP 15.00 40.00

2023-24 Upper Deck Team Canada Juniors Patterned Foilboard Gold

*PAT FOIL GOLD/25: 5X TO 12X BASIC

2023-24 Upper Deck Team Canada Juniors Patterned Foilboard Red

*PAT FOIL RED: 1X TO 2.5X BASIC
8 Connor Bedard U20 15.00 40.00
26 Macklin Celebrini U18 8.00 20.00
65 Connor Bedard POP 15.00 40.00
97 Macklin Celebrini POP 8.00 20.00

2023-24 Upper Deck Team Canada Juniors Red Foil

*RED: .5X TO 1.2X BASIC

2023-24 Upper Deck Team Canada Juniors Rose Gold

*ROSE GOLD: .6X TO 1.5X BASIC

2023-24 Upper Deck Team Canada Juniors Go to the Top

GT1 Sarah Fillier 3.00 8.00
GT2 Matthew Wood 3.00 8.00
GT3 Olen Zellweger 4.00 10.00
GT4 Cameron Allen 4.00 10.00
GT5 Zack Ostapchuk 4.00 10.00
GT6 Brennan Othmann 4.00 10.00
GT7 Zach Dean 3.00 8.00
GT8 Logan Stankoven 8.00 20.00
GT9 Caedan Bankier 3.00 8.00
GT10 Marie-Philip Poulin 10.00 25.00
GT11 Berkly Catton 8.00 20.00
GT12 Angus MacDonell 3.00 8.00
GT13 Macklin Celebrini 12.00 30.00
GT14 Thomas Milic 2.50 6.00
GT15 Gabriel D'Aigle 8.00 20.00
GT16 Reid Schaefer 4.00 10.00
GT17 Kevin Korchinski 5.00 12.00
GT18 Tyson Hinds 3.00 8.00
GT19 Andrew Gibson 4.00 10.00
GT20 Carter Yakemchuk 3.00 8.00
GT21 Adam Fantilli 10.00 25.00
GT22 Renata Fast 3.00 8.00
GT23 Andrew Cristall 4.00 10.00
GT24 Nolan Allan 4.00 10.00
GT25 Benjamin Gaudreau 4.00 10.00
GT26 Lukas Dragicevic 5.00 12.00
GT27 Quinton Burns 3.00 8.00
GT28 Tristan Bertucci 3.00 8.00
GT29 Nathan Gaucher 4.00 10.00
GT30 Porter Martone 8.00 20.00
GT31 Caden Price 3.00 8.00
GT32 Ty Halaburda 3.00 8.00
GT33 Sarah Nurse 8.00 20.00
GT34 Tanner Howe 4.00 10.00
GT35 Nick Lardis 3.00 8.00
GT36 Calum Ritchie 4.00 10.00
GT37 Connor Bedard 20.00 50.00
GT38 Natalie Spooner 8.00 20.00
GT39 Alex Pharand 3.00 8.00
GT40 Colby Barlow 3.00 8.00

2023-24 Upper Deck Team Canada Juniors Jerseys

1 Thomas Milic U20 1.50 4.00
2 Nolan Allan U20 2.50 6.00
3 Olen Zellweger U20 2.50 6.00
4 Brennan Othmann U20 2.50 6.00
5 Joshua Roy U20 2.50 6.00
6 Logan Stankoven U20 5.00 12.00
7 Zach Dean U20 2.00 5.00
8 Connor Bedard U20 12.00 30.00
9 Adam Fantilli U20 6.00 15.00
10 Nathan Gaucher U20 2.50 6.00
11 Ethan Del Mastro U20 2.00 5.00
12 Jack Matier U20 2.00 5.00
13 Benjamin Gaudreau U20 2.50 6.00
14 Tyson Hinds U20 2.00 5.00
15 Reid Schaefer U20 2.50 6.00
16 Caedan Bankier U20 2.00 5.00
17 Zack Ostapchuk U20 2.50 6.00
18 Kevin Korchinski U20 3.00 8.00
19 Tanner Howe U18 2.50 6.00
20 Matthew Wood U18 2.00 5.00
21 Ty Halaburda U18 2.00 5.00
22 Colby Barlow U18 2.50 6.00
23 Berkly Catton U18 5.00 12.00
24 Andrew Cristall U18 2.50 6.00
25 Nick Lardis U18 2.00 5.00
26 Macklin Celebrini U18 8.00 20.00
27 Angus MacDonell U18 2.00 5.00
28 Calum Ritchie U18 2.50 6.00
29 Porter Martone U18 5.00 12.00
30 Alex Pharand U18 2.00 5.00
31 Lukas Dragicevic U18 3.00 8.00
32 Caden Price U18 2.00 5.00
33 Andrew Gibson U18 2.50 6.00
34 Cameron Allen U18 2.50 6.00
35 Quinton Burns U18 2.00 5.00
36 Carter Yakemchuk U18 2.00 5.00
37 Tristan Bertucci U18 2.00 5.00
38 Gabriel D'Aigle U18 5.00 12.00
39 Carson Bjarnason U18 2.00 5.00
40 Riley Heidt U18 3.00 8.00
41 Emerance Maschmeyer WWC 2.50 6.00
42 Ann-Renee Desbiens WWC 5.00 12.00
43 Kristen Campbell WWC 3.00 8.00
44 Jocelyne Larocque WWC 2.00 5.00
45 Renata Fast WWC 2.00 5.00
46 Micah Zandee-Hart WWC 2.50 6.00
47 Ella Shelton WWC 2.50 6.00
48 Erin Ambrose WWC 3.00 8.00
49 Jaime Bourbonnais WWC 2.00 5.00
50 Claire Thompson WWC 2.00 5.00
51 Rebecca Johnston WWC 2.50 6.00
52 Laura Stacey WWC 2.50 6.00
53 Sarah Fillier WWC 2.00 5.00
54 Brianne Jenner WWC 3.00 8.00
55 Sarah Nurse WWC 5.00 12.00
56 Natalie Spooner WWC 5.00 12.00
57 Emily Clark WWC 4.00 10.00
58 Emma Maltais WWC 4.00 10.00
59 Marie-Philip Poulin WWC 6.00 15.00
60 Blayre Turnbull WWC 2.00 5.00
61 Kristin O'Neill WWC 2.00 5.00
62 Jamie Lee Rattray WWC 2.50 6.00
63 Danielle Serdachny WWC 2.00 5.00
64 Tyson Hinds POP 2.00 5.00
65 Connor Bedard POP 12.00 30.00
66 Brennan Othmann POP 2.50 6.00
67 Caedan Bankier POP 2.00 5.00
68 Nathan Gaucher POP 2.50 6.00
69 Olen Zellweger POP 2.50 6.00
70 Ethan Del Mastro POP 2.00 5.00
71 Zach Dean POP 2.00 5.00
72 Kevin Korchinski POP 3.00 8.00
73 Reid Schaefer POP 2.50 6.00
74 Zack Ostapchuk POP 2.50 6.00
75 Adam Fantilli POP 6.00 15.00
76 Nolan Allan POP 2.50 6.00
77 Jack Matier POP 2.00 5.00
78 Logan Stankoven POP 5.00 12.00
79 Benjamin Gaudreau POP 2.50 6.00
80 Joshua Roy POP 2.50 6.00
81 Thomas Milic POP 1.50 4.00
82 Colby Barlow POP 2.50 6.00
83 Tristan Bertucci POP 2.00 5.00
84 Angus MacDonell POP 2.00 5.00
85 Alex Pharand POP 2.00 5.00
86 Tanner Howe POP 2.50 6.00
87 Caden Price POP 2.00 5.00
88 Andrew Gibson POP 2.50 6.00
89 Andrew Cristall POP 2.50 6.00
90 Porter Martone POP 5.00 12.00
91 Cameron Allen POP 2.50 6.00
92 Berkly Catton POP 5.00 12.00
93 Carter Yakemchuk POP 2.00 5.00
94 Nick Lardis POP 2.00 5.00
95 Calum Ritchie POP 2.50 6.00
96 Lukas Dragicevic POP 3.00 8.00
97 Macklin Celebrini POP 8.00 20.00
98 Quinton Burns POP 2.00 5.00
99 Matthew Wood POP 2.00 5.00
100 Ty Halaburda POP 2.00 5.00

2023-24 Upper Deck Team Canada Juniors License to Ice

*RED/23: .6X TO 1.5X BASIC
LI1 Brennan Othmann 10.00 25.00
LI2 Tristan Bertucci 8.00 20.00
LI3 Ty Halaburda 8.00 20.00
LI4 Zach Dean 8.00 20.00
LI5 Sarah Fillier 8.00 20.00
LI6 Carson Bjarnason 8.00 20.00
LI7 Caden Price 8.00 20.00
LI8 Ann-Renee Desbiens 20.00 50.00
LI9 Logan Stankoven 20.00 50.00
LI10 Jack Matier 8.00 20.00
LI11 Alex Pharand 8.00 20.00
LI12 Joey Costanzo 8.00 20.00
LI13 Brianne Jenner 12.00 30.00
LI14 Nick Lardis 8.00 20.00
LI15 Ethan Del Mastro 8.00 20.00
LI16 Andrew Gibson 10.00 25.00
LI17 Macklin Celebrini 30.00 80.00
LI18 Laura Stacey 10.00 25.00
LI19 Nolan Allan 10.00 25.00
LI20 Colby Barlow 8.00 20.00
LI21 Olen Zellweger 10.00 25.00
LI22 Zack Ostapchuk 10.00 25.00
LI23 Gabriel D'Aigle 20.00 50.00
LI24 Emerance Maschmeyer 10.00 25.00
LI25 Tanner Howe 10.00 25.00
LI26 Natalie Spooner 20.00 50.00
LI27 Joshua Roy 10.00 25.00
LI28 Connor Bedard 50.00 125.00
LI29 Sarah Nurse 20.00 50.00
LI30 Tyson Hinds 8.00 20.00
LI31 Berkly Catton 20.00 50.00
LI32 Matthew Wood 8.00 20.00
LI33 Renata Fast 8.00 20.00
LI34 Carter Yakemchuk 8.00 20.00
LI35 Thomas Milic 6.00 15.00
LI36 Quinton Burns 8.00 20.00
LI37 Nathan Gaucher 10.00 25.00
LI38 Kevin Korchinski 12.00 30.00
LI39 Andrew Cristall 10.00 25.00
LI40 Cameron Allen 10.00 25.00
LI41 Porter Martone 20.00 50.00
LI42 Caedan Bankier 8.00 20.00
LI43 Angus MacDonell 8.00 20.00
LI44 Adam Fantilli 25.00 60.00
LI45 Blayre Turnbull 8.00 20.00
LI46 Benjamin Gaudreau 10.00 25.00
LI47 Lukas Dragicevic 12.00 30.00
LI48 Reid Schaefer 10.00 25.00
LI49 Erin Ambrose 12.00 30.00
LI50 Calum Ritchie 10.00 25.00

2023-24 Upper Deck Team Canada Juniors Patch Autographs

1 Thomas Milic U20/175 10.00 25.00
2 Nolan Allan U20/175 15.00 40.00
3 Olen Zellweger U20/125 15.00 40.00
4 Brennan Othmann U20/175 15.00 40.00
5 Joshua Roy U20/175 15.00 40.00
6 Logan Stankoven U20/175 30.00 80.00
9 Adam Fantilli U20/125 40.00 100.00
10 Nathan Gaucher U20/175 15.00 40.00
11 Ethan Del Mastro U20/175 12.00 30.00
12 Jack Matier U20/175 12.00 30.00
13 Benjamin Gaudreau U20/175 15.00 40.00
14 Tyson Hinds U20/175 12.00 30.00
15 Reid Schaefer U20/175 15.00 40.00
16 Caedan Bankier U20/175 12.00 30.00
18 Kevin Korchinski U20/175 20.00 50.00
19 Tanner Howe U18/125 15.00 40.00
21 Ty Halaburda U18/175 12.00 30.00
22 Colby Barlow U18/125 15.00 40.00
23 Berkly Catton U18/175 30.00 80.00
24 Andrew Cristall U18/125 15.00 40.00
25 Nick Lardis U18/175 12.00 30.00
27 Angus MacDonell U18/175 12.00 30.00
28 Calum Ritchie U18/125 15.00 40.00
29 Porter Martone U18/175 30.00 80.00
30 Alex Pharand U18/175 12.00 30.00
31 Lukas Dragicevic U18/175 20.00 50.00
32 Caden Price U18/175 12.00 30.00
33 Andrew Gibson U18/175 15.00 40.00
34 Cameron Allen U18/175 15.00 40.00
35 Quinton Burns U18/175 12.00 30.00
36 Carter Yakemchuk U18/175 12.00 30.00
37 Tristan Bertucci U18/175 12.00 30.00
38 Gabriel D'Aigle U18/175 30.00 80.00
39 Carson Bjarnason U18/175 12.00 30.00
41 Emerance Maschmeyer WWC/175 15.00 40.00
42 Ann-Renee Desbiens WWC/175 30.00 80.00
43 Kristen Campbell WWC/175 20.00 50.00
44 Jocelyne Larocque WWC/175 12.00 30.00
45 Renata Fast WWC/175 12.00 30.00
47 Ella Shelton WWC/175 15.00 40.00
48 Erin Ambrose WWC/175 20.00 50.00
49 Jaime Bourbonnais WWC/175 12.00 30.00
50 Claire Thompson WWC/175 12.00 30.00
51 Rebecca Johnston WWC/175 12.00 30.00
52 Laura Stacey WWC/175 15.00 40.00
53 Sarah Fillier WWC/175 12.00 30.00
54 Brianne Jenner WWC/175 20.00 50.00
55 Sarah Nurse WWC/175 30.00 80.00
56 Natalie Spooner WWC/175 30.00 80.00
57 Emily Clark WWC/175 25.00 60.00
58 Emma Maltais WWC/175 25.00 60.00
59 Marie-Philip Poulin WWC/175 40.00 100.00
60 Blayre Turnbull WWC/175 12.00 30.00
61 Kristin O'Neill WWC/175 12.00 30.00
62 Jamie Lee Rattray WWC/175 15.00 40.00
63 Danielle Serdachny WWC/175 12.00 30.00
64 Tyson Hinds POP/25 20.00 50.00
66 Brennan Othmann POP/25 25.00 60.00
67 Caedan Bankier POP/25 20.00 50.00
68 Nathan Gaucher POP/25 25.00 60.00
69 Olen Zellweger POP/25 25.00 60.00
70 Ethan Del Mastro POP/25 20.00 50.00
72 Kevin Korchinski POP/25 30.00 80.00
73 Reid Schaefer POP/25 25.00 60.00
75 Adam Fantilli POP/25 60.00 150.00
76 Nolan Allan POP/25 25.00 60.00
77 Jack Matier POP/25 20.00 50.00
78 Logan Stankoven POP/25 50.00 125.00
79 Benjamin Gaudreau POP/25 25.00 60.00
80 Joshua Roy POP/25 25.00 60.00
81 Thomas Milic POP/25 15.00 40.00
82 Colby Barlow POP/25 25.00 60.00
83 Tristan Bertucci POP/25 20.00 50.00
84 Angus MacDonell POP/25 20.00 50.00
85 Alex Pharand POP/25 20.00 50.00
86 Tanner Howe POP/25 25.00 60.00
87 Caden Price POP/25 20.00 50.00
88 Andrew Gibson POP/25 25.00 60.00
89 Andrew Cristall POP/25 25.00 60.00
90 Porter Martone POP/25 50.00 120.00
91 Cameron Allen POP/25 25.00 60.00
92 Berkly Catton POP/25 50.00 125.00
93 Carter Yakemchuk POP/25 20.00 50.00
94 Nick Lardis POP/25 20.00 50.00
95 Calum Ritchie POP/25 25.00 60.00
96 Lukas Dragicevic POP/25 30.00 80.00
98 Quinton Burns POP/25 20.00 50.00
100 Ty Halaburda POP/25 20.00 50.00

2023-24 Upper Deck Team Canada Juniors Prospectus Momentous

*RED/549: .5X TO 1.2X BASIC
*BLUE/349: .6X TO 1.5X BASIC
*YELLOW/149: .75X TO 2X BASIC
*GOLD/99: 1X TO 2.5X BASIC
*ORANGE/75: 1.2X TO 3X BASIC
*GREEN/49: 1.5X TO 4X BASIC
*PURPLE/25: 2.5X TO 6X BASIC
PM1 Calum Ritchie 1.25 3.00
PM2 Brennan Othmann 1.25 3.00
PM3 Logan Stankoven 2.50 6.00
PM4 Carter Yakemchuk 1.00 2.50
PM5 Gabriel D'Aigle 2.50 6.00
PM6 Olen Zellweger 1.25 3.00
PM7 Alex Pharand 1.00 2.50
PM8 Macklin Celebrini 4.00 10.00
PM9 Andrew Gibson 1.25 3.00
PM10 Berkly Catton 2.50 6.00
PM11 Andrew Cristall 1.25 3.00
PM12 Quinton Burns 1.00 2.50
PM13 Kevin Korchinski 1.50 4.00
PM14 Zach Dean 1.00 2.50
PM15 Caden Price 1.00 2.50
PM16 Adam Fantilli 3.00 8.00
PM17 Caedan Bankier 1.00 2.50
PM18 Porter Martone 2.50 6.00
PM19 Cameron Allen 1.25 3.00
PM20 Carson Bjarnason 1.00 2.50
PM21 Tyson Hinds 1.00 2.50
PM22 Jack Matier 1.00 2.50
PM23 Nick Lardis 1.00 2.50
PM24 Riley Heidt 1.50 4.00
PM25 Ty Halaburda 1.00 2.50
PM26 Joshua Roy 1.25 3.00
PM27 Reid Schaefer 1.25 3.00
PM28 Matthew Wood 1.00 2.50
PM29 Ethan Del Mastro 1.00 2.50
PM30 Lukas Dragicevic 1.50 4.00
PM31 Thomas Milic .75 2.00
PM32 Tanner Howe 1.25 3.00
PM33 Angus MacDonell 1.00 2.50
PM34 Nathan Gaucher 1.25 3.00
PM35 Zack Ostapchuk 1.25 3.00
PM36 Connor Bedard 6.00 15.00
PM37 Nolan Allan 1.25 3.00
PM38 Colby Barlow 1.00 2.50
PM39 Tristan Bertucci 1.00 2.50
PM40 Benjamin Gaudreau 1.25 3.00
PM41 Adam Fantilli 3.00 8.00
PM42 Brennan Othmann 1.25 3.00
PM43 Zach Dean 1.00 2.50
PM44 Kevin Korchinski 1.50 4.00
PM45 Tanner Howe 1.25 3.00
PM46 Berkly Catton 2.50 6.00
PM47 Calum Ritchie 1.25 3.00
PM48 Lukas Dragicevic 1.50 4.00
PM49 Nick Lardis 1.00 2.50
PM50 Colby Barlow 1.00 2.50

2023-24 Upper Deck Team Canada Juniors Prospectus Momentous Autographs

PM1 Calum Ritchie 12.00 30.00
PM5 Gabriel D'Aigle 25.00 60.00
PM6 Olen Zellweger 12.00 30.00
PM7 Alex Pharand 10.00 25.00
PM11 Andrew Cristall 12.00 30.00
PM12 Quinton Burns 10.00 25.00
PM19 Cameron Allen 12.00 30.00
PM20 Carson Bjarnason 10.00 25.00
PM21 Tyson Hinds 10.00 25.00
PM34 Nathan Gaucher 12.00 30.00
PM39 Tristan Bertucci 10.00 25.00

2023-24 Upper Deck Team Canada Juniors Signatures

1 Thomas Milic U20 B 8.00 20.00
2 Nolan Allan U20 A 12.00 30.00
3 Olen Zellweger U20 B 12.00 30.00
4 Brennan Othmann U20 B 12.00 30.00
5 Joshua Roy U20 B 12.00 30.00
6 Logan Stankoven U20 B 25.00 60.00
10 Nathan Gaucher U20 A 12.00 30.00
11 Ethan Del Mastro U20 B 10.00 25.00
12 Jack Matier U20 B 10.00 25.00
13 Benjamin Gaudreau U20 B 12.00 30.00
14 Tyson Hinds U20 A 10.00 25.00
15 Reid Schaefer U20 A 12.00 30.00
16 Caedan Bankier U20 A 10.00 25.00
18 Kevin Korchinski U20 B 15.00 40.00
19 Tanner Howe U18 B 12.00 30.00
21 Ty Halaburda U18 B 10.00 25.00
22 Colby Barlow U18 B 12.00 30.00
23 Berkly Catton U18 B 25.00 60.00
24 Andrew Cristall U18 C 12.00 30.00
25 Nick Lardis U18 B 10.00 25.00
27 Angus MacDonell U18 B 10.00 25.00
28 Calum Ritchie U18 B 12.00 30.00
29 Porter Martone U18 B 25.00 60.00
30 Alex Pharand U18 B 10.00 25.00
31 Lukas Dragicevic U18 B 15.00 40.00
32 Caden Price U18 B 10.00 25.00
33 Andrew Gibson U18 B 12.00 30.00
34 Cameron Allen U18 A 12.00 30.00
35 Quinton Burns U18 A 10.00 25.00
36 Carter Yakemchuk U18 B 10.00 25.00
37 Tristan Bertucci U18 D 10.00 25.00
38 Gabriel D'Aigle U18 C 25.00 60.00
39 Carson Bjarnason U18 C 10.00 25.00
43 Kristen Campbell WWC C 15.00 40.00
44 Jocelyne Larocque WWC C 10.00 25.00
45 Renata Fast WWC C 10.00 25.00
46 Micah Zandee-Hart WWC C 12.00 30.00
47 Ella Shelton WWC C 12.00 30.00
48 Erin Ambrose WWC C 15.00 40.00
49 Jaime Bourbonnais WWC D 10.00 25.00
50 Claire Thompson WWC D 10.00 25.00
51 Rebecca Johnston WWC D 10.00 25.00
52 Laura Stacey WWC C 12.00 30.00
53 Sarah Fillier WWC C 10.00 25.00
54 Brianne Jenner WWC D 15.00 40.00
55 Sarah Nurse WWC D 25.00 60.00
56 Natalie Spooner WWC C 25.00 60.00
58 Emma Maltais WWC D 20.00 50.00
59 Marie-Philip Poulin WWC D 30.00 80.00
60 Blayre Turnbull WWC C 10.00 25.00
61 Kristin O'Neill WWC D 10.00 25.00
62 Jamie Lee Rattray WWC D 12.00 30.00
63 Danielle Serdachny WWC D 10.00 25.00

64 Tyson Hinds POP A 10.00 25.00
66 Brennan Othmann POP A 12.00 30.00
67 Caedan Bankier POP A 10.00 25.00
68 Nathan Gaucher POP A 12.00 30.00
69 Olen Zellweger POP B 12.00 30.00
70 Ethan Del Mastro POP B 10.00 25.00
72 Kevin Korchinski POP A 15.00 40.00
76 Nolan Allan POP A 12.00 30.00
77 Jack Matier POP B 10.00 25.00
78 Logan Stankoven POP A 25.00 60.00
79 Benjamin Gaudreau POP B 12.00 30.00
80 Joshua Roy POP B 12.00 30.00
81 Thomas Milic POP A 8.00 20.00
82 Colby Barlow POP B 10.00 25.00
83 Tristan Bertucci POP C 10.00 25.00
84 Angus MacDonell POP B 10.00 25.00
85 Alex Pharand POP B 10.00 25.00
86 Tanner Howe POP B 12.00 30.00
87 Caden Price POP B 10.00 25.00
88 Andrew Gibson POP B 12.00 30.00
89 Andrew Cristall POP B 12.00 30.00
90 Porter Martone POP A 25.00 60.00
91 Cameron Allen POP A 12.00 30.00
92 Berkly Catton POP B 25.00 60.00
93 Carter Yakemchuk POP A 10.00 25.00
94 Nick Lardis POP A 10.00 25.00
95 Calum Ritchie POP A 12.00 30.00
96 Lukas Dragicevic POP A 15.00 40.00
98 Quinton Burns POP A 10.00 25.00
100 Ty Halaburda POP A 10.00 25.00
104 Tanner Howe POE 12.00 30.00
109 Gabriel D'Aigle POE 25.00 60.00
111 Quinton Burns POE 10.00 25.00
116 Tristan Bertucci POE 10.00 25.00
120 Calum Ritchie POE 12.00 30.00
122 Alex Pharand POE 10.00 25.00
124 Olen Zellweger POE 12.00 30.00
131 Tyson Hinds POE 10.00 25.00
132 Carson Bjarnason POE 10.00 25.00
136 Cameron Allen POE 12.00 30.00

2023-24 Upper Deck Team Canada Juniors Skating the Wave

SW1 Porter Martone 20.00 50.00
SW2 Joshua Roy 10.00 25.00
SW3 Marie-Philip Poulin 25.00 60.00
SW4 Tanner Howe 10.00 25.00
SW5 Carson Bjarnason 8.00 20.00
SW6 Jack Matier 8.00 20.00
SW7 Zach Dean 8.00 20.00
SW8 Lukas Dragicevic 12.00 30.00
SW9 Ethan Del Mastro 8.00 20.00
SW10 Macklin Celebrini 30.00 80.00
SW11 Zack Ostapchuk 10.00 25.00
SW12 Gabriel D'Aigle 20.00 50.00
SW13 Colby Barlow 8.00 20.00
SW14 Caedan Bankier 8.00 20.00
SW15 Brennan Othmann 10.00 25.00
SW16 Angus MacDonell 8.00 20.00
SW17 Berkly Catton 20.00 50.00
SW18 Ty Halaburda 8.00 20.00
SW19 Jocelyne Larocque 8.00 20.00
SW20 Riley Heidt 12.00 30.00
SW21 Caden Price 8.00 20.00
SW22 Jamie Lee Rattray 10.00 25.00
SW23 Nick Lardis 8.00 20.00
SW24 Tristan Bertucci 8.00 20.00
SW25 Nolan Allan 10.00 25.00
SW26 Danielle Serdachny 8.00 20.00
SW27 Reid Schaefer 10.00 25.00
SW28 Tyson Hinds 8.00 20.00
SW29 Calum Ritchie 10.00 25.00
SW30 Claire Thompson 8.00 20.00
SW31 Emily Clark 15.00 40.00
SW32 Cameron Allen 10.00 25.00
SW33 Rebecca Johnston 8.00 20.00
SW34 Benjamin Gaudreau 10.00 25.00
SW35 Alex Pharand 8.00 20.00
SW36 Thomas Milic 6.00 15.00
SW37 Carter Yakemchuk 10.00 25.00
SW38 Olen Zellweger 10.00 25.00
SW39 Emma Maltais 15.00 40.00
SW40 Quinton Burns 8.00 20.00
SW41 Andrew Gibson 10.00 25.00
SW42 Connor Bedard 50.00 125.00
SW43 Micah Zandee-Hart 10.00 25.00
SW44 Nathan Gaucher 10.00 25.00
SW45 Logan Stankoven 20.00 50.00
SW46 Kevin Korchinski 12.00 30.00
SW47 Andrew Cristall 10.00 25.00
SW48 Kristin O'Neill 8.00 20.00
SW49 Matthew Wood 8.00 20.00
SW50 Adam Fantilli 25.00 60.00

2023-24 Upper Deck Team Canada Juniors Team Canada FX

FX1 Nolan Allan 8.00 20.00
FX2 Thomas Milic 5.00 12.00
FX3 Zack Ostapchuk 8.00 20.00
FX4 Brianne Jenner 10.00 25.00
FX5 Cameron Allen 8.00 20.00
FX6 Sarah Nurse 15.00 40.00
FX7 Kevin Korchinski 10.00 25.00
FX8 Zach Dean 6.00 15.00
FX9 Reid Schaefer 8.00 20.00
FX10 Adam Fantilli 20.00 50.00
FX11 Matthew Wood 6.00 15.00
FX12 Berkly Catton 15.00 40.00
FX13 Andrew Cristall 8.00 20.00
FX14 Brennan Othmann 8.00 20.00
FX15 Nathan Gaucher 8.00 20.00
FX16 Tanner Howe 8.00 20.00
FX17 Connor Bedard 60.00 150.00
FX18 Ann-Renee Desbiens 15.00 40.00
FX19 Macklin Celebrini 25.00 60.00
FX20 Calum Ritchie 8.00 20.00

2024-25 Upper Deck Team Canada Juniors

1 Jake Furlong .50 1.25
2 Oliver Bonk .50 1.25
3 Maveric Lamoureux .75 2.00
4 Carson Rehkopf .50 1.25
5 Matthew Wood .50 1.25
6 Jordan Dumais .75 2.00
7 Denton Mateychuk 1.00 2.50
8 Nate Danielson .75 2.00
9 Brayden Yager .75 2.00
10 Samuel St-Hilaire .40 1.00
11 Macklin Celebrini 2.50 6.00
12 Noah Warren .75 2.00
13 Easton Cowan 1.50 4.00
14 Owen Allard .50 1.25
15 Conor Geekie 1.00 2.50
16 Ty Nelson .60 1.50
17 Mathis Rousseau .40 1.00
18 Jorian Donovan .60 1.50
19 Carter George .40 1.00
20 Porter Martone 1.25 3.00
21 Ryder Ritchie .60 1.50
22 Ollie Josephson .40 1.00
23 Caleb Desnoyers 1.50 4.00
24 Liam Greentree .60 1.50
25 Matthew Schaefer 1.50 4.00
26 Ryerson Leenders .50 1.25
27 Tij Iginla 1.00 2.50
28 Carson Wetsch .50 1.25
29 Jack Ivankovic .75 2.00
30 Charlie Elick .40 1.00
31 Kashawn Aitcheson .50 1.25
32 Henry Mews .50 1.25
33 Marek Vanacker .50 1.25
34 Cole Beaudoin .60 1.50
35 Spencer Gill .60 1.50
36 Gavin McKenna 2.00 5.00
37 Jett Luchanko 1.00 2.50
38 Malcolm Spence .60 1.50
39 Frankie Marrelli .50 1.25
40 Maxim Masse .75 2.00
41 Harrison Brunicke .75 2.00
42 Denton Mateychuk 1.00 2.50
43 Maveric Lamoureux .75 2.00
44 Oliver Bonk .50 1.25
45 Macklin Celebrini 2.50 6.00
46 Nate Danielson .75 2.00
47 Brayden Yager .75 2.00
48 Owen Allard .50 1.25
49 Conor Geekie 1.00 2.50
50 Carson Rehkopf .50 1.25
51 Matthew Wood .50 1.25
52 Jake Furlong .50 1.25
53 Noah Warren .75 2.00
54 Jordan Dumais .75 2.00
55 Ty Nelson .60 1.50
56 Easton Cowan 1.50 4.00
57 Mathis Rousseau .40 1.00
58 Maxim Masse .75 2.00
59 Porter Martone 1.25 3.00
60 Gavin McKenna 2.00 5.00
61 Henry Mews .50 1.25
62 Carter George .40 1.00
63 Ryder Ritchie .60 1.50
64 Jett Luchanko 1.00 2.50
65 Caleb Desnoyers 1.50 4.00
66 Cole Beaudoin .60 1.50
67 Tij Iginla 1.00 2.50
68 Malcolm Spence .60 1.50
69 Matthew Schaefer 1.50 4.00
70 Macklin Celebrini POP 2.50 6.00
71 Jordan Dumais POP .75 2.00
72 Ty Nelson POP .60 1.50
73 Carson Rehkopf POP .50 1.25
74 Denton Mateychuk POP 1.00 2.50
75 Mathis Rousseau POP .40 1.00
76 Nate Danielson POP .75 2.00
77 Matthew Wood POP .50 1.25
78 Oliver Bonk POP .50 1.25
79 Owen Allard POP .50 1.25
80 Brayden Yager POP .75 2.00
81 Easton Cowan POP 1.50 4.00
82 Conor Geekie POP 1.00 2.50
83 Jett Luchanko POP 1.00 2.50
84 Ryder Ritchie POP .60 1.50
85 Matthew Schaefer POP 1.50 4.00
86 Cole Beaudoin POP .60 1.50
87 Gavin McKenna POP 2.00 5.00
88 Porter Martone POP 1.25 3.00
89 Ollie Josephson POP .40 1.00
90 Carson Wetsch POP .50 1.25
91 Caleb Desnoyers POP 1.50 4.00
92 Tij Iginla POP 1.00 2.50
93 Malcolm Spence POP .60 1.50
94 Henry Mews POP .50 1.25
95 Kashawn Aitcheson POP .50 1.25
96 Maxim Masse POP .75 2.00
97 Harrison Brunicke POP .75 2.00
98 Liam Greentree POP .60 1.50
99 Carter George POP .40 1.00
100 Charlie Elick POP .40 1.00
101 Samuel St-Hilaire POE .40 1.00
102 Denton Mateychuk POE 1.00 2.50
103 Oliver Bonk POE .50 1.25
104 Matthew Wood POE .50 1.25
105 Owen Allard POE .50 1.25
106 Carson Rehkopf POE .50 1.25
107 Jordan Dumais POE .75 2.00
108 Ty Nelson POE .60 1.50
109 Brayden Yager POE .75 2.00
110 Jake Furlong POE .50 1.25
111 Macklin Celebrini POE 2.50 6.00
112 Noah Warren POE .75 2.00
113 Maveric Lamoureux POE .75 2.00
114 Jorian Donovan POE .60 1.50
115 Conor Geekie POE 1.00 2.50
116 Easton Cowan POE 1.50 4.00
117 Nate Danielson POE .75 2.00
118 Mathis Rousseau POE .40 1.00
119 Tij Iginla POE 1.00 2.50
120 Malcolm Spence POE .60 1.50
121 Caleb Desnoyers POE 1.50 4.00
122 Ryder Ritchie POE .60 1.50
123 Gavin McKenna POE 2.00 5.00
124 Ollie Josephson POE .40 1.00
125 Roger McQueen POE .60 1.50
126 Maxim Masse POE .75 2.00
127 Porter Martone POE 1.25 3.00
128 Carter George POE .40 1.00
129 Ryerson Leenders POE .50 1.25
130 Kashawn Aitcheson POE .50 1.25
131 Harrison Brunicke POE .75 2.00
132 Frankie Marrelli POE .50 1.25
133 Cole Beaudoin POE .60 1.50
134 Spencer Gill POE .60 1.50
135 Matthew Schaefer POE 1.50 4.00
136 Jett Luchanko POE 1.00 2.50
137 Charlie Elick POE .40 1.00
138 Henry Mews POE .50 1.25
139 Liam Greentree POE .60 1.50
140 Carson Wetsch POE .50 1.25
141 Marek Vanacker POE .50 1.25
142 Brayden Yager POE .75 2.00
143 Porter Martone POE 1.25 3.00
144 Easton Cowan POE 1.50 4.00
145 Carter George POE .40 1.00
146 Conor Geekie POE 1.00 2.50
147 Tij Iginla POE 1.00 2.50
148 Mathis Rousseau POE .40 1.00
149 Gavin McKenna POE 2.00 5.00
150 Macklin Celebrini POE 2.50 6.00

2024-25 Upper Deck Team Canada Juniors Clear Cut

*CLEAR CUT: 3X TO 8X BASIC
36 Gavin McKenna 50.00 125.00
60 Gavin McKenna 50.00 125.00
87 Gavin McKenna POP 50.00 125.00
123 Gavin McKenna POE 50.00 125.00
149 Gavin McKenna POE 50.00 125.00

2024-25 Upper Deck Team Canada Juniors Exclusives

*EXCLUSIVES/100: 4X TO 10X BASIC

2024-25 Upper Deck Team Canada Juniors Metal

*METAL: 4X TO 10X BASIC

2024-25 Upper Deck Team Canada Juniors Outburst

*OUTBURST: 3X TO 8X BASIC
11 Macklin Celebrini 25.00 60.00
36 Gavin McKenna 40.00 100.00
45 Macklin Celebrini 25.00 60.00
60 Gavin McKenna 40.00 100.00
70 Macklin Celebrini POP 25.00 60.00
87 Gavin McKenna POP 40.00 100.00

2024-25 Upper Deck Team Canada Juniors Outburst Red

*OUT RED/25: 6X TO 15X BASIC
11 Macklin Celebrini 50.00 125.00
25 Matthew Schaefer 15.00 40.00
45 Macklin Celebrini 50.00 125.00
69 Matthew Schaefer 15.00 40.00
70 Macklin Celebrini POP 50.00 125.00
85 Matthew Schaefer POP 15.00 40.00

2024-25 Upper Deck Team Canada Juniors Patterned Foilboard

*PAT FOIL: .8X TO 2X BASIC

2024-25 Upper Deck Team Canada Juniors Patterned Foilboard Blue

*PAT FOIL BLUE: 2X TO 5X BASIC

2024-25 Upper Deck Team Canada Juniors Patterned Foilboard Gold

*PAT FOIL GOLD/25: 6X TO 15X BASIC
11 Macklin Celebrini 50.00 125.00
36 Gavin McKenna 60.00 150.00
45 Macklin Celebrini 50.00 125.00
60 Gavin McKenna 60.00 150.00
70 Macklin Celebrini POP 50.00 125.00
87 Gavin McKenna POP 60.00 150.00

2024-25 Upper Deck Team Canada Juniors Patterned Foilboard Purple

*PAT FOIL PURPLE: 1X TO 2.5X BASIC

2024-25 Upper Deck Team Canada Juniors Red Foil

*RED: .5X TO 1.2X BASIC

2024-25 Upper Deck Team Canada Juniors Rose Gold Foil

*ROSE GOLD: .6X TO 1.5X BASIC

2024-25 Upper Deck Team Canada Juniors Bound for Greatness

BG1 Noah Warren 2.50 6.00
BG2 Matthew Wood 1.50 4.00
BG3 Conor Geekie 3.00 8.00
BG4 Easton Cowan 5.00 12.00
BG5 Scott Ratzlaff 1.50 4.00
BG6 Macklin Celebrini 8.00 20.00
BG7 Nate Danielson 2.50 6.00
BG8 Oliver Bonk 1.50 4.00
BG9 Carson Rehkopf 1.50 4.00
BG10 Mathis Rousseau 1.25 3.00
BG11 Denton Mateychuk 3.00 8.00
BG12 Brayden Yager 2.50 6.00
BG13 Jordan Dumais 2.50 6.00
BG14 Ty Nelson 2.00 5.00
BG15 Owen Allard 1.50 4.00
BG16 Jake Furlong 1.50 4.00
BG17 Maveric Lamoureux 2.50 6.00
BG18 Samuel St-Hilaire 1.25 3.00
BG19 Jorian Donovan 2.00 5.00
BG20 Matthew Wood 1.50 4.00
BG21 Conor Geekie 3.00 8.00
BG22 Easton Cowan 5.00 12.00
BG23 Macklin Celebrini 8.00 20.00
BG24 Nate Danielson 2.50 6.00
BG25 Brayden Yager 2.50 6.00

2024-25 Upper Deck Team Canada Juniors Future Stardom

*RED: .6X TO 1.5X BASIC
FS1 Macklin Celebrini 15.00 40.00
FS2 Samuel St-Hilaire 2.50 6.00
FS3 Carson Rehkopf 3.00 8.00
FS4 Noah Warren 5.00 12.00
FS5 Jorian Donovan 4.00 10.00
FS6 Matthew Wood 3.00 8.00
FS7 Brayden Yager 5.00 12.00
FS8 Nate Danielson 5.00 12.00
FS9 Ty Nelson 4.00 10.00
FS10 Jordan Dumais 5.00 12.00
FS11 Easton Cowan 10.00 25.00
FS12 Mathis Rousseau 2.50 6.00
FS13 Owen Allard 2.50 6.00
FS14 Jake Furlong 3.00 8.00
FS15 Maveric Lamoureux 5.00 12.00
FS16 Conor Geekie 6.00 15.00
FS17 Oliver Bonk 3.00 8.00
FS18 Denton Mateychuk 6.00 15.00
FS19 Gavin McKenna 12.00 30.00
FS20 Jett Luchanko 6.00 15.00
FS21 Matthew Schaefer 10.00 25.00
FS22 Spencer Gill 4.00 10.00
FS23 Tij Iginla 6.00 15.00
FS24 Charlie Elick 2.50 6.00
FS25 Maxim Masse 5.00 12.00
FS26 Harrison Brunicke 5.00 12.00
FS27 Ryerson Leenders 3.00 8.00
FS28 Caleb Desnoyers 10.00 25.00
FS29 Marek Vanacker 3.00 8.00
FS30 Cole Beaudoin 4.00 10.00
FS31 Ryder Ritchie 4.00 10.00
FS32 Henry Mews 3.00 8.00
FS33 Frankie Marrelli 3.00 8.00
FS34 Porter Martone 8.00 20.00
FS35 Carter George 2.50 6.00
FS36 Malcolm Spence 4.00 10.00
FS37 Liam Greentree 4.00 10.00
FS38 Ollie Josephson 2.50 6.00
FS39 Roger McQueen 4.00 10.00
FS40 Carson Wetsch 3.00 8.00
FS41 Kashawn Aitcheson 3.00 8.00
FS42 Brayden Yager 5.00 12.00
FS43 Carter George 2.50 6.00
FS44 Nate Danielson 5.00 12.00
FS45 Gavin McKenna 12.00 30.00
FS46 Easton Cowan 10.00 25.00
FS47 Tij Iginla 6.00 15.00
FS48 Macklin Celebrini 15.00 40.00
FS49 Porter Martone 8.00 20.00
FS50 Conor Geekie 6.00 15.00

2024-25 Upper Deck Team Canada Juniors Jerseys

1 Jake Furlong 2.00 5.00
2 Oliver Bonk 2.00 5.00
3 Maveric Lamoureux 3.00 8.00
4 Carson Rehkopf 2.00 5.00
5 Matthew Wood 2.00 5.00
6 Jordan Dumais 3.00 8.00
7 Denton Mateychuk 4.00 10.00
8 Nate Danielson 3.00 8.00
9 Brayden Yager 3.00 8.00
10 Samuel St-Hilaire 1.50 4.00
11 Macklin Celebrini 10.00 25.00
12 Noah Warren 3.00 8.00
13 Easton Cowan 6.00 15.00
14 Owen Allard 2.00 5.00
15 Conor Geekie 4.00 10.00
16 Ty Nelson 2.50 6.00
17 Mathis Rousseau 1.50 4.00
18 Jorian Donovan 2.50 6.00
19 Carter George 1.50 4.00
20 Porter Martone 5.00 12.00
21 Ryder Ritchie 2.50 6.00
22 Ollie Josephson 1.50 4.00
23 Caleb Desnoyers 6.00 15.00
24 Liam Greentree 2.50 6.00
25 Matthew Schaefer 6.00 15.00
26 Ryerson Leenders 2.00 5.00
27 Tij Iginla 4.00 10.00
28 Carson Wetsch 2.00 5.00
29 Jack Ivankovic 3.00 8.00
30 Charlie Elick 1.50 4.00
31 Kashawn Aitcheson 2.00 5.00
32 Henry Mews 2.00 5.00
33 Marek Vanacker 2.00 5.00
34 Cole Beaudoin 2.50 6.00
35 Spencer Gill 2.50 6.00
36 Gavin McKenna 8.00 20.00
37 Jett Luchanko 4.00 10.00
38 Malcolm Spence 2.50 6.00
39 Frankie Marrelli 2.00 5.00
40 Maxim Masse 3.00 8.00
41 Harrison Brunicke 3.00 8.00
42 Denton Mateychuk 4.00 10.00
43 Maveric Lamoureux 3.00 8.00
44 Oliver Bonk 2.00 5.00
45 Macklin Celebrini 10.00 25.00
46 Nate Danielson 3.00 8.00
47 Brayden Yager 3.00 8.00
48 Owen Allard 2.00 5.00
49 Conor Geekie 4.00 10.00
50 Carson Rehkopf 2.00 5.00
51 Matthew Wood 2.00 5.00
52 Jake Furlong 2.00 5.00
53 Noah Warren 3.00 8.00
54 Jordan Dumais 3.00 8.00
55 Ty Nelson 2.50 6.00
56 Easton Cowan 6.00 15.00
57 Mathis Rousseau 1.50 4.00
58 Maxim Masse 3.00 8.00
59 Porter Martone 5.00 12.00
60 Gavin McKenna 8.00 20.00
61 Henry Mews 2.00 5.00
62 Carter George 1.50 4.00
63 Ryder Ritchie 2.50 6.00
64 Jett Luchanko 4.00 10.00
65 Caleb Desnoyers 6.00 15.00
66 Cole Beaudoin 2.50 6.00
67 Tij Iginla 4.00 10.00
68 Malcolm Spence 2.50 6.00
69 Matthew Schaefer 6.00 15.00
70 Macklin Celebrini POP 10.00 25.00
71 Jordan Dumais POP 3.00 8.00
72 Ty Nelson POP 2.50 6.00
73 Carson Rehkopf POP 2.00 5.00
74 Denton Mateychuk POP 4.00 10.00
75 Mathis Rousseau POP 1.50 4.00
76 Nate Danielson POP 3.00 8.00
77 Matthew Wood POP 2.00 5.00
78 Oliver Bonk POP 2.00 5.00
79 Owen Allard POP 2.00 5.00
80 Brayden Yager POP 3.00 8.00
81 Easton Cowan POP 6.00 15.00
82 Conor Geekie POP 4.00 10.00
83 Jett Luchanko POP 4.00 10.00
84 Ryder Ritchie POP 2.50 6.00
85 Matthew Schaefer POP 6.00 15.00
86 Cole Beaudoin POP 2.50 6.00
87 Gavin McKenna POP 20.00 50.00
88 Porter Martone POP 5.00 12.00
89 Ollie Josephson POP 1.50 4.00
90 Carson Wetsch POP 2.00 5.00
91 Caleb Desnoyers POP 6.00 15.00
92 Tij Iginla POP 4.00 10.00
93 Malcolm Spence POP 2.50 6.00
94 Henry Mews POP 2.00 5.00
95 Kashawn Aitcheson POP 2.00 5.00
96 Maxim Masse POP 3.00 8.00
97 Harrison Brunicke POP 3.00 8.00
98 Liam Greentree POP 2.50 6.00
99 Carter George POP 1.50 4.00
100 Charlie Elick POP 1.50 4.00

2024-25 Upper Deck Team Canada Juniors Patch Autographs

1 Jake Furlong/175 12.00 30.00
2 Oliver Bonk/175 12.00 30.00
3 Maveric Lamoureux/175 20.00 50.00
4 Carson Rehkopf/175 12.00 30.00
5 Matthew Wood/175 12.00 30.00
6 Jordan Dumais/175 20.00 50.00
7 Denton Mateychuk/175 25.00 60.00
8 Nate Danielson/175 20.00 50.00
9 Brayden Yager/125 20.00 50.00
10 Samuel St-Hilaire/175 10.00 25.00
11 Macklin Celebrini/125 150.00 400.00
12 Noah Warren/175 20.00 50.00
13 Easton Cowan/125 40.00 100.00
14 Owen Allard/175 12.00 30.00
15 Conor Geekie/175 25.00 60.00
16 Ty Nelson/175 15.00 40.00
17 Mathis Rousseau/175 10.00 25.00
18 Jorian Donovan/175 15.00 40.00
19 Carter George/125 10.00 25.00
20 Porter Martone/175 30.00 80.00
21 Ryder Ritchie/175 15.00 40.00
22 Ollie Josephson/175 10.00 25.00
23 Caleb Desnoyers/175 40.00 100.00
24 Liam Greentree/175 15.00 40.00
25 Matthew Schaefer/175 40.00 100.00
26 Ryerson Leenders/175 12.00 30.00
27 Tij Iginla/125 25.00 60.00
28 Carson Wetsch/175 12.00 30.00
29 Jack Ivankovic/175 20.00 50.00
30 Charlie Elick/175 10.00 25.00
31 Kashawn Aitcheson/175 12.00 30.00
32 Henry Mews/175 12.00 30.00
33 Marek Vanacker/175 12.00 30.00
34 Cole Beaudoin/175 15.00 40.00
35 Spencer Gill/175 15.00 40.00
36 Gavin McKenna/125 50.00 125.00
37 Jett Luchanko/175 25.00 60.00
39 Frankie Marrelli/175 12.00 30.00
40 Maxim Masse/175 20.00 50.00
41 Harrison Brunicke/175 20.00 50.00
42 Denton Mateychuk/175 25.00 60.00
44 Oliver Bonk/175 12.00 30.00
46 Nate Danielson/175 20.00 50.00
47 Brayden Yager/175 20.00 50.00
48 Owen Allard/175 12.00 30.00
49 Conor Geekie/175 25.00 60.00
51 Matthew Wood/175 12.00 30.00
52 Jake Furlong/175 12.00 30.00
53 Noah Warren/175 20.00 50.00
54 Jordan Dumais/175 20.00 50.00
56 Easton Cowan/175 40.00 100.00
57 Mathis Rousseau/175 10.00 25.00
58 Maxim Masse/175 20.00 50.00
59 Porter Martone/175 30.00 80.00
60 Gavin McKenna/175 50.00 125.00
61 Henry Mews/175 12.00 30.00
62 Carter George/175 10.00 25.00
63 Ryder Ritchie/175 15.00 40.00
64 Jett Luchanko/175 25.00 60.00
65 Caleb Desnoyers/175 40.00 100.00
66 Cole Beaudoin/175 15.00 40.00
69 Matthew Schaefer/175 40.00 100.00
71 Jordan Dumais POP/25 30.00 80.00
72 Ty Nelson POP/25 25.00 60.00
73 Carson Rehkopf POP/25 20.00 50.00
74 Denton Mateychuk POP/25 40.00 100.00
75 Mathis Rousseau POP/25 15.00 40.00
76 Nate Danielson POP/25 30.00 80.00
77 Matthew Wood POP/25 20.00 50.00
78 Oliver Bonk POP/25 20.00 50.00
79 Owen Allard POP/25 20.00 50.00
80 Brayden Yager POP/25 30.00 80.00
81 Easton Cowan POP/25 60.00 150.00
82 Conor Geekie POP/25 40.00 100.00
83 Jett Luchanko POP/25 40.00 100.00
84 Ryder Ritchie POP/25 25.00 60.00
85 Matthew Schaefer POP/25 60.00 150.00
86 Cole Beaudoin POP/25 25.00 60.00
87 Gavin McKenna POP/25 80.00 200.00
88 Porter Martone POP/25 50.00 120.00
89 Ollie Josephson POP/25 15.00 40.00
90 Carson Wetsch POP/25 20.00 50.00
91 Caleb Desnoyers POP/25 60.00 150.00
92 Tij Iginla POP/25 40.00 100.00
94 Henry Mews POP/25 20.00 50.00
95 Kashawn Aitcheson POP/25 20.00 50.00
96 Maxim Masse POP/25 30.00 80.00
97 Harrison Brunicke POP/25 30.00 80.00
98 Liam Greentree POP/25 25.00 60.00
99 Carter George POP/25 15.00 40.00
100 Charlie Elick POP/25 15.00 40.00

2024-25 Upper Deck Team Canada Juniors Prospectus Momentous

*RED/399: .6X TO 1.5X BASIC
*BLUE/199: .8X TO 2X BASIC
*PINK/99: 1X TO 2.5X BASIC
*GOLD/65: 1.5X TO 4X BASIC
*ORANGE/35: 2X TO 5X BASIC
PM1 Easton Cowan 3.00 8.00
PM2 Jorian Donovan 1.25 3.00
PM3 Matthew Wood 1.00 2.50
PM4 Ty Nelson 1.25 3.00
PM5 Conor Geekie 2.00 5.00
PM6 Oliver Bonk 1.00 2.50
PM7 Maveric Lamoureux 1.50 4.00
PM8 Jordan Dumais 1.50 4.00
PM9 Nate Danielson 1.50 4.00
PM10 Denton Mateychuk 2.00 5.00
PM11 Carson Rehkopf 1.00 2.50
PM12 Macklin Celebrini 5.00 12.00
PM13 Jake Furlong 1.00 2.50
PM14 Brayden Yager 1.50 4.00
PM15 Noah Warren 1.50 4.00
PM16 Spencer Gill 1.25 3.00
PM17 Liam Greentree 1.25 3.00
PM18 Marek Vanacker 1.00 2.50
PM19 Frankie Marrelli 1.00 2.50
PM20 Carter George .75 2.00
PM21 Henry Mews 1.00 2.50
PM22 Kashawn Aitcheson 1.00 2.50
PM23 Jett Luchanko 2.00 5.00
PM24 Maxim Masse 1.50 4.00
PM25 Roger McQueen 1.25 3.00
PM26 Charlie Elick .75 2.00
PM27 Ollie Josephson .75 2.00
PM28 Harrison Brunicke 1.50 4.00
PM29 Matthew Schaefer 3.00 8.00
PM30 Caleb Desnoyers 3.00 8.00
PM31 Porter Martone 2.50 6.00
PM32 Ryerson Leenders 1.00 2.50
PM33 Gavin McKenna 4.00 10.00
PM34 Malcolm Spence 1.25 3.00
PM35 Cole Beaudoin 1.25 3.00
PM36 Ryder Ritchie 1.25 3.00
PM37 Carson Wetsch 1.00 2.50
PM38 Tij Iginla 2.00 5.00
PM39 Maveric Lamoureux 1.50 4.00
PM40 Denton Mateychuk 2.00 5.00
PM41 Oliver Bonk 1.00 2.50
PM42 Carter George .75 2.00
PM43 Matthew Wood 1.00 2.50
PM44 Brayden Yager 1.50 4.00
PM45 Macklin Celebrini 5.00 12.00
PM46 Tij Iginla 2.00 5.00
PM47 Conor Geekie 2.00 5.00
PM48 Nate Danielson 1.50 4.00
PM49 Gavin McKenna 4.00 10.00
PM50 Easton Cowan 3.00 8.00

2024-25 Upper Deck Team Canada Juniors Signatures

1 Jake Furlong SP 10.00 25.00
2 Oliver Bonk SP 10.00 25.00
3 Maveric Lamoureux SP 15.00 40.00
4 Carson Rehkopf SP 10.00 25.00
5 Matthew Wood SP 10.00 25.00
6 Jordan Dumais SP 15.00 40.00
7 Denton Mateychuk 20.00 50.00
8 Nate Danielson 15.00 40.00
9 Brayden Yager 15.00 40.00
10 Samuel St-Hilaire SP 8.00 20.00
11 Macklin Celebrini SP 80.00 200.00
12 Noah Warren SP 15.00 40.00
13 Easton Cowan SP 30.00 80.00
14 Owen Allard SP 10.00 25.00
15 Conor Geekie 20.00 50.00
16 Ty Nelson SP 12.00 30.00
17 Mathis Rousseau SP 8.00 20.00
18 Jorian Donovan SP 12.00 30.00
19 Carter George SP 8.00 20.00
20 Porter Martone 25.00 60.00
21 Ryder Ritchie 12.00 30.00
22 Ollie Josephson 8.00 20.00
23 Caleb Desnoyers 30.00 80.00
24 Liam Greentree 12.00 30.00
25 Matthew Schaefer 30.00 80.00
26 Ryerson Leenders 10.00 25.00
28 Carson Wetsch 10.00 25.00
29 Jack Ivankovic 15.00 40.00
30 Charlie Elick 8.00 20.00
31 Kashawn Aitcheson 10.00 25.00
32 Henry Mews 10.00 25.00
33 Marek Vanacker 10.00 25.00
34 Cole Beaudoin 12.00 30.00
35 Spencer Gill 12.00 30.00
36 Gavin McKenna 150.00 400.00
37 Jett Luchanko SP 20.00 50.00
39 Frankie Marrelli 10.00 25.00
40 Maxim Masse 15.00 40.00
41 Harrison Brunicke 15.00 40.00
61 Henry Mews 10.00 25.00
62 Carter George SP 8.00 20.00
70 Macklin Celebrini POP 80.00 200.00
73 Carson Rehkopf POP 10.00 25.00
77 Matthew Wood POP SP 10.00 25.00
80 Brayden Yager POP 15.00 40.00
82 Conor Geekie POP 20.00 50.00
83 Jett Luchanko POP SP 20.00 50.00
85 Matthew Schaefer POP 30.00 80.00
86 Cole Beaudoin POP 12.00 30.00
89 Ollie Josephson POP 8.00 20.00
90 Carson Wetsch POP 10.00 25.00
91 Caleb Desnoyers POP 30.00 80.00
94 Henry Mews POP 10.00 25.00
95 Kashawn Aitcheson POP 10.00 25.00
96 Maxim Masse POP SP 15.00 40.00
97 Harrison Brunicke POP 15.00 40.00
98 Liam Greentree POP 12.00 30.00
100 Charlie Elick POP 8.00 20.00
101 Samuel St-Hilaire POE SP 8.00 20.00
102 Denton Mateychuk POE SP 20.00 50.00
104 Matthew Wood POE SP 10.00 25.00
106 Carson Rehkopf POE SP 10.00 25.00
108 Ty Nelson POE SP 12.00 30.00
109 Brayden Yager POE 15.00 40.00
110 Jake Furlong POE SP 10.00 25.00
111 Macklin Celebrini POE SP 80.00 200.00
112 Noah Warren POE SP 15.00 40.00
113 Maveric Lamoureux POE SP 15.00 40.00
115 Conor Geekie POE SP 20.00 50.00
117 Nate Danielson POE SP 15.00 40.00
118 Mathis Rousseau POE SP 8.00 20.00
121 Caleb Desnoyers POE 30.00 80.00
122 Ryder Ritchie POE 12.00 30.00
123 Gavin McKenna POE 150.00 400.00
124 Ollie Josephson POE 8.00 20.00
125 Roger McQueen POE 10.00 25.00
126 Maxim Masse POE 15.00 40.00
127 Porter Martone POE 25.00 60.00
128 Carter George POE 8.00 20.00
129 Ryerson Leenders POE 10.00 25.00
130 Kashawn Aitcheson POE 10.00 25.00
131 Harrison Brunicke POE 15.00 40.00
132 Frankie Marrelli POE 10.00 25.00
133 Cole Beaudoin POE 12.00 30.00
134 Spencer Gill POE 12.00 30.00
135 Matthew Schaefer POE 30.00 80.00
136 Jett Luchanko POE 20.00 50.00
137 Charlie Elick POE 8.00 20.00
138 Henry Mews POE 10.00 25.00
139 Liam Greentree POE 12.00 30.00
140 Carson Wetsch POE 10.00 25.00
141 Marek Vanacker POE 10.00 25.00
145 Carter George POE 8.00 20.00
146 Conor Geekie POE SP 20.00 50.00

2024-25 Upper Deck Team Canada Juniors Team Canada FX

FX1 Macklin Celebrini 30.00 80.00
FX2 Nate Danielson 10.00 25.00
FX3 Mathis Rousseau 5.00 12.00
FX4 Easton Cowan 20.00 50.00
FX5 Brayden Yager 10.00 25.00
FX6 Noah Warren 10.00 25.00
FX7 Jorian Donovan 8.00 20.00
FX8 Jake Furlong 6.00 15.00
FX9 Jordan Dumais 10.00 25.00
FX10 Matthew Wood 6.00 15.00
FX11 Oliver Bonk 6.00 15.00
FX12 Samuel St-Hilaire 5.00 12.00
FX13 Scott Ratzlaff 6.00 15.00
FX14 Conor Geekie 12.00 30.00
FX15 Maveric Lamoureux 10.00 25.00
FX16 Carson Rehkopf 6.00 15.00
FX17 Denton Mateychuk 12.00 30.00
FX18 Ty Nelson 8.00 20.00
FX19 Owen Allard 6.00 15.00
FX20 Easton Cowan 20.00 50.00
FX21 Matthew Wood 6.00 15.00
FX22 Conor Geekie 12.00 30.00
FX23 Nate Danielson 10.00 25.00
FX24 Brayden Yager 10.00 25.00
FX25 Macklin Celebrini 30.00 80.00

2024-25 Upper Deck Team Canada Juniors Team Canada Logo Metal Die-Cut

TC1 Maveric Lamoureux 12.00 30.00
TC2 Denton Mateychuk 15.00 40.00
TC3 Owen Allard 8.00 20.00
TC4 Carson Rehkopf 8.00 20.00
TC5 Samuel St-Hilaire 6.00 15.00
TC6 Jake Furlong 8.00 20.00
TC7 Macklin Celebrini 40.00 100.00
TC8 Noah Warren 12.00 30.00
TC9 Matthew Wood 8.00 20.00
TC10 Easton Cowan 25.00 60.00
TC11 Scott Ratzlaff 8.00 20.00
TC12 Ty Nelson 10.00 25.00
TC13 Jorian Donovan 10.00 25.00
TC14 Brayden Yager 12.00 30.00
TC15 Oliver Bonk 8.00 20.00
TC16 Jordan Dumais 12.00 30.00
TC17 Mathis Rousseau 6.00 15.00
TC18 Nate Danielson 12.00 30.00
TC19 Conor Geekie 15.00 40.00

2015-16 Upper Deck Tim Hortons

COMPLETE SET (100) 30.00 60.00
1 Tim Horton .50 1.25
2 Eric Staal .60 1.50
3 Andrew Hammond .60 1.50
4 Shea Weber .40 1.00
5 Mark Giordano .50 1.25
6 Bobby Ryan .40 1.00
7 Kyle Turris .40 1.00
8 Alexander Ovechkin 2.00 5.00
9 Tyler Johnson .30 .75
10 Corey Perry .75 2.00
11 Zach Parise .50 1.25
12 Jarome Iginla .60 1.50
13 Pavel Datsyuk .75 2.00
14 Jamie Benn .50 1.25
15 Ryan Getzlaf .50 1.25
16 Andrew Ladd .30 .75
17 Radim Vrbata .30 .75
18 Ryan Strome .50 1.25
19 Jonathan Toews .75 2.00
20 Alexander Steen .20 .50
21 James van Riemsdyk .40 1.00
22 Daniel Sedin .60 1.50
23 Sean Monahan .30 .75
24 Jiri Hudler .25 .60
25 Oliver Ekman-Larsson .50 1.25
26 Blake Wheeler .50 1.25
27 Matt Moulson .30 .75
28 Claude Giroux .50 1.25
29 Jason Pominville .30 .75
30 Henrik Lundqvist 1.25 3.00
31 Carey Price 1.00 2.50
32 Jonathan Quick .60 1.50
33 Henrik Sedin .60 1.50
34 Filip Forsberg .75 2.00
35 Pekka Rinne .60 1.50
36 Tuukka Rask .60 1.50
37 Patrice Bergeron .60 1.50
38 Bryan Little .40 1.00
39 Logan Couture .60 1.50
40 Henrik Zetterberg .60 1.50
41 Jaroslav Halak .50 1.25
42 Tyler Bozak .30 .75
43 Adam Henrique .40 1.00
44 Marian Hossa .50 1.25
45 Jonathan Bernier .40 1.00
46 Shane Doan .40 1.00
47 Taylor Hall .60 1.50
48 Brian Elliott .40 1.00
49 Vladimir Tarasenko .60 1.50
50 Corey Crawford .60 1.50
51 Teddy Purcell .30 .75
52 Aaron Ekblad .60 1.50
53 Jeff Skinner .60 1.50
54 Nicklas Backstrom .50 1.25
55 Roberto Luongo .75 2.00
56 Milan Lucic .40 1.00
57 Drew Doughty .60 1.50
58 Kris Letang .60 1.50

59 Gustav Nyquist .30 .75
60 Frederik Andersen .60 1.50
61 Rick Nash .50 1.25
62 Johnny Gaudreau .75 2.00
63 Tyler Ennis .30 .75
64 Marc-Andre Fleury 1.00 2.50
65 Erik Karlsson .60 1.50
66 Brian Gionta .30 .75
67 Max Pacioretty .50 1.25
68 Jaden Schwartz .60 1.50
69 Kyle Okposo .30 .75
70 Braden Holtby .60 1.50
71 Evgeni Malkin 1.00 2.50
72 Sergei Bobrovsky .75 2.00
73 Nick Foligno .40 1.00
74 Derick Brassard .30 .75
75 Nathan MacKinnon 2.00 5.00
76 P.K. Subban .60 1.50
77 Jeff Carter .40 1.00
78 Jordan Eberle .50 1.25
79 Kari Lehtonen .40 1.00
80 Ryan Johansen .40 1.00
81 Phil Kessel .50 1.25
82 Tomas Plekanec .30 .75
83 Anze Kopitar .75 2.00
84 Ryan Nugent-Hopkins .60 1.50
85 Steve Mason .40 1.00
86 Joe Pavelski .60 1.50
87 Sidney Crosby 2.00 5.00
88 Patrick Kane 1.00 2.50
89 Tyler Seguin .60 1.50
90 Steven Stamkos 1.00 2.50
91 John Tavares .75 2.00
92 Gabriel Landeskog .60 1.50
93 Jakub Voracek .40 1.00
94 Cory Schneider .50 1.25
95 Tomas Tatar .30 .75
96 Ryan Miller .50 1.25
97 Derek Stepan .30 .75
98 Devan Dubnyk .40 1.00
99 Dustin Byfuglien .50 1.25
100 Michael Cammalleri .40 1.00
SP1 Connor McDavid Draft 400.00 700.00
NNO Draft Pick/McDvd EXCH 400.00 700.00
SC S.Crosby AU/87 EXCH 1250.00 1750.00

2015-16 Upper Deck Tim Hortons Above the Ice

AIAO Alexander Ovechkin 10.00 25.00
AICG Claude Giroux 2.50 6.00
AICP Carey Price 5.00 12.00
AIDD Drew Doughty 3.00 8.00
AIEK Erik Karlsson 3.00 8.00
AIHL Henrik Lundqvist 6.00 15.00
AIHZ Henrik Zetterberg 3.00 8.00
AIJT John Tavares 4.00 10.00
AIPK Patrick Kane 5.00 12.00
AIRM Ryan Miller 2.50 6.00
AIRNH Ryan Nugent-Hopkins 3.00 8.00
AISC Sidney Crosby 10.00 25.00
AISS Steven Stamkos 5.00 12.00
AITS Tyler Seguin 3.00 8.00

2015-16 Upper Deck Tim Hortons Autographs

AAH Andrew Hammond EXCH 60.00 150.00
AAO Alexander Ovechkin EXCH 150.00 300.00
ABS Brayden Schenn EXCH 60.00 150.00
ACP Carey Price EXCH 350.00 450.00
ADP Dion Phaneuf EXCH 150.00 250.00
ADU Matt Duchene EXCH 100.00 250.00
AJI Jarome Iginla EXCH 60.00 150.00
AKH Kevin Hayes EXCH 60.00 150.00
ALB Lance Bouma EXCH 60.00 150.00
AMD Mathew Dumba EXCH 50.00 125.00
AMP Max Pacioretty EXCH 60.00 150.00
AMS Mark Scheifele EXCH 60.00 150.00
APH Patric Hornqvist EXCH 50.00 125.00
ARN Ryan Nugent-Hopkins EXCH 60.00 150.00
ASW Shea Weber EXCH 150.00 250.00

2015-16 Upper Deck Tim Hortons Die Cuts

COMPLETE SET (15) 8.00 20.00
TH1 Carey Price 1.25 3.00
TH2 Andrew Ladd .40 1.00
TH3 Jonathan Bernier .50 1.25
TH4 Erik Karlsson .75 2.00
TH5 Jordan Eberle .60 1.50
TH6 Jiri Hudler .50 1.25
TH7 Alexander Ovechkin 2.50 6.00
TH8 Henrik Lundqvist 1.50 4.00
TH9 John Tavares 1.00 2.50
TH10 Jonathan Toews 1.00 2.50
TH11 Sidney Crosby 2.50 6.00
TH12 Steven Stamkos 1.25 3.00
TH13 Zach Parise .60 1.50
TH14 Vladimir Tarasenko .75 2.00
TH15 Jamie Benn .60 1.50

2015-16 Upper Deck Tim Hortons Franchise Force

COMPLETE SET (12) 90.00 150.00
FF1 Mark Messier 8.00 20.00
FF2 Mario Lemieux 25.00 60.00
FF3 Patrick Roy 15.00 40.00
FF4 Johnny Gaudreau 10.00 25.00
FF5 Taylor Hall 6.00 15.00
FF6 Carey Price 12.00 30.00
FF7 Bobby Ryan 6.00 15.00
FF8 Phil Kessel 6.00 15.00
FF9 Ryan Miller 8.00 20.00
FF10 Blake Wheeler 6.00 15.00
FF11 Sidney Crosby 25.00 60.00
FF12 Alexander Ovechkin 25.00 60.00

2015-16 Upper Deck Tim Hortons Jerseys

JRAB Alexandre Burrows 8.00 20.00
JRAO Alexander Ovechkin 20.00 50.00
JRBW Blake Wheeler 12.00 30.00
JREK Erik Karlsson 15.00 40.00
JRHZ Henrik Zetterberg 15.00 40.00
JRJE Jordan Eberle 15.00 40.00
JRJG Johnny Gaudreau 15.00 40.00
JRJI Jarome Iginla 15.00 40.00
JRJP Jason Pominville 8.00 20.00
JRJT John Tavares 15.00 40.00
JRMM Matt Moulson 8.00 20.00
JRPK Phil Kessel 12.00 30.00
JRPS P.K. Subban 15.00 40.00
JRRJ Ryan Johansen 10.00 25.00
JRRN Rick Nash 12.00 30.00
JRSC Sidney Crosby 40.00 100.00
JRSS Steven Stamkos 15.00 40.00

2015-16 Upper Deck Tim Hortons Platinum Profiles

SS1 Mark Messier 8.00 20.00
SS2 Darryl Sittler 5.00 12.00
SS3 Peter Forsberg 8.00 20.00
SS4 Guy Lafleur 5.00 12.00
SS5 Theoren Fleury 5.00 12.00
SS6 Patrick Roy 10.00 25.00
SS7 Henrik Zetterberg 5.00 12.00
SS8 Alexander Ovechkin 15.00 40.00
SS9 John Tavares 6.00 15.00
SS10 Steven Stamkos 8.00 20.00
SS11 Henrik Lundqvist 10.00 25.00
SS12 Sidney Crosby 15.00 40.00

2015-16 Upper Deck Tim Hortons Season Highlights

COMPLETE SET (7) 2.00 5.00
SH1 Johnny Gaudreau .50 1.25
SH2 Jordan Eberle .30 .75
SH3 Carey Price .60 1.50
SH4 Erik Karlsson .40 1.00
SH5 James van Riemsdyk .25 .60
SH6 Bo Horvat .40 1.00
SH7 Ondrej Pavelec .30 .75

2015-16 Upper Deck Tim Hortons Shining Futures

COMPLETE SET (12) 10.00 25.00
SF1 Malcolm Subban 1.50 4.00
SF2 Kevin Fiala 1.25 3.00
SF3 Johnny Gaudreau 1.50 4.00
SF4 Vladimir Tarasenko 1.25 3.00
SF5 Nathan MacKinnon 4.00 10.00
SF6 Evgeny Kuznetsov 1.25 3.00
SF7 Ryan Johansen .75 2.00
SF8 Filip Forsberg 1.50 4.00
SF9 Aaron Ekblad 1.25 3.00
SF10 Mark Stone 1.25 3.00
SF11 Sean Monahan .60 1.50
SF12 Jacob de la Rose 1.00 2.50

2016-17 Upper Deck Tim Hortons

1 Tim Horton 1.00 2.50
2 Duncan Keith .40 1.00
3 Roberto Luongo .75 2.00
4 Taylor Hall .50 1.25
5 Aaron Ekblad .60 1.50
6 Joe Pavelski .60 1.50
7 Drew Doughty .60 1.50
8 Alex Ovechkin 2.00 5.00
9 Matt Duchene .50 1.25
10 Corey Perry .75 2.00
11 Anze Kopitar .75 2.00
12 Jarome Iginla .60 1.50
13 Pavel Datsyuk .75 2.00
14 Jamie Benn .50 1.25
15 Ryan Getzlaf .50 1.25
16 Max Domi .50 1.25
17 Wayne Simmonds .60 1.50
18 Bryan Little .40 1.00
19 Jonathan Toews .75 2.00
20 Brandon Saad .40 1.00
21 James van Riemsdyk .40 1.00
22 Daniel Sedin .60 1.50
23 Oliver Ekman-Larsson .50 1.25
24 Filip Forsberg .75 2.00
25 Mikko Koivu .40 1.00
26 Blake Wheeler .50 1.25
27 Alex Galchenyuk .30 .75
28 Claude Giroux .50 1.25
29 Nathan MacKinnon 2.00 5.00
30 Henrik Lundqvist 1.25 3.00
31 Carey Price 1.00 2.50
32 Jonathan Quick .60 1.50
33 Henrik Sedin .60 1.50
34 Dustin Byfuglien .50 1.25
35 Pekka Rinne .50 1.25
36 Cory Schneider .50 1.25
37 Patrice Bergeron .60 1.50
38 Boone Jenner .50 1.25
39 Tuukka Rask .60 1.50
40 Henrik Zetterberg .60 1.50
41 Jaroslav Halak .50 1.25
42 Devan Dubnyk .40 1.00
43 Nazem Kadri .60 1.50
44 Craig Anderson .50 1.25
45 Jonathan Bernier .40 1.00
46 David Krejci .50 1.25
47 Brayden Schenn .50 1.25
48 Zach Parise .50 1.25
49 Eric Staal .60 1.50
50 Johnny Gaudreau .75 2.00
51 Frans Nielsen .30 .75
52 Jeff Skinner .60 1.50
53 Bo Horvat .60 1.50
54 Adam Henrique .40 1.00
55 Justin Faulk .40 1.00
56 Robby Fabbri .30 .75
57 Rasmus Ristolainen .30 .75
58 P.A. Parenteau .30 .75
59 Roman Josi .50 1.25
60 Joe Thornton .75 2.00
61 Rick Nash .50 1.25
62 Mark Stone .60 1.50
63 Brad Marchand 1.00 2.50
64 Nicklas Backstrom .50 1.25
65 Erik Karlsson .60 1.50
66 Marc-Andre Fleury 1.00 2.50
67 Max Pacioretty .50 1.25
68 Jaromir Jagr 1.50 4.00
69 Mike Hoffman .30 .75
70 Braden Holtby .60 1.50
71 Evgeni Malkin 1.00 2.50
72 Artemi Panarin 1.00 2.50
73 Dylan Larkin .60 1.50
74 Sergei Bobrovsky .75 2.00
75 Alexander Steen .30 .75
76 P.K. Subban .60 1.50
77 Victor Hedman .60 1.50
78 Tomas Tatar .30 .75
79 Sean Monahan .30 .75
80 Sam Reinhart 1.00 2.50
81 Phil Kessel .50 1.25
82 Connor Hellebuyck 1.00 2.50
83 Ben Bishop .40 1.00
84 Ryan Miller .50 1.25
85 Karri Ramo .40 1.00
86 Cam Talbot .50 1.25
87 Sidney Crosby 2.00 5.00
88 Patrick Kane 1.00 2.50
89 Brent Burns .50 1.25
90 Evander Kane .50 1.25
91 Steven Stamkos 1.00 2.50
92 Evgeny Kuznetsov .60 1.50
93 Sam Bennett .75 2.00
94 Jason Spezza .50 1.25
95 Jordan Eberle .50 1.25
96 Jack Eichel .75 2.00
97 Connor McDavid 2.50 6.00
98 Tyler Seguin .60 1.50
99 John Tavares .75 2.00
100 Vladimir Tarasenko .60 1.50
DP1 Auston Matthews Draft 250.00 400.00

2016-17 Upper Deck Tim Hortons Clear Cut Phenoms

CC1 Max Domi 2.50 6.00
CC2 Jack Eichel 4.00 10.00
CC3 Sam Bennett 4.00 10.00
CC4 Artemi Panarin 5.00 12.00
CC5 Dylan Larkin 3.00 8.00
CC6 Connor McDavid 12.00 30.00
CC7 Alex Galchenyuk 1.50 4.00
CC8 Filip Forsberg 4.00 10.00
CC9 Mark Stone 3.00 8.00
CC10 Robby Fabbri 1.50 4.00
CC11 Nikita Kucherov 5.00 12.00
CC12 Shayne Gostisbehere 2.50 6.00
CC13 Bo Horvat 3.00 8.00
CC14 Nikolaj Ehlers 2.50 6.00

2016-17 Upper Deck Tim Hortons Franchise Force

FF1 Johnny Gaudreau 10.00 25.00
FF2 Jonathan Toews 10.00 25.00
FF3 Henrik Zetterberg 8.00 20.00
FF4 Connor McDavid 30.00 80.00
FF5 Carey Price 12.00 30.00
FF6 Henrik Lundqvist 15.00 40.00
FF7 Erik Karlsson 8.00 20.00
FF8 Sidney Crosby 25.00 60.00
FF9 Nazem Kadri 8.00 20.00
FF10 Ryan Miller 6.00 15.00
FF11 Alex Ovechkin 25.00 60.00
FF12 Dustin Byfuglien 6.00 15.00

2016-17 Upper Deck Tim Hortons Game Day Action

GDA1 Tuukka Rask 1.25 3.00
GDA2 Jack Eichel 1.50 4.00
GDA3 Johnny Gaudreau 1.50 4.00
GDA4 Jonathan Toews 1.50 4.00
GDA5 Jamie Benn 1.00 2.50
GDA6 Henrik Zetterberg 1.25 3.00
GDA7 Connor McDavid 5.00 12.00
GDA8 Carey Price 2.00 5.00
GDA9 Erik Karlsson 1.25 3.00
GDA10 Sidney Crosby 4.00 10.00
GDA11 Steven Stamkos 2.00 5.00
GDA12 Nazem Kadri 1.25 3.00
GDA13 Ryan Miller 1.00 2.50
GDA14 Alex Ovechkin 4.00 10.00
GDA15 Dustin Byfuglien 1.00 2.50

2016-17 Upper Deck Tim Hortons Local Leaders

LL1 Mark Giordano 1.00 2.50
LL2 Taylor Hall 1.00 2.50
LL3 Max Pacioretty 1.00 2.50
LL4 Erik Karlsson 1.25 3.00
LL5 Tyler Bozak .60 1.50
LL6 Henrik Sedin 1.25 3.00
LL7 Blake Wheeler 1.00 2.50

2016-17 Upper Deck Tim Hortons NHL Jersey Relic Cards

JAO Alexander Ovechkin 20.00 50.00
JCM Connor McDavid 40.00 100.00
JCP Carey Price 20.00 50.00
JDB Dustin Byfuglien 12.00 30.00
JDD Drew Doughty 15.00 40.00
JDK Duncan Keith 10.00 25.00
JDS Daniel Sedin 15.00 40.00
JEK Erik Karlsson 15.00 40.00
JHL Henrik Lundqvist 12.00 30.00
JJB Jonathan Bernier 10.00 25.00
JJE Jack Eichel 12.00 30.00
JJG Johnny Gaudreau 12.00 30.00
JNM Nathan MacKinnon 20.00 50.00
JPD Pavel Datsyuk 15.00 40.00
JRL Roberto Luongo 12.00 30.00
JSC Sidney Crosby 30.00 80.00
JSS Steven Stamkos 12.00 30.00
JZC Zdeno Chara 12.00 30.00

2016-17 Upper Deck Tim Hortons Platinum Profiles

PP1 Johnny Gaudreau 3.00 8.00
PP2 Jonathan Toews 3.00 8.00
PP3 Jarome Iginla 2.50 6.00
PP4 Pavel Datsyuk 3.00 8.00
PP5 Connor McDavid 10.00 25.00
PP6 Jaromir Jagr 6.00 15.00
PP7 Carey Price 4.00 10.00
PP8 Henrik Lundqvist 5.00 12.00
PP9 Erik Karlsson 2.50 6.00
PP10 James van Riemsdyk 1.50 4.00
PP11 Ryan Miller 2.00 5.00
PP12 Blake Wheeler 2.00 5.00

2016-17 Upper Deck Tim Hortons Pure Gold

PG1 Ryan Getzlaf 1.00 2.50
PG2 Patrice Bergeron 1.25 3.00
PG3 Sean Monahan .60 1.50
PG4 Patrick Kane 2.00 5.00
PG5 Tyler Seguin 1.25 3.00
PG6 Dylan Larkin 1.25 3.00
PG7 Jordan Eberle 1.00 2.50
PG8 Anze Kopitar 1.50 4.00
PG9 Zach Parise 1.00 2.50
PG10 Max Pacioretty 1.00 2.50
PG11 John Tavares 1.50 4.00
PG12 Rick Nash 1.00 2.50
PG13 Mike Hoffman .60 1.50
PG14 Daniel Sedin 1.25 3.00
PG15 Bryan Little .75 2.00

2016-17 Upper Deck Tim Hortons Timbits Autograps

2000 Nathan MacKinnon 500.00 800.00

2017-18 Upper Deck Tim Hortons

COMMON CARD .30 .75
SEMISTARS .40 1.00
UNLISTED STARS .50 1.25
1 Tim Horton .50 1.25
2 Duncan Keith .40 1.00
3 Charlie Coyle .50 1.25
4 Dougie Hamilton .40 1.00
5 Aaron Ekblad .60 1.50
6 Shea Weber .40 1.00
7 Joe Pavelski .60 1.50
8 Alexander Ovechkin 2.00 5.00
9 Taylor Hall .50 1.25
10 Corey Perry .75 2.00
11 Anze Kopitar .75 2.00
12 Cam Atkinson .50 1.25
13 Johnny Gaudreau .75 2.00
14 Jamie Benn .50 1.25
15 Jack Eichel .75 2.00
16 Mitch Marner .75 2.00
17 Ryan Kesler .50 1.25
18 Filip Forsberg .75 2.00
19 Jonathan Toews .75 2.00
20 Sebastian Aho .75 2.00
21 Kyle Okposo .30 .75
22 Daniel Sedin .60 1.50
23 Oliver Ekman-Larsson .50 1.25
24 Aleksander Barkov .75 2.00
25 William Nylander 1.00 2.50
26 Kyle Palmieri .40 1.00
27 Patrik Laine .60 1.50
28 Claude Giroux .50 1.25
29 Nathan MacKinnon 2.00 5.00
30 Henrik Lundqvist 1.25 3.00
31 Carey Price 1.00 2.50
32 Leon Draisaitl 1.50 4.00
33 Henrik Sedin .60 1.50
34 Auston Matthews 2.00 5.00
35 Josh Bailey .40 1.00
36 Matthew Tkachuk 1.00 2.50
37 Matt Duchene .50 1.25
38 Nikolaj Ehlers .50 1.25
39 Frederik Andersen .60 1.50
40 Henrik Zetterberg .60 1.50
41 Craig Anderson .50 1.25
42 Vincent Trocheck .50 1.25
43 Blake Wheeler .50 1.25
44 Mike Smith .50 1.25
45 Morgan Reilly .75 2.00
46 Devan Dubnyk .40 1.00
47 Sergei Bobrovsky .75 2.00
48 Matt Murray .75 2.00
49 Bo Horvat .60 1.50
50 Zach Werenski .75 2.00
51 Evgeny Kuznetsov .60 1.50
52 Eric Staal .60 1.50
53 Jeff Skinner .60 1.50
54 Patrice Bergeron .60 1.50
55 Mark Scheifele .75 2.00
56 Wayne Simmonds .60 1.50
57 Alex Galchenyuk .30 .75
58 Chris Kreider .60 1.50
59 Loui Eriksson .30 .75
60 Thomas Greiss .40 1.00
61 Mark Stone .60 1.50
62 Mike Hoffman .30 .75
63 Brad Marchand 1.00 2.50
64 Mikael Granlund .40 1.00
65 Erik Karlsson .60 1.50
66 Andreas Athanasiou .50 1.25
67 Max Pacioretty .50 1.25
68 Jaden Schwartz .60 1.50
69 Milan Lucic .50 1.25
70 Braden Holtby .60 1.50
71 Evgeni Malkin 1.00 2.50
72 Artemi Panarin 1.00 2.50
73 Dylan Larkin .60 1.50
74 Nicklas Backstrom .50 1.25
75 Phil Kessel .50 1.25
76 P.K. Subban .60 1.50
77 Jeff Carter .40 1.00
78 Drew Doughty .60 1.50
79 Dustin Byfuglien .50 1.25
80 Victor Hedman .60 1.50
81 Martin Jones .40 1.00
82 J.T. Miller .60 1.50
83 Tuukka Rask .60 1.50
84 Steven Stamkos 1.00 2.50
85 Colton Parayko .40 1.00
86 Nikita Kucherov 1.00 2.50
87 Sidney Crosby 2.00 5.00
88 Patrick Kane 1.00 2.50
89 Frans Nielsen .30 .75
90 Ryan O'Reilly .50 1.25
91 John Tavares .75 2.00
92 Ryan Johnson .40 1.00
93 Jakub Voracek .40 1.00
94 Sam Reinhart 1.00 2.50
95 Tyler Seguin .60 1.50
96 Sean Monahan .30 .75
97 Connor McDavid 2.50 6.00
98 David Pastrnak 1.25 3.00
99 Vladimir Tarasenko .60 1.50
100 Brent Burns .50 1.25

2017-18 Upper Deck Tim Hortons '17 NHL Draft NO.1 Draft Pick

DP1 Nico Hischier 150.00 250.00

2017-18 Upper Deck Tim Hortons Aaron Ekblad Timbits Autograph

1 Aaron Ekblad 500.00 600.00

2017-18 Upper Deck Tim Hortons Clear Cut Phenoms

COMMON CARD 1.50 4.00
SEMISTARS 2.00 5.00
UNLISTED STARS 2.50 6.00
CCP1 Connor McDavid 12.00 30.00
CCP2 Dylan Larkin 3.00 8.00
CCP3 Patrik Laine 3.00 8.00
CCP4 Jack Eichel 4.00 10.00
CCP5 Matthew Tkachuk 5.00 12.00
CCP6 Zach Werenski 4.00 10.00
CCP7 Mitch Marner 4.00 10.00
CCP8 William Nylander 5.00 12.00
CCP9 Thomas Chabot 2.50 6.00
CCP10 Nikolaj Ehlers 2.50 6.00
CCP11 Travis Konecny 2.50 6.00
CCP12 Matt Murray 4.00 10.00
CCP13 Colton Parayko 2.00 5.00
CCP14 Auston Matthews 10.00 25.00

2017-18 Upper Deck Tim Hortons Game Day Action

COMMON CARD .60 1.50
SEMISTARS .75 2.00
UNLISTED STARS 1.00 2.50
GDA1 Sidney Crosby 4.00 10.00
GDA2 Erik Karlsson 1.25 3.00
GDA3 Johnny Gaudreau 1.50 4.00
GDA4 Auston Matthews 4.00 10.00
GDA5 Tyler Seguin 1.25 3.00
GDA6 Bo Horvat 1.25 3.00
GDA7 Connor McDavid 5.00 12.00
GDA8 Max Pacioretty 1.00 2.50
GDA9 Brent Burns 1.00 2.50
GDA10 Mark Scheifele 1.50 4.00
GDA11 Aaron Ekblad 1.25 3.00
GDA12 Vladimir Tarasenko 1.25 3.00
GDA13 Mitch Marner 1.50 4.00
GDA14 Braden Holtby 1.25 3.00
GDA15 Alex Ovechkin 4.00 10.00

2017-18 Upper Deck Tim Hortons NHL Autograph Jersey

1 Brendan Gallagher 500.00 600.00
2 Bo Horvat 90.00 200.00
3 Mike Hoffman 90.00 200.00
5 Mats Zuccarello 350.00 450.00

2017-18 Upper Deck Tim Hortons NHL Jersey

1 Alex Ovechkin 60.00 150.00
2 Brent Burns 60.00 150.00
3 Bo Horvat 60.00 150.00
4 Brad Marchand 60.00 150.00
5 Connor McDavid 200.00 350.00
6 Devan Dubnyk 40.00 100.00
7 Evgeni Malkin 50.00 120.00
8 Frederik Andersen 60.00 150.00
9 John Tavares 50.00 120.00
10 Mike Hoffman 50.00 120.00
11 Max Pacioretty 60.00 150.00
12 Mark Scheifele 60.00 150.00
13 Sidney Crosby 200.00 350.00
14 Sean Monahan 50.00 120.00
15 Jonathan Toews 60.00 150.00
16 Tyler Seguin 40.00 100.00
17 Vladimir Tarasenko 50.00 120.00
18 Wayne Simmonds 60.00 150.00

2017-18 Upper Deck Tim Hortons NHL Signatures

1 Artem Anisimov 100.00 200.00
2 Anthony Mantha 100.00 200.00
3 Andrew Shaw 100.00 200.00
4 Bo Horvat 100.00 200.00
5 Jakub Voracek 50.00 125.00
6 Leon Draisaitl 200.00 300.00
7 Mark Giordano 100.00 200.00
8 Morgan Rielly 150.00 250.00
9 Mark Stone 150.00 250.00
10 Mats Zuccarello 100.00 200.00
11 Nikolaj Ehlers 150.00 250.00
14 Ryan Kesler 150.00 250.00
15 Taylor Hall 150.00 250.00

2017-18 Upper Deck Tim Hortons Platinum Profiles

PP1 Alex Ovechkin 6.00 15.00
PP2 Carey Price 3.00 8.00
PP3 Johnny Gaudreau 2.50 6.00
PP4 Brad Marchand 3.00 8.00
PP5 Henrik Lundqvist 4.00 10.00
PP6 Jonathan Toews 2.50 6.00
PP7 Auston Matthews 6.00 15.00
PP8 Nathan MacKinnon 6.00 15.00
PP9 Connor McDavid 8.00 20.00
PP10 Vladimir Tarasenko 2.00 5.00
PP11 Henrik Zetterberg 2.00 5.00
PP12 Sidney Crosby 6.00 15.00

2017-18 Upper Deck Tim Hortons Stat Makers

SM1 Connor McDavid 8.00 20.00
SM2 Auston Matthews 6.00 15.00
SM3 Mark Scheifele 2.50 6.00
SM4 Vladimir Tarasenko 2.00 5.00
SM5 Evgeni Malkin 3.00 8.00
SM6 Sean Monahan 1.00 2.50
SM7 Erik Karlsson 2.00 5.00
SM8 Alex Ovechkin 6.00 15.00
SM9 Henrik Sedin 2.00 5.00
SM10 Max Pacioretty 1.50 4.00
SM11 Patrick Kane 3.00 8.00
SM12 Nicklas Backstrom 1.50 4.00
SM13 Jeff Carter 1.25 3.00
SM14 Brent Burns 1.50 4.00
SM15 Sidney Crosby 6.00 15.00

2017-18 Upper Deck Tim Hortons Top 100

TOP1 Sidney Crosby 5.00 12.00
TOP2 Jonathan Toews 2.00 5.00
TOP3 Alex Ovechkin 5.00 12.00
TOP4 Patrick Kane 2.50 6.00
TOP5 Jaromir Jagr 4.00 10.00
TOP6 Duncan Keith 1.00 2.50
TOP7 Tim Horton 1.25 3.00

2017-18 Upper Deck Tim Hortons Triple Exposure

TE1 Sidney Crosby 25.00 60.00
TE2 Johnny Gaudreau 10.00 25.00
TE3 Max Pacioretty 6.00 15.00
TE4 Jamie Benn 6.00 15.00
TE5 Auston Matthews 25.00 60.00
TE6 Patrik Laine 8.00 20.00
TE7 Brad Marchand 12.00 30.00
TE8 Alex Ovechkin 25.00 60.00
TE9 Vladimir Tarasenko 8.00 20.00
TE10 Patrick Kane 12.00 30.00
TE11 Jeff Carter 5.00 12.00
TE12 Connor McDavid 30.00 80.00

2018-19 Upper Deck Tim Hortons

1 Tim Horton .75 2.00
2 Duncan Keith .40 1.00
3 John Klingberg .50 1.25
4 Artemi Panarin 1.00 2.50
5 Mathew Barzal .60 1.50
6 Brock Boeser .60 1.50
7 Andrei Vasilevskiy .75 2.00
8 Alex Ovechkin 2.00 5.00
9 Taylor Hall .50 1.25
10 Marc-Andre Fleury 1.00 2.50
11 Anze Kopitar .75 2.00
12 Patrick Marleau .50 1.25
13 Johnny Gaudreau .75 2.00
14 Jamie Benn .50 1.25
15 Ryan Getzlaf .50 1.25
16 Mitch Marner .75 2.00
17 Jack Eichel .75 2.00
18 Henrik Sedin .60 1.50
19 Jonathan Toews .75 2.00
20 Corey Crawford .40 1.00
21 Niklas Backstrom .50 1.25
22 Brayden Schenn .50 1.25
23 Oliver Ekman-Larsson .50 1.25
24 Tyler Seguin .60 1.50
25 Zdeno Chara .50 1.25
26 Blake Wheeler .50 1.25
27 Seth Jones .50 1.25
28 Claude Giroux .50 1.25
29 Nathan MacKinnon 2.00 5.00
30 Henrik Lundqvist 1.25 3.00
31 Carey Price 1.00 2.50
32 Aaron Ekblad .60 1.50
33 Devan Dubnyk .40 1.00
34 Auston Matthews 2.00 5.00
35 Pekka Rinne .50 1.25
36 Mats Zuccarello .50 1.25
37 Patrice Bergeron .60 1.50
38 Sean Couturier .40 1.00
39 Anthony Mantha .40 1.00
40 Henrik Zetterberg .60 1.50
41 Nico Hischier .75 2.00
42 Ryan Johansen .40 1.00
43 Max Pacioretty .50 1.25
44 Eric Staal .50 1.25
45 Mike Smith .40 1.00
46 Aleksander Barkov .75 2.00
47 Gabriel Landeskog .60 1.50
48 Josh Bailey .40 1.00
49 Sebastian Aho .75 2.00
50 Patrik Laine .60 1.50
51 Ryan O'Reilly .50 1.25
52 Logan Couture .60 1.50
53 Bo Horvat .60 1.50
54 Clayton Keller .60 1.50
55 Mark Scheifele .75 2.00
56 Jaden Schwartz .60 1.50
57 Mark Stone .60 1.50
58 Kris Letang .60 1.50
59 Roman Josi .50 1.25
60 Leon Draisaitl 1.50 4.00
61 Corey Perry .75 2.00
62 Daniel Sedin .60 1.50
63 Brad Marchand 1.00 2.50
64 Mikael Granlund .40 1.00
65 Erik Karlsson .60 1.50
66 Shayne Gostisbehere .50 1.25
67 Rickard Rakell .40 1.00
68 Mike Hoffman .30 .75
69 Kevin Shattenkirk .30 .75
70 Braden Holtby .60 1.50
71 Evgeni Malkin 1.00 2.50
72 Ryan Nugent-Hopkins .60 1.50
73 Kyle Palmieri .40 1.00
74 Nikolaj Ehlers .50 1.25
75 Patrick Kane 1.00 2.50
76 P.K. Subban .60 1.50
77 Victor Hedman .60 1.50
78 David Pastrnak 1.25 3.00
79 Darnell Nurse .40 1.00
80 Matt Murray .50 1.25
81 Phil Kessel .50 1.25
82 Jeff Carter .40 1.00
83 Jonathan Marchessault .60 1.50
84 Jonathan Huberdeau .60 1.50
85 Shea Weber .50 1.25
86 Nikita Kucherov 1.00 2.50
87 Sidney Crosby 2.00 5.00
88 Brent Burns .50 1.25
89 Joe Pavelski .60 1.50
90 Dylan Larkin .60 1.50
91 Steven Stamkos 1.00 2.50
92 Jonathan Drouin .40 1.00
93 Jakub Voracek .40 1.00
94 Evgeny Kuznetsov .60 1.50
95 Matt Duchene .50 1.25
96 Mikko Rantanen 1.25 3.00
97 Connor McDavid 2.50 6.00
98 Reilly Smith .50 1.25
99 William Karlsson .60 1.50
100 Drew Doughty .60 1.50
101 Noah Hanifin .50 1.25
102 Mark Giordano .50 1.25
103 Sven Baertschi .40 1.00
104 Brayden Point .60 1.50
105 Alex Galchenyuk .30 .75
106 Roberto Luongo .75 2.00
107 Connor Hellebuyck 1.00 2.50
108 Morgan Rielly .50 1.25
109 Teuvo Teravainen .50 1.25
110 Vladimir Tarasenko .60 1.50
111 Brendan Gallagher .50 1.25
112 Sean Monahan .30 .75
113 Anders Lee .40 1.00
114 Mika Zibanejad .60 1.50
115 William Nylander 1.00 2.50
116 Rasmus Ristolainen .30 .75
117 Pierre-Luc Dubois .40 1.00
118 Max Domi .50 1.25
119 Jonathan Quick .60 1.50
120 John Tavares .75 2.00

2018-19 Upper Deck Tim Hortons '18 NHL Draft No.1 Draft Pick

DP1 Rasmus Dahlin 40.00 100.00

2018-19 Upper Deck Tim Hortons Brad Marchand Timbits Autograph

1993 Brad Marchand 400.00 500.00

2018-19 Upper Deck Tim Hortons Clear Cut Phenoms

CC1 Connor McDavid 12.00 30.00
CC2 Jack Eichel 4.00 10.00
CC3 Mathew Barzal 3.00 8.00
CC4 Mitch Marner 4.00 10.00
CC5 Jonathan Drouin 2.00 5.00
CC6 David Pastrnak 6.00 15.00
CC7 Patrik Laine 3.00 8.00
CC8 Matthew Tkachuk 5.00 12.00
CC9 Leon Draisaitl 8.00 20.00
CC10 Dylan Larkin 3.00 8.00
CC11 Nikolaj Ehlers 2.50 6.00
CC12 William Nylander 5.00 12.00
CC13 Nathan MacKinnon 10.00 25.00
CC14 Brock Boeser 3.00 8.00
CC15 Auston Matthews 10.00 25.00

2018-19 Upper Deck Tim Hortons Game Day Action

GDA1 Brock Boeser 1.25 3.00
GDA2 Connor McDavid 5.00 12.00
GDA3 Patrik Laine 1.25 3.00
GDA4 Johnny Gaudreau 1.50 4.00
GDA5 Carey Price 2.00 5.00
GDA6 Erik Karlsson 1.25 3.00
GDA7 Steven Stamkos 2.00 5.00
GDA8 Nikita Kucherov 2.00 5.00
GDA9 Sidney Crosby 4.00 10.00
GDA10 Auston Matthews 4.00 10.00
GDA11 Evgeni Malkin 2.00 5.00
GDA12 Brad Marchand 2.00 5.00
GDA13 Mathew Barzal 1.25 3.00
GDA14 P.K. Subban 1.25 3.00
GDA15 Nathan MacKinnon 4.00 10.00

2018-19 Upper Deck Tim Hortons Golden Etchings

GE1 Sidney Crosby 4.00 10.00
GE2 Auston Matthews 4.00 10.00
GE3 Erik Karlsson 1.25 3.00
GE4 Patrik Laine 1.25 3.00
GE5 Johnny Gaudreau 1.50 4.00
GE6 John Tavares 1.50 4.00
GE7 Carey Price 2.00 5.00
GE8 Steven Stamkos 2.00 5.00
GE9 Nathan MacKinnon 4.00 10.00
GE10 Connor McDavid 5.00 12.00

2018-19 Upper Deck Tim Hortons NHL Jerseys

JAM Auston Matthews 25.00 60.00
JAO Alex Ovechkin 25.00 60.00
JBB Brock Boeser 8.00 20.00
JCM Connor McDavid 30.00 80.00
JCP Carey Price 12.00 30.00
JDD Drew Doughty 8.00 20.00
JEK Erik Karlsson 8.00 20.00
JHL Henrik Lundqvist 15.00 40.00
JHZ Henrik Zetterberg 8.00 20.00
JJG Johnny Gaudreau 10.00 25.00
JJT Jonathan Toews 10.00 25.00
JMF Marc-Andre Fleury 12.00 30.00
JNM Nathan MacKinnon 25.00 60.00
JPL Patrik Laine 8.00 20.00
JPS P.K. Subban 8.00 20.00
JSC Sidney Crosby 25.00 60.00
JSS Steven Stamkos 12.00 30.00
JTA John Tavares 10.00 25.00

2018-19 Upper Deck Tim Hortons Superstar Showcase

SS1 Connor McDavid 5.00 12.00
SS2 Brock Boeser 1.25 3.00
SS3 Blake Wheeler 1.00 2.50
SS4 Carey Price 2.00 5.00
SS5 Taylor Hall 1.00 2.50
SS6 Claude Giroux 1.00 2.50
SS7 Erik Karlsson 1.25 3.00
SS8 Sidney Crosby 4.00 10.00
SS9 Johnny Gaudreau 1.50 4.00
SS10 Alex Ovechkin 4.00 10.00
SS11 Evgeni Malkin 2.00 5.00
SS12 Nikita Kucherov 2.00 5.00
SS13 Drew Doughty 1.25 3.00
SS14 P.K. Subban 1.25 3.00
SS15 Auston Matthews 4.00 10.00

2018-19 Upper Deck Tim Hortons Top Line Talents

TLT1 Connor McDavid 20.00 50.00
TLT2 Brock Boeser 5.00 12.00
TLT3 Nikita Kucherov 8.00 20.00
TLT4 Carey Price 8.00 20.00
TLT5 Sidney Crosby 15.00 40.00
TLT6 Johnny Gaudreau 6.00 15.00
TLT7 Erik Karlsson 5.00 12.00
TLT8 Patrik Laine 5.00 12.00
TLT9 Alex Ovechkin 15.00 40.00
TLT10 Claude Giroux 4.00 10.00
TLT11 Henrik Lundqvist 10.00 25.00
TLT12 Auston Matthews 15.00 40.00

2019-20 Upper Deck Tim Hortons

1 Tim Horton .75 2.00
2 Duncan Keith .40 1.00
3 Filip Zadina RC .75 2.00
4 Miro Heiskanen .60 1.50
5 Mark Giordano .50 1.25
6 Brock Boeser .60 1.50

7 Brady Tkachuk .75 2.00
8 Alexander Ovechkin 2.00 5.00
9 Jack Eichel .75 2.00
10 Jordan Binnington .75 2.00
11 Zach Parise .50 1.25
12 Josh Bailey .40 1.00
13 Johnny Gaudreau .75 2.00
14 Jamie Benn .50 1.25
15 Ryan Getzlaf .50 1.25
16 Mitch Marner .75 2.00
17 Victor Hedman .60 1.50
18 Pierre-Luc Dubois .40 1.00
19 Jonathan Toews .75 2.00
20 Sebastian Aho .75 2.00
21 Brayden Point .60 1.50
22 Carter Hart .50 1.25
23 Sean Monahan .30 .75
24 Jonathan Huberdeau .60 1.50
25 Nico Hischier .75 2.00
26 Blake Wheeler .50 1.25
27 Filip Forsberg .75 2.00
28 Claude Giroux .50 1.25
29 Nathan MacKinnon 2.00 5.00
30 Henrik Lundqvist 1.25 3.00
31 Carey Price 1.00 2.50
32 Sean Couturier .40 1.00
33 Sam Reinhart 1.00 2.50
34 Auston Matthews 2.00 5.00
35 Pekka Rinne .50 1.25
36 John Gibson .50 1.25
37 Patrice Bergeron .60 1.50
38 Joe Pavelski .60 1.50
39 Aleksander Barkov .75 2.00
40 Taylor Hall .50 1.25
41 Jake Guentzel .75 2.00
42 Elias Lindholm .50 1.25
43 Anthony Mantha .40 1.00
44 Morgan Rielly .50 1.25
45 Joe Thornton .75 2.00
46 Cale Makar RC 2.50 6.00
47 Kyle Connor .75 2.00
48 Connor Hellebuyck 1.00 2.50
49 Aaron Ekblad .60 1.50
50 Patrik Laine .60 1.50
51 Rasmus Dahlin .60 1.50
52 Chris Kreider .60 1.50
53 Bo Horvat .60 1.50
54 Jonathan Quick .60 1.50
55 Mark Scheifele .75 2.00
56 Devan Dubnyk .40 1.00
57 Ryan Poehling RC .75 2.00
58 Kris Letang .60 1.50
59 Roman Josi .50 1.25
60 Drew Doughty .60 1.50
61 Colin White .30 .75
62 David Krejci .50 1.25
63 Brad Marchand 1.00 2.50
64 Eric Staal .50 1.25
65 Erik Karlsson .60 1.50
66 Alexander Radulov .50 1.25
67 Max Pacioretty .50 1.25
68 Anders Lee .40 1.00
69 Cam Atkinson .50 1.25
70 Braden Holtby .60 1.50
71 Evgeni Malkin 1.00 2.50
72 Andreas Athanasiou .40 1.00
73 Mark Stone .60 1.50
74 John Carlson .50 1.25
75 Frederik Andersen .60 1.50
76 P.K. Subban .60 1.50
77 Ryan Nugent-Hopkins .60 1.50
78 William Karlsson .60 1.50
79 Elias Pettersson .75 2.00
80 Artemi Panarin 1.00 2.50
81 Phil Kessel .50 1.25
82 Logan Couture .60 1.50
83 Quinn Hughes RC 2.50 6.00
84 Evgeny Kuznetsov .60 1.50
85 Leon Draisaitl 1.50 4.00
86 Nikita Kucherov 1.00 2.60
87 Sidney Crosby 2.00 5.00
88 Patrick Kane 1.00 2.50
89 Alex DeBrincat .60 1.50
90 Ryan O'Reilly .50 1.25
91 John Tavares .75 2.00
92 Gabriel Landeskog .60 1.50
93 Mika Zibanejad .60 1.50
94 Martin Jones .40 1.00
95 Dylan Strome .60 1.50
96 Mikko Rantanen 1.25 3.00
97 Connor McDavid 2.50 6.00
98 Shea Weber .50 1.25
99 Brendan Gallagher .50 1.25
100 Brent Burns .50 1.25
101 Tyler Seguin .60 1.50
102 Jeff Skinner .50 1.25
103 Thomas Chabot .50 1.25
104 Kyle Palmieri .40 1.00
105 David Pastrnak 1.25 3.00
106 Max Domi .50 1.25
107 Nicklas Backstrom .50 1.25
108 Teuvo Teravainen .50 1.25
109 Matthew Tkachuk 1.00 2.50
110 Dylan Larkin .60 1.50
111 Clayton Keller .60 1.50
112 Marc-Andre Fleury 1.00 2.50
113 Jakub Voracek .40 1.00
114 Vladimir Tarasenko .60 1.50
115 Mathew Barzal .60 1.50
116 Oliver Ekman-Larsson .50 1.25
117 Andrei Vasilevskiy .75 2.00
118 Jonathan Drouin .40 1.00
119 Anze Kopitar .75 2.00
120 Steven Stamkos 1.00 2.50

2019-20 Upper Deck Tim Hortons Clear Cut Phenoms

CC1 Connor McDavid 10.00 25.00
CC2 Carter Hart 2.00 5.00
CC3 Mitch Marner 3.00 8.00
CC4 Jack Eichel 3.00 8.00
CC5 David Pastrnak 5.00 12.00
CC6 Mikko Rantanen 5.00 12.00
CC7 Dylan Larkin 2.50 6.00
CC8 Patrik Laine 2.50 6.00
CC9 Rasmus Dahlin 2.50 6.00
CC10 Elias Pettersson 3.00 8.00
CC11 Miro Heiskanen 2.50 6.00
CC12 Brady Tkachuk 3.00 8.00
CC13 Mathew Barzal 2.50 6.00
CC14 Matthew Tkachuk 4.00 10.00
CC15 Auston Matthews 8.00 20.00

2019-20 Upper Deck Tim Hortons Franchise Duos

D1 A.Matthews/J.Tavares 20.00 50.00
D2 E.Pettersson/B.Boeser 8.00 20.00
D3 C.Price/M.Domi 10.00 25.00
D4 M.Scheifele/B.Wheeler 8.00 20.00
D5 T.Chabot/B.Tkachuk 6.00 15.00
D6 J.Gaudreau/S.Monahan 8.00 20.00
D7 C.McDavid/L.Draisaitl 25.00 60.00
D8 P.Kane/J.Toews 10.00 25.00
D9 S.Stamkos/N.Kucherov 10.00 25.00
D10 N.MacKinnon/M.Rantanen 20.00 50.00
D11 M.Fleury/M.Stone 10.00 25.00
D12 E.Karlsson/B.Burns 6.00 15.00
D13 P.Subban/P.Rinne 6.00 15.00
D14 A.Ovechkin/N.Backstrom 20.00 50.00
D15 B.Marchand/D.Pastrnak 12.00 30.00
D16 J.Eichel/R.Dahlin 8.00 20.00
D17 C.Giroux/C.Hart 5.00 12.00
D18 S.Crosby/E.Malkin 20.00 50.00

2019-20 Upper Deck Tim Hortons Gold Etchings

GE1 Connor McDavid 5.00 12.00
GE2 Nathan MacKinnon 4.00 10.00
GE3 Carey Price 2.00 5.00
GE4 Patrick Kane 2.00 5.00
GE5 Johnny Gaudreau 1.50 4.00
GE6 Elias Pettersson 1.50 4.00
GE7 Patrik Laine 1.25 3.00
GE8 Alexander Ovechkin 4.00 10.00
GE9 Steven Stamkos 2.00 5.00
GE10 Sidney Crosby 4.00 10.00

2019-20 Upper Deck Tim Hortons Highly Decorated

HD1 Sidney Crosby 4.00 10.00
HD2 Patrick Kane 2.00 5.00
HD3 Carey Price 2.00 5.00
HD4 Anze Kopitar 1.50 4.00
HD5 Duncan Keith .75 2.00
HD6 Drew Doughty 1.25 3.00
HD7 Jonathan Toews 1.50 4.00
HD8 Alexander Ovechkin 4.00 10.00
HD9 Jonathan Quick 1.25 3.00
HD10 Zdeno Chara 1.00 2.50
HD11 Evgeni Malkin 2.00 5.00
HD12 Joe Thornton 1.50 4.00
HD13 Steven Stamkos 2.00 5.00
HD14 Braden Holtby 1.25 3.00
HD15 Connor McDavid 5.00 12.00

2019-20 Upper Deck Tim Hortons Historic Game Day Action

HGD1 Connor McDavid 5.00 12.00
HGD2 Carey Price 2.00 5.00
HGD3 Brock Boeser 1.25 3.00
HGD4 Mark Scheifele 1.50 4.00
HGD5 Thomas Chabot 1.00 2.50
HGD6 Johnny Gaudreau 1.50 4.00
HGD7 John Tavares 1.50 4.00
HGD8 Jonathan Toews 1.50 4.00
HGD9 Elias Pettersson 1.50 4.00
HGD10 Auston Matthews 4.00 10.00
HGD11 Patrik Laine 1.25 3.00
HGD12 Alexander Ovechkin 4.00 10.00
HGD13 Steven Stamkos 2.00 5.00
HGD14 Nathan MacKinnon 4.00 10.00
HGD15 Sidney Crosby 4.00 10.00

2019-20 Upper Deck Tim Hortons Jerseys

JAM Auston Matthews EXCH 60.00 150.00
JBB Brent Burns EXCH 15.00 40.00
JBO Brock Boeser EXCH 20.00 50.00
JCM Connor McDavid EXCH 80.00 200.00
JCP Carey Price EXCH 30.00 80.00
JDL Dylan Larkin EXCH 20.00 50.00
JEP Elias Pettersson EXCH 25.00 60.00
JJG Johnny Gaudreau EXCH 25.00 60.00
JJT Jonathan Toews EXCH 25.00 60.00
JMD Max Domi EXCH 15.00 40.00
JMF Marc-Andre Fleury EXCH 30.00 80.00
JPB Patrice Bergeron EXCH 20.00 50.00
JPL Patrik Laine EXCH 20.00 50.00
JPS P.K. Subban EXCH 20.00 50.00
JSC Sidney Crosby EXCH 60.00 150.00
JSS Steven Stamkos EXCH 30.00 80.00
JTA John Tavares EXCH 25.00 60.00
JTC Thomas Chabot EXCH 15.00 40.00

2019-20 Upper Deck Tim Hortons Key Season Events

SE1 Jake DeBrusk 2.50 6.00
SE2 Tuukka Rask 3.00 8.00
SE3 Nico Hischier 4.00 10.00
SE4 Patrik Laine 3.00 8.00
SE5 Patrice Bergeron 3.00 8.00
SE6 Sidney Crosby 10.00 25.00
SE7 Claude Giroux 2.50 6.00

2019-20 Upper Deck Tim Hortons No. 1 Draft Pick Redemption

R1 No. 1 Draft Pick 50.00 125.00

2019-20 Upper Deck Tim Hortons Red Die Cuts

DC1 Brady Tkachuk 1.50 4.00
DC2 Alexander Ovechkin 4.00 10.00
DC3 Jack Eichel 1.50 4.00
DC4 Jordan Binnington 1.50 4.00
DC5 Johnny Gaudreau 1.50 4.00
DC6 Jamie Benn 1.00 2.50
DC7 Ryan Getzlaf 1.00 2.50
DC8 Pierre-Luc Dubois .75 2.00
DC9 Jonathan Toews 1.50 4.00
DC10 Sebastian Aho 1.50 4.00
DC11 Carter Hart 1.00 2.50
DC12 Nathan MacKinnon 4.00 10.00
DC13 Henrik Lundqvist 2.50 6.00
DC14 Carey Price 2.00 5.00
DC15 Auston Matthews 4.00 10.00
DC16 Patrice Bergeron 1.25 3.00
DC17 Brent Burns 1.00 2.50
DC18 Taylor Hall 1.00 2.50
DC19 Cale Makar 5.00 12.00
DC20 Aaron Ekblad 1.25 3.00
DC21 Mark Scheifele 1.50 4.00
DC22 Drew Doughty 1.25 3.00
DC23 Eric Staal 1.00 2.50
DC24 P.K. Subban 1.25 3.00
DC25 Elias Pettersson 1.50 4.00
DC26 Ryan Poehling 1.50 4.00
DC27 Sidney Crosby 4.00 10.00
DC28 Connor McDavid 5.00 12.00
DC29 Dylan Larkin 1.25 3.00
DC30 Clayton Keller 1.25 3.00
DC31 Marc-Andre Fleury 2.00 5.00
DC32 Mathew Barzal 1.25 3.00
DC33 Steven Stamkos 2.00 5.00
DCSP1 Tim Horton 30.00 80.00

2020-21 Upper Deck Tim Hortons

1 Tim Horton .75 2.00
2 Zdeno Chara .50 1.25
3 Seth Jones .50 1.25
4 Aaron Ekblad .60 1.50
5 Mark Giordano .50 1.25
6 Brock Boeser .60 1.50
7 Brady Tkachuk .75 2.00
8 Alex Ovechkin 2.00 5.00
9 Jack Eichel .75 2.00
10 Artemi Panarin 1.00 2.50
11 Jonathan Huberdeau .60 1.50
12 Anze Kopitar .75 2.00
13 Mathew Barzal .60 1.50
14 Sean Couturier .40 1.00
15 Johnny Gaudreau .75 2.00
16 Mitch Marner .75 2.00
17 Cale Makar 1.25 3.00
18 Pierre-Luc Dubois .40 1.00
19 Jonathan Toews .75 2.00
20 Matthew Tkachuk 1.00 2.50
21 Brayden Point .60 1.50
22 Sergei Bobrovsky .75 2.00
23 David Perron .40 1.00
24 P.K. Subban .60 1.50
25 Matt Murray .50 1.25
26 Blake Wheeler .50 1.25
27 Max Domi .50 1.25
28 Claude Giroux .50 1.25
29 Nathan MacKinnon 2.00 5.00
30 Patrik Laine .60 1.50
31 Carey Price 1.00 2.50
32 Bo Horvat .60 1.50
33 Dougie Hamilton .40 1.00
34 Auston Matthews 2.00 5.00
35 Ryan Getzlaf .50 1.25
36 Nico Hischier .75 2.00
37 Connor Hellebuyck 1.00 2.50
38 Sebastian Aho .75 2.00
39 Shea Weber .50 1.25
40 Elias Pettersson .75 2.00
41 Brendan Gallagher .50 1.25
42 Alex DeBrincat .60 1.50
43 Quinn Hughes 1.25 3.00
44 Eric Staal .50 1.25
45 James Neal .30 .75
46 Nicklas Backstrom .50 1.25
47 Jack Hughes 1.25 3.00
48 Zach Parise .50 1.25
49 Sean Monahan .30 .75
50 Jordan Binnington .75 2.00
51 Jaden Schwartz .60 1.50
52 Brayden Schenn .50 1.25
53 John Gibson .50 1.25
54 Morgan Rielly .50 1.25
55 Mark Scheifele .75 2.00
56 Kaapo Kakko .40 1.00
57 Tuukka Rask .60 1.50
58 Kris Letang .60 1.50
59 Jake Guentzel .75 2.00
60 Evgeni Malkin 1.00 2.50
61 Mark Stone .60 1.50
62 Anthony Mantha .40 1.00
63 Brad Marchand 1.00 2.50
64 Drew Doughty .60 1.50
65 Roman Josi .50 1.25
66 Thomas Chabot .50 1.25
67 Andrei Svechnikov .60 1.50
68 David Pastrnak 1.25 3.00
69 Miro Heiskanen .60 1.50
70 Erik Karlsson .60 1.50
71 Dylan Larkin .60 1.50
72 Ben Bishop .40 1.00
73 Zach Werenski .75 2.00
74 John Carlson .50 1.25
75 Patrice Bergeron .60 1.50
76 Anthony Duclair .40 1.00
77 Victor Hedman .60 1.50
78 Tom Wilson .50 1.25
79 Carter Hart .50 1.25
80 Leon Draisaitl 1.50 4.00
81 Phil Kessel .50 1.25
82 Kyle Connor .75 2.00
83 Max Pacioretty .50 1.25
84 Rasmus Dahlin .60 1.50
85 Connor Brown .40 1.00
86 Nikita Kucherov 1.00 2.50
87 Sidney Crosby 2.00 5.00
88 Patrick Kane 1.00 2.50
89 Reilly Smith .50 1.25
90 Ryan O'Reilly .50 1.25
91 John Tavares .75 2.00
92 Evgeny Kuznetsov .60 1.50
93 Ryan Nugent-Hopkins .60 1.50
94 Mika Zibanejad .60 1.50
95 Matt Duchene .50 1.25
96 Mikko Rantanen 1.25 3.00
97 Connor McDavid 2.50 6.00
98 Tyler Bertuzzi .40 1.00
99 Brock Nelson .50 1.25
100 Marc-Andre Fleury 1.00 2.50
101 Tyler Seguin .60 1.50
102 Joe Thornton .75 2.00
103 Tomas Tatar .30 .75
104 Gabriel Landeskog .60 1.50
105 Taylor Hall .50 1.25
106 Teuvo Teravainen .50 1.25
107 Clayton Keller .60 1.50
108 Travis Konecny .50 1.25
109 Ryan Suter .40 1.00
110 Andrei Vasilevskiy .75 2.00
111 J.T. Miller .60 1.50
112 Vladimir Tarasenko .60 1.50
113 Sam Reinhart 1.00 2.50
114 William Karlsson .60 1.50
115 Frederik Andersen .60 1.50
116 Henrik Lundqvist 1.25 3.00
117 Jamie Benn .50 1.25
118 Anthony Deangelo .30 .75
119 Brent Burns .50 1.25
120 Steven Stamkos 1.00 2.50
121 Adam Henrique .40 1.00
122 Pekka Rinne .50 1.25
123 Jeff Carter .40 1.00
124 Aleksander Barkov .75 2.00
125 Anders Lee .40 1.00

2020-21 Upper Deck Tim Hortons All Star Standouts

AS1 Connor McDavid 1.50 4.00
AS2 Elias Pettersson .50 1.25
AS3 Shea Weber .30 .75
AS4 Matthew Tkachuk .60 1.50
AS5 David Pastrnak .75 2.00
AS6 Brady Tkachuk .50 1.25
AS7 Ryan O'Reilly .30 .75
AS8 Connor Hellebuyck .60 1.50
AS9 Patrick Kane .60 1.50
AS10 Nathan MacKinnon 1.25 3.00
AS11 Jordan Binnington .50 1.25
AS12 Leon Draisaitl 1.00 2.50
AS13 Mathew Barzal .40 1.00
AS14 Quinn Hughes .75 2.00
AS15 Mitch Marner .50 1.25

2020-21 Upper Deck Tim Hortons Canvas

C1 Connor McDavid 1.50 4.00
C2 Brad Marchand .60 1.50
C3 Leon Draisaitl 1.00 2.50
C4 Patrick Kane .60 1.50
C5 Nathan MacKinnon 1.25 3.00
C6 Artemi Panarin .60 1.50
C7 Alex Ovechkin 1.25 3.00
C8 David Pastrnak .75 2.00
C9 Steven Stamkos .60 1.50
C10 Auston Matthews 1.25 3.00
C11 Carey Price .60 1.50
C12 Mitch Marner .50 1.25
C13 Jack Eichel .50 1.25
C14 Mika Zibanejad .40 1.00
C15 Sidney Crosby 1.25 3.00

2020-21 Upper Deck Tim Hortons Clear Cut Phenoms

CC1 Connor McDavid 5.00 12.00
CC2 Elias Pettersson 1.50 4.00
CC3 Patrik Laine 1.25 3.00
CC4 Matthew Tkachuk 2.00 5.00
CC5 Mitch Marner 1.50 4.00
CC6 Cale Makar 2.50 6.00
CC7 Auston Matthews 4.00 10.00
CC8 Thomas Chabot 1.00 2.50
CC9 Brock Boeser 1.25 3.00
CC10 Quinn Hughes 2.50 6.00
CC11 Kyle Connor 1.50 4.00
CC12 Rasmus Dahlin 1.25 3.00
CC13 Mathew Barzal 1.25 3.00
CC14 Brady Tkachuk 1.50 4.00
CC15 Jack Eichel 1.50 4.00

2020-21 Upper Deck Tim Hortons Cup Winners

CW1 Sidney Crosby 1.50 4.00
CW2 Drew Doughty .50 1.25
CW3 Patrice Bergeron .50 1.25
CW4 Evgeni Malkin .75 2.00
CW5 Jonathan Toews .60 1.50
CW6 John Carlson .40 1.00
CW7 Duncan Keith .30 .75
CW8 Anze Kopitar .60 1.50
CW9 Ryan Getzlaf .40 1.00
CW10 Patrick Kane .75 2.00
CW11 Jordan Binnington .60 1.50
CW12 Zdeno Chara .40 1.00
CW13 Brad Marchand .75 2.00
CW14 Nicklas Backstrom .40 1.00
CW15 Alex Ovechkin 1.50 4.00

2020-21 Upper Deck Tim Hortons Franchise Trios

T1 Draisaitl/McDavid/Nugent-Hopkins 15.0040.00
T2 Scheifele/Laine/Hellebuyck 12.00 30.00
T3 Binnington/O'Reilly/Tarasenko 10.00 25.00
T4 Kucherov/Stamkos/Hedman 12.00 30.00
T5 Boeser/Pettersson/Hughes 15.00 40.00
T6 Tkachuk/Gaudreau/Monahan 12.00 30.00
T7 Backstrom/Ovechkin/Carlson 15.00 40.00
T8 Rantanen/MacKinnon/Makar 25.00 60.00
T9 Stone/Fleury/Pacioretty 12.00 30.00
T10 Matthews/Tavares/Marner 15.00 40.00
T11 Tkachuk/Chabot/Duclair 8.00 20.00
T12 Mantha/Larkin/Bertuzzi 8.00 20.00
T13 Panarin/Zibanejad/Kakko 12.00 30.00
T14 Kane/Toews/DeBrincat 12.00 30.00
T15 Price/Weber/Domi 15.00 40.00
T16 Dahlin/Eichel/Olofsson 10.00 25.00
T17 Couturier/Giroux/Hart 6.00 15.00
T18 Seguin/Benn/Bishop 8.00 20.00
T19 Duchene/Josi/Rinne 6.00 15.00
T20 Malkin/Crosby/Letang 15.00 40.00

2020-21 Upper Deck Tim Hortons Gold Etchings

G1 Connor McDavid 1.50 4.00
G2 John Tavares .50 1.25
G3 Elias Pettersson .50 1.25
G4 Johnny Gaudreau .50 1.25
G5 Nathan MacKinnon 1.25 3.00
G6 David Pastrnak .75 2.00
G7 Ryan O'Reilly .30 .75
G8 Auston Matthews 1.25 3.00
G9 Carey Price .60 1.50
G10 Alex Ovechkin 1.25 3.00
G11 Artemi Panarin .60 1.50
G12 Jack Eichel .50 1.25
G13 Steven Stamkos .60 1.50
G14 Leon Draisaitl 1.00 2.50
G15 Sidney Crosby 1.25 3.00

2020-21 Upper Deck Tim Hortons Jerseys

JAM Auston Matthews 100.00 250.00
JAO Alex Ovechkin 80.00 200.00
JAP Artemi Panarin 50.00 125.00
JBM Brad Marchand 50.00 125.00
JBT Brady Tkachuk 50.00 125.00
JCH Connor Hellebuyck 30.00 80.00
JCM Connor McDavid 125.00 300.00
JCP Carey Price 50.00 125.00
JDP David Pastrnak 60.00 150.00
JEP Elias Pettersson 40.00 100.00
JJE Jack Eichel 40.00 100.00
JJG Johnny Gaudreau 40.00 100.00
JLD Leon Draisaitl 80.00 200.00
JMM Mitch Marner 40.00 100.00
JMS Mark Scheifele 40.00 100.00
JRO Ryan O'Reilly 30.00 80.00
JSC Sidney Crosby 100.00 250.00
JSS Steven Stamkos 40.00 100.00

2020-21 Upper Deck Tim Hortons No. 1 Draft Pick Redemption

AL Alexis Lafreniere 250.00 600.00

2020-21 Upper Deck Tim Hortons Red Die Cuts

DC1 Tim Horton 4.00 10.00
DC2 Brock Boeser .60 1.50
DC3 Brady Tkachuk .75 2.00
DC4 Alex Ovechkin 2.00 5.00
DC5 Jack Eichel .75 2.00
DC6 Artemi Panarin 1.00 2.50
DC7 Mathew Barzal .60 1.50
DC8 Johnny Gaudreau .75 2.00
DC9 Mitch Marner .75 2.00
DC10 Cale Makar 1.25 3.00
DC11 Jonathan Toews .75 2.00
DC12 Matthew Tkachuk 1.00 2.50
DC13 Mark Scheifele .75 2.00
DC14 Max Domi .50 1.25
DC15 Claude Giroux .50 1.25
DC16 Nathan MacKinnon 2.00 5.00
DC17 Patrik Laine .60 1.50
DC18 Carey Price 1.00 2.50
DC19 Auston Matthews 2.00 5.00
DC20 Shea Weber .50 1.25
DC21 Elias Pettersson .75 2.00
DC22 Quinn Hughes 1.25 3.00
DC23 Nicklas Backstrom .50 1.25
DC24 Jordan Binnington .75 2.00
DC25 Sidney Crosby 2.00 5.00
DC26 Connor Hellebuyck 1.00 2.50
DC27 Evgeni Malkin 1.00 2.50
DC28 Mark Stone .60 1.50
DC29 Brad Marchand 1.00 2.50
DC30 Drew Doughty .60 1.50
DC31 Roman Josi .50 1.25
DC32 David Pastrnak 1.25 3.00
DC33 Erik Karlsson .60 1.50
DC34 Dylan Larkin .60 1.50
DC35 John Carlson .50 1.25
DC36 Patrice Bergeron .60 1.50
DC37 Carter Hart .50 1.25
DC38 Leon Draisaitl 1.50 4.00
DC39 Nikita Kucherov 1.00 2.50
DC40 Patrick Kane 1.00 2.50
DC41 Ryan O'Reilly .50 1.25
DC42 John Tavares .75 2.00
DC43 Mikko Rantanen 1.25 3.00
DC44 Connor McDavid 2.50 6.00
DC45 Marc-Andre Fleury 1.00 2.50
DC46 Taylor Hall .50 1.25
DC47 Andrei Vasilevskiy .75 2.00
DC48 Mika Zibanejad .60 1.50
DC49 Henrik Lundqvist 1.25 3.00
DC50 Steven Stamkos 1.00 2.50

2020-21 Upper Deck Tim Hortons Signatures

SAL Adam Lowry 40.00 100.00
SBT Brady Tkachuk 60.00 150.00
SCM Cale Makar 125.00 300.00
SDH Danton Heinen 50.00 125.00
SFZ Filip Zadina 60.00 150.00
SJV Jimmy Vesey 40.00 100.00
SMF Micheal Ferland 40.00 100.00
SMP Max Pacioretty 50.00 125.00
SMS Mark Scheifele 80.00 200.00
SNH Noah Hanifin 50.00 125.00
SNP Nicolas Petan 30.00 80.00
SPD Phillip Danault 50.00 125.00
SQH Quinn Hughes 125.00 300.00
SRP Ryan Poehling 50.00 125.00
STP Tanner Pearson 50.00 125.00

2020-21 Upper Deck Tim Hortons Superstar Signatures

SSNM Nathan MacKinnon 600.00 1500.00
SSSC Sidney Crosby 400.00 1000.00

2020-21 Upper Deck Tim Hortons Wayne Gretzky Tribute

WG Wayne Gretzky 150.00 400.00

2021-22 Upper Deck Tim Hortons

1 Tim Horton .75 2.00
2 Duncan Keith .40 1.00
3 Seth Jones .50 1.25
4 Bowen Byram .60 1.50
5 Aaron Ekblad .60 1.50
6 Brock Boeser .60 1.50
7 Brady Tkachuk .75 2.00
8 Alex Ovechkin 2.00 5.00
9 Jack Eichel .75 2.00
10 Artemi Panarin 1.00 2.50
11 Anze Kopitar .75 2.00
12 Alex DeBrincat .60 1.50
13 Mathew Barzal .60 1.50
14 Jamie Benn .50 1.25
15 Ryan Getzlaf .50 1.25
16 Mitch Marner .75 2.00
17 Josh Anderson .40 1.00
18 Tim Stutzle .60 1.50
19 Nicklas Backstrom .50 1.25
20 Sebastian Aho .75 2.00
21 Brayden Point .60 1.50
22 Kevin Shattenkirk .30 .75
23 Sean Monahan .30 .75
24 Dylan Cozens .50 1.25
25 Jordan Kyrou .50 1.25
26 Jeff Petry .50 1.25
27 Shea Theodore .60 1.50
28 Claude Giroux .50 1.25
29 Nathan Mackinnon 2.00 5.00
30 Matt Murray .50 1.25
31 Carey Price 1.00 2.50
32 Jonathan Huberdeau .60 1.50
33 Viktor Arvidsson .30 .75
34 Auston Matthews 2.00 5.00
35 Patrik Laine .60 1.50
36 John Gibson .50 1.25
37 Patrice Bergeron .60 1.50
38 Boone Jenner .50 1.25
39 Anthony Mantha .40 1.00
40 Semyon Varlamov .50 1.25
41 Gabe Vilardi .50 1.25
42 Alex Pietrangelo .40 1.00
43 Quinn Hughes 1.25 3.00
44 Morgan Rielly .50 1.25
45 Kevin Hayes .40 1.00
46 Jared Spurgeon .50 1.25
47 Torey Krug .40 1.00
48 Tomas Hertl .50 1.25
49 Samuel Girard .30 .75
50 Miro Heiskanen .60 1.50
51 Zach Parise .50 1.25
52 Darnell Nurse .40 1.00
53 Bo Horvat .60 1.50
54 Pierre-Luc Dubois .40 1.00
55 Mark Scheifele .75 2.00
56 Rasmus Dahlin .60 1.50
57 Oliver Bjorkstrand .40 1.00
58 Jake Guentzel .75 2.00
59 Roman Josi .50 1.25
60 Aleksander Barkov .75 2.00
61 Mark Stone .60 1.50
62 Jordan Greenway .30 .75
63 Brad Marchand 1.00 2.50
64 Jordan Staal .40 1.00
65 Elias Lindholm .50 1.25
66 Jason Zucker .50 1.25
67 Max Pacioretty .50 1.25
68 Connor Hellebuyck 1.00 2.50
69 Joe Pavelski .60 1.50
70 Andrei Svechnikov .60 1.50
71 Evgeni Malkin 1.00 2.50
72 Thomas Chabot .50 1.25
73 Tyler Toffoli .50 1.25
74 John Carlson .50 1.25
75 Charlie McAvoy .60 1.50
76 Dylan Larkin .60 1.50
77 Victor Hedman .60 1.50
78 Andrei Vasilevskiy .75 2.00
79 Carter Hart .50 1.25
80 Brent Burns .50 1.25
81 Kyle Connor .75 2.00
82 Cale Makar 1.25 3.00
83 John Klingberg .50 1.25
84 Christian Dvorak .40 1.00
85 Patrick Kane 1.00 2.50
86 Jack Hughes 1.25 3.00
87 Sidney Crosby 2.00 5.00
88 David Pastrnak 1.25 3.00
89 Pavel Buchnevich .40 1.00
90 Ryan O'Reilly .50 1.25
91 John Tavares .75 2.00
92 Shea Weber .50 1.25
93 Ryan Nugent-Hopkins .60 1.50
94 J.T. Miller .60 1.50
95 Johnny Gaudreau .75 2.00
96 Mikko Rantanen 1.25 3.00
97 Connor McDavid 2.50 6.00
08 Kirill Kaprizov 1.50 4.00
99 Leon Draisaitl 1.50 4.00
100 William Nylander 1.00 2.50
101 Victor Olofsson .50 1.25
102 Matthew Tkachuk 1.00 2.50
103 Blake Wheeler .50 1.25
104 Nick Schmaltz .40 1.00
105 Joel Farabee .50 1.25
106 Steven Stamkos 1.00 2.50
107 Maxime Comtois .40 1.00
108 Alexis Lafreniere .75 2.00
109 Jakob Chychrun .50 1.25
110 Ty Smith .50 1.25
111 Jacob Markstrom .50 1.25
112 Drew Doughty .60 1.50
113 Elias Pettersson .75 2.00
114 Mackenzie Blackwood .50 1.25
115 Filip Forsberg .75 2.00
116 Brayden Schenn .50 1.25
117 Nikolaj Ehlers .50 1.25
118 Tyler Bertuzzi .40 1.00
119 Logan Couture .60 1.50
120 Sergei Bobrovsky .75 2.00
121 Nick Suzuki 1.00 2.50
122 Noah Dobson .60 1.50
123 Dominik Kubalik .50 1.25
124 Josh Norris .50 1.25
125 Kris Letang .60 1.50

2021-22 Upper Deck Tim Hortons Gold Etchings

G1 Connor McDavid 2.00 5.00
G2 Sidney Crosby 1.50 4.00
G3 Alex Ovechkin 1.50 4.00
G4 Auston Matthews 1.50 4.00
G5 Elias Lindholm .40 1.00
G6 Kyle Connor .60 1.50
G7 Tyler Toffoli .40 1.00
G8 John Gibson .40 1.00
G9 Brock Boeser .50 1.25
G10 Dylan Larkin .50 1.25
G11 David Pastrnak 1.00 2.50
G12 William Nylander .75 2.00
G13 Jack Eichel .60 1.50
G14 Brady Tkachuk .60 1.50
G15 Nathan MacKinnon 1.50 4.00

2021-22 Upper Deck Tim Hortons Hockey Heroes

H1 Jack Hughes 12.00 30.00
H2 Auston Matthews 15.00 40.00
H3 Alex Ovechkin 15.00 40.00
H4 Alex DeBrincat 10.00 25.00
H5 Carey Price 12.00 30.00
H6 Claude Giroux 8.00 20.00
H7 Connor McDavid 20.00 50.00
H8 Quinn Hughes 12.00 30.00
H9 Thomas Chabot 8.00 20.00
H10 Alexis Lafreniere 12.00 30.00
H11 Patrik Laine 10.00 25.00
H12 Sean Monahan 5.00 12.00
H13 Sidney Crosby 15.00 40.00
H14 Mathew Barzal 10.00 25.00
H15 Jack Eichel 12.00 30.00
H16 Dylan Larkin 10.00 25.00
H17 Blake Wheeler 8.00 20.00
H18 David Pastrnak 12.00 30.00
H19 Kirill Kaprizov 12.00 30.00
H20 Nathan MacKinnon 12.00 30.00

2021-22 Upper Deck Tim Hortons Jerseys

NNO Thomas Chabot 25.00 60.00
NNO Kyle Connor 40.00 100.00
NNO Sidney Crosby 100.00 250.00
NNO Leon Draisaitl 80.00 200.00
NNO Johnny Gaudreau 40.00 100.00
NNO Quinn Hughes 60.00 150.00
NNO Jesperi Kotkaniemi 25.00 60.00
NNO Nathan MacKinnon 100.00 250.00
NNO Auston Matthews 100.00 250.00
NNO Connor McDavid 125.00 300.00
NNO J.T. Miller 30.00 80.00
NNO William Nylander 50.00 125.00
NNO David Pastrnak 60.00 150.00
NNO Elias Pettersson 40.00 100.00
NNO Carey Price 50.00 125.00
NNO John Tavares 40.00 100.00
NNO Brady Tkachuk 40.00 100.00
NNO Blake Wheeler 25.00 60.00

2021-22 Upper Deck Tim Hortons NHL Canvas

C1 Tyler Toffoli .40 1.00
C2 Patrice Bergeron .50 1.25
C3 Connor McDavid 2.00 5.00
C4 Sidney Crosby 1.50 4.00
C5 Alex Ovechkin 1.50 4.00
C6 Quinn Hughes 1.00 2.50
C7 Artemi Panarin .75 2.00
C8 Matthew Tkachuk .75 2.00
C9 Mark Scheifele .60 1.50
C10 Alex Pietrangelo .30 .75
C11 Andrei Vasilevskiy .60 1.50
C12 Auston Matthews 1.50 4.00
C13 Nathan MacKinnon 1.50 4.00
C14 Jordan Binnington .60 1.50
C15 Patrick Kane .75 2.00

2021-22 Upper Deck Tim Hortons Photo Finish

PF1 Sebastian Aho .60 1.50
PF2 Carey Price .75 2.00
PF3 Brayden Point .50 1.25
PF4 Victor Hedman .50 1.25
PF5 Robin Lehner .30 .75
PF6 Joel Kiviranta .25 .60
PF7 Denis Gurianov .50 1.25
PF8 Anthony Cirelli .30 .75
PF9 Steven Stamkos .75 2.00
PF10 Jordan Binnington .60 1.50
PF11 Leon Draisaitl 1.25 3.00
PF12 Patrik Laine .50 1.25
PF13 Connor McDavid 2.00 5.00
PF14 Philipp Grubauer .40 1.00
PF15 Sidney Crosby 1.50 4.00

2021-22 Upper Deck Tim Hortons ProMotion

PP1 Tim Stutzle 1.00 2.50
PP2 Quinn Hughes 2.00 5.00
PP3 Jordan Kyrou .75 2.00
PP4 Josh Norris .75 2.00
PP5 Alexis Lafreniere 1.25 3.00
PP6 Dylan Cozens .75 2.00
PP7 Elias Pettersson 1.25 3.00
PP8 Kirill Kaprizov 2.50 6.00
PP9 Miro Heiskanen 1.00 2.50
PP10 Andrei Svechnikov 1.00 2.50
PP11 Joel Farabee .75 2.00
PP12 Nick Suzuki 1.50 4.00
PP13 Pierre-Luc Dubois .60 1.50
PP14 Jack Hughes 2.00 5.00
PP15 Cale Makar 2.00 5.00

2021-22 Upper Deck Tim Hortons Red Die Cuts

DC1 Tim Horton .75 2.00
DC2 Mathew Barzal .60 1.50
DC3 John Carlson .50 1.25
DC4 Sidney Crosby 2.00 5.00
DC5 Claude Giroux .50 1.25
DC6 Patrice Bergeron .60 1.50
DC7 Tim Stutzle .60 1.50
DC8 John Tavares .75 2.00
DC9 Tyler Toffoli .50 1.25
DC10 John Gibson .50 1.25
DC11 Patrick Kane 1.00 2.50
DC12 Mark Scheifele .75 2.00
DC13 Jack Hughes 1.25 3.00
DC14 Cale Makar 1.25 3.00
DC15 Brent Burns .50 1.25
DC16 Elias Pettersson .75 2.00
DC17 Anze Kopitar .75 2.00
DC18 Leon Draisaitl 1.50 4.00
DC19 Jack Eichel .75 2.00
DC20 Miro Heiskanen .60 1.50
DC21 Connor McDavid 2.50 6.00
DC22 Brad Marchand 1.00 2.50
DC23 Steven Stamkos 1.00 2.50
DC24 Mitch Marner .75 2.00
DC25 Jonathan Huberdeau .60 1.50
DC26 Kirill Kaprizov 1.50 4.00
DC27 Ryan O'Reilly .50 1.25
DC28 Brady Tkachuk .75 2.00

DC29 Auston Matthews 2.00 5.00
DC30 Blake Wheeler .50 1.25
DC31 Dylan Larkin .60 1.50
DC32 Johnny Gaudreau .75 2.00
DC33 Andrei Vasilevskiy .75 2.00
DC34 Roman Josi .50 1.25
DC35 Alex Ovechkin 2.00 5.00
DC36 Matthew Tkachuk 1.00 2.50
DC37 David Pastrnak 1.25 3.00
DC38 Evgeni Malkin 1.00 2.50
DC39 Patrik Laine .60 1.50
DC40 Sebastian Aho .75 2.00
DC41 Alexis Lafreniere .75 2.00
DC42 Mark Stone .60 1.50
DC43 Victor Hedman .60 1.50
DC44 Nathan MacKinnon 2.00 5.00
DC45 Artemi Panarin 1.00 2.50
DC46 Kyle Connor .75 2.00
DC47 Thomas Chabot .50 1.25
DC48 Carey Price 1.00 2.50
DC49 Jakob Chychrun .50 1.25
DC50 Quinn Hughes 1.25 3.00

2021-22 Upper Deck Tim Hortons Superstar Showcase

SS1 Connor McDavid 2.50 6.00
SS2 Mark Scheifele .75 2.00
SS3 Mitch Marner .75 2.00
SS4 Andrei Vasilevskiy .75 2.00
SS5 Leon Draisaitl 1.50 4.00
SS6 Alex Ovechkin 2.00 5.00
SS7 Artemi Panarin 1.00 2.50
SS8 Connor Hellebuyck 1.00 2.50
SS9 Quinn Hughes 1.25 3.00
SS10 Nathan MacKinnon 2.00 5.00
SS11 Auston Matthews 2.00 5.00
SS12 Patrice Bergeron .60 1.50
SS13 Patrick Kane 1.00 2.50
SS14 Jonathan Huberdeau .60 1.50
SS15 Sidney Crosby 2.00 5.00

2021-22 Upper Deck Tim Hortons Superstar Signatures

SSNM Nathan MacKinnon/100 150.00 400.00
SSSC Sidney Crosby/87 400.00 1000.00

2021-22 Upper Deck Tim Hortons Wayne Gretzky Tribute

WGT1 Wayne Gretzky 150.00 400.00

2022-23 Upper Deck Tim Hortons

1 Tim Horton .75 2.00
2 Timo Meier .50 1.25
3 John Klingberg .50 1.25
4 Miro Heiskanen .60 1.50
5 Aaron Ekblad .60 1.50
6 Brock Boeser .60 1.50
7 Brady Tkachuk .75 2.00
8 Alex Ovechkin 2.00 5.00
9 Sam Reinhart 1.00 2.50
10 Artemi Panarin 1.00 2.50
11 Jonathan Huberdeau .60 1.50
12 Alex Debrincat .60 1.50
13 Alexis Lafreniere .75 2.00
14 Nick Suzuki 1.00 2.50
15 Frederik Andersen .60 1.50
16 Mitch Marner .75 2.00
17 Vladimir Tarasenko .60 1.50
18 Tim Stutzle .60 1.50
19 Marc-Andre Fleury 1.00 2.50
20 Sebastian Aho .75 2.00
21 Brayden Point .60 1.50
22 Tyson Barrie .30 .75
23 Adam Fox .60 1.50
24 Matt Dumba .30 .75
25 Darnell Nurse .40 1.00
26 Charlie McAvoy .60 1.50
27 Nikolaj Ehlers .50 1.25
28 Elias Lindholm .50 1.25
29 Nathan MacKinnon 2.00 5.00
30 Jack Campbell .50 1.25
31 Carey Price 1.00 2.50
32 Johnny Gaudreau .75 2.00
33 Cam Talbot .50 1.25
34 Auston Matthews 2.00 5.00
35 Thatcher Demko .60 1.50
36 Mats Zuccarello .50 1.25
37 Patrice Bergeron .60 1.50
38 Boone Jenner .50 1.25
39 Alex Nedeljkovic .40 1.00
40 Elias Pettersson .75 2.00
41 Leon Draisaitl 1.50 4.00
42 Brendan Gallagher .50 1.25
43 Quinn Hughes 1.25 3.00
44 Andrew Mangiapane .50 1.25
45 Devon Toews .40 1.00
46 Trevor Zegras .50 1.25
47 Tomas Hertl .50 1.25
48 Gabriel Landeskog .60 1.50
49 Jordan Binnington .75 2.00
50 John Carlson .50 1.25
51 Rasmus Dahlin .60 1.50
52 Moritz Seider .60 1.50
53 Dylan Larkin .60 1.50
54 Nazem Kadri .60 1.50
55 Mark Scheifele .75 2.00
56 Kris Letang .60 1.50
57 Erik Karlsson .60 1.50
58 Roman Josi .50 1.25
59 Jake Guentzel .75 2.00
60 Jakob Chychrun .50 1.25
61 Mark Stone .60 1.50
62 Mikael Granlund .40 1.00
63 Brad Marchand 1.00 2.50
64 Alex Tuch .50 1.25
65 John Gibson .50 1.25
66 Lucas Raymond .75 2.00
67 Jacob Markstrom .50 1.25
68 Taylor Hall .50 1.25
69 Thomas Chabot .50 1.25
70 Tyler Toffoli .50 1.25
71 Evgeni Malkin 1.00 2.50
72 Anthony Duclair .40 1.00
73 P.K. Subban .60 1.50
74 Alex Pietrangelo .40 1.00
75 Drake Batherson .50 1.25
76 Carter Hart .50 1.25
77 Victor Hedman .60 1.50
78 Kyle Connor .75 2.00
79 Jack Eichel .75 2.00
80 Joel Farabee .50 1.25
81 Teuvo Teravainen .50 1.25
82 Jack Hughes 1.25 3.00
83 Nikita Kucherov 1.00 2.50
84 Matt Duchene .50 1.25
85 Evgeny Kuznetsov .60 1.50
86 Ryan O'Reilly .50 1.25
87 Sidney Crosby 2.00 5.00
88 Patrick Kane 1.00 2.50
89 Blake Wheeler .50 1.25
90 David Pastrnak 1.25 3.00
91 Steven Stamkos 1.00 2.50
92 Jack Roslovic .30 .75
93 Jordan Kyrou .50 1.25
94 Andrei Vasilevskiy .75 2.00
95 William Nylander 1.00 2.50
96 Brent Burns .50 1.25
97 Connor McDavid 2.50 6.00
98 Chandler Stephenson .40 1.00
99 Drew Doughty .60 1.50
100 Seth Jones .50 1.25
101 Dylan Cozens .50 1.25
102 Igor Shesterkin 1.00 2.50
103 Dawson Mercer .60 1.50
104 Cale Makar 1.25 3.00
105 Matthew Tkachuk 1.00 2.50
106 Nico Hischier .75 2.00
107 Clayton Keller .60 1.50
108 Troy Terry .40 1.00
109 Connor Hellebuyck 1.00 2.50
110 Jason Robertson .75 2.00
111 Mathew Barzal .60 1.50
112 Aleksander Barkov .75 2.00
113 Cole Caufield 1.00 2.50
114 Sean Couturier .40 1.00
115 Kirill Kaprizov 1.50 4.00
116 Andrei Svechnikov .60 1.50
117 Anze Kopitar .75 2.00
118 John Tavares .75 2.00
119 Brock Nelson .50 1.25
120 Phil Kessel .50 1.25

2022-23 Upper Deck Tim Hortons '22 Draft Pick Redemption

NNO TBA 100.00 250.00

2022-23 Upper Deck Tim Hortons Flow of Time

NT1 Sidney Crosby 10.00 25.00
NT2 Brent Burns 2.50 6.00
NT3 Jonathan Toews 4.00 10.00
NT4 Patrick Kane 5.00 12.00
NT5 Patrice Bergeron 3.00 8.00
NT6 Brad Marchand 5.00 12.00
NT7 Kris Letang 3.00 8.00
NT8 Anze Kopitar 4.00 10.00
NT9 Nathan MacKinnon 10.00 25.00
NT10 Connor McDavid 12.00 30.00
NT11 Auston Matthews 10.00 25.00
NT12 Nikita Kucherov 5.00 12.00
NT13 Jamie Benn 2.50 6.00
NT14 Steven Stamkos 5.00 12.00
NT15 Jonathan Huberdeau 3.00 8.00
NT16 Drew Doughty 3.00 8.00
NT17 Alex Ovechkin 10.00 25.00
NT18 Carey Price 5.00 12.00

2022-23 Upper Deck Tim Hortons Gold Etchings

G1 Nathan MacKinnon 1.50 4.00
G2 Sidney Crosby 1.50 4.00
G3 Alex Ovechkin 1.50 4.00
G4 Andrei Svechnikov .50 1.25
G5 Carey Price .75 2.00
G6 Connor McDavid 2.00 5.00
G7 Auston Matthews 1.50 4.00
G8 David Pastrnak 1.00 2.50
G9 Artemi Panarin .75 2.00
G10 Mark Scheifele .60 1.50
G11 Elias Pettersson .60 1.50
G12 Quinn Hughes 1.00 2.50
G13 Nick Suzuki .75 2.00
G14 Tim Stutzle .50 1.25
G15 Leon Draisaitl 1.25 3.00
G16 Steven Stamkos .75 2.00
G17 Johnny Gaudreau .60 1.50
G18 Jonathan Huberdeau .50 1.25

2022-23 Upper Deck Tim Hortons Hockey Triumphs

HT1 Auston Matthews 2.00 5.00
HT2 Sidney Crosby 2.00 5.00
HT3 Alex Ovechkin 2.00 5.00
HT4 Mark Stone .60 1.50
HT5 Patrick Kane 1.00 2.50
HT6 Steven Stamkos 1.00 2.50
HT7 Brady Tkachuk .75 2.00
HT8 Connor McDavid 2.50 6.00
HT9 Kevin Fiala .40 1.00
HT10 Darnell Nurse .40 1.00
HT11 Mitch Marner .75 2.00
HT12 Andrei Vasilevskiy .75 2.00
HT13 Nikolaj Ehlers .50 1.25
HT14 Cole Caufield 1.00 2.50
HT15 Lucas Raymond .75 2.00
HT16 Trevor Zegras .50 1.25
HT17 Marc-Andre Fleury 1.00 2.50
HT18 Joe Thornton .75 2.00

2022-23 Upper Deck Tim Hortons InMotion Phenoms

PM1 Arthur Kaliyev .75 2.00
PM2 Tim Stutzle 1.00 2.50
PM3 Jason Robertson 1.25 3.00
PM4 Cole Caufield 1.50 4.00
PM5 Tanner Jeannot .50 1.25
PM6 Trevor Zegras .75 2.00
PM7 Moritz Seider 1.00 2.50
PM8 Dawson Mercer 1.00 2.50
PM9 Michael Bunting .75 2.00
PM10 Lucas Raymond 1.25 3.00
PM11 Cale Makar 2.00 5.00
PM12 Lukas Reichel 1.50 4.00
PM13 Jamie Drysdale .60 1.50
PM14 Jack Quinn 1.25 3.00
PM15 Jonathan Dahlen .50 1.25
PM16 Jeremy Swayman 1.25 3.00
PM17 Spencer Knight .75 2.00
PM18 Alexis Lafreniere 1.25 3.00

2022-23 Upper Deck Tim Hortons Jerseys

JAK Anze Kopitar 40.00 100.00
JBB Brent Burns 25.00 60.00
JBG Brendan Gallagher 25.00 60.00
JBT Brady Tkachuk 40.00 100.00
JCH Carter Hart 25.00 60.00
JCK Chris Kreider 30.00 80.00
JCP Carey Price 50.00 125.00
JEL Elias Lindholm 25.00 60.00
JEP Elias Pettersson 40.00 100.00
JJT John Tavares 40.00 100.00
JKK Kirill Kaprizov 80.00 200.00
JLD Leon Draisaitl 80.00 200.00
JMR Mikko Rantanen 60.00 150.00
JMS Mark Scheifele 40.00 100.00
JRO Ryan O'Reilly 25.00 60.00
JSC Sidney Crosby 100.00 250.00
JSS Steven Stamkos 50.00 125.00
JTB Tyler Bertuzzi 20.00 50.00

2022-23 Upper Deck Tim Hortons Red Die Cuts

DC1 Connor McDavid 2.50 6.00
DC2 Sidney Crosby 2.00 5.00
DC3 Nathan MacKinnon 2.00 5.00
DC4 Alex Ovechkin 2.00 5.00
DC5 Patrick Kane 1.00 2.50
DC6 Steven Stamkos 1.00 2.50
DC7 Cale Makar 1.25 3.00
DC8 Mitch Marner .75 2.00
DC9 Brady Tkachuk .75 2.00
DC10 Quinn Hughes 1.25 3.00
DC11 Jack Hughes 1.25 3.00
DC12 Carey Price 1.00 2.50
DC14 Artemi Panarin 1.00 2.50
DC15 David Pastrnak 1.25 3.00
DC16 Adam Fox .60 1.50
DC17 Andrei Svechnikov .60 1.50
DC18 Brent Burns .50 1.25
DC19 Jaden Schwartz .40 1.00
DC20 Kirill Kaprizov 1.50 4.00
DC21 Ryan O'Reilly .50 1.25
DC22 Jake Guentzel .75 2.00
DC23 Brad Marchand 1.00 2.50
DC24 Andrei Vasilevskiy .75 2.00
DC25 Brayden Point .60 1.50
DC26 Mark Scheifele .75 2.00
DC27 Miro Heiskanen .60 1.50
DC28 Auston Matthews 2.00 5.00
DC29 Troy Terry .40 1.00
DC30 Leon Draisaitl 1.50 4.00
DC31 Chris Kreider .60 1.50
DC32 Kyle Connor .75 2.00
DC33 Matthew Tkachuk 1.00 2.50
DC34 Johnny Gaudreau .75 2.00
DC35 Jordan Kyrou .50 1.25
DC36 John Tavares .75 2.00
DC37 Aleksander Barkov .75 2.00
DC38 Nick Suzuki 1.00 2.50
DC39 Rasmus Dahlin .60 1.50
DC40 Marc-Andre Fleury 1.00 2.50
DC41 Lucas Raymond .75 2.00
DC42 Moritz Seider .60 1.50

2022-23 Upper Deck Tim Hortons Spectrum Standouts

C1 Sidney Crosby 2.00 5.00
C2 Connor McDavid 2.50 6.00
C3 Nathan MacKinnon 2.00 5.00
C4 Alex Ovechkin 2.00 5.00
C6 Patrick Kane 1.00 2.50
C7 Elias Pettersson .75 2.00
C8 Brad Marchand 1.00 2.50
C9 Nikita Kucherov 1.00 2.50
C10 Mitch Marner .75 2.00
C11 Quinn Hughes 1.25 3.00
C12 Lucas Raymond .75 2.00
C13 Marco Rossi 1.25 3.00
C14 Jack Quinn .75 2.00
C15 Matt Boldy 1.50 4.00
C16 William Nylander 1.00 2.50
C17 Nazem Kadri .60 1.50
C18 Tyler Bertuzzi .40 1.00

2022-23 Upper Deck Tim Hortons Superstar Showcase

SS1 Connor McDavid 2.50 6.00
SS2 Leon Draisaitl 1.50 4.00
SS3 Auston Matthews 2.00 5.00
SS4 Sidney Crosby 2.00 5.00
SS5 Alex Ovechkin 2.00 5.00
SS6 Patrick Kane 1.00 2.50
SS7 Nathan MacKinnon 2.00 5.00
SS8 Elias Pettersson .75 2.00
SS9 Brad Marchand 1.00 2.50
SS10 Cale Makar 1.25 3.00
SS11 Mitch Marner .75 2.00
SS12 Mark Scheifele .75 2.00
SS13 Brady Tkachuk .75 2.00
SS14 Matthew Tkachuk 1.00 2.50
SS15 Nick Suzuki 1.00 2.50
SS16 Brayden Point .60 1.50
SS17 Morgan Rielly .50 1.25
SS18 Chris Kreider .60 1.50

2022-23 Upper Deck Tim Hortons Superstar Signatures

SSNM Nathan MacKinnon/100 150.00 400.00
SSSC Sidney Crosby/87 400.00 1000.00

2022-23 Upper Deck Tim Hortons Wayne Gretzky Tribute

WGT1 Wayne Gretzky 125.00 300.00

2023-24 Upper Deck Tim Hortons

1 Tim Horton .75 2.00
2 Travis Konecny .50 1.25
3 Brent Burns .50 1.25
4 Seth Jones .50 1.25
5 Aaron Ekblad .60 1.50
6 Dylan Guenther .60 1.50
7 Brady Tkachuk .75 2.00
8 Cale Makar 1.25 3.00
9 Jack Eichel .75 2.00
10 Jonathan Huberdeau .60 1.50
11 Trevor Zegras .50 1.25
12 Alex DeBrincat .60 1.50
13 Carter Verhaeghe .50 1.25
14 Nick Suzuki 1.00 2.50
15 Aleksander Barkov .75 2.00
16 Mitch Marner .75 2.00
17 Darcy Kuemper .50 1.25
18 Tim Stutzle .60 1.50
19 Jonathan Toews .75 2.00
20 Sebastian Aho .75 2.00
21 Jason Robertson .75 2.00
22 Cole Caufield 1.00 2.50
23 Lucas Raymond .75 2.00
24 Dylan Cozens .50 1.25
25 Jordan Kyrou .50 1.25
26 Rasmus Dahlin .60 1.50
27 Cole Perfetti .50 1.25
28 Claude Giroux .50 1.25
29 Nathan MacKinnon 2.00 5.00
30 Ilya Sorokin .75 2.00
31 Igor Shesterkin 1.00 2.50
32 Drew Doughty .50 1.25
33 Jake Guentzel .75 2.00
34 Auston Matthews 2.00 5.00
35 Kris Letang .60 1.50
36 Matt Boldy .75 2.00
37 Patrice Bergeron .60 1.50
38 Tyler Seguin .60 1.50
39 Alexandar Georgiev .50 1.25
40 Elias Pettersson .75 2.00
41 Mason McTavish .50 1.25
42 Matthew Tkachuk 1.00 2.50
43 Quinn Hughes 1.25 3.00
44 Nikita Kucherov 1.00 2.50
45 Patrik Laine .60 1.50
46 Jared Spurgeon .50 1.25
47 Robert Thomas .50 1.25
48 Tomas Hertl .50 1.25
49 Anze Kopitar .75 2.00
50 Jordan Binnington .75 2.00
51 Logan Thompson .60 1.50
52 Jacob Markstrom .50 1.25
53 Bo Horvat .60 1.50
54 Artemi Panarin 1.00 2.50
55 Mark Scheifele .75 2.00
56 Zach Hyman .75 2.00
57 Jakob Chychrun .50 1.25
58 Evgeni Malkin 1.00 2.50
59 Dylan Larkin .60 1.50
60 Dougie Hamilton .40 1.00
61 Mark Stone .60 1.50
62 Timo Meier .50 1.25
63 Brad Marchand 1.00 2.50
64 Roope Hintz .60 1.50
65 Erik Karlsson .60 1.50
66 Andre Burakovsky .30 .75
67 Martin Necas .75 2.00
68 Juraj Slafkovsky 1.00 2.50
69 Jordan Eberle .50 1.25
70 Karel Vejmelka .30 .75
71 Linus Ullmark .50 1.25
72 Tage Thompson .60 1.50
73 Tyler Toffoli .50 1.25
74 John Carlson .50 1.25
75 David Perron .40 1.00
76 Andrei Vasilevskiy .75 2.00
77 Kirby Dach .50 1.25
78 Morgan Rielly .50 1.25
79 Carter Hart .50 1.25
80 Josh Morrissey .60 1.50
81 Kyle Connor .75 2.00
82 Noah Dobson .60 1.50
83 Brock Boeser .60 1.50
84 Troy Terry .40 1.00
85 Elias Lindholm .50 1.25
86 Jack Hughes 1.25 3.00
87 Sidney Crosby 2.00 5.00
88 William Nylander 1.00 2.50
89 Connor Hellebuyck 1.00 2.50
90 Matty Beniers .60 1.50
91 John Tavares .75 2.00
92 Gabriel Landeskog .60 1.50
93 Ryan Nugent-Hopkins .60 1.50
94 Nico Hischier .75 2.00
95 Matt Duchene .50 1.25
96 Mikko Rantanen 1.25 3.00
97 Connor McDavid 2.50 6.00
98 Filip Forsberg .75 2.00
99 J.T. Miller .60 1.50
100 Frederik Andersen .60 1.50
101 Alex Tuch .50 1.25
102 Brayden Point .60 1.50
103 Darnell Nurse .40 1.00
104 Leon Draisaitl 1.50 4.00
105 Marc-Andre Fleury 1.00 2.50
106 Quinton Byfield .60 1.50
107 Mathew Barzal .60 1.50
108 Alex Ovechkin 2.00 5.00
109 Nazem Kadri .60 1.50
110 Steven Stamkos 1.00 2.50
111 Mika Zibanejad .60 1.50
112 Kirill Kaprizov 1.50 4.00
113 Roman Josi .50 1.25
114 Moritz Seider .60 1.50
115 Clayton Keller .60 1.50
116 Kevin Fiala .40 1.00
117 Adam Fox .60 1.50
118 Johnny Gaudreau .75 2.00
119 David Pastrnak 1.25 3.00
120 Patrick Kane 1.00 2.50

2023-24 Upper Deck Tim Hortons '23 Draft Pick Redemption

NNO TBA 400.00 1000.00

2023-24 Upper Deck Tim Hortons Hockey Triumphs

HT1 Mark Scheifele .75 2.00
HT2 Mark Stone .60 1.50
HT3 Elias Lindholm .50 1.25
HT4 Drew Doughty .50 1.25
HT5 Jake Guentzel .75 2.00
HT6 Tim Stutzle .60 1.50
HT7 Jonathan Toews .75 2.00
HT8 Aleksander Barkov .75 2.00
HT9 Johnny Gaudreau .75 2.00
HT10 Tyler Toffoli .50 1.25
HT11 Patrik Laine .60 1.50
HT12 Dougie Hamilton .40 1.00
HT13 Mathew Barzal .60 1.50
HT14 Jordan Kyrou .50 1.25
HT15 Matt Duchene .50 1.25
HT16 Clayton Keller .60 1.50
HT17 Timo Meier .50 1.25
HT18 William Nylander 1.00 2.50

2023-24 Upper Deck Tim Hortons Ice Gems

IG1 Sidney Crosby 30.00 80.00
IG2 Alex Ovechkin 30.00 80.00
IG3 Mitch Marner 12.00 30.00
IG4 Cale Makar 20.00 50.00
IG5 Adam Fox 10.00 25.00
IG6 Andrei Vasilevskiy 12.00 30.00

2023-24 Upper Deck Tim Hortons In Motion Phenoms

MP1 Cale Makar 2.00 5.00
MP2 Juraj Slafkovsky 1.50 4.00
MP3 Jason Robertson 1.25 3.00
MP4 Matty Beniers 1.00 2.50
MP5 Matt Boldy 1.25 3.00
MP6 Shane Wright 1.00 2.50
MP7 Adam Fox 1.00 2.50
MP8 Rasmus Dahlin 1.00 2.50
MP9 Jack Hughes 2.00 5.00
MP10 Kent Johnson .75 2.00
MP11 Nick Suzuki 1.50 4.00
MP12 Brady Tkachuk 1.25 3.00
MP13 Owen Power .75 2.00
MP14 Trevor Zegras .75 2.00
MP15 Jake Sanderson 1.00 2.50
MP16 Elias Pettersson 1.25 3.00
MP17 Moritz Seider 1.00 2.50
MP18 Jack Quinn .60 1.50

2023-24 Upper Deck Tim Hortons Jerseys

JAE Aaron Ekblad 30.00 80.00
JBB Brock Boeser 30.00 80.00
JBM Brad Marchand 50.00 125.00
JBT Brady Tkachuk 40.00 100.00
JBW Blake Wheeler 25.00 60.00
JCH Connor Hellebuyck 50.00 125.00
JCM Connor McDavid 125.00 300.00
JCP Carey Price 50.00 125.00
JEL Elias Lindholm 25.00 60.00
JJM Jacob Markstrom 25.00 60.00
JJN Josh Norris 25.00 60.00
JJT Jonathan Toews 40.00 100.00
JLD Leon Draisaitl 80.00 200.00
JMM Mitch Marner 40.00 100.00
JNS Nick Suzuki 50.00 125.00
JRN Ryan Nugent-Hopkins 30.00 80.00
JWN William Nylander 50.00 125.00

2023-24 Upper Deck Tim Hortons Net Keepers

NK1 Igor Shesterkin 1.50 4.00
NK2 Stuart Skinner 1.00 2.50
NK3 John Gibson .75 2.00
NK4 Connor Hellebuyck 1.50 4.00
NK5 Linus Ullmark .75 2.00
NK6 Andrei Vasilevskiy 1.25 3.00
NK7 Jacob Markstrom .75 2.00
NK8 Cam Talbot .75 2.00
NK9 Logan Thompson 1.00 2.50
NK10 Ilya Sorokin 1.25 3.00
NK11 Jake Oettinger 1.25 3.00
NK12 Darcy Kuemper .75 2.00
NK13 Jordan Binnington 1.25 3.00
NK14 Vitek Vanecek .75 2.00
NK15 Matt Murray .75 2.00
NK16 Juuse Saros 1.00 2.50
NK17 Tristan Jarry .75 2.00
NK18 Marc-Andre Fleury 1.50 4.00

2023-24 Upper Deck Tim Hortons Point Leaders

PL1 Connor McDavid 4.00 10.00
PL2 Mitch Marner 1.25 3.00
PL3 Ryan Nugent-Hopkins 1.00 2.50
PL4 Jason Robertson 1.25 3.00
PL5 David Pastrnak 2.00 5.00
PL6 Mikko Rantanen 2.00 5.00
PL7 Kyle Connor 1.25 3.00
PL8 Nathan MacKinnon 3.00 8.00
PL9 Tage Thompson 1.00 2.50
PL10 Jack Hughes 2.00 5.00
PL11 Matthew Tkachuk 1.50 4.00
PL12 Artemi Panarin 1.50 4.00
PL13 Kirill Kaprizov 2.50 6.00
PL14 Alex Ovechkin 3.00 8.00
PL15 Sidney Crosby 3.00 8.00
PL16 Brady Tkachuk 1.25 3.00
PL17 Nikita Kucherov 1.50 4.00
PL18 Auston Matthews 3.00 8.00

2023-24 Upper Deck Tim Hortons Superstar Showcase

SS1 Sidney Crosby 2.00 5.00
SS2 Auston Matthews 2.00 5.00
SS3 Connor McDavid 2.50 6.00
SS4 Alex Ovechkin 2.00 5.00
SS5 Kirill Kaprizov 1.50 4.00
SS6 Nathan MacKinnon 2.00 5.00
SS7 Patrice Bergeron .60 1.50
SS8 Aaron Ekblad .60 1.50
SS9 Cale Makar 1.25 3.00
SS10 Elias Pettersson .75 2.00
SS11 Jonathan Huberdeau .60 1.50
SS12 Trevor Zegras .50 1.25
SS13 Quinn Hughes 1.25 3.00
SS14 Leon Draisaitl 1.50 4.00
SS15 Jack Hughes 1.25 3.00
SS16 Kyle Connor .75 2.00
SS17 Cole Caufield 1.00 2.50
SS18 Mitch Marner .75 2.00

2023-24 Upper Deck Tim Hortons Symmetry Standout

3D1 Cale Makar 6.00 15.00
3D2 Alex Ovechkin 10.00 25.00
3D3 Nazem Kadri 4.00 10.00
3D4 Mitch Marner 4.00 10.00
3D5 Connor McDavid 12.00 30.00
3D6 Jason Robertson 4.00 10.00
3D7 David Pastrnak 6.00 15.00
3D8 Moritz Seider 3.00 8.00
3D9 Tage Thompson 3.00 8.00
3D10 Jack Eichel 4.00 10.00
3D11 Patrick Kane 5.00 12.00
3D12 Matty Beniers 3.00 8.00
3D13 Adam Fox 3.00 8.00
3D14 Sidney Crosby 10.00 25.00
3D15 Kirill Kaprizov 8.00 20.00
3D16 Auston Matthews 10.00 25.00
3D17 Kyle Connor 4.00 10.00
3D18 Leon Draisaitl 8.00 20.00

2023-24 Upper Deck Tim Hortons Timbits Autograph

JM Josh Morrissey 250.00 600.00

2023-24 Upper Deck Tim Hortons Wayne Gretzky Tribute

WGT1 Wayne Gretzky 125.00 300.00

2024-25 Upper Deck Tim Hortons

1 Tim Horton .75 2.00
2 Cale Makar 1.25 3.00
3 Jack Hughes 1.25 3.00
4 David Pastrnak 1.25 3.00
5 Cole Caufield 1.00 2.50
6 Adam Fantilli .75 2.00
7 Morgan Rielly .50 1.25
8 Alex Ovechkin 2.00 5.00
9 Steven Stamkos 1.00 2.50
10 Elias Pettersson .75 2.00
11 Quinton Byfield .60 1.50
12 Brent Burns .50 1.25
13 Kyle Connor .75 2.00
14 Jake Oettinger .75 2.00
15 Mitch Marner .75 2.00
16 Moritz Seider .60 1.50
17 Erik Karlsson .60 1.50
18 Nick Suzuki 1.00 2.50
19 Mason McTavish .50 1.25
20 Adam Fox .60 1.50
21 Brady Tkachuk .75 2.00
22 Ryan O'Reilly .50 1.25
23 Jake Sanderson .60 1.50
24 Marc-Andre Fleury 1.00 2.50
25 Alexis Lafreniere .75 2.00
26 Jonathan Huberdeau .60 1.50
27 Brendan Gallagher .50 1.25
28 Tage Thompson .60 1.50
29 Nathan MacKinnon 2.00 5.00
30 Leon Draisaitl 1.50 4.00
31 Nico Hischier .75 2.00
32 Igor Shesterkin 1.00 2.50
33 Tim Stutzle .60 1.50
34 Auston Matthews 2.00 5.00
35 Clayton Keller .60 1.50
36 Tomas Hertl .50 1.25
37 Jordan Binnington .75 2.00
38 Cole Perfetti .50 1.25
39 Vince Dunn .40 1.00
40 Nikita Kucherov 1.00 2.50
41 Anze Kopitar .75 2.00
42 Sebastian Aho .75 2.00
43 Juraj Slafkovsky 1.00 2.50
44 Claude Giroux .50 1.25
45 Drew Doughty .50 1.25
46 Brad Marchand 1.00 2.50
47 Connor Hellebuyck 1.00 2.50
48 Johnny Gaudreau .75 2.00
49 Philipp Kurashev .40 1.00
50 Filip Forsberg .75 2.00
51 Jack Eichel .75 2.00
52 Zach Hyman .75 2.00
53 Nick Schmaltz .40 1.00
54 Bo Horvat .60 1.50
55 Travis Konecny .50 1.25
56 Roman Josi .50 1.25
57 Mats Zuccarello .50 1.25
58 Quinn Hughes 1.25 3.00
59 Logan Cooley .75 2.00
60 Jordan Eberle .50 1.25
61 Tom Wilson .50 1.25
62 Mikko Rantanen 1.25 3.00
63 Sam Reinhart 1.00 2.50
64 Mark Stone .60 1.50
65 Jason Robertson .75 2.00
66 Aleksander Barkov .75 2.00
67 Kris Letang .60 1.50
68 Brayden Point .60 1.50
69 Alex Tuch .50 1.25
70 Kirill Kaprizov 1.50 4.00
71 Mathew Barzal .60 1.50
72 Sean Couturier .40 1.00
73 Seth Jones .50 1.25
74 Logan Couture .60 1.50
75 Matty Beniers .60 1.50
76 Wyatt Johnston 1.00 2.50
77 Evgeni Malkin 1.00 2.50
78 Alex DeBrincat .60 1.50
79 Robert Thomas .50 1.25
80 Alex Newhook .40 1.00
81 Trevor Zegras .50 1.25
82 Luke Hughes .75 2.00
83 Dylan Strome .60 1.50
84 Joseph Woll .60 1.50
85 Rasmus Dahlin .60 1.50
86 J.T. Miller .60 1.50
87 Sidney Crosby 2.00 5.00
88 Artemi Panarin 1.00 2.50
89 Ryan Nugent-Hopkins .60 1.50
90 Owen Tippett .30 .75
91 Lucas Raymond .75 2.00
92 Martin Necas .75 2.00
93 Mika Zibanejad .60 1.50
94 Zach Werenski .75 2.00
95 Josh Morrissey .60 1.50
96 Timo Meier .50 1.25
97 Connor McDavid 2.50 6.00
98 Connor Bedard 1.50 4.00
99 Jordan Kyrou .50 1.25
100 Linus Ullmark .50 1.25
101 John Tavares .75 2.00
102 Jakob Chychrun .50 1.25
103 Dylan Larkin .60 1.50
104 Mark Scheifele .75 2.00
105 Evan Bouchard .60 1.50
106 Mikael Backlund .40 1.00
107 Thatcher Demko .60 1.50
108 Andrei Vasilevskiy .75 2.00
109 Lukas Reichel .50 1.25
110 Brock Boeser .60 1.50
111 Matthew Tkachuk 1.00 2.50
112 William Eklund .60 1.50
113 Jacob Markstrom .50 1.25
114 MacKenzie Weegar .40 1.00
115 Pierre-Luc Dubois .40 1.00
116 Ilya Sorokin .75 2.00
117 Jonathan Marchessault .60 1.50
118 Leo Carlsson .75 2.00
119 Miro Heiskanen .60 1.50
120 Owen Power .50 1.25

2024-25 Upper Deck Tim Hortons Above the Ice

AI1 Connor McDavid 2.00 5.00
AI2 Kirill Kaprizov 1.25 3.00
AI3 Brayden Point .50 1.25
AI4 Mason McTavish .40 1.00
AI5 Igor Shesterkin .75 2.00
AI6 Thatcher Demko .50 1.25
AI7 Alex Ovechkin 1.50 4.00
AI8 Sidney Crosby 1.50 4.00
AI9 Auston Matthews 1.50 4.00
AI10 John Tavares .60 1.50
AI11 Robert Thomas .40 1.00
AI12 Carter Verhaeghe .40 1.00
AI13 Dylan Larkin .50 1.25
AI14 Elias Pettersson .60 1.50
AI15 Artemi Panarin .75 2.00
AI16 Pierre-Luc Dubois .30 .75
AI17 Aleksander Barkov .60 1.50
AI18 Nazem Kadri .50 1.25

2024-25 Upper Deck Tim Hortons Franchise Trios

FT1 Pastrnak/Marchand/McAvoy 40.00 100.00
FT2 Miller/Pettersson/Hughes 40.00 100.00
FT3 Nylander/Matthews/Marner 40.00 100.00
FT4 Draisaitl/McDavid/Hyman 40.00 100.00
FT5 Caufield/Suzuki/Slafkovsky 40.00 100.00
FT6 Stutzle/Tkachuk/Giroux 40.00 100.00

2024-25 Upper Deck Tim Hortons Frozen Hotshots

FH1 Sidney Crosby 1.00 2.50
FH2 Jack Hughes .60 1.50
FH3 Leon Draisaitl .75 2.00
FH4 Alex DeBrincat .30 .75
FH5 Connor Bedard .75 2.00
FH6 Jack Eichel .40 1.00
FH7 Kyle Connor .40 1.00
FH8 David Pastrnak .60 1.50
FH9 Matty Beniers .30 .75
FH10 Cole Caufield .50 1.25
FH11 Mikko Rantanen .60 1.50
FH12 Alex Ovechkin 1.00 2.50
FH13 Quinn Hughes .60 1.50
FH14 Nikita Kucherov .50 1.25
FH15 Bo Horvat .30 .75
FH16 Jason Robertson .40 1.00
FH17 Auston Matthews 1.00 2.50
FH18 Connor McDavid 1.25 3.00

2024-25 Upper Deck Tim Hortons InMotion Phenoms

MP1 Cale Makar 2.00 5.00
MP2 Luke Hughes 1.25 3.00
MP3 Adam Fantilli 1.25 3.00
MP4 Jake Sanderson 1.00 2.50
MP5 Cole Caufield 1.50 4.00
MP6 Zach Benson .60 1.50
MP7 Quinton Byfield 1.00 2.50
MP8 Logan Cooley 1.25 3.00
MP9 Matty Beniers 1.00 2.50
MP10 Jack Hughes 2.00 5.00
MP11 Pavel Mintyukov .60 1.50
MP12 Wyatt Johnston 1.50 4.00
MP13 Bobby Brink .50 1.25
MP14 Matthew Knies 1.50 4.00
MP15 Tim Stutzle 1.00 2.50
MP16 Leo Carlsson 1.25 3.00
MP17 Matthew Poitras .75 2.00
MP18 Connor Bedard 2.50 6.00

2024-25 Upper Deck Tim Hortons Jerseys

JAM Auston Matthews 100.00 250.00
JBP Brayden Point 30.00 80.00
JCC Cole Caufield 50.00 125.00
JCH Connor Hellebuyck 50.00 125.00
JDL Dylan Larkin 30.00 80.00
JJH Jonathan Huberdeau 30.00 80.00
JJP Joe Pavelski 30.00 80.00
JJS Jeremy Swayman 40.00 100.00
JMF Marc-Andre Fleury 50.00 125.00
JMN Martin Necas 40.00 100.00
JMR Mikko Rantanen 60.00 150.00
JMZ Mika Zibanejad 30.00 80.00
JNH Nico Hischier 40.00 100.00
JOP Owen Power 25.00 60.00
JPB Pavel Buchnevich 20.00 50.00
JPL Patrik Laine 30.00 80.00
JSA Juuse Saros 30.00 80.00
JTC Thomas Chabot 25.00 60.00

2024-25 Upper Deck Tim Hortons Pure Gold

PG1 Quinn Hughes 1.50 4.00
PG2 Brady Tkachuk 1.00 2.50
PG3 Pavel Zacha .50 1.25
PG4 Ryan O'Reilly .60 1.50
PG5 Joseph Woll .75 2.00
PG6 Miro Heiskanen .75 2.00
PG7 Jake Guentzel 1.00 2.50
PG8 Johnny Gaudreau 1.00 2.50
PG9 Travis Konecny .60 1.50
PG10 Moritz Seider .75 2.00
PG11 Tomas Hertl .60 1.50
PG12 Matthew Tkachuk 1.25 3.00
PG13 Seth Jones .60 1.50
PG14 Filip Forsberg 1.00 2.50
PG15 Juraj Slafkovsky 1.25 3.00
PG16 Clayton Keller .75 2.00

PG17 Anze Kopitar 1.00 2.50
PG18 Shane Wright .75 2.00

2024-25 Upper Deck Tim Hortons Sidney Crosby Retrospective
SC1 Sidney Crosby 2.50 6.00
SC2 Sidney Crosby 2.50 6.00
SC3 Sidney Crosby 2.50 6.00
SC4 Sidney Crosby 2.50 6.00
SC5 Sidney Crosby 2.50 6.00
SC6 Sidney Crosby 2.50 6.00
SC7 Sidney Crosby 2.50 6.00
SC8 Sidney Crosby 2.50 6.00
SC9 Sidney Crosby 2.50 6.00

2024-25 Upper Deck Tim Hortons Signatures
SAS Andrei Svechnikov 80.00 200.00
SAX Arber Xhekaj 60.00 150.00
SBC Brandt Clarke 60.00 150.00
SCP Cole Perfetti 60.00 150.00
SDJ Dakota Joshua 40.00 100.00
SJG John Gibson 60.00 150.00
SJK Jordan Kyrou 60.00 150.00
SJS Jake Sanderson 80.00 200.00
SLR Lukas Reichel 60.00 150.00
SPM Pavel Mintyukov 50.00 125.00
SRH Roope Hintz 80.00 200.00
STD Thatcher Demko 80.00 200.00
STJ Tristan Jarry 60.00 150.00
STM Timo Meier 60.00 150.00
SWK William Karlsson 80.00 200.00

2024-25 Upper Deck Tim Hortons Timbits to NHL
1993 Sidney Crosby 40.00 100.00
1993 Brad Marchand 30.00 80.00
1999 Colton Parayko 12.00 30.00
1999 Brendan Gallagher 15.00 40.00
2000 Brayden Point 20.00 50.00
2000 Nathan MacKinnon 25.00 60.00
2001 Aaron Ekblad 20.00 50.00
2002 Josh Morrissey 20.00 50.00
2008 Dawson Mercer 20.00 50.00

2024-25 Upper Deck Tim Hortons True North Future
TN1 Connor Bedard 1.50 4.00
TN2 Steven Stamkos 1.00 2.50
TN3 Brad Marchand 1.00 2.50
TN4 Nathan MacKinnon 2.00 5.00
TN5 Connor McDavid 2.50 6.00
TN6 Mark Stone .60 1.50
TN7 Dylan Cozens .50 1.25
TN8 John Tavares .75 2.00
TN9 Brent Burns .50 1.25
TN11 Nick Suzuki 1.00 2.50
TN12 Mitch Marner .75 2.00
TN13 Mason McTavish .50 1.25
TN14 Owen Power .50 1.25
TN15 Logan Thompson .60 1.50
TN16 Sidney Crosby 2.00 5.00
TN17 Jordan Kyrou .50 1.25
TN18 Marc-Andre Fleury 1.00 2.50

2023-24 Upper Deck Tim Hortons Greatest Duos
1 T.Horton/F.Mahovlich .75 2.00
2 K.Kaaprizov/M.Boldy 1.50 4.00
3 C.Caufield/K.Dach 1.00 2.50
4 M.Seider/D.Perron .60 1.50
5 C.McDavid/L.Draisaitl 2.50 6.00
6 M.Beniers/J.McCann .60 1.50
7 A.Ovechkin/E.Kuznetsov 2.00 5.00
8 M.Weegar/E.Lindholm .50 1.25
9 J.Saros/R.Josi .60 1.50
10 M.Stone/C.Stephenson .60 1.50
11 B.Horvat/M.Barzal .60 1.50
12 J.Kyrou/B.Schenn .50 1.25
13 T.Stutzle/C.Giroux .60 1.50
14 J.Eichel/J.Marchessault .75 2.00
15 B.Burns/J.Slavin .50 1.25
16 M.Sundin/D.Gilmour .60 1.50
17 D.Larkin/L.Raymond .75 2.00
18 B.Tkachuk/M.Tkachuk 1.00 2.50
19 I.Shesterkin/A.Panarin 1.00 2.50
20 T.Wilson/T.Oshie .50 1.25
21 M.Ekholm/D.Nurse .40 1.00
22 S.Aho/S.Jarvis .75 2.00
23 J.Huberdeau/N.Kadri .60 1.50
24 L.Ullmark/H.Lindholm .50 1.25
25 S.Crosby/N.MacKinnon 2.00 5.00
26 N.Suzuki/J.Slafkovsky 1.00 2.50
27 B.Leetch/M.Messier 1.00 2.50
28 A.Vasilevskiy/N.Kucherov 1.00 2.50
29 R.Dahlin/O.Power .60 1.50
30 S.Bobrovsky/C.Verhaeghe .75 2.00
31 D.Pastrnak/C.McAvoy 1.25 3.00
32 C.Perfetti/M.Scheifele .75 2.00
33 A.Kopitar/A.Kempe .75 2.00
34 A.Kerikonen/M.Rantanen 1.25 3.00
35 T.Thompson/D.Cozens .60 1.50
36 J.Oettinger/M.Heiskanen .75 2.00
37 T.Jarry/K.Letang .60 1.50
38 M.Lemieux/P.Coffey 2.00 5.00
39 R.Thomas/P.Buchnevich .50 1.25
40 A.Svechnikov/M.Necas .75 2.00
41 T.Hertl/A.Barabanov .50 1.25
42 L.Couture/M.Ferraro .60 1.50
43 C.Kreidr/M.Zibanejad .60 1.50
44 S.Pinto/J.Norris .50 1.25
45 M.Marner/W.Nylander 1.00 2.50
46 S.Jones/C.Jones .50 1.25
47 A.Burakovsky/J.Eberle .50 1.25
48 Q.Hughes/J.Miller 1.25 3.00
49 R.Bourque/A.Oates .75 2.00
50 T.Barrie/F.Forsberg .75 2.00
51 O.Palat/N.Hischier .75 2.00
52 R.Hartman/J.Spurgeon .50 1.25
53 T.Chabot/J.Chychrun .50 1.25
54 A.Ekblad/B.Montour .60 1.50
55 K.Fiala/V.Arvidsson .40 1.00
56 J.Hughes/D.Mercer 1.25 3.00
57 L.Reichel/T.Raddysh .50 1.25
58 C.Makar/G.Landeskog 1.25 3.00
59 J.Guentzel/E.Malkin 1.00 2.50
60 T.Linden/M.Naslund .50 1.25
61 T.Zegras/M.McTavish .50 1.25
62 A.Matthews/J.Tavares 2.00 5.00
63 C.Keller/N.Schmaltz .60 1.50
64 V.Hedman/M.Sergachev .60 1.50
65 N.Neiderreiter/J.Morrissey .60 1.50
66 P.Laine/K.Johnson .60 1.50
67 C.Bedard/A.Athanasiou 3.00 8.00
68 T.Konecny/J.Farabee .50 1.25
69 I.Sorokin/B.Nelson .75 2.00
70 W.Gretzky/J.Kurri 3.00 8.00
71 E.Pettersson/A.Kuzmenko .75 2.00
72 S.Stamkos/B.Point 1.00 2.50
73 J.Gaudreau/K.Marchenko .75 2.00
74 A.Fox/K.Miller .60 1.50
75 M.Backlund/J.Markstrom .50 1.25
76 J.Sakic/P.Stastny 1.00 2.50
77 L.Crouse/D.Guenther .60 1.50
78 R.Nugent-Hopkins/Z.Hyman .75 2.00
79 M.Modano/M.Turco .75 2.00
80 B.Marchand/J.DeBrusk 1.00 2.50
81 T.Terry/J.Gibson .50 1.25
82 J.Robertson/W.Johnson 1.00 2.50
83 O.Tippett/T.Foerster 1.00 2.50
84 J.Beliveau/H.Richard .50 1.25
85 K.Connor/N.Ehlers .75 2.00
86 S.Nurse/L.Stacey 1.25 3.00
87 M.Rooney/A.Frankel .75 2.00
88 J.Larocque/K.O'Neill .50 1.25
89 R.Fast/J.Saulnier .60 1.50
90 L.Steckelin/H.Scamurra .50 1.25
91 E.Clark/J.Rattray 1.00 2.50
92 S.Harmon/A.Desbiens 1.25 3.00
93 M.Poulin/J.Eldridge 1.50 4.00
94 E.Maschmeyer/K.Campbell .75 2.00
95 B.Turnbull/V.Bach .50 1.25
96 E.Shelton/A.Carpenter .60 1.50
97 J.Bourbonnais/M.Keller .50 1.25
98 B.Jenner/H.Brandt .75 2.00
99 A.Roque/H.Knight 1.25 3.00
100 N.Hensley/E.Ambrose .75 2.00

2023-24 Upper Deck Tim Hortons Greatest Duos Autographs
NNO1 A.Xhekaj/B.Gallagher 80.00 200.00
NNO3 B.Byram/D.Toews 100.00 250.00
NNO4 B.Tkachuk/S.Pinto 125.00 300.00
NNO5 B.Point/B.Hagel 100.00 250.00
NNO7 C.Mittelstadt/A.Tuch 80.00 200.00
NNO8 E.Kuznetsov/T.Wilson 100.00 250.00
NNO9 J.Markstrom/B.Coleman 80.00 200.00
NNO11 M.Duchene/J.Saros 100.00 250.00
NNO12 M.Heiskanen/J.Pavelski 100.00 250.00
NNO13 N.Ehlers/C.Perfetti 80.00 200.00
NNO14 R.Thomas/J.Kyrou 80.00 200.00
NNO15 S.Reinhart/A.Barkov 150.00 400.00
NNO16 S.Theodore/W.Karlsson 100.00 250.00

2023-24 Upper Deck Tim Hortons Greatest Duos Bounded by Honour
BH1 W.Gretzky/A.Ovechkin 40.00 100.00
BH2 P.Roy/D.Hasek 30.00 80.00
BH3 C.McDavid/M.Lemieux 30.00 80.00
BH4 S.Crosby/E.Malkin 30.00 80.00
BH5 M.Poulin/S.Nurse 30.00 80.00

2023-24 Upper Deck Tim Hortons Greatest Duos Captains
C1 C.McDavid/W.Gretzky 25.00 60.00
C2 P.Bergeron/A.Barkov 8.00 20.00
C3 R.Josi/J.Trouba 5.00 12.00
C4 M.St. Louis/N.Suzuki 10.00 25.00
C5 S.Stamkos/A.Ovechkin 20.00 50.00
C6 J.Sakic/G.Landeskog 10.00 25.00
C7 A.Kopitar/M.Stone 8.00 20.00
C8 J.Tavares/M.Sundin 8.00 20.00
C9 D.Larkin/N.Hischier 8.00 20.00
C10 S.Crosby/M.Lemieux 20.00 50.00
C11 B.Tkachuk/K.Tkachuk 8.00 20.00
C12 K.Okposo/L.Couture 6.00 15.00
C13 J.Staal/J.Benn 5.00 12.00
C14 M.Poulin/H.Knight 15.00 40.00
C15 S.Nurse/M.Keller 12.00 30.00

2023-24 Upper Deck Tim Hortons Greatest Duos Crosby McKinnon Autographs
NNO S.Crosby/N.MacKinnon 600.00 1500.00

2023-24 Upper Deck Tim Hortons Greatest Duos Family Foundations
FF1 B.Tkachuk/M.Tkachuk 2.00 5.00
FF2 W.Nylander/A.Nylander 2.00 5.00
FF3 D.Nurse/S.Nurse 2.50 6.00
FF4 J.Hughes/Q.Hughes 2.50 6.00
FF5 J.Van Riemsdyk/T.Van Riemsdyk .75 2.00
FF6 E.Staal/J.Staal .75 2.00
FF7 T.Thompson/T.Thompson 1.25 3.00
FF8 R.Strome/D.Strome 1.25 3.00
FF9 D.Potvin/J.Potvin 1.00 2.50
FF10 C.Jarnkrok/E.Lindholm 1.00 2.50
FF11 S.Jones/C.Jones 1.00 2.50
FF12 B.Hull/B.Hull 2.00 5.00
FF13 M.Barron/J.Barron .75 2.00
FF14 M.Domi/T.Domi 1.00 2.50
FF15 F.Mahovlich/P.Mahovlich 1.00 2.50

2023-24 Upper Deck Tim Hortons Greatest Duos Linked by Numbers
LN1 B.Tkachuk/K.Tkachuk 1.25 3.00
LN2 C.Makar/A.Ovechkin 3.00 8.00
LN3 J.Eichel/C.Keller 1.25 3.00
LN4 M.Beniers/J.Huberdeau 1.00 2.50
LN5 A.Roque/S.Kunin .75 2.00
LN6 M.Sundin/T.Selanne 1.50 4.00
LN7 M.Marner/D.Tucker 1.25 3.00
LN8 S.Nurse/H.Brandt 2.00 5.00
LN9 E.Clark/K.Schofield 2.00 5.00
LN10 N.MacKinnon/P.Laine 3.00 8.00
LN11 R.Josi/J.Guentzel 1.25 3.00
LN12 J.Hughes/N.Kucherov 2.00 5.00
LN13 S.Stamkos/J.Tavares 1.50 4.00
LN14 M.Zibanejad/R.Nugent-Hopkins 1.00 2.50
LN15 C.Caufield/K.Fiala 1.50 4.00

2023-24 Upper Deck Tim Hortons Greatest Duos Rink Rivals
RR1 C.McDavid/A.Matthews 4.00 10.00
RR2 B.Gallagher/B.Marchand 1.50 4.00
RR3 M.Tkachuk/S.Stamkos 1.50 4.00
RR4 L.Draisaitl/N.Kadri 2.50 6.00
RR5 J.Eichel/M.Beniers 1.25 3.00
RR6 S.Jones/C.Parayko .75 2.00
RR7 E.Maschmeyer/A.Desbiens 2.00 5.00
RR8 S.Crosby/A.Ovechkin 3.00 8.00
RR9 K.Connor/K.Kaprizov 2.50 6.00
RR10 J.Hughes/T.Konecny 2.00 5.00
RR11 K.O'Neil/H.Knight 2.00 5.00
RR12 A.Kopitar/L.Couture 1.25 3.00
RR13 I.Shesterkin/I.Sorokin 1.50 4.00
RR14 M.Poulin/A.Roque 2.50 6.00
RR15 S.Yzerman/J.Sakic 2.00 5.00

2023-24 Upper Deck Tim Hortons Greatest Duos Rookie Connection
RC1 A.Ovechkin/E.Malkin 3.00 8.00
RC2 S.Crosby/K.Letang 3.00 8.00
RC3 J.Tavares/V.Hedman 1.25 3.00
RC4 N.MacKinnon/A.Barkov 3.00 8.00
RC5 L.Draisaitl/D.Larkin 2.50 6.00
RC6 C.McDavid/J.Eichel 4.00 10.00
RC7 A.Matthews/T.Thompson 3.00 8.00
RC8 J.Robertson/N.Suzuki 1.50 4.00
RC9 R.Dahlin/Q.Hughes 2.00 5.00
RC10 J.Hughes/T.Zegras 2.00 5.00
RC11 T.Stutzle/L.Raymond 1.25 3.00
RC12 O.Power/M.Beniers 1.00 2.50
RC13 M.Lemieux/P.Roy 3.00 8.00
RC14 R.Fast/L.Stacey 1.00 2.50
RC15 S.Nurse/V.Bach 2.00 5.00

2022-23 Upper Deck Tim Hortons Legends
1 Tim Horton .60 1.50
2 Jean Beliveau .40 1.00
3 Jacques Plante .40 1.00
4 Glenn Hall .40 1.00
5 Andy Bathgate .30 .75
6 Johnny Bower .40 1.00
7 Henri Richard .40 1.00
8 Frank Mahovlich .40 1.00
9 Johnny Bucyk .40 1.00
10 Stan Mikita .40 1.00
11 Bobby Hull .75 2.00
12 Bobby Clarke .60 1.50
13 Brad Park .30 .75
14 Tony Esposito .40 1.00
15 Mark Howe .40 1.00
16 Larry Robinson .40 1.00
17 Denis Potvin .40 1.00
18 Marcel Dionne .50 1.25
19 Wendel Clark .60 1.50
20 Butch Goring .40 1.00
21 Lanny McDonald .40 1.00
22 Bernie Federko .30 .75
23 Billy Smith .40 1.00
24 Chris Pronger .40 1.00
25 Chris Chelios .40 1.00
26 Pat Lafontaine .40 1.00
27 Peter Stastny .30 .75
28 Martin Biron .30 .75
29 Phil Housley .30 .75
30 Kevin Lowe .40 1.00
31 Scott Gomez .30 .75
32 Bryan Trottier .40 1.00
33 Glenn Anderson .30 .75
34 Wayne Gretzky 2.50 6.00
35 Grant Fuhr .60 1.50
36 Paul Coffey .40 1.00
37 Steve Yzerman 1.00 2.50
38 Doug Gilmour .50 1.25
39 Dave Andreychuk .40 1.00
40 Denis Savard .40 1.00
41 Al MacInnis .50 1.25
42 Dale Hawerchuk .50 1.25
43 Mike Gartner .50 1.25
44 Michel Goulet .40 1.00
45 Andy Moog .40 1.00
46 Ray Bourque .60 1.50
47 Brian Bellows .30 .75
48 Steve Larmer .30 .75
49 Igor Larionov .40 1.00
50 Patrick Roy 1.00 2.50
51 Joe Nieuwendyk .30 .75
52 Mario Lemieux 1.50 4.00
53 Luc Robitaille .40 1.00
54 Adam Oates .40 1.00
55 Vincent Damphousse .30 .75
56 Theoren Fleury .40 1.00
57 Brian Leetch .30 .75
58 Mats Sundin .40 1.00
59 Peter Forsberg .75 2.00
60 Mike Modano .60 1.50
61 Teemu Selanne .75 2.00
62 Sergei Zubov .30 .75
63 Trevor Linden .40 1.00
64 Brendan Shanahan .40 1.00
65 Mark Recchi .40 1.00
66 Joe Sakic .75 2.00
67 Ed Belfour .40 1.00
68 Chris Osgood .40 1.00
69 Rod Brind'Amour .40 1.00
70 Ray Whitney .25 .60
71 Jason Arnott .30 .75
72 Scott Niedermayer .40 1.00
73 Martin St.Louis .40 1.00
74 Brad Richards .40 1.00
75 Alex Tanguay .25 .60
76 Angela James .30 .75
77 France Saint-Louis .30 .75
78 Vicky Sunohara .30 .75
79 Cassie Campbell .40 1.00
80 Caroline Ouellette .40 1.00
81 Becky Kellar .30 .75
82 Therese Brisson .30 .75
83 Jayna Hefford .40 1.00
84 Kim St-Pierre .40 1.00
85 Charline Labonte .40 1.00
86 Shannon Szabados .30 .75
87 Hayley Wickenheiser .30 .75
88 Danielle Goyette .30 .75
89 Manon Rheaume 1.00 2.50
90 Nancy Drolet .30 .75
91 Jennifer Botterill .40 1.00
92 Meghan Agosta .30 .75
93 Geraldine Heaney .30 .75
94 Cheryl Pounder .40 1.00
95 Cherie Piper .30 .75
96 Gillian Apps .40 1.00
97 Sarah Vaillancourt .30 .75
98 Tessa Bonhomme .40 1.00
99 Colleen Sostorics .30 .75
100 Catherine Ward .30 .75

2022-23 Upper Deck Tim Hortons Legends Autographs
HW Hayley Wickenheiser JSY/22 400.00 1000.00
WG Wayne Gretzky/99 800.00 2000.00

2022-23 Upper Deck Tim Hortons Legends Canvas Legends
CL1 Tim Horton 1.25 3.00
CL2 Mike Gartner 1.00 2.50
CL3 Al MacInnis 1.00 2.50
CL4 Stan Mikita .75 2.00
CL5 Bobby Hull 1.50 4.00
CL6 Johnny Bower .75 2.00
CL7 Steve Yzerman 2.00 5.00
CL8 Grant Fuhr 1.25 3.00
CL9 Luc Robitaille .75 2.00
CL10 Mario Lemieux 3.00 8.00
CL11 Joe Sakic 1.50 4.00
CL12 Mark Recchi .75 2.00
CL13 Hayley Wickenheiser .60 1.50
CL14 Jayna Hefford .75 2.00
CL15 Manon Rheaume 2.00 5.00

2022-23 Upper Deck Tim Hortons Legends Championship Resume
CR1 Tim Horton .75 2.00
CR2 Frank Mahovlich .50 1.25
CR3 Teemu Selanne 1.00 2.50
CR4 Johnny Bucyk .50 1.25
CR5 Jean Beliveau .50 1.25
CR6 Jacques Plante .50 1.25
CR7 Bernie Parent .60 1.50
CR8 Adam Graves .40 1.00
CR9 Patrick Roy 1.25 3.00
CR10 Bryan Trottier .50 1.25
CR11 Theoren Fleury .50 1.25
CR12 Mario Lemieux 2.00 5.00
CR13 Scott Niedermayer .50 1.25
CR14 Kim St-Pierre .50 1.25
CR15 Geraldine Heaney .40 1.00

2022-23 Upper Deck Tim Hortons Legends Legendary Celebrations
LC1 Wayne Gretzky 15.00 40.00
LC2 Grant Fuhr 6.00 15.00
LC3 Denis Potvin 8.00 20.00
LC4 Bobby Clarke 8.00 20.00
LC5 Steve Yzerman 8.00 20.00
LC6 Dave Andreychuk 8.00 20.00
LC7 Guy Carbonneau 8.00 20.00
LC8 Joe Nieuwendyk 6.00 15.00
LC9 Ray Bourque 8.00 20.00
LC10 Mark Recchi 8.00 20.00
LC11 Brendan Shanahan 8.00 20.00
LC12 Rod Brind'Amour 8.00 20.00
LC13 Brad Richards 8.00 20.00
LC14 Danielle Goyette 6.00 15.00
LC15 Jayna Hefford 8.00 20.00

2022-23 Upper Deck Tim Hortons Legends Record Books
RB1 Wayne Gretzky 3.00 8.00
RB2 Larry Robinson .50 1.25
RB3 Patrick Roy 1.25 3.00
RB4 Terry Sawchuk .50 1.25
RB5 Mario Lemieux 2.00 5.00
RB6 Pat Lafontaine .50 1.25
RB7 Ray Bourque .75 2.00
RB8 Ed Belfour .50 1.25
RB9 Paul Coffey .50 1.25
RB10 Bobby Hull 1.00 2.50
RB11 Marcel Dionne .60 1.50
RB12 Brendan Shanahan .50 1.25
RB13 Joe Sakic 1.00 2.50
RB14 Manon Rheaume 1.25 3.00
RB15 Hayley Wickenheiser .40 1.00

2022-23 Upper Deck Tim Hortons Legends Trendsetters
T1 Wayne Gretzky 5.00 12.00
T2 Mario Lemieux 3.00 8.00
T3 Martin St. Louis .75 2.00
T4 Patrick Roy 2.00 5.00
T5 Borje Salming .75 2.00
T6 Ted Lindsay .75 2.00
T7 Stan Mikita .75 2.00
T9 Dale Hawerchuk 1.00 2.50
T10 Jacques Plante .75 2.00
T11 Igor Larionov .75 2.00
T12 Al MacInnis 1.00 2.50
T13 Ray Bourque 1.25 3.00
T14 Angela James .60 1.50
T15 Geraldine Heaney .60 1.50

2022-23 Upper Deck Tim Hortons Legends World's Best
WB1 Wayne Gretzky 60.00 150.00
WB2 Brett Hull 25.00 60.00
WB3 Nicklas Lidstrom 25.00 60.00
WB4 Teemu Selanne 25.00 60.00
WB5 Hayley Wickenheiser 25.00 60.00

2024-25 Upper Deck Tim Hortons Rookie Retrospective
1 Tim Horton .25 .60
2 Mitch Marner .25 .60
3 Mathew Barzal .20 .50
4 Miro Heiskanen .20 .50
5 Tage Thompson .20 .50
6 Sam Reinhart .30 .75
7 Patrick Kane .30 .75
8 Auston Matthews .60 1.50
9 Leon Draisaitl .50 1.25
10 Owen Tippett .10 .25
11 Aleksander Barkov .25 .60
12 Vince Dunn .12 .30
13 Brady Tkachuk .25 .60
14 Vincent Trocheck .15 .40
15 Connor McDavid .75 2.00
16 Bo Horvat .20 .50
17 Jason Robertson .25 .60
18 Cole Caufield .30 .75
19 Igor Shesterkin .30 .75
20 Claude Giroux .15 .40
21 Frank Vatrano .12 .30
22 Robert Thomas .15 .40
23 Jonathan Marchessault .20 .50
24 Matthew Tkachuk .30 .75
25 Brent Burns .15 .40
26 Anze Kopitar .25 .60
27 Artemi Panarin .30 .75
28 Sebastian Aho .25 .60
29 Travis Konecny .15 .40
30 Mason McTavish .15 .40
31 Nazem Kadri .20 .50
32 Jake Guentzel .25 .60
33 Jordan Kyrou .15 .40
34 J.T. Miller .20 .50
35 Jack Eichel .25 .60
36 Tim Stutzle .20 .50
37 Filip Forsberg .25 .60
38 Nick Suzuki .30 .75
39 Zach Werenski .25 .60
40 Marc-Andre Fleury .30 .75
41 Brayden Point .20 .50
42 Adrian Kempe .15 .40
43 Jamie Benn .15 .40
44 David Pastrnak .40 1.00
45 Connor Bedard .50 1.25
46 Jeremy Swayman .25 .60
47 Mark Stone .20 .50
48 Wyatt Johnston .30 .75
49 Nathan MacKinnon .60 1.50
50 Nikita Kucherov .30 .75
51 Alex Tuch .15 .40
52 Mark Scheifele .25 .60
53 William Nylander .30 .75
54 Logan Cooley .25 .60
55 Sam Bennett .25 .60
56 Clayton Keller .20 .50
57 Zach Hyman .25 .60
58 Connor Hellebuyck .30 .75
59 Jack Hughes .40 1.00
60 Sidney Crosby .60 1.50
61 Alex Ovechkin .60 1.50
62 Evgeni Malkin .30 .75
63 Thatcher Demko .20 .50
64 Evan Bouchard .20 .50
65 Dylan Strome .20 .50
66 Boone Jenner .15 .40
67 Steven Stamkos .30 .75
68 John Tavares .25 .60
69 Logan Couture .20 .50
70 Dylan Larkin .20 .50
71 Kirill Kaprizov .50 1.25
72 Cale Makar .40 1.00
73 Roman Josi .15 .40
74 William Eklund .20 .50
75 Quinn Hughes .40 1.00
76 Sarah Nurse .50 1.25
77 Erin Ambrose .40 1.00
78 Corinne Schroeder .15 .40
79 Taylor Heise .60 1.50
80 Emily Clark .50 1.25
81 Marie-Philip Poulin .75 2.00
82 Blayre Turnbull .15 .40
83 Emma Maltais .50 1.25
84 Ann-Renee Desbiens .60 1.50
85 Brianne Jenner .30 .75
86 Alina Muller .30 .75
87 Grace Zumwinkle .25 .60
88 Alex Carpenter .30 .75
89 Aerin Frankel .30 .75
90 Kendall Coyne Schofield .40 1.00
91 Wayne Gretzky 1.00 2.50
92 Mario Lemieux .60 1.50
93 Steve Yzerman .40 1.00
94 Joe Sakic .30 .75
95 Dominik Hasek .25 .60
96 Doug Gilmour .20 .50
97 Patrick Roy .40 1.00
98 Brad Marchand .30 .75
99 Ray Bourque .25 .60
100 Grant Fuhr .25 .60

2024-25 Upper Deck Tim Hortons Rookie Retrospective Celebrated Prodigies
CP1 Steven Stamkos 1.25 3.00
CP2 Blake Wheeler .60 1.50
CP3 Drew Doughty .60 1.50
CP4 Luke Schenn .60 1.50
CP5 Connor Bedard 2.00 5.00
CP6 Nicklas Backstrom .60 1.50
CP7 Evgeni Malkin 1.25 3.00
CP8 Quinn Hughes 1.50 4.00
CP9 Auston Matthews 2.50 6.00
CP10 Elias Pettersson 1.00 2.50
CP11 Steve Yzerman 1.50 4.00
CP12 Jordan Staal .50 1.25
CP13 Rick Nash .60 1.50
CP14 Emily Clark 2.00 5.00
CP15 Marie-Philip Poulin 3.00 8.00

2024-25 Upper Deck Tim Hortons Rookie Retrospective Dynamic Debuts
DD1 Taylor Heise 30.00 80.00
DD2 Mario Lemieux 30.00 80.00
DD3 Alex Ovechkin 30.00 80.00
DD4 Sidney Crosby 30.00 80.00
DD5 Igor Shesterkin 25.00 60.00

2024-25 Upper Deck Tim Hortons Rookie Retrospective In the Books
ITB1 Ryan Nugent-Hopkins .50 1.25
ITB2 Lucas Raymond .60 1.50
ITB3 Aaron Ekblad .50 1.25
ITB4 Brock Boeser .50 1.25
ITB5 Trevor Zegras .40 1.00
ITB6 Alexis Lafreniere .60 1.50
ITB7 Timo Meier .40 1.00
ITB8 Kyle Connor .60 1.50
ITB9 Drake Batherson .40 1.00
ITB10 Juraj Slafkovsky .75 2.00
ITB11 Blake Coleman .30 .75
ITB12 Roope Hintz .50 1.25
ITB13 Mike Modano .60 1.50
ITB14 Sarah Nurse 1.25 3.00
ITB15 Brianne Jenner .75 2.00

2024-25 Upper Deck Tim Hortons Rookie Retrospective Initial Strides
IS1 Kevin Fiala .40 1.00
IS2 Andrei Vasilevskiy .75 2.00
IS3 Zach Hyman .75 2.00
IS4 Mikko Rantanen 1.25 3.00
IS5 Alex DeBrincat .60 1.50
IS6 Chris Kreider .60 1.50
IS7 Ilya Sorokin .75 2.00
IS8 Elias Pettersson .75 2.00
IS9 Luke Hughes .75 2.00
IS10 Juuse Saros .60 1.50
IS11 Troy Terry .40 1.00
IS12 Connor Bedard 1.50 4.00
IS13 William Karlsson .60 1.50
IS14 Seth Jarvis .60 1.50
IS15 Carter Verhaeghe .50 1.25

2024-25 Upper Deck Tim Hortons Rookie Retrospective Starting Success
SS1 Auston Matthews 12.00 30.00
SS2 Keith Tkachuk 8.00 20.00
SS3 Morgan Geekie 8.00 20.00
SS4 Jake Guentzel 8.00 20.00
SS5 Vladimir Tarasenko 8.00 20.00
SS6 Anze Kopitar 8.00 20.00
SS7 Alex Ovechkin 12.00 30.00
SS8 Mason McTavish 8.00 20.00
SS9 Kirill Kaprizov 8.00 20.00
SS10 Logan Cooley 8.00 20.00
SS11 Elias Pettersson 8.00 20.00
SS12 Dylan Larkin 8.00 20.00
SS13 Charlie McAvoy 8.00 20.00
SS14 Shane Doan 8.00 20.00
SS15 Alex Carpenter 8.00 20.00

2024-25 Upper Deck Tim Hortons Rookie Retrospective Take a Bow
TB1 Connor McDavid 1.50 4.00
TB2 Igor Shesterkin .60 1.50
TB3 Aleksander Barkov .50 1.25
TB4 Sidney Crosby 1.25 3.00
TB5 Natalie Spooner 1.25 3.00
TB6 Nick Suzuki .60 1.50
TB7 Nathan MacKinnon 1.25 3.00
TB8 Patrick Kane .60 1.50
TB9 Cale Makar .75 2.00
TB10 Tim Stutzle .40 1.00
TB11 Mark Scheifele .50 1.25
TB12 Ella Shelton .50 1.25
TB13 William Nylander .60 1.50
TB14 Scott Niedermayer .30 .75
TB15 Martin St. Louis .30 .75

2021-22 Upper Deck Tim Hortons Team Canada
1 Connor McDavid 1.50 4.00
2 Sidney Crosby 1.25 3.00
3 Darcy Kuemper .30 .75
4 Sean Couturier .25 .60
5 Ryan Getzlaf .30 .75
6 Mathew Barzal .40 1.00
7 Anthony Mantha .25 .60
8 Patrick Marleau .25 .60
9 Colton Parayko .25 .60
10 Carey Price .60 1.50
11 Dylan Cozens .30 .75
12 Shea Weber .30 .75
13 Brad Marchand .60 1.50
14 Nick Suzuki .60 1.50
15 John Tavares .50 1.25
16 Pierre-Luc Dubois .25 .60
17 Claude Giroux .30 .75
18 Taylor Hall .30 .75
19 Maxime Comtois .25 .60
20 Patrice Bergeron .40 1.00
21 Brent Burns .30 .75
22 Wayne Simmonds .30 .75
23 Aaron Ekblad .40 1.00
24 Mark Scheifele .50 1.25
25 Alex Pietrangelo .25 .60
26 Carter Hart .30 .75
27 Eric Staal .30 .75
28 Mark Stone .40 1.00
29 Andrew Mangiapane .30 .75
30 Cam Talbot .30 .75
31 Nathan MacKinnon 1.25 3.00
32 Joe Thornton .50 1.25
33 Brayden Schenn .30 .75
34 Tyson Jost .25 .60
35 Peyton Krebs .25 .60
36 Marc-Andre Fleury .60 1.50
37 Connor Brown .25 .60
38 Jordan Eberle .30 .75
39 Adam Henrique .25 .60
40 Corey Perry .50 1.25
41 Bowen Byram .40 1.00
42 Ryan Nugent-Hopkins .40 1.00
43 Cale Makar .75 2.00
44 Ryan Ellis .20 .50
45 Jason Spezza .30 .75
46 Ryan O'Reilly .30 .75
47 Matt Duchene .30 .75
48 Steven Stamkos .60 1.50
49 Mitch Marner .50 1.25
50 Alexis Lafreniere .50 1.25
51 Kirby Dach .30 .75
52 Quinton Byfield .75 2.00
53 Kris Letang .40 1.00
54 Travis Konecny .30 .75
55 Sam Reinhart .60 1.50
56 Marc-Edouard Vlasic .20 .50
57 Tyler Seguin .40 1.00
58 Tyler Toffoli .30 .75
59 Jonathan Huberdeau .40 1.00
60 Jeff Skinner .30 .75
61 Barrett Hayton .30 .75
62 Brendan Gallagher .30 .75
63 Dylan Strome .40 1.00
64 Jonathan Toews .50 1.25
65 Jeff Carter .25 .60
66 Matt Dumba .25 .60
67 Max Domi .30 .75
68 Thomas Chabot .30 .75
69 Brayden Point .40 1.00
70 Jonathan Marchessault .40 1.00
71 Sarah Nurse .75 2.00
72 Natalie Spooner .75 2.00
73 Rebecca Johnston .30 .75
74 Jocelyne Larocque .30 .75
75 Brianne Jenner .50 1.25
76 Emerance Maschmeyer .40 1.00
77 Melodie Daoust .30 .75
78 Erin Ambrose .50 1.25
79 Renata Fast .30 .75
80 Jamie Lee Rattray .40 1.00
81 Marie-Philip Poulin 1.00 2.50
82 Victoria Bach .30 .75
83 Blayre Turnbull .30 .75
84 Jillian Saulnier .40 1.00
85 Ann-Renee Desbiens .75 2.00
86 Steve Yzerman .75 2.00
87 Mark Messier .60 1.50
88 Martin Brodeur .75 2.00
89 Phil Esposito .50 1.25
90 Bobby Hull .50 1.25
91 Guy Lafleur .40 1.00
92 Joe Sakic .60 1.50
93 Eric Lindros .50 1.25
94 Shayne Corson .25 .60
95 Marcel Dionne .40 1.00
96 Jarome Iginla .40 1.00
97 Grant Fuhr .50 1.25
98 Paul Coffey .40 1.00
99 Mario Lemieux 1.25 3.00
100 Wayne Gretzky 2.00 5.00

2021-22 Upper Deck Tim Hortons Team Canada Canada Moments Canvas
CM1 Sidney Crosby 2.00 5.00
CM2 Carey Price 1.00 2.50
CM3 Jeff Carter .40 1.00
CM4 Brayden Schenn .50 1.25
CM5 Brianne Jenner .75 2.00
CM6 Patrice Bergeron .60 1.50
CM7 Jordan Eberle .50 1.25
CM8 Carter Hart .50 1.25
CM9 Max Domi .50 1.25
CM10 Matt Duchene .50 1.25
CM11 John Tavares .75 2.00
CM12 Mario Lemieux 2.00 5.00
CM13 Jonathan Toews .75 2.00
CM14 Eric Lindros .75 2.00
CM15 Wayne Gretzky 3.00 8.00

2021-22 Upper Deck Tim Hortons Team Canada Canada's Captains
CC1 Adam Henrique .40 1.00
CC2 Kyle Turris .40 1.00
CC3 Connor McDavid 2.50 6.00
CC4 Claude Giroux .50 1.25
CC5 Sidney Crosby 2.00 5.00
CC6 Corey Perry .75 2.00
CC7 Marie-Philip Poulin 1.50 4.00
CC8 Ryan Getzlaf .50 1.25
CC9 Mario Lemieux 2.00 5.00
CC10 Eric Lindros .75 2.00
CC11 Dylan Strome .60 1.50
CC12 Maxime Comtois .40 1.00
CC13 Ryan Nugent-Hopkins .60 1.50
CC14 Jaden Schwartz .40 1.00
CC15 Wayne Gretzky 3.00 8.00

2021-22 Upper Deck Tim Hortons Team Canada Championship Medals
M1 Patrice Bergeron .60 1.50
M2 Connor Brown .40 1.00
M3 Cale Makar 1.25 3.00
M4 Connor McDavid 2.50 6.00
M5 Sidney Crosby 2.00 5.00
M6 Sam Reinhart 1.00 2.50
M7 Eric Staal .50 1.25
M8 Alexis Lafreniere .75 2.00
M9 Marie-Philip Poulin 1.50 4.00
M10 Jonathan Toews .75 2.00
M11 Shayne Corson .40 1.00
M12 Jordan Eberle .50 1.25
M13 P.K. Subban .60 1.50
M14 Kris Letang .60 1.50
M15 Wayne Gretzky 3.00 8.00

2021-22 Upper Deck Tim Hortons Team Canada Jerseys
JAC Anthony Cirelli 30.00 80.00
JAE Aaron Ekblad 50.00 125.00
JBP Brayden Point 50.00 125.00
JCH Carter Hart 40.00 100.00
JDC Dylan Cozens 40.00 100.00
JJT Joe Thornton 60.00 150.00
JKD Kirby Dach 40.00 100.00
JMB Mathew Barzal 50.00 125.00
JMC Maxime Comtois 30.00 80.00
JMP Marie-Philip Poulin 120.00 300.00
JPD Pierre-Luc Dubois 30.00 80.00
JPK Peyton Krebs 30.00 80.00
JPM Patrick Marleau 30.00 80.00
JQB Quinton Byfield 100.00 250.00
JRG Ryan Getzlaf 40.00 100.00
JRJ Rebecca Johnston 40.00 100.00
JTC Thomas Chabot 40.00 100.00
JTK Travis Konecny 40.00 100.00

2021-22 Upper Deck Tim Hortons Team Canada Program of Excellence Heroes
POE1 Connor McDavid 2.50 6.00
POE2 Carey Price 1.00 2.50
POE3 Patrice Bergeron .60 1.50
POE4 Joe Thornton .75 2.00
POE5 Alex Pietrangelo .40 1.00

Card	Low	High
POE6 Marie-Philip Poulin	1.50	4.00
POE7 Steve Yzerman	1.25	3.00
POE8 Brayden Point	.60	1.50
POE9 Joe Sakic	1.00	2.50
POE10 Corey Perry	.75	2.00
POE11 Eric Lindros	.75	2.00
POE12 Jarome Iginla	.60	1.50
POE13 Mike Gartner	.60	1.50
POE14 Drew Doughty	.60	1.50
POE15 Brent Seabrook	.30	.75

2021-22 Upper Deck Tim Hortons Team Canada Signature Jerseys

Card	Low	High
AJAL Alexis Lafreniere	100.00	250.00
AJCM Connor McDavid	300.00	800.00
AJJI Jarome Iginla	80.00	200.00
AJJT Jonathan Toews	100.00	250.00
AJNS Nick Suzuki	125.00	300.00
AJQB Quinton Byfield	150.00	400.00

2021-22 Upper Deck Tim Hortons Team Canada Signatures

Card	Low	High
SBB Bowen Byram	40.00	100.00
SBH Barrett Hayton	30.00	80.00
SBS Brayden Schenn	30.00	80.00
SCH Carter Hart	30.00	80.00
SCM Connor McMichael	30.00	80.00
SCT Cam Talbot	30.00	80.00
SDC Dylan Cozens	30.00	80.00
SKD Kirby Dach	30.00	80.00
SMA Cale Makar	80.00	200.00
SMC Maxime Comtois	25.00	60.00
SMM Mitch Marner	50.00	125.00
SPD Pierre-Luc Dubois	25.00	60.00
SPK Peyton Krebs	25.00	60.00
SQB Quinton Byfield	80.00	200.00
STH Thomas Harley	30.00	80.00

2021-22 Upper Deck Tim Hortons Team Canada Team Canada Trios

Card	Low	High
T1 Ryan Nugent-Hopkins		
Connor McDavid		
Pierre-Luc Dubois	15.00	40.00
T2 Taylor Hall		
Claude Giroux		
Jason Spezza	1.25	3.00
T3 Jonathan Toews		
Carey Price		
Kris Letang	2.50	6.00
T4 Nathan MacKinnon		
Ryan O'Reilly		
Mitch Marner	5.00	12.00
T5 Andrew Mangiapane		
Connor Brown		
Adam Henrique	1.25	3.00
T6 Marie-Philip Poulin		
Natalie Spooner		
Rebecca Johnston	15.00	40.00
T7 Sidney Crosby		
Patrice Bergeron		
Ryan Getzlaf	5.00	12.00
T8 Alexis Lafreniere		
Quinton Byfield		
Dylan Cozens	15.00	40.00
T9 Guy Lafleur		
Bobby Hull		
Phil Esposito	2.00	5.00
T10 Anthony Mantha		
Mark Stone		
Kyle Turris	1.50	4.00
T11 Thomas Chabot		
Travis Konecny		
Mathew Barzal	1.50	4.00
T12 Wayne Gretzky		
Paul Coffey		
Eric Lindros	25.00	60.00
T13 P.K. Subban		
Jordan Eberle		
John Tavares	2.00	5.00
T14 Shea Weber		
Jordan Staal		
Jonathan Toews	2.00	5.00
T15 Mark Messier		
Wayne Gretzky		
Mario Lemieux	8.00	20.00

2021-22 Upper Deck Tim Hortons Team Canada Timbits to Team Canada

Card	Low	High
1993 Sidney Crosby	60.00	150.00
1993 Brad Marchand	50.00	125.00
1999 Brendan Gallagher	40.00	100.00
2000 Brayden Point	30.00	80.00
2000 Nathan MacKinnon	50.00	125.00

2003-04 Upper Deck Toronto Fall Expo Priority Signings

Card	Low	High
CJ Curtis Joseph/41	20.00	50.00
DH Dany Heatley/25	30.00	80.00
GH Gordie Howe/40	60.00	150.00
IK Ilya Kovalchuk/78	20.00	50.00
JI Jarome Iginla/57	20.00	50.00
JS Jason Spezza/110	15.00	40.00
JT Joe Thornton/107	15.00	40.00
MB Martin Brodeur/70	50.00	125.00
PB Pavel Bure/29	25.00	60.00
PR Patrick Roy/44	75.00	200.00
RB Ray Bourque/75	25.00	60.00

2004 UD Toronto Fall Expo Pride of Canada

Card	Low	High
COMPLETE SET (26)	125.00	250.00
1 Martin Brodeur	15.00	40.00
2 Roberto Luongo	6.00	15.00
3 Jose Theodore	8.00	20.00
4 Jay Bouwmeester	4.00	10.00
5 Eric Brewer	4.00	10.00
6 Adam Foote	4.00	10.00
7 Scott Hannan	4.00	10.00
8 Ed Jovanovski	4.00	10.00
9 Scott Niedermayer	4.00	10.00
10 Wade Redden	4.00	10.00
11 Robyn Regehr	4.00	10.00
12 Shane Doan	4.00	10.00
13 Kris Draper	4.00	10.00
14 Simon Gagne	5.00	12.00
15 Dany Heatley	6.00	15.00
16 Jarome Iginla	8.00	20.00
17 Vincent Lecavalier	8.00	20.00
18 Mario Lemieux	15.00	40.00
19 Kirk Maltby	4.00	10.00
20 Patrick Marleau	4.00	10.00
21 Brenden Morrow	4.00	10.00
22 Brad Richards	4.00	10.00
23 Joe Sakic	10.00	25.00
24 Martin St. Louis	4.00	10.00
25 Ryan Smyth	4.00	10.00
26 Joe Thornton	6.00	15.00

2004-05 Upper Deck Toronto Fall Expo Priority Signings

Card	Low	High
AH Ales Hemsky/50	10.00	25.00
AY Alexei Yashin/50	10.00	25.00
CK Chuck Kobasew/49	10.00	25.00
GR Wayne Gretzky/25	200.00	300.00
HO Marian Hossa/52	12.50	30.00
JL John LeClair/50	10.00	25.00
JR Jeremy Roenick/31	40.00	80.00
JS Jason Spezza/39	25.00	60.00
MH Martin Havlat/50	12.50	30.00
MN Markus Naslund/50	12.50	30.00
MP Mark Parrish/50	8.00	20.00
MT Marty Turco/35	20.00	50.00
PB Pavel Bure/60	12.50	30.00
PE Mike Peca/27	20.00	50.00
PR Patrick Roy/33	75.00	150.00
RL Roberto Luongo/50	12.50	30.00
RN Rick Nash/61	30.00	80.00
SH Scott Hartnell/78	8.00	20.00
TB Todd Bertuzzi/44	20.00	50.00

2005-06 Upper Deck Toronto Fall Expo Priority Signings

Card	Low	High
PSBO Brooks Orpik/40	6.00	15.00
PSAR Andrew Raycroft/63	10.00	25.00
PSES Eric Staal/62	25.00	60.00
PSLU Joffrey Lupul/64	10.00	25.00
PSJC Jonathan Cheechoo/61	12.00	30.00
PSST Matt Stajan/70	10.00	25.00
PSML Matthew Lombardi/61	6.00	15.00
PSRY Michael Ryder/60	20.00	50.00
PSNZ Nikolai Zherdev/61	10.00	25.00
PSBE Patrice Bergeron/62	12.00	30.00
PSPS Philippe Sauve/63	6.00	15.00
PSRT Raffi Torres/60	10.00	25.00
PSRM Ryan Malone/62	10.00	25.00
PSTH Trent Hunter/61	10.00	25.00
PSAF Alexander Frolov/40	20.00	50.00
PSGR Wayne Gretzky/25	300.00	800.00
PSTR Tuomo Ruutu/62	10.00	25.00
PSPB P-M Bouchard/61	8.00	20.00

2006-07 Upper Deck Toronto Spring Expo Priority Signings

Card	Low	High
PSAM Andrej Meszaros/40	8.00	20.00
PSAS Alexander Steen/40	15.00	30.00
PSPK Phil Kessel/40	10.00	25.00
PSTV Thomas Vanek/40	8.00	20.00
PSZP Zach Parise/40	10.00	25.00

2006-07 Upper Deck Toronto Fall Expo Priority Signings

Card	Low	High
PSAA Aaron Asham/75	4.00	10.00
PSAS Alexander Steen/50	12.00	30.00
PSBB Brad Boyes/50	10.00	25.00
PSBO Jay Bouwmeester/26	12.00	30.00
PSBR Brad Richardson/41	8.00	20.00
PSCH Chris Higgins/82	12.00	30.00
PSDP Dion Phaneuf/15	50.00	80.00
PSFS Fredrik Sjostrom/94	4.00	10.00
PSGB Gilbert Brule/21	20.00	50.00
PSHL Henrik Lundqvist/26	30.00	60.00
PSJB Jason Blake/75	6.00	15.00
PSJT Jeff Tambellini/52	4.00	10.00
PSRN Robert Nilsson/57	4.00	10.00
PSRW Ryan Whitney/65	8.00	20.00
PSSC Sidney Crosby/35	175.00	250.00
PSTV Thomas Vanek/42	20.00	40.00

2007-08 Upper Deck Toronto Spring Expo Priority Signings

Card	Low	High
PSBB Brad Boyes/75	5.00	12.00
PSBO Bobby Orr/25	150.00	250.00
PSCP Corey Perry/15	30.00	60.00
PSFM Frank Mahovlich/42	25.00	50.00

2008-09 Upper Deck Toronto Fall Expo Priority Signings

Card	Low	High
PSAO Adam Oates/75	6.00	15.00
PSBB Brad Boyes/75	6.00	15.00
PSCP Corey Perry/50	6.00	15.00
PSPA Daniel Paille/75	6.00	15.00
PSEM Evgeni Malkin/25	40.00	80.00
PSME Matt Ellis/75	6.00	15.00
PSMF Mark Fraser/75	6.00	15.00
PSMP Michael Peca/75	6.00	15.00
PSMR Mason Raymond/75	6.00	15.00
PSRC Ryane Clowe/75	6.00	15.00
PSRE Ron Ellis/40	6.00	15.00
PSRV Rogie Vachon/15	20.00	40.00
PSST Stefan Meyer/75	6.00	15.00

2010-11 Upper Deck Toronto Fall Expo Priority Signings

Card	Low	High
PSJB Jamie Benn/50	8.00	20.00
PSJT John Tavares/25	25.00	60.00
PSNZ Nazem Kadri/25	20.00	50.00
PSSM Stan Mikita/15	20.00	40.00
PSTS Tyler Seguin/25	25.00	50.00
PSYZ Steve Yzerman/15	40.00	80.00

2012-13 Upper Deck Toronto Fall Expo Priority Signings

Card	Low	High
PSAH Adam Henrique/75	8.00	20.00
PSBG Blake Geoffrion/75	12.00	30.00
PSBO Bobby Orr/75	60.00	125.00
PSBS Brayden Schenn/25	15.00	40.00
PSCA Carter Ashton/75	4.00	10.00
PSCC Casey Cizikas/75	4.00	10.00
PSCT Colten Teubert/75	10.00	25.00
PSJB Jamie Benn/75	10.00	25.00
PSJN Jonathan Bernier/75	5.00	12.00
PSMF Marcus Foligno/70	15.00	40.00
PSMS Mark Scheifele/75	10.00	25.00
PSNK Nikolai Kulemin/75	4.00	10.00
PSRE Ryan Ellis/30	15.00	40.00
PSTB Tyson Barrie/75	4.00	10.00

2013-14 Upper Deck Toronto Spring Expo Priority Signings

Card	Low	High
COMPLETE SET (36)		
SBN Brock Nelson/50	5.00	12.00
SEP Edward Pasquale/50	4.00	10.00
SFA Frederick Andersen/30	12.00	30.00
SJF Justin Fontaine/50	5.00	12.00
SJG John Gibson/25	12.00	30.00
SMB Michael Bournival/50	3.00	8.00
SMD Mathew Dumba/15	12.00	30.00
SMG Mikael Granlund/25	10.00	25.00
SNB Nathan Beaulieu/15	8.00	20.00
SNY Nail Yakupov/25	30.00	60.00
SRE Max Reinhart/30	8.00	20.00
SRS Ryan Strome/25	12.00	30.00
STH Tomas Hertl/25	25.00	50.00
STJ Tomas Jurco/15	15.00	40.00
STJ Tyler Johnson/30	8.00	20.00
STP Tanner Pearson/40	8.00	20.00

2013-14 Upper Deck Toronto Fall Expo Priority Signings

Card	Low	High
FBB Beau Bennett/75	12.00	30.00
FCT Christian Thomas/75	6.00	15.00
FDH Dougie Hamilton/15	10.00	25.00
FJB Boone Jenner/75	5.00	12.00
FNB Nathan Beaulieu/25	10.00	25.00
FNM Nathan MacKinnon/25	100.00	200.00
FRS Ryan Spooner/45	6.00	15.00
FSC Jordan Schroeder/75	4.00	10.00
FTT Tyler Toffoli/75	8.00	20.00
FTW Tom Wilson/75	6.00	15.00
FJTI Jarred Tinordi/45	5.00	12.00

2003-04 Upper Deck Trilogy

Card	Low	High
COMP.SET w/o SP's	50.00	100.00
1 Sergei Fedorov	1.25	3.00
2 Stanislav Chistov	.50	1.25
3 Jean-Sebastien Giguere	.75	2.00
4 Dany Heatley	.60	1.50
5 Ilya Kovalchuk	.75	2.00
6 Joe Thornton	1.25	3.00
7 Glen Murray	.60	1.50
8 Bobby Orr	6.00	15.00
9 Miroslav Satan	.60	1.50
10 Maxim Afinogenov	.50	1.25
11 Chris Drury	.60	1.50
12 Jarome Iginla	1.00	2.50
13 Lanny McDonald	.60	1.50
14 Roman Turek	.60	1.50
15 Ron Francis	1.00	2.50
16 Jeff O'Neill	.50	1.25
17 Kyle Calder	.50	1.25
17 Alexei Zhamnov	.60	1.50
19 Jocelyn Thibault	.60	1.50
20 Teemu Selanne	1.50	4.00
21 Peter Forsberg	1.50	4.00
22 Paul Kariya	.75	2.00
23 Joe Sakic	1.50	4.00
24 Patrick Roy	2.00	5.00
25 Rick Nash	.75	2.00
26 Marc Denis	.60	1.50
27 Todd Marchant	.50	1.25
28 Mike Modano	1.25	3.00
29 Bill Guerin	.75	2.00
30 Marty Turco	.75	2.00
31 Brendan Shanahan	.75	2.00
32 Gordie Howe	3.00	8.00
33 Steve Yzerman	2.00	5.00
34 Dominik Hasek	1.25	3.00
35 Ryan Smyth	.60	1.50
36 Mike Comrie	.60	1.50
37 Ales Hemsky	.75	2.00
38 Wayne Gretzky	5.00	12.00
39 Olli Jokinen	.75	2.00
40 Stephen Weiss	.50	1.25
41 Jay Bouwmeester	.50	1.25
42 Roberto Luongo	1.25	3.00
43 Zigmund Palffy	.75	2.00
44 Alexander Frolov	.60	1.50
45 Roman Cechmanek	.60	1.50
46 Marian Gaborik	.75	2.00
47 Pierre-Marc Bouchard	.75	2.00
48 Manny Fernandez	.50	1.25
49 Dwayne Roloson	.60	1.50
50 Saku Koivu	.75	2.00
51 Marcel Hossa	.50	1.25
52 Jose Theodore	.75	2.00
53 Guy Lafleur	1.00	2.50
54 David Legwand	.60	1.50
55 Tomas Vokoun	.60	1.50
56 Patrik Elias	.75	2.00
57 Jamie Langenbrunner	.60	1.50
58 Scott Stevens	.75	2.00
59 Martin Brodeur	2.00	5.00
60 Alexei Yashin	.60	1.50
61 Rick DiPietro	.60	1.50
62 Alex Kovalev	.60	1.50
63 Eric Lindros	1.25	3.00
64 Pavel Bure	.75	2.00
65 Mike Dunham	.60	1.50
66 Marian Hossa	.75	2.00
67 Daniel Alfredsson	.75	2.00
68 Jason Spezza	.75	2.00
69 Patrick Lalime	.60	1.50
70 Jeremy Roenick	1.25	3.00
71 Tony Amonte	.60	1.50
72 John LeClair	.75	2.00
73 Bobby Clarke	1.25	3.00
74 Mike Johnson	.50	1.25
75 Chris Gratton	.50	1.25
76 Sean Burke	.50	1.25
77 Mario Lemieux	3.00	8.00
78 Martin Straka	.50	1.25
79 Sebastien Caron	.60	1.50
80 Mike Ricci	.50	1.25
81 Niko Dimitrakos	.50	1.25
82 Evgeni Nabokov	.60	1.50
83 Al MacInnis	1.00	2.50
84 Keith Tkachuk	.75	2.00
85 Chris Pronger	.75	2.00
86 Chris Osgood	.75	2.00
87 Vincent Lecavalier	.75	2.00
88 Martin St. Louis	.75	2.00
89 Nikolai Khabibulin	.75	2.00
90 Alexander Mogilny	.60	1.50
91 Mats Sundin	.75	2.00
92 Owen Nolan	.75	2.00
93 Ed Belfour	.75	2.00
94 Alexander Auld	.50	1.25
95 Markus Naslund	.75	2.00
96 Todd Bertuzzi	.75	2.00
97 Ed Jovanovski	.60	1.50
98 Jaromir Jagr	2.50	6.00
99 Peter Bondra	.75	2.00
100 Olaf Kolzig	.75	2.00
101 Joe Thornton COH	8.00	20.00
102 Sergei Fedorov COH	8.00	20.00
103 Dany Heatley COH	4.00	10.00
104 Steve Yzerman COH	12.00	30.00
105 Henrik Zetterberg COH	6.00	15.00
106 Patrick Roy COH	12.00	30.00
107 Peter Forsberg COH	10.00	25.00
108 Jean-Sebastien Giguere COH	5.00	12.00
109 Marian Gaborik COH	5.00	12.00
110 Markus Naslund COH	5.00	12.00
111 Jeremy Roenick COH	8.00	20.00
112 Mario Lemieux COH	12.00	30.00
113 Mats Sundin COH	5.00	12.00
114 Ed Belfour COH	5.00	12.00
115 Ilya Kovalchuk COH	5.00	12.00
116 Marian Hossa COH	5.00	12.00
117 Eric Lindros COH	8.00	20.00
118 Jocelyn Thibault COH	4.00	10.00
119 Jose Theodore COH	5.00	12.00
120 Mike Modano COH	8.00	20.00
121 Jason Spezza COH	5.00	12.00
122 Rick Nash COH	5.00	12.00
123 Jean Beliveau COH	6.00	15.00
124 Mike Bossy COH	5.00	12.00
125 Johnny Bucyk COH	5.00	12.00
126 Marcel Dionne COH	6.00	15.00
127 Grant Fuhr COH	8.00	20.00
128 Michel Goulet COH	4.00	10.00
129 Jari Kurri COH	5.00	12.00
130 Guy Lafleur COH	6.00	15.00
131 Ted Lindsay COH	5.00	12.00
132 Scotty Bowman COH	5.00	12.00
133 Lanny McDonald COH	4.00	10.00
134 Stan Mikita COH	6.00	15.00
135 Denis Potvin COH	5.00	12.00
136 Ray Bourque COH	8.00	20.00
137 Don Cherry COH	10.00	25.00
138 Bobby Orr COH	20.00	50.00
139 Gordie Howe COH	15.00	40.00
140 Bobby Clarke COH	8.00	20.00
141 Phil Esposito COH	8.00	20.00
142 Jiri Hudler RC	4.00	10.00
143 Patrice Bergeron RC	15.00	40.00
144 Matthew Lombardi RC	2.00	5.00
145 Lasse Kukkonen RC	1.50	4.00
146 John-Michael Liles RC	2.00	5.00
147 Marek Svatos RC	3.00	8.00
148 Cody McCormick RC	2.00	5.00
149 Dan Fritsche RC	1.50	4.00
150 Antti Miettinen RC	2.50	6.00
151 Esa Pirnes RC	1.50	4.00
152 Tim Gleason RC	2.00	5.00
153 Brent Burns RC	5.00	12.00
154 Christoph Brandner RC	2.00	5.00
155 Chris Higgins RC	3.00	8.00
156 Dan Hamhuis RC	2.00	5.00
157 Marek Zidlicky RC	1.50	4.00
158 Wade Brookbank RC	2.00	5.00
159 David Hale RC	1.50	4.00
160 Paul Martin RC	2.00	5.00
161 Sean Bergenheim RC	2.00	5.00
162 Antoine Vermette RC	3.00	8.00
163 Matthew Spiller RC	2.00	5.00
164 Ryan Malone RC	3.00	8.00
165 Christian Ehrhoff RC	2.00	5.00
166 Alexander Semin RC	5.00	12.00
167 Tom Preissing RC	2.00	5.00
168 Peter Sejna RC	2.00	5.00
169 Maxim Kondratiev RC	1.50	4.00
170 Matt Stajan RC	2.50	6.00
171 Boyd Gordon RC	2.00	5.00
172 Joffrey Lupul RC	5.00	12.00
173 Eric Staal RC	10.00	25.00
174 Tuomo Ruutu RC	3.00	8.00
175 Pavel Vorobiev RC	2.50	6.00
176 Nathan Horton RC	5.00	12.00
177 Dustin Brown RC	5.00	12.00
178 Jordin Tootoo RC	4.00	10.00
179 Joni Pitkanen RC	3.00	8.00
180 Marc-Andre Fleury RC	12.00	30.00
181 Milan Michalek RC	4.00	10.00
182 Mikhail Yakubov RC	1.50	4.00
183 Trevor Daley RC	2.50	6.00
184 Ryan Kesler RC	6.00	15.00
185 Fredrik Sjostrom RC	2.50	6.00
186 Nikolai Zherdev RC	3.00	8.00
187 Timofei Shishkanov RC	1.50	4.00
188 Niklas Kronwall RC	3.00	8.00
189 Fedor Tyutin RC	1.50	4.00

2003-04 Upper Deck Trilogy Limited

*1-100 VETS/30: 4X TO 10X BASIC CARDS
*101-141 CREST/30: 1X TO 2.5X BASIC COH
*ROOKIE/30: 1.2X TO 3X RC/999
*ROOKIE/30: 1X TO 2.5X RC/499

2003-04 Upper Deck Trilogy Limited Threads

Card	Low	High
LT1 Jaromir Jagr	30.00	80.00
LT2 Scott Stevens	15.00	40.00
LT3 Mario Lemieux	75.00	150.00
LT4 Jarome Iginla	40.00	100.00
LT5 Roman Turek	15.00	40.00
LT6 Patrick Roy	60.00	120.00
LT7 Steve Yzerman	60.00	120.00
LT8 Mats Sundin	15.00	40.00
LT9 Mike Modano	25.00	60.00
LT10 Zigmund Palffy	15.00	40.00
LT11 Peter Forsberg	25.00	60.00
LT12 Pavel Bure	20.00	50.00
LT13 Todd Bertuzzi	20.00	50.00
LT14 Jason Spezza	25.00	60.00
LT15 Scott Stevens	15.00	40.00
LT16 Jocelyn Thibault	15.00	40.00
LT17 Joe Sakic	30.00	80.00
LT18 Henrik Zetterberg	25.00	60.00
LT19 Joe Thornton	25.00	60.00
LT20 Patrick Lalime	15.00	40.00
LT21 Adam Deadmarsh	20.00	50.00
LT22 Markus Naslund	15.00	40.00
LT23 Ed Belfour	25.00	60.00
LT24 Scott Gomez	15.00	40.00
LT25 Marian Hossa	15.00	40.00
LT26 Alexei Yashin	15.00	40.00
LT27 Sergei Samsonov	15.00	40.00
LT28 Martin Brodeur	30.00	80.00
LT29 Martin Brodeur	30.00	80.00

2003-04 Upper Deck Trilogy Authentic Patches

Card	Low	High
AP1 Wayne Gretzky	100.00	200.00
AP2 Jean-Sebastien Giguere	8.00	20.00
AP3 Mike Modano	20.00	50.00
AP4 Jaromir Jagr	12.00	30.00
AP5 Steve Yzerman	20.00	50.00
AP6 Jose Theodore	20.00	50.00
AP7 Joe Sakic	20.00	50.00
AP8 Mario Lemieux	25.00	60.00
AP9 Marian Hossa	12.50	30.00
AP10 Martin Brodeur	25.00	60.00
AP11 Dominik Hasek	15.00	40.00
AP12 Mats Sundin	12.50	30.00
AP13 Milan Hejduk	12.50	30.00
AP14 Jeremy Roenick	12.50	30.00
AP15 Ray Bourque	25.00	60.00
AP16 Markus Naslund	12.50	30.00
AP17 Pavol Demitra	12.00	30.00
AP18 Doug Gilmour	12.50	30.00
AP19 Joe Thornton	20.00	50.00
AP20 Peter Forsberg	15.00	40.00
AP21 Scott Gomez	12.50	30.00
AP22 Sergei Fedorov	20.00	50.00
AP23 Pavel Bure	12.50	30.00
AP24 Dany Heatley	15.00	40.00
AP25 Teemu Selanne	12.50	30.00
AP26 John LeClair	12.50	30.00
AP27 Zigmund Palffy	12.50	30.00
AP28 Guy Lafleur	20.00	50.00
AP29 Ed Belfour	12.50	30.00
AP30 Jari Kurri	25.00	60.00
AP31 Marcel Dionne	10.00	25.00
AP32 Tony Amonte	12.50	30.00
AP33 Patrick Roy	40.00	100.00
AP34 Eric Lindros	15.00	40.00
AP35 Sergei Samsonov	12.50	30.00
AP36 Keith Tkachuk	12.50	30.00
AP37 Grant Fuhr	15.00	40.00
AP38 Guy Lafleur	15.00	40.00
AP39 Wayne Gretzky	100.00	200.00
AP40 Nicklas Lidstrom	15.00	40.00
AP41 Ray Bourque	25.00	60.00
AP42 Patrick Roy	25.00	60.00

2003-04 Upper Deck Trilogy Crest Variations

Card	Low	High
101 Joe Thornton JSY#/19*	15.00	40.00
102 Sergei Fedorov JSY#/91*	15.00	40.00
104 Steve Yzerman JSY#/19*	50.00	120.00
105 H.Zetterberg JSY#/40*	20.00	50.00
106 Patrick Roy JSY#/33*	50.00	120.00
107 Peter Forsberg JSY#/21*	20.00	50.00
108 J.Giguere JSY#/35*	30.00	60.00
110 Markus Naslund JSY#/19*	20.00	50.00
111 Jeremy Roenick JSY#/97*	12.50	30.00
112 Mario Lemieux JSY#/66*	30.00	80.00
114 Ed Belfour JSY#/20*	25.00	60.00
116 Marian Hossa JSY#/18*	20.00	40.00
117 Eric Lindros JSY#/88*	12.50	30.00
118 Jocelyn Thibault JSY#/41*	15.00	40.00
119 Jose Theodore JSY#/60*	15.00	40.00
121 Jason Spezza JSY#/39*	30.00	60.00
122 Rick Nash JSY#/61*	15.00	40.00
123 Jean Beliveau SC/72*	12.50	30.00
124 Mike Bossy SC/91*	10.00	25.00
125 Johnny Bucyk SC/81*	12.50	30.00
126 Marcel Dionne DET/92*	12.50	30.00
128 Michel Goulet QUE/98*	12.50	30.00
130 Guy Lafleur SC/88*	15.00	40.00
131 Ted Lindsay SC/66*	12.50	30.00
132 Scotty Bowman SC/91*	15.00	40.00
133 L.McDonald SC/92*	12.50	30.00
134 Stan Mikita SC/83*	12.50	30.00
135 Denis Potvin SC/91*	12.50	30.00
136 Ray Bourque SC/77*	20.00	50.00
137 D.Cherry Cherries/99*	20.00	50.00
138 Bobby Orr SC/79*	15.00	40.00
139 Gordie Howe SC/72*	25.00	60.00
140 Bobby Clarke SC/87*	12.50	30.00
141 Wayne Gretzky SC/99*	150.00	250.00
141 Phil Esposito SC/84*	12.50	30.00

2003-04 Upper Deck Trilogy Scripts

Card	Low	High
S1AH Ales Hemsky	6.00	15.00
S1BO Brooks Orpik	6.00	15.00
S1HL Adam Hall	3.00	8.00
S1HZ Henrik Zetterberg	12.50	30.00
S1JA Jared Aulin	3.00	8.00
S1JB Jay Bouwmeester	6.00	15.00
S1JL Jordan Leopold	3.00	8.00
S1JS Jason Spezza	12.50	30.00
S1PB P-M Bouchard	5.00	12.00
S1PL Pascal Leclaire	3.00	8.00
S1RH Ron Hainsey	3.00	8.00
S1SO Steve Ott	5.00	12.00
S2CJ Curtis Joseph	10.00	25.00
S2EC Erik Cole	3.00	8.00
S2JG Jean-Sebastien Giguere	5.00	12.00
S2JL John LeClair	6.00	15.00
S2JT Jose Theodore	10.00	25.00
S2JT Joe Thornton	25.00	60.00
S2JW Justin Williams	5.00	12.00
S2MA Maxim Afinogenov	5.00	12.00
S2MB Martin Brodeur	60.00	150.00
S2MH Martin Havlat	6.00	15.00
S2MH Marian Hossa	8.00	20.00
S2MN Markus Naslund	6.00	15.00
S2MT Marty Turco	8.00	20.00
S2PR Patrick Roy	75.00	200.00
S2SS Sergei Samsonov	5.00	12.00
S2TB Todd Bertuzzi	10.00	25.00
S3BC Bobby Clarke	12.50	30.00
S3BK Johnny Bucyk AS	8.00	20.00
S3BO Bobby Orr	100.00	200.00
S3BY Mike Bossy AS	10.00	25.00
S3DC Don Cherry	15.00	40.00
S3DP Denis Potvin NYI	6.00	15.00
S3G1 Wayne Gretzky AS	150.00	400.00
S3GF Grant Fuhr	8.00	20.00
S3GH Gordie Howe HAR	30.00	80.00
S3GL Guy Lafleur	12.50	30.00
S3GR Wayne Gretzky AS	150.00	400.00
S3GT Michel Goulet AS	5.00	12.00
S3GY Wayne Gretzky NYR	150.00	400.00
S3JB Jean Beliveau	30.00	60.00
S3JK Jari Kurri	10.00	25.00
S3JK Johnny Bucyk BOS	8.00	20.00
S3LM Lanny McDonald	6.00	15.00
S3MB Mike Bossy NYI	10.00	25.00
S3MD Marcel Dionne	5.00	12.00
S3MG Michel Goulet CHI	5.00	12.00
S3MH Gordie Howe DET	50.00	125.00
S3PE Phil Esposito	15.00	40.00
S3PN Denis Potvin AS	6.00	15.00
S3RB Ray Bourque	15.00	40.00
S3SB Scotty Bowman	15.00	40.00
S3SM Stan Mikita	12.00	30.00
S3TL Ted Lindsay	10.00	25.00
S3WA Wayne Gretzky LA	150.00	400.00
S3WG Wayne Gretzky EDM	150.00	400.00
S399 Wayne Gretzky HOF	150.00	400.00
CSBC Bobby Clarke HOF	20.00	50.00
CSBC2 B.Clarke Broad St.	30.00	80.00
CSBU J.Beliveau LeGros Bill	25.00	60.00
CSBU2 J.Beliveau HOF	25.00	60.00
CSBY M.Bossy HOF	10.00	25.00
CSBY2 M.Bossy SC	25.00	60.00
CSDC D.Cherry Grapes	20.00	50.00
CSGH Gordie Howe	50.00	100.00
CSGL Guy Lafleur HOF	20.00	50.00
CSJB J.Bucyk Chief	15.00	40.00
CSJG J.Giguere Jiggy	12.50	30.00
CSMC Mike Comrie	6.00	15.00
CSMH G.Howe HOF	50.00	125.00
CSMH2 G.Howe Mr.Elbows	50.00	125.00
CSMH3 G.Howe SC	50.00	125.00
CSMH4 G.Howe Prod.Line	50.00	125.00
CSRN R.Nash #1 Pick	20.00	50.00
CSSB S.Bowman HOF	30.00	80.00
CSSO S.Ott Otter	6.00	15.00
CSTB T.Bertuzzi Bert	20.00	50.00
CSTL T.Lindsay Prod.Line	15.00	40.00
CSTL2 T.Lindsay Art Ross	15.00	40.00
CSTL3 T.Lindsay HOF	15.00	40.00
CSTL4 T.Lindsay SC Winner	15.00	40.00
CSZP Z.Palffy Ziggy	15.00	40.00

2003-04 Upper Deck Trilogy Scripts Limited

Card	Low	High
S1AH Ales Hemsky	12.00	30.00
S1BO Brooks Orpik	10.00	25.00
S1HL Adam Hall	10.00	25.00
S1HZ Henrik Zetterberg	25.00	60.00
S1JA Jared Aulin	8.00	20.00
S1JB Jay Bouwmeester	12.00	30.00
S1JL Jordan Leopold	10.00	25.00
S1JS Jason Spezza	25.00	60.00
S1PB P-M Bouchard	10.00	25.00
S1PL Pascal Leclaire	10.00	25.00
S1RH Ron Hainsey	8.00	20.00
S1SO Steve Ott	12.00	30.00
S2CJ Curtis Joseph	20.00	50.00
S2EC Erik Cole	10.00	25.00
S2JG Jean-Sebastien Giguere	12.00	30.00
S2JL John LeClair	12.00	30.00
S2JT Joe Thornton	20.00	50.00
S2JT Jose Theodore	15.00	40.00
S2JW Justin Williams	10.00	25.00
S2MA Maxim Afinogenov	10.00	25.00
S2MB Martin Brodeur	100.00	200.00
S2MH Martin Havlat	12.00	30.00
S2MH Marian Hossa	20.00	40.00
S2MN Markus Naslund	12.00	30.00
S2MT Marty Turco	12.00	30.00
S2PR Patrick Roy	100.00	200.00
S2SS Sergei Samsonov	10.00	25.00
S2TB Todd Bertuzzi	12.00	30.00
S3BC Bobby Clarke	20.00	50.00
S3BK Johnny Bucyk AS	12.00	30.00
S3BO Bobby Orr	125.00	250.00
S3BY Mike Bossy AS	20.00	50.00
S3DC Don Cherry	30.00	80.00
S3DP Denis Potvin NYI	12.00	30.00
S3G1 Wayne Gretzky AS	150.00	400.00
S3GF Grant Fuhr	12.00	30.00
S3GH Gordie Howe HAR	75.00	150.00
S3GL Guy Lafleur	15.00	40.00
S3GR Wayne Gretzky AS	150.00	400.00
S3GT Michel Goulet AS	10.00	25.00
S3GY Wayne Gretzky NYR	200.00	500.00
S3JB Jean Beliveau	30.00	80.00
S3JK Jari Kurri	15.00	40.00
S3JK Johnny Bucyk BOS	12.00	30.00
S3LM Lanny McDonald	12.00	30.00
S3MB Mike Bossy NYI	20.00	50.00
S3MD Marcel Dionne	12.00	30.00
S3MG Michel Goulet CHI	12.00	30.00
S3MH Gordie Howe DET	100.00	200.00
S3PE Phil Esposito	30.00	60.00
S3PN Denis Potvin AS	12.00	30.00
S3RB Ray Bourque	30.00	60.00
S3SB Scotty Bowman	30.00	80.00
S3SM Stan Mikita	15.00	40.00
S3TL Ted Lindsay	20.00	50.00
S3WA Wayne Gretzky LA	200.00	500.00
S3WG Wayne Gretzky EDM	200.00	500.00
S399 Wayne Gretzky HOF	200.00	500.00

2003-04 Upper Deck Trilogy Scripts Red

Card	Low	High
S1HL Adam Hall/31	10.00	25.00
S1JB Jay Bouwmeester/31	12.00	30.00
S1PL Pascal Leclaire/31	10.00	25.00
S2CJ Curtis Joseph/30	20.00	50.00
S2IK Ilya Kovalchuk/30	30.00	80.00
S2MN Markus Naslund/30	15.00	40.00
S2PR Patrick Roy/27	150.00	250.00
S2TB Todd Bertuzzi/22	15.00	40.00
S3BC Bobby Clarke/30	20.00	50.00
S3BO Bobby Orr/30	125.00	250.00
S3DC Don Cherry/30	20.00	50.00
S3DP Denis Potvin/30	12.00	30.00
S3GF Grant Fuhr/30	12.00	30.00
S3GL Guy Lafleur/30	15.00	40.00
S3JB Jean Beliveau/30	30.00	80.00
S3JB Johnny Bucyk/30	12.00	30.00
S3JK Jari Kurri/30	15.00	40.00
S3LM Lanny McDonald/30	12.00	30.00
S3MB Mike Bossy/30	20.00	50.00
S3MD Marcel Dionne/30	12.00	30.00
S3MG Michel Goulet/30	12.00	30.00
S3MH Gordie Howe/30	60.00	125.00
S3RB Ray Bourque/30	30.00	60.00
S3SB Scotty Bowman/30	30.00	80.00
S3SM Stan Mikita/30	25.00	50.00
S3TL Ted Lindsay/30	25.00	50.00
S3WG W.Gretzky EDM Blu/30	300.00	800.00

2005-06 Upper Deck Trilogy

Card	Low	High
COMP.SET w/o SP's (90)	20.00	40.00
1 Jean-Sebastien Giguere	.60	1.50
2 Joffrey Lupul	.40	1.00
3 Sergei Fedorov	1.00	2.50
4 Marian Hossa	.60	1.50
5 Ilya Kovalchuk	.60	1.50
6 Kari Lehtonen	.50	1.25
7 Andrew Raycroft	.50	1.25
8 Joe Thornton	1.00	2.50
9 Patrice Bergeron	.75	2.00
10 Glen Murray	.50	1.25
11 Brian Leetch	.50	1.25
12 Daniel Briere	.60	1.50
13 Chris Drury	.50	1.25
14 Maxim Afinogenov	.40	1.00
15 Jarome Iginla	.75	2.00
16 Jordan Leopold	.40	1.00
17 Miikka Kiprusoff	.60	1.50
18 Eric Staal	.75	2.00
19 Erik Cole	.40	1.00
20 Nikolai Khabibulin	.60	1.50
21 Tuomo Ruutu	.60	1.50
22 David Aebischer	.50	1.25
23 Joe Sakic	1.25	3.00
24 Rob Blake	.60	1.50
25 Milan Hejduk	.50	1.25
26 Alex Tanguay	.60	1.50
27 Rick Nash	.60	1.50
28 Nikolai Zherdev	.40	1.00
29 Mike Modano	1.00	2.50
30 Bill Guerin	.60	1.50
31 Marty Turco	.60	1.50
32 Manny Legace	.60	1.50
33 Pavel Datsyuk	1.00	2.50
34 Brendan Shanahan	.60	1.50
35 Steve Yzerman	1.50	4.00
36 Henrik Zetterberg	.75	2.00
37 Ty Conklin	.50	1.25
38 Ryan Smyth	.50	1.25
39 Chris Pronger	.60	1.50
40 Roberto Luongo	1.00	2.50
41 Stephen Weiss	.40	1.00
42 Luc Robitaille	.60	1.50
43 Jeremy Roenick	1.00	2.50
44 Marian Gaborik	.60	1.50
45 Mike Ribeiro	.40	1.00
46 Michael Ryder	.50	1.25
47 Jose Theodore	.60	1.50
48 Saku Koivu	.60	1.50
49 Paul Kariya	.60	1.50
50 Steve Sullivan	.40	1.00
51 Tomas Vokoun	.50	1.25
52 Martin Brodeur	1.50	4.00
53 Scott Gomez	.50	1.25
54 Patrik Elias	.60	1.50
55 Jaromir Jagr	2.00	5.00
56 Kevin Weekes	.50	1.25
57 Alexei Yashin	.50	1.25
58 Miroslav Satan	.50	1.25
59 Rick DiPietro	.50	1.25
60 Daniel Alfredsson	.60	1.50
61 Dany Heatley	.50	1.25
62 Jason Spezza	.60	1.50
63 Martin Havlat	.60	1.50
64 Peter Forsberg	1.25	3.00
65 Keith Primeau	.50	1.25
66 Simon Gagne	.60	1.50
67 Robert Esche	.50	1.25
68 Ladislav Nagy	.40	1.00
69 Curtis Joseph	.75	2.00
70 Shane Doan	.50	1.25
71 Zigmund Palffy	.60	1.50
72 Mario Lemiuex	2.50	6.00
73 Mark Recchi	.75	2.00
74 Evgeni Nabokov	.50	1.25
75 Patrick Marleau	.60	1.50
76 Jonathan Cheechoo	.50	1.25
77 Patrick Lalime	.50	1.25
78 Doug Weight	.60	1.50
79 Keith Tkachuk	.60	1.50
80 Brad Richards	.60	1.50
81 Sean Burke	.40	1.00
82 Martin St. Louis	.60	1.50
83 Vincent Lecavalier	.60	1.50
84 Ed Belfour	.60	1.50
85 Mats Sundin	.60	1.50
86 Eric Lindros	1.00	2.50
87 Kyle Wellwood	.50	1.25
88 Markus Naslund	.60	1.50
89 Ed Jovanovski	.50	1.25
90 Olaf Kolzig	.60	1.50
91 Jean-Sebastien Giguere FIT	4.00	10.00
92 Sergei Fedorov FIT	6.00	15.00
93 Sergei Fedorov FIT	3.00	8.00
94 Ilya Kovalchuk FIT	4.00	10.00
95 Joe Thornton FIT	4.00	10.00
96 Ray Bourque FIT	6.00	15.00
97 Chris Drury FIT	3.00	8.00
98 Jarome Iginla FIT	5.00	12.00
99 Miikka Kiprusoff FIT	4.00	10.00
100 Eric Staal FIT	5.00	12.00
101 Tuomo Ruutu FIT	4.00	10.00
102 Joe Sakic FIT	8.00	20.00
103 Patrick Roy FIT	10.00	25.00
104 Paul Kariya FIT	4.00	10.00

105 Peter Forsberg FIT 8.00 20.00
106 Nikolai Zherdev FIT 2.50 6.00
107 Rick Nash FIT 4.00 10.00
108 Mike Modano FIT 6.00 15.00
109 Gordie Howe FIT 12.00 30.00
110 Pavel Datsyuk FIT 6.00 15.00
111 Steve Yzerman FIT 10.00 25.00
112 Henrik Zetterberg FIT 5.00 12.00
113 Wayne Gretzky FIT 25.00 60.00
114 Marian Gaborik FIT 4.00 10.00
115 Jose Theodore FIT 4.00 10.00
116 Saku Koivu FIT 4.00 10.00
117 Martin Brodeur FIT 10.00 25.00
118 Jaromir Jagr FIT 12.00 30.00
119 Mark Messier FIT 8.00 20.00
120 Jason Spezza FIT 4.00 10.00
121 Jeremy Roenick FIT 6.00 15.00
122 Marc-Andre Fleury FIT 8.00 20.00
123 Mario Lemieux FIT 15.00 40.00
124 Chris Pronger FIT 4.00 10.00
125 Brad Richards FIT 4.00 10.00
126 Martin St. Louis FIT 4.00 10.00
127 Vincent Lecavalier FIT 4.00 10.00
128 Ed Belfour FIT 4.00 10.00
129 Mats Sundin FIT 4.00 10.00
130 Markus Naslund FIT 4.00 10.00
131 Kari Lehtonen FIT 3.00 8.00
132 Andrew Raycroft FIT 3.00 8.00
133 Patrice Bergeron FIT 5.00 12.00
134 Alex Tanguay FIT 4.00 10.00
135 Milan Hejduk FIT 3.00 8.00
136 Marty Turco FIT 4.00 10.00
137 Bill Guerin FIT 4.00 10.00
138 Brendan Shanahan FIT 3.00 8.00
139 Ryan Smyth FIT 3.00 8.00
140 Roberto Luongo FIT 6.00 15.00
141 Luc Robitaille FIT 4.00 10.00
142 Michael Ryder FIT 3.00 8.00
143 Tomas Vokoun FIT 3.00 8.00
144 Patrik Elias FIT 4.00 10.00
145 Rick DiPietro FIT 3.00 8.00
146 Daniel Alfredsson FIT 4.00 10.00
147 Marian Hossa FIT 4.00 10.00
148 Keith Primeau FIT 3.00 8.00
149 Brett Hull FIT 8.00 20.00
150 Evgeni Nabokov FIT 3.00 8.00
151 Patrick Marleau FIT 4.00 10.00
152 Doug Weight FIT 4.00 10.00
153 Keith Tkachuk FIT 4.00 10.00
154 Todd Bertuzzi FIT 4.00 10.00
155 Olaf Kolzig FIT 4.00 10.00
156 Cam Neely FIT 4.00 10.00
157 Gilbert Perreault FIT 4.00 10.00
158 Denis Savard FIT 4.00 10.00
159 Tony Esposito FIT 4.00 10.00
160 Jari Kurri FIT 4.00 10.00
161 Grant Fuhr FIT 6.00 15.00
162 Mike Ribeiro FIT 2.50 6.00
163 Guy LaFleur FIT 5.00 12.00
164 Mike Bossy FIT 4.00 10.00
165 Alexei Yashin FIT 3.00 8.00
166 Phil Esposito FIT 6.00 15.00
167 Dominik Hasek FIT 6.00 15.00
168 Martin Havlat FIT 4.00 10.00
169 Simon Gagne FIT 4.00 10.00
170 Ed Jovanovski FIT 3.00 8.00
171 Corey Perry RC 12.00 30.00
172 Ryan Getzlaf RC 8.00 20.00
173 Braydon Coburn RC 4.00 10.00
174 Jim Slater RC 3.00 8.00
175 Hannu Toivonen RC 4.00 10.00
176 Milan Jurcina RC 3.00 8.00
177 Andrew Alberts RC 2.50 6.00
178 Thomas Vanek RC 8.00 20.00
179 Dion Phaneuf RC 12.00 30.00
180 Eric Nystrom RC 3.00 8.00
181 Cam Ward RC 6.00 15.00
182 Brent Seabrook RC 8.00 20.00
183 Rene Bourque RC 4.00 10.00
184 Cam Barker RC 3.00 8.00
185 Wojtek Wolski RC 3.00 8.00
186 Peter Budaj RC 5.00 12.00
187 Gilbert Brule RC 4.00 10.00
188 Jussi Jokinen RC 4.00 10.00
189 Jim Howard RC 6.00 15.00
190 Johan Franzen RC 8.00 20.00
191 Brett Lebda RC 2.50 6.00
192 Rostislav Olesz RC 3.00 8.00
193 Anthony Stewart RC 3.00 8.00
194 Alexander Perezhogin RC 3.00 8.00
195 Yann Danis RC 3.00 8.00
196 Mark Streit RC 2.50 6.00
197 Ryan Suter RC 5.00 12.00
198 Zach Parise RC 6.00 15.00
199 Robert Nilsson RC 4.00 10.00
200 Petteri Nokelainen RC 2.50 6.00
201 Chris Campoli RC 2.50 6.00
202 Henrik Lundqvist RC 12.00 30.00
203 Petr Prucha RC 4.00 10.00
204 Al Montoya RC 4.00 10.00
205 Andrej Meszaros RC 3.00 8.00
206 Brandon Bochenski RC 4.00 10.00
207 Jeff Carter RC 6.00 15.00
208 Mike Richards RC 8.00 20.00
209 David Leneveu RC 3.00 8.00
210 Keith Ballard RC 3.00 8.00
211 Sidney Crosby RC 100.00 300.00
212 Maxime Talbot RC 4.00 10.00
213 Ryane Clowe RC 5.00 12.00
214 Jeff Woywitka RC 2.50 6.00
215 Jay McClement RC 2.50 6.00
216 Lee Stempniak RC 4.00 10.00
217 Jeff Hoggan RC 2.50 6.00
218 Alexander Steen RC 6.00 15.00
219 Andrew Wozniewski RC 3.00 8.00
220 Alexander Ovechkin RC 200.00 500.00
221 Dustin Penner RC 4.00 10.00
222 Zenon Konopka RC 2.50 6.00
223 Michael Wall RC 3.00 8.00
224 Adam Berkhoel RC 3.00 8.00
225 Jordan Sigalet RC 2.50 6.00
226 Ben Walter RC 2.50 6.00
227 Chris Thorburn RC 3.00 8.00
228 Daniel Paille RC 4.00 10.00
229 Nathan Paetsch RC 3.00 8.00
230 Jiri Novotny RC 3.00 8.00
231 Richie Regehr RC 2.50 6.00
232 Mark Giordano RC 5.00 12.00
233 Andrew Ladd RC 5.00 12.00
234 Chad Larose RC 2.50 6.00
235 Niklas Nordgren RC 4.00 10.00
236 Danny Richmond RC 2.50 6.00
237 Martin St. Pierre RC 2.50 6.00
238 Corey Crawford RC 12.00 30.00
239 James Wisniewski RC 3.00 8.00
240 Duncan Keith RC 8.00 20.00
241 Brad Richardson RC 4.00 10.00
242 Vitaly Kolesnik RC 3.00 8.00
243 Andrew Penner RC 3.00 8.00
244 Ole-Kristian Tollefsen RC 3.00 8.00
245 Alexandre Picard RC 2.50 6.00
246 Joakim Lindstrom RC 2.50 6.00
247 Steven Goertzen RC 2.50 6.00
248 Geoff Platt RC 3.00 8.00
249 Jaroslav Balastik RC 2.50 6.00
250 Junior Lessard RC 2.50 6.00
251 Vojtech Polak RC 2.50 6.00
252 Kyle Quincey RC 3.00 8.00
253 Valtteri Filppula RC 5.00 12.00
254 Brad Winchester RC 4.00 10.00
255 Matt Greene RC 2.50 6.00
256 Kyle Brodziak RC 2.50 6.00
257 J-F Jacques RC 2.50 6.00
258 Mathieu Roy RC 4.00 10.00
259 Danny Syvret RC 2.50 6.00
260 Greg Jacina RC 2.50 6.00
261 Rob Globke RC 2.50 6.00
262 Petr Taticek RC 3.00 8.00
263 Jeff Tambellini RC 2.50 6.00
264 Petr Kanko RC 3.00 8.00
265 Yanick Lehoux RC 4.00 10.00
266 Richard Petiot RC 3.00 8.00
267 Matt Ryan RC 3.00 8.00
268 Connor James RC 3.00 8.00
269 Mikko Koivu RC 5.00 12.00
270 Derek Boogaard RC 6.00 15.00
271 Maxim Lapierre RC 4.00 10.00
272 Andrei Kostitsyn RC 5.00 12.00
273 J-P Cote RC 2.50 6.00
274 Jonathan Ferland RC 3.00 8.00
275 Kevin Klein RC 2.50 6.00
276 Pekka Rinne RC 8.00 20.00
277 Barry Tallackson RC 3.00 8.00
278 Cam Janssen RC 3.00 8.00
279 Jason Ryznar RC 2.50 6.00
280 Jeremy Colliton RC 2.50 6.00
281 Bruno Gervais RC 2.50 6.00
282 Ryan Hollweg RC 2.50 6.00
283 Chris Holt RC 2.50 6.00
284 Patrick Eaves RC 4.00 10.00
285 Christoph Schubert RC 2.50 6.00
286 Brian McGrattan RC 2.50 6.00
287 R.J. Umberger RC 4.00 10.00
288 Ben Eager RC 3.00 8.00
289 Alexandre Picard RC 2.50 6.00
290 Stefan Ruzicka RC 2.50 6.00
291 Matt Jones RC 2.50 6.00
292 Ryan Whitney RC 4.00 10.00
293 Erik Christensen RC 2.50 6.00
294 Colby Armstrong RC 4.00 10.00
295 Steve Bernier RC 4.00 10.00
296 Dimitri Patzold RC 2.50 6.00
297 Grant Stevenson RC 2.50 6.00
298 Doug Murray RC 2.50 6.00
299 Josh Gorges RC 3.00 8.00
300 Dennis Wideman RC 2.50 6.00
301 Chris Beckford-Tseu RC 3.00 8.00
302 Colin Hemingway RC 2.50 6.00
303 Jon DiSalvatore RC 3.00 8.00
304 Evgeny Artyukhin RC 3.00 8.00
305 Gerald Coleman RC 2.50 6.00
306 Ryan Craig RC 2.50 6.00
307 Nick Tarnasky RC 2.50 6.00
308 Paul Ranger RC 2.50 6.00
309 Darren Reid RC 2.50 6.00
310 Doug O'Brien RC 2.50 6.00
311 Staffan Kronwall RC 2.50 6.00
312 Jay Harrison RC 3.00 8.00
313 Kevin Bieksa RC 6.00 15.00
314 Rob McVicar RC 3.00 8.00
315 Tomas Mojzis RC 2.50 6.00
316 Tomas Fleischmann RC 4.00 10.00
317 Jakub Klepis RC 2.50 6.00
318 Mike Green RC 5.00 12.00
319 David Steckel RC 3.00 8.00
320 Joey Tenute RC 3.00 8.00

2005-06 Upper Deck Trilogy Crystal

*FIT/25: 2X TO 5X BASIC CARDS
119 Mark Messier FIT 30.00 80.00

2005-06 Upper Deck Trilogy Honorary Swatches

HSRN Rick Nash 6.00 15.00
HSMT Marty Turco 6.00 15.00
HSSY Steve Yzerman 10.00 25.00
HSAH Ales Hemsky 5.00 12.00
HSRS Ryan Smyth 5.00 12.00
HSRL Roberto Luongo 10.00 25.00
HSAF Alexander Frolov 4.00 10.00
HSMG Marian Gaborik 6.00 15.00
HSJO Jose Theodore 6.00 15.00
HSSK Saku Koivu 6.00 15.00
HSMB Martin Brodeur 10.00 25.00
HSPE Patrik Elias 6.00 15.00
HSJJ Jaromir Jagr 20.00 50.00
HSMM Mark Messier 12.00 30.00
HSSP Jason Spezza 6.00 15.00
HSHO Marian Hossa 6.00 15.00
HSHA Martin Havlat 6.00 15.00
HSJR Jeremy Roenick 10.00 25.00
HSSG Simon Gagne 6.00 15.00
HSML Mario Lemieux 15.00 40.00
HSJC Jonathan-Cheechoo 4.00 10.00
HSCP Chris Pronger 6.00 15.00
HSVL Vincent Lecavalier 6.00 15.00
HSMS Mats Sundin 6.00 15.00
HSEJ Ed Jovanovski 5.00 12.00
HSMN Markus Naslund 6.00 15.00
HSLU Jeffrey Lupul 5.00 12.00
HSSF Sergei Fedorov 10.00 25.00
HSGM Glen Murray 5.00 12.00
HSTK Keith Tkachuk 6.00 15.00
HSAM Al MacInnis 8.00 20.00
HSAT Alex Tanguay 6.00 15.00
HSEL Eric Lindros 10.00 25.00
HSDW Doug Weight 6.00 15.00
HSDC Dan Cloutier 5.00 12.00
HSTB Todd Bertuzzi 6.00 15.00
HSJG Jean-Sebastien Giguere 6.00 15.00
HSMK Miikka Kiprusoff 4.00 10.00
HSBR Brad Richards SP 6.00 15.00
HSSV Sergei Samsonov 5.00 12.00
HSED Eric Daze 5.00 12.00
HSJW Justin Williams 5.00 12.00
HSNK Nikolai Khabibulin 6.00 15.00
HSDA David Aebischer 5.00 12.00
HSMD Marc Denis 5.00 12.00
HSBG Bill Guerin 6.00 15.00
HSMO Mike Modano 10.00 25.00
HSCC Chris Chelios 6.00 15.00
HSNL Nicklas Lidstrom 6.00 15.00
HSKD Kris Draper 8.00 20.00
HSWG Wayne Gretzky 30.00 80.00
HSTC Ty Conklin 5.00 12.00
HSMP Michael Peca 5.00 12.00
HSJB Jay Bouwmeester 4.00 10.00
HSNH Nathan Horton 6.00 15.00
HSRE Robert Esche 5.00 12.00
HSRY Michael Ryder 5.00 12.00
HSRI Mike Ribeiro 4.00 10.00
HSDL David Legwand 5.00 12.00
HSPK Paul Kariya 6.00 15.00
HSOK Olaf Kolzig 6.00 15.00
HSSS Scott Stevens 6.00 15.00
HSAL Daniel Alfredsson 6.00 15.00
HSHK Dominik Hasek 8.00 20.00
HSKP Keith Primeau 5.00 12.00
HSCJ Curtis Joseph 8.00 20.00
HSBL Brian Leetch 5.00 12.00
HSJL John LeClair 6.00 15.00
HSZP Zigmund Palffy 6.00 15.00
HSIK Ilya Kovalchuk 6.00 15.00
HSKL Kari Lehtonen 5.00 12.00
HSAR Andrew Raycroft 5.00 12.00
HSJT Joe Thornton 10.00 25.00
HSDB Daniel Briere 6.00 15.00
HSJI Jarome Iginla 8.00 20.00
HSTR Tuomo Ruutu 6.00 15.00
HSJS Joe Sakic 12.00 30.00
HSMH Milan Hejduk 5.00 12.00
HSPF Peter Forsberg 6.00 15.00
HSNZ Nikolai Zherdev 4.00 10.00

2005-06 Upper Deck Trilogy Ice Scripts

ISAH Ales Hemsky 8.00 20.00
ISAT Alex Tanguay 8.00 20.00
ISAR Andrew Raycroft 8.00 20.00
ISBC Bobby Clarke 25.00 60.00
ISCN Cam Neely 12.00 30.00
ISAL Daniel Alfredsson 75.00 150.00
ISDB Daniel Briere 10.00 25.00
ISDH Dany Heatley 12.50 30.00
ISDA David Aebischer 6.00 15.00
ISDC Don Cherry 20.00 50.00
ISGC Gerry Cheevers 12.00 30.00
ISGP Gilbert Perreault 10.00 25.00
ISHL Glenn Hall 20.00 50.00
ISGH Gordie Howe 60.00 125.00
ISIK Ilya Kovalchuk 30.00 60.00
ISJI Jarome Iginla 10.00 25.00
ISJT Joe Thornton 12.50 30.00
ISJO Jose Theodore 12.00 30.00
ISJG Jean-Sebastien Giguere 8.00 20.00
ISLR Luc Robitaille 10.00 25.00
ISMF Marc-Andre Fleury 12.00 30.00
ISHS Marcel Hossa 6.00 15.00
ISMG Marian Gaborik 15.00 40.00
ISHO Marian Hossa 10.00 25.00
ISMN Markus Naslund 10.00 25.00
ISMB Martin Brodeur 100.00 200.00
ISHA Martin Havlat 8.00 20.00
ISSL Martin St. Louis 12.00 30.00
ISMT Marty Turco 8.00 20.00
ISMS Mats Sundin SP 150.00 250.00
ISBO Mike Bossy 15.00 40.00
ISMM Mike Modano 12.00 30.00
ISMH Milan Hejduk 8.00 20.00
ISRB Ray Bourque SP 25.00 60.00
ISRN Rick Nash 15.00 40.00
ISRS Ryan Smyth 10.00 25.00
ISSK Saku Koivu SP 150.00 250.00
ISSW Stephen Weiss 6.00 15.00
ISVL Vincent Lecavalier SP 40.00 100.00
ISWG Wayne Gretzky 250.00 600.00

2005-06 Upper Deck Trilogy Legendary Scripts

LEGBC Bobby Clarke 12.00 30.00
LEGBH Bobby Hull SP 30.00 80.00
LEGCG Clark Gillies 6.00 15.00
LEGCN Cam Neely 10.00 25.00
LEGDC Don Cherry 15.00 40.00
LEGDS Denis Savard 6.00 15.00
LEGGA Glenn Anderson 6.00 15.00
LEGGC Gerry Cheevers 12.00 30.00
LEGGH Gordie Howe SP 60.00 125.00
LEGGL Guy Lafleur SP 60.00 125.00
LEGGP Gilbert Perreault 12.00 30.00
LEGJK Jari Kurri 12.00 30.00
LEGLM Lanny McDonald 6.00 15.00
LEGMD Marcel Dionne 10.00 25.00
LEGPE Phil Esposito SP 30.00 80.00
LEGRB Ray Bourque SP 60.00 125.00
LEGRR Rene Robert 6.00 15.00
LEGSM Stan Mikita SP 12.00 30.00
LEGTE Tony Esposito SP 20.00 50.00
LEGTL Ted Lindsay 12.00 30.00
LEGWG Wayne Gretzky SP 400.00 1000.00

2005-06 Upper Deck Trilogy Personal Scripts

PERBC Bobby Clarke SP 20.00 50.00
PERBH Bobby Hull SP 25.00 60.00
PERCN Cam Neely SP 20.00 50.00
PERDS Denis Savard SP 10.00 25.00
PERGF Grant Fuhr 15.00 40.00
PERGH Gordie Howe 75.00 200.00
PERGL Guy Lafleur SP 50.00 100.00
PERGP Gilbert Perreault SP 25.00 50.00
PERLM Lanny McDonald 10.00 25.00
PERMB Martin Brodeur SP 200.00 300.00
PERMD Marcel Dionne 12.00 30.00
PERMF Marc-Andre Fleury 15.00 40.00
PERPE Phil Esposito SP 40.00 80.00
PERRB Ray Bourque SP 75.00 200.00
PERRH Ron Hextall 20.00 50.00
PERRN Rick Nash 15.00 40.00
PERRR Rene Robert SP 10.00 25.00
PERSM Stan Mikita SP 25.00 60.00
PERSP Jason Spezza 10.00 25.00
PERTE Tony Esposito SP 30.00 60.00
PERGC1 G.Cheevers No Inscrip. 12.50 30.00
PERGC2 G.Cheevers Cheesy 20.00 50.00

2005-06 Upper Deck Trilogy Scripts

SCSAY Alexei Yashin 5.00 12.00
SCSCD Chris Drury 5.00 12.00
SCSJG Jean-Sebastien Giguere 8.00 20.00
SCSJL John LeClair 5.00 12.00
SCSJS Jason Spezza 10.00 25.00
SCSMN Markus Naslund 6.00 15.00
SCSMP Mark Parrish 5.00 12.00
SCSMT Marty Turco 4.00 10.00
SCSPB Pavel Bure 6.00 15.00
SCSPE Michael Peca 5.00 12.00
SCSRL Roberto Luongo 6.00 15.00
SCSRN Rick Nash 12.00 30.00
SCSRS Ryan Smyth 8.00 20.00
SCSTB Todd Bertuzzi 8.00 20.00
SCSTR Tuomo Ruutu 5.00 12.00
SFSAF Alexander Frolov 4.00 10.00
SFSAH Ales Hemsky 3.00 8.00
SFSAM Antti Miettinen 3.00 8.00
SFSAR Andrew Raycroft 4.00 10.00
SFSBB Brad Boyes 3.00 8.00
SFSBG Boyd Gordon 3.00 8.00
SFSBM Brenden Morrow 4.00 10.00
SFSCK Chuck Kobasew 3.00 8.00
SFSDA David Aebischer 4.00 10.00
SFSDB Dustin Brown 3.00 8.00
SFSFS Fredrik Sjostrom 3.00 8.00
SFSJB Jay Bouwmeester 3.00 8.00
SFSJL Joffrey Lupul 5.00 12.00
SFSJP Joni Pitkanen 3.00 8.00
SFSKL Kari Lehtonen 5.00 12.00
SFSLN Ladislav Nagy 3.00 8.00
SFSMA Maxim Afinogenov 3.00 8.00
SFSMC Mike Cammalleri 3.00 8.00
SFSMF Marc-Andre Fleury 12.00 30.00
SFSMH Martin Havlat 4.00 10.00
SFSMR Mike Ribeiro 3.00 8.00
SFSMS Matt Stajan 3.00 8.00
SFSNA Nik Antropov 3.00 8.00
SFSNH Nathan Horton 3.00 8.00
SFSNS Nathan Smith 3.00 8.00
SFSNZ Nikolai Zherdev 4.00 10.00
SFSPS Philippe Sauve 4.00 10.00
SFSRF Ruslan Fedotenko 3.00 8.00
SFSRK Ryan Kesler 10.00 25.00
SFSRM Ryan Miller 6.00 15.00
SFSSB Sean Bergenheim 3.00 8.00
SFSTC Ty Conklin 4.00 10.00
SFSTH Trent Hunter 3.00 8.00
SFSTM Travis Moen 3.00 8.00
SFSTP Tom Poti 3.00 8.00
SSSDH Dominik Hasek 25.00 60.00
SSSGL Guy Lafleur 20.00 50.00
SSSIK Ilya Kovalchuk 20.00 50.00
SSSJI Jarome Iginla 20.00 50.00
SSSJO Jose Theodore 12.50 30.00
SSSJT Joe Thornton 15.00 40.00
SSSMB Martin Brodeur 75.00 150.00
SSSMG Marian Gaborik 15.00 40.00
SSSRB Ray Bourque 30.00 80.00
SSSWG Wayne Gretzky 200.00 500.00

2006-07 Upper Deck Trilogy

1 Chris Pronger .60 1.50
2 Teemu Selanne 1.25 3.00
3 Jean-Sebastien Giguere .60 1.50
4 Ilya Kovalchuk .60 1.50
5 Kari Lehtonen .50 1.25
6 Marian Hossa .60 1.50
7 Hannu Toivonen .50 1.25
8 Zdeno Chara .60 1.50
9 Patrice Bergeron .75 2.00
10 Brad Boyes .40 1.00
11 Ryan Miller .60 1.50
12 Chris Drury .50 1.25
13 Daniel Briere .60 1.50
14 Miikka Kiprusoff .60 1.50
15 Jarome Iginla .75 2.00
16 Alex Tanguay .40 1.00
17 Dion Phaneuf .50 1.25
18 Eric Staal .75 2.00
19 Cam Ward .60 1.50
20 Rod Brind'Amour .60 1.50
21 Martin Havlat .40 1.00
22 Nikolai Khabibulin .60 1.50
23 Tuomo Ruutu .60 1.50
24 Joe Sakic 1.25 3.00
25 Jose Theodore .60 1.50
26 Milan Hejduk .50 1.25
27 Marek Svatos .40 1.00
28 Pascal Leclaire .50 1.25
29 Rick Nash .60 1.50
30 Fredrik Modin .40 1.00
31 Sergei Fedorov 1.00 2.50
32 Mike Modano 1.00 2.50
33 Marty Turco .60 1.50
34 Eric Lindros 1.00 2.50
35 Pavel Datsyuk 1.00 2.50
36 Henrik Zetterberg .75 2.00
37 Nicklas Lidstrom .60 1.50
38 Dominik Hasek 1.00 2.50
39 Ryan Smyth .50 1.25
40 Joffrey Lupul .40 1.00
41 Ales Hemsky .50 1.25
42 Dwayne Roloson .50 1.25
43 Todd Bertuzzi .60 1.50
44 Olli Jokinen .60 1.50
45 Ed Belfour .60 1.50
46 Rob Blake .60 1.50
47 Alexander Frolov .40 1.00
48 Marian Gaborik .60 1.50
49 Pavol Demitra .75 2.00
50 Manny Fernandez .40 1.00
51 Saku Koivu .60 1.50
52 Cristobal Huet .50 1.25
53 Michael Ryder .40 1.00
54 Alex Kovalev .50 1.25
55 Tomas Vokoun .50 1.25
56 Paul Kariya .60 1.50
57 Jason Arnott .50 1.25
58 Martin Brodeur 1.50 4.00
59 Patrik Elias .60 1.50
60 Brian Gionta .40 1.00
61 Miroslav Satan .50 1.25
62 Rick DiPietro .50 1.25
63 Alexei Yashin .50 1.25
64 Jaromir Jagr 2.00 5.00
65 Henrik Lundqvist 1.50 4.00
66 Brendan Shanahan .60 1.50
67 Daniel Alfredsson .60 1.50
68 Jason Spezza .60 1.50
69 Dany Heatley .50 1.25
70 Martin Gerber .50 1.25
71 Peter Forsberg 1.25 3.00
72 Jeff Carter .50 1.25
73 Simon Gagne .60 1.50
74 Mike Richards .50 1.25
75 Shane Doan .50 1.25
76 Curtis Joseph .75 2.00
77 Jeremy Roenick 1.00 2.50
78 Mark Recchi .75 2.00
79 Sidney Crosby 2.50 6.00
80 Marc-Andre Fleury 1.25 3.00
81 Joe Thornton 1.00 2.50
82 Vesa Toskala .50 1.25
83 Patrick Marleau .60 1.50
84 Jonathan Cheechoo .50 1.25
85 Keith Tkachuk .60 1.50
86 Doug Weight .60 1.50
87 Manny Legace .50 1.25
88 Brad Richards .60 1.50
89 Vincent Lecavalier .60 1.50
90 Martin St. Louis .60 1.50
91 Mats Sundin .60 1.50
92 Andrew Raycroft .50 1.25
93 Michael Peca .50 1.25
94 Alexander Steen .40 1.00
95 Roberto Luongo 1.00 2.50
96 Markus Naslund .60 1.50
97 Henrik Sedin .75 2.00
98 Daniel Sedin .75 2.00
99 Alexander Ovechkin 2.50 6.00
100 Olaf Kolzig .60 1.50
101 Shane O'Brien RC 1.50 4.00
102 Ryan Shannon RC 1.50 4.00
103 Yan Stastny RC 1.50 4.00
104 Mark Stuart RC 1.50 4.00
105 Phil Kessel RC 5.00 12.00
106 Carsen Germyn RC 1.50 4.00
107 Dustin Byfuglien RC 4.00 10.00
108 Paul Stastny RC 4.00 10.00
109 Filip Novak RC 1.50 4.00
110 Fredrik Norrena RC 1.50 4.00
111 Loui Eriksson RC 3.00 8.00
112 Tomas Kopecky RC 2.00 5.00
113 M-A Pouliot RC 1.50 4.00
114 Patrick Thoresen RC 1.50 4.00
115 Ladislav Smid RC 1.50 4.00
116 K. Pushkarev RC 2.00 5.00
117 Patrick O'Sullivan RC 2.50 6.00
118 Anze Kopitar RC 8.00 20.00
119 Erik Reitz RC 1.50 4.00
120 Miroslav Kopriva RC 1.50 4.00
121 Niklas Backstrom RC 3.00 8.00
122 Dan Janoovoki RC 1.60 4.00
123 G. Latendresse RC 2.50 6.00
124 Shea Weber RC 4.00 10.00
125 Mikko Lehtonen RC 2.00 5.00
126 Frank Doyle RC 2.00 5.00
127 John Oduya RC 2.50 6.00
128 Travis Zajac RC 3.00 8.00
129 Rob Collins RC 1.50 4.00
130 Steve Regier RC 1.50 4.00
131 Matt Koalska RC 1.50 4.00
132 Ryan Caldwell RC 1.50 4.00
133 Masi Marjamaki RC 1.50 4.00
134 Keith Yandle RC 4.00 10.00
135 Enver Lisin RC 1.50 4.00
136 Jarkko Immonen RC 2.00 5.00
137 David Liffiton RC 1.50 4.00
138 Nigel Dawes RC 1.50 4.00
139 Alexei Kaigorodov RC 1.50 4.00
140 Ryan Potulny RC 1.50 4.00
141 David Printz RC 1.50 4.00
142 Bill Thomas RC 1.50 4.00
143 Joel Perrault RC 1.50 4.00
144 Patrick Fischer RC 1.50 4.00
145 Noah Welch RC 1.50 4.00
146 Michel Ouellet RC 2.00 5.00
147 Jordan Staal RC 4.00 10.00
148 Kristopher Letang RC 8.00 20.00
149 Evgeni Malkin RC 15.00 40.00
150 Matt Carle RC 1.50 4.00
151 M-E Vlasic RC 2.50 6.00
152 D.J. King RC 1.50 4.00
153 Roman Polak RC 2.00 5.00
154 Ben Ondrus RC 1.50 4.00
155 Brendan Bell RC 1.50 4.00
156 Ian White RC 2.00 5.00
157 Jeremy Williams RC 1.50 4.00
158 Luc Bourdon RC 2.50 6.00
159 Eric Fehr RC 2.50 6.00
160 Jonas Johansson RC 1.50 4.00

2006-07 Upper Deck Trilogy Combo Clearcut Autographs

C2AR Smyth/Hemsky 12.00 30.00
C2BB Boyes/Bergeron 12.00 30.00
C2CK Calder/Khabibulin 12.00 30.00
C2EE P.Espo/T.Espo 30.00 80.00
C2GP Gomez/Parise EXCH 15.00 40.00
C2HS Hejduk/Svatos 12.00 30.00
C2KK S.Koivu/M.Koivu 15.00 40.00
C2KN Kiprusoff/Niittymaki 20.00 50.00
C2LJ Luongo/Jokin EXCH 10.00 25.00
C2LS Lecav/St. Lou EXCH 20.00 50.00
C2LZ Legace/Zetter EXCH 25.00 50.00
C2MM Lanny/Mullen 12.00 30.00
C2MV Miller/Vanek 15.00 40.00
C2NM Naslund/Morrison 12.00 30.00
C2PG Perry/Getzlaf 20.00 50.00
C2PM Marleau/Michalek 15.00 40.00
C2RC Redden/Chara 15.00 40.00
C2SH Smith/Hextall EXCH 25.00 60.00
C2VS Vokoun/Sully EXCH 20.00 50.00
C3BLS Beliv/Laf/Shutt EXCH 90.00 150.00
C3BPS Bossy/Potvin/Smith 50.00 100.00
C3CGS Cole/Gerb/Staal EXCH 25.00 60.00
C3FCB Frolov/Cam/Brown 50.00 100.00
C3FEC Fuhr/Espo/Cheev EXCH 60.00 125.00
C3HTT Hejd/Theo/Tang EXCH 60.00 120.00
C3IKP Iggy/Kipper/Dion 40.00 100.00
C3LDZ Leg/Draper/Zett EXCH 100.00 200.00
C3MSS McDonald/Sittler/Salming 40.00 80.00
C3MTM Mo/Turco/Morrow 40.00 80.00
C3NOB Cam/Terry/Ray EXCH 75.00 150.00
C3PGC Primeau/Gagne/Carter 30.00 60.00
C3RBH Roy/Brod/Hasek 125.00 250.00
C3RHH Red/Hav/Heat 40.00 80.00

2006-07 Upper Deck Trilogy Frozen In Time

COMPLETE SET (20) 150.00 250.00
FT1 Alexander Ovechkin 15.00 40.00
FT2 Bobby Clarke 6.00 15.00
FT3 Brendan Shanahan 4.00 10.00
FT4 Cam Neely 4.00 10.00
FT5 Dominik Hasek 6.00 15.00
FT6 Gordie Howe 8.00 20.00
FT7 Guy Lafleur 5.00 12.00
FT8 Jaromir Jagr 12.00 30.00
FT9 Jean Beliveau 4.00 10.00
FT10 Joe Sakic 8.00 20.00
FT11 Martin Brodeur 10.00 25.00
FT12 Mats Sundin 4.00 10.00
FT13 Mike Bossy 4.00 10.00
FT14 Mike Modano 6.00 15.00
FT15 Patrick Roy 8.00 20.00
FT16 Ray Bourque 6.00 15.00
FT17 Sidney Crosby 15.00 40.00
FT18 Steve Yzerman 10.00 25.00
FT19 Tony Esposito 4.00 10.00
FT20 Wayne Gretzky 15.00 40.00

2006-07 Upper Deck Trilogy Honorary Scripted Swatches

HSAH Ales Hemsky 15.00 40.00
HSSAF Alexander Frolov 12.00 30.00
HSSAO Alexander Ovechkin 200.00 500.00
HSSAR Andrew Raycroft 15.00 40.00
HSSAT Alex Tanguay 12.00 30.00
HSSBB Brad Boyes 12.00 30.00
HSSBG Brian Gionta 12.00 30.00
HSSBL Rob Blake 20.00 50.00
HSSBM Brenden Morrow 15.00 40.00
HSSBO Borje Salming 20.00 50.00
HSSBR Bill Ranford 20.00 50.00
HSSBS Billy Smith 20.00 50.00
HSSCA Jeff Carter 15.00 40.00
HSSCD Chris Drury 15.00 40.00
HSSCK Chuck Kobasew 12.00 30.00
HSSCN Cam Neely 20.00 50.00
HSSCO Corey Perry 30.00 80.00
HSSDA David Aebischer 15.00 40.00
HSSDB Dustin Brown 20.00 50.00
HSSDC Dan Cloutier 15.00 40.00
HSSDG Doug Gilmour 25.00 60.00
HSSDH Dany Heatley 20.00 50.00
HSSDR Dwayne Roloson 15.00 40.00
HSSDS Darryl Sittler 25.00 60.00
HSSDW Doug Weight 20.00 50.00
HSSEB Ed Belfour 20.00 50.00
HSSES Eric Staal 25.00 60.00
HSSGA Simon Gagne 20.00 50.00
HSSGH Gordie Howe 75.00 150.00
HSSGL Guy Lafleur 25.00 60.00
HSSHA Dominik Hasek 30.00 80.00
HSSHE Milan Hejduk 12.00 30.00
HSSHV Martin Havlat 12.00 30.00
HSSHZ Henrik Zetterberg 25.00 60.00
HSSIK Ilya Kovalchuk 20.00 50.00
HSSJA Jarret Stoll 15.00 40.00
HSSJB Jay Bouwmeester 12.00 30.00
HSSJI Jarome Iginla 12.00 30.00
HSSJL Joffrey Lupul 12.00 30.00
HSSJP Joni Pitkanen 12.00 30.00
HSSJR Jeremy Roenick 25.00 60.00
HSSJS Jason Spezza 20.00 50.00
HSSJT Joe Thornton 30.00 80.00
HSSJW Justin Williams 15.00 40.00
HSSKC Kyle Calder 12.00 30.00
HSSKD Kris Draper 12.00 30.00
HSSKL Kari Lehtonen 15.00 40.00
HSSKP Keith Primeau 15.00 40.00
HSSLE Mario Lemieux 75.00 200.00
HSSLM Lanny McDonald 20.00 50.00
HSSMB Martin Brodeur 60.00 125.00
HSSMC Mike Cammalleri 12.00 30.00
HSSMG Martin Gerber 15.00 40.00
HSSMH Marian Hossa 20.00 50.00
HSSMK Miikka Kiprusoff 20.00 50.00
HSSML Manny Legace 15.00 40.00
HSSMN Markus Naslund 20.00 50.00
HSSMP Michael Peca 15.00 40.00
HSSMR Michael Ryder 12.00 30.00
HSSMS Marek Svatos 12.00 30.00
HSSMT Marty Turco 20.00 50.00
HSSNH Nathan Horton 20.00 50.00
HSSNK Nikolai Khabibulin 20.00 50.00
HSSNL Nicklas Lidstrom 20.00 50.00
HSSON Owen Nolan 20.00 50.00
HSSPB Patrice Bergeron 25.00 60.00
HSSPE Patrik Elias 20.00 50.00
HSSPI Pierre-Marc Bouchard 20.00 50.00
HSSPM Patrick Marleau 20.00 50.00
HSSPR Patrick Roy 50.00 120.00
HSSRB Ray Bourque 40.00 100.00
HSSRE Robert Esche 15.00 40.00
HSSRL Roberto Luongo 50.00 100.00
HSSRM Ryan Miller 20.00 50.00
HSSRN Rick Nash 20.00 50.00
HSSRS Ryan Smyth 20.00 50.00
HSSSA Miroslav Satan 15.00 40.00
HSSSC Sidney Crosby 150.00 300.00
HSSSD Shane Doan 15.00 40.00
HSSSG Scott Gomez 15.00 40.00
HSSSK Saku Koivu 20.00 50.00
HSSSN Scott Niedermayer 20.00 50.00
HSSSS Sergei Samsonov 15.00 40.00
HSSST Martin St. Louis 20.00 50.00
HSSSU Steve Sullivan 12.00 30.00
HSSTB Todd Bertuzzi 20.00 50.00
HSSTV Tomas Vokoun 15.00 40.00
HSSVL Vincent Lecavalier 50.00 100.00
HSSWG Wayne Gretzky 250.00 600.00
HSSWI Doug Wilson 15.00 40.00

2006-07 Upper Deck Trilogy Honorary Swatches

HSAH Ales Hemsky 4.00 10.00
HSAO Alexander Ovechkin SP 10.00 25.00
HSBM Brenden Morrow 4.00 10.00
HSBO Ray Bourque 8.00 20.00
HSBR Bill Ranford 5.00 12.00
HSBS Borje Salming 5.00 12.00
HSCD Chris Drury 4.00 10.00
HSCN Cam Neely 5.00 12.00
HSCW Cam Ward 5.00 12.00
HSDG Doug Gilmour 6.00 15.00
HSDH Dany Heatley 4.00 10.00
HSDS Darryl Sittler 6.00 15.00
HSEB Ed Belfour 5.00 12.00
HSES Eric Staal 6.00 15.00
HSGH Gordie Howe SP 12.00 30.00
HSGL Guy Lafleur SP 6.00 15.00
HSGO Scott Gomez 4.00 10.00
HSHA Dominik Hasek SP 8.00 20.00
HSHO Marian Hossa 5.00 12.00
HSHZ Henrik Zetterberg 6.00 15.00
HSIK Ilya Kovalchuk 5.00 12.00
HSIM Jarkko Immonen 4.00 10.00
HSIW Ian White 4.00 10.00
HSJG Jean-Sebastien Giguere 5.00 12.00
HSJI Jarome Iginla 6.00 15.00
HSJS Jason Spezza 5.00 12.00
HSJT Joe Thornton 8.00 20.00
HSJW Justin Williams 4.00 10.00
HSKD Kris Draper 3.00 8.00
HSKL Kari Lehtonen SP 4.00 10.00
HSKP Keith Primeau 4.00 10.00
HSLE Manny Legace 4.00 10.00
HSLM Lanny McDonald 5.00 12.00
HSMA Marc-Antoine Pouliot 3.00 8.00
HSMB Martin Brodeur SP 12.00 30.00
HSMH Milan Hejduk 4.00 10.00
HSMK Miikka Kiprusoff 5.00 12.00
HSML Mario Lemieux SP 12.00 30.00
HSMN Markus Naslund 5.00 12.00
HSMR Michael Ryder 3.00 8.00
HSMS Marek Svatos 3.00 8.00
HSMT Marty Turco 5.00 12.00
HSOK Olaf Kolzig 5.00 12.00
HSPB Patrice Bergeron 6.00 15.00
HSPR Patrick Roy 10.00 30.00
HSRB Rob Blake 5.00 12.00
HSRL Roberto Luongo 8.00 20.00
HSRM Ryan Miller 5.00 12.00
HSRN Rick Nash 5.00 12.00
HSRS Ryan Smyth 4.00 10.00
HSSA Miroslav Satan 4.00 10.00
HSSC Sidney Crosby SP 20.00 50.00
HSSG Simon Gagne 5.00 12.00
HSSK Saku Koivu 5.00 12.00
HSSM Billy Smith 5.00 12.00
HSSN Scott Niedermayer 5.00 12.00
HSST Martin St. Louis 5.00 12.00
HSVL Vincent Lecavalier 5.00 12.00
HSWG Wayne Gretzky SP 40.00 80.00

2006-07 Upper Deck Trilogy Ice Scripts

ISAH Ales Hemsky 6.00 15.00
ISAK Andrei Kostitsyn 6.00 15.00
ISAL Andrew Ladd 5.00 12.00
ISAN Antero Niittymaki 6.00 15.00
ISAO Alexander Ovechkin 250.00 600.00
ISBB Brad Boyes 5.00 12.00
ISBH Bobby Hull EXCH 30.00 80.00
ISBR Dustin Brown 8.00 20.00
ISCD Chris Drury 6.00 15.00
ISCK Chuck Kobasew 5.00 12.00
ISCP Chris Pronger 8.00 20.00
ISDA David Aebischer 6.00 15.00
ISDB Daniel Briere 8.00 20.00
ISDC Don Cherry 20.00 50.00
ISDH Dominik Hasek 25.00 60.00
ISDR Dwayne Roloson 6.00 15.00
ISGF Grant Fuhr 15.00 40.00
ISGH Gordie Howe 60.00 150.00
ISGL Guy Lafleur SP 30.00 80.00
ISHE Dany Heatley 6.00 15.00
ISJB Johnny Bucyk 12.00 30.00
ISJC Jonathan Cheechoo 6.00 15.00
ISJI Jarome Iginla 10.00 25.00
ISJL Joffrey Lupul 5.00 12.00
ISJO Joe Thornton 12.00 30.00
ISJT Jose Theodore 8.00 20.00
ISKD Kris Draper 5.00 12.00
ISMA Martin Brodeur SP 60.00 150.00
ISMB Mike Bossy 8.00 20.00
ISMC Mike Cammalleri 5.00 12.00
ISMF Marc-Andre Fleury 15.00 40.00
ISMG Marian Gaborik 8.00 20.00
ISMH Milan Hejduk 6.00 15.00
ISMI Miikka Kiprusoff 8.00 20.00
ISMK Mikko Koivu 6.00 15.00
ISMM Milan Michalek 5.00 12.00
ISMN Markus Naslund 8.00 20.00
ISMR Mike Ribeiro 5.00 12.00
ISMS Marek Svatos 5.00 12.00
ISOJ Olli Jokinen 8.00 20.00
ISPB Patrice Bergeron 50.00 125.00
ISPE Phil Esposito 20.00 50.00
ISPR Patrick Roy EXCH 60.00 150.00
ISRB Ray Bourque 25.00 60.00
ISRM Ryan Malone 5.00 12.00
ISRY Ryan Miller 8.00 20.00
ISSB Scotty Bowman SP 40.00 100.00
ISSC Sidney Crosby SP 80.00 200.00

ISSH Shawn Horcoff 5.00 12.00
ISSK Saku Koivu 12.00 30.00
ISTV Thomas Vanek 6.00 15.00
ISVL Vincent Lecavalier 8.00 20.00
ISVO Tomas Vokoun 6.00 15.00
ISWG Wayne Gretzky SP 200.00 500.00

2006-07 Upper Deck Trilogy Legendary Scripts

LSBC Bobby Clarke 25.00 60.00
LSBR Richard Brodeur 20.00 50.00
LSBS Billy Smith 15.00 40.00
LSCN Cam Neely 25.00 60.00
LSDC Don Cherry 25.00 60.00
LSDS Denis Savard 10.00 25.00
LSGA Glenn Anderson 6.00 15.00
LSGC Gerry Cheevers 15.00 40.00
LSGF Grant Fuhr 15.00 40.00
LSGH Gordie Howe/25 75.00 150.00
LSGL Guy Lafleur/25 30.00 80.00
LSJB Jean Beliveau 30.00 80.00
LSJM Joe Mullen 6.00 15.00
LSMB Mike Bossy 20.00 50.00
LSML Mario Lemieux/25 75.00 200.00
LSPE Phil Esposito 20.00 50.00
LSRB Ray Bourque/25 40.00 80.00
LSRH Ron Hextall 25.00 60.00
LSRL Reggie Leach 20.00 50.00
LSSB Scotty Bowman 25.00 50.00
LSTE Tony Esposito 15.00 40.00
LSTL Ted Lindsay 10.00 25.00
LSWG Wayne Gretzky/25 250.00 600.00

2006-07 Upper Deck Trilogy Scripts

S1GH Gordie Howe/26 75.00 150.00
S1GL Guy Lafleur/17 100.00 200.00
S1ML Mario Lemieux/17 80.00 200.00
S1PR Patrick Roy/19 100.00 200.00
S1RB Ray Bourque/23 40.00 80.00
S1WG Wayne Gretzky/20 300.00 800.00
S2ES Eric Staal/28 20.00 50.00
S2HZ Henrik Zetterberg/39 20.00 50.00
S2IK Ilya Kovalchuk/27 20.00 50.00
S3AR Andrew Raycroft/25 20.00 40.00
S3DH Dany Heatley/25 25.00 60.00
S3ES Eric Staal/25 20.00 50.00
S3HA Dominik Hasek/25 40.00 80.00
S3HZ Henrik Zetterberg/25 30.00 60.00
S3IK Ilya Kovalchuk/25 25.00 60.00
S3JC Jonathan Cheechoo/25 20.00 50.00
S3JI Jarome Iginla/25 15.00 40.00
S3JR Jeremy Roenick/25 25.00 60.00
S3JT Joe Thornton/25 25.00 60.00
S3MB Martin Brodeur/25 50.00 100.00
S3MG Marian Gaborik/25 20.00 50.00
S3MK Miikka Kiprusoff/25 25.00 50.00
S3MN Markus Naslund/25 25.00 50.00
S3NL Nicklas Lidstrom/25 25.00 60.00
S3PB Patrice Bergeron/25 15.00 40.00
S3RB Rob Blake/25 20.00 50.00
S3RL Roberto Luongo/25 25.00 60.00
S3RN Rick Nash/25 20.00 50.00
S3SC Sidney Crosby/25 250.00 400.00
S3SK Saku Koivu/25 20.00 50.00
S3TH Jose Theodore/25 20.00 40.00
S3TV Tomas Vokoun/25 20.00 50.00
S3VL Vincent Lecavalier/25 40.00 80.00
TSAA Adrian Aucoin 3.00 8.00
TSAF Alexander Frolov 5.00 12.00
TSAH Ales Hemsky 5.00 12.00
TSAL Andrew Ladd 3.00 8.00
TSAN Antero Niittymaki 6.00 15.00
TSAP Alexandre Picard 6.00 15.00
TSBB Brad Boyes 8.00 20.00
TSBR Dustin Brown 12.00 30.00
TSBS Billy Smith SP 15.00 40.00
TSCD Chris Drury 10.00 25.00
TSCK Chuck Kobasew 6.00 15.00
TSCN Cam Neely SP 15.00 40.00
TSDA David Aebischer 12.00 30.00
TSDB Daniel Briere SP 30.00 80.00
TSDC Dan Cloutier 8.00 20.00
TSDL David Leneveu 8.00 20.00
TSDO Doug Wilson 6.00 15.00
TSDP Dion Phaneuf SP 20.00 50.00
TSDR Danny Richmond 3.00 8.00
TSDS Derek Sanderson 8.00 20.00
TSDT Dave Taylor 4.00 10.00
TSDW Doug Weight 10.00 25.00
TSED Eric Daze 3.00 8.00
TSGH Gordie Howe SP 30.00 60.00
TSHO Shawn Horcoff 8.00 20.00
TSHZ Henrik Zetterberg 12.00 30.00
TSJB Johnny Bucyk 6.00 15.00
TSJC Jonathan Cheechoo 10.00 25.00
TSJH Jeff Halpern 6.00 15.00
TSJI Jarome Iginla SP 25.00 60.00
TSJL Jason Labarbera 4.00 10.00
TSJM Joe Mullen SP 8.00 20.00
TSJP Joni Pitkanen 8.00 20.00
TSJT Jose Theodore SP 15.00 40.00
TSKC Kyle Calder 6.00 15.00
TSKD Kris Draper 8.00 20.00
TSKL Kari Lehtonen SP 20.00 50.00
TSKM Kirk Muller SP 8.00 20.00
TSKU Chris Kunitz 8.00 20.00
TSLI John-Michael Liles 6.00 15.00
TSLN Ladislav Nagy 6.00 15.00
TSLS Lee Stempniak 6.00 15.00
TSLU Joffrey Lupul SP 12.00 30.00
TSMB Martin Biron 8.00 20.00
TSMC Mike Cammalleri 10.00 25.00
TSMF Marc-Andre Fleury SP 25.00 50.00
TSMG Marian Gaborik SP 20.00 50.00
TSMH Marcel Hossa 6.00 15.00
TSMI Ryan Miller 15.00 40.00
TSML Manny Legace 8.00 20.00
TSMM Milan Michalek 8.00 20.00
TSMN Markus Naslund SP 20.00 50.00
TSMP Mark Parrish 6.00 15.00
TSMR Mike Ribeiro 6.00 15.00
TSMS Marc Savard 8.00 20.00
TSMT Mikael Tellqvist 10.00 25.00
TSNA Nikolai Antropov 8.00 20.00
TSPM Patrick Marleau SP 30.00 80.00
TSPO Denis Potvin SP 30.00 80.00
TSPS Philippe Sauve 4.00 10.00
TSRB Richard Brodeur SP 12.00 30.00
TSRF Ruslan Fedotenko 6.00 15.00
TSRG Ryan Getzlaf 15.00 40.00
TSRH Ron Hextall 10.00 25.00
TSRL Reggie Leach SP 15.00 40.00
TSRM Ryan Malone 12.00 30.00
TSRV Rogie Vachon 15.00 40.00
TSRY Michael Ryder 6.00 15.00
TSSA Denis Savard 5.00 12.00
TSSC Sidney Crosby SP 125.00 250.00
TSSG Scott Gomez 8.00 20.00
TSSH Scott Hartnell 6.00 15.00
TSSS Steve Shutt 15.00 40.00
TSSW Stephen Weiss 6.00 15.00
TSTA Jeff Tambellini 6.00 15.00
TSTC Ty Conklin 8.00 20.00
TSTL Ted Lindsay SP 15.00 40.00
TSTV Tomas Vokoun 10.00 25.00
TSVA Rick Vaive 12.00 30.00
TSWC Wayne Cashman 10.00 25.00
TSWG Wayne Gretzky SP 200.00 500.00
TSWI Dave Williams 6.00 15.00
TSWR Wade Redden 8.00 20.00
TSZC Zdeno Chara 12.00 30.00

2007-08 Upper Deck Trilogy

COMP.SET w/o SPs (100) 20.00 50.00
1 Ryan Getzlaf .60 1.50
2 Jean-Sebastien Giguere .60 1.50
3 Chris Pronger .60 1.50
4 Teemu Selanne 1.25 3.00
5 Ilya Kovalchuk .60 1.50
6 Kari Lehtonen .50 1.25
7 Marian Hossa .60 1.50
8 Phil Kessel .60 1.50
9 Manny Fernandez .40 1.00
10 Patrice Bergeron .75 2.00
11 Ryan Miller .60 1.50
12 Thomas Vanek .50 1.25
13 Jason Pominville .40 1.00
14 Drew Stafford .40 1.00
15 Miikka Kiprusoff .60 1.50
16 Dion Phaneuf .50 1.25
17 Jarome Iginla .75 2.00
18 Alex Tanguay .50 1.25
19 Cam Ward .60 1.50
20 Eric Staal .75 2.00
21 Justin Williams .50 1.25
22 Nikolai Khabibulin .60 1.50
23 Martin Havlat .60 1.50
24 Tuomo Ruutu .60 1.50
25 Joe Sakic 1.25 3.00
26 Ryan Smyth .50 1.25
27 Paul Stastny .50 1.25
28 Milan Hejduk .50 1.25
29 Rick Nash .60 1.50
30 David Vyborny .40 1.00
31 Sergei Fedorov 1.00 2.50
32 Mike Modano 1.00 2.50
33 Marty Turco .60 1.50
34 Mike Ribeiro .40 1.00
35 Henrik Zetterberg .75 2.00
36 Kris Draper .40 1.00
37 Pavel Datsyuk 1.00 2.50
38 Nicklas Lidstrom .60 1.50
39 Dwayne Roloson .50 1.25
40 Joni Pitkanen .40 1.00
41 Shawn Horcoff .40 1.00
42 Ales Hemsky .50 1.25
43 Tomas Vokoun .50 1.25
44 Olli Jokinen .50 1.25
45 Nathan Horton .60 1.50
46 Alexander Frolov .40 1.00
47 Anze Kopitar 1.00 2.50
48 Rob Blake .60 1.50
49 Marian Gaborik .60 1.50
50 Niklas Backstrom .60 1.50
51 Mikko Koivu .50 1.25
52 Saku Koivu .60 1.50
53 Cristobal Huet .50 1.25
54 Michael Ryder .40 1.00
55 Guillaume Latendresse .50 1.25
56 Alexander Radulov .60 1.50
57 Chris Mason .50 1.25
58 Steve Sullivan .40 1.00
59 Martin Brodeur 1.50 4.00
60 Zach Parise .60 1.50
61 Patrik Elias .60 1.50
62 Rick DiPietro .50 1.25
63 Miroslav Satan .50 1.25
64 Trent Hunter .40 1.00
65 Jaromir Jagr 2.00 5.00
66 Chris Drury .50 1.25
67 Henrik Lundqvist 1.50 4.00
68 Dany Heatley .50 1.25
69 Ray Emery .50 1.25
70 Daniel Alfredsson .60 1.50
71 Jason Spezza .60 1.50
72 Daniel Briere .60 1.50
73 Simon Gagne .60 1.50
74 Jeff Carter .50 1.25
75 Shane Doan .50 1.25
76 Ed Jovanovski .50 1.25
77 Sidney Crosby 2.50 6.00
78 Evgeni Malkin 1.25 3.00
79 Marc-Andre Fleury 1.25 3.00
80 Jordan Staal .50 1.25
81 Joe Thornton 1.00 2.50
82 Patrick Marleau .60 1.50
83 Jonathan Cheechoo .50 1.25
84 Paul Kariya .60 1.50
85 Doug Weight .60 1.50
86 Keith Tkachuk .60 1.50
87 Martin St. Louis .60 1.50
88 Vincent Lecavalier .60 1.50
89 Brad Richards .60 1.50
90 Mats Sundin .60 1.50
91 Darcy Tucker .50 1.25
92 Vesa Toskala .50 1.25
93 Jason Blake .40 1.00
94 Henrik Sedin .75 2.00
95 Daniel Sedin .75 2.00
96 Roberto Luongo 1.00 2.50
97 Markus Naslund .60 1.50
98 Alexander Semin .60 1.50
99 Olaf Kolzig .60 1.50
100 Alexander Ovechkin 2.50 6.00
101 Alex Ovechkin/799 10.00 25.00
102 Bobby Hull/799 5.00 12.00
103 Bobby Orr/799 10.00 25.00
104 Evgeni Malkin/799 5.00 12.00
105 Gordie Howe/799 8.00 20.00
106 Jarome Iginla/799 3.00 8.00
107 Jaromir Jagr/799 8.00 20.00
108 Joe Sakic/799 5.00 12.00
109 Joe Thornton/799 4.00 10.00
110 Larry Robinson/799 2.50 6.00
111 Mario Lemieux/799 10.00 25.00
112 Martin Brodeur/799 6.00 15.00
113 Mats Sundin/799 2.50 6.00
114 Nicklas Lidstrom/799 2.50 6.00
115 Patrick Roy/799 6.00 15.00
116 Phil Esposito/799 4.00 10.00
117 Roberto Luongo/799 4.00 10.00
118 Sidney Crosby/799 10.00 25.00
119 Vincent Lecavalier/799 2.50 6.00
120 Wayne Gretzky/799 15.00 40.00
121 Bobby Ryan RC 6.00 15.00
122 Drew Miller RC 3.00 8.00
123 Ryan Carter RC 2.50 6.00
124 Jonas Hiller RC 5.00 12.00
125 Bryan Little RC 4.00 10.00
126 Brett Sterling RC 2.50 6.00
127 Tobias Enstrom RC 4.00 10.00
128 David Krejci RC 8.00 20.00
129 Milan Lucic RC 10.00 25.00
130 Jonathan Sigalet RC 2.50 6.00
131 Curtis McElhinney RC 4.00 10.00
132 Jonathan Toews RC 20.00 40.00
133 Patrick Kane RC 20.00 50.00
134 Magnus Johansson RC 2.50 6.00
135 Tyler Weiman RC 3.00 8.00
136 Jaroslav Hlinka RC 3.00 8.00
137 Kris Russell RC 4.00 10.00
138 Jared Boll RC 3.00 8.00
139 Marc Methot RC 2.50 6.00
140 Matt Niskanen RC 4.00 10.00
141 Tobias Stephan RC 3.00 8.00
142 Matt Ellis RC 3.00 8.00
143 Sam Gagner RC 5.00 12.00
144 Andrew Cogliano RC 3.00 8.00
145 Rob Schremp RC 3.00 8.00
146 Tom Gilbert RC 3.00 8.00
147 Cory Murphy RC 2.50 6.00
148 Jack Johnson RC 3.00 8.00
149 Jonathan Bernier RC 5.00 12.00
150 Lauri Tukonen RC 2.50 6.00
151 Brady Murray RC 2.50 6.00
152 Petr Kalus RC 2.50 6.00
153 James Sheppard RC 2.50 6.00
154 Carey Price RC 15.00 40.00
155 Kyle Chipchura RC 4.00 10.00
156 Jaroslav Halak RC 8.00 20.00
157 Ville Koistinen RC 2.50 6.00
158 Nicklas Bergfors RC 2.50 6.00
159 Andy Greene RC 3.00 8.00
160 Frans Nielsen RC 4.00 10.00
161 Marc Staal RC 4.00 10.00
162 Brandon Dubinsky RC 5.00 12.00
163 Ryan Callahan RC 5.00 12.00
164 Daniel Girardi RC 3.00 8.00
165 Nick Foligno RC 5.00 12.00
166 Brian Elliott RC 5.00 12.00
167 Ryan Parent RC 2.50 6.00
168 Denis Tolpeko RC 2.50 6.00
169 Peter Mueller RC 3.00 8.00
170 Martin Hanzal RC 3.00 8.00
171 Craig Weller RC 2.50 6.00
172 Daniel Winnik RC 3.00 8.00
173 Torrey Mitchell RC 3.00 8.00
174 Erik Johnson RC 4.00 10.00
175 Steve Wagner RC 2.50 6.00
176 Matt Smaby RC 2.50 6.00
177 Mike Lundin RC 2.50 6.00
178 Mason Raymond RC 4.00 10.00
179 Jannik Hansen RC 3.00 8.00
180 Nicklas Backstrom RC 8.00 20.00

2007-08 Upper Deck Trilogy Combo Clearcut Autographs

CC2BH Brodeur/Huet/25 50.00 125.00
CC2GL Mario/Gretz/25 EXCH 500.00 1200.00
CC2HE T.Esposito/B.Hull/25 40.00 100.00
CC2HL Lindsay/Howe/100 60.00 150.00
CC2IC Iginla/Cheechoo/25 25.00 60.00
CC2MS Miller/Stafford/100 12.00 30.00
CC2MT Modano/Turco/25 30.00 80.00
CC2OC Orr/Cherry/100 100.00 200.00
CC2OM Ovechkin/Malkin/25 100.00 200.00
CC2RF Roy/Fuhr/25 75.00 150.00
CC2RP Potvin/Robinson/100 12.00 30.00
CC2SD Stastny/Dionne/100 15.00 40.00
CC2SR Shutt/Ryder/100 10.00 25.00
CC2SS Staal/Staal/100 15.00 40.00
CC2ZL Zettrbrg/Lidstrom/100 15.00 40.00

2007-08 Upper Deck Trilogy Honorary Scripted Swatches

SSAH Ales Hemsky 10.00 25.00
SSAM Al MacInnis 15.00 40.00
SSAO Alexander Ovechkin 50.00 120.00
SSAR Andrew Raycroft 10.00 25.00
SSBE Patrice Bergeron 15.00 40.00
SSBG Brian Gionta 8.00 20.00
SSCN Cam Neely 12.00 30.00
SSDH Dale Hawerchuk 15.00 40.00
SSGF Grant Fuhr 20.00 50.00
SSHA Dominik Hasek 20.00 50.00
SSHE Dany Heatley 10.00 25.00
SSHL Henrik Lundqvist 30.00 80.00
SSIK Ilya Kovalchuk 12.00 30.00
SSJC Jonathan Cheechoo 10.00 25.00
SSJI Jarome Iginla 15.00 40.00
SSJT Joe Thornton 20.00 50.00
SSKL Kari Lehtonen 10.00 25.00
SSMB Martin Brodeur 30.00 80.00
SSMF Marc-Andre Fleury 25.00 60.00
SSMG Marian Gaborik 12.00 30.00
SSMR Michael Ryder 8.00 20.00
SSMT Marty Turco 12.00 30.00
SSNL Nicklas Lidstrom 12.00 30.00
SSPB Pierre-Marc Bouchard 12.00 30.00
SSPM Patrick Marleau 12.00 30.00
SSPS Peter Stastny 10.00 25.00
SSRB Ray Bourque 20.00 50.00
SSRM Ryan Miller 12.00 30.00
SSRN Rick Nash 12.00 30.00
SSSC Sidney Crosby 50.00 125.00
SSSG Simon Gagne 12.00 30.00
SSTV Tomas Vokoun 10.00 25.00
SSVL Vincent Lecavalier 12.00 30.00

2007-08 Upper Deck Trilogy Honorary Swatches

HSAH Ales Hemsky 4.00 10.00
HSAM Al MacInnis 6.00 15.00
HSAO Alexander Ovechkin 20.00 50.00
HSAR Andrew Raycroft 4.00 10.00
HSAY Alexei Yashin 4.00 10.00
HSBC Bobby Clarke 8.00 20.00
HSBF Bernie Federko 4.00 10.00
HSBG Bill Guerin 5.00 12.00
HSBL Rob Blake 5.00 12.00
HSBO Pierre-Marc Bouchard 5.00 12.00
HSBR Brad Richards 5.00 12.00
HSBS Billy Smith 5.00 12.00
HSCH Jonathan Cheechoo 4.00 10.00
HSCJ Curtis Joseph 6.00 15.00
HSCN Cam Neely 5.00 12.00
HSCP Chris Pronger 5.00 12.00
HSCW Cam Ward 5.00 12.00
HSDA Daniel Alfredsson 5.00 12.00
HSDB Daniel Briere 5.00 12.00
HSDC Dino Ciccarelli 5.00 12.00
HSDE Denis Savard 5.00 12.00
HSDG Doug Gilmour 6.00 15.00
HSDH Dale Hawerchuk 6.00 15.00
HSDS Darryl Sittler 6.00 15.00
HSDW Doug Weight 5.00 12.00
HSEB Ed Belfour 5.00 12.00
HSEL Eric Lindros 8.00 20.00
HSES Eric Staal 6.00 15.00
HSFL Marc-Andre Fleury 10.00 25.00
HSGF Grant Fuhr 8.00 20.00
HSGH Gordie Howe 15.00 40.00
HSGI Brian Gionta 3.00 8.00
HSGL Guy Lafleur 6.00 15.00
HSHA Dominik Hasek 8.00 20.00
HSHE Dany Heatley 4.00 10.00
HSHL Henrik Lundqvist 12.00 30.00
HSIK Ilya Kovalchuk 5.00 12.00
HSJC Jeff Carter 4.00 10.00
HSJG Jean-Sebastien Giguere 5.00 12.00
HSJI Jarome Iginla 6.00 15.00
HSJJ Jaromir Jagr 15.00 40.00
HSJO Joe Sakic 10.00 25.00
HSJS Jason Spezza 5.00 12.00
HSJT Joe Thornton 8.00 20.00
HSKL Kari Lehtonen 4.00 10.00
HSKO Mikko Koivu 4.00 10.00
HSKT Keith Tkachuk 5.00 12.00
HSLM Lanny McDonald 5.00 12.00
HSLR Larry Robinson 5.00 12.00
HSMB Martin Brodeur 12.00 30.00
HSMF Manny Fernandez 3.00 8.00
HSMG Marian Gaborik 5.00 12.00
HSMH Marian Hossa 5.00 12.00
HSMK Miikka Kiprusoff 5.00 12.00
HSML Mario Lemieux 20.00 50.00
HSMM Mike Modano 8.00 20.00
HSMN Markus Naslund 5.00 12.00
HSMR Mark Recchi 6.00 15.00
HSMS Marek Svatos 3.00 8.00
HSMT Marty Turco 5.00 12.00
HSNH Nathan Horton 5.00 12.00
HSNK Nikolai Khabibulin 5.00 12.00
HSNL Nicklas Lidstrom 5.00 12.00
HSOK Olaf Kolzig 5.00 12.00
HSPB Patrice Bergeron 6.00 15.00
HSPD Pavel Datsyuk 8.00 20.00
HSPE Patrik Elias 5.00 12.00
HSPF Peter Forsberg 10.00 25.00
HSPK Paul Kariya 5.00 12.00
HSPM Patrick Marleau 5.00 12.00
HSPR Patrick Roy 12.00 30.00
HSPS Peter Stastny 4.00 10.00
HSRB Ray Bourque 8.00 20.00
HSRD Rick DiPietro 4.00 10.00
HSRH Ron Hextall 5.00 12.00
HSRL Roberto Luongo 8.00 20.00
HSRM Ryan Miller 5.00 12.00
HSRN Rick Nash 5.00 12.00
HSRS Ryan Smyth 4.00 10.00
HSRY Michael Ryder 3.00 8.00
HSSA Borje Salming 5.00 12.00
HSSC Sidney Crosby 20.00 50.00
HSSD Shane Doan 4.00 10.00
HSSF Sergei Fedorov 8.00 20.00
HSSG Simon Gagne 5.00 12.00
HSSH Brendan Shanahan 5.00 12.00
HSSK Saku Koivu 5.00 12.00
HSSN Scott Niedermayer 5.00 12.00
HSSS Steve Shutt 4.00 10.00
HSST Jordan Staal 4.00 10.00
HSSU Mats Sundin 5.00 12.00
HSSZ Sergei Zubov 4.00 10.00
HSTB Todd Bertuzzi 5.00 12.00
HSTS Teemu Selanne 10.00 25.00
HSTV Thomas Vanek 4.00 10.00
HSVL Vincent Lecavalier 5.00 12.00
HSVO Tomas Vokoun 4.00 10.00
HSWG Wayne Gretzky 30.00 80.00
HSWI Doug Wilson 4.00 10.00
HSZC Zdeno Chara 5.00 12.00

2007-08 Upper Deck Trilogy Ice Scripts

ISAH Ales Hemsky 6.00 15.00
ISAK Anze Kopitar 12.00 30.00
ISAM Al MacInnis 10.00 25.00
ISAO Alexander Ovechkin 30.00 80.00
ISAR Andrew Raycroft 6.00 15.00
ISBH Bobby Hull 15.00 40.00
ISBO Bobby Orr 60.00 150.00
ISBP Benoit Pouliot 5.00 12.00
ISCH Cristobal Huet 6.00 15.00
ISCI Dino Ciccarelli 8.00 20.00
ISCP Corey Perry EXCH 12.00 30.00
ISDH Dany Heatley 6.00 15.00
ISDP Denis Potvin 8.00 20.00
ISDS Drew Stafford 5.00 12.00
ISEM Evgeni Malkin 15.00 40.00
ISES Eric Staal 10.00 25.00
ISGF Grant Fuhr 12.00 30.00
ISGH Gordie Howe 60.00 150.00
ISGP Gilbert Perreault 8.00 20.00
ISJB Johnny Bower 8.00 20.00
ISJC Jonathan Cheechoo 6.00 15.00
ISJG Jean-Sebastien Giguere 8.00 20.00
ISJH Jaroslav Halak 15.00 40.00
ISJI Jarome Iginla 10.00 25.00
ISJK Jari Kurri 8.00 20.00
ISJS Jordan Staal 6.00 15.00
ISJT Joe Thornton 12.00 30.00
ISLR Larry Robinson 8.00 20.00
ISLT Lauri Tukonen 5.00 12.00
ISMB Martin Brodeur 20.00 50.00
ISMD Marcel Dionne 10.00 25.00
ISMF Marc-Andre Fleury 15.00 40.00
ISMG Marian Gaborik EXCH 8.00 20.00
ISML Mario Lemieux 50.00 125.00
ISMR Michael Ryder 5.00 12.00
ISMT Marty Turco 8.00 20.00
ISND Nigel Dawes 5.00 12.00
ISNL Nicklas Lidstrom 8.00 20.00
ISPK Phil Kessel 8.00 20.00
ISPR Patrick Roy 50.00 125.00
ISRH Ron Hextall 8.00 20.00
ISRM Ryan Miller 8.00 20.00
ISRN Rick Nash 8.00 20.00
ISSC Sidney Crosby 60.00 150.00
ISSG Simon Gagne 8.00 20.00
ISSS Steve Shutt 6.00 15.00
ISSV Marek Svatos 5.00 12.00
ISTE Tony Esposito 8.00 20.00
ISTL Ted Lindsay 8.00 20.00
ISTV Tomas Vokoun 6.00 15.00
ISVL Vincent Lecavalier 8.00 20.00
ISWG Wayne Gretzky 250.00 600.00
ISWW Wojtek Wolski 6.00 15.00

2007-08 Upper Deck Trilogy Personal Scripts

PSAH Ales Hemsky 25.00 50.00
PSAK Anze Kopitar 50.00 100.00
PSAT Alex Tanguay 15.00 40.00
PSBC Bobby Clarke 30.00 60.00
PSBF Bernie Federko 15.00 40.00
PSBH Bobby Hull 40.00 100.00
PSBN Bob Nystrom 12.00 30.00
PSBO Bobby Orr 300.00 500.00
PSCP Corey Perry 30.00 60.00
PSCW Cam Ward 20.00 50.00
PSDH Dany Heatley 15.00 40.00
PSEM Evgeni Malkin 75.00 125.00
PSGF Grant Fuhr 30.00 80.00
PSGH Gordie Howe 75.00 150.00
PSGP Gilbert Perreault 20.00 50.00
PSHA Dominik Hasek 30.00 80.00
PSHO Gordie Howe 75.00 150.00
PSJC Jonathan Cheechoo 15.00 40.00
PSJG Jean-Sebastien Giguere 15.00 40.00
PSJI Jarome Iginla 40.00 80.00
PSJK Jari Kurri 30.00 60.00
PSJS Jordan Staal 15.00 40.00
PSJT Joe Thornton 30.00 80.00
PSLM Lanny McDonald 20.00 50.00
PSLR Larry Robinson 20.00 50.00
PSMB Martin Brodeur 75.00 150.00
PSME Mark Messier/10 150.00 300.00
PSMF Marc-Andre Fleury 40.00 100.00
PSML Mario Lemieux 125.00 200.00
PSMM Mark Messier/25 150.00 300.00
PSMR Michael Ryder 12.00 30.00
PSMS Martin St. Louis 20.00 50.00
PSMT Marty Turco 20.00 50.00
PSNL Nicklas Lidstrom 75.00 150.00
PSPE Phil Esposito 40.00 80.00
PSPK Phil Kessel 30.00 60.00
PSPR Patrick Roy 75.00 150.00
PSRB Ray Bourque 30.00 80.00
PSRH Ron Hextall 20.00 50.00
PSRM Ryan Miller 20.00 50.00
PSSC Sidney Crosby 250.00 400.00
PSSG Simon Gagne 20.00 50.00
PSTE Tony Esposito 40.00 80.00
PSVL Vincent Lecavalier 20.00 50.00

2007-08 Upper Deck Trilogy Scripts

S1AB Alex Brooks 5.00 12.00
S1AD Adam Dennis SP 6.00 15.00
S1AK Anze Kopitar 12.00 30.00
S1BC Blake Comeau 5.00 12.00
S1BE Benoit Pouliot 5.00 12.00
S1BJ Blair Jones 5.00 12.00
S1BO Dave Bolland 6.00 15.00
S1BP Brandon Prust 5.00 12.00
S1BR Brad Boyes 5.00 12.00
S1CH Chris Higgins 5.00 12.00
S1CK Chris Kunitz 8.00 20.00
S1CP Corey Perry 12.00 30.00
S1CW Cam Ward 8.00 20.00
S1DB Dustin Boyd 5.00 12.00
S1DS Drew Stafford 5.00 12.00
S1EC Erik Christensen 5.00 12.00
S1EF Eric Fehr 5.00 12.00
S1EM Evgeni Malkin SP 15.00 40.00
S1HL Henrik Lundqvist SP 20.00 50.00
S1HT Hannu Toivonen 6.00 15.00
S1IW Ian White 5.00 12.00
S1JC Jeff Carter 6.00 15.00
S1JG Josh Gorges 5.00 12.00
S1JH Josh Hennessy 5.00 12.00
S1JO Johnny Oduya 6.00 15.00
S1JP Joe Pavelski 10.00 25.00
S1JS Jordan Staal 6.00 15.00
S1MC Matt Carle 5.00 12.00
S1MJ Milan Jurcina 5.00 12.00
S1MP Marc-Antoine Pouliot SP 5.00 12.00
S1MR Mike Richards 6.00 15.00
S1MS Marek Svatos 5.00 12.00
S1NW Noah Welch SP 5.00 12.00
S1PK Phil Kessel SP 8.00 20.00
S1PN Petteri Nokelainen 5.00 12.00
S1PO Patrick O'Sullivan 6.00 15.00
S1PP Petr Prucha 5.00 12.00
S1PR Paul Ranger 5.00 12.00
S1PS Paul Stastny 6.00 15.00
S1RG Ryan Getzlaf 8.00 20.00
S1RK Ryan Kesler 8.00 20.00
S1RM Ryan Miller 8.00 20.00
S1RO Roman Polak 5.00 12.00
S1RP Ryan Potulny SP 5.00 12.00
S1RS Ryan Shannon 5.00 12.00
S1SB Steve Bernier 5.00 12.00
S1SO Shane O'Brien 5.00 12.00
S1TK Tomas Kopecky 6.00 15.00
S1TZ Travis Zajac SP 5.00 12.00
S1VF Valtteri Filppula 5.00 12.00
S1WW Wojtek Wolski 6.00 15.00
S1YS Yan Stastny 5.00 12.00
S2AF Alexander Frolov 5.00 12.00
S2AO Alex Ovechkin SP 60.00 150.00
S2AT Alex Tanguay 6.00 15.00
S2DH Dominik Hasek SP 12.00 30.00
S2DR Dwayne Roloson 6.00 15.00
S2ES Eric Staal 10.00 25.00
S2GO Scott Gomez 6.00 15.00
S2HE Dany Heatley 6.00 15.00
S2IK Ilya Kovalchuk 8.00 20.00
S2JC Jonathan Cheechoo 6.00 15.00
S2JG Jean-Sebastien Giguere SP 8.00 20.00
S2JI Jarome Iginla 10.00 25.00
S2JT Joe Thornton SP 12.00 30.00
S2MB Martin Brodeur SP 30.00 80.00
S2MF Marc-Andre Fleury 15.00 40.00
S2MG Marian Gaborik EXCH 8.00 20.00
S2MR Michael Ryder 5.00 12.00
S2NL Nicklas Lidstrom 8.00 20.00
S2PB Patrice Bergeron 10.00 25.00
S2RN Rick Nash 8.00 20.00
S2SC Sidney Crosby 60.00 150.00
S2SD Shane Doan SP 6.00 15.00
S2SG Simon Gagne 8.00 20.00
S2ST Martin St. Louis 8.00 20.00
S2TV Tomas Vokoun 6.00 15.00
S2VL Vincent Lecavalier 8.00 20.00
S2VT Vesa Toskala 6.00 15.00
S3AM Al MacInnis 10.00 25.00
S3BC Bobby Clarke 12.00 30.00
S3CN Cam Neely 8.00 20.00
S3GC Gerry Cheevers 8.00 20.00
S3GF Grant Fuhr 12.00 30.00
S3GH Gordie Howe SP 60.00 150.00
S3JK Jari Kurri 8.00 20.00
S3LM Lanny McDonald 8.00 20.00
S3LR Larry Robinson 8.00 20.00

2008-09 Upper Deck Trilogy

COMP.SET w/o SPs (100) 15.00 40.00
1 Ales Hemsky .75 2.00
2 Alex Kovalev .75 2.00
3 Alexander Frolov .60 1.50
4 Alexander Ovechkin 4.00 10.00
5 Andrew Cogliano .60 1.50
6 Anze Kopitar 1.50 4.00
7 Brad Boyes .60 1.50
8 Brad Richards 1.00 2.50
9 Brenden Morrow .75 2.00
10 Brian Campbell .75 2.00
11 Cam Ward 1.00 2.50
12 Carey Price 2.00 5.00
13 Chris Drury .75 2.00
14 Chris Osgood 1.00 2.50
15 Chris Pronger 1.00 2.50
16 Corey Perry 1.50 4.00
17 Cristobal Huet .75 2.00
18 Daniel Alfredsson 1.00 2.50
19 Daniel Briere 1.00 2.50
20 Daniel Sedin 1.25 3.00
21 Dany Heatley .75 2.00
22 Derek Roy .60 1.50
23 Dion Phaneuf .75 2.00
24 Eric Staal 1.25 3.00
25 Evgeni Malkin 2.00 5.00
26 Evgeni Nabokov .75 2.00
27 Henrik Lundqvist 2.50 6.00
28 Henrik Sedin 1.25 3.00
29 Henrik Zetterberg 1.25 3.00
30 Ilya Kovalchuk 1.00 2.50
31 J.P. Dumont .60 1.50
32 Jarome Iginla 1.25 3.00
33 Jason Arnott .75 2.00
34 Jason Pominville .60 1.50
35 Jason Spezza 1.00 2.50
36 Jean-Sebastien Giguere 1.00 2.50
37 Joe Sakic 2.00 5.00
38 Joe Thornton 1.50 4.00
39 Jonathan Cheechoo .75 2.00
40 Jonathan Toews 1.50 4.00
41 Jordan Staal .75 2.00
42 Jose Theodore 1.00 2.50
43 Justin Williams .75 2.00
44 Kari Lehtonen 1.25 3.00
45 Manny Legace 1.00 2.50
46 Marc-Andre Fleury 2.00 5.00
47 Marian Gaborik 1.00 2.50
48 Marian Hossa 1.00 2.50
49 Mark Streit .60 1.50
50 Markus Naslund 1.00 2.50
51 Martin Brodeur 2.50 6.00
52 Martin St. Louis 1.00 2.50
53 Marty Turco 1.00 2.50
54 Mats Sundin 1.00 2.50
55 Miikka Kiprusoff 1.00 2.50
56 Mike Comrie .75 2.00
57 Mike Green .75 2.00
58 Mike Modano 1.50 4.00
59 Mike Ribeiro .60 1.50
60 Mike Richards .75 2.00
61 Mikko Koivu .75 2.00
62 Nathan Horton .75 2.00
63 Nicklas Backstrom 1.00 2.50
64 Nicklas Lidstrom 1.00 2.50
65 Nik Antropov .75 2.00
66 Niklas Backstrom 1.00 2.50
67 Nikolai Zherdev .60 1.50
68 Olli Jokinen .75 2.00
69 Pascal Leclaire .75 2.00
70 Patrice Bergeron 1.25 3.00
71 Patrick Kane 2.00 5.00
72 Patrick Sharp 1.00 2.50
73 Patrik Elias 1.00 2.50
74 Paul Kariya 1.00 2.50
75 Paul Stastny .75 2.00
76 Pavel Datsyuk 1.50 4.00
77 Peter Mueller .75 2.00
78 Phil Kessel 1.00 2.50
79 Rick DiPietro .75 2.00
80 Rick Nash 1.00 2.50
81 Roberto Luongo 1.50 4.00
82 Ryan Getzlaf 1.00 2.50
83 Ryan Malone .60 1.50
84 Ryan Miller 1.00 2.50
85 Ryan Smyth .75 2.00
86 Saku Koivu 1.00 2.50
87 Sam Gagner .60 1.50
88 Scott Gomez .75 2.00
89 Shane Doan .75 2.00
90 Shawn Horcoff .60 1.50
91 Sidney Crosby 4.00 10.00
92 Simon Gagne 1.00 2.50
93 Thomas Vanek .75 2.00
94 Tim Thomas 1.00 2.50
95 Tobias Enstrom .60 1.50
96 Tomas Kaberle .60 1.50
97 Tomas Vokoun .75 2.00
98 Vesa Toskala 1.25 3.00
99 Vincent Lecavalier 1.00 2.50
100 Zach Parise 1.00 2.50
101 Sami Lepisto RC 3.00 8.00
102 Mike Brown RC 4.00 10.00
103 Zach Fitzgerald RC 4.00 10.00
104 Alex Foster RC 3.00 8.00
105 Darryl Boyce RC 3.00 8.00
106 John Mitchell RC 3.00 8.00
107 Robbie Earl RC 2.50 6.00
108 Jonas Frogren RC 2.50 6.00
109 Vladimir Mihalik RC 2.50 6.00
110 Janne Niskala RC 4.00 10.00
111 Tom Cavanagh RC 3.00 8.00
112 Alex Goligoski RC 5.00 12.00
113 Jon Filewich RC 3.00 8.00
114 Ryan Stone RC 2.50 6.00
115 Kevin Porter RC 3.00 8.00
116 Kyle Turris RC 6.00 15.00
117 Claude Giroux RC 8.00 20.00
118 Tim Ramholt RC 3.00 8.00
119 Brian Lee RC 3.00 8.00
120 Ilya Zubov RC 3.00 8.00
121 Jesse Winchester RC 2.50 6.00
122 Kyle Okposo RC 5.00 12.00
123 Mike Iggulden RC 3.00 8.00
124 Anssi Salmela RC 4.00 10.00
125 Ryan Jones RC 4.00 10.00
126 Matt D'Agostini RC 3.00 8.00
127 James Neal RC 8.00 20.00
128 Brian Boyle RC 3.00 8.00
129 Oscar Moller RC 3.00 8.00
130 Danny Taylor RC 3.00 8.00
131 Erik Ersberg RC 3.00 8.00
132 Wayne Simmonds RC 6.00 15.00
133 Michael Frolik RC 4.00 10.00
134 Shawn Matthias RC 4.00 10.00
135 Viktor Tikhonov RC 3.00 8.00
136 Patrik Berglund RC 3.00 8.00
137 Darren Helm RC 4.00 10.00
138 Jonathan Ericsson RC 4.00 10.00
139 Justin Abdelkader RC 6.00 15.00
140 Mattias Ritola RC 3.00 8.00
141 B.J. Crombeen RC 2.50 6.00
142 Garrett Stafford RC 4.00 10.00
143 Mark Fistric RC 3.00 8.00
144 Adam Pineault RC 3.00 8.00
145 Andrew Murray RC 3.00 8.00
146 Dan LaCosta RC 4.00 10.00
147 Derick Brassard RC 4.00 10.00
148 Derek Dorsett RC 5.00 12.00
149 Steve Mason RC 6.00 15.00
150 Tom Sestito RC 4.00 10.00
151 Cody McLeod RC 3.00 8.00
152 Jordan Hendry RC 3.00 8.00
153 Brandon Nolan RC 3.00 8.00
154 Joe Jensen RC 4.00 10.00
155 Tim Conboy RC 3.00 8.00
156 Kyle Greentree RC 4.00 10.00
157 Luca Sbisa RC 2.50 6.00
158 Pascal Pelletier RC 2.50 6.00
159 Boris Valabik RC 4.00 10.00
160 Andrew Ebbett RC 2.50 6.00
161 Luke Schenn RC 6.00 15.00
162 Nikolai Kulemin RC 5.00 12.00
163 Steven Stamkos RC 25.00 60.00
164 Alex Pietrangelo RC 8.00 20.00
165 T.J. Oshie RC 12.00 30.00
166 Zach Boychuk RC 5.00 12.00
167 Mikkel Boedker RC 6.00 15.00
168 Nikita Filatov RC 5.00 12.00
169 Fabian Brunnstrom RC 4.00 10.00
170 Drew Doughty RC 12.00 30.00
171 Colton Gillies RC 4.00 10.00
172 Jakub Voracek RC 10.00 25.00
173 Brandon Sutter RC 5.00 12.00
174 Blake Wheeler RC 12.00 30.00
175 Zach Bogosian RC 6.00 15.00

2008-09 Upper Deck Trilogy Combo Clearcut Autographs

CC2BG Bossy/Gillies/25 15.00 40.00
CC2BO Orr/Bucyk/25 75.00 150.00
CC2BT Tkaczuk/Bathgate 15.00 40.00
CC2HD H.Sedin/D.Sedin 20.00 50.00
CC2HN Heatley/Nash/25 15.00 40.00
CC2JJ E.Johnson/J.Johnson 10.00 25.00
CC2KP Price/Koivu/25 30.00 80.00
CC2LM Messier/Leetch/25 30.00 80.00
CC2LS Lidstrom/Salming/25 15.00 40.00
CC2OB Ovech/Backstrm/25 60.00 150.00
CC2PG Getzlaf/Perry 25.00 60.00
CC2SB St. Louis/Boyle 15.00 40.00
CC2SS Stastny/Stastny 12.00 30.00
CC2TK Kane/Toews 60.00 120.00
CC2TN Thornton/Nabokov/25 25.00 60.00
CC2VH Vokoun/Horton 12.00 30.00

2008-09 Upper Deck Trilogy Frozen in Time

COMPLETE SET (20) 150.00 300.00
101 Bobby Orr 12.00 30.00
102 Alexander Ovechkin 12.00 30.00

103 Patrick Roy 8.00 20.00
104 Henrik Zetterberg 4.00 10.00
105 Ilya Kovalchuk 3.00 8.00
106 Mark Messier 6.00 15.00
107 Evgeni Malkin 6.00 15.00
108 Mats Sundin 3.00 8.00
109 Vincent Lecavalier 3.00 8.00
110 Carey Price 6.00 15.00
111 Gordie Howe 10.00 25.00
112 Jarome Iginla 4.00 10.00
113 Mike Richards 2.50 6.00
114 Marian Gaborik 3.00 8.00
115 Mario Lemieux 12.00 30.00
116 Joe Thornton 5.00 12.00
117 Jonathan Toews 5.00 12.00
118 Joe Sakic 6.00 15.00
119 Sidney Crosby 12.00 30.00
120 Wayne Gretzky 20.00 50.00

2008-09 Upper Deck Trilogy Honorary Swatches

HSBD Rod Brind'Amour 4.00 10.00
HSBS Brendan Shanahan 4.00 10.00
HSCP Carey Price 8.00 20.00
HSEM Evgeni Malkin 8.00 20.00
HSES Eric Staal 5.00 12.00
HSHL Henrik Lundqvist 10.00 25.00
HSIK Ilya Kovalchuk 4.00 10.00
HSJS Jason Spezza 4.00 10.00
HSJT Joe Thornton 6.00 15.00
HSKN Patrick Kane 8.00 20.00
HSMB Martin Brodeur 10.00 25.00
HSMG Marian Gaborik 4.00 10.00
HSMH Marian Hossa 4.00 10.00
HSMM Mike Modano 6.00 15.00
HSMS Martin St. Louis 4.00 10.00
HSNB Nicklas Backstrom 4.00 10.00
HSNZ Nikolai Zherdev 2.50 6.00
HSPK Phil Kessel 4.00 10.00
HSPM Pierre-Marc Bouchard 4.00 10.00
HSPS Paul Stastny 3.00 8.00
HSRB Rob Blake 4.00 10.00
HSRD Rick DiPietro 3.00 8.00
HSRL Roberto Luongo 6.00 15.00
HSRM Ryan Miller 4.00 10.00
HSRN Rick Nash 4.00 10.00
HSSC Sidney Crosby 15.00 40.00
HSSK Saku Koivu 4.00 10.00
HSSU Mats Sundin 4.00 10.00
HSSW Shea Weber 3.00 8.00
HSTO Jonathan Toews 6.00 15.00

2008-09 Upper Deck Trilogy Ice Scripts

ISGI Clark Gillies 8.00 20.00
ISAC Andrew Cogliano 5.00 12.00
ISAD Alex Delvecchio 8.00 20.00
ISAO Alexander Ovechkin 30.00 80.00
ISBB Brad Boyes 5.00 12.00
ISBO Bobby Orr 30.00 80.00
ISCD Chris Drury 6.00 15.00
ISCG Claude Giroux 15.00 40.00
ISCP Carey Price 15.00 40.00
ISDB Derick Brassard 8.00 20.00
ISDC Don Cherry 20.00 50.00
ISDP David Perron 6.00 15.00
ISDS Daniel Sedin 10.00 25.00
ISEJ Erik Johnson 5.00 12.00
ISEM Evgeni Malkin 15.00 40.00
ISGH Gordie Howe 50.00 125.00
ISGP Gilbert Perreault 8.00 20.00
ISHS Henrik Sedin 10.00 25.00
ISHZ Henrik Zetterberg 10.00 25.00
ISJB Johnny Bucyk 8.00 20.00
ISJC Jeff Carter 6.00 15.00
ISJH Josh Harding 8.00 20.00
ISJJ Jack Johnson 5.00 12.00
ISJO Joe Thornton 12.00 30.00
ISJS Jordan Staal 6.00 15.00
ISJT Jonathan Toews 12.00 30.00
ISKE Phil Kessel 8.00 20.00
ISLI Ted Lindsay 8.00 20.00
ISMB Martin Brodeur 20.00 50.00
ISML Mario Lemieux 30.00 80.00
ISMM Mark Messier 15.00 40.00
ISMO Mike Modano 12.00 30.00
ISMR Mike Ribeiro 5.00 12.00
ISMS Marc Staal 5.00 12.00
ISMT Marty Turco 8.00 20.00
ISNB Nicklas Backstrom 8.00 20.00
ISNF Nick Foligno 8.00 20.00
ISNH Nathan Horton 6.00 15.00
ISPK Patrick Kane 15.00 40.00
ISPM Peter Mueller 6.00 15.00
ISPO Denis Potvin 8.00 20.00
ISPR Patrick Roy 20.00 50.00
ISPS Paul Stastny 6.00 15.00
ISRB Ray Bourque 12.00 30.00
ISRE Robbie Earl 5.00 12.00
ISRG Ryan Getzlaf 8.00 20.00
ISRL Rod Langway 6.00 15.00
ISSB Scotty Bowman 8.00 20.00
ISSC Sidney Crosby 100.00 250.00
ISSG Sam Gagner 5.00 12.00
ISSM Steve Mason 12.00 30.00
ISSS Steve Shutt 8.00 20.00
ISST Peter Stastny 6.00 15.00
ISTE Tony Esposito 8.00 20.00
ISTL Jiri Tlusty 5.00 12.00
ISTR Tuukka Rask 10.00 25.00
ISTV Tomas Vokoun 6.00 15.00
ISWG Wayne Gretzky 100.00 250.00
ISWT Walt Tkaczuk 5.00 12.00

2008-09 Upper Deck Trilogy Rivals

ANACOL Ducks/Avalanche 15.00 40.00
ANASJS Ducks/Sharks 12.00 30.00
BOSNYR Bruins/Rangers 10.00 25.00
CARTBY Hurricanes/Lightning 10.00 25.00
CGYEDM Flames/Oilers 8.00 20.00
CGYVAN Flames/Canucks 12.00 30.00
DETCHI Red Wings/Blackhawks 15.00 40.00
EDMCGY Oilers/Flames legends 15.00 40.00
EDMVAN Oilers/Canucks 12.00 30.00
LAKANA Kings/Ducks 15.00 40.00
MONBOS Canadiens/Bruins 15.00 40.00
NJDNYR Devils/Rangers 20.00 50.00
NYRNYI Rangers/Islanders 20.00 50.00
NYRPIT Rangers/Penguins 20.00 50.00
OTTMON Senators/Canadiens 15.00 40.00
PITPHI Penguins/Flyers 30.00 80.00
SJSDAL Sharks/Stars 12.00 30.00
TORBUF Leafs/Sabers 10.00 25.00
TORMON Leafs/Canadiens 15.00 40.00

2008-09 Upper Deck Trilogy Scripted Swatches Second Star

*SECOND STAR: .6X TO 1.5X THIRD STAR

2008-09 Upper Deck Trilogy Scripted Swatches Third Star

3RDAM Al MacInnis 12.00 30.00
3RDAO Alexander Ovechkin 40.00 100.00
3RDCP Carey Price 20.00 50.00
3RDCW Cam Ward 10.00 25.00
3RDDC Dino Ciccarelli 10.00 25.00
3RDEM Evgeni Malkin 30.00 80.00
3RDES Eric Staal 12.00 30.00
3RDGP Gilbert Perreault 10.00 25.00
3RDHA Dominik Hasek 15.00 40.00
3RDHE Milan Hejduk 8.00 20.00
3RDHZ Henrik Zetterberg 15.00 40.00
3RDIK Ilya Kovalchuk 10.00 25.00
3RDJC Jonathan Cheechoo 8.00 20.00
3RDJG Jean-Sebastien Giguere 10.00 25.00
3RDJL Joffrey Lupul 6.00 15.00
3RDJT Joe Thornton 15.00 40.00
3RDKL Kari Lehtonen 12.00 30.00
3RDLR Luc Robitaille 10.00 25.00
3RDMB Martin Brodeur 25.00 60.00
3RDMF Marc-Andre Fleury 20.00 50.00
3RDMH Marian Hossa 10.00 25.00
3RDMM Mike Modano 15.00 40.00
3RDMN Markus Naslund 10.00 25.00
3RDMT Marty Turco 10.00 25.00
3RDNH Nathan Horton 8.00 20.00
3RDNL Nicklas Lidstrom 10.00 25.00
3RDNZ Nikolai Zherdev 6.00 15.00
3RDPK Patrick Kane 40.00 80.00
3RDPS Paul Stastny 8.00 20.00
3RDRG Ryan Getzlaf 10.00 25.00
3RDRM Ryan Miller 10.00 25.00
3RDRN Rick Nash 10.00 25.00
3RDSC Sidney Crosby 40.00 100.00
3RDSG Simon Gagne 10.00 25.00
3RDSK Saku Koivu 10.00 25.00
3RDSM Sam Gagner 6.00 15.00
3RDTO Jonathan Toews 15.00 40.00
3RDVO Tomas Vokoun 8.00 20.00

2008-09 Upper Deck Trilogy Superstar Scripts

SSAO Alexander Ovechkin 30.00 80.00
SSAT Alex Tanguay 5.00 12.00
SSBB Brad Boyes 5.00 12.00
SSBM Brenden Morrow 6.00 15.00
SSCD Chris Drury 6.00 15.00
SSCN Cam Neely 8.00 20.00
SSCP Corey Perry 12.00 30.00
SSCW Cam Ward 8.00 20.00
SSDB Dan Boyle 5.00 12.00
SSDC Dan Cleary 6.00 15.00
SSDS Daniel Sedin 10.00 25.00
SSDT Darcy Tucker 6.00 15.00
SSEM Evgeni Malkin 15.00 40.00
SSES Eric Staal 10.00 25.00
SSGO Scott Gomez 6.00 15.00
SSHE Dany Heatley 6.00 15.00
SSHL Henrik Lundqvist 20.00 50.00
SSHO Marian Hossa 8.00 20.00
SSHS Henrik Sedin 10.00 25.00
SSHZ Henrik Zetterberg 12.00 30.00
SSJA Jason Arnott 6.00 15.00
SSJC Jonathan Cheechoo 6.00 15.00
SSJG Jean-Sebastien Giguere 8.00 20.00
SSJI Jarome Iginla 10.00 25.00
SSJT Joe Thornton 12.00 30.00
SSLR Luc Robitaille 8.00 20.00
SSMH Milan Hejduk 6.00 15.00
SSMK Mike Knuble 5.00 12.00
SSMM Milan Michalek 6.00 15.00
SSMN Markus Naslund 8.00 20.00
SSMO Mike Modano 12.00 30.00
SSMR Mike Ribeiro 5.00 12.00
SSMT Marty Turco 8.00 20.00
SSNL Nicklas Lidstrom 8.00 20.00
SSOA Adam Oates 8.00 20.00
SSPE Patrik Elias 8.00 20.00
SSPM Pierre-Marc Bouchard 8.00 20.00
SSPS Paul Stastny 6.00 15.00
SSRG Ryan Getzlaf 8.00 20.00
SSRM Ryan Miller 8.00 20.00
SSRS Ryan Smyth 6.00 15.00
SSSC Sidney Crosby 60.00 150.00
SSSG Simon Gagne 8.00 20.00
SSTV Tomas Vokoun 6.00 15.00
SSVA Thomas Vanek 6.00 15.00

2008-09 Upper Deck Trilogy Three Star Spotlights

3SADW Arnott/Dumont/Weber 5.00 12.00
3SBPP Bourque/Phaneuf/Pronger 10.00 25.00
3SCNT Crosby/Nash/Thornton 25.00 60.00
3SCOM Crosby/Ovechkin/Malkin 25.00 60.00
3SDMF Fleury/DiPietro/Miller 12.00 30.00
3SDSL Luongo/Sedin/Demitra 10.00 25.00
3SFMM Fleury/MacIns/McDonald 8.00 20.00
3SFSS Fleury/Staal/Sykora 12.00 30.00
3SGHL Gretzky/Howe/Lemieux 40.00 100.00
3SGNB Gaborik/Nolan/Bouchard 6.00 15.00
3SGSP Getzlaf/Selanne/Perry 12.00 30.00
3SHGP Hossa/Gaborik/Parise 6.00 15.00
3SHSG Heatley/Spezza/Gerber 6.00 15.00
3SKAA Koval/Afinogy/Antropov 6.00 15.00
3SKMF Messier/Kurri/Fuhr 12.00 30.00
3SKPM Kane/Parise/Mueller 12.00 30.00
3SKSK Koivu/Shutt/Kovalev 6.00 15.00
3SLBN Luongo/Brodeur/Nabokov 15.00 40.00
3SLLN St. Louis/Lecavalier/Nash 6.00 15.00
3SLMP Lundqvist/Miller/DiPietro 15.00 40.00
3SLNK Luongo/Nabokov/Kiprus 10.00 25.00
3SLPP Lidstrom/Phaneuf/Pronger 6.00 15.00
3SMKA Messier/Kurri/Anderson 12.00 30.00
3SMKG Malkin/Kovalev/Gonchar 12.00 30.00
3SMRL Modano/Ribeiro/Leht 10.00 25.00
3SNGS Naslnd/Gomez/Shanahn 6.00 15.00
3SNPL Nash/Peca/Leclaire 6.00 15.00
3SOMK Ovech/Malkin/Koval 25.00 60.00
3SPBC Phaneuf/Bertuz/Cammalri 6.00 15.00
3SRBG Richards/Briere/Gagne 6.00 15.00
3SRBP Roy/Price/Brodeur 15.00 40.00
3SSFS Stastny/Sakic/Forsberg 12.00 30.00
3SSGS Salming/Gilmour/Sundin 8.00 20.00
3SSSF Sundin/Sakic/Forsberg 12.00 30.00
3SSSG Staal/Getzlaf/St. Louis 8.00 20.00
3SSTA Sundin/Toskala/Antropov 8.00 20.00
3SSTC Savard/Thomas/Chara 6.00 15.00
3STKB Toews/Kane/Backstrom 12.00 30.00
3STTN Toews/Thornton/Nash 10.00 25.00
3SZHL Zetter/Holmstrm/Lidstrm 8.00 20.00

2008-09 Upper Deck Trilogy Tri-Color Tandems

TCTBF M.Brodeur/M.Fleury 30.00 80.00
TCTCM S.Crosby/E.Malkin 50.00 125.00
TCTCO S.Crosby/A.Ovechkin 50.00 125.00
TCTDM S.Doan/P.Mueller 10.00 25.00
TCTEP Z.Parise/P.Elias 12.00 30.00
TCTGB M.Gaborik/P.Bouchard 12.00 30.00
TCTHG D.Heatley/M.Gerber 10.00 25.00
TCTJM E.Malkin/J.Staal 25.00 60.00
TCTJP D.Perron/E.Johnson 8.00 20.00
TCTJS J.Staal/P.Stastny 25.00 60.00
TCTKJ A.Kopitar/J.Johnson 20.00 50.00
TCTKK S.Koivu/A.Kovalev 10.00 25.00
TCTKL I.Kovalchuk/K.Lehtonen 15.00 40.00
TCTKM E.Malkin/I.Kovalchuk 20.00 50.00
TCTKS P.Kariya/T.Selanne 25.00 60.00
TCTLD R.Luongo/P.Demitra 20.00 50.00
TCTLP N.Lidstrom/D.Phaneuf 12.00 30.00
TCTMD R.Miller/R.DiPietro 12.00 30.00
TCTNC E.Nabokov/J.Cheechoo 10.00 25.00
TCTOB A.Ovechkin/N.Backstrom 50.00 125.00
TCTPG R.Getzlaf/D.Phaneuf 40.00 100.00
TCTPL C.Price/H.Lundqvist 25.00 60.00
TCTPN C.Pronger/S.Niedermayer 12.00 30.00
TCTRP P.Forsberg/R.Blake 25.00 60.00
TCTRB M.Richards/D.Briere 12.00 30.00
TCTSD D.Sedin/P.Demitra 15.00 40.00
TCTSF M.Sundin/P.Forsberg 25.00 60.00
TCTSK M.Savard/P.Kessel 12.00 30.00
TCTSN R.Nash/J.Spezza 20.00 40.00
TCTTD J.Thornton/S.Doan 20.00 50.00
TCTTK P.Kane/J.Toews 20.00 50.00
TCTVH N.Horton/T.Vokoun 10.00 25.00
TCTWA S.Weber/J.Arnott 10.00 25.00
TCTZD H.Zetterberg/P.Datsyuk 15.00 40.00

2008-09 Upper Deck Trilogy Two-Way Threads

2WAO Alexander Ovechkin 8.00 20.00
2WAR Jason Arnott 5.00 12.00
2WBM Brendan Morrison 4.00 10.00
2WCP Chris Pronger 6.00 15.00
2WDP Dion Phaneuf 5.00 12.00
2WDW Doug Weight 6.00 15.00
2WEC Erik Cole 4.00 10.00
2WHZ Henrik Zetterberg 8.00 20.00
2WJL Jere Lehtinen 4.00 10.00
2WJS Jordan Staal 6.00 15.00
2WJT Joe Thornton 10.00 25.00
2WKD Kris Draper 4.00 10.00
2WMP Michael Peca 5.00 12.00
2WNH Nathan Horton 5.00 12.00
2WNL Nicklas Lidstrom 6.00 15.00
2WOJ Olli Jokinen 5.00 12.00
2WPE Patrik Elias 6.00 15.00
2WPF Peter Forsberg 12.00 30.00
2WPM Patrick Marleau 6.00 15.00
2WPS Patrick Sharp 6.00 15.00
2WRD Rod Brind'Amour 6.00 15.00
2WRG Ryan Getzlaf 6.00 15.00
2WSD Shane Doan 5.00 12.00
2WSF Sergei Fedorov 10.00 25.00
2WSK Joe Sakic 10.00 25.00
2WTH Tomas Holmstrom 5.00 12.00
2WVL Vincent Lecavalier 5.00 12.00
2WZC Zdeno Chara 6.00 15.00
2WZP Zach Parise 6.00 15.00

2008-09 Upper Deck Trilogy Young Star Scripts

YSAB Adam Burish 6.00 15.00
YSAC Andrew Cogliano 5.00 12.00
YSBC Blake Comeau 5.00 12.00
YSBD Brandon Dubinsky 5.00 12.00
YSBE Jonathan Bernier 6.00 15.00
YSCB Cam Barker 5.00 12.00
YSCK Chris Kunitz 8.00 20.00
YSCL David Clarkson 5.00 12.00
YSCP Carey Price 15.00 40.00
YSDC Daniel Carcillo 5.00 12.00
YSDP Dustin Penner 5.00 12.00
YSDS Devin Setoguchi 6.00 15.00
YSEC Erik Christensen 5.00 12.00
YSEJ Erik Johnson 5.00 12.00
YSJB Jared Boll 5.00 12.00
YSJC Jeff Carter 6.00 15.00
YSJH Josh Harding 8.00 20.00
YSJJ Jack Johnson 5.00 12.00
YSJP Jason Pominville 5.00 12.00
YSJS Jordan Staal 6.00 15.00
YSJT Jiri Tlusty 5.00 12.00
YSKC Kyle Chipchura 5.00 12.00
YSKL Kari Lehtonen 5.00 12.00
YSKO Kyle Okposo 10.00 25.00
YSKT Kyle Turris 12.00 30.00
YSMF Marc-Andre Fleury 15.00 40.00
YSML Milan Lucic 12.00 30.00
YSMR Mike Richards 6.00 15.00
YSNB Nicklas Backstrom 8.00 20.00
YSND Nigel Dawes 5.00 12.00
YSNZ Nikolai Zherdev 5.00 12.00
YSPK Patrick Kane 15.00 40.00
YSPM Peter Mueller 6.00 15.00
YSPN David Perron 6.00 15.00
YSPS Paul Stastny 6.00 15.00
YSRS Rob Schremp 6.00 15.00
YSSB Steve Bernier 5.00 12.00
YSSG Sam Gagner 5.00 12.00
YSSM Steve Mason 12.00 30.00
YSST Drew Stafford 5.00 12.00
YSSW Shea Weber 6.00 15.00
YSTE Tobias Enstrom 5.00 12.00
YSTH T.J. Hensick 6.00 15.00
YSTK Tyler Kennedy 6.00 15.00
YSTO Jonathan Toews 12.00 30.00
YSVF Vallteri Filppula 5.00 12.00

2009-10 Upper Deck Trilogy

COMP.SET w/o SPS (100)
1 Roberto Luongo 1.50 4.00
2 Luke Schenn 1.00 2.50
3 Dion Phaneuf .75 2.00
4 Bobby Orr 4.00 10.00
5 Nicklas Lidstrom .60 1.50
6 Shea Weber .75 2.00
7 Phil Esposito 1.50 4.00
8 Alexander Ovechkin 4.00 10.00
9 Zach Parise 1.00 2.50
10 Corey Perry 1.50 4.00
11 Jordan Staal .75 2.00
12 Jarome Iginla 1.25 3.00
13 Pavel Datsyuk 1.50 4.00
14 Jonathan Cheechoo .75 2.00
15 Ryan Getzlaf 1.00 2.50
16 Devin Setoguchi .75 2.00
17 Jeff Carter .75 2.00
18 Mike Richards .75 2.00
19 Jonathan Toews 1.50 4.00
20 Evgeni Nabokov .75 2.00
21 Olli Jokinen .75 2.00
22 Dan Boyle .60 1.50
23 Chris Drury .75 2.00
24 Nathan Horton 1.00 2.50
25 Chris Pronger 1.00 2.50
26 Paul Stastny .75 2.00
27 Ilya Kovalchuk 1.00 2.50
28 Alexander Semin 1.00 2.50
29 Marc-Andre Fleury 2.00 5.00
30 Martin Brodeur 2.50 6.00
31 Carey Price 2.00 5.00
32 Niklas Backstrom 1.00 2.50
33 Patrick Roy 2.50 6.00
34 Miikka Kiprusoff 1.00 2.50
35 Marty Turco 1.00 2.50
36 Jussi Jokinen .60 1.50
37 J.P. Dumont .60 1.50
38 Daniel Sedin 1.25 3.00
39 Rick DiPietro .75 2.00
40 Henrik Zetterberg 1.25 3.00
41 Nikolai Kulemin .60 1.50
42 Josh Bailey .75 2.00
43 Mikko Koivu 1.00 2.50
44 Sheldon Souray .60 1.50
45 Marian Hossa 1.00 2.50
46 Daniel Alfredsson 1.00 2.50
47 Marian Gaborik 1.00 2.50
48 Daniel Briere 1.00 2.50
49 Thomas Vanek .75 2.00
50 Chris Mason .75 2.00
51 Brian Campbell .75 2.00
52 Mike Green .75 2.00
53 Bobby Ryan .75 2.00
54 Eric Staal 1.25 3.00
55 Jason Blake .60 1.50
56 Shane Doan .75 2.00
57 David Perron .75 2.00
58 James Neal .60 1.50
59 Joe Thornton 1.50 4.00
60 Henrik Sedin 1.25 3.00
61 Rick Nash 1.00 2.50
62 Martin St. Louis 1.00 2.50
63 Kris Versteeg .60 1.50
64 Mike Modano 1.50 4.00
65 Andrew Cogliano .60 1.50
66 Mario Lemieux 4.00 10.00
67 Michael Frolik .75 2.00
68 Bryan Little .60 1.50
69 Henrik Lundqvist 2.50 6.00
70 Derek Roy .60 1.50
71 Evgeni Malkin 2.00 5.00
72 Patrik Elias 1.00 2.50
73 Michael Ryder .60 1.50
74 T.J. Oshie 1.00 2.50
75 Tomas Vokoun .75 2.00
76 Kyle Okposo .60 1.50
77 Ray Bourque 1.50 4.00
78 Cam Ward 1.00 2.50
79 Andrei Markov 1.00 2.50
80 Jason Arnott .75 2.00
81 Phil Kessel 1.00 2.50
82 Mike Cammalleri .75 2.00
83 Ales Hemsky .75 2.00
84 Mikhail Grabovski .60 1.50
85 Dany Heatley .75 2.00
86 Scott Gomez .75 2.00
87 Sidney Crosby 4.00 10.00
88 Patrick Kane 2.00 5.00
89 Sam Gagner .60 1.50
90 Ryan Miller 1.00 2.50
91 Steven Stamkos 2.00 5.00
92 Simeon Varlamov 1.00 2.50
93 Jakub Voracek .75 2.00
94 Ryan Smyth .75 2.00
95 Patrik Berglund .60 1.50
96 Pierre-Marc Bouchard .60 1.50
97 Steve Mason .75 2.00
98 Peter Mueller .75 2.00
99 Wayne Gretzky 6.00 15.00
100 Jason Spezza 1.00 2.50
101 Alexander Ovechkin FIT 12.00 30.00
102 Bobby Orr FIT 12.00 30.00
103 Carey Price FIT 6.00 15.00
104 Evgeni Malkin FIT 12.00 30.00
105 Gordie Howe FIT 10.00 25.00
106 Ilya Kovalchuk FIT 3.00 8.00
107 Joe Thornton FIT 5.00 12.00
108 Jonathan Toews FIT 10.00 25.00
109 Mario Lemieux FIT 12.00 30.00
110 Mark Messier FIT 6.00 15.00
111 Martin Brodeur FIT 8.00 20.00
112 Mike Richards FIT 2.50 6.00
113 Nicklas Backstrom FIT 3.00 8.00
114 Patrick Kane FIT 6.00 15.00
115 Patrick Roy FIT 8.00 20.00
116 Roberto Luongo FIT 5.00 12.00
117 Ron Hextall FIT 3.00 8.00
118 Sidney Crosby FIT 12.00 30.00
119 Vincent Lecavalier FIT 3.00 8.00
120 Wayne Gretzky FIT 12.50 30.00
121 Michael Sauer RC 3.00 8.00
122 Tyler Bozak RC 6.00 15.00
123 Spencer Machacek RC 4.00 10.00
124 Jhonas Enroth RC 5.00 12.00
125 Benn Ferriero RC 4.00 10.00
126 Matt Hendricks RC 3.00 8.00
127 Cal O'Reilly RC 3.00 8.00
128 Michael Grabner RC 4.00 10.00
129 Mike Santorelli RC 4.00 10.00
130 Tom Wandell RC 4.00 10.00
131 Jay Rosehill RC 4.00 10.00
132 Luca Caputi RC 4.00 10.00
133 T.J. Galiardi RC 4.00 10.00
134 Frazer McLaren RC 3.00 8.00
135 Riku Helenius RC 1.00 2.50
136 Joel Rechlicz RC 2.50 6.00
137 Alec Martinez RC 5.00 12.00
138 Dmitry Kulikov RC 4.00 10.00
139 Matt Beleskey RC 3.00 8.00
140 Ivan Vishnevskiy RC 2.50 6.00
141 Antti Niemi RC 6.00 15.00
142 James Wright RC 4.00 10.00
143 Mikael Backlund RC 6.00 15.00
144 Teemu Laakso RC 2.50 6.00
145 Erik Karlsson RC 12.00 30.00
146 Michal Neuvirth RC 6.00 15.00
147 Mika Pyorala RC 3.00 8.00
148 Jason Demers RC 6.00 15.00
149 Taylor Chorney RC 4.00 10.00
150 John Negrin RC 4.00 10.00
151 Matt Gilroy RC 4.00 10.00
152 Yannick Weber RC 4.00 10.00
153 Christian Hanson RC 4.00 10.00
154 Artem Anisimov RC 2.50 6.00
155 Sergei Shirokov RC 2.50 6.00
156 Colin Wilson RC 5.00 12.00
157 Ryan O'Reilly RC 10.00 25.00
158 Brad Marchand RC 8.00 20.00
159 Ville Leino RC 4.00 10.00
160 Michael Del Zotto RC 5.00 12.00
161 Victor Hedman RC 12.00 30.00
162 Evander Kane RC 10.00 25.00
163 Matt Duchene RC 12.00 30.00
164 James van Riemsdyk RC 10.00 25.00
165 Jonas Gustavsson RC 6.00 15.00
166 Jamie Benn RC 15.00 40.00
167 Viktor Stalberg RC 5.00 12.00
168 Tyler Myers RC 10.00 25.00
169 Logan Couture RC 10.00 25.00
170 John Tavares RC 15.00 40.00

2009-10 Upper Deck Trilogy Classic Confrontations

CCBOBU Boston/Buffalo 20.00 50.00
CCCANJ Carolina/New Jersey 30.00 80.00
CCCHSL Chicago/St. Louis 20.00 50.00
CCCODA Colorado/Dallas 25.00 60.00
CCCONJ Colorado/New Jersey 30.00 80.00
CCDECH Detroit/Chicago 25.00 60.00
CCDECO Detroit/Colorado 25.00 60.00
CCDEPH Detroit/Philadelphia 20.00 50.00
CCDEPI Detroit/Pittsburgh 30.00 80.00
CCDESL Detroit/St. Louis 20.00 50.00
CCDETO Detroit/Toronto 20.00 50.00
CCEDCG Edmonton/Calgary 25.00 60.00
CCEDDA Edmonton/Dallas 20.00 50.00
CCEDNY Edmonton/NYI 20.00 50.00
CCHABO Hartford/Boston 20.00 50.00
CCLAED LA/Edmonton 40.00 100.00
CCLATO LA/Toronto 40.00 100.00
CCMTBO Montreal/Boston 20.00 50.00
CCMTCG Montreal/Calgary 15.00 40.00
CCNJPH New Jersey/Philly 30.00 80.00
CCNYNJ NYR/New Jersey 30.00 80.00
CCNYPH NYI/Philly 20.00 50.00
CCPHNY Philly/Rangers 25.00 60.00
CCPIPH Pittsburgh/Philly 50.00 125.00
CCPIWA Pittsburgh/Wash 20.00 50.00
CCTOMT Toronto/Montreal 25.00 60.00
CCWANY Washington/NYR 30.00 80.00

2009-10 Upper Deck Trilogy Combo Clearcut Autographs

CC2BP Potvin/Bossy/25 EXCH 15.00 40.00
CC2CG Gagner/Cogliano/100 8.00 20.00
CC2EB Bourque/Esposito/25 25.00 60.00
CC2GB Backstrom/Green/100 12.00 30.00
CC2GG C.Gillies/C.Gillies/100 12.00 30.00
CC2GR Getzlaf/Ryan/100 12.00 30.00
CC2IP Iginla/Phaneuf/25 20.00 50.00
CC2JD Johnson/Doughty/100 15.00 40.00
CC2LD Delvecchio/Lindsay/100 12.00 30.00
CC2MS McDonald/Salming/25 15.00 40.00
CC2NK Kessel/Neely/25 EXCH 20.00 50.00
CC2NL Lundqvist/Naslund/25 EXCH 20.00 50.00
CC2NM Nash/Mason/25 15.00 40.00
CC2OB K.Okposo/J.Bailey/100 10.00 25.00
CC2PS Pogge/Schenn/100 15.00 40.00
CC2RC Richards/Carter/25 12.00 30.00
CC2SW Wishart/Stamkos/100 20.00 50.00
CC2TK Kane/Toews/25 EXCH 50.00 100.00
CC2TS Thornton/Setoguchi/25 25.00 60.00

2009-10 Upper Deck Trilogy Hat Trick Heroes

HTHAK Andrei Kostitsyn 5.00 12.00
HTHAO Alexander Ovechkin 25.00 60.00
HTHBL Bryan Little 6.00 15.00
HTHBW Blake Wheeler 6.00 15.00
HTHCD Chris Drury 5.00 12.00
HTHDB David Booth 4.00 10.00
HTHDU Dustin Brown 6.00 15.00
HTHEM Evgeni Malkin 12.00 30.00
HTHES Eric Staal 8.00 20.00
HTHIK Ilya Kovalchuk 6.00 15.00
HTHJC Jeff Carter 5.00 12.00
HTHJN James Neal 6.00 15.00
HTHJS Jason Spezza 6.00 15.00
HTHKE Phil Kessel 6.00 15.00
HTHMC Mike Cammalleri 5.00 12.00
HTHML Milan Lucic 5.00 12.00
HTHMM Mark Messier 12.00 30.00
HTHOJ Olli Jokinen 5.00 12.00
HTHPK Patrick Kane 12.00 30.00
HTHPS Petr Sykora 5.00 12.00
HTHRN Rick Nash 6.00 15.00
HTHSC Sidney Crosby 15.00 40.00
HTHSG Sam Gagner 4.00 10.00
HTHST Jordan Staal 5.00 12.00
HTHTS Teemu Selanne 12.00 30.00
HTHTV Thomas Vanek 5.00 12.00
HTHWG Wayne Gretzky 40.00 100.00

2009-10 Upper Deck Trilogy Hat Trick Heroes Gold

*SINGLES: .5X TO 1.2X BASIC INSERTS

2009-10 Upper Deck Trilogy Honorary Swatches

HSAO Alexander Ovechkin 10.00 25.00
HSBL Brian Leetch 4.00 10.00
HSBS Borje Salming 5.00 12.00
HSCN Cam Neely 5.00 12.00
HSCP Carey Price 10.00 25.00
HSDC Dino Ciccarelli 5.00 12.00
HSDG Doug Gilmour 6.00 15.00
HSDH Dale Hawerchuk 6.00 15.00
HSDS Denis Savard 6.00 15.00
HSEM Evgeni Malkin 10.00 25.00
HSES Eric Staal 6.00 15.00
HSFM Frank Mahovlich 5.00 12.00
HSGA Glenn Anderson 4.00 10.00
HSGF Grant Fuhr 8.00 20.00
HSGH Gordie Howe 15.00 40.00
HSGP Gilbert Perreault 5.00 12.00
HSIK Ilya Kovalchuk 5.00 12.00
HSJB Johnny Bucyk 5.00 12.00
HSJK Jari Kurri 5.00 12.00
HSJT Jonathan Toews 8.00 20.00
HSLM Lanny McDonald 5.00 12.00
HSLR Larry Robinson 5.00 12.00
HSMB Martin Brodeur 12.00 30.00
HSMK Miikka Kiprusoff 5.00 12.00
HSML Mario Lemieux 20.00 50.00
HSMM Mark Messier 10.00 25.00
HSMO Mike Modano 8.00 20.00
HSMT Marty Turco 5.00 12.00
HSNL Nicklas Lidstrom 3.00 8.00
HSPE Phil Esposito 8.00 20.00
HSPK Patrick Kane 10.00 25.00
HSPR Patrick Roy 12.00 30.00
HSRB Ray Bourque 8.00 20.00
HSRH Ron Hextall 5.00 12.00
HSRL Roberto Luongo 8.00 20.00
HSRN Rick Nash 5.00 12.00
HSRO Luc Robitaille 5.00 12.00
HSSC Sidney Crosby 12.00 30.00
HSTE Tony Esposito 10.00 25.00
HSWG Wayne Gretzky 15.00 40.00

2009-10 Upper Deck Trilogy Honorary Swatches Gold

*SINGLES: .5X TO 1.2X BASIC INSERTS

2009-10 Upper Deck Trilogy Ice Scripts

ISAC Andrew Cogliano 6.00 15.00
ISBA Josh Bailey 6.00 15.00
ISBH Bobby Hull SP 20.00 50.00
ISBL Brian Leetch 6.00 15.00
ISBO Bobby Orr SP 150.00 250.00
ISBR Bobby Ryan 6.00 15.00
ISBS Brandon Sutter 5.00 12.00
ISCN Cam Neely SP 25.00 60.00
ISDD Drew Doughty 15.00 40.00
ISDH Dany Heatley 6.00 15.00
ISDP Dion Phaneuf 6.00 15.00
ISES Eric Staal 8.00 20.00
ISGH Gordie Howe SP 75.00 150.00
ISHL Henrik Lundqvist 20.00 50.00
ISHZ Henrik Zetterberg SP 12.00 30.00
ISIK Ilya Kovalchuk SP 10.00 25.00
ISJB Jean Beliveau SP 75.00 150.00
ISJI Jarome Iginla SP 12.00 30.00
ISJK Jari Kurri 8.00 20.00
ISJN James Neal 6.00 15.00
ISJP Justin Pogge 8.00 20.00
ISJT Joe Thornton SP 15.00 40.00
ISKA Karl Alzner 5.00 12.00
ISKM Kenndal McArdle 6.00 15.00
ISLS Luke Schenn 8.00 20.00
ISMB Martin Brodeur SP 50.00 100.00
ISMF Marc-Andre Fleury 12.00 30.00
ISML Mario Lemieux SP 60.00 120.00
ISMP Max Pacioretty 8.00 20.00
ISMR Mike Richards 8.00 20.00
ISNB Nicklas Backstrom 8.00 20.00
ISNL Nicklas Lidstrom 12.00 30.00
ISPB Patrice Bergeron 40.00 100.00
ISPD Pavel Datsyuk SP 25.00 50.00
ISPE Phil Esposito SP 25.00 60.00
ISPH Chris Phillips 5.00 12.00
ISPK Patrick Kane 15.00 40.00
ISPR Patrick Roy SP 125.00 250.00
ISPS Paul Stastny 6.00 15.00
ISRB Ray Bourque SP 25.00 60.00
ISRM Ryan Miller 20.00 40.00
ISRN Rick Nash 8.00 20.00
ISSB Scotty Bowman SP 50.00 100.00
ISSC Sidney Crosby 60.00 120.00
ISSK Saku Koivu 15.00 40.00
ISSM Steve Mason 6.00 15.00
ISSS Steven Stamkos 25.00 50.00
ISTE Tony Esposito SP 25.00 60.00
ISTO Jonathan Toews 25.00 50.00
ISWG Wayne Gretzky SP EXCH 300.00 800.00
ISZB Zach Bogosian 6.00 15.00

2009-10 Upper Deck Trilogy Line Mates

*GOLD/50: .5X TO 1.2X BASIC INSERTS
LMAD J.Dumont/J.Arnott 5.00 12.00
LMAM M.Messier/G.Anderson 12.00 30.00
LMBK A.Kopitar/D.Brown 10.00 25.00
LMCG S.Gagner/A.Cogliano 4.00 10.00
LMHD P.Datsyuk/T.Holmstrom 10.00 25.00
LMHS M.Hejduk/P.Stastny 5.00 12.00
LMJI O.Jokinen/J.Iginla 8.00 20.00
LMKL I.Kovalchuk/B.Little 6.00 15.00
LMLL V.Lecavalier/M.St. Louis 6.00 15.00
LMLS S.Shutt/G.Lafleur 8.00 20.00
LMMN M.Modano/J.Neal 10.00 25.00
LMMS L.McDonald/D.Sittler 8.00 20.00
LMMT J.Thornton/P.Marleau 10.00 25.00
LMNO A.Oates/C.Neely 6.00 15.00
LMOB A.Ovechkin/N.Backstrom 15.00 40.00
LMRG M.Richards/S.Gagne 6.00 15.00
LMRL B.Rafalski/N.Lidstrom 4.00 10.00
LMRS T.Ruutu/E.Staal 8.00 20.00
LMRV T.Vanek/D.Roy 5.00 12.00
LMRW B.Wheeler/M.Ryder 6.00 15.00
LMSC J.Spezza/J.Cheechoo 6.00 15.00
LMSM M.Satan/S.Crosby 12.00 30.00
LMSS P.Stastny/M.Svatos 5.00 12.00
LMTK P.Kane/J.Toews 12.00 30.00
LMWF M.Frolik/S.Weiss 5.00 12.00
LMWL L.Robitaille/W.Gretzky 15.00 40.00

2009-10 Upper Deck Trilogy Superstar Scripts

SSAC Andrew Cogliano 6.00 15.00
SSAM Al MacInnis 10.00 25.00
SSAO Alexander Ovechkin 30.00 80.00
SSCB Cam Barker 5.00 12.00
SSCC Cal Clutterbuck 6.00 15.00
SSCK Chris Kunitz 8.00 20.00
SSCL David Clarkson 6.00 15.00
SSCW Cam Ward 8.00 20.00
SSDC Dan Cleary 6.00 15.00
SSDP David Perron 6.00 15.00
SSEL Patrik Elias 8.00 20.00
SSEM Evgeni Malkin 15.00 40.00
SSHZ Henrik Zetterberg 10.00 25.00
SSJA Jason Arnott 6.00 15.00
SSJC Jeff Carter 6.00 15.00
SSJD J.P. Dumont 5.00 12.00
SSJH Josh Harding 8.00 20.00
SSJI Jarome Iginla 10.00 25.00
SSJJ Jack Johnson 5.00 12.00
SSJP Jason Pominville 5.00 12.00
SSMF Marc-Andre Fleury 12.00 30.00
SSMG Mike Green 6.00 15.00
SSMR Mike Richards 6.00 15.00
SSMS Matt Stajan 5.00 12.00
SSMT Maxime Talbot 5.00 12.00
SSNB Nicklas Backstrom 8.00 20.00
SSPB Peter Budaj 6.00 15.00
SSPD Pavel Datsyuk 20.00 40.00
SSPE Dustin Penner 5.00 12.00
SSPH Dion Phaneuf 6.00 15.00
SSPK Phil Kessel 8.00 20.00
SSPO Denis Potvin 8.00 20.00
SSRS Ryan Smyth 6.00 15.00
SSSB Steve Bernier 5.00 12.00
SSSC Sidney Crosby 75.00 150.00
SSSG Simon Gagne 8.00 20.00
SSSS Steve Shutt 8.00 20.00
SSSW Stephen Weiss 5.00 12.00
SSTH Tomas Holmstrom 6.00 15.00
SSTV Thomas Vanek 6.00 15.00

2009-10 Upper Deck Trilogy Young Star Scripts

YSAE Andrew Ebbett 4.00 10.00
YSAN Andreas Nodl 5.00 12.00
YSBB Ben Bishop 5.00 12.00
YSBL Brian Lee 6.00 15.00
YSBM Brendan Mikkelson 4.00 10.00
YSBO Brian Boyle 4.00 10.00
YSBS Brandon Sutter 6.00 15.00
YSBV Boris Valabik 6.00 15.00
YSBW Blake Wheeler 6.00 15.00
YSCG Colton Gillies 5.00 12.00
YSCS Chris Stewart 5.00 12.00
YSDD Drew Doughty 15.00 40.00
YSDL Dan LaCosta 5.00 12.00
YSDO Derek Dorsett 5.00 12.00
YSDT Danny Taylor 5.00 12.00
YSEE Erik Ersberg 5.00 12.00
YSFB Fabian Brunnstrom 5.00 12.00
YSGI Claude Giroux 20.00 40.00
YSJB Josh Bailey 5.00 12.00
YSJF Jonathan Ericsson 4.00 10.00
YSJG Jonas Frogren 5.00 12.00
YSJM John Mitchell 4.00 10.00
YSJP Justin Pogge 6.00 15.00
YSJT John Tavares 30.00 80.00
YSJV Jakub Voracek 5.00 12.00
YSKA Karl Alzner 4.00 10.00
YSKM Kenndal McArdle 4.00 10.00
YSKO Kyle Okposo 4.00 10.00
YSKP Kevin Porter 4.00 10.00
YSLS Luke Schenn 6.00 15.00
YSMA Ben Maxwell 5.00 12.00
YSMB Mikkel Boedker 4.00 10.00
YSMC Jamie McGinn 5.00 12.00
YSMD Matt D'Agostini 5.00 12.00
YSMH Matthew Halischuk 5.00 12.00
YSMP Max Pacioretty 6.00 15.00
YSMR Michal Repik 5.00 12.00
YSNF Nikita Filatov 5.00 12.00
YSNO Nathan Oystrick 4.00 10.00
YSOM Oscar Moller 4.00 10.00
YSPI Alex Pietrangelo 5.00 12.00
YSPV Petr Vrana 8.00 20.00
YSRJ Ryan Jones 5.00 12.00
YSRY Bobby Ryan 5.00 12.00
YSSC Cory Schneider 6.00 15.00
YSSM Shawn Matthias 6.00 15.00
YSSS Steven Stamkos 12.00 30.00
YSST Steve Mason 5.00 12.00
YSTK Tim Kennedy 5.00 12.00
YSTL Trevor Lewis 4.00 10.00
YSTO T.J. Oshie 6.00 15.00
YSTP Tyler Plante 5.00 12.00
YSTS Tom Sestito 4.00 10.00
YSTW Ty Wishart 5.00 12.00
YSVT Viktor Tikhonov 5.00 12.00
YSWS Wayne Simmonds 8.00 20.00
YSZA Zach Boychuk 5.00 12.00
YSZB Zach Bogosian 5.00 12.00

2013-14 Upper Deck Trilogy

COMP.SET w/o RC's (100) 20.00 40.00
1 Bobby Ryan .60 1.50
2 Ryan Getzlaf .75 2.00
3 Jonas Hiller .60 1.50
4 Teemu Selanne 1.50 4.00
5 Bobby Orr 3.00 8.00

6 Cam Neely .75 2.00
7 Brad Marchand 1.50 4.00
8 Tuukka Rask 1.00 2.50
9 Patrice Bergeron 1.00 2.50
10 Ray Bourque 1.25 3.00
11 Terry O'Reilly .60 1.50
12 Tyler Seguin 1.00 2.50
13 Zdeno Chara .75 2.00
14 Ryan Miller .75 2.00
15 Dominik Hasek 1.25 3.00
16 Doug Gilmour 1.00 2.50
17 Jarome Iginla 1.00 2.50
18 Jeff Skinner 1.00 2.50
19 Eric Staal 1.00 2.50
20 Jordan Staal .60 1.50
21 Denis Savard .75 2.00
22 Doug Wilson .60 1.50
23 Ed Belfour .75 2.00
24 Jonathan Toews 1.25 3.00
25 Marian Hossa .75 2.00
26 Patrick Kane 1.50 4.00
27 Joe Sakic 1.50 4.00
28 Matt Duchene .75 2.00
29 Gabriel Landeskog 1.00 2.50
30 Derek Roy .50 1.25
31 Jamie Benn .75 2.00
32 Jaromir Jagr 2.50 6.00
33 Johan Franzen .60 1.50
34 Nicklas Lidstrom .75 2.00
35 Pavel Datsyuk 1.25 3.00
36 Grant Fuhr 1.25 3.00
37 Bill Ranford .75 2.00
38 Jordan Eberle .75 2.00
39 Jari Kurri .75 2.00
40 Paul Coffey .75 2.00
41 Ryan Nugent-Hopkins 1.00 2.50
42 Taylor Hall .75 2.00
43 Wayne Gretzky 5.00 12.00
44 Stephen Weiss .60 1.50
45 Ron Francis 1.00 2.50
46 Anze Kopitar 1.25 3.00
47 Drew Doughty 1.00 2.50
48 Mike Richards .60 1.50
49 Luc Robitaille .75 2.00
50 Jonathan Quick 1.00 2.50
51 Dino Ciccarelli .75 2.00
52 Mike Modano 1.25 3.00
53 Jean Beliveau .75 2.00
54 Larry Robinson .75 2.00
55 P.K. Subban 1.00 2.50
56 Carey Price 1.50 4.00
57 Pekka Rinne .75 2.00
58 Ilya Kovalchuk .75 2.00
59 Martin Brodeur 2.00 5.00
60 Mike Bossy .75 2.00
61 John Tavares 1.25 3.00
62 Bryan Trottier .75 2.00
63 Rick Nash .75 2.00
64 Brad Richards .75 2.00
65 Theoren Fleury 1.00 2.50
66 Marian Gaborik .75 2.00
67 Mark Messier 1.50 4.00
68 Henrik Lundqvist 2.00 5.00
69 Erik Karlsson 1.00 2.50
70 Jason Spezza .75 2.00
71 Claude Giroux .75 2.00
72 Eric Lindros 1.25 3.00
73 Bernie Parent 1.00 2.50
74 Brayden Schenn .75 2.00
75 Dave Schultz .75 2.00
76 Shane Doan .60 1.50
77 Evgeni Malkin 1.50 4.00
78 Marc-Andre Fleury 1.50 4.00
79 Mario Lemieux 3.00 8.00
80 Sidney Crosby 3.00 8.00
81 Patrick Marleau .75 2.00
82 Joe Pavelski 1.00 2.50
83 Antti Niemi .60 1.50
84 Logan Couture 1.00 2.50
85 Curtis Joseph 1.00 2.50
86 Brett Hull 1.50 4.00
87 David Backes .50 1.25
88 Jaroslav Halak .75 2.00
89 Steven Stamkos 1.50 4.00
90 Vincent Lecavalier .75 2.00
91 Dion Phaneuf .60 1.50
92 Phil Kessel .75 2.00
93 Markus Naslund .75 2.00
94 Ryan Kesler .75 2.00
95 Trevor Linden .75 2.00
96 Alexander Ovechkin 3.00 8.00
97 Braden Holtby 1.00 2.50
98 Nicklas Backstrom .75 2.00
99 Dale Hawerchuk 1.00 2.50
100 Evander Kane .75 2.00
101 Nail Yakupov AU/699 RC 12.00 30.00
102 Nail Yakupov AU/399 20.00 50.00
103 Nail Yakupov AU/49 150.00 300.00
104 Tarasenko AU/699 RC EXCH 25.00 60.00
105 Vladimir Tarasenko AU/399 30.00 80.00
106 Vladimir Tarasenko AU/49 150.00 250.00
107 A.Galchenyuk AU/699 RC 15.00 40.00
108 Alex Galchenyuk AU/399 20.00 50.00
109 Alex Galchenyuk AU/49 150.00 300.00
110 Justin Schultz AU/699 RC 4.00 10.00
111 Justin Schultz AU/399 5.00 12.00
112 Justin Schultz AU/49 150.00 250.00
113 Mikael Granlund AU/699 RC 6.00 15.00
114 Mikael Granlund AU/399 8.00 20.00
115 Mikael Granlund AU/49 40.00 100.00
116 M.Grigorenko AU/699 RC 2.50 6.00
117 Mikhail Grigorenko AU/399 3.00 8.00
118 Mikhail Grigorenko AU/49 75.00 150.00
119 J.Huberdeau AU/699 RC 10.00 25.00
120 Jonathan Huberdeau AU/399 10.00 25.00
121 Jonathan Huberdeau AU/49 100.00 200.00
122 Nathan Beaulieu AU/699 RC 2.50 6.00
123 Nathan Beaulieu AU/399 3.00 8.00
124 Nathan Beaulieu AU/49 12.00 30.00
125 B.Gallagher AU/699 RC 12.00 30.00
126 Brendan Gallagher AU/399 20.00 50.00
127 Brendan Gallagher AU/49 125.00 250.00
128 Charlie Coyle AU/699 RC 6.00 15.00
129 Charlie Coyle AU/399 8.00 20.00
130 Charlie Coyle AU/49 20.00 50.00
131 Cory Conacher AU/699 RC 2.50 6.00
132 Cory Conacher AU/399 3.00 8.00
133 Cory Conacher AU/49 15.00 40.00
134 D.Brunner AU/699 RC EXCH 3.00 8.00
135 D.Brunner AU/399 EXCH 4.00 10.00
136 D.Brunner AU/49 EXCH 15.00 40.00
137 Dougie Hamilton AU/699 RC 8.00 20.00
138 Dougie Hamilton AU/399 10.00 25.00
139 Dougie Hamilton AU/49 50.00 100.00
140 Emerson Etem AU/699 RC 4.00 10.00
141 Emerson Etem AU/399 5.00 12.00
142 Emerson Etem AU/49 20.00 50.00
143 Jonas Brodin AU/699 RC 5.00 12.00
144 Jonas Brodin AU/399 6.00 15.00
145 Jonas Brodin AU/49 25.00 60.00
146 J.Schroeder AU/699 RC 4.00 10.00
147 Jordan Schroeder AU/399 5.00 12.00
148 Jordan Schroeder AU/49 15.00 40.00
149 Petr Mrazek AU/699 RC 6.00 15.00
150 Petr Mrazek AU/399 8.00 20.00
151 Petr Mrazek AU/49 40.00 100.00
152 Quinton Howden AU/699 RC 3.00 8.00
153 Quinton Howden AU/399 4.00 10.00
154 Quinton Howden AU/49 15.00 40.00
155 Ryan Spooner AU/699 RC 4.00 10.00
156 Ryan Spooner AU/399 5.00 12.00
157 Ryan Spooner AU/49 25.00 60.00
158 Scott Laughton AU/699 RC 5.00 12.00
159 Scott Laughton AU/399 6.00 15.00
160 Scott Laughton AU/49 25.00 60.00
161 Stefan Matteau AU/699 RC 3.00 8.00
162 Stefan Matteau AU/399 4.00 10.00
163 Stefan Matteau AU/49 15.00 40.00
164 Viktor Fasth AU/699 RC 4.00 10.00
165 Viktor Fasth AU/399 5.00 12.00
166 Viktor Fasth AU/49 20.00 50.00
167 Jarred Tinordi AU/699 RC 4.00 10.00
168 Jarred Tinordi AU/399 5.00 12.00
169 Jarred Tinordi AU/49 30.00 80.00
170 R.Cervenka AU/699 RC 3.00 8.00
171 Roman Cervenka AU/399 4.00 10.00
172 Roman Cervenka AU/49 15.00 40.00
173 Jamie Oleksiak AU/699 RC 3.00 8.00
174 Jamie Oleksiak AU/399 4.00 10.00
175 Jamie Oleksiak AU/49 15.00 40.00
176 Beau Bennett AU/699 RC 5.00 12.00
177 Beau Bennett AU/399 6.00 15.00
178 Beau Bennett AU/49 30.00 80.00
179 Jack Campbell AU/699 RC 15.00 40.00
180 Jack Campbell AU/399 20.00 50.00
181 Jack Campbell AU/49 30.00 80.00
182 Leo Komarov AU/699 RC 4.00 10.00
183 Leo Komarov AU/399 5.00 12.00
184 Leo Komarov AU/49 20.00 50.00
185 Ryan Murphy AU/699 RC 4.00 10.00
186 Ryan Murphy AU/399 5.00 12.00
187 Ryan Murphy AU/49 20.00 50.00
188 Nick Petrecki AU/699 RC 2.50 6.00
189 Nick Petrecki AU/399 3.00 8.00
190 Nick Petrecki AU/49 12.00 30.00
191 Rickard Rakell AU/699 RC 4.00 10.00
192 Rickard Rakell AU/399 5.00 12.00
193 Rickard Rakell AU/49 15.00 40.00
194 T.Hickey AU/699 RC 3.00 8.00
195 Thomas Hickey AU/399 4.00 10.00
196 Thomas Hickey AU/49 15.00 40.00
197 Tyler Toffoli AU/699 RC 8.00 20.00
198 Tyler Toffoli AU/399 10.00 25.00
199 Tyler Toffoli AU/49 50.00 100.00
200 Ykp/Trsk/Glch AU/25 EX 300.00 500.00
201 Nathan MacKinnon AU/149 RC 100.00200.00
202 Nathan MacKinnon AU/49 200.00 500.00
203 Nathan MacKinnon AU/25 250.00 600.00
204 Seth Jones AU/149 RC 15.00 40.00
205 Seth Jones AU/49 30.00 80.00
206 Seth Jones AU/25 75.00 150.00
207 Tomas Hertl AU/149 RC 30.00 60.00
208 Tomas Hertl AU/49 75.00 150.00
209 Tomas Hertl AU/25 125.00 250.00
210 Aleksander Barkov AU/149 RC 15.00 40.00
211 Aleksander Barkov AU/49 40.00 80.00
212 Aleksander Barkov AU/25 40.00 100.00
213 Morgan Rielly AU/149 RC 20.00 50.00
214 Morgan Rielly AU/49 40.00 100.00
215 Morgan Rielly AU/25 75.00 150.00
216 Sean Monahan AU/149 RC 12.00 30.00
217 Sean Monahan AU/49 60.00 120.00
218 Sean Monahan AU/25 100.00 200.00

2013-14 Upper Deck Trilogy Autographs

1 Bobby Ryan C 8.00 20.00
2 Ryan Getzlaf B 10.00 25.00
3 Jonas Hiller C 8.00 20.00
5 Bobby Orr D 40.00 100.00
6 Cam Neely B 10.00 25.00
7 Brad Marchand B 20.00 50.00
8 Tuukka Rask C 12.00 30.00
10 Ray Bourque B 15.00 40.00
11 Terry O'Reilly C 8.00 20.00
12 Tyler Seguin C 12.00 30.00
14 Ryan Miller C 10.00 25.00
15 Dominik Hasek B 15.00 40.00
16 Doug Gilmour B 12.00 30.00
17 Jarome Iginla B 12.00 30.00
18 Jeff Skinner C 12.00 30.00
19 Eric Staal D 12.00 30.00
20 Jordan Staal C 8.00 20.00
21 Denis Savard D 10.00 25.00
22 Doug Wilson C 8.00 20.00
23 Ed Belfour C 10.00 25.00
24 Jonathan Toews B 15.00 40.00
26 Patrick Kane C 20.00 50.00
27 Joe Sakic A 20.00 50.00
28 Matt Duchene C 10.00 25.00
29 Gabriel Landeskog C 12.00 30.00
30 Derek Roy D 6.00 15.00
31 Jamie Benn C 10.00 25.00
32 Jaromir Jagr B 30.00 80.00
33 Johan Franzen C 8.00 20.00
34 Nicklas Lidstrom D 10.00 25.00
35 Pavel Datsyuk B 15.00 40.00
36 Grant Fuhr C 15.00 40.00
37 Bill Ranford C 10.00 25.00
39 Jari Kurri C 10.00 25.00
40 Paul Coffey B 10.00 25.00
41 Ryan Nugent-Hopkins C 12.00 30.00
42 Taylor Hall B 10.00 25.00
43 Wayne Gretzky C 200.00 500.00
44 Stephen Weiss C 8.00 20.00
45 Ron Francis B 12.00 30.00
46 Anze Kopitar C 15.00 40.00
48 Mike Richards B 8.00 20.00
49 Luc Robitaille B 10.00 25.00
50 Jonathan Quick C 12.00 30.00
52 Mike Modano B 15.00 40.00
53 Jean Beliveau B 10.00 25.00
54 Larry Robinson D 10.00 25.00
55 P.K. Subban C 12.00 30.00
56 Carey Price C 20.00 50.00
57 Pekka Rinne C 10.00 25.00
58 Ilya Kovalchuk A 10.00 25.00
59 Martin Brodeur B 25.00 60.00
60 Mike Bossy D 10.00 25.00
61 John Tavares D 15.00 40.00
62 Bryan Trottier C 10.00 25.00
63 Rick Nash B 10.00 25.00
65 Theoren Fleury D 12.00 30.00
67 Mark Messier B 20.00 50.00
69 Erik Karlsson C 12.00 30.00
72 Eric Lindros A 15.00 40.00
74 Brayden Schenn D 10.00 25.00
75 Dave Schultz C 10.00 25.00
77 Evgeni Malkin C 20.00 50.00
78 Marc-Andre Fleury C 20.00 50.00
79 Mario Lemieux A 40.00 100.00
80 Sidney Crosby A 60.00 150.00
81 Patrick Marleau C 10.00 25.00
82 Joe Pavelski C 12.00 30.00
84 Logan Couture C 12.00 30.00
85 Curtis Joseph C 12.00 30.00
86 Brett Hull B 20.00 50.00
87 David Backes C 6.00 15.00
88 Jaroslav Halak C 10.00 25.00
89 Steven Stamkos C 20.00 50.00
91 Dion Phaneuf B 8.00 20.00
92 Phil Kessel C 10.00 25.00
93 Markus Naslund D 10.00 25.00
94 Ryan Kesler C 10.00 25.00
95 Trevor Linden C 10.00 25.00
96 Alexander Ovechkin B 40.00 100.00
97 Braden Holtby C 12.00 30.00
98 Nicklas Backstrom C 10.00 25.00
99 Dale Hawerchuk C 12.00 30.00
100 Evander Kane C 10.00 25.00

2013-14 Upper Deck Trilogy Clear Cut Combo Autographs

CC2RW P.Rinne/S.Weber 10.00 25.00
CCCBH J.Halak/D.Backes C 10.00 25.00
CCCBS T.Seguin/Bergeron C 12.00 30.00
CCCBT M.Bossy/J.Tavares B 30.00 80.00
CCCCG B.Clarke/C.Giroux B 15.00 40.00
CCCGO W.Gretzky/B.Orr A 250.00 600.00
CCCHE T.Hall/J.Eberle B 10.00 25.00
CCCLB R.Leach/B.Barber C 10.00 25.00
CCCLJ M.Lemieux/J.Jagr A 100.00 200.00
CCCML M.Messier/E.Lindros A 20.00 50.00
CCCMR B.Marchand/T.Rask C 20.00 50.00
CCCNS Nugent-Hpkns/Smyth C 12.00 30.00
CCCRP P.Roy/C.Price A 60.00 150.00
CCCSC B.Schenn/Couturier C 10.00 25.00
CCCSK C.Schneider/Kassian C 10.00 25.00
CCCSL Subban/L.Leblanc C 12.00 30.00
CCCSO D.Schultz/T.O'Reilly C 10.00 25.00
CCCTK J.Toews/P.Kane B 60.00 150.00

2013-14 Upper Deck Trilogy Crystal

C1 Patrick Kane 8.00 20.00
C2 Tyler Seguin 5.00 12.00
C3 Ryan Nugent-Hopkins 5.00 12.00
C4 Drew Doughty 5.00 12.00
C5 Phil Kessel 4.00 10.00
C6 Erik Karlsson 5.00 12.00
C7 James Neal 2.50 6.00
C8 Jonathan Quick 5.00 12.00
C9 Corey Perry 6.00 15.00
C10 Jeff Skinner 5.00 12.00
C11 Henrik Lundqvist 10.00 25.00
C12 Evgeni Malkin 8.00 20.00
C13 Taylor Hall 4.00 10.00
C14 Jordan Eberle 4.00 10.00
C15 Martin Brodeur 10.00 25.00
C16 Sidney Crosby 15.00 40.00
C17 Carey Price 12.00 30.00
C18 Alexander Ovechkin 25.00 60.00
C19 Steven Stamkos 12.00 30.00
C20 Jonathan Toews 10.00 25.00
C21 Paul Coffey 5.00 12.00
C22 Nicklas Lidstrom 5.00 12.00
C23 Mats Sundin 5.00 12.00
C24 Ray Bourque 8.00 20.00
C25 Larry Robinson 5.00 12.00
C26 Jean Beliveau 6.00 15.00
C27 Guy Lafleur 6.00 15.00
C28 Howie Morenz 4.00 10.00
C29 Pelle Lindbergh 4.00 10.00
C30 Mark Messier 10.00 25.00
C31 Eric Lindros 6.00 15.00
C32 Brett Hull 10.00 25.00
C33 Bobby Hull 10.00 25.00
C34 Ron Francis 6.00 15.00
C35 Pavel Bure 8.00 20.00
C36 Patrick Roy 20.00 50.00
C37 Joe Sakic 15.00 40.00
C38 Mario Lemieux 30.00 80.00
C39 Bobby Orr 30.00 80.00
C40 Wayne Gretzky 25.00 60.00
C41 Petr Mrazek/225 8.00 20.00
C42 Viktor Fasth/225 4.00 10.00
C43 Quinton Howden/225 3.00 8.00
C44 Jonas Brodin/225 5.00 12.00
C45 Emerson Etem/225 4.00 10.00
C46 Charlie Coyle/125 8.00 20.00
C47 Brendan Gallagher/125 12.00 30.00
C48 Ryan Spooner/125 5.00 12.00
C49 Scott Laughton/125 8.00 20.00
C50 Damien Brunner/125 8.00 20.00
C51 Cory Conacher/75 4.00 10.00
C52 J.T. Miller/75 15.00 40.00
C53 Dougie Hamilton/75 25.00 50.00
C54 Mikhail Grigorenko/75 15.00 40.00
C55 Jonathan Huberdeau/75 15.00 40.00
C56 Mikael Granlund/75 10.00 25.00
C57 Justin Schultz/75 6.00 15.00
C58 Alex Galchenyuk/75 40.00 100.00
C59 Vladimir Tarasenko/75 30.00 80.00
C60 Nail Yakupov/75 50.00 100.00

2013-14 Upper Deck Trilogy Ice Scripts

ISAO Alexander Ovechkin A 40.00 100.00
ISBB Bill Barber D 10.00 25.00
ISBC Bobby Clarke B 15.00 40.00
ISBH Brett Hull A 20.00 50.00
ISBM Brad Marchand D 20.00 50.00
ISBO Bobby Orr C 50.00 125.00
ISCG Claude Giroux C EXCH 10.00 25.00
ISCH Cody Hodgson D 6.00 15.00
ISCJ Curtis Joseph B 12.00 30.00
ISCK Chris Kreider D 12.00 30.00
ISCP Carey Price B 20.00 50.00
ISCS Cory Schneider D 10.00 25.00
ISDG Doug Gilmour A 12.00 30.00
ISDH Dominik Hasek A EXCH 15.00 40.00
ISEB Ed Belfour A 10.00 25.00
ISEK Erik Karlsson D 12.00 30.00
ISEL Eric Lindros A 15.00 40.00
ISJA Jake Allen D 10.00 25.00
ISJB Jean Beliveau A 10.00 25.00
ISJE Jordan Eberle D 10.00 25.00
ISJH Jaroslav Halak D 10.00 25.00
ISJI Jarome Iginla A 12.00 30.00
ISJJ Jaromir Jagr A 30.00 80.00
ISJM Jacob Markstrom D 10.00 25.00
ISJS Joe Sakic A 20.00 50.00
ISKA Evander Kane D EXCH 10.00 25.00
ISKN Patrick Kane B 20.00 50.00
ISLE Lars Eller D 6.00 15.00
ISMB Mike Bossy A 10.00 25.00
ISMB Martin Brodeur A 25.00 60.00
ISMF Marc-Andre Fleury C 20.00 50.00
ISMG Mike Gartner D 12.00 30.00
ISML Mario Lemieux A 40.00 100.00
ISMM Mark Messier A 20.00 50.00
ISPB Patrice Bergeron C 12.00 30.00
ISPD Pavel Datsyuk B 15.00 40.00
ISPK Phil Kessel C EXCH 10.00 25.00
ISPR Patrick Roy A 25.00 60.00
ISPS P.K. Subban C EXCH 12.00 30.00
ISRA Bill Ranford C 10.00 25.00
ISRB Ray Bourque A 15.00 40.00
ISRF Ron Francis A 12.00 30.00
ISRK Ryan Kesler D 10.00 25.00
ISRN Ryan Nugent-Hopkins B 12.00 30.00
ISSB Sven Baertschi D 8.00 20.00
ISSC Sean Couturier D 8.00 20.00
ISSD Sidney Crosby A 40.00 100.00
ISSW Jaden Schwartz D 12.00 30.00
ISTA Maxime Talbot D 6.00 15.00
ISTH Taylor Hall C 10.00 25.00
ISTL Trevor Linden D 10.00 25.00
ISTO Terry O'Reilly C 8.00 20.00
ISTS Tyler Seguin B 12.00 30.00
ISTV John Tavares C 15.00 40.00
ISTW Jonathan Toews B 15.00 40.00
ISWC Wendel Clark B 15.00 40.00
ISWG Wayne Gretzky A 200.00 500.00
ISZK Zack Kassian D 6.00 15.00

2013-14 Upper Deck Trilogy Signature Pucks

SPAG Alex Galchenyuk E 25.00 60.00
SPAL Anders Lindback E 6.00 15.00
SPAO Alexander Ovechkin A 40.00 100.00
SPAS Andrew Shaw E 6.00 15.00
SPBE Jean Beliveau A 10.00 25.00
SPBG Brendan Gallagher D 25.00 60.00
SPBH Bobby Hull B 20.00 50.00
SPBM Brad Marchand E 20.00 50.00
SPBO Bobby Orr C 40.00 100.00
SPBR Bobby Ryan D 8.00 20.00
SPBS Brayden Schenn D 10.00 25.00
SPBT Bryan Trottier C 10.00 25.00
SPCA Carl Hagelin D 6.00 15.00
SPCC Cory Conacher E 6.00 15.00
SPCH Cody Hodgson E 6.00 15.00
SPCK Chris Kreider D 12.00 30.00
SPCN Cam Neely B 10.00 25.00
SPCP Carey Price B 20.00 50.00
SPCS Cory Schneider B 10.00 25.00
SPDA Dale Hawerchuk B 12.00 30.00
SPDG Doug Gilmour B 12.00 30.00
SPDH Dougie Hamilton E 15.00 40.00
SPDS Darryl Sittler B 12.00 30.00
SPEK Erik Karlsson A 12.00 30.00
SPEL Eric Lindros A 15.00 40.00
SPGA Jake Gardiner E 6.00 15.00
SPGF Grant Fuhr B 15.00 40.00
SPGG Mikhail Grigorenko E 6.00 15.00
SPGL Gabriel Landeskog E EXCH 12.00 30.00
SPGR Mikael Granlund E 15.00 40.00
SPHA Dominik Hasek A 15.00 40.00
SPHB Jonathan Huberdeau D 25.00 60.00
SPHU Brett Hull A 20.00 50.00
SPJA Jaden Schwartz E 12.00 30.00
SPJB Jamie Benn E 10.00 25.00
SPJD Jordan Schroeder D 10.00 25.00
SPJE Jordan Eberle C 10.00 25.00
SPJG Josh Gorges A 8.00 20.00
SPJH Jaroslav Halak D 10.00 25.00
SPJI Jarome Iginla A 12.00 30.00
SPJJ Jaromir Jagr A 30.00 80.00
SPJK Jake Allen E 10.00 25.00
SPJQ Jonathan Quick D 12.00 30.00
SPJS Jeff Skinner D 12.00 30.00
SPJT Jonathan Toews B EXCH 15.00 40.00
SPKE Phil Kessel C 10.00 25.00
SPKU Jari Kurri A 10.00 25.00
SPLA Guy Lafleur A 12.00 30.00
SPLC Logan Couture D 12.00 30.00
SPLL Louis Leblanc C 6.00 15.00
SPMB Mikkel Boedker C 6.00 15.00
SPMF Marc-Andre Fleury C 20.00 50.00
SPMG Mike Gartner E 12.00 30.00
SPMI Mike Bossy B 10.00 25.00
SPML Mario Lemieux A 60.00 150.00
SPMM Mark Messier A 20.00 50.00
SPMS Marc Staal D 6.00 15.00
SPNH Ryan Nugent-Hopkins B EXCH 12.0030.00
SPNL Nicklas Lidstrom A 10.00 25.00
SPNY Nail Yakupov E EXCH 20.00 50.00
SPPB Patrice Bergeron C 60.00 150.00
SPPC Paul Coffey A 10.00 25.00
SPPD Pavel Datsyuk B 15.00 40.00
SPPR Patrick Roy A 25.00 60.00
SPPS P.K. Subban C 12.00 30.00
SPRA Bill Ranford C 10.00 25.00
SPRD Raphael Diaz C 6.00 15.00
SPRE Ryan Ellis D 8.00 20.00
SPRF Ron Francis B 12.00 30.00
SPRH Ron Hextall B 10.00 25.00
SPRI Pekka Rinne C 10.00 25.00
SPRJ Ryan Johansen D 8.00 20.00
SPRN Rick Nash C 10.00 25.00
SPRS Ryan Spooner D 10.00 25.00
SPRY Ryan Smyth B 8.00 20.00
SPSA Joe Sakic A 20.00 50.00
SPSB Sven Baertschi E 8.00 20.00
SPSC Sidney Crosby A EXCH 150.00 250.00
SPSH Brendan Smith E 6.00 15.00
SPSM Stan Mikita B 12.00 30.00
SPSV Jakob Silfverberg E 6.00 15.00
SPSZ Justin Schultz E 10.00 25.00
SPTA John Tavares E 15.00 40.00
SPTH Taylor Hall B 10.00 25.00
SPTL Trevor Linden A 10.00 25.00
SPTS Tyler Seguin C EXCH 12.00 30.00
SPTT Tony Tanti B 6.00 15.00
SPVT Vladimir Tarasenko E EXCH 25.00 60.00
SPWG Wayne Gretzky A 200.00 500.00
SPZP Zach Parise B 10.00 25.00

2013-14 Upper Deck Trilogy Three Star International Jerseys

CANGR8 Grtzky/Lmieux/Sakic A 40.00 80.00
CANNET Lngo/Brdr/Fleury D 5.00 12.00
CANYNG Hbrdeau/Lghtn/Cncher D 5.00 12.00
CZRFWD Jagr/Plknc/Elias D 12.00 30.00
CZRNET Vkoun/Hsek/Pvlec C 6.00 15.00
FINNET Rnne/Kprsft/Lhtnen C 4.00 10.00
RUSFWD Ovchkn/Dtsyk/Ykpv D 10.00 25.00
RUSNET Bryzglv/Vrlmv/Khbblin B 4.00 10.00
SLVGR8 Hssa/Gbrk/Chara C 5.00 12.00
SWEDEF Slmng Ldstrm/Ekmn-Lrssn D 4.00 10.00
SWEDET Zttrbrg/Ldstrm/Frnzn B 5.00 12.00
SWEFWD Lndskg/Brglnd/Pjrvi D 5.00 12.00
SWEPTS Sndin/Ldstrm/Alfrdssn A 8.00 20.00
USAFWD Ststny/Drry/Brwn B 4.00 10.00
USANET Quick/Mller/Thmas C 5.00 12.00
USAYNG Glchnyk/Cyle/Etem D 5.00 12.00
RUSSTAR Bure/Ovchkn/Malkin C 15.00 40.00
SWEROOK Fsth/Brdin/Rkell C 4.00 10.00
SWESTAR Krlssn/Bckstrm/Zttrbrg B 5.00 12.00
SWEYDEF Ekmn-Lrssn/Lrssn/Brdn B 5.00 12.00
USASTAR Kne/Pvlski/Parise A 12.00 30.00
CANROOKD Hmltn/Olksk/Schltz D 4.00 10.00
CANROOKF Hbrdeau/Lghtn/Spner D 4.00 10.00

2013-14 Upper Deck Trilogy Three Star Past Present Future Jerseys

PPFANA Ndrmyr/Gtzlf/Rkell F 4.00 10.00
PPFBOS Espsto/Brgrn/Sgin F 6.00 15.00
PPFCAR Frncs/Staal/Skner D 5.00 12.00
PPFCGY McDnld/Ignla/Crvnka F 5.00 12.00
PPFDAL Mdno/Benn/Olksk D 6.00 15.00
PPFDRW Hsek/Hwrd/Mrzk E 8.00 20.00
PPFEDM Grtzky/Hall/Ykpv B 30.00 60.00
PPFFLA Bre/Vrstg/Hwdn C 4.00 10.00
PPFMON Koivu/Ellr/Glchnyk E 6.00 15.00
PPFMTL Rbnsn/Mrkv/Sbban F 5.00 12.00
PPFOIL Cffey/Whtny/Schltz F 4.00 10.00
PPFPHI Lndrs/Groux/Lghtn E 6.00 15.00
PPFSJS Thrntn/Cture/Ptrcki E 6.00 15.00
PPFSTL Fdrko/Brglnd/Trsnko D 5.00 12.00
PPFVAN Bure/Sdin/Schrder F 5.00 12.00
PPFBEES Bcyk/Hrtn/Spner F 4.00 10.00
PPFBOST Brque/Chra/Hmltn D 4.00 10.00
PPFEDMF Krri/Smyth/Ebrle D 4.00 10.00
PPFMINN Gbrik/Prise/Cyle E 6.00 15.00
PPFDUCKS Giguere/Hller/Fsth F 4.00 10.00
PPFPNTHR Bure/Flschmnn/Hbrd A 10.00 25.00
PPFWINGS Ldstrm/Zttrbrg/Brnner D 5.00 12.00

2014-15 Upper Deck Trilogy

COMP.SET w/o RC's (100) 15.00 40.00
1 Morgan Rielly .75 2.00
2 Anze Kopitar 1.25 3.00
3 Pekka Rinne .75 2.00
4 Sidney Crosby 3.00 8.00
5 Jonathan Quick 1.00 2.50
6 Chris Kunitz .75 2.00
7 Joe Thornton 1.25 3.00
8 Gabriel Landeskog 1.00 2.50
9 Milan Lucic .75 2.00
10 Sergei Bobrovsky 1.25 3.00
11 Alex Galchenyuk .50 1.25
12 Claude Giroux .75 2.00
13 Ryan Getzlaf .75 2.00
14 Cody Hodgson .50 1.25
15 Jacob Trouba .60 1.50
16 Jordan Eberle .75 2.00
17 Jamie Benn .75 2.00
18 Ryan Johansen .60 1.50
19 Pavel Datsyuk 1.25 3.00
20 Ryan McDonagh .50 1.25
21 Alexander Ovechkin 3.00 8.00
22 Vladimir Tarasenko 1.00 2.50
23 Nicklas Backstrom .75 2.00
24 Blake Wheeler .75 2.00
25 Corey Crawford 1.00 2.50
26 Rick Nash .75 2.00
27 Jonathan Bernier .60 1.50
28 Alexander Steen .50 1.25
29 Henrik Sedin 1.00 2.50
30 Joe Pavelski 1.00 2.50
31 Tuukka Rask 1.00 2.50
32 Antti Niemi .60 1.50
33 Henrik Lundqvist 2.00 5.00
34 Brent Seabrook .50 1.25
35 Taylor Hall .75 2.00
36 Zach Parise .75 2.00
37 Brendan Gallagher .75 2.00
38 Brad Marchand 1.50 4.00
39 Evgeni Malkin 1.50 4.00
40 Kyle Okposo .50 1.25
41 Logan Couture 1.00 2.50
42 Ryan Nugent-Hopkins 1.00 2.50
43 David Backes .50 1.25
44 Jonathan Huberdeau 1.00 2.50
45 Carey Price 1.50 4.00
46 P.K. Subban 1.00 2.50
47 Drew Doughty 1.00 2.50
48 Nazem Kadri 1.00 2.50
49 Corey Perry 1.25 3.00
50 John Gibson .75 2.00
51 Phil Kessel .75 2.00
52 James van Riemsdyk .60 1.50
53 Jeff Carter .60 1.50
54 Patrice Bergeron 1.00 2.50
55 Aleksander Barkov 1.25 3.00
56 Kari Lehtonen .60 1.50
57 Shea Weber .60 1.50
58 Daniel Sedin 1.00 2.50
59 Eric Staal 1.00 2.50
60 Ryan Suter .60 1.50
61 Patrick Kane 1.50 4.00
62 Jonathan Toews 1.25 3.00
63 Cam Ward .75 2.00
64 Cory Schneider .75 2.00
65 Boone Jenner .75 2.00
66 Dustin Byfuglien .75 2.00
67 John Tavares 1.25 3.00
68 Ryan Callahan .50 1.25
69 Steven Stamkos 1.50 4.00
70 Erik Karlsson 1.00 2.50
71 Martin St. Louis .75 2.00
72 Zemgus Girgensons .60 1.50
73 Tomas Hertl .75 2.00
74 Kyle Turris .75 2.00
75 Roberto Luongo 1.25 3.00
76 Max Pacioretty .75 2.00
77 Brandon Dubinsky .50 1.25
78 Mark Giordano .75 2.00
79 Semyon Varlamov .75 2.00
80 Nathan MacKinnon 3.00 8.00
81 Bryan Little .75 2.00
82 Henrik Zetterberg 1.00 2.50
83 Patrick Sharp .75 2.00
84 Sean Monahan .50 1.25
85 Mike Smith .75 2.00
86 T.J. Oshie .75 2.00
87 Jaromir Jagr 2.50 6.00
88 Matt Duchene .75 2.00
89 Tyler Seguin 1.00 2.50
90 Arturs Irbe .60 1.50
91 Bobby Orr 3.00 8.00
92 Teemu Selanne 1.50 4.00
93 Patrick Roy 2.00 5.00
94 Jeremy Roenick 1.25 3.00
95 Rob Blake .75 2.00
96 Mats Sundin .75 2.00
97 Mario Lemieux 3.00 8.00
98 Mike Bossy .75 2.00
99 Wayne Gretzky 5.00 12.00
100 Steve Yzerman 2.00 5.00
101 Oscar Klefbom/799 RC 4.00 10.00
102 Johnny Gaudreau/799 RC 6.00 15.00
103 Jonathan Drouin/799 RC 4.00 10.00
104 Teuvo Teravainen/799 RC 3.00 8.00
105 Greg McKegg/799 RC 1.50 4.00
106 Joey Hishon/799 RC 2.50 6.00
107 Marko Dano/799 RC 2.00 5.00
108 Ryan Sproul/799 RC 2.00 5.00
109 Evgeny Kuznetsov/799 RC 5.00 12.00
110 Brandon Gormley/799 RC 2.00 5.00
111 Aaron Ekblad/799 RC 5.00 12.00
112 Andre Burakovsky/799 RC 3.00 8.00
113 Curtis Lazar/799 RC 2.00 5.00
114 Victor Rask/799 RC 2.00 5.00
115 A.Khokhlachev/799 RC 2.00 5.00
116 Mark Visentin/799 RC 2.00 5.00
117 Vincent Trocheck/799 RC 4.00 10.00
118 Sam Reinhart/799 RC 8.00 20.00
119 Damon Severson/799 RC 2.00 5.00
120 Alexander Wennberg/799 RC 3.00 8.00
121 Colton Sissons/799 RC 2.00 5.00
122 William Karlsson/799 RC 6.00 15.00
123 Calle Jarnkrok/799 RC 2.00 5.00
124 Stuart Percy/799 RC 2.00 5.00
125 Anthony Duclair/799 RC 3.00 8.00
126 Griffin Reinhart/799 RC 2.00 5.00
127 Chris Tierney/799 RC 2.00 5.00
128 Jake McCabe/799 RC 2.00 5.00
129 Mirco Mueller/799 RC 2.00 5.00
130 V.Namestnikov/799 RC 3.00 8.00
131 Leon Draisaitl/799 RC 10.00 25.00
132 Bo Horvat/799 RC 5.00 12.00
133 Ty Rattie/799 RC 2.00 5.00
134 Oscar Klefbom AU/399 10.00 25.00
135 Johnny Gaudreau AU/399 60.00 150.00
136 Jonathan Drouin AU/399 10.00 25.00
137 Teuvo Teravainen AU/399 8.00 20.00
138 Greg McKegg AU/399 4.00 10.00
139 Joey Hishon AU/399 6.00 15.00
140 Marko Dano AU/399 5.00 12.00
141 Ryan Sproul AU/399 5.00 12.00
142 Evgeny Kuznetsov AU/399 15.00 30.00
143 Brandon Gormley AU/399 5.00 12.00
144 Aaron Ekblad AU/399 12.00 30.00
145 Andre Burakovsky AU/399 8.00 20.00
146 Curtis Lazar AU/399 5.00 12.00
147 Victor Rask AU/399 5.00 12.00
148 A.Khokhlachev AU/399 5.00 12.00
149 Mark Visentin AU/399 5.00 12.00
150 Vincent Trocheck AU/399 10.00 25.00
151 Sam Reinhart AU/399 20.00 50.00
152 Damon Severson AU/399 5.00 12.00
153 Alexander Wennberg AU/399 8.00 20.00
154 Colton Sissons AU/399 5.00 12.00
155 William Karlsson AU/399 15.00 40.00
156 Calle Jarnkrok AU/399 EXCH 5.00 12.00
157 Stuart Percy AU/399 5.00 12.00
158 Anthony Duclair AU/399 EXCH 8.00 20.00
159 Griffin Reinhart AU/399 5.00 12.00
160 Chris Tierney AU/399 5.00 12.00
161 Jake McCabe AU/399 EXCH 5.00 12.00
162 Mirco Mueller AU/399 5.00 12.00
163 V.Namestnikov AU/399 6.00 15.00
164 Leon Draisaitl AU/399 50.00 125.00
165 Bo Horvat AU/399 10.00 25.00
166 Ty Rattie AU/399 5.00 12.00
167 Oscar Klefbom AU/49 25.00 60.00
168 Johnny Gaudreau AU/49 125.00 300.00
169 Jonathan Drouin AU/49 60.00 120.00
170 Teuvo Teravainen AU/49 20.00 50.00
171 Greg McKegg AU/49 10.00 25.00
172 Joey Hishon AU/49 15.00 40.00
173 Marko Dano AU/49 12.00 30.00
174 Ryan Sproul AU/49 12.00 30.00
175 Evgeny Kuznetsov AU/49 30.00 80.00
176 Brandon Gormley AU/49 12.00 30.00
177 Aaron Ekblad AU/49 40.00 80.00
178 Andre Burakovsky AU/49 20.00 50.00
179 Curtis Lazar AU/49 20.00 50.00
180 Victor Rask AU/49 12.00 30.00
181 A.Khokhlachev AU/49 12.00 30.00
182 Mark Visentin AU/49 12.00 30.00
183 Vincent Trocheck AU/49 25.00 60.00
184 Sam Reinhart AU/49 50.00 125.00
185 Damon Severson AU/49 12.00 30.00
186 Alexander Wennberg AU/49 20.00 50.00
187 Colton Sissons AU/49 12.00 30.00
188 William Karlsson AU/49 40.00 100.00
189 Calle Jarnkrok AU/49 EXCH 12.00 30.00
190 Stuart Percy AU/49 12.00 30.00
191 Anthony Duclair AU/49 EXCH 20.00 50.00
192 Griffin Reinhart AU/49 12.00 30.00
193 Chris Tierney AU/49 12.00 30.00
194 Jake McCabe AU/49 EXCH 12.00 30.00
195 Mirco Mueller AU/49 12.00 30.00
196 V.Namestnikov AU/49 15.00 40.00
197 Leon Draisaitl AU/49 60.00 150.00
198 Bo Horvat AU/49 25.00 60.00
199 Ty Rattie AU/49 12.00 30.00
200 Drn/Ekb/Rnhrt AU/25 200.00 350.00

2014-15 Upper Deck Trilogy Radiant Blue

*VETS/200-367: 1.5X TO 4X BASIC CARDS
*VETS/102-196: 2X TO 5X BASIC CARDS
*VETS/54-99: 2.5X TO 6X BASIC CARDS
*101-133 ROOK/499: .4X TO 1X BASIC RC/799
*134-166 ROOK.AU/225: .5X TO 1.2X AUTO/399
*167-199 ROOK.AU/15: X TO X AUTO/49
23 Nicklas Backstrom/367 3.00 8.00
25 Corey Crawford/115 5.00 12.00
135 Johnny Gaudreau AU/225 60.00 150.00
164 Leon Draisaitl AU/225 40.00 100.00
169 Jonathan Drouin AU/15 175.00 300.00
177 Aaron Ekblad AU/15 60.00 150.00

2014-15 Upper Deck Trilogy Radiant Green

*VETS/54-99: 2.5X TO 6X BASIC CARDS
*VETS/30-48: 3X TO 8X BASIC CARDS
*VETS/15-29: 4X TO 10X BASIC CARDS
*101-133 ROOK/199: .5X TO 1.2X BASIC RC/799
*134-166 ROOK.AU/99: .6X TO 1.5X AUTO/399
23 Nicklas Backstrom/61 5.00 12.00
25 Corey Crawford/32 8.00 20.00
99 Wayne Gretzky/20 40.00 80.00
135 Johnny Gaudreau AU/99 80.00 200.00
164 Leon Draisaitl AU/99 40.00 100.00

2014-15 Upper Deck Trilogy Crystal

TCAK Anze Kopitar/275 6.00 15.00
TCAO Alexander Ovechkin/275 15.00 40.00
TCCG Claude Giroux/275 5.00 12.00
TCCP Carey Price/275 10.00 25.00
TCEM Evgeni Malkin/275 8.00 20.00
TCHL Henrik Lundqvist/275 10.00 25.00
TCHZ Henrik Zetterberg/275 5.00 12.00
TCJJ Jaromir Jagr/275 12.00 30.00
TCJQ Jonathan Quick/275 5.00 12.00
TCJT Jonathan Toews/275 8.00 20.00
TCMD Matt Duchene/275 4.00 10.00
TCPB Patrice Bergeron/275 5.00 12.00
TCPD Pavel Datsyuk/275 5.00 12.00
TCPK Phil Kessel/275 4.00 10.00
TCPS P.K. Subban/275 6.00 15.00
TCRG Ryan Getzlaf/275 4.00 10.00
TCSC Sidney Crosby/275 12.00 30.00
TCSS Steven Stamkos/275 8.00 20.00
TCTA John Tavares/275 6.00 15.00
TCZP Zach Parise/275 4.00 10.00
TCRAE1 Aaron Ekblad/399 8.00 20.00
TCRAE2 Aaron Ekblad/249 10.00 25.00
TCRAE3 Aaron Ekblad/125 12.00 30.00
TCRAK1 Alexander Khokhlachev/399 3.00 8.00
TCRAK2 Alexander Khokhlachev/249 4.00 10.00
TCRAK3 Alexander Khokhlachev/125 5.00 12.00
TCRBG1 Brandon Gormley/399 3.00 8.00
TCRBG2 Brandon Gormley/249 4.00 10.00
TCRBG3 Brandon Gormley/125 5.00 12.00
TCRBH1 Bo Horvat/399 6.00 15.00
TCRBH2 Bo Horvat/249 8.00 20.00
TCRBH3 Bo Horvat/125 10.00 25.00
TCRCJ1 Calle Jarnkrok/399 3.00 8.00
TCRCJ2 Calle Jarnkrok/249 4.00 10.00
TCRCJ3 Calle Jarnkrok/125 5.00 12.00
TCRCL1 Curtis Lazar/399 3.00 8.00
TCRCL2 Curtis Lazar/249 4.00 10.00
TCRCL3 Curtis Lazar/125 5.00 12.00
TCREK1 Evgeny Kuznetsov/399 8.00 20.00
TCREK2 Evgeny Kuznetsov/249 10.00 25.00
TCREK3 Evgeny Kuznetsov/125 12.00 30.00
TCRJD1 Jonathan Drouin/399 8.00 20.00
TCRJD2 Jonathan Drouin/249 10.00 25.00
TCRJD3 Jonathan Drouin/125 12.00 30.00
TCRJG1 Johnny Gaudreau/399 10.00 25.00
TCRJG2 Johnny Gaudreau/249 12.00 30.00
TCRJG3 Johnny Gaudreau/125 15.00 40.00
TCRJH1 Joey Hishon/399 4.00 10.00
TCRJH2 Joey Hishon/249 5.00 12.00
TCRJH3 Joey Hishon/125 6.00 15.00
TCRLD1 Leon Draisaitl/399 15.00 40.00
TCRLD2 Leon Draisaitl/249 20.00 50.00
TCRLD3 Leon Draisaitl/125 25.00 60.00
TCRMV1 Mark Visentin/399 3.00 8.00
TCRMV2 Mark Visentin/249 4.00 10.00
TCRMV3 Mark Visentin/125 5.00 12.00
TCRSR1 Sam Reinhart/399 12.00 30.00
TCRSR2 Sam Reinhart/249 15.00 40.00
TCRSR3 Sam Reinhart/125 20.00 50.00
TCRTR1 Ty Rattie/399 4.00 10.00
TCRTR2 Ty Rattie/249 5.00 12.00

TCRTR3 Ty Rattie/125 6.00 15.00
TCRTT1 Teuvo Teravainen/399 5.00 12.00
TCRTT2 Teuvo Teravainen/249 6.00 15.00
TCRTT3 Teuvo Teravainen/125 8.00 20.00
TCRVN1 V.Namestnikov/399 5.00 12.00
TCRVN2 V.Namestnikov/249 6.00 15.00
TCRVN3 Vladislav Namestnikov/125 8.00 20.00

2014-15 Upper Deck Trilogy Ice Scripts

ISAO Alexander Ovechkin A 50.00 100.00
ISAT Alex Tanguay D 6.00 15.00
ISBH Bobby Hull A 30.00 60.00
ISBO Bobby Orr A 60.00 120.00
ISBO Sergei Bobrovsky D 15.00 40.00
ISBR Bobby Ryan B 10.00 25.00
ISCG Claude Giroux Upd. B 10.00 25.00
ISCL Claude Lemieux D 8.00 20.00
ISCN Cam Neely C 12.00 30.00
ISDB David Backes C 6.00 15.00
ISDG Doug Gilmour B 15.00 40.00
ISDS Darryl Sittler C 12.00 30.00
ISEK Evgeny Kuznetsov D 15.00 40.00
ISEM Evgeni Malkin A 30.00 60.00
ISJB Jonathan Bernier B 10.00 25.00
ISJB Johnny Bucyk C 10.00 25.00
ISJJ Jaromir Jagr C 40.00 80.00
ISJS Jaden Schwartz C 12.00 30.00
ISJT John Tavares D 15.00 40.00
ISLR Larry Robinson B 12.00 30.00
ISMB Mike Bossy B 12.00 30.00
ISMG Marian Gaborik D 10.00 25.00
ISMP Max Pacioretty D 10.00 25.00
ISNK Niklas Kronwall D 8.00 20.00
ISNL Nicklas Lidstrom B 12.00 30.00
ISPE Phil Esposito A 20.00 40.00
ISPS Patrick Sharp Upd. A 10.00 25.00
ISRB Ray Bourque A 25.00 50.00
ISRF Ron Francis D 12.00 30.00
ISRM Ryan McDonagh Upd. B 8.00 20.00
ISSB Scotty Bowman A 12.00 30.00
ISSM Stan Mikita B 30.00 60.00
ISSY Steve Yzerman A 60.00 100.00
ISTL Trevor Linden B 12.00 30.00
ISTT Teuvo Teravainen D 15.00 40.00
ISVL Vincent Lecavalier B 12.00 30.00
ISWG Wayne Gretzky A 200.00 500.00
ISZP Zach Parise A 12.00 30.00

2014-15 Upper Deck Trilogy Signature Pucks

SPAB Aleksander Barkov D 12.00 30.00
SPAG Alex Galchenyuk D 5.00 12.00
SPAI Arturs Irbe B 6.00 15.00
SPAO Alexander Ovechkin A EXCH 30.00 80.00
SPAR Antti Raanta E 8.00 20.00
SPBA David Backes D 5.00 12.00
SPBB Brian Bellows D 6.00 15.00
SPBG Brandon Gormley E 8.00 20.00
SPBH Bobby Hull B 15.00 40.00
SPBL Brian Leetch C 6.00 15.00
SPBO Bobby Orr B 60.00 150.00
SPBP Brad Park C 6.00 15.00
SPBR Martin Brodeur A 30.00 80.00
SPCG Claude Giroux B 8.00 20.00
SPCJ Calle Jarnkrok E EXCH 8.00 20.00
SPCP Corey Perry D EXCH 12.00 30.00
SPDB Dustin Brown D 8.00 20.00
SPDD Danny DeKeyser E 5.00 12.00
SPDG Doug Gilmour B 10.00 25.00
SPDI Dion Phaneuf C 6.00 15.00
SPDK Darcy Kuemper E 8.00 20.00
SPDS Denis Savard D 8.00 20.00
SPEK Evgeny Kuznetsov E 20.00 50.00
SPFP Felix Potvin C 12.00 30.00
SPGC Guy Carbonneau C 8.00 20.00
SPGF Grant Fuhr A 12.00 30.00
SPJA Jacob Trouba E 6.00 15.00
SPJB Jonathan Bernier C 6.00 15.00
SPJD Jonathan Drouin C EXCH 15.00 40.00
SPJG Johnny Gaudreau E 40.00 100.00
SPJH Joey Hishon D 10.00 25.00
SPJJ Jaromir Jagr A 30.00 80.00
SPJO Jonathan Toews A 30.00 80.00
SPJP Joe Pavelski E 10.00 25.00
SPJR Jeremy Roenick B 12.00 30.00
SPJS Joe Sakic A EXCH 30.00 80.00
SPJV James van Riemsdyk E EXCH 6.00 15.00
SPKD David Krejci B 8.00 20.00
SPKL Kari Lehtonen C 6.00 15.00
SPKO Olaf Kolzig C 8.00 20.00
SPLC Logan Couture D 10.00 25.00
SPLE John LeClair C 8.00 20.00
SPLR Larry Robinson C 8.00 20.00
SPLU Luc Robitaille B 8.00 20.00
SPMA Steve Mason E 6.00 15.00
SPMB Mike Bossy B 8.00 20.00
SPMD Matt Duchene C 8.00 20.00
SPMG Marian Gaborik C 8.00 20.00
SPMI Stan Mikita A 10.00 25.00
SPML Mario Lemieux B EXCH 30.00 80.00
SPMM Mike Modano B 12.00 30.00
SPMR Mike Richter C 8.00 20.00
SPMS Martin St. Louis B 8.00 20.00
SPNL Nicklas Lidstrom B 8.00 20.00
SPNM Nathan MacKinnon D 30.00 80.00
SPOA Adam Oates D 8.00 20.00
SPOM Olli Maatta D EXCH 5.00 12.00
SPPD Pavel Datsyuk B 12.00 30.00
SPPE Phil Esposito A 25.00 60.00
SPPJ Jason Pominville B 5.00 12.00
SPPK Phil Kessel B 8.00 20.00
SPPR Patrick Roy A 30.00 80.00
SPPT Pierre Turgeon C 6.00 15.00
SPRH Ron Hextall C 8.00 20.00
SPRM Ryan McDonagh E EXCH 5.00 12.00
SPRN Rick Nash B 8.00 20.00
SPRS Ryan Suter E 6.00 15.00
SPRV Rogie Vachon B 10.00 25.00
SPRY Bobby Ryan E 6.00 15.00
SPSC Sidney Crosby A EXCH 100.00 200.00
SPSM Sean Monahan E EXCH 5.00 12.00
SPST Ryan Strome E 8.00 20.00
SPSY Steve Yzerman A 30.00 80.00
SPTA John Tavares D EXCH 12.00 30.00
SPTE Teuvo Teravainen E 12.00 30.00
SPTJ Tomas Jurco E 5.00 12.00
SPTL Trevor Linden C 8.00 20.00
SPTO Terry O'Reilly C 6.00 15.00
SPTP Tomas Plekanec E 5.00 12.00
SPTR Ty Rattie E 8.00 20.00
SPTS Teemu Selanne B EXCH 15.00 40.00
SPTT Tomas Tatar E 5.00 12.00
SPTW Tom Wilson E 8.00 20.00
SPTY Tyler Toffoli E EXCH 8.00 20.00
SPVN Vladislav Namestnikov E 12.00 30.00
SPWG Wayne Gretzky B 250.00 600.00
SPZP Zach Parise B 8.00 20.00

2014-15 Upper Deck Trilogy Tryptichs

T1ST1 John Tavares JSY/400 6.00 15.00
T1ST2 Taylor Hall JSY/400 4.00 10.00
TANA1 Corey Perry AU/60 EXCH 15.00 40.00
TANA2 Ryan Getzlaf JSY/400 4.00 10.00
TAVS1 Patrick Roy JSY/250 10.00 25.00
TAVS2 Joe Sakic JSY/600 8.00 20.00
TAVS3 Alex Tanguay PATCH/100 5.00 12.00
TBB1 Bobby Orr AU/40 50.00 125.00
TBB2 Phil Esposito JSY/400 6.00 15.00
TBB3 Ray Bourque GLV/50 12.00 30.00
TBEES1 Ray Bourque STK/50 12.00 30.00
TBEES2 Cam Neely STK/50 8.00 20.00
TBEES3 Adam Oates JSY/400 4.00 10.00
TBH1 Brett Hull AU/60 20.00 50.00
TBH2 Brett Hull JSY/600 8.00 20.00
TBOS1 Tuukka Rask JSY/481 5.00 12.00
TBOS2 Zdeno Chara PATCH/150 8.00 20.00
TBOS3 P.Bergeron PATCH/100 10.00 25.00
TCAPS1 Braden Holtby JSY/400 5.00 12.00
TCAPS2 A.Ovechkin STK/150 30.00 80.00
TCAPS3 E.Kuznetsov AU/120 10.00 25.00
TCHI1 Corey Crawford JSY/600 5.00 12.00
TCHI2 Jonathan Toews AU/60 15.00 40.00
TCHI3 Duncan Keith JSY/400 3.00 8.00
TCP1 Carey Price JSY/600 8.00 20.00
TCP2 Carey Price GLV/50 15.00 40.00
TCP3 Carey Price BLK/300 8.00 20.00
TDAL1 Kari Lehtonen JSY/400 3.00 8.00
TDAL2 Tyler Seguin JSY/300 5.00 12.00
TDAL3 Jamie Benn PATCH/75 8.00 20.00
TDRW1 Nicklas Lidstrom JSY/103 5.00 12.00
TDRW2 Steve Yzerman JSY/400 10.00 25.00
TDRW3 Henrik Zetterberg JSY/400 5.00 12.00
TFLY1 Sean Couturier JSY/62 5.00 12.00
TFLY2 Claude Giroux JSY/600 4.00 10.00
TFLY3 Steve Mason JSY/400 3.00 8.00
TGOALIE1 Martin Brodeur JSY/600 10.00 25.00
TGOALIE2 Patrick Roy JSY/250 10.00 25.00
TGOALIE3 Dominik Hasek JSY/400 6.00 15.00
THL1 Henrik Lundqvist BLK/300 10.00 25.00
THL2 H.Lundqvist PATCH/50 20.00 50.00
THL3 Henrik Lundqvist BLK/50 20.00 50.00
THZ1 H.Zetterberg PATCH/50 10.00 25.00
THZ2 Henrik Zetterberg STK/150 10.00 25.00
THZ3 Henrik Zetterberg JSY/400 5.00 12.00
TJR1 Jeremy Roenick AU/60 15.00 40.00
TJR2 Jeremy Roenick JSY/600 6.00 15.00
TJR3 J.Roenick PATCH/100 12.00 30.00
TKINGS1 Wayne Gretzky AU/40 150.00 400.00
TKINGS2 Jari Kurri STK/150 8.00 20.00
TKINGS3 Luc Robitaille JSY/600 4.00 10.00
TLAK1 Jonathan Quick JSY/421 5.00 12.00
TLAK2 Anze Kopitar JSY/400 6.00 15.00
TLAK3 Dustin Brown JSY/400 4.00 10.00
TML1 Mario Lemieux GLV/50 30.00 80.00
TML2 Mario Lemieux AU/40 50.00 125.00
TML3 Mario Lemieux JSY/250 15.00 40.00
TMON1 P.K. Subban PATCH/25 12.00 30.00
TMON3 Max Pacioretty AU/90 8.00 20.00
TNET1 Curtis Joseph PAD/600 8.00 20.00
TNET2 Dominik Hasek PAD/600 10.00 25.00
TNET3 Grant Fuhr PAD/600 10.00 25.00
TNJD1 Adam Henrique JSY/400 3.00 8.00
TNJD2 Jaromir Jagr AU/40 40.00 100.00
TNJD3 Cory Schneider JSY/400 4.00 10.00
TNYR1 Rick Nash STK/142 8.00 20.00
TNYR2 Mats Zuccarello JSY/400 4.00 10.00
TNYR3 Chris Kreider JSY/90 6.00 15.00
TPB1 Pavel Bure AU/40 EXCH 12.00 30.00
TPB2 Pavel Bure TAG/25 10.00 25.00
TPB3 Pavel Bure PATCH/50 8.00 20.00
TPIT1 Ron Francis JSY/400 5.00 12.00
TPIT3 Rob Brown PATCH/50 6.00 15.00
TPR1 Patrick Roy PAD/100 12.00 30.00
TPR2 Patrick Roy JSY/250 10.00 25.00
TPR3 Patrick Roy JSY/250 10.00 25.00
TRAN1 Mike Richter PATCH/25 10.00 25.00
TRAN2 Mark Messier STK/100 15.00 40.00
TRAN3 Henrik Lundqvist BLK/300 10.00 25.00
TRB1 Ray Bourque JSY/400 6.00 15.00
TRB2 Ray Bourque JSY/400 6.00 15.00
TRB3 Ray Bourque AU/60 15.00 40.00
TROOK1 Evgeny Kuznetsov JSY/600 6.00 15.00
TROOK2 Teuvo Teravainen JSY/600 4.00 10.00
TROOK3 Brandon Gormley JSY/600 4.00 10.00
TRUS1 A.Ovechkin JSY/400 15.00 40.00
TRUS2 Evgeni Malkin JSY/400 8.00 20.00
TRUS3 Pavel Datsyuk JSY/100 8.00 20.00
TSC1 Sidney Crosby JSY/400 15.00 40.00
TSC2 Sidney Crosby STK/150 30.00 80.00
TSJS1 Joe Thornton PATCH/50 12.00 30.00
TSJS2 Joe Pavelski AU/100 EXCH 10.00 25.00
TSJS3 Antti Niemi JSY/444 3.00 8.00
TSTAR1 Bobby Orr AU/40 50.00 125.00
TSTAR2 Wayne Gretzky BAG/75 40.00 100.00
TSTAR3 Mario Lemieux PATCH/25 40.00 100.00
TSY1 Steve Yzerman JSY/400 10.00 25.00
TSY2 Steve Yzerman AU/40 30.00 80.00
TSY3 Steve Yzerman STK/50 20.00 50.00
TTBL1 Jonathan Drouin JSY/400 8.00 20.00
TTBL3 Ben Bishop JSY/400 3.00 8.00
TTOR1 Nazem Kadri JSY/400 5.00 12.00
TTOR2 Phil Kessel STK/50 8.00 20.00
TTOR3 J.van Riemsdyk AU/80 6.00 15.00
TVET1 Jaromir Jagr STK/88 25.00 60.00
TVET2 Evgeni Malkin AU/60 20.00 50.00
TWG1 Wayne Gretzky BIB/100 30.00 80.00
TWG2 Wayne Gretzky AU/40 150.00 400.00
TWG3 Wayne Gretzky STK/50 60.00 150.00
TWINGS1 Henrik Zetterberg JSY/400 5.00 12.00
TWINGS3 Pavel Datsyuk AU/60 15.00 40.00

2015-16 Upper Deck Trilogy

COMP.SET w/o RC's (100) 12.00 30.00
1 Ryan Getzlaf .60 1.50
2 Corey Perry 1.00 2.50
3 Frederik Andersen .75 2.00
4 Shane Doan .50 1.25
5 Oliver Ekman-Larsson .60 1.50
6 Mikkel Boedker .40 1.00
7 Zdeno Chara .60 1.50
8 Patrice Bergeron .75 2.00
9 Tuukka Rask .75 2.00
10 Sam Reinhart 1.25 3.00
11 Zemgus Girgensons .50 1.25
12 Matt Moulson .40 1.00
13 Johnny Gaudreau 1.00 2.50
14 Sean Monahan .40 1.00
15 Jiri Hudler .50 1.25
16 Eric Staal .75 2.00
17 Cam Ward .60 1.50
18 Elias Lindholm .60 1.50
19 Jonathan Toews 1.00 2.50
20 Duncan Keith .50 1.25
21 Corey Crawford .75 2.00
22 Nathan MacKinnon 2.50 6.00
23 Gabriel Landeskog .75 2.00
24 Matt Duchene .60 1.50
25 Ryan Johansen .50 1.25
26 Brandon Dubinsky .40 1.00
27 Scott Hartnell .40 1.00
28 Tyler Seguin .75 2.00
29 Jason Spezza .60 1.50
30 Kari Lehtonen .50 1.25
31 Henrik Zetterberg .75 2.00
32 Pavel Datsyuk 1.00 2.50
33 Gustav Nyquist .40 1.00
34 Taylor Hall .60 1.50
35 Ryan Nugent-Hopkins .75 2.00
36 Jordan Eberle .60 1.50
37 Aaron Ekblad .75 2.00
38 Jaromir Jagr 2.00 5.00
39 Jonathan Huberdeau .75 2.00
40 Jonathan Quick .75 2.00
41 Jeff Carter .50 1.25
42 Anze Kopitar 1.00 2.50
43 Zach Parise .60 1.50
44 Ryan Suter .50 1.25
45 Jason Pominville .40 1.00
46 Carey Price 1.25 3.00
47 P.K. Subban .75 2.00
48 Max Pacioretty .60 1.50
49 Shea Weber .50 1.25
50 Pekka Rinne .60 1.50
51 Calle Jarnkrok .50 1.25
52 Cory Schneider .60 1.50
53 Adam Henrique .50 1.25
54 Michael Cammalleri .50 1.25
55 John Tavares 1.00 2.50
56 Kyle Okposo .40 1.00
57 Ryan Strome .60 1.50
58 Henrik Lundqvist 1.50 4.00
59 Rick Nash .60 1.50
60 Mats Zuccarello .60 1.50
61 Mika Zibanejad .75 2.00
62 Craig Anderson .60 1.50
63 Erik Karlsson .75 2.00
64 Sean Couturier .50 1.25
65 Jakub Voracek .50 1.25
66 Claude Giroux .60 1.50
67 Sidney Crosby 2.50 6.00
68 Marc-Andre Fleury 1.25 3.00
69 Evgeni Malkin 1.25 3.00
70 Joe Thornton 1.00 2.50
71 Joe Pavelski .75 2.00
72 Logan Couture .75 2.00
73 Jake Allen .60 1.50
74 Vladimir Taraconko .75 2.00
75 Jaden Schwartz .75 2.00
76 Steven Stamkos 1.25 3.00
77 Ben Bishop .50 1.25
78 Tyler Johnson .40 1.00
79 Jonathan Bernier .50 1.25
80 James van Riemsdyk .50 1.25
81 Nazem Kadri .75 2.00
82 Henrik Sedin .75 2.00
83 Ryan Miller .60 1.50
84 Bo Horvat .75 2.00
85 Alexander Ovechkin 2.50 6.00
86 Braden Holtby .75 2.00
87 Nicklas Backstrom .60 1.50
88 Blake Wheeler .60 1.50
89 Jacob Trouba .50 1.25
90 Mark Scheifele 1.00 2.50
91 Steve Yzerman 1.50 4.00
92 Felix Potvin 1.00 2.50
93 Mark Messier 1.25 3.00
94 Glenn Hall .60 1.50
95 Martin Brodeur 1.50 4.00
96 Ray Bourque 1.00 2.50
97 Mike Liut .40 1.00
98 Patrick Roy 1.50 4.00
99 Brett Hull 1.25 3.00
100 Wayne Gretzky 2.00 5.00
101 Connor McDavid RC 125.00 300.00
102 Henrik Samuelsson RC 1.00 2.50
103 Oscar Lindberg RC 1.50 4.00
104 Shane Prince RC 1.00 2.50
105 Robby Fabbri RC 2.00 5.00
106 Jacob de la Rose RC 1.50 4.00
107 Max Domi RC 3.00 8.00
108 Kevin Fiala RC 2.00 5.00
109 Emile Poirier RC 1.25 3.00
110 Sam Bennett RC 5.00 12.00
111 Brock McGinn RC 1.50 4.00
112 Antoine Bibeau RC 1.50 4.00
113 Derek Forbort RC 1.25 3.00
114 Noah Hanifin RC 2.50 6.00
115 Artemi Panarin RC 6.00 15.00
116 Ryan Hartman RC 2.00 5.00
117 Nick Cousins RC 1.50 4.00
118 Kyle Baun RC 1.50 4.00
119 Slater Koekkoek RC 1.00 2.50
120 Dylan Larkin RC 10.00 25.00
121 Daniel Sprong RC 2.00 5.00
122 Josh Anderson RC 3.00 8.00
123 Brendan Ranford RC 1.25 3.00
124 Nikolaj Ehlers RC 3.00 8.00
125 Stefan Noesen RC 1.00 2.50
126 Nicolas Petan RC 1.50 4.00
127 Nikolay Goldobin RC 1.50 4.00
128 Connor Hellebuyck RC 6.00 15.00
129 Anthony Stolarz RC 4.00 10.00
130 Matt Puempel RC 1.25 3.00
131 Jake Virtanen RC 2.00 5.00
132 Mikko Rantanen RC 8.00 20.00
133 Jack Eichel RC 12.00 30.00
134 Connor McDavid AU/499 150.00 250.00
135 Henrik Samuelsson AU/499 2.00 5.00
136 Oscar Lindberg AU/499 3.00 8.00
137 Shane Prince AU/499 2.00 5.00
138 Robby Fabbri AU/499 4.00 10.00
139 Jacob de la Rose AU/499 3.00 8.00
140 Max Domi AU/499 12.00 30.00
141 Kevin Fiala AU/499 4.00 10.00
142 Emile Poirier AU/499 2.50 6.00
143 Sam Bennett AU/499 10.00 25.00
144 Brock McGinn AU/499 3.00 8.00
145 Antoine Bibeau AU/499 3.00 8.00
146 Derek Forbort AU/499 2.50 6.00
147 Noah Hanifin AU/499 5.00 12.00
148 Artemi Panarin AU/499 30.00 60.00
149 Ryan Hartman AU/499 4.00 10.00
150 Nick Cousins AU/499 3.00 8.00
151 Kyle Baun AU/499 3.00 8.00
152 Slater Koekkoek AU/499 2.00 5.00
153 Dylan Larkin AU/499 50.00 100.00
154 Daniel Sprong AU/499 5.00 12.00
155 Josh Anderson AU/499 6.00 15.00
156 Brendan Ranford AU/499 2.50 6.00
157 Nikolaj Ehlers AU/499 6.00 15.00
158 Stefan Noesen AU/499 2.00 5.00
159 Nicolas Petan AU/499 3.00 8.00
160 Nikolay Goldobin AU/499 3.00 8.00
161 Connor Hellebuyck AU/499 10.00 25.00
162 Anthony Stolarz AU/499 8.00 20.00
163 Matt Puempel AU/499 2.50 6.00
164 Jake Virtanen AU/499 6.00 15.00
165 Mikko Rantanen AU/499 30.00 80.00
166 Jack Eichel/499 15.00 40.00
167 Connor McDavid AU/49 500.00 800.00
168 Henrik Samuelsson AU/49 6.00 15.00
169 Oscar Lindberg AU/49 10.00 25.00
170 Shane Prince AU/49 6.00 15.00
171 Robby Fabbri AU/49 12.00 30.00
172 Jacob de la Rose AU/49 10.00 25.00
173 Max Domi AU/49 20.00 50.00
174 Kevin Fiala AU/49 12.00 30.00
175 Emile Poirier AU/49 8.00 20.00
176 Sam Bennett AU/49 30.00 80.00
177 Brock McGinn AU/49 10.00 25.00
178 Antoine Bibeau AU/49 10.00 25.00
179 Derek Forbort AU/49 8.00 20.00
180 Noah Hanifin AU/49 15.00 40.00
181 Artemi Panarin AU/49 EXCH 125.00 200.00
182 Ryan Hartman AU/49 12.00 30.00
183 Nick Cousins AU/49 10.00 25.00
184 Kyle Baun AU/49 10.00 25.00
185 Slater Koekkoek AU/49 6.00 15.00
186 Dylan Larkin AU/49 200.00 350.00
187 Daniel Sprong AU/49 20.00 40.00
188 Josh Anderson AU/49 20.00 50.00
189 Brendan Ranford AU/49 8.00 20.00
190 Nikolaj Ehlers AU/49 20.00 50.00
191 Stefan Noesen AU/49 6.00 15.00
192 Nicolas Petan AU/49 10.00 25.00
193 Nikolay Goldobin AU/49 10.00 25.00
194 Connor Hellebuyck AU/49 40.00 80.00
195 Anthony Stolarz AU/49 25.00 60.00
196 Matt Puempel AU/49 8.00 20.00
197 Jake Virtanen AU/49 30.00 60.00
198 Mikko Rantanen AU/49 50.00 125.00
199 Jack Eichel/49 60.00 120.00
200 McDv/Lrkn/Dmi AU/25 000.00 1200.00
201 Colton Parayko/799 RC 4.00 10.00
202 Zachary Fucale/799 RC 2.00 5.00
203 Ben Hutton/799 RC 2.50 6.00
204 Matt O'Connor/799 RC 2.00 5.00
205 Jordan Weal/799 RC 1.50 4.00
206 Mattias Janmark/799 RC 2.50 6.00
207 Jared McCann/799 RC 3.00 8.00
208 Hunter Shinkaruk/799 RC 2.50 6.00
209 Andreas Athanasiou/799 RC 6.00 15.00
210 Mike Condon/799 RC 2.50 6.00
211 Colton Parayko AU/399 6.00 15.00
212 Zachary Fucale AU/399 3.00 8.00
213 Ben Hutton AU/399 4.00 10.00
214 Matt O'Connor AU/399 3.00 8.00
215 Jordan Weal AU/399 2.50 6.00
216 Mattias Janmark AU/399 4.00 10.00
217 Jared McCann AU/399 5.00 12.00
218 Hunter Shinkaruk AU/399 4.00 10.00
219 Andreas Athanasiou AU/399 10.00 25.00
220 Mike Condon AU/399 4.00 10.00
221 Colton Parayko AU/49 20.00 50.00
222 Zachary Fucale AU/49 10.00 25.00
223 Ben Hutton AU/49 12.00 30.00
224 Matt O'Connor AU/49 10.00 25.00
225 Jordan Weal AU/49 8.00 20.00
226 Mattias Janmark AU/49 12.00 30.00
227 Jared McCann AU/49 15.00 40.00
228 Hunter Shinkaruk AU/49 12.00 30.00
229 Andreas Athanasiou AU/49 30.00 80.00
230 Mike Condon AU/49 12.00 30.00

2015-16 Upper Deck Trilogy Rainbow Black

COMMON PATCH/40-78 6.00 15.00
PATCH UNL.STAR/40-78 8.00 20.00
COMMON PATCH/30-39 6.00 15.00
PATCH SEMISTAR/30-39 8.00 20.00
PATCH UNL.STAR/30-39 10.00 25.00
COMMON PATCH/15-29 8.00 20.00
PATCH SEMISTAR/15-29 10.00 25.00
PATCH UNL.STAR/15-29 12.00 30.00
*101-133 ROOK/49: 1.5X TO 4X BASIC RC/999
*ROOK.AU/130-209: .6X TO 1.5X BASIC AU/499
*ROOK.AU/57-95: .8X TO 2X BASIC AU/499
*ROOK.AU/30-47: 1X TO 2.5X BASIC AU/499
*ROOK.AU/15-27: 1.2X TO 3X BASIC AU/499
13 Johnny Gaudreau PATCH/40 12.00 30.00
19 Jonathan Toews PATCH/28 20.00 50.00
21 Corey Crawford PATCH/32 12.00 30.00
46 Carey Price PATCH/44 30.00 60.00
58 Henrik Lundqvist PATCH/33 25.00 60.00
67 Sidney Crosby PATCH/28 50.00 125.00
68 Marc-Andre Fleury PATCH/34 20.00 50.00
76 Steven Stamkos PATCH/29 25.00 60.00
87 Nicklas Backstrom PATCH/18 12.00 30.00
95 Martin Brodeur PATCH/17 30.00 80.00
96 Ray Bourque PATCH/57 12.00 30.00
100 Wayne Gretzky PATCH/18 75.00 125.00
116 Ryan Hartman/49 8.00 20.00
148 Artemi Panarin AU/15 EXCH 125.00 200.00
149 Ryan Hartman AU/30 10.00 25.00
153 Dylan Larkin AU/15 200.00 350.00
161 Connor Hellebuyck AU/130 25.00 50.00

2015-16 Upper Deck Trilogy Rainbow Blue

*1-100 VETS/401-898: 1.2X TO 3X BASIC CARDS
*1-100 VETS/202-395: 1.5X TO 4X BASIC CARDS
*1-100 VETS/108-179: 2X TO 5X BASIC CARDS
*1-100 VETS/60-91: 2.5X TO 6X BASIC CARDS
*101-133 ROOK/399: .5X TO 1.2X BASIC RC/999
*134-166 RK.AU/199: .5X TO 1.2X BASIC AU/499
*167-198 RK.AU/64-97: .25X TO .6X BASIC AU/49
*167-198 RK.AU/41-56: .3X TO .8X BASIC AU/49
*167-198 RK.AU/30-39: .4X TO 1X BASIC AU/49
*167-198 RK.AU/15-29: .5X TO 1.2X BASIC AU/49
21 Corey Crawford/147 4.00 10.00
87 Nicklas Backstrom/572 2.00 5.00
100 Wayne Gretzky/91 20.00 40.00
116 Ryan Hartman/399 2.50 6.00
134 Connor McDavid AU/199 175.00 300.00
143 Sam Bennett AU/199 12.00 30.00
148 Artemi Panarin AU/199 50.00 100.00
149 Ryan Hartman AU/199 5.00 12.00
153 Dylan Larkin AU/199 90.00 150.00
165 Mikko Rantanen AU/199 40.00 100.00
166 Jack Eichel/199 15.00 40.00
167 Connor McDavid AU/97 350.00 600.00
176 Sam Bennett AU/93 20.00 50.00
181 Artemi Panarin AU/72 90.00 150.00
182 Ryan Hartman AU/38 12.00 30.00
186 Dylan Larkin AU/71 125.00 250.00
198 Mikko Rantanen AU/96 40.00 100.00

2015-16 Upper Deck Trilogy Rainbow Green

*134-166 PATCH/35: 1X TO 2.5X JSY/599
1 Ryan Getzlaf JSY/105 4.00 10.00
2 Corey Perry JSY/105 6.00 15.00
3 Frederik Andersen JSY/113 5.00 12.00
4 Shane Doan JSY/95 3.00 8.00
5 Oliver Ekman-Larsson JSY/110 4.00 10.00
6 Mikkel Boedker JSY/108 2.50 6.00
7 Zdeno Chara JSY/97 4.00 10.00
8 Patrice Bergeron JSY/103 5.00 12.00
9 Tuukka Rask JSY/107 5.00 12.00
10 Sam Reinhart JSY/114 8.00 20.00
11 Zemgus Girgensons JSY/113 3.00 8.00
12 Matt Moulson JSY/107 2.50 6.00
13 Johnny Gaudreau JSY/114 6.00 15.00
14 Sean Monahan JSY/113 2.50 6.00
15 Jiri Hudler JSY/103 3.00 8.00
16 Eric Staal JSY/103 5.00 12.00
17 Cam Ward JSY/105 4.00 10.00
18 Elias Lindholm JSY/113 4.00 10.00
19 Jonathan Toews JSY/107 6.00 15.00
20 Duncan Keith JSY/105 3.00 8.00
21 Corey Crawford JSY/105 5.00 12.00
22 Nathan MacKinnon JSY/113 15.00 40.00
23 Gabriel Landeskog JSY/111 5.00 12.00
24 Matt Duchene JSY/109 4.00 10.00
25 Ryan Johansen JSY/111 3.00 8.00
26 Brandon Dubinsky JSY/106 2.50 6.00
27 Scott Hartnell JSY/100 2.50 6.00
28 Tyler Seguin JSY/110 5.00 12.00
29 Jason Spezza JSY/102 4.00 10.00
30 Kari Lehtonen JSY/103 3.00 8.00
31 Henrik Zetterberg JSY/102 5.00 12.00
32 Pavel Datsyuk JSY/101 6.00 15.00
33 Gustav Nyquist JSY/111 2.50 6.00
34 Taylor Hall JSY/110 4.00 10.00
35 Ryan Nugent-Hopkins JSY/111 5.00 12.00
36 Jordan Eberle JSY/110 4.00 10.00
37 Aaron Ekblad JSY/114 5.00 12.00
39 Jonathan Huberdeau JSY/112 5.00 12.00
40 Jonathan Quick JSY/107 5.00 12.00
41 Jeff Carter JSY/105 3.00 8.00
42 Anze Kopitar JSY/106 6.00 15.00
43 Zach Parise JSY/105 4.00 10.00
45 Jason Pominville JSY/103 2.50 6.00
46 Carey Price JSY/107 8.00 20.00
47 P.K. Subban JSY/109 5.00 12.00
48 Max Pacioretty JSY/108 4.00 10.00
49 Shea Weber JSY/105 3.00 8.00
50 Pekka Rinne JSY/105 4.00 10.00
51 Calle Jarnkrok JSY/113 3.00 8.00
52 Cory Schneider JSY/108 4.00 10.00
53 Adam Henrique JSY/110 3.00 8.00
54 Michael Cammalleri JSY/102 3.00 8.00
55 John Tavares JSY/109 6.00 15.00
56 Kyle Okposo JSY/107 2.50 6.00
57 Ryan Strome JSY/113 4.00 10.00
58 Henrik Lundqvist JSY/105 10.00 25.00
59 Rick Nash JSY/102 4.00 10.00
60 Mats Zuccarello JSY/110 4.00 10.00
61 Mika Zibanejad JSY/111 5.00 12.00
62 Craig Anderson JSY/102 4.00 10.00
63 Erik Karlsson JSY/109 5.00 12.00
64 Sean Couturier JSY/111 3.00 8.00
65 Jakub Voracek JSY/108 3.00 8.00
66 Claude Giroux JSY/107 4.00 10.00
67 Sidney Crosby JSY/105 15.00 40.00
68 Marc-Andre Fleury JSY/103 8.00 20.00
69 Evgeni Malkin JSY/106 8.00 20.00
70 Joe Thornton JSY/97 6.00 15.00
71 Joe Pavelski JSY/106 5.00 12.00
72 Logan Couture JSY/109 5.00 12.00
73 Jake Allen JSY/112 4.00 10.00
74 Vladimir Tarasenko JSY/112 5.00 12.00
75 Jaden Schwartz JSY/111 5.00 12.00
76 Steven Stamkos JSY/108 8.00 20.00
77 Ben Bishop JSY/108 3.00 8.00
79 Jonathan Bernier JSY/107 3.00 8.00
80 James van Riemsdyk JSY/109 3.00 8.00
81 Nazem Kadri JSY/109 5.00 12.00
82 Henrik Sedin JSY/100 5.00 12.00
83 Ryan Miller JSY/102 4.00 10.00
85 Alexander Ovechkin JSY/105 15.00 40.00
86 Braden Holtby JSY/110 5.00 12.00
87 Nicklas Backstrom JSY/107 4.00 10.00
88 Blake Wheeler JSY/108 4.00 10.00
89 Jacob Trouba JSY/113 3.00 8.00
90 Mark Scheifele JSY/111 6.00 15.00
91 Steve Yzerman JSY/83 10.00 25.00
93 Mark Messier JSY/79 8.00 20.00
94 Glenn Hall JSY/52 4.00 10.00
95 Martin Brodeur JSY/91 10.00 25.00
96 Ray Bourque JSY/79 6.00 15.00
98 Patrick Roy JSY/84 10.00 25.00
99 Brett Hull JSY/86 8.00 20.00
100 Wayne Gretzky JSY/79 12.00 30.00
101 Connor McDavid JSY/599 150.00 400.00
102 Henrik Samuelsson JSY/599 1.50 4.00
104 Shane Prince JSY/599 1.50 4.00
105 Robby Fabbri JSY/599 3.00 8.00
106 Jacob de la Rose JSY/599 2.50 6.00
107 Max Domi JSY/599 5.00 12.00
108 Kevin Fiala JSY/599 3.00 8.00
109 Emile Poirier JSY/599 2.00 5.00
110 Sam Bennett JSY/599 8.00 20.00
111 Brock McGinn JSY/599 2.50 6.00
112 Antoine Bibeau JSY/599 2.50 6.00
113 Derek Forbort JSY/599 2.00 5.00
114 Noah Hanifin JSY/599 4.00 10.00
116 Ryan Hartman JSY/599 3.00 8.00
117 Nick Cousins JSY/599 2.50 6.00
118 Kyle Baun JSY/599 2.50 6.00
119 Slater Koekkoek JSY/599 1.50 4.00
120 Dylan Larkin JSY/599 12.00 30.00
122 Josh Anderson JSY/599 5.00 12.00
124 Nikolaj Ehlers JSY/599 5.00 12.00
125 Stefan Noesen JSY/599 1.50 4.00
126 Nicolas Petan JSY/599 2.50 6.00
128 Connor Hellebuyck JSY/599 10.00 25.00
130 Matt Puempel JSY/599 2.00 5.00
131 Jake Virtanen JSY/599 3.00 8.00
133 Jack Eichel JSY/599 10.00 25.00
149 Ryan Hartman Patch/35 8.00 20.00

2015-16 Upper Deck Trilogy Ice Scripts

ISAG Alex Galchenyuk B 5.00 12.00
ISAK Anze Kopitar C EXCH 12.00 30.00
ISAO Alexander Ovechkin A 60.00 100.00
ISBG Brendan Gallagher D 8.00 20.00
ISBO Bobby Orr A 60.00 100.00
ISBS Brandon Saad D 6.00 15.00
ISCC Chris Chelios B 12.00 30.00
ISCK Chris Kreider D 10.00 25.00
ISCM Connor McDavid D 175.00 300.00
ISCP Carey Price B 30.00 60.00
ISDP Derrick Pouliot E 5.00 12.00
ISDS Darryl Sittler B 10.00 25.00
ISFA Frederik Andersen B 10.00 25.00
ISGL Gabriel Landeskog D 10.00 25.00
ISJB Jamie Benn A 8.00 20.00
ISJB Jonathan Bernier C 6.00 15.00
ISJJ Jaromir Jagr A 30.00 60.00
ISJP Joe Pavelski B 10.00 25.00
ISJR James van Riemsdyk D 6.00 15.00
ISJT John Tavares B 12.00 30.00
ISJT John Tavares C 12.00 30.00
ISJV Jakub Voracek C 6.00 15.00
ISKT Kyle Turris D 6.00 15.00
ISMG Mike Gartner D 10.00 25.00
ISML Mario Lemieux A 60.00 150.00
ISMN Markus Naslund D 8.00 20.00
ISMR Morgan Rielly B 8.00 20.00
ISMS Mats Sundin A 20.00 40.00
ISNB Nick Bjugstad E 5.00 12.00
ISNM Nathan MacKinnon A 30.00 80.00
ISPD Pavel Datsyuk B 12.00 30.00
ISPM Patrick Marleau A 8.00 20.00
ISRB Rob Blake B 12.00 30.00
ISRJ Ryan Johansen D 6.00 15.00
ISRM Ryan Miller A 8.00 20.00
ISRN Rick Nash B 8.00 20.00
ISSC Sidney Crosby A 75.00 125.00
ISSP Jason Spezza B 10.00 25.00
ISSU Malcolm Subban E 10.00 25.00
ISSY Steve Yzerman A 60.00 100.00
ISTH Taylor Hall D 12.00 30.00
ISTJ Tyler Johnson E 5.00 12.00
ISWG Wayne Gretzky B 200.00 500.00

2015-16 Upper Deck Trilogy Signature Pucks

SPAD Anthony Duclair B 8.00 20.00
SPAE Aaron Ekblad B 20.00 40.00
SPAI Arturs Irbe C 8.00 20.00
SPAO Alexander Ovechkin B 30.00 60.00
SPAV Andrei Vasilevskiy F 10.00 25.00
SPBB Ben Bishop E 5.00 12.00
SPBE Jonathan Bernier C 8.00 20.00
SPBG Brendan Gallagher D 10.00 25.00
SPBH Bo Horvat E 10.00 25.00
SPBR Brett Ritchie D 4.00 10.00
SPCC Chris Chelios B 10.00 25.00
SPCH Charles Hudon F 8.00 20.00
SPCM Connor McDavid C 150.00 250.00
SPCP Carey Price B 30.00 60.00
SPCS Cory Schneider C 10.00 25.00
SPDG Doug Gilmour B 15.00 40.00
SPDO Max Domi F 12.00 30.00
SPDP Derrick Pouliot F 4.00 10.00
SPFA Frederik Andersen D 8.00 20.00
SPFP Felix Potvin D 10.00 25.00
SPGA Mike Gartner D 8.00 20.00
SPGN Gustav Nyquist B 6.00 15.00
SPJB Jordan Binnington F 10.00 25.00
SPJI Jarome Iginla B 12.00 30.00
SPJK John Klingberg F 8.00 20.00
SPJL Jori Lehtera E 4.00 10.00
SPJP Joe Pavelski C 12.00 30.00
SPJT Jonathan Toews B 30.00 60.00
SPJV John Vanbiesbrouck C 10.00 25.00
SPKO Kyle Okposo B 6.00 15.00
SPKT Kyle Turris F 5.00 12.00
SPKY Keith Yandle B 6.00 15.00
SPLD Leon Draisaitl E 12.00 30.00
SPLE Mario Lemieux A 60.00 100.00
SPMA Martin Brodeur B 40.00 80.00
SPMB Martin Biron E 5.00 12.00
SPMC Marty McSorley D 10.00 25.00
SPMD Marcel Dionne C 12.00 30.00
SPMF Marc-Andre Fleury B 15.00 40.00
SPMG Mikael Granlund E 5.00 12.00
SPMK Mike Keane D 5.00 12.00
SPML Mike Liut E 4.00 10.00
SPMS Malcolm Subban F 10.00 25.00
SPMZ Mats Zuccarello D 6.00 15.00
SPNB Nick Bjugstad F 4.00 10.00
SPNE Nikolaj Ehlers F 8.00 20.00
SPNH Noah Hanifin C 15.00 40.00
SPNK Nikita Kucherov F EXCH 12.00 30.00
SPOR Bobby Orr B 60.00 120.00
SPPA David Pastrnak E 12.00 30.00
SPPD Pavel Datsyuk B 15.00 40.00
SPPM Patrick Marleau B 10.00 25.00
SPPO Jason Pominville D 4.00 10.00
SPPR Patrick Roy A 60.00 100.00
SPPS Patrick Sharp B 10.00 25.00
SPRB Rob Blake B 10.00 25.00
SPRJ Ryan Johansen D 5.00 12.00
SPRK Ryan Kesler D 8.00 20.00
SPRM Ryan Miller B 10.00 25.00
SPRN Rick Nash B 10.00 25.00
SPRY Bobby Ryan C 8.00 20.00
SPSB Sam Bennett E 20.00 50.00
SPSC Sidney Crosby A 60.00 100.00
SPSE Sean Couturier E 5.00 12.00
SPSL Steve Larmer D 5.00 12.00
SPSR Sam Reinhart C 20.00 50.00
SPSV Semyon Varlamov C 10.00 25.00
SPTA John Tavares B 15.00 40.00
SPTB Tom Barrasso D 6.00 15.00
SPTJ Tyler Johnson F 4.00 10.00
SPTK Torey Krug F 5.00 12.00
SPVI Jake Virtanen E 8.00 20.00
SPVO Jakub Voracek E 5.00 12.00
SPWG Wayne Gretzky B 250.00 600.00
SPZG Zemgus Girgensons F 5.00 12.00
SPZP Zach Parise B 10.00 25.00

2015-16 Upper Deck Trilogy Signature Pucks Draft Logo

SPCM1 Connor McDavid/21 300.00 450.00

2015-16 Upper Deck Trilogy Signature Pucks Dual

SP2BK Burakovsky/Kuznetsov C 15.00 40.00
SP2FP Fleury/C.Price A EXCH 50.00 100.00
SP2GM Gretzky/C.McDavid B 750.00 2000.00
SP2JK T.Johnson/Kucherov C 25.00 60.00
SP2LM Lndeskg/McKinn B EXCH 40.00 80.00
SP2PG Pacioretty/Galchenyuk B 30.00 60.00
SP2RT B.Ryan/K.Turris C 10.00 25.00
SP2RW P.Rinne/S.Weber B 15.00 40.00
SP2SN R.Strome/B.Nelson C 12.00 30.00
SP2ST P.Sharp/J.Toews A 40.00 80.00
SP2TN T.Tatar/G.Nyquist C 8.00 20.00
SP2WR Wennberg/Rychel C EXCH 8.00 20.00

2015-16 Upper Deck Trilogy Tryptichs

TJJ1 Jaromir Jagr PATCH/50 25.00 50.00
TJJ2 Jaromir Jagr STK/25 30.00 80.00
TJJ3 Jaromir Jagr STK/75 25.00 60.00
TMB1 Martin Brodeur BLKR/50 25.00 60.00
TMB2 Martin Brodeur PATCH/25 20.00 50.00
TMB3 Martin Brodeur GLV/25 15.00 40.00
TON1 Owen Nolan PATCH/25 10.00 25.00
TON2 Owen Nolan AU/60 8.00 20.00
TON3 Owen Nolan JSY/150 3.00 8.00
TSC1 Sidney Crosby JSY/100 12.00 30.00
TSC2 Sidney Crosby AU/20 75.00 150.00
TSC3 Sidney Crosby STK/50 30.00 80.00
TWG1 Wayne Gretzky STK/25 60.00 120.00
TWG2 Wayne Gretzky AU/20 200.00 500.00
TWG3 Wayne Gretzky Socks/15 60.00 120.00
TBOS2 Ray Bourque AU/40 15.00 40.00
TBOS3 Zdeno Chara PATCH/75 8.00 20.00
TCBH1 Bobby Hull AU/40 12.00 30.00
TCBH2 Glenn Hall JSY/50 6.00 15.00
TCBH3 Tony Esposito AU/40 10.00 25.00
TCGY1 Jiri Hudler JSY/250 2.50 6.00
TCGY2 Sean Monahan JSY/200 2.00 5.00
TCGY3 Johnny Gaudreau JSY/150 5.00 12.00
TCHI1 Corey Crawford JSY/200 4.00 10.00
TCHI2 Patrick Kane PATCH/25 20.00 50.00
TCOL1 Matt Duchene JSY/200 3.00 8.00
TCOL2 Gabriel Landeskog AU/60 10.00 25.00
TEDM1 Jari Kurri STK/25 10.00 25.00
TEDM2 Glenn Anderson AU/40 8.00 20.00
TEDM3 Grant Fuhr STK/25 15.00 40.00
TFLY1 Jakub Voracek AU/60 6.00 15.00
TFLY2 Claude Giroux PATCH/25 10.00 25.00
TFLY3 Steve Mason JSY/250 2.50 6.00
TLAK1 Drew Doughty GLV/25 10.00 25.00
TLAK3 Jeff Carter GLV/25 6.00 15.00
TNET1 Terry Sawchuk STK/25 20.00 40.00
TNET3 Patrick Roy STK/50 20.00 50.00
TNYI1 Kyle Okposo PATCH/25 6.00 15.00
TNYI2 John Tavares GLV/25 12.00 30.00
TNYI3 Ryan Strome JSY/250 3.00 8.00
TOIL1 Nail Yakupov PATCH/50 5.00 12.00
TOIL2 Taylor Hall AU/80 10.00 25.00
TOIL3 Ryan Nugent-Hopkins JSY/200 4.00 10.00
TPHI1 Bobby Clarke AU/60 20.00 40.00
TPHI3 Dave Schultz AU/80 8.00 20.00
TRC11 Connor McDavid JSY/250 100.00 250.00
TRC12 Jack Eichel JSY/250 10.00 25.00
TRC13 Sam Bennett JSY/250 8.00 20.00
TRC21 Kevin Fiala JSY/250 4.00 10.00
TRC22 Ryan Hartman JSY/250 4.00 10.00
TRC23 Henrik Samuelsson JSY/250 2.00 5.00
TRC31 Emile Poirier JSY/250 2.50 6.00
TRC32 Matt Puempel JSY/250 2.50 6.00
TRC33 Connor Hellebuyck JSY/250 10.00 25.00
TRUS1 Alexander Ovechkin AU/20 40.00 80.00
TRUS2 Evgeni Malkin PATCH/25 20.00 50.00
TRUS3 Pavel Datsyuk PAD/15 25.00 50.00
TTBL1 Steven Stamkos JSY/150 6.00 15.00
TTBL2 Jonathan Drouin AU/60 10.00 25.00
TTBL3 Ondrej Palat PATCH/50 6.00 15.00
TTML1 Nazem Kadri JSY/150 4.00 10.00
TTML2 Jonathan Bernier AU/60 6.00 15.00

TTML3 James van
Riemsdyk PATCH/50 6.00 15.00
TTOR1 Felix Potvin AU/40 15.00 40.00
TTOR2 Doug Gilmour STK/25 12.00 30.00
TTOR3 Borje Salming AU/40 12.00 30.00
TVAN1 Henrik Sedin STK/50 10.00 25.00
TVAN2 Bo Horvat AU/80 12.00 30.00
TVAN3 Ryan Miller JSY/150 3.00 8.00
TGOON1 Marty McSorley STK/25 8.00 20.00
TGOON2 Dave Schultz AU/60 8.00 20.00
TGOON3 Wendel Clark STK/50 15.00 40.00
TPENS2 Tom Barrasso AU/80 8.00 20.00
TPENS3 Paul Coffey PATCH/15 15.00 40.00
TSTAR2 Wayne Gretzky AU/20 200.00 500.00
TSTAR3 Connor McDavid AU/60 750.00 2000.00
TDRAFT1 Nathan MacKinnon
PATCH/25 40.00 100.00
TDRAFT2 Aleksander Barkov JSY/250 5.00 12.00
TDRAFT3 Jonathan Drouin AU/80 6.00 15.00
TISLES1 Bob Bourne AU/40 6.00 15.00
TISLES2 Billy Smith PATCH/25 10.00 25.00
TISLES3 Mike Bossy AU/20 25.00 50.00
TWINGS1 Chris Chelios AU/40 10.00 25.00
TWINGS2 Nicklas Lidstrom AU/40 12.00 30.00
TWINGS3 Steve Yzerman AU/20 40.00 80.00
TGOALIE1 Carey Price BLKR/50 20.00 50.00
TGOALIE2 Jonathan Quick BLKR/50 12.00 30.00

2016-17 Upper Deck Trilogy

1 Patrick Kane 1.25 3.00
2 Steven Stamkos 1.25 3.00
3 Tyler Toffoli .60 1.50
4 Martin Jones .50 1.25
5 John Tavares 1.00 2.50
6 Joe Pavelski .75 2.00
7 Henrik Lundqvist 1.50 4.00
8 Ryan Getzlaf .60 1.50
9 Dylan Larkin .75 2.00
10 Evgeni Malkin 1.25 3.00
11 Braden Holtby .75 2.00
12 Jaromir Jagr 2.00 5.00
13 Morgan Rielly .60 1.50
14 Jarome Iginla .75 2.00
15 Jonathan Toews 1.00 2.50
16 Tuukka Rask .75 2.00
17 Erik Karlsson .75 2.00
18 Anze Kopitar 1.00 2.50
19 Matt Duchene .60 1.50
20 Carey Price 1.25 3.00
21 Tyler Seguin .75 2.00
22 Max Pacioretty .60 1.50
23 Filip Forsberg 1.00 2.50
24 Jaden Schwartz .75 2.00
25 Connor McDavid 3.00 8.00
26 John Klingberg .60 1.50
27 Duncan Keith .50 1.25
28 Aleksander Barkov 1.00 2.50
29 Nikita Kucherov 1.25 3.00
30 Alexander Ovechkin 2.50 6.00
31 Sam Bennett 1.00 2.50
32 Torey Krug .50 1.25
33 Claude Giroux .60 1.50
34 Noah Hanifin .60 1.50
35 Cory Schneider .60 1.50
36 Daniel Sedin .75 2.00
37 Jamie Benn .60 1.50
38 Ryan Kesler .60 1.50
39 Zach Parise .60 1.50
40 Johnny Gaudreau 1.00 2.50
41 Jack Eichel 1.00 2.50
42 Henrik Zetterberg .75 2.00
43 Blake Wheeler .60 1.50
44 Max Domi .60 1.50
45 Nick Leddy .40 1.00
46 Phil Kessel .60 1.50
47 Jack Johnson .40 1.00
48 Brent Burns .60 1.50
49 Vladimir Tarasenko .75 2.00
50 Sidney Crosby 2.50 6.00
51 Auston Matthews RC 30.00 80.00
52 Patrik Laine RC 12.00 30.00
53 Mitch Marner RC 12.00 30.00
54 Jesse Puljujarvi RC 3.00 8.00
55 Jimmy Vesey RC 2.50 6.00
56 Kyle Connor RC 5.00 12.00
57 Matthew Tkachuk RC 6.00 15.00
58 Ivan Provorov RC 2.50 6.00
59 Sebastian Aho RC 5.00 12.00
60 Travis Konecny RC 3.00 8.00
61 Christian Dvorak RC 2.00 5.00
62 Mathew Barzal RC 10.00 25.00
63 Thomas Chabot RC 3.00 8.00
64 Dylan Strome RC 4.00 10.00
65 Anthony Beauvillier RC 1.50 4.00
66 Zach Werenski RC 5.00 12.00
67 Pavel Buchnevich RC 2.50 6.00
68 Brayden Point RC 4.00 10.00
69 Danton Heinen RC 1.25 3.00
70 Nick Schmaltz RC 2.00 5.00
71 William Nylander RC 10.00 25.00
72 Oliver Bjorkstrand RC 2.00 5.00
73 Nikita Soshnikov RC 1.00 2.50
74 Anthony Mantha RC 3.00 8.00
75 Charlie Lindgren RC 2.50 6.00
76 Hudson Fasching RC 1.50 4.00
77 Ryan Pulock RC 1.50 4.00
78 Kasperi Kapanen RC 2.50 6.00
79 Sonny Milano RC 2.00 5.00
80 Daniel Altshuller RC 1.25 3.00
81 Connor Brown RC 2.50 6.00
82 Justin Bailey RC 1.50 4.00
83 Pavel Zacha RC 2.50 6.00
84 Auston Matthews AU/99 300.00 800.00
85 Patrik Laine AU/175 100.00 250.00
86 Mitch Marner AU/175 100.00 250.00
87 Jesse Puljujarvi AU/275 6.00 15.00
88 Jimmy Vesey AU/275 12.00 30.00
89 Kyle Connor AU/275 25.00 60.00
90 Matthew Tkachuk AU/275 30.00 80.00
91 Ivan Provorov AU/275 12.00 30.00
92 Sebastian Aho AU/275 25.00 60.00
93 Travis Konecny AU/275 15.00 40.00
94 Christian Dvorak AU/275 10.00 25.00
95 Mathew Barzal AU/275 25.00 60.00
96 Thomas Chabot AU/275 15.00 40.00
97 Dylan Strome AU/275 20.00 50.00
98 Anthony Beauvillier AU/275 8.00 20.00
99 Zach Werenski AU/275 20.00 50.00
100 Pavel Buchnevich AU/275 12.00 30.00
101 Brayden Point AU/275 20.00 50.00
102 Danton Heinen AU/275 6.00 15.00
103 Nick Schmaltz AU/275 10.00 25.00
104 William Nylander AU/275 30.00 80.00
105 Oliver Bjorkstrand AU/275 10.00 25.00
106 Nikita Soshnikov AU/275 5.00 12.00
107 Anthony Mantha AU/275 15.00 40.00
108 Charlie Lindgren AU/275 12.00 30.00
109 Hudson Fasching AU/275 8.00 20.00
110 Ryan Pulock AU/275 8.00 20.00
111 Kasperi Kapanen AU/275 12.00 30.00
112 Sonny Milano AU/275 10.00 25.00
113 Daniel Altshuller AU/275 6.00 15.00
114 Connor Brown AU/275 12.00 30.00
115 Justin Bailey AU/275 8.00 20.00
116 Pavel Zacha AU/275 12.00 30.00
117 Auston Matthews AU/25 500.00 900.00
118 Patrik Laine AU/49 150.00 300.00
119 Mitch Marner AU/49 150.00 300.00
120 Jesse Puljujarvi AU/49 10.00 25.00
121 Jimmy Vesey AU/49 20.00 50.00
122 Kyle Connor AU/49 40.00 100.00
123 Matthew Tkachuk AU/49 50.00 125.00
124 Ivan Provorov AU/49 20.00 50.00
125 Sebastian Aho AU/49 40.00 100.00
126 Travis Konecny AU/49 25.00 60.00
127 Christian Dvorak AU/49 15.00 40.00
128 Mathew Barzal AU/49 40.00 100.00
129 Thomas Chabot AU/49 25.00 60.00
130 Dylan Strome AU/49 30.00 80.00
131 Anthony Beauvillier AU/49 12.00 30.00
132 Zach Werenski AU/49 40.00 100.00
133 Pavel Buchnevich AU/49 20.00 50.00
134 Brayden Point AU/49 30.00 80.00
135 Danton Heinen AU/49 10.00 25.00
136 Nick Schmaltz AU/49 15.00 40.00
137 William Nylander AU/49 50.00 125.00
138 Oliver Bjorkstrand AU/49 15.00 40.00
139 Nikita Soshnikov AU/49 8.00 20.00
140 Anthony Mantha AU/49 25.00 60.00
141 Charlie Lindgren AU/49 20.00 50.00
142 Hudson Fasching AU/49 12.00 30.00
143 Ryan Pulock AU/49 12.00 30.00
144 Kasperi Kapanen AU/49 20.00 50.00
145 Sonny Milano AU/49 15.00 40.00
146 Daniel Altshuller AU/49 10.00 25.00
147 Connor Brown AU/49 20.00 50.00
148 Justin Bailey AU/49 12.00 30.00
149 Pavel Zacha AU/49 20.00 50.00

2016-17 Upper Deck Trilogy Rainbow Black

1 Patrick Kane PATCH/17 8.00 20.00
3 Tyler Toffoli STK/58 10.00 25.00
4 Martin Jones PATCH/37 10.00 25.00
7 Henrik Lundqvist PATCH/65 25.00 60.00
9 Dylan Larkin PATCH/23 15.00 40.00
11 Braden Holtby PATCH/48 12.00 30.00
13 Morgan Rielly PATCH/36 12.00 30.00
14 Jarome Iginla STK/22 15.00 40.00
16 Tuukka Rask PATCH/64 12.00 30.00
17 Erik Karlsson GLV/66 12.00 30.00
18 Anze Kopitar STK/18 12.00 30.00
19 Matt Duchene PATCH/30 12.00 30.00
21 Tyler Seguin STK/40 12.00 30.00
22 Max Pacioretty SKATE/30 12.00 30.00
23 Filip Forsberg PATCH/64 15.00 40.00
24 Jaden Schwartz PATCH/33 15.00 40.00
25 Connor McDavid SOCK/16 25.00 60.00
26 John Klingberg PATCH/48 10.00 25.00
27 Duncan Keith PATCH/43 8.00 20.00
28 Aleksander Barkov PATCH/66 15.00 40.00
29 Nikita Kucherov PATCH/66 20.00 50.00
31 Sam Bennett PATCH/36 20.00 50.00
32 Torey Krug PATCH/44 8.00 20.00
33 Claude Giroux PATCH/67 10.00 25.00
34 Noah Hanifin PATCH/22 12.00 30.00
35 Cory Schneider PATCH/27 12.00 30.00
36 Daniel Sedin PATCH/33 15.00 40.00
37 Jamie Benn GLV/30 12.00 30.00
38 Ryan Kesler PATCH/50 10.00 25.00
39 Zach Parise PATCH/53 10.00 25.00
41 Jack Eichel PATCH/56 15.00 40.00
43 Blake Wheeler PATCH/82 10.00 25.00
44 Max Domi PATCH/18 10.00 25.00
45 Nick Leddy PATCH/40 6.00 15.00
46 Phil Kessel STK/26 12.00 30.00
47 Jack Johnson PATCH/86 6.00 15.00
48 Brent Burns PATCH/48 10.00 25.00
51 Auston Matthews 60.00 150.00
52 Patrik Laine 15.00 40.00
53 Mitch Marner 20.00 50.00
54 Jesse Puljujarvi 12.00 30.00
55 Jimmy Vesey 10.00 25.00
56 Kyle Connor 20.00 50.00
57 Matthew Tkachuk 25.00 60.00
58 Ivan Provorov 10.00 25.00
59 Sebastian Aho 20.00 50.00
60 Travis Konecny 12.00 30.00
61 Christian Dvorak 8.00 20.00
62 Mathew Barzal 20.00 50.00
63 Thomas Chabot 12.00 30.00
64 Dylan Strome 15.00 40.00
65 Anthony Beauvillier 6.00 15.00
66 Zach Werenski 20.00 50.00
67 Pavel Buchnevich 10.00 25.00
68 Brayden Point 15.00 40.00
69 Danton Heinen 5.00 12.00
70 Nick Schmaltz 8.00 20.00
71 William Nylander 25.00 60.00
72 Oliver Bjorkstrand 8.00 20.00
73 Nikita Soshnikov 4.00 10.00
74 Anthony Mantha 12.00 30.00
75 Charlie Lindgren 10.00 25.00
76 Hudson Fasching 6.00 15.00
77 Ryan Pulock 6.00 15.00
78 Kasperi Kapanen 10.00 25.00
79 Sonny Milano 8.00 20.00
80 Daniel Altshuller 5.00 12.00
81 Connor Brown 10.00 25.00
82 Justin Bailey 6.00 15.00
83 Pavel Zacha 10.00 25.00
88 Jimmy Vesey AU/66 15.00 40.00
93 Travis Konecny AU/24 25.00 60.00
94 Christian Dvorak AU/58 12.00 30.00
95 Mathew Barzal AU/16 20.00 50.00
96 Thomas Chabot AU/18 25.00 60.00
100 Pavel Buchnevich AU/75 15.00 40.00
101 Brayden Point AU/79 25.00 60.00
102 Danton Heinen AU/116 8.00 20.00
103 Nick Schmaltz AU/20 15.00 40.00
105 Oliver Bjorkstrand AU/89 12.00 30.00
107 Anthony Mantha AU/20 25.00 60.00
109 Hudson Fasching AU/118 10.00 25.00
111 Kasperi Kapanen AU/22 20.00 50.00
113 Daniel Altshuller AU/69 8.00 20.00
114 Connor Brown AU/156 15.00 40.00
115 Justin Bailey AU/52 10.00 25.00

2016-17 Upper Deck Trilogy Rainbow Green

1 Patrick Kane JSY/44 15.00 40.00
2 Steven Stamkos JSY/198 10.00 25.00
3 Tyler Toffoli JSY/230 4.00 10.00
4 Martin Jones JSY/205 3.00 8.00
5 John Tavares JSY/36 15.00 40.00
6 Joe Pavelski JSY/212 5.00 12.00
7 Henrik Lundqvist JSY/59 20.00 50.00
8 Ryan Getzlaf JSY/520 3.00 8.00
9 Dylan Larkin JSY/45 10.00 25.00
10 Evgeni Malkin JSY/108 10.00 25.00
11 Braden Holtby JSY/244 5.00 12.00
12 Jaromir Jagr JSY/133 15.00 40.00
13 Morgan Rielly JSY/236 4.00 10.00
14 Jarome Iginla JSY/190 6.00 15.00
15 Jonathan Toews JSY/51 12.00 30.00
16 Tuukka Rask JSY/167 6.00 15.00
18 Anze Kopitar JSY/243 6.00 15.00
19 Matt Duchene JSY/221 4.00 10.00
20 Carey Price JSY/36 20.00 50.00
21 Tyler Seguin JSY/163 6.00 15.00
22 Max Pacioretty JSY/84 6.00 15.00
23 Filip Forsberg JSY/182 8.00 20.00
24 Jaden Schwartz JSY/491 4.00 10.00
25 Connor McDavid JSY/48 40.00 100.00
26 John Klingberg JSY/269 4.00 10.00
27 Duncan Keith JSY/374 3.00 8.00
28 Aleksander Barkov JSY/381 6.00 15.00
29 Nikita Kucherov JSY/211 8.00 20.00
30 Alexander Ovechkin JSY/88 25.00 60.00
31 Sam Bennett JSY/137 8.00 20.00
33 Claude Giroux JSY/351 4.00 10.00
34 Noah Hanifin JSY/79 6.00 15.00
35 Cory Schneider JSY/270 4.00 10.00
36 Daniel Sedin JSY/123 6.00 15.00
37 Jamie Benn JSY/45 8.00 20.00
38 Ryan Kesler JSY/223 4.00 10.00
39 Zach Parise JSY/299 4.00 10.00
40 Johnny Gaudreau JSY/88 10.00 25.00
41 Jack Eichel JSY/81 10.00 25.00
42 Henrik Zetterberg JSY/97 8.00 20.00
43 Blake Wheeler JSY/440 3.00 8.00
44 Max Domi JSY/81 6.00 15.00
45 Nick Leddy JSY/417 2.00 5.00
46 Phil Kessel JSY/70 6.00 15.00
47 Jack Johnson JSY/629 2.00 5.00
49 Vladimir Tarasenko JSY/106 6.00 15.00
50 Sidney Crosby JSY/46 30.00 80.00
51 Auston Matthews JSY 30.00 80.00
52 Patrik Laine JSY 10.00 25.00
53 Mitch Marner JSY 12.00 30.00
54 Jesse Puljujarvi JSY 6.00 15.00
55 Jimmy Vesey JSY 6.00 15.00
56 Kyle Connor JSY 12.00 30.00
57 Matthew Tkachuk JSY 15.00 40.00
58 Ivan Provorov JSY 6.00 15.00
59 Sebastian Aho JSY 12.00 30.00
60 Travis Konecny JSY 8.00 20.00
61 Christian Dvorak JSY 5.00 12.00
62 Mathew Barzal JSY 12.00 30.00
63 Thomas Chabot JSY 8.00 20.00
64 Dylan Strome JSY 10.00 25.00
65 Anthony Beauvillier JSY 4.00 10.00
66 Zach Werenski JSY 12.00 30.00
67 Pavel Buchnevich JSY 6.00 15.00
68 Brayden Point JSY 10.00 25.00
70 Nick Schmaltz JSY 5.00 12.00
71 William Nylander JSY 15.00 40.00
72 Oliver Bjorkstrand JSY 5.00 12.00
73 Nikita Soshnikov JSY 2.50 6.00
74 Anthony Mantha JSY 8.00 20.00
75 Charlie Lindgren JSY 6.00 15.00
76 Hudson Fasching JSY 4.00 10.00
77 Ryan Pulock JSY 4.00 10.00
78 Kasperi Kapanen JSY 6.00 15.00
79 Sonny Milano JSY 5.00 12.00
80 Daniel Altshuller JSY 3.00 8.00
81 Connor Brown JSY 6.00 15.00
82 Justin Bailey JSY 4.00 10.00
83 Pavel Zacha JSY 6.00 15.00
84 Auston Matthews PATCH 100.00 200.00
85 Patrik Laine PATCH 25.00 60.00
86 Mitch Marner PATCH 30.00 80.00
87 Jesse Puljujarvi PATCH 8.00 20.00
88 Jimmy Vesey PATCH 15.00 40.00
89 Kyle Connor PATCH 30.00 80.00
90 Matthew Tkachuk PATCH 40.00 100.00
91 Ivan Provorov PATCH 15.00 40.00
92 Sebastian Aho PATCH 30.00 80.00
93 Travis Konecny PATCH 20.00 50.00
94 Christian Dvorak PATCH 12.00 30.00
95 Mathew Barzal PATCH 30.00 80.00
96 Thomas Chabot PATCH 20.00 50.00
97 Dylan Strome PATCH 25.00 60.00
98 Anthony Beauvillier PATCH 10.00 25.00
99 Zach Werenski PATCH 30.00 80.00
100 Pavel Buchnevich PATCH 15.00 40.00
101 Brayden Point PATCH 25.00 60.00
103 Nick Schmaltz PATCH 12.00 30.00
104 William Nylander PATCH 40.00 100.00
105 Oliver Bjorkstrand PATCH 12.00 30.00
106 Nikita Soshnikov PATCH 6.00 15.00
107 Anthony Mantha PATCH 20.00 50.00
108 Charlie Lindgren PATCH 15.00 40.00
109 Hudson Fasching PATCH 10.00 25.00
110 Ryan Pulock PATCH 10.00 25.00
111 Kasperi Kapanen PATCH 15.00 40.00
112 Sonny Milano PATCH 12.00 30.00
113 Daniel Altshuller PATCH 8.00 20.00
114 Connor Brown PATCH 15.00 40.00
115 Justin Bailey PATCH 10.00 25.00
116 Pavel Zacha PATCH 15.00 40.00

2016-17 Upper Deck Trilogy Hall of Fame Signature Pucks

HOFIBO Bobby Orr B 80.00 150.00
HOFIBS Borje Salming C 8.00 20.00
HOFIDG Doug Gilmour C 25.00 60.00
HOFIDH Dominik Hasek C 30.00 80.00
HOFIGH Glenn Hall A 20.00 50.00
HOFIJS Joe Sakic B 25.00 60.00
HOFILM Lanny McDonald C 15.00 40.00
HOFIML Mario Lemieux A 80.00 150.00
HOFIMM Mark Messier A 50.00 120.00
HOFINL Nicklas Lidstrom B 25.00 60.00
HOFIPB Pavel Bure B 30.00 80.00
HOFIPR Patrick Roy A 60.00 150.00
HOFISY Steve Yzerman A 50.00 120.00
HOFIWG Wayne Gretzky A 250.00 600.00

2016-17 Upper Deck Trilogy Ice Scripts

ISAH Adam Henrique D 10.00 25.00
ISAM Anthony Mantha D 25.00 60.00
ISBO Bobby Orr B 60.00 150.00
ISCM Connor McDavid B 120.00 300.00
ISLM Larry Murphy C 10.00 25.00
ISMF Marc-Andre Fleury D 12.00 30.00
ISMM Mark Messier A 60.00 150.00
ISOV Alexander Ovechkin A 40.00 100.00
ISPB Pavel Bure C 25.00 60.00
ISPZ Pavel Zacha D 12.00 30.00
ISTO Jonathan Toews B 30.00 80.00
ISTT Tyler Toffoli D 5.00 12.00
ISWG Wayne Gretzky A 250.00 600.00
ISWN William Nylander C 20.00 50.00

2016-17 Upper Deck Trilogy Signature Pucks

SPAA Andreas Athanasiou G 6.00 15.00
SPAH Adam Henrique E 5.00 12.00
SPAK Anze Kopitar C 15.00 40.00
SPAM Auston Matthews A 80.00 200.00
SPBB Brent Burns E 15.00 40.00
SPBJ Boone Jenner G 6.00 15.00
SPBS Brayden Schenn E 6.00 15.00
SPCM Connor McDavid C 100.00 250.00
SPCS Cory Schneider D 6.00 15.00
SPCW Cam Ward E 6.00 15.00
SPDK David Krejci E 6.00 15.00
SPDS Derek Stepan F 4.00 10.00
SPEK Aaron Ekblad G 8.00 20.00
SPGH Glenn Hall A 20.00 50.00
SPGI John Gibson G 6.00 15.00
SPHL Henrik Lundqvist B 30.00 80.00
SPHZ Henrik Zetterberg C 15.00 40.00
SPJA Jake Allen G 6.00 15.00
SPJH Jonathan Huberdeau D 8.00 20.00
SPJM Josh Morrissey G 15.00 40.00
SPJP Jesse Puljujarvi F 12.00 30.00
SPJT Joe Thornton C 10.00 25.00
SPJV James van Riemsdyk F 5.00 12.00
SPKP Kyle Palmieri F 5.00 12.00
SPLD Leon Draisaitl F 12.00 30.00
SPMA Anthony Mantha F 12.00 30.00
SPMB Matt Beleskey G 5.00 12.00
SPMD Matt Duchene C 6.00 15.00
SPMH Mike Hoffman G 4.00 10.00
SPMM Mark Messier B 15.00 40.00
SPMU Matt Murray E 15.00 40.00
SPNK Nikita Kucherov G 12.00 30.00
SPPB Peter Bondra C 8.00 20.00
SPPL Patrik Laine E 15.00 40.00
SPRF Robby Fabbri F 4.00 10.00
SPRM Ryan Miller D 6.00 15.00
SPRO Ryan O'Reilly G 6.00 15.00
SPSH Scott Hartnell D 4.00 10.00
SPSI Roman Josi G 6.00 15.00
SPSM Sean Monahan F 4.00 10.00
SPTL Trevor Linden C 10.00 25.00
SPTO Tyler Toffoli E 6.00 15.00
SPTS Tyler Seguin C 10.00 25.00
SPVR Victor Rask G 4.00 10.00
SPWG Wayne Gretzky B 200.00 500.00
SPWN William Nylander F 25.00 60.00

2016-17 Upper Deck Trilogy Signature Pucks Dual

SP2AL A.Athanasiou/D.Larkin D 30.00 80.00
SP2BL P.Bure/T.Linden B 50.00 120.00
SP2DI J.Iginla/M.Duchene D 15.00 40.00
SP2MD C.McDavid/L.Draisaitl C 150.00 250.00
SP2MN A.Matthews/W.Nylander C 175.00 300.00
SP2SN R.Nash/D.Stepan C 20.00 50.00

2016-17 Upper Deck Trilogy Signature Pucks Team Logo

COMMON CARD 15.00 40.00
SEMISTARS 20.00 50.00
UNLISTED STARS 25.00 60.00
SPAM Auston Matthews 250.00 400.00
SPCM Connor McDavid 175.00 300.00
SPWG Wayne Gretzky 250.00 600.00

2016-17 Upper Deck Trilogy Triple Relics

TRBSS Benn/Seguin/Spezza/49 15.00 40.00
TRBTB Bergeron/Thornton
Backstrom/125 12.00 30.00
TRCRS Carbonneau/Roy/Savard/25 40.00 100.00
TRDGR Dionne/Gretzky
Robitaille/25 100.00 250.00
TRHCL Hextall/Clarke/LeClair/49 20.00 50.00
TRHYH Hull/Yzerman/Hasek/25 40.00 100.00
TRJBL Jagr/Bure/Luongo/49 40.00 100.00
TRJSS Milano/Dickinson/Bailey/125 10.00 25.00
TRKDB Karlsson/Doughty/Burns/49 15.00 40.00
TRKML Kessel/Malkin/Letang/25 30.00 80.00
TRKOT Kane/Ovechkin/Tavares/25 60.00 150.00
TRLCJ Brown/Lindgren
Morrissey/125 20.00 50.00
TRPGP Price/Galchenyuk
Pacioretty/49 25.00 60.00
TRPSG Perry/Selanne/Getzlaf/49 25.00 60.00
TRQKC Quick/Kopitar/Carter/49 20.00 50.00
TRSMS Sedin/Miller/Sedin/49 15.00 40.00
TRZWS Zacha/Wood/Santini/125 12.00 30.00

2017-18 Upper Deck Trilogy

*BLUE/999: 1X TO 2.5X BASIC CARDS
1 Connor McDavid 2.00 5.00
2 Oliver Ekman-Larsson .40 1.00
3 David Pastrnak 1.00 2.50
4 Alex Galchenyuk .25 .60
5 Alexander Ovechkin 1.50 4.00
6 Mats Zuccarello .40 1.00
7 Wayne Simmonds .50 1.25
8 Brent Burns .40 1.00
9 Mark Scheifele .60 1.50
10 John Tavares .60 1.50
11 Henrik Zetterberg .50 1.25
12 Ryan Johansen .30 .75
13 Aaron Ekblad .50 1.25
14 Jamie Benn .40 1.00
15 Sidney Crosby 1.50 4.00
16 Corey Perry .60 1.50
17 Mikael Granlund .30 .75
18 Ryan O'Reilly .40 1.00
19 Sean Monahan .25 .60
20 Auston Matthews 1.50 4.00
21 Jeff Carter .30 .75
22 Nathan MacKinnon 1.50 4.00
23 Artemi Panarin .75 2.00
24 Nikita Kucherov .75 2.00
25 Patrick Kane .75 2.00
26 Erik Karlsson .50 1.25
27 Bo Horvat .50 1.25
28 Vladimir Tarasenko .50 1.25
29 Jordan Staal .30 .75
30 Taylor Hall .40 1.00
31 Marc-Andre Fleury .75 2.00
32 Anze Kopitar .60 1.50
33 P.K. Subban .50 1.25
34 Milan Lucic .40 1.00
35 Jonathan Toews .60 1.50
36 William Karlsson .50 1.25
37 Jonathan Quick .50 1.25
38 Evgeny Kuznetsov .50 1.25
39 Leon Draisaitl 1.25 3.00
40 Carey Price .75 2.00
41 Mitch Marner .60 1.50
42 Sergei Bobrovsky .60 1.50
43 Tyler Seguin .50 1.25
44 Patrice Bergeron .50 1.25
45 Evgeni Malkin .75 2.00
46 Corey Crawford .50 1.25
47 Jonathan Drouin .30 .75
48 Jack Eichel .60 1.50
49 Matt Murray .60 1.50
50 Wayne Gretzky 2.50 6.00
51 Christian Fischer RC 2.00 5.00
52 Jack Roslovic RC 2.00 5.00
53 Samuel Morin RC 1.00 2.50
54 Haydn Fleury RC 1.50 4.00
55 Colin White RC 2.00 5.00
56 Adrian Kempe RC 3.00 8.00
57 Alex Tuch RC 4.00 10.00
58 Nikita Scherbak RC 2.00 5.00
59 J.T. Compher RC 1.50 4.00
60 Vladislav Kamenev RC 1.50 4.00
61 Gabriel Carlsson RC 1.25 3.00
62 Riley Barber RC 1.50 4.00
63 Lucas Wallmark RC 1.50 4.00
64 Jon Gillies RC 1.50 4.00
65 Ivan Barbashev RC 2.00 5.00
66 Luke Kunin RC 1.50 4.00
67 Anders Bjork RC 2.00 5.00
68 Alex DeBrincat RC 4.00 10.00
69 Owen Tippett RC 3.00 8.00
70 Alexander Nylander RC 2.50 6.00
71 Jake DeBrusk RC 4.00 10.00
72 Tage Thompson RC 4.00 10.00
73 Tyson Jost RC 3.00 8.00
74 Logan Brown RC 1.50 4.00
75 Vadim Shipachyov RC 2.00 5.00
76 Evgeny Svechnikov RC 3.00 8.00
77 Josh Ho-Sang RC 2.00 5.00
78 Brock Boeser RC 4.00 10.00
79 Pierre-Luc Dubois RC 2.50 6.00
80 Charlie McAvoy RC 4.00 10.00
81 Clayton Keller RC 4.00 10.00
82 Nolan Patrick RC 3.00 8.00
83 Nico Hischier RC 5.00 12.00
84 Christian Fischer AU/349 10.00 25.00
85 Jack Roslovic AU/349 10.00 25.00
86 Samuel Morin AU/349 5.00 12.00
87 Haydn Fleury AU/349 8.00 20.00
88 Colin White AU/349 10.00 25.00
89 Adrian Kempe AU/349 15.00 40.00
90 Alex Tuch AU/349 20.00 50.00
91 Nikita Scherbak AU/349 10.00 25.00
92 J.T. Compher AU/349 8.00 20.00
93 Vladislav Kamenev AU/349 8.00 20.00
94 Gabriel Carlsson AU/349 6.00 15.00
95 Riley Barber AU/349 8.00 20.00
97 Jon Gillies AU/349 8.00 20.00
98 Ivan Barbashev AU/349 10.00 25.00
99 Luke Kunin AU/249 8.00 20.00
100 Anders Bjork AU/249 10.00 25.00
101 Alex DeBrincat AU/249 20.00 50.00
102 Owen Tippett AU/249 15.00 40.00
103 Alexander Nylander AU/249 12.00 30.00
105 Tage Thompson AU/249 20.00 50.00
106 Tyson Jost AU/249 15.00 40.00
108 Vadim Shipachyov AU/249 10.00 25.00
109 Evgeny Svechnikov AU/249 15.00 40.00
110 Josh Ho-Sang AU/249 10.00 25.00
111 Brock Boeser AU/149 150.00 300.00
112 Pierre-Luc Dubois 12.00 30.00
113 Charlie McAvoy AU/149 20.00 50.00
114 Clayton Keller AU/149 20.00 50.00
115 Nolan Patrick/149 12.00 30.00
116 Nico Hischier/149 20.00 50.00
117 Christian Fischer AU/49 20.00 50.00
118 Jack Roslovic AU/49 20.00 50.00
119 Samuel Morin AU/49 10.00 25.00
120 Haydn Fleury AU/49 15.00 40.00
121 Colin White AU/49 20.00 50.00
122 Adrian Kempe AU/49 30.00 80.00
123 Alex Tuch AU/49 40.00 100.00
124 Nikita Scherbak AU/49 20.00 50.00
125 J.T. Compher AU/49 15.00 40.00
126 Vladislav Kamenev AU/49 15.00 40.00
127 Gabriel Carlsson AU/49 12.00 30.00
128 Riley Barber AU/49 15.00 40.00
129 Lucas Wallmark AU/49 15.00 40.00
130 Jon Gillies AU/49 15.00 40.00
131 Ivan Barbashev AU/49 20.00 50.00
132 Luke Kunin AU/49 15.00 40.00
133 Anders Bjork AU/49 20.00 50.00
134 Alex DeBrincat AU/49 40.00 100.00
135 Owen Tippett AU/49 30.00 80.00
136 Alexander Nylander AU/49 25.00 60.00
138 Tage Thompson AU/49 40.00 100.00
139 Tyson Jost AU/49 30.00 80.00
141 Vadim Shipachyov AU/49 20.00 50.00
142 Evgeny Svechnikov AU/49 30.00 80.00
143 Josh Ho-Sang AU/49 20.00 50.00
144 Brock Boeser AU/49 350.00 500.00
145 Pierre-Luc Dubois AU/49 25.00 60.00
146 Charlie McAvoy AU/49 40.00 100.00
147 Clayton Keller AU/49 40.00 100.00
148 Nolan Patrick/25 20.00 50.00
149 Nico Hischier/25 30.00 80.00
150 Luc-DuBois AU/Keller
AU/McAvoy AU/25 40.00 100.00

2017-18 Upper Deck Trilogy Black

5 Alexander Ovechkin PATCH/17 20.00 50.00
15 Sidney Crosby PATCH/17 30.00 80.00
31 Marc-Andre Fleury PAD/18 25.00 60.00
41 Mitch Marner PATCH/42 15.00 40.00
78 Brock Boeser 25.00 60.00

2017-18 Upper Deck Trilogy Green

COMMON CARD (1-83) 2.50 6.00
SEMISTARS 3.00 8.00
UNLISTED STARS 4.00 10.00
COMMON CARD (84-113) 6.00 15.00
SEMISTARS 8.00 20.00
UNLISTED STARS 10.00 25.00
78 Brock Boeser JSY/399 20.00 50.00
111 Brock Boeser PATCH/35 80.00 150.00

2017-18 Upper Deck Trilogy Combo Signature Pucks

SP2CS D.Sanderson/G.Cheevers B 15.00 40.00
SP2DT M.Dionne/D.Taylor B 20.00 50.00
SP2FB I.Barbashev/R.Fabbri C 20.00 50.00
SP2FS J.Sakic/P.Forsberg A 30.00 80.00
SP2KF C.Fischer/C.Keller B 40.00 100.00
SP2MK F.Mahovlich/R.Kelly A 15.00 40.00
SP2MM E.Malkin/M.Murray B 30.00 80.00
SP2SK S.Stamkos/N.Kucherov A 30.00 80.00
SP2SL M.Scheifele/P.Laine B 25.00 60.00
SP2ST B.Salming/I.Turnbull C 15.00 40.00
SP2TK J.Toews/P.Kane A 30.00 80.00

2017-18 Upper Deck Trilogy Hall of Fame Signature Pucks

HOFICN Cam Neely C 15.00 40.00
HOFIJB Johnny Bower B 15.00 40.00
HOFIPF Peter Forsberg A 50.00 120.00
HOFIPH Phil Housley C 10.00 25.00
HOFIPL Pat LaFontaine B 10.00 25.00
HOFIRV Rogie Vachon C 12.00 330.00

2017-18 Upper Deck Trilogy Honorary Triple Swatches

HTSAE Aaron Ekblad/49 8.00 20.00
HTSAK Anze Kopitar/49 10.00 25.00
HTSAN Alexander Nylander/49 10.00 25.00
HTSCK Clayton Keller/25 15.00 40.00
HTSEK Erik Karlsson/25 8.00 20.00
HTSHA Noah Hanifin/25 6.00 15.00
HTSJB Jamie Benn/25 6.00 15.00
HTSJQ Jonathan Quick/49 8.00 20.00
HTSJS Jason Spezza/25 6.00 15.00
HTSLU Milan Lucic/25 6.00 15.00
HTSRL Roberto Luongo/25 10.00 25.00
HTSTJ Tyson Jost/49 12.00 30.00
HTSVT Vladimir Tarasenko/25 8.00 20.00

2017-18 Upper Deck Trilogy Ice Scripts

ISCK Clayton Keller C 25.00 60.00
ISCP Carey Price A 50.00 120.00
ISDS Derek Sanderson C 10.00 25.00
ISEM Evgeni Malkin A 20.00 50.00
ISHZ Henrik Zetterberg A 12.00 30.00
ISJJ Jaromir Jagr A 80.00 150.00
ISJK Jari Kurri B 10.00 25.00
ISJT John Tavares 15.00 40.00
ISLD Leon Draisaitl C 30.00 80.00
ISML Mario Lemieux A 40.00 100.00
ISNK Nikita Kucherov C 20.00 50.00
ISNS Nikita Scherbak C 12.00 30.00
ISPK Patrick Kane A 20.00 50.00
ISPL Patrik Laine B 12.00 30.00
ISRK Ryan Kesler B 10.00 25.00
ISSY Steve Yzerman A 80.00 150.00
ISTH Taylor Hall B 10.00 25.00
ISWS Wayne Simmonds C 12.00 30.00

2017-18 Upper Deck Trilogy Personal Scripts

PSAG Alex Galchenyuk C 5.00 12.00
PSAO Alexander Ovechkin A 30.00 80.00
PSBO Bobby Orr B 80.00 200.00
PSCM Connor McDavid A 250.00 400.00
PSDS Dave Schultz C 8.00 20.00
PSEB Ed Belfour C 10.00 25.00
PSHL Henrik Lundqvist B 25.00 60.00
PSJT Jonathan Toews B 25.00 60.00
PSSS Steven Stamkos B 30.00 80.00
PSTA John Tavares B 25.00 60.00
PSTH Joe Thornton C 25.00 60.00
PSWG Wayne Gretzky A 250.00 600.00

2017-18 Upper Deck Trilogy Scripted Hall of Fame Plaques

SHOFMB Mike Bossy 30.00 80.00
SHOFPR Patrick Roy 250.00 350.00
SHOFTS Teemu Selanne 80.00 200.00
SHOFWG Wayne Gretzky 250.00 600.00

2017-18 Upper Deck Trilogy Signature Pucks

SPAB Aleksander Barkov B 12.00 30.00
SPAV Andrei Vasilevskiy C 12.00 30.00
SPBB Brock Boeser C 20.00 50.00
SPBC Bobby Clarke A 12.00 30.00
SPBR Bobby Ryan C 6.00 15.00
SPCA Cam Atkinson B 8.00 20.00
SPCB Connor Brown C 6.00 15.00
SPCH Carl Hagelin B 5.00 12.00
SPCS Conor Sheary B 8.00 20.00
SPDA Dave Andreychuk A 8.00 20.00
SPDS Darryl Sittler A 10.00 25.00
SPES Evgeny Svechnikov C 15.00 40.00
SPFA Robby Fabbri B 5.00 12.00
SPFP Felix Potvin A 12.00 30.00
SPGF Grant Fuhr A 12.00 30.00
SPGI Mark Giordano B 8.00 20.00
SPGN Gustav Nyquist B 5.00 12.00
SPIB Ivan Barbashev C 10.00 25.00
SPIP Ivan Provorov C 6.00 15.00
SPJC John Carlson C 8.00 20.00
SPJH Jaroslav Halak B 8.00 20.00
SPJK Jari Kurri A 8.00 20.00
SPJM Jake Muzzin C 8.00 20.00
SPJP Joe Pavelski A 10.00 25.00
SPJR Jack Roslovic A 10.00 25.00
SPJV Jimmy Vesey B 6.00 15.00
SPKM Kirk Muller C 6.00 15.00
SPKP Kyle Palmieri C 6.00 15.00
SPLC Logan Couture B 10.00 25.00
SPLM Larry Murphy A 6.00 15.00
SPMI Mikael Granlund C 6.00 15.00
SPMM Michael Matheson C 6.00 15.00
SPMR Mikko Rantanen C 20.00 50.00
SPMS Mark Scheifele A 12.00 30.00
SPMT Matthew Tkachuk C 15.00 40.00
SPNE Nikolaj Ehlers C 8.00 20.00
SPNN Nino Niederreiter C 5.00 12.00
SPNU Norm Ullman C 8.00 20.00
SPON Owen Nolan A 8.00 20.00
SPPL Pierre-Luc Dubois A 12.00 30.00
SPPM Petr Mrazek B 8.00 20.00
SPRB Rod Brind'Amour C 8.00 20.00
SPRF Radek Faksa C 6.00 15.00
SPRH Ryan Hartman C 5.00 12.00
SPRK Ryan Kesler A 8.00 20.00
SPRS Ryan Spooner C 6.00 15.00
SPSI Charlie Simmer B 5.00 12.00
SPTB Tom Barrasso A 6.00 15.00
SPTH Taylor Hall A 8.00 20.00
SPTT Teuvo Teravainen C 8.00 20.00
SPVA John Vanbiesbrouck A 8.00 20.00
SPVH Victor Hedman A 10.00 25.00
SPWS Wayne Simmonds A 10.00 25.00

2017-18 Upper Deck Trilogy Stanley Cup Champions Signature Pucks

SCCAD Alex Delvecchio C 8.00 20.00
SCCBO Bobby Orr A 60.00 150.00
SCCGA Glenn Anderson A 8.00 20.00
SCCLR Larry Robinson B 10.00 25.00
SCCMB Mike Bossy B 20.00 50.00
SCCWG Wayne Gretzky A 250.00 600.00

2017-18 Upper Deck Trilogy Triple Relics

TRBDK Blake/Dionne/Kopitar/25 10.00 25.00
TRBKJ Boeser/Keller/Jost/49 15.00 40.00
TRCSR Clarke/Schultz/Recchi/25 10.00 25.00
TRDAW Dubinsky/Atkinson
Wennberg/49 6.00 15.00
TREKD Ekblad/Karlsson/Doughty/25 8.00 20.00
TRHBC Hasek/Belfour/Crawford/25 10.00 25.00
TRKTS Kane/Toews/Saad/25 12.00 30.00
TRLBC Lemieux/Barrasso/Coffey/25 25.00 60.00
TRLHH LaFontaine
Hawerchuk/Hasek/25 25.00 60.00
TRMDH McDavid/Draisaitl
Nugent-Hopkins/25 30.00 80.00
TRMGF Messier/Gretzky/Fuhr/25 30.00 80.00
TRNSB Nylander/Svechnikov
Barbashev/99 12.00 30.00
TROBM Ovechkin/Bure/Malkin/25 25.00 60.00
TRPLP Price/Lafleur/Roy/25 15.00 40.00
TRPSB Forsberg/Sakic/Bourque/25 12.00 30.00
TRSDT Shipachyov
DeBrincat/Tippett/49 15.00 40.00
TRSMW Ho-Sang/McAvoy/White/49 15.00 40.00
TRTBS Tarasenko/Bouwmeester
Steen/49 8.00 20.00
TRVMD Varlamov/MacKinnon
Duchene/49 25.00 60.00

2017-18 Upper Deck Trilogy Trophy Winners Signature Pucks

TWSBO Bobby Orr B 50.00 125.00
TWSCM Connor McDavid A 150.00 250.00
TWSCP Carey Price B 25.00 60.00
TWSHL Henrik Lundqvist C 30.00 80.00
TWSPK Patrick Kane 25.00 60.00
TWSSS Steven Stamkos B 25.00 60.00

2017-18 Upper Deck Trilogy Tryptichs

TBOS1 Bobby Orr AU/49 80.00 150.00
TCAP2 Evgeny Kuznetsov PATCH/49 6.00 15.00
TCAP3 Braden Holtby JSY/149 5.00 12.00
TCBJ1 Cam Atkinson AU/199 10.00 25.00
TCBJ2 Alexander
Wennberg PATCH/25 15.00 40.00
TCBJ3 Sergei Bobrovsky JSY/149 6.00 15.00
TDET1 Anthony Mantha AU/199 8.00 20.00
TDET2 Henrik Zetterberg PATCH/25 10.00 25.00
TDET3 Tomas Tatar JSY/149 2.50 6.00
TFLO1 Aaron Ekblad AU/99 6.00 15.00
TFLO2 Roberto Luongo STK/25 10.00 25.00
TFLO3 Aleksander Barkov JSY/149 6.00 15.00
THOF1 Mario Lemieux AU/20 80.00 200.00
THOF3 Joe Sakic JSY/25 10.00 25.00
TLAK1 Anze Kopitar AU/99 8.00 20.00
TLAK2 Jonathan Quick BLKR/49 6.00 15.00
TLAK3 Jeff Carter JSY/149 3.00 8.00
TOTT1 Mike Hoffman AU/199 6.00 15.00
TOTT2 Erik Karlsson GLV/25 15.00 40.00
TOTT3 Mark Stone JSY/149 5.00 12.00
TPEN2 Phil Kessel JSY/49 5.00 12.00
TPEN3 Conor Sheary AU/199 10.00 25.00
TPRE1 P.K. Subban PATCH/49 6.00 15.00
TPRE2 Filip Forsberg JSY/149 6.00 15.00
TPRE3 Roman Josi JSY/149 4.00 10.00
TRC11 Nolan Patrick JSY/49 10.00 25.00
TRC12 Nico Hischier JSY/49 15.00 40.00

TRC13 Vadim Shipachyov JSY/149 5.00 12.00
TRC21 Brock Boeser JSY/149 10.00 25.00
TRC22 Clayton Keller JSY/49 12.00 30.00
TRC23 Charlie McAvoy JSY/149 10.00 25.00
TSTL1 Vladimir Tarasenko JSY/49 6.00 15.00
TSTL2 Alex Pietrangelo PATCH/49 4.00 10.00
TSTL3 Jake Allen PATCH/49 5.00 12.00
TTML3 Doug Gilmour JSY/25 25.00 60.00
TUSA2 Mike Modano PATCH/25 15.00 40.00
TVAN2 Henrik Sedin PATCH/49 6.00 15.00
TVAN3 Daniel Sedin JSY/49 6.00 15.00
TLEAF2 Mitch Marner PATCH/25 20.00 50.00
TLEAF3 William Nylander PATCH/49 10.00 25.00
TSTAR1 Connor McDavid AU/20 200.00 350.00
TSTAR3 Auston Matthews JSY/25 20.00 50.00

2018-19 Upper Deck Trilogy

*BLUE: 1X TO 2.5X BASIC CARDS
*GREEN: 1.25X TO 3X BASIC CARDS
1 Alexander Ovechkin 1.50 4.00
2 Brock Boeser .40 1.00
3 Patrick Kane .75 2.00
4 Phil Kessel .40 1.00
5 Marc-Andre Fleury .75 2.00
6 Taylor Hall .40 1.00
7 Dylan Larkin .40 1.00
8 Mathew Barzal .40 1.00
9 Alex Galchenyuk .20 .50
10 Filip Forsberg .60 1.50
11 Erik Karlsson .40 1.00
12 Brad Marchand .75 2.00
13 Vladimir Tarasenko .40 1.00
14 Cam Atkinson .40 1.00
15 Henrik Lundqvist .75 2.00
16 Johnny Gaudreau .60 1.50
17 Steven Stamkos .75 2.00
18 Aleksander Barkov .60 1.50
19 Drew Doughty .40 1.00
20 Auston Matthews 1.50 4.00
21 Jamie Benn .40 1.00
22 Sean Couturier .30 .75
23 Patrik Laine .40 1.00
24 Ryan Suter .30 .75
25 Connor McDavid 1.50 4.00
26 Jack Eichel .60 1.50
27 Mark Stone .40 1.00
28 Sebastian Aho .60 1.50
29 Carey Price .75 2.00
30 Nathan MacKinnon 1.50 4.00
31 Ryan Getzlaf .40 1.00
32 T.J. Oshie .40 1.00
33 P.K. Subban .40 1.00
34 Reilly Smith .40 1.00
35 Sidney Crosby 1.50 4.00
36 Mitch Marner .60 1.50
37 Connor Hellebuyck .75 2.00
38 Kevin Shattenkirk .20 .50
39 Mike Hoffman .20 .50
40 Jonathan Toews .60 1.50
41 Jake Guentzel .60 1.50
42 Tuukka Rask .40 1.00
43 Ryan Nugent-Hopkins .40 1.00
44 Anze Kopitar .60 1.50
45 Nikita Kucherov .75 2.00
46 Jonathan Marchessault .40 1.00
47 Max Domi .40 1.00
48 John Tavares .60 1.50
49 Braden Holtby .40 1.00
50 Patrick Roy .75 2.00
51 Rasmus Dahlin RC 4.00 10.00
52 Sam Steel RC 1.50 4.00
53 Lias Andersson RC 2.50 6.00
54 Dillon Dube RC 2.00 5.00
55 Dylan Sikura RC 2.00 5.00
56 Kristian Vesalainen RC 2.00 5.00
57 Jordan Greenway RC 1.50 4.00
58 Jordan Kyrou RC 3.00 8.00
59 Anthony Cirelli RC 2.50 6.00
60 Maxime Comtois RC 1.50 4.00
61 Andreas Johnsson RC 2.00 5.00
62 Evan Bouchard RC 4.00 10.00
63 Travis Dermott RC 2.50 6.00
64 Juuso Valimaki RC 1.50 4.00
65 Henrik Borgstrom RC 2.50 6.00
66 Brett Howden RC 2.00 5.00
67 Warren Foegele RC 1.50 4.00
68 Adam Gaudette RC 2.50 6.00
69 Henri Jokiharju RC 1.25 3.00
70 Eeli Tolvanen RC 3.00 8.00
71 Noah Juulsen RC 1.50 4.00
72 Brady Tkachuk RC 5.00 12.00
73 Miro Heiskanen RC 4.00 10.00
74 Robert Thomas RC 3.00 8.00
75 Michael Rasmussen RC 2.00 5.00
76 Ryan Donato RC 2.50 6.00
77 Casey Mittelstadt RC 3.00 8.00
78 Jesperi Kotkaniemi RC 3.00 8.00
79 Andrei Svechnikov RC 4.00 10.00
80 Elias Pettersson RC 15.00 40.00
81 Rasmus Dahlin/399 8.00 20.00
82 Sam Steel AU/399 6.00 15.00
83 Lias Andersson AU/399 10.00 25.00
84 Dillon Dube AU/399 8.00 20.00
85 Dylan Sikura AU/399 8.00 20.00
86 Kristian Vesalainen AU/399 8.00 20.00
87 Jordan Greenway AU/399 6.00 15.00
88 Jordan Kyrou AU/399 12.00 30.00
89 Anthony Cirelli AU/399 10.00 25.00
90 Maxime Comtois AU/399 6.00 15.00
91 Andreas Johnsson AU/399 8.00 20.00
92 Evan Bouchard AU/399 15.00 40.00
93 Travis Dermott AU/399 10.00 25.00
94 Juuso Valimaki AU/399 6.00 15.00
95 Henrik Borgstrom AU/399 10.00 25.00
96 Brett Howden AU/399 8.00 20.00
97 Warren Foegele AU/399 6.00 15.00
98 Adam Gaudette AU/399 10.00 25.00
99 Henri Jokiharju AU/399 5.00 12.00
100 Eeli Tolvanen AU/399 12.00 30.00
101 Noah Juulsen AU/399 6.00 15.00
102 Brady Tkachuk AU/249 20.00 50.00
103 Miro Heiskanen AU/249 15.00 40.00
104 Robert Thomas AU/249 12.00 30.00
105 Michael Rasmussen AU/249 8.00 20.00
107 Casey Mittelstadt AU/249 12.00 30.00
108 Jesperi Kotkaniemi AU/149 12.00 30.00
109 Andrei Svechnikov AU/149 15.00 40.00
110 Elias Pettersson AU/149 80.00 200.00
111 Rasmus Dahlin/49 40.00 100.00
112 Sam Steel AU/49 15.00 40.00
113 Lias Andersson AU/49 25.00 60.00
114 Dillon Dube AU/49 20.00 50.00
115 Dylan Sikura AU/49 20.00 50.00
116 Kristian Vesalainen AU/49 20.00 50.00
117 Jordan Greenway AU/49 15.00 40.00
118 Jordan Kyrou AU/49 30.00 80.00
119 Anthony Cirelli AU/49 25.00 60.00
120 Maxime Comtois AU/49 15.00 40.00
121 Andreas Johnsson AU/49 20.00 50.00
122 Evan Bouchard AU/49 40.00 100.00
123 Travis Dermott AU/49 25.00 60.00
124 Juuso Valimaki AU/49 15.00 40.00
125 Henrik Borgstrom AU/49 25.00 60.00
126 Brett Howden AU/49 20.00 50.00
127 Warren Foegele AU/49 15.00 40.00
128 Adam Gaudette AU/49 25.00 60.00
129 Henri Jokiharju AU/49 12.00 30.00
130 Eeli Tolvanen AU/49 30.00 80.00
131 Noah Juulsen AU/49 15.00 40.00
132 Brady Tkachuk AU/49 50.00 125.00
133 Miro Heiskanen AU/49 40.00 100.00
134 Robert Thomas AU/49 30.00 80.00
135 Michael Rasmussen AU/49 20.00 50.00
136 Ryan Donato AU/49 25.00 60.00
137 Casey Mittelstadt AU/49 30.00 80.00
138 Jesperi Kotkaniemi AU/49 30.00 80.00
139 Andrei Svechnikov AU/49 40.00 100.00
140 Elias Pettersson AU/49 200.00 400.00

2018-19 Upper Deck Trilogy '03-04 15th Anniversary Retro Rookie Autographs

03ABT Brady Tkachuk 20.00 50.00
03AEP Elias Pettersson 150.00 250.00
03AJK Jesperi Kotkaniemi 12.00 30.00

2018-19 Upper Deck Trilogy '03-04 15th Anniversary Retro Rookie Jerseys

03AS Andrei Svechnikov 5.00 12.00
03BT Brady Tkachuk 6.00 15.00
03CM Casey Mittelstadt 4.00 10.00
03EP Elias Pettersson 25.00 60.00
03JK Jesperi Kotkaniemi 4.00 10.00
03RD Rasmus Dahlin 5.00 12.00

2018-19 Upper Deck Trilogy '03-04 15th Anniversary Retro Rookies

03AS Andrei Svechnikov 5.00 12.00
03BT Brady Tkachuk 6.00 15.00
03CM Casey Mittelstadt 4.00 10.00
03EP Elias Pettersson 15.00 40.00
03JK Jesperi Kotkaniemi 4.00 10.00
03RD Rasmus Dahlin 5.00 12.00

2018-19 Upper Deck Trilogy '03-04 15th Anniversary Retro Rookies Black

*BLACK/25: 1.25X TO 3X BASIC INSERTS
03BT Brady Tkachuk 30.00 80.00

2018-19 Upper Deck Trilogy All Star Signature Pucks

ASPCM Connor McDavid A 200.00 300.00
ASPPR Patrick Roy A 60.00 150.00
ASPVT Vladimir Tarasenko B 25.00 60.00
ASPWG Wayne Gretzky A 250.00 600.00

2018-19 Upper Deck Trilogy Auto Focus

AFBO Bobby Orr B 80.00 150.00
AFCM Connor McDavid A 200.00 300.00
AFMM Mark Messier A 40.00 100.00
AFWG Wayne Gretzky A 250.00 600.00

2018-19 Upper Deck Trilogy Hall of Fame Signature Pucks

HOFICC Chris Chelios B 8.00 20.00
HOFIGF Grant Fuhr C 12.00 30.00
HOFILR Larry Robinson B 8.00 20.00
HOFIMM Mike Modano B 15.00 40.00
HOFINU Norm Ullman C 8.00 20.00
HOFITS Teemu Selanne A 30.00 80.00

2018-19 Upper Deck Trilogy Honorary Triple Swatches

HTSDA Rasmus Dahlin/25 25.00 60.00
HTSDD Drew Doughty/49 12.00 30.00
HTSEB Ed Belfour/25 10.00 25.00
HTSEM Evgeni Malkin/25 20.00 50.00
HTSEP Elias Pettersson/49 30.00 80.00
HTSHZ Henrik Zetterberg/25 12.00 30.00
HTSMI Casey Mittelstadt/25 20.00 50.00
HTSMR Mark Recchi/25 12.00 30.00
HTSPR Chris Pronger/49 6.00 15.00
HTSRD Ryan Donato/49 15.00 40.00
HTSTD Tie Domi/25 8.00 20.00
HTSTS Tyler Seguin/25 12.00 30.00
HTSVT Vladimir Tarasenko/25 12.00 30.00
HTSWN William Nylander/49 40.00 100.00

2018-19 Upper Deck Trilogy Ice Scripts

ISAV Andrei Vasilevskiy C 15.00 40.00
ISCM Casey Mittelstadt C 20.00 50.00
ISET Eeli Tolvanen C 20.00 50.00
ISJG Jake Guentzel B 15.00 40.00
ISJP Joe Pavelski B 12.00 30.00
ISKS Kevin Shattenkirk B 6.00 15.00
ISKU Evgeny Kuznetsov A 12.00 30.00
ISMP Max Pacioretty A 10.00 25.00
ISRL Roberto Luongo A 15.00 40.00

2018-19 Upper Deck Trilogy Personal Scripts

PSCP Carey Price A 100.00 250.00
PSMA Marc-Andre Fleury C 60.00 150.00
PSSB Scotty Bowman B 25.00 60.00
PSSZ Steve Yzerman A 40.00 100.00
PSTS Teemu Selanne A 50.00 120.00
PSVT Vladimir Tarasenko C 30.00 80.00

2018-19 Upper Deck Trilogy Scripted Hall of Fame Plaques

SHOFAD Alex Delvecchio 25.00 60.00
SHOFBH Brett Hull 50.00 120.00
SHOFDS Darryl Sittler 40.00 100.00

2018-19 Upper Deck Trilogy Triple Relics

TRBPT Bossy/Potvin/Trottier/25 10.00 25.00
TRBSB Benn/Seguin/Bishop/49 12.00 30.00
TRDRB Dionne/Robitaille/Blake/25 12.00 30.00
TREBC Esposito/Bucyk/Cheevers/25 15.00 40.00
TRFMM Fleury/MacInnis McDonald/49 12.00 30.00
TRFQG Fleury/Quick/Gibson/49 20.00 50.00
TRGSD Gilmour/Sundin/Domi/25 12.00 30.00
TRHMK Hall/Malkin/Kopitar/25 20.00 50.00
TRHMN Hull/Modano/Nieuwendyk/25 20.00 50.00
TRMDG Mittelstadt/Donato Greenway/99 20.00 50.00
TRMOT McDavid/Ovechkin Toews/25 50.00 120.00
TRPAB Panarin/Atkinson Bobrovsky/99 20.00 50.00
TRPSD Pettersson/Svechnikov Dahlin/25 30.00 80.00
TRSCA Savard/Chelios/Amonte/25 10.00 25.00
TRSFB Subban/Forsberg/Bonino/99 15.00 40.00
TRSSN Sakic/Stastny/Nolan/25 20.00 50.00
TRTBS Tolvanen/Borgstrom/Sikura/99 20.00 50.00
TRYLP Yzerman/Lidstrom/Probert/25 25.00 60.00

2018-19 Upper Deck Trilogy Trophy Winners Signature Pucks

TWSNM Nathan MacKinnon B 60.00 150.00
TWSPR Patrick Roy A 40.00 100.00
TWSVH Victor Hedman B 20.00 50.00

2018-19 Upper Deck Trilogy Tryptichs

TCHI1 Patrick Kane PATCH/25 10.00 25.00
TCHI2 Brandon Saad JSY/99 4.00 10.00
TCHI3 Duncan Keith AU/49 4.00 10.00
TCOL2 Peter Forsberg JSY/49 10.00 25.00
TCOL3 Claude Lemieux STK/25 5.00 12.00
TEDM1 Leon Draisaitl STK/25 15.00 40.00
TEDM2 Milan Lucic GLV/49 4.00 10.00
TEDM3 Adam Larsson STK/49 10.00 25.00
TLAK1 Jonathan Quick BLKR/49 6.00 15.00
TLAK2 Dustin Brown GLV/25 5.00 12.00
TLAK3 Tyler Toffoli STK/25 5.00 12.00
TMTL2 Chris Chelios FS/25 5.00 12.00
TMTL3 Bobby Smith STK/25 5.00 12.00
TNET2 Ed Belfour PAD/25 5.00 12.00
TNET3 Roberto Luongo BLKR/25 8.00 20.00
TNYI2 Billy Smith PAD/49 5.00 12.00
TNYI3 Derek King STK/25 5.00 12.00
TNYR2 Mark Messier JSY/49 10.00 25.00
TNYR3 Brian Leetch TAPE/25 4.00 10.00
TRC11 Rasmus Dahlin JSY/99 12.00 30.00
TRC12 Elias Pettersson PATCH/25 30.00 80.00
TRC13 Andrei Svechnikov PATCH/49 12.00 30.00
TRC21 Casey Mittelstadt PATCH/49 10.00 25.00
TRC22 Ryan Donato JSY/99 8.00 20.00
TRC23 Adam Gaudette GLV/49 8.00 20.00
TSTL1 Al MacInnis STK/25 6.00 15.00
TSTL2 Pierre Turgeon STK/25 4.00 10.00
TSTL3 Chris Pronger PATCH/49 5.00 12.00
TTML1 Auston Matthews JSY/99 20.00 50.00
TTML3 Mitch Marner AU/49 8.00 20.00
TVGK1 Marc-Andre Fleury PATCH/25 10.00 25.00
TVGK2 William Karlsson PATCH/25 6.00 15.00
TVGK3 Jonathan Marchessault PATCH/49 6.00 15.00
TBLUE1 Vladimir Tarasenko GLV/25 6.00 15.00
TBLUE2 Brayden Schenn SKT/49 5.00 12.00
TBLUE3 Jaden Schwartz PATCH/49 6.00 15.00
TCAPS2 Evgeny Kuznetsov AU/49 6.00 15.00
TCAPS3 Nicklas Backstrom JSY/99 5.00 12.00
THABS2 Jonathan Drouin PATCH/25 4.00 10.00
THABS3 Brendan Gallagher JSY/99 5.00 12.00

2019-20 Upper Deck Trilogy

*VETS.RED: 5X TO 12X BASIC CARDS
*RC.RED/499: 1X TO 2.5X BASIC CARDS
*RC.RED/49: 2X TO 5X BASIC CARDS
1 Connor McDavid 1.50 4.00
2 Steven Stamkos .75 2.00
3 Brad Marchand .75 2.00
4 Jack Eichel .60 1.50
5 Jonathan Drouin .30 .75
6 Nathan MacKinnon 1.50 4.00
7 Mark Stone .40 1.00
8 Ryan O'Reilly .40 1.00
9 Brady Tkachuk .60 1.50
10 Patrick Kane .75 2.00
11 Tyler Seguin .40 1.00
12 Nico Hischier .60 1.50
13 Anders Lee .30 .75
14 John Gibson .40 1.00
15 Alexander Ovechkin 1.50 4.00
16 Carter Hart .40 1.00
17 Teuvo Teravainen .40 1.00
18 Pierre-Luc Dubois .30 .75
19 Dylan Larkin .40 1.00
20 Henrik Lundqvist .75 2.00
21 Matt Dumba .20 .50
22 Matthew Tkachuk .75 2.00
23 Matt Murray .40 1.00
24 Brock Boeser .40 1.00
25 Mark Scheifele .60 1.50
26 Viktor Arvidsson .20 .50
27 Aleksander Barkov .60 1.50
28 Brent Burns .40 1.00
29 Clayton Keller .40 1.00
30 Auston Matthews 1.50 4.00
31 Jonathan Quick .40 1.00
32 Marc-Andre Fleury .75 2.00
33 Mitch Marner .60 1.50
34 Jonathon Toews .60 1.50
35 Carey Price .75 2.00
36 Ben Bishop .30 .75
37 Alex DeBrincat .40 1.00
38 Brayden Point .40 1.00
39 Taylor Hall .40 1.00
40 John Tavares .60 1.50
41 Mathew Barzal .40 1.00
42 Tomas Hertl .40 1.00
43 Artemi Panarin .75 2.00
44 Leon Draisaitl 1.00 3.00
45 Johnny Gaudreau .60 1.50
46 Elias Pettersson .60 1.50
47 Sergei Bobrovsky .60 1.50
48 David Pastrnak .75 2.00
49 Jordan Binnington .60 1.50
50 Sidney Crosby 1.50 4.00
51 Nico Sturm RC 1.25 3.00
52 Adam Fox RC 4.00 10.00
53 Karson Kuhlman RC 1.50 4.00
54 Blake Lizotte RC 1.50 4.00
55 Dante Fabbro RC 1.50 4.00
56 Ilya Mikheyev RC 2.50 6.00
57 Max Jones RC 1.50 4.00
58 Kirby Dach RC 3.00 8.00
59 Taro Hirose RC 1.50 4.00
60 Jesper Boqvist RC 1.25 3.00
61 Philippe Myers RC 1.25 3.00
62 Ryan Poehling RC 2.50 6.00
63 Vitaly Abramov RC 1.50 4.00
64 Rasmus Sandin RC 2.50 6.00
65 Alexandre Texier RC 1.50 4.00
66 Oliver Wahlstrom RC 2.50 6.00
67 Victor Olofsson RC 3.00 8.00
68 Noah Dobson RC 4.00 10.00
69 Erik Brannstrom RC 1.50 4.00
70 Jimmy Schuldt RC 1.25 3.00
71 Carl Grundstrom RC 1.50 4.00
72 Joel Farabee RC 2.50 6.00
73 Teddy Blueger RC 1.50 4.00
74 Zach Senyshyn RC 1.50 4.00
75 Barrett Hayton RC 3.00 8.00
76 Nikita Gusev RC 2.50 6.00
77 Cody Glass RC 2.50 6.00
78 Filip Zadina RC 2.50 6.00
79 Nick Suzuki RC 6.00 15.00
80 Quinn Hughes RC 8.00 20.00
81 Cale Makar RC 8.00 20.00
82 Kaapo Kakko RC 2.50 6.00
83 Jack Hughes RC 8.00 20.00
84 Nico Sturm 6.00 15.00
85 Adam Fox 6.00 15.00
86 Karson Kuhlman 2.00 5.00
87 Blake Lizotte 2.50 6.00
88 Dante Fabbro 2.50 6.00
89 Ilya Mikheyev 4.00 10.00
90 Max Jones 2.50 6.00
91 Kirby Dach 5.00 12.00
92 Taro Hirose 2.50 6.00
93 Jesper Boqvist 2.00 5.00
94 Philippe Myers 2.00 5.00
95 Ryan Poehling 4.00 10.00
96 Vitaly Abramov 2.50 6.00
97 Rasmus Sandin 4.00 10.00
98 Alexandre Texier 2.50 6.00
99 Oliver Wahlstrom 4.00 10.00
100 Victor Olofsson 5.00 12.00
101 Noah Dobson 6.00 15.00
102 Erik Brannstrom 2.50 6.00
103 Jimmy Schuldt 2.00 5.00
104 Carl Grundstrom 2.50 6.00
105 Joel Farabee 4.00 10.00
106 Teddy Blueger 2.50 6.00
107 Zach Senyshyn 2.50 6.00
108 Barrett Hayton 5.00 12.00
109 Nikita Gusev 4.00 10.00
110 Cody Glass 4.00 10.00
111 Filip Zadina 4.00 10.00
112 Nick Suzuki 10.00 25.00
113 Quinn Hughes 12.00 30.00
114 Cale Makar 12.00 30.00
115 Kaapo Kakko 4.00 10.00
116 Jack Hughes 12.00 30.00
117 Nico Sturm 2.00 5.00
118 Adam Fox 6.00 15.00
119 Karson Kuhlman 2.00 5.00
120 Blake Lizotte 2.00 5.00
121 Dante Fabbro 2.00 5.00
122 Ilya Mikheyev 4.00 10.00
123 Max Jones 2.00 5.00
124 Kirby Dach 5.00 12.00
125 Taro Hirose 2.00 5.00
126 Jesper Boqvist 2.00 5.00
127 Philippe Myers 2.00 5.00
128 Ryan Poehling 4.00 10.00
129 Vitaly Abramov 2.00 5.00
130 Rasmus Sandin 4.00 10.00
131 Alexandre Texier 2.50 6.00
132 Oliver Wahlstrom 4.00 10.00
133 Victor Olofsson 5.00 12.00
134 Noah Dobson 6.00 15.00
135 Erik Brannstrom 2.50 6.00
136 Jimmy Schuldt 2.00 5.00
137 Carl Grundstrom 2.50 6.00
138 Joel Farabee 4.00 10.00
139 Teddy Blueger 2.50 6.00
140 Zach Senyshyn 2.50 6.00
141 Barrett Hayton 5.00 12.00
142 Nikita Gusev 4.00 10.00
143 Cody Glass 4.00 10.00
144 Filip Zadina 4.00 10.00
145 Nick Suzuki 10.00 25.00
146 Quinn Hughes 12.00 30.00
147 Cale Makar 12.00 30.00
148 Kaapo Kakko 4.00 10.00
149 Jack Hughes 20.00 50.00
150 Hughes/Hughes/Makar 30.00 80.00

2019-20 Upper Deck Trilogy Blue

3 Brad Marchand JSY AU/25 30.00 80.00
5 Jonathan Drouin JSY AU/25 12.00 30.00
6 Nathan MacKinnon JSY/25 20.00 50.00
8 Ryan O'Reilly JSY AU/25 15.00 40.00
9 Brady Tkachuk JSY AU/25 25.00 60.00
11 Tyler Seguin JSY/25 10.00 25.00
12 Nico Hischier JSY AU/25 25.00 60.00
13 Anders Lee JSY AU/25 12.00 30.00
14 John Gibson JSY AU/25 15.00 40.00
17 Teuvo Teravainen JSY AU/25 15.00 40.00
18 Pierre-Luc Dubois JSY AU/25 12.00 30.00
21 Matt Dumba JSY AU/25 10.00 25.00
22 Matthew Tkachuk JSY AU/25 30.00 80.00
23 Matt Murray JSY AU/25 15.00 40.00
24 Brock Boeser JSY AU/25 20.00 50.00
25 Mark Scheifele JSY AU/25 25.00 60.00
26 Viktor Arvidsson JSY AU/25 10.00 25.00
27 Aleksander Barkov JSY AU/25 25.00 60.00
28 Brent Burns JSY AU/25 15.00 40.00
29 Clayton Keller JSY/25 8.00 20.00
31 Jonathan Quick JSY AU/25 20.00 50.00
33 Mitch Marner JSY AU/25 25.00 60.00
36 Ben Bishop JSY AU/25 12.00 30.00
37 Alex DeBrincat JSY AU/25 20.00 50.00
39 Taylor Hall JSY AU/25 12.00 30.00
41 Mathew Barzal JSY AU/25 25.00 60.00
42 Tomas Hertl JSY AU/25 15.00 40.00
44 Leon Draisaitl JSY AU/25 50.00 125.00
48 David Pastrnak JSY/25 20.00 50.00

2019-20 Upper Deck Trilogy Silver

1 Connor McDavid AU A 150.00 250.00
2 Steven Stamkos AU B 15.00 40.00
3 Brad Marchand AU C 15.00 40.00
4 Jack Eichel AU B 12.00 30.00
7 Mark Stone AU C 10.00 25.00
8 Ryan O'Reilly AU D 8.00 20.00
9 Brady Tkachuk AU E 12.00 30.00
10 Patrick Kane AU B 15.00 40.00
12 Nico Hischier AU B 12.00 30.00
13 Anders Lee AU E 6.00 15.00
14 John Gibson AU C 8.00 20.00
16 Carter Hart AU A 8.00 20.00
17 Teuvo Teravainen AU D 8.00 20.00
20 Henrik Lundqvist AU B 20.00 50.00
21 Matt Dumba AU E 5.00 12.00
22 Matthew Tkachuk AU E 15.00 40.00
24 Brock Boeser AU C 10.00 25.00
25 Mark Scheifele AU D 12.00 30.00
26 Viktor Arvidsson AU E 5.00 12.00
27 Aleksander Barkov AU D 12.00 30.00
28 Brent Burns AU C 8.00 20.00
30 Auston Matthews AU A 30.00 80.00
32 Marc-Andre Fleury AU B 15.00 40.00
33 Mitch Marner AU C 12.00 30.00
34 Jonathon Toews AU B 12.00 30.00
36 Ben Bishop AU D 6.00 15.00
37 Alex DeBrincat AU C 10.00 25.00
40 John Tavares AU B 12.00 30.00
42 Tomas Hertl AU E 8.00 20.00
43 Artemi Panarin AU A 15.00 40.00
44 Leon Draisaitl AU D 25.00 60.00
45 Johnny Gaudreau AU B 12.00 30.00
46 Elias Pettersson AU A 12.00 30.00
47 Sergei Bobrovsky AU B 12.00 30.00
49 Jordan Binnington AU B 12.00 30.00
50 Sidney Crosby AU A 30.00 80.00
51 Nico Sturm AU/399 6.00 15.00
52 Adam Fox AU/399 20.00 50.00
53 Karson Kuhlman AU/399 8.00 20.00
54 Blake Lizotte AU/399 8.00 20.00
55 Dante Fabbro AU/399 8.00 20.00
56 Ilya Mikheyev AU/399 12.00 30.00
57 Max Jones AU/399 8.00 20.00
58 Kirby Dach AU/399 15.00 40.00
59 Taro Hirose AU/399 8.00 20.00
60 Jesper Boqvist AU/399 6.00 15.00
61 Philippe Myers AU/399 6.00 15.00
62 Ryan Poehling AU/399 12.00 30.00
64 Rasmus Sandin AU/399 12.00 30.00
65 Alexandre Texier AU/399 8.00 20.00
66 Oliver Wahlstrom AU/399 12.00 30.00
67 Victor Olofsson AU/399 15.00 40.00
68 Noah Dobson AU/399 20.00 50.00
69 Erik Brannstrom AU/399 8.00 20.00
70 Jimmy Schuldt AU/399 6.00 15.00
71 Carl Grundstrom AU/399 8.00 20.00
72 Joel Farabee AU/399 12.00 30.00
73 Teddy Blueger AU/399 8.00 20.00
74 Zach Senyshyn AU/399 8.00 20.00
77 Cody Glass AU/249 12.00 30.00
78 Filip Zadina AU/249 12.00 30.00
79 Nick Suzuki AU/249 30.00 80.00
80 Quinn Hughes AU/249 40.00 100.00
81 Cale Makar AU/249 40.00 100.00
83 Jack Hughes AU/249 40.00 100.00
84 Nico Sturm AU/199 8.00 20.00
85 Adam Fox AU/199 25.00 60.00
86 Karson Kuhlman AU/199 10.00 25.00
87 Blake Lizotte AU/199 10.00 25.00
88 Dante Fabbro AU/199 10.00 25.00
89 Ilya Mikheyev AU/199 15.00 40.00
90 Max Jones AU/199 10.00 25.00
91 Kirby Dach AU/199 20.00 50.00
92 Taro Hirose AU/199 10.00 25.00
93 Jesper Boqvist AU/199 8.00 20.00
94 Philippe Myers AU/199 8.00 20.00
95 Ryan Poehling AU/199 15.00 40.00
96 Vitaly Abramov AU/199 10.00 25.00
97 Rasmus Sandin AU/199 15.00 40.00
98 Alexandre Texier AU/199 10.00 25.00
99 Oliver Wahlstrom AU/199 15.00 40.00
100 Victor Olofsson AU/199 20.00 50.00
101 Noah Dobson AU/199 25.00 60.00
102 Erik Brannstrom AU/199 10.00 25.00
103 Jimmy Schuldt AU/199 8.00 20.00
104 Carl Grundstrom AU/199 10.00 25.00
105 Joel Farabee AU/199 15.00 40.00
106 Teddy Blueger AU/199 10.00 25.00
107 Zach Senyshyn AU/199 10.00 25.00
108 Barrett Hayton AU/199 20.00 50.00
110 Cody Glass AU/99 15.00 40.00
111 Filip Zadina AU/99 15.00 40.00
112 Nick Suzuki AU/99 40.00 100.00
113 Quinn Hughes AU/99 50.00 125.00
114 Cale Makar AU/99 50.00 125.00
116 Jack Hughes AU/99 50.00 125.00
117 Nico Sturm AU/49 12.00 30.00
118 Adam Fox AU/49 30.00 80.00
119 Karson Kuhlman AU/49 15.00 40.00
120 Blake Lizotte AU/49 12.00 30.00
121 Dante Fabbro AU/49 12.00 30.00
122 Ilya Mikheyev AU/49 20.00 50.00
123 Max Jones AU/49 12.00 30.00
124 Kirby Dach AU/49 25.00 60.00
125 Taro Hirose AU/49 12.00 30.00
126 Jesper Boqvist AU/49 10.00 25.00
127 Philippe Myers AU/49 10.00 25.00
128 Ryan Poehling AU/49 20.00 50.00
129 Vitaly Abramov AU/49 12.00 30.00
130 Rasmus Sandin AU/49 20.00 50.00
131 Alexandre Texier AU/49 12.00 30.00
132 Oliver Wahlstrom AU/49 20.00 50.00
133 Victor Olofsson AU/49 25.00 60.00
134 Noah Dobson AU/49 30.00 80.00
135 Erik Brannstrom AU/49 12.00 30.00
136 Jimmy Schuldt AU/49 10.00 25.00
137 Carl Grundstrom AU/49 12.00 30.00
138 Joel Farabee AU/49 20.00 50.00
139 Teddy Blueger AU/49 12.00 30.00
140 Zach Senyshyn AU/49 12.00 30.00
141 Barrett Hayton AU/49 25.00 60.00
143 Cody Glass AU/25 20.00 50.00
144 Filip Zadina AU/25 20.00 50.00
145 Nick Suzuki AU/25 50.00 125.00
146 Quinn Hughes AU/25 60.00 150.00
147 Cale Makar AU/25 60.00 150.00
149 Jack Hughes AU/25 60.00 150.00

2019-20 Upper Deck Trilogy All Star Signature Pucks

ASPBM Brad Marchand 15.00 40.00
ASPLD Leon Draisaitl 25.00 60.00
ASPMH Miro Heiskanen 10.00 25.00

2019-20 Upper Deck Trilogy Auto Focus

AFAV Andrei Vasilevskiy C 20.00 50.00
AFBM Brad Marchand B 25.00 60.00
AFHL Henrik Lundqvist A 60.00 150.00
AFJT Joe Thornton B 20.00 50.00
AFMF Marc-Andre Fleury B 25.00 60.00

2019-20 Upper Deck Trilogy Crystallized Signatures

CAL Anders Lee B 6.00 15.00
CBB Brent Burns A 8.00 20.00
CBI Ben Bishop A 6.00 15.00
CCA Cam Atkinson B 8.00 20.00
CCM Connor McDavid A 150.00 250.00
CES Eric Staal B 12.00 30.00
CHE Connor Hellebuyck B 15.00 40.00
CJT John Tavares A 12.00 30.00
CLD Leon Draisaitl A 25.00 60.00
CNH Nico Hischier A 12.00 30.00

2019-20 Upper Deck Trilogy Hall of Fame Signature Pucks

HOFIBH Brett Hull 25.00 60.00
HOFIMB Martin Brodeur 30.00 80.00
HOFISB Scotty Bowman 12.00 30.00
HOFIWR Willie O'Ree 15.00 40.00

2019-20 Upper Deck Trilogy Honorary Triple Swatches

HTSAE Aaron Ekblad/35 12.00 30.00
HTSAK Anze Kopitar/25 15.00 40.00
HTSAL Adam Larsson/35 8.00 20.00
HTSBH Brett Hull/25 20.00 50.00
HTSCC Claude Giroux/35 10.00 25.00
HTSCP Carey Price/25 20.00 50.00
HTSFZ Filip Zadina/35 15.00 40.00
HTSHO Bo Horvat/35 12.00 30.00
HTSJG Jake Guentzel/35 15.00 40.00
HTSJH Jack Hughes/25 50.00 125.00
HTSKK Kaapo Kakko/35 15.00 40.00
HTSMA Cale Makar/35 50.00 125.00
HTSNH Noah Hanifin/35 10.00 25.00
HTSPD Pierre-Luc Dubois/35 8.00 20.00
HTSTB Tom Barrasso/25 8.00 20.00

2019-20 Upper Deck Trilogy Rookie Renditions

*RED/799: .6X TO 1.5X BASIC INSERTS
*BLUE/399: 1X TO 2.5X BASIC INSERTS
RR1 Cale Makar 2.50 6.00
RR2 Vitaly Abramov .50 1.25
RR3 Mackenzie MacEachern .50 1.25
RR4 Brady Keeper .50 1.25
RR5 Erik Brannstrom .50 1.25
RR6 Jimmy Schuldt .40 1.00
RR7 Aleksi Saarela .50 1.25
RR8 Zach Senyshyn .50 1.25
RR9 Ryan Kuffner .40 1.00
RR10 Ryan Poehling .75 2.00
RR11 Riley Stillman .50 1.25
RR12 Carl Grundstrom .50 1.25
RR13 Kole Sherwood .50 1.25
RR14 Rem Pitlick .50 1.25
RR15 Teddy Blueger .50 1.25
RR16 Nico Sturm .40 1.00
RR17 Blake Lizotte .50 1.25
RR18 Dante Fabbro .50 1.25
RR19 Brandon Gignac .40 1.00
RR20 Alexandre Texier .50 1.25
RR21 Karson Kuhlman .50 1.25
RR22 Trent Frederic .50 1.25
RR23 Zack MacEwen .40 1.00
RR24 Libor Hajek .40 1.00
RR25 Filip Zadina .75 2.00
RR26 Philippe Myers .40 1.00
RR27 Max Veronneau .40 1.00
RR28 Victor Olofsson 1.00 2.50
RR29 Joey Daccord 1.00 2.50
RR30 Quinn Hughes 2.50 6.00
RR31 Guillaume Brisebois .50 1.25
RR32 Nathan Bastian .50 1.25
RR33 Taro Hirose .50 1.25
RR34 Rudolfs Balcers .50 1.25
RR35 Ryan Lindgren .50 1.25
RR36 Max Jones .50 1.25
RR37 Kaden Fulcher .50 1.25
RR38 Noah Dobson 1.25 3.00
RR39 Nikita Gusev .75 2.00
RR40 Nick Suzuki 2.00 5.00
RR41 Adam Fox 1.25 3.00
RR42 Ilya Mikheyev .75 2.00
RR43 Dominik Kubalik 1.00 2.50
RR44 Cody Glass .75 2.00
RR45 Kaapo Kakko .75 2.00
RR46 Elvis Merzlikins 1.00 2.50
RR47 Barrett Hayton 1.00 2.50
RR48 Rasmus Sandin .75 2.00
RR49 Oliver Wahlstrom .75 2.00
RR50 Jack Hughes 2.50 6.00

2019-20 Upper Deck Trilogy Rookie Renditions Autographs Gold

RR1 Cale Makar A 40.00 100.00
RR2 Vitaly Abramov B 8.00 20.00
RR3 Mackenzie MacEachern D 8.00 20.00
RR4 Brady Keeper D 8.00 20.00
RR5 Erik Brannstrom B 8.00 20.00
RR6 Jimmy Schuldt B 6.00 15.00
RR8 Zach Senyshyn C 8.00 20.00
RR9 Ryan Kuffner D 6.00 15.00
RR10 Ryan Poehling B 12.00 30.00
RR11 Riley Stillman D 8.00 20.00
RR12 Carl Grundstrom B 8.00 20.00
RR13 Kole Sherwood D 8.00 20.00
RR14 Rem Pitlick D 8.00 20.00
RR15 Teddy Blueger C 8.00 20.00
RR16 Nico Sturm C 6.00 15.00
RR17 Blake Lizotte D 8.00 20.00
RR18 Dante Fabbro B 8.00 20.00
RR19 Brandon Gignac D 6.00 15.00
RR20 Alexandre Texier C 8.00 20.00
RR21 Karson Kuhlman C 8.00 20.00
RR22 Trent Frederic C 8.00 20.00
RR23 Zack MacEwen D 6.00 15.00
RR24 Libor Hajek D 6.00 15.00
RR25 Filip Zadina B 12.00 30.00
RR26 Philippe Myers A 6.00 15.00
RR27 Max Veronneau D 6.00 15.00
RR28 Victor Olofsson B 15.00 40.00
RR29 Joey Daccord D 15.00 40.00
RR30 Quinn Hughes A 40.00 100.00
RR31 Guillaume Brisebois D 8.00 20.00
RR32 Nathan Bastian C 8.00 20.00
RR33 Taro Hirose B 8.00 20.00
RR34 Rudolfs Balcers C 8.00 20.00
RR35 Ryan Lindgren D 8.00 20.00
RR36 Max Jones B 8.00 20.00
RR37 Kaden Fulcher D 8.00 20.00
RR38 Noah Dobson A 20.00 50.00
RR40 Nick Suzuki A 30.00 80.00
RR41 Adam Fox C 20.00 50.00
RR42 Ilya Mikheyev A 12.00 30.00
RR44 Cody Glass B 12.00 30.00
RR46 Elvis Merzlikins D 15.00 40.00
RR47 Barrett Hayton A 15.00 40.00
RR48 Rasmus Sandin B 12.00 30.00
RR49 Oliver Wahlstrom A 12.00 30.00
RR50 Jack Hughes A 40.00 100.00

2019-20 Upper Deck Trilogy Rookie Renditions Patch Autographs Gold

RR1 Cale Makar/25 80.00 200.00
RR2 Vitaly Abramov/49 15.00 40.00
RR3 Mackenzie MacEachern/49 15.00 40.00
RR4 Brady Keeper/49 15.00 40.00
RR5 Erik Brannstrom/49 15.00 40.00
RR6 Jimmy Schuldt/49 15.00 40.00
RR8 Zach Senyshyn/49 15.00 40.00
RR9 Ryan Kuffner/49 12.00 30.00
RR10 Ryan Poehling/25 25.00 60.00
RR11 Riley Stillman/49 15.00 40.00
RR12 Carl Grundstrom/49 15.00 40.00
RR13 Kole Sherwood/49 15.00 40.00
RR14 Rem Pitlick/49 15.00 40.00
RR15 Teddy Blueger/49 15.00 40.00
RR16 Nico Sturm/49 12.00 30.00
RR17 Blake Lizotte/49 15.00 40.00
RR18 Dante Fabbro/49 15.00 40.00
RR19 Brandon Gignac/49 12.00 30.00
RR20 Alexandre Texier/49 15.00 40.00
RR21 Karson Kuhlman/49 15.00 40.00
RR22 Trent Frederic/49 15.00 40.00
RR23 Zack MacEwen/49 12.00 30.00
RR24 Libor Hajek/49 12.00 30.00
RR25 Filip Zadina/25 25.00 60.00
RR26 Philippe Myers/49 12.00 30.00
RR27 Max Veronneau/49 12.00 30.00
RR28 Victor Olofsson/25 30.00 80.00
RR29 Joey Daccord/49 30.00 80.00
RR30 Quinn Hughes/25 80.00 200.00
RR31 Guillaume Brisebois/49 15.00 40.00
RR33 Taro Hirose/49 15.00 40.00
RR34 Rudolfs Balcers/49 15.00 40.00
RR35 Ryan Lindgren/49 15.00 40.00
RR36 Max Jones/49 15.00 40.00
RR37 Kaden Fulcher/49 15.00 40.00
RR38 Noah Dobson/49 40.00 100.00
RR40 Nick Suzuki/25 60.00 150.00
RR41 Adam Fox/49 40.00 100.00
RR42 Ilya Mikheyev/49 25.00 60.00
RR44 Cody Glass/25 25.00 60.00
RR46 Elvis Merzlikins/49 30.00 80.00
RR47 Barrett Hayton/49 30.00 80.00
RR48 Rasmus Sandin/25 25.00 60.00
RR49 Oliver Wahlstrom/49 25.00 60.00
RR50 Jack Hughes/25 80.00 200.00

2019-20 Upper Deck Trilogy Rookie Signature Pucks

*TEAM.LOGO/25: .8X TO 2X BASIC INSERTS
RSPDF Dante Fabbro C 8.00 20.00
RSPEB Erik Brannstrom C 8.00 20.00
RSPJH Jack Hughes A 40.00 100.00
RSPKD Kirby Dach B 15.00 40.00
RSPQH Quinn Hughes A 40.00 100.00
RSPRP Ryan Poehling B 12.00 30.00

2019-20 Upper Deck Trilogy Scripted Hall of Fame Plaques

SHOFJL Jacques Lemaire 50.00 125.00
SHOFMM Mark Messier 60.00 150.00
SHOFNL Nicklas Lidstrom 50.00 125.00

2019-20 Upper Deck Trilogy Signature Pucks

*TEAM.LOGO/20: .6X TO 1.5X BASIC INSERTS
SPAL Anders Lee C 6.00 15.00
SPAM Anthony Mantha C 6.00 15.00
SPBB Ben Bishop B 6.00 15.00
SPDB Drake Batherson D 8.00 20.00
SPDS Dylan Strome C 10.00 25.00
SPES Eric Staal B 8.00 20.00
SPHB Henrik Borgstrom D 6.00 15.00
SPJV Jakub Vrana C 8.00 20.00
SPKT Kyle Turris D 6.00 15.00
SPMG Mikael Granlund C 6.00 15.00
SPMM Matt Murray B 8.00 20.00
SPMW Miles Wood D 5.00 12.00
SPNH Nico Hischier A 12.00 30.00
SPOB Oliver Bjorkstrand D 6.00 15.00
SPRD Ryan Dzingel D 6.00 15.00

SPSJ Seth Jones D 8.00 20.00
SPTB Tyler Bertuzzi D 6.00 15.00
SPTH Tomas Hertl B 8.00 20.00

2019-20 Upper Deck Trilogy Triple Relics

TRAFD Atkinson/Foligno/Dubois/35 15.00 40.00
TRDBF Doughty/Burns/Fowler/35 20.00 50.00
TRFTP Fleury/Tuch/Pacioretty/25 30.00 80.00
TRHHP Hughes/Hughes/Poehling/35 80.00 200.00
TRHLN Nugent-Hopkins
Larsson/Nurse/35 20.00 50.00
TRMZH Makar/Zadina/Hughes/35 80.00 200.00
TRSSS Staal/Staal/Staal/35 15.00 40.00
TRTBO Tarasenko/Bouwmeester
O'Reilly/25 20.00 50.00

2019-20 Upper Deck Trilogy Trophy Winner Signature Pucks

TWSAV Andrei Vasilevskiy B 25.00 60.00
TWSBB Brent Burns B 15.00 40.00
TWSBO Bobby Orr B 60.00 150.00
TWSWG Wayne Gretzky A 200.00 500.00

2020-21 Upper Deck Trilogy

1 Sidney Crosby 1.50 4.00
2 Quinn Hughes .75 2.00
3 Matthew Tkachuk .75 2.00
4 Nikita Kucherov .75 2.00
5 Nathan MacKinnon 1.50 4.00
6 William Karlsson .40 1.00
7 Sebastian Aho .60 1.50
8 Brendan Gallagher .40 1.00
9 Travis Konecny .40 1.00
10 Jonathan Toews .60 1.50
11 Roman Josi .40 1.00
12 Artemi Panarin .75 2.00
13 Dylan Larkin .40 1.00
14 Joe Pavelski .40 1.00
15 Auston Matthews 1.50 4.00
16 Martin Jones .30 .75
17 Nico Hischier .60 1.50
18 Sam Reinhart .75 2.00
19 Alex Ovechkin 1.50 4.00
20 Connor McDavid 1.50 4.00
21 Ryan Suter .30 .75
22 Connor Hellebuyck .75 2.00
23 Colton Parayko .30 .75
24 Nick Schmaltz .30 .75
25 Anze Kopitar .60 1.50
26 Brady Tkachuk .60 1.50
27 Nick Foligno .30 .75
28 Jonathan Huberdeau .40 1.00
29 Josh Bailey .30 .75
30 Brad Marchand .75 2.00
31 Adam Henrique .30 .75
32 Elias Pettersson .60 1.50
33 Carey Price .75 2.00
34 Carter Hart .40 1.00
35 Cale Makar .75 2.00
36 Jake Guentzel .60 1.50
37 John Tavares .60 1.50
38 Leon Draisaitl 1.00 3.00
39 Brayden Schenn .40 1.00
40 Jason Spezza .40 1.00
41 Brock Boeser .40 1.00
42 Marc Staal .20 .50
43 Patrick Kane .75 2.00
44 Evgeni Malkin .75 2.00
45 Jack Eichel .60 1.50
46 Marc-Andre Fleury .75 2.00
47 Jakub Vrana .40 1.00
48 Andrei Svechnikov .40 1.00
49 Patrice Bergeron .40 1.00
50 Andrei Vasilevskiy .60 1.50
51 Alexander Yelesin/999 RC 1.50 4.00
52 Pierre-Olivier Joseph/999 RC 2.00 5.00
53 Gustav Lindstrom/999 RC 1.50 4.00
54 Joel Kiviranta/999 RC 2.00 5.00
55 Maxim Letunov/999 RC 1.50 4.00
56 Kieffer Bellows/999 RC 1.50 4.00
57 Michael DiPietro/999 RC 2.50 6.00
58 Morgan Geekie/999 RC 2.00 5.00
59 Tyler Benson/999 RC 2.00 5.00
59 Lucas Carlsson/999 RC 1.50 4.00
60 Alex Belzile/999 RC 1.50 4.00
61 Alexander Alexeyev/999 RC 1.50 4.00
62 Jake Evans/999 RC 2.00 5.00
64 Vitali Kravtsov/999 RC 4.00 10.00
65 Brandon Hagel/999 RC 2.50 6.00
66 Jake Oettinger/999 RC 5.00 12.00
67 Egor Zamula/999 RC 1.50 4.00
68 Mikey Anderson/999 RC 2.00 5.00
69 Shane Bowers/999 RC 1.50 4.00
70 Gabe Vilardi/999 RC 3.00 8.00
71 Martin Kaut/999 RC 2.00 5.00
72 Liam Foudy/999 RC 2.00 5.00
73 Timothy Liljegren/999 RC 2.00 5.00
74 Josh Norris/999 RC 3.00 8.00
75 Thomas Harley/999 RC 3.00 8.00
76 Jason Robertson/999 RC 5.00 12.00
77 Victor Soderstrom/999 RC 1.50 4.00
78 Ty Dellandrea/999 RC 2.00 5.00
79 Peyton Krebs/999 RC 3.00 8.00
80 Nick Robertson/999 RC 3.00 8.00
81 Bowen Byram/999 RC 4.00 10.00
82 Connor McMichael/999 RC 3.00 8.00
83 Alexis Lafreniere/999 RC 15.00 40.00
84 Alexander Yelesin/499 2.50 6.00
85 Pierre-Olivier Joseph/499 3.00 8.00
86 Gustav Lindstrom/499 2.50 6.00
87 Joel Kiviranta/499 3.00 8.00
88 Maxim Letunov/499 2.50 6.00
89 Kieffer Bellows/499 2.50 6.00
90 Michael DiPietro/499 4.00 10.00
91 Morgan Geekie/499 3.00 8.00
92 Tyler Benson/499 3.00 8.00
93 Lucas Carlsson/499 2.50 6.00
94 Alex Belzile/499 2.50 6.00
95 Alexander Alexeyev/499 2.50 6.00
96 Jake Evans/499 3.00 8.00
97 Vitali Kravtsov/499 6.00 15.00
98 Brandon Hagel/499 4.00 10.00
99 Jake Oettinger/499 8.00 20.00
AR Alexander Romanov/299 4.00 10.00
AR Alexander Romanov/499 4.00 10.00
AR Alexander Romanov/999 RC 2.50 6.00
DC Dylan Cozens/999 RC 3.00 8.00
DC Dylan Cozens/499 5.00 12.00
DC Dylan Cozens/299 5.00 12.00
IS Ilya Sorokin/499 8.00 20.00
IS Ilya Sorokin/999 RC 5.00 12.00
IS Ilya Sorokin/299 8.00 20.00
KK Kirill Kaprizov/999 RC 30.00 80.00
KK Kirill Kaprizov/499 40.00 100.00
KK Kirill Kaprizov/299 60.00 150.00
ST Tim Stutzle/499 15.00 40.00
ST Tim Stutzle/999 RC 10.00 25.00
ST Tim Stutzle/299 20.00 50.00
TS Ty Smith/999 RC 3.00 8.00
TS Ty Smith/499 5.00 12.00
TS Ty Smith/299 5.00 12.00
100 Egor Zamula/499 2.50 6.00
101 Mikey Anderson/499 3.00 8.00
102 Shane Bowers/499 2.50 6.00
103 Gabe Vilardi/499 5.00 12.00
104 Martin Kaut/499 3.00 8.00
105 Liam Foudy/499 3.00 8.00
106 Timothy Liljegren/499 3.00 8.00
107 Josh Norris/499 5.00 12.00
108 Thomas Harley/499 5.00 12.00
109 Jason Robertson/499 8.00 20.00
110 Victor Soderstrom/499 2.50 6.00
111 Ty Dellandrea/499 3.00 8.00
112 Peyton Krebs/499 5.00 12.00
113 Nick Robertson/499 5.00 12.00
114 Bowen Byram/499 6.00 15.00
115 Connor McMichael/499 5.00 12.00
116 Alexis Lafreniere/499 20.00 50.00
117 Alexander Yelesin/299 2.50 6.00
118 Pierre-Olivier Joseph/299 3.00 8.00
119 Gustav Lindstrom/299 2.50 6.00
120 Joel Kiviranta/299 3.00 8.00
121 Maxim Letunov/299 2.50 6.00
122 Kieffer Bellows/299 2.50 6.00
123 Michael DiPietro/299 4.00 10.00
124 Morgan Geekie/299 3.00 8.00
125 Tyler Benson/299 3.00 8.00
126 Lucas Carlsson/299 2.50 6.00
127 Alex Belzile/299 2.50 6.00
128 Alexander Alexeyev/299 2.50 6.00
129 Jake Evans/299 3.00 8.00
130 Vitali Kravtsov/299 6.00 15.00
131 Brandon Hagel/299 4.00 10.00
132 Jake Oettinger/299 8.00 20.00
133 Egor Zamula/299 2.50 6.00
134 Mikey Anderson/299 3.00 8.00
135 Shane Bowers/299 2.50 6.00
136 Gabe Vilardi/299 5.00 12.00
137 Martin Kaut/299 3.00 8.00
138 Liam Foudy/299 3.00 8.00
139 Timothy Liljegren/299 3.00 8.00
140 Josh Norris/299 5.00 12.00
141 Thomas Harley/299 5.00 12.00
142 Jason Robertson/299 8.00 20.00
143 Victor Soderstrom/299 2.50 6.00
144 Ty Dellandrea/299 3.00 8.00
145 Peyton Krebs/299 5.00 12.00
146 Nick Robertson/299 5.00 12.00
147 Bowen Byram/299 6.00 15.00
148 Connor McMichael/299 5.00 12.00
149 Alexis Lafreniere/299 30.00 80.00
150 McMichael/Byram/Lafreniere 60.00 150.00

2020-21 Upper Deck Trilogy Red

*VETS.RED: 5X TO 12X BASIC
*RC.RED/499: 1X TO 2.5X BASIC
*RC.RED/49: 1.25X TO 3X BASIC

2020-21 Upper Deck Trilogy Silver

6 William Karlsson AU D 10.00 25.00
8 Brendan Gallagher AU D 8.00 20.00
10 Jonathan Toews AU A 12.00 30.00
11 Roman Josi AU D 8.00 20.00
14 Joe Pavelski AU D 10.00 25.00
16 Martin Jones AU C 6.00 15.00
17 Nico Hischier AU C 12.00 30.00
18 Sam Reinhart AU E 15.00 40.00
21 Ryan Suter AU E 6.00 15.00
22 Connor Hellebuyck AU D 15.00 40.00
23 Colton Parayko AU E 6.00 15.00
25 Anze Kopitar AU B 12.00 30.00
27 Nick Foligno AU C 6.00 15.00
29 Josh Bailey AU C 6.00 15.00
30 Brad Marchand AU B 15.00 40.00
33 Carey Price AU A 15.00 40.00
36 Jake Guentzel AU C 12.00 30.00
37 John Tavares AU B 12.00 30.00
39 Brayden Schenn AU C 8.00 20.00
40 Jason Spezza AU D 8.00 20.00
41 Brock Boeser AU B 10.00 25.00
42 Marc Staal AU E 5.00 12.00
44 Evgeni Malkin AU A 15.00 40.00
45 Jack Eichel AU B 12.00 30.00
46 Marc-Andre Fleury AU B 15.00 40.00
47 Jakub Vrana AU E 8.00 20.00
48 Andrei Svechnikov AU E 10.00 25.00
50 Andrei Vasilevskiy AU C 12.00 30.00
53 Gustav Lindstrom AU/399 8.00 20.00
54 Joel Kiviranta AU/399 10.00 25.00
55 Maxim Letunov AU/399 8.00 20.00
56 Kieffer Bellows AU/399 8.00 20.00
58 Morgan Geekie AU/399 10.00 25.00
59 Tyler Benson AU/399 10.00 25.00
59 Lucas Carlsson AU/399 8.00 20.00
60 Alex Belzile AU/399 8.00 20.00
62 Jake Evans AU/399 10.00 25.00
65 Brandon Hagel AU/399 12.00 30.00
66 Jake Oettinger AU/399 25.00 60.00
68 Mikey Anderson AU/399 10.00 25.00
69 Shane Bowers AU/399 8.00 20.00
70 Gabe Vilardi AU/399 15.00 40.00
71 Martin Kaut AU/399 10.00 25.00
72 Liam Foudy AU/399 10.00 25.00
73 Timothy Liljegren AU/399 10.00 25.00
74 Josh Norris AU/249 15.00 40.00
75 Thomas Harley AU/249 15.00 40.00
76 Jason Robertson AU/249 60.00 150.00
77 Victor Soderstrom AU/249 8.00 20.00
78 Ty Dellandrea AU/249 10.00 25.00
79 Peyton Krebs AU/249 15.00 40.00
80 Nick Robertson AU/249 15.00 40.00
81 Bowen Byram AU/249 20.00 50.00
82 Connor McMichael AU/249 15.00 40.00
83 Alexis Lafreniere AU/249 150.00 400.00
84 Alexander Yelesin AU/199 10.00 25.00
85 Pierre-Olivier Joseph AU/199 12.00 30.00
86 Gustav Lindstrom AU/199 10.00 25.00
87 Joel Kiviranta AU/199 12.00 30.00
88 Maxim Letunov AU/199 10.00 25.00
89 Kieffer Bellows AU/199 10.00 25.00
91 Morgan Geekie AU/199 12.00 30.00
92 Tyler Benson AU/199 12.00 30.00
93 Lucas Carlsson AU/199 10.00 25.00
94 Alex Belzile AU/199 10.00 25.00
96 Jake Evans AU/199 12.00 30.00
98 Brandon Hagel AU/199 15.00 40.00
99 Jake Oettinger AU/199 30.00 80.00
AR Alexander Romanov AU/199 15.00 40.00
AR Alexander Romanov AU/25 25.00 60.00
DC Dylan Cozens AU/399 15.00 40.00
DC Dylan Cozens AU/25 30.00 80.00
DC Dylan Cozens AU/199 20.00 50.00
IS Ilya Sorokin AU/199 60.00 150.00
KK Kirill Kaprizov AU/249 150.00 400.00
KK Kirill Kaprizov AU/99 200.00 500.00
KK Kirill Kaprizov AU/25 300.00 800.00
ST Tim Stutzle AU/249 50.00 125.00
TS Ty Smith AU/399 15.00 40.00
TS Ty Smith AU/25 30.00 80.00
TS Ty Smith AU/99 20.00 50.00
101 Mikey Anderson AU/199 12.00 30.00
102 Shane Bowers AU/199 10.00 25.00
103 Gabe Vilardi AU/199 20.00 50.00
104 Martin Kaut AU/199 12.00 30.00
105 Liam Foudy AU/199 12.00 30.00
106 Timothy Liljegren AU/199 12.00 30.00
107 Josh Norris AU/199 20.00 50.00
108 Thomas Harley AU/199 20.00 50.00
109 Jason Robertson AU/99 80.00 200.00
110 Victor Soderstrom AU/99 10.00 25.00
111 Ty Dellandrea AU/99 12.00 30.00
112 Peyton Krebs AU/99 20.00 50.00
113 Nick Robertson AU/99 20.00 50.00
114 Bowen Byram AU/99 25.00 60.00
115 Connor McMichael AU/99 20.00 50.00
116 Alexis Lafreniere AU/99 200.00 500.00
117 Alexander Yelesin AU/49 12.00 30.00
118 Pierre-Olivier Joseph AU/49 15.00 40.00
119 Gustav Lindstrom AU/49 12.00 30.00
120 Joel Kiviranta AU/49 15.00 40.00
121 Maxim Letunov AU/49 12.00 30.00
122 Kieffer Bellows AU/49 12.00 30.00
124 Morgan Geekie AU/49 15.00 40.00
125 Tyler Benson AU/49 15.00 40.00
126 Lucas Carlsson AU/49 12.00 30.00
127 Alex Belzile AU/49 12.00 30.00
129 Jake Evans AU/49 15.00 40.00
131 Brandon Hagel AU/49 20.00 50.00
132 Jake Oettinger AU/49 40.00 100.00
134 Mikey Anderson AU/49 15.00 40.00
135 Shane Bowers AU/49 12.00 30.00
136 Gabe Vilardi AU/49 25.00 60.00
137 Martin Kaut AU/49 15.00 40.00
138 Liam Foudy AU/49 15.00 40.00
139 Timothy Liljegren AU/49 15.00 40.00
140 Josh Norris AU/25 30.00 80.00
141 Thomas Harley AU/25 30.00 80.00
142 Jason Robertson AU/25 150.00 400.00
143 Victor Soderstrom AU/25 15.00 40.00
144 Ty Dellandrea AU/25 20.00 50.00
145 Peyton Krebs AU/25 30.00 80.00
146 Nick Robertson AU/25 30.00 80.00
147 Bowen Byram AU/25 40.00 100.00
148 Connor McMichael AU/25 30.00 80.00
149 Alexis Lafreniere AU/25 250.00 600.00

2020-21 Upper Deck Trilogy All Star Signature Pucks

ASPAK Anze Kopitar B 12.00 30.00
ASPCH Connor Hellebuyck B 15.00 40.00
ASPJS Jaccob Slavin C 6.00 15.00
ASPMF Marc-Andre Fleury A 15.00 40.00
ASPNH Nico Hischier A 12.00 30.00
ASPTC Thomas Chabot C 8.00 20.00
ASPTK Travis Konecny B 8.00 20.00
ASPTS Tyler Seguin A 10.00 25.00

2020-21 Upper Deck Trilogy Auto Focus

AFAD Alex DeBrincat C 15.00 40.00
AFBG Brendan Gallagher B 12.00 30.00
AFBH Bo Horvat B 15.00 40.00
AFJG Jake Guentzel A 40.00 100.00
AFJS Jordan Staal C 10.00 25.00
AFJT John Tavares A 20.00 50.00
AFMS Mark Stone B 40.00 100.00
AFRK Ryan Kesler C 12.00 30.00

2020-21 Upper Deck Trilogy Auto Focus Rookies

AFRAL Alexis Lafreniere 200.00 500.00

2020-21 Upper Deck Trilogy Crystallized Signatures

CAK Anze Kopitar B 15.00 40.00
CBM Brad Marchand B 20.00 50.00
CJV Jakub Vrana D 12.00 30.00
CKK Kasperi Kapanen D 8.00 20.00
CMS Mark Scheifele C 15.00 40.00
CMZ Mats Zuccarello D 30.00 80.00
CPR Pekka Rinne B 20.00 50.00
CSR Sam Reinhart C 15.00 40.00
CTJ Tyler Johnson C 6.00 15.00
CTS Tyler Seguin A 12.00 30.00
CVR James van Riemsdyk C 8.00 20.00

2020-21 Upper Deck Trilogy Honorary Triple Swatches

HTSAV Andrei Vasilevskiy 15.00 40.00
HTSCK Chris Kreider 12.00 30.00
HTSEM Evgeni Malkin 20.00 50.00
HTSJH Jack Hughes 25.00 60.00
HTSKK Kasperi Kapanen 8.00 20.00
HTSMS Mark Scheifele 15.00 40.00
HTSNF Nick Foligno 8.00 20.00
HTSPK Patrick Kane 20.00 50.00
HTSPS Paul Stastny 8.00 20.00
HTSRN Ryan Nugent-Hopkins 12.00 30.00
HTSSG Scott Gomez 8.00 20.00
HTSSK Saku Koivu 10.00 25.00
HTSTL Timothy Liljegren 12.00 30.00

2020-21 Upper Deck Trilogy Rookie Renditions

*RED/799: .6X TO 1.5X BASIC
*BLUE/399: 1X TO 2.5X BASIC
RR1 Alexis Lafreniere 2.00 5.00
RR2 Nick Robertson 1.00 2.50
RR3 Thomas Harley 1.00 2.50
RR4 Alex Belzile .50 1.25
RR5 Vitali Kravtsov 1.25 3.00
RR6 Gabe Vilardi 1.00 2.50
RR7 Ty Dellandrea .60 1.50
RR8 Peyton Krebs 1.00 2.50
RR9 Jake Oettinger 1.50 4.00
RR10 Tyler Benson .60 1.50
RR11 Philipp Kurashev .75 2.00
RR12 Pierre-Olivier Joseph .60 1.50
RR13 Dylan Coghlan .60 1.50
RR14 Alexander Yelesin .50 1.25
RR15 Jake Evans .60 1.50
RR16 Martin Kaut .60 1.50
RR17 Nicolas Beaudin .60 1.50
RR18 Connor Ingram .50 1.25
RR19 Josh Norris 1.00 2.50
RR20 Morgan Geekie .60 1.50
RR21 Shane Bowers .50 1.25
RR22 Kieffer Bellows .50 1.25
RR23 Ryan McLeod .50 1.25
RR24 Olli Juolevi .60 1.50
RR25 Alexander Alexeyev .50 1.25
RR26 Timothy Liljegren .60 1.50
RR27 Reid Duke .60 1.50
RR28 Victor Soderstrom .50 1.25
RR29 Connor McMichael 1.00 2.50
RR30 Bowen Byram 1.25 3.00

2020-21 Upper Deck Trilogy Rookie Renditions Autographs Gold

RR2 Nick Robertson D 12.00 30.00
RR3 Thomas Harley C 12.00 30.00
RR4 Alex Belzile C 6.00 15.00
RR6 Gabe Vilardi C 12.00 30.00
RR7 Ty Dellandrea E 8.00 20.00
RR8 Peyton Krebs C 12.00 30.00
RR9 Jake Oettinger D 20.00 50.00
RR10 Tyler Benson C 8.00 20.00
RR11 Philipp Kurashev D 10.00 25.00
RR13 Dylan Coghlan E 8.00 20.00
RR15 Jake Evans E 8.00 20.00
RR16 Martin Kaut E 8.00 20.00
RR17 Nicolas Beaudin B 8.00 20.00
RR19 Josh Norris B 12.00 30.00
RR20 Morgan Geekie B 8.00 20.00
RR21 Shane Bowers E 6.00 15.00
RR22 Kieffer Bellows B 6.00 15.00
RR24 Olli Juolevi E 8.00 20.00
RR26 Timothy Liljegren E 8.00 20.00
RR27 Reid Duke E 8.00 20.00
RR28 Victor Soderstrom D 6.00 15.00
RR29 Connor McMichael B 20.00 50.00
RR30 Bowen Byram B 30.00 80.00

2020-21 Upper Deck Trilogy Rookie Renditions Jerseys Silver

RR1 Alexis Lafreniere A 12.00 30.00
RR2 Nick Robertson A 6.00 15.00
RR3 Thomas Harley C 6.00 15.00
RR4 Alex Belzile C 3.00 8.00
RR6 Gabe Vilardi A 6.00 15.00
RR7 Ty Dellandrea C 4.00 10.00
RR8 Peyton Krebs A 6.00 15.00
RR9 Jake Oettinger C 10.00 25.00
RR10 Tyler Benson B 4.00 10.00
RR11 Philipp Kurashev C 5.00 12.00
RR12 Pierre-Olivier Joseph C 4.00 10.00
RR14 Alexander Yelesin C 3.00 8.00
RR15 Jake Evans B 4.00 10.00
RR16 Martin Kaut B 4.00 10.00
RR17 Nicolas Beaudin C 4.00 10.00
RR18 Connor Ingram B 3.00 8.00
RR19 Josh Norris A 6.00 15.00
RR20 Morgan Geekie B 4.00 10.00
RR21 Shane Bowers B 3.00 8.00
RR22 Kieffer Bellows B 3.00 8.00
RR23 Ryan McLeod C 3.00 8.00
RR24 Olli Juolevi B 4.00 10.00
RR25 Alexander Alexeyev C 3.00 8.00
RR26 Timothy Liljegren C 4.00 10.00
RR28 Victor Soderstrom B 3.00 8.00
RR29 Connor McMichael B 6.00 15.00
RR30 Bowen Byram A 8.00 20.00

2020-21 Upper Deck Trilogy Rookie Renditions Patch Autographs Gold

RR2 Nick Robertson/25 30.00 80.00
RR3 Thomas Harley/25 (No Auto) 30.00 80.00
RR4 Alex Belzile/49 15.00 40.00
RR6 Gabe Vilardi/49 30.00 80.00
RR7 Ty Dellandrea/49 20.00 50.00
RR8 Peyton Krebs/49 30.00 80.00
RR9 Jake Oettinger/49 50.00 125.00
RR10 Tyler Benson/49 20.00 50.00
RR11 Philipp Kurashev/25 (No Auto) 25.00 60.00
RR12 Pierre-Olivier Joseph/49 20.00 50.00
RR14 Alexander Yelesin/49 15.00 40.00
RR15 Jake Evans/49 20.00 50.00
RR16 Martin Kaut/49 20.00 50.00
RR17 Nicolas Beaudin/49 20.00 50.00
RR18 Connor Ingram/49 15.00 40.00
RR19 Josh Norris/49 30.00 80.00
RR20 Morgan Geekie/49 20.00 50.00
RR21 Shane Bowers/49 15.00 40.00
RR22 Kieffer Bellows/49 15.00 40.00
RR23 Ryan McLeod/49 15.00 40.00
RR24 Olli Juolevi/49 20.00 50.00
RR26 Timothy Liljegren/49 20.00 50.00
RR28 Victor Soderstrom/49 15.00 40.00
RR29 Connor McMichael/49 30.00 80.00
RR30 Bowen Byram/25 40.00 100.00

2020-21 Upper Deck Trilogy Rookie Signature Pucks

*TEAM.LOGO/25: .75X TO 2X BASIC
RSPAL Alexis Lafreniere A 80.00 200.00
RSPBB Bowen Byram C 20.00 50.00
RSPGV Gabe Vilardi C 15.00 40.00
RSPJR Jason Robertson D 60.00 150.00
RSPKK Kirill Kaprizov B 250.00 600.00
RSPLF Liam Foudy D 10.00 25.00
RSPTB Tyler Benson D 10.00 25.00
RSPTL Timothy Liljegren C 10.00 25.00

2020-21 Upper Deck Trilogy Rookie Super Stage

*RED/999: .75X TO 2X BASIC
*BLUE/499: 1X TO 2.5X BASIC
RSS1 Alexis Lafreniere 1.50 4.00
RSS2 Gage Quinney .30 .75
RSS3 Gabe Vilardi .75 2.00
RSS4 Calvin Thurkauf .40 1.00
RSS5 Vitek Vanecek .75 2.00
RSS6 Lucas Carlsson .40 1.00
RSS7 Alexander True .40 1.00
RSS8 Matiss Kivlenieks 6.00 15.00
RSS9 Jani Hakanpaa .30 .75
RSS10 Gustav Lindstrom .40 1.00
RSS11 Jonas Johansson .50 1.25
RSS12 Egor Korshkov .30 .75
RSS13 Keegan Kolesar .40 1.00
RSS14 Anthony Angello .40 1.00
RSS15 Mikey Anderson .50 1.25
RSS16 Steven Lorentz .40 1.00
RSS17 Liam Foudy .50 1.25
RSS18 Jason Robertson 1.25 3.00
RSS19 Nick Robertson .75 2.00
RSS20 Bowen Byram 1.00 2.50

2020-21 Upper Deck Trilogy Rookie Super Stage Autographs Gold

RSS1 Alexis Lafreniere 150.00 400.00
RSS2 Gage Quinney 6.00 15.00
RSS3 Gabe Vilardi 15.00 40.00
RSS4 Calvin Thurkauf 8.00 20.00
RSS5 Vitek Vanecek 15.00 40.00
RSS6 Lucas Carlsson 8.00 20.00
RSS7 Alexander True 8.00 20.00
RSS10 Gustav Lindstrom 8.00 20.00
RSS11 Jonas Johansson 10.00 25.00
RSS14 Anthony Angello 8.00 20.00
RSS15 Mikey Anderson 10.00 25.00
RSS16 Steven Lorentz 8.00 20.00
RSS17 Liam Foudy 10.00 25.00
RSS18 Jason Robertson 80.00 200.00
RSS19 Nick Robertson 15.00 40.00
RSS20 Bowen Byram 20.00 50.00

2020-21 Upper Deck Trilogy Rookie Super Stage Jerseys Silver

RSS1 Alexis Lafreniere 8.00 20.00
RSS2 Gage Quinney 1.50 4.00
RSS3 Gabe Vilardi 4.00 10.00
RSS4 Calvin Thurkauf 2.00 5.00
RSS5 Vitek Vanecek 4.00 10.00
RSS6 Lucas Carlsson 2.00 5.00
RSS7 Alexander True 2.00 5.00
RSS8 Matiss Kivlenieks 8.00 20.00
RSS9 Jani Hakanpaa 1.50 4.00
RSS10 Gustav Lindstrom 2.00 5.00
RSS11 Jonas Johansson 2.50 6.00
RSS12 Egor Korshkov 1.50 4.00
RSS13 Keegan Kolesar 2.00 5.00
RSS14 Anthony Angello 2.00 5.00
RSS15 Mikey Anderson 2.50 6.00
RSS16 Steven Lorentz 2.00 5.00
RSS17 Liam Foudy 2.50 6.00
RSS18 Jason Robertson 6.00 15.00
RSS19 Nick Robertson 4.00 10.00
RSS20 Bowen Byram 5.00 12.00

2020-21 Upper Deck Trilogy Signature Pucks

SPAG Andy Greene C 5.00 12.00
SPAM Alec Martinez C 5.00 12.00
SPAT Alex Tuch A 8.00 20.00
SPBA Tyson Barrie B 5.00 12.00
SPCA Craig Anderson B 6.00 15.00
SPCC Connor Clifton C 5.00 12.00
SPCP Colton Parayko A 6.00 15.00
SPDB Dustin Brown B 8.00 20.00
SPDH Darren Helm C 5.00 12.00
SPDO Dmitry Orlov C 8.00 20.00
SPDS Dylan Strome A 10.00 25.00
SPHA Dougie Hamilton A 6.00 15.00
SPJB Jay Bouwmeester A 5.00 12.00
SPJG John Gibson A 8.00 20.00
SPJM John Marino C 8.00 20.00
SPJP Jean-Gabriel Pageau C 5.00 12.00
SPJT Jacob Trouba A 6.00 15.00
SPKK Kasperi Kapanen B 6.00 15.00
SPKL Kevin Labanc C 5.00 12.00
SPKP Kyle Palmieri B 6.00 15.00
SPKY Keith Yandle B 5.00 12.00
SPMF Morgan Frost C 6.00 15.00
SPMK Mikko Koivu B 6.00 15.00
SPMN Martin Necas C 12.00 30.00
SPMO Josh Morrissey B 10.00 25.00
SPMS Mikhail Sergachev B 6.00 15.00
SPNH Niklas Hjalmarsson C 5.00 12.00
SPNS Nick Suzuki A 40.00 100.00
SPPB Pavel Buchnevich C 6.00 15.00
SPRH Roope Hintz B 10.00 25.00
SPRS Roman Josi A 8.00 20.00
SPSM Sean Monahan A 5.00 12.00
SPST Marc Staal B 5.00 12.00
SPSU Ryan Suter A 6.00 15.00
SPTB Teddy Blueger C 5.00 12.00
SPTT Tyler Toffoli A 8.00 20.00
SPVO Victor Olofsson B 8.00 20.00
SPYG Yanni Gourde C 6.00 15.00

2020-21 Upper Deck Trilogy Triple Relics

TREKG Jack Eichel
Patrick Kane
Johnny Gaudreau 30.00 80.00
TRHHK Kevin Hayes
Carter Hart
Travis Konecny 15.00 40.00
TRKBM David Krejci
Patrice Bergeron
Brad Marchand 30.00 80.00
TRKVH Nikita Kucherov
Andrei Vasilevskiy
Victor Hedman 30.00 80.00
TRSAA Jordan Staal
Sebastian Aho
Jaccob Slavin 25.00 60.00
TRSBS Henrik Sedin
Alexandre Burrows
Daniel Sedin 20.00 50.00
TRTTT Keith Tkachuk
Matthew Tkachuk
Brady Tkachuk 30.00 80.00
TRVBF Gabe Vilardi
Tyler Benson
Liam Foudy 30.00 80.00

2021-22 Upper Deck Trilogy

1 Brett Leason 4.00 10.00
2 Thomas Novak 4.00 10.00
3 Tyce Thompson 4.00 10.00
4 Parker Kelly 4.00 10.00
5 Joey Keane 3.00 8.00
6 Mike Hardman 4.00 10.00
7 Matthew Phillips 4.00 10.00
8 Wade Allison 4.00 10.00
9 Fabian Zetterlund 4.00 10.00
10 Daniil Tarasov 4.00 10.00
11 Riley Damiani 4.00 10.00
12 Vladimir Tkachev 4.00 10.00
13 Axel Jonsson-Fjallby 4.00 10.00
14 Markus Niemelainen 4.00 10.00
15 Hugo Alnefelt 4.00 10.00
16 Josiah Slavin 4.00 10.00
17 Nico Daws 6.00 15.00
18 Logan Thompson 10.00 25.00
19 Scott Reedy 3.00 8.00
20 Felix Sandstrom 4.00 10.00
21 Taylor Raddysh 6.00 15.00
22 Michael Pezzetta 4.00 10.00
23 Mattias Samuelsson 4.00 10.00
24 Zac Jones 5.00 12.00
25 Boris Katchouk 3.00 8.00
26 Marian Studenic 4.00 10.00
27 Adam Ruzicka 4.00 10.00
28 Arttu Ruotsalainen 4.00 10.00
29 Garrett Pilon 5.00 12.00
30 Riley Tufte 4.00 10.00
31 Wyatt Kalynuk 4.00 10.00
32 Sean Day 4.00 10.00
33 Jasper Weatherby 4.00 10.00
34 Egor Sokolov 6.00 15.00
35 Karel Vejmelka 8.00 20.00
36 Filip Gustavsson 12.00 30.00
37 Robin Salo 6.00 15.00
38 Scott Perunovich 6.00 15.00
39 Aliaksei Protas 6.00 15.00
40 Adam Beckman 6.00 15.00
41 Cole Schwindt 6.00 15.00
42 Alex Barre-Boulet 6.00 15.00
43 Jesse Ylonen 6.00 15.00
44 Kole Lind 8.00 20.00
45 Jan Jenik 8.00 20.00
46 Jonathan Dahlen 6.00 15.00
47 Jake Leschyshyn 6.00 15.00
48 Gabriel Fortier 6.00 15.00
49 Connor Dewar 6.00 15.00
50 Jacob Bernard-Docker 6.00 15.00
51 David Farrance 6.00 15.00
52 Joe Veleno 8.00 20.00
53 Yegor Chinakhov 10.00 25.00
54 Cam York 6.00 15.00
55 Artemi Kniazev 6.00 15.00
56 Sean Durzi 6.00 15.00
57 Ross Colton 8.00 20.00
58 Morgan Barron 5.00 12.00
59 Hendrix Lapierre 6.00 15.00
60 Mattias Norlinder 6.00 15.00
61 Ryan Merkley 8.00 20.00
62 Rafael Harvey-Pinard 6.00 15.00
63 Lassi Thomson 6.00 15.00
64 Jake Neighbours 12.00 30.00
65 Pavel Dorofeyev 8.00 20.00
66 Justus Annunen 8.00 20.00
67 Moritz Seider 20.00 50.00
68 Jamie Drysdale 12.00 30.00
69 Dawson Mercer 20.00 50.00
70 Grigori Denisenko 10.00 25.00
71 Tanner Jeannot 8.00 20.00
72 Sampo Ranta 8.00 20.00
73 Cole Perfetti 15.00 40.00
74 Alex Turcotte 10.00 25.00
75 Jeremy Swayman 25.00 60.00
76 Spencer Knight 15.00 40.00
77 Michael Bunting 8.00 20.00
78 Benoit-Olivier Groulx 8.00 20.00
79 Quinton Byfield 20.00 50.00
80 Mason McTavish 15.00 40.00
81 Rasmus Kupari 8.00 20.00
82 Alex Newhook 12.00 30.00
83 Philip Tomasino 10.00 25.00
84 Seth Jarvis 20.00 50.00
85 Lucas Raymond 25.00 60.00
86 Nils Lundkvist 8.00 20.00
87 Calen Addison 8.00 20.00
88 Justin Barron 12.00 30.00
89 Cole Caufield 30.00 80.00
90 Anton Lundell 15.00 40.00
91 Alexander Holtz 12.00 30.00
92 Shane Pinto 12.00 30.00
93 Trevor Zegras 15.00 40.00
94 John-Jason Peterka 15.00 40.00
95 William Eklund 20.00 50.00
96 Cole Sillinger 12.00 30.00
97 Jack Drury 12.00 30.00
98 Vasily Podkolzin 10.00 25.00
99 Ukko-Pekka Luukkonen 12.00 30.00
100 Lucas Raymond
Trevor Zegras
Quinton Byfield 30.00 80.00

2021-22 Upper Deck Trilogy Autographs

67 Moritz Seider/25 40.00 100.00
68 Jamie Drysdale/49 25.00 60.00
69 Dawson Mercer/49 40.00 100.00
70 Grigori Denisenko/49 20.00 50.00
71 Tanner Jeannot/49 15.00 40.00
72 Sampo Ranta/49 15.00 40.00
73 Cole Perfetti/49 30.00 80.00
74 Alex Turcotte/25 20.00 50.00
75 Jeremy Swayman/49 50.00 125.00
76 Spencer Knight/49 30.00 80.00
78 Benoit-Olivier Groulx/49 15.00 40.00
79 Quinton Byfield/25 40.00 100.00
80 Mason McTavish/25 30.00 80.00
81 Rasmus Kupari/49 15.00 40.00
82 Alex Newhook/49 25.00 60.00
83 Philip Tomasino/49 20.00 50.00
85 Lucas Raymond/25 50.00 125.00
86 Nils Lundkvist/49 15.00 40.00
87 Calen Addison/49 15.00 40.00
89 Cole Caufield/25 60.00 150.00
90 Anton Lundell/25 30.00 80.00
91 Alexander Holtz/49 25.00 60.00
92 Shane Pinto/49 25.00 60.00
93 Trevor Zegras/25 30.00 80.00
94 John-Jason Peterka/49 30.00 80.00
95 William Eklund/49 40.00 100.00
96 Cole Sillinger/49 25.00 60.00
98 Vasily Podkolzin/49 20.00 50.00
99 Ukko-Pekka Luukkonen/49 25.00 60.00

2022-23 Upper Deck Trilogy

1 Tim Stutzle .50 1.25
2 Cole Caufield .75 2.00
3 Tanner Jeannot .25 .60
4 Tom Wilson .40 1.00
5 Conor Garland .30 .75
6 Rasmus Dahlin .50 1.25
7 Joe Veleno .30 .75
8 Jamie Drysdale .30 .75
9 Tomas Hertl .40 1.00
10 Anze Kopitar .60 1.50
11 Jordan Eberle .40 1.00
12 Pavel Buchnevich .30 .75
13 Jesper Bratt .40 1.00
14 Troy Terry .30 .75
15 Cole Sillinger .30 .75
16 Jonathan Toews .60 1.50
17 Clayton Keller .50 1.25
18 Nico Hischier .60 1.50
19 Jonathan Marchessault .50 1.25
20 Carey Price .75 2.00
21 Ryan McLeod .25 .60
22 Mathew Barzal .50 1.25
23 Cam York .25 .60
24 Roope Hintz .50 1.25
25 Yanni Gourde .30 .75
26 Patrik Laine .50 1.25
27 Nick Schmaltz .30 .75
28 Evgeni Malkin .75 2.00
29 Tage Thompson .50 1.25
30 Quinton Byfield .50 1.25
31 James van Riemsdyk .30 .75
32 Jordan Kyrou .40 1.00
33 Mats Zuccarello .40 1.00
34 Mark Scheifele .60 1.50
35 Jason Robertson .60 1.50
36 John Tavares .60 1.50
37 Rasmus Kupari .25 .60
38 Nikolaj Ehlers .40 1.00
39 Moritz Seider .50 1.25
40 Alex DeBrincat .50 1.25
41 Jack Eichel .60 1.50
42 Connor McMichael .40 1.00
43 Brad Marchand .75 2.00
44 Shane Pinto .30 .75
45 Sam Reinhart .75 2.00
46 Trevor Zegras .40 1.00
47 Filip Forsberg .60 1.50
48 Vladimir Tarasenko .50 1.25
49 Timo Meier .40 1.00
50 Quinn Hughes 1.00 2.50
51 Ilya Sorokin .60 1.50
52 Andrei Svechnikov .50 1.25
53 Mark Stone .50 1.25
54 Jake Oettinger .60 1.50
55 Jack Hughes 1.00 2.50
56 Jacob Markstrom .40 1.00
57 Elias Pettersson .60 1.50
58 Marc-Andre Fleury .75 2.00
59 Lucas Raymond .60 1.50
60 Juuse Saros .50 1.25
61 Lane Pederson .25 .60
62 Mattias Samuelsson .25 .60
63 Joe Pavelski .50 1.25
64 Martin Necas .60 1.50
65 John Carlson .40 1.00
66 Patrice Bergeron .50 1.25
67 Taylor Hall .40 1.00
68 Andrew Mangiapane .40 1.00
69 Adam Fox .50 1.25
70 Jake Guentzel .60 1.50
71 Kirill Kaprizov 1.25 3.00
72 Mikko Rantanen 1.00 2.50
73 Sebastian Aho .60 1.50
74 Victor Hedman .50 1.25
75 Aaron Ekblad .50 1.25
76 Roman Josi .40 1.00
77 David Pastrnak 1.00 2.50
78 Kyle Connor .60 1.50
79 Johnny Gaudreau .60 1.50
80 Mika Zibanejad .50 1.25
81 Patrick Kane .75 2.00
82 Leon Draisaitl 1.25 3.00
83 Aleksander Barkov .60 1.50
84 Andrei Vasilevskiy .60 1.50
85 J.T. Miller .50 1.25
86 Brady Tkachuk .60 1.50
87 Sidney Crosby 1.50 4.00
88 Steven Stamkos .75 2.00
89 Artemi Panarin .75 2.00
90 Igor Shesterkin .75 2.00
91 Alex Ovechkin 1.50 4.00
92 Jonathan Huberdeau .50 1.25
93 Nikita Kucherov .75 2.00
94 Auston Matthews 1.50 4.00
95 Matthew Tkachuk .75 2.00
96 Nathan MacKinnon 1.50 4.00
97 Cale Makar 1.00 2.50
98 Mitch Marner .60 1.50
99 Gabriel Landeskog .50 1.25
100 Connor McDavid 2.00 5.00

101 Nathan Smith/999 RC 1.25 3.00
102 Elmer Soderblom/999 RC 3.00 8.00
103 Trey Fix-Wolansky/999 RC 1.50 4.00
104 Erik Kallgren/999 RC 1.50 4.00
105 Marc McLaughlin/999 RC 1.50 4.00
106 Michael Eyssimont/999 RC 1.50 4.00
107 Chase Pearson/999 RC 1.25 3.00
108 Noah Cates/999 RC 1.50 4.00
109 Mark Kastelic/999 RC 1.25 3.00
110 Reilly Walsh/999 RC 1.50 4.00
111 Nick Abruzzese/999 RC 1.50 4.00
112 Matias Maccelli/999 RC 2.50 6.00
113 Jordan Spence/999 RC 1.50 4.00
114 Jack McBain/999 RC 1.50 4.00
115 Lukas Dostal/999 RC 3.00 8.00
116 Valtteri Puustinen/999 RC 1.25 3.00
117 Jack LaFontaine/999 RC 1.50 4.00
118 Ronnie Attard/999 RC 1.50 4.00
119 Jordan Harris/999 RC 2.00 5.00
120 Jacob Moverare/999 RC 1.25 3.00
121 Filip Hallander/999 RC 1.50 4.00
122 Bokondji Imama/999 RC 1.25 3.00
123 Alex Vlasic/999 RC 1.25 3.00
124 Dylan Samberg/999 RC 1.50 4.00
125 Samuel Fagemo/999 RC 1.25 3.00
126 Thomas Bordeleau/999 RC 1.50 4.00
127 Kaedan Korczak/999 RC 1.25 3.00
128 Vladislav Kolyachonok/999 RC 1.25 3.00
129 Isaac Ratcliffe/999 RC 1.50 4.00
130 Pyotr Kochetkov/999 RC 3.00 8.00
131 Bobby Brink/999 RC 1.50 4.00
132 Jacob Perreault/999 RC 1.50 4.00
133 Viktor Lodin/999 RC 1.50 4.00
134 Fredrik Karlstrom/999 RC 1.25 3.00
135 Nikita Okhotiuk/999 RC 1.25 3.00
136 Lukas Reichel/999 RC 3.00 8.00
137 Brayden Tracey/999 RC 1.25 3.00
138 Mads Sogaard/999 RC 2.00 5.00
139 Dylan Guenther/999 RC 4.00 10.00
140 Jake Sanderson/999 RC 4.00 10.00
141 Marco Rossi/999 RC 4.00 10.00
142 Jack Quinn/999 RC 2.50 6.00
143 Dylan Holloway/999 RC 3.00 8.00
144 Braden Schneider/999 RC 2.50 6.00
145 Kent Johnson/999 RC 3.00 8.00
146 Juraj Slafkovsky/999 RC 8.00 20.00
147 Shane Wright/999 RC 4.00 10.00
148 Matt Boldy/999 RC 5.00 12.00
149 Matty Beniers/999 RC 8.00 20.00
150 Owen Power/999 RC 3.00 8.00
151 Nathan Smith/699 1.25 3.00
152 Elmer Soderblom/699 3.00 8.00
153 Trey Fix-Wolansky/699 1.50 4.00
154 Erik Kallgren/699 1.50 4.00
155 Marc McLaughlin/699 1.50 4.00
156 Michael Eyssimont/699 1.50 4.00
157 Chase Pearson/699 1.25 3.00
158 Noah Cates/699 1.50 4.00
159 Mark Kastelic/699 1.25 3.00
160 Reilly Walsh/699 1.50 4.00
161 Nick Abruzzese/699 1.50 4.00
162 Matias Maccelli/699 2.50 6.00
163 Jordan Spence/699 1.50 4.00
164 Jack McBain/699 1.50 4.00
165 Lukas Dostal/699 3.00 8.00
166 Valtteri Puustinen/699 1.25 3.00
167 Jack LaFontaine/699 1.50 4.00
168 Ronnie Attard/699 1.50 4.00
169 Jordan Harris/699 2.00 5.00
170 Jacob Moverare/699 1.25 3.00
171 Filip Hallander/699 1.50 4.00
172 Bokondji Imama/699 1.25 3.00
173 Alex Vlasic/699 1.25 3.00
174 Dylan Samberg/699 1.50 4.00
175 Samuel Fagemo/699 1.25 3.00
176 Thomas Bordeleau/699 1.50 4.00
177 Kaedan Korczak/699 1.25 3.00
178 Vladislav Kolyachonok/699 1.25 3.00
179 Isaac Ratcliffe/699 1.50 4.00
180 Pyotr Kochetkov/699 3.00 8.00
181 Bobby Brink/699 1.50 4.00
182 Jacob Perreault/699 1.50 4.00
183 Viktor Lodin/699 1.50 4.00
184 Fredrik Karlstrom/699 1.25 3.00
185 Nikita Okhotiuk/699 1.25 3.00
186 Lukas Reichel/699 3.00 8.00
187 Brayden Tracey/699 1.25 3.00
188 Mads Sogaard/699 2.00 5.00
189 Dylan Guenther/699 4.00 10.00
190 Jake Sanderson/699 4.00 10.00
191 Marco Rossi/699 4.00 10.00
192 Jack Quinn/699 2.50 6.00
193 Dylan Holloway/699 3.00 8.00
194 Braden Schneider/699 2.50 6.00
195 Kent Johnson/699 3.00 8.00
196 Juraj Slafkovsky/699 8.00 20.00
197 Shane Wright/699 4.00 10.00
198 Matt Boldy/699 5.00 12.00
199 Matty Beniers/699 8.00 20.00
200 Owen Power/699 3.00 8.00
201 Nathan Smith/299 2.00 5.00
202 Elmer Soderblom/299 5.00 12.00
203 Trey Fix-Wolansky/299 2.50 6.00
204 Erik Kallgren/299 2.50 6.00
205 Marc McLaughlin/299 2.50 6.00
206 Michael Eyssimont/299 2.50 6.00
207 Chase Pearson/299 2.00 5.00
208 Noah Cates/299 2.50 6.00
209 Mark Kastelic/299 2.00 5.00
210 Reilly Walsh/299 2.50 6.00
211 Nick Abruzzese/299 2.50 6.00
212 Matias Maccelli/299 4.00 10.00
213 Jordan Spence/299 2.50 6.00
214 Jack McBain/299 2.50 6.00
215 Lukas Dostal/299 5.00 12.00
216 Valtteri Puustinen/299 2.00 5.00
217 Jack LaFontaine/299 2.50 6.00
218 Ronnie Attard/299 2.50 6.00
219 Jordan Harris/299 3.00 8.00
220 Jacob Moverare/299 2.00 5.00
221 Filip Hallander/299 2.50 6.00
222 Bokondji Imama/299 2.00 5.00
223 Alex Vlasic/299 2.00 5.00
224 Dylan Samberg/299 2.50 6.00
225 Samuel Fagemo/299 2.00 5.00
226 Thomas Bordeleau/299 2.50 6.00
227 Kaedan Korczak/299 2.00 5.00
228 Vladislav Kolyachonok/299 2.00 5.00
229 Isaac Ratcliffe/299 2.50 6.00
230 Pyotr Kochetkov/299 5.00 12.00
231 Bobby Brink/299 2.50 6.00
232 Jacob Perreault/299 2.50 6.00
233 Viktor Lodin/299 2.50 6.00
234 Fredrik Karlstrom/299 2.00 5.00
235 Nikita Okhotiuk/299 2.00 5.00
236 Lukas Reichel/299 5.00 12.00
237 Brayden Tracey/299 2.00 5.00
238 Mads Sogaard/299 3.00 8.00
239 Dylan Guenther/299 6.00 15.00
240 Jake Sanderson/299 6.00 15.00
241 Marco Rossi/299 6.00 15.00
242 Jack Quinn/299 4.00 10.00
243 Dylan Holloway/299 5.00 12.00
244 Braden Schneider/299 4.00 10.00
245 Kent Johnson/299 5.00 12.00
246 Juraj Slafkovsky/299 12.00 30.00
247 Shane Wright/299 6.00 15.00
248 Matt Boldy/299 8.00 20.00
249 Matty Beniers/299 15.00 40.00
250 Owen Power/299 5.00 12.00

2022-23 Upper Deck Trilogy Blue
*BLUE: 2X TO 5X BASIC
*BLUE RC/99-199: .75X TO 2X BASIC
*BLUE RC/25: 1X TO 2.5X BASIC
149 Matty Beniers/199 30.00 80.00
199 Matty Beniers/99 30.00 80.00
246 Juraj Slafkovsky/25 60.00 150.00
249 Matty Beniers/25 50.00 125.00

2022-23 Upper Deck Trilogy Gold
*GOLD: 8X TO 20X BASIC
*GOLD RC/149-449: 3X TO 8X BASIC
*GOLD RC/33-49: 2.5X TO 6X BASIC
91 Alex Ovechkin AU 125.00 300.00
100 Connor McDavid AU 150.00 400.00
146 Juraj Slafkovsky AU/149 60.00 150.00
147 Shane Wright AU/149 60.00 150.00
148 Matt Boldy AU/149 60.00 150.00
149 Matty Beniers AU/149 150.00 400.00
150 Owen Power AU/49 60.00 150.00
196 Juraj Slafkovsky AU/49 80.00 200.00
197 Shane Wright AU/49 80.00 200.00
198 Matt Boldy AU/49 60.00 150.00
199 Matty Beniers AU/49 200.00 500.00
200 Owen Power AU/49 60.00 150.00

2022-23 Upper Deck Trilogy Green
*GREEN: 4X TO 10X BASIC
*GREEN RC/99: 1X TO 2.5X BASIC
*GREEN RC/25: 1.5X TO 4X BASIC
149 Matty Beniers/99 40.00 100.00
199 Matty Beniers/25 80.00 200.00

2022-23 Upper Deck Trilogy Orange
*ORANGE: 4X TO 10X BASIC

2022-23 Upper Deck Trilogy Red
*RED: .6X TO 1.5X BASIC
*RED RC/149-299: .5X TO 1.2X BASIC
*RED RC/49: .6X TO 1.5X BASIC
149 Matty Beniers/299 12.00 30.00
199 Matty Beniers/149 12.00 30.00
246 Juraj Slafkovsky/49 30.00 80.00
249 Matty Beniers/49 40.00 100.00

2022-23 Upper Deck Trilogy Rookie Year Photo Variations
*PHOTO YEAR: 5X TO 12X BASIC
74 Victor Hedman 12.00 30.00
76 Roman Josi 10.00 25.00
87 Sidney Crosby 15.00 40.00
91 Alex Ovechkin 15.00 40.00
94 Auston Matthews 15.00 40.00
97 Cale Makar 15.00 40.00
100 Connor McDavid 30.00 80.00

2022-23 Upper Deck Trilogy '05-06 Rookie Premieres Tribute
05AV Alex Vlasic 8.00 20.00
05BB Bobby Brink 10.00 25.00
05BE Matty Beniers 80.00 200.00
05BT Brayden Tracey 8.00 20.00
05DG Dylan Guenther 25.00 60.00
05DH Dylan Holloway 20.00 50.00
05DS Dylan Samberg 10.00 25.00
05IR Isaac Ratcliffe 10.00 25.00
05JP Jacob Perreault 10.00 25.00
05JQ Jack Quinn 15.00 40.00
05JS Jordan Spence 10.00 25.00
05JY Juraj Slafkovsky 50.00 125.00
05KJ Kent Johnson 20.00 50.00
05KK Kaedan Korczak 8.00 20.00
05LR Lukas Reichel 20.00 50.00
05MB Matt Boldy 30.00 80.00
05MR Marco Rossi 25.00 60.00
05MS Mads Sogaard 12.00 30.00
05NO Nikita Okhotiuk 8.00 20.00
05OP Owen Power 20.00 50.00
05PK Pyotr Kochetkov 20.00 50.00
05SA Jake Sanderson 25.00 60.00
05SF Samuel Fagemo 8.00 20.00
05SW Shane Wright 25.00 60.00
05TB Thomas Bordeleau 10.00 25.00

2022-23 Upper Deck Trilogy Auto Focus
AFBM Brad Marchand 30.00 80.00
AFCM Connor McDavid 200.00 500.00
AFIS Igor Shesterkin 60.00 150.00
AFJH Jonathan Huberdeau 20.00 50.00
AFMK Cale Makar 80.00 200.00
AFNS Nick Suzuki 30.00 80.00
AFTH Tomas Hertl 15.00 40.00

2022-23 Upper Deck Trilogy Auto Focus Rookies
AFRBY Matt Boldy 60.00 150.00
AFRJQ Jack Quinn 30.00 80.00
AFRKJ Kent Johnson 40.00 100.00
AFRMB Matty Beniers 150.00 400.00
AFROP Owen Power 40.00 100.00
AFRSW Shane Wright 50.00 125.00

2022-23 Upper Deck Trilogy Crystalized Signatures
CAB Aleksander Barkov 30.00 80.00
CAS Andrei Svechnikov 25.00 60.00
CBT Brady Tkachuk 30.00 80.00
CIS Ilya Sorokin 30.00 80.00
CMT Matthew Tkachuk 40.00 100.00
CQH Quinn Hughes 30.00 80.00
CTJ Tanner Jeannot 12.00 30.00

2022-23 Upper Deck Trilogy Frozen in Time
FTAB Aleksander Barkov 3.00 8.00
FTAM Auston Matthews 8.00 20.00
FTAO Alex Ovechkin 8.00 20.00
FTAP Artemi Panarin 4.00 10.00
FTAV Andrei Vasilevskiy 3.00 8.00
FTBH Bobby Hull 4.00 10.00
FTBO Bobby Orr 8.00 20.00
FTCM Connor McDavid 15.00 40.00
FTDP David Pastrnak 5.00 12.00
FTGH Gordie Howe 6.00 15.00
FTIS Igor Shesterkin 4.00 10.00
FTJE Jack Eichel 3.00 8.00
FTJG Johnny Gaudreau 3.00 8.00
FTJH Jonathan Huberdeau 2.50 6.00
FTJJ Jaromir Jagr 6.00 15.00
FTJM J.T. Miller 2.50 6.00
FTKC Kyle Connor 3.00 8.00
FTKK Kirill Kaprizov 6.00 15.00
FTLD Leon Draisaitl 6.00 15.00
FTMA Cale Makar 5.00 12.00
FTMB Martin Brodeur 5.00 12.00
FTME Mark Messier 4.00 10.00
FTML Mario Lemieux 8.00 20.00
FTMM Mitch Marner 3.00 8.00
FTMR Mikko Rantanen 5.00 12.00
FTMT Matthew Tkachuk 4.00 10.00
FTNK Nikita Kucherov 4.00 10.00
FTNM Nathan MacKinnon 8.00 20.00
FTPK Patrick Kane 4.00 10.00
FTPR Patrick Roy 5.00 12.00
FTSC Sidney Crosby 8.00 20.00
FTSY Steve Yzerman 5.00 12.00
FTTM Timo Meier 2.00 5.00
FTVH Victor Hedman 2.50 6.00
FTWG Wayne Gretzky 15.00 40.00

2022-23 Upper Deck Trilogy Frozen in Time Blue Frost
*BLUE/50: 1.2X TO 3X BASIC
FTCM Connor McDavid 30.00 80.00
FTWG Wayne Gretzky 40.00 100.00

2022-23 Upper Deck Trilogy Generations
*RED: .5X TO 1.2X BASIC
*BLUE/299: .6X TO 1.5X BASIC
*GREEN/75: .8X TO 2X BASIC
TG1A Dany Heatley .60 1.50
TG1B Brady Tkachuk 1.25 3.00
TG1C Tim Stutzle 1.00 2.50
TG2A Cam Neely .75 2.00
TG2B Taylor Hall .75 2.00
TG2C Jeremy Swayman 1.25 3.00
TG3A Doug Gilmour 1.00 2.50
TG3B John Tavares 1.25 3.00
TG3C Michael Bunting .75 2.00
TG4A Dominik Hasek 1.25 3.00
TG4B Victor Olofsson .75 2.00
TG4C Jack Quinn 1.25 3.00
TG5A Jonathan Cheechoo .60 1.50
TG5B Tomas Hertl .75 2.00
TG5C William Eklund 1.00 2.50
TG6A Rod Brind'Amour .75 2.00
TG6B Sebastian Aho 1.25 3.00
TG6C Seth Jarvis 1.00 2.50
TG7A Doug Wilson .60 1.50
TG7B Patrick Kane 1.50 4.00
TG7C Lukas Reichel 1.50 4.00
TG8A Saku Koivu .75 2.00
TG8B Nick Suzuki 1.50 4.00
TG8C Cole Caufield 1.50 4.00
TG9A Teemu Selanne 1.50 4.00
TG9B John Gibson .75 2.00
TG9C Trevor Zegras .75 2.00
TG10A Pekka Rinne .75 2.00
TG10B Roman Josi .75 2.00
TG10C Philip Tomasino .50 1.25
TG11A Henrik Zetterberg 1.00 2.50
TG11B Tyler Bertuzzi .60 1.50
TG11C Lucas Raymond 1.25 3.00
TG12A Peter Forsberg 1.50 4.00
TG12B Gabriel Landeskog 1.00 2.50
TG12C Alex Newhook .60 1.50
TG13A Doug Weight .75 2.00
TG13B Connor McDavid 4.00 10.00
TG13C Dylan Holloway 1.50 4.00
TG14A Eric Lindros 1.25 3.00
TG14B James van Riemsdyk .60 1.50
TG14C Isaac Ratcliffe .75 2.00
TG15A Brooks Orpik .50 1.25
TG15B Kris Letang 1.00 2.50
TG15C Tristan Jarry .75 2.00
TG16A John Vanbiesbrouck .75 2.00
TG16B Sam Bennett 1.25 3.00
TG16C Anton Lundell .75 2.00
TG17A Marcel Dionne 1.00 2.50
TG17B Kevin Fiala .60 1.50
TG17C Quinton Byfield 1.00 2.50
TG18A Scott Gomez .60 1.50
TG18B Dougie Hamilton .60 1.50
TG18C Dawson Mercer 1.00 2.50
TG19A Zach Parise .75 2.00
TG19B Mats Zuccarello .75 2.00
TG19C Matt Boldy 2.50 6.00
TG20A Mike Richter .75 2.00
TG20B Adam Fox 1.00 2.50
TG20C Braden Schneider 1.25 3.00

2022-23 Upper Deck Trilogy Generations Autographs
TG1A Dany Heatley/25 8.00 20.00
TG1B Brady Tkachuk/25 15.00 40.00
TG1C Tim Stutzle/25 12.00 30.00
TG2A Cam Neely/25 10.00 25.00
TG2B Taylor Hall/25 10.00 25.00
TG2C Jeremy Swayman/49 15.00 40.00
TG3A Doug Gilmour/25 12.00 30.00
TG3B John Tavares/25 15.00 40.00
TG3C Michael Bunting/49 10.00 25.00
TG4C Jack Quinn/49 15.00 40.00
TG5A Jonathan Cheechoo/25 8.00 20.00
TG5B Tomas Hertl/25 10.00 25.00
TG5C William Eklund/49 12.00 30.00
TG6A Rod Brind'Amour/25 10.00 25.00
TG6C Seth Jarvis/49 8.00 20.00
TG7A Doug Wilson/49 8.00 20.00
TG7C Lukas Reichel/49 20.00 50.00
TG8A Saku Koivu/25 10.00 25.00
TG8B Nick Suzuki/25 20.00 50.00
TG9C Trevor Zegras/25 10.00 25.00
TG10B Roman Josi/25 10.00 25.00
TG10C Philip Tomasino/49 6.00 15.00
TG11A Henrik Zetterberg/25 12.00 30.00
TG12A Peter Forsberg/25 20.00 50.00
TG12B Gabriel Landeskog/25 12.00 30.00
TG12C Alex Newhook/25 8.00 20.00
TG13A Doug Weight/49 10.00 25.00
TG13C Dylan Holloway/49 20.00 50.00
TG14A Eric Lindros/25 15.00 40.00
TG14C Isaac Ratcliffe/49 10.00 25.00
TG15A Brooks Orpik/25 6.00 15.00
TG15B Kris Letang/25 12.00 30.00
TG16A John Vanbiesbrouck/49 10.00 25.00
TG16B Sam Bennett/49 15.00 40.00
TG16C Anton Lundell/49 10.00 25.00
TG17A Marcel Dionne/25 12.00 30.00
TG17B Kevin Fiala/49 8.00 20.00
TG17C Quinton Byfield/49 12.00 30.00
TG18B Dougie Hamilton/49 8.00 20.00
TG18C Dawson Mercer/49 12.00 30.00
TG19A Zach Parise/49 10.00 25.00
TG19B Mats Zuccarello/49 10.00 25.00
TG19C Matt Boldy/49 30.00 80.00
TG20A Mike Richter/25 10.00 25.00
TG20B Adam Fox/25 12.00 30.00
TG20C Braden Schneider/25 15.00 40.00

2022-23 Upper Deck Trilogy Generations Jerseys
TG1A Dany Heatley 2.50 6.00
TG1B Brady Tkachuk 5.00 12.00
TG1C Tim Stutzle 4.00 10.00
TG2B Taylor Hall 3.00 8.00
TG2C Jeremy Swayman 5.00 12.00
TG3A Doug Gilmour 4.00 10.00
TG3B John Tavares 5.00 12.00
TG3C Michael Bunting 3.00 8.00
TG4B Victor Olofsson 3.00 8.00
TG4C Jack Quinn 5.00 12.00
TG5A Jonathan Cheechoo 2.50 6.00
TG5B Tomas Hertl 3.00 8.00
TG5C William Eklund 4.00 10.00
TG6A Rod Brind'Amour 3.00 8.00
TG6B Sebastian Aho 8.00 20.00
TG6C Seth Jarvis 4.00 10.00
TG7A Doug Wilson 2.50 6.00
TG7B Patrick Kane 6.00 15.00
TG7C Lukas Reichel 6.00 15.00
TG8A Saku Koivu 3.00 8.00
TG8B Nick Suzuki 6.00 15.00
TG8C Cole Caufield 6.00 15.00
TG9A Teemu Selanne 6.00 15.00
TG9B John Gibson 3.00 8.00
TG9C Trevor Zegras 3.00 8.00
TG10A Pekka Rinne 3.00 8.00
TG10B Roman Josi 3.00 8.00
TG10C Philip Tomasino 2.00 5.00
TG11A Henrik Zetterberg 4.00 10.00
TG11B Tyler Bertuzzi 2.50 6.00
TG11C Lucas Raymond 5.00 12.00
TG12A Peter Forsberg 6.00 15.00
TG12B Gabriel Landeskog 4.00 10.00
TG12C Alex Newhook 2.50 6.00
TG13A Doug Weight 3.00 8.00
TG13B Connor McDavid 15.00 40.00
TG13C Dylan Holloway 6.00 15.00
TG14A Eric Lindros 5.00 12.00
TG14B James van Riemsdyk 2.50 6.00
TG14C Isaac Ratcliffe 3.00 8.00
TG15A Brooks Orpik 2.00 5.00
TG15B Kris Letang 4.00 10.00
TG15C Tristan Jarry 3.00 8.00
TG16B Sam Bennett 5.00 12.00
TG16C Anton Lundell 3.00 8.00
TG17B Kevin Fiala 2.50 6.00
TG17C Quinton Byfield 4.00 10.00
TG18A Scott Gomez 2.50 6.00
TG18B Dougie Hamilton 2.50 6.00
TG18C Dawson Mercer 4.00 10.00
TG19A Zach Parise 3.00 8.00
TG19B Mats Zuccarello 3.00 8.00
TG19C Matt Boldy 10.00 25.00
TG20A Mike Richter 3.00 8.00
TG20B Adam Fox 4.00 10.00
TG20C Braden Schneider 5.00 12.00

2022-23 Upper Deck Trilogy Honorary Triple Swatches
HTSDD Drew Doughty/35 12.00 30.00
HTSDN Darnell Nurse/35 8.00 20.00
HTSEM Evgeni Malkin/25 40.00 100.00
HTSMB Matty Beniers/25 80.00 200.00
HTSMR Marco Rossi/35 25.00 60.00
HTSSC Mark Scheifele/35 8.00 20.00
HTSTS Tyler Seguin/35 12.00 30.00
HTSVT Vladimir Tarasenko/25 8.00 20.00

2022-23 Upper Deck Trilogy Rookie Premier
RPAV Alex Vlasic 4.00 10.00
RPBB Bobby Brink 5.00 12.00
RPBE Matty Beniers 12.00 30.00
RPBI Bokondji Imama 4.00 10.00
RPBS Braden Schneider 8.00 20.00
RPBT Brayden Tracey 4.00 10.00
RPDG Dylan Guenther 12.00 30.00
RPDH Dylan Holloway 10.00 25.00
RPDS Dylan Samberg 5.00 12.00
RPFH Filip Hallander 5.00 12.00
RPIR Isaac Ratcliffe 5.00 12.00
RPJH Jordan Harris 6.00 15.00
RPJM Jacob Moverare 5.00 12.00
RPJP Jacob Perreault 5.00 12.00
RPJQ Jack Quinn 8.00 20.00
RPJS Jordan Spence 5.00 12.00
RPKJ Kent Johnson 10.00 25.00
RPKK Kaedan Korczak 4.00 10.00
RPLR Lukas Reichel 10.00 25.00
RPMB Matt Boldy 15.00 40.00
RPMR Marco Rossi 12.00 30.00
RPMS Mads Sogaard 6.00 15.00
RPNC Noah Cates 5.00 12.00
RPNO Nikita Okhotiuk 4.00 10.00
RPOP Owen Power 10.00 25.00
RPPK Pyotr Kochetkov 10.00 25.00
RPSF Samuel Fagemo 4.00 10.00
RPSW Shane Wright 12.00 30.00
RPTB Thomas Bordeleau 5.00 12.00
RPVK Vladislav Kolyachonok 4.00 10.00

2022-23 Upper Deck Trilogy Rookie Premier Gold Tint
*GOLD/50: .6X TO 1.5X BASIC
RPBE Matty Beniers 200.00 500.00

2022-23 Upper Deck Trilogy Rookie Renditions
*RED/799: .6X TO 1.5X BASIC
*BLUE/399: 1X TO 2.5X BASIC
*GREEN/99: 1.5X TO 4X BASIC
*PINK/25: 4X TO 10X BASIC
RR1 Erik Kallgren .50 1.25
RR2 Marco Rossi 1.25 3.00
RR3 Dylan Holloway 1.00 2.50
RR4 Nick Abruzzese .50 1.25
RR5 Braden Schneider .75 2.00
RR6 Nathan Smith .40 1.00
RR7 Chase Pearson .40 1.00
RR8 Dylan Guenther 1.25 3.00
RR9 Mark Kastelic .40 1.00
RR10 Brayden Tracey .40 1.00
RR11 Bobby Brink .50 1.25
RR12 Filip Hallander .50 1.25
RR13 Mads Sogaard .60 1.50
RR15 Matias Maccelli .75 2.00
RR16 Noah Cates .50 1.25
RR17 Nikita Okhotiuk .40 1.00
RR18 Jacob Perreault .50 1.25
RR19 Isaac Ratcliffe .50 1.25
RR20 Thomas Bordeleau .50 1.25
RR21 Lukas Dostal 1.00 2.50
RR22 Kaedan Korczak .40 1.00
RR23 Pyotr Kochetkov 1.00 2.50
RR24 Alex Vlasic .40 1.00
RR25 Dylan Samberg .50 1.25
RR26 Reilly Walsh .50 1.25
RR27 Samuel Fagemo .40 1.00
RR28 Trey Fix-Wolansky .50 1.25
RR29 Marc McLaughlin .50 1.25
RR30 Jack McBain .50 1.25
RR31 Jordan Harris .60 1.50
RR32 Jack LaFontaine .50 1.25
RR33 Ronnie Attard .50 1.25
RR34 Jordan Spence .50 1.25
RR35 Jack Quinn .75 2.00
RR36 Kent Johnson 1.00 2.50
RR37 Owen Power 1.00 2.50
RR38 Matty Beniers 1.25 3.00
RR39 Matt Boldy 1.50 4.00
RR40 Shane Wright 1.25 3.00

2022-23 Upper Deck Trilogy Rookie Renditions Autographs
RR1 Erik Kallgren 8.00 20.00
RR2 Marco Rossi 20.00 50.00
RR3 Dylan Holloway 15.00 40.00
RR4 Nick Abruzzese 8.00 20.00
RR5 Braden Schneider 12.00 30.00
RR6 Nathan Smith 6.00 15.00
RR7 Chase Pearson 6.00 15.00
RR8 Dylan Guenther 20.00 50.00
RR9 Mark Kastelic 6.00 15.00
RR10 Brayden Tracey 6.00 15.00
RR11 Bobby Brink 8.00 20.00
RR12 Filip Hallander 8.00 20.00
RR13 Mads Sogaard 10.00 25.00
RR14 Lukas Reichel 15.00 40.00
RR15 Matias Maccelli 12.00 30.00
RR16 Noah Cates 8.00 20.00
RR18 Jacob Perreault 8.00 20.00
RR19 Isaac Ratcliffe 8.00 20.00
RR20 Thomas Bordeleau 8.00 20.00
RR21 Lukas Dostal 15.00 40.00
RR22 Kaedan Korczak 6.00 15.00
RR23 Pyotr Kochetkov 15.00 40.00
RR24 Alex Vlasic 6.00 15.00
RR25 Dylan Samberg 8.00 20.00
RR27 Samuel Fagemo 6.00 15.00
RR28 Trey Fix-Wolansky 8.00 20.00
RR29 Marc McLaughlin 8.00 20.00
RR30 Jack McBain 8.00 20.00
RR31 Jordan Harris 10.00 25.00
RR33 Ronnie Attard 8.00 20.00
RR34 Jordan Spence 8.00 20.00
RR35 Jack Quinn 12.00 30.00
RR36 Kent Johnson 15.00 40.00
RR37 Owen Power 15.00 40.00
RR38 Matty Beniers 125.00 300.00
RR39 Matt Boldy 25.00 60.00
RR40 Shane Wright 40.00 100.00

2022-23 Upper Deck Trilogy Rookie Renditions Jerseys
RR2 Marco Rossi 5.00 12.00
RR3 Dylan Holloway 4.00 10.00
RR4 Nick Abruzzese 2.50 6.00
RR5 Braden Schneider 3.00 8.00
RR6 Nathan Smith 1.50 4.00
RR7 Chase Pearson 1.50 4.00
RR8 Dylan Guenther 5.00 12.00
RR9 Mark Kastelic 1.50 4.00
RR10 Brayden Tracey 1.50 4.00
RR11 Bobby Brink 2.00 5.00
RR12 Filip Hallander 2.00 5.00
RR13 Mads Sogaard 2.50 6.00
RR14 Lukas Reichel 4.00 10.00
RR15 Matias Maccelli 3.00 8.00
RR16 Noah Cates 2.00 5.00
RR18 Jacob Perreault 2.00 5.00
RR19 Isaac Ratcliffe 2.00 5.00
RR21 Lukas Dostal 4.00 10.00
RR22 Kaedan Korczak 1.50 4.00
RR23 Pyotr Kochetkov 4.00 10.00
RR24 Alex Vlasic 1.50 4.00
RR25 Dylan Samberg 2.00 5.00
RR26 Reilly Walsh 2.00 5.00
RR28 Trey Fix-Wolansky 2.00 5.00
RR31 Jordan Harris 2.50 6.00
RR33 Ronnie Attard 2.00 5.00
RR35 Jack Quinn 3.00 8.00
RR36 Kent Johnson 4.00 10.00
RR37 Owen Power 4.00 10.00
RR38 Matty Beniers 5.00 12.00
RR39 Matt Boldy 6.00 15.00
RR40 Shane Wright 6.00 15.00

2022-23 Upper Deck Trilogy Rookie Renditions Patch Autographs
RR2 Marco Rossi/49 50.00 125.00
RR3 Dylan Holloway/49 40.00 100.00
RR4 Nick Abruzzese/25 20.00 50.00
RR5 Braden Schneider/49 30.00 80.00
RR6 Nathan Smith/25 (No Auto) 8.00 20.00
RR7 Chase Pearson/49 15.00 40.00
RR8 Dylan Guenther/49 50.00 125.00
RR9 Mark Kastelic/49 15.00 40.00
RR10 Brayden Tracey/49 15.00 40.00
RR11 Bobby Brink/49 20.00 50.00
RR12 Filip Hallander/25 (No Auto) 10.00 25.00
RR13 Mads Sogaard/49 25.00 60.00
RR14 Lukas Reichel/49 40.00 100.00
RR15 Matias Maccelli/49 30.00 80.00
RR16 Noah Cates/49 20.00 50.00
RR17 Nikita Okhotiuk/25 (No Auto) 8.00 20.00
RR18 Jacob Perreault/49 20.00 50.00
RR19 Isaac Ratcliffe/49 20.00 50.00
RR20 Thomas Bordeleau/49 20.00 50.00
RR21 Lukas Dostal/49 40.00 100.00
RR22 Kaedan Korczak/49 15.00 40.00
RR23 Pyotr Kochetkov/49 40.00 100.00
RR24 Alex Vlasic/49 15.00 40.00
RR25 Dylan Samberg/49 20.00 50.00
RR26 Reilly Walsh/25 (No Auto) 8.00 20.00
RR27 Samuel Fagemo/25 15.00 40.00
RR28 Trey Fix-Wolansky/25 20.00 50.00
RR31 Jordan Harris/25 25.00 60.00
RR33 Ronnie Attard/25 20.00 50.00
RR35 Jack Quinn/25 30.00 80.00
RR36 Kent Johnson/25 40.00 100.00
RR37 Owen Power/25 40.00 100.00
RR39 Matt Boldy/25 60.00 150.00
RR40 Shane Wright/25 50.00 125.00

2022-23 Upper Deck Trilogy Rookie Signature Pucks
*TEAM LOGO/23: 1X TO 2.5X BASIC
RSPAV Alex Vlasic 8.00 20.00
RSPBE Matty Beniers 200.00 500.00
RSPBT Brayden Tracey 8.00 20.00
RSPDG Dylan Guenther 25.00 60.00
RSPDH Dylan Holloway 20.00 50.00
RSPDS Dylan Samberg 10.00 25.00
RSPJB Jonatan Berggren 15.00 40.00
RSPJP Jacob Perreault 10.00 25.00
RSPJQ Jack Quinn 15.00 40.00
RSPJS Jordan Spence 10.00 25.00
RSPKJ Kent Johnson 20.00 50.00
RSPLD Lukas Dostal 20.00 50.00
RSPLR Lukas Reichel 20.00 50.00
RSPMB Matt Boldy 30.00 80.00
RSPMR Marco Rossi 25.00 60.00
RSPMS Mads Sogaard 12.00 30.00
RSPNA Nick Abruzzese 10.00 25.00
RSPOP Owen Power 20.00 50.00
RSPSW Shane Wright 25.00 60.00

2022-23 Upper Deck Trilogy Rookie Triptychs
RTAV Alex Vlasic 4.00 10.00
RTBB Bobby Brink 5.00 12.00
RTBO Matt Boldy 15.00 40.00
RTBS Braden Schneider 8.00 20.00
RTBT Brayden Tracey 4.00 10.00
RTDG Dylan Guenther 12.00 30.00
RTDH Dylan Holloway 10.00 25.00
RTDS Dylan Samberg 5.00 12.00
RTIR Isaac Ratcliffe 5.00 12.00
RTJP Jacob Perreault 5.00 12.00
RTJQ Jack Quinn 8.00 20.00
RTJS Juraj Slafkovsky 25.00 60.00
RTKJ Kent Johnson 10.00 25.00
RTKK Kaedan Korczak 4.00 10.00
RTLR Lukas Reichel 10.00 25.00
RTMB Matty Beniers 40.00 100.00
RTMR Marco Rossi 12.00 30.00
RTMS Mads Sogaard 6.00 15.00
RTOP Owen Power 10.00 25.00
RTPK Pyotr Kochetkov 10.00 25.00
RTSA Jake Sanderson 12.00 30.00
RTSW Shane Wright 12.00 30.00
RTTD Thomas Bordeleau 5.00 12.00

2022-23 Upper Deck Trilogy Scripted Hall of Fame Plaques
SHFTS Teemu Selanne 125.00 300.00
SHFEL Eric Lindros 150.00 400.00

2022-23 Upper Deck Trilogy Signature Pucks
*TEAM LOGO/23: .75X TO 2X BASIC
SPAF Adam Fox 10.00 25.00
SPAI Alex Iafallo 5.00 12.00
SPAL Alexis Lafreniere 25.00 60.00
SPBJ Boone Jenner 8.00 20.00
SPBN Brock Nelson 8.00 20.00
SPBT Brady Tkachuk 12.00 30.00
SPBU Brent Burns 8.00 20.00
SPCM Connor McDavid 200.00 500.00
SPCS Cole Sillinger 6.00 15.00
SPDC Dylan Cozens 8.00 20.00
SPDS Dylan Strome 10.00 25.00
SPHZ Henrik Zetterberg 10.00 25.00
SPJH Jonathan Huberdeau 10.00 25.00
SPJI Jarome Iginla 10.00 25.00
SPJM Jared McCann 6.00 15.00
SPJP Joe Pavelski 8.00 20.00
SPKC Kyle Connor 12.00 30.00
SPKF Kevin Fiala 6.00 15.00
SPKM K'Andre Miller 6.00 15.00
SPKP Kyle Palmieri 6.00 15.00
SPKT Keith Tkachuk 8.00 20.00
SPLD Leon Draisaitl 25.00 60.00
SPMH Miro Heiskanen 10.00 25.00
SPMI J.T. Miller 10.00 25.00
SPMO Janis Moser 5.00 12.00
SPMS Mark Stone 10.00 25.00
SPMT Matthew Tkachuk 15.00 40.00
SPNE Nikolaj Ehlers 8.00 20.00
SPPS Pius Suter 6.00 15.00
SPQH Quinn Hughes 20.00 50.00
SPRC Ross Colton 6.00 15.00
SPRH Roope Hintz 10.00 25.00
SPSK Saku Koivu 8.00 20.00
SPTE Troy Terry 6.00 15.00
SPTL Trevor Linden 8.00 20.00
SPTO Tyler Toffoli 8.00 20.00
SPTS Tim Stutzle 25.00 60.00
SPTT Teuvo Teravainen 8.00 20.00
SPTW Tom Wilson 8.00 20.00
SPYG Yanni Gourde 6.00 15.00

2022-23 Upper Deck Trilogy Signature Puckstoppers
SPUAV Andrei Vasilevskiy 20.00 50.00
SPUJC Jack Campbell 12.00 30.00
SPUJM Jacob Markstrom 12.00 30.00
SPUJO Jake Oettinger 20.00 50.00
SPUMA Marc-Andre Fleury 30.00 80.00
SPURH Ron Hextall 12.00 30.00

2022-23 Upper Deck Trilogy Signature Puckstoppers Team Logo
*TEAM LOGO/23: .6X TO 1.5X BASIC
SPUJO Jake Oettinger 30.00 80.00
SPUMA Marc-Andre Fleury 80.00 200.00
SPURH Ron Hextall 30.00 80.00

2022-23 Upper Deck Trilogy Triple Relics
TRAAS Aho/Svechnikov/Andersen/25 25.00 60.00
TRBMP Pastrnak Marchand/Bergeron/25 40.00 100.00
TRBSZ Zegras/Byfield/Seider/25 20.00 50.00
TRDQP Dahlin/Power/Quinn/35 30.00 80.00
TRGTZ Zegras/Gibson/Terry/35 15.00 40.00
TRHKP Hedman/Kucherov/Point/25 30.00 80.00
TRHMH Hughes/Hischier/Mercer/35 50.00 125.00
TRKQD Kopitar/Doughty/Quick/35 20.00 50.00
TRLBS Sorokin/Lee/Barzal/35 25.00 60.00
TRPJB Power/Beniers/Johnson/25 125.00 300.00
TRPSC Suzuki/Caufield/Price/35 100.00 250.00
TRSEC Scheifele/Connor/Ehlers/25 25.00 60.00
TRTMB Bunting/Marner/Tavares/35 25.00 60.00

2023-24 Upper Deck Trilogy
1 Martin Necas .75 2.00
2 Kent Johnson .50 1.25
3 John Carlson .50 1.25
4 Seth Jones .50 1.25
5 Kirby Dach .50 1.25
6 Tomas Hertl .50 1.25
7 Travis Konecny .50 1.25
8 Kevin Fiala .40 1.00
9 Wyatt Johnston 1.00 2.50
10 Nick Schmaltz .40 1.00
11 Juuso Parssinen .30 .75
12 Mika Zibanejad .60 1.50
13 Jared McCann .40 1.00
14 Taylor Raddysh .40 1.00
15 Elias Lindholm .50 1.25
16 Tyler Toffoli .50 1.25
17 Anton Lundell .50 1.25
18 Jonathan Marchessault .60 1.50
19 Noah Dobson .60 1.50
20 Gabe Vilardi .50 1.25
21 Carter Hart .50 1.25
22 Jake Guentzel .75 2.00
23 Claude Giroux .50 1.25
24 Colton Parayko .40 1.00
25 Matias Maccelli .40 1.00
26 Yegor Sharangovich .50 1.25
27 Troy Terry .40 1.00
28 Evan Bouchard .60 1.50
29 Noah Cates .30 .75
30 Andrew Copp .30 .75
31 Brayden Schenn .50 1.25
32 Anders Lee .40 1.00
33 Cole Perfetti .50 1.25
34 J.T. Miller .60 1.50
35 Matt Boldy .75 2.00
36 Mason McTavish .50 1.25
37 Jonathan Huberdeau .60 1.50
38 Mikko Rantanen 1.25 3.00
39 Dylan Larkin .60 1.50
40 Miro Heiskanen .60 1.50
41 Patrik Laine .60 1.50
42 Erik Karlsson .60 1.50
43 William Nylander 1.00 2.50
44 Lucas Raymond .75 2.00
45 Jordan Kyrou .50 1.25
46 Mark Stone .60 1.50
47 Kyle Connor .75 2.00
48 Roman Josi .50 1.25
49 Quinn Hughes 1.25 3.00
50 Ryan Nugent-Hopkins .60 1.50
51 Mathew Barzal .60 1.50
52 Owen Power .50 1.25
53 Moritz Seider .60 1.50
54 Alexis Lafreniere .75 2.00
55 Brady Tkachuk .75 2.00
56 Brayden Point .60 1.50
57 Nick Suzuki 1.00 2.50
58 Dylan Cozens .50 1.25
59 Tage Thompson .60 1.50
60 Joe Pavelski .60 1.50
61 Johnny Gaudreau .75 2.00
62 Matt Duchene .50 1.25
63 Nico Hischier .75 2.00
64 Sebastian Aho .75 2.00
65 Clayton Keller .60 1.50
66 Jordan Eberle .50 1.25
67 Mark Scheifele .75 2.00
68 Tim Stutzle .60 1.50
69 Connor McDavid 2.50 6.00
70 Leon Draisaitl 1.50 4.00

71 Anze Kopitar .75 2.00
72 Nikita Kucherov 1.00 2.50
73 Cale Makar 1.25 3.00
74 Marc-Andre Fleury 1.00 2.50
75 Mitch Marner .75 2.00
76 Jason Robertson .75 2.00
77 Patrice Bergeron .60 1.50
78 Aleksander Barkov .75 2.00
79 Alex Ovechkin 2.00 5.00
80 Auston Matthews 2.00 5.00
81 Steven Stamkos 1.00 2.50
82 Elias Pettersson .75 2.00
83 Brad Marchand 1.00 2.50
84 Artemi Panarin 1.00 2.50
85 Evgeni Malkin 1.00 2.50
86 Kirill Kaprizov 1.50 4.00
87 Andrei Vasilevskiy .75 2.00
88 Cole Caufield 1.00 2.50
89 Igor Shesterkin 1.00 2.50
90 Sidney Crosby 2.00 5.00
91 Rasmus Dahlin .60 1.50
92 Matthew Tkachuk 1.00 2.50
93 Jack Eichel .75 2.00
94 John Tavares .75 2.00
95 Andrei Svechnikov .60 1.50
96 Jack Hughes 1.25 3.00
97 Trevor Zegras .50 1.25
98 David Pastrnak 1.25 3.00
99 Nathan MacKinnon 2.00 5.00
100 Matty Beniers .60 1.50
101 Owen Beck/999 RC 2.50 6.00
102 Connor Bedard/999 RC 50.00 125.00
103 Olle Eriksson Ek/999 RC 1.50 4.00
104 Jonathan Gruden/999 RC 1.50 4.00
105 Leevi Merilainen/999 RC 1.50 4.00
106 Tye Kartye/999 RC 2.50 6.00
107 Logan Cooley/999 RC 5.00 12.00
108 Hunter McKown/999 RC 1.50 4.00
109 Samuel Bolduc/999 RC 1.50 4.00
110 Marco Kasper/999 RC 4.00 10.00
111 Jakob Pelletier/999 RC 2.00 5.00
112 Luke Philp/999 RC 1.50 4.00
113 Hugh McGing/999 RC 1.50 4.00
114 Cole McWard/999 RC 1.50 4.00
115 Billy Sweezey/999 RC 1.50 4.00
116 William Dufour/999 RC 1.25 3.00
117 Akito Hirose/999 RC 1.25 3.00
118 Jiri Patera/999 RC 2.50 6.00
119 Milos Kelemen/999 RC 1.50 4.00
120 David Gust/999 RC 1.50 4.00
121 Matt Murray/999 RC 1.50 4.00
122 Sean Farrell/999 RC 1.50 4.00
123 Will Cuylle/999 RC 2.50 6.00
124 Bobby McMann/999 RC 2.50 6.00
125 Matthew Kessel/999 RC 1.25 3.00
126 Danil Gushchin/999 RC 1.50 4.00
127 Henry Thrun/999 RC 1.50 4.00
128 Joona Koppanen/999 RC 1.25 3.00
129 Michael Kesselring/999 RC 1.50 4.00
130 Egor Afanasyev/999 RC 1.50 4.00
131 Arnaud Durandeau/999 RC 1.50 4.00
132 Vincent Iorio/999 RC 1.50 4.00
133 Aidan McDonough/999 RC 1.25 3.00
134 Adam Fantilli/999 RC 5.00 12.00
135 Matthew Knies/999 RC 6.00 15.00
136 Luke Evangelista/999 RC 2.50 6.00
137 Dustin Wolf/999 RC 5.00 12.00
138 Lukas Rousek/999 RC 1.25 3.00
139 Ridly Greig/999 RC 2.50 6.00
140 Tyson Foerster/999 RC 3.00 8.00
141 Elliot Desnoyers/999 RC 1.50 4.00
142 Nikita Nesterenko/999 RC 1.50 4.00
143 Devon Levi/999 RC 4.00 10.00
144 Matthew Coronato/999 RC 2.50 6.00
145 Yaroslav Askarov/999 RC 4.00 10.00
146 Tyler Kleven/999 RC 1.50 4.00
147 Luke Hughes/999 RC 5.00 12.00
148 Vincent Desharnais/999 RC 2.00 5.00
149 Brock Faber/999 RC 4.00 10.00
150 Simon Edvinsson/999 RC 3.00 8.00
151 Owen Beck/699 2.50 6.00
152 Connor Bedard/699 50.00 125.00
153 Olle Eriksson Ek/699 1.50 4.00
154 Jonathan Gruden/699 1.50 4.00
155 Leevi Merilainen/699 1.50 4.00
156 Tye Kartye/699 2.50 6.00
157 Logan Cooley/699 5.00 12.00
158 Hunter McKown/699 1.50 4.00
159 Samuel Bolduc/699 1.50 4.00
160 Marco Kasper/699 4.00 10.00
161 Jakob Pelletier/699 2.00 5.00
162 Luke Philp/699 1.50 4.00
163 Hugh McGing/699 1.50 4.00
164 Cole McWard/699 1.50 4.00
165 Billy Sweezey/699 1.50 4.00
166 William Dufour/699 1.25 3.00
167 Akito Hirose/699 1.25 3.00
168 Jiri Patera/699 2.50 6.00
169 Milos Kelemen/699 1.50 4.00
170 David Gust/699 1.50 4.00
171 Matt Murray/699 1.50 4.00
172 Sean Farrell/699 1.50 4.00
173 Will Cuylle/699 2.50 6.00
174 Bobby McMann/699 2.50 6.00
175 Matthew Kessel/699 1.25 3.00
176 Danil Gushchin/699 1.50 4.00
177 Henry Thrun/699 1.50 4.00
178 Joona Koppanen/699 1.25 3.00
179 Michael Kesselring/699 1.50 4.00
180 Egor Afanasyev/699 1.50 4.00
181 Arnaud Durandeau/699 1.50 4.00
182 Vincent Iorio/699 1.50 4.00
183 Aidan McDonough/699 1.25 3.00
184 Adam Fantilli/699 5.00 12.00
185 Matthew Knies/699 6.00 15.00
186 Luke Evangelista/699 2.50 6.00
187 Dustin Wolf/699 5.00 12.00
188 Lukas Rousek/699 1.25 3.00
189 Ridly Greig/699 2.50 6.00
190 Tyson Foerster/699 3.00 8.00
191 Elliot Desnoyers/699 1.50 4.00
192 Nikita Nesterenko/699 1.50 4.00
193 Devon Levi/699 4.00 10.00
194 Matthew Coronato/699 2.50 6.00
195 Yaroslav Askarov/699 4.00 10.00
196 Tyler Kleven/699 1.50 4.00
197 Luke Hughes/699 5.00 12.00
198 Vincent Desharnais/699 2.00 5.00
199 Brock Faber/699 4.00 10.00
200 Simon Edvinsson/699 3.00 8.00
201 Owen Beck/299 4.00 10.00
202 Connor Bedard/299 125.00 300.00
203 Olle Eriksson Ek/299 2.50 6.00
204 Jonathan Gruden/299 2.50 6.00
205 Leevi Merilainen/299 2.50 6.00
206 Tye Kartye/299 4.00 10.00
207 Logan Cooley/299 8.00 20.00
208 Hunter McKown/299 2.50 6.00
209 Samuel Bolduc/299 2.50 6.00
210 Marco Kasper/299 6.00 15.00
211 Jakob Pelletier/299 3.00 8.00
212 Luke Philp/299 2.50 6.00
213 Hugh McGing/299 2.50 6.00
214 Cole McWard/299 2.50 6.00
215 Billy Sweezey/299 2.50 6.00
216 William Dufour/299 2.00 5.00
217 Akito Hirose/299 2.00 5.00
218 Jiri Patera/299 4.00 10.00
219 Milos Kelemen/299 2.50 6.00
220 David Gust/299 2.50 6.00
221 Matt Murray/299 2.50 6.00
222 Sean Farrell/299 2.50 6.00
223 Will Cuylle/299 4.00 10.00
224 Bobby McMann/299 4.00 10.00
225 Matthew Kessel/299 2.00 5.00
226 Danil Gushchin/299 2.50 6.00
227 Henry Thrun/299 2.50 6.00
228 Joona Koppanen/299 2.00 5.00
229 Michael Kesselring/299 2.50 6.00
230 Egor Afanasyev/299 2.50 6.00
231 Arnaud Durandeau/299 2.50 6.00
232 Vincent Iorio/299 2.50 6.00
233 Aidan McDonough/299 2.00 5.00
234 Adam Fantilli/299 8.00 20.00
235 Matthew Knies/299 10.00 25.00
236 Luke Evangelista/299 4.00 10.00
237 Dustin Wolf/299 8.00 20.00
238 Lukas Rousek/299 2.00 5.00
239 Ridly Greig/299 4.00 10.00
240 Tyson Foerster/299 5.00 12.00
241 Elliot Desnoyers/299 2.50 6.00
242 Nikita Nesterenko/299 2.50 6.00
243 Devon Levi/299 6.00 15.00
244 Matthew Coronato/299 4.00 10.00
245 Yaroslav Askarov/299 6.00 15.00
246 Tyler Kleven/299 2.50 6.00
247 Luke Hughes/299 8.00 20.00
248 Vincent Desharnais/299 3.00 8.00
249 Brock Faber/299 6.00 15.00
250 Simon Edvinsson/299 5.00 12.00

2023-24 Upper Deck Trilogy Blue

*BLUE: 2.5X TO 6X BASIC
*BLUE RC: 1X TO 2.5X BASIC
102 Connor Bedard/99 125.00 300.00
202 Connor Bedard/25 400.00 1000.00

2023-24 Upper Deck Trilogy Gold

*GOLD: 6X TO 15X BASIC
*GOLD RC: 3X TO 8X BASIC
69 Connor McDavid SP AU 200.00 500.00
77 Patrice Bergeron SP AU 50.00 125.00
80 Auston Matthews SP AU 60.00 150.00
95 Andrei Svechnikov SP AU 15.00 40.00
96 Jack Hughes SP AU 60.00 150.00
100 Matty Beniers SP AU 20.00 50.00
102 Connor Bedard AU/49 1000.00 2500.00
152 Connor Bedard AU/49 1000.00 2500.00
184 Adam Fantilli AU/49 100.00 250.00
185 Matthew Knies AU/49 60.00 150.00
197 Luke Hughes AU/49 60.00 150.00
199 Brock Faber AU/49 60.00 150.00

2023-24 Upper Deck Trilogy Green

*GREEN: 2.5X TO 6X BASIC
*GREEN RC: 1.2X TO 3X BASIC
152 Connor Bedard/25 200.00 500.00

2023-24 Upper Deck Trilogy Red

*RED: 1.5X TO 4X BASIC

2023-24 Upper Deck Trilogy Auto Focus

AFAB Aleksander Barkov 25.00 60.00
AFBT Brady Tkachuk 25.00 60.00
AFCM Cale Makar SP 100.00 250.00
AFDG Dylan Guenther 50.00 125.00
AFJK Jordan Kyrou 15.00 40.00
AFJM Jonathan Marchessault 20.00 50.00
AFNS Nick Suzuki 30.00 80.00
AFPK Peyton Krebs 12.00 30.00
AFRO Ryan O'Reilly 15.00 40.00
AFSW Shane Wright 20.00 50.00
AFVP Vasily Podkolzin 10.00 25.00

2023-24 Upper Deck Trilogy Auto Focus Rookies

AFRCB Connor Bedard SP 1200.00 3000.00
AFRMK Marco Kasper 50.00 125.00
AFRSE Simon Edvinsson 50.00 125.00
AFRYA Yaroslav Askarov 60.00 150.00

2023-24 Upper Deck Trilogy Crystallized Signatures

CAM Auston Matthews SP 125.00 300.00
CAV Andrei Vasilevskiy 30.00 80.00
CCM Connor McDavid SP 200.00 500.00
CIS Ilya Sorokin 30.00 80.00
CKU Andrei Kuzmenko 20.00 50.00
CLD Leon Draisaitl SP 60.00 150.00
CMF Marc-Andre Fleury SP 40.00 100.00
CTS Tim Stutzle 25.00 60.00
CWJ Wyatt Johnston 40.00 100.00

2023-24 Upper Deck Trilogy Generations

TG1A Nicklas Lidstrom .75 2.00
TG1B Moritz Seider 1.00 2.50
TG1C Simon Edvinsson 1.50 4.00
TG2A Henrik Lundqvist 2.00 5.00
TG2B Artemi Panarin 1.50 4.00
TG2C Alexis Lafreniere 1.25 3.00
TG3A Brett Hull 1.50 4.00
TG3B Jordan Kyrou .75 2.00
TG3C Jake Neighbours .75 2.00
TG4A Martin Brodeur 2.00 5.00
TG4B Jack Hughes 2.00 5.00
TG4C Luke Hughes 2.50 6.00
TG5A Scott Mellanby .60 1.50
TG5B Matthew Tkachuk 1.50 4.00
TG5C Anton Lundell .75 2.00
TG6A Pekka Rinne .75 2.00
TG6B Juuse Saros 1.00 2.50
TG6C Yaroslav Askarov 2.00 5.00
TG7A Dominik Hasek 1.25 3.00
TG7B Tage Thompson 1.00 2.50
TG7C Owen Power .75 2.00
TG8A Doug Gilmour 1.00 2.50
TG8B Auston Matthews 3.00 8.00
TG8C Michael Bunting .75 2.00
TG9A Shane Doan .60 1.50
TG9B Clayton Keller 1.00 2.50
TG9C Dylan Guenther 1.00 2.50
TG10A Bobby Orr 3.00 8.00
TG10C Jeremy Swayman 1.25 3.00
TG11A Peter Forsberg 1.50 4.00
TG11B Mikko Rantanen 2.00 5.00
TG11C Cale Makar 2.00 5.00
TG12A Eric Lindros 1.25 3.00
TG12B Carter Hart .75 2.00
TG12C Tyson Foerster 1.50 4.00
TG13A Maurice Richard 1.50 4.00
TG13B Cole Caufield 1.50 4.00
TG13C Juraj Slafkovsky 1.50 4.00
TG14A Mike Modano 1.25 3.00
TG14B Joe Pavelski 1.00 2.50
TG14C Jake Oettinger 1.25 3.00
TG15A Jarome Iginla 1.00 2.50
TG15B Jonathan Huberdeau 1.00 2.50
TG15C Jakob Pelletier 1.00 2.50
TG16A Wayne Gretzky 5.00 12.00
TG16B Anze Kopitar 1.25 3.00
TG16C Gabe Vilardi .75 2.00
TG17A Mike Gartner 1.00 2.50
TG17B Alex Ovechkin 3.00 8.00
TG17C Dylan Strome 1.00 2.50
TG18A Ron Francis 1.00 2.50
TG18B Sebastian Aho 1.25 3.00
TG18C Seth Jarvis 1.00 2.50
TG19A Billy Smith .75 2.00
TG19B Brock Nelson .75 2.00
TG19C Ilya Sorokin 1.25 3.00
TG20A Mario Lemieux 3.00 8.00
TG20B Connor McDavid 4.00 10.00
TG20C Connor Bedard 8.00 20.00

2023-24 Upper Deck Trilogy Generations Blue

*BLUE/349: .6X TO 1.5X BASIC
TG20C Connor Bedard 40.00 100.00

2023-24 Upper Deck Trilogy Generations Green

*GREEN/99: .8X TO 2X BASIC
TG20C Connor Bedard 125.00 300.00

2023-24 Upper Deck Trilogy Generations Pink

*PINK/25: 2.5X TO 6X BASIC
TG4A Martin Brodeur 20.00 50.00
TG20B Connor McDavid 40.00 100.00
TG20C Connor Bedard 200.00 500.00

2023-24 Upper Deck Trilogy Generations Red

*RED/799: .5X TO 1.2X BASIC
TG20C Connor Bedard 25.00 60.00

2023-24 Upper Deck Trilogy Generations Autographs

TG1C Simon Edvinsson/49 20.00 50.00
TG3B Jordan Kyrou/49 10.00 25.00
TG4A Martin Brodeur/25 60.00 150.00
TG5C Anton Lundell/49 10.00 25.00
TG6B Juuse Saros/49 12.00 30.00
TG6C Yaroslav Askarov/25 25.00 60.00
TG7B Tage Thompson/25 12.00 30.00
TG8A Doug Gilmour/25 12.00 30.00
TG8C Michael Bunting/49 10.00 25.00
TG9C Dylan Guenther/49 12.00 30.00
TG11B Mikko Rantanen/25 25.00 60.00
TG12B Carter Hart/49 10.00 25.00
TG12C Tyson Foerster/49 20.00 50.00
TG14A Mike Modano/25 15.00 40.00
TG14B Joe Pavelski/25 12.00 30.00
TG15B Jonathan Huberdeau/49 12.00 30.00
TG15C Jakob Pelletier/25 12.00 30.00
TG16C Gabe Vilardi/49 10.00 25.00
TG17A Mike Gartner/49 12.00 30.00
TG17C Dylan Strome/49 12.00 30.00
TG18A Ron Francis/25 12.00 30.00
TG18C Seth Jarvis/25 12.00 30.00
TG19C Ilya Sorokin/25 15.00 40.00

2023-24 Upper Deck Trilogy Generations Jerseys

TG1B Moritz Seider 4.00 10.00
TG1C Simon Edvinsson 6.00 15.00
TG2A Henrik Lundqvist 8.00 20.00
TG2B Artemi Panarin 6.00 15.00
TG2C Alexis Lafreniere 5.00 12.00
TG3A Brett Hull 6.00 15.00
TG3B Jordan Kyrou 3.00 8.00
TG3C Jake Neighbours 3.00 8.00
TG4A Martin Brodeur 8.00 20.00
TG4B Jack Hughes 8.00 20.00
TG4C Luke Hughes 10.00 25.00
TG5B Matthew Tkachuk 6.00 15.00
TG5C Anton Lundell 3.00 8.00
TG6A Pekka Rinne 3.00 8.00
TG6B Juuse Saros 4.00 10.00
TG6C Yaroslav Askarov 8.00 20.00
TG7B Tage Thompson 4.00 10.00
TG7C Owen Power 3.00 8.00
TG8B Auston Matthews 12.00 30.00
TG8C Michael Bunting 3.00 8.00
TG9A Shane Doan 2.50 6.00
TG9B Clayton Keller 4.00 10.00
TG9C Dylan Guenther 4.00 10.00
TG10B Brad Marchand 6.00 15.00
TG10C Jeremy Swayman 5.00 12.00
TG11B Mikko Rantanen 8.00 20.00
TG11C Cale Makar 8.00 20.00
TG12B Carter Hart 3.00 8.00
TG12C Tyson Foerster 6.00 15.00
TG13B Cole Caufield 6.00 15.00
TG13C Juraj Slafkovsky 6.00 15.00
TG14B Joe Pavelski 4.00 10.00
TG14C Jake Oettinger 5.00 12.00
TG15A Jarome Iginla 4.00 10.00
TG15B Jonathan Huberdeau 4.00 10.00
TG15C Jakob Pelletier 4.00 10.00
TG16B Anze Kopitar 5.00 12.00
TG16C Gabe Vilardi 3.00 8.00
TG17B Alex Ovechkin 12.00 30.00
TG17C Dylan Strome 4.00 10.00
TG18B Sebastian Aho 5.00 12.00
TG18C Seth Jarvis 4.00 10.00
TG19B Brock Nelson 3.00 8.00
TG19C Ilya Sorokin 5.00 12.00
TG20B Connor McDavid 15.00 40.00
TG20C Connor Bedard 80.00 200.00

2023-24 Upper Deck Trilogy Honorary Triple Swatches

HTSAK Aaron Ekblad/35 12.00 30.00
HTSAK Anze Kopitar/25 15.00 40.00
HTSAP Artemi Panarin/25 20.00 50.00
HTSAS Andrei Svechnikov/35 12.00 30.00
HTSAV Andrei Vasilevskiy/25 15.00 40.00
HTSBM Brad Marchand/25 20.00 50.00
HTSCC Cole Caufield/25 20.00 50.00
HTSCM Cale Makar/25 25.00 60.00
HTSDC Dylan Cozens/35 10.00 25.00
HTSDD Drew Doughty/35 10.00 25.00
HTSEM Evgeni Malkin/25 20.00 50.00
HTSEP Elias Pettersson/35 15.00 40.00
HTSJB Jamie Benn/35 10.00 25.00
HTSJH Jack Hughes/25 25.00 60.00
HTSJT John Tavares/25 15.00 40.00
HTSLH Luke Hughes/35 30.00 80.00
HTSMB Matty Beniers/25 12.00 30.00
HTSMM Mitch Marner/25 15.00 40.00
HTSMS Moritz Seider/35 12.00 30.00
HTSMT Matthew Tkachuk/35 20.00 50.00
HTSMZ Mika Zibanejad/35 12.00 30.00
HTSNK Nikita Kucherov/25 20.00 50.00
HTSNS Nick Suzuki/35 12.00 30.00
HTSOP Owen Power/35 10.00 25.00
HTSRD Rasmus Dahlin/35 12.00 30.00
HTSSE Simon Edvinsson/35 20.00 50.00
HTSSS Steven Stamkos/25 20.00 50.00
HTSTS Tim Stutzle/25 15.00 40.00
HTSTZ Trevor Zegras/25 10.00 25.00
HTSYA Yaroslav Askarov/35 25.00 60.00

2023-24 Upper Deck Trilogy Jerseys

1 Martin Necas 5.00 12.00
2 Kent Johnson 3.00 8.00
3 John Carlson 3.00 8.00
4 Seth Jones 3.00 8.00
5 Kirby Dach 3.00 8.00
6 Tomas Hertl 3.00 8.00
7 Travis Konecny 3.00 8.00
8 Kevin Fiala 2.50 6.00
10 Nick Schmaltz 2.50 6.00
11 Juuso Parssinen 2.00 5.00
12 Mika Zibanejad 4.00 10.00
13 Jared McCann 2.50 6.00
14 Taylor Raddysh 2.50 6.00
15 Elias Lindholm 3.00 8.00
16 Tyler Toffoli 3.00 8.00
17 Anton Lundell 3.00 8.00
18 Jonathan Marchessault 4.00 10.00
20 Gabe Vilardi 3.00 8.00
21 Carter Hart 3.00 8.00
22 Jake Guentzel 5.00 12.00
23 Claude Giroux 3.00 8.00
24 Colton Parayko 2.50 6.00
25 Matias Maccelli 2.50 6.00
26 Yegor Sharangovich 3.00 8.00
27 Troy Terry 2.50 6.00
30 Andrew Copp 2.00 5.00
31 Brayden Schenn 3.00 8.00
32 Anders Lee 2.50 6.00
33 Cole Perfetti 3.00 8.00
34 J.T. Miller 4.00 10.00
35 Matt Boldy 5.00 12.00
36 Mason McTavish 3.00 8.00
37 Jonathan Huberdeau 4.00 10.00
38 Mikko Rantanen 8.00 20.00
39 Dylan Larkin 4.00 10.00
40 Miro Heiskanen 3.00 8.00
41 Patrik Laine 4.00 10.00
42 Erik Karlsson 4.00 10.00
43 William Nylander 6.00 15.00
44 Lucas Raymond 5.00 12.00
45 Jordan Kyrou 3.00 8.00
46 Mark Stone 4.00 10.00
47 Kyle Connor 5.00 12.00
48 Roman Josi 3.00 8.00
49 Quinn Hughes 8.00 20.00
50 Ryan Nugent-Hopkins 4.00 10.00
51 Mathew Barzal 4.00 10.00
52 Owen Power 3.00 8.00
53 Moritz Seider 4.00 10.00
54 Alexis Lafreniere 5.00 12.00
55 Brady Tkachuk 6.00 15.00
56 Brayden Point 5.00 12.00
57 Nick Suzuki 6.00 15.00
58 Dylan Cozens 3.00 8.00
59 Tage Thompson 4.00 10.00
60 Joe Pavelski 4.00 10.00
61 Johnny Gaudreau 5.00 12.00
62 Matt Duchene 3.00 8.00
63 Nico Hischier 5.00 12.00
64 Sebastian Aho 5.00 12.00
65 Clayton Keller 4.00 10.00
66 Jordan Eberle 3.00 8.00
67 Mark Scheifele 5.00 12.00
68 Tim Stutzle 4.00 10.00
69 Connor McDavid 15.00 40.00
70 Leon Draisaitl 10.00 25.00
71 Anze Kopitar 5.00 12.00
72 Nikita Kucherov 6.00 15.00
73 Cale Makar 8.00 20.00
74 Marc-Andre Fleury 6.00 15.00
75 Mitch Marner 5.00 12.00
76 Jason Robertson 5.00 12.00
77 Patrice Bergeron 4.00 10.00
78 Aleksander Barkov 5.00 12.00
79 Alex Ovechkin 12.00 30.00
80 Auston Matthews 12.00 30.00
81 Steven Stamkos 6.00 15.00
82 Elias Pettersson 5.00 12.00
83 Brad Marchand 6.00 15.00
84 Artemi Panarin 6.00 15.00
85 Evgeni Malkin 6.00 15.00
86 Kirill Kaprizov 10.00 25.00
87 Andrei Vasilevskiy 5.00 12.00
88 Cole Caufield 6.00 15.00
89 Igor Shesterkin 6.00 15.00
90 Sidney Crosby 12.00 30.00
91 Rasmus Dahlin 4.00 10.00
92 Matthew Tkachuk 6.00 15.00
93 Jack Eichel 5.00 12.00
94 John Tavares 5.00 12.00
95 Andrei Svechnikov 4.00 10.00
96 Jack Hughes 8.00 20.00
97 Trevor Zegras 3.00 8.00
98 David Pastrnak 8.00 20.00
99 Nathan MacKinnon 12.00 30.00
100 Matty Beniers 4.00 10.00
101 Owen Beck 3.00 8.00
102 Connor Bedard 60.00 150.00
103 Olle Eriksson Ek 3.00 8.00
104 Jonathan Gruden 3.00 8.00
105 Leevi Merilainen 3.00 8.00
106 Tye Kartye 5.00 12.00
107 Logan Cooley 10.00 25.00
108 Hunter McKown 3.00 8.00
109 Samuel Bolduc 3.00 8.00
110 Marco Kasper 8.00 20.00
111 Jakob Pelletier 4.00 10.00
112 Luke Philp 3.00 8.00
113 Hugh McGing 3.00 8.00
114 Cole McWard 3.00 8.00
115 Billy Sweezey 3.00 8.00
116 William Dufour 2.50 6.00
117 Akito Hirose 2.50 6.00
118 Jiri Patera 5.00 12.00
119 Milos Kelemen 3.00 8.00
120 David Gust 3.00 8.00
121 Matt Murray 3.00 8.00
122 Sean Farrell 3.00 8.00
123 Will Cuylle 5.00 12.00
124 Bobby McMann 5.00 12.00
125 Matthew Kessel 2.50 6.00
127 Henry Thrun 3.00 8.00
128 Joona Koppanen 2.50 6.00
129 Michael Kesselring 3.00 8.00
130 Egor Afanasyev 3.00 8.00
131 Arnaud Durandeau 3.00 8.00
132 Vincent Iorio 3.00 8.00
133 Aidan McDonough 2.50 6.00
134 Adam Fantilli 10.00 25.00
135 Matthew Knies 12.00 30.00
136 Luke Evangelista 5.00 12.00
137 Dustin Wolf 10.00 25.00
138 Lukas Rousek 2.50 6.00
139 Ridly Greig 5.00 12.00
140 Tyson Foerster 6.00 15.00
141 Elliot Desnoyers 3.00 8.00
142 Nikita Nesterenko 3.00 8.00
143 Devon Levi 8.00 20.00
144 Matthew Coronato 5.00 12.00
145 Yaroslav Askarov 8.00 20.00
146 Tyler Kleven 3.00 8.00
147 Luke Hughes 10.00 25.00
148 Vincent Desharnais 4.00 10.00
149 Brock Faber 8.00 20.00
150 Simon Edvinsson 6.00 15.00

2023-24 Upper Deck Trilogy Jerseys Patch

*PATCH/49: .8X TO 2X BASIC
102 Connor Bedard/49 300.00 800.00

2023-24 Upper Deck Trilogy Rookie Premieres Plexi

RP1 Connor Bedard 125.00 300.00
RP2 Owen Beck 6.00 15.00
RP3 Matthew Kessel 3.00 8.00
RP4 Brock Faber 10.00 25.00
RP5 Joona Koppanen 3.00 8.00
RP6 Olle Eriksson Ek 4.00 10.00
RP7 Yaroslav Askarov 10.00 25.00
RP8 Marco Kasper 10.00 25.00
RP9 Matt Murray 4.00 10.00
RP10 Luke Hughes 12.00 30.00
RP11 Jakob Pelletier 5.00 12.00
RP12 Sean Farrell 4.00 10.00
RP13 David Gust 4.00 10.00
RP14 Matthew Coronato 6.00 15.00
RP15 Devon Levi 10.00 25.00
RP16 Jiri Patera 6.00 15.00
RP17 Adam Fantilli 12.00 30.00
RP18 Luke Philp 4.00 10.00
RP19 Dustin Wolf 12.00 30.00
RP20 Jonathan Gruden 4.00 10.00
RP21 Aidan McDonough 4.00 10.00
RP22 Tyson Foerster 8.00 20.00
RP23 Leevi Merilainen 4.00 10.00
RP24 Lukas Rousek 4.00 10.00
RP25 Bobby McMann 6.00 15.00
RP26 Nikita Nesterenko 4.00 10.00
RP27 Matthew Knies 15.00 40.00
RP28 Danil Gushchin 4.00 10.00
RP29 Akito Hirose 4.00 10.00
RP30 Simon Edvinsson 8.00 20.00
RP31 Logan Cooley 12.00 30.00
RP32 Hunter McKown 4.00 10.00
RP33 Tye Kartye 6.00 15.00
RP34 Michael Kesselring 4.00 10.00
RP35 William Dufour 3.00 8.00
RP36 Ridly Greig 6.00 15.00
RP37 Luke Evangelista 6.00 15.00
RP38 Vincent Desharnais 5.00 12.00
RP39 Hugh McGing 4.00 10.00
RP40 Vincent Iorio 4.00 10.00

2023-24 Upper Deck Trilogy Rookie Premieres Plexi Gold Tint

*GOLD/49: .8X TO 2X BASIC
RP4 Brock Faber 40.00 100.00
RP10 Luke Hughes 80.00 200.00
RP17 Adam Fantilli 50.00 125.00
RP27 Matthew Knies 40.00 100.00
RP31 Logan Cooley 40.00 100.00

2023-24 Upper Deck Trilogy Rookie Renditions

*RED/799: .6X TO 1.5X BASIC
*BLUE/499: 1X TO 2.5X BASIC
*GREEN/99: 1.5X TO 4X BASIC
*PINK/25: 4X TO 10X BASIC
RR1 Owen Beck .75 2.00
RR2 Matthew Kessel .40 1.00
RR3 Brock Faber 1.25 3.00
RR4 Yaroslav Askarov 1.25 3.00
RR5 Marco Kasper 1.25 3.00
RR6 Luke Hughes 1.50 4.00
RR7 Jakob Pelletier .60 1.50
RR8 Sean Farrell .50 1.25
RR9 David Gust .50 1.25
RR10 Connor Bedard 20.00 50.00
RR11 Joona Koppanen .40 1.00
RR12 Olle Eriksson Ek .50 1.25
RR13 Matt Murray .50 1.25
RR14 Matthew Coronato .75 2.00
RR15 Devon Levi 1.25 3.00
RR16 Jiri Patera .75 2.00
RR17 Billy Sweezey .50 1.25
RR18 Luke Philp .50 1.25
RR19 Dustin Wolf 1.50 4.00
RR20 Jonathan Gruden .50 1.25
RR21 Aidan McDonough .40 1.00
RR22 Tyson Foerster 1.00 2.50
RR23 Leevi Merilainen .50 1.25
RR24 Lukas Rousek .40 1.00
RR25 Bobby McMann .75 2.00
RR26 Nikita Nesterenko .50 1.25
RR27 Matthew Knies 2.00 5.00
RR28 Danil Gushchin .50 1.25
RR29 Akito Hirose .40 1.00
RR30 Simon Edvinsson 1.00 2.50
RR31 Milos Kelemen .50 1.25
RR32 Hunter McKown .50 1.25
RR33 Tye Kartye .75 2.00
RR34 Michael Kesselring .50 1.25
RR35 William Dufour .40 1.00
RR36 Ridly Greig .75 2.00
RR37 Luke Evangelista .75 2.00
RR38 Vincent Desharnais .60 1.50
RR39 Hugh McGing .50 1.25
RR40 Vincent Iorio .50 1.25

2023-24 Upper Deck Trilogy Rookie Renditions Autographs

RR1 Owen Beck/99 12.00 30.00
RR2 Matthew Kessel/99 6.00 15.00
RR3 Brock Faber/99 50.00 125.00
RR4 Yaroslav Askarov/49 20.00 50.00
RR5 Marco Kasper/99 20.00 50.00
RR6 Luke Hughes/49 50.00 125.00
RR7 Jakob Pelletier/99 10.00 25.00
RR8 Sean Farrell/99 8.00 20.00
RR9 David Gust/99 8.00 20.00
RR11 Joona Koppanen/99 6.00 15.00
RR12 Olle Eriksson Ek/99 8.00 20.00
RR13 Matt Murray/99 8.00 20.00
RR14 Matthew Coronato/99 12.00 30.00
RR16 Jiri Patera/99 12.00 30.00
RR17 Billy Sweezey/99 8.00 20.00
RR18 Luke Philp/99 8.00 20.00
RR19 Dustin Wolf/99 25.00 60.00
RR21 Aidan McDonough/99 6.00 15.00
RR22 Tyson Foerster/99 15.00 40.00
RR23 Leevi Merilainen/99 8.00 20.00
RR24 Lukas Rousek/99 6.00 15.00
RR25 Bobby McMann/99 12.00 30.00
RR26 Nikita Nesterenko/99 8.00 20.00
RR27 Matthew Knies/49 50.00 125.00
RR28 Danil Gushchin/99 8.00 20.00
RR29 Akito Hirose/99 6.00 15.00
RR30 Simon Edvinsson/49 15.00 40.00
RR31 Milos Kelemen/99 8.00 20.00
RR33 Tye Kartye/99 12.00 30.00
RR34 Michael Kesselring/99 8.00 20.00
RR35 William Dufour/99 6.00 15.00
RR36 Ridly Greig/99 12.00 30.00
RR37 Luke Evangelista/99 12.00 30.00
RR38 Vincent Desharnais/99 10.00 25.00
RR39 Hugh McGing/99 8.00 20.00
RR40 Vincent Iorio/99 8.00 20.00

2023-24 Upper Deck Trilogy Rookie Renditions Jerseys

RR1 Owen Beck 3.00 8.00
RR2 Matthew Kessel 1.50 4.00
RR3 Brock Faber 5.00 12.00
RR4 Yaroslav Askarov 5.00 12.00
RR5 Marco Kasper 5.00 12.00
RR6 Luke Hughes 6.00 15.00
RR7 Jakob Pelletier 2.50 6.00
RR8 Sean Farrell 2.00 5.00
RR9 David Gust 2.00 5.00
RR10 Connor Bedard 40.00 100.00
RR11 Joona Koppanen 1.50 4.00
RR12 Olle Eriksson Ek 2.00 5.00
RR13 Matt Murray 2.00 5.00
RR14 Matthew Coronato 3.00 8.00
RR15 Devon Levi 5.00 12.00
RR16 Jiri Patera 3.00 8.00
RR17 Billy Sweezey 2.00 5.00
RR18 Luke Philp 2.00 5.00
RR19 Dustin Wolf 6.00 15.00
RR20 Jonathan Gruden 2.00 5.00
RR21 Aidan McDonough 1.50 4.00
RR22 Tyson Foerster 4.00 10.00
RR23 Leevi Merilainen 2.00 5.00
RR24 Lukas Rousek 1.50 4.00
RR25 Bobby McMann 3.00 8.00
RR26 Nikita Nesterenko 2.00 5.00
RR27 Matthew Knies 8.00 20.00
RR29 Akito Hirose 1.50 4.00
RR30 Simon Edvinsson 4.00 10.00
RR32 Hunter McKown 2.00 5.00
RR33 Tye Kartye 3.00 8.00
RR34 Michael Kesselring 2.00 5.00
RR35 William Dufour 1.50 4.00
RR36 Ridly Greig 3.00 8.00
RR37 Luke Evangelista 3.00 8.00
RR38 Vincent Desharnais 2.50 6.00
RR39 Hugh McGing 2.00 5.00
RR40 Vincent Iorio 2.00 5.00

2023-24 Upper Deck Trilogy Rookie Renditions Patch Autographs

RR2 Matthew Kessel/25 12.00 30.00
RR3 Brock Faber/25 100.00 250.00
RR7 Jakob Pelletier/25 20.00 50.00
RR8 Sean Farrell/25 15.00 40.00
RR9 David Gust/25 15.00 40.00
RR11 Joona Koppanen/25 12.00 30.00
RR12 Olle Eriksson Ek/25 15.00 40.00
RR13 Matt Murray/25 15.00 40.00
RR16 Jiri Patera/25 25.00 60.00
RR17 Billy Sweezey/25 15.00 40.00
RR18 Luke Philp/25 15.00 40.00
RR21 Aidan McDonough/25 12.00 30.00
RR22 Tyson Foerster/25 30.00 80.00
RR23 Leevi Merilainen/25 15.00 40.00
RR24 Lukas Rousek/25 12.00 30.00
RR25 Bobby McMann/25 25.00 60.00
RR26 Nikita Nesterenko/25 15.00 40.00
RR29 Akito Hirose/25 12.00 30.00
RR33 Tye Kartye/25 25.00 60.00
RR34 Michael Kesselring/25 15.00 40.00
RR35 William Dufour/25 12.00 30.00
RR36 Ridly Greig/25 25.00 60.00
RR37 Luke Evangelista/25 25.00 60.00
RR38 Vincent Desharnais/25 20.00 50.00
RR39 Hugh McGing/25 15.00 40.00
RR40 Vincent Iorio/25 15.00 40.00

2023-24 Upper Deck Trilogy Rookie Signature Pucks

RSPCB Connor Bedard 300.00 800.00
RSPCZ Connor Zary 20.00 50.00
RSPJP Jakob Pelletier 12.00 30.00
RSPLC Logan Cooley 30.00 80.00
RSPLE Luke Evangelista 15.00 40.00
RSPLH Luke Hughes 40.00 100.00
RSPMA Matthew Knies 40.00 100.00
RSPMK Marco Kasper 25.00 60.00
RSPMS Matt Savoie 20.00 50.00
RSPOB Owen Beck 15.00 40.00
RSPRG Ridly Greig 15.00 40.00
RSPSE Simon Edvinsson 20.00 50.00
RSPTF Tyson Foerster 20.00 50.00
RSPWD William Dufour 8.00 20.00
RSPYA Yaroslav Askarov 40.00 100.00

2023-24 Upper Deck Trilogy Rookie Signature Pucks Team Logo

*TEAM LOGO/24: 1X TO 2.5X BASIC
RSPCB Connor Bedard 4000.00 10000.00

2023-24 Upper Deck Trilogy Scripted Hall of Fame Plaques

SHFDH Dominik Hasek 150.00 400.00
SHFJK Jari Kurri 80.00 200.00
SHFMB Martin Brodeur 250.00 600.00
SHFMR Mark Recchi 150.00 400.00

2023-24 Upper Deck Trilogy Signature Pucks

SPAS Andrei Svechnikov 12.00 30.00
SPBJ Boone Jenner 10.00 25.00
SPCA Cam Atkinson 10.00 25.00
SPCC Chris Chelios SP 10.00 25.00
SPCM Connor McDavid SP 200.00 500.00
SPCP Cole Perfetti 10.00 25.00
SPDC Dylan Cozens 10.00 25.00
SPEB Jordan Eberle 10.00 25.00
SPET Eeli Tolvanen 10.00 25.00
SPJA Josh Anderson 8.00 20.00
SPJN Jake Neighbours 10.00 25.00
SPKC Kyle Connor 15.00 40.00
SPKM K'Andre Miller 8.00 20.00
SPLR Luc Robitaille SP 20.00 50.00
SPMM Mike Modano SP 20.00 50.00
SPMP Max Pacioretty 10.00 25.00
SPPA Joe Pavelski 12.00 30.00
SPRF Ron Francis SP 12.00 30.00
SPRJ Roman Josi 10.00 25.00
SPRM Rick Middleton 10.00 25.00
SPRO Larry Robinson SP 10.00 25.00
SPRT Robert Thomas SP 10.00 25.00
SPSG Samuel Girard 6.00 15.00
SPSR Sam Reinhart 20.00 50.00
SPTE Teuvo Teravainen 10.00 25.00
SPTH Tomas Hertl 10.00 25.00
SPTO Tyler Toffoli 10.00 25.00
SPTR Taylor Raddysh 8.00 20.00
SPTS Tim Stutzle SP 12.00 30.00

2023-24 Upper Deck Trilogy Signature Pucks Team Logo

*TEAM LOGO/24: .6X TO 1.5X BASIC
SPCC Chris Chelios 25.00 60.00
SPCP Cole Perfetti 60.00 150.00
SPJN Jake Neighbours 25.00 60.00
SPMM Mike Modano 60.00 150.00
SPTH Tomas Hertl 25.00 60.00

2023-24 Upper Deck Trilogy Signature Puckstoppers

SPUBR Bill Ranford 8.00 20.00
SPUCH Carter Hart 10.00 25.00
SPUGC Gerry Cheevers 10.00 25.00
SPUHE Connor Hellebuyck 20.00 50.00
SPUPG Philipp Grubauer 10.00 25.00

2023-24 Upper Deck Trilogy Signature Puckstoppers Team Logo

*TEAM LOGO/24: .6X TO 1.5X BASIC
SPUJS Juuse Saros 25.00 60.00

2023-24 Upper Deck Trilogy Team Canada Signature Pucks

TCSPAL Alexis Lafreniere 15.00 40.00
TCSPDC Dylan Cozens 10.00 25.00
TCSPSW Shane Wright SP 15.00 40.00
TCSPTC Thomas Chabot 10.00 25.00

2023-24 Upper Deck Trilogy Team Canada Signature Pucks Retro Logo 1

TCSPAL Alexis Lafreniere 80.00 200.00

2023-24 Upper Deck Trilogy Triple Gold Club

TGCBS Brendan Shanahan 10.00 25.00
TGCCP Chris Pronger 10.00 25.00
TGCHZ Henrik Zetterberg 12.00 30.00
TGCIL Igor Larionov 10.00 25.00
TGCJJ Jaromir Jagr 25.00 60.00
TGCJS Joe Sakic 20.00 50.00
TGCNL Nicklas Lidstrom 10.00 25.00
TGCPB Patrice Bergeron 12.00 30.00
TGCPF Peter Forsberg 20.00 50.00
TGCRB Rob Blake 10.00 25.00
TGCSC Sidney Crosby 40.00 100.00
TGCSN Scott Niedermayer 10.00 25.00

2023-24 Upper Deck Trilogy Trivium

*GOLD/49: .8X TO 2X BASIC
TR1 Lindsay/Howe/Delvecchio 15.00 40.00
TR2 Richard/Richard/Beliveau 10.00 25.00
TR3 Pappin/Mahovlich/Stemkowski 5.00 12.00
TR4 Orr/Cheevers/Esposito 20.00 50.00
TR5 Barber/Clarke/Leach 8.00 20.00
TR6 Lafleur/Shutt/Mahovlich 6.00 15.00
TR7 Trottier/Bossy/Potvin 5.00 12.00
TR8 Lemieux/Robinson/Richer 5.00 12.00
TR9 Messier/Gretzky/Kurri 20.00 50.00
TR10 Hrdina/Gilmour/Nieuwendyk 6.00 15.00
TR11 Francis/Lemieux/Jagr 20.00 50.00
TR12 Zubov/Messier/Leetch 10.00 25.00
TR13 Shanahan/Yzerman/Larionov 12.00 30.00
TR14 Modano/Hull/Nieuwendyk 10.00 25.00
TR15 Arnott/Brodeur/Holik 12.00 30.00
TR16 Selanne/Getzlaf/Pronger 10.00 25.00
TR17 Bergeron/Marchand/Lucic 10.00 25.00
TR18 Kopitar/Quick/Doughty 8.00 20.00
TR19 Kane/Crawford/Hossa 10.00 25.00
TR20 Malkin/Crosby/Kessel 10.00 25.00
TR21 Ovechkin/Kuznetsov/Backstrom 20.0050.00
TR22 O'Reilly/Tarasenko/Schenn 6.00 15.00
TR23 Kucherov/Stamkos/Hedman 10.00 25.00
TR24 Makar/MacKinnon/Rantanen 20.00 50.00
TR25 Eichel/Marchessault/Stone 8.00 20.00

1996 Upper Deck U.S. Olympic

COMPLETE SET (135) 8.00 20.00
68 Jim Craig .20 .50
69 Mike Eruzione .25 .60

1996 Upper Deck U.S. Olympic Reflections of Gold

COMPLETE SET (10) 8.00 20.00
RG2 Mike Eruzione .60 1.50

1996 Upper Deck U.S. Olympic Reflections of Gold Signatures

COMPLETE SET (9) 3000.00 5000.00
RG2 Mike Eruzione 12.00 30.00

1999-00 Upper Deck Victory

COMPLETE SET (440) 20.00 50.00
1 Paul Kariya CL .10 .25
2 Paul Kariya .10 .25
3 Teemu Selanne .20 .50
4 Matt Cullen .05 .15
5 Steve Rucchin .05 .15
6 Oleg Tverdovsky .05 .15
7 Guy Hebert .10 .25
8 Fredrik Olausson .05 .15
9 Ted Donato .05 .15
10 Marty McInnis .05 .15
11 Damian Rhodes CL .05 .15
12 Jody Hull .05 .15
13 Damian Rhodes .05 .15
14 Kelly Buchberger .05 .15
15 Scott Langkow RC .05 .15
16 Norm Maracle .05 .15
17 Jason Botterill .05 .15
18 Randy Robitaille .05 .15
19 Ray Ferraro .05 .15
20 Ray Bourque CL .15 .40
21 Ray Bourque .15 .40
22 Sergei Samsonov .07 .20
23 Joe Thornton .15 .40
24 Shawn Bates .05 .15
25 Byron Dafoe .07 .20
26 Jonathan Girard .05 .15
27 Jason Allison .07 .20
28 Anson Carter .07 .20
29 Hal Gill .05 .15
30 Kyle McLaren .05 .15
31 Don Sweeney .05 .15
32 Dominik Hasek CL .15 .40
33 Dominik Hasek .15 .40
34 Michael Peca .07 .20
35 Miroslav Satan .07 .20
36 Dixon Ward .05 .15
37 Martin Biron .07 .20
38 Joe Juneau .05 .15
39 Cory Sarich .05 .15
40 Brian Holzinger .05 .15
41 Rhett Warrener .05 .15
42 Alexei Zhitnik .05 .15
43 Jean-Sebastien Giguere CL .10 .25
44 Valeri Bure .05 .15
45 Jean-Sebastien Giguere .10 .25
46 Jarome Iginla .12 .30
47 Rico Fata .05 .15
48 Derek Morris .05 .15
49 Rene Corbet .05 .15
50 Phil Housley .07 .20
51 Tyrone Garner RC .05 .15
52 Marc Savard .05 .15
53 Keith Primeau CL .07 .20
54 Sami Kapanen .05 .15
55 Bates Battaglia .05 .15
56 Arturs Irbe .07 .20
57 Keith Primeau .07 .20
58 Gary Roberts .05 .15
59 Ron Francis .12 .30
60 Paul Coffey .10 .25
61 Martin Gelinas .05 .15
62 Jeff O'Neill .05 .15
63 Glen Wesley .05 .15
64 Tony Amonte CL .07 .20
65 Tony Amonte .07 .20
66 J-P Dumont .07 .20
67 Doug Gilmour .12 .30
68 Ty Jones .05 .15
69 Anders Eriksson .05 .15
70 Remi Royer .05 .15
71 Jocelyn Thibault .07 .20
72 Alexei Zhamnov .05 .15
73 Eric Daze .07 .20
74 Bryan McCabe .07 .20
75 Peter Forsberg CL .20 .50
76 Chris Drury .07 .20
77 Peter Forsberg .20 .50
78 Patrick Roy .25 .60
79 Joe Sakic .20 .50
80 Milan Hejduk .07 .20
81 Adam Deadmarsh .05 .15
82 Adam Foote .07 .20
83 Sandis Ozolinsh .05 .15
84 Claude Lemieux .07 .20
85 Brett Hull CL .20 .50
86 Ed Belfour .10 .25
87 Brett Hull .20 .50
88 Mike Modano .15 .40
89 Derian Hatcher .07 .20
90 Jamie Langenbrunner .05 .15
91 Joe Nieuwendyk .07 .20
92 Jon Sim RC .10 .25
93 Jere Lehtinen .07 .20
94 Darryl Sydor .07 .20
95 Sergei Zubov .07 .20
96 Steve Yzerman CL .25 .60
97 Brendan Shanahan .10 .25
98 Steve Yzerman .25 .60
99 Chris Chelios .10 .25
100 Sergei Fedorov .15 .40
101 Vyacheslav Kozlov .05 .15
102 Igor Larionov .10 .25
103 Nicklas Lidstrom .10 .25
104 Tomas Holmstrom .05 .15
105 Chris Osgood .10 .25
106 Kris Draper .07 .20
107 Darren McCarty .05 .15
108 Doug Weight CL .10 .25
109 Bill Guerin .10 .25
110 Tom Poti .05 .15
111 Mike Grier .05 .15
112 Tommy Salo .07 .20
113 Doug Weight .10 .25
114 Josef Beranek .05 .15
115 Fredrik Lindquist .05 .15
116 Roman Hamrlik .05 .15
117 Todd Marchant .05 .15
118 Janne Niinimaa .05 .15
119 Pavel Bure CL .10 .25
120 Pavel Bure .10 .25
121 Mark Parrish .05 .15
122 Scott Mellanby .05 .15
123 Viktor Kozlov .05 .15
124 Oleg Kvasha .05 .15
125 Rob Niedermayer .05 .15
126 Bret Hedican .05 .15
127 Trevor Kidd .05 .15
128 Robert Svehla .05 .15
129 Peter Worrell .05 .15
130 Rob Blake CL .10 .25
131 Rob Blake .10 .25
132 Pavel Rosa .05 .15
133 Donald Audette .05 .15
134 Luc Robitaille .10 .25
135 Vladimir Tsyplakov .05 .15
136 Jozef Stumpel .05 .15
137 Nathan Lafayette .05 .15
138 Glen Murray .07 .20
139 Zigmund Palffy .10 .25
140 Bryan Smolinski .05 .15
141 Jamie Storr .05 .15
142 Saku Koivu CL .10 .25
143 Saku Koivu .10 .25
144 Arron Asham .05 .15
145 Jeff Hackett .05 .15
146 Trevor Linden .10 .25
147 Eric Weinrich .05 .15
148 Vladimir Malakhov .05 .15
149 Martin Rucinsky .05 .15
150 Brian Savage .05 .15
151 Shayne Corson .07 .20
152 Scott Lachance .05 .15
153 Jose Theodore .10 .25
154 David Legwand CL .05 .15
155 Mike Dunham .05 .15
156 David Legwand .05 .15
157 Sergei Krivokrasov .05 .15
158 Cliff Ronning .05 .15
159 Kimmo Timonen .05 .15
160 Bob Boughner .05 .15
161 Mark Mowers RC .05 .15
162 Patrick Cote .05 .15
163 Tomas Vokoun .10 .25
164 Jan Vopat .05 .15
165 Martin Brodeur CL .25 .60
166 Martin Brodeur .25 .60
167 John Madden RC .10 .25
168 Vadim Sharifijanov .05 .15
169 Patrik Elias .10 .25
170 Scott Stevens .10 .25
171 Petr Sykora .07 .20
172 Jason Arnott .07 .20
173 Brendan Morrison .07 .20
174 Scott Niedermayer .10 .25
175 Bobby Holik .05 .15
176 Eric Brewer CL .05 .15
177 Eric Brewer .05 .15
178 Zdeno Chara .10 .25
179 Kenny Jonsson .05 .15
180 Dmitri Nabokov .05 .15
181 Mariusz Czerkawski .05 .15
182 Brad Isbister .05 .15
183 Olli Jokinen .07 .20
184 Felix Potvin .15 .40
185 Mike Watt .05 .15
186 Claude Lapointe .07 .20
187 Brian Leetch CL .07 .20
188 Manny Malhotra .07 .20
189 Mike Richter .10 .25
190 Theo Fleury .12 .30
191 Adam Graves .07 .20
192 Brian Leetch .07 .20
193 Petr Nedved .05 .15
194 Brent Fedyk .05 .15
195 Barry Richter .05 .15
196 Valeri Kamensky .05 .15
197 Kirk McLean .07 .20
198 Kevin Stevens .07 .20
199 Alexei Yashin CL .07 .20
200 Marian Hossa .10 .25
201 Alexei Yashin .07 .20
202 Shawn McEachern .05 .15
203 Sami Salo .07 .20
204 Daniel Alfredsson .10 .25
205 Magnus Arvedson .05 .15
206 Wade Redden .05 .15
207 Ron Tugnutt .07 .20
208 Chris Phillips .05 .15
209 Vaclav Prospal .05 .15
210 Eric Lindros CL .15 .40
211 John LeClair .10 .25
212 Eric Lindros .15 .40
213 Mark Recchi .12 .30
214 Rod Brind'Amour .10 .25
215 Eric Desjardins .07 .20
216 Jean-Marc Pelletier .05 .15
217 Ryan Bast RC .05 .15
218 Keith Jones .05 .15
219 John Vanbiesbrouck .10 .25
220 Brian Wesenberg RC .05 .15
221 Dan McGillis .05 .15
222 Keith Tkachuk CL .10 .25
223 Robert Esche RC .10 .25
224 Keith Tkachuk .10 .25
225 Nikolai Khabibulin .07 .20
226 Trevor Letowski .05 .15
227 Robert Reichel .05 .15
228 Jeremy Roenick .15 .40
229 Greg Adams .05 .15
230 Daniel Briere .07 .20
231 Rick Tocchet .07 .20
232 Stanislav Neckar .05 .15
233 Teppo Numminen .05 .15
234 Jaromir Jagr CL .30 .75
235 Jaromir Jagr .30 .75
236 Matthew Barnaby .05 .15
237 Tom Barrasso .10 .25
238 Jan Hrdina .05 .15
239 Martin Straka .05 .15
240 Jean-Sebastien Aubin .07 .20
241 Alexei Kovalev .07 .20
242 German Titov .05 .15
243 Kevin Hatcher .05 .15
244 Kip Miller .05 .15
245 Alexei Morozov .07 .20
246 Jeff Friesen CL .07 .20
247 Vincent Damphousse .07 .20
248 Jeff Friesen .07 .20
249 Scott Hannan .05 .15
250 Patrick Marleau .10 .25
251 Mike Ricci .05 .15
252 Owen Nolan .10 .25
253 Marco Sturm .05 .15
254 Gary Suter .05 .15
255 Jeff Norton .05 .15
256 Steve Shields .07 .20
257 Mike Vernon .07 .20
258 Al MacInnis CL .12 .30
259 Pavol Demitra .12 .30
260 Al MacInnis .12 .30
261 Lubos Bartecko .05 .15
262 Jochen Hecht RC .15 .40
263 Chris Pronger .10 .25
264 Grant Fuhr .15 .40
265 Michal Handzus .07 .20
266 Pierre Turgeon .07 .20
267 Jim Campbell .05 .15
268 Roman Turek .07 .20
269 Vincent Lecavalier CL .10 .25
270 Vincent Lecavalier .10 .25
271 Paul Mara .05 .15
272 Kevin Hodson .05 .15
273 Dan Cloutier .05 .15
274 Chris Gratton .05 .15
275 Pavel Kubina .05 .15
276 Darcy Tucker .05 .15
277 Alexandre Daigle .05 .15
278 Stephane Richer .07 .20
279 Niklas Sundstrom .05 .15
280 Mats Sundin CL .10 .25
281 Mats Sundin .10 .25
282 Bryan Berard .05 .15
283 Sergei Berezin .05 .15
284 Curtis Joseph .12 .30
285 Tomas Kaberle .05 .15
286 Daniil Markov .05 .15
287 Steve Thomas .05 .15
288 Mike Johnson .07 .20
289 Tie Domi .07 .20
290 Yanic Perreault .05 .15
291 Derek King .05 .15
292 Mark Messier CL .20 .50
293 Mark Messier .20 .50
294 Bill Muckalt .05 .15
295 Josh Holden .05 .15
296 Markus Naslund .10 .25
297 Kevin Weekes .05 .15
298 Ed Jovanovski .07 .20
299 Alexander Mogilny .07 .20
300 Mattias Ohlund .05 .15
301 Todd Bertuzzi .07 .20
302 Peter Schaefer .05 .15
303 Peter Bondra CL .10 .25
304 Peter Bondra .10 .25
305 Adam Oates .10 .25
306 Jan Bulis .05 .15
307 Jaroslav Svejkovsky .05 .15
308 Sergei Gonchar .05 .15
309 Olaf Kolzig .10 .25
310 Richard Zednik .05 .15
311 Benoit Gratton RC .05 .15
312 Matt Herr .05 .15
313 Nolan Baumgartner .05 .15
314 Peter Forsberg .20 .50
315 Jaromir Jagr .30 .75
316 Paul Kariya .10 .25
317 Ray Bourque .15 .40
318 Al MacInnis .12 .30
319 Dominik Hasek .15 .40
320 Steve Yzerman .25 .60
321 Teemu Selanne .20 .50
322 Brett Hull .20 .50
323 Chris Pronger .10 .25
324 Nicklas Lidstrom .10 .25
325 Patrick Roy .25 .60
326 Teemu Selanne .20 .50
327 Tony Amonte .07 .20
328 Jaromir Jagr .30 .75
329 Alexei Yashin .07 .20
330 John LeClair .10 .25
331 Jaromir Jagr .30 .75
332 Peter Forsberg .20 .50
333 Paul Kariya .10 .25
334 Teemu Selanne .20 .50
335 Joe Sakic .20 .50
336 Jaromir Jagr .30 .75
337 Teemu Selanne .20 .50
338 Paul Kariya .10 .25
339 Peter Forsberg .20 .50
340 Joe Sakic .20 .50
341 Al MacInnis .12 .30
342 Nicklas Lidstrom .10 .25
343 Ray Bourque .15 .40
344 Fredrik Olausson .05 .15
345 Brian Leetch .07 .20
346 Martin Brodeur .25 .60
347 Ed Belfour .10 .25
348 Curtis Joseph .12 .30
349 Chris Osgood .10 .25
350 Patrick Roy .25 .60
351 Milan Hejduk .07 .20
352 Brendan Morrison .07 .20
353 Chris Drury .07 .20
354 Jan Hrdina .05 .15
355 Mark Parrish .05 .15
356 Oleg Saprykin RC .10 .25
357 Patrik Stefan RC .10 .25
358 Pavel Brendl RC .15 .40
359 Roberto Luongo .15 .40
360 Scott Gomez .07 .20
361 Sheldon Keefe RC .10 .25
362 Simon Gagne .10 .25
363 Steve Kariya RC .10 .25
364 Alex Tanguay .07 .20
365 Brad Stuart .07 .20
366 Branislav Mezei RC .05 .15
367 Brian Campbell RC .10 .25
368 Daniel Sedin .25 .60
369 Henrik Sedin .25 .60
370 Mike Ribiero .05 .15
371 Ivan Novoseltsev RC .12 .30
372 Nick Boynton .07 .20
373 Nikos Tselios .05 .15
374 Tim Connolly .05 .15
375 J.F. Damphousse RC .05 .15
376 Patrick Roy .25 .60
377 Ed Belfour .10 .25
378 Chris Osgood .10 .25
379 Arturs Irbe .07 .20
380 Nikolai Khabibulin .07 .20
381 Dominik Hasek .15 .40
382 Byron Dafoe .07 .20
383 Jean-Sebastien Giguere .10 .25
384 Olaf Kolzig .10 .25
385 John Vanbiesbrouck .10 .25
386 Martin Brodeur .25 .60
387 Dan Cloutier .05 .15
388 Damian Rhodes .05 .15
389 Curtis Joseph .12 .30
390 Mike Richter .10 .25
391 Wayne Gretzky .60 1.50
392 Wayne Gretzky .60 1.50
393 Wayne Gretzky .60 1.50
394 Wayne Gretzky .60 1.50
395 Wayne Gretzky .60 1.50
396 Wayne Gretzky .60 1.50
397 Wayne Gretzky .60 1.50
398 Wayne Gretzky .60 1.50
399 Wayne Gretzky .60 1.50
400 Wayne Gretzky .60 1.50
401 Wayne Gretzky .60 1.50
402 Wayne Gretzky .60 1.50
403 Wayne Gretzky .60 1.50
404 Wayne Gretzky .60 1.50
405 Wayne Gretzky .60 1.50
406 Wayne Gretzky .60 1.50
407 Wayne Gretzky .60 1.50
408 Wayne Gretzky .60 1.50
409 Wayne Gretzky .60 1.50
410 Wayne Gretzky .60 1.50
411 Wayne Gretzky .60 1.50
412 Wayne Gretzky .60 1.50
413 Wayne Gretzky .60 1.50
414 Wayne Gretzky .60 1.50
415 Wayne Gretzky .60 1.50
416 Wayne Gretzky .60 1.50
417 Wayne Gretzky .60 1.50
418 Wayne Gretzky .60 1.50
419 Wayne Gretzky .60 1.50
420 Wayne Gretzky .60 1.50
421 Wayne Gretzky .60 1.50
422 Wayne Gretzky .60 1.50
423 Wayne Gretzky .60 1.50
424 Wayne Gretzky .60 1.50
425 Wayne Gretzky .60 1.50
426 Wayne Gretzky .60 1.50
427 Wayne Gretzky .60 1.50
428 Wayne Gretzky .60 1.50
429 Wayne Gretzky .60 1.50
430 Wayne Gretzky .60 1.50
431 Wayne Gretzky .60 1.50
432 Wayne Gretzky .60 1.50
433 Wayne Gretzky .60 1.50
434 Wayne Gretzky .60 1.50
435 Wayne Gretzky .60 1.50
436 Wayne Gretzky .60 1.50
437 Wayne Gretzky .60 1.50
438 Wayne Gretzky .60 1.50
439 Wayne Gretzky .60 1.50
440 Wayne Gretzky .60 1.50

2000-01 Upper Deck Victory

1 Paul Kariya CL .12 .30
2 Ladislav Kohn .07 .20
3 Vitali Vishnevsky .07 .20
4 Steve Rucchin .07 .20
5 Oleg Tverdovsky .07 .20
6 Guy Hebert .10 .25
7 Teemu Selanne .25 .60
8 Paul Kariya .12 .30
9 Patrik Stefan CL .10 .25
10 Andrew Brunette .07 .20
11 Patrik Stefan .10 .25
12 Donald Audette .10 .25
13 Damian Rhodes .07 .20
14 Maxim Galanov .07 .20
15 Dean Sylvester .07 .20
16 Ray Ferraro .07 .20
17 Joe Thornton CL .20 .50
18 Brian Rolston .10 .25
19 Sergei Samsonov .10 .25
20 Joe Thornton .20 .50
21 Byron Dafoe .10 .25
22 Jason Allison .10 .25
23 Anson Carter .10 .25
24 Hal Gill .07 .20
25 Dominik Hasek CL .20 .50
26 Dominik Hasek .20 .50
27 Michael Peca .10 .25
28 Miroslav Satan .07 .20
29 Doug Gilmour .15 .40
30 Chris Gratton .07 .20
31 Curtis Brown .07 .20
32 Maxim Afinogenov .07 .20
33 Jay McKee .07 .20
34 Valeri Bure CL .10 .25
35 Valeri Bure .10 .25
36 Fred Brathwaite .10 .25
37 Jarome Iginla .15 .40
38 Phil Housley .10 .25
39 Derek Morris .07 .20
40 Cory Stillman .07 .20
41 Marc Savard .07 .20
42 Ron Francis CL .15 .40
43 Sami Kapanen .07 .20
44 Arturs Irbe .10 .25
45 Rod Brind'Amour .12 .30
46 Gary Roberts .07 .20
47 Ron Francis .15 .40
48 Paul Coffey .12 .30
49 Jeff O'Neill .10 .25
50 Tony Amonte CL .10 .25
51 Tony Amonte .10 .25
52 Steve Sullivan .07 .20
53 Michal Grosek .07 .20
54 Boris Mironov .07 .20
55 Jocelyn Thibault .10 .25
56 Alexei Zhamnov .10 .25
57 Eric Daze .10 .25
58 Peter Forsberg CL .25 .60
59 Chris Drury .10 .25
60 Peter Forsberg .25 .60
61 Patrick Roy .30 .75
62 Joe Sakic .25 .60
63 Ray Bourque .20 .50
64 Adam Deadmarsh .07 .20
65 Milan Hejduk .10 .25
66 Sandis Ozolinsh .07 .20
67 Alex Tanguay .10 .25
68 Adam Foote .10 .25
69 Blue Jackets CL .05 .15
70 Mike Modano CL .20 .50
71 Ed Belfour .12 .30
72 Brett Hull .25 .60
73 Sergei Zubov .10 .25
74 Brenden Morrow .10 .25
75 Jamie Langenbrunner .10 .25
76 Joe Nieuwendyk .10 .25
77 Mike Modano .20 .50
78 Derian Hatcher .10 .25
79 Jere Lehtinen .10 .25
80 Roman Lyashenko .07 .20
81 Steve Yzerman CL .30 .75
82 Brendan Shanahan .12 .30
83 Steve Yzerman .30 .75
84 Chris Chelios .12 .30
85 Sergei Fedorov .20 .50
86 Slava Kozlov .10 .25
87 Pat Verbeek .10 .25
88 Nicklas Lidstrom .12 .30
89 Tomas Holmstrom .10 .25
90 Chris Osgood .12 .30
91 Martin Lapointe .10 .25
92 Doug Weight CL .12 .30
93 Bill Guerin .12 .30
94 Tom Poti .07 .20
95 Mike Grier .07 .20
96 Tommy Salo .10 .25
97 Doug Weight .12 .30
98 Ryan Smyth .10 .25
99 Alexander Selivanov .07 .20
100 Pavel Bure CL .12 .30
101 Pavel Bure .12 .30
102 Mark Parrish .07 .20
103 Scott Mellanby .07 .20
104 Viktor Kozlov .10 .25
105 Oleg Kvasha .07 .20
106 Ray Whitney .10 .25
107 Trevor Kidd .07 .20
108 Rob Blake CL .12 .30
109 Rob Blake .12 .30
110 Jere Karalahti .07 .20
111 Luc Robitaille .12 .30
112 Jozef Stumpel .07 .20
113 Glen Murray .10 .25
114 Zigmund Palffy .12 .30
115 Bryan Smolinski .10 .25
116 Minnesota Wild CL .05 .15
117 Saku Koivu CL .12 .30
118 Saku Koivu .12 .30
119 Sergei Zholtok .07 .20
120 Eric Weinrich .07 .20
121 Jose Theodore .12 .30
122 Martin Rucinsky .07 .20
123 Brian Savage .07 .20
124 Shayne Corson .10 .25
125 Dainius Zubrus .07 .20
126 David Legwand CL .05 .15
127 Mike Dunham .07 .20
128 David Legwand .12 .30
129 Greg Johnson .07 .20
130 Cliff Ronning .07 .20
131 Kimmo Timonen .07 .20
132 Patric Kjellberg .07 .20
133 Drake Berehowsky .07 .20
134 Martin Brodeur CL .30 .75
135 Martin Brodeur .30 .75
136 John Madden .10 .25
137 Scott Gomez .10 .25
138 Patrik Elias .12 .30
139 Scott Stevens .12 .30
140 Jason Arnott .10 .25
141 Alexander Mogilny .10 .25
142 Tim Connolly CL .05 .15
143 Dave Scatchard .07 .20
144 Tim Connolly .07 .20
145 Kenny Jonsson .07 .20
146 Claude Lapointe .07 .20
147 Mariusz Czerkawski .07 .20
148 Brad Isbister .07 .20
149 Olli Jokinen .10 .25
150 Theo Fleury CL .15 .40
151 Mike Richter .12 .30
152 Theo Fleury .15 .40
153 Adam Graves .10 .25
154 Brian Leetch .10 .25
155 Petr Nedved .10 .25
156 Radek Dvorak .10 .25
157 Mike York .07 .20
158 Marian Hossa CL .12 .30
159 Marian Hossa .12 .30
160 Radek Bonk .10 .25
161 Shawn McEachern .07 .20
162 Vaclav Prospal .07 .20
163 Daniel Alfredsson .12 .30
164 Magnus Arvedson .07 .20
165 Wade Redden .07 .20
166 John LeClair CL .12 .30
167 John LeClair .12 .30
168 Eric Lindros .20 .50
169 Mark Recchi .15 .40
170 Keith Primeau .10 .25
171 Eric Desjardins .10 .25
172 Brian Boucher .10 .25
173 Daymond Langkow .07 .20
174 Simon Gagne .12 .30
175 Jeremy Roenick CL .20 .50
176 Daniel Briere .07 .20
177 Keith Tkachuk .12 .30
178 Sean Burke .07 .20
179 Trevor Letowski .07 .20
180 Shane Doan .10 .25
181 Jeremy Roenick .20 .50
182 Travis Green .07 .20
183 Jaromir Jagr CL .40 1.00
184 Jaromir Jagr .40 1.00
185 Matthew Barnaby .07 .20
186 Robert Lang .07 .20
187 Jan Hrdina .07 .20
188 Martin Straka .10 .25
189 Ron Tugnutt .10 .25
190 Alexei Kovalev .10 .25
191 Jeff Friesen CL .05 .15
192 Vincent Damphousse .10 .25
193 Jeff Friesen .07 .20
194 Brad Stuart .10 .25
195 Patrick Marleau .12 .30
196 Mike Ricci .07 .20
197 Owen Nolan .12 .30
198 Steve Shields .07 .20
199 Chris Pronger CL .12 .30
200 Pavol Demitra .15 .40
201 Al MacInnis .15 .40
202 Lubos Bartecko .07 .20
203 Jochen Hecht .07 .20
204 Chris Pronger .12 .30
205 Roman Turek .10 .25
206 Michal Handzus .07 .20
207 Pierre Turgeon .10 .25
208 Vincent Lecavalier CL .12 .30
209 Vincent Lecavalier .12 .30
210 Paul Mara .07 .20
211 Mike Johnson .07 .20
212 Dan Cloutier .10 .25
213 Wayne Primeau .07 .20
214 Pavel Kubina .07 .20
215 Fredrik Modin .07 .20
216 Mats Sundin CL .12 .30
217 Mats Sundin .12 .30
218 Darcy Tucker .07 .20
219 Sergei Berezin .07 .20
220 Curtis Joseph .15 .40
221 Jonas Hoglund .07 .20
222 Nikolai Antropov .10 .25
223 Steve Thomas .07 .20
224 Tie Domi .10 .25
225 Mark Messier CL .25 .60
226 Mark Messier .25 .60
227 Andrew Cassels .07 .20
228 Brendan Morrison .12 .30
229 Markus Naslund .12 .30
230 Felix Potvin .20 .50
231 Ed Jovanovski .10 .25
232 Harold Druken .07 .20
233 Olaf Kolzig CL .12 .30
234 Peter Bondra .12 .30
235 Adam Oates .12 .30
236 Jan Bulis .07 .20
237 Jeff Halpern .07 .20
238 Sergei Gonchar .07 .20
239 Olaf Kolzig .12 .30
240 Chris Simon .07 .20
241 P.Bure/V.Bure HL .12 .30
242 P.Kariya/S.Kariya HL .12 .30
243 Dominik Hasek HL .20 .50
244 Patrick Roy HL .30 .75
245 Joe Sakic HL .25 .60
246 Ray Bourque HL .20 .50
247 Brett Hull HL .25 .60
248 Brendan Shanahan HL .12 .30
249 Steve Yzerman HL .30 .75
250 Pat Verbeek HL .10 .25
251 Pavel Bure HL .12 .30
252 Scott Gomez HL .10 .25
253 John LeClair HL .12 .30
254 Brian Boucher HL .10 .25
255 Jeremy Roenick HL .20 .50
256 Jaromir Jagr HL .40 1.00
257 Chris Pronger HL .12 .30
258 Roman Turek HL .10 .25
259 Curtis Joseph HL .15 .40
260 Wayne Gretzky HL .75 2.00
261 S.Aubin RC/D.Hinote .10 .25
262 Brandon Smith RC
Andre Savage .07 .20
263 Keith Aldridge RC
Ryan Christie .07 .20
264 S.Reinprecht RC/B.Chartrand .12 .30
265 Petr Mika RC
Jason Krog .07 .20
266 Steve Valiquette RC
Vladimir Orszagh .10 .25
267 Kyle Freadrich RC
Corey Sarich .07 .20
268 Eric Nickulas RC
Joel Prpic .07 .20
269 David Gosselin RC
Richard Lintner .10 .25
270 Greg Andrusak RC
Nathan Dempsey .10 .25
271 Brent Sopel RC
Alfie Michaud .12 .30
272 Jeremy Stevenson RC
Maxim Balmochnykh .07 .20
273 Andreas Karlsson
Scott Fankhouser .07 .20
274 Dave Tanabe
Byron Ritchie .07 .20
275 Steven McCarthy
Kyle Calder .07 .20
276 Petr Schastlivy
Mike Fisher .07 .20
277 Andy Delmore
Mark Eaton .07 .20
278 Evgeni Nabokov
Scott Hannan .10 .25
279 D.Heatley RC/J.Svoboda RC 1.00 2.50
280 Matt Pettinger RC
Chris Nielsen RC .07 .20
281 Teemu Selanne NB .25 .60
282 Paul Kariya NB .12 .30
283 Patrik Stefan NB .10 .25
284 Sergei Samsonov NB .10 .25
285 Joe Thornton NB .20 .50
286 Dominik Hasek NB .20 .50
287 Doug Gilmour NB .15 .40
288 Valeri Bure NB .10 .25
289 Ron Francis NB .15 .40
290 Tony Amonte NB .10 .25
291 Peter Forsberg NB .25 .60
292 Patrick Roy NB .30 .75
293 Joe Sakic NB .25 .60
294 Ray Bourque NB .20 .50
295 Milan Hejduk NB .10 .25
296 Ed Belfour NB .12 .30
297 Brett Hull NB .25 .60
298 Mike Modano NB .20 .50
299 Brendan Shanahan NB .12 .30
300 Steve Yzerman NB .30 .75
301 Sergei Fedorov NB .20 .50
302 Chris Osgood NB .12 .30
303 Doug Weight NB .12 .30
304 Pavel Bure NB .12 .30
305 Zigmund Palffy NB .12 .30
306 Rob Blake NB .12 .30
307 Saku Koivu NB .12 .30
308 David Legwand NB .05 .15
309 Martin Brodeur NB .30 .75
310 Scott Gomez NB .10 .25
311 Tim Connolly NB .05 .15
312 Theo Fleury NB .15 .40
313 Marian Hossa NB .12 .30
314 John LeClair NB .12 .30
315 Eric Lindros NB .20 .50
316 Keith Tkachuk NB .12 .30
317 Jeremy Roenick NB .20 .50
318 Jaromir Jagr NB .40 1.00
319 Jeff Friesen NB .05 .15
320 Owen Nolan NB .12 .30
321 Al MacInnis NB .15 .40
322 Pavol Demitra NB .05 .15
323 Chris Pronger NB .12 .30
324 Roman Turek NB .10 .25
325 Vincent Lecavalier NB .12 .30
326 Mats Sundin NB .12 .30
327 Curtis Joseph NB .15 .40
328 Mark Messier NB .25 .60
329 Peter Bondra NB .12 .30
330 Olaf Kolzig NB .12 .30
WCB Pavel Bure Jer Contest .05 .15

2001-02 Upper Deck Victory

COMPLETE SET (453) 50.00 100.00
COMP.SERIES I (440) 30.00 60.00
1 Jean-Sebastien Giguere CL .12 .30
2 Steve Rucchin .10 .25
3 Oleg Tverdovsky .10 .25
4 Matt Cullen .10 .25
5 Vitali Vishnevsky .10 .25
6 Jean-Sebastien Giguere .15 .40
7 Mike LeClerc .10 .25
8 Petr Tenkrat .10 .25
9 Paul Kariya .15 .40
10 Samuel Pahlsson .10 .25
11 Jeff Friesen .10 .25
12 Milan Hnilicka CL .10 .25
13 Patrik Stefan .12 .30
14 Andrew Brunette .10 .25
15 Hnat Domenichelli .10 .25
16 Jiri Slegr .10 .25
17 Tomi Kallio .10 .25
18 Steve Staios .10 .25
19 Steve Guolla .10 .25
20 Milan Hnilicka .12 .30
21 Ray Ferraro .10 .25
22 Frantisek Kaberle .10 .25
23 Ladislav Kohn .10 .25
24 Byron Dafoe CL .10 .25
25 Sergei Samsonov .12 .30
26 Joe Thornton .25 .60
27 Per Johan Axelsson .10 .25
28 Brian Rolston .12 .30
29 Mikko Eloranta .10 .25
30 Jason Allison .12 .30
31 Mike Knuble .10 .25

Card	Low	High
32 Eric Weinrich	.10	.25
33 Byron Dafoe	.12	.30
34 Bill Guerin	.15	.40
35 Kyle McLaren	.10	.25
36 Dominik Hasek CL	.20	.50
37 Curtis Brown	.10	.25
38 Miroslav Satan	.12	.30
39 Dominik Hasek	.25	.60
40 Maxim Afinogenov	.10	.25
41 Stu Barnes	.12	.30
42 J-P Dumont	.10	.25
43 Martin Biron	.12	.30
44 Alexei Zhitnik	.10	.25
45 Dimitri Kalinin	.10	.25
46 Chris Gratton	.10	.25
47 Denis Hamel	.10	.25
48 Mike Vernon CL	.10	.25
49 Jarome Iginla	.20	.50
50 Marc Savard	.10	.25
51 Jeff Cowan	.10	.25
52 Derek Morris	.10	.25
53 Dave Lowry	.10	.25
54 Craig Conroy	.10	.25
55 Robyn Regehr	.10	.25
56 Oleg Saprykin	.10	.25
57 Clarke Wilm	.10	.25
58 Toni Lydman	.10	.25
59 Arturs Irbe CL	.10	.25
60 Rod Brind'Amour	.15	.40
61 Ron Francis	.20	.50
62 Sami Kapanen	.10	.25
63 Jeff O'Neill	.12	.30
64 Sandis Ozolinsh	.10	.25
65 Arturs Irbe	.12	.30
66 Dave Tanabe	.10	.25
67 Shane Willis	.10	.25
68 Josef Vasicek	.10	.25
69 Tommy Westlund	.10	.25
70 Bates Battaglia	.10	.25
71 Jocelyn Thibault CL	.10	.25
72 Steve Sullivan	.10	.25
73 Tony Amonte	.12	.30
74 Eric Daze	.12	.30
75 Steven McCarthy	.10	.25
76 Alexei Zhamnov	.12	.30
77 Jaroslav Spacek	.10	.25
78 Jocelyn Thibault	.12	.30
79 Michael Nylander	.10	.25
80 Kyle Calder	.10	.25
81 Chris Herperger	.10	.25
82 Ryan Vandenbussche	.10	.25
83 Patrick Roy CL	.30	.75
84 Peter Forsberg	.30	.75
85 Ray Bourque	.25	.60
86 Milan Hejduk	.12	.30
87 Alex Tanguay	.12	.30
88 David Aebischer	.12	.30
89 Chris Drury	.12	.30
90 Rob Blake	.15	.40
91 Joe Sakic	.30	.75
92 Patrick Roy	.40	1.00
93 Ville Nieminen	.10	.25
94 Steven Reinprecht	.10	.25
95 Adam Foote	.12	.30
96 Ron Tugnutt CL	.10	.25
97 Geoff Sanderson	.10	.25
98 Serge Aubin	.10	.25
99 David Vyborny	.10	.25
100 Ron Tugnutt	.12	.30
101 Espen Knutsen	.10	.25
102 Tyler Wright	.10	.25
103 Lyle Odelein	.10	.25
104 Marc Denis	.12	.30
105 Blake Sloan	.10	.25
106 Jean-Luc Grand-Pierre	.10	.25
107 Mike Maneluk	.10	.25
108 Ed Belfour CL	.12	.30
109 Mike Modano	.25	.60
110 Brett Hull	.30	.75
111 Brenden Morrow	.12	.30
112 Joe Nieuwendyk	.12	.30
113 Sergei Zubov	.12	.30
114 Ed Belfour	.15	.40
115 Derian Hatcher	.10	.25
116 Jamie Langenbrunner	.10	.25
117 Grant Marshall	.10	.25
118 Marty Turco	.15	.40
119 Jere Lehtinen	.12	.30
120 Darryl Sydor	.10	.25
121 Chris Osgood CL	.12	.30
122 Sergei Fedorov	.25	.60
123 Steve Yzerman	.40	1.00
124 Nicklas Lidstrom	.15	.40
125 Mathieu Dandenault	.10	.25
126 Slava Kozlov	.12	.30
127 Chris Osgood	.15	.40
128 Darren McCarty	.10	.25
129 Kirk Maltby	.10	.25
130 Boyd Devereaux	.10	.25
131 Manny Legace	.12	.30
132 Brendan Shanahan	.15	.40
133 Tomas Holmstrom	.10	.25
134 Tommy Salo CL	.10	.25
135 Anson Carter	.12	.30
136 Todd Marchant	.10	.25
137 Ryan Smyth	.12	.30
138 Tommy Salo	.12	.30
139 Doug Weight	.15	.40
140 Janne Niinimaa	.10	.25
141 Rem Murray	.12	.30
142 Daniel Cleary	.12	.30
143 Tom Poti	.10	.25
144 Georges Laraque	.12	.30
145 Mike Grier	.10	.25
146 Roberto Luongo CL	.20	.50
147 Kevyn Adams	.10	.25
148 Viktor Kozlov	.10	.25
149 Marcus Nillson	.10	.25
150 Robert Svehla	.10	.25
151 Pavel Bure	.15	.40
152 Anders Eriksson	.10	.25
153 Vaclav Prospal	.10	.25
154 Roberto Luongo	.25	.60
155 Denis Shvidki	.10	.25
156 Peter Worrell	.10	.25
157 Olli Jokinen	.12	.30
158 Felix Potvin CL	.20	.50
159 Luc Robitaille	.15	.40
160 Zigmund Palffy	.15	.40
161 Jozef Stumpel	.10	.25
162 Bryan Smolinski	.10	.25
163 Glen Murray	.12	.30
164 Aaron Miller	.10	.25
165 Adam Deadmarsh	.10	.25
166 Jaroslav Modry	.10	.25
167 Felix Potvin	.25	.60
168 Eric Belanger	.10	.25
169 Ian Laperriere	.10	.25
170 Manny Fernandez CL	.07	.20
171 Marian Gaborik	.15	.40
172 Stacy Roest	.10	.25
173 Wes Walz	.10	.25
174 Lubomir Sekeras	.10	.25
175 Manny Fernandez	.10	.25
176 Darby Hendrickson	.10	.25
177 Aaron Gavey	.10	.25
178 Roman Simicek	.10	.25
179 Jamie McLennan	.10	.25
180 Antti Laaksonen	.10	.25
181 Andy Sutton	.10	.25
182 Jose Theodore CL	.12	.30
183 Richard Zednik	.12	.30
184 Martin Rucinsky	.10	.25
185 Saku Koivu	.15	.40
186 Jose Theodore	.15	.40
187 Brian Savage	.10	.25
188 Oleg Petrov	.10	.25
189 Patrice Brisebois	.10	.25
190 Chad Kilger	.10	.25
191 Craig Darby	.10	.25
192 Andrei Markov	.15	.40
193 Mike Dunham CL	.10	.25
194 Cliff Ronning	.10	.25
195 Vitali Yachmenev	.10	.25
196 Scott Walker	.10	.25
197 Kimmo Timonen	.10	.25
198 Patric Kjellberg	.10	.25
199 Mike Dunham	.12	.30
200 Greg Johnson	.10	.25
201 David Legwand	.12	.30
202 Scott Hartnell	.10	.25
203 Tom Fitzgerald	.10	.25
204 Tomas Vokoun	.12	.30
205 Martin Brodeur CL	.30	.75
206 Scott Stevens	.15	.40
207 Patrik Elias	.15	.40
208 Randy McKay	.10	.25
209 Jason Arnott	.12	.30
210 Alexander Mogilny	.12	.30
211 Petr Sykora	.10	.25
212 Scott Gomez	.12	.30
213 Sergei Brylin	.10	.25
214 Bobby Holik	.10	.25
215 Martin Brodeur	.40	1.00
216 John Madden	.12	.30
217 Scott Niedermayer	.15	.40
218 Rick DiPietro CL	.10	.25
219 Mariusz Czerkawski	.10	.25
220 Jason Krog	.10	.25
221 Roman Hamrlik	.10	.25
222 Jason Blake	.10	.25
223 Rick DiPietro	.12	.30
224 Dave Scatchard	.10	.25
225 Brad Isbister	.10	.25
226 Mark Parrish	.10	.25
227 Kenny Jonsson	.10	.25
228 Oleg Kvasha	.10	.25
229 Mike Richter CL	.12	.30
230 Mark Messier	.30	.75
231 Mike York	.10	.25
232 Theo Fleury	.20	.50
233 Brian Leetch	.12	.30
234 Petr Nedved	.12	.30
235 Radek Dvorak	.12	.30
236 Jan Hlavac	.10	.25
237 Mike Richter	.15	.40
238 Manny Malhotra	.12	.30
239 Tomas Kloucek	.10	.25
240 Sandy McCarthy	.10	.25
241 Patrick Lalime CL	.10	.25
242 Marian Hossa	.15	.40
243 Shawn McEachern	.10	.25
244 Wade Redden	.10	.25
245 Daniel Alfredsson	.15	.40
246 Radek Bonk	.10	.25
247 Martin Havlat	.12	.30
248 Patrick Lalime	.12	.30
249 Magnus Arvedson	.10	.25
250 Karel Rachunek	.10	.25
251 Sami Salo	.10	.25
252 Jani Hurme	.12	.30
253 Roman Cechmanek CL	.10	.25
254 John LeClair	.15	.40
255 Daymond Langkow	.12	.30
256 Keith Primeau	.12	.30
257 Justin Williams	.12	.30
258 Simon Gagne	.15	.40
259 Roman Cechmanek	.12	.30
260 Mark Recchi	.20	.50
261 Ruslan Fedotenko	.10	.25
262 Dan McGillis	.10	.25
263 Eric Desjardins	.12	.30
264 Brian Boucher	.12	.30
265 Sean Burke CL	.07	.20
266 Shane Doan	.12	.30
267 Mike Johnson	.10	.25
268 Michal Handzus	.10	.25
269 Landon Wilson	.10	.25
270 Jeremy Roenick	.25	.60
271 Mika Alatalo	.10	.25
272 Sean Burke	.10	.25
273 Daniel Briere	.12	.30
274 Trevor Letowski	.10	.25
275 Teppo Numminen	.10	.25
276 Ladislav Nagy	.10	.25
277 Johan Hedberg CL	.10	.25
278 Jaromir Jagr	.50	1.25
279 Jan Hrdina	.10	.25
280 Mario Lemieux	.60	1.50
281 Alexei Kovalev	.12	.30
282 Robert Lang	.10	.25
283 Martin Straka	.10	.25
284 Alexei Morozov	.10	.25
285 Janne Laukkanen	.10	.25
286 Rene Corbet	.10	.25
287 Jean-Sebastien Aubin	.12	.30
288 Darius Kasparaitis	.10	.25
289 Evgeni Nabokov CL	.10	.25
290 Teemu Selanne	.30	.75
291 Patrick Marleau	.15	.40
292 Owen Nolan	.15	.40
293 Marcus Ragnarsson	.10	.25
294 Brad Stuart	.10	.25
295 Mike Ricci	.10	.25
296 Vincent Damphousse	.12	.30
297 Scott Thornton	.12	.30
298 Mike Rathje	.10	.25
299 Marco Sturm	.10	.25
300 Evgeni Nabokov	.12	.30
301 Alexander Korolyuk	.10	.25
302 Brent Johnson CL	.10	.25
303 Keith Tkachuk	.15	.40
304 Cory Stillman	.10	.25
305 Chris Pronger	.15	.40
306 Scott Young	.10	.25
307 Pavol Demitra	.20	.50
308 Al MacInnis	.20	.50
309 Jochen Hecht	.10	.25
310 Pierre Turgeon	.12	.30
311 Tyson Nash	.10	.25
312 Jamal Mayers	.10	.25
313 Dallas Drake	.10	.25
314 Kevin Weekes CL	.10	.25
315 Vincent Lecavalier	.15	.40
316 Brad Richards	.15	.40
317 Brian Holzinger	.10	.25
318 Fredrik Modin	.10	.25
319 Kevin Weekes	.12	.30
320 Pavel Kubina	.10	.25
321 Andrei Zyuzin	.10	.25
322 Martin St. Louis	.15	.40
323 Matthew Barnaby	.10	.25
324 Nikolai Khabibulin	.15	.40
325 Curtis Joseph CL	.15	.40
326 Mats Sundin	.15	.40
327 Gary Roberts	.10	.25
328 Bryan McCabe	.12	.30
329 Curtis Joseph	.20	.50
330 Tomas Kaberle	.10	.25
331 Jonas Hoglund	.10	.25
332 Darcy Tucker	.10	.25
333 Nikolai Antropov	.10	.25
334 Tie Domi	.12	.30
335 Aki Berg	.10	.25
336 Dimitri Yushkevich	.10	.25
337 Dan Cloutier CL	.10	.25
338 Markus Naslund	.15	.40
339 Donald Brashear	.10	.25
340 Andrew Cassels	.10	.25
341 Todd Bertuzzi	.15	.40
342 Ed Jovanovski	.12	.30
343 Brendan Morrison	.12	.30
344 Daniel Sedin	.20	.50
345 Henrik Sedin	.20	.50
346 Dan Cloutier	.12	.30
347 Peter Schaefer	.10	.25
348 Harold Druken	.10	.25
349 Olaf Kolzig CL	.12	.30
350 Peter Bondra	.15	.40
351 Sergei Gonchar	.10	.25
352 Steve Konowalchuk	.10	.25
353 Chris Simon	.10	.25
354 Adam Oates	.15	.40
355 Olaf Kolzig	.15	.40
356 Jeff Halpern	.10	.25
357 Trevor Linden	.15	.40
358 Calle Johansson	.12	.30
359 Dainius Zubrus	.10	.25
360 Andrei Nikolishin	.10	.25
361 Gregg Naumenko	.10	.25
362 Tappr/Vigier/Snyder RC	.12	.30
363 Kutlak RC/Goren/Kolarik	.10	.25
364 Mika Noronen	.10	.25
365 Murray/Fata/Petrovicky	.10	.25
366 Hnkinsn RC/Lrcq RC/Bell	.10	.25
367 Y.Babenko/R.Shearer	.10	.25
368 Steve Gainey	.10	.25
369 J.Williams/M.Kuznetsov	.10	.25
370 Chimera RC/Comrie/Hait	.12	.30
371 Shelley RC/Spnhl RC/Kles	.12	.30
372 M.Darche RC/M.Davidson	.15	.40
373 Podkonicky RC/Thompson	.10	.25
374 T.Scott/A.Lilja	.10	.25
375 Pascal Dupuis RC	.15	.40
376 Matteucci RC/Gustafson	.10	.25
377 Francis Belanger RC	.12	.30
378 C.Mason/P.Skrbek RC	.10	.25
379 Dagenais/M.Jefferson RC	.10	.25
380 Juraj Kolnik	.10	.25
381 P.Smrek RC/Ulmer/Yerem	.10	.25
382 Joel Kwiatkowski RC	.10	.25
383 Maxime Ouellet	.15	.40
384 David Cullen RC	.10	.25
385 Tibb/Croz/Hedberg RC	.12	.30
386 Kiprusoff/Samuelsson RC	.15	.40
387 J.Obsut RC/M.Van Ryn	.10	.25
388 Ziegler RC/Afanasenkov	.12	.30
389 A.Ponikarovsky/J.Farkas	.10	.25
390 K.Beech/M.Pettinger	.10	.25
391 Mario Lemieux MHG	.75	2.00
392 Jaromir Jagr MHG	.30	.75
393 Chris Pronger MHG	.15	.40
394 Peter Forsberg MHG	.25	.60
395 Pavel Bure MHG	.20	.50
396 Patrick Roy MHG	1.00	2.50
397 Joe Sakic MHG	.40	1.00
398 Dominik Hasek MHG	.30	.75
399 John Leclair MHG	.20	.50
400 Sergei Fedorov MHG	.30	.75
401 Nicklas Lidstrom MHG	.20	.50
402 Martin Brodeur MHG	.50	1.25
403 Ed Belfour MHG	.20	.50
404 Steve Yzerman MHG	.60	1.50
405 Owen Nolan MHG	.15	.40
406 Keith Tkachuk MHG	.20	.50
407 Olaf Kolzig MHG	.15	.40
408 Rob Blake MHG	.15	.40
409 Brett Hull MHG	.25	.60
410 Brian Leetch MHG	.15	.40
411 Ray Bourque MHG	.30	.75
412 Pierre Turgeon MHG	.15	.40
413 Alexei Yashin MHG	.12	.30
414 Mike Modano MHG	.20	.50
415 Curtis Joseph MHG	.20	.50
416 Alexei Kovalev MHG	.15	.40
417 Marian Hossa MHG	.20	.50
418 Milan Hejduk MHG	.20	.50
419 Markus Naslund MHG	.20	.50
420 Theo Fleury MHG	.20	.50
421 Bill Guerin MHG	.15	.40
422 Doug Weight MHG	.15	.40
423 Luc Robitaille MHG	.15	.40
424 Zigmund Palffy MHG	.15	.40
425 Jeremy Roenick MHG	.25	.60
426 Mats Sundin MHG	.20	.50
427 Alexander Mogilny MHG	.15	.40
428 Ed Jovanovski MHG	.15	.40
429 Adam Foote MHG	.15	.40
430 Peter Bondra MHG	.20	.50
431 Mark Recchi MHG	.15	.40
432 Radek Bonk MHG	.12	.30
433 Simon Gagne MHG	.20	.50
434 Scott Stevens MHG	.15	.40
435 Steve Sullivan MHG	.12	.30
436 Martin Straka MHG	.12	.30
437 Evgeni Nabokov MHG	.15	.40
438 Keith Primeau MHG	.15	.40
439 Brendan Shanahan MHG	.20	.50
440 Vincent Lecavalier MHG	.20	.50
441 Ilya Kovalchuk RC	5.00	12.00
442 Erik Cole RC	2.00	5.00
443 Pavel Datsyuk RC	5.00	12.00
444 Kristian Huselius RC	1.50	4.00
445 Marcel Hossa RC	1.50	4.00
446 Martin Erat RC	1.25	3.00
447 Christian Berglund RC	1.25	3.00
448 Raffi Torres RC	1.50	4.00
449 Dan Blackburn RC	1.25	3.00
451 Krys Kolanos RC	1.00	2.50
452 Brian Sutherby RC	1.00	2.50
453 Olivier Michaud RC	1.50	4.00

2001-02 Upper Deck Victory Gold

*GOLD: 1X TO 2.5X BASIC CARDS

Card	Low	High
230 Mark Messier	.75	2.00

2002-03 Upper Deck Victory

Card	Low	High
1 Vitali Vishnevsky	.05	.15
2 Paul Kariya	.10	.25
3 Jeff Friesen	.05	.15
4 Jean-Sebastien Giguere	.10	.25
5 Oleg Tverdovsky	.05	.15
6 Matt Cullen	.05	.15
7 Mike LeClerc	.05	.15
8 Pasi Nurminen	.05	.15
9 Dany Heatley	.07	.20
10 Ilya Kovalchuk	.12	.30
11 Pascal Rheaume	.05	.15
12 Lubos Bartecko	.05	.15
13 Mark Hartigan	.05	.15
14 Frederic Cassivi	.05	.15
15 Jozef Stumpel	.05	.15
16 Sergei Samsonov	.07	.20
17 P.J. Stock	.05	.15
18 Joe Thornton	.15	.40
19 Nick Boynton	.05	.15
20 Brian Rolston	.07	.20
21 Martin Lapointe	.07	.20
22 Maxim Afinogenov	.05	.15
23 Martin Biron	.07	.20
24 J-P Dumont	.05	.15
25 Stu Barnes	.05	.15
26 Tim Connolly	.05	.15
27 Miroslav Satan	.10	.25
28 Taylor Pyatt	.05	.15
29 Craig Conroy	.05	.15
30 Roman Turek	.10	.25
31 Jarome Iginla	.12	.30
32 Dean McAmmond	.05	.15
33 Marc Savard	.05	.15
34 Derek Morris	.05	.15
35 Micki Dupont RC	.05	.15
36 Sami Kapanen	.05	.15
37 Jeff O'Neill	.05	.15
38 Ron Francis	.12	.30
39 Rod Brind'Amour	.10	.25
40 Erik Cole	.05	.15
41 Bates Battaglia	.05	.15
42 Arturs Irbe	.07	.20
43 Alexei Zhamnov	.07	.20
44 Jocelyn Thibault	.07	.20
45 Eric Daze	.05	.15
46 Steve Sullivan	.05	.15
47 Phil Housley	.07	.20
48 Kyle Calder	.05	.15
49 Bob Probert	.10	.25
50 Patrick Roy	.25	.60
51 Radim Vrbata	.05	.15
52 Chris Drury	.10	.25
53 Joe Sakic	.20	.50
54 Milan Hejduk	.07	.20
55 Alex Tanguay	.07	.20
56 Peter Forsberg	.20	.50
57 Rob Blake	.10	.25
58 Ray Whitney	.07	.20
59 Espen Knutsen	.05	.15
60 Marc Denis	.07	.20
61 Rostislav Klesla	.05	.15
62 Ron Tugnutt	.07	.20
63 Mike Sillinger	.05	.15
64 Chris Nielsen	.05	.15
65 Jason Arnott	.07	.20
66 Marty Turco	.10	.25
67 Jere Lehtinen	.10	.25
68 Sergei Zubov	.07	.20
69 Mike Modano	.15	.40
70 Brenden Morrow	.07	.20
71 Pierre Turgeon	.07	.20
72 Derian Hatcher	.07	.20
73 Brendan Shanahan	.10	.25
74 Dominik Hasek	.15	.40
75 Sergei Fedorov	.15	.40
76 Pavel Datsyuk	.15	.40
77 Steve Yzerman	.25	.60
78 Brett Hull	.20	.50
79 Chris Chelios	.10	.25
80 Luc Robitaille	.10	.25
81 Mike Comrie	.10	.25
82 Anson Carter	.07	.20
83 Ryan Smyth	.07	.20
84 Tommy Salo	.07	.20
85 Jochen Hecht	.05	.15
86 Eric Brewer	.05	.15
87 Mike York	.05	.15
88 Kristian Huselius	.05	.15
89 Stephen Weiss	.10	.25
90 Roberto Luongo	.15	.40
91 Sandis Ozolinsh	.05	.15
92 Valeri Bure	.07	.20
93 Marcus Nilsson	.05	.15
94 Niklas Hagman	.05	.15
95 Adam Deadmarsh	.05	.15
96 Felix Potvin	.15	.40
97 Jason Allison	.07	.20
98 Eric Belanger	.05	.15
99 Zigmund Palffy	.10	.25
100 Cliff Ronning	.05	.15
101 Mathieu Schneider	.05	.15
102 Andrew Brunette	.05	.15
103 Sylvain Blouin RC	.05	.15
104 Marian Gaborik	.10	.25
105 Wes Walz	.05	.15
106 Filip Kuba	.05	.15
107 Manny Fernandez	.05	.15
108 Tony Virta	.05	.15
109 Jose Theodore	.10	.25
110 Saku Koivu	.10	.25
111 Mike Ribeiro	.05	.15
112 Yanic Perreault	.05	.15
113 Oleg Petrov	.05	.15
114 Joe Juneau	.05	.15
115 Marcel Hossa	.05	.15
116 Denis Arkhipov	.05	.15
117 Scott Hartnell	.05	.15
118 David Legwand	.07	.20
119 Mike Dunham	.07	.20
120 Kimmo Timonen	.05	.15
121 Greg Johnson	.05	.15
122 Andy Delmore	.05	.15
123 Petr Sykora	.07	.20
124 Scott Stevens	.10	.25
125 Brian Gionta	.05	.15
126 Scott Niedermayer	.10	.25
127 Martin Brodeur	.25	.60
128 Patrik Elias	.10	.25
129 Joe Nieuwendyk	.07	.20
130 Scott Gomez	.07	.20
131 Ray Schultz RC	.05	.15
132 Mark Parrish	.05	.15
133 Raffi Torres	.05	.15
134 Alexei Yashin	.07	.20
135 Chris Osgood	.10	.25
136 Michael Peca	.07	.20
137 Shawn Bates	.05	.15
138 Pavel Bure	.10	.25
139 Mark Messier	.20	.50
140 Eric Lindros	.15	.40
141 Brian Leetch	.07	.20
142 Petr Nedved	.05	.15
143 Tom Poti	.05	.15
144 Dan Blackburn	.07	.20
145 Mike Richter	.10	.25
146 Martin Havlat	.07	.20
147 Patrick Lalime	.07	.20
148 Daniel Alfredsson	.10	.25
149 Marian Hossa	.10	.25
150 Radek Bonk	.07	.20
151 Wade Redden	.05	.15
152 Magnus Arvedson	.05	.15
153 Todd White	.05	.15
154 Roman Cechmanek	.07	.20
155 Mark Recchi	.12	.30
156 Simon Gagne	.10	.25
157 Jeremy Roenick	.15	.40
158 John LeClair	.10	.25
159 Keith Primeau	.07	.20
160 Justin Williams	.07	.20
161 Brian Boucher	.07	.20
162 Krys Kolanos	.05	.15
163 Sean Burke	.05	.15
164 Teppo Numminen	.05	.15
165 Shane Doan	.07	.20
166 Ladislav Nagy	.05	.15
167 Daymond Langkow	.07	.20
168 Daniel Briere	.07	.20
169 Kris Beech	.05	.15
170 Johan Hedberg	.10	.25
171 Martin Straka	.07	.20
172 Mario Lemieux	.40	1.00
173 Alexei Kovalev	.07	.20
174 Jan Hrdina	.05	.15
175 Alexei Morozov	.05	.15
176 Vincent Damphousse	.07	.20
177 Owen Nolan	.10	.25
178 Patrick Marleau	.10	.25
179 Evgeni Nabokov	.07	.20
180 Brad Stuart	.05	.15
181 Mike Ricci	.05	.15
182 Scott Thornton	.05	.15
183 Al MacInnis	.12	.30
184 Pavol Demitra	.12	.30
185 Chris Pronger	.10	.25
186 Brent Johnson	.07	.20
187 Doug Weight	.10	.25
188 Keith Tkachuk	.10	.25
189 Scott Young	.05	.15
190 Cory Stillman	.05	.15
191 Sheldon Keefe	.05	.15
192 Brad Richards	.10	.25
193 Nikolai Khabibulin	.10	.25
194 Martin St. Louis	.10	.25
195 Vincent Lecavalier	.10	.25
196 Fredrik Modin	.05	.15
197 Pavel Kubina	.05	.15
198 Alexander Mogilny	.07	.20
199 Tomas Kaberle	.05	.15
200 Mats Sundin	.10	.25
201 Gary Roberts	.05	.15
202 Mikael Renberg	.05	.15
203 Tie Domi	.07	.20
204 Darcy Tucker	.05	.15
205 Brendan Morrison	.07	.20
206 Brent Sopel	.05	.15
207 Trevor Linden	.10	.25
208 Dan Cloutier	.07	.20
209 Todd Bertuzzi	.10	.25
210 Ed Jovanovski	.07	.20
211 Markus Naslund	.10	.25
212 Sergei Gonchar	.07	.20
213 Jaromir Jagr	.30	.75
214 Peter Bondra	.10	.25
215 Steve Konowalchuk	.05	.15
216 Dainius Zubrus	.05	.15
217 Brian Sutherby	.05	.15
218 Olaf Kolzig	.10	.25
219 Patrick Roy CL	.25	.60
220 Pavel Bure CL	.10	.25

2002-03 Upper Deck Victory Bronze

*BRONZE: 1.2X TO 3X BASIC CARDS

Card	Low	High
139 Mark Messier	.75	2.00

2002-03 Upper Deck Victory Gold

*GOLD: 8X TO 20X BASIC CARDS

Card	Low	High
139 Mark Messier	5.00	12.00

2002-03 Upper Deck Victory Silver

*SILVER: 4X TO 10X BASIC CARDS

Card	Low	High
139 Mark Messier	2.50	6.00

2002-03 Upper Deck Victory National Pride

Card	Low	High
NP1 Ruslan Salei	.20	.50
NP2 Paul Kariya	.30	.75
NP3 Jarome Iginla	.40	1.00
NP4 Joe Sakic	.60	1.50
NP5 Rob Blake	.30	.75
NP6 Steve Yzerman	.75	2.00
NP7 Brendan Shanahan	.30	.75
NP8 Martin Brodeur	.75	2.00
NP9 Eric Lindros	.50	1.25
NP10 Simon Gagne	.30	.75
NP11 Mario Lemieux	1.25	3.00
NP12 Chris Pronger	.30	.75
NP13 Curtis Joseph	.40	1.00
NP14 Milan Hejduk	.25	.60
NP15 Dominik Hasek	.50	1.25
NP16 Patrik Elias	.30	.75
NP17 Petr Sykora	.25	.60
NP18 Martin Rucinsky	.20	.50
NP19 Martin Havlat	.25	.60
NP20 Robert Lang	.20	.50
NP21 Jaromir Jagr	1.00	2.50
NP22 Sami Kapanen	.20	.50
NP23 Ville Nieminen	.20	.50
NP24 Jere Lehtinen	.30	.75
NP25 Jani Hurme	.25	.60
NP26 Teppo Numminen	.20	.50
NP27 Teemu Selanne	.60	1.50
NP28 Jochen Hecht	.20	.50
NP29 Marco Sturm	.20	.50
NP30 Olaf Kolzig	.30	.75
NP31 Ilya Kovalchuk	.40	1.00
NP32 Sergei Samsonov	.25	.60
NP33 Alexei Zhamnov	.25	.60
NP34 Sergei Fedorov	.50	1.25
NP35 Pavel Bure	.30	.75
NP36 Alexei Yashin	.25	.60
NP37 Alexei Kovalev	.25	.60
NP38 Nikolai Khabibulin	.30	.75
NP39 Sergei Gonchar	.25	.60
NP40 Miroslav Satan	.30	.75
NP41 Zigmund Palffy	.30	.75
NP42 Marian Hossa	.30	.75
NP43 Pavol Demitra	.40	1.00
NP44 Nicklas Lidstrom	.30	.75
NP45 Tomas Holmstrom	.20	.50
NP46 Tommy Salo	.25	.60
NP47 Daniel Alfredsson	.30	.75
NP48 Kim Johnsson	.20	.50
NP49 Mats Sundin	.30	.75
NP50 Markus Naslund	.30	.75
NP51 Bill Guerin	.30	.75
NP52 Tony Amonte	.25	.60
NP53 Chris Drury	.30	.75
NP54 Mike Modano	.50	1.25
NP55 Chris Chelios	.30	.75
NP56 Mike Dunham	.25	.60
NP57 Mike Richter	.30	.75
NP58 Jeremy Roenick	.50	1.25
NP59 Keith Tkachuk	.30	.75
NP60 Doug Weight	.30	.75

2003-04 Upper Deck Victory

Card	Low	High
1 Paul Kariya	.10	.25
2 Petr Sykora	.07	.20
3 Adam Oates	.10	.25
4 Stanislav Chistov	.05	.15
5 Jean-Sebastien Giguere	.10	.25
6 Dany Heatley	.07	.20
7 Ilya Kovalchuk	.10	.25
8 Marc Savard	.05	.15
9 Patrik Stefan	.05	.15
10 Simon Gamache	.05	.15
11 Joe DiPenta RC	.07	.20
12 Joe Thornton	.15	.40
13 Glen Murray	.07	.20
14 Bryan Berard	.07	.20
16 P.J. Stock	.05	.15
17 Jeff Hackett	.07	.20
18 Steve Shields	.07	.20
19 Miroslav Satan	.07	.20
20 Daniel Briere	.10	.25
21 Ales Kotalik	.05	.15
22 Milan Bartovic RC	.07	.20
23 Maxim Afinogenov	.05	.15
24 Martin Biron	.07	.20
25 Ryan Miller	.10	.25
26 Rick Mrozik RC	.05	.15
27 Sergei Samsonov	.07	.20
27 Jarome Iginla	.12	.30
28 Chris Drury	.07	.20
29 Jordan Leopold	.05	.15
30 Roman Turek	.07	.20
31 Jamie McLennan	.05	.15
32 Jeff O`Neill	.05	.15
33 Ron Francis	.12	.30
34 Rod Brind`Amour	.10	.25
35 Erik Cole	.05	.15
36 Pavel Brendl	.05	.15
37 Steve Sullivan	.05	.15
38 Alexei Zhamnov	.07	.20
39 Eric Daze	.07	.20
40 Kyle Calder	.05	.15
41 Igor Radulov	.05	.15
42 Jocelyn Thibault	.07	.20
43 Peter Forsberg	.20	.50
44 Milan Hejduk	.07	.20
45 Alex Tanguay	.07	.20
46 Joe Sakic	.20	.50
47 Rob Blake	.10	.25
48 David Aebischer	.07	.20
49 Patrick Roy	.25	.60
50 Ray Whitney	.07	.20
51 Andrew Cassels	.05	.15
52 Geoff Sanderson	.05	.15
53 Rick Nash	.10	.25
54 Marc Denis	.07	.20
55 Kent McDonell RC	.07	.20
56 Mike Modano	.15	.40
57 Bill Guerin	.10	.25
58 Jere Lehtinen	.07	.20
59 Jason Arnott	.07	.20
60 Steve Ott	.05	.15
61 Marty Turco	.10	.25
62 Sergei Fedorov	.15	.40
63 Brett Hull	.20	.50
64 Brendan Shanahan	.10	.25
65 Nicklas Lidstrom	.10	.25
66 Pavel Datsyuk	.15	.40
67 Henrik Zetterberg	.12	.30
68 Steve Yzerman	.25	.60
69 Manny Legace	.05	.15
70 Curtis Joseph	.12	.30
71 Ryan Smyth	.07	.20
72 Todd Marchant	.05	.15
73 Mike Comrie	.07	.20
74 Ales Hemsky	.10	.25
75 Eric Brewer	.05	.15
76 Fernando Pisani	.05	.15
77 Tommy Salo	.07	.20
78 Olli Jokinen	.10	.25
79 Viktor Kozlov	.05	.15
80 Stephen Weiss	.05	.15
81 Jay Bouwmeester	.05	.15
82 Roberto Luongo	.15	.40
83 Zigmund Palffy	.10	.25
84 Alexander Frolov	.07	.20
85 Jason Allison	.07	.20
86 Adam Deadmarsh	.05	.15
87 Jamie Storr	.07	.20
88 Cristobal Huet	.07	.20
89 Marian Gaborik	.10	.25
90 Pascal Dupuis	.05	.15
91 P-M Bouchard	.10	.25
92 Manny Fernandez	.05	.15
93 Dwayne Roloson	.07	.20
94 Wes Walz	.05	.15
95 Saku Koivu	.10	.25
96 Richard Zednik	.05	.15
97 Marcel Hossa	.05	.15
98 Jose Theodore	.10	.25
99 Michael Komisarek	.05	.15
100 Mathieu Garon	.05	.15
101 Ron Hainsey	.05	.15
102 David Legwand	.07	.20
103 Denis Arkhipov	.05	.15
104 Scott Hartnell	.05	.15
105 Scottie Upshall	.07	.20
106 Tomas Vokoun	.07	.20
107 Patrik Elias	.10	.25
108 Jamie Langenbrunner	.07	.20
109 Scott Gomez	.07	.20
110 Joe Nieuwendyk	.07	.20
111 John Madden	.05	.15
112 Scott Stevens	.10	.25
113 Martin Brodeur	.25	.60
114 Alexei Yashin	.07	.20
115 Jason Blake	.05	.15
116 Dave Scatchard	.05	.15
117 Michael Peca	.07	.20
118 Janne Niinimaa	.05	.15
119 Rick DiPietro	.07	.20
120 Garth Snow	.07	.20
121 Alex Kovalev	.07	.20
122 Anson Carter	.07	.20
123 Eric Lindros	.15	.40
124 Tom Poti	.05	.15
125 Mark Messier	.20	.50
126 Pavel Bure	.10	.25
127 Brian Leetch	.07	.20
128 Mike Dunham	.07	.20
129 Dan Blackburn	.07	.20
130 Marian Hossa	.10	.25
131 Daniel Alfredsson	.10	.25
132 Todd White	.05	.15
133 Zdeno Chara	.10	.25
134 Jason Spezza	.10	.25
135 Patrick Lalime	.07	.20
136 Ray Emery	.07	.20
137 Jeremy Roenick	.15	.40
138 Mark Recchi	.12	.30
139 Tony Amonte	.07	.20
140 Keith Primeau	.07	.2
141 John LeClair	.10	.25
142 Simon Gagne	.10	.25
143 Robert Esche	.05	.15
144 Mike Johnson	.05	.15
145 Shane Doan	.07	.2
146 Ladislav Nagy	.05	.1
147 Chris Gratton	.05	.1
148 Sean Burke	.05	.1
149 Mario Lemieux	.40	1.0
150 Martin Straka	.05	.1
151 Rico Fata	.05	.1
152 Johan Hedberg	.07	.2
153 Sebastien Caron	.07	.2
154 Brooks Orpik	.05	.1
155 Teemu Selanne	.20	.5
156 Vincent Damphousse	.07	.2
157 Patrick Marleau	.10	.2

158 Jim Fahey .05 .15
159 Niko Dimitrakos .05 .15
160 Kyle McLaren .05 .15
161 Evgeni Nabokov .07 .20
162 Peter Sejna RC .07 .20
163 Pavol Demitra .12 .30
164 Al MacInnis .12 .30
165 Doug Weight .10 .25
166 Keith Tkachuk .10 .25
167 Chris Pronger .10 .25
168 Chris Osgood .10 .25
169 Barret Jackman .05 .15
170 Vaclav Prospal .05 .15
171 Vincent Lecavalier .10 .25
172 Martin St. Louis .10 .25
173 Alexander Svitov .05 .15
174 Nikolai Khabibulin .10 .25
175 Matt Stajan RC .60 1.50
176 Alexander Mogilny .07 .20
177 Mats Sundin .10 .25
178 Owen Nolan .10 .25
179 Nik Antropov .07 .20
180 Doug Gilmour .12 .30
181 Tie Domi .07 .20
182 Gary Roberts .05 .15
183 Ed Belfour .10 .25
184 Carlo Colaiacovo .05 .15
185 Alexander Auld .05 .15
186 Markus Naslund .10 .25
187 Todd Bertuzzi .10 .25
188 Brendan Morrison .07 .20
189 Ed Jovanovski .07 .20
190 Matt Cooke .05 .15
191 Trevor Linden .10 .25
192 Henrik Sedin .12 .30
193 Daniel Sedin .12 .30
194 Dan Cloutier .07 .20
195 Jaromir Jagr .30 .75
196 Sergei Gonchar .05 .15
197 Michael Nylander .05 .15
198 Peter Bondra .10 .25
199 Mike Grier .05 .15
200 Olaf Kolzig .10 .25
201 Joffrey Lupul RC 1.50 4.00
202 Eric Staal RC 3.00 8.00
203 Tuomo Ruutu RC 1.00 2.50
204 Nathan Horton RC 1.50 4.00
205 Dustin Brown RC 1.50 4.00
206 Jordin Tootoo RC 1.25 3.00
207 Joni Pitkanen RC 1.00 2.50
208 Milan Michalek RC 1.25 3.00
209 Sean Bergenheim RC .75 2.00
210 Marc-Andre Fleury RC 4.00 10.00

2003-04 Upper Deck Victory Bronze

*VETS/199: 4X TO 10X BASIC CARDS
*ROOKIES/199: 2.5X TO 6X BASIC RC

2003-04 Upper Deck Victory Gold

*VETS/25: 12X TO 30X BASIC CARDS
*ROOKIES: 1.5X TO 4X

2003-04 Upper Deck Victory Silver

*VETS50: 8X TO 20X BASIC CARDS
*ROOKIES/50: 5X TO 12X BASIC RC

2003-04 Upper Deck Victory Freshman Flashback

FF1 Paul Kariya .25 .60
FF2 Stanislav Chistov .15 .40
FF3 Ilya Kovalchuk .25 .60
FF4 Dany Heatley .20 .50
FF5 Joe Thornton .40 1.00
FF6 Sergei Samsonov .20 .50
FF7 Ryan Miller .25 .60
FF8 Jarome Iginla .30 .75
FF9 Jordan Leopold .15 .40
FF10 Jocelyn Thibault .20 .50
FF11 Igor Radulov .15 .40
FF12 Peter Forsberg .50 1.25
FF13 Joe Sakic .50 1.25
FF14 Patrick Roy .60 1.50
FF15 Rick Nash .25 .60
FF16 Mike Modano .40 1.00
FF17 Henrik Zetterberg .30 .75
FF18 Brett Hull .50 1.25
FF19 Brendan Shanahan .25 .60
FF20 Dmitri Bykov .15 .40
FF21 Roberto Luongo .40 1.00
FF22 Jay Bouwmeester .15 .40
FF23 Zigmund Palffy .25 .60
FF24 Cristobal Huet .20 .50
FF25 Marian Gaborik .25 .60
FF26 Mike Komisarek .15 .40
FF27 Martin Brodeur .60 1.50
FF28 Alex Kovalev .20 .50
FF29 Pavel Bure .25 .60
FF30 Marian Hossa .25 .60
FF31 Jason Spezza .25 .60
FF32 Ray Emery .20 .50
FF33 John LeClair .25 .60
FF34 Tony Amonte .20 .50
FF35 Jeremy Roenick .40 1.00
FF36 Mario Lemieux 1.00 2.50
FF37 Teemu Selanne .50 1.25
FF38 Jim Fahey .15 .40
FF39 Niko Dimitrakos .15 .40
FF40 Chris Pronger .25 .60
FF41 Keith Tkachuk .25 .60
FF42 Vincent Lecavalier .25 .60
FF43 Owen Nolan .25 .60
FF44 Mats Sundin .25 .60
FF45 Alexander Mogilny .20 .50
FF46 Jaromir Jagr .75 2.00
FF47 Bobby Orr 1.00 2.50
FF48 Ray Bourque .40 1.00
FF49 Wayne Gretzky 1.50 4.00
FF50 Gordie Howe .75 2.00

2003-04 Upper Deck Victory Game Breakers

GB1 Peter Forsberg .40 1.00
GB2 Paul Kariya .20 .50
GB3 Ilya Kovalchuk .20 .50
GB4 Martin Brodeur .50 1.25
GB5 Sean Burke .12 .30
GB6 Bill Guerin .20 .50
GB7 Owen Nolan .20 .50
GB8 Alexei Yashin .15 .40
GB9 Marty Turco .20 .50
GB10 Dany Heatley .15 .40
GB11 Joe Sakic .40 1.00
GB12 Mike Comrie .15 .40
GB13 Jason Blake .12 .30
GB14 Nikolai Khabibulin .20 .50
GB15 Ed Belfour .20 .50
GB16 Chris Pronger .20 .50
GB17 Rick Nash .20 .50
GB18 Jaromir Jagr .60 1.50
GB19 Vincent Lecavalier .20 .50
GB20 Olli Jokinen .20 .50
GB21 Alex Kovalev .15 .40
GB22 Mike Modano .30 .75
GB23 Henrik Zetterberg .25 .60
GB24 Roberto Luongo .30 .75
GB25 Teemu Selanne .40 1.00
GB26 John LeClair .20 .50
GB27 Tie Domi .15 .40
GB28 Todd Bertuzzi .20 .50
GB29 Pavel Bure .20 .50
GB30 Mario Lemieux .75 2.00
GB31 Al MacInnis .25 .60
GB32 Joe Thornton .30 .75
GB33 Mats Sundin .20 .50
GB34 Keith Tkachuk .20 .50
GB35 Alexander Mogilny .15 .40
GB36 Marian Hossa .20 .50
GB37 Brett Hull .40 1.00
GB38 Marian Gaborik .20 .50
GB39 Tony Amonte .15 .40
GB40 Zigmund Palffy .20 .50
GB41 Patrick Roy .50 1.25
GB42 Sergei Samsonov .15 .40
GB43 Sergei Fedorov .30 .75
GB44 Markus Naslund .20 .50
GB45 Brendan Shanahan .20 .50
GB46 Saku Koivu .20 .50
GB47 Jarome Iginla .25 .60
GB48 Jocelyn Thibault .15 .40
GB49 Jason Spezza .20 .50
GB50 Jeremy Roenick .30 .75

2005-06 Upper Deck Victory

1 Jean-Sebastien Giguere .20 .50
2 Joffrey Lupul .12 .30
3 Sergei Fedorov .30 .75
4 Stanislav Chistov .12 .30
5 Sandis Ozolinsh .12 .30
6 Steve Rucchin .12 .30
7 Dany Heatley .15 .40
8 Ilya Kovalchuk .20 .50
9 Kari Lehtonen .15 .40
10 Shawn McEachern .12 .30
11 Marc Savard .12 .30
12 Patrik Stefan .12 .30
13 Glen Murray .15 .40
14 Patrice Bergeron .25 .60
15 Andrew Raycroft .15 .40
16 Nick Boynton .12 .30
17 Sergei Gonchar .12 .30
18 Sergei Samsonov .15 .40
19 Joe Thornton .30 .75
20 Miroslav Satan .15 .40
21 Chris Drury .15 .40
22 Martin Biron .15 .40
23 Jochen Hecht .12 .30
24 Daniel Briere .20 .50
25 Maxim Afinogenov .12 .30
26 Mike Grier .12 .30
27 Jarome Iginla .25 .60
28 Martin Gelinas .12 .30
29 Jordan Leopold .12 .30
30 Miikka Kiprusoff .20 .50
31 Chris Simon .12 .30
32 Ville Nieminen .12 .30
33 Jeff O'Neill .12 .30
34 Martin Gerber .15 .40
35 Rod Brind'Amour .20 .50
36 Erik Cole .12 .30
37 Eric Staal .25 .60
38 Josef Vasicek .12 .30
39 Bryan Berard .12 .30
40 Eric Daze .15 .40
41 Jocelyn Thibault .15 .40
42 Tyler Arnason .12 .30
43 Mark Bell .12 .30
44 Tuomo Ruutu .20 .50
45 Joe Sakic .40 1.00
46 Peter Forsberg .40 1.00
47 David Aebischer .15 .40
48 Rob Blake .20 .50
49 Milan Hejduk .15 .40
50 Alex Tanguay .20 .50
51 Paul Kariya .20 .50
52 Adam Foote .12 .30
53 Teemu Selanne .40 1.00
54 Rick Nash .20 .50
55 Rostislav Klesla .12 .30
56 Geoff Sanderson .12 .30
57 Nikolai Zherdev .12 .30
58 Marc Denis .15 .40
59 Pascal LeClaire .15 .40
60 Mike Modano .30 .75
61 Bill Guerin .20 .50
62 Marty Turco .20 .50
63 Brenden Morrow .15 .40
64 Jere Lehtinen .15 .40
65 Jason Arnott .15 .40
66 Sergei Zubov .15 .40
67 Steve Yzerman .50 1.25
68 Brendan Shanahan .20 .50
69 Chris Chelios .20 .50
70 Pavel Datsyuk .30 .75
71 Henrik Zetterberg .25 .60
72 Robert Lang .12 .30
73 Nicklas Lidstrom .20 .50
74 Kris Draper .25 .60
75 Curtis Joseph .25 .60
76 Gordie Howe .60 1.50
77 Wayne Gretzky 1.25 3.00
78 Raffi Torres .12 .30
79 Ty Conklin .15 .40
80 Ryan Smyth .15 .40
81 Jason Smith .12 .30
82 Georges Laraque .15 .40
83 Mike York .12 .30
84 Stephen Weiss .12 .30
85 Roberto Luongo .30 .75
86 Olli Jokinen .20 .50
87 Mike Van Ryn .12 .30
88 Kristian Huselius .12 .30
89 Jay Bouwmeester .12 .30
90 Eric Belanger .12 .30
91 Luc Robitaille .20 .50
92 Mathieu Garon .15 .40
93 Zigmund Palffy .20 .50
94 Lubomir Visnovsky .12 .30
95 Mike Cammalleri .20 .50
96 Marian Gaborik .20 .50
97 Pascal Dupuis .12 .30
98 Andrew Brunette .12 .30
99 Brian Rolston .15 .40
100 Manny Fernandez .12 .30
101 Dwayne Roloson .15 .40
102 Jose Theodore .20 .50
103 Saku Koivu .20 .50
104 Michael Ryder .15 .40
105 Mike Ribeiro .12 .30
106 Sheldon Souray .12 .30
107 Richard Zednik .12 .30
108 Yanic Perreault .12 .30
109 David Legwand .15 .40
110 Scott Walker .12 .30
111 Tomas Vokoun .15 .40
112 Steve Sullivan .12 .30
113 Kimmo Timonen .12 .30
114 Martin Erat .12 .30
115 Martin Brodeur .50 1.25
116 Scott Stevens .20 .50
117 Scott Gomez .15 .40
118 Brian Rafalski .15 .40
119 Scott Niedermayer .20 .50
120 Patrik Elias .20 .50
121 Rick DiPietro .15 .40
122 Alexei Yashin .15 .40
123 Mark Parrish .12 .30
124 Michael Peca .15 .40
125 Trent Hunter .12 .30
126 Adrian Aucoin .12 .30
127 Bobby Holik .12 .30
128 Mark Messier .40 1.00
129 Mike Dunham .12 .30
130 Jaromir Jagr .60 1.50
131 Jamie Lundmark .12 .30
132 Tom Poti .12 .30
133 Daniel Alfredsson .20 .50
134 Martin Havlat .20 .50
135 Dominik Hasek .30 .75
136 Jason Spezza .20 .50
137 Marian Hossa .20 .50
138 Peter Bondra .20 .50
139 Wade Redden .12 .30
140 Jeremy Roenick .30 .75
141 Simon Gagne .20 .50
142 Keith Primeau .15 .40
143 John LeClair .20 .50
144 Robert Esche .15 .40
145 Tony Amonte .15 .40
146 Donald Brashear .12 .30
147 Michal Handzus .15 .40
148 Brett Hull .40 1.00
149 Shane Doan .15 .40
150 Ladislav Nagy .12 .30
151 Brian Boucher .15 .40
152 Mike Comrie .15 .40
153 Mike Ricci .12 .30
154 Milan Kraft .12 .30
155 Mario Lemieux .75 2.00
156 Marc-Andre Fleury .40 1.00
157 Mark Recchi .25 .60
158 Dick Tarnstrom .12 .30
159 Ryan Malone .12 .30
160 Patrick Marleau .20 .50
161 Nils Ekman .12 .30
162 Jonathan Cheechoo .15 .40
163 Evgeni Nabokov .15 .40
164 Marco Sturm .12 .30
165 Alyn McCauley .12 .30
166 Doug Weight .20 .50
167 Keith Tkachuk .20 .50
168 Chris Pronger .20 .50
169 Al MacInnis .25 .60
170 Patrick Lalime .15 .40
171 Pavol Demitra .25 .60
172 Barret Jackman .12 .30
173 Brad Richards .20 .50
174 Vincent Lecavalier .20 .50
175 Fredrik Modin .12 .30
176 Nikolai Khabibulin .20 .50
177 Ruslan Fedotenko .12 .30
178 Cory Stillman .15 .40
179 Martin St. Louis .20 .50
180 Dan Boyle .12 .30
181 Mats Sundin .20 .50
182 Bryan McCabe .12 .30
183 Joe Nieuwendyk .15 .40
184 Gary Roberts .12 .30
185 Tie Domi .15 .40
186 Ed Belfour .20 .50
187 Brian Leetch .15 .40
188 Darcy Tucker .15 .40
189 Markus Naslund .20 .50
190 Brendan Morrison .12 .30
191 Dan Cloutier .15 .40
192 Ed Jovanovski .15 .40
193 Matt Cooke .12 .30
194 Brent Sopel .12 .30
195 Trevor Linden .20 .50
196 Olaf Kolzig .20 .50
197 Jeff Halpern .12 .30
198 Alexander Semin .20 .50
199 Rastislav Stana .12 .30
200 Brendan Witt .12 .30
201 Teemu Selanne .40 1.00
202 Scott Niedermayer .20 .50
203 Marian Hossa .20 .50
204 Peter Bondra .20 .50
205 Brian Leetch .15 .40
206 Brad Boyes .15 .40
207 Ryan Miller .20 .50
208 Tony Amonte .15 .40
209 Justin Williams .15 .40
210 Nikolai Khabibulin .20 .50
211 Pavel Vorobiev .12 .30
212 Pierre Turgeon .15 .40
213 Sergei Fedorov .30 .75
214 Antti Miettinen .12 .30
215 Niko Kapanen .12 .30
216 Manny Legace .20 .50
217 Jason Williams .12 .30
218 Chris Pronger .20 .50
219 Ales Hemsky .15 .40
220 Joe Nieuwendyk .15 .40
221 Nathan Horton .20 .50
222 Jeremy Roenick .30 .75
223 Pavol Demitra .25 .60
224 Pierre-Marc Bouchard .20 .50
225 Alex Kovalev .15 .40
226 Paul Kariya .20 .50
227 Scott Hartnell .12 .30
228 Brian Gionta .12 .30
229 Jamie Langenbrunner .12 .30
230 Miroslav Satan .15 .40
231 Alexei Zhitnik .12 .30
232 Steve Rucchin .12 .30
233 Kevin Weekes .15 .40
234 Dany Heatley .15 .40
235 Zdeno Chara .20 .50
236 Peter Forsberg .40 1.00
237 Joni Pitkanen .12 .30
238 Curtis Joseph .25 .60
239 Geoff Sanderson .12 .30
240 Sergei Gonchar .12 .30
241 John LeClair .20 .50
242 Milan Michalek .12 .30
243 Petr Cajanek .12 .30
244 Sean Burke .12 .30
245 Vaclav Prospal .12 .30
246 Eric Lindros .30 .75
247 Jason Allison .15 .40
248 Jeff O'Neill .12 .30
249 Todd Bertuzzi .20 .50
250 Jeff Friesen .12 .30
251 Peter Budaj RC 1.00 2.50
252 Wojtek Wolski RC .60 1.50
253 Brent Seabrook RC 1.50 4.00
254 Cam Barker RC .60 1.50
255 Gilbert Brule RC .75 2.00
256 Jay McClement RC .50 1.25
257 Jeff Woywitka RC .50 1.25
258 Andrew Alberts RC .50 1.25
259 Hannu Toivonen RC .75 2.00
260 Yann Danis RC .60 1.50
261 Alexander Perezhogin RC .60 1.50
262 Brad Winchester RC .75 2.00
263 Kyle Brodziak RC .50 1.25
264 Alexander Ovechkin RC 40.00 100.00
265 Jakub Klepis RC .50 1.25
266 Keith Ballard RC .60 1.50
267 David Leneveu RC .60 1.50
268 Zach Parise RC 2.00 5.00
269 Dion Phaneuf RC 1.25 3.00
270 Eric Nystrom RC .60 1.50
271 Mike Richards RC 1.50 4.00
272 Jeff Carter RC 1.25 3.00
273 R.J. Umberger RC .75 2.00
274 Cam Ward RC 1.25 3.00
275 Robert Nilsson RC .75 2.00
276 Chris Campoli RC .50 1.25
277 George Parros RC .50 1.25
278 Evgeny Artyukhin RC .60 1.50
279 Alexander Steen RC 1.25 3.00
280 Ryan Getzlaf RC 2.00 5.00
281 Corey Perry RC 2.50 6.00
282 Rostislav Olesz RC .60 1.50
283 Anthony Stewart RC .60 1.50
284 Ryan Whitney RC .75 2.00
285 Sidney Crosby RC 25.00 60.00
286 Maxime Talbot RC .75 2.00
287 Ryan Suter RC 1.00 2.50
288 Henrik Lundqvist RC 4.00 10.00
289 Alvaro Montoya RC .75 2.00
290 Jim Howard RC 2.00 5.00
291 Johan Franzen RC 1.25 3.00
292 Thomas Vanek RC 1.50 4.00
293 Andrej Meszaros RC .60 1.50
294 Christoph Schubert RC .50 1.25
295 Patrick Eaves RC .75 2.00
296 Steve Bernier RC .75 2.00
297 Jussi Jokinen RC .75 2.00
298 Braydon Coburn RC .75 2.00
299 Matt Foy RC .50 1.25
300 Mikko Koivu RC 1.00 2.50

2005-06 Upper Deck Victory Gold

*1-250 VETS/100: 6X TO 15X BASIC CARDS
*251-300 ROOKIES/100 : 3X TO 8X BASE RC
128 Mark Messier 8.00 20.00
264 Alexander Ovechkin RC 250.00 600.00
269 Dion Phaneuf RC 10.00 25.00
285 Sidney Crosby RC 150.00 400.00

2005-06 Upper Deck Victory Silver

*1-200 SILVER/250: 3X TO 8X BASIC CARDS
128 Mark Messier 4.00 10.00

2005-06 Upper Deck Victory Jumbos

BU1 Jean-Sebastien Giguere .75 2.00
BU2 Dany Heatley .60 1.50
BU3 Ilya Kovalchuk .75 2.00
BU4 Patrice Bergeron 1.00 2.50
BU5 Joe Thornton 1.25 3.00
BU6 Jarome Iginla 1.00 2.50
BU7 Miikka Kiprusoff .75 2.00
BU8 Joe Sakic 1.50 4.00
BU9 Peter Forsberg 1.50 4.00
BU10 Paul Kariya .75 2.00
BU11 Rick Nash .75 2.00
BU12 Mike Modano 1.25 3.00
BU13 Gordie Howe 2.50 6.00
BU14 Steve Yzerman 2.00 5.00
BU15 Brendan Shanahan .75 2.00
BU16 Wayne Gretzky 5.00 12.00
BU17 Ryan Smyth .60 1.50
BU18 Marian Gaborik .75 2.00
BU19 Jose Theodore .75 2.00
BU20 Saku Koivu .75 2.00
BU21 Michael Ryder .60 1.50
BU22 Martin Brodeur 2.00 5.00
BU23 Mark Messier 1.50 4.00
BU24 Jaromir Jagr 2.50 6.00
BU25 Dominik Hasek 1.25 3.00
BU26 Marian Hossa .75 2.00
BU27 Jason Spezza .75 2.00
BU28 Jeremy Roenick 1.25 3.00
BU29 Keith Primeau .60 1.50
BU30 Brett Hull 1.50 4.00
BU31 Mario Lemieux 3.00 8.00
BU32 Evgeni Nabokov .60 1.50
BU33 Patrick Marleau .75 2.00
BU34 Chris Pronger .75 2.00
BU35 Martin St. Louis .75 2.00
BU36 Vincent Lecavalier .75 2.00
BU37 Nikolai Khabibulin .75 2.00
BU38 Ed Belfour .75 2.00
BU39 Mats Sundin .75 2.00
BU40 Bryan McCabe .50 1.25
BU41 Markus Naslund .75 2.00
BU42 Ed Jovanovski .60 1.50

2005-06 Upper Deck Victory Game Breakers

COMPLETE SET (45) 8.00 20.00
GB1 Sergei Fedorov .40 1.00
GB2 Dany Heatley .20 .50
GB3 Ilya Kovalchuk .25 .60
GB4 Glen Murray .20 .50
GB5 Joe Thornton .40 1.00
GB6 Chris Drury .20 .50
GB7 Eric Daze .20 .50
GB8 Tuomo Ruutu .25 .60
GB9 Peter Forsberg .50 1.25
GB10 Joe Sakic .50 1.25
GB11 Milan Hejduk .20 .50
GB12 Paul Kariya .25 .60
GB13 Rick Nash .25 .60
GB14 Mike Modano .40 1.00
GB15 Bill Guerin .25 .60
GB16 Brendan Shanahan .25 .60
GB17 Steve Yzerman .60 1.50
GB18 Kris Draper .30 .75
GB19 Henrik Zetterberg .30 .75
GB20 Ryan Smyth .20 .50
GB21 Olli Jokinen .25 .60
GB22 Zigmund Palffy .25 .60
GB23 Marian Gaborik .25 .60
GB24 Michael Ryder .20 .50
GB25 Saku Koivu .25 .60
GB26 Steve Sullivan .15 .40
GB27 Alexei Yashin .20 .50
GB28 Jaromir Jagr .75 2.00
GB29 Marian Hossa .25 .60
GB30 Martin Havlat .25 .60
GB31 Peter Bondra .25 .60
GB32 Keith Primeau .20 .50
GB33 Simon Gagne .25 .60
GB34 Brett Hull .50 1.25
GB35 Shane Doan .20 .50
GB36 Mario Lemieux 1.00 2.50
GB37 Patrick Marleau .25 .60
GB38 Pavol Demitra .30 .75
GB39 Keith Tkachuk .25 .60
GB40 Martin St. Louis .25 .60
GB41 Vincent Lecavalier .25 .60
GB42 Brad Richards .25 .60
GB43 Alexander Mogilny .20 .50
GB44 Mats Sundin .25 .60
GB45 Markus Naslund .25 .60

2005-06 Upper Deck Victory Stars on Ice

COMPLETE SET (45) 8.00 20.00
SI1 Jean-Sebastien Giguere .25 .60
SI2 Dany Heatley .20 .50
SI3 Ilya Kovalchuk .25 .60
SI4 Joe Thornton .40 1.00
SI5 Andrew Raycroft .20 .50
SI6 Miroslav Satan .20 .50
SI7 Jarome Iginla .30 .75
SI8 Miikka Kiprusoff .25 .60
SI9 Jeff O'Neill .15 .40
SI10 Jocelyn Thibault .20 .50
SI11 Joe Sakic .50 1.25
SI12 Peter Forsberg .50 1.25
SI13 Alex Tanguay .25 .60
SI14 Rob Blake .25 .60
SI15 David Aebischer .20 .50
SI16 Rick Nash .25 .60
SI17 Marty Turco .25 .60
SI18 Sergei Zubov .20 .50
SI19 Mike Modano .40 1.00
SI20 Nicklas Lidstrom .25 .60
SI21 Steve Yzerman .60 1.50
SI22 Robert Lang .15 .40
SI23 Roberto Luongo .40 1.00
SI24 Luc Robitaille .25 .60
SI25 Jose Theodore .25 .60
SI26 Martin Brodeur .60 1.50
SI27 Scott Stevens .25 .60
SI28 Eric Lindros .40 1.00
SI29 Dominik Hasek .40 1.00
SI30 Daniel Alfredsson .25 .60
SI31 Jason Spezza .25 .60
SI32 Jeremy Roenick .40 1.00
SI33 John LeClair .25 .60
SI34 Brett Hull .50 1.25
SI35 Mario Lemieux 1.00 2.50
SI36 Evgeni Nabokov .20 .50
SI37 Keith Tkachuk .25 .60
SI38 Doug Weight .25 .60
SI39 Martin St. Louis .25 .60
SI40 Nikolai Khabibulin .25 .60
SI41 Ed Belfour .25 .60
SI42 Brian Leetch .20 .50
SI43 Mats Sundin .25 .60
SI44 Markus Naslund .25 .60
SI45 Ed Jovanovski .20 .50

2006-07 Upper Deck Victory

1 Jean-Sebastien Giguere .15 .40
2 Joffrey Lupul .10 .25
3 Teemu Selanne .30 .75
4 Andy McDonald .12 .30
5 Scott Niedermayer .15 .40
6 Ilya Bryzgalov .15 .40
7 Ilya Kovalchuk .15 .40
8 Kari Lehtonen .12 .30
9 Marian Hossa .15 .40
10 Marc Savard .10 .25
11 Slava Kozlov .10 .25
12 Patrice Bergeron .20 .50
13 Tim Thomas .15 .40
14 Brian Leetch .12 .30
15 Glen Murray .12 .30
16 Brad Boyes .10 .25
17 Marco Sturm .10 .25
18 Brad Stuart .10 .25
19 Andrew Raycroft .12 .30
20 Chris Drury .12 .30
21 Ryan Miller .15 .40
22 Thomas Vanek .12 .30
23 Tim Connolly .10 .25
24 Maxim Afinogenov .10 .25
25 Martin Biron .12 .30
26 Ales Kotalik .10 .25
27 Daniel Briere .15 .40
28 Miikka Kiprusoff .15 .40
29 Jarome Iginla .20 .50
30 Dion Phaneuf .12 .30
31 Daymond Langkow .10 .25
32 Chuck Kobasew .10 .25
33 Kristian Huselius .10 .25
34 Cam Ward .15 .40
35 Eric Staal .20 .50
36 Mark Recchi .20 .50
37 Doug Weight .15 .40
38 Justin Williams .12 .30
39 Erik Cole .10 .25
40 Rod Brind`Amour .15 .40
41 Tuomo Ruutu .15 .40
42 Nikolai Khabibulin .15 .40
43 Kyle Calder .10 .25
44 Brent Seabrook .10 .25
45 Mark Bell .10 .25
46 Pavel Vorobiev .10 .25
47 Joe Sakic .30 .75
48 Jose Theodore .15 .40
49 Marek Svatos .10 .25
50 Milan Hejduk .12 .30
51 Alex Tanguay .10 .25
52 Rob Blake .15 .40
53 Andrew Brunette .10 .25
54 Rick Nash .15 .40
55 David Vyborny .10 .25
56 Marc Denis .12 .30
57 Nikolai Zherdev .10 .25
58 Sergei Fedorov .25 .60
59 Pascal Leclaire .12 .30
60 Mike Modano .25 .60
61 Marty Turco .15 .40
62 Jussi Jokinen .12 .30
63 Brenden Morrow .12 .30
64 Sergei Zubov .12 .30
65 Jere Lehtinen .10 .25
66 Bill Guerin .15 .40
67 Jason Arnott .12 .30
68 Steve Yzerman .40 1.00
69 Pavel Datsyuk .25 .60
70 Brendan Shanahan .15 .40
71 Manny Legace .12 .30
72 Nicklas Lidstrom .15 .40
73 Henrik Zetterberg .20 .50
74 Tomas Holmstrom .12 .30
75 Kris Draper .10 .25
76 Ryan Smyth .12 .30
77 Shawn Horcoff .10 .25
78 Ales Hemsky .12 .30
79 Chris Pronger .15 .40
80 Dwayne Roloson .12 .30
81 Michael Peca .12 .30
82 Raffi Torres .10 .25
83 Roberto Luongo .25 .60
84 Nathan Horton .15 .40
85 Olli Jokinen .15 .40
86 Jay Bouwmeester .10 .25
87 Mike Van Ryn .10 .25
88 Joe Nieuwendyk .12 .30
89 Mathieu Garon .12 .30
90 Dustin Brown .15 .40
91 Alexander Frolov .10 .25
92 Pavol Demitra .20 .50
93 Craig Conroy .10 .25
94 Mike Cammalleri .10 .25
95 Lubomir Visnovsky .10 .25
96 Marian Gaborik .15 .40
97 Manny Fernandez .10 .25
98 Brian Rolston .12 .30
99 Pierre-Marc Bouchard .15 .40
100 Wes Walz .10 .25
101 Mikko Koivu .12 .30
102 David Aebischer .12 .30
103 Saku Koivu .15 .40
104 Alex Kovalev .12 .30
105 Michael Ryder .10 .25
106 Chris Higgins .10 .25
107 Mike Ribeiro .10 .25
108 Cristobal Huet .12 .30
109 Paul Kariya .15 .40
110 Tomas Vokoun .12 .30
111 Steve Sullivan .10 .25
112 Martin Erat .10 .25
113 Kimmo Timonen .10 .25
114 Scott Hartnell .10 .25
115 David Legwand .12 .30
116 Martin Brodeur .40 1.00
117 Brian Gionta .10 .25
118 Scott Gomez .12 .30
119 Patrik Elias .15 .40
120 Brian Rafalski .12 .30
121 Zach Parise .15 .40
122 Alexei Yashin .12 .30
123 Rick DiPietro .12 .30
124 Miroslav Satan .12 .30
125 Jason Blake .10 .25
126 Mike York .10 .25
127 Alexei Zhitnik .10 .25
128 Trent Hunter .10 .25
129 Henrik Lundqvist .40 1.00
130 Jaromir Jagr .50 1.25
131 Martin Straka .10 .25
132 Petr Prucha .12 .30
133 Michael Nylander .10 .25
134 Fedor Tyutin .10 .25
135 Jason Spezza .15 .40
136 Dany Heatley .12 .30
137 Dominik Hasek .25 .60
138 Daniel Alfredsson .15 .40
139 Zdeno Chara .15 .40
140 Wade Redden .10 .25
141 Martin Havlat .10 .25
142 Ray Emery .12 .30
143 Peter Forsberg .30 .75
144 Antero Niittymaki .12 .30
145 Simon Gagne .15 .40
146 Joni Pitkanen .10 .25
147 Keith Primeau .12 .30
148 Jeff Carter .12 .30
149 Mike Richards .12 .30
150 Robert Esche .12 .30
151 Shane Doan .12 .30
152 Curtis Joseph .20 .50
153 Ladislav Nagy .10 .25
154 Mike Comrie .12 .30
155 Geoff Sanderson .10 .25
156 Keith Ballard .10 .25
157 Sidney Crosby .60 1.50
158 Ryan Malone .10 .25
159 Marc-Andre Fleury .30 .75
160 Sergei Gonchar .10 .25
161 Colby Armstrong .12 .30
162 Ryan Whitney .12 .30
163 Joe Thornton .25 .60
164 Evgeni Nabokov .12 .30
165 Patrick Marleau .15 .40
166 Jonathan Cheechoo .12 .30
167 Vesa Toskala .12 .30
168 Steve Bernier .10 .25
169 Curtis Sanford .12 .30
170 Lee Stempniak .10 .25
171 Keith Tkachuk .15 .40
172 Scott Young .10 .25
173 Petr Cajanek .10 .25
174 Barret Jackman .10 .25
175 Evgeni Artyukhin .10 .25
176 Vaclav Prospal .10 .25
177 Martin St. Louis .15 .40
178 Vincent Lecavalier .15 .40
179 Sean Burke .10 .25
180 Brad Richards .15 .40
181 Fredrik Modin .10 .25
182 Tie Domi .12 .30
183 Mats Sundin .15 .40
184 Ed Belfour .15 .40
185 Eric Lindros .25 .60
186 Bryan McCabe .10 .25
187 Alexander Steen .10 .25
188 Darcy Tucker .12 .30
189 Jason Allison .12 .30
190 Henrik Sedin .20 .50
191 Alex Auld .10 .25
192 Markus Naslund .15 .40
193 Brendan Morrison .10 .25
194 Ed Jovanovski .12 .30
195 Mattias Ohlund .10 .25
196 Daniel Sedin .20 .50
197 Jeff Halpern .10 .25
198 Dainius Zubrus .10 .25
199 Alexander Ovechkin .60 1.50
200 Olaf Kolzig .15 .40
201 Tomas Kopecky RC .40 1.00
202 Billy Thompson RC .30 .75
203 Dustin Byfuglien RC .75 2.00
204 Yan Stastny RC .30 .75
205 Eric Fehr RC .50 1.25
206 Bon Ondrus RC .30 .75
207 Rob Collins RC .30 .75
208 Brendan Bell RC .30 .75
209 Frank Doyle RC .40 1.00
210 Noah Welch RC .30 .75
211 Filip Novak RC .30 .75
212 Ian White RC .40 1.00
213 Konstantin Pushkarev RC .40 1.00
214 Dan Jancevski RC .30 .75
215 Shea Weber RC .75 2.00
216 Michel Ouellet RC .40 1.00
217 Marc-Antoine Pouliot RC .30 .75
218 Carsen Germyn RC .30 .75
219 Matt Carle RC .30 .75
220 Steve Regier RC .30 .75
221 Mark Stuart RC .30 .75
222 Bill Thomas RC .30 .75
223 Jarkko Immonen RC .40 1.00
224 Erik Reitz RC .30 .75
225 Joel Perrault RC .30 .75
226 Ryan Potulny RC .30 .75
227 Jeremy Williams RC .30 .75
228 Masi Marjamaki RC .30 .75
229 Miroslav Kopriva RC .30 .75
230 Matt Koalska RC .30 .75
231 Chris Pronger .50 1.25
232 Zdeno Chara .50 1.25
233 Marc Savard .30 .75
234 Hannu Toivonen .12 .30
235 Alex Tanguay .10 .25
236 Martin Havlat .10 .25
237 Michal Handzus .12 .30
238 Wojtek Wolski .12 .30
239 Jordan Leopold .10 .25
240 Fredrik Modin .10 .25
241 Gilbert Brule .12 .30
242 Anson Carter .12 .30
243 Mike Ribeiro .10 .25
244 Eric Lindros .25 .60
245 Patrik Stefan .10 .25
246 Jeff Halpern .10 .25
247 Dominik Hasek .25 .60
248 Joffrey Lupul .10 .25
249 Petr Sykora .12 .30
250 Todd Bertuzzi .15 .40
251 Ed Belfour .15 .40

252 Alexander Auld .10 .25
253 Rob Blake .15 .40
254 Dan Cloutier .12 .30
255 Pavol Demitra .20 .50
256 Mark Parrish .10 .25
257 Sergei Samsonov .12 .30
258 Jason Arnott .12 .30
259 Mike Sillinger .10 .25
260 Brendan Shanahan .15 .40
261 Matt Cullen .10 .25
262 Martin Gerber .12 .30
263 Kyle Calder .10 .25
264 Geoff Sanderson .10 .25
265 Owen Nolan .15 .40
266 Ed Jovanovski .12 .30
267 Jeremy Roenick .25 .60
268 Mark Recchi .20 .50
269 Nils Ekman .10 .25
270 Mark Bell .10 .25
271 Mike Grier .10 .25
272 Doug Weight .15 .40
273 Bill Guerin .15 .40
274 Manny Legace .12 .30
275 Marc Denis .12 .30
276 Andrew Raycroft .12 .30
277 Michael Peca .12 .30
278 Kyle Wellwood .12 .30
279 Roberto Luongo .25 .60
280 Alexander Semin .15 .40
281 Shane O'Brien RC .30 .75
282 Jonas Johansson RC .30 .75
283 Ryan Shannon RC .30 .75
284 Patrick O'Sullivan RC .50 1.25
285 Anze Kopitar RC 2.50 6.00
286 John Oduya RC .50 1.25
287 Travis Zajac RC .60 1.50
288 Fredrik Norrena RC .30 .75
289 Phil Kessel RC 2.50 6.00
290 Guillaume Latendresse RC .50 1.25
291 Nigel Dawes RC .30 .75
292 Jordan Staal RC .75 2.00
293 Kristopher Letang RC 1.25 3.00
294 Paul Stastny RC .75 2.00
295 Niklas Backstrom RC .60 1.50
296 D.J. King RC .30 .75
297 Marc-Edouard Vlasic RC .50 1.25
298 Patrick Thoresen RC .30 .75
299 Ladislav Smid RC .30 .75
300 Loui Eriksson RC .60 1.50
301 Patrick Fischer RC .30 .75
302 Mikko Lehtonen RC .40 1.00
303 Roman Polak RC .40 1.00
304 Evgeni Malkin RC 6.00 15.00
305 Luc Bourdon RC .50 1.25
306 Alexei Kaigorodov RC .30 .75
307 Alex Brooks RC .30 .75
308 Nate Thompson RC .30 .75
309 Janis Sprukts RC .30 .75
310 Alexander Radulov RC .60 1.50
311 Keith Yandle RC .75 2.00
312 Enver Lisin RC .30 .75
313 Cole Jarrett RC .30 .75
314 Ryan Caldwell RC .30 .75
315 David Printz RC .30 .75
316 David Liffiton RC .30 .75
317 Adam Burish RC .50 1.25
318 Dave Bolland RC .50 1.25
319 Michael Blunden RC .30 .75
320 Matt Lashoff RC .30 .75
321 Alexei Mikhnov RC .30 .75
322 Jan Hejda RC .30 .75
323 Lars Jonsson RC .30 .75
324 Triston Grant RC .30 .75
325 Alexander Edler RC .50 1.25
326 Brandon Prust RC .30 .75
327 Dustin Boyd RC .30 .75
328 Drew Stafford RC .50 1.25
329 Kelly Guard RC .40 1.00
330 Nathan McIver RC .30 .75

2006-07 Upper Deck Victory Gold

*1-200 VETS: 5X TO 12X BASIC CARDS
*201-230 ROOK: 1.5X TO 4X BASIC RC

2006-07 Upper Deck Victory Game Breakers

COMPLETE SET (50) 60.00 125.00
GB1 Jean-Sebastien Giguere 1.25 3.00
GB2 Ilya Kovalchuk 1.25 3.00
GB3 Marian Hossa 1.25 3.00
GB4 Patrice Bergeron 1.50 4.00
GB5 Jarome Iginla 1.50 4.00
GB6 Miikka Kiprusoff 1.25 3.00
GB7 Eric Staal 1.50 4.00
GB8 Martin Gerber 1.00 2.50
GB9 Nikolai Khabibulin 1.25 3.00
GB10 Joe Sakic 2.50 6.00
GB11 Alex Tanguay .75 2.00
GB12 Marek Svatos .75 2.00
GB13 Rick Nash 1.25 3.00
GB14 Mike Modano 2.00 5.00
GB15 Marty Turco 1.25 3.00
GB16 Henrik Zetterberg 1.50 4.00
GB17 Pavel Datsyuk 2.00 5.00
GB18 Brendan Shanahan 1.25 3.00
GB19 Roberto Luongo 2.00 5.00
GB20 Olli Jokinen 1.25 3.00
GB21 Alexander Frolov .75 2.00
GB22 Marian Gaborik 1.25 3.00
GB23 Saku Koivu 1.25 3.00
GB24 Alex Kovalev 1.00 2.50
GB25 Michael Ryder .75 2.00
GB26 Paul Kariya 1.25 3.00
GB27 Tomas Vokoun 1.00 2.50
GB28 Martin Brodeur 3.00 8.00
GB29 Patrik Elias 1.25 3.00
GB30 Jaromir Jagr 4.00 10.00
GB31 Henrik Lundqvist 3.00 8.00
GB32 Jason Spezza 1.25 3.00
GB33 Dany Heatley 1.00 2.50
GB34 Daniel Alfredsson 1.25 3.00
GB35 Dominik Hasek 2.00 5.00
GB36 Simon Gagne 1.25 3.00
GB37 Jeff Carter 1.00 2.50
GB38 Peter Forsberg 2.50 6.00
GB39 Shane Doan 1.00 2.50
GB40 Sidney Crosby 5.00 12.00
GB41 Marc-Andre Fleury 2.50 6.00
GB42 Joe Thornton 2.00 5.00
GB43 Patrick Marleau 1.25 3.00
GB44 Jonathan Cheechoo 1.00 2.50
GB45 Martin St. Louis 1.25 3.00
GB46 Vincent Lecavalier 1.25 3.00
GB47 Ed Belfour 1.25 3.00
GB48 Mats Sundin 1.25 3.00
GB49 Markus Naslund 1.25 3.00
GB50 Alexander Ovechkin 5.00 12.00

2006-07 Upper Deck Victory Next In Line

COMPLETE SET (50) 25.00 60.00
NL1 Corey Perry 1.50 4.00
NL2 Joffrey Lupul .60 1.50
NL3 Ryan Getzlaf 1.00 2.50
NL4 Ilya Kovalchuk 1.00 2.50
NL5 Kari Lehtonen .75 2.00
NL6 Patrice Bergeron 1.25 3.00
NL7 Andrew Raycroft .75 2.00
NL8 Brad Boyes .60 1.50
NL9 Thomas Vanek .75 2.00
NL10 Ryan Miller 1.00 2.50
NL11 Dion Phaneuf .75 2.00
NL12 Eric Staal 1.25 3.00
NL13 Cam Ward 1.00 2.50
NL14 Tuomo Ruutu 1.00 2.50
NL15 Marek Svatos .60 1.50
NL16 Rick Nash 1.00 2.50
NL17 Nikolai Zherdev .60 1.50
NL18 Gilbert Brule .75 2.00
NL19 Jussi Jokinen .75 2.00
NL20 Henrik Zetterberg 1.25 3.00
NL21 Ales Hemsky .75 2.00
NL22 Jarret Stoll .75 2.00
NL23 Nathan Horton 1.00 2.50
NL24 Rostislav Olesz .60 1.50
NL25 Alexander Frolov .60 1.50
NL26 Mike Cammalleri .60 1.50
NL27 Marian Gaborik 1.00 2.50
NL28 Mikko Koivu .75 2.00
NL29 Yann Danis .75 2.00
NL30 Alexander Perezhogin .60 1.50
NL31 Zach Parise 1.00 2.50
NL32 Rick DiPietro .75 2.00
NL33 Henrik Lundqvist 2.50 6.00
NL34 Petr Prucha .75 2.00
NL35 Jason Spezza 1.00 2.50
NL36 Dany Heatley .75 2.00
NL37 Jeff Carter .75 2.00
NL38 Mike Richards .75 2.00
NL39 Joni Pitkanen .60 1.50
NL40 Marc-Andre Fleury 2.00 5.00
NL41 Sidney Crosby 4.00 10.00
NL42 Jonathan Cheechoo .75 2.00
NL43 Evgeni Artyukhin .60 1.50
NL44 Matt Stajan .60 1.50
NL45 Alexander Steen .60 1.50
NL46 Ryan Kesler 1.00 2.50
NL47 Alex Auld .60 1.50
NL48 Alexander Ovechkin 4.00 10.00
NL49 Erik Cole .60 1.50
NL50 Kyle Wellwood .75 2.00

2006-07 Upper Deck Victory Jumbos

AF Alexander Frolov 2.00 5.00
AH Ales Hemsky 2.50 6.00
AO Alexander Ovechkin 12.00 30.00
AT Alex Tanguay 2.00 5.00
BB Brad Boyes 2.00 5.00
CP Chris Pronger 3.00 8.00
DA Daniel Alfredsson 3.00 8.00
DH Dany Heatley 2.50 6.00
ES Eric Staal 4.00 10.00
HL Henrik Lundqvist 8.00 20.00
HZ Henrik Zetterberg 4.00 10.00
IK Ilya Kovalchuk 3.00 8.00
JC Jonathan Cheechoo 2.50 6.00
JG Jean-Sebastien Giguere 3.00 8.00
JI Jarome Iginla 4.00 10.00
JJ Jaromir Jagr 10.00 25.00
JS Joe Sakic 6.00 15.00
JT Joe Thornton 5.00 12.00
KL Kari Lehtonen 2.50 6.00
MB Martin Brodeur 8.00 20.00
MG Marian Gaborik 3.00 8.00
MK Miikka Kiprusoff 3.00 8.00
MM Mike Modano 5.00 12.00
MN Markus Naslund 3.00 8.00
MR Michael Ryder 2.00 5.00
MS Martin St. Louis 3.00 8.00
MT Marty Turco 3.00 8.00
NK Nikolai Khabibulin 3.00 8.00
PB Patrice Bergeron 4.00 10.00
PD Pavel Datsyuk 5.00 12.00
PF Peter Forsberg 6.00 15.00
PK Paul Kariya 5.00 12.00
RL Roberto Luongo 5.00 12.00
RM Ryan Miller 3.00 8.00
RN Rick Nash 3.00 8.00
SC Sidney Crosby 12.00 30.00
SD Shane Doan 2.50 6.00
SG Simon Gagne 3.00 8.00
SK Saku Koivu 3.00 8.00
SP Jason Spezza 3.00 8.00
SU Mats Sundin 3.00 8.00
VL Vincent Lecavalier 3.00 8.00

2007-08 Upper Deck Victory

COMPLETE SET (345) 30.00 60.00
COMP.SET w/o SPs (200) 12.00 30.00
1 Martin Brodeur .60 1.50
2 Zach Parise .25 .60
3 Brian Rafalski .20 .50
4 Scott Gomez .20 .50
5 Brian Gionta .15 .40
6 Travis Zajac .15 .40
7 Patrik Elias .25 .60
8 Marc-Andre Fleury .50 1.25
9 Evgeni Malkin .50 1.25
10 Mark Recchi .30 .75
11 Jordan Staal .20 .50
12 Ryan Whitney .20 .50
13 Sergei Gonchar .15 .40
14 Sidney Crosby 1.00 2.50
15 Rick DiPietro .20 .50
16 Jason Blake .15 .40
17 Viktor Kozlov .15 .40
18 Ryan Smyth .20 .50
19 Alexei Yashin .20 .50
20 Miroslav Satan .20 .50
21 Henrik Lundqvist .60 1.50
22 Martin Straka .15 .40
23 Brendan Shanahan .25 .60
24 Michael Nylander .15 .40
25 Sean Avery .15 .40
26 Jaromir Jagr .75 2.00
27 Martin Biron .20 .50
28 Jeff Carter .20 .50
29 Joni Pitkanen .15 .40
30 Mike Knuble .15 .40
31 Mike Richards .20 .50
32 Simon Gagne .25 .60
33 Ryan Miller .25 .60
34 Maxim Afinogenov .15 .40
35 Thomas Vanek .20 .50
36 Drew Stafford .15 .40
37 Jason Pominville .15 .40
38 Chris Drury .20 .50
39 Derek Roy .15 .40
40 Daniel Briere .25 .60
41 Ray Emery .20 .50
42 Jason Spezza .25 .60
43 Mike Fisher .15 .40
44 Wade Redden .15 .40
45 Daniel Alfredsson .25 .60
46 Dany Heatley .20 .50
47 Cristobal Huet .20 .50
48 Alex Kovalev .20 .50
49 Guillaume Latendresse .20 .50
50 Sheldon Souray .15 .40
51 Michael Ryder .15 .40
52 Chris Higgins .15 .40
53 Saku Koivu .25 .60
54 Andrew Raycroft .20 .50
55 Alexander Steen .15 .40
56 Tomas Kaberle .15 .40
57 Darcy Tucker .20 .50
58 Jeff O'Neill .15 .40
59 Bryan McCabe .15 .40
60 Mats Sundin .25 .60
61 Tim Thomas .25 .60
62 Marc Savard .15 .40
63 Marco Sturm .15 .40
64 Zdeno Chara .25 .60
65 Glen Murray .20 .50
66 Phil Kessel .25 .60
67 Patrice Bergeron .30 .75
68 Johan Holmqvist .20 .50
69 Dan Boyle .15 .40
70 Brad Richards .25 .60
71 Vaclav Prospal .15 .40
72 Vincent Lecavalier .25 .60
73 Martin St. Louis .25 .60
74 Kari Lehtonen .20 .50
75 Slava Kozlov .15 .40
76 Keith Tkachuk .25 .60
77 Marian Hossa .25 .60
78 Scott Mellanby .15 .40
79 Ilya Kovalchuk .25 .60
80 Cam Ward .25 .60
81 Erik Cole .15 .40
82 Justin Williams .20 .50
83 Cory Stillman .15 .40
84 Rod Brind'Amour .25 .60
85 Eric Staal .30 .75
86 Ed Belfour .25 .60
87 Nathan Horton .25 .60
88 Jay Bouwmeester .15 .40
89 Stephen Weiss .15 .40
90 Jozef Stumpel .15 .40
91 Olli Jokinen .20 .50
92 Olaf Kolzig .25 .60
93 Alexander Semin .25 .60
94 Chris Clark .15 .40
95 Matt Pettinger .15 .40
96 Eric Fehr .15 .40
97 Alexander Ovechkin 1.00 2.50
98 Dominik Hasek .40 1.00
99 Tomas Holmstrom .20 .50
100 Pavel Datsyuk .40 1.00
101 Nicklas Lidstrom .25 .60
102 Dan Cleary .20 .50
103 Kris Draper .15 .40
104 Henrik Zetterberg .30 .75
105 Tomas Vokoun .20 .50
106 Paul Kariya .25 .60
107 Chris Mason .20 .50
108 Kimmo Timonen .15 .40
109 Jason Arnott .20 .50
110 Steve Sullivan .15 .40
111 Peter Forsberg .50 1.25
112 Manny Legace .20 .50
113 Brad Boyes .15 .40
114 Doug Weight .25 .60
115 Lee Stempniak .15 .40
116 Barret Jackman .15 .40
117 Jay McClement .15 .40
118 Nikolai Khabibulin .25 .60
119 Jason Williams .15 .40
120 Tuomo Ruutu .25 .60
121 Duncan Keith .20 .50
122 Radim Vrbata .15 .40
123 Martin Havlat .25 .60
124 Fredrik Norrena .15 .40
125 David Vyborny .15 .40
126 Sergei Fedorov .40 1.00
127 Fredrik Modin .15 .40
128 Pascal Leclaire .20 .50
129 Gilbert Brule .20 .50
130 Rick Nash .25 .60
131 Roberto Luongo .40 1.00
132 Daniel Sedin .30 .75
133 Brendan Morrison .15 .40
134 Henrik Sedin .30 .75
135 Sami Salo .15 .40
136 Trevor Linden .25 .60
137 Markus Naslund .25 .60
138 Manny Fernandez .15 .40
139 Brian Rolston .20 .50
140 Pierre-Marc Bouchard .25 .60
141 Mikko Koivu .20 .50
142 Pavol Demitra .30 .75
143 Niklas Backstrom .25 .60
144 Marian Gaborik .25 .60
145 Miikka Kiprusoff .25 .60
146 Daymond Langkow .15 .40
147 Craig Conroy .15 .40
148 Dion Phaneuf .20 .50
149 Alex Tanguay .20 .50
150 Matthew Lombardi .15 .40
151 Jarome Iginla .30 .75
152 Peter Budaj .20 .50
153 Paul Stastny .20 .50
154 Milan Hejduk .20 .50
155 Wojtek Wolski .20 .50
156 Andrew Brunette .15 .40
157 Marek Svatos .15 .40
158 Jose Theodore .25 .60
159 Joe Sakic .50 1.25
160 Dwayne Roloson .20 .50
161 Raffi Torres .15 .40
162 Jarret Stoll .20 .50
163 Shawn Horcoff .15 .40
164 Joffrey Lupul .15 .40
165 Petr Sykora .20 .50
166 Ales Hemsky .20 .50
167 Jean-Sebastien Giguere .25 .60
168 Andy McDonald .20 .50
169 Scott Niedermayer .25 .60
170 Chris Kunitz .25 .60
171 Ryan Getzlaf .25 .60
172 Chris Pronger .25 .60
173 Corey Perry .40 1.00
174 Teemu Selanne .50 1.25
175 Vesa Toskala .20 .50
176 Jonathan Cheechoo .20 .50
177 Bill Guerin .25 .60
178 Evgeni Nabokov .20 .50
179 Milan Michalek .15 .40
180 Patrick Marleau .25 .60
181 Joe Thornton .40 1.00
182 Marty Turco .25 .60
183 Philippe Boucher .15 .40
184 Mike Ribeiro .15 .40
185 Eric Lindros .40 1.00
186 Brenden Morrow .20 .50
187 Ladislav Nagy .15 .40
188 Mike Modano .40 1.00
189 Mathieu Garon .20 .50
190 Lubomir Visnovsky .15 .40
191 Rob Blake .25 .60
192 Anze Kopitar .40 1.00
193 Mike Cammalleri .20 .50
194 Alexander Frolov .15 .40
195 Curtis Joseph .30 .75
196 Owen Nolan .25 .60
197 Shane Doan .20 .50
198 Ed Jovanovski .20 .50
199 Mikael Tellqvist .20 .50
200 Zbynek Michalek .15 .40
201 Jack Johnson RC .60 1.50
202 Mark Mancari RC .50 1.25
203 Daniel Girardi RC .60 1.50
204 Rich Peverley RC .50 1.25
205 David Clarkson RC .50 1.25
206 Tomi Maki RC .50 1.25
207 Petr Kalus RC .50 1.25
208 Bryan Bickell RC 1.00 2.50
209 Marc Methot RC .50 1.25
210 Robbie Schremp RC .60 1.50
211 Yutaka Fukufuji RC .60 1.50
212 Frans Nielsen RC .75 2.00
213 Colin Fraser RC .50 1.25
214 Aaron Rome RC .60 1.50
215 Martin Lojek RC .50 1.25
216 Ryan Parent RC .50 1.25
217 David Moss RC .75 2.00
218 Ryan Callahan RC 1.00 2.50
219 Patrick Kaleta RC .50 1.25
220 Mark Fraser RC .50 1.25
221 Tobias Stephan RC .60 1.50
222 Tomas Popperle RC .50 1.25
223 Jeff Schultz RC .60 1.50
224 Tom Gilbert RC .60 1.50
225 Jonathan Sigalet RC .50 1.25
226 Brandon Dubinsky RC 1.00 2.50
227 Jaroslav Halak RC 1.50 4.00
228 David Krejci RC 1.50 4.00
229 Andy Greene RC .60 1.50
230 Lauri Tukonen RC .50 1.25
231 Jeff Finger RC .50 1.25
232 Daniel Carcillo RC .60 1.50
233 Kent Huskins RC .50 1.25
234 John Zeiler RC .50 1.25
235 Zack Stortini RC .50 1.25
236 Matt Ellis RC .60 1.50
237 Joel Lundqvist RC .50 1.25
238 Duncan Milroy RC .50 1.25
239 Bryan Young RC .50 1.25
240 Danny Bois RC .50 1.25
241 Drew Fata RC .50 1.25
242 Krys Barch RC .60 1.50
243 Pierre Parenteau RC .60 1.50
244 Mathieu Roy RC .50 1.25
245 Jannik Hansen RC .60 1.50
246 Dainius Zubrus .15 .40
247 Petr Sykora .20 .50
248 Darryl Sydor .15 .40
249 Bill Guerin .25 .60
250 Mike Comrie .20 .50
251 Chris Drury .20 .50
252 Scott Gomez .20 .50
253 Daniel Briere .25 .60
254 Joffrey Lupul .15 .40
255 Tim Connolly .15 .40
256 Andrew Peters .15 .40
257 Patrick Eaves .15 .40
258 Chris Neil .15 .40
259 Bryan Smolinski .15 .40
260 Roman Hamrlik .15 .40
261 Vesa Toskala .20 .50
262 Jason Blake .15 .40
263 Manny Fernandez .15 .40
264 Michel Ouellet .15 .40
265 Todd White .15 .40
266 Ray Whitney .20 .50
267 Mike Commodore .15 .40
268 Tomas Vokoun .20 .50
269 Richard Zednik .15 .40
270 Viktor Kozlov .15 .40
271 Michael Nylander .15 .40
272 Brian Rafalski .20 .50
273 Mikael Samuelsson .15 .40
274 Alexander Radulov .25 .60
275 Paul Kariya .25 .60
276 Keith Tkachuk .25 .60
277 Robert Lang .15 .40
278 Sergei Samsonov .20 .50
279 Nikolai Zherdev .15 .40
280 Brendan Morrison .15 .40
281 Mark Parrish .15 .40
282 Owen Nolan .25 .60
283 Adrian Aucoin .15 .40
284 Ryan Smyth .20 .50
285 Joni Pitkanen .15 .40
286 Geoff Sanderson .15 .40
287 Todd Bertuzzi .25 .60
288 Mathieu Schneider .15 .40
289 Matt Carle .15 .40
290 Jere Lehtinen .15 .40
291 Jussi Jokinen .15 .40
292 Ladislav Nagy .15 .40
293 Kyle Calder .15 .40
294 Fredrik Sjostrom .15 .40
295 Nick Boynton .15 .40
296 Andrew Cogliano RC .75 2.00
297 Anton Stralman RC .60 1.50
298 Bobby Ryan RC 1.50 4.00
299 Brett Sterling RC .60 1.50
300 Brian Elliott RC 1.25 3.00
301 Bryan Little RC 1.00 2.50
302 Cal Clutterbuck RC 1.00 2.50
303 Carey Price RC 8.00 20.00
304 Cory Murphy RC .60 1.50
305 Curtis McElhinney RC 1.00 2.50
306 Daniel Winnik RC .75 2.00
307 David Perron RC 1.25 3.00
308 Denis Tolpeko RC .60 1.50
309 Devin Setoguchi RC 1.00 2.50
310 Erik Johnson RC 1.00 2.50
311 James Sheppard RC .60 1.50
312 Jared Boll RC .75 2.00
313 Jaroslav Hlinka RC .75 2.00
314 Jiri Tlusty RC 1.00 2.50
315 Jonathan Bernier RC 1.25 3.00
316 Jonathan Toews RC 5.00 12.00
317 Kris Russell RC 1.00 2.50
318 Kyle Chipchura RC 1.00 2.50
319 Lukas Kaspar RC .60 1.50
320 Marc Staal RC 1.00 2.50
321 Martin Hanzal RC .75 2.00
322 Mason Raymond RC 1.00 2.50
323 Matt Keetley RC .60 1.50
324 Matt Moulson RC 1.00 2.50
325 Matt Niskanen RC 1.00 2.50
326 Matt Smaby RC .60 1.50
327 Mike Lundin RC .60 1.50
328 Mike Weber RC .60 1.50
329 Milan Lucic RC 2.50 6.00
330 Nick Foligno RC 1.25 3.00
331 Nicklas Backstrom RC 2.00 5.00
332 Nicklas Bergfors RC .60 1.50
333 Olli Malmivaara RC .60 1.50
334 Ondrej Pavelec RC 1.25 3.00
335 Patrick Kane RC 10.00 25.00
336 Peter Mueller RC .75 2.00
337 Petteri Wirtanen RC .60 1.50
338 Sam Gagner RC 1.25 3.00
339 Stefan Meyer RC .75 2.00
340 Steve Wagner RC .60 1.50
341 Tobias Stephan RC .75 2.00
342 Torrey Mitchell RC .75 2.00
343 Tyler Kennedy RC .60 1.50
344 Tyler Weiman RC .75 2.00
345 Ville Koistinen RC .60 1.50

2007-08 Upper Deck Victory Gold

*GOLD VETS: 6X TO 15X BASIC CARDS
*GOLD ROOKIES: 3X TO 8X RC

2007-08 Upper Deck Victory EA Sports Face-Off

COMPLETE SET (6) 1.50 4.00
FO1 Jarome Iginla .60 1.50
FO2 Henrik Lundqvist 1.25 3.00
FO3 Eric Staal .60 1.50
FO4 Kris Draper .30 .75
FO5 Chris Pronger .50 1.25
FO6 Dion Phaneuf .40 1.00

2007-08 Upper Deck Victory GameBreakers

COMPLETE SET (50) 15.00 40.00
GB1 Sidney Crosby 2.50 6.00
GB2 Martin Brodeur 1.50 4.00
GB3 Joe Thornton 1.00 2.50
GB4 Saku Koivu .60 1.50
GB5 Daniel Alfredsson .60 1.50
GB6 Roberto Luongo 1.00 2.50
GB7 Chris Drury .50 1.25
GB8 Henrik Zetterberg .75 2.00
GB9 Ilya Kovalchuk .60 1.50
GB10 Jean-Sebastien Giguere .60 1.50
GB11 Mike Modano 1.00 2.50
GB12 Daniel Briere .60 1.50
GB13 Kari Lehtonen .50 1.25
GB14 Simon Gagne .60 1.50
GB15 Paul Kariya .60 1.50
GB16 Milan Hejduk .50 1.25
GB17 Dominik Hasek 1.00 2.50
GB18 Jonathan Cheechoo .50 1.25
GB19 Joe Sakic 1.25 3.00
GB20 Vincent Lecavalier .60 1.50
GB21 Cam Ward .60 1.50
GB22 Mats Sundin .60 1.50
GB23 Patrik Elias .60 1.50
GB24 Ryan Miller .60 1.50
GB25 Teemu Selanne 1.25 3.00
GB26 Jason Spezza .60 1.50
GB27 Tomas Vokoun .50 1.25
GB28 Ales Hemsky .50 1.25
GB29 Marian Hossa .60 1.50
GB30 Marc-Andre Fleury 1.25 3.00
GB31 Evgeni Malkin 1.25 3.00
GB32 Anze Kopitar 1.00 2.50
GB33 Olli Jokinen .50 1.25
GB34 Patrick Marleau .60 1.50
GB35 Dany Heatley .50 1.25
GB36 Paul Stastny .50 1.25
GB37 Marty Turco .60 1.50
GB38 Jarome Iginla .75 2.00
GB39 Eric Staal .75 2.00
GB40 Peter Forsberg 1.25 3.00
GB41 Andrew Raycroft .50 1.25
GB42 Martin St. Louis .60 1.50
GB43 Thomas Vanek .50 1.25
GB44 Pavel Datsyuk 1.00 2.50
GB45 Markus Naslund .60 1.50
GB46 Jaromir Jagr 2.00 5.00
GB47 Miikka Kiprusoff .60 1.50
GB48 Patrice Bergeron .75 2.00
GB49 Henrik Lundqvist 1.50 4.00
GB50 Alexander Ovechkin 2.50 6.00

2007-08 Upper Deck Victory Oversize Cards

COMPLETE SET (42) 30.00 60.00
OS1 Martin Brodeur 2.00 5.00
OS2 Marc-Andre Fleury 1.50 4.00
OS3 Evgeni Malkin 1.50 4.00
OS4 Sidney Crosby 3.00 8.00
OS5 Rick DiPietro .60 1.50
OS6 Henrik Lundqvist 2.00 5.00
OS7 Brendan Shanahan .75 2.00
OS8 Jaromir Jagr 2.50 6.00
OS9 Simon Gagne .75 2.00
OS10 Ryan Miller .75 2.00
OS11 Thomas Vanek .60 1.50
OS12 Jason Spezza .75 2.00
OS13 Dany Heatley .60 1.50
OS14 Michael Ryder .50 1.25
OS15 Saku Koivu .75 2.00
OS16 Andrew Raycroft .60 1.50
OS17 Mats Sundin .75 2.00
OS18 Patrice Bergeron 1.00 2.50
OS19 Vincent Lecavalier .75 2.00
OS20 Martin St. Louis .75 2.00
OS21 Kari Lehtonen .60 1.50
OS22 Ilya Kovalchuk .75 2.00
OS23 Eric Staal 1.00 2.50
OS24 Alexander Ovechkin 3.00 8.00
OS25 Dominik Hasek 1.25 3.00
OS26 Pavel Datsyuk 1.25 3.00
OS27 Henrik Zetterberg 1.00 2.50
OS28 Paul Kariya .75 2.00
OS29 Peter Forsberg 1.50 4.00
OS30 Rick Nash .75 2.00
OS31 Roberto Luongo 1.25 3.00
OS32 Markus Naslund .75 2.00
OS33 Marian Gaborik .75 2.00
OS34 Miikka Kiprusoff .75 2.00
OS35 Jarome Iginla 1.00 2.50
OS36 Joe Sakic 1.50 4.00
OS37 Dwayne Roloson .60 1.50
OS38 Jean-Sebastien Giguere .75 2.00
OS39 Jonathan Cheechoo .60 1.50
OS40 Joe Thornton 1.25 3.00
OS41 Mike Modano 1.25 3.00
OS42 Shane Doan .60 1.50

2007-08 Upper Deck Victory Stars on Ice

COMPLETE SET (50) 12.00 30.00
SI1 Roberto Luongo .75 2.00
SI2 Joe Thornton .75 2.00
SI3 Dion Phaneuf .40 1.00
SI4 Ryan Miller .50 1.25
SI5 Nicklas Lidstrom .50 1.25
SI6 Phil Kessel .50 1.25
SI7 Sergei Fedorov .75 2.00
SI8 Alexander Ovechkin 2.00 5.00
SI9 Jason Spezza .50 1.25
SI10 Brian Gionta .30 .75
SI11 Dany Heatley .40 1.00
SI12 Eric Staal .60 1.50
SI13 Teemu Selanne 1.00 2.50
SI14 Jonathan Cheechoo .40 1.00
SI15 Cristobal Huet .40 1.00
SI16 Jaromir Jagr 1.50 4.00
SI17 Ilya Kovalchuk .50 1.25
SI18 Saku Koivu .50 1.25
SI19 Joe Sakic 1.00 2.50
SI20 Andy McDonald .40 1.00
SI21 Jay Bouwmeester .30 .75
SI22 Ryan Getzlaf .50 1.25
SI23 Dominik Hasek .75 2.00
SI24 Scott Niedermayer .50 1.25
SI25 Simon Gagne .50 1.25
SI26 Martin St. Louis .50 1.25
SI27 Marian Hossa .50 1.25
SI28 Mats Sundin .50 1.25
SI29 Ryan Smyth .40 1.00
SI30 Martin Brodeur 1.25 3.00
SI31 Jordan Staal .40 1.00
SI32 Milan Hejduk .40 1.00
SI33 Rick Nash .50 1.25
SI34 Miikka Kiprusoff .50 1.25
SI35 Marty Turco .50 1.25
SI36 Patrice Bergeron .60 1.50
SI37 Vincent Lecavalier .50 1.25
SI38 Markus Naslund .50 1.25
SI39 Jarome Iginla .60 1.50
SI40 Henrik Zetterberg .60 1.50
SI41 Evgeni Malkin 1.00 2.50
SI42 Martin Havlat .50 1.25
SI43 Brendan Shanahan .50 1.25
SI44 Michael Ryder .30 .75
SI45 Patrick Marleau .50 1.25
SI46 Zach Parise .50 1.25
SI47 Daniel Briere .50 1.25
SI48 Marc-Andre Fleury 1.00 2.50
SI49 Tomas Kaberle .30 .75
SI50 Sidney Crosby 2.00 5.00

2008-09 Upper Deck Victory

COMPLETE SET (350) 25.00 60.00
COMP.SET w/o SPs (200) 12.00 30.00
COMP.UPDATE SET (100) 12.00 30.00
1 Olaf Kolzig .25 .60
2 Alexander Ovechkin 1.00 2.50
3 Nicklas Backstrom .25 .60
4 Alexander Semin .25 .60
5 Cristobal Huet .20 .50
6 Sergei Fedorov .40 1.00
7 Roberto Luongo .40 1.00
8 Daniel Sedin .30 .75
9 Henrik Sedin .30 .75
10 Ryan Kesler .25 .60
11 Alexander Edler .15 .40
12 Markus Naslund .25 .60
13 Brendan Morrison .15 .40
14 Mats Sundin .25 .60
15 Vesa Toskala .30 .75
16 Matt Stajan .15 .40
17 Darcy Tucker .20 .50
18 Tomas Kaberle .15 .40
19 Nikolai Antropov .20 .50
20 Alexander Steen .15 .40
21 Vincent Lecavalier .25 .60
22 Mike Smith .25 .60
23 Martin St. Louis .25 .60
24 Paul Ranger .15 .40
25 Jussi Jokinen .15 .40
26 Paul Kariya .25 .60
27 Manny Legace .25 .60
28 Lee Stempniak .15 .40
29 Erik Johnson .15 .40
30 Keith Tkachuk .25 .60
31 Brad Boyes .15 .40
32 Joe Thornton .40 1.00
33 Milan Michalek .15 .40
34 Evgeni Nabokov .20 .50
35 Jonathan Cheechoo .20 .50
36 Patrick Marleau .25 .60
37 Brian Campbell .20 .50
38 Sidney Crosby 1.00 2.50
39 Marc-Andre Fleury .50 1.25
40 Ryan Malone .15 .40
41 Evgeni Malkin .50 1.25
42 Jordan Staal .20 .50
43 Ty Conklin .20 .50
44 Marian Hossa .25 .60
45 Ilya Bryzgalov .20 .50
46 Shane Doan .20 .50
47 Peter Mueller .20 .50
48 Radim Vrbata .15 .40
49 Ed Jovanovski .20 .50
50 Martin Hanzal .20 .50
51 Mike Richards .20 .50
52 Daniel Briere .25 .60
53 Mike Knuble .15 .40
54 Martin Biron .20 .50
55 Jeff Carter .20 .50
56 R.J. Umberger .15 .40
57 Simon Gagne .25 .60
58 Daniel Alfredsson .25 .60
59 Jason Spezza .25 .60
60 Ray Emery .20 .50
61 Wade Redden .15 .40
62 Dany Heatley .20 .50
63 Martin Gerber .20 .50
64 Henrik Lundqvist .60 1.50
65 Scott Gomez .20 .50
66 Jaromir Jagr .75 2.00
67 Chris Drury .20 .50
68 Brendan Shanahan .25 .60
69 Marc Staal .15 .40
70 Michal Rozsival .15 .40
71 Rick DiPietro .20 .50
72 Bill Guerin .25 .60
73 Miroslav Satan .25 .60
74 Trent Hunter .15 .40
75 Mike Comrie .20 .50
76 Ruslan Fedotenko .15 .40
77 Martin Brodeur .60 1.50
78 Brian Gionta .15 .40
79 Travis Zajac .15 .40
80 Patrik Elias .25 .60
81 John Madden .15 .40
82 Zach Parise .25 .60
83 Jason Arnott .20 .50
84 Dan Ellis .15 .40
85 David Legwand .20 .50
86 J.P. Dumont .15 .40
87 Alexander Radulov .25 .60
88 Martin Erat .15 .40
89 Carey Price .50 1.25
90 Saku Koivu .25 .60
91 Andrei Kostitsyn .20 .50
92 Guillaume Latendresse .15 .40
93 Michael Ryder .15 .40
94 Alex Kovalev .20 .50
95 Chris Higgins .15 .40
96 Marian Gaborik .25 .60
97 Josh Harding .25 .60
98 Mikko Koivu .20 .50
99 Pierre-Marc Bouchard .25 .60
100 Brian Rolston .20 .50
101 Niklas Backstrom .25 .60
102 Anze Kopitar .40 1.00
103 Jack Johnson .15 .40
104 Patrick O'Sullivan .20 .50
105 Alexander Frolov .15 .40
106 Mike Cammalleri .20 .50
107 Dustin Brown .25 .60
108 Jason LaBarbera .20 .50
109 Olli Jokinen .20 .50
110 Tomas Vokoun .20 .50
111 Jay Bouwmeester .15 .40
112 Nathan Horton .20 .50
113 Stephen Weiss .15 .40
114 David Booth .15 .40
115 Dustin Penner .20 .50
116 Ales Hemsky .20 .50
117 Dwayne Roloson .20 .50
118 Sam Gagner .15 .40
119 Shawn Horcoff .15 .40
120 Jarret Stoll .20 .50
121 Andrew Cogliano .15 .40
122 Dominik Hasek .40 1.00
123 Nicklas Lidstrom .25 .60
124 Dan Cleary .20 .50
125 Pavel Datsyuk .40 1.00
126 Chris Osgood .25 .60

127 Valtteri Filppula .15 .40
128 Tomas Holmstrom .20 .50
129 Henrik Zetterberg .30 .75
130 Johan Holmqvist .20 .50
131 Brad Richards .25 .60
132 Mike Modano .40 1.00
133 Marty Turco .25 .60
134 Brenden Morrow .20 .50
135 Jere Lehtinen .15 .40
136 Sergei Zubov .20 .50
137 Mike Ribeiro .15 .40
138 Pascal Leclaire .20 .50
139 Rick Nash .25 .60
140 Nikolai Zherdev .15 .40
141 Gilbert Brule .15 .40
142 Michael Peca .20 .50
143 Peter Budaj .20 .50
144 Ryan Smyth .20 .50
145 Joe Sakic .50 1.25
146 Peter Forsberg .50 1.25
147 Milan Hejduk .20 .50
148 Paul Stastny .20 .50
149 Wojtek Wolski .20 .50
150 Patrick Kane .50 1.25
151 Nikolai Khabibulin .25 .60
152 Martin Havlat .25 .60
153 Jonathan Toews .40 1.00
154 Patrick Sharp .25 .60
155 Duncan Keith .20 .50
156 Robert Lang .15 .40
157 Cam Ward .25 .60
158 Ray Whitney .20 .50
159 Eric Staal .30 .75
160 Justin Williams .20 .50
161 Rod Brind`Amour .25 .60
162 Erik Cole .15 .40
163 Miikka Kiprusoff .25 .60
164 Jarome Iginla .30 .75
165 Matthew Lombardi .15 .40
166 Dion Phaneuf .20 .50
167 Kristian Huselius .15 .40
168 Daymond Langkow .15 .40
169 Alex Tanguay .15 .40
170 Steve Bernier .15 .40
171 Derek Roy .15 .40
172 Ryan Miller .25 .60
173 Drew Stafford .15 .40
174 Jason Pominville .15 .40
175 Thomas Vanek .20 .50
176 Ales Kotalik .15 .40
177 Tim Thomas .25 .60
178 Patrice Bergeron .30 .75
179 Milan Lucic .40 1.00
180 Zdeno Chara .25 .60
181 Phil Kessel .25 .60
182 Glen Murray .20 .50
183 Marc Savard .15 .40
184 Colby Armstrong .15 .40
185 Ilya Kovalchuk .25 .60
186 Kari Lehtonen .30 .75
187 Slava Kozlov .15 .40
188 Bobby Holik .15 .40
189 Todd White .15 .40
190 Johan Hedberg .20 .50
191 Teemu Selanne .50 1.25
192 Ryan Getzlaf .25 .60
193 Scott Niedermayer .25 .60
194 Jean-Sebastien Giguere .25 .60
195 Corey Perry .40 1.00
196 Chris Kunitz .25 .60
197 Chris Pronger .25 .60
198 George Parros .15 .40
199 Sidney Crosby CL 1.00 2.50
200 Alexander Ovechkin CL 1.00 2.50
201 Derick Brassard RC .60 1.50
202 Mark Fistric RC .50 1.25
203 Alex Goligoski RC .75 2.00
204 Claude Giroux RC 1.25 3.00
205 Jon Filewich RC .50 1.25
206 Robbie Earl RC .40 1.00
207 Ilya Zubov RC .50 1.25
208 Steve Mason RC 1.00 2.50
209 Brian Boyle RC .50 1.25
210 Shawn Matthias RC .60 1.50
211 Ryan Stone RC .40 1.00
212 Teddy Purcell RC .50 1.25
213 Mike Iggulden RC .50 1.25
214 Tim Ramholt RC .50 1.25
215 Dan LaCosta RC .60 1.50
216 Sami Lepisto RC .50 1.25
217 Danny Taylor RC .50 1.25
218 Tom Cavanagh RC .50 1.25
219 Andrew Murray RC .50 1.25
220 Kevin Doell RC .40 1.00
221 Tim Conboy RC .50 1.25
222 Pascal Pelletier RC .40 1.00
223 Chris Minard RC .60 1.50
224 Joey Mormina RC .50 1.25
225 Darryl Boyce RC .50 1.25
226 Cody McLeod RC .50 1.25
227 Jordan Hendry RC .50 1.25
228 Corey Locke RC .50 1.25
229 Mike Brown RC .50 1.25
230 B.J. Crombeen RC .40 1.00
231 David Brine RC .40 1.00
232 Joe Jensen RC .60 1.50
233 Kyle Greentree RC .60 1.50
234 Peter Vandermeer RC .40 1.00
235 Marc-Andre Gragnani RC .50 1.25
236 Andrew Ebbett RC .40 1.00
237 Erik Ersberg RC .50 1.25
238 Jonathan Ericsson RC .60 1.50
239 Theo Peckham RC .50 1.25
240 Darren Helm RC .60 1.50
241 Mattias Ritola RC .50 1.25
242 Clay Wilson RC .40 1.00
243 Brian Lee RC .50 1.25
244 Alex Foster RC .50 1.25
245 Kyle Okposo RC .75 2.00
246 Kyle Turris RC 1.00 2.50
247 Tyler Plante RC .50 1.25
248 Matt D'Agostini RC .50 1.25
249 Adam Pineault RC .50 1.25
250 Boris Valabik RC .60 1.50
251 Brendan Morrison .15 .40
252 Mathieu Schneider .15 .40
253 Ron Hainsey .15 .40
254 Patrick Lalime .20 .50
255 Todd Bertuzzi .25 .60
256 Mike Cammalleri .20 .50
257 Joni Pitkanen .15 .40
258 Brian Campbell .20 .50
259 Cristobal Huet .20 .50
260 Adam Foote .15 .40
261 Darcy Tucker .20 .50
262 Andrew Raycroft .20 .50
263 Kristian Huselius .15 .40
264 R.J. Umberger .15 .40
265 Sean Avery .15 .40
266 Marian Hossa .25 .60
267 Ty Conklin .20 .50
268 Lubomir Visnovsky .15 .40
269 Erik Cole .15 .40
270 Keith Ballard .15 .40
271 Cory Stillman .15 .40
272 Jarret Stoll .20 .50
273 Andrew Brunette .15 .40
274 Owen Nolan .25 .60
275 Marek Zidlicky .15 .40
276 Georges Laraque .20 .50
277 Alex Tanguay .15 .40
278 Brian Rolston .20 .50
279 Doug Weight .25 .60
280 Mark Streit .15 .40
281 Markus Naslund .25 .60
282 Nikolai Zherdev .15 .40
283 Wade Redden .15 .40
284 Olli Jokinen .20 .50
285 Eric Godard .15 .40
286 Miroslav Satan .25 .60
287 Ruslan Fedotenko .15 .40
288 Rob Blake .25 .60
289 Chris Mason .20 .50
290 Mark Recchi .30 .75
291 Radim Vrbata .15 .40
292 Ryan Malone .15 .40
293 Andrej Meszaros .15 .40
294 Matt Carle .15 .40
295 Gary Roberts .15 .40
296 Olaf Kolzig .25 .60
297 Curtis Joseph .30 .75
298 Pavol Demitra .30 .75
299 Steve Bernier .15 .40
300 Jose Theodore .25 .60
301 Steve MacIntyre RC .60 1.50
302 Jason Garrison RC .60 1.50
303 Darroll Powe RC .60 1.50
304 Mitch Fritz RC .50 1.25
305 Fabian Brunnstrom RC .50 1.25
306 Petr Vrana RC .40 1.00
307 Nathan Oystrick RC .60 1.50
308 Brett Skinner RC .50 1.25
309 Matthew Halischuk RC .40 1.00
310 Pierre-Luc Letourneau-Leblond RC .40 1.00
311 Paul Bissonnette RC .75 2.00
312 Brad Staubitz RC .50 1.25
313 Tyler Sloan RC .75 2.00
314 Andreas Nodl RC .40 1.00
315 Derek Dorsett RC .75 2.00
316 Nikita Filatov RC .60 1.50
317 Dwight Helminen RC .60 1.50
318 Nikolai Kulemin RC .60 1.50
319 Viktor Tikhonov RC .50 1.25
320 Kevin Porter RC .50 1.25
321 Zach Boychuk RC .60 1.50
322 Patrik Berglund RC .50 1.25
323 Mikkel Boedker RC .75 2.00
324 Zach Bogosian RC .75 2.00
325 Drew Doughty RC 1.50 4.00
326 Michael Frolik RC .60 1.50
327 Colton Gillies RC .50 1.25
328 Jamie McGinn RC .60 1.50
329 Patric Hornqvist RC .60 1.50
330 Ryan Jones RC .60 1.50
331 Steve Mason RC 1.00 2.50
332 Ben Bishop RC 1.00 2.50
333 Vladimir Mihalik RC .40 1.00
334 Jonas Frogren RC .40 1.00
335 Oscar Moller RC .50 1.25
336 James Neal RC 1.25 3.00
337 Janne Niskala RC .60 1.50
338 T.J. Oshie RC 1.25 3.00
339 Adam Pardy RC .50 1.25
340 Alex Pietrangelo RC 1.00 2.50
341 Chris Porter RC .60 1.50
342 Jared Ross RC .60 1.50
343 Anssi Salmela RC .60 1.50
344 Luca Sbisa RC .40 1.00
345 Luke Schenn RC .75 2.00
346 Wayne Simmonds RC 1.00 2.50
347 Blake Wheeler RC 1.50 4.00
348 Brandon Sutter RC .60 1.50
349 Jakub Voracek RC 1.25 3.00
350 Steven Stamkos RC 4.00 10.00

2008-09 Upper Deck Victory Black

*VETS: 8X TO 20X BASIC CARDS
*ROOKIES: 2.5X TO 6X BASIC RC
3 Nicklas Backstrom 5.00 12.00

2008-09 Upper Deck Victory Gold

*VETS: 4X TO 10X BASIC CARDS
*ROOKIES: 2X TO 5X BASIC RC
3 Nicklas Backstrom 2.50 6.00

2008-09 Upper Deck Victory Game Breakers

COMPLETE SET (50) 15.00 40.00
GB1 Sidney Crosby 2.00 5.00
GB2 Alexander Ovechkin 2.00 5.00
GB3 Roberto Luongo .75 2.00
GB4 Vincent Lecavalier .50 1.25
GB5 Miikka Kiprusoff .50 1.25
GB6 Joe Thornton .75 2.00
GB7 Ilya Kovalchuk .50 1.25
GB8 Martin Brodeur 1.25 3.00
GB9 Marian Gaborik .50 1.25
GB10 Henrik Zetterberg .60 1.50
GB11 Eric Staal .60 1.50
GB12 Mats Sundin .50 1.25
GB13 Anze Kopitar .75 2.00
GB14 Jaromir Jagr 1.50 4.00
GB15 Rick Nash .50 1.25
GB16 Patrick Kane 1.00 2.50
GB17 Dany Heatley .40 1.00
GB18 Paul Kariya .50 1.25
GB19 Jarome Iginla .60 1.50
GB20 Joe Sakic 1.00 2.50
GB21 Evgeni Malkin 1.00 2.50
GB22 Peter Mueller .40 1.00
GB23 Patrik Elias .50 1.25
GB24 Jean-Sebastien Giguere .50 1.25
GB25 Marian Hossa .50 1.25
GB26 Josh Harding .50 1.25
GB27 Marc-Andre Fleury 1.00 2.50
GB28 Nicklas Backstrom .50 1.25
GB29 Michael Ryder .30 .75
GB30 Carey Price 1.00 2.50
GB31 Sam Gagner .30 .75
GB32 Jonathan Cheechoo .40 1.00
GB33 Patrice Bergeron .60 1.50
GB34 Tomas Vokoun .40 1.00
GB35 Daniel Sedin .60 1.50
GB36 Phil Kessel .50 1.25
GB37 Daniel Alfredsson .50 1.25
GB38 Olli Jokinen .40 1.00
GB39 Jack Johnson .30 .75
GB40 Paul Stastny .40 1.00
GB41 Ryan Miller .50 1.25
GB42 Pavel Datsyuk .75 2.00
GB43 Jonathan Toews .75 2.00
GB44 Simon Gagne .50 1.25
GB45 Teemu Selanne 1.00 2.50
GB46 Mike Richards .40 1.00
GB47 Shane Doan .40 1.00
GB48 Martin St. Louis .50 1.25
GB49 Henrik Lundqvist 1.25 3.00
GB50 Alexander Radulov .50 1.25

2008-09 Upper Deck Victory Jumbos

COMPLETE SET (42) 40.00 100.00
OS1 Alexander Ovechkin 4.00 10.00
OS2 Roberto Luongo 1.50 4.00
OS3 Mats Sundin 1.00 2.50
OS4 Vincent Lecavalier 1.00 2.50
OS5 Martin St. Louis 1.00 2.50
OS6 Paul Kariya 1.00 2.50
OS7 Joe Thornton 1.50 4.00
OS8 Sidney Crosby 4.00 10.00
OS9 Evgeni Malkin 2.00 5.00
OS10 Peter Mueller .75 2.00
OS11 Simon Gagne 1.00 2.50
OS12 Jason Spezza 1.00 2.50
OS13 Dany Heatley .75 2.00
OS14 Jaromir Jagr 3.00 8.00
OS15 Brendan Shanahan 1.00 2.50
OS16 Martin Brodeur 2.50 6.00
OS17 Carey Price 2.00 5.00
OS18 Saku Koivu 1.00 2.50
OS19 Marian Gaborik 1.00 2.50
OS20 Anze Kopitar 1.50 4.00
OS21 Ales Hemsky .75 2.00
OS22 Sam Gagner .60 1.50
OS23 Dominik Hasek 1.50 4.00
OS24 Pavel Datsyuk 1.50 4.00
OS25 Henrik Zetterberg 1.25 3.00
OS26 Mike Modano 1.50 4.00
OS27 Marty Turco 1.00 2.50
OS28 Rick Nash 1.00 2.50
OS29 Joe Sakic 2.00 5.00
OS30 Peter Forsberg 2.00 5.00
OS31 Paul Stastny .75 2.00
OS32 Patrick Kane 2.00 5.00
OS33 Jonathan Toews 1.50 4.00
OS34 Eric Staal 1.25 3.00
OS35 Miikka Kiprusoff 1.00 2.50
OS36 Jarome Iginla 1.25 3.00
OS37 Ryan Miller 1.00 2.50
OS38 Thomas Vanek .75 2.00
OS39 Patrice Bergeron 1.25 3.00
OS40 Ilya Kovalchuk 1.00 2.50
OS41 Teemu Selanne 2.00 5.00
OS42 Ryan Getzlaf 1.00 2.50

2008-09 Upper Deck Victory Stars of the Game

COMPLETE SET (50) 20.00 50.00
SG1 Teemu Selanne 1.00 2.50
SG2 Ilya Kovalchuk .50 1.25
SG3 Jonathan Toews .75 2.00
SG4 Jarome Iginla .60 1.50
SG5 Dominik Hasek .75 2.00
SG6 Marian Gaborik .50 1.25
SG7 Jason Spezza .50 1.25
SG8 Thomas Vanek .40 1.00
SG9 Henrik Lundqvist 1.25 3.00
SG10 Simon Gagne .50 1.25
SG11 Brad Boyes .30 .75
SG12 Sidney Crosby 2.00 5.00
SG13 Anze Kopitar .75 2.00
SG14 Martin Brodeur 1.25 3.00
SG15 Patrice Bergeron .60 1.50
SG16 Vincent Lecavalier .50 1.25
SG17 Saku Koivu .50 1.25
SG18 Roberto Luongo .75 2.00
SG19 Rick Nash .50 1.25
SG20 Henrik Zetterberg .60 1.50
SG21 Michael Ryder .30 .75
SG22 Joe Sakic 1.00 2.50
SG23 Jaromir Jagr 1.50 4.00
SG24 Dany Heatley .40 1.00
SG25 Ryan Miller .50 1.25
SG26 Eric Staal .60 1.50
SG27 Mats Sundin .50 1.25
SG28 Sam Gagner .30 .75
SG29 Joe Thornton .75 2.00
SG30 Alexander Ovechkin 2.00 5.00
SG31 Miikka Kiprusoff .50 1.25
SG32 Mike Modano .75 2.00
SG33 Rick DiPietro .40 1.00
SG34 Paul Kariya .50 1.25
SG35 Patrick Kane 1.00 2.50
SG36 Alexander Radulov .50 1.25
SG37 Marty Turco .50 1.25
SG38 Ryan Getzlaf .50 1.25
SG39 Shane Doan .40 1.00
SG40 Evgeni Malkin 1.00 2.50
SG41 Pavel Datsyuk .75 2.00
SG42 Markus Naslund .50 1.25
SG43 Martin St. Louis .50 1.25
SG44 Paul Stastny .40 1.00
SG45 Tomas Vokoun .40 1.00
SG46 Zach Parise .50 1.25
SG47 Daniel Alfredsson .50 1.25
SG48 Marian Hossa .50 1.25
SG49 Carey Price 1.00 2.50
SG50 Brendan Shanahan .50 1.25

2009-10 Upper Deck Victory

COMPLETE SET (340) 75.00 150.00
COMP.SERIES 1 (250) 40.00 100.00
COMP.SET w/o SPs (200) 15.00 40.00
COMP.UPDATE SET (90) 20.00 50.00
1 Ryan Getzlaf .25 .60
2 Scott Niedermayer .25 .60
3 Jean-Sebastien Giguere .25 .60
4 Corey Perry .40 1.00
5 Chris Pronger .25 .60
6 Bryan Little .25 .60
7 Ilya Kovalchuk .25 .60
8 Kari Lehtonen .20 .50
9 Colby Armstrong .15 .40
10 Todd White .15 .40
11 Slava Kozlov .15 .40
12 Michael Ryder .15 .40
13 David Krejci .25 .60
14 Patrice Bergeron .30 .75
15 Blake Wheeler .25 .60
16 Zdeno Chara .25 .60
17 Phil Kessel .25 .60
18 Tim Thomas .25 .60
19 Marc Savard .15 .40
20 Clarke MacArthur .15 .40
21 Derek Roy .15 .40
22 Ryan Miller .25 .60
23 Drew Stafford .15 .40
24 Jason Pominville .15 .40
25 Thomas Vanek .20 .50
26 David Moss .20 .50
27 Mike Cammalleri .20 .50
28 Jarome Iginla .30 .75
29 Todd Bertuzzi .25 .60
30 Dion Phaneuf .20 .50
31 Miikka Kiprusoff .25 .60
32 Daymond Langkow .15 .40
33 Rene Bourque .15 .40
34 Olli Jokinen .20 .50
35 Cam Ward .25 .60
36 Ray Whitney .20 .50
37 Eric Staal .30 .75
38 Brandon Sutter .15 .40
39 Rod Brind`Amour .25 .60
40 Tuomo Ruutu .15 .40
41 Patrick Kane .50 1.25
42 Nikolai Khabibulin .25 .60
43 Martin Havlat .20 .50
44 Jonathan Toews .40 1.00
45 Patrick Sharp .25 .60
46 Brian Campbell .20 .50
47 Kris Versteeg .15 .40
48 John-Michael Liles .15 .40
49 Ryan Smyth .20 .50
50 T.J. Hensick .15 .40
51 Peter Budaj .20 .50
52 Milan Hejduk .20 .50
53 Paul Stastny .20 .50
54 Wojtek Wolski .15 .40
55 Jakub Voracek .20 .50
56 Derick Brassard .15 .40
57 Rick Nash .25 .60
58 Steve Mason .20 .50
59 R.J. Umberger .20 .50
60 Kristian Huselius .15 .40
61 Marty Turco .25 .60
62 Brad Richards .25 .60
63 Mike Modano .40 1.00
64 Loui Eriksson .15 .40
65 Brendon Morrow .20 .50
66 Mike Ribeiro .15 .40
67 Fabian Brunnstrom .20 .50
68 Johan Franzen .20 .50
69 Nicklas Lidstrom .15 .40
70 Jiri Hudler .20 .50
71 Pavel Datsyuk .40 1.00
72 Ty Conklin .20 .50
73 Marian Hossa .25 .60
74 Tomas Holmstrom .20 .50
75 Henrik Zetterberg .30 .75
76 Ales Kotalik .15 .40
77 Andrew Cogliano .15 .40
78 Ales Hemsky .20 .50
79 Sheldon Souray .15 .40
80 Sam Gagner .15 .40
81 Shawn Horcoff .15 .40
82 Dustin Penner .15 .40
83 Dwayne Roloson .20 .50
84 Michael Frolik .20 .50
85 Tomas Vokoun .20 .50
86 Jay Bouwmeester .15 .40
87 Nathan Horton .25 .60
88 Stephen Weiss .15 .40
89 David Booth .15 .40
90 Anze Kopitar .40 1.00
91 Jack Johnson .15 .40
92 Alexander Frolov .20 .50
93 Drew Doughty .30 .75
94 Dustin Brown .25 .60
95 Erik Ersberg .20 .50
96 Marian Gaborik .25 .60
97 Marek Zidlicky .15 .40
98 Mikko Koivu .25 .60
99 Andrew Brunette .15 .40
100 Niklas Backstrom .25 .60
101 Antti Miettinen .15 .40
102 Andrei Kostitsyn .20 .50
103 Carey Price .50 1.25
104 Saku Koivu .25 .60
105 Andrei Markov .25 .60
106 Robert Lang .15 .40
107 Alex Tanguay .15 .40
108 Alex Kovalev .20 .50
109 Max Pacioretty .25 .60
110 Jason Arnott .20 .50
111 Dan Ellis .15 .40
112 Ryan Suter .20 .50
113 J.P. Dumont .15 .40
114 Shea Weber .20 .50
115 Martin Erat .15 .40
116 Martin Brodeur .60 1.50
117 Brian Gionta .15 .40
118 Travis Zajac .15 .40
119 Patrik Elias .25 .60
120 Scott Clemmensen .20 .50
121 Zach Parise .25 .60
122 Josh Bailey .20 .50
123 Rick DiPietro .20 .50
124 Doug Weight .25 .60
125 Kyle Okposo .15 .40
126 Mark Streit .15 .40
127 Henrik Lundqvist .60 1.50
128 Scott Gomez .20 .50
129 Wade Redden .15 .40
130 Chris Drury .20 .50
131 Marc Staal .15 .40
132 Nikolai Zherdev .15 .40
133 Markus Naslund .25 .60
134 Nik Antropov .20 .50
135 Daniel Alfredsson .25 .60
136 Jason Spezza .25 .60
137 Filip Kuba .15 .40
138 Antoine Vermette .15 .40
139 Dany Heatley .20 .50
140 Alex Auld .20 .50
141 Mike Richards .20 .50
142 Martin Biron .20 .50
143 Mike Knuble .15 .40
144 Daniel Briere .25 .60
145 Jeff Carter .20 .50
146 Scott Hartnell .15 .40
147 Simon Gagne .25 .60
148 Shane Doan .20 .50
149 Peter Mueller .20 .50
150 Mikkel Boedker .15 .40
151 Ilya Bryzgalov .20 .50
152 Kyle Turris .25 .60
153 Chris Kunitz .25 .60
154 Bill Guerin .25 .60
155 Petr Sykora .20 .50
156 Marc-Andre Fleury .50 1.25
157 Miroslav Satan .15 .40
158 Evgeni Malkin .50 1.25
159 Jordan Staal .20 .50
160 Sidney Crosby 1.00 2.50
161 Alex Goligoski .20 .50
162 Devin Setoguchi .20 .50
163 Joe Pavelski .30 .75
164 Ryane Clowe .15 .40
165 Evgeni Nabokov .20 .50
166 Patrick Marleau .25 .60
167 Dan Boyle .15 .40
168 Joe Thornton .40 1.00
169 Manny Legace .20 .50
170 Paul Kariya .25 .60
171 Patrik Berglund .15 .40
172 Keith Tkachuk .25 .60
173 Brad Boyes .15 .40
174 Vincent Lecavalier .25 .60
175 Vaclav Prospal .15 .40
176 Steven Stamkos .50 1.25
177 Martin St. Louis .25 .60
178 Mike Smith .25 .60
179 Luke Schenn .25 .60
180 Matt Stajan .15 .40
181 Mikhail Grabovski .15 .40
182 Vesa Toskala .25 .60
183 Tomas Kaberle .15 .40
184 Alexei Ponikarovsky .15 .40
185 Nikolai Kulemin .15 .40
186 Kevin Bieksa .20 .50
187 Daniel Sedin .30 .75
188 Henrik Sedin .30 .75
189 Ryan Kesler .25 .60
190 Roberto Luongo .40 1.00
191 Mats Sundin .25 .60
192 Steve Bernier .15 .40
193 Mike Green .20 .50
194 Alexander Ovechkin 1.00 2.50
195 Nicklas Backstrom .25 .60
196 Alexander Semin .25 .60
197 Semen Varlamov .25 .60
198 Sergei Fedorov .40 1.00
199 Sidney Crosby CL .75 2.00
200 Alexander Ovechkin CL .75 2.00
201 Chris Durno RC .50 1.25
202 Peter Regin RC .50 1.25
203 Kevin Quick RC .40 1.00
204 Taylor Chorney RC .60 1.50
205 Mike Santorelli RC .60 1.50
206 Alexander Sulzer RC .40 1.00
207 Troy Bodie RC .50 1.25
208 Matt Beleskey RC .50 1.25
209 Kevin Westgarth RC .50 1.25
210 John Scott RC .60 1.50
211 Mikael Backlund RC 1.00 2.50
212 Byron Bitz RC .50 1.25
213 Matt Pelech RC .60 1.50
214 Tim Wallace RC .40 1.00
215 Ben Lovejoy RC .60 1.50
216 Riley Armstrong RC .50 1.25
217 Christian Hanson RC .60 1.50
218 Sean Collins RC .50 1.25
219 Riku Helenius RC .60 1.50
220 Ville Leino RC .50 1.25
221 Michal Neuvirth RC 1.00 2.50
222 Artem Anisimov RC .40 1.00
223 Davis Drewiske RC .60 1.50
224 David Schlemko RC .50 1.25
225 Luca Caputi RC .60 1.50
226 Jakub Petruzalek RC .60 1.50
227 Ryan Vesce RC .50 1.25
228 Jay Beagle RC .75 2.00
229 Jhonas Enroth RC .75 2.00
230 Brandon Segal RC .50 1.25
231 Tim Stapleton RC .60 1.50
232 Jesse Joensuu RC .50 1.25
233 John Negrin RC .60 1.50
234 Grant Lewis RC .50 1.25
235 Cal O'Reilly RC .50 1.25
236 Brian Salcido RC .40 1.00
237 Phil Oreskovic RC .60 1.50
238 Kris Chucko RC .40 1.00
239 Joel Rechlicz RC .40 1.00
240 Andrew MacDonald RC .40 1.00
241 Antti Niemi RC 1.00 2.50
242 Ivan Vishnevsky RC .40 1.00
243 Mike McKenna RC .50 1.25
244 Spencer Machacek RC .60 1.50
245 Tom Wandell RC .60 1.50
246 Michael Vernace RC .50 1.25
247 Yannick Weber RC .60 1.50
248 Matt Hendricks RC .50 1.25
249 Scott Lehman RC .40 1.00
250 T.J. Galiardi RC .60 1.50
251 Saku Koivu .25 .60
252 Joffrey Lupul .15 .40
253 Nik Antropov .20 .50
254 Maxim Afinogenov .15 .40
255 Mark Recchi .30 .75
256 Daniel Paille .20 .50
257 Tim Connolly .15 .40
258 Jay Bouwmeester .15 .40
259 Nigel Dawes .15 .40
260 Jussi Jokinen .15 .40
261 Marian Hossa .25 .60
262 Dustin Byfuglien .25 .60
263 Craig Anderson .25 .60
264 Antoine Vermette .15 .40
265 James Neal .15 .40
266 Jimmy Howard .30 .75
267 Dan Cleary .25 .60
268 Nikolai Khabibulin .25 .60
269 Patrick O'Sullivan .20 .50
270 Jordan Leopold .15 .40
271 Ryan Smyth .20 .50
272 Jonathan Quick .30 .75
273 Owen Nolan .25 .60
274 Martin Havlat .20 .50
275 Mike Cammalleri .20 .50
276 Scott Gomez .20 .50
277 Brian Gionta .15 .40
278 Pekka Rinne .25 .60
279 Jamie Langenbrunner .15 .40
280 Matt Moulson .20 .50
281 Dwayne Roloson .20 .50
282 Marian Gaborik .25 .60
283 Vaclav Prospal .15 .40
284 Jonathan Cheechoo .20 .50
285 Alex Kovalev .20 .50
286 Milan Michalek .15 .40
287 Chris Pronger .25 .60
288 Ray Emery .20 .50
289 Matthew Lombardi .15 .40
290 Tyler Kennedy .20 .50
291 Dany Heatley .20 .50
292 Chris Mason .20 .50
293 Alex Tanguay .15 .40
294 Mattias Ohlund .15 .40
295 Mike Komisarek .20 .50
296 Francois Beauchemin .15 .40
297 Christian Ehrhoff .15 .40
298 Mikael Samuelsson .15 .40
299 Mike Knuble .15 .40
300 Brendan Morrison .20 .50
301 Evander Kane RC 1.00 2.50
302 Brad Marchand RC 2.50 6.00
303 Tyler Myers RC 1.00 2.50
304 Chris Butler RC .60 1.50
305 Matt Duchene RC 1.25 3.00
306 Ryan O'Reilly RC 1.25 3.00
307 Ryan Wilson RC .60 1.50
308 Jamie Benn RC 2.00 5.00
309 Perttu Lindgren RC .50 1.25
310 Aaron Gagnon RC .40 1.00
311 Francis Wathier RC .50 1.25
312 Dmitry Kulikov RC .60 1.50
313 Jakub Kindl RC .60 1.50
314 Teemu Laakso RC .40 1.00
315 Colin Wilson RC .60 1.50
316 Cody Franson RC .60 1.50
317 Ilkka Pikkarainen RC .60 1.50
318 John Tavares RC 4.00 10.00
319 Matt Gilroy RC .60 1.50
320 Michael Del Zotto RC .60 1.50
321 Erik Karlsson RC 2.00 5.00
322 James van Riemsdyk RC 1.25 3.00
323 Johan Backlund RC .60 1.50
324 Lars Eller RC .60 1.50
325 Jason Demers RC 1.00 2.50
326 Benn Ferriero RC .60 1.50
327 Frazer McLaren RC .50 1.25
328 Steven Zalewski RC .50 1.25
329 Logan Couture RC 1.25 3.00
330 James Wright RC .60 1.50
331 Victor Hedman RC 1.50 4.00
332 Viktor Stalberg RC .60 1.50
333 Jay Rosehill RC .60 1.50
334 Jonas Gustavsson RC 2.00 5.00
335 Tyler Bozak RC 1.00 2.50
336 James Reimer RC 2.50 6.00
337 Sergei Shirokov RC .40 1.00
338 Guillaume Desbiens RC .60 1.50
339 Michael Grabner RC .60 1.50
340 Braden Holtby RC 1.50 4.00

2009-10 Upper Deck Victory Black

*1-200 VETS: 15X TO 40X BASIC CARDS
*201-250 ROOK: 6X TO 15X BASIC CARDS
*251-300 VETS: 12X TO 30X BASIC CARDS
*301-350 ROOK: 4X TO 10X BASIC CARDS
195 Nicklas Backstrom 10.00 25.00

2009-10 Upper Deck Victory Gold

*GOLD: 4X TO 10X BASE
*GOLD RCs: 1.5X TO 4X BASE
*GOLD UPDATE: 4X TO 10X BASE
*GOLD UPDATE RCs: 1.2X TO 3X BASE
121 Zach Parise 2.50 6.00
195 Nicklas Backstrom 2.50 6.00
318 John Tavares 8.00 20.00
334 Jonas Gustavsson 2.50 6.00
336 James Reimer 5.00 12.00

2009-10 Upper Deck Victory Game Breakers

COMPLETE SET (50) 15.00 40.00
GB1 Sidney Crosby 2.00 5.00
GB2 Patrick Sharp .50 1.25
GB3 Rick Nash .50 1.25
GB4 Phil Kessel .50 1.25
GB5 Brad Richards .50 1.25
GB6 Joe Thornton .75 2.00
GB7 Eric Staal .60 1.50
GB8 Simon Gagne .50 1.25
GB9 Paul Stastny .40 1.00
GB10 Thomas Vanek .40 1.00
GB11 Vincent Lecavalier .50 1.25
GB12 Martin St. Louis .50 1.25
GB13 Ilya Kovalchuk .50 1.25
GB14 David Krejci .50 1.25
GB15 Brad Boyes .30 .75
GB16 Alex Tanguay .30 .75
GB17 Jeff Carter .40 1.00
GB18 Patrick Kane 1.00 2.50
GB19 Devin Setoguchi .40 1.00
GB20 Jarome Iginla .60 1.50
GB21 Marian Gaborik .50 1.25
GB22 Pavel Datsyuk .75 2.00
GB23 Mikko Koivu .50 1.25
GB24 Markus Naslund .50 1.25
GB25 Loui Eriksson .30 .75
GB26 Chris Drury .40 1.00
GB27 Dany Heatley .40 1.00
GB28 Jason Arnott .40 1.00
GB29 Evgeni Malkin 1.00 2.50
GB30 Peter Mueller .40 1.00
GB31 Bryan Little .50 1.25
GB32 Patrik Elias .50 1.25
GB33 Mats Sundin .50 1.25
GB34 Patrick Marleau .50 1.25
GB35 Patrice Bergeron .60 1.50
GB36 Shane Doan .40 1.00
GB37 Marian Hossa .50 1.25
GB38 Nicklas Backstrom .50 1.25
GB39 Alex Kovalev .40 1.00
GB40 Ryan Getzlaf .50 1.25
GB41 Mike Cammalleri .40 1.00
GB42 David Booth .30 .75
GB43 Jason Spezza .50 1.25
GB44 Jonathan Toews .75 2.00
GB45 Zach Parise .50 1.25
GB46 Ryane Clowe .30 .75
GB47 Daniel Sedin .60 1.50
GB48 Henrik Zetterberg .60 1.50
GB49 Paul Kariya .50 1.25
GB50 Alexander Ovechkin 2.00 5.00

2009-10 Upper Deck Victory Jumbos

COMPLETE SET (42) 40.00 100.00
OS1 Ryan Getzlaf 1.00 2.50
OS2 Ilya Kovalchuk 1.00 2.50
OS3 Phil Kessel 1.00 2.50
OS4 Ryan Miller 1.00 2.50
OS5 Thomas Vanek .75 2.00
OS6 Jarome Iginla 1.25 3.00
OS7 Dion Phaneuf .75 2.00
OS8 Eric Staal 1.25 3.00
OS9 Patrick Kane 2.00 5.00
OS10 Jonathan Toews 1.50 4.00
OS11 Paul Stastny .75 2.00
OS12 Rick Nash 1.00 2.50
OS13 Steve Mason .75 2.00
OS14 Marty Turco 1.00 2.50
OS15 Mike Modano 1.50 4.00
OS16 Nicklas Lidstrom .60 1.50
OS17 Pavel Datsyuk 1.50 4.00
OS18 Henrik Zetterberg 1.25 3.00
OS19 Sam Gagner .60 1.50
OS20 Anze Kopitar 1.50 4.00
OS21 Drew Doughty 1.25 3.00
OS22 Marian Gaborik 1.00 2.50
OS23 Carey Price 2.00 5.00
OS24 Saku Koivu 1.00 2.50
OS25 Shea Weber .75 2.00
OS26 Martin Brodeur 2.50 6.00
OS27 Zach Parise 1.00 2.50
OS28 Rick DiPietro .75 2.00
OS29 Henrik Lundqvist 2.50 6.00
OS30 Jason Spezza 1.00 2.50
OS31 Dany Heatley .75 2.00
OS32 Mike Richards .75 2.00
OS33 Jeff Carter .75 2.00
OS34 Peter Mueller .75 2.00
OS35 Marc-Andre Fleury 2.00 5.00
OS36 Evgeni Malkin 2.00 5.00
OS37 Sidney Crosby 4.00 10.00
OS38 Joe Thornton 1.50 4.00
OS39 Vincent Lecavalier 1.00 2.50
OS40 Luke Schenn 1.00 2.50
OS41 Roberto Luongo 1.50 4.00
OS42 Alexander Ovechkin 4.00 10.00

2009-10 Upper Deck Victory Stars of the Game

COMPLETE SET (50) 20.00 50.00
SG1 Carey Price 1.00 2.50
SG2 Patrice Bergeron .60 1.50
SG3 Ilya Kovalchuk .50 1.25
SG4 Zach Parise .50 1.25
SG5 Vincent Lecavalier .50 1.25
SG6 Nicklas Lidstrom .30 .75
SG7 Jean-Sebastien Giguere .50 1.25
SG8 Alexander Ovechkin 2.00 5.00
SG9 Joe Thornton .75 2.00
SG10 Patrick Kane 1.00 2.50
SG11 Marty Turco .50 1.25
SG12 Simon Gagne .50 1.25
SG13 Dany Heatley .40 1.00
SG14 Mats Sundin .50 1.25
SG15 Henrik Lundqvist 1.25 3.00
SG16 Eric Staal .60 1.50
SG17 Evgeni Malkin 1.00 2.50
SG18 Peter Mueller .40 1.00
SG19 Tomas Vokoun .40 1.00
SG20 Alex Kovalev .40 1.00
SG21 Henrik Zetterberg .60 1.50
SG22 Marian Gaborik .50 1.25
SG23 Martin Brodeur 1.25 3.00
SG24 Marc Savard .30 .75

SG25 Jarome Iginla .60 1.50
SG26 Vesa Toskala .50 1.25
SG27 Rick Nash .50 1.25
SG28 Pavel Datsyuk .75 2.00
SG29 Miikka Kiprusoff .50 1.25
SG30 Alex Tanguay .30 .75
SG31 Patrick Marleau .50 1.25
SG32 Jonathan Toews .75 2.00
SG33 Roberto Luongo .75 2.00
SG34 Thomas Vanek .40 1.00
SG35 Martin St. Louis .50 1.25
SG36 Jason Spezza .50 1.25
SG37 Paul Stastny .40 1.00
SG38 Marc-Andre Fleury 1.00 2.50
SG39 Alexander Semin .50 1.25
SG40 Mike Richards .40 1.00
SG41 Ryan Getzlaf .50 1.25
SG42 Mike Modano .75 2.00
SG43 Steve Mason .40 1.00
SG44 Markus Naslund .50 1.25
SG45 Marian Hossa .50 1.25
SG46 Anze Kopitar .75 2.00
SG47 Rick DiPietro .40 1.00
SG48 Saku Koivu .50 1.25
SG49 Paul Kariya .50 1.25
SG50 Sidney Crosby 2.00 5.00

2010-11 Upper Deck Victory

COMP.BASE SET (250) 25.00 60.00
COMP.SET w/o SPs (200) 12.00 30.00
COMP.UPD.SET (100) 15.00 40.00
COMP.UPD.w/o SPs (50) 8.00 20.00
1 Ryan Getzlaf .25 .60
2 Jonas Hiller .20 .50
3 Corey Perry .40 1.00
4 Bobby Ryan .20 .50
5 Lubomir Visnovsky .15 .40
6 Nik Antropov .20 .50
7 Zach Bogosian .20 .50
8 Evander Kane .25 .60
9 Bryan Little .25 .60
10 Rich Peverley .25 .60
11 Patrice Bergeron .30 .75
12 Zdeno Chara .25 .60
13 David Krejci .25 .60
14 Milan Lucic .25 .60
15 Marc Savard .15 .40
16 Tim Thomas .25 .60
17 Blake Wheeler .25 .60
18 Tim Connolly .15 .40
19 Ryan Miller .25 .60
20 Tyler Myers .15 .40
21 Jason Pominville .15 .40
22 Derek Roy .15 .40
23 Drew Stafford .15 .40
24 Thomas Vanek .20 .50
25 Erik Cole .15 .40
26 Jussi Jokinen .15 .40
27 Joni Pitkanen .20 .50
28 Eric Staal .30 .75
29 Brandon Sutter .15 .40
30 Cam Ward .25 .60
31 Jay Bouwmeester .15 .40
32 Rene Bourque .15 .40
33 Niklas Hagman .15 .40
34 Jarome Iginla .30 .75
35 Miikka Kiprusoff .25 .60
36 Daymond Langkow .15 .40
37 Matt Stajan .15 .40
38 Marian Hossa .25 .60
39 Patrick Kane .50 1.25
40 Duncan Keith .20 .50
41 Brent Seabrook .15 .40
42 Patrick Sharp .25 .60
43 Jonathan Toews .40 1.00
44 Kris Versteeg .15 .40
45 Derick Brassard .15 .40
46 Kristian Huselius .15 .40
47 Steve Mason .20 .50
48 Rick Nash .25 .60
49 Antoine Vermette .15 .40
50 Jakub Voracek .20 .50
51 Craig Anderson .25 .60
52 Matt Duchene .25 .60
53 T.J. Galiardi .20 .50
54 Milan Hejduk .20 .50
55 Ryan O'Reilly .25 .60
56 Paul Stastny .20 .50
57 Chris Stewart .20 .50
58 Jamie Benn .30 .75
59 Loui Eriksson .15 .40
60 Kari Lehtonen .20 .50
61 Brenden Morrow .20 .50
62 James Neal .15 .40
63 Mike Ribeiro .15 .40
64 Brad Richards .25 .60
65 Dan Cleary .25 .60
66 Pavel Datsyuk .40 1.00
67 Johan Franzen .20 .50
68 Jim Howard .30 .75
69 Nicklas Lidstrom .25 .60
70 Brian Rafalski .15 .40
71 Henrik Zetterberg .30 .75
72 Andrew Cogliano .15 .40
73 Sam Gagner .15 .40
74 Ales Hemsky .20 .50
75 Shawn Horcoff .15 .40
76 Nikolai Khabibulin .20 .50
77 Dustin Penner .15 .40
78 David Booth .15 .40
79 Michael Frolik .15 .40
80 Nathan Horton .20 .50
81 Cory Stillman .15 .40
82 Tomas Vokoun .20 .50
83 Stephen Weiss .20 .50
84 Dustin Brown .25 .60
85 Drew Doughty .30 .75
86 Michal Handzus .20 .50
87 Anze Kopitar .40 1.00
88 Jonathan Quick .30 .75
89 Wayne Simmonds .30 .75
90 Ryan Smyth .20 .50
91 Niklas Backstrom .25 .60
92 Andrew Brunette .15 .40
93 Brent Burns .25 .60
94 Cal Clutterbuck .15 .40
95 Martin Havlat .20 .50
96 Mikko Koivu .25 .60
97 Guillaume Latendresse .20 .50
98 Mike Cammalleri .25 .60
99 Scott Gomez .20 .50
100 Brian Gionta .15 .40
101 Jaroslav Halak .25 .60
102 Andrei Markov .25 .60
103 Tomas Plekanec .15 .40
104 Carey Price .50 1.25
105 Jason Arnott .20 .50
106 J.P. Dumont .15 .40
107 Martin Erat .15 .40
108 Patric Hornqvist .15 .40
109 Pekka Rinne .25 .60
110 Steve Sullivan .15 .40
111 Shea Weber .20 .50
112 Martin Brodeur .60 1.50
113 Patrik Elias .25 .60
114 Ilya Kovalchuk .25 .60
115 Jamie Langenbrunner .15 .40
116 Zach Parise .25 .60
117 Brian Rolston .20 .50
118 Travis Zajac .15 .40
119 Josh Bailey .20 .50
120 Blake Comeau .15 .40
121 Matt Moulson .20 .50
122 Kyle Okposo .15 .40
123 Mark Streit .15 .40
124 John Tavares .40 1.00
125 Ryan Callahan .15 .40
126 Chris Drury .20 .50
127 Brandon Dubinsky .15 .40
128 Marian Gaborik .25 .60
129 Henrik Lundqvist .60 1.50
130 Vaclav Prospal .15 .40
131 Marc Staal .15 .40
132 Daniel Alfredsson .25 .60
133 Mike Fisher .15 .40
134 Alex Kovalev .20 .50
135 Filip Kuba .15 .40
136 Brian Elliott .20 .50
137 Milan Michalek .15 .40
138 Jason Spezza .25 .60
139 Daniel Briere .25 .60
140 Jeff Carter .20 .50
141 Claude Giroux .25 .60
142 Scott Hartnell .15 .40
143 Chris Pronger .25 .60
144 Mike Richards .20 .50
145 James van Riemsdyk .20 .50
146 Ilya Bryzgalov .20 .50
147 Shane Doan .20 .50
148 Scottie Upshall .15 .40
149 Radim Vrbata .15 .40
150 Wojtek Wolski .15 .40
151 Keith Yandle .15 .40
152 Sidney Crosby 1.00 2.50
153 Marc-Andre Fleury .50 1.25
154 Tyler Kennedy .15 .40
155 Kristopher Letang .30 .75
156 Evgeni Malkin .50 1.25
157 Jordan Staal .20 .50
158 Maxime Talbot .15 .40
159 Dan Boyle .15 .40
160 Ryane Clowe .15 .40
161 Dany Heatley .20 .50
162 Patrick Marleau .25 .60
163 Joe Pavelski .30 .75
164 Devin Setoguchi .20 .50
165 Joe Thornton .40 1.00
166 David Backes .15 .40
167 Brad Boyes .15 .40
168 Erik Johnson .15 .40
169 Andy McDonald .20 .50
170 T.J. Oshie .25 .60
171 David Perron .20 .50
172 Steve Downie .15 .40
173 Victor Hedman .30 .75
174 Vincent Lecavalier .25 .60
175 Ryan Malone .15 .40
176 Martin St. Louis .25 .60
177 Steven Stamkos .50 1.25
178 Tyler Bozak .15 .40
179 Jean-Sebastien Giguere .25 .60
180 Jonas Gustavsson .30 .75
181 Phil Kessel .25 .60
182 Nikolai Kulemin .15 .40
183 Dion Phaneuf .20 .50
184 Luke Schenn .25 .60
185 Alexandre Burrows .15 .40
186 Alexander Edler .15 .40
187 Ryan Kesler .25 .60
188 Roberto Luongo .40 1.00
189 Mason Raymond .15 .40
190 Daniel Sedin .30 .75
191 Henrik Sedin .30 .75
192 Nicklas Backstrom .25 .60
193 Tomas Fleischmann .15 .40
194 Mike Green .20 .50
195 Mike Knuble .15 .40
196 Alexander Ovechkin 1.00 2.50
197 Alexander Semin .25 .60
198 Semyon Varlamov .25 .60
199 Ryan Miller CL .20 .50
200 Steven Stamkos CL .40 1.00
201 Nick Bonino RC .60 1.50
202 Arturs Kulda RC .50 1.25
203 Andrew Bodnarchuk RC .50 1.25
204 Zach Hamill RC .50 1.25
205 Adam McQuaid RC .60 1.50
206 Jeff Penner RC .75 2.00
207 Jamie McBain RC .50 1.25
208 Jerome Samson RC .50 1.25
209 Justin Mercier RC .50 1.25
210 Brandon Yip RC .50 1.25
211 Grant Clitsome RC .50 1.25
212 Tomas Kana RC .50 1.25
213 Maxime Fortunus RC .40 1.00
214 Philip Larsen RC .50 1.25
215 Raymond Sawada RC .40 1.00
216 Dean Arsene RC .50 1.25
217 Johan Motin RC .40 1.00
218 Bryan Pitton RC .60 1.50
219 Alex Plante RC .50 1.25
220 Evgeny Dadonov RC .60 1.50
221 Mike Duco RC .50 1.25
222 Richard Clune RC .60 1.50
223 Cody Almond RC .50 1.25
224 Justin Falk RC .40 1.00
225 Maxim Noreau RC .40 1.00
226 Clayton Stoner RC .50 1.25
227 Casey Wellman RC .50 1.25
228 P.K. Subban RC 1.50 4.00
229 Brock Trotter RC 1.00 2.50
230 J.T. Wyman RC .50 1.25
231 Nick Spaling RC .50 1.25
232 Nick Palmieri RC .50 1.25
233 Dustin Kohn RC .50 1.25
234 Dylan Reese RC .50 1.25
235 Ilkka Heikkinen RC .75 2.00
236 Matt Zaba RC .60 1.50
237 Bobby Butler RC .50 1.25
238 Jared Cowen RC .50 1.25
239 Kaspars Daugavins RC .60 1.50
240 Derek Smith RC .50 1.25
241 Jeremy Duchesne RC .60 1.50
242 Nick Johnson RC .40 1.00
243 Alexander Pechurski RC .60 1.50
244 Eric Tangradi RC .50 1.25
245 John McCarthy RC .50 1.25
246 Dustin Tokarski RC .50 1.25
247 Brayden Irwin RC .50 1.25
248 Nazem Kadri RC 1.50 4.00
249 Evan Oberg RC .60 1.50
250 Kyle Wilson RC .60 1.50
251 Dustin Byfuglien .25 .60
252 Sergei Kostitsyn .15 .40
253 Ruslan Salei .15 .40
254 Marty Turco .25 .60
255 Zenon Konopka .20 .50
256 Alexei Ponikarovsky .15 .40
257 Ethan Moreau .15 .40
258 Nathan Horton .20 .50
259 Antero Niittymaki .20 .50
260 Raffi Torres .15 .40
261 Dominic Moore .15 .40
262 Jason Arnott .20 .50
263 Derek Boogaard .15 .40
264 Dan Ellis .20 .50
265 Milan Jurcina .15 .40
266 Andrew Raycroft .20 .50
267 Brent Sopel .15 .40
268 Olli Jokinen .20 .50
269 Matt Cullen .15 .40
270 Sergei Gonchar .15 .40
271 Dan Hamhuis .20 .50
272 Keith Ballard .15 .40
273 Sean O'Donnell .15 .40
274 Matt Hunwick .15 .40
275 Nikolai Zherdev .15 .40
276 Colby Armstrong .15 .40
277 Jeff Tambellini .15 .40
278 Chris Higgins .15 .40
279 Daniel Winnik .15 .40
280 Matthew Lombardi .15 .40
281 Todd White .15 .40
282 Alexander Frolov .15 .40
283 Brett Lebda .15 .40
284 Anton Volchenkov .15 .40
285 Jaroslav Halak .25 .60
286 Dennis Wideman .15 .40
287 Andrew Ladd .15 .40
288 Alex Tanguay .15 .40
289 Chris Mason .20 .50
290 Mike Modano .40 1.00
291 Manny Malhotra .20 .50
292 Martin Biron .20 .50
293 Paul Martin .15 .40
294 Pavel Kubina .15 .40
295 Sean Bergenheim .15 .40
296 Lars Eller .15 .40
297 John Madden .15 .40
298 Steve Bernier .15 .40
299 Jordan Leopold .15 .40
300 Willie Mitchell .15 .40
301 Kevin Shattenkirk RC 1.00 2.50
302 Mattias Tedenby RC .50 1.25
303 Ian Cole RC .50 1.25
304 Matt Kassian RC .50 1.25
305 Travis Hamonic RC .60 1.50
306 Eric Wellwood RC .60 1.50
307 Jeremy Morin RC .50 1.25
308 Keith Aulie RC .50 1.25
309 Stephen Gionta RC .60 1.50
310 Evgeny Grachev RC .50 1.25
311 Marco Scandella RC .50 1.25
312 Alexander Burmistrov RC .50 1.25
313 Ryan Reaves RC .60 1.50
314 Mike Moore RC .50 1.25
315 Tommy Wingels RC .50 1.25
316 Robin Lehner RC 1.00 2.50
317 Luke Adam RC .50 1.25
318 Derek Stepan RC .60 1.50
319 Mark Dekanich RC .50 1.25
320 Anders Lindback RC .50 1.25
321 Dana Tyrell RC .50 1.25
322 Jake Muzzin RC 1.25 3.00
323 Kyle Clifford RC .60 1.50
324 Brayden Schenn RC 1.25 3.00
325 Nino Niederreiter RC .75 2.00
326 Zac Dalpe RC .60 1.50
327 Jeff Skinner RC 3.00 8.00
328 Sergei Bobrovsky RC 2.00 5.00
329 T.J. Brodie RC .50 1.25
330 Henrik Karlsson RC .50 1.25
331 Cam Fowler RC 1.25 3.00
332 Alexander Vasyunov RC .50 1.25
333 Matt Taormina RC .50 1.25
334 Alexander Urbom RC .50 1.25
335 Olivier Magnan-Grenier RC .50 1.25
336 Jacob Josefson RC .50 1.25
337 Oliver Ekman-Larsson RC .75 2.00
338 Brian Fahey RC .50 1.25
339 Marcus Johansson RC .75 2.00
340 Tyler Seguin RC 3.00 8.00
341 Jordan Caron RC .60 1.50
342 Nick Holden RC .50 1.25
343 Evan Brophey RC .50 1.25
344 Brandon Pirri RC .50 1.25
345 Nick Leddy RC .60 1.50
346 Jonas Holos RC .50 1.25
347 Mark Olver RC .50 1.25
348 Magnus Paajarvi RC .60 1.50
349 Jordan Eberle RC 3.00 8.00
350 Taylor Hall RC 3.00 8.00

2010-11 Upper Deck Victory Black

*1-200 VETS: 15X TO 40X BASIC CARDS
*201-250 ROOK: 6X TO 15X BASIC CARDS
*251-300 VETS: 15X TO 40X BASIC CARDS
*301-350 ROOK: 5X TO 12X BASIC CARDS
192 Nicklas Backstrom 10.00 25.00

2010-11 Upper Deck Victory Gold

COMP.UPD.SET (100) 75.00 150.00
*GOLD VETS: 4X TO 10X BASE
*GOLD ROOKIE: 1.5X TO 4X BASE
*GOLD UPD 251-300: 3X TO 8X BASE
*GOLD UPD ROOKIE 301-350: 1.5X TO 4X
192 Nicklas Backstrom 2.50 6.00
248 Nazem Kadri 8.00 20.00

2010-11 Upper Deck Victory Red

*RED: 6X TO 15X BASE
*RED RCs: 4X TO 10X BASE
192 Nicklas Backstrom 4.00 10.00

2010-11 Upper Deck Victory Game Breakers

GBAK Anze Kopitar .50 1.25
GBAO Alexander Ovechkin 1.25 3.00
GBAS Alexander Semin .30 .75
GBBA Nicklas Backstrom .30 .75
GBCP Corey Perry .50 1.25
GBDA Daniel Alfredsson .30 .75
GBDD Drew Doughty .40 1.00
GBDH Dany Heatley .25 .60
GBDR Derek Roy .20 .50
GBDS Daniel Sedin .40 1.00
GBDU Pascal Dupuis .20 .50
GBEM Evgeni Malkin .60 1.50
GBES Eric Staal .40 1.00
GBGL Guillaume Latendresse .25 .60
GBHS Henrik Sedin .40 1.00
GBHZ Henrik Zetterberg .40 1.00
GBIK Ilya Kovalchuk .30 .75
GBJC Jeff Carter .25 .60
GBJI Jarome Iginla .40 1.00
GBJJ Jussi Jokinen .20 .50
GBJT John Tavares .50 1.25
GBJV James van Riemsdyk .25 .60
GBKA Patrick Kane .60 1.50
GBMC Mike Cammalleri .30 .75
GBMD Matt Duchene .30 .75
GBMF Mike Fisher .20 .50
GBMG Marian Gaborik .30 .75
GBMH Michal Handzus .25 .60
GBMK Mikko Koivu .30 .75
GBMM Matt Moulson .25 .60
GBMR Mike Richards .25 .60
GBMS Martin St. Louis .30 .75
GBNB Nicklas Bergfors .25 .60
GBPB Patrice Bergeron .40 1.00
GBPD Pavel Datsyuk .50 1.25
GBPH Patric Hornqvist .20 .50
GBPK Phil Kessel .30 .75
GBPM Patrick Marleau .30 .75
GBRG Ryan Getzlaf .30 .75
GBRM Ryan Malone .20 .50
GBRN Rick Nash .30 .75
GBRP Rich Peverley .30 .75
GBSC Sidney Crosby 1.25 3.00
GBSD Shane Doan .25 .60
GBSS Steven Stamkos .60 1.50
GBTB Troy Brouwer .20 .50
GBTH Joe Thornton .50 1.25
GBTO Jonathan Toews .50 1.25
GBWW Wojtek Wolski .20 .50
GBZP Zach Parise .30 .75

2010-11 Upper Deck Victory Stars of the Game

COMPLETE SET (50) 20.00 50.00
SOGAK Anze Kopitar .60 1.50
SOGAM Andrei Markov .40 1.00
SOGAO Alexander Ovechkin 1.50 4.00
SOGBB Brad Boyes .25 .60
SOGBR Bobby Ryan .30 .75
SOGCP Carey Price .75 2.00
SOGDA Daniel Alfredsson .40 1.00
SOGDD Drew Doughty .50 1.25
SOGDH Dany Heatley .30 .75
SOGDS Daniel Sedin .50 1.25
SOGEM Evgeni Malkin .75 2.00
SOGES Eric Staal .50 1.25
SOGGA Marian Gaborik .40 1.00
SOGHL Henrik Lundqvist 1.00 2.50
SOGHS Henrik Sedin .50 1.25
SOGHZ Henrik Zetterberg .50 1.25
SOGIB Ilya Bryzgalov .30 .75
SOGJC Jeff Carter .30 .75
SOGJI Jarome Iginla .50 1.25
SOGJS Jason Spezza .40 1.00
SOGJT John Tavares .60 1.50
SOGKE Phil Kessel .40 1.00
SOGMB Martin Brodeur 1.00 2.50
SOGMD Matt Duchene .40 1.00
SOGMF Marc-Andre Fleury .75 2.00
SOGMG Mike Green .30 .75
SOGMK Mikko Koivu .40 1.00
SOGMR Mike Richards .30 .75
SOGMS Martin St. Louis .40 1.00
SOGNB Nicklas Backstrom .40 1.00
SOGPB Patrice Bergeron .50 1.25
SOGPD Pavel Datsyuk .60 1.50
SOGPE Corey Perry .60 1.50
SOGPK Patrick Kane .75 2.00
SOGPR Chris Pronger .40 1.00
SOGPS Paul Stastny .30 .75
SOGRG Ryan Getzlaf .40 1.00
SOGRI Brad Richards .40 1.00
SOGRL Roberto Luongo .60 1.50
SOGRM Ryan Miller .40 1.00
SOGRN Rick Nash .40 1.00
SOGSC Sidney Crosby 1.50 4.00
SOGSD Shane Doan .30 .75
SOGSS Steven Stamkos .75 2.00
SOGSW Shea Weber .30 .75
SOGTH Joe Thornton .60 1.50
SOGTM Tyler Myers .25 .60
SOGTO Jonathan Toews .60 1.50
SOGZC Zdeno Chara .40 1.00
SOGZP Zach Parise .40 1.00

2011-12 Upper Deck Victory

COMPLETE SET (250) 25.00 60.00
COMP.SET w/o SPs (200) 12.00 30.00
COMP.UPDATE SET (60) 15.00 30.00
1 Ryan Getzlaf .25 .60
2 Corey Perry .40 1.00
3 Teemu Selanne .50 1.25
4 Bobby Ryan .20 .50
5 Cam Fowler .25 .60
6 Jonas Hiller .20 .50
7 Lubomir Visnovsky .15 .40
8 Evander Kane .25 .60
9 Dustin Byfuglien .25 .60
10 Alexander Burmistrov .20 .50
11 Ondrej Pavelec .25 .60
12 Andrew Ladd .15 .40
13 David Krejci .25 .60
14 Zdeno Chara .25 .60
15 Nathan Horton .25 .60
16 Patrice Bergeron .30 .75
17 Tyler Seguin .30 .75
18 Tomas Kaberle .15 .40
19 Tim Thomas .25 .60
20 Milan Lucic .25 .60
21 Derek Roy .15 .40
22 Thomas Vanek .20 .50
23 Tyler Myers .15 .40
24 Tyler Ennis .15 .40
25 Drew Stafford .15 .40
26 Tim Connolly .15 .40
27 Ryan Miller .25 .60
28 Brad Boyes .15 .40
29 Jarome Iginla .30 .75
30 Alex Tanguay .15 .40
31 Rene Bourque .15 .40
32 Matt Stajan .15 .40
33 Jay Bouwmeester .15 .40
34 Miikka Kiprusoff .25 .60
35 Mikael Backlund .20 .50
36 Eric Staal .30 .75
37 Jeff Skinner .30 .75
38 Jussi Jokinen .15 .40
39 Cam Ward .25 .60
40 Joni Pitkanen .20 .50
41 Brandon Sutter .15 .40
42 Patrick Kane .50 1.25
43 Patrick Sharp .25 .60
44 Jonathan Toews .40 1.00
45 Marian Hossa .25 .60
46 Duncan Keith .20 .50
47 Brent Seabrook .15 .40
48 Michael Frolik .15 .40
49 Corey Crawford .30 .75
50 Milan Hejduk .20 .50
51 Matt Duchene .25 .60
52 Paul Stastny .20 .50
53 John-Michael Liles .15 .40
54 Erik Johnson .15 .40
55 David Jones .15 .40
56 Rick Nash .25 .60
57 Derick Brassard .15 .40
58 R.J. Umberger .15 .40
59 Antoine Vermette .15 .40
60 Jakub Voracek .20 .50
61 Steve Mason .20 .50
62 Brad Richards .25 .60
63 Loui Eriksson .15 .40
64 Mike Ribeiro .15 .40
65 Jamie Benn .25 .60
66 Kari Lehtonen .20 .50
67 Pavel Datsyuk .40 1.00
68 Henrik Zetterberg .30 .75
69 Nicklas Lidstrom .15 .40
70 Dan Cleary .25 .60
71 Johan Franzen .20 .50
72 Jonathan Ericsson .15 .40
73 Jim Howard .30 .75
74 Jordan Eberle .25 .60
75 Sam Gagner .15 .40
76 Taylor Hall .25 .60
77 Ales Hemsky .20 .50
78 Magnus Paajarvi .20 .50
79 Linus Omark .25 .60
80 Niclas Bergfors .20 .50
81 David Booth .15 .40
82 Tomas Vokoun .20 .50
83 Stephen Weiss .20 .50
84 Dustin Penner .20 .50
85 Anze Kopitar .40 1.00
86 Ryan Smyth .20 .50
87 Drew Doughty .30 .75
88 Jonathan Quick .30 .75
89 Dustin Brown .25 .60
90 Jonathan Bernier .20 .50
91 Jack Johnson .15 .40
92 Mikko Koivu .20 .50
93 Martin Havlat .20 .50
94 Matt Cullen .15 .40
95 Brent Burns .25 .60
96 Niklas Backstrom .25 .60
97 Pierre-Marc Bouchard .25 .60
98 Andrei Kostitsyn .20 .50
99 Tomas Plekanec .15 .40
100 Brian Gionta .15 .40
101 Michael Cammalleri .20 .50
102 Benoit Pouliot .15 .40
103 P.K. Subban .30 .75
104 Carey Price .50 1.25
105 Lars Eller .15 .40
106 Shea Weber .20 .50
107 Patric Hornqvist .15 .40
108 Cal O'Reilly .15 .40
109 Steve Sullivan .15 .40
110 Pekka Rinne .25 .60
111 Mike Fisher .15 .40
112 Zach Parise .25 .60
113 Patrik Elias .25 .60
114 Ilya Kovalchuk .25 .60
115 Martin Brodeur .60 1.50
116 Travis Zajac .15 .40
117 John Tavares .40 1.00
118 Blake Comeau .15 .40
119 Kyle Okposo .15 .40
120 Matt Moulson .15 .40
121 Michael Grabner .20 .50
122 Marian Gaborik .25 .60
123 Brandon Dubinsky .15 .40
124 Ryan Callahan .15 .40
125 Henrik Lundqvist .60 1.50
126 Marc Staal .15 .40
127 Derek Stepan .15 .40
128 Wojtek Wolski .15 .40
129 Craig Anderson .25 .60
130 Jason Spezza .25 .60
131 Daniel Alfredsson .25 .60
132 Erik Karlsson .30 .75
133 Mike Richards .20 .50
134 Jeff Carter .20 .50
135 Chris Pronger .25 .60
136 Claude Giroux .25 .60
137 Daniel Briere .25 .60
138 James van Riemsdyk .20 .50
139 Sergei Bobrovsky .40 1.00
140 Scott Hartnell .15 .40
141 Kris Versteeg .15 .40
142 Kyle Turris .15 .40
143 Oliver Ekman-Larsson .25 .60
144 Shane Doan .20 .50
145 Ilya Bryzgalov .25 .60
146 Keith Yandle .15 .40
147 James Neal .15 .40
148 Sidney Crosby 1.00 2.50
149 Evgeni Malkin .50 1.25
150 Kristopher Letang .30 .75
151 Marc-Andre Fleury .50 1.25
152 Jordan Staal .20 .50
153 Maxime Talbot .15 .40
154 Tyler Kennedy .15 .40
155 Logan Couture .30 .75
156 Dany Heatley .20 .50
157 Joe Thornton .40 1.00
158 Patrick Marleau .25 .60
159 Dan Boyle .15 .40
160 Joe Pavelski .30 .75
161 Ryane Clowe .15 .40
162 Antti Niemi .20 .50
163 Alex Pietrangelo .20 .50
164 Chris Stewart .20 .50
165 David Backes .15 .40
166 Patrik Berglund .15 .40
167 Jaroslav Halak .25 .60
168 David Perron .20 .50
169 Victor Hedman .30 .75
170 Steven Stamkos .50 1.25
171 Martin St. Louis .25 .60
172 Ryan Malone .15 .40
173 Vincent Lecavalier .25 .60
174 Luke Schenn .25 .60
175 Nazem Kadri .30 .75
176 Clarke MacArthur .15 .40
177 Phil Kessel .25 .60
178 Nikolai Kulemin .15 .40
179 Jean-Sebastien Giguere .25 .60
180 Dion Phaneuf .20 .50
181 Alexander Edler .15 .40
182 Cory Schneider .25 .60
183 Christian Ehrhoff .15 .40
184 Daniel Sedin .30 .75
185 Henrik Sedin .30 .75
186 Ryan Kesler .25 .60
187 Roberto Luongo .40 1.00
188 Alexandre Burrows .15 .40
189 Mason Raymond .15 .40
190 Michal Neuvirth .20 .50
191 Brooks Laich .15 .40
192 Jason Arnott .20 .50
193 Alexander Ovechkin 1.00 2.50
194 Alexander Semin .25 .60
195 Nicklas Backstrom .25 .60
196 Mike Green .20 .50
197 Semyon Varlamov .25 .60
198 John Carlson .25 .60
199 Steven Stamkos CL .40 1.00
200 Sidney Crosby CL .75 2.00
201 Timo Pielmeier .60 1.50
202 Jean-Philippe Levasseur .50 1.25
203 Paul Postma RC .50 1.25
204 Andrei Zubarev RC .60 1.50
205 Carl Klingberg RC .50 1.25
206 Greg Nemisz RC .50 1.25
207 Lance Bouma RC .50 1.25
208 Marcus Kruger RC .75 2.00
209 Cameron Gaunce RC .40 1.00
210 John Moore RC .50 1.25
211 Tomas Kubalik RC .50 1.25
212 Tomas Vincour RC .50 1.25
213 Colton Sceviour RC .50 1.25
214 Teemu Hartikainen RC .50 1.25
215 Chris Vande Velde RC .75 2.00
216 Hugh Jessiman RC .50 1.25
217 Scott Timmins RC .50 1.25
218 Drew Bagnall RC .50 1.25
219 Carson McMillan RC .60 1.50
220 Aaron Palushaj RC .50 1.25
221 Brendon Nash RC .50 1.25
222 Jonathon Blum RC .50 1.25
223 Blake Geoffrion RC .50 1.25
224 Adam Henrique RC 1.25 3.00
225 Matt Campanale RC .50 1.25
226 Shane Sims RC .50 1.25
227 Mikko Koskinen RC .60 1.50
228 Todd Ford RC .60 1.50
229 Jamie Doornbosch RC .50 1.25
230 Mark Katic RC .50 1.25
231 Justin DiBenedetto RC .40 1.00
232 Cam Talbot RC 1.25 3.00
233 Patrick Wiercioch RC .50 1.25
234 Erik Condra RC .50 1.25
235 Roman Wick RC .60 1.50
236 Colin Greening RC .50 1.25
237 Andre Benoit RC .60 1.50
238 Stephane Da Costa RC .50 1.25
239 Erik Gustafsson RC .60 1.50
240 Ben Holmstrom RC .50 1.25
241 Zac Rinaldo RC .50 1.25
242 Brian Strait RC .60 1.50
243 Joe Vitale RC .50 1.25
244 Alex Stalock .40 1.00
245 Ben Scrivens RC .50 1.25
246 Matt Frattin RC .50 1.25
247 Joe Colborne RC .50 1.25
248 Yann Suave RC .50 1.25
249 Cody Hodgson RC 4.00 10.00
250 Cody Hodgson CL .75 2.00
251 Ville Leino .30 .75
252 Christian Ehrhoff .25 .60
253 Semyon Varlamov .40 1.00
254 Jean-Sebastien Giguere .40 1.00
255 Jeff Carter .30 .75
256 Tomas Fleischmann .25 .60
257 Kris Versteeg .25 .60
258 Jose Theodore .40 1.00
259 Mike Richards .30 .75
260 Dany Heatley .30 .75
261 Devin Setoguchi .30 .75
262 Evgeni Nabokov .30 .75
263 Brad Richards .40 1.00
264 Ilya Bryzgalov .40 1.00
265 Jaromir Jagr 1.25 3.00
266 Maxime Talbot .25 .60
267 Brent Burns .40 1.00
268 Martin Havlat .30 .75
269 John-Michael Liles .25 .60
270 David Booth .25 .60
271 Tomas Vokoun .30 .75
272 Ondrej Pavelec .40 1.00
273 Evander Kane .40 1.00
274 Alexander Burmistrov .30 .75
275 Wayne Simmonds .50 1.25
276 Brayden Schenn .40 1.00
277 Dustin Byfuglien .40 1.00
278 Ryan Smyth .30 .75
279 Robyn Regehr .25 .60
280 Brian Campbell .25 .60
281 Devante Smith-Pelly RC .75 2.00
282 Peter Holland RC .60 1.50
283 Zack Kassian RC .75 2.00
284 Justin Faulk RC 1.00 2.50
285 Brandon Saad RC 1.25 3.00
286 Gabriel Landeskog RC 2.00 5.00
287 Ryan Johansen RC 2.00 5.00
288 Gustav Nyquist RC 1.50 4.00
289 Ryan Nugent-Hopkins RC 5.00 12.00
290 Anton Lander RC .60 1.50
291 Lennart Petrell RC .75 2.00
292 Colten Teubert RC .60 1.50
293 Erik Gudbranson RC .75 2.00
294 Louis Leblanc RC .60 1.50
295 Raphael Diaz RC .60 1.50
296 Alexei Emelin RC .60 1.50
297 Craig Smith RC .75 2.00
298 Adam Larsson RC .75 2.00
299 Keith Kinkaid RC .60 1.50
300 Tim Erixon RC .60 1.50
301 Calvin de Haan RC .60 1.50
302 Mika Zibanejad RC 2.00 5.00
303 Sean Couturier RC 1.25 3.00
304 Matt Read RC .75 2.00
305 Andy Miele RC .60 1.50
306 Brett Connolly RC .60 1.50
307 Jake Gardiner RC 1.00 2.50
308 Eddie Lack RC .60 1.50
309 Cody Eakin RC 1.00 2.50
310 Mark Scheifele RC 2.50 6.00

2011-12 Upper Deck Victory Black

*1-200 VETS: 15X TO 40X BASIC CARDS
*201-250 ROOK: 6X TO 15X BASIC CARDS
*251-280 VETS: 12X TO 30X BASIC CARDS
*281-310 ROOK: 4X TO 10X BASIC CARDS
49 Corey Crawford 12.00 30.00
195 Nicklas Backstrom 10.00 25.00

2011-12 Upper Deck Victory Red

*RED 1-200: 6X TO 15X BASE
*RED 201-250: 3X TO 8X BASE
49 Corey Crawford 5.00 12.00
195 Nicklas Backstrom 4.00 10.00
249 Cody Hodgson 6.00 15.00
250 Cody Hodgson CL 10.00 25.00

2011-12 Upper Deck Victory Game Breakers

COMPLETE SET (25) 10.00 25.00
GBAK Anze Kopitar .60 1.50
GBAO Alexander Ovechkin 1.50 4.00
GBAS Alexander Semin .40 1.00
GBBR Brad Richards .40 1.00
GBCG Claude Giroux .40 1.00
GBCP Chris Pronger .40 1.00
GBDA Daniel Alfredsson .40 1.00
GBDB Dustin Byfuglien .40 1.00
GBDS Daniel Sedin .50 1.25
GBEM Evgeni Malkin .75 2.00
GBES Eric Staal .50 1.25
GBHZ Henrik Zetterberg .50 1.25
GBJI Jarome Iginla .50 1.25
GBJS Jeff Skinner .50 1.25
GBJT John Tavares .60 1.50
GBMK Mikko Koivu .30 .75
GBMS Martin St. Louis .40 1.00
GBNB Nicklas Backstrom .40 1.00
GBPK Phil Kessel .40 1.00
GBPS Patrick Sharp .40 1.00
GBRG Ryan Getzlaf .40 1.00
GBSC Sidney Crosby 1.50 4.00
GBSS Steven Stamkos .75 2.00
GBTH Taylor Hall .40 1.00
GBTO Jonathan Toews .60 1.50

2011-12 Upper Deck Victory Stars of the Game

COMPLETE SET (25) 10.00 25.00
SOGAO Alexander Ovechkin 1.50 4.00
SOGCP Carey Price .75 2.00
SOGDD Drew Doughty .50 1.25
SOGDH Dany Heatley .30 .75
SOGEM Evgeni Malkin .75 2.00
SOGES Eric Staal .50 1.25
SOGHS Henrik Sedin .50 1.25
SOGJT Jonathan Toews .60 1.50
SOGMB Martin Brodeur 1.00 2.50
SOGMD Matt Duchene .40 1.00
SOGMF Marc-Andre Fleury .75 2.00

SOGMG Marian Gaborik .40 1.00
SOGMR Mike Richards .30 .75
SOGMS Martin St. Louis .40 1.00
SOGNB Nicklas Backstrom .40 1.00
SOGPD Pavel Datsyuk .60 1.50
SOGPK Patrick Kane .75 2.00
SOGRG Ryan Getzlaf .40 1.00
SOGRM Ryan Miller .40 1.00
SOGRN Rick Nash .40 1.00
SOGSC Sidney Crosby 1.50 4.00
SOGSS Steven Stamkos .75 2.00
SOGTH Joe Thornton .60 1.50
SOGTT Tim Thomas .40 1.00
SOGZP Zach Parise .40 1.00

2015-16 Upper Deck Victory Black

VB1 Shane Prince .75 2.00
VB2 Sam Bennett 4.00 10.00
VB3 Ryan Hartman 1.50 4.00
VB4 Ronalds Kenins .75 2.00
VB5 Matt Puempel 1.00 2.50
VB6 Malcolm Subban 2.00 5.00
VB7 Kevin Fiala 1.50 4.00
VB8 Jacob de la Rose 1.25 3.00
VB9 Emile Poirier 1.00 2.50
VB10 Antoine Bibeau 1.25 3.00
VB11 Brendan Ranford 1.00 2.50
VB12 Henrik Samuelsson .75 2.00
VB13 Stefan Noesen .75 2.00
VB14 Kyle Baun 1.25 3.00
VB15 Josh Anderson 2.50 6.00
VB16 Andrew Copp 1.25 3.00
VB17 Connor McDavid 100.00 250.00
VB18 Jake Virtanen 3.00 8.00
VB19 Nikolaj Ehlers 5.00 12.00
VB20 Robby Fabbri 3.00 8.00
VB21 Max Domi 5.00 12.00
VB22 Dylan Larkin 20.00 40.00
VB23 Artemi Panarin 10.00 25.00
VB24 Mike Condon 2.50 6.00
VB25 Noah Hanifin 4.00 10.00
VB26 Jack Eichel 20.00 40.00

2016-17 Upper Deck Victory Black

V1 William Nylander 8.00 20.00
V2 Miles Wood 1.50 4.00
V3 Kasperi Kapanen 3.00 8.00
V4 Sonny Milano 2.50 6.00
V5 Brendan Leipsic 1.50 4.00
V6 Nikita Soshnikov 1.25 3.00
V7 Tobias Lindberg 3.00 8.00
V8 Connor Brown 3.00 8.00
V9 Frederik Gauthier 1.50 4.00
V10 Zach Hyman 6.00 15.00
V11 Pavel Zacha 3.00 8.00
V12 Jason Dickinson 1.50 4.00
V13 Anthony Mantha 4.00 10.00
V14 Josh Morrissey 5.00 12.00
V15 Charlie Lindgren 3.00 8.00
V16 Hudson Fasching 2.00 5.00
V17 Auston Matthews 30.00 80.00
V18 Patrik Laine 20.00 50.00
V19 Matthew Tkachuk 8.00 20.00
V20 Mikhail Sergachev 3.00 8.00
V21 Mitch Marner 15.00 40.00
V22 Tyler Motte 2.00 5.00
V23 Nick Schmaltz 2.50 6.00
V24 Zach Werenski 6.00 15.00
V25 Ivan Provorov 3.00 8.00
V26 Jimmy Vesey 3.00 8.00

2021-22 Upper Deck Victory Black

V1 Spencer Knight 2.50 6.00
V2 Cam York 1.25 3.00
V3 Calen Addison 1.25 3.00
V4 Ukko-Pekka Luukkonen 2.00 5.00
V5 Cole Caufield 5.00 12.00
V6 Joe Veleno 1.50 4.00
V7 Quinton Byfield 3.00 8.00
V8 Grigori Denisenko 1.50 4.00
V9 Jeremy Swayman 4.00 10.00
V10 Shane Pinto 2.00 5.00
V11 Trevor Zegras 2.50 6.00
V12 Alex Newhook 2.00 5.00
V13 Jamie Drysdale 2.00 5.00

2021-22 Upper Deck Victory Stars

VS1 Ryan Getzlaf 1.25 3.00
VS2 Lawson Crouse .75 2.00
VS3 Patrice Bergeron 1.50 4.00
VS4 Jeff Skinner 1.25 3.00
VS5 Andrew Mangiapane 1.25 3.00
VS6 Jordan Staal 1.00 2.50
VS7 Marc-Andre Fleury 2.50 6.00
VS8 Nathan MacKinnon 5.00 12.00
VS9 Boone Jenner 1.25 3.00
VS10 Tyler Seguin 1.50 4.00
VS11 Tyler Bertuzzi 1.00 2.50
VS12 Connor McDavid 6.00 15.00
VS13 Jonathan Huberdeau 1.50 4.00
VS14 Drew Doughty 1.50 4.00
VS15 Cam Talbot 1.25 3.00
VS16 Nick Suzuki 2.50 6.00
VS17 Matt Duchene 1.25 3.00
VS18 Dougie Hamilton 1.00 2.50
VS19 Mathew Barzal 1.50 4.00
VS20 Alexis Lafreniere 2.00 5.00
VS21 Connor Brown 1.00 2.50
VS22 Claude Giroux 1.25 3.00
VS23 Sidney Crosby 5.00 12.00
VS24 Brent Burns 1.25 3.00
VS25 Jordan Eberle 1.25 3.00
VS26 Ryan O'Reilly 1.25 3.00
VS27 Steven Stamkos 2.50 6.00
VS28 Mitch Marner 2.00 5.00
VS29 Bo Horvat 1.50 4.00
VS30 Mark Stone 1.50 4.00
VS31 Tom Wilson (NHL) 1.25 3.00
VS32 Mark Scheifele 2.00 5.00

2000-01 Upper Deck Vintage

1 German Titov .07 .20
2 Teemu Selanne .25 .60
3 Matt Cullen .07 .20
4 Oleg Tverdovsky .07 .20
5 Jean-Sebastien Giguere .12 .30
6 Guy Hebert .10 .25
7 Mike Leclerc .07 .20
8 Jason Marshall .07 .20
9 Paul Kariya .12 .30
10 Steve Rucchin .07 .20
11 Paul Kariya
Guy Hebert
Teemu Selanne .25 .60
12 Paul Kariya
Guy Hebert .12 .30
13 Patrik Stefan .10 .25
14 Damian Rhodes .07 .20
15 Donald Audette .10 .25
16 Yannick Tremblay .07 .20
17 Hnat Domenichelli .07 .20
18 Dean Sylvester .07 .20
19 Steve Guolla .07 .20
20 Petr Buzek .07 .20
21 Andrew Brunette .07 .20
22 Ray Ferraro .07 .20
23 Patrik Stefan
Damian Rhodes
Denny Lambert .10 .25
24 Patrik Stefan
Damian Rhodes .10 .25
25 Joe Thornton .20 .50
26 Brian Rolston .10 .25
27 Kyle McLaren .07 .20
28 Sergei Samsonov .10 .25
29 Paul Coffey .12 .30
30 Andrei Kovalenko .07 .20
31 Jason Allison .10 .25
32 Bill Guerin .12 .30
33 Byron Dafoe .10 .25
34 Mikko Eloranta .07 .20
35 Don Sweeney .07 .20
36 Thrntn/Dafoe/McLar .20 .50
37 J.Thornton/Dafoe .20 .50
38 Miroslav Satan .07 .20
39 Dominik Hasek .20 .50
40 Stu Barnes .10 .25
41 Chris Gratton .07 .20
42 Doug Gilmour .15 .40
43 Curtis Brown .07 .20
44 James Patrick .07 .20
45 Alexei Zhitnik .10 .25
46 Rhett Warrener .07 .20
47 Dave Andreychuk .12 .30
48 Maxim Afinogenov .07 .20
49 Satan/Hasek/Ray CL .20 .50
50 M.Satan/D.Hasek .20 .50
51 Valeri Bure .10 .25
52 Mike Vernon .10 .25
53 Marc Savard .07 .20
54 Clarke Wilm .07 .20
55 Phil Housley .10 .25
56 Fred Brathwaite .10 .25
57 Cory Stillman .07 .20
58 Derek Morris .07 .20
59 Robyn Regehr .07 .20
60 Jarome Iginla .15 .40
61 Valeri Bure
Fred Brathwaite
Jason Wiemer .10 .25
62 Valeri Bure
Fred Brathwaite .10 .25
63 Bates Battaglia .07 .20
64 Sandis Ozolinsh .07 .20
65 Jeff O'Neill .07 .20
66 Ron Francis .15 .40
67 Sami Kapanen .07 .20
68 Martin Gelinas .07 .20
69 Arturs Irbe .10 .25
70 Dave Tanabe .07 .20
71 Rod Brind'Amour .12 .30
72 Glen Wesley .07 .20
73 Jeff O'Neill
Arturs Irbe
Ron Francis .15 .40
74 Ron Francis
Arturs Irbe .15 .40
75 Tony Amonte .10 .25
76 Steve Sullivan .07 .20
77 Eric Daze .10 .25
78 Boris Mironov .07 .20
79 Jocelyn Thibault .10 .25
80 Jean-Yves Leroux .07 .20
81 Valeri Zelepukin .07 .20
82 Alexei Zhamnov .10 .25
83 Josef Marha .07 .20
84 Michael Nylander .07 .20
85 Tony Amonte
Jocelyn Thibault
Bob Probert .12 .30
86 Tony Amonte
Jocelyn Thibault .10 .25
87 Patrick Roy .30 .75
88 Joe Sakic .25 .60
89 Jon Klemm .07 .20
90 Adam Deadmarsh .07 .20
91 Ray Bourque .20 .50
92 Peter Forsberg .25 .60
93 Milan Hejduk .10 .25
94 Chris Drury .10 .25
95 Alex Tanguay .10 .25
96 Adam Foote .10 .25
97 Dave Reid .07 .20
98 Sakic/Roy/Bourque CL .30 .75
99 J.Sakic/P.Roy .30 .75
100 Marc Denis .10 .25
101 Geoff Sanderson .07 .20
102 Ron Tugnutt .10 .25
103 Lyle Odelein .07 .20
104 Krzysztof Oliwa .07 .20
105 Kevyn Adams .07 .20
106 Steve Heinze .07 .20
107 Jamie Pushor .07 .20
108 Bruce Gardiner .07 .20
109 Jan Caloun .07 .20
110 Kevyn Adams
Marc Denis
Krzysztof Oliwa .10 .25
111 Geoff Sanderson
Ron Tugnutt .10 .25
112 Mike Modano .20 .50
113 Jere Lehtinen .10 .25
114 Brett Hull .25 .60
115 Sergei Zubov .10 .25
116 Jamie Langenbrunner .10 .25
117 Shaun Van Allen .07 .20
118 Ed Belfour .12 .30
119 Brenden Morrow .10 .25
120 Darryl Sydor .10 .25
121 Joe Nieuwendyk .10 .25
122 Derian Hatcher .10 .25
123 Mike Modano
Ed Belfour
Derian Hatcher .20 .50
124 Mike Modano
Ed Belfour .20 .50
125 Steve Yzerman .30 .75
126 Nicklas Lidstrom .12 .30
127 Sergei Fedorov .20 .50
128 Chris Osgood .12 .30
129 Brendan Shanahan .12 .30
130 Larry Murphy .10 .25
131 Darren McCarty .07 .20
132 Chris Chelios .12 .30
133 Kris Draper .07 .20
134 Tomas Holmstrom .10 .25
135 Slava Kozlov .10 .25
136 Yzerm/Osgood/Shanahn CL .30 .75
137 S.Yzerman/C.Osgood .30 .75
138 Doug Weight .12 .30
139 Todd Marchant .07 .20
140 Eric Brewer .07 .20
141 Mike Grier .07 .20
142 Tom Poti .07 .20
143 Ryan Smyth .10 .25
144 Tommy Salo .10 .25
145 Janne Niinimaa .07 .20
146 Daniel Cleary .10 .25
147 Bill Guerin .12 .30
148 Doug Weight
Tommy Salo
Georges Laraque .12 .30
149 Doug Weight
Tommy Salo .12 .30
150 Pavel Bure .12 .30
151 Ray Whitney .10 .25
152 Viktor Kozlov .10 .25
153 Igor Larionov .12 .30
154 Scott Mellanby .07 .20
155 Trevor Kidd .07 .20
156 Rob Niedermayer .10 .25
157 Robert Svehla .07 .20
158 Roberto Luongo .20 .50
159 Mike Sillinger .07 .20
160 Pavel Bure
Roberto Luongo
Peter Worrell .20 .50
161 Pavel Bure
Trevor Kidd .12 .30
162 Zigmund Palffy .12 .30
163 Luc Robitaille .12 .30
164 Stephane Fiset .07 .20
165 Rob Blake .12 .30
166 Bryan Smolinski .10 .25
167 Glen Murray .10 .25
168 Mattias Norstrom .07 .20
169 Jamie Storr .10 .25
170 Craig Johnson .07 .20
171 Nelson Emerson .07 .20
172 Zigmund Palffy
Jamie Storr
Rob Blake .12 .30
173 Luc Robitaille
Stephane Fiset .12 .30
174 Stacy Roest .07 .20
175 Manny Fernandez .07 .20
176 Jim Dowd .07 .20
177 Curtis Leschyshyn .07 .20
178 Jeff Nielsen .07 .20
179 Aaron Gavey .07 .20
180 Sergei Krivokrasov .07 .20
181 Brad Bombardir .07 .20
182 Cam Stewart .07 .20
183 Scott Pellerin .07 .20
184 Pell/Frndz/Gabrk CL .25 .60
185 Sergei Krivokrasov
Manny Fernandez .07 .20
186 Saku Koivu .12 .30
187 Eric Weinrich .07 .20
188 Sergei Zholtok .07 .20
189 Dainius Zubrus .07 .20
190 Brian Savage .07 .20
191 Jeff Hackett .07 .20
192 Patrick Poulin .07 .20
193 Jose Theodore .12 .30
194 Christian Laflamme .07 .20
195 Martin Rucinsky .07 .20
196 Trevor Linden
Jose Theodore
Saku Koivu CL .12 .30
197 Saku Koivu
Jose Theodore .12 .30
198 Greg Johnson .07 .20
199 Cliff Ronning .07 .20
200 Drake Berehowsky .07 .20
201 Mike Dunham .07 .20
202 David Legwand .12 .30
203 Tom Fitzgerald .07 .20
204 Patric Kjellberg .07 .20
205 Scott Walker .07 .20
206 Kimmo Timonen .07 .20
207 Bill Houlder .07 .20
208 David Legwand
Mike Dunham
Todd Fitzgerald .12 .30
209 David Legwand
Mike Dunham .12 .30
210 Scott Stevens .12 .30
211 Martin Brodeur .30 .75
212 Jason Arnott .10 .25
213 Patrik Elias .12 .30
214 Alexander Mogilny .10 .25
215 Scott Gomez .10 .25
216 John Madden .10 .25
217 Bobby Holik .07 .20
218 Petr Sykora .10 .25
219 Ken Sutton .07 .20
220 Randy McKay .07 .20
221 Gomz/Brodr/Stvns .30 .75
222 S.Gomez/M.Brodeur .30 .75
223 Tim Connolly .07 .20
224 Kevin Haller .07 .20
225 Brad Isbister .07 .20
226 Mariusz Czerkawski .07 .20
227 Roman Hamrlik .07 .20
228 Claude Lapointe .07 .20
229 Bill Muckalt .07 .20
230 John Vanbiesbrouck .12 .30
231 Kenny Jonsson .07 .20
232 Mark Parrish .07 .20
233 Tim Connolly
John Vanbiesbrouck
Kenny Jonsson .12 .30
234 Tim Connolly
John Vanbiesbrouck .12 .30
235 Theo Fleury .15 .40
236 Brian Leetch .12 .30
237 Mark Messier .25 .60
238 Adam Graves .10 .25
239 Mike Richter .12 .30
240 Vladimir Malakhov .07 .20
241 Mike York .07 .20
242 Radek Dvorak .10 .25
243 Petr Nedved .10 .25
244 Jan Hlavac .07 .20
245 Tim Taylor .07 .20
246 Mark Messier
Mike Richter
Adam Graves .25 .60
247 Mark Messier
Mike Richter .25 .60
248 Radek Bonk .10 .25
249 Marian Hossa .12 .30
250 Jason York .07 .20
251 Wade Redden .07 .20
252 Patrick Lalime .10 .25
253 Daniel Alfredsson .12 .30
254 Shawn McEachern .07 .20
255 Sami Salo .07 .20
256 Petr Schastlivy .07 .20
257 Vaclav Prospal .07 .20
258 Alexei Yashin
Patrick Lalime
Marian Hossa .12 .30
259 Marian Hossa
Patrick Lalime .12 .30
260 John LeClair .12 .30
261 Rick Tocchet .07 .20
262 Daymond Langkow .07 .20
263 Simon Gagne .12 .30
264 Keith Primeau .10 .25
265 Eric Desjardins .10 .25
266 Brian Boucher .10 .25
267 Andy Delmore .07 .20
268 Mark Recchi .15 .40
269 Keith Jones .07 .20
270 Chris Therien .07 .20
271 John LeClair
Brian Boucher
Rick Tocchet .12 .30
272 John LeClair
Brian Boucher .12 .30
273 Jeremy Roenick .20 .50
274 Teppo Numminen .07 .20
275 Brad May .07 .20
276 Keith Tkachuk .12 .30
277 Trevor Letowski .07 .20
278 Shane Doan .10 .25
279 Jyrki Lumme .07 .20
280 Joe Juneau .07 .20
281 Sean Burke .10 .25
282 Travis Green .07 .20
283 Jeremy Roenick
Sean Burke
Keith Tkachuk .20 .50
284 Keith Tkachuk
Sean Burke .12 .30
285 Jean-Sebastien Aubin .10 .25
286 Jaromir Jagr .40 1.00
287 Alexei Morozov .07 .20
288 Josef Beranek .07 .20
289 Jan Hrdina .07 .20
290 Milan Kraft .07 .20
291 Alexei Kovalev .10 .25
292 Robert Lang .07 .20
293 Janne Laukkanen .07 .20
294 Martin Straka .10 .25
295 J.Jagr/Aubin/Kasp .40 1.00
296 J.Jagr/J-S Aubin .40 1.00
297 Niklas Sundstrom .07 .20
298 Owen Nolan .12 .30
299 Jeff Friesen .07 .20
300 Vincent Damphousse .10 .25
301 Brad Stuart .10 .25
302 Marco Sturm .07 .20
303 Alexander Korolyuk .07 .20
304 Mike Ricci .07 .20
305 Patrick Marleau .12 .30
306 Steve Shields .07 .20
307 Jeff Friesen
Steve Shields
Owen Nolan .12 .30
308 Jeff Friesen
Steve Shields .07 .20
309 Chris Pronger .12 .30
310 Pavol Demitra .15 .40
311 Marty Reasoner .07 .20
312 Jochen Hecht .07 .20
313 Michal Handzus .07 .20
314 Al MacInnis .15 .40
315 Roman Turek .10 .25
316 Lubos Bartecko .07 .20
317 Jamal Mayers .07 .20
318 Dallas Drake .07 .20
319 Pierre Turgeon .10 .25
320 Pavol Demitra
Roman Turek
Chris Pronger .15 .40
321 Chris Pronger
Roman Turek .12 .30
322 Vincent Lecavalier .12 .30
323 Mike Johnson .07 .20
324 Brad Richards .12 .30
325 Dan Cloutier .10 .25
326 Paul Mara .07 .20
327 Fredrik Modin .07 .20
328 Bryan Muir .07 .20
329 Jassen Cullimore .07 .20
330 Todd Warriner .07 .20
331 Petr Svoboda .07 .20
332 Vincent Lecavalier
Dan Cloutier
Petr Svoboda .12 .30
333 Vincent Lecavalier
Dan Cloutier .12 .30
334 Mats Sundin .12 .30
335 Sergei Berezin .07 .20
336 Nikolai Antropov .10 .25
337 Steve Thomas .07 .20
338 Curtis Joseph .15 .40
339 Jonas Hoglund .07 .20
340 Dimitri Yushkevich .07 .20
341 Darcy Tucker .07 .20
342 Gary Roberts .07 .20
343 Jeff Farkas .07 .20
344 Tie Domi .10 .25
345 Mats Sundin
Curtis Joseph
Tie Domi .15 .40
346 Mats Sundin
Curtis Joseph .15 .40
347 Markus Naslund .12 .30
348 Brendan Morrison .12 .30
349 Todd Bertuzzi .10 .25
350 Adrian Aucoin .07 .20
351 Donald Brashear .07 .20
352 Murray Baron .07 .20
353 Daniel Sedin .15 .40
354 Andrew Cassels .07 .20
355 Henrik Sedin .15 .40
356 Mattias Ohlund .07 .20
357 Naslund/Potvin/Brash .20 .50
358 M.Naslund/F.Potvin .20 .50
359 Chris Simon .07 .20
360 Olaf Kolzig .12 .30
361 Jeff Halpern .07 .20
362 Andrei Nikolishin .07 .20
363 Steve Konowalchuk .07 .20
364 Peter Bondra .12 .30
365 Adam Oates .12 .30
366 Richard Zednik .07 .20
367 Sergei Gonchar .07 .20
368 Brendan Witt .07 .20
369 Peter Bondra
Olaf Kolzig
Chris Simon .12 .30
370 Adam Oates
Olaf Kolzig .12 .30
371 Rostislav Klesla RC .40 1.00
372 Jonas Ronnqvist RC .15 .40
373 Eric Nickulas RC .15 .40
374 Andrew Raycroft RC .40 1.00
375 Jeff Cowan RC .15 .40
376 Reto Von Arx RC .20 .50
377 Serge Aubin RC .20 .50
378 Tyler Bouck RC .15 .40
379 Michel Riesen RC .20 .50
380 Eric Belanger RC .20 .50
381 Marian Gaborik RC .50 1.25
382 Scott Hartnell RC .40 1.00
383 Greg Classen RC .15 .40
384 Willie Mitchell RC .25 .60
385 Colin White RC .15 .40
386 Steve Valiquette RC .20 .50
387 Jani Hurme RC .15 .40
388 Martin Havlat RC .50 1.25
389 Justin Williams RC .40 1.00
390 Petr Hubacek RC .15 .40
391 Roman Simicek RC .15 .40
392 Matt Elich RC .20 .50
393 Brent Sopel RC .25 .60
394 Marc-Andre Thinel RC .15 .40
395 Zdenek Blatny RC .15 .40
396 Michael Ryder RC 3.00 8.00
397 Jason Jaspers RC .15 .40
398 Jordan Krestanovich RC .15 .40
399 Fedor Fedorov RC .20 .50
400 Jeff Bateman RC .15 .40
31S Curtis Joseph SAMPLE .40 1.00

2000-01 Upper Deck Vintage All UD Team

COMPLETE SET (10) 6.00 15.00
UD1 Patrick Roy 2.00 5.00
UD2 Martin Brodeur 1.00 2.50
UD3 Chris Pronger .25 .60
UD4 Ray Bourque .75 2.00
UD5 Paul Kariya .25 .60
UD6 John LeClair .50 1.25
UD7 Steve Yzerman 2.00 5.00
UD8 Peter Forsberg 1.00 2.50
UD9 Jaromir Jagr .60 1.50
UD10 Pavel Bure .50 1.25

2000-01 Upper Deck Vintage Dynasty A Piece of History

*GOLD/50: .6X TO 1.5X BASIC INSERTS
BG B.Bourne/C.Gillies 8.00 20.00
BK M.Bossy/A.Kallur 8.00 20.00
GC B.Goring/B.Carroll 8.00 20.00
GH C.Gillies/M.Hallin 8.00 20.00
GK W.Gretzky/M.Messier 30.00 80.00
LJ M.Lemieux/J.Jagr 25.00 60.00
LL P.Lafontaine/D.Langevin 8.00 20.00
NS B.Nystrom/B.Sutter 8.00 20.00
PR D.Potvin/C.Resch 8.00 20.00
TP B.Trottier/S.Persson 8.00 20.00
YO S.Yzerman/C.Osgood 10.00 25.00

2000-01 Upper Deck Vintage Great Gloves

COMPLETE SET (20) 4.00 10.00
GG1 Guy Hebert .40 1.00
GG2 Byron Dafoe .40 1.00
GG3 Dominik Hasek 1.25 2.50
GG4 Fred Brathwaite .40 1.00
GG5 Arturs Irbe .40 1.00
GG6 Patrick Roy 2.50 6.00
GG7 Ed Belfour .50 1.25
GG8 Chris Osgood .40 1.00
GG9 Tommy Salo .40 1.00
GG10 Trevor Kidd .40 1.00
GG11 Jose Theodore .60 1.50
GG12 Mike Richter .40 1.00
GG13 Brian Boucher .40 1.00
GG14 Jean-Sebastien Aubin .40 1.00
GG15 Steve Shields .40 1.00
GG16 Roman Turek .40 1.00
GG17 Dan Cloutier .40 1.00
GG18 Curtis Joseph .50 1.25
GG19 Felix Potvin .60 1.50
GG20 Olaf Kolzig .40 1.00

2000-01 Upper Deck Vintage Messier Heroes of Hockey

COMPLETE SET (10) 10.00 20.00
COMMON MESSIER 1.25 3.00

2000-01 Upper Deck Vintage National Heroes

COMPLETE SET (20) 6.00 15.00
NH1 Paul Kariya .25 .60
NH2 Teemu Selanne .25 .60
NH3 Patrik Stefan .20 .50
NH4 Sergei Samsonov .20 .50
NH5 Dominik Hasek .50 1.25
NH6 Valeri Bure .20 .50
NH7 Tony Amonte .20 .50
NH8 Patrick Roy 1.25 3.00
NH9 Peter Forsberg .60 1.50
NH10 Mike Modano .40 1.00
NH11 Steve Yzerman 1.25 3.00
NH12 Pavel Bure .30 .75
NH13 Saku Koivu .25 .60
NH14 Martin Brodeur .60 1.50
NH15 Scott Gomez .20 .50
NH16 Mark Messier .30 .75
NH17 John LeClair .30 .75
NH18 Jeremy Roenick .30 .75
NH19 Jaromir Jagr .40 1.00
NH20 Mats Sundin .25 .60

2000-01 Upper Deck Vintage Original 6 Piece of History

*GOLD/67: 1.2X TO 3X BASIC
OCJ Curtis Joseph 6.00 15.00
OJT Jose Theodore 8.00 20.00
OMY Mike York 6.00 15.00
OSS Sergei Samsonov 6.00 15.00
OSY Steve Yzerman 12.00 30.00
OTE Tony Esposito 10.00 25.00

2000-01 Upper Deck Vintage Star Tandems

COMPLETE SET (10) 10.00 20.00
S1A Paul Kariya .50 1.25
S1B Teemu Selanne .50 1.25
S2A Joe Sakic .75 2.00
S2B Patrick Roy 2.00 5.00
S3A Steve Yzerman 2.00 5.00
S3B Brendan Shanahan .60 1.50
S4A Scott Gomez .50 1.25
S4B Martin Brodeur 1.00 2.50
S5A John LeClair .50 1.25
S5B Brian Boucher .50 1.25

2001-02 Upper Deck Vintage

COMPLETE SET (300) 40.00 80.00
1 Jean-Sebastien Giguere .25 .60
2 Jeff Friesen .15 .40
3 Paul Kariya .25 .60
4 Oleg Tverdovsky .15 .40
5 Steve Rucchin .15 .40
6 Mike Leclerc .15 .40
7 Dan Bylsma .15 .40
8 Paul Kariya .25 .60
9 Mighty Ducks CL .15 .40
10 Patrik Stefan .20 .50
11 Tomi Kallio .15 .40
12 Chris Tamer .15 .40
13 Milan Hnilicka .20 .50
14 Ray Ferraro .15 .40
15 Stephen Guolla .15 .40
16 Ray Ferraro .15 .40
17 Thrashers CL .15 .40
18 Kyle McLaren .15 .40
19 Brian Rolston .20 .50
20 Byron Dafoe .20 .50
21 Mikko Eloranta .15 .40
22 Sergei Samsonov .20 .50
23 Joe Thornton .40 1.00
24 Bill Guerin .20 .50
25 Joe Thornton .40 1.00
26 Bruins CL .25 .60
27 Martin Biron .20 .50
28 Maxim Afinogenov .15 .40
29 J-P Dumont .15 .40
30 Chris Gratton .15 .40
31 Rhett Warrener .15 .40
32 Miroslav Satan .20 .50
33 Curtis Brown .15 .40
34 Miroslav Satan .20 .50
35 Sabres CL .15 .40
36 Marc Savard .15 .40
37 Jarome Iginla .30 .75
38 Derek Morris .15 .40
39 Oleg Saprykin .15 .40
40 Jeff Shantz .15 .40
41 Craig Conroy .15 .40
42 Jarome Iginla .30 .75
43 Flames CL .20 .50
44 Jeff O'Neill .15 .40
45 Arturs Irbe .20 .50
46 Shane Willis .15 .40
47 Dave Tanabe .15 .40
48 Rod Brind'Amour .25 .60
49 Sami Kapanen .15 .40
50 Ron Francis .30 .75
51 Jeff O'Neill .20 .50
52 Hurricanes CL .15 .40
53 Eric Daze .15 .40
54 Alexei Zhamnov .20 .50
55 Jaroslav Spacek .15 .40
56 Michael Nylander .15 .40
57 Tony Amonte .20 .50
58 Steve Sullivan .15 .40
59 Kevin Dean .15 .40
60 Steve Sullivan .15 .40
61 Blackhawks CL .15 .40
62 Chris Drury .20 .50
63 Rob Blake .25 .60
64 Joe Sakic .50 1.25
65 Peter Forsberg .50 1.25
66 Ray Bourque .40 1.00
67 Milan Hejduk .20 .50
68 Patrick Roy .60 1.50
69 Joe Sakic .50 1.25
70 Avalanche CL .40 1.00
71 Ron Tugnutt .20 .50
72 Geoff Sanderson .15 .40
73 Espen Knutsen .15 .40
74 Tyler Wright .15 .40
75 Rostislav Klesla .15 .40
76 Jamie Heward .15 .40
77 Geoff Sanderson .15 .40
78 Blue Jackets CL .15 .40
79 Mike Modano .40 1.00
80 Ed Belfour .25 .60
81 Pierre Turgeon .20 .50
82 Joe Nieuwendyk .20 .50
83 Sergei Zubov .20 .50
84 Jere Lehtinen .20 .50
85 Donald Audette .15 .40
86 Mike Modano .40 1.00
87 Stars CL .25 .60
88 Steve Yzerman .60 1.50
89 Brendan Shanahan .25 .60
90 Sergei Fedorov .40 1.00
91 Luc Robitaille .25 .60
92 Dominik Hasek .40 1.00
93 Nicklas Lidstrom .25 .60
94 Darren McCarty .15 .40
95 Brendan Shanahan .25 .60
96 Red Wings CL .40 1.00
97 Tommy Salo .20 .50
98 Mike Comrie .20 .50
99 Tom Poti .15 .40
100 Mike Grier .15 .40
101 Janne Niinimaa .15 .40
102 Ryan Smyth .20 .50
103 Anson Carter .20 .50
104 Ryan Smyth .20 .50
105 Oilers CL .15 .40
106 Pavel Bure .25 .60
107 Viktor Kozlov .15 .40
108 Marcus Nilsson .15 .40
109 Denis Shvidki .15 .40
110 Bret Hedican .15 .40
111 Roberto Luongo .40 1.00
112 Pavel Bure .25 .60
113 Panthers CL .25 .60
114 Zigmund Palffy .25 .60
115 Felix Potvin .40 1.00
116 Adam Deadmarsh .15 .40
117 Glen Murray .20 .50
118 Eric Belanger .15 .40
119 Jason Holland .15 .40
120 Jozef Stumpel .15 .40
121 Zigmund Palffy .25 .60
122 Kings CL .25 .60
123 Marian Gaborik .25 .60
124 Manny Fernandez .15 .40
125 Brad Bombardir .15 .40
126 Lubomir Sekeras .15 .40
127 Wes Walz .15 .40
128 Antti Laaksonen .15 .40
129 Marian Gaborik .25 .60
130 Wild CL .15 .40
131 Saku Koivu .25 .60
132 Oleg Petrov .15 .40
133 Martin Rucinsky .15 .40
134 Jose Theodore .25 .60
135 Brian Savage .15 .40
136 Andrei Markov .25 .60
137 Richard Zednik .20 .50
138 Saku Koivu .25 .60
139 Canadiens CL .15 .40
140 David Legwand .20 .50
141 Mike Dunham .20 .50
142 Scott Walker .15 .40
143 Cliff Ronning .15 .40
144 Patric Kjellberg .15 .40
145 Greg Johnson .15 .40
146 Vitali Yachmenev .15 .40
147 Cliff Ronning .15 .40
148 Predators CL .15 .40
149 Martin Brodeur .60 1.50
150 Patrik Elias .25 .60
151 Jason Arnott .20 .50
152 Scott Niedermayer .25 .60
153 Petr Sykora .15 .40
154 Scott Gomez .20 .50
155 Scott Stevens .25 .60
156 Patrik Elias .25 .60
157 Devils CL .40 1.00
158 Michael Peca .20 .50
159 Rick DiPietro .20 .50
160 Mariusz Czerkawski .15 .40
161 Roman Hamrlik .15 .40
162 Dave Scatchard .15 .40
163 Brad Isbister .15 .40
164 Mark Parrish .15 .40
165 Islanders CL .15 .40
166 Mark Messier .50 1.25
167 Theo Fleury .25 .60
168 Mike Richter .25 .60
169 Brian Leetch .20 .50
170 Kim Johnsson .15 .40
171 Radek Dvorak .15 .40
172 Theo Fleury .30 .75
173 Rangers CL .30 .75
174 Marian Hossa .25 .60
175 Radek Bonk .15 .40
176 Martin Havlat .20 .50
177 Daniel Alfredsson .25 .60
178 Magnus Arvedson .15 .40
179 Patrick Lalime .20 .50
180 Shawn McEachern .15 .40
181 Radek Bonk .15 .40
182 Senators CL .15 .40
183 Jeremy Roenick .40 1.00
184 Roman Cechmanek .20 .50
185 Keith Primeau .20 .50

186 John LeClair .25 .60
187 Kent Manderville .15 .40
188 Mark Recchi .30 .75
189 Eric Desjardins .20 .50
190 Mark Recchi .30 .75
191 Flyers CL .20 .50
192 Sean Burke .15 .40
193 Shane Doan .20 .50
194 Michal Handzus .15 .40
195 Teppo Numminen .15 .40
196 Ladislav Nagy .15 .40
197 Landon Wilson .15 .40
198 Sean Burke .15 .40
199 Coyotes CL .15 .40
200 Alexei Kovalev .20 .50
201 Mario Lemieux 1.00 2.50
202 Johan Hedberg .20 .50
203 Robert Lang .15 .40
204 Martin Straka .15 .40
205 Andrew Ference .15 .40
206 Kevin Stevens .20 .50
207 Alexei Kovalev .20 .50
208 Penguins CL .60 1.50
209 Evgeni Nabokov .20 .50
210 Teemu Selanne .50 1.25
211 Owen Nolan .25 .60
212 Mike Ricci .15 .40
213 Scott Thornton .20 .50
214 Vincent Damphousse .20 .50
215 Brad Stuart .15 .40
216 Evgeni Nabokov .20 .50
217 Sharks CL .30 .75
218 Chris Pronger .25 .60
219 Keith Tkachuk .25 .60
220 Doug Weight .25 .60
221 Pavol Demitra .30 .75
222 Cory Stillman .15 .40
223 Al MacInnis .30 .75
224 Bryce Salvador .15 .40
225 Scott Young .15 .40
226 Blues CL .20 .50
227 Brad Richards .25 .60
228 Vincent Lecavalier .25 .60
229 Nikolai Khabibulin .25 .60
230 Fredrik Modin .15 .40
231 Martin St. Louis .25 .60
232 Pavel Kubina .15 .40
233 Brad Richards .25 .60
234 Lightning CL .15 .40
235 Curtis Joseph .25 .60
236 Mats Sundin .25 .60
237 Shayne Corson .20 .50
238 Darcy Tucker .15 .40
239 Nikolai Antropov .15 .40
240 Gary Roberts .15 .40
241 Bryan McCabe .20 .50
242 Mats Sundin .25 .60
243 Maple Leafs CL .20 .50
244 Markus Naslund .25 .60
245 Daniel Sedin .30 .75
246 Peter Schaefer .15 .40
247 Andrew Cassels .15 .40
248 Brendan Morrison .20 .50
249 Todd Bertuzzi .25 .60
250 Markus Naslund .25 .60
251 Canucks CL .20 .50
252 Steve Konowalchuk .15 .40
253 Sergei Gonchar .15 .40
254 Calle Johansson .20 .50
255 Peter Bondra .25 .60
256 Jaromir Jagr .75 2.00
257 Olaf Kolzig .25 .60
258 Andrei Nikolishin .15 .40
259 Olaf Kolzig .25 .60
260 Capitals CL .25 .60
261 P.Bure/J.Sakic/J.Jagr LL 1.25 3.00
262 J.Jagr/A.Oates/M.Straka LL 1.25 3.00
263 J.Jagr/J.Sakic/P.Elias LL 1.25 3.00
264 P.Bondra/P.Bure/J.Sakic LL .75 2.00
265 J.Sakic/P.Elias/S.Stevens LL .75 2.00
266 Barnaby/Worrell/Grimson LL .25 .60
267 Brodeur/Roy/Hasek LL 1.00 2.50
268 Turco/Cechmanek/Legace LL .40 1.00
269 Dunham/Burke/Turco LL .40 1.00
270 Hasek/Cechmanek/Brodeur LL 1.00 2.50
271 Timo Parssinen RC .60 1.50
272 Ilja Bryzgalov RC 1.25 3.00
273 Kevin Sawyer RC .50 1.25
274 Kamil Piros RC .50 1.25
275 Ilya Kovalchuk RC 2.50 6.00
276 Brian Pothier RC .50 1.25
277 Zdenek Kutlak RC .50 1.25
278 Vaclav Nedorost RC .50 1.25
279 Jaroslav Obsut RC .50 1.25
280 Niko Kapanen RC .75 2.00
281 Kristian Huselius RC .75 2.00
282 Jaroslav Bednar RC .50 1.25
283 Martin Erat RC .60 1.50
284 Josef Boumedienne RC .50 1.25
285 Scott Clemmensen RC .50 1.25
286 Andreas Salomonsson RC .50 1.25
287 Radek Martinek RC .50 1.25
288 Mikael Samuelsson RC .60 1.50
289 Peter Smrek RC .50 1.25
290 Ivan Ciernik RC .50 1.25
291 Chris Neil RC .60 1.50
292 Jiri Dopita RC .50 1.25
293 David Cullen RC .50 1.25
294 Krys Kolanos RC .50 1.25
295 Jeff Jillson RC .50 1.25
296 Mark Rycroft RC .60 1.50
297 Nikita Alexeev RC .50 1.25
298 Thomas Ziegler RC .60 1.50
299 Bob Wren RC .50 1.25
300 Brian Sutherby RC .50 1.25

2001-02 Upper Deck Vintage Jerseys

GGAM Andy Moog 10.00 25.00
GGBS Billy Smith 12.50 30.00
GGGC Gerry Cheevers 10.00 25.00
GGGF Grant Fuhr 10.00 25.00
GGRV Rogie Vachon 12.50 30.00
SCBS Billy Smith 10.00 25.00
SCBT Bryan Trottier 10.00 25.00
SCMB Mike Bossy 10.00 25.00
SCSY Steve Yzerman 6.00 15.00
SCWG Wayne Gretzky 40.00 100.00
SDBC Bobby Clarke 15.00 40.00
SDGH Gordie Howe 12.50 30.00
SDGL Guy Lafleur 10.00 25.00
SDGP Gilbert Perreault 10.00 25.00
SDMB Mike Bossy 10.00 25.00
SDPE Phil Esposito 10.00 25.00

2001-02 Upper Deck Vintage Next In Line

NLBL R.Bourque/N.Lidstrom 50.00 100.00
NLCO G.Cheevers/M.Ouellet 20.00 50.00
NLGS W.Gretzky/J.Sakic 100.00 200.00
NLHY G.Howe/S.Yzerman 125.00 250.00
NLLK G.Lafleur/P.Kariya 25.00 60.00
NLSC B.Smith/R.Cechmanek 15.00 40.00

2001-02 Upper Deck Vintage Sweaters of Honor

SHGL Guy Lafleur 8.00 20.00
SHLA Guy Lapointe 8.00 20.00
SHML Michel Larocque 6.00 15.00
SHSS Steve Shutt 6.00 15.00

2002-03 Upper Deck Vintage

COMPLETE SET (350) 50.00 100.00
1 Vitali Vishnevski .12 .30
2 Paul Kariya SP .40 1.00
3 Samuel Pahlsson .12 .30
4 Mike LeClerc .12 .30
5 Matt Cullen .12 .30
6 Ruslan Salei .12 .30
7 Jean-Sebastien Giguere .20 .50
8 Andy McDonald .20 .50
9 Patrik Stefan .15 .40
10 Milan Hnilicka .15 .40
11 Lubos Bartecko .12 .30
12 Jeff Cowan .12 .30
13 Ilya Kovalchuk .25 .60
14 Frantisek Kaberle .12 .30
15 Dany Heatley .25 .60
16 Daniel Tjarnqvist .12 .30
17 Sergei Samsonov .15 .40
18 P.J. Stock .12 .30
19 Nick Boynton .12 .30
20 Martin Lapointe .15 .40
21 Jozef Stumpel .12 .30
22 John Grahame .12 .30
23 Joe Thornton SP .60 1.50
24 Glen Murray .15 .40
25 Brian Rolston .15 .40
26 Hal Gill .12 .30
27 Stu Barnes .12 .30
28 Tim Connolly .12 .30
29 Miroslav Satan .20 .50
30 Maxim Afinogenov .20 .50
31 Martin Biron .15 .40
32 Jay McKee .12 .30
33 J-P Dumont .12 .30
34 Curtis Brown .12 .30
35 Alexei Zhitnik .15 .40
36 Roman Turek .20 .50
37 Rob Niedermayer .15 .40
38 Marc Savard .12 .30
39 Jarome Iginla SP .50 1.25
40 Derek Morris .12 .30
41 Denis Gauthier .12 .30
42 Dave Lowry .12 .30
43 Craig Conroy .12 .30
44 Sami Kapanen .12 .30
45 Ron Francis .25 .60
46 Rod Brind'Amour .20 .50
47 Niclas Wallin .12 .30
48 Josef Vasicek .12 .30
49 Jeff O'Neill .12 .30
50 Erik Cole .12 .30
51 Dave Tanabe .12 .30
52 Arturs Irbe .15 .40
53 Steve Sullivan .12 .30
54 Ryan VandenBussche .12 .30
55 Michael Nylander .12 .30
56 Mark Bell .12 .30
57 Kyle Calder .12 .30
58 Jocelyn Thibault .15 .40
59 Eric Daze .12 .30
60 Alexei Zhamnov .15 .40
61 Steve Reinprecht .12 .30
62 Stephane Yelle .12 .30
63 Rob Blake .20 .50
64 Peter Forsberg .40 1.00
65 Patrick Roy SP 1.00 2.50
66 Milan Hejduk .15 .40
67 Joe Sakic SP .75 2.00
68 Greg DeVries .12 .30
69 Chris Drury .20 .50
70 Alex Tanguay .15 .40
71 Adam Foote .12 .30
72 David Vyborny .12 .30
73 Rostislav Klesla .12 .30
74 Marc Denis .15 .40
75 Ray Whitney .15 .40
76 Jody Shelley .12 .30
77 Jean-Luc Grand-Pierre .12 .30
78 Geoff Sanderson .15 .40
79 Espen Knutsen .12 .30
80 Pierre Turgeon .15 .40
81 Mike Modano SP .60 1.50
82 Marty Turco .20 .50
83 Bill Guerin .20 .50
84 Jere Lehtinen .20 .50
85 Jason Arnott .15 .40
86 Derian Hatcher .15 .40
87 Brenden Morrow .15 .40
88 Steve Yzerman SP 1.00 2.50
89 Sergei Fedorov .30 .75
90 Pavel Datsyuk .30 .75
91 Nicklas Lidstrom .20 .50
92 Luc Robitaille .20 .50
93 Kris Draper .12 .30
94 Curtis Joseph .25 .60
95 Dominik Hasek SP .60 1.50
96 Brett Hull .40 1.00
97 Brendan Shanahan .20 .50
98 Boyd Devereaux .12 .30
99 Tommy Salo .15 .40
100 Ryan Smyth .15 .40
101 Mike York .12 .30
102 Mike Comrie SP .40 1.00
103 Georges Laraque .15 .40
104 Ethan Moreau .12 .30
105 Daniel Cleary .15 .40
106 Anson Carter .15 .40
107 Viktor Kozlov .12 .30
108 Valeri Bure .15 .40
109 Olli Jokinen .20 .50
110 Sandis Ozolinsh .20 .50
111 Roberto Luongo .30 .75
112 Peter Worrell .12 .30
113 Niklas Hagman .12 .30
114 Kristian Huselius .12 .30
115 Zigmund Palffy .20 .50
116 Mattias Norstrom .12 .30
117 Mathieu Schneider .12 .30
118 Jason Allison .15 .40
119 Felix Potvin .30 .75
120 Bryan Smolinski .15 .40
121 Adam Deadmarsh .12 .30
122 Aaron Miller .12 .30
123 Richard Park .12 .30
124 Nick Schultz .12 .30
125 Marian Gaborik SP .40 1.00
126 Jim Dowd .12 .30
127 Hnat Domenichelli .12 .30
128 Filip Kuba .12 .30
129 Manny Fernandez .12 .30
130 Andrew Brunette .12 .30
131 Yanic Perreault .12 .30
132 Saku Koivu .20 .50
133 Richard Zednik .12 .30
134 Jose Theodore SP .20 .50
135 Donald Audette .12 .30
136 Craig Rivet .12 .30
137 Andrei Markov .20 .50
138 Andreas Dackell .12 .30
139 Stu Grimson .12 .30
140 Scott Hartnell .12 .30
141 Mike Dunham .15 .40
142 Martin Erat .12 .30
143 Kimmo Timonen .12 .30
144 Denis Arkhipov .12 .30
145 David Legwand .15 .40
146 Andy Delmore .12 .30
147 Sergei Brylin .12 .30
148 Scott Stevens .20 .50
149 Scott Niedermayer .20 .50
150 John Madden .12 .30
151 Patrik Elias .20 .50
152 Martin Brodeur SP 1.00 2.50
153 Joe Nieuwendyk .15 .40
154 Brian Rafalski .12 .30
155 Roman Hamrlik .12 .30
156 Raffi Torres .12 .30
157 Michael Peca .15 .40
158 Mark Parrish .12 .30
159 Oleg Kvasha .12 .30
160 Eric Cairns .12 .30
161 Dave Scatchard .12 .30
162 Chris Osgood .20 .50
163 Alexei Yashin SP .30 .75
164 Tom Poti .12 .30
165 Sandy McCarthy .12 .30
166 Radek Dvorak .15 .40
167 Petr Nedved .12 .30
168 Pavel Bure SP .40 1.00
169 Matthew Barnaby .12 .30
170 Mark Messier SP .40 1.00
171 Eric Lindros .30 .75
172 Dan Blackburn .15 .40
173 Brian Leetch .15 .40
174 Wade Redden .12 .30
175 Radek Bonk .12 .30
176 Patrick Lalime .15 .40
177 Mike Fisher .12 .30
178 Martin Havlat .15 .40
179 Marian Hossa .20 .50
180 Magnus Arvedson .12 .30
181 Daniel Alfredsson .20 .50
182 Simon Gagne SP .40 1.00
183 Kim Johnsson .12 .30
184 Roman Cechmanek .15 .40
185 Mark Recchi .25 .60
186 Keith Primeau .15 .40
187 Justin Williams .15 .40
188 John LeClair .20 .50
189 Jeremy Roenick .30 .75
190 Eric Weinrich .12 .30
191 Donald Brashear .12 .30
192 Teppo Numminen .12 .30
193 Shane Doan .15 .40
194 Sean Burke .12 .30
195 Ladislav Nagy .12 .30
196 Daymond Langkow .15 .40
197 Daniel Briere .15 .40
198 Claude Lemieux .15 .40
199 Tony Amonte .15 .40
200 Ville Nieminen .12 .30
201 Martin Straka .15 .40
202 Mario Lemieux SP 1.50 4.00
203 Johan Hedberg .20 .50
204 Jan Hrdina .12 .30
205 Andrew Ference .12 .30
206 Alexei Kovalev .15 .40
207 Alexei Morozov .15 .40
208 Vincent Damphousse .12 .30
209 Scott Thornton .12 .30
210 Patrick Marleau .20 .50
211 Owen Nolan .20 .50
212 Mike Ricci .12 .30
213 Marcus Ragnarsson .12 .30
214 Marco Sturm .12 .30
215 Evgeni Nabokov SP .30 .75
216 Brad Stuart .12 .30
217 Tyson Nash .12 .30
218 Shjon Podein .12 .30
219 Pavol Demitra .25 .60
220 Keith Tkachuk SP .40 1.00
221 Doug Weight .20 .50
222 Cory Stillman .12 .30
223 Chris Pronger .20 .50
224 Brent Johnson .15 .40
225 Al MacInnis .25 .60
226 Vincent Lecavalier .20 .50
227 Vaclav Prospal .12 .30
228 Shane Willis .12 .30
229 Pavel Kubina .12 .30
230 Nikolai Khabibulin .20 .50
231 Martin St. Louis .20 .50
232 Fredrik Modin .12 .30
233 Brad Richards .20 .50
234 Tomas Kaberle .12 .30
235 Tie Domi .15 .40
236 Shayne Corson .15 .40
237 Mats Sundin SP .40 1.00
238 Gary Roberts .12 .30
239 Darcy Tucker .12 .30
240 Ed Belfour .20 .50
241 Bryan McCabe .12 .30
242 Alyn McCauley .12 .30
243 Alexander Mogilny .15 .40
244 Trevor Linden .20 .50
245 Todd Bertuzzi .20 .50
246 Markus Naslund .20 .50
247 Henrik Sedin .25 .60
248 Ed Jovanovski .15 .40
249 Daniel Sedin .25 .60
250 Dan Cloutier .15 .40
251 Brendan Morrison .15 .40
252 Brendan Witt .12 .30
253 Steve Konowalchuk .12 .30
254 Sergei Gonchar .15 .40
255 Peter Bondra .20 .50
256 Olaf Kolzig .20 .50
257 Jeff Halpern .12 .30
258 Jaromir Jagr SP 1.25 3.00
259 Andrei Nikolishin .12 .30
260 Robert Lang .12 .30
261 Mighty Ducks CL .12 .30
262 Thrashers CL .15 .40
263 Bruins CL .20 .50
264 Sabres CL .12 .30
265 Flames CL .15 .40
266 Hurricanes CL .15 .40
267 Blackhawks CL .10 .25
268 Avalanche CL .30 .75
269 Blue Jackets CL .10 .25
270 Stars CL .20 .50
271 Red Wings CL .30 .75
272 Oilers CL .12 .30
273 Panthers CL .20 .50
274 Kings CL .20 .50
275 Wild CL .12 .30
276 Canadiens CL .12 .30
277 Predators CL .10 .25
278 Devils CL .30 .75
279 Islanders CL .12 .30
280 Rangers CL .25 .60
281 Senators CL .12 .30
282 Flyers CL .20 .50
283 Coyotes CL .10 .25
284 Penguins CL .50 1.25
285 Sharks CL .12 .30
286 Blues CL .15 .40
287 Lightning CL .12 .30
288 Maple Leafs CL .12 .30
289 Canucks CL .12 .30
290 Capitals CL .40 1.00
291 Joe Sakic AA .50 1.25
292 Patrick Roy AA .60 1.50
293 Mike Modano AA .40 1.00
294 Brendan Shanahan AA .25 .60
295 Steve Yzerman AA .60 1.50
296 Detroit Red Wings AA .30 .75
297 Joe Nieuwendyk AA .20 .50
298 Martin Brodeur AA .60 1.50
299 Pavel Bure AA .25 .60
300 Brian Leetch AA .20 .50
301 Jeremy Roenick AA .40 1.00
302 Mark Recchi AA .30 .75
303 Mario Lemieux AA 1.00 2.50
304 Teemu Selanne AA .50 1.25
305 Peter Bondra AA .25 .60
306 Iginla/Murray/Sundin SL .25 .60
307 Oates/Allison/Sakic SL .40 1.00
308 Iginla/Naslund/Bertuzzi SL .25 .60
309 Bondra/Iginla/Yashin SL .25 .60
310 Gonchar/Lidstrom/Blake SL .20 .50
311 Rolston/Peca/Satan SL .20 .50
312 Chelios/Roenick/Gagne SL .30 .75
313 Worrell/Ference/Neil SL .12 .30
314 Briere/Hrdina/Deadmarsh SL .15 .40
315 Heatley/Kovlchk/Huslius SL .25 .60
316 Hasek/Brodeur/Nabokov SL .50 1.25
317 Roy/Cechmanek/Turco SL .50 1.25
318 Thdore/Roy/Cechmanek SL .50 1.25
319 Roy/Theodore/Khabibulin SL .50 1.25
320 Blckbrn/Kiprusof/Nornen SL .20 .50
321 Pasi Nurminen .12 .30
322 Mark Hartigan .12 .30
323 Henrik Tallinder .12 .30
324 Micki Dupont RC .30 .75
325 Jaroslav Svoboda .12 .30
326 Jordan Krestanovich .12 .30
327 Kelly Fairchild .12 .30
328 Riku Hahl .12 .30
329 Andrej Nedorost .12 .30
330 Blake Bellefeuille .12 .30
331 Ales Pisa .12 .30
332 Jani Rita .12 .30
333 Stephen Weiss .12 .30
334 Lukas Krajicek .15 .40
335 Sylvain Blouin RC .30 .75
336 Marcel Hossa .12 .30
337 Adam Hall RC .30 .75
338 Jonas Andersson .15 .40
339 Jan Lasak .15 .40
340 Ray Schultz RC .30 .75
341 Trent Hunter .12 .30
342 Martin Prusek .12 .30
343 Branko Radivojevic .12 .30
344 Shane Endicott .12 .30
345 Sebastien Centomo .12 .30
346 Karel Pilar .12 .30
347 Sebastien Charpentier .12 .30
348 Jean-Francois Fortin .12 .30
349 Ales Kotalik .12 .30
350 Kyle Rossiter .12 .30

2002-03 Upper Deck Vintage Green Backs

*GREEN BACK/199: 5X TO 12X BASIC CARDS

2002-03 Upper Deck Vintage Jerseys

*GOLD/50: 1.2X TO 3X BASE JSY
EEBB Brian Boucher 3.00 8.00
EEDA David Aebischer 3.00 8.00
EEFP Felix Potvin 5.00 12.00
EEMB Martin Biron 3.00 8.00
EEMD Mike Dunham 3.00 8.00
EEMO Maxime Ouellet 3.00 8.00
EEMT Marty Turco 5.00 12.00
EEOK Olaf Kolzig 5.00 12.00
EERC Roman Cechmanek 3.00 8.00
EERT Ron Tugnutt 3.00 8.00
FSBM Brenden Morrow 5.00 12.00
FSCD Chris Drury 5.00 12.00
FSJJ Jaromir Jagr 6.00 15.00
FSKP Keith Primeau 3.00 8.00
FSMH Milan Hejduk 3.00 8.00
FSSY Steve Yzerman 12.00 30.00
HSJD J-P Dumont 3.00 8.00
HSJW Justin Williams 3.00 8.00
HSMD Marc Denis 3.00 8.00
HSPB Peter Bondra 5.00 12.00
HSRB Ray Bourque 8.00 20.00
HSRF Ruslan Fedotenko 3.00 8.00
HSRK Rostislav Klesla 3.00 8.00
HSSG Simon Gagne 5.00 12.00
HSSK Steve Konowalchuk 3.00 8.00
HSVN Ville Nieminen 3.00 8.00
OSED Eric Daze 3.00 8.00
OSGM Glen Murray 3.00 8.00
OSJT Jose Theodore SP 8.00 20.00
OSMS Mats Sundin 5.00 12.00
OSRD Radek Dvorak 3.00 8.00
OSSY Steve Yzerman 12.00 30.00
SOCD Chris Drury 5.00 12.00
SOEL Eric Lindros 6.00 15.00
SOJH Jeff Halpern 3.00 8.00
SOJI Jarome Iginla SP 8.00 20.00
SOJJ Jaromir Jagr SP 8.00 20.00
SOJL John LeClair 3.00 8.00
SOKP Keith Primeau 3.00 8.00
SOMR Mark Recchi 3.00 8.00
SOPF Peter Forsberg 5.00 15.00
SOPK Paul Kariya 5.00 12.00

2002-03 Upper Deck Vintage Tall Boys

*GOLD/99: 1.5X TO 4X BASIC INSERTS
T1 Paul Kariya .75 2.00
T2 Jean-Sebastien Giguere .60 1.50
T3 Dany Heatley 1.50 4.00
T4 Ilya Kovalchuk 1.00 2.50
T5 Joe Thornton 3.00 6.00
T6 Sergei Samsonov .60 1.50
T7 Miroslav Satan .60 1.50
T8 Maxim Afinogenov 1.50 4.00
T9 Roman Turek .60 1.50
T10 Jarome Iginla 1.00 2.50
T11 Arturs Irbe .60 1.50
T12 Ron Francis 1.00 2.50
T13 Eric Daze .60 1.50
T14 Jocelyn Thibault .60 1.50
T15 Patrick Roy 5.00 12.00
T16 Peter Forsberg 2.00 5.00
T17 Joe Sakic 1.50 4.00
T18 Chris Drury .60 1.50
T19 Alex Tanguay .60 1.50
T20 Espen Knutsen .60 1.50
T21 Rostislav Klesla .60 1.50
T22 Mike Modano 1.25 3.00
T23 Jason Arnott .60 1.50
T24 Steve Yzerman 3.00 8.00
T25 Brendan Shanahan .75 2.00
T26 Sergei Fedorov 1.25 3.00
T27 Curtis Joseph .75 2.00
T28 Mike Comrie .60 1.50
T29 Tommy Salo 1.00 2.50
T30 Roberto Luongo 1.50 4.00
T31 Stephen Weiss .60 1.50
T32 Jason Allison .60 1.50
T33 Zigmund Palffy .60 1.50
T34 Marian Gaborik 1.50 4.00
T35 Jose Theodore 1.00 2.50
T36 Saku Koivu .75 2.00
T37 Mike Dunham .60 1.50
T38 Scott Hartnell .60 1.50
T39 Martin Brodeur 2.00 5.00
T40 Patrik Elias .60 1.50
T41 Michael Peca .60 1.50
T42 Chris Osgood .60 1.50
T43 Eric Lindros .75 2.00
T44 Pavel Bure .75 2.00
T45 Daniel Alfredsson .60 1.50
T46 Marian Hossa .75 2.00
T47 Jeremy Roenick 1.00 2.50
T48 Simon Gagne .75 2.00
T49 Sean Burke .60 1.50
T50 Daniel Briere .60 1.50
T51 Tony Amonte .60 1.50
T52 Mario Lemieux 4.00 10.00
T53 Johan Hedberg .60 1.50
T54 Owen Nolan .60 1.50
T55 Evgeni Nabokov 1.00 2.50
T56 Keith Tkachuk .75 2.00
T57 Chris Pronger .60 1.50
T58 Vincent Lecavalier .75 2.00
T59 Nikolai Khabibulin .75 2.00
T60 Mats Sundin .75 2.00
T61 Alexander Mogilny .60 1.50
T62 Markus Naslund .75 2.00
T63 Todd Bertuzzi .75 2.00
T64 Jaromir Jagr 1.25 3.00
T65 Olaf Kolzig .60 1.50
T66 Gordie Howe 3.00 8.00
T67 Gordie Howe 3.00 8.00
T68 Gordie Howe 3.00 8.00
T69 Gordie Howe 3.00 8.00
T70 Gordie Howe 3.00 8.00

2000 Upper Deck Wayne Gretzky Master Collection

COMPLETE SET (18) 200.00 400.00
COMMON GRETZKY (1-18) 12.00 30.00
*CANADIAN: .4X TO 1X US

2000 Upper Deck Wayne Gretzky Master Collection Inserts

1 Gretzky Ed.AU/50 Can 500.00 1200.00
2 Gretzky Ed.AU/50 Can 500.00 1200.00
3 Gretzky Ed.AU/50 Can 500.00 1200.00
4 Gretzky Ed/50 USA 100.00 200.00
5 Gretzky Ed/50 USA 100.00 200.00
6 Gretzky Ed/50 USA 100.00 200.00
7 Gretzky LA/50 100.00 200.00
8 Gretzky LA/50 100.00 200.00
9 Gretzky LA/50 100.00 200.00
10 Gretzky AS/50 100.00 200.00
11 Gretzky AS/50 100.00 200.00
12 Gretzky AS/50 100.00 200.00
13 Gretzky NY AU/50 USA 500.00 1200.00
14 Gretzky NY AU/50 USA 500.00 1200.00
15 Gretzky NY AU/50 USA 500.00 1200.00
16 Gretzky NY/50 Can 100.00 200.00
17 Gretzky NY/50 Can 100.00 200.00
18 Gretzky NY/50 Can 100.00 200.00

2000 Upper Deck Wayne Gretzky Master Collection Mystery Pack

19 Gretzky Jersey/99 175.00 300.00

2011-12 Upper Deck Winter Classic

1 Sidney Crosby 8.00 20.00
2 Evgeni Malkin 4.00 10.00
3 Pascal Dupuis 1.25 3.00
4 Jordan Staal 1.50 4.00
5 Brooks Orpik 1.25 3.00
6 Chris Kunitz 2.00 5.00
7 Paul Martin 1.25 3.00
8 Eric Tangradi 1.25 3.00
9 Marc-Andre Fleury 4.00 10.00
10 Alex Ovechkin 8.00 20.00
11 Mike Green 1.50 4.00
12 Nicklas Backstrom 2.00 5.00
13 Alexander Semin 2.00 5.00
14 Mike Knuble 1.25 3.00
15 Brooks Laich 1.25 3.00
16 Tomas Fleischmann 1.25 3.00
17 Marcus Johansson 1.50 4.00
18 Semyon Varlamov 2.00 5.00
19 Pittsburgh 2011 1.25 3.00
20 City of Pittsburgh 1.25 3.00

2013-14 Upper Deck Winter Classic

COMPLETE SET (20) 40.00 80.00
WC1 Jimmy Howard 2.50 6.00
WC2 Henrik Zetterberg 2.50 6.00
WC3 Jonathan Ericsson 1.25 3.00
WC4 Dan Cleary 2.00 5.00
WC5 Johan Franzen 1.50 4.00
WC6 Daniel Alfredsson 2.00 5.00
WC7 Niklas Kronwall 1.50 4.00
WC8 Pavel Datsyuk 3.00 8.00
WC9 Danny DeKeyser 1.50 4.00
WC10 Petr Mrazek 2.50 6.00
WC11 Jonathan Bernier 1.50 4.00
WC12 Phil Kessel 2.00 5.00
WC13 James van Riemsdyk 1.50 4.00
WC14 Tyler Bozak 1.25 3.00
WC15 Nazem Kadri 2.50 6.00
WC16 Dion Phaneuf 1.50 4.00
WC17 Joffrey Lupul 1.25 3.00
WC18 James Reimer 2.00 5.00
WC19 Josh Leivo 1.50 4.00
WC20 Morgan Rielly 3.00 8.00

2015-16 Upper Deck Winter Classic Bruins

COMPLETE SET (5) 5.00 10.00
WCB1 Brad Marchand 2.00 5.00
WCB2 David Krejci 1.00 2.50
WCB3 David Pastrnak 2.50 6.00
WCB4 Tuukka Rask 1.25 3.00
WCB5 Zdeno Chara 1.00 2.50

2015-16 Upper Deck Winter Classic Canadiens

COMPLETE SET (5) 5.00 10.00
WCM1 P.K. Subban 1.25 3.00
WCM2 Andrei Markov .60 1.50
WCM3 Lars Eller .60 1.50
WCM4 Max Pacioretty 1.00 2.50
WCM5 Mike Condon .75 2.00

2016 Upper Deck World Cup of Hockey

WCH1 Jonathan Toews .40 1.00
WCH2 Carey Price .50 1.25
WCH3 Jamie Benn .30 .75
WCH4 John Tavares .40 1.00
WCH5 Sidney Crosby 1.00 2.50
WCH6 David Krejci .25 .60
WCH7 Radko Gudas .20 .50
WCH8 Petr Mrazek .30 .75
WCH9 Tomas Plekanec .25 .60
WCH10 Pavel Zacha .30 .75
WCH11 Leon Draisaitl .50 1.25
WCH12 Marian Hossa .30 .75
WCH13 Tomas Tatar .30 .75
WCH14 Frederik Andersen .30 .75
WCH15 Roman Josi .20 .50
WCH16 Joe Pavelski .25 .60
WCH17 Patrick Kane .40 1.00
WCH18 Ben Bishop .25 .60
WCH19 Justin Abdelkader .20 .50
WCH20 John Carlson .25 .60
WCH21 Teuvo Teravainen .25 .60
WCH22 Joonas Donskoi .15 .40
WCH23 Aleksander Barkov .40 1.00
WCH24 Pekka Rinne .30 .75
WCH25 Patrik Laine .60 1.50
WCH26 Connor McDavid .75 2.00
WCH27 Auston Matthews 1.50 4.00
WCH28 Matt Murray .30 .75
WCH29 Dylan Larkin .30 .75
WCH30 Johnny Gaudreau .30 .75
WCH31 Alexander Ovechkin 1.00 2.50
WCH32 Dmitry Orlov .25 .60
WCH33 Pavel Datsyuk .40 1.00
WCH34 Nikita Kucherov .50 1.25
WCH35 Evgeni Malkin .60 1.50
WCH36 Erik Karlsson .30 .75
WCH37 Henrik Zetterberg .30 .75
WCH38 Henrik Sedin .30 .75
WCH39 Nicklas Backstrom .40 1.00
WCH40 Henrik Lundqvist .60 1.50

2016 Upper Deck World Cup of Hockey Autographs

WCHAAB Aleksander Barkov 40.00 100.00
WCHACP Carey Price 50.00 125.00
WCHADK David Krejci 25.00 60.00
WCHADL Dylan Larkin 30.00 80.00
WCHAFA Frederik Andersen 30.00 80.00
WCHAJD Joonas Donskoi 15.00 40.00
WCHAJP Joe Pavelski 25.00 60.00
WCHAMM Matt Murray 30.00 80.00
WCHAPZ Pavel Zacha 30.00 80.00
WCHASB Dmitry Orlov 25.00 60.00

2010 Upper Deck World of Sports

COMPLETE SET (375) 100.00 150.00
COMP.SET w/o SPs (300) 30.00 60.00
159 Sarah Davis .15 .40
160 Hannah Armstrong .15 .40
161 Jillian Saulnier .15 .40
162 Laurie Kingsbury .15 .40
163 Melodie Daoust .15 .40
164 Jamie Lee Rattray .15 .40
165 Jenna McParland .15 .40
166 Kelly Terry .15 .40
167 Emily Fulton .15 .40
168 Christine Bestland .15 .40
169 Carly Mercer .15 .40
170 Jessica Campbell 8.00 20.00
171 Hayleigh Cudmore .15 .40
172 Brigette Lacquette .15 .40
173 Erin Ambrose .15 .40
174 Cassandra Poudrier .15 .40
175 Caitlin MacDonald .15 .40
176 Shannon Doyle .15 .40
177 Carmen MacDonald .15 .40
178 Erica Howe .15 .40
179 Stefan Elliott .15 .40
180 Curtis Hamilton .15 .40
181 Joey Hishon .25 .60
182 Stefan Della Rovere .15 .40
183 Brandon Kozun .15 .40
184 Zack Kassian .25 .60
185 Calvin Pickard .40 1.00
186 Olivier Roy .25 .60
187 Adam Henrique .25 .60
188 Erik Gudbranson .25 .60
189 Taylor Doherty .15 .40
190 Gabriel Bourque .25 .60
191 Taylor Hall 2.00 5.00
192 Scott Glennie .15 .40
193 Calvin de Haan .15 .40
194 Ethan Werek .15 .40
195 Ryan Ellis .15 .40
196 Cody Eakin .15 .40
197 Travis Hamonic .15 .40
198 Colten Teubert .15 .40
199 Martin Jones .25 .60
200 Jake Allen .40 1.00
236 Jennifer Botterill .25 .60
237 Cassie Campbell .40 1.00
238 Cammi Granato .25 .60
240 Hayley Wickenheiser .25 .60
242 Julie Chu .15 .40
246 Natalie Darwitz .15 .40
248 Kim St. Pierre .40 1.00
303 Taylor Hall SP 1.50 4.00
304 Sidney Crosby SP 2.00 5.00
305 Wayne Gretzky SP 2.00 5.00
306 Bobby Orr SP 1.00 2.50
307 John Tavares SP 1.50 4.00
308 Mark Messier SP 1.00 2.50
309 Gordie Howe SP 1.50 4.00
310 Mario Lemieux SP 1.00 2.50
311 Patrick Roy SP 1.50 4.00
312 Steve Yzerman SP 1.50 4.00
313 Phil Esposito SP 1.00 2.50
314 Tony Esposito SP 1.00 2.50
315 Ray Bourque SP 1.00 2.50
316 Luc Robitaille SP 1.00 2.50
317 Al MacInnis SP 1.00 2.50
318 Brian Leetch SP 1.00 2.50
319 Steven Stamkos SP 1.00 2.50
320 Grant Fuhr SP 1.00 2.50
321 Marc-Andre Fleury SP 1.00 2.50
322 Bobby Hull SP 1.00 2.50
323 Gilbert Perreault SP 1.00 2.50
324 Guy Lafleur SP 1.00 2.50
325 Joe Mullen SP 1.00 2.50
326 Lanny McDonald SP 1.00 2.50
327 Dale Hawerchuk SP 1.00 2.50
328 Denis Potvin SP 1.00 2.50
329 Dino Ciccarelli SP 1.00 2.50
330 Glenn Anderson SP 1.00 2.50

2010 Upper Deck World of Sports All-Sport Apparel Memorabilia

ASA33 John Tavares 5.00 12.00
ASA34 Sidney Crosby 12.00 30.00
ASA35 Wayne Gretzky 25.00 60.00
ASA36 Lanny McDonald 4.00 10.00
ASA37 Dale Hawerchuk 5.00 12.00
ASA38 Stefan Della Rovere 5.00 12.00
ASA39 Ryan Ellis 6.00 15.00
ASA40 Colten Teubert 4.00 10.00

2010 Upper Deck World of Sports All-Sport Apparel Memorabilia Autographs

ASA40 Colten Teubert 10.00 25.00

2010 Upper Deck World of Sports Athletes of the World Autographs

AW91 Billy Smith 4.00 10.00
AW92 Dominik Hasek 10.00 25.00
AW93 Harry Howell 8.00 20.00

AW94 Elmer Lach 10.00 25.00
AW97 Jeremy Roenick 15.00 40.00
AW98 Michael Peca 6.00 15.00

2010 Upper Deck World of Sports Autographs

182 Stefan Della Rovere 5.00 12.00
192 Scott Glennie 5.00 12.00
193 Calvin de Haan 5.00 12.00
195 Ryan Ellis 12.00 30.00
198 Colten Teubert 5.00 12.00
237 Cassie Campbell 25.00 50.00
238 Cammi Granato 10.00 25.00
242 Julie Chu 6.00 15.00
246 Natalie Darwitz 6.00 15.00
304 Sidney Crosby 100.00 175.00
308 Mark Messier 25.00 50.00
309 Gordie Howe 60.00 120.00
312 Steve Yzerman 40.00 80.00
313 Phil Esposito 15.00 30.00
324 Guy Lafleur 15.00 30.00
327 Dale Hawerchuk 10.00 25.00

2010 Upper Deck World of Sports Clear Competitors

CC15 Sidney Crosby 5.00 12.00
CC16 Wayne Gretzky 12.00 30.00
CC17 Mark Messier 5.00 12.00
CC18 Taylor Hall 6.00 15.00
CC19 Patrick Roy 6.00 15.00
CC20 Steve Yzerman 5.00 12.00
CC21 John Tavares 4.00 10.00
CC22 Steven Stamkos 4.00 10.00
CC32 Cassie Campbell 3.00 8.00

1980 USA Olympic Team Mini Pics

COMPLETE SET (15) 25.00 50.00
1 Jim Craig 5.00 10.00
2 Mike Eruzione 5.00 10.00
3 John Harrington .75 2.00
4 Mark Johnson 1.25 3.00
5 Rob McClanahan .75 2.00
6 Jack O'Callahan .75 2.00
7 Phil Verchota .75 2.00
8 Bob Suter .75 2.00
9 Eric Strobel .75 2.00
10 Dave Silk .75 2.00
11 Mike Ramsey 1.25 3.00
12 Marty Pavelich .75 2.00
13 Steve Christoff 1.25 3.00
14 Dave Christian 1.25 3.00
15 Herb Brooks CO 2.50 5.00
NNO Score Card 2.50 5.00

1980 USSR Olympic Team Mini Pics

COMPLETE SET (10) 17.50 35.00
1 Juri Fedorov .75 2.00
2 Irek Gimayev .75 2.00
3 Alexander Golikov .75 2.00
4 Sergei Kapustin .75 2.00
5 V.Kovin .75 2.00
6 Boris Mikhailov 2.50 5.00
7 V.Myshkin 2.50 5.00
8 Vladimir Petrov 2.50 5.00
9 Vladislav Tretiak 5.00 10.00
10 Valeri Vasilijev 2.50 5.00

1983-84 Vachon

COMPLETE SET (140) 80.00 200.00
1 Paul Baxter .30 .75
2 Ed Beers .20 .50
3 Steve Bozek .20 .50
4 Mike Eaves .20 .50
5 Don Edwards .40 1.00
6 Kari Eloranta .20 .50
7 Dave Hindmarch .20 .50
8 Jamie Hislop .20 .50
9 Steve Konroyd .20 .50
10 Reggie Lemelin .40 1.00
11 Hakan Loob .75 2.00
12 Jamie Macoun .20 .50
13 Lanny McDonald 1.25 3.00
14 Kent Nilsson .75 2.00
15 Colin Patterson .20 .50
16 Jim Peplinski .40 1.00
17 Paul Reinhart .40 1.00
18 Doug Risebrough .40 1.00
19 Steve Tambellini .20 .50
20 Mickey Volcan .20 .50
21 Glenn Anderson 1.50 4.00
22 Paul Coffey 5.00 12.00
23 Lee Fogolin .20 .50
24 Grant Fuhr 2.00 5.00
25 Randy Gregg .20 .50
26 Wayne Gretzky 20.00 50.00
27 Charlie Huddy .30 .75
28 Pat Hughes .20 .50
29 Dave Hunter .20 .50
30 Don Jackson .20 .50
31 Jari Kurri 3.00 8.00
32 Willy Lindstrom .20 .50
33 Ken Linseman .30 .75
34 Kevin Lowe .60 1.50
35 Dave Lumley .20 .50
36 Mark Messier 10.00 25.00
37 Andy Moog 2.00 5.00
38 Jaroslav Pouzar .20 .50
39 Tom Roulston .20 .50
40 Dave Semenko .30 .75
41 Guy Carbonneau 1.25 3.00
42 Kent Carlson .20 .50
43 Gilbert Delorme .20 .50
44 Bob Gainey .75 2.00
45 Jean Hamel .20 .50
46 Mark Hunter .20 .50
47 Guy Lafleur 2.50 6.00
48 Craig Ludwig .20 .50
49 Pierre Mondou .20 .50
50 Mats Naslund .75 2.00
51 Chris Nilan .40 1.00
52 Greg Paslawski .20 .50
53 Larry Robinson .75 2.00
54 Richard Sevigny .40 1.00
55 Steve Shutt .75 2.00
56 Bobby Smith .40 1.00
57 Mario Tremblay .30 .75
58 Ryan Walter .30 .75
59 Rick Wamsley .40 1.00
60 Doug Wickenheiser .20 .50
61 Bo Berglund .20 .50
62 Dan Bouchard .40 1.00
63 Alain Cote .20 .50
64 Brian Ford .20 .50
65 Michel Goulet 1.00 2.50
66 Dale Hunter .75 2.00
67 Mario Marois .30 .75
68 Tony McKegney .30 .75
69 Randy Moller .20 .50
70 Wilf Paiement .40 1.00
71 Pat Price .20 .50
72 Normand Rochefort .20 .50
73 Andre Savard .20 .50
74 Louis Sleigher .20 .50
75 Anton Stastny .30 .75
76 Marian Stastny .30 .75
77 Peter Stastny 2.50 6.00
78 John Van Boxmeer .20 .50
79 Wally Weir .20 .50
80 Blake Wesley .20 .50
81 John Anderson .30 .75
82 Jim Benning .20 .50
83 Dan Daoust .20 .50
84 Bill Derlago .30 .75
85 Dave Farrish .20 .50
86 Miroslav Frycer .20 .50
87 Stewart Gavin .30 .75
88 Gaston Gingras .20 .50
89 Billy Harris .20 .50
90 Peter Inhacak .40 1.00
91 Jim Korn .20 .50
92 Terry Martin .20 .50
93 Dale McCourt .20 .50
94 Gary Nylund .20 .50
95 Mike Palmateer .75 2.00
96A Walt Poddubny ERR (Photo actually Peter Inhacek 4.00 10.00
96B Walt Poddubny COR (With mustache) 1.00 2.50
97 Borje Salming 1.25 3.00
98 Rick St.Croix .40 1.00
99 Greg P. Terrion .20 .50
100 Rick Vaive .40 1.00
101 Richard Brodeur .60 1.50
102 Jiri Bubla .20 .50
103 Garth Butcher .20 .50
104 Ron Delorme .20 .50
105 John Garrett .60 1.50
106 Jere Gillis .20 .50
107 Thomas Gradin .40 1.00
108 Doug Halward .20 .50
109 Mark Kirton .20 .50
110 Rick Lanz .20 .50
111 Gary Lupul .20 .50
112 Kevin McCarthy .20 .50
113 Lars Molin .20 .50
114 Jim Nill .20 .50
115 Darcy Rota .20 .50
116 Stan Smyl .40 1.00
117 Harold Snepsts .60 1.50
118 Patrik Sundstrom .40 1.00
119 Tony Tanti .40 1.00
120 Tiger Williams .75 2.00
121 Scott Arniel .20 .50
122 Dave Babych .40 1.00
123 Laurie Boschman .20 .50
124 Wade Campbell .20 .50
125 Lucien DeBlois .20 .50
126 Dale Hawerchuk 3.00 8.00
127 Brian Hayward .40 1.00
128 Jim Kyte .30 .75
129 Morris Lukowich .20 .50
130 Bengt Lundholm .20 .50
131 Paul MacLean .40 1.00
132 Moe Mantha .20 .50
133 Andrew McBain .20 .50
134 Brian Mullen .20 .50
135 Robert Picard .20 .50
136 Doug Smail .40 1.00
137 Doug Soetaert .40 1.00
138 Thomas Steen .60 1.50
139 Tim Watters .20 .50
140 Tim Young .30 .75

2000-01 Vanguard

1 Guy Hebert .20 .50
2 Paul Kariya .25 .60
3 Teemu Selanne .50 1.25
4 Ray Ferraro .15 .40
5 Damian Rhodes .15 .40
6 Patrik Stefan .20 .50
7 Jason Allison .20 .50
8 Bill Guerin .25 .60
9 Sergei Samsonov .20 .50
10 Joe Thornton .40 1.00
11 Maxim Afinogenov .15 .40
12 Doug Gilmour .30 .75
13 Dominik Hasek .40 1.00
14 Miroslav Satan .15 .40
15 Valeri Bure .20 .50
16 Jarome Iginla .30 .75
17 Marc Savard .15 .40
18 Rod Brind'Amour .25 .60
19 Ron Francis .30 .75
20 Arturs Irbe .20 .50
21 Sami Kapanen .15 .40
22 Tony Amonte .20 .50
23 Jocelyn Thibault .20 .50
24 Alexei Zhamnov .20 .50
25 Ray Bourque .40 1.00
26 Chris Drury .20 .50
27 Peter Forsberg .50 1.25
28 Milan Hejduk .20 .50
29 Patrick Roy .60 1.50
30 Joe Sakic .50 1.25
31 Geoff Sanderson .20 .50
32 Ron Tugnutt .20 .50
33 Ed Belfour .25 .60
34 Brett Hull .50 1.25
35 Mike Modano .40 1.00
36 Joe Nieuwendyk .20 .50
37 Sergei Fedorov .40 1.00
38 Nicklas Lidstrom .25 .60
39 Chris Osgood .25 .60
40 Brendan Shanahan .25 .60
41 Steve Yzerman .60 1.50
42 Anson Carter .20 .50
43 Tommy Salo .20 .50
44 Doug Weight .25 .60
45 Pavel Bure .25 .60
46 Viktor Kozlov .20 .50
47 Ray Whitney .20 .50
48 Ziggy Palffy .25 .60
49 Luc Robitaille .25 .60
50 Sergei Krivokrasov .15 .40
51 Saku Koivu .25 .60
52 Trevor Linden .25 .60
53 Jose Theodore .25 .60
54 David Legwand .25 .60
55 Randy Robitaille .15 .40
56 Jason Arnott .20 .50
57 Martin Brodeur .60 1.50
58 Patrik Elias .25 .60
59 Scott Gomez .20 .50
60 Alexander Mogilny .20 .50
61 Tim Connolly .15 .40
62 Mariusz Czerkawski .15 .40
63 John Vanbiesbrouck .25 .60
64 Theo Fleury .30 .75
65 Brian Leetch .20 .50
66 Mark Messier .50 1.25
67 Mike Richter .25 .60
68 Daniel Alfredsson .25 .60
69 Marian Hossa .25 .60
70 Alexei Yashin .20 .50
71 Brian Boucher .20 .50
72 Simon Gagne .25 .60
73 John LeClair .25 .60
74 Eric Lindros .40 1.00
75 Shane Doan .20 .50
76 Jeremy Roenick .40 1.00
77 Keith Tkachuk .25 .60
78 Jean-Sebastien Aubin .20 .50
79 Jan Hrdina .15 .40
80 Jaromir Jagr .75 2.00
81 Martin Straka .20 .50
82 Al MacInnis .30 .75
83 Chris Pronger .25 .60
84 Roman Turek .20 .50
85 Pierre Turgeon .20 .50
86 Vincent Damphousse .20 .50
87 Jeff Friesen .15 .40
88 Owen Nolan .25 .60
89 Mike Johnson .15 .40
90 Vincent Lecavalier .25 .60
91 Nik Antropov .20 .50
92 Tie Domi .20 .50
93 Curtis Joseph .30 .75
94 Mats Sundin .25 .60
95 Andrew Cassels .15 .40
96 Markus Naslund .25 .60
97 Felix Potvin .40 1.00
98 Peter Bondra .25 .60
99 Olaf Kolzig .25 .60
100 Adam Oates .25 .60
101 Samuel Pahlsson 1.00 2.50
102 Jonas Ronnqvist RC 1.00 2.50
103 Milan Hnilicka 1.00 2.50
104 Andrew Raycroft RC 2.50 6.00
105 Dimitri Kalinin 1.00 2.50
106 Mika Noronen 1.00 2.50
107 Oleg Saprykin 1.00 2.50
108 Josef Vasicek RC 2.50 6.00
109 Shane Willis 1.00 2.50
110 Steve McCarthy 1.00 2.50
111 David Aebischer RC 2.00 5.00
112 Serge Aubin RC 1.25 3.00
113 Marc Denis 1.25 3.00
114 Rostislav Klesla RC 2.50 6.00
115 David Vyborny 1.00 2.50
116 Tyler Bouck RC 1.00 2.50
117 Marty Turco RC 2.00 5.00
118 Joaquin Gage 1.00 2.50
119 Michel Riesen RC 1.25 3.00
120 Brian Swanson RC 1.00 2.50
121 Roberto Luongo 2.50 6.00
122 Ivan Novoseltsev 1.00 2.50
123 Eric Belanger RC 1.25 3.00
124 Steven Reinprecht RC 1.50 4.00
125 Lubomir Visnovsky RC 2.00 5.00
126 Manny Fernandez 1.00 2.50
127 Marian Gaborik RC 3.00 8.00
128 Filip Kuba 1.00 2.50
129 Mathieu Garon 1.00 2.50
130 Andrei Markov 2.00 5.00
131 Scott Hartnell RC 2.50 6.00
132 Colin White RC 1.00 2.50
133 Rick DiPietro RC 2.00 5.00
134 Taylor Pyatt 1.00 2.50
135 Martin Havlat RC 3.00 8.00
136 Jani Hurme RC 1.00 2.50
137 Roman Cechmanek RC 1.25 3.00
138 Justin Williams RC 2.50 6.00
139 Robert Esche 1.00 2.50
140 Wyatt Smith 1.00 2.50
141 Ossi Vaananen RC 1.25 3.00
142 Milan Kraft 1.00 2.50
143 Brent Johnson 1.25 3.00
144 Ladislav Nagy 1.00 2.50
145 Evgeni Nabokov 1.25 3.00
146 Sheldon Keefe 1.00 2.50
147 Brad Richards 1.50 4.00
148 Petr Svoboda RC 1.25 3.00
149 Daniel Sedin 2.00 5.00
150 Henrik Sedin 2.00 5.00
151 Mario Lemieux 1.00 2.50

2000-01 Vanguard Holographic Gold

*1-151 VETS/60: 3X TO 8X BASIC CARDS

2000-01 Vanguard Holographic Purple

*1-151 VETS/105: 2.5X TO 6X BASIC CARDS

2000-01 Vanguard Premiere Date

*1-150 VETS/100: 2.5X TO 6X BASIC CARDS

2000-01 Vanguard Cosmic Force

1 Paul Kariya 2.00 5.00
2 Dominik Hasek 3.00 8.00
3 Peter Forsberg 4.00 10.00
4 Patrick Roy 5.00 12.00
5 Steve Yzerman 5.00 12.00
6 Pavel Bure 2.00 5.00
7 Martin Brodeur 5.00 12.00
8 Eric Lindros 3.00 8.00
9 Jaromir Jagr 6.00 15.00
10 Curtis Joseph 2.50 6.00

2000-01 Vanguard Dual Game-Worn Jerseys

1 J.Thrnton S.Samsnov/1500 5.00 12.00
2 P.Forsberg/M.Sundin/125 6.00 15.00
3 J.Sakic/E.Lindros/250 6.00 15.00
4 D.Hatcher/M.Modano/1500 5.00 12.00
5 B.Shanahan/C.Chelios/1500 3.00 8.00
6 S.Fedorov/C.Osgood/400 5.00 12.00
7 D.Weight/R.Smyth/1500 3.00 8.00
8 B.Holik/M.Czerkawski/1500 2.00 5.00
9 Vanbiesbrouck/Richter/50 3.00 8.00
10 A.Zhamnov/C.Stillman/1500 2.50 6.00
11 C.Ronning/V.Ychmnev/1500 2.00 5.00
12 T.Fitzgerald/K.Timonen/1400 2.00 5.00
13 B.Dafoe/D.McCarty/1400 2.50 6.00
14 K.McLarn/D.Sweeny/1400 2.00 5.00
15 J.Lehtinen/J.Lngnbrnnr/400 2.50 6.00
16 E.Daze/M.McInnis/300 2.50 6.00
17 A.Dackell/U.Dahlen/400 2.00 5.00
18 S.Corson/J.Hackett/400 2.50 6.00
19 C.Terreri/G.Hebert/400 2.50 6.00
20 S.Niedrmyr/M.Lapointe/400 3.00 8.00

2000-01 Vanguard Dual Game-Worn Patches

1 J.Thornton/S.Samsnov/300 8.00 20.00
2 P.Forsberg/M.Sundin/100 10.00 25.00
3 J.Sakic/E.Lindros/100 10.00 25.00
4 D.Hatcher/M.Modano/300 8.00 20.00
5 B.Shanahan/C.Chelios/125 5.00 12.00
6 S.Fedorov/C.Osgood/25 8.00 20.00
7 D.Weight/R.Smyth/300 5.00 12.00
8 B.Holik/M.Czerkawski/300 3.00 8.00
10 A.Zhamnov/C.Stillman/300 4.00 10.00
11 C.Ronning/V.Yachmnev/300 3.00 8.00
12 T.Fitzgerald/K.Timonen/300 3.00 8.00
13 B.Dafoe/D.McCarty/300 4.00 10.00
14 K.McLaren/D.Sweeney/300 3.00 8.00
15 J.Lehtinen/J.Langnbrnnr/100 4.00 10.00
17 A.Dackell/U.Dahlen/75 3.00 8.00
18 S.Corson/J.Hackett/75 4.00 10.00
19 C.Terreri/G.Hebert/75 4.00 10.00
20 S.Niedrmyr/M.Lapointe/100 5.00 12.00

2000-01 Vanguard High Voltage

*RED/299: .75X TO 2X BASIC INSERTS
*GOLD/199: 1X TO 2.5X BASIC INSERTS
*GREEN/99: 1.5X TO 4X BASIC INSERTS
1 Paul Kariya .30 .75
2 Teemu Selanne .60 1.50
3 Joe Thornton .50 1.25
4 Jason Allison .25 .60
5 Dominik Hasek .50 1.25
6 Ray Bourque .50 1.25
7 Peter Forsberg .60 1.50
8 Patrick Roy .75 2.00
9 Joe Sakic .60 1.50
10 Ed Belfour .30 .75
11 Brett Hull .60 1.50
12 Mike Modano .50 1.25
13 Brendan Shanahan .30 .75
14 Steve Yzerman .75 2.00
15 Doug Weight .30 .75
16 Pavel Bure .30 .75
17 Zigmund Palffy .30 .76
18 Marian Gaborik .60 1.50
19 Martin Brodeur .75 2.00
20 Scott Gomez .25 .60
21 Rick DiPietro .40 1.00
22 Theo Fleury .40 1.00
23 Mark Messier .60 1.50
24 Marian Hossa .30 .75
25 John LeClair .30 .75
26 Eric Lindros .50 1.25
27 Jeremy Roenick .50 1.25
28 Keith Tkachuk .30 .75
29 Jaromir Jagr 1.00 2.50
30 Pierre Turgeon .25 .60
31 Vincent Lecavalier .30 .75
32 Curtis Joseph .40 1.00
33 Mats Sundin .30 .75
34 Daniel Sedin .40 1.00
35 Henrik Sedin .40 1.00
36 Peter Bondra .30 .75

2000-01 Vanguard In Focus

1 Paul Kariya .60 1.50
2 Teemu Selanne 1.25 3.00
3 Jason Allison .50 1.25
4 Ray Bourque 1.00 2.50
5 Peter Forsberg 1.25 3.00
6 Patrick Roy 1.50 4.00
7 Brett Hull 1.25 3.00
8 Sergei Fedorov 1.00 2.50
9 Steve Yzerman 1.50 4.00
10 Pavel Bure .60 1.50
11 Marian Gaborik 1.25 3.00
12 Martin Brodeur 1.50 4.00
13 Theo Fleury .75 2.00
14 John LeClair .60 1.50
15 Jaromir Jagr 2.00 5.00
16 Vincent Lecavalier .60 1.50
17 Curtis Joseph .75 2.00
18 Mats Sundin .60 1.50
19 Daniel Sedin .75 2.00
20 Henrik Sedin .75 2.00

2000-01 Vanguard Press East/West

1 Paul Kariya .60 1.50
2 Teemu Selanne 1.25 3.00
3 Peter Forsberg 1.25 3.00
4 Patrick Roy 1.50 4.00
5 Brett Hull 1.25 3.00
6 Sergei Fedorov 1.00 2.50
7 Steve Yzerman 1.50 4.00
8 Zigmund Palffy .60 1.50
9 Jeremy Roenick 1.00 2.50
10 Pierre Turgeon .50 1.25
11 Joe Thornton 1.00 2.50
12 Dominik Hasek 1.00 2.50
13 Pavel Bure .60 1.50
14 Martin Brodeur 1.50 4.00
15 Mark Messier 1.25 3.00
16 Alexei Yashin .50 1.25
17 Eric Lindros 1.00 2.50
18 Jaromir Jagr 2.00 5.00
19 Vincent Lecavalier .60 1.50
20 Curtis Joseph .75 2.00

2001-02 Vanguard

1 Jeff Friesen .20 .50
2 Paul Kariya .30 .75
3 Dany Heatley .25 .60
4 Milan Hnilicka .25 .60
5 Byron Dafoe .25 .60
6 Glen Murray .25 .60
7 Sergei Samsonov .25 .60
8 Joe Thornton .50 1.25
9 Martin Biron .25 .60
10 Tim Connolly .20 .50
11 J-P Dumont .20 .50
12 Jarome Iginla .40 1.00
13 Marc Savard .20 .50
14 Roman Turek .25 .60
15 Ron Francis .40 1.00
16 Arturs Irbe .25 .60
17 Jeff O'Neill .25 .60
18 Tony Amonte .25 .60
19 Mark Bell .20 .50
20 Kyle Calder .20 .50
21 Eric Daze .25 .60
22 Jocelyn Thibault .25 .60
23 Rob Blake .30 .75
24 Chris Drury .25 .60
25 Milan Hejduk .25 .60
26 Patrick Roy .75 2.00
27 Joe Sakic .60 1.50
28 Alex Tanguay .25 .60
29 Rostislav Klesla .20 .50
30 Ron Tugnutt .25 .60
31 Ed Belfour .30 .75
32 Mike Modano .50 1.25
33 Pierre Turgeon .25 .60
34 Sergei Fedorov .50 1.25
35 Dominik Hasek .50 1.25
36 Brett Hull .60 1.50
37 Brendan Shanahan .30 .75
38 Steve Yzerman .75 2.00
39 Mike Comrie .25 .60
40 Tommy Salo .25 .60
41 Ryan Smyth .25 .60
42 Pavel Bure .30 .75
43 Roberto Luongo .50 1.25
44 Jason Allison .25 .60
45 Zigmund Palffy .30 .75
46 Felix Potvin .50 1.25
47 Manny Fernandez .20 .50
48 Marian Gaborik .30 .75
49 Doug Gilmour .40 1.00
50 Yanic Perreault .20 .50
51 Brian Savage .20 .50
52 Jose Theodore .30 .75
53 Mike Dunham .25 .60
54 David Legwand .25 .60
55 Jason Arnott .25 .60
56 Martin Brodeur .75 2.00
57 Patrik Elias .30 .75
58 Rick DiPietro .25 .60
59 Chris Osgood .30 .75
60 Mark Parrish .20 .50
61 Michael Peca .25 .60
62 Alexei Yashin .25 .60
63 Brian Leetch .25 .60
64 Eric Lindros .50 1.25
65 Mark Messier .60 1.50
66 Mike Richter .30 .75
67 Daniel Alfredsson .30 .75
68 Martin Havlat .25 .60
69 Marian Hossa .30 .75
70 Patrick Lalime .25 .60
71 Pavel Brendl .20 .50
72 Roman Cechmanek .25 .60
73 John LeClair .30 .75
74 Jeremy Roenick .50 1.25
75 Sean Burke .20 .50
76 Shane Doan .25 .60
77 Daymond Langkow .25 .60
78 Kris Beech .20 .50
79 Johan Hedberg .25 .60
80 Mario Lemieux 1.25 3.00
81 Brent Johnson .25 .60
82 Chris Pronger .30 .75
83 Keith Tkachuk .30 .75
84 Doug Weight .30 .75
85 Patrick Marleau .30 .75
86 Evgeni Nabokov .25 .60
87 Owen Nolan .30 .75
88 Teemu Selanne .60 1.50
89 Vincent Lecavalier .30 .75
90 Brad Richards .30 .75
91 Martin St. Louis .30 .75
92 Curtis Joseph .40 1.00
93 Alexander Mogilny .25 .60
94 Mats Sundin .30 .75
95 Dan Cloutier .25 .60
96 Brendan Morrison .25 .60
97 Markus Naslund .30 .75
98 Peter Bondra .30 .75
99 Jaromir Jagr 1.00 2.50
100 Olaf Kolzig .30 .75
101 Ilja Bryzgalov RC 2.50 6.00
102 Timo Parssinen RC 1.25 3.00
103 Ilya Kovalchuk RC 5.00 12.00
104 Brian Pothier RC 1.00 2.50
105 Jukka Hentunen RC 1.00 2.50
106 Erik Cole RC 2.00 5.00
107 Vaclav Nedorost RC 1.00 2.50
108 Niko Kapanen RC 1.50 4.00
109 Pavel Datsyuk RC 15.00 40.00
110 Jason Chimera RC 1.00 2.50
111 Ty Conklin RC 1.50 4.00
112 Jussi Markkanen SP 1.00 2.50
113 Niklas Hagman RC 1.25 3.00
114 Kristian Huselius RC 1.50 4.00
115 Jaroslav Bednar RC 1.00 2.50
116 Pascal Dupuis RC 1.50 4.00
117 Nick Schultz RC 1.00 2.50
118 Martin Erat RC 1.25 3.00
119 Andreas Salomonsson RC 1.00 2.50
120 Radek Martinek RC 1.00 2.50
121 Raffi Torres RC 1.50 4.00
122 Dan Blackburn RC 1.25 3.00
123 Chris Neil RC 1.25 3.00
124 Jiri Dopita RC 1.00 2.50
125 David Cullen RC 1.00 2.50
126 Krystofer Kolanos RC 1.00 2.50
127 Mark Rycroft RC 1.25 3.00
128 Jeff Jillson RC 1.00 2.50
129 Nikita Alexeev RC 1.00 2.50
130 Brian Sutherby RC 1.00 2.50

2001-02 Vanguard Blue

*1-100 VETS: 3X TO 8X BASIC CARDS
*101-130 ROOK: .3X TO .8X BASIC RC/404

2001-02 Vanguard Premiere Date

*1-100 VETS: 3X TO 8X BASIC CARDS
*101-130 ROOK: .3X TO .8X BASIC RC/404

2001-02 Vanguard Red

*1-100 VETS: 5X TO 12X BASIC CARDS
*101-130 ROOK: .4X TO 1X BASIC RC/404

2001-02 Vanguard East Meets West

COMPLETE SET (10) 15.00 40.00
1 M.Lemieux/J.Jagr 5.00 12.00
2 P.Roy/D.Hasek 5.00 12.00
3 J.Sakic/P.Forsberg 4.00 10.00
4 M.Brodeur/J.Hedberg 4.00 10.00
5 E.Lindros/A.Yashin 2.00 5.00
6 P.Kariya/T.Selanne 2.00 5.00
7 S.Yzerman/S.Fedorov 4.00 10.00
8 B.Shanahan/P.Bure 2.00 5.00
9 J.Iginla/M.Sundin 2.50 6.00
10 C.Pronger/N.Lidstrom 2.00 5.00

2001-02 Vanguard In Focus

1 Patrick Roy 15.00 40.00
2 Joe Sakic 12.50 30.00
3 Dominik Hasek 12.50 30.00
4 Brendan Shanahan 10.00 25.00
5 Steve Yzerman 15.00 40.00
6 Pavel Bure 8.00 20.00
7 Martin Brodeur 15.00 40.00
8 Mario Lemieux 20.00 50.00
9 Mats Sundin 8.00 10.00
10 Jaromir Jagr 10.00 25.00

2001-02 Vanguard Memorabilia

1 P.Kariya/O.Tverdovsky 3.00 8.00
2 P.Kariya/G.Hebert 3.00 8.00
3 S.Samsonov/D.Sweeney 2.50 6.00
4 J.Iginla/M.Savard 3.00 8.00
5 F.Brathwaite/R.Turek 2.50 6.00
6 C.Stillman/C.Conroy 2.50 6.00
7 B.Mironov/M.Nylander 2.50 6.00
8 T.Amonte/S.Sullivan SP 5.00 12.00
9 J.Sakic/P.Forsberg 10.00 20.00
10 P.Roy/J.Sakic 8.00 20.00
11 M.Modano/D.Hatcher 5.00 12.00
12 J.Langenbrunner/D.Sydor 2.50 6.00
13 S.Yzerman/C.Chelios 8.00 20.00
14 N.Lidstrom/S.Fedorov SP 12.00 30.00
15 S.Koivu/T.Selanne 6.00 15.00
16 C.Ronning/V.Yachmenev 2.50 6.00
17 B.Holik/S.Niedermayer SP 2.50 6.00
18 M.Czerkawski/S.Bates 2.50 6.00
19 E.Lindros/P.Brendl 3.00 8.00
20 M.Richter/M.York 10.00 25.00
21 J.Roenick/E.Weinrich 8.00 20.00
22 J.Lehtinen/J.Lumme 2.50 6.00
23 M.Straka/J.Beranek 2.50 6.00
24 J.Hrdina/B.Boughner 2.50 6.00
25 A.Kovalev/D.Kasparaitis 2.50 6.00
26 M.Lemieux/R.Lang 8.00 20.00
27 M.Straka/R.Parent 2.50 6.00
28 D.Drake/M.Eastwood 2.50 6.00
29 J.Hecht/J.McLennan 2.50 6.00
30 P.Turgeon/V.Lecavalier 5.00 12.00
31 J.Dumont/S.Young 2.50 6.00
32 C.Joseph/J.Theodore 8.00 20.00
33 J.Jagr/P.Bondra 10.00 25.00
34 M.Sundin/A.Cassels 3.00 8.00
35 O.Kolzig/D.Cloutier SP 5.00 12.00
36 C.Lapointe/M.Lindgren 2.50 6.00
37 G.DeVries/E.Messier SP 5.00 12.00
38 S.Yzerman/E.Lindros SP 20.00 50.00
39 A.Kovalev/K.Miller 2.50 6.00
40 L.Odelein/A.Savage 2.50 6.00
41 M.Savard/R.Turek 2.50 6.00
42 J.Jagr JSY/I.Kovalchuk STK 12.50 30.00
43 P.Roy/J.Theodore 10.00 25.00
44 M.Lemieux/M.Sundin 10.00 25.00
45 T.Fleury/M.Hossa NET 12.50 30.00
46 B.Hull/P.Bure NET 20.00 50.00
47 D.Weight/P.Forsberg NET 10.00 25.00
48 J.Allsion/Z.Palffy NET 10.00 25.00
49 R.Blake/M.Hejduk NET 10.00 25.00
50 M.Brodeur/D.Hasek NET 25.00 60.00

2001-02 Vanguard Patches

3 Samsonov/Sweeney 12.50 30.00
5 Brathwaite/R.Turek 12.50 30.00
6 C.Stillman/C.Conroy 12.50 30.00
10 P.Roy/J.Sakic 20.00 50.00
12 Langenbrunner/Sydor 12.50 30.00
21 J.Roenick/E.Weinrich 20.00 50.00
22 J.Lehtinen/J.Lumme 12.50 30.00
23 M.Straka/J.Beranek 12.50 30.00
25 Kovalev/D.Kasparaitis 12.50 30.00
27 M.Straka/R.Parent 12.50 30.00
28 D.Drake/M.Eastwood 12.50 30.00
33 J.Jagr/P.Bondra 15.00 40.00
37 G.DeVries/E.Messier 12.50 30.00
38 Yzerman/E.Lindros 30.00 80.00
39 A.Kovalev/K.Miller 12.50 30.00
41 M.Savard/R.Turek 12.50 30.00

2001-02 Vanguard Prime Prospects

COMPLETE SET (20) 15.00 40.00
1 Dany Heatley 3.00 8.00
2 Ilya Kovalchuk 4.00 10.00
3 Vaclav Nedorost .75 2.00
4 Rostislav Klesla .75 2.00
5 Pavel Datsyuk 10.00 25.00
6 Mike Comrie 1.25 3.00
7 Kristian Huselius .75 2.00
8 Jaroslav Bednar .75 2.00
9 Marian Gaborik 3.00 8.00
10 Martin Erat .75 2.00
11 Rick DiPietro 2.00 5.00
12 Dan Blackburn .75 2.00
13 Martin Havlat 2.00 5.00
14 Pavel Brendl .75 2.00
15 Krystofer Kolanos .75 2.00
16 Brent Johnson 1.25 3.00
17 Jeff Jillson .75 2.00
18 Nikita Alexeev .75 2.00
19 Daniel Sedin 2.00 5.00
20 Henrik Sedin 2.00 5.00

2001-02 Vanguard Quebec Tournament Heroes

COMPLETE HOBBY SET (10) 20.00 40.00
1 Brett Hull 1.25 3.00
2 Mario Lemieux 5.00 12.00
3 Patrick Roy 4.00 10.00
4 Steve Yzerman 4.00 10.00
5 Mike Modano 1.50 4.00
6 Jeremy Roenick 1.25 3.00
7 Brendan Shanahan 1.50 4.00
8 Felix Potvin 1.00 2.50
9 Doug Weight 1.00 2.50
10 Eric Lindros 1.50 4.00
11 Jocelyn Thibault 4.00 10.00
12 Jason Allison 2.00 5.00
13 Chris Drury 2.00 5.00
14 Jeff O'Neill 2.00 5.00
15 Sergei Samsonov 10.00 25.00
16 Alex Tanguay 4.00 10.00
17 Marian Hossa 10.00 25.00
18 Simon Gagne 10.00 25.00
19 Vincent Lecavalier 6.00 15.00
20 Rick DiPietro 6.00 15.00

2001-02 Vanguard Stonewallers

COMPLETE SET (20) 40.00 80.00
1 Milan Hnilicka 1.25 3.00
2 Byron Dafoe 1.25 3.00
3 Martin Biron 1.25 3.00
4 Roman Turek 1.25 3.00
5 Patrick Roy 6.00 15.00
6 Ed Belfour 1.50 4.00
7 Dominik Hasek 3.00 8.00
8 Tommy Salo 1.25 3.00
9 Roberto Luongo 2.00 5.00
10 Jose Theodore 2.00 5.00
11 Martin Brodeur 4.00 10.00
12 Chris Osgood 1.25 3.00
13 Mike Richter 1.50 4.00
14 Patrick Lalime 1.25 3.00
15 Roman Cechmanek 1.25 3.00
16 Johan Hedberg 1.25 3.00
17 Evgeni Nabokov 1.25 3.00
18 Nikolai Khabibulin 1.50 4.00
19 Curtis Joseph 1.50 4.00
20 Olaf Kolzig 1.25 3.00

2001-02 Vanguard V-Team

COMPLETE SET (20) 12.00 30.00
1 Roman Turek .60 1.50
2 Patrick Roy 4.00 10.00
3 Ed Belfour .75 2.00
4 Dominik Hasek 1.50 4.00
5 Martin Brodeur 2.00 5.00
6 Chris Osgood .60 1.50
7 Roman Cechmanek .60 1.50
8 Johan Hedberg .60 1.50
9 Evgeni Nabokov .60 1.50
10 Curtis Joseph .75 2.00
11 Jarome Iginla 1.00 2.50
12 Joe Sakic 1.50 4.00
13 Brendan Shanahan 1.25 3.00
14 Steve Yzerman 4.00 10.00
15 Pavel Bure 1.00 2.50
16 Eric Lindros 1.25 3.00
17 Mario Lemieux 5.00 12.00
18 Teemu Selanne .75 2.00
19 Mats Sundin .75 2.00
20 Jaromir Jagr 1.25 3.00

2002-03 Vanguard

1 Jean-Sebastien Giguere .20 .50
2 Paul Kariya .20 .50
3 Steve Rucchin .12 .30
4 Byron Dafoe .15 .40
5 Dany Heatley .15 .40
6 Ilya Kovalchuk .25 .60
7 Glen Murray .15 .40
8 Brian Rolston .15 .40
9 Steve Shields .15 .40
10 Joe Thornton .30 .75
11 Martin Biron .15 .40
12 Chris Gratton .12 .30
13 Jochen Hecht .12 .30
14 Chris Drury .20 .50
15 Jarome Iginla .25 .60
16 Roman Turek .20 .50
17 Rod Brind'Amour .20 .50
18 Ron Francis .25 .60
19 Jeff O'Neill .12 .30
20 Kevin Weekes .15 .40
21 Tyler Arnason .20 .50
22 Eric Daze .12 .30
23 Theo Fleury .25 .60
24 Jocelyn Thibault .15 .40
25 Peter Forsberg .40 1.00
26 Milan Hejduk .15 .40
27 Patrick Roy .50 1.25
28 Joe Sakic .40 1.00
29 Andrew Cassels .12 .30
30 Marc Denis .15 .40
31 Geoff Sanderson .15 .40
32 Bill Guerin .20 .50
33 Mike Modano .30 .75

34 Marty Turco .20 .50
35 Sergei Fedorov .30 .75
36 Brett Hull .40 1.00
37 Curtis Joseph .25 .60
38 Nicklas Lidstrom .20 .50
39 Brendan Shanahan .20 .50
40 Steve Yzerman .50 1.25
41 Anson Carter .15 .40
42 Mike Comrie .20 .50
43 Tommy Salo .15 .40
44 Kristian Huselius .12 .30
45 Olli Jokinen .20 .50
46 Roberto Luongo .30 .75
47 Jason Allison .15 .40
48 Adam Deadmarsh .12 .30
49 Ziggy Palffy .20 .50
50 Felix Potvin .30 .75
51 Andrew Brunette .12 .30
52 Marian Gaborik .20 .50
53 Dwayne Roloson .12 .30
54 Jeff Hackett .15 .40
55 Saku Koivu .20 .50
56 Yanic Perreault .12 .30
57 Jose Theodore .20 .50
58 Andreas Johansson .12 .30
59 David Legwand .15 .40
60 Martin Brodeur .50 1.25
61 Patrik Elias .20 .50
62 Jamie Langenbrunner .15 .40
63 Mark Parrish .12 .30
64 Michael Peca .15 .40
65 Alexei Yashin .15 .40
66 Dan Blackburn .15 .40
67 Pavel Bure .20 .50
68 Eric Lindros .30 .75
69 Daniel Alfredsson .20 .50
70 Marian Hossa .20 .50
71 Patrick Lalime .15 .40
72 Roman Cechmanek .15 .40
73 Simon Gagne .20 .50
74 John LeClair .20 .50
75 Jeremy Roenick .30 .75
76 Tony Amonte .15 .40
77 Brian Boucher .15 .40
78 Mike Johnson .15 .40
79 Johan Hedberg .20 .50
80 Alexei Kovalev .15 .40
81 Mario Lemieux .75 2.00
82 Eric Boguniecki .12 .30
83 Cory Stillman .12 .30
84 Doug Weight .20 .50
85 Evgeni Nabokov .15 .40
86 Owen Nolan .20 .50
87 Teemu Selanne .40 1.00
88 Nikolai Khabibulin .20 .50
89 Vincent Lecavalier .20 .50
90 Martin St. Louis .20 .50
91 Ed Belfour .20 .50
92 Alexander Mogilny .15 .40
93 Mats Sundin .20 .50
94 Todd Bertuzzi .20 .50
95 Dan Cloutier .15 .40
96 Brendan Morrison .15 .40
97 Markus Naslund .20 .50
98 Peter Bondra .20 .50
99 Jaromir Jagr .60 1.50
100 Olaf Kolzig .20 .50
101 Stanislav Chistov RC .60 1.50
102 Martin Gerber RC 1.00 2.50
103 Alexei Smirnov RC .75 2.00
104 Tim Thomas RC 2.50 6.00
105 Ryan Miller RC 4.00 10.00
106 Chuck Kobasew RC .75 2.00
107 Jordan Leopold RC 1.00 2.50
108 Pascal Leclaire RC .75 2.00
109 Rick Nash RC 4.00 10.00
110 Lasse Pirjeta RC .60 1.50
111 Steve Ott RC .60 1.50
112 Dmitri Bykov RC .60 1.50
113 Henrik Zetterberg RC 6.00 15.00
114 Ales Hemsky RC 2.50 6.00
115 Jay Bouwmeester RC 2.00 5.00
116 Mike Cammalleri RC 2.00 5.00
117 Alexander Frolov RC 1.50 4.00
118 P-M Bouchard RC 1.00 2.50
119 Stephane Veilleux RC .60 1.50
120 Sylvain Blouin RC .60 1.50
121 Ron Hainsey RC .60 1.50
122 Adam Hall RC .60 1.50
123 Scottie Upshall RC .75 2.00
124 Jason Spezza RC 4.00 10.00
125 Anton Volchenkov RC .60 1.50
126 Dennis Seidenberg RC 1.00 2.50
127 Patrick Sharp RC 2.00 5.00
128 Radovan Somik RC .60 1.50
129 Jeff Taffe RC .60 1.50
130 Dick Tarnstrom RC .60 1.50
131 Tom Koivisto RC .60 1.50
132 Curtis Sanford RC 1.00 2.50
133 Lynn Loyns RC .60 1.50
134 Alexander Svitov RC .60 1.50
135 Carlo Colaiacovo RC 1.00 2.50
136 Steve Eminger RC .60 1.50

2002-03 Vanguard LTD

*1-100 VETS: 3X TO 8X BASIC CARDS
*101-136 ROOKIES: .5X TO 1.2X

2002-03 Vanguard East Meets West

COMPLETE SET (10) 15.00 30.00
1 I.Kovalchuk/M.Naslund 2.00 5.00
2 J.Thornton/J.Iginla 2.50 6.00
3 M.Lemieux/S.Yzerman 4.00 10.00
4 P.Bure/S.Fedorov 2.00 5.00
5 J.LeClair/M.Modano 2.00 5.00
6 M.Sundin/P.Forsberg 2.00 5.00
7 V.Lecavalier/J.Sakic 2.00 5.00
8 M.Hossa/M.Gaborik 2.00 5.00
9 M.Brodeur/P.Roy 4.00 10.00
10 E.Belfour/M.Turco 2.00 5.00

2002-03 Vanguard In Focus

COMPLETE SET (10) 12.00 30.00
1 Paul Kariya 1.25 3.00
2 Ilya Kovalchuk 2.00 5.00
3 Peter Forsberg 2.00 5.00
4 Joe Sakic 2.00 5.00
5 Rick Nash 3.00 8.00
6 Steve Yzerman 4.00 10.00
7 Marian Gaborik 2.00 5.00
8 Jason Spezza 3.00 8.00
9 Mario Lemieux 4.00 10.00
10 Jaromir Jagr 1.50 4.00

2002-03 Vanguard Jerseys

*GOLD/50: 1X TO 2.5X BASIC JSY
1 Adam Oates 2.50 6.00
2 Dany Heatley 5.00 12.00
3 Ilya Kovalchuk 5.00 12.00
4 Patrik Stefan 2.50 6.00
5 Joe Thornton 6.00 15.00
6 J-P Dumont 2.50 6.00
7 Chris Drury 2.50 6.00
8 Jamie McLennan 2.50 6.00
9 Rod Brind'Amour 2.50 6.00
10 Sergei Berezin 2.50 6.00
11 Theo Fleury 3.00 8.00
12 Alexei Zhamnov SP 3.00 8.00
13 Joe Sakic 6.00 15.00
14 Rostislav Klesla 2.50 6.00
15 Mike Modano 6.00 15.00
16 Pierre Turgeon 2.50 6.00
17 Sergei Fedorov 4.00 10.00
18 Brett Hull 4.00 10.00
19 Curtis Joseph 3.00 8.00
20 Ryan Smyth 3.00 8.00
21 Kristian Huselius 2.50 6.00
22 Ziggy Palffy 3.00 8.00
23 Yanic Perreault 2.50 6.00
24 Jose Theodore 4.00 10.00
25 Scott Walker 2.50 6.00
26 Martin Brodeur 10.00 25.00
27 Scott Gomez 2.50 6.00
28 Michael Peca 2.50 6.00
29 Pavel Bure 3.00 8.00
30 Mark Messier 3.00 8.00
31 Daniel Alfredsson 3.00 8.00
32 Patrick Lalime 2.50 6.00
33 Tomi Kallio 2.50 6.00
34 John LeClair 2.50 6.00
35 Krystofer Kolanos 2.50 6.00
36 Johan Hedberg 2.50 6.00
37 Mario Lemieux 12.50 30.00
38 Pavol Demitra 2.50 6.00
39 Keith Tkachuk 2.50 6.00
40 Patrick Marleau 3.00 8.00
41 Evgeni Nabokov 3.00 8.00
42 Nikolai Khabibulin 3.00 8.00
43 Alexander Mogilny 2.50 6.00
44 Gary Roberts 2.50 6.00
45 Darcy Tucker 2.50 6.00
46 Dan Cloutier 2.50 6.00
47 Brendan Morrison 2.50 6.00
48 Markus Naslund 3.00 8.00
49 Peter Bondra 3.00 8.00
50 Jaromir Jagr 6.00 15.00

2002-03 Vanguard Prime Prospects

COMPLETE SET (20) 15.00 40.00
1 Stanislav Chistov .75 2.00
2 Alexei Smirnov .75 2.00
3 Ivan Huml .75 2.00
4 Ryan Miller 2.00 5.00
5 Chuck Kobasew 1.25 3.00
6 Jordan Leopold .75 2.00
7 Tyler Arnason .75 2.00
8 Rick Nash 4.00 10.00
9 Henrik Zetterberg 3.00 8.00
10 Ales Hemsky 1.50 4.00
11 Jay Bouwmeester 1.50 4.00
12 Stephen Weiss .75 2.00
13 Alexander Frolov 1.50 4.00
14 P-M Bouchard 1.50 4.00
15 Scottie Upshall .75 2.00
16 Justin Mapletoft .75 2.00
17 Jamie Lundmark .75 2.00
18 Jason Spezza 3.00 8.00
19 Petr Cajanek .75 2.00
20 Barret Jackman .75 2.00

2002-03 Vanguard Stonewallers

COMPLETE SET (12) 10.00 20.00
1 Patrick Roy 4.00 10.00
2 Marty Turco .60 1.50
3 Curtis Joseph .75 2.00
4 Roberto Luongo 1.00 2.50
5 Felix Potvin .75 2.00
6 Jose Theodore 1.00 2.50
7 Martin Brodeur 2.00 5.00
8 Mike Richter .75 2.00
9 Patrick Lalime .60 1.50
10 Roman Cechmanek .60 1.50
11 Nikolai Khabibulin .75 2.00
12 Ed Belfour .75 2.00

2002-03 Vanguard V-Team

COMPLETE SET (12) 20.00 40.00
1 Patrick Roy 4.00 10.00
2 Marty Turco .60 1.50
3 Curtis Joseph .75 2.00
4 Jose Theodore 1.00 2.50
5 Martin Brodeur 2.00 5.00
6 Ed Belfour .75 2.00
7 Ilya Kovalchuk 1.00 2.50
8 Joe Thornton 1.25 3.00
9 Joe Sakic 1.50 4.00
10 Steve Yzerman 4.00 10.00
11 Mario Lemieux 5.00 12.00
12 Jaromir Jagr 1.25 3.00

1924-26 V128-1 Paulin's Candy

COMPLETE SET (70) 4500.00 9000.00
1 Bill Borland 75.00 150.00
2 Pete Speirs 50.00 100.00
3 Jack Hughes 50.00 100.00
4 Errol Gillis 50.00 100.00
5 Cecil Browne 50.00 100.00
6 W. Roberts 50.00 100.00
7 Howard Brandon 50.00 100.00
8 Fred Comfort 50.00 100.00
9 Cliff O'Meara 50.00 100.00
10 Leo Benard 50.00 100.00
11 Lloyd Harvey 50.00 100.00
12 Bobby Connors 50.00 100.00
13 Daddy Dalman 50.00 100.00
14 Dub Mackie 50.00 100.00
15 Lorne Chabot 150.00 300.00
16 Phat Wilson 75.00 125.00
17 Wilf L'Heureux 50.00 100.00
18 Danny Cox 50.00 100.00
19 Bill Brydge 50.00 100.00
20 Alex Gray 50.00 100.00
21 Albert Pudas 50.00 100.00
22 Jack Irwin 50.00 100.00
23 Puss Traub 50.00 100.00
24 Red McCusker 75.00 125.00
25 Jack Asseltine 75.00 125.00
26 Duke Dutkowski 50.00 100.00
27 Charley McVeigh 50.00 100.00
28 George Hay 125.00 250.00
29 Amby Moran 50.00 100.00
30 Barney Stanley 150.00 300.00
31 Art Gagne 50.00 100.00
32 Louis Berlinquette 50.00 100.00
33 P.C. Stevens 50.00 100.00
34 W.D. Elmer 50.00 100.00
35 Bill Cook 200.00 350.00
36 Leo Reise 50.00 100.00
37 Curly Headley 125.00 250.00
38 Newsy Lalonde 350.00 600.00
39 George Hainsworth 350.00 600.00
40 Laurie Scott 50.00 100.00
41 Joe Simpson 200.00 350.00
42 Bob Trapp 50.00 100.00
43 Joe McCormick 50.00 100.00
44 Ty Arbour 50.00 100.00
45 Duke Keats 75.00 125.00
46 Hal Winkler 50.00 100.00
47 Johnny Sheppard 50.00 100.00
48 Crutchy Morrison 50.00 100.00
49 Spunk Sparrow 50.00 100.00
50 Percy McGregor 50.00 100.00
51 Harry Tuckwell 50.00 100.00
52 Chubby Scott 50.00 100.00
53 Scotty Fraser 50.00 100.00
54 Bob Davis 50.00 100.00
55 Clucker White 50.00 100.00
56 Bob Armstrong 50.00 100.00
57 Doc Longtry 50.00 100.00
58 Darb Sommers 50.00 100.00
59 Frank Hacquoil 50.00 100.00
60 Stan Evans 50.00 100.00
61 Ed Oatman 50.00 100.00
62 Red Dutton 250.00 400.00
63 Herb Gardiner 125.00 250.00
64 Bernie Morris 50.00 100.00
65 Bobbie Benson 50.00 100.00
66 Ernie Anderson 50.00 100.00
67 Cully Wilson 50.00 100.00
68 Charlie Reid 75.00 125.00
69 Harry Oliver 125.00 250.00
70 Rusty Crawford 100.00 200.00

1928-29 V128-2 Paulin's Candy

COMPLETE SET (90) 2750.00 5500.00
1 Univ. of Man. Girls Hockey Team 50.00 100.00
2 Elgin Hockey Team 40.00 80.00
3 Brandon Schools Boy Champions 40.00 80.00
4 Port Arthur Hockey Team 40.00 80.00
5 Enderby Hockey Team 40.00 80.00
6 Humboldt High School Team 40.00 80.00
7 Regina Collegiate Hockey Team 40.00 80.00
8 Weyburn Beavers 40.00 80.00
9 Moose Jaw College Junior Hockey Team 50.00 100.00
10 M.A.C. Junior Hockey 40.00 80.00
11 Vermillion Agri-cultural School 40.00 80.00
12 Rovers& Cranbrook B.C. 40.00 80.00
13 Empire School& Moose Jaw 40.00 80.00
14 Arts Senior Hockey 40.00 80.00
15 Juvenile Varsity Hockey 40.00 80.00
16 St. Peter's College Hockey 40.00 80.00
17 Arts Girls Hockey 50.00 100.00
18 Swan River Hockey Team 40.00 80.00
19 U.M.S.U. Junior Hockey Team 40.00 80.00
20 Campion College Hockey Team 50.00 100.00
21 Drinkwater Hockey Team 40.00 80.00
22 Elks Hockey Team Biggar, Saskatchewan 40.00 80.00
23 South Calgary High School 40.00 80.00
24 Meota Hockey 40.00 80.00
25 Chartered Accountants 50.00 100.00
26 Nutana Collegiate Hockey Team 40.00 80.00
27 MacLeod Hockey Team 50.00 100.00
28 Arts Junior Hockey 40.00 80.00
29 Fort William Juniors 40.00 80.00
30 Swan Lake Hockey Team 40.00 80.00
31 Dauphin Hockey Team 40.00 80.00
32 Mount Royal Hockey Team 40.00 80.00
33 Port Arthur W. End Junior Hockey 40.00 80.00
34 Hanna Hockey Club 40.00 80.00
35 Vermillion Junior Hockey 40.00 80.00
36 Smithers Hockey Team 40.00 80.00
37 Lloydminster High School 40.00 80.00
38 Winnipeg Rangers 50.00 100.00
39 Delisle Intermediate Hockey 40.00 80.00
40 Moose Jaw College Senior Hockey 40.00 80.00
41 Art Bonneyman 25.00 50.00
42 Jimmy Graham 25.00 50.00
43 Pat O'Hunter 25.00 50.00
44 Leo Moret 25.00 50.00
45 Blondie McLennen 25.00 50.00
46 Red Beattie 40.00 80.00
47 Frank Peters 40.00 80.00
48 Lloyd McIntyre 25.00 50.00
49 Art Somers 40.00 80.00
50 Ikey Morrison 25.00 50.00
51 Calgary Jimmies 25.00 50.00
52 Don Cummings 25.00 50.00
53 Calgary Jimmies 25.00 50.00
54 P. Gerlitz 25.00 50.00
55 A. Kay 25.00 50.00
56 Paul Runge 40.00 80.00
57 J. Gerlitz 25.00 50.00
58 H. Gerlitz 25.00 50.00
59 C. Biles 25.00 50.00
60 Jimmy Evans 25.00 50.00
61 Ira Stuart 25.00 50.00
62 Berg Irving 50.00 100.00
63 Cecil Browne 40.00 80.00
64 Nick Wasnie 40.00 80.00
65 Gordon Teal 40.00 80.00
66 Jack Hughes 40.00 80.00
67 D. Yeatman 40.00 80.00
68 Connie Johanneson 25.00 50.00
69 S. Walters 25.00 50.00
70 Harold McMunn 40.00 80.00
71 Smokey Harris 25.00 50.00
72 Calgary Jimmies 25.00 50.00
73 Bernie Morris 25.00 50.00
74 J. Fowler 40.00 80.00
75 Calgary Jimmies 25.00 50.00
76 Pete Spiers 25.00 50.00
77 Bill Borland 40.00 80.00
78 Cliff O'Meara 40.00 80.00
79 F. Porteous 40.00 80.00
80 W. Brooks 40.00 80.00
81 Everett McGowan 25.00 50.00
82 Calgary Jimmies 25.00 50.00
83 George Dame 25.00 50.00
84 Calgary Jimmies 25.00 50.00
85 Calgary Jimmies 25.00 50.00
86 Calgary Jimmies 25.00 50.00
87 Norman Hec Fowler 40.00 80.00
88 Jimmy Hoyle 25.00 50.00
89 Charlie Gardiner 75.00 150.00
90 Calgary Jimmies 40.00 80.00

1933-34 V129

COMPLETE SET (49) 7500.00 15000.00
1 Red Horner RC 250.00 500.00
2 Hap Day 175.00 350.00
3 Ace Bailey RC 250.00 500.00
4 Buzz Boll RC 75.00 150.00
5 Charlie Conacher RC 500.00 1000.00
6 Busher Jackson RC 250.00 500.00
7 Joe Primeau RC 250.00 500.00
8 King Clancy 500.00 1000.00
9 Alex Levinsky RC 100.00 200.00
10 Bill Thoms RC 75.00 150.00
11 Andy Blair RC 75.00 150.00
12 Harold Cotton RC 100.00 200.00
13 George Hainsworth 250.00 500.00
14 Ken Doraty RC 75.00 150.00
15 Fred Robertson RC 75.00 150.00
16 Charlie Sands RC 75.00 150.00
17 Hec Kilrea RC 75.00 150.00
18 John Roach 100.00 200.00
19 Larry Aurie RC 75.00 150.00
20 Ebbie Goodfellow RC 150.00 300.00
21 Normie Himes RC 100.00 200.00
22 Bill Brydge RC 75.00 150.00
23 Red Dutton RC 150.00 300.00
24 Cooney Weiland RC 200.00 400.00
25 Bill Beveridge RC 100.00 200.00
26 Frank Finnigan 100.00 200.00
27 Albert Leduc RC 100.00 200.00
28 Babe Siebert RC 200.00 400.00
29 Murray Murdoch RC 75.00 150.00
30 Butch Keeling RC 75.00 150.00
31 Bill Cook RC 150.00 300.00
32 Cecil Dillon RC 75.00 150.00
33 Ivan Johnson RC 200.00 400.00
34 Ott Heller RC 100.00 200.00
35 Red Beattie RC 75.00 150.00
36 Dit Clapper 300.00 600.00
37 Eddie Shore RC 1000.00 2000.00
38 Marty Barry RC 150.00 300.00
39 Harry Oliver SP RC 7500.00 15000.00
40 Bob Gracie RC 75.00 150.00
41 Howie Morenz 1500.00 3000.00
42 Pit Lepine RC 75.00 150.00
43 Johnny Gagnon RC 75.00 150.00
44 Armand Mondou RC 75.00 150.00
45 Lorne Chabot RC 150.00 300.00
46 Bun Cook RC 150.00 300.00
47 Alex Smith RC 75.00 150.00
48 Danny Cox RC 75.00 150.00
49 Baldy Northcott RC UER 100.00 200.00
50 Paul Thompson RC 100.00 200.00

1924-25 V130 Maple Crispette

COMPLETE SET (29) 4000.00 8000.00
1 Dunc Munro RC 100.00 200.00
2 Clint Benedict 200.00 400.00
3 Norman Hec Fowler RC 100.00 200.00
4 Curly Headley RC 75.00 150.00
5 Alf Skinner RC 75.00 150.00
6 Lloyd Cook RC 150.00 300.00
7 Smokey Harris RC 75.00 150.00
8 Jim Herberts RC 75.00 150.00
9 Carson Cooper RC 75.00 150.00
10 Red Green 75.00 150.00
11 Billy Boucher 75.00 150.00
12 Howie Morenz 1000.00 2000.00
13 Georges Vezina 700.00 1400.00
14 Aurel Joliat 400.00 800.00
15 Sprague Cleghorn SP 6000.00 12000.00
16 Dutch Cain RC 75.00 150.00
17 Charlie Dinsmore RC 75.00 150.00
18 Punch Broadbent 150.00 300.00
19 Sam Rothschild RC -125.00 200.00
20 George Carroll RC 75.00 150.00
21 Billy Burch 150.00 300.00
22 Shorty Green 150.00 300.00
23 Mickey Roach 75.00 150.00
24 Ken Randall 75.00 150.00
25 Vernon Forbes 100.00 200.00
26 Charlie Langlois RC 75.00 150.00
27 Newsy Lalonde 300.00 600.00
28 Fred Lowrey RC 75.00 150.00
29 Ganton Scott RC 75.00 150.00
30 Louis Berlinquette RC (spelled Berlinguette on front) 100.00 200.00

1923-24 V145-1

COMPLETE SET (39) 6000.00 12000.00
1 Eddie Gerard 125.00 250.00
2 Frank Nighbor RC 175.00 350.00
3 King Clancy RC 900.00 1800.00
4 Jack Darragh 100.00 200.00
5 Harry Helman RC 50.00 100.00
6 George Boucher RC 100.00 200.00
7 Clint Benedict 150.00 300.00
8 Lionel Hitchman RC 100.00 200.00
9 Punch Broadbent 125.00 250.00
10 Cy Denneny RC 200.00 400.00
11 Sprague Cleghorn 150.00 300.00
12 Sylvio Mantha RC 125.00 250.00
13 Joe Malone 200.00 400.00
14 Aurel Joliat RC 650.00 1300.00
15 Howie Morenz RC 1500.00 3000.00
16 Billy Boucher RC 60.00 125.00
17 Billy Coutu RC 60.00 125.00
18 Odie Cleghorn 60.00 125.00
19 Georges Vezina 750.00 1500.00
20 Amos Arbour RC 50.00 100.00
21 Lloyd Andrews RC 50.00 100.00
22 Red Stuart RC 60.00 125.00
23 Cecil Dye RC 150.00 300.00
24 Jack Adams RC 200.00 400.00
25 Bert Corbeau RC SP 10000.00 20000.00
26 Reg Noble RC 150.00 300.00
27 Stan Jackson RC 50.00 100.00
28 John Roach RC 60.00 125.00
29 Vernon Forbes RC 60.00 125.00
30 Shorty Green RC 100.00 200.00
31 Red Green RC 50.00 100.00
32 Goldie Prodgers 50.00 100.00
33 Leo Reise RC 50.00 100.00
34 Ken Randall RC 50.00 100.00
35 Billy Burch RC 100.00 200.00
36 Jesse Spring RC 50.00 100.00
37 Eddie Bouchard RC 50.00 100.00
38 Mickey Roach RC 50.00 100.00
39 Chas. Fraser RC 50.00 100.00
40 Corbett Denneny RC 100.00 200.00

1924-25 V145-2

COMPLETE SET (60) 6000.00 12000.00
1 Joe Ironstone RC 250.00 500.00
2 George Boucher 100.00 200.00
3 King Clancy 750.00 1500.00
4 Lionel Hitchman 75.00 150.00
5 Hooley Smith RC 125.00 250.00
6 Frank Nighbor 100.00 200.00
7 Cy Denneny 125.00 250.00
8 Spiff Campbell RC 50.00 100.00
9 Frank Finnigan RC 75.00 150.00
10 Alex Connell RC 125.00 250.00
11 Vernon Forbes 60.00 125.00
12 Ken Randall 50.00 100.00
13 Billy Burch 100.00 200.00
14 Shorty Green 100.00 200.00
15 Red Green 50.00 100.00
16 Alex McKinnon RC 50.00 100.00
17 Charlie Langlois RC 50.00 100.00
18 Mickey Roach 50.00 100.00
19 Eddie Bouchard 50.00 100.00
20 Jesse Spring 50.00 100.00
21 Carson Cooper RC 50.00 100.00
22 Smokey Harris RC 50.00 100.00
23 Curly Headley RC 50.00 100.00
24 Lloyd Cook UER RC (Bill on front) 200.00 400.00
25 Jim Herberts RC 50.00 100.00
26 Werner Schnarr RC 50.00 100.00
27 Alf Skinner RC 50.00 100.00
28 George Redding RC 50.00 100.00
29 Herbie Mitchell RC 50.00 100.00
30 Norman Hec Fowler RC 60.00 125.00
31 Red Stuart 50.00 100.00
32 Clint Benedict 100.00 200.00
33 Gerald Munro RC 50.00 100.00
34 Dunc Munro RC 60.00 125.00
35 Dutch Cain RC 50.00 100.00
36 Fred Lowrey RC 50.00 100.00
37 Sam Rothschild RC 75.00 135.00
38 Ganton Scott RC 50.00 100.00
39 Punch Broadbent 125.00 250.00
40 Charlie Dinsmore RC 50.00 100.00
41 Louis Berlinquette RC 50.00 100.00
42 George Carroll RC 50.00 100.00
43 Georges Vezina 600.00 1200.00
44 Billy Coutu 50.00 100.00
45 Odie Cleghorn 60.00 125.00
46 Billy Boucher 75.00 150.00
47 Howie Morenz 1000.00 2000.00
48 Aurel Joliat 500.00 1000.00
49 Sprague Cleghorn 125.00 250.00
50 Billy Mantha RC 75.00 150.00
51 Reg Noble 100.00 200.00
52 John Roach 60.00 125.00
53 Jack Adams 125.00 250.00
54 Cecil Dye 100.00 200.00
55 Reg Reid RC 50.00 100.00
56 Albert Holway RC 50.00 100.00
57 Bert McCaffery RC 50.00 100.00
58 Bert Corbeau 100.00 200.00
59 Lloyd Andrews RC 50.00 100.00
60 Stan Jackson 75.00 150.00

1933-34 V252 Canadian Gum

COMPLETE SET (50) 4500.00 9000.00
1 Clarence Abel RC 100.00 200.00
2 Larry Aurie RC 90.00 150.00
3 Ace Bailey RC 200.00 400.00
4 Helge Bostrom RC 50.00 100.00
5 Bill Brydge RC 50.00 100.00
6 Glyn Brydson RC 50.00 100.00
7 Marty Burke RC 50.00 100.00
8 Gerald Carson RC 75.00 125.00
9 Lorne Chabot RC 200.00 400.00
10 King Clancy 450.00 800.00
11 Dit Clapper RC 200.00 400.00
12 Charlie Conacher RC 400.00 750.00
13 Lionel Conacher RC 200.00 400.00
14 Alex Connell 100.00 175.00
15 Bun Cook RC 100.00 175.00
16 Danny Cox RC 50.00 100.00
17 Hap Day 100.00 200.00
18 Cecil Dillon RC 50.00 100.00
19 Lorne Duguid RC 75.00 125.00
20 Duke Dutkowski RC 50.00 100.00
21 Red Dutton RC 100.00 175.00
22 Happy Emms RC 75.00 125.00
23 Frank Finnigan 75.00 125.00
24 Chuck Gardiner RC 100.00 175.00
25 Ebbie Goodfellow RC 100.00 175.00
26 Johnny Gottselig RC 75.00 125.00
27 Bob Gracie RC 50.00 100.00
28 George Hainsworth 200.00 400.00
29 Ott Heller RC 50.00 100.00
30 Normie Himes RC 75.00 125.00
31 Red Horner RC 150.00 300.00
32 Busher Jackson RC 200.00 400.00
33 Walter Jackson RC 50.00 100.00
34 Aurel Joliat 400.00 750.00
35 Dave Kerr RC 75.00 125.00
36 Pit Lepine RC 50.00 100.00
37 Georges Mantha RC 50.00 100.00
38 Howie Morenz 1000.00 2000.00
39 Murray Murdoch RC 50.00 100.00
40 Baldy Northcott RC 75.00 125.00
41 John Roach 90.00 150.00
42 Johnny Sheppard 50.00 100.00
43 Babe Siebert RC 125.00 250.00
44 Alex Smith RC 50.00 100.00
45 John Sorrell RC 90.00 150.00
46 Nelson Stewart RC 200.00 400.00
47 Dave Trottier RC 50.00 100.00
48 Bill Touhey RC 50.00 100.00
49 Jimmy Ward RC 50.00 100.00
50 Nick Wasnie RC 50.00 100.00

1933-34 V288 Hamilton Gum

COMPLETE SET (21) 3000.00 6000.00
1 Nick Wasnie 62.50 125.00
2 Joe Primeau 200.00 400.00
3 Marty Burke 50.00 100.00
7 Bill Thoms 50.00 100.00
8 Howie Morenz 1000.00 2000.00
9 Andy Blair 50.00 100.00
11 Ace Bailey 175.00 350.00
14 Wildor Larochelle 50.00 100.00
17 King Clancy 400.00 800.00
18 Sylvio Mantha 87.50 175.00
21 Red Horner 150.00 300.00
23 Pit Lepine 50.00 100.00
27 Aurel Joliat 400.00 800.00
29 Harvey(Busher) Jackson 175.00 350.00
30 Lorne Chabot 100.00 200.00
33 Hap Day 100.00 200.00
36 Alex Levinsky 62.50 125.00
39 Harold Cotton 75.00 150.00
42 Ebbie Goodfellow 87.50 175.00
44 Larry Aurie 50.00 100.00
49 Charlie Conacher 400.00 800.00

1937-38 V356 World Wide Gum

COMPLETE SET (135) 11000.00 22000.00
1 Charlie Conacher 500.00 1000.00
2 Jimmy Ward 50.00 100.00
3 Babe Siebert 175.00 350.00
4 Marty Barry 100.00 200.00
5 Eddie Shore 750.00 1500.00
6 Paul Thompson 50.00 100.00
7 Roy Worters 150.00 300.00
8 Red Horner 100.00 200.00
9 Wilfred Cude 75.00 150.00
10 Lionel Conacher 175.00 350.00
11 Ebbie Goodfellow 125.00 250.00
12 Tiny Thompson 150.00 300.00
13 Mush March RC 60.00 125.00
14 Red Dutton 100.00 200.00
15 Butch Keeling 50.00 100.00
16 Frank Boucher RC 100.00 200.00
17 Tommy Gorman RC 50.00 100.00
18 Howie Morenz 1250.00 2500.00
19 Marvin Wentworth 75.00 150.00
20 Hooley Smith 100.00 200.00
21 Ivan Johnson RC 150.00 300.00
22 Baldy Northcott 75.00 150.00
23 Syl Apps 400.00 800.00
24 Hec Kilrea 50.00 100.00
25 John Sorrell 50.00 100.00
26 Lorne Carr RC 50.00 100.00
27 Charlie Sands 50.00 100.00
28 Nick Metz 50.00 100.00
29 King Clancy 500.00 1000.00
30 Russ Blinco 50.00 100.00
31 Pete Martin RC 50.00 100.00
32 Walter Buswell RC 50.00 100.00
33 Paul Haynes 50.00 100.00
34 Wildor Larochelle 60.00 125.00
35 Harold Cotton 60.00 125.00
36 Dit Clapper 200.00 400.00
37 Joe Lamb 50.00 100.00
38 Bob Gracie 50.00 100.00
39 Jack Shill 50.00 100.00
40 Buzz Boll 50.00 100.00
41 John Gallagher 50.00 100.00
42 Art Chapman 50.00 100.00
43 Tom Cook RC 50.00 100.00
44 Bill MacKenzie 50.00 100.00
45 Georges Mantha 50.00 100.00
46 Herb Cain 60.00 125.00
47 Mud Bruneteau RC 75.00 150.00
48 Bob Davidson 50.00 100.00
49 Doug Young RC 50.00 100.00
50 Paul Drouin RC 50.00 100.00
51 Busher Jackson 200.00 400.00
52 Hap Day 150.00 300.00
53 Dave Kerr 100.00 200.00
54 Al Murray 50.00 100.00
55 Johnny Gottselig 60.00 125.00
56 Andy Blair 50.00 100.00
57 Lynn Patrick 200.00 400.00
58 Sweeney Schriner 125.00 250.00
59 Happy Emms 60.00 125.00
60 Allan Shields 50.00 100.00
61 Alex Levinsky 60.00 125.00
62 Flash Hollett 50.00 100.00
63 Peggy O'Neil RC 50.00 100.00
64 Herbie Lewis RC 100.00 200.00
65 Aurel Joliat 400.00 800.00
66 Carl Voss RC 100.00 200.00
67 Stewart Evans 50.00 100.00
68 Bun Cook 125.00 250.00
69 Cooney Weiland 125.00 250.00
70 Dave Trottier 50.00 100.00
71 Louis Trudel RC 50.00 100.00
72 Marty Burke 50.00 100.00
73 Leroy Goldsworthy 50.00 100.00
74 Normie Smith RC 50.00 100.00
75 Syd Howe 150.00 300.00
76 Gordon Pettinger RC 50.00 100.00
77 Jack McGill 50.00 100.00
78 Pit Lepine 50.00 100.00
79 Sammy McManus RC 50.00 100.00
80 Phil Watson RC 75.00 150.00
81 Paul Runge 50.00 100.00
82 Bill Beveridge 60.00 125.00
83 Johnny Gagnon 50.00 100.00
84 Bucko MacDonald RC 60.00 125.00
85 Earl Robinson 50.00 100.00
86 Pep Kelly 50.00 100.00
87 Ott Heller 50.00 100.00
88 Murray Murdoch 50.00 100.00
89 Mac Colville RC 50.00 100.00
90 Alex Shibicky 75.00 150.00
91 Neil Colville 125.00 250.00
92 Normie Himes 60.00 125.00
93 Charley McVeigh 50.00 100.00
94 Lester Patrick 200.00 400.00
95 Connie Smythe 200.00 400.00
96 Art Ross 200.00 400.00
97 Cecil M.Hart RC 125.00 250.00
98 Dutch Gainor RC 50.00 100.00
99 Jack Adams 150.00 300.00
100 Howie Morenz Jr. 150.00 300.00
101 Buster Mundy RC 50.00 100.00
102 Johnny Wing RC 50.00 100.00
103 Morris Croghan RC 50.00 100.00
104 Pete Jotkus RC 50.00 100.00
105 Doug MacQuisten RC 50.00 100.00
106 Lester Brennan RC 50.00 100.00
107 Jack O'Connell RC 50.00 100.00
108 Ray Malenfant RC 50.00 100.00
109 Ken Murray RC 50.00 100.00
110 Frank Stangle RC 50.00 100.00
111 Dave Neville RC 50.00 100.00
112 Claude Burke RC 50.00 100.00
113 Herman Murray RC 50.00 100.00
114 Buddy O'Connor RC 125.00 250.00
115 Albert Perreault RC 50.00 100.00
116 Johnny Taugher RC 50.00 100.00
117 Rene Boudreau RC 50.00 100.00
118 Kenny McKinnon RC 50.00 100.00
119 Alex Bolduc RC 50.00 100.00
120 Jimmy Keiller RC 50.00 100.00
121 Lloyd McIntyre RC 50.00 100.00
122 Emile Fortin RC 50.00 100.00
123 Mike Karakas 60.00 125.00
124 Art Wiebe 50.00 100.00
125 Louis St. Denis RC 50.00 100.00
126 Stan Pratt RC 50.00 100.00
127 Jules Cholette RC 50.00 100.00
128 Jimmy Muir RC 50.00 100.00
129 Pete Morin RC 50.00 100.00
130 Jimmy Heffernan RC 50.00 100.00
131 Morris Bastien RC 50.00 100.00
132 Tuffy Griffiths RC 50.00 100.00
133 Johnny Mahaffey RC 50.00 100.00
134 Trueman Donnelly RC 50.00 100.00
135 Bill Stewart RC 75.00 150.00

1933-34 V357 Ice Kings

COMP.SET (72) 9000.00 15000.00
*ENGLISH ONLY BACK: .5X TO 1X
1 Dit Clapper RC 350.00 600.00
2 Bill Brydge RC 50.00 100.00
3 Aurel Joliat UER 500.00 800.00
4 Andy Blair 50.00 100.00
5 Earl Robinson RC 50.00 100.00
6 Paul Haynes RC 50.00 100.00
7 Ronnie Martin RC 50.00 100.00
8 Babe Siebert RC 175.00 300.00
9 Archie Wilcox RC 50.00 100.00
10 Hap Day 150.00 250.00
11 Roy Worters RC 200.00 350.00
12 Nels Stewart RC 350.00 600.00
13 King Clancy 600.00 1000.00
14 Marty Burke RC 125.00 200.00
15 Cecil Dillon RC 50.00 100.00
16 Red Horner RC 175.00 300.00
17 Armand Mondou RC 50.00 100.00
18 Paul Raymond RC 50.00 100.00
19 Dave Kerr RC 75.00 125.00
20 Butch Keeling RC 50.00 100.00
21 Johnny Gagnon RC 50.00 100.00
22 Ace Bailey RC 300.00 500.00
23 Harry Oliver RC 150.00 250.00
24 Gerald Carson RC 50.00 100.00
25 Red Dutton RC 150.00 250.00
26 Georges Mantha RC 50.00 100.00
27 Marty Barry RC 150.00 250.00
28 Wildor Larochelle RC 75.00 125.00
29 Red Beattie RC 50.00 100.00
30 Bill Cook RC 150.00 250.00
31 Hooley Smith 150.00 250.00
32 Art Chapman RC 50.00 100.00
33 Harold Cotton RC 125.00 200.00
34 Lionel Hitchman 125.00 200.00
35 George Patterson RC 50.00 100.00
36 Howie Morenz 1200.00 2000.00
37 Jimmy Ward RC 50.00 100.00
38 Charley McVeigh RC 75.00 125.00
39 Glen Brydson RC 75.00 125.00
40 Joe Primeau RC 300.00 500.00
41 Joe Lamb RC 90.00 150.00
42 Sylvio Mantha 125.00 200.00
43 Cy Wentworth RC 75.00 125.00
44 Normie Himes RC 75.00 125.00
45 Doug Brennan RC 50.00 100.00
46 Pit Lepine RC 50.00 100.00
47 Alex Levinsky RC 75.00 125.00
48 Baldy Northcott RC 75.00 125.00
49 Ken Doraty RC 75.00 125.00
50 Bill Thoms RC 75.00 125.00
51 Vernon Ayres RC 75.00 125.00

52 Lorne Duguid RC 75.00 125.00
53 Wally Kilrea RC 75.00 125.00
54 Vic Ripley RC 75.00 125.00
55 Happy Emms RC 75.00 125.00
56 Duke Dutkowski RC 75.00 125.00
57 Tiny Thompson RC 600.00 1500.00
58 Charlie Sands RC 75.00 125.00
59 Larry Aurie RC 75.00 125.00
60 Bill Beveridge RC 75.00 125.00
61 Bill McKenzie RC 75.00 125.00
62 Earl Roche RC 75.00 125.00
63 Bob Gracie RC 75.00 125.00
64 Hec Kilrea RC 75.00 125.00
65 Cooney Weiland RC 250.00 400.00
66 Bun Cook RC 200.00 350.00
67 John Roach 90.00 150.00
68 Murray Murdoch RC 75.00 125.00
69 Danny Cox RC 75.00 125.00
70 Desse Roche RC 75.00 125.00
71 Lorne Chabot RC 250.00 400.00
72 Syd Howe RC 250.00 400.00

1933-34 V357-2 Ice Kings Premiums

COMPLETE SET (6) 2000.00 4000.00
1 King Clancy 500.00 1000.00
2 Hap Day 175.00 350.00
3 Aurel Joliat 400.00 800.00
4 Howie Morenz 1000.00 2000.00
5 Allan Shields 87.50 175.00
6 Reginald Smith 125.00 250.00

1999-00 Wayne Gretzky Hockey

1 Paul Kariya .15 .40
2 Guy Hebert .15 .40
3 Steve Rucchin .10 .25
4 Teemu Selanne .30 .75
5 Oleg Tverdovsky .10 .25
6 Matt Cullen .10 .25
7 Jeff Nielsen .10 .25
8 Patrik Stefan RC .15 .40
9 Kelly Buchberger .10 .25
10 Andrew Brunette .10 .25
11 Ray Ferraro .10 .25
12 Nelson Emerson .10 .25
13 Damian Rhodes .10 .25
14 Sergei Samsonov .12 .30
15 John Grahame RC .12 .30
16 Joe Thornton .25 .60
17 Jason Allison .12 .30
18 Kyle McLaren .10 .25
19 Rob DiMaio .10 .25
20 Ray Bourque .25 .60
21 Dominik Hasek .25 .60
22 Miroslav Satan .12 .30
23 Alexei Zhitnik .10 .25
24 Stu Barnes .12 .30
25 Curtis Brown .10 .25
26 Brian Campbell RC .15 .40
27 Michael Peca .12 .30
28 Marc Savard .10 .25
29 Valeri Bure .10 .25
30 Phil Housley .12 .30
31 Grant Fuhr .25 .60
32 Cory Stillman .10 .25
33 Oleg Saprykin RC .15 .40
34 Sami Kapanen .10 .25
35 Bates Basttaglia .10 .25
36 Dave Tanabe .10 .25
37 Ron Francis .20 .50
38 Arturs Irbe .12 .30
39 Keith Primeau .12 .30
40 Doug Gilmour .20 .50
41 J-P Dumont .12 .30
42 Eric Daze .12 .30
43 Tony Amonte .12 .30
44 Alexei Zhamnov .10 .25
45 Kyle Calder RC .12 .30
46 Joe Sakic .30 .75
47 Chris Drury .12 .30
48 Milan Hejduk .12 .30
49 Adam Deadmarsh .10 .25
50 Patrick Roy .40 1.00
51 Peter Forsberg .30 .75
52 Alex Tanguay .12 .30
53 Mike Modano .25 .60
54 Brett Hull .30 .75
55 Ed Belfour .15 .40
56 Jamie Langenbrunner .10 .25
57 Pavel Patera RC .10 .25
58 Joe Nieuwendyk .12 .30
59 Jere Lehtinen .12 .30
60 Steve Yzerman .40 1.00
61 Jiri Fischer .10 .25
62 Brendan Shanahan .15 .40
63 Chris Osgood .15 .40
64 Chris Chelios .15 .40
65 Sergei Fedorov .25 .60
66 Nicklas Lidstrom .15 .40
67 Doug Weight .15 .40
68 Mike Grier .10 .25
69 Ryan Smyth .12 .30
70 Jason Smith .10 .25
71 Tom Poti .10 .25
72 Pavel Bure .15 .40
73 Mark Parrish .10 .25
74 Ivan Novoseltsev RC .20 .50
75 Trevor Kidd .10 .25
76 Viktor Kozlov .10 .25
77 Scott Mellanby .10 .25
78 Rob Blake .15 .40
79 Ian Lapperiere .10 .25
80 Zigmund Palffy .15 .40
81 Luc Robitaille .15 .40
82 Jozef Stumpel .10 .25
83 Aki Berg .10 .25
84 Stephane Fiset .12 .30
85 Saku Koivu .15 .40
86 Brian Savage .10 .25
87 Trevor Linden .15 .40
88 Jeff Hackett .10 .25
89 Eric Weinrich .10 .25
90 David Legwand .10 .25
91 Sergei Krivokrasov .10 .25
92 Randy Robitaille .10 .25
93 Kimmo Timonen .10 .25
94 Mike Dunham .10 .25
95 Brendan Morrison .12 .30
96 Scott Stevens .15 .40
97 Sheldon Souray .10 .25
98 Petr Sykora .12 .30
99 Wayne Gretzky 1.00 2.50
100 Martin Brodeur .40 1.00
101 Scott Niedermayer .15 .40
102 Patrik Elias .15 .40
103 Tim Connolly .10 .25
104 Jorgen Jonsson RC .10 .25
105 Mathieu Biron .10 .25
106 Claude Lapointe .12 .30
107 Kenny Jonsson .10 .25
108 Roberto Luongo .25 .60
109 Theo Fleury .20 .50
110 Petr Nedved .10 .25
111 Valeri Kamensky .10 .25
112 Adam Graves .12 .30
113 Manny Malhotra .12 .30
114 Brian Leetch .12 .30
115 Mike Richter .15 .40
116 Marian Hossa .15 .40
117 Radek Bonk .10 .25
118 Joe Juneau .10 .25
119 Wade Redden .10 .25
120 Ron Tugnutt .12 .30
121 Daniel Alfredsson .15 .40
122 Eric Lindros .25 .60
123 John LeClair .15 .40
124 Marc Bureau .10 .25
125 Simon Gagne .15 .40
126 Mark Recchi .20 .50
127 Rod Brind'Amour .15 .40
128 John Vanbiesbrouck .15 .40
129 Keith Tkachuk .15 .40
130 Jeremy Roenick .25 .60
131 Daniel Briere .12 .30
132 Bob Essensa .10 .25
133 J.J. Daigneault .10 .25
134 Mika Alatalo RC .12 .30
135 Travis Green .10 .25
136 Jaromir Jagr .50 1.25
137 Martin Straka .10 .25
138 Alexei Morozov .12 .30
139 Jan Hrdina .10 .25
140 Alexei Kovalev .12 .30
141 Peter Skudra .12 .30
142 John Slaney .10 .25
143 Pierre Turgeon .12 .30
144 Roman Turek .12 .30
145 Pavol Demitra .20 .50
146 Al MacInnis .20 .50
147 Chris Pronger .15 .40
148 Jochen Hecht RC .25 .60
149 Jeff Friesen .12 .30
150 Steve Shields .12 .30
151 Patrick Marleau .15 .40
152 Vincent Damphousse .12 .30
153 Marco Sturm .10 .25
154 Brad Stuart .12 .30
155 Darcy Tucker .10 .25
156 Vincent Lecavalier .15 .40
157 Andrei Zyuzin .10 .25
158 Chris Gratton .10 .25
159 Fredrik Modin .10 .25
160 Mats Sundin .15 .40
161 Steve Thomas .10 .25
162 Sergei Berezin .10 .25
163 Mike Johnson .12 .30
164 Dimitri Khristich .10 .25
165 Bryan Berard .10 .25
166 Curtis Joseph .20 .50
167 Mark Messier .30 .75
168 Alexander Mogilny .12 .30
169 Garth Snow .12 .30
170 Markus Naslund .15 .40
171 Steve Kariya RC .15 .40
172 Peter Schaefer .10 .25
173 Peter Bondra .15 .40
174 Joe Sacco .10 .25
175 Adam Oates .15 .40
176 Olaf Kolzig .15 .40
177 Jan Bulis .10 .25
178 Alexander Volchkov RC .10 .25
179 Wayne Gretzky CL 1.00 2.50
180 Curtis Joseph CL .20 .50
GM1P Wayne Gretzky PUCK 25.00 60.00
GM1S Wayne Gretzky STICK 30.00 80.00

1999-00 Wayne Gretzky Hockey Changing The Game

COMPLETE SET (10) 15.00 30.00
CG1 Peter Forsberg 1.50 4.00
CG2 Eric Lindros 1.25 3.00
CG3 Paul Kariya 1.25 3.00
CG4 Jaromir Jagr 1.50 4.00
CG5 Dominik Hasek 2.00 5.00
CG6 Sergei Samsonov 1.00 2.50
CG7 Theo Fleury 1.25 3.00
CG8 Al MacInnis 1.00 2.50
CG9 Pavel Bure 1.25 3.00
CG10 Patrick Roy 5.00 12.00

1999-00 Wayne Gretzky Hockey Elements of the Game

COMPLETE SET (15) 8.00 15.00
EG1 Teemu Selanne .40 1.00
EG2 Mike Peca .30 .75
EG3 Sergei Samsonov .30 .75
EG4 Sergei Fedorov .60 1.50
EG5 Peter Forsberg 1.00 2.50
EG6 Brett Hull .50 1.25
EG7 Eric Lindros .40 1.00
EG8 Pavel Bure .40 1.00
EG9 Theo Fleury .30 .75
EG10 Martin Brodeur 1.00 2.50
EG11 Jaromir Jagr .60 1.50
EG12 Keith Tkachuk .40 1.00
EG13 Peter Bondra .40 1.00
EG14 Joe Sakic .75 2.00
EG15 Curtis Joseph .40 1.00

1999-00 Wayne Gretzky Hockey Great Heroes

COMPLETE SET (10) 20.00 40.00
GH1 Jaromir Jagr 2.00 5.00
GH2 Paul Kariya 2.00 5.00
GH3 Joe Sakic 2.50 6.00
GH4 Dominik Hasek 2.50 6.00
GH5 Patrick Roy 5.00 12.00
GH6 Steve Yzerman 5.00 12.00
GH7 Eric Lindros 2.00 5.00
GH8 Patrik Stefan 1.50 4.00
GH9 Teemu Selanne 2.00 5.00
GH10 Pavel Bure 1.50 4.00

1999-00 Wayne Gretzky Hockey Hall of Fame Career

COMPLETE SET (30) 12.00 25.00
COMMON GRETZKY .40 1.00

1999-00 Wayne Gretzky Hockey Signs of Greatness

AI Arturs Irbe 6.00 15.00
BH Brett Hull SP 30.00 60.00
CD Chris Drury 6.00 15.00
CJ Curtis Joseph SP 40.00 80.00
CO Chris Osgood 6.00 15.00
DL David Legwand 6.00 15.00
MP Mark Parrish 5.00 12.00
NK Nikolai Khabibulin 8.00 20.00
PB Pavel Bure SP 25.00 60.00
PM Paul Mara 5.00 12.00
PS Patrik Stefan 6.00 15.00
RB Ray Bourque 25.00 60.00
SS Sergei Samsonov SP 15.00 40.00
VS Vadim Sharifijanov 6.00 15.00
WG Wayne Gretzky SP 300.00 800.00

1999-00 Wayne Gretzky Hockey Tools of Greatness

TGAI Arturs Irbe 10.00 25.00
TGBH Brett Hull 12.50 30.00
TGBS Brendan Shanahan 10.00 25.00
TGCJ Curtis Joseph 10.00 25.00
TGDW Doug Weight 10.00 25.00
TGEB Ed Belfour 10.00 25.00
TGEL Eric Lindros 10.00 25.00
TGLR Luc Robitaille 10.00 25.00
TGMR Mike Richter 10.00 25.00
TGMS Mats Sundin 10.00 25.00
TGNK Nikolai Khabibulin 10.00 25.00
TGPB Pavel Bure 10.00 25.00
TGPF Peter Forsberg 12.00 30.00
TGPK Paul Kariya 10.00 25.00
TGPR Patrick Roy 20.00 50.00
TGRB Ray Bourque 15.00 40.00
TGSS Sergei Samsonov 8.00 20.00
TGTA Tony Amonte 8.00 20.00
TGTS Teemu Selanne 10.00 25.00

1999-00 Wayne Gretzky Hockey Visionary

COMPLETE SET (10) 75.00 150.00
COMMON GRETZKY (V1-V10) 10.00 25.00

1999-00 Wayne Gretzky Hockey Will to Win

COMPLETE SET (10) 12.00 25.00
W1 Paul Kariya .60 1.50
W2 Steve Yzerman 3.00 8.00
W3 Jaromir Jagr 1.00 2.50
W4 Dominik Hasek 1.25 3.00
W5 Patrick Roy 3.00 8.00
W6 Jeremy Roenick .75 2.00
W7 Ray Bourque 1.00 2.50
W8 John LeClair .75 2.00
W9 Mats Sundin .60 1.50
W10 Mark Messier .75 2.00

1927 Werner and Mertz Field Hockey

COMPLETE SET (6) 62.50 125.00
1 Womens Field Hockey 12.50 25.00
2 Womens Field Hockey 12.50 25.00
3 Mens Field Hockey
Scrum at midfield 12.50 25.00
4 Mens Field Hockey
Chasing the ball 12.50 25.00
5 Mens Field Hockey
Pileup 12.50 25.00
6 Mens Field Hockey
Goalie action shot 12.50 25.00

1982-83 Whalers Junior Hartford Courant

COMPLETE SET (22) 14.00 75.00
1 Greg Adams 1.50 4.00
2 Russ Anderson .75 2.00
3 Ron Francis 10.00 25.00
4 Michel Galarneau .75 2.00
5 Dan Fridgen .75 2.00
6 Archie Henderson .75 2.00
7 Ed Hospodar .75 2.00
8 Mark Johnson 1.25 3.00
9 Chris Kotsopoulos .75 2.00
10 Pierre Larouche 1.50 4.00
11 George Lyle .75 2.00
12 Greg Millen 2.00 5.00
13 Warren Miller .75 2.00
14 Ray Neufeld 1.25 3.00
15 Mark Renaud .75 2.00
16 Risto Siltanen 1.25 3.00
17 Stuart Smith .75 2.00
18 Blaine Stoughton 1.50 4.00
19 Doug Sulliman .75 2.00
20 Bob Sullivan .75 2.00
21 Mike Veisor 1.25 3.00
22 Mickey Volcan .75 2.00
23 Blake Wesley .75 2.00

1983-84 Whalers Junior Hartford Courant

COMPLETE SET (22) 10.00 25.00
1 Bob Crawford .40 1.00
2 Mike Crombeen .40 1.00
3 Richie Dunn .40 1.00
4 Normand Dupont .40 1.00
5 Ron Francis 3.00 8.00
6 Ed Hospodar .40 1.00
7 Marty Howe .75 2.00
8 Mark Johnson .60 1.50
9 Chris Kotsopoulos .40 1.00
10 Pierre Lacroix .60 1.50
11 Greg Malone .60 1.50
12 Greg Malone .60 1.50
13 Ray Neufeld .40 1.00
14 Joel Quenneville .60 1.50
15 Torrie Robertson .60 1.50
16 Risto Siltanen .40 1.00
17 Blaine Stoughton .75 2.00
18 Steve Stoyanovich .40 1.00
19 Doug Sulliman .40 1.00
20 Sylvain Turgeon .60 1.50
21 Mike Veisor .60 1.50
22 Mike Zuke .40 1.00

1984-85 Whalers Junior Wendy's

COMPLETE SET (22) 10.00 25.00
1 Jack Brownschidle .40 1.00
2 Sylvain Cote .40 1.00
3 Bob Crawford .40 1.00
4 Mike Crombeen .40 1.00
5 Tony Currie .40 1.00
6 Ron Francis 2.50 6.00
7 Mark Fusco .40 1.00
8 Dave Jensen .40 1.00
9 Mark Johnson .60 1.50
10 Chris Kotsopoulos .40 1.00
11 Greg Malone .60 1.50
12 Greg Millen .75 2.00
13 Ray Neufeld .40 1.00
14 Randy Pierce .40 1.00
15 Joel Quenneville .60 1.50
16 Torrie Robertson .60 1.50
17 Ulf Samuelsson 1.50 4.00
18 Risto Siltanen .40 1.00
19 Dave Tippett .40 1.00
20 Sylvain Turgeon .40 1.00
21 Steve Weeks .75 2.00
22 Mike Zuke .60 1.50

1985-86 Whalers Junior Wendy's

COMPLETE SET (23) 12.00 30.00
1 Jack Brownschidle .40 1.00
2 Sylvain Cote .40 1.00
3 Bob Crawford .40 1.00
4 Kevin Dineen 1.50 4.00
5 Paul Fenton .40 1.00
6 Ray Ferraro 1.25 3.00
7 Ron Francis 2.00 5.00
8 Scott Kleinendorst .40 1.00
9 Paul Lawless .40 1.00
10 Mike Liut 1.25 3.00
11 Paul MacDermid .40 1.00
12 Greg Malone .40 1.00
13 Dana Murzyn .40 1.00
14 Ray Neufeld .40 1.00
15 Jorgen Pettersson .40 1.00
16 Joel Quenneville .40 1.00
17 Torrie Robertson .60 1.50
18 Ulf Samuelsson 1.25 3.00
19 Risto Siltanen .40 1.00
20 Dave Tippett .40 1.00
21 Sylvain Turgeon .60 1.50
22 Steve Weeks .60 1.50
23 Mike Zuke .40 1.00

1986-87 Whalers Junior Thomas'

COMPLETE SET (23) 12.00 30.00
1 John Anderson .40 1.00
2 Dave Babych .75 2.00
3 Wayne Babych .40 1.00
4 Sylvain Cote .40 1.00
5 Kevin Dineen 1.25 3.00
6 Dean Evason .40 1.00
7 Ray Ferraro .40 1.00
8 Ron Francis 2.50 6.00
9 Bill Gardner .40 1.00
10 Stewart Gavin .40 1.00
11 Doug Jarvis .40 1.00
12 Scot Kleinendorst .40 1.00
13 Paul Lawless .40 1.00
14 Mike Liut 1.25 3.00
15 Paul MacDermid .40 1.00
16 Mike McEwen .40 1.00
17 Dana Murzyn .40 1.00
18 Joel Quenneville .40 1.00
19 Torrie Robertson .50 1.25
20 Ulf Samuelsson 1.25 3.00
21 Dave Tippett .40 1.00
22 Sylvain Turgeon .40 1.00
23 Steve Weeks .60 1.50

1987-88 Whalers Jr. Burger King/Pepsi

COMPLETE SET (21) 10.00 25.00
1 John Anderson .40 1.00
2 Dave Babych .75 2.00
3 Sylvain Cote .40 1.00
4 Kevin Dineen 1.00 2.50
5 Dean Evason .40 1.00
6 Ray Ferraro 1.00 2.50
7 Ron Francis 1.50 4.00
8 Stew Gavin .40 1.00
9 Doug Jarvis .40 1.00
10 Scott Kleinendorst .40 1.00
11 Randy Ladouceur .40 1.00
12 Paul Lawless .40 1.00
13 Mike Liut 1.00 2.50
14 Paul MacDermid .40 1.00
15 Dana Murzyn .40 1.00
16 Joel Quenneville .40 1.00
17 Torrie Robertson .40 1.00
18 Ulf Samuelsson .75 2.00
19 Dave Tippett .40 1.00
20 Sylvain Turgeon .40 1.00
21 Steve Weeks .60 1.50

1988-89 Whalers Junior Ground Round

COMPLETE SET (18) 8.00 20.00
1 John Anderson .40 1.00
2 Dave Babych .60 1.50
3 Sylvain Cote .40 1.00
4 Kevin Dineen .75 2.00
5 Dean Evason .40 1.00
6 Ray Ferraro .75 2.00
7 Ron Francis 1.50 4.00
8 Scot Kleinendorst .40 1.00
9 Randy Ladouceur .40 1.00
10 Mike Liut .75 2.00
11 Paul MacDermid .40 1.00
12 Brent Peterson .40 1.00
13 Joel Quenneville .40 1.00
14 Torrie Robertson .40 1.00
15 Ulf Samuelsson .75 2.00
16 Dave Tippett .40 1.00
17 Sylvain Turgeon .40 1.00
18 Carey Wilson .40 1.00

1989-90 Whalers Junior Milk

COMPLETE SET (23) 8.00 20.00
1 Mikael Andersson .20 .50
2 Dave Babych .30 .75
3 Sylvain Cote .20 .50
4 Randy Cunneyworth .20 .50
5 Kevin Dineen .60 1.50
6 Dean Evason .20 .50
7 Ray Ferraro .40 1.00
8 Ron Francis 1.25 3.00
9 Jody Hull .20 .50
10 Grant Jennings .20 .50
11 Ed Kastelic SP .75 2.00
12 Todd Krygier SP .75 2.00
13 Randy Ladouceur .20 .50
14 Mike Liut .60 1.50
15 Paul MacDermid .20 .50
16 Joel Quenneville .20 .50
17 Ulf Samuelsson .60 1.50
18 Brad Shaw .30 .75
19 Peter Sidorkiewicz .30 .75
20 Dave Tippett .20 .50
21 Mike Tomlak SP .75 2.00
22 Pat Verbeek .60 1.50
23 Scott Young .40 1.00

1990-91 Whalers Jr. 7-Eleven

COMPLETE SET (27) 12.00 30.00
1 Mikael Andersson .20 .50
2 Dave Babych .30 .75
3 Rob Brown SP .75 2.00
4 Yvon Corriveau .20 .50
5 Sylvain Cote .20 .50
6 Doug Crossman .20 .50
7 Randy Cunneyworth .20 .50
8 Paul Cyr .20 .50
9 Kevin Dineen .40 1.00
10 Dean Evason .20 .50
11 Ron Francis 1.00 2.50
12 Chris Govedaris SP .75 2.00
13 Bobby Holik .40 1.00
14 Gordie Howe 2.00 5.00
15 Grant Jennings .20 .50
16 Ed Kastelic .20 .50
17 Todd Krygier .20 .50
18 Randy Ladouceur .20 .50
19 Jim McKenzie SP .75 2.00
20 Daryl Reaugh SP 1.00 2.50
21 Ulf Samuelsson .40 1.00
22 Brad Shaw .30 .75
23 Peter Sidorkiewicz .30 .75
24 Mike Tomlak .20 .50
25 Pat Verbeek .60 1.50
26 Carey Wilson .20 .50
27 Scott Young .30 .75

1991-92 Whalers Jr. 7-Eleven

COMPLETE SET (28) 8.00 20.00
1 Mikael Andersson .20 .50
2 Marc Bergevin .20 .50
3 James Black SP .60 1.50
4 Rob Brown .25 .60
5 Adam Burt .20 .50
6 Andrew Cassels SP 1.25 3.00
7 Murray Craven .30 .75
8 John Cullen .40 1.00
9 Randy Cunneyworth .20 .50
10 Paul Cyr SP .60 1.50
11 Joe Day .20 .50
12 Paul Gillis SP .60 1.50
13 Mark Greig .20 .50
14 Bobby Holik .30 .75
15 Doug Houda .20 .50
16 Mark Hunter .20 .50
17 Ed Kastelic .20 .50
18 Dan Keczmer SP .75 2.00
19 Steve Konroyd SP .60 1.50
20 Randy Ladouceur .20 .50
21 Jim McKenzie .20 .50
22 Michel Picard .20 .50
23 Geoff Sanderson 2.00 5.00
24 Brad Shaw .25 .60
25 Peter Sidorkiewicz .30 .75
26 Pat Verbeek .60 1.50
27 Kay Whitmore .30 .75
28 Zarley Zalapski .30 .75

1992-93 Whalers Dairymart

COMPLETE SET (26) 7.20 18.00
1 Jim Agnew .20 .50
2 Sean Burke .60 1.50
3 Adam Burt .20 .50
4 Andrew Cassels .40 1.00
5 Murray Craven .25 .60
6 Randy Cunneyworth .20 .50
7 Paul Gillis .20 .50
8 Paul Holmgren CO .20 .50
9 Doug Houda .20 .50
10 Mark Janssens .20 .50
11 Tim Kerr .30 .75
12 Steve Konroyd .20 .50
13 Nick Kypreos .20 .50
14 Randy Ladouceur .20 .50
15 Jim McKenzie .20 .50
16 Michael Nylander .40 1.00
17 Allen Pedersen .20 .50
18 Robert Petrovicky .20 .50
19 Frank Pietrangelo .30 .75
20 Patrick Poulin .20 .50
21 Geoff Sanderson 1.50 4.00
22 Pat Verbeek .60 1.50
23 Eric Weinrich .20 .50
24 Terry Yake .20 .50
25 Zarley Zalapski .20 .50
26 Junior Whalers
Member Card .08 .25

1993-94 Whalers Coke

COMPLETE SET (24) 7.20 18.00
1 Sean Burke .75 2.00
2 Adam Burt .20 .50
3 Andrew Cassels .40 1.00
4 Randy Cunneyworth .20 .50
5 Alexander Godynyuk .20 .50
6 Mark Greig .20 .50
7 Mark Janssens .20 .50
8 Robert Kron .20 .50
9 Bryan Marchment .20 .50
10 Brad McCrimmon .20 .50
11 Pierre McGuire CO .08 .25
12 Michael Nylander .30 .75
13 James Patrick .20 .50
14 Frank Pietrangelo .30 .75
15 Marc Potvin .20 .50
16 Chris Pronger 1.25 3.00
17 Brian Propp .30 .75
18 Jeff Reese .30 .75
19 Geoff Sanderson .75 2.00
20 Jim Sandlak .20 .50
21 Jim Storm .20 .50
22 Darren Turcotte .30 .75
23 Pat Verbeek .60 1.50
24 Zarley Zalapski .20 .50

1995-96 Whalers Bob's Stores

COMPLETE SET (27) 4.80 12.00
1 Sean Burke .30 .75
2 Adam Burke .15 .40
3 Andrew Cassels .15 .40
4 Kelly Chase .15 .40
5 Scott Daniels .15 .40
6 Gerald Diduck .15 .40
7 Nelson Emerson .25 .60
8 Glen Featherstone .15 .40
9 Brian Glynn .15 .40
10 Mark Janssens .15 .40
11 Robert Kron .15 .40
12 Frantisek Kucera .15 .40
13 Jocelyn Lemieux .15 .40
14 Marek Malik .15 .40
15 Steve Martins .15 .40
16 Paul Maurice CO .08 .25
17 Brad McCrimmon .15 .40
18 Jason Muzzatti .15 .40
19 Andrei Nikolishin .15 .40
20 Jeff O'Neill .15 .40
21 Paul Ranheim .15 .40
22 Steven Rice .15 .40
23 Geoff Sanderson .25 .60
24 Brendan Shanahan 1.25 3.00
25 Kevin Smyth .15 .40
26 Glen Wesley .25 .60
27 Kids Club Discount Card .02 .10

1996-97 Whalers Kid's Club

COMPLETE SET (28) 14.00 35.00
1 Sean Burke .75 2.00
2 Jason Muzzatti .60 1.50
3 Kevin Dineen .60 1.50
4 Geoff Sanderson .60 1.50
5 Keith Primeau .75 2.00
6 Jeff O'Neill .75 2.00
7 Marek Malik .40 1.00
8 Paul Ranheim .40 1.00
9 Alexander Godynyuk .40 1.00
10 Robert Kron .40 1.00
11 Gerald Diduck .40 1.00
12 Kelly Chase .40 1.00
13 Glen Wesley .40 1.00
14 Andrew Cassels .60 1.50
15 Hnat Domenichelli .40 1.00
16 Sami Kapanen .75 2.00
17 Nelson Emerson .60 1.50
18 Mark Janssens .40 1.00
19 Stu Grimson .75 2.00
20 Nolan Pratt .40 1.00
21 Glen Featherstone .40 1.00
22 Curtis Leschyshyn .40 1.00
23 Jeff Brown .40 1.00
24 Adam Burt .40 1.00
25 Steven Rice .40 1.00
26 Kevin Brown 1.25 3.00
27 Steve Chiasson 1.25 3.00
28 Kent Manderville 1.25 3.00

2001-02 Wild Crime Prevention

COMPLETE SET (8) 8.00 20.00
17 Willie Mitchell .40 1.00
18 Marian Gaborik 6.00 15.00
19 Darby Hendrickson .40 1.00
20 Andrew Brunette .40 1.00
21 Sergei Zholtok .40 1.00
22 Jim Dowd .40 1.00
23 Manny Fernandez .60 1.50
24 Nick Schultz .40 1.00

2001-02 Wild Team Issue

COMPLETE SET
1 Manny Fernandez .75 2.00
2 Stacy Roest .40 1.00
3 Willie Mitchell .40 1.00

2003-04 Wild Law Enforcement Cards

COMPLETE SET (11)
1 Brad Bombardir .40 1.00
2 Pierre-Marc Bouchard 1.25 3.00
3 Marian Gaborik 1.25 3.00
4 Filip Kuba .40 1.00
5 Willie Mitchell .40 1.00
6 Richard Park .40 1.00
7 Dwayne Roloson .75 2.00
8 Nick Schultz .40 1.00
9 Wes Walz .40 1.00
10 Sergei Zholtok .40 1.00
11 McGruff the Crime Dog .04 .10

2006-07 Wild Crime Prevention

1 Pavol Demitra .40 1.00
2 Kim Johnsson .40 1.00
3 Keith Carney .40 1.00
4 Mark Parrish .40 1.00
5 Brian Rolston .40 1.00
6 Kurtis Foster .40 1.00
7 Mikko Koivu .75 2.00
8 Marian Gaborik 2.00 5.00
9 McGruff the Crime Dog .10 .25

2007-08 Wild Crime Prevention

COMPLETE SET (9) 5.00 10.00
1 McGruff The Crime Dog .10 .25
2 Niklas Backstrom .75 2.00
3 Brent Burns .60 1.50
4 Pierre-Marc Bouchard .60 1.50
5 Nick Schultz .60 1.50
6 Stephane Veilleux .40 1.00
7 Josh Harding .75 2.00
8 Petteri Nummelin .40 1.00
9 Branko Radivojevic .40 1.00

2011-12 Minnesota Wild Team Issue Jumbo

1 Cody Almond .30 .75
2 Niklas Backstrom .50 1.25
3 Pierre-Marc Bouchard .50 1.25
4 Kyle Brodziak .30 .75
5 Cal Clutterbuck .30 .75
6 Matt Cullen .30 .75
7 Justin Falk .30 .75
8 Josh Harding .50 1.25
9 Dany Heatley .40 1.00
10 Nick Johnson .40 1.00
11 Matt Kassian .30 .75
12 Mikko Koivu .40 1.00
13 Guillaume Latendresse .40 1.00
14 Warren Peters .50 1.25
15 Darroll Powe .30 .75
16 Nate Prosser .30 .75
17 Marco Scandella .30 .75
18 Devin Setoguchi .40 1.00
19 Jared Spurgeon .50 1.25

2011-12 Wild Team Issue Sony

1 Matt Cullen .50 1.25
2 Cal Clutterbuck .50 1.25
3 Devin Setoguchi .60 1.50
4 Mikko Koivu .60 1.50
5 Niklas Backstrom .75 2.00

1960-61 Wonder Bread Premium Photos

COMPLETE SET (4) 300.00 600.00
1 Gordie Howe 150.00 300.00
2 Bobby Hull 100.00 200.00
3 Dave Keon 40.00 80.00
4 Maurice Richard 100.00 200.00

1960-61 York Photos

COMPLETE SET (37) 1200.00 2400.00
1 George Armstrong TML 30.00 60.00
2 Ralph Backstrom MC 25.00 50.00
3 Bob Baun TML 30.00 60.00
4 Jean Beliveau MC 87.50 175.00
5 Marcel Bonin MC 17.50 35.00
6 Johnny Bower TML 62.50 125.00
7 Carl Brewer TML 25.00 50.00
8 Dick Duff TML 25.00 50.00
9 Jean-Guy Gendron MC 17.50 35.00
10 Boom Boom Geoffrion MC 62.50 125.00
11 Phil Goyette MC 17.50 35.00
12 Billy Harris TML 17.50 35.00
13 Doug Harvey MC 50.00 100.00
14 Bill Hicke MC 17.50 35.00
15 Larry Hillman TML 17.50 35.00
16 Charlie Hodge MC 25.00 50.00
17 Tim Horton TML 87.50 175.00
18 Tom Johnson MC 25.00 50.00
19 Red Kelly TML 30.00 60.00
20 Dave Keon TML 62.50 125.00
21 Albert Langlois MC 17.50 35.00
22 Frank Mahovlich TML 62.50 125.00
23 Don Marshall MC 25.00 50.00
24 Dickie Moore MC 30.00 60.00
25 Bob Nevin TML 17.50 35.00
26 Bert Olmstead TML 30.00 60.00
27 Jacques Plante MC 175.00 350.00
28 Claude Provost MC 25.00 50.00
29 Bob Pulford TML 30.00 60.00
30 Larry Regan TML 17.50 35.00
31 Henri Richard MC 62.50 125.00
32 Eddie Shack TML 50.00 100.00
33 Allan Stanley TML 30.00 60.00
34 Ron Stewart TML 17.50 35.00
35 Jean-Guy Talbot MC 25.00 50.00
36 Gilles Tremblay MC 25.00 50.00
37 Bob Turner MC 17.50 35.00

1961-62 York Yellow Backs

COMPLETE SET (42) 300.00 600.00
1 Bob Baun 7.50 15.00
2 Dick Duff 6.00 12.00
3 Frank Mahovlich 12.50 25.00
4 Gilles Tremblay 5.00 10.00
5 Dickie Moore 7.50 15.00
6 Don Marshall 5.00 10.00
7 Tim Horton 15.00 30.00
8 Johnny Bower 10.00 20.00
9 Allan Stanley 7.50 15.00
10 Jean Beliveau 20.00 40.00
11 Tom Johnson 7.50 15.00
12 Jean-Guy Talbot 6.00 12.00
13 Carl Brewer 5.00 10.00
14 Bob Pulford 7.50 15.00
15 Billy Harris 5.00 10.00
16 Bill Hicke 5.00 10.00
17 Claude Provost 6.00 12.00
18 Henri Richard 12.50 25.00
19 Bert Olmstead 7.50 15.00
20 Ron Stewart 5.00 10.00
21 Red Kelly 7.50 15.00
22 Toe Blake CO 7.50 15.00
23 Jacques Plante 25.00 50.00
24 Ralph Backstrom 6.00 12.00
25 Eddie Shack 10.00 20.00
26 Bob Nevin 5.00 10.00
27 Dave Keon 20.00 40.00
28 Boom Boom Geoffrion 10.00 20.00
29 Marcel Bonin 5.00 10.00
30 Phil Goyette 5.00 10.00
31 Larry Hillman 5.00 10.00
32 Larry Keenan 5.00 10.00
33 Al Arbour 7.50 15.00
34 J.C. Tremblay 6.00 12.00
35 Bobby Rousseau 5.00 10.00
36 Al McNeil 5.00 10.00
37 George Armstrong 7.50 15.00
38 Punch Imlach CO 6.00 12.00
39 King Clancy 10.00 20.00
40 Lou Fontinato 5.00 10.00
41 Cesare Maniago 7.50 15.00
42 Jean Gauthier 5.00 10.00
xx Album 20.00 40.00

1962-63 York Iron-On Transfers
COMPLETE SET (36) 900.00 1800.00
1 Johnny Bower 25.00 50.00
2 Jacques Plante 75.00 150.00
3 Tim Horton 50.00 100.00
4 Jean-Guy Talbot 15.00 30.00
5 Carl Brewer 15.00 30.00
6 J.C. Tremblay 15.00 30.00
7 Dick Duff 15.00 30.00
8 Jean Beliveau 50.00 100.00
9 Dave Keon 25.00 50.00
10 Henri Richard 40.00 80.00
11 Frank Mahovlich 40.00 80.00
12 BoomBoom Geoffrion 25.00 50.00
13 Kent Douglas 12.50 25.00
14 Claude Provost 15.00 30.00
15 Bob Pulford 15.00 30.00
16 Ralph Backstrom 15.00 30.00
17 George Armstrong 20.00 40.00
18 Bobby Rousseau 12.50 25.00
19 Gordie Howe 125.00 250.00
20 Red Kelly 20.00 40.00
21 Alex Delvecchio 20.00 40.00
22 Dickie Moore 20.00 40.00
23 Marcel Pronovost 15.00 30.00
24 Doug Barkley 12.50 25.00
25 Terry Sawchuk 50.00 100.00
26 Billy Harris 12.50 25.00
27 Parker MacDonald 12.50 25.00
28 Don Marshall 12.50 25.00
29 Norm Ullman 25.00 50.00
30A Andre Pronovost 12.50 25.00
30B Vic Stasiuk 12.50 25.00
31 Bill Gadsby 15.00 30.00
32 Eddie Shack 25.00 50.00
33 Larry Jeffrey 12.50 25.00
34 Gilles Tremblay 12.50 25.00
35 Howie Young 12.50 25.00
36 Bruce MacGregor 12.50 25.00

1963-64 York White Backs
COMPLETE SET (54) 375.00 750.00
1 Tim Horton 20.00 40.00
2 Johnny Bower 12.50 25.00
3 Ron Stewart 7.50 15.00
4 Eddie Shack 12.50 25.00
5 Frank Mahovlich 15.00 30.00
6 Dave Keon 15.00 30.00
7 Bob Baun 7.50 15.00
8 Bob Nevin 7.50 15.00
9 Dick Duff 7.50 15.00
10 Billy Harris 7.50 15.00
11 Larry Hillman 7.50 15.00
12 Red Kelly 10.00 20.00
13 Kent Douglas 7.50 15.00
14 Allan Stanley 7.50 15.00
15 Don Simmons 7.50 15.00
16 George Armstrong 10.00 20.00
17 Carl Brewer 7.50 15.00
18 Bob Pulford 7.50 15.00
19 Henri Richard 15.00 30.00
20 BoomBoom Geoffrion 12.50 25.00
21 Gilles Tremblay 7.50 15.00
22 Gump Worsley 12.50 25.00
23 Jean-Guy Talbot 7.50 15.00
24 J.C. Tremblay 7.50 15.00
25 Bobby Rousseau 7.50 15.00
26 Jean Beliveau 20.00 40.00
27 Ralph Backstrom 7.50 15.00
28 Claude Provost 7.50 15.00
29 Jean Gauthier 7.50 15.00
30 Bill Hicke 7.50 15.00
31 Terry Harper 7.50 15.00
32 Marc Reaume 7.50 15.00
33 Dave Balon 7.50 15.00
34 Jacques Laperriere 10.00 20.00
35 John Ferguson 10.00 20.00
36 Red Berenson 7.50 15.00
37 Terry Sawchuk 25.00 50.00
38 Marcel Pronovost 7.50 15.00
39 Bill Gadsby 10.00 20.00
40 Parker MacDonald 7.50 15.00
41 Larry Jeffrey 7.50 15.00
42 Floyd Smith 7.50 15.00
43 Andre Pronovost 7.50 15.00
44 Art Stratton 7.50 15.00
45 Gordie Howe 50.00 100.00
46 Doug Barkley 7.50 15.00
47 Norm Ullman 10.00 20.00
48 Eddie Joyal 7.50 15.00
49 Alex Faulkner 15.00 30.00
50 Alex Delvecchio 10.00 20.00
51 Bruce MacGregor 7.50 15.00
52 Ted Hampson 7.50 15.00
53 Pete Goegan 7.50 15.00
54 Ron Ingram 7.50 15.00
xx Album 20.00 40.00

1967-68 York Action Octagons
COMPLETE SET (36) 300.00 600.00
1 Brian Conacher 22
Allan Stanley 26
Leon Rochefort 7.50 15.00
2 Terry Harper 19
Gump Worsley 30
Mike Walton 16 10.00 20.00
3 Tim Horton 7
George Armstrong 10
Jean Beliveau 4 20.00 40.00
4 Dave Keon 14
George Armstrong 10
Claude Provost 14 10.00 20.00
5 Jacques Laperriere 2
Rogatien Vachon 29
Bob Pulford 20 10.00 20.00
6 Bob Pulford 20
Brian Conacher 22
Claude Provost 14 6.00 12.00
7 Bob Pulford 20
Jim Pappin 18
Terry Harper 19 6.00 12.00
8 Pete Stemkowski 12
Jim Pappin 18
Harris 10 6.00 12.00
9 J.C. Tremblay 3
Rogatien Vachon 29
Pete Stemkowski 12 7.50 15.00
10 Rogatien Vachon 29
Ralph Backstrom 6
Bob Pulford 20 10.00 20.00
11 Rogatien Vachon 29
Jacques Laperriere 2
Mike Walton 16 10.00 20.00
12 Mike Walton 16
Pete Stemkowski 12
J.C. Tremblay 3 6.00 12.00
13 Dave Keon 16
Mike Walton 16
J.C. Tremblay 3 7.50 15.00
14 Pete Stemkowski 12
Ralph Backstrom 6 5.00 10.00
15 Rogatien Vachon 29
Bob Pulford 20 7.50 15.00
16 Johnny Bower 1
Ron Ellis 8
John Ferguson 22 7.50 15.00
17 Ron Ellis 8
Gump Worsley 30 7.50 15.00
18 Gump Worsley 30
Jacques Laperriere 2
Frank Mahovlich 27 12.50 25.00
19 J.C. Tremblay 3
Dave Keon 14 7.50 15.00
20 Claude Provost 14
Frank Mahovlich 27 10.00 20.00
21 John Ferguson 22
Tim Horton 7 10.00 20.00
22 Gump Worsley 30
Ron Ellis 8 7.50 15.00
23 Johnny Bower 1
Mike Walton 16
Jean Beliveau 4 10.00 20.00
24 J.C. Tremblay 3
Gump Worsley 30
Bob Pulford 20 7.50 15.00
25 Tim Horton 7
Johnny Bower 1
Jean Beliveau 4 15.00 30.00
26 Allan Stanley 26
Johnny Bower 1
Dick Duff 8 7.50 15.00
27 Ralph Backstrom 6
Johnny Bower 1 7.50 15.00
28 Yvan Cournoyer 12
Jean Beliveau 4
Frank Mahovlich 27 20.00 40.00
29 Johnny Bower 1
Larry Hillman 2
Yvan Cournoyer 12 10.00 20.00
30 Johnny Bower 1
Yvan Cournoyer 12 10.00 20.00
31 Tim Horton 7
Rogatien Vachon 29 10.00 20.00
32 Jim Pappin 18
Bob Pulford 20
Rogatien Vachon 29 7.50 15.00
33 Terry Harper 19
Bobby Rousseau 15
Pronovost 3 5.00 10.00
34 Johnny Bower 1
Pronovost 3
Ralph Backstrom 6 6.00 12.00
35 Frank Mahovlich 27
Gump Worsley 30 12.50 25.00
36 Claude Provost 14
Johnny Bower 1 6.00 12.00

1992-93 Zeller's Masters of Hockey
COMPLETE SET (7) 8.00 20.00
1 Johnny Bower 1.25 3.00
2 Rod Gilbert 1.25 3.00
3 Ted Lindsay 1.25 3.00
4 Frank Mahovlich 1.50 4.00
5 Stan Mikita 1.50 4.00
6 Maurice Richard 2.50 6.00

1992-93 Zeller's Masters of Hockey Signed
COMPLETE SET (7) 50.00 125.00
1 Johnny Bower 6.00 15.00
2 Rod Gilbert 6.00 15.00
3 Ted Lindsay 6.00 15.00
4 Frank Mahovlich 8.00 20.00
5 Stan Mikita 8.00 20.00
6 Maurice Richard 25.00 60.00

1993-94 Zeller's Masters of Hockey
COMPLETE SET (8) 6.00 15.00
1 Andy Bathgate .40 1.00
2 Johnny Bucyk .75 2.00
3 Yvan Cournoyer .75 2.00
4 Marcel Dionne .75 2.00
5 Bobby Hull 1.50 4.00
6 Brad Park .75 2.00
7 Jean Ratelle .75 2.00
8 Gump Worsley 1.00 2.50
NNO Marcel Dionne Large .40 1.00

1993-94 Zeller's Masters of Hockey Signed
COMPLETE SET (8) 60.00 150.00
1 Andy Bathgate 6.00 15.00
2 Johnny Bucyk 10.00 25.00
3 Yvan Cournoyer 10.00 25.00
4 Marcel Dionne 10.00 25.00
5 Bobby Hull 15.00 40.00
6 Brad Park 10.00 25.00
7 Jean Ratelle 6.00 15.00
8 Gump Worsley 10.00 25.00

1994-95 Zeller's Masters of Hockey
COMPLETE SET (8) 4.00 10.00
1 Jean Beliveau 1.50 4.00
2 Gerry Cheevers .75 2.00
3 Red Kelly .75 2.00
4 Dave Keon .75 2.00
5 Lanny McDonald .40 1.00
6 Pierre Pilote .40 1.00
7 Henri Richard .75 2.00
8 Norm Ullman .75 2.00
NNO Jean Beliveau Large .75 2.00

1994-95 Zeller's Masters of Hockey Signed
COMPLETE SET (8) 50.00 125.00
1 Jean Beliveau 25.00 50.00
2 Gerry Cheevers 6.00 15.00
3 Red Kelly 6.00 15.00
4 Dave Keon 6.00 15.00
5 Lanny McDonald 6.00 15.00
6 Pierre Pilote 6.00 15.00
7 Henri Richard 8.00 20.00
8 Norm Ullman 6.00 15.00

1995-96 Zeller's Masters of Hockey Signed
COMPLETE SET (8) 70.00 175.00
1 Mike Bossy 10.00 25.00
2 Eddie Giacomin 6.00 15.00
3 Gordie Howe 20.00 50.00
4 Jacques Laperriere 6.00 15.00
5 Gilbert Perreault 8.00 20.00
6 Serge Savard 6.00 15.00
7 Steve Shutt 6.00 15.00
8 Darryl Sittler 8.00 20.00

1995-96 Zenith
1 Brett Hull .30 .75
2 Paul Coffey .15 .40
3 Jaromir Jagr .50 1.25
4 Joe Murphy .10 .25
5 Jim Carey .12 .30
6 Eric Lindros .25 .60
7 Ulf Dahlen .10 .25
8 Mark Recchi .20 .50
9 Pavel Bure .15 .40
10 Adam Oates .15 .40
11 Theo Fleury .20 .50
12 Martin Brodeur .40 1.00
13 Wayne Gretzky 1.00 2.50
14 Geoff Sanderson .10 .25
15 Chris Gratton .10 .25
16 Owen Nolan .15 .40
17 Paul Kariya .15 .40
18 Mark Messier .30 .75
19 Mats Sundin .15 .40
20 Brian Savage .10 .25
21 Mathieu Schneider .10 .25
22 Alexandre Daigle .10 .25
23 Jason Arnott .12 .30
24 Mike Modano .25 .60
25 Scott Mellanby .12 .30
26 Alexei Zhamnov .15 .40
27 Scott Niedermayer .15 .40
28 Chris Pronger .15 .40
29 Ray Bourque .25 .60
30 Sergei Fedorov .25 .60
31 Alexander Mogilny .15 .40
32 Brian Leetch .12 .30
33 Adam Graves .12 .30
34 Jocelyn Thibault .12 .30
35 Ron Francis .20 .50
36 John Vanbiesbrouck .15 .40
37 Chris Chelios .15 .40
38 Pierre Turgeon .12 .30
39 Stephane Richer .12 .30
40 Al MacInnis .20 .50
41 Dave Andreychuk .15 .40
42 Mikael Renberg .12 .30
43 Nelson Emerson .10 .25
44 Kevin Hatcher .12 .30
45 Kirk Muller .12 .30
46 Bernie Nicholls .12 .30
47 Bill Ranford .15 .40
48 Luc Robitaille .15 .40
49 Peter Bondra .15 .40
50 Jari Kurri .15 .40
51 Dino Ciccarelli .12 .30
52 Kevin Stevens .12 .30
53 Mike Richter .15 .40
54 Doug Gilmour .20 .50
55 Kelly Hrudey .15 .40
56 Dave Gagner .10 .25
57 Kirk McLean .12 .30
58 Geoff Courtnall .10 .25
59 John LeClair .15 .40
60 Mike Vernon .12 .30
61 Cam Neely .15 .40
62 Mike Gartner .20 .50
63 Igor Korolev .10 .25
64 Joe Sakic .30 .75
65 Jeff Friesen .10 .25
66 Sergei Zubov .12 .30
67 Trevor Kidd .12 .30
68 Rod Brind'Amour .15 .40
69 John MacLean .12 .30
70 Peter Forsberg .30 .75
71 Oleg Tverdovsky .15 .40
72 Jeremy Roenick .25 .60
73 Gary Suter .10 .25
74 Keith Tkachuk .15 .40
75 Todd Harvey .10 .25
76 Felix Potvin .25 .60
77 Vincent Damphousse .12 .30
78 Blaine Lacher .12 .30
79 Tomas Sandstrom .12 .30
80 Chris Osgood .20 .50
81 Arturs Irbe .12 .30
82 Pat Verbeek .12 .30
83 Keith Primeau .12 .30
84 Brett Lindros .12 .30
85 Pat LaFontaine .15 .40
86 Brendan Shanahan .12 .30
87 Trevor Linden .12 .30
88 Rob Blake .12 .30
89 Scott Stevens .15 .40
90 Tom Barrasso .12 .30
91 Mike Ricci .10 .25
92 Ray Sheppard .12 .30
93 Steve Yzerman .40 1.00
94 Wendel Clark .25 .60
95 Ed Belfour .20 .50
96 Joe Juneau .10 .25
97 Ron Hextall .15 .40
98 Shayne Corson .12 .30
99 Guy Hebert .10 .25
100 Sean Burke .10 .25
101 Sandis Ozolinsh .10 .25
102 Teemu Selanne .30 .75
103 Petr Nedved .12 .30
104 Phil Housley .12 .30
105 Andy Moog .15 .40
106 Larry Murphy .12 .30
107 Grant Fuhr .25 .60
108 Mario Lemieux .60 1.50
109 Dominik Hasek .25 .60
110 Rob Niedermayer .12 .30
111 Steve Duchesne .10 .25
112 Joe Nieuwendyk .12 .30
113 Yanic Perreault .10 .25
114 Steve Thomas .12 .30
115 Russ Courtnall .10 .25
116 Claude Lemieux .15 .40
117 Patrick Roy .40 1.00
118 Rick Tocchet .12 .30
119 Stephane Fiset .12 .30
120 Daren Puppa .12 .30
121 Ed Jovanovski .12 .30
122 Eric Daze .30 .75
123 Cory Stillman .10 .25
124 Brendan Witt .15 .40
125 Valeri Bure .10 .25
126 Brian Holzinger RC .30 .75
127 Kyle McLaren RC .10 .25
128 Niklas Sundstrom .15 .40
129 Jamie Langenbrunner .10 .25
130 Jeff O'Neill .15 .40
131 Vitali Yachmenev .15 .40
132 Shane Doan RC .50 1.25
133 Byron Dafoe .12 .30
134 Corey Hirsch .12 .30
135 Antti Tormanen RC .10 .25
136 Jason Bonsignore .10 .25
137 Ryan Smyth .12 .30
138 Bryan McCabe .15 .40
139 Chad Kilger RC .15 .40
140 Todd Bertuzzi RC .20 .50
141 Marcus Ragnarsson RC .20 .50
142 Marty Murray .15 .40
143 Daymond Langkow RC .15 .40
144 Saku Koivu .12 .30
145 Jere Lehtinen .12 .30
146 Aki Berg RC .15 .40
147 Radek Dvorak RC .20 .50
148 Robert Svehla RC .10 .25
149 Daniel Alfredsson RC .75 2.00
150 Miroslav Satan RC .20 .50

1995-96 Zenith Gifted Grinders
COMPLETE SET (18) 6.00 15.00
1 Keith Tkachuk .60 1.50
2 Kevin Stevens .40 1.00
3 Wendel Clark .60 1.50
4 Claude Lemieux .40 1.00
5 Rick Tocchet .40 1.00
6 Trevor Linden .60 1.50
7 John LeClair .40 1.00
8 Mikael Renberg .40 1.00
9 Owen Nolan .40 1.00
10 Todd Harvey .40 1.00
11 Dave Gagner .40 1.00
12 Dale Hunter .40 1.00
13 Dave Andreychuk .40 1.00
14 Mark Recchi .40 1.00
15 Jason Arnott .40 1.00
16 Dino Ciccarelli .40 1.00
17 Adam Graves .40 1.00
18 Steve Thomas .40 1.00

1995-96 Zenith Rookie Roll Call
COMPLETE SET (18) 8.00 20.00
1 Saku Koivu 1.25 3.00
2 Radek Dvorak .40 1.00
3 Brendan Witt .40 1.00
4 Antti Tormanen .40 1.00
5 Brian Holzinger .40 1.00
6 Aki Berg .40 1.00
7 Ed Jovanovski .75 2.00
8 Marcus Ragnarsson .40 1.00
9 Todd Bertuzzi 1.25 3.00
10 Daniel Alfredsson 1.25 3.00
11 Vitali Yachmenev .40 1.00
12 Chad Kilger .40 1.00
13 Eric Daze .40 1.00
14 Niklas Sundstrom .40 1.00
15 Shane Doan 1.25 3.00
16 Cory Stillman .40 1.00
17 Kyle McLaren .40 1.00
18 Jeff O'Neill .40 1.00

1995-96 Zenith Z-Team
1 Patrick Roy 25.00 60.00
2 Martin Brodeur 25.00 60.00
3 Mario Lemieux 40.00 100.00
4 Wayne Gretzky 60.00 150.00
5 Mark Messier 20.00 50.00
6 Jeremy Roenick 15.00 40.00
7 Eric Lindros 15.00 40.00
8 Peter Forsberg 20.00 50.00
9 Sergei Fedorov 15.00 40.00
10 Mike Modano 15.00 40.00
11 Jaromir Jagr 30.00 80.00
12 Pavel Bure 10.00 25.00
13 Joe Sakic 20.00 50.00
14 Paul Kariya 10.00 25.00
15 Brett Hull 20.00 50.00
16 Brendan Shanahan 10.00 25.00
17 Felix Potvin 15.00 40.00
18 Jim Carey 8.00 20.00
S2 Martin Brodeur SAMPLE 25.00 60.00

1996-97 Zenith
COMPLETE SET (150) 12.00 30.00
1 Mike Modano .30 .75
2 Martin Brodeur .50 1.25
3 Pavel Bure .20 .50
4 Ray Bourque .30 .75
5 Steve Yzerman .50 1.25
6 Keith Tkachuk .20 .50
7 Jim Carey .20 .50
8 Valeri Kamensky .15 .40
9 Valeri Bure .12 .30
10 Ron Francis .25 .60
11 Trevor Kidd .12 .30
12 Doug Weight .20 .50
13 Wayne Gretzky 1.25 3.00
14 Todd Gill .15 .40
15 Dominik Hasek .30 .75
16 Scott Mellanby .15 .40
17 John LeClair .20 .50
18 Al MacInnis .25 .60
19 Derian Hatcher .12 .30
20 Stephane Fiset .15 .40
21 Alexander Selivanov .12 .30
22 Vyacheslav Kozlov .12 .30
23 Alexei Yashin .15 .40
24 Wendel Clark .30 .75
25 Ed Belfour .20 .50
26 Travis Green .15 .40
27 Joe Juneau .12 .30
28 Teemu Selanne .40 1.00
29 Jeff O'Neill .12 .30
30 Jeremy Roenick .30 .75
31 Felix Potvin .30 .75
32 Bernie Nicholls .15 .40
33 Steve Thomas .12 .30
34 Alexander Mogilny .15 .40
35 Patrick Roy .50 1.25
36 Luc Robitaille .20 .50
37 Owen Nolan .20 .50
38 Sergei Zubov .12 .30
39 Pierre Turgeon .15 .40
40 Nikolai Khabibulin .15 .40
41 Adam Oates .20 .50
42 Stephane Richer .15 .40
43 Daren Puppa .12 .30
44 Joe Sakic .40 1.00
45 Ed Jovanovski .15 .40
46 Ron Hextall .20 .50
47 Doug Gilmour .25 .60
48 Paul Coffey .20 .50
49 Craig Janney .15 .40
50 Brendan Witt .12 .30
51 Jere Lehtinen .12 .30
52 Vitali Yachmenev .12 .30
53 Damian Rhodes .15 .40
54 Petr Nedved .15 .40
55 Theo Fleury .40 1.00
56 Petr Sykora .12 .30
57 Kelly Hrudey .15 .40
58 Saku Koivu .20 .50
59 Brian Bradley .12 .30
60 Arturs Irbe .15 .40
61 Eric Lindros .30 .75
62 Michal Pivonka .12 .30
63 Joe Nieuwendyk .15 .40
64 Mats Sundin .20 .50
65 Jason Arnott .12 .30
66 Mike Richter .20 .50
67 Brett Hull .40 1.00
68 Chris Chelios .20 .50
69 Jocelyn Thibault .12 .30
70 Oleg Tverdovsky .15 .40
71 Peter Bondra .20 .50
72 Bill Ranford .15 .40
73 Scott Stevens .20 .50
74 Jaromir Jagr .60 1.50
75 Corey Hirsch .15 .40
76 Peter Forsberg .40 1.00
77 Brendan Shanahan .20 .50
78 Antti Tormanen .12 .30
79 Marcus Ragnarsson .12 .30
80 Sergei Fedorov .30 .75
81 Todd Bertuzzi .12 .30
82 Grant Fuhr .30 .75
83 Pat LaFontaine .20 .50
84 Rob Niedermayer .15 .40
85 Brian Leetch .15 .40
86 Yanic Perreault .12 .30
87 Dino Ciccarelli .20 .50
88 Dimitri Khristich .12 .30
89 Jeff Friesen .12 .30
90 Paul Kariya .20 .50
91 John Vanbiesbrouck .20 .50
92 Roman Hamrlik .12 .30
93 Pat Verbeek .12 .30
94 Mark Messier .40 1.00
95 Trevor Linden .20 .50
96 Igor Larionov .20 .50
97 Zigmund Palffy .20 .50
98 Tom Barrasso .15 .40
99 Eric Daze .15 .40
100 Vincent Damphousse .12 .30
101 Keith Primeau .15 .40
102 Claude Lemieux .15 .40
103 Daniel Alfredsson .15 .40
104 Ryan Smyth .20 .50
105 Chris Osgood .20 .50
106 Bill Guerin .20 .50
107 Shayne Corson .12 .30
108 Alexei Zhamnov .15 .40
109 Mikael Renberg .15 .40
110 Andy Moog .20 .50
111 Larry Murphy .15 .40
112 Curtis Joseph .25 .60
113 Cory Stillman .12 .30
114 Mario Lemieux .75 2.00
115 Scott Young .12 .30
116 Eric Fichaud .15 .40
117 Jonas Hoglund .12 .30
118 Tomas Holmstrom RC .60 1.50
119 Jarome Iginla .25 .60
120 Richard Zednik RC .25 .60
121 Andreas Dackell RC .20 .50
122 Anson Carter .15 .40
123 Dainius Zubrus RC .25 .60
124 Janne Niinimaa .20 .50
125 Jason Allison .15 .40
126 Bryan Berard .20 .50
127 Sergei Berezin RC .30 .75
128 Wade Redden .12 .30
129 Jim Campbell .12 .30
130 Darcy Tucker .20 .50
131 Harry York RC .20 .50
132 Brandon Convery .12 .30
133 Ethan Moreau RC .20 .50
134 Mattias Timander RC .12 .30
135 Christian Dube .12 .30
136 Kevin Hodson RC .20 .50
137 Anders Eriksson .12 .30
138 Chris O'Sullivan .12 .30
139 Jamie Langenbrunner .12 .30
140 Steve Sullivan RC .15 .40
141 Daymond Langkow .15 .40
142 Landon Wilson .12 .30
143 Scott Bailey .12 .30
144 Terry Ryan RC .20 .50
145 Curtis Brown .12 .30
146 Rem Murray RC .20 .50
147 Jamie Pushor .12 .30
148 Daniel Goneau RC .20 .50
149 Mike Prokopec RC .15 .40
150 Brad Smyth RC .15 .40

1996-97 Zenith Artist's Proofs
*VETS: 20X TO 50X BASIC CARDS
*ROOKIES: 8X TO 20X

1996-97 Zenith Assailants
COMPLETE SET (15) 10.00 25.00
1 Alexei Yashin .75 2.00
2 Mike Modano 2.00 5.00
3 Jason Arnott .75 2.00
4 Mikael Renberg .75 2.00
5 Saku Koivu 1.25 3.00
6 Todd Bertuzzi 1.25 3.00
7 Zigmund Palffy 1.25 3.00
8 Eric Lindros 1.25 3.00
9 Pat LaFontaine .75 2.00
10 John LeClair .75 2.00
11 Theo Fleury .75 2.00
12 Pierre Turgeon .75 2.00
13 Petr Nedved .75 2.00
14 Owen Nolan 1.25 3.00
15 Valeri Bure .75 2.00

1996-97 Zenith Champion Salute
COMPLETE SET (15) 25.00 60.00
*DIAMOND: 2X TO 5X BASIC INSERTS
1 Mark Messier 1.50 4.00
2 Wayne Gretzky 10.00 25.00
3 Grant Fuhr .75 2.00
4 Paul Coffey .75 2.00
5 Mario Lemieux 6.00 15.00
6 Jaromir Jagr 1.25 3.00
7 Ron Francis .75 2.50
8 Joe Sakic 2.50 6.00
9 Peter Forsberg 1.50 4.00
10 Claude Lemieux .75 2.00
11 Patrick Roy 5.00 12.00
12 Chris Chelios .75 2.00
13 Doug Gilmour .75 2.00
14 Mike Richter .75 2.00
15 Martin Brodeur 3.00 8.00
P3 Grant Fuhr PROMO 1.50 4.00
P9 Peter Forsberg PROMO 3.00 8.00
P15 Martin Brodeur PROMO 4.00 10.00

1996-97 Zenith Z-Team
COMPLETE SET (18) 40.00 100.00
1 Eric Lindros 6.00 15.00
2 Paul Kariya 5.00 12.00
3 Teemu Selanne 8.00 20.00
4 Brendan Shanahan 6.00 15.00
5 Sergei Fedorov 6.00 15.00
6 Steve Yzerman 12.00 30.00
7 Brett Hull 6.00 15.00
8 Pavel Bure 5.00 12.00
9 Alexander Mogilny 4.00 10.00
10 Jeremy Roenick 5.00 12.00
11 Jocelyn Thibault 4.00 10.00
12 Keith Tkachuk 4.00 10.00
13 Daniel Alfredsson 4.00 10.00
14 Eric Daze 4.00 10.00
15 Jim Carey 4.00 10.00
16 Felix Potvin 6.00 15.00
17 John Vanbiesbrouck 4.00 10.00
18 Chris Osgood 5.00 12.00

1997-98 Zenith
1 Jarome Iginla .30 .75
2 Peter Forsberg .50 1.25
3 Brendan Shanahan .25 .60
4 Wayne Gretzky 1.50 4.00
5 Steve Yzerman .60 1.50
6 Eric Lindros .40 1.00
7 Keith Tkachuk .25 .60
8 John LeClair .25 .60
9 John Vanbiesbrouck .25 .60
10 Patrick Roy .60 1.50
11 Ray Bourque .40 1.00
12 Theo Fleury .30 .75
13 Brian Leetch .20 .50
14 Chris Chelios .25 .60
15 Paul Kariya .25 .60
16 Mark Messier .50 1.25
17 Curtis Joseph .30 .75
18 Mike Richter .25 .60
19 Jeremy Roenick .40 1.00
20 Dominik Hasek .40 1.00
21 Martin Brodeur .60 1.50
22 Sergei Fedorov .40 1.00
23 Pierre Turgeon .20 .50
24 Teemu Selanne .50 1.25
25 Brett Hull .50 1.25
26 Saku Koivu .25 .60
27 Owen Nolan .25 .60
28 Jozef Stumpel .15 .40
29 Joe Sakic .50 1.25
30 Zigmund Palffy .25 .60
31 Jaromir Jagr .75 2.00
32 Adam Oates .25 .60
33 Jeff Friesen .20 .50
34 Pavel Bure .25 .60
35 Chris Osgood .25 .60
36 Mark Recchi .30 .75
37 Mike Modano .40 1.00
38 Felix Potvin .40 1.00
39 Vincent Damphousse .20 .50
40 Byron Dafoe .20 .50
41 Luc Robitaille .25 .60
42 Peter Bondra .25 .60
43 Daniel Alfredsson .25 .60
44 Pat LaFontaine .25 .60
45 Mikael Renberg .20 .50
46 Doug Gilmour .30 .75
47 Dino Ciccarelli .25 .60
48 Mats Sundin .25 .60
49 Ed Belfour .25 .60
50 Ron Francis .30 .75
51 Miroslav Satan .15 .40
52 Cory Stillman .20 .50
53 Bryan Berard .15 .40
54 Keith Primeau .20 .50
55 Eric Daze .15 .40
56 Chris Gratton .15 .40
57 Claude Lemieux .20 .50
58 Nicklas Lidstrom .25 .60
59 Olaf Kolzig .25 .60
60 Grant Fuhr .40 1.00
61 Jamie Langenbrunner .20 .50
62 Doug Weight .25 .60
63 Joe Nieuwendyk .20 .50
64 Yanic Perreault .20 .50
65 Jocelyn Thibault .20 .50
66 Guy Hebert .20 .50
67 Shayne Corson .20 .50
68 Bobby Holik .15 .40
69 Sami Kapanen .20 .50
70 Robert Reichel .20 .50
71 Ryan Smyth .20 .50
72 Alexei Yashin .20 .50
73 Trevor Linden .25 .60
74 Rod Brind'Amour .25 .60
75 Dave Gagner .15 .40
76 Nikolai Khabibulin .25 .60
77 Tom Barrasso .20 .50
78 Tony Amonte .20 .50
79 Alexander Mogilny .20 .50
80 Jason Allison .20 .50
81 Patrik Elias RC 2.00 5.00
82 Mike Johnson RC .20 .50
83 Richard Zednik .20 .50
84 Patrick Marleau .25 .60
85 Mattias Ohlund .20 .50
86 Sergei Samsonov .20 .50
87 Marco Sturm RC .25 .60
88 Alyn McCauley .20 .50
89 Chris Phillips .20 .50
90 Brendan Morrison RC .30 .75
91 Vaclav Prospal RC .20 .50
92 Joe Thornton .40 1.00
93 Boyd Devereaux .20 .50
94 Alexei Morozov .20 .50
95 Vincent Lecavalier RC 8.00 20.00
96 Manny Malhotra RC .30 .75
97 Roberto Luongo RC 10.00 25.00
98 Mathieu Garon .25 .60
99 Alex Tanguay RC 3.00 8.00
100 Josh Holden .20 .50

1997-98 Zenith Z-Gold
*VETS: 15X TO 40X BASIC CARDS
*PROSPECTS: 10X TO 25X
4 Wayne Gretzky 150.00 300.00
9 John Vanbiesbrouck 20.00 50.00
95 Vincent Lecavalier 100.00 200.00
97 Roberto Luongo 100.00 200.00

1997-98 Zenith Z-Silver
COMPLETE SET (100)
*VETS: 2X TO 5X BASIC CARDS
*PROSPECTS: 1X TO 2.5X
4 Wayne Gretzky 15.00 40.00
95 Vincent Lecavalier 15.00 40.00
97 Roberto Luongo 20.00 50.00

1997-98 Zenith 5x7
COMPLETE SET (80) 75.00 150.00
1 Wayne Gretzky 4.00 10.00
2 Eric Lindros .60 1.50
3 Patrick Roy 3.00 8.00
4 John Vanbiesbrouck .50 1.25
5 Martin Brodeur 1.50 4.00
6 Teemu Selanne .60 1.50
7 Joe Sakic 1.25 3.00
8 Jaromir Jagr 1.00 2.50
9 Brendan Shanahan .60 1.50
10 Ed Belfour .60 1.50
11 Guy Hebert .50 1.25
12 Doug Gilmour .50 1.25
13 Keith Primeau .25 .60
14 Grant Fuhr .25 .60
15 Joe Nieuwendyk .50 1.25
16 Ryan Smyth .50 1.25
17 Chris Osgood .50 1.25
18 Keith Tkachuk .60 1.50
19 Peter Forsberg 1.50 4.00
20 Jarome Iginla .75 2.00
21 Steve Yzerman 3.00 8.00
22 Jeremy Roenick .75 2.00
23 Jozef Stumpel .50 1.25
24 Mark Recchi .50 1.25
25 Daniel Alfredsson .50 1.25
26 Pat LaFontaine .60 1.50
27 Zigmund Palffy .50 1.25
28 Jason Allison .25 .60
29 Yanic Perreault .25 .60
30 Olaf Kolzig .50 1.25
31 Mikael Renberg .50 1.25
32 Bryan Berard .50 1.25
33 Jocelyn Thibault .50 1.25
34 Shayne Corson .50 1.25
35 Dave Gagner .25 .60
36 Claude Lemieux .25 .60
37 Saku Koivu .60 1.50
38 Curtis Joseph .60 1.50
39 Chris Chelios .60 1.50
40 Ray Bourque 1.00 2.50
41 Adam Oates .50 1.25
42 Felix Potvin .50 1.25
43 Peter Bondra .50 1.25
44 Sergei Fedorov 1.00 2.50
45 Paul Kariya .60 1.50
46 Theo Fleury .25 .60
47 John LeClair .60 1.50
48 Brett Hull .75 2.00
49 Rod Brind'Amour .60 1.50
50 Doug Weight .50 1.25
51 Jamie Langenbrunner .25 .60
52 Mats Sundin .60 1.50
53 Ron Francis .50 1.25
54 Eric Daze .50 1.25
55 Nicklas Lidstrom .60 1.50
56 Luc Robitaille .50 1.25
57 Vincent Damphousse .25 .60
58 Mike Modano 1.00 2.50
59 Pavel Bure .60 1.50
60 Owen Nolan .50 1.25
61 Pierre Turgeon .50 1.25

62 Dominik Hasek 1.25 3.00
63 Mike Richter .60 1.50
64 Mark Messier .60 1.50
65 Brian Leetch .60 1.50
66 Sergei Samsonov .30 .75
67 Alexei Morozov .30 .75
68 Marco Sturm 1.25 3.00
69 Patrik Elias 1.00 2.50
70 Eric Messier .30 .75
71 Mike Johnson .30 .75
72 Richard Zednik .30 .75
73 Mattias Ohlund .30 .75
74 Joe Thornton 1.50 4.00
75 Vincent Lecavalier 8.00 20.00
76 Manny Malhotra .75 2.00
77 Roberto Luongo 12.50 25.00
78 Mathieu Garon .30 .75
79 Alex Tanguay 2.50 6.00
80 Josh Holden .30 .75

1997-98 Zenith 5x7 Gold Impulse

*VETS: 10X TO 25X BASIC 5x7
*PROJECTS: 2X TO 5X BASIC 5x7

1997-98 Zenith 5x7 Silver Impulse

*VETS: 2X TO 5X BASIC 5x7
*PROSPECTS: .3X TO .8X BASIC 5x7

1997-98 Zenith Chasing The Cup

COMPLETE SET (15) 50.00 125.00
1 Patrick Roy 10.00 25.00
2 Wayne Gretzky 15.00 40.00
3 Jaromir Jagr 4.00 10.00
4 Eric Lindros 2.00 5.00
5 Mike Modano 4.00 10.00
6 Brendan Shanahan 2.00 5.00
7 Brett Hull 3.00 8.00
8 John LeClair 1.25 3.00
9 Jocelyn Thibault 1.25 3.00
10 Ed Belfour 2.00 5.00
11 Martin Brodeur 10.00 25.00
12 Peter Forsberg 6.00 15.00
13 Saku Koivu 2.00 5.00
14 Pat LaFontaine 1.25 3.00
15 Steve Yzerman 12.00 30.00

1997-98 Zenith Rookie Reign

COMPLETE SET (15) 30.00 60.00
1 Sergei Samsonov 4.00 10.00
2 Joe Thornton 8.00 20.00
3 Erik Rasmussen 1.25 3.00
4 Brendan Morrison 2.00 5.00
5 Magnus Arvedson 1.25 3.00
6 Vaclav Prospal 1.25 3.00
7 Brad Isbister 1.25 3.00
8 Alexei Morozov 1.25 3.00
9 Marco Sturm 2.00 5.00
10 Patrick Marleau 4.00 10.00
11 Alyn McCauley 2.00 5.00
12 Mike Johnson 1.25 3.00
13 Mattias Ohlund 1.25 3.00
14 Patrik Elias 2.00 5.00
15 Richard Zednik 1.25 3.00

1997-98 Zenith Z-Team

COMPLETE SET (18) 100.00 200.00
*5X7: .5X TO 1.2X BASIC INSERTS
*GOLDS: 1X TO 2.5X BASIC INSERTS
1 Teemu Selanne 3.00 8.00
2 Wayne Gretzky 20.00 50.00
3 Patrick Roy 8.00 20.00
4 Eric Lindros 3.00 8.00
5 Peter Forsberg 6.00 15.00
6 Paul Kariya 3.00 8.00
7 John LeClair 2.00 5.00
8 Martin Brodeur 8.00 20.00
9 Brendan Shanahan 3.00 8.00
10 Joe Thornton 6.00 16.00
11 Mattias Ohlund 2.00 5.00
12 Mike Johnson 2.00 5.00
13 Vaclav Prospal 2.00 5.00
14 Sergei Samsonov 2.00 5.00
15 Marco Sturm 2.00 5.00
16 Patrik Elias 2.00 5.00
17 Richard Zednik 2.00 5.00
18 Alexei Morozov 2.00 5.00

2010-11 Zenith

*RED: 1X TO 2.5X BASE
*WHITE: 6X TO 15X BASE
1 Claude Giroux .30 .75
2 Erik Johnson .20 .50
3 Roberto Luongo .50 1.25
4 Joe Thornton .50 1.25
5 Henrik Zetterberg .40 1.00
6 Dion Phaneuf .25 .60
7 Patrice Bergeron .40 1.00
8 Carey Price .60 1.50
9 Dustin Brown .30 .75
10 Martin Brodeur .75 2.00
11 Nicklas Backstrom .30 .75
12 Patrick Marleau .30 .75
13 Sam Gagner .20 .50
14 Tomas Vokoun .25 .60
15 Teemu Selanne .60 1.50
16 Jonathan Quick .40 1.00
17 Steven Stamkos .60 1.50
18 Zach Parise .30 .75
19 Ryan Miller .30 .75
20 Henrik Sedin .40 1.00
21 Alex Ovechkin 1.25 3.00
22 Shane Doan .25 .60
23 Phil Kessel .30 .75
24 Patrick Sharp .30 .75
25 Sidney Crosby 1.25 3.00
26 Daniel Sedin .40 1.00
27 Dany Heatley .25 .60
28 David Backes .20 .50
29 Tim Thomas .30 .75
30 Evgeni Malkin .60 1.50
31 Derick Brassard .20 .50
32 Simon Gagne .30 .75
33 Eric Staal .40 1.00
34 Tim Jackman .20 .50
35 Duncan Keith .25 .60
36 James Reimer .30 .75
37 Vincent Lecavalier .30 .75
38 Nicklas Lidstrom .30 .75
39 Jussi Jokinen .20 .50
40 Brad Marchand .60 1.50
41 Marc-Andre Fleury .60 1.50
42 Ryan Getzlaf .30 .75
43 Steve Mason .25 .60
44 Ales Hemsky .25 .60
45 Niklas Backstrom .30 .75
46 Jonathan Toews .50 1.25
47 Rick Nash .30 .75
48 Jamie Langenbrunner .20 .50
49 Jimmy Howard .40 1.00
50 Mike Richards .25 .60
51 Jarome Iginla .40 1.00
52 Pekka Rinne .30 .75
53 Mikko Koivu .30 .75
54 Brad Richards .30 .75
55 Ilya Bryzgalov .25 .60
56 Thomas Vanek .25 .60
57 Marian Gaborik .30 .75
58 Jaroslav Halak .30 .75
59 Paul Stastny .25 .60
60 Michael Cammalleri .30 .75
61 Nikolai Khabibulin .25 .60
62 Anze Kopitar .50 1.25
63 Dustin Byfuglien .30 .75
64 Daniel Alfredsson .30 .75
65 David Booth .20 .50
66 Wojtek Wolski .20 .50
67 Henrik Lundqvist .75 2.00
68 Craig Anderson .30 .75
69 Jeff Carter .25 .60
70 Jordan Leopold .20 .50
71 Ryan Kesler .30 .75
72 Mike Green .25 .60
73 Miikka Kiprusoff .30 .75
74 Jason Spezza .30 .75
75 Shea Weber .25 .60
76 Pierre-Alexandre Parenteau .20 .50
77 Antti Niemi .25 .60
78 Semyon Varlamov .30 .75
79 Matt Duchene .30 .75
80 Cam Ward .30 .75
81 John Tavares .50 1.25
82 Patrick Kane .60 1.50
83 Jordan Staal .25 .60
84 Brian Boucher .25 .60
85 T.J. Oshie .30 .75
86 Corey Perry .50 1.25
87 Clarke MacArthur .20 .50
88 Rick DiPietro .25 .60
89 Kari Lehtonen .25 .60
90 Brandon Dubinsky .20 .50
91 Stephen Weiss .20 .50
92 James Wisniewski .20 .50
93 Patrik Elias .30 .75
94 Rene Bourque .20 .50
95 Milan Lucic .30 .75
96 Andrew Ladd .30 .75
97 Bobby Ryan .25 .60
98 Dan Hamhuis .25 .60
99 Martin St. Louis .25 .60
100 Jason Pominville .20 .50
101 Brent Burns .30 .75
102 Dwayne Roloson .25 .60
103 Peter Forsberg .60 1.50
104 Kris Letang .40 1.00
105 Evander Kane .30 .75
106 Matthew Lombardi .20 .50
107 Corey Crawford .40 1.00
108 Dan Boyle .20 .50
109 Tomas Kaberle .20 .50
110 Andrej Meszaros .20 .50
111 Loui Eriksson .20 .50
112 Ryan Malone .20 .50
113 Mikhail Grabovski .20 .50
114 Michael Grabner .25 .60
115 Theo Peckham .20 .50
116 Rod Gilbert .30 .75
117 Steve Yzerman .75 2.00
118 Cam Neely .30 .75
119 Joe Sakic .60 1.50
120 Brian Leetch .25 .60
121 Darren Pang .30 .75
122 Curtis Joseph .40 1.00
123 Eric Lindros .50 1.25
124 Jeremy Roenick .50 1.25
125 Mario Lemieux 1.25 3.00
126 Ray Bourque .50 1.25
127 Tiger Williams .20 .50
128 Doug Gilmour .40 1.00
129 Guy Lafleur .40 1.00
130 Felix Potvin .50 1.25
131 Dave Schultz .30 .75
132 Derek Sanderson .30 .75
133 Brett Hull .60 1.50
134 Dale Hawerchuk .40 1.00
135 Kelly Hrudey .25 .60
136 Nick Fotiu .40 1.00
137 Patrick Roy .75 2.00
138 Trevor Linden .30 .75
139 Jean Beliveau .30 .75
140 Ed Belfour .30 .75
141 Patrice Cormier RC 2.50 6.00
142 Jamie Arniel RC 2.00 5.00
143 Trevor Gillies RC 2.00 5.00
144 Nazem Kadri RC 10.00 25.00
145 Marcel Mueller RC 2.50 6.00
146 Jan Mursak RC 4.00 10.00
147 Cedrick Desjardins RC 2.50 6.00
148 Jon Matsumoto RC 2.00 5.00
149 Richard Bachman RC 2.50 6.00
150 Matt Calvert RC 3.00 8.00
151 Mark Dekanich RC 2.00 5.00
152 Matt Hackett RC 2.50 6.00
153 Chris Tanev RC 5.00 12.00
154 Eric Tangradi RC 2.00 5.00
155 Jim O'Brien RC 2.50 6.00
156 Andrew Desjardins RC 2.00 5.00
157 Brett MacLean RC 2.50 6.00
158 Brandon Mashinter RC 2.50 6.00
159 Dana Tyrell RC 2.00 5.00
160 Dale Weise RC 2.50 6.00
161 Linus Klasen RC 2.00 5.00
162 Brodie Dupont RC 2.50 6.00
163 Travis Hamonic RC 2.50 6.00
164 Alex Urbom RC 2.00 5.00
165 Jeff Petry RC 4.00 10.00
166 Aaron Volpatti RC 2.50 6.00
167 Cory Emmerton RC 2.50 6.00
168 Jordan Pearce RC 3.00 8.00
169 Timo Pielmeier RC 2.50 6.00
170 J.P. Anderson RC 2.50 6.00
171 Alex Stalock RC 2.00 5.00
172 Evgeny Grachev RC 2.00 5.00
173 Nathan Lawson RC 2.00 5.00
174 Andreas Engqvist RC 3.00 8.00
175 Alexander Vasyunov RC 2.00 5.00
176 Dwight King RC 2.00 5.00
177 Colby Cohen RC 2.00 5.00
178 Rhett Rakhshani RC 2.00 5.00
179 Travis Morin RC 1.50 4.00
180 Paul Byron RC 2.50 6.00
181 Brandon Pirri RC 2.00 5.00
182 Ian Cole RC 2.00 5.00
183 Stefan Della Rovere RC 2.00 5.00
184 Keith Aulie RC 2.00 5.00
185 Chris Mueller RC 2.00 5.00
186 Philip McRae AU RC 4.00 10.00
187 T.J. Brodie AU RC 4.00 10.00
188 Marcus Johansson AU RC 6.00 15.00
189 Eric Wellwood AU RC 5.00 12.00
190 Tommy Wingels AU RC 4.00 10.00
191 Robin Lehner AU RC 8.00 20.00
192 Mats Zuccarello AU RC 8.00 20.00
193 Mattias Tedenby AU RC 4.00 10.00
194 Ryan McDonagh AU RC 10.00 25.00
195 Tomas Tatar AU RC 10.00 25.00
196 Kyle Clifford AU RC 5.00 12.00
197 Matt Bartkowski AU RC 5.00 12.00
198 Kevin Poulin AU RC 5.00 12.00
199 Luke Adam AU RC 4.00 10.00
200 Anders Lindback AU RC 4.00 10.00
201 Zac Dalpe AU RC 5.00 12.00
202 Steven Kampfer AU RC 6.00 15.00
203 Jeremy Morin AU RC 4.00 10.00
204 Kyle Palmieri AU RC 8.00 20.00
205 Henrik Karlsson AU RC 4.00 10.00
206 Nick Leddy AU RC 5.00 12.00
207 Ekman-Larsson AU/499 RC 6.00 15.00
208 Nino Niederreiter AU RC 6.00 15.00
209 Jacob Markstrom AU RC 10.00 25.00
210 Jacob Josefson AU RC 4.00 10.00
211 Tyler Seguin AU/199 RC 12.00 30.00
212 Cam Fowler AU/199 RC 10.00 25.00
213 Jordan Eberle AU/199 RC 10.00 25.00
214 Jordan Caron AU/199 RC 5.00 12.00
215 Sergei Bobrovsky AU/199 RC 15.00 40.00
216 Taylor Hall AU/199 RC 10.00 25.00
217 Derek Stepan AU/199 RC 5.00 12.00
218 Magnus Paajarvi AU/99 RC 5.00 12.00
219 Jeff Skinner AU/199 RC 10.00 25.00
220 Brayden Schenn AU/199 RC 10.00 25.00
221 A.Burmistrov AU/199 RC 4.00 10.00
222 P.K. Subban AU/199 RC 12.00 30.00
223 K.Shattenkirk AU/199 RC 8.00 20.00
224 T.McCollum AU/199 RC 4.00 10.00
225 Linus Omark AU/199 RC 5.00 12.00

2010-11 Zenith Rookie Parallel

141 Patrice Cormier AU 5.00 12.00
142 Jamie Arniel AU 4.00 10.00
143 Trevor Gillies AU 4.00 10.00
144 Nazem Kadri AU 12.00 30.00
145 Marcel Mueller AU 5.00 12.00
146 Jan Mursak AU 8.00 20.00
147 Cedrick Desjardins AU 6.00 15.00
148 Jon Matsumoto AU 4.00 10.00
149 Richard Bachman AU 5.00 12.00
150 Matt Calvert AU 6.00 15.00
151 Mark Dekanich AU 4.00 10.00
152 Matt Hackett AU 5.00 12.00
153 Chris Tanev AU 10.00 25.00
154 Eric Tangradi AU 4.00 10.00
155 Jim O'Brien AU 5.00 12.00
156 Andrew Desjardins AU 4.00 10.00
157 Brett MacLean AU 5.00 12.00
158 Brandon Mashinter AU 5.00 12.00
159 Dana Tyrell AU 4.00 10.00
160 Dale Weise AU 5.00 12.00
161 Linus Klasen AU 4.00 10.00
162 Brodie Dupont AU 5.00 12.00
163 Travis Hamonic AU 5.00 12.00
164 Alex Urbom AU 4.00 10.00
165 Jeff Petry AU 8.00 20.00
166 Aaron Volpatti AU 5.00 12.00
167 Cory Emmerton AU 5.00 12.00
168 Jordan Pearce AU 6.00 15.00
169 Timo Pielmeier AU 5.00 12.00
170 J.P. Anderson AU 5.00 12.00
171 Alex Stalock AU 4.00 10.00
172 Evgeny Grachev AU 5.00 12.00
173 Nathan Lawson AU 5.00 12.00
174 Andreas Engqvist AU 6.00 15.00
175 Alexander Vasyunov AU 5.00 12.00
176 Dwight King AU 4.00 10.00
177 Colby Cohen AU 4.00 10.00
178 Rhett Rakhshani AU 4.00 10.00
179 Travis Morin AU 3.00 8.00
180 Paul Byron AU 4.00 10.00
181 Brandon Pirri AU 4.00 10.00
182 Ian Cole AU 4.00 10.00
183 Stefan Della Rovere AU 5.00 12.00
184 Keith Aulie AU 4.00 10.00
185 Chris Mueller AU 4.00 10.00
186 Philip McRae 4.00 10.00
187 T.J. Brodie 4.00 10.00
188 Marcus Johansson 6.00 15.00
189 Eric Wellwood 5.00 12.00
190 Tommy Wingels 4.00 10.00
191 Robin Lehner 8.00 20.00
192 Mats Zuccarello 8.00 20.00
193 Mattias Tedenby 4.00 10.00
194 Ryan McDonagh 10.00 25.00
195 Tomas Tatar 10.00 25.00
196 Kyle Clifford 5.00 12.00
197 Matt Bartkowski 5.00 12.00
198 Kevin Poulin 5.00 12.00
199 Luke Adam 4.00 10.00
200 Anders Lindback 4.00 10.00
201 Zac Dalpe 5.00 12.00
202 Steven Kampfer 6.00 15.00
203 Jeremy Morin 4.00 10.00
204 Kyle Palmieri 8.00 20.00
205 Henrik Karlsson 4.00 10.00
206 Nick Leddy 5.00 12.00
207 Oliver Ekman-Larsson 6.00 15.00
208 Nino Niederreiter 6.00 15.00
209 Jacob Markstrom 10.00 25.00
210 Jacob Josefson 4.00 10.00

2010-11 Zenith Behind The Bench Autographs

1 Joel Quenneville 15.00 40.00
2 Mike Babcock 15.00 40.00
3 Ron Wilson 6.00 15.00
4 Barry Trotz 15.00 40.00
5 Bruce Boudreau 8.00 20.00
6 Lindy Ruff 6.00 15.00
7 Alain Vigneault 6.00 15.00
8 Peter Laviolette 6.00 15.00
9 Claude Julien 15.00 40.00
10 Jacques Martin 10.00 25.00

2010-11 Zenith Chasing The Cup

1 Roberto Luongo 1.50 4.00
2 Daniel Sedin 1.25 3.00
3 Jimmy Howard 1.25 3.00
4 Nicklas Lidstrom 1.00 2.50
5 Pekka Rinne 1.00 2.50
6 Brad Richards 1.00 2.50
7 Jonathan Toews 1.50 4.00
8 Corey Crawford 1.25 3.00
9 Joe Thornton 1.50 4.00
10 Ryane Clowe .60 1.50
11 Mike Richards .75 2.00
12 Claude Giroux 1.00 2.50
13 Tim Thomas 1.00 2.50
14 Patrice Bergeron 1.25 3.00
15 Sidney Crosby 4.00 10.00
16 Marc-Andre Fleury 2.00 5.00
17 Alex Ovechkin 4.00 10.00
18 Semyon Varlamov 1.00 2.50
19 Steven Stamkos 2.00 5.00
20 Carey Price 2.00 5.00

2010-11 Zenith Crease Is The Word

1 Jonas Hiller 1.00 2.50
2 Tim Thomas 1.25 3.00
3 Carey Price 2.50 6.00
4 Jimmy Howard 1.50 4.00
5 Kari Lehtonen 1.00 2.50
6 Marc-Andre Fleury 2.50 6.00
7 Cam Ward 1.25 3.00
8 Henrik Lundqvist 3.00 8.00
9 Ondrej Pavelec 1.25 3.00
10 Corey Crawford 1.50 4.00

2010-11 Zenith Dare To Tear Jumbo

UNTORN CARD 15.00 40.00
226 Sidney Crosby 6.00 15.00
227 Steven Stamkos 3.00 8.00
228 Carey Price 3.00 8.00
229 Alex Ovechkin 6.00 15.00
230 Henrik Lundqvist 4.00 10.00
231 Martin St. Louis 1.50 4.00
232 Martin Brodeur 4.00 10.00
233 Henrik Sedin 2.00 5.00
234 Henrik Zetterberg 2.00 5.00
235 Roberto Luongo 2.50 6.00
236 Steve Yzerman 4.00 10.00
237 Joe Sakic 3.00 8.00
238 Mario Lemieux 6.00 15.00
239 Patrick Roy 4.00 10.00
240 Eric Lindros 2.50 6.00
241 Mark Messier 3.00 8.00
242 Ray Bourque 2.50 6.00
243 Tony Esposito 1.50 4.00
244 Jeremy Roenick 2.50 6.00
245 Felix Potvin 2.50 6.00
246 Ed Belfour 1.50 4.00
247 Doug Gilmour 2.00 5.00
248 Brian Leetch 1.50 4.00
249 Brendan Shanahan 1.50 4.00
250 Cam Neely 1.50 4.00

2010-11 Zenith Donruss Elite Autographs

201 Taylor Hall 12.00 30.00
202 Tyler Seguin 15.00 40.00
203 Jeff Skinner 12.00 30.00
204 Jordan Eberle 12.00 30.00
205 Mattias Tedenby 5.00 12.00
206 P.K. Subban 15.00 40.00
207 Derek Stepan 6.00 15.00
208 Nino Niederreiter 8.00 20.00
209 Sergei Bobrovsky 20.00 50.00
210 Tomas Tatar 12.00 30.00
211 Cam Fowler 12.00 30.00
212 Robin Lehner 10.00 25.00
213 Mats Zuccarello 10.00 25.00
214 Nazem Kadri 15.00 40.00
215 Anders Lindback 5.00 12.00
216 Patrice Cormier 6.00 15.00
217 Jeremy Morin 5.00 12.00
218 Philip Larsen 5.00 12.00
219 Luke Adam 5.00 12.00
220 Linus Omark 5.00 12.00
221 Kyle Clifford 6.00 15.00
222 Keith Aulie 5.00 12.00
223 John McCarthy 5.00 12.00
224 Jacob Markstrom 12.00 30.00
225 Alexander Vasyunov 5.00 12.00
226 Brandon Pirri 5.00 12.00
227 Cory Emmerton 6.00 15.00
228 Evgeny Grachev 5.00 12.00
229 Kevin Shattenkirk 10.00 25.00
230 Maxim Noreau 4.00 10.00

2010-11 Zenith Epix

1 Loui Eriksson 1.50 4.00
2 Anze Kopitar 4.00 10.00
3 Ryan Kesler 2.50 6.00
4 Sidney Crosby 10.00 25.00
5 Daniel Sedin 3.00 8.00
6 Henrik Zetterberg 3.00 8.00
7 Brad Richards 2.50 6.00
8 Jarome Iginla 3.00 8.00
9 Milan Hejduk 2.00 5.00
10 Kris Letang 3.00 8.00
11 Thomas Vanek 2.00 5.00
12 Tyler Myers 1.50 4.00
13 Evgeni Malkin 5.00 12.00
14 Dustin Brown 2.50 6.00
15 Patrice Bergeron 3.00 8.00
16 Tobias Enstrom 1.50 4.00
17 Tomas Plekanec 1.50 4.00
18 James Neal 1.50 4.00
19 John Tavares 4.00 10.00
20 Stephen Weiss 1.50 4.00
21 Ryan Malone 1.50 4.00
22 Shane Doan 2.00 5.00
23 Patrik Elias 2.00 5.00
24 Phil Kessel 2.50 6.00
25 Milan Lucic 2.50 6.00
26 Ryan Smyth 2.00 5.00
27 Dustin Penner 1.50 4.00
28 Nikolai Kulemin 1.50 4.00
29 Danny Briere 2.50 6.00
30 Blake Comeau 1.50 4.00
31 Tomas Fleischmann 1.50 4.00
32 Michal Neuvirth 2.00 5.00
33 Ville Leino 2.00 5.00
34 Matthew Lombardi 1.50 4.00
35 Nikolay Zherdev 1.50 4.00
36 Sergei Gonchar 1.50 4.00
37 David Krejci 2.50 6.00
38 George Parros 2.00 5.00
39 Bryan Little 2.50 6.00
40 Tyler Ennis 2.00 5.00
41 Robyn Regehr 1.50 4.00
42 Duncan Keith 2.00 5.00
43 Ryan O'Reilly 2.50 6.00
44 Taylor Hall 5.00 12.00
45 Jacob Markstrom 5.00 12.00
46 Tomas Tatar 5.00 12.00
47 Mats Zuccarello 4.00 10.00
48 Ryan McDonagh 5.00 12.00
49 Jeff Skinner 5.00 12.00
50 Jordan Eberle 5.00 12.00

2010-11 Zenith Epix Materials

1 Loui Eriksson 2.00 5.00
2 Anze Kopitar 5.00 12.00
3 Ryan Kesler 3.00 8.00
4 Sidney Crosby 12.00 30.00
5 Daniel Sedin 4.00 10.00
6 Henrik Zetterberg 4.00 10.00
7 Brad Richards 3.00 8.00
8 Jarome Iginla 4.00 10.00
9 Milan Hejduk 2.50 6.00
10 Kris Letang 4.00 10.00
11 Thomas Vanek 2.50 6.00
12 Tyler Myers 2.00 5.00
13 Evgeni Malkin 6.00 15.00
14 Dustin Brown 3.00 8.00
15 Patrice Bergeron 4.00 10.00
16 Tobias Enstrom 2.00 5.00
17 Tomas Plekanec 2.00 5.00
18 James Neal 2.00 5.00
19 John Tavares 5.00 12.00
20 Stephen Weiss 2.50 6.00
21 Ryan Malone 2.00 5.00
22 Shane Doan 2.50 6.00
23 Patrik Elias 2.00 5.00
24 Phil Kessel 3.00 8.00
25 Milan Lucic 3.00 8.00
26 Ryan Smyth 2.50 6.00
27 Dustin Penner 2.00 5.00
28 Nikolai Kulemin 2.00 5.00
29 Danny Briere 3.00 8.00
30 Blake Comeau 2.00 5.00
31 Tomas Fleischmann 2.00 5.00
32 Michal Neuvirth 3.00 8.00
33 Ville Leino 2.50 6.00
34 Matthew Lombardi 2.00 5.00
35 Nikolay Zherdev 2.00 5.00
36 Sergei Gonchar 2.00 5.00
37 David Krejci 3.00 8.00
38 George Parros 2.50 6.00
39 Bryan Little 3.00 8.00
40 Tyler Ennis 2.00 5.00
41 Robyn Regehr 2.00 5.00
42 Duncan Keith 2.50 6.00
43 Ryan O'Reilly 3.00 8.00
44 Taylor Hall 6.00 15.00
45 Jacob Markstrom 6.00 15.00
46 Tomas Tatar 6.00 15.00
47 Mats Zuccarello 5.00 12.00
48 Ryan McDonagh 6.00 15.00
49 Jeff Skinner 6.00 15.00
50 Jordan Eberle 6.00 15.00

2010-11 Zenith Gifted Grinders

1 Troy Brouwer .75 2.00
2 Alex Ovechkin 5.00 12.00
3 Luke Schenn 1.25 3.00
4 Brian Boyle .75 2.00
5 Chris Neil .75 2.00
6 Brenden Morrow 1.00 2.50
7 Shea Weber 1.00 2.50
8 David Backes .75 2.00
9 Cal Clutterbuck .75 2.00
10 Milan Lucic 1.25 3.00
11 James Neal .75 2.00
12 Ryan Getzlaf 1.25 3.00
13 Ryan Malone .75 2.00
14 Scott Hartnell .75 2.00
15 Shane Doan 1.00 2.50
16 Shawn Thornton .75 2.00
17 Dustin Brown 1.25 3.00
18 Derek Dorsett .75 2.00
19 Ryan Callahan .75 2.00
20 Marc Staal .75 2.00

2010-11 Zenith Gifted Grinders Scraps Jerseys

*PRIME/24-50: .6X TO 1.5X JERSEYS
2 Alex Ovechkin 8.00 20.00
3 Luke Schenn 3.00 8.00
4 Brian Boyle 2.50 6.00
5 Chris Neil 2.00 5.00
6 Brenden Morrow 3.00 8.00
7 Shea Weber 3.00 8.00
8 David Backes 2.50 6.00
9 Cal Clutterbuck 2.50 6.00
10 Milan Lucic/99 5.00 12.00
11 James Neal 2.50 6.00
12 Ryan Getzlaf 4.00 10.00
13 Ryan Malone 2.50 6.00
14 Scott Hartnell 2.50 6.00
15 Shane Doan 3.00 8.00
16 Shawn Thornton 2.50 6.00
17 Dustin Brown/99 5.00 12.00
18 Derek Dorsett 2.50 6.00
19 Ryan Callahan 2.50 6.00
20 Marc Staal 2.50 6.00

2010-11 Zenith Mozaics

1 Pavelec/Boulton/Antropov 1.00 2.50
2 Thornton/Chara/Rask 1.25 3.00
3 Vanek/Pominville/Stafford .75 2.00
4 Kiprusoff/Iginla/Backlund 1.25 3.00
5 Galiardi/Stastny/Duchene 1.00 2.50
6 Vermette/Mason/Voracek .75 2.00
7 Richards/Benn/Daley 1.25 3.00
8 Tatar/Zetterberg/Lidstrom 2.00 5.00
9 Eberle/Hall/Paajarvi 2.00 5.00
10 Schenn/Kopitar/Doughty 2.00 5.00
11 Clutterbuck/Backstrom/Koivu 1.00 2.50
12 Price/Pouliot/Pacioretty 2.00 5.00
13 Weber/Rinne/Suter 1.00 2.50
14 Parise/Brodeur/Tedenby 2.50 6.00
15 Lundqvist/Callahan/Zuccarello 2.50 6.00
16 Malkin/Staal/Tangradi 2.00 5.00
17 Stamkos/Hedman/Malone 2.00 5.00
18 Kessel/Gustavsson/Kadri 2.50 6.00
19 Burrows/Kesler/Luongo 1.50 4.00
20 Knuble/Ovechkin/Fehr 4.00 10.00

2010-11 Zenith Mozaics Materials

*DOUBLE JSY: .5X TO 1.2X SINGLE JSY
1 Pavelec/Boulton/Antropov 3.00 8.00
2 Thornton/Chara/Rask 4.00 10.00
3 Vanek/Pominville/Stafford 2.50 6.00
4 Kiprusoff/Iginla/Backlund 4.00 10.00
5 Galiardi/Stastny/Duchene 3.00 8.00
6 Vermette/Mason/Voracek 2.50 6.00
7 Richards/Benn/Daley 4.00 10.00
8 Tatar/Zetterberg/Lidstrom 6.00 15.00
9 Eberle/Hall/Paajarvi 6.00 15.00
10 Schenn/Kopitar/Doughty 6.00 15.00
11 Clutterbuck/Backstrom/Koivu 3.00 8.00
12 Price/Pouliot/Pacioretty 6.00 15.00
13 Weber/Rinne/Suter 3.00 8.00
14 Parise/Brodeur/Tedenby 8.00 20.00
15 Lundqvist/Callahan/Zuccarello 8.00 20.00
16 Malkin/Staal/Tangradi 6.00 15.00
17 Stamkos/Hedman/Malone 6.00 15.00
18 Kessel/Gustavsson/Kadri 8.00 20.00
19 Burrows/Kesler/Luongo 5.00 12.00
20 Knuble/Ovechkin/Fehr 12.00 30.00

2010-11 Zenith Mozaics Materials Triple

*TRIPLE JSY: .6X TO 1.5X SINGLE JSY

2010-11 Zenith National Treasures Autographs

201 Zac Dalpe 12.00 30.00
202 Ryan McDonagh 20.00 50.00
203 Mats Zuccarello 25.00 60.00
205 Cam Fowler 25.00 60.00
206 Ian Cole 20.00 50.00
207 Tyler Seguin 60.00 120.00
208 Jacob Markstrom 25.00 60.00
209 Jeff Skinner 30.00 80.00
210 Anders Lindback 10.00 25.00
211 Tomas Tatar 25.00 50.00
212 P.K. Subban 50.00 120.00
213 Taylor Hall 40.00 100.00
214 Nazem Kadri 30.00 80.00
215 Jordan Eberle 60.00 120.00
216 Kevin Shattenkirk 20.00 50.00
217 Mattias Tedenby 10.00 25.00
218 Jordan Caron 12.00 30.00
219 Nino Niederreiter 25.00 60.00
220 Jeremy Morin 10.00 25.00
222 Alexander Burmistrov 10.00 25.00
224 Robin Lehner 15.00 40.00
225 Sergei Bobrovsky 40.00 80.00

2010-11 Zenith Rookie Roll Call

1 Logan Couture 1.25 3.00
2 Jeff Skinner 2.00 5.00
3 Taylor Hall 2.00 5.00
4 Derek Stepan 1.00 2.50
5 Cam Fowler 2.00 5.00
6 Jordan Eberle 2.00 5.00
7 Kevin Shattenkirk 1.50 4.00
8 Tyler Seguin 2.50 6.00
9 Tyler Ennis .60 1.50
10 Magnus Paajarvi 1.00 2.50
11 Mats Zuccarello 1.50 4.00
12 Tomas Tatar 2.00 5.00
13 Brad Marchand 2.00 5.00
14 Mark Letestu 1.00 2.50
15 Oliver Ekman-Larsson 1.25 3.00
16 Corey Crawford 1.25 3.00
17 Jonathan Bernier .75 2.00
18 Sergei Bobrovsky 3.00 8.00
19 Anders Lindback .75 2.00
20 James Reimer 1.00 2.50

2010-11 Zenith Rookie Roll Call Jerseys

2 Jeff Skinner 4.00 10.00
3 Taylor Hall 4.00 10.00
4 Derek Stepan 2.00 5.00
5 Cam Fowler 4.00 10.00
6 Jordan Eberle 4.00 10.00
7 Kevin Shattenkirk 3.00 8.00
8 Tyler Seguin 5.00 12.00
9 Tyler Ennis 1.25 3.00
10 Magnus Paajarvi 2.00 5.00
11 Mats Zuccarello 3.00 8.00
12 Tomas Tatar 4.00 10.00
14 Mark Letestu 2.00 5.00
15 Oliver Ekman-Larsson 2.50 6.00
16 Corey Crawford 2.50 6.00
17 Jonathan Bernier 2.00 5.00
18 Sergei Bobrovsky 6.00 15.00
19 Anders Lindback 1.50 4.00
20 James Reimer 2.50 6.00

2010-11 Zenith Team Logo Die-Cut Jerseys

AT Alex Tanguay 2.00 5.00
AV Antoine Vermette 2.00 5.00
BB Brian Boucher 2.50 6.00
BJ Brent Johnson 2.50 6.00
BS Brayden Schenn 6.00 15.00
CC Cal Clutterbuck 2.00 5.00
CG Claude Giroux 3.00 8.00
DB Dustin Brown 3.00 8.00
DC Daniel Carcillo 2.00 5.00
DK Duncan Keith 2.50 6.00
DKU Dmitry Kulikov 2.50 6.00
DL David Legwand 2.50 6.00
DP Dion Phaneuf 2.50 6.00
DS Drew Stafford 2.00 5.00
EM Evgeni Malkin 6.00 15.00
IB Ilya Bryzgalov 2.50 6.00
JB Jared Boll 2.00 5.00
JBO Jay Bouwmeester 2.00 5.00
JG Josh Gorges 2.00 5.00
JM Jacob Markstrom 6.00 15.00
JS Jordan Staal 2.50 6.00
JV Jakub Voracek 2.50 6.00
KL Kris Letang 4.00 10.00
LC Luca Caputi 2.50 6.00
ME Martin Erat 2.00 5.00
MH Martin Havlat 2.50 6.00
MP Max Pacioretty 3.00 8.00
MS Mikael Samuelsson 2.00 5.00
MSL Martin St. Louis 3.00 8.00
NB Niklas Backstrom 3.00 8.00
NL Nicklas Lidstrom 3.00 8.00
OE Oliver Ekman-Larsson 4.00 10.00
PB Peter Budaj 2.50 6.00
PD Pavel Datsyuk 5.00 12.00
PH Patric Hornqvist 2.00 5.00
PK Phil Kessel 3.00 8.00
RB Rene Bourque 2.00 5.00
RK Ryan Kesler 3.00 8.00
RL Roberto Luongo 5.00 12.00
RM Ryan Malone 2.00 5.00
RMI Ryan Miller 3.00 8.00
SD Shane Doan 2.50 6.00
SM Steve Mason 2.50 6.00
TC Tim Connolly 2.00 5.00
TE Tyler Ennis 2.00 5.00
TG T.J. Galiardi 2.50 6.00
TH Tomas Holmstrom 2.00 5.00
TP Tomas Plekanec 2.00 5.00
TPU Teddy Purcell 2.00 5.00
WS Wayne Simmonds 4.00 10.00

2010-11 Zenith Winter Warriors Materials

*PRIME/25-50: .6X TO 1.5X MATERIALS
AF Alexander Frolov 1.25 3.00
AK Anze Kopitar 3.00 8.00
AK Andrei Kostitsyn 1.50 4.00
AV Antoine Vermette 1.25 3.00
BB Brent Burns 2.00 5.00
BS Brayden Schenn 4.00 10.00
CK Chris Kunitz 2.00 5.00
CP Carey Price 4.00 10.00
DB David Backes 1.25 3.00
DK David Krejci 2.00 5.00
DS Daniel Sedin 2.50 6.00
EB Eric Boulton 1.25 3.00
EK Evander Kane 2.50 6.00
GC Gregory Campbell 1.25 3.00
JB Jared Boll 1.25 3.00
JE Jordan Eberle 4.00 10.00
JI Jarome Iginla 2.50 6.00
JM Jacob Markstrom 4.00 10.00
JQ Jonathan Quick 2.50 6.00
KL Kris Letang 2.50 6.00
KL Kari Lehtonen 1.50 4.00
LE Loui Eriksson 1.25 3.00
MD Michael Del Zotto 1.50 4.00
MG Mark Giordano 2.00 5.00
MG Michael Grabner 1.50 4.00
MH Milan Hejduk 1.50 4.00
MH Martin Havlat 1.50 4.00
MP Magnus Paajarvi 2.00 5.00
MZ Mats Zuccarello 3.00 8.00
NK Nikolai Kulemin 1.25 3.00
PE Patrik Elias 2.00 5.00
PR Peter Regin 1.50 4.00
PR Pekka Rinne 2.00 5.00
RM Ryan McDonagh 2.50 6.00
SC Sidney Crosby 8.00 20.00
SG Sergei Gonchar 1.25 3.00
SG Scott Gomez 1.50 4.00
TE Tyler Ennis 1.25 3.00
TF Tomas Fleischmann 1.25 3.00
TH Tomas Holmstrom 1.25 3.00
TH Taylor Hall 4.00 10.00
TV Thomas Vanek 1.50 4.00
TZ Travis Zajac 1.25 3.00
VL Ville Leino 1.50 4.00
VL Vincent Lecavalier 2.00 5.00
WB Wade Belak 1.50 4.00
WS Wayne Simmonds 2.50 6.00
ZB Zach Bogosian 1.50 4.00

2010-11 Zenith Yours Truly Autographs

AA Artem Anisimov 4.00 10.00
AB Alexandre Burrows 4.00 10.00
AK Anze Kopitar 15.00 40.00
AO Alex Ovechkin Upd. 30.00 80.00
BB Brian Boucher 5.00 12.00
BE Jamie Benn 8.00 20.00
BK Mikael Backlund Upd. 5.00 12.00
BO Drayson Bowman 5.00 12.00
BS Brandon Sutter Upd. 5.00 12.00
BW Jay Bouwmeester 4.00 10.00
CM Chris Mason Upd. 5.00 12.00
CN Chris Neil 4.00 10.00
DB Dustin Brown 6.00 15.00
DC Daniel Carcillo 4.00 10.00
DP David Perron 5.00 12.00
DR Dwayne Roloson 5.00 12.00
EB Emile Bouchard 6.00 15.00
EK Evander Kane 6.00 15.00
EM Evgeni Malkin 12.00 30.00
GI Rod Gilbert 6.00 15.00

GP George Parros 5.00 12.00
GR Michael Grabner 5.00 12.00
GZ Greg Zanon 4.00 10.00
HO Tomas Holmstrom Upd. 4.00 10.00
JB Johnny Bower 6.00 15.00
JD Jeff Deslauriers 4.00 10.00
JF Johan Franzen 5.00 12.00
JG Jonas Gustavsson 8.00 20.00
JH Jimmy Howard 8.00 20.00
JM Joe Mullen 5.00 12.00
JN James Neal 4.00 10.00
JO Jonas Hiller 5.00 12.00
JT John Tavares 15.00 40.00
KA Erik Karlsson Upd. 15.00 40.00
KB Krys Barch 4.00 10.00
KL Kari Lehtonen 5.00 12.00
LC Luca Caputi 5.00 12.00
LE Loui Eriksson Upd. 4.00 10.00
LS Lee Stempniak 4.00 10.00
MB Mikkel Boedker Upd. 4.00 10.00
MF Michael Frolik Upd. 4.00 10.00
MG Marian Gaborik Upd. 6.00 15.00
MH Matt Hunwick 4.00 10.00
MM Matt Moulson 5.00 12.00
MR Mike Richards 5.00 12.00
MS Mikael Samuelsson 4.00 10.00
MT Max Talbot Upd. 4.00 10.00
NG Nathan Gerbe 4.00 10.00
NK Nikolai Khabibulin 5.00 12.00
NZ Nikolay Zherdev 4.00 10.00
OP Ondrej Pavelec Upd. 6.00 15.00
PH Patric Hornqvist 4.00 10.00
PK Patrick Kane 25.00 60.00
PM Peter Mueller Upd. 5.00 12.00
PR Patrick Roy Upd. 40.00 100.00
PS Paul Stastny Upd. 5.00 12.00
RB Ray Bourque Upd. 15.00 40.00
RC Ryan Callahan 4.00 10.00
RG Ryan Getzlaf 6.00 15.00
RI Pekka Rinne 6.00 15.00
RK Ryan Kesler Upd. 6.00 15.00
RM Ryan Miller Upd. 6.00 15.00
RP Rich Peverley 6.00 15.00
RR Rick Rypien 6.00 15.00
RS Ryan Smyth 5.00 12.00
RY Bobby Ryan 5.00 12.00
SA Sam Gagner Upd. 4.00 10.00
SC Sidney Crosby Upd. 50.00 120.00
SD Shane Doan Upd. 5.00 12.00
SG Scott Gomez 5.00 12.00
SM1 Steve Mason 5.00 12.00
SM2 Stan Mikita 8.00 20.00
SS Steven Stamkos 15.00 40.00
SW Stephen Weiss 5.00 12.00
TB Tyler Bozak Upd. 4.00 10.00
TH Jose Theodore 6.00 15.00
TM Tyler Myers 4.00 10.00
TT Tim Thomas 6.00 15.00
TU Marty Turco 6.00 15.00
TV Tomas Vokoun 5.00 12.00
TZ Travis Zajac Upd. 4.00 10.00
VA Semyon Varlamov 6.00 15.00
VL Vincent Lecavalier 6.00 15.00
VS Viktor Stalberg Upd. 5.00 12.00
WE Shea Weber Upd. 5.00 12.00
WW Wojtek Wolski 4.00 10.00
ZA Zach Bogosian Upd. 5.00 12.00
ZB Zach Boychuk 5.00 12.00
ZP Zach Parise 6.00 15.00
ZS Zack Stortini 4.00 10.00

2010-11 Zenith Z-Team

*RED HOT: .6X TO 1.5X Z-TEAM
*WHITE HOT/25: 1.2X TO 3X Z-TEAM
1 Steven Stamkos 2.50 6.00
2 Peter Forsberg 2.50 6.00
3 Sidney Crosby 5.00 12.00
4 Tim Thomas 1.25 3.00
5 Alex Ovechkin 5.00 12.00
6 Jarome Iginla 1.50 4.00
7 Jonathan Toews 2.00 5.00
8 Roberto Luongo 2.00 5.00
9 Taylor Hall 2.50 6.00
10 Jeff Skinner 2.50 6.00

1956 Austrian Platnik and Shone

NNO Ice Hockey 12.50 25.00

1995-96 Austrian National Team

COMPLETE SET (28) 6.00 15.00
1 Christoph Brander .40 1.00
2 Thomas Cijan .20 .50
3 Claus Dalpiaz .30 .75
4 Reinhard Divis 1.25 3.00
5 Konrad Dorn .20 .50
6 Robin Doyle .20 .50
7 Michael Guntner .20 .50
8 Karl Heinzle .20 .50
9 Herbert Hohenberger .30 .75
10 Dieter Kalt .20 .50
11 Peter Kasper .20 .50
12 Werner Kerth .20 .50
13 Martin Krainz .20 .50
14 Gunter Lanzinger .20 .50
15 Engelbert Linder .20 .50
16 Arthur Marczell .20 .50
17 Manfred Muhr .20 .50
18 Rick Nasheim .20 .50
19 Kraig Nienhuis .40 1.00
20 Christian Perthaler .20 .50
21 Michael Puschacher .20 .50
22 Gerhard Puschnik .20 .50
23 Andreas Puschnig .20 .50
24 Gerald Ressmann .20 .50
25 Mario Schaden .20 .50
26 Michael Shea .20 .50
27 Wolfgang Strauss .20 .50
28 Martin Ulrich .20 .50

1937 British Sporting Personalities

37 Joe Beaton 10.00 20.00

1994-95 Czech APS Extraliga

COMPLETE SET (303) 60.00 150.00
1 Pavel Cagas .30 .75
2 Ladislav Blazek .20 .50
3 Ales Flasar .08 .25
4 Petr Tejkl .08 .25
5 Jaromir Latal .08 .25
6 Ales Tomasek .08 .25
7 Jiri Kuntos .08 .25
8 Jan Vavrecka .08 .25
9 Martin Smetak .08 .25
10 Patrik Rimmel .08 .25
11 Michal Slavik .08 .25
12 Milan Navratil .08 .25
13 Petr Fabian .15 .40
14 Zdenek Eichenmann .08 .25
15 Miroslav Chalanek .08 .25
16 Pavel Nohel .08 .25
17 Radim Radevic .08 .25
18 Tomas Martinec .08 .25
19 Ales Zima .08 .25
20 Ivo Hrstka .08 .25
21 Richard Brancik .08 .25
22 Martin Jenacek .08 .25
23 Robert Holy .08 .25
24 Radovan Biegl .20 .50
25 Dusan Salficky .30 .75
26 Jiri Malinsky .08 .25
27 Jan Filip .08 .25
28 Jaroslav Spelda .08 .25
29 Petr Jancarik .08 .25
30 Robert Kostka .08 .25
31 Kamil Toupal .08 .25
32 Tomas Pacal .08 .25
33 Ales Pisa .15 .40
34 Milan Hejduk 15.00 40.00
35 Josef Zajic .20 .50
36 Stanislav Prochazka .08 .25
37 Jiri Sejba .20 .50
38 Marek Zadina .08 .25
39 Milan Filipi .08 .25
40 David Pospisil .08 .25
41 Tomas Blazek .20 .50
42 Patrik Weber .15 .40
43 Richard Kral .15 .40
44 Martin Sekera .08 .25
45 Ladislav Lubina .08 .25
46 Jiri Provaznik .08 .25
47 Martin Chlad .20 .50
48 Tomas Vokoun 4.00 10.00
49 Pavel Trnka .30 .75
50 Petr Kuda .08 .25
51 Frantisek Kaberle .30 .75
52 Libor Prochazka .30 .75
53 Jan Dlouhy .08 .25
54 Otakar Cerny .08 .25
55 Martin Ancicka .08 .25
56 Marek Zidlicky .75 2.00
57 Martin Prochazka .20 .50
58 Pavel Patera .30 .75
59 Otakar Vejvoda .30 .75
60 Jan Blaha .08 .25
61 David Cermak .15 .40
62 Petr Ton .08 .25
63 Miroslav Mach .08 .25
64 Patrik Elias 6.00 15.00
65 Martin Stepanek .08 .25
66 Tomas Mikolasek .08 .25
67 Milan Ruchar .15 .40
68 Jaromir Jagr 20.00 50.00
69 Milos Kajer .08 .25
70 Jaromir Sindel .40 1.00
71 Ivo Capek .20 .50
72 Jan Bohacek .08 .25
73 Zdenek Touzimsky .08 .25
74 Jan Krulis .08 .25
75 Frantisek Musil .20 .50
76 Jaroslav Nedved .08 .25
77 Frantisek Ptacek .08 .25
78 Pavel Taborsky .08 .25
79 Frantisek Kucera .20 .50
80 Pavel Srek .08 .25
81 Martin Simek .08 .25
82 Zbynek Kukacka .08 .25
83 Jiri Zelenka .15 .40
84 Jan Hlavac .75 2.00
85 Patrik Martinec .08 .25
86 David Bruk .08 .25
87 Pavel Geffert .20 .50
88 Michal Sup .08 .25
89 Jaromir Kverka .08 .25
90 Miroslav Hlinka .08 .25
91 Milan Kastner .20 .50
92 Andrej Potajcuk .08 .25
93 Roman Turek 2.00 5.00
94 Ladislav Gula .20 .50
95 Robert Slavik .20 .50
96 Jiri Hala .08 .25
97 Jaroslav Modry .20 .50
98 Petr Sedy .08 .25
99 Petr Hodek .08 .25
100 Petr Mainer .08 .25
101 Michael Kubicek .08 .25
102 Milan Nedoma .20 .50
103 Rudolf Suchanek .08 .25
104 Libor Zabransky .20 .50
105 Jaroslav Brabec .08 .25
106 Lubos Rob .15 .40
107 Zdenek Sperger .08 .25
108 Ondrej Vosta .08 .25
109 Filip Turek .08 .25
110 Radek Belohlav .20 .50
111 Frantisek Sevcik .08 .25
112 Roman Bozek .15 .40
113 Roman Horak .20 .50
114 Pavel Pycha .08 .25
115 Arpad Gyori .08 .25
116 Tomas Vasicek .20 .50
117 Michal Hlinka .20 .50
118 Daniel Kysela .08 .25
119 Rudolf Wolf .08 .25
120 Antonin Planovsky .08 .25
121 Tomas Kramny .08 .25
122 Vitezslav Skuta .20 .50
123 Pavel Marecek .08 .25
124 Miroslav Javin .08 .25
125 Kamil Pribyla .08 .25
126 Michal Cerny .08 .25
127 Juris Opulskis .08 .25
128 Richard Smehlik .30 .75
129 Ales Badal .08 .25
130 Robert Simicek .08 .25
131 Vladimir Vujtek .20 .50
132 Tomas Chlubna .08 .25
133 Michal Piskor .15 .40
134 Petr Folta .15 .40
135 Roman Kadera .15 .40
136 Lumir Kotala .08 .25
137 Jan Peterek .15 .40
138 Roman Rysanek .08 .25
139 Rudolf Pejchar .20 .50
140 Jiri Kucera .20 .50
141 Stanislav Benes .08 .25
142 Karel Smid .20 .50
143 Martin Kovarik .08 .25
144 Jiri Jonak .08 .25
145 Alexander Savickij .08 .25
146 Vaclav Ruprecht .08 .25
147 Ivan Vlcek .08 .25
148 Jaroslav Spacek .20 .50
149 Peter Veselovsky .08 .25
150 Milan Cerny .08 .25
151 Milan Volak .08 .25
152 Dusan Huml .08 .25
153 Tomas Kucharcik .08 .25
154 Martin Zivny .08 .25
155 Martin Straka .75 2.00
156 Michal Straka .08 .25
157 Jiri Beranek .15 .40
158 Ondrej Steiner .20 .50
159 Josef Rybar .40 1.00
160 Jaroslav Kreuzmann .08 .25
161 David Trachta .08 .25
162 Marek Novotny .20 .50
163 Pavel Falta .20 .50
164 Antonin Necas .08 .25
165 Roman Cech .08 .25
166 Pavel Zmrhal .08 .25
167 Petr Buzek .20 .50
168 Jaroslav Benak .20 .50
169 Michael Vyhlidal .08 .25
170 Petr Kuchyna .08 .25
171 Josef Marha .40 1.00
172 Leos Pipa .08 .25
173 Jiri Poukar .08 .25
174 Libor Dolana .08 .25
175 Viktor Ujcik .30 .75
176 Ladislav Prokupek .20 .50
177 Jiri Cihlar .20 .50
178 Patrik Fink .08 .25
179 Oldrich Valek .08 .25
180 Zdenek Cely .08 .25
181 Jaroslav Kames .30 .75
182 Pavel Malac .20 .50
183 Martin Maskarinec .08 .25
184 Pavel Rajnoha .15 .40
185 Pavel Kowalczyk .08 .25
186 Miloslav Guren .20 .50
187 Radim Tesarik .08 .25
188 Jan Krajicek .08 .25
189 Patrik Hucko .08 .25
190 Roman Kankovsky .08 .25
191 Jaroslav Hub .08 .25
192 Petr Kankovsky .08 .25
193 Pavel Janku .20 .50
194 Miroslav Okal .08 .25
195 Zdenek Okal .08 .25
196 Roman Mejzlik .15 .40
197 Juraj Jurik .08 .25
198 Roman Meluzin .08 .25
199 Josef Straub .20 .50
200 Martin Kotasek .08 .25
201 Zdenek Sedlak .08 .25
202 Petr Cajanek 1.25 3.00
203 Zdenek Orct .40 1.00
204 Petr Franek .20 .50
205 Petr Svoboda .40 1.00
206 Angel Nikolov .20 .50
207 Petr Molnar .08 .25
208 Kamil Prachar .20 .50
209 Jiri Slegr .40 1.00
210 Radek Mrazek .08 .25
211 Jan Vopat .20 .50
212 Ondrej Zetek .08 .25
213 Martin Stelcich .08 .25
214 Zdenek Skorepa .08 .25
215 Stanislav Rosa .08 .25
216 Radek Sip .20 .50
217 Martin Rousek .08 .25
218 Tomas Vlasak .20 .50
219 Radim Piroutek .08 .25
220 Robert Kysela .20 .50
221 Martin Rucinsky .40 1.00
222 Robert Lang .75 2.00
223 Ivo Prorok .08 .25
224 Jan Alinc .15 .40
225 Vladimir Machulda .08 .25
226 Kamil Kolacek .08 .25
227 David Balazs .08 .25
228 Roman Cechmanek 4.00 10.00
229 Ivo Pesat .20 .50
230 Antonin Stavjana .20 .50
231 Pavel Augusta .08 .25
232 Daniel Vrla .08 .25
233 Alexej Jaskin .08 .25
234 Radek Mesicek .08 .25
235 Marek Tichy .08 .25
236 Stanislav Pavelec .08 .25
237 Jan Srdinko .08 .25
238 Zbynek Marak .08 .25
239 Andrej Galkin .08 .25
240 Miroslav Stavjana .08 .25
241 Libor Forch .08 .25
242 Roman Stantien .08 .25
243 Josef Beranek .30 .75
244 Lubos Jenacek .08 .25
245 Michal Tomek .08 .25
246 Rostislav Vlach .08 .25
247 Miroslav Barus .08 .25
248 Josef Podlaha .08 .25
249 Pavel Rohlik .08 .25
250 Martin Altrichter .20 .50
251 Radek Toth .30 .75
252 Vladimir Hudacek .20 .50
253 Miloslav Horava .20 .50
254 Petr Macek .08 .25
255 Pavel Blaha .08 .25
256 Radomir Brazda .08 .25
257 Jiri Hes .08 .25
258 Tomas Arnost .08 .25
259 Miroslav Hosek .08 .25
260 Jan Penk .08 .25
261 Tomas Jelinek .20 .50
262 Jiri Hlinka .08 .25
263 Lubos Pazler .08 .25
264 Roman Blazek .08 .25
265 Vladimir Ruzicka .40 1.00
266 Tomas Kupka .08 .25
267 Lubos Dopita .08 .25
268 Ladislav Slizek .08 .25
269 Milan Antos .08 .25
270 Vadim Kulabuchov .08 .25
271 Anatolij Najda .08 .25
272 Tomas Hyka .08 .25
273 Vaclav Eiselt .08 .25
274 Tomas Placatka .08 .25
275 Jan Nemecek .20 .50
276 Josef Augusta CO .08 .25
277 Lubomir Fischer CO .08 .25
278 Jaromir Precechtel CO .08 .25
279 Marek Sykora CO .08 .25
280 Petr Hemsky CO .08 .25
281 Jan Neliba CO .08 .25
282 Zdenek Muller CO .08 .25
283 Frantisek Vyborny CO .08 .25
284 Stanislav Berger CO .08 .25
285 Karel Prazak CO .08 .25
286 Vladimir Caldr CO .08 .25
287 Alois Hadamczik CO .08 .25
288 Bretislav Bochensky CO .08 .25
289 Karel Trachta CO .08 .25
290 Jindrich Setikovsky CO .08 .25
291 Jaroslav Holik CO .08 .25
292 Jan Hrbaty CO .08 .25
293 Vladimir Vujtek CO .08 .25
294 Zdenek Cech CO .08 .25
295 Frantisek Vorlicek CO .08 .25
296 Ondrej Weissmann CO .08 .25
297 Horst Valasek CO .08 .25
298 Zdislav Tabara CO .08 .25
299 Pavel Richter CO .08 .25
300 Bretislav Kopriva CO .08 .25
NNO Checklist 1 .02 .10
NNO Checklist 2 .02 .10
NNO Checklist 3 .02 .10

1995-96 Czech APS Extraliga

COMPLETE SET (400) 50.00 125.00
1 Horst Valasek .08 .25
2 Zdislav Tabara .08 .25
3 Roman Cechmanek 1.50 4.00
4 Ivo Pesat .30 .75
5 Alexej Jaskin .08 .25
6 Stanislav Pavelec .08 .25
7 Jan Srdinko .08 .25
8 Antonin Stavjana .20 .50
9 Pavel Taborsky .08 .25
10 Jiri Veber .08 .25
11 Daniel Vrla .08 .25
12 Miroslav Barus .08 .25
13 Ivan Padelek .08 .25
14 Libor Forch .08 .25
15 Andrej Galkin .08 .25
16 Lubos Jenacek .08 .25
17 Tomas Srsen .08 .25
18 Rostislav Vlach .08 .25
19 Zbynek Marak .08 .25
20 Jiri Dopita .40 1.00
21 Ales Polcar .30 .75
22 Roman Stantien .08 .25
23 Michal Tomek .08 .25
24 Jiri Zadrazil .08 .25
25 Pavel Augusta .08 .25
26 Tomas Jakes .08 .25
27 Vladimir Vujtek .20 .50
28 Zdenek Cech .08 .25
29 Jaroslav Kames .30 .75
30 Pavel Malac .30 .75
31 Jan Vavrecka .08 .25
32 Miroslav Javin .08 .25
33 Stanislav Medrik .08 .25
34 Pavel Kowalczyk .08 .25
35 Miloslav Guren .20 .50
36 Radim Tesarik .08 .25
37 Jan Krajicek .08 .25
38 Jiri Marusak .08 .25
39 Josef Straub .30 .75
40 Pavel Janku .08 .25
41 Roman Meluzin .30 .75
42 Miroslav Okal .08 .25
43 Zdenek Okal .08 .25
44 David Bruk .08 .25
45 Jaroslav Hub .08 .25
46 Petr Cajanek .40 1.00
47 Tomas Nemcicky .08 .25
48 Martin Kotasek .08 .25
49 Zdenek Sedlak .08 .25
50 Petr Leska .08 .25
51 Vladimir Caldr .08 .25
52 Jaroslav Liska .08 .25
53 Oldrich Svoboda .08 .25
54 Robert Slavik .20 .50
55 Rudolf Suchanek .08 .25
56 Milan Nedoma .30 .75
57 Lukas Zib .08 .25
58 Karel Soudek .08 .25
59 Petr Sedy .08 .25
60 Libor Zabransky .20 .50
61 Kamil Toupal .08 .25
62 Michal Kubicek .08 .25
63 Martin Masak .08 .25
64 Radek Belohlav .20 .50
65 Radek Toupal .15 .40
66 Pavel Pycha .08 .25
67 Lubos Rob .15 .40
68 Filip Turek .08 .25
69 Ondrej Vosta .08 .25
70 Roman Bozek .15 .40
71 Jaroslav Brabec .08 .25
72 Petr Sailer .08 .25
73 Martin Strba .08 .25
74 Zdenek Sperger .08 .25
75 Jan Neliba .08 .25
76 Zdenek Muller .08 .25
77 Martin Chlad .30 .75
78 Jiri Kucera .08 .25
79 Jan Dlouhy .08 .25
80 Tomas Kaberle .75 2.00
81 Petr Kasik .08 .25
82 Jan Krulis .08 .25
83 Petr Kuda .08 .25
84 Libor Prochazka .20 .50
85 Martin Stepanek .08 .25
86 Marek Zidlicky .40 1.00
87 Jiri Beranek .15 .40
88 Jiri Burger .08 .25
89 David Cermak .08 .25
90 Milos Kajer .08 .25
91 Miroslav Mach .08 .25
92 Tomas Mikolasek .08 .25
93 Pavel Patera .30 .75
94 Martin Prochazka .30 .75
95 Petr Ton .08 .25
96 Otakar Vejvoda .30 .75
97 Josef Zajic .30 .75
98 Josef Augusta .08 .25
99 Lubomir Fischer .08 .25
100 Jaromir Precechtel .08 .25
101 Pavel Cagas .20 .50
102 Ladislav Blazek .20 .50
103 Jaromir Latal .08 .25
104 Jiri Latal .15 .40
105 Petr Tejkl .08 .25
106 Jiri Kuntos .08 .25
107 Patrik Rimmel .08 .25
108 Robert Machalek .08 .25
109 Jiri Polak .08 .25
110 Martin Bakula .08 .25
111 Michal Slavik .08 .25
112 Pavel Nohel .08 .25
113 Igor Cikl .08 .25
114 Zdenek Eichenmann .08 .25
115 Milan Navratil .08 .25
116 Ales Zima .08 .25
117 Tomas Martinec .15 .40
118 Richard Brancik .08 .25
119 Ondrej Kratena .30 .75
120 Michal Bros .20 .50
121 Juraj Jurik .08 .25
122 Jan Tomajko .08 .25
123 Richard Farda .15 .40
124 Bretislav Kopriva .08 .25
125 Martin Altrichter .30 .75
126 Radek Toth .20 .50
127 Miloslav Horava .30 .75
128 Martin Maskarinec .08 .25
129 Jakub Ficenec .20 .50
130 Jiri Hes .08 .25
131 Andrej Jakovenko .15 .40
132 Petr Macek .08 .25
133 Jan Penk .08 .25
134 Robert Kostka .08 .25
135 Vladimir Ruzicka .30 .75
136 Viktor Ujcik .30 .75
137 Ivo Prorok .08 .25
138 Tomas Jelinek .20 .50
139 Michal Sup .08 .25
140 Milan Antos .08 .25
141 Roman Blazek .08 .25
142 Jiri Hlinka .08 .25
143 Tomas Kupka .08 .25
144 Vaclav Eiselt .08 .25
145 Jaroslav Bednar .75 2.00
146 Ladislav Svoboda .08 .25
147 Ladislav Kudrna .08 .25
148 Josef Beranek .20 .50
149 Vladimir Kyhos .08 .25
150 Zdenek Orct .30 .75
151 Petr Franek .30 .75
152 Kamil Prachar .15 .40
153 Angel Nikolov .20 .50
154 Ondrej Zetek .08 .25
155 Tomas Arnost .08 .25
156 Normunds Sejejs .08 .25
157 Petr Kratky .08 .25
158 Sergej Butko .08 .25
159 Petr Molnar .08 .25
160 Radek Mrazek .08 .25
161 Radim Piroutek .08 .25
162 David Balazs .08 .25
163 Jindrich Kotrla .08 .25
164 Jaroslav Buchal .08 .25
165 Josef Straka .30 .75
166 Michail Fadejev .08 .25
167 Radek Sip .08 .25
168 Martin Rousek .08 .25
169 Tomas Vlasak .20 .50
170 Robert Kysela .30 .75
171 Jan Alinc .15 .40
172 Vladimir Machulda .08 .25
173 Vladimir Jerabek .08 .25
174 Frantisek Vorlicek .08 .25
175 Jan Hrbaty .08 .25
176 Marek Novotny .20 .50
177 Lukas Sablik .08 .25
178 Roman Kankovsky .08 .25
179 Michael Vyhlidal .08 .25
180 Jan Bohacek .08 .25
181 Roman Cech .30 .75
182 Zdenek Touzimsky .08 .25
183 Marek Posmyk .20 .50
184 Pavel Rajnoha .15 .40
185 Martin Tupa .08 .25
186 Libor Dolana .08 .25
187 Petr Vlk .15 .40
188 Petr Kankovsky .08 .25
189 Jiri Cihlar .30 .75
190 Jiri Poukar .08 .25
191 Jaromir Kverka .08 .25
192 Leos Pipa .08 .25
193 Ladislav Prokupek .30 .75
194 Patrik Fink .08 .25
195 Marek Melenovsky .30 .75
196 Jiri Holik .08 .25
197 Miroslav Bruna .08 .25
198 Jaroslav Walter .08 .25
199 Otto Zelezny .08 .25
200 Libor Barta .08 .25
201 Pavel Nestak .08 .25
202 Leo Gudas .08 .25
203 Karel Beran .08 .25
204 Richard Adam .08 .25
205 Pavel Zubicek .08 .25
206 Alexandr Elsner .08 .25
207 Robert Kantor .08 .25
208 Ladislav Tresl .20 .50
209 Frantisek Sevcik .20 .50
210 Michal Konecny .08 .25
211 Richard Sebestu .08 .25
212 Roman Mejzlik .15 .40
213 Zdenek Cely .08 .25
214 Jiri Vitek .08 .25
215 Radek Haman .08 .25
216 Tomas Krasny .08 .25
217 Jiri Suhrada .08 .25
218 Jaroslav Smolik .08 .25
219 Alois Hadamczik CO .08 .25
220 Karel Suchanek .08 .25
221 Michal Hlinka .30 .75
222 Josef Lucak .08 .25
223 Karel Pavlik .08 .25
224 Stanislav Meciar .30 .75
225 Petr Mainer .08 .25
226 Petr Pavlas .08 .25
227 Lubomir Sekeras .40 1.00
228 Roman Sindel .20 .50
229 Vaclav Slaby .08 .25
230 Miroslav Cihal .08 .25
231 Martin Palinek .08 .25
232 Petr Zajonc .08 .25
233 Michal Piskor .15 .40
234 Roman Kadera .30 .75
235 Marek Zadina .08 .25
236 Richard Kral .15 .40
237 Miroslav Skovira .08 .25
238 Vladimir Michalek .08 .25
239 Libor Zatopek .08 .25
240 Dusan Adamcik .08 .25
241 Jiri Novotny .08 .25
242 Karel Trachta .08 .25
243 Jindrich Setikovsky .08 .25
244 Rudolf Pejchar .30 .75
245 Michal Marik .08 .25
246 Karel Smid .30 .75
247 Martin Kovarik .08 .25
248 Jiri Hanzlik .08 .25
249 Jaroslav Spacek .20 .50
250 Stanislav Benes .08 .25
251 Robert Jindrich .20 .50
252 Vaclav Ruprecht .08 .25
253 Tomas Kucharcik .08 .25
254 Michal Straka .08 .25
255 Ondrej Steiner .20 .50
256 Tomas Klimt .20 .50
257 Martin Zivny .08 .25
258 Milan Volak .08 .25
259 Pavel Metlicka .08 .25
260 Josef Rybar .30 .75
261 Jaroslav Kreuzmann .08 .25
262 David Trachta .08 .25
263 Anatolij Najda .08 .25
264 Tomas Ruprecht .08 .25
265 Dalibor Sanda .08 .25
266 Jaroslav Brabec .08 .25
267 Frantisek Vyborny .08 .25
268 Stanislav Berger .08 .25
269 Ivo Capek .30 .75
270 David Volek .30 .75
271 Jiri Vykoukal .20 .50
272 Vaclav Burda .08 .25
273 Petr Kuchyna .08 .25
274 Pavel Srek .08 .25
275 Frantisek Ptacek .08 .25
276 Radek Hamr .15 .40
277 Jiri Krocak .08 .25
278 Jaroslav Nedved .08 .25
279 Jiri Zelenka .15 .40
280 David Vyborny .30 .75
281 Checklist 1 .02 .10
282 Checklist 2 .02 .10
283 Checklist 3 .02 .10
284 Checklist 4 .02 .10
285 Zbynek Kukacka .08 .25
286 Miroslav Hlinka .08 .25
287 Jaroslav Hlinka .08 .25
288 Jan Hlavac .40 1.00
289 Andrej Potajcuk .08 .25
290 Richard Zemlicka .40 1.00
291 Vladimir Stransky .08 .25
292 Ladislav Svozil .08 .25
293 Martin Prusek 4.00 10.00
294 Vladimir Hudacek .15 .50
295 Pavel Marecek .08 .25
296 Rudolf Wolf .08 .25
297 Tomas Kramny .08 .25
298 Pavel Kubina 1.25 3.00
299 Rene Sevecek .08 .25
300 Filip Kuba .30 .75
301 Ales Tomasek .08 .25
302 Roman Rysanek .08 .25
303 Vladimir Vujtek .20 .50
304 Petr Folta .08 .25
305 Jan Peterek .08 .25
306 Roman Simicek .20 .50
307 Pavel Zdrahal .08 .25
308 Pavel Sebesta .08 .25
309 David Moravec .40 1.00
310 Tomas Chlubna .08 .25
311 Ludek Krayzel .08 .25
312 Waldemar Klisiak .08 .25
313 Petr Fabian .08 .25
314 Josef Palacek .08 .25
315 Florian Strida .08 .25
316 Radovan Biegl .08 .25
317 Dusan Salficky .30 .75
318 Petr Jancarik .08 .25
319 Tomas Pacal .08 .25
320 Radomir Brazda .08 .25
321 Radek Mesicek .08 .25
322 Jiri Antonin .08 .25
323 Alexander Terechov .08 .25
324 Milan Beranek .08 .25
325 Ladislav Lubina .08 .25
326 David Pospisil .08 .25
327 Milan Kastner .08 .25
328 Stanislav Prochazka .08 .25
329 Patrik Weber .08 .25
330 Milan Hejduk 10.00 20.00
331 Tomas Blazek .08 .25
332 Jiri Jantovsky .08 .25
333 Jaroslav Kudrna .08 .25
334 Tomas Pisa .08 .25
335 Ales Pisa .08 .25
336 Ivan Vasilev .08 .25
337 Milan Hnilicka 2.00 5.00
338 Ales Flasar .08 .25
339 Martin Smetak .08 .25
340 Libor Polasek .20 .50
341 Vitezslav Skuta .08 .25
342 Ladislav Benysek .40 1.00
343 Jaroslav Smolik .08 .25
344 Igor Cikl .08 .25
345 Jan Czerlinski .08 .25
346 Marek Vorel .08 .25
347 Martin Ancicka .08 .25
348 Pavel Skrbek .20 .50
349 Petr Kadlec .08 .25
350 Tomas Kucharcik .08 .25
351 Ludek Bukac .30 .75
352 Zdenek Uher .08 .25
353 Roman Cechmanek 1.50 4.00
354 Roman Turek .75 2.00
355 Petr Briza .75 2.00
356 Jaroslav Kames .30 .75
357 Antonin Stavjana .20 .50
358 Bedrich Scerban .30 .75
359 Petr Kuchyna .08 .25
360 Jiri Vykoukal .30 .75
361 Frantisek Kaberle .30 .75
362 Jan Vopat .30 .75
363 Libor Prochazka .20 .50
364 Jiri Kucera .20 .50
365 Tomas Jelinek .20 .50
366 Richard Zemlicka .40 1.00
367 Martin Hostak .20 .50
368 Tomas Srsen .08 .25
369 Jiri Dopita .40 1.00
370 Martin Prochazka .30 .75
371 Pavel Patera .20 .50
372 Otakar Vejvoda .30 .75
373 Roman Horak .08 .25
374 Radek Belohlav .20 .50
375 Pavel Geffert .08 .25
376 Jan Alinc .08 .25
377 Roman Kadera .08 .25
378 Viktor Ujcik .30 .75
379 Roman Meluzin .20 .50
380 Pavel Janku .08 .25
381 Tomas Kucharcik .08 .25
382 Zbynek Marak .08 .25
383 Ales Zima .08 .25
384 Jaromir Jagr 10.00 25.00
385 Pavel Patera .30 .75
386 Martin Prochazka .30 .75
387 Pavel Janku .08 .25
388 Roman Cechmanek 1.50 4.00
389 Antonin Stavjana .20 .50
390 Rostislav Vlach .08 .25
391 Lubos Jenacek .08 .25
392 Dominik Hasek 6.00 15.00
393 Jiri Holik .08 .25
394 Frantisek Pospisil .08 .25
395 Ivan Hlinka .30 .75
396 Vladimir Martinec .08 .25
397 Jaroslav Pouzar .08 .25
398 Karel Gut .08 .25
399 Jan Benda .30 .75
400 unknown .08 .25

1996-97 Czech APS Extraliga

COMPLETE SET (350) 36.00 90.00
1 Marek Sykora CO .02 .10
2 Vladimir Kolek .02 .10
3 Rudolf Pejchar .15 .40
4 Ladislav Kudrna .15 .40
5 Miloslav Horava .08 .25
6 Petr Kadlec .08 .25
7 Jaromir Latal .08 .25
8 Jiri Hes .08 .25
9 Andrei Jakovenko .08 .25
10 Martin Maskarinec .08 .25
11 Jaroslav Horacek .08 .25
12 Robert Kostka .08 .25
13 Jiri Dolezal .08 .25
14 Tomas Kucharcik .08 .25
15 Ivo Prorok .08 .25
16 Roman Kadera .08 .25
17 Jiri Hlinka .08 .25
18 Tomas Kupka .08 .25
19 Viktor Ujcik .30 .75
20 Vladimir Ruzicka .15 .40
21 Ladislav Slizek .08 .25
22 Jaroslav Bednar .40 1.00
23 Michal Sup .08 .25
24 Radek Matejovsky .08 .25
25 Horst Valasek .02 .10
26 Jiri Vodak .02 .10
27 Jaroslav Kames .30 .75
28 Petr Kubena .15 .40
29 Petr Kuchyna .08 .25
30 Jiri Marusak .08 .25
31 Radim Tesarik .08 .25
32 Vadim Podrezov .08 .25
33 Stanislav Medrik .08 .25
34 Jan Krajicek .08 .25
35 Pavel Kowalczyk .08 .25
36 David Bruk .08 .25
37 Tomas Nemcicky .08 .25
38 Zdenek Sedlak .08 .25
39 Ales Zima .08 .25
40 Zbynek Marak .08 .25
41 Ales Polcar .08 .25
42 Roman Meluzin .08 .25
43 Pavel Janku .08 .25
44 Miroslav Okal .08 .25
45 Petr Cajanek .40 1.00
46 Martin Kotasek .08 .25
47 Petr Leska .08 .25
48 Alois Hadamczik CO .02 .10
49 Ales Mach .02 .10
50 Radovan Biegl .20 .50
51 Josef Lukac .20 .50
52 Petr Jancarik .08 .25
53 Lubomir Sekeras .40 1.00

54 Jiri Kuntos .08 .25
55 Stanislav Pavelec .08 .25
56 Patrik Hucko .08 .25
57 Miroslav Cihal .08 .25
58 Karel Pavlik .08 .25
59 Ondrej Zetek .08 .25
60 Richard Kral .08 .25
61 Petr Folta .08 .25
62 Josef Straub .08 .25
63 Petr Zajonc .08 .25
64 Roman Kontsek .08 .25
65 Marek Zadina .08 .25
66 Roman Blazek .08 .25
67 Michal Piskor .08 .25
68 Jozef Dano .08 .25
69 Vladimir Machulda .08 .25
70 Jiri Novotny .08 .25
71 Petr Lipina .08 .25
72 Jan Novotny CO .02 .10
73 Lubomir Bauer .02 .10
74 Milan Hnilicka 2.00 5.00
75 Martin Chlad .20 .50
76 Petr Kasik .08 .25
77 Jan Krulis .08 .25
78 Libor Prochazka .20 .50
79 Jan Dlouhy .08 .25
80 Marek Zidlicky .40 1.00
81 Tomas Kaberle .60 1.50
82 Pavel Skrbek .20 .50
83 Tomas Trachta .08 .25
84 Zdenek Eichenmann .08 .25
85 Josef Zajic .20 .50
86 David Cermak .08 .25
87 Ladislav Svoboda .08 .25
88 Tomas Mikolasek .08 .25
89 Petr Ton .08 .25
90 Jiri Beranek .15 .40
91 Vaclav Eiselt .08 .25
92 Jiri Burger .08 .25
93 Petr Tenkrat .30 .75
94 Petr Vogeltanz .08 .25
95 Filip Klapac .08 .25
96 Karel Suchanek .08 .25
97 Kamil Konecny .08 .25
98 Rostislav Haas .08 .25
99 Roman Slupina .08 .25
100 Milos Hrubes .08 .25
101 Petr Tejkl .08 .25
102 Martin Bakula .08 .25
103 Radek Mesicek .08 .25
104 Karel Frydl .08 .25
105 David Galvas .08 .25
106 Denis Tsygurov .15 .40
107 Juraj Jurik .08 .25
108 Petr Fabian .08 .25
109 Radim Radevic .08 .25
110 Jiri Zadrazil .08 .25
111 Martin Filip .08 .25
112 Karel Horny .08 .25
113 Zdenek Pavelek .08 .25
114 Eduard Gorbachev .15 .40
115 Valerij Belov .08 .25
116 Dalibor Rimsky .08 .25
117 Marek Harazim .08 .25
118 David Dostal .08 .25
119 Slavomir Lener .15 .40
120 Vaclav Sykora .08 .25
121 Robert Schistad .15 .40
122 Martin Cinibulk .08 .25
123 Jiri Vykoukal .20 .50
124 Jan Bohacek .08 .25
125 Jaroslav Nedved .08 .25
126 Jiri Krocak .08 .25
127 Vaclav Burda .08 .25
128 Radek Hamr .15 .40
129 Frantisek Ptacek .08 .25
130 Roman Horak .08 .25
131 Pavel Geffert .08 .25
132 Richard Zemlicka .20 .50
133 Jiri Zelenka .15 .40
134 Patrik Martinec .08 .25
135 David Vyborny .20 .50
136 Miroslav Hlinka .08 .25
137 Martin Hostak .15 .40
138 Jan Hlavac .40 1.00
139 Jaroslav Hinka .08 .25
140 Jan Benda .15 .40
141 Josef Palecek .08 .25
142 Milos Riha CO .08 .25
143 Libor Barta .08 .25
144 Dusan Salficky .30 .75
145 Radomir Brazda .08 .25
146 Pavel Augusta .08 .25
147 Jiri Malinsky .08 .25
148 Tomas Pacal .08 .25
149 Ales Pisa .08 .25
150 Pavel Kriz .15 .40
151 Alexander Tsyplakov .20 .50
152 Petr Mudroch .08 .25
153 Ladislav Lubina .08 .25
154 David Pospisil .08 .25
155 Stanislav Prochazka .08 .25
156 Tomas Martinec .08 .25
157 Milan Hejduk 7.50 15.00
158 Tomas Martinec .08 .25
159 Jiri Jantovsky .08 .25
160 Martin Koudelka .08 .25
161 Pavel Kabrt .08 .25
162 Petr Sykora .20 .50
163 Milan Prochazka .15 .40
164 Karel Plasek .08 .25
165 Josef Beranek .20 .50
166 Vladimir Kyhos .08 .25
167 Zdenek Orct .30 .75
168 Richard Hrazdira .08 .25
169 Kamil Prachar .15 .40
170 Radek Mrazek .08 .25
171 Roman Cech .20 .50
172 Angel Nikolov .20 .50
173 Martin Stepanek .08 .25
174 Sergej Butko .08 .25
175 Normunds Sejejs .08 .25
176 Petr Kratky .08 .25
177 Vladimir Jerabek .08 .25
178 Kamil Kastak .15 .40
179 Robert Kysela .08 .25
180 Petr Hrbek .08 .25
181 Martin Rousek .08 .25
182 Tomas Krasny .08 .25
183 Tomas Vlasak .20 .50
184 David Balazs .08 .25
185 Jindrich Kotrla .08 .25
186 Josef Straka .20 .50
187 Jaroslav Buchal .08 .25
188 Kamil Piros .60 1.50
189 Vladimir Vujtek .08 .25
190 Ladislav Svozil .08 .25
191 Martin Prusek 2.00 5.00
192 Tomas Vasicek .08 .25
193 Jiri Jonak .08 .25
194 Ales Tomasek .08 .25
195 Daniel Kysela .08 .25
196 Vitezslav Skuta .08 .25
197 Tomas Kramny .08 .25
198 Rene Sevecek .08 .25
199 Dmitrij Jerofejev .08 .25
200 Pavel Kumstat .08 .25
201 Roman Rysanek .08 .25
202 Roman Simicek .20 .50
203 Martin Smetak .08 .25
204 Tomas Chlubna .08 .25
205 Ludek Krayzel .08 .25
206 David Moravec .20 .50
207 Alexander Prokopjev .08 .25
208 Ales Kratoska .08 .25
209 Libor Pavlis .08 .25
210 Radek Klauda .08 .25
211 Libor Polasek .15 .40
212 Jan Neliba .08 .25
213 Zdislav Tabara .08 .25
214 Roman Cechmanek .75 2.00
215 Ivo Pesat .20 .50
216 Antonin Stavjana .20 .50
217 Bedrich Scerban .15 .40
218 Jiri Veber .08 .25
219 Alexej Jaskin .08 .25
220 Jan Srdinko .08 .25
221 Tomas Jakes .08 .25
222 Petr Kubox .08 .25
223 Michal Divisek .08 .25
224 Rostislav Vlach .08 .25
225 Michal Tomek .08 .25
226 Oto Hascak .20 .50
227 Tomas Kapusta .20 .50
228 Tomas Srsen .08 .25
229 Roman Stantien .08 .25
230 Jiri Dopita .30 .75
231 Ivan Padelek .08 .25
232 Andrej Galkin .08 .25
233 Ondrej Kratena .20 .50
234 David Hruska .08 .25
235 Daniel Tesarik .08 .25
236 Lukas Duba .08 .25
237 Vladimir Caldr .08 .25
238 Jaroslav Liska .08 .25
239 Oldrich Svoboda .08 .25
240 Robert Slavik .20 .50
241 Rudolf Suchanek .08 .25
242 Karel Soudek .08 .25
243 Milan Nedoma .20 .50
244 Kamil Toupal .08 .25
245 Petr Sedy .08 .25
246 Lukas Zib .08 .25
247 Martin Masak .08 .25
248 Radek Martinek .40 1.00
249 Vladimir Antipin .08 .25
250 Radek Toupal .15 .40
251 Pavel Pycha .08 .25
252 Lubos Rob .15 .40
253 Filip Turek .08 .25
254 Arpad Gyori .08 .25
255 Radek Belohlav .20 .50
256 Ondrej Vosta .08 .25
257 Milan Navratil .08 .25
258 Frantisek Sevcik .08 .25
259 Petr Sailer .08 .25
260 Michal Horak .08 .25
261 Kamil Brabenec .15 .40
262 Miroslav Barus .08 .25
263 Jiri Latal .15 .40
264 Miroslav Venkrbec .08 .25
265 Ladislav Blazek .20 .50
266 Robert Horyna .15 .40
267 Petr Pavlas .08 .25
268 Roman Veber .08 .25
269 Marek Tichy .08 .25
270 Jergus Baca .15 .40
271 Ladislav Benysek .20 .50
272 Jiri Polak .08 .25
273 Marek Cernosek .08 .25
274 Michal Slavik .08 .25
275 Pavel Nohel .08 .25
276 Radek Sip .08 .25
277 Jan Tomajko .08 .25
278 Michal Bros .15 .40
279 Radek Prochazka .08 .25
280 Radek Svoboda .08 .25
281 Michal Dvorak .08 .25
282 Ales Lipensky .08 .25
283 Filip Dvorak .08 .25
284 Milan Jurak .08 .25
285 Adam Drabek .08 .25
286 Bohuslav Ebermann .08 .25
287 Radim Rulik .08 .25
288 Martin Altrichter .20 .50
289 Michal Marik .08 .25
290 Ivan Vlcek .08 .25
291 Josef Reznicek .08 .25
292 Karel Smid .20 .50
293 Vaclav Ruprecht .08 .25
294 Jaroslav Spacek .20 .50
295 Jiri Hanzlik .08 .25
296 Robert Jindrich .20 .50
297 Tomas Jelinek .08 .25
298 Milan Volak .08 .25
299 Radek Kampf .08 .25
300 Miroslav Mach .08 .25
301 Petr Korinek .20 .50
302 Jiri Kucera .15 .40
303 Michal Straka .08 .25
304 Tomas Klimt .20 .50
305 Josef Rybar .20 .50
306 Dalibor Sanda .08 .25
307 Jiri Novotny .08 .25
308 Pavel Vostrak .08 .25
309 Frantisek Vorlicek .08 .25
310 Jan Hrbaty .08 .25
311 Ivo Capek .20 .50
312 Marek Novotny .08 .25
313 Roman Kankovsky .08 .25
314 Miroslav Javin .08 .25
315 Michael Vyhlidal .08 .25
316 Zdenek Touzimsky .08 .25
317 Martin Tupa .08 .25
318 Marian Morava .08 .25
319 Filip Vanecek .08 .25
320 Marek Posmyk .20 .50
321 Libor Dolana .08 .25
322 Petr Vlk .15 .40
323 Petr Kankovsky .08 .25
324 Jaroslav Hub .08 .25
325 Jiri Poukar .08 .25
326 Leos Pipa .08 .25
327 Ladislav Prokupek .20 .50
328 Patrik Fink .08 .25
329 Marek Melenovsky .15 .40
330 Milan Antos .08 .25
331 Jiri Holik .08 .25
332 Miroslav Bruna .08 .25
333 Michail Fadejev .08 .25
334 Ludek Bukac .15 .40
335 Slavomir Lener .15 .40
336 Zdenek Uher .08 .25
337 Roman Cechmanek .75 2.00
338 Roman Turek .75 2.00
339 Robert Sysela .08 .25
340 Jiri Veber .08 .25
341 Pavel Patera .20 .50
342 Radek Bonk .40 1.00
343 Radek Belohlav .20 .50
344 Drahomir Kadlec .15 .40
345 Michal Sykora .20 .50
346 Jiri Vykoukal .20 .50
347 Viktor Ujcik .20 .50
348 Stanislav Neckar .20 .50
349 Robert Reichel .30 .75
350 Roman Meluzin .15 .40

1997-98 Czech APS Extraliga

COMPLETE SET (380) 50.00 125.00
1 Slavomir Lener CO .20 .50
2 Vaclav Sykora CO .08 .25
3 Milan Hnilicka 2.00 5.00
4 Martin Cinibulk .08 .25
5 Frantisek Ptacek .08 .25
6 Frantisek Kucera .08 .25
7 Jaroslav Nedved .08 .25
8 Jiri Krocak .08 .25
9 Martin Holy .08 .25
10 Jaromir Kverka .08 .25
11 Jiri Zelenka .08 .25
12 Richard Zemlicka .20 .50
13 Jaroslav Hlinka .08 .25
14 Jaroslav Bednar .40 1.00
15 Ivo Novotny .08 .25
16 Radek Duda .20 .50
17 Michal Sivek .75 2.00
18 Jan Hlavac .40 1.00
19 Miroslav Hlinka .08 .25
20 Patrik Stefan ERC 1.25 3.00
21 Vaclav Burda .08 .25
22 Patrik Martinec .08 .25
23 Ladislav Benysek .20 .50
24 Jiri Vykoukal .20 .50
25 Petr Nedved .75 2.00
26 Jan Neliba CO .08 .25
27 Zdislav Tabara CO .08 .25
28 Roman Cechmanek 2.00 5.00
29 Ivo Pesat .30 .75
30 Radim Tesarik .08 .25
31 Antonin Stavjana .20 .50
32 Jiri Veber .08 .25
33 Michal Bros .08 .25
34 Alexej Jaskin .08 .25
35 Andrej Galkin .08 .25
36 Rostislav Vlach .08 .25
37 Ivan Padelek .08 .25
38 Tomas Srsen .08 .25
39 Jiri Dopita .30 .75
40 Ondrej Kratena .08 .25
41 Tomas Kapusta .08 .25
42 Pavel Zubicek .08 .25
43 Radek Belohlav .20 .50
44 Tomas Demel .08 .25
45 Michal Divisek .08 .25
46 Michal Safarik .08 .25
47 Josef Beranek .20 .50
48 Jan Tomajko .08 .25
49 Jan Srdinko .08 .25
50 Roman Stantien .08 .25
51 Eduard Novak CO .08 .25
52 Zdenek Cech CO .08 .25
53 Jaroslav Kames .40 1.00
54 Robert Hamrla .08 .25
55 Pavel Kowalczyk .08 .25
56 Jan Krajicek .08 .25
57 Petr Kuchyna .08 .25
58 Pavel Rajnoha .08 .25
59 Martin Hamrlik .08 .25
60 Jiri Marusak .08 .25
61 Karel Rachunek .40 1.00
62 Roman Meluzin .20 .50
63 Ales Zima .08 .25
64 Pavel Janku .20 .50
65 Tomas Nemcicky .08 .25
66 Petr Cajanek .30 .75
67 Miroslav Okal .08 .25
68 Zdenek Sedlak .08 .25
69 Ales Polcar .08 .25
70 Petr Leska .08 .25
71 Martin Spanhel .30 .75
72 Branislav Janos .08 .25
73 Marek Vorel .08 .25
74 Tomas Zizka .08 .25
75 Ondrej Weissman CO .08 .25
76 Vladimir Jerabek CO .08 .25
77 Zdenek Orct .30 .75
78 Richard Hrazdira .08 .25
79 Angel Nikolov .08 .25
80 Drahomir Kadlec .30 .75
81 Frantisek Prochazka .08 .25
82 Radek Mrazek .08 .25
83 Petr Molnar .08 .25
84 Martin Stepanek .08 .25
85 Roman Cech .08 .25
86 Vladimir Gyna .08 .25
87 Tomas Vlasak .08 .25
88 Robert Kysela .08 .25
89 Martin Rousek .08 .25
90 Petr Hrbek .08 .25
91 Vladimir Petrovka .08 .25
92 Ivo Prorok .08 .25
93 Tomas Krasny .08 .25
94 David Balazs .08 .25
95 Josef Straka .08 .25
96 Kamil Piros .40 1.00
97 Denis Afinogenov .20 .50
98 Rail Muftijev .08 .25
99 Dmitrij Denisov .08 .25
100 Karel Franek CO .08 .25
101 Petr Pelucha CO .08 .25
102 Rostislav Haas .08 .25
103 Pavel Nestak .08 .25
104 Martin Maskarinec .08 .25
105 David Galvas .08 .25
106 Milos Hrubes .08 .25
107 Pavel Sebesta .08 .25
108 Tomas Kramny .08 .25
109 Pavel Marecek .08 .25
110 Vaclav Slaby .08 .25
111 Petr Suchanek .08 .25
112 Zbynek Marak .08 .25
113 Michal Tomek .08 .25
114 Michal Piskor .08 .25
115 Juraj Jurik .08 .25
116 Karel Horny .08 .25
117 Jiri Zurek .08 .25
118 Martin Sychra .08 .25
119 Zdenek Pavelek .08 .25
120 Richard Brancik .08 .25
121 Milan Ministr .08 .25
122 Martin Sekera .08 .25
123 Vladimir Vujtek CO .20 .50
124 Ladislav Svozil CO .08 .25
125 Martin Prusek 1.50 4.00
126 Zdenek Dobes .08 .25
127 Jiri Jonak .08 .25
128 Vitezslav Skuta .08 .25
129 Dmitrij Jerofejev .08 .25
130 Petr Jurecka .08 .25
131 Pavel Kumstat .08 .25
132 Roman Simicek .20 .50
133 Roman Rysanek .08 .25
134 David Moravec .30 .75
135 Alexander Prokopjev .08 .25
136 Alexander Cherbajev .08 .25
137 Libor Pavlis .08 .25
138 Jan Matejny .08 .25
139 Libor Polasek .08 .25
140 Martin Kotasek .08 .25
141 Petr Zajonc .08 .25
142 Martin Lamich .08 .25
143 Daniel Vilasek .08 .25
144 Martin Tomasek .08 .25
145 Ales Kratoska .08 .25
146 Richard Farda CO .08 .25
147 Ladislav Slizek CO .08 .25
148 Martin Altrichter .08 .25
149 Ladislav Blazek .20 .50
150 Robert Kostka .08 .25
151 Jiri Hes .08 .25
152 Andrej Jakovenko .08 .25
153 Pavel Kolarik .20 .50
154 Martin Bakula .08 .25
155 Petr Kadlec .08 .25
156 Jan Novak .08 .25
157 Jan Hejda .08 .25
158 Vladimir Ruzicka .20 .50
160 Viktor Ujcik .20 .50
160 Jiri Dolezal .08 .25
161 Jiri Poukar .08 .25
162 Tomas Kucharcik .08 .25
163 Michal Sup .08 .25
164 Jiri Hlinka .08 .25
165 Tomas Kupka .08 .25
166 Radek Matejovsky .08 .25
167 Robert Kucera .08 .25
168 Jan Fadrny .08 .25
169 Jan Sochor .08 .25
170 Marek Sykora CO .08 .25
171 Radim Rulik CO .08 .25
172 Michal Marik .08 .25
173 Dusan Salficky .40 1.00
174 Josef Reznicek .08 .25
175 Ivan Vlcek .08 .25
176 Robert Jindrich .20 .50
177 Jiri Hanzlik .08 .25
178 Pavel Srek .08 .25
179 Ondrej Zetek .08 .25
180 Pavel Geffert .08 .25
181 David Pospisil .08 .25
182 Martin Filip .08 .25
183 Tomas Jelinek .08 .25
184 Michal Straka .08 .25
185 Milan Volak .08 .25
186 Pavel Vostrak .08 .25
187 Dalibor Sanda .08 .25
188 Milan Navratil .08 .25
189 Mojmir Musil .08 .25
190 Milan Kraft 2.00 5.00
191 Jiri Jelen .08 .25
192 Martin Cech .08 .25
193 Jan Novotny CO .08 .25
194 Lubomir Bauer CO .08 .25
195 Radek Toth .08 .25
196 Martin Bilek .08 .25
197 Jan Krulis .08 .25
198 Marek Zidlicky .08 .25
199 Tomas Kaberle 1.25 3.00
200 Pavel Skrbek .20 .50
201 Jan Penk .08 .25
202 Jan Dlouhy .08 .25
203 Jan Hranac .08 .25
204 Josef Zajic .08 .25
205 Zdenek Eichenmann .08 .25
206 Petr Ton .08 .25
207 Jiri Beranek .08 .25
208 Ladislav Svoboda .08 .25
209 Vaclav Eiselt .08 .25
210 Jiri Burger .08 .25
211 Petr Tenkrat .30 .75
212 Jiri Kuchler .08 .25
213 Tomas Trachta .08 .25
214 Jiri Holsan .08 .25
215 Milan Novy .08 .25
216 Jiri Kloboucek .08 .25
217 Tomas Mikolasek .08 .25
218 Milan Kasparek CO .08 .25
219 Karel Trachta CO .08 .25
220 Vladimir Hudacek .08 .25
221 Robert Horyna CO .08 .25
222 Petr Pavlas .08 .25
223 Petr Mainer .08 .25
224 Ales Tomasek .08 .25
225 Pavel Blaha .08 .25
226 Jiri Polak .08 .25
227 Martin Richter .08 .25
228 Martin Rejthar .08 .25
229 Michal Cerny .08 .25
230 Zbynek Kukacka .08 .25
231 Ondrej Steiner .08 .25
232 Pavel Metlicka .08 .25
233 Martin Streit .08 .25
234 Radek Prochazka .08 .25
235 Radek Svoboda .08 .25
236 Michal Porak .08 .25
237 Michal Horak .08 .25
238 Jan Lipiansky .08 .25
239 Jaroslav Buchal .08 .25
240 Tomas Klimt .20 .50
241 Petr Fical .08 .25
242 Milos Riha CO .08 .25
243 Josef Palecek CO .08 .25
244 Libor Barta .08 .25
245 Adam Svoboda .40 1.00
246 Patrik Rozsival .08 .25
247 Jiri Malinsky .08 .25
248 Ales Pisa .08 .25
249 Tomas Pacal .08 .25
250 Pavel Kriz .20 .50
251 Pavel Augusta .08 .25
252 Petr Murdoch .08 .25
253 Robert Pospisil .08 .25
254 Tomas Blazek .20 .50
255 Milan Hejduk 8.00 20.00
256 Jiri Jantovsky .08 .25
257 Stanislav Prochazka .08 .25
258 Tomas Martinec .08 .25
259 Pavel Kabrt .08 .25
260 Jaroslav Kudrna .20 .50
261 Karel Plasek .08 .25
262 Petr Sykora 2.00 5.00
263 Lukas Palecek .08 .25
264 Vladimir Caldr CO .08 .25
265 Jaroslav Liska CO .08 .25
266 Oldrich Svoboda .40 1.00
267 Robert Slavik .08 .25
268 Rudolf Suchanek .08 .25
269 Karel Soudek .08 .25
270 Milan Nedoma .08 .25
271 Kamil Toupal .08 .25
272 Lukas Zib .08 .25
273 Jan Bohacek .08 .25
274 Filip Vanecek .08 .25
275 Radek Martinek .30 .75
276 Radek Toupal .08 .25
277 Lubos Rob .08 .25
278 Pavel Pycha .08 .25
279 David Bruk .08 .25
280 Filip Turek .08 .25
281 Ondrej Vosta .08 .25
282 Arpad Györi .08 .25
283 Petr Sailer .08 .25
284 Martin Strba .08 .25
285 Petr Sachl .08 .25
286 Miroslav Barus .08 .25
287 Vaclav Kral .08 .25
288 Ales Kotalik ERC 2.00 5.00
289 Josef Augusta CO .20 .50
290 Karel Dvorak CO .08 .25
291 Marek Novotny .20 .50
292 Lukas Sablik .08 .25
293 Michael Vyhlidal .08 .25
294 Miroslav Javin .08 .25
295 Martin Tupa .08 .25
296 Marian Morava .08 .25
297 Jaroslav Horacek .08 .25
298 Tomas Jakes .08 .25
299 Daniel Zapotocny .08 .25
300 Miroslav Duben .08 .25
301 Petr Vlk .08 .25
302 Roman Mejzlik .08 .25
303 Jiri Cihlar .08 .25
304 Jaroslav Hub .08 .25
305 Leos Pipa .08 .25
306 Ladislav Prokupek .08 .25
307 Marek Melenovsky .08 .25
308 Milan Antos .08 .25
309 Vaclav Adamec .08 .25
310 Ales Sochorec .08 .25
311 Ales Polcar .08 .25
312 Daniel Hodek .08 .25
313 Alois Hadamczik CO .08 .25
314 Kamil Konecny CO .08 .25
315 Radovan Biegl .20 .50
316 Vlastimil Lakosil .08 .25
317 Lubomir Sekeras .30 .75
318 Miroslav Cihal .08 .25
319 Petr Jancarik .08 .25
320 Stanislav Pavelec .08 .25
321 Jiri Kuntos .08 .25
322 Patrik Hucko .08 .25
323 Petr Gregorek .08 .25
324 Filip Stefanka .08 .25
325 Vladimir Machulda .08 .25
326 Marek Zadina .08 .25
327 Richard Kral .08 .25
328 Jozef Dano .08 .25
329 Ladislav Lubina .08 .25
330 Tomas Chlubna .08 .25
331 Jan Peterek .08 .25
332 Petr Folta .08 .25
333 Josef Straub .08 .25
334 Roman Kadera .08 .25
335 Marian Kacir .08 .25
336 Robert Kantor .08 .25
337 Roman Kontsek .08 .25
338 Miloslav Horava .08 .25
339 Ladislav Kudrna .08 .25
340 Ivan Hlinka CO .30 .75
341 Slavomir Lener CO .20 .50
342 Roman Cechmanek 2.00 5.00
343 Milan Hnilicka 2.00 5.00
344 Martin Prusek 1.50 4.00
345 Frantisek Kaberle .20 .50
346 Jiri Slegr .20 .50
347 Jiri Vykoukal .20 .50
348 Jiri Veber .08 .25
349 Ladislav Benysek .20 .50
350 Frantisek Kucera .08 .25
351 Libor Prochazka .08 .25
352 Jaroslav Spacek .20 .50
353 Vlastimil Kroupa .08 .25
354 Robert Reichel .30 .75
355 Robert Lang .40 1.00
356 Pavel Patera .20 .50
357 Martin Prochazka .20 .50
358 Jiri Dopita .30 .75
359 Josef Beranek .20 .50
360 Viktor Ujcik .20 .50
361 David Vyborny .20 .50
362 Vladimir Vujtek .20 .50
363 Roman Simicek .20 .50
364 Jan Alinc .08 .25
365 Rostislav Vlach .08 .25
366 Ondrej Kratena .08 .25
367 Richard Zemlicka .20 .50
368 Dominik Hasek POY 4.00 10.00
369 Jiri Dopita .30 .75
370 Roman Cechmanek 2.00 5.00
371 Roman Horak .08 .25
372 Richard Zemlicka .20 .50
373 Antonin Stavjana .20 .50
374 Ondrej Kratena .08 .25
375 Richard Farda .08 .25
376 Frantisek Cernik .08 .25
377 Ludek Cajka .08 .25
378 Vlastimil Bubnik .08 .25
379 Josef Mikolas .08 .25
380 Stanislav Konopasek .08 .25

1997-98 Czech DS Extraliga

COMPLETE SET (120) 20.00 75.00
1 Roman Cechmanek 4.00 10.00
2 Milan Hnilicka 4.00 10.00
3 Josef Beranek .30 .75
4 Milan Nedoma .40 1.00
5 Lubomir Sekeras .40 1.00
6 Jiri Vykoukal .75 2.00
7 Jiri Dopita .75 2.00
8 Robert Kysela .40 1.00
9 Roman Meluzin .75 2.00
10 Roman Simicek .20 .50
11 Petr Ton .40 1.00
12 Viktor Ujcik .75 2.00
13 Vladimir Hudacek .20 .50
14 Petr Pavlas .08 .25
15 Ales Tomasek .08 .25
16 Pavel Blaha .08 .25
17 Pavel Nohel .08 .25
18 Tomas Klimt .20 .50
19 Radek Prochazka .08 .25
20 Rostislav Haas .08 .25
21 Karel Smid .20 .50
22 Milos Hrubes .08 .25
23 Martin Maskarinec .08 .25
24 Zbynek Marak .08 .25
25 Michal Tomek .08 .25
26 Juraj Jurik .08 .25
27 Oldrich Svoboda .40 1.00
28 Rudolf Suchanek .08 .25
29 Karel Soudek .08 .25
30 Radek Martinek .30 .75
31 Radek Toupal .08 .25
32 Lubos Rob .08 .25
33 Pavel Pycha .08 .25
34 Marek Novotny .08 .25
35 Michael Vyhlidal .08 .25
36 Petr Vlk .08 .25
37 Roman Mejzlik .08 .25
38 Jiri Cihlar .08 .25
39 Jaroslav Hub .08 .25
40 Marek Melenovsky .08 .25
41 Zdenek Orct .30 .75
42 Angel Nikolov .20 .50
43 Frantisek Prochazka .08 .25
44 Martin Stepanek .08 .25
45 Tomas Vlasak .08 .25
46 Martin Rousek .08 .25
47 Petr Hrbek .08 .25
48 Ivo Prorok .08 .25
49 Dusan Salficky .30 .75
50 Josef Reznicek .08 .25
51 Ivan Vlcek .08 .25
52 Robert Jindrich .20 .50
53 Pavel Geffert .08 .25
54 Tomas Jelinek .08 .25
55 David Pospisil .08 .25
56 Milan Volak .08 .25
57 Antonin Stavjana .20 .50
58 Radim Tesarik .08 .25
59 Alexej Jaskin .08 .25
60 Tomas Srsen .08 .25
61 Tomas Kapusta .08 .25
62 Radek Belohlav .20 .50
63 Ondrej Kratena .08 .25
64 Jan Tomajko .08 .25
65 Michal Bros .08 .25
66 Rostislav Vlach .08 .25
67 Libor Barta .08 .25
68 Pavel Augusta .08 .25
69 Tomas Blazek .08 .25
70 Milan Hejduk 4.00 10.00
71 Stanislav Prochazka .08 .25
72 Tomas Martinec .08 .25
73 Jaroslav Kudrna .20 .50
74 Ladislav Blazek .08 .25
75 Martin Bakula .08 .25
76 Vladimir Ruzicka .20 .50
77 Jiri Dolezal .08 .25
78 Jiri Poukar .08 .25
79 Tomas Kucharcik .08 .25
80 Frantisek Kucera .08 .25
81 Vaclav Burda .08 .25
82 Jaroslav Nedved .08 .25
83 Richard Zemlicka .20 .50
84 Jiri Zelenka .08 .25
85 Patrik Martinec .08 .25
86 Jan Hlavac .40 1.00
87 Patrik Stefan ERC .75 2.00
88 Jaroslav Bednar .40 1.00
89 Radek Toth .08 .25
90 Jan Krulis .08 .25
91 Pavel Skrbek .20 .50
92 Josef Zajic .08 .25
93 Zdenek Eichenmann .08 .25
94 Ladislav Svoboda .08 .25
95 Martin Prusek .75 2.00
96 Jiri Jonak .08 .25
97 Vitezslav Skuta .08 .25
98 Dimitri Jerofejev .08 .25
99 Roman Rysanek .08 .25
100 David Moravec .20 .50
101 Alexander Prokopjev .08 .25
102 Jaroslav Kames .30 .75
103 Pavel Kowalczyk .08 .25
104 Petr Kuchyna .08 .25
105 Ales Zima .08 .25
106 Pavel Janku .08 .25
107 Tomas Nemcicky .08 .25
108 Petr Cajanek .40 1.00
109 Branislav Janos .08 .25
110 Radovan Biegl .20 .50
111 Richard Kral .08 .25
112 Roman Kontsek .08 .25
113 Jozef Dano .08 .25
114 Ladislav Lubina .08 .25
115 Tomas Chlubna .08 .25
116 Jozef Straub .08 .25
117 Roman Kadera .08 .25
118 Marek Zadina .08 .25
119 Checklist .02 .10

1997-98 Czech DS Stickers

COMPLETE SET (283) 35.00 90.00
1 Roman Cechmanek .60 1.50
2 Jiri Veber .08 .25
3 Jiri Vykoukal .20 .50
4 Miloslav Horava .08 .25
5 Martin Stepanek .08 .25
6 Antonin Stavjana .20 .50
7 Bedrich Scerban .08 .25
8 Radek Belohlav .20 .50
9 League Logo .08 .25
10 Jiri Dopita .30 .75
11 David Vyborny .20 .50
12 Josef Beranek .20 .50
13 Vladimir Jerabek .08 .25
14 Viktor Ujcik .20 .50
15 Roman Meluzin .20 .50
16 Jiri Kucera .08 .25
17 Robert Lang .40 1.00
18 Roman Cechmanek .60 1.50
19 Antonin Stavjana .20 .50
20 Tomas Jakes .08 .25
21 Alexej Jaskin .08 .25
22 Jan Srdinko .08 .25
23 Jiri Veber .08 .25
24 Bedrich Scerban .08 .25
25 Ivan Padelek .08 .25
26 HC Petra Vsetin Logo .08 .25
27 HC Petra Vsetin Team Card .08 .25
28 HC Petra Vsetin Team Card .08 .25
29 Rostislav Vlach .08 .25
30 Josef Beranek .20 .60
31 Ondrej Kratena .08 .25
32 Jiri Dopita .30 .75
33 Tomas Kapusta .08 .25
34 Tomas Srsen .08 .25
35 Andrej Galkin .08 .25
36 Oto Hascak .08 .25
37 Zdenek Orct .30 .75
38 Martin Stepanek .08 .25
39 Normunds Sejejs .08 .25
40 Sergej Butko .08 .25
41 Roman Cech .08 .25
42 Radek Mrazek .08 .25
43 Angel Nikolov .20 .50
44 Robert Kysela .08 .25
45 HC Litvinov Logo .08 .25
46 HC Litvinov Team Card .08 .25
47 HC Litvinov Team Card .08 .25
48 Vladimir Jerabek .08 .25
49 Martin Rousek .08 .25
50 Jaroslav Buchal .08 .25
51 Petr Hrbek .08 .25
52 Tomas Vlasak .08 .25
53 Tomas Krasny .08 .25
54 Josef Straka .08 .25
55 Kamil Kastak .08 .25
56 Robert Schistad .08 .25
57 Radek Hamr .08 .25
58 Jaroslav Nedved .08 .25
59 Jan Bohacek .08 .25
60 Vaclav Burda .08 .25
61 Jiri Vykoukal .20 .50
62 Frantisek Ptacek .08 .25
63 Jan Benda .08 .25
64 HC Sparta Praha Logo .08 .25
65 HC Sparta Praha Team Card .08 .25
66 HC Sparta Praha Team Card .08 .25
67 Richard Zemlicka .20 .50
68 Roman Horak .20 .50
69 Patrik Martinec .08 .25
70 Martin Hostak .08 .25
71 David Vyborny .20 .50
72 Pavel Geffert .08 .25
73 Robert Lang .40 1.00
74 Andrej Potajcuk .08 .25
75 Oldrich Svoboda .40 1.00
76 Karel Soudek .08 .25
77 Kamil Toupal .08 .25
78 Milan Nedoma .08 .25
79 Radek Martinek .20 .50
80 Vladimir Antipin .08 .25

81 Rudolf Suchanek .08 .25
82 Pavel Pycha .08 .25
83 HC Ceske Budejovice Logo .08 .25
84 HC Ceske Budejovice Team .08 .25
85 HC Ceske Budejovice Team .08 .25
86 Radek Toupal .08 .25
87 Lubos Rob .08 .25
88 Milan Navratil .08 .25
89 Filip Turek .08 .25
90 Radek Belohlav .20 .50
91 Miroslav Barus .08 .25
92 Frantisek Sevcik .08 .25
93 Arpad Györi .08 .25
94 Jaroslav Kames .30 .75
95 Petr Kuchyna .08 .25
96 Pavel Kowalczyk .08 .25
97 Stanislav Medrik .08 .25
98 Jan Krajicek .08 .25
99 Radim Tesarik .08 .25
100 Jiri Marusak .08 .25
101 Pavel Janku .08 .25
102 HC ZPS Zlin Logo .08 .25
103 HC ZPS Zlin Team Card .08 .25
104 HC ZPS Zlin Team Card .08 .25
105 Ales Polcar .08 .25
106 David Bruk .08 .25
107 Zbynek Marak .08 .25
108 Ales Zima .08 .25
109 Roman Meluzin .20 .50
110 Miroslav Okal .08 .25
111 Petr Cajanek .40 1.00
112 Tomas Nemcicky .08 .25
113 Rudolf Pejchar .08 .25
114 Jaromir Latal .08 .25
115 Robert Kostka .08 .25
116 Jiri Hes .08 .25
117 Petr Kadlec .08 .25
118 Martin Maskarinec .08 .25
119 Miloslav Horava .08 .25
120 Roman Kadera .08 .25
121 HC Slavia Praha Logo .08 .25
122 HC Slavia Praha Team Card .08 .25
123 HC Slavia Praha Team Card .08 .25
124 Tomas Kucharcik .08 .25
125 Jiri Dolezal .08 .25
126 Jaroslav Bednar .40 1.00
127 Ladislav Slizek .08 .25
128 Tomas Kupka .08 .25
129 Viktor Ujcik .20 .50
130 Vladimir Ruzicka .20 .50
131 Ivo Prorok .08 .25
132 Milan Hnilicka .60 1.50
133 Jan Krulis .08 .25
134 Jan Dlouhy .08 .25
135 Libor Prochazka .08 .25
136 Tomas Kaberle .60 1.50
137 Marek Zidlicky .40 1.00
138 Petr Kasik .08 .25
139 Jiri Beranek .08 .25
140 HC Poldi Kladno Logo .08 .25
141 HC Poldi Kladno Team Card .08 .25
142 HC Poldi Kladno Team Card .08 .25
143 Josef Zajic .08 .25
144 Tomas Mikolasek .08 .25
145 Ladislav Svoboda .08 .25
146 Zdenek Eichenmann .08 .25
147 Vaclev Eiselt .08 .25
148 Petr Ton .08 .25
149 Jiri Burger .08 .25
150 David Cermak .08 .25
151 Ivo Capek .08 .25
152 Marian Morava .08 .25
153 Michael Vyhlidal .08 .25
154 Roman Kankovsky .08 .25
155 Zdenek Touzimsky .08 .25
156 Marek Posmyk .08 .25
157 Miroslav Javin .08 .25
158 Miroslav Bruna .08 .25
159 HC Dukla Jihlava Logo .08 .25
160 HC Dukla Jihlava Team Card .08 .25
161 HC Dukla Jihlava Team Card .08 .25
162 Jaroslav Hub .08 .25
163 Petr Vlk .08 .25
164 Jiri Poukar .08 .25
165 Petr Kankovsky .08 .25
166 Ladislav Prokupek .08 .25
167 Milan Antos .08 .25
168 Leos Pipa .08 .25
169 Michail Fadejev .08 .25
170 Ladislav Blazek .08 .25
171 Petr Pavlas .20 .50
172 Marek Cernosek .08 .25
173 Ladislav Benysek .20 .50
174 Jergus Baca .08 .25
175 Marek Tichy .08 .25
176 Roman Veber .08 .25
177 Martin Streit .08 .25
178 Hockey Olomouc Logo .08 .25
179 Hockey Olomouc Team Card .08 .25
180 Hockey Olomouc Team Card .08 .25
181 Michal Bros .08 .25
182 Radek Svoboda .08 .25
183 Pavel Nohel .08 .25
184 Radek Prochazka .08 .25
185 Jan Tomajko .08 .25
186 Michal Slavik .08 .25
187 Radek Sip .08 .25
188 Filip Dvorak .08 .25
189 Martin Prusek .60 1.50
190 Jiri Jonak .08 .25
191 Pavel Kumstat .08 .25
192 Vitezslav Skuta .08 .25
193 Dmitri Jerofejev .08 .25
194 Rene Sevecek .08 .25
195 Ales Tomasek .08 .25
196 Roman Simicek .20 .50
197 HC Vitkovice Logo .08 .25
198 HC Vitkovice Team Card .08 .25
199 HC Vitkovice Team Card .08 .25
200 Alexander Prokopjev .08 .25
201 Jan Peterek .08 .25
202 David Moravec .20 .50
203 Tomas Chlubna .08 .25
204 Libor Polasek .08 .25
205 Ales Kratoska .08 .25
206 Roman Rysanek .08 .25
207 Martin Smetak .08 .25
208 Martin Altrichter .08 .25
209 Karel Smid .20 .50
210 Josef Reznicek .08 .25
211 Jaroslav Spacek .20 .50
212 Ivan Vlcek .08 .25
213 Jiri Hanzlik .08 .25
214 Robert Jindrich .20 .50
215 Milan Volak .08 .25
216 HC ZKZ Plzen Logo .08 .25
217 HC ZKZ Plzen Team Card .08 .25
218 HC ZKZ Plzen Team Card .08 .25
219 Jiri Kucera .08 .25
220 Tomas Klimt .20 .50
221 Tomas Jelinek .08 .25
222 Michal Straka .08 .25
223 Miroslav Mach .08 .25
224 Pavel Vostrak .08 .25
225 Petr Korinek .08 .25
226 Radek Kampf .08 .25
227 Radovan Biegl .20 .50
228 Jiri Kuntos .08 .25
229 Lubomir Sekeras .30 .75
230 Petr Jancarik .08 .25
231 Stanislav Pavelec .08 .25
232 Ondrej Zetek .08 .25
233 Patrik Hucko .08 .25
234 Vladimir Machulda .08 .25
235 HC Zelezarny Trinec Logo .08 .25
236 HC Zelezarny Trinec Team .08 .25
237 HC Zelezarny Trinec Team .08 .25
238 Jozef Dano .08 .25
239 Roman Blazek .08 .25
240 Marek Zadina .08 .25
241 Richard Kral .08 .25
242 Petr Folta .08 .25
243 Michal Piskor .08 .25
244 Josef Straub .08 .25
245 Petr Zajonc .08 .25
246 Dusan Salficky .30 .75
247 Pavel Augusta .08 .25
248 Tomas Pacal .08 .25
249 Jiri Malinsky .08 .25
250 Pavel Kriz .08 .25
251 Radomir Brazda .08 .25
252 Ales Pisa .08 .25
253 Ladislav Lubina .08 .25
254 HC IB Pardubice Logo .08 .25
255 HC IB Pardubice Team .08 .25
256 HC IB Pardubice Team .08 .25
257 Tomas Blazek .08 .25
258 Jiri Jantovsky .08 .25
259 Milan Hejduk 4.00 10.00
260 Tomas Martinec .08 .25
261 David Pospisil .08 .25
262 Stanislav Prochazka .08 .25
263 Milan Prochazka .08 .25
264 Milan Kastner .08 .25
265 Rostislav Haas .08 .25
266 Denis Tsygurov .08 .25
267 Martin Bakula .08 .25
268 David Galvas .08 .25
269 Petr Tejkl .08 .25
270 Radek Mesicek .08 .25
271 Milos Hrubes .08 .25
272 Eduard Gorbachev .08 .25
273 HC Slezan Opava Logo .08 .25
274 HC Slezan Opava Team .08 .25
275 HC Slezan Opava Team .08 .25
276 Petr Fabian .08 .25
277 Zdenek Pavelek .08 .25
278 Karel Horny .08 .25
279 Martin Filip .08 .25
280 Juraj Jurik .08 .25
281 Radim Radevic .08 .25
282 Jan Zurek .08 .25
283 Valerij Belov .08 .25

1998-99 Czech DS

COMPLETE SET (125) 75.00 150.00
1 Jiri Dopita 10.00 25.00
2 Pavel Patera 2.00 5.00
3 Martin Prochazka 2.00 5.00
4 Martin Rucinsky 2.00 5.00
5 Vladimir Vujtek 2.00 5.00
6 David Moravec 2.00 5.00
7 Libor Prochazka 2.00 5.00
8 Viktor Ujcik 2.00 5.00
9 Vladimir Ruzicka 2.00 5.00
10 Frantisek Kucera 2.00 5.00
11 David Vyborny 2.00 5.00
12 Rudolf Pejchar 4.00 10.00
13 Oldrich Svoboda 2.00 5.00
14 Marek Novotny 2.00 5.00
15 Zdenek Orct 2.00 5.00
16 Libor Barta 2.00 5.00
17 Dusan Salficky 2.00 5.00
18 Pavel Cagas 2.00 5.00
19 Ladislav Blazek 2.00 5.00
20 Roman Cechmanek 2.00 5.00
21 Milan Hnilicka 2.00 5.00
22 Martin Cinibulk 2.00 5.00
23 Martin Prusek 2.00 5.00
24 Jaroslav Kames 2.00 5.00
25 Radovan Biegl 2.00 5.00
26 Petr Pavlas .08 .25
27 Ondrej Steiner .08 .25
28 Pavel Janku .08 .25
29 Jaromir Kverka .08 .25
30 Martin Rousek .08 .25
31 Milan Nedoma .08 .25
32 Radek Martinek .20 .50
33 Rudolf Suchanek .08 .25
34 Radek Toupal .15 .40
35 Filip Turek .08 .25
36 Miroslav Barus .08 .25
37 Miroslav Duben .08 .25
38 Petr Vlk .08 .25
39 Marek Melenovsky .08 .25
40 Jiri Cihlar .08 .25
41 Roman Mejzlik .08 .25
42 Ales Polcar .08 .25
43 Angel Nikolov .20 .50
44 Martin Stepanek .08 .25
45 Petr Hrbek .08 .25
46 Ivo Prorok .08 .25
47 Vladimir Petrovka .08 .25
48 Robert Kysela .08 .25
49 Josef Straka .08 .25
50 Ales Pisa .08 .25
51 Pavel Kriz .08 .25
52 Tomas Blazek .08 .25
53 Tomas Martinec .08 .25
54 Jiri Jantovsky .08 .25
55 Stanislav Prochazka .08 .25
56 Jaroslav Kudrna .08 .25
57 Josef Reznicek .08 .25
58 Pavel Geffert .08 .25
59 Petr Korinek .15 .40
60 Pavel Vostrak .08 .25
61 Michal Straka .08 .25
62 David Pospisil .08 .25
63 Milan Volak .08 .25
64 Milan Navratil .08 .25
65 Vitezslav Skuta .08 .25
66 Michael Vyhlidal .08 .25
67 Petr Kuchyna .08 .25
68 Drahomir Kadlec .08 .25
69 Petr Kadlec .08 .25
70 Martin Bakula .08 .25
71 Andrej Jakovenko .08 .25
72 Marian Kacir .20 .50
73 Vladimir Machulda .08 .25
74 Michal Sup .08 .25
75 Jiri Dolezal .15 .40
76 Tomas Kucharcik .08 .25
77 Jiri Veber .08 .25
78 Jan Srdinko .08 .25
79 Radim Tesarik .08 .25
80 Ondrej Kratena .08 .25
81 Michal Bros .08 .25
82 Jan Tomajko .08 .25
83 Tomas Srsen .08 .25
84 Zbynek Marak .08 .25
85 Radek Belohlav .15 .40
86 Roman Stantien .08 .25
87 Alexej Jaskin .08 .25
88 Vaclav Burda .08 .25
89 Ladislav Benysek .20 .50
90 Frantisek Ptacek .08 .25
91 Roman Horak .08 .25
92 Richard Zemlicka .20 .50
93 Jan Hlavac .40 1.00
94 Jiri Zelenka .08 .25
95 Patrik Martinec .08 .25
96 Jaroslav Bednar .40 1.00
97 Marek Zidlicky .40 1.00
98 Ladislav Svoboda .08 .25
99 Vaclav Eiselt .08 .25
100 Zdenek Eichenmann .08 .25
101 Jiri Burger .08 .25
102 Ales Tomasek .08 .25
103 Tomas Jelinek .08 .25
104 Rene Sevecek .08 .25
105 Pavel Kowalczyk .08 .25
106 Alexander Cherbajev .08 .25
107 Martin Kotasek .08 .25
108 Ales Kratoska .08 .25
109 Martin Hamrlik .08 .25
110 Roman Meluzin .08 .25
111 Petr Cajanek .40 1.00
112 Tomas Nemcicky .15 .40
113 Josef Straub .08 .25
114 Miroslav Okal .08 .25
115 Lubomir Sekeras .30 .75
116 Jiri Kuntos .08 .25
117 Stanislav Pavelec .08 .25
118 Richard Kral .08 .25
119 Ladislav Lubina .08 .25
120 Roman Kadera .08 .25
121 Jozef Dano .08 .25
122 Tomas Chlubna .08 .25
123 Ales Zima .08 .25
124 Branislav Janos .08 .25
125 Checklist .02 .10

1998-99 Czech DS Stickers

COMPLETE SET 30.00 60.00
1 HC Petra Vsetin .08 .25
2 HC Petra Vsetin .08 .25
3 HC Petra Vsetin .08 .25
4 HC Petra Vsetin .08 .25
5 HC Petra Vsetin .08 .25
6 HC Petra Vsetin .08 .25
7 League Logo .08 .25
8 Roman Cechmanek .40 1.00
10 Antonin Stavjana .15 .40
11 Milan Nedoma .08 .25
12 Jiri Vykoukal .20 .50
14 Martin Stepanek .08 .25
15 Vitezslav Skuta .08 .25
16 Jiri Zelenka .08 .25
17 Robert Lang .40 1.00
18 Ondrej Kratena .08 .25
19 Viktor Ujcik .15 .40
24 Team Logo .02 .10
25 Team Photo .08 .25
26 Team Photo .08 .25
27 Vladimir Hudacek .20 .50
28 Robert Horyna .08 .25
29 Petr Pavlas .08 .25
30 Ales Tomasek .08 .25
31 Pavel Blaha .08 .25
32 Jiri Polak .08 .25
33 Martin Richter .08 .25
34 Marek Cernosek .08 .25
35 Pavel Nohel .08 .25
36 Michal Cerny .08 .25
37 Tomas Klimt .20 .50
38 Ondrej Steiner .08 .25
39 Zbynek Kukacka .08 .25
40 Martin Streit .08 .25
41 Radek Prochazka .08 .25
42 Radek Svoboda .08 .25
43 Jan Lipiansky .08 .25
44 Team Logo .02 .10
45 Team Photo .08 .25
46 Team Photo .08 .25
47 Rostislav Haas .08 .25
48 Pavel Nestak .08 .25
49 Martin Maskarinec .08 .25
50 David Galvas .08 .25
51 Milos Hrubes .08 .25
52 Karel Smid .20 .50
53 Tomas Kramny .08 .25
54 Pavel Marecek .08 .25
55 Zbynek Marak .08 .25
56 Michal Tomek .08 .25
57 Juraj Jurik .08 .25
58 Michal Piskor .08 .25
59 Karel Horny .08 .25
60 Pavel Sebesta .08 .25
61 Martin Sychra .08 .25
62 Zdenek Pavelek .08 .25
63 Milan Kubis .08 .25
64 Team Logo .02 .10
65 Team Photo .08 .25
66 Team Photo .08 .25
67 Oldrich Svoboda .20 .50
68 Rudolf Suchanek .08 .25
69 Karel Soudek .08 .25
70 Milan Nedoma .08 .25
71 Radek Martinek .20 .50
72 Jan Bohacek .08 .25
73 Kamil Toupal .08 .25
74 Radek Toupal .08 .25
75 Lubos Rob .08 .25
76 Pavel Pycha .08 .25
77 Filip Turek .08 .25
78 David Bruk .08 .25
79 Ondrej Vosta .08 .25
80 Arpad Györi .08 .25
81 Miroslav Barus .08 .25
82 Petr Sailer .08 .25
83 Petr Sachl .08 .25
84 Team Logo .02 .10
85 Team Photo .08 .25
86 Team Photo .08 .25
87 Zdenek Orct .30 .75
88 Richard Hrazdira .08 .25
89 Frantisek Prochazka .08 .25
90 Angel Nikolov .20 .50
91 Martin Stepanek .08 .25
92 Roman Cech .08 .25
93 Radek Mrazek .08 .25
94 Robert Kysela .08 .25
95 Tomas Vlasak .08 .25
96 Martin Rousek .08 .25
97 Petr Hrbek .08 .25
98 Vladimir Petrovka .08 .25
99 Ivo Prorok .08 .25
100 Denis Afinogenov .20 .50
101 Rail Muftijev .08 .25
102 Dmitrij Denisov .08 .25
103 Kamil Piros .40 1.00
104 Team Logo .02 .10
105 Team Photo .08 .25
106 Team Photo .08 .25
107 Marek Novotny .08 .25
108 Lukas Sablik .08 .25
109 Michael Vyhlidal .08 .25
110 Miroslav Javin .08 .25
111 Martin Tupa .08 .25
112 Marian Morava .08 .25
113 Tomas Jakes .08 .25
114 Miroslav Duben .08 .25
115 Petr Vlk .08 .25
116 Roman Mejzlik .08 .25
117 Jiri Cihlar .08 .25
118 Jaroslav Hub .08 .25
119 Leos Pipa .08 .25
120 Ladislav Prokupek .08 .25
121 Marek Melenovsky .08 .25
122 Milan Antos .08 .25
123 Miroslav Stavjana .08 .25
124 Team Logo .02 .10
125 Team Photo .08 .25
126 Team Photo .08 .25
127 Libor Barta .08 .25
128 Adam Svoboda .30 .75
129 Michal Sykora .15 .40
130 Pavel Augusta .08 .25
131 Tomas Pacal .08 .25
132 Ales Pisa .08 .25
133 Petr Mudroch .08 .25
134 Alexander Cypljakov .08 .25
135 Jiri Malinsky .08 .25
136 Milan Hejduk 4.00 10.00
137 Tomas Blazek .08 .25
138 Jaroslav Kudrna .08 .25
139 Tomas Maskarinec .08 .25
140 Stanislav Prochazka .08 .25
141 Jiri Jantovsky .08 .25
142 Pavel Kabrt .08 .25
143 Martin Koudelka .08 .25
144 Team Logo .02 .10
145 Team Photo .08 .25
146 Team Photo .08 .25
147 Dusan Salficky .30 .75
148 Michal Marik .08 .25
149 Josef Reznicek .08 .25
150 Ivan Vlcek .08 .25
151 Robert Jindrich .20 .50
152 Martin Cech .08 .25
153 Jiri Hanzlik .08 .25
154 Pavel Srek .08 .25
155 Tomas Jelinek .08 .25
156 Pavel Geffert .08 .25
157 David Pospisil .08 .25
158 Martin Filip .08 .25
159 Milan Volak .08 .25
160 Michal Straka .08 .25
161 Milan Navratil .08 .25
162 Mojmir Musil .08 .25
163 Pavel Vostrak .08 .25
164 Team Logo .02 .10
165 Team Photo .08 .25
166 Team Photo .08 .25
167 Roman Cechmanek .40 1.00
168 Antonin Stavjana .15 .40
169 Jan Srdinko .08 .25
170 Radim Tesarik .08 .25
171 Alexej Jaskin .08 .25
172 Michal Divisek .08 .25
173 Pavel Zubicek .08 .25
174 Rostislav Vlach .08 .25
175 Jiri Dopita .30 .75
176 Tomas Srsen .08 .25
177 Radek Belohlav .15 .40
178 Tomas Kapusta .08 .25
179 Ondrej Kratena .08 .25
180 Michal Bros .08 .25
181 Jan Tomajko .08 .25
182 Andrej Galkin .08 .25
183 Josef Beranek .20 .50
184 Team Logo .02 .10
185 Team Photo .08 .25
186 Team Photo .08 .25
187 Ladislav Blazek .20 .50
188 Martin Altrichter .08 .25
189 Robert Kostka .08 .25
190 Andrej Jakovenko .08 .25
191 Pavel Kolarik .20 .50
192 Martin Bakula .08 .25
193 Petr Kadlec .08 .25
194 Jan Hejda .08 .25
195 Vladimir Ruzicka .20 .50
196 Viktor Ujcik .15 .40
197 Jiri Dolezal .15 .40
198 Jiri Poukar .08 .25
199 Tomas Kucharcik .08 .25
200 Michal Sup .08 .25
201 Jiri Hlinka .08 .25
202 Tomas Kupka .08 .25
203 Radek Matejovsky .08 .25
204 Team Logo .02 .10
205 Team Photo .08 .25
206 Team Photo .08 .25
207 Milan Hnilicka .75 2.00
208 Martin Cinibulk .08 .25
209 Jiri Vykoukal .20 .50
210 Vaclav Burda .08 .25
211 Frantisek Kucera .08 .25
212 Jaroslav Nedved .08 .25
213 Frantisek Ptacek .08 .25
214 Richard Zemlicka .20 .50
215 Jiri Zelenka .08 .25
216 Patrik Martinec .08 .25
217 Jaroslav Bednar .40 1.00
218 Jaromir Kverka .08 .25
219 Jan Hlavac .40 1.00
220 Miroslav Hlinka .08 .25
221 Jaroslav Hlinka .08 .25
222 Patrik Stefan .75 2.00
223 Petr Nedved .40 1.00
224 Team Logo .02 .10
225 Team Photo .08 .25
226 Team Photo .08 .25
227 Radek Toth .08 .25
228 Martin Bilek .20 .50
229 Jan Krulis .08 .25
230 Marek Zidlicky .40 1.00
231 Tomas Kaberle .40 1.00
232 Pavel Skrbek .20 .50
233 Jan Penk .08 .25
234 Jan Dlouhy .08 .25
235 Josef Zajic .08 .25
236 Zdenek Eichenmann .08 .25
237 Petr Ton .08 .25
238 Jiri Beranek .08 .25
239 Tomas Mikolasek .08 .25
240 Ladislav Svoboda .08 .25
241 Vaclav Eiselt .08 .25
242 Jiri Burger .08 .25
243 Petr Tenkrat .40 1.00
244 Team Logo .02 .10
245 Team Photo .08 .25
246 Team Photo .08 .25
247 Martin Prusek .75 2.00
248 Zdenek Dobes .08 .25
249 Vitezslav Skuta .08 .25
250 Pavel Kumstat .08 .25
251 Jiri Jonak .08 .25
252 Rene Sevecek .08 .25
253 Dmitrij Jerofejev .08 .25
254 Petr Jurecka .08 .25
255 Roman Simicek .20 .50
256 Roman Rysanek .08 .25
257 David Moravec .20 .50
258 Alexander Prokopjev .08 .25
259 Libor Polasek .08 .25
260 Martin Kotasek .08 .25
261 Alexander Cherbajev .08 .25
262 Libor Pavlis .08 .25
263 Petr Zajonc .08 .25
264 Team Logo .02 .10
265 Team Photo .08 .25
266 Team Photo .08 .25
267 Radovan Biegl .20 .50
268 Lubomir Sekeras .30 .75
269 Jiri Kuntos .08 .25
270 Stanislav Pavelec .08 .25
271 Patrik Hucko .08 .25
272 Petr Jancarik .08 .25
273 Robert Kantor .08 .25
274 Richard Kral .08 .25
275 Ladislav Lubina .08 .25
276 Tomas Chlubna .08 .25
277 Roman Kadera .08 .25
278 Josef Straub .08 .25
279 Jozef Dano .08 .25
280 Roman Kontsek .08 .25
281 Marek Zadina .08 .25
282 Petr Folta .08 .25
283 Jan Peterek .08 .25
284 Team Logo .02 .10
285 Team Photo .08 .25
286 Team Photo .08 .25
287 Jaroslav Kames .30 .75
288 Pavel Kowalczyk .08 .25
289 Jan Krajicek .08 .25
290 Petr Kuchyna .08 .25
291 Martin Hamrlik .08 .25
292 Pavel Rajnoha .08 .25
293 Jiri Marusak .08 .25
294 Roman Meluzin .20 .50
295 Pavel Janku .08 .25
296 Ales Zima .08 .25
297 Miroslav Okal .08 .25
298 Petr Cajanek .40 1.00
299 Tomas Nemcicky .08 .25
300 Branislav Janos .08 .25
301 Ales Polcar .08 .25
302 Zdenek Sedlak .08 .25
303 Petr Leska .08 .25

1998-99 Czech OFS

COMPLETE SET (490) 60.00 150.00
1 Ondrej Weissmann .08 .25
2 Zdenek Orct .20 .50
3 Angel Nikolov .20 .50
4 Radek Mrazek .08 .25
5 Martin Stepanek .08 .25
6 Sergej Butko .08 .25
7 Oleg Romanov .08 .25
8 Marian Menhart .20 .50
9 Vladimir Petrovka .08 .25
10 Ivo Prorok .08 .25
11 Jindrich Kotrla .08 .25
12 Josef Straka .08 .25
13 Vadim Bekbulatov .08 .25
14 Daniel Branda .08 .25
15 Vojtech Kubincak .08 .25
16 Michal Travnicek .20 .50
17 Zdenek Venera .08 .25
18 Jaroslav Kames .30 .75
19 Pavel Augusta .08 .25
20 Patrik Hucko .08 .25
21 Martin Hamrlik .08 .25
22 Jiri Marusak .08 .25
23 Pavel Mojzis .08 .25
24 Tomas Zizka .08 .25
25 Roman Meluzin .08 .25
26 Michal Tomek .08 .25
27 Josef Straub .08 .25
28 Tomas Nemcicky .15 .40
29 Petr Cajanek .40 1.00
30 Miroslav Okal .08 .25
31 Petr Leska .08 .25
32 Petr Vala .08 .25
33 Radim Rulik .08 .25
34 Dusan Salficky .30 .75
35 Josef Reznicek .08 .25
36 Robert Jindrich .20 .50
37 Jiri Hanzlik .08 .25
38 Ondrej Kriz .08 .25
39 Vladimir Zajic .08 .25
40 Pavel Geffert .08 .25
41 David Pospisil .08 .25
42 Milan Antos .08 .25
43 Petr Korinek .15 .40
44 Michal Straka .08 .25
45 Milan Volak .08 .25
46 Pavel Vostrak .08 .25
47 Milan Navratil .08 .25
48 Martin Spanhel .40 1.00
49 Josef Augusta .08 .25
50 Jaroslav Suchan .08 .25
51 Martin Tupa .08 .25
52 Marian Morava .08 .25
53 Michal Divisek .08 .25
54 Petr Svoboda .15 .40
55 Zdenek Fuksa .08 .25
56 Petr Vlk .08 .25
57 Jiri Cihlar .08 .25
58 Leos Pipa .08 .25
59 Marek Melenovsky .08 .25
60 Miroslav Bruna .08 .25
61 Petr Mokrejs .08 .25
62 Vaclav Adamec .08 .25
63 Richard Cachnin .08 .25
64 Jan Kloboucek .08 .25
65 Stanislav Nevesely .08 .25
66 Radek Masny .08 .25
67 Jan Krajicek .08 .25
68 Ales Tomasek .08 .25
69 Vladimir Holik .08 .25
70 Tomas Jelinek .08 .25
71 Pavel Nohel .08 .25
72 Jaroslav Hub .08 .25
73 Robert Kucera .08 .25
74 Andrej Galkin .08 .25
75 Pavel Selingr .08 .25
76 Pavel Bacho .08 .25
77 Jiri Zurek .08 .25
78 Pavel Zdrahal .08 .25
79 Bogdan Savenko .08 .25
80 Zdenek Sedlak .08 .25
81 Karel Trachta .08 .25
82 Rudolf Pejchar .20 .50
83 Petr Pavlas .08 .25
84 Pavel Blaha .08 .25
85 Martin Richter .08 .25
86 Jan Snopek .15 .40
87 Martin Filip .08 .25
88 Jaromir Kverka .08 .25
89 Pavel Janku .08 .25
90 Martin Rousek .08 .25
91 Ondrej Steiner .08 .25
92 Pavel Metlicka .08 .25
93 Streit Martin .08 .25
94 Ladislav Prokupek .08 .25
95 Richard Richter .08 .25
96 Martin Maskarinec .08 .25
97 Zdislav Tabara .08 .25
98 Miroslav Venkrbec .08 .25
99 Roman Cechmanek .40 1.00
100 Jiri Veber .08 .25
101 Radim Tesarik .08 .25
102 Jan Srdinko .08 .25
103 Alexej Jaskin .08 .25
104 Pavel Zubicek .08 .25
105 Jiri Dopita .30 .75
106 Martin Prochazka .20 .50
107 Pavel Patera .20 .50
108 Radek Belohlav .15 .40
109 Ondrej Kratena .08 .25
110 Michal Bros .08 .25
111 Jan Tomajko .08 .25
112 Roman Stantien .08 .25
113 Ladislav Svozil .08 .25
114 Jiri Trvaj .08 .25
115 Rene Sevecek .08 .25
116 Vitezslav Skuta .08 .25
117 Pavel Kowalczyk .08 .25
118 Radek Philipp .08 .25
119 Vladimir Vujtek .20 .50
120 Alexander Cherbajev .08 .25
121 Libor Pavlis .08 .25
122 Libor Polasek .08 .25
123 Martin Kotasek .08 .25
124 Zdenek Pavelek .08 .25
125 Martin Lamich .08 .25
126 Igor Varickij .08 .25
127 Petr Hubacek .08 .25
128 Zbynek Irgl .08 .25
129 Julius Supler .08 .25
130 Milan Hnilicka .40 1.00
131 Frantisek Ptacek .08 .25
132 Ladislav Benysek .20 .50
133 Richard Adam .08 .25
134 Frantisek Kucera .08 .25
135 Pavel Srek .08 .25
136 Jiri Zelenka .08 .25
137 David Vyborny .20 .50
138 Patrik Martinec .08 .25
139 Jaroslav Bednar .40 1.00
140 Jan Hlavac .40 1.00
141 Miroslav Hlinka .08 .25
142 Jaroslav Hlinka .08 .25
143 Martin Chabada .08 .25
144 Vaclav Novak .08 .25
145 Michal Chalupa .08 .25
146 Adam Svoboda .30 .75
147 Jiri Malinsky .08 .25
148 Ales Pisa .08 .25
149 Tomas Pacal .08 .25
150 Pavel Kriz .08 .25
151 Petr Jancarik .08 .25
152 Petr Mudroch .08 .25
153 Tomas Blazek .08 .25
154 Jiri Jantovsky .08 .25
155 Stanislav Prochazka .08 .25
156 Tomas Martinec .08 .25
157 Pavel Kabrt .08 .25
158 Jaroslav Kudrna .20 .50
159 Karel Plasek .08 .25
160 Michal Mikeska .08 .25
161 Zdenek Sindler .08 .25
162 Martin Cinibulk .20 .50
163 Marek Zidlicky .40 1.00
164 Jan Dlouhy .08 .25
165 Pavel Taborsky .08 .25
166 Michal Madl .08 .25
167 Jiri Jelinek .08 .25
168 Tomas Mikolasek .08 .25
169 Ladislav Svoboda .08 .25
170 Jiri Burger .08 .25
171 Petr Tenkrat .40 1.00
172 Tomas Kupka .08 .25
173 Marke Vorel .08 .25
174 Michal Kanka .08 .25
175 Tomas Horna .08 .25
176 Zdenek Mraz .08 .25
177 Kamil Konecny .08 .25
178 Radovan Biegl .20 .50
179 Stanislav Pavelec .08 .25
180 Jiri Kuntos .08 .25
181 Petr Gregorek .08 .25
182 Miroslav Cihal .08 .25
183 Robert Prochazka .08 .25
184 Viktor Ujcik .20 .50
185 Ladislav Lubina .08 .25
186 Jan Peterek .08 .25
187 Petr Folta .08 .25
188 Ales Zima .08 .25
189 Roman Kadera .08 .25
190 Vaclav Pletka .20 .50
191 Patrik Moskal .08 .25
192 David Appel .08 .25
193 Jaroslav Parizek CO .08 .25
194 Michal Marik .08 .25
195 Rudolf Suchanek .08 .25
196 Milan Nedoma .08 .25
197 Kamil Toupal .08 .25
198 Roman Cech .08 .25
199 Radek Martinek .20 .50
200 Vladimir Sicak .08 .25
201 Radek Toupal .15 .40
202 Filip Turek .08 .25
203 Petr Sailer .08 .25
204 Martin Strba .08 .25
205 Miroslav Barus .08 .25
206 Vaclav Kral .08 .25
207 Milan Filipi .08 .25
208 Peter Bartos .08 .25
209 Richard Farda .08 .25
210 Roman Malek .08 .25
211 Robert Kostka .08 .25
212 Pavel Kolarik .20 .50
213 Martin Bakula .08 .25
214 Petr Kadlec .08 .25
215 Jan Novak .08 .25
216 Vladimir Ruzicka .20 .50
217 Jiri Dolezal .15 .40
218 Tomas Kucharcik .08 .25
219 Michal Sup .08 .25
220 Vladimir Machulda .08 .25
221 Petr Mika .30 .75
222 Tomas Divisek .30 .75
223 Jan Kopecky .08 .25
224 Jiri Polak .08 .25
225 Ivan Hlinka OLY .30 .75
226 Slavomir Lener OLY .15 .40
227 Dominik Hasek OLY 4.00 10.00
228 Roman Cechmanek OLY .40 1.00
229 Milan Hnilicka OLY .40 1.00
230 Richard Smehlik OLY .15 .40
231 Petr Svoboda OLY .15 .40
232 Roman Hamrlik OLY .30 .75
233 Jiri Slegr OLY .15 .40
234 Frantisek Kucera OLY .08 .25
235 Libor Prochazka OLY .20 .50
236 Jaroslav Spacek OLY .20 .50
237 Robert Reichel OLY .40 1.00
238 Robert Lang OLY .40 1.00
239 Pavel Patera OLY .30 .75
240 Martin Prochazka OLY .20 .50
241 Jiri Dopita OLY .30 .75
242 Josef Beranek OLY .20 .50
243 David Moravec OLY .30 .75
244 Jan Caloun OLY .20 .50
245 Martin Rucinsky OLY .30 .75
246 Martin Straka OLY .40 1.00
247 Jaromir Jagr OLY 8.00 20.00
248 Vladimir Ruzicka OLY .20 .50
249 Milan Hejduk OLY 4.00 10.00
250 Ladislav Slizek .08 .25

Card	Low	High
251 Ladislav Blazek	.08	.25
252 Andrej Jakovenko	.08	.25
253 Jan Hejda	.08	.25
254 Marian Kacir	.20	.50
255 Robin Bacul	.08	.25
256 Jan Sochor	.08	.25
257 Petr Hrbek	.08	.25
258 Jan Sebor	.08	.25
259 Michal Slavik	.08	.25
260 Vladimir Jerabek	.08	.25
261 Marek Pinc	.08	.25
262 Vladimir Gyna	.08	.25
263 Martin Znojemsky	.08	.25
264 Robert Kysela	.08	.25
265 Petr Hrbek	.08	.25
266 Kamil Piros	.40	1.00
267 Viktor Hubl	.08	.25
268 Marian Kacir	.20	.50
269 Miloslav Horava	.08	.25
270 Michal Pinc	.08	.25
271 Zdenek Skorepa	.08	.25
272 Vaclav Sykora	.08	.25
273 Antonin Stavjana	.15	.40
274 Richard Hrazdira	.08	.25
275 Karel Rachunek	.40	1.00
276 David Brezik	.08	.25
277 Marek Zadina	.08	.25
278 Jaroslav Balastik	.08	.25
279 Martin Ambruz	.08	.25
280 Ondrej Vesely	.08	.25
281 Tomas Kapusta	.08	.25
282 Tomas Martinek	.08	.25
283 Ivan Rachunek	.20	.50
284 Karel Sefcik	.08	.25
285 Marek Sykora	.08	.25
286 Vladimir Hudacek	.20	.50
287 Ivan Vlcek	.08	.25
288 Martin Cech	.08	.25
289 Michal Vasicek	.08	.25
290 Michal Jelinek	.08	.25
291 Vladimir Bednar	.08	.25
292 Pavel Augusta	.08	.25
293 Ladislav Slizek	.08	.25
294 Karel Dvorak	.08	.25
295 Marek Novotny	.08	.25
296 Lukas Sablik	.08	.25
297 Daniel Zapotocny	.08	.25
298 Miroslav Duben	.08	.25
299 Ales Polcar	.08	.25
300 Roman Mejzlik	.08	.25
301 Radek Matejovsky	.08	.25
302 Daniel Hodek	.08	.25
303 Ales Padelek	.08	.25
304 Ivan Padelek	.08	.25
305 Pavel Rajnoha	.08	.25
306 Richard Adam	.08	.25
307 Vladimir Caldr	.08	.25
308 Jiri Dobrovolny	.08	.25
309 Lukas Novak	.08	.25
310 Ivo Novotny	.08	.25
311 Jan Smarda	.08	.25
312 Lubomir Oslizlo	.08	.25
313 Pavel Cagas	.20	.50
314 Petr Kuchyna	.08	.25
315 Drahomir Kadlec	.08	.25
316 Michael Vyhlidal	.08	.25
317 Miroslav Javin	.08	.25
318 Petr Suchanek	.08	.25
319 Vitezslav Skuta	.08	.25
320 Libor Polasek	.08	.25
321 Jiri Poukal	.08	.25
322 Michal Cech	.08	.25
323 Lukas Fiala	.08	.25
324 Milota Florian	.08	.25
325 Milan Kubis	.08	.25
326 Jiri Latal	.08	.25
327 Libor Pavlis	.08	.25
328 Ivan Puncochar	.08	.25
329 Rostislav Vlach	.08	.25
330 Tomas Zapletal	.08	.25
331 Josef Beranek	.20	.50
332 Robert Hamrla	.08	.25
333 Marek Cernosek	.08	.25
334 Normunds Sejejs	.08	.25
335 Tomas Klimt	.08	.25
336 Radek Prochazka	.08	.25
337 Radek Svoboda	.08	.25
338 Michal Horak	.08	.25
339 Jakub Kraus	.08	.25
340 Ivo Pesat	.08	.25
341 Tomas Jakes	.08	.25
342 Michal Safarik	.08	.25
343 Tomas Srsen	.08	.25
344 Zbynek Marak	.08	.25
345 Tomas Demel	.08	.25
346 Ondrej Kavulic	.08	.25
347 Petr Suchy	.08	.25
348 Libor Zabransky	.15	.40
349 Vladimir Vujtek	.20	.50
350 Martin Prusek	.40	1.00
351 Lukas Galvas	.08	.25
352 Petr Jurecka	.08	.25
353 Vadim Brezgunov	.08	.25
354 Lukas Zatopek	.08	.25
355 David Moravec	.20	.50
356 Ludek Krayzel	.08	.25
357 Ales Kratoska	.08	.25
358 Ales Tomasek	.08	.25
359 Milos Holan	.15	.40
360 Roman Kelner	.08	.25
361 Frantisek Vyborny	.08	.25
362 Petr Prikryl	.08	.25
363 Zdenek Touzimsky	.08	.25
364 Vaclav Burda	.08	.25
365 Vaclav Benak	.08	.25
366 Michal Dobron	.08	.25
367 Richard Zemlicka	.20	.50
368 Roman Horak	.08	.25
369 Michal Sivek	.40	1.00
370 Jaroslav Kalla	.08	.25
371 Pavel Richter	.08	.25
372 Jaroslav Roubik	.08	.25
373 Michal Sykora	.15	.40
374 Milos Riha	.08	.25
375 Libor Barta	.08	.25
376 Alexander Cypljakov	.08	.25
377 Robert Pospisil	.08	.25
378 Petr Caslava	.08	.25
379 Martin Koudelka	.08	.25
380 Patrik Rozsival	.08	.25
381 Michal Tvrdik	.08	.25
382 Tomas Vak	.08	.25
383 Alois Hadamczik CO	.08	.25
384 Vlastimil Lakosil	.08	.25
385 Lubomir Sekeras	.20	.50
386 Libor Prochazka	.20	.50
387 Robert Kantor	.08	.25
388 Mario Cartelli	.08	.25
389 Richard Kral	.08	.25
390 Jozef Dano	.08	.25
391 Branislav Janos	.08	.25
392 Tomas Chlubna	.08	.25
393 Martin Havlat	10.00	25.00
394 Jaroslav Jagr	.20	.50
395 Lubomir Bauer	.08	.25
396 Martin Bilek	.20	.50
397 Lubos Horcicka	.08	.25
398 Jiri Krocak	.08	.25
399 Martin Taborsky	.08	.25
400 Zdenek Eichenmann	.08	.25
401 Vaclav Eiselt	.08	.25
402 Premysl Sedlak	.08	.25
403 Jiri Holsan	.08	.25
404 Jiri Kames	.08	.25
405 Jiri Habacek	.08	.25
406 Stanislav Lapacek	.08	.25
407 Lukas Poznik	.08	.25
408 Otakar Vejvoda	.15	.40
409 Jaroslav Liska	.08	.25
410 Oldrich Svoboda	.20	.50
411 Lukas Zib	.08	.25
412 Michal Klimes	.08	.25
413 Kamil Brabenec	.08	.25
414 Ales Kotalik	1.00	2.50
415 Jiri Broz	.08	.25
416 Zdenek Kutlak	.20	.50
417 Vaclav Nedorost	.40	1.00
418 Lubos Rob	.10	.25
419 Martin Prusek	.40	1.00
420 Frantisek Kaberle	.20	.50
421 Jiri Vykoukal	.20	.50
422 Jiri Veber	.08	.25
423 Ladislav Benysek	.20	.50
424 Martin Stepanek	.08	.25
425 Jan Srdinko	.08	.25
426 Radek Belohlav	.15	.40
427 David Vyborny	.20	.50
428 Viktor Ujcik	.20	.50
429 Roman Meluzin	.08	.25
430 Vladimir Vujtek	.20	.50
431 Ondrej Kratena	.08	.25
432 Michal Bros	.08	.25
433 Marian Kacir	.20	.50
434 Jan Hlavac	.40	1.00
435 Richard Kral	.08	.25
436 Roman Kadera	.08	.25
437 Ivan Hlinka	.40	1.00
438 Roman Cechmanek	.40	1.00
439 Milan Hnilicka	.40	1.00
440 Libor Prochazka	.20	.50
441 Pavel Patera	.20	.50
442 Martin Prochazka	.20	.50
443 Josef Augusta	.08	.25
444 Pavel Richter	.08	.25
445 Marek Sykora	.08	.25
446 Milan Hnilicka	.40	1.00
447 Dusan Salficky	.30	.75
448 Frantisek Kucera	.08	.25
449 Ladislav Benysek	.20	.50
450 Josef Reznicek	.08	.25
451 Martin Richter	.08	.25
452 Ales Pisa	.08	.25
453 Ivan Vlcek	.08	.25
454 Martin Stepanek	.08	.25
455 Petr Jancarik	.08	.25
456 David Vyborny	.20	.50
457 Jan Hlavac	.40	1.00
458 Jiri Zelenka	.08	.25
459 Petr Tenkrat	.40	1.00
460 Vaclav Kral	.08	.25
461 David Pospisil	.08	.25
462 Vaclav Eiselt	.08	.25
463 Tomas Kucharcik	.08	.25
464 Petr Korinek	.15	.40
465 Pavel Janku	.08	.25
466 Radek Toupal	.15	.40
467 Ivo Prorok	.08	.25
468 Zdislav Tabara	.08	.25
469 Jaroslav Jagr	.20	.50
470 Roman Cechmanek	.40	1.00
471 Libor Prochazka	.20	.50
472 Jiri Veber	.08	.25
473 Milos Holan	.15	.40
474 Jan Srdinko	.08	.25
475 Robert Kantor	.08	.25
476 Ales Tomasek	.08	.25
477 Miroslav Duben	.08	.25
478 Jiri Dopita	.30	.75
479 Martin Prochazka	.20	.50
480 Pavel Patera	.20	.50
481 Radek Belohlav	.15	.40
482 David Moravec	.20	.50
483 Roman Meluzin	.08	.25
484 Jiri Poukar	.08	.25
485 Andrej Galkin	.08	.25
486 Ivo Padelek	.08	.25
487 Marek Zadina	.08	.25
488 Petr Cajanek	.40	1.00
489 Miroslav Javin	.08	.25
490 Ondrej Kratena	.08	.25
NNO Checklist	.02	.10
NNO Checklist	.02	.10
NNO Checklist	.02	.10
NNO Checklist	.02	.10
NNO Checklist	.02	.10
NNO Checklist	.02	.10
NNO Checklist	.02	.10
NNO Checklist	.02	.10

1998-99 Czech OFS Legends

Card	Low	High
COMPLETE SET (20)	12.00	30.00
1 Vaclav Nedomansky	.75	2.00
2 Miroslav Horava	.75	2.00
3 Peter Stastny	4.00	10.00
4 Jiri Sejba	.40	1.00
5 Ivan Hlinka	1.25	3.00
6 Vladimir Martinec	.40	1.00
7 Jaroslav Pouzar	.40	1.00
8 Jiri Holecek	.40	1.00
9 Ludek Cajka	.40	1.00
10 Ludek Bukac	.40	1.00
11 Milan Novy	.75	2.00
12 Jiri Kralik	.40	1.00
13 Jiri Hrdina	.40	1.00
14 Frantisek Cernik	.40	1.00
15 Frantisek Pospisil	.40	1.00
16 Jiri Lala	.40	1.00
17 Antonin Stavjana	.75	2.00
18 Jaromir Sindel	.75	2.00
19 Vincent Lukac	.40	1.00
20 Dusan Pasek	1.25	3.00

1998-99 Czech OFS Olympic Winners

Card	Low	High
COMPLETE SET (20)	30.00	75.00
1 Jiri Dopita	.75	2.00
2 Dominik Hasek	8.00	20.00
3 Jaromir Jagr	15.00	40.00
4 Frantisek Kucera	.75	2.00
5 Pavel Patera	.75	2.00
6 Robert Reichel	.75	2.00
7 Martin Rucinsky	.75	2.00
8 Vladimir Ruzicka	.75	2.00
9 Jiri Slegr	.75	2.00
10 Petr Svoboda	.75	2.00
11 David Moravec	.75	2.00
12 Richard Smehlik	.75	2.00
13 Jaroslav Spacek	.75	2.00
14 Martin Prochazka	.75	2.00
15 Roman Hamrlik	.75	2.00
16 Ivan Hlinka	.75	2.00
17 Roman Cechmanek	1.25	3.00
18 Josef Beranek	.75	2.00
19 Robert Lang	1.25	3.00
20 Martin Straka	1.25	3.00

1998 Czech Bonaparte

Card	Low	High
COMPLETE SET (33)	14.00	35.00
1A Martin Prochazka	.20	.50
1B Robert Reichel	.20	.50
1C Robert Lang	.20	.50
1D Milan Hejduk	1.50	4.00
2A Martin Rucinsky	.20	.50
2B Jaromir Jagr	2.00	5.00
2C Richard Smehlik	.20	.50
2D Dominik Hasek	1.25	3.00
3A Josef Beranek	.20	.50
3B Jaroslav Spacek	.20	.50
3C Jaromir Jagr	2.00	5.00
3D Jiri Slegr	.20	.50
4A Vladimir Ruzicka	.20	.50
4B Roman Cechmanek	.40	1.00
4C Jan Caloun	.20	.50
4D Milan Hnilicka	.75	2.00
5A Jiri Dopita	.30	.75
5B Frantisek Kucera	.20	.50
5C Jaromir Jagr	2.00	5.00
5D Petr Svoboda	.20	.50
6A Petr Svoboda	.20	.50
6B Ivan Hlinka	.20	.50
6C Slavomir Lener	.20	.50
6D Jaromir Jagr	2.00	5.00
7A Jiri Slegr	.20	.50
7B Martin Straka	.20	.50
7C Pavel Patera	.20	.50
7D David Moravec	.20	.50
8A Vladimir Ruzicka	.20	.50
8B Libor Prochazka	.20	.50
8C Roman Hamrlik	.20	.50
8D Dominik Hasek	1.25	3.00

1998 Czech Bonaparte Tall

COMPLETE SET ?

1998 Czech Pexeso

Card	Low	High
COMPLETE SET (28)	8.00	20.00
1 Martin Prochazka	.08	.25
2 Robert Reichel	.20	.50
3 Robert Lang	.20	.50
4 Milan Hejduk	1.50	4.00
5 Martin Rucinsky	.08	.25
6 Richard Smehlik	.08	.25
7 Dominik Hasek	1.25	3.00
8 Josef Beranek	.08	.25
9 Jaroslav Spacek	.08	.25
10 Jaromir Jagr	2.00	5.00
11 Roman Cechmanek	.40	1.00
12 Martin Rucinsky	.08	.25
13 Jiri Slegr	.08	.25
14 Jan Caloun	.08	.25
15 Milan Hnilicka	.75	2.00
16 Jiri Dopita	.20	.50
17 Jiri Kucera	.08	.25
18 Jaromir Jagr	2.00	5.00
19 Petr Svoboda	.08	.25
20 Ivan Hlinka	.08	.25
21 Slavomir Lener	.08	.25
22 Jiri Slegr	.08	.25
23 Martin Straka	.08	.25
24 Pavel Patera	.08	.25
25 David Moravec	.08	.25
26 Libor Prochazka	.08	.25
27 Roman Hamrlik	.08	.25
28 Dominik Hasek	1.25	3.00

1998 Czech Spaghetti

Card	Low	High
COMPLETE SET (12)	8.00	20.00
1 Jaromir Jagr	4.00	10.00
2 Dominik Hasek	2.00	5.00
3 Josef Beranek	.40	1.00
4 Roman Hamrlik	.40	1.00
5 Robert Lang	.60	1.50
6 Martin Straka	.60	1.50
7 Robert Reichel	.60	1.50
8 Martin Rucinsky	.60	1.50
9 Jiri Slegr	.40	1.00
10 Petr Svoboda	.40	1.00
11 Richard Smehlik	.40	1.00
12 Martin Prochazka	.40	1.00

1999-00 Czech DS

Card	Low	High
COMPLETE SET (196)	30.00	75.00
1 Richard Hrazdira	.20	.50
2 Vladimir Hudacek	.20	.50
3 Roman Hamrlik	.30	.75
4 Martin Hamrlik	.08	.25
5 Jiri Marusak	.08	.25
6 Tomas Zizka	.20	.50
7 Petr Cajanek	.30	.75
8 Miroslav Okal	.08	.25
9 Josef Straub	.08	.25
10 Petr Leska	.08	.25
11 Michal Tomek	.08	.25
12 Martin Kotasek	.08	.25
13 Ondrej Vesely	.08	.25
14 Petr Vala	.08	.25
15 Rudolf Pejchar	.08	.25
16 Zdenek Smid	.30	.75
17 Martin Richter	.08	.25
18 Petr Pavlas	.08	.25
19 Martin Maskarinec	.08	.25
20 Jan Snopek	.08	.25
21 Michal Divisek	.08	.25
22 Pavel Janku	.08	.25
23 Jaromir Kverka	.08	.25
24 Martin Rousek	.08	.25
25 Miroslav Barus	.08	.25
26 Martin Streit	.08	.25
27 Martin Filip	.08	.25
28 Radek Prochazka	.08	.25
29 Ivo Capek	.20	.50
30 Michal Marik	.08	.25
31 Milan Nedoma	.08	.25
32 Radek Martinek	.20	.50
33 Rudolf Suchanek	.20	.50
34 Roman Cech	.08	.25
35 Vaclav Kral	.08	.25
36 Filip Turek	.08	.25
37 Peter Bartos	.08	.25
38 Radek Toupal	.08	.25
39 Lubos Rob	.08	.25
40 Martin Strba	.08	.25
41 Petr Sailer	.08	.25
42 Kamil Brabenec	.08	.25
43 Pavel Cagas	.20	.50
44 Robert Horyna	.20	.50
45 Michael Vyhlidal	.08	.25
46 Miroslav Javin	.08	.25
47 Libor Pivko	.08	.25
48 Ales Tomasek	.08	.25
49 Roman Horak	.20	.50
50 Pavel Nohel	.08	.25
51 Ales Aima	.08	.25
52 Marek Melanovsky	.08	.25
53 Jaroslav Hub	.08	.25
54 Pavel Zdrahal	.08	.25
55 Bogdan Savenko	.08	.25
56 Robert Kantor	.08	.25
57 Zdenek Orct	.20	.50
58 Marek Pinc	.08	.25
59 Miloslav Horava	.08	.25
60 Angel Nikolov	.08	.25
61 Petr Kratky	.08	.25
62 Radek Mrazek	.08	.25
63 Robert Reichel	.20	.50
64 Robert Kysela	.08	.25
65 Ivo Prorok	.08	.25
66 Jan Alinc	.20	.50
67 Jindrich Kotrla	.08	.25
68 Zdenek Skorepa	.20	.50
69 Josef Straka	.08	.25
70 Michal Travnicek	.20	.50
71 Libor Barta	.08	.25
72 Adam Svoboda	.30	.75
73 Ales Pisa	.08	.25
74 Tomas Pacal	.08	.25
75 Jiri Malinsky	.08	.25
76 Petr Jancarik	.08	.25
77 Patrik Elias	.75	2.00
78 Brendan Morrison	1.25	3.00
79 Radek Bonk	.40	1.00
80 Jaroslav Kudrna	.20	.50
81 Tomas Blazek	.08	.25
82 Ladislav Lubina	.08	.25
83 Stanislav Prochazka	.08	.25
84 Jiri Jantovsky	.08	.25
85 Dusan Salficky	.30	.75
86 Radek Masny	.08	.25
87 Josef Reznicek	.08	.25
88 Ivan Vlcek	.08	.25
89 Martin Cech	.08	.25
90 Jiri Hanzlik	.08	.25
91 Martin Spanhel	.30	.75
92 Michal Straka	.08	.25
93 Zdenek Sedlak	.08	.25
94 Pavel Vostrak	.08	.25
95 Petr Korinek	.20	.50
96 Pavel Geffert	.08	.25
97 David Pospisil	.08	.25
98 Milan Volak	.08	.25
99 Vlastimil Lakosil	.20	.50
100 Marek Novotny	.08	.25
101 Jiri Kuntos	.08	.25
102 Petr Gregorek	.08	.25
103 Milos Holan	.20	.50
104 Lubomir Sekeras	.20	.50
105 Richard Kral	.08	.25
106 Marek Zadina	.08	.25
107 Martin Havlat	6.00	15.00
108 Roman Dadera	.08	.25
109 Tomas Chlubna	.08	.25
110 Petr Folta	.08	.25
111 Ondrej Zetek	.08	.25
112 Branislav Janos	.08	.25
113 Ladislav Blazek	.08	.25
114 Roman Malek	.08	.25
115 Vitezslav Skuta	.08	.25
116 Jan Krajicek	.08	.25
117 Pavel Kolarik	.20	.50
118 Martin Bakula	.08	.25
119 Vladimir Ruzicka	.08	.25
120 Tomas Kucharcik	.08	.25
121 Michal Sup	.08	.25
122 Jiri Dolezal	.08	.25
123 Jan Kopecky	.08	.25
124 Petr Hrbek	.08	.25
125 Radek Matejovsky	.08	.25
126 Vladimir Machulda	.08	.25
127 Roman Cechmanek	.40	1.00
128 Ivo Pesat	.08	.25
129 Jan Srdinko	.08	.25
130 Libor Zabransky	.08	.25
131 Jiri Veber	.08	.25
132 Radim Tesarik	.08	.25
133 Jiri Dopita	.20	.50
134 Radek Belohlav	.15	.40
135 Jan Tomajko	.08	.25
136 Jan Pardavy	.08	.25
137 Roman Stantien	.08	.25
138 Zbynek Marak	.08	.25
139 Alexei Jaskin	.08	.25
140 Pavel Zubicek	.08	.25
141 Petr Briza	.30	.75
142 Petr Prikryl	.08	.25
143 Frantisek Kucera	.07	.20
144 Ladislav Benysek	.20	.50
145 Michal Sykora	.20	.50
146 Jaroslav Nedved	.08	.25
147 David Vyborny	.20	.50
148 Patrik Martinec	.08	.25
149 Jaroslav Hlinka	.08	.25
150 Ondrej Kratena	.08	.25
151 Michal Bros	.08	.25
152 Richard Zemlicka	.20	.50
153 Jiri Zelenka	.08	.25
154 Vaclav Eiselt	.08	.25
155 Martin Bilek	.20	.50
156 Lubos Horcicka	.08	.25
157 Michal Madl	.08	.25
158 Jan Krulis	.08	.25
159 Jiri Krocak	.08	.25
160 Jan Dlouhy	.08	.25
161 Tomas Horna	.08	.25
162 Ladislav Svoboda	.08	.25
163 Zdenek Eichenmann	.08	.25
164 Jiri Burger	.08	.25
165 Tomas Kupka	.08	.25
166 Jiri Kames	.20	.50
167 Juri Holdan	.08	.25
168 Ondrej Kriz	.08	.25
169 Martin Prusek	.75	2.00
170 Jiri Trvaj	.08	.25
171 Dmitrij Jerofejev	.08	.25
172 Lukas Galvas	.08	.25
173 Pavel Kowalczyk	.08	.25
174 Petr Jurecka	.08	.25
175 Ludik Krayzel	.08	.25
176 Libor Polasek	.08	.25
177 Martin Lamich	.08	.25
178 Petr Hubacek	.08	.25
179 Serej Petrenko	.08	.25
180 Zdenek Pavelek	.08	.25
181 Martin Tomasek	.08	.25
182 Zbynik Irgi	.08	.25
183 Ladislav Kudrna	.20	.50
184 Pavol Rybar	.20	.50
185 Pavel Kumstat	.08	.25
186 Tomas Jakes	.08	.25
187 Karel Soudek	.08	.25
188 Jiri Hes	.08	.25
189 Petr Kankovsky	.08	.25
190 Milan Kastner	.08	.25
191 Jiri Poukar	.08	.25
192 Peter Pucher	.08	.25
193 Marek Vorel	.08	.25
194 Radek Haman	.08	.25
195 Karel Plasek	.08	.25
196 Milan Prochazka	.08	.25
GC Jaromir Jagr Gold	20.00	50.00

1999-00 Czech DS Goalies

Card	Low	High
COMPLETE SET (14)	16.00	40.00
G1 Richard Hrazdira	1.25	3.00
G2 Rudolf Pejchar	1.25	3.00
G3 Ivo Capek	1.25	3.00
G4 Pavel Cagas	1.25	3.00
G5 Zdenek Orct	1.25	3.00
G6 Libor Barta	1.25	3.00
G7 Dusan Salficky	1.50	4.00
G8 Vlastimil Lakosil	1.25	3.00
G9 Ladislav Blazek	1.25	3.00
G10 Roman Cechmanek	1.50	4.00
G11 Petr Briza	1.50	4.00
G12 Martin Bilek	1.25	3.00
G13 Martin Prusek	4.00	10.00
G14 Pavol Rybar	1.25	3.00

1999-00 Czech DS National Stars

Card	Low	High
COMPLETE SET (23)	50.00	125.00
NS1 Dominik Hasek	8.00	20.00
NS2 Milan Hnilicka	2.00	5.00
NS3 Jaromir Jagr	15.00	40.00
NS4 Jiri Slegr	1.25	3.00
NS5 Jaroslav Spacek	1.25	3.00
NS6 Frantisek Kucera	1.25	3.00
NS7 Roman Hamrlik	1.50	4.00
NS8 Petr Svoboda	1.50	4.00
NS9 Viktor Ujcik	1.25	3.00
NS10 Frantisek Kaberle	1.25	3.00
NS11 Libor Prochazka	1.25	3.00
NS12 Robert Reichel	1.25	3.00
NS13 Martin Rucinsky	1.25	3.00
NS14 Martin Straka	1.50	4.00
NS15 Martin Prochazka	1.25	3.00
NS16 Pavel Patera	1.25	3.00
NS17 Vladimir Ruzicka	1.25	3.00
NS18 Josef Beranek	1.25	3.00
NS19 David Moravec	1.25	3.00
NS20 Jan Hlavac	1.50	4.00
NS21 David Vyborny	1.25	3.00
NS22 Jiri Dopita	1.25	3.00
NS23 Petr Sykora	2.00	5.00

1999-00 Czech DS Premium

Card	Low	High
COMPLETE SET (12)	36.00	75.00
P1 Dominik Hasek	10.00	25.00
P2 Roman Turek	1.50	4.00
P3 Roman Cechmanek	1.50	4.00
P4 Milan Hnilicka	2.00	5.00
P5 Martin Prochazka	1.25	3.00
P6 Jaromir Jagr	20.00	50.00
P7 Jiri Slegr	1.25	3.00
P8 Jaroslav Spacek	1.25	3.00
P9 Pavel Patera	1.25	3.00
P10 Jiri Dopita	1.25	3.00
P11 Robert Reichel	1.25	3.00
P12 Martin Rucinsky	1.50	4.00

1999-00 Czech OFS

Card	Low	High
COMPLETE SET (560)	30.00	75.00
1 Libor Barta	.08	.25
2 Martin Bilek	.20	.50
3 Ladislav Blazek	.08	.25
4 Petr Briza	.30	.75
5 Ivo Capek	.20	.50
6 Roman Cechmanek	.40	1.00
7 Robert Horyna	.20	.50
8 Vladimir Hudacek	.20	.50
9 Ladislav Kudrna	.20	.50
10 Vlastimil Lakosil	.20	.50
11 Michal Marik	.20	.50
12 Zdenek Orct	.20	.50
13 Rudolf Pejchar	.20	.50
14 Martin Prusek	.75	2.00
15 Dusan Salficky	.30	.75
16 Richard Farda	.07	.20
17 Marian Jelinek	.07	.20
18 Josef Beranek	.07	.20
19 Leo Gudas	.07	.20
20 Milan Hnilicka	.40	1.00
21 Milos Holan	.07	.20
22 Jan Hrdina	.75	2.00
23 Jaromir Jagr	4.00	10.00
24 Frantisek Kaberle	.20	.50
25 Tomas Kaberle	.30	.75
26 Pavel Kubina	.40	1.00
27 Marek Malik	.07	.20
28 Pavel Patera	.20	.50
29 Martin Prochazka	.07	.20
30 Vaclav Prospal	.20	.50
31 Robert Reichel	.20	.50
32 Martin Rucinsky	.20	.50
33 Vladimir Ruzicka	.20	.50
34 Pavel Skrbek	.20	.50
35 Jiri Slegr	.20	.50
36 Jaroslav Spacek	.20	.50
37 Martin Straka	.40	1.00
38 Vaclav Varada	.20	.50
39 David Volek	.20	.50
40 Jan Vopat	.20	.50
41 Vladimir Caldr	.07	.20
42 Martin Bakula	.07	.20
43 Miroslav Hajek	.07	.20
44 Petr Hrbek	.07	.20
45 Petr Kadlec	.07	.20
46 Jan Kopecky	.07	.20
47 Jan Krajicek	.07	.20
48 Angel Krstev	.07	.20
49 Radek Matejovsky	.07	.20
50 Jan Novak	.07	.20
51 Vladimir Pojkar	.07	.20
52 Vladimir Ruzicka	.20	.50
53 Jan Slavik	.07	.20
54 Jan Sochor	.07	.20
55 Michal Sup	.07	.20
56 Zdislav Tabara	.07	.20
57 Jiri Dopita	.20	.50
58 Ondrej Kavulic	.07	.20
59 Petr Kubos	.07	.20
60 Radim Kucharczyk	.07	.20
61 Marko Palo	.07	.20
62 Jukka Seppo	.07	.20
63 Lukas Slaby	.07	.20
64 Roman Stantien	.07	.20
65 Petr Suchy	.07	.20
66 Radim Tesarik	.07	.20
67 Jan Tomajko	.07	.20
68 Martin Vozdecky	.07	.20
69 Petr Zajgla	.07	.20
70 Pavel Zubicek	.07	.20
71 Pavel Pazourek	.07	.20
72 Petr Belohlavek	.07	.20
73 Radim Freibauer	.07	.20
74 Radek Haman	.07	.20
75 David Havir	.07	.20
76 Jiri Hes	.07	.20
77 Jiri Hradecky	.07	.20
78 Jan Kloboucek	.07	.20
79 David Pazourek	.07	.20
80 David Petlak	.07	.20
81 Karel Plasek	.07	.20
82 Jiri Poukar	.07	.20
83 Milan Prochazka	.07	.20
84 Peter Pucher	.07	.20
85 Marek Vorel	.07	.20
86 Pavel Mara	.07	.20
87 Martin Barek	.07	.20
88 Tomas Blazek	.07	.20
89 Jan Dusanek	.07	.20
90 Patrik Elias	.75	2.00
91 Petr Jancarik	.20	.50
92 Jaroslav Kudrna	.20	.50
93 Tomas Martinec	.07	.20
94 Brendan Morrison	.40	1.00
95 Andrej Novotny	.07	.20
96 Tomas Pacal	.07	.20
97 Rastislav Palov	.07	.20
98 Patrik Rozsival	.07	.20
99 Michael Tvrdik	.07	.20
100 Tomas Vak	.07	.20
101 Pavel Richter	.07	.20
102 Michal Bros	.07	.20
103 Vaclav Eiselt	.07	.20
104 Petr Havelka	.07	.20
105 Martin Holy	.07	.20
106 Pavel Kasparik	.07	.20
107 Ondrej Kratena	.07	.20
108 Frantisek Kucera	.07	.20
109 Jaroslav Nedved	.07	.20
110 Frantisek Ptacek	.07	.20
111 Miha Rebolj	.07	.20
112 Pavel Srek	.07	.20
113 David Vyborny	.07	.20
114 Jiri Zelenka	.07	.20
115 Richard Zemlicka	.20	.50
116 Marek Sykora	.07	.20
117 Milan Antos	.07	.20
118 Martin Cech	.07	.20
119 Marek Cernosek	.07	.20
120 Petr Chvojka	.07	.20
121 Pavel Geffert	.07	.20
122 Jiri Hanzlik	.07	.20
123 Jiri Jelen	.07	.20
124 Michal Jelinek	.07	.20
125 Petr Korinek	.20	.50
126 Josef Reznicek	.07	.20
127 Radek Svoboda	.07	.20
128 Petr Ulehla	.07	.20
129 Ivan Vlcek	.07	.20
130 Pavel Vostrak	.07	.20
131 Martin Pesout	.07	.20
132 Michal Dobron	.07	.20
133 Martin Filip	.07	.20
134 Pavel Janku	.07	.20
135 Jaroslav Kalla	.07	.20
136 Jan Kostal	.07	.20
137 Jaromir Kverka	.07	.20
138 Petr Macek	.07	.20
139 Martin Maskarinec	.07	.20
140 Petr Pavlas	.07	.20
141 Josef Podlaha	.07	.20
142 Michal Porak	.07	.20
143 Martin Richter	.07	.20
144 Jan Snopek	.07	.20
145 Martin Streit	.07	.20
146 Vaclav Sykora	.07	.20
147 David Balazs	.07	.20
148 Viktor Hubl	.07	.20
149 Petr Kratky	.07	.20
150 Vojtech Kubincak	.07	.20
151 Robert Kysela	.07	.20
152 Marian Menhart	.20	.50
153 Radek Mrazek	.07	.20
154 Angel Nikolov	.20	.50
155 Karel Pilar	.40	1.00
156 Ivo Prorok	.07	.20
157 Robert Reichel	.20	.50
158 Zdenek Skorepa	.20	.50
159 Josef Straka	.07	.20
160 Martin Strbak	.07	.20
161 Otakar Vejvoda	.07	.20
162 Jan Dlouhy	.07	.20
163 Zdenek Eichenmann	.07	.20
164 Jiri Holsan	.07	.20
165 Tomas Horna	.07	.20
166 Ondrej Kriz	.07	.20
167 Jiri Krocak	.07	.20
168 Tomas Kupka	.07	.20
169 Michal Madl	.07	.20
170 Milan Novy	.07	.20
171 Tomas Polansky	.07	.20
172 Lukas Poznik	.07	.20
173 Ladislav Svoboda	.07	.20
174 Tomas Ullrych	.07	.20
175 Martin Vejvoda	.07	.20
176 Jaroslav Liska	.07	.20
177 Kamil Brabenec	.07	.20
178 Roman Cech	.07	.20
179 Milan Filipi	.07	.20
180 Stanislav Jasecko	.07	.20
181 Josef Jindra	.07	.20
182 Michal Klimes	.07	.20
183 Zdenek Kutlak	.20	.50
184 Milan Nedoma	.07	.20
185 David Nedorost	.07	.20
186 Lubos Rob	.07	.20
187 Petr Sailer	.07	.20
188 Jiri Simanek	.07	.20
189 Rudolf Suchanek	.07	.20
190 Radek Toupal	.07	.20
191 Alois Hadamczik CO	.07	.20
192 Mario Cartelli	.07	.20
193 Petr Gregorek	.07	.20
194 Martin Havlat	6.00	15.00
195 Branislav Janos	.07	.20
196 Roman Kadera	.07	.20
197 Richard Kral	.07	.20
198 Jiri Kuntos	.07	.20
199 David Nosek	.07	.20
200 Vaclav Pletka	.20	.50
201 Pavel Selinger	.07	.20
202 Petr Svoboda	.15	.40
203 Viktor Ujcik	.15	.40
204 Marek Zadina	.07	.20
205 Jiri Zurek	.07	.20
206 Antonin Stavjana	.07	.20
207 Jaroslav Balastik	.07	.20
208 Roman Hamrlik	.30	.75
209 Lubomir Korhon	.07	.20
210 Martin Kotasek	.07	.20
211 Petr Leska	.07	.20
212 Patrik Luza	.07	.20
213 Jiri Marusak	.07	.20
214 Pavel Mojzis	.07	.20
215 Milan Navratil	.07	.20
216 Miroslav Okal	.07	.20
217 Michal Tomek	.07	.20
218 Petr Vala	.07	.20
219 Pavol Valko	.07	.20
220 Tomas Zizka	.07	.20
221 Vladimir Vujtek	.07	.20
222 Lukas Galvas	.07	.20
223 Dmitrij Gogolev	.07	.20
224 Zbynek Irgl	.07	.20
225 Dmitri Jerofejev	.07	.20
226 Petr Jurecka	.07	.20
227 Ludek Krayzel	.07	.20
228 Daniel Kysela	.07	.20
229 Zdenek Pavelek	.07	.20
230 Sergei Petrenko	.07	.20
231 Daniel Seman	.07	.20
232 Lukas Smolka	.07	.20
233 Vaclav Varada	.20	.50
234 Jan Vytisk	.07	.20
235 Lukas Zatopek	.07	.20
236 Richard Farda	.07	.20
237 Michal Cech	.07	.20
238 Vladimir Holik	.07	.20
239 Andrei Yakovenko	.07	.20
240 Marek Melenovsky	.07	.20
241 Martin Miklik	.07	.20
242 Pavel Nohel	.07	.20
243 Libor Pivko	.07	.20
244 Bogdan Savenko	.07	.20
245 Petr Suchanek	.07	.20
246 Kamil Suchanek	.07	.20
247 Petr Tejkl	.07	.20

248 Petr Vlasanek .07 .20
249 Michael Vyhlidal .07 .20
250 Tomas Zapletal .07 .20
251 Josef Augusta .07 .20
252 Ivan Hlinka .20 .50
253 Vladimir Martinec .07 .20
254 Roman Cechmanek .40 1.00
255 Martin Prusek .75 2.00
256 Radek Belohlav .15 .40
257 Ladislav Benysek .20 .50
258 Petr Cajanek .30 .75
259 Jan Caloun .20 .50
260 Jiri Dopita .20 .50
261 Vaclav Kral .07 .20
262 Frantisek Kucera .07 .20
263 Tomas Kucharcik .07 .20
264 Radek Martinek .20 .50
265 Ales Pisa .07 .20
266 Robert Reichel .20 .50
267 Martin Richter .07 .20
268 Roman Simicek .20 .50
269 Jan Srdinko .07 .20
270 Martin Stepanek .07 .20
271 Petr Tenkrat .30 .75
272 Jan Tomajko .07 .20
273 Viktor Ujcik .15 .40
274 Tomas Vlasak .07 .20
275 David Vyborny .07 .20
276 Jiri Vykoukal .07 .20
277 Jaroslav Parizek CO .07 .20
278 Peter Bartos .07 .20
279 Jiri Broz .07 .20
280 Ales Kotalik 1.25 3.00
281 Lukas Zib .07 .20
282 Vaclav Kral .07 .20
283 Radek Martinek .20 .50
284 Vaclav Nedorost .75 2.00
285 Martin Strba .07 .20
286 Filip Turek .07 .20
287 Ivo Pestuka CO .07 .20
288 Jaroslav Hub .07 .20
289 Miroslav Javin .07 .20
290 Roman Kontsek .07 .20
291 Rostislav Pilavka .07 .20
292 Ivan Puncochar .07 .20
293 Roman Rysanek .07 .20
294 Petr Sykora .07 .20
295 Ales Tomasek .07 .20
296 Daniel Vilasek .07 .20
297 David Kriz .07 .20
298 Michal Mikeska .07 .20
299 Pavol Pekarik .07 .20
300 Jan Peterek .07 .20
301 Radek Philipp .07 .20
302 Pavel Zdrahal .07 .20
303 Ales Zima .07 .20
304 Filip Stefanka .07 .20
305 Tomas Sykora .07 .20
306 Marcel Hanzal .07 .20
307 Roman Horak .07 .20
308 Milos Riha CO .07 .20
309 Ladislav Prokupek .07 .20
310 Roman Prosek .07 .20
311 Martin Rousek .07 .20
312 Miroslav Barus .07 .20
313 Michal Divisek .07 .20
314 David Hruska .07 .20
315 Pavel Metlicka .07 .20
316 Radek Prochazka .07 .20
317 Tomas Martinec .07 .20
318 Zdenek Pavelek .07 .20
319 Jiri Polak .07 .20
320 Tomas Chlubna .07 .20
321 Jiri Malinsky .07 .20
322 Petr Fiala .07 .20
323 Eduard Novak CO .07 .20
324 Lubomir Bauer .07 .20
325 Petr Bohunicky .07 .20
326 Jiri Burger .07 .20
327 Jiri Hubacek .07 .20
328 Jiri Kames .07 .20
329 Michal Kanka .07 .20
330 Petr Kounovsky .07 .20
331 Jan Krulis .07 .20
332 Radim Skuhrovec .07 .20
333 Martin Taborsky .07 .20
334 Ladislav Vlcek .07 .20
335 Radek Gardon .07 .20
336 Vladimir Jerabek CO .07 .20
337 Jan Alinc .07 .20
338 Vladimir Gyna .07 .20
339 Jindrich Kotrla .07 .20
340 Michal Travnicek .07 .20
341 Lukas Bednarik .07 .20
342 Daniel Branda .07 .20
343 Marek Cernosek .07 .20
344 Jan Liska .07 .20
345 Kamil Piros .40 1.00
346 Petr Rosol .07 .20
347 Josef Palecek CO .07 .20
348 Petr Hemsky CO .07 .20
349 Milan Chalupa CO .07 .20
350 Ales Hemsky 8.00 20.00
351 Jiri Jantovsky .07 .20
352 Robert Kantor .07 .20
353 Marek Cernosek .07 .20
354 Jiri Malinsky .07 .20
355 Miroslav Mosnar .07 .20
356 Ales Pisa .07 .20
357 Stanislav Prochazka .07 .20
358 Petr Sykora .07 .20
359 Jan Archalous .07 .20
360 Martin Filip .07 .20
361 Pavel Kabrt .07 .20
362 Jan Kolar .07 .20
363 Martin Koudelka .07 .20
364 Radek Matejovsky .07 .20
365 Michal Mikeska .07 .20
366 Petr Mudroch .07 .20
367 Petr Caslava .07 .20
368 Radim Rulik CO .07 .20
369 Jiri Dobrovolny .07 .20
370 Mojmir Musil .07 .20
371 David Pospisil .07 .20
372 Martin Spanhel .40 1.00
373 Jaroslav Spelda .07 .20
374 Michal Straka .07 .20
375 Milan Volak .07 .20
376 Zdenek Sedlak .07 .20
377 Jan Fiala .07 .20
378 Petr Kadlec .07 .20
379 Josef Straka .07 .20
380 Jiri Kalous CO .07 .20
381 Josef Beranek CO .07 .20
382 Jiri Dolezal .07 .20
383 Jan Hejda .07 .20
384 Pavel Kolarik .07 .20
385 Tomas Kucharcik .07 .20
386 Vladimir Machulda .07 .20
387 Jan Bohac .07 .20
388 Pavel Geffert .07 .20
389 Jiri Jantovsky .07 .20
390 Zdenek Skorepa .20 .50
391 Vitezslav Skuta .07 .20
392 Robin Bacul .07 .20
393 Marek Tomica .07 .20
394 Frantisek Vyborny CO .07 .20
395 Ladislav Benysek .20 .50
396 Jaroslav Hlinka .07 .20
397 Vaclav Novak .07 .20
398 Patrik Martinec .07 .20
399 Vaclav Novak .07 .20
400 Josef Slanec .07 .20
401 Michal Sykora .08 .25
402 Vladimir Vujtek .07 .20
403 Kamil Konecny CO .07 .20
404 Jozef Dano .07 .20
405 Petr Folta .07 .20
406 Tomas Chlubna .07 .20
407 Robert Kantor .07 .20
408 Jan Marek .07 .20
409 Lubomir Sekeras .20 .50
410 Ondrej Zetek .07 .20
411 David Appel .07 .20
412 Pavel Janku .07 .20
413 Dmitrij Jerofejev .07 .20
414 David Nosek .07 .20
415 Vladimir Vlk .07 .20
416 Kamil Konecny .07 .20
417 Jan Sterbak CO .07 .20
418 Mojmir Trlicik .07 .20
419 Pavel Bacho .07 .20
420 Ondrej Zetek .07 .20
421 Roman Kadera .07 .20
422 Petr Hubacek .07 .20
423 Roman Kelner .07 .20
424 Pavel Kowalczyk .07 .20
425 Martin Lamich .07 .20
426 Jan Matejny .07 .20
427 Libor Pavlis .07 .20
428 Radek Philipp .07 .20
429 Libor Polasek .07 .20
430 Martin Tomasek .07 .20
431 Libor Gelacek .07 .20
432 Martin Louzek .07 .20
433 Martin Maskarinec .07 .20
434 David Moravec .20 .50
435 Ivan Padelek .07 .20
436 Martin Streit .07 .20
437 Miroslav Venkrbec .07 .20
438 Radek Belohlav .15 .40
439 Alexej Jaskin .07 .20
440 Zbynek Marak .07 .20
441 Oleg Antonenko .07 .20
442 Josef Mikes .07 .20
443 Jan Pardavy .07 .20
444 Jan Srdinko .07 .20
445 Jiri Veber .07 .20
446 Libor Zabransky .07 .20
447 Pavel Patera .20 .50
448 Martin Prochazka .20 .50
449 Zbynek Spitzer .07 .20
450 S. Prikryl CO .07 .20
451 Petr Cajanek .30 .75
452 Jiri David .07 .20
453 Martin Hamrlik .07 .20
454 Marek Ivan .07 .20
455 Josef Straub .07 .20
456 Ondrej Vesely .07 .20
457 Martin Ambruz .07 .20
458 Jan Homer .07 .20
459 Rostislav Malena .07 .20
460 S. Barada CO .07 .20
461 Pavol Valko .07 .20
462 Marek Uram .07 .20
463 Patrik Fink .07 .20
464 Tomas Hradecky .07 .20
465 Tomas Jakes .07 .20
466 Petr Kankovsky .07 .20
467 Milan Kastner .07 .20
468 David Kudelka .07 .20
469 Pavel Kumstat .07 .20
470 Karel Soudek .07 .20
471 Jan Kopecky .07 .20
472 Michal Bros .08 .25
473 Martin Cech .07 .20
474 Petr Gregorek .07 .20
475 Jiri Hanzlik .07 .20
476 Jaroslav Hlinka .07 .20
477 Petr Korinek .07 .20
478 Ludek Krayzel .07 .20
479 David Moravec .20 .50
480 Angel Nikolov .07 .20
481 Pavel Patera .20 .50
482 Kamil Piros .40 1.00
483 Vaclav Pletka .20 .50
484 Martin Spanhel .40 1.00
485 Radim Tesarik .07 .20
486 Libor Zabransky .07 .20
487 Petr Briza .30 .75
488 Dusan Salficky .30 .75
489 Roman Cechmanek .40 1.00
490 Vladimir Hudacek .20 .50
491 Peter Bartos .07 .20
492 Vladimir Vujtek .07 .20
493 David Vyborny .07 .20
494 Ladislav Benysek .20 .50
495 Tomas Blazek .08 .25
496 Frantisek Kucera .07 .20
497 Jiri Burger .07 .20
498 Jan Kopecky .07 .20
499 Vaclav Kral .07 .20
500 Jan Krulis .07 .20
501 Ivo Prorok .07 .20
502 Radek Martinek .20 .50
503 Jaroslav Nedved .07 .20
504 Petr Pavlas .07 .20
505 Ales Pisa .07 .20
506 Michal Sykora .08 .25
507 Robert Reichel .20 .50
508 Miroslav Buras .07 .20
509 Martin Spanhel .40 1.00
510 Michal Sup .07 .20
511 Petr Cajanek .40 1.00
512 Jiri Dopita .20 .50
513 Martin Hamrlik .07 .20
514 Roman Horak .07 .20
515 Zbynek Irgl .07 .20
516 Tomas Jakes .07 .20
517 Ludek Krayzel .07 .20
518 Jiri Kuntos .07 .20
519 Petr Leska .07 .20
520 Jiri Marusak .07 .20
521 David Moravec .20 .50
522 Jan Pardavy .07 .20
523 Pavel Patera .20 .50
524 Jan Peterek .07 .20
525 Martin Prochazka .20 .50
526 Karel Soudek .07 .20
527 Jan Srdinko .07 .20
528 Radim Tesarik .07 .20
529 Viktor Ujcik .15 .40
530 Libor Zabransky .08 .25
531 Pavel Cagas .20 .50
532 Zdenek Smid .30 .75
533 Lubos Horcicka .20 .50
534 Pavel Krizek .20 .50
535 Marek Pinc .20 .50
536 Petr Jez .08 .25
537 Radek Masny .20 .50
538 Roman Malek .20 .50
539 Tomas Duba .20 .50
540 Petr Prikryl .20 .50
541 Jiri Kratochvil .20 .50
542 Marek Novotny .08 .25
543 Jiri Trvaj .20 .50
544 Ivo Pesat .20 .50
545 Richard Hrazdira .20 .50
546 Petr Kubena .20 .50
547 Pavol Rybar .20 .50
548 Adam Svoboda .30 .75
549 Radek Masny .20 .50
550 Petr Tucek .20 .50
551 Vladimir Hudacek .20 .50
552 Dusan Salficky .30 .75
NNO Ladislav Blazek CL .08 .25
NNO Martin Prusek CL .40 1.00
NNO Zdenek Orct CL .40 1.00
NNO Petr Briza CL .30 .75
NNO Vladimir Hudacek CL .20 .50
NNO Roman Cechmanek CL .40 1.00
NNO Rudolf Pejchar CL .40 1.00
NNO Dusan Salficky CL .30 .75

1999-00 Czech OFS All-Star Game Blue

COMPLETE SET (44) 15.00 25.00
487 Petr Briza .40 1.00
488 Dusan Salficky .40 1.00
489 Roman Cechmanek .75 2.00
490 Vladimir Hudacek .20 .50
491 Peter Bartos .20 .50
492 Vladimir Vujtek .20 .50
493 David Vyborny .20 .50
494 Ladislav Benysek .40 1.00
495 Tomas Blazek .40 1.00
496 Frantisek Kucera .20 .50
497 Jiri Burger .20 .50
498 Jan Kopecky .20 .50
499 Vaclav Kral .20 .50
500 Jan Krulis .20 .50
501 Ivo Prorok .20 .50
502 Radek Martinek .40 1.00
503 Jaroslav Nedved .20 .50
504 Petr Pavlas .20 .50
505 Ales Pisa .20 .50
506 Michal Sykora .20 .50
507 Robert Reichel .40 1.00
508 Miroslav Buras .20 .50
509 Martin Spanhel .30 .75
510 Michal Sup .20 .50
511 Petr Cajanek 1.25 3.00
512 Jiri Dopita .40 1.00
513 Martin Hamrlik .20 .50
514 Roman Horak .20 .50
515 Zbynek Irgl .20 .50
516 Tomas Jakes .20 .50
517 Ludek Krayzel .20 .50
518 Jiri Kuntos .20 .50
519 Petr Leska .20 .50
520 Jiri Marusak .20 .50
521 David Moravec .20 .50
522 Jan Pardavy .20 .50
523 Pavel Patera .20 .50
524 Jan Peterek .20 .50
525 Martin Prochazka .20 .50
526 Karel Soudek .20 .50
527 Jan Srdinko .20 .50
528 Radim Tesarik .20 .50
529 Viktor Ujcik .20 .50
530 Libor Zabransky .30 .75

1999-00 Czech OFS Goalie Die-Cuts

COMPLETE SET (15) 40.00 80.00
1 Libor Barta 2.00 5.00
2 Martin Bilek 2.00 5.00
3 Ladislav Blazek 2.00 5.00
4 Petr Briza 3.00 8.00
5 Ivo Capek 2.00 5.00
6 Roman Cechmanek 4.00 10.00
7 Robert Horyna 2.00 5.00
8 Vladimir Hudacek 2.00 5.00
9 Ladislav Kudrna 2.00 5.00
10 Vlastimil Lakosil 2.00 5.00
11 Michal Marik 2.00 5.00
12 Zdenek Orct 2.00 5.00
13 Rudolf Pejchar 2.00 5.00
14 Martin Prusek 8.00 20.00
15 Dusan Salficky 3.00 8.00

1999-00 Czech OFS Jagr Team Embossed

COMPLETE SET (25) 15.00 30.00
16 Richard Farda .20 .50
17 Marian Jelinek .20 .50
18 Josef Beranek .20 .50
19 Leo Gudas .20 .50
20 Milan Hnilicka 1.25 3.00
21 Milos Holan .20 .50
22 Jan Hrdina .75 2.00
23 Jaromir Jagr 8.00 20.00
24 Frantisek Kaberle .20 .50
25 Tomas Kaberle .60 1.50
26 Pavel Kubina .75 2.00
27 Marek Malik .20 .50
28 Pavel Patera .20 .50
29 Martin Prochazka .20 .50
30 Vaclav Prospal .40 1.00
31 Robert Reichel .40 1.00
32 Martin Rucinsky .40 1.00
33 Vladimir Ruzicka .40 1.00
34 Pavel Skrbek .40 1.00
35 Jiri Slegr .40 1.00
36 Jaroslav Spacek .40 1.00
37 Martin Straka .75 2.00
38 Vaclav Varada .40 1.00
39 David Volek .40 1.00
40 Jan Vopat .40 1.00

1999-00 Czech Score Blue 2000

COMPLETE SET (165) 20.00 50.00
1 Roman Malek .30 .75
2 Roman Hrubes .20 .50
3 Ladislav Slizek .20 .50
4 Jaroslav Roubik .20 .50
5 Jiri Kuchler .20 .50
6 Petr Mudroch .20 .50
7 Jiri Cmunt .20 .50
8 Lukas Palecek .20 .50
9 Pavel Malecek .20 .50
10 Vaclav Drabek .20 .50
11 Dalibor Sanda .20 .50
12 Jiri Novotny .20 .50
13 Dalimil Svoboda .20 .50
14 Petr Kubena .20 .50
15 Martin Svetlik .20 .50
16 Jakub Ziska .20 .50
17 Richard Kolacek .20 .50
18 Tomas Trachta .20 .50
19 Patrik Weber .20 .50
20 Ales Sochorec .20 .50
21 Alexandr Elsner .20 .50
22 Michal Safarik .20 .50
23 Michal Safarik .20 .50
24 Tomas Mikolasek .20 .50
25 Pavel Malac .20 .50
26 Kamil Jarina .20 .50
27 Petr Martinek .20 .50
28 Ladislav Bousek .20 .50
29 Kamil Kolacek .20 .50
30 Jiri Gombar .20 .50
31 David Hajek .20 .50
32 Martin Tupa .20 .50
33 Stanislav Stavensky .20 .50
34 Martin Stelcich .20 .50
35 Radek Sip .20 .50
36 Petr Altrichter .20 .50
37 Lukas Stabl .20 .50
38 Lukas Sablik .20 .50
39 Marian Morava .20 .50
40 Zdenek Fuksa .20 .50
41 Petr Mokrejs .20 .50
42 Miroslav Duben .20 .50
43 Jiri Cihlar .20 .50
44 Vaclav Adamec .20 .50
45 Daniel Hodek .20 .50
46 Ales Polcar .20 .50
47 Daniel Zapotocny .20 .50
48 Richard Cachnin .20 .50
49 Roman Spiler .20 .50
50 Filip Sindelar .20 .50
51 Petr Jaros .20 .50
52 Marek Dvorak .20 .50
53 Jaroslav Mares .20 .50
54 Robert Vavroch .20 .50
55 Vratislav Hreben .20 .50
56 Petr Cerveny .20 .50
57 Jaroslav Kocar .20 .50
58 Ales Skokan .20 .50
59 Michal Horak .20 .50
60 Jakub Kraus .20 .50
61 Marcel Kucera .20 .50
62 Miroslav Sedlacek .20 .50
63 Richard Richter .20 .50
64 Rudolf Mudra .20 .50
65 Jaroslav Muller .20 .50
66 Evzen Gal .20 .50
67 Petr Spojcar .20 .50
68 Jaroslav Kreuzman .20 .50
69 Premysl Sedlak .20 .50
70 Martin Nosek .20 .50
71 Tomas Vyskocil .20 .50
72 Michal Lanicek .20 .50
73 Pavel Malac .20 .50
74 Ales Vala .20 .50
75 Martin Vyborny .20 .50
76 Tomas Vozka .20 .50
77 Petr Hocicka .20 .50
78 Jan Plodek .20 .50
79 Oldrich Nyc .20 .50
80 Filip Pesan .20 .50
81 Milan Plodek .20 .50
82 Jiri Matousek .20 .50
83 Vitezslav Jankovych .20 .50
84 Petr Kus .20 .50
85 Martin Chlad .20 .50
86 Hiroyuki Murakami .20 .50
87 Lukas Bednarik .20 .50
88 Michal Oliverius .20 .50
89 Tomas Pisa .20 .50
90 Jan Hranac .20 .50
91 Jan Bohacek .20 .50
92 Tomas Klimt .20 .50
93 Martin Zivny .20 .50
94 Michal Havel .20 .50
95 Martin Rejthar .20 .50
96 Karl Rakovsky .20 .50
97 Martin Vojtek .20 .50
98 Robert Prochazka .20 .50
99 Daniel Vilasek .20 .50
100 Jan Kasik .20 .50
101 Jevgenij Alipov .20 .50
102 Ales Kretinsky .20 .50
103 Pavel Sebesta .20 .50
104 David Kostelnak .20 .50
105 Karel Harazim .20 .50
106 Richard Brancik .20 .50
107 Petr Rozum .20 .50
108 Michal Pinkas .20 .50
109 Robert Slavik .20 .50
110 Josef Vachulka .20 .50
111 Lubos Pindiak .20 .50
112 Robert Zak .20 .50
113 David Mika .20 .50
114 Jiri Kudrna .20 .50
115 Vaclav Benak .20 .50
116 Roman Bezpalec .20 .50
117 Pavel Hejl .20 .50
118 Michal Janiga .20 .50
119 Vladimir Mizera .20 .50
120 David Pisek .20 .50
121 Petr Tucek .20 .50
122 Martin Palinek .20 .50
123 Jiri Polak .20 .50
124 Michal Cerny .20 .50
125 Milan Ministr .20 .50
126 Tomas Hradecky .20 .50
127 David Svec .20 .50
128 Filip Janecek .20 .50
129 Tomas Hradecky .20 .50
130 Radomir Brazda .20 .50
131 Petr Hrachovina .20 .50
132 Martin Altrichter .20 .50
133 Jaromir Pichal .20 .50
134 Jiri Bures .20 .50
135 Jiri Mifek .20 .50
136 Jaroslav Smolik .20 .50
137 Milota Florian .20 .50
138 Robert Holy .20 .50
139 Josef Drabek .20 .50
140 Michal Slavik .20 .50
141 Tomas Kramny .20 .50
142 Jan Konecny .20 .50
143 Radek Lukes .20 .50
144 Robert Hamrla .20 .50
145 Petr Lustinec .20 .50
146 Radek Kucera .20 .50
147 Petr Sakarov .20 .50
148 Pavel Kormunda .20 .50
149 Petr Suchy .20 .50
150 David Brezik .20 .50
151 Michal Nohejl .20 .50
152 Martin Jenacek .20 .50
153 Dusan Barica .20 .50
154 Zdenek Kucirek .20 .50
155 Stanislav Neruda .20 .50
156 Robert Pospisil .20 .50
157 Brendan Morrison .75 2.00
158 Frantisek Sevcik .20 .50
159 Roman Hlouch .20 .50
160 Patrik Elias .75 2.00
161 Oldrich Bakus .20 .50
162 Jiri Oliva .20 .50
163 Karel Selcik .20 .50
164 Marcel Hrbacek .20 .50
165 Rostislav Malena .20 .50

2000 Czech Stadion

COMPLETE SET (216) 100.00 200.00
5 Dominik Hasek 1.25 3.00
13 Roman Turek .20 .50
57 Jaromir Jagr 2.00 5.00
61 Mike Ricci .20 .50
64 Marty McSorley .20 .50
65 Martin Brodeur 4.00 10.00
66 Olaf Kolzig .60 1.50
67 Mark Messier 1.50 4.00
68 Eric Lindros 1.25 3.00
69 Robert Lang .20 .50
71 Milan Hejduk 1.25 3.00
72 Alexei Yashin .20 .50
74 Owen Nolan .40 1.00
75 Patrick Roy 6.00 15.00
76 Petr Svoboda .10 .25
77 Martin Straka .20 .50
79 Mario Lemieux 6.00 15.00
80 Petr Nedved .20 .50
81 Mats Sundin 1.25 3.00
82 Wayne Gretzky 10.00 25.00
83 Jaromir Jagr 2.00 5.00
84 Saku Koivu 1.25 3.00
85 Steve Yzerman 6.00 15.00
87 Mike Modano 1.25 3.00
90 Brian Leetch .75 2.00
91 Patrik Stefan .20 .50
92 Ed Belfour 1.50 4.00
93 Curtis Joseph 1.25 3.00
94 Brett Hull 1.50 4.00
95 Scott Stevens .40 1.00
96 Patrik Elias .40 1.00
99 Pavel Bure 1.25 3.00
109 Roman Turek .30 .50
110 Arturs Irbe .20 .50
111 Radek Dvorak .20 .50
112 Valeri Kamensky .20 .50
113 Jiri Slegr .20 .50
114 Alexander Mogilny .40 1.00
115 Peter Forsberg 2.00 5.00
116 Martin Havlat 4.00 10.00
117 Daniel Alfredsson .40 1.00
118 Theo Fleury .75 2.00
119 Sergei Brylin .10 .25
120 Patrick Roy 6.00 15.00
121 Patrick Lalime .60 1.50
122 Tomas Vokoun .60 1.50
123 Marian Hossa 1.25 3.00
124 Zigmund Palffy .40 1.00
125 Evgeni Nabokov .75 2.00
126 Jaroslav Modry .10 .25
145 Rob Blake .40 1.00
146 Jaromir Jagr 2.00 5.00
147 Mario Lemieux 6.00 15.00
148 Mario Lemieux 6.00 15.00
149 Al MacInnis .40 1.00
150 Mark Messier 1.50 4.00
151 Chris Pronger .75 2.00
152 Mike Richter 1.25 3.00
153 Brian Savage .20 .50
154 Maxim Afinogenov .40 1.00
155 Martin Biron .75 2.00
156 Martin Brodeur 4.00 10.00
157 Paul Coffey .75 2.00
158 Mariusz Czerkawski .20 .50
159 Wayne Gretzky 10.00 25.00
160 Michal Grosek .10 .25
161 Adam Graves .20 .50
162 J.Jagr
M.Lemieux 6.00 15.00
190 Dominik Hasek 1.25 3.00
191 Milan Hnilicka .40 1.00
192 Joe Sakic 2.00 5.00
193 Jocelyn Thibault .75 2.00
194 Vladimir Chebaturkin .10 .25
195 Bill Guerin .40 1.00
196 Krzysztof Oliwa .40 1.00
197 Bob Probert .75 2.00
198 Rick Tocchet .40 1.00

2000-01 Czech DS Extraliga

COMPLETE SET (168) 25.00 60.00
1 Petr Briza .40 1.00
2 Petr Prikryl .20 .50
3 Libor Zabransky .20 .50
4 Vlastimil Kroupa .20 .50
5 Frantisek Ptacek .20 .50
6 Michal Dobron .20 .50
7 Vladimir Vujtek .20 .50
8 Jaroslav Hlinka .20 .50
9 Martin Chabada .20 .50
10 Ondrej Kratena .20 .50
11 Michal Bros .20 .50
12 Richard Zemlicka .30 .75
13 Jaroslav Kames .40 1.00
14 Ivo Pesat .20 .50
15 Jan Srdinko .20 .50
16 Milan Nedoma .20 .50
17 Martin Strbak .20 .50
18 Radim Tesarik .20 .50
19 Jan Pardavy .20 .50
20 Jiri Dopita .40 1.00
21 Jan Sochor .20 .50
22 Jan Lipiansky .20 .50
23 Jiri Hudler 6.00 15.00
24 Ondrej Vesely .20 .50
25 Dusan Salficky .40 1.00
26 Petr Kus .20 .50
27 Josef Reznicek .20 .50
28 Martin Cech .20 .50
29 Ivan Vlcek .20 .50
30 Jiri Hanzlik .20 .50
31 Pavel Vostrak .20 .50
32 Petr Korinek .20 .50
33 Milan Volak .20 .50
34 Michal Straka .20 .50
35 David Pospisil .20 .50
36 Milan Antos .20 .50
37 Zdenek Orct .40 1.00
38 Michal Podolka .40 1.00
39 Angel Nikolov .30 .75
40 Karel Pilar .40 1.00
41 Radek Mrazek .20 .50
42 Vladimir Gyna .20 .50
43 Robert Reichel .30 .75
44 Petr Rosol .20 .50
45 Vojtech Kubincak .20 .50
46 Kamil Piros .40 1.00
47 Vesa Karjalainen .20 .50
48 Robert Kysela .20 .50
49 Vladimir Hudacek .40 1.00
50 Richard Hrazdira .20 .50
51 Tomas Zizka .40 1.00
52 Jiri Marusak .20 .50
53 Martin Hamrlik .20 .50
54 Miroslav Barus .20 .50
55 Miroslav Okal .20 .50
56 Petr Cajanek .30 .75
57 Jaroslav Balastik .20 .50
58 Petr Vala .20 .50
59 Martin Ambruz .20 .50
60 Petr Leska .20 .50
61 Marek Novotny .20 .50
62 Vlastimil Lakosil .40 1.00
63 Marek Zadina .20 .50
64 Mario Cartelli .20 .50
65 Vladimir Vlk .20 .50
66 Jiri Kuntos .20 .50
67 Richard Kral .20 .50
68 Viktor Ujcik .30 .75
69 Jozef Dano .20 .50
70 Petr Gregorek .20 .50
71 Richard Kapus .20 .50
72 Pavel Janku .20 .50
73 Michal Marik .20 .50
74 Ivo Capek .40 1.00
75 Radek Martinek .40 1.00
76 Rudolf Suchanek .20 .50
77 Stanislav Jasecko .20 .50
78 Vaclav Kral .20 .50
79 Filip Turek .20 .50
80 Lubos Rob .20 .50
81 Radek Belohlav .30 .75
82 Jiri Simanek .20 .50
83 Ales Kotalik .20 .50
84 Kamil Brabenec .20 .50
85 Libor Barta .20 .50
86 Adam Svoboda .40 1.00
87 Ales Pisa .40 1.00
88 Jiri Malinsky .20 .50
89 Petr Jancarik .20 .50
90 Otakar Janecky .30 .75
91 Ladislav Lubina .20 .50
92 Tomas Blazek .20 .50
93 Jaroslav Kudrna .30 .75
94 Michal Mikeska .20 .50
95 Stanislav Prochazka .20 .50
96 Michal Tvrdik .20 .50
97 Oldrich Svoboda .40 1.00
98 Ladislav Kudrna .20 .50
99 Tomas Jakes .20 .50
100 Jiri Hes .20 .50
101 Pavel Kumstat .20 .50
102 Karel Soudek .20 .50
103 Peter Pucher .20 .50
104 David Havir .20 .50
105 Zbynek Marak .20 .50
106 Milan Prochazka .20 .50
107 Radek Haman .20 .50
108 David Pazourek .20 .50
109 Ladislav Blazek .20 .50
110 Roman Malek .40 1.00
111 Petr Kadlec .20 .50
112 Jan Novak .20 .50
113 Angel Krstev .20 .50
114 Jan Snopek .20 .50
115 Daniel Branda .20 .50
116 Jan Alinc .20 .50
117 Viktor Hubl .20 .50
118 Petr Hrbek .20 .50
119 Jan Bohac .20 .50
120 Zdenek Skorepa .20 .50
121 Petr Franek .20 .50
122 Zdenek Smid .40 1.00
123 Libor Prochazka .20 .50
124 Normunds Sejejs .20 .50
125 Jiri Polak .20 .50
126 Roman Zak .20 .50
127 Jaromir Kverka .20 .50
128 Tomas Chlubna .20 .50
129 Radek Prochazka .20 .50
130 David Hruska .20 .50
131 Robert Tomik .20 .50
132 Pavel Kasparik .20 .50
133 Lubos Horcicka .20 .50
134 Marek Pinc .30 .75
135 Jan Krulis .20 .50
136 Michal Madl .20 .50
137 Radek Gardon .20 .50
138 Jan Bohacek .20 .50
139 Ladislav Svoboda .20 .50
140 Tomas Horna .20 .50
141 Jiri Holsan .20 .50
142 Ondrej Kriz .20 .50
143 Ladislav Vlcek .20 .50
144 Jozef Voskar .20 .50
145 Radovan Biegl .30 .75
146 Radek Masny .20 .50
147 Michael Vyhlidal .20 .50
148 Miroslav Javin .20 .50
149 Petr Pavlas .20 .50
150 Tomas Srsen .20 .50
151 Petr Folta .20 .50
152 Libor Pivko .20 .50
153 Daniel Bohac .20 .50
154 Roman Horak .20 .50
155 Jan Peterek .20 .50
156 Richard Pavlikovsky .20 .50
157 Martin Prusek .40 1.00
158 Jiri Trvaj .20 .50
159 Zdenek Pavelek .20 .50
160 Vitezslav Skuta .20 .50
161 Dmitri Jerofejev .20 .50
162 David Moravec .40 1.00
163 Roman Kadera .20 .50
164 Zbynek Irgl .20 .50
165 Marek Ivan .20 .50
166 Martin Prochazka .30 .75
167 Josef Straub .20 .50
168 Ivan Padelek .20 .50

2000-01 Czech DS Extraliga Best of the Best

COMPETE SET (4) 25.00 60.00
BBH1 Dominik Hasek 4.00 10.00
BBH2 Dominik Hasek 4.00 10.00
BBJ1 Jaromir Jagr 6.00 15.00
BBJ2 Jaromir Jagr 6.00 15.00
BBH1 D.Hasek AU/200 40.00 100.00
BBJ2 J.Jagr AU/200 60.00 150.00

2000-01 Czech DS Extraliga Goalies

COMPLETE SET (14) 25.00 60.00
G1 Petr Briza 3.00 8.00
G2 Jaroslav Kames 2.00 5.00
G3 Dusan Salficky 2.00 5.00
G4 Zdenek Orct 2.00 5.00
G5 Vladimir Hudacek 2.00 5.00
G6 Vlastimil Lakosil 2.00 5.00
G7 Ivo Capek 2.00 5.00
G8 Adam Svoboda 2.00 5.00
G9 Oldrich Svoboda 2.00 5.00
G10 Roman Malek 2.00 5.00
G11 Zdenek Smid 2.00 5.00
G12 Marek Pinc 2.00 5.00
G13 Radovan Biegl 2.00 5.00
G14 Martin Prusek 4.00 10.00

2000-01 Czech DS Extraliga National Team

COMPLETE SET (10) 25.00 60.00
NT1 Dusan Salficky 2.00 5.00
NT2 Roman Cechmanek 3.00 7.50
NT3 Martin Stepanek 1.25 3.00
NT4 Vladimir Vujtek 1.25 3.00
NT5 Robert Reichel 2.00 5.00
NT6 Jiri Dopita 2.00 5.00
NT7 Martin Rucinsky 2.00 5.00
NT8 Martin Havlat 10.00 25.00
NT9 Tomas Vlasak 1.25 3.00
NT10 Michal Bros 1.25 3.00

2000-01 Czech DS Extraliga Team Jagr

COMPETE SET (16) 40.00 80.00
JT1 Roman Turek 2.00 5.00
JT2 Milan Hnilicka 2.00 5.00
JT3 Petr Sykora 1.50 4.00
JT4 Roman Hamrlik 1.25 3.00
JT5 Martin Straka 1.50 4.00
JT6 Pavel Kubina 1.25 3.00
JT7 Petr Nedved 1.50 4.00
JT8 Martin Prochazka 1.25 3.00
JT9 Vaclav Prospal 1.25 3.00
JT10 David Volek 1.25 3.00
JT11 Milan Hejduk 6.00 15.00

JT12 Jaromir Jagr 8.00 25.00
JT13 Jan Hlavac 1.50 4.00
JT14 Pavel Patera 1.25 3.00
JT15 Tomas Vlasak 1.25 3.00
JT16 Vaclav Varada 1.25 3.00

2000-01 Czech DS Extraliga Team Jagr Parallel

COMPLETE SET (9) 50.00 125.00
JT1 Roman Turek 8.00 20.00
JT2 Milan Hnilicka 4.00 10.00
JT3 Petr Sykora 4.00 15.00
JT4 Roman Hamrlik 4.00 10.00
JT5 Martin Straka 4.00 10.00
JT6 Petr Nedved 4.00 10.00
JT7 Milan Hejduk 12.50 30.00
JT8 Jaromir Jagr 20.00 50.00
JT9 Jan Hlavac 4.00 10.00

2000-01 Czech DS Extraliga Top Stars

TS1 Petr Briza 3.00 8.00
TS2 Radek Martinek 2.00 5.00
TS3 Petr Cajanek 2.00 5.00
TS4 Jiri Dopita 3.00 8.00
TS5 Robert Reichel 3.00 8.00
TS6 Martin Prochazka 2.00 5.00

2000-01 Czech DS Extraliga Valuable Players

COMPLETE SET (6) 12.00 20.00
VP1 Vladimir Hudacek 2.00 5.00
VP2 Frantisek Kucera 1.00 3.00
VP3 Michal Sykora 1.00 3.00
VP4 Robert Reichel 2.00 5.00
VP5 Jiri Dopita 2.00 5.00
VP6 Petr Cajanek 1.00 3.00

2000-01 Czech DS Extraliga World Champions

COMPLETE SET (11) 30.00 75.00
WCH1 Roman Cechmanek 6.00 8.00
WCH2 Dusan Salficky 2.00 5.00
WCH3 Radek Martinek 2.00 5.00
WCH4 Martin Stepanek 2.00 5.00
WCH5 Frantisek Kucera 2.00 5.00
WCH6 Michal Sykora 2.00 5.00
WCH7 Martin Havlat 10.00 25.00
WCH8 Robert Reichel 2.00 5.00
WCH9 Tomas Vlasak 2.00 5.00
WCH10 David Vyborny 2.00 5.00
WCH11 Michal Bros 2.00 5.00

2000-01 Czech OFS

COMPLETE SET (421) 32.00 80.00
1 Team Logo .04 .10
2 Jaroslav Liska CO .04 .10
3 Jaroslav Parizek CO .04 .10
4 Jan Tlacil CO .04 .10
5 Jaroslav Pouzar CO .04 .10
6 Michal Marik .10 .25
7 Ivo Capek .20 .50
8 Radek Martinek .30 .75
9 Rudolf Suchanek .20 .50
10 Stanislav Jasecko .10 .25
11 Pavel Mojzis .10 .25
12 Vaclav Benak .10 .25
13 Ladislav Cierny .20 .50
14 Josef Jindra .10 .25
15 Vaclav Kral .10 .25
16 Filip Turek .10 .25
17 Lubos Rob .10 .25
18 Radek Belohlav .15 .40
19 Ales Kotalik .75 2.00
20 Kamil Brabenec .10 .25
21 Jiri Simanek .10 .25
22 Martin Strba .10 .25
23 Petr Sailer .10 .25
24 Milan Filipi .04 .25
25 Jiri Broz .10 .25
26 Jiri Novotny .20 .50
27 Michal Vondrka .10 .25
28 Team Logo .04 .10
29 Josef Palacek CO .04 .10
30 Petr Hemsky CO .04 .10
31 Libor Barta .20 .25
32 Adam Svoboda .30 .75
33 Martin Barek .10 .25
34 Ales Pisa .10 .25
35 Jiri Malinsky .10 .25
36 Petr Jancarik .10 .25
37 Miroslav Duben .10 .25
38 Tomas Pacal .10 .25
39 Michal Divisek .10 .25
40 Andrej Novotny .10 .25
41 Petr Mudroch .10 .25
42 Otakar Janecky .20 .50
43 Ladislav Lubina .10 .25
44 Tomas Blazek .10 .25
45 Jaroslav Kudrna .20 .50
46 Michal Mikeska .10 .25
47 Stanislav Prochazka .10 .25
48 Michal Tvrdik .10 .25
49 Martin Filip .10 .25
50 Martin Koudelka .10 .25
51 Pavel Kabrt .10 .25
52 Petr Sykora .20 .50
53 Tomas Rolinek .10 .25
54 Jan Kolar .10 .25
55 Team Logo .04 .10
56 Marek Sykora CO .04 .10
57 Dusan Salficky .30 .75
58 Petr Kus .10 .25
59 Josef Reznicek .10 .25
60 Martin Cech .10 .25
61 Ivan Vlcek .10 .25
62 Jiri Hanzlik .10 .25
63 Jaroslav Spelda .10 .25
64 Zdenek Touzimsky .10 .25
65 Jiri Dobrovolny .10 .25
66 Jan Choteborsky .10 .25
67 Pavel Vostrak .10 .25
68 Petr Korinek .20 .50
69 Milan Volak .10 .25
70 Michal Straka .10 .25
71 David Pospisil .10 .25
72 Josef Straka .10 .25
73 Milan Antos .10 .25
74 Andrej Nedorost .40 1.00
75 Vaclav Eiselt .10 .25
76 Jiri Jelen .10 .25
77 Michal Dvorak .10 .25
78 Jiri Zurek .10 .25
79 Dusan Andrasovsky .10 .25
80 Team Logo .04 .10
81 Jaromir Sindel CO .10 .25
82 Ondrej Weissmann CO .04 .10
83 Ladislav Blazek .20 .50
84 Roman Malek .10 .25
85 Petr Kadlec .10 .25
86 Jan Novak .10 .25
87 Angel Krstev .10 .25
88 Jan Snopek .10 .25
89 Jan Kloboucek .10 .25
90 Jan Hejda .10 .25
91 Petr Martinek .10 .25
92 Jan Slavik .10 .25
93 Daniel Branda .10 .25
94 Jan Alinc .20 .50
95 Viktor Hubl .10 .25
96 Jan Kopecky .10 .25
97 Jan Bohac .10 .25
98 Zdenek Skorepa .20 .50
99 Michal Sup .10 .25
100 Radek Matejovsky .10 .25
101 Robin Bacul .10 .25
102 Leos Cermak .10 .25
103 Petr Jira .10 .25
104 Marek Tomica .10 .25
105 Petr Hrbek .10 .25
106 Team Logo .04 .10
107 Eduard Novak CO .04 .10
108 Petr Fiala CO .04 .10
109 Lubos Horcicka .10 .25
110 Marek Pinc .10 .25
111 Jan Pospisil .10 .25
112 Jan Krulis .10 .25
113 Michal Madl .10 .25
114 Ondrej Kriz .10 .25
115 Jan Bohacek .10 .25
116 David Hajek .10 .25
117 Jan Dlouhy .10 .25
118 Martin Taborsky .10 .25
119 Jiri Kames .20 .50
120 Ladislav Svoboda .10 .25
121 Pavel Geffert .10 .25
122 Tomas Horna .10 .25
123 Jiri Holsan .10 .25
124 Radek Gardon .10 .25
125 Ladislav Vlcek .10 .25
126 Jozef Voskar .10 .25
127 Tomas Klimt .20 .50
128 Premysl Sedlak .10 .25
129 Tomas Plekanec ERC .10 .25
130 Michal Havel .10 .25
131 Vaclav Skuhravy .10 .25
132 Team Logo .04 .10
133 Vaclav Sykora CO .04 .10
134 Otakar Vejvoda CO .04 .10
135 Zdenek Orct .20 .50
136 Michal Podolka .30 .75
137 Angel Nikolov .20 .50
138 Karel Pilar .40 1.00
139 Radek Mrazek .10 .25
140 Marek Cernosek .10 .25
141 Vladimir Gyna .10 .25
142 Martin Tupa .10 .25
143 Jan Hranac .10 .25
144 Petr Suchy .10 .25
145 Robert Reichel .31 .50
146 Petr Rosol .10 .25
147 Vojtech Kubincak .10 .25
148 Kamil Piros .40 1.00
149 Jindrich Kotrla .10 .25
150 Vesa Karjalainen .10 .25
151 Robert Kysela .10 .25
152 Stanislav Stavensky .10 .25
153 Tomas Martinec .10 .25
154 Zdenek Zak .10 .25
155 Martin Tvrznik .10 .25
156 Lukas Bednarik .10 .25
157 Team Logo .04 .10
158 Radim Rulik CO .04 .10
159 Martin Pesout CO .04 .10
160 Petr Franek .10 .25
161 Zdenek Smid .30 .75
162 Pavel Csipka .10 .25
163 Libor Prochazka .10 .25
164 Robert Kantor .10 .25
165 Jiri Polak .10 .25
166 Normunds Sejejs .10 .25
167 Roman Prosek .10 .25
168 Roman Zak .10 .25
169 Ivan Puncochar .10 .25
170 Petr Puncochar .10 .25
171 Jakub Grof .10 .25
172 Jaromir Kverka .10 .25
173 Tomas Chlubna .10 .25
174 Radek Prochazka .10 .25
175 David Hruska .10 .25
176 Robert Tomik .10 .25
177 Pavel Kasparik .10 .25
178 Martin Rousek .10 .25
179 Jaroslav Kalla .10 .25
180 Petr Bohunicky .10 .25
181 Jan Kostal .10 .25
182 Petr Domin .10 .25
183 Petr Sinagl .10 .25
184 Team Logo .04 .10
185 Milan Chalupa CO .10 .25
186 Pavel Pazourek CO .04 .10
187 Oldrich Svoboda .10 .25
188 Ladislav Kudrna .20 .50
189 Miloslav Bahensky .10 .25
190 Tomas Jakes .10 .25
191 Jiri Hes .10 .25
192 Pavel Kumstat .10 .25
193 Karel Soudek .10 .25
194 Pavol Valko .10 .25
195 David Havir .10 .25
196 David Petlak .10 .25
197 Vladimir Holik .10 .25
198 Peter Pucher .10 .25
199 Marek Uram .10 .25
200 Karel Plasek .10 .25
201 Zbynek Marak .10 .25
202 Milan Prochazka .10 .25
203 Patrik Fink .10 .25
204 David Pazourek .10 .25
205 Marek Vorel .10 .25
206 Radek Haman .10 .25
207 Petr Lipina .10 .25
208 Petr Kumstat .10 .25
209 Team Logo .04 .10
210 Vladimir Vujtek CO .04 .10
211 Ales Mach CO .04 .10
212 Marek Novotny .10 .25
213 Vlastimil Lakosil .20 .50
214 Mario Cartelli .10 .25
215 Vladimir Vlk .10 .25
216 Jiri Kuntos .10 .25
217 Petr Gregorek .10 .25
218 Robert Prochazka .10 .25
219 Ondrej Zetek .10 .25
220 David Nosek .10 .25
221 Tomas Houdek .10 .25
222 Tomas Harant .10 .25
223 Richard Kral .10 .25
224 Viktor Ujcik .15 .40
225 Jozef Dano .10 .25
226 Richard Kapus .10 .25
227 Pavel Janku .20 .25
228 Marek Zadina .10 .25
229 Branislav Janos .10 .25
230 Tomas Nemcicky .10 .25
231 Patrik Moskal .10 .25
232 David Appel .10 .25
233 Jan Marek .10 .25
234 Jiri Hasek .10 .25
235 Team Logo .04 .10
236 Alois Hadamczik CO .04 .10
237 Kamil Konecny CO .04 .10
238 Mojmir Trlicik CO .04 .10
239 Martin Prusek .75 2.00
240 Jiri Trvaj .10 .25
241 Lukas Smolka .10 .25
242 Vitezslav Skuta .10 .25
243 Dmitrij Jerofejev .10 .25
244 Daniel Kapotocny .10 .25
245 Petr Jurecka .10 .25
246 Radek Philipp .10 .25
247 Lukas Zatopek .10 .25
248 Daniel Seman .10 .25
249 Jan Vytisk .10 .25
250 David Moravec .20 .50
251 Martin Prochazka .10 .25
252 Ivan Padelek .10 .25
253 Josef Straub .10 .25
254 Roman Kadera .10 .25
255 Marek Ivan .10 .25
256 Zdenek Pavelek .10 .25
257 Martin Tomasek .10 .25
258 Pavel Selinger .10 .25
259 Jan Pleva .10 .25
260 Ales Padelek .10 .25
261 Team Logo .04 .10
262 Ivo Pestuka CO .04 .10
263 Jiri Reznar CO .04 .10
264 Radovan Biegl .10 .25
265 Radek Masny .10 .25
266 Michael Vyhlidal .10 .25
267 Miroslav Javin .10 .25
268 Richard Pavlikovsky .10 .25
269 Petr Pavlas .10 .25
270 Patrik Rimmel .10 .25
271 Ales Tomasek .10 .25
272 Petr Suchanek .10 .25
273 Tomas Srsen .10 .25
274 Petr Folta .10 .25
275 Libor Pivko .10 .25
276 Daniel Bohac .10 .25
277 Roman Horak .20 .50
278 Jan Peterek .10 .25
279 Marek Melenovsky .10 .25
280 Pavel Zdrahal .10 .25
281 Roman Kontsek .10 .25
282 Michal Cech .10 .25
283 Tomas Sykora .10 .25
284 Martin Streit .10 .25
285 Milos Melicherik .10 .25
286 Team Logo .04 .10
287 Milos Riha CO .04 .10
288 Frantisek Vyborny CO .04 .10
289 Pavel Hynek CO .04 .10
290 Petr Briza .30 .75
291 Petr Prikryl .10 .25
292 Tomas Duba .10 .25
293 Libor Zabransky .20 .25
294 Vlastimil Kroupa .20 .50
295 Frantisek Ptacek .10 .25
296 Michal Dobron .10 .25
297 Pavel Srek .10 .25
208 Jaroslav Nedved .10 .25
299 Martin Holy .10 .25
300 Miha Rebolj .10 .25
301 Jan Hanzlik .10 .25
302 Vladimir Vujtek .20 .50
303 Jaroslav Hlinka .10 .25
304 Martin Chabada .10 .25
305 Ondrej Kratena .10 .25
306 Michal Bros .20 .25
307 Patrik Martinec .10 .25
308 Richard Zemlicka .20 .50
309 Jiri Zelenka .10 .25
310 Vaclav Novak .10 .25
311 Petr Havelka .10 .25
312 Michal Sivek .60 1.50
313 Petr Hrbek .10 .25
314 Radek Duda .10 .25
315 Josef Slanec .10 .25
316 Petr Kanko .75 2.00
317 Team Logo .04 .10
318 Zdislav Tabara CO .04 .10
319 Miroslav Venkrbec CO .04 .10
320 Jaroslav Kames .30 .75
321 Ivo Pesat .10 .25
322 Lukas Plsek .10 .25
323 Jan Srdinko .10 .25
324 Milan Nedoma .10 .25
325 Martin Strbak .10 .25
326 Radim Tesarik .10 .25
327 Pavel Zubicek .10 .25
328 Alexej Jaskin .10 .25
329 Petr Kubos .10 .25
330 Zbynek Spitzer .10 .25
331 Michal Safarik .10 .25
332 Pavel Augusta .10 .25
333 Jan Pardavy .10 .25
334 Jiri Dopita .20 .50
335 Jan Tomajko .10 .25
336 Roman Stantien .10 .25
337 Jan Sochor .10 .25
338 Martin Paroulek .10 .25
339 Jan Lipiansky .10 .25
340 Jiri Hudler ERC 6.00 15.00
341 Ondrej Vesely .10 .25
342 Jiri Jantovsky .10 .25
343 Petr Zajgla .10 .25
344 Tomas Demel .10 .25
345 Petr Vampola .10 .25
346 Team Logo .04 .10
347 Antonin Stavjana CO .10 .25
348 Zdenek Venera CO .04 .10
349 Vladimir Hudacek .20 .50
350 Richard Hrazdira .20 .50
351 Petr Tucek .10 .25
352 Tomas Zizka .10 .25
353 Jiri Marusak .10 .25
354 Martin Hamrlik .10 .25
355 Patrik Luza .10 .25
356 Rostislav Malena .08 .20
357 Jan Homer .10 .25
358 Lukas Zib .10 .25
359 Boris Zabka .10 .25
360 Miroslav Okal .08 .20
361 Petr Cajanek .30 .75
362 Jaroslav Balastik .10 .25
363 Petr Vala .10 .25
364 Martin Ambruz .10 .25
365 Petr Leska .10 .25
366 Miroslav Barus .10 .25
367 Martin Kotasek .10 .25
368 Lubomir Korhon .20 .50
369 Ivan Rachunek .40 1.00
370 Radovan Somik .10 .25
371 Filip Cech .10 .25
372 Martin Jenacek .10 .25
373 Pavel Mojzis .10 .25
374 Milan Navratil .10 .25
375 Michal Safarik .10 .25
376 Miroslav Blatak .20 .50
377 Team Logo .04 .10
378 Roman Turek .40 1.00
379 Milan Hnilicka .40 1.00
380 Tomas Kaberle .30 .75
381 Frantisek Kaberle .20 .50
382 Roman Hamrlik .30 .75
383 Pavel Kubina .40 1.00
384 Jaromir Jagr 2.00 5.00
385 Patrik Elias .75 2.00
386 Milan Hejduk 2.00 5.00
387 Radek Dvorak .40 1.00
388 Petr Nedved .30 .75
389 Vaclav Prospal .40 1.00
390 Pavel Patera .20 .50
391 Petr Sykora 1.25 3.00
392 Vaclav Varada .20 .50
393 Martin Straka .40 1.00
394 Jan Hrdina .40 1.00
395 David Volek .20 .50
396 Tomas Vlasak .30 .75
397 Michal Rozsival .30 .75
398 Team Logo .04 .10
399 Ladislav Blazek .10 .25
400 Miloslav Horava .10 .25
401 Frantisek Kucera .20 .50
402 Lubomir Sekeras .20 .50
403 Petr Kadlec .10 .25
404 Jaroslav Spacek .20 .50
405 Frantisek Prochazka .20 .50
406 Antonin Stavjana .10 .25
407 Vladimir Ruzicka .20 .50
408 Petr Rosol .10 .25
409 Robert Reichel .31 .50
410 Martin Rucinsky .20 .50
411 Josef Beranek .20 .50
412 Viktor Ujcik .15 .40
413 Michal Sup .10 .25
414 Ivo Prorok .10 .25
415 Zdeno Ciger .20 .50
416 Jiri Hrdina .10 .25
417 J.Jagr/V.Ruzicka 2.00 5.00
418 Checklist .04 .10
419 Checklist .04 .10
420 Checklist .04 .10
421 Checklist .04 .10

2000-01 Czech OFS Star Emerald

COMPLETE SET (36) 10.00 25.00
*VIOLET PARALLELS: 1X to 2X
PINK PARALLELS : 2X to 3X
1 Jaroslav Kames .40 1.00
2 Jiri Dopita .40 1.00
3 Jan Pardavy .20 .50
4 Vladimir Hudacek .20 .50
5 Petr Cajanek .75 2.00
6 Richard Hrazdira .40 1.00
7 Petr Briza .75 2.00
8 Jiri Zelenka .20 .50
9 Richard Zemlicka .40 1.00
10 Libor Barta .40 1.00
11 Adam Svoboda .40 1.00
12 Otakar Janecky .40 1.00
13 Vaclav Kral .20 .50
14 Rudolf Suchanek .40 1.00
15 Michal Marik .20 .50
16 Dusan Salficky .60 1.50
17 Petr Korinek .40 1.00
18 Ivan Vlcek .20 .50
19 Zdenek Orct .40 1.00
20 Robert Reichel .40 1.00
21 Petr Franek .20 .50
22 Libor Prochazka .20 .50
23 Vlastimil Lakosil .40 1.00
24 Richard Kral .20 .50
25 Viktor Ujcik .20 .50
26 Martin Prusek 1.00 2.50
27 Martin Prochazka .20 .50
28 Josef Straub .20 .50
29 Radek Gardon .20 .50
30 Lubos Horcicka .20 .50
31 Tomas Srsen .20 .50
32 Radovan Biegl .20 .50
33 Oldrich Svoboda .20 .50
34 Marek Uram .20 .50
35 Ladislav Blazek .40 1.00
36 Roman Malek .20 .50

2001 Czech Stadion

COMPLETE SET (45) 30.00 60.00
217 Ray Bourque 2.00 5.00
218 Patrik Elias .75 2.00
219 Milan Hejduk .75 2.00
220 Bobby Holik .40 1.00
221 Tomas Kaberle .40 1.00
222 Nick Lidstrom 1.25 3.00
223 Petr Sykora .40 1.00
224 Martin Skoula .40 1.00
225 Alex Tanguay .75 2.00
226 Daniel Alfredsson .75 2.00
227 Jason Allison .40 1.00
228 Adam Deadmarsh .40 1.00
229 Chris Drury .75 2.00
230 Bob Essensa .40 1.00
231 Scott Gomez .40 1.00
233 Tomas Holmstrom .75 2.00
234 Darius Kasparaitis .40 1.00
235 Pavel Brendl .40 1.00
236 Eric Lindros 1.25 3.00
237 Rostislav Klesla .40 1.00
238 Scott Niedermayer .40 1.00
239 Brett Hull 1.25 3.00
240 Paul Kariya 1.25 3.00
241 Chris Gratton .40 1.00
242 Doug Gilmour .75 2.00
243 Alexei Yashin .40 1.00
244 Saku Koivu .75 2.00
245 Randy McKay .40 1.00
246 Markus Naslund .75 2.00
247 Keith Primeau .40 1.00
248 Dainius Zubrus .40 1.00
249 Dominik Hasek 1.50 4.00
250 Frantisek Kaberle .40 1.00
251 Jaromir Jagr 2.00 5.00
252 Jaromir Jagr (Tennis) 2.00 5.00
253 Rob Blake .40 1.00
254 Adam Oates .40 1.00
255 Joe Sakic 2.00 5.00
256 Alexei Kovalev .40 1.00
257 Ivan Hlinka .40 1.00
258 Martin Straka .40 1.00
259 Milan Hnilicka .40 1.00
260 Miroslav Satan .40 1.00
261 Peter Bondra .40 1.00
324 John Leclair .40 1.00

2001-02 Czech DS

COMPLETE SET (61) 15.00 30.00
1 Dominik Hasek 2.00 5.00
2 Vladimir Hudacek .20 .50
3 Roman Malek .10 .25
4 Mario Cartelli .10 .25
5 Tomas Kaberle .30 .75
6 Petr Kadlec .10 .25
7 Angel Nikolov .20 .50
8 Radek Philipp .10 .25
9 Libor Prochazka .10 .25
10 Michal Sykora .10 .25
11 Libor Zabransky .10 .25
12 Kamil Brabenec .10 .25
13 Michal Bros .10 .25
14 Jiri Burger .10 .25
15 Petr Cajanek .30 .75
16 Jaroslav Hlinka .10 .25
17 Viktor Hubl .10 .25
18 David Moravec .20 .50
19 Martin Prochazka .10 .25
20 Petr Sykora .10 .25
21 Jan Tomajko .10 .25
22 Viktor Ujcik .15 .35
23 Pavel Vostrak .10 .25
24 Jaroslav Bednar .20 .50
25 Martin Rucinsky .20 .50
26 Tomas Vokoun 1.25 3.00
27 Milan Hnilicka .20 .50
28 Josef Melichar .20 .50
29 Michal Rozsival .20 .50
30 Karel Pilar .20 .50
31 Jan Horacek .10 .25
32 Robert Schnabel .20 .50
33 Pavel Kolarik .20 .50
34 Petr Mika .20 .50
35 Petr Tenkrat .20 .50
36 Jaromir Jagr 2.00 5.00
37 Pavel Patera .20 .50
38 Josef Beranek .20 .50
39 Martin Straka .30 .75
40 Petr Nedved .30 .75
41 Martin Rucinsky .20 .50
42 Robert Reichel .20 .50
43 David Vyborny .40 1.00
44 Roman Hamrlik .30 .75
45 Milan Hejduk 1.25 3.00
46 Patrik Elias .75 2.00
47 Vaclav Prospal .20 .50
48 Vaclav Varada .20 .50
49 Petr Sykora .10 .25
50 Dusan Salficky .30 .75
51 Petr Briza .30 .75
52 Martin Prusek .40 1.00
53 Radek Martinek .20 .50
54 Karel Pilar .20 .50
55 Viktor Ujcik .15 .35
56 Vaclav Nedorost .40 1.00
57 Ales Kotalik .60 1.50
58 Jiri Dopita .20 .50
59 Robert Reichel .20 .50
60 Petr Cajanek .30 .75
61 David Moravec .20 .50

2001-02 Czech DS Best of the Best

COMPLETE SET (9) 5.00 10.00
BB1 Dominik Hasek 2.00 5.00
BB2 Tomas Kaberle .60 1.50
BB3 Michal Sykora .20 .50
BB4 Petr Cajanek .60 1.50
BB5 David Moravec .40 1.00
BB6 Martin Prochazka .20 .50
BB7 Martin Rucinsky .40 1.00
BB8 Robert Reichel .40 1.00
BB9 Jiri Dopita .40 1.00

2001-02 Czech DS Goalies

COMPLETE SET (5) 6.00 15.00
G1 Dominik Hasek 4.00 10.00
G2 Milan Hnilicka .75 2.00
G3 Petr Briza .75 2.00
G4 Roman Cechmanek .75 2.00
G5 Roman Malek .75 2.00

2001-02 Czech DS Ice Heroes

COMPLETE SET (10) 8.00 15.00
IH1 Tomas Vokoun 2.00 5.00
IH2 Jaromir Jagr 3.00 8.00
IH3 Pavel Patera .40 1.00
IH4 Josef Beranek .40 1.00
IH5 Martin Straka .75 2.00
IH6 Petr Nedved .60 1.50
IH7 Martin Rucinsky .40 1.00
IH8 Robert Reichel .40 1.00
IH9 David Vyborny .20 .50
IH10 Petr Tenkrat .60 1.50

2001-02 Czech DS Legends

COMPLETE SET (12) 3.00 6.00
L1 Jiri Holocek .40 1.00
L2 Jiri Kralik .20 .50
L3 Vlastimil Bubnik .40 1.00
L4 Vaclav Rozinak .20 .50
L5 Vladimir Zabrodsky .40 1.00
L6 Vladimir Martinec .40 1.00
L7 Ivan Hlinka .40 1.00
L8 Jan Havel .20 .50
L9 Frantisek Pospisil .20 .50
L10 Jaroslav Holik .20 .50
L11 Milan Novy .40 1.00
L12 Jiri Lala .20 .50

2001-02 Czech DS Top Gallery

COMPLETE SET (2) 8.00 15.00
1 Jaromir Jagr 4.00 10.00
2 Jaromir Jagr 4.00 10.00

2001-02 Czech National Team Postcards

COMPLETE SET (17) 20.00 40.00
1 Josef Beranek .75 2.00
2 Petr Briza .75 2.00
3 Josef Beranek .75 2.00
4 Radek Duda .75 2.00
5 Jiri Hudler 2.00 5.00
6 Jaromir Jagr 4.00 10.00
7 Richard Kral .75 2.00
8 Frantisek Kucera .75 2.00
9 David Moravec .75 2.00
10 Karel Rachunek .75 2.00
11 Martin Richter .75 2.00
12 Dusan Salficky .75 2.00
13 Michal Sykora .75 2.00
14 Viktor Ujcik .75 2.00
15 Tomas Vlasak .75 2.00
16 Vladimir Vujtek .75 2.00
17 Michal Bros .75 2.00

2001-02 Czech OFS

COMPLETE SET (284) 25.00 50.00
1 Lukas Hronek .08 .20
2 Petr Martinek .08 .20
3 Petr Kadlec .08 .20
4 Roman Malek .08 .20
5 Jan Alinc .20 .50
6 Josef Beranek .20 .50
7 Viktor Hubl .08 .20
8 Martin Rousek .08 .20
9 Radek Matejovsky .08 .20
10 Jan Kloboucek .08 .20
11 Daniel Brandl .08 .20
12 Viktor Ujcik .20 .60
13 Milan Antos .08 .20
14 Radek Belohlav .08 .20
15 Michal Bros .20 .50
16 Petr Briza .20 .50
17 Radek Hamr .08 .20
18 Jaroslav Hlinka .08 .20
19 Martin Chabada .08 .20
20 Pavel Kasparik .08 .20
21 Marek Ivan .08 .20
22 Lukas Galvas .08 .20
23 Radek Simicek .08 .20
24 Robert Tomanek .08 .20
25 Jan Tomajko .08 .20
26 Ivan Padelek .08 .20
27 Zdenek Pavelek .08 .20
28 Radek Philipp .08 .20
29 Pavel Srek .08 .20
30 David Moravec .20 .50
31 Jan Srdinko .08 .20
32 Marek Melenovsky .20 .50
33 Frantisek Ptacek .08 .20
34 Vaclav Novak .08 .20
35 Jaroslav Nedved .20 .50
36 Ludek Krayzel .08 .20
37 Roman Kadera .08 .20
38 Petr Jurecka .08 .20
39 Lukas Smolka .08 .20
40 Vitezslav Skuta .08 .20
41 Josef Straub .08 .20
42 Jiri Trvaj .08 .20
43 Jan Vytisk .08 .20
44 Daniel Zapotocny .08 .20
45 Pavel Selingr .08 .20
46 Martin Prochazka .20 .50
47 Vlastimil Lakosil .08 .20
48 Petr Gregorek .08 .20
49 Mario Cartelli .08 .20
50 Miloslav Guren .20 .50
51 Petr Jancarik .08 .20
52 Libor Prochazka .20 .50
53 Jan Slavik .08 .20
54 Pavel Janku .08 .20
55 Branislav Janos .08 .20
56 Marek Zadina .08 .20
57 Jiri Polak .08 .20
58 Ondrej Nemec .08 .20
59 Petr Kubos .08 .20
60 Slavomir Hrina .08 .20
61 Ivo Pesat .08 .20
62 Radovan Biegl .20 .50
63 Zdenek Skorepa .20 .50
64 Roman Meluzin .08 .20
65 Jan Marek .08 .20
66 Richard Kral .08 .20
67 Rostislav Vlach .08 .20
68 Ondrej Vetchy .08 .20
69 Petr Vampola .08 .20
70 Lukas Valko .08 .20
71 Michal Sararcik .08 .20
72 Martin Streit .08 .20
73 Radim Kucharczyk .08 .20
74 Jiri Hudler 8.00 20.00
75 Jiri Burger .08 .20
76 Martin Strbak .08 .20
77 Martin Ambruz .08 .20
78 Jakub Blazek .08 .20
79 Pavel Mojzis .08 .20
80 Jiri Marusak .08 .20
81 Rostislav Malena .08 .20
82 Jan Homer .08 .20
83 Martin Hamrlik .08 .20
84 Petr Tucek .08 .20
85 Vladimir Hubacek .08 .20
86 Ales Zacha .08 .20
87 Radovan Somik .40 1.00
88 Ivan Rachunek .08 .20
89 Libor Pivko .08 .20
90 Milan Ministr .08 .20
91 Petr Leska .08 .20
92 Martin Jenacek .08 .20
93 Petr Cajanek .30 .75
94 Karol Bartanus .20 .50
95 Jaroslav Balastik .08 .20
96 Petr Havelka .08 .20
97 Jan Hanzlik .08 .20
98 Petr Prikryl .08 .20
99 Libor Zabransky .20 .50
100 David Hnat .08 .20
101 David Pazourek .08 .20
102 Zbynek Marak .08 .20
103 Radek Haman .08 .20
104 Karel Soudek .08 .20
105 Pavel Kumstat .08 .20
106 Tomas Jakes .08 .20
107 Vladimir Holik .08 .20
108 Jiri Hes .08 .20
109 David Havir .08 .20
110 Oldrich Svoboda .20 .50
111 Ladislav Kudrna .20 .50
112 Valdemar Jirus .08 .20
113 Miroslav Okal .08 .20
114 Peter Bohunicky .08 .20
115 Patrik Hucko .08 .20
116 Miroslav Blatak .08 .20
117 Tomas Netik .08 .20
118 Richard Zemlicka .20 .50
119 Marek Uram .08 .20
120 Peter Pucher .08 .20
121 Lukas Krajicek ERC .75 2.00
122 Michal Klimes .08 .20
123 Josef Jindra .08 .20
124 Ladislav Cierny .08 .20
125 Michal Marik .08 .20
126 Josef Kucera .08 .20
127 Michal Kolarik .08 .20
128 Jiri Hasek .08 .20
129 David Nosek .08 .20
130 Martin Vojtek .08 .20
131 Milan Nedoma .08 .20
132 Rudolf Suchanek .08 .20
133 Filip Vanecek .08 .20
134 Pavel Zubicek .08 .20
135 Kamil Brabenec .08 .20
136 Jiri Broz .08 .20
137 Dan Hlavka .08 .20
138 Stepan Hrobojk .08 .20
139 Roman Horak .08 .20
140 Milan Michalek ERC 6.00 15.00
141 Peter Bartos .20 .50
142 Michal Vondrka .08 .20
143 Jiri Simanek .08 .20
144 Petr Sailer .08 .20
145 Lubos Rob .08 .20
146 Jan Rehor .08 .20
147 Martin Strba .08 .20
148 Marek Pinc .08 .20
149 Vladimir Gyna .08 .20
150 Jan Hranac .08 .20
151 Martin Nosek .08 .20
152 Lukas Pozivil .08 .20
153 Vojtech Kubincak .08 .20
154 Anton Lezo .08 .20
155 Martin Tupa .08 .20
156 Vlastimil Kroupa .20 .50
157 Jindrich Kotrla .08 .20
158 David Hruska .08 .20
159 Petr Jira .08 .20
160 Michal Oliverius .08 .20
161 Lukas Havel .08 .20
162 Jaroslav Buchal .08 .20
163 Jan Sulc .08 .20
164 Pavol Rieciciar .08 .20
165 Petr Klima .20 .50
166 Jiri Gombar .08 .20
167 Tomas Kaberle .20 .50
168 Ladislav Svoboda .08 .20
169 Pavel Geffert .08 .20
170 Tomas Horna .08 .20
171 Zdenek Orct .20 .50
172 Robert Kysela .08 .20
173 Radek Gardon .08 .20
174 Ondrej Kriz .20 .50
175 Tomas Klimt .20 .50
176 Jan Bohacek .20 .50
177 Michal Havel .08 .20
178 David Hajek .08 .20
179 Vaclav Skuhravy .08 .20
180 Radim Skuhrovec .08 .20
181 Tomas Plekanec .40 1.00
182 Jan Dlouhy .08 .20
183 David Patera .08 .20

184 Jan Krulis .08 .20
185 Jan Pospisil .08 .20
186 David Appel .08 .20
187 Jakub Kraus .08 .20
188 Petr Machulda .08 .20
189 Petr Franek .08 .20
190 Jaromir Kverka .08 .20
191 Michal Madl .08 .20
192 Marcel Kucera .08 .20
193 Jakub Grof .08 .20
194 Michal Dobron .08 .20
195 Jan Kopecky .08 .20
196 Dmitrij Rodine .08 .20
197 David Balasz .08 .20
198 Roman Prosek .08 .20
199 Jan Kostal .08 .20
200 Petr Domin .08 .20
201 Jan Choteborsky .08 .20
202 Vaclav Benak .08 .20
203 Miroslav Simonovic .08 .20
204 Jiri Hanzlik .08 .20
205 Josef Reznicek .08 .20
206 Ivan Vlcek .08 .20
207 Libor Barta .08 .20
208 Ondrej Steiner .08 .20
209 Dusan Andrasovsky .08 .20
210 Martin Vyborny .08 .20
211 Juraj Stefanka .08 .20
212 Radek Duda .08 .20
213 Josef Slanec .08 .20
214 Michal Dvorak .08 .20
215 Libor Pavlis .08 .20
216 Vaclav Eiselt .08 .20
217 Tomas Nemcicky .08 .20
218 Petr Mudroch .08 .20
219 Patrik Moskal .08 .20
220 Zdenek Sedlak .08 .20
221 Pavel Vostrak .08 .20
222 Milan Volak .08 .20
223 Petr Mudroch .08 .20
224 Jiri Malinsky .08 .20
225 Jan Svik .08 .20
226 Petr Caslava .08 .20
227 Michal Straka .08 .20
228 Adam Svoboda .20 .50
229 Josef Straka .20 .50
230 Patrik Rimmel .08 .20
231 Petr Pavlas .08 .20
232 Michael Prochazka .20 .50
233 Miroslav Javin .08 .20
234 Robin Bacul .08 .20
235 Marek Cernosek .08 .20
236 Petr Folta .08 .20
237 Pavel Malac .08 .20
238 Radek Krestan .08 .20
239 Lubomir Korhon .08 .20
240 Pavel Cagas .20 .50
241 Radoslav Kropac .08 .20
242 Dusan Pohorelec .08 .20
243 Petr Vala .08 .20
244 Pavel Zdrahal .08 .20
245 Otakar Janecky .20 .50
246 Tomas Blazek .20 .50
247 Michael Vyhlidal .20 .50
248 Michal Sykora .20 .50
249 Tomas Pacal .08 .20
250 Andrej Novotny .08 .20
251 Tomas Rolinek .08 .20
252 Stanislav Prochazka .08 .20
253 David Pospisil .08 .20
254 Michal Mikeska .08 .20
255 Ladislav Lubina .08 .20
256 Jaroslav Kudrna .20 .50
257 Tomas Vak .08 .20
258 Michal Tvrdik .08 .20
259 Petr Sykora .20 .50
260 Jan Bokoc .08 .20
261 Milan Prochazka .08 .20
262 Patrik Fink .08 .20
263 Richard Kuckrek .08 .20
264 Marek Vorel .08 .20
265 Tomas Klimes .08 .20
266 Premysl Sedlak .08 .20
267 David Hajek .08 .20
268 Ladislav Vlcek .08 .20
269 Jiri Kames .20 .50
270 Radek Krestan .08 .20
271 Jan Hejda .08 .20
272 Borek Stagma .08 .20
273 Leos Cermak .08 .20
274 Jan Novak .08 .20
275 Zbynek Tuma .08 .20
276 Daniel Bohac .08 .20
277 Michal Sup .08 .20
278 Jan Snopek .08 .20
279 Adam Saffer .08 .20
280 David Pojkar .08 .20
281 Marek Tomica .08 .20
282 Petr Jurecka .08 .20
283 Lukas Krenzelok .08 .20
284 Michael Prochazka .20 .50

2001-02 Czech OFS All Stars

COMPLETE SET (41) 20.00 40.00
1 Martin Hamrlik .40 1.00
2 Petr Gregorek .40 1.00
3 Oldrich Svoboda .75 2.00
4 Radim Tesarik .40 1.00
5 Jiri Dopita 1.25 3.00
6 Petr Cajanek .75 2.00
7 Marek Uram .40 1.00
8 Michael Vyhlidal .40 1.00
9 Mario Cartelli .40 1.00
10 Pavel Zdrahal .40 1.00
11 Libor Prochazka .75 2.00
12 Ales Pisa .75 2.00
13 Robert Reichel .75 2.00
14 Josef Reznicek .40 1.00
15 Karel Pilar 1.25 3.00
16 Dusan Salficky .75 2.00
17 Patrik Martinec .40 1.00
18 Rudolf Suchanek .40 1.00
19 Jaromir Kverka .40 1.00
20 Ladislav Svoboda .40 1.00
21 Daniel Branda .40 1.00
22 Jan Pardavy .40 1.00
23 David Moravec .75 2.00
24 Zbynek Marak .40 1.00
25 Petr Leska .40 1.00
26 Jiri Marusak .40 1.00
27 Roman Stantien .40 1.00
28 Jan Srdinko .40 1.00
29 Martin Prusek 2.00 5.00
30 Libor Pivko .40 1.00
31 Zdenek Pavelek .40 1.00
32 Jaroslav Hlinka .40 1.00
33 Otakar Janecky .75 2.00
34 Petr Kadlec .75 2.00
35 Ales Kotalik 1.25 3.00
36 Jan Krulis .40 1.00
37 Robert Tomik .40 1.00
38 Petr Sykora .75 2.00
39 Ivan Vlcek .40 1.00
40 Pavel Vostrak .40 1.00
41 Vladimir Vujtek .40 1.00

2001-02 Czech OFS Gold Inserts

COMPLETE SET (11) 20.00 40.00
G1 Roman Malek 2.00 5.00
G2 Petr Franek 2.00 5.00
G3 Petr Prikryl 2.00 5.00
G4 Vlastimil Lakosil 2.00 5.00
G5 Radovan Biegl 2.00 5.00
G6 Vladimir Hudacek 2.00 5.00
G7 Oldrich Svoboda 2.00 5.00
G8 Josef Kucera 2.00 5.00
G9 Michal Marik 2.00 5.00
G10 Miroslav Simonovic 2.00 5.00
G11 Pavel Malac 2.00 5.00

2001-02 Czech OFS H Inserts

COMPLETE SET (15) 25.00 50.00
H1 Lukas Hronek 1.50 4.00
H2 Marcel Kucera 1.50 4.00
H3 Zdenek Orct 2.00 5.00
H4 Martin Vojtek 1.50 4.00
H5 Jan Pospisil 1.50 4.00
H6 Lukas Smolka 1.50 4.00
H7 Jiri Trvaj 1.50 4.00
H8 Ivo Pesat 1.50 4.00
H9 Petr Tucek 1.50 4.00
H10 Ladislav Kudrna 1.50 4.00
H11 Marek Pinc 1.50 4.00
H12 Pavel Cagas 1.50 4.00
H13 Adam Svoboda 2.00 5.00
H14 Libor Barta 1.50 4.00
H15 Petr Briza 2.50 6.00

2001-02 Czech OFS Red Inserts

COMPLETE SET (24) 25.00 50.00
RE1D Viktor Ujcik .75 2.00
RE2D Josef Beranek .75 2.00
RE3D Tomas Plekanec .75 2.00
RE4D Tomas Kaberle 1.25 3.00
RE5D Jiri Zelenka .75 2.00
RE6D Martin Prochazka .75 2.00
RE7D David Moravec .75 2.00
RE8D Petr Klima .75 2.00
RE9D Rudolf Suchanek .75 2.00
RE10D Frantisek Kucera .75 2.00
RE11D Michal Sykora .75 2.00
RE12D Otakar Janecky .75 2.00
RE13D Pavel Zdrahal .75 2.00
RE14D Radoslav Kropac .75 2.00
RE15D Rostislav Vlach .75 2.00
RE16D Marek Uram .75 2.00
RE17D Petr Leska .75 2.00
RE18D Petr Cajanek 1.25 3.00
RE19D Ondrej Kratena 1.25 3.00
RE20D Petr Korinek .75 2.00
RE21D Jiri Hudler 6.00 15.00
RE22D Pavel Janku .75 2.00
RE23D Richard Kral .75 2.00
RE24D Miloslav Guren .75 2.00

2002 Czech National Team Postcards

COMPLETE SET (15) 10.00 20.00
1 Jaroslav Balastik .75 2.00
2 Jaroslav Bednar .75 2.00
3 Petr Briza .75 2.00
4 Jan Hlavac .75 2.00
5 Jindrich Kotrla .40 1.00
6 Tomas Kucharcik .40 1.00
7 Jan Marek .40 1.00
8 Zbynek Michalek 1.25 3.00
9 Jaroslav Modry .40 1.00
10 Vaclav Pletka .40 1.00
11 Jaroslav Spacek .40 1.00
12 Petr Tenkrat .40 1.00
13 Radim Tesarik .40 1.00
14 Marek Vorel .40 1.00
15 David Vyborny .75 2.00

2002 Czech Stadion Cup Finals

COMPLETE SET (9)
484 Scotty Bowman .75 2.00
485 Jiri Fischer .75 2.00
486 Ron Francis .75 2.00
487 Dominik Hasek 2.00 5.00
488 Arturs Irbe .75 2.00
489 Marek Malik .40 1.00
490 Jaroslav Svoboda .40 1.00
491 Jiri Slegr .40 1.00
492 Josef Vasicek .40 1.00

2002 Czech Stadion Olympics

325 Petr Cajanek .75 2.00
326 Roman Cechmanek .40 1.00
327 Jiri Dopita .40 1.00
328 Radek Dvorak .40 1.00
329 Patrik Elias 1.25 3.00
330 Roman Hamrlik .40 1.00
331 Milan Hejduk 1.25 3.00
332 Martin Havlat 2.00 5.00
333 Dominik Hasek 2.00 5.00
334 Jan Hrdina .40 1.00
335 Jaromir Jagr 2.00 5.00
336 Tomas Kaberle .75 2.00
337 Pavel Patera .40 1.00
338 Robert Lang .40 1.00
339 Pavel Kubina .40 1.00
340 Petr Sykora .40 1.00
341 Martin Rucinsky .40 1.00
342 Robert Reichel .40 1.00
347 Roman Turek .40 1.00
348 Jaroslav Spacek .40 1.00
349 Richard Smehlik .40 1.00
350 Martin Skoula .40 1.00
351 Michal Sykora .40 1.00

2002-03 Czech DS

COMPLETE SET (100) 30.00 60.00
1 Milan Hnilicka .40 1.00
2 Dusan Salficky .30 .75
3 Petr Briza .30 .75
4 Adam Svoboda .30 .75
5 Frantisek Kucera .10 .25
6 Petr Kadlec .10 .25
7 Karel Rachunek .30 .75
8 Richard Kral .10 .25
9 Josef Beranek .20 .50
10 Radek Duda .10 .25
11 Petr Mudroch .10 .25
12 Milan Michalek 2.00 5.00
13 Tomas Kucharcik .10 .25
14 Frantisek Kaberle .10 .25
15 Rostislav Klesla .75 2.00
16 Filip Kuba .20 .50
17 Pavel Kubina .30 .75
18 Jaroslav Spacek .20 .50
19 Michal Sykora .10 .25
20 Martin Richter .10 .25
21 Michal Bros .10 .25
22 Petr Cajanek .30 .75
23 Jaroslav Hlinka .10 .25
24 Jan Hrdina .40 1.00
25 Jaromir Jagr 2.00 5.00
26 David Moravec .20 .50
27 Pavel Patera .20 .50
28 Martin Prochazka .10 .25
29 Zdenek Sedlak .10 .25
30 Viktor Ujcik .20 .50
31 Tomas Vlasak .10 .25
32 Ondrej Kratena .10 .25
33 David Vyborny .10 .25
34 Vladimir Vujtek .20 .50
35 Petr Leska .10 .25
36 Marek Zidlicky .30 .75
37 Jaroslav Balastik .10 .25
38 Libor Pivko .10 .25
39 David Hruska .10 .25
40 Jiri Marusak .10 .25
41 Milan Hnilicka 2.00 5.00
42 Tomas Vokoun .20 .50
43 Jaroslav Spacek .10 .25
44 Jaroslav Bednar .10 .25
45 Martin Rucinsky .10 .25
46 Jaromir Jagr .20 .50
47 Karel Pilar 2.00 5.00
48 David Vyborny .10 .25
49 Frantisek Kaberle .20 .50
50 Tomas Kaberle .10 .25
51 Vaclav Prospal .40 1.00
52 Jan Hrdina .10 .25
53 Robert Reichel .20 .50
54 Josef Melichar .10 .25
55 Jan Hlavac .40 1.00
56 Jiri Fischer .75 2.00
57 Milan Hejduk .20 .50
58 Jiri Dopita .40 1.00
59 Vaclav Varada .20 .50
60 Patrik Stefan 2.00 5.00
61 Milan Kraft .20 .50
62 Jiri Hudler .10 .25
63 Libor Ustrnul .10 .25
64 Lukas Hronek .30 .75
65 Miroslav Blatak .20 .50
66 Jan Hanzlik .40 1.00
67 Jiri Novotny .20 .50
68 Ales Hemsky .20 .50
69 Tomas Plekanec .40 1.00
70 Filip Novak .75 2.00
71 Miloslav Horava 1.50 4.00
72 Lukas Krajicek .20 .50
73 Tomas Mojzis .20 .50
74 Jiri Jakes .40 1.00
75 Jan Bohac .40 1.00
76 Milan Hnilicka .40 1.00
77 Dusan Salficky .30 .75
78 Roman Malek .10 .25
79 Tomas Vokoun .75 2.00
80 Lukas Hronek .10 .25
81 Petr Briza .30 .75
82 Adam Svoboda .30 .75
83 Viktor Ujcik .20 .50
84 Martin Prochazka .10 .25
85 Petr Cajanek .30 .75
86 Pavel Patera .20 .50
87 Radek Duda .10 .25
88 Tomas Vlasak .10 .25
89 Jaromir Jagr 2.00 5.00
90 Jaromir Jagr 2.00 5.00
91 Robert Reichel .20 .50
92 Frantisek Kaberle .10 .25
93 Jaroslav Spacek .20 .50
94 Jan Hlavac .20 .50
95 Martin Rucinsky .20 .50
96 Tomas Kaberle .30 .75
97 Dominik Hasek 1.25 3.00
98 Dominik Hasek 1.25 3.00
99 Dominik Hasek 1.25 3.00
100 Checklist .10 .25

2002-03 Czech OFS Plus

COMPLETE SET (369) 75.00 125.00
1 Daniel Branda .20 .50
2 Michal Bros .20 .50
3 Petr Briza .30 .75
4 Jan Hanzlik .20 .50
5 Petr Havelka .20 .50
6 Valdemar Jirus .20 .50
7 Pavel Kasparik .20 .50
8 Ondrej Kratena .20 .50
9 Petr Leska .20 .50
10 Patrik Martinec .20 .50
11 Jaroslav Nedved .20 .50
12 Petr Prikryl .20 .50
13 Frantisek Ptacek .20 .50
14 Martin Richter .20 .50
15 Jan Srdinko .20 .50
16 Martin Spanhel .20 .50
17 Pavel Srek .20 .50
18 Jan Tomajko .20 .50
19 Robert Tomik .20 .50
20 Roman Vondracek .20 .50
21 Jiri Zelenka .20 .50
22 Richard Zemlicka .20 .50
23 Jaroslav Balastik .60 1.50
24 Miroslav Blatak .20 .50
25 Martin Cech .20 .50
26 Lukas Galvas .20 .50
27 Martin Hamrlik .20 .50
28 Jan Homer .20 .50
29 Slavomir Hrina .20 .50
30 Petr Hubacek .20 .50
31 Patrik Hucko .20 .50
32 Martin Jenacek .20 .50
33 Jiri Marusak .20 .50
34 Milan Ministr .20 .50
35 Petr Mokrejs .20 .50
36 Miroslav Okal .20 .50
37 Ivo Pesat .20 .50
38 Libor Pivko .20 .50
39 Ivan Rachunek .20 .50
40 Petr Tucek .20 .50
41 Ondrej Vesely .20 .50
42 Rostislav Vlach .20 .50
43 Ladislav Vlcek .20 .50
44 Martin Zahorovsky .20 .50
45 Pavel Zubicek .20 .50
46 Jiri Burger .20 .50
47 Marek Cernosek .20 .50
48 Martin Falter .20 .50
49 Stanislav Gron .40 1.00
50 Jakub Hulva .20 .50
51 Lukas Chmelir .20 .50
52 Zbynek Irgl .30 .75
53 Petr Jurecka .20 .50
54 Roman Kadera .20 .50
55 Ludek Krayzel .20 .50
56 Leszek Laszkiewicz .20 .50
57 Marek Melenovsky .20 .50
58 David Moravec .20 .50
59 Ales Padelek .20 .50
60 Ivan Padelek .20 .50
61 Radek Philipp .20 .50
62 Martin Ambruz .20 .50
63 Peter Bartek .20 .50
64 Radovan Biegl .30 .75
65 Tomas Demel .20 .50
66 Marek Dubec .20 .50
67 Jiri Hudler 10.00 25.00
68 Alexej Jaskin .20 .50
69 Petr Kubos .20 .50
70 Radim Kucharczyk .20 .50
71 Patrik Luza .20 .50
72 Ondrej Nemec .20 .50
73 Lukas Plsek .20 .50
74 Jiri Polak .20 .50
75 Bohuslav Ptacek .20 .50
76 Jan Sochor .20 .50
77 Roman Stantien .20 .50
78 Martin Streit .20 .50
79 Tomas Vak .20 .50
80 Lukas Valko .20 .50
81 Petr Vampola .20 .50
82 Jiri Hasek .20 .50
83 Lubos Horcicka .20 .50
84 Tomas Houdek .20 .50
85 Jiri Hunkes .20 .50
86 Marek Ivan .20 .50
87 Petr Jancarik .20 .50
88 Pavel Janku .20 .50
89 Richard Kral .20 .50
90 Vlastimil Lakosil .20 .50
91 Jiri Malinsky .20 .50
92 Jan Marek .20 .50
93 Rostislav Martynek .20 .50
94 Roman Meluzin .20 .50
95 Marian Morava .20 .50
96 David Nosek .20 .50
97 Zdenek Pavelek .20 .50
98 Gregor Poloncic .20 .50
99 Libor Prochazka .20 .50
100 Marek Zadina .20 .50
101 Tomas Zboril .20 .50
102 Boris Zabka .20 .50
103 Martin Altrichter .20 .50
104 Miroslav Barus .20 .50
105 Vaclav Benak .20 .50
106 Roman Erat .20 .50
107 Radek Haman .20 .50
108 David Havir .20 .50
109 Ales Kretinsky .20 .50
110 Pavel Kumstat .20 .50
111 Petr Kumstat .20 .50
112 David Ludvik .20 .50
113 Jan Mikulik .20 .50
114 Karel Plasek .20 .50
115 Jan Plch .20 .50
116 Milan Prochazka .20 .50
117 Peter Pucher .20 .50
118 Jaroslav Sklenar .20 .50
119 Jan Snopek .20 .50
120 Karel Soudek .20 .50
121 Oldrich Svoboda .20 .50
122 Milan Toman .20 .50
123 Marek Uram .20 .50
124 Marek Vorel .20 .50
125 Lukas Bednarik .20 .50
126 Daniel Bohac .20 .50
127 Jakub Cech .20 .50
128 Michal Cech .20 .50
129 Vratislav Cech .20 .50
130 Ales Cerny .20 .50
131 Juraj Durco .20 .50
132 Martin Filip .20 .50
133 Petr Folta .20 .50
134 Tomas Harant .20 .50
135 Martin Holy .20 .50
136 Jan Kopecky .20 .50
137 Jiri Kucera .20 .50
138 Michal Marik .20 .50
139 Petr Pavlas .20 .50
140 Albin Podstavek .20 .50
141 Radek Prochazka .20 .50
142 Rene Pucher .20 .50
143 Tomas Srsen .20 .50
144 Ales Stanek .20 .50
145 Vaclav Studeny .20 .50
146 Filip Stefanka .20 .50
147 Milan Beranek .20 .50
148 Martin Cakajik .20 .50
149 Pavel Falta .20 .50
150 Miroslav Hajek .20 .50
151 Jan Holub .20 .50
152 Vitezslav Jankovych .20 .50
153 Pavel Kabrt .20 .50
154 Vaclav Koci .20 .50
155 Radoslav Kropac .20 .50
156 Angel Krstev .20 .50
157 Vojtech Kubincak .20 .50
158 Jiri Kudrna .20 .50
159 Pavel Malecek .20 .50
160 Jiri Moravec .20 .50
161 Mojmir Musil .20 .50
162 Vaclav Novak .20 .50
163 Jan Plodek .20 .50
164 Robert Pospisil .20 .50
165 Stanislav Prochazska .20 .50
166 Patrik Rozsival .20 .50
167 Michal Straka .20 .50
168 Daniel Babka .20 .50
169 Michal Barinka .20 .50
170 Peter Bartos .20 .50
171 Jiri Broz .20 .50
172 Petr Gregorek .20 .50
173 Stepan Hrebejk .20 .50
174 Vladimir Hudacek .20 .50
175 Josef Jindra .20 .50
176 Ivo Kotaska .20 .50
177 Josef Kucera .20 .50
178 Milan Michalek 4.00 10.00
179 Frantisek Mrazek .20 .50
180 Jan Mucha .20 .50
181 Milan Nedoma .20 .50
182 Zdenek Ondrej .20 .50
183 Lubos Rob .20 .50
184 Petr Sailer .20 .50
185 Rudolf Suchanek .20 .50
186 Jiri Simanek .20 .50
187 Martin Strba .20 .50
188 Filip Turek .20 .50
189 Michal Vondrka .20 .50
190 Jan Alinc .20 .50
191 Jiri Gombar .20 .50
192 Vladimir Gyna .20 .50
193 Lukas Havel .20 .50
194 Jan Hranac .20 .50
195 Petr Klima .20 .50
196 Jan Kloboucek .20 .50
197 Jindrich Kotrla .20 .50
198 Vlastimil Kroupa .20 .50
199 Jiri Kuntos .20 .50
200 Petr Macholda .20 .50
201 Tomas Martinec .20 .50
202 Marek Pinc .20 .50
203 Michal Podolka .20 .50
204 Lukas Pozivil .20 .50
205 Ivo Prorok .20 .50
206 Lukas Riha .20 .50
207 Stanislav Stavensky .20 .50
208 Jiri Slegr .20 .50
209 Jan Sulc .20 .50
210 Martin Tupa .20 .50
211 Martin Barek .20 .50
212 Jakub Barton .20 .50
213 Tomas Blazek .20 .50
214 Tomas Divisek .40 1.00
215 Miroslav Duben .20 .50
216 Otakar Janecky .20 .50
217 Jan Kolar .20 .50
218 Petr Koukal .20 .50
219 Ladislav Lubina .20 .50
220 Michal Mikeska .20 .50
221 Petr Mocek .20 .50
222 Petr Mudroch .20 .50
223 Andrej Novotny .20 .50
224 Lubomir Pistek .20 .50
225 David Pospisil .20 .50
226 Petr Prucha 6.00 15.00
227 Tomas Rolinek .20 .50
228 Petr Caslava .20 .50
229 Adam Svoboda .30 .75
230 Michal Sykora .20 .50
231 Petr Sykora .20 .50
232 Michael Vyhlidal .20 .50
233 Milan Antos .20 .50
234 Josef Beranek .20 .50
235 Dominik Granak .20 .50
236 Jan Hejda .40 1.00
237 Lukas Hronek .20 .50
238 David Hruska .20 .50
239 Petr Jaros .20 .50
240 Petr Kadlec .20 .50
241 Jakub Klepis ERC 1.25 3.00
242 Pavel Kolarik .20 .50
243 Frantisek Kucera .20 .50
244 Roman Malek .20 .50
245 Petr Mika .30 .75
246 Jan Novak .20 .50
247 Marek Posmyk .20 .50
248 Ondrej Steiner .20 .50
249 Michal Sup .20 .50
250 Adam Saffer .20 .50
251 Josef Straub .20 .50
252 Marek Tomica .20 .50
253 Viktor Ujcik .20 .50
254 Dusan Andrasovsky .20 .50
255 Libor Barta .20 .50
256 Michal Dobron .20 .50
257 Radek Duda .20 .50
258 Michal Dvorak .20 .50
259 Robert Hamrla .20 .50
260 Jiri Hanzlik .20 .50
261 Petr Chvojka .20 .50
262 Vaclav Kral .20 .50
263 Ales Kratoska .20 .50
264 Radek Matejovsky .20 .50
265 Josef Reznicek .20 .50
266 Josef Straka .20 .50
267 Jaroslav Spelda .20 .50
268 Juraj Stefanka .20 .50
269 Jan Svik .20 .50
270 Ivan Vlcek .20 .50
271 Milan Voboril .20 .50
272 Milan Volak .20 .50
273 Josef Voskar .20 .50
274 Martin Vyborny .20 .50
275 Robin Bacul .20 .50
276 David Balasz .20 .50
277 Richard Bauer .20 .50
278 Petr Franek .20 .50
279 Jakub Grof .20 .50
280 Martin Hlavacka .20 .50
281 Jan Kostal .20 .50
282 Lukas Krajicek .60 1.50
283 Jakub Kraus .20 .50
284 Marcel Kucera .20 .50
285 Jaromir Kverka .20 .50
286 Michal Madl .20 .50
287 Tomas Nemcicky .20 .50
288 Martin Opatovsky .20 .50
289 Libor Pavlis .20 .50
290 Petr Puncochar .20 .50
291 Dmitri Rodine .20 .50
292 Vaclav Skuhravy .20 .50
293 Ladislav Svoboda .20 .50
294 Petr Sinagl .20 .50
295 Marek Topoli .20 .50
296 Kamil Tvrdek .20 .50
297 Pavel Selinger .20 .50
298 Radim Tesarik .20 .50
299 Jiri Trvaj .20 .50
300 Jan Vytisk .20 .50
301 Danniel Zapotocny .20 .50
302 Michal Divisek .20 .50
303 Jiri Dobrovolny .20 .50
304 Michal Kello .20 .50
305 Radek Krestan .20 .50
306 Tomas Micka .20 .50
307 Petr Mika .20 .50
308 Jan Dresler .20 .50
309 Rostislav Olesz ERC 4.00 10.00
310 Lukas Zatopek .20 .50
311 Vaclav Pletka .30 .75
312 Lukas Krenzelok .20 .50
313 Lukas Smolka .20 .50
314 Jaroslav Sklenar .20 .50
315 Richard Bordowski .20 .50
316 Mario Cartelli .20 .50
317 Tomas Horna .20 .50
318 Petr Hrbek .20 .50
319 Martin Kotasek .20 .50
320 Jan Korotvicka .20 .50
321 Michal Tvrdik .20 .50
322 David Pojkar .20 .50
323 Martin Adamsky .20 .50
324 Jaroslav Kracik .20 .50
325 Miloslav Topol .20 .50
326 Vojtech Polak .20 .50
327 Lukas Pech .20 .50
328 Jaroslav Hasek .20 .50
329 Jan Kudrna .20 .50
330 Jan Visek .20 .50
331 Patrik Moskal .20 .50
332 Zdenek Smid .20 .50
333 Michal Travnicek .20 .50
334 Martin Nosek .20 .50
335 Zdenek Skorepa .20 .50
336 Jan Horacek .20 .50
337 David Appel .20 .50
338 Petr Svoboda .20 .50
339 Jan Nemecek .20 .50
340 Jan Kotatko .20 .50
341 Ales Vala .20 .50
342 Radek Mrazek .20 .50
343 Viktor Hubl .20 .50
344 Jaroslav Kudrna .20 .50
345 Tomas Pacal .20 .50
346 David Mazanec .20 .50
347 Radek Prochazka .20 .50
348 Ales Kratoska .20 .50
349 Michal Marik .20 .50
350 Ladislav Vlcek .20 .50
351 Jiri Hanzlik .20 .50
352 Jaroslav Hubl .20 .50
353 Martin Tuma .20 .50
354 Petr Martinek .20 .50
355 Michal Divisek .20 .50
356 Lubomir Hurtaj .20 .50
357 Jakub Koreis ERC .75 2.00
358 Ondrej Kubes .20 .50
359 Viktor Ujcik .20 .50
360 Radek Dlouhy .20 .50
361 Radek Duda .20 .50
362 Milan Kopecky .20 .50
363 Patrik Stejskal .20 .50
364 Vaclav Pletka .30 .75
365 Radek Masny .20 .50
366 Zbynek Spitzer .20 .50
367 Tomas Frolo .20 .50
368 Martin Filip .20 .50
369 Ivan Rachunek .20 .50
370 Tomas Klimes .20 .50

2002-03 Czech OFS Plus All-Star Game

COMPLETE SET (43) 30.00 75.00
H1 Jaroslav Balastik 2.00 5.00
H2 Jiri Burger .75 2.00
H3 Petr Cajanek 1.25 3.00
H4 Petr Gregorek .75 2.00
H5 Miloslav Guren .75 2.00
H6 Martin Hamrlik .75 2.00
H7 Vladimir Hudacek .75 2.00
H8 Jiri Hudler 4.00 10.00
H9 Tomas Jakes .75 2.00
H10 Miroslav Javin .75 2.00
H11 Lubomir Korhon .75 2.00
H12 Richard Kral .75 2.00
H13 Petr Leska .75 2.00
H14 Jiri Marusak .75 2.00
H15 Marek Melenovsky .75 2.00
H16 David Moravec .75 2.00
H17 David Nosek .75 2.00
H18 Karel Soudek .75 2.00
H19 Jiri Trvaj .75 2.00
H20 Marek Uram .75 2.00
H21 Petr Vala .75 2.00
H22 Ondrej Vesely .75 2.00
H23 Peter Bartos .75 2.00
H24 Petr Briza 1.25 3.00
H25 Vladimir Gyna .75 2.00
H26 Martin Hlavacka .75 2.00
H27 Jaroslav Hlinka .75 2.00
H28 Otakar Janecky .75 2.00
H29 Petr Kadlec .75 2.00
H30 Ladislav Lubina .75 2.00
H31 Jaroslav Nedved .75 2.00
H32 Tomas Nemcicky .75 2.00
H33 Josef Reznicek .75 2.00
H34 Vaclav Skuhravy .75 2.00
H35 Jan Srdinko .75 2.00
H36 Josef Straka .75 2.00
H37 Adam Svoboda 1.25 3.00
H38 Ladislav Svoboda .75 2.00
H39 Michal Sykora .75 2.00
H40 Viktor Ujcik .75 2.00
H41 Unknown .75 2.00
H42 Jiri Zelenka .75 2.00
H43 Daniel Branda .75 2.00

2002-03 Czech OFS Plus Checklists

COMPLETE SET (12) 5.00 10.00
C1 Jakub Cech .40 1.00
C2 Marek Pinc .40 1.00
C3 Pavel Falta .40 1.00
C4 Petr Prikril .40 1.00
C5 Lukas Hronek .40 1.00
C6 Robert Hamrla .40 1.00
C7 Adam Svoboda .75 2.00
C8 Petr Franek .40 1.00
C9 Petr Tucek .40 1.00
C10 Lubos Horcicka .40 1.00
C11 Jiri Trvaj .40 1.00
C12 Radovan Biegl .75 2.00

2002-03 Czech OFS Plus Masks

M2 Ivo Pesat 4.00 10.00
M3 Petr Tucek 4.00 10.00
M4 Jiri Trvaj 4.00 10.00
M5 Lukas Plsek 4.00 10.00
M6 Radovan Biegl 4.00 10.00
M7 Marek Pinc 4.00 10.00
M8 Petr Prikril 4.00 10.00
M9 Lukas Hronek 4.00 10.00
M10 Roman Malek 4.00 10.00
M11 Pavel Falta 4.00 10.00
M14 Vladimir Hudacek 4.00 10.00
M16 Adam Svoboda 6.00 15.00
M17 Robert Hamrla 4.00 10.00
M18 Marcel Kucera 4.00 10.00
M24 Jakub Cech 4.00 10.00

2002-03 Czech OFS Plus Trios

T1 Vladimir Hudacek
Rudolf Suchanek
Peter Bartos 2.50 6.00
T2 Michal Marik
Filip Stefanka
Michal Cech 2.50 6.00
T3 Jakub Cech
Tomas Harant
Daniel Bohac 2.50 6.00
T4 Petr Franek
Dmitri Rodine
TomasNemcicky 2.50 6.00
T5 Pavel Falta
Angel Krstev
Vitezslav Jankovych 2.50 6.00
T6 Marek Pinc
Jiri Slegr
Martin Rucinsky 2.50 6.00
T7 Michal Podolka
Petr Martinek
Petr Klima 2.50 6.00
T8 Adam Svoboda
Michal Sykora
Petr Sykora 2.50 6.00
T9 Tomas Maly
Michael Vyhlidal
Ladislav Lubina 2.50 6.00
T10 Libor Barta
Josef Reznicek
Radek Duda 2.50 6.00
T11 Robert Hamrla
Ivan Vlcek
Josef Straka 2.50 6.00
T12 Roman Malek
Frantisek Kucera
Josef Beranek 2.50 6.00
T13 Lukas Hronek
Petr Kadlec
Viktor Ujcik 2.50 6.00
T14 Petr Briza
Jaroslav Nedved
Richard Zemlicka 2.50 6.00
T15 Petr Prikril
Jan Srdinko
Petr Leska 2.50 6.00
T16 Vlastimil Lakosil
Libor Prochazka
Richard Kral 2.50 6.00
T17 Lubos Horcicka
David Nosek
Vaclav Pletka 2.50 6.00
T18 Jiri Trvaj
Radim Tesarik
David Moravec 2.50 6.00
T19 Martin Falter
Marek Cernosek
Roman Kadera 2.50 6.00
T20 Radovan Biegl
Alexej Jaskin
Jiri Hudler 8.00 20.00
T21 Radek Masny
Petr Kubos
Radim Kucharczyk 2.50 6.00
T22 Ivo Pesat
Martin Hamrlik
Miroslav Okal 2.50 6.00
T23 Petr Tucek
Jirin Marusak
Ladislav Vlach 2.50 6.00
T24 Petr Svoboda
Jan Snopek

Peter Pucher 2.50 6.00
T25 Martin Altrichter
Karel Soudek
Marek Uram 2.50 6.00

2002-03 Czech OFS Plus Znaky Klubu

COMPLETE SET (14) 5.00 10.00
Z1 Ceske Budejovice .40 1.00
Z2 Havirov Panthers .40 1.00
Z3 Energie Karlovy Vary .40 1.00
Z4 Bili Tygri Liberec .40 1.00
Z5 Chemopetrol Litvinov .40 1.00
Z6 IPB Pojistovna Pardubice .40 1.00
Z7 Keramika Plzen .40 1.00
Z8 Slavia Praha .40 1.00
Z9 Sparta Praha .40 1.00
Z10 Ocelari Trinec .40 1.00
Z11 Vitkovice .40 1.00
Z12 Vsetin .40 1.00
Z13 Hame Zlin .40 1.00
Z14 ME Znojemsti Orli .40 1.00

2002-03 Czech OFS Plus Duos

COMPLETE SET (25) 40.00 80.00
D1 Radovan Biegl
Jiri Hudler 6.00 15.00
D2 Petr Briza
Jiri Zelenka 2.00 5.00
D3 Martin Richter
Jan Tomajko 2.00 5.00
D4 Josef Beranek
Roman Malek 2.00 5.00
D5 Frantisek Kucera
Viktor Ujcik 2.00 5.00
D6 Jiri Trvaj
David Moravec 2.00 5.00
D7 Jiri Burger
Roman Kadera 2.00 5.00
D8 Libor Prochazka
Richard Kral 2.00 5.00
D9 Vaclav Pletka
Vlastimil Lakocil 2.00 5.00
D10 Adam Svoboda
Michal Vyhlidal 2.00 5.00
D11 Michal Sykora
Ladislav Lubina 2.00 5.00
D12 Oldrich Svoboda
Marek Uram 3.00 8.00
D13 Peter Pucher
Martin Altrichter 2.00 5.00
D14 Martin Vyborny
Libor Barta 2.00 5.00
D15 Radek Duda
Robert Hamrla 2.00 5.00
D16 Martin Hamrlik
Jiri Marusak 2.00 5.00
D17 Rostislav Vlach
Petr Tucek 2.00 5.00
D18 Petr Ranek
Robin Bacul 2.00 5.00
D19 Vladimir Hudacek
Milan Nedoma 2.00 5.00
D20 Vlastimil Kroupa
Marek Pinc 2.00 5.00
D21 Martin Rucinsky
Jiri Slegr 2.00 5.00
D22 Radoslav Kropac
Pavel Falta 2.00 5.00
D23 Angel Krstev
Vitezslav Jankovych 2.00 5.00
D24 Tomas Srsen
Jakub Cech 2.00 5.00
D25 Jan Kopecky
Michal Marik 2.00 5.00

2003 Czech National Team Postcards

COMPLETE SET (17) 20.00 40.00
17 David Vyborny 1.25 3.00
1 Jaroslav Balastik 1.25 3.00
2 Jan Hejda .75 2.00
3 Milan Hejduk 2.00 5.00
4 Jan Hlavac .75 2.00
5 Ivan Hlinka CO .40 1.00
6 Jiri Hudler 4.00 10.00
7 Frantisek Kaberle .75 2.00
8 Jindrich Kotrla .75 2.00
9 Jaroslav Modry .75 2.00
10 Robert Reichel .75 2.00
11 Martin Straka .75 2.00
12 Radek Sup .75 2.00
13 Martin Tomasek .75 2.00
14 Josef Vasicek .75 2.00
15 Tomas Vokoun 2.00 5.00
16 Radim Vrbata 1.25 3.00
18 Tomas Kaberle 2.00 5.00
19 Michal Sup .75 2.00
20 Jaroslav Hlinka .75 2.00

2003 Czech Stadion

COMPLETE SET 15.00 40.00
529 Anson Carter .40 1.00
530 Peter Bondra .40 1.00
531 Magnus Arvedson .40 1.00
532 Sandy McCarthy .40 1.00
533 Mikko Eloranta .40 1.00
534 Tie Domi .75 2.00
535 Bates Battaglia .40 1.00
536 Jaromir Jagr
Mario Lemieux 4.00 10.00
537 Darcy Tucker .40 1.00
538 Brian Rafalski .40 1.00
539 Jozef Stumpel .40 1.00
540 Marco Sturm .40 1.00
541 Eric Lindros 1.25 3.00
542 Ed Jovanovski .40 1.00
543 Darren McCarty .40 1.00
544 Zigmund Palffy .40 1.00
545 Luc Robitaille 1.25 3.00
546 Keith Primeau .40 1.00
547 Bobby Clarke .40 1.00
548 Marcel Dionne .40 1.00
549 Ken Dryden 2.00 5.00
550 Frank Mahovlich .75 2.00
551 Valeri Kharlamov .75 2.00
552 Phil Esposito 2.00 5.00
553 Boris Mikhailov .75 2.00
554 Stan Mikita .75 2.00
555 Bobby Orr 4.00 10.00
556 Vladimir Petrov .40 1.00
557 Vladislav Tretiak 1.25 3.00
562 Chuck Kobasew .40 1.00
565 Bobby Holik .40 1.00

2003-04 Czech National Team

COMPLETE SET
1 Dusan Salficky .40 1.00
2 Jan Hejda .20 .50
3 Martin Cech .20 .50
4 Pavel Patera .20 .50

2003-04 Czech OFS Plus

COMPLETE SET (398) 40.00 80.00
1 Jiri Burger .20 .50
2 Marek Cernosek .20 .50
3 Jan Dresler .20 .50
4 Martin Falter .20 .50
5 Petr Hubacek .20 .50
6 Jakub Hulva .20 .50
7 Lukas Chmelir .20 .50
8 Zbynek Irgl .20 .50
9 Roman Kadera .20 .50
10 Rostislav Olesz 1.25 3.00
11 Ludek Krayzel .20 .50
12 Lukas Krenzelok .20 .50
13 Pavel Kumstat .20 .50
14 Jiri Trvaj .20 .50
15 Petr Vala .20 .50
16 Ales Padelek .20 .50
17 Ivan Padelek .20 .50
18 Tomas Ficenc .20 .50
19 Pavel Kowalczyk .20 .50
20 Petr Mika .20 .50
21 Daniel Zapotocny .20 .50
22 Daniel Seman .20 .50
23 Martin Tomasek .20 .50
24 Martin Ambruz .20 .50
25 Marek Dubec .20 .50
26 Radovan Biegl .30 .75
27 Michal Horak .20 .50
28 Tomas Demel .20 .50
29 Radim Hruska .20 .50
30 Petr Kubos .20 .50
31 Alexej Jaskin .20 .50
32 Ondrej Nemec .20 .50
33 Jiri Polak .20 .50
34 Roman Stantien .20 .50
35 Jan Sochor .20 .50
36 Radek Masny .20 .50
37 Tomas Vak .20 .50
38 Petr Vampola .20 .50
39 Pavel Selinger .20 .50
40 Jiri Hasek .20 .50
41 Michal Hudec .20 .50
42 Lubomir Stach .20 .50
43 Martin Vyrubalik .20 .50
44 Patrik Luza .20 .50
45 Otakar Janecky .20 .50
46 Martin Barek .20 .50
47 Tomas Blazek .20 .50
48 Petr Caslava .20 .50
49 Tomas Divisek .20 .50
50 Miroslav Duben .20 .50
51 Petr Koukal .20 .50
52 Jaroslav Kudrna .20 .50
53 Frantisek Mrazek .20 .50
54 Petr Mudroch .20 .50
55 Andrej Novotny .20 .50
56 Tomas Pacal .20 .50
57 Lubomir Pistek .20 .50
58 Petr Prucha 2.00 5.00
59 Adam Svoboda .30 .75
60 Jan Kolar .20 .50
61 Michal Sykora .20 .50
62 Petr Sykora .20 .50
63 Jiri Dopita .20 .50
64 Peter Podhradsky .20 .50
65 Tomas Razingar .20 .50
66 Jan Alinc .20 .50
67 Robin Bacul .20 .50
68 Richard Bauer .20 .50
69 Lukas Bednarik .20 .50
70 Jakub Kraus .20 .50
71 Lukas Galvas .20 .50
72 Jan Kostal .20 .50
73 Lukas Krajicek .40 1.00
74 Petr Kumstat .20 .50
75 Tomas Mencicky .20 .50
76 Rudolf Pejchar .20 .50
77 Dmitrij Rodin .20 .50
78 Vaclav Skuhravy .20 .50
79 Frantisek Ptacek .20 .50
80 Vojtech Polak .20 .50
81 Ladislav Svoboda .20 .50
82 Michal Tvrdik .20 .50
83 Lukas Sablik .20 .50
84 Tomas Netik .20 .50
85 Miroslav Vantroba .20 .50
86 Martin Kivon .20 .50
87 Jan Lipiansky .20 .50
88 David Balaze .20 .50
89 Frantisek Bojnic .20 .50
90 Viktor Hubl .20 .50
91 Jan Hranac .20 .50
92 Jiri Gombar .20 .50
93 Lukas Havel .20 .50
94 Marian Kacir .20 .50
95 Lukas Kaspar .20 .50
96 Jan Kloboucek .20 .50
97 Vlastimil Kroupa .20 .50
98 Vojtech Kubincak .20 .50
99 Tomas Martinec .20 .50
100 Petr Martinek .20 .50
101 Lukas Riha .20 .50
102 Richard Zemlicka .20 .50
103 Tomas Rolinek .20 .50
104 Miha Rebolj .20 .50
105 Michal Travnicek .20 .50
106 Marek Pinc .20 .50
107 Lukas Pozivil .20 .50
108 Ivo Prorok .20 .50
109 Martin Cakajik .20 .50
110 Miroslav Hajek .20 .50
111 Jan Holub .20 .50
112 Richard Jares .20 .50
113 Waldemar Jirus .20 .50
114 Pavel Kasparik .20 .50
115 Vaclav Koci .20 .50
116 Radoslav Kropac .20 .50
117 Angel Krstev .20 .50
118 Vaclav Novak .20 .50
119 Jiri Moravec .20 .50
120 Lukas Pabiska .20 .50
121 Mojmir Musil .20 .50
122 Jan Plodek .20 .50
123 Stanislav Prochazka .20 .50
124 Patrik Rozsival .20 .50
125 Michal Straka .20 .50
126 Oldrich Svoboda .20 .50
127 Ladislav Smid ERC 2.00 5.00
128 Lubomir Korhon .20 .50
129 Rudolf Vercik .20 .50
130 Jaroslav Balastik .40 1.00
131 Miroslav Blatak .20 .50
132 Martin Cech .20 .50
133 Martin Cech .20 .50
134 Martin Hamrlik .20 .50
135 Martin Jenacek .20 .50
136 Petr Leska .20 .50
137 Petr Macholda .20 .50
138 Petr Mokrejs .20 .50
139 Martin Nosek .20 .50
140 Miroslav Okal .20 .50
141 Martin Altrichter .20 .50
142 Radim Tesarik .20 .50
143 Petr Tucek .20 .50
144 Ondrej Vesely .20 .50
145 Rostislav Vlach .20 .50
146 Martin Zahorovsky .20 .50
147 Pavel Zubicek .20 .50
148 Peter Barinka .20 .50
149 Erik Weissemann .20 .50
150 Pavel Zavrtalek .20 .50
151 Michal Bros .20 .50
152 Petr Briza .30 .75
153 Jan Hanzlik .20 .50
154 Jaroslav Mrazek .20 .50
155 Jakub Sindel .30 .75
156 Ondrej Kratena .30 .75
157 Jan Marek .20 .50
158 Martin Paroulek .20 .50
159 Petr Ton .20 .50
160 David Vrbata .20 .50
161 Libor Prochazka .20 .50
162 Josef Reznicek .20 .50
163 Marek Schwarz ERC 2.00 5.00
164 Jan Srdinko .20 .50
165 Jan Tomajko .20 .50
166 Roman Vondracek .20 .50
167 Jan Vytisk .20 .50
168 Karel Hromas .20 .50
169 Jiri Jakes .20 .50
170 Radek Mika .20 .50
171 Milan Antos .20 .50
172 Josef Beranek .20 .50
173 Radek Dlouhy .20 .50
174 Jan Fadrny .20 .50
175 Dominik Granak .20 .50
176 Lukas Hronek .20 .50
177 David Hruska .20 .50
178 Jiri Kuntos .20 .50
179 Roman Malek .20 .50
180 Patrik Martinec .20 .50
181 Petr Jaros .20 .50
182 Jakub Klepis .40 1.00
183 Pavel Kolarik .20 .50
184 Milan Kopecky .20 .50
185 Frantisek Kucera .20 .50
186 Jan Novak .20 .50
187 David Pojkar .20 .50
188 Ondrej Stanek .20 .50
189 Michal Sup .20 .50
190 Adam Saffer .20 .50
191 Stanislav Gron .40 1.00
192 Petr Kadlec .20 .50
193 Marek Tomica .20 .50
194 Leos Cermak .20 .50
195 Ivan Dropa .20 .50
196 Martin Adamsky .20 .50
197 Michal Dobron .20 .50
198 Michal Dvorak .20 .50
199 Libor Barta .20 .50
200 Mario Cartelli .20 .50
201 Jiri Hanzlik .20 .50
202 Ales Kratoska .20 .50
203 Ondrej Kubes .20 .50
204 Josef Straka .20 .50
205 Radek Matejovsky .20 .50
206 Jan Svik .20 .50
207 Milan Voboril .20 .50
208 Milan Volak .20 .50
209 Zdenek Smid .20 .50
210 David Pospisil .20 .50
211 Roman Bilek .20 .50
212 Jiri Dobrovolny .20 .50
213 Michal Duraz .20 .50
214 Patrik Rimmel .20 .50
215 Zdenek Sedlak .20 .50
216 Vitezslav Bilek .20 .50
217 Jakub Evan .20 .50
218 Martin Frolik .20 .50
219 Radek Gardon .20 .50
220 Tomas Horna .20 .50
221 Miloslav Horava .20 .50
222 Vitezslav Jankovych .20 .50
223 Jaroslav Kalla .20 .50
224 David Pazourek .20 .50
225 Jan Pospisil .20 .50
226 Tomas Klimt .20 .50
227 Jan Krulis .20 .50
228 Robert Kysela .20 .50
229 Rostislav Malena .20 .50
230 Zdenek Orct .20 .50
231 Jiri Zeman .20 .50
232 Jan Dlouhy .20 .50
233 Petr Hrava .20 .50
234 Petr Kasik .20 .50
235 Miroslav Lazo .20 .50
236 Martin Prochazka .20 .50
237 Juraj Stefanka .20 .50
238 Miroslav Barus .20 .50
239 Vaclav Benak .20 .50
240 Roman Erat .20 .50
241 Radek Haman .20 .50
242 David Havir .20 .50
243 Ales Kretinsky .20 .50
244 David Ludvik .20 .50
245 Roman Nemecek .20 .50
246 Karel Plasek .20 .50
247 Jan Snopek .20 .50
248 Milan Prochazka .20 .50
249 Peter Pucher .20 .50
250 Robert Slavik .20 .50
251 Pavel Mojzis .20 .50
252 Tomas Duba .20 .50
253 Igor Rataj .20 .50
254 Jan Pardavy .20 .50
255 Lukas Vomela .20 .50
256 Daniel Babka .20 .50
257 Radek Belohlav .20 .50
258 Stepan Hrebejk .20 .50
259 Vladimir Hudacek .20 .50
260 Stanislav Jasecko .20 .50
261 Josef Jindra .20 .50
262 Vaclav Koci .20 .50
263 Jaroslav Kristek .20 .50
264 Josef Kucera .20 .50
265 Lukas Kveton .20 .50
266 Jan Mucha .20 .50
267 Zbynek Neckar .20 .50
268 Zdenek Ondrej .20 .50
269 Ivan Rachunek .20 .50
270 Lubos Rob .20 .50
271 Petr Sailer .20 .50
272 Jiri Simanek .20 .50
273 Vladimir Skoda .20 .50
274 Rudolf Suchanek .20 .50
275 Filip Turek .20 .50
276 Michal Vondra .20 .50
277 Robert Prochazka .20 .50
278 Marek Schwarz 2.00 5.00
279 Zdenek Skorepa .20 .50
280 Filip Stefanka .20 .50
281 Richard Bordowski .20 .50
282 Michal Holes .20 .50
283 Lubos Horcicka .20 .50
284 Tomas Houdek .20 .50
285 Jiri Hunkes .20 .50
286 Marek Ivan .20 .50
287 Petr Jancarik .20 .50
288 Pavel Janku .20 .50
289 Richard Kral .20 .50
290 Jan Kudrna .20 .50
291 Vlastimil Lakosil .20 .50
292 Marek Melenovsky .20 .50
293 Jiri Malinsky .20 .50
294 Rostislav Martynek .20 .50
295 Roman Meluzin .20 .50
296 Zdenek Pavelek .20 .50
297 Vaclav Pletka .20 .50
298 Michal Podolka .20 .50
299 Jiri Polansky .20 .50
300 Gregor Poloncic .20 .50
301 Josef Vitek .20 .50
302 Boris Zabka .20 .50
303 Marek Zadina .20 .50
304 Tomas Zboril .20 .50
305 Tomas Frolo .20 .50
306 Martin Vyborny .20 .50
307 Marek Posmyk .20 .50
308 Milan Nedoma .20 .50
309 Dusan Andrasovsky .20 .50
310 Ladislav Lubina .20 .50
311 Alexandr Hylak .20 .50
312 Jaroslav Nedved .20 .50
313 Pavel Falta .20 .50
314 Leos Cermak .20 .50
315 Tomas Vlcek .20 .50
316 Igor Murin .20 .50
317 Tomas Karny .20 .50
318 Patrik Hucko .20 .50
319 Michal Mikeska .20 .50
320 Pavel Srek .20 .50
321 Gabriel Spilar .20 .50
322 Petr Havelka .20 .50
323 Martin Richter .20 .50
324 Radovan Sloboda .20 .50
325 Peter Bartos .20 .50
326 Vladimir Gyna .20 .50
327 Jan Chabera .20 .50
328 Andrej Mezin .20 .50
329 Jan Rehor .20 .50
330 Martin Strba .20 .50
331 Miroslav Durak .20 .50
332 Kamil Jarina .20 .50
333 Roman Kadera .20 .50
334 Angel Krstev .20 .50
335 Michal Marik .20 .50
336 Jakub Petruzalek .20 .50
337 Lubos Bartecko .20 .50
338 Petr Buzek .20 .50
339 Vaclav Eiselt .20 .50
340 Martin Chabada .20 .50
341 Tomas Popperle .20 .50
342 Zdenek Sedlak .20 .50
343 Ladislav Svoboda .20 .50
344 Roman Simicek .20 .50
345 Martin Havlat 2.00 5.00
346 Martin Vojtek .20 .50
347 Martin Jurecka .20 .50
348 Petr Jurecka .20 .50
349 David Mocek .20 .50
350 Patrik Rimmel .20 .50
351 Juraj Stefanka .20 .50
352 Filip Turek .20 .50
353 Pavel Zdrahal .20 .50
354 Daniel Mracka .20 .50
355 Libor Pavlis .20 .50
356 Tomaz Razingar .20 .50
357 Pavel Sebesta .20 .50
358 Dalibor Sochorek .20 .50
359 Radim Tesarik .20 .50
360 Juraj Prokop .20 .50
361 Josef Hrabal .20 .50
362 Stefan Zigardy .20 .50
363 Jan Kudrna .20 .50
364 Vaclav Skuhravy .20 .50
365 Ivan Dropa .20 .50
366 Michal Hreus .20 .50
367 Radim Skuhrovec .20 .50
368 Jiri Veber .20 .50
369 Jan Dlouhy .20 .50
370 Marek Dubec .20 .50
371 Miroslav Hlinka .20 .50
372 Jiri Beroun .20 .50
373 Tomas Duba .20 .50
374 Tomas Hradecky .20 .50
375 Jaroslav Mares .20 .50
376 Petr Puncochar .20 .50
377 Michal Straka .20 .50
378 Marek Uram .20 .50
379 Jakub Kindl .20 .50
380 Libor Zabransky .20 .50
381 Lubomir Jurtaj .20 .50
382 Petr Jez .20 .50
383 Robert Jindrich .20 .50
384 Roman Malek .20 .50
385 Martin Paroulek .20 .50
386 Adam Saffer .20 .50
387 Michal Straka .20 .50
388 Martin Klaus .20 .50
389 Tomas Kapusta .20 .50
390 Lubomir Vosatko .20 .50
391 Jiri Hanzlik .20 .50
392 Jiri Hasek .20 .50
393 Ctibor Jech .20 .50
394 Ctirad Ovcacik .20 .50
395 Tomas Rolinek .20 .50
396 Martin Tupa .20 .50
397 Libor Barta .20 .50
398 Jiri Jantovsky .20 .50
399 Petr Jaros .20 .50
400 Martin Havlat CL .75 2.00

2003-04 Czech OFS Plus All-Star Game

COMPLETE SET (45) 30.00 75.00
H1 Miroslav Simonovic .75 2.00
H2 Normunds Sejejs .75 2.00
H3 Jiri Hes .75 2.00
H4 Marcel Hanzal .75 2.00
H5 Roman Kukumberg .75 2.00
H6 Arne Krotak .75 2.00
H7 Karol Krizan .75 2.00
H8 Juraj Kledrowetz .75 2.00
H9 Miroslav Vantroba .75 2.00
H10 Miroslav Skovira .75 2.00
H11 Jaroslav Kmit .75 2.00
H12 Lubomir Kolnik .75 2.00
H13 Pavel Kowalczyk .75 2.00
H14 Martin Ivicic .75 2.00
H15 Branislav Janos .75 2.00
H16 Zdeno Ciger .75 2.00
H17 Petr Korinek .75 2.00
H18 Tomas Starosta .75 2.00
H19 Tomas Nadazdi .75 2.00
H20 Igor Rataj .75 2.00
H21 Richard Kapus .75 2.00
H22 Erik Weissmann .75 2.00
H23 Adam Svoboda 1.25 3.00
H24 Michal Sykora .75 2.00
H25 Petr Sykora .75 2.00
H26 Roman Malek 1.25 3.00
H27 Petr Kadlec .75 2.00
H28 Jan Hejda .75 2.00
H29 Michal Sup .75 2.00
H30 Frantisek Kucera .75 2.00
H31 Frantisek Ptacek .75 2.00
H32 Ondrej Kratena .75 2.00
H33 Libor Prochazka .75 2.00
H34 Richard Kral .75 2.00
H35 Marek Zadina .75 2.00
H36 Jan Marek .75 2.00
H37 Vaclav Pletka .75 2.00
H38 Martin Hlavacka .75 2.00
H39 Jan Vytisk .75 2.00
H40 David Moravec .75 2.00
H41 Jiri Burger .75 2.00
H42 Jiri Hudler 6.00 15.00
H43 Marek Uram .75 2.00
H44 Peter Pucher .75 2.00
H45 A.Svoboda
M.Sykora CL .75 2.00

2003-04 Czech OFS Plus Checklists

COMPLETE SET (14) 15.00 30.00
1 Jiri Trvaj 1.25 3.00
2 Radovan Biegl 1.25 3.00
3 Adam Svoboda 1.25 3.00
4 Petr Franek 1.25 3.00
5 Marek Pinc 1.25 3.00
6 Oldrich Svoboda 1.25 3.00
7 Petr Tucek 1.25 3.00
8 Petr Briza 1.25 3.00
9 Roman Malek 1.25 3.00
10 Libor Barta 1.25 3.00
11 Josef Kucera 1.25 3.00
12 Martin Altrichter 1.25 3.00
13 Josef Kucera 1.25 3.00
14 Vlastimil Lakosil 1.25 3.00

2003-04 Czech OFS Plus MS Praha

COMPLETE SET (50) 30.00 75.00
SE1 Martin Havlat 4.00 10.00
SE2 Roman Simicek .75 2.00
SE3 Petr Briza 1.25 3.00
SE4 Jan Marek .75 2.00
SE5 Petr Buzek .75 2.00
SE6 Ondrej Kratena .75 2.00
SE7 Michal Sykora .75 2.00
SE8 Petr Sykora .75 2.00
SE9 Adam Svoboda 1.25 3.00
SE10 Jiri Dopita .75 2.00
SE11 Michal Mikeska .75 2.00
SE12 Petr Prucha 4.00 10.00
SE13 Martin Prochazka .75 2.00
SE14 Zdenek Orct 1.25 3.00
SE15 Petr Leska .75 2.00
SE16 Jaroslav Balastik 1.25 3.00
SE17 Jan Snopek .75 2.00
SE18 Jiri Burger .75 2.00
SE19 Rostislav Olesz 4.00 10.00
SE20 Jiri Trvaj .75 2.00
SE21 Zdenek Pavelek .75 2.00
SE22 Frantisek Ptacek .75 2.00
SE23 Roman Malek .75 2.00
SE24 Marek Posmyk .75 2.00
SE25 Petr Kadlec .75 2.00
SE26 Oldrich Svoboda .75 2.00
SE27 Josef Beranek .75 2.00
SE28 Michal Travnicek .75 2.00
SE29 Lukas Havel .75 2.00
SE30 Jiri Hudler 4.00 10.00
SE31 David Moravec .75 2.00
SE32 Radim Tesarik .75 2.00
SE33 Jan Hejda .75 2.00
SE34 Vlastimil Lakosil .75 2.00
SE35 Martin Chabada .75 2.00
SE36 Petr Franek .75 2.00
SE37 Radovan Biegl 1.25 3.00
SE38 Tomas Duba .75 2.00
SE39 Lukas Hronek .75 2.00
SE40 Jan Novak .75 2.00
SE41 Martin Altrichter .75 2.00
SE42 Marek Schwarz 2.00 5.00
SE43 Josef Kucera .75 2.00
SE44 Tomas Divisek .75 2.00
SE45 Jakub Klepis 2.00 5.00
SE46 Michal Sup .75 2.00
SE47 Michal Marik .75 2.00
SE48 Richard Kral .75 2.00
SE49 Marek Pinc .75 2.00
SE50 Pavel Falta .75 2.00

2003-04 Czech Pardubice Postcards

COMPLETE SET (16) 8.00 15.00
1 Martin Barek .40 1.00
2 Tomas Blazek .40 1.00
3 Tomas Divisek .40 1.00
4 Jiri Dopita .40 1.00
5 Otakar Janecky .40 1.00
6 Petr Koukal .40 1.00
7 Jaroslav Kudrna .40 1.00
8 Ladislav Lubina .40 1.00
9 Michal Mikeska .40 1.00
10 Frantisek Mrazek .40 1.00
11 Andrej Novotny .40 1.00
12 Tomas Pacal .40 1.00
13 Petr Prucha 2.00 5.00
14 Tomaz Razingar .40 1.00
15 Adam Svoboda .75 2.00
16 Michal Sykora .40 1.00

2003-04 Czech Stadion

601 Scott Stevens .75 2.00
603 Patrik Elias .75 2.00
604 Jeff Friesen .40 1.00
605 Grant Marshall .40 1.00
606 Jamie Langenbrunner .40 1.00
607 Martin Brodeur 4.00 10.00
608 Scott Niedermayer .40 1.00
609 Mike Rupp .40 1.00
610 Ruslan Salei .40 1.00
611 Guy Lafleur 1.50 4.00
612 Petr Sykora .40 1.00
613 Steve Rucchin .40 1.00
614 Jean-Sebastien Giguere 1.25 3.00
615 Adam Oates .40 1.00
616 Paul Kariya 1.50 4.00
617 Steve Thomas .40 1.00
618 Rob Niedermayer .40 1.00
622 Vladimir Zabrodsky .40 1.00
637 Vsevolod Bobrov .40 1.00
638 Vlastimil Bubnik .40 1.00
639 Leif Holmqvist .40 1.00
640 Vladimir Dzurilla .75 2.00
641 Anatoli Firsov .40 1.00
642 Josef Golonka .40 1.00
643 Jiri Holecek .40 1.00
644 Jaroslav Holik .40 1.00
645 Jiri Holik .40 1.00
646 Dobby Hull 2.00 5.00
647 Alexander Yakushev .75 2.00
648 Sven Tumba Johansson .40 1.00
649 Alexander Maltsev .75 2.00
650 Vaclav Nedomansky .40 1.00
651 Alexander Ragulin .75 2.00
652 Maurice Richard 2.00 5.00
653 Vladimir Martinek .40 1.00
654 Frantisek Pospisil .40 1.00

2004 Czech World Championship Postcards

COMPLETE SET (24) 10.00 25.00
1 Josef Beranek .40 1.00
2 Roman Cechmanek .60 1.50
3 Jiri Dopita .40 1.00
4 Radek Dvorak .40 1.00
5 Radek Hamr .40 1.00
6 Roman Hamrlik .40 1.00
7 Jan Hejda .40 1.00
8 Jan Hlavac .40 1.00
9 Jaroslav Hlinka .40 1.00
10 Jaromir Jagr 2.00 5.00
11 Frantisek Kaberle .40 1.00
12 Milan Kraft .40 1.00
13 Jan Novak .40 1.00
14 Vaclav Prospal .40 1.00
15 Petr Prucha 1.50 4.00
16 Martin Rucinsky .40 1.00
17 Dusan Salficky .60 1.50
18 Jiri Slegr .40 1.00
19 Jaroslav Spacek .40 1.00
20 Martin Straka .40 1.00
21 Michal Sup .40 1.00
22 Tomas Vokoun 1.50 4.00
23 David Vyborny .60 1.50

2004-05 Czech HC Plzen Postcards

COMPLETE SET (23) 10.00 20.00
1 Martin Adamsky .40 1.00
2 Dusan Andrasovsky .40 1.00
3 Mario Cartelli .40 1.00
4 Martin Cibak .60 1.50
5 Tomas Duba .40 1.00
6 Michal Duras .40 1.00
7 Robert Jindrich .60 1.50
8 Jaroslav Kracik .40 1.00
9 Jaroslav Kudrna .40 1.00
10 Radek Matejovsky .40 1.00
11 Frank Mrazek .40 1.00
12 Milan Nedoma .40 1.00
13 Martin Paroulek .40 1.00
14 Rudolf Pejchar .40 1.00
15 David Pospisil .40 1.00
16 Jaroslav Spacek .40 1.00
17 Pavel Srek .40 1.00
18 Josef Straka .40 1.00
19 Martin Straka .60 1.50
20 Michal Straka .40 1.00
21 Pavel Trnka .40 1.00
22 Martin Vyborny .40 1.00
23 Jan Vytisk .40 1.00

2004-05 Czech HC Slavia Praha Postcards

COMPLETE SET (22) 15.00 25.00
1 Milan Antos .40 1.00
2 Radek Duda .40 1.00
3 Petr Franek .40 1.00
4 Petr Kadlec .40 1.00
5 Tomas Kloucek .60 1.50
6 Zigmund Palffy 1.50 4.00
7 Vladimir Ruzicka .40 1.00
8 Jozef Stumpel .60 1.50
9 Radek Sup .40 1.00
10 Josef Vasicek .60 1.50
11 Tomas Vlasak .40 1.00
12 Team Card .60 1.50
13 Josef Beranek .40 1.00
14 Jan Novak .40 1.00
15 Pavel Kolarik .40 1.00
16 David Hruska .40 1.00
17 Michal Sup .40 1.00
18 Jaroslav Spacek .40 1.00
19 Dominik Granak .40 1.00
20 Lukas Havel .40 1.00
21 Zdenek Smid .40 1.00
22 Tomas Zizka .40 1.00

2004-05 Czech HC Sparta Praha Postcards

COMPLETE SET (24) 15.00 30.00
1 Petr Briza .75 2.00
2 Michal Bros .40 1.00
3 Martin Chabada .40 1.00
4 Michal Dobron .40 1.00
5 Michal Dragoun .40 1.00
6 Jan Hanzlik .40 1.00
7 Jan Hlavac .75 2.00
8 Pavel Kasparik .40 1.00
9 Jindrich Kotrla .40 1.00
10 Ondrej Kratena .40 1.00
11 Jan Marek .40 1.00
12 Petr Nedved .75 2.00
13 Tomas Netik .40 1.00
14 Rostislav Olesz 1.25 3.00
15 Karel Pilar .75 2.00
16 Tomas Popperle .40 1.00
17 Libor Prochazka .40 1.00
18 Jozef Reznicek .40 1.00
19 Martin Richter .40 1.00
20 Robert Schnabel .40 1.00
21 Jakub Sindel .40 1.00
22 Michal Sivek .75 2.00
23 Petr Ton .40 1.00
24 David Vyborny .75 2.00

2004-05 Czech NHL ELH Postcards

COMPLETE SET (16) 15.00 30.00
1 Jan Bulis .75 2.00
2 Petr Cajanek .75 2.00
3 Roman Hamrlik .75 2.00
4 Milan Hejduk 1.50 4.00
5 Ales Hemsky 1.50 4.00
6 Jan Hlavac .75 2.00
7 Jaromir Jagr 2.00 5.00
8 Ales Kotalik .75 2.00
9 Petr Nedved .75 2.00
10 Karel Pilar .75 2.00
11 Robert Reichel .75 2.00
12 Martin Rucinsky .75 2.00
13 Jiri Slegr .75 2.00
14 Jaroslav Spacek .75 2.00
15 Martin Straka .75 2.00
16 David Vyborny .75 2.00

2004-05 Czech OFS

COMPLETE SET (372) 40.00 100.00
1 Petr Altrichter .08 .20
2 Oldrich Bakus .08 .20
3 Petr Buzek .08 .20
4 Tomas Cachotsky .08 .20
5 Dusan Devecka .08 .20
6 Jiri Dobrovolny .08 .20
7 Tomas Ficenc .08 .20
8 Marian Havel .08 .20
9 Roman Hlouch .08 .20
10 Lukas Hronek .08 .20
11 Jiri Jantovsky .08 .20
12 Petr Kuchyna .08 .20
13 Rostislav Malena .08 .20
14 Jaroslav Mares .08 .20
15 Ales Padelek .08 .20
16 Vojtech Polak .08 .20
17 Petr Puncochar .08 .20
18 Ladislav Rytnauer .08 .20
19 Jaroslav Suchan .08 .20
20 Petr Vala .08 .20
21 Rudolf Vercik .08 .20
22 Martin Zajac .08 .20
23 Richard Bauer .08 .20
24 Michal Dvorak .08 .20
25 Martin Hlavacka .08 .20
26 Martin Kivon .08 .20
27 Jan Kostal .08 .20
28 Petr Kumstat .08 .20
29 Edgars Masalskis .08 .20
30 Petr Mika .08 .20
31 Lukas Pech .08 .20
32 Milan Prochazka .08 .20
33 Frantisek Ptacek .08 .20
34 Vaclav Skuhravy .08 .20
35 Zdenek Smid .08 .20

36 Dmitrij Suur .08 .20
37 Robert Tomik .08 .20
38 Jiri Polak .08 .20
39 Lukas Krajicek .40 1.00
40 Lukas Bednarik .08 .20
41 Jakub Kraus .08 .20
42 Jan Alinc .08 .20
43 Jan Lipiansky .08 .20
44 Lubomir Hurtaj .08 .20
45 Zdenek Kutlak .08 .20
46 Lukas Mensator .20 .50
47 Vitezslav Bilek .08 .20
48 Vratislav Cech .08 .20
49 Jakub Evan .08 .20
50 Martin Frolik .08 .20
51 Michael Frolik 2.00 5.00
52 Radek Gardon .08 .20
53 Miloslav Horava .08 .20
54 Petr Horava .08 .20
55 Tomas Horna .08 .20
56 Jaromir Jagr 2.00 5.00
57 Jiri Jelinek .08 .20
58 Tomas Kaberle .20 .50
59 Jaroslav Kalla .08 .20
60 Tomas Klimt .08 .20
61 Jakub Lev .08 .20
62 Zdenek Orct .20 .50
63 Pavel Patera .08 .20
64 Martin Prochazka .08 .20
65 Martin Sevc .08 .20
66 Jaroslav Spelda .08 .20
67 Josef Zajic .08 .20
68 Jan Holub .08 .20
69 Richard Jares .08 .20
70 Valdemar Jirus .08 .20
71 Ales Kotalik .60 1.50
72 Jiri Moravec .08 .20
73 Vaclav Nedorost .40 1.00
74 Vaclav Novak .08 .20
75 Jan Plodek .08 .20
76 Andrej Podkonicky .08 .20
77 Stanislav Prochazka .08 .20
78 Igor Rataj .08 .20
79 Patrik Rozsival .08 .20
80 Ladislav Smid ERC .75 2.00
81 Jan Tomajko .08 .20
82 Lubomir Vaic .20 .50
83 Radim Vrbata .40 1.00
84 Pavel Falta .08 .20
85 Leos Cermak .08 .20
86 Miroslav Duben .08 .20
87 Milan Hnilicka .40 1.00
88 Jiri Hanzlik .08 .20
89 David Balaze .08 .20
90 Frantisek Bombic .08 .20
91 Daniel Branda .08 .20
92 Jiri Gombar .08 .20
93 Lukas Havel .08 .20
94 Viktor Hubl .08 .20
95 Kamil Jarina .08 .20
96 Jan Kloboucek .08 .20
97 Vlastimil Kroupa .08 .20
98 Vojtech Kubincak .08 .20
99 Tomas Kurka .08 .20
100 Michal Marik .08 .20
101 Lukas Pozivil .08 .20
102 Robert Reichel .20 .50
103 Lukas Riha .08 .20
104 Martin Rucinsky .20 .50
105 Zbynek Sklenicka .08 .20
106 Martin Skoula .20 .50
107 Radim Skuhrovec .08 .20
108 Jiri Slegr .08 .20
109 Michal Travnicek .08 .20
110 Martin Tupa .08 .20
111 Tomas Blazek .08 .20
112 Jan Bulis .08 .20
113 Petr Caslava .08 .20
114 Tomas Divisek .20 .50
115 Jiri Dopita .20 .50
116 David Havir .08 .20
117 Milan Hejduk .75 2.00
118 Alexandr Hylak .08 .20
119 Jaroslav Kames .20 .50
120 Jan Kolar .08 .20
121 Petr Koukal .08 .20
122 Tomas Linhart .08 .20
123 Ladislav Lubina .08 .20
124 Michal Mikeska .08 .20
125 Petr Mudroch .08 .20
126 Andrej Novotny .08 .20
127 Tomas Pacal .08 .20
128 Petr Prucha .75 2.00
129 Tomaz Razingar .08 .20
130 Tomas Rolinek .08 .20
131 Jan Snopek .08 .20
132 Petr Sykora .40 1.00
133 Jan Lasak .75 2.00
134 Ales Hemsky 1.25 3.00
135 Michal Tvrdik .08 .20
136 Lubomir Korhon .08 .20
137 Martin Adamsky .08 .20
138 Dusan Andrasovsky .08 .20
139 Mario Cartelli .08 .20
140 Tomas Duba .08 .20
141 Michal Duraz .08 .20
142 Petr Havelka .08 .20
143 Robert Jindrich .20 .50
144 Josef Straka .08 .20
145 Jaroslav Kracik .08 .20
146 Milan Kraft .40 1.00
147 Martin Straka .40 1.00
148 Radek Matejovsky .08 .20
149 Michal Straka .08 .20
150 Milan Nedoma .08 .20
151 Rudolf Pejchar .08 .20
152 David Pospisil .08 .20
153 Adam Saffer .08 .20
154 Jaroslav Spacek .08 .20
155 Pavel Trnka .08 .20
156 Martin Vyborny .08 .20
157 Jan Vytisk .08 .20
158 Milan Antos .08 .20
159 Radek Dlouhy .08 .20
160 Radek Duda .08 .20
161 Petr Franek .08 .20
162 Dominik Granak .08 .20
163 David Hruska .08 .20
164 Petr Kadlec .08 .20
165 Tomas Kloucek .20 .50
166 Pavel Kolarik .08 .20
167 Milan Kopecky .08 .20
168 Ales Kratoska .08 .20
169 Frantisek Kucera .08 .20
170 Lukas Musil .08 .20
171 Jan Novak .08 .20
172 Zigmund Palffy .75 2.00
173 Jozef Stumpel .20 .50
174 Michal Sup .08 .20
175 Marek Tomica .08 .20
176 Josef Vasicek .20 .50
177 Michal Vondrka .08 .20
178 Boris Zabka .08 .20
179 Petr Jaros .08 .20
180 David Pojkar .08 .20
181 Patrik Martinec .08 .20
182 Vladimir Sobotka .08 .20
183 Petr Briza .20 .50
184 Michal Dobron .08 .20
185 Jan Hanzlik .08 .20
186 Jan Hlavac .20 .50
187 Martin Chabada .08 .20
188 Pavel Kasparik .08 .20
189 Jindrich Kotrla .08 .20
190 Jan Marek .08 .20
191 Petr Nedved .20 .50
192 Tomas Netik .08 .20
193 Rostislav Olesz 1.25 3.00
194 Karel Pilar .20 .50
195 Tomas Popperle .08 .20
196 Libor Prochazka .08 .20
197 Josef Reznicek .08 .20
198 Martin Richter .08 .20
199 Robert Schnabel .08 .20
200 Jakub Sindel .08 .20
201 Michal Sivek .08 .20
202 Petr Ton .08 .20
203 David Vyborny .20 .50
204 Radek Bonk .20 .50
205 Richard Bordowski .08 .20
206 Martin Cakajik .08 .20
207 Miroslav Durak .08 .20
208 Jiri Hasek .08 .20
209 Pavel Janku .08 .20
210 Vladislav Koutsky .08 .20
211 Richard Kral .08 .20
212 Vlastimil Lakosil .08 .20
213 Jiri Malinsky .08 .20
214 Rostislav Martynek .08 .20
215 Marek Melenovsky .08 .20
216 Zdenek Pavelek .08 .20
217 Jan Peterek .08 .20
218 Vaclav Pletka .20 .50
219 Peter Podhradsky .08 .20
220 Jiri Polansky .08 .20
221 Michal Rozsival .20 .50
222 Zdenek Skorepa .08 .20
223 Filip Stefanka .08 .20
224 Jiri Burger .08 .20
225 Marek Cernosek .08 .20
226 Petr Hubacek .08 .20
227 Stanislav Hudec .08 .20
228 Jakub Hulva .08 .20
229 Zbynek Irgl .08 .20
230 Martin Krayzel .08 .20
231 Lukas Krenzelok .08 .20
232 Pavel Kumstat .08 .20
233 Marek Malik .08 .20
234 David Moravec .08 .20
235 Ivan Padelek .08 .20
236 Radek Philipp .08 .20
237 Marek Pinc .08 .20
238 Martin Prusek .40 1.00
239 Patrik Rimmel .08 .20
240 Martin Tomasek .08 .20
241 Filip Turek .08 .20
242 Vaclav Varada .20 .50
243 Kamil Brabenec .08 .20
244 Roman Cechmanek .20 .50
245 Tomas Demel .08 .20
246 Marek Dubec .08 .20
247 Tomas Frolo .08 .20
248 Ladislav Gengel .08 .20
249 Josef Hrabal .08 .20
250 Alexej Jaskin .08 .20
251 Rostislav Klesla .40 1.00
252 Robin Kovar .08 .20
253 Pavel Kowalczyk .08 .20
254 Radek Masny .08 .20
255 Ondrej Nemec .08 .20
256 Libor Pavlis .08 .20
257 Lukas Plsek .08 .20
258 Branko Radivojevic .40 1.00
259 Pavel Selingr .08 .20
260 Roman Stantien .08 .20
261 Tomas Vak .08 .20
262 Martin Vasut .08 .20
263 Rostislav Vlach .08 .20
264 Marek Zadina .08 .20
265 Robert Horak .08 .20
266 Radovan Somik .08 .20
267 Jan Koroptvicka .08 .20
268 Ondrej Vesely .08 .20
269 Martin Altrichter .08 .20
270 Martin Ambruz .08 .20
271 Jaroslav Balastik .40 1.00
272 Peter Barinka .20 .50
273 Miroslav Blatak .08 .20
274 Petr Cajanek .20 .50
275 Martin Cech .08 .20
276 Martin Erat .40 1.00
277 Lukas Galvas .08 .20
278 Roman Hamrlik .20 .50
279 Martin Jenacek .08 .20
280 Miroslav Kovacik .08 .20
281 Jaroslav Kristek .08 .20
282 Tomas Kudelka .08 .20
283 Petr Leska .08 .20
284 Petr Mokrejs .08 .20
285 Igor Murin .08 .20
286 David Nosek .08 .20
287 Miroslav Okal .08 .20
288 Radim Tesarik .08 .20
289 Martin Vosatko .08 .20
290 Martin Zahorovsky .08 .20
291 Pavel Zubicek .08 .20
292 Vaclav Benak .08 .20
293 Radim Bicanek .08 .20
294 Roman Erat .08 .20
295 Radek Haman .08 .20
296 Tomas Kucharcik .08 .20
297 Branislav Kvetan .08 .20
298 Zdenek Ondrej .08 .20
299 Jan Pardavy .08 .20
300 Peter Pucher .08 .20
301 Ivan Rachunek .08 .20
302 Milan Toman .08 .20
303 Marek Vorel .08 .20
304 Marek Uram .08 .20
305 Karel Plasek .08 .20
306 Ales Kretinsky .08 .20
307 Miroslav Barus .08 .20
308 David Ludvik .08 .20
309 Robert Slavik .08 .20
310 Pavel Mojzis .08 .20
311 Tomas Vokoun 1.25 3.00
312 Patrik Elias .40 1.00
313 Martin Havlat .75 2.00
314 David Vsetecka .08 .20
315 Josef Vitek .08 .20
316 Jiri Hunkes .08 .20
317 Radim Kucharczyk .08 .20
318 Branislav Mezei .20 .50
319 Karel Rachunek .20 .50
320 Ivan Majesky .20 .50
321 David Vrbata .08 .20
322 Jaroslav Kasik .08 .20
323 Ondrej Malinsky .08 .20
324 Michal Dragoun .08 .20
325 Michal Bros .08 .20
326 Ondrej Kratena .08 .20
327 Petr Kasik .08 .20
328 Jiri Zeman .08 .20
329 Miroslav Kopriva .08 .20
330 Robert Kysela .08 .20
331 Frantisek Kaberle .08 .20
332 Jan Hrdina .20 .50
333 Jiri Jelinek .08 .20
334 Milan Hluchy .08 .20
335 Jiri Stejskal .08 .20
336 Jiri Fischer .20 .50
337 Angel Krstev .08 .20
338 Tomas Klimenta .08 .20
339 Lukas Pabiska .08 .20
340 Petr Vampola .08 .20
341 Jan Visek .08 .20
342 Jaroslav Modry .20 .50
343 Martin Strba .08 .20
344 David Stich .08 .20
345 Jakub Korinek .08 .20
346 Martin Paroulek .08 .20
347 Frantisek Mrazek .08 .20
348 Martin Cibak .20 .50
349 David Moravec .08 .20
350 Lukas Pulpan .08 .20
351 Josef Beranek .08 .20
352 Tomas Vlasak .08 .20
353 Tomas Zizka .08 .20
354 Vladimir Vujtek .08 .20
355 Daniel Seman .08 .20
356 Roman Simicek .08 .20
357 Juraj Stefanka .08 .20
358 Tomas Dolana .08 .20
359 Pavel Vostrak .08 .20
360 Radovan Biegl .20 .50
361 Karol Sloboda .08 .20
362 Vladimir Gyna .08 .20
363 Petr Gregorek .08 .20
364 Jiri Hudler 1.50 4.00
365 Pavel Kubina .40 1.00
366 Ludek Krayzel .08 .20
367 Martin Hamrlik .08 .20
368 Michal Hrazdira .08 .20
369 Connor Dunlop .40 1.00
370 Miroslav Hanuljak .08 .20
371 Miroslav Zalesak .40 1.00
372 Radovan Biegl .20 .50
373 Martin Vojtek .08 .20
374 TomÃ¡Ã¡ Zboril .08 .20
375 TomÃ¡Ã¡ Kloucek .20 .50
376 TomÃ¡Ã¡ PospÃÃ¡il .20 .50
377 Jaroslav Kudrna .20 .50
378 TomÃ¡Ã¡ Harant .20 .50
379 Milan Kraft .20 .50
380 Radim Kucharczyk .08 .20
381 Roman MÃ¡lek .20 .50
382 Andrej Nedorost .20 .50
383 Vojtech PolÃ¡k .30 .75
384 FrantiÃ¡ek MrÃ¡zek .08 .20
385 Jan Caloun .08 .20
386 Radek Fiala .08 .20
387 Martin Heinisch .08 .20
388 Peter Jansky .08 .20
389 Jindrich Kotrla .08 .20
390 Jaroslav Å pacek .08 .20
391 Matej Badiura .08 .20
392 Å tepÃ¡n Hrebejk .08 .20
393 Radek HubÃ¡cek .08 .20
394 Radek HubÃ¡cek .08 .20
395 MojmÃr Musil .08 .20
396 Robert Najdek .08 .20
397 Michal NedbÃ¡lek .08 .20
398 Michal Å afarÃk .08 .20
399 Radek Bonk .20 .50
400 Ondrej VeselÃ½ .08 .20
401 Martin Ambruz .08 .20
402 JirÃ Beroun .08 .20
403 Martin CakajÃk .08 .20
404 Petr KuboÃ¡ .08 .20
405 Milan MikulÃk .08 .20
406 Roman Nemecek .08 .20
407 Ondrej Å mach .08 .20
408 Josef Straka .08 .20
409 RÃ³bert Filc .08 .20
410 Pavel MojzÃÃ¡ .08 .20
411 Jan Peterek .08 .20
412 Radek ProchÃ¡zka .08 .20
NNO Frantisek Kaberle CL .08 .20

2004-05 Czech OFS Assist Leaders

COMPLETE SET (15) 15.00 35.00
1 Josef Beranek 1.25 3.00
2 Petr Leska 1.25 3.00
3 Peter Pucher 1.25 3.00
4 Josef Straka 1.25 3.00
5 Jan Marek 1.25 3.00
6 Zdenek Pavelek 1.25 3.00
7 Jiri Dopita 1.25 3.00
8 Jiri Burger 1.25 3.00
9 Martin Hamrlik 1.25 3.00
10 Michal Bros 1.25 3.00
11 Pavel Janku 1.25 3.00
12 Marek Uram 1.25 3.00
13 Tomas Divisek 1.25 3.00
14 Dusan Andrasovsky 1.25 3.00
15 Petr Sykora 1.25 3.00

2004-05 Czech OFS Checklist Cards

COMPLETE SET 10.00 25.00
1 Petr Buzek .75 2.00
2 Frantisek Ptacek .75 2.00
3 Jaromir Jagr 2.00 5.00
4 Patrik Rozsival .75 2.00
5 Martin Skoula .75 2.00
6 Milan Hejduk 1.25 3.00
7 Jaroslav Spacek .75 2.00
8 Zigmund Palffy 1.25 3.00
9 Petr Nedved .75 2.00
10 Radek Bonk .75 2.00
11 David Moravec .75 2.00
12 Rostislav Klesla .75 2.00
13 Petr Cajanek .75 2.00
14 Patrik Elias 1.25 3.00

2004-05 Czech OFS Czech/Slovak

COMPLETE SET (46) 20.00 40.00
1 Jaroslav Balastik .75 2.00
2 Jiri Burger .40 1.00
3 Tomas Demel .40 1.00
4 Michal Dobron .40 1.00
5 Jiri Dopita .40 1.00
6 Tomas Duba .40 1.00
7 Martin Chabada .40 1.00
8 Waldemar Jirus .40 1.00
9 Jiri Malinsky .40 1.00
10 Jan Novak .40 1.00
11 Frantisek Ptacek .40 1.00
12 Peter Pucher .40 1.00
13 Petr Sailer .40 1.00
14 Jan Srdinko .40 1.00
15 Josef Straka .40 1.00
16 Michal Sup .40 1.00
17 Adam Svoboda .75 2.00
18 Michal Sykora .40 1.00
19 Petr Sykora .40 1.00
20 Michal Travnicek .40 1.00
21 Marek Uram .40 1.00
22 Libor Zabransky .40 1.00
23 Daniel Babka .40 1.00
24 Martin Bartek .40 1.00
25 Zdeno Ciger .40 1.00
26 Peter Fabus .40 1.00
27 Miroslav Hala .40 1.00
28 Juraj Halaj .40 1.00
29 Richard Hartmann .40 1.00
30 Jiri Hes .40 1.00
31 Martin Ivicic .40 1.00
32 Juraj Kledrowetz .40 1.00
33 Jaroslav Kmit .40 1.00
34 Arne Krotak .40 1.00
35 Roman Kukumberg .40 1.00
36 Igor Majesky .40 1.00
37 Petr Pavlas .40 1.00
38 Slavomir Pavlicko .40 1.00
39 Pavol Rybar .40 1.00
40 Michal Segla .40 1.00
41 Richard Sechny .40 1.00
42 Marcel Simurda .40 1.00
43 Tomas Starosta .40 1.00
44 Rastislav Stork .40 1.00
45 Adam Svoboda CL .75 2.00
46 Pavol Rybar CL .40 1.00

2004-05 Czech OFS Defence Points

COMPLETE SET (15) 15.00 25.00
1 Martin Hamrlik 1.00 2.50
2 David Havir 1.00 2.50
3 Jan Novak 1.00 2.50
4 Stanislav Jasecko 1.00 2.50
5 Michal Sykora 1.00 2.50
6 Josef Reznicek 1.00 2.50
7 Frantisek Ptacek 1.00 2.50
8 Alexej Jaskin 1.00 2.50
9 Valdemar Jirus 1.00 2.50
10 Petr Kadlec 1.00 2.50
11 Jiri Malinsky 1.00 2.50
12 Patrik Luza 1.00 2.50
13 Radim Tesarik 1.00 2.50
14 Pavel Kowalczyk 1.00 2.50
15 Petr Jancarik 1.00 2.50

2004-05 Czech OFS Goals-Against Leaders

COMPLETE SET (16) 25.00 60.00
1 Igor Murin 2.00 5.00
2 Adam Svoboda 2.50 6.00
3 Petr Briza 2.00 5.00
4 Jiri Trvaj 2.00 5.00
5 Roman Malek 2.00 5.00
6 Petr Franek 2.00 5.00
7 Radovan Biegl 2.00 5.00
8 Tomas Duba 2.00 5.00
9 Zdenek Orct 2.00 5.00
10 Lukas Hronek 2.00 5.00
11 Martin Vojtek 2.00 5.00
12 Martin Altrichter 2.00 5.00
13 Oldrich Svoboda 2.00 5.00
14 Michal Marik 2.00 5.00
15 Marek Pinc 2.00 5.00
NNO Altrichter
Murin CL 2.00 5.00

2004-05 Czech OFS Goals Leaders

COMPLETE SET (15) 12.00 30.00
1 Jaroslav Balastik 1.50 4.00
2 Michal Sup 1.00 2.50
3 Marek Uram 1.00 2.50
4 Josef Straka 1.00 2.50
5 Jiri Burger 1.00 2.50
6 Petr Sykora 1.00 2.50
7 Marek Melenovsky 1.00 2.50
8 Jan Marek 1.00 2.50
9 Lukas Havel 1.00 2.50
10 Jiri Dopita 1.00 2.50
11 Tomas Divisek 1.00 2.50
12 Peter Barinka 1.00 2.50
13 Zbynek Irgl 1.00 2.50
14 David Hruska 1.00 2.50
15 Ondrej Vesely 1.00 2.50

2004-05 Czech OFS Jaromir Jagr

COMPLETE SET (6) 20.00 50.00
J01 Jaromir Jagr 4.00 10.00
J02 Jaromir Jagr 4.00 10.00
J03 Jaromir Jagr 4.00 10.00
J04 Jaromir Jagr 4.00 10.00
J05 Jaromir Jagr 4.00 10.00
J06 Jaromir Jagr 4.00 10.00

2004-05 Czech OFS Points Leaders

COMPLETE SET (15) 20.00 40.00
1 Josef Beranek 1.25 3.00
2 Petr Leska 1.25 3.00
3 Josef Straka 1.25 3.00
4 Peter Pucher 1.25 3.00
5 Jan Marek 1.25 3.00
6 Marek Uram 1.25 3.00
7 Jiri Burger 1.25 3.00
8 Jiri Dopita 1.25 3.00
9 Jaroslav Balastik 1.25 3.00
10 Petr Sykora 1.25 3.00
11 Michal Sup 1.25 3.00
12 Tomas Divisek 1.25 3.00
13 Marek Melenovsky 1.25 3.00
14 Zdenek Pavelek 1.25 3.00
15 Michal Bros 1.25 3.00

2004-05 Czech OFS Save Percentage Leaders

COMPLETE SET (15) 25.00 60.00
1 Igor Murin 2.00 5.00
2 Petr Briza 2.00 5.00
3 Zdenek Orct 2.00 5.00
4 Petr Franek 2.00 5.00
5 Roman Malek 2.00 5.00
6 Jiri Trvaj 2.00 5.00
7 Adam Svoboda 2.50 6.00
8 Radovan Biegl 2.00 5.00
9 Martin Vojtek 2.00 5.00
10 Tomas Duba 2.00 5.00
11 Martin Altrichter 2.00 5.00
12 Marek Pinc 2.00 5.00
13 Lukas Hronek 2.00 5.00
14 Libor Barta 2.00 5.00
15 Michal Marik 2.00 5.00

2004-05 Czech OFS Stars

COMPLETE SET (51) 30.00 60.00
1 Tomas Kaberle .75 2.00
2 Jaromir Jagr 4.00 10.00
3 Radim Vrbata 1.25 3.00
4 Vaclav Nedorost .75 2.00
5 Tomas Kurka .40 1.00
6 Martin Rucinsky .40 1.00
7 Martin Skoula .40 1.00
8 Robert Reichel .40 1.00
9 Jiri Slegr .40 1.00
10 Jan Bulis .40 1.00
11 Milan Hejduk 1.50 4.00
12 Ales Hemsky 2.00 5.00
13 Jiri Dopita .40 1.00
14 Jan Lasak .75 2.00
15 Martin Straka .40 1.00
16 Jaroslav Spacek .40 1.00
17 Milan Kraft .75 2.00
18 Zigmund Palffy 1.25 3.00
19 Josef Stumpel .40 1.00
20 Josef Vasicek .40 1.00
21 Tomas Kloucek .40 1.00
22 Radek Duda .40 1.00
23 Jan Hlavac .40 1.00
24 Karel Pilar .40 1.00
25 David Vyborny .75 2.00
26 Petr Nedved .40 1.00
27 Michal Rozsival .40 1.00
28 Radek Bonk .40 1.00
29 Branislav Mezei .40 1.00
30 Martin Prusek .75 2.00
31 Marek Malik .40 1.00
32 Pavel Kubina .40 1.00
33 Vaclav Varada .40 1.00
34 Rostislav Klesla .40 1.00
35 Roman Cechmanek .40 1.00
36 Branko Radivojevic .40 1.00
37 Radovan Somik .40 1.00
38 Martin Erat .40 1.00
39 Roman Hamrlik .40 1.00
40 Petr Cajanek .40 1.00
41 Patrik Elias .75 2.00
42 Martin Havlat 1.50 4.00
43 Karel Rachunek .40 1.00
44 Tomas Vokoun 2.00 5.00
45 Petr Buzek .40 1.00
46 David Moravec .40 1.00
47 Martin Hlavacka .40 1.00
48 Ales Kotalik 1.25 3.00
49 Robert Schnabel .40 1.00
50 Michal Sivek .40 1.00
51 Jaromir Jagr CL 4.00 10.00

2004-05 Czech OFS Stars II

COMPLETE SET (16) 20.00 50.00
1 Frantisek Kaberle 1.50 4.00
2 Jan Hrdina 1.50 4.00
3 Ivan Majesky 1.50 4.00
4 Jiri Hudler 6.00 15.00
5 Connor Dunlop 1.50 4.00
6 Vladimir Vujtek 1.50 4.00
7 Josef Beranek 1.50 4.00
8 Tomas Vlasak 1.50 4.00
9 Roman MÃ¡lek 1.50 4.00
10 Jan Caloun 1.50 4.00
11 JirÃ Fischer 2.00 5.00
12 Jaroslav ModrÃ½ 1.50 4.00
13 Roman Å imÃcek 1.50 4.00
14 TomÃ¡Ã¡ Harant 1.50 4.00
15 Martin HamrlÃk 1.50 4.00
16 Pavel Kubina CL 1.50 4.00

2004-05 Czech OFS Team Cards

COMPLETE SET (14) 6.00 15.00
1 Jaroslav Suchan .40 1.00
2 Zdenek Smid .40 1.00
3 Zdenek Orct .75 2.00
4 Milan Hnilicka .75 2.00
5 Michal Marik .40 1.00
6 Jan Lasak 1.25 3.00
7 Tomas Duba .40 1.00
8 Petr Franek .40 1.00
9 Petr Briza .75 2.00
10 Vlastimil Lakosil .40 1.00
11 Martin Prusek .75 2.00
12 Roman Cechmanek .75 2.00
13 Martin Altrichter .40 1.00
14 Robert Slavik .40 1.00

2005 Czech World Champions Postcards

COMPLETE SET (23) 15.00 40.00
1 Frantisek Kaberle .40 1.00
2 Jiri Slegr .40 1.00
3 David Vyborny .40 1.00
4 Jiri Fischer .40 1.00
5 Jan Hlavac .40 1.00
6 Josef Vasicek .40 1.00
7 Vaclav Prospal .40 1.00
8 Vaclav Varada .40 1.00
9 Pavel Kubina .40 1.00
10 Radek Dvorak .40 1.00
11 Ales Hemsky 1.50 4.00
12 Radim Vrbata .75 2.00
13 Martin Rucinsky .40 1.00
14 Martin Straka .40 1.00
15 Jaromir Jagr 4.00 10.00
16 Marek Zidlicky .40 1.00
17 Milan Hnilicka .75 2.00
18 Petr Sykora .40 1.00
19 Tomas Kaberle .40 1.00
20 Petr Cajanek .40 1.00
21 Tomas Vokoun 2.00 5.00
22 Jaroslav Spacek .40 1.00
23 Jan Hejda .40 1.00

2005-06 Czech HC Ceski Budejovice

COMPLETE SET (16) 8.00 20.00
1 Kamil Brabenec .60 1.50
2 Petr Gregorek .60 1.50
3 Tomas Harant .60 1.50
4 Stepan Hrebejk .60 1.50
5 Viktor Hubl .60 1.50
6 Michal Hudec .60 1.50
7 Milan Kopecky .60 1.50
8 Jindrich Kotrla .60 1.50
9 Ales Kratoska .60 1.50
10 Zdenek Kutlak .60 1.50
11 Jan Mucha .60 1.50
12 Marek Posmyk .60 1.50
13 Petr Sailer .60 1.50
14 Roman Turek .75 2.00
15 Tomas Vak .60 1.50
16 Rene Vydareny .60 1.50

2005-06 Czech HC Hame Zlin

COMPLETE SET (16) 8.00 20.00
1 Martin Altrichter .60 1.50
2 Petr Barinka .60 1.50
3 Jan Benda .60 1.50
4 Miroslav Blatak .60 1.50
5 Lukas Galvas .60 1.50
6 Martin Hamrlik .60 1.50
7 Richard Kral .60 1.50
8 Petr Leska .60 1.50
9 Marek Melenovsky .60 1.50
10 Petr Mokrejs .60 1.50
11 Igor Murin .60 1.50
12 David Nosek .60 1.50
13 Miroslav Okal .60 1.50
14 Ivan Rachunek .60 1.50
15 Michal Travnicek .60 1.50
16 Martin Zahorovsky .60 1.50

2005-06 Czech HC Karlovy Vary

COMPLETE SET (16) 8.00 20.00
1 Jan Alinc .60 1.50
2 Roman Cechmanek .75 2.00
3 Miroslav Duben .60 1.50
4 Michal Dvorak .60 1.50
5 Lubomir Hurtaj .60 1.50
6 Jan Kostal .60 1.50
7 Lukas Krajicek .60 1.50
8 Petr Kumstat .60 1.50
9 Lukas Mensator .60 1.50
10 Andrej Nedorost .60 1.50
11 Ondrej Nemec .60 1.50
12 Lukas Pech .60 1.50
13 Frantisek Ptacek .60 1.50
14 Josef Reznicek .60 1.50
15 Vaclav Skuhravy .60 1.50
16 Libor Ustrnul .60 1.50

2005-06 Czech HC Kladno

COMPLETE SET (15) 10.00 25.00
1 Jan Besser .60 1.50
2 Martin Frolik .60 1.50
3 Michael Frolik 2.00 5.00
4 Radek Gardon .60 1.50
5 Tomas Horna .60 1.50
6 Ivan Huml 1.00 2.50
7 Jaroslav Kalla .60 1.50
8 Jakub Lev .60 1.50
9 Zdenek Orct .75 2.00
10 Libor Prochazka .60 1.50
11 Martin Prochazka .60 1.50
12 Jaroslav Spelda .60 1.50
13 Ladislav Vlcek .60 1.50
14 Josef Zajic .60 1.50
15 Jiri Zeman .60 1.50

2005-06 Czech HC Liberec

COMPLETE SET (16) 8.00 20.00
1 Leos Cermak .60 1.50
2 Pavel Falta .60 1.50
3 Jiri Hanzlik .60 1.50
4 Milan Hnilicka .75 2.00
5 Valdemar Jirus .60 1.50
6 Angel Krstev .60 1.50
7 Lukas Pabiska .60 1.50
8 Andrej Podkonicky .60 1.50
9 Stanislav Prochazka .60 1.50
10 Igor Rataj .60 1.50
11 Martin Richtr .60 1.50
12 Patrik Rozsival .60 1.50
13 Martin Rygl .60 1.50
14 Jan Tomajko .60 1.50
15 Lubomir Vaic .60 1.50
16 Petr Vampola .60 1.50

2005-06 Czech HC Pardubice

COMPLETE SET (16) 8.00 20.00
1 Tomas Blazek .60 1.50
2 Jan Caloun .60 1.50
3 Petr Caslava .60 1.50
4 David Havir .60 1.50
5 Robert Kantor .60 1.50
6 Jan Kolar .60 1.50
7 Lubomir Korhon .60 1.50
8 Jan Lasak 1.25 3.00
9 Ladislav Lubina .60 1.50
10 Michal Mikeska .60 1.50
11 Frantisek Mrazek .60 1.50
12 Petr Mudroch .75 2.00
13 Andrej Novotny .75 2.00
14 Tomas Rolinek .60 1.50
15 Jan Snopek .60 1.50
16 Michal Tvrdik .60 1.50

2005-06 Czech HC Plzen

COMPLETE SET (16) 8.00 20.00
1 Martin Adamsky .60 1.50
2 Mario Cartelli .60 1.50
3 Michal Duras .60 1.50
4 Petr Jez .60 1.50
5 Robert Jindrich .60 1.50
6 Jaroslav Kracik .60 1.50
7 Roman Malek .60 1.50
8 Radek Matejovsky .60 1.50
9 David Moravec .60 1.50
10 Martin Stepanek .60 1.50
11 Josef Straka .60 1.50
12 Michal Straka .60 1.50
13 Pavel Trnka .60 1.50
14 Matej Trojovsky .60 1.50
15 Roman Tvrdon .60 1.50
16 Marek Vorel .60 1.50

2005-06 Czech HC Slavia Praha

COMPLETE SET (16) 8.00 20.00
1 Jaroslav Bednar .60 1.50
2 Josef Beranek .60 1.50
3 Roman Cervenka .60 2.00
4 Radek Dlouhy .60 1.50
5 Jiri Drtina .60 1.50
6 Radek Duda .60 1.50
7 Petr Franek .60 1.50
8 David Hruska .60 1.50
9 Petr Kadlec .60 1.50
10 Pavel Kolarik .60 1.50
11 Jan Novak .60 1.50
12 Michal Sup .60 1.50
13 Tomas Vlasak .60 1.50
14 Michal Vondrka .60 1.50
15 Boris Zabka .60 1.50
16 Tomas Zizka .60 1.50

2005-06 Czech HC Sparta Praha

COMPLETE SET (16) 8.00 20.00
1 Petr Briza 1.25 3.00
2 Marek Cernosek .60 1.50
3 Michal Dobron .60 1.50
4 Jan Hanzlik .60 1.50
5 Martin Hlavacka .60 1.50
6 Martin Chabada .60 1.50
7 Ondrej Kratena .60 1.50
8 Jan Marek .60 1.50
9 Jakub Sindel .60 1.50
10 Michal Sivek .75 2.00
11 Martin Spanhel .75 2.00
12 Josef Straka .60 1.50
13 Milan Toman .60 1.50
14 Petr Ton .60 1.50
15 Roman Vopat .60 1.50
16 Jiri Vykoukal .60 1.50

2005-06 Czech HC Trinec

COMPLETE SET (15) 8.00 20.00
1 Richard Bordowski .60 1.50
2 Lukas Danecek .60 1.50
3 Jiri Hasek .60 1.50
4 Jiri Hunkes .60 1.50
5 Tomas Jurdic .60 1.50
6 Jaroslav Kudrna .60 1.50
7 Tomas Pacal .60 1.50
8 Jan Peterek .60 1.50
9 Lubomir Pistek .60 1.50
10 Vaclav Pletka 1.00 2.50
11 Jiri Polansky .60 1.50
12 Radim Tesarik .60 1.50
13 David Vsetecka .60 1.50
14 Martin Vojtek .60 1.50
15 Tomas Zboril .60 1.50

2005-06 Czech HC Vitkovice

COMPLETE SET (16) 8.00 20.00
1 Jiri Burger .60 1.50
2 Jan Dresler .60 1.50
3 Petr Hubacek .60 1.50
4 Stanislav Hudec .60 1.50
5 Jakub Hulva .60 1.50
6 Zbynek Irgl .60 1.50
7 Petr Jurecka .60 1.50
8 Jaroslav Kames .75 2.00
9 Bedrich Kohler .60 1.50
10 Lukas Krenzelok .60 1.50
11 Radoslav Kropac .60 1.50

12 Radek Philipp .60 1.50
13 Marek Pinc .75 2.00
14 Radek Prochazka .60 1.50
15 Roman Simicek .60 1.50
16 Martin Tomasek .60 1.50

2005-06 Czech HC Vsetin

COMPLETE SET (15) 8.00 20.00
1 Richard Bauer .60 1.50
2 Tomas Demel .60 1.50
3 Roman Gorev .60 1.50
4 Michal Horak .60 1.50
5 Josef Hrabal .60 1.50
6 Ondrej Hruska .60 1.50
7 Radim Hruska .60 1.50
8 Josef Kucera .60 1.50
9 David Kveton .60 1.50
10 Havi Sasu .60 1.50
11 Zdenek Spitzer .60 1.50
12 Roman Stantien .60 1.50
13 Filip Stefanka .60 1.50
14 Ondrej Steiner .60 1.50
15 Patrik Luza .60 1.50

2005-06 Czech HC Znojmo

COMPLETE SET (14) 8.00 20.00
1 Radim Bicanek .60 1.50
2 Martin Cakajik .60 1.50
3 Jiri Dopita .60 1.50
4 Roman Erat .60 1.50
5 Radek Haman .60 1.50
6 Richard Jares .60 1.50
7 Ales Kretinsky .60 1.50
8 Milan Ministr .60 1.50
9 Pavel Mojzis .60 1.50
10 Zdenek Ondrej .60 1.50
11 Karel Plasek .60 1.50
12 Peter Pucher .60 1.50
13 Jiri Trvaj .60 1.50
14 Marek Uram .60 1.50

2006-07 Czech CP Cup Postcards

COMPLETE SET (23) 20.00 40.00
1 Miroslav Blatak .75 2.00
2 Jiri Burger .75 2.00
3 Radek Hamr .75 2.00
4 Jaroslav Hlinka .75 2.00
5 Milan Hnilicka 1.25 3.00
6 Miloslav Horava .75 2.00
7 Petr Hubacek .75 2.00
8 Jiri Hunkes .75 2.00
9 Martin Chabada .75 2.00
10 Zbynek Irgl .75 2.00
11 Zdenek Kutlak .75 2.00
12 Roman Malek .75 2.00
13 Jan Marek .75 2.00
14 Josef Marha .75 2.00
15 Vaclav Pletka .75 2.00
16 Tomas Rolinek .75 2.00
17 Michal Sivek .75 2.00
18 Vaclav Skuhravy .75 2.00
19 Petr Sykora .75 2.00
20 Martin Sevc .75 2.00
21 Ivan Rachunek .75 2.00
22 Lukas Zib .75 2.00
23 Tomas Zizka .75 2.00

2006-07 Czech HC Ceske Budejovice Postcards

COMPLETE SET (14) 15.00 25.00
1 Petr Gregorek .75 2.00
2 Viktor Hubl .75 2.00
3 Michal Hudec .75 2.00
4 Jindrich Kotrla .75 2.00
5 Jan Mucha .75 2.00
6 Vaclav Nedorost 1.25 3.00
7 Petr Sailer .75 2.00
8 Jiri Simanek .75 2.00
9 Milan Toman .75 2.00
10 Roman Turek 1.25 3.00
11 Martin Vagner .75 2.00
12 Tomas Vak .75 2.00
13 Ondrej Vesely .75 2.00
14 Rene Vydareny .75 2.00

2006-07 Czech HC Kladno Postcards

COMPLETE SET (11) 10.00 20.00
1 Ales Pavlas .75 2.00
2 Jakub Lev .75 2.00
3 Jaroslav Kalla .75 2.00
4 Martin Frolik .75 2.00
5 Martin Prochazka .75 2.00
6 Martin Sevc .75 2.00
7 Michal Havel .75 2.00
8 Milan Hluchy .75 2.00
9 Pavel Patera .75 2.00
10 Radek Gardon .75 2.00
11 Zdenek Orct 1.25 3.00

2006-07 Czech HC Liberec Postcards

COMPLETE SET (12) 10.00 20.00
1 Jakub Cutta .75 2.00
2 Ondrej Hruska .75 2.00
3 Waldemar Jirus .75 2.00
4 Angel Krstev .75 2.00
5 Michal Nedvidek .75 2.00
6 Vaclav Novak .75 2.00
7 Vaclav Pletka .75 2.00
8 Filip Sindelar .75 2.00
9 Jan Tomajko .75 2.00
10 Lubomir Vaic .75 2.00
11 Jan Visek .75 2.00
12 Lukas Zib .75 2.00

2006-07 Czech HC Pardubice Postcards

COMPLETE SET (23) 20.00 40.00
1 Dusan Andrasovsky .75 2.00
2 Tomas Blazek 1.25 3.00
3 Jan Caloun 1.25 3.00
4 Petr Caslava .75 2.00
5 David Havir .75 2.00
6 Miroslav Hlinka .75 2.00
7 Jan Kolar .75 2.00
8 Jaroslav Koma .75 2.00
9 Petr Koukal .75 2.00
10 Vladislav Koutsky .75 2.00
11 Jan Lasak 1.25 3.00
12 Tomas Linhart .75 2.00
13 Frantisek Mrazek .75 2.00
14 Andrej Novotny .75 2.00
15 Ales Pisa .75 2.00
16 Libor Pivko .75 2.00
17 Tomas Rolinek .75 2.00
18 Michal Seda .75 2.00
19 Jan Snopek .75 2.00
20 Adam Svoboda 1.25 3.00
21 Petr Sykora .75 2.00
22 Michal Tvrdik .75 2.00
23 Jan Stary .75 2.00

2006-07 Czech HC Plzen Postcards

COMPLETE SET (16) 15.00 30.00
1 Adam Saffer .75 2.00
2 Ales Padelek .75 2.00
3 David Ludvik .75 2.00
4 Jiri Malinsky .75 2.00
5 Jiri Zelenka .75 2.00
6 Lukas Derner .75 2.00
7 Lukas Pulpan .75 2.00
8 Roman Malek 1.25 3.00
9 Martin Adamsky .75 2.00
10 Michal Duras .75 2.00
11 Milan Nedoma .75 2.00
12 Peter Fabus .75 2.00
13 Petr Jez .75 2.00
14 Tomas Divisek .75 2.00
15 Tomas Kubalik .75 2.00
16 Vaclav Benak .75 2.00

2006-07 Czech HC Slavia Praha Postcards

COMPLETE SET (16) 15.00 30.00
1 Jaroslav Bednar .75 2.00
2 Josef Beranek .75 2.00
3 Leos Cermak .75 2.00
4 Roman Cervenka .75 2.00
5 Radek Dlouhy .75 2.00
6 Jiri Drtina .75 2.00
7 Dominik Granak .75 2.00
8 Martin Hlavacka .75 2.00
9 David Hruska .75 2.00
10 Pavel Kolarik .75 2.00
11 Igor Rataj .75 2.00
12 Vladimir Sobotka .75 2.00
13 Michal Sup .75 2.00
14 Adam Svoboda 1.25 3.00
15 Tomas Vlasak .75 2.00
16 Tomas Zizka .75 2.00

2006-07 Czech HC Sparta Praha Postcards

COMPLETE SET (15) 15.00 30.00
1 Ladislav Benysek .75 2.00
2 Marek Cernosek .75 2.00
3 David Vrbata .75 2.00
4 Dusan Salficky 1.25 3.00
5 Frantisek Ptacek .75 2.00
6 Jan Hanzlik .75 2.00
7 Jan Hlavac 1.25 3.00
8 Jaroslav Hlinka .75 2.00
9 Jakub Langhammer .75 2.00
10 Michal Sivek 1.25 3.00
11 Ondrej Kratena .75 2.00
12 Petr Ton .75 2.00
13 Martin Strba .75 2.00
14 Tomas Netik .75 2.00
15 Tomas Protivny .75 2.00

2006-07 Czech HC Vsetin Postcards

COMPLETE SET (12) 10.00 25.00
1 Lukas Bolf .75 2.00
2 Guntis Galvins .75 2.00
3 Josef Hrabal .75 2.00
4 Jiri Kucny .75 2.00
5 Lukas Duba .75 2.00
6 Lubos Rob .75 2.00
7 Lubomir Sabol .75 2.00
8 Vladimir Skoda .75 2.00
9 Lubomir Stach .75 2.00
10 Roman Stantien .75 2.00
11 Martin Stefl .75 2.00
12 Tomas Demel .75 2.00

2006-07 Czech HC Zlin Hame Postcards

COMPLETE SET (15) 15.00 30.00
1 Martin Cech .75 2.00
2 Martin Hamrlik .75 2.00
3 Jan Horacek .75 2.00
4 Robin Kovar .75 2.00
5 Jaroslav Kristek .75 2.00
6 Pavel Kubis .75 2.00
7 Petr Leska .75 2.00
8 Marek Melenovsky 1.25 3.00
9 Igor Murin .75 2.00
10 Roman Psurny .75 2.00
11 Ivan Rachunek .75 2.00
12 Robert Tomik .75 2.00
13 Lubomir Sekeras .75 2.00
14 Martin Zahorovsky .75 2.00
15 Pavel Zubicek .75 2.00

2006-07 Czech IIHF World Championship Postcards

COMPLETE SET (23) 20.00 40.00
1 Jaroslav Balastik .75 2.00
2 Jaroslav Bednar .60 1.50
3 Jan Bulis .60 1.50
4 Martin Erat .75 2.00
5 Jan Hejda .60 1.50
6 Jan Hlavac .60 1.50
7 Jaroslav Hlinka .60 1.50
8 Milan Hnilicka .75 2.00
9 Petr Hubacek .60 1.50
10 Zbynek Irgl .60 1.50
11 Tomas Kaberle .75 2.00
12 Lukas Krajicek .75 2.00
13 Zdenek Kutlak .60 1.50
14 Zbynek Michalek .60 1.50
15 Tomas Plekanec 1.25 3.00
16 Ivo Prorok .60 1.50
17 Martin Richter .60 1.50
18 Tomas Rolinek .60 1.50
19 Martin Skoula .60 1.50
20 Patrik Stefan .60 1.50
21 Adam Svoboda .60 1.50
22 Petr Tenkrat .60 1.50
23 David Vyborny .75 2.00

2006-07 Czech LG Hockey Games Postcards

COMPLETE SET (22) 15.00 30.00
1 Jaroslav Balastik .75 2.00
2 Jaroslav Bednar .40 1.00
3 Miroslav Blatak .40 1.00
4 Petr Hubacek .40 1.00
5 Jiri Hunkes .40 1.00
6 Zbynek Irgl .75 2.00
7 Jaroslav Kracik .40 1.00
8 Lukas Krajicek .75 2.00
9 Jaroslav Kudrna .75 2.00
10 Zdenek Kutlak .40 1.00
11 Jan Marek .40 1.00
12 Zbynek Michalek .40 1.00
13 Jan Novak .40 1.00
14 Jan Peterek .40 1.00
15 Tomas Popperle .75 2.00
16 Ivo Prorok .40 1.00
17 Tomas Rolinek .40 1.00
18 Martin Sevc .40 1.00
19 Martin Skoula .40 1.00
20 Patrik Stefan .40 1.00
21 Adam Svoboda .75 2.00
22 Petr Tenkrat .40 1.00

2006-07 Czech OFS

COMPLETE SET (326) 75.00 125.00
1 Kamil Brabenec .20 .50
2 Petr Gregorek .20 .50
3 Milan Gulas .20 .50
4 Stepan Hrebejk .20 .50
5 Viktor Hubl .20 .50
6 Michal Hudec .20 .50
7 Jan Chabera .30 .75
8 Jindrich Kotrla .20 .50
9 Zdenek Kutlak .30 .75
10 Lukas Kveton .20 .50
11 Petr Machacek .20 .50
12 Jan Mucha .20 .50
13 Vaclav Nedorost .40 1.00
14 Marek Posmyk .30 .75
15 Petr Sailer .20 .50
16 Jiri Simanek .20 .50
17 Milan Toman .20 .50
18 Roman Turek .40 1.00
19 Martin Vagner .30 .75
20 Tomas Vak .20 .50
21 Ondrej Vesely .20 .50
22 Rene Vydareny .20 .50
23 David Balasz .20 .50
24 Michal Borovansky .20 .50
25 Michal Dobron .20 .50
26 Miroslav Duben .20 .50
27 Michal Dvorak .20 .50
28 Jiri Hanzlik .20 .50
29 Vojtech Kloz .20 .50
30 Jan Kostal .20 .50
31 Milan Kraft .40 1.00
32 Petr Kumstat .20 .50
33 Vladimir Machulda .20 .50
34 Lukas Mensator .30 .75
35 Petr Mudroch .20 .50
36 Ondrej Nemec .20 .50
37 Lukas Pech .20 .50
38 Milan Prochazka .20 .50
39 Josef Reznicek .20 .50
40 Lukas Sablik .30 .75
41 Frantisek Skladany .20 .50
42 Vaclav Skuhravy .20 .50
43 Kamil Tvrdek .20 .50
44 Libor Ustrnul .30 .75
45 Jiri Burger .20 .50
46 Jan Dresler .20 .50
47 Michal Gulasi .20 .50
48 Petr Hubacek .20 .50
49 Stanislav Hudec .20 .50
50 Lukas Chmelir .20 .50
51 Zbynek Irgl .30 .75
52 Stanislav Jasecko .20 .50
53 Petr Jurecka .20 .50
54 Tomas Kana .20 .50
55 Bedrich Kohler .20 .50
56 Lukas Krenzelok .20 .50
57 Radoslav Kropac .20 .50
58 Petr Kubos .20 .50
59 Milan Mikulik .20 .50
60 Marek Pinc .30 .75
61 Radek Prochazka .20 .50
62 Filip Seman .20 .50
63 Roman Simicek .20 .50
64 Jakub Stepanek .30 .75
65 Martin Tomasek .20 .50
66 Lukas Klimek .20 .50
67 Jiri Vykoukal .20 .50
68 David Vrbata .20 .50
69 Petr Ton .20 .50
70 Jan Tabacek .20 .50
71 Michal Sivek .40 1.00
72 Dusan Salficky .60 1.50
73 Frantisek Ptacek .20 .50
74 Petr Prikryl .30 .75
75 Tomas Protivny .20 .50
76 Martin Podlesak .20 .50
77 Tomas Netik .20 .50
78 Jaroslav Mrazek .20 .50
79 Jakub Langhammer .20 .50
80 Ondrej Kratena .30 .75
81 Karel Hromas .20 .50
82 Jaroslav Hlinka .20 .50
83 Jan Hlavac .40 1.00
84 Jan Hanzlik .20 .50
85 Michal Dragoun .20 .50
86 Marek Cernosek .20 .50
87 Ladislav Benysek .20 .50
88 Jan Holub .20 .50
89 Ondrej Hruska .20 .50
90 Ctibor Jech .20 .50
91 Valdemar Jirus .20 .50
92 Tomas Klimenta .20 .50
93 Vaclav Koci .20 .50
94 Angel Krstev .20 .50
95 Jiri Moravec .20 .50
96 Michal Nedvidek .30 .75
97 Lukas Pabiska .20 .50
98 Rok Pajic .20 .50
99 Vaclav Pletka .30 .75
100 Jan Plodek .20 .50
101 Andrej Podkonicky .20 .50
102 Stanislav Prochazka .20 .50
103 Jiri Stejskal .30 .75
104 Petr Sachl .20 .50
105 Lubomir Vaic .20 .50
106 Petr Vampola .20 .50
107 Jan Visek .20 .50
108 Lukas Zib .20 .50
109 Boris Zabka .20 .50
110 Dusan Andrasovsky .20 .50
111 Tomas Blazek .20 .50
112 Jan Caloun .30 .75
113 Petr Caslava .20 .50
114 David Havir .20 .50
115 Miroslav Hlinka .20 .50
116 Jan Kolar .20 .50
117 Jaroslav Koma .20 .50
118 Petr Koukal .20 .50
119 Vladislav Koutsky .30 .75
120 Jan Lasak .75 2.00
121 Tomas Linhart .20 .50
122 Andrej Novotny .20 .50
123 Zdenek Ondrej .20 .50
124 Tomas Rolinek .20 .50
125 Jan Snopek .20 .50
126 Petr Sykora .20 .50
127 Michal Seda .20 .50
128 Lukas Bednarik .20 .50
129 Jan Benda .20 .50
130 Frantisek Bombic .20 .50
131 Daniel Branda .20 .50
132 Jakub Cerny .20 .50
133 Vladimir Gyna .20 .50
134 Jan Hranac .20 .50
135 Jaroslav Hubl .30 .75
136 Peter Jansky .20 .50
137 Martin Jenacek .20 .50
138 Milan Kopecky .20 .50
139 Vojtech Kubincak .20 .50
140 Frantisek Lukes .20 .50
141 Marian Morava .20 .50
142 Angel Nikolov .20 .50
143 Lukas Pozivil .20 .50
144 Ivo Prorok .20 .50
145 Robert Reichel .40 1.00
146 Zbynek Sklenicka .20 .50
147 Radim Skuhrovec .20 .50
148 Jiri Slegr .30 .75
149 Michal Travnicek .20 .50
150 Michal Podolka .40 1.00
151 Jaroslav Barton .20 .50
152 Radovan Biegl .30 .75
153 Jan Danecek .20 .50
154 Lukas Danecek .40 1.00
155 Tomas Frolo .20 .50
156 Jiri Hasek .20 .50
157 Alexandr Hegegy .20 .50
158 Marcin Kolusz .20 .50
159 Lubomir Korhon .20 .50
160 Vlastimil Kroupa .20 .50
161 Jaroslav Kudrna .20 .50
162 Rostislav Martynek .20 .50
163 Tomas Pacal .20 .50
164 Jan Peterek .20 .50
165 Jiri Polansky .20 .50
166 Tomaz Razingar .20 .50
167 Zdenek Skorepa .20 .50
168 Radim Tesarik .20 .50
169 Roman Tomas .20 .50
170 Tomas Vrba .20 .50
171 Jan Vytisk .20 .50
172 Stefan Zigardy .30 .75
173 Armands Berzins .20 .50
174 Lukas Bolf .20 .50
175 Martin Davidek .20 .50
176 Tomas Demel .20 .50
177 Lukas Duba .20 .50
178 Marek Dubec .20 .50
179 Guntis Galvins .20 .50
180 Marek Grill .20 .50
181 Michal Horak .20 .50
182 Josef Hrabal .20 .50
183 Jakub Kraus .20 .50
184 Jiri Kucny .20 .50
185 David Kveton .20 .50
186 Radim Ostrcil .20 .50
187 Lubos Rob .20 .50
188 Lubomir Sabol .20 .50
189 Petr Sakrajda .20 .50
190 Roman Stantien .20 .50
191 Matej Stritesky .20 .50
192 Vladimir Skoda .20 .50
193 Lubomir Stach .20 .50
194 Martin Stefl .20 .50
195 Simo Vehvilainen .30 .75
196 Dusan Brincko .20 .50
197 Waldemar Pelikovsky .20 .50
198 Jiri Beroun .20 .50
199 Radim Bicanek .20 .50
200 Martin Cakajik .20 .50
201 Jiri Dopita .30 .75
202 Roman Erat .20 .50
203 Radek Haman .20 .50
204 Christoph Harand .20 .50
205 Richard Jares .20 .50
206 Ivo Kotaska .20 .50
207 Radim Kucharczyk .20 .50
208 Pavel Mojzis .20 .50
209 Roman Nemecek .20 .50
210 Karel Plasek .20 .50
211 Peter Pucher .20 .50
212 Martin Ruzicka .20 .50
213 Pavel Selingr .20 .50
214 Jaroslav Svoboda .20 .50
215 Ondrej Smach .20 .50
216 Jiri Trvaj .30 .75
217 David Turon .20 .50
218 Lubomir Vaskovic .20 .50
219 David Adamec .30 .75
220 Stanislav Balan .20 .50
221 Jakub Cech .30 .75
222 Martin Cech .20 .50
223 Lukas Galvas .20 .50
224 Martin Hamrlik .20 .50
225 Jan Horacek .20 .50
226 Pavel Kasparik .20 .50
227 Robin Kovar .20 .50
228 Jaroslav Kristek .20 .50
229 Pavel Kubis .20 .50
230 Petr Leska .20 .50
231 Martin Lucka .20 .50
232 Jiri Marusak .20 .50
233 Marek Melenovsky .20 .50
234 Pavel Mokrejs .20 .50
235 Igor Murin .30 .75
236 David Nosek .20 .50
237 Miroslav Okal .20 .50
238 Michal Psurny .20 .50
239 Roman Psurny .20 .50
240 Ivan Rachunek .20 .50
241 Dalibor Sedlar .30 .75
242 Lubomir Sekeras .20 .50
243 Robert Tomik .20 .50
244 Lubomir Vosatko .20 .50
245 Martin Zahorovsky .20 .50
246 Pavel Zubicek .20 .50
247 Vitezslav Bilek .20 .50
248 Vratislav Cech .20 .50
249 Marek Curilla .20 .50
250 Richard Divis .20 .50
251 Martin Frolik .20 .50
252 Radek Gardon .20 .50
253 David Hajek .20 .50
254 Michal Havel .20 .50
255 Milan Hluchy .20 .50
256 Tomas Horna .20 .50
257 Petr Jaros .20 .50
258 Jaroslav Kalla .20 .50
259 Jiri Kuchler .20 .50
260 Jakub Lev .30 .75
261 Zdenek Orct .30 .75
262 Pavel Patera .20 .50
263 Ales Pavlas .20 .50
264 Libor Prochazka .20 .50
265 Martin Prochazka .20 .50
266 Martin Sevc .20 .50
267 Martin Stepanek .20 .50
268 Jiri Zeman .20 .50
269 Vaclav Benak .20 .50
270 Mario Cartelli .20 .50
271 Michal Duraz .20 .50
272 Jan Herman .20 .50
273 Petr Jez .30 .75
274 Richard Kepl .20 .50
275 Richard Kral .20 .50
276 Roman Malek .30 .75
277 Jiri Malinsky .20 .50
278 Radek Matejovsky .20 .50
279 David Mazanec .20 .50
280 Milan Nedoma .20 .50
281 Ales Padelek .20 .50
282 Igor Rataj .20 .50
283 Adam Saffer .20 .50
284 Jakub Sindel .20 .50
285 Pavel Trnka .20 .50
286 Milan Voboril .20 .50
287 Jiri Zelenka .20 .50
288 Jaroslav Bednar .40 1.00
289 Josef Beranek .20 .50
290 Roman Cervenka .20 .50
291 Tomas Divisek .40 1.00
292 Radek Dlouhy .20 .50
293 Jiri Drtina .20 .50
294 Petr Franek .30 .75
295 Dominik Granak .20 .50
296 Lukas Hronek .30 .75
297 David Hruska .20 .50
298 Jiri Jebavy .20 .50
299 Petr Kadlec .20 .50
300 David Pojkar .20 .50
301 Vladimir Ruzicka .20 .50
302 Jakub Sklenar .20 .50
303 Vladimir Sobotka .20 .50
304 Michal Sup .20 .50
305 Tomas Spila .20 .50
306 Tomas Vlasak .20 .50
307 Michal Vondrka .20 .50
308 Tomas Zizka .20 .50
309 Radek Hubacek .20 .50
310 Petr Tucek .30 .75
311 Andrej Novotny .20 .50
312 Petr Puncochar .20 .50
313 Jan Stary .20 .50
314 Michal Tvrdik .20 .50
315 Libor Pivko .20 .50
316 Jan Kolar .20 .50
317 Martin Cech .20 .50
318 Jan Kana .20 .50
319 Tomas Voracek .20 .50
320 Marek Novotny .20 .50
321 Tomas Brnak .20 .50
322 Martin Zatovic .30 .75
323 Tomas Chrenko .20 .50
324 Ales Pisa .20 .50
325 Frantisek Mrazek .20 .50
326 Josef Kucera .20 .50
327 Frantisek Mrazek .20 .50
328 Josef Kucera .20 .50

2006-07 Czech OFS All Stars

1 Milan Hnilicka 2.00 5.00
2 Roman Malek 2.00 5.00
3 Jan Novak 1.50 4.00
4 Miroslav Blatak 1.50 4.00
5 Frantisek Ptacek 1.50 4.00
6 Josef Reznicek 1.50 4.00
7 Radim Tesarik 1.50 4.00
8 Stanislav Hudec 1.50 4.00
9 Valdemar Jirus 1.50 4.00
10 Martin Richter 1.50 4.00
11 Ivan Rachunek 1.50 4.00
12 Lubomir Vaic 1.50 4.00
13 Petr Sykora 1.50 4.00
14 Michal Mikeska 1.50 4.00
15 Jan Marek 1.50 4.00
16 Marek Tomica 1.50 4.00
17 Jiri Burger 1.50 4.00
18 Michal Travnicek 1.50 4.00
19 Radek Gardon 1.50 4.00
20 David Moravec 1.50 4.00
21 Jan Peterek 1.50 4.00
22 Ales Kretinsky 1.50 4.00

2006-07 Czech OFS Brothers

1 M.Herman/J.Herman 2.00 5.00
2 J.Kana/T.Kana 2.00 5.00
3 L.Danecek/J.Danecek 2.00 5.00
4 R.Hubacek/P.Hubacek 2.00 5.00
5 M.Psurny/R.Psurny 2.00 5.00

2006-07 Czech OFS Coaches

1 Ernest Bokros .40 1.00
2 Milos Holan .40 1.00
3 Miloslav Horava .40 1.00
4 Josef Jandac .40 1.00
5 Jiri Jurik .40 1.00
6 Zdenek Müller .40 1.00
7 Josef Palecek .40 1.00
8 Vladimir Ruzicka .40 1.00
9 Milos Riha .40 1.00
10 Marek Sykora .40 1.00
11 Vaclav Sykora .40 1.00
12 Zdenek Venera .40 1.00
13 Rostislav Vlach .40 1.00
14 Frantisek Vyborny .40 1.00

2006-07 Czech OFS Defenders

1 Martin Hamrlik .75 2.00
2 Jan Novak .75 2.00
3 Stanislav Hudec .75 2.00
4 Martin Richter .75 2.00
5 Valdemar Jirus .75 2.00
6 Petr Gregorek .75 2.00
7 Marek Posmyk .75 2.00
8 Martin Sevc .75 2.00
9 Josef Reznicek .75 2.00
10 Miroslav Blatak .75 2.00
11 Petr Kadlec .75 2.00
12 Radim Tesarik .75 2.00
13 Angel Krstev .75 2.00
14 Radim Bicanek .75 2.00
15 Frantisek Ptacek .75 2.00

2006-07 Czech OFS Goalies I

1 Igor Murin 2.00 5.00
2 Lukas Mensator 2.00 5.00
3 Petr Franek 2.00 5.00
4 Milan Hnilicka 2.00 5.00
5 Jiri Trvaj 2.00 5.00
6 Marek Pinc 2.00 5.00
7 Roman Malek 2.00 5.00
8 Jan Chabera 2.00 5.00
9 Radek Fiala 2.00 5.00
10 Sasu Hovi 2.00 5.00
11 Jan Lasak 2.50 6.00
12 Kamil Jarina 2.00 5.00
13 Petr Briza 2.50 6.00
14 Martin Altrichter 2.00 5.00
15 Roman Turek 2.00 5.00

2006-07 Czech OFS Goalies II

1 Milan Hnilicka 2.00 5.00
2 Igor Murin 2.00 5.00
3 Petr Franek 2.00 5.00
4 Jan Chabera 2.00 5.00
5 Jiri Trvaj 2.00 5.00
6 Lukas Mensator 2.00 5.00
7 Marek Pinc 2.00 5.00
8 Roman Turek 2.00 5.00
9 Radek Fiala 2.00 5.00
10 Roman Malek 2.00 5.00
11 Kamil Jarina 2.00 5.00
12 Martin Altrichter 2.00 5.00
13 Jan Lasak 2.50 6.00
14 Petr Briza 2.50 6.00
15 Radovan Biegl 2.00 5.00

2006-07 Czech OFS Goals Leaders

1 Petr Ton 1.25 3.00
2 Michal Sup 1.25 3.00
3 Jan Marek 1.25 3.00
4 Jaroslav Kudrna 1.25 3.00
5 Jaroslav Bednar 1.25 3.00
6 Ales Padelek 1.25 3.00
7 Lubomir Vaic 1.25 3.00
8 Jan Caloun 1.25 3.00
9 Igor Rataj 1.25 3.00
10 Peter Pucher 1.25 3.00
11 Radek Duda 1.25 3.00
12 Petr Hubacek 1.25 3.00
13 Ondrej Kratena 1.25 3.00
14 Jiri Zelenka 1.25 3.00
15 Jan Benda 1.25 3.00

2006-07 Czech OFS Jagr Team

1 Marek Schwarz 3.00 8.00
2 Jaroslav Kames 1.25 3.00
3 Jiri Tlusty 4.00 10.00
4 Petr Taticek 1.25 3.00
5 Jakub Koreis 2.00 5.00
6 Jiri Novotny 1.25 3.00
7 Lukas Krajicek 1.25 3.00
8 Martin Richter 1.25 3.00
9 Rostislav Klesla 1.25 3.00
10 Josef Melichar 1.25 3.00
11 Michal Rozsival 1.25 3.00
12 Petr Tenkrat 1.25 3.00
13 Tomas Plekanec 2.50 6.00
14 Jaroslav Hlinka 1.25 3.00
15 Jan Hrdina 1.25 3.00
16 Ales Kotalik 2.00 5.00
17 Tomas Kaberle 2.00 5.00
18 David Vyborny 1.25 3.00
19 Martin Straka 1.25 3.00
20 Martin Rucinsky 1.25 3.00
21 Jaromir Jagr 4.00 10.00
22 Jaroslav Svoboda 1.25 3.00
23 Jiri Hudler 2.50 6.00

2006-07 Czech OFS Points Leaders

1 Jan Marek 1.25 3.00
2 Lubomir Vaic 1.25 3.00
3 Josef Beranek 1.25 3.00
4 Petr Ton 1.25 3.00
5 Jaroslav Kudrna 1.25 3.00
6 Jaroslav Bednar 1.25 3.00
7 Radek Duda 1.25 3.00
8 Jan Peterek 1.25 3.00
9 Peter Pucher 1.25 3.00
10 Jan Benda 1.25 3.00
11 Petr Hubacek 1.25 3.00
12 Jan Caloun 1.25 3.00
13 Tomas Vlasak 1.25 3.00
14 Martin Strba 1.25 3.00
15 Michal Sup 1.25 3.00

2006-07 Czech OFS Stars

1 Jiri Stejskal 1.25 3.00
2 Andrej Podkonicky 1.25 3.00
3 Daniel Branda 1.25 3.00
4 Lukas Mensator 1.25 3.00
5 Milan Kraft 1.25 3.00
6 Igor Murin 1.25 3.00
7 Petr Leska 1.25 3.00
8 Martin Hamrlik 1.25 3.00
9 Roman Malek 1.25 3.00
10 Richard Kral 1.25 3.00
11 Petr Sykora 1.25 3.00
12 Miroslav Hlinka 1.25 3.00
13 Roman Turek 1.50 4.00
14 Vaclav Nedorost 1.25 3.00
15 Jiri Polansky 1.25 3.00
16 Zdenek Orct 1.50 4.00
17 Jaroslav Bednar 1.25 3.00
18 Dusan Salficky 1.50 4.00
19 Jiri Vykoukal 1.25 3.00
20 Tomas Demel 1.25 3.00
21 Martin Stefl 1.25 3.00
22 Roman Erat 1.25 3.00
23 Pavel Mojzis 1.25 3.00
24 Jiri Trvaj 1.50 4.00
25 Zbynek Irgl 1.50 4.00

2006-07 Czech OFS Team Cards

1 R.Turek/V.Nedorost 1.50 4.00
2 L.Mansator/P.Kumstat 1.50 4.00
3 P.Patera/Z.Orct 1.50 4.00
4 J.Stejskal/J.Plodek 1.50 4.00
5 R.Reichel/J.Hubl 1.50 4.00
6 P.Sykora/J.Lasak 2.00 5.00
7 J.Zelenka/R.Malek 1.50 4.00
8 T.Vlasak/P.Franek 1.50 4.00
9 D.Salficky/J.Hlinka 1.50 4.00
10 R.Biegl/J.Vytisk 1.50 4.00
11 M.Pinc/J.Burger 1.50 4.00
12 M/Stefl/R.Stantien 1.50 4.00
13 I.Murin/P.Leska 1.50 4.00
14 J.Trvaj/J.Dopita 1.50 4.00

2006-07 Czech NHL ELH Postcards

COMPLETE SET (15) 15.00 30.00
1 Martin Havlat .75 2.00
2 Milan Hnilicka .75 2.00
3 Jan Hrdina .75 2.00
4 Milan Kraft .75 2.00
5 Pavel Kubina .75 2.00
6 Jason Marshall .75 2.00
7 Vaclav Nedorost .75 2.00
8 Zigmund Palffy 1.25 3.00
9 Michal Rozsival .75 2.00
10 Jaroslav Spacek .75 2.00
11 Josef Stumpel .75 2.00
12 Pavel Trnka .75 2.00
13 Vaclav Varada .75 2.00
14 Radim Vrbata .75 2.00
15 Josef Vasicek .75 2.00

2006-07 Czech Super Six Postcards

1 Niklas Backstrom 2.00 5.00
2 Michal Bros .75 2.00
3 Mikhail Grabovskij 1.25 3.00
4 David Havir .75 2.00
5 Miroslav Hlinka .75 2.00
6 Robert Kantor .75 2.00
7 Jan Lasak 1.25 3.00
8 Michal Mikeska .75 2.00
9 Vaclav Pletka .75 2.00
10 Tomasz Razingar 1.25 3.00
11 Tomas Rolinek .75 2.00
12 Pavel Rosa .75 2.00
13 Maxim Susinskij .75 2.00
14 Petr Tenkrat .75 2.00
15 Viktor Ujcik .75 2.00
16 Jari Viuhkola .75 2.00

1999-00 Danish Hockey League

COMPLETE SET (225)

2005-06 Dutch Vadeko Flyers

COMPLETE SET (20) 8.00 15.00
1 Kevin Bruijsten .30 .75
2 Andriy Butochnov .30 .75
3 Anton Butochnov .30 .75
4 Sander Dijkstra .30 .75
5 James Easter .30 .75
6 Brent Janssen .30 .75
7 Matt Korthuis .30 .75
8 Petr Kratky .30 .75
9 Hans Kroon .30 .75
10 Paul Kroon .30 .75
11 Jacco Landman .30 .75
12 Don Nichols .30 .75
13 Marcel Nijland .30 .75
14 Tyler Palmiscno .30 .75
15 Marco Postma .30 .75
16 Brad Smulders .30 .75
17 Ruud vander Holst .30 .75
18 Jeroen van Olphen .30 .75
19 Stanislav Vernikov .30 .75
20 Brain de Bruijn HC .10 .25

1966 Finnish Jaakiekkosarja

COMPLETE SET (220)

1971-72 Finnish Suomi Stickers

COMPLETE SET (384) 200.00 500.00
1 Vitaly Davydov .30 .75
2 Anatoli Firsov 2.00 5.00
3 Valeri Kharlamov 20.00 50.00
4 Viktor Konovalenko .30 .75
5 Viktor Kuzkin .30 .75

6 Yuri Liapkin .40 1.00
7 Vladimir Lutchenko .30 .75
8 Alexander Maltsev 2.00 5.00
9 Alexander Martiniuk .40 1.00
10 Boris Mikhailov 2.00 5.00
11 Evgeni Mishakov .30 .75
12 Vladimir Petrov 2.00 5.00
13 Alexander Ragulin .75 2.00
14 Igor Romishevski .30 .75
15 Vladimir Shadrin .40 1.00
16 Viatjeslav Starshinov .40 1.00
17 Vladislav Tretiak 10.00 20.00
18 Gennady Tsygankov .40 1.00
19 Vladimir Vikulov .40 1.00
20 Evgeni Zimin .40 1.00
21 Bedrich Brunschk .20 .50
22 Jiri Bubla .75 2.00
23 Josef Cerny .30 .75
24 Richard Farda .30 .75
25 Jan Havel .20 .50
26 Ivan Hnlicka .20 .50
27 Jiri Holecek .40 1.00
28 Jiri Holik .30 .75
29 Josef Horesovsky .20 .50
30 Jiri Kochta .20 .50
31 Oldrich Machac .20 .50
32 Vladimir Martinec .30 .75
33 Vaclav Nedomansky .75 2.00
34 Eduard Novak .20 .50
35 Frantisek Panchartek .20 .50
36 Frantisek Pospisil .30 .75
37 Marcel Sakac .20 .50
38 Bohuslav Stastny .40 1.00
39 Jan Suchy .30 .75
40 Christer Abrahamsson .75 2.00
41 Thommy Abrahamsson .40 1.00
42 Thommie Bergman 1.25 3.00
43 Arne Carlsson .20 .50
44 Inge Hammarstrom 4.00 10.00
45 Anders Hedberg 3.00 8.00
46 Leif Holmqvist .75 2.00
47 Stig-Goran Johansson .40 1.00
48 Stefan Karlsson .20 .50
49 Hans Lindberg .20 .50
50 Tord Lundstrom .20 .50
51 William Lofqvist .40 1.00
52 Kjell-Rune Milton .20 .50
53 Lars-Goran Nilsson .20 .50
54 Bert-Ola Nordlander .40 1.00
55 Hakan Nygren .20 .50
56 Bjorn Palmqvist .20 .50
57 Hakan Pettersson .20 .50
58 Ulf Sterner .20 .50
59 Lennart Svedberg .40 1.00
60 Hakan Wickberg .20 .50
61 Esa Isaksson .20 .50
62 Heikki Jarn .20 .50
63 Veli-Pekka Ketola .75 2.00
64 Ilpo Koskela .20 .50
65 Seppo Lindstrom .20 .50
66 Harri Linnonmaa .20 .50
67 Hannu Luojola .20 .50
68 Pekka Mononen .20 .50
69 Erkki Mononen .20 .50
70 Lauri Mononen .20 .50
71 Matti Murto .40 1.00
72 Lasse Oksanen .20 .50
73 Esa Peltonen .20 .50
74 Seppo Repo .20 .50
75 Tommi Salmelainen .20 .50
76 Juhani Tamminen .20 .50
77 Jorma Valtonen .40 1.00
78 Jorma Vehmanen .20 .50
79 Urpo Ylonen .40 1.00
80 Jouko Oystila .20 .50
81 Tapio Flinck .20 .50
82 Antti Heikkila .20 .50
83 Reijo Heinonen .20 .50
84 Jaakko Honkanen .20 .50
85 Veli-Pekka Ketola .75 2.00
86 Raimo Kilpio .20 .50
87 Tapio Koskinen .20 .50
88 Kaj Matalamaki .20 .50
89 Pertti Makela .20 .50
90 Pekka Rautakallio .20 .50
91 Markku Riihimaki .20 .50
92 Matti Salmi .20 .50
93 Jorma Valtonen .40 1.00
94 Anto Virtanen .20 .50
95 Erkki Vakiparta .20 .50
96 Pertti Ahokas .20 .50
97 Pertti Arvaja .20 .50
98 Olli Hietanen .20 .50
99 Pentti Hiiros .20 .50
100 Eero Holopainen .20 .50
101 Kari Kinnunen .20 .50
102 Ilpo Koskela .20 .50
103 Timo Kyntola .20 .50
104 Henry Leppa .20 .50
105 Erkki Mononen .20 .50
106 Pertti Nurmi .20 .50
107 Timo Relas .20 .50
108 Timo Sutinen .20 .50
109 Timo Turunen .20 .50
110 Jouko Oystila .20 .50
111 Juhani Bostrom .20 .50
112 Kimmo Heino .20 .50
113 Esa Isaksson .20 .50
114 Juhani Jylha .20 .50
115 Heikki Jarn .20 .50
116 Mauri Kaukorari .20 .50
117 Vaino Kolkka .20 .50
118 Harri Linnonmaa .20 .50
119 Jaakko Marttinen .20 .50
120 Matti Murto .40 1.00
121 Lalli Partinen .20 .50
122 Juha Rantasila .20 .50
123 Heikki Riihiranta .20 .50
124 Jorma Rikala .20 .50
125 Tommi Salmelainen .20 .50
126 Jorma Thusberg .20 .50
127 Matti Vaisanen .20 .50
128 Jukka Alkula .20 .50
129 Pertti Ansakorpi .20 .50
130 Keijo Jarvinen .20 .50
131 Pertti Koivulahti .20 .50
132 Ilpo Kuisma .20 .50
134 Antti Leppanen .20 .50
135 Pekka Marjamaki .20 .50
136 Mikko Myntiien .20 .50
137 Pekka Makinen .20 .50
138 Seppo Makinen .20 .50
139 Keijo Mannisto .20 .50
140 Antti Perttula .20 .50
141 Tuomo Rautiainen .20 .50
142 Juhani Saarelainen .20 .50
143 Jorma Saarikorpi .20 .50
144 Risto Seesvuori .20 .50
145 Jorma Siitarinen .20 .50
146 Raimo Suoniemi .20 .50
147 Juhani Aaltonen .20 .50
148 Matti Ahvenharju .20 .50
149 Hannu Auvinen .20 .50
150 Jorma Borgstrom .20 .50
151 Martti Immonen .20 .50
152 Matti Keinonen .20 .50
153 Seppo Laakkio .20 .50
154 Timo Lahtinen .20 .50
155 Esa Peltonen .20 .50
156 Keijo Puhakka .20 .50
157 Antti Ravi .20 .50
158 Timo Saari .20 .50
159 Esa Siren .20 .50
160 Erkki Suni .20 .50
161 Seppo Suoraniemi .20 .50
162 Juhani Tamminen .20 .50
163 Jorma Vehmanen .20 .50
164 Stig Wetzell .20 .50
165 Olli Viilma .20 .50
166 Leo Aikas .20 .50
167 Sakari Ahlberg .20 .50
168 Seppo Ahokainen .20 .50
169 Jorma Aro .20 .50
170 Esko Eriksson .20 .50
171 Marku Hakanen .20 .50
172 Matti Hakanen .20 .50
173 Reijo Hakanen .20 .50
174 Martti Helle .20 .50
175 Timo Hirsimaki .20 .50
176 Jorma Kallio .20 .50
177 Esko Kaonpaa .20 .50
178 Pentti Koskela .20 .50
179 Pekka Kuusisto .20 .50
180 Pekka Leimu .20 .50
181 Jukka Mattila .20 .50
182 Lasse Oksanen .20 .50
183 Kari Palooja .20 .50
184 Jorma Peltonen .40 1.00
185 Tuomo Sillman .20 .50
186 Jaakko Siren .20 .50
187 Veikkoi Suominen .20 .50
188 Matti Jakonen .20 .50
189 Kari Johansson .20 .50
190 Arto Kaunonen .20 .50
191 Timo Kokkonen .20 .50
192 Reijo Leppanen .20 .50
193 Seppo Lindstrom .20 .50
194 Hannu Luojola .20 .50
195 Hannu Niittoaho .20 .50
196 Reijo Paksal .20 .50
197 Seppo Parikka .20 .50
198 Jarmo Rantanen .20 .50
199 Veijo Saarinen .20 .50
200 Martti Salonen .20 .50
201 Voitto Soini .20 .50
202 Kari Torkkel .20 .50
203 Risto Vainio .20 .50
204 Pentti Vihanto .20 .50
205 Seppo Wikstrom .20 .50
206 Urpo Ylonen .40 1.00
207 Hannu Haapalainen .20 .50
208 Jukka-Pekka Jarvenpaa .20 .50
209 Timo Jarvinen .20 .50
210 Heikki Keinonen .20 .50
211 Heimo Keinonen .20 .50
212 Rauno Lehtio .20 .50
213 Markku Moisio .20 .50
214 Seppo Nurmi .20 .50
215 Esko Rantanen .20 .50
216 Juhani Ruohonen .20 .50
217 Mikko Raikkonen .20 .50
218 Lauri Salomaa .20 .50
219 Veikko Savolainen .20 .50
220 Leo Seppanen .20 .50
221 Pekka Uitus .20 .50
222 Jorma Vilen .20 .50
223 Tapio Virhimo .20 .50
224 Kauko Fomin .20 .50
225 Heikki Hurme .20 .50
226 Eero Juntunen .20 .50
227 Lauri Jamsen .20 .50
228 Lasse Kiili .20 .50
229 Hannu Koivunen .20 .50
230 Jarmo Koivunen .20 .50
231 Pekka Lahtela .20 .50
232 Ilkka Mesikammen .20 .50
233 Timo Nummelin .20 .50
234 Rauli Ottila .20 .50
235 Matti Rautee .20 .50
236 Pekka Rautee .20 .50
237 Jari Rosberg .20 .50
238 Jouni Samuli .20 .50
239 Harry Silver .20 .50
240 Rauli Tammelin .20 .50
241 Bengt Wilenius .20 .50
242 Mikko Erholm .20 .50
243 Veikko Ihalainen .20 .50
244 Heikki Kauhanen .20 .50
245 Tapani Koskimaki .20 .50
246 Antti Laine .20 .50
247 Arto Laine .20 .50
248 Timo Lehtorinne .20 .50
249 Hannu Lunden .20 .50
250 Teppo Rastio .20 .50
251 Pentti Rautalin .20 .50
252 Kai Rosvall .20 .50
253 Ilkka Saarikko .20 .50
254 Jari Sarronlahti .20 .50
255 Matti Saurio .20 .50
256 Hannu Siivonen .20 .50
257 Erkki Sundelin .20 .50
258 Simo Suoknuuti .20 .50
259 Martti Haapala .20 .50
260 Yrjo Hakulinen .20 .50
261 Pentti Hirvonen .20 .50
262 Antero Honkanen .20 .50
263 Pekka Lavkainen .20 .50
264 Pentti Lavkainen .20 .50
265 Pertti Martikainen .20 .50
266 Pentti Martikainen .20 .50
267 Seppo Nevalainen .20 .50
268 Tapio Pohtinen .20 .50
269 Kari Puustinen .20 .50
270 Markku Rouhiainen .20 .50
271 Jarmo Sahlmann .20 .50
272 Seppo Saros .20 .50
273 Juha Silvennoinen .20 .50
274 Unto Turpeinen .20 .50
275 Kari Viitakahti .20 .50
276 Erkki Airaksinen .20 .50
277 Kauko Alkunen .20 .50
278 Jarmo Gummerus .20 .50
279 Bjorn Herbert .20 .50
280 Jarmo Jaakkola .20 .50
281 Hannu Kapanen .20 .50
282 Matti Koskinen .20 .50
283 Martti Kuokkanen .20 .50
284 Juhani Laine .20 .50
285 Heikki Leppik .20 .50
286 Juhani Langstrom .20 .50
287 Osmo Lotjonen .20 .50
288 Lauri Mononen .20 .50
289 Christer Nordblad .20 .50
290 Juha Poikolainen .20 .50
291 Kimmo Rantanen .20 .50
292 Seppo Repo .20 .50
293 Ilpo Ruokosalmi .20 .50
294 Arto Siisala .20 .50
295 Bo Sjostedt .20 .50
296 Pentti Viitanen .20 .50
297 Pekka Arbelius .40 1.00
298 Olli Enqvist .20 .50
299 Hannu Hiltunen .20 .50
300 Paavo Holopainen .20 .50
301 Juha Huikari .20 .50
302 Ari Jalonen .20 .50
303 Kari Jalonen .20 .50
304 Ari Kaikkonen .20 .50
305 Ari Kalmokoski .20 .50
306 Arto Lehtinen .20 .50
307 Markku Narhi .20 .50
308 Ilkka Okkonen .20 .50
309 Matti Perhonma .20 .50
310 Juha-Pekka Porvari .20 .50
311 Arto Ruotanen .20 .50
312 Reijo Ruotsalainen .20 .50
313 Matti Ruutti .20 .50
314 Pertti Raisanen .20 .50
315 Ari Timosaari .20 .50
316 Janne Oro .20 .50
317 Anssi Eronen .20 .50
318 Seppo Hirvonen .20 .50
319 Jari Hannu Hamalainen .20 .50
320 Jari Pekka Hamalainen .20 .50
321 Timo Harkonen .40 1.00
322 Jouko Ikonen .20 .50
323 Lasse Kaiponen .20 .50
324 Jyri Kemppinen .20 .50
325 Jouni Kostiainen .20 .50
326 Kai Kulhoranta .20 .50
327 Olli Lemola .20 .50
328 Jari Lopponen .20 .50
329 Pasi Makkonen .20 .50
330 Vesa Massinen .20 .50
331 Timo Minkkila .20 .50
332 Petri Pellinen .20 .50
333 Juhan Rasanen .20 .50
334 Pasi Sallinen .20 .50
335 Kauko Tamminen .20 .50
336 Olli Teijonmaa .20 .50
337 Ismo Tolvanen .20 .50
338 Timo Vaahtoluoto .20 .50
339 Kari Heikkila .20 .50
340 Pekka Helander .20 .50
341 Jari Hirsimaki .20 .50
342 Jari Huotari .20 .50
343 Ilkka Huura .20 .50
344 Tero Juojarvi .20 .50
345 Jari Jarvinen .20 .50
346 Mika Laine .20 .50
347 Marko Lepaus .20 .50
348 Pertti Lundberg .20 .50
349 Tino Minetti .20 .50
350 Jarom Partanen .20 .50
351 Olli-Pekka Perala .20 .50
352 Ari Ruuska .20 .50
353 Kai Saario .20 .50
354 Olli-Pekka Turunen .20 .50
355 Veli-Matti Uusimaa .20 .50
356 Mauri Viita .20 .50
357 Timo Virtanen .20 .50
358 Jarmo Viteli .20 .50
359 Petri Viteli .20 .50
360 Ari Havukainen .20 .50
361 Ismo Heinonen .20 .50
362 Riku Hoyden .20 .50
363 Jari Jokinen .20 .50
364 Timo Joutsenvuori .20 .50
365 Jyrki Jantti .20 .50
366 Kimmo Jantti .20 .50
367 Toni Ketola .20 .50
368 Juha Korhonen .20 .50
369 Ari Laine .20 .50
370 Kari Lainio .20 .50
371 Juha Makinen .20 .50
372 Reima Numminen .20 .50
373 Mika Pirila .20 .50
374 Kai Pulli .20 .50
375 Tero Tommila .20 .50
376 Harri Tuohimaa .20 .50
377 Pasi Tuohimaa .20 .50
378 Ari Veijalainen .20 .50
379 Jean Beliveau 10.00 25.00
380 Phil Esposito 15.00 40.00
381 Tony Esposito 15.00 40.00
382 Gordie Howe 30.00 60.00
383 Bobby Hull 15.00 40.00
384 Bobby Orr 50.00 100.00

1972-73 Finnish Jaakiekko

COMPLETE SET (360) 100.00 250.00
1 Vladimir Bednar .40 1.00
2 Jiri Bubla .40 1.00
3 Vladimir Dzurilla 1.25 3.00
4 Richard Farda .20 .50
5 Julius Haas .20 .50
6 Ivan Hlinka .75 2.00
7 Jiri Holecek .75 2.00
8 Jaroslav Holik .40 1.00
9 Jiri Holik .40 1.00
10 Josef Horesovsky .20 .50
11 Jan Klapac .20 .50
12 Jiri Kochta .20 .50
13 Milan Kuzela .20 .50
14 Oldrich Machac .20 .50
15 Vladimir Martinec .20 .50
16 Vaclav Nedomansky 2.00 5.00
17 Josef Palecek .20 .50
18 Frantisek Pospisil .20 .50
19 Bohuslav Stastny .20 .50
20 Rudolf Tajcnar .20 .50
21 Vjatsjeslav Anisin .40 1.00
22 Juri Blinov .40 1.00
23 Aleksandr Gusev .75 2.00
24 Valeri Kharlamov 20.00 50.00
25 Aleksandr Yakushev 4.00 10.00
26 Viktor Kuzkin .40 1.00
27 Vladimir Lutshenko .40 1.00
28 Aleksandr Maltsev 2.00 5.00
29 Boris Mikhailov 2.00 5.00
30 Jevgeni Mishakov .75 2.00
31 Vladimir Petrov 2.00 5.00
32 Aleksandr Ragulin .75 2.00
33 Igor Romishevski .40 1.00
34 Vladimir Shadrin .75 2.00
35 Vladimir Shepovalov .40 1.00
36 Vjatsjeslav Solodukhin .40 1.00
37 Vladislav Tretjak 8.00 20.00
38 Gennadi Tsigankov .40 1.00
39 Valeri Vasiljev 2.00 5.00
40 Vladimir Vikulov .40 1.00
41 Christer Abrahamsson 1.25 3.00
42 Tommy Abrahamsson 1.25 3.00
43 Thommie Bergman 2.00 5.00
44 Inge Hammarstrom 3.00 8.00
45 Anders Hedberg 3.00 8.00
46 Leif Holmqvist .75 2.00
47 Bjorn Johansson .20 .50
48 Stig-Goran Johansson .40 1.00
49 Stefan Karlsson .20 .50
50 Stig Larsson .20 .50
51 Mats Lind .20 .50
52 Tord Lundstrom .20 .50
53 Lars-Goran Johansson .20 .50
54 Bjorn Palmqvist .20 .50
55 Hakan Pettersson .20 .50
56 Borje Salming 8.00 20.00
57 Lars-Erik Sjoberg 1.25 3.00
58 Carl Sundqvist .20 .50
59 Hakan Wickberg .20 .50
60 Stig Ostling .20 .50
61 Seppo Ahokainen .20 .50
62 Matti Keinonen .20 .50
63 Veli-Pekka Ketola 1.25 3.00
64 Harri Linnonmaa .20 .50
65 Pekka Marjamaki .20 .50
66 Lauri Mononen .20 .50
67 Matti Murto .20 .50
68 Timo Nummelin .20 .50
69 Lasse Oksanen .20 .50
70 Esa Peltonen .20 .50
71 Juha Rantasila .20 .50
72 Pekka Rautakallio 1.25 3.00
73 Seppo Repo .20 .50
74 Heikki Riihiranta .20 .50
75 Juhani Tamminen .40 1.00
76 Timo Turunen .20 .50
77 Pertti Valkeapaa .20 .50
78 Jorma Valtonen .20 .50
79 Stig Wetzell .20 .50
80 Jouko Oystila .20 .50
81 Juhani Bostrom .20 .50
82 Kimmo Heino .20 .50
83 Penti Karlsson .20 .50
84 Mauri Kaukokari .20 .50
85 Jarmo Koivunen .20 .50
86 Heikki Kojola .20 .50
87 Vaino Kolkka .20 .50
88 Harri Linnonmaa .20 .50
89 Jaakko Marttinen .20 .50
90 Matti Murto .20 .50
91 Lalli Partinen .20 .50
92 Juha Rantasila .20 .50
93 Heikki Riihiranta .20 .50
94 Jorma Rikala .20 .50
95 Henry Saleva .20 .50
96 Tommi Salmelainen .20 .50
97 Jorma Thusberg .20 .50
98 Jorma Virtanen .20 .50
99 Matti Vainionen .20 .50
100 Juhani Aaltonen .20 .50
101 Jorma Immonen .20 .50
102 Martti Immonen .20 .50
103 Heikki Jarn .20 .50
104 Matti Keinonen .20 .50
105 Seppo Laakkio .20 .50
106 Timo Lahtinen .20 .50
107 Esa Peltonen .20 .50
108 Keijo Puhakka .20 .50
109 Seppo Railio .20 .50
110 Antti Ravi .20 .50
111 Timo Saari .20 .50
112 Esa Siren .20 .50
113 Seppo Suoraniemi .20 .50
114 Juhani Tamminen .20 .50
115 Jorma Vehmanen .20 .50
116 Stig Wetzell .20 .50
117 Leo Aikas .20 .50
118 Sakari Ahlberg .20 .50
119 Seppo Ahokainen .20 .50
120 Jorma Aro .20 .50
121 Esko Eriksson .20 .50
122 Markku Hakanen .20 .50
123 Timo Hirsimaki .20 .50
124 Jorma Kallio .20 .50
125 Esko Kaonpaa .20 .50
126 Pentti Koskela .20 .50
127 Pekka Kuusisto .20 .50
128 Pekka Leimu .20 .50
129 Len Lunde .20 .50
130 Jukka Mattila .20 .50
131 Lasse Oksanen .20 .50
132 Hannu Palmu .20 .50
133 Kari Palo-oja .20 .50
134 Jorma Peltonen .20 .50
135 Tuomo Sillman .20 .50
136 Veikko Suominen .20 .50
137 Pertti Ahokass .20 .50
138 Pertti Arvaja .20 .50
139 Christer Bergenheim .20 .50
140 Jarmo Borgstrom .20 .50
141 Olli Hietanen .20 .50
142 Pentti Hiiros .20 .50
143 Eero Holopainen .20 .50
144 Kari Kinnunen .20 .50
145 Keijo Koivunen .20 .50
146 Ilpo Koskela .20 .50
147 Timo Kyntola .20 .50
148 Henry Leppa .20 .50
149 Erkki Mononen .20 .50
150 Pertti Nurmi .20 .50
151 Tero Raty .20 .50
152 Timo Sutinen .20 .50
153 Timo Turunen .20 .50
154 Jouko Oystila .20 .50
155 Hannu Haapalainen .20 .50
156 Olavi Haapalainen .20 .50
157 Jukka-Pekka Jarvenpaa .20 .50
158 Heimo Keinonen .20 .50
159 Markku Moisio .20 .50
160 Heikki Nurmi .20 .50
161 Seppo Nurmi .20 .50
162 Oiva Oijennus .20 .50
163 Reino Pulkkinen .20 .50
164 Esko Rantanen .20 .50
165 Juhani Ruohonen .20 .50
166 Mikko Raikkonen .20 .50
167 Lauri Salomaa .20 .50
168 Leo Seppanen .20 .50
169 Pekka Uitus .20 .50
170 Jorma Vilen .20 .50
171 Tapio Virhimo .20 .50
172 Leo Haakana .20 .50
173 Seppo Hyvonen .20 .50
174 Heikki Juselius .20 .50
175 Hannu Lemander .20 .50
176 Kyosti Lahde .20 .50
177 Ari Mikkola .20 .50
178 Martti Makia .20 .50
179 Martti Narinen .20 .50
180 Pekka Nieminen .20 .50
181 Teijo Rasanen .20 .50
182 Timo Sartiala .20 .50
183 Pekka Sartjarvi .20 .50
184 Reijo Sinkkonen .20 .50
185 Martti Sinkkonen .20 .50
186 Arto Summanen .20 .50
187 Erkki Suni .20 .50
188 Seppo Urpalainen .20 .50
189 Matti Vaatamoinen .20 .50
190 Timo Vaatamoinen .20 .50
191 Jukka Alkula .20 .50
192 Pertti Ansakorpi .20 .50
193 Keijo Jarvinen .20 .50
194 Pertti Koivulahti .20 .50
195 Ilpo Kuisma .20 .50
196 Vesa Lehtoranta .20 .50
197 Antti Leppanen .20 .50
198 Pekka Marjamaki .20 .50
199 Mikko Myntinen .20 .50
200 Pekka Makinen .20 .50
201 Seppo Makinen .20 .50
202 Antti Perttula .20 .50
203 Tuomo Rautiainen .20 .50
204 Jorma Saarikorpi .20 .50
205 Jorma Siitarinen .20 .50
206 Raimo Suoniemi .20 .50
207 Pertti Valkeapaa .20 .50
208 Kari Horkko .20 .50
209 Eero Juntunen .20 .50
210 Lauri Jamsen .20 .50
211 Kari Kauppila .20 .50
212 Lasse Kiili .20 .50
213 Olli Kokkonen .20 .50
214 Pekka Lahtela .20 .50
215 Robert Lamoureux .20 .50
216 Ilkka Mesikammen .20 .50
217 Timo Nummelin .20 .50
218 Rauli Ottila .20 .50
219 Matti Rautee .20 .50
220 Pekka Rautee .20 .50
221 Jari Rosberg .20 .50
222 Jouni Samuli .20 .50
223 Harri Silver .20 .50
224 Rauli Tammelin .20 .50
225 Bengt Wilenius .20 .50
226 Pertti Hasanen .20 .50
227 Kari Johansson .20 .50
228 Arto Kaunonen .20 .50
229 Timo Kokkonen .20 .50
230 Reijo Leppanen .20 .50
231 Seppo Lindstrom .20 .50
232 Hannu Luojola .20 .50
233 Hannu Niittoaho .20 .50
234 Reijo Paksal .20 .50
235 Seppo Parikka .20 .50
236 Jarmo Rantanen .20 .50
237 Kari Salonen .20 .50
238 Tapani Sura .20 .50
239 Kari Torkkel .20 .50
240 Risto Vainio .20 .50
241 Pentti Vihanto .20 .50
242 Seppo Wikstrom .20 .50
243 Urpo Ylonen .20 .50
244 Tapio Flinck .20 .50
245 Antti Heikkila .20 .50
246 Reijo Heinonen .20 .50
247 Jaakko Honkanen .20 .50
248 Veli-Pekka Ketola 1.25 3.00
249 Raimo Kilpio .20 .50
250 Tapio Koskinen .20 .50
251 Jarkko Levonen .20 .50
252 Kaj Matalamaki .20 .50
253 Pertti Makela .20 .50
254 Hannu Pulkkinen .20 .50
255 Pekka Rautakallio 1.25 3.00
256 Markku Riihimaki .20 .50
257 Matti Salmi .20 .50
258 Jorma Valtonen .20 .50
259 Anto Virtanen .20 .50
260 Erkki Vakiparta .20 .50
261 Matti Jarkko .20 .50
262 Torsti Jarvenpaa .20 .50
263 Tapio Kallio .20 .50
264 Jussi Kiansten .20 .50
265 Kimmo Korpela .20 .50
266 Jarmo Kuisma .20 .50
267 Antero Lehtonen .20 .50
268 Mikko Leinonen .20 .50
269 Tuomas Leinonen .20 .50
270 Lasse Litma .20 .50
271 Seppo Makinen .20 .50
272 Heikki Niemi .20 .50
273 Reijo Narvanen .20 .50
274 Kalevi Paakkonen .20 .50
275 Reijo Rossi .20 .50
276 Seppo Sevon .20 .50
277 Jorma Siren .20 .50
278 Risto Sirkkola .20 .50
279 Risto Hevonkorpi .20 .50
280 Veijo Hukkanen .20 .50
281 Timo Hytti .20 .50
282 Kalle Impola .20 .50
283 Pertti Jarvenpaa .20 .50
284 Rauno Jarvinen .20 .50
285 Antti Kaivola .20 .50
286 Jorma Karvonen .20 .50
287 Pekka Karvonen .20 .50
288 Seppo Kettunen .20 .50
289 Kari Niemi .20 .50
290 Timo Niiniviita .20 .50
291 Jari Nurminen .20 .50
292 Pentti Poussu .20 .50
293 Matti Rautiainen .20 .50
294 Vesa Ronkainen .20 .50
295 Mauri Salminen .20 .50
296 Kari Silius .20 .50
297 Kimo Turtiainen .20 .50
298 Juha Wikman .20 .50
299 Juha-Pekka Aho .20 .50
300 Matti Estola .20 .50
301 Markku Heinonen .20 .50
302 Mauri Heinonen .20 .50
303 Jukka Hirsimaki .20 .50
304 Jarmo Huhtala .20 .50
305 Harri Huotari .20 .50
306 Kari Jarvinen .20 .50
307 Jari Kaarela .20 .50
308 Kai Lehto .20 .50
309 Jari Leppanen .20 .50
310 Jarmo Liitus .20 .50
311 Markus Matsson .20 .50
312 Jari Niinimaki .20 .50
313 Hannu Oksanen .20 .50
314 Sakari Pehu .20 .50
315 Mika Rajala .20 .50
316 Risto Siltanen .20 .50
317 Jarmo Siro .20 .50
318 Jukka Siro .20 .50
319 Jari Uusikartano .20 .50
320 Seppo Vartiainen .20 .50
321 Mika Weissman .20 .50
322 Seppo Aro .20 .50
323 Jari Huotari .20 .50
324 Ilkka Huura .20 .50
325 Jari Hytti .20 .50
326 Jarmo Jamalainen .20 .50
327 Jari Jokinen .20 .50
328 Tero Juojarvi .20 .50
329 Jari Jarvinen .20 .50
330 Lauri Kosonen .20 .50
331 Aki Laakso .20 .50
332 Ismo Laine .20 .50
333 Matti Lisko .20 .50
334 Dale Lunde .20 .50
335 Markku Pirkkalanniemi .20 .50
336 Rauno Saarnio .20 .50
337 Jukka Silander .20 .50
338 Olli-Pekka Turunen .20 .50
339 Mauri Unkila .20 .50
340 Jarmo Viteli .20 .50
341 Jukka Ahonen .20 .50
342 Jari Hallila .20 .50
343 Jari Helle .20 .50
344 Jari Hirsimaki .20 .50
345 Petri Jokinen .20 .50
346 Kari Jarvinen .20 .50
347 Arto Laine .20 .50
348 Ari Leinonen .20 .50
349 Jukka Oksanen .20 .50
350 Sten Pakarinen .20 .50
351 Jyrki Seppa .20 .50
352 Jari Simola .20 .50
353 Olli Sarkilahti .20 .50
354 Kari-Pekka Tarko .20 .50
355 Timo Toivonen .20 .50
356 Veli-Matti Uusimaa .20 .50
357 Risto Viljanen .20 .50
358 Timo Virtanen .20 .50
359 Teppo Valimaki .20 .50
360 Juha Yrjola .20 .50

1972 Finnish Hellas

COMPLETE SET (99) 50.00 125.00
1 Seppo Ahokainen .20 .50
2 Veli-Pekka Ketola .60 1.50
3 Henry Leppa .20 .50
4 Harri Linnonmaa .20 .50
5 Pekka Marjamaki .20 .50
6 Lauri Mononen .20 .50
7 Matti Murto .20 .50
8 Timo Nummelin .20 .50
9 Lasse Oksanen .20 .50
10 Esa Peltonen .20 .50
11 Pekka Rautakallio .60 1.50
12 Seppo Repo .20 .50
13 Heikki Riihiranta .40 1.00
14 Tommi Salmelainen .20 .50
15 Leo Seppanen .20 .50
16 Juhani Tamminen .40 1.00
17 Timo Turunen .20 .50
18 Pertti Valkeapaa .20 .50
19 Jorma Valtonen .40 1.00
20 Jouko Oystila .20 .50
21 Timo Saari .20 .50
22 Seppo Suoraniemi .20 .50
23 Leif Holmqvist .40 1.00
24 Thommy Abrahamsson .40 1.00
25 Thommie Bergman .75 2.00
26 Stig Ostling .20 .50
27 Lars Sjoberg .75 2.00
28 Carl Sundquist .20 .50
29 Bjorn Johansson .20 .50
30 Tord Lundstrom .20 .50
31 Stig-Goran Johansson .20 .50
32 Stefan Karlsson .20 .50
33 Lars-Goran Nilsson .20 .50
34 Stig Larsson .20 .50
35 Mats Lindh .20 .50
36 Bjorn Palmqvist .20 .50
37 Inge Hammarstrom 4.00 10.00
38 Anders Hedberg 2.00 5.00
39 Kurt Larsson .20 .50
40 Hakan Pettersson .20 .50
41 Hakan Wickberg .20 .50
42 Borje Salming 6.00 15.00
43 Franz Funk .20 .50
44 Otto Schneitberger .20 .50
45 Josef Volk .20 .50
46 Rudolph Thanner .20 .50
47 Paul Langner .20 .50
48 Harald Kadow .20 .50
49 Anton Pohl .20 .50
50 Karl-Heinz Egger 2.00 5.00
51 Lorenz Funk .20 .50
52 Alois Schloder .20 .50
53 Gustav Hanig .20 .50
54 Philips Reiner .20 .50
55 Bernd Kuhn .20 .50
56 Johan Eimansberger .20 .50
57 Rainer Makatsch .20 .50
58 Michael Eibl .20 .50
59 Hans Schichtl .20 .50
60 Anton Hoffher .20 .50
61 Valdimir Lutchenko .40 1.00
62 Aleksandr Gusev .30 .75
63 Vladimir Lutchenko .40 1.00
64 Viktor Kuzkin .20 .50
65 Aleksandr Ragulin .40 1.00
66 Igor Romishevski .20 .50
67 Gennadi Tsigankov .40 1.00
68 Valeri Vasiliev .40 1.00
69 Yuri Blinov .20 .50
70 Alexander Maltsev 2.00 5.00
71 Evgeny Mishakov .30 .75
72 Boris Mikhailov 2.00 5.00
73 Vjatseslav Anisin .30 .75
74 Alexander Yakushev 2.00 5.00
75 Vladimir Petrov 1.25 3.00
76 Valeri Kharlamov 10.00 25.00
77 Vladimir Vikulov .30 .75
78 Vladimir Shadrin .30 .75
79 Vladislav Tretiak 6.00 15.00
80 Vladimir Dzurilla .60 1.50
81 Jiri Holecek .40 1.00
82 Josef Horesovsky .20 .50
83 Oldrich Machac .20 .50
84 Jaroslav Holik .30 .75
85 Rudolf Tajcnar .20 .50
86 Frantisek Pospisil .30 .75
87 Jiri Kochta .20 .50
88 Jan Klapac .20 .50
89 Vladimir Martinec .20 .50
90 Richard Farda .30 .75
91 Bohuslav Stastny .30 .75
92 Vaclav Nedomansky .60 1.50
93 Julius Haas .20 .50
94 Josef Palecek .20 .50
95 Jiri Bubla .40 1.00
96 Milan Kuzela .20 .50
97 Vladimir Bednar .20 .50
98 Jiri Holik .40 1.00
99 Ivan Hlinka .30 .75

1972 Finnish Panda Toronto

COMPLETE SET (118) 50.00 100.00
1 Juhani Bostrom .40 1.00
2 Gary Engberg .40 1.00
3 Kimmo Heino .40 1.00
4 Mauri Kaukokari .40 1.00
5 Vaino Kolkka .40 1.00
6 Harri Linnonmaa .40 1.00
7 Jaakko Marttinen .40 1.00
8 Matti Murto .40 1.00
9 Lalli Partinen .40 1.00
10 Juha Rantasila .40 1.00
11 Heikki Riihiranta .40 1.00
12 Jorma Rikala .40 1.00
13 Tommi Salmelainen .40 1.00
14 Jorma Thusberg .40 1.00
15 Jorma Virtanen .40 1.00
16 Matti Vaisanen .40 1.00
17 Sakari Ahlberg .40 1.00
18 Jorma Aro .40 1.00
19 Esko Eriksson .40 1.00
20 Markku Hakanen .40 1.00
21 Matti Hakanen .40 1.00
22 Reijo Hakanen .40 1.00
23 Timo Hirsimaki .40 1.00
24 Jorma Kallio .40 1.00
25 Esko Kaonpaa .40 1.00
26 Pentti Koskela .40 1.00
27 Pekka Kuusisto .40 1.00
28 Pekka Leimu .40 1.00
29 Lasse Oksanen .40 1.00
30 Kari Palo-oja .40 1.00
31 Jorma Peltonen .40 1.00
32 Veikko Suominen .40 1.00
33 Tapio Flinck .40 1.00
34 Pentti Hakamaki .40 1.00
35 Antti Heikkila .40 1.00
36 Reijo Heinonen .40 1.00
37 Jaakko Honkanen .40 1.00
38 Veli-Pekka Ketola .40 1.00
39 Raimo Kilpio .40 1.00

40 Tapio Koskinen .40 1.00
41 Kaj Matalamaki .40 1.00
42 Pekka Rautakallio .40 1.00
43 Matti Salmi .40 1.00
44 Kari-Pekka Toivonen .40 1.00
45 Jorma Valtonen .40 1.00
46 Anto Virtanen .40 1.00
47 Erkki Vakiparta .40 1.00
48 Vitaly Davydov .75 2.00
49 Anatoly Firsov .75 2.00
50 Valeri Kharlamov 8.00 20.00
51 Victor Konovalenko .75 2.00
52 Victor Kuzkin .75 2.00
53 Yuri Liapkin .75 2.00
54 Vladimir Lutchenko .75 2.00
55 Alexander Maltsev 2.00 5.00
56 Alexander Martyniuk .75 2.00
57 Boris Mikhailov 2.00 5.00
58 Aleksander Ragulin .75 2.00
59 Igor Romishevskyi .75 2.00
60 Vladimir Shadrin .75 2.00
61 Viacheslav Starshinov .75 2.00
62 Vladislav Tretiak 8.00 20.00
63 Evgenyi Zimin .75 2.00
64 Christer Abrahamsson .75 2.00
65 Tommy Abrahamsson .75 2.00
66 Arne Carlsson .40 1.00
67 Inge Hammarstrom 2.00 5.00
68 Leif Holmqvist .75 2.00
69 Stig-Goran Johansson .40 1.00
70 Stefan Karlsson .40 1.00
71 Hans Lindberg .40 1.00
72 Tord Lundstrom .40 1.00
73 Lars-Goran Nilsson .40 1.00
74 Bert-Ola Nordlander .40 1.00
75 Hakan Nygren .40 1.00
76 Bjorn Palmqvist .40 1.00
77 Ulf Sterner .40 1.00
78 Lennart Svedberg .40 1.00
79 Hakan Wickberg .40 1.00
80 Josef Cerny .40 1.00
81 Richard Farda .40 1.00
82 Ivan Hlinka .40 1.00
83 Jiri Holecek .40 1.00
84 Jiri Holik .40 1.00
85 Josef Horesovsky .40 1.00
86 Milan Kuzela .40 1.00
87 Oldrich Machac .40 1.00
88 Vladimir Martinec .40 1.00
89 Vladimir Nadrchal .40 1.00
90 Vaclav Nedomansky 1.50 4.00
91 Frantisek Panchartek .40 1.00
92 Frantisek Pospisil .40 1.00
93 Marcel Sakac .40 1.00
94 Bohuslav Stastny .40 1.00
95 Rudolf Tajcnar .40 1.00
96 Esa Isaksson .40 1.00
97 Heikki Jarn .40 1.00
98 Veli-Pekka Ketola 1.50 4.00
99 Ilpo Koskela .40 1.00
100 Seppo Lindstrom .40 1.00
101 Harri Linnonmaa .40 1.00
102 Pekka Marjamaki .40 1.00
103 Erkki Mononen .40 1.00
104 Lauri Mononen 1.00
105 Matti Murto .40 1.00
106 Lasse Oksanen .40 1.00
107 Esa Peltonen .40 1.00
108 Seppo Repo .40 1.00
109 Tommi Salmelainen .40 1.00
110 Jorma Valtonen .40 1.00
111 Urpo Ylonen .40 1.00
112 Jouko Oystila .40 1.00
113 Sovjet - Finland .40 1.00
114 Sverige - Tjeckoslovakien .40 1.00
115 Finland - Sverige .40 1.00
116 Tjeckoslovakien - Sovjet .40 1.00
117 USA - Sovjet .40 1.00
118 Hockey Sticks .40 1.00

1972 Finnish Semic World Championship

17 Valeri Kharlamov 20.00 50.00

1973-74 Finnish Jaakiekko

COMPLETE SET (325) 125.00 250.00
1 Vjatsjeslav Anisin .75 2.00
2 Aleksandr Bodunov .75 2.00
3 Aleksandr Gusev .75 2.00
4 Valeri Kharlamov 6.00 15.00
5 Aleksandr Yakushev 2.00 5.00
6 Juri Lebedev .75 2.00
7 Juri Liapkin .75 2.00
8 Vladimir Lutshenko .75 2.00
9 Aleksandr Maltsev 2.00 5.00
10 Aleksandr Martiniuk .75 2.00
11 Boris Mikhailov 2.00 5.00
12 Jevgeni Paladiev .75 2.00
13 Vladimir Petrov 2.00 5.00
14 Aleksandr Ragulin .75 2.00
15 Vladimir Shadrin .75 2.00
16 Aleksandr Sidelnikov .75 2.00
17 Vladislav Tretiak 8.00 20.00
18 Gennadi Tsigankov .75 2.00
19 Valeri Vasiljev 2.00 5.00
20 Vladimir Vikulov .75 2.00
21 Aleksandr Voltshkov .75 2.00
22 Christer Abrahamsson 1.25 3.00
23 Thommy Abrahamsson 1.25 3.00
24 Roland Bond .40 1.00
25 Arne Carlsson .40 1.00
26 Inge Hammarstrom 2.00 5.00
27 Anders Hedberg 2.00 5.00
28 Bjorn Johansson .40 1.00
29 Stefan Karlsson .40 1.00
30 Curt Larsson .40 1.00
31 Tord Lundstrom .40 1.00
32 William Lofqvist .40 1.00
33 Ulf Nilsson 2.00 5.00
34 Borje Salming 6.00 15.00
35 Lars-Erik Sjoberg 1.25 3.00
36 Ulf Sterner .40 1.00
37 Karl-Johan Sundqvist .40 1.00
38 Dan Soderstrom .40 1.00
39 Hakan Wickberg .40 1.00
40 Kjell-Arne Wickstrom .40 1.00
41 Dick Yderstrom .40 1.00
42 Mats Ahlberg .40 1.00
43 Peter Adamik .40 1.00
44 Jiri Bubla .40 1.00
45 Jiri Crha 1.25 3.00
46 Richard Farda .40 1.00
47 Ivan Hlinka .75 2.00
48 Jiri Holecek .75 2.00
49 Jaroslav Holik .40 1.00
50 Jiri Holik .40 1.00
51 Josef Horesovsky .40 1.00
52 Jan Klapac .40 1.00
53 Jiri Kochta .40 1.00
54 Milan Kuzela .40 1.00
55 Oldrich Machac .40 1.00
56 Vladimir Martinec .40 1.00
57 Vaclav Nedomansky 1.25 3.00
58 Jiri Novak .40 1.00
59 Josef Palecek .40 1.00
60 Frantisek Pospisil .40 1.00
61 Bohuslav Stastny .40 1.00
62 Karel Vohralik .40 1.00
63 Seppo Ahokainen .40 1.00
64 Matti Keinonen .40 1.00
65 Veli-Pekka Ketola 1.25 3.00
66 Ilpo Koskela .40 1.00
67 Ilpo Kuisma .40 1.00
68 Pekka Kuusisto .40 1.00
69 Henry Leppa .40 1.00
70 Antti Leppanen .40 1.00
71 Seppo Lindstrom .40 1.00
72 Lauri Mononen .40 1.00
73 Timo Nummelin .40 1.00
74 Lalli Partinen .40 1.00
75 Esa Peltonen .40 1.00
76 Pekka Rautakallio 1.25 3.00
77 Seppo Repo .40 1.00
78 Heikki Riihiranta .40 1.00
79 Timo Sutinen .40 1.00
80 Juhani Tamminen .40 1.00
81 Timo Turunen .40 1.00
82 Jorma Valtonen .40 1.00
83 Jorma Vehmanen .40 1.00
84 Jouko Oystila .40 1.00
85 Josef Batkeiwicz .40 1.00
86 Krzysztof Bialynicki .40 1.00
87 Stefan Chowaniec .40 1.00
88 Ludwik Czachovski .40 1.00
89 Andrzej Czczepaniec .40 1.00
90 Stanislav Fryzlewicz .40 1.00
91 Robert Goralczyk .40 1.00
92 Mieczyslaw Jaskierski .40 1.00
93 Tadeusz Kacik .40 1.00
94 Adam Kopczynski .40 1.00
95 Valery Kosyl .40 1.00
96 Tadeusz Obloj .40 1.00
97 Jerzy Potz .40 1.00
98 Andrzej Slowakiewicz .40 1.00
99 Josef Slowakiewicz .40 1.00
100 Jan Szeja .40 1.00
101 Leszek Tokarz .40 1.00
102 Wieslaw Tokarz .40 1.00
103 Henryk Vojtynek .40 1.00
104 Walenty Zietara .40 1.00
105 Pertti Arvaja .40 1.00
106 Olli J. Hietanen .40 1.00
107 Olli T. Hietanen .40 1.00
108 Pentti Hiiros .40 1.00
109 Eero Holopainen .40 1.00
110 Kari Kinnunen .40 1.00
111 Ilpo Koskela .40 1.00
112 Timo Kyntola .40 1.00
113 Henry Leppa .40 1.00
114 Jan Lindberg .40 1.00
115 Lauri Mononen .40 1.00
116 Mika Rajala .40 1.00
117 Pertti Nurmi .40 1.00
118 Jyrki Seivo .40 1.00
119 Jorma Siitarinen .40 1.00
120 Seppo Suoraniemi .40 1.00
121 Timo Sutinen .40 1.00
122 Timo Turunen .40 1.00
123 Jorma Valtonen .40 1.00
124 Seppo Vartiainen .40 1.00
125 Jouko Oystila .40 1.00
126 Juhani Bostrom .40 1.00
127 Matti Hagman 1.25 3.00
128 Kimmo Heino .40 1.00
129 Jorma Immonen .40 1.00
130 Pentti Karlsson .40 1.00
131 Mauri Kaukokari .40 1.00
132 Jarmo Koivunen .40 1.00
133 Vaino Kolkka .40 1.00
134 Harri Linnonmaa .40 1.00
135 Jaakko Marttinen .40 1.00
136 Matti Murto .40 1.00
137 Lalli Partinen .40 1.00
138 Esa Peltonen .40 1.00
139 Juha Rantasila .40 1.00
140 Heikki Riihiranta .40 1.00
141 Jorma Rikala .40 1.00
142 Tommi Salmelainen .40 1.00
143 Henry Saleva .40 1.00
144 Juhani Tamminen .75 2.00
145 Jorma Thusberg .40 1.00
146 Jorma Virtanen .40 1.00
147 Matti Vaisanen .40 1.00
148 Stig Wetzell .40 1.00
149 Jukka Alkula .40 1.00
150 Pertti Ansakorpi .40 1.00
151 Hannu Haapalainen .40 1.00
152 Martti Jarkko .40 1.00
153 Keijo Jarvinen .40 1.00
154 Pertti Koivulahti .40 1.00
155 Ilpo Kuisma .40 1.00
156 Antero Lehtonen .40 1.00
157 Antti Leppanen .40 1.00
158 Lasse Litma .40 1.00
159 Pekka Marjamaki .40 1.00
160 Mikko Mynttinen .40 1.00
161 Pekka Makinen .40 1.00
162 Seppo I. Makinen .40 1.00
163 Seppo S. Makinen .40 1.00
164 Keijo Mannisto .40 1.00
165 Antti Perttula .40 1.00
166 Tuomo Rautiainen .40 1.00
167 Jorma Saarikorpi .40 1.00
168 Juha Silvennoinen .40 1.00
169 Jorma Siren .40 1.00
170 Raimo Suoniemi .40 1.00
171 Pertti Valkeapaa .40 1.00
172 Sakari Ahlberg .40 1.00
173 Seppo Ahokainen .40 1.00
174 Jorma Aro .40 1.00
175 Esko Eriksson .40 1.00
176 Markku Hakanen .40 1.00
177 Reijo Hakanen .40 1.00
178 Martti Helle .40 1.00
179 Erkki Jarvinen .40 1.00
180 Jorma Kallio .40 1.00
181 Erkki Kesalainen .40 1.00
182 Pekka Kuusisto .40 1.00
183 Pekka Leimu .40 1.00
184 Jukka Mattila .40 1.00
185 Esko Makinen .40 1.00
186 Lassse Oksanen .40 1.00
187 Kari Palo-oja .40 1.00
188 Jorma Peltonen .40 1.00
189 Pekka Rampa .40 1.00
190 Heikki Salminen .40 1.00
191 Tuomo Sillman .40 1.00
192 Veikko Suominen .40 1.00
193 Tapio Virhimo .40 1.00
194 Juhani Aaltonen .40 1.00
195 Bjorn Herbert .40 1.00
196 Hannu Kapanen .40 1.00
197 Matti Keinonen .40 1.00
198 Lasse Kiili .40 1.00
199 Matti Koskinen .40 1.00
200 Martti Kuokkanen .40 1.00
201 Urpo Kuukauppi .40 1.00
202 Seppo Laakkio .40 1.00
203 Timo Lahtinen .40 1.00
204 Juhani Laine .40 1.00
205 Heikki Leppik .40 1.00
206 Osmo Lotjonen .40 1.00
207 Kyosti Majava .40 1.00
208 Keijo Puhakka .40 1.00
209 Antti Ravi .40 1.00
210 Seppo Repo .40 1.00
211 Timo Saari .40 1.00
212 Arto Siissala .40 1.00
213 Jorma Vehmanen .40 1.00
214 Pentti Viitanen .40 1.00
215 Leo Aikas .40 1.00
216 Raine Heinonen .40 1.00
217 Vladimir Jursinov .40 1.00
218 Jukka-Pekka Jarvenpaa .40 1.00
219 Pertti Jarvenpaa .40 1.00
220 Heimo Keinonen .40 1.00
221 Seppo Kettunen .40 1.00
222 Veikko Kirveskoski .40 1.00
223 Reijo Laksola .40 1.00
224 Raimo Majapuro .40 1.00
225 Markku Moisio .40 1.00
226 Heikki Nurmi .40 1.00
227 Seppo Nurmi .40 1.00
228 Oiva Oijennus .40 1.00
229 Esko Rantanen .40 1.00
230 Matti Rautiainen .40 1.00
231 Juhani Ruohonen .40 1.00
232 Mikko Raikkonen .40 1.00
233 Lauri Salomaa .40 1.00
234 Veikko Savolainen .40 1.00
235 Leo Seppanen .40 1.00
236 Veikko Seppanen .40 1.00
237 Pekka Uitus .40 1.00
238 Kari Viitalahti .40 1.00
239 Jorma Vilen .40 1.00
240 Asko Ahonen .40 1.00
241 Tapio Flinck .40 1.00
242 Matti Hakanen .40 1.00
243 Antti Heikkila .40 1.00
244 Reijo Heinonen .40 1.00
245 Jaakko Honkanen .40 1.00
246 Jari Kaski .40 1.00
247 Veli-Pekka Ketola .40 1.00
248 Raimo Kilpio .40 1.00
249 Tapio Koskinen .40 1.00
250 Jarkko Levonen .40 1.00
251 Kaj Matalamaki .40 1.00
252 Pertti Makela .40 1.00
253 Jaakko Niemi .40 1.00
254 Hannu Pulkkinen .40 1.00
255 Pekka Rautakallio .40 1.00
256 Markku Riihimaki .40 1.00
257 Anto Virtanen .40 1.00
258 Erkki Vakiparta .40 1.00
259 Pertti Hasanen .40 1.00
260 Rainer Holmroos .40 1.00
261 Kari Johansson .40 1.00
262 Arto Kaunonen .40 1.00
263 Timo Kokkonen .40 1.00
264 Reijo Leppanen .40 1.00
265 Seppo Lindstrom .40 1.00
266 Hannu Luojola .40 1.00
267 Hannu Niittoaho .40 1.00
268 Reijo Paksal .40 1.00
269 Seppo Parikka .40 1.00
270 Jarmo Rantanen .40 1.00
271 Kari Hyokki .40 1.00
272 Kari Salonen .40 1.00
273 Tapani Sura .40 1.00
274 Kari Torkkel .40 1.00
275 Risto Vainio .40 1.00
276 Pentti Vihanto .40 1.00
277 Urpo Ylonen .40 1.00
278 Lars Elfolk .40 1.00
279 Kari Horkko .40 1.00
280 Hannu Jortikka .40 1.00
281 Eero Juntunen .40 1.00
282 Lauri Jamsen .40 1.00
283 Jari Kapanen .40 1.00
284 Jari Kauppila .40 1.00
285 Matti Kauppila .40 1.00
286 Jukka Koskilahti .40 1.00
287 Jukka Koivu .40 1.00
288 Ilkka Laaksonen .40 1.00
289 Robert Lamoureux .40 1.00
290 Hannu Lunden .40 1.00
291 Ilkka Mesikammen .40 1.00
292 Timo Nummelin .40 1.00
293 Timo Nurminen .40 1.00
294 Rauli Ottila .40 1.00
295 Matti Rautee .40 1.00
296 Pekka Rautee .40 1.00
297 Jari Rosberg .40 1.00
298 Tarmo Saarni .40 1.00
299 Asko Salminen .40 1.00
300 Jouni Samuli .40 1.00
301 Rauli Tammelin .40 1.00
302 Veijo Wahlsten .40 1.00
303 Bengt Wilenius .40 1.00
304 Denis Bavaudin .40 1.00
305 Mikko Erholm .40 1.00
306 Matti Forss .40 1.00
307 Esa Hakkarainen .40 1.00
308 Veikko Ihalainen .40 1.00
309 Esa Isaksson .40 1.00
310 Juhani Jylha .40 1.00
311 Heikki Kauhanen .40 1.00
312 Jari Laiho .40 1.00
313 Arto Laine .40 1.00
314 Jouni Peltonen .40 1.00
315 Jouni Rinne .40 1.00
316 Kai Rosvall .40 1.00
317 Seppo Santala .40 1.00
318 Jari Sarronlahti .40 1.00
319 Matti Saurio .40 1.00
320 Ari Sjoman .40 1.00
321 Erkki Sundelin .40 1.00
322 Ismo Villa .40 1.00
323 Mikko Ylaja .40 1.00
324 Veijo Ylanen .40 1.00
NNO Album 25.00 50.00

1974 Finnish Jenkki

COMPLETE SET (120) 50.00 100.00
1 Sakari Ahlberg .30 .75
2 Seppo Ahokainen .30 .75
3 Jukka Alkula .30 .75
4 Jorma Aro .30 .75
5 Hannu Haapalainen .30 .75
6 Veli-Pekka Ketola 1.25 3.00
7 Tapio Koskinen .30 .75
8 Henry Leppa .30 .75
9 Antti Leppanen .30 .75
10 Reijo Leppanen .30 .75
11 Pekka Marjamaki .30 .75
12 Matti Murto .30 .75
13 Esa Peltonen .30 .75
14 Pekka Rautakallio 1.25 3.00
15 Leo Seppanen .30 .75
16 Juha Silvennoinen .30 .75
17 Raimo Suoniemi .30 .75
18 Seppo Suoraniemi .30 .75
19 Timo Sutinen .30 .75
20 Juhani Tamminen .75 2.00
21 Pertti Valkeapaa .30 .75
22 Christer Abrahamsson 1.25 3.00
23 Thommie Bergman 1.25 3.00
24 Roland Bond .30 .75
25 Anders Hedberg 2.00 5.00
26 Bjorn Johansson .30 .75
27 Stefan Karlsson .30 .75
28 Mats Lind .30 .75
29 Tord Lundstrom .30 .75
30 William Lofqvist .30 .75
31 Ulf Nilsson 2.00 5.00
32 Bjorn Palmqvist .30 .75
33 Hakan Pettersson .30 .75
34 Lars-Erik Sjoberg .75 2.00
35 Ulf Sterner .30 .75
36 Karl-Johan Sundqvist .30 .75
37 Hakan Wickberg .30 .75
38 Kjell-Arne Wickstrom .30 .75
39 Dick Yderstrom .30 .75
40 Mats Ahlberg .30 .75
41 Stig Ostling .30 .75
42 Vjatseslav Anisin .40 1.00
43 Aleksandr Bodunov .40 1.00
44 Aleksandr Gusev .40 1.00
45 Valeri Kharlamov 6.00 15.00
46 Aleksandr Yakushev 2.00 5.00
47 Juri Liapkin .40 1.00
48 Vladimir Lutshenko .40 1.00
49 Aleksandr Maltsev 2.00 5.00
50 Aleksandr Martiniuk .40 1.00
51 Boris Mikhailov 2.00 5.00
52 Jevgeni Paladiev .40 1.00
53 Vladimir Petrov 2.00 5.00
54 Aleksandr Ragulin .40 1.00
55 Vladimir Shadrin .40 1.00
56 Aleksandr Sidelnikov .40 1.00
57 Vladislav Tretiak 6.00 15.00
58 Gennadi Tsigankov .40 1.00
59 Valeri Vasiljev 2.00 5.00
60 Vladimir Vikulov .40 1.00
61 Aleksandr Voltshkov .40 1.00
62 Julij Blinov .40 1.00
63 Vladimir Sepovalov .40 1.00
64 Josef Horesovsky .30 .75
65 Peter Adamik .30 .75
66 Vladimir Bednar .30 .75
67 Jiri Bubla .75 2.00
68 Richard Farda .30 .75
69 Julius Haas .30 .75
70 Ivan Hlinka .75 2.00
71 Jiri Holecek .75 2.00
72 Jaroslav Holik .30 .75
73 Jiri Holik .30 .75
74 Jan Klapac .30 .75
75 Jiri Kochta .30 .75
76 Milan Kuzela .30 .75
77 Oldrich Machac .30 .75
78 Vladimir Martinec .30 .75
79 Vaclav Nedomansky 1.50 4.00
80 Josef Palecek .30 .75
81 Frantisek Pospisil .30 .75
82 Bohuslav Stastny .30 .75
83 Rudolf Tajcnar .30 .75
84 Karl Vohralik .30 .75
85 Jerzy Potz .30 .75
86 Andrzej Slowakiewicz .30 .75
87 Josef Slowakiewicz .30 .75
88 Leszek Tokarz .30 .75
89 Wieslaw Tokarz .30 .75
90 Henryk Vojtynek .30 .75
91 Walenty Zietara .30 .75
92 Josef Batkiewicz .30 .75
93 Stefan Chowaniec .30 .75
94 Ludvik Czachovski .30 .75
95 Andrzej Czczepaniec .30 .75
96 Robert Goralczyk .30 .75
97 Mieczyslaw Jaskierski .30 .75
98 Tadeusz Kacik .30 .75
99 Adam Kopczynski .30 .75
100 Valery Kosyl .30 .75
101 Tadeusz Obloj .30 .75
102 Joachim Stasche .30 .75
103 Roland Peters .30 .75
104 Dietmar Peters .30 .75
105 Bernd Karrenbauer .30 .75
106 Peter Prusa .30 .75
107 Rainer Patschinski .30 .75
108 Hartmut Nickel .30 .75
109 Dieter Dewitz .30 .75
110 Harald Felber .30 .75
111 Joachim Hurbanek .30 .75
112 Wolfgang Fischer .30 .75
113 Frank Braun .30 .75
114 Dieter Huschto .30 .75
115 Ruediger Hoack .30 .75
116 Dieter Simon .30 .75
117 Hartwig Schur .30 .75
118 Jochen Philip .30 .75
119 Rolf Bielas .30 .75
120 Peter Slapke .30 .75

1974 Finnish Typotor

COMPLETE SET (120) 30.00 80.00
1 Matti Murto .40 1.00
2 Esa Peltonen .20 .50
3 Juha Rantasila .40 1.00
4 Heikki Riihiranta .75 2.00
5 Juhani Tamminen .75 2.00
6 Jorma Virtanen .40 1.00
7 Seppo Ahokainen .40 1.00
8 Jorma Kallio .20 .50
9 Ari Kankaanpera .20 .50
10 Lasse Oksanen .20 .50
11 Jorma Peltonen .40 1.00
12 Tapio Virhimo .20 .50
13 Ilpo Kokela .20 .50
14 Henry Leppa .20 .50
15 Seppo Suoraniemi .20 .50
16 Timo Sutinen .20 .50
17 Timo Turunen .20 .50
18 Jorma Valtonen .40 1.00
19 Mikko Erholm .20 .50
20 Esa Isaksson .20 .50
21 Juhani Jylha .20 .50
22 Tapani Koskimaki .20 .50
23 Hannu Siivonen .20 .50
24 Jorma Vehmanen .40 1.00
25 Jukka Alkula .20 .50
26 Hannu Haapalainen .20 .50
27 Martti Jarkko .20 .50
28 Antti Leppanen .20 .50
29 Pekka Marjamaki .20 .50
30 Raimo Suoniemi .20 .50
31 Lasse Litma .20 .50
32 Timo Nummelin .20 .50
33 Matti Rautee .20 .50
34 Pekka Rautee .20 .50
35 Seppo Repo .20 .50
36 Jouko Oystila .20 .50
37 Kari Johansson .20 .50
38 Reijo Leppanen .20 .50
39 Seppo Lindstrom .20 .50
40 Hannu Niittoaho .20 .50
41 Pentti Vihanto .20 .50
42 Urpo Ylonen .20 .50
43 Antti Heikkila .20 .50
44 Reijo Heinonen .20 .50
45 Veli-Pekka Ketola .60 1.50
46 Raimo Kilpio .20 .50
47 Tapio Koskinen .20 .50
48 Pekka Rautakallio .75 2.00
49 Seppo Ahokainen .20 .50
50 Henry Leppa .20 .50
51 Antti Leppanen .20 .50
52 Pekka Marjamaki .20 .50
53 Matti Murto .20 .50
54 Esa Peltonen .20 .50
55 Heikki Riihiranta .40 1.00
56 Timo Sutinen .20 .50
57 Juhani Tamminen .75 2.00
58 Rolf Bielas .20 .50
59 Joachim Hurbanek .20 .50
60 Reinhard Karger .20 .50
61 Hartmut Nickel .20 .50
62 Rudiger Noack .20 .50
63 Helmut Novy .20 .50
64 Dietmar Peters .20 .50
65 Peter Prusa .20 .50
66 Peter Slapke .20 .50
67 Vakeri Kharlamov 20.00 50.00
68 Alexander Yakushev 1.50 4.00
69 Alexander Maltsev 1.50 4.00
70 Boris Mikhailov 1.50 4.00
71 Vladimir Petrov 1.50 4.00
72 Vladimir Shadrin .40 1.00
73 Vladislav Tretiak 6.00 15.00
74 Gennady Tsygankov .40 1.00
75 Valeri Vasiljev 1.25 3.00
76 Per-Erik Ingier .20 .50
77 Morten Johansen .20 .50
78 Hakan Lundenes .20 .50
79 N. Nilsen .20 .50
80 Morten Sethereng .20 .50
81 T. Skar .20 .50
82 J-E. Solberg .20 .50
83 K. Thorkildsen .20 .50
84 T. Troymark .20 .50
85 J. Borovicz .20 .50
86 L. Czachovski .20 .50
87 Michael Jaskierski .20 .50
88 Tadeusz Kacik .20 .50
89 Adam Kopczynski .20 .50
90 Tadeusz Obloj .20 .50
91 Jan Szeja .20 .50
92 Leszek Tokarz .20 .50
93 Walenty Zietara .20 .50
94 Christer Abrahamsson .50 1.50
95 Tommy Abrahamsson .75 2.00
96 Anders Hedberg 1.50 4.00
97 Stefan Karlsson .20 .50
98 Kjell-Rune Milton .20 .50
99 Ulf Nilsson 1.50 4.00
100 Bjorn Palmqvist .20 .50
101 Dan Soderstrom .20 .50
102 Mats Ahlberg .30 .75
103 Guy Dubois .40 1.00
104 C. Friedrich .20 .50
105 Charly Henzen .20 .50
106 Ueli Hofmann .20 .50
107 Mirco Horisberger .20 .50
108 M. Lindenmann .20 .50
109 Alfio Molina .20 .50
110 Tony Neininger .20 .50
111 U. Williman .20 .50
112 Richard Farda .20 .50
113 Ivan Hlinka .40 1.00
114 Jiri Holecek .40 1.00
115 Jiri Holik .40 1.00
116 Josef Horesovsky .20 .50
117 Jiri Kochta .20 .50
118 Oldrich Machac .20 .50
119 Vladimir Martinec .20 .50
120 Bohuslav Stastny .30 .75

1978-79 Finnish SM-Liiga

COMPLETE SET (240) 50.00 125.00
1 Hannu Kamppuri .40 1.00
2 Pekka Rautakallio .75 2.00
3 Timo Nummelin .20 .50
4 Pertti Valkeapaa .20 .50
5 Risto Siltanen .40 1.00
6 Hannu Haapalainen .20 .50
7 Markku Kiimalainen .20 .50
8 Tapio Levo .40 1.00
9 Lasse Litma .20 .50
10 Reijo Ruotsalainen .75 2.00
11 Jukka Porvari .20 .50
12 Matti Rautiainen .20 .50
13 Veli-Pekka Ketola .75 2.00
14 Antero Lehtonen .20 .50
15 Martti Jarkko .20 .50
16 Juhani Tamminen .75 2.00
17 Pertti Koivulahti .20 .50
18 Kari Makkonen .20 .50
19 Antero Kivela .20 .50
20 Veli-Matti Ruisma .20 .50
21 Stig Wetzell .20 .50
22 Kyosti Majava .20 .50
23 Seppo Pakelo .20 .50
24 Reijo Laksola .20 .50
25 Heikki Riihiranta .20 .50
26 Raimo Hirvonen .20 .50
27 Jorma Immonen .20 .50
28 Terry Ball .20 .50
29 Pertti Lehtonen .20 .50
30 Jaakko Marttinen .20 .50
31 Esa Peltonen .40 1.00
32 Lauri Mononen .40 1.00
33 Tommi Salmelainen .20 .50
34 Hannu Kapanen .20 .50
35 Matti Forss .20 .50
36 Harri Linnonmaa .20 .50
37 Matti Murto .20 .50
38 Juhani Bostrom .20 .50
39 Matti Hagman .40 1.00
40 Ilkka Sinisalo .75 2.00
41 Tomi Taimio .20 .50
42 Ari Lahteenmaki .20 .50
43 Tapio Virhimo .20 .50
44 Jukka Airaksinen .20 .50
45 Hannu Helander .20 .50
46 Jorma Aro .20 .50
47 Jouko Urvikko .20 .50
48 Hannu Pulkkinen .20 .50
49 Olli Pennanen .20 .50
50 Ari Kankaanpera .20 .50
51 Risto Siltanen .40 1.00
52 Jari Jarvinen .20 .50
53 Sakari Ahlberg .20 .50
54 Keijo Kivela .20 .50
55 Lasse Oksanen .20 .50
56 Risto Kankaanpera .20 .50
57 Kari Jarvinen .20 .50
58 Pekka Orimus .20 .50
59 Jarmo Huhtala .20 .50
60 Hannu Oksanen .20 .50
61 Jari Viitala .20 .50
62 Veikko Suominen .20 .50
63 Antti Heikkila .20 .50
64 Seppo Hiitela .20 .50
65 Hannu Kamppuri .40 1.00
66 Patrik Wainio .20 .50
67 Timo Blomqvist .40 1.00
68 Ilmo Uotila .20 .50
69 Pertti Savolainen .20 .50
70 Jussi Lepisto .20 .50
71 Jorma Piisinen .20 .50
72 Robert Barnes .20 .50
73 Ari Makinen .20 .50
74 David Conte .40 1.00
75 Juha Jyrkkio .20 .50
76 Jari Kurri 20.00 40.00
77 Matti Heikkila .20 .50
78 Henry Leppa .20 .50
79 Pekka Kaski .20 .50
80 Jari Kapanen .20 .50
81 Ari Mikkola .20 .50
82 Vesa Rajaniemi .20 .50
83 Ari Blomqvist .20 .50
84 Erkki Korhonen .20 .50
85 Rainer Risku .20 .50
86 Henry Saleva .20 .50
87 Leo Seppanen .20 .50
88 Rauli Sohlman .20 .50
89 Juhani Ruohonen .20 .50
90 Tuomo Martin .20 .50
91 Reijo Mansikka .20 .50
92 Reino Pulkkinen .20 .50
93 Mauri Kultakuusi .20 .50
94 Kari Saarikko .20 .50
95 Kari Viitalahti .20 .50
96 Barry Salovaara .20 .50
97 Auvo Vaananen .20 .50
98 Pauli Pyykko .20 .50
99 Ari Jortikka .20 .50
100 Jukka-Pekka Jarvenpaa .20 .50
101 Seppo Sevon .20 .50
102 Pekka Koskela .20 .50
103 Arto Jokinen .20 .50
104 Timo Niinivirta .20 .50
105 Matti Rautiainen .20 .50
106 Pertti Jarvenpaa .20 .50
107 Reima Pullinen .20 .50
108 Jukka-Pekka Vuorinen .20 .50
109 Petteri Kanerva .20 .50
110 Kalevi Rantanen .20 .50
111 Jorma Virtanen .20 .50
112 Matti Kaario .20 .50
113 Frank Neal .20 .50
114 Eero Mantere .20 .50
115 Harri Nyman .20 .50
116 Olli Saarinen .20 .50
117 Jari Saarela .20 .50
118 Pasi Virta .20 .50
119 Dave Chalk .20 .50
120 Hannu Koskinen .20 .50
121 Harri Toivonen .20 .50
122 Jarmo Makitalo .20 .50
123 Kari Makitalo .20 .50
124 Olavi Niemenranta .20 .50
125 Pekka Laine .20 .50
126 Markku Hakulinen .20 .50
127 Pekka Nissinen .20 .50
128 Yrjo Hakulinen .20 .50
129 Timo Heino .20 .50
130 Hannu Savolainen .20 .50
131 Ari Hellgren .20 .50
132 Matti Saikkonen .20 .50
133 Ilpo Kukkola .20 .50
134 Pentti Karlsson .20 .50
135 Pekka Karjala .20 .50
136 Juha Tuohimaa .20 .50
137 Pekka Makinen .20 .50
138 Reijo Ruotsalainen .75 2.00
139 Seppo Tenhunen .20 .50
140 Hannu Jalonen .20 .50
141 Jari Virtanen .20 .50
142 Juha Huikuri .20 .50
143 Veikko Torkkeli .20 .50
144 Markku Kiimalainen .20 .50
145 Kalevi Hongisto .20 .50
146 Eero Vartiainen .20 .50
147 Jouko Kamarainen .20 .50
148 Kai Suikkanen .20 .50
149 Ilkka Alatalo .20 .50
150 Markku Perkkio .20 .50
151 Jorma Torkkeli .20 .50
152 Kari Jalonen .20 .50
153 Hannu Siivonen .20 .50
154 Kari Kaupinsalo .20 .50
155 Teppo Mattsson .20 .50
156 Esa Hakkarainen .20 .50
157 Jouni Peltonen .20 .50
158 Timo Peltonen .20 .50
159 Hannu Luojola .20 .50
160 Tapani Koskimaki .20 .50
161 Tuomo Jormakka .20 .50
162 Mika Rajala .20 .50
163 Pekka Santanen .20 .50
164 Jorma Vehmanen .20 .50
165 Olli Tuominen .20 .50
166 Hannu Kemppainen .20 .50
167 Ismo Villa .20 .50
168 Matti Tynkkynen .20 .50
169 Jouni Rinne .20 .50
170 Jari Rastio .20 .50
171 Harri Tuohimaa .20 .50
172 Jari Laiho .20 .50
173 Juhani Wallenius .20 .50
174 Pekka Strander .20 .50
175 Pertti Hasanen .20 .50
176 Pertti Karjalainen .20 .50
177 Jorma Kallio .20 .50
178 Pekka Marjamaki .20 .50
179 Hannu Haapalainen .20 .50
180 Pertti Valkeapaa .20 .50
181 Lasse Litma .20 .50
182 Jarkko Hirsimaki .20 .50
183 Oiva Oijennus .20 .50
184 Jukka Aikula .20 .50
185 Timo Susi .20 .50
186 Jukka Porvari .20 .50
187 Erkki Lehtonen .20 .50
188 Antero Lehtonen .20 .50
189 Juha Solvennoinen .20 .50
190 Pertti Koivulahti .20 .50
191 Keijo Mannisto .20 .50
192 Jorma Sevon .20 .50
193 Martti Jarkko .20 .50
194 Jari Lindgren .20 .50
195 Tapio Kallio .20 .50
196 Tero Kapynen .20 .50
197 Urpo Ylonen .20 .50
198 Jorma Valtonen .20 .50
199 Harri Kari .20 .50
200 Hannu Jortikka .20 .50
201 Timo Nummelin .20 .50
202 Seppo Suoraniemi .20 .50
203 Ilkka Mesikammen .20 .50
204 Pertti Ahokas .20 .50
205 Hannu Niitoaho .20 .50
206 Arto Kaunonen .20 .50
207 Pekka Rautee .20 .50
208 Juhani Tamminen .20 .50
209 Timo Viljanen .20 .50
210 Kari Kauppila .20 .50
211 Bengt Willenius .20 .50
212 Reijo Leppanen .20 .50
213 Rauli Tammelin .20 .50
214 Jukka Koskilahti .20 .50
215 Markku Haapaniemi .20 .50
216 Kari Horkko .20 .50
217 Kalevi Aho .20 .50
218 Hakan Hjerpe .20 .50
219 Antero Kivela .20 .50
220 Pertti Lehti .20 .50
221 Antti Heikkila .20 .50
222 Tapio Flinck .20 .50
223 Pekka Rautakallio .75 2.00
224 Jaakko Niemi .20 .50
225 Tapio Levo .40 1.00
226 Jyrki Levonen .20 .50

227 Harry Nikander .20 .50
228 Arto Javanainen .20 .50
229 Pekka Makela .20 .50
230 Tapio Koskinen .20 .50
231 Pekka Stenfors .20 .50
232 Ari Peltola .20 .50
233 Veli-Pekka Ketola .75 2.00
234 Erkki Vakiparta .20 .50
235 Rauli Levonen .20 .50
236 Martti Nenonen .20 .50
237 Jouni Makitalo .20 .50
238 Veli-Matti Ruisma .20 .50
239 Tauno Makela .20 .50
240 Kari Makkonen .20 .50

1982 Finnish Skopbank

COMPLETE SET (8) 24.00 60.00
1 Pekka Arbelius 2.00 5.00
2 Ari Hellgren 2.00 5.00
3 Raimo Hirvonen 2.00 5.00
4 Hannu Kamppuri 3.00 8.00
5 Markku Kiimalainen 2.00 5.00
6 Pertti Koivulahti 2.00 5.00
7 Hannu Koskinen 2.00 5.00
8 Mikko Leinonen 2.00 5.00
9 Reijo Leppanen 2.00 5.00
10 Tapio Levo 2.00 5.00
11 Timo Nummelin 2.00 5.00
12 Jukka Porvari 2.00 5.00
13 Reijo Ruotsalainen 3.00 8.00
14 Seppo Suoraniemi 2.00 5.00
15 Timo Susi 2.00 5.00
16 Juhani Tamminen 3.00 8.00

1989 Finnish Pelimiehen

COMPLETE SET (6) 12.00 30.00
1 Kari Eloranta 1.25 3.00
2 Jari Kurri 6.00 15.00
3 Reijo Ruotsalainen 1.25 3.00
4 Christian Ruuttu 1.25 3.00
5 Kari Takko 2.00 5.00
6 Esa Tikkanen 3.00 8.00

1990-91 Finnish Jyvas-Hyva Stickers

COMPLETE SET (12) 10.00 25.00
NNO Hockey Reipas Lahti .75 2.00
NNO Saipa Lappeenranta .75 2.00
NNO Tappara Tampere .75 2.00
NNO TPS Turku .75 2.00
NNO Assat Pori .75 2.00
NNO JypHT Jyvaskyla .75 2.00
NNO Jokerit .75 2.00
NNO Lukko Rauma 1.25 3.00
NNO Kalpa Kuopio .75 2.00
NNO HIFK .75 2.00
NNO HPK Hameenlinna .75 2.00
NNO Ilves Tampere .75 2.00

1991 Finnish Semic World Championship Stickers

COMPLETE SET (250) 50.00 100.00
1 Finnish Emblem .02 .10
2 Markus Ketterer .20 .50
3 Sakari Lindfors .20 .50
4 Jukka Tammi .20 .50
5 Timo Jutila .08 .25
6 Hannu Virta .08 .25
7 Simo Saarinen .08 .25
8 Jukka Marttila .08 .25
9 Ville Siren .08 .25
10 Pasi Huura .08 .25
11 Hannu Henriksson .08 .25
12 Arto Ruotanen .08 .25
13 Ari Haanpaa .08 .25
14 Pauli Jarvinen .08 .25
15 Teppo Kivela .08 .25
16 Risto Kurkinen .08 .25
17 Mika Nieminen .08 .25
18 Jari Kurri .75 2.00
19 Esa Keskinen .08 .25
20 Raimo Summanen .08 .25
21 Teemu Selanne 4.00 10.00
22 Jari Torkki .08 .25
23 Hannu Jarvenpaa .08 .25
24 Raimo Helminen .08 .25
25 Timo Peltomaa .08 .25
26 Swedish Emblem .02 .10
27 Peter Lindmark .20 .50
28 Rolf Ridderwall .20 .50
29 Tommy Soderstrom .20 .50
30 Thomas Eriksson .08 .25
31 Nicklas Lidstrom 4.00 10.00
32 Tomas Jonsson .08 .25
33 Tommy Samuelsson .08 .25
34 Fredrik Stillman .08 .25
35 Peter Andersson .08 .25
36 Peter Andersson .08 .25
37 Kenneth Kennholt .08 .25
38 Hakan Loob .40 1.00
39 Thomas Rundqvist .08 .25
40 Hakan Ahlund .08 .25
41 Jan Viktorsson .08 .25
42 Charles Berglund .08 .25
43 Mikael Johansson .08 .25
44 Robert Burakovsky .08 .25
45 Bengt-Ake Gustafsson .08 .25
46 Patrik Carnback .08 .25
47 Patrik Erickson .08 .25
48 Anders Carlsson .08 .25
49 Mats Naslund .75 2.00
50 Kent Nilsson .75 2.00
51 Canadian Emblem .40 1.00
52 Patrick Roy 10.00 25.00
53 Ed Belfour 2.00 5.00
54 Daniel Berthiaume .40 1.00
55 Ray Bourque 4.00 10.00
56 Scott Stevens .40 1.00
57 Al MacInnis .75 2.00
58 Paul Coffey .75 2.00
59 Paul Cavallini .40 1.00
60 Zarley Zalapski .40 1.00
61 Steve Duchesne .40 1.00
62 Dave Ellett .40 1.00
63 Mark Messier 4.00 10.00
64 Wayne Gretzky 12.00 30.00
65 Steve Yzerman 8.00 20.00
66 Pierre Turgeon .40 1.00
67 Bernie Nicholls .40 1.00
68 Cam Neely 2.00 5.00
69 Joe Nieuwendyk .40 1.00
70 Luc Robitaille 2.00 5.00
71 Kevin Dineen .40 1.00
72 John Cullen .40 1.00
73 Steve Larmer .40 1.00
74 Mark Recchi .75 2.00
75 Joe Sakic 4.00 10.00
76 Soviet Emblem .02 .10
77 Arturs Irbe .40 1.00
78 Alexei Marin .20 .50
79 Mikhail Shtalenkov .20 .50
80 Vladimir Malakhov .08 .25
81 Vladimir Konstantinov 1.25 3.00
82 Igor Kravchuk .08 .25
83 Ilya Byakin .08 .25
84 Dimitri Mironov .08 .25
85 Vladimir Turikov .08 .25
86 Vjatjeslav Uvajev .08 .25
87 Vladimir Fedosov .08 .25
88 Valeri Kamensky .08 .25
89 Pavel Bure 2.00 5.00
90 Vyacheslav Butsayev .08 .25
91 Igor Maslennikov .08 .25
92 Evgeny Davydov .08 .25
93 Andrei Kovalev .08 .25
94 Alexander Semak .08 .25
95 Alexei Zhamnov .08 .25
96 Sergei Nemchinov .08 .25
97 Viktor Gordijuk .08 .25
98 Vyacheslav Kozlov .08 .25
99 Andrei Khomotov .08 .25
100 Vyacheslav Bykov .08 .25
101 Czech Emblem .02 .10
102 Petr Briza .20 .50
103 Dominik Hasek 4.00 10.00
104 Eduard Hartmann .20 .50
105 Bedrich Scerban .08 .25
106 Jiri Slegr .08 .25
107 Josef Reznicek .08 .25
108 Petr Pavlas .08 .25
109 Peter Slanina .08 .25
110 Martin Maskarinec .08 .25
111 Antonin Stavjana .08 .25
112 Stanislav Medrik .08 .25
113 Dusan Pasek .08 .25
114 Jiri Lala .08 .25
115 Darius Rusnak .08 .25
116 Oto Hascak .08 .25
117 Radek Toupal .08 .25
118 Pavel Pycha .08 .25
119 Lubomir Kolnik .08 .25
120 Libor Dolana .08 .25
121 Ladislav Lubina .08 .25
122 Tomas Jelinek .08 .25
123 Petr Vlk .08 .25
124 Vladimir Petrovka .08 .25
125 Richard Zemlička .08 .25
126 U.S.A. Emblem .02 .10
127 John Vanbiesbrouck .75 2.00
128 Mike Richter .75 2.00
129 Chris Terreri .40 1.00
130 Chris Chelios 2.00 5.00
131 Brian Leetch 1.25 3.00
132 Gary Suter .40 1.00
133 Phil Housley .40 1.00
134 Mark Howe .40 1.00
135 Al Iafrate .40 1.00
136 Kevin Hatcher .40 1.00
137 Mathieu Schneider .40 1.00
138 Pat LaFontaine .75 2.00
139 Darren Turcotte .40 1.00
140 Neal Broten .75 2.00
141 Mike Modano 2.00 5.00
142 Dave Christian .40 1.00
143 Craig Janney .40 1.00
144 Brett Hull 2.00 5.00
145 Kevin Stevens .40 1.00
146 Joe Mullen .40 1.00
147 Tony Granato .40 1.00
148 Ed Olczyk .40 1.00
149 Jeremy Roenick 2.00 5.00
150 Jimmy Carson .40 1.00
151 West German Emblem .02 .10
152 Helmut De Raaf .20 .50
153 Josef Heiss .20 .50
154 Karl Friesen .20 .50
155 Uli Hiemer .08 .25
156 Harold Kreis .08 .25
157 Udo Kiessling .08 .25
158 Michael Schmidt .08 .25
159 Michael Heidt .08 .25
160 Andreas Pokorny .08 .25
161 Bernd Wagner .08 .25
162 Uwe Krupp .08 .25
163 Gerd Truntschka .08 .25
164 Bernd Truntschka .08 .25
165 Thomas Brandl .08 .25
166 Peter Draisaitl .08 .25
167 Andreas Brockmann .08 .25
168 Ulrich Liebsch .08 .25
169 Ralf Hantschke .08 .25
170 Thomas Schinko .08 .25
171 Anton Krinner .08 .25
172 Thomas Werner .08 .25
173 Dieter Hegen .08 .25
174 Helmut Steiger .08 .25
175 Georg Franz .08 .25
176 Swiss Emblem .02 .10
177 Renato Tosio .20 .50
178 Reto Pavoni .20 .50
179 Dino Stecher .20 .50
180 Sven Leuenberger .08 .25
181 Rick Tschumi .08 .25
182 Patrice Brasey .08 .25
183 Didier Massy .08 .25
184 Sandro Bertaggia .08 .25
185 Samuel Balmer .08 .25
186 Martin Rauch .08 .25
187 Marc Leuenberger .08 .25
188 Jorg Eberle .08 .25
189 Fredy Luthi .08 .25
190 Andy Ton .08 .25
191 Raymond Walder .08 .25
192 Manuele Celio .08 .25
193 Roman Wager .08 .25
194 Felix Hollenstein .08 .25
195 Andre Rotheli .08 .25
196 Christian Weber .08 .25
197 Peter Jaks .08 .25
198 Gil Montandon .08 .25
199 Oliver Hoffmann .08 .25
200 Thomas Vrabec .08 .25
201 Teppo Numminen .08 .25
202 Jyrki Lumme .08 .25
203 Esa Tikkanen .08 .25
204 Petri Skriko .08 .25
205 Christian Ruutu .08 .25
206 Ilkka Sinisalo .08 .25
207 Calle Johansson .08 .25
208 Tomas Sandstrom .08 .25
209 Thomas Steen .08 .25
210 Per-Erik Eklund .08 .25
211 Mats Sundin 1.25 3.00
212 Johan Garpenlov .08 .25
213 Slava Fetisov .08 .25
214 Alexei Kasatonov .08 .25
215 Mikhail Tatarinov .08 .25
216 Sergei Makarov .20 .50
217 Igor Larionov .40 1.00
218 Alexander Mogilny .40 1.00
219 Sergei Fedorov 1.25 3.00
220 Petr Klima .08 .25
221 David Volek .08 .25
222 Michal Pivonka .08 .25
223 Robert Reichel .08 .25
224 Robert Holik .08 .25
225 Jaromir Jagr 4.00 10.00
226 Urpo Ylonen .08 .25
227 Ilpo Koskela .08 .25
228 Pekka Rautakallio .20 .50
229 Lasse Oksanen .08 .25
230 Veli-Pekka Ketola .20 .50
231 Leif Holmqvist .20 .50
232 Lennart Svedberg .08 .25
233 Sven Tumba Johansson .08 .25
234 Ulf Sterner .08 .25
235 Anders Hedberg .20 .50
236 Ken Dryden 2.00 5.00
237 Bobby Orr 10.00 25.00
238 Gordie Howe 4.00 10.00
239 Bobby Hull 3.00 8.00
240 Phil Esposito 2.00 5.00
241 Vladislav Tretiak 4.00 10.00
242 Alexander Ragulin .08 .25
243 Anatoli Firsov .08 .25
244 Valeri Kharlamov 2.00 5.00
245 Alexander Maltsev .75 2.00
246 Jiri Holecek .08 .25
247 Jan Suchy .08 .25
248 Jozef Golonka .08 .25
249 Vaclav Nedomansky .08 .25
250 Ivan Hlinka .08 .25

1991-92 Finnish Jyvas-Hyva Stickers

COMPLETE SET (84) 30.00 80.00
1 Sakari Lindfors .40 1.00
2 Jukka Seppo .08 .25
3 Pekka Tuomisto .05 .15
4 Harri Tuohimaa .05 .15
5 Pertti Lehtonen .05 .15
6 Simo Saarinen .05 .15
7 Timo Lehkonen .05 .15
8 Teppo Kivela .05 .15
9 Markku Piikkila .05 .15
10 Pekka Peltola .05 .15
11 Hannu Henriksson .05 .15
12 Jari Haapamaki .05 .15
13 Jukka Tammi .40 1.00
14 Risto Jalo .05 .15
15 Timo Peltomaa .05 .15
16 Raimo Summanen .40 1.00
17 Ville Siren .20 .50
18 Risto Siltanen .40 1.00
19 Markus Ketterer .30 .75
20 Pekka Jarvela .05 .15
21 Teemu Selanne 30.00 80.00
22 Keijo Sailynoja .05 .15
23 Mika Stromberg .08 .25
24 Waltteri Immonen .05 .15
25 Ari-Pekka Siekkinen .08 .25
26 Jari Lindroos .08 .25
27 Ari Haanpaa .05 .15
28 Jiri Dolezal .08 .25
29 Harri Laurila .05 .15
30 Leo Gudas .08 .25
31 Mika Rautio .05 .15
32 Pekka Tirkkonen .05 .15
33 Jarmo Kekalainen .20 .50
34 Juha Jokiharju .05 .15
35 Juha Tuohimaa .05 .15
36 Erik Hamalainen .08 .25
37 Juha Jaaskelainen .05 .15
38 Rostislav Vlach .05 .15
39 Jouni Mustonen .05 .15
40 Marku Kyllonen .05 .15
41 Antonin Stavjana .08 .25
42 Ossi Piitulainen .05 .15
43 Petr Briza .40 1.00
44 Mika Nieminen .20 .50
45 Jari Torkki .05 .15
46 Tommi Pullola .05 .15
47 Jarmo Kuusisto .05 .15
48 Pasi Huura .05 .15
49 Jaromir Sindel .20 .50
50 Marko Jantunen .08 .25
51 Erkki Laine .05 .15
52 Erkki Makela .05 .15
53 Niko Marttila .05 .15
54 Erik Kakko .05 .15
55 Jari Halme .05 .15
56 Kari Heikkinen .05 .15
57 Jiri Kucera .08 .25
58 Vesa Viitakoski .20 .50
59 Jukka Marttila .05 .15
60 Pekka Laksola .05 .15
61 Jouni Rokama .08 .25
62 Esa Keskinen .20 .50
63 Jukka Vilander .05 .15
64 Jari Pulliainen .05 .15
65 Jouko Narvanmaa .05 .15
66 Hannu Virta .08 .25
67 Kari Takko .40 1.00
68 Janne Virtanen .05 .15
69 Arto Javanainen .05 .15
70 Oleg Znarok .08 .25
71 Tapio Levo .05 .15
72 Harry Nikander .05 .15
NNO Hockey Reipat Lahti .05 .15
NNO Joensuun Kiekkopojat .05 .15
NNO Rauman Luoko .05 .15
NNO Turun Palloseura .05 .15
NNO Jokerit Helsinki .08 .25
NNO HPK Hameenlinna .05 .15
NNO JyPHT Jyvaskyla .05 .15
NNO KaiPa Kupio .05 .15
NNO Assat Pori .05 .15
NNO Ilves Tampere .05 .15
NNO Tappara Tampere .05 .15
NNO HIFK Helsinki .05 .15

1992 Finnish Semic

COMPLETE SET (288) 100.00 250.00
1 Finland .02 .10
2 Pentti Matikainen .20 .50
3 Markus Ketterer .20 .50
4 Sakari Lindfors .20 .50
5 Teppo Numminen .08 .25
6 Jyrki Lumme .08 .25
7 Janne Laukkanen .08 .25
8 Ville Siren .08 .25
9 Mikko Haapakoski .08 .25
10 Simo Saarinen .08 .25
11 Teemu Selanne 20.00 50.00
12 Petri Skriko .08 .25
13 Iiro Jarvi .08 .25
14 Esa Tikkanen .08 .25
15 Christian Ruuttu .08 .25
16 Raimo Summanen .08 .25
17 Jari Kurri .75 2.00
18 Timo Peltomaa .08 .25
19 Mika Nieminen .08 .25
20 Mikko Makela .08 .25
21 Janne Ojanen .08 .25
22 Jarmo Kekalainen .08 .25
23 Keijo Sailynoja .08 .25
24 Esa Keskinen .08 .25
25 Norge .02 .10
26 Bengt Ohlsson .20 .50
27 Jim Marthinsen .20 .50
28 Steve Allman .20 .50
29 Petter Salsten .08 .25
30 Age Ellingsen .08 .25
31 Kim Sogaard .08 .25
32 Jan Roar Fagerli .08 .25
33 Tommy Jakobsen .08 .25
34 Cato Tom Andersen .08 .25
35 Arne Billkvam .08 .25
36 Oystein Olsen .08 .25
37 Geir Hoff .08 .25
38 Erik Kristiansen .08 .25
39 Orjan Lovdal .08 .25
40 Espen Knutsen .75 2.00
41 Ole Eskild Dahlstrom .08 .25
42 Rune Gulliksen .08 .25
43 Marius Rath .08 .25
44 Petter Thoresen .08 .25
45 Tom Johansen .08 .25
46 Stephen Foyn .08 .25
47 Stig Johansen .08 .25
48 Per Christian Knold .08 .25
49 Svierge .02 .10
50 Conny Evensson .02 .10
51 Tommy Soderstrom .20 .50
52 Fredrik Andersson .20 .50
53 Thomas Eriksson .08 .25
54 Peter Andersson .08 .25
55 Peter Andersson .08 .25
56 Nicklas Lidstrom 2.00 5.00
57 Calle Johansson .08 .25
58 Ulf Samuelsson .08 .25
59 Fredrik Olausson .08 .25
60 Borje Salming .40 1.00
61 Hakan Loob .08 .25
62 Thomas Rundqvist .08 .25
63 Mats Naslund .08 .25
64 Mikael Johansson .08 .25
65 Bengt-Ake Gustavsson .08 .25
66 Peter Ottosson .08 .25
67 Markus Naslund .08 .25
68 Daniel Rydmark .08 .25
69 Tomas Sandstrom .08 .25
70 Thomas Steen .08 .25
71 Per-Erik Eklund .08 .25
72 Mats Sundin .75 2.00
73 Kanada .20 .50
74 Dave King .02 .10
75 Bill Ranford .75 2.00
76 Ed Belfour 1.25 3.00
77 Al MacInnis .75 2.00
78 Scott Stevens .40 1.00
79 Steve Smith .40 1.00
80 Ray Bourque 3.00 8.00
81 Paul Coffey .75 2.00
82 Larry Murphy .40 1.00
83 Mark Tinordi .40 1.00
84 Wayne Gretzky 10.00 25.00
85 Mark Messier 3.00 8.00
86 Mario Lemieux 8.00 20.00
87 Steve Yzerman 6.00 15.00
88 Eric Lindros 8.00 20.00
89 Luc Robitaille 1.25 3.00
90 Theoren Fleury .75 2.00
91 Steve Larmer .40 1.00
92 Brent Sutter .40 1.00
93 Shayne Corson .40 1.00
94 Dale Hawerchuk .75 2.00
95 Russ Courtnall .40 1.00
96 Rick Tocchet .40 1.00
97 Soviet .02 .10
98 Victor Tikhonov .02 .10
99 Andrei Trefilov .20 .50
100 Mikhail Shtalenkov .20 .50
101 Alexei Kasatonov .08 .25
102 Mikhail Tatarinov .08 .25
103 Igor Kravchuk .08 .25
104 Vladimir Malakhov .08 .25
105 Alex Gusarov .08 .25
106 Dimitri Filimonov .08 .25
107 Dimitri Mironov .08 .25
108 Vladimir Konstantinov .75 2.00
109 Sergei Fedorov 1.25 3.00
110 Alexei Zhamnov .08 .25
111 Vyatcheslav Kozlov .08 .25
112 Valery Kamesky .08 .25
113 Alexander Semak .08 .25
114 Vjatcheslav Butsayev .08 .25
115 Andrei Lomakin .08 .25
116 Pavel Bure 2.00 5.00
117 Andrei Kovalenko .08 .25
118 Ravil Khaidarov .08 .25
119 Victor Gordiuk .08 .25
120 Vitali Prokhorov .08 .25
121 Tjeckoslovakien .02 .10
122 Ivan Hlinka .02 .10
123 Oldrich Svoboda .20 .50
124 Dominik Hasek 4.00 10.00
125 Leo Gudas .08 .25
126 Frantisek Musil .08 .25
127 Kamil Prachar .08 .25
128 Frantisek Kucera .08 .25
129 Richard Smehlik .08 .25
130 Jergus Baca .08 .25
131 Jiri Slegr .08 .25
132 Petr Hrbek .08 .25
133 Kamil Kastak .08 .25
134 Richard Zemlicka .08 .25
135 Jaromir Jagr 3.00 8.00
136 Martin Rucinsky .08 .25
137 Josef Beranek .08 .25
138 Michael Pivonka .08 .25
139 Robert Kron .08 .25
140 Zigmund Palffy .75 2.00
141 Tomas Jelinek .08 .25
142 Robert Reichel .08 .25
143 Lubomir Kolnik .08 .25
144 Zdeno Ciger .08 .25
145 USA .02 .10
146 Tim Taylor .02 .10
147 John Vanbiesbrouck .75 2.00
148 Mike Richter .75 2.00
149 Phil Housley .08 .25
150 Brian Leetch .40 1.00
151 Kevin Hatcher .08 .25
152 Gary Suter .08 .25
153 Chris Chelios .75 2.00
154 Eric Weinrich .08 .25
155 Jim Johnson .08 .25
156 Brett Hull 2.00 5.00
157 Mike Modano 2.00 5.00
158 Jeremy Roenick 2.00 5.00
159 Pat LaFontaine .40 1.00
160 Craig Janney .08 .25
161 Ed Olczyk .08 .25
162 Tony Granato .08 .25
163 Joe Mullen .08 .25
164 Dave Christian .08 .25
165 Doug Brown .08 .25
166 Kevin Miller .08 .25
167 Joel Otto .08 .25
168 Randy Wood .08 .25
169 Tyskland .02 .10
170 Ludek Bukac .08 .25
171 Klaus Merk .08 .25
172 Josef Heiss .08 .25
173 Harold Kreiss .08 .25
174 Michael Heidt .08 .25
175 Jorg Mayr .08 .25
176 Marco Rentzsch .08 .25
177 Heinrich Schiffel .08 .25
178 Stefan Steinecker .08 .25
179 Torsten Kienass .08 .25
180 Raimund Hilger .08 .25
181 Ernst Kopf .08 .25
182 Peter Draisatl .08 .25
183 Axel Kammerer .08 .25
184 Michael Rumrich .08 .25
185 Jurgen Rumrich .08 .25
186 Georg Holzmann .08 .25
187 Lorenz Funk .08 .25
188 Thomas Schinko .08 .25
189 Andreas Lupzig .08 .25
190 Tobias Abstreiter .08 .25
191 Michael Pohl .08 .25
192 Antony Vogel .08 .25
193 Schweiz .02 .10
194 Juhani Tamminen .02 .10
195 Renato Tosio .20 .50
196 Reto Pavoni .20 .50
197 Rick Tschumi .08 .25
198 Patrice Brasey .08 .25
199 Didier Massy .08 .25
200 Sandro Bertaggia .08 .25
201 Sven Leuenberger .08 .25
202 Samuel Palmer .08 .25
203 Martin Rauch .08 .25
204 Dino Kessler .08 .25
205 Raymond Walder .08 .25
206 Peter Jaks .08 .25
207 Andy Ton .08 .25
208 Jorg Eberle .08 .25
209 Felix Hollenstein .08 .25
210 Fredy Luthi .08 .25
211 Manuele Celio .08 .25
212 Christian Weber .08 .25
213 Andre Rotheli .08 .25
214 Gil Montandon .08 .25
215 Thomas Vrabec .08 .25
216 Patrick Howald .08 .25
217 Frankrike .02 .10
218 Kjell Larsson .02 .10
219 Jean-Marc Djian .20 .50
220 Petri Ylonen .20 .50
221 Stephane Botteri .08 .25
222 Michel Leblanc .08 .25
223 Jean-Philippe Lemoine .08 .25
224 Denis Perez .08 .25
225 Bruno Saunier .08 .25
226 Steven Woodburn .08 .25
227 Serge Poudrier .08 .25
228 Michael Babin .08 .25
229 Stephane Barin .08 .25
230 Philippe Bozon .40 1.00
231 Arnaud Briand .08 .25
232 Yves Crettenand .08 .25
233 Patrick Dunn .08 .25
234 Yannick Goicoechea .08 .25
235 Benoit Laporte .08 .25
236 Christian Pouget .08 .25
237 Antoine Richer .08 .25
238 Christophe Ville .08 .25
239 Peter Almasy .08 .25
240 Pierre Pousse .08 .25
241 Italien .02 .10
242 Gene Ubriaco .02 .10
243 David Delfino .40 1.00
244 Mike Zanier .40 1.00
245 Erwin Kostner .08 .25
246 Roberto Oberrauch .08 .25
247 Jim Camazzola .08 .25
248 Anthony Circelli .08 .25
249 Michael de Angelis .08 .25
250 Giovanni Marchetti .08 .25
251 Alessandro Batiani .08 .25
252 Georg Comploi .08 .25
253 Gaetano Orlando .08 .25
254 Bruno Zarrillo .08 .25
255 Emilio Iovio .08 .25
256 Frank Nigro .08 .25
257 Marco Scapinello .08 .25
258 Giuseppe Foglietta .08 .25
259 Rick Morocco .08 .25
260 Santino Pellegrino .08 .25
261 Lucio Topatigh .08 .25
262 Mario Simioni .08 .25
263 Ivano Cloch .08 .25
264 Martino Soracreppa .08 .25
265 Polen .02 .10
266 Leszek Lejcyk .02 .10
267 Andrzej Hanisz .20 .50
268 Mariusz Kieca .20 .50
269 Henryk Gruth .08 .25
270 Janusz Syposz .08 .25
271 Robert Szopinski .08 .25
272 Mark Cholewa .08 .25
273 Jacek Zamojski .08 .25
274 Rafal Stroka .08 .25
275 Dariusz Garbocz .08 .25
276 Stanislaw Cyrwus .08 .25
277 Janusz Adamiec .08 .25
278 Miloslaw Copija .08 .25
279 Piotr Zdunek .08 .25
280 Krzysztof Bujar .08 .25
281 Ludwik Czapka .08 .25
282 Andrzej Kotonski .08 .25
283 Janusz Hajnos .08 .25
284 Slawomir Wieloch .08 .25
285 Wojciech Matczak .08 .25
286 Jedrzej Kasperczyk .08 .25
287 Wojciech Tkacs .08 .25
288 Mariusz Czerkawski .20 .50

1992-93 Finnish Jyvas-Hyva Stickers

COMPLETE SET (204) 19.56 48.89
1 Harri Rindell .05 .15
2 Sakari Lindfors .40 1.00
3 Simo Saarinen .05 .15
4 Pertti Lehtonen .05 .15
5 Kari Laitinen .05 .15
6 Teppo Kivela .05 .15
7 Darren Boyko .20 .50
8 Kai Rautio .08 .25
9 Drahomir Kadlec .08 .25
10 Mika Kortelainen .05 .15
11 Jukka Seppo .08 .25
12 Pekka Tuomisto .05 .15
13 Pasi Sormunen .05 .15
14 Kai Tervonen .05 .15
15 Ville Peltonen .40 1.00
16 Valeri Krykov .05 .15
17 Iiro Jarvi .20 .50
18 Hannu Jortikka .05 .15
19 Timo Lehkonen .05 .15
20 Timo Nykopp .05 .15
21 Janne Laukkanen .40 1.00
22 Marko Palo .08 .25
23 Juha Ylonen 1.25 3.00
24 Jarkko Varvio .20 .50
25 Marko Allen .05 .15
26 Marko Tuulola .05 .15
27 Jarkko Nikander .08 .25
28 Radek Toupal .05 .15
29 Tommi Varjonen .05 .15
30 Niko Marttila .05 .15
31 Jari Haapamaki .05 .15
32 Pasi Kivela .05 .15
33 Tony Virta .05 .15
34 Markku Piikkila .05 .15
35 Anatoli Bogdanov .05 .15
36 Jukka Tammi .40 1.00
37 Jani Nikko .08 .25
38 Jukka Ollila .05 .15
39 Tommi Kiiski .05 .15
40 Mikko Luovi .08 .25
41 Juha Jarvenpaa .05 .15
42 Juha Lampinen .05 .15
43 Janne Siva .05 .15
44 Timo Peltomaa .08 .25
45 Mika Arvaja .05 .15
46 Esa Tommila .05 .15
47 Kristian Taubert .05 .15
48 Jarkko Glad .05 .15
49 Hannu Mattila .05 .15
50 Pasi Maattanen .05 .15
51 Petri Sullamaa .05 .15
52 Boris Majorov .05 .15
53 Markus Ketterer .40 1.00
54 Waltteri Immonen .05 .15
55 Mika Stromberg .08 .25
56 Keijo Sailynoja .05 .15
57 Otakar Janecky .08 .25
58 Jiri Sejba .08 .25
59 Kari Martikainen .05 .15
60 Erik Hamalainen .08 .25
61 Timo Norppa .05 .15
62 Pekka Jarvela .05 .15
63 Juha Salo .05 .15
64 Heikki Riihijarvi .05 .15
65 Ari Salo .05 .15
66 Hannu Jarvenpaa .20 .50
67 Jali Wahlsten .05 .15
68 Juha Jokiharju .05 .15
69 Hannu Aravirta .05 .15
70 Ari-Pekka Siekkinen .08 .25
71 Jarmo Jokilahti .05 .15
72 Harri Laurila .05 .15
73 Juha Riihijarvi .20 .50
74 Jari Lindroos .08 .25
75 Marko Virtanen .05 .15
76 Jari Munck .05 .15
77 Markku Heikkinen .05 .15
78 Lasse Nieminen .05 .15
79 Tero Lehikoinen .05 .15
80 Ari Haanpaa .05 .15
81 Jarmo Rantanen .05 .15
82 Veli-Pekka Hard .05 .15
83 Mika Paananen .05 .15
84 Joni Lius .08 .25
85 Risto Kurkinen .05 .15
86 Juha Junno .05 .15
87 Pasi Kuivalainen .20 .50
88 Jari Jarvinen .05 .15
89 Vesa Salo .05 .15
90 Vesa Karjalainen .05 .15
91 Darius Rusnak .05 .15
92 Arto Sirvio .05 .15
93 Vesa Ruotsalainen .05 .15
94 Juha Tuohimaa .05 .15
95 Jari Hamalainen .05 .15
96 Pekka Tirkkonen .05 .15
97 Jari Laukkanen .05 .15
98 Antti Tuomenoksa .05 .15
99 Janne Leppanen .05 .15
100 Marko Jantunen .08 .25
101 Dusan Pasek .40 1.00
102 Sami Kapanen 1.25 3.00
103 Martti Merra .05 .15
104 Sami Aikaa .05 .15
105 Teemu Sillanpaa .05 .15
106 Sami Nuutinen .05 .15
107 Jere Lehtinen 3.00 8.00
108 Jan Langbacka .05 .15
109 Tero Lehtera .08 .25
110 Robert Salo .05 .15
111 Jimi Helin .05 .15
112 Sami Kokko .05 .15
113 Riku Kuusisto .05 .15
114 Markku Tiinus .05 .15
115 Pasi Heinisto .05 .15
116 Petri Pulkkinen .05 .15
117 Tom Laaksonen .05 .15
118 Jarmo Muukkonen .05 .15
119 Petro Koivunen .08 .25
120 Matti Keinonen .05 .15
121 Petr Briza .40 1.00
122 Timo Kulonen .05 .15
123 Allan Measures .05 .15
124 Harri Suvanto .05 .15
125 Timo Saarikoski .05 .15
126 Mika Alatalo .75 2.00
127 Kari-Pekka Friman .05 .15
128 Jarmo Kuusisto .05 .15
129 Mika Valila .05 .15
130 Jari Torkki .05 .15
131 Pekka Peltola .05 .15
132 Pasi Huura .05 .15
133 Matti Forss .05 .15
134 Kalle Sahlstedt .08 .25
135 Tommi Pullola .05 .15
136 Tero Arkiomaa .05 .15
137 Esko Nokelainen .05 .15
138 Petri Engman .05 .15
139 Timo Kahelin .05 .15
140 Pasi Ruponen .05 .15
141 Petteri Sihvonen .05 .15
142 Toni Sihvonen .05 .15
143 Sami Wikstrom .05 .15
144 Erik Kakko .05 .15
145 Jari Parviainen .05 .15
146 Jonni Vauhkonen .08 .25
147 Jari Kauppila .05 .15
148 Erkki Makela .05 .15
149 Jarkko Hamalainen .05 .15
150 Petri Koski .05 .15
151 Sami Lekkerimaki .05 .15
152 Toni Koivunen .05 .15
153 Jani Uski .05 .15
154 Pertti Hasanen .05 .15
155 Jaromir Sindel .20 .50
156 Tommi Haapsaari .05 .15
157 Jukka Marttila .05 .15
158 Jarmo Kekalainen .20 .50
159 Tommi Pohja .05 .15
160 Pauli Jarvinen .05 .15
161 Timo Jutila .20 .50
162 Janne Gronvall .08 .25
163 Jussi-Pekka Jarvinen .05 .15
164 Kari Heikkinen .05 .15
165 Marko Ek .05 .15
166 Veli-Pekka Kautonen .05 .15
167 Pekka Laksola .05 .15
168 Pasi Forsberg .05 .15
169 Marko Lapinkoski .05 .15
170 Mikko Peltola .05 .15
171 Vladimir Jursinov .05 .15
172 Jouni Rokama .08 .25
173 Mikko Haapakoski .05 .15
174 Kari Harila .05 .15
175 Kari Kanervo .05 .15
176 Esa Keskinen .20 .50
177 Saku Koivu 6.00 15.00
178 Jouko Narvanmaa .05 .15
179 Alexander Smirnov .05 .15
180 Reijo Mikkolainen .05 .15
181 Mikko Makela .30 .75
182 Raimo Summanen .20 .50
183 Hannu Virta .08 .25
184 Jukka Virtanen .05 .15
185 German Titov .20 .50
186 Jukka Vilander .05 .15
187 Ari Vuori .05 .15
188 Vasili Tikhonov .20 .50
189 Kari Takko .40 1.00
190 Sami Saarinen .05 .15

191 Marko Sten .05 .15
192 Arto Javanainen .05 .15
193 Janne Virtanen .05 .15
194 Arto Heiskanen .05 .15
195 Jouni Vento .05 .15
196 Olli Kaski .05 .15
197 Vyacheslav Fandul .05 .15
198 Jokke Hainanen .05 .15
199 Petri Varis .20 .50
200 Harry Nikander .05 .15
201 Jarno Miikkulainen .05 .15
202 Jari Korpisalo .08 .25
203 Rauli Raitanen .05 .15
204 Jari Levonen .05 .15

1993-94 Finnish Jyvas-Hyva Stickers

COMPLETE SET (359) 24.00 60.00
1 HIFK Team Photo .02 .10
2 HIFK Team Photo .02 .10
3 HIFK Team Photo .02 .10
4 HIFK Team Photo .02 .10
5 HIFK Team Photo .02 .10
6 HIFK Team Photo .02 .10
7 HIFK Team Photo .02 .10
8 HIFK Team Photo .02 .10
9 HIFK Team Photo .02 .10
10 HIFK Team Photo .02 .10
11 HIFK Team Photo .02 .10
12 HIFK Team Photo .02 .10
13 Harri Rindell .05 .15
14 Sakari Lindfors .40 1.00
15 Simo Saarinen .05 .15
16 Pertti Lehtonen .05 .15
17 Jari Laukkanen .05 .15
18 Valeri Krykov .05 .15
19 Iiro Jarvi .20 .50
20 Jari Munck .05 .15
21 Pasi Sormunen .05 .15
22 Pekka Peltola .05 .15
23 Teppo Kivela .05 .15
24 Pekka Tuomisto .05 .15
25 Kai Tervonen .05 .15
26 Dan Lambert .20 .50
27 Marco Poulsen .05 .15
28 Ville Peltonen .40 1.00
29 Kim Ahlroos .05 .15
31 HPK Team Photo .02 .10
32 HPK Team Photo .02 .10
33 HPK Team Photo .02 .10
34 HPK Team Photo .02 .10
35 HPK Team Photo .02 .10
36 HPK Team Photo .02 .10
37 HPK Team Photo .02 .10
38 HPK Team Photo .02 .10
39 HPK Team Photo .02 .10
40 HPK Team Photo .02 .10
41 HPK Team Photo .02 .10
42 HPK Team Photo .02 .10
43 Pentti Matikainen .05 .15
44 Kari Rosenberg .08 .25
45 Mikko Myllykoski .05 .15
46 Janne Laukkanen .40 1.00
47 Jarkko Nikander .08 .25
48 Tomas Kapusta .05 .15
49 Mika Lartama .05 .15
50 Niko Marttila .05 .15
51 Jari Haapamaki .05 .15
52 Tommi Varjonen .05 .15
53 Tony Virta .05 .15
54 Marko Palo .08 .25
55 Marko Allen .05 .15
56 Miikka Ruokonen .05 .15
57 Jani Hassinen .05 .15
58 Pasi Kivila .05 .15
59 Markku Piikkila .05 .15
61 Ilves Team Photo .02 .10
62 Ilves Team Photo .02 .10
63 Ilves Team Photo .02 .10
64 Ilves Team Photo .02 .10
65 Ilves Team Photo .02 .10
66 Ilves Team Photo .02 .10
67 Ilves Team Photo .02 .10
68 Ilves Team Photo .02 .10
69 Ilves Team Photo .02 .10
70 Ilves Team Photo .02 .10
71 Ilves Team Photo .02 .10
72 Ilves Team Photo .02 .10
73 Jukka Jalonen .05 .15
74 Jukka Tammi .40 1.00
75 Jani Nikko .08 .25
76 Hannu Henriksson .05 .15
77 Juha Jarvenpaa .05 .15
78 Hannu Mattila .05 .15
79 Timo Peltomaa .08 .25
80 Jukka Ollila .05 .15
81 Juha-Matti Marijarvi .05 .15
82 Mikko Louvi .08 .25
83 Jarno Peltonen .05 .15
84 Pasi Maattanen .05 .15
85 Juha Lampinen .05 .15
86 Allan Measures .05 .15
87 Janne Seva .05 .15
88 Risto Jalo .05 .15
89 Esa Tommila .05 .15
91 Jokerit Team Photo .02 .10
92 Jokerit Team Photo .02 .10
93 Jokerit Team Photo .02 .10
94 Jokerit Team Photo .02 .10
95 Jokerit Team Photo .02 .10
96 Jokerit Team Photo .02 .10
97 Jokerit Team Photo .02 .10
98 Jokerit Team Photo .02 .10
99 Jokerit Team Photo .02 .10
100 Jokerit Team Photo .02 .10
101 Jokerit Team Photo .02 .10
102 Jokerit Team Photo .02 .10
103 Alpo Suhonen .20 .50
104 Ari Sulander .40 1.00
105 Kari Martikainen .08 .25
106 Erik Hamalainen .08 .25
107 Juha Jokiharju .05 .15
108 Otakar Janecky .08 .25
109 Petri Varis .20 .50
110 Waltteri Immonen .05 .15
111 Mika Stromberg .08 .25
112 Keijo Sailynoja .05 .15
113 Timo Saarikoski .05 .15
114 Juha Ylonen .75 2.00
115 Ari Salo .05 .15
116 Heikki Riihijarvi .05 .15
117 Timo Norppa .05 .15
118 Jali Wahlsten .05 .15
119 Rami Koivisto .05 .15
121 JYP HT Team Photo .02 .10
122 JYP HT Team Photo .02 .10
123 JYP HT Team Photo .02 .10
124 JYP HT Team Photo .02 .10
125 JYP HT Team Photo .02 .10
126 JYP HT Team Photo .02 .10
127 JYP HT Team Photo .02 .10
128 JYP HT Team Photo .02 .10
129 JYP HT Team Photo .02 .10
130 JYP HT Team Photo .02 .10
131 JYP HT Team Photo .02 .10
132 JYP HT Team Photo .02 .10
133 Kari Savolainen .05 .15
134 Ari-Pekka Siekkinen .08 .25
135 Harri Laurila .05 .15
136 Markku Heikkinen .05 .15
137 Jari Lindroos .08 .25
138 Lasse Nieminen .05 .15
139 Risto Kurkinen .05 .15
140 Jarmo Jokilahti .06 .15
141 Veli-Pekka Hard .05 .15
142 Joni Lius .08 .25
143 Jyrki Jokinen .05 .15
144 Mika Arvaja .05 .15
145 Vesa Ponto .05 .15
146 Jarmo Rantanen .05 .15
147 Mika Paananen .05 .15
148 Marko Virtanen .08 .25
149 Marko Ek .05 .15
151 Kalpa Team Photo .02 .10
152 Kalpa Team Photo .02 .10
153 Kalpa Team Photo .02 .10
154 Kalpa Team Photo .02 .10
155 Kalpa Team Photo .02 .10
156 Kalpa Team Photo .02 .10
157 Kalpa Team Photo .02 .10
158 Kalpa Team Photo .02 .10
159 Kalpa Team Photo .02 .10
160 Kalpa Team Photo .02 .10
161 Kalpa Team Photo .02 .10
162 Kalpa Team Photo .02 .10
163 Hannu Kapanen .05 .15
164 Pasi Kuivalainen .08 .25
165 Kimmo Timonen .60 1.50
166 Vesa Salo .05 .15
167 Jani Rautio .05 .15
168 Pekka Tirkkonen .05 .15
169 Dimitri Zinine .05 .15
170 Antti Tuomenoksa .05 .15
171 Jari Jarvinen .05 .15
172 Tuomas Kalliomaki .05 .15
173 Tommi Miettinen .08 .25
174 Sami Kapanen .75 2.00
175 Vesa Ruotsalainen .05 .15
176 Mikko Tavi .05 .15
177 Sami Mettovaara .05 .15
178 Veli-Pekka Pekkarinen .05 .15
179 Arto Sirvio .05 .15
181 Kiekko-Espoo Team Photo .02 .10
182 Kiekko-Espoo Team Photo .02 .10
183 Kiekko-Espoo Team Photo .02 .10
184 Kiekko-Espoo Team Photo .02 .10
185 Kiekko-Espoo Team Photo .02 .10
186 Kiekko-Espoo Team Photo .02 .10
187 Kiekko-Espoo Team Photo .02 .10
188 Kiekko-Espoo Team Photo .02 .10
189 Kiekko-Espoo Team Photo .02 .10
190 Kiekko-Espoo Team Photo .02 .10
191 Kiekko-Espoo Team Photo .02 .10
192 Kiekko-Espoo Team Photo .02 .10
193 Martti Merra .05 .15
194 Timo Maki .05 .15
195 Sami Nuutinen .05 .15
196 Teemu Sillanpaa .05 .15
197 Tero Lehtera .08 .25
198 Jan Langbacka .05 .15
199 Jukka Tiilikainen .05 .15
200 Petri Pulkkinen .05 .15
201 Robert Salo .05 .15
202 Petro Koivunen .08 .25
203 Juha Ikonen .05 .15
204 Mikko Lempiainen .40 1.00
205 Marko Halonen .05 .15
206 Jimi Helin .05 .15
207 Timo Hirvonen .05 .15
208 Mikko Halonen .05 .15
209 Kimmo Maki-Kokkila .05 .15
211 Lukko Team Photo .02 .10
212 Lukko Team Photo .02 .10
213 Lukko Team Photo .02 .10
214 Lukko Team Photo .02 .10
215 Lukko Team Photo .02 .10
216 Lukko Team Photo .02 .10
217 Lukko Team Photo .02 .10
218 Lukko Team Photo .02 .10
219 Lukko Team Photo .02 .10
220 Lukko Team Photo .02 .10
221 Lukko Team Photo .02 .10
222 Lukko Team Photo .02 .10
223 Vaclav Sykora .05 .15
224 Jarmo Myllys .40 1.00
225 Kari-Pekka Friman .05 .15
226 Timo Kulonen .05 .15
227 Pasi Saarela .05 .15
228 Kalle Sahlstedt .08 .25
229 Kimmo Rintanen .20 .50
230 Jarmo Kuusisto .05 .15
231 Tuomas Gronman .08 .25
232 Tero Arkiomaa .05 .15
233 Petr Korinek .08 .25
234 Mika Alatalo .60 1.50
235 Marko Tuulola .05 .15
236 Pasi Huura .05 .15
237 Tommi Pullola .05 .15
238 Mika Valila .05 .15
239 Jari Torkki .05 .15
241 Reipas Lahti Team Photo .02 .10
242 Reipas Lahti Team Photo .02 .10
243 Reipas Lahti Team Photo .02 .10
244 Reipas Lahti Team Photo .02 .10
245 Reipas Lahti Team Photo .02 .10
246 Reipas Lahti Team Photo .02 .10
247 Reipas Lahti Team Photo .02 .10
248 Reipas Lahti Team Photo .02 .10
249 Reipas Lahti Team Photo .02 .10
250 Reipas Lahti Team Photo .02 .10
251 Reipas Lahti Team Photo .02 .10
252 Reipas Lahti Team Photo .02 .10
253 Kari Makinen .05 .15
254 Oldrich Svoboda .05 .15
255 Timo Kahelin .05 .15
256 Pasi Ruponen .05 .15
257 Tommy Kiviaho .05 .15
258 Jari Multanen .05 .15
259 Erkki Makela .05 .15
260 Jari Parviainen .05 .15
261 Petri Koski .05 .15
262 Jouni Vauhkonen .08 .25
263 Toni Koivunen .05 .15
264 Sami Wikstrom .05 .15
265 Jarkko Hamalainen .05 .15
266 Sami Helenius .20 .50
267 Sami Lekkerimaki .05 .15
268 Jari Kauppila .05 .15
269 Jani Uski .05 .15
271 Tappara Team Photo .02 .10
272 Tappara Team Photo .02 .10
273 Tappara Team Photo .02 .10
274 Tappara Team Photo .02 .10
275 Tappara Team Photo .02 .10
276 Tappara Team Photo .02 .10
277 Tappara Team Photo .02 .10
278 Tappara Team Photo .02 .10
279 Tappara Team Photo .02 .10
280 Tappara Team Photo .02 .10
281 Tappara Team Photo .02 .10
282 Tappara Team Photo .02 .10
283 Boris Majorov .05 .15
284 Timo Hankela .05 .15
285 Timo Jutila .20 .50
286 Samuli Rautio .05 .15
287 Ari Haanpaa .05 .15
288 Mikko Peltola .05 .15
289 Pauli Jarvinen .05 .15
290 Pekka Laksola .05 .15
291 Janne Gronvall .08 .25
292 Kari Heikkinen .05 .15
293 Tommi Pohja .05 .15
294 Petri Aaltonen .05 .15
295 Petri Kalteva .05 .15
296 Tommi Haapsaari .05 .15
297 Teemu Numminen .05 .15
298 Pasi Forsberg .05 .15
299 Veli-Pekka Kautonen .05 .15
301 TPS Team Photo .02 .10
302 TPS Team Photo .02 .10
303 TPS Team Photo .02 .10
304 TPS Team Photo .02 .10
305 TPS Team Photo .02 .10
306 TPS Team Photo .02 .10
307 TPS Team Photo .02 .10
308 TPS Team Photo .02 .10
309 TPS Team Photo .02 .10
310 TPS Team Photo .02 .10
311 TPS Team Photo .02 .10
312 TPS Team Photo .02 .10
313 Vladimir Jursinov .05 .15
314 Jouni Rokama .08 .25
315 Hannu Virta .08 .25
316 Erik Kakko .05 .15
317 Jukka Vilander .05 .15
318 Esa Keskinen .20 .50
319 Ari Vuori .05 .15
320 Jouko Narvanmaa .05 .15
321 Marko Kiprusoff .08 .25
322 Jere Lehtinen 2.00 5.00
323 Saku Koivu 4.00 10.00
324 Marko Jantunen .08 .25
325 Kari Harila .05 .15
326 Alexander Smirnov .05 .15
327 Toni Sihvonen .05 .15
328 Harri Sillgren .05 .15
329 Kai Nurminen .40 1.00
331 Assat Team Photo .02 .10
332 Assat Team Photo .02 .10
333 Assat Team Photo .02 .10
334 Assat Team Photo .02 .10
335 Assat Team Photo .02 .10
336 Assat Team Photo .02 .10
337 Assat Team Photo .02 .10
338 Assat Team Photo .02 .10
339 Assat Team Photo .02 .10
340 Assat Team Photo .02 .10
341 Assat Team Photo .02 .10
342 Assat Team Photo .02 .10
343 Veli-Pekka Ketola .08 .25
344 Kari Takko .40 1.00
345 Olli Kaski .05 .15
346 Karri Kivi .05 .15
347 Arto Heiskanen .05 .15
348 Janne Virtanen .05 .15
349 Mikael Kotkaniemi .05 .15
350 Stanislav Meciar .05 .15
351 Jarmo Miikkulainen .05 .15
352 Jokke Heinanen .05 .15
353 Vjatseslav Fandul .08 .25
354 Ari Saarinen .05 .15
355 Jouni Vento .05 .15
356 Arto Javanainen .05 .15
357 Jari Korpisalo .08 .25
358 Rauli Raitanen .05 .15
359 Jari Levonen .05 .15
NNO Binder 4.00 10.00

1993-94 Finnish SISU

COMPLETE SET (396) 20.00 50.00
1 Jokerit Team Card .08 .25
2 Alpo Suhonen .20 .50
3 Ari Sulander .40 1.00
4 Marko Rantanen .05 .15
5 Ari Salo .02 .10
6 Kalle Koskinen .05 .15
7 Sebastian Sulku .02 .10
8 Waltteri Immonen .05 .15
9 Mika Stromberg .08 .25
10 Heikki Riihijarvi .02 .10
11 Kari Martikainen .05 .15
12 Erik Hamalainen .08 .25
13 Juha Jokiharju .05 .15
14 Timo Norppa .02 .10
15 Rami Koivisto .02 .10
16 Antti Tormanen .30 .75
17 Keijo Sailynoja .05 .15
18 Jere Keskinen .02 .10
19 Jali Wahlsten .02 .10
20 Mikko Kontilla .02 .10
21 Juha Ylonen .60 1.50
22 Jussi Vienonen ERR wrong photo .02 .10
22B Jussi Vienonen COR .08 .25
23 Petri Varis .20 .50
24 Juha Lind .40 1.00
25 Timo Saarikoski .02 .10
26 Otakar Janecky .08 .25
27 TPS Team Card .05 .15
28 Vladimir Jursinov CO .02 .10
29 Jouni Rokama .05 .15
30 Kimmo Lecklin .02 .10
31 Jouko Narvanmaa .02 .10
32 Petteri Nummelin .05 .15
33 Erik Kakko .02 .10
34 Tom Koivisto .02 .10
35 Marko Kiprusoff .08 .25
36 Kari Harila .02 .10
37 Hannu Virta .08 .25
38 Aki Berg .40 1.00
39 Aleksander Smirnov .02 .10
40 Esa Keskinen .08 .25
41 Saku Koivu 4.00 10.00
42 Jukka Vilander .02 .10
43 Antti Aalto .40 1.00
44 Mika Karapuu ERR wrong photo .02 .10
44B Mika Karapuu COR .08 .25
45 Toni Sihvonen .02 .10
46 Pavel Torgajev .08 .25
47 Jere Lehtinen 1.25 3.00
48 Kai Nurminen .08 .25
49 Harri Sillgren .02 .10
50 Niko Mikkola .02 .10
51 Ari Vuori .02 .10
52 Lasse Pirjeta .02 .10
53 Reijo Mikkolainen .02 .10
54 Marko Jantunen .08 .25
55 Mikko Virolainen ERR wrong photo .02 .10
55B Mikko Virolainen COR .08 .25
56 Tappara Team Card .05 .15
57 Boris Majorov CO .02 .10
58 Jaromir Sindel .08 .25
59 Timo Hankela .02 .10
60 Teemu Kivinen .02 .10
61 Petri Kalteva .02 .10
62 Jari Harjumaki .02 .10
63 Timo Jutila .08 .25
64 Janne Gronvall .08 .25
65 Jari Gronstrand .05 .15
66 Pekka Laksola .02 .10
67 Tommi Haapsaari .02 .10
68 Veli-Pekka Kautonen .02 .10
69 Mikko Peltola .02 .10
70 Kari Heikkinen .02 .10
71 Teemu Numminen .02 .10
72 Jiri Kucera .05 .15
73 Pauli Jarvinen .02 .10
74 Pasi Forsberg .02 .10
75 Tero Toivola .02 .10
76 Ari Haanpaa .05 .15
77 Tommi Pohja .02 .10
78 Samuli Rautio .02 .10
79 Markus Oijennus .02 .10
80 Petri Aaltonen .02 .10
81 HIFK Team Card .05 .15
82 Harri Rindell CO .02 .10
83 Sakari Lindfors .08 .25
84 Mikael Granlund .02 .10
85 Kimmo Hyttinen .02 .10
86 Jere Karalahti .20 .50
87 Dan Lambert .20 .50
88 Simo Saarinen .02 .10
89 Pasi Sormunen .02 .10
90 Tommi Hamalainen .02 .10
91 Pertti Lehtonen .02 .10
92 Jari Munck .02 .10
93 Kai Tervonen .02 .10
94 Kim Ahlroos .02 .10
95 Teppo Kivela .02 .10
96 Darren Boyko .05 .15
97 Pekka Peltola .02 .10
98 Marco Poulsen .02 .10
99 Valeri Krykov .02 .10
100 Jari Laukkanen .02 .10
101 Ville Peltonen .40 1.00
102 Pekka Tuomisto .02 .10
103 Miro Haapaniemi .02 .10
104 Mika Kortelainen .02 .10
105 Marko Ojanen .02 .10
106 Iiro Jarvi .05 .15
107 Ilves Tampere Team Card .05 .15
108 Jukka Jalonen CO .02 .10
109 Jukka Tammi .20 .50
110 Mika Manninen .05 .15
111 Jani Nikko .08 .25
112 Jukka Ollila .02 .10
113 Juha Lampinen .02 .10
114 Hannu Henriksson .02 .10
115 Sami Lehtonen .02 .10
116 Mikko Niemi .02 .10
117 Juha-Matti Marijarvi .02 .10
118 Jarkko Glad .02 .10
119 Allan Measures .02 .10
120 Mikko Luovi .02 .10
121 Risto Jalo .05 .15
122 Juha Jarvenpaa .05 .15
123 Jarno Peltonen .02 .10
124 Matti Kaipainen .02 .10
125 Timo Peltomaa .05 .15
126 Esa Tommila .02 .10
127 Hannu Mattila .02 .10
128 Jari Neuvonen .02 .10
129 Pasi Maattanen .02 .10
130 Juha Hautamaa .02 .10
131 Janne Seva .02 .10
132 Sami Ahlberg .02 .10
133 Jari Virtanen .02 .10
134 JyP HT Team Card .05 .15
135 Kari Savolainen CO .02 .10
136 Ari-Pekka Siekkinen .05 .15
137 Marko Leinonen .02 .10
138 Jan Latvala .02 .10
139 Markku Heikkinen .02 .10
140 Jarmo Jokilahti .02 .10
141 Veli-Pekka Hard .02 .10
142 Kalle Koskinen .02 .10
143 Vesa Ponto .02 .10
144 Petri Kujala .02 .10
145 Jarmo Rantanen .02 .10
146 Harri Laurila .02 .10
147 Lasse Nieminen .02 .10
148 Mika Paananen .02 .10
149 Mika Arvaja .02 .10
150 Marko Virtanen .05 .15
151 Marko Ek .02 .10
152 Joni Lius .02 .10
153 Teemu Kohvakka .02 .10
154 Jari Lindroos .05 .15
155 Marko Kupari .02 .10
156 Markku Ikonen .02 .10
157 Jyrki Jokinen .02 .10
158 Risto Kurkinen .02 .10
159 KalPa Team Card .05 .15
160 Hannu Kapanen CO .02 .10
161 Pasi Kuivalainen .05 .15
162 Kimmo Kapanen .02 .10
163 Kimmo Timonen .40 1.00
164 Jari Jarvinen .02 .10
165 Mikko Tavi .02 .10
166 Jermu Pisto .02 .10
167 Antti Tuomenoksa .02 .10
168 Vesa Ruotsalainen .02 .10
169 Vesa Salo .02 .10
170 Veli-Pekka Pekkarinen .02 .10
171 Tuomas Kalliomaki .02 .10
172 Dimitri Zinine .02 .10
173 Jani Rautio .02 .10
173B Marko Virtanen ERR incorrect numbering .08 .25
174 Janne Kekalainen .02 .10
174B Marko Ek ERR incorrect numbering .08 .25
175 Arto Sirvio .02 .10
176 Sami Mettovaara .02 .10
177 Sami Simonen .02 .10
178 Pekka Tirkkonen .05 .15
179 Sami Kapanen .75 2.00
180 Jussi Tarvainen .02 .10
181 Lukko Team Card .05 .15
182 Vaclav Sykora .02 .10
183 Jarmo Myllys .40 1.00
183B Pasi Kujala ERR incorrect numbering .08 .25
184 Kimmo Vesa .02 .10
185 Mika Yli-Maenpaa .05 .15
185B Jarmo Rantanen ERR incorrect numbering .08 .25
186 Jarmo Kuusisto .02 .10
187 Marko Tuulola .02 .10
188 Tuomas Gronman .08 .25
189 Timo Kulonen .02 .10
189B Mika Arvaja ERR incorrect numbering .08 .25
190 Kari-Pekka Friman VAR name on front smaller font .02 .10
190B Kari-Pekka Friman VAR name on front larger font .08 .25
191 Pasi Huura .05 .15
192 Harri Suvanto .02 .10
193 Kamil Kastak .02 .10
194 Jari Torkki .02 .10
195 Kalle Sahlstedt .05 .15
196 Tommi Pullola .02 .10
197 Mika Valila .02 .10
198 Tero Arkiomaa .02 .10
199 Pasi Saarela .02 .10
200 Matti Forss .02 .10
201 Jussi Kiuru ERR wrong photo .02 .10
201B Jussi Kiuru COR .08 .25
202 Mika Alatalo .75 2.00
203 Kimmo Rintanen .08 .25
204 Petri Latti ERR wrong photo .02 .10
204B Petri Latti COR .08 .25
205 Petr Korinek .05 .15
206 Assat Team Card .05 .15
207 Veli-Pekka Ketola CO .05 .15
208 Kari Takko .08 .25
209 Timo Jarvinen .02 .10
210 Marko Sten .02 .10
211 Pasi Peltonen .02 .10
212 Olli Kaski .02 .10
213 Jarno Miikkulainen .02 .10
214 Jouni Vento .02 .10
215 Karri Kivi .05 .15
215B HIFK Team Card ERR incorrect numbering .02 .10
215C Jouni Vento ERR incorrect numbering .08 .25
216 Stanislav Meciar .05 .15
217 Nemo Nokkosmaki .02 .10
218 Arto Javanainen .02 .10
219 Janne Virtanen .02 .10
220 Vjatseslav Fandul .05 .15
221 Jari Levonen .02 .10
222 Jarno Levonen .02 .10
223 Jari Korpisalo .08 .25
224 Jokke Heinanen .02 .10
225 Harri Lonnberg .02 .10
226 Ari Saarinen .02 .10
227 Kari Syvasalmi .02 .10
228 Jarno Makela .02 .10
229 Rauli Raitanen .02 .10
230 Arto Heiskanen .02 .10
231 Mikael Kotkaniemi .02 .10
232 HPK Team Card .05 .15
233 Pentti Matikainen .02 .10
234 Kari Rosenberg .05 .15
235 Petri Vilen .02 .10
236 Marko Allen .02 .10
237 Mikko Myllykoski .02 .10
238 Kim Vahanen .02 .10
239 Janne Laukkanen .30 .75
240 Jari Haapamaki .02 .10
241 Niko Marttila .02 .10
242 Esa Saleri .02 .10
243 Toni Virta .02 .10
244 Marko Palo .05 .15
245 Markku Piikkila .02 .10
246 Jani Hassinen .02 .10
247 Jarkko Nikander .05 .15
248 Pasi Kivila .02 .10
249 Mika Lartama .02 .10
250 Tomas Kapusta .05 .15
251 Tommi Varjonen .02 .10
252 Teemu Tamminen .02 .10
253 Jukka Seppo .05 .15
254 Kiekko-Espoo Team Card .05 .15
255 Martti Merra .02 .10
256 Scott Brower .20 .50
257 Timo Maki .02 .10
258 Petri Pulkkinen .02 .10
259 Robert Salo .02 .10
260 Sami Nuutinen .02 .10
261 Teemu Sillanpaa .02 .10
262 Marko Halonen .02 .10
263 Jimi Helin .02 .10
264 Kari Haakana .02 .10
265 Jukka Tiilikainen .02 .10
266 Jan Langbacka .02 .10
267 Jarmo Muukkonen .02 .10
268 Timo Hirvonen .05 .15
269 Pasi Heinisto .05 .15
270 Kimmo Maki-Kokkila .02 .10
271 Mikko Lempiainen .02 .10
272 Tero Lehtera .05 .15
273 Hannu Jarvenpaa .05 .15
274 Riku Kuusisto .02 .10
275 Mikko Halonen .02 .10
276 Markku Takala .02 .10
277 Petro Koivunen .05 .15
278 Reipas Lahti Team Card .05 .15
279 Kari Makinen CO .05 .15
280 Oldrich Svoboda .02 .10
281 Pekka Ilmivalta .02 .10
282 Matti Vuorio .02 .10
283 Jari Parviainen .02 .10
284 Timo Kahelin .02 .10
285 Ville Skinnari .02 .10
286 Petri Koski .02 .10
287 Jarkko Hamalainen .02 .10
288 Pasi Ruponen .02 .10
289 Oldrich Valek .02 .10
290 Juha Nurminen .02 .10
291 Erkki Laine .02 .10
292 Sami Lekkerimaki .02 .10
293 Tommy Kiviaho .02 .10
293B Ville Skinnari ERR incorrect numbering .08 .25
294 Jyrki Poikolainen .02 .10
295 Sami Wikstrom .02 .10
296 Jonni Vauhkonen .08 .25
297 Erkki Laine .02 .10
298 Jani Uski .02 .10
299 Jari Multanen .02 .10
300 Toni Koivunen .02 .10
301 Runkosarjan 1 .02 .10
302 Runkosarjan 2 .02 .10
303 Runkosarjan 3 .02 .10
304 Runkosarjan 4 .02 .10
305 Runkosarjan 5 .02 .10
306 Runkosarjan 6 .02 .10
307 Runkosarjan 7 .02 .10
308 Runkosarjan 8 .02 .10
309 Runkosarjan 9 .02 .10
310 Runkosarjan 10 .02 .10
311 Runkosarjan 11 .02 .10
312 Runkosarjan 12 .02 .10
313 Runkosarjan 13 .02 .10
314 Runkosarjan 14 .02 .10
315 Runkosarjan 15 .02 .10
316 Runkosarjan 16 .02 .10
317 Runkosarjan 17 .02 .10
318 Runkosarjan 18 .02 .10
319 Runkosarjan 19 .02 .10
320 Runkosarjan 20 .02 .10
321 Runkosarjan 21 .02 .10
322 Runkosarjan 22 .02 .10
323 Runkosarjan 23 .02 .10
324 Runkosarjan 24 .02 .10
325 Runkosarjan 25 .02 .10
326 Runkosarjan 26 .02 .10
327 Runkosarjan 27 .02 .10
328 Runkosarjan 28 .02 .10
329 Runkosarjan 29 .02 .10
330 Runkosarjan 30 .02 .10
331 Runkosarjan 31 .02 .10
332 Runkosarjan 32 .02 .10
333 Runkosarjan 33 .02 .10
334 Runkosarjan 34 .02 .10
335 Runkosarjan 35 .02 .10
336 Runkosarjan 36 .02 .10
337 Runkosarjan 37 .02 .10
338 Runkosarjan 38 .02 .10
339 Runkosarjan 39 .02 .10
340 Runkosarjan 40 .02 .10
341 Runkosarjan 41 .02 .10
342 Runkosarjan 42 .02 .10
343 Runkosarjan 43 .02 .10
344 Runkosarjan 44 .02 .10
345 Paikallisottelut (HIFK/ .02 .10
346 Paikallisottelut (Lukko .02 .10
347 Paikallisottelut (HPK
348 Paikallisottelut (JyP H .02 .10
349 Puolivaliera (HPK Lukko) .02 .10
350 Puolivaliera (Jokerit A .02 .10
351 Puolivaliera (Jokerit Assat) .02 .10
352 Puolivaliera (TPS Ilves .02 .10
353 Valiera (HPK JyP HT) .02 .10
354 Valiera (TPS Assat) .02 .10
355 Pronssiottelu .02 .10
356 1.Finaali (TPS 9& HPK 3 .02 .10
357 2. Finaali .02 .10
358 3.Finaali (TPS 3& HPK 2 .02 .10
360 Esa Keskinen LL .08 .25
361 Tomas Kapusta LL .02 .10
362 Erik Hamalainen LL .05 .15
363 Brian Tutt LL .02 .10
364 Otakar Janecky LL ERR .05 .15
364B Otakar Janecky LL COR .08 .25
365 Ville Peltonen LL .40 1.00
366 Petr Briza AS .40 1.00
367 Janne Laukkanen AS .20 .50
368 Timo Jutila AS .08 .25
369 Juha Riihijarvi AS ERR card back from 384 .08 .25
369B Juha Riihijarvi AS COR .20 .50
370 Esa Keskinen AS ERR card back from 372 .08 .25
371 Jarkko Varvio AS .05 .15
372 Esa Keskinen AW Fair Pl .08 .25
372B Esa Keskinen AW COR .20 .50
373 Vladimir Jursinov AW Be .02 .10
374 Erik Hamalainen AW Best .05 .15
375 Timo Lehkonen AW Best G .05 .15
376 German Titov AW Most Pl .08 .25
377 Raimo Summanen AW .05 .15
378 Mikko Haapakoski AW Bes .02 .10
379 Marko Palo AW .02 .10
380 Seppo Makela AW .02 .10
381 TPS, Turku Team Card .02 .10
382 HPK Hameenlinna Hopeami .02 .10
383 JyP HT Jyvaskyla .02 .10
384 Juha Riihijarvi MVP ERR card back from 369 .05 .15
384B Juha Riihijarvi MVP COR .08 .25
385 Jukka Tammi .02 .10
386 Kari Jalonen .05 .15
387 Matti Forss .02 .10
388 Arto Javanainen .02 .10
389 Saku Koivu/1993 NHL Dra 4.00 10.00
390 Janne Niinimaa/1993 NHL .40 1.00
391 Ville Peltonen/1993 NHL .40 1.00
392 Jonni Vauhkonen .08 .25
393 Petri Varis/1993 NHL Dr .20 .50
394 Antti Aalto/1993 NHL Dr .40 1.00
395 Jere Karalahti/1993 NHL .20 .50
396 Kimmo Timonen/1993 NHL .40 1.00

1993-94 Finnish SISU Autographs

COMPLETE SET (12) 90.00 150.00
8 Waltteri Immonen 4.00 10.00
41 Saku Koivu 20.00 50.00
73 Pauli Jarvinen 4.00 10.00
83 Sakari Lindfors 10.00 25.00
121 Risto Jalo 4.00 10.00
173 Marko Virtanen 4.00 10.00
178 Pekka Tirkkonen 6.00 15.00
203 Kimmo Rintanen 4.00 10.00
223 Jari Korpisalo 4.00 10.00
239 Janne Laukkanen 6.00 15.00
260 Sami Nuutinen 4.00 10.00
296 Jonni Vauhkonen 4.00 10.00

1993-94 Finnish SISU Promos

COMPLETE SET (12) 4.00 125.00
NNO Timo Peltomaa 4.00 10.00
NNO Jari Lindroos 4.00 10.00
NNO Petri Skriko 6.00 15.00
NNO Mika Alatalo 6.00 15.00
NNO Timo Jutila 4.00 10.00
NNO Pasi Ruponen 4.00 10.00
NNO German Titov 4.00 10.00
NNO Rauli Raitanen 4.00 10.00
NNO Simo Saarinen 4.00 10.00
NNO Rami Koivisto 4.00 10.00
NNO Janne Laukkanen 6.00 15.00
NNO Pekka Tirkkonen 6.00 15.00

1994 Finnish Jaa Kiekko

COMPLETE SET (360) 30.00 50.00
1 Jarmo Myllys .08 .25
2 Pasi Kuivalainen .02 .10
3 Jukka Tammi .07 .20
4 Markus Ketterer .08 .25
5 Timo Jutila .05 .15
6 Mikko Haapakoski .02 .10
7 Marko Tuulola .02 .10
8 Jyrki Lumme .08 .25
9 Kari Harila .02 .10
10 Teppo Numminen .08 .25
11 Pasi Sormunen .02 .10
12 Petteri Nummelin .02 .10
13 Harri Laurila .02 .10
14 Mika Stromberg .05 .15
15 Ville Siren .05 .15
16 Pekka Laksola .02 .10
17 Janne Laukkanen .07 .20
18 Marko Kiprusoff .05 .15
19 Waltteri Immonen .05 .15
20 Teemu Selanne .60 1.50
21 Mika Alatalo .08 .25
22 Vesa Viitakoski .05 .15
23 Tero Arkiomaa .02 .10
24 Jari Kurri .20 .50

25 Pekka Tirkkonen .02 .10
26 Jarmo Kekalainen .05 .15
27 Saku Koivu .40 1.00
28 Antti Tormanen .07 .20
29 Jere Lehtinen .20 .50
30 Raimo Helminen .05 .15
31 Mikko Makela .05 .15
32 Marko Jantunen .05 .15
33 Ville Peltonen .08 .25
34 Esa Tikkanen .08 .25
35 Janne Ojanen .05 .15
36 Mika Nieminen .02 .10
37 Marko Palo .02 .10
38 Rauli Raitanen .02 .10
39 Sami Kapanen .40 1.00
40 Juha Riihijarvi .02 .10
41 Esa Keskinen .02 .10
42 Jari Korpisalo .02 .10
43 Christian Ruuttu .05 .15
44 Jarkko Varvio .05 .15
45 Sami Wahlsten .02 .10
46 Petri Varis .08 .25
47 Timo Saarikoski .02 .10
48 Timo Norppa .02 .10
49 Marko Virtanen .02 .10
50 Pauli Jarvinen .02 .10
51 Hakan Algotsson .07 .20
52 Tommy Soderstrom .08 .25
53 Rolf Ridderwall .05 .15
54 Tomas Jonsson .05 .15
55 Christian Due-Boje .02 .10
56 Peter Popovic .05 .15
57 Fredrik Stillman .02 .10
58 Magnus Svensson .07 .20
59 Fredrik Nilsson .02 .10
60 Tommy Albelin .05 .15
61 Joacim Esbjors .02 .10
62 Roger Johansson .05 .15
63 Stefan Nilsson .02 .10
64 Hakan Loob .08 .25
65 Peter Ottosson .02 .10
66 Daniel Rydmark .02 .10
67 Mikael Renberg .08 .25
68 Patrik Juhlin .07 .20
69 Thomas Rundqvist .05 .15
70 Andreas Johansson .08 .25
71 Stefan Ornskog .05 .15
72 Nillas Eriksson .02 .10
73 Jonas Bergqvist .08 .25
74 Mats Sundin .40 1.00
75 Peter Forsberg .75 2.00
76 Stefan Elvenes .02 .10
77 Tomas Forslund .05 .15
78 Patric Kjellberg .08 .25
79 Bill Ranford .20 .50
80 Corey Hirsch .08 .25
81 Larry Murphy .08 .25
82 Mark Tinordi .05 .15
83 Scott Stevens .20 .50
84 Al Macinnis .40 1.00
85 Steve Smith .08 .25
86 Paul Coffey .40 1.00
87 Eric Desjardins .08 .25
88 Eric Lindros .60 1.50
89 Dale Hawerchuk .20 .50
90 Steve Larmer .08 .25
91 Brent Sutter .07 .20
92 Luc Robitaille .40 1.00
93 Shayne Corson .08 .25
94 Mark Messier .60 1.50
95 Rick Tocchet .20 .50
96 Theo Fleury .40 1.00
97 Dirk Graham .08 .25
98 Russ Courtnall .08 .25
99 Wayne Gretzky 2.00 5.00
100 Brendan Shanahan .60 1.50
101 Mark Recchi .40 1.00
102 David Harlock .05 .15
103 Craig Woodcroft .02 .10
104 Paul Kariya .75 2.00
105 Jason Marshall .05 .15
106 Brett Lindros .08 .25
107 Mike Richter .40 1.00
108 Mike Dunham .20 .50
109 Craig Wolanin .05 .15
110 Jim Johnson .05 .15
111 Chris Chelios .40 1.00
112 Eric Weinrich .05 .15
113 Brian Leetch .40 1.00
114 Kevin Hatcher .08 .25
115 Ed Olczyk .08 .25
116 Kevin Miller .07 .20
117 Doug Brown .02 .10
118 Joe Mullen .08 .25
119 Craig Janney .08 .25
120 Pat LaFontaine .20 .50
121 Gary Suter .08 .25
122 Jeremy Roenick .40 1.00
123 Brett Hull .60 1.50
124 Joel Otto .08 .25
125 Mike Modano .60 1.50
126 Tony Granato .08 .25
127 Dave Christian .07 .20
128 Brian Mullen .05 .15
129 Chris Ferraro .07 .20
130 John Lilley .05 .15
131 Jeff Lazaro .05 .15
132 Peter Ferraro .08 .25
133 Brian Rolston .08 .25
134 David Roberts .05 .15
135 Nikolai Khabibulin .40 1.00
136 Andrei Trefilov .08 .25
137 Vladimir Malakhov .08 .25
138 Alexander Karpovtsev .07 .20
139 Alexander Kmirnov .02 .10
140 Sergei Zubov .08 .25
141 Sergei Seljanin .02 .10
142 Sergei Shendelev .02 .10
143 Alexei Kasatonov .07 .20
144 Sergei Sorokin .02 .10
145 Vjatseslav Bykov .02 .10
146 Sergei Fedorov .60 1.50
147 Alexei Yashin .08 .25
148 Vjatseslav Butsajev .05 .15
149 Konstantin Astrahantsev .02 .10
150 Alexei Zhamnov .08 .25
151 Dimitri Frolov .02 .10
152 Slava Kozlov .08 .25
153 Sergei Pushkov .02 .10
154 Andrei Khomutov .02 .10
155 Sergei Makarov .08 .25
156 Igor Larionov .20 .50
157 Valeri Kamenski .08 .25
158 Alexander Semak .05 .15
159 Alexei Gusarov .05 .15
160 Andrei Lomakin .05 .15
161 Igor Korolev .05 .15
162 Ravil Haidarov .02 .10
163 Dominik Hasek .60 1.50
164 Oldrich Svoboda .02 .10
165 Petr Briza .08 .25
166 Leo Gudas .02 .10
167 Kamil Prachar .02 .10
168 Richard Smehlik .07 .20
169 Frantisek Kucera .05 .15
170 Drahomir Kadlec .05 .15
171 Jan Vopat .02 .10
172 Frantisek Prochazka .02 .10
173 Antonin Stavjana .02 .10
174 Bedrich Scerban .02 .10
175 Kamil Kastak .02 .10
176 Josef Beranek .08 .25
177 Martin Rucinsky .08 .25
178 Michal Pivonka .08 .25
179 Tomas Jelinek .02 .10
180 Richard Zemlicka .02 .10
181 Robert Kron .07 .20
182 Jiri Slegr .08 .25
183 Jaromir Jagr .75 2.00
184 Robert Reichel .08 .25
185 David Vyborny .05 .15
186 Robert Lang .08 .25
187 Petr Rosol .02 .10
188 Otakar Janecky .05 .15
189 Martin Hostak .02 .10
190 Jiri Kucera .05 .15
191 Eduard Hartmann .08 .25
192 Lubomir Sekeras .02 .10
193 Marian Smerciak .02 .10
194 Jan Varholik .02 .10
195 Lubomir Rybovic .02 .10
196 Miroslav Marcinko .02 .10
197 Stanislav Medrik .02 .10
198 Zdeno Ciger .07 .20
199 Jergus Baca .05 .15
200 Peter Stastny .08 .25
201 Peter Veselovsky .02 .10
202 Anton Stastny .07 .20
203 Lubomir Kolnik .05 .15
204 Roman Kontsek .02 .10
205 Rene Pucher .02 .10
206 Slavomir Ilvasky .02 .10
207 Zigmund Palffy .40 1.00
208 Vlastimil Plavucha .02 .10
209 Dusan Pohorelec .02 .10
210 Robert Petrovicky .05 .15
211 Michel Valliere .02 .10
212 Petri Ylonen .08 .25
213 Jean-Philippe Lemoine .02 .10
214 Christophe Moyon .02 .10
215 Denis Perez .02 .10
216 Bruno Saunier .02 .10
217 Stephane Botteri .02 .10
218 Michel Breistroff .02 .10
219 Geralf Guennelon .02 .10
220 Serge Poudrier .02 .10
221 Benjamin Agnel .02 .10
222 Stephane Arcangeloni .02 .10
223 Pierrick Maia .02 .10
224 Antoine Richer .02 .10
225 Christoph Ville .02 .10
226 Michael Babin .02 .10
227 Lionel Orsolini .02 .10
228 Stephane Barin .02 .10
229 Arnaud Briand .02 .10
230 Franck Pajonkowski .07 .20
231 Claus Dalpiaz .07 .20
232 Brian Stankiewicz .02 .10
233 Rob Doyle .02 .10
234 Michael Guntner .02 .10
235 Martin Krainz .02 .10
236 Michael Shea .02 .10
237 Martin Ulrich .02 .10
238 Erich Solderer .02 .10
239 Wayne Groulx .02 .10
240 Andreas Puschnig .02 .10
241 Dieter Kalt .02 .10
242 Gerhard Puschnik .02 .10
243 Werner Kerth .02 .10
244 Richard Nasheim .02 .10
245 Arno Maier .02 .10
246 Mario Schaden .02 .10
247 Reinhard Lampert .02 .10
248 Karl Heinzle .02 .10
249 Wolfgang Kromp .02 .10
250 Marty Dallman .02 .10
251 Jim Marthinsen .07 .20
252 Rob Schistad .02 .10
253 Tom Cato Andersen .02 .10
254 Anders Myrvold .07 .20
255 Svein Enok Norstebo .02 .10
256 Tommy Jakobsen .02 .10
257 Pal Kristiansen .02 .10
258 Petter Salsten .02 .10
259 Ole Eskild Dahlstrom .02 .10
260 Morten Finstad .02 .10
261 Espen Knutsen .08 .25
262 Erik Kristiansen .02 .10
263 Geir Hoff .02 .10
264 Roy Johansen .02 .10
265 Trond Magnussen .02 .10
266 Marius Rath .02 .10
267 Vegar Barlie .02 .10
268 Arne Billkvam .02 .10
269 Tom Johansen .02 .10
270 Petter Thoresen .02 .10
271 Klaus Merk .08 .25
272 Josef Heiss .07 .20
273 Rikhard Amann .02 .10
274 Torsten Kienass .02 .10
275 Mirco Ludemann .02 .10
276 Jason Meyer .02 .10
277 Uli Hiemer .02 .10
278 Karsten Mende .02 .10
279 Andreas Niederberger .02 .10
280 Thomas Brandl .02 .10
281 Benoit Doucet .05 .15
282 Robert Hock .02 .10
283 Georg Franz .02 .10
284 Ernst Kopf, Jr. .02 .10
285 Reemt Pyka .05 .15
286 Jurgen Rumrich .02 .10
287 Dieter Hegen .02 .10
288 Raimund Hilger .02 .10
289 Thomas Schinko .02 .10
290 Leo Stefan .02 .10
291 David Delfino .07 .20
292 Elmar Parth .02 .10
293 Luigi Da Corte .02 .10
294 Phil De Gaetano .02 .10
295 Ralph Di Fiore .02 .10
296 Giorgio Comploi .02 .10
297 Alexander Thaler .02 .10
298 Giovanni Marchetti .02 .10
299 Gaetano Orlando .05 .15
300 Frank Di Muzio .02 .10
301 Giuseppe Foglietta .02 .10
302 Stefano Figliuzzi .02 .10
303 John Vecchiarelli .02 .10
304 Maurizio Mansi .02 .10
305 Santino Pellegrino .02 .10
306 Lino De Toni .02 .10
307 Mario Chitarroni .02 .10
308 Bruno Zarillo .02 .10
309 Armando Chelodi .02 .10
310 Carmine Vani .02 .10
311 Martin McKay .02 .10
312 Scott O'Connor .02 .10
313 John McCrone .02 .10
314 Stephen Cooper .02 .10
315 Mike O'Connor .02 .10
316 Chris Kelland .02 .10
317 Graham Waghorn .02 .10
318 Nicky Chinn .02 .10
319 Damian Smith .02 .10
320 Tim Cranston .02 .10
321 Scott Morrisson .02 .10
322 Antony Johnson .02 .10
323 Tony Hand .05 .15
324 Kevin Conway .02 .10
325 Rick Fera .02 .10
326 Doug McEwen .02 .10
327 Scott Neil .02 .10
328 John Iredale .02 .10
329 Iain Robertson .02 .10
330 Ian Cooper .02 .10
331 Bill Ranford DT .08 .25
332 Jarmo Myllys DT .08 .25
333 Dominik Hasek DT .60 1.50
334 Tommy Soderstrom DT .08 .25
335 Teppo Numminen DT .08 .25
336 Mihail Tatarinov DT .05 .15
337 Paul Coffey DT .40 1.00
338 Chris Chelios DT .40 1.00
339 Brian Leetch DT .40 1.00
340 Al MacInnis DT .40 1.00
341 Vladimir Malakhov DT .08 .25
342 Kevin Hatcher DT .08 .25
343 Jiri Slegr DT .05 .15
344 Wayne Gretzky DT 2.00 5.00
345 Teemu Selanne DT .60 1.50
346 Jari Kurri DT .20 .50
347 Brett Hull DT .60 1.50
348 Sergei Fedorov DT .60 1.50
349 Esa Tikkanen DT .08 .25
350 Mark Messier DT .60 1.50
351 Jaromir Jagr DT .75 2.00
352 Jeremy Roenick DT .40 1.00
353 Luc Robitaille DT .40 1.00
354 Tomas Sandstrom DT .08 .25
355 Peter Forsberg DT .75 2.00
356 Alexei Zhamnov DT .08 .25
357 Theo Fleury DT .40 1.00
358 Rick Tocchet DT .20 .50
359 Pat LaFontaine DT .20 .50
360 Eric Lindros DT .60 1.50
NNO Album 4.00 10.00

1994-95 Finnish SISU

COMPLETE SET (400) 20.00 50.00
COMPLETE SERIES 1 (200) 6.00 15.00
COMPLETE SERIES 2 (200) 14.00 35.00
1 Pasi Kuivolainen .07 .20
2 Jere Karalahti .20 .50
3 Markku Heikkinen .02 .10
4 Marko Allen .02 .10
5 Jarmo Kuusisto .02 .10
6 Marko Tuulola .02 .10
7 Marko Kiprusoff .08 .25
8 Vesa Ponto .02 .10
9 Tero Lehtera .07 .20
10 Darren Boyko .02 .10
11 Kari Heikkinen .02 .10
12 Niko Marttila .02 .10
13 Jari Torkki .02 .10
14 Jiri Kucera .07 .20
15 Jari Levonen .02 .10
16 Juha Ikonen .02 .10
17 Joni Lius .02 .10
18 Pekka Tuomisto .02 .10
19 Petri Kokku .02 .10
20 Jere Lehtinen 1.25 3.00
21 Janne Kekalainen .02 .10
22 Ari Haanpaa .02 .10
23 Hannu Jarvenpaa .07 .20
24 Waltteri Immonen .07 .20
25 Jari Lindroos .07 .20
26 Jan Langbacka .02 .10
27 Kari Takko .20 .50
28 Pasi Maattanen .02 .10
29 Jan Latvala .02 .10
30 Arto Heiskanen .02 .10
31 Iiro Jarvi .08 .25
32 Igor Boldin .02 .10
33 Sami Simonen .02 .10
34 Kari Rosenberg .07 .20
35 Sakari Lindfors .20 .50
36 Veli-Pekka Hard .02 .10
37 Jari Halme .08 .25
38 Jukka Tammi .20 .50
39 Kalle Koskinen .02 .10
40 Pekka Tirkkonen .02 .10
41 Ari Sulander .20 .50
42 Joni Hassinen .02 .10
43 Timo Peltomaa .02 .10
44 Sami Mettovaara .02 .10
45 Mika Yli-Maenpaa .08 .25
46 Toni Virta .02 .10
47 Kimmo Lecklin .07 .20
48 Rauli Raitanen .02 .10
49 Juha Lind .20 .50
50 Ari-Pekka Siekkinen .07 .20
51 Kim Ahlroos .02 .10
52 Jarkko Nikander .02 .10
53 Jouni Vento .02 .10
54 Juha Lampinen .02 .10
55 Kalle Sahlstedt .02 .10
56 Teemu Sillanpaa .02 .10
57 Lasse Nieminen .02 .10
58 Janne Niinimaa .40 1.00
59 Timo Jutila .07 .20
60 Tommi Haapsaari .02 .10
61 Allan Measures .02 .10
62 Petteri Nummelin .02 .10
63 Antti Tormanen .08 .25
64 Pekka Laksola .02 .10
65 Esa Sateri .02 .10
66 Petro Koivunen .02 .10
67 Janne Virtanen .02 .10
68 Pekka Peltola .02 .10
69 Matti Kaipainen .02 .10
70 Semi Pekki .02 .10
71 Jussi Tarvainen .02 .10
72 Jari Virtanen .02 .10
73 Kimmo Salminen .02 .10
74 Tommi Varjonen .02 .10
75 Pauli Jarvinen .02 .10
76 Hannu Mattila .02 .10
77 Aleksander Smirnov .02 .10
78 Arto Kulmala .02 .10
79 Roland Carlsson .02 .10
80 Jarma Miikkulainen .02 .10
81 Jarmo Muukkonen .02 .10
82 Mika Paananen .02 .10
83 Pasi Kivila .02 .10
84 Jari Laukkanen .02 .10
85 Tero Arkiomaa .02 .10
86 Tommi Miettinen .07 .20
87 Juha Jarvenpaa .02 .10
88 Niko Mikkola .02 .10
89 Antti Tuomenoksa .02 .10
90 Ilkka Sinisalo .08 .25
91 Otakar Janecky .07 .20
92 Arto Sirvio .02 .10
93 Robert Salo .02 .10
94 Ari Saarinen .02 .10
95 Kari Martikainen .02 .10
96 Miro Haapaniemi .02 .10
97 Fredrik Norrena .07 .20
98 Erik Hamalainen .07 .20
99 Simo Saarinen .02 .10
100 Harri Suvanto .02 .10
101 Kai Nurminen .20 .50
102 Rami Koivisto .02 .10
103 Pasi Peltonen .02 .10
104 Kari-Pekka Friman .02 .10
105 Mika Kortelainen .07 .20
106 Timo Hirvanen .02 .10
107 Jari Haapamaki .02 .10
108 Mika Manninen .02 .10
109 Ari Vuori .02 .10
110 Markku Ikonen .02 .10
111 Mikko Konttila .02 .10
112 Harri Sillgren .02 .10
113 Mikko Teui .02 .10
114 Markus Oijennus .02 .10
115 Kimmo Hyttinen .02 .10
116 Jokke Heinanen .02 .10
117 Sami Ahlberg .02 .10
118 Mika Rautio .07 .20
119 Ari Salo .07 .20
120 Juha Hautamaa .02 .10
121 Kari Haakana .02 .10
122 Sami Nuutinen .02 .10
123 Lasse Pirjeta .02 .10
124 Koijo Sailynoja .07 .20
125 Mikael Kotkaniemi .02 .10
126 Samuli Rautio .02 .10
127 Veli-Pekka Pekkarinen .02 .10
128 Hannu Henriksson .02 .10
129 Antti Aalto .30 .75
130 Jyrki Jokinen .02 .10
131 Marko Ek .02 .10
132 Marko Ojanen .02 .10
133 Mika Arvaja .02 .10
134 Karri Kivi .02 .10
135 Timo Saarikoski .02 .10
136 Toni Sihvonen .02 .10
137 Mika Laaksonen .02 .10
138 HIFK Helsinki Team Card .02 .10
139 HPK Team Card .02 .10
140 Ilves Team Card .02 .10
141 Jokerit Team Card .08 .25
142 JyP HT Team Card .02 .10
143 KalPa Team Card .02 .10
144 Kiekko-Espoo Team Card .02 .10
145 Lukko Team Card .02 .10
146 Tappara Team Card .02 .10
147 TPS Turku Team Card .02 .10
148 TuTo Turku Team Card .02 .10
149 Assat Team Card .02 .10
150 Petteri Nummelin CL .02 .10
151 Kari Takko CL .08 .25
152 Vladimir Jursinov CL .02 .10
153 Juha Lind CL .08 .25
154 Marko Jantunen
Goals
R .07 .20
155 Jere Lehtinen
Goals
Pl .75 2.00
156 Esa Keskinen
Points
Re .08 .25
157 Jere Lehtinen
Points
P .75 2.00
158 Timo Peltomaa
Penalties .08 .25
159 Janne Gronvall Pena .08 .25
160 Jarmo Myllys
All Stars# .20 .50
161 Markko Kiprusoff
All St .08 .25
162 Timo Jutila
All Stars/ .07 .20
163 Sami Kapanen
All Stars# .40 1.00
164 Esa Keskinen
All Stars# .08 .25
165 Mika Alatalo
All Stars# .20 .50
166 Ville Peltonen
HIFK
Te .20 .50
167 Igor Boldin .02 .10
168 Sami Lehtonen .02 .10
169 Juha Jokiharju .02 .10
170 Harri Laurila .02 .10
171 Pekka Tirkkonen
KalPa/ .02 .10
172 Mikko Halonen .02 .10
173 Tero Arkiomaa .02 .10
174 Jonni Vauhkonen
Reipas# .08 .25
175 Janne Gronvall
Tappara# .08 .25
176 Marko Jantunen .02 .10
177 Jouni Vento
Assat
Team .07 .20
178 HIFK .02 .10
179 HPK .02 .10
180 Ilves Tampere
Team Performance
Final Position 7t .02 .10
181 JyP HT .02 .10
182 Jokerit .02 .10
183 KalPa .02 .10
184 Kiekko-Espoo .02 .10
185 Lukko .02 .10
186 Tappara .02 .10
187 TPS .02 .10
188 Reipas .02 .10
189 Assat .02 .10
190 Jokerit
Finnish Champio .08 .25
191 Lukko/2nd Place Nationa .02 .10
192 TPS
European Champions .08 .25
193 TPS
European Cup Champi .08 .25
194 Playoffs .02 .10
195 Playoffs .02 .10
196 Playoffs .02 .10
197 Finals Game 1 .02 .10
198 Finals Game 2 .02 .10
199 Finals Game 3 .02 .10
200 Finals Game 4 .02 .10
201 Jouni Rokama .07 .20
202 Sami Leinonen .02 .10
203 Jani Nikko .08 .25
204 Arto Vuoti .02 .10
205 Petr Pavlas .02 .10
206 Reijo Mikkolainen .02 .10
207 Jari Kurri .75 2.00
208 Janne Ojanen .20 .50
209 Sami Kapanen .75 2.00
210 Teppo Kivela .02 .10
211 Saku Koivu 2.00 5.00
212 Pekka Virta .02 .10
213 Risto Jalo .07 .20
214 Sergei Prjakhin .08 .25
215 Aleksander Barkov .02 .10
216 Ville Peltonen .30 .75
217 Jari Korpisalo .07 .20
218 Jari Liikkanen .02 .10
219 Timo Lehkonen .07 .20
220 Juha Ylonen .20 .50
221 Harri Lonnberg .02 .10
222 Teemu Vuorinen .02 .10
223 Pertti Lehtonen .02 .10
224 Tommi Pullola .02 .10
225 Tomas Kapusta .07 .20
226 Joonas Jaaskelainen .02 .10
227 Jukka Tiilikainen .02 .10
228 Jarno Kultanen .20 .50
229 Kimmo Kapanen .08 .25
230 Jari Kauppila .02 .10
231 Jarkko Glad .02 .10
232 Nemo Nokkosmaki .02 .10
233 Petri Matikainen .02 .10
234 Christian Ruutu .20 .50
235 Martti Jarventie .30 .75
236 Sami Salo .20 .50
237 Timo Kulonen .02 .10
238 Pasi Sormunen .02 .10
239 Timo Nurmberg .02 .10
240 Jari Hirsimaki .02 .10
241 Tommi Hamalainen .02 .10
242 Vesa Salo .08 .25
243 Juha Nurminen .02 .10
244 Petr Korinek .02 .10
245 Kimmo Vesa .07 .20
246 Jukka Seppo .02 .10
247 Jarno Makela .02 .10
248 Petri Varis .20 .50
249 Marko Virtanen .02 .10
250 Risto Siltanen .08 .25
251 Juha Jarvenpaa .02 .10
252 Raimo Summanen .08 .25
253 Markus Hatinen .02 .10
254 Kimmo Nurro .02 .10
255 Timo Salonen .02 .10
256 Jari Munck .02 .10
257 Kimmo Rintanen .08 .25
258 Jarno Levonen .02 .10
259 Jarno Peltonen .02 .10
260 Valeri Krykov .02 .10
261 Kai Rautio .02 .10
262 Timo Blomqvist .08 .25
263 Teemu Selanne 2.00 5.00
264 Juha Virtanen .02 .10
265 Veli-Pekka Kautonen .02 .10
266 Mikko Koivunoro .02 .10
267 Mikko Luovi .08 .25
268 Jaroslav Otevrel .02 .10
269 Erik Kakko .02 .10
270 Peter Ahola .07 .20
271 Miikka Kemppi .02 .10
272 Toni Makiaho .02 .10
273 Pekka Poikolainen .02 .10
274 Timo Norppa .02 .10
275 Sebastian Sulku .02 .10
276 Esa Tikkanen .40 1.00
277 Pasi Saarela .02 .10
278 Ilpo Kauhanen .20 .50
279 Mika Alatalo .20 .50
280 Jukka Suomalainen .02 .10
281 Tony Arima .02 .10
282 Mika Puhakka .02 .10
283 Jussi Kiuru .02 .10
284 Jarkko Isotalo .02 .10
285 Esa Tommila .02 .10
286 Jouni Loponen .02 .10
287 Jermu Pisto .02 .10
288 Pasi Heinisto .02 .10
289 Toni Porkka .02 .10
290 Juha Vuorivirta .08 .25
291 Vesa Karjalainen .02 .10
292 Tom Koivisto .02 .10
293 Markku Hurme .02 .10
294 Mika Kannisto .02 .10
295 Marko Rantanen .07 .20
296 Petri Kalteva .02 .10
297 Pasi Huura .02 .10
298 Miikka Ruokonen .02 .10
299 Tuomo Raty .02 .10
300 Vadim Shaidullin .02 .10
301 Juha Riihijarvi .07 .20
302 Brad Turner .02 .10
303 Marko Toivola .02 .10
304 Kimmo Timonen .30 .75
305 Kai Nurminen .20 .50
306 Vesa Lehtonen .02 .10
307 Mika Niittymaki .02 .10
308 Sami Wahlsten .02 .10
309 Pavel Torgajev .08 .25
310 Pasi Kemppainen .02 .10
311 Markku Kallio .02 .10
312 Timo Maki .07 .20
313 Mika Stromberg .08 .25
314 Tuomas Gronman .08 .25
315 Tommi Rajamaki .08 .25
316 Juri Kuznetsov .07 .20
317 Mikko Myllykoski .02 .10
318 Brian Tutt .02 .10
319 Teemu Numminen .07 .20
320 Juha Jokiharju .02 .10
321 Mika Lehtinen .02 .10
322 Jari Pulliainen .02 .10
323 Kimmo Maki-Kokkila .02 .10
324 Mikko Peltola .02 .10
325 Risto Kurkinen .02 .10
326 Harri Laurila .02 .10
327 Vjatcheslav Fandul .02 .10
328 Niklas Hede .02 .10
329 Boris Rousson .20 .50
330 Jukka Ollila .08 .25
331 Jouni Tuominen .02 .10
332 Marko Harkonen .07 .20
333 Petri Engman .07 .20
334 Mikko Halonen .02 .10
335 Aki Berg .30 .75
336 Kristian Fagerstrom .02 .10
337 Jiri Veber .02 .10
338 Tommy Kiviaho .02 .10
339 Konstantin Astrahantsev .02 .10
340 Jukka Makitalo .07 .20
341 Timo Nykopp .02 .10
342 Sami Lehtonen .02 .10
343 Joni Lehto .07 .20
344 Jouko Myrra .02 .10
345 Mikko Makela .20 .50
346 Marco Poulsen .02 .10
347 Janne Seva .02 .10
348 Shawn McEachern .20 .50
349 Jarkko Varvio .07 .20
350 Mikko Konttila .02 .10
351 Veli-Pekka Ahonen .02 .10
352 Michael Nylander .30 .75
353 Kristian Taubert .02 .10
354 Ismo Kuoppala .02 .10
355 Kimmo Hyttinen .02 .10
356 Petri Latti .02 .10
357 Ted Donato .20 .50
358 Jari Harjumaki .02 .10
359 Teppo Numminen .20 .50
360 Jyrki Lumme .20 .50
361 German Titov .20 .50
362 Kari Eloranta .08 .25
363 Raimo Helminen .08 .25
364 Marko Jantunen .08 .25
365 Olli Kaski .02 .10
366 Jarmo Kekalainen .07 .20
367 Esa Keskinen .08 .25
368 Jarmo Makitalo .02 .10
369 Mika Nieminen .08 .25
370 Marko Palo .02 .10
371 Ville Siren .08 .25
372 Kari Suoraniemi .02 .10
373 Otakar Janecky
Playmake .08 .25
374 Jari Lindroos PM .02 .10
375 Teppo Kivela PM .02 .10
376 Petri Varis PM .08 .25
377 Pekka Laksola PM .02 .10
378 Jari Korpisalo PM .07 .20
379 Iiro Jarvi PM .08 .25
380 Timo Saarikoski PM .02 .10
381 Rauli Raitanen PM .02 .10
382 Juha Riihijarvi
Playmak .02 .10
383 Juha Jokiharju PM .02 .10
384 Vesa Salo PM .02 .10
385 Mika Nieminen CL .08 .25
386 Marko Jantunen CL .02 .10
387 Checklist 301-350
Mika .40 1.00
388 Checklist 351-400
Ari S .08 .25
389 Hannu Kapanen CO .02 .10
390 Hannu Savolainen CO .02 .10
391 Heikki Vesala CO .02 .10
392 Hannu Aravirta CO .02 .10
393 Kari Savolainen CO .02 .10
394 Anatoli Bogdanov CO .02 .10
395 Harri Rindell CO .02 .10
396 Vaclav Sykora CO .02 .10
397 Boris Majorov CO .02 .10
398 Vladimir Jursinov CO .05 .15
399 Seppo Suoraniemi CO .02 .10
400 Veli-Pekka Ketola CO .08 .25
NNO1 Canada Bowl
Super Chase 8.00 20.00
NNO2 Saku Koivu
Super Chase 20.00 50.00

1994-95 Finnish SISU Fire On Ice

COMPLETE SET (20) 12.00 30.00
1 Tero Arkiomoa .40 1.00
2 Igor Boldin .40 1.00
3 Vjatseslav Fandul .40 1.00
4 Otakar Janecky .75 2.00
5 Marko Jantunen .75 2.00
6 Timo Jutila .40 1.00
7 Pauli Jarvinen .40 1.00
8 Sami Kapanen 1.25 3.00
9 Tomas Kapusta .40 1.00
10 Esa Keskinen .75 2.00
11 Saku Koivu 4.00 10.00
12 Petro Koivunen .40 1.00
13 Petr Korinek .40 1.00
14 Jari Karpisolo .40 1.00
15 Risto Kurkinen .40 1.00
16 Tero Lehtera .75 2.00
17 Juha Nurminen .40 1.00
18 Kai Nurminen .75 2.00
19 Janne Ojanen .75 2.00
20 Jari Torkki .40 1.00

1994-95 Finnish SISU Guest Specials

COMPLETE SET (12) 16.00 30.00
1 Ted Donato .75 2.00
2 Jari Kurri 2.00 5.00
3 Jyrki Lumme .75 2.00
4 Shawn McEachern .75 2.00
5 Mikko Makela .75 2.00
6 Teppo Numminen .75 2.00
7 Michael Nylander .75 2.00
8 Christian Ruuttu .75 2.00
9 Teemu Selanne 10.00 20.00
10 Esa Tikkanen .75 2.00
11 German Titov .40 1.00
12 Jarkko Varvio .40 1.00

1994-95 Finnish SISU Horoscopes

COMPLETE SET (20) 4.80 12.00
1 Juha Lind .40 1.00
2 Jukka Seppo .40 1.00
3 Antti Tuomenoksa .20 .50
4 Tuomas Gronman .40 1.00
5 Peter Ahola .20 .50
6 Ville Peltonen .75 2.00
7 Timo Saarikoski .20 .50
8 Timo Peltomaa .40 1.00
9 Jari Levonen .20 .50
10 Teppo Kivela .20 .50
11 Valeri Krykov .20 .50
12 Juha Riihijarvi .20 .50
13 Kai Nurminen .40 1.00
14 Mikko Luovi .20 .50
15 Raimo Summanen .40 1.00
16 Tommy Kiviaho .20 .50
17 Hannu Jarvenpaa .20 .50
18 Marko Virtanen .20 .50
19 Sami Lehtonen .20 .50
20 Mika Alatalo .75 2.00

1994-95 Finnish SISU Junior

COMPLETE SET (10) 6.00 15.00
1 Saku Koivu 3.00 8.00
2 Jekke Heimanen .40 1.00
3 Tommi Miettinen .40 1.00
4 Jere Karalahti .75 2.00
5 Kalle Koskinen .40 1.00
6 Kari Rosenberg .40 1.00
7 Mika Manninen .40 1.00
8 Jussi Tarvainen .40 1.00
9 Mika Stromberg .40 1.00
10 Kalle Sahlstedt .40 1.0

1994-95 Finnish SISU Magic Numbers

COMPLETE SET (10) 4.80 12.0
1 Pasi Kuivalainen .40 1.0
2 Petteri Nummelin .75 2.0
3 Jarmo Kuusisto .40 1.0
4 Janne Ojanen .40 1.0
5 Sami Kapanen 1.25 3.0
6 Pekka Virta .40 1.0
7 Antti Tormanen .40 1.0
8 Jari Korpisalo .40 1.0
9 Kimmo Salminen .40 1.0
10 Jukka Tammi 1.25 3.0

1994-95 Finnish SISU NHL Draf

COMPLETE SET (8) 2.00 5.0
1 Title Card .20 .5
2 Marko Kiprusoff .40 1.0
3 Jussi Tarvainen .40 1.0
4 Arto Kuki .40 1.0
5 Tommi Rajamaki .40 1.0
6 Tero Lehtera .40 1.0
7 Tommi Miettinen .40 1.0
8 Antti Tormanen .40 1.0

1994-95 Finnish SISU NIL Phenoms

COMPLETE SET (10) 12.00 30.0
1 Mika Manninen 1.25 3.0
2 Kari Takko 2.00 5.0
3 Ari Sulander 2.00 5.0
4 Jouni Rokama 1.25 3.0

5 Kari Rosenberg 1.25 3.00
6 Mika Rautio 1.25 3.00
7 Ari-Pekka Siekkinen 1.25 3.00
8 Allain Roy 1.25 3.00
9 Pasi Kuivalainen 1.25 3.00
10 Sakari Lindfors 1.25 3.00

1994-95 Finnish SISU Specials

COMPLETE SET (10) 8.00 20.00
1 Mika Alatalo .75 2.00
2 Jari Korpisalo .40 1.00
3 Petteri Nummelin .75 2.00
4 Janne Ojanen .40 1.00
5 Sami Kapanen 1.25 3.00
6 Kari Takko .75 2.00
7 Esa Keskinen .40 1.00
8 Ari Sulander .75 2.00
9 Jarmo Myllys .75 2.00
10 Saku Koivu 4.00 10.00

1995 Finnish Karjala World Championship Labels

COMPLETE SET (24) 16.00 40.00
1 Erik Hamalainen .40 1.00
2 Raimo Helminen .40 1.00
3 Timo Jutila .60 1.50
4 Sami Kapanen .75 2.00
5 Esa Keskinen .40 1.00
6 Marko Kiprusoff .40 1.00
7 Saku Koivu 2.00 5.00
8 Tero Lehtera .40 1.00
9 Jere Lehtinen 1.25 3.00
10 Curt Lindstrom .40 1.00
11 Jarmo Myllys .75 2.00
12 Mika Nieminen .40 1.00
13 Janne Niinimaa .75 2.00
14 Petteri Nummelin .40 1.00
15 Janne Ojanen .40 1.00
16 Marko Palo .40 1.00
17 Ville Peltonen .60 1.50
18 Mika Stromberg .40 1.00
19 Ari Sulander .75 2.00
20 Raimo Summanen .40 1.00
21 Jukka Tammi .75 2.00
22 Antti Tormanen .40 1.00
23 Hannu Virta .60 1.50
24 Juha Ylonen .60 1.50

1995 Finnish Kellogg's

COMPLETE SET (6) 12.00 30.00
1 Jarmo Myllys 2.00 5.00
2 Marko Kiprusoff 1.25 3.00
3 Hannu Virta 1.25 3.00
4 Ville Peltonen 1.25 3.00
5 Saku Koivu 6.00 15.00
6 Sami Kapanen 2.00 5.00

1995 Finnish Semic World Championships

COMPLETE SET (240) 20.00 50.00
1 Pasi Kuivalainen .07 .20
2 Marko Kiprusoff .05 .15
3 Tuomas Gronman .05 .15
4 Erik Hamalainen .02 .10
5 Timo Jutila .05 .15
6 Pasi Sormunen .02 .10
7 Waltteri Immonen .05 .15
8 Janne Ojanen .05 .15
9 Esa Keskinen .05 .15
10 Kimmo Timonen .08 .25
11 Saku Koivu .40 1.00
12 Janne Laukkanen .08 .25
13 Marko Palo .02 .10
14 Raimo Helminen .05 .15
15 Mika Alatalo .08 .25
16 Ville Peltonen .15 .40
17 Jari Kurri .30 .75
18 Jari Korpisalo .05 .15
19 Kimmo Rintanen .05 .15
20 Jere Lehtinen .40 1.00
21 Kalle Sahlstedt .05 .15
22 Christian Ruuttu .05 .15
23 Hannu Virta .05 .15
24 Sami Kapanen .20 .50
25 Marko Tuulola .02 .10
26 Mika Stromberg .05 .15
27 Tero Lehtera .05 .15
28 Petri Varis .05 .15
29 Mikko Peltola .02 .10
30 Jukka Tammi .08 .25
31 Tero Arkiomaa .02 .10
32 Olli Kaski .02 .10
33 Pekka Laksola .02 .10
34 Mika Valila .02 .10
35 Jarmo Myllys .08 .25
36 Harri Laurila .02 .10
37 Teppo Numminen .08 .25
38 Jyrki Lumme .07 .20
39 Petteri Nummelin .02 .10
40 Mika Nieminen .08 .25
41 Teemu Selanne .60 1.50
42 Mikko Makela .05 .15
43 Esa Tikkanen .15 .40
44 Jarkko Varvio .05 .15
45 Vesa Viitakoski .05 .15
46 Juha Riihijarvi .05 .15
47 Markus Ketterer .08 .25
48 Mikko Haapakoski .02 .10
49 Antti Tormanen .05 .15
50 Timo Peltomaa .02 .10
51 Rauli Raitanen .02 .10
52 Roger Nordstrom .02 .10
53 Tommy Salo .20 .50
54 Tommy Soderstrom .20 .50
55 Magnus Svensson .05 .15
56 Fredrik Stillman .02 .10
57 Nicklas Lidstrom .40 1.00
58 Roger Johansson .02 .10
59 Kenny Jonsson .20 .50
60 Peter Andersson .02 .10
61 Tommy Sjodin .05 .15
62 Mats Sundin .40 1.00
63 Jonas Bergqvist .05 .15
64 Peter Forsberg .75 2.00
65 Roger Hansson .02 .10
66 Jorgen Jonsson .02 .10
67 Charles Berglund .02 .10
68 Mikael Johansson .02 .10
69 Tomas Forslund .05 .15
70 Andreas Dackell .08 .25
71 Stefan Ornskog .02 .10
72 Mikael Andersson .05 .15
73 Jan Larsson .02 .10
74 Patrik Carnback .05 .15
75 Hakan Loob .08 .25
76 Patrik Juhlin .08 .25
77 Bill Ranford .20 .50
78 Ed Belfour .60 1.50
79 Rob Blake .20 .50
80 Yves Racine .05 .15
81 Steve Smith .05 .15
82 Paul Coffey .40 1.00
83 Larry Murphy .20 .50
84 Mark Tinordi .05 .15
85 Al MacInnis .40 1.00
86 Paul Kariya .75 2.00
87 Joe Sakic .75 2.00
88 Brendan Shanahan .60 1.50
89 Luc Robitaille .40 1.00
90 Rod Brind'Amour .30 .75
91 Shayne Corson .08 .25
92 Mike Ricci .08 .25
93 Mario Lemieux ERR Name 2.00 5.00
94 Eric Lindros .75 2.00
95 Russ Courtnall .08 .25
96 Theo Fleury .40 1.00
97 Mark Messier .60 1.50
98 Rick Tocchet .20 .50
99 Wayne Gretzky 2.00 5.00
100 Steve Larmer .08 .25
101 Brett Lindros .08 .25
102 John Vanbiesbrouck .40 1.00
103 Craig Wolanin .05 .15
104 Chris Chelios .40 1.00
105 Brian Leetch .40 1.00
106 Kevin Hatcher .07 .20
107 Craig Janney .08 .25
108 Tim Sweeney .05 .15
109 Shawn Chambers .05 .15
110 Scott Young .08 .25
111 John Lilley .05 .15
112 Joe Sacco .05 .15
113 Brett Hull .60 1.50
114 Pat LaFontaine .20 .50
115 Joel Otto .08 .25
116 Mike Modano .60 1.50
117 Tony Granato .05 .15
118 Jeremy Roenick .60 1.50
119 Jeff Lazaro .05 .15
120 Brian Mullen .05 .15
121 Mihail Shtalenkov .20 .50
122 Valeri Ivannikov .02 .10
123 Andrei Nikolishin .08 .25
124 Ilya Byakin Spelled Ilj .05 .15
125 Alexander Smirnov .02 .10
126 Dimitri Yushkevich .08 .25
127 Sergei Shendelev .02 .10
128 Alexei Zhitnik Spelled .05 .15
129 Igor Ulanov .05 .15
130 Dmitri Frolov .02 .10
131 Valeri Kamensky Spelled .15 .40
132 Igor Fedulov .02 .10
133 Andrei Kovalenko .08 .25
134 Valeri Bure .20 .50
135 Sergei Berezin .15 .40
136 Alexei Yashin Spelled A .20 .50
137 Vyatcheslav Kozlov Spel .15 .40
138 Vyatcheslav Bykov Spell .08 .25
139 Andrei Khomutov Spelled .08 .25
140 Petr Briza .08 .25
141 Dominik Hasek .60 1.50
142 Roman Turek .30 .75
143 Jan Vopat .05 .15
144 Drahomir Kadlec .05 .15
145 Petr Pavlas .02 .10
146 Frantisek Kucera .05 .15
147 Jiri Veber .02 .10
148 David Vyborny .05 .15
149 Radek Toupal .05 .15
150 Jiri Kucera .05 .15
151 Richard Zemlicka .05 .15
152 Martin Rucinsky .08 .25
153 Jiri Dolezal .02 .10
154 Josef Beranek .05 .15
155 Martin Prochazka .02 .10
156 Tomas Srsen .05 .15
157 David Bruk .02 .10
158 Jaromir Jagr .75 2.00
159 Jan Caloun .05 .15
160 Martin Straka .20 .50
161 Roman Horak .02 .10
162 Frantisek Musil .05 .15
163 Peter Hrbek .02 .10
164 Jan Alino .02 .10
165 Joseph Heiss .07 .20
166 Peter Gulda .02 .10
167 Jayson Meyer .02 .10
168 Ernst Kopf .02 .10
169 Raimund Hilger .02 .10
170 Richard Bohm .02 .10
171 Michael Rosati .08 .25
172 Michael DeAngelis .02 .10
173 Anthony Circelli .02 .10
174 Gaetano Orlando .02 .10
175 Lucio Topatigh .02 .10
176 Martin Pavlu .02 .10
177 Jim Marthinsen .08 .25
178 Petter Salsten .02 .10
179 Tommy Jacobson .02 .10
180 Morten Finsted .02 .10
181 Tom Andersen .02 .10
182 Manus Rath .02 .10
183 Michael Puschacher .05 .15
184 James Burton .02 .10
185 Michael Shea .02 .10
186 Dieter Kalt .02 .10
187 Manfred Muhr .02 .10
188 Andreas Puschnig .02 .10
189 Renato Tosio .02 .10
190 Doug Honneger .02 .10
191 Felix Hollenstein .02 .10
192 Jorg Eberle .02 .10
193 Gil Montandon .02 .10
194 Roberto Triulzi .02 .10
195 Petri Ylonen .05 .15
196 Bruno Maynort .02 .10
197 Michel LeBlanc .02 .10
198 Benoit Laborte .04 .10
199 Christophe Ville .02 .10
200 Antoine Richer .02 .10
201 Bill Ranford MM 94 All .20 .50
202 Timo Jutila AS .05 .15
203 Magnus Svensson AS .05 .15
204 Jari Kurri MM 94 All St .30 .75
205 Saku Koivu MM 94 All St .40 1.00
206 Paul Kariya MM 94 All S .75 2.00
207 Jarmo Myllys Maalivahti .08 .25
208 Bill Ranford Maalivahti .20 .50
209 Roger Nordstrom ME .02 .10
210 Guy Hebert Maalivahti E .30 .75
211 Mihail Shtalenkov Maali .20 .50
212 Tommy Soderstrom Maaliv .20 .50
213 Petr Briza Maalivahti E .08 .25
214 Dominik Hasek Maalivaht .60 1.50
215 Tom Barrasso Maalivahti .15 .40
216 Jukka Tammi ME .05 .15
217 John Vanbiesbrouck Maal .40 1.00
218 Mike Richter Maalivahti .40 1.00
219 Saku Koivu Special .40 1.00
220 Saku Koivu Special .40 1.00
221 Saku Koivu Special .40 1.00
222 Saku Koivu Special .40 1.00
223 Saku Koivu Special .40 1.00
224 Saku Koivu Special .40 1.00
225 Tuomas Gronman FS .05 .15
226 Jani Nikko FS .02 .10
227 Janne Niinimaa Future S .40 1.00
228 Jukka Tiilikainen FS .02 .10
229 Kimmo Rintanen FS .05 .15
230 Ville Peltonen Future S .15 .40
231 Sami Kapanen Future Sta .30 .75
232 Jere Lehtinen Future St .40 1.00
233 Kimmo Timonen Future St .05 .15
234 Jonni Vauhkonen Future .05 .15
235 Juha Lind FS .08 .25
236 Tommi Miettinen FS .05 .15
237 Jere Karalahti Future S .08 .25
238 Antti Aalto Future Star .08 .25
239 Teemu Kohvakka FS .02 .10
240 Niko Mikkola FS .02 .10

1995-96 Finnish Beckett Ad Cards

COMPLETE SET (8) 10.00 25.00
1 Saku Koivu 4.00 10.00
2 Jere Lehtinen 2.00 5.00
3 Ville Peltonen .75 2.00
4 Erik Hamalainen .75 2.00
5 Sami Kapanen 2.00 5.00
6 Marko Kiprusoff .75 2.00
7 Mika Stromberg .75 2.00
8 Marko Palo .75 2.00

1995-96 Finnish Jaa Kiekko Lehti Ad Cards

COMPLETE SET (8) 14.00 35.00
1 Jarmo Myllys 1.25 3.00
2 Jari Kurri 1.50 4.00
3 Saku Koivu 3.00 8.00
4 Teemu Selanne 6.00 15.00
5 Esa Tikkanen 1.25 3.00
6 Christian Ruuttu .75 2.00
7 Mika Nieminen .75 2.00
8 Timo Jutila .75 2.00

1995-96 Finnish SISU

COMPLETE SET (400) 20.00 50.00
COMPLETE SERIES 1 (200) 12.00 30.00
COMPLETE SERIES 2 (200) 8.00 20.00
1 HIFK, Team Card .02 .10
2 Kimmo Kapanen .02 .10
3 Juri Kuznetsov .02 .10
4 Simo Saarinen .02 .10
5 Roland Carlsson .02 .10
6 Veli-Pekka Fagerstrom .02 .10
7 Kristian Fagerstrom .02 .10
8 Mika Kortelainen .02 .10
9 Jari Laukkanen .02 .10
10 Juha Nurminen .02 .10
11 Markku Hurme .02 .10
12 Sami Kapanen .40 1.00
13 Darren Boyko .02 .10
14 Marko Ojanen .02 .10
15 HPK, Team Card .02 .10
16 Kari Rosenberg .08 .25
17 Petri Engman .02 .10
18 Niko Marttila .02 .10
19 Jari Haapamaki .02 .10
20 Marko Allen .02 .10
21 Erik Kakko .02 .10
22 Mikko Myllykoski .02 .10
23 Jani Hassinen .02 .10
24 Risto Jalo .08 .25
25 Juha Jarvenpaa .02 .10
26 Jari Kauppila .02 .10
27 Toni Makiaho .02 .10
28 Ilves, Team Card .02 .10
29 Mika Manninen .08 .25
30 Hannu Henriksson .02 .10
31 Petri Kokko .02 .10
32 Martti Jarventie .20 .50
33 Allan Measures .02 .10
34 Pasi Huura .02 .10
35 Janne Seva .02 .10
36 Tommy Kiviaho .02 .10
37 Reijo Mikkolainen .02 .10
38 Hannu Mattila .02 .10
39 Jari Virtanen .02 .10
40 Sami Ahlberg .02 .10
41 Juha Hautamaa .02 .10
42 Jokerit, Team Card .02 .10
43 Ari Sulander .20 .50
44 Santeri Immonen .02 .10
45 Pasi Sormunen .02 .10
46 Waltteri Immonen .02 .10
47 Mika Stromberg .08 .25
48 Kari Martikainen .02 .10
49 Tommi Sova .08 .25
50 Juha Lind .20 .50
51 Niko Halttunen .02 .10
52 Keijo Sailynoja .08 .25
53 Otakar Janecky .08 .25
54 Timo Saarikoski .02 .10
55 JYP HT, Team Card .02 .10
56 Ari-Pekka Siekkinen .08 .25
57 Vesa Ponto .02 .10
58 Kalle Koskinen .02 .10
59 Jouni Loponen .02 .10
60 Miska Kangasniemi .08 .25
61 Mika Paananen .02 .10
62 Markku Ikonen .02 .10
63 Kimmo Salminen .02 .10
64 Joni Lius .02 .10
65 Lasse Nieminen .02 .10
66 Janne Kurjenniemi .02 .10
67 Marko Virtanen .02 .10
68 KalPa, Team Card .02 .10
69 Jarkko Kortesoja .02 .10
70 Petri Matikainen .02 .10
71 Mika Laaksonen .02 .10
72 Kai Rautio .02 .10
73 Jarno Kultanen .20 .50
74 Miikka Ruokonen .02 .10
75 Jussi Tarvainen .02 .10
76 Mikko Honkonen .02 .10
77 Sami Simonen .02 .10
78 Petr Korinek .02 .10
79 Veli-Pekka Pekkarinen .02 .10
80 Pekka Tirkkonen .02 .10
81 Kiekko-Espoo, Team Card .02 .10
82 Iiro Itamies .08 .25
83 Tommi Nyyssonen .02 .10
84 Robert Salo .02 .10
85 Sami Nuutinen .02 .10
86 Timo Blomqvist .02 .10
87 Ismo Kuoppala .02 .10
88 Mikko Koivunoro .02 .10
89 Petro Koivunen .08 .25
90 Jarmo Muukkonen .02 .10
91 Sergei Prjahin .02 .10
92 Teemu Riihijarvi .08 .25
93 Juha Ikonen .02 .10
94 Lukko, Team Card .02 .10
95 Boris Rousson .20 .50
96 Vesa Salo .08 .25
97 Toni Porkka .02 .10
98 Mika Yli-Maenpaa .08 .25
99 Juha Riihijarvi .08 .25
100 Petri Latti .02 .10
101 Veli-Pekka Ahonen .02 .10
102 Mikko Poltola .02 .10
103 Kalle Sahlstedt .08 .25
104 Jari Torkki .02 .10
105 Jussi Kiuru .02 .10
106 Sakari Palsola .02 .10
107 Tappara, Team Card .02 .10
108 Ilpo Kauhanen .20 .50
109 Sami Lehtonen .02 .10
110 Pasi Petrilainen .02 .10
111 Pekka Laksola .02 .10
112 Tommi Haapsaari .02 .10
113 Ville Nieminen 1.25 3.00
114 Arto Kulmala .02 .10
115 Valeri Krykov .02 .10
116 Timo Nurmberg .02 .10
117 Aleksander Barkov .02 .10
118 Miikka Kemppi .02 .10
119 Marko Toivola .02 .10
120 Juha Vuorivirta .08 .25
121 TPS, Team Card .02 .10
122 Miikka Kiprusoff 4.00 10.00
123 Kimmo Timonen .20 .50
124 Sami Salo .02 .10
125 Kari Harila .02 .10
126 Tuomas Gronman .08 .25
127 Vjatsheslav Fandul .02 .10
128 Mika Alatalo .20 .50
129 Jukka Tiilikainen .02 .10
130 Kimmo Rintanen .15 .40
131 Hannes Hyvonen .20 .50
132 Simo Rouvali .02 .10
133 Harri Sillgren .02 .10
134 Harri Suvanto .02 .10
135 TuTo, Team Card .02 .10
136 Markus Korhonen .02 .10
137 Sebastian Sulku .02 .10
138 Jukka Suomalainen .02 .10
139 Timo Kulonen .02 .10
140 Risto Siltanen .08 .25
141 Sami Leinonen .02 .10
142 Juha Virtanen .02 .10
143 Jari Hirsimaki .02 .10
144 Jouni Tuominen .02 .10
145 Vesa Karjalainen .02 .10
146 Pekka Virta .02 .10
147 Jouko Myrra .02 .10
148 Assat, Team Card .02 .10
149 Kari Takko .20 .50
150 Timo Nykopp .02 .10
151 Harri Laurila .02 .10
152 Jarno Miikkulainen .02 .10
153 Pasi Peltonen .02 .10
154 Jari Korpisalo .02 .10
155 Teppo Kivela .02 .10
156 Jari Levonen .02 .10
157 Janne Virtanen .02 .10
158 Jarno Makela .02 .10
159 Mikael Kotkaniemi .02 .10
160 Ari Saarinen .02 .10
161 Boris Rousson AS .20 .50
162 Joni Lehto AS .05 .15
163 Marko Kiprusoff AS .08 .25
164 Jere Lehtinen AS .40 1.00
165 Saku Koivu AS 1.25 3.00
166 Kai Nurminen AS .20 .50
167 Ari Sulander AS .20 .50
168 Mika Stromberg AS .08 .25
169 All Stars Kuusisto .02 .10
170 All Stars Arkiomaa .02 .10
171 Otakar Janecky AS .08 .25
172 Ville Peltonen AS .20 .50
173 Milestones Arima .02 .10
174 Milestones Boyko .02 .10
175 Milestones Friman .02 .10
176 Milestones Heiskanen .02 .10
177 Milestones Henriksson .02 .10
178 Milestones Hamalainen .02 .10
179 Milestones Jalo .02 .10
180 Timo Jutila AS .07 .20
181 Milestones Jarvenpaa .02 .10
182 Milestones Kuusisto .02 .10
183 Milestones Laksola .02 .10
184 Milestones Laurila .02 .10
185 Milestones Lehtonen .02 .10
186 Milestones Lindroos .02 .10
187 Milestones Mikkolainen .02 .10
188 Milestones Tommila .02 .10
189 Milestones Torkki .02 .10
190 Milestones Tuomenoksa .02 .10
191 Milestones Vuori .02 .10
192 TPS, SM-kultaa .02 .10
193 Jokerit, SM-hopeaa .02 .10
194 Assat, SM-pronssia .02 .10
195 Jokerit, EM-kultaa .02 .10
196 TPS, EM-pronssia .02 .10
197 Checklist 1-50, Nurminen .15 .40
198 Veli-Pekka Kautonen CL .02 .10
199 Koivu Checklist .40 1.00
200 Kiprusoff Checklist .08 .25
201 HIFK, Fan Card .02 .10
202 Sakari Lindfors .20 .50
203 Lauri Puolanne .02 .10
204 Pertti Lehtonen .02 .10
205 Peter Ahola .02 .10
206 Jere Karalahti .20 .50
207 Kimmo Maki-Kokkila .02 .10
208 Tom Laaksonen .02 .10
209 Tero Hamalainen .02 .10
210 Miro Haapaniemi .02 .10
211 Toni Sihvonen .02 .10
212 Sami Laine .02 .10
213 Iiro Jarvi .08 .25
214 Pekka Tuomisto .02 .10
215 HPK, Fan Card .02 .10
216 Mika Pictila .08 .25
217 Tom Koivisto .02 .10
218 Tommi Hamalainen .02 .10
219 Kai Rautio .02 .10
220 Jani Nikko .08 .25
221 Mika Kannisto .02 .10
222 Jason Miller .02 .10
223 Niklas Hede .02 .10
224 Tony Virta .02 .10
225 Aleksander Andrijevski .02 .10
226 Mika Puhakka .02 .10
227 Timo Peltomaa .02 .10
228 Toni Saarinen .02 .10
229 Ilves, Fan Card .02 .10
230 Vesa Toskala 1.25 3.00
231 Pekka Kangasalusta .02 .10
232 Juha Lampinen .02 .10
233 Pasi Saarinen .02 .10
234 Teemu Vuorinen .02 .10
235 Jarno Peltonen .02 .10
236 Matti Kaipainen .02 .10
237 Semi Pekki .02 .10
238 Sami Karjalainen .02 .10
239 Juoni Lahtinen .02 .10
240 Pasi Maatanen .02 .10
241 Petri Murtovaara .02 .10
242 Tomi Hirvonen .02 .10
243 Mikko Eloranta .20 .50
244 Mika Arvaja .02 .10
245 Juha Jarvenpaa .08 .25
246 Jokerit, Fan Card .02 .10
247 Marko Rantanen .02 .10
248 Marko Tuulola .02 .10
249 Jani-Matti Loikala .02 .10
250 Antti-Jussi Niemi .20 .50
251 Janne Niinimaa .30 .75
252 Jari Lindroos .02 .10
253 Paso Saarela .02 .10
254 Juha Ylonen .30 .75
255 Mika Asikainen .08 .25
256 Eero Somervuori .40 1.00
257 Tero Lehtera .02 .10
258 Jukka Penttinen .02 .10
259 Petri Varis .20 .50
260 JyP HT, Fan Card .02 .10
261 Marko Leinonen .02 .10
262 Jan Latvala .02 .10
263 Jukka Laamanen .02 .10
264 Pekka Poikolainen .02 .10
265 Thomas Sjogren .02 .10
266 Pasi Kangas .08 .25
267 Tini Koivunen .02 .10
268 Lasse Jamsen .02 .10
269 Petri Kujala .02 .10
270 Mikko Inkinen .02 .10
271 Kalpa, Fan Card .02 .10
272 Pasi Kuivalainen .20 .50
273 Pasi Kolehmainen .02 .10
274 Reijo Ruotsalainen .08 .25
275 Jarkko Glad .02 .10
276 Ivan Vizek .02 .10
277 Jarmo Levonen .02 .10
278 Janne Kekalainen .02 .10
279 Veli-Pekka Nutikka .20 .50
280 Mikko Konttila .08 .25
281 Janne Virtanen .02 .10
282 Pasi Kemppainen .02 .10
283 Kiekko-Espoo, Fan Card .02 .10
284 Mika Rautio .08 .25
285 Kari Haakana .02 .10
286 Teemu Sillanpaa .02 .10
287 Timo Nykopp .02 .10
288 Miikka Teimonen .02 .10
289 Tero Tiainen .02 .10
290 Joonas Jaaskelainen .02 .10
291 Lubomir Kolnik .08 .25
292 Arto Sirvio .02 .10
293 Iikka Sinisalo .08 .25
294 Timo Hirvonen .02 .10
295 Arto Kuki .02 .10
296 Timo Norppa .02 .10
297 Lukko, Fan Card .02 .10
298 Timo Kauharren .02 .10
299 Joni Lehto .02 .10
300 Jarno Miikkulainen .02 .10
301 Kimmo Lotvonen .02 .10
302 Robert Nordmark .02 .10
303 Riku Kallioniemi .02 .10
304 Matti Raunio .02 .10
305 Tommi Turunen .02 .10
306 Jarkko Varvio .05 .15
307 Tero Arkiomaa .02 .10
308 Harri Lonnberg .08 .25
309 Mikko Luovi .02 .10
310 Tappara, Fan Card .02 .10
311 Jussi Markkanen .75 2.00
312 Timo Jutila .02 .10
313 Jukka Ollila .02 .10
314 Antti Rahkonen .02 .10
315 Derek Mayer .02 .10
316 Petri Kalteva .02 .10
317 Jarkko Nikander .02 .10
318 Pauli Jarvinen .02 .10
319 Mikko Helisten .02 .10
320 Ari Haanpaa .02 .10
321 Markus Oijennus .02 .10
322 Janne Ojanen .15 .40
323 TPS, Fan Card .02 .10
324 Fredrik Norrena .15 .40
325 Mika Lehtinen .02 .10
326 Karlis Skrastins .20 .50
327 Marru Laapas .02 .10
328 Antti Aalto .20 .50
329 Teemu Numminen .02 .10
330 Tommi Miettinen .02 .10
331 Lasse Pirjeta .02 .10
332 Miikka Rousu .02 .10
333 Marko Makinen .02 .10
334 Mikko Markkanen .02 .10
335 Tomi Kallio .40 1.00
336 Miika Elomo .20 .50
337 Sami Mettovaara .02 .10
338 TuTo, Fan Card .02 .10
339 Jukka Tammi .15 .40
340 Kari-Pekka Friman .02 .10
341 Veli-Pekka Hard .02 .10
342 Antti Tirkkonen .02 .10
343 Jukka Seppo .02 .10
344 Kim Ahlroos .02 .10
345 Marto Poulsen .02 .10
346 Juha Kuusisaari .02 .10
347 Mikko Laaksonen .02 .10
348 Tuomas Jalava .02 .10
349 Tommi Pullola .08 .25
350 Tuomas Kalliomaki .02 .10
351 Assat, Fan Card .02 .10
352 Karri Kivi .02 .10
353 Olli Kaski .02 .10
354 Jouni Vento .02 .10
355 Tommi Rajamaki .08 .25
356 Jokke Heinanen .02 .10
357 Tomas Kapusta .02 .10
358 Jaroslav Otevrel .02 .10
359 Timo Salonen .02 .10
360 Pekka Virta .02 .10
361 Vesa Goman .02 .10
362 Pekka Peltola .02 .10
363 Rauli Raitanen .02 .10
364 Pasi Tuominen .02 .10
365 Kari Syvasalmi .02 .10
366 Timo Hakanen .02 .10
367 Foreigners Andrijevski .02 .10
368 Foreigners Barkov .02 .10
369 Foreigners Boyko .02 .10
370 Foreigners Fandul .02 .10
371 Foreigners Janecky .02 .10
372 Foreigners Kapusta .02 .10
373 Foreigners Kolnik .02 .10
374 Foreigners Korinek .02 .10
375 Foreigners Mayer .02 .10
376 Foreigners Measures .02 .10
377 Foreigners Miller .02 .10
378 Foreigners Nordmark .02 .10
379 Foreigners Otevrel .02 .10
380 Foreigners Prjahin .02 .10
381 Foreigners Rousson .08 .25
382 Foreigners Sjogren .02 .10
383 Foreigners Skrastins .02 .10
384 Foreigners Vlzek .02 .10
385 Vladimir Jursinov .02 .10
386 Hannu Aravirta .02 .10
387 Veli-Pekka Ketola .08 .25
388 Vaclav Sykora .02 .10
389 Hannu Kapanen .02 .10
390 Kari Savolainen .02 .10
391 Harri Rindell .02 .10
392 Anatoli Bogdanov .02 .10
393 Sakari Pietilla .02 .10
394 Jukka Rautakorpi .02 .10
395 Harri Jalava .02 .10
396 Vladimir Jursinov Jr. .02 .10
397 Checklist 201-250 .20 .50
398 Checklist 251-300 .02 .10
399 Checklist 301-350 .02 .10
400 Koivu Checklist .40 1.00
NNOA Saku Koivu Super Bonus SISU logo upper right 10.00 20.00
NNO Saku Koivu Jumbo 2.00 5.00
NNO Saku Koivu Super Chase 10.00 25.00
NNO Janne Niinimaa Super Chase 4.00 10.00

1995-96 Finnish SISU Double Trouble

COMPLETE SET (8) 8.00 20.00
1 T.Gronman K.Timonen 1.25 3.00
2 W.Immonen M.Stromberg 1.25 3.00
3 O.Kaski K.Kivi 1.25 3.00
4 J.Lehto R.Nordmark 1.25 3.00
5 P.Ahola P.Lehtonen 1.25 3.00
6 T.Blomqvist S.Nuutinen 1.25 3.00
7 R.Ruotsalainen I.Vizek 1.25 3.00
8 T.Jutila P.Laksola 1.25 3.00

1995-96 Finnish SISU Drafted Dozen

COMPLETE SET (12) 8.00 25.00
1 Aki Berg .75 2.00
2 Teemu Riihijarvi .40 1.00
3 Miika Elomo .75 2.00
4 Marko Makinen .40 1.00
5 Tomi Kallio 1.25 3.00
6 Sami Kapanen 1.50 4.00
7 Vesa Toskala 2.00 5.00
8 Miikka Kiprusoff 6.00 15.00
9 Timo Hakanen .40 1.00
10 Juha Vuorivirta .40 1.00
11 Tomi Hirvonen .40 1.00
12 Mikko Markkanen .40 1.00

1995-96 Finnish SISU Ghost Goalies

COMPLETE SET (10) 16.00 40.00
1 Sakari Lindfors 2.00 5.00
2 Boris Rousson 1.50 4.00
3 Ari Sulander 2.00 5.00
4 Kari Takko 1.50 4.00
5 Fredrik Norrena 1.50 4.00
6 Kari Rosenberg 1.50 4.00
7 Ari-Pekka Siekkinen 1.50 4.00
8 Jukka Tammi 1.50 4.00
9 Pasi Kuivalainen 1.50 4.00
10 Ilpo Kauhanen 1.50 4.00

1995-96 Finnish SISU Gold Cards

COMPLETE SET (24) 24.00 60.00
1 Title Card .75 2.00
2 Jarmo Myllys 1.50 4.00
3 Ari Sulander 1.50 4.00
4 Jukka Tammi 1.50 4.00
5 Erik Hamalainen .75 2.00
6 Timo Jutila .75 2.00
7 Marko Kiprusoff .75 2.00
8 Janne Niinimaa 1.50 4.00
9 Petteri Nummelin .75 2.00
10 Mika Stromberg .75 2.00
11 Hannu Virta .75 2.00
12 Raimo Helminen .75 2.00
13 Sami Kapanen 2.00 5.00
14 Esa Keskinen .75 2.00
15 Saku Koivu 6.00 15.00
16 Tero Lehtera .75 2.00
17 Jere Lehtinen 3.00 8.00
18 Mika Nieminen .75 2.00
19 Janne Ojanen .75 2.00
20 Marko Palo .75 2.00
21 Ville Peltonen 1.25 3.00
22 Raimo Summanen .75 2.00
23 Antti Tormanen .75 2.00
24 Juha Ylonen 1.25 3.00

1995-96 Finnish SISU Limited

COMPLETE SET (108) 20.00 40.00
1 Fredrik Norrena .20 .50
2 Hannu Virta .15 .40
3 Petteri Nummelin .07 .20
4 Tuomas Gronman .15 .40
5 Marko Kiprusoff .15 .40

6 Saku Koivu 2.00 5.00
7 Raimo Summanen .15 .40
8 Esa Keskinen .15 .40
9 Jere Lehtinen 1.25 3.00
10 Ari Sulander .30 .75
11 Waltteri Immonen .07 .20
12 Mika Stromberg .15 .40
13 Janne Niinimaa .40 1.00
14 Otakar Janecky .15 .40
15 Teemu Selanne 4.00 10.00
16 Jari Kurri 1.25 3.00
17 Antti Tormanen .15 .40
18 Petri Varis .30 .75
19 Kari Takko .30 .75
20 Olli Kaski .07 .20
21 Rauli Raitanen .07 .20
22 Jari Korpisalo .07 .20
23 Teppo Kivela .07 .20
24 Jokke Heinanen .07 .20
25 Arto Javanainen .07 .20
26 Jari Levonen .07 .20
27 Arto Heiskanen .07 .20
28 Jarmo Myllys .40 1.00
29 Boris Rousson .20 .50
30 Jarmo Kuusisto .07 .20
31 Joni Lehto .07 .20
32 Robert Nordmark .07 .20
33 Tero Arkiomaa .07 .20
34 Jari Torkki .07 .20
35 Juha Riihijarvi .15 .40
36 Matti Forss .07 .20
37 Sakari Lindfors .30 .75
38 Pertti Lehtonen .07 .20
39 Simo Saarinen .07 .20
40 Esa Tikkanen .40 1.00
41 Ville Peltonen .40 1.00
42 Christian Ruuttu .15 .40
43 Mika Kortelainen .07 .20
44 Darren Boyko .07 .20
45 Iiro Jarvi .15 .40
46 Ari-Pekka Siekkinen .20 .50
47 Harri Laurila .07 .20
48 Jouni Loponen .07 .20
49 Joni Lius .07 .20
50 Jari Lindroos .07 .20
51 Risto Kurkinen .07 .20
52 Thomas Sjorgren .07 .20
53 Marko Virtanen .07 .20
54 Michael Nylander .40 1.00
55 Mika Rautio .20 .50
56 Sami Nuutinen .07 .20
57 Peter Ahola .07 .20
58 Timo Blomqvist .07 .20
59 Ikka Sinisalo .15 .40
60 Petro Koivunen .15 .40
61 Sergei Prjahin .07 .20
62 Tero Lehtera .07 .20
63 Mariusz Czerkawski .40 1.00
64 Pasi Kuivalainen .30 .75
65 Kimmo Timonen .40 1.00
66 Reijo Ruotsalainen .15 .40
67 Vesa Salo .15 .40
68 Petr Korinek .07 .20
69 Marko Jantunen .15 .40
70 Pekka Tirkkonen .07 .20
71 Janne Kekalainen .07 .20
72 Sami Kapanen .75 2.00
73 Timo Jutila .07 .20
74 Pekka Laksola .07 .20
75 Janne Gronvall .15 .40
76 Jiri Kucera .07 .20
77 Janne Ojanen .20 .50
78 Pauli Jarvinen .07 .20
79 Ari Haanpaa .07 .20
80 Aleksander Barkov .07 .20
81 Theo Fleury 1.25 3.00
82 Kari Rosenberg .15 .40
83 Janne Laukkanen .20 .50
84 Jani Nikko .15 .40
85 Mika Lartama .07 .20
86 Kai Nurminen .30 .75
87 Tomas Kapusta .07 .20
88 Marko Palo .07 .20
89 Jarkko Varvio .15 .40
90 Risto Jalo .15 .40
91 Jukka Tammi .20 .50
92 Risto Siltanen .15 .40
93 Teppo Numminen .30 .75
94 Marco Poulsen .07 .20
95 Jukka Seppo .07 .20
96 Vesa Karjalainen .07 .20
97 Ted Donato .15 .40
98 Juha Virtanen .07 .20
99 Jari Hirsimaki .07 .20
100 Vesa Toskala 2.50 5.00
101 Jyrki Lumme .40 1.00
102 Hannu Henriksson .07 .20
103 Allan Measures .07 .20
104 Timo Peltomaa .07 .20
105 Juha Hautamaa .07 .20
106 Mikko Makela .15 .40
107 Juha Jarvenpaa .07 .20
108 Semi Pekki .07 .20
NNO Koivu Line Super Chase 10.00 25.00

1995-96 Finnish SISU Limited Leaf Gallery

COMPLETE SET (9) 10.00 15.00
1 Jyrki Lumme .75 2.00
2 Janne Laukkanen .75 2.00
3 Michael Nylander 1.25 3.00
4 Janne Ojanen .75 2.00
5 Peter Ahola .75 2.00
6 Kari Takko 1.25 3.00
7 Hannu Virta .75 2.00
8 Juha Lind .75 2.00
9 Sakari Lindfors 1.25 3.00

1995-96 Finnish SISU Limited Signed and Sealed

COMPLETE SET (9) 20.00 25.00
1 Sami Kapanen 1.25 3.00
2 Christian Ruuttu .75 2.00
3 Teemu Selanne 7.50 15.00
4 Aki Berg .75 2.00
5 Joni Lehto .75 2.00
6 Teppo Numminen .75 2.00
7 Jari Kurri 2.00 5.00
8 Esa Tikkanen 1.25 3.00
9 Theo Fleury 2.00 5.00

1995-96 Finnish SISU Painkillers

COMPLETE SET (8) 3.00 8.00
1 Jokke Heinanen .40 1.00
2 Mika Alatalo .40 1.00
3 Joni Lehto .40 1.00
4 Harri Lonnberg .40 1.00
5 Ville Peltonen .75 2.00
6 Harri Sillgren .40 1.00
7 Petri Varis .75 2.00
8 Marko Virtanen .40 1.00

1995-96 Finnish SISU Specials

COMPLETE SET (10) 16.00 40.00
1 Petri Varis 1.25 3.00
2 Boris Rousson 1.25 3.00
3 Saku Koivu 6.00 15.00
4 Jari Kurri 3.00 8.00
5 Jarmo Kuusisto .75 2.00
6 Janne Ojanen .75 2.00
7 Jere Lehtinen 3.00 8.00
8 Peter Ahola .75 2.00
9 Jukka Seppo .75 2.00
10 Michael Nylander 1.25 3.00

1995-96 Finnish SISU Spotlights

COMPLETE SET (8) 2.00 5.00
1 Otakar Janecky .40 1.00
2 Jari Korpisalo .40 1.00
3 Juha Riihijarvi .40 1.00
4 Iiro Jarvi .40 1.00
5 Thomas Sjogren .40 1.00
6 Risto Jalo .40 1.00
7 Jari Hirsimaki .40 1.00
8 Juha Hautamaa .40 1.00

1996-97 Finnish SISU Redline

COMPLETE SET (200) 8.00 20.00
1 Checklist (1-50) .02 .10
2 Sakari Lindfors .20 .50
3 Peter Ahola .05 .15
4 Jere Karalahti .20 .50
5 Pertti Lehtonen .02 .10
6 Lauri Puolanne .02 .10
7 Sami Laine .08 .25
8 Tommy Kiviaho .02 .10
9 Markku Hurme .02 .10
10 Jari Laukkanen .02 .10
11 Tero Nyman .02 .10
12 Toni Sihvonen .02 .10
13 Mika Kortelainen .05 .15
14 Tero Hamalainen .02 .10
15 Mika Pietila .08 .25
16 Erik Kakko .02 .10
17 Tom Koivisto .02 .10
18 Jani Nikko .08 .25
19 Risto Jalo .08 .25
20 Aleksander Andrievski .05 .15
21 Jari Kauppila .02 .10
22 Jarkko Savijoki .02 .10
23 Toni Makiaho .02 .10
24 Mika Kannisto .02 .10
25 Mika Puhakka .02 .10
26 Toni Saarinen .02 .10
27 Vesa Toskala .40 1.00
28 Teemu Vuorinen .02 .10
29 Petri Kokko .02 .10
30 Pekka Kangasalusta .02 .10
31 Tommi Kahiluoto .02 .10
32 Jarno Peltonen .02 .10
33 Mika Arvaja .02 .10
34 Matti Kaipainen .02 .10
35 Hannu Mattila .02 .10
36 Tomi Hirvonen .02 .10
37 Jouni Lahtinen .02 .10
38 Jari Suorsa .02 .10
39 Juha Jarvenpaa .07 .20
40 Semi Pekki .02 .10
41 Ari Sulander .20 .50
42 Mika Stromberg .08 .25
43 Marko Tuulola .02 .10
44 Pasi Sormunen .02 .10
45 Waltteri Immonen .05 .15
46 Jukka Penttinen .02 .10
47 Petri Varis .20 .50
48 Keijo Sailynoja .08 .25
49 Tero Lehtera .05 .15
50 Checklist (51-100) .02 .10
51 Jari Lindroos .05 .15
52 Ismo Kuoppala .02 .10
53 Juha Ylonen .20 .50
54 Pasi Saarela .05 .15
55 Marko Leinonen .02 .10
56 Kalle Koskinen .02 .10
57 J-P Laamanen .02 .10
58 Jouni Loponen .02 .10
59 Pekka Poikolainen .02 .10
60 Jan Latvala .02 .10
61 Timo Ahmaoja .02 .10
62 Mika Paananen .02 .10
63 Kimmo Salminen .02 .10
64 Lasse Jamsen .02 .10
65 Thomas Sjogren .07 .20
66 Juha Viinikainen .02 .10
67 Mikko Inkinen .02 .10
68 Toni Koivunen .02 .10
69 Pasi Kuivalainen .08 .25
70 Tommi Kovanen .02 .10
71 Jermu Pisto .02 .10
72 Ivan Vlzek .02 .10
73 Mika Laaksonen .02 .10
74 Miikka Ruokonen .02 .10
75 Sami Simonen .02 .10
76 Mikko Honkonen .02 .10
77 Veli-Pekka Nutikka .20 .50
78 Arto Sirvio .02 .10
79 Janne Kekalainen .02 .10
80 Jarno Levonne .02 .10
81 Jussi Tarvainen .02 .10
82 Iiro Itamies .08 .25
83 Tommi Nyyssonen .02 .10
84 Kari Haakana .02 .10
85 Jarmo Muukkonen .02 .10
86 Tero Nissinen .02 .10
87 Tero Tiainen .02 .10
88 Joonas Jaaskelainen .02 .10
89 Juha Ikonen .02 .10
90 Timo Norppa .02 .10
91 Teemu Riihijarvi .08 .25
92 Mikko Koivunoro .02 .10
93 Sergei Priakhin .05 .15
94 Timo Hirvonen .02 .10
95 Boris Rousson .20 .50
96 Kimmo Lotvonen .02 .10
97 Riku Kallioniemi .02 .10
98 Martti Jarventie .15 .40
99 Mikko Luovi .07 .20
100 Checklist (101-150) .02 .10
101 Kalle Sahlstedt .08 .25
102 Sakari Palsola .02 .10
103 Tommi Turunen .02 .10
104 Petri Latti .02 .10
105 Jonni Vauhkonen .05 .15
106 Veli-Pekka Ahonen .02 .10
107 Jari Torkki .05 .15
108 Jarkko Varvio .05 .15
109 Matti Viitakoski .02 .10
110 Mikko Myllykoski .02 .10
111 Petri Peronmaa .02 .10
112 Vesa Ruotsalainen .02 .10
113 Timo Lohko .02 .10
114 Simo Liukka .02 .10
115 Juha-Pekka Rinkinen .02 .10
116 Timo Makinen .02 .10
117 Marko Ek .05 .15
118 Matti Nevalainen .02 .10
119 Ari Santanen .02 .10
120 Jonas Hemming .02 .10
121 Mika Karapuu .02 .10
122 Ilpo Kauhanen .20 .50
123 Sami-Ville Salomaa .02 .10
124 Antti Rahkonen .02 .10
125 Harri Laurilla .02 .10
126 Sami Lehtonen .02 .10
127 Pasi Petrilainen .08 .25
128 Arto Kulmala .02 .10
129 Jarkko Nikander .02 .10
130 Timo Nurmberg .02 .10
131 Tuomas Reijonen .02 .10
132 Aleksander Barkov .02 .10
133 Mika Niittymaki .02 .10
134 Valeri Krykov .02 .10
135 Fredrik Norrena .20 .50
136 Mika Lehtinen .02 .10
137 Sami Salo .20 .50
138 Riku-Petteri Lehtonen .02 .10
139 Mikko Sokka .02 .10
140 Manu Laapas .02 .10
141 Hannes Hyvonen .15 .40
142 Miikka Rousu .02 .10
143 Simo Rouvali .02 .10
144 Tommi Miettinen .02 .10
145 Kimmo Rintanen .20 .50
146 Tomi Kallio .20 .50
147 Antti Aalto .20 .50
148 Miika Elomo .20 .50
149 Kari Takko .20 .50
150 Checklist (151-200) .02 .10
151 Tommi Rajemaki .08 .25
152 Pasi Peltonen .02 .10
153 Karri Kivi .07 .20
154 Jokke Heinanen .02 .10
155 Teppo Kivela .02 .10
156 Vesa Goman .02 .10
157 Pekka Virta .02 .10
158 Pasi Tuominen .02 .10
159 Timo Hakanen .02 .10
160 Jari Levonen .02 .10
161 Jari Korpisalo .05 .15
162 Timo Salonen .02 .10
163 Jokerit .08 .25
164 Jokerit .02 .10
165 Jokerit .02 .10
166 Jokerit .02 .10
167 Jokerit .02 .10
168 Jokerit .02 .10
169 Jokerit .02 .10
170 Jokerit .02 .10
171 Jokerit .02 .10
172 Jokerit .02 .10
173 Jokerit .02 .10
174 Jokerit .02 .10
175 Ari Sulander .20 .50
176 Joni Lehto .05 .15
177 Timo Jutila .05 .15
178 Mikko Peltola .02 .10
179 Juha Riihijarvi .08 .25
180 Petri Varis .20 .50
181 Boris Rousson .20 .50
182 Kimmo Timonen .20 .50
183 Mika Stromberg .08 .25
184 Jari Korpisalo .05 .15
185 Otakar Janecky .08 .25
186 Juha Lind .08 .25
187 Aarne Honkavaara .20 .50
188 Esko Niemi .02 .10
189 Raimo Kilpio .02 .10
190 Jarmo Wasama .02 .10
191 Lalli Partinen .02 .10
192 Urpo Ylonen .08 .25
193 Ilpo Koskela .20 .50
194 Jorma Vehmanen .02 .10
195 Pekka Marjamaki .02 .10
196 Veli-Pekka Ketola .08 .25
197 Matti Murto .02 .10
198 Juhani Tamminen .08 .25
199 Matti Hagman .07 .20
200 Checklist (inserts) .08 .25
NNO Kari Takko Super Bonus 2.00 5.00
NNO Juha Riihijarvi Chase 2.00 5.00

1996-97 Finnish SISU Redline At The Gala

COMPLETE SET (8) 5.00 10.00
1 Petri Varis .75 2.00
2 Juha Riihijarvi .40 1.00
3 Waltteri Immonen .40 1.00
4 Jani Hurme 1.25 3.00
5 Pasi Kuivalainen .75 2.00
6 Mika Stromberg .40 1.00
7 Sakari Pietila .40 1.00
8 Ari Sulander .75 2.00

1996-97 Finnish SISU Redline Keeping It Green

COMPLETE SET (4) 15.00 30.00
1 Ari Sulander 4.00 10.00
2 Jani Hurme 7.50 15.00
3 Boris Rousson 4.00 10.00
4 Mika Pietila 4.00 10.00

1996-97 Finnish SISU Redline Mighty Adversaries

COMPLETE SET (9) 10.00 25.00
1 K.Takko
K.Rintanen 1.25 3.00
2 B.Rousson
P.Saarela 1.25 3.00
3 I.Kauhanen
A.Andrijevski 1.25 3.00
4 A.Sulander
M.Kortelainen 1.25 3.00
5 P.Kuivalainen
T.Sjogren 1.25 3.00
6 V.Toskala
J.Ojanen 2.00 5.00
7 F.Norrena
O.Janecky 1.25 3.00
8 S.Lindfors
J.Korpisalo 1.25 3.00
9 A.Siekkinen
J.Lindroos 1.25 3.00

1996-97 Finnish SISU Redline Promos

COMPLETE SET (12) 15.00
1 Mika Kortelainen .40 1.00
2 Alexander Andrievski .40 1.00
3 Vesa Toskala 1.25 3.00
4 Jari Lindroos .40 1.00
5 Thomas Sjogren .40 1.00
6 Pasi Kuivalainen .75 2.00
7 Iiro Itamies .75 2.00
8 Kalle Sahlstedt .75 2.00
9 Mika Karapuu .40 1.00
10 Valeri Krykov .40 1.00
11 Kimmo Rintanen .40 1.00
12 Jari Levonen .40 1.00

1996-97 Finnish SISU Redline Rookie Energy

COMPLETE SET (9) 8.00 15.00
1 Jani Hurme 2.00 5.00
2 Mikko Eloranta .75 2.00
3 Sami Salo .75 2.00
4 Tero Hamalainen .40 1.00
5 Miika Elomo .75 2.00
6 Mika Pietila .40 1.00
7 Arto Kuki .40 1.00
8 Vesa Toskala 2.00 5.00
9 Miikka Rousu .40 1.00

1996-97 Finnish SISU Redline Silver Signatures

COMPLETE SET (5) 60.00 125.00
1 Jani Hurme 12.00 30.00
2 Pasi Kuivalainen 8.00 20.00
3 Boris Rousson 12.00 30.00
4 Ari Sulander 12.00 30.00
5 Vesa Toskala 15.00 40.00

1996-97 Finnish SISU Redline Sledgehammers

COMPLETE SET (9) 2.00 5.00
1 Hannu Henriksson .40 1.00
2 Robert Nordmark .40 1.00
3 Pasi Sormunen .40 1.00
4 Tuomas Gronman .40 1.00
5 Derek Mayer .40 1.00
6 Toni Porkka .40 1.00
7 Timo Peltomaa .40 1.00
8 Iiro Jarvi .40 1.00
9 Joni Lehto .40 1.00

1998-99 Finnish Kerailysarja

COMPLETE SET (270) 16.00 40.00
1 Checklist 1-60 .07 .20
2 Checklist 61-120 .07 .20
3 Checklist 121-180 .07 .20
4 Checklist 181-240 .07 .20
5 Checklist 241-270 .07 .20
6 Inserts Checklist .07 .20
7 Ari-Pekka Siekkinen .15 .40
8 Jani Riihinen .07 .20
9 Riku Varjamo .07 .20
10 Jiri Vykoukal .07 .20
11 Jonas Andersson-Junkka .15 .40
12 Riku-Petteri Lehtonen .07 .20
13 Pasi Sormunen .07 .20
14 Robert Salo .07 .20
15 Juha Gustafsson .15 .40
16 Christian Ruuttu .15 .40
17 Tero Hamalainen .07 .20
18 Juha Ikonen .07 .20
19 Hannes Hyvonen .20 .50
20 Timo Hirvonen .20 .50
21 Petr Ton .07 .20
22 Nils Ekman .30 .75
23 Joonas Jaaskelainen .07 .20
24 Tommy Kiviaho .07 .20
25 Tomas Kapusta .07 .20
26 Tero Tiainen .07 .20
27 Teemu Riihijarvi .15 .40
28 Jan Lundell .07 .20
29 Niklas Backstrom .07 .20
30 Ville Siren .07 .20
31 Marko From .07 .20
32 Brian Rafalski .40 1.00
33 Jarno Kultanen .20 .50
34 Toni Lydman .20 .50
35 Jani Nikko .15 .40
36 Jere Karalahti .15 .40
37 Kari Rajala .07 .20
38 Kari Kalto .07 .20
39 Kimmo Kuhta .07 .20
40 Jan Caloun .15 .40
41 Markku Hurme .07 .20
42 Tom Laaksonen .07 .20
43 Niklas Hagman .40 1.00
44 Luciano Borsato .07 .20
45 Toni Sihvonen .07 .20
46 Mika Kortelainen .15 .40
47 Toni Makiaho .07 .20
48 Mika Nieminen .15 .40
49 Jarkko Ruutu .30 .75
50 Marko Tuomainen .15 .40
51 Pasi Nurminen 1.50 4.00
52 Kari Rosenberg .07 .20
53 Aki Heino .07 .20
54 Erik Kakko .07 .20
55 Tom Koivisto .07 .20
56 Ari Vallin .07 .20
57 Tomi Kallarsson .07 .20
58 Jaroslav Nedved .07 .20
59 Kai Rautio .07 .20
60 Mikko Kuparinen .15 .40
61 Mika Kannisto .07 .20
62 Juha Virtanen .07 .20
63 Jani Keinanen .07 .20
64 Jyrki Louhi .07 .20
65 Roman Simicek .20 .50
66 Semi Pekki .07 .20
67 Timo Parssinen .07 .20
68 Jarkko Savijoki .07 .20
69 Marko Palo .07 .20
70 Antti Virtanen .07 .20
71 Niko Kapanen .75 2.00
72 Tomas Vlasak .15 .40
73 Riku Hahl .40 1.00
74 Vesa Toskala .75 2.00
75 Markus Korhonen .07 .20
76 Timo Willman .07 .20
77 Veli-Pekka Hard .07 .20
78 Pekka Kangasalusta .07 .20
79 Oscar Ackestrom .07 .20
80 Allan Measures .07 .20
81 Pasi Puistola .07 .20
82 Pasi Saarinen .15 .40
83 Mikko Haapakoski .07 .20
84 Martti Jarventie .20 .50
85 Mika Arvaja .07 .20
86 Juha Hautamaa .07 .20
87 Raimo Helminen .15 .40
88 Tomi Hirvonen .07 .20
89 Matti Kaipainen .07 .20
90 Peter Larsson .07 .20
91 Vesa Viitakoski .15 .40
92 Mikko Peltola .07 .20
93 Timo Peltomaa .07 .20
94 Hannu Mattila .07 .20
95 Sami Ahlberg .07 .20
96 Juha Jarvenpaa .07 .20
97 Markus Ketterer .15 .40
98 Ari Kumpula .07 .20
99 Waltteri Immonen .07 .20
100 Antti-Jussi Niemi .15 .40
101 Sami Nuutinen .07 .20
102 Yves Racine .15 .40
103 Rami Alanko .07 .20
104 Mika Stromberg .15 .40
105 Ossi Vaananen .40 1.00
106 Jani Rita .40 1.00
107 Sami Mettovaara .07 .20
108 Fredrik Nilsson .07 .20
109 Kimmo Rintanen .15 .40
110 Jari Kauppila .07 .20
111 Pasi Saarela .15 .40
112 Timo Saarikoski .07 .20
113 Eero Somervuori .15 .40
114 Jukka Tiilikainen .07 .20
115 Jarkko Vaananen .07 .20
116 Otakar Janecky .15 .40
117 Patrik Juhlin .15 .40
118 Juha Lind .20 .50
119 Marko Leinonen .07 .20
120 Tommi Satosaari .07 .20
121 Mikko Luoma .07 .20
122 Jan Latvala .07 .20
123 Kevin Wortman .07 .20
124 Kalle Koskinen .07 .20
125 Jyrki Valivaara .07 .20
126 Markus Kankaanpera .07 .20
127 Jarkko Glad .07 .20
128 Marko Kauppinen .07 .20
129 Robert Nordberg .07 .20
130 Juha Viinikainen .07 .20
131 Marko Ojanen .07 .20
132 Toni Koivunen .07 .20
133 Mikko Rantala .07 .20
134 Jussi Tarvainen .07 .20
135 Tommi Turunen .07 .20
136 Timo Vertala .07 .20
137 Veli-Pekka Nutikka .15 .40
138 Stefan Ornskog .07 .20
139 Marko Virtanen .07 .20
140 Lasse Jamsen .07 .20
141 Kimmo Kapanen .07 .20
142 Ari Luostarinen .07 .20
143 Tobias Ablad .07 .20
144 Derry Menard .07 .20
145 Jermu Pisto .07 .20
146 Sebastian Sulku .07 .20
147 Timo Ahmaoja .07 .20
148 Teemu Tuomainen .07 .20
149 Pekka Poikolainen .07 .20
150 Aki Korhonen .07 .20
151 Pekka Tirkkonen .07 .20
152 Petro Koivunen .07 .20
153 Marko Levanen .07 .20
154 Janne Kekalainen .07 .20
155 Antti Riekkinen .07 .20
156 Mikko Honkonen .07 .20
157 Timo Sikkula .07 .20
158 Sami Simonen .07 .20
159 Mikko Konttila .07 .20
160 Jaakko Uhlback .07 .20
161 Lubos Rob .07 .20
162 Kimmo Vesa .07 .20
163 Sinuhe Wallinheimo .07 .20
164 Jaakko Harikkala .15 .40
165 Atvars Tribuntsovs .07 .20
166 Ismo Kuoppala .07 .20
167 Kimmo Lotvonen .07 .20
168 Marko Toivonen .07 .20
169 Erik Hamalainen .15 .40
170 Mikael Tjallden .07 .20
171 Roland Carlsson .07 .20
172 Niko Halttunen .07 .20
173 Jouni Vauhkonen .07 .20
174 Matti Raunio .07 .20
175 Ville Mikkonen .07 .20
176 Petri Pakaslahti .07 .20
177 Janne Seva .07 .20
178 Harri Sillgren .07 .20
179 Leonids Tambijevs .07 .20
180 Jari Hyvarinen .07 .20
181 Patrik Wallenberg .07 .20
182 Jarkko Nikander .07 .20
183 Aigars Cipruss .07 .20
184 Jussi Markkanen .60 1.50
185 Pasi Hakkinen .07 .20
186 Harri Tikkanen .07 .20
187 Juri Kuznetsov .07 .20
188 Riku Kallioniemi .07 .20
189 Jussi Pekkala .07 .20
190 Mikko Myllykoski .07 .20
191 Vesa Ruotsalainen .07 .20
192 Tommi Sova .07 .20
193 Dale McTavish .07 .20
194 Pasi Maattanen .07 .20
195 Aleksander Matsijevski .07 .20
196 Sami Kaartinen .07 .20
197 Ari Saarinen .07 .20
198 Joel Salonen .07 .20
199 Ari Santanen .07 .20
200 Mika Skytta .07 .20
201 Mika Kauppinen .07 .20
202 Keijo Sailynoja .07 .20
203 Eric Weilleux .07 .20
204 Ville Immonen .07 .20
205 Mika Noronen 2.00 5.00
206 Iiro Itamies .07 .20
207 Josef Boumedienne .20 .50
208 Miska Kangasniemi .15 .40
209 Mikko Tamminen .07 .20
210 Timo Jutila .07 .20
211 Janne Gronvall .15 .40
212 Sami-Ville Salomaa .07 .20
213 Janne Vuorela .07 .20
214 Pasi Petrilainen .15 .40
215 Pasi Tuominen .07 .20
216 Jani Hassinen .07 .20
217 Valeri Krykov .07 .20
218 Juha Vuorivirta .07 .20
219 Aleksander Barkov .07 .20
220 Harri Lonnberg .07 .20
221 Arto Kumala .07 .20
222 Janne Ojanen .15 .40
223 Lasse Pirjeta .07 .20
224 Sami Salonen .07 .20
225 Johannes Alanen .07 .20
226 Mikko Makela .15 .40
227 Fredrik Norrena .15 .40
228 Miikka Kiprusoff 2.00 5.00
229 Kimmo Eronen .07 .20
230 Marko Kiprusoff .07 .20
231 Jouni Loponen .07 .20
232 Ilkka Mikkola .15 .40
233 Aki Berg .20 .50
234 Tommi Rajamaki .15 .40
235 Peter Ahola .07 .20
236 Mika Lehtinen .07 .20
237 Tony Virta .07 .20
238 Joni Lius .07 .20
239 Mikko Eloranta .20 .50
240 Marco Tuokko .07 .20
241 Juha Joninen .07 .20
242 Tomi Kallio .15 .40
243 Mikko Rautio .07 .20
244 Jani Kiviharju .07 .20
245 Tommi Miettinen .20 .50
246 Simo Rouvali .07 .20
247 Kalle Sahlstedt .15 .40
248 Teemu Elomo .15 .40
249 Mika Alatalo .20 .50
250 Miika Elomo .15 .40
251 Pasi Kuivalainen .15 .40
252 Mika Lehto .07 .20
253 Joachim Esbjors .07 .20
254 Mikko Sokka .07 .20
255 Pasi Peltonen .15 .40
256 Vesa Salo .07 .20
257 Mika Laaksonen .07 .20
258 Santeri Immonen .07 .20
259 Jonas Esbjors .07 .20
260 Vjatcheslav Fandul .07 .20
261 Kimmo Salminen .07 .20
262 Jokke Heinanen .07 .20
263 Jari Levonen .07 .20
264 Niko Mikkola .07 .20
265 Andrei Potaitshuk .07 .20
266 Rauli Raitanen .07 .20
267 Timo Hakanen .07 .20
268 Jan Benda .07 .20
269 Tero Arkiomaa .15 .40
270 Marko Kivenmaki .07 .20

1998-99 Finnish Kerailysarja 90's Top 12

COMPLETE SET (12) 16.00 30.00
1 Jere Lehtinen 1.25 3.00
2 Pertti Lehtonen .75 2.00
3 Janne Laukkanen .75 2.00
4 Jukka Tammi .75 2.00
5 Teemu Selanne 4.00 10.00
6 Jari Lindroos .75 2.00
7 Sami Kapanen 1.25 3.00
8 Jarmo Kuusisto .75 2.00
9 Ari Santanen .75 2.00
10 Timo Jutila .75 2.00
11 Saku Koivu 2.00 5.00
12 Kari Takko .75 2.00

1998-99 Finnish Kerailysarja Dream Team

COMPLETE SET (7) 16.00 20.00
1 Jari Kurri 2.00 5.00
2 Ari Sulander 1.25 3.00
3 Jyrki Lumme .75 2.00
4 Janne Niinimaa .75 2.00
5 Jere Lehtinen 1.50 4.00
6 Saku Koivu 2.00 5.00
7 Teemu Selanne 4.00 10.00

1998-99 Finnish Kerailysarja Leijonat

COMPLETE SET (47) 6.00 15.00
1 Markus Ketterer .20 .50
2 Jarmo Myllys .20 .50
3 Jukka Tammi .20 .50
4 Peter Ahola .08 .25
5 Erik Hamalainen .08 .25
6 Timo Jutila .08 .25
7 Jere Karalahti .20 .50
8 Marko Kiprusoff .08 .25
9 Janne Laukkanen .20 .50
10 Joni Lehto .08 .25
11 Kaj Linna .08 .25
12 Jouni Loponen .08 .25
13 Toni Lydman .15 .40
14 Antti-Jussi Niemi .20 .50
15 Petteri Nummelin .08 .25
16 Mika Stromberg .08 .25
17 Kimmo Timonen .20 .50
18 Hannu Virta .08 .25
19 Mika Alatalo .20 .50
20 Mikko Eloranta .20 .50
21 Raimo Helminen .08 .25
22 Juha Ikonen .08 .25
23 Marko Jantunen .08 .25
24 Olli Jokinen .75 2.00
25 Joonas Jaaskelainen .08 .25
26 Sami Kapanen .75 2.00
27 Esa Keskinen .08 .25
28 Jari Korpisalo .08 .25
29 Tero Lehtera .08 .25
30 Juha Lind .08 .25
31 Joni Lius .08 .25
32 Toni Maklaho .08 .25
33 Mika Nieminen .20 .50
34 Janne Ojanen .08 .25
35 Marko Palo .08 .25
36 Ville Peltonen .30 .75
37 Juha Riihijarvi .08 .25
38 Kimmo Rintanen .08 .25
39 Christian Ruuttu .15 .40
40 Jarkko Ruutu .08 .25
41 Jukka Seppo .08 .25
42 Raimo Summanen .08 .25
43 Esa Tikkanen .40 1.00
44 Marko Tuomainen .08 .25
45 Antti Tormanen .08 .25
46 Jarkko Varvio .08 .25
47 Juha Ylonen .20 .50

1998-99 Finnish Kerailysarja Mad Masks

COMPLETE SET (12) 24.00 75.00
1 Ari-Pekka Siekkinen 2.00 5.00
2 Jan Lundell 2.00 5.00
3 Pasi Nurminen 6.00 15.00
4 Vesa Toskala 4.00 10.00
5 Markus Ketterer 2.00 5.00
6 Marko Leinonen 2.00 5.00
7 Kimmo Kapanen 2.00 5.00
8 Sinuhe Wallinheimo 2.00 5.00
9 Jussi Markkanen 4.00 10.00
10 Mika Noronen 6.00 15.00
11 Fredrik Norrena 2.00 5.00
12 Pasi Kuivalainen 2.00 5.00

1998-99 Finnish Kerailysarja Off Duty

COMPLETE SET (12) 8.00 20.00
1 Juha Ikonen .75 2.00
2 Toni Sihvonen .75 2.00
3 Tom Koivisto .75 2.00
4 Juha Hautamaa .75 2.00
5 Kimmo Rintanen .75 2.00
6 Marko Leinonen .75 2.00
7 Sami Simonen .75 2.00
8 Sinuhe Wallinheimo 1.25 3.00
9 Jussi Markkanen 1.50 4.00
10 Arto Kulmala .75 2.00
11 Marko Kiprusoff .75 2.00
12 Pasi Kuivalainen .75 2.00

1999 Finnish Valio World Championships

COMPLETE SET (6) 6.00 15.00
1 Kari Eloranta .75 2.00
2 Jari Kurri 3.00 8.00
3 Tapio Levo .75 2.00
4 Markus Mattsson 1.25 3.00
5 Jukka Porvari .75 2.00
6 Pekka Rautakallio .75 2.00

1999-00 Finnish Cardset

COMPLETE SET (346) 30.00 75.00
1 Checklist 1-40 .07 .20
2 Checklist 41-80 .07 .20
3 Checklist 81-120 .07 .20
4 Checklist 121-160 .07 .20
5 Checklist 161-200 .07 .20
6 Inserts Checklist .07 .20
7 Ari-Pekka Siekkinen .15 .40
8 Jiri Vykoukal .07 .20
9 Riku Varjamo .07 .20
10 Riku-Petteri Lehtonen .07 .20
11 Juha Gustafsson .15 .40
12 Arto Laatikainen .30 .75
13 Hannes Hyvonen .20 .50
14 Timo Hirvonen .20 .50
15 Tommy Kiviaho .07 .20
16 Tero Tiainen .07 .20
17 Joonas Jaaskelainen .07 .20
18 Teemu Riihijarvi .15 .40
19 Olli Ahonen .07 .20
20 Santeri Heiskanen .07 .20
21 Jarno Kultanen .20 .50
22 Marko From .07 .20
23 Kimmo Kuhta .07 .20
24 Tom Laaksonen .07 .20
25 Kari Kalto .07 .20
26 Jan Caloun .15 .40
27 Markku Hurme .07 .20
28 Toni Makiaho .07 .20
29 Mika Nieminen .15 .40
30 Luciano Borsato .07 .20

31 Aki Heino .07 .20
32 Jonas Andersson-Junkka .15 .40
33 Tomi Kallarsson .07 .20
34 Roman Simicek .20 .50
35 Juha Virtanen .07 .20
36 Antti Virtanen .07 .20
37 Jyrki Louhi .07 .20
38 Jarkko Savijoki .07 .20
39 Jukka Hentunen .20 .50
40 Timo Parssinen .40 1.00
41 Niko Kapanen .40 1.00
42 Tomas Vlasak .15 .40
43 Kristian Antila .07 .20
44 Pasi Puistola .07 .20
45 Pasi Saarinen .15 .40
46 Pekka Kangasalusta .07 .20
47 Martti Jarventie .07 .20
48 Sami Karjalainen .07 .20
49 Riku Niemela .07 .20
50 Mikko Peltola .07 .20
51 Juha Hautamaa .07 .20
52 Raimo Helminen .15 .40
53 Tomi Hirvonen .07 .20
54 Sami Ahlberg .07 .20
55 Vesa Viitakoski .07 .20
56 Mika Arvaja .07 .20
57 Rami Alanko .07 .20
58 Antti-Jussi Niemi .15 .40
59 Antti Hulkkonen .10 .30
60 Jani Rita .40 1.00
61 Jarkko Vaananen .07 .20
62 Fredrik Nilsson .07 .20
63 Jari Kauppila .07 .20
64 Eero Somervuori .20 .50
65 Jukka Tiilikainen .07 .20
66 Patrik Juhlin .15 .40
67 Tommi Satosaari .07 .20
68 Jarkko Glad .07 .20
69 Jyrki Valivaara .07 .20
70 Markus Kankaanpera .07 .20
71 Kalle Koskinen .07 .20
72 Juha Viinikainen .07 .20
73 Marko Ojanen .07 .20
74 Toni Koivunen .07 .20
75 Veli-Pekka Nutikka .15 .40
76 Stefan Ornskog .07 .20
77 Marko Virtanen .07 .20
78 Lasse Jamsen .07 .20
79 Petri Vehanen .07 .20
80 Kimmo Lotvonen .07 .20
81 Jaakko Harikkala .15 .40
82 Ismo Kuoppala .07 .20
83 Erik Hamalainen .15 .40
84 Zdenek Nedved .07 .20
85 Harri Suvanto .07 .20
86 Jouni Vauhkonen .07 .20
87 Ville Mikkonen .07 .20
88 Janne Seva .07 .20
89 Petri Latti .07 .20
90 Harri Sillgren .07 .20
91 Leonids Tambijevs .07 .20
92 Sami Lehtinen .07 .20
93 Jussi-Antti Reimari .07 .20
94 Marko Ahonen .07 .20
95 Veli-Pekka Laitinen .07 .20
96 Mika Niskanen .07 .20
97 Jan Latvala .07 .20
98 Mika Asikainen .07 .20
99 Aigars Cipruss .07 .20
100 Michael Johansson .07 .20
101 Tomi-Pekka Kolu .07 .20
102 Jarkko Ollikainen .07 .20
103 Toni Saarinen .07 .20
104 Jussi Vienonen .07 .20
105 Jouko Mytta .07 .20
106 Jussi Markkanen .40 1.00
107 Harri Tikkanen .07 .20
108 Riku Kallioniemi .07 .20
109 Jussi Pekkala .07 .20
110 Mikko Myllykoski .07 .20
111 Vesa Ruotsalainen .07 .20
112 Tommi Sova .07 .20
113 Ari Santanen .07 .20
114 Pasi Maattanen .07 .20
115 Tero Hamalainen .07 .20
116 Mika Skytta .07 .20
117 Ville Immonen .07 .20
118 Keijo Sailynoja .07 .20
119 Miska Kangasniemi .15 .40
120 Josef Boumedienne .20 .50
121 Janne Vuorela .07 .20
122 Janne Gronvall .15 .40
123 Valeri Krykov .07 .20
124 Arto Kumala .07 .20
125 Aleksander Barkov .07 .20
126 Johannes Alanen .07 .20
127 Jani Hassinen .07 .20
128 Janne Ojanen .15 .40
129 Tuomas Reijonen .07 .20
130 Sami Salonen .07 .20
131 Fredrik Norrena .15 .40
132 Kimmo Eronen .07 .20
133 Marko Kiprusoff .08 .25
134 Jouni Loponen .07 .20
135 Ilkka Mikkola .15 .40
136 Jani Kiviharju .07 .20
137 Tony Virta .07 .20
138 Kalle Sahlstedt .15 .40
139 Tomi Kallio .40 1.00
140 Joni Lius .07 .20
141 Teemu Elomo .15 .40
142 Ville Vahalahti .07 .20
143 Marco Tuokko .07 .20
144 Kai Nurminen .15 .40
145 Petr Kuchyna .07 .20
146 Tuomo Kyha .07 .20
147 Pasi Peltonen .15 .40
148 Santeri Immonen .07 .20
149 Pauli Levokari .07 .20
150 Vesa Salo .07 .20
151 Timo Salonen .07 .20
152 Marko Kivenmaki .07 .20
153 Niko Mikkola .07 .20
154 Andrei Potaitshuk .07 .20
155 Tero Arkiomaa .15 .40
156 Timo Hakanen .07 .20
157 Jan Peterek .07 .20
158 Jan Caloun .15 .40
159 Pasi Saarela .15 .40
160 Tomas Vlasak .15 .40
161 Brian Rafalski .40 1.00
162 Peter Larsson .07 .20
163 Roman Simicek .20 .50
164 Raimo Helminen .15 .40
165 Leonids Tambijevs .07 .20
166 Mika Nieminen .15 .40
167 Janne Ojanen .15 .40
168 Otakar Janecky .15 .40
169 Juha Ikonen .07 .20
170 Jari Kauppila .07 .20
171 Jan Benda .07 .20
172 Tony Virta .07 .20
173 Niko Kapanen .40 1.00
174 Aleksander Barkov .07 .20
175 Hannes Hyvonen .20 .50
176 Lasse Pirjeta .07 .20
177 Jussi Tarvainen .07 .20
178 Miikka Kiprusoff 2.00 5.00
179 Ari Sulander .30 .75
180 Vesa Toskala .75 2.00
181 Aki Berg .20 .50
182 Jere Karalahti .20 .50
183 Marko Kiprusoff .08 .25
184 Toni Lydman .20 .50
185 Kari Martikainen .07 .20
186 Antti-Jussi Niemi .15 .40
187 Petteri Nummelin .15 .40
188 Kimmo Timonen .30 .75
189 Mikko Eloranta .20 .50
190 Raimo Helminen .15 .40
191 Olli Jokinen .40 1.00
192 Tomi Kallio .40 1.00
193 Saku Koivu 1.25 3.00
194 Juha Lind .20 .50
195 Ville Peltonen .20 .50
196 Kimmo Rintanen .15 .40
197 Teemu Selanne 2.00 5.00
198 Toni Sihvonen .07 .20
199 Marko Tuomainen .15 .40
200 Antti Tormanen .20 .50
201 Tom Draper .15 .40
202 Timo Leinonen .07 .20
203 Pasi Nurminen 1.25 3.00
204 Tommi Satosaari .07 .20
205 Mika Oksa .07 .20
206 Jermu Pisto .07 .20
207 Niclas Hedberg .15 .40
208 Peter Ahola .07 .20
209 Aki Korhonen .07 .20
210 Mikko Kaukokari .07 .20
211 Esa Pirnes .07 .20
212 Arto Kuki .07 .20
213 Dale McTavish .15 .40
214 Ari Katavisto .07 .20
215 Teemu Siren .07 .20
216 Mikael Jamsanen .07 .20
217 Otakar Janecky .15 .40
218 Niklas Backstrom .07 .20
219 Ari Ahonen ERC 1.25 3.00
220 Jere Karalahti .20 .50
221 Marek Zidlicky .07 .20
222 Toni Lydman .07 .20
223 Pekka Kangasalusta .07 .20
224 Kari Rajala .07 .20
225 Mike Gaffney .07 .20
226 Timo Ahmaoja .07 .20
227 Aki Tuominen .07 .20
228 Aki Uusikartano .07 .20
229 Mika Kortelainen .15 .40
230 Toni Sihvonen .07 .20
231 Pasi Nielikainen .07 .20
232 Lasse Pirjeta .07 .20
233 Kimmo Kapanen .07 .20
234 Ari Kumpula .07 .20
235 Kimmo Peltonen .07 .20
236 Sebastian Sulku .07 .20
237 Harri Laurila .07 .20
238 Teemu Aalto .07 .20
239 Oscar Ackestrom .07 .20
240 Antti Miettinen ERC .30 .75
241 Marko Palo .07 .20
242 Riku Hahl .40 1.00
243 Petr Tenkrat .30 .75
244 Pasi Kuivalainen .15 .40
245 Arto Tukio .07 .20
246 Hannu Henriksson .07 .20
247 Teemu Kesa .07 .20
248 Antti Bruun .07 .20
249 Tomi Pettinen .07 .20
250 Tapio Sammalkangas .07 .20
251 Rodrigo Lavins .15 .40
252 Ilkka Laitinen .07 .20
253 Tommi Miettinen .15 .40
254 Jarkko Nikander .07 .20
255 Daniel Marois .15 .40
256 Antti Hilden .07 .20
257 Kimmo Vesa .07 .20
258 Pasi Nurminen 1.25 3.00
259 Ossi Vaananen .40 1.00
260 Sean Gagnon .15 .40
261 Marko Kauppinen .15 .40
262 Tuomas Gronman .07 .20
263 Tom Koivisto .07 .20
264 Tomek Valtonen .07 .20
265 Esa Tikkanen .40 1.00
266 Jan Benda .07 .20
267 Tommi Santala .07 .20
268 Petri Varis .15 .40
269 Tuomas Eskelinen .07 .20
270 Tero Lehtera .15 .40
271 Markus Hatinen .07 .20
272 Pekka Poikolainen .07 .20
273 Mikko Luoma .07 .20
274 Vesa Ponto .07 .20
275 Nik Zupancic .07 .20
276 Pasi Kangas .15 .40
277 Topi Riutta .07 .20
278 Jussi Pesonen .07 .20
279 Petr Ton .07 .20
280 Jaroslav Bednar .30 .75
281 Tom Draper .20 .50
282 Mika Laaksonen .07 .20
283 Allan Measures .07 .20
284 Martin Stepanek .07 .20
285 Marko Toivonen .07 .20
286 Petteri Lotila .07 .20
287 Jari Hyvarinen .07 .20
288 Timo Peltomaa .07 .20
289 Petri Pakaslahti .07 .20
290 Jokke Heinanen .07 .20
291 Matti Kaipainen .07 .20
292 Ville Koivula .07 .20
293 Veli-Pekka Kautonen .07 .20
294 Daniel Johansson .07 .20
295 Tommi Kovanen .07 .20
296 Roland Carlsson .07 .20
297 Jani Keinanen .07 .20
298 Mikko Juutilainen .07 .20
299 Aki Kaskinen .07 .20
300 Tommi Turunen .07 .20
301 Mathias Bosson .07 .20
302 Teemu Riihijarvi .07 .20
303 Pasi Hakkinen .07 .20
304 Jani-Matti Loikala .07 .20
305 Juri Kuznetsov .15 .40
306 Mikko Jokela .07 .20
307 Ville Hamalainen .07 .20
308 Joel Salonen .07 .20
309 Timo Saarikoski .07 .20
310 Pekka Tirkkonen .07 .20
311 Mika Kauppinen .15 .40
312 Sami Kaartinen .07 .20
313 Timo Jarvinen .07 .20
314 Jason Muzzatti .20 .50
315 Per Lofstrom .07 .20
316 Ari Vallin .07 .20
317 Asko Rantanen .07 .20
318 Tuukka Mantyla .07 .20
319 Pasi Petrilainen .20 .50
320 Pasi Tuominen .07 .20
321 Roman Meluzin .07 .20
322 Miikka Mannikko .07 .20
323 Jussi Tarvainen .07 .20
324 Timo Vertala .07 .20
325 Jaakko Uhlback .07 .20
326 Antero Niittymaki ERC 1.25 3.00
327 Kimmo Lecklin .07 .20
328 Tommi Rajamaki .07 .20
329 Mika Lehtinen .07 .20
330 Kari Harila .07 .20
331 Petri Tahtisalo .07 .20
332 Esa Keskinen .07 .20
333 Kimmo Rintanen .15 .40
334 Michael Holmkvist .20 .50
335 Mikko Rautee .07 .20
336 Mika Lehto .07 .20
337 Timo Leinonen .07 .20
338 Timo Willman .07 .20
339 Olli Kaski .07 .20
340 Samu Wesslin .07 .20
341 Mika Kannisto .07 .20
342 Ales Kratoska .07 .20
343 Marko Luomala .07 .20
344 Jaakko Makela .07 .20
345 Ondreji Steiner .07 .20
346 Markku Tahtinen .07 .20
NNO Teemu Selanne GG 10.00 25.00
NNO Jere Lehtinen TT 4.00 10.00

1999-00 Finnish Cardset Aces High

COMPLETE SET (54) 8.00 25.00
J1 Jari Kurri .75 2.00
J2 Teemu Selanne 2.00 5.00
C2 Peter Ahola .07 .20
C3 Teppo Numminen .20 .50
C4 Janne Laukkanen .07 .20
C5 Risto Siltanen .07 .20
C6 Iiro Jarvi .07 .20
C7 Antti Aalto .07 .20
C8 Theo Fleury .75 2.00
C9 Ilkka Sinisalo .07 .20
C10 Michael Nylander .07 .20
D2 Timo Blomqvist .07 .20
D3 Sami Salo .07 .20
D4 Marko Kiprusoff .07 .20
D5 Aki Berg .20 .50
D6 Jan Caloun .07 .20
D7 Olli Jokinen .40 1.00
D8 Patrik Juhlin .07 .20
D9 Dale McTavish .07 .20
D10 Sami Kapanen .40 1.00
H2 Hannu Virta .07 .20
H3 Tuomas Gronman .07 .20
H4 Timo Jutila .07 .20
H5 Jyrki Lumme .20 .50
H6 Juha Ylonen .30 .75
H7 Janne Ojanen .07 .20
H8 Juha Lind .20 .50
H9 Antti Tormanen .07 .20
H10 Jarkko Varvio .07 .20
S2 Reijo Ruotsalainen .07 .20
S3 Janne Niinimaa .20 .50
S4 Brian Rafalski .20 .50
S5 Kimmo Timonen .20 .50
S6 Kai Nurminen .07 .20
S7 Raimo Helminen .07 .20
S8 Raimo Summanen .07 .20
S9 Petri Varis .15 .40
S10 Christian Ruuttu .07 .20
CA Jani Hurme .40 1.00
CJ Mika Alatalo .20 .50
CK Ville Peltonen .15 .40
CQ Paivi Ylitite .40 1.00
DA Jarmo Myllys .20 .50
DJ Mikko Eloranta .20 .50
DK Jere Lehtinen .60 1.50
DQ Carissa Chan .40 1.00
HA Boris Rousson .20 .50
HJ Jan Benda .07 .20
HK Saku Koivu 1.50 4.00
HQ Ann Bjorklof .40 1.00
SA Kari Takko .20 .50
SJ Marko Tuomainen .07 .20
SK Esa Tikkanen .40 1.00
SQ Satu Jokinen .40 1.00

1999-00 Finnish Cardset Blazing Patriots

COMPLETE SET (6) 20.00 30.00
1 Miikka Kiprusoff 4.00 10.00
2 Jere Karalahti 1.25 3.00
3 Kimmo Timonen 1.25 3.00
4 Teemu Selanne 4.00 10.00
5 Saku Koivu 4.00 8.00
6 Marko Tuomainen 1.25 3.00

1999-00 Finnish Cardset Jere Lehtinen Triple Threat

1 Jere Lehtinen 4.00 10.00

1999-00 Finnish Cardset Most Wanted

COMPLETE SET (12) 20.00 30.00
1 Aki Berg .75 2.00
2 Olli Jokinen .75 2.00
3 Teemu Selanne 4.00 10.00
4 Teemu Riihuarvi .40 1.00
5 Jani Rita .75 2.00
6 Saku Koivu 4.00 8.00
7 Mika Noronen 2.00 5.00
8 Miika Elomo .75 2.00
9 Jukka Seppo .40 1.00
10 Ari Ahonen 2.00 5.00
11 Tuomas Gronman .40 1.00
12 Ville Siren .40 1.00

1999-00 Finnish Cardset Par Avion

COMPLETE SET (12) 14.00 25.00
1 Mika Alatalo .75 2.00
2 Toni Lydman .75 2.00
3 Brian Rafalski .75 2.00
4 Jere Karalahti .75 2.00
5 Juha Lind .75 2.00
6 Mikko Kuparinen .40 1.00
7 Marko Tuomainen .40 1.00
8 Miikka Kiprusoff 4.00 10.00
9 Mika Noronen 2.00 5.00
10 Vesa Toskala 2.00 5.00
11 Mikko Eloranta .75 2.00
12 Jarkko Ruutu .75 2.00

1999-00 Finnish Cardset Puck Stoppers

COMPLETE SET (6) 12.00 25.00
1 Antero Niittymaki 4.00 10.00
2 Ari-Pekka Siekkinen 2.00 5.00
3 Pasi Kuivalainen 2.00 5.00
4 Sami Lehtinen 2.00 5.00
5 Jason Muzzatti 2.00 5.00
6 Kimmo Kapanen 2.00 5.00

2000-01 Finnish Cardset

COMPLETE SET (360) 30.00 60.00
1 Checklist .04 .10
2 Checklist .04 .10
3 Checklist .04 .10
4 Mika Oksa .04 .10
5 Peter Ahola .04 .10
6 Jermu Pisto .04 .10
7 Jiri Vykoukal .04 .10
8 Niclas Hedberg .04 .10
9 Teemu Siren .04 .10
10 Joonas Jaaskelainen .20 .50
11 Timo Hirvonen .04 .10
12 Mikko Kaukokari .04 .10
13 Ari Ahonen 1.25 3.00
14 Marek Zidlicky .04 .10
15 Jarno Kultanen .08 .20
16 Toni Sihvonen .04 .10
17 Aki Uusikartano .04 .10
18 Pasi Nielikainen .04 .10
19 Hannes Hyvonen .20 .50
20 Mika Nieminen .20 .50
21 Mika Kortelainen .04 .10
22 Kimmo Kapanen .04 .10
23 Jonas Andersson-Junkka .08 .20
24 Kimmo Peltonen .04 .10
25 Sebastian Sulku .04 .10
26 Teemu Aalto .04 .10
27 Antti Miettinen .30 .75
28 Riku Hahl .40 1.00
29 Marko Palo .04 .10
30 Juha Pitkamaki .04 .10
31 Arto Tukio .20 .50
32 Tapio Sammalkangas .04 .10
33 Tomi Pettinen .04 .10
34 Jarkko Nikander .04 .10
35 Raimo Helminen .08 .20
36 Juha Hautamaa .04 .10
37 Sami Karjalainen .04 .10
38 Pasi Nurminen .75 2.00
39 Ossi Vaananen .30 .75
40 Marko Kauppinen .20 .50
41 Tom Koivisto .04 .50
42 Rami Alanko .04 .10
43 Petri Varis .20 .50
44 Jan Benda .08 .20
45 Jani Rita .40 1.00
46 Markus Kankaanpera .20 .50
47 Jarkko Glad .04 .10
48 Jyrki Valivaara .04 .10
49 Tuomas Pihlman ERC .04 .10
50 Jussi Pesonen .04 .10
51 Petr Ton .04 .10
52 Markus Korhonen .20 .50
53 Harri Aho .04 .10
54 Karri Kivi .08 .20
55 Mikko Haapakoski .04 .10
56 Jakko Niskavaara .08 .20
57 Niklas Hagman .40 1.00
58 Sakari Palsola .04 .10
59 Jari Laukkanen .04 .10
60 Petri Isotalus .20 .50
61 Jari Viuhkola .04 .10
62 Allan Measures .04 .10
63 Mika Laaksonen .04 .10
64 Marko Toivonen .04 .10
65 Matti Kaipainen .04 .10
66 Petri Latti .04 .10
67 Sami Torkki .04 .10
68 Jokke Hainanen .04 .10
69 Sami Lehtinen .20 .50
70 Veli-Pekka Laitinen .04 .10
71 Kaj Lindstrom .04 .10
72 Mika Niskanen .04 .10
73 Jani Keinanen .04 .10
74 Tommi Turunen .04 .10
75 Mikko Juutilainen .04 .10
76 Veli-Pekka Nutikka .08 .20
77 Mikko Jokela .20 .50
78 Martin Richter .04 .10
79 Pekka Tirkkonen .08 .20
80 Vladimir Machulda .04 .10
81 Ville Hamalainen .04 .10
82 Mika Skytta .04 .10
83 Ville Immonen .04 .10
84 Sami Kaartinen .04 .10
85 Tuukka Mantyla .20 .50
86 Miska Kangasniemi .08 .20
87 Janne Gronvall .08 .20
88 Jussi Tarvainen .08 .20
89 Janne Ojanen .04 .10
90 Jaakko Uhlback .04 .10
91 Johannes Alanen .04 .10
92 Jani Hassinen .04 .10
93 Fredrik Norrena .20 .50
94 Jouni Loponen .04 .10
95 Tommi Rajamaki .04 .10
96 Kimmo Eronen .04 .10
97 Kimmo Rintanen .04 .10
98 Tony Virta .04 .10
99 Jani Kiviharju .04 .10
100 Teemu Elomo .04 .10
101 Mikko Rautee .04 .10
102 Jim Hrivnak .20 .50
103 Pasi Peltonen .04 .10
104 Timo Willman .04 .10
105 Pauli Levokari .04 .10
106 Tuomo Kyha .04 .10
107 Janne Laitila .04 .10
108 Janne Makela .04 .10
109 Samu Wesslin .04 .10
110 Hannu Tala .04 .10
111 Vesa Toskala .40 1.00
112 Aki Berg .20 .50
113 Antti-Jussi Niemi .08 .20
114 Janne Niinimaa .20 .50
115 Ville Peltonen .30 .75
116 Olli Jokinen .40 1.00
117 Teemu Selanne 1.25 3.00
118 Marko Tuomainen .08 .20
119 Juha Lind .20 .50
120 Niko Kapanen .40 1.00
121 Checklist 1 .04 .10
122 Checklist 2 .04 .10
123 Checklist 3 .04 .10
124 Arto Laatikainen .20 .50
125 Tero Maatta .30 .50
126 Juha Gustafsson .04 .10
127 Toni Koivunen .04 .10
128 Teemu Virkkunen .04 .10
129 Valeri Krykov .04 .10
130 Frank Banham .20 .50
131 Semir Ben-Amor .04 .10
132 Jiri Burger .04 .10
133 Aki Tuominen .04 .10
134 Ray Giroux .08 .20
135 Mikko Kurvinen .04 .10
136 Patrik Hucko .04 .10
137 Jari Kauppila .04 .10
138 Tony Salmelainen .04 .10
139 Kimmo Kuhta .04 .10
140 Jaroslav Bednar .40 .50
141 Ari Vallin .04 .10
142 Sami Nuutinen .04 .10
143 Jani Virtanen .04 .10
144 Timo Ahmaoja .04 .10
145 Tomi Suoniemi .04 .10
146 Jari Kesti .04 .10
147 Tommi Santala .04 .10
148 Pavel Rosa .20 .50
149 Eero Somervuori .08 .20
150 Mika Pietila .04 .10
151 Ivan Majesky FRC .04 .10
152 Antti Bruun .04 .10
153 Matt Smith .08 .20
154 Jari-Pekka Pajula .04 .10
155 Kimmo Vaha-Ruohola .04 .10
156 Toni Dahlman .04 .10
157 Antti Hilden .04 .10
158 Timo Koskela .04 .10
159 Vesa Viitakoski .08 .20
160 Kari Haakana .04 .10
161 Pasi Saarinen .08 .20
162 Santeri Heiskanen .04 .10
163 Antti Tormanen .08 .20
164 Juha Virtanen .04 .10
165 Tuomo Ruutu ERC 4.00 10.00
166 Niko Mikkola .04 .10
167 Aigars Cipruss .04 .10
168 Mika Lehto .04 .10
169 Chris MacKenzie .08 .20
170 Pekka Poikolainen .04 .10
171 Riku Varjamo .04 .10
172 Markku Paukkunen .04 .10
173 Mika Paananen .04 .10
174 Juha-Pekka Hytonen .04 .10
175 Janne Hauhtonen .04 .10
176 Jouni Kulonen .04 .10
177 Antti Virtanen .04 .10
178 Kristian Taubert .04 .10
179 Mikko Lehtonen .20 .50
180 Lasse Kukkonen ERC .04 .10
181 Kimmo Koskenkorva .04 .10
182 Tuomo Harjula .04 .10
183 Juha Joenvaara .04 .10
184 Brett Lievers .04 .10
185 Miikka Rousu .04 .10
186 Bruce Racine .20 .50
187 Ismo Kuoppala .04 .10
188 Topi Lehtonen .04 .10
189 Toni Koivisto .04 .10
190 Jouni Vauhkonen .08 .20
191 Jimmy Provencher .04 .10
192 Pasi Saarela .04 .10
193 Pasi Kuivalainen .20 .50
194 Jussi-Antti Reimari .04 .10
195 Jan Latvala .04 .10
196 Roman Vopat .08 .20
197 Janne Sinkkonen .04 .10
198 Ales Kratoska .04 .10
200 Niklas Backstrom .04 .10
201 Oleg Romanov .04 .10
202 Riku Kallioniemi .04 .10
203 Petri Kokko .04 .10
204 Juha Pursiainen .04 .10
205 Joni Yli-Torkko .04 .10
206 Pasi Tuominen .04 .10
207 Ludek Krayzel .04 .10
208 Mika Kauppinen .08 .20
209 Jussi Markkanen .40 1.00
210 Alain Cote .08 .20
211 Pekka Saravo .04 .10
212 Niki Siren .04 .10
213 Timo Vertala .04 .10
214 Tero Lehtera .08 .20
216 Henrik Tallinder .20 .50
217 Martti Jarventie .30 .50
218 Marco Tuokko .04 .10
219 Joni Lius .04 .10
220 Jarkko Varvio .08 .20
222 Mikko Koivu ERC 6.00 15.00
223 Ari Vapola .04 .10
224 Curtis Sheptak .04 .10
225 Marcus Kristoffersson .40 1.00
226 Jari Korpisalo .04 .10
227 Gabriel Karlsson .20 .50
228 Sami Salonen .04 .10
229 Jarkko Vaananen .04 .10
230 Niklas Hede .04 .10
231 Ari Sulander .20 .50
232 Jere Karalahti .20 .50
233 Toni Lydman .20 .50
234 Petteri Nummelin .20 .50
235 Raimo Helminen .20 .50
236 Tomi Kallio .30 .50
237 Toni Sihvonen .04 .10
238 Jukka Hentunen .20 .50
239 Tony Virta .04 .10
240 Esa Tikkanen .20 .50
241 Checklist 1 .04 .10
242 Checklist 2 .04 .10
243 Checklist 3 .04 .10
244 Tom Draper .20 .50
245 Timo Willman .04 .10
246 Asko Rantanen .04 .10
247 Jukka Tiilikainen .04 .10
248 Mikael Jamsanen .04 .10
249 Kari Kalto .04 .10
250 Esa Pirnes .04 .10
251 Johan Davidsson .20 .50
252 Shayne Toporowski .20 .50
253 Sakari Lindfors .20 .50
254 Tomi Nyman .04 .10
255 Kari Rajala .04 .10
256 Martin Stepanek .04 .10
257 Veli-Pekka Kautonen .04 .10
258 Toni Makiaho .04 .10
259 Lasse Pirjeta .04 .10
260 Markku Hurme .04 .10
261 Erkki Rajamaki .04 .10
262 Jan Caloun .20 .50
263 Joonas Vihko .04 .10
264 Jan Lundell .04 .10
265 Dan Ratushny .08 .20
266 Darcy Werenka .08 .20
267 Timo Parssinen .30 .50
268 Tomas Vlasak .04 .10
269 Jyrki Louhi .04 .10
270 Pasi Maattanen .04 .10
271 Petr Kuchyna .04 .10
272 Jani Nikko .04 .10
273 Tommi Miettinen .30 .50
274 Jesse Welling .04 .10
275 Oliver Setzinger .04 .50
276 Jarno Peltonen .04 .10
277 Tony Salmelainen .04 .10
278 Kari Lehtonen ERC 8.00 20.00
279 Pauli Levokari .04 .10
280 Thomas Johansson .04 .10
281 Lee Sorochan .20 .50
282 Tomek Valtonen .04 .10
283 Jukka Hentunen .20 .50
284 Mikko Ruutu .20 .50
285 Timo Saarikoski .04 .10
286 Teemu Sainomaa .04 .10
287 Ari-Pekka Siekkinen .04 .10
288 Tomi Hirvonen .04 .10
289 Jarno Tiilikainen .04 .10
290 Radoslav Kropac .04 .10
291 Zdenek Sedlak .04 .10
292 Tuomo Jaaskelainen .04 .10
293 Antti Kangas .04 .10
294 Steve Shierreffs .04 .10
295 Pekka Kangasalusta .04 .10
296 Vjatsheslav Fandul .04 .10
297 Kimmo Salminen .04 .10
298 Sami Alalauri .04 .10
299 Andrei Potaitshuk .04 .10
300 Petri Vehanen .04 .10
301 Erik Hamalainen .04 .10
302 Tuomas Gronman .04 .10
303 Kimmo Lotvonen .04 .10
304 Janne Siivonen .04 .10
305 Marko Kivenmaki .04 .10
306 Zdenek Nedved .04 .10
307 Petri Pakaslahti .04 .10
308 Harri Sillgren .04 .10
309 Samu Isosalo .04 .10
310 Henri Laurila .04 .10
311 Jussi Salminen .04 .10
312 Kalle Koskinen .04 .10
313 Jarkko Ollikainen .04 .10
314 Toni Saarinen .04 .10
315 Teemu Riihijarvi .08 .20
316 Lasse Jamsen .04 .10
317 Jouko Myrra .04 .10
318 Pasi Hakkinen .04 .10
319 Juha Kuokkanen .04 .10
320 Roland Carlsson .04 .10
321 Harri Tikkanen .04 .10
322 Juri Kuznetsov .20 .50
323 Ville Kiiskinen .04 .10
324 Olli Sipilainen .04 .10
325 Tuomas Reijonen .04 .10
326 Joel Salonen .04 .10
327 Sami Ahlberg .04 .10
328 Sasu Hovi .04 .10
329 Janne Vourela .04 .10
330 Mikko Luoma .04 .10
331 Miro Laitinen .04 .10
332 Sami Venalainen .04 .10
333 Marko Ojanen .04 .10
334 Marko Makinen .04 .10
335 Aleksander Barkov .04 .10
336 Antero Niittymaki 1.25 3.00
337 Markus Seikola .04 .10
338 Ilkka Mikkola .04 .10
339 Mika Lehtinen .04 .10
340 Niko Kapanen .40 1.00
341 Ville Vahalahti .04 .10
342 Kalle Sahlstedt .20 .50
343 Kristian Antila .04 .10
344 Pasi Puistola .04 .10
345 Vesa Salo .04 .10
346 Veli-Pekka Hard .04 .10
347 Eric Perrin .04 .10
348 Tomas Kucharcik .04 .10
349 Markku Tahtinen .04 .10
350 Mikko Konttila .04 .10
351 Pasi Nurminen .75 2.00
352 Kimmo Timonen .20 .50
353 Jyrki Lumme .20 .50
354 Janne Laukkanen .20 .50
355 Kimmo Rintanen .20 .50
356 Saku Koivu .75 2.00
357 Jere Lehtinen .40 1.00
358 Sami Kapanen .40 1.00
359 Antti Aalto .20 .50
360 Mika Alatalo .20 .50
NNO Ari Ahonen MM 8.00 20.00
NNO Saku Koivu MT 10.00 25.00
NNO Pasi Nurminen MM 10.00 25.00

2000-01 Finnish Cardset Masquerade

COMPLETE SET (9) 24.00 40.00
1 Mika Pietila 2.00 5.00
2 Bruce Racine 4.00 10.00
3 Sami Lehtinen 2.00 5.00
4 Niklas Backstrom 2.00 5.00
5 Antero Niittymaki 6.00 15.00
6 Markus Korhonen 2.00 5.00
7 Jussi Markkanen 6.00 15.00
8 Tom Draper 4.00 10.00
9 Kristian Antila 2.00 5.00

2000-01 Finnish Cardset Master Blasters

COMPLETE SET (9) 12.50 20.00
1 Kai Nurminen 1.20 3.00
2 Jan Caloun 1.20 3.00
3 Petr Tenkrat 2.00 5.00
4 Jaroslav Bednar 2.00 5.00
5 Dale McTavish .80 2.00
6 Kalle Sahlstedt 1.20 3.00
7 Zdenek Nedved .80 2.00
8 Tomi Kallio 2.00 5.00
9 Timo Parssinen 2.00 5.00

2000-01 Finnish Cardset Next Generation

COMPLETE SET (9) 30.00 30.00
1 Mikko Koivu 4.00 10.00
2 Tuukka Mantyla .60 1.50
3 Tuomo Ruutu 3.00 8.00
4 Jani Rita 1.00 2.50
5 Ari Ahonen 1.50 4.00
6 Arto Tukio .60 1.50
7 Antti Miettinen 1.50 4.00
8 Markus Kankaanpera .60 1.50
9 Antero Niittymaki 2.00 5.00

2001 Finnish Cardset Teemu Selanne

NNO Teemu Selanne 8.00 20.00

2001-02 Finnish Cardset

COMPLETE SET (380) 35.00 70.00
1 Espoo Blues .04 .10
2 Mika Oksa .08 .20
3 Tero Maatta .20 .50
4 Jermu Pisto .08 .20
5 Niclas Hedberg .08 .20
6 Arto Laatikainen .20 .50
7 Valeri Krykov .08 .20
8 Teemu Virkkunen .08 .20
9 Teemu Siren .08 .20
10 Timo Hirvonen .08 .20
11 Mikael Jamsanen .08 .20
12 Kari Kalto .08 .20
13 HIFK Helsinki .04 .10
14 Sakari Lindfors .20 .50
15 Marek Zidlicky .40 1.00
16 Tuomas Eskelinen .08 .20
17 Aki Tuominen .08 .20
18 Mikko Kurvinen .08 .20
19 Hannes Hyvonen .20 .50
20 Kimmo Kuhta .08 .20
21 Toni Happola .08 .20
22 Pasi Nielikainen .08 .20
23 Mika Nieminen .20 .50
24 Toni Makiaho .08 .20
25 Jaroslav Bednar .20 .50
26 HPK Hameenlinna .04 .10
27 Kimmo Peltonen .08 .20
28 Teemu Aalto .08 .20
29 Eero Somervuori .08 .20
30 Riku Hahl .20 .50
31 Antti Miettinen .75 2.00
32 Tommi Santala .08 .20
33 Kasper Kenig .08 .20
34 Pasi Maattanen .08 .20
35 Ilves Tampere .04 .10
36 Mika Pietila .08 .20
37 Jani Nikko .08 .20
38 Antti Bruun .08 .20
39 Tomi Pettinen .08 .20
40 Matt Smith .08 .20
41 Oliver Setzinger .20 .50
42 Toni Dahlman .08 .20
43 Timo Koskela .08 .20
44 Kimmo Vaha-Ruohola .08 .20

45 Jarkko Nikander .08 .20
46 Jari-Pekka Pajula .08 .20
47 Antti Hilden .08 .20
48 Jokerit Helsinki .04 .10
49 Pasi Nurminen .60 1.50
50 Kari Haakana .20 .50
51 Rami Alanko .08 .20
52 Tomek Valtonen .08 .20
53 Teemu Sainomaa .08 .20
54 Antti Tormanen .08 .20
55 Timo Saarikoski .08 .20
56 Teemu Laine .20 .50
57 Mikko Ruutu .08 .20
58 Tuomo Ruutu 1.50 4.00
59 Niko Mikkola .08 .20
60 JYP Jyvaskala .04 .10
61 Mika Lehto .08 .20
62 Pekka Poikolainen .08 .20
63 Jarkko Glad .08 .20
64 Tuomo Jaaskelainen .08 .20
65 Juha-Pekka Hytonen .08 .20
66 Tuomas Pihlman .20 .50
67 Janne Hauhtonen .08 .20
68 Jouni Kulonen .08 .20
69 Tomi Hirvonen .08 .20
70 Antti Virtanen .08 .20
71 Oulun Karpat .04 .10
72 Antti Kangas .08 .20
73 Lasse Kukkonen .20 .50
74 Joni Pitkanen ERC .75 2.00
75 Harri Aho .08 .20
76 Kristian Taubert .08 .20
77 Mikko Lehtonen .20 .50
78 Kimmo Koskenkorva .08 .20
79 Jari Laukkanen .08 .20
80 Juha Joenvaara .08 .20
81 Brett Lievers .08 .20
82 Jari Viuhkola .08 .20
83 Andrei Potaitshuk .08 .20
84 Rauman Lukko .04 .10
85 Mika Laaksonen .08 .20
86 Topi Lehtonen .08 .20
87 Marko Toivonen .08 .20
88 Tuomas Gronman .08 .20
89 Petteri Lotila .08 .20
90 Toni Koivisto .08 .20
91 Sami Torkki .08 .20
92 Samu Isosalo .08 .20
93 Petri Latti .08 .20
94 Janne Siivonen .08 .20
95 Matti Kaipainen .08 .20
96 Lahden Pelicans .04 .10
97 Pasi Kuivalainen .20 .50
98 Mika Niskanen .08 .20
99 Jan Latvala .08 .20
100 Kaj Lindstrom .08 .20
101 Mikko Peltola .08 .20
102 Teemu Riihijarvi .08 .20
103 Jani Keinanen .08 .20
104 Lasse Jamsen .08 .20
105 Toni Saarinen .08 .20
106 Veli-Pekka Nutikka .08 .20
107 SaiPa Lappeenranta .04 .10
108 Harri Tikkanen .08 .20
109 Riku Kallioniemi .08 .20
110 Juri Kuznetsov .20 .50
111 Petri Kokko .08 .20
112 Mikko Jokela .20 .50
113 Ville Hamalainen .08 .20
114 Pasi Tuominen .08 .20
115 Pekka Tirkkonen .08 .20
116 Mika Kauppinen .08 .20
117 Vladimir Machulda .20 .50
118 Olli Sipilainen .08 .20
119 Joni Yli-Torkko .08 .20
120 Tappara Tampere .04 .10
121 Jussi Markkanen .40 1.00
122 Miska Kangasniemi .08 .20
123 Miikko Luoma .08 .20
124 Pekka Saravo .08 .20
125 Miro Laitinen .08 .20
126 Aleksander Barkov .08 .20
127 Jussi Tarvainen .08 .20
128 Marko Ojanen .08 .20
129 Johannes Alanen .08 .20
130 Timo Vertala .08 .20
131 Jaakko Uhlback .08 .20
132 Arto Kuki .08 .20
133 TPS Turku .04 .10
134 Antero Niittymaki .75 2.00
135 Tuomo Karjalainen .08 .20
136 Mika Lehtinen .08 .20
137 Henrik Tallinder .20 .50
138 Markus Seikola .08 .20
139 Kimmo Eronen .08 .20
140 Martti Jarventie .20 .50
141 Mikko Rautee .08 .20
142 Mikko Koivu 2.00 5.00
143 Marco Tuokko .08 .20
144 Michael Holmqvist .40 1.00
145 Ville Vahalahti .08 .20
146 Porin Assat .04 .10
147 Kristian Antila .08 .20
148 Pasi Peltonen .08 .20
149 Curtis Sheptak .08 .20
150 Sami Karjalainen .08 .20
151 Jari Korpisalo .08 .20
152 Mikko Konttila .08 .20
153 Juha Viinikainen .08 .20
154 Eric Perrin .08 .20
155 Markku Tahtinen .08 .20
156 Finnish National Team .04 .10
157 Pasi Nurminen .60 1.50
158 Miikka Kiprusoff .75 2.00
159 Jarmo Myllys .20 .50
160 Marko Kiprusoff .08 .20
161 Petteri Nummelin .20 .50
162 Kimmo Timonen .20 .50
163 Sami Salo .20 .50
164 Ossi Vaananen .20 .50
165 Aki Berg .20 .50
166 Antti-Jussi Niemi .08 .20
167 Janne Gronvall .08 .20
168 Raimo Helminen .08 .20
169 Antti Laaksonen .20 .50
170 Tomi Kallio .20 .50
171 Niko Kapanen .40 1.00
172 Sami Kapanen .40 1.00
173 Jukka Hentunen .20 .50
174 Timo Parssinen .20 .50
175 Juha Lind .20 .50
176 Toni Sihvonen .08 .20
177 Kimmo Rintanen .08 .20
178 Tony Virta .08 .20
179 Juha Ylonen .20 .50
180 Jarkko Ruutu .20 .50
181 Espoo Blues .04 .10
182 Jarmo Myllys .20 .50
183 Juha Gustafsson .08 .20
184 Matti Kuusisto .08 .20
185 Jani Virtanen .08 .20
186 Jiri Vykoukal .08 .20
187 Jan Caloun .20 .50
188 Markku Hurme .08 .20
189 Jiri Zelenka .08 .20
190 Tero Lehtera .08 .20
191 Janne Seva .08 .20
192 Teemu Elomo .08 .20
193 Filip Turek .08 .20
194 HIFK Helsinki .04 .10
195 Mikko Stromberg .08 .20
196 Antti-Pekka Lamberg .08 .20
197 Robert Kantor .08 .20
198 Jonas Junkka .08 .20
199 Mikko Ilkka .08 .20
200 Pauli Levokari .08 .20
201 Kari Rajala .08 .20
202 Joonas Vihko .08 .20
203 Carlo Grunn .08 .20
204 Jonni Vauhkonen .20 .50
205 Mika Kortelainen .08 .20
206 Kimmo Salminen .08 .20
207 Aigars Cipruss .08 .20
208 Ilkka Pikkarainen .08 .20
209 Andrej Podkonicky .20 .50
210 Kim Hirschovits .08 .20
211 HPK Hameenlinna .04 .10
212 Zdenek Smid .20 .50
213 Hannu Toivonen ERC 1.25 3.00
214 Joni Puurula .08 .20
215 Vladimir Sicak .08 .20
216 Janne Juppo .08 .20
217 Sebastian Sulku .08 .20
218 Markus Kankaanpera .20 .50
219 Marko Tuulola .08 .20
220 Tuukka Makela .40 1.00
221 Erkki Rajamaki .08 .20
222 Olli Sillanpaa .08 .20
223 Vladimir Vujtek .08 .20
224 Tomas Kucharcik .08 .20
225 Harri Suutarinen .08 .20
226 Jarkko Savijoki .08 .20
227 Zdenek Nedved .08 .20
228 Janne Lahti .08 .20
229 Ilves Tampere .04 .10
230 Bruce Racine .20 .50
231 Juha Pitkamaki .08 .20
232 Kari Takko .20 .50
233 Ville Koistinen .08 .20
234 Arto Tukio .20 .50
235 Teemu Jaaskelainen .08 .20
236 Ivan Majesky .20 .50
237 Roman Vopat .08 .20
238 Tommi Miettinen .20 .50
239 Riku Rahikainen .08 .20
240 Ville Hirvonen .08 .20
241 Tony Salmelainen .08 .20
242 Vesa Viitakoski .08 .20
243 Mika Nieminen .20 .50
244 Raimo Helminen .08 .20
245 Jokerit Helsinki .04 .10
246 Markus Helanen .08 .20
247 Jamie Ram .20 .50
248 Kari Lehtonen 4.00 10.00
249 Ari Vallin .08 .20
250 Pasi Saarinen .08 .20
251 Tuomas Luotonen .08 .20
252 Ilkka Mikkola .08 .20
253 Tom Koivisto .08 .20
254 Olli Malmivaara .08 .20
255 Rob Cowie .20 .50
256 Alex Brooks .08 .20
257 Sean Bergenheim ERC .60 1.50
258 Antti Aalto .20 .50
259 Ville Peltonen .20 .50
260 Petri Pakaslahti .08 .20
261 Petri Varis .20 .50
262 Jussi Pesonen .08 .20
263 Frank Banham .20 .50
264 Pavel Rosa .20 .50
265 JYP Jyvaskyla .04 .10
266 Tero Leinonen .08 .20
267 Jani-Matti Loikala .08 .20
268 Martin Cech .08 .20
269 Sami Siltavirta .08 .20
270 Jyri Marttinen .08 .20
271 Petri Virolainen .08 .20
272 Angel Nikolov .20 .50
273 Olli Ahonen .08 .20
274 Jari Jaaskelainen .08 .20
275 Harri Sillgren .08 .20
276 Petr Ton .08 .20
277 Tomas Chlubna .08 .20
278 Oulun Karpat .04 .10
279 Markus Korhonen .20 .50
280 Kimmo Lotvonen .08 .20
281 Mikko Myllykoski .08 .20
282 Pekka Saarenheimo .08 .20
283 Mika Pyorala .08 .20
284 Tuomo Harjula .08 .20
285 Harri Korpela .08 .20
286 Janne Pesonen .08 .20
287 Juha-Pekka Haataja .08 .20
288 Sakari Palsola .08 .20
289 Lasse Pirjeta .08 .20
290 Jussi Jokinen ERC 2.00 5.00
291 Rauman Lukko .04 .10
292 Petri Vehanen .08 .20
293 Jaakko Harikkala .08 .20
294 Mikko Purontakanen .08 .20
295 Ville Piekkola .20 .50
296 Janne Niskala .08 .20
297 Teemu Kesa .08 .20
298 Jaakko Hagelberg .08 .20
299 Jari Hyvarinen .08 .20
300 Mika Viinanen .08 .20
301 Joel Salonen .08 .20
302 Teemu Normio .08 .20
303 Hermani Vidman .08 .20
304 Aki Uusikartano .08 .20
305 Pasi Saarela .08 .20
306 Markus Jamsa .08 .20
307 Lahden Pelicans .04 .10
308 Mikko Ramo .08 .20
309 Kalle Koskinen .08 .20
310 Jussi-Antti Reimari .08 .20
311 Veli-Pekka Laitinen .08 .20
312 Henri Laurila .08 .20
313 Teemu Viherva .08 .20
314 Jussi Saarinen .08 .20
315 Olli Sinkkonen .08 .20
316 Jarkko Vaananen .08 .20
317 Jarkko Ollikainen .08 .20
318 Joonas Jaaskelainen .20 .50
319 Niki Siren .08 .20
320 Tommi Turunen .08 .20
321 Toni Koivunen .08 .20
322 SaiPa Lappeenranta .04 .10
323 Juha Kuokkanen .08 .20
324 Sami Lehtinen .20 .50
325 Tomas Duba .08 .20
326 Antti Hulkkonen .08 .20
327 Juha Pursiainen .08 .20
328 Jan Huokko .08 .20
329 Ville Immonen .08 .20
330 Mikko Kinnunen .08 .20
331 Mika Skytta .08 .20
332 Juuso Vakkilainen .08 .20
333 Jesse Welling .08 .20
334 Ville Koho .08 .20
335 Tappara Tampere .04 .10
336 Tom Draper .20 .50
337 Tuukka Mantyla .20 .50
338 Pasi Puistola .08 .20
339 Jyrki Valivaara .08 .20
340 Janne Gronvall .08 .20
341 Esa Pirnes .08 .20
342 Christian Sjogren .08 .20
343 Marko Makinen .08 .20
344 Sami Venalainen .08 .20
345 Janne Ojanen .08 .20
346 Tuomas Reijonen .08 .20
347 Jani Hassinen .08 .20
348 TPS Turku .04 .10
349 Fredrik Norrena .20 .50
350 Matti Tahkapaa .08 .20
351 Marko Kauppinen .20 .50
352 Pasi Petrilainen .08 .20
353 Pekka Kangasalusta .08 .20
354 Markku Paukkunen .08 .20
355 Chris Joseph .20 .50
356 Peter Schaefer .20 .50
357 Kai Nurminen .20 .50
358 Miika Elomo .20 .50
359 Janne Jokila .08 .20
360 Mikko Kankaanpera .08 .20
361 Tommi Hannus .08 .20
362 Mika Alatalo .20 .50
363 Rob Shearer .20 .50
364 Jani Kiviharju .08 .20
365 Porin Assat .04 .10
366 Tommi Satosaari .08 .20
367 Matti Jarvinen .08 .20
368 Mika Rontti .08 .20
369 Timo Willman .08 .20
370 Stanislav Jasecko .08 .20
371 Jukka-Pekka Laamanen .08 .20
372 Timo Ahmaoja .08 .20
373 Tapio Sammalkangas .08 .20
374 Jan Lipiansky .08 .20
375 Jani Vaananen .08 .20
376 Jarkko Immonen .08 .20
377 Sandy Moger .20 .50
378 Marko Palo .08 .20
379 Semir Ben-Amor .08 .20
380 Samu Wesslin .08 .20
NNO Jari Kurri HOF 8.00 20.00
NNO Mikko Koivu AU 30.00 80.00
NNO Antero Niittymaki AU 12.00 30.00
NNO Tuomo Ruutu AU 25.00 60.00
NNO Ville Nieminen DREAM 2.00 5.00
NNO Kari Lehtonen AU 60.00 125.00

2001-02 Finnish Cardset Adrenaline Rush

COMPLETE SET (6) 16.00 35.00
1 Kari Lehtonen 6.00 15.00
2 Tero Maatta 1.25 3.00
3 Tuukka Mantyla 1.25 3.00
4 Tony Salmelainen 1.25 3.00
5 Mikko Koivu 4.00 10.00
6 Tuomo Ruutu 4.00 10.00

2001-02 Finnish Cardset Dueling Aces

COMPLETE SET (8) 6.00 15.00
1 Joonas Jaaskelainen
Vladimir Machulda .75 2.00
2 Ville Peltonen
Janne Ojanen 1.25 3.00
3 Jan Caloun
Kai Nurminen .75 2.00
4 Toni Happola
Mika Viinanen .75 2.00
5 Vladimir Vujtek
Raimo Helminen .75 2.00
6 Petr Ton
Pavel Rosa .75 2.00
7 Marek Zidlicky
Jiri Vykoukal .75 2.00
8 Tom Draper
Jari Korpisalo 1.25 3.00

2001-02 Finnish Cardset Haltmeisters

COMPLETE SET (12) 30.00 75.00
1 Pasi Nurminen 4.00 10.00
2 Miikka Kiprusoff 6.00 15.00
3 Jani Hurme 4.00 10.00
4 Vesa Toskala 4.00 10.00
5 Mika Noronen 4.00 10.00
6 Jarmo Myllys 2.00 5.00
7 Ari Sulander 2.00 5.00
8 Ari Ahonen 4.00 10.00
9 Jussi Markkanen 4.00 10.00
10 Fredrik Norrena 2.00 5.00
11 Sakari Lindfors 2.00 5.00
12 Pasi Kuivalainen 2.00 5.00

2001-02 Finnish Cardset Salt Lake City

COMPLETE SET (12) 20.00 30.00
1 Jani Hurme 1.25 3.00
2 Miikka Kiprusoff 3.00 8.00
3 Teppo Numminen .75 2.00
4 Kimmo Timonen .75 2.00
5 Janne Niinimaa .75 2.00
6 Jyrki Lumme .75 2.00
7 Teemu Selanne 4.00 10.00
8 Juha Ylonen .75 2.00
9 Jere Lehtinen 1.25 3.00
10 Tomi Kallio .75 2.00
11 Raimo Helminen .75 2.00
12 Sami Kapanen 1.25 3.00

2002-03 Finnish Cardset

COMPLETE SET (300) 30.00 80.00
1 Peter Ahola .08 .20
2 Mika Alatalo .08 .20
3 Kristian Antila .08 .20
4 Frank Banham .25 .60
5 Jaroslav Bednar .25 .60
6 Jan Benda .08 .20
7 Frantisek Bombic .08 .20
8 Jan Caloun .08 .20
9 Martin Cech .08 .20
10 Tomas Chlubna .08 .20
11 Toni Dahlman .08 .20
12 Johan Davidsson .08 .20
13 Tom Draper .25 .60
14 Tomas Duba .08 .20
15 Miika Elomo .25 .60
16 Mikko Eloranta .25 .60
17 Vjatsheslav Fandul .08 .20
18 Theo Fleury .40 1.00
19 Janne Gronvall .08 .20
20 Kari Haakana .08 .20
21 Niklas Hagman .25 .60
22 Riku Hahl .40 1.00
23 Jaakko Harikkala .25 .60
24 Jani Hassinen .08 .20
25 Timo Hirvonen .08 .20
26 Sasu Hovi .08 .20
27 Markku Hurme .08 .20
28 Ville Immonen .08 .20
29 Otakar Janecky .25 .60
30 Olli Jokinen .25 .60
31 Martti Jarventie .25 .60
32 Erik Kakko .08 .20
33 Tomi Kallio .25 .60
34 Kimmo Kapanen .08 .20
35 Niko Kapanen .25 .60
36 Sami Kapanen .25 .60
37 Jari Kauppila .08 .20
38 Markus Ketterer .25 .60
39 Marko Kiprusoff .08 .20
40 Miikka Kiprusoff .40 1.00
41 Tom Koivisto .25 .60
42 Markus Korhonen .25 .60
43 Jari Korpisalo .08 .20
44 Mika Kortelainen .08 .20
45 Kimmo Koskenkorva .08 .20
46 Valeri Krykov .08 .20
47 Kimmo Kuhta .08 .20
48 Pasi Kuivalainen .25 .60
49 Jarno Kultanen .08 .20
50 Mikko Kuparinen .08 .20
51 Jari Kurri .40 1.00
52 Jarmo Kuusisto .08 .20
53 Juri Kuznetsov .08 .20
54 Arto Laatikainen .25 .60
55 Veli-Pekka Laitinen .08 .20
56 Peter Larsson .08 .20
57 Mikko Lehtonen .08 .20
58 Pertti Lehtonen .08 .20
59 Jari Levonen .08 .20
60 Brett Lievers .08 .20
61 Juha Lind .08 .20
62 Sakari Lindfors .25 .60
63 Kimmo Lotvonen .08 .20
64 Jyrki Lumme .25 .60
65 Petri LÃ¤tti .08 .20
66 Vladimir Machulda .08 .20
67 Ivan Majesky .25 .60
68 Olli Malmivaara .08 .20
69 Jussi Markkanen .25 .60
70 Kari Martikainen .08 .20
71 Dale McTavish .08 .20
72 Sami Mettovaara .08 .20
73 Antti Miettinen 3.00 8.00
74 Niko Mikkola .08 .20
75 Cory Murphy .08 .20
76 Jason Muzzatti .25 .60
77 Tuukka Makela .25 .60
78 Marko MÃ¤kinen .25 .60
79 David Nemirovsky .08 .20
80 Ville Nieminen .25 .60
81 Antero Niittymaki .40 1.00
82 Angel Nikolov .08 .20
83 Janne Niskala .25 .60
84 Fredrik Norrena .25 .60
85 Petteri Nummelin .25 .60
86 Kai Nurminen .25 .60
87 Janne Ojanen .08 .20
88 Mika Oksa .08 .20
89 Petri Pakaslahti .08 .20
90 Mikko Peltola .08 .20
91 Kimmo Peltonen .08 .20
92 Pasi Peltonen .08 .20
93 Tomi Pettinen .08 .20
94 Tuomas Pihlman .40 1.00
95 Ilkka Pikkarainen .08 .20
96 Lasse Pirjeta .08 .20
97 Esa Pirnes .08 .20
98 Andrei Potaitshuk .08 .20
99 Pasi Puistola .08 .20
100 Joni Puurula .40 1.00
101 Timo Parssinen .08 .20
102 Bruce Racine .25 .60
103 Brian Rafalski .25 .60
104 Jamie Ram .25 .60
105 Martin Richter .25 .60
106 Juha Riihijarvi .08 .20
107 Teemu Riihijarvi .08 .20
108 Kimmo Rintanen .08 .20
109 Pavel Rosa .08 .20
110 Boris Rousson .25 .60
111 Christian Ruuttu .08 .20
112 Pasi Saarela .08 .20
113 Peter Schaefer .08 .20
114 Markus Seikola .08 .20
115 Teemu Selanne .75 2.00
116 Oliver Setzinger .25 .60
117 Vladimir Sicak .08 .20
118 Ari-Pekka Siekkinen .08 .20
119 Toni Sihvonen .08 .20
121 Ari Sulander .25 .60
122 Sebastian Sulku .08 .20
123 Mike Stapleton .08 .20
123 Kari Takko .25 .60
124 Jussi Tarvainen .08 .20
125 Esa Tikkanen .25 .60
126 Harri Tikkanen .08 .20
127 Petr Ton .08 .20
128 Vesa Toskala .25 .60
129 Arto Tukio .08 .20
130 Tommi Turunen .08 .20
131 Marko Tuulola .08 .20
132 Markku TÃ¤htinen .08 .20
133 Antti Tormanen .08 .20
134 Ville Vahalahti .08 .20
135 Ari Vallin .08 .20
136 Petri Varis .25 .60
137 Timo Vertala .08 .20
138 Joonas Vihko .08 .20
139 Mika Viinanen .08 .20
140 Vesa Viitakoski .08 .20
141 Tony Virta .08 .20
142 Tomas Vlasak .08 .20
143 Pavel Vostrak .08 .20
144 Vladimir Vujtek .08 .20
145 Jiri Vykoukal .08 .20
146 Marek Zidlicky .08 .20
147 Kari Lehtonen CL 2.50 6.00
148 Niklas Backstrom CL .08 .20
149 Petri Vehanen CL .08 .20
150 Tomas Duba CL .08 .20
151 Antti Aalto .25 .60
152 Teemu Aalto .08 .20
153 Ari Ahonen .75 2.00
154 Rami Alanko .08 .20
155 Drew Bannister .08 .20
156 Aleksander Barkov .08 .20
157 Aki Berg .25 .60
158 Sean Bergenheim .25 .60
159 Tom Bissett .25 .60
160 Niklas Backstrom .08 .20
161 Aigars Cipruss .08 .20
162 Parris Duffus .25 .60
163 Jason Elliott .25 .60
164 Teemu Elomo .08 .20
165 Jarkko Glad .08 .20
166 Carlo Grunn .08 .20
167 Tuomas Gronman .08 .20
168 Juha Gustafsson .08 .20
169 Timo Hakanen .08 .20
170 Quinn Hancock .08 .20
171 Markus Helanen .08 .20
172 Raimo Helminen .08 .20
173 Jukka Hentunen .08 .20
174 Michael Holmkvist .25 .60
175 Antti Hulkkonen .08 .20
176 Jani Hurme .40 1.00
177 Hannes Hyvonen .25 .60
178 Erik Hamalainen .08 .20
179 Toni Happola .08 .20
180 Juha Ikonen .08 .20
181 Jarkko Immonen .08 .20
182 Mikko Jokela .25 .60
183 Jussi Jokinen .40 1.00
184 Timo Jutila .08 .20
185 Lasse Jamsen .08 .20
186 Joonas Jaaskelainen .08 .20
187 Matti Kaipainen .08 .20
188 Robert Kantor .08 .20
189 Jere Karalahti .08 .20
190 Marko Kauppinen .08 .20
191 Mika Kauppinen .08 .20
192 Jani Keinanen .08 .20
193 Max Kenig .08 .20
194 Esa Keskinen .08 .20
195 Jani Kiviharju .08 .20
196 Toni Koivisto .08 .20
197 Mikko Koivu 2.00 5.00
198 Saku Koivu 1.25 3.00
199 Toni Koivunen .08 .20
200 Tomas Kucharcik .08 .20
201 Arto Kuki .08 .20
202 Lasse Kukkonen .08 .20
203 Juha Kuokkanen .08 .20
204 Janne Laakkonen .08 .20
205 Antii Laaksonen .25 .60
206 Jukka-Pekka Laamanen .08 .20
207 Scott Langkow .25 .60
208 Jan Latvala .08 .20
209 Janne Laukkanen .08 .20
210 Jari Laukkanen .08 .20
211 Tero Lehtera .25 .60
212 Jere Lehtinen .40 1.00
213 Mika Lehto .08 .20
214 Kari Lehtonen 5.00 12.00
215 Tero Leinonen .08 .20
216 Pauli Levokari .08 .20
217 Joni Lius .08 .20
218 Jouni Loponen .08 .20
219 Mikko Luoma .08 .20
220 Toni Lydman .08 .20
221 Jyri Marttinen .08 .20
222 Ilkka Mikkola .08 .20
223 Mikko Myllykoski .08 .20
224 Jere Myllyniemi .08 .20
225 Jarmo Myllys .25 .60
226 Toni Makiaho .08 .20
227 Tuuka Mantyla .08 .20
228 Tero Maatta .25 .60
229 Antti-Jussi Niemi .08 .20
230 Mika Nieminen .08 .20
231 Janne Niinimaa .25 .60
232 Jesse Niinimaki .40 1.00
233 Tuomas Nissinen .08 .20
234 Mika Noronen .40 1.00
235 Teppo Numminen .25 .60
236 Pasi Nurminen .25 .60
237 Michael Nylander .25 .60
238 Matti Naatanen .08 .20
239 Marko Ojanen .08 .20
240 Marko Palo .08 .20
241 Sakari Palsola .08 .20
242 Jan Pardavy .08 .20
243 Timo Peltomaa .08 .20
244 Ville Peltonen .08 .20
245 Eric Perrin .08 .20
246 Jussi Pesonen .08 .20
247 Pasi Petrilainen .08 .20
248 Juha Pitkamaki .08 .20
249 Joni Pitkanen 1.25 3.00
250 Toni Porkka .08 .20
251 Mika Pyorala .08 .20
252 Erkki Rajamaki .08 .20
253 Jani Rita .25 .60
254 Jarkko Ruutu .25 .60
255 Mikko Ruutu .40 1.00
256 Tuomo Ruutu 1.00 2.50
257 Mikko Ramo .08 .20
258 Timo Saarikoski .08 .20
259 Pasi Saarinen .08 .20
260 Kalle Sahlstedt .08 .20
261 Teemu Sainomaa .08 .20
262 Tony Salmelainen .08 .20
263 Sami Salo .25 .60
264 Timo Salonen .08 .20
265 Tommi Santala .08 .20
266 Peter Sarno .25 .60
267 Tommi Satosaari .08 .20
268 Steve Shirreffs .08 .20
269 Harri Sillgren .08 .20
270 Roman Simicek .08 .20
271 Eero Somervuori .25 .60
272 Dave Stathos .08 .20
273 Mika Stromberg .25 .60
274 Raimo Summanen .25 .60
275 Henrik Tallinder .25 .60
276 Petr Tenkrat .25 .60
277 Tim Thomas .40 1.00
278 Kimmo Timonen .08 .20
279 Pekka Tirkkonen .08 .20
280 Hannu Toivonen 1.00 2.50
281 Sami Torkki .08 .20
282 Marco Tuokko .08 .20
283 Marko Tuomainen .08 .20
284 Aki Uusikartano .08 .20
285 Lubomir Vaic .08 .20
286 Tomek Valtonen .08 .20
287 Petri Vehanen .08 .20
288 Samu Wesslin .08 .20
289 Hannu Virta .08 .20
290 Antii Virtanen .08 .20
291 Jari Viuhkola .08 .20
292 Roman Vopat .08 .20
293 Julkka Voutilainen .08 .20
294 Jyrki Valivaara .08 .20
295 Ossi Vaananen .25 .60
296 Juha Ylonen .25 .60
297 Dave Stathos .08 .20
298 Scott Langkow .25 .60
299 Tero Leinonen .08 .20
300 Mika Lehto .08 .20

2002-03 Finnish Cardset Bound for Glory

COMPLETE SET (10) 12.00 30.00
1 Sean Bergenheim .75 2.00
2 Jussi Jokinen 1.50 4.00
3 Mikko Koivu 3.00 8.00
4 Kari Lehtonen 4.00 10.00
5 Jesse Niinimaki .40 1.00
6 Joni Pitkanen 1.25 3.00
7 Tuomo Ruutu 2.00 5.00
8 Oliver Setzinger .40 1.00
9 Jussi Timonen .75 2.00
10 Hannu Toivonen 2.00 5.00

2002-03 Finnish Cardset Dynamic Duos

COMPLETE SET (10) 15.00 40.00
1 Saku Koivu
Mikko Koivu 4.00 10.00
2 Pasi Nurminen
Kari Lehtonen 4.00 10.00
3 Sami Kapanen
Tuomo Ruutu 2.00 5.00
4 Janne Niinimaa
Joni Pitkanen 1.25 3.00
5 Olli Jokinen
Jukka Voutilainen 1.25 3.00
6 Ville Nieminen
Tuukka Mantyla 1.25 3.00
7 Tomi Kallio
Tuomas Pihlman 1.25 3.00
8 Jani Hurme
Tomas Duba 1.25 3.00
9 Niko Kapanen
Antti Miettinen 2.00 5.00
10 Teemu Selanne
Sean Bergenheim 4.00 10.00

2002-03 Finnish Cardset Kari Lehtonen Honors

COMPLETE SET (3) 10.00 25.00
1 Kari Lehtonen
U-18 top goalie 4.00 10.00
2 Kari Lehtonen
U-18 All-Stars 4.00 10.00
3 Kari Lehtonen
U-20 top goalie 4.00 10.00

2002-03 Finnish Cardset Kari Lehtonen Trophies

COMPLETE SET (3) 10.00 25.00
1 Kari Lehtonen 4.00 10.00
2 Kari Lehtonen 4.00 10.00
3 Kari Lehtonen 4.00 10.00

2002-03 Finnish Cardset Signatures

1 Sean Bergenheim 10.00 25.00
2 Jussi Jokinen 15.00 40.00
3 Mikko Koivu 20.00 50.00
4 Kari Lehtonen 100.00 200.00
6 Joni Pitkanen 20.00 50.00
7 Tuomo Ruutu 25.00 60.00
8 Oliver Setzinger 10.00 25.00
9 Jussi Timonen 10.00 25.00
10 Hannu Toivonen 15.00 40.00

2002-03 Finnish Cardset Solid Gold

COMPLETE SET (6) 6.00 15.00
1 Pasi Nurminen .75 2.00
2 Janne Niinimaa .75 2.00
3 Sami Salo .75 2.00
4 Sami Kapanen .75 2.00
5 Saku Koivu 2.00 5.00
6 Teemu Selanne 2.00 5.00

2002-03 Finnish Cardset Solid Gold Six-Pack

COMPLETE SET (6) 3.00 8.00
1 Jussi Markkanen 1.25 3.00
2 Toni Lydman .40 1.00
3 Ossi Vaananen .40 1.00
4 Niklas Hagman .40 1.00
5 Olli Jokinen 1.25 3.00
6 Niko Kapanen 1.25 3.00

2003-04 Finnish Cardset

COMPLETE SET (182) 20.00 40.00
1 Jere Myllyniemi .20 .50
2 Sami Heinonen .20 .50
3 Sebastien Sulku .08 .20
4 Tero Maatta .08 .20
5 Rami Alanko .08 .20
6 Arto Laatikainen .08 .20
7 Jan Caloun .08 .20
8 Markku Hurme .08 .20
9 Jukka Tiilikainen .08 .20
10 Ladislav Kohn .08 .20
11 Miika Elomo .08 .20
12 Bruce Gardiner .20 .50
13 Marko Tuomainen .08 .20
14 Teemu Elomo .08 .20
15 Dave Stathos .30 .75
16 Ladislav Benysek .08 .20
17 Jere Karalahti .08 .20
18 Jarno Kultanen .08 .20
19 Toni Soderholm .08 .20
20 Pasi Saarinen .08 .20
21 Kim Hirschovits .08 .20
22 Kimmo Kuhta .08 .20
23 Joonas Vihko .08 .20
24 Toni Happola .08 .20
25 Carlo Grunn .08 .20
26 Timo Parssinen .20 .50
27 Brett Harkins .20 .50
28 Martin Spanhel .08 .20
29 Joni Puurula .20 .50
30 Rob Tallas .20 .50
31 Vladimir Sicak .08 .20
32 Aki Heino .08 .20
33 Tomas Eskeleinen .08 .20
34 Marko Tuulola .08 .20
35 Teemu Aalto .08 .20
36 Jyrki Louhi .08 .20
37 Tony Virta .08 .20
38 Vladimir Vujtek .08 .20
39 Tomas Kucharcik .08 .20
40 Janne Laakkonen .08 .20
41 Janne Lahti .08 .20
42 Anders Burstrom .08 .20
43 Juha Pitkamaki .20 .50
44 Tuomas Nissinen .20 .50
45 Cory Murphy .08 .20
46 Ismo Siren .08 .20
47 Martin Hlavacka .08 .20
48 Jukka-Pekka Laamanen .08 .20
49 Jesse Niinimaki .30 .75
50 Ville Snellman .08 .20
51 Toni Dahlman .08 .20
52 Erkki Rajamaki .08 .20
53 Marek Vorel .08 .20
54 Mikko Suvanto .08 .20
55 Vesa Viitakoski .08 .20
56 Raimo Helminen .08 .20
57 Markus Helanen .20 .50
58 Pasi Hakkinen .20 .50
59 Sami Helenius .20 .50
60 Jan Latvala .08 .20
61 Martti Jarventie .20 .50
62 Arto Tukio .08 .20
63 Tomek Valtonen .08 .20
64 Petri Pakaslahti .08 .20
65 Jussi Pesonen .08 .20
66 Timo Vertala .08 .20
67 Tommi Turunen .08 .20
68 Glen Metropolit .30 .75
69 Marko Jantunen .08 .20
70 Teemu Laine .08 .20
71 Tero Leinonen .20 .50
72 Tommi Nikkila .20 .50
73 Tuomo Kortelainen .08 .20
74 Tommi Kovanen .08 .20
75 Jari Korhonen .08 .20
76 Jyri Marttinen .08 .20
77 Ilari Filppula .08 .20
78 Tuomo Jaaskelainen .08 .20
79 Alexandre Tremblay .08 .20
80 Jari Jaaskelainen .08 .20
81 Jarkko Immonen .08 .20
82 Jaakko Uhlback .08 .20
83 Antti Virtanen .08 .20
84 P.C. Drouin .20 .50
85 Niklas Backstrom .30 .75
86 Ari Vallin .08 .20
87 Ilkka Mikkola .08 .20
88 Martin Stepanek .08 .20
89 Mikko Lehtonen .08 .20
90 Kimmo Lotvonen .08 .20
91 Mikko Myllykoski .08 .20

92 Jussi Jokinen .08 .20
93 Lasse Jamsen .08 .20
94 Mika Pyorala .08 .20
95 Janne Pesonen .08 .20
96 Brett Lievers .08 .20
97 Jari Viuhkola .08 .20
98 Sakari Palsola .08 .20
99 Antti Jokela .20 .50
100 Petri Vehanen .20 .50
101 Jaakko Harikkala .08 .20
102 Toni Porkka .08 .20
103 Janne Niskala .08 .20
104 Erik Hamalainen .08 .20
105 Mikko Luovi .08 .20
106 Mika Viinanen .08 .20
107 Toni Koivisto .08 .20
108 Sami Torkki .08 .20
109 Joe Murphy .20 .50
110 Markku Tahtinen .08 .20
111 Quinn Hancock .20 .50
112 Pasi Saarela .08 .20
113 Mikko Ramo .08 .20
114 Martin Cech .08 .20
115 Tero Paappanen .08 .20
116 Santeri Heiskanen .08 .20
117 Jermu Pisto .08 .20
118 Radek Philipp .08 .20
119 Tommi Hannus .08 .20
120 Daniel Widing .08 .20
121 Jari Kauppila .08 .20
122 Ville Hirvonen .08 .20
123 Toni Saarinen .08 .20
124 Toni Makiaho .08 .20
125 Shayne Toporowski .20 .50
126 Oliver Setzinger .20 .50
127 Juha Kuokkanen .08 .20
128 Jarmo Myllys .20 .50
129 Jussi Pekkala .08 .20
130 Petri Kokko .08 .20
131 Antti Bruun .08 .20
132 Sami Kaartinen .08 .20
133 Ville Immonen .08 .20
134 Kalle Kerman .08 .20
135 Mika Kauppinen .08 .20
136 Vladimir Machulda .08 .20
137 Pasi Nielikainen .08 .20
138 Petr Sachl .08 .20
139 Aki Uusikartano .08 .20
140 Timo Hirvonen .08 .20
141 Sasu Hovi .20 .50
142 Mika Lehto .20 .50
143 Pekka Saravo .08 .20
144 Pasi Puistola .08 .20
145 Pasi Petrilainen .08 .20
146 Miska Kangasniemi .08 .20
147 Janne Ojanen .08 .20
148 Aleksander Barkov .08 .20
149 Petri Varis .08 .20
150 Marko Ojanen .08 .20
151 Marko Makinen .08 .20
152 Sami Venalainen .08 .20
153 Stefan Ohman .08 .20
154 Arto Kuki .08 .20
155 Teemu Lassila .20 .50
156 Tuomo Karjalainen .20 .50
157 Kimmo Peltonen .08 .20
158 Marko Kauppinen .08 .20
159 David Schneider .08 .20
160 Jiri Vykoukal .08 .20
161 Antti Hulkkonen .08 .20
162 Mikko Koivu 1.25 3.00
163 Marko Tuokko .08 .20
164 Antti Aalto .08 .20
165 Kai Nurminen .08 .20
166 Ville Vahalahti .08 .20
167 Mikko Eloranta .08 .20
168 Niko Mikkola .08 .20
169 Scott Langkow .30 .75
170 Steve Shierrefs .20 .50
171 Pasi Peltonen .08 .20
172 Oleg Sorokin .08 .20
173 Jarkko Glad .08 .20
174 Samu Wesslin .08 .20
175 Vyacheslav Fandul .08 .20
176 Jari Korpisalo .08 .20
177 Pasi Tuominen .08 .20
178 Marko Kivenmaki .08 .20
179 Tomi Pollanen .08 .20
180 Timo Salonen .08 .20
181 Juha Kiilholma .08 .20
182 Martin Bergeron .20 .50

2003-04 Finnish Cardset D-Day

COMPLETE SET (16) 15.00 40.00
D1 Sean Bergenheim .75 2.00
D2 Mikael Holmqvist .75 2.00
D3 Lasse Kukkonen .75 2.00
D4 Kari Lehtonen 5.00 12.00
D5 Mikko Luoma .40 1.00
D6 Antti Miettinen .75 2.00
D7 Eric Perrin 1.25 3.00
D8 Tuomas Pihlman .75 2.00
D9 Ilkka Pikkarainen .40 1.00
D10 Esa Pirnes .40 1.00
D11 Joni Pitkanen 1.25 3.00
D12 Tuomo Ruutu 3.00 8.00
D13 Tomi Santala .40 1.00
D14 Eero Somervuori .40 1.00
D15 Hannu Toivonen 3.00 8.00
D16 Marek Zidlicky 1.25 3.00

2003-04 Finnish Cardset Globetrotters

COMPLETE SET (9) 6.00 15.00
R1 Toni Dahlman .75 2.00
R2 Mikko Eloranta .75 2.00
R3 Sami Helenius .75 2.00
R4 Marko Jantunen .75 2.00
R5 Jere Karalahti .75 2.00
R6 Martin Stepanek .75 2.00
R7 Petri Varis .75 2.00
R8 Tony Virta .75 2.00
R9 Vladimir Vujtek .75 2.00

2003-04 Finnish Cardset Vintage 1983

COMPLETE SET (3) 10.00 25.00
V1 Mikko Koivu 6.00 15.00
V2 Joni Pitkanen 2.00 5.00
V3 Tuomo Ruutu 4.00 10.00

2004-05 Finnish Cardset

COMPLETE SET (317) 30.00 60.00
1 Jere Myllyniemi .20 .50
2 Mika Oksa .20 .50
3 Kari Haakana .08 .20
4 Arto Laatikainen .08 .20
5 Mika Lehtinen .08 .20
6 Landon Wilson .20 .50
7 Donald MacLean .20 .50
8 Krystofer Kolanos .20 .50
9 Joni Toykkala .08 .20
10 Olli Ahonen .08 .20
11 Ladislav Kohn .08 .20
12 Lauri Tukonen ERC 1.25 3.00
13 Teemu Elomo .08 .20
14 Dave Stathos .20 .50
15 Marek Zidlicky .20 .50
16 Jere Karalahti .08 .20
17 Jarno Kultanen .08 .20
18 Toni Soderholm .08 .20
19 Pasi Saarinen .08 .20
20 Kim Hirschovits .08 .20
21 Kimmo Kuhta .08 .20
22 Joonas Vihko .08 .20
23 Jarkko Ruutu .20 .50
24 Timo Parssinen .08 .20
25 Arttu Luttinen .08 .20
26 Lennart Petrell .08 .20
27 Brett Harkins .20 .50
28 Eetu Holma .08 .20
29 Roman Vopat .08 .20
30 Miika Wiikman .20 .50
31 Vladimir Sicak .20 .50
32 Tuomas Eskelinen .08 .20
33 Mikko Jokela .08 .20
34 Veli-Pekka Laitinen .08 .20
35 Tuukka Makela .08 .20
36 Jyrki Louhi .08 .20
37 Jani Hassinen .08 .20
38 Hannu Vaisanen .08 .20
39 Riku Hahl .20 .50
40 Jani Keinanen .08 .20
41 Janne Laakkonen .08 .20
42 Jani Rita .20 .50
43 Jukka Voutilainen .08 .20
44 Toni Makiaho .08 .20
45 Oliver Setzinger .20 .50
46 Juha Pitkamaki .08 .20
47 Tuukka Rask ERC 2.00 5.00
48 Ville Koistinen .08 .20
49 Cory Murphy .20 .50
50 Sami Helenius .20 .50
51 Ismo Kuoppala .08 .20
52 Jesse Niinimaki .20 .50
53 Marko Luomala .08 .20
54 Timo Peltomaa .08 .20
55 Ville Leino .08 .20
56 Steve Kariya .40 1.00
57 Patrik Stefan .20 .50
58 Jussi Pesonen .08 .20
59 Tommi Turunen .08 .20
60 Raimo Helminen .08 .20
61 Simo Vidgren .08 .20
62 Pasi Hakkinen .20 .50
63 Tim Thomas .40 1.00
64 Kevin Kantee .08 .20
65 Kari Martikainen .08 .20
66 Jan Latvala .08 .20
67 Sami Lepisto .08 .20
68 Martti Jarventie .08 .20
69 Marko Jantunen .08 .20
70 Tomek Valtonen .08 .20
71 Toni Dahlman .08 .20
72 Petri Pakaslahti .08 .20
73 Petri Varis .08 .20
74 Juha Lind .08 .20
75 Timo Vertala .08 .20
76 Quinn Hancock .08 .20
77 Glen Metropolit .20 .50
78 Valtteri Filppula ERC .50 1.25
79 Tommi Nikkila .20 .50
80 Sinuhe Wallinheimo .20 .50
81 Tommi Kovanen .08 .20
82 Duvie Westcott .20 .50
83 Jari Korhonen .08 .20
84 Ilari Filppula .08 .20
85 Arsi Piispanen .08 .20
86 Steve Martins .20 .50
87 Jarkko Immonen .08 .20
88 Janne Hauhtonen .08 .20
89 Jaakko Uhlback .08 .20
90 Antti Virtanen .08 .20
91 Niklas Backstrom .40 1.00
92 Oskari Korpikari .08 .20
93 Lasse Kukkonen .20 .50
94 Ari Vallin .08 .20
95 Mikko Lehtonen .20 .50
96 Janne Niinimaa .20 .50
97 Jussi Jokinen .40 1.00
98 Viktor Ujcik .08 .20
99 Pekka Saarenheimo .08 .20
100 Mika Pyorala .08 .20
101 Janne Pesonen .08 .20
102 Jari Viuhkola .08 .20
103 Toni Sihvonen .08 .20
104 Sakari Palsola .08 .20
105 Petr Tenkrat .08 .20
106 Eero Somervuori .08 .20
107 Michael Nylander .20 .50
108 Dwayne Roloson .75 2.00
109 Petri Vehanen .08 .20
110 Toni Porkka .08 .20
111 Tomi Pettinen .08 .20
112 Janne Niskala .08 .20
113 Otto Honkaheimo .08 .20
114 Erik Hamalainen .08 .20
115 Steve Larouche .20 .50
116 Esa Pirnes .20 .50
117 Ville Snellman .08 .20
118 Shayne Toporowski .08 .20
119 Martin Bartek .08 .20
120 Toni Koivisto .08 .20
121 Sami Torkki .08 .20
122 Markku Tahtinen .08 .20
123 Pasi Saarela .08 .20
124 Pasi Nurminen .20 .50
125 Santeri Heiskanen .08 .20
126 Topi Lehtonen .08 .20
127 Erik Kakko .08 .20
128 Daniel Widing .08 .20
129 Sami Salonen .08 .20
130 Lasse Jamsen .08 .20
131 Ville Hirvonen .08 .20
132 Toni Saarinen .08 .20
133 Jesse Saarinen .08 .20
134 Jesse Welling .08 .20
135 Toni Koivunen .08 .20
136 Jarmo Myllys .20 .50
137 Jussi Pekkala .08 .20
138 Jussi Timonen .08 .20
139 Olli Malmivaara .08 .20
140 Petri Kokko .08 .20
141 Justin D. Forrest .08 .20
142 Eetu Qvist .08 .20
143 Kalle Kerman .08 .20
144 Mika Kauppinen .08 .20
145 Petr Sachl .08 .20
146 Petteri Nokelainen ERC 1.25 3.00
147 Timo Hirvonen .08 .20
148 Frank Banham .20 .50
149 Ville Viitaluoma .08 .20
150 Mika Lehto .20 .50
151 Anssi Salmela .08 .20
152 Pekka Saravo .08 .20
153 Juha Gustafsson .08 .20
154 Pasi Puistola .08 .20
155 Robert Kantor .08 .20
156 Mikko Myllykoski .08 .20
157 Janne Ojanen .08 .20
158 Johannes Alanen .08 .20
159 Mika Viinanen .08 .20
160 Marko Ojanen .08 .20
161 Petri Kontiola .08 .20
162 Ville Nieminen .20 .50
163 Sami Venalainen .08 .20
164 Stefan Ohman .08 .20
165 Tomas Chlubna .08 .20
166 Teemu Laine .08 .20
167 Teemu Lassila .20 .50
168 Tuomo Karjalainen .08 .20
169 Marko Kiprusoff .08 .20
170 Kimmo Eronen .08 .20
171 Markus Seikola .08 .20
172 David Schneider .08 .20
173 Jiri Vykoukal .08 .20
174 Antti Hulkkonen .08 .20
175 Marco Tuokko .08 .20
176 Antti Aalto .08 .20
177 Joni Lius .08 .20
178 Kai Nurminen .08 .20
179 Ville Vahalahti .08 .20
180 Lauri Korpikoski ERC 1.25 3.00
181 Mika Alatalo .08 .20
182 Jari Kauppila .08 .20
183 Arttu Virtanen .08 .20
184 Tuomas Nissinen .08 .20
185 Scott Langkow .20 .50
186 Pasi Peltonen .08 .20
187 Olegs Sorokins .08 .20
188 Pauli Levokari .08 .20
189 Greg Classen .20 .50
190 Samu Wesslin .08 .20
191 Mika Niemi .08 .20
192 Jari Korpisalo .08 .20
193 Jesse Joensuu .08 .20
194 Pasi Tuominen .08 .20
195 Marko Kivenmaki .08 .20
196 Teemu Virkkunen .08 .20
197 Pasi Nielikainen .08 .20
198 Jason Williams .20 .50
199 Aki Uusikartano .08 .20
200 Juha Kiilholma .08 .20
201 Janne Jalasvaara .08 .20
202 Tommi Pelkonen .08 .20
203 Tero Maatta .08 .20
204 Antti Pihlstrom .08 .20
205 Miika Elomo .08 .20
206 Jarkko Almmonen .08 .20
207 Mike Ribeiro .20 .50
208 Matti Naatanen .08 .20
209 Jani Nieminen .08 .20
210 Tomas Vokoun .75 2.00
211 Mikko Turunen .08 .20
212 Mikko Kurvinen .08 .20
213 Hannu Pikkarainen .08 .20
214 Lasse Pirjeta .08 .20
215 Juha Fagerstedt .08 .20
216 Jermu PorthÃ´n .08 .20
217 Mikko Laine .08 .20
218 Mika Noronen .20 .50
219 Jarno Virkki .08 .20
220 Tuomas Immonen .08 .20
221 Jukka-Pekka Laamanen .08 .20
222 Josh Holden .08 .20
223 Petteri Virtanen .08 .20
224 Joni Lappalainen .08 .20
225 Joni Lindlof .08 .20
226 Juha-Pekka Loikas .08 .20
227 Janne Lahti .08 .20
228 Juuso Riksman .08 .20
229 Teemu Jaaskelainen .08 .20
230 Henri Laurila .08 .20
231 Ossi Pellinen .08 .20
232 Antti Miettinen .40 1.00
233 Hannes Hyvonen .08 .20
234 Jukka Tiilikainen .08 .20
235 Tommi Jaminki .08 .20
236 Mikko Suvanto .08 .20
237 Samuli Jalkanen .08 .20
238 Brian Campbell .20 .50
239 Mikko Kalteva .08 .20
240 Markus Kankaanpera .08 .20
241 Tero Konttinen .08 .20
242 Ossi Vaananen .08 .20
243 Tomi Maki .08 .20
244 Arto Koivisto .08 .20
245 Arto Kuki .08 .20
246 Roni Andersson .08 .20
247 Teemu Kuusisto .08 .20
248 Petri Virolainen .08 .20
249 Ilkka Vaarasuo .08 .20
250 Carlo Grünn .20 .50
251 Juha-Pekka Hytonen .08 .20
252 Jari Jaaskelainen .08 .20
253 Ossi Louhivaara .08 .20
254 Tuomas Mikkonen .08 .20
255 Eero Hyvarinen .08 .20
256 Jody Shelley .40 1.00
257 Pekka Rinne 4.00 10.00
258 Ilkka Mikkola .08 .20
259 Topi Jaakola .08 .20
260 Kimmo Lotvonen .08 .20
261 Josef Boumedienne .08 .20
262 Juha-Pekka Haataja .08 .20
263 Antti Aarnio .08 .20
264 Mikael Vuorio .08 .20
265 Jaakko Harikkala .08 .20
266 Antti Bruun .08 .20
267 Ilkka Saarela .08 .20
268 Jarkko Kauvosaari .08 .20
269 Teemu Normio .08 .20
270 Janne Silvonen .08 .20
271 Juhamatti Yli-Junnila .08 .20
272 Joni Yli-Torkko .08 .20
273 Jaakko Suomalainen .08 .20
274 Karri Ramo .08 .20
275 Markus Helanen .08 .20
276 Olli Korkeavuori .08 .20
277 Antti-Pekka Lamberg .08 .20
278 Mikko Niinikoski .08 .20
279 Petri Koskinen .08 .20
280 Tommi Hannus .08 .20
281 Tuomas Santavuori .08 .20
282 Juha Kuokkanen .08 .20
283 Thomas Innerwinkler .08 .20
284 Harri Tikkanen .08 .20
285 Matti Hana .08 .20
286 Ossi-Petteri Gronholm .08 .20
287 Mike Gabinet .20 .50
288 Kalle Kaijomaa .08 .20
289 Ville Koho .08 .20
290 Mika Skytta .08 .20
291 Tuomas Vanttinen .08 .20
292 Andrew Raycroft .60 1.50
293 Sasu Hovi .08 .20
294 Mikko Pukka .08 .20
295 Kimmo Koskenkorva .08 .20
296 Teemu Nurmi .08 .20
297 Robert Tomik .08 .20
298 Jarkko Pyymaki .08 .20
299 Marko Makinen .08 .20
300 Timo Vertala .08 .20
301 Juho Santanen .08 .20
302 Simon Backman .08 .20
303 Markku Paukkunen .08 .20
304 Craig Rivet .08 .20
305 Tomi Sykko .08 .20
306 Saku Koivu .75 2.00
307 Matias Metsaranta .08 .20
308 Markus Ojala .08 .20
309 Tyler Bouck .20 .50
310 Matti Aho .08 .20
311 Marko Toivonen .08 .20
312 Mika Rontti .08 .20
313 Atte Pentikainen .20 .50
314 Aki Heino .08 .20
315 Kristian Kuusela .08 .20
316 Matti Kuparinen .08 .20
317 Juha-Pekka Ketola .08 .20

2004-05 Finnish Cardset Parallel

2X to 5X BASE CARD VALUE

2004-05 Finnish Cardset Saku Koivu Golden Signatures

COMPLETE SET (3) 10.00 25.00
1 Saku Koivu 4.00 10.00
2 Saku Koivu 4.00 10.00
3 Saku Koivu 4.00 10.00

2004-05 Finnish Cardset Signatures

1 Joni Toykkala 8.00 20.00
2 Ladislav Kohn 8.00 20.00
3 Lauri Tukonen 12.00 30.00
4 Marek Zidlicky 12.00 30.00
5 Jere Karalahti 8.00 20.00
6 Jarno Kultanen 8.00 20.00
7 Brett Harkins 8.00 20.00
8 Vladimir Sicak 8.00 20.00
9 Tuomas Eskelinen 8.00 20.00
10 Riku Hahl 8.00 20.00
11 Jani Rita 8.00 20.00
12 Tuukka Rask 25.00 60.00
13 Jussi Pesonen 8.00 20.00
14 Simo Vidgren 8.00 20.00
15 Toni Dahlman 8.00 20.00
16 Valtteri Filppula 15.00 30.00
17 Duvie Westcott 12.00 30.00
18 Arsi Piispanen 8.00 20.00
19 Steve Martins 8.00 20.00
20 Jarkko Immonen 12.00 30.00
21 Niklas Backstrom 15.00 40.00
22 Jussi Jokinen 25.00 60.00
23 Dwayne Roloson 15.00 40.00
24 Esa Pirnes 8.00 20.00
25 Erik Kakko 8.00 20.00
26 Jarmo Myllys 8.00 20.00
27 Petteri Nokelainen 12.00 30.00
28 Frank Banham 8.00 20.00
29 Pekka Saravo 8.00 20.00
30 Pasi Puistola 8.00 20.00
31 Mikko Myllykoski 8.00 20.00
32 Petri Kontiola 8.00 20.00
33 Ville Nieminen 8.00 20.00
34 Marko Kiprusoff 8.00 20.00
35 David Schneider 8.00 20.00
36 Lauri Korpikoski 12.00 30.00
37 Olegs Sorokins 8.00 20.00
38 Mika Niemi 8.00 20.00
39 Jesse Joensuu 8.00 20.00
40 Teemu Virkkunen 8.00 20.00
41 Jason Williams 12.00 30.00

2004-05 Finnish Cardset Stars of the Game

COMPLETE SET (14) 10.00 25.00
1 Riku Hahl 1.25 3.00
2 Hannes Hyvonen .40 1.00
3 Jarkko Immonen 1.25 3.00
4 Scott Langkow .75 2.00
5 Teemu Lassila .40 1.00
6 Ville Nieminen .75 2.00
7 Janne Niinimaa .75 2.00
8 Mika Noronen 1.25 3.00
9 Pasi Nurminen 1.25 3.00
10 Michael Nylander .75 2.00
11 Jarkko Ruutu .75 2.00
12 Patrik Stefan .75 2.00
13 Tim Thomas 1.25 3.00
14 Marek Zidlicky .75 2.00

2004-05 Finnish Cardset Tribute to Koivu

COMPLETE SET (3) 10.00 25.00
1 Saku Koivu 4.00 10.00
2 Saku Koivu 4.00 10.00
3 Saku Koivu 4.00 10.00

2004-05 Finnish Cardset Tribute to Nieminen

COMMON CARD 1.25 3.00

2005 Finnish Tappara Legendat

COMPLETE SET (32) 10.00 25.00
1 Antti Leppanen .40 1.00
2 Seppo Liitsola .40 1.00
3 Aleksander Barkov .40 1.00
4 Jukka Porvari .40 1.00
5 Mikko Leinonen .40 1.00
6 Martti Jarkko .40 1.00
7 Kiira Korpi .40 1.00
8 Ville Nieminen .40 1.00
9 Esko Niemi .40 1.00
10 Teppo Numminen .40 1.00
11 Erkki Lehtonen .40 1.00
12 Jarl Ohlson .40 1.00
13 Timo Susi .40 1.00
14 Kiira Korpi .40 1.00
15 Timo Jutila .40 1.00
16 Hannu Kamppuri .75 2.00
17 Lasse Litma .40 1.00
18 Pertti Valkeapaa .40 1.00
19 Yrjo Hakala .40 1.00
20 Jouni Seistamo .40 1.00
21 Kiira Korpi .40 1.00
22 Pekka Marjamaki .40 1.00
23 Markus Mattsson .40 1.00
24 Seppo Ahokainen .40 1.00
25 Hannu Haapalainen .40 1.00
26 Esko Luostarinen .40 1.00
27 Pertti Koivulahti .40 1.00
28 Kiira Korpi .40 1.00
29 Janne Ojanen .40 1.00
30 Kalevi Numminen .40 1.00
31 Jukka Rautakorpi .40 1.00
32 Rauno Korpi .40 1.00

2005-06 Finnish Cardset

COMPLETE SET (352) 25.00 60.00
1 Janne Jalasvaara .10 .25
2 Kari Haakana .10 .25
3 Arto Laatikainen .10 .25
4 Joni TöykkÃ¤lÃ¤ .10 .25
5 Olli Ahonen .10 .25
6 Ladislav Kohn .10 .25
7 Lauri Tukonen .20 .50
8 Mike Ribeiro .20 .50
9 Niko Nieminen .10 .25
10 Jan Lundell .10 .25
11 Marek Zidlicky .20 .50
12 Mikko Turunen .10 .25
13 Toni Lydman .10 .25
14 Mikko Kurvinen .10 .25
15 Pasi Saarinen .10 .25
16 Kim Hirschovits .10 .25
17 Joonas Vihko .10 .25
18 Toni HÃ¤ppÃ¶lÃ¤ .10 .25
19 Juha Fagerstedt .10 .25
20 Turo JÃ¤rvinen .10 .25
21 Arttu Luttinen .10 .25
22 Eetu Holma .10 .25
23 Olli Jokinen .20 .50
24 Mika Noronen .20 .50
25 Miika Wiikman .10 .25
26 Tuomas Immonen .10 .25
27 Mikko Jokela .10 .25
28 Veli-Pekka Laitinen .10 .25
29 Jyrki Louhi .10 .25
30 Petteri Wirtanen .10 .25
31 Joni Lappalainen .10 .25
32 Hannu VÃ¤isÃ¤nen .10 .25
33 Riku Hahl .10 .25
34 Jani KeinÃ¤nen .10 .25
35 Juha-Pekka Loikas .10 .25
36 Janne Lahti .10 .25
37 Oliver Setzinger .10 .25
38 Juha PitkÃ¤mÃ¤ki .10 .25
39 Vesa Toskala .40 1.00
40 Tuukka Rask 1.25 3.00
41 Joonas Rönnberg .10 .25
42 Ville Koistinen .20 .50
43 Ossi Pellinen .10 .25
44 Marko Anttila .10 .25
45 Marko Luomala .10 .25
46 Patrik Stefan .10 .25
47 Jussi Pesonen .10 .25
48 Raimo Helminen .10 .25
49 Simo Vidgren .10 .25
50 Pasi HÃ¤kkinen .10 .25
51 Tim Thomas .75 2.00
52 Brian Campbell .20 .50
53 Markus KankaanperÃ¤ .10 .25
54 Kevin Kantee .10 .25
55 Kari Martikainen .10 .25
56 Ossi VÃ¤Ã¤nÃ¤nen .10 .25
57 Martti JÃ¤rventie .10 .25
58 Tomi MÃ¤ki .10 .25
59 Toni Dahlman .10 .25
60 Petri Pakaslahti .10 .25
61 Petri Varis .10 .25
62 Teemu Kuusisto .10 .25
63 Tommi NikkilÃ¤ .10 .25
64 Tommi Kovanen .10 .25
65 Duvie Westcott .20 .50
66 Ilkka Vaarasuo .10 .25
67 Carlo Grunn .10 .25
68 Juha-Pekka Hytönen .10 .25
69 Arsi Piispanen .10 .25
70 Jari JÃ¤Ã¤skelÃ¤inen .10 .25
71 Ossi Louhivaara .10 .25
72 Tuomas Mikkonen .10 .25
73 Jarkko Immonen .20 .50
74 Antti Virtanen .10 .25
75 Ari Luostarinen .10 .25
76 Jermu Pisto .10 .25
77 Mikko Saavinen .10 .25
78 Samuli Suhonen .10 .25
79 Ville HÃ¤mÃ¤lÃ¤inen .10 .25
80 Tuomas Kiiskinen .10 .25
81 Henri Huohvanainen .10 .25
82 Sami Salonen .10 .25
83 Max Kenig .10 .25
84 Saku KekÃ¤lÃ¤inen .10 .25
85 Sami Kaartinen .10 .25
86 Timo Kuuluvainen .10 .25
87 Pekka Rinne .60 1.50
88 Oskari Korpikari .10 .25
89 Lasse Kukkonen .10 .25
90 Ilkka Mikkola .10 .25
91 Topi Jaakola .10 .25
92 Janne Niinimaa .10 .25
93 Jussi Jokinen .40 1.00
94 Viktor Ujcik .10 .25
95 Pekka Saarenheimo .10 .25
96 Mika PyÃ¶rÃ¤lÃ¤ .10 .25
97 Juha-Pekka Haataja .10 .25
98 Petr Tenkrat .10 .25
99 Antti Jokela .10 .25
100 Dwayne Roloson .40 1.00
101 Toni Porkka .10 .25
102 Antti Bruun .10 .25
103 Otto Honkaheimo .10 .25
104 Ilkka Heikkinen .10 .25
105 Tommi Hannus .10 .25
106 Ville Snellman .10 .25
107 Jarkko Kauvosaari .10 .25
108 Jaakko Hagelberg .10 .25
109 Teemu Normio .10 .25
110 Markku TÃ¤htinen .10 .25
111 Juhamatti Yli-Junnila .10 .25
112 Pasi Nurminen .15 .40
113 Olli Korkeavuori .10 .25
114 Kimmo Pikkarainen .10 .25
115 Santeri Heiskanen .10 .25
116 Matias Loppi .10 .25
117 Tuomas Santavuori .10 .25
118 Toni Sihvonen .10 .25
119 Henri Heino .10 .25
120 Marcus Paulsson .10 .25
121 Tommi Turunen .10 .25
122 Ville-Matti Koponen .10 .25
123 Jesse Saarinen .10 .25
124 Jussi Timonen .10 .25
125 Harri Tikkanen .10 .25
126 Olli Malmivaara .10 .25
127 Ossi-Petteri Grönholm .10 .25
128 Petri Kokko .10 .25
129 Kalle Kaijomaa .10 .25
130 Ville Koho .10 .25
131 Teemu Paakkarinen .10 .25
132 Mika SkyttÃ¤ .10 .25
133 Tuomas VÃ¤nttinen .10 .25
134 Eetu Qvist .10 .25
135 Ville Viitaluoma .10 .25
136 Mikko Silvennoinen .10 .25
137 Mika Lehto .10 .25
138 Anssi Salmela .10 .25
139 Ville MÃ¤ntymaa .10 .25
140 Pasi Puistola .10 .25
141 Mikko Pukka .10 .25
142 Janne Ojanen .10 .25
143 Mika Viinanen .10 .25
144 Marko Ojanen .10 .25
145 Petri Kontiola .10 .25
146 Marko MÃ¤kinen .10 .25
147 Ville Nieminen .10 .25
148 Sami VenÃ¤lÃ¤inen .10 .25
149 Stefan Ã–hman .10 .25
150 Teemu Laine .10 .25
151 Juho Santanen .10 .25
152 Tuomo Karjalainen .10 .25
153 Marko Kiprusoff .10 .25
154 Kimmo Eronen .10 .25
155 Antti Hulkkonen .10 .25
156 Saku Koivu .40 1.00
157 Antti Aalto .10 .25
158 Kai Nurminen .10 .25
159 Ville Vahalahti .10 .25
160 Lauri Korpikoski .40 1.00
161 Jari Kauppila .10 .25
162 Arttu Virtanen .10 .25
163 Matti Aho .10 .25
164 Tuomas Nissinen .10 .25
165 Pasi Peltonen .10 .25
166 Marko Toivonen .10 .25
167 Kristian Kuusela .10 .25
168 Mika Niemi .10 .25
169 Matti Kuparinen .10 .25
170 Marko KivenmÃ¤ki .10 .25
171 Pasi NielikÃ¤inen .10 .25
172 Jason Williams .40 1.00
173 Aki Uusikartano .10 .25
174 Juha Kiilholma .10 .25
175 Neil Little .40 1.00
176 Matti Kaltiainen .10 .25
177 Tuomas Eskelinen .10 .25
178 Tero Maatta .10 .25
179 Kimmo Peltonen .10 .25
180 Joakim Eriksson .10 .25
181 Esa Pirnes .10 .25
182 Markku Hurme .10 .25
183 Pentti Noyranen .10 .25
184 Steve Kariya .10 .25
185 Timo Hirvonen .10 .25
186 Jaakko Uhlback .10 .25
187 Kari Kalto .10 .25
188 Tom Askey .20 .50
189 Robert Schnabel .10 .25
190 Jere Karalahti .10 .25
191 Hannu Pikkarainen .10 .25
192 Patrik Lostedt .10 .25
193 Tony Salmelainen .20 .50
194 Miika Jouhkimainen .10 .25
195 Jermu Porthen .10 .25
196 Janne Hauhtonen .10 .25
197 Tobias Salmelainen .10 .25
198 Lennart Petrell .10 .25
199 Pasi Salonen .10 .25
200 Heikki Laine .10 .25
201 Juha Toivonen .10 .25
202 David Schneider .10 .25
203 Juuso Hietanen .10 .25
204 Jukka-Pekka Laamanen .10 .25
205 Kaspars Astashenko .10 .25
206 Jani Hassinen .10 .25
207 Jari Sailio .10 .25
208 Mikko Laine .10 .25
209 Antti Hilden .10 .25
210 Jukka Voutilainen .10 .25
211 Janis Sprukts .10 .25
212 Ville Leino .10 .25
213 Toni Niemi .10 .25
214 Jyrki Lumme .10 .25
215 Juha Alen .10 .25
216 Mikko Kuukka .10 .25
217 Jonas Andersson .10 .25
218 Perttu Lindgren .40 1.00
219 Ville Korhonen .10 .25
220 Tommi Huhtala .10 .25
221 Toni Koivisto .10 .25
222 Jason Guerriero .10 .25
223 Tomi Hirvonen .10 .25
224 Henrik Juntunen .10 .25
225 Vesa Viitakoski .10 .25
226 Joonas Hallikainen .10 .25
227 Samuli Jalkanen .10 .25
228 Mikko Kalteva .10 .25
229 Jan Latvala .10 .25
230 Sami Lepisto .10 .25
231 Tero Konttinen .10 .25
232 Tony Virta .10 .25
233 Marko Jantunen .10 .25
234 Tomek Valtonen .10 .25
235 Jesse Niinimaki .10 .25
236 Arto Koivisto .10 .25
237 Ilari Filppula .10 .25
238 Tommi Santala .10 .25
239 Arto Kuki .10 .25
240 Sinuhe Wallinheimo .20 .50
241 Miika Huczkowski .10 .25
242 Jaako Niskavaara .10 .25
243 Eerikki Koivu .10 .25
244 Juha Salmu .10 .25
245 Jyri Marttinen .10 .25
246 Johannes Alanen .10 .25
247 Filip Riska .10 .25
248 Miikka Mannikko .10 .25
249 Valtteri Tenkanen .10 .25
250 Lucas Lawson .10 .25
251 Tero Koponen .10 .25
252 Miika Lahti .10 .25
253 Juha Jaaskelainen .10 .25
254 Kimmo Kapanen .10 .25
255 Juha Alastalo .10 .25
256 Juho Kuronen .10 .25
257 Jussi Savolainen .10 .25
258 Matti Kuusisto .10 .25
259 Mikko Hakkarainen .10 .25
260 Jani Tuppurainen .10 .25
261 Tomi Pollanen .10 .25
262 Kasper Kenig .10 .25
263 Tomas Kurka .10 .25
264 Matti Tiihonen .10 .25
265 Niklas Backstrom .75 2.00
266 Mika Pietila .10 .25
267 Antti Ylonen .10 .25
268 Ari Vallin .10 .25
269 Mikko Lehtonen .15 .40
270 Jouni Loponen .10 .25
271 Janne Pesonen .10 .25
272 Tommi Paakkolanvaara .10 .25
273 Jari Viuhkola .10 .25
274 Mikko Alikoski .10 .25
275 Michal Bros .10 .25
276 Kalle Sahlstedt .10 .25
277 Juhamatti Aaltonen .10 .25
278 Tomi Mustonen .10 .25
279 Scott Langkow .20 .50
280 Topi Lehtonen .10 .25
281 Markku Paukkunen .10 .25
282 Tuukka Makela .10 .25
283 Pauli Levokari .10 .25
284 Erik Hamalainen .10 .25
285 Jamie Wright .10 .25
286 Petri Lammassaari .10 .25
287 Shayne Toporowski .10 .25
288 Miikka Tuomainen .10 .25
289 Pasi Saarela .10 .25
290 Joni Yli-Torkko .10 .25
291 Antti Niemi .10 .25
292 Esa Saksinen .10 .25
293 Sami Helenius .10 .25
294 Jarkko Glad .10 .25
295 Erik Kakko .10 .25
296 Kari Sihvonen .10 .25
297 Toni Koivunen .10 .25
298 Olli Julkunen .10 .25
299 Jussi Saarinen .10 .25
300 Lasse Jamsen .10 .25
301 Mikko Stromberg .10 .25
302 Rob Zepp .20 .50
303 Mikko Palomaki .10 .25
304 Juha Jokiraita .10 .25
305 Joni Tuominen .10 .25
306 Kristian Kudroc .10 .25
307 Antti Pihlstrom .10 .25
308 Kimmo Koskenkorva .10 .25
309 Jaska Vilen .10 .25
310 Morten Ask .10 .25

Card	Low	High
311 Jarkko Immonen	.20	.50
312 Peter Nylander	.10	.25
313 Janne Kolehmainen	.10	.25
314 Teemu Seppanen	.10	.25
315 Pekka Tuokkola	.10	.25
316 Brian White	.10	.25
317 Marko Kauppinen	.10	.25
318 Tuukka Mantyla	.10	.25
319 Jussi Halme	.10	.25
320 Greg Hawgood	.20	.50
321 Janne Gronvall	.10	.25
322 Teemu Nurmi	.10	.25
323 Jarkko Pyymaki	.10	.25
324 Teemu Virkkunen	.10	.25
325 Timo Vertala	.10	.25
326 Quinn Hancock	.10	.25
327 Mika Lehtinen	.10	.25
328 Henri Palmroth	.10	.25
329 Simon Backman	.10	.25
330 Markus Seikola	.10	.25
331 Tomi Sykko	.10	.25
332 Joni Lius	.10	.25
333 Jussi Makkonen	.10	.25
334 Mika Alatalo	.10	.25
335 Jarmo Jokila	.10	.25
336 Daniel Widing	.10	.25
337 Andreas Jamtin	.10	.25
338 Tuukka Pulliainen	.10	.25
339 Juuso Riksman	.10	.25
340 Jussi Rynnas	.10	.25
341 Justin Forrest	.10	.25
342 Atte Pentikainen	.10	.25
343 Matt Nickerson	.20	.50
344 Jesse Saarinen	.10	.25
345 Mikko Rautee	.10	.25
346 Jesse Joensuu	.20	.50
347 Tuomas Takala	.10	.25
348 Rob Hisey	.10	.25
349 Patrik Forsbacka	.10	.25
350 Petteri Tasku	.10	.25
351 Leo Komarov	.10	.25
352 Matti Kaipainen	.10	.25

2005-06 Finnish Cardset Magicmakers

Card	Low	High
COMPLETE SET (18)	15.00	40.00
1 Mike Ribeiro	.75	2.00
2 Toni Lydman	.75	2.00
3 Olli Jokinen	1.25	3.00
4 Jarkko Ruutu	.75	2.00
5 Riku Hahl	.75	2.00
6 Josh Holden	.75	2.00
7 Steve Kariya	1.25	3.00
8 Patrik Stefan	.75	2.00
9 Sami Lepistö	.75	2.00
10 Ossi VÃ¤Ã¤nÃ¤nen	.75	2.00
11 Valtteri Filppula	2.00	5.00
12 Jarkko Immonen	1.50	4.00
13 Jussi Jokinen	2.00	5.00
14 Jari Viuhkola	.75	2.00
15 Ville Nieminen	.75	2.00
16 Saku Koivu	2.00	5.00
17 Craig Rivet	.75	2.00
18 Jason Williams	1.50	4.00

2005-06 Finnish Cardset Super Snatchers

Card	Low	High
COMPLETE SET (18)	20.00	50.00
1 Jan Lundell	1.25	3.00
2 Tomas Vokoun	2.50	6.00
3 Mika Noronen	1.25	3.00
4 Miika Wiikman	1.25	3.00
5 Juha PitkÃ¤mÃ¤ki	1.25	3.00
6 Vesa Toskala	2.50	6.00
7 Tim Thomas	2.50	6.00
8 Sinuhe Wallinheimo	1.25	3.00
9 Kimmo Kapanen	1.25	3.00
10 Niklas Backstrom	1.50	4.00
11 Dwayne Roloson	1.50	4.00
12 Pasi Nurminen	1.25	3.00
13 Jarmo Myllys	1.25	3.00
14 Andrew Raycroft	2.00	5.00
15 Mika Lehto	1.25	3.00
16 Tuomo Karjalainen	1.25	3.00
17 Teemu Lassila	1.25	3.00
18 Tuomas Nissinen	1.25	3.00

2006-07 Finnish Cardset

Card	Low	High
COMPLETE SERIES 1 (180)	40.00	80.00
1 Juha Gustafsson	.20	.50
2 Tuomas Eskelinen	.20	.50
3 Arto Laatikainen	.20	.50
4 Kimmo Peltonen	.20	.50
5 Jari Korhonen	.20	.50
6 Markku Hurme	.20	.50
7 Olli Ahonen	.20	.50
8 Ladislav Kohn	.20	.50
9 Erkki RajamÃ¤ki	.20	.50
10 Mikko Lehtonen	.20	.50
11 Pentti NöyrÃ¤nen	.20	.50
12 Kari Kalto	.20	.50
13 Jan Lundell	.30	.75
14 Teemu Laakso	.20	.50
15 Jere Karalahti	.20	.50
16 Mikko Turunen	.20	.50
17 Hannu Pikkarainen	.20	.50
18 Tony Salmelainen	.20	.50
19 Turo JÃ¤rvinen	.20	.50
20 Jermu PorthÃ©n	.20	.50
21 Janne Hauhtonen	.20	.50
22 Arttu Luttinen	.20	.50
23 Pasi Salonen	.20	.50
24 Heikki Laine	.20	.50
25 Karri RÃ¤mö	.75	2.00
26 Juha Toivonen	.20	.50
27 David Schneider	.20	.50
28 Juuso Hietanen	.20	.50
29 Mikko Jokela	.20	.50
30 Veli-Pekka Laitinen	.20	.50
31 Jani Hassinen	.20	.50
32 Jari Sailio	.20	.50
33 Petteri Wirtanen	.20	.50
34 Iivo Hokkanen	.20	.50
35 Joni Lappalainen	.20	.50
36 Hannu VÃ¤isÃ¤nen	.20	.50
37 Juha-Pekka Loikas	.20	.50
38 Ville Leino	.20	.50
39 Tuukka Rask	2.00	5.00
40 Toni Niemi	.20	.50
41 Jyrki Lumme	.20	.50
42 Ville Koistinen	.20	.50
43 Juha AlÃ©n	.20	.50
44 Juho Mielonen	.20	.50
45 Perttu Lindgren	.60	1.50
46 Marko Anttila	.20	.50
47 Ville Korhonen	.20	.50
48 Toni Koivisto	.20	.50
49 Jussi Pesonen	.20	.50
50 Tomi Hirvonen	.20	.50
51 Vesa Viitakoski	.20	.50
52 Raimo Helminen	.20	.50
53 Joonas Hallikainen	.20	.50
54 Mikko Kalteva	.20	.50
55 Markus KankaanperÃ¤	.20	.50
56 Kevin Kantee	.20	.50
57 Jan Latvala	.20	.50
58 Sami Lepistö	.20	.50
59 Tony Virta	.20	.50
60 Tomek Valtonen	.20	.50
61 Arto Koivisto	.20	.50
62 Petri Pakaslahti	.20	.50
63 Tommi Santala	.20	.50
64 Petri Varis	.20	.50
65 Jesse Uronen	.20	.50
66 Roni Andersson	.20	.50
67 Sinuhe Wallinheimo	.30	.75
68 Miika Huczkowski	.20	.50
69 Jaako Niskavaara	.20	.50
70 Erkka LeppÃ¤nen	.20	.50
71 Eerikki Koivu	.20	.50
72 Juha Salmu	.20	.50
73 Jyrki Marttinen	.20	.50
74 Carlo Grünn	.20	.50
75 Johannes Alanen	.20	.50
76 Miikka MÃ¤nnikkö	.20	.50
77 Juha-Pekka Hytönen	.20	.50
78 Arsi Piispanen	.20	.50
79 Jari JÃ¤Ã¤skelÃ¤inen	.20	.50
80 Ossi Louhivaara	.20	.50
81 Kimmo Kapanen	.30	.75
82 Jermu Pisto	.20	.50
83 Matti Kuusisto	.20	.50
84 Juha Alastalo	.20	.50
85 Ville HÃ¤mÃ¤lÃ¤inen	.20	.50
86 Jani Tuppurainen	.20	.50
87 Kasper Kenig	.20	.50
88 Henri Huohvanainen	.20	.50
89 Sami Salonen	.20	.50
90 Tuomas Kiiskinen	.20	.50
91 Sami Kaartinen	.20	.50
92 Niklas Backstrom	1.50	4.00
93 Oskari Korpikari	.20	.50
94 Ari Vallin	.20	.50
95 Ilkka Mikkola	.20	.50
96 Mikko Lehtonen	.20	.50
97 Jouni Loponen	.20	.50
98 Viktor Ujcik	.20	.50
99 Janne Pesonen	.20	.50
100 Tommi Paakkolanvaara	.20	.50
101 Jyri Junnila	.20	.50
102 Jari Viuhkola	.20	.50
103 Michal Bros	.20	.50
104 Kalle Sahlstedt	.20	.50
105 Tomi Mustonen	.20	.50
106 Markus Nordlund	.20	.50
107 Otto Honkaheimo	.20	.50
108 Tuukka MÃ¤kelÃ¤	.20	.50
109 Ilkka Heikkinen	.20	.50
110 Pauli Levokari	.20	.50
111 Erik HÃ¤mÃ¤lÃ¤inen	.20	.50
112 Tommi Hannus	.20	.50
113 Ville-Vesa Vainiola	.20	.50
114 Petri Lammassaari	.20	.50
115 Shayne Toporowski	.20	.50
116 Jarkko Kauvosaari	.20	.50
117 Miikka Tuomainen	.20	.50
118 Juhamatti Yli-Junnila	.20	.50
119 Antti Niemi	.30	.75
120 Esa Saksinen	.20	.50
121 Olli Korkeavuori	.20	.50
122 Sami Helenius	.20	.50
123 Jarkko Glad	.20	.50
124 Erik Kakko	.20	.50
125 Matias Loppi	.20	.50
126 Olli Julkunen	.20	.50
127 Jesse Saarinen	.20	.50
128 Jussi Saarinen	.20	.50
129 Tuomas Santavuori	.20	.50
130 Henri Heino	.20	.50
131 Ville-Matti Koponen	.20	.50
132 Toni Koivunen	.20	.50
133 Mikko Strömberg	.20	.50
134 Jussi Timonen	.30	.75
135 Harri Tikkanen	.20	.50
136 Mikko PalomÃ¤ki	.20	.50
137 Ossi-Petteri Grönholm	.20	.50
138 Ville Koho	.20	.50
139 Kimmo Koskenkorva	.20	.50
140 Teemu Paakkarinen	.20	.50
141 Jaska Vilen	.20	.50
142 Jarkko Immonen	.30	.75
143 Janne Kolehmainen	.20	.50
144 Mika Lehto	.30	.75
145 Marko Kauppinen	.20	.50
146 Ville MÃ¤ntymaa	.20	.50
147 Tuukka MÃ¤ntylÃ¤	.20	.50
148 Mikko Pukka	.20	.50
149 Janne Grönvall	.20	.50
150 Teemu Nurmi	.20	.50
151 Mika Viinanen	.20	.50
152 Petri Kontiola	.20	.50
153 Sami VenÃ¤lÃ¤inen	.20	.50
154 Stefan Ã–hman	.20	.50
155 Quinn Hancock	.20	.50
156 Teemu Laine	.20	.50
157 Marko Kiprusoff	.20	.50
158 Simon Backman	.20	.50
159 Tomi Sykkö	.20	.50
160 Kai Nurminen	.20	.50
161 Jussi Makkonen	.20	.50
162 Ville Vahalahti	.20	.50
163 Lauri Korpikoski	.60	1.50
164 Mika Alatalo	.20	.50
165 Arttu Virtanen	.20	.50
166 Matti Aho	.20	.50
167 Tuukka Pulliainen	.20	.50
168 Jussi RynnÃ¤s	.20	.50
169 Pasi Peltonen	.20	.50
170 Marko Toivonen	.20	.50
171 Mika Rontti	.20	.50
172 Juhamatti HietamÃ¤ki	.20	.50
173 Matt Nickerson	.40	1.00
174 Kristian Kuusela	.20	.50
175 Jesse Joensuu	.20	.50
176 Marko KivenmÃ¤ki	.20	.50
177 Matti Kuparinen	.20	.50
178 Tuomas Takala	.20	.50
179 Rob Hisey	.20	.50
180 Patrik Forsbacka	.20	.50
181 Bernd Brückler	.30	.75
182 Ari Ahonen	.40	1.00
183 Tomi KÃ¤llarsson	.20	.50
184 Kimmo Pikkarainen	.20	.50
185 Ismo Kuoppala	.20	.50
186 Samuli Suhonen	.20	.50
187 Tomas Sinisalo	.20	.50
188 Joni TöykkÃ¤lÃ¤	.20	.50
189 Jari Tolsa	.20	.50
190 Semir Ben-Amor	.20	.50
191 Ville Viitaluoma	.20	.50
192 Mikko Laine	.20	.50
193 Martin Kariya	.20	.50
194 Toni KÃ¤hkönen	.20	.50
195 Aleksis Ahlqvist	.30	.75
196 Robert Schnabel	.20	.50
197 Cory Murphy	.20	.50
198 Patrik Lostedt	.20	.50
199 Pasi Saarinen	.20	.50
200 Kimmo Kuhta	.20	.50
201 Miikka Jouhkimainen	.20	.50
202 Raymond Murray	.20	.50
203 Juha Fagerstedt	.20	.50
204 Janne Laakkonen	.20	.50
205 Lennart Petrell	.20	.50
206 Ilkka Pikkarainen	.20	.50
207 Jan Hrdina	.20	.50
208 Pasi NielikÃ¤inen	.20	.50
209 Mika Oksa	.30	.75
210 Miika Wiikman	.30	.75
211 Risto Korhonen	.20	.50
212 Mikko MÃ¤enpÃ¤Ã¤	.20	.50
213 Philippe Seydoux	.20	.50
214 Mika Strömberg	.30	.75
215 Fredrik Svensson	.20	.50
216 Jani KeinÃ¤nen	.20	.50
217 Janne Lahti	.20	.50
218 Joonas Vihko	.20	.50
219 Aki Uusikartano	.20	.50
220 Antti Pihlström	.20	.50
221 Jonas Andersson	.20	.50
222 Toni MÃ¤kiaho	.20	.50
223 Riku Helenius	.60	1.50
224 Teemu JÃ¤Ã¤skelÃ¤inen	.20	.50
225 Mikko Kuukka	.20	.50
226 Teppo Tuomanen	.20	.50
227 Kristian Kudroc	.20	.50
228 Pasi PetrilÃ¤inen	.20	.50
229 Mikko Peltola	.20	.50
230 Sami Sandell	.20	.50
231 Tommi Huhtala	.20	.50
232 Pasi MÃ¤Ã¤ttÃ¤nen	.20	.50
233 Lauris Darzins	.20	.50
234 Tomas Kurka	.20	.50
235 Niko Hovinen	.30	.75
236 Juuso Riksman	.30	.75
237 Mikko Kuparinen	.20	.50
238 Marko Tuulola	.20	.50
239 Martti JÃ¤rventie	.20	.50
240 Tim Stapleton	.20	.50
241 Jyrki Louhi	.20	.50
242 Jani Rita	.20	.50
243 Arto Kuki	.20	.50
244 Kim Hirschovits	.20	.50
245 Ryan VandenBussche	.40	1.00
246 Jori LehterÃ¤	.20	.50
247 Samuli Jalkanen	.20	.50
248 Pekka Tuokkola	.20	.50
249 Miska Kangasniemi	.20	.50
250 Henrik Forsberg	.20	.50
251 Valtteri Tenkanen	.20	.50
252 Miika Lahti	.20	.50
253 Tuomas VÃ¤nttinen	.20	.50
254 Samuli Piiroinen	.20	.50
255 Olli SipilÃ¤inen	.20	.50
256 Riku Rahikainen	.20	.50
257 Ilari Filppula	.20	.50
258 Tuomas Nissinen	.30	.75
259 Janne Jalasvaara	.20	.50
260 Kyle Peto	.20	.50
261 Mats Hansson	.20	.50
262 Mikko Purontakanen	.20	.50
263 Eetu Qvist	.20	.50
264 Timo Koskela	.20	.50
265 Martin Sonnenberg	.20	.50
266 Matt Davidson	.20	.50
267 Aatu HÃ¤mÃ¤lÃ¤inen	.20	.50
268 Jaakko Suomalainen	.30	.75
269 Tuomas Tarkki	.30	.75
270 Tommi Leinonen	.20	.50
271 Topi Jaakola	.20	.50
272 Ivan Majesky	.20	.50
273 Atvars Tribuncovs	.20	.50
274 Jukka-Pekka Laamanen	.20	.50
275 Antti Ylönen	.20	.50
276 Teemu Normio	.20	.50
277 Veikko Karppinen	.20	.50
278 Mika PyörÃ¤lÃ¤	.20	.50
279 Antti Aarnio	.20	.50
280 Juhamatti Aaltonen	.20	.50
281 Markus Korhonen	.30	.75
282 Petri TÃ¤htisalo	.20	.50
283 Kari Martikainen	.20	.50
284 Jiri Hunkes	.20	.50
285 Otto Honkaheimo	.20	.50
286 Jan Platil	.20	.50
287 Pekka Saarenheimo	.20	.50
288 Toni Dahlman	.20	.50
289 Juha-Pekka Haataja	.20	.50
290 Henrik Juntunen	.20	.50
291 Marko Luomala	.20	.50
292 Josef Straka	.20	.50
293 Tommi Satosaari	.20	.50
294 Jani Forsström	.20	.50
295 Mikko Heiskanen	.20	.50
296 Anssi Salmela	.20	.50
297 Ville Uusitalo	.20	.50
298 Vili Sopanen	.20	.50
299 Karo Koivunen	.20	.50
300 Toni Sihvonen	.20	.50
301 Kari Sihvonen	.20	.50
302 Leo Komarov	.20	.50
303 Marko Jantunen	.20	.50
304 Rob Zepp	.30	.75
305 Jarno Virkki	.20	.50
306 Joonas Rönnberg	.20	.50
307 Pauli Levokari	.20	.50
308 Kalle Kaijomaa	.20	.50
309 Henrik PetrÃ©	.20	.50
310 Sami RyhÃ¤nen	.20	.50
311 Petri Koskinen	.20	.50
312 Mikko Hakkarainen	.20	.50
313 Janne Jokila	.20	.50
314 Eetu Holma	.20	.50
315 Emil Lundberg	.20	.50
316 Ville Snellman	.20	.50
317 Jens Bergenström	.20	.50
318 Tommi NikkilÃ¤	.30	.75
319 Burke Henry	.20	.50
320 Matti Koistinen	.20	.50
321 Harri Ilvonen	.20	.50
322 Dale Clarke	.20	.50
323 Teemu Aalto	.20	.50
324 Janne Ojanen	.20	.50
325 Niko Nieminen	.20	.50
326 Jarkko PyymÃ¤ki	.20	.50
327 Marko Ojanen	.20	.50
328 Jonas Enlund	.20	.50
329 Antti Hölli	.20	.50
330 Teemu Virkkunen	.20	.50
331 Juho Santanen	.20	.50
332 Jani Hurme	.40	1.00
333 Juho Jokinen	.20	.50
334 Aki Berg	.20	.50
335 Vladimir Sicak	.20	.50
336 Jesse Saarinen	.20	.50
337 Mikko Rautee	.20	.50
338 Tommi Laine	.20	.50
339 Layne Ulmer	.20	.50
340 Tuomas Suominen	.20	.50
341 Ivan Huml	.30	.75
342 Teemu Ramstedt	.20	.50
343 Joni Yli-Torkko	.20	.50
344 Matti Kaltiainen	.30	.75
345 Eero KilpelÃ¤inen	.30	.75
346 Peter Aston	.20	.50
347 Anssi Tieranta	.20	.50
348 Eetu Heikkinen	.20	.50
349 Ilkka Törnvall	.20	.50
350 Tapio Sammalkangas	.20	.50
351 Toni HÃ¤ppölÃ¤	.20	.50
352 Tom Wandell	.20	.50
353 Aleksandr Naurov	.20	.50
354 Joonas Kemppainen	.20	.50
355 Ville Hirvonen	.20	.50
356 Brandon Crombeen	.30	.75

2006-07 Finnish Cardset Between the Pipes

Card	Low	High
1 Ari Ahonen	3.00	8.00
2 Bernd Brückler	2.00	5.00
3 Aleksis Ahlqvist	2.00	5.00
4 Jan Lundell	2.00	5.00
5 Mika Oksa	2.00	5.00
6 Miika Wiikman	2.00	5.00
7 Riku Helenius	2.50	6.00
8 Tuukka Rask	5.00	12.00
9 Niko Hovinen	2.00	5.00
10 Juuso Riksman	2.00	5.00
11 Sinuhe Wallinheimo	2.00	5.00
12 Kimmo Kapanen	2.00	5.00
13 Tuomas Nissinen	2.00	5.00
14 Jaakko Suomalainen	2.00	5.00
15 Tuomas Tarkki	2.00	5.00
16 Markus Korhonen	2.00	5.00
17 Antti Niemi	4.00	10.00
18 Mikko Strömberg	2.00	5.00
19 Rob Zepp	2.00	5.00
20 Mika Lehto	2.00	5.00
21 Tommi NikkilÃ¤	2.00	5.00
22 Jani Hurme	2.50	6.00
23 Matti Kaltiainen	2.00	5.00
24 Eero KilpelÃ¤inen	2.00	5.00

2006-07 Finnish Cardset Enforcers

Card	Low	High
1 Sami Helenius	1.25	3.00
2 Kristian Kudroc	1.25	3.00
3 Ryan VandenBussche	2.00	5.00
4 Robert Schnabel	1.25	3.00
5 Burke Henry	1.25	3.00
6 Jan Platil	1.25	3.00
7 Toni MÃ¤kiaho	1.25	3.00
8 Markus KankaanperÃ¤	1.25	3.00
9 Aki Berg	1.25	3.00
10 Pasi Peltonen	1.25	3.00
11 Pasi NielikÃ¤inen	1.25	3.00
12 Jere Karalahti	1.25	3.00

2006-07 Finnish Cardset Playmakers Rookies

Card	Low	High
1 Perttu Lindgren	2.00	5.00
2 Juhamatti Aaltonen	1.25	3.00
3 Jussi Makkonen	1.25	3.00
4 Pasi Salonen	1.25	3.00
5 Juuso Hietanen	1.25	3.00
6 Petteri Wirtanen	1.25	3.00
7 Petri Lammassaari	1.25	3.00
8 Patrick Forsbacka	1.25	3.00
9 Juha AlÃ©n	1.25	3.00
10 Miika Lahti	1.25	3.00
11 Jari Sailio	1.25	3.00
12 Leo Komarov	1.25	3.00

2006-07 Finnish Cardset Playmakers Rookies Gold

Card	Low	High
COMPLETE SET (12)	40.00	80.00
1 Perttu Lindgren	6.00	15.00
2 Juhamatti Aaltonen	4.00	10.00
3 Jussi Makkonen	4.00	10.00
4 Pasi Salonen	4.00	10.00
5 Juuso Hietanen	4.00	10.00
6 Petteri Wirtanen	4.00	10.00
7 Petri Lammassaari	4.00	10.00
8 Patrick Forsbacka	4.00	10.00
9 Juha AlÃ©n	4.00	10.00
10 Miika Lahti	4.00	10.00
11 Jari Sailio	4.00	10.00
12 Perttu Lindgren	4.00	10.00

2006-07 Finnish Cardset Playmakers Rookies Silver

Card	Low	High
COMPLETE SET (12)	15.00	40.00
1 Perttu Lindgren	4.00	10.00
2 Juhamatti Aaltonen	2.00	5.00
3 Jussi Makkonen	2.00	5.00
4 Pasi Salonen	2.00	5.00
5 Juuso Hietanen	2.00	5.00
6 Petteri Wirtanen	2.00	5.00
7 Petri Lammassaari	2.00	5.00
8 Patrick Forsbacka	2.00	5.00
9 Juha AlÃ©n	2.00	5.00
10 Miika Lahti	2.00	5.00
11 Jari Sailio	2.00	5.00
12 Leo Komarov	2.00	5.00

2006-07 Finnish Cardset Signature Sensations

Card	Low	High
1 Mikko Lehtonen	15.00	40.00
2 Erkki RajamÃ¤ki	15.00	40.00
3 Miika Wiikman	15.00	40.00
4 Juuso Hietanen	15.00	40.00
5 Petteri Wirtanen	15.00	40.00
6 Tuukka Rask	40.00	80.00
7 Ville Koistinen	15.00	40.00
8 Perttu Lindgren	25.00	60.00
9 Joonas Hallikainen	15.00	40.00
10 Sami Lepistö	15.00	40.00
11 Tommi Santala	15.00	40.00
12 Sinuhe Wallinheimo	15.00	40.00
13 Miika Lahti	15.00	40.00
14 Arsi Piispanen	15.00	40.00
15 Kimmo Kapanen	15.00	40.00
16 Tuomas Kiiskinen	15.00	40.00
17 Mikko Alikoski	15.00	40.00
18 Lasse Kukkonen	15.00	40.00
19 Juhamatti Aaltonen	15.00	40.00
20 Otto Honkaheimo	15.00	40.00
21 Petri Lammassaari	15.00	40.00
22 Miikka Tuomainen	15.00	40.00
23 Antti Niemi	30.00	60.00
24 Jesse Saarinen	15.00	40.00
25 Mikko Strömberg	15.00	40.00
26 Jarkko Immonen	15.00	40.00
27 Mika Lehto	15.00	40.00
28 Petri Kontiola	15.00	40.00
29 Juho Santanen	15.00	40.00
30 Jussi Makkonen	15.00	40.00
31 Tuukka Pulliainen	15.00	40.00
32 Kristian Kuusela	15.00	40.00
33 Jesse Joensuu	15.00	40.00
34 Marko KivenmÃ¤ki	15.00	40.00
35 Patrick Forsbacka	15.00	40.00

2006-07 Finnish Cardset Superior Snatchers

Card	Low	High
1 Niklas Backstrom	4.00	10.00
2 Joonas Hallikainen	2.00	5.00
3 Kimmo Kapanen	2.00	5.00
4 Mika Lehto	2.00	5.00
5 Jan Lundell	2.00	5.00
6 Antti Niemi	4.00	10.00
7 Tuukka Rask	5.00	12.00
8 Juuso Riksman	2.00	5.00
9 Karri RÃ¤mö	3.00	8.00
10 Sinuhe Wallinheimo	2.00	5.00
11 Miika Wiikman	2.00	5.00
12 Rob Zepp	2.00	5.00

2006-07 Finnish Cardset Superior Snatchers Gold

Card	Low	High
COMPLETE SET (12)	60.00	150.00
1 Niklas Backstrom	12.00	30.00
2 Joonas Hallikainen	6.00	15.00
3 Kimmo Kapanen	6.00	15.00
4 Mika Lehto	6.00	15.00
5 Jan Lundell	6.00	15.00
6 Antti Niemi	6.00	15.00
7 Tuukka Rask	15.00	40.00
8 Juuso Riksman	6.00	15.00
9 Karri RÃ¤mö	8.00	20.00
10 Sinuhe Wallinheimo	6.00	15.00
11 Miika Wiikman	6.00	15.00
12 Rob Zepp	6.00	15.00

2006-07 Finnish Cardset Superior Snatchers Silver

Card	Low	High
COMPLETE SET (12)	50.00	100.00
1 Niklas Backstrom	8.00	20.00
2 Joonas Hallikainen	4.00	10.00
3 Kimmo Kapanen	4.00	10.00
4 Mika Lehto	4.00	10.00
5 Jan Lundell	4.00	10.00
6 Antti Niemi	4.00	10.00
7 Tuukka Rask	12.00	30.00
8 Juuso Riksman	4.00	10.00
9 Karri RÃ¤mö	6.00	15.00
10 Sinuhe Wallinheimo	4.00	10.00
11 Miika Wiikman	4.00	10.00
12 Rob Zepp	4.00	10.00

2006-07 Finnish Cardset Trophy Winners

Card	Low	High
COMPLETE SET (7)	6.00	15.00
1 Jukka Jalonen	1.25	3.00
2 Perttu Lindgren	2.00	5.00
3 Esa Pirnes	1.25	3.00
4 Juuso Riksman	1.25	3.00
5 Lasse Kukkonen	1.25	3.00
6 Miika Wiikman	1.25	3.00
7 Tony Salmelainen	1.25	3.00

2006-07 Finnish Ilves Team Set

Card	Low	High
1 Juha Alen	.20	.50
2 Juuso Antonen	.20	.50
3 Marko Anttila	.20	.50
4 Lauris Darzins	.20	.50
5 Riku Helenius	.75	2.00
6 Tomi Hirvonen	.20	.50
7 Tommi Huhtala	.20	.50
8 Teemu Jaaskelainen	.20	.50
9 Toni Koivisto	.20	.50
10 Ville Korhonen	.20	.50
11 Kristian Kudroc	.20	.50
12 Tomas Kurka	.20	.50
13 Mikko Kuukka	.20	.50
14 Jarno Laitinen	.20	.50
15 Joonas Lehtivuori	.20	.50
16 Perttu Lindgren	.60	1.50
17 Juho Mielonen	.20	.50
18 Pasi Maattanen	.20	.50
19 Toni Niemi	.20	.50
20 Mikko Peltola	.20	.50
21 Jussi Pesonen	.20	.50
22 Pasi Petrilainen	.20	.50
23 Tuukka Rask	4.00	10.00
24 Sami Sandell	.20	.50
25 Teppo Tuomanen	.20	.50
26 Vesa Viitakoski	.20	.50
27 Kari Eloranta CO	.10	.25
28 Petteri Hirvonen CO	.10	.25

2006-07 Finnish Porin Assat Pelaajakortit

Card	Low	High
COMPLETE SET (32)	10.00	25.00
1 Matti Kaltiainen	.30	.75
2 Eero Kilpelainen	.60	1.50
3 Jussi Rynnas	.30	.75
4 Pasi Peltonen	.30	.75
5 Marko Toivonen	.30	.75
6 Mika Rontti	.30	.75
7 Peter Aston	.30	.75
8 Tero Konttinen	.30	.75
9 Juhamatti Hietamaki	.30	.75
10 Anssi Tieranta	.30	.75
11 Eetu Heikkinen	.30	.75
12 Iikka Tornvall	.30	.75
13 Tapio Samalkangas	.30	.75
14 Toni Happola	.30	.75
15 Kristian Kuusela	.30	.75
16 Tom Wandell	.30	.75
17 Tuomas Huhtanen	.30	.75
18 Jesse Joensuu	.30	.75
19 Marko Kivenmaki	.30	.75
20 Matti Kuparinen	.30	.75
21 Tuomas Takala	.30	.75
22 Patrick Forsbacka	.30	.75
23 Petteri Tasku	.30	.75
24 Alexander Naurov	.30	.75
25 Joonas Kemppainen	.30	.75
26 Jussi Peltomaa	.30	.75
27 Ville Hirvonen	.30	.75
28 Brandon BJ Crombeen	.40	1.00
29 Teemu Kesa	.30	.75
30 Tobias Salmelainen	.30	.75
31 David Bararuk	.30	.75
32 Jari Harkala	.30	.75

2007-08 Finnish Cardset MVP

Card	Low	High
1 Martin Kariya	1.00	2.50
2 Cory Murphy	1.00	2.50
3 Mikko MÃ¤enpÃ¤Ã¤	1.00	2.50
4 Tuukka Rask	2.50	6.00
5 Jani Rita	1.00	2.50
6 Sinuhe Wallinheimo	1.00	2.50
7 Jani Tuppurainen	1.00	2.50
8 Jari Viuhkola	1.00	2.50
9 Juha-Pekka Haataja	1.00	2.50
10 Antti Niemi	4.00	10.00
11 Kimmo Koskenkorva	1.00	2.50
12 Petri Kontiola	1.00	2.50
13 Aki Berg	1.00	2.50
14 Marko KivenmÃ¤ki	1.00	2.50

2007-08 Finnish Cardset Twirls

Card	Low	High
1 Bernd Brückler	1.00	2.50
2 Jere Karalahti	1.00	2.50
3 Antti Pihlström	1.00	2.50
4 Perttu Lindgren	1.25	3.00
5 Kim Hirschovits	1.00	2.50
6 Juuso Riksman	1.00	2.50
7 Janne Pesonen	1.00	2.50
8 Tuomas Tarkki	1.00	2.50
9 Tuomas Suominen	1.00	2.50

2009-10 Finnish Upper Deck Victory

Card	Low	High
COMPLETE SET (250)	75.00	150.00
COMP.SET w/o SPS (200)	30.00	60.00
*FINNISH: .6X TO 1.5X BASIC VICTORY		
195 Nicklas Backstrom	.40	1.00

2009-10 Finnish Upper Deck Victory Suomalaisia Supertahtia

Card	Low	High
COMPLETE SET (20)	10.00	25.00
FF1 Kari Lehtonen	.60	1.50
FF2 Niklas Hagman	.50	1.25
FF3 Niklas Backstrom	.75	2.00
FF4 Sami Salo	.75	2.00
FF5 Jarkko Ruutu	.50	1.25
FF6 Vesa Toskala	.75	2.00
FF7 Antti Miettinen	.50	1.25
FF8 Jere Lehtinen	.60	1.50
FF9 Mikko Koivu	.75	2.00
FF10 Teppo Numminen	.50	1.25
FF11 Saku Koivu	.75	2.00
FF12 Olli Jokinen	.60	1.50
FF13 Teemu Selanne	1.50	4.00
FF14 Kimmo Timonen	.60	1.50
FF15 Tuomo Ruutu	.50	1.25
FF16 Miikka Kiprusoff	.75	2.00
FF17 Joni Pitkanen	.60	1.50
FF18 Valtteri Filppula	.50	1.25
FF19 Pekka Rinne	.75	2.00
FF20 Jussi Jokinen	.50	1.25

1994-95 French National Team

Card	Low	High
COMPLETE SET (35)	8.00	20.00
1 Benjamin Agnel	.20	.50
2 Richard Aimonetto	.20	.50
3 Stephane Arcangeloni	.20	.50
4 Mickael Babin	.20	.50
5 Alain Beaule	.20	.50
6 J. Francois Bonnard	.20	.50
7 Arnaud Briand	.20	.50
8 Karl DeWolf	.20	.50
9 Serge Djelloul	.20	.50
10 Roger Dube	.20	.50
11 Patrick Dunn	.20	.50
12 J. Christophe Filippin	.20	.50
13 Michel Galarneau	.20	.50
14 Gerald Guennelon	.20	.50
15 Eric Lemarque	.20	.50
16 J. Philippe Lemoine	.20	.50
17 Fabrice LHenry	.30	.75
18 Pierrick Maia	.20	.50
19 Antoine Mindjimba	.75	2.00
20 Christophe Moyon	.20	.50
21 Lionel Orsolini	.20	.50
22 Franck Pajonkowski	.30	.75
23 Denis Perez	.20	.50
24 Eric Pinard	.20	.50
25 Serge Poudrier	.30	.75
26 Christian Pouget	.20	.50
27 Pierre Pousse	.20	.50
28 Antoine Richer	.20	.50
29 Franck Saunier	.20	.50
30 J. Marc Soghomonian	.20	.50
31 Juhani Tamminen	.30	.75
32 Michel Valliere	.30	.75
33 Andre Vittenberg	.20	.50
34 Steven Woodburn	.20	.50
35 Petri Ylonen	.60	1.50

1936 German Jaszmatzi

Card	Low	High
208 Ice Hockey	15.00	30.00

1994-95 German DEL

Card	Low	High
COMPLETE SET (440)	20.00	50.00
1 International Hockey Association	.02	.10
2 DEL 1994/95	.02	.10
3 Season 1994-95	.02	.10
4 Augsburger Panther Team	.02	.10
5 Gunnar Leidborg	.02	.10
6 Gary Prior	.08	.25
7 Scott Campbell	.02	.10
8 Dieter Medicus	.02	.10
9 Duanne Moeser	.02	.10
10 Daniel Naud	.02	.10
11 Andy Romer	.02	.10
12 Thomas Groger	.02	.10
13 Sven Zywitza	.02	.10
14 Fritz Meyer	.02	.10
15 Christian Curth	.02	.10
16 Toni Krinner	.02	.10
17 Patrik Pysz	.02	.10
18 Heinrich Romer	.02	.10
19 Ales Polcar	.02	.10
20 Philip Kukuk	.02	.10
21 Dietrich Adam	.02	.10
22 Tim Schnobrich	.02	.10
23 Tim Ferguson	.08	.25
24 Robert Heidt	.02	.10
25 Alfred Burkhard	.02	.10
26 Charly Fliegauf	.02	.10
27 Robert Paclik	.02	.10
28 Stefan Mayer	.02	.10
29 Reinhard Haider	.02	.10
30 Dennis Schrapp	.02	.10
31 Eisbaren Berlin Team Card	.02	.10
32 Walter Jaroslav	.02	.10
33 Klaus Schroder	.02	.10
34 Andre Dietzsch	.02	.10
35 Juri Stumpf	.02	.10
36 Torsten Deutscher	.02	.10
37 Frank Kannewurf	.02	.10
38 Thomas Graul	.02	.10
39 Sven Felski	.02	.10
40 Moritz Schmidt	.02	.10
41 Marco Swibenko	.02	.10
42 Holger Mix	.02	.10
43 Jiri Dopita	.40	1.00
44 Dirk Perschau	.02	.10
45 Guido Hiller	.02	.10
46 Daniel Held	.02	.10
47 Richard Zemlicka	.08	.25
48 Jan Schertz	.02	.10
49 Mike Losch	.02	.10
50 Patrick Solf	.02	.10
51 Rupert Meister	.02	.10
52 BSC Preussen Team Card	.02	.10
53 Billy Flynn	.08	.25
54 Tony Tanti	.08	.25
55 Jochen Molling	.02	.10
56 Andreas Schubert	.02	.10
57 Stefan Steinecker	.02	.10
58 Josef Lehner	.02	.10
59 Tom O'Regan	.08	.25
60 Gaetan Malo	.02	.10
61 Michael Komma	.02	.10
62 Marco Schinko	.02	.10
63 Marco Rentzsch	.02	.10
64 Georg Holzmann	.02	.10
65 Mark Kosturik	.02	.10
66 Jurgen Rumrich	.02	.10
67 John Chabot	.20	.50
68 Harald Windler	.02	.10
69 Mark Teevens	.08	.25
70 Klaus Merk	.08	.25
71 Stephan Sinner	.02	.10
72 Mark Gronau	.02	.10
73 Bruce Hardy	.08	.25
74 Fabian Brannstrom	.02	.10
75 Daniel Poudrier	.08	.25
76 Dusseldorfer EG Team Card	.02	.1
77 Hans Zach	.02	.1
78 Helmut DeRaaf	.02	.1
79 Markus Kehle	.02	.1
80 Christian Schmitz	.02	.1
81 Lorenz Funk	.02	.1
82 Chris Valentine	.20	.5
83 Rafael Jedamzik	.02	.1
84 Torsten Kienass	.08	.2
85 Christopher Kreutzer	.02	.1
86 Benoit Doucet	.08	.2
87 Bernd Kuhnhauser	.02	.1
88 Andreas Niederberger	.02	.1
89 Rick Amann	.08	.2
90 Thorsten Van Leyen	.02	.1
91 Bruce Eakin	.02	.1
92 Pierre Rioux	.08	.2
93 Andreas Brockmann	.02	.1
94 Uli Hiemer	.02	.1

95 Bernd Truntschka .08 .25
96 Wolfgang Kummer .02 .10
97 Carsten Gossmann .02 .10
98 Ernst Kopf .08 .25
99 Robert Sterflinger .02 .10
100 Kevin LaVallee .08 .25
101 Rainer Zerwesz .02 .10
102 Frankfurt Lions Team Card .02 .10
103 Pjotr Vorobjev .02 .10
104 Peter Obresa .02 .10
105 Vladimir Quapp .02 .10
106 Florian Storf .02 .10
107 Alexander Wedl .02 .10
108 Olaf Scholz .02 .10
109 Ilya Vorobjev .02 .10
110 Ladislav Strompf .02 .10
111 Udo Dohler .02 .10
112 Alexander Wunsch .02 .10
113 Jiri Lala .02 .10
114 Andrej Jaufmann .02 .10
115 Thomas Muhlbauer .02 .10
116 Markus Kempf .02 .10
117 Igor Schultz .02 .10
118 Martin Schultz .02 .10
119 Michael Raubal .02 .10
120 Rudi Gorgenlander .02 .10
121 Jurgen Schaal .02 .10
122 Patrick Vozar .02 .10
123 Rochus Schneider .02 .10
124 Toni Raubal .02 .10
125 Stefan Koniger .02 .10
126 EC Hannover Team Card .02 .10
127 Hartmut Nickel .02 .10
128 Joachim Lempio .02 .10
129 Torsten Hanusch .02 .10
130 Thomas Jungwirth .02 .10
131 David Reierson .02 .10
132 Friedhelm Bogelsack .02 .10
133 Thomas Werner .02 .10
134 Dirk Rohrbach .02 .10
135 Harald Kuhnke .02 .10
136 Florian Funk .02 .10
137 Mark Maroste .02 .10
138 Anton Maidl .02 .10
139 Rene Reuter .02 .10
140 Rene Ledock .02 .10
141 Marco Herbst .02 .10
142 Milos Vanik .02 .10
143 Gunther Preuss .02 .10
144 Troy Tumbach .02 .10
145 Marc Wittbrock .02 .10
146 Roger Mede .02 .10
147 Craig Topolnisky .02 .10
148 Josef Schlickenrieder .02 .10
149 Marcus Bleicher .02 .10
150 EC Kassel Team Card .02 .10
151 Ross Yates .02 .10
152 Josef Kontny .02 .10
153 Milan Mokros .02 .10
154 Alexander Engel .02 .10
155 Greg Johnston .08 .25
156 Jedrzej Kasperczyk .02 .10
157 Dave Morrison .02 .10
158 Jaro Mucha .02 .10
159 Mike Millar .08 .25
160 Ireneusz Pacula .02 .10
161 Vitalij Grossmann .02 .10
162 Murray McIntosh .02 .10
163 Manfred Ahne .02 .10
164 Peter Kwasigroch .02 .10
165 Georg Guttler .02 .10
166 Falk Ozellis .02 .10
167 Mario Naster .02 .10
168 Sergej Wikulow .02 .10
169 Gerhard Hegen .02 .10
170 Brian Hannon .02 .10
171 Tino Boos .02 .10
172 Kaufbeurer Adler Team Card .02 .10
173 Peter Kathan .02 .10
174 Kenneth Karouk .02 .10
175 Michael Olbrich .02 .10
176 Drahomir Kadlec .08 .25
177 Christian Seeberger .02 .10
178 Elmar Boiger .02 .10
179 Oto Hascak .02 .10
180 Thorsten Rau .02 .10
181 Tomas Martinec .02 .10
182 Norbert Zabel .02 .10
183 Daniel Kunce .02 .10
184 Hans-Jorg Mayer .02 .10
185 Manfred Jorde .02 .10
186 Roland Timoschuk .02 .10
187 Jim Hoffmann .02 .10
188 Andreas Volland .02 .10
189 Rolf Hammer .02 .10
190 Manuel Hess .02 .10
191 Timo Gschwill .02 .10
192 Marc Pethke .02 .10
193 Axel Kammerer .02 .10
194 Jurgen Simon .02 .10
195 Patrick Lange .02 .10
196 Ronny Martin .02 .10
197 Kolner EC Team Card .02 .10
198 Vladimir Vassiliev .02 .10
199 Bernd Haake .02 .10
200 Joseph Heiss .30 .75
201 Jorg Mayr .02 .10
202 Thomas Brandl .02 .10
203 Stephan Mann .02 .10
204 Tonny Reddo .02 .10
205 Mirco Ludemann .08 .25
206 Leo Stefan .08 .25
207 Andreas Pokorny .02 .10
208 Peter Draisaitl .08 .25
209 Ralf Dobrzynski .02 .10
210 Andreas Lupzig .02 .10
211 Karsten Mende .02 .10
212 Frank Hohenadl .02 .10
213 Marco Heinrichs .02 .10
214 Michael Rumrich .02 .10
215 Martin Ondrejka .02 .10
216 Herbert Hohenberger .08 .25
217 Thorsten Sendt .02 .10
218 Thorsten Koslowski .02 .10
219 Olaf Grundmann .02 .10
220 Franz Demmel .02 .10
221 Sergej Berezin .75 2.00
222 Krefelder EV Team Card .02 .10
223 Michael Zettel .02 .10
224 Frank Brunsing .02 .10
225 Karel Lang .02 .10
226 Markus Kranwinkel .02 .10
227 Earl Spry .02 .10
228 Andre Grein .02 .10
229 Greg Evtushevski .08 .25
230 Herberts Vasiljevs .02 .10
231 Ken Petrash .02 .10
232 Greg Thomson .02 .10
233 Reemt Pyka .08 .25
234 Brad Bergen .08 .25
235 Chris Lindberg .08 .25
236 Markus Kranwinkel .02 .10
237 Martin Gebel .02 .10
238 Francois Sills .02 .10
239 Klaus Micheller .02 .10
240 Peter Ihnacak .20 .50
241 Marek Stebnicki .02 .10
242 Johnny Walker .02 .10
243 Gunter Oswald .02 .10
244 James Hanlon .02 .10
245 Rene Bielke .02 .10
246 EV Landshut Team Card .02 .10
247 Bernahrd Johnston .02 .10
248 Mark Stuckey .02 .10
249 Michael Bresagk .02 .10
250 Bernd Wagner .02 .10
251 Eduard Uvria .02 .10
252 Mike Smazal .02 .10
253 Jacek Plachta .02 .10
254 Georg Franz .02 .10
255 Stephan Retzer .02 .10
256 Henri Marcoux .02 .10
257 Andreas Loth .02 .10
258 Mike Bullard .02 .10
259 Markus Berwanger .02 .10
260 Petr Briza .40 1.00
261 Wally Schreiber .20 .50
262 Peter Gulda .02 .10
263 Ralf Hantschke .02 .10
264 Steve McNeil .02 .10
265 Christian Kunast .02 .10
266 Jorg Hendrick .02 .10
267 Helmut Steiger .02 .10
268 Udo Kiessling .02 .10
269 Mike Lay .02 .10
270 Adler Mannheim Team Card .02 .10
271 Lance Nethery .08 .25
272 Marcus Kuhl .02 .10
273 Joachim Appel .02 .10
274 Harold Kreis .02 .10
275 Mike Heidt .02 .10
276 Mario Gehrig .02 .10
277 Pavel Gross .02 .10
278 Steffen Michel .02 .10
279 Daniel Korber .02 .10
280 Robert Cimetta .08 .25
281 Dale Krentz .08 .25
282 Jochen Hecht 4.00 10.00
283 Till Feser .02 .10
284 Lars Bruggemann .02 .10
285 Toni Plattner .02 .10
286 Alexander Schuster .02 .10
287 Dieter Willmann .02 .10
288 Markus Flemming .02 .10
289 Rick Goldmann .20 .50
290 Damian Adamus .02 .10
291 Frederik Ledlin .02 .10
292 David Musial .02 .10
293 Michael Gabler .02 .10
294 Sven Valenti .02 .10
295 Maddogs Munchen Team Card .02 .10
296 Robert Murdoch .02 .10
297 Alexander Genze .02 .10
298 Greg Muller .02 .10
299 Mike Schmidt .02 .10
300 Zdenek Travnicek .02 .10
301 Christian Lukes .02 .10
302 Gordon Sherven .08 .25
303 Anthony Vogel .02 .10
304 Michael Hreuss .02 .10
305 Dale Derkatch .08 .25
306 Sergej Schendelew .02 .10
307 Christian Brittig .02 .10
308 Harald Waibel .02 .10
309 Rainer Lutz .02 .10
310 Ewald Steiger .02 .10
311 Didi Hegen .02 .10
312 Ralf Reisinger .02 .10
313 Henrik Holscher .02 .10
314 Karl Friesen .20 .50
315 Christian Frutel .02 .10
316 Tobias Abstreiter .02 .10
317 Christopher Sandner .02 .10
318 Harald Birk .02 .10
319 Chris Straube .02 .10
320 EHC 80 Nurnberg Team Card .02 .10
321 Josef Golonka .02 .10
322 Christian Gerum .02 .10
323 Paul Geddes .02 .10
324 Ian Young .02 .10
325 Stefan Steinbock .02 .10
326 Doug Irwin .02 .10
327 Christian Flugge .02 .10
328 Klaus Birk .02 .10
329 Jurgen Lechl .02 .10
330 Thomas Popiesch .02 .10
331 Miroslav Maly .02 .10
332 Stephan Eder .02 .10
333 Arno Brux .02 .10
334 Jiri Dolezal .08 .25
335 Reiner Vorderbruggen .02 .10
336 Thomas Sterflinger .02 .10
337 Bernhard Engelbrecht .02 .10
338 Michael Weinfurter .02 .10
339 Sepp Wassermann .02 .10
340 Stephan Bauer .02 .10
341 Otto Sykora .02 .10
342 Ratingen Die Lowen Team Card .02 .10
343 Bill Lochead .08 .25
344 Pavel Mann .02 .10
345 Christian Kohmann .02 .10
346 Sven Prusa .02 .10
347 Otto Keresztes .02 .10
348 Frank Kovacs .02 .10
349 Jiri Smicek .02 .10
350 Richard Brodnicke .02 .10
351 Andrej Fuchs .02 .10
352 Oliver Kasper .02 .10
353 Michael Kratz .02 .10
354 Klaus Striemitzer .02 .10
355 Oliver Schwarz .02 .10
356 Boris Fuchs .02 .10
357 Christian Althoff .02 .10
358 Waldemar Novosjolov .02 .10
359 Thomas Imdahl .02 .10
360 Helmut Elters .02 .10
361 Andrej Hanisz .02 .10
362 Peter Lutter .02 .10
363 Martem Janov .02 .10
364 Mark Bassen .02 .10
365 Udo Schmid .02 .10
366 Mark Bassen .08 .25
367 Rosenheim Star Bulls Team Card .02 .10
368 Ernst Hofner .02 .10
369 Ludek Bukac .02 .10
370 Markus Wieland .02 .10
371 Andreas Schneider .02 .10
372 Raphael Kruger .02 .10
373 Michael Tattner .02 .10
374 Rick Boehm .02 .10
375 Robert Hock .02 .10
376 Joachim Reil .02 .10
377 Radek Toupal .02 .10
378 Martin Reichel .02 .10
379 Ron Fischer .02 .10
380 Raimund Hilger .08 .25
381 Petr Hrbek .02 .10
382 Oliver Hausler .02 .10
383 Christian Gegenfurther .02 .10
384 Marc Seliger .08 .25
385 Venci Sebek .02 .10
386 Florian Keller .08 .25
387 Heinrich Schiffl .02 .10
388 Michael Pohl .02 .10
389 Fuchse Sachsen Team Card .02 .10
390 Jiri Kochta .02 .10
391 Boris Capla .02 .10
392 Matthias Kliemann .02 .10
393 Josef Rednicek .02 .10
394 Branjo Heisig .02 .10
395 Jens Schwabe .08 .25
396 Frank Peschke .02 .10
397 Thomas Schubert .02 .10
398 Torsten Eisebitt .02 .10
399 Marcel Lichnovsky .02 .10
400 Jari Gronstrand .08 .25
401 Thomas Knobloch .02 .10
402 Falk Herzig .02 .10
403 Thomas Wagner .02 .10
404 Jan Tabor .02 .10
405 Sebastian Klenner .02 .10
406 Peter Hofmann .02 .10
407 Terry Cambell .08 .25
408 Antonio Fonso .02 .10
409 Thomas Bresagk .02 .10
410 Peter Franke .02 .10
411 Andreas Ott .02 .10
412 Michael Flemming .02 .10
413 Janusz Janikowski .02 .10
414 Schwenningen Wild Wings Team Card .02 .10
415 Miroslav Berek .02 .10
416 Bob Burns .02 .10
417 Thomas Gaus .02 .10
418 Richard Trojan .02 .10
419 Ilmar Toman .02 .10
420 Alan Young .02 .10
421 Michael Pastika .02 .10
422 Thomas Schadler .02 .10
423 Andrei Kovalev .02 .10
424 Alexander Horn .02 .10
425 Petr Kopta .02 .10
426 Robert Brezina .02 .10
427 Wayne Hynes .08 .25
428 Frantisek Frosch .02 .10
429 Carsten Solbach .02 .10
430 George Fritz .02 .10
431 Mike Bader .02 .10
432 Thomas Deiter .02 .10
433 Daniel Nowak .08 .25
434 Peter Heinold .02 .10
435 Matthias Hoppe .08 .25
436 Grant Martin .08 .25
437 Roger Bruns .08 .25
438 Andreas Renz .02 .10
439 Karsten Schulz .02 .10
440 Alfie Turcotte .08 .25

1994-95 German First League

COMPLETE SET (665) 30.00 80.00
33 Jorn Seuthe .08 .25
34 Pietro Vacca .08 .25
35 Gunther Eisenhut .08 .25
36 Thomas Kulzer .08 .25
37 Christian Zessak .08 .25
38 Peter Sterz .08 .25
39 Michael Maass .08 .25
40 Thomas Brandl .08 .25
41 Thomas Daffner .08 .25
42 Volker Kollmeder .08 .25
43 Thomas Haiti .08 .25
44 Hans Eberhard .08 .25
45 Enrico Kock .08 .25
46 Peter Hampl .08 .25
47 German Wolgin .08 .25
48 Andrej Balandin .08 .25
49 Rainer Wohlmann .08 .25
50 Teamcard Checklist .08 .25
51 Michael Eibl .08 .25
52 Sven Schubert .08 .25
53 Franz Steer .08 .25
54 Ottmar Schluttenhofer .08 .25
55 Wolfgang Oswald .08 .25
56 John Samanski .08 .25
57 Marty Irvine .08 .25
58 Herbert Schadler .08 .25
59 Jeff Vaive .08 .25
60 Markus Neumuller .08 .25
61 Norbert Arians .08 .25
62 Alfred Weiss .08 .25
63 Gert Heubach .08 .25
64 Hans-Georg Eder .08 .25
65 Hansi Bader .08 .25
66 Franz Futtner .08 .25
67 Klaus Pillmaier .08 .25
68 Donar Dotzauer .08 .25
69 Bertil Filgis .08 .25
70 Roman Zaborowski .08 .25
71 Thomas Dahlem .08 .25
72 Markus Faistenhammer .08 .25
73 Teamcard Checklist .08 .25
74 Thomas Dolak .08 .25
75 Oliver Kratt .08 .25
76 Klaus Muller .08 .25
77 Ralf Lux .08 .25
78 Igor Dorochin .08 .25
79 Ravil Khaidarov .08 .25
80 Peter Hejma .08 .25
81 Thomas Geldreich .08 .25
82 Christian Helber .08 .25
83 Marc Schonfeld .08 .25
84 Christian Wolfgramm .08 .25
85 Leos Zajic .08 .25
86 Rick Laycock .08 .25
87 Stefan Lahn .08 .25
88 Thomas Steinberg .08 .25
89 Jan Repka .08 .25
90 Joseph Peroutka .08 .25
91 Andreas Mockl .08 .25
92 Peter Salmik .08 .25
93 Jorg Lettgen .08 .25
94 Frank Furderer .08 .25
95 Christian Ott .08 .25
96 Teamcard Checklist .08 .25
97 Rodion Pauels .08 .25
98 Aaron Strasser .08 .25
99 Ernst Messthaler .08 .25
100 Juri Starkhov .08 .25
101 Nikolai Varianov .08 .25
102 Tomas Krejcir .08 .25
103 Stefan Zellhuber .08 .25
104 Markus Gmeiner .08 .25
105 Richard Schnetz .08 .25
106 Wolfgang Koziol .08 .25
107 Christian Hauserer .08 .25
108 Gerhard Dittrich .08 .25
109 Christopher Zweng .08 .25
110 Peter Hartung .08 .25
111 Robert Scharpf .08 .25
112 Florian Schneider .08 .25
113 Tauno Zobel .08 .25
114 Matthias Sanger .08 .25
115 Peter Asanger .08 .25
116 Christian Ganseneder .08 .25
117 Hans-Jorg Stetter .08 .25
118 Thomas Frohlich .08 .25
119 Karl Streit .08 .25
120 Stefan Bardzinski .08 .25
121 Teamcard Checklist .08 .25
122 Josef Capla .08 .25
123 Jorg Zinnecker .08 .25
124 Peter Harrer .08 .25
125 Heinrich Korph .08 .25
126 Martin Kirsch .08 .25
127 Michael Freissmann .08 .25
128 Peter Rappold .08 .25
129 Daniel Piechaczek .08 .25
130 Bernd Gessinger .08 .25
131 Michael Hogl .08 .25
132 Hubert Jellen .08 .25
133 Hans Hansch .08 .25
134 Steven Schafer .08 .25
135 Harald Wust .08 .25
136 Jean-Claude Brehm .08 .25
137 Olaf Bjorner .08 .25
138 Dusan Canik .08 .25
139 Martin Gessinger .08 .25
140 Martin Tschichoflos .08 .25
141 Ullrich Liebsch .08 .25
142 Svyatoslav Khalizov .08 .25
143 Michael Pescheck .08 .25
144 Roland Seckler .08 .25
145 Teamcard Checklist .08 .25
146 Gerd Wittmann .08 .25
147 Vladimir Macholda .08 .25
148 Sascha Bernhardt .08 .25
149 Michael Thurner .08 .25
150 Norbert Haslach .08 .25
151 Vitus ner Mitterfell .08 .25
152 Thorsten Haaf .08 .25
153 Michael Stejskal .08 .25
154 Klaus Jansen .08 .25
155 Oliver Hackert .08 .25
156 Ladislav Svozil .08 .25
157 Karsten Neumann .08 .25
158 Alexander Ulmer .08 .25
159 Joseph West .08 .25
160 Oliver Weissenberger .08 .25
161 Manfred Schuster .08 .25
162 Oliver Vost .08 .25
163 Peter Stankovic .08 .25
164 Uwe Geisert .08 .25
165 Peter Holdschick .08 .25
166 Ralf Hartfuss .08 .25
167 Bernhard Kopf .08 .25
168 Teamcard Checklist .08 .25
169 Kim Collins .08 .25
170 Josef Wieser .08 .25
171 Frank Fischer .08 .25
172 Peter Geier .08 .25
173 Glenn Goodall .40 1.00
174 Patrick Fertich .08 .25
175 Mathias Wieser .08 .25
176 Maximilian Schindler .08 .25
177 Bastian Kammerloher .08 .25
178 James Quinlan .08 .25
179 Dirk Heick .08 .25
180 Walter Deisenberger .08 .25
181 Christoph Sauter .08 .25
182 Christian Walleitner .08 .25
183 Martin Sauter .08 .25
184 Oliver Mayer .08 .25
185 Roland Floss .08 .25
186 Maximilian Ahammer .08 .25
187 Robert Schumacher .08 .25
188 Ludvik Kopecky .08 .25
189 Florian Eder .10 .25
190 Teamcard Checklist .08 .25
191 Ewalds Grabowskis .08 .25
192 Gerhard Petrussek .08 .25
193 Robert Bockler .08 .25
194 Markus Epple .08 .25
195 Mivhael Weisenbach .08 .25
196 Michael Billmaier .08 .25
197 Joachim Ried .08 .25
198 Holger Micheller .08 .25
199 Igor Pavlov .08 .25
200 Rudiger Weis .08 .25
201 Alexander Zittlau .08 .25
202 Michael Schaeufl .08 .25
203 Oleg Znarok .08 .25
204 Armin Fohry .08 .25
205 Franz-Xaver Ibelherr .08 .25
206 Karl Sajdl .08 .25
207 Daniel Schury .08 .25
208 Manfred Korb .08 .25
209 Christian Baier .08 .25
210 Christian Reuter .08 .25
211 Paul Haringer .08 .25
212 Erwin Haiusa .08 .25
213 Roland Hanemann .08 .25
214 Joachim Jais .08 .25
215 Teamcard Checklist .08 .25
216 Eduard Giblak .08 .25
217 Robert Bohm .08 .25
218 Paul Greiter .08 .25
219 Max Ostermeier .08 .25
220 Florian Schmid .08 .25
221 Alexander Meyer .08 .25
222 Michael Lehmann .08 .25
223 Andi Ostermeier .08 .25
224 Manfred Braun .08 .25
225 Franz Daxner .08 .25
226 Michael Hock .08 .25
227 Oliver Kleininger .08 .25
228 Chris Clarke .08 .25
229 Andreas Paukner .08 .25
230 Florian Jager .08 .25
231 Patrick Gerber .08 .25
232 Karl Huttl .08 .25
233 Brad Belland .08 .25
234 Christian Lex .08 .25
235 Anton Hager .08 .25
236 Uli Stadler .08 .25
237 Teamcard Checklist .08 .25
238 Florian Strida .08 .25
239 Peter Freissl .08 .25
240 Peter Engel .08 .25
241 Georg Weckerle .08 .25
242 Reiner Bauerle .08 .25
243 Johann Fischer .08 .25
244 Christian Kratzmeier .08 .25
245 Martin Strida .08 .25
246 Wolfgang Obermeier .08 .25
247 Franz Bruckl .08 .25
248 Robert Schmidt .08 .25
249 Jiri Jiroutek .08 .25
250 Bjorn Lehner .08 .25
251 Florian Rohde .08 .25
252 Paul Ruzicka .08 .25
253 Andreas Kraus .08 .25
254 Oliver Ciganovic .08 .25
255 Christian Steidl .08 .25
256 Klaus Strobl .08 .25
257 Robert Hauck .08 .25
258 Thomas Reitmeir .08 .25
259 Joachim Hagelsperger .08 .25
260 Florian Steidl .08 .25
261 Teamcard Checklist .08 .25
262 Alexej Sulak .08 .25
263 Markus Mayer .08 .25
264 Thomas Brenzig .08 .25
265 Sven Erhart .08 .25
266 Holger Lieb .08 .25
267 Josef Maier .08 .25
268 Paul Huber .08 .25
269 Rainer Hain .08 .25
270 Peter Kothmayr .08 .25
271 Denis Hanko .08 .25
272 Manfred Muhlegger .08 .25
273 James Johannsen .08 .25
274 Michael Kteitl .08 .25
275 Reiner Sangl .08 .25
276 Rainer Hirschvogel .08 .25
277 Markus Weiss .08 .25
278 Herbert Gmeinder .08 .25
279 Gunther Hartmann .08 .25
280 Jorg Peters .08 .25
281 Sergej Boldavesko .08 .25
282 Peter Dorn .08 .25
283 Markus Kothmayr .08 .25
284 Teamcard Checklist .08 .25
285 Georg Kink .08 .25
286 Gerhard Stranka .08 .25
287 Michael Pump .08 .25
288 Tom Gobel .08 .25
289 Vladimir Fedossov .08 .25
290 Andreas Oswald .08 .25
291 Andreas Ludwig .08 .25
292 Martin Leuthner .08 .25
293 Jurgen Reindl .08 .25
294 Karl Ostler .08 .25
295 Martin Holzer .08 .25
296 Peter Fischer .08 .25
297 Jens Feller .08 .25
298 Henry Domke .08 .25
299 Markus Kossig .08 .25
300 Andreas Maurer .08 .25
301 Georg Grunauer .08 .25
302 Andreas Wittig .08 .25
303 Andreas Gebauer .08 .25
304 Hubert Buchwieser .08 .25
305 Andreas Raubal .08 .25
306 Christian Winkler .08 .25
307 Brett Stewart .08 .25
308 Christoph Sandner .08 .25
309 Rainer Lutz .08 .25
310 Alfred Burkhard .08 .25
311 Dale Derkatch .20 .50
312 Teamcard Checklist .08 .25
313 Rudolf Sindelar .08 .25
314 Thomas Hobek .08 .25
315 Jason Hall .08 .25
316 Jochen Hordler .08 .25
317 Mark Armstrong .08 .25
318 Peter Netsch .08 .25
319 Armin Hanke .08 .25
320 Jaroslav Peska .08 .25
321 Steve Neumann .08 .25
322 Markus Trendl .08 .25
323 Daniel Gardner .08 .25
324 Marek Kurowski .08 .25
325 Markus Albrecht .08 .25
326 Sascha Groger .08 .25
327 Stefan Leuschner .08 .25
328 Andreas Kimker .08 .25
329 Roland Schneider .08 .25
330 Elko Porzi .08 .25
331 Stefan Wegmann .08 .25
332 Holger Cecco .08 .25
333 Ralf Gaess .08 .25
334 EHC Straubing .08 .25
335 Franz Hejcik .08 .25
337 Achim Sipmeier .08 .25
338 Christian Penzkofer .08 .25
339 Thomas Schambeck .08 .25
340 Douglas Kirton .08 .25
341 Rainer Schuster .08 .25
342 Vaclav Mandous .08 .25
343 Christian Knott .08 .25
344 Edward Zawatsky .08 .25
345 Christian Heitzer .08 .25
346 Rüdiger Metsch .08 .25
347 Christian Setz .08 .25
348 Sascha Werner .08 .25
349 Martin Ebenburger .08 .25
350 Daniel Vogl .08 .25
351 Stephan Meier .08 .25
352 Sven Barnet .08 .25
353 Robert Steinmann .08 .25
354 1. EV Weiden .08 .25
355 Wilbert Duszenko .08 .25
356 Alexander Becker .08 .25
357 Frank Gentges .08 .25
358 Anton Doll .08 .25
359 Stefan Peschek .08 .25
360 Oliver Hecht .08 .25
361 Dirk Salinger .08 .25
362 Yuri Chipitsyn .08 .25
363 Marco Zimmermann .08 .25
364 Christian Martin .08 .25
365 Lubos Thur .08 .25
366 Andreas Frysztacki .08 .25
367 Sergej Agejkin .08 .25
368 Roman Bartosch .08 .25
369 Ales Volek .08 .25
370 Josef PreuÃŸ .08 .25
371 Thomas Pokorny .08 .25
372 Roman Zilka .08 .25
373 Dietmar Habnitt .08 .25
374 Horst BÃ¤rnreuther .08 .25
375 Stefan Breitner .08 .25
376 Teamcard Checklist .08 .25
377 Ricki Alexander .08 .25
378 Ingo Schwarz .08 .25
379 Serge Lajoie .08 .25
380 Thomas Barczikowski .08 .25
381 Rik Schaefer .08 .25
382 Markus Reiter .08 .25
383 Todd Goodwin .08 .25
384 Thorsten Wolf .08 .25
385 Volker Lindenzweig .08 .25
386 Sven Paschek .08 .25
387 Markus Jehner .08 .25
388 Jurgen Engels .08 .25
389 Martin Prada .08 .25
390 Norbert Scholz .08 .25
391 Gregory Pruden .08 .25
392 Oliver Vieten .08 .25
393 Robert Vozar .08 .25
394 Martin Williams .08 .25
395 Jan Schier .08 .25
396 Michael Eckert .08 .25
397 Thomas Krebs .08 .25
398 Teamcard Checklist .08 .25
399 Gerald Mull .08 .25
400 Juris Kruminsch .08 .25
401 Frank Strauss .08 .25
402 Peter Kaluza .08 .25
403 Dirk Sobottka .08 .25
404 Alwin Wever .08 .25
405 Jerzey Christ .08 .25
406 Andreas Kemper .08 .25
407 Andre Wilmshofer .08 .25
408 Olaf Busch .08 .25
409 Rico Petrick .08 .25
410 Kurt Wickenheiser .20 .50
411 Marc Muller .20 .50
412 Steffen Klau .08 .25
413 Zsolt Heffler .08 .25
414 Martin Bergeron .08 .25
415 Willi Tesch .08 .25
416 Frank Fischoder .08 .25
417 Darius Wonschweski .08 .25
418 Teamcard Checklist .08 .25
419 Eduard Nocak .08 .25
420 Stephan Schaller .08 .25
421 Michael Schmitz .08 .25
422 Jochen Hecker .08 .25
423 Axel Gessner .08 .25
424 Heinz-Gerd Albers .08 .25
425 Markus Bak .08 .25
426 Bernd Deske .08 .25
427 Ron Noak .08 .25
428 Darren Colbourne .08 .25
429 Frank Pribil .08 .25
430 Holger Rimroth .08 .25
431 Lars Tannhof .08 .25
432 Ulrik Kuhnekath .08 .25
433 Jorg Deske .08 .25
434 Guy Phillips .08 .25
435 Jorg Bohme .08 .25
436 Udo Solan .08 .25
437 Matthias Starke .08 .25
438 Oliver Walde .08 .25
439 Teamcard Checklist .08 .25
440 Dieter Bruggemann .08 .25
441 Julian Binavince .08 .25
442 Kai Kemper .08 .25
443 Raimund Peschke .08 .25
444 Frank Besser .08 .25
445 Frank Blanke .08 .25
446 John Neeld .08 .25
447 Alexander Knoff .08 .25
448 Brad Scott .08 .25
449 Bodo Mischer .08 .25
450 Jiri Kovarik .08 .25
451 Markus Kolloch .08 .25
452 Carsten Plate .08 .25
453 Thomas Hesse .08 .25
454 Jorg Loschek .08 .25
455 Dirk Voss .08 .25
456 Detlev Eltermann .08 .25
457 Volker Loscheck .08 .25
458 Richard Drewniak .08 .25
459 Teamcard Checklist .08 .25
460 Erwin Materna .08 .25
461 Ingmar Kracht .08 .25
462 Michael Meixner .08 .25
463 Dirk Rossbach .08 .25
464 Karsten Scherping .08 .25
465 Mark Mahon .08 .25
466 Wolfgang Hofbauer .08 .25
467 Uwe Geiselmann .08 .25
468 Sean Krakivsky .08 .25
469 Douglas Murray .08 .25
470 Marek Gajewski .08 .25
471 Mario Feigl .08 .25
472 Frank Liebert .08 .25
473 Miroslav Mago .08 .25
474 Mirsolav Sakmirda .08 .25
475 Dirk Nieleck .08 .25
476 Jan Furd .08 .25
477 Ralf Kubiak .08 .25
478 Marek Adamec .08 .25
479 Douglas Murray .08 .25
480 Teamcard Checklist .08 .25
481 Sergej Svetlov .08 .25
482 Christian Berlin .08 .25
483 Marek Adamek .08 .25
484 Ralf Cassebaum .08 .25
485 Ingo Rdurch .08 .25
486 Sergej Hatkevitsch .08 .25
487 Thomas Otto .08 .25
488 Riccardo Siegert .08 .25
489 Willy Reinhard .08 .25
490 Jorn Sigmansky .08 .25
491 Guido Drongowski .08 .25
492 Carsten Boss .08 .25
493 Jacek Piechutta .08 .25
494 Thorsten Peters .08 .25
495 Lutz Bongers .08 .25
496 Armin Schnitzler .08 .25
497 Teamcard Checklist .08 .25
498 Walter Koberle .08 .25
499 Carsten Lange .08 .25
500 Jurgen Schultz .08 .25
501 Jan Raspel .08 .25
502 Christoph Gelzinus .08 .25
503 Markus Kamman .08 .25
504 Markus Buchhart .08 .25
505 Holger Schmitz .08 .25
506 Ladislav Kolda .08 .25
507 Arndt Kons .08 .25
508 Boris Morsch .08 .25
509 Darius Wonschewski .08 .25
510 Benedikt Kons .08 .25
511 James Dressler .08 .25
512 Dirk Scholz .08 .25
513 Marco Scharf .08 .25
514 Mike van Hauten .08 .25
515 Max Bander .08 .25
516 Gilbert Schroder .08 .25
517 Teamcard Checklist .08 .25
518 Alexander Wolkow .08 .25
519 Sven Schmitz .08 .25
520 Andrej Ovtschinnikov .08 .25
521 Boguslav Kuta .08 .25
522 Sergej Zaitsev .08 .25
523 Rene Naroska .08 .25
524 Markus Menschig .08 .25
525 Milos Piperski .08 .25
526 Andreas Halfmann .08 .25
527 Marcus Golabek .08 .25
528 Peter Kraus .08 .25
529 Peter Juchem .08 .25
530 Marius Cissewski .08 .25
531 Falk Elzner .08 .25
532 Jens Herget .08 .25
533 Fabian Dahlem .08 .25
534 Jurgen Trattner .08 .25
535 Daniel Walther .08 .25
536 Peter Burfant .08 .25
537 Eduard Lorer .08 .25
538 Andreas Keiler .08 .25
539 Haie Schalker GEV .08 .25
540 Charly Stenner CO .08 .25
541 Thomas Blasche .08 .25
542 Dietmar Schramm .08 .25
543 Achim Blaar .08 .25
544 Graischa Pietsch .08 .25
545 Robert Simon .08 .25
546 Bruce Bonner .08 .25

547 Ladislav Hospodar	.08	.25
548 Martin Jilek	.08	.25
549 Michael Scanu	.08	.25
550 Phil Berger	.08	.25
551 Christoph Kleckers	.08	.25
552 Patrick Schmitz	.08	.25
553 Gregor Wilk	.08	.25
554 Jens Casten	.08	.25
555 Andre Jucknischke	.08	.25
556 Vladimir Kames	.08	.25
557 Petr Fiala	.08	.25
558 Marco Blazyczek	.08	.25
559 Trajan Cazacu	.08	.25
560 Robert Schutz	.08	.25
561 Jaromir Jágr	20.00	50.00
562 ETC Timmendorf	.08	.25
563 Jeff Pyle	.08	.25
564 Gerd Vogel	.08	.25
565 Andrzej Bielenink	.08	.25
566 Marvin Glaser	.08	.25
567 Harald Bolke	.08	.25
568 Christian Spaan	.08	.25
569 Henry Thom	.08	.25
570 Matthias Schnabel	.08	.25
571 Mike Bukowski	.08	.25
572 Jeff Tomlinson	.20	.50
573 Steffen Thau	.08	.25
574 Mark MacKay	.20	.50
575 Olaf Brull	.08	.25
576 Moe Lemay	.40	1.00
577 Michael Mai	.08	.25
578 Peter Hiller	.08	.25
579 Christoph Hadraschek	.08	.25
580 Mike Wehrmann	.08	.25
581 Lars Wunsche	.08	.25
582 Maj Boguslaw	.08	.25
583 Sven Rampf	.08	.25
584 Teamcard Checklist	.08	.25
585 Helmut Bauer	.08	.25
586 Guido Titzhoff	.08	.25
587 Lubomir Lang	.08	.25
588 Guy Rouleau	.08	.25
589 Andreas Naumann	.20	.50
590 Marc Otten	.08	.25
591 Kenneth Filgis	.08	.25
592 Dimitri Matuschow	.08	.25
593 Markus Pollock	.08	.25
594 Mario Plack	.08	.25
595 Herbert Plattner	.08	.25
596 Roman Sindelar	.20	.50
597 Herbert Ott	.08	.25
598 Reik Blasche	.08	.25
599 Vladimir Lukscheider	.08	.25
600 Christof Grunthal	.08	.25
601 Hermann Retzer	.08	.25
602 Adam Gedyk	.08	.25
603 Ralf Lamberty	.08	.25
604 Teamcard Checklist	.08	.25
605 Kevin Gaudet	.08	.25
606 Dale Reinig	.08	.25
607 Jorg Meyer	.08	.25
608 Bruce Keller	.08	.25
609 Laszlo Csata	.08	.25
610 Douglas Murray	.08	.25
611 Garry Schwindt	.08	.25
612 Fred Carroll	.08	.25
613 Len Soccio	.20	.50
614 Michail Lemmer	.08	.25
615 Dieter Reiss	.08	.25
616 Jirko Seib	.08	.25
617 Matthias Kuhnel	.08	.25
618 Heinrich Synowietz	.08	.25
619 Paul Synowietz	.08	.25
620 Justyn Denisiuk	.08	.25
621 Slawomir Osinski	.08	.25
622 Jari Pasanen	.08	.25
623 Marcus Beeck	.08	.25
624 Vladimir Konstantinov	4.00	10.00
625 Teamcard Checklist	.08	.25
626 Josef Vimmer	.08	.25
627 Torsten Kluin	.08	.25
628 Dieter Frenzel	.08	.25
629 Harald Hebig	.08	.25
630 Jorg Volkle	.08	.25
631 Alexander Gorsdorf	.08	.25
632 Roman Slezak	.08	.25
633 Jan Baron	.08	.25
634 Sergej Jaschin	.08	.25
635 Robert Eylert	.08	.25
636 Anatoli Antipov	.08	.25
637 Heiko Tabor	.08	.25
638 Jan-Hans Pokorny	.08	.25
639 Roman Blazek	.08	.25
640 Alexander Purschel	.08	.25
641 Bernd Timmer	.08	.25
642 Tomasz Mieszkowski	.08	.25
643 Vaclav Drobny	.08	.25
644 Teamcard Checklist	.08	.25
645 Nikolai Besprosvannych	.08	.25
646 Dimitri Ritthaler	.08	.25
647 Dimitri Konjuchov	.08	.25
648 Erwin Forster	.08	.25
649 Olaf-Bjorn Kolle	.08	.25
650 Gary Cummins	.08	.25
651 Garth Bannatyne	.08	.25
652 Jamie Hartnett	.08	.25
653 Cory Holden	.08	.25
654 Andreas Henkel	.08	.25
655 Janusz Wielgus	.08	.25
656 Douglas Morton	.08	.25
657 Kebin McGibney	.08	.25
658 Daniel Poudrier	.20	.50
659 Peter Just	.08	.25
660 Lumir Mikesz	.08	.25
661 Kenneth Filbey	.08	.25
662 Richard Jelsovsky	.08	.25
663 Petr Klima	.40	1.00
664 Jiri Jiroutek	.08	.25
665 Mark MacKay	.20	.50

1995-96 German DEL

COMPLETE SET (450)	50.00	125.00
1 Gary Prior	.05	.15
2 R. Meister	.02	.10
3 D. Schrapp	.02	.10
4 S. Campbell	.02	.10
5 F. Meyer	.02	.10
6 R. Mendel	.02	.10
7 K. Collins	.05	.15
8 S. Mayer	.02	.10
9 T. Fendt	.02	.10
10 Andrei Skopintsev	.05	.15
11 B. Wilkie	.02	.10
12 D. Moeser	.02	.10
13 Martin Nagler	.02	.10
14 Sven Zywitza	.02	.10
15 Marc Habscheid	.08	.25
16 D. Held	.02	.10
17 H.Romer	.02	.10
18 Rick Laycock	.02	.10
19 Robert Francz	.02	.10
20 Tim Ferguson	.02	.10
21 R. Heidt	.05	.15
22 Eric Dylla	.02	.10
23 H. Birk	.02	.10
24 R. Schneider	.02	.10
25 B. Flynn	.02	.10
26 A. Dietzsch	.02	.10
27 U. Dohler	.02	.10
28 J. Stumpf	.02	.10
29 T. Deutscher	.02	.10
30 F. Kannewurf	.02	.10
31 T. Graul	.02	.10
32 D. Perschau	.02	.10
33 P. Solf	.02	.10
34 D. Poudrier	.02	.10
35 Bernhard Kaminski	.02	.10
36 Christoph Hadraschek	.02	.10
37 S. Felski	.02	.10
38 M. Swibenko	.02	.10
39 H. Mix	.02	.10
40 M. Maroste	.02	.10
41 T. Tumbach	.02	.10
42 J. Schertz	.02	.10
43 M. Losch	.02	.10
44 Andreas Naumann	.05	.15
45 Marc Garthe	.02	.10
46 I. Dorochin	.02	.10
47 Thomas Mitew	.02	.10
48 Claes Lundmark	.02	.10
49 C. Panek	.02	.10
50 K. Merk	.20	.50
51 M. Gronau	.02	.10
52 S. Steinecker	.02	.10
53 J. Lehner	.02	.10
54 T. O'Regan	.05	.15
55 F. Stillmann	.02	.10
56 M. Rentzsch	.02	.10
57 S. Sinner	.02	.10
58 A. Schubert	.05	.15
59 T. Tanti	.08	.25
60 G. Malo	.02	.10
61 M. Komma	.02	.10
62 T. Schinko	.02	.10
63 G. Holzmann	.02	.10
64 M. Kosturik	.02	.10
65 C. Brittig	.02	.10
66 J. Rumrich	.02	.10
67 J. Chabot	.20	.50
68 A. Dimbat	.02	.10
69 U. Liebsch	.02	.10
70 M. Teevens	.05	.15
71 F. Brannstom	.02	.10
72 Dennis Meyer	.02	.10
73 Lars Hoffmann	.02	.10
74 H. Nilsson	.02	.10
75 M. Karlsson	.02	.10
76 Helmut De Raaf	.08	.25
77 K. Fischer	.30	.75
78 C. Gossmann	.02	.10
79 T. Kienas	.08	.25
80 C. Kreutzer	.02	.10
81 B. Bergen	.02	.10
82 A. Niederberger	.05	.15
83 R. Amann	.02	.10
84 U. Hiemer	.05	.15
85 S. Sorokin	.05	.15
86 R. Sterflinger	.02	.10
87 L. Funk	.02	.10
88 C. Valentine	.20	.50
89 G. Sherven	.05	.15
90 B. Lingemann	.02	.10
91 B. Doucet	.08	.25
92 B. Kuhnhauser	.02	.10
93 B. Eakin	.05	.15
94 D. Hegen	.08	.25
95 A. Brockmann	.02	.10
96 B. Truntschka	.08	.25
97 W. Kummer	.02	.10
98 M. Makela	.08	.25
99 N. Mondt	.02	.10
100 P. Vorobjew	.05	.15
101 P. Obresa	.02	.10
102 T. Mayer	.02	.10
103 M. Seliger	.40	1.00
104 F. Storf	.02	.10
105 L. Strompf	.02	.10
106 G. Thomson	.02	.10
107 S. Schendelev	.02	.10
108 Martin Duris	.02	.10
109 Rudi Gorgenlander	.02	.10
110 Andreas Raubal	.02	.10
111 S. Ziesche	.05	.15
112 P. Kopta	.02	.10
113 T. Popiesch	.02	.10
114 F. Sills	.02	.10
115 J. Lala	.05	.15
116 R. Reichel	.40	1.00
117 M. Kempf	.02	.10
118 I. Schultz	.02	.10
119 M. Schultz	.02	.10
120 B. Hannon	.02	.10
121 J. Schaal	.02	.10
122 P. Vozar	.02	.10
123 R. Kennedy	.02	.10
124 F. Bogelsack	.05	.15
125 M. Herbst	.02	.10
126 J. Schlickenrieder	.02	.10
127 T. Hanusch	.02	.10
128 T. Jungwirth	.02	.10
129 D. Reierson	.02	.10
130 C. Curth	.02	.10
131 A. Maidl	.02	.10
132 M. Wittbrock	.02	.10
133 B. Schlegel	.08	.25
134 T. Werner	.02	.10
135 D. Rohrbach	.02	.10
136 B. Hardy	.02	.10
137 H. Kuhnke	.02	.10
138 F. Funk	.02	.10
139 R. Reuter	.02	.10
140 M. Vanik	.02	.10
141 G. Preuss	.02	.10
142 K. LaVallee	.05	.15
143 M. Bleicher	.02	.10
144 A. Krinner	.02	.10
145 H. Waibel	.02	.10
146 H. Zach	.02	.10
147 J. Kontny	.02	.10
148 G. Hegen	.02	.10
149 M. Mokros	.02	.10
150 V. Sebek	.02	.10
151 A. Engel	.02	.10
152 A. Wedl	.02	.10
153 J. Mucha	.02	.10
154 M. McIntosh	.02	.10
155 G. Guttler	.02	.10
156 G. Johnston	.05	.15
157 J. Kaspercyk	.02	.10
158 D. Morrison	.02	.10
159 M. Millar	.05	.15
160 I. Pacula	.02	.10
161 Vitalij Grossmann	.02	.10
162 Igor Varitsky	.02	.10
163 P. Kwasigroch	.02	.10
164 B. Heisig	.02	.10
165 G. Evtushevski	.05	.15
166 F. Ozellis	.02	.10
167 T. Boos	.02	.10
168 J. Tolvanen	.02	.10
169 D. Medicus	.02	.10
170 M. Olbrich	.02	.10
171 M. Pethke	.02	.10
172 D. Kadlec	.05	.15
173 C. Seeberger	.02	.10
174 G. Kunce	.02	.10
175 D. Kunce	.02	.10
176 T. Gschwill	.02	.10
177 Marco Eltner	.02	.10
178 J. Simon	.02	.10
179 Alexander Herbst	.02	.10
180 E. Boiger	.02	.10
181 O. Hascak	.08	.25
182 T. Schnobrich	.02	.10
183 A. Vogel	.02	.10
184 T. Martinec	.02	.10
185 H. Mayer	.05	.15
186 R. Timoschuk	.02	.10
187 J. Hoffmann	.02	.10
188 A. Volland	.02	.10
189 R. Hammer	.02	.10
190 M. Hess	.02	.10
191 D. Derkatch	.20	.50
192 Sebastian Schwele	.02	.10
193 R.J. Murdoch	.08	.25
194 B. Haake	.02	.10
195 J. Heiss	.30	.75
196 O. Grundmann	.02	.10
197 A. Genze	.02	.10
198 A. von Trzcinski	.02	.10
199 J. Mayr	.05	.15
200 M. Ludemann	.08	.25
201 A. Pokorny	.02	.10
202 J. Meyer	.02	.10
203 K. Mende	.02	.10
204 H. Hohenberger	.20	.50
205 T. Brandl	.02	.10
206 S. Mann	.02	.10
207 L. Borsato	.08	.25
208 L. Stefan	.08	.25
209 P. Draisaitl	.08	.25
210 A. Lupzig	.08	.25
211 R. Reisinger	.02	.10
212 R. Zerwesz	.02	.10
213 M. Rumrich	.02	.10
214 M. Ondrejka	.02	.10
215 T. Abstreiter	.02	.10
216 F. Demmel	.02	.10
217 Sergei Berezin	.40	1.00
218 M. Berek	.02	.10
219 K. Lang	.02	.10
220 R. Bieike	.02	.10
221 M. Krawinkel	.02	.10
222 K. Karpuk	.02	.10
223 K. Micheller	.02	.10
224 E. Spry	.02	.10
225 A. Ott	.02	.10
226 P. Limatainen	.02	.10
227 A. Grein	.02	.10
228 K. Petrash	.02	.10
229 J. Hanlon	.02	.10
230 R. Pyka	.08	.25
231 T. Imdahl	.02	.10
232 C. Lindberg	.08	.25
233 Jay Luknowsky	.02	.10
234 P. Ihnacak	.08	.25
235 M. Stebnicki	.02	.10
236 J. Walker	.02	.10
237 A. Brux	.02	.10
238 Robert Busch	.02	.10
239 M. Bassen	.02	.10
240 M. Gebel	.02	.10
241 B. Johnston	.02	.10
242 P. Briza	.30	.75
243 C. Kunast	.02	.10
244 M. Bresagk	.02	.10
245 E. Uvira	.02	.10
246 M. Heidt	.02	.10
247 P. Gulda	.02	.10
248 U. KieBling	.08	.25
249 D. Bloem	.02	.10
250 T. Vogl	.02	.10
251 J. Plachta	.02	.10
252 G. Franz	.02	.10
253 S. Retzer	.02	.10
254 H. Marcoux	.02	.10
255 A. Loth	.02	.10
256 M. Bullard	.08	.25
257 J. Charbonneau	.08	.25
258 W. Schreiber	.08	.25
259 J. Handrick	.02	.10
260 H. Steiger	.02	.10
261 Marco Sturm	6.00	15.00
262 L. Nethery	.05	.15
263 M. Kuhl	.02	.10
264 J. Appel	.02	.10
265 M. Flemming	.02	.10
266 H. Kreis	.02	.10
267 P. Stanton	.08	.25
268 C. Lukes	.02	.10
269 S. Michel	.02	.10
270 S. Richer	.05	.15
271 J. Hanft	.02	.10
272 E. Goldmann	.02	.10
273 M. Gehrig	.02	.10
274 P. Gross	.02	.10
275 D. Korber	.02	.10
276 R. Cimetta	.08	.25
277 Jochen Hecht	1.25	3.00
278 T. Feser	.02	.10
279 Alexander Serikow	.40	1.00
280 P. Pysz	.05	.15
281 D. Adamus	.02	.10
282 David Musial	.02	.10
283 M. Hreus	.02	.10
284 C. Straube	.02	.10
285 S. Valenti	.02	.10
286 S. Thivierge	.02	.10
287 J. Eysselt	.02	.10
288 Richard Neubauer	.02	.10
289 Roman Turek	.40	1.00
290 S. Lahn	.02	.10
291 C. Gerum	.02	.10
292 H. Smazal	.02	.10
293 M. Maly	.02	.10
294 T. Sterflinger	.02	.10
295 Michael Weinfurter	.02	.10
296 S. Bauer	.02	.10
297 L. Bruggemann	.02	.10
298 M. Kehle	.02	.10
299 P. Geddes	.02	.10
300 I. Young	.02	.10
301 S. Steinbock	.02	.10
302 J. Lechl	.02	.10
303 Markus Goerlitz	.02	.10
304 J. Dolozal	.08	.25
305 H. Holscher	.02	.10
306 S. Wassermann	.02	.10
307 O. Sykora	.02	.10
308 B. Lochead	.05	.15
309 P. Lange	.02	.10
310 I. Wood	.02	.10
311 H. Thorn	.02	.10
312 D. Irwin	.02	.10
313 C. Schmitz	.02	.10
314 A. Wunsch	.02	.10
315 C. Holden	.02	.10
316 Jamie Bartman	.02	.10
317 P. Lutter	.02	.10
318 P. Mann	.02	.10
319 G. Muller	.02	.10
320 C. Kohmann	.02	.10
321 P. Beraldo	.05	.15
322 T. Groger	.02	.10
323 A. Fuchs	.02	.10
324 K. Birk	.02	.10
325 Dave Rich	.02	.10
326 B. Fuchs	.02	.10
327 T. Muhlbauer	.02	.10
328 A. Kammerer	.02	.10
329 J. Lazaro	.20	.50
330 O. Scholz	.02	.10
331 B. Reynolds	.02	.10
332 J. Sevcik	.08	.25
333 P.M. Arnholt	.02	.10
334 Gerhard Stranka	.02	.10
335 V. Riendeau	.20	.50
336 M. Schmidt	.02	.10
337 T. Gobel	.02	.10
338 V. Fedosov	.02	.10
339 R. Jadamzik	.02	.10
340 F. Hohendahl	.02	.10
341 Anton Raubal	.02	.10
342 C. Schonmoser	.02	.10
343 Andreas Ludwig	.02	.10
344 Karl Ostler	.02	.10
345 M. Berwanger	.02	.10
346 Martin Holzer	.02	.10
347 Jens Feller	.02	.10
348 Henry Domke	.02	.10
349 Andreas Maurer	.02	.10
350 Andreas Gebauer	.02	.10
351 G. Oswald	.02	.10
352 Hubert Buchwieser	.02	.10
353 Brett Stewart	.02	.10
354 C. Sandner	.02	.10
355 Joachim Hagelsperger	.02	.10
356 R. Hock	.02	.10
357 Mark Jooris	.02	.10
358 E. Hofner	.02	.10
359 G. Clark	.02	.10
360 K. Friesen	.30	.75
361 K. Dalpiaz	.08	.25
362 M. Wieland	.02	.10
363 C. Clarke	.02	.10
364 M. Pottinger	.02	.10
365 R. Kruger	.02	.10
366 R. Fischer	.02	.10
367 C. Gegenfurter	.02	.10
368 H. Schiffl	.02	.10
369 A. Schneider	.02	.10
370 Vitus Mitterfellner	.02	.10
371 R. Bohm	.02	.10
372 D. Krentz	.08	.25
373 Tobias Schraven	.02	.10
374 F. Keller	.40	1.00
375 D. Derraugh	.04	.10
376 M. Reichel	.05	.15
377 Markus Draxler	.02	.10
378 R. Hilger	.05	.15
379 M. Pohl	.02	.10
380 M. Kropf	.02	.10
381 J. Savage	.20	.50
382 J. Eckmaier	.02	.10
383 R.R. Burns	.02	.10
384 G. Leidborg	.02	.10
385 C. Solbach	.02	.10
386 M. Hoppe	.02	.10
387 G. Hynes	.08	.25
388 T. Gaus	.02	.10
389 Z. Travnicek	.02	.10
390 R. Trojan	.02	.10
391 F. Frosch	.02	.10
392 D. Nowak	.02	.10
393 A. Renz	.02	.10
394 A. Young	.02	.10
395 R. Brezina	.02	.10
396 W. Hynes	.02	.10
397 G. Fritz	.02	.10
398 M. Bader	.02	.10
399 G. Martin	.02	.10
400 K. Schulz	.02	.10
401 M. Lay	.02	.10
402 J. Penney	.05	.15
403 R. Cernomaz	.05	.15
404 M. MacKay	.30	.75
405 S. Hasan	.02	.10
406 J. Kochta	.02	.10
407 T. Bresagk	.02	.10
408 P. Franke	.02	.10
409 J. Molling	.02	.10
410 F. Prochazka	.02	.10
411 J. Reznicek	.02	.10
412 T. Schubert	.02	.10
413 R. Martin	.02	.10
414 M. Lichnovsky	.02	.10
415 M. Kliemann	.02	.10
416 Ronny Reddo	.02	.10
417 F. Peschke	.02	.10
418 T. Eisebitt	.02	.10
419 J. Janikowski	.02	.10
420 T. Knobloch	.02	.10
421 F. Herzig	.02	.10
422 T. Wagner	.02	.10
423 J. Tabor	.05	.15
424 Jorg Pohling	.02	.10
425 R. Vit	.02	.10
426 V. Kulabuchov	.02	.10
427 D. Cup Meister 1995	.08	.25
428 Kingston Kuhnhauser Genze	.08	.25
429 Heib Lupzig	.08	.25
430 Brandl Mann	.08	.25
431 Doucet Nowak	.08	.25
432 Meyer Pyka	.08	.25
433 Hegen Kunce	.08	.25
434 Rumrich Ludemann	.08	.25
435 Benda Kosturik	.08	.25
436 Kienass Brockmann Hanft	.05	.15
437 Draisaitl Simon Schneider	.08	.25
438 Niederberger	.08	.25
439 Martin Reichel	.05	.15
440 Klaus Merk	.20	.50
441 Glenn Anderson	1.25	3.00
442 Pavel Bure	12.00	30.00
443 Vincent Damphousse	2.00	5.00
444 Uwe Krupp	.20	.50
445 Robert Reichel	.40	1.00
446 Jeremy Roenick	12.00	30.00
447 Brendan Shanahan	12.00	30.00
448 Jozef Stumpel	.75	2.00
449 Doug Weight	2.00	5.00
450 Scott Young	.75	2.00
NNO Hologram Karte	4.00	10.00

1996-97 German DEL

COMPLETE SET (360)	16.00	40.00
1 Gary Prior CO	.05	.15
2 Bruno Campese	.08	.25
3 Leonardo Conti	.05	.15
4 Scott Campbell	.05	.15
5 Robert Mendel	.05	.15
6 Serge Poudrier	.05	.15
7 Torsten Fendt	.05	.15
8 Shawn Rivers	.05	.15
9 Stefan Mayer	.05	.15
10 Michael Bakos	.05	.15
11 Tommy Jakobsen	.05	.15
12 Duanne Moeser	.05	.15
13 Tero Arkiomaa	.05	.15
14 Sven Zywitza	.05	.15
15 Craig Streu	.05	.15
16 Terry Campbell	.05	.15
17 Timothy Ferguson	.05	.15
18 Yves Heroux	.05	.15
19 Max Boldt	.05	.15
20 Andre Faust	.05	.15
21 Rochus Schneider	.05	.15
22 Ron Kennedy CO	.05	.15
23 Barry Lewis ASST CO	.05	.15
24 Mario Brunetta	.20	.50
25 Udo Dohler	.05	.15
26 Dirk Perschau	.05	.15
27 Darren Durdle	.05	.15
28 Greg Andrusak	.08	.25
29 Leif Carlsson	.05	.15
30 Derek Mayer	.08	.25
31 Rob Leask	.05	.15
32 Chad Biafore	.05	.15
33 Thomas Steen	.05	.15
34 Lorenz Funk	.05	.15
35 Florian Funk	.05	.15
36 Sven Felski	.05	.15
37 Peter John Lee	.08	.25
38 Andrew McKim	.20	.50
39 Andrei Lomakin	.08	.25
40 Pelle Svensson	.05	.15
41 Jan Schertz	.05	.15
42 Kraig Nienhuis	.20	.50
43 Niklas Hede	.05	.15
44 Mario Chitarroni	.08	.25
45 Chris Govedaris	.20	.50
46 Pentti Matikainen CO	.05	.15
47 Jukka Tammi	.08	.25
48 Rupert Meister	.05	.15
49 Florian Storf	.05	.15
50 Greg Thomson	.05	.15
51 Toni Porkka	.05	.15
52 Sergej Schendelev	.05	.15
53 Kai Rautio	.05	.15
54 Rudi Gorgenlander	.05	.15
55 Petr Kopta	.05	.15
56 Tony Virta	.08	.25
57 Ilja Vorobjev	.05	.15
58 Thomas Popiesch	.05	.15
59 Francois Sills	.05	.15
60 JIro Jarvi	.05	.15
61 Jurgen Schaal	.05	.15
62 Pavel Vit	.05	.15
63 Timo Peltomaa	.05	.15
64 Igor Schultz	.05	.15
65 Dave Archibald	.08	.25
66 Joni Lehto	.05	.15
67 Brad Jones	.05	.15
68 Miroslav Berek CO	.05	.15
69 Karel Lang	.05	.15
70 Peter Franke	.05	.15
71 Markus Krawinkel	.05	.15
72 Zdenek Travnicek	.05	.15
73 Martin Gebel	.05	.15
74 Klaus Micheller	.05	.15
75 Earl Spry	.05	.15
76 Frantisek Frosch	.05	.15
77 Petri Liimatainen	.05	.15
78 Andre Grein	.05	.15
79 Ken Petrash	.05	.15
80 James Hanlon	.05	.15
81 Andrej Kovalev	.05	.15
82 Reemt Pyka	.05	.15
83 Chris Lindberg	.08	.25
84 Jay Luknowsky	.05	.15
85 Peter Ihnacak	.08	.25
86 Marek Stebnicki	.05	.15
87 Johnny Walker	.05	.15
88 Danton Cole	.08	.25
89 Michael Hreus	.05	.15
90 Damian Adamus	.05	.15
91 Bill Lochead CO	.08	.25
92 Joakim Persson	.08	.25
93 Ian Wood	.05	.15
94 Pierre Jonsson	.05	.15
95 Juha Lampinen	.05	.15
96 Christian Schmitz	.05	.15
97 Cory Holden	.05	.15
98 Peter Lutter	.05	.15
99 Dieter Bloem	.05	.15
100 Maurizio Catenacci	.05	.15
101 Andrej Fuchs	.05	.15
102 Mark Montanari	.05	.15
103 Boris Fuchs	.05	.15
104 Andreas Salomonsson	.05	.15
105 Robert Reynolds	.05	.15
106 Axel Kammerer	.05	.15
107 Jeffrey Lazaro	.08	.25
108 Olaf Scholz	.05	.15
109 Tony Cimellaro	.05	.15
110 Kenneth Hodge	.08	.25
111 Gregory Burke	.05	.15
112 Tom Coolen CO	.05	.15
113 Marc Pethke	.05	.15
114 Christian Kunast	.05	.15
115 Drahomir Kadlec	.08	.25
116 Florian Kuhn	.08	.25
117 Erich Goldmann	.08	.25
118 Jurgen Simon	.05	.15
119 Jeff Winstanley	.05	.15
120 Stefano Figliuzzi	.05	.15
121 Maurice Mansi	.05	.15
122 Agostino Casale	.05	.15
123 Hans-Jorg Mayer	.05	.15
124 Dino Felicetti	.05	.15
125 Roland Timoschuk	.05	.15
126 Jim Hoffmann	.05	.15
127 John Porco	.05	.15
128 Rolf Hammer	.05	.15
129 Manuel Hess	.05	.15
130 Andy Rymsha	.08	.25
131 Wolfgang Kummer	.05	.15
132 Trevor Burgess	.05	.15
133 Daniel Kunce	.05	.15
134 Timo Sutinen	.05	.15
135 Petr Briza	.30	.75
136 Markus Nachtmann	.05	.15
137 Markus Wieland	.05	.15
138 Mike Heidt	.05	.15
139 Peter Gulda	.05	.15
140 Jacek Plachta	.05	.15
141 Georg Franz	.05	.15
142 Stephan Retzer	.05	.15
143 Henry Marcoux	.05	.15
144 Mike Bullard	.30	.75
145 Jose Charbonneau	.08	.25
146 Wally Schreiber	.08	.25
147 Jorg Handrick	.05	.15
148 Helmut Steiger	.05	.15
149 Marco Sturm	4.00	10.00
150 Jonas Johnsson	.05	.15
151 Vesa Salo	.05	.15
152 Gino Cavallini	.08	.25
153 Lars Hurtig	.05	.15
154 Olli Kaski	.05	.15
155 007 Charly	.05	.15
156 Lance Nethery CO	.05	.15
157 Ross Yates ASST CO	.05	.15
158 Joachim Appel	.05	.15
159 Mike Rosati	.20	.50
160 Harold Kreis	.05	.15
161 Paul Stanton	.08	.25
162 Christian Lukes	.05	.15
163 Robert Nardella	.05	.15
164 Alexander Erdmann	.05	.15
165 Stephane J.G. Richer	.08	.25
166 Martin Ulrich	.05	.15
167 Mike Pellegrims	.05	.15
168 Mario Gehrig	.05	.15
169 Pavel Gross	.05	.15
170 Dave Tomlinson	.08	.25
171 Daniel Korber	.05	.15
172 Francois Guay	.05	.15
173 Jochen Hecht	1.25	3.00
174 Florian Keller	.20	.50
175 Till Feser	.05	.15
176 Alexander Serikow	.20	.50
177 Christian Pouget	.05	.15
178 Dieter Kalt	.05	.15
179 Paul Beraldo	.05	.15
180 Steven Thornton	.05	.15
181 Robert Cimetta	.20	.50
182 Gary Clark CO	.05	.15
183 Bjorn Leonhardt	.05	.15
184 Claus Dalpiaz	.08	.25
185 Jesper Duus	.05	.15
186 Manuel Hiemer	.05	.15
187 Markus Pottinger	.05	.15
188 Chris Bartolone	.05	.15
189 Christian Gegenfurther	.05	.15
190 Heinrich Schiffl	.05	.15
191 Per Lundell	.05	.15
192 Joel Savage	.08	.25
193 Josef Muller	.05	.15
194 Jari Torkki	.05	.15
195 James Hiller	.05	.15
196 Doug Derraugh	.05	.15
197 Pekka Tirkkonen	.05	.15
198 Martin Reichel	.05	.15
199 Raimond Hilger	.08	.25
200 Michael Schneidawind	.05	.15
201 Scott Beattie	.05	.15
202 Paris Proft	.05	.15
203 Kevin Gaudet	.05	.15
204 Wayne Cowley	.05	.15
205 Marco Herbst	.05	.15
206 Andreas Schubert	.05	.15
207 Stephan Sinner	.05	.15
208 Heinrich Synowietz	.05	.15
209 Paul Synowietz	.05	.15
210 Dimitri Frolov	.05	.15
211 Andrej Saposhnikov	.05	.15
212 Jedrzej Kasperczyk	.05	.15
213 Joseph West	.05	.15
214 Fabian Ahrens	.05	.15
215 Maurice Lemay	.05	.15
216 Mark Kosturik	.05	.15
217 Mark Jooris	.05	.15
218 Len Soccio	.05	.15
219 Mark Mahon	.05	.15
220 Frank LaScala	.05	.15
221 Jari Pasanen	.05	.15
222 Ralph Vos	.05	.15
223 Anthony Cirelli	.05	.15
224 Emilio Iovio	.05	.15
225 Gerhard Brunner CO	.05	.15
226 Pavel Cagas	.05	.15
227 Jonas Eriksson	.05	.15
228 Alexander Engel	.05	.15
229 Gregory Johnston	.08	.25
230 Alexander Wedl	.05	.15
231 Jouni Vento	.05	.15
232 Roger Ohman	.05	.15
233 David Morrison	.05	.15
234 Bruce Eakin	.05	.15
235 Michael Millar	.05	.15
236 Roger Hansson	.02	.10
237 Peter Kwasigroch	.05	.15
238 Branjo Heisig	.05	.15
239 Jukka Seppo	.05	.15
240 Greg Evtushevski	.05	.15
241 Falk Ozellis	.05	.15
242 Daniel Larin	.05	.15
243 Tino Boos	.05	.15
244 Toni Krinner	.05	.15
245 Milan Mokros	.05	.15
246 Peter Ustorf CO	.05	.15
247 Klaus Merk	.08	.25
248 David Berge	.05	.15
249 Georg Holzmann	.05	.15
250 Tom O'Regan	.05	.15
251 Jochen Molling	.05	.15
252 Joseph Lehner	.05	.15
253 Marco Rentzsch	.05	.15
254 Pekka Laksola	.05	.15
255 Petri Matikainen	.05	.15
256 Tony Tanti	.30	.75
257 Gaetan Malo	.05	.15
258 Thomas Schinko	.05	.15
259 Vitali Karamnow	.05	.15
260 Gunther Oswald	.05	.15
261 Christian Brittig	.05	.15
262 Jurgen Rumrich	.05	.15
263 John Chabot	.20	.50
264 Andreas Dimbat	.05	.15
265 Mark Teevens	.05	.15
266 Veli-Pekka Kautonen	.05	.15
267 Jarno-Sakari Peltonen	.05	.15
268 Hardy Nilsson CO	.05	.15
269 Martin Karlsson ASST CO	.05	.15
270 Ake Lilljebjorn	.05	.15
271 Kai Fischer	.08	.25
272 Brad Bergen	.05	.15
273 Andreas Niederberger	.05	.15
274 Sergej Sorokin	.05	.15
275 Robert Sterflinger	.05	.15
276 Peter Andersson	.05	.15
277 Viktor Gordiouk	.08	.25
278 Gordon Sherven	.08	.25
279 Benoit Doucet	.20	.50
280 Bernd Kuhnhauser	.08	.25
281 Dieter Hegen	.05	.15
282 Andreas Brockmann	.05	.15
283 Ernst Kopf	.05	.15
284 Alexej Kudashov	.05	.15
285 Bernd Truntschka	.08	.25
286 Mikko Makela	.05	.15
287 Nikolaus Mondt	.05	.15
288 Boris Lingemann	.05	.15
289 Thomas Brandl	.08	.25
290 Leo Stefan	.08	.25
291 Bob Burns	.05	.15

292 Carsten Solbach .05 .15
293 Matthias Hoppe .05 .15
294 Sascha Goc .20 .50
295 Gordon Hynes .20 .50
296 Thomas Gaus .05 .15
297 Brian Tutt .05 .15
298 Richard Trojan .05 .15
299 Daniel Nowak .05 .15
300 Andreas Renz .05 .15
301 Sana Hassan .05 .15
302 Alan Young .05 .15
303 Mike Bader .05 .15
304 Robert Brezina .05 .15
305 Wayne Hynes .05 .15
306 Mark Bassen .05 .15
307 Andrew Clark .05 .15
308 Grant Martin .05 .15
309 Michael Lay .05 .15
310 Jackson Penney .05 .15
311 Rich Chernomaz .15 .40
312 Mark MacKay .20 .50
313 Vladimir Fedosov .05 .15
314 Emanuel Viveiros .08 .25
315 Jan Eysselt CO .05 .15
316 Michel Valliere .05 .15
317 Stefan Lahn .05 .15
318 Christian Gerum .05 .15
319 Heiko Smazal .05 .15
320 Christian Curth .05 .15
321 Miroslav Maly .05 .15
322 Torsten Kienass .05 .15
323 Thomas Sterflinger .05 .15
324 Lars Bruggemann .05 .15
325 Paul Geddes .05 .15
326 Rolan Ramoser .05 .15
327 Martin Jiranek .05 .15
328 Stefan Steinbock .05 .15
329 Martin Ekrt .05 .15
330 Jurgen Lechl .05 .15
331 Dion Del Monte .05 .15
332 Markus Welz .05 .15
333 Henrik Holscher .05 .15
334 Otto Sykora .05 .15
335 Milos Vanik .05 .15
336 Robert Murdoch CO .05 .15
337 Bernd Haake ASST CO .05 .15
338 Joseph Heiss .08 .25
339 Olaf Grundmann .05 .15
340 Alexander Genze .05 .15
341 Jorg Mayr .05 .15
342 Mirco Ludemann .05 .15
343 Jayson Meyer .05 .15
344 Karsten Mende .05 .15
345 Herbert Hohenberger .08 .25
346 Joe Cirella .08 .25
347 Petter Nilsson .05 .15
348 Jim Montgomery .20 .50
349 Stefan Mann .05 .15
350 Luciano Borsato .08 .25
351 Dwayne Norris .08 .25
352 Bruno Zarrillo .05 .15
353 Peter Draisaitl .08 .25
354 Joe Busillo .05 .15
355 Andreas Lupzig .05 .15
356 Rainer Zerwesz .05 .15
357 Thomas Forslund .08 .25
358 Tobias Abstreiter .05 .15
359 Patrick Carnback .08 .25
360 Franz Demmel .05 .15

1998-99 German DEL

COMPLETE SET (344) 20.00 50.00
1 Burke Murphy .07 .20
2 Marc Seliger .20 .50
3 Jason Clark .07 .20
4 Mike McNeill .07 .20
5 Norm Matherson .07 .20
6 Jeff Sebastien .07 .20
7 Phil Huber .07 .20
8 Todd Wtzel .07 .20
9 Jesper Morin .07 .20
10 Marc Pellike .07 .20
11 Jacek Plachta .07 .20
12 Marcus Adolfson .07 .20
13 Christian Schmitz .07 .20
14 Bob Marshall .07 .20
15 Peter Lutter .07 .20
16 Stefan Mayer .07 .20
17 Daniel Korber .07 .20
18 Carsten Gosdeck .07 .20
19 Jiri Kochta .07 .20
20 Petri Liimatainen .07 .20
21 Thomas Brandl .07 .20
22 Andrej Kovalev .08 .25
23 Johnny Walker .07 .20
24 Neil Eisenhut .20 .50
25 Karel Lang .07 .20
26 Marek Stebnicki .07 .20
27 Chris Bartolone .07 .20
28 John Van Kessel .07 .20
29 Lars Bruggemann .07 .20
30 Jason Meyer .07 .20
31 Reemt Pyka .07 .20
32 Mark Pederson .07 .20
33 Veli-Pekka Kautonen .07 .20
34 Tommie Hartogs .07 .20
35 Frantisek Frosch .07 .20
36 Leo van den Thillart .07 .20
37 Vitali Karamnov .08 .25
38 Stephane Barin .07 .20
39 Roger Nordstrom .07 .20
40 Robert Ouellet .07 .20
41 Doug Mason .07 .20
42 Francois Guay .07 .20
43 Greg Johnston .20 .50
44 Greg Evtushevski .07 .20
45 Shane Peacock .07 .20
46 Chris Rogles .30 .75
47 Gunter Oswald .07 .20
48 Jukka Seppo .07 .20
49 Jurgen Rumrich .07 .20
50 Roger Hansson .07 .20
51 Stephane Robitaille .07 .20
52 Orjan Lindmark .07 .20
53 Jeff MacLeod .07 .20
54 Alexander Wedl .07 .20
55 Jochen Molling .07 .20
56 Paul Cohen .07 .20
57 Daniel Kreutzer .07 .20
58 Nikolaus Mondt .07 .20
59 John Lilley .20 .50
60 Roland Ramoser .07 .20
61 Thomas Dolak .07 .20
62 Tino Boos .07 .20
63 Tobias Abstreiter .07 .20
64 Hans Zach .07 .20
65 Petr Briza .30 .75
66 Wally Schreiber .20 .50
67 Chris Luongo .20 .50
68 Dean Evason .20 .50
69 David Bruce .20 .50
70 Peter Douris .20 .50
71 Jason Herter .20 .50
72 Jorg Hendrick .07 .20
73 Rob Murphy .20 .50
74 Mike Casselmann .07 .20
75 Steve Junker .07 .20
76 Zbynek Kukacka .07 .20
77 Mark Krys .07 .20
78 Markus Wieland .07 .20
79 Evan Marble .07 .20
80 Jari Korpisalo .07 .20
81 Peter Gulda .07 .20
82 Bob Joyce .20 .50
83 Johan Rosen .07 .20
84 Christian Kunast .07 .20
85 Olli Kaski .07 .20
86 Chris Valentine .30 .75
87 Corey Millen .20 .50
88 Tomas Forslund .15 .40
89 Bruno Zarrillo .20 .50
90 Igor Alexandrov .07 .20
91 Bob Halkidis .20 .50
92 Petri Varis .20 .50
93 Joseph Heiss .20 .50
94 Greg Brown .20 .50
95 Dwayne Norris .20 .50
96 Mirko Ludemann .07 .20
97 John Miner .07 .20
98 Boris Rousson .30 .75
99 Craig Woodcroft .07 .20
100 Jorg Mayr .07 .20
101 Steve Wilson .07 .20
102 Rainer Zerwesz .07 .20
103 Brian McReynolds .07 .20
104 Andreas Lupzig .07 .20
105 Giuseppe Busillo .07 .20
106 Jeff Ricciardi .07 .20
107 Mike Hartman .20 .50
108 Timo Lahtinen .07 .20
109 Stephane Morin .20 .50
110 Paul Broten .20 .50
111 Robert Guillet .07 .20
112 Clayton Beddoes .15 .40
113 Robert Cimetta .20 .50
114 Dave MacIntyre .07 .20
115 Johan Norgren .07 .20
116 Todd Nelson .07 .20
117 Guy Phillips .07 .20
118 Craig Martin .20 .50
119 Parris Duffus .30 .75
120 Christian Brittig .07 .20
121 Thomas Schinko .07 .20
122 Mario Gehrig .07 .20
123 Fredrik Ytfeldt .07 .20
124 Lawrence Rucchin .07 .20
125 Heinz Ehlers .07 .20
126 Heinrich Schiffl .07 .20
127 Sylvain Couturier .08 .25
128 Hakan Galiamoutsas .07 .20
129 David Berge .07 .20
130 Marc Savard .07 .20
131 Dale McCourt .20 .50
132 Jukka Tammi .20 .50
133 Chris Snell .20 .50
134 John Chabot .20 .50
135 Len Barrie .20 .50
136 Lija Vorobjov .07 .20
137 Steve Palmer .07 .20
138 Fabrice L'Henry .07 .20
139 Rob Doyle .07 .20
140 Victor Gervais .07 .20
141 Jose Charbonneau .08 .25
142 Thorsten Apel .07 .20
143 Michael Bresagk .07 .20
144 Rick Hayward .08 .25
145 Phil von Steffenelli .07 .20
146 Martin Williams .07 .20
147 Toni Porkka .07 .20
148 Jean-Marc Richard .07 .20
149 Douglas Kirton .07 .20
150 Joel Savage .20 .50
151 Ralf Hantschke .07 .20
152 Ken Quinney .15 .40
153 Marcus Bleicher .07 .20
154 Bob Manno .08 .25
155 Rob Cowie .07 .20
156 Mike Bullard .30 .75
157 Maren Valenti .07 .20
158 Sven Felski .07 .20
159 Andrew McKim .20 .50
160 Derek Mayer .08 .25
161 Niklas Hede .07 .20
162 Thomas Steen .20 .50
163 Mario Brunetta .20 .50
164 Marc Fortier .20 .50
165 Thomas Rhodin .07 .20
166 Nico Pyka .07 .20
167 Chris Govedaris .08 .25
168 Lorenz Funk .07 .20
169 Florian Funk .07 .20
170 Yvon Corriveau .20 .50
171 Mikael Wahlberg .07 .20
172 Darren Durdle .07 .20
173 Pelle Svensson .07 .20
174 Greg Andrusak .08 .25
175 Leif Carlsson .07 .20
176 Andreas Brockmann .07 .20
177 Robert Leask .07 .20
178 Mario Chitaroni .07 .20
179 Chad Biafore .07 .20
180 Peter John Lee .07 .20
181 Len Soccio .20 .50
182 Jason Lafreniere .20 .50
183 Joe West .07 .20
184 Brent Tully .20 .50
185 Mark Kosturik .07 .20
186 David Haas .07 .20
187 Darcy Martini .07 .20
188 Gary Leeman .20 .50
189 Lee Davidson .07 .20
190 Scott Metcalfe .20 .50
191 Tom Pederson .20 .50
192 Francois Gravel .07 .20
193 Bjorn Leonhardt .07 .20
194 Mike Johnson .07 .20
195 Claudio Scremin .07 .20
196 Mike Ware .07 .20
197 Jurgen Trattner .07 .20
198 Dan Currie .20 .50
199 Patrick Curcio .07 .20
200 Patrick Senger .07 .20
201 Frank Di Muzio .07 .20
202 Kevin Gaudet .07 .20
203 Mark MacKay .20 .50
204 Claude Vilgrain .20 .50
205 Rich Chernomaz .07 .20
206 Daniel Laperriere .20 .50
207 Wayne Hynes .07 .20
208 Todd Harkins .07 .20
209 Scott McCrory .20 .50
210 Andrew Rymsha .15 .40
211 Daniel Nowak .07 .20
212 Andy Schneider .15 .40
213 David Marcinshyn .07 .20
214 Marc Laniel .07 .20
215 Guy Lehoux .07 .20
216 Matthias Vater .07 .20
217 Jens Stramkowski .07 .20
218 Alexander Dexheimer .07 .20
219 Mark Bassen .07 .20
220 Steffen Karg .07 .20
221 Randy Perry .07 .20
222 Robert Schistad .20 .50
223 Andreas Renz .07 .20
224 Matthias Hoppe .07 .20
225 Ron Ivany .07 .20
226 Phillippe Bozon .40 1.00
227 Dave Tomlinson .20 .50
228 Stephane Richer .07 .20
229 Paul Stanton .20 .50
230 Pavel Gross .07 .20
231 Christian Pouget .07 .20
232 Jackson Penney .07 .20
233 Gordon Hynes .20 .50
234 Jason Young .07 .20
235 Alexander Serikow .20 .50
236 Mike Stevens .07 .20
237 Mike Pellegrims .07 .20
238 Reid Simonton .07 .20
239 Christian Lukes .07 .20
240 Ron Pasco .07 .20
241 Mike Hudson .30 .75
242 Denis Perez .07 .20
243 Svan Rampf .07 .20
244 Danny Lorenz .20 .50
245 Brian Tutt .07 .20
246 Jan Alston .07 .20
247 Lance Nethery .07 .20
248 Sergio Momesso .20 .50
249 Andrej Mezin .40 1.00
250 Jarno Peltonen .07 .20
251 Martin Reichel .07 .20
252 Sergej Stas .07 .20
253 Martin Jiranek .07 .20
254 Jason Miller .07 .20
255 Jozef Cierny .07 .20
256 Liam Garvey .07 .20
257 Kevin Grant .07 .20
258 Chris Straube .07 .20
259 Heiko Smazal .07 .20
260 Vadim Shakhraichuk .07 .20
261 Leszek Laszkiewicz .07 .20
262 Sven Valenti .07 .20
263 Michel Valliere .07 .20
264 Per Lundell .07 .20
265 Dimitri Dudik .07 .20
266 Daniel Kunce .07 .20
267 Ivan Droppa .07 .20
268 Peter Ihnacak .20 .50
269 Harald Birk .07 .20
270 Bradley Bergen .07 .20
271 Pierre Rioux .07 .20
272 Jim Camazzola .07 .20
273 Klaus Merk .20 .50
274 Rick Girard .07 .20
275 Andre Faust .07 .20
276 Hakan Ahlund .07 .20
277 Kyosti Karjalainen .20 .50
278 Leonardo Conti .07 .20
279 Leo Gudas .07 .20
280 Mathias Ahxner .07 .20
281 Francols Groleau .07 .20
282 Michael Bakos .07 .20
283 Alan Reader .07 .20
284 Nordin Harfaoui .07 .20
285 Dale Craigwell .20 .50
286 Dimitri Gromling .07 .20
287 Duanne Moeser .07 .20
288 Tommy Jakobsen .07 .20
289 Patrik Degerstedt .07 .20
290 Greg Bullock .07 .20
291 Gunnar Leidborg .07 .20
292 Dieter Hegen .07 .20
293 Derek Cormier .07 .20
294 Jim Hiller .07 .20
295 Gordon Sherven .08 .25
296 Eric Murana .07 .20
297 Robert Muller .07 .20
298 Klaus Kathan .07 .20
299 Raimond Hilger .07 .20
300 Christian Due-Boje .07 .20
301 Jesper Duus .07 .20
302 Michael Pohl .07 .20
303 Bernd Kuhnhauser .15 .40
304 Frank Hohenadl .07 .20
305 Alexander Jansen .07 .20
306 Teemu Sillanpaa .07 .20
307 Hans Abranamsson .07 .20
308 Claus Dalpiaz .08 .25
309 Kari Haakana .07 .20
310 Christian Gegenfurtner .07 .20
311 Peter Ottosson .07 .20
312 Wolfgang Kummer .07 .20
313 Beppi Eckmaier .07 .20
314 Gerhard Brunner .07 .20
315 Mirko Ludemann .08 .25
316 Sven Felski .07 .20
317 Reemt Pyka .07 .20
318 Jorg Mayr .07 .20
319 Michael Bresagk .07 .20
320 Andraes Lupzig .07 .20
321 Jurgen Rumrich .07 .20
322 Josef Lehner .07 .20
323 Peter Draisaitl .07 .20
324 Leo Stefan .07 .20
325 Joseph Heiss .08 .25
326 Klaus Kathan .07 .20
327 Klaus Merk .08 .25
328 Peter Gulda .07 .20
329 Daniel Nowak .07 .20
330 Bradley Bergen .07 .20
331 Thomas Dolak .07 .20
332 Martin Reichel .07 .20
333 Alexander Serikow .20 .50
334 Harold Birk .07 .20
335 Michael Bakos .07 .20
336 Mario Gehrig .07 .20
337 Mark Mackay .20 .50
338 Dieter Hegen .15 .40
339 Hans Zach .07 .20
340 Erich Kuhnackl .15 .40
341 Ernst Hofner .07 .20
NNO Gerhard Leinauer CL .07 .20
NNO Rick Amann CL .08 .25
NNO Robert Muller CL .07 .20

1999-00 German DEL

COMPLETE SET (434) 24.00 60.00
1 Mannheim .05 .15
2 Gordon Hynes .20 .50
3 Paul Stanton .20 .50
4 Christian Lukes .05 .15
5 Clayton Beddoes .20 .50
6 Shawn McCosh .05 .15
7 Dave Tomlinson .20 .50
8 Patrice Lefebvre .20 .50
9 Steve Junker .20 .50
10 Ralph Intranuovo .20 .50
11 Joel Savage .20 .50
12 Stephane J.G. Richer .20 .50
13 Rainer Zerwesz .05 .15
14 Yves Racine .20 .50
15 Mike Stevens .20 .50
16 Markus Wieland .05 .15
17 Bjorn Leonhardt .05 .15
18 Mike Rosati .20 .50
19 Philip Schumacher .05 .15
20 Jan Alston .05 .15
21 Kevin Grant .05 .15
22 Chris Straube .05 .15
23 Dennis Seidenberg .05 .15
24 Chris Valentine TR .20 .50
25 Nürnberg .05 .15
26 Stefan Mann .05 .15
27 Vadim Shakhraichuk .05 .15
28 Roland Ramoser .05 .15
29 Martin Jiranek .05 .15
30 Hannes Körber .05 .15
31 Jarno Peltonen .05 .15
32 Dimitri Dudik .05 .15
33 Viktors Ignatjevs .05 .15
34 Alexander Cherbayev .08 .25
35 Martin Reichel .05 .15
36 Russ Romaniuk .08 .25
37 Jason Miller .05 .15
38 Sergej Dautin .05 .15
39 Jozef Cierny .05 .15
40 Marc Seliger .40 1.00
41 Daniel Kunce .05 .15
42 Pasi Sormunen .05 .15
43 Christian Schönmoser .05 .15
44 Stefan Mayer .05 .15
45 Alain Cote .08 .25
46 Liam Garvey .05 .15
47 John Craighead .05 .15
48 Petr Franek .05 .15
49 Peter Ihnacak TR .20 .50
50 Eisbaren .05 .15
51 Nico Pyka .05 .15
52 Robert Leask .20 .50
53 Alexander Godynyuk .08 .25
54 Lorenz Funk .05 .15
55 Sven Felski .05 .15
56 Giuseppe Busillo .05 .15
57 Yvon Corriveau .20 .50
58 Mikael Wahlberg .05 .15
59 Udo Dohler .05 .15
60 Sandy Smith .20 .50
61 Jaroslav Kames .05 .15
62 Rob Murphy .08 .25
63 Marc Fortier .20 .50
64 Mario Chitaroni .05 .15
65 Leif Carlsson .05 .15
66 Derek Mayer .20 .50
67 Sebastian Elwing .05 .15
68 Thomas Schinko .05 .15
69 Rob Cowie .05 .15
70 Thomas Rhodin .05 .15
71 Peter Hammarstrom .05 .15
72 Chris Govedaris .20 .50
73 Mike Bullard .20 .50
74 Peter John Lee TR .05 .15
75 Frankfurt .05 .15
76 Michael Bresagk .05 .15
77 Joachim Appel .05 .15
78 Rick Hayward .20 .50
79 Robin Doyle .05 .15
80 Christian Langer .05 .15
81 Bob Bassen .20 .50
82 John Chabot .20 .50
83 Devin Edgerton .05 .15
84 Toni Porkka .05 .15
85 Jean-Marc Richard .05 .15
86 Jose Charbonneau .08 .25
87 Douglas Kirton .05 .15
88 Andrej Vasilyev .05 .15
89 Ralf Hantschke .05 .15
90 Steve Palmer .05 .15
91 Jason Ruff .20 .50
92 Bastian Niedermeier .05 .15
93 Chris Hynes .05 .15
94 Victor Gervais .05 .15
95 Ken Quinney .20 .50
96 Mark Bassen .05 .15
97 Chris Snell .20 .50
98 Eldon Reddick .20 .50
99 Peter Obresa TR .05 .15
100 Koln .05 .15
101 Joseph Heiss .20 .50
102 Steve Wilson .05 .15
103 Mario Doyon .20 .50
104 Jorg Mayr .05 .15
105 Marty Murray .20 .50
106 Mirko Ludemann .05 .15
107 Dwayne Norris .20 .50
108 Christoph Paepke .05 .15
109 Bruno Zarrillo .20 .50
110 Dan Lambert .20 .50
111 Anders Huusko .05 .15
112 George Zajankala .05 .15
113 Andreas Lupzig .05 .15
114 Jean-Yves Roy .20 .50
115 Tomas Forslund .08 .25
116 Jason Young .08 .25
117 Todd Hlushko .20 .50
118 Andrew Verner .20 .50
119 Corey Millen .20 .50
120 Greg Brown .05 .15
121 John Miner .08 .25
122 Sergio Momesso .20 .50
123 Lance Nethery TR .05 .15
124 Krefeld .05 .15
125 Karel Lang .05 .15
126 Andy Roach .05 .15
127 Tomas Brandl .05 .15
128 Neil Eisenhut .20 .50
129 Ilja Vorobjev .05 .15
130 Andrey Kovalev .05 .15
131 Mark Pederson .08 .25
132 Shayne Wright .05 .15
133 Reemt Pyka .05 .15
134 Andrew Rymsha .05 .15
135 Lars Bruggemann .05 .15
136 Tommie Hartogs .05 .15
137 Marek Stebnicki .05 .15
138 Johnny Walker .05 .15
139 Chris Bartolone .05 .15
140 Stephane Barin .05 .15
141 Mickey Elick .05 .15
142 Phil von Stefenelli .08 .25
143 Jean-Francois Jomphe .20 .50
144 Robert Ouellet .05 .15
145 Roger Nordstrom .05 .15
146 Martin Lindman .05 .15
147 Doug Mason TR .05 .15
148 Augsburg .05 .15
149 Vladislav Boulin .05 .15
150 Leo Gudas .05 .15
151 Duane Moeser .05 .15
152 Sergej Vostrikov .05 .15
153 Igor Maslennikov .05 .15
154 Kyosti Karjalainen .05 .15
155 Kurtis Miller .05 .15
156 Bradley Bergen .05 .15
157 Scott Allison .05 .15
158 Hakan Ahlund .05 .15
159 Peter Larsson .05 .15
160 Brian Loney .05 .15
161 Michael Bakos .05 .15
162 Sven Rampf .05 .15
163 Jim Camazzola .05 .15
164 Andre Faust .05 .15
165 Harald Birk .05 .15
166 Tommy Jakobsen .05 .15
167 Sergej Klimovich .05 .15
168 Klaus Merk .20 .50
169 Bob Manno TR .08 .25
170 Kassel .05 .15
171 Jochen Molling .05 .15
172 David Cooper .20 .50
173 Thomas Dolak .05 .15
174 Stephane Robitaille .05 .15
175 Jeff MacLeod .05 .15
176 Roger Hansson .05 .15
177 Francois Guay .05 .15
178 Nikolaus Mondt .05 .15
179 Andreas Loth .05 .15
180 Ron Pasco .05 .15
181 Jurgen Rumrich .05 .15
182 Greg Evtushevski .05 .15
183 Daniel Kreutzer .05 .15
184 Brent Tully .05 .15
185 Ivan Droppa .05 .15
186 Tobias Abstreiter .05 .15
187 Sylvain Turgeon .20 .50
188 Chris Rogles .20 .50
189 Leonardo Conti .05 .15
190 Tino Boos .05 .15
191 Benjamin Hinterstocker .05 .15
192 Craig Woodcroft .20 .50
193 Orjan Lindmark .05 .15
194 Hans Zach TR .05 .15
195 Schwenningen .05 .15
196 Kevin Wortman .05 .15
197 Marc Laniel .20 .50
198 Daniel Laperriere .20 .50
199 Marcel Goc 1.25 3.00
200 Guy Lehoux .05 .15
201 Steffen Oder .05 .15
202 Jens Stramkowski .05 .15
203 Mark Kolesar .15 .40
204 Scott McCrory .05 .15
205 John Lilley .20 .50
206 Patrik Augusta .05 .15
207 Randy Perry .05 .15
208 Daniel Nowak .05 .15
209 Todd Harkins .05 .15
210 Robert Schistad .05 .15
211 Andreas Renz .05 .15
212 Stephane Beauregard .20 .50
213 Rick Girard .05 .15
214 Iain Fraser .20 .50
215 Andy Schneider .20 .50
216 Mark Mackay .20 .50
217 Rich Chernomaz TR .20 .50
218 Hannover .05 .15
219 Lars Jansson .05 .15
220 Tom Pederson .20 .50
221 Juri Gunko .05 .15
222 Mattias Loof .05 .15
223 Joseph West .05 .15
224 Egor Bashkatov .08 .25
225 Grigori Panteleyev .20 .50
226 Mark Kosturik .05 .15
227 Len Soccio .05 .15
228 Dominic Lavoie .20 .50
229 Peter Willmann .05 .15
230 Wally Schreiber .20 .50
231 Scott Metcalfe .20 .50
232 David Haas .05 .15
233 Ildar Mukhometov .20 .50
234 Igor Chibirev .08 .25
235 Michael Thurner .05 .15
236 Jan Munster .05 .15
237 Jakob Karlsson .05 .15
238 David Sulkovsky .05 .15
239 Brian Tutt .05 .15
240 Igor Alexandrov .05 .15
241 Kevin Gaudet TR .05 .15
242 Rosenheim .05 .15
243 Hakan Algotsson .20 .50
244 Trevor Burgess .05 .15
245 Christian Due-Boje .05 .15
246 Teemu Sillanpaa .05 .15
247 Curtis Fry .05 .15
248 Gordon Sherven .20 .50
249 Frank Hohenadl .05 .15
250 Bernd Kuhnhauser .05 .15
251 Michael Pohl .05 .15
252 Derek Cormier .05 .15
253 Jean-Francois Quintin .20 .50
254 Dieter Hegen .05 .15
255 Peter Ottosson .05 .15
256 Raimond Hilger .08 .25
257 Niklas Brannstrom .05 .15
258 Wolfgang Kummer .05 .15
259 Kari Haakana .05 .15
260 Paul Weismann .05 .15
261 Klaus Kathan .05 .15
262 Sami Nuutinen .05 .15
263 Patrik Hucko .05 .15
264 Robert Muller .05 .15
265 Gerhard Brunner TR .05 .15
266 Capitals .05 .15
267 Andrej Mezin .40 1.00
268 Fredrik Stillman .20 .50
269 Fredrik Ytfeldt .05 .15
270 Markus Pottinger .05 .15
271 Niklas Hede .05 .15
272 Alexander Kuzminski .05 .15
273 Thomas Sjogren .05 .15
274 Dennis Meyer .05 .15
275 Robert Cimetta .20 .50
276 Jim Hiller .05 .15
277 Doug Derraugh .05 .15
278 Patrick Senger .05 .15
279 Pavel Gross .05 .15
280 Robert Guillet .05 .15
281 Sylvain Couturier .05 .15
282 Heinrich Schiffl .05 .15
283 Heinz Ehlers .05 .15
284 Larry Rucchin .05 .15
285 Gregory Johnston .20 .50
286 David Berge .05 .15
287 Johan Norgren .05 .15
288 Martin Ulrich .05 .15
289 Benjamin Hecker .05 .15
290 Mike Pellegrims .05 .15
291 Michael Komma TR .05 .15
292 Oberhausen .05 .15
293 Peter Gulda .05 .15
294 Jergus Baca .05 .15
295 Bob Marshall .05 .15
296 Mike Sullivan .20 .50
297 Jacek Plachta .05 .15
298 Andrej Fuchs .05 .15
299 Mike McNeill .20 .50
300 Aleksandrs Kerch .05 .15
301 Robert Hock .05 .15
302 Albert Malgin .05 .15
303 Kai Fischer .20 .50
304 Burke Murphy .05 .15
305 Jeff Sebastian .05 .15
306 Sergej Stas .05 .15
307 Sebastian Klenner .05 .15
308 Boris Fuchs .05 .15
309 Ivo Jan .05 .15
310 Francois Gravel .05 .15
311 Alexander Makritzky .05 .15
312 Viktor Karatchun .05 .15
313 Gunnar Loidborg TR .05 .15
314 Munchen .05 .15
315 Boris Rousson .20 .50
316 Hans Lodin .05 .15
317 Chris Luongo .20 .50
318 Mike Casselman .05 .15
319 Heiko Smazal .05 .15
320 Peter Abstreiter .05 .15
321 Simon Wheeldon .20 .50
322 Phil Huber .05 .15
323 Peter Douris .20 .50
324 Jari Korpisalo .05 .15
325 Kent Fearns .05 .15
326 Markus Jocher .05 .15
327 Pelle Svensson .05 .15
328 Sven Wiele .05 .15
329 Wayne Hynes .05 .15
330 Bill McDougall .20 .50
331 Alexander Serikow .20 .50
332 Robert Joyce .20 .50
333 Jorg Handrick .05 .15
334 Jason Herter .08 .25
335 Johan Rosen .05 .15
336 Mike Kennedy .20 .50
337 Christian Kunast .05 .15
338 Shane Peacock .05 .15
339 Sean Simpson TR .05 .15
340 Essen .05 .15
341 Oldrich Svoboda .05 .15
342 Bodo Mueller-Boenigk .05 .15
343 Vlastimil Kroupa .05 .15
344 Zdenek Touzimsky .05 .15
345 Pavel Augusta .05 .15
346 Christian Kohmann .05 .15
347 Martin Sychra .05 .15
348 Torsten Kienass .08 .25
349 Peter Draisaitl .05 .15
350 Marian Kacir .05 .15
351 Terry Campbell .05 .15
352 Roland Verwey .05 .15
353 Radek Toth .05 .15
354 Josef Zajic .05 .15
355 Jochen Vollmer .05 .15
356 Jiri Sejba .05 .15
357 Jukka Seppo .05 .15
358 Marc Savard .20 .50
359 Enrico Ciccone .08 .25
360 Michael Dvorak .05 .15
361 Tomas Nemcicky .05 .15
362 Andrej Nederost .40 1.00
363 Tomas Srsen .05 .15
364 Bedrich Scerban .05 .15
365 Jan Benda TR .15 .40
366 3ffi National .05 .15
367 Robert Muller .05 .15
368 Torsten Kienass .08 .25
369 Markus Pottinger .05 .15
370 Lorenz Funk .05 .15
371 Nico Pyka .05 .15
372 Sven Felski .05 .15
373 Jochen Molling .05 .15
374 Christian Langer .05 .15
375 Nikolaus Mondt .05 .15
376 Bernd Kuhnhauser .05 .15
377 Jurgen Rumrich .05 .15
378 Lars Bruggemann .05 .15
379 Alexander Serikow .20 .50
380 Klaus Kathan .05 .15
381 Terry Campbell .05 .15
382 Tino Boos .05 .15
383 Michael Bresagk .05 .15
384 Christian Lukes .05 .15
385 Heiko Smazal .05 .15
386 Tobias Abstreiter .05 .15
387 Thomas Dolak .05 .15
388 Udo Dohler .05 .15
389 Andreas Loth .05 .15
390 David Berge .05 .15
391 Mark MacKay .20 .50
392 Hans Zach TR .05 .15
393 Moderatoren .05 .15
394 Marc Hindelang .05 .15
395 Peter Kohl .05 .15
396 Sven Kukulies .05 .15
397 Claus Muller .05 .15
398 Gerhard Leinauer .05 .15
399 Michael Leopold .05 .15
400 Rick Amann .05 .15
401 Schiris .05 .15
402 Holger Gerstberger .05 .15
403 Ralph Dimmers .05 .15
404 Harald Deubert .05 .15
405 Petr Chvatal .05 .15
406 Frank Awizus .05 .15
407 Axel Rademaker .05 .15
408 Wolfgang Hellwig .05 .15
409 Gerhard Muller .05 .15
410 Gerhard Lichtnecker .05 .15
411 Rainer Kluge .05 .15
412 Stefan TR .05 .15
413 Richard Schütz .05 .15
414 Willi Schimm .05 .15
415 Peter Slapke .05 .15
416 TW 1 .05 .15
417 TW 2 .05 .15
418 TW 3 .05 .15
419 TW 4 .05 .15
420 TW 5 .05 .15
421 TW 6 .05 .15
422 TW 7 .05 .15
423 TW 8 .05 .15
424 TW 9 .05 .15
425 RS 1 .05 .15
426 RS 2 .05 .15
427 RS 3 .05 .15
428 RS 4 .05 .15
429 RS 5 .05 .15
430 RS 6 .05 .15
431 RS 7 .05 .15
432 RS 8 .05 .15
433 RS 9 .05 .15
434 SK .05 .15

1999-00 German Bundesliga 2

COMPLETE SET (330) 30.00 60.00
1 EC Bad Nauheim Team Card .02 .10
2 Darryl Olsen .20 .50
3 Sven Gerbig .08 .25
4 Gaetan Malo .08 .25
5 Steffen Michel .08 .25
6 Dennis Cardona .08 .25
7 Marco Rentzsch .08 .25
8 Dino Felicetti .08 .25
9 David Matsos .08 .25
10 Sven Paschek .08 .25
11 Marco Heinrichs .08 .25
12 Larry Mitchell .08 .25
13 Ingo Schwarz .08 .25
14 Dale Jago .08 .25
15 Claus Dalpiaz .20 .50
16 Marc West .08 .25
17 Christian Seeberger .08 .25
18 Olaf Scholz .08 .25
19 Carsten Gosdeck .08 .25
20 Dan Olsen .08 .25
21 EC Bad Tölz Team Card .02 .10
22 Christian Proulx .20 .50
23 Michael Teltscher .08 .25
24 Florian Keller .08 .25
25 Christian Curth .08 .25
26 Yanick Dube .20 .50
27 Markus Witting .08 .25
28 Axel Kammerer .08 .25
29 Dave Flanagan .08 .25

30 Ilpo Kauhanen .20 .50
31 Johan SÃ¶lle .08 .25
32 Ambrosius Fichtner .08 .25
33 David St. Pierre .08 .25
34 Mathias Hart .08 .25
35 Franz Demmel .08 .25
36 Markus Feierabend .08 .25
37 Florian Zeller .08 .25
38 Sven Valenti .08 .25
39 Christian Gegenfurtner .08 .25
40 Josef Schlickenrieder .08 .25
41 SC Bietigheim-Bissingen Team Card .02 .10
42 David Belitski .20 .50
43 Frank Appel .08 .25
44 Markus Rohde .08 .25
45 Milos Vanik .08 .25
46 Marc Mundil .08 .25
47 Ulrich Liebsch .08 .25
48 Darren Ritchie .08 .25
49 Mike Bader .08 .25
50 Daniel Held .08 .25
51 Andrej Jaufmann .08 .25
52 Tim Leahy .08 .25
53 Martin Ancicka .08 .25
54 Christian Baader .08 .25
55 Craig Teeple .08 .25
56 Ralf StÃ¤rk .08 .25
57 Andreas Naumann .08 .25
58 Stephan Sinner .08 .25
59 Timo Nykopp .08 .25
60 Vaclav Drobny .08 .25
61 Thomas Mieszkowski .08 .25
62 Tom Pokel .08 .25
63 Braunlager EHC Harz Team Card .02 .10
64 Jarno Miikkulainen .20 .50
65 Peter Lundmark .20 .50
66 Josef Beppi Eckmair .08 .25
67 Douglas Murray .08 .25
68 Chris Clarke .08 .25
69 Ron Gaudet .08 .25
70 Sven Gerike .08 .25
71 Marek Gajewski .08 .25
72 Markus Draxler .08 .25
73 Frederik Andersson .08 .25
74 Timo Gschwill .08 .25
75 Georg Gailer .08 .25
76 Frank Richardt .08 .25
77 Johan Silfwerplatz .08 .25
78 Marcus Bleicher .08 .25
79 Anton Krinner .08 .25
80 Sebastian Buchwieser .08 .25
81 Bastian Niedermeier .08 .25
82 Anton Raubal .08 .25
83 Peter Gailer .08 .25
84 Düsseldorfer EG Team Card .02 .10
85 Chad Biafore .20 .50
86 Fabian BrÃ¤nnström .20 .50
87 Zdenek Travnicek .08 .25
88 Victor Gordiouk .08 .25
89 Leo Stefan .08 .25
90 Till Feser .08 .25
91 Andreas Pokorny .08 .25
92 Andreas Brockmann .08 .25
93 Ralf Reisinger .08 .25
94 Marc Dillmann .08 .25
95 Sergej Sorokin .08 .25
96 Peter Franke .08 .25
97 Udo Schmid .08 .25
98 Rafael Jedamzik .08 .25
99 Jouni Vento .08 .25
100 Torsten Kunz .08 .25
101 Sebastian Odenthal .08 .25
102 Anders Gozzi .08 .25
103 Maurizio Mansi .08 .25
104 Boris Lingemann .08 .25
105 Czeslaw Panek .08 .25
106 EHC Freiburg Team Card .02 .10
107 Rostislav Haas .20 .50
108 Alexander Semak .08 .25
109 Oleg Znarok .08 .25
110 David Danner .08 .25
111 Igor Dorochin .08 .25
112 Tobias Samendinger .08 .25
113 Ravil Khaidarov .08 .25
114 Evgeni Sultanowitsch .08 .25
115 Thomas Jetter .08 .25
116 Rudolf GorgenlÃ¤nder .08 .25
117 Andrej Strakhov .08 .25
118 Vitalij Grossmann .08 .25
119 Max Bauer .08 .25
120 Peter Mares .08 .25
121 Josef Peroutka .08 .25
122 Peter Precan .08 .25
123 Michael Vasicek .08 .25
124 Patrick Vozar .08 .25
125 Frantisek Frosch .08 .25
126 Thomas Dolak sen. .08 .25
127 Grefrather EV Team Card .02 .10
128 Frank Gentges .20 .50
129 Jochen Hecker .08 .25
130 Dirk Kuhnekath .08 .25
131 Bill Trew .08 .25
132 Thomas Popiesch .08 .25
133 Christoph Kleckers .08 .25
134 Henrik Hölscher .08 .25
135 Arno Brux .08 .25
136 Ashlin Halfnight .08 .25
137 Nolan McDonald .08 .25
138 Gilbert Schröder .08 .25
139 Nicklas Norlander .08 .25
140 Steve Smillie .08 .25
141 Tobias Grossecker .08 .25
142 Marcel Sakac .08 .25
143 Elmar Schmitz .08 .25
144 Hamburg Crocodiles Team Card .02 .10
145 Alexander Genze .08 .25
146 Derek Booth .08 .25
147 Alexander Engel .08 .25
148 John Johnson .08 .25
149 Jason Dunham .08 .25
150 Mike Millar .08 .25
151 Jay Luknowsky .08 .25
152 Andy Pritchard .08 .25
153 Mark Mahon .08 .25
154 Patrick Pysz .08 .25
155 Karsten Mende .08 .25
156 Phil Bourque .20 .50
157 Jürgen Trattner .08 .25
158 Carsten Solbach .08 .25
159 Maurice Lemay .30 .75
160 Jayson Meyer .08 .25
161 Marius Cissewski .08 .25
162 Christoph Sandner .08 .25
163 Harald Waibel .08 .25
164 Mario Gehrig .08 .25
165 Ross Yates .08 .25
166 Heilbronner EC Team Card .02 .10
167 Mikael Granlund .20 .50
168 Alexander Schuster .08 .25
169 Niklas Rinaldo .08 .25
170 Todd Sparks .08 .25
171 Thomas SchÃ¤dler .08 .25
172 Martin Williams .08 .25
173 Kenneth Filbey .08 .25
174 Ronny Martin .08 .25
175 Henri Marcoux .08 .25
176 Christian Martin .08 .25
177 Felix Feeser .08 .25
178 Brad Scott .08 .25
179 Alexander Semjonov .08 .25
180 Michael Rumrich .08 .25
181 Layne Roland .08 .25
182 Björn Barta .08 .25
183 Markus Eberl .08 .25
184 Rainer Suchan .08 .25
185 Johan Lindh .08 .25
186 Gary Prior .08 .25
187 ERC Ingolstadt Team Card .02 .10
188 Marco Thommes .08 .25
189 Stephane Julien .08 .25
190 Agostino Casale .08 .25
191 Kevin Ryan .08 .25
192 Harald SchÃ¤fler .08 .25
193 Markus Welz .08 .25
194 Wolfgang Fries .08 .25
195 Petr Bares .08 .25
196 Thomas Daffner .08 .25
197 Clayton Young .08 .25
198 Samuel Groleau .08 .25
199 Philippe DeRouville .30 .75
200 Cory Holden .08 .25
201 Sven Zywitza .08 .25
202 Frank Kannewurf .08 .25
203 Fabian Dahlem .08 .25
204 Jürgen Simon .08 .25
205 Roland Timoschuk .08 .25
206 Glenn Goodall .40 1.00
207 Giacinto Boni .08 .25
208 Iserlohner EC Team Card .02 .10
209 Cory Laylin .08 .25
210 Oliver Bernhardt .08 .25
211 Robert Gratza .08 .25
212 Collin Danielsmeier .08 .25
213 Pat Mikesch .08 .25
214 Tomas Martinec .08 .25
215 Teal Fowler .08 .25
216 Michael Hackert .08 .25
217 Mike Muller .08 .25
218 Oliver Hackert .08 .25
219 Peter Hellmann .08 .25
220 Steve Potvin .08 .25
221 Torsten Fendt .08 .25
222 Manuel Kofler .08 .25
223 Lars Müller .08 .25
224 Elvis Beslagic .08 .25
225 Ronny Arendt .08 .25
226 Christian Franz .08 .25
227 Ian Wood .20 .50
228 Greg Poss .08 .25
229 EHC Neuwied Team Card .02 .10
230 Juri Stumpf .08 .25
231 Dean Fedorchuk .08 .25
232 Andrej Teljukin .08 .25
233 Alexander Andrievsky .08 .25
234 Ladislav Strompf .08 .25
235 Richard Baptist .08 .25
236 Otto Keresztes .08 .25
237 Klaus Micheller .08 .25
238 Todd Johnson .08 .25
239 Mario Naster .08 .25
240 Jens Hergt .08 .25
241 Falk Ozellis .08 .25
242 Craig Streu .08 .25
243 Marc Gronau .08 .25
244 Ole Kopitz .08 .25
245 Vitalij Semenchenko .08 .25
246 Radek Vit .08 .25
247 Sinuhe Wallinheimo .30 .75
248 Michael Weinfurter .08 .25
249 Petteri Lehmussaari .08 .25
250 GEC Nordhorn Team Card .02 .10
251 Christian von Trzcinski .08 .25
252 Jedrzej Kasperczyk .08 .25
253 Peter Kwasigroch .08 .25
254 Christian Spaan .08 .25
255 Gabriel Krüger .08 .25
256 Moritz Schmidt .08 .25
257 Alexej Pogodin .08 .25
258 Markus Kempf .08 .25
259 Sergej Zvyagin .08 .25
260 Christian Brittig .08 .25
261 Juris Opulskis .08 .25
262 Andreas Morczinietz .08 .25
263 Andrzej Hanisz .08 .25
264 Sami Leinonen .08 .25
265 Sergej Tchoudinov .08 .25
266 Mikka Kemppi .08 .25
267 Anton Weissgerber .08 .25
268 SC Riessersee Team Card .02 .10
269 Michael Pump .08 .25
270 Georg Güttler .08 .25
271 Christoph Klotz .08 .25
272 Tim Regan .08 .25
273 Alexander Wedl .08 .25
274 Mika Puhakka .08 .25
275 Martin Holzer .08 .25
276 Hubert Buchwieser .08 .25
277 Michael Raubal .08 .25
278 Josef Lehner .08 .25
279 Christian Mayr .08 .25
280 Tobias Netter .08 .25
281 Tom OÂ´Grady .08 .25
282 Samuli Peltosara .08 .25
283 Leonhard Wild .08 .25
284 Florian Brandl .08 .25
285 Duane Dennis .08 .25
286 Mark Zdan .08 .25
287 Florian Storf .08 .25
288 Ron Chyzowski .08 .25
289 ES Weisswasser Team Card .02 .10
290 Torsten Hanusch .08 .25
291 Daniel Sikorski .08 .25
292 Alexej Jefimov .08 .25
293 Alexandre Vinogradov .08 .25
294 Ronny Reddo .08 .25
295 Frank Peschke .08 .25
296 Ronny Glaser .08 .25
297 Jörgen Hermansson .08 .25
298 Robert Brezina .08 .25
299 Sven Steinecke .08 .25
300 David Musial .08 .25
301 Pekka Virta .08 .25
302 Thomas Knobloch .08 .25
303 Daniel Bartell .08 .25
304 Falk Herzig .08 .25
305 Dimitri Alekhin .08 .25
306 Joakim Wiberg .08 .25
307 Martin Wiita .08 .25
308 Jörg Pohling .08 .25
309 Bror Hansson .08 .25
310 EC Wilhelmshaven-Stickhausen Team Card .02 .10
311 Vadim Finko .08 .25
312 Harald Hebig .08 .25
313 Kai Ahlroth .08 .25
314 Boris Blank .08 .25
315 Eduard Lewandowski .08 .25
316 Alexander Rusch .08 .25
317 Dimitry Dudarev .08 .25
318 Vitali Janke .08 .25
319 Ilia Stachenkov .08 .25
320 Jürgen Schaal .08 .25
321 Andrej Dmitriev .08 .25
322 Iiro ItÃ¤mies .08 .25
323 Sergej Jaschin .08 .25
324 Martin Ekrt .08 .25
325 Marian Horvarth .08 .25
326 Mario Schüssel .08 .25
327 Alexander Herbst .08 .25
328 Andrej Naumann .08 .25
329 Peter Kalinowski .08 .25
330 Anatoli Antipov .08 .25

2000-01 German Berlin Polar Bears Postcards

COMPLETE SET (22) 10.00 20.00
1 John Chabot .40 1.00
2 Derek Cormier .40 1.00
3 Rob Cowie .40 1.00
4 Uli Egen .40 1.00
5 Sven Felski .40 1.00
6 Marc Fortier .40 1.00
7 Alexander Godynyuk .40 1.00
8 Rich Gosselin .40 1.00
9 Peter Hammarstrom .40 1.00
10 Todd Harkins .40 1.00
11 Alex Hicks .40 1.00
12 Alexander Jung .40 1.00
13 Daniel Laperriere .40 1.00
14 Rob Leask .40 1.00
15 Martin Lindman .40 1.00
16 Derek Mayer .40 1.00
17 Klaus Merk .40 1.00
18 Nico Pyka .40 1.00
19 Sandy Smith .40 1.00
20 Jeff Tomlinson .40 1.00
21 Lubomir Vaic .40 1.00
22 Steve Walker .40 1.00

2000-01 German DEL Upper Deck

COMPLETE SET (240) 15.00 40.00
1 Gordon Hynes .10 .25
2 Dave Tomlinson .20 .50
3 Stephane Richer .05 .15
4 Steve Junker .05 .15
5 Wayne Hynes .05 .15
6 Bradley Bergen .05 .15
7 Devin Edgerton .05 .15
8 Ron Pasco .05 .15
9 Francois Groleau .05 .15
10 Todd Hlushko .20 .50
11 Mike Rosati .20 .50
12 Chris Straube .05 .15
13 Jean-Francois Jomphe .20 .50
14 Jan Alston .05 .15
15 Sven Rampf .05 .15
16 Sergej Vostrikov .05 .15
17 Igor Maslennikov .05 .15
18 Reemt Pyka .05 .15
19 Dave Chyzowski .20 .50
20 Arnaud Briand .05 .15
21 Sergej Stas .05 .15
22 Sebastian Klenner .05 .15
23 Vasily Pankov .05 .15
24 Duane Moeser .05 .15
25 Jason Muzzatti .40 1.00
26 Herbert Hohenberger .20 .50
27 Ryan Savoia .05 .15
28 Jim Camazzola .05 .15
29 Tommy Jakobsen .05 .15
30 Andrei Mezin .40 1.00
31 Markus Pottinger .05 .15
32 Thomas Sjogren .05 .15
33 Jim Hiller .05 .15
34 Pavel Gross .05 .15
35 Robert Guillet .05 .15
36 Udo Dohler .05 .15
37 Anders Huusko .05 .15
38 Heinz Ehlers .05 .15
39 Gregory Johnston .20 .50
40 Petri Liimatainen .05 .15
41 Johan Norgren .05 .15
42 Martin Ulrich .05 .15
43 Iain Fraser .10 .25
44 Gary Shuchuk .10 .25
45 Torsten Kienass .10 .25
46 Niki Mondt .05 .15
47 Bernd Kuhnhauser .05 .15
48 Craig Reichert .10 .25
49 Niclas Sundblad .10 .25
50 Sergey Sorokin .05 .15
51 Peter Franke .05 .15
52 Ivan Droppa .05 .15
53 Christopher Bartolone .05 .15
54 Leo Stefan .05 .15
55 Victor Gordiouk .10 .25
56 Lorenz Funk .05 .15
57 Boris Lingemann .05 .15
58 Andrei Trefilov .20 .50
59 Nico Pyka .05 .15
60 Alexander Jung .05 .15
61 Alexander Godynyuk .10 .25
62 Derek Mayer .10 .25
63 Sven Felski .05 .15
64 Marc Fortier .10 .25
65 John Chabot .20 .50
66 Derek Cormier .05 .15
67 Steve Walker .05 .15
68 Lubomir Vaic .10 .25
69 Klaus Merk .20 .50
70 Dan Laperriere .20 .50
71 Rob Cowie .05 .15
72 Martin Lindman .05 .15
73 Chris Govedaris .20 .50
74 Michael Bresagk .05 .15
75 Leonardo Conti .05 .15
76 Robin Doyle .05 .15
77 Toni Porkka .05 .15
78 John Walker .05 .15
79 Jean-Marc Richard .05 .15
80 Jason Ruff .10 .25
81 Jason Cirone .10 .25
82 Jose Charbonneau .10 .25
83 Victor Gervais .05 .15
84 Patrice Lefebvre .20 .50
85 Martin Gendron .20 .50
86 Ken Quinney .20 .50
87 Keith Aldridge .20 .50
88 Eldon Reddick .20 .50
89 Oscar Ackestrom .05 .15
90 Mattias Loof .05 .15
91 Egor Bashkatov .10 .25
92 Mark Kosturik .05 .15
93 Wallace Schreiber .20 .50
94 Dominic Lavoie .10 .25
95 Rob Murphy .10 .25
96 Pavel Cagas .05 .15
97 Igor Chibirev .10 .25
98 Kevin Grant .05 .15
99 Jan Munster .05 .15
100 Chris Snell .10 .25
101 Patrik Zetterberg .05 .15
102 Colin Beardsmore .05 .15
103 Calle Carlsson .05 .15
104 Tomas Martinec .05 .15
105 Teal Fowler .05 .15
106 Alexander Kuzminski .05 .15
107 Terence Campbell .05 .15
108 Duane Derksen .20 .50
109 Peter Roed .05 .15
110 Torsten Fendt .05 .15
111 Shawn Anderson .05 .15
112 Manuel Kofler .05 .15
113 Radek Toth .05 .15
114 Steve Potvin .05 .15
115 Brent Tully .05 .15
116 Ted Crowley .05 .15
117 Pat Mikesch .05 .15
118 Stephane Robitaille .05 .15
119 Francois Guay .05 .15
120 Andreas Loth .05 .15
121 Patrice Tardif .20 .50
122 Scott Levins .05 .15
123 Joachim Appel .05 .15
124 Chris Rogles .20 .50
125 Thomas Daffner .05 .15
126 Klaus Kathan .05 .15
127 Sylvain Turgeon .10 .25
128 Andrew Verner .20 .50
129 Bruno Zarrillo .05 .15
130 Dwayne Norris .20 .50
131 Christoph Paepke .05 .15
132 Mirko Ludemann .05 .15
133 Andreas Lupzig .05 .15
134 Jason Young .10 .25
135 Joseph Heiss .20 .50
136 Tomas Forslund .10 .25
137 Andre Faust .05 .15
138 Tino Boos .05 .15
139 John Miner .10 .25
140 Dave McIlwain .20 .50
141 Dieter Kalt .05 .15
142 Corey Millen .20 .50
143 Marc Hussey .05 .15
144 Brent Severyn .20 .50
145 Christian Ehrhoff .05 .15
146 Neil Eisenhut .10 .25
147 Ilja Vorobjev .05 .15
148 Shayne Wright .05 .15
149 Dan Lambert .20 .50
150 Brad Purdie .05 .15
151 Christoph Brandner .05 .15
152 Roger Nordstrom .05 .15
153 Jeff Christian .10 .25
154 Karel Lang .05 .15
155 Thomas Brandl .05 .15
156 Martin Sychra .05 .15
157 Jason McBain .05 .15
158 Ralph Intranuovo .20 .50
159 Jarkko Savijoki .05 .15
160 Marc Savard .20 .50
161 Roman Meluzin .05 .15
162 Todd Simon .10 .25
163 Jean-Francois Quintin .10 .25
164 Scott Pearson .20 .50
165 Kevin Wortman .05 .15
166 Geoff Sarjeant .20 .50
167 Leonard Wild .05 .15
168 Erich Goldmann .20 .50
169 Marc Laniel .20 .50
170 Esa Tikkanen .75 2.00
171 Hans Lodin .05 .15
172 Rick Girard .05 .15
173 Christian Kunast .05 .15
174 Simon Wheeldon .15 .40
175 Shane Peacock .05 .15
176 Christoph Schubert .05 .15
177 Peter Douris .10 .25
178 Alexander Serikow .20 .50
179 Peter Larsson .05 .15
180 Thomas Dolak .05 .15
181 Jorg Handrick .05 .15
182 Jason Herter .10 .25
183 Andrew Schneider .10 .25
184 Parris Duffus .20 .50
185 Luciano Borsato .10 .25
186 Jurgen Rumrich .05 .15
187 Dimitri Dudik .05 .15
188 Alexander Cherbayev .10 .25
189 Martin Jiranek .05 .15
190 Martin Reichel .05 .15
191 Mario Chitarroni .05 .15
192 Jason Miller .05 .15
193 Bjorn Nord .05 .15
194 Kevin Miehm .10 .25
195 Marc Seliger .20 .50
196 Daniel Kunce .05 .15
197 Paul Stanton .10 .25
198 Peter Gulda .05 .15
199 Christian Kohmann .05 .15
200 Mika Arvaja .05 .15
201 Carsten Gosdeck .05 .15
202 Aleksandrs Kercs .05 .15
203 Alexandre Andrievski .10 .25
204 Robert Hock .05 .15
205 Josef Zajic .05 .15
206 Marek Stebnicki .05 .15
207 Andrej Kovalev .05 .15
208 Ladislav Karabin .05 .15
209 Peter Draisaitl .05 .15
210 Sinuhe Wallinheimo .10 .25
211 Jergus Baca .05 .15
212 Peter Allen .05 .15
213 Alexander Duck .05 .15
214 Marcel Goc .60 1.50
215 Jens Stramkowski .05 .15
216 Mark MacKay .10 .25
217 Vadym Slivchenko .05 .15
218 Jacek Plachta .05 .15
219 Alexei Yegorov .20 .50
220 Patrik Augusta .05 .15
221 Brad Schlegel .10 .25
222 Andreas Renz .05 .15
223 Thomas Greilinger .05 .15
224 Ian Gordon .10 .25
225 Mike Bullard .20 .50
226 Robert Muller .05 .15
227 Mike Pellegrims .05 .15
228 Mike Casselman .05 .15
229 Leonardo Soccio .05 .15
230 Andreas Pokorny .10 .25
231 Tim Schnelle .05 .15
232 Daniel Kreutzer .05 .15
233 Tobias Abstreiter .05 .15
234 Tomas Hartogs .05 .15
235 Stephane Barin .05 .15
236 Boris Rousson .20 .50
237 Mike Kennedy .10 .25
238 John Craighead .05 .15
239 Marc Pethke .05 .15
240 Markus Janka .05 .15

2000-01 German DEL Upper Deck All-Star Class

COMPLETE SET (10) 8.00 20.00
A1 Martin Jiranek .80 2.00
A2 Patrice Lefebvre 1.60 4.00
A3 Peter Douris .80 2.00
A4 Sergej Vostrikov .80 2.00
A5 Gregory Johnston 1.20 3.00
A6 Chris Govedaris .80 2.00
A7 Mike Casselman .80 2.00
A8 Corey Millen 1.20 3.00
A9 Shawn Anderson 1.20 3.00
A10 Sylvain Turgeon 1.20 3.00

2000-01 German DEL Upper Deck Game Jersey

COMPLETE SET (16) 160.00 400.00
BZ Bruno Zarrillo 16.00 40.00
DM Duane Moeser 10.00 25.00
JB Jergus Baca 12.00 30.00
JR Jurgen Rumrich 10.00 25.00
LE Leonard Soccio 12.00 30.00
LS Leo Stefan 12.00 30.00
MF Marc Fortier 12.00 30.00
MM Mark MacKay 12.00 30.00
MS Marc Savard 20.00 50.00
PG Pavel Gross 12.00 30.00
SR Stephane Richer 12.00 30.00
SW Simon Wheeldon 16.00 40.00
TA Tobias Abstreiter 16.00 40.00
TF Teal Fowler 12.00 30.00
TH Tomas Hartogs 12.00 30.00
TP Toni Porkka 10.00 25.00

2000-01 German DEL Upper Deck Profiles

COMPLETE SET (11) 8.00 20.00
P1 Jan Alston .80 2.00
P2 Andrei Mezin 2.00 5.00
P3 John Chabot 1.20 3.00
P4 Wallace Schreiber 1.20 3.00
P5 Shane Peacock .80 2.00
P6 Mike Bullard 1.20 3.00
P7 Mirko Ludemann .80 2.00
P8 Boris Rousson 1.25 3.00
P9 Andrej Kovalev .80 2.00
P10 Mike Pellegrims .40 1.00
P11 Andrei Trefilov .80 2.00

2000-01 German DEL Upper Deck Star Attractions

COMPLETE SET (10) 10.00 25.00
S1 Ivan Droppa 1.25 3.00
S2 Gordon Hynes 1.20 3.00
S3 Marek Stebnicki 1.20 3.00
S4 Daniel Kreutzer 1.20 3.00
S5 Thomas Brandl 1.20 3.00
S6 Esa Tikkanen 2.00 5.00
S7 Bob Sweeney 1.20 3.00
S8 Paul Stanton 1.20 3.00
S9 Dave Tomlinson 1.20 3.00
S10 Brent Severyn 2.00 5.00

2001-02 German Adler Mannheim Eagles Postcards

1 Robert Muller .75 2.00
2 Eric Charron .75 2.00
3 Devin Edgerton .75 2.00
4 Mike Rosati .75 2.00
5 Chris Straube .75 2.00
6 Francois Groleau .75 2.00
7 Rene Corbet .75 2.00
8 Stephane Richer 1.25 3.00
9 Stefan Ustorf .75 2.00

2001-02 German Berlin Polar Bears Postcards

COMPLETE SET (27) 10.00 25.00
1 Keith Aldridge .40 1.00
2 Alex Barta .40 1.00
3 Boris Blank .40 1.00
4 David Cooper .40 1.00
5 Patrick Czajka .40 1.00
6 Uli Egen .40 1.00
7 Sven Felski .40 1.00
8 Marc Fortier .40 1.00
9 Daniel Laperriere .40 1.00
10 Steve Larouche .40 1.00
11 Rob Leask .40 1.00
12 Scott Levins .40 1.00
13 Eduard Lewandoski .40 1.00
14 Martin Lindman .40 1.00
15 Chris Marinucci .40 1.00
16 Klaus Merk .40 1.00
17 Hartmut Nickel .40 1.00
18 Fabio Patrzek .40 1.00
19 Ed Patterson .40 1.00
20 Nico Pyka .40 1.00
21 David Roberts .40 1.00
22 Jan Schertz .40 1.00
23 Richard Shulmistra .40 1.00
24 Tom Skinner .40 1.00
25 Lee Sorochan .40 1.00
26 Jeff Tomlinson .40 1.00
27 Steve Walker .40 1.00

2001-02 German DEL Upper Deck

COMPLETE SET (270) 15.00 40.00
1 Igor Alexandrov .08 .20
2 Marc Beaucage .15 .40
3 Eric Dylla .20 .50
4 Mickey Elick .15 .40
5 Magnus Eriksson .08 .20
6 Jakub Ficenec .20 .50
7 Robert Guillet .08 .20
8 Tommy Jakobsen .08 .20
9 Christian Lukes .08 .20
10 Igor Maslennikov .08 .20
11 Duanne Moeser .15 .40
12 Vasily Pankov .08 .20
13 Reemt Pyka .08 .20
14 Reid Simonton .15 .40
15 Sergej Vostrikov .08 .20
16 Alexander Cherbayev .08 .20
17 Heinz Ehlers .08 .20
18 Ronny Arendt .08 .20
19 Andrej Vassilyev .08 .20
20 Francois Leroux .20 .50
21 Andrei Mezin .40 1.00
22 Jan Münster .08 .20
23 Markus Pöttinger .08 .20
24 Patrick Senger .08 .20
25 Aleksandrs Kercs .08 .20
26 Gordon Hynes .20 .50
27 Greg Andrusak .20 .50
28 Vjatcheslav Fanduls .08 .20
29 Yvon Corriveau .20 .50
30 Frederik Ã–berg .08 .20
31 Keith Aldridge .20 .50
32 David Cooper .15 .40
33 Sven Felski .08 .20
34 Marc Fortier .20 .50
35 Dan Laperriere .20 .50
36 Steve LaRouche .20 .50
37 Scott Levins .20 .50
38 Chris Marinucci .20 .50
39 Klaus Merk .20 .50
40 Nico Pyka .08 .20
41 David Roberts .20 .50
42 Jan Schertz .08 .20
43 Richard Shulmistra .20 .50
44 Lee Sorochan .20 .50
45 Steve Walker .15 .40
46 Chris Bartolone .15 .40
48 Ivan Droppa .08 .20
49 Neil Eisenhut .15 .40
50 Tore Vikingstad .08 .20
51 Torsten Kienass .08 .20
52 Bernd Kühnhauser .08 .20
53 Trond Magnussen .08 .20
54 Mike Pellegrims .15 .40
55 Jean-Francois Quintin .15 .40
56 Ralf Reisinger .08 .20
57 Leo Stefan .08 .20
58 Andrej Trefilov .20 .50
59 Martin Ulrich .08 .20
60 Rainer Zerwesz .08 .20
61 Frank Appel .15 .40
62 Lars Brüggemann .08 .20
63 Mike Casselman .15 .40
64 Ted Crowley .15 .40
65 Liam Garvey .08 .20
66 Erich Goldmann .20 .50
67 Todd Hawkins .15 .40
68 Ralph Intranuovo .20 .50
69 Martin Sychra .08 .20
70 Riku-Petteri Lehtonen .08 .20
71 Doug MacDonald .15 .40
72 Marc Savard .20 .50
73 Todd Simon .15 .40
74 Jimmy Waite .30 .75
75 Craig Woodcroft .15 .40
76 Michael Bresagk .08 .20
77 Brent Cullaton .15 .40
78 Rob Doyle .08 .20
79 Greg Evtushevski .15 .40
80 Victor Gervais .15 .40
81 Rick Girard .15 .40
82 Stewart Malgunas .15 .40
83 Rob Pearson .20 .50
84 Eldon Reddick .20 .50
85 Ian Fraser .15 .40
86 Alexander Selivanov .08 .20
87 Vadim Slivchenko .08 .20
88 Chris Snell .15 .40
89 Brent Tully .15 .40
90 John Walker .15 .40
91 Oscar Ackeström .20 .50
92 Egor Bashkatov .08 .20
93 Igor Chibirev .08 .20
94 Kevin Grant .15 .40
95 David Haas .15 .40
96 Peter Jakobsson .08 .20
97 Dominic Lavoie .20 .50
98 Mattias Lööf .08 .20
99 Rob Murphy .15 .40
100 Mark Pederson .15 .40
101 Wally Schreiber .15 .40
102 Len Soccio .20 .50
103 Andrew Verner .20 .50
104 Steve Wilson .15 .40
105 Patrik Zetterberg .08 .20
106 Doug Ast .15 .40
107 Colin Beardsmore .15 .40
108 Guy Dupuis .15 .40
109 Oliver Bernhardt .08 .20
110 Rusty Fitzgerald .20 .50
111 Terry Hollinger .20 .50
112 Kimmo Kapanen .08 .20
113 Dmitrij Kotschnew .08 .20
114 Cory Laylin .15 .40
115 Paul Dyck .20 .50
116 Tomas Martinec .08 .20
117 Colin Danielsmeier .08 .20
118 David Musial .15 .40
119 Andreas Pokorny .08 .20
120 Sean Tallaire .15 .40
121 Tobias Abstreiter .20 .50
122 Thomas Daffner .08 .20
123 Doug Derraugh .15 .40
124 Leonid Fatikov .08 .20
125 Tommie Hartogs .08 .20
126 Klaus Kathan .08 .20
127 Ilpo Kauhanen .20 .50
128 Ã–rjan Lindmark .08 .20
129 Andreas Loth .08 .20
130 Jeff MacLeod .15 .40
131 Pat Mikesch .08 .20
132 Jochen Molling .08 .20
133 Brent Peterson .20 .50
134 Shayne Wright .15 .40
135 Jeff Tory .15 .40
136 Tino Boos .08 .20
137 AndrÃ© Faust .20 .50
138 Alex Hicks .20 .50
139 Petri Liimatainen .08 .20
140 Mirko Lüdemann .20 .50
141 Jörg Mayr .08 .20
142 Dave McLlwain .20 .50
143 Corey Millen .20 .50
144 John Miner .15 .40
145 Dwayne Norris .15 .40
146 Toni Porkka .08 .20
147 Andreas Renz .08 .20
148 Chris Rogles .20 .50
149 Niklas Sundblad .20 .50
150 Jason Young .15 .40
151 Patrik Augusta .08 .20
152 StÃ©phane Barin .08 .20
153 Thomas Brandl .08 .20
154 Steffen Ziesche .08 .20
156 Jeff Christian .15 .40
157 Gilbert Dionne .20 .50
158 Mario Doyon .20 .50
159 Daniel Kunce .08 .20
160 Dan Lambert .30 .75
161 Roger Nordström .08 .20
162 Brad Purdie .20 .50
163 Gary Shuchuk .20 .50
164 Sergej Stas .08 .20
165 Phil von Stefenelli .20 .50
166 Brad Bergen .15 .40
167 Fabian BrÃ¤nnström .08 .20
168 Devin Edgerton .15 .40
169 Todd Hlushko .20 .50
170 Wayne Hynes .15 .40
171 FranÃ§ois Groleau .15 .40
172 Michel Picard .20 .50
173 Yves Racine .20 .50
174 StÃ©phane Richer .15 .40
175 Andy Roach .15 .40
176 Mike Rosati .30 .75
177 Mike Stevens .15 .40
178 Dave Tomlinson .15 .40
179 Steve Junker .15 .40
180 Stefan Ustorf .20 .50
181 Kent Fearns .15 .40
182 Jason Herter .15 .40
183 Mike Kennedy .20 .50
184 Derek King .20 .50
185 Christian Künast .08 .20
186 Hans Lodin .08 .20
187 David Oliver .15 .40
188 Shane Peacock .15 .40
189 Derek PlantÃ© .20 .50
190 Johan RosÃ©n .08 .20
191 Boris Rousson .20 .50
192 Andy Schneider .15 .40
193 Peter Douris .20 .50
194 Heiko Smazal .08 .20
195 Simon Wheeldon .20 .50
196 Shawn Anderson .15 .40
197 Luciano Borsato .20 .50
198 Frederic Chabot .60 1.50
199 Mario Chitarroni .20 .50
200 Kevin Dahl .15 .40
201 David Emma .20 .50
202 Martin Jiranek .08 .20
203 Chris Luongo .20 .50
204 Guy Lehoux .20 .50
205 Jacek Plachta .08 .20
206 Martin Reichel .08 .20

207 Jürgen Rumrich .08 .20
208 Christian Schönmoser .08 .20
209 Jan Nemecek .08 .20
210 Bruno Zarrillo .20 .50
211 Andreas Lupzig .08 .20
212 Jergus Baca .08 .20
213 Derek Cormier .15 .40
214 John Craighead .30 .75
215 Jesper Damgaard .08 .20
216 Peter Gulda .08 .20
217 Robert Hock .08 .20
218 Martin Hohenberger .08 .20
219 Ladislav Karabin .08 .20
220 Christian Kohmann .08 .20
221 Andrej Kovalev .08 .20
222 Jason McBain .15 .40
223 Andrei Teljukin .08 .20
224 Sinuhe Wallinheimo .20 .50
225 Josef Zajic .08 .20
226 Micah Aivazoff .30 .75
227 Peter Allen .15 .40
228 Mike Bullard .20 .50
229 Dave Chyzowski .20 .50
230 Eric Dubois .15 .40
231 Ian Gordon .15 .40
232 Markus Janka .08 .20
233 Mark MacKay .20 .50
234 Neal Martin .15 .40
235 Jeff Nelson .15 .40
236 Jackson Penney .15 .40
237 Kent Simpson .15 .40
238 Jason Deleurme .15 .40
239 Gerhard Unterluggauer .08 .20
240 Darcy Werenka .20 .50
241 Andreas Morczinietz .08 .20
242 Christian Rohde .08 .20
243 Jonas Lanier .08 .20
244 Boris Blank .08 .20
245 Eduard Lewandowski .08 .20
246 Niki Mondt .08 .20
247 Leonard Wild .08 .20
248 Leonardo Conti .08 .20
249 Philip Schumacher .08 .20
250 Björn Leonhardt .20 .50
251 Christian Franz .20 .50
252 Manuel Kofler .20 .50
253 Daniel Kreutzer .20 .50
254 Markus Guggemos .20 .50
255 Dimitri PAtzold .20 .50
256 Benjamin Hinterstocker .20 .50
257 Christian Ehrhoff .40 1.00
258 Adrian Grygiel .20 .50
259 Benjamin Voigt .20 .50
260 Robert Müller .20 .50
261 Dennis Seidenberg .60 1.50
262 Peter Abstreiter .20 .50
263 Christoph Schubert .20 .50
264 Andrej Strakhov .20 .50
265 Benjamin Hecker .20 .50
266 Vitalij Aab .20 .50
267 Carsten Gosdeck .20 .50
268 Lasse Kopitz .20 .50
269 Marcel Goc .75 2.00
270 Alexander Dück .20 .50

2001-02 German DEL Upper Deck Gate Attractions

COMPLETE SET (10) 10.00 25.00
GA1 Sergej Vostrikov 1.25 3.00
GA2 Aleksandrs Kercs 1.25 3.00
GA3 Sven Felski 1.25 3.00
GA4 Mark MacKay 1.25 3.00
GA5 Alexander Selivanov 1.25 3.00
GA6 Len Soccio 2.00 5.00
GA7 Ivan Droppa 1.25 3.00
GA8 Gilbert Dionne 2.00 5.00
GA9 Stefan Ustorf 1.25 3.00
GA10 Jason Miller 1.25 3.00

2001-02 German DEL Upper Deck Goalies in Action

COMPLETE SET (10) 20.00 40.00
G1 Andrei Mezin 2.50 6.00
G2 Klaus Merk 2.00 5.00
G3 Andrej Trefilov 2.50 6.00
G4 Andrew Verner 2.00 5.00
G5 Chris Rogles 2.00 5.00
G6 Roger Nordstrom 2.00 5.00
G7 Mike Rosati 2.00 5.00
G8 Christian Kunast 2.00 5.00
G9 Marc Seliger 3.00 8.00
G10 Sinuhe Wallinheimo 2.00 5.00

2001-02 German DEL Upper Deck Jerseys

COMPLETE SET (6) 150.00 400.00
AMJ Andrei Mezin 20.00 50.00
ATJ Andrej Trefilov 12.00 30.00
AVJ Andrew Verner 12.00 30.00
CKJ Christian Kunast 8.00 20.00
CRJ Chris Rogles 12.00 30.00
ERJ Eldon Reddick 12.00 30.00
FCJ Frederic Chabot 20.00 50.00
GJ Ian Gordon 8.00 20.00
WJ Jimmy Waite 20.00 50.00
KKJ Kimmo Kapanen 8.00 20.00
FJ Leonid Fatikov 8.00 20.00
MEJ Magnus Eriksson 8.00 20.00
MRJ Mike Rosati 12.00 30.00
NJ Roger Nordstrom 8.00 20.00
SJ Richard Shulmistra 12.00 30.00
WJ Sinuhe Wallinheimo 12.00 30.00

2001-02 German DEL Upper Deck Skilled Stars

COMPLETE SET (11) 6.00 15.00
S1 Robert Hock .75 2.00
S2 David Cooper 1.25 3.00
S3 Brad Purdie 1.25 3.00
S4 Todd Simon .75 2.00
S5 Oscar Ackestrom .75 2.00
S6 Tomas Martinec .75 2.00
S7 Pat Mikesch .75 2.00
S8 Mirko Ludemann .75 2.00
S9 Stephane Richer .75 2.00
S10 Shane Peacock .75 2.00
S11 Paul Stanton .75 2.00

2002-03 German Adler Mannheim Eagles Postcards

1 Todd Hlushko .40 1.00
2 Thomas Schenkel .40 1.00
3 Danny Aus Den Birken .40 1.00
4 Mike Rosati .40 1.00
5 Thomas Fischer .40 1.00
6 Klaus Kathan .40 1.00
7 Sachar Blank .40 1.00
8 Yannic Seidenberg .40 1.00
9 Rico Rossi .40 1.00
10 Bill Stewart .40 1.00
11 Fabio Carciola .40 1.00
12 Rene Corbet .40 1.00
13 Sascha Goc .40 1.00
14 Nick Naumenko .40 1.00
15 Ilja Vorobiev .40 1.00
16 Steve Junker .40 1.00
17 Wayne Hynes .40 1.00
18 Devin Edgerton .40 1.00

2002-03 German Berlin Polar Bears Postcards

COMPLETE SET (28) 10.00 25.00
1 Keith Aldridge .40 1.00
2 Alex Barta .40 1.00
3 Marc Beaufait .40 1.00
4 Brad Bergen .40 1.00
5 Boris Blank .40 1.00
6 David Cooper .40 1.00
7 Yvon Corriveau .40 1.00
8 Kelly Fairchild .40 1.00
9 Sven Felski .40 1.00
10 John Gruden .40 1.00
11 Thorsten Heine .40 1.00
12 Martin Hoffmann .40 1.00
13 Oliver Jonas .40 1.00
14 Florian Katz .40 1.00
15 Florian Keller .40 1.00
16 Mark Kosick .40 1.00
17 Rob Leask .40 1.00
18 Klaus Merk .40 1.00
19 Hartmut Nickel .40 1.00
20 Pierre Page CO .40 1.00
21 Ricard Persson .40 1.00
22 Daniel Pyka .40 1.00
23 Nico Pyka .40 1.00
24 David Roberts .40 1.00
25 Rob Shearer .40 1.00
26 Richard Shulmistra .40 1.00
27 Jeff Tomlinson .40 1.00
28 Steve Walker .40 1.00

2002-03 German DEL City Press

COMPLETE SET (290) 50.00 100.00
1 Ronny Arendt .20 .50
2 Philippe Audet .20 .50
3 Bjorn Barta .20 .50
4 Frederic Bouchard .20 .50
6 Shawn Carter .20 .50
7 Igor Dorochin .20 .50
8 P.C. Drouin .40 1.00
9 Magnus Eriksson .20 .50
10 Thorsten Fendt .20 .50
11 Maxim Galanov .20 .50
12 Patrick Koslow .20 .50
13 Greg Leeb .40 1.00
14 Christian Lukes .20 .50
15 Shayne McCosh .20 .50
16 Duanne Moeser .20 .50
17 Christopher Oravec .20 .50
18 Reid Simonton .20 .50
19 Andrej Strakhov .20 .50
20 Chris Straube .20 .50
21 Sergej Vostrikov .20 .50
22 Keith Aldridge .20 .50
23 Alexander Barta .20 .50
24 Mark Beaufait .20 .50
25 Bradley Bergen .20 .50
26 Boris Blank .20 .50
27 David Cooper .20 .50
28 Yvon Corriveau .20 .50
29 Kelly Fairchild .20 .50
30 Sven Felski .20 .50
31 John Gruden .20 .50
32 Oliver Jonas .20 .50
33 Florian Keller .20 .50
34 Robert Leask .20 .50
35 Ricard Persson .20 .50
36 Nico Pyka .20 .50
37 David Roberts .20 .50
38 Rob Shearer .20 .50
39 Richard Shulmistra .20 .50
40 Jeff Tomlinson .20 .50
41 Steve Walker .20 .50
42 Marc Beaucage .20 .50
43 Fabian Brannstrom .20 .50
44 Jeff Christian .20 .50
45 Neil Eisenhut .20 .50
46 Jakub Ficenec .40 1.00
47 Michael Hackert .20 .50
48 Mathias Hart .20 .50
49 Tommy Jakobsen .20 .50
50 Alexander Jung .20 .50
51 Torsten Kienass .20 .50
52 Daniel Kreutzer .20 .50
53 Bernd Kuhnhauser .20 .50
54 Trond Magnussen .20 .50
55 Nikolaus Mondt .20 .50
56 Mike Pellegrims .20 .50
57 Markus Pottinger .20 .50
58 Jean-Francois Quintin .20 .50
59 Leo Stefan .20 .50
60 Andrei Trefilov .20 .50
61 Martin Ulrich .20 .50
62 Gerhard Unterluggauer .20 .50
63 Tore Vikingstad .20 .50
64 Rainer Zerwesz .20 .50
65 Greg Adams .20 .50
66 Pascal Appel .20 .50
67 Michael Bresagk .20 .50
68 Robert Busch .20 .50
69 Collin Danielsmeier .20 .50
70 Jason Dunham .20 .50
71 Rusty Fitzgerald .20 .50
72 Marc Fortier .20 .50
73 Robert Francz .20 .50
74 Matthias Frenzel .20 .50
75 Victor Gervais .20 .50
76 Rick Girard .20 .50
77 Cory Laylin .20 .50
78 Stewart Malgunas .20 .50
79 Jackson Penney .20 .50
80 Marc Pethke .20 .50
81 Stephane Richer .20 .50
82 Dominic Roussel .40 1.00
83 Christoph Sandner .20 .50
84 Chris Snell .20 .50
85 Paul Stanton .20 .50
86 Jonas Stopfgeshoff .20 .50
87 Peter Abstreiter .20 .50
88 Greg Andrusak .20 .50
89 Ted Crowley .20 .50
90 Thomas Dolak .20 .50
91 Ted Drury .20 .50
92 Bobby House .20 .50
93 Manuel Kofler .20 .50
94 Patrick Koppchen .20 .50
95 Christian Kunast .20 .50
96 Bob Lachance .20 .50
97 Jason Miller .20 .50
98 Jacek Plachta .20 .50
99 Boris Rousson .40 1.00
100 Andrew Schneider .20 .50
101 Heiko Smazal .20 .50
102 Mike Stevens .20 .50
103 David Sulkovsky .20 .50
104 Jeff Tory .20 .50
105 Christian Volk .20 .50
106 Phil von Stefenelli .20 .50
107 Gilbert Dionne .20 .50
108 Patrick Ehelechner .20 .50
109 Edvin Frylen .20 .50
110 Lorenz Funk Jr. .20 .50
111 Todd Hawkins .20 .50
112 Stefan Hellkvist .20 .50
113 Peter Jakobsson .20 .50
114 Peter Johansson .20 .50
115 Torbjorn Johansson .20 .50
116 Jakob Karlsson .20 .50
117 Sebastian Klenner .20 .50
118 Mattias Loof .20 .50
119 Rob Murphy .20 .50
120 Fredrik Oberg .20 .50
121 Daniel Reiss .20 .50
122 Wallace Schreiber .20 .50
123 Patrick Senger .20 .50
124 Leonard Soccio .20 .50
125 Andrew Verner .20 .50
126 Steve Wilson .20 .50
127 Chad Allan .20 .50
128 Mike Bales .40 1.00
129 Petr Bares .20 .50
130 Francois Bouchard .20 .50
131 Brad Burym .20 .50
132 Terry Campbell .20 .50
133 Kent Fearns .20 .50
134 Alexander Genze .20 .50
135 Erich Goldman .20 .50
136 Glen Goodall .40 1.00
137 Samuel Groleau .20 .50
138 Jean-Francois Jomphe .20 .50
139 Ilpo Kauhanen .20 .50
140 Steve Lingren .20 .50
141 Christoph Melischko .20 .50
142 Neville Rautert .20 .50
143 Jason Ruff .20 .50
144 Reiner Suchan .20 .50
145 Sean Tallaire .20 .50
146 Shayne Toporowski .20 .50
147 Jason Young .20 .50
148 Igor Alexandrov .20 .50
149 Doug Ast .20 .50
150 Christopher Dartolone .20 .50
151 Colin Beardsmore .20 .50
152 Oliver Bernhardt .20 .50
153 Lars Bruggemann .20 .50
154 Markus Draxler .20 .50
155 Jorgen Eriksson .20 .50
156 Petr Fical .20 .50
157 Christian Franz .20 .50
158 Carsten Gosdeck .20 .50
159 Justin Harney .20 .50
160 Christian Hommel .20 .50
161 Scott King .20 .50
162 Lasse Kopitz .20 .50
163 Dimitrij Kotschnew .20 .50
164 Chris Lipsett .20 .50
165 Andrej Podkonicky .20 .50
166 Roland Verwey .20 .50
167 Jimmy Waite .40 1.00
168 Steve Washburn .20 .50
169 Tobias Abstreiter .20 .50
170 Gert Acker .20 .50
171 Frank Appel .20 .50
172 Alexander Cherbayev .20 .50
173 Thomas Daffner .20 .50
174 Doug Deraugh .20 .50
175 Markus Janka .20 .50
176 Lars Jansson .20 .50
177 Orjan Lindmark .20 .50
178 Andreas Loth .20 .50
179 Jeffrey John MacLeod .20 .50
180 Pat Mikesch .20 .50
181 Zdenek Nedved .20 .50
182 Rich Parent .40 1.00
183 Brent Peterson .20 .50
184 Stephan Retzer .20 .50
185 StÃ©phane Robitaille .20 .50
186 Alexander Serikow .20 .50
187 Andrej Teljukin .20 .50
188 Sven Valenti .20 .50
189 Mikael Wahlberg .20 .50
190 Shayne Wright .20 .50
191 Tino Boos .20 .50
192 Mickey Elick .20 .50
193 Sebastian Furchner .20 .50
194 Alex Hicks .20 .50
195 Robert Hock .20 .50
196 Markus Jocher .20 .50
197 Eduard Lewandowski .20 .50
198 Mirko Ludemann .20 .50
199 Dave McLlwain .20 .50
200 Andreas Morczinietz .20 .50
201 Frederik Nilsson .20 .50
202 Dwayne Norris .20 .50
203 Ron Pasco .20 .50
204 Shane Peacock .20 .50
205 Andreas Renz .20 .50
206 Chris Rogles .40 1.00
207 Stefan Schauer .20 .50
208 Brad Schlegel .20 .50
209 Niklas Sundblad .20 .50
210 Christoph Ullmann .20 .50
211 Darcy Werenka .20 .50
212 Leonard Wild .20 .50
213 Patrick Augusta .20 .50
214 Stephane Barin .20 .50
215 Thomas Brandl .20 .50
216 Christoph Brandner .20 .50
217 Mario Doyon .20 .50
218 Paul Dyck .20 .50
219 Christian Ehrhoff 1.25 3.00
220 Adrian Grygiel .20 .50
221 Daniel Kunce .20 .50
222 Dan Lambert .20 .50
223 Jonas Lanier .20 .50
224 Sandy Moger .20 .50
225 Robert Muller .20 .50
226 David Musial .20 .50
227 Roger Nordstrom .20 .50
228 Gunther Oswald .20 .50
229 Brad Purdie .20 .50
230 Andreas Raubal .20 .50
231 Darryl Shannon .20 .50
232 Gary Shuchuk .20 .50
233 Sergej Stas .20 .50
234 Steffen Ziesche .20 .50
235 Michael Bakos .20 .50
236 Rene Corbet .20 .50
237 Devin Edgerton .20 .50
238 Sascha Goc .20 .50
239 Marcel Goc .75 2.00
240 Francois Groleau .20 .50
241 Todd Hlushko .20 .50
242 Wayne Hynes .20 .50
243 Chris Joseph .20 .50
244 Steve Junker .20 .50
245 Klaus Kathan .20 .50
246 Mike Kennedy .20 .50
247 Tomas Martinec .20 .50
248 Anders Myrvold .20 .50
249 Nick Naumenko .20 .50
250 Dimitri Patzold .75 2.00
251 Jason Podollan .20 .50
252 Yves Racine .20 .50
253 Andy Roach .40 1.00
254 Mike Rosati .40 1.00
255 Yannic Seidenberg .20 .50
256 Stefan Ustorf .20 .50
257 Ilja Vorobiev .20 .50
258 Vitalij Aab .20 .50
259 Shawn Anderson .20 .50
260 Frederic Chabot .75 2.00
261 Kevin Dahl .20 .50
262 Ivan Droppa .20 .50
263 Thomas Greilinger .20 .50
264 Robert Guillet .20 .50
265 Martin Jiranek .20 .50
266 Steve Larouche .20 .50
267 Guy Lehoux .20 .50
268 Christopher Luongo .20 .50
269 Martin Reichel .20 .50
270 Jurgen Rumrich .20 .50
271 Marc Savard .20 .50
272 Thomas Schinko .20 .50
273 Christian Schonmoser .20 .50
274 Marc Seliger .20 .50
275 Martin Sychra .20 .50
276 Dave Tomlinson .20 .50
277 Terry Yake .20 .50
278 Paul Brousseau .20 .50
279 Markus Busch .20 .50
280 Dave Chyzowski .20 .50
281 Alexander Duck .20 .50
282 Mark Etz .20 .50
283 Francois Fortier .20 .50
284 Ian Gordon .20 .50
285 Eric Houde .20 .50
286 Ladislav Karabin .20 .50
287 Steffen Karg .20 .50
288 Rainer Kosttstorfer .20 .50
289 Christian Kohmann .20 .50
290 Alexander Kuzminski .20 .50
291 Neal Martin .20 .50
292 Jochen Molling .20 .50
293 Curtis Sheptak .20 .50
294 Vadim Slivchenko .20 .50
295 Ralf Stark .20 .50
296 Jens Stramkowski .20 .50
297 Mathias Svedberg .20 .50
298 Lukas Zib .20 .50

2002-03 German DEL City Press Top Stars

COMPLETE SET (10)

2003-04 German Berlin Polar Bears Postcards

COMPLETE SET (31) 10.00 25.00
1 Keith Aldridge .40 1.00
2 Nils Antons .40 1.00
3 Alex Barta .40 1.00
4 Jens Baxmann .40 1.00
5 Mark Beaufait .40 1.00
6 Brad Bergen .40 1.00
7 Florian Busch .40 1.00
8 Yvon Corriveau .40 1.00
9 Tobias Draxinger .40 1.00
10 Micki DuPont .40 1.00
11 Kelly Fairchild .40 1.00
12 Sven Felski .40 1.00
13 Tom Fiedler .40 1.00
14 Patrick Flynn .40 1.00
15 Mathias Forster .40 1.00
16 Martin Hoffmann .40 1.00
17 Frank Hordler .40 1.00
18 Oliver Jonas .40 1.00
19 Florian Keller .40 1.00
20 Rob Leask .40 1.00
21 Hartmut Nickel .40 1.00
22 Pierre Page CO .40 1.00
23 Rich Parent .75 2.00
24 Denis Pederson .40 1.00
25 Ricard Persson .40 1.00
26 Andre Rankel .40 1.00
27 David Roberts .40 1.00
28 Darryl Shannon .40 1.00
29 Rob Shearer .40 1.00
30 Jeff Tomlinson .40 1.00
31 Steve Walker .40 1.00

2003-04 German Deg Metro Stars

COMPLETE SET (23) 10.00 20.00
1 Fabian Brannstrom .40 1.00
2 Christian Brittig .40 1.00
3 Mathias Hart .40 1.00
4 Tommy Jakobsen .40 1.00
5 Thomas Jorg .40 1.00
6 Alexander Jung .40 1.00
7 Florian Jung .40 1.00
8 Walter Koberle .40 1.00
9 Michael Komma .40 1.00
10 Daniel Kreutzer .40 1.00
11 Bobo Kuhnhauser .40 1.00
12 Trond Magnussen .40 1.00
13 Pat Mikesch .40 1.00
14 Johan Molin .40 1.00
15 Mike Pellegrims .40 1.00
16 Markus Pottinger .40 1.00
17 Alexander Sulzer .40 1.00
18 Jeff Tory .40 1.00
19 Andrej Trefilov .40 1.00
20 Martin Ulrich .40 1.00
21 Gerhard Unterluggauer .40 1.00
22 Tore Vikingstad .40 1.00
23 Clayton Young .40 1.00

2003-04 German DEL

COMPLETE SET (210) 15.00 40.00
1 Rene Corbet .10 .25
2 Devin Edgerton .10 .25
3 Sascha Goc .10 .25
4 Francois Groleau .10 .25
5 Robert Hock .10 .25
6 Chris Joseph .10 .25
7 Klaus Kathan .10 .25
8 Tomas Martinec .10 .25
9 Jochen Molling .10 .25
10 Derek Plante .10 .25
11 Jason Podollan .10 .25
12 Andy Roach .20 .50
13 Marc Seliger .10 .25
14 Richard Shulmistra .10 .25
15 Christoph Ullmann .10 .25
16 Ronny Arendt .10 .25
17 Bjorn Barta .10 .25
18 Colin Beardsmore .10 .25
19 Shawn Carter .10 .25
20 Eric Dandenault .10 .25
21 Xavier Delisle .10 .25
22 Magnus Eriksson .10 .25
23 Francois Fortier .10 .25
24 Rick Girard .10 .25
25 John Miner .10 .25
26 Duanne Moeser .10 .25
27 Arvids Rekis .10 .25
28 Marc Savard .10 .25
29 Andrej Strakhov .10 .25
30 Bob Wren .10 .25
31 Fabian Brannstrom .10 .25
32 Christian Brittig .10 .25
33 Tommy Jakobsen .10 .25
34 Alexander Jung .10 .25
35 Daniel Kreutzer .10 .25
36 Trond Magnussen .10 .25
37 Pat Mikesch .10 .25
38 Mike Pellegrims .10 .25
39 Marcus Thuresson .10 .25
40 Jeff Tory .10 .25
41 Andrej Trefilov .10 .25
42 Martin Ulrich .10 .25
43 Gerhard Unterluggauer .10 .25
44 Tore Vikingstad .10 .25
45 Clayton Young .10 .25
46 Peter Boon .10 .25
47 Dany Bousquet .10 .25
48 Olivier Coqueux .10 .25
49 David Danner .10 .25
50 Juraj Faith .10 .25
51 Dusan Frosch .10 .25
52 Rudolf Gorgenlander .10 .25
53 Rostislav Haas .10 .25
54 Henrik Holscher .10 .25
55 Thomas Jetter .10 .25
56 Ravil Khaidarov .10 .25
57 Vadim Slivchenko .10 .25
58 Sergej Stas .10 .25
59 Bastian Steingross .10 .25
60 Jiri Zelenka .10 .25
61 Keith Aldridge .10 .25
62 Alexander Barta .10 .25
63 Mark Beaufait .10 .25
64 Micki Dupont .10 .25
65 Kelly Fairchild .10 .25
66 Sven Felski .10 .25
67 Oliver Jonas .10 .25
68 Florian Keller .10 .25
69 Robert Leask .10 .25
70 Rich Parent .40 1.00
71 Denis Pederson .10 .25
72 Ricard Persson .10 .25
73 David Roberts .10 .25
74 Rob Shearer .10 .25
75 Steve Walker .10 .25
76 Doug Ast .10 .25
77 Craig Ferguson .10 .25
78 Jakub Ficenec .20 .50
79 Glenn Goodall .40 1.00
80 Samuel Groleau .10 .25
81 Justin Harney .10 .25
82 Cameron Mann .40 1.00
83 Nikolaus Mondt .10 .25
84 Gunther Oswald .10 .25
85 Yves Racine .10 .25
86 Thomas Schinko .10 .25
87 Ken Sutton .10 .25
88 Sean Tallaire .10 .25
89 Phil von Stefenelli .10 .25
90 Jimmy Waite .40 1.00
91 Christian Kohmann .10 .25
92 Jesse Belanger .10 .25
93 Francois Bouchard .10 .25
94 Michael Bresagk .10 .25
95 Ian Gordon .10 .25
96 David Gosselin .10 .25
97 Michael Hackert .10 .25
98 Mike Harder .10 .25
99 Sebastian Klenner .10 .25
100 Patrick Lebeau .40 1.00
101 Dwayne Norris .10 .25
102 Peter Ratchuk .10 .25
103 Martin Reichel .10 .25
104 Paul Stanton .10 .25
105 Jason Young .10 .25
106 Darren van Impe .10 .25
107 Mark Greig .10 .25
108 Robert House .10 .25
109 Wayne Hynes .10 .25
110 Christian Kunast .10 .25
111 Patrick Koppchen .10 .25
112 Dan Lambert .10 .25
113 Paul Manning .10 .25
114 Shane Peacock .10 .25
115 Jacek Plachta .10 .25
116 Brad Purdie .10 .25
117 Boris Rousson .40 1.00
118 Andrew Schneider .10 .25
119 Heiko Smazal .10 .25
120 Dave Tomlinson .10 .25
121 Patrik Augusta .10 .25
122 Bjorn Bombis .10 .25
123 Jeff Christian .10 .25
124 Gordon Borberg .10 .25
125 Edvin Frylen .10 .25
126 Lorenz Funk .10 .25
127 David Haas .10 .25
128 Peter Jakobsson .10 .25
129 Ilpo Kauhanen .10 .25
130 Mattias Loof .10 .25
131 Zdenek Nedved .10 .25
132 Frederik Oberg .10 .25
133 Leonard Soccio .10 .25
134 Andrej Teljukin .10 .25
135 Steve Wilson .10 .25
136 David Cooper .10 .25
137 Bryan Adams .10 .25
138 Chris Bartolone .10 .25
139 James Black .10 .25
140 Lars Bruggemann .10 .25
141 Jason Cipolla .10 .25
142 Michael Fountain .10 .25
143 Erich Goldmann .10 .25
144 Matt Henderson .10 .25
145 Matt Higgins .10 .25
146 Christian Hommel .10 .25
147 Scott King .10 .25
148 Dimitrij Kotschnew .10 .25
149 Rob Sandrock .10 .25
150 Roland Verwey .10 .25
151 Tobias Abstreiter .10 .25
152 Paul Brousseau .10 .25
153 Ted Crowley .10 .25
154 Josh DeWolf .10 .25
155 Ted Drury .10 .25
156 Joaquin Gage .10 .25
157 Orjan Lindmark .10 .25
158 Andreas Loth .10 .25
159 Jeff MacLeod .10 .25
160 Brent Peterson .10 .25
161 Stephan Retzer .10 .25
162 Stephane Robitaille .10 .25
163 Alexander Serikow .10 .25
164 Matthias Trattnig .10 .25
165 Mikael Wahlberg .10 .25
166 Jeremy Adduono .10 .25
167 Tino Boos .10 .25
168 Jeff Dessner .10 .25
169 Mickey Elick .10 .25
170 Sebastian Furchner .10 .25
171 Alex Hicks .10 .25
172 Mirko Ludemann .10 .25
173 Eduard Lewandowski .10 .25
174 Dave McLlwain .10 .25
175 Andreas Morczinietz .10 .25
176 Andreas Renz .10 .25
177 Chris Rogles .10 .25
178 Jean-Yves Roy .10 .25
179 Brad Schlegel .10 .25
180 Leo Stefan .10 .25
181 Pascal Appel .10 .25
182 Marc Beaucage .10 .25
183 Eric Bertrand .10 .25
184 Adrian Grygiel .10 .25
185 Robert Guillet .10 .25
186 Christopher Kelleher .10 .25
187 Daniel Kunce .10 .25
188 Justin Kurtz .10 .25
189 Chris Luongo .10 .25
190 Robert Muller .10 .25
191 Alexander Selivanov .10 .25
192 Stefan Ustorf .10 .25
193 Shayne Wright .10 .25
194 Terry Yake .10 .25
195 Steffen Ziesche .10 .25
196 Vitalij Aab .10 .25
197 Frederic Chabot .40 1.00
198 Marian Cisar .10 .25
199 Petr Fical .10 .25
200 Liam Garvey .10 .25
201 Thomas Greilinger .10 .25
202 Martin Jiranek .10 .25
203 Stephane Julien .10 .25
204 Lasse Kopitz .10 .25
205 Steve Larouche .10 .25
206 Greg Leeb .20 .50
207 Guy Lehoux .10 .25
208 Alfie Michaud .10 .25
209 Yan Stastny ERC 1.25 3.00
210 Robert Tomik .10 .25

2003-04 German DEL All-Stars

COMPLETE SET (22) 15.00 30.00
AS1 Jimmy Waite 1.25 3.00
AS2 Andrej Trefilov 1.25 3.00
AS3 Chris Rogles 1.25 3.00
AS4 Justin Harney .75 2.00
AS5 Paul Stanton .75 2.00
AS6 Andy Roach 1.25 3.00
AS7 Christoph Brandner .75 2.00
AS8 Dwayne Norris .75 2.00
AS9 Francois Fortier .75 2.00
AS10 Philippe Audet .75 2.00
AS11 Doug Ast .75 2.00
AS12 Brad Purdie .75 2.00
AS13 Kelly Fairchild .75 2.00
AS14 Wally Schreiber .75 2.00
AS15 Terry Yake .75 2.00
AS16 Jean-Francois Jomphe .75 2.00
AS17 Andrew Schneider .75 2.00
AS18 Tommy Jakobsen .75 2.00
AS19 Dave McLlwain .75 2.00
AS20 Trond Magnussen .75 2.00
AS21 Shawn Anderson .75 2.00
AS22 Jeff Tory .75 2.00

2003-04 German Mannheim Eagles Postcards

COMPLETE SET (29) 30.00 75.00
1 Richard Shulmistra 1.50 4.00
2 Marc Seliger 1.50 4.00
3 Marco Schutz 1.50 4.00
4 Sachar Blank .40 1.00
5 Yannic Seidenberg 1.50 4.00
6 Bill Stewart 1.50 4.00
7 Christoph Ullmann 1.50 4.00
8 Stefan Ustorf 1.50 4.00
9 Rico Rossi 1.50 4.00
10 Andy Roach 2.50 6.00
11 Yves Racine 1.50 4.00
12 Nico Pyka 1.50 4.00
13 Jason Podollan 2.50 6.00
14 Derek Plante 2.50 6.00
15 Jochen Molling 1.50 4.00
16 Tomas Martinec 1.50 4.00
17 Mike Kennedy 1.50 4.00
18 Klaus Kathan 1.50 4.00
19 Steve Junker 1.50 4.00
20 Chris Joseph 1.50 4.00
21 Robert Hock 1.50 4.00
22 Todd Hlushko 1.50 4.00
23 Francois Groleau 1.50 4.00
24 Sascha Goc 1.50 4.00
25 Devin Edgerton 1.50 4.00
26 Rene Corbet 1.50 4.00
27 Fabio Carciola 1.50 4.00
28 Michael Bakos 1.50 4.00
29 Danny Aus.Den Birken 1.50 4.00
30 Marc Bruns 1.50 4.00
31 Markus Koch 1.50 4.00
32 Andy Roach 2.50 6.00
33 Christoph Ullmann 1.50 4.00

2003-04 German Nuremberg Ice Tigers Postcards

COMPLETE SET (26) 10.00 25.00
1 Vitalij Aab .40 1.00
2 Benjamin Barz .40 1.00
3 Frederic Chabot 1.25 3.00
4 Marian Cisar .40 1.00
5 Kevin Dahl .40 1.00
6 Jon DiSalvatore .40 1.00
7 Petr Fical .40 1.00
8 Konstantin Firsanov .40 1.00
9 Liam Garvey .40 1.00
10 Thomas Greilinger .40 1.00
11 Tobias Guttner .40 1.00
12 Martin Jiranek .40 1.00
13 Stephane Julien .40 1.00
14 Lasse Kopitz .40 1.00
15 Steve Larouche .40 1.00
16 Greg Leeb .75 2.00
17 Guy Lehoux .40 1.00
18 Josef Menauer .40 1.00
19 Alfie Michaud .40 1.00
20 Sebastian Osterloh .40 1.00
21 Felix Petermann .40 1.00
22 Greg Poss .40 1.00
23 Jurgen Rumrich .40 1.00
24 Christian Schonmoser .40 1.00
25 Otto Sykora GM .40 1.00
26 Robert Tomik .40 1.00

2004-05 German Augsburg Panthers Postcards

COMPLETE SET (27) 10.00 25.00
1 Pascal Appel .40 1.00
2 Ronny Arendt .40 1.00
3 Steve Bancroft .40 1.00
4 Bjorn Barta .40 1.00
5 Rich Brennan .40 1.00
6 Robert Brezina .40 1.00
7 Marc Brown .40 1.00
8 Robert Busch .40 1.00
9 Shawn Carter .40 1.00
10 David Danner .40 1.00
11 Dennis Endras .40 1.00
12 Brian Felsner .40 1.00
13 Torsten Fendt .40 1.00
14 Francois Fortier .40 1.00
15 Rick Girard .40 1.00
16 Manuel Kopfler .40 1.00
17 Jean-Francois Labbe .75 2.00
18 Benoit Laporte CO .20 .50
19 Roland Mayr .40 1.00
20 Francois Methot .40 1.00
21 John Miner .40 1.00
22 Duanne Moeser .40 1.00
23 Mike Pudlick .40 1.00
24 Daniel Rau .40 1.00
25 Arvids Rekis .40 1.00
26 Steffen Tolzer .40 1.00
27 Benjamin Voigt .40 1.00

2004-05 German Berlin Eisbarens 50th Anniversary

COMPLETE SET (75) 15.00 30.00
1 Header .04 .10
2 Mike Losch .20 .50

3 Dave Morrison .20 .50
4 Roland Peters .20 .50
5 Mario Plack .20 .50
6 Joachim Stasche .20 .50
7 Detlef Radant .20 .50
8 Pelle Svensson .20 .50
9 Egon Schmeisser .20 .50
10 Klaus Merk .20 .50
11 Rainer Patschinski .20 .50
12 Franz Steer .20 .50
13 Sergej Jaschin .20 .50
14 Steffen Ziesche .20 .50
15 Wolfgang Kraske .20 .50
16 Torsten Deutscher .20 .50
17 Magnus Roupe .20 .50
18 Heinz Pohland .20 .50
19 Mark Jooris .20 .50
20 Wolfgang Beuthner .20 .50
21 Uwe Geisert .20 .50
22 Rene Bielke .20 .50
23 Reinhard Fengler .20 .50
24 Dietmar Peters .20 .50
25 Helmut Senftleben .20 .50
26 Peter Prusa .20 .50
27 Thomas Swibenko .20 .50
28 Marc Fortier .20 .50
29 Andre Dietzch .20 .50
30 Holger Mix .20 .50
31 Werner Thomas .20 .50
32 Hanne Frenzel .20 .50
33 Thomas Mitew .20 .50
34 Jeff Tomlinson .20 .50
35 Fred Freitag .20 .50
36 Bernd Karrenbauer .20 .50
37 Friedhelm Bogelsack .20 .50
38 Thomas Graul .20 .50
39 Sven Felski .20 .50
40 Dirk Perschau .20 .50
41 Gerhard Muller .20 .50
42 Jurgen Schmutzler .20 .50
43 Wilhelm Kopatz .20 .50
44 Dieter Janke .20 .50
45 Jurgen Geisert .20 .50
46 Rob Cowie .20 .50
47 Dieter Dewitz .20 .50
48 Joachim Lempio .20 .50
49 Leif Carlsson .20 .50
50 Joachim Hurbanek .20 .50
51 Gerhard Klugel .20 .50
52 Udo Dohler .20 .50
53 Frank Proske .20 .50
54 Wolfgang Plotka .20 .50
55 Hartmut Nickel .20 .50
56 Andrew McKim .20 .50
57 Jens Ziesche .20 .50
58 Wilfried Rohrbach .20 .50
59 Dieter Frenzel .20 .50
60 Jurgen Breitschuh .20 .50
61 Peter-John Lee .20 .50
62 Mike Bullard .20 .50
63 Guido Hiller .20 .50
64 Gunther Katzur .20 .50
65 Peter Lehnigk .20 .50
66 Matthias Dietz .20 .50
67 Harald Kuhnke .20 .50
68 Frank Krause .20 .50
69 Joachim Ziesche .20 .50
70 Dieter Voigt .20 .50
71 Thomas Steen .20 .50
72 Daniel Held .20 .50
73 Derek Mayer .20 .50
74 Nico Pyka .20 .50
75 Checklist .04 .10

2004-05 German Berlin Polar Bears Postcards

COMPLETE SET (32) 10.00 25.00
1 Alexander Barta .30 .75
2 Jens Baxmann .30 .75
3 Mark Beaufait .30 .75
4 Florian Busch .30 .75
5 Erik Cole .75 2.00
6 Nathan Dempsey .40 1.00
7 Tobias Draxinger .30 .75
8 Danier Dshunussow .30 .75
9 Micki Dupont .40 1.00
10 Kelly Fairchild .40 1.00
11 Sven Felski .30 .75
12 Christoph Gawlik .30 .75
13 Shawn Heins .40 1.00
14 Martin Hoffmann .30 .75
15 Frank Hordler .30 .75
16 Kay Hurbanek .30 .75
17 Oliver Jonas .30 .75
18 Florian Keller .30 .75
19 Olaf Kolzig 2.00 5.00
20 Rob Leask .30 .75
21 Hartmut Nickel ACO .10 .25
22 Pierre Page CO .10 .25
23 Denis Pederson .40 1.00
24 Ricard Persson .30 .75
25 Andre Rankel .30 .75
26 Rob Shearer .30 .75
27 Stefan Ustorf .30 .75
28 Steve Walker .30 .75
29 Derrick Walser .40 1.00
30 Yourri Ziffzer .30 .75
31 Bully MASCOT .10 .25
32 Team Photo .10 .25

2004-05 German Cologne Sharks Postcards

COMPLETE SET (28) 10.00 25.00
1 Jeremy Adduono .40 1.00
2 Colin Beardsmore .40 1.00
3 Markus Berwanger CO .10 .25
4 Dan Bjornlie .40 1.00
5 Boris Blank .40 1.00
6 Tino Boos .40 1.00
7 Jon Coleman .40 1.00
8 Thomas Fischer .40 1.00
9 Sebastian Furchner .40 1.00
10 Philip Gogulla .40 1.00
11 Thomas Greiss .40 1.00
12 Mattias Hart .40 1.00
13 Alex Hicks .40 1.00
14 Kai Hospelt .40 1.00
15 Michael Hrstka .40 1.00
16 Stephane Julien .40 1.00
17 Eduard Lewandowski .40 1.00
18 Mirko Ludemann .40 1.00
19 Dave McLlwain .40 1.00
20 Rupert Meister ACO .10 .25
21 Moritz Muller .40 1.00
22 Andreas Renz .40 1.00
23 Chris Rogles .60 1.50
24 Jean-Yves Roy .40 1.00
25 Brad Schlegel .40 1.00
26 Yannic Seidenberg .40 1.00
27 Paul Traynor .40 1.00
28 Hans Zach CO .10 .25

2004-05 German DEL

COMPLETE SET (283) 25.00 50.00
1 Vitalij Aab .10 .25
2 Danny aus den Birken .10 .25
3 Michael Bakos .10 .25
4 Sven Butenschon .10 .25
5 Rene Corbet .20 .50
6 Andy Delmore .20 .50
7 Devin Edgerton .10 .25
8 Sascha Goc .20 .50
9 Francois Groleau .10 .25
10 Eric Healey .20 .50
11 Jochen Hecht .40 1.00
12 Christopher Joseph .10 .25
13 Steve Kelly .10 .25
14 Markus Kink .10 .25
15 Derek Plante .10 .25
16 Jason Podollan .10 .25
17 Nico Pyka .10 .25
18 John Tripp .10 .25
19 Cristobal Huet 1.25 3.00
20 Thomas Greilinger .10 .25
21 Christoph Ullmann .10 .25
22 Ronny Arendt .10 .25
23 Bjorn Barta .10 .25
24 Robert Brezina .10 .25
25 Marc Brown .10 .25
26 Shawn Carter .10 .25
27 Brian Felsner .10 .25
28 Thorsten Fendt .10 .25
29 Francois Fortier .10 .25
30 Rick Girard .10 .25
31 Manuel Kofler .10 .25
32 Jean Francois Labbe .20 .50
33 Roland Mayr .10 .25
34 Francois Methot .10 .25
35 John Miner .10 .25
36 Duanne Moeser .10 .25
37 Arvids Rekis .10 .25
38 Steve Bancroft .10 .25
39 Mike Pudlick .10 .25
40 David Danner .10 .25
41 Daniel Rau .10 .25
42 Christian Brittig .10 .25
43 Fabian Brannstrom .10 .25
44 Eric Dandenault .10 .25
45 Matt Davidson .10 .25
46 Matt Herr .20 .50
47 Tommy Jakobsen .10 .25
48 Alexander Jung .10 .25
49 Klaus Kathan .10 .25
50 Bernd Kuhnhauser .10 .25
51 Daniel Kreutzer .10 .25
52 Trond Magnussen .10 .25
53 Mike Pellegrims .10 .25
54 Andrew Schneider .10 .25
55 Jeff Tory .10 .25
56 Andrej Trefilov .20 .50
57 Martin Ulrich .10 .25
58 Tore Vikingstad .10 .25
59 Clayton Young .10 .25
60 Florian Jung .10 .25
61 Alexander Sulzer .10 .25
62 Jens Baxmann .10 .25
63 Mark Beaufait .10 .25
64 Tobias Draxinger .10 .25
65 Micki DuPont .20 .50
66 Kelly Fairchild .20 .50
67 Sven Felski .10 .25
68 Shawn Heins .20 .50
69 Frank Hordler .10 .25
70 Oliver Jonas .10 .25
71 Florian Keller .10 .25
72 Robert Leask .10 .25
73 Denis Pederson .10 .25
74 Ricard Persson .10 .25
75 Rob Shearer .10 .25
76 Stefan Ustorf .10 .25
77 Steve Walker .10 .25
78 Derrick Walser .20 .50
79 Youri Ziffzer .10 .25
80 Alexander Barta .10 .25
81 Florian Busch .10 .25
82 Chris Armstrong .10 .25
83 Doug Ast .20 .50
84 Brad Burym .10 .25
85 Craig Ferguson .10 .25
86 Jakub Ficenec .20 .50
87 Glenn Goodall .20 .50
88 Justin Harney .10 .25
89 Martin Jiranek .10 .25
90 Andreas Loth .10 .25
91 Cameron Mann .40 1.00
92 Nikolaus Mondt .10 .25
93 Gunther Oswald .10 .25
94 Aleksander Polaczek .10 .25
95 Marco Sturm .40 1.00
96 Ken Sutton .10 .25
97 Phil von Stefenelli .10 .25
98 Jimmy Waite .20 .50
99 Andy McDonald .40 1.00
100 Daniel Hilpert .10 .25
101 Christoph Melischko .10 .25
102 Boris Ackers .10 .25
103 Marc Beaucage .10 .25
104 Francois Bouchard .10 .25
105 Mihael Bresagk .10 .25
106 Ian Gordon .10 .25
107 Markus Jocher .10 .25
108 Sebastian Klenner .10 .25
109 Christian Kohmann .10 .25
110 Patrick Lebeau .20 .50
111 Mikael Magnusson .10 .25
112 Dwayne Norris .10 .25
113 Sean Pronger .10 .25
114 Peter Ratchuk .10 .25
115 Martin Reichel .10 .25
116 Andrej Strakhov .10 .25
117 David Sulkovsky .10 .25
118 Jason Young .10 .25
119 Stephane Robidas .20 .50
120 Michael Hackert .10 .25
121 Neville Rautert .10 .25
122 Nils Antons .10 .25
123 Robert Francz .10 .25
124 Robert House .10 .25
125 Wayne Hynes .10 .25
126 Craig Johnson .10 .25
127 Alan Letang .10 .25
128 Paul Manning .10 .25
129 Jochen Molling .10 .25
130 Shane Peacock .10 .25
131 Jacek Plachta .10 .25
132 Brad Purdie .10 .25
133 Brandon Reid .40 1.00
134 Boris Rousson .40 1.00
135 Jurgen Rumrich .10 .25
136 Heiko Smazal .10 .25
137 Dave Tomlinson .10 .25
138 Darren van Impe .10 .25
139 Leonhard Wild .10 .25
140 Jim Dowd .20 .50
141 Christopher Oravec .10 .25
142 Martin Walter .10 .25
143 Peter Abstreiter .10 .25
144 Patrick Augusta .10 .25
145 Gordon Borberg .10 .25
146 Lars Bruggemann .10 .25
147 Jason Cipolla .10 .25
148 Thomas Dolak .10 .25
149 Edvin Frylen .10 .25
150 Robert Hock .10 .25
151 Christian Kunast .10 .25
152 Lipo Kauhanen .10 .25
153 Patrick Koppchen .10 .25
154 Dan Lambert .10 .25
155 Andreas Morczienitz .10 .25
156 Frederik Oberg .10 .25
157 Len Soccio .10 .25
158 Andrej Teljukin .10 .25
159 Steve Wilson .10 .25
160 Michael Nemirovski .10 .25
161 Rene Rothke .10 .25
162 Benedikt Schopper .10 .25
163 Bryan Adams .10 .25
164 Igor Alexandrov .10 .25
165 Oliver Bernhardt .10 .25
166 Leonardo Conti .10 .25
167 Collin Danielsmeier .10 .25
168 Sven Gerbig .10 .25
169 Erich Goldmann .10 .25
170 Rhett Gordon .10 .25
171 Matt Higgins .20 .50
172 Ralph Intrnuovo .20 .50
173 Martin Knold .10 .25
174 Dimitij Kotschew .10 .25
175 Brett Lysak .10 .25
176 Mike Martin .10 .25
177 Kevin Mitchell .10 .25
178 Roland Verwey .10 .25
179 Brian White .10 .25
180 Mike York .20 .50
181 Mark Etz .10 .25
182 Franz Fritzmeier .10 .25
183 Tobias Abstreiter .10 .25
184 Gert Acker .10 .25
185 Dany Bousquet .20 .50
186 Daniel Corso .20 .50
187 Kirk Furey .10 .25
188 Joaquin Gage .20 .50
189 David Gosselin .10 .25
190 Christian Hommel .10 .25
191 Sebastian Jones .10 .25
192 Mark Greig .10 .25
193 Christian Laflamme .10 .25
194 Jan Munster .10 .25
195 Dean Melanson .10 .25
196 Alexander Serikow .10 .25
197 Brian Swanson .10 .25
198 Martin Sychra .10 .25
199 Sven Valent .10 .25
200 Nick Schultz .20 .50
201 Stephan Retzer .10 .25
202 Petr Macholda .10 .25
203 Christian Retzer .10 .25
204 Jeremy Adduono .20 .50
205 Colin Beardsmore .10 .25
206 Dan Bjornlie .10 .25
207 Boris Blank .10 .25
208 Tino Boos .10 .25
209 Thomas Fischer .10 .25
210 Thomas Greiss .10 .25
211 Matthias Hart .10 .25
212 Alex Hicks .10 .25
213 Stephane Julien .10 .25
214 Mirko Ludemann .10 .25
215 Eduard Lewandowski .10 .25
216 Dave McLlwain .10 .25
217 Andreas Renz .10 .25
218 Chris Rogles .20 .50
219 Jean-Yves Roy .10 .25
220 Brad Schlegel .10 .25
221 Leo Stefan .10 .25
222 Yannic Seidenberg .10 .25
223 Sebastian Furchner .10 .25
224 Steve Brule .10 .25
225 Alexander Dueck .10 .25
226 Paul Dyck .10 .25
227 Carsten Gosdeck .10 .25
228 Robert Guillet .10 .25
229 Chris Herperger .10 .25
230 Christian Rhode .10 .25
231 Ivo Jan .10 .25
232 Markus Janka .10 .25
233 Scott King .10 .25
234 Daniel Kunce .10 .25
235 Justin Kurtz .10 .25
236 Guy Lehoux .10 .25
237 Robert Muller .10 .25
238 Florian Schnitzer .10 .25
239 Alexander Selivanov .10 .25
240 Shayne Wright .10 .25
241 Steffen Ziesche .10 .25
242 Adrian Grygiel .10 .25
243 Rainer Kottstorfer .10 .25
244 Drew Bannister .10 .25
245 Benjamin Barz .10 .25
246 Petr Fical .10 .25
247 Konstantin Firsanov .10 .25
248 Christian Franz .10 .25
249 Mike Green .10 .25
250 Lasse Kopitz .10 .25
251 Greg Leeb .10 .25
252 Tomas Martinec .10 .25
253 Ulrich Maurer .10 .25
254 Josef Menauer .10 .25
255 Stefan Schauer .10 .25
256 Lubomir Sekeras .10 .25
257 Yan Stastny 1.25 3.00
258 Adam Svoboda .20 .50
259 Sean Tallaire .10 .25
260 Brad Tapper .20 .50
261 Pascal Trepanier .20 .50
262 Bjorn Bombis .10 .25
263 Felix Petermann .10 .25
264 Ivan Ciernik .10 .25
265 Dale Clarke .10 .25
266 Xavier Delisle .10 .25
267 Alexander Genze .10 .25
268 Ladislav Karabin .10 .25
269 Andrej Kaufmann .10 .25
270 Boris Lingemann .10 .25
271 Per-Anton Lundstrom .10 .25
272 Marek Mastic .10 .25
273 David Musial .10 .25
274 Christoph Paepke .10 .25
275 Richard Pavlikovsky .10 .25
276 Marc Seliger .10 .25
277 Todd Simon .10 .25
278 Peter Smrek .10 .25
279 Rainer Suchan .10 .25
280 Roman Veber .10 .25
281 Jan Zurek .10 .25
282 Markus Guggemos .10 .25
283 Tobias Samendinger .10 .25
NNO Deutscher Meister
2004 Frankfurt Lions 4.00 10.00

2004-05 German DEL All-Stars

COMPLETE SET (19) 15.00 30.00
AS1 Jimmy Waite 2.00 5.00
AS2 Andrej Trefilov .75 2.00
AS3 Stephane Julien .75 2.00
AS4 Ricard Persson .75 2.00
AS5 Peter Ratchuk .75 2.00
AS6 Jakub Ficenec 1.25 3.00
AS7 Mike Pellegrims .75 2.00
AS8 John Miner .75 2.00
AS9 Cameron Mann 1.25 3.00
AS10 Marian Cisar .75 2.00
AS11 Ted Drury .75 2.00
AS12 Rene Corbet .75 2.00
AS13 Kelly Fairchild .75 2.00
AS14 Danny Bousquet .75 2.00
AS15 Patrick Augusta .75 2.00
AS16 Alexander Selivanov .75 2.00
AS17 Dave McLlwain .75 2.00
AS18 Brad Purdie .75 2.00
AS19 Scott King .75 2.00

2004-05 German DEL Global Players

COMPLETE SET (5) 10.00 20.00
GP1 Olaf Kolzig 4.00 10.00
GP2 Christian Ehrhoff 1.25 3.00
GP3 Jochen Hecht 1.25 3.00
GP4 Marco Sturm 1.25 3.00
GP5 Dennis Seidenberg 1.25 3.00
GP6 Checklist .40 1.00

2004-05 German DEL Superstars

COMPLETE SET (23) 20.00 40.00
SU01 Sven Butenschön .75 2.00
SU02 Jochen Hecht 1.25 3.00
SU03 Cristobal Huet 2.00 5.00
SU04 Yannick Tremblay .75 2.00
SU05 Erik Cole 1.25 3.00
SU06 Olaf Kölzig 2.00 5.00
SU07 Nathan Dempsey .75 2.00
SU08 Stephane Robidas .75 2.00
SU09 Doug Weight .75 2.00
SU10 Andy McDonald .75 2.00
SU11 Marco Sturm 1.25 3.00
SU12 Jamie Langenbrunner .75 2.00
SU13 Aaron Ward .75 2.00
SU14 Mike York .75 2.00
SU15 John-Michael Liles .75 2.00
SU16 Jean-Sebastien Giguere .75 2.00
SU17 Paul Mara .75 2.00
SU18 Nick Schultz .75 2.00
SU19 Tom Preissing .75 2.00
SU20 Krys Kolanos .75 2.00
SU21 Ty Conklin 1.25 3.00
SU22 Kevyn Adams .75 2.00
SU23 Superstars Checklist .40 1.00

2004-05 German DEL Update

284 Fabio Carciola .10 .25
285 Steven Passmore .20 .50
286 Adler Manheim CL .04 .10
287 Richard Brennan .10 .25
288 Augsburger Panther CL .04 .10
289 Markus Pottinger .10 .25
290 Patrick Reimer .10 .25
291 Thomas Jorg .10 .25
292 DEG Metro Stars CL .04 .10
293 Andre Rankel .10 .25
294 Norman Martens .10 .25
295 Christoph Gawlik .10 .25
296 Daniar Dshunussov .10 .25
297 Richard Mueller .10 .25
298 Marcus Sommerfeld .10 .25
299 Ehc EisBaren Berlin CL .04 .10
300 Mike Harder .10 .25
301 Markus Schroder .10 .25
302 Steffen Karg .10 .25
303 ERC Ingolstadt CL .04 .10
304 Joseph Murray .10 .25
305 Chad Bassen .10 .25
306 Frankfurt Lions CL .04 .10
307 Sasha Martinovic .10 .25
308 Clayton Young .10 .25
309 Hamburg Freezers CL .04 .10
310 Todd Hlushko .10 .25
311 Marian Cisar .10 .25
312 Bastian Steingrog .04 .10
313 Alexander Serikow .10 .25
314 Jonas Lanier .10 .25
315 Michael Kozhenikov .10 .25
316 Wayne Hynes .10 .25
317 Rich Parent .40 1.00
318 Hannover Scorpions CL .04 .10
319 Tobias Schwab .10 .25
320 Iserluhn Roosters CL .04 .10
321A Paul Traynor .10 .25
322A John Coleman .10 .25
322B Ted Drury .20 .50
323A Kai Hospelt .10 .25
323B Corey Hirsch .20 .50
324A Andreas Loth .10 .25
324B Peter Abstreiter .10 .25
325A Marquis Mathieu .40 1.00
325B Mark Kosick .10 .25
326 Manuel Klinge .10 .25
326A Manuel Klinge .10 .25
326b Kolner Haie CL .04 .10
327 Kassel Huskies CL .04 .10
334 Stefan Schroder .10 .25
335 Martin Hyun .10 .25
336 Martin Schymainski .10 .25
337 Vadim Slivchenko .10 .25
338 Krefeld Checklist .04 .10
339 Herbert Vasiljievs .10 .25
340 Lukas Lang .10 .25
341 Robert Tomik .10 .25
342 Nuremberg Checklist .04 .10
343 Sebastian Osterioh .10 .25
344 Lars Bruggemann .10 .25
345 Artjom Kostyrev .10 .25
346 Eric Wolfsburg CL .04 .10
NNO Kolner Haie Checklist .04 .10

2004-05 German Dusseldorf Metro Stars Postcards

COMPLETE SET (25) 10.00 20.00
1 Fabian Brannstrom .40 1.00
2 Christian Brittig .40 1.00
3 Eric Dandenault .40 1.00
4 Matt Davidson .40 1.00
5 Matt Herr .75 2.00
6 Tommy Jakobsen .40 1.00
7 Thomas Jorg .40 1.00
8 Alexander Jung .40 1.00
9 Florian Jung .40 1.00
10 Klaus Kathan .40 1.00
11 Walter Koberle CO .10 .25
12 Daniel Kreutzer .40 1.00
13 Bernd Kuhnhauser .40 1.00
14 Trond Magnussen .40 1.00
15 Mike Pellegrims .40 1.00
16 Markus Pottinger .40 1.00
17 Patrick Reimer .40 1.00
18 Andy Schneider .40 1.00
19 Alexander Sulzer .40 1.00
20 Jeff Tory .40 1.00
21 Andrei Trefilov .60 1.50
22 Martin Ulrich .40 1.00
23 Tore Vikingstad .40 1.00
24 Clayton Young .40 1.00
25 Dussi MASCOT .04 .10

2004-05 German Hamburg Freezers Postcards

COMPLETE SET (22) 10.00 20.00
1 Nils Antons .40 1.00
2 Robert Francz .40 1.00
3 Jean-Sebastien Giguere 2.00 5.00
4 Bobby House .40 1.00
5 Craig Johnson .40 1.00
6 Alan Letang .40 1.00
7 Paul Manning .40 1.00
8 Sasha Martinovic .40 1.00
9 Jochen Molling .40 1.00
10 Christopher Oravec .40 1.00
11 Shane Peacock .40 1.00
12 Jacek Plachta .40 1.00
13 Brad Purdie .40 1.00
14 Brandon Reid .75 2.00
15 Boris Rousson .75 2.00
16 Jorgen Rumrich .40 1.00
17 Mike Schmidt CO .40 1.00
18 Mike Smazal .40 1.00
19 Dave Tomlinson .40 1.00
20 Darren Van Impe .40 1.00
21 Martin Walter .40 1.00
22 Clayton Young .40 1.00

2004-05 German Hannover Scorpions Postcards

COMPLETE SET (29) 10.00 25.00
1 Peter Abstreiter .40 1.00
2 Patrik Augusta .40 1.00
3 Gordon Borberg .40 1.00
4 Lars Bruggemann .40 1.00
5 Jason Cipolla .40 1.00
6 Marian Cisar .40 1.00
7 Thomas Dolak .40 1.00
8 Edvin Frylen .40 1.00
9 Axel Hackert .40 1.00
10 Todd Hlushko .40 1.00
11 Robert Hock .40 1.00
12 Wayne Hynes .40 1.00
13 Ilpo Kauhanen .75 2.00
14 Patrick Koppchen .40 1.00
15 Mikhail Kozhevnikov .40 1.00
16 Christian Kunast .40 1.00
17 Dan Lambert .40 1.00
18 Jonas Lanier .40 1.00
19 Paul Mara .75 2.00
20 Andreas Morczinietz .40 1.00
21 Fredrik Oberg .40 1.00
22 Andy Reiss .40 1.00
23 Rene Rothke .40 1.00
24 Benedikt Schopper .40 1.00
25 Alexander Serikow .40 1.00
26 Lenny Soccio .40 1.00
27 Bastian Steingross .40 1.00
28 Andrei Teljukin .40 1.00
29 Steve Wilson .40 1.00

2004-05 German Ingolstadt Panthers

COMPLETE SET (29) 10.00 25.00
1 Chris Armstrong .30 .75
2 Doug Ast .30 .75
3 Jamie Bartman CO .10 .25
4 Brad Burym .30 .75
5 Craig Ferguson .30 .75
6 Jakub Ficenec .30 .75
7 Glen Goodall .30 .75
8 Mike Harder .30 .75
9 Justin Harney .30 .75
10 Daniel Hilpert .30 .75
11 Martin Jiranek .30 .75
12 Steffen Karg .30 .75
13 Ron Kennedy CO .10 .25
14 Jamie Langenbrunner .30 .75
15 Cameron Mann .75 2.00
16 Andy McDonald .75 2.00
17 Christoph Melischko .30 .75
18 Nikolaus Mondt .30 .75
19 Gunther Oswald .30 .75
20 Alexander Polaczek .30 .75
21 Markus Schroder .30 .75
22 Marco Sturm 1.25 3.00
23 Ken Sutton .30 .75
24 Phil von Stefenelli .30 .75
25 Jimmy Waite .75 2.00
26 Aaron Ward .75 2.00
27 Xavier MASCOT .04 .10
28 Drew Omicioli .30 .75
29 Andreas Loth .30 .75

2004-05 German Krefeld Penguins Postcards

COMPLETE SET (24) 12.00 30.00
1 Steve Brule .60 1.50
2 Alexander Duck .60 1.50
3 Paul Dyck .60 1.50
4 Franz Fritzmeier CO .10 .25
5 Carsten Gosdeck .60 1.50
6 Adrien Grygiel .60 1.50
7 Robert Guillet .60 1.50
8 Chris Herperger .60 1.50
9 Martin Hyun .60 1.50
10 Ivo Jan .60 1.50
11 Markus Janka .60 1.50
12 Scott King .60 1.50
13 Rainer Kottstorfer .60 1.50
14 Daniel Kunce .60 1.50
15 Justin Kurtz .60 1.50
16 Guy Lehoux .60 1.50
17 Robert Muller .60 1.50
18 Christian Rohde .60 1.50
19 Florian Schnitzer .60 1.50
20 Alexander Selivanov .60 1.50
21 Mario Simioni CO .10 .25
22 Ferdinand Stradter MD .10 .25
23 Shayne Wright .60 1.50
24 Steffen Ziesche .60 1.50

2004-05 German Nuremburg Ice Tigers Postcards

COMPLETE SET (19) 10.00 25.00
1 Drew Bannister .60 1.50
2 Benjamin Barz .60 1.50
3 Bjorn Bombis .60 1.50
4 Robert Dietrich .60 1.50
5 Petr Fical .60 1.50
6 Konstantin Firsanov .60 1.50
7 Christian Franz .60 1.50
8 Mike Green .60 1.50
9 Lasse Kopitz .60 1.50
10 Lukas Lang .60 1.50
11 Tomas Martinec .60 1.50
12 Ulrich Maurer .60 1.50
13 Felix Petermann .60 1.50
14 Greg Poss CO .10 .25
15 Stefan Schauer .60 1.50
16 Yan Stastny 1.25 3.00
17 Adam Svoboda 1.25 3.00
18 Otto Sykora MG .10 .25
19 Brad Tapper .60 1.50

2004-05 German Weiden Blue Devils

COMPLETE SET (27) 10.00 20.00
1 Florian Bartels .30 .75
2 Michal Bartosch .30 .75
3 J.F. Boutin .30 .75
4 Christian Franz .30 .75
5 Roman Goeldner .30 .75
6 Christian Grosch .30 .75
7 Peter Gruhle .30 .75
8 Benjamin Grunwald .30 .75
9 Stephan Hagn .30 .75
10 Reinhard Haider .30 .75
11 Alexander Herbst .30 .75
12 Michael Hoeck .30 .75
13 Thomas Kastner .30 .75
14 Stefan Keski-Kungas .30 .75
15 Christian Kinateder .30 .75
16 Holger Koenig .30 .75
17 Christian Meiler .30 .75
18 Florian Ondruschka .30 .75
19 Jan Penk .30 .75
20 Michal Piskor .30 .75
21 Daniel Rappl .30 .75
22 Samuel St. Pierre .30 .75
23 Damiel Strom .30 .75
24 Sebastian Wolsch .30 .75
25 Florian Zellner .30 .75
26 Josef Hefner ACO .10 .25
27 Leos Sulak CO .10 .25

2005-06 German DEL

COMPLETE SET (381) 30.00 60.00
1 Patrick Aufiero .10 .25
2 Christian Eklund .10 .25
3 Dennis Endrass .10 .25
4 Thorsten Fendt .10 .25
5 Rick Girard .10 .25
6 Scott King .20 .50
7 Manuel Kofler .10 .25
8 Martin Lindmann .10 .25
9 Roland Mayr .10 .25
10 Josef Menauer .10 .25
11 Steve Potvin .10 .25
12 Daniel Rau .10 .25
13 Arvids Rekis .10 .25
14 Rainer Suchan .10 .25
15 Jayme Filipowicz .10 .25
16 Rolf Wanhainen .10 .25
17 Stefan Endrass .10 .25
18 Brendan Yarema .10 .25
19 David Danner .10 .25
20 Konstantin Firsanov .10 .25
21 Jens Baxmann .10 .25
22 Mark Beaufait .10 .25
23 Tobias Draxinger .10 .25
24 Daniar Dshunussow .10 .25
25 Micki DuPont .20 .50
26 Kelly Fairchild .20 .50
27 Sven Felski .10 .25
28 Steve Walker .10 .25
29 Christoph Gawlik .10 .25
30 Frank Hördler .10 .25
31 Rob Leask .10 .25
32 Norman Martens .10 .25
33 Richard Mueller .10 .25
34 Rene Kramer .10 .25
35 Stefan Ustorf .10 .25
36 Derrick Walser .20 .50
37 Denis Pederson .20 .50
38 Youri Ziffzer .10 .25
39 Florian Busch .10 .25
40 Andre Rankel .10 .25
41 Steve Brule .10 .25
42 Mathieu Darche .20 .50
43 Robert Francz .10 .25
44 Thorsten Kienass .10 .25
45 Patrick Koslow .10 .25
46 Petri Kujala .10 .25
47 Trond Magnussen .10 .25
48 Shawn McNeill .20 .50
49 Stephane Robitaille .10 .25
50 Christian Rohde .10 .25
51 Martin Schymainski .10 .25
52 Niklas Sundblad .10 .25
53 Andrej Teljukin .10 .25
54 Michael Waginger .10 .25
55 Jean-Luc Grand-Pierre .20 .50
56 Radek Vit .10 .25
57 Francois Groleau .10 .25
58 Mika Puhakka .10 .25
59 Björn Reiser .10 .25
60 Anton Bader .10 .25
61 Alexander Jung .10 .25
62 Marian Bazany .10 .25
63 Fabian BrÅonnström .10 .25
64 Chris Ferraro .20 .50
65 Florian Jung .10 .25
66 Thomas Jörg .10 .25
67 Craig Johnson .20 .50
68 Klaus Kathan .10 .25
69 Daniel Kreutzer .10 .25
70 Peter Ferraro .20 .50
71 Mike Pellegrims .10 .25
72 Chris Schmidt .10 .25
73 Andrew Schneider .20 .50
74 Jeff Tory .10 .25
75 Andrej Trefilov .20 .50
76 Tore Vikingstad .10 .25
77 Todd Reirden .10 .25
78 Tommy Jakobsen .10 .25
79 Patrick Reimer .10 .25
80 Alexander Sulzer .10 .25
81 Patrick Boileau .10 .25
82 Francois Bouchard .10 .25
83 Michael Bresagk .10 .25
84 Daniel Corso .20 .50
85 Ian Gordon .10 .25
86 David Gosselin .20 .50
87 Markus Jocher .10 .25
88 Sebastian Klenner .10 .25
89 Christian Kohmann .10 .25
90 Patrick Lebeau .20 .50
91 Dwayne Norris .20 .50
92 Philippe Plante .10 .25
93 Neville Rautert .10 .25
94 Jonas Stöpfgeshoff .10 .25
95 David Sulkovsky .10 .25
96 Jason Young .10 .25
97 Boris Ackers .10 .25
98 Chad Bassen .10 .25
99 Simon Danner .10 .25
100 Jan Barta .10 .25
101 Marc Beaucage .10 .25
102 Björn Bombis .10 .25
103 Francois Fortier .10 .25
104 Benoit Gratton .20 .50
105 Tobias Güttner .10 .25
106 Benjamin Hinterstocker .10 .25
107 Martin Hinterstocker .10 .25
108 Christian Hommel .10 .25
109 Alan Letang .10 .25
110 Paul Manning .10 .25
111 Sasa Martinovic .10 .25
112 Shane Peacock .10 .25
113 Jacek Plachta .10 .25
114 Boris Rousson .20 .50
115 Heiko Smazal .10 .25
116 Christopher Oravec .10 .25
117 Jeff Ulmer .10 .25
118 Darren van Impe .10 .25
119 Alexander Barta .10 .25
120 Martin Walter .10 .25
121 Patrick Augusta .10 .25
122 Brad Burym .10 .25
123 Jason Cipolla .10 .25
124 Thomas Dolak .10 .25
125 Sascha Goc .20 .50
126 Mike Green .20 .50
127 Shawn Heins .20 .50
128 Robert Hock .10 .25
129 Marcel Juhasz .10 .25
130 Trevor Kidd .20 .50

131 Patrick Köppchen .10 .25
132 Christian Künast .10 .25
133 Dan Lambert .20 .50
134 Andreas Morczinietz .10 .25
135 Brad Tapper .20 .50
136 Todd Warriner .20 .50
137 Jeff Finley .10 .25
138 Steve Guolla .20 .50
139 Rene Röthke .10 .25
140 Michael Höck .10 .25
141 Chris Armstrong .10 .25
142 Doug Ast .10 .25
143 Björn Barta .10 .25
144 Craig Ferguson .10 .25
145 Jakub Ficenec .20 .50
146 Glenn Goodall .20 .50
147 Daniel Hilpert .10 .25
148 Jason Holland .10 .25
149 Martin Jiranek .10 .25
150 Florian Keller .10 .25
151 Cameron Mann .20 .50
152 Christoph Melischko .10 .25
153 Günther Oswald .10 .25
154 Sebastian Vogl .10 .25
155 Ken Sutton .10 .25
156 Sean Tallaire .10 .25
157 Phil von Stefenelli .20 .50
158 Jimmy Waite .20 .50
159 Christoph Höhenleitner .10 .25
160 Yannic Seidenberg .10 .25
161 Vitalij Aab .10 .25
162 Bryan Adams .10 .25
163 Collin Danielsmeier .10 .25
164 Mark Etz .10 .25
165 Linus Fagemo .10 .25
166 Kirk Furey .10 .25
167 Erich Goldmann .10 .25
168 Michael Wolf .10 .25
169 Matt Higgins .20 .50
170 Raffaele Intranuovo .20 .50
171 Sebastian Jonas .10 .25
172 Ladislav Karabin .10 .25
173 Martin Knold .10 .25
174 Leonardo Conti .10 .25
175 Dimitrij Kotschnew .10 .25
176 Markus Pöttinger .10 .25
177 Bruce Richardson .10 .25
178 Mats Trygg .10 .25
179 Tobias Schwab .10 .25
180 Alexej Dmitriev .10 .25
181 Tobias Abstreiter .10 .25
182 Drew Bannister .20 .50
183 Eric Bertrand .10 .25
184 Joaquin Gage .20 .50
185 Sven Gerbig .10 .25
186 Dommink Hammer .10 .25
187 Justin Harney .10 .25
188 Guy Lehoux .10 .25
189 Alexander Serikow .10 .25
190 Martin Sychra .10 .25
191 Sven Valenti .10 .25
192 Steffen Ziesche .10 .25
193 Dale Clarke .10 .25
194 Danny Groulx .10 .25
195 Ryan Kraft .10 .25
196 Adam Ondraschek .10 .25
197 Jason Ulmer .10 .25
198 Alexander Heinrich .10 .25
199 Manuel Klinge .10 .25
200 Tobias Wörle .10 .25
201 Jeremy Adduono .10 .25
202 Tino Boos .10 .25
203 Ivan Ciernik .10 .25
204 Sebastian Furchner .10 .25
205 Thomas Greiss .10 .25
206 Kai Hospelt .10 .25
207 Oliver Jonas .10 .25
208 Stephane Julien .10 .25
209 Lasse Kopitz .10 .25
210 Eduard Lewandowski .10 .25
211 Mirko Lüdemann .10 .25
212 Dave McLlwain .10 .25
213 Nikolaus Mondt .10 .25
214 Andreas Renz .10 .25
215 Jean-Yves Roy .10 .25
216 Paul Traynor .10 .25
217 Brad Schlegel .10 .25
218 Alex Hicks .10 .25
219 Philip Gogulla .10 .25
220 Moritz Müller .10 .25
221 Boris Blank .10 .25
222 Alexander Dück .10 .25
223 Franz Fritzmeier .10 .25
224 Robert Guillet .10 .25
225 Chris Herperger .10 .25
226 Andre Huebscher .10 .25
227 Ivo Jan .10 .25
228 Rainer Köttsdorfer .10 .25
229 Daniel Kunce .10 .25
230 Richard Pavlikovski .10 .25
231 Ken Passmann .10 .25
232 Alexander Selivanov .10 .25
233 Herberts Vasiljevs .10 .25
234 Roland Verwey .10 .25
235 Markus Witting .10 .25
236 Robert Müller .10 .25
237 Philip Hendle .10 .25
238 Andy Hedlund .10 .25
239 Adrian Grygiel .10 .25
240 Daniel Pietta .10 .25
241 Ronny Arendt .10 .25
242 Patrick Ehelechner .20 .50
243 Michael Bakos .10 .25
244 Lonny Bohonos .20 .50
245 Shawn Carter .10 .25
246 Karl Dykhuis .10 .25
247 Devin Edgerton .10 .25
248 Pierre Hedin .10 .25
249 Steve Kelly .20 .50
250 Marcus Kink .10 .25
251 Peter Ratchuk .10 .25
252 Sefan Retzer .10 .25
253 Jeff Shantz .10 .25
254 John Tripp .10 .25
255 Marco Schütz .10 .25
256 Sachar Blank .10 .25
257 Fredrik Chabot .20 .50
258 Rene Corbet .20 .50
259 Fabio Carciola .10 .25
260 Christoph Ullmann .10 .25
261 Benjamin Barz .10 .25
262 Colin Beardsmore .10 .25
263 Rich Brennan .10 .25
264 Matt Davidson .20 .50
265 Robert Döme .20 .50
266 Petr Fical .10 .25
267 Christian Franz .10 .25
268 Lukas Lang .10 .25
269 Jean-Francois Labbe .20 .50
270 Christian Laflamme .10 .25
271 Greg Leeb .10 .25
272 Thomas Martinec .10 .25
273 Francois Methot .10 .25
274 Michel Periard .10 .25
275 Alexander Polaczek .10 .25
276 Jame Pollock .10 .25
277 Christian Retzer .10 .25
278 Brian Swanson .10 .25
279 Felix Petermann .10 .25
280 Stefan Schauer .10 .25
281 Olaf Kölzig 2.00 5.00
282 Alexander Jung .10 .25
283 Rob Leask .10 .25
284 Christian Erhoff .30 .75
285 Chritoph Schubert .10 .25
286 Andreas Renz .10 .25
287 Lasse Kopitz .10 .25
288 Dennis Seidenberg .20 .50
289 Sven Felski .10 .25
290 Jochen Hecht .40 1.00
291 Marco Sturm .40 1.00
292 Stefan Ustorf .10 .25
293 Daniel Kreutzer .10 .25
294 Alexander Barta .10 .25
295 Thomas Martinec .10 .25
296 Klaus Kathan .10 .25
297 Michael Hackert .10 .25
298 Tino Boos .10 .25
299 Andreas Morczinietz .10 .25
300 Jan Benda .10 .25
301 Patrick Buzas .10 .25
302 Jay Henderson .20 .50
303 Marc Savard .10 .25
304 Steffen Tölzer .10 .25
305 Drake Berehowsky .10 .25
306 Constantin Braun .10 .25
307 Sean Fischer .10 .25
308 Patrick Jarrett .20 .50
309 TomÃ¡s Pöpperle .10 .25
310 Deron Quint .20 .50
311 Thomas Schenkel .10 .25
312 Hugo Boisvert .10 .25
313 Patrick Ehelechner .20 .50
314 Kari Haakana .10 .25
315 Martin Hamann .10 .25
316 Michael Henrich .10 .25
317 Markus Schmidt .10 .25
318 Chris Bright .10 .25
319 Michael Hackert .10 .25
320 Steve Kelly .10 .25
321 James Patrick .10 .25
322 Martin Reichel .10 .25
323 Andrej Strakhov .10 .25
324 Roman Cechmanek .20 .50
325 Matthias Forster .10 .25
326 Niklas Hede .10 .25
327 Ryan Jardine .10 .25
328 Steffen Karg .10 .25
329 Max Lingemann .10 .25
330 Florian Schnitzer .10 .25
331 Lukas Slavetinsky .10 .25
332 Björn Bombis .10 .25
333 Dominik Hammer .10 .25
334 Jonas Lanier .10 .25
335 Marty Murray .10 .25
336 AndrÃ© Reiss .10 .25
337 Benedikt Schopper .10 .25
338 Wally Schreiber .10 .25
339 Matt Kinch .10 .25
340 Bastian Steingrog .10 .25
341 Rob Valicevic .20 .50
342 Mark Greig .10 .25
343 Brad Purdie .10 .25
344 Rich Parent .40 1.00
345 Steve Brule .10 .25
346 Brad Burym .10 .25
347 Martin Hlinka .10 .25
348 Sinsa Martinovic .10 .25
349 Chris Nielsen .10 .25
350 Sebastian Osterloh .10 .25
351 Torsten Ankert .10 .25
352 Daniel Hatterscheid .10 .25
353 William Lindsay .10 .25
354 Henry Martens .10 .25
355 Ted Drury .10 .25
356 Mike Pudlick .10 .25
357 Igor Alexandrov .10 .25
358 Anthony Aquino .10 .25
359 David Cespiva .10 .25
360 Daniel Del Monte .10 .25
361 Ilpo Kauhanen .20 .50
362 Stefan Langwieder .10 .25
363 Thomas Pielmeier .10 .25
364 Yannick Tremblay .10 .25
365 Gert Acker .10 .25
366 Ulrich Maurer .10 .25
367 Florian Ondruschka .10 .25
368 Björn Barta .10 .25
369 Michael Bresagk .20 .50
370 Petr Fical .10 .25
371 Sebastian Furchner .10 .25
372 Marcel Goc .20 .50
373 Dimitrij Kotschnew .10 .25
374 Eduard Lewandowski .10 .25
375 Robert Müller .20 .50
376 Alexander Sulzer .10 .25
377 Christoph Ullmann .10 .25
378 Thomas Greiss .10 .25
379 Nico Pyka .10 .25
NNO EisbÃ¤ren Berlin Deutscher Meister 2005 4.00 10.00
NNO DEG Metro Stars DEB Pokalsieger 2006 4.00 10.00

2005-06 German DEL All-Star Jerseys

AS01 Andy Delmore 8.00 20.00
AS02 Micki DuPont 8.00 20.00
AS03 Jakub Ficenec 8.00 20.00
AS04 Darren van Impe 8.00 20.00
AS05 Stepahne Julien 8.00 20.00
AS06 Ladislav Karabin 8.00 20.00
AS07 Ivan Ciernik 8.00 20.00
AS08 Patrick Lebeau 8.00 20.00
AS09 Dave McIlwain 8.00 20.00
AS10 Francois Methot 8.00 20.00
AS11 Duanne Moeser 8.00 20.00
AS12 Dwayne Norris 8.00 20.00
AS13 Mike Pellegrims 8.00 20.00
AS14 Brad Purdie 8.00 20.00
AS15 Chris Rogles 8.00 20.00
AS16 Boris Rousson 10.00 25.00
AS17 Alexander Selivanov 8.00 20.00
AS18 Yan Stastny 12.00 30.00
AS19 Steve Walker 8.00 20.00
AS20 Pascal Trepanier 8.00 20.00
AS21 All Star Game 2006 20.00 50.00

2005-06 German DEL DEB-Jerseys

TR01 Jan Benda 8.00 20.00
TR02 Jochen Hecht 12.00 30.00
TR03 Olaf Kölzig 20.00 50.00
TR04 Marco Sturm 12.00 30.00

2005-06 German DEL Goalies

COMPLETE SET (14) 20.00 40.00
G01 Roman Cechmanek 1.25 3.00
G02 Patrick Ehelechner 2.00 5.00
G03 Joaquin Gage 1.25 3.00
G04 Ian Gordon 1.25 3.00
G05 Thomas Greiss 1.25 3.00
G06 Trevor Kidd 2.00 5.00
G07 Alexander Jung 1.25 3.00
G08 Ilpo Kauhanen 1.25 3.00
G09 Jean-Francois LabbÃ© 1.25 3.00
G10 Robert Müller 1.25 3.00
G11 Rich Parent 2.00 5.00
G12 TomÃ¡s Pöpperle 1.25 3.00
G13 Jimmy Waite 2.00 5.00
G14 Rolf Wanhainen 1.25 3.00

2005-06 German DEL Star Attack

COMPLETE SET (10) 8.00 20.00
ST01 Ivan Ciernik .75 2.00
ST02 Jochen Hecht 1.25 3.00
ST03 Daniel Kreutzer .75 2.00
ST04 Patrick Lebeau .75 2.00
ST05 Dwayne Norris .75 2.00
ST06 Yan Stastny 1.50 4.00
ST07 Brad Tapper .75 2.00
ST08 Pascal Trepanier .75 2.00
ST09 Mike York 1.25 3.00
ST10 Jason Young .75 2.00

2005-06 German DEL Team Checklists

COMPLETE SET (20) 6.00 15.00
CL01 Augsburger Panther Checklist .40 1.00
CL02 EisbÃ¤ren Berlin Checklist .40 1.00
CL03 DEG Metro Stars Checklist .40 1.00
CL04 EV Duisburg Checklist .40 1.00
CL05 Frankfurt Lions Checklist .40 1.00
CL06 Hamburg Freezers Checklist .40 1.00
CL07 Hannover Scorpions Checklist .40 1.00
CL08 ERC Ingolstadt Checklist .40 1.00
CL09 Iserlohn Roosters Checklist .40 1.00
CL10 Kassel Huskies Checklist .40 1.00
CL11 Kölner Haie Checklist .40 1.00
CL12 Krefeld Pinguine Checklist .40 1.00
CL13 Adler Mannheim Checklist .40 1.00
CL14 Nürnberg Ice Tigers Checklist .40 1.00
CL15 Nationalmannschaft Checklist .40 1.00
CL16 Defender Checklist .40 1.00
CL17 Star Attack Checklist .40 1.00
CL18 Allstars 05 Checklist .40 1.00
CL19 Goalies Checklist .40 1.00
CL20 Trikotkarten DEB Checklist .40 1.00

2006-07 German DEL All-Star Jerseys

AS1 Doug Ast 10.00 25.00
AS2 Francois Bouchard 10.00 25.00
AS3 Ivan Ciernik 10.00 25.00
AS4 Ted Drury 10.00 25.00
AS5 Jakub Ficenec 15.00 40.00
AS6 Andy Hedlund 10.00 25.00
AS7 Matt Higgins 10.00 25.00
AS8 Martin Hlinka 10.00 25.00
AS9 Stephane Julien 10.00 25.00
AS10 Trevor Kidd 15.00 40.00

2006-07 German DEL German Forwards

GF1 Tomas Martinec 1.25 3.00
GF2 Michael Hackert 1.25 3.00
GF3 Andreas Morczinietz 1.25 3.00
GF4 Daniel Kreutzer 1.25 3.00
GF5 Manuel Kofler 1.25 3.00
GF6 Sven Felski 1.25 3.00
GF7 Markus Jocher 1.25 3.00
GF8 Robert Hock 1.25 3.00
GF9 Robert Francz 1.25 3.00
GF10 Petr Fical 1.25 3.00
GF11 Tino Boos 1.25 3.00
GF12 Boris Blank 1.25 3.00
GF13 Alexander Barta 1.25 3.00
GF14 Michael Waginger 1.25 3.00

2006-07 German DEL New Arrivals

NA1 Travis Brigley 1.25 3.00
NA2 Cory Cross 1.25 3.00
NA3 Per Eklund 1.25 3.00
NA4 Scott King 1.25 3.00
NA5 Jason Marshall 1.25 3.00
NA6 Dusan Milo 1.25 3.00
NA7 Eric Nickulas 2.00 5.00
NA8 Andy Roach 2.00 5.00
NA9 Nathan Robinson 2.00 5.00
NA10 Jamie Storr 1.50 4.00
NA11 Levente Szuper 1.50 4.00
NA12 Chris Taylor 1.25 3.00
NA13 Brad Tiley 1.25 3.00
NA14 Daniel Tkaczuk 1.25 3.00

2006-07 German DEL Team Leaders

TL1 Craig Darby 1.25 3.00
TL2 Ted Drury 1.25 3.00
TL3 Glen Goodall 2.00 5.00
TL4 Torsten Kienass 1.25 3.00
TL5 Alan Letang 1.25 3.00
TL6 Greg Leeb 1.25 3.00
TL7 Dave McIlwain 1.25 3.00
TL8 Jimmy Roy 1.25 3.00
TL9 William Trew 1.25 3.00
TL10 Stefan Ustorf 1.25 3.00
TL11 Todd Warriner 1.50 4.00
TL12 Pascal Trepanier 1.25 3.00
TL13 Craig Johnson 1.25 3.00
TL14 Jason Young 1.25 3.00

2007-08 German DEL Cologne Sharks

COMPLETE SET (27)

2007-08 German DEL Masked Marvels

COMPLETE SET (16)

2007-08 German DEL Playmakers

COMPLETE SET (15)

2007-08 Italian Ritten Renon Team Set

COMPLETE SET (23) 4.00 10.00
1 Josh Olson .25 .60
2 Mark Smith .25 .60
3 Enrico Dorigatti .25 .60
4 Shawn Mather .25 .60
5 Dan Tudin .25 .60
6 Alex Egger .25 .60
7 Tony Tuzzolino .25 .60
8 Ingemar Gruber .25 .60
9 Kaspars Astashenko .25 .60
10 Emanuel Scelfo .25 .60
11 Jan Vodrazka .25 .60
12 Paolo Bustreo .25 .60
13 Matteo Rasom .25 .60
14 Alex Rottensteiner .25 .60
15 Lorenz Daccordo .25 .60
16 Marcus Hafner .25 .60
17 Fritz Ploner .25 .60
18 Thomas Unterfrauner .25 .60
19 Benjamin Bregenzer .25 .60
20 Frederic Cloutier .25 .60
21 Niederstaetter .25 .60
22 Paul Adey .25 .60
23 Herbert Frisch .25 .60

1992-93 Norwegian Elite Series

COMPLETE SET (242) 20.00 50.00
1 Jim Marthinsen .20 .50
2 Jarl Eriksen .07 .20
3 Erik Tveten .07 .20
4 Carl Gunnar Gundersen .07 .20
5 Nick Carone .07 .20
6 Jaromir Latal .07 .20
7 Tom Johansen .07 .20
8 Asgaut Moe .07 .20
9 Oystein Olsen .07 .20
10 Atle Olsen .07 .20
11 Roy Johansen .07 .20
12 Marius Rath .07 .20
13 Svenn Erik Bjornstad .07 .20
14 Jon Magne Karlstad .07 .20
15 Pal Kristiansen .07 .20
16 Espen Knutsen 2.00 5.00
17 Stig Johansen .07 .20
18 Geir Myhre .07 .20
19 Remo Martinsen .07 .20
20 Jan Tore Ronningen .07 .20
21 Jon Hroar Nordstrom .07 .20
22 Tom Erik Olsen .07 .20
23 Peter Madach .07 .20
24 Rune Gulliksen .07 .20
25 Carl Oscar Boe Andersen .07 .20
26 Martin Ahlberg .07 .20
27 Erik Kristiansen .07 .20
28 Tommy Larsen .07 .20
29 Age Ellingsen .07 .20
30 Patric Eide .07 .20
31 Svein Harald Arnesen .07 .20
32 Petter Thoresen .07 .20
33 Pal Marthinsen .07 .20
34 Ole Eskild Dahlstrom .07 .20
35 Nikolai Davydkin .07 .20
36 Lennart Ahlberg .07 .20
37 Tommie Eriksen .07 .20
38 Jan Roar Fagerli .07 .20
39 Erik Nerell .07 .20
40 Knut Walbye .07 .20
41 Pal Dahlstrom .07 .20
42 Martin Andresen .07 .20
43 Geir Hoff .07 .20
44 Cato Andersen .07 .20
45 Per Oddvar Walbye .07 .20
46 Cato Tom Andersen .07 .20
47 Frode Hansen .07 .20
48 Petter Salsten .20 .50
49 Arne Billkvam .07 .20
50 Jarle Friis .07 .20
51 Steve Allmann .07 .20
52 Torbjorn Orskau .07 .20
53 Christian Kjeldsberg .07 .20
54 Bjorn Mathisrud .07 .20
55 Pal Gjermundsen .07 .20
56 Ketil Martinsen .07 .20
57 Vidar Andersen .07 .20
58 Rene Hansen .07 .20
59 Martin Friis .07 .20
60 Orjan Lovdal .07 .20
61 Lars Hakon Andersen .07 .20
62 Robert Sundt .07 .20
63 Henrik Buskoven .07 .20
64 Morten Finstad .20 .50
65 Magnus Christoffersen .07 .20
66 Roar Larsen .07 .20
67 Zdenek Albrecht .07 .20
68 Oldrich Valek .07 .20
69 Fredrik Jacobsen .07 .20
70 Rune Hansen .07 .20
71 Lars Jacobsen .07 .20
72 Staffan Tholsson .07 .20
73 Lase Syversen .07 .20
74 Kim Sogaard .07 .20
75 Jan Erik Thoresen .07 .20
76 Pal Andre Eriksen .07 .20
77 Bjorn Freddy Bekkerud .07 .20
78 Kjell Erik Myreng .07 .20
79 Lars Eilertsen .07 .20
80 Reino Johansen .07 .20
81 Igor Mishukov .07 .20
82 Ole Petter Dalene .07 .20
83 Jon Gundersen .07 .20
84 Pal Raab Lien .07 .20
85 Vadim Tunikov .07 .20
86 Tommy Skaarberg .07 .20
87 Per Christian Knold .07 .20
88 Stephen Foyn .07 .20
89 Glenn Asland .07 .20
90 Bjorte Olsson .07 .20
91 Gorm Gundersen .07 .20
92 Morgan Andersen .07 .20
93 Vegar Barlie .07 .20
94 Oystein Tronrud .07 .20
95 Kim Fagerhoi .07 .20
96 Tor Nilsen .07 .20
97 Arne Bergseng .07 .20
98 Timo Laituri .07 .20
99 Sjur Robert Nilsen .07 .20
100 Mattis Haakensen .07 .20
101 Lars Bergseng .07 .20
102 Svein Enok Norstebo .20 .50
103 Tor Anders Jacobsen .07 .20
104 Jorgen Salsten .07 .20
105 Tommy Jakobsen .07 .20
106 Tim Budy .07 .20
107 Martin Wiita .07 .20
108 Lenny Eriksson .07 .20
109 Stale Berg .07 .20
110 Bjorn Anders Dahl .07 .20
111 Geir Tore Dahl .07 .20
112 Dallas Gaume .07 .20
113 Geir Haugen .07 .20
114 Roar Husby .07 .20
115 Robert Nielsen .07 .20
116 Lars Erik Lunde .07 .20
117 Kare Nordnes .07 .20
118 Magne Nordnes .07 .20
119 Geir Leknes .07 .20
120 Rob Doroshuk .07 .20
121 Roger Olsen .07 .20
122 Oyvind Sorli .07 .20
123 Gunnar Bye .07 .20
124 Per Kristian Vellan .07 .20
125 Marc Laniel .20 .50
126 Dallas Gaume .07 .20
127 Robert Schistad .07 .20
128 Jan Petter Loschbrandt .07 .20
129 Tore Kristensen .07 .20
130 Eskil Eide .07 .20
131 Eirik Brodahl .07 .20
132 Morten Nordhus .07 .20
133 Erik Pettersen .07 .20
134 Hans Bekken .07 .20
135 Jan Bekken .07 .20
136 Jon Erik Haaland .07 .20
137 Richard Little .07 .20
138 Eivind Olsen .07 .20
139 Morten Gilje .07 .20
140 Sverre Hogemark .07 .20
141 Eirik Paulsen .07 .20
142 Kyle McDonough .07 .20
143 Steffen Trettenes .07 .20
144 Richard David .07 .20
145 Odd Nilsen .07 .20
146 Per Marthinsen .07 .20
147 Johnny Nilsen .07 .20
148 Per Christian Fjeldstad .07 .20
149 Christian Hafsmoe .07 .20
150 Raymond Lunde .07 .20
151 Rene Lemire .07 .20
152 Thomas Kristiansen .07 .20
153 Vidar Wold .07 .20
154 Hans Petter Halla .07 .20
155 Michael Smithurst .07 .20
156 Lars Erik Solberg .07 .20
157 Kenneth Fjell .07 .20
158 Morten Hem .07 .20
159 Dag Hoyem .07 .20
160 Vince Guidotti .07 .20
161 Glen Engevik .07 .20
162 Joe Clarke .07 .20
163 Lars Erik Kjaer .07 .20
164 Gorm Laursen .07 .20
165 Per Reidar Johansen .07 .20
166 Anders Martinsen .07 .20
167 Jorn Arild Flatha .07 .20
168 Rune Hansen .07 .20
169 Stian Kraft .07 .20
170 Geir Svendsberget .07 .20
171 Andre Aas .07 .20
172 Erik Skoglund Nilsen .07 .20
173 Frode Sletner .07 .20
174 Petter Syversne .07 .20
175 Jarle Gundersen .07 .20
176 Terje Wikstrom .07 .20
177 Steve MacDonald .07 .20
178 Sjur Kinder .07 .20
179 Morten Fjeldstad .07 .20
180 George Tower .07 .20
181 Espen Knutsen 2.00 5.00
182 Jon Magne Karlstad .07 .20
183 Tommy Jakobsen .07 .20
184 Valerengen .02 .10
185 Trondheim .02 .10
186 Dallas Gaume .02 .10
187 Bjorn Anders Dahl .02 .10
188 Jarl Eriksen .07 .20
189 Mark Fioretti .02 .10
190 Brian Tutt .20 .50
191 Jim Marthinsen .20 .50
192 Brian Tutt .20 .50
193 Jaromir Latal .07 .20
194 Espen Knutsen 2.00 5.00
195 Dallas Gaume .20 .50
196 Oldrich Valek .07 .20
197 Bjorn Skaare .07 .20
198 Knut Walbye .07 .20
199 Age Ellingsen .07 .20
200 Espen Knutsen 2.00 5.00
201 Ole Eskild Dahlstrom .07 .20
202 Tommie Eriksen .07 .20
203 Vegar Barlie .07 .20
204 Glenn Jessesen .07 .20
205 Tor Arne Alseth .07 .20
206 Per Kristian Vellan .07 .20
207 Jone Hatteland .07 .20
208 Henrik Aaby .07 .20
209 Johnny Nilsen .07 .20
210 Geir Svendsberget .07 .20
211 Pal Kristian Eggen .07 .20
212 Andreas Brunvoll .07 .20
213 Andre Manscov Hansen .07 .20
214 Frode Christiansen .07 .20
215 Jan Morten Dahl .07 .20
216 Stian Kraft .07 .20
217 Lubos Sikela .07 .20
218 Rune Fjeldstad .07 .20
219 Sven Arild Olsen .07 .20
220 Kent Inge Kristiansen .07 .20
221 Sjur Rakstad Larsen .07 .20
222 Borre Ostvang .07 .20
223 Harald Bastiansen .07 .20
224 Jon Warset .07 .20
225 Jo Espen Leibnitz .07 .20
226 Arild Syversen .07 .20
227 Terje Haukali .07 .20
228 Geir Dalene .07 .20
229 Jonas Larsen .07 .20
230 Thomas Hansen .07 .20
231 Stig Olsen .07 .20
232 Lars Hansen .07 .20
233 Hans M. Anonsen .07 .20
234 Ketil Kristiansen .07 .20
235 Bjornar Sorensen .07 .20
236 Tom Jostne .07 .20
237 John Klears .07 .20
238 Arve Jansen .07 .20
239 Orjan Gjertsen .07 .20
240 Checklist (1-81) .02 .10
241 Checklist (82-162) .02 .10
242 Checklist (163-242) .02 .10

1999-00 Norwegian National Team

COMPLETE SET (24) 10.00 25.00
1 Robert Schistad .75 2.00
2 Geir Svendsberget .40 1.00
3 Henrik Aaby .40 1.00
4 Tommy Jacobsen .40 1.00
5 Tommy Jacobsen .40 1.00
6 Andre Manskov Hansen .40 1.00
7 Morten Fjeldstad .40 1.00
8 Lars Hakon Andersen .40 1.00
9 Marius Trygg .40 1.00
10 Svein Enok Norstebo .75 2.00
11 Carl Oscar Boe Andersen .40 1.00
12 Ole Eskild Dalstrom .40 1.00
13 Per Age Skroder .40 1.00
14 Pal Johnsen .40 1.00
15 Trond Vegar Magnussen .40 1.00
16 Mats Trygg .40 1.00
17 Ketil Wold .40 1.00
18 Sjur Robert Nilsen .40 1.00
19 Anders Myrvold .75 2.00
20 Tore Vikingstad .40 1.00
21 Bjorge Josefsen .40 1.00
22 Oyvind Sorli .40 1.00
23 Bard Sorlie .40 1.00
24 Leif Boork CO .20 .50

1969-70 Russian National Team Postcards

COMPLETE SET (27) 75.00 150.00
1 Viktor Zinger 1.50 4.00
2 Vitali Davydov 1.50 4.00
3 Vladimir Lutchenko 1.50 4.00
4 Viktor Kuzkin 1.50 4.00
5 Alexander Ragulin 4.00 10.00
6 Igor Romishevski 1.50 4.00
7 Boris Mikhailov 6.00 15.00
8 Viacheslav Starshinov 1.50 4.00
9 Evgeny Zimin 1.50 4.00
10 Alexander Maltsev 6.00 15.00
11 Anatoli Firsov 4.00 10.00
12 Evgeny Paladiev 1.50 4.00
13 Alexander Yakushev 6.00 15.00
14 Vladimir Petrov 6.00 15.00
15 Valeri Kharlamov 10.00 25.00
16 Evgeny Mishakov 1.50 4.00
17 Vladimir Vikulov 1.50 4.00
18 Vladimir Yursinov 1.50 4.00
19 Viktor Pushkov 1.50 4.00
20 Arkady Chernishev 1.50 4.00
21 Anatoli Tarasov 4.00 10.00
22 USSR vs Sweden .75 2.00
23 USSR vs Sweden .75 2.00
24 USSR vs Sweden .75 2.00
25 USSR vs Finland, Sweden .75 2.00
26 USSR vs Canada, Sweden 1.50 4.00
27 Team Photo 1.50 4.00

1970-71 Russian National Team Postcards

COMPLETE SET (20) 100.00 150.00
1 Viktor Konovalenko 2.00 5.00
2 Vitali Davydov 2.00 5.00
3 Vladimir Lutchenko 2.00 5.00
4 Valeri Nikitin 2.00 5.00
5 Alexander Ragulin 4.00 10.00
6 Igor Romishevski 2.00 5.00
7 Evgeny Paladiev 2.00 5.00
8 Viacheslav Starshinov 2.00 5.00
9 Viktor Polupanov 2.00 5.00
10 Alexander Maltsev 6.00 15.00
11 Anatoli Firsov 6.00 15.00
12 Evgeni Mishakov 2.00 5.00
13 Boris Mikhailov 6.00 15.00
14 Valeri Vasiliev 4.00 10.00
15 Alexander Yakushev 6.00 15.00
16 Vladimir Petrov 6.00 15.00
17 Valeri Kharlamov 10.00 25.00
18 Vladimir Vikulov 2.00 5.00
19 Vladimir Shadrin 2.00 5.00
20 Vladislav Tretiak 10.00 25.00

1973-74 Russian National Team

COMPLETE SET (25) 60.00 125.00
1 Team Photo 1.50 4.00
2 Vladislav Tretiak 8.00 20.00
3 Alexander Sidelnikov 1.50 4.00
4 Alexander Gusev 1.50 4.00
5 Valeri Vasiliev 3.00 8.00
6 Boris Mikhailov 3.00 8.00
7 Vladimir Petrov 3.00 8.00
8 Valeri Kharlamov 6.00 15.00
9 Kharlamov, Petrov, Mikhailov 4.00 10.00
10 Vladimir Lutchenko 1.50 4.00
11 Gennady Tsygankov 1.50 4.00
12 Alexander Ragulin 1.50 4.00
13 Alexander Volchkov 1.50 4.00
14 Vlacheslav Anisin 1.50 4.00
15 Yuri Lebedev 1.50 4.00
16 Alexander Bodunov 1.50 4.00
17 Alexander Martinyuk 1.50 4.00
18 Vladimir Shadrin 1.50 4.00
19 Alexander Yakushev 3.00 8.00
20 Alexander Maltsev 3.00 8.00
21 Evgeny Paladiev 1.50 4.00
22 Yuri Liapkin 1.50 4.00
23 Bobrov Kulagin CO .75 2.00
24 Boris Mikhailov 3.00 8.00
25 Viktor Kuzkin 1.50 4.00

1974 Russian National Team

COMPLETE SET (25) 50.00 100.00
1 Vyacheslav Anisin 1.50 4.00
2 Vsevolod Bobrov CO 1.50 4.00
3 Alexander Bodunov 1.50 4.00
4 Alexander Gusev 1.50 4.00
5 Sergei Kapustin 1.50 4.00
6 Valeri Kharlamov 5.00 12.00
7 Boris Kulagin CO 1.50 4.00
8 Viktor Kuzkin 1.50 4.00
9 Yuri Lebedev 1.50 4.00
10 Yuri Liapkin 1.50 4.00
11 Vladimir Lutchenko 1.50 4.00
12 Alexander Maltsev 3.00 8.00
13 Boris Mikhailov 3.00 8.00
14 Boris Mikhailov 3.00 8.00
15 Vladimir Petrov 3.00 8.00
16 Vladimir Repneev 1.50 4.00
17 Vladimir Shadrin 1.50 4.00
18 Yuri Shatalov 1.50 4.00
19 Alexander Sidelnikov 1.50 4.00
20 Vladislav Tretiak 6.00 15.00
21 Gennady Tsygankov 1.50 4.00
22 Valeri Vasiliev 3.00 8.00
23 Alexander Yakushev 3.00 8.00
24 USSR .40 1.00
25 USSR .40 1.00

1979 Russian National Team

COMPLETE SET (24) 37.50 100.00
1 Team Photo .50 1.00
2 Viktor Tikhonov CO 1.00 2.00
3 Vladimir Yursinov CO .50 2.00
4 Vladislav Tretiak 5.00 15.00
5 Alexander Pashkov 1.50 3.00
6 Vladimir Lutchenko 1.00 3.00
7 Valeri Vasiliev 1.00 5.00
8 Gennady Tsygankov 1.00 3.00
9 Yuri Fedorov 1.00 2.00
10 Slava Fetisov 5.00 15.00
11 Zinetula Bilyaletinov 2.50 5.00
12 Vasili Pervukhin 1.00 3.00
13 Boris Mikhailov 2.50 8.00
14 Vladimir Petrov 2.50 8.00
15 Valeri Kharlamov 5.00 15.00
16 Alexander Maltsev 2.50 8.00
17 Sergei Kapustin 1.00 3.00
18 Yuri Lebedev 1.00 2.00
19 Viktor Zhluktov 1.00 3.00
20 Helmut Balderis 1.50 5.00
21 Alexander Golikov 1.00 2.00
22 Sergei Makarov 4.00 15.00
23 Vladimir Golikov 1.00 2.00
24 Team Photo .50 1.00

1984 Russian National Team

COMPLETE SET (23) 40.00 80.00
1 Sergei Babinov .75 2.00
2 Helmut Balderis 1.25 3.00
3 Zinetula Bilyaletinov 1.25 3.00
4 Vyacheslav Bykov 2.00 5.00
5 Slava Fetisov 4.00 10.00
6 Irek Gimaev .75 2.00
7 Sergei Kapustin .75 2.00
8 Alexei Kasatonov 2.00 5.00
9 Andrei Khomotov 2.00 5.00
10 Vladimir Krutov 4.00 10.00
11 Igor Larionov 6.00 15.00
12 Sergei Makarov 4.00 10.00
13 Alexander Maltsev 2.00 5.00
14 Vladimir Myshkin 2.00 5.00
15 Vasily Pervukhin .75 2.00
16 Sergei Shepelev .75 2.00
17 Alexander Skvorstsov .75 2.00
18 Sergei Starikov 1.25 3.00
19 Viktor Tikhonov CO .75 2.00
20 Vladislav Tretiak 4.00 10.00
21 Mikhael Vasiliev .75 2.00
22 Vladimir Yursinov CO .40 1.00
23 Viktor Zhluktov .75 2.00
24 Vladimir Zubkov .75 2.00

1987 Russian National Team

COMPLETE SET (24) 18.00 45.00
1 Sergei Ageikin .40 1.00
2 Evgeny Belosheikin .75 2.00
3 Zinetula Belyaletdinov .40 1.00
4 Viacheslav Bykov .75 2.00
5 Slava Fetisov 2.00 5.00
6 Alexei Gusarov .60 1.50
7 Valeri Kamensky 1.25 3.00
8 Alexei Kasatonov .75 2.00
9 Yuri Khmylev .60 1.50
10 Andrei Khomutov .75 2.00
11 Vladimir Konstantinov 2.00 5.00
12 Vladimir Krutov 1.25 3.00

13 Igor Larionov 2.00 5.00
14 Sergei Makarov 1.25 3.00
15 Sergei Mylnikov .75 2.00
16 Vasili Pervukhin .40 1.00
17 Sergei Starikov .40 1.00
18 Igor Stelnov .40 1.00
19 Sergei Svetlov .40 1.00
20 Viktor Tikhonov CO .75 2.00
21 Viktor Tjumenev .40 1.00
22 Michael Varnakov .40 1.00
23 Sergei Yashin .40 1.00
24 Vladimir Yursinov CO .40 1.00

1989 Russian National Team

COMPLETE SET (24) 14.00 35.00
1 Ilya Byakin .30 .75
2 Viacheslav Bykov .40 1.00
3 Alexandr Chernik .20 .50
4 Igor Dmitriev CO .20 .50
5 Sergei Fedorov 3.00 8.00
6 Slava Fetisov 1.25 3.00
7 Alexei Gusarov .30 .75
8 Arturs Irbe 2.00 5.00
9 Valeri Kamensky .75 2.00
10 Alexei Kasatonov .60 1.50
11 Svatoslav Khalizov .20 .50
12 Yuri Khmylev .30 .75
13 Andrei Khomutov .40 1.00
14 Vladimir Konstantinov 2.00 5.00
15 Vladimir Krutov .75 2.00
16 Dimitri Kvartalnov .40 1.00
17 Igor Larionov 1.50 4.00
18 Sergei Makarov .75 2.00
19 Vladimir Mishkin .40 1.00
20 Sergei Mylnikov .40 1.00
21 Sergei Nemchinov .40 1.00
22 Valeri Shirjaev .20 .50
23 Viktor Tikhonov CO .40 1.00
24 Sergei Yashin .20 .50

1991 Russian Sports Unite Hearts

COMPLETE SET (10) 6.00 15.00
1 Sergei Fedorov 2.00 5.00
2 Viacheslav Fetisov .75 2.00
3 Alexei Gusarov .40 1.00
4 Alexei Kasatonov .40 1.00
5 Vladimir Konstantinov .75 2.00
6 Igor Larionov .75 2.00
7 Sergei Makarov .40 1.00
8 Alexander Mogilny .75 2.00
9 Mikhail Tatarinov .40 1.00
10 Vladislav Tretiak 1.25 3.00

1991 Russian Stars in NHL

COMPLETE SET (11) 3.00 8.00
1 Sergei Fedorov 1.50 4.00
2 Slava Fetisov .40 1.00
3 Alexei Gusarov .08 .25
4 Alexei Kasatonov .20 .50
5 Vladimir Konstantinov .40 1.00
6 Igor Larionov .40 1.00
7 Sergei Makarov .40 1.00
8 Alexander Mogilny .60 1.50
9 Mikhail Tatarinov .08 .25
10 Vladislav Tretiak .75 2.00
11 Team Photo
USSR National Team .15 .40

1991-92 Russian Stars Red Ace

COMPLETE SET (17) 4.00 10.00
1 Pavel Bure 1.25 3.00
2 Evgeny Davydov .08 .25
3 Sergei Fedorov 1.25 3.00
4 Slava Fetisov .40 1.00
5 Alexei Gusarov .08 .25
6 Valeri Kamensky .30 .75
7 Alexei Kasatonov .20 .50
8 Ravil Khaidarov .08 .25
9 Vladimir Konstantinov .40 1.00
10 Igor Kravchuk .15 .40
11 Igor Larionov .40 1.00
12 Andrei Lomakin .08 .25
13 Sergei Makarov .30 .75
14 Alexander Mogilny .40 1.00
15 Sergei Nemchinov .15 .40
16 Anatoli Semenov .08 .25
17 Mikhail Tatarinov .08 .25

1991-92 Russian Tri-Globe Bure

COMPLETE SET (6) 3.00 8.00
COMMON CARD (6-10) .60 1.50
NNO Sergei Fedorov
Checklist .20 .50

1991-92 Russian Tri-Globe Fedorov

COMPLETE SET (5) 2.50 6.00
COMMON CARD (1-5) .50 1.25

1991-92 Russian Tri-Globe Irbe

COMPLETE SET (6) 1.50 4.00
COMMON CARD (16-20) .30 .75
NNO Sergei Fedorov
Checklist .20 .50

1991-92 Russian Tri-Globe Kamensky

COMPLETE SET (6) .60 1.50
COMMON CARD (1-5) .30 .75
NNO Sergei Fedorov
Checklist .20 .50

1991-92 Russian Tri-Globe Semenov

COMPLETE SET (6) .60 1.50
COMMON CARD (11-15) .08 .25
NNO Sergei Fedorov
Checklist .20 .50

1992 Russian Stars Red Ace

COMPLETE SET (36) 2.00 5.00
1 Darius Kasparaitis .10 .25
2 Alexei Zhamnov .10 .25
3 Dimitri Khristich .20 .50
4 Andrei Trefilov .20 .50
5 Vitali Prokhorov .02 .10
6 Dmitri Filimonov .02 .10
7 Valeri Zelepukin .10 .25
8 Alexei Kovalev .30 .75
9 Dmitri Kvartalnov .10 .25
10 Igor Korolev .10 .25
11 Nikolai Borschevsky .10 .25
12 Igor Boldin .02 .10
13 Arturs Irbe .30 .75
14 Viachesiav Butsayev .02 .10
15 Boris Mironov .10 .25
16 Sergei Bautin .02 .10
17 Alexander Kharlamov .10 .25
18 Viacheslav Kozlov .20 .50
19 Mikhail Shtalenkov .20 .50
20 Roman Oksyuta .02 .10
21 Sandis Ozolinsh .20 .50
22 Dmitri Mironov .10 .25
23 Sergei Brylin .10 .25
24 Vladimir Grachev .02 .10
25 Dmitri Starostenko .02 .10
26 Andrei Nazarov .10 .25
27 Alexei Yashin .20 .50
28 Vladimir Malakhov .10 .25
29 Ravil Jakubov .02 .10
30 Sergei Klimovich .02 .10
31 Artur Oktjabrev .02 .10
32 Lev Berdichevski .02 .10
33 Ian Kaminski .10 .25
34 Andrei Kovalenko .10 .25
35 Dmitri Yushkevich .10 .25
36 Checklist .02 .10

1992 Russian Tri-Globe From Russia With Puck

COMPLETE SET (24) 4.00 10.00
1 Igor Larionov .20 .50
2 Igor Larionov .20 .50
3 Andrei Lomakin .08 .25
4 Andrei Lomakin .08 .25
5 Pavel Bure .75 2.00
6 Pavel Bure .75 2.00
7 Alexei Zhamnov .08 .25
8 Alexei Zhamnov .08 .25
9 Sergei Krivokrasov .08 .25
10 Sergei Krivokrasov .08 .25
11 Valeri Kamensky .08 .25
12 Valeri Kamensky .08 .25
13 Viacheslav Kozlov .20 .50
14 Viacheslav Kozlov .20 .50
15 Valeri Zelepukhin .08 .25
16 Valeri Zelepukhin .08 .25
17 Igor Kravchuk .08 .25
18 Igor Kravchuk .08 .25
19 Vladimir Malakhov .08 .25
20 Vladimir Malakhov .08 .25
21 Boris Mironov .08 .25
22 Boris Mironov .08 .25
23 Arturs Irbe .20 .50
24 Arturs Irbe .20 .50

1992-93 Russian Stars Red Ace

COMPLETE SET (37) 2.00 5.00
1 Aleksander Barkov .02 .10
2 Sergei Bautin .02 .10
3 Igor Boldin .02 .10
4 Nikolai Borchevsky .08 .25
5 Sergei Brylin .08 .25
6 Viacheslav Butsayev .02 .10
7 Alexander Cherbajev .02 .10
8 Evgeny Garanin .02 .10
9 Sergei Gonchar .20 .50
10 Alexander Karpovtsev .08 .25
11 Darius Kasparaitis .08 .25
12 Alexander Kharlamov .08 .25
13 Yuri Khmylev .08 .25
14 Sergei Klimovich .02 .10
15 Igor Korolev .08 .25
16 Andrei Kovalenko .08 .25
17 Alexei Kovalev UER
(Bac .30 .75
18 Dmitri Kvartalnov .08 .25
19 Vladimir Malakhov .08 .25
20 Maxim Mikhailovsky .02 .10
21 Boris Mironov .08 .25
22 Dmitri Mironov .08 .25
23 Andrei Nazarov .08 .25
24 Roman Oksyuta .02 .10
25 Artur Oktyabrev .02 .10
26 Sergei Petrenko .02 .10
27 Oleg Petrov .08 .25
28 Andrei Potaichuk .02 .10
29 Vitali Prokhorov .02 .10
30 Alexander Semak .08 .25
31 Dmitri Starostenko .02 .10
32 Ravil Yakubov .02 .10
33 Alexei Yashin .20 .50
34 Dmitri Yushkevich .08 .25
35 Alexei Zhamnov .08 .25
36 Alexei Zhitnik .08 .25
NNO Checklist Card .02 .10

1998-99 Russian Hockey League

COMPLETE SET (167) 24.00 60.00
1 Sergei Gomolyako .20 .50
2 Sergei Zemchenok .20 .50
3 Oleg Mikulchik .20 .50
4 Evgueni Koreshkov .20 .50
5 Andrei Razin .20 .50
6 Ravil Gusmanov .20 .50
7 Dmitri Popov .20 .50
8 Valeri Karpov .30 .75
9 Andrei Sokolov .20 .50
10 Makhail Borodulin .20 .50
11 Konstantin Shafranov .30 .75
12 Vladimir Antipin .20 .50
13 Igor Zemlyanoi .20 .50
14 Sergei Tertyshny .20 .50
15 Vadim Glovatski .20 .50
16 Alexander Golts .30 .75
17 Alexander Koreshkov .20 .50
18 Boris Tortunov .20 .50
19 Valeri Nikulin .20 .50
20 Andrei Sapoznikov .20 .50
21 Dmitri Maksimov .20 .50
22 Dmitri Mylnikov .75 2.00
23 Maxim Sushinski .40 1.00
24 Yuri Panov .20 .50
25 Alexander Terekhov .20 .50
26 Vladimir Zorkin .20 .50
27 Eduard Gorbachev .20 .50
28 Leonid Kanarekin .20 .50
29 Alexander Savchenkov .20 .50
30 Maxim Chukanov .20 .50
31 Evgueni Fedorov .20 .50
32 Yaroslav Lyuzenkov .20 .50
33 Oleg Leontiev .20 .50
34 Sergei Osipov .20 .50
35 Andrei Kudinov .20 .50
36 Dmitri Krasotkin .20 .50
37 Ravil Yakubov .40 1.00
38 Dmitri Zatonski .20 .50
39 Konstantin Maslyukov .20 .50
40 Andrei Subbotin .30 .75
41 Pavel Kamentsev .20 .50
42 Evgueni Tarasov .20 .50
43 Oleg Kryazhev .20 .50
44 Igor Nikitin .20 .50
45 Denis Arkhipov 1.25 3.00
46 Albert Loginov .20 .50
47 Andrei Samokhvalov .20 .50
48 Igor Dorofeev .20 .50
49 Sergei Bautin .20 .50
50 Evgueni Varlamov .20 .50
51 Sergei Korobkin .20 .50
52 Rafik Yakubov .20 .50
53 Alexei Chupin .20 .50
54 Dmitri Ryabikin .20 .50
55 Alexei Kudashav .20 .50
56 Alexander Trofimov .20 .50
57 Igor Andryushchenko .20 .50
58 Igor Gorbenko .20 .50
59 Dmitri Gorenko .20 .50
60 Alexander Kazakov .20 .50
61 Evgueni Kuveko .20 .50
62 Igor Nikolaev .20 .50
63 Mikhail Pereyaslov .20 .50
64 Alexander Filippov .20 .50
65 Igor Mikhailov .20 .50
66 Roman Shipulin .20 .50
67 Dmitri Shpakovski .20 .50
68 Dmitri Shulakov .20 .50
69 Konstantin Golokhvastov .20 .50
70 Yuri Fimin .20 .50
71 Sergei Yasakov .20 .50
72 Oleg Filimonov .20 .50
73 Anatoli Ustyugov .20 .50
74 Andrei Skabelka .30 .75
75 Sergei Zolotov .20 .50
76 Dmitri Bezrukov .20 .50
77 Dmitri Vanyasov .20 .50
78 Evgueni Zakharov .20 .50
79 Arat Kadyekin .20 .50
80 Evgueni Mlinchenko .20 .50
81 Leonid Labzov .20 .50
82 Andrei Mazhugin .20 .50
83 Vladislav Makarov .20 .50
84 Remir Khaidarov .20 .50
85 Pavel Agarkov .20 .50
86 Igor Belyavski .20 .50
87 Dmitri Dubrovski .20 .50
88 Vyacheslav Zavalnyuk .20 .50
89 Yuri Zuev .20 .50
90 Andrei Evstafiev .20 .50
91 Vadim Epanchintsev .40 1.00
92 Igor Zelenchev .20 .50
93 Dmitri Klevakin .20 .50
94 Alexei Koledaev .20 .50
95 Nikolai Kurochkin .20 .50
96 Boris Kuzmin .20 .50
97 Roman Kukhtinov .20 .50
98 Sergei Moskalev .20 .50
99 Evgueni Pupkov .20 .50
100 Alexei Tkachuk .20 .50
101 Rinat Khasanov .20 .50
102 Sergei Shalamai .20 .50
103 Vadim Tarasov .75 2.00
104 Vladislav Morozov .20 .50
105 Almaz Garifullin .30 .75
106 Ilnur Gizatullin .20 .50
107 Alexander Zavyalov .20 .50
108 Oleg Vevcherenko .20 .50
109 Alexander Savitski .20 .50
110 Mikhail Sarmatin .20 .50
111 Igor Stepanov .20 .50
112 Konstantin Butsenko .20 .50
113 Alexei Murzin .20 .50
114 Andrei Nikolaev .20 .50
115 Dmitri Plekhanov .20 .50
116 Roman Salnikov .20 .50
117 Vyacheslav Timchenko .20 .50
118 Anitoli Stepanishev .20 .50
119 Roman Baranov .20 .50
120 Artem Anisimov .20 .50
121 Yuri Guniko .20 .50
122 Eduard Kudermetov .20 .50
123 Dmitri Balmin .20 .50
124 Igor Dyakiv .20 .50
125 Ramil Saifullin .20 .50
126 Alexander Vyukhin .20 .50
127 Oleg Leontiev .20 .50
128 Evgueni Koreshkov .20 .50
129 Sergei Gomolyako .20 .50
130 Oleg Mikulchik .20 .50
131 Andrei Petrakov .20 .50
132 Alexei Stepanov .20 .50
133 Dmitri Verzhinin .20 .50
134 Artem Ostroushko .20 .50
135 Sergei Berdnikov .20 .50
136 Konstantin Koltsov .20 .50
137 Vladimir Tarasov .20 .50
138 Sergei Shimkovski .20 .50
139 Oleg Pchelyakov .20 .50
140 Oleg Burlutski .20 .50
141 Oleg Bratash .20 .50
142 Sergei Voronov .20 .50
143 Uldar Mukhometov .30 .75
144 Alexei Egorov .40 1.00
145 Vladimir Kopat .20 .50
146 Vladimir Kochin .20 .50
147 Alexei Putilin .20 .50
148 Andrei Rasolko .20 .50
149 Vadim Molotilov .20 .50
150 Dmitri Nazarov .20 .50
151 Igor Vyazmikin .20 .50
152 Alexei Kalyukhny .20 .50
153 Denis Kartsev .20 .50
154 Alexander Kuvaldin .20 .50
155 Alexei Troschinsky .20 .50
156 Alexander Kharitonov .40 1.00
157 Valeri Cherny .20 .50
158 Yuri Dobrishkin .20 .50
159 Evgueni Pavlov .20 .50
160 Nikolai Antropov 1.25 3.00
161 Alexander Zhurik .20 .50
162 Valeri Belousov .20 .50
163 Artem Chubarov .40 1.00
164 Boris Zelenko .20 .50
165 Dmitri Frolov .40 1.00
166 Vladimir Kirik .20 .50
167 Alexei Danilov .20 .50

1999 Russian Fetisov Tribute

COMPLETE SET (41) 6.00 15.00
1 Alexander Korolyuk .07 .20
2 Pavel Bure .75 2.00
3 Alexei Morozov .07 .20
4 Viktor Kozlov .07 .20
5 Sergei Makarov .20 .50
6 Valeri Kamensky .07 .20
7 Maxim Afinogenov .20 .50
8 Slava Fetisov .20 .50
9 Maxim Sokolov .20 .50
10 Vladimir Malakhov .07 .20
11 Alexei Yashin .07 .20
12 Sergei Vyshedkevich .07 .20
13 Oleg Tverdovsky .07 .20
14 Sergei Brylin .07 .20
15 Vladimir Krutov .20 .50
16 Gennadi Tsygankov .07 .20
17 Egor Podomatski .20 .50
18 Vitali Vishnevski .07 .20
19 Sergei Nemchinov .07 .20
20 Daniil Markov .07 .20
21 Alexander Kharitonov .07 .20
22 Slava Bykov .07 .20
23 Bobby Carpenter .07 .20
24 Scott Stevens .20 .50
25 Ken Daneyko .07 .20
26 Jari Kurri .75 2.00
27 Slava Kozlov .20 .50
28 Anders Eriksson .07 .20
29 Darius Kasparaitis .07 .20
30 Doug Brown .07 .20
31 Ilkka Sinisalo .07 .20
32 Valeri Shiryaev .07 .20
33 Martin Brodeur 2.00 5.00
34 Christian Ruuttu .07 .20
35 Randy McKay .07 .20
36 Gino Odjick .20 .50
37 Igor Larionov .20 .50
38 Martin Lapointe .07 .20
39 Larry Robinson CO .20 .50
40 Viktor Tikhonov CO .07 .20
41 Scotty Bowman CO .20 .50

1999-00 Russian Dynamo Moscow

COMPLETE SET (27) 6.00 15.00
1 Alexei Tereshenko .20 .50
2 Igor Shadilov .20 .50
3 Alexei Ponikarovski .30 .75
4 Alexei Litvinenko .20 .50
5 Roman Zolotov .20 .50
6 Andrei Markov .75 2.00
7 Alexander Khavanov .30 .75
8 Vitali Proshkin .20 .50
9 Alexei Troschinsky .20 .50
10 Oleg Orekhovski .20 .50
11 Marat Davydov .20 .50
12 Dmitri Kokorev .20 .50
13 Alexander Kharitonov .30 .75
14 Alexander Prokopiev .20 .50
15 Mikhail Ivanov .20 .50
16 Alexei Kudashov .30 .75
17 Alexander Kuvaldin .20 .50
18 Denis Kartsev .20 .50
19 Stanislav Romanov .20 .50
20 Alexander Savchenkov .20 .50
21 Lev Berdichevski .20 .50
22 Alexei Kalyuzhni .20 .50
23 Alexander Stepanov .20 .50
24 Boris Zelenko .20 .50
25 Vitali Yeremeev .60 1.50
26 Alexei Yegorov .40 1.00
NNO Team Photo .20 .50

1999-00 Russian Hockey League

COMPLETE SET (270) 60.00 100.00
1 Valeri Karpov .40 1.00
2 Igor Zemlyanoi .08 .25
3 Mikhail Borodulin .08 .25
4 Vladimir Antipin .08 .25
5 Vadim Glovatskin .08 .25
6 Alexei Stepanov .08 .25
7 Sergei Gomolyako .08 .25
8 Andrei Sokolov .08 .25
9 Andrei Razin .08 .25
10 Dmitri Popov .08 .25
11 Valeri Nikulin .08 .25
12 Andrei Petrakov .08 .25
13 Evgueni Koreshkov .08 .25
14 Alexander Koreshkov .08 .25
15 Andrei Sapozhnikov .20 .50
16 Oleg Mikulchik .40 1.00
17 Ravil Gusmanov .30 .75
18 Vitali Prokhorov .20 .50
19 Boris Tortunov .08 .25
20 Sergei Zemchenok .08 .25
21 Sergei Tertyshny .08 .25
22 Yuri Kuznetsov .08 .25
23 Maxim Bets .40 1.00
24 Sergei Osipov .08 .25
25 Oleg Leontiev .08 .25
26 Andrei Kudinov .08 .25
27 Konstantin Bezborodov .08 .25
28 Maxim Stepanov .08 .25
29 Alexei Lazarenko .08 .25
30 Vladimir Tyurikov .08 .25
31 Alexei Komarov .08 .25
32 Oleg Polkovinkov .08 .25
33 Dmitri Vershinin .08 .25
34 Vladimir Dumnov .08 .25
35 Oleg Smirnov .08 .25
36 Denis Ivanov .08 .25
37 Alexander Grishin .08 .25
38 Sergei Luchinkin .08 .25
39 Sergei Reshetnikov .08 .25
40 Denis Martiniuk .08 .25
41 Igor Boldin .08 .25
42 Nikolai Semin .08 .25
43 Alexander Zhdan .30 .75
44 Denis Metliuk .08 .25
45 Sergei Zolotov .08 .25
46 Yuri Dobryshkin .08 .25
47 Sergei Milnikov .40 1.00
48 Anton Ulyanov .08 .25
49 Yakov Deev .08 .25
50 Dmitri Bykov .08 .25
51 Dmitri Milnikov .40 1.00
52 Rinat Kasyanov .08 .25
53 Dmitri Balmin .08 .25
54 Alexei Chupin .08 .25
55 Artem Anisimov .08 .25
56 Sergei Smirnov .08 .25
57 Ivan Andriyashev .08 .25
58 Sergei Shilov .08 .25
59 Vladislav Makarov .08 .25
60 Dmitri Mylnikov
Sergei Mylnikov Jr. .75 2.00
61 Rafik Yakubov .08 .25
62 Dmitri Shandurov .08 .25
63 Vladimir Pozdnyakov .08 .25
64 Alexei Ivashkin .08 .25
65 Valeri Ivannikov .08 .25
66 Egor Mikhailov .08 .25
67 Alexander Zibin .08 .25
68 Igor Averchenkov .08 .25
69 Alexei Sheblanov .08 .25
70 Dmitri Yachanov .08 .25
71 Oleg Romanov .08 .25
72 Denis Arkhipov 1.25 3.00
73 Almaz Garifullin .08 .25
74 Evgueni Varlamov .08 .25
75 Igor Stepanov .08 .25
76 Alexander Zavyalov .08 .25
77 Ilinur Gizhatullin .08 .25
78 Alexander Trofimov .08 .25
79 Eduard Kudermetov .08 .25
80 Remir Khaidarov .08 .25
81 Nikolai Pronin .08 .25
82 Andrei Glebov .08 .25
83 Andrei Savchenko .08 .25
84 Andrei Mukhachev .08 .25
85 Maxim Ossipov .20 .50
86 Sergei Mozyakin .08 .25
87 Alexei Gubarev .08 .25
88 Oleg Filimonov .30 .75
89 Igor Nikolaev .08 .25
90 Eduard Polyakov .08 .25
91 Konstantin Tatarintsev .08 .25
92 Anitoli Ustyugov .08 .25
93 Victor Dronov .08 .25
94 Sergei Yasakov .08 .25
95 Oleg Gorbenko .08 .25
96 Igor Andryushenko .08 .25
97 Alexei Plotinkov .08 .25
98 Igor Bakhmutov .08 .25
99 Dmitri Shandurov .08 .25
100 Dmitri Bezrukov .08 .25
101 Airat Kadeikin .08 .25
102 Leonid Labzov .08 .25
103 Alexei Vakhrushev .08 .25
104 Denis Tsigurov .08 .25
105 Roman Baranov .08 .25
106 Vladimir Zorkin .08 .25
107 Dmitri Maksimov .08 .25
108 Dmitri Kulikov .08 .25
109 Alexander Guskov .08 .25
110 Dmitri Khomutov .08 .25
111 Alexander Skugarev .08 .25
112 Mikhail Pereyaslov .08 .25
113 Artem Argokov .08 .25
114 Alexei Strakhov .08 .25
115 Dmitri Shulakov .08 .25
116 Oleg Vevcherenko .08 .25
117 Yuri Fimin .08 .25
118 Ruslan Bernikov .08 .25
119 Alexander Titov .08 .25
120 Dmitri Gorenko .08 .25
121 Alexander Filippov .08 .25
122 Konstantin Mitroshkin .08 .25
123 Alexander Zevakhin .08 .25
124 Steve Plouffe .40 1.00
125 Nikolai Tsulgin .30 .75
126 Alexei Tertyshny .08 .25
127 Nikolai Zavarykhin .30 .75
128 Evgueni Zakharov .08 .25
129 Sergei Klimentiev .20 .50
130 Pavel Duma .30 .75
131 Maxim Vasyuchkov .08 .25
132 Rustem Amirov .08 .25
133 Matvei Belousov .08 .25
134 Alexander Schev .08 .25
135 Evgueni Muratov .08 .25
136 Andrei Buldakov .08 .25
137 Andrei Tsareev .08 .25
138 Vladimir Zavyalov .08 .25
139 Andrei Pchelyakov .08 .25
140 Igor Knyazev 1.25 3.00
141 Ilya Kovalchuk 25.00 50.00
142 Alexei Chervyakov .08 .25
143 Vladimir Kulikov .08 .25
144 Andrei Bushan .08 .25
145 Ravil Yakubov .20 .50
146 Sergei Shitkovski .08 .25
147 Sergei Berdnikov .08 .25
148 Ramil Saifullin .08 .25
149 Konstantin Golokhvastov .08 .25
150 Konstantin Maslyukov .08 .25
151 Alexei Bulatov .08 .25
152 Dmitri Kirilenko .08 .25
153 Sergei Makarov .08 .25
154 Rustem Kamaletdinov .08 .25
155 Maxim Mikhailovski .30 .75
156 Denis Khlopotnov .40 1.00
157 Albert Loginov .08 .25
158 Dmitri Nazarov .08 .25
159 Alexei Miroshnikov .08 .25
160 Sergei Zimakov .08 .25
161 Valeri Belov .08 .25
162 Alexei Kochegarov .08 .25
163 Alexei Pogonin .08 .25
164 Andrei Rasolko .08 .25
165 Dmitri Denisov .20 .50
166 Dmitri Tarasov .08 .25
167 Vadim Pokotilo .08 .25
168 Evgueni Fedorov .08 .25
169 Maxim Sushinski .30 .75
170 Alexander Popov .08 .25
171 Dmitri Parkhomenko .08 .25
172 Oleg Kryazhev .08 .25
173 Vitali Lyutkevich .08 .25
174 Dmitri Zatonski .08 .25
175 Oleg Ugolnikov .08 .25
176 Alexander Svitov 1.50 4.00
177 Dmitri Ryabkin .08 .25
178 Nikolai Babenko .08 .25
179 Yuri Panov .08 .25
180 Andrei Samokhvalov .08 .25
181 Alexander Ermakov .08 .25
182 Sergei Kagaikin .08 .25
183 Anvar Gatiyatulin .08 .25
184 Vladimir Tarasov .08 .25
185 Igor Varitskin .08 .25
186 Oleg Bolkov .08 .25
187 Rail Muftiev .08 .25
188 Vitali Yeremeev 1.25 3.00
189 Vladislav Brizgalov .30 .75
190 Dmitri Teplyakov .08 .25
191 Vladimir Kopat .08 .25
192 Denis Kuzmenko .08 .25
193 Evgueni Petrochinin .08 .25
194 Sergei Arekaev .08 .25
195 Pavel Agarkov .08 .25
196 Evgueni Pupkov .08 .25
197 Vadim Tarasov .40 1.00
198 Andrei Smirnov .08 .25
199 Alexander Maksimov .08 .25
200 Vitali Valui .08 .25
201 Sergei Petrenko .08 .25
202 Alexei Chistyakov .08 .25
203 Alexei Murzin .08 .25
204 Oleg Komissarov .08 .25
205 Mikhail Buturlin .08 .25
206 Konstantin Frolov .08 .25
207 Igor Zhelenchev .08 .25
208 Oleg Shargorodski .40 1.00
209 Sergei Selyutin .08 .25
210 Alexei Kupreenkov .08 .25
211 Roman Kukhtinov .08 .25
212 Vladislav Morozov .08 .25
213 Igor Belyavski .08 .25
214 Sergei Moskalev .08 .25
215 Alexei Tkachuk .08 .25
216 Sergei Chernyavski .08 .25
217 Vitali Kabanov .08 .25
218 Dmitri Klevakin .08 .25
219 Alexei Koledaev .08 .25
220 Oleg Glebov .08 .25
221 Georgi Evtyukhin .08 .25
222 Alexei Koznev .08 .25
223 Alexei Rubov .08 .25
224 Sergei Zinovjev 2.00 5.00
225 Evgueni Petrochinin .08 .25
226 Valeri Pokrovski .08 .25
227 Sergei Fedotov .08 .25
228 Vyacheslav Kurochkin .08 .25
229 Oleg Boltunov .08 .25
230 Alexei Baranov .08 .25
231 Igor Emeleev .08 .25
232 Roman Krivomazov .08 .25
233 Sergei Tikhonov .08 .25
234 Vladislav Brizgalov .30 .75
235 Dmitri Dubrovski .08 .25
236 Stepan Mokhov .08 .25
237 Dmitri Gogolev .08 .25
238 Evgueni Filinov .08 .25
239 Alexander Yudin .20 .50
240 Alexander Drozdetskin .08 .25
241 Sergei Shalamai .08 .25
242 Timofei Shishkanov .40 1.00
243 Alexander Sivov .08 .25
244 Vadim Musatov .08 .25
245 Andrei Chernoskutov .08 .25
246 Ruslan Shafikov .08 .25
247 Maxim Sokolov .20 .50
248 Alexander Matvichuk .08 .25
249 Andrei Evstafiev .08 .25
250 Vyacheslav Zavalnyuk .08 .25
251 Andrei Korolev .08 .25
252 Alexander Yudin .20 .50
253 Dmitri Mikhailov .08 .25
254 Artem Ostroushko .08 .25
255 Rinat Khasanov .08 .25
256 Vadim Epanchintsev .30 .75
257 Pavel Komarov .08 .25
258 Alexander Vyukhin .08 .25
259 Alfred Fatkullin .08 .25
260 Danis Zaripov .08 .25
261 Andrei Zubkov .08 .25
262 Marat Askarov .08 .25
263 Alexei Myagkikh .08 .25
264 Alexander Yudin .20 .50
265 Eduard Dmitriev .08 .25
266 Oleg Saltikov .08 .25
267 Oleg Grachev .08 .25
268 Valeri Oleinik .08 .25
269 Konstantin Koltsov .40 1.00
NNO Andrei Raiski .08 .25
NNO I.Koreshkov
Alexander Koreshkov
Evgeni Koreshk .20 .50

1999-00 Russian Metallurg Magnetogorsk

COMPLETE SET 6.00 15.00
27 Sergei Gomolyako .20 .50
28 Vadim Glovatski .20 .50
29 Sergei Tertyshny .20 .50
30 Igor Zemlyanoi .20 .50
31 Valeri Nikulin .20 .50
32 Andrei Sapozhnikov .30 .75
33 Boris Tortunov .20 .50
34 Sergei Zemchenok .20 .50
35 Oleg Mikulchuk .30 .75
36 Andrei Razin .30 .75
37 Ravil Gusmanov .30 .75
38 Maxim Bets .30 .75
39 Andrei Petrakov .20 .50
40 Andrei Kudinov .20 .50
41 Mikhail Borodulin .20 .50
42 Sergei Osipov .20 .50
43 Valeri Karpov .30 .75
44 Evgeni Koreshkov .20 .50
45 Alexander Koreshkov .20 .50
46 Dmitri Popov .20 .50
47 Andrei Sokolov .20 .50
48 Oleg Leontiev .20 .50
49 Vladimir Antipin .20 .50
50 Alexei Stelanov .20 .50
51 Vitali Prokhorov .30 .75
52 Alexander Golts .20 .50
53 Konstantin Shafranov .40 1.00
54 Team Card .20 .50

1999-00 Russian Stars of Hockey

COMPLETE SET (42) 12.00 30.00
1 Alexei Chupin .08 .25
2 Alexander Prokopiev .08 .25
3 Alexei Kudashov .08 .25
4 Alexander Khavanov .20 .50
5 Andrei Markov .60 1.50
6 Maxim Sushinski .08 .25
7 Dmitri Krasotkin .08 .25
8 Sergei Petrenko .08 .25
9 Valeri Karpov .08 .25
10 Sergei Tertyshny .08 .25
11 Ravil Gusmanov .08 .25
12 Egor Podomatski .20 .50
13 Alexei Chervyakov .08 .25
14 Valeri Ivannikov .08 .25
15 Maxim Mikhailovski .08 .25
16 Alexander Kharitonov .20 .50
17 Denis Arkhipov .30 .75
18 Yuri Dobryshkin .08 .25
19 Alexander Kuvaldin .08 .25
20 Dmitri Vlasenkov .08 .25
21 Evgeny Petrochinin .08 .25
22 Alexei Koznev .08 .25
23 Oleg Shargorodski .08 .25
24 Maxim Bets .08 .25
25 Dmitri Filimonov .08 .25
26 Alexei Yashin .20 .50
27 Pavel Bure 1.00 2.50
28 Sergei Fedorov 1.25 3.00
29 Alexander Mogilny .40 1.00
30 Alexei Kovalev .40 1.00
31 Maxim Sokolov .08 .25
32 Vyacheslav Kozlov .30 .75
33 Alexander Yakushev .40 1.00
34 Valeri Kharlamov 1.00 2.50
35 Alexei Kasatonov .20 .50
36 Vladislav Tretiak 2.00 5.00
37 Vyacheslav Fetisov .75 2.00
38 Valeri Vasiliev .40 1.00
39 Boris Mikhailov .40 1.00
40 Vyacheslav Anisin .08 .25
41 Vladimir Petrov .40 1.00
42 Alexander Maltsev .40 1.00

1999-00 Russian Stars Postcards

1 Maxim Afinogenov .75 2.00
2 Maxim Balmochnykh .40 1.00
3 Maxim Bets .40 1.00
4 Alexander Boikov .40 1.00
5 Victor Chistov .40 1.00
6 Marat Davydov .40 1.00
7 Kirill Golubev .40 1.00
8 Alexei Gorshkov .40 1.00
9 Airat Kadeikin .40 1.00
10 Svyatoslav Khalizov .40 1.00
11 Igor Khatsej .40 1.00
12 Viacheslav Kurochkin .40 1.00
13 Evgeny Kuveko .40 1.00
14 Albert Lecshev .40 1.00
15 Egor Mikhailov .75 2.00
16 Ildar Mukhametov .75 2.00
17 Andrei Pchelyakov .40 1.00
18 Sergey Petrenko .40 1.00
19 Alexander Prokopiev .40 1.00
20 Maxim Rybin .40 1.00
21 Vener Safin .40 1.00
22 Evgeny Shtepa .40 1.00
23 Dmitry Starostenko .40 1.00
24 Maxim Stepanov .40 1.00
25 Andrei Subbotin .40 1.00
26 Vadim Tarasov .75 2.00
27 Alexei Tkachuk .40 1.00
28 Andrei Tsarev .40 1.00
29 Vasily Turkovsky .40 1.00
30 Vladimir Tyurikov .40 1.00
31 Alexander Vyukhin .40 1.00
32 Sergei Yasakov .40 1.00

2000 Russian Champions

COMPLETE SET (6) 4.00 10.00
1 Alexander Khavanov .80 2.00
2 Alexei Troschinsky .80 2.00
3 Andrei Markov 1.25 3.00
4 Alexander Kharitonov .80 2.00
5 Alexander Prokopiev .40 1.00
6 Vitali Yeremeyev 1.20 3.00

2000-01 Russian Dynamo Moscow

COMPLETE SET (33) 6.00 15.00
1 Alexey Yegorov .30 .75
2 Oleg Shevtsov .20 .50
3 Alexander Yeremenko .30 .75
4 Mikhail Shtalenkov .40 1.00
5 Roman Zolotov .20 .50
6 Oleg Orekhovsky .20 .50
7 Igor Stchadilov .20 .50
8 Oleg Polkovnikov .20 .50
9 Ilya Nikulin .30 .75
10 Evgeny Gribko .20 .50
11 Marat Davydov .20 .50
12 Mikhail Donika .20 .50
13 Andrei Kuzmin .20 .50
14 Mikhail Ivanov .20 .50
15 Alexander Kuvaldin .20 .50
16 Sergei Klimovich .20 .50
17 Alexander Kharlamov .30 .75
18 Alexander Savchenkov .20 .50
19 Alexei Smirnov .40 1.00

Card	Low	High
20 Oleg Smirnov	.20	.50
21 Stanislav Romanov	.20	.50
22 Alexei Kudashov	.30	.75
23 Boris Zelenko	.20	.50
24 Alexei Tereshenko	.20	.50
25 Alexander Stepanov	.20	.50
26 Dmitri Dudarev	.20	.50
27 Denis Kartsev	.20	.50
28 Dmitri Subbotin	.20	.50
29 Igor Bakhmutov	.20	.50
30 Alexander Karpovtsev	.30	.75
31 Alexander Klebnikov	.20	.50
32 Dmitri Semenov	.20	.50
33 Dmitriy Kokorev	.30	.75

2000-01 Russian Dynamo Moscow Blue-White

Card	Low	High
COMPLETE SET (5)	2.50	6.00
1 Mikhail Shtalenkov	1.25	3.00
2 Alexei Kudashov	.75	2.00
3 Oleg Orekhovsky	.40	1.00
4 Mikhail Ivanov	.40	1.00
5 Dmitri Subbotin	.40	1.00

2000-01 Russian Goalkeepers

Card	Low	High
COMPLETE SET (9)	5.00	12.00
1 Maxim Sokolov	.40	1.00
2 Mikhail Shtalenkov	.75	2.00
3 Ilja Bryzgalov	1.50	4.00
4 Andrei Tsareev	.40	1.00
5 Oleg Shevtsov	.40	1.00
6 Andrei Malkov	.40	1.00
7 Sergey Nikolaev	.40	1.00
8 Alexei Yegorov	.40	1.00
9 Maxim Mikhailovsky	.40	1.00

2000-01 Russian Hockey League

Card	Low	High
COMPLETE SET (394)	75.00	175.00
COMMON CARD (1-394)	.10	.25
SEMISTARS	.20	.50
UNLISTED STARS	.30	.75
1 Oleg Filimonov	.10	.25
2 Alexei Lazarenko	.10	.25
3 Sergei Yasakov	.10	.25
4 Steve Plouffe	.30	.75
5 Alexander Tichkin	.10	.25
6 Igor Boldin	.10	.25
7 Vitali Evdokimov	.10	.25
8 Igor Andryiotshenko	.10	.25
9 Alexander Grishin	.10	.25
10 Andrei Kyselev	.10	.25
11 Dmitri Tarasov	.10	.25
12 Anatoli Ustyugov	.10	.25
13 Ruslan Bernikov	.10	.25
14 Oleg Naumenko	.10	.25
15 Igor Nikolaev	.10	.25
16 Renat Khairetdinov	.10	.25
17 Vadim Pokotilo	.10	.25
18 Vladimir Tyorikov	.10	.25
19 Dmitri Uchaikin	.10	.25
20 Konstantin Mitroshkin	.10	.25
21 Alexei Plotnikov	.10	.25
22 Oleg Vevcherenko	.10	.25
23 Dmitri Shulakov	.10	.25
24 Sergei Butko	.10	.25
25 Dmitri Levinski	.10	.25
26 Vladimir Gusev	.30	.75
27 Denis Martiniuk	.10	.25
28 Ross Harris	.10	.25
29 Nikolai Pronin	.10	.25
30 Sergei Zholotov	.10	.25
31 Dmitri Bykov	.75	2.00
32 Remir Khaidarov	.10	.25
33 Eduard Kudermetov	.10	.25
34 Dmitri Yachanov	.10	.25
35 Dmitri Balmin	.10	.25
36 Alexander Zhdan	.30	.75
37 Alexei Chupin	.10	.25
38 Almaz Gariffilin	.10	.25
39 Alexander Zavyalov	.10	.25
40 Ilnur Gizhatullin	.10	.25
41 Alexei Tertyshny	.10	.25
42 Evgeni Varlamov	.10	.25
43 Oleg Glebov	.10	.25
44 Sergei Mylnikov Jr.	.30	.75
45 Leonid Kanaryekin	.10	.25
46 Ildar Yobin	.10	.25
47 Anton Volchenkov ERC	2.00	5.00
48 Andrei Loginov	.10	.25
49 Vitali Drindeyen	.10	.25
50 Pavel Khanarski	.10	.25
51 Vladimir Kramskoy	.10	.25
52 Oleg Mikulchik	.10	.25
53 Vyacheslav Zhavaliuk	.10	.25
54 Sergei Soin ERC	.75	2.00
55 Andrei Galkin	.10	.25
56 Valeri Cherni	.10	.25
57 Andrei Posnov	.10	.25
58 Alexander Ardashev	.10	.25
59 Roman Salnikov	.10	.25
60 Eduard Gorbachev	.10	.25
61 Sergei Martinov	.10	.25
62 Dmitri Perozhkov	.10	.25
63 Alexander Frolov ERC	6.00	15.00
64 Vladimir Zhavyalov	.10	.25
65 Lev Berdischevski	.10	.25
66 Andrei Maximenko	.10	.25
67 Dmitri Teplyakov	.10	.25
68 Boris Kuzmin	.10	.25
69 Nikolai Ruzhenikov	.10	.25
70 Maxim Ossipov	.20	.50
71 Vladimir Loginov	.10	.25
72 Andrei Kuzmin	.20	.50
73 Ilya Dokshin	.10	.25
74 Sergei Yakimovich	.10	.25
75 Oleg Kuzmin	.10	.25
76 Yuri Truvacheev	.10	.25
77 Fedor Tjutin ERC	.10	.25
78 Alexei Tsvetkov	.10	.25
79 Alexander Shenkar	.10	.25
80 Gyori Kabanov	.10	.25
81 Vitali Chumicheev	.10	.25
82 Artem Chernov	.30	.75
83 Dmitri Khramchenko	.20	.50
84 Andrei Sharapov	.10	.25
85 Oleg Antonenko	.10	.25
86 Oleg Namestnikov	.10	.25
87 Andrei Poddyakon	.10	.25
88 Vasili Smirnov	.10	.25
89 Vitali Novopashin	.10	.25
90 Roman Malov	.10	.25
91 Vadim Averkin	.10	.25
92 Nikolai Voevodin	.10	.25
93 Vladimir Fedosov	.10	.25
94 Vasili Chestokletov	.10	.25
95 Anatoli Filatov	.10	.25
96 Igor Safonov	.10	.25
97 Mikhail Belobragin	.10	.25
98 Maxim Ovchinikov	.10	.25
99 Alexei Vorobiev	.10	.25
100 Igor Shevtsov	.10	.25
101 Sergei Fadeyev	.10	.25
102 Dmitri Pankov	.10	.25
103 Sergei Berdnikov	.10	.25
104 Georgi Evtyiokhin	.10	.25
105 Sergei Voronov	.10	.25
106 Alexei Kaliozhni	.10	.25
107 Yuri Kuznetsov	.10	.25
108 Alexander Golts	.20	.50
109 Sergei Klyshin	.10	.25
110 Igor Melyakov	.10	.25
111 Sergei Kiseleev	.10	.25
112 Igor Karpenko	.30	.75
113 Igor Karpenko	.30	.75
114 Sergei Nikolayev	.10	.25
115 Igor Sipchenko	.10	.25
116 Valeri Pokrovski	.10	.25
117 Sergei Gubernatorov	.10	.25
118 Igor Samoylov	.10	.25
119 Alexander Urakin	.10	.25
120 Oleg Eremeyev	.10	.25
121 Paolo Della Bella	.20	.50
122 Slava Bezhukladnikov	.10	.25
123 Alexei Troschinsky	.20	.50
124 Vladimir Antipin	.10	.25
125 Alexander Yudin	.10	.25
126 Vitali Proshkin	.10	.25
127 Ilya Kovalchuk	6.00	15.00
128 Dmitri Ryabikin	.10	.25
129 Alexander Zhurik	.10	.25
130 Igor Shastin	.10	.25
131 Mikhail Shukaev	.10	.25
132 Anvar Gatiyatulin	.10	.25
133 Andrei Anisimov	.10	.25
134 Maxim Soloviev	.10	.25
135 Konstantin Bezborodov	.10	.25
136 Ravil Yakubov	.10	.25
137 Alexander Prokopiev	.10	.25
138 Oleg Shargorodsky	.20	.50
139 Ruslan Batyrshin	.20	.50
140 Alexei Kypreyenkov	.10	.25
141 Pavel Komarov	.10	.25
142 Alexei Sharnin	.10	.25
143 Sergei Fedotov	.10	.25
144 Denis Khlistov	.10	.25
145 Mikhail Potapov	.10	.25
146 Alexander Semak	.20	.50
147 Andrei Vasilesvki	.30	.75
148 Azhat Sharipov	.10	.25
149 Andrei Sidyakin	.10	.25
150 Sergei Shikhanov	.10	.25
151 Sergei Gomolyako	.10	.25
152 Dmitri Nabokov	.20	.50
153 Valentin Morozov	.10	.25
154 Denis Metliuk	.20	.50
155 Ilja Bryzgalov ERC	2.00	5.00
156 Alexander Lyubimov	.20	.50
157 Ilya Byakin	.20	.50
158 Sergei Tertyshny	.10	.25
159 Valeri Karpov	.20	.50
160 Andrei Tarasenko	.10	.25
161 Alexander Yudin	.20	.50
162 Nikolai Zavarukin	.20	.50
163 Oleg Belkin	.10	.25
164 Andrei Skabelka	.10	.25
165 Leonid Fatikov	.10	.25
166 Oleg Khmylev	.10	.25
167 Denis Afinogenov	.10	.25
168 Alexander Nesterov	.10	.25
169 Andrei Kruchinin	.10	.25
170 Andrei Petrunin	.20	.50
171 Vladimir Malenkikh	.10	.25
172 Sergei Shabanov	.10	.25
173 Vadim Tarasov	.30	.75
174 Igor Zhelenchev	.10	.25
175 Sergei Shalamai	.10	.25
176 Yuri Zhuev	.10	.25
177 Artem Argokov	.10	.25
178 Evgeni Pupkov	.10	.25
179 Sergei Moskaleev	.10	.25
180 Alexander Filippov	.10	.25
181 Igor Dyakiv	.10	.25
182 Stanislav Pinevski	.10	.25
183 Alexander Agnevtshikov	.10	.25
184 Sergei Sherevtsov	.10	.25
185 Roman Kuhtinov	.10	.25
186 Evgeni Lapin	.10	.25
187 Nikolai Kurochkin	.10	.25
188 Alexei Alekeev	.10	.25
189 Alexei Koledaev	.10	.25
190 Sergei Berenikin	.10	.25
191 Denis Tyurin	.10	.25
192 Rail Rozakov	.10	.25
193 Vladimir Pozdnyakov	.10	.25
194 Pavel Desyatkov	.10	.25
195 Alexei Krovopuskov	.10	.25
196 Sergei Sevastyanov	.10	.25
197 Mikhail Yakubov ERC	1.50	4.00
198 Mikhail Sevastyanov	.10	.25
199 Pavel Torgaev	.10	.25
200 Denis Tyulyapkin	.10	.25
201 Dmitri Altareev	.10	.25
202 Maxim Savosin	.10	.25
203 Leonid Toropchenko	.10	.25
204 Stanislav Timakov	.10	.25
205 Valeri Emelyanov	.10	.25
206 Igor Gracheev	.10	.25
207 Stanislav Udyachski	.10	.25
208 Yuris Ozols	.10	.25
209 Alexander Galkin	.10	.25
210 Sergei C. Makarov	.10	.25
211 Sergei Seliutin	.10	.25
212 Alexander Popov	.10	.25
213 Sergei Zhadeleyenov	.10	.25
214 Alexei Litvinenko	.10	.25
215 Dmitri Shulga	.10	.25
216 Denis Sokolov	.10	.25
217 Maxim Krayev	.10	.25
218 Renat Hasanov	.10	.25
219 Boris Tortunov	.10	.25
220 Dmitri Krasotkin	.10	.25
221 Maxim Velikov	.10	.25
222 Yuri Panov	.10	.25
223 Alexander Vyukhin	.10	.25
224 Vadim Shakhraichuk	.10	.25
225 Alexei Badyukov	.10	.25
226 Alexander Korobolin	.10	.25
227 Dmitri Zatonski	.10	.25
228 Kirill Koltsov	.75	2.00
229 Alexander Svitov	1.25	3.00
230 Ilya Gorbushin	.10	.25
231 Andrei Samokhvalov	.10	.25
232 Igor Nikitin	.10	.25
233 Ramil Saifullin	.10	.25
234 Viktor Chistov	.10	.25
235 Vladimir Vorobiev	.10	.25
236 Igor Niklulin	.10	.25
237 Alexander Sidorovski	.10	.25
238 Oleg Polkovnikov	.10	.25
239 Dmitri Dudarev	.10	.25
240 Andrei Sapozhnikov	.10	.25
241 Andrei Kudinov	.10	.25
242 Alik Gareev	.10	.25
243 Ruslan Nurtdinov	.10	.25
244 Alexander Ageev	.10	.25
245 Andrei Yakhanov	.10	.25
246 Vener Safin	.10	.25
247 Sergei Komarov	.10	.25
248 Nail Shayakhmetov	.10	.25
249 Vladislav Ozolin	.10	.25
250 Nikolai Tsuligin	.10	.25
251 Albert Letsvheyev	.10	.25
252 Stanislav Shalnov	.10	.25
253 Maxim Orlov	.10	.25
254 Alexei Chernikov	.10	.25
255 Sergei B. Makarov	.10	.25
256 Sergei Zimakov	.20	.50
257 Gennady Savilov	.10	.25
258 Vasili Turkovski	.10	.25
259 Igor Mikhailov	.10	.25
260 Vadim Glovatskin	.10	.25
261 Alexei Tkachuk	.10	.25
262 Mikhail Volkov	.10	.25
263 Dmitri Gogolev	.10	.25
264 Pavel Agarkov	.10	.25
265 Vladimir Korsunov	.10	.25
266 Andrei Medvedev	1.50	4.00
267 Dmitri Bykov	.75	2.00
268 Ruslan Zainullin	.20	.50
269 Dmitri Starostenko	.10	.25
270 Alexander Schev	.10	.25
271 Andrei Petrakov	.10	.25
272 Sergei Klimentiev	.10	.25
273 Yuri Kuznetsov	.10	.25
274 Igor Knyazev	.60	1.50
275 Vladimir Tikhomirov	.10	.25
276 Vladimir Repneev	.10	.25
277 Alexander Boikov	.10	.25
278 Sergei Voronov	.10	.25
279 Rustem Kamaletdinov	.10	.25
280 Konstantin Molodstov	.10	.25
281 Andrei Frolkin	.10	.25
282 Vladimir Terekhov	.10	.25
283 Dmitri Klevakin	.10	.25
284 Denis Denisov	.20	.50
285 Vladislav Korneev	.20	.50
286 Evgeni Muratov	.20	.50
287 Pavel Duma	.30	.75
288 Egor Shastin	.75	2.00
289 Artem Chernov	.30	.75
290 Rail Rozakov	.30	.75
291 Alexander Chagodaev	.30	.75
292 Alexander Buturlin	.75	2.00
293 Mikhail Yakubov	1.50	4.00
294 Alexei Petrov	.30	.75
295 Pavel Vorobiev ERC	1.50	4.00
296 Ilya Kovalchuk	6.00	15.00
297 Vladimir Tikhomirov	.20	.50
298 Igor Bakhmutov	.20	.50
299 Sergei Zholotov	.20	.50
300 Vadim Tarasov	.30	.75
301 Andrei Medvedev	1.50	4.00
302 Anton Volchenkov ERC	2.00	5.00
303 Denis Grebeshkov ERC	.40	1.00
304 Andrei Shefer	.75	2.00
305 Alexander Seluyanov	.20	.50
306 Ivan Nepryaev	.30	.75
307 Stanislav Chistov ERC	2.00	5.00
308 Alexander Barkunov	.30	.75
309 Alexander Svitov	1.25	3.00
310 Igor Boriskov	.20	.50
311 Alexander Zhdan	.30	.75
312 Ilya Nikulin	.20	.50
313 Mikhail Donika	.20	.50
314 Andrei Kuzmin	.20	.50
315 Alexei Smirnov	.75	2.00
316 Vadim Brezhgunov	.75	2.00
317 Mikhail Shtalenkov	.30	.75
318 Sergei Klimovich	.20	.50
319 Alexander Kharlamov	.20	.50
320 Dmitri Subbotin	.10	.25
321 Alexander Karpovstev	.10	.25
322 Oleg Shevtsov	.10	.25
323 Evgeni Gribko	.10	.25
324 Denis Khlopotnov	.30	.75
325 Pavel Boichenko	.10	.25
326 Alexander Stepanov	.10	.25
327 Nikolai Ignatov	.10	.25
328 Alexander Skoptsov	.10	.25
329 Mikhail Mikhailovski	.10	.25
330 Sergei Semin	.10	.25
331 Pavel Trakhanov	.10	.25
332 Dmitri Riabkin	.10	.25
333 Ravil Yakubov	.10	.25
334 Pavel Datsyuk ERC	15.00	40.00
335 Andrei Evstafiev	.10	.25
336 Andrei Razin	.10	.25
337 Denis Afinogenov	.10	.25
338 Oleg Orekhovsky	.10	.25
339 Ilya Gorbushin	.10	.25
340 Viktor Tchistov	.10	.25
341 Valeri Oleinik	.10	.25
342 Sergei Shumykin	.10	.25
343 Oleg Romashko	.10	.25
344 Yuri Bogusevich	.10	.25
345 Nikolai Koptin	.10	.25
346 Vladislav Pustovalov	.10	.25
347 Andrei Gavrylin	.10	.25
348 Dmitri Chikin	.10	.25
349 Evgeni Letov	.10	.25
350 Vadim Navrotskin	.10	.25
351 Vitali Chumichev	.10	.25
352 Sergei Mozyakin	.10	.25
353 Alexei Simakov	.10	.25
354 Vadim Gusev	.10	.25
355 Sergei Kutyavin	.10	.25
356 Lev Trifonov	.10	.25
357 Roman Oksiuta	.10	.25
358 Alexei Chervyakov	.10	.25
359 Sergei Erkovich	.10	.25
360 Oleg Volkov	.10	.25
361 Sergei Gomolyako	.10	.25
362 Evgeni Bobariko	.10	.25
363 Evgeni Bobariko	.10	.25
364 Igor Boldin	.10	.25
365 Oleg Komissarov	.10	.25
366 Yuri Zlov	.10	.25
367 Andrei Pchelyakov	.10	.25
368 Oleg Boltunov	.10	.25
369 Nikolai Babenko	.10	.25
370 Igor Varitskin	.10	.25
371 Andrei Rasolko	.10	.25
372 Dmitri Denisov	.10	.25
373 Konstantin Maslyukov	.10	.25
374 Vadim Epanchintsev	.20	.50
375 Alexei Krivchenkov	.10	.25
376 Maxim Sokolov	.10	.25
377 Alexei Koznev	.10	.25
378 Evgeni Petrochinin	.10	.25
379 Vladislav Luchkin	.10	.25
380 Artur Oktyabriev	.10	.25
381 Vladimir Kopat	.10	.25
382 Vladimir Kochin	.10	.25
383 Igor Emeleev	.10	.25
384 Sergei Shitkovski	.10	.25
385 Andrei Kozrev	.10	.25
386 Alexander Smagin	.10	.25
387 Rafik Yakubov	.10	.25
388 Ildar Mukhometov	.30	.75
389 Ivan Tkachenko	.10	.25
390 Evgeni Akhmetov	.10	.25
391 Vitali Lyutkevich	.10	.25
392 Alexander Vinogradov	.10	.25
393 Evgeni Artyukhin	.10	.25
394 Andrei Tsareev	.10	.25

2001-02 Russian Dynamo Moscow

Card	Low	High
COMPLETE SET (22)	15.00	35.00
1 Oleg Orekhovskiy	.20	.50
2 Alexei Troschinsky	.30	.75
3 Andrey Razin	.20	.50
4 Dmitriy Starostenko	.20	.50
5 Andrey Skopintsev	.20	.50
6 Evgeniy Gribko	.20	.50
7 Alexey Kudashov	.20	.50
8 Evgeniy Lapin	.20	.50
9 Iliy Nikulin	.20	.50
10 Valeriy Karpov	.20	.50
11 Alexander Kuvaldin	.20	.50
12 Ravil Yakubov	.20	.50
13 Alexander Nizivij	.20	.50
14 Dmitriy Semenov	.20	.50
15 Alexander Ovechkin	10.00	25.00
16 Marat Davydov	.20	.50
17 Mikhail Shtalenkov	.30	.75
10 Vladimir Korolkov	.20	.60
19 Igor Mirnov	.20	.50
20 Vitaliy Yeremeev	.40	1.00
21 Alexander Savchenkov	.30	.75
22 Sergei Vishedkevich	.30	.75

2001-02 Russian Dynamo Moscow Mentos

Card	Low	High
COMPLETE SET (16)	3.00	8.00
1 Sergey Vishedkevich	.20	.50
2 Evgeniy Lapin	.20	.50
3 Alexander Savtchenkov	.20	.50
4 Alexander Stepanov	.20	.50
5 Mikhail Ivanov	.20	.50
6 Mikhail Shtalenkov	.30	.75
7 Dmitriy Starostenko	.20	.50
8 Alexei Troschinsky	.20	.50
9 Ravil Yakubov	.20	.50
10 Oleg Orekhovskiy	.20	.50
11 Andrey Skopintsev	.20	.50
12 Andrey Razin	.20	.50
13 Marat Davydov	.20	.50
14 Iliy Nikulin	.20	.50
15 Alexander Yudin	.20	.50
16 Evgeniy Gribko	.20	.50

2001-02 Russian Hockey League

Card	Low	High
COMPLETE SET (173)	30.00	60.00
1 Dmitri Spirin	.08	.20
2 Alexander Yakovenko	.08	.20
3 Ivan Sakharov	.08	.20
4 Andrei Mukhachev	.08	.20
5 Anatoli Stepanov	.08	.20
6 Nikolai Pronin	.08	.20
7 Igor Boiko	.08	.20
8 Alexander Borovkov	.08	.20
9 Dmitri Sergeev	.08	.20
10 Stepanov Brothers	.08	.20
11 Renat Kharetdinov	.08	.20
12 Alexander Andrievsky	.08	.20
13 Evgeni Bobariko	.08	.20
14 Andrei Galkin	.08	.20
15 Evgeni Gamalei	.08	.20
16 Oleg Grachev	.08	.20
17 Dmitri Yevdokimov	.08	.20
18 Andrei Yershov	.08	.20
19 Sergei Kiselev	.08	.20
20 Maxim Korobov	.08	.20
21 Denis Kuzmenko	.08	.20
22 Denis Makarov	.08	.20
23 Sergei Makarov	.08	.20
24 Oleg Mikulchik	.08	.20
25 Roman Oksiuta	.08	.20
26 Slava Polikarkin	.08	.20
27 Andrei Ponomarev	.08	.20
28 Dmitri Popov	.08	.20
29 Vitali Prokhorov	.08	.20
30 Alexander Romanov	.08	.20
31 Sergei Selyutin	.08	.20
32 Alexander Smirnov	.75	2.00
33 Sergei Sorokin	.08	.20
34 Mikhail Strelkov	.08	.20
35 Stanislav Timakov	.08	.20
36 Dmitri Timofeev	.08	.20
37 Vladimir Fedossov	.08	.20
38 Alexei Chrevyakov	.08	.20
39 Vitali Chinakhov	.08	.20
40 Oleg Yashin	.08	.20
41 Sergei Gomolyako	.08	.20
42 Vasili Chistokletov	.08	.20
43 Alexander Yudin	.08	.20
44 Alexander Yudin	.08	.20
45 Alexander Yudin	.08	.20
46 Artem Anisimov	.08	.20
47 Sergei Shikhanov	.08	.20
48 Evgeni Akhmetov	.08	.20
49 Igor Varitsky	.08	.20
50 Vladimir Antipin	.08	.20
51 Vadim Sharifjanov	.20	.50
52 Rail Muftiev	.08	.20
53 Maxim Bets	.20	.50
54 Viktor Ignatiev	.20	.50
55 Yuri Trubachev	.08	.20
56 Igor Shadilov	.08	.20
57 Sergei Gusev	.08	.20
58 Viktor Chistov	.20	.50
59 Maxim Sokolov	.40	1.00
60 Alexander Semak	.08	.20
61 Ruslan Akhmadullin	.08	.20
62 Igor Volkov	.08	.20
63 Sergei Shalamai	.08	.20
64 Vitali Karamnov	.08	.20
65 Vladislav Ozolin	.08	.20
66 Vladislav Makarov	.08	.20
67 Igor Karpenko	.40	1.00
68 Parris Duffus	.75	2.00
69 Igor Shastin	.08	.20
70 Evgeny Muratov	.08	.20
71 Nikolai Bardin	.08	.20
72 Roman Baranov	.08	.20
73 Artem Chernov	.08	.20
74 Konstantin Mikhailov	.08	.20
75 Dmitri Parkhomenko	.08	.20
76 Igor Mikhailov	.08	.20
77 Vladimir Korsunov	.08	.20
78 Alexei Livinenko	.08	.20
79 Alexander Vyukhin	.20	.50
80 Dmitri Zatonski	.08	.20
81 Kirill Koltsov	.75	2.00
82 Alexander Kharitonov	.08	.20
83 Renat Kharetdinov	.08	.20
84 Alexander Levenyuk	.08	.20
85 Alexei Volkov	.40	1.00
86 Sergei Yasakov	.08	.20
87 Andrei Dylevsky	.08	.20
88 Sergei Kutyavin	.08	.20
89 Sergei Yerkovich	.08	.20
90 Sergei Berdnikov	.08	.20
91 Oleg Shargorodsky	.20	.50
92 Oleg Vevcherenko	.08	.20
93 Stanislav Shalnov	.08	.20
94 Alexei Gorshkov	.08	.20
95 Andrei Subbotin	.60	1.50
96 Ramil Saifullin	.08	.20
97 Ilya Gorbushin	.08	.20
98 Alexander Svitov	1.25	3.00
99 Sergei Tertyshny	.08	.20
100 Alexander Popov	.00	.20
101 Alexander Korobolin	.08	.20
102 Denis Zaripov	.08	.20
103 Sergei Klimentiev	.08	.20
104 Dmitri Kirilenko	.08	.20
105 Maxim Rybin	.08	.20
106 Konstantin Gorovikov	.08	.20
107 Denis Khlystov	.08	.20
108 Andrei Tsareev	.20	.50
109 Alexei Chupin	.08	.20
111 Alexander Drozdetski	.08	.20
113 Vadim Brezgunov	.08	.20
114 Alexei Podalinski	.08	.20
115 Konstantin Shafronov	.08	.20
116 Alexander Golts	.08	.20
117 Ilya Gorokhov	.08	.20
118 Dmitri Zatonski	.08	.20
119 Vadim Epanchinsev	.08	.20
120 Dmitri Gogolev	.08	.20
121 Alexander Yudin	.08	.20
122 Maxim Sokolov	.40	1.00
123 Boris Tortunov	.20	.50
124 Vladimir Antipov	.08	.20
125 Vladimir Kretchin	.08	.20
126 Sergei Zinovjev	1.25	3.00
127 Andrei Kruchinin	.08	.20
128 Sergei Zhukov	.08	.20
129 Yuri Kuznetsov	.08	.20
130 Anton But	.08	.20
131 Denis Khlopotnov	.20	.50
132 Yuri Kuznetsov	.08	.20
133 Oleg Shvetsov	.20	.50
134 Andrei Loginov	.08	.20
135 Stanislav Udiansky	.08	.20
136 Denis Baev	.08	.20
137 Sergei Semin	.08	.20
138 Maxim Soloviev	.08	.20
139 Dmitri Dubrovsky	.08	.20
140 Vitali Drynin	.08	.20
141 Lev Berdischevski	.08	.20
142 Alexei Sergievsky	.08	.20
143 Evgeni Artyukhin	.08	.20
144 Alexei Kochegarov	.08	.20
145 Evgeny Lapenkov	.08	.20
146 Alexander Borozenko	.08	.20
147 Dmitri Vershinin	.08	.20
148 Yaroslav Lyuzenkov	.08	.20
149 Artem Rybin	.08	.20
150 Alexander Skoptsev	.08	.20
151 Alexei Pogonin	.08	.20
152 Vladislav Poperechny	.08	.20
153 Dmitri Plekhanov	.08	.20
154 Alexei Krovopuskov	.08	.20
155 Alexei Yegorov	.20	.50
156 Oleg Voschenikin	.08	.20
157 Vitali Trigubov	.20	.50
158 Jan Benda	.08	.20
159 Patrik Martinec	.08	.20
160 Dmitri Yachanov	.20	.50
161 Almaz Garifullin	.08	.20
162 Alexei Murzin	.08	.20
163 Vladimir Loginov	.08	.20
164 Khalim Nigmatullin	.08	.20
165 Alexander Dolishnya	.08	.20
166 Igor Fadeev	.08	.20
167 Dmitri Kulikov	.08	.20
168 Andrei Yemelin	.08	.20
169 Oleg Yashin	.08	.20
170 Andrei Zabolotnov	.08	.20
171 Alexander Semak	.08	.20
172 Sergei Askimov	.08	.20
173 Rinat Khasanov	.08	.20

2001-02 Russian Legions

Card	Low	High
COMPLETE SET (3)	.75	2.00
1 Alexei Troschinsky	.40	1.00
2 Dmitriy Starostenko	.40	1.00
3 Vladimir Tsiplakov	.40	1.00

2001-02 Russian Lightnings

Card	Low	High
COMPLETE SET (8)	2.00	5.00
1 Maxim Sushinskiy	.40	1.00
2 Igor Varitskiy	.40	1.00
3 Alexey Kudashov	.40	1.00
4 Andrey Razin	.40	1.00
5 Dmitriy Gogolev	.40	1.00
6 Dmitriy Kvartalnov	.40	1.00
7 Denis Metlyuk	.40	1.00
8 Andrei Kovalenko	.40	1.00

2001-02 Russian Ultimate Line

Card	Low	High
COMPLETE SET (5)		
1 Vitaliy Yeremeev	.75	2.00
2 Egor Podomatskiy	.75	2.00
3 Mike Fountain	.75	2.00
4 Jaroslav Kamesh	.40	1.00
5 Alexander Yeremenko	.40	1.00

2001-02 Russian Young Lions

Card	Low	High
COMPLETE SET (11)	10.00	40.00
1 Ilya Kovalchuk	6.00	15.00
2 Alexander Svitov	.75	2.00
3 Alexander Ovechkin	6.00	15.00
4 Igor Grigorenko	1.50	4.00
5 Kirill Koltsov	.75	2.00
6 Anton Babchuk	.75	2.00
7 Alexander Frolov	1.25	3.00
8 Nikolai Zherdev	1.25	3.00
9 Alexander Perezhogin	.40	1.00
10 Ilya Nikulin	.40	1.00
11 Maxim Sheviev	.40	1.00

2002 Russian Olympic Faces

Card	Low	High
COMPLETE SET (4)	2.76	6.89
1 Nikolai Khabibulin	.80	2.00
2 Nikolai Khabibulin	.80	2.00
3 Sergei Fedorov	1.20	2.50
4 Sergei Fedorov	1.20	2.50

2002 Russian Olympic Team

Card	Low	High
COMPLETE SET (9)	6.00	15.00
1 Sergei Samsonov	.80	2.00
2 Sergei Fedorov	1.25	3.00
3 Pavel Bure	1.00	2.50
4 Ilya Kovalchuk	3.00	8.00
5 Valeri Bure	.20	.50
6 Alexei Kovalev	.20	.50
7 Nikolai Khabibulin	.80	2.00
8 Maxim Afinogenov	.75	2.00
9 Darius Kasparaitis	.10	.25

2002 Russian World Championships

Card	Low	High
COMPLETE SET (20)	3.00	8.00
1 Egor Podomatski	.40	1.00
2 Alexander Yudin	.20	.50
3 Maxim Sushinski	.20	.50
4 Maxim Sokolov	.40	1.00
5 Ivan Tkachenko	.20	.50
6 Vladimir Antipov	.20	.50
7 Roman Lyashenko	.30	.75
8 Maxim Afinogenov	.75	2.00
9 Alexander Guskov	.20	.50
10 Alexei Koznev	.20	.50
11 Sergei Gusev	.20	.50
12 Slava Butsayev	.20	.50
13 Ravil Gusmanov	.20	.50
14 Dmitri Kalinin	.20	.50
15 Valeri Karpov	.20	.50
16 Andrei Kovalenko	.20	.50
17 Alexander Prokopiev	.20	.50
18 Sergei Vyshedkevich	.20	.50
19 Dmitri Zatonsky	.20	.50
20 Sergei Zhukov	.20	.50

2002-03 Russian Future Stars

Card	Low	High
COMPLETE SET (20)	10.00	25.00
1 Alexander Ovechkin	6.00	15.00
2 Igor Grigorenko	1.25	3.00
3 Vladislav Evseev	.75	2.00
4 Konstantin Glazachev	.40	1.00
5 Fedor Tyutin	.40	1.00
6 Denis Grebeshkov	.40	1.00
7 Alexander Perezhogin	.75	2.00
8 Kiril Koltsov	.40	1.00
9 Yuri Trubachev	.20	.50
10 Andrei Taratukhin	.20	.50
11 Igor Mirnov	.20	.50
12 Dmitri Chernykh	.20	.50
13 Dmitri Shitikov	.20	.50
14 Dmitri Semin	.20	.50
15 Andrei Medvedev	.40	1.00
16 Alexei Volkov	.30	.75
17 Sergei Zinovjev	.75	2.00
18 Sergei Soin	.40	1.00
19 Alexei Mikhnov	.20	.50
20 Ilya Nikulin	.20	.50

2002-03 Russian Hockey League

Card	Low	High
COMPLETE SET (273)	75.00	150.00
COMMON CARD (1-273)	.08	.20
SEMISTARS	.20	.50
UNLISTED STARS	.40	1.00
1 Evgeni Krutov	.08	.20
2 Sergei Zhurikov	.08	.20
3 Alexei Medvedev	.08	.20
4 Juri Bogusevich	.08	.20
5 Gleb Klimenko	.08	.20
6 Alexei Petrov	.08	.20
7 Andrei Tsarev	.20	.50
8 Victor Lee	.08	.20
9 Slava Zavalnyuk ENG	.20	.50
10 Slava Zavalnyuk RUS	.20	.50
11 Dmitri Klevakin	.20	.50
12 Dmitri Semin	.08	.20
13 Evgeny Fedorov	.08	.20
14 Evgeny Fedorov	.08	.20
15 Dmitri Yachanov	.20	.50
16 Dmitri Balmin	.08	.20
17 Konstantin Maslyukov	.08	.20
18 Vitali Atyushov	.08	.20
19 Denis Metliuk	.08	.20
20 Andrei Kudinov	.08	.20
21 Anton Babchuk ERC	1.25	3.00
22 Alexei Badyukov	.08	.20
23 Dmitri Gogolev	.08	.20
24 Alexei Chupin	.08	.20
25 Denis Platonov	.08	.20
26 Sergei Zolotov	.08	.20
27 Jan Benda	.08	.20
28 Steve Plouffe	.75	2.00
29 Artem Chernov	.08	.20
30 Dmitri Khomutov	.20	.50
31 Sergei Zvyagin	.20	.50
32 Vladimir Malenjkih	.08	.20
33 Oleg Minakov	.08	.20
34 Stanislav Yasechko	.08	.20
35 Mike Fountain	.75	2.00
36 Oleg Volkov	.08	.20
37 Maxim Mikhailovsky	.20	.50
38 Oleg Belkin	.08	.20
39 Alexander Buturlin	.08	.20
40 Alexander Bobkin	.08	.20
41 Sergei Sevostjanov	.08	.20
42 Andrei Frolkin	.08	.20
43 Alexander Boikov	.08	.20
44 Richard Shekhny	.08	.20
45 Petr Vorobiev CO	.04	.10
46 Andrei Esipov	.08	.20
47 Mikhail Sevostjanov	.08	.20
48 Alexander Semin ERC	6.00	15.00
49 Alexander Yudin	.08	.20
50 Rail Rozakov	.08	.20
51 Sergei Berdnikov	.08	.20
52 Philip Metliuk	.08	.20
53 Vadim Averkin	.08	.20
54 Alexander Gutov	.08	.20
55 Ilya Gorokov	.08	.20
56 Maxim Kondratiev	.20	.50
57 Alexander Nesterov	.08	.20
58 Igor Grigorenko ERC	5.00	12.00
59 Vladislav Boulin	.08	.20
60 Artur Oktyabrev	.08	.20
61 Ladislav Chierny	.08	.20
62 Alexander Yudin	.08	.20
63 Alex Westlund	.75	2.00
64 Alexander Fomitchev	.40	1.00
65 David MacIsaac	.20	.50
66 Andrei Tsarev	.20	.50
67 Maxim Spiridonov	.08	.20
68 Vadim Pokotilo	.08	.20
69 Konstantin Chaschukhin	.20	.50
70 Evgeni Safronov	.08	.20
71 Albert Vishnyakov	.08	.20
72 Christian Bronsard	.75	2.00
73 Alexei Mikhnov	.20	.50
74 Askhat Rakhmatullin	.08	.20
75 Andrei Tarasenko	.08	.20
76 Alexei Korshkov	.08	.20
77 Leo Chermak	.08	.20
78 Kirill Sidorenko	.08	.20
79 Sergei Gomolyako	.08	.20
80 Ildar Mukhometov	.20	.50
81 Dmitri Dudarev	.08	.20
82 Artem Ternavsky	.08	.20
83 Igor Kamaev	.08	.20
84 Sergei Rozin	.08	.20
85 Roman Gorev	.08	.20
86 Dmitri Kokorev	.08	.20
87 Martin Tomasek	.08	.20
88 Roman Popov	.08	.20
89 Vladimir Antipin	.08	.20
90 Vadim Tarasov	.20	.50
91 Sergei Mikhailev CO	.04	.10
92 Nikolai Zherdev ERC	6.00	15.00
93 Andrei Mukhachev	.08	.20
94 Ilya Byakin	.08	.20
95 Miroslav Guren	.08	.20
96 Nikolai Pronin	.08	.20
97 Sergei Mozyakin	.08	.20
98 Maxim Ossipov	.08	.20
99 Alexei Kolkunov	.08	.20
100 Albert Leschev	.08	.20
101 Alexander Polushin ERC	2.00	5.00
102 Igor Emeleev	.08	.20
103 Sergei Luchinkin	.08	.20
104 Rail Muftiev	.08	.20
105 Nikolai Semin	.08	.20
106 Sergei Anshakov	.20	.50
107 Vadim Khomitsky	.08	.20
108 Pavel Trakhanov	.08	.20
109 Yan Golubovsky	.20	.50
110 Dusan Salficky	.40	1.00
111 Dmitri Kosmachev	.08	.20
112 Vladimir Kramskoy	.08	.20
113 Alexander Drozdetsky	.08	.20
114 Alexei Shotkov	.08	.20
115 Maxim Velikov	.08	.20
116 Evgeni Akhmetov	.08	.20
117 Vladimir Gorbunov	.08	.20
118 Pavel Patera	.08	.20
119 Maxim Sokolov	.40	1.00
120 Martin Prochazka	.08	.20
121 Tomas Vlasak	.08	.20
122 Alexander Perezhogin	.75	2.00
123 Dmitri Zatonsky	.08	.20
124 Andrei Subbotin	.40	1.00

125 Ravil Yakubov .08 .20
126 Valeri Pokrovsky .08 .20
127 Kirill Koltsov 1.25 3.00
128 Ramil Saifullin .08 .20
129 Maxim Sokolov .40 1.00
130 Igor Varitsky .08 .20
131 Maxim Balmochnykh .20 .50
132 Marcel Cousineau .75 2.00
133 Yuri Kuznetsov .08 .20
134 Ruslan Nurtdinov .08 .20
135 Andrei Sidyakin .08 .20
136 Sergei Zvyagin .20 .50
137 Patrik Guchko .08 .20
138 Andrei Yakhanov .08 .20
139 Evgeni Muratov .08 .20
140 Alexei Simakov .08 .20
141 Roman Baranov .08 .20
142 Alexander Zavyalov .08 .20
143 Evgeni Varlamov .08 .20
144 Alexei Tertyshny .08 .20
145 Danis Zaripov .08 .20
146 Vasili Turkovsky .08 .20
147 Alexander Guskov .08 .20
148 Alexander Zhurik .08 .20
149 Yuri Kuznetsov .08 .20
150 Maxim Balmochnykh .20 .50
151 Marat Davydov .08 .20
152 Alexei Koznev .08 .20
153 Valeri Karpov .08 .20
154 Oleg Shargorodsky .20 .50
155 Sergei Gomolyako .08 .20
156 Vladimir Tikhomirov .20 .50
157 Alexei Yegorov .20 .50
158 Konstantin Simchuk .20 .50
159 Sergei Shalamai .08 .20
160 Alexei Danilov .08 .20
161 Vadim Epanchintsev .08 .20
162 Vasily Tikhonov ACO .04 .10
163 Viktor Tikhonov CO .08 .20
164 Andrei Sapozhnikov .08 .20
165 Yuri Dobryshkin .08 .20
166 Vasili Turkovsky .08 .20
167 Evgeni Petrochinin .08 .20
168 Sergei Gimaev .08 .20
169 Alexander Yudin .08 .20
170 Alexander Shinin .08 .20
171 Yuri Trubachev .08 .20
172 Evgeny Isakov .08 .20
173 Andrei Nikitenko .08 .20
174 Alexander Shinkar .08 .20
175 Viktor Chistov .20 .50
176 Andrei Shefer .20 .50
177 Igor Shadilov .08 .20
178 Martin Brochu .75 2.00
179 Alexei Kalyuzhny .08 .20
180 Alexander Shinin .08 .20
181 Maxim Balmochnykh .20 .50
182 Vladimir Antipov .08 .20
183 Boris Tortunov .08 .20
184 Vadim Epanchintsev .08 .20
184B Yuri Trubachev .08 .20
185 Fedor Tyutin 1.25 3.00
186 Sergei Anshakov .20 .50
187 Timofei Shishkanov 2.00 5.00
188 Igor Grigorenko ERC 6.00 15.00
189 Maxim Kondratiev ERC .20 .50
190 Kirill Koltsov .75 2.00
191 Evgeny Artyukhin .08 .20
192 Konstantin Barulin ERC .40 1.00
193 Andrei Taratukhin .08 .20
194 Dmitri Fakhrutdinov .08 .20
195 Dmitri Pestunov .08 .20
196 Andrei Medvedev .75 2.00
197 Nikolai Zherdev ERC 6.00 15.00
198 Alexander Ovechkin ERC 25.00 60.00
199 Alexander Polushin ERC 2.00 5.00
200 Alexei Kaigorodov .08 .20
201 Alexander Perezhogin ERC .75 2.00
202 Mikhail Lyubushin .08 .20
203 Konstantin Korneev .20 .50
204 Denis Grebeshkov 1.25 3.00
205 Konstantin Gorovikov .08 .20
206 Vitali Proshkin .08 .20
207 Alexander Suglobov ERC .40 1.00
208 Alexei Chupin .08 .20
209 Sergei Soin .20 .50
210 Andrei Subbotin .40 1.00
211 Dmitri Vlasenkov .08 .20
212 Sergei Gusev .08 .20
213 Vladimir Vujtek .08 .20
214 Vasily Turkovsky .08 .20
215 Igor Shadilov .08 .20
216 Yuri Dobryshin .08 .20
217 Igor Podomatski .40 1.00
218 Alexander Semak .08 .20
219 Ilya Byakin .08 .20
220 Alexander Guskov .08 .20
221 Alexander Guskov .08 .20
222 Nikolai Zavarukhin .08 .20
223 Andrei Petrunin .08 .20
224 Konstantin Gorovikov .08 .20
225 Alexei Gorshkov .08 .20
226 Rustem Kamaletdinov .08 .20
227 Alexander Zavakhin .08 .20
228 Vladislav Ozolin .08 .20
229 Dmitri Krasotkin .08 .20
230 Sergei Nemchinov .20 .50
231 Alexei Chupin .08 .20
232 Andrei Kovalenko .08 .20
233 Sergei Gomolyako .08 .20
234 Vitali Yeremeyev .40 1.00
235 Sergei Zholotov .08 .20
236 Dmitri Kirilenko .08 .20
237 Sergei Askimov .08 .20
238 Ruslan Berdnikov .08 .20
239 Yuri Butsayev .08 .20
240 Sergei Zinovjev 2.00 5.00
241 Radim Tesarik .08 .20
242 Dmitri Zatonsky .08 .20
243 Konstantin Baranov .08 .20
244 Vladimir Popov CO .04 .10
245 Sergei Piskunov .08 .20
246 Vladimir Antipin .08 .20
247 Alexander Drozdetksy .08 .20
248 Sergei Vyshedkevich .20 .50
249 Timofei Shishkanov 2.00 5.00
250 Alexander Kharitonov .08 .20
251 Dmitri Fakhrutdinov .08 .20
252 Vladimir Tsyplakov .08 .20
253 Evgeni Namestnikov .20 .50
254 Vitali Atyushov .08 .20
255 Dmitri Erofeev .08 .20
256 Sergei Korolev .08 .20
257 Dmitri Erofeev .08 .20
258 Vladislav Gushin .08 .20
259 Vadim Glovatskin .08 .20
260 Renat Khasanov .08 .20
261 Nikolai Zherdev ERC 6.00 15.00
262 Dmitri Zatonsky .08 .20
263 Yan Peterik .08 .20
264 Alexei Petrov .08 .20
265 Lev Trifonov .08 .20
266 Almaz Garifullin .08 .20
267 Mikhail Sarmatin .08 .20
268 Rail Rozakov .08 .20
269 Patrick Labrecque .75 2.00
270 Oleg Khmyl .08 .20
271 Alexander Blokhin .08 .20
272 Leonid Labzov .08 .20

2002-03 Russian Lightnings

COMPLETE SET (3) 10.00 25.00
1 Alexander Ovechkin 10.00 25.00
2 Alexander Polushin .75 2.00
3 Alexander Stepanov .20 .50

2002-03 Russian SL

COMPLETE SET (52) 20.00 40.00
1 Andrei Razin .20 .50
2 Dusan Salficky .40 1.00
3 Alexander Polushin .75 2.00
4 Alexander Guskov .20 .50
5 Vladimir Vujtek CO .04 .10
6 Evgeni Varlamov .20 .50
7 Andrei Skopintsev .20 .50
8 Vladimir Plyustchev CO .04 .10
9 Valeri Karpov .20 .50
10 Igor Mirnov .20 .50
11 Egor Podomatskiy .30 .75
12 Mike Fountain .30 .75
13 Mikhail Donika .20 .50
14 Vyacheslav Butsaev .20 .50
15 Andrei Esipov .20 .50
16 Igor Grigorenko 1.25 3.00
17 Yuri Moiseev CO .04 .10
18 Alexander Zhdan .20 .50
19 Maxim Sokolov .20 .50
20 Alexander Selivanov .20 .50
21 Mikhail Ivanov .20 .50
22 Ivan Hlinka CO .10 .25
23 Andrei Tsareev .20 .50
24 Dmitri Ryabykin .20 .50
25 Jiri Slegr .20 .50
26 Sergei Soin .30 .75
27 Anton But .20 .50
28 Alexander Ovechkin 10.00 25.00
29 Vladimir Antipov .20 .50
30 Evgeni Makarov .20 .50
31 Sergei Naumov .20 .50
32 Andrei Pyatanov CO .04 .10
33 Sergei Gusev .20 .50
34 Viktor Tikhonov CO .04 .10
35 Mikhail Lyubushin .20 .50
36 Dmitri Yachanov .20 .50
37 Tomas Vlasak .20 .50
38 Alex Westlund .40 1.00
39 Vladislav Boulin .20 .50
40 Jan Peterek .20 .50
41 Vladimir Vorobiev .20 .50
42 Petr Vorobiev CO .04 .10
43 Vasily Turkovski .20 .50
44 Nikolai Zherdev 1.50 4.00
45 Andrei Taratukhin .20 .50
46 Viktor Aleksandrov .20 .50
47 Yuri Dobryshkin .20 .50
48 Alexander Savchenkov .20 .50
49 Sergei Voronov .20 .50
50 Alexei Terestchenko .20 .50
51 Alexei Shkotov .20 .50
52 Alexander Zevakhin .20 .50

2002-03 Russian Transfert

COMPLETE SET (31) 6.00 15.00
1 Alexander Semin .40 1.00
2 Alexander Golts .20 .50
3 Georgi Evtyukhin .20 .50
4 Alexander Korolyuk .20 .50
5 Marcel Cousineau .30 .75
6 Sergei Bautin .20 .50
7 Vitali Lutkevich .20 .50
8 Valeri Zelepukin .20 .50
9 Nikolai Zherdev 1.25 3.00
10 Vladimir Vorobiev .20 .50
11 Sergei Petrenko .20 .50
12 Osmo Soutukorva .20 .50
13 Sergei Korolev .20 .50
14 Alex Westlund .20 .50
15 Denis Afinogenov .20 .50
16 Vadim Tarasov .40 1.00
17 Alexander Zhdan .20 .50
18 Alexander Selivanov .20 .50
19 Vladislav Boulin .20 .50
20 Maxim Sokolov .20 .50
21 Dmitri Gogolev .20 .50
22 Alexei Volkov .30 .75
23 Ravil Yakubov .20 .50
24 Mikhail Ivanov .20 .50
25 Alexei Egorov .20 .50
26 Viktor Gordiyuk .20 .50
27 Alexander Semak .20 .50
28 Bruce Gardiner .20 .50
29 Rodrigo Lavins .20 .50
30 Steve Plouffe .30 .75
31 Sergei Krivokrasov .20 .50

2002-03 Russian Transfert Promos

COMPLETE SET (6) 2.00 5.00
1 Vladimir Vorobiev .40 1.00
2 Osmo Soutukorvo .40 1.00
3 Vitali Lutkevich .40 1.00
4 Denis Afinogenov .40 1.00
5 Alexei Volkov .75 2.00
6 Maxim Sokolov .75 2.00

2002-03 Russian Ultimate Line

COMPLETE SET (13) 6.00 15.00
1 Sergei Zvyagin .40 1.00
2 Dusan Salficky .75 2.00
3 Alexander Yeremenko .40 1.00
4 Sergei Nikolaev .40 1.00
5 Mike Fountain 1.25 3.00
6 Steve Plouffe 1.25 3.00
7 Igor Karpenko .75 2.00
8 Oleg Glebov .40 1.00
9 Patrick Labrecque 1.25 3.00
10 Alexei Volkov .75 2.00
11 Vadim Tarasov .75 2.00
12 Andrei Medvedev .75 2.00
13 Vitali Yeremeyev .75 2.00

2002-03 Russian Young Lions

COMPLETE SET (17) 10.00 25.00
1 Dmitri Kazionov .20 .50
2 Alexander Ovechkin 6.00 15.00
3 Igor Mirnov .20 .50
4 Alexander Semin .40 1.00
5 Igor Grigorenko 1.25 3.00
6 Sergei Soin .30 .75
7 Denis Grebeshkov .40 1.00
8 Alexei Kaigorodov .20 .50
9 Dmitry Pestunov .20 .50
10 Alexander Polushin .75 2.00
11 Konstantin Mikhailov .20 .50
12 Iliy Nikulin .20 .50
13 Alexander Perezhogin .75 2.00
14 Alexei Mikhnov .20 .50
15 Nikolai Zherdev 1.25 3.00
16 Fedor Tyutin .40 1.00
NNO Alexander Ovechkin PROMO 6.00 15.00

2003 Russian Under-18 Team

COMPLETE SET (22) 15.00 35.00
1 Grigori Shafigulin .20 .50
2 Dmitri Petrov .20 .50
3 Alexei Ivanov .20 .50
4 Evgeni Malkin 6.00 15.00
5 Dmitri Pestunov .20 .50
6 Vitali Anikienko .20 .50
7 Dmitri Chernykh .20 .50
8 Anton Dubinin .20 .50
9 Rustan Sidikov .30 .75
10 Alexander Naurov .20 .50
11 Denis Pervyshin .20 .50
12 Alexander Ovechkin 6.00 15.00
13 Denis Ezhov .20 .50
14 Georgi Misharin .20 .50
15 Anton Belov .20 .50
16 Artem Nosov .20 .50
17 Denis Loginov .20 .50
18 Dmitri Kosmachev .20 .50
19 Konstantin Makarov .20 .50
20 Sergei Gorelov .30 .75
21 Konstantin Glazachev .60 1.50
22 Dmitri Shitikov .20 .50

2003 Russian World Championship Stars

COMPLETE SET (35) 10.00 25.00
1 Jan Benda .10 .25
2 Leonid Tambievs .10 .25
3 Jan Lasak .30 .75
4 Miroslav Hlinka .10 .25
5 Sergei Naumov .20 .50
6 Atvars Tribuntsovs .10 .25
7 Peter Forsberg 1.25 3.00
8 Tommy Salo .30 .75
9 Mats Sundin .60 1.50
10 Henrik Zetterberg .60 1.50
11 Mikael Tellqvist .60 1.50
12 Dany Heatley .75 2.00
13 Sean Burke .40 1.00
14 Mike Comrie .30 .75
15 Kris Draper .40 1.00
16 Roberto Luongo 1.25 3.00
17 Anson Carter .40 1.00
18 Miroslav Satan .40 1.00
19 Peter Bondra .40 1.00
20 Zigmund Palffy .40 1.00
21 Robert Svehla .10 .25
22 Richard Zednik .10 .25
23 Arturs Irbe .40 1.00
24 Milan Hejduk .60 1.50
25 Jiri Hudler .75 2.00
26 Robert Reichel .10 .25
27 Martin Straka .20 .50
28 Radek Duda .10 .25
29 Alexander Khavanov .10 .25
30 Ilya Kovalchuk 1.00 2.50
31 Maxim Sokolov .20 .50
32 Tomas Vokoun .60 1.50
33 Ryan Smith .60 1.50
34 Rodrigo Lavins .10 .25
35 Eric Brewer .20 .50

2003 Russian World Championship Team 2003

COMPLETE SET (24) 6.00 15.00
1 Maxim Sokolov .20 .50
2 Igor Podomatski .20 .50
3 Alexander Frolov .75 2.00
4 Alexander Semin 1.00 2.50
5 Pavel Datsyuk 1.25 3.00
6 Ivan Novoseltsev .10 .25
7 Sergei Zinovjev .40 1.00
8 Vladimir Antipov .10 .25
9 Dmitri Kalinin .10 .25
10 Vitali Proshkin .10 .25
11 Sergei Soin .10 .25
12 Alexander Suglobov .20 .50
13 Alexander Zhdan .10 .25
14 Sergei Vyshedkevich .10 .25
15 Sergei Gusev .10 .25
16 Oleg Saprykin .20 .50
17 Denis Arkhipov .20 .50
18 Dmitri Erofeev .10 .25
19 Igor Grigorenko .75 2.00
20 Alexander Guskov .10 .25
21 Vasily Turkovsky .10 .25
22 Alexander Khavanov .10 .25
23 Ilya Kovalchuk 2.00 5.00
24 Alexei Kaigorodov .40 1.00

2003 Russian World Championships Preview

COMPLETE SET (5) 6.00 15.00
1 Alexander Ovechkin 6.00 15.00
2 Pavel Datsyuk .75 2.00
3 Denis Loginov .20 .50
4 Denis Arkhipov .20 .50
5 Ilya Kovalchuk 1.50 4.00

2003-04 Russian Avangard Omsk

COMPLETE SET (28) 4.00 10.00
1 Maxim Sokolov .20 .50
2 Konstantin Baranov .10 .25
3 Maxim Sushinski .10 .25
4 Dmitri Zatonsky .10 .25
5 Tomas Vlasak .10 .25
6 Oleg Tverdovsky .10 .25
7 Sergei Krivokrasov .10 .25
8 Stanislav Shalnov .10 .25
9 Dmitri Subbotin .10 .25
10 Dmitri Ryabikin .10 .25
11 Valeri Belousov CO .04 .10
12 Igor Nikitin .10 .25
13 Pavel Patera .10 .25
14 Alexander Popov .10 .25
15 Ramil Saifullin .10 .25
16 Yuri Yermolin .10 .25
17 Alexander Golovin .10 .25
18 Alexander Prokopiev .10 .25
19 Evgeni Khatsei .10 .25
20 Oleg Grachev .10 .25
21 Jaroslav Bednar .20 .50
22 Oleg Orekhovsky .10 .25
23 Yuri Panov .10 .25
24 Anton Kuzmin .10 .25
25 Vladimir Antipin .10 .25
26 Vitali Semenchenko .20 .50
27 Anatoli Bardin GM .04 .10
28 Checklist .04 .10

2003-04 Russian Hockey League

COMPLETE SET (283) 50.00 125.00
1 Roman Salnikov .08 .20
2 Denis Tyrin .08 .20
3 Almaz Garifullin .08 .20
4 Sergei Shalamai .08 .20
5 Andrei Evstafiev .08 .20
6 Nikolai Zherdev 2.00 5.00
7 Mikhail Sarmatin .08 .20
8 Dusan Salficky .40 1.00
9 Sergei Mozyakin .08 .20
10 Andrei Razin .08 .20
11 Yuri Butsayev .08 .20
12 Oleg Romashko .20 .50
13 Evgeny Fedorov .08 .20
14 Danis Zaripov .08 .20
15 Gennady Razin .08 .20
16 Oleg Filimonov .20 .50
17 Dmitri Tarasov .08 .20
18 Vitali Shulakov .08 .20
19 Oleg Minakov .08 .20
20 Jan Benda .08 .20
21 Alexander Zevakhin .08 .20
22 Alexander Yudin .08 .20
23 Alexander Yudin .08 .20
24 SKA St. Pete's .04 .10
25 Dynamo Moscow .04 .10
26 Vitali Yeremeev .20 .50
27 Alexei Volkov .20 .50
28 Alexander Yeremenko .20 .50
29 Mikhail Lyubishin .08 .20
30 Ilya Nikulin .08 .20
31 Alexei Troschinsky .08 .20
32 Igor Mirnov .08 .20
33 Alexander Kuvaldin .08 .20
34 Igor Schyadilov .08 .20
35 Andrei Skopintsev .08 .20
36 Alexander Kharitonov .08 .20
37 Alexei Chupin .08 .20
38 Vadim Shakhrajchuk .08 .20
39 Alexander Savchenkov .08 .20
40 Vladislav Boulin .08 .20
41 Alexei Kudashov .08 .20
42 Alexander Zhdan .08 .20
43 Alexei Tereschenko .08 .20
44 Alexander Stepanov .08 .20
45 Alexander Ovechkin 10.00 25.00
46 Sergei Vyshedkevich .20 .50
47 Miroslav Hlinka .08 .20
48 Dmitri Starostenko .08 .20
49 Alexander Stepanov .08 .20
50 Alexander Ovechkin 10.00 25.00
51 Tomas Garant .20 .50
52 Vladimir Vorobiev .08 .20
53 Yuri Babenko .08 .20
54 Ruslan Zainullin .20 .50
55 Robert Kantor .08 .20
56 Denis Kartsev .08 .20
57 Vladislav Evseev .40 1.00
58 Zinatula Bilyaletdinov CO .08 .20
59 Alexei Yegorov .20 .50
60 Sergei Naumov .40 1.00
61 Sergei Semin .08 .20
62 Valeri Pokrovski .08 .20
63 Torbjorn Johansson .08 .20
64 Artem Ostroushko .08 .20
65 Andrei Spiridonov .08 .20
66 Marat Davydov .08 .20
67 Nikolai Syrtsov .08 .20
68 Vyacheslav Zavalnyuk .08 .20
69 Andrei Kozyrev .08 .20
70 Yan Golubovsky .20 .50
71 Jan Lasak .75 2.00
72 Konstantin Kasjyanchuk .08 .20
73 Egor Bashkatov .08 .20
74 Andrei Potaichuk .08 .20
75 Egor Mikhailov .08 .20
76 Andrei Galushkin .08 .20
77 Mike Watt .20 .50
78 Alexei Akifjev .08 .20
79 Andrei Pchelyakov .08 .20
80 Evgeni Tunik .08 .20
81 Pavel Boichenko .08 .20
82 Valeri Zelepukin .08 .20
83 Oleg Boltunov .08 .20
84 Alexei Tsvetkov .08 .20
85 Boris Mikhailov CO .20 .50
86 Eduard Kudermetov .08 .20
87 Sergei Berdnikov .08 .20
88 Vladimir Antipin .08 .20
89 Oleg Tverdovsky .08 .20
90 Denis Khlopotnov .08 .20
91 Fedor Tyutin .40 1.00
92 Andrei Shurupov .08 .20
93 Evgeny Koronov .08 .20
94 Albert Leschev .08 .20
95 Sergei Yerkovich .08 .20
96 Vladimir Tyurikov .08 .20
97 Dmitri Vershinin .08 .20
98 Alexei Krutov .08 .20
99 German Titov .08 .20
100 Igor Nikolaev .08 .20
101 Maxim Shevyev .08 .20
102 Andrei Ershov .08 .20
103 Ilya Krikunov .08 .20
104 Peter Skudra .40 1.00
105 Andrei Galkin .08 .20
106 Andei Dylevski .08 .20
107 Ondrej Steiner .08 .20
108 Vadim Brezgunov .08 .20
109 Roman Oksiuta .08 .20
110 Oleg Belkin .08 .20
111 Alexander Boikov .08 .20
112 Dmitri Kazionov .08 .20
113 Vladimir Malenkikh .08 .20
114 Ruslan Bernikov .08 .20
115 Alexander Buturlin .08 .20
116 Andrei Esipov .08 .20
117 Maxim Semenov .08 .20
118 Yakov Rachinsky .08 .20
119 Mikhail Balandin .08 .20
120 Dmitri Vorobiev .08 .20
121 J.F. Labbe .40 1.00
122 Rinat Khasanov .08 .20
123 Vladimir Loginov .08 .20
124 Alexei Deev .08 .20
125 Alexander Grishin .08 .20
126 Sergei Gomolyako .08 .20
127 Anatoli Filatov .08 .20
128 Vasili Koshechkin .20 .50
129 Alexander Seluyanov .08 .20
130 Ladislav Cherny .08 .20
131 Igor Varitski .08 .20
132 Maxim Yakutsenya .08 .20
133 Alexander Gutov .08 .20
134 Stanislav Zhmakin .08 .20
135 Mikhail Sevostjanov .08 .20
136 Alexander Skugarev .08 .20
137 Sergei Sevostjanov .08 .20
138 Petr Vorobiev CO .04 .10
139 Yevgeni Safronov .08 .20
140 Ilya Vorobiev .08 .20
141 Alexander Titov .08 .20
142 Ruslan Nurtdinov .08 .20
143 Alexander Zavjalov .08 .20
144 Vadim Epanchinsev .08 .20
145 Jamie Ram .75 2.00
146 Viktor Chistov CO .04 .10
147 Tomas Hlubna .08 .20
148 Alexander Semak .08 .20
149 Sergei Gimaev .08 .20
150 Nikolai Makarov CO .04 .10
151 Atvars Tribuntsovs .08 .20
152 Vladislav Ozolin .08 .20
153 Nikolai Semin .08 .20
154 Vitali Proshkin .08 .20
155 Vassiliy Turkovsky .08 .20
156 Denis Platonov .08 .20
157 Radek Duda .08 .20
158 Sergei Korolev .08 .20
159 Konstantin Korneev .20 .50
160 Sergei Arakaev .08 .20
161 Denis Denisov .08 .20
162 Alexander Drozdetsky .08 .20
163 Alexander Cherbayev .08 .20
164 Maxim Mikhailovsky .20 .50
165 Mikhail Tyulyapkin .08 .20
166 Valeri Kamensky .08 .20
167 Vladimir Vujtek .08 .20
168 Konstanin Glazachev .20 .50
169 Konstantin Mikhailov .08 .20
170 Egor Shastin .08 .20
171 Alexei Mikhnov .40 1.00
172 Alexander Fomitchev .30 .75
173 Daniel Branda .08 .20
174 Eric Charron .20 .50
175 Miroslav Guren .08 .20
176 Ravil Yakubov .08 .20
177 Dmitri Dudarev .08 .20
178 Ruslan Batyrshin .08 .20
179 Ruslan Shafikov .08 .20
180 Martin Cech .08 .20
181 Tero Lehtera .08 .20
182 Egor Mikhailov .08 .20
183 Valeri Pokrovsky .08 .20
184 Vadim Sharifjanov .20 .50
185 David Pospisil .08 .20
186 Yan Golubovsky .20 .50
187 Angel Nikolov .20 .50
188 Viktor Alexandrov .20 .50
189 Dmitri Pankov .08 .20
190 Jiri Marushak .08 .20
191 Oleg Gross CO .04 .10
192 Sergei Moskalev .08 .20
193 Alexei Medvedev .08 .20
194 Vadim Tarasov .30 .75
195 Evgeny Shtaiger .08 .20
196 Nikolai Soloviev CO .04 .10
197 Evgeny Lapin .08 .20
198 Mikhail Chernov .08 .20
199 Zdenek Skorepa .08 .20
200 Sergei Mikhailev CO .04 .10
201 Sergei Naumov .40 1.00
202 Evgeny Korolev .08 .20
203 Rail Rozakov .08 .20
204 Yuri Kuznetsov .20 .50
205 Sergei Berdnikov .08 .20
206 Yuri Kuznetsov .20 .50
207 Andrei Sapozhnikov .08 .20
208 Andrei Nikitenko .08 .20
209 Andrei Petrunin .08 .20
210 Yuri Dobryshkin .08 .20
211 Sergei Gimaev .08 .20
212 Alexander Astashev CO .04 .10
213 Vadim Khomitsky .08 .20
214 Maxim Yakutsenya .08 .20
215 Martin Richter .08 .20
216 Sergei Anshakov .20 .50
217 Denis Parshin .20 .50
218 Sergei Berezin .08 .20
219 Jan Hejda .08 .20
220 Dmitri Levinsky .08 .20
221 Norm Maracle .75 2.00
222 Pavel Patera .08 .20
223 Tomas Vlasak .08 .20
224 Jaroslav Bednar .20 .50
225 Konstantin Baranov .08 .20
226 Maxim Sokolov .30 .75
227 Denis Kuzmenko .20 .50
228 Oleg Burlitsky .08 .20
229 Alexei Potemkin .08 .20
230 Alexander Zhukov .08 .20
231 Ilnaz Zagitov .08 .20
232 Dmitri Yushkevich .08 .20
233 Martin Hlavacka .08 .20
234 Alexander Guskov .08 .20
235 Robert Kantor .08 .20
236 Marat Vailullin .08 .20
237 Zdenek Orct .20 .50
238 David Nemirovsky .20 .50
239 Jiri Hudler 2.00 5.00
240 Maxim Krivonozhkin .08 .20
241 Yuri Butsayev .20 .50
242 Andrei Esipov .08 .20
243 Rudolf Guna .08 .20
244 Philip Metliuk .08 .20
245 Alexander Lyubimov .08 .20
246 Jiri Trvaj .20 .50
247 Dmitri Cherhukh .08 .20
248 Renat Khairetdinov .08 .20
249 Artem Vostrikov .08 .20
250 Peter Skudra .40 1.00
251 Evgeny Malkin 15.00 40.00
252 Nikolai Tsulygin .08 .20
253 Andrei Kostitsyn 4.00 10.00
254 Denis Belsky .08 .20
255 Andrei Davletov .08 .20
256 Sergei Konkov .08 .20
257 Denis Loginov .08 .20
258 Michael Martin .08 .20
259 David Moravec .08 .20
260 Yan Peterik .08 .20
261 Lubomir Sekeras .08 .20
262 Toivo Suursoo .08 .20
263 Marat Salimov .08 .20
264 Sergei Fadeev .08 .20
265 Mikhail Shukaev .08 .20
266 Dmitri Yachanov .20 .50
267 Lukas Zib .08 .20
268 Butsayev Brothers .08 .20
269 Sergei Sevostjanov .08 .20
270 Mikhail Sevostjanov .08 .20
271 Ruslan Nurtdinov .08 .20
272 Frank Banham .20 .50
273 Herbert Vasiliev .08 .20
274 Dave Karpa .20 .50
275 Kirill Lyamin .20 .50
276 Mikhail Chernov .08 .20
277 Ildar Mukhometov .20 .50
278 Ilya Zubov .08 .20
279 Sergei Shinkar .08 .20
280 Sergei Voronov .08 .20
281 Sergei Borisov .20 .50
282 Yuri Trubachev .08 .20
283 Sergei Bernatsky .08 .20

2003-04 Russian Metallurg Magnitogorsk

COMPLETE SET (9) 3.00 8.00
1 Vitali Atyushov .40 1.00
2 Alexander Boikov .40 1.00
3 Evgeni Gladskikh .40 1.00
4 Oleg Davydov .40 1.00
5 Nikolia Ignatov .40 1.00
6 Dmitri Pestunov .40 1.00
7 Ivan Sidorov .40 1.00
8 Martin Cech .40 1.00
9 Lubomir Vaic .40 1.00

2003-04 Russian National Team

COMPLETE SET (36) 10.00 25.00
1 Alexei Badyukov .20 .50
2 Danis Zaripov .20 .50
3 Sergei Mozyakin .20 .50
4 Andrei Mukhachev .20 .50
5 Igor Emeleev .20 .50
6 Denis Gusmanov .20 .50
7 Maxim Spiridonov .20 .50
8 Alexei Yegorov .20 .50
9 Alexander Stepanov .20 .50
10 Nikolai Semin .20 .50
11 Alexander Drozdetsky .20 .50
12 Alexander Skugarev .20 .50
13 Sergei Korolev .20 .50
14 Vladimir Chebaturkin .20 .50
15 Andrei Kovalenko .20 .50
16 Vitali Yachmenev .20 .50
17 Igor Volkov .20 .50
18 Alexander Boikov .20 .50
19 Yuri Dobryshkin .20 .50
20 Alexander Ryazantsev .20 .50
21 Maxim Sushinsky .30 .75
22 Alexander Prokopiev .20 .50
23 Oleg Tverdovsky .20 .50
24 Alexander Ovechkin 6.00 15.00
25 Viktor Tikhonov .20 .50
26 Vladimir Malenkikh .20 .50
27 Valeri Zelepukin .20 .50
28 Dmitri Yushkevich .20 .50
29 Andrei Bashkirov .20 .50
30 Alexander Buturlin .20 .50
31 Leonid Kanareikin .20 .50
32 Artur Oktyabrev .20 .50
33 Maxim Kondratiev .20 .50
34 Vyacheslav Butsayev .20 .50
35 Alexander Savchenkov .20 .50
36 Sergei Krivokrasov .20 .50

2003-04 Russian Postcards

COMPLETE SET (12) 8.00 20.00
1 Viacheslav Butsayev .75 2.00
2 Alexander Guskov .75 2.00
3 Andrei Kovalenko .75 2.00
4 Sergei Mozyakin .75 2.00
5 Egor Podomatsky .75 2.00
6 Alexander Prokopiev .75 2.00
7 Maxim Sokolov .75 2.00
8 Maxim Sushinsky .75 2.00
9 Oleg Tverdovsky .75 2.00
10 Igor Volkov .75 2.00
11 Vitali Yachmenev .75 2.00
12 Dmitry Zatonsky .75 2.00

2003-04 Russian SL

COMPLETE SET (40) 15.00 30.00
1 Alexei Chupin .20 .50
2 Radek Duda .20 .50
3 Alexei Yegorov .40 1.00
4 Tomas Harant .20 .50
5 Miroslav Hlinka .20 .50
6 Tomas Hlubna .20 .50
7 J.F. Labbe .30 .75
8 Oleg Orekhovsky .20 .50
9 Alexander Ovechkin 4.00 10.00
10 Andrei Razin .20 .50
11 Dmitri Ryabykin .20 .50
12 Konstantin Simchuk .40 1.00
13 Andrei Subbotin .20 .50
14 Yuri Trubachev .20 .50
15 Ravil Yakubov .20 .50
16 Nikolai Zherdev 1.25 3.00
17 Vadim Tarasov .40 1.00
18 Sergei Naumovs .40 1.00
19 Christian Bronsard .40 1.00
20 Dmitri Kazionov .20 .50
21 Sergei Gomolyako .20 .50
22 Alexander Kuvaldin .20 .50
23 Peter Skudra .40 1.00
24 Alex Westlund .40 1.00
25 Sergei Shalamai .20 .50
26 Atvars Tribuntsovs .20 .50
27 Alexei Kudashov .20 .50
28 Ruslan Nurtdinov .20 .50
29 David Moravec .20 .50
30 Alexei Tertyshny .20 .50
31 Mikhail Shukaev .40 1.00
32 Alexei Vasiliev .20 .50
33 Kirill Lyamin .40 1.00
34 Daniel Branda .20 .50
35 Vadim Khomitsky .20 .50
36 Vitali Yeremeev .40 1.00
37 Lubomir Vaic .20 .50
38 Ruslan Zainullin .20 .50
39 Alexander Savchenkov .20 .50
40 Sergei Mozyakin .20 .50

2003-04 Russian Young Lions

COMPLETE SET (7) 5.00 12.00
1 Dmitri Chernykh .40 1.00
2 Alexander Semin .60 1.50
3 Alexander Ovechkin 4.00 10.00
4 Maxim Shevjev .40 1.00
5 Dmitri Pestunov .40 1.00
6 Maxim Krivonozhkin .40 1.00
7 Kirill Lyamin .40 1.00

2004 Russian Super League All-Stars

COMPLETE SET (31) 6.00 15.00
1 Egor Podomatsky .40 1.00
2 Viktor Chistov .40 1.00
3 Dmitry Krasotkin .20 .50
4 Alexei Troschinsky .20 .50
5 Vladimir Tyurikov .20 .50
6 Alexander Yudin .20 .50
7 Alexander Semak .20 .50
8 Marat Davydov .20 .50
9 Dmitry Gogolev .20 .50
10 Andrei Razin .20 .50
11 Valeri Zelepukin .20 .50
12 Egor Mikhailov .20 .50
13 Pavel Boichenko .20 .50
14 Vladimir Samylin .20 .50
15 Vladimir Vorobiev .20 .50
16 Alexei Chupin .20 .50
17 Konstantin Simchuk .40 1.00
18 Alexander Fomitchev .40 1.00
19 Sergei Klimentiev .20 .50
20 Andrei Evstafiev .20 .50
21 Jiri Marushak .20 .50
22 Nikolai Tsulygin .20 .50
23 Oleg Khmylev .20 .50
24 Jan Benda .20 .50
25 Sergei Gomolyako .20 .50
26 Igor Varitsky .20 .50
27 Andrei Skabelka .20 .50
28 Evgeny Koreshkov .20 .50
29 Sergei Moskalev .20 .50
30 Dmitri Kvartalnov .20 .50
31 Vadim Epanchintsev .20 .50

2004 Russian Under-18 Team

COMPLETE SET (23) 15.00 40.00
1 Adgur Dzhugelia .20 .50
2 Evgeni Biryukov .20 .50
3 Sergei Salnikov .20 .50
4 Kirill Lyamin .30 .75
5 Dmitri Shitikov UER
first name listed as Sergei .20 .50
6 Rinat Ibragimov .20 .50
7 Anton Belov .20 .50
8 Sergei Shirokov .20 .50
9 Nikolai Kulemin .20 .50
10 Ivan Kasutin .30 .75
11 Evgeni Malkin 10.00 25.00
12 Roman Voloshenko .40 1.00
13 Alexander Aksenenko .20 .50
14 Sergei Karetin .20 .50
15 Enver Lisin .40 1.00
16 Denis Parshin .20 .50
17 Alexander Plyuschev .20 .50
18 Mikhail Yunkov .20 .50
19 Sergei Ogorodnikov .20 .50
20 Anton Khudobin .30 .75
21 Alexei Yemelin .40 1.00
22 Alexander Radulov 4.00 10.00
NNO Checklist .02 .10

2004 Russian World Championship Team
COMPLETE SET (25) 15.00 30.00
1 Maxim Afinogenov .60 1.50
2 Alexei Yashin .20 .50
3 Nikolai Pronin .20 .50
4 Maxim Kondratiev .20 .50
5 Andrei Skopintsev .20 .50
6 Alexander Prokopiev .20 .50
7 Alexei Morozov .20 .50
8 Alexander Ovechkin 8.00 20.00
9 Maxim Sushinski .20 .50
10 Alexander Guskov .20 .50
11 Alexander Skugarev .20 .50
12 Vasili Turkovski .20 .50
13 Alexander Fomitchev .30 .75
14 Andrei Bashkirov .20 .50
15 Valeri Zelepukin .20 .50
16 Vitali Proshkin .20 .50
17 Ilya Kovalchuk 2.00 5.00
18 Maxim Sokolov .20 .50
19 Dmitri Bykov .20 .50
20 Oleg Tverdovsky .20 .50
21 Slava Butsayev .20 .50
22 Dmitri Yushkevich .20 .50
23 Dmitri Kalinin .20 .50
24 Vladimir Antipov .20 .50
25 Egor Podomatski .30 .75

2004 Russian World Junior Team
COMPLETE SET (22) 15.00 40.00
1 Konstantin Korneev .20 .50
2 Denis Grot .20 .50
3 Alexander Ovechkin 8.00 20.00
4 Dmitry Pestunov .20 .50
5 Alexei Shkotov .20 .50
6 Sergei Gimaev .20 .50
7 Andrei Spiridonov .20 .50
8 Ilya Krikunov .20 .50
9 Evgeni Malkin 8.00 20.00
10 Sergei Anshakov .20 .50
11 Mikhail Tyulyapkin .20 .50
12 Sergei Karpov .20 .50
13 Grigory Shafigulin .20 .50
14 Alexander Kozhevnikov .20 .50
15 Yuri Ermolin .20 .50
16 Dmitry Kosmachev .20 .50
17 Denis Ezhov .20 .50
18 Evgeny Tunik .20 .50
19 Dmitry Kazionov .20 .50
20 Alexander Semin 1.25 3.00
21 Konstantin Barulin .40 1.00
22 Denis Khudyakov .40 1.00

2004-05 Russian Back to Russia
COMPLETE SET (41) 12.00 30.00
1 Alexander Frolov .75 2.00
2 Pavel Datsyuk 1.50 4.00
3 Konstantin Koltsov .20 .50
4 Andrei Markov .40 1.00
5 Slava Kozlov .40 1.00
6 Dmitri Afanasenkov .20 .50
7 Igor Korolev .20 .50
8 Ilya Kovalchuk 4.00 10.00
9 Artem Chubarov .20 .50
10 Nikolai Zherdev 1.00 2.50
11 Alexander Semin 1.50 4.00
12 Maxim Kuznetsov .20 .50
13 Andrei Nikolishin .20 .50
14 Alexei Ponikarovsky .40 1.00
15 Maxim Afinogenov .75 2.00
16 Oleg Saprykin .20 .50
17 Viktor Kozlov .40 1.00
18 Andrei Nazarov .20 .50
19 Fedor Fedorov .40 1.00
20 Maxim Kondratiev .20 .50
21 Alexei Morozov .20 .50
22 Dmitry Kalinin .20 .50
23 Alexander Karpovtsev .20 .50
24 Nikolai Khabibulin .75 2.00
25 Oleg Kvasha .20 .50
26 Vitaly Vishnevsky .40 1.00
27 Sergei Gonchar .40 1.00
28 Darius Kasparaitis .20 .50
29 Alexander Perezhogin .40 1.00
30 Kirill Safronov .20 .50
31 Fedor Tyutin .20 .50
32 Nikolai Antropov .40 1.00
33 Evgeny Nabokov 1.00 2.50
34 Sergei Brylin .20 .50
35 Alexei Kovalev .40 1.00
36 Alexei Yashin .40 1.00
37 Ruslan Salei .20 .50
38 Sergei Samsonov 1.00 2.50
39 Alexei Zhitnik .20 .50
40 Igor Radulov .20 .50
41 Denis Arkhipov .40 1.00

2004-05 Russian Hope
COMPLETE SET (6) 15.00 30.00
1 Alexander Ovechkin 8.00 20.00
3 Enver Lisin .40 1.00
4 Anton Belov .40 1.00
5 Yakov Rylov .40 1.00
6 Viachesav Seluyanov .40 1.00

2004-05 Russian Legion
COMPLETE SET (41) 15.00 40.00
1 Pavel Rosa .20 .50
2 Jaromir Jagr 6.00 15.00
3 Lubomir Bartecko .20 .50
4 Martin Strbak .20 .50
5 Martin Havlat 1.50 4.00
6 Fred Brathwaite .75 2.00
7 Tomas Harant .20 .50
8 Vladimir Tsyplakov .20 .50
9 Joni Puurula .20 .50
10 Dainius Zubrus .20 .50
11 Vadim Shakhraichuk .20 .50
12 Jussi Markkanen .40 1.00
13 Vladimir Hudacek .20 .50
14 Curtis Murphy .20 .50
15 Roman Tomas .20 .50
16 Jiri Trvaj .20 .50
17 Jaroslav Bednar .20 .50
18 Miroslav Lipovsky .20 .50
19 Martin Cech .20 .50
20 Jaroslav Hlinka .20 .50
21 Lukas Zib .20 .50
23 Jan Hejda .20 .50
24 Vincent Lecavalier 6.00 15.00
25 Miroslav Guren .20 .50
27 Petr Sykora .40 1.00
28 Kamil Piros .20 .50
29 Patrik Elias .40 1.00
30 Petr Kubos .20 .50
31 Marc Lamothe .40 1.00
32 Roman Malek .20 .50
33 Aigars Cipruss .20 .50
34 Markus Korhonen .20 .50
35 Jan Benda .20 .50
36 Dusan Salficky .40 1.00
37 Dany Heatley 6.00 15.00
38 Mika Pietila .20 .50
39 Pauli Jaks .20 .50
41 Atvars Tribuntsovs .20 .50

2004-05 Russian Moscow Dynamo
COMPLETE SET (36) 15.00 35.00
1 Maxim Afinogenov .75 2.00
2 Yuri Babenko .20 .50
3 Lubomir Bartecko .20 .50
4 Vladislav Boulin .20 .50
5 Albert Vishnyakov .20 .50
6 Vladimir Vorobiev .20 .50
7 Sergey Vyshedkevich .20 .50
8 Martin Havlat 1.50 4.00
9 Tomas Harant .20 .50
10 Pavel Datsyuk 1.25 3.00
11 Vladislav Evseev .20 .50
12 Vitaly Yeremeev .40 1.00
13 Alexander Yeremenko .40 1.00
14 Vladimir Karpov .20 .50
15 Denis Kartsev .20 .50
16 Alexei Komarov .20 .50
17 Alexei Kudashov .20 .50
18 Maxim Kuznetsov .20 .50
19 Andrei Markov .20 .50
20 Igor Mirnov .20 .50
21 Ilya Nikulin .20 .50
22 Alexander Ovechkin 8.00 20.00
23 Oleg Orekhovsky .20 .50
24 Konstantin Romanov .20 .50
25 Pavel Rosa .20 .50
26 Yakov Rylov .20 .50
27 Alexander Savchenkov .20 .50
28 Andrei Skopintsev .20 .50
29 Alexander Stepanov .20 .50
30 Alexei Tereschenko .20 .50
31 Alexei Troschinsky .20 .50
32 Alexander Kharitonov .20 .50
33 Artem Chubarov .20 .50
34 Alexei Chupin .20 .50
35 Igor Shadilov .20 .50
36 Vladimir Krikunov CO .20 .50

2004-05 Russian RHL
COMPLETE SET (22) 15.00 30.00
1 Sergey Borisov .20 .50
2 Andrei Kovalenko .20 .50
3 Maxim Potapov .20 .50
4 Roman Sychev .20 .50
5 Andrei Taratukhin .20 .50
6 Maxim Ovchinikov .20 .50
7 Denis Mashanov .20 .50
8 Alexander Zavyzlov .20 .50
9 Andrei Petrunin .20 .50
10 Mikhail Varnakov .20 .50
11 Sergey Zhurikov .20 .50
12 Evgeni Malkin 10.00 25.00
13 Igor Grigorenko 1.25 3.00
14 Vladimir Popov .20 .50
15 Ruslan Khasanshin .20 .50
16 Dmitry Dudarev .20 .50
17 Valery Pokrovsky .20 .50
18 Andrei Tsareev .20 .50
19 Roman Malov .20 .50
20 Sergey Korolev .20 .50
21 Maxim Ossipov .20 .50
22 Vladimir Antipin .20 .50

2005 Russian Avangard Omsk Calendars
COMPLETE SET (5) 4.00 8.00
1 Alexander Prokopiev .75 2.00
2 Dmitry Subbotin .75 2.00
3 Maxim Sushinsky .75 2.00
4 Oleg Tverdovsky .75 2.00
5 Team photo .75 2.00

2005-06 Russian Hockey League RHL
COMPLETE SET (60) 20.00 40.00
1 Denis Kulyash .20 .50
2 Alexander Bumagin .20 .50
3 Alexei Kaigorodov .40 1.00
4 Anton Krysanov .20 .50
5 Alexander Budkin .20 .50
6 Denis Bodrov .20 .50
7 Stanislav Chistov .30 .75
8 Mikhail Grabovsky .30 .75
9 Nikita Alexeev .30 .75
10 Dmitri Shitikov .20 .50
11 Igor Ignatushkin .20 .50
12 Vladislav Bouljin .20 .50
13 Fred Brathwaite .40 1.00
14 Alexander Korolyuk .30 .75
15 Alexei Troschinsky .20 .50
16 Alexei Shkotov .20 .50
17 Evgeni Birukov .20 .50
18 Alexei Chupin .20 .50
19 Dmitri Bykov .20 .50
19B Alexander Ryazantsev .20 .50
20 Vadim Epanchintsev .20 .50
21 Milan Kraft .30 .75
22 Andrei Mukhachev .20 .50
23 Eugeni Fedorov .30 .75
24 Alexander Semin 1.25 3.00
25 Vladimir Vorobiev .20 .50
26 Eugeni Ryasenski .20 .50
28 Travis Scott .40 1.00
30 Maxim Sushinsky .30 .75
31 David Nemirovsky .30 .75
32 David Ling .30 .75
33 Vyacheslav Buravchikov .20 .50
34 Sergei Zvyagin .20 .50
35 Raymond Giroux .30 .75
36 Kirill Koltsov .40 1.00
37 Eugeni Malkin 8.00 20.00
38 Atrem Bikkinyaev .20 .50
39 Ilya Zubov .40 1.00
40 Nikolai Kulemin .40 1.00
41 Oleg Romashko .20 .50
42 Alexander Rybakov .20 .50
43 Dusan Sakficky .40 1.00
44 Maxim Yakutsenya .20 .50
45 Boris Tortunov .20 .50
46 Ilya Nikulin .20 .50
48 Radik Zakiyev .20 .50
49 Ruslan Nurtdinov .20 .50
50 Tyler Moss .40 1.00
51 Dmitri Obukhov .20 .50
52 Andrei Nikolishin .20 .50
53 Alexander Yunkov / Mikhail Yunkov .20 .50
54 Alexander Yudin .20 .50
55 Eugeni Konstantinov .40 1.00
C1 Milos Rziga .20 .50
C2 Jan Zachurla .20 .50
C3 Vladimir Kapulovsky .20 .50

2006 Russian Sport Collection Olympic Stars
1 Maxim Afinogenov 1.00 2.50
2 Ilya Bryzgalov 1.00 2.50
3 Anton Volchenkov 1.00 2.50
4 Sergei Gonchar 1.00 2.50
5 Pavel Datsyuk 2.00 5.00
6 Darius Kasparaitis 1.00 2.50
7 Alexei Kovalev 1.00 2.50
8 Ilya Kovalchuk 4.00 10.00
9 Evgeny Malkin 8.00 20.00
10 Andrei Markov 1.00 2.50
11 Evgeny Nabokov 2.00 5.00
12 Alexander Ovechkin 8.00 20.00
13 Maxim Sokolov 1.00 2.50
14 Fedor Tyutin 1.00 2.50
15 Alexei Yashin 1.00 2.50
16 Daniel Alfredson 2.00 5.00
17 Henrik Zetterberg 2.00 5.00
18 Nicklas Lidstrom 2.00 5.00
19 Henrik Lundqvist 4.00 10.00
20 Mats Sundin 2.00 5.00
21 Peter Forsberg 4.00 10.00
22 Jussi Jokinen 1.00 2.50
23 Saku Koivu 2.00 5.00
24 Jere Lehtinen 1.00 2.50
25 Antero Niittymaki 2.00 5.00
26 Ville Peltonen 1.00 2.50
27 Teemu Selanne 4.00 10.00
28 Tomas Vokoun 2.00 5.00
29 Tomas Kaberle 1.00 2.50
30 Martin Straka 1.00 2.50
31 Milan Hejduk 2.00 5.00
32 Ales Hemsky 2.00 5.00
33 Jaromir Jagr 4.00 10.00
34 Martin Brodeur 6.00 15.00
35 Jarome Iginla 4.00 10.00
36 Vincent Lecavalier 4.00 10.00
37 Rick Nash 4.00 10.00
38 Brad Richards 2.00 5.00
39 Joe Sakic 6.00 15.00
40 Joe Thornton 4.00 10.00
41 Dany Heatley 4.00 10.00
42 Peter Bondra 1.00 2.50
43 Peter Budaj 1.00 2.50
44 Marian Gaborik 4.00 10.00
45 Pavol Demitra 1.00 2.50
46 Richard Zednik 1.00 2.50
47 Zdeno Chara 1.00 2.50
48 Marian Hossa 2.00 5.00
49 Miroslav Satan 1.00 2.50
50 Rick Dipietro 2.00 5.00
51 Mike Modano 3.00 8.00
52 Keith Tkachuk 2.00 5.00
53 Vitali Yeremeyev 1.00 2.50

2006 Russian Torino Olympic Team
COMPLETE SET (26) 15.00 25.00
1 Alexander Ovechkin 4.00 10.00
2 Evgeny Malkin 4.00 10.00
3 Maxim Sokolov .20 .50
4 Ilya Bryzgalov .40 1.00
5 Fedor Tyutin .20 .50
6 Vitaly Vishenvsky .20 .50
7 Maxim Sushinski .20 .50
8 Alexei Yashin .20 .50
9 Alexei Kovalev .40 1.00
10 Alexander Korolyuk .20 .50
11 Ilya Kovalchuk 1.25 3.00
12 Maxim Afinogenov .40 1.00
13 Alexander Kharitonov .20 .50
14 Pavel Datsyuk .75 2.00
15 Viktor Kozlov .20 .50
16 Ivan Nepryaev .20 .50
17 Andrei Markov .20 .50
18 Alexander Frolov .40 1.00
19 Sergei Zhukov .20 .50
20 Evgeny Nabokov .40 1.00
21 Darius Kasparaitis .20 .50
22 Andrei Taratukhin .20 .50
23 Sergei Gonchar .20 .50
24 Anton Volchenkov .20 .50
25 Daniil Markov .20 .50
26 Russian Team CL .02 .10

1995-96 Slovakian APS National Team
COMPLETE SET (28) 20.00 40.00
1 Dr. Jan Mitosinka CO .02 .10
2 Dusan Pasek CO .08 .25
3 Julius Supler CO .08 .25
4 Jan Selvek .08 .25
5 Jaromir Dragan .08 .25
6 Eduard Hartmann .08 .25
7 Roman Cunderlik .08 .25
8 Stanislav Jasecko .08 .25
9 Lubomir Sekeras .40 1.00
10 Stanislav Medrik .08 .25
11 Jan Varholik .08 .25
12 Marian Smerciak .08 .25
13 Robert Svehla .40 1.00
14 Slavomir Vorobel .20 .50
15 Vlastimil Plavucha .08 .25
16 Oto Hascak .20 .50
17 Peter Bondra 6.00 15.00
18 Rene Pucher .08 .25
19 Miroslav Satan 6.00 15.00
20 Branislav Janos .08 .25
21 Lubomir Kolnik .08 .25
22 Peter Stastny 2.00 5.00
23 Zdeno Ciger .20 .50
24 Zigmund Palffy 6.00 15.00
25 Josef Dano .08 .25
26 Robert Petrovicky .20 .50
27 Dusan Pohorelec .08 .25
28 Jozef Stumpel .75 2.00

1995 Slovakian-Quebec Pee-Wee Tournament
COMPLETE SET (29) 3.00 8.00
1 Jozef Balej 1.25 3.00
2 Patrik Behan .08 .25
3 Michal Bela .08 .25
4 Ivan Dobry .08 .25
5 Milan Dornic CO .02 .10
6 Vladimir Dubek .08 .25
7 Ladislav Gero CO .02 .10
8 Marian Hutyra .08 .25
9 Peter Hutyra .08 .25
10 Dr. Leopold Karafiat MG .02 .10
11 Miroslav Karafiat CO .02 .10
12 Vladimir Kulich .08 .25
13 Marek Laco .08 .25
14 Michal Loksa .08 .25
15 Igor Martak .08 .25
16 Branislav Medzihorsky .08 .25
17 Miroslav Micuda .08 .25
18 Tomas Mihalik .08 .25
19 Stanislav Mistrik .08 .25
20 Andrej Mrena .08 .25
21 Marian Nemeth .08 .25
22 Vladimir Polacek .08 .25
23 Rastislav Sendrey .08 .25
24 Norbert Skorvaga .08 .25
25 Tomas Surovy .60 1.50
26 Michal Turcer .08 .25
27 Sponsor Card .10 .25
28 Team Card .02 .10
29 Title Card .10 .25

1996 Slovakian Quebec Pee-Wee Tournament Team
COMPLETE SET (30) 5.60 15.00
1 Jozef Balej .75 2.00
2 Michal Baranka .20 .50
3 Jan Behan CO .02 .10
4 Martin Bonda .20 .50
5 Robert Cerny .20 .50
6 Peter Duris .20 .50
7 Jan Frkan .20 .50
8 Milan Fujerik CO .02 .10
9 Michal Gunis .20 .50
10 Stefan Hlusek .20 .50
11 Peter Holecko .20 .50
12 Dr. Leopold Karafiat GM .02 .10
13 Lukas Krejci .20 .50
14 Miroslav Kristin .20 .50
15 Andrej Kucko .20 .50
16 Roman Kyndl .20 .50
17 Michal Macho .20 .50
18 Tomas Mikus .30 .75
19 Juraj Nemcek .30 .75
20 Viliam Ondrejik .20 .50
21 Miroslav Pistek .20 .50
22 Marek Pollak .30 .75
23 Tomas Psenka .20 .50
24 Milan Sitar CO .02 .10
25 Frantisek Skladany .40 1.00
26 Peter Steklac .20 .50
27 Richard Svrbik .20 .50
28 Michal Sykora .20 .50
29 Martin Wala .20 .50
30 Team Picture .02 .10

1998-99 Slovakian Eurotel
COMPLETE SET (29) 32.00 80.00
1 Peter Bondra 1.25 3.00
2 Sergei Fedorov 2.00 5.00
3 Peter Forsberg 3.00 8.00
4 Wayne Gretzky 8.00 20.00
5 Bill Guerin .75 2.00
6 Brett Hull 1.50 4.00
7 Jaromir Jagr 2.00 5.00
8 Saku Koivu 1.25 3.00
9 Jari Kurri .75 2.00
10 Pat Lafontaine .75 2.00
11 Janne Laukkanen .40 1.00
12 Robert Lang .40 1.00
13 John LeClair .75 2.00
14 Eric Lindros 1.50 4.00
15 Al MacInnis .75 2.00
16 Joe Nieuwendyk .75 2.00
17 Zigmund Palffy .75 2.00
18 Mike Richter 1.25 3.00
19 Patrick Roy 6.00 15.00
20 Joe Sakic 2.00 5.00
21 Tommy Salo .75 2.00
22 Miroslav Satan .75 2.00
23 Teemu Selanne 1.50 4.00
24 Mikhail Shtalenkov .40 1.00
25 Martin Straka .40 1.00
26 Mats Sundin .75 2.00
27 Alexei Yashin .40 1.00
28 Steve Yzerman 6.00 15.00
29 Alexei Zhamnov .40 1.00

1999-00 Slovakian Challengers
COMPLETE SET (30) 30.00 60.00
1 Rob Niedermayer .20 .50
2 Robert Svehla .20 .50
3 Richard Zednik .20 .50
4 Steve Sullivan .20 .50
5 Alexei Yashin .20 .50
6 Alexander Mogilny .30 .75
7 Zigmund Palffy .40 1.00
8 Martin Brodeur 6.00 15.00
9 Sandis Ozolinsh .20 .50
10 Adam Deadmarsh .30 .75
11 Peter Forsberg 2.50 6.00
12 Martin Rucinsky .20 .50
13 Shayne Corson .20 .50
14 Grant Fuhr .75 2.00
15 Al MacInnis .75 2.00
16 Paul Kariya 2.00 5.00
17 Teemu SelÃonne 2.00 5.00
18 Steve Yzerman 8.00 20.00
19 Chris Osgood .75 2.00
20 Brendan Shanahan 1.25 3.00
21 Vaclav Varada .20 .50
22 Brian Holzinger .20 .50
23 Dominik Hasek 2.50 6.00
24 Michael Peca .30 .75
25 Ed Belfour 1.25 3.00
26 Jere Lehtinen .75 2.00
27 Jaromir Jagr 3.00 8.00
28 Kevin Hatcher .20 .50
29 John LeClair .75 2.00
30 Alexei Zhamnov .20 .50

2001 Slovakian Kvarteto
COMPLETE SET (33) 10.00 25.00
1A Jergus Baca .20 .50
1B Josef Dano .20 .50
1C Peter Bondra .40 2.00
1D Jaromir Dragan .40 1.00
2A Zdeno Ciger .20 .50
2B Peter Bondra .60 2.00
2C Pavol Demitra .60 2.00
2D Stanislav Jasecko .20 .50
3A Ivan Droppa .20 .50
3B Otto Hascak .20 .50
3C Branislav Janos .20 .50
3D Peter Bondra .60 2.00
4A Stanislav Jasecko .20 .50
4B Lubomir Kolnik .20 .50
4C Zigmund Palffy .60 2.00
4D Roman Kontsek .20 .50
5A Igor Murin .20 .50
5B Lubomir Visnovsky .30 .75
5C Lubomir Kolnik .20 .50
5D Jan Pardavy .20 .50
6A Robert Petrovicky .20 .50
6B Vlastimil Plavucha .20 .50
6C Peter Pucher .20 .50
6D Rene Pucher .20 .50
7A Pavol Rybar .20 .75
7B Miroslav Satan .60 2.00
7C Lubomir Sekeras .30 .75
7D Roman Stantien .20 .50
8A Roman Stantien .20 .50
8B Jozef Stumpel .30 .75
8C Robert Svehla .20 .50
8D Marian Varolik .20 .50
HOKEJ Peter Bondra 2.00 5.00

2002 Slovakian Kvarteto
COMPLETE SET (32) 8.00 20.00
1 Miroslav Satan .75 2.00
2 Peter Bondra .75 2.00
3 Zigmund Palffy .75 2.00
4 Jan Lasak .40 1.00
5 Rastislav Stana .40 1.00
6 Radoslav Hecl .20 .50
7 Richard Lintner .20 .50
8 Dusan Milo .20 .50
9 Peter Smrek .20 .50
10 Martin Strbak .20 .50
11 Lubomir Visnovsky .20 .50
12 Jergus Baca .20 .50
13 Michael Handzus .20 .50
14 Rastislav Pavlikovsky .20 .50
15 Robert Petrovicky .20 .50
16 Jozef Stumpel .20 .50
17 Radovan Somik .20 .50
18 Robert Tomik .20 .50
19 Miroslav Hlinka .20 .50
20 Lubos Bartecko .20 .50
21 Ladislav Nagy .40 1.00
22 Vladimir Orszagh .20 .50
23 Peter Stastny GM .20 .50
24 Samuel Petras .20 .50
25 Dalimir Jancovic .20 .50
26 Ernest Bokros .20 .50
27 Marek Uram .20 .50
28 Peter Pucher .20 .50
29 Ladislav Cierny .20 .50
30 Vladimir Stastny .20 .50
31 Miroslav Simonovic .20 .50
32 Jan Filc .20 .50

2004-05 Slovakian Poprad Team Set
COMPLETE SET (30) 10.00 25.00
1 Ladislav Svozil .30 .75
2 Vladimir Klinga .30 .75
3 Stanislav Kozuch .30 .75
4 Radovan Hurajt .30 .75
5 Miroslav Javin .30 .75
6 Stefan Rusnak .30 .75
7 Miroslav Turan .30 .75
8 Lukas Bambuch .30 .75
9 Stefan Fabian .30 .75
10 Ridvan Sadiki .30 .75
11 Tomas Jurco .30 .75
12 Radoslav Suchy .30 .75
13 Tomas Valecko .30 .75
14 Pavol Gurcik .30 .75
15 Peter Bondra 1.25 3.00
16 Miroslav Skovira .30 .75
17 Slavomir Pavlicko .30 .75
18 Juraj Halaj .30 .75
19 Pavol Zavacky .30 .75
20 Miroslav Ihnacak .30 .75
21 Juraj Faith .30 .75
22 Peter Misal .30 .75
23 Ludovit Jurinyi .30 .75
24 Jozef Slaninak .30 .75
25 Richard Zemlicka .30 .75
26 Stefan Rusnak .30 .75
27 Miroslav Stolc .30 .75
28 Viktor Kubenko .30 .75
29 Erik Piatak .30 .75
30 Roman Soltys .30 .75

2004-05 Slovakian Skalica Team Set
COMPLETE SET (28) 10.00 25.00
1 Martin Kucera .40 1.00
2 Matej Bukna .40 1.00
3 Tibor Visnovsky .40 1.00
4 Josef Mrena .40 1.00
5 Jaroslav Prosvic .40 1.00
6 Roman Chatrnuch .40 1.00
7 Milan Carsky .40 1.00
8 Miroslav Zalesak .60 1.50
9 Davis Galvas .40 1.00
10 Rene Jarolin .40 1.00
11 Richard Hartmann .40 1.00
12 Peter Kocak .40 1.00
13 Roman Kelner .40 1.00
14 Milan Malik .40 1.00
15 Marek Grill .40 1.00
16 Robert Liscak .40 1.00
17 Zigmund Palffy 1.25 3.00
18 Ladislav Paciga .40 1.00
19 Jozef Liska .40 1.00
20 Radovan Sloboda .40 1.00
21 Boris Flamik .40 1.00
22 Juraj Mikus .40 1.00
23 Peter Ivicic .40 1.00
24 Richard Stehlik .40 1.00
25 Martin Ivicic .40 1.00
26 Petr Tucek .40 1.00
27 Lukas Komarek .40 1.00
28 Martin Skadra .40 1.00

2004-05 South Surrey Eagles
COMPLETE SET (30) 15.00
1 Tyson Angus .50
2 Tim Crowder .50
3 Chris Defrancescanto .50
4 Korey Diehl .50
5 Korey Diehl PROMO 1.00
6 Tyler Eckford .50
7 Tyler Eckford PROMO 1.00
8 Matthew Girling .50
9 Daniel Idema .50
10 Andrew Kozek .50
11 Andrew Kozek PROMO 1.00
12 Kyle Kuehner .50
13 Aaron McKenzie .50
14 Brock Meadows .50
15 T.J. Miller .50
16 David Moncur .50
17 Tyrell Moulton .50
18 T.J. Mulock .50
19 T.J. Mulock PROMO 1.00
20 Kyle Nason .50
21 Blake Rielly PROMO 1.00
22 Blake Rielly PROMO 1.00
23 David Rutherford .50
24 David Rutherford PROMO 1.00
25 Cody Rymut .50
26 Dustin Slade .50
27 Stewart Thiessen .50
28 Matt Wiest .50
29 Rick Hillier HC .10
30 Team Card .10

1932-33 Swedish Marabou
Hockey players in set (6)

1964 Swedish Coralli ISHockey
COMPLETE SET (165) 150.00 300.00
1 Sven Johansson 1.50 3.00
2 Ove Malmberg 1.00 2.00
3 Bjorn Larsson 1.00 2.00
4 Ulf Sterner 1.00 2.00
5 Bertil Karlsson 1.00 2.00
6 Leif Holmqvist 5.00 10.00
7 Uno Ohrlund 1.00 2.00
8 Mats Lonn 1.00 2.00
9 Bjorn Palmqvist 1.00 2.00
10 Nils Johansson 1.00 2.00
11 Ander Andersson 1.00 2.00
12 Lennart Haggroth 2.00 4.00
13 Hans Svedberg 1.00 2.00
14 Ronald Pettersson 1.00 2.00
15 Lars Eric Lundvall 1.00 2.00
16 Gert Blome 1.00 2.00
17 Bo Englund 1.00 2.00
18 Folke Bengtsson 1.00 2.00
19 Nils Nilsson 1.00 2.00
20 Lennart Johansson 1.00 2.00
21 Lennart Svedberg 2.50 5.00
22 Lars Ake Sivertsson 1.00 2.00
23 Hakan Wickberg 1.00 2.00
24 Tord Lundstrom 1.00 2.00
25 Ove Andersson 1.00 2.00
26 Bert Ola Nordlander 1.50 3.00
27 Jan Erik Nilsson 1.00 2.00
28 Ellert Maatta 1.00 2.00
29 Roland Stoltz 1.00 2.00
30 Kurt Thulin 1.00 2.00
31 Ove Andersson 1.00 2.00
32 Ingemar Johansson 1.00 2.00
33 Rune Lind 1.00 2.00
34 Bert-Ola Nordlander 1.50 3.00
35 Hans Eriksson 1.00 2.00
36 Antik Johansson 1.00 2.00
37 Bo Hansson 1.00 2.00
38 Jan Back 1.00 2.00
39 Lennart Soderberg 1.00 2.00
40 Benny Soderling 1.00 2.00
41 Anders Parmstrom 1.00 2.00
42 Lennart Selinder 1.00 2.00
43 Bjorn Larsson 1.00 2.00
44 Jorma Salmi 1.00 2.00
45 Berndt Arvidsson 1.00 2.00
46 P.A. Karlstrom 1.00 2.00
47 Lars Erik Sjoberg 5.00 10.00
48 Vilgot Larsson 1.00 2.00
49 Gunnar Andersson 1.00 2.00
50 Roland Bond 1.00 2.00
51 Goran Lysen 1.00 2.00
52 Bosse Englund 1.00 2.00
53 Stig Pavels 1.00 2.00
54 Bengt Bornstrom 1.00 2.00
55 Nisse Nilsson 1.00 2.00
56 Lennart Lange 1.00 2.00
57 Des Moroney 1.00 2.00
58 Folke Bengtsson 1.00 2.00
59 Olle Sjogren 1.00 2.00
60 Knut Knutsson 1.00 2.00
61 Kjell Svensson 1.00 2.00
62 Rickard Eagerlund 2.50 5.00
63 Arne Loong 1.00 2.00
64 Stig Carlsson 1.00 2.00
65 Lars Hagg 1.00 2.00
66 Olle Stenar 1.00 2.00
67 Einar Granath 1.00 2.00
68 Leif Andersson 1.00 2.00
69 Hans Soderstrom 1.00 2.00
70 Kalle Lilja 1.00 2.00
71 Soren Maatta 1.00 2.00
72 Sven Bystrom 1.00 2.00
73 Hans Karlsson 1.00 2.00
74 Stig Goran Johansson 1.50 3.00
75 Jan Allinger 1.00 2.00
76 Kjell Larsson 1.00 2.00
77 Hakan Wickberg 1.00 2.00
78 Tord Lundstrom 1.00 2.00
79 Lennart Svedberg 2.50 5.00
80 Jan Erik Lyck 1.00 2.00
81 Hans Eriksson 1.00 2.00
82 Kjell Jonsson 1.00 2.00
83 Lars Hedenstrom 1.00 2.00
84 Lars Ake Sivertsson 1.00 2.00
85 Lennart Johansson 1.00 2.00
86 Hans Sjoberg 1.00 2.00
87 Hans Dahllof 1.00 2.00
88 Leif Jansson 1.00 2.00
89 Lars Byling 1.00 2.00
90 Bertil Lindstrom 1.00 2.00
91 Arne Eriksson 1.00 2.00
92 Gert Blomer 1.00 2.00
93 Kjell Adrian 1.00 2.00
94 Jan Olsen 1.00 2.00
95 Benny Karlsson 1.00 2.00
96 Tommy Carlsson 1.00 2.00
97 Ulf Sterner 1.00 2.00
98 Kjell-Ove Gustafsson 1.00 2.00
99 Lars Erik Lundvall 1.00 2.00
100 Kjell-Ronny Pettersson 1.00 2.00
101 Ronald Pettersson 1.00 2.00
102 Kjell Jonsson 1.00 2.00
103 Gote Hansson 1.00 2.00
104 Rolf Eklof 1.00 2.00
105 Eine Olsson 1.00 2.00
106 Hans-Erik Fernstrom 1.00 2.00
107 Leif Holmkvist 1.00 2.00
108 Bo Zetterberg 1.00 2.00
109 Ake Zattlin 1.00 2.00
110 Bengt-Olov Andreasson 1.00 2.00
111 Borje Mohlander 1.00 2.00
112 Sture Sundin 1.00 2.00
113 Bertil Karlsson 1.00 2.00
114 Lars Molander 1.00 2.00
115 Benno Persson 1.00 2.00
116 Gert Nystrom 1.00 2.00
117 Sune Bohlin 1.00 2.00
118 Olle Westlund 1.00 2.00
119 Goran Wallin 1.00 2.00
120 Ingemar Persson 1.00 2.00
121 Tommy Bjorkman 1.00 2.00
122 Eddie Wingren 1.00 2.00
123 Lars Bjorn 1.00 2.00
124 Roland Stoltz 1.00 2.00
125 Sven Johansson 1.50 3.00
126 Leif Skold 1.00 2.00
127 Hans Mild 1.00 2.00
128 Kurt Thulin 1.00 2.00
129 Ake Rydberg 1.00 2.00
130 Ove Malmberg 1.00 2.00
131 Lars Lundqvist 1.00 2.00
132 Kurt Svensson 1.00 2.00
133 Gosta Westerlund 1.00 2.00
134 Lars Andersson 1.00 2.00
135 Ulf Rydin 1.00 2.00
136 Lennart Haggroth 2.00 4.00
137 Jan Hedberg 1.00 2.00
138 Karl Soren Hedlund 1.00 2.00
139 Hans Svedberg 1.00 2.00
140 Sture Hoverberg 1.00 2.00
141 Anders Ronnblom 1.00 2.00
142 Ulf Eriksson 1.00 2.00
143 Anders Andersson 1.00 2.00
144 Henrik Hedlund 1.00 2.00
145 Per Lundstrom 1.00 2.00
146 Hakan Nygren 1.00 2.00
147 Bo Berglund, Sr 2.00 4.00
148 Lars Ake Warning 1.00 2.00
149 Sven-Olov Johansson 1.00 2.00
150 Ove Stenlund 1.00 2.00
151 Ivar Larsson 1.00 2.00
152 Nils Johansson 1.00 2.00
153 Sten Olsen 1.00 2.00
154 Lars Gidlund 1.00 2.00
155 Tor Haarstad 1.00 2.00
156 K-O Barrefjord 1.00 2.00
157 Bjorn Palmqvist 1.00 2.00
158 Soren Lindstrom 1.00 2.00
159 Henna Svensson 1.00 2.00
160 Lars Hagstrom 1.00 2.00
161 Ake Eklof 1.00 2.00
162 Ulf Lundstrom 1.00 2.00
163 Ronny Nordstrom 1.00 2.00
164 Paul Stahl 1.00 2.00
165 Kenneth Sahlen 1.50 3.00

1965 Swedish Coralli ISHockey
COMPLETE SET (214) 125.00 300.00
1 Sven Johansson 1.25 3.00
2 Ove Malmberg .75 2.00
3 Bjorn Larsson .75 2.00
4 Ulf Sterner .75 2.00
5 Bertil Karlsson 1.00 3.00
6 Leif Holmqvist 4.00 8.00
7 Uno Ohrlund .75 2.00
8 Mats Lonn .75 2.00
9 Bjorn Palmqvist .75 2.00
10 Nils Johansson .75 2.00
11 Anders Andersson .75 2.00
12 Lennart Haggroth 1.50 4.00
13 Hans Svedberg .75 2.00
14 Ronald Pettersson .75 2.00
15 Lars Eric Lundvall .75 2.00
16 Gert Blome .75 2.00

17 Bo Englund .75 2.00
18 Folke Bengtsson .75 2.00
19 Nils Nilsson .75 2.00
20 Lennart Johansson .75 2.00
21 Lennart Svedberg 1.75 4.00
22 Lars Ake Sivertsson .75 2.00
23 Hakan Wickberg .75 2.00
24 Tord Lundstrom .75 2.00
25 Ove Andersson .75 2.00
26 Bert Ola Nordlander 1.25 3.00
27 Jan Erik Nilsson .75 2.00
28 Eilert Maatta .75 2.00
29 Roland Stoltz .75 2.00
30 Kurt Thulin .75 2.00
31 Leif Holmqvist 4.00 8.00
32 Ingemar Johansson 1.00 3.00
33 Rune Lind .75 2.00
34 Bert-Ola Nordlander 1.25 3.00
35 Hans Eriksson .75 2.00
36 Antik Johansson .75 2.00
37 Bo Hansson .75 2.00
38 Hans-Ake Carlsson .75 2.00
39 Lennart Soderberg .75 2.00
40 Benny Soderling .75 2.00
41 Anders Parmstrom .75 2.00
42 Lennart Selinder .75 2.00
43 Bjorn Larsson .75 2.00
44 Ove Hedberg .75 2.00
45 Berndt Arvidsson .75 2.00
46 P.A. Carlstrom .75 2.00
47 Lars Erik Sjoberg 4.00 8.00
48 Kjell Fhinn .75 2.00
49 Gunnar Andersson .75 2.00
50 Roland Bond .75 2.00
51 Goran Lysen .75 2.00
52 Bosse Englund .75 2.00
53 Stig Pavels .75 2.00
54 Bengt Bornstrom .75 2.00
55 Nisse Nilsson .75 2.00
56 Lennart Lange .75 2.00
57 Tommy Abrahamsson 4.00 8.00
58 Folke Bengtsson .75 2.00
59 Olle Sjogren .75 2.00
60 Knut Knutsson .75 2.00
61 Kjell Svensson .75 2.00
62 Rickard Fagerlund 1.75 4.00
63 Eilert Maatta .75 2.00
64 Stig Carlsson .75 2.00
65 Lars Hagg .75 2.00
66 Olle Stenar .75 2.00
67 Einar Andersson .75 2.00
68 Leif Andersson .75 2.00
69 Percy Lind .75 2.00
70 Gunnar Tallberg .75 2.00
71 Soren Maatta .75 2.00
72 Sven Bystrom .75 2.00
73 Hans Carlsson .75 2.00
74 Stig Goran Johansson 1.25 3.00
75 Thomas Warming .75 2.00
76 Kjell Larsson .75 2.00
77 Hakan Wickberg .75 2.00
78 Tord Lundstrom .75 2.00
79 Lennart Svedberg 2.00 4.00
80 Jan Erik Lyck .75 2.00
81 Stefan Carlsson .75 2.00
82 Kjell Jonsson .75 2.00
83 Lars Hedenstrom .75 2.00
84 Lars Ake Sivertsson .75 2.00
85 Lennart Johansson .75 2.00
86 Hans Sjoberg .75 2.00
87 Hans Dahllof .75 2.00
88 Hans Lindberg .75 2.00
89 Lars Bylund .75 2.00
90 Sten Edqvist .75 2.00
91 Arne Ericsson .75 2.00
92 Gert Blomer .75 2.00
93 Kjell Adrian .75 2.00
94 Jan Olsen .75 2.00
95 Berny Karlsson .75 2.00
96 Jorma Salmi .75 2.00
97 Ulf Sterner .75 2.00
98 Kjell-Ove Gustafsson .75 2.00
99 Lars Erik Lundvall .75 2.00
100 Kjell-Ronny Pettersson 1.00 3.00
101 Ronald Pettersson .75 2.00
102 Kjell Jonsson .75 2.00
103 Gote Hansson .75 2.00
104 Ove Sterner .75 2.00
105 Eine Olsson .75 2.00
106 Hans-Erik Fernstrom .75 2.00
107 Per-Olov Hardin .75 2.00
108 Bo Zetterberg .75 2.00
109 Ake Zettlin .75 2.00
110 Bengt-Olov Andreasson .75 2.00
111 Borje Molander .75 2.00
112 Sture Sundin .75 2.00
113 Bertil Karlsson 1.00 3.00
114 Lars Molander .75 2.00
115 Benno Persson .75 2.00
116 Rolf Larsson .75 2.00
117 Ronny Francis .75 2.00
118 Olle Westlund .75 2.00
119 Goran Wallin .75 2.00
120 Ingemar Persson .75 2.00
121 Tommy Bjorkman .75 2.00
122 Eddie Wingren .75 2.00
123 Lars Bjorn .75 2.00
124 Roland Stoltz .75 2.00
125 Sven Johansson 1.25 3.00
126 Arne Loong .75 2.00
127 Hans Mild .75 2.00
127 Per Lundstrom .75 2.00
128 Kurt Thulin .75 2.00
129 Ake Rydberg .75 2.00
130 Ove Malmberg .75 2.00
131 Lars Lundqvist .75 2.00
132 Kurt Svensson .75 2.00
133 Gosta Westerlund .75 2.00
134 Lars Andersson .75 2.00
135 Ulf Rydin .75 2.00
136 Lennart Haggroth 1.50 4.00
137 Jan Hedberg .75 2.00
138 Anders Carlberg .75 2.00
139 Hans Svedberg .75 2.00
140 Sture Hofverberg .75 2.00
141 Anders Ronnblom .75 2.00
142 Ulf Eriksson .75 2.00
143 Anders Andersson .75 2.00
144 Henrik Hedlund .75 2.00
145 Roger Boman .75 2.00
146 Bo Astrom .75 2.00
147 Bo Berglund 1.50 3.00
148 Lars Ake Warning .75 2.00
149 Sven-Olov Johansson .75 2.00
150 Ove Stenlund .75 2.00
151 Ivar Larsson .75 2.00
152 Nicke Johansson .75 2.00
153 Sten Olsen .75 2.00
154 Lars Gidlund .75 2.00
155 Tor Haarstad .75 2.00
156 Hakan Nygren .75 2.00
157 Bjorn Palmqvist .75 2.00
158 Soren Lindstrom .75 2.00
159 Henry Svensson .75 2.00
160 Lars Hagstrom .75 2.00
161 Ake Eklof .75 2.00
162 Ulf Lundstrom .75 2.00
163 Ronny Nordstrom .75 2.00
164 Paul Stahl .75 2.00
165 Kenneth Sahlen 1.25 3.00
166 Anders Hedlund .75 2.00
167 Ingemar Caris .75 2.00
168 Arne Carlsson .75 2.00
169 Gote Bostrom .75 2.00
170 Roger Olsson .75 2.00
171 Ole Jacobson .75 2.00
172 Curt Edenvik .75 2.00
173 Goran Svensson .75 2.00
174 Eje Lindstrom .75 2.00
175 Curt Larsson 2.50 5.00
176 Gunnar Backman .75 2.00
177 Anders Nordin .75 2.00
178 Ulf Torstensson .75 2.00
179 Kent Lindgren .75 2.00
180 Kent Sjalin .75 2.00
181 Lars Goran Nilsson .75 2.00
182 Heimo Klockare .75 2.00
183 Lars Sattare .75 2.00
184 Lars-Ake Lundell .75 2.00
185 Kjell Savstrom .75 2.00
186 Carl-Goran Oberg .75 2.00
187 Bjorn Larsson .75 2.00
188 Leif Eriksson .75 2.00
189 Dag Olsson .75 2.00
190 Lars Lohman .75 2.00
191 unknown .75 2.00
192 unknown .75 2.00
193 unknown .75 2.00
194 unknown .75 2.00
195 unknown .75 2.00
196 unknown .75 2.00
197 unknown .75 2.00
198 unknown .75 2.00
199 unknown .75 2.00
200 Hans Aleblad .75 2.00
201 Karl Soren Hedlund .75 2.00
202 Clarence Carlsson .75 2.00
203 Bjorn Johansson .75 2.00
204 Kent Persson .75 2.00
205 Goran Thelin .75 2.00
206 Leif Ohrlund .75 2.00
207 Mats Davidsson .75 2.00
208 Leif Artursson .75 2.00
209 Karl Gunnar Backman .75 2.00
210 Hans Mellinger .75 2.00
211 Hans Inge Lund .75 2.00
212 Kent Jansson .75 2.00
213 Anders Ronnkvist .75 2.00
214 Bo Olofsson .75 2.00

1967-68 Swedish Hockey

COMPLETE SET (300) 62.50 150.00
1 Christer Abrahamsson 2.00 4.00
2 Tommy Abrahamsson 1.00 2.00
3 Folke Bengtsson .25 1.00
4 Arne Carlsson .25 1.00
5 Bengt-Ake Gustavsson .25 1.00
6 Anders Hagstrom .25 1.00
7 Inge Hammarstrom 2.50 5.00
8 Leif Henriksson .25 1.00
9 Leif Holmqvist 1.00 2.00
10 Per-Arne Hubinette .25 1.00
11 Mats Hysing .25 1.00
12 Nils Johansson .25 1.00
13 Stig-Goran Johansson .25 1.00
14 Hans Lindberg .25 1.00
15 Tord Lundstrom .25 1.00
16 Lars-Goran Nilsson .25 1.00
17 Anders Nordin .25 1.00
18 Bert-Ola Nordlander .25 1.00
19 Roger Olsson .25 1.00
20 Bjorn Palmquist .25 1.00
21 Kjell Sundstrom .25 1.00
22 Lennart Svedberg .50 2.00
23 Hakan Wickberg .25 1.00
24 Carl-Goran Oberg .25 1.00
25 Lasse Ohman .25 1.00
26 Curt Edenvik .25 1.00
27 Hans Eriksson .25 1.00
28 Rolf Hallgren .25 1.00
29 Bo Hansson .25 1.00
30 Ove Hedberg .25 1.00
31 Kjell Hedman .50 2.00
32 Leif Holmqvist 1.00 2.00
33 Anders Johansson .25 1.00
34 Bengt Larsson .25 1.00
35 Bjorn Larsson .25 1.00
36 Rune Lindh .25 1.00
37 Borje Molander .25 1.00
38 Kjell Nilsson .25 1.00
39 Bert-Ola Nordlander .25 1.00
40 Anders Parmstrom .25 1.00
41 Lennart Selinder .25 1.00
42 Kjell Savstrom .25 1.00
43 Lars Bylund .25 1.00
44 Hans Dahllof .50 2.00
45 Lennart Gustafsson .25 1.00
46 Lars Hedenstrom .25 1.00
47 Lennart Johansson .25 1.00
48 Kjell Johnsson .25 1.00
49 Stefan Karlsson .25 1.00
50 Nisse Larsson .25 1.00
51 Lennart Lind .25 1.00
52 Hans Lindberg .25 1.00
53 Tord Lundstrom .25 1.00
54 Jan-Erik Lyck .25 1.00
55 Lars-Goran Nilsson .25 1.00
56 Anders Sahlin .50 2.00
57 Lars-Ake Sivertsson .25 1.00
58 Hans Sjoberg .25 1.00
59 Hakan Wickberg .25 1.00
60 Tommy Bjorkman .50 2.00
61 Lasse Bjorn .25 1.00
62 Thomas Carlsson .25 1.00
63 Roland Einarsson .50 2.00
64 Kjell Keijser .25 1.00
65 Stig Larsson .25 1.00
66 Kent Lindgren .25 1.00
67 Tommie Lindgren .25 1.00
68 Lars-Ake Lundell .25 1.00
69 Per Lundstrom .25 1.00
70 Bjorn Palmquist .25 1.00
71 Ulf Rydin .25 1.00
72 Lars-Eric Sjoberg 2.00 4.00
73 Lars Starck .25 1.00
74 Roland Stoltz .25 1.00
75 Henry Svensson .25 1.00
76 Kurt Thulin .25 1.00
77 Gosta Westerlund .25 1.00
78 Eddie Wingren .25 1.00
79 Carl-Goran Oberg .25 1.00
80 Anders Andersson .25 1.00
81 Hasse Andersson .25 1.00
82 Hakan Andersson .25 1.00
83 Anders Asplund .25 1.00
84 Hans Bergqvist .25 1.00
85 Hans Bostrom .25 1.00
86 Kjell Eriksson .50 2.00
87 Conny Evensson .50 2.00
88 Bjorn Fagerlund .50 2.00
89 Ingemar Magnusson .25 1.00
90 Hans-Ake Nilsson .25 1.00
91 Rune Nilsson .25 1.00
92 Kent Olsson .25 1.00
93 Lars Stalberg .25 1.00
94 Christer Sundqvist .25 1.00
95 Christer Abrahamsson 2.00 4.00
96 Tommy Abrahamsson 1.00 2.00
97 Bosse Andersson .25 1.00
98 Gunnar Andersson .25 1.00
99 Lars Andersson .25 1.00
100 Folke Bengtsson .25 1.00
101 Roland Bond .25 1.00
102 Kjell Fihnn .25 1.00
103 Jan-Olof Kroon .25 1.00
104 Lennart Lange .25 1.00
105 Sture Leksell .50 2.00
106 Goran Lysen .25 1.00
107 Ulf Martensson .25 1.00
108 Nisse Nilsson .25 1.00
109 Dag Ohlsson .25 1.00
110 Olle Sjogren .25 1.00
111 Ake Sunesson .25 1.00
112 Dan Soderstrom .25 1.00
113 Goran Winge .25 1.00
114 Mats Ahlberg .25 1.00
115 Olle Ost .25 1.00
116 Gunnar Backman .50 2.00
117 Lage Edin .25 1.00
118 Ake Eklof .25 1.00
119 Torbjorn Hubinette .25 1.00
120 Nils Johansson .25 1.00
121 Ulf Kroon .25 1.00
122 Ivar Larsson .50 2.00
123 Christer Nilsson .25 1.00
124 Anders Nordin .25 1.00
125 Hakan Nygren .25 1.00
126 Sten Olsen .25 1.00
127 Paul Stahl .25 1.00
128 Gunnar Safsten .25 1.00
129 Ulf Torstensson .25 1.00
130 Ulf Wigren .25 1.00
131 Lars Ohman .25 1.00
132 Tore Ohman .25 1.00
133 Bengt Andersson .25 1.00
134 Nils Carlsson .25 1.00
135 Kjell Eklind .25 1.00
136 Allan Fernstrom .25 1.00
137 Bengt Gustavsson .25 1.00
138 Bengt-Ake Gustavsson .50 2.00
139 Gote Hansson .25 1.00
140 Per-Arne Hubinette .25 1.00
141 Sven-Ake Jakobsson .25 1.00
142 Goran Johansson .50 2.00
143 Mats Lind .25 1.00
144 Mats Lonn .25 1.00
145 Ulf Nises .25 1.00
146 Bo Olsson .25 1.00
147 Lennart Svedberg .50 2.00
148 Evert Tysk .25 1.00
149 Stig Ostling .25 1.00
150 Ulf Berglund .25 1.00
151 Clarence Carlsson .25 1.00
152 Arne Ekenberg .25 1.00
153 Kenneth Ekman .25 1.00
154 Tom Haugh .50 2.00
155 Rolf Joelsson .25 1.00
156 Bjorn Johanesson .25 1.00
157 Arne Johansson .25 1.00
158 Bengt-Goran Karlsson .25 1.00
159 Kjell Larsson .25 1.00
160 Lasse Larsson .25 1.00
161 Barry Murman .25 1.00
162 Klas Goran Nilsson .25 1.00
163 Rolf Norell .25 1.00
164 Lennart Skordaker .25 1.00
165 Ulf Sterner .50 2.00
166 Arne Wickstrom .25 1.00
167 Bengt-Olov Andreasson .50 2.00
168 Leif Eriksson .25 1.00
169 Ove Evaldson .25 1.00
170 Hans-Erik Fernstrom .25 1.00
171 Kenneth Hillgren .25 1.00
172 Per-Olof Hardin .25 1.00
173 Bertil Karlsson .25 1.00
174 Torsten Karlsson .25 1.00
175 Rolf Larsson .25 1.00
176 William Lofqvist 1.00 2.00
177 Lars Mollander .25 1.00
178 Gert Nystrom .25 1.00
179 Olle Westlund .25 1.00
180 Bo Zetterberg .25 1.00
181 Leif Andersson .25 1.00
182 Borje Burlin .25 1.00
183 Hans Carlsson .25 1.00
184 Stig Carlsson .25 1.00
185 Einar Granath .25 1.00
186 Kjell-Ake Hedstrom .25 1.00
187 Mats Hysing .25 1.00
188 Stig-Goran Johansson .25 1.00
189 Curt Larsson 1.25 2.50
190 Eilert Maatta .25 1.00
191 Soren Maatta .25 1.00
192 Nils-Olof Schilstrom .25 1.00
193 Jan Schullstrom .25 1.00
194 Kjell Svensson .50 2.00
195 Gunnar Tallberg .25 1.00
196 Dick Yderstrom .25 1.00
197 Sten Andersson .50 2.00
198 Lars Arne Bergkvist .25 1.00
199 Anders Edstrom .25 1.00
200 Lars Bertil Eriksson .25 1.00
201 Charles Gustavsson .25 1.00
202 Ake Johansson .25 1.00
203 Lars Karestal .25 1.00
204 Rolf Karlsson .25 1.00
205 Erik Lindahl .25 1.00
206 Freddy Lindfors .50 2.00
207 Lennart Lindkvist .25 1.00
208 Kjell Rune Milton .25 1.00
209 Olle Nilsater .25 1.00
210 Birger Nordlund .25 1.00
211 Inge Tornlund .25 1.00
212 Jan Roger Oberg .25 1.00
213 Kjell Sture Oberg .25 1.00
214 Tommy Andersson .25 1.00
215 Soren Bostrom .25 1.00
216 Anders Bryner .25 1.00
217 Anders Claesson .50 2.00
218 Svante Granholm .25 1.00
219 Inge Hammarstrom 2.50 5.00
220 Borje Holmstrom .25 1.00
221 Jan Johansson .25 1.00
222 Antero Jonasson .25 1.00
223 Ove Jonsson .25 1.00
224 Lennart Lind .50 2.00
225 Jan-Erik Nilsson .25 1.00
226 Kurt Olofsson .25 1.00
227 Gosta Sjokvist .25 1.00
228 Jan Stolpe .25 1.00
229 Kjell Westerlund .25 1.00
230 Olle Ahman .25 1.00
231 Jan-Ivar Bergqvist .25 1.00
232 Lars-Ake Brannlund .50 2.00
233 Hans Bohlmark .25 1.00
234 Jan Christiansson .25 1.00
235 Bengt Eriksson .25 1.00
236 Arne Grenemo .25 1.00
237 Lars-Olof Henriksson .25 1.00
238 Kurt Jakobsson .25 1.00
239 Leif Jakobsson .25 1.00
240 Lars-Goran Johansson .25 1.00
241 Kimo Kivela .25 1.00
242 Borje Maatta .25 1.00
243 Anders Rapp .25 1.00
244 Tommy Sahlsten .25 1.00
245 Stig-Olof Zetterbrg .25 1.00
246 Lennart Abrahamsson .25 1.00
247 John Andersson .25 1.00
248 Ove Andersson .50 2.00
249 Kjell-olov Barrefjord .25 1.00
250 Ulf Barrefjord .25 1.00
251 Kent Bjork .25 1.00
252 Lars Dahlgren .25 1.00
253 Karl-Ove Eriksson .25 1.00
254 Osten Folkesson .25 1.00
255 Anders Hagstrom .25 1.00
256 Eric Jarvholm .25 1.00
257 Ulf Larsson .25 1.00
258 Bengt Lovgren .25 1.00
259 Roger Nilsson .25 1.00
260 Bengt Persson .50 2.00
261 Kjell Sundstrom .25 1.00
262 Roger Osterlund .25 1.00
263 Hans Aleblad .50 2.00
264 Ake Bolander .25 1.00
265 Karl-Gunnar Backman .25 1.00
266 Mats Davidsson .25 1.00
267 Bosse Englund .25 1.00
268 Tommy Eriksson .25 1.00
269 Karl-Soren Hedlund .25 1.00
270 Don Hughes .25 1.00
271 Krister Lindgren .25 1.00
272 Hans Mellinger .25 1.00
273 Des Moroney .25 1.00
274 Bo Olofsson .25 1.00
275 Hakan Olsson .25 1.00
276 Kent Persson .25 1.00
277 Ove Stenlund .25 1.00
278 Goran Thelin .25 1.00
279 Ove Thelin .25 1.00
280 Leif Ohrlund .25 1.00
281 Uno Ohrlund .25 1.00
282 Jan Ostling .25 1.00
283 Gert Blome .25 1.00
284 Ingemar Caris .50 2.00
285 Arne Carlsson .25 1.00
286 Kjell-Ove Gustafsson .25 1.00
287 Henric Hedlund .25 1.00
288 Leif Henriksson .25 1.00
289 Kjell Jonsson .25 1.00
290 Berny Karlsson .25 1.00
291 Goran Lindberg .25 1.00
292 Bernt Lundqvist .25 1.00
293 Lars Eric Lundvall .25 1.00
294 Carl-Fredrik Montan .25 1.00
295 Eine Ohlsson .50 2.00
296 Jan Olsen .25 1.00
297 Roger Olsson .25 1.00
298 Kjell-Ronnie Pettersson .50 2.00
299 Ronald Pettersson .25 1.00
300 Roland Sarnholm .25 1.00

1969-70 Swedish Hockey

COMPLETE SET (384) 200.00 500.00
1 Valerij Charlamov 40.00 100.00
2 Vitalij Davydov .75 2.00
3 Anatolij Firsov 3.00 8.00
4 Alexander Jakusjev 5.00 12.00
5 Vladimir Jursinov 1.00 2.50
6 Victor Kuzkin .40 1.00
7 Vladimir Lutjenko 1.00 2.50
8 Alexander Maltsev 5.00 12.00
9 Boris Michailov 5.00 12.00
10 Jevgenij Misjakov 1.50 4.00
11 Vladimir Petrov 5.00 12.00
12 Jevgenij Poladjev .40 1.00
13 Victor Putjkov .50 1.25
14 Alexander Ragulin 1.50 4.00
15 Igor Romisjevskij .40 1.00
16 Vjatjeslav Starsjinov 1.25 3.00
17 Vladimir Vikulov .75 2.00
18 Jevgenij Zimin .75 2.00
19 Victor Zinger .50 1.25
20 Josef Augusta .40 1.00
21 Vladimir Bednar .40 1.00
22 Josef Cerny .50 1.25
23 Vladimir Dzurilla 5.00 12.00
24 Richard Farda .40 1.00
25 Josef Golonka .75 2.00
26 Jan Havel .40 1.00
27 Jaroslav Holik .75 2.00
28 Jiri Holik .50 1.25
29 Josef Horesovsky .40 1.00
30 Jan Hrbaty .40 1.00
31 Jaroslav Jirik .40 1.00
32 Jan Klapac .40 1.00
33 Miroslav Lacky .75 2.00
34 Oldrich Machac .40 1.00
35 Vaclav Nedomansky 2.50 6.00
36 Frantisek Pospisil 1.00 2.50
37 Frantisek Sevcik .50 1.25
38 Jan Suchy .50 1.25
39 Ake Carlsson .40 1.00
40 Curt Edenvik .40 1.00
41 Hans Eriksson .40 1.00
42 Bo Hansson .40 1.00
43 Ove Hedberg .40 1.00
44 Kjell Hedman .75 2.00
45 Leif Holmqvist 1.50 4.00
46 Anders Johansson .40 1.00
47 Bjorn Larsson .40 1.00
48 Borje Molander .40 1.00
49 Ulf Nilsson 10.00 25.00
50 Bert-Ola Nordlander .50 1.25
51 Bo Olofsson .40 1.00
52 Anders Parmstrom .40 1.00
53 Lennart Selinder .40 1.00
54 Hans Stromberg .40 1.00
55 Kjell Savstrom .40 1.00
56 Lars-Ake Warning .40 1.00
57 Lars Bylund .40 1.00
58 Inge Hammarstrom 2.50 6.00
59 Hans Dahllof .40 1.00
60 Lars Hedenstrom .40 1.00
61 Kjell Johnsson .40 1.00
62 Lennart Johansson .40 1.00
63 Bertil Karlsson .40 1.00
64 Stefan Karlsson .40 1.00
65 Lennart Lind .40 1.00
66 Hans Lindberg .40 1.00
67 Tord Lundstrom .40 1.00
68 Jan-Erik Lyck .40 1.00
69 William Lovqvist 1.00 2.50
70 Lars-Goran Nilsson .40 1.00
71 Stig Salming .50 1.25
72 Lars-Ake Sivertsson .40 1.00
73 Lars-Goran Tano .40 1.00
74 Hakan Wickberg .40 1.00
75 Rolf Berglund .40 1.00
76 Lars Alserydh .75 2.00
77 Tage Blom .40 1.00
78 Alf Granstrom .40 1.00
79 Lennart Haggroth .75 2.00
80 Bertil Karlsson .40 1.00
81 Sven-Bertil Lindstrom .40 1.00
82 Anders Lundberg .40 1.00
83 Goran Lundmark .75 2.00
84 Sven-Erik Lundqvist .40 1.00
85 Hans Lundstrom .40 1.00
86 Kjell Lang .40 1.00
87 Borje Lofstedt .40 1.00
88 Olle Nilsson .40 1.00
89 Jan-Olof Nordin .40 1.00
90 Kjell Rehnstrom .40 1.00
91 Peder Rehnstrom .40 1.00
92 Leif Tjernstrom .40 1.00
93 Kjell-Arne Wikstrom .40 1.00
94 Anders Andren .40 1.00
95 Thomas Carlsson .40 1.00
96 Roland Einarsson 1.00 2.50
97 Lars Granlund .40 1.00
98 Stig Larsson .40 1.00
99 Lars-Ake Lundell .40 1.00
100 Per Lundstrom .40 1.00
101 Bjorn Palmquist .40 1.00
102 Ulf Rydin .40 1.00
103 Christer Sehlstedt .75 2.00
104 Lars Starck .40 1.00
105 Roland Stoltz .40 1.00
106 Billy Sundstrom .40 1.00
107 Henry Svensson .40 1.00
108 Ove Svensson .40 1.00
109 Ulf Torstensson .40 1.00
110 Christer Abrahamsson 2.50 6.00
111 Tommy Abrahamsson 1.00 2.50
112 Gunnar Andersson .40 1.00
113 Folke Bengtsson .40 1.00
114 Kjell Brus .40 1.00
115 Ake Danielsson .40 1.00
116 Bo Englund .40 1.00
117 Lennart Gustavsson .40 1.00
118 Hans Jax .40 1.00
119 Jan-Olov Kroon .40 1.00
120 Roger Lindqvist .40 1.00
121 Gunnar Mars .75 2.00
122 Ulf Martensson .40 1.00
123 Nisse Nilsson .40 1.00
124 Lars-Erik Sjoberg 2.50 6.00
125 Olle Sjogren .40 1.00
126 Dan Soderstrom .40 1.00
127 Mats Ahlberg .40 1.00
128 Gunnar Backman 1.00 2.50
129 Ulf Croon .40 1.00
130 Lage Edin .40 1.00
131 Ake Eklof .40 1.00
132 Anders Hedberg 10.00 25.00
133 Torbjorn Hubinette .40 1.00
134 Nils Johansson .40 1.00
135 Ivar Larsson 1.00 2.50
136 Christer Nilsson .40 1.00
137 Lennart Norberg .40 1.00
138 Anders Nordin .40 1.00
139 Hakan Nygren .40 1.00
140 Sten Olsen .40 1.00
141 Anders Schahlin .40 1.00
142 Gunnar Safsten .40 1.00
143 Ulf Wigren .40 1.00
144 Lars Ohman .40 1.00
145 Tore Ohman .40 1.00
146 Nils Carlsson .40 1.00
147 Kjell Eklund .40 1.00
148 Bengt Gustavsson .40 1.00
149 Bengt-Ake Gustavsson 1.00 2.50
150 Gote Hansson .40 1.00
151 Hans Hansson .40 1.00
152 Per-Arne Hubinette .40 1.00
153 Sven-Ake Jakobsson .40 1.00
154 Goran Johansson .75 2.00
155 Mats Lind .40 1.00
156 Mats Lonn .40 1.00
157 Borje Marcus .40 1.00
158 Lars Mjoberg .40 1.00
159 Ulf Nises .40 1.00
160 Bo Olsson .40 1.00
161 Erling Sundblad .40 1.00
162 Lennart Svedberg 1.00 2.50
163 Evert Tysk .40 1.00
164 Stig Ostling .40 1.00
165 Magnus Andersson .40 1.00
166 Erling Bergmark .40 1.00
167 Kenneth Hellman .40 1.00
168 Bjorn Johansson .40 1.00
169 Ulf Johansson .40 1.00
170 Berny Karlsson .40 1.00
171 Nils-Erik Karlsson .40 1.00
172 Rolf Larsson .40 1.00
173 Tore Larsson .40 1.00
174 Roland Lestander .75 2.00
175 Lennart Lindgren .40 1.00
176 Finn Lundstrom .40 1.00
177 Kenneth Manberg .40 1.00
178 Lars Molander .40 1.00
179 Lennart Rudby .40 1.00
180 Sven-Ake Rudby .40 1.00
181 Curt Svensson .40 1.00
182 Sverker Torstensson .40 1.00
183 Gunnar Backman 1.00 2.50
184 Arne Carlsson .40 1.00
185 Leif Henriksson .40 1.00
186 Leif Holmqvist 1.50 4.00
187 Mats Hysing .40 1.00
188 Nils Johansson .40 1.00
189 Stig-Goran Johansson .75 2.00
190 Stefan Karlsson .40 1.00
191 Tord Lundstrom .40 1.00
192 Kjell-Rune Milton .40 1.00
193 Lars-Goran Nilsson .40 1.00
194 Bert-Ola Nordlander .50 1.25
195 Hakan Nygren .40 1.00
196 Roger Olsson .40 1.00
197 Bjorn Palmquist .40 1.00
198 Lars-Erik Sjoberg 2.00 5.00
199 Ulf Sterner .40 1.00
200 Lennart Svedberg .75 2.00
201 Dick Yderstrom .40 1.00
202 Lennart Abrahamsson .40 1.00
203 Anders Bengtsson .75 2.00
204 Agne Bylund .40 1.00
205 Jan Edlund .40 1.00
206 Goran Hedberg .40 1.00
207 Christer Johansson .40 1.00
208 Rolf Jager .40 1.00
209 Per-Erik Kall .40 1.00
210 Anders Norberg .40 1.00
211 Janne Pettersson .75 2.00
212 Bo Sjostrom .40 1.00
213 Dick Sjostrom .40 1.00
214 Lasse Sjostrom .40 1.00
215 Ulf Steckser .40 1.00
216 Lennart Strohm .40 1.00
217 Kurt Tillander .40 1.00
218 Roger Osterlund .40 1.00
219 Hans-Ake Andersson .40 1.00
220 Hans Bejbom .40 1.00
221 Carl-Axel Berglund .40 1.00
222 Goran Borell .40 1.00
223 Bjarne Brostrom .40 1.00
224 Per Backman .40 1.00
225 Kennet Calen .40 1.00
226 Lennart Carlsson .40 1.00
227 Mats Davidsson .40 1.00
228 Curt Ferding .40 1.00
229 Lars-Olof Granstrom .40 1.00
230 Rolf Hansson .40 1.00
231 Rune Holmgren .40 1.00
232 Rune Norrstrom .40 1.00
233 Bert-Ake Olsson .40 1.00
234 Olle Olsson .40 1.00
235 Jan Svedman .40 1.00
236 Walter Winsth .40 1.00
237 Goran Akerlund .40 1.00
238 Borje Burlin .40 1.00
239 Hans Carlsson .40 1.00
240 Stig Carlsson .40 1.00
241 Gunnar Granberg .40 1.00
242 Allan Helenefors .40 1.00
243 Mats Hysing .40 1.00
244 Bertil Jacobsson .40 1.00
245 Stig-Goran Johansson .75 2.00
246 Curt Larsson 1.25 3.00
247 Eilert Maatta .40 1.00
248 Soren Maatta .40 1.00
249 Tommy Bergman .40 1.00
250 Nils-Olof Schilstrom .40 1.00
251 Jan Schullstrom .40 1.00
252 Kjell Svensson .75 2.00
253 Gunnar Tallberg .40 1.00
254 Borje Ulweback .40 1.00
255 Dick Yderstrom .40 1.00
256 Tommy Andersson .40 1.00
257 Bulla Berggren .40 1.00
258 Anders Bryner .40 1.00
259 Anders Claesson .75 2.00
260 Jan Johansson .40 1.00
261 Ove Jonsson .40 1.00
262 Lennart Lind .40 1.00
263 Arne Lundstrom .40 1.00
264 Ake Lundstrom .40 1.00
265 Jan-Erik Nilsson .40 1.00
266 Lennart Norberg .40 1.00
267 Sten-Olov Olsson .40 1.00
268 Hakan Pettersson .40 1.00
269 Stefan Pettersson .40 1.00
270 Gosta Sjokvist .40 1.00
271 Jan Stolpe .40 1.00
272 Ake Soderberg .40 1.00
273 Kjell Westerlund .40 1.00
274 Olle Ahman .40 1.00
275 Krister Andersson .75 2.00
276 Bert Danielsson .40 1.00
277 Gert Danielsson .40 1.00
278 Bengt Eriksson .40 1.00
279 Lars-Anders Gustavsson .40 1.00
280 Curt Jacobsson .40 1.00
281 Leif Jacobsson .40 1.00
282 Lars-Erik Jakobsson .40 1.00
283 Lars-Goran Johansson .40 1.00
284 Des Moroney .40 1.00
285 Borje Maatta .40 1.00
286 Lars-Ake Nordin .40 1.00
287 Kenneth Pedersen .40 1.00
288 Anders Rapp .40 1.00
289 Benny Runesson .40 1.00
290 Jonny Ryman .40 1.00
291 Ake Ryman .40 1.00
292 Goran Ahsten .75 2.00
293 John Andersson .40 1.00
294 Kjell-Olov Barrefjord .40 1.00
295 Ulf Barrefjord .40 1.00
296 Kent Bjork .40 1.00
297 Lars Dahlgren .40 1.00
298 Karl-Olof Eriksson .40 1.00
299 Osten Folkesson .40 1.00
300 Anders Hagstrom .40 1.00
301 Eric Jarvholm .40 1.00
302 Ulf Larsson .40 1.00
303 Bo Leong .75 2.00
304 Bengt Lofgren .40 1.00
305 Roger Nilsson .40 1.00
306 Bengt Persson .75 2.00
307 Ulf Stromsoe .40 1.00
308 Kjell Sundstrom .40 1.00
309 Leif Andersson .40 1.00
310 Bernt Augustsson .40 1.00
311 Kjell Augustsson .40 1.00
312 Tommy Eriksson 1.00 2.50
313 Lars-Olof Feltendahl .40 1.00
314 Karl-Soren Hedlund .40 1.00
315 Pentti Hyytiainen .40 1.00
316 Arne Johansson .40 1.00
317 Bengt-Goran Karlsson .40 1.00
318 Curt Lundmark 1.00 2.50
319 Hakan Olsson .75 2.00
320 Kent Persson .40 1.00
321 Ove Stenlund .40 1.00
322 Goran Thelin .40 1.00
323 Ove Thelin .40 1.00
324 Bo Astrom .40 1.00
325 Hasse Mellinger .40 1.00
326 Uno Ohrlund .40 1.00
327 Jan Ostling .40 1.00
328 Kjell Andersson .40 1.00
329 Ronny Andersson 1.00 2.50
330 Gert Blome .40 1.00
331 Ingemar Caris 1.00 2.50
332 Arne Carlsson .40 1.00
333 Svante Granholm .40 1.00
334 Henric Hedlund .40 1.00
335 Leif Henriksson .40 1.00
336 Anders Johansson .40 1.00
337 Kjell Jonsson .40 1.00
338 Bjorn Lindberg .40 1.00
339 Goran Lindberg .40 1.00
340 Carl-Fredrik Montan .40 1.00
341 Leif Nilsson .40 1.00
342 Kurt Olofsson .40 1.00
343 Jan Olsen .40 1.00
344 Roger Olsson .40 1.00
345 Kjell-Ronnie Petterson .40 1.00
346 Ulf Sterner .40 1.00
347 Rickie Bayes 1.25 3.00
348 Gary Begg .75 2.00
349 Roger Bourbonnais 1.00 2.50
350 Jack Bownass 1.00 2.50
351 Terry Caffery 1.25 3.00
352 Steve Carlyle 1.25 3.00
353 Ab Demarco 1.50 4.00
354 Ted Hargreaves 1.00 2.50
355 Bill Heindl 1.25 3.00
356 Fran Huck .75 2.00
357 Steve King 1.25 3.00
358 Chuck Lefley 2.00 5.00
359 Morris Mott 1.25 3.00
360 Terry O'Malley 1.00 2.50
361 Kevin O'Shea 1.25 3.00
362 Gerry Pinder 2.00 5.00
363 Steve Rexe 1.50 4.00
364 Ken Stephenson 1.25 3.00
365 Wayne Stephenson 5.00 12.00
366 Matti Harju .40 1.00
367 Esa Isaksson .40 1.00
368 Kari Johansson .40 1.00
369 Juhani Jylha .40 1.00
370 Matti Keinonen .40 1.00
371 Veli-Pekka Ketola 1.50 4.00
372 Lasse Kiili .75 2.00
373 Ilpo Koskela .40 1.00
374 Pekka Leimu .40 1.00
375 Seppo Lindstrom .40 1.00
376 Pekka Marjamaki .40 1.00
377 Lauri Mononen .40 1.00
378 Lasse Oksanen .40 1.00
379 Lalli Partanen .40 1.00

Card	Low	High
380 Esa Peltonen	.40	1.00
381 Jorma Peltonen	.40	1.00
382 Juhani Rantasila	.40	1.00
383 Juhani Wahlsten	.40	1.00
384 Urpo Ylonen	1.25	3.00

1970-71 Swedish Mastar Serien

Card	Low	High
COMPLETE SET (200)	500.00	1200.00
1 Vladimir Dzurila	15.00	40.00
2 Jozef Golonka	1.50	4.00
3 Jiri Holik	1.25	3.00
4 Vaclav Nedomansky	4.00	10.00
5 Vaclav Nedomansky	4.00	10.00
6 Jaroslav Holik	1.50	4.00
7 Jozef Golonka	1.50	4.00
8 Vaclav Nedomansky	4.00	10.00
9 Vladimir Bednar	.75	2.00
10 Jan Havel	.75	2.00
11 Jan Hrbaty	.75	2.00
12 Jan Suchy	1.25	3.00
13 Lasse Oksanen	.75	2.00
14 Urpo Ylonen	1.50	4.00
15 Michael Curran	2.50	6.00
16 Gary Begg	1.50	4.00
17 Carl Lackey	1.50	4.00
18 Terry O'Malley	2.50	6.00
19 Gary Gamuicci	1.50	4.00
20 Seppo Lindstrom	.75	2.00
21 Lucenko		
Misjakov		
Davidov	2.50	6.00
22 Victor Putjkov	1.25	3.00
23 Alexandr Ragulin	3.00	8.00
24 Gerry Pinder	4.00	10.00
25 Fran Huck	1.50	4.00
26 Ken Dryden	50.00	120.00
27 Viktor Zinger	1.25	3.00
28 Vladimir Petrov	8.00	20.00
29 Igor Romisjevsky		
Viktor Zinger	1.50	4.00
30 Valerij Charlamov	20.00	50.00
31 Alexandr Ragulin	3.00	8.00
32 Ab Demarco	3.00	8.00
33 Morris Mott	2.50	6.00
34 Fran Huck	1.50	4.00
35 Vjatjeslav Starsinov	2.50	6.00
36 Lars-Goran Nilsson	1.50	4.00
37 Stig-Goran Stisse Johansson	1.50	4.00
38 Leif Honken Holmqvist	3.00	8.00
39 Hakan Nygren	.75	2.00
40 Tord Lundstrom	.75	2.00
41 Ulf Sterner	.75	2.00
42 Lars-Erik Sjoberg	5.00	12.00
43 Kjell-Rune Milton	.75	2.00
44 Leif Honken Holmqvist	3.00	8.00
45 Stefan Lill-Prosten Karlsson	.75	2.00
46 Lennart Lill-Strimma Svedberg	1.50	4.00
47 Tord Lundstrom	.75	2.00
48 Ulf Sterner	.75	2.00
49 Tord Lundstrom	.75	2.00
50 Lennart Lill-Strimma Svedberg	1.50	4.00
51 Sverige (12 st)	.75	2.00
52 Bert-Ola Nordlander	1.25	3.00
53 Leif Honken Holmqvist	3.00	8.00
54 Lars-Erik Sjoberg	5.00	12.00
55 Lars-Erik Sjoberg	5.00	12.00
56 Nils Nicke Johansson	.75	2.00
57 Ulf Sterner	.75	2.00
58 Ulf Sterner		
Leif Blixten Henriksson	.75	2.00
59 Tord Lundstrom	.75	2.00
60 Mats Hysing		
Nils Johansson	.75	2.00
61 Lars-Goran Nilsson	.75	2.00
62 Hakan Nygren	.75	2.00
63 USSR vs. Team Canada		
Gerry Pinder		
Anatolij Firsov		
Alexandre Jakusjev		
Alexandr Ragulin		
Igor Romisjevsky		
Stephenson		
Ken Dryden		
Bill Heindl		
Vitalij Misjakov	10.00	25.00
64 Evgenij Misjakov	1.50	4.00
65 Vjatjaslav Starsinov	2.50	6.00
66 Alexandr Ragulin	3.00	8.00
67 Alexandr Maltsev	8.00	20.00
68 Anatolij Firsov	6.00	15.00
69 Vladimir Lucenko	2.50	6.00
70 Vladimir Petrov	8.00	20.00
71 Vladimir Petrov	8.00	20.00
72 Vjatjeslav Starsinov	2.50	6.00
73 Vladimir Vikulov	1.50	4.00
74 Vitaly Davidov	1.50	4.00
75 Evgenij Zimin	1.25	3.00
76 Vladimir Bednar		
Vladimir Dzurila	4.00	10.00
77 Jan Suchy	1.25	3.00
78 Jaroslav Holik	1.50	4.00
79 Josef Horesovsky	.75	2.00
80 Jozef Golonka	1.50	4.00
81 Richard Farda	.75	2.00
82 Frantisek Pospisil		
Oldrich Machac	1.50	4.00
83 Ilop Koskela	.75	2.00
84 Juhani Jylha	.75	2.00
85 Esa Peltonen	.75	2.00
86 Lasse Oksanen	.75	2.00
87 Juhani Wahlsten	.75	2.00
88 Juha Rantasila	.75	2.00
89 Bob Paradise	1.50	4.00
90 Bob Paradise	1.50	4.00
91 Tim Sheehy	1.50	4.00
92 Michael Curran	4.00	10.00
93 Ken Dryden	50.00	120.00
94 Morris Mott	2.50	6.00
95 Fran Huck	1.50	4.00
96 unknown	.75	2.00
97 unknown	.75	2.00
98 unknown	.75	2.00
99 unknown	.75	2.00
100 unknown	.75	2.00
101 Arne Carlsson	.75	2.00
102 Nils Nicke Johansson	.75	2.00
103 Leif Holmqvist	3.00	8.00
104 Leif Henriksson	.75	2.00
105 Lennart Svedberg	1.50	4.00
106 Hakan Wickberg	.75	2.00
107 Gennar Backman	.75	2.00
108 Roger Olsson	.75	2.00
109 Kjell-Rune Milton	.75	2.00
110 Mats Hysing	.75	2.00
111 Lars-Erik Sjoberg	5.00	12.00
112 Anders Hedberg	20.00	50.00
113 Bjorn Palmqvist	.75	2.00
114 Tord Lundstrom	.75	2.00
115 Ulf Sterner	.75	2.00
116 Stig-Goran Johansson	1.50	4.00
117 Lars-Goran Nilsson	.75	2.00
118 Stefan Karlsson	.75	2.00
119 Anders Nordin	.75	2.00
120 Hans Virus Lindberg	.75	2.00
121 Davidov		
Starshinov		
Polupanov		
Jakushev		
Maltsev		
Firsov	15.00	40.00
122 Vitaly Davidov	1.50	4.00
123 Alexandr Jakusjev		
Valtonen O. Rantasila	8.00	20.00
124 Alexandr Maltsev	8.00	20.00
125 Valerij Charlamov	20.00	50.00
126 Alexandr Ragulin	3.00	8.00
127 Igor Romisjevskij	.75	2.00
128 Boris Michailov	8.00	20.00
129 Vyatcheslav Starsinov		
Victor Polupanov		
Alexander Ragulin		
Vladimir Lucenko	10.00	25.00
130 Victor Konovalenko	.75	2.00
131 Jakusjev		
Vitalij Davidov		
Boris Michailov		
Vladislav Tretiak		
Alexander Maltsev		
Evgenji Paladjev	10.00	25.00
132 Vladimir Lucenko		
Vladimir Petrov		
Anatoli Firsov		
Valerij Nikitin		
Igor Romishevski		
Vikulov		
Alexander Yakushev	10.00	25.00
133 Alexandr Maltsev	8.00	20.00
134 Valerij Nikitin	.75	2.00
135 Vladimir Vikulov	1.50	4.00
136 Vjatjeslav Starsinov	2.50	6.00
137 Evgenij Paladjev	.75	2.00
138 Vladimir Shapovalov	.75	2.00
139 Anatolij Firsov	6.00	15.00
140 Victor Polupanov	.75	2.00
141 Jaroslav Jirik	.75	2.00
142 Miroslav Lacky	1.50	4.00
143 Jan Suchy	1.25	3.00
144 Lubomir Ujvary	.75	2.00
145 Vladimir Bednar	.75	2.00
146 Richard Farda	.75	2.00
147 Josef Cernyh	1.25	3.00
148 Vaclav Nedomansky	4.00	10.00
149 Jaroslav Holik	2.50	6.00
150 Jiri Holik	1.25	3.00
151 Julius Haas		
Vladislav Martinec	1.25	3.00
152 Vaclav Nedomansky	4.00	10.00
153 Josef Horesovsky	.75	2.00
154 Oldrich Machac	.75	2.00
155 Tommy Abrahamsson		
Jiri Kochta	1.50	4.00
156 Vladimir Dzurila		
Jan Suchy		
Vladimir Bednar	4.00	10.00
157 Jorma Valtonen	1.50	4.00
158 Veli-Pekka Ketola	3.00	8.00
159 Malli Murto		
Lauri Mononen	.75	2.00
160 Heikki Riihiranta	1.50	4.00
161 Pekka Leimu	.75	2.00
162 Lasse Oksanen	.75	2.00
163 Jorma Valtonen		
Vaino Kolkka		
Pekka Marjamaki	8.00	20.00
164 Urpo Ylonen	8.00	20.00
165 Matti Keinonen	.75	2.00
166 Juha Rantasila		
Anatolij Firsov	4.00	10.00
167 Jorma Vehmanen	.75	2.00
168 Matti Murto	.75	2.00
169 Peter Slapke	.75	2.00
170 Claus Hirche	.75	2.00
171 Frank Braun	.75	2.00
172 Rolf Bielas	.75	2.00
173 Kargar		
Hiller		
Ziesche		
Braun	.75	2.00
174 Beilas		
Braun		
Hirche		
Kolbe	.75	2.00
175 Wilfried Rohrbach		
Hartmut Nickel	.75	2.00
176 Plotka		
Karrenbauer		
Rohrbach		
Patschinski	.75	2.00
177 John Mayasich		
James Branch	.75	2.00
178 Larry Skime	1.50	4.00
179 Paul Coppo	1.50	4.00
180 Larry Pleau	1.50	4.00
181 Bruce Riutta		
Ron Nasland		
John Lothrop	1.50	4.00
182 Jerry Lackey	1.50	4.00
183 Bob Paradise		
Michael Curran		
Carl Lackey	2.50	6.00
184 Paul Coppo		
Peter Markle	1.50	4.00
185 Roger Bourbonnais	2.50	6.00
186 Ted Hargreaves	2.50	6.00
187 Fran Huck	1.50	4.00
188 Wayne Stephenson	8.00	20.00
189 Morris Mott	2.50	6.00
190 Gerry Pinder	4.00	10.00
191 Gary Begg	1.50	4.00
192 Ken Dryden		
Blank Back	50.00	120.00
193 Felix Goralczyk	.75	2.00
194 Andrzej Tkacz	.75	2.00
195 Jan Modzelewski	.75	2.00
196 Marian Kajzerek	.75	2.00
197 Josef Stefaniak	.75	2.00
198 Walery Kosyl	.75	2.00
199 Jan Modzelewski	.75	2.00
200 Pajerski		
Goralzcyk		
Chachowski		
Polen	.75	2.00

1970-71 Swedish Hockey

Card	Low	High
COMPLETE SET (384)	200.00	500.00
1 Leif (Honken) Holmqvist	1.25	3.00
2 Kjell Hedman	.75	2.00
3 Lars Danielsson	.40	1.00
4 Ake Fagerstrom	.40	1.00
5 Per-Arne Hubinette	.40	1.00
6 Hakan Lindgren	.40	1.00
7 Bert-Ola Nordlander	.50	1.25
8 Rolf (Rattan) Edberg	.40	1.00
9 Bo Hansson	.40	1.00
10 Jan-Olov Kroon	.40	1.00
11 Ulf Nilsson	5.00	12.00
12 Bosse Olofsson	.40	1.00
13 Lennart Selinder	.40	1.00
14 Hans Stromberg	.40	1.00
15 Kjell Savstrom	.40	1.00
16 Lars-Ake Warning	.40	1.00
17 Lars-Goran Nilsson		
Alexander Yakushev	.75	2.00
18 William Lofqvist	.75	2.00
19 Hans Dahllof	.75	2.00
20 Lars Bylund	.40	1.00
21 Lars Hedenstrom	.40	1.00
22 Kjell Johnsson	.40	1.00
23 Borje Salming	12.50	30.00
24 Stig Salming	.40	1.00
25 Stig Ostling	.40	1.00
26 Inge Hammarstrom	2.50	6.00
27 Lennart Johansson	.40	1.00
28 Stefan Karlsson	.40	1.00
29 Lennart Lind	.40	1.00
30 Hans (Virus) Lindberg	.40	1.00
31 Tord Lundstrom	.40	1.00
32 Jan-Erik Lyck	.40	1.00
33 Lars-Goran Nilsson	.40	1.00
34 Lars-Ake Sivertsson	.40	1.00
35 Hakan Wickberg	.40	1.00
36 puzzle	.40	1.00
37 puzzle	.40	1.00
38 puzzle	.40	1.00
39 puzzle	.40	1.00
40 puzzle	.40	1.00
41 puzzle	.40	1.00
42 puzzle	.40	1.00
43 puzzle	.40	1.00
44 puzzle	.40	1.00
45 puzzle	.40	1.00
46 puzzle	.40	1.00
47 puzzle	.40	1.00
48 Roland Einarsson	.75	2.00
49 Ake Eklof	.40	1.00
50 Christer Ahlstrand	.40	1.00
51 Thomas Carlsson	.40	1.00
52 Anders Rylin	.40	1.00
53 Billy Sundstrom	.40	1.00
54 Folke Bengtsson	.40	1.00
55 Stig Larsson	.40	1.00
56 Lars-Ake Lundell	.40	1.00
57 Per Lundstrom	.40	1.00
58 Bjorn Palmqvist	.40	1.00
59 Ulf Rydin	.40	1.00
60 Ove Svensson	.40	1.00
61 Jan Zabrodsky	.40	1.00
62 Leif Holmqvist PUZ	1.00	2.50
63 Leif Holmqvist PUZ	1.00	2.50
64 Leif Holmqvist PUZ	1.00	2.50
65 Leif Holmqvist PUZ	1.00	2.50
66 Christer Abrahamsson	1.50	4.00
67 Christer Sterner	.75	2.00
68 Thommy Abrahamsson	.75	2.00
69 Karl-Gustaf Alander	.40	1.00
70 Gunnar Andersson	.40	1.00
71 Roland Bond	.40	1.00
72 Ake Danielsson	.40	1.00
73 Per-Olov Brasar	1.50	4.00
74 Kjell Brus	.40	1.00
75 Hans Jax	.40	1.00
76 Dan Labraaten	1.50	4.00
77 Roger Lindqvist	.40	1.00
78 Ulf Martensson	.40	1.00
79 Olle Sjogren	.40	1.00
80 Ingemar Snis	.40	1.00
81 Dan Soderstrom	.40	1.00
82 Mats Ahlberg	.40	1.00
83 Gunnar Backman	.75	2.00
84 Ivar Larsson	.75	2.00
85 Lage Edin	.40	1.00
86 Kjell-Rune Milton	.40	1.00
87 Ulf Torstensson	.40	1.00
88 Ulf Wigren	.40	1.00
89 Ulf Croon	.40	1.00
90 Hakan Dahllof	.40	1.00
91 Anders Hedberg	5.00	12.00
92 Torbjorn Hubinette	.40	1.00
93 Christer Nilsson	.40	1.00
94 Lennart Norberg	.40	1.00
95 Anders Nordin	.40	1.00
96 Hakan Nygren	.40	1.00
97 Per-Olof Uusitalo	.40	1.00
98 Lars Ohman	.40	1.00
99 Tore Ohman	.40	1.00
100 V. Dzurilla PUZ	.75	2.00
101 V. Dzurilla PUZ	.75	2.00
102 V. Dzurilla PUZ	.75	2.00
103 V. Dzurilla PUZ	.75	2.00
104 V. Dzurilla PUZ	.75	2.00
105 V. Dzurilla PUZ	.75	2.00
106 V. Dzurilla PUZ	.75	2.00
107 V. Dzurilla PUZ	.75	2.00
108 V. Dzurilla PUZ	.75	2.00
109 V. Dzurilla PUZ	.75	2.00
110 V. Dzurilla PUZ	.75	2.00
111 V. Dzurilla PUZ	.75	2.00
112 Bengt-Ake Gustavsson	.75	2.00
113 Lars Gustavsson	.75	2.00
114 Tommy Andersson	.40	1.00
115 Hans-Olov Ernlund	.40	1.00
116 Lars Mjoberg	.40	1.00
117 Gote Hansson	.40	1.00
118 L. Svedberg PUZ	.50	1.25
119 B. Mikhailov PUZ	1.50	4.00
120 L. Holmqvist PUZ	1.00	2.50
121 Hans Hansson	.40	1.00
122 Sven-Ake Jakobsson	.40	1.00
123 Mats Lind	.40	1.00
124 Mats Lonn	.40	1.00
125 Borje Marcus	.40	1.00
126 Ulf Nises	.40	1.00
127 Borje Skoog	.40	1.00
128 Erling Sundblad	.40	1.00
129 Kent Sundkvist	.40	1.00
130 Curt Larsson	1.00	2.50
131 Torbjorn Hellsing	.75	2.00
132 Tommie Bergman	2.00	5.00
133 Arne Carlsson	.40	1.00
134 Allan Helenefors	.40	1.00
135 Eilert Maatta	.40	1.00
136 Jan Schullstrom	.40	1.00
137 Hans Carlsson	.40	1.00
138 Tommy Carlsson	.40	1.00
139 Gunnar Granberg	.40	1.00
140 Mats Hysing	.40	1.00
141 Bertil Jacobsson	.40	1.00
142 Stig-Goran Johansson	.40	1.00
143 Soren Maatta	.40	1.00
144 Nils-Olov Schilstrom	.40	1.00
145 Dick Yderstrom	.40	1.00
146 Carl-Goran Oberg	.40	1.00
147 Lennart Svedberg	.50	1.25
148 Anders Claesson	.75	2.00
149 Kent Othberg	.75	2.00
150 Jan Johansson	.40	1.00
151 Jan-Erik Nilsson	.40	1.00
152 Stefan Pettersson	.40	1.00
153 Lennart Svedberg	.75	2.00
154 Bo Berggren	.40	1.00
155 Arne Lundstrom	.40	1.00
156 Finn Lundstrom	.40	1.00
157 I. Romisjevskij PUZ	.40	1.00
158 I. Romisjevskij PUZ	.50	1.25
159 Ake Lundstrom	.40	1.00
160 V. Tretiak PUZ	4.00	10.00
161 V. Tretiak PUZ	4.00	10.00
162 Lennart Norberg	.40	1.00
163 Hakan Pettersson	.40	1.00
164 Ake Soderberg	.50	1.25
165 Olle Ahman	.40	1.00
166 puzzle	.40	1.00
167 puzzle	.40	1.00
168 puzzle	.40	1.00
169 puzzle	.40	1.00
170 puzzle	.40	1.00
171 puzzle	.40	1.00
172 puzzle	.40	1.00
173 puzzle	.40	1.00
174 puzzle	.40	1.00
175 puzzle	.40	1.00
176 puzzle	.40	1.00
177 puzzle	.40	1.00
178 Christer Andersson	.75	2.00
179 Goran Astrom	.75	2.00
180 Kenneth Ekman	.40	1.00
181 Lars Erik Jakobsson	.40	1.00
182 Des Moroney	.40	1.00
183 Borje Maatta	.40	1.00
184 Kenneth Pederson	.40	1.00
185 Anders Rapp	.40	1.00
186 Sven Crabo	.40	1.00
187 Lars Anders Gustavsson	.40	1.00
188 Kurt Jacobsson	.40	1.00
189 Leif Jacobsson	.40	1.00
190 Lars Goran Johansson	.40	1.00
191 Bernt Karlsson	.40	1.00
192 Benny Runesson	.40	1.00
193 Jonny Ryman	.40	1.00
194 Ake Ryman	.40	1.00
195 Christer Grahn	.75	2.00
196 Ronny Sandstrom	.40	1.00
197 John Andersson	.40	1.00
198 Karl-Olof Eriksson	.40	1.00
199 Anders Hagstrom	.40	1.00
200 Rolf Jager	.40	1.00
201 Erik Jarvholm	.40	1.00
202 Lars Nordin	.40	1.00
203 Ulf Barrefjord	.40	1.00
204 Lars Dahlgren	.40	1.00
205 Ulf Ingvarsson	.40	1.00
206 Ulf Larsson	.40	1.00
207 Jan Lundqvist	.40	1.00
208 Ulf Lundstrom	.40	1.00
209 Bengt Lovgren	.40	1.00
210 Lars SJostrom	.40	1.00
211 Kjell Sundstrom	.40	1.00
212 Ulf Stromsoe	.40	1.00
213 Hakan Olsson	.75	2.00
214 Leif Andersson	.40	1.00
215 Tommy Eriksson	.75	2.00
216 Karl-Soren Hedlund	.40	1.00
217 Curt Lundmark	.75	2.00
218 Ove Nystrom	.40	1.00
219 Gote Gustavsson	.40	1.00
220 Hans Hjelm	.40	1.00
221 Pennti Hyytiainen	.40	1.00
222 Arne Johansson	.40	1.00
223 Bengt-Goran Karlsson	.40	1.00
224 Kent Persson	.40	1.00
225 Ove Stenlund	.40	1.00
226 Goran Thelin	.40	1.00
227 Ove Thelin	.40	1.00
228 Bo Astrom	.40	1.00
229 Jan Ostling	.40	1.00
230 V. Tretiak action	10.00	25.00
231 V. Konovalenko PUZ	.40	1.00
232 V. Konovalenko PUZ	.40	1.00
233 V. Konovalenko PUZ	.40	1.00
234 V. Konovalenko PUZ	.40	1.00
235 V. Konovalenko PUZ	.40	1.00
236 V. Konovalenko PUZ	.40	1.00
237 V. Konovalenko PUZ	.40	1.00
238 V. Konovalenko PUZ	.40	1.00
239 V. Konovalenko PUZ	.40	1.00
240 V. Konovalenko PUZ	.40	1.00
241 V. Konovalenko PUZ	.40	1.00
242 V. Konovalenko PUZ	.40	1.00
243 Ingemar Caris	.75	2.00
244 Ronny Andersson	.75	2.00
245 Gert Blome	.40	1.00
246 Anders Johansson	.40	1.00
247 Goran Lindberg	.40	1.00
248 Jan Olsen	.40	1.00
249 Lars-Erik Sjoberg	2.00	5.00
250 Kjell Andersson	.40	1.00
251 Svante Granholm	.40	1.00
252 Henrik Hedlund	.40	1.00
253 Leif Henriksson	.40	1.00
254 Bjorn Lindberg	.40	1.00
255 Billy Lindstrom	.40	1.00
256 Carl-Fredrik Montan	.40	1.00
257 Leif Nilsson	.40	1.00
258 Kurt Olofsson	.40	1.00
259 Roger Olsson	.40	1.00
260 Kjell-Ronnie Pettersson	.40	1.00
261 Soviet team PUZ	.40	1.00
262 Soviet team PUZ	.40	1.00
263 Soviet team PUZ	.40	1.00
264 Soviet team PUZ	.40	1.00
265 Soviet team PUZ	.40	1.00
266 Soviet team PUZ	.40	1.00
267 Soviet team PUZ	.40	1.00
268 Soviet team PUZ	.40	1.00
269 Soviet team PUZ	.40	1.00
270 Soviet team PUZ	.40	1.00
271 Soviet team PUZ	.40	1.00
272 Soviet team PUZ	.40	1.00
273 Leif Holmqvist	1.00	2.50
274 Gunnar Backman	.75	2.00
275 Christer Abrahamsson	1.50	4.00
276 Thommy Abrahamsson	.75	2.00
277 Arne Carlsson	.40	1.00
278 Nils Johansson	.40	1.00
279 Ljell-Rune Milton	.40	1.00
280 Lars-Erik Sjoberg	2.00	5.00
281 Lennart Svedberg	.75	2.00
282 Anders Hedberg	5.00	12.00
283 Stig-Goran Johansson	.40	1.00
284 Stefan Karlsson	.40	1.00
285 Hans Lindberg	.40	1.00
286 Tord Lundstrom	.40	1.00
287 Lars-Goran Nilsson	.40	1.00
288 Anders Nordin	.40	1.00
289 Roger Olsson	.40	1.00
290 Bjorn Palmqvist	.40	1.00
291 Ulf Sterner	.40	1.00
292 Hakan Wickberg	.40	1.00
293 Urpo Ylonen	1.00	2.50
294 Jorma Valtonen	.75	2.00
295 Ilpo Koskela	.40	1.00
296 Seppo Lindstrom	.40	1.00
297 Pekka Marjamaki	.40	1.00
298 Lalli Partinen	.40	1.00
299 Juha Rantasila	.40	1.00
300 Heikki Riihiranta	1.00	2.50
301 Pekka Keimu	.40	1.00
302 Matti Keinonen	.40	1.00
303 Veli-Pekka Ketola	1.50	4.00
304 Vaino Kolkka	.40	1.00
305 Harri Linnonmaa	.40	1.00
306 Lauri Mononen	.40	1.00
307 Matti Murto	.75	2.00
308 Lasse Oksanen	.40	1.00
309 Esa Peltonen	.40	1.00
310 Jorma Poltonon	.40	1.00
311 Juhani Tamminen	.75	2.00
312 Jorma Vehmanen	.40	1.00
313 Viktor Konovalenko	.75	2.00
314 Vladislav Tretjak	20.00	50.00
315 Vitalij Davidov	.75	2.00
316 Vladimir Lutjenko	.75	2.00
317 Jevgenij Paladjev	.40	1.00
318 Alexander Ragulin	1.50	4.00
319 Igor Romisjevski	.50	1.25
320 Valerij Vasiljev	2.50	6.00
321 Valerij Nikitin	.50	1.25
322 Valerij Charlamov	20.00	50.00
323 Anatolij Firsov	4.00	10.00
324 Alexander Jakusjev	4.00	10.00
325 Alexander Maltsev	4.00	10.00
326 Boris Michailov	4.00	10.00
327 Jevgenij Misjakov	1.25	3.00
328 Vladimir Petrov	2.50	6.00
329 Viktor Polupanov	.40	1.00
330 Vladimir Sjadrin	1.50	4.00
331 Vjatjeslav Starsinov	1.25	3.00
332 Vladimir Vikulov	.50	1.25
333 puzzle	.40	1.00
334 puzzle	.40	1.00
335 puzzle	.40	1.00
336 puzzle	.40	1.00
337 puzzle	.40	1.00
338 puzzle	.40	1.00
339 puzzle	.40	1.00
340 puzzle	.40	1.00
341 puzzle	.40	1.00
342 puzzle	.40	1.00
343 puzzle	.40	1.00
344 puzzle	.40	1.00
345 Vladimir Dzurilla	2.50	6.00
346 Miroslav Lacky	.75	2.00
347 Vladimir Bednar	.40	1.00
348 Josef Horesovsky	.40	1.00
349 Oldrich Machac	.40	1.00
350 Frantisek Pospisil	.75	2.00
351 Jan Suchy	.50	1.25
352 Lubomir Ujvary	.40	1.00
353 Josef Cerny	.50	1.25
354 Richard Farda	.40	1.00
355 Julius Haas	.40	1.00
356 Ivan Hlinka	.75	2.00
357 Jaroslav Holik	.50	1.25
358 Jiri Holik	.50	1.25
359 Jan Hrbaty	.40	1.00
360 Jiri Kochta	.40	1.00
361 Vladislav Martinec	.40	1.00
362 Vaclav Nedomansky	1.50	4.00
363 Stanislav Pryl	.40	1.00
364 Frantisek Sevcik	.40	1.00
365 Klaus Hirche	.75	2.00
366 Diter Purschel	.75	2.00
367 Frank Braun	.40	1.00
368 Dieter Dewitz	.40	1.00
369 Bernd Karrenbauer	.40	1.00
370 Helmut Novy	.40	1.00
371 Dietmar Peters	.40	1.00
372 Wolfgang Plotka	.40	1.00
373 Peter Slapke	.40	1.00
374 Rolf Bielas	.40	1.00
375 Lothar Fuchs	.40	1.00
376 Bernd Hiller	.40	1.00
377 Reinhard Karger	.40	1.00
378 Hartmut Nickel	.40	1.00
379 Rudiger Noack	.40	1.00
380 Rainer Patschinski	.40	1.00
381 Peter Prusa	.40	1.00
382 Wilfried Rohrbach	.40	1.00
383 Dieter Rohl	.40	1.00
384 Joachim Ziesche	.40	1.00

1971-72 Swedish Hockey

Card	Low	High
COMPLETE SET (400)	200.00	500.00
1 Christer Abrahamsson	1.00	2.00
2 Leif (Honken) Holmqvist	.50	1.00
3 William (Loken) Lofqvist	.50	1.00
4 Thommy Abrahamsson	.50	1.00
5 Gunnar Andersson	.25	.50
6 Thommie Bergman	1.50	3.00
7 Arne Carlsson	.25	.50
8 Kjell-Rune Milton	.25	.50
9 Bert-Ola Nordlander	.50	1.00
10 Lennart Svedberg	.50	1.00
11 Lars-Erik Sjoberg	1.00	2.00
12 Stig Ostling	.25	.50
13 Inge Hammarstrom	1.50	10.00
14 Anders Hedberg	4.00	8.00
15 Stig-Goran Johansson	.50	1.00
16 Stefan Karlsson	.25	.50
17 Dan Labraaten	1.00	2.00
18 Hans (Virus) Lindberg	.25	.50
19 Tord Lundstrom	.25	.50
20 Lars-Goran Nilsson	.25	.50
21 Hakan Nygren	.25	.50
22 Bjorn Palmqvist	.25	.50
23 Hakan Pettersson	.25	.50
24 Ulf Sterner	.25	.50
25 Hakan Wickberg	.25	.50
26 Viktor Konovalenko	.30	.75
27 Vladislav Tretjak	10.00	20.00
28 Gennadij Cigannkov	.30	.75
29 Vitali Davidov	.30	.75
30 Victor Kuskin	.25	.50
31 Vladimir Lutjenko	.30	.75
32 Alexander Ragulin	1.00	2.00
33 Igor Romisjevskij	.30	.75
34 Valerij Kharlamov	20.00	50.00
35 Anatolij Firsov	2.50	5.00
36 Alexander Maltsev	2.50	5.00
37 Boris Michailov	2.50	5.00
38 Jevgenij Misjakov	1.00	2.00
39 Vladimir Petrov	2.50	5.00
40 Vjatjeslav Starshinov	.50	1.00
41 Vladimir Vikulov	.30	.75
42 Evgenij Zimin	.50	1.00
43 Jiri Holecek	.50	1.00
44 Josef Horesovsky	.25	.50
45 Oldrich Machac	.25	.50
46 Frantisek Panchartek	.25	.50
47 Frantisek Pospisil	.30	.75
48 Jan Suchy	.30	.75
49 Josef Cerny	.30	.75
50 Richard Farda	.25	.50
51 Jan Havel	.25	.50
52 Ivan Hlinka	.50	1.00
53 Jiri Holik	.30	.75
54 Jiri Kochta	.25	.50
55 Vladimir Martinec	.30	.75
56 Vaclav Nedomansky	1.00	2.00
57 Eduard Novak	.25	.50
58 Bohuslav Stastny	.50	1.00
59 Jorma Valtonen	.50	1.00
60 Urpo Ylonen	.50	1.00
61 Ilpo Koskela	.25	.50
62 Seppo Lindstrom	.25	.50
63 Hannu Luojola	.25	.50
64 Pekka Marjamaki	.25	.50
65 Esa Isaksson	.25	.50
66 Veli-Pekka Ketola	1.00	2.00
67 Harri Linnonmaa	.25	.50
68 Erkki Mononen	.25	.50
69 Lauri Mononen	.25	.50
70 Matti Murto	.50	1.00
71 Lasse Oksanen	.25	.50
72 Esa Peltonen	.25	.50
73 Juhanni Tamminen	.50	1.00
74 Jorma Vehmanen	.25	.50
75 Leif (Honken) Holmqvist	.50	1.00
76 Bert Jattne	.50	1.00
77 Lars Danielsson	.25	.50
78 Ake Fagerstrom	.25	.50
79 Per-Arne (Hybbe) Hubinette	.25	.50
80 Hakan (Flamman) Lindgren	.25	.50
81 Bert-Ola Nordlander	.50	1.00
82 Lennart (Petter) Pettersson	.25	.50
83 Rolf (Rattan) Edberg	.25	.50
84 Bo Hansson	.25	.50
85 Jan-Olov Kroon	.25	.50
86 Gunnar (Gurra) Lindkvist	.25	.50
87 Christer Lundberg	.25	.50
88 Ulf (Projsarn) Nilsson	4.00	8.00
89 Bo Olofsson	.25	.50
90 Jan Olsson	.25	.50
91 Lennart (Sillen) Selinder	.25	.50
92 Soren Sjogren	.25	.50
93 Hans (Strumpan) Stromberg	.25	.50
94 Jan Ostling	.25	.50
95 Kjell Helling	.50	1.00
96 William (Loken) Lofqvist	.50	1.00
97 Lars (Bylle) Bylund	.25	.50
98 Kjell (Kulan) Johnsson	.25	.50
99 Par Malmstrom	.25	.50
100 Borje Salming	5.00	10.00
101 Stig Salming	.25	.50
102 Stig Ostling	.25	.50
103 Inge Hammarstrom	1.50	10.00
104 Lennart Johansson	.25	.50
105 Stefan Karlsson	.25	.50
106 Lennart (Huppa) Lind	.25	.50
107 Hans (Virus) Lindberg	.25	.50
108 Tord Lundstrom	.25	.50
109 Jan-Erik Lyck	.25	.50
110 Lars-Goran Nilsson	.25	.50
111 Leif Olsson	.25	.50
112 Lars-Ake (Sivert) Sivertsson	.25	.50
113 Hakan Wickberg	.25	.50
114 Lars Oberg	.25	.50
115 Roland Einarsson	.50	1.00
116 Peder Nilsson	.50	1.00
117 Kent Olsson	.50	1.00
118 Thomas Carlsson	.25	.50
119 Lars-Ake Lundell	.25	.50
120 Jorgen Palm	.25	.50
121 Anders Rylin	.25	.50
122 Billy Sundstrom	.25	.50
123 Kent Soderlund	.25	.50
124 Folke (Totte) Bengtsson	.25	.50
125 Ake Eklof	.25	.50
126 Stig Larsson	.25	.50
127 Sven-Bertil Lindstrom	.25	.50
128 Thomas Palm	.25	.50
129 Bjorn Palmqvist	.25	.50
130 Ulf Rydin	.25	.50
131 Ove Svensson	.25	.50
132 Per-Allan Wikstrom	.25	.50
133 Anders Andren	.25	.50
134 Per Lundstrom	.25	.50
135 Lennart Andersson	.50	1.00
136 Kent Bodin	.50	1.00
137 Bjorn Fagerlund	.50	1.00
138 Ake Carlsson	.25	.50
139 Nils (Nicke) Johansson	.25	.50
140 Lars-Goran Nilsson	.25	.50
141 Kent Olsson	.50	1.00
142 Hans-Ake Rosendahl	.25	.50
143 Karl-Johan Sundqvist	.25	.50
144 Benny Andersson	.25	.50
145 Hasse Andersson	.25	.50
146 Kent-Erik Andersson	.25	.50
147 Berndt Augustsson	.25	.50
148 Kjell Augustsson	.25	.50
149 Per-Ole Backman	.25	.50
150 Conny Evensson	.50	1.00
151 Sten Johansson	.25	.50
152 Leif Labraaten	.25	.50
153 Sven-Ove (Nutte) Olsson	.25	.50
154 Ulf Sterner	.25	.50
155 Christer Abrahamsson	1.00	2.00
156 Krister Sterner	.50	1.00
157 Thommy Abrahamsson	.50	1.00
158 Karl-Gustaf Alander	.25	.50
159 Gunnar Andersson	.25	.50
160 Roland Bond	.25	.50
161 Ake Danielsson	.25	.50
162 Ulf Weinstock	.25	.50
163 Per-Olov Brasar	1.00	2.00
164 Kjell Brus	.25	.50
165 Hans (Jacken) Jax	.25	.50
166 Dan Labraaten	1.00	2.00
167 Roger (Stoarn) Lindqvist	.25	.50
168 Ulf (Marten) Martensson	.25	.50
169 Stig Nordin	.25	.50
170 Olle (Mapa) Sjogren	.25	.50
171 Ingemar Snis	.25	.50
172 Dan Soderstrom	.25	.50
173 Bo Theander	.30	.75
174 Mats (Matta) Ahlberg	.25	.50
175 Gunnar (Backis) Backman	.25	.50
176 Ivar Larsson	.50	1.00
177 Sture Andersson	.25	.50
178 Lage Edin	.25	.50
179 Kjell-Rune (Mille) Milton	.25	.50
180 Per-Olof Uusitalo	.25	.50
181 Ulf Wigren	.25	.50
182 Hakan Dahlof	.25	.50
183 Anders Hedberg	4.00	8.00
184 Torbjorn Hubinette	.25	.50
185 Assar Lundgren	.25	.50
186 Per Lundqvist	.25	.50
187 Christer Nilsson	.25	.50
188 Kenneth Nordenberg	.25	.50
189 Anders (Ante) Nordin	.25	.50
190 Hakan Nygren	.25	.50
191 Ulf Thors	.25	.50
192 Ulf Torstensson	.25	.50
193 Lars Ohman	.25	.50
194 Tore Ohman	.25	.50
195 Tony Esposito	17.50	35.00
196 Bobby Orr	50.00	100.00
197 Jean Beliveau	12.50	35.00
198 Gordie Howe	40.00	75.00
199 Phil Esposito	12.50	35.00
200 Bobby Hull	20.00	40.00
201 Bengt-Ake Gustavsson	.50	1.00
202 Lars Gustavsson	.50	1.00
203 Tommy Andersson	.25	.50
204 Hans-Olov Ernlund	.25	.50
205 Tord Johansson	.25	.50
206 Lars Mjoberg	.25	.50
207 Per-Erik (Plattis) Olsson	.25	.50
208 Tord Svensson	.25	.50
209 Jan (Bambis) Danielsson	.25	.50
210 Tommy Eriksson	.50	1.00
211 Gote Hansson	.25	.50
212 Hans Hansson	.25	.50
213 Sven-Ake (Saja) Jacobsson	.25	.50
214 Mats (Tuppen) Lonn	.25	.50
215 Borje Marcus	.25	.50
216 Lars Munther	.25	.50
217 Ulf Nises	.25	.50
218 Anders Rosen	.25	.50
219 Borje Skogs	.25	.50
220 Kent Sundkvist	.25	.50

221 Mikael Collin .50 1.00
222 Bjorn Jansson .50 1.00
223 Curt Larsson .50 1.00
224 Tommie Bergman 1.50 3.00
225 Arne Carlsson .25 .50
226 Christer Karlsson .25 .50
227 Eilert (Garvis) Maatta .25 .50
228 Jan Schullstrom .25 .50
229 Borje (Poppen) Burlin .25 .50
230 Hans Carlsson .25 .50
231 Tommy Carlsson .25 .50
232 Mats Hysing .25 .50
233 Bertil Jacobsson .25 .50
234 Stig-Goran Johansson .50 1.00
235 Dan Landegren .25 .50
236 Kjell Landstrom .25 .50
237 Soren Maatta .25 .50
238 Nils-Olov Schilstrom .25 .50
239 Dick Yderstrom .25 .50
240 Carl Goran (Lillstoveln) Oberg .25 .50
241 Anders Claesson .50 1.00
242 Kent Othberg .50 1.00
243 Jan Johansson .25 .50
244 Jan-Erik (Biffen) Nilsson .25 .50
245 Stefan Pettersson .25 .50
246 Tord Salomonsson .25 .50
247 Lennart Svedberg .50 1.00
248 Bo (Bulla) Berggren .25 .50
249 Bjorn Broman .25 .50
250 Lennart Broman .25 .50
251 Ove Larsson .25 .50
252 Rolf Larsson .25 .50
253 Orjan Lindstrom .25 .50
254 Arne Lundstrom .25 .50
255 Fhinn Lundstrom .25 .50
256 Ake Lundstrom .25 .50
257 Lennart Norberg .25 .50
258 Hakan Pettersson .25 .50
259 Ake (Taget) Soderberg .25 .50
260 Olle Ahman .25 .50
261 Christer Andersson .50 1.00
262 Bengt Gustavsson .25 .50
263 Goran (Klasse) Astrom .25 .50
264 Anders Brostrom .25 .50
265 Kenneth Ekman .25 .50
266 Soren Gunnarsson .25 .50
267 Lars-Erik Jacobsson .25 .50
268 Des Moroney .25 .50
269 Borje Maatta .25 .50
270 Tommy Pettersson .25 .50
271 Bengt Alm .25 .50
272 Sven Crabo .25 .50
273 Bengt (Benken) Eriksson .25 .50
274 Kurt Jakobsson .25 .50
275 Leif (Tvilling) Jakobsson .25 .50
276 Lars-Goran Johansson .25 .50
277 Bert (Berra) Karlsson .25 .50
278 Benny (Nacka) Runesson .25 .50
279 Ake Ryman .25 .50
280 Jan Roger (Joje) Strand .25 .50
281 Christer (Slim) Grahn .30 .75
282 Ronny (Centis) Sandstrom .25 .50
283 John Andersson .25 .50
284 Karl-Olov (Kalle) Eriksson .25 .50
285 Anders (Hagge) Hagstrom .25 .50
286 Ulf (Ingo) Ingvarsson .25 .50
287 Rolf Jager .25 .50
288 Erik (Jarvis) Jarvholm .25 .50
289 Bo Westling .25 .50
290 Ulf (Lill-Barre) Barrefjord .25 .50
291 Kent Bjork .25 .50
292 Lars (Dallas) Dahlgren .25 .50
293 Ulf (Pygge) Larsson .25 .50
294 Jan Lundqvist .25 .50
295 Ulf Lundstrom .25 .50
296 Bengt (Lovet) Lovgren .25 .50
297 Leif Martensson .25 .50
298 Lars-Ake (Nollan) Nordin .25 .50
299 Lars Sjostrom .25 .50
300 Kjell Sundstrom .25 .50
301 Ronny Andersson .50 1.00
302 Ingemar (Sparris) Caris .50 1.00
303 Anders (Johan) Johansson .25 .50
304 Hakan (Norsen) Norstrom .25 .50
305 Jan Olsen .25 .50
306 Lars-Erik Sjoberg .50 1.00
307 Bengt (Bengan) Sjoholm .25 .50
308 Kjell Andersson .25 .50
309 Svante Granholm .25 .50
310 Kjell-Ove Gustavsson .25 .50
311 Henrik (Tosse) Hedlund .25 .50
312 Leif (Blixten) Henriksson .25 .50
313 Lars-Erik Johansson .25 .50
314 Bjorn (Nalle) Lindberg .25 .50
315 Evert Lindstrom .25 .50
316 Willy Lindstrom 1.00 2.00
317 Leif (Nisse) Nilsson .25 .50
318 Kurt (Kulle) Olofsson .25 .50
319 Roger (Viking) Olsson .25 .50
320 Kjell-Ronnie Pettersson .25 .50
321 Kenneth Holmstedt .50 1.00
322 Lars-Erik Larsson .25 .50
323 Lennart (Sly) Eriksson .25 .50
324 Lennart Gustavsson .25 .50
325 Jan-Ake Karlsson .25 .50
326 Rolf Karlsson .25 .50
327 Bengt Lundberg .25 .50
328 Anders Thelander .25 .50
329 Kent Bengtsson .25 .50
330 Gunnar Backman .50 1.00
331 Stefan Canderyd .25 .50
332 Curt Edenvik .25 .50
333 Per Edenvik .25 .50
334 Weine Gullberg .25 .50
335 Nils-Arne Hedqvist .25 .50
336 Bengt-Ake Karlsson .25 .50
337 Christer Kihlstrom .25 .50
338 Stig-Olof (Bullen) Persson .25 .50
339 Christer Sjoberg .25 .50
340 Roddy Skyllqvist .25 .50
341 Lars Blomqvist .50 1.00
342 Bjorn Forsberg .50 1.00
343 Anders Hedlund .25 .50
344 Lennart Johansson .25 .50
345 Martin Kruger .25 .50
346 Harry Namd .25 .50
347 Lennart Strohm .25 .50
348 Peter Bejemark .25 .50
349 Bertil Bond .25 .50
350 Nils Carlsson .25 .50
351 Ulf Pilo .25 .50
352 Claes-Ove Fjallby .25 .50
353 Lars Granlund .25 .50
354 Kjell Keijser .25 .50
355 Lennart Lange .25 .50
356 Bo Mellbin .25 .50
357 Lars Starck .25 .50
358 Leif Svensson .25 .50
359 Kjell Ahlen .25 .50
360 Henry (Henna) Svensson .25 .50
361 Sven-Allan Ellstrom .50 1.00
362 Tommy Eriksson .50 1.00
363 Walter Winsth .50 1.00
364 Hans-Ake Andersson .25 .50
365 Jan Andersson .25 .50
366 Hans Bejbom .25 .50
367 Goran Borell .25 .50
368 Bo Schilstrom .25 .50
369 Bjarne Brostrom .25 .50
370 Kenneth Calen .25 .50
371 Lennart Carlsson .25 .50
372 Mats Davidsson .25 .50
373 Rolf Hansson .25 .50
374 Rune Norrstrom .25 .50
375 Gunther Rauch .25 .50
376 Jan Vestberg .25 .50
377 Bengt Wistling .25 .50
378 Kent Zetterberg .25 .50
379 Goran Akerlund .25 .50
380 Uno (Garvis) Ohrlund .25 .50
381 Goran Hogosta .60 1.50
382 Juha Raninen .50 1.00
383 Bert Backman .25 .50
384 Christer Collin .25 .50
385 Dag Olsson .25 .50
386 Bjorn Resare .25 .50
387 Lars Thoreus .25 .50
388 Stig Andersson .25 .50
389 Borje Engblom .25 .50
390 Christer Englund .25 .50
391 Bo Eriksson .25 .50
392 Mats Eriksson .25 .50
393 Roland Eriksson .25 .50
394 Olle Henriksson .25 .50
395 Yngve Hindrikes .25 .50
396 Kjell Jansson .25 .50
397 Jan Johansson .25 .50
398 Jan Karlsson .25 .50
399 Agne Norberg .25 .50
400 Christian Reuthie .25 .50

1972 Swedish Semic World Championship

COMPLETE SET (233) 200.00 400.00
1 Viktor Konovalenko .38 .75
2 Vitalij Davydov .38 .75
3 Vladimir Lutjenko .38 .75
4 Viktor Kuskin .38 .75
5 Alexander Ragulin .75 3.00
6 Igor Romitjevskij .38 .75
7 Gennadij Tsigankov .38 .75
8 Vjatsjeslav Starsjinov .75 1.50
9 Evgenij Zimin .50 1.00
10 Alexander Maltsev 2.50 5.00
11 Anatolij Firsov 1.25 2.00
12 Evgenij Misjakov .38 .75
13 Boris Michailov 2.00 4.00
14 Juri Ljapkin .50 1.00
15 Alexander Martinyk .38 .75
16 Vladimir Petrov 2.00 4.00
17 Valeri Kharlamov 20.00 50.00
18 Vladimir Vikulov .38 .75
19 Vladimir Sjadrin .50 1.00
20 Vladislav Tretiak 10.00 20.00
21 Marcel Sakac .25 .50
22 Jiri Holecek .50 1.00
23 Josef Horesovsky .25 .50
24 Oldrich Machac .25 .50
25 Rudolf Tajcnar .25 .50
26 Frantisek Panchartek .25 .50
27 Frantisek Pospisil .38 .75
28 Jiri Kochta .25 .50
29 Jan Havel .25 .50
30 Vladimir Martinec .25 .50
31 Richard Farda .25 .50
32 Bohuslav Stastny .38 .75
33 Vaclav Nedomansky .75 1.50
34 Josef Cerny .25 .50
35 Bedrich Brunchk .25 .50
36 Jan Suchy .25 .50
37 Eduard Novak .25 .50
38 Jiri Bubla .75 1.50
39 Jiri Holik .38 .75
40 Ivan Hlinka 1.00 2.00
41 Vladimir Bednar .25 .50
42 Leif Holmqvist .50 1.00
43 Christer Abrahamsson 1.00 2.00
44 Christer Andersson .50 1.00
45 Lars-Erik Sjoberg .75 1.50
46 Lennart Svedberg .50 1.00
47 Stig-Goran Johansson .25 .50
48 Bert-Ola Nordlander .25 .50
49 Thommy Abrahamsson .50 1.00
50 Arne Carlsson .25 .50
51 Stefan Karlsson .25 .50
52 Hakan Wickberg .25 .50
53 Hakan Nygren .25 .50
54 Lars-Goran Nilsson .25 .50
55 Thommie Bergman 1.00 2.00
56 Ulf Sterner .38 .75
57 Hans Lindberg .25 .50
58 Tord Lundstrom .25 .50
59 Gunnar Andersson .25 .50
60 Bjorn Palmqvist .25 .50
61 Inge Hammarstrom 1.00 2.00
62 Kjell-Rune Milton .25 .50
63 Kjell Brus .25 .50
64 Kenneth Ekman .25 .50
65 Bengt-Goran Karlsson .25 .50
66 Hakan Pettersson .25 .50
67 Dan Labraaten .75 1.50
68 Dan Soderstrom .25 .50
69 Anders Hedberg 2.50 5.00
70 Ake Soderberg .25 .50
71 Urpo Ylonen .25 .50
72 Ilpo Koskela .25 .50
73 Seppo Lindstrom .25 .50
74 Hannu Luojola .25 .50
75 Pekka Marjamaki .25 .50
76 Jouko Oystila .25 .50
77 Heikki Jarn .25 .50
78 Esa Isaksson .25 .50
79 Veli-Pekka Ketola .75 1.50
80 Harri Linnonmaa .25 .50
81 Erkki Mononen .25 .50
82 Lauri Mononen .25 .50
83 Matti Murto .25 .50
84 Lasse Oksanen .25 .50
85 Esa Peltonen .25 .50
86 Seppo Repo .25 .50
87 Tommi Salmelainen .25 .50
88 Juhani Tamminen .25 .50
89 Jorma Vehmanen .25 .50
90 Jorma Valtonen .38 .75
91 Matti Keinonen .25 .50
92 Juha Rantasila .25 .50
93 Toni Kehle .25 .50
94 Josef Schramm .25 .50
95 Walter Stadler .25 .50
96 Josef Volk .25 .50
97 Hans Schichtl .25 .50
98 Erwin Riedmeier .25 .50
99 Werner Modes .25 .50
100 Johann Eimannsberger .25 .50
101 Karlheinz Egger .25 .50
102 Lorenz Funk, Sr. .25 .50
103 Klaus Ego .25 .50
104 Anton Hofherr .25 .50
105 Otto Schneitberger .25 .50
106 Heinz Weisenbach .25 .50
107 Alois Schloder .25 .50
108 Gustav Hanig .25 .50
109 Rainer Philipp .25 .50
110 Bernd Kuhn .25 .50
111 Paul Langner .25 .50
112 Franz Hofherr .25 .50
113 Reinhold Bauer .25 .50
114 Johann Rotkirch .25 .50
115 Walter Koberle .25 .50
116 Rainer Makatsch .25 .50
117 Carl Wetzel .38 .75
118 Mike Curran .38 .75
119 Jim McElmury .38 .75
120 Bruce Riutta .38 .75
121 Tom Mellor .38 .75
122 Don Ross .38 .75
123 Gary Gambucci .38 .75
124 Keith Christiansen .38 .75
125 Len Lilyholm .38 .75
126 Henry Boucha .75 3.00
127 Craig Falkman .38 .75
128 Tim Sheehy .38 .75
129 Kevin Ahearn .38 1.00
130 Craig Patrick 1.00 2.00
131 Pete Fichuk .38 1.00
132 George Konik .38 1.00
133 Dick McGlynn .38 1.00
134 Dick Toomey .38 1.00
135 Paul Schilling .38 1.00
136 Bob Lindberg .38 1.00
137 Dick Tomasoni .38 1.00
138 Nando Mathieu .25 .50
139 Francis Reinhard .25 .50
140 Gaston Furrer .25 .50
141 Bruno Wittwer .25 .50
142 Andre Berra .25 .50
143 Hans Keller .25 .50
144 Peter Luthi .25 .50
145 Peter Aeschlimann .25 .50
146 Werner Kuenzi .25 .50
147 Tony Neininger .25 .50
148 Jacques Pousaz .25 .50
149 Roger Chappot .25 .50
150 Charly Henzen .25 .50
151 Paul Probst .25 .50
152 Guy Dubois .25 .50
153 Rene Squaldo .25 .50
154 Rene Hueguenin .25 .50
155 Gaston Pelletier .25 .50
156 Beat Kaufmann .25 .50
157 Alfio Molina .25 .50
158 Gerald Rigolet .25 .50
159 Harald Jones .25 .50
160 Gilbert Mathieu .25 .50
161 Michel Turler .25 .50
162 Reto Taillens .25 .50
163 Norm Ullman 1.50 5.00
164 Dave Keon 2.50 10.00
165 Roger Crozier 2.50 5.00
166 Ron Ellis 1.50 5.00
167 Paul Henderson 2.50 10.00
168 Jim Dorey .50 1.00
169 Jacques Plante 15.00 30.00
170 Jean-Guy Gendron .50 1.00
171 Gary Smith 1.50 3.00
172 Dennis Hextall .50 2.00
173 Norm Ferguson .50 1.00
174 Simon Nolet .50 1.00
175 Bernie Parent 5.00 10.00
176 Ted Hampson .50 1.00
177 Earl Ingarfield .50 1.00
178 Larry Hillman .50 2.00
179 Gary Dornhoefer 1.00 3.00
180 Gary Croteau .50 1.00
181 Carol Vadnais .50 2.00
182 Jim Roberts .50 2.00
183 Red Berenson 1.50 5.00
184 Phil Esposito 12.50 25.00
185 John McKenzie 1.00 3.00
186 Barclay Plager 1.00 3.00
187 Glenn Hall 7.50 15.00
188 Gerry Cheevers 7.50 15.00
189 Jim McKenny .50 1.00
190 Gordie Howe 25.00 50.00
191 Garry Unger 1.00 3.00
192 Roy Edwards 1.50 5.00
193 Alex Delvecchio 2.50 5.00
194 Brad Park 2.50 10.00
195 Frank Mahovlich 5.00 10.00
196 Phil Goyette .50 1.00
197 Don Marshall .50 1.00
198 Henri Richard 5.00 10.00
199 Claude Larose .50 1.00
200 Bobby Rousseau .50 1.00
201 Lorne Worsley 5.00 10.00
202 Gilles Marotte .75 1.50
203 Bob Pulford 1.50 5.00
204 Yvan Cournoyer 2.50 5.00
205 Eddie Joyal .50 1.00
206 Ross Lonsberry .50 1.00
207 Jean Beliveau 10.00 20.00
208 Jacques Lemaire 2.50 5.00
209 Orland Kurtenbach .75 1.50
210 Andre Boudrias .50 1.00
211 Jim Neilson .50 2.00
212 Walter Tkaczuk 1.00 3.00
213 Ed Giacomin 5.00 10.00
214 Jean Ratelle 2.50 5.00
215 Les Binkley 1.50 5.00
216 Jean Pronovost .50 1.00
217 Bryan Watson .50 2.00
218 Dean Prentice .50 1.00
219 Jean-Paul Parise 1.00 3.00
220 Bill Goldsworthy .75 3.00
221 Wayne Maki .50 2.00
222 Dale Tallon .75 3.00
223 Bobby Orr 37.50 75.00
224 Pit Martin .50 2.00
225 Jacques Laperriere 1.50 3.00
226 Bill Flett .50 2.00
227 Stan Mikita 7.50 15.00
228 Bobby Hull 15.00 30.00
229 Larry Pleau .50 2.00
230 Keith Magnuson 1.00 2.00
231 Tony Esposito 7.50 15.00
232 Rogatien Vachon 4.00 10.00
233 Mickey Redmond 7.50 15.00

1972-73 Swedish Stickers

COMPLETE SET (300) 150.00 400.00
1 Christer Abrahamsson 1.00 2.00
2 Leif Holmqvist .50 1.00
3 Tommy Abrahamsson .50 1.00
4 Thommie Bergman 1.00 2.00
5 Bjorn Johansson .25 .50
6 Kjell-Rune Milton .25 .50
7 Borje Salming 5.00 10.00
8 Lars-Erik Sjoberg 1.00 2.00
9 Karl-Johan Sundqvist .25 .50
10 Stig Ostling .25 .50
11 Inge Hammarstrom 1.00 2.00
12 Anders Hedberg 2.50 5.00
13 Stig-Goran Johansson .25 .50
14 Stefan Karlsson .25 .50
15 Hans Lindberg .25 .50
16 Mats Lindh .25 .50
17 Tord Lundstrom .25 .50
18 Lars-Goran Nilsson .25 .50
19 Bjorn Palmqvist .25 .50
20 Hakan Wickberg .25 .50
21 Jiri Holecek .50 1.00
22 Josef Horesovsky .25 .50
23 Frantisek Pospisil .38 .75
24 Jaroslav Holik .25 .50
25 Jiri Holik .38 .75
26 Vaclav Nedomansky 1.00 2.00
27 Vladislav Tretiak 10.00 20.00
28 Gennadi Tsigankov .38 .75
29 Igor Romisjevskij .38 .75
30 Valeri Kharlamov 20.00 50.00
31 Alexander Maltsev 2.50 5.00
32 Vladimir Vikulov .38 .75
33 Jorma Valtonen .38 .75
34 Pekka Marjamaki .25 .50
35 Matti Keinonen .25 .50
36 Veli-Pekka Ketola 1.00 2.00
37 Lauri Mononen .25 .50
38 Lasse Oksanen .25 .50
39 Krister Sterner .50 1.00
40 Sten-Ake Bark .25 .50
41 Jan-Erik Silfverberg .25 .50
42 Steffan Andersson .25 .50
43 Roland Eriksson .25 .50
44 Gunnar Johansson .25 .50
45 Jiri Holecek .50 1.00
46 Thommie Bergman 1.00 2.00
47 Josef Horesovsky .25 .50
48 Vladimir Vikulov .38 .75
49 Alexander Maltsev 2.50 5.00
50 Valeri Kharlamov 20.00 50.00
51 Leif Holmqvist .50 1.00
52 Lars Danielsson .25 .50
53 Ake Fagerstrom .25 .50
54 Per-Arne Hubinette .25 .50
55 Hakan Lindgren .25 .50
56 Bert-Ola Nordlander .25 .50
57 Bo Olofsson .25 .50
58 Soren Sjogren .25 .50
59 Jan Olsson .25 .50
60 Lennart Selinder .25 .50
61 Jan Olof Kroon .25 .50
62 Rolf Edberg .25 .50
63 Ulf Nilsson 2.50 5.00
64 Leif Holmgren .25 .50
65 Jan Ostling .25 .50
66 Christer Grahn .50 1.00
67 Karl-Olov Grahn .50 1.00
68 Anders Hagstrom .25 .50
69 Erik Jarvholm .25 .50
70 Bo Westling .25 .50
71 Ulf Ingvarsson .25 .50
72 Bengt Lovgren .25 .50
73 Kjell Sundstrom .25 .50
74 Kent Bjork .25 .50
75 Ulf Lundstrom .25 .50
76 Mats Lundmark .25 .50
77 Ulf Barrefjord .25 .50
78 Lars Dahlgren .25 .50
79 Olle Nilsson .25 .50
80 Roger Nilsson .25 .50
81 Willie Lofqvist .50 1.00
82 Jan-Erik Silfverberg .25 .50
83 Kjell Johnsson .25 .50
84 Jan-Olof Svensson .25 .50
85 Stig Salming .25 .50
86 Borje Salming 5.00 10.00
87 Stig Ostling .25 .50
88 Tord Lundstrom .25 .50
89 Inge Hammarstrom 1.00 2.00
90 Lars-Göran Nilsson .25 .50
91 Hans Lindberg .25 .50
92 Hakan Wickberg .25 .50
93 Jan-Erik Lyck .25 .50
94 Stefan Karlsson .25 .50
95 Lars Oberg .25 .50
96 Roland Einarsson .50 1.00
97 Billy Sundstrom .25 .50
98 Anders Rylin .25 .50
99 Tomas Carlsson .25 .50
100 Ulf Ojerklint .25 .50
101 L-A Gustavsson .50 1.00
102 Jorgen Palm .25 .50
103 Lars-Ake Lundell .25 .50
104 Ake Eklof .25 .50
105 Bengt-Ake Karlsson .25 .50
106 Bjorn Palmqvist .25 .50
107 Per-Allan Wickstrom .25 .50
108 Sven-Bertil Lindstrom .25 .50
109 Totte Bengtsson .25 .50
110 Stig Larsson .25 .50
111 Ken Dryden 20.00 40.00
112 Jacques Laperriere 1.50 3.00
113 Bobby Orr 37.50 75.00
114 Brad Park 2.50 5.00
115 Phil Esposito 10.00 20.00
116 Rod Gilbert 2.50 5.00
117 Vic Hadfield 1.50 3.00
118 Bobby Hull 15.00 30.00
119 Frank Mahovlich 5.00 10.00
120 Jean Ratelle 2.50 5.00
121 Lennart Andersson .50 1.00
122 Karl-Johan Sundqvist .25 .50
123 Nicke Johansson .25 .50
124 Lars-Goran Nilsson .25 .50
125 Ake Carlsson .25 .50
126 Hans-Ake Rosendahl .25 .50
127 Sten-Ake Bark .25 .50
128 Par Backman .25 .50
129 Leif Labraaten .25 .50
130 Berndt Augustsson .25 .50
131 Uffe Sterner .25 .50
132 Benny Andersson .25 .50
133 Conny Evensson .50 1.00
134 Kjell Augustsson .25 .50
135 Hans Andersson .25 .50
136 Kenneth Holmstedt .50 1.00
137 Lennart Gustavsson .25 .50
138 Lennart Eriksson .25 .50
139 Rolf Carlsson .25 .50
140 Bengt Lundberg .25 .50
141 Jan-Ake Karlsson .25 .50
142 Curt Edenvik .25 .50
143 Per Edenvik .25 .50
144 Weine Gullberg .25 .50
145 Gunnar Backman .50 1.00
146 Roddy Skyllqvist .25 .50
147 Stefan Canderyd .25 .50
148 Christer Kihlstrom .25 .50
149 Nils-Arne Hedqvist .25 .50
150 Stig-Olof Persson .25 .50
151 Christer Abrahamsson 1.00 2.00
152 Thommy Abrahamsson .50 1.00
153 Roland Bond .25 .50
154 Gunnar Andersson .25 .50
155 Ulf Weinstock .25 .50
156 Ake Danielsson .25 .50
157 Peter Gudmundsson .25 .50
158 Olle Sjogren .25 .50
159 Hans Jax .25 .50
160 Mats Ahlberg .25 .50
161 Dan Labraaten 1.00 2.00
162 Ulf Martensson .25 .50
163 Kjell Brus .25 .50
164 Dan Soderstrom .25 .50
165 Per Olof Brasar 1.00 2.00
166 Ivar Larsson .50 1.00
167 Sture Andersson .25 .50
168 Lage Edin .25 .50
169 Kjell Rune Milton .25 .50
170 Ulf Wigren .25 .50
171 Hakan Dahllof .25 .50
172 Anders Hedberg 2.50 5.00
173 Assar Lundgren .25 .50
174 Christer Nilsson .25 .50
175 Anders Nordin .25 .50
176 Hakan Nygren .25 .50
177 Ulf Thors .25 .50
178 Ulf Torstensson .25 .50
179 Lasse Ohman .25 .50
180 Tore Ohman .25 .50
181 Bengt Ake Gustafsson .38 .75
182 Tommy Andersson .25 .50
183 Hans-Olof Ernlund .25 .50
184 Tord Johansson .25 .50
185 Tord Svensson .25 .50
186 Jan Danielsson .25 .50
187 Tommy Eriksson .50 1.00
188 Gote Hansson .25 .50
189 Hans Hansson .25 .50
190 Sven-Ake Jacobsson .25 .50
191 Mats Lonn .25 .50
192 Lars Mjoberg .25 .50
193 Lars Munther .25 .50
194 Ulf Nises .25 .50
195 Borje Skogs .25 .50
196 Roland Lestander .25 .50
197 Bosse Andersson .25 .50
198 Hakan Dahlin .25 .50
199 Martin Johansson .25 .50
200 Anders Lindberg .25 .50
201 Lars-Fredrik Nystrom .25 .50
202 Hans Gunnar Skarin .25 .50
203 Jerry Aberg .25 .50
204 Anders Almqvist .25 .50
205 Christer Johansson .25 .50
206 Per Johansson .25 .50
207 Martin Karlsson .25 .50
208 Lars-Gunnar Lundberg .25 .50
209 Hardy Nilsson .25 .50
210 Kjell-Arne Wikstrom .25 .50
211 Mikael Collin .50 1.00
212 Curt Larsson .50 1.00
213 Arne Carlsson .25 .50
214 Bjorn Johansson .25 .50
215 Nils-Olov Schilstrom .25 .50
216 Jan Schullstrom .25 .50
217 Borje Burlin .25 .50
218 Hans Carlsson .25 .50
219 Mats Hysing .25 .50
220 Bertil Jacobsson .25 .50
221 Stisse Johansson .25 .50
222 Dan Landegren .25 .50
223 Kjell Landstrom .25 .50
224 Dick Yderstrom .25 .50
225 Carl-Goran Oberg .25 .50
226 Christer Sehlstedt .25 .50
227 Tommie Lindgren .25 .50
228 Jan-Erik Nilsson .25 .50
229 Stefan Pettersson .25 .50
230 Tord Nansen .25 .50
231 Bo Berggren .25 .50
232 Bjorn Broman .25 .50
233 Ove Larsson .25 .50
234 Kent Lindgren .25 .50
235 Orjan Lindstrom .25 .50
236 Lennart Norberg .25 .50
237 Arne Lundstrom .25 .50
238 Hakan Pettersson .25 .50
239 Ake Soderberg .25 .50
240 Olle Ahman .25 .50
241 Christer Andersson 1.00 2.00
242 Anders Brostrom .25 .50
243 Kenneth Ekman .25 .50
244 Soren Gunnarsson .25 .50
245 Borje Maatta .25 .50
246 Tommy Pettersson .25 .50
247 Kurt Jakobsson .25 .50
248 Leif Jakobsson .25 .50
249 Lars-Goran Johansson .25 .50
250 Bengt-Goran Karlsson .25 .50
251 Berndt Karlsson .25 .50
252 Tadeusz Niedomyst .25 .50
253 Benny Runesson .25 .50
254 Ake Ryman .25 .50
255 Jan-Roger Strand .25 .50
256 Goran Hogosta .50 1.00
257 Bert Backman .25 .50
258 Christer Collin .25 .50
259 Bo Eriksson .25 .50
260 Hakan Norstrom .25 .50
261 Lars Thoreus .25 .50
262 Stig Andersson .25 .50
263 Mats Eriksson .25 .50
264 Roland Eriksson .25 .50
265 Kjell Fhinn .25 .50
266 Olle Henriksson .25 .50
267 Yngve Hindrikes .25 .50
268 Jan Karlsson .25 .50
269 Kjell Jansson .25 .50
270 Ingemar Snis .25 .50
271 Christer Stahl .25 .50
272 Leif Andersson .25 .50
273 Tommy Eriksson .50 1.00
274 Christer Holmstrom .25 .50
275 Curt Lundmark 1.00 2.00
276 Dennis Pettersson .25 .50
277 Ove Thelin .25 .50
278 Bo Wahlberg .25 .50
279 Gote Gustavsson .25 .50
280 Christer Lindgren .25 .50
281 Kent Persson .25 .50
282 Par Marts .25 .50
283 Ove Stenlund .25 .50
284 Bo Olsson .25 .50
285 Bo Astrom .25 .50
286 Ronny Andersson .50 1.00
287 Roger Bergman .25 .50
288 Thommie Bergman 1.00 2.00
289 Anders Johansson .25 .50
290 Jan Olsen .25 .50
291 Lars Erik Sjoberg 1.00 2.00
292 Kjell Andersson .25 .50
293 Svante Granholm .25 .50
294 Henrik Hedlund .25 .50
295 Leif Henriksson .25 .50
296 Mats Lindh .25 .50
297 Evert Lindstrom .25 .50
298 Willy Lindstrom 1.00 2.00
299 Roger Olsson .25 .50
300 Kjell-Ronnie Pettersson .25 .50

1973-74 Swedish Stickers

COMPLETE SET (243) 75.00 200.00
1 Christer Abrahamsson 1.00 2.00
2 William Lofqvist .50 1.00
3 Arne Karlsson .25 .50
4 Lars-Erik Sjoberg 1.00 2.00
5 Bjorn Johansson .25 .50
6 Thommy Abrahamsson .50 1.00
7 Borje Salming 5.00 10.00
8 Karl Johan Sundqvist .25 .50
9 Ulf Sterner .25 .50
10 Ulf Nilsson 2.50 5.00
11 Kjell-Arne Wickstrom .25 .50
12 Inge Hammarstrom 2.50 5.00
13 Hakan Wickberg .25 .50
14 Tord Lundstrom .25 .50
15 Dan Soderstrom .25 .50
16 Mats Ahlberg .50 1.00
17 Anders Hedberg 2.50 5.00
18 Dick Yderstrom .30 .75
19 Stefan Karlsson .25 .50
20 Roland Bond .25 .50
21 Kjell-Rune Milton .25 .50
22 Willy Lindstrom .75 1.50
23 Kurt Carlsson .30 .75
24 Mats Walltin .25 .50
25 Roland Eriksson .25 .50
26 Martin Karlsson .25 .50
27 Jiri Holecek .50 1.00
28 Josef Horesovsky .25 .50
29 Oldrich Machac .25 .50
30 Vladimir Martinec .50 1.00
31 Vaclav Nedomansky .75 1.50
32 Jiri Kochta .25 .50
33 Jorma Waltonen .50 1.00
34 Heikki Riihiranta .50 1.00
35 Lauri Mononen .25 .50
36 Timo Turunen .25 .50
37 Matti Keinonen .25 .50
38 Seppo Repo .25 .50
39 Christer Abrahamsson .75 1.50
40 Lars Stenvall .25 .50
41 Per Karlsson .25 .50
42 Roland Bond .25 .50
43 Thommy Abrahamsson .50 1.00
44 Ulf Weinstock .25 .50
45 Gunnar Andersson .25 .50
46 Hans Eriksson .25 .50
47 Peter Gudmundsson .25 .50
48 Mats Ahlberg .50 1.00
49 Per-Olov Brasar .75 1.50
50 Roger Lindqvist .25 .50
51 Dan Soderstrom .25 .50
52 Ulf Martensson .25 .50
53 Kjell Brus .25 .50
54 Hans Jax .25 .50
55 Dan Labraaten .75 1.50
56 Nils-Olov Olsson .25 .50
57 Stig Nordin .25 .50
58 Bo Theander .25 .50
59 Curt Larsson .50 1.00
60 Mikael Collin .50 1.00
61 Arne Carlsson .25 .50
62 Leif Svensson .25 .50
63 Sverker Torstensson .25 .50
64 Bjorn Johansson .25 .50
65 Stisse Johansson .25 .50
66 Carl-Goran Oberg .25 .50
67 Mats Hysing .25 .50
68 Mats Walltin .25 .50
69 Hans Carlsson .25 .50
70 Nils-Olov Schilstrom .25 .50
71 Kjell-Arne Wickstrom .25 .50
72 Jan Schullstrom .25 .50
73 Borje Burlin .25 .50
74 Dick Yderstrom .30 .75
75 Dan Landegren .25 .50
76 Kjell Landstrom .25 .50
77 Vladislav Tretjak 10.00 20.00
78 Alexander Sidelnikov 1.00 2.00
79 Alexander Ragulin 1.25 2.50
80 Vladimir Luttjenko 1.00 2.00
81 Gennadij Tsygankov .75 1.50
82 Alexander Gusev .50 1.00
83 Jevgenij Poladiev .30 .75
84 Jurij Liapkin .75 1.50
85 Valerij Vasiljev 1.50 3.00
86 Boris Michailov 2.50 5.00
87 Valeri Kharlamov 10.00 25.00
88 Vladimir Petrov 2.50 5.00
89 Alexander Maltsev 2.50 5.00
90 Vladimir Sjadrin 1.25 2.50
91 Alexander Yakusjev 2.50 5.00
92 Alexander Martynjuk .30 .75
93 Vjateslav Anissin .50 1.00
94 Jurij Lebedev 1.00 2.00
95 Alexander Bodunov .50 1.00
96 Alexander Volchkov 1.00 2.00
97 Vsevolod Bobrov 2.00 4.00
98 Konstantin Loktev .25 .50
99 Anatolij Firsov 1.50 3.00
100 Viktor Kuzkin .50 1.00
101 Jurij Blochin .25 .50
102 Vladimir Vikulov .50 1.00
103 Jurij Blinov .50 1.00
104 Jevgenij Misjakov 1.00 2.00
105 Vladimir Trunov .25 .50
106 Sergej Glazov .25 .50
107 Vladimir Popov .75 1.50
108 Viktor Zinger .50 1.00
109 Viktor Krivolapov .30 .75
110 Jevgenij Kazatjkin .25 .50
111 Viktor Korotkov .75 1.50
112 Valentin Markov .25 .50
113 Alexander Sapjolkin .25 .50
114 Leonid Borzov .25 .50
115 Gennadij Krylov .25 .50
116 Konstantin Klimov .25 .50
117 Jevgenij Zimin .50 1.00
118 Vladimir Gurejev .25 .50
119 Viktor Jaroslavtsev .25 .50
120 Alexander Pasjkov .30 .75
121 Vladimir Polupanov .50 1.00
122 Vitalij Davydov .75 1.50
123 Michail Alexeenko .25 .50
124 Alexander Filippov .50 1.00
125 Valerij Nazarov .25 .50
126 Vladimir Orlov .25 .50
127 Stanislav Sitjegolev .25 .50
128 Anatolij Bjelonozjkin .25 .50
129 Vladimir Devjatov .25 .50
130 Jevgenij Kotlov .25 .50
131 Anatolij Motovilov .25 .50
132 Jurij Reps .25 .50
133 Igor Samotjernov .25 .50
134 Alexander Sevidov .25 .50
135 Viktor Sjilov .25 .50
136 Jurij Tjitjurin .30 .75
137 Sune Odling .25 .50
138 Lars-Erik Sjoberg 1.00 2.00
139 Bengt Sjoholm .25 .50
140 Leif Henriksson .25 .50
141 Henric Hedlund .25 .50
142 Roger Olsson .25 .50
143 Kjell-Rune Milton .25 .50
144 Kjell-Ronnie Pettersson .25 .50
145 Svante Granholm .25 .50
146 Kjell Andersson .25 .50
147 Lars-Erik Esbjorn .25 .50
148 Bjorn Lindberg .25 .50
149 Willy Lindstrom .75 1.50
150 Evert Lindstrom .25 .50
151 Lars-Erik Johansson .25 .50
152 Krister Sterner .30 .75
153 Mats Lindh .25 .50
154 Roger Bergman .25 .50
155 Willie Lofqvist .50 1.00
156 Jan Olov Svensson .25 .50
157 Jan Erik Silfverberg .25 .50
158 Stig Ostling .50 1.00
159 Kjell Johansson .25 .50
160 Borje Salming 5.00 10.00
161 Stig Salming .50 1.00

162 Tord Lundstrom .25 .50
163 Hakan Wickberg .25 .50
164 Inge Hammarstrom 2.50 5.00
165 Lars Goran Nilsson .25 .50
166 Jan Erik Lyck .25 .50
167 Stefan Karlsson .25 .50
168 Lennart Lind .50 1.00
169 Hans Ake Persson .25 .50
170 Lars Oberg .25 .50
171 Lars Erik Eriksson .25 .50
172 Bjorn Fagerlund .30 .75
173 Nicke Johansson .25 .50
174 Lars Goran Nilsson .25 .50
175 Hans Erik Jansson .25 .50
176 Per Backman .25 .50
177 Jorgen Palm .25 .50
178 Conny Evensson .30 .75
179 Ulf Sterner .25 .50
180 Sven Ake Rudby .25 .50
181 Lennart Andersson .30 .75
182 Kent Erik Andersson .25 .50
183 Hans Ake Rosendahl .25 .50
184 Karl Johan Sundqvist .25 .50
185 Hasse Andersson .25 .50
186 Benny Andersson .25 .50
187 Gunnar Johansson .25 .50
188 Sten Ake Bark .25 .50
189 Lasse Zetterstrom .25 .50
190 Leif Holmqvist .50 1.00
191 Bert Jattne .50 1.00
192 Lars Danielsson .50 1.00
193 Hakan Lindgren .25 .50
194 Ake Fagerstrom .25 .50
195 Bert-Ola Nordlander .30 .75
196 Leif Holmgren .25 .50
197 Soren Sjogren .25 .50
198 Hans Lindberg .25 .50
199 Jan-Olov Kroon .25 .50
200 Rolf Edberg .25 .50
201 Lennart Selinder .50 1.00
202 Ulf Nilsson 2.50 5.00
203 Jan Olsson .25 .50
204 Jan Ostling .25 .50
205 Christer Lundberg .25 .50
206 Christer Englund .25 .50
207 Bo Olofsson .25 .50
208 Roland Einarsson .50 1.00
209 Ake Danielsson .25 .50
210 Billy Sundstrom .25 .50
211 Thomas Carlsson .25 .50
212 Stig Larsson .25 .50
213 Lars Ake Gustavsson .50 1.00
214 Bjorn Palmqvist .25 .50
215 Anders Hedberg 2.50 5.00
216 Anders Rylin .25 .50
217 Sven Bertil Lindstrom .25 .50
218 Kjell Nilsson .25 .50
219 Claes Goran Wallin .25 .50
220 Ake Eklof .25 .50
221 Peder Nilsson .30 .75
222 Lars Ake Lundell .25 .50
223 Bengt Ake Karlsson .25 .50
224 Ove Svensson .25 .50
225 Soren Johansson .25 .50
226 Christer Sehlstedt .30 .75
227 Lage Edin .25 .50
228 Tommy Andersson .25 .50
229 Janerik Nilsson .25 .50
230 Tommie Lindgren .25 .50
231 Bo Bergman .25 .50
232 Lennart Norberg .25 .50
233 Olle Ahman .25 .50
234 Arne Lundstrom .30 .75
235 Kent Lindgren .25 .50
236 Orjan Lindstrom .25 .50
237 Kent Ohberg .30 .75
238 Finn Lundstrom .25 .50
239 Ake Soderberg .25 .50
240 Jan Kock .25 .50
241 Ove Larsson .25 .50
242 Hakan Pettersson .25 .50
243 Stefan Pettersson .25 .50

1974 Swedish Semic World Championship Stickers

COMPLETE SET (100) 40.00 80.00
1 Christer Abrahamsson .75 1.50
2 William Lofqvist .50 1.00
3 Arne Carlsson .25 .50
4 Lars-Erik Sjoberg 1.00 2.00
5 Bjorn Johansson .25 .50
6 Tommy Abrahamsson .50 1.00
7 Karl-Johan Sundqvist .25 .50
8 Ulf Nilsson 2.00 4.00
9 Hakan Wickberg .25 .50
10 Dan Soderstrom .25 .50
11 Mats Ahlberg .30 .75
12 Anders Hedberg 2.00 4.00
13 Dick Yderstrom .25 .50
14 Stefan Karlsson .25 .50
15 Roland Bond .25 .50
16 Kjell-Rune Milton .25 .50
17 Willy Lindstrom .50 1.00
18 Mats Waltin .25 .50
19 Lars-Goran Nilsson .25 .50
20 Bjorn Palmquist .25 .50
21 Stig-Goran Johansson .25 .50
22 Bo Berggren .25 .50
23 Dan Labraaten .75 1.50
24 Curt Larsson .30 .75
25 Mats Lindh .25 .50
26 Vladislav Tretiak 7.50 15.00
27 Alexander Ragulin .50 1.00
28 Vladimir Luttjenko .50 1.00
29 Gennadij Tsygankov .50 1.00
30 Alexander Gusev .50 1.00
31 Jevgenij Poladiev .25 .50
32 Jurij Ljapkin .50 1.00
33 Boris Michailov 2.00 4.00
34 Valeri Kharlamov 10.00 25.00
35 Vladimir Petrov 2.00 3.00
36 Alexander Maltsev 2.00 4.00
37 Vladimir Sjadrin .30 .75
38 Alexander Yakusjev 2.00 4.00
39 Alexander Martynjuk .30 .75
40 Jurij Lebedev .75 1.50

41 Alexander Bodunov .50 1.00
42 Anatolij Firsov .75 1.50
43 Vitalij Davydov .30 .75
44 Vjateslav Starsjinov .30 .75
45 Viktor Kuzkin .25 .50
46 Igor Romitjevskij .25 .50
47 Jevgenij Zimin .30 .75
48 Jevgenij Misjakov .50 1.00
49 Vladimir Vikulov .30 .75
50 Viktor Konovalenko .50 1.00
51 Jiri Holecek .50 1.00
52 Frantisek Pospisil .30 .75
53 Jiri Bubla .50 1.00
54 Josef Horesovsky .25 .50
55 Oldrich Machac .25 .50
56 Vladimir Martinec .50 1.00
57 Vaclav Nedomansky .75 1.50
58 Jiri Kochta .25 .50
59 Milan Novy .50 1.00
60 Jaroslav Holik .25 .50
61 Jiri Holik .50 1.00
62 Jiri Klapac .25 .50
63 Richard Farda .30 .75
64 Bohuslav Stastny .30 .75
65 Jiri Novak .25 .50
66 Ivan Hlinka .30 .75
67 Jan Suchy .30 .75
68 Vladimir Bednar .25 .50
69 Rudolf Tajcnar .25 .50
70 Josef Cerny .25 .50
71 Jan Havel .30 .75
72 Marcel Sakac .25 .50
73 Frantisek Pancharek .25 .50
74 Bedrich Brunchk .25 .50
75 Edvard Novak .25 .50
76 Jorma Valtonen .50 1.00
77 Seppo Lindstrom .25 .50
78 Pekka Marjamaki .25 .50
79 Pekka Rautakallio .75 1.50
80 Heikki Riihiranta .50 1.00
81 Seppo Suoraniemi .25 .50
82 Jouko Oystila .25 .50
83 Veli-Pekka Ketola .75 1.50
84 Henry Leppa .25 .50
85 Harri Linnonmaa .25 .50
86 Matti Murto .25 .50
87 Lasse Oksanen .25 .50
88 Esa Peltonen .25 .50
89 Seppo Repo .25 .50
90 Raimo Suoniemi .25 .50
91 Timo Sutinen .25 .50
92 Juhani Tamminen .50 1.00
93 Leo Seppanen .25 .50
94 Hannu Haapalainen .25 .50
95 Pertti Valkeapaa .25 .50
96 Sakari Ahlberg .25 .50
97 Antti Leppanen .25 .50
98 Kalevi Numminen .25 .50
99 Lauri Mononen .25 .50
100 Ilpo Koskela .30 .75

1974-75 Swedish Stickers

COMPLETE SET (324) 75.00 200.00
1 Vladislav Tretiak 7.50 15.00
2 Gennadij Tsigannkov .50 1.00
3 Valerij Vasiljev 1.50 3.00
4 Alexander Gusev .50 1.00
5 Valeri Kharlamov 10.00 25.00
6 Vladimir Petrov 2.00 4.00
7 Boris Michailov 2.00 4.00
8 Alexander Maltsev 2.00 4.00
9 Alexander Yakusjev 2.00 4.00
10 Jiri Chra 1.50 3.00
11 Jiri Bubla .50 1.00
12 Milan Kuzela .25 .50
13 Oldrich Machac .25 .50
14 Ivan Hlinka .50 1.00
15 Vaclav Nedomansky .75 1.50
16 Boshulav Stastny .75 1.50
17 Vladimir Martinec .75 1.50
18 Richard Farda .25 .50
19 Curt Larsson .30 .75
20 Lars-Erik Sjoberg 1.00 2.00
21 Thommy Abrahamsson .50 1.00
22 Kjell-Rune Milton .25 .50
23 Anders Hedberg 2.00 4.00
24 Mats Ahlberg .30 .75
25 Dan Soderstrom .25 .50
26 Ulf Nilsson 2.00 4.00
27 Per-Olof Brassar .75 1.50
28 Stig Wetzell .25 .50
29 Juha Rantasila .25 .50
30 Heikki Riihiranta .50 1.00
31 Timo Saari .25 .50
32 Seppo Repo .25 .50
33 Esa Peltonen .25 .50
34 Juhani Tamminen .50 1.00
35 Matti Murto .25 .50
36 Harri Linnonmaa .25 .50
37 Gennadij Lapsjenkov .50 1.00
38 Pjotr Zjulin .25 .50
39 Vladimir Merinov .25 .50
40 Sergej Tyznych 1.00 2.00
41 Valerij Kostin .25 .50
42 Valerij Nikitin .50 1.00
43 Sergej Gusev .50 1.00
44 Valentin Kozin .25 .50
45 Viktor Liksiutkin .25 .50
46 Alexander Golikov .50 1.00
47 Viktor Zhluktov .50 1.00
48 Anatolij Frolov .75 1.50
49 Vladimir Golikov 1.00 2.00
50 Nikolaj Epstein .25 .50
51 Alexander Kasjajev .25 .50
52 Alexander Sidelnikov 1.00 2.00
53 Valerij Kuzmin .50 1.00
54 Viktor Kuznetsov .50 1.00
55 Jurij Terechin .30 .75
56 Jurij Tjitjurin .30 .75
57 Jurij Sjalavalov .30 .75
58 Vjateslav Anissin .30 .75
59 Alexander Bodunov .50 1.00
60 Jurij Lebedev .75 1.50
61 Igor Dmitriev 2.00 4.00
62 Konstantin Klimov .30 .75
63 Sergej Kapustin .30 .75
64 Vladimir Repnjov .30 .75

65 Jevgenij Kucharzj .30 .75
66 Boris Kulagin 1.00 2.00
67 Viktor Afonin .25 .50
68 Juris Liberts .30 .75
69 Igor Kobzev .30 .75
70 Valerij Odintsov .30 .75
71 Vjatjeslav Nazarov .50 1.00
72 Andris Hendelis .30 .75
73 Alexander Sokolovskij .30 .75
74 Michail Denisov .30 .75
75 Helmut Balderis 2.00 4.00
76 Vladimir Sorokin .25 .50
77 Vladimir Sernjajev .25 .50
78 Viktor Verizjnikov .25 .50
79 Vladimir Markov .25 .50
80 Viktor Tichonov 2.50 5.00
81 Edgar Rosenberg .25 .50
82 Alexander Kotomkin .25 .50
83 Vladimir Astafjev .50 1.00
84 Alexander Kulikov .25 .50
85 Sergej Mosjkarov .25 .50
86 Vjatjeslav Usjmakov .25 .50
87 Jurij Fjodorov .50 1.00
88 Victor Dobrochotov .25 .50
89 Vitalij Krajov .25 .50
90 Alexej Masjin .25 .50
91 Vladimir Orlov .25 .50
92 Vladimir Smagin .25 .50
93 Alexander Usov .25 .50
94 Alexander Fedotov .50 1.00
95 Alexander Prilepskij .25 .50
96 Alexander Rogov .25 .50
97 Seppo Ahokainen .25 .50
98 Lasse Oksanen .25 .50
99 Jorma Peltonen .50 1.00
100 Henry Leppa .25 .50
101 Seppo Suoraniemi .25 .50
102 Timi Sutinen .25 .50
103 Jorma Valtonen .50 1.00
104 Antti Leppanen .25 .50
105 Pekka Marjamaki .25 .50
106 Jouko Oystila .25 .50
107 Seppo Lindstrom .25 .50
108 Veli-Pekka Ketola .75 1.50
109 Jiri Holecek .50 1.00
110 Jiri Kochta .25 .50
111 Josef Horesovsky .25 .50
112 Jaroslav Sima .25 .50
113 Frantisek Vorlicek .25 .50
114 Vladimir Kostka .25 .50
115 Jaroslav Holik .30 .75
116 Jiri Holik .50 1.00
117 Jan Suchy .30 .75
118 Josef Augusta .25 .50
119 Miroslav Dvorak .50 1.00
120 Jan Hrbaty .25 .50
121 AIK .25 .50
122 If Bjorkloven .25 .50
123 Brynas IF .25 .50
124 Djurgardens IF .25 .50
125 Farjestads BK .25 .50
126 IF Karlskoga .25 .50
127 Leksands IF .25 .50
128 MoDo AIK .25 .50
129 Mora IK .25 .50
130 Skelleftea AIK .25 .50
131 Sodertalje SK .25 .50
132 Timra IK .25 .50
133 Tingsryds AIF .25 .50
134 V. Frolunda IF .25 .50
135 Vasteras IK .25 .50
136 Orebro IK .25 .50
137 Christer Abrahamsson .75 1.50
138 Christer Andersson .25 .50
139 Mikael Collin .50 1.00
140 Bjorn Fagerlund .25 .50
141 Christer Grahn .50 1.00
142 Kenneth Holmstedt .25 .50
143 Goran Hogosta .50 1.00
144 Bert Jattne .25 .50
145 Curt Larsson .30 .75
146 Ivar Larsson .25 .50
147 Wille Lofqvist .50 1.00
148 Peder Nilsson .25 .50
149 Christer Sehlstedt .25 .50
150 Krister Sterner .30 .75
151 Christer Stahl .25 .50
152 Sune Odling .25 .50
153 Thommy Abrahamsson .50 1.00
154 Gunnar Andersson .25 .50
155 Jan Andersson .25 .50
156 Leif Andersson .25 .50
157 Sture Andersson .25 .50
158 Tommy Andersson .25 .50
159 Sten Ake Bark .25 .50
160 Roger Bergman .25 .50
161 Roland Bond .25 .50
162 Arne Carlsson .25 .50
163 Thomas Carlsson .25 .50
164 Lasse Danielsson .25 .50
165 Ake Danielsson .25 .50
166 Kenneth Ekman .25 .50
167 Lars Erik Esbjors .25 .50
168 Soren Gunnarsson .25 .50
169 Mats Hysing .25 .50
170 Bjorn Johansson .25 .50
171 Martin Johansson .25 .50
172 Jan Kock .25 .50
173 Hakan Lindgren .25 .50
174 Larsake Lundell .25 .50
175 Mats Lundmark .25 .50
176 Kjell-Rune Milton .25 .50
177 Jan Erik Nilsson .25 .50
178 Lars Goran Nilsson .25 .50
179 Hakan Nygren .25 .50
180 Jan Olsson .25 .50
181 Jorgen Palm .25 .50
182 Dennis Pettersson .25 .50
183 Stefan Pettersson .25 .50
184 Anders Rylin .25 .50
185 Stig Salming .30 .75
186 Nils-Olof Schilstrom .25 .50
187 Jan Erik Silfverberg .25 .50
188 Lars Erik Sjoberg 1.50 3.00
189 Karl-Johan Sundqvist .25 .50
190 Jan-Olof Svensson .25 .50

191 Leif Svensson .25 .50
192 Tord Svensson .25 .50
193 Sverker Torstensson .25 .50
194 Mats Waltin .25 .50
195 Ulf Weinstock .25 .50
196 Jan Ove Wiberg .25 .50
197 Lars Zetterstrom .25 .50
198 Stig Ostling .30 .75
199 Hans Andersson .25 .50
200 Kent-Erik Andersson .25 .50
201 Kjell Andersson .25 .50
202 Ulf Barrefjord .25 .50
203 Kent Bengtsson .25 .50
204 Bo Berggren .25 .50
205 Kjell Brus .25 .50
206 Per-Olof Brasar .75 1.50
207 Borje Burlin .25 .50
208 Per Backman .25 .50
209 Stefan Canderyd .25 .50
210 Hans Carlsson .25 .50
211 Hakan Dahlov .25 .50
212 Rolf Edberg .25 .50
213 Ake Eklof .25 .50
214 Roland Eriksson .25 .50
215 Conny Evensson .50 1.00
216 Svante Granholm .25 .50
217 Peter Gudmundsson .25 .50
218 Hans Hansson .25 .50
219 Anders Hedberg 2.00 4.00
220 Henric Hedlund .25 .50
221 Nils Arne Hedqvist .25 .50
222 Leif Henriksson .25 .50
223 Leif Holmgren .25 .50
224 Sven-Ake Jacobsson .25 .50
225 Hans Jax .25 .50
226 Christer Johansson .25 .50
227 Gunnar Johansson .25 .50
228 Lars Erik Johansson .25 .50
229 Stig-Goran Johansson .25 .50
230 Soren Johansson .25 .50
231 Bengt Goran Karlsson .25 .50
232 Bengt-Ake Karlsson .25 .50
233 Martin Karlsson .25 .50
234 Stefan Karlsson .25 .50
235 Jan-Olov Kroon .25 .50
236 Dan Labraaten .75 1.50
237 Dan Landegren .25 .50
238 Kjell Landstrom .25 .50
239 Ove Larsson .25 .50
240 Stig Larsson .25 .50
241 Hans Lindberg .25 .50
242 Mats Lindh .25 .50
243 Willy Lindstrom .50 1.00
244 Orjan Lindstrom .25 .50
245 Christer Lundberg .25 .50
246 Lars-Gunnar Lundberg .25 .50
247 Per Lundqvist .25 .50
248 Arne Lundstrom .50 1.00
249 Fhinn Lundstrom .25 .50
250 Bengt Lovgren .25 .50
251 Ulf Martensson .25 .50
252 Par Marts .25 .50
253 Tadeusz Niedomysl .25 .50
254 Hardy Nilsson .25 .50
255 Lars Goran Nilsson .25 .50
256 Ulf Nilsson 2.00 4.00
257 Anders Nordin .25 .50
258 Nils-Olof Olsson .25 .50
259 Bjorn Palmqvist .25 .50
260 Kent Persson .25 .50
261 Hakan Pettersson .25 .50
262 Sven-Ake Rudby .25 .50
263 Benny Runesson .25 .50
264 Jan Roger Strand .25 .50
265 Ake Soderberg .50 1.00
266 Dan Soderstrom .25 .50
267 Ulf Torstensson .25 .50
268 Claes Goran Wallin .25 .50
269 Hakan Wickberg .25 .50
270 Kjell Arne Wickstrom .25 .50
271 Per Allan Wickstrom .25 .50
272 Dick Yderstrom .25 .50
273 Mats Ahlberg .30 .75
274 Olle Ahman .25 .50
275 Lars Oberg .25 .50
276 Jan Ostling .25 .50
277 Akning .25 .50
278 Akning .25 .50
279 Akning .25 .50
280 Skott .25 .50
281 Skott .25 .50
282 Skott .25 .50
283 Puckforing .25 .50
284 Tekning .25 .50
285 Malvaktsspel .25 .50
286 Malvaktsspel .50 1.00
287 Forsvarsspel .25 .50
288 Forsvarsspel .25 .50
289 Forsvarsspel .25 .50
290 Forsvarsspel .25 .50
291 Forsvarsspel .25 .50
292 Forsvarsspel .25 .50
293 Forsvarsspel .25 .50
294 Forsvarsspel .25 .50
295 Forsvarsspel .25 .50
296 Forsvarsspel .25 .50
297 Forsvarsspel .25 .50
298 Forsvarsspel .25 .50
299 Forsvarsspel .25 .50
300 Forsvarsspel .25 .50
301 Forsvarsspel .25 .50
302 Forsvarsspel .25 .50
303 Anfallsspel .25 .50
304 Anfallsspel .25 .50
305 Anfallsspel .25 .50
306 Anfallsspel .25 .50
307 Anfallsspel .25 .50
308 Anfallsspel .25 .50
309 Anfallsspel .25 .50
310 Anfallsspel .25 .50
311 Anfallsspel .25 .50
312 Anfallsspel .25 .50
313 Inge Hammarstrom 1.00 2.00
314 Borje Salming 3.00 6.00
315 Thommie Bergman 1.25 2.50
316 Leif Holmqvist .50 1.00

317 Ulf Sterner .25 .50
318 Tord Lundstrom .25 .50
319 Tre Kroner puzzle .25 .50
320 Tre Kroner puzzle .25 .50
321 Tre Kroner puzzle .25 .50
322 Tre Kroner puzzle .25 .50
323 Tre Kroner puzzle .25 .50
324 Tre Kroner puzzle .25 .50

1981 Swedish Semic Hockey VM Stickers

COMPLETE SET (144) 50.00 125.00
1 Goran Hogosta .20 .50
2 Tomas Jonsson .20 .50
3 Ulf Weinstock .08 .25
4 Goran Nilsson .08 .25
5 Jan Eriksson .08 .25
6 Tommy Samuelsson .08 .25
7 Mats Waltin .08 .25
8 Peter Helander .08 .25
9 Per Lundqvist .08 .25
10 Conny Silfverberg .08 .25
11 Mats Naslund 2.00 5.00
12 Lennart Norberg .08 .25
13 Bengt Lundholm .40 1.00
14 Leif Holmgren .08 .25
15 Bo Berglund .40 1.00
16 Dan Soderstrom .08 .25
17 Lars Molin .30 .75
18 Tore Oqvist .08 .25
19 Ari Hellgren .08 .25
20 Hannu Lassila .08 .25
21 Kari Eloranta .40 1.00
22 Lasse Litma .08 .25
23 Seppo Suoraniemi .08 .25
24 Tapio Levo .20 .50
25 Timo Nummelin .08 .25
26 Reijo Ruotsalainen .60 1.50
27 Markku Kiimalainen .08 .25
28 Mikko Leinonen .30 .75
29 Reijo Leppanen .08 .25
30 Hannu Koskinen .08 .25
31 Timo Susi .08 .25
32 Jukka Porvari .08 .25
33 Arto Javanainen .08 .25
34 Juhanni Tamminen .40 1.00
35 Pertti Koivulahti .08 .25
36 Antero Lehtonen .08 .25
37 Vladislav Tretiak 4.00 10.00
38 Vladimir Mysjkin .60 1.50
39 Slava Fetisov 2.50 6.00
40 Vladimir Luttjenko .30 .75
41 Sergei Babinov .20 .50
42 Vasilij Pervuchin .30 .75
43 Sergej Starikov .30 .75
44 Zinetula Biljaletdinov .30 .75
45 Vladimir Krutov 2.00 5.00
46 Alexander Maltsev 1.25 3.00
47 Jurij Lebedev .30 .75
48 Viktor Tiumenev .20 .50
49 Nikolaj Drozdetskij .08 .25
50 Valeri Kharlamov 2.50 6.00
51 Sergej Makarov 2.00 5.00
52 Vladimir Golikov .30 .75
53 Alexander Skvortsov .20 .50
54 Michail Varnakov .30 .75
55 Jiri Kralik .20 .50
56 Jaromir Sindel .60 1.50
57 Miroslav Dvorak .30 .75
58 Frantisek Kaberle .20 .50
59 Arnold Kadlec .20 .50
60 Jan Neliba .08 .25
61 Radoslav Svoboda .08 .25
62 Jaroslav Lycka .08 .25
63 Milan Novy .40 1.00
64 Jaroslav Pouzar .40 1.00
65 Miroslav Frycer .60 1.50
66 Karel Holy .08 .25
67 Ladislav Svozil .08 .25
68 Marian Bezak .08 .25
69 Jindrich Kokrment .08 .25
70 Jiri Lala .30 .75
71 Ludos Penicka .08 .25
72 Ivan Hlinka .75 2.00
73 Wayne Stephenson .75 2.00
74 Ron Paterson .30 .75
75 Warren Anderson .30 .75
76 Brad Pirie .30 .75
77 Randy Gregg .60 1.50
78 Tim Watters .40 1.00
79 Joe Grant .30 .75
80 Don Spring .30 .75
81 Ron Davidson .30 .75
82 Glenn Anderson 4.00 10.00
83 Kevin Maxwell .30 .75
84 Jim Nill .40 1.00
85 John Devaney .30 .75
86 Paul MacLean .60 1.50
87 Dan D'Alvise .30 .75
88 Ken Berry .30 .75
89 David Hindmarch .30 .75
90 Kevin Primeau .40 1.00
91 Steve Janaszak 2.00 5.00
92 Bob Suter 2.00 5.00
93 Ken Morrow 2.00 5.00
94 Mike Ramsey 2.00 5.00
95 Bill Baker 2.00 5.00
96 Dave Christian 2.00 5.00
97 Les Auge .40 1.00
98 Dave Silk 2.00 5.00
99 Neal Broten 2.00 5.00
100 Mark Johnson 2.00 5.00
101 Steve Christoff 2.00 5.00
102 Mark Pavelich 2.00 5.00
103 Eric Strobel 2.00 5.00
104 Mike Eruzione 10.00 25.00
105 Rob McClanahan 2.00 5.00
106 Buzz Schneider 2.00 5.00
107 Phil Verchota 2.00 5.00
108 John Harrington 2.00 5.00
109 Leif Holmqvist .40 1.00
110 Kjell Svensson .30 .75
111 Roland Stoltz .08 .25
112 Bert-Ola Nordlander .08 .25
113 Nils Johansson .08 .25
114 Lennart Svedberg .20 .50

115 Ulf Sterner .08 .25
116 Hakan Wickberg .08 .25
117 Tord Lundstrom .08 .25
118 Carl-Goran Oberg .08 .25
119 Eilert Maatta .08 .25
120 Lars-Goran Nilsson .08 .25
121 Nils Nilsson .08 .25
122 Hans Oberg .08 .25
123 Lars-Erik Lundvall .08 .25
124 Sven Tumba Johansson .20 .50
125 Lars Bjorn .08 .25
126 Ronald Pettersson .08 .25
127 World Championships 1981 .08 .25
128 Sweden .08 .25
129 Finland .08 .25
130 Soviet Union .08 .25
131 CSSR .08 .25
132 Canada .30 .75
133 U.S.A. .30 .75
134 West Germany .08 .25
135 Holland .08 .25
136 Referee's Signs .08 .25
137 Referee's Signs .08 .25
138 Referee's Signs .08 .25
139 Referee's Signs .08 .25
140 Referee's Signs .08 .25
141 Referee's Signs .08 .25
142 Referee's Signs .08 .25
143 Referee's Signs .08 .25
144 Referee's Signs .08 .25

1982 Swedish Semic VM Stickers

COMPLETE SET (162) 24.00 60.00
1 Peter Lindmark .40 1.00
2 Gote Walitalo .08 .25
3 Gunnar Leidborg .08 .25
4 Goran Lindblom .08 .25
5 Thomas Eriksson .08 .25
6 Mats Waltin .08 .25
7 Jan Eriksson .08 .25
8 Mats Thelin .30 .75
9 Peter Helander .08 .25
10 Tommy Samuelsson .08 .25
11 Bo Ericsson .08 .25
12 Peter Andersson .20 .50
13 Mats Naslund 2.00 5.00
14 Ulf Isaksson .08 .25
15 Patrik Sundstrom .75 2.00
16 Peter Sundstrom .60 1.50
17 Thomas Rundqvist .30 .75
18 Mats Ulander .08 .25
19 Tommy Morth .08 .25
20 Ove Olsson .08 .25
21 Rolf Edberg .08 .25
22 Hakan Loob 1.50 4.00
23 Leif Holmgren .40 1.00
24 Jan Erixon .60 1.50
25 Harald Luckner .08 .25
26 Hannu Kamppuri .40 1.00
27 Hannu Issila .20 .50
28 Kari Heikkila .08 .25
29 Timo Nummelin .08 .25
30 Pertti Lehtonen .08 .25
31 Raimo Hirvonen .08 .25
32 Seppo Suoraniemi .08 .25
33 Juha Huikari .08 .25
34 Hannu Helander .08 .25
35 Lasse Litma .08 .25
36 Hakan Hjerpe .08 .25
37 Kari Jalonen .20 .50
38 Arto Javanainen .08 .25
39 Jari Lindgren .08 .25
40 Markku Kiimalainen .08 .25
41 Jarmo Makitalo .08 .25
42 Jorma Sevon .08 .25
43 Erkki Laine .08 .25
44 Hannu Koskinen .08 .25
45 Reijo Leppanen .08 .25
46 Pekka Arbelius .08 .25
47 Markku Hakulinen .08 .25
48 Timo Susi .08 .25
49 Esa Peltonen .08 .25
50 Juhani Tamminen .75 2.00
51 Vladislav Tretiak 4.00 10.00
52 Vladimir Mysjkin .30 .75
53 Slava Fetisov 2.00 5.00
54 Sergej Babinov .20 .50
55 Vasilij Pervuchin .20 .50
56 Valerij Vasiljev .30 .75
57 Alexei Kasatonov .75 2.00
58 Zinetula Biljaletdinov .40 1.00
59 Sergej Starikov .30 .75
60 Sergej Makarov 1.25 3.00
61 Sergej Sjepelev .30 .75
62 Vladimir Krutov 1.25 3.00
63 Nikolaj Drozdetskij .30 .75
64 Viktor Zjluktov .20 .50
65 Viktor Sjalimov .20 .50
66 Vladimir Golikov .30 .75
67 Aleksandr Maltsev 1.00 2.50
68 Andrej Khomutov .75 2.00
69 Sergej Svetlov .20 .50
70 Helmut Balderis .30 .75
71 Sergej Kapustin .20 .50
72 Vladimir Zubkov .20 .50
73 Aleksandr Kozjevnikov .20 .50
74 Jurij Lebedev .20 .50
75 Nikolaj Makarov .20 .50
76 Jiri Kralik .20 .50
77 Karel Lang .20 .50
78 Jaromir Sindel .40 1.00
79 Miroslav Horava .20 .50
80 Milan Chalupa .20 .50
81 Stanislav Hajdusek .08 .25
82 Arnold Kadlec .20 .50
83 Miroslav Dvorak .20 .50
84 Jan Neliba .08 .25
85 Petr Misek .08 .25
86 Eduard Uvira .08 .25
87 Milan Novy .20 .50
88 Frantisek Cerny .20 .50
89 Jiri Lala .20 .50
90 Jindrich Kokrment .08 .25
91 Frantisek Cernik .20 .50
92 Darius Rusnak .08 .25

93 Dusan Pasek .20 .50
94 Lubomir Penicka .08 .25
95 Jaroslav Korbela .08 .25
96 Peter Ihnacak .40 1.00
97 Jaroslav Hrdina .08 .25
98 Igor Liba .20 .50
99 Peter Slania .08 .25
100 Vincent Lukac .08 .25
101 Erich Weishaupt .20 .50
102 Bernhard Engelbrecht .20 .50
103 Robert Murray .20 .50
104 Peter Gailer .08 .25
105 Udo Kiessling .20 .50
106 Harold Kreis .20 .50
107 Joachim Reil .08 .25
108 Harald Krull .08 .25
109 Ulrich Egen .08 .25
110 Marcus Kuhl .08 .25
111 Peter Schiller .08 .25
112 Erich Kuhnhackl .20 .50
113 Holger Meitinger .08 .25
114 Ernst Hofner .08 .25
115 Vladimir Vacatko .08 .25
116 Manfred Wolf .08 .25
117 Johann Morz .08 .25
118 Franz Reindl .08 .25
119 Helmut Steiger .08 .25
120 Georg Holzmann .08 .25
121 Roy Roedger .08 .25
122 Jim Corsi .40 1.00
123 Nick Sanza .08 .25
124 Guido Tenisi 8.00 20.00
125 Erwin Kostner .08 .25
126 Mike Amodeo .20 .50
127 John Bellio .08 .25
128 Dave Tomassoni .08 .25
129 Daniel Pupillo .08 .25
130 Giulio Francella .08 .25
131 Fabio Polloni .08 .25
132 Adolf Insam .08 .25
133 Patrick Dell'Jannone .08 .25
134 Rick Bragnalo .08 .25
135 Michael Mair .08 .25
136 Alberto DiFazio .08 .25
137 Cary Farelli .08 .25
138 Tom Milani .08 .25
139 Martin Pavlu .08 .25
140 Bob De Piero .08 .25
141 Grant Goegan .08 .25
142 Jerry Ciarcia .08 .25
143 Borje Salming 2.00 5.00
144 Lars Lindgren .20 .50
145 Ulf Nilsson .75 2.00
146 Bengt-Ake Gustavsson .60 1.50
147 Kent Nilsson 1.50 4.00
148 Thomas Gradin 1.25 3.00
149 Lars Molin .30 .75
150 Thomas Steen 1.25 3.00
151 Bengt Lundholm .30 .75
152 Jorgen Pettersson .30 .75
153 Jukka Porvari .20 .50
154 Tapio Levo .20 .50
155 Reijo Ruotsalainen .30 .75
156 Matti Hagman .30 .75
157 Risto Siltanen .30 .75
158 Ilkka Sinisalo .40 1.00
159 Markus Mattsson .30 .75
160 Mikko Leinonen .20 .50
161 Pekka Rautakallio .40 1.00
162 Veli-Pekka Ketola .40 1.00

1983 Swedish Semic VM Stickers

COMPLETE SET (162) 40.00 80.00
1 Peter Lindmark .40 1.00
2 Gote Walitalo .08 .25
3 Lars Eriksson .08 .25
4 Roger Hagglund .08 .25
5 Thomas Eriksson .30 .75
6 Mats Waltin .08 .25
7 Jan Eriksson .08 .25
8 Mats Thelin .30 .75
9 Michael Thelven .20 .50
10 Peter Andersson .40 1.00
11 Bo Ericson .08 .25
12 Bo Berglund .20 .50
13 Tomas Sandstrom 1.25 3.00
14 Per-Erik Eklund .75 2.00
15 Roland Eriksson .08 .25
16 Peter Sundstrom .40 1.00
17 Thomas Rundqvist .60 1.50
18 Mats Ulander .08 .25
19 Tommy Morth .08 .25
20 Ove Olsson .08 .25
21 Hakan Sodergren .08 .25
22 Håkan Loob 2.00 5.00
23 Leif Holmgren .08 .25
24 Jan Erixon .40 1.00
25 Tom Eklund .08 .25
26 Hannu Kamppuri .40 1.00
27 Rauli Sohlman .08 .25
28 Kari Takko .40 1.00
29 Pekka Rautakallio .40 1.00
30 Pertti Lehtonen .08 .25
31 Hannu Haapalainen .08 .25
32 Markus Lehto .08 .25
33 Juha Huikari .08 .25
34 Hannu Helander .08 .25
35 Lasse Litma .08 .25
36 Arto Routanen .08 .25
37 Raimo Summanen .20 .50
38 Arto Javaninen .08 .25
39 Jari Lindgren .08 .25
40 Risto Jalo .20 .50
41 Petri Skriko .08 .25
42 Juha Nurmi .08 .25
43 Erkki Laine .20 .50
44 Anssi Melametsa .08 .25
45 Reijo Leppanen .08 .25
46 Matti Hagman .40 1.00
47 Kari Makkonen .08 .25
48 Timo Susi .08 .25
49 Harri Touhimaa .08 .25
50 Arto Jokinen .08 .25
51 Vladislav Tretiak 6.00 15.00
52 Vladimir Mysjkin .40 1.00

Card	Low	High
53 Vjatjeslav Fetisov	2.00	5.00
54 Sergej Babinov	.08	.25
55 Vasilij Pervuchin	.30	.75
56 Sergej Gimajev	.08	.25
57 Aleksej Kasatonov	.40	1.00
58 Zinetula Biljaletdinov	.20	.50
59 Sergej Starikov	.08	.25
60 Sergej Makarov	2.00	5.00
61 Sergej Sjepelev	.08	.25
62 Vladimir Krutov	2.00	5.00
63 Nikolaj Drozdetskij	.08	.25
64 Viktor Zjluktov	.08	.25
65 Viktor Sjalimov	.08	.25
66 Vladimir Golikov	.08	.25
67 Aleksandr Maltsev	1.25	3.00
68 Andrej Chomutov	.40	1.00
69 Vjatjeslav Bykov	.30	.75
70 Michail Vasiljev	.08	.25
71 Sergej Kapustin	.20	.50
72 Aleksandr Gerasimov	.08	.25
73 Aleksandr Kozjevnikov	.08	.25
74 Igor Larionov	4.00	10.00
75 Vladimir Zubkov	.08	.25
76 Jiri Kralik	.08	.25
77 Karel Lang	.20	.50
78 Jaromir Sindel	.20	.50
79 Miloslav Horava	.20	.50
80 Milan Chalupa	.20	.50
81 Stanislav Hajdusek	.08	.25
82 Arnold Kadlec	.20	.50
83 Ladislav Kolda	.08	.25
84 Jaroslav Benak	.08	.25
85 Radoslav Svoboda	.08	.25
86 Eduard Uvira	.08	.25
87 Antonin Planovsky	.08	.25
88 Petr Slanina	.08	.25
89 Jiri Lala	.20	.50
90 Jindrich Kokrment	.08	.25
91 Frantisek Cernik	.08	.25
92 Darius Rusnak	.08	.25
93 Dusan Pasek	.30	.75
94 Pavel Richtr	.08	.25
95 Jaroslav Korbela	.08	.25
96 Ivan Dornic	.08	.25
97 Jiri Hrdina	.08	.25
98 Igor Liba	.20	.50
99 Jiri Dudacek	.20	.50
100 Vincent Lukac	.08	.25
101 Erich Weishaupt	.08	.25
102 Bernhard Engelbrecht	.08	.25
103 Karl-Heinz Friesen	.30	.75
104 Ignaz Berndaner	.08	.25
105 Udo Kiessling	.20	.50
106 Harold Kreis	.08	.25
107 Joachim Reil	.08	.25
108 Gerd Truntschka	.20	.50
109 Ulrich Egen	.08	.25
110 Marcus Kuhl	.08	.25
111 Peter Schiller	.08	.25
112 Erich Kühnhackl	.20	.50
113 Holger Meitinger	.08	.25
114 Ernst Hofner	.08	.25
115 Dieter Hegen	.08	.25
116 Manfred Wolf	.08	.25
117 Johann Morz	.08	.25
118 Franz Reindl	.08	.25
119 Helmut Steiger	.08	.25
120 Horst-Peter Kretschmer	.08	.25
121 Roy Roedger	.08	.25
122 Jim Corsi	.08	.25
123 Nick Sanza	.08	.25
124 Guido Tenisi	8.00	20.00
125 Erwin Kostner	.08	.25
126 Mike Amodeo	.20	.50
127 John Bellio	.08	.25
128 Dave Tomassoni	.08	.25
129 Bob Manno	.30	.75
130 Gino Pasqualotto	.08	.25
131 Fabio Polloni	.08	.25
132 Adolf Insam	.08	.25
133 Constant Priondolo	.08	.25
134 Rick Bragnalo	.08	.25
135 Michael Mair	.08	.25
136 Alberto Di Fazio	.08	.25
137 Cary Farelli	.08	.25
138 Tom Milani	.08	.25
139 Martin Pavlu	.08	.25
140 Bob De Piero	.08	.25
141 Grant Goegan	.08	.25
142 Jerry Ciarcia	.08	.25
143 Rene Bielke	.08	.25
144 Ingolf Spantig	.08	.25
145 Frank Braun	.08	.25
146 Joachim Lempio	.08	.25
147 Reinhardt Fengler	.08	.25
148 Dieter Frenzel	.08	.25
149 Klaus Schroder	.08	.25
150 Dietmar Peters	.08	.25
151 Dieter Simon	.08	.25
152 Andreas Ludwig	.08	.25
153 Detlef Radant	.08	.25
154 Friedhelm Bogelsack	.08	.25
155 Thomas Graul	.08	.25
156 Roland Peters	.08	.25
157 Frank Proske	.08	.25
158 Fred Bartell	.08	.25
159 Harald Kuhnke	.08	.25
160 Gerhard Müller	.08	.25
161 Harald Bolke	.08	.25
162 Dieter Kinzel	.08	.25

1983-84 Swedish Semic Elitserien

Card	Low	High
COMPLETE SET (243)	24.00	60.00
1 Gunnar Leidborg	.20	.50
2 Peter Aslin	.40	1.00
3 Mats Thelin	.40	1.00
4 Jan Eriksson	.08	.25
5 Hans Cederholm	.08	.25
6 Bo Ericsson	.08	.25
7 Bjorn Hellman	.08	.25
8 Tomas Nord	.08	.25
9 Anders Wallin	.08	.25
10 Mats Alba	.08	.25
11 Ronny Jansson	.08	.25
12 Roger Lindstrom	.08	.25
13 Mats Hessel	.08	.25
14 Peter Gradin	.08	.25
15 Mats Ulander	.08	.25
16 Per-Erik Eklund	1.25	3.00
17 Ulf Isaksson	.08	.25
18 Rolf Eriksson	.08	.25
19 Michael Wikstrom	.08	.25
20 Leif Holmgren	.08	.25
21 Per Martinelle	.08	.25
22 Tommy Lehmann	.30	.75
23 Hans Norberg	.08	.25
24 Jan Ericsson	.08	.25
25 Per Backman	.08	.25
26 Gote Walitalo	.08	.25
27 Jakob Gustavsson	.08	.25
28 Staffan Andersson	.08	.25
29 Torbjorn Andersson	.08	.25
30 Anders Bostrom	.08	.25
31 Jan Lindholm	.08	.25
32 Ulf Nilsson	2.00	5.00
33 Par Sjolander	.08	.25
34 Lennart Dahlberg	.08	.25
35 Rolf Berglund	.08	.25
36 Patrik Aberg	.08	.25
37 Tom Eklund	.08	.25
38 Stefan Nilsson	.08	.25
39 Matti Pauna	.08	.25
40 Jan Lundstrom	.08	.25
41 Mikael Andersson	1.25	3.00
42 Hans Edlund	.08	.25
43 Jon Lundstrom	.08	.25
44 Tony Lundgren	.08	.25
45 Ulf Wikgren	.08	.25
46 Tomas Hedin	.08	.25
47 Lars-Gunnar Pettersson	.08	.25
48 Peter Edstrom	.08	.25
49 Tore Okvist	.08	.25
50 Tommy Sandlin	.30	.75
51 Lars Eriksson	.08	.25
52 Ake Lilljebjorn	.20	.50
53 Anders Backstrom	.08	.25
54 Goran Grundstrom	.08	.25
55 Jan Kock	.08	.25
56 Gunnar Persson	.08	.25
57 Torbjorn Mattsson	.08	.25
58 Stig Ostling	.08	.25
59 Hans Johansson	.08	.25
60 Robert Nordmark	.40	1.00
61 Mikael Sandstrom	.08	.25
62 Anders Carlsson	.08	.25
63 Christer Andersson	.08	.25
64 Per Hedenstrom	.08	.25
65 Bjorn Akerblom	.08	.25
66 Conny Silfverberg	.08	.25
67 Jonny Stridh	.08	.25
68 Goran Sjoberg	.08	.25
69 Kenneth Andersson	.08	.25
70 Fredrik Lundstrom	.08	.25
71 Henrik Cedergren	.08	.25
72 Tomas Sandstrom	1.25	3.00
73 Anders Huss	.08	.25
74 Stig Salming	.20	.50
75 Rolf Ridderwall	.40	1.00
76 Bo Larsson	.08	.25
77 Mikael Westling	.08	.25
78 Tord Nansen	.08	.25
79 Tommy Albelin	1.25	3.00
80 Orvar Stambert	.08	.25
81 Karl-Erik Lilja	.08	.25
82 Mats Waltin	.08	.25
83 Stefan Perlstrom	.08	.25
84 Michael Thelven	.20	.50
85 Stefan Jansson	.08	.25
86 Jens Ohling	.08	.25
87 Peter Nilsson	.08	.25
88 Hakan Eriksson	.08	.25
89 Jorgen Holmberg	.08	.25
90 Tommy Morth	.08	.25
91 Jan Claesson	.08	.25
92 Per Goransson	.08	.25
93 Martin Linse	.08	.25
94 Bjorn Carlsson	.08	.25
95 Hakan Sodergren	.08	.25
96 Anders Johnsson	.08	.25
97 Jan Viktorsson	.20	.50
98 Jeff Hallegard	.08	.25
99 Leif Boork	.08	.25
100 Hakan Hermansson	.08	.25
101 Thomas Blom	.08	.25
102 Christer Dalgard	.08	.25
103 Tommy Samuelsson	.08	.25
104 Lars-Goran Nilsson	.08	.25
105 Peter Andersson	.40	1.00
106 Mats Lusth	.08	.25
107 Tommy Moller	.08	.25
108 Leif Carlsson	.08	.25
109 Urban Larsson	.08	.25
110 Hakan Nordin	.08	.25
111 Harald Luckner	.08	.25
112 Thomas Rundqvist	.60	1.50
113 Kjell Dahlin	.75	2.00
114 Robin Eriksson	.08	.25
115 Jan Ingman	.08	.25
116 Stefan Persson	.08	.25
117 Peter Berndtsson	.08	.25
118 Anders Steen	.08	.25
119 Claes-HEnrik Silfver	.08	.25
120 Magnus Roupe	.40	1.00
121 Jan Wickberg	.08	.25
122 Dan Mohlin	.08	.25
123 Kent Olsson	.08	.25
124 Stefan Lunner	.08	.25
125 Niklas Holmberg	.08	.25
126 Anders Alverud	.08	.25
127 Stefan Svensson	.08	.25
128 Lars Karlsson	.08	.25
129 Ulf Weinstock	.08	.25
130 Kjell Samuelsson	1.25	3.00
131 Magnus Svensson	.40	1.00
132 Ove Pettersson	.08	.25
133 Hans Eriksson	.08	.25
134 Ulf Samuelsson	1.25	3.00
135 Roland Eriksson	.08	.25
136 Kjell Bond	.08	.25
137 Per Nordlinder	.08	.25
138 Ivan Hansen	.08	.25
139 Sivert Andersson	.08	.25
140 Jonas Bergkvist	.40	1.00
141 Per-Olof Carlsson	.08	.25
142 Dan Labraaten	.60	1.50
143 Ulf Skoglund	.08	.25
144 Ove Olsson	.08	.25
145 Mikael Leek	.08	.25
146 Mats Loov	.08	.25
147 Lennart Ahlberg	.08	.25
148 Hardy Astrom	2.00	5.00
149 Anders Bergman	.08	.25
150 Per Forsberg	.08	.25
151 Sture Andersson	.08	.25
152 Mikael Good	.08	.25
153 Jan Nyman	.08	.25
154 Roger Eliasson	.08	.25
155 Jan Karlsson	.08	.25
156 Lennart Jonsson	.08	.25
157 Robert Frestadius	.08	.25
158 Juha Tuohimaa	.08	.25
159 Jerry Lundberg	.08	.25
160 Tommy Sjalin	.08	.25
161 Ulf Norberg	.08	.25
162 Michael Hjalm	.08	.25
163 Per Nilsson	.08	.25
164 Lars Nyberg	.08	.25
165 Ulf Odmark	.08	.25
166 Ingemar Strom	.08	.25
167 Erik Holmberg	.08	.25
168 Lars Bystrom	.08	.25
169 Lars Hellstrom	.08	.25
170 Henry Saleva	.08	.25
171 Hardy Nilsson	.08	.25
172 Mats Abrahamsson	.08	.25
173 Ulf Nilsson	2.00	5.00
174 Jens Johansson	.08	.25
175 Lars Marklund	.08	.25
176 Robert Ohman	.08	.25
177 Goran Lindblom	.08	.25
178 Ola Stenlund	.08	.25
179 Ulf Agren	.08	.25
180 Thomas Ahlen	.08	.25
181 Tomas Jonsson	.75	2.00
182 Mikael Granstedt	.08	.25
183 Mats Lundstrom	.08	.25
184 Per Andersson	.08	.25
185 Johnny Forsman	.10	.25
186 Lars Nystrom	.08	.25
187 Niklas Mannberg	.08	.25
188 Peter Lundmark	.75	2.00
189 Claes Lindblom	.08	.25
190 Leif Hedlund	.08	.25
191 Roland Stoltz	.08	.25
192 Martin Pettersson	.08	.25
193 Jorgen Marklund	.08	.25
194 Mats Lundstrom	.08	.25
195 Tommy Andersson	.08	.25
196 Ake Andersson	.08	.25
197 Lars Fernqvist	.08	.25
198 Anders Eldebrink	.40	1.00
199 Ulf Borg	.08	.25
200 Mats Kihlstrom	.30	.75
201 Bo Andersson	.08	.25
202 Peter Ekroth	.08	.25
203 Jukka Hirsimaki	.08	.25
204 Stefan Jonsson	.08	.25
205 Peter Loob	.20	.50
206 Tomas Jernberg	.08	.25
207 Dan Hermansson	.08	.25
208 Glenn Johansson	.08	.25
209 Leif R. Carlsson	.08	.25
210 Johan Mellstrom	.08	.25
211 Tomas Gustavsson	.08	.25
212 Olof Johansson	.08	.25
213 Peter Wallin	.08	.25
214 Hans Sarkijarvi	.08	.25
215 Reine Karlsson	.08	.25
216 Conny Jansson	.08	.25
217 Jarmo Makitalo	.08	.25
218 Mikael Johansson	.08	.25
219 Timo Lahtinen	.08	.25
220 Goran Nilsson	.08	.25
221 Joakim Hokegard	.08	.25
222 Peter Pettersson	.08	.25
223 Goran Nilsson	.08	.25
224 Jan Carlsson	.08	.25
225 Soren Johansson	.08	.25
226 Thomas Lundin	.08	.25
227 Calle Johansson	.75	2.00
228 Anders Brostrom	.08	.25
229 Stefan Larsson	.08	.25
230 Thomas Karrbrandt	.08	.25
231 Roger Hagglund	.08	.25
232 Christer Kellgren	.08	.25
233 Kent Eriksson	.08	.25
234 Mikael Andersson	1.25	3.00
235 Ove Karlsson	.08	.25
236 Peter Elander	.08	.25
237 Hans Jonsson	.08	.25
238 Hasse Sjoo	.08	.25
239 Ulf Labraaten	.08	.25
240 Jens Hellgren	.08	.25
241 Roger Ahsberg	.08	.25
242 Kurt Carlsson	.08	.25
243 Peter Gustavsson	.08	.25

1984-85 Swedish Semic Elitserien

Card	Low	High
COMPLETE SET (243)	20.00	50.00
1 Gunnar Leidborg	.20	.50
2 Thomas Ostlund	.75	2.00
3 Jan Eriksson	.08	.25
4 Tomas Nord	.08	.25
5 Bjorn Hellman	.08	.25
6 Hans Cederholm	.08	.25
7 Mats Alba	.08	.25
8 Roger Hellgren	.08	.25
9 Peter Zetterholm	.08	.25
10 Tony Barthelsson	.08	.25
11 Roger Lindstrom	.08	.25
12 Mats Hessel	.08	.25
13 Peter Gradin	.08	.25
14 Per-Erik Eklund	.75	2.00
15 Ulf Isaksson	.08	.25
16 Harri Tiala	.08	.25
17 Michael Wikstrom	.08	.25
18 Per Backe	.08	.25
19 Per Martinelle	.08	.25
20 Tommy Lehmann	.20	.50
21 Hans Norberg	.08	.25
22 Odd Nilsson	.08	.25
23 Henrik Cedergren	.08	.25
24 Stefan Sandin	.08	.25
25 Per Backman	.08	.25
26 Gote Walitalo	.08	.25
27 Jakob Gustavsson	.08	.25
28 Torbjorn Andersson	.08	.25
29 Anders Bostrom	.08	.25
30 Jan Lindholm	.08	.25
31 Lars Karlsson	.08	.25
32 Rolf Berglund	.08	.25
33 Lennart Dahlberg	.08	.25
34 Patric Aberg	.08	.25
35 Ulf Nilsson	1.50	4.00
36 Mats Jacobsson	.08	.25
37 Michael Hjalm	.08	.25
38 Stefan Nilsson	.08	.25
39 Matti Pauna	.08	.25
40 Jan Lundstrom	.08	.25
41 Mikael Andersson	.40	1.00
42 Hans Edlund	.08	.25
43 Jon Lundstrom	.08	.25
44 Tony Lundgren	.08	.25
45 Ulf Wikgren	.08	.25
46 Thomas Hedin	.08	.25
47 Lars-Gunnar Pettersson	.08	.25
48 Peter Edstrom	.08	.25
49 Tommy Sandlin	.20	.50
50 Lars Eriksson	.08	.25
51 Ake Lilljebjorn	.20	.50
52 Mats Kihlstrom	.20	.50
53 Anders Backstrom	.08	.25
54 Lars Ivarsson	.40	1.00
55 Jan Kock	.08	.25
56 Gunnar Persson	.08	.25
57 Torbjorn Mattsson	.08	.25
58 Per Jarnberg	.08	.25
59 Hans Johansson	.08	.25
60 Anders Huss	.08	.25
61 Per Nilsson	.08	.25
62 Owe Eriksson	.08	.25
63 Christer Andersson	.08	.25
64 Per Hedenstrom	.08	.25
65 Jan Larsson	.08	.25
66 Conny Silfverberg	.08	.25
67 Jonny Stridh	.08	.25
68 Erik Holmberg	.08	.25
69 Kenneth Andersson	.08	.25
70 Fredrik Lundstrom	.08	.25
71 Peter Eriksson	.08	.25
72 Peter Eriksson	.08	.25
73 Stig Salming	.20	.50
74 Rolf Ridderwall	.40	1.00
75 Mats Ytter	.08	.25
76 Michael Thelven	.30	.75
77 Stefan Perlstrom	.08	.25
78 Tord Nansen	.08	.25
79 Tommy Albelin	.75	2.00
80 Orvar Stambert	.08	.25
81 Karl-Erik Lilja	.08	.25
82 Kristian Henriksson	.08	.25
83 Arto Blomsten	.30	.75
84 Anders Johnsson	.08	.25
85 Pontus Molander	.08	.25
86 Jens Ohling	.08	.25
87 Peter Nilsson	.08	.25
88 Hakan Sodergren	.08	.25
89 Jorgen Holmberg	.08	.25
90 Tommy Morth	.08	.25
91 Jan Claesson	.08	.25
92 Per Goransson	.08	.25
93 Jan Viktorsson	.20	.50
94 Bjorn Carlsson	.08	.25
95 Erik Ahlstrom	.08	.25
96 Peter Schank	.08	.25
97 Ake Eksell	.08	.25
98 Gunnar Svensson	.08	.25
99 Peter Lindmark	.08	.25
100 Christer Dalgard	.08	.25
101 Hakan Nordin	.08	.25
102 Fredrik Olausson	1.25	3.00
103 Tommy Samuelsson	.08	.25
104 Anders Svensson	.08	.25
105 Peter Andersson	.30	.75
106 Mats Lusth	.08	.25
107 Tommy Moller	.08	.25
108 Leif Carlsson	.08	.25
109 Kent-Erik Andersson	.08	.25
110 Erkki Laine	.08	.25
111 Harald Luckner	.08	.25
112 Staffan Lundh	.08	.25
113 Kjell Dahlin	.75	2.00
114 Dan Mohlin	.08	.25
115 Jan Ingman	.08	.25
116 Stefan Persson	.40	1.00
117 Peter Berndtsson	.08	.25
118 Lars Karlsson	.08	.25
119 Claes-Henrik Silfver	.08	.25
120 Magnus Roupe	.30	.75
121 Conny Evensson	.30	.75
122 Bo Larsson	.08	.25
123 Hans-Goran Elo	.08	.25
124 Carsten Bokstrom	.08	.25
125 Claes Norstrom	.08	.25
126 Alf Tornqvist	.08	.25
127 Bruno Ohlzon	.08	.25
128 Peter Lindgren	.08	.25
129 Christian Due-Boije	.20	.50
130 Tony Landeskog	.08	.25
131 Tomas Lunden	.08	.25
132 Lars Lindskog	.08	.25
133 Anders Karlsson	.08	.25
134 Morgan Craas	.08	.25
135 Ulf Andersson	.08	.25
136 Timo Salomaa	.08	.25
137 Ulf Radbjer	.08	.25
138 Hans Segerberg	.08	.25
139 Roger Melin	.08	.25
140 Rolf Edberg	.08	.25
141 Lasse Bjork	.08	.25
142 Robin Eriksson	.08	.25
143 Thomas Jagenstedt	.08	.25
144 Jan Lindberg	.08	.25
145 Bjorn Berggren	.08	.25
146 Tommy Nilsson	.08	.25
147 Stefan Lunner	.08	.25
148 Niklas Holmberg	.08	.25
149 Anders Alverud	.08	.25
150 Stefan Svensson	.08	.25
151 Jussi Lepisto	.08	.25
152 Kjell Samuelsson	.75	2.00
153 Magnus Svensson	.30	.75
154 Ove Pettersson	.08	.25
155 Stefan Nilsson	.08	.25
156 Jens Christiansson	.08	.25
157 Orjan Lindmark	.08	.25
158 Tomas Gustafsson	.08	.25
159 Jan Segersten	.08	.25
160 Jonas Bergqvist	.40	1.00
161 Per-Olof Carlsson	.08	.25
162 Hannu Oksanen	.08	.25
163 Dan Labraaten	.60	1.50
164 Ulf Skoglund	.08	.25
165 Ove Olsson	.08	.25
166 Mats Loov	.08	.25
167 Hakan Olsson	.08	.25
168 Carl-Erik Larsson	.08	.25
169 Dan Soderstrom	.08	.25
170 Mats Blomqvist	.08	.25
171 Robert Skoog	.08	.25
172 Lars Lindgren	.08	.25
173 Robert Nordmark	.30	.75
174 Kjell-Ake Johansson	.08	.25
175 Kari Heikkila	.08	.25
176 Torbjorn Wirf	.08	.25
177 Lars Modig	.08	.25
178 Bo Eriksson	.08	.25
179 Roger Ohman	.30	.75
180 Mats Ohman	.08	.25
181 Matti Ruisma	.08	.25
182 Erik Stalnacke	.08	.25
183 Jari Lindgren	.08	.25
184 Jens Hellgren	.08	.25
185 Lars-Goran Niemi	.08	.25
186 Tore Okvist	.08	.25
187 Ingemar Mikko	.08	.25
188 Roger Mikko	.08	.25
189 Rolf Karlsson	.08	.25
190 Petter Antti	.08	.25
191 Johan Stromvall	.08	.25
192 Tomas Backstrom	.08	.25
193 Jan Nilsson	.08	.25
194 Freddy Lindfors	.08	.25
195 Mats Abrahamsson	.08	.25
196 Ulf Nilsson	1.50	4.00
197 Goran Lindblom	.08	.25
198 Thomas Ahlen	.08	.25
199 Jens Johansson	.08	.25
200 Lars Marklund	.08	.25
201 Ola Stenlund	.08	.25
202 Ulf Lindblom	.08	.25
203 Olle Haggstrom	.08	.25
204 Ulf Agren	.08	.25
205 Mikael Granstedt	.08	.25
206 Hans Nilsson	.08	.25
207 Per Andersson	.08	.25
208 Jonny Forsman	.08	.25
209 Lars Nystrom	.08	.25
210 Niklas Mannberg	.08	.25
211 Peter Lundmark	.40	1.00
212 Claes Lindblom	.08	.25
213 Leif Hedlund	.08	.25
214 Roland Stoltz	.08	.25
215 Martin Pettersson	.08	.25
216 Jorgen Marklund	.08	.25
217 Mats Lundstrom	.08	.25
218 Tommy Andersson	.08	.25
219 Hardy Astrom	1.25	3.00
220 Sam Lindstahl	.30	.75
221 Jari Luoma	.08	.25
222 Anders Eldebrink	.30	.75
223 Ulf Borg	.08	.25
224 Bo Ericson	.08	.25
225 Tomas Jernberg	.08	.25
226 Peter Ekroth	.08	.25
227 Stefan Jonsson	.08	.25
228 Niklas Gallstedt	.08	.25
229 Jonas Heed	.08	.25
230 Jarmo Makitalo	.08	.25
231 Thom Eklund	.08	.25
232 Dan Hermansson	.08	.25
233 Glenn Johansson	.08	.25
234 Leif R. Carlsson	.08	.25
235 Johan Mellstrom	.08	.25
236 Niclas Lindgren	.08	.25
237 Peter Wallin	.08	.25
238 Hans Sarkijarvi	.08	.25
239 Anders Carlsson	.08	.25
240 Reine Karlsson	.08	.25
241 Conny Jansson	.08	.25
242 Stefan Karlsson	.08	.25
243 Timo Lahtinen	.08	.25

1985-86 Swedish Panini Stickers

Card	Low	High
1 AIK Team Emblem	.08	.25
2 Per Backman	.08	.25
3 Tomas Ostlund	.75	2.00
4 Gunnar Leidborg	.08	.25
5 Jari Munck	.08	.25
6 Jan Eriksson	.08	.25
7 Hans Cederholm	.08	.25
8 Bjorn Hellman	.08	.25
9 Tomas Ahlen	.08	.25
10 Roger Hellgren	.08	.25
11 Mats Alba	.08	.25
12 Roger Lindstrom	.08	.25
13 Team Picture Left	.08	.25
14 Team Picture Right	.08	.25
15 Mats Hessel	.08	.25
16 Peter Gradin	.08	.25
17 Thomas Bjuhr	.08	.25
18 Per Martinelle	.08	.25
19 Tommy Lehman	.20	.50
20 Thomas Jagenstedt	.08	.25
21 Hans Segerberg	.08	.25
22 Odd Nilsson	.08	.25
23 Bjorkloven Team Picture L	.08	.25
24 Bjorkloven Team Picture U	.08	.25
25 Jakob Gustavsson	.08	.25
26 Gote Walitalo	.08	.25
27 Torbjorn Andersson	.08	.25
28 Jan Lindholm	.08	.25
29 Lars Karlsson	.08	.25
30 Calle Johansson	.75	2.00
31 Ulf Nilsson	1.25	3.00
32 Rolf Berglund	.08	.25
33 Matti Pauna	.08	.25
34 Mikael Andersson	.75	2.00
35 Tommy Sandlin	.08	.25
36 Team Emblem	.08	.25
37 Hans Edlund	.08	.25
38 Ulf Dahlen	1.25	3.00
39 Mikael Hjalm	.08	.25
40 Jon Lundstrom	.08	.25
41 Lars-Gunnar Pettersson	.08	.25
42 Peter Edstrom	.08	.25
43 Tore Oqvist	.08	.25
44 Par Edlund	.08	.25
45 Brynas Team Emblem	.08	.25
46 Stig Salming	.08	.25
47 Lars Eriksson	.08	.25
48 Ake Lilljebjorn	.08	.25
49 Anders Backstrom	.08	.25
50 Lars Ivarsson	.08	.25
51 Mats Kihlstrom	.08	.25
52 Jan Ove Mettavainio	.08	.25
53 Gunnar Persson	.08	.25
54 Torbjorn Mattsson	.08	.25
55 Christer Andersson	.08	.25
56 Per Hedenstrom	.08	.25
57 Team Picture L	.08	.25
58 Team Picture R	.08	.25
59 Per Nilsson	.08	.25
60 Conny Silfverberg	.08	.25
61 Jonny Stridh	.08	.25
62 Owe Eriksson	.08	.25
63 Kenneth Andersson	.08	.25
64 Erik Holmberg	.08	.25
65 Joakim Pehrson	.08	.25
66 Anders Huss	.20	.50
67 Djurgarden Team Picture L	.08	.25
68 Djurgarden Team Picture R	.08	.25
69 Rolf Ridderwall	.40	1.00
70 Mats Ytter	.20	.50
71 Orvar Stambert	.08	.25
72 Karl-Erik Lilja	.08	.25
73 Arto Blomsten	.20	.50
74 Stefan Perlstrom	.08	.25
75 Peter Lindgren	.08	.25
76 Tommy Albelin	.30	.75
77 Jens Ohling	.08	.25
78 Peter Nilsson	.08	.25
79 Gunnar Svenson	.08	.25
80 Team Emblem	.08	.25
81 Jorgen Holmberg	.08	.25
82 Tommy Morth	.08	.25
83 Bjorn Carlsson	.08	.25
84 Hakan Sodergren	.20	.50
85 Anders Johnson	.08	.25
86 Mikael Johansson	.08	.25
87 Jan Viktorsson	.08	.25
88 Erik Ahlstrom	.08	.25
89 Farjestad Team Emblem	.08	.25
90 Conny Evensson	.20	.50
91 Peter Lindmark	.60	1.50
92 Christer Dalgard	.08	.25
93 Tommy Samuelsson	.08	.25
94 Peter Andersson	.30	.75
95 Mats Lusth	.08	.25
96 Leif Karlsson	.08	.25
97 Fredrik Olausson	.75	2.00
98 Hakan Nordin	.08	.25
99 Harald Luckner	.08	.25
100 Tomas Rundqvist	.20	.50
101 Team Picture L	.08	.25
102 Team Picture R	.08	.25
103 Jan Ingman	.08	.25
104 Erkki Laine	.08	.25
105 Stefan Persson	.40	1.00
106 Claes-Henrik Silfver	.08	.25
107 Magnus Roupe	.30	.75
108 Mikael Holmberg	.08	.25
109 Kent-Erik Andersson	.08	.25
110 Staffan Lundh	.08	.25
111 Kjell Dahlin U	.20	.50
112 Kjell Dahlin L	.20	.50
113 Kjell Samuelsson U	.40	1.00
114 Kjell Samuelsson L	.40	1.00
115 Peter Lindmark U	.20	.50
116 Peter Lindmark L	.20	.50
117 Pelle Lindberg U	4.00	10.00
118 Pelle Lindberg L	4.00	10.00
119 Per-Erik Eklund U	.30	.75
120 Per-Erik Eklund L	.30	.75
121 Anders Eldebrink L	.15	.40
122 Anders Eldebrink R	.15	.40
123 Michael Thelven U	.15	.40
124 Michael Thelven L	.15	.40
125 Dan Labraaten L	.20	.50
126 Dan Labraaten R	.20	.50
127 Ove Olsson L	.08	.25
128 Ove Olsson R	.08	.25
129 Kent-E Andersson L	.08	.25
130 Kent-E Andersson R	.08	.25
131 Leksand Team Emblem	.08	.25
132 Dan Soderstrom	.08	.25
133 Stefan Lunner	.08	.25
134 Peter Aslin	.40	1.00
135 Jussi Lepisto	.08	.25
136 Magnus Svensson	.30	.75
137 Owe Pettersson	.08	.25
138 Stefan Nilsson	.08	.25
139 Orjan Lindmark	.08	.25
140 Tomas Nord	.08	.25
141 Robert Burakovsky	.20	.50
142 Jan Segersten	.08	.25
143 Team Picture L	.08	.25
144 Team Picture R	.08	.25
145 Jonas Bergkvist	.30	.75
146 Per-Olof Carlsson	.08	.25
147 Dan Labraaten	.40	1.00
148 Ulf Skoglund	.08	.25
149 Ove Olsson	.08	.25
150 Heinz Ehlers	.08	.25
151 Mats Loov	.08	.25
152 Jarmo Makitalo	.08	.25
153 Lulea Team Picture L	.08	.25
154 Lulea Team Picture R	.08	.25
155 Mats Blomqvist	.08	.25
156 Robert Skoog	.08	.25
157 Lars Modig	.08	.25
158 Kjell-Ake Johansson	.08	.25
159 Bo Eriksson	.08	.25
160 Robert Nordmark	.20	.50
161 Kari Heikkila	.08	.25
162 Lars Lindgren	.08	.25
163 Roger Mikko	.08	.25
164 Kari Jaako	.08	.25
165 Hans Lindberg	.08	.25
166 Team Emblem	.08	.25
167 Petter Antti	.08	.25
168 Johan Stromvall	.08	.25
169 Juha Nurmi	.08	.25
170 Erik Stalnacke	.08	.25
171 Lars Hurtig	.08	.25
172 Jari Lindgren	.08	.25
173 Jens Hellgren	.08	.25
174 Hans Norberg	.08	.25
175 HV 71 Team Emblem	.08	.25
176 Curt Lundmark	.40	1.00
177 Kenneth Johansson	.08	.25
178 Tomas Javeblad	.08	.25
179 Nils-G Svensson	.08	.25
180 Bert-Roland Naslund	.08	.25
181 Kevan Beaton	.08	.25
182 Jan Hedell	.08	.25
183 Fredrik Stillman	.15	.40
184 Kari Eloranta	.30	.75
185 Klas Heed	.08	.25
186 Hans Sallin	.08	.25
187 Team Picture L	.08	.25
188 Team Picture R	.08	.25
189 Ove Tornberg	.08	.25
190 Thomas Ljungberg	.08	.25
191 Bengt Kinell	.08	.25
192 Roland Eriksson	.08	.25
193 Uno Johansson	.08	.25
194 Ivan Hansen	.08	.25
195 Thomas Lindster	.08	.25
196 Per Martinsson	.08	.25
197 MoDo Team Picture L	.08	.25
198 MoDo Team Picture R	.08	.25
199 Anders Bergman	.08	.25
200 Goran Arnmark	.08	.25
201 Thomas Olofsson	.08	.25
202 Jorgen Palm	.08	.25
203 Ulf Agren	.08	.25
204 Roger Eliasson	.08	.25
205 Juha Tuohimaa	.08	.25
206 Jan Karlsson	.08	.25
207 Lennart Jonsson	.08	.25
208 Ulf Norberg	.08	.25
209 Hakan Nygren	.08	.25
210 Team Emblem	.08	.25
211 Hakan Hjerpe	.08	.25
212 Anders Wikberg	.08	.25
213 P-A Alexandersson	.08	.25
214 Ingemar Strom	.08	.25
215 Tommy Eriksson	.08	.25
216 Lars Molin	.20	.50
217 Lars Bystrom	.08	.25
218 Pekka Arbelius	.08	.25
219 Sodertalje Team Emblem	.08	.25
220 Kjell Larsson	.08	.25
221 Sam Lindstal	.08	.25
222 Hardy Astrom	1.25	3.00
223 Anders Eldebrink	.30	.75
224 Niklas Gallstedt	.08	.25
225 Jonas Heed	.08	.25
226 Peter Ekroth	.08	.25
227 Bo Eriksson	.08	.25
228 Stefan Jonsson	.08	.25
229 Thom Eklund	.08	.25
230 Glenn Johansson	.08	.25
231 Team Picture L	.08	.25
232 Team Picture R	.08	.25
233 Leif Carlsson	.08	.25
234 Jan Claesson	.08	.25
235 Niclas Lindgren	.08	.25
236 Peter Wallin	.08	.25
237 Hans Sarkijarvi	.08	.25
238 Reine Karlsson	.08	.25
239 Conny Jansson	.08	.25
240 Anders Carlsson	.08	.25

1986-87 Swedish Panini Stickers

Card	Low	High
COMPLETE SET (270)	20.00	50.00
1 Bjorkloven Team Emblem	.08	.25
2 Hans Lindberg	.08	.25
3 Gote Walitalo	.08	.25
4 Jakob Gustavsson	.08	.25
5 Torbjorn Andersson	.08	.25
6 Lars Karlsson	.08	.25
7 Calle Johansson	.40	1.00
8 Rolf Berglund	.08	.25
9 Patrik Aberg	.08	.25
10 Niclas Holmgren	.08	.25
11 Roger Hagglund	.08	.25
12 Team Picture Left	.08	.25
13 Team Picture Right	.08	.25
14 Peter Andersson	.30	.75
15 Tore Oqvist	.08	.25
16 Johan Tornqvist	.08	.25
17 Par Edlund	.08	.25
18 Stefan Nilsson	.08	.25
19 Matti Pauna	.08	.25
20 Lars-Gunnar Pettersson	.08	.25
21 Mikael Hjalm	.08	.25
22 Hans Edlund	.08	.25
23 Peter Sundstrom	.40	1.00
24 Jon Lundstrom	.08	.25
25 Peter Edstrom	.08	.25
26 Mikael Andersson	.40	1.00
27 Ulf Dahlen	.75	2.00
28 Brynas Team Emblem	.08	.25
29 Stig Salming	.08	.25
30 Ake Lilljebjorn	.08	.25
31 Lars Eriksson	.08	.25
32 Christer Lundqvist	.08	.25
33 Lars Ivarsson	.08	.25
34 Torbjorn Mattsson	.08	.25
35 Gunnar Persson	.08	.25

36 Anders Backstrom .08 .25
37 Team Picture L .08 .25
38 Team Picture R .08 .25
39 Jan Ove Mettavainio .08 .25
40 Par Djoos .20 .50
41 Tommy Sjodin .40 1.00
42 Conny Silfverberg .08 .25
43 Christer Andersson .08 .25
44 Kenneth Andersson .08 .25
45 Lars Andersson .08 .25
46 Anders Huss .08 .25
47 Joakim Pehrson .08 .25
48 Jonny Stridh .08 .25
49 Patrik Eriksson .08 .25
50 Anders Ivarsson .08 .25
51 Mikael Lindholm .08 .25
52 Jan Larsson .08 .25
53 Peter Eriksson .08 .25
54 Jan Gronberg .08 .25
55 Djurgarden Team Emblem .08 .25
56 Leif Boork .08 .25
57 Rolf Ridderwall .40 1.00
58 Hans-Goran Elo .08 .25
59 Tommy Albelin .40 1.00
60 Orvar Stambert .08 .25
61 Tomas Eriksson .08 .25
62 Stefan Perlstrom .08 .25
63 Arto Blomsten .20 .50
64 Christian Due-Boije .20 .50
65 Kalle Lilja .08 .25
66 Team Picture L .08 .25
67 Team Picture R .08 .25
68 Stefan Jansson .08 .25
69 Hakan Sodergren .08 .25
70 Jens Ohling .08 .25
71 Peter Nilsson .08 .25
72 Tommy Morth .08 .25
73 Bjorn Carlsson .08 .25
74 Per Goransson .08 .25
75 Pontus Molander .08 .25
76 Jeff Hallegard .08 .25
77 Tomaz Eriksson .08 .25
78 Mikael Johansson .08 .25
79 Anders Johnson .08 .25
80 Jan Viktorsson .08 .25
81 Johan Garpenlov .40 1.00
82 Farjestad Team Emblem .08 .25
83 Conny Evensson .20 .50
84 Peter Lindmark .40 1.00
85 Christer Dalgard .08 .25
86 Tommy Samuelsson .08 .25
87 Mats Lusth .08 .25
88 Peter Andersson .08 .25
89 Hakan Nordin .08 .25
90 Leif Carlsson .08 .25
91 Team Picture L .08 .25
92 Team Picture R .08 .25
93 Patrik Lundback .08 .25
94 Anders Berglund .08 .25
95 Roger Johansson .08 .25
96 Thomas Rundqvist .20 .50
97 Harald Luckner .08 .25
98 Erkki Laine .08 .25
99 Jan Ingman .08 .25
100 Staffan Lund .08 .25
101 Claes-Henrik Silfver .08 .25
102 Magnus Roupe .20 .50
103 Stefan Persson .40 1.00
104 Daniel Rydmark .08 .25
105 Bo Svanberg .08 .25
106 Mikael Holmberg .08 .25
107 Tomas Tallberg .08 .25
108 Kjell Augustsson .08 .25
109 HV 71 Team Emblem .08 .25
110 Curt Lundmark .20 .50
111 Thomas Javeblad .08 .25
112 Kenneth Johansson .08 .25
113 Kari Eloranta .30 .75
114 Jan Hedell .08 .25
115 Arto Routanen .08 .25
116 Klas Heed .08 .25
117 Bert-Roland Naslund .08 .25
118 Nils-Gunnar Svensson .08 .25
119 Fredrik Stillman .08 .25
120 Team Picture L .08 .25
121 Team Picture R .08 .25
122 Nicklas Carlsson .08 .25
123 Ivan Hansen .08 .25
124 Thomas Ljungberg .08 .25
125 Peter Eriksson .08 .25
126 Hans Wallin .08 .25
127 Ove Thornberg .08 .25
128 Per Martinsson .08 .25
129 Mats Loov .08 .25
130 Stefan Nilsson .08 .25
131 Peter Eriksson .08 .25
132 Thomas Lindster .08 .25
133 Boo Peterzen .08 .25
134 Stefan Falk .08 .25
135 Torgny Karlsson .08 .25
136 Leksand Team Emblem .08 .25
137 Kalle Alander .08 .25
138 Peter Aslin .30 .75
139 Bengt-Ake Pers .08 .25
140 Magnus Svensson .20 .50
141 Ove Pettersson .08 .25
142 Stefan Nilsson .08 .25
143 Jens Christiansson .08 .25
144 Leif Eriksson .08 .25
145 Team Picture L .08 .25
146 Team Picture R .08 .25
147 Orjan Lindmark .08 .25
148 Thomas Nord .08 .25
149 Peter Imhauser .08 .25
150 Dan Labraaten .40 1.00
151 Ulf Skoglund .08 .25
152 Jarmo Makitalo .08 .25
153 Per-Olof Carlsson .08 .25
154 Ove Olsson .08 .25
155 Heinz Ehlers .08 .25
156 Jonas Bergqvist .20 .50
157 Robert Burakovsky .20 .50
158 Carl-Erik Larsson .08 .25
159 Cenneth Soderlund .08 .25
160 Ola Sundberg .08 .25
161 Ronny Reichenberg .08 .25
162 Hans Jax .08 .25
163 Lulea Team Emblem .08 .25
164 Freddy Lindfors .08 .25
165 Mats Blomqvist .08 .25
166 Robert Skoog .08 .25
167 Robert Nordmark .20 .50
168 Lars Lindgren .08 .25
169 Lars Modig .08 .25
170 Bo Eriksson .08 .25
171 Kjell-Ake Johansson .08 .25
172 Roger Akerstrom .08 .25
173 Juha Tuohimaa .08 .25
174 Team Picture L .08 .25
175 Team Picture R .08 .25
176 Mats Ohman .08 .25
177 Erik Stalnacke .08 .25
178 Juha Nurmi .08 .25
179 Lars-Goran Niemi .08 .25
180 Hans Norberg .08 .25
181 Jari Lindgren .08 .25
182 Roger Mikko .08 .25
183 Lars Hurtig .08 .25
184 Johan Stromvall .08 .25
185 Jens Hellgren .08 .25
186 Kari Jaako .08 .25
187 Stefan Nilsson .08 .25
188 Ulf Taavola .08 .25
189 Tomas Edstrom .08 .25
190 MoDo Team Emblem .08 .25
191 Hakan Nygren .08 .25
192 Anders Bergman .08 .25
193 Fredrik Andersson .08 .25
194 Robert Frestadius .08 .25
195 Jouko Narvanmaa .08 .25
196 Jan Asplund .08 .25
197 Ulf Agren .08 .25
198 Jorgen Palm .08 .25
199 Team Picture L .08 .25
200 Team Picture R .08 .25
201 Per Forsberg .08 .25
202 Jens Johansson .08 .25
203 Hans Lodin .08 .25
204 Lars Molin .08 .25
205 Per-Arne Alexandersson .08 .25
206 Pecka Arbelius .08 .25
207 Per Nilsson .08 .25
208 Anders Wikberg .08 .25
209 Lars Bystrom .08 .25
210 Ulf Odmark .08 .25
211 Robert Tedenby .08 .25
212 Kent Lantz .08 .25
213 Ulf Sandstrom .08 .25
214 Mikael Pettersson .08 .25
215 Peter Smedberg .08 .25
216 Mikael Stahl .08 .25
217 Skelleftea Team Emblem .08 .25
218 Christer Abrahamsson .40 1.00
219 Mats Abrahamsson .08 .25
220 Ulf Nilsson 1.00 2.50
221 Goran Lindblom .08 .25
222 Lars Marklund .08 .25
223 Ola Stenlund .08 .25
224 Serge Roy .20 .50
225 Mikael Lindman .08 .25
226 Robert Larsson .08 .25
227 Stefan Svensson .08 .25
228 Team Picture L .08 .25
229 Team Picture R .08 .25
230 Roland Stoltz .08 .25
231 Martin Pettersson .08 .25
232 Jonny Forsman .08 .25
233 Tomas Hedin .08 .25
234 Mikael Granstedt .08 .25
235 Randy Heath .08 .25
236 Peter Lundmark .30 .75
237 Niklas Mannberg .08 .25
238 Claes Lindblom .20 .50
239 Mats Lundmark .08 .25
240 Jorgen Marklund .08 .25
241 Daniel Pettersson .08 .25
242 Mats Lundstrom .08 .25
243 Hans Hjalmar .08 .25
244 Sodertalje Team Emblem .08 .25
245 Dan Hober .08 .25
246 Sam Lindstahl .08 .25
247 Reino Sundberg .08 .25
248 Anders Eldebrink .20 .50
249 Mats Kihlstrom .08 .25
250 Ulf Borg .08 .25
251 Bo Ericsson .08 .25
252 Peter Ekroth .08 .25
253 Team Picture L .08 .25
254 Team Picture R .08 .25
255 Jonas Heed .08 .25
256 Stefan Jonsson .08 .25
257 Hans Pettersson .08 .25
258 Hans Sarkijarvi .08 .25
259 Thom Eklund .08 .25
260 Glenn Johansson .08 .25
261 Peter Loob .08 .25
262 Niklas Lindgren .08 .25
263 Conny Jansson .08 .25
264 Tomas Jernberg .08 .25
265 Reine Karlsson .08 .25
266 Anders Frykbo .08 .25
267 Jan Loob .08 .25
268 Peter Larsson .08 .25
269 Erik Holmberg .08 .25
270 Jorgen Winborg .08 .25

1987-88 Swedish Panini Stickers

COMPLETE SET (270) 20.00 50.00
1 AIK Team Emblem .08 .25
2 AIK Team Picture Left .08 .25
3 AIK Team Picture Right .08 .25
4 Lars-Gunnar Jansson .20 .50
5 Ake Liljebjorn .08 .25
6 Thomas Ostlund .40 1.00
7 Jan Eriksson .08 .25
8 Hans Cederholm .08 .25
9 Rickard Franzen .08 .25
10 Thomas Ahlen .08 .25
11 Mats Thelin .20 .50
12 Bjorn Hellman .08 .25
13 Peter Gradin .20 .50
14 Bjorn Carlsson .08 .25
15 Anders Gozzi .08 .25
16 Per Martinelle .08 .25
17 Bo Berglund .20 .50
18 Thomas Gradin .40 1.00
19 Hans Segerberg .08 .25
20 Odd Nilsson .08 .25
21 Mats Hessel .08 .25
22 IF Bjorkloven Team Emblem .08 .25
23 IF Bjorkloven Team Picture Left .08 .25
24 IF Bjorkloven Team Picture Right .08 .25
25 Rolf Jager .08 .25
26 Gote Walitalo .08 .25
27 Staffan Andersson .08 .25
28 Torbjorn Andersson .08 .25
29 Lars Karlsson .08 .25
30 Roger Hagglund .08 .25
31 Rolf Berglund .08 .25
32 Peter Andersson .08 .25
33 Age Ellingsen .08 .25
34 Matti Pauna .08 .25
35 Tore Oqvist .08 .25
36 Mikael Andersson .40 1.00
37 Hans Edlund .08 .25
38 Johan Tornqvist .08 .25
39 Peter Edstrom .08 .25
40 Par Edlund .08 .25
41 Erik Kristiansen .08 .25
42 Ulf Andersson .08 .25
43 Brynas IF Team Emblem .08 .25
44 Brynas IF Team Picture Left .08 .25
45 Brynas IF Team Picture Right .08 .25
46 Tord Lundstrom .08 .25
47 Lars Eriksson .08 .25
48 Michael Sundlov .40 1.00
49 Lars Ivarsson .08 .25
50 Par Djoos .20 .50
51 Jan Ove Mettavainio .08 .25
52 Anders Backstrom .08 .25
53 Gunnar Persson .08 .25
54 Christer Andersson .08 .25
55 Conny Silfverberg .08 .25
56 Jonny Stridh .08 .25
57 Kyosti Karjalainen .20 .50
58 Willy Lindstrom .30 .75
59 Joakim Pehrson .08 .25
60 Patrik Erickson .08 .25
61 Anders Huss .08 .25
62 Peter Eriksson .08 .25
63 Jan Larsson .08 .25
64 Djurgardens IF Team Emblem .08 .25
65 Djurgardens IF Team Picture Left .08 .25
66 Djurgardens IF Team Picture Right .08 .25
67 Ingvar Karlsson .08 .25
68 Rolf Ridderwall .40 1.00
69 Hans-Goran Elo .08 .25
70 Orvar Stambert .08 .25
71 Kalle Lilja .08 .25
72 Arto Blomsten .20 .50
73 Stefan Jansson .08 .25
74 Tomas Eriksson .08 .25
75 Christian Due-Boije .20 .50
76 Jens Ohling .08 .25
77 Pontus Molander .08 .25
78 Tommy Morth .08 .25
79 Johan Garpenlov .40 1.00
80 Hakan Sodergren .08 .25
81 Anders Johnson .08 .25
82 Mikael Johansson .08 .25
83 Jan Viktorsson .08 .25
84 Peter Nilsson .08 .25
85 Farjestads BK Team Emblem .08 .25
86 Farjestads BK Team Picture Left .08 .25
87 Farjestads BK Team Picture Right .08 .25
88 Per Backman .08 .25
89 Peter Lindmark .40 1.00
90 Christer Dalgard .08 .25
91 Tommy Samuelsson .08 .25
92 Peter Andersson .08 .25
93 Mats Lusth .08 .25
94 Leif Carlsson .08 .25
95 Jesper Duus .08 .25
96 Hakan Nordin .08 .25
97 Thomas Rundqvist .20 .50
98 Staffan Lund .08 .25
99 Harald Luckner .08 .25
100 Erkki Laine .08 .25
101 Stefan Persson .30 .75
102 Bo Svanberg .08 .25
103 Claes-Henrik Silfver .08 .25
104 Mikael Holmberg .08 .25
105 Roger Johansson .08 .25
106 HV 71 Team Emblem .08 .25
107 HV 71 Team Picture Left .08 .25
108 HV 71 Team Picture Right .08 .25
109 Curt Lundmark .40 1.00
110 Kenneth Johansson .08 .25
111 Boo Peterzen .08 .25
112 Arto Routanen .08 .25
113 Jan Hedell .08 .25
114 Fredrik Stillman .08 .25
115 Reijo Ruotsalainen .40 1.00
116 Bert-Roland Naslund .08 .25
117 Peter Eriksson .08 .25
118 Hans Wallin .08 .25
119 Peter Berndtsson .08 .25
120 Mats Loov .08 .25
121 Thomas Lindster .08 .25
122 Peter Eriksson .08 .25
123 Hasse Sjoo .08 .25
124 Stefan Nilsson .08 .25
125 Stefan Falk .08 .25
126 Ove Thornberg .08 .25
127 Wash Out .08 .25
128 Butt-Ending .08 .25
129 Fordrojd Signal .08 .25
130 Hakning .08 .25
131 Charging .08 .25
132 Olampligt Uppträdande .08 .25
133 Fasthallning .08 .25
134 Hog Klubba .08 .25
135 Tripping .08 .25
136 Cross Checking .08 .25
137 Armbagstackling .08 .25
138 Icing .08 .25
139 Icing .08 .25
140 Boarding .08 .25
141 Slashing .08 .25
142 Roughing .08 .25
143 Spearing .08 .25
144 Interference .08 .25
145 Leksands IF Team Emblem .08 .25
146 Leksands IF Team Picture Left .08 .25
147 Leksands IF Team Picture Right .08 .25
148 Christer Abrahamsson .40 1.00
149 Peter Aslin .20 .50
150 Bengt-Ake Pers .08 .25
151 Magnus Svensson .20 .50
152 Stefan Nilsson .08 .25
153 Orjan Lindmark .08 .25
154 Thomas Nord .08 .25
155 Peter Imhauser .08 .25
156 Stefan Larsson .08 .25
157 Robert Burakovsky .20 .50
158 Jonas Bergqvist .20 .50
159 Heinz Ehlers .08 .25
160 Ivan Hansen .08 .25
161 Jarmo Makitalo .08 .25
162 Dan Labraaten .30 .75
163 Per-Olof Carlsson .08 .25
164 Carl-Erik Larsson .08 .25
165 Ulf Skoglund .08 .25
166 Lulea Hockey Team Emblem .08 .25
167 Lulea Hockey Team Picture Left .08 .25
168 Lulea Hockey Team Picture Right .08 .25
169 Freddy Lindfors .08 .25
170 Tomas Javeblad .08 .25
171 Robert Skoog .08 .25
172 Juha Tuohimaa .08 .25
173 Bo Eriksson .08 .25
174 Roger Akerstrom .08 .25
175 Lars Lindgren .08 .25
176 Lars Modig .08 .25
177 Erik Stalnacke .08 .25
178 Johan Stromvall .08 .25
179 Juha Nurmi .08 .25
180 Lars-Goran Niemi .08 .25
181 Jari Lindgren .08 .25
182 Lars-Gunnar Pettersson .08 .25
183 Hans Norberg .08 .25
184 Kari Jaako .08 .25
185 Lars Hurtig .08 .25
186 Jens Hellgren .08 .25
187 MoDo Hockey Team Emblem .08 .25
188 MoDo Hockey Team Picture Left .08 .25
189 MoDo Hockey Team Picture Right .08 .25
190 Anders Nordin .08 .25
191 Anders Bergman .08 .25
192 Fredrik Andersson .08 .25
193 Hans Lodin .08 .25
194 Jens Johansson .08 .25
195 Jouko Narvanmaa .08 .25
196 Robert Frestadius .08 .25
197 Per Forsberg .08 .25
198 Mikael Hjalm .08 .25
199 Ulf Sandstrom .08 .25
200 Ulf Odmark .08 .25
201 Per Nilsson .08 .25
202 Anders Wikberg .08 .25
203 Lars Molin .20 .50
204 Per-Arne Alexandersson .08 .25
205 Lars Bystrom .08 .25
206 Mikael Stahl .08 .25
207 Ove Pettersson .08 .25
208 Skelleftea Hockey Team Emblem .08 .25
209 Skelleftea Hockey Team Picture Left .08 .25
210 Skelleftea Hockey Team Picture Right .08 .25
211 Tommie Bergman .40 1.00
212 Ulf Nilsson .75 2.00
213 Sam Lindstahl .08 .25
214 Lars Marklund .08 .25
215 Goran Lindblom .08 .25
216 Ola Stenlund .08 .25
217 Stefan Svensson .08 .25
218 Kari Suoraniemi .08 .25
219 Hans Hjalmar .08 .25
220 Mikael Granstedt .08 .25
221 Mats Lundstrom .08 .25
222 Jonny Forsman .08 .25
223 Kari Jalonen .20 .50
224 Claes Lindblom .20 .50
225 Tomas Hedin .08 .25
226 Martin Pettersson .08 .25
227 Jorgen Marklund .08 .25
228 Niklas Mannberg .08 .25
229 Sodertalje SK Team Emblem .08 .25
230 Sodertalje SK Team Picture Left .08 .25
231 Sodertalje SK Team Picture Right .08 .25
232 John Pettersson .08 .25
233 Reino Sundberg .08 .25
234 Jari Luoma .08 .25
235 Anders Eldebrink .20 .50
236 Mats Kihlstrom .08 .25
237 Jonas Heed .08 .25
238 Bo Ericsson .08 .25
239 Ulf Borg .08 .25
240 Stefan Jonsson .08 .25
241 Mats Hallin .08 .25
242 Glenn Johansson .08 .25
243 Thomas Ljungberg .08 .25
244 Hans Sarkijarvi .08 .25
245 Thom Eklund .08 .25
246 Peter Larsson .08 .25
247 Conny Jansson .08 .25
248 Niklas Lindgren .08 .25
249 Reine Karlsson .08 .25
250 Vasby IK Team Emblem .08 .25
251 Vasby IK Team Picture Left .08 .25
252 Vasby IK Team Picture Right .08 .25
253 Anders Jacobsen .08 .25
254 Jorgen Larsson .08 .25
255 Stefan Sohlin .08 .25
256 Torbjorn Mattsson .08 .25
257 Hakan Persson .08 .25
258 Kenneth Lindqvist .08 .25
259 Jens Mackegard .08 .25
260 Anders Lindberg .08 .25
261 Mats Edholm .08 .25
262 Mats Poppler .08 .25
263 Claes Gustafsson .08 .25
264 Per Bergman .08 .25
265 Peter Wallen .08 .25
266 Hans-Rickard Andersson .08 .25
267 Arto Heinola .08 .25
268 Mats Lindberg .08 .25
269 Urban Jakobsson .08 .25
270 Stefan Sandin .08 .25

1989 Swedish Semic World Championship Stickers

COMPLETE SET (200) 100.00 250.00
1 Sweden National Emblem .02 .10
2 Tommy Sandlin .08 .25
3 Peter Lindmark .08 .25
4 Rolf Ridderwall .08 .25
5 Tomas Jonsson .08 .25
6 Tommy Albelin .08 .25
7 Mats Kihlstrom .02 .10
8 Tommy Samuelsson .02 .10
9 Anders Eldebrink .05 .15
10 Fredrik Olausson .08 .25
11 Peter Andersson .05 .15
12 Thomas Eriksson .02 .10
13 Thom Eklund .02 .10
14 Bo Berglund .05 .15
15 Thomas Steen .15 .40
16 Ulf Sandstrom .02 .10
17 Jonas Bergkvist .08 .25
18 Thomas Rundqvist .05 .15
19 Per-Erik Eklund .20 .50
20 Bengt-Ake Gustavsson .05 .15
21 Patrik Sundstrom .15 .40
22 Mikael Johansson .05 .15
23 Hakan Sodergren .02 .10
24 Kent Nilsson .20 .50
25 Lars-Gunnar Pettersson .02 .10
26 Finland National Emblem .02 .10
27 Pentti Matikainen .02 .10
28 Jukka Tammi .08 .25
29 Sakari Lindfors .08 .25
30 Reijo Ruotsalainen .08 .25
31 Kari Eloranta .08 .25
32 Timo Blomqvist .08 .25
33 Simo Saarinen .02 .10
34 Hannu Virta .08 .25
35 Jouko Narvanmaa .02 .10
36 Jarmo Kuusisto .02 .10
37 Kari Suoraniemi .02 .10
38 Reijo Mikkolainen .02 .10
39 Raimo Helminen .08 .25
40 Raimo Summanen .08 .25
41 Mikko Makela .08 .25
42 Kari Jalonen .02 .10
43 Kari Laitinen .02 .10
44 Petri Skriko .15 .40
45 Erkki Laine .02 .10
46 Pauli Jarvinen .02 .10
47 Jukka Vilander .02 .10
48 Esa Keskinen .15 .40
49 Ari Vuori .02 .10
50 Mika Nieminen .15 .40
51 Canada National Emblem .08 .25
52 Dave King .08 .25
53 Grant Fuhr 4.00 10.00
54 Patrick Roy 4.00 10.00
55 Ron Hextall .75 2.00
56 Al MacInnis .60 1.50
57 Ray Bourque 4.00 10.00
58 Scott Stevens .20 .50
59 Paul Coffey 1.25 3.00
60 Zarley Zalapski .15 .40
61 James Patrick .15 .40
62 Kevin Lowe .15 .40
63 Brad McCrimmon .15 .40
64 Mario Lemieux 12.00 30.00
65 Wayne Gretzky 20.00 50.00
66 Denis Savard .30 .75
67 Dale Hawerchuk .40 1.00
68 Luc Robitaille .75 2.00
69 Mark Messier 4.00 10.00
70 Michel Goulet .20 .50
71 Cam Neely 2.00 5.00
72 Steve Yzerman 10.00 25.00
73 Bernie Nicholls .30 .75
74 Joe Nieuwendyk .40 1.00
75 Mike Gartner .40 1.00
76 USSR National Emblem .08 .25
77 Viktor Tichonov .07 .20
78 Jevgenij Belosjejkin .20 .50
79 Sergei Mylnikov .20 .50
80 Sergei Golosjumov .08 .25
81 Alexei Kasatonov .20 .50
82 Aleksej Gusarov .08 .25
83 Andrej Smirnov .05 .15
84 Valerij Sjirjajev .05 .15
85 Igor Stelnov .05 .15
86 Vladimir Konstantinov 1.25 3.00
87 Slava Fetisov .40 1.00
88 Sergei Jasjin .05 .15
89 Vladimir Krutov .30 .75
90 Igor Larionov .75 2.00
91 Valerij Kamenskij .20 .50
92 Vjatjeslav Bykov .20 .50
93 Andrej Chomutov .20 .50
94 Yuri Khmylev .20 .50
95 Sergei Nemchinov .20 .50
96 Sergei Makarov .40 1.00
97 Igor Jesmantovitj .05 .15
98 Andrei Lomakin .07 .20
99 Anatolij Semjonov .08 .25
100 Aleksandr Tjernych .05 .15
101 West Germany National Emblem .02 .10
102 Xaver Unsinn .08 .25
103 Karl Friesen .08 .25
104 Josef Schlickenrieder .02 .10
105 Matthias Hoppe .02 .10
106 Andreas Niederberger .02 .10
107 Udo Kiessling .05 .15
108 Uli Hiemer .05 .15
109 Harold Kreis .05 .15
110 Manfred Schuster .02 .10
111 Jorg Hanft .02 .10
112 Ron Fischer .02 .10
113 Michael Heidt .05 .15
114 Dieter Hegen .05 .15
115 Gerd Truntschka .05 .15
116 Helmut Steiger .02 .10
117 Georg Franz .02 .10
118 Georg Holzmann .02 .10
119 Peter Obresa .02 .10
120 Bernd Truntschka .05 .15
121 Manfred Wolf .02 .10
122 Roy Roedger .02 .10
123 Axel Kammerer .02 .10
124 Peter Draisaitl .07 .20
125 Daniel Held .02 .10
126 Poland National Emblem .02 .10
127 Leszek Lejczyk .07 .20
128 Jerzy Mruk .07 .20
129 Andrezej Hanisz .02 .10
130 Dariusz Wieczorek .02 .10
131 Jacek Zamojski .02 .10
132 Marek Cholewa .02 .10
133 Henryk Gruth .02 .10
134 Robert Szopinski .02 .10
135 Jerzy Potz .02 .10
136 Andrzej Swiatek .02 .10
137 Ludvik Czapka .02 .10
138 Piotr Zdunek .02 .10
139 Jedrzej Kasperczyk .02 .10
140 Krzysztof Podsiadlo .02 .10
141 Miroslaw Copija .02 .10
142 Krzysztof Bujar .02 .10
143 Janusz Adamiec .02 .10
144 Jacek Solinski .02 .10
145 Roman Steblecki .02 .10
146 Adam Fraszko .02 .10
147 Leszek Minge .02 .10
148 Piotr Kwasigroch .02 .10
149 Ireneusz Pacula .02 .10
150 1989 World Championship Emblem .02 .10
151 USA National Emblem .08 .25
152 Art Berglund .02 .10
153 Tom Barrasso 2.00 5.00
154 John Vanbiesbrouck 2.00 5.00
155 Gary Suter .20 .50
156 Phil Housley .20 .50
157 Chris Chelios 1.25 3.00
158 Mike Ramsey .08 .25
159 Rod Langway .08 .25
160 Mark Howe .15 .40
161 Brian Leetch 2.00 5.00
162 Al Iafrate .15 .40
163 Jimmy Carson .05 .15
164 Pat LaFontaine .40 1.00
165 Neal Broten .20 .50
166 Dave Christian .15 .40
167 Brett Hull 4.00 10.00
168 Bob Carpenter .08 .25
169 Ed Olczyk .08 .25
170 Joe Mullen .20 .50
171 Bob Brooke .05 .15
172 Brian Lawton .05 .15
173 Craig Janney .20 .50
174 Mark Johnson .08 .25
175 Chris Nilan .08 .25
176 CSSR National Emblem .02 .10
177 Pavel Wohl .02 .10
178 Dominik Hasek 40.00 100.00
179 Jaromir Sindel .08 .25
180 Petr Briza .40 1.00
181 Antonin Staviana .08 .25
182 Bedrich Scerban .07 .20
183 Petr Slanina .02 .10
184 Frantisek Kucera .07 .20
185 Jergus Baca .05 .15
186 Leo Gudas .05 .15
187 Drahomir Kadlec .05 .15
188 Mojmir Bozik .02 .10
189 Petr Vlk .02 .10
190 Vladimir Ruzicka .08 .25
191 Otakar Janecky .08 .25
192 Jan Vodila .02 .10
193 Jiri Dolezal .02 .10
194 Rostislav Vlach .02 .10
195 Jiri Kucera .07 .20
196 Jiri Sejba .05 .15
197 Oldrich Valek .02 .10
198 Jiri LaLa .05 .15
199 Robert Kron .08 .25
200 Petr Rosol .05 .15
NNO Sticker Album 4.00 10.00

1989-90 Swedish Semic Elitserien Stickers

COMPLETE SET (285) 60.00 150.00
1 AIK .08 .25
2 Ake Lilljebjorn .08 .25
3 Thomas Ostlund .30 .75
4 Mats Thelin .08 .25
5 Thomas Ahlen .08 .25
6 Petri Liimatainen .08 .25
7 Roger Ohman .08 .25
8 Rikard Franzen .08 .25
9 Stefan Claesson .08 .25
10 Tommy Hedlund .08 .25
11 Stefan Jansson .08 .25
12 Peter Gradin .08 .25
13 Thomas Gradin .20 .50
14 Bo Berglund .08 .25
15 Heinz Ehlers .08 .25
16 Robert Burakovsky .08 .25
17 Alexander Kozjevnikov .08 .25
18 Peter Hammarstrom .08 .25
19 Anders Gozzi .08 .25
20 Thomas Bjuhr .08 .25
21 Patric Englund .08 .25
22 Odd Nilsson .08 .25
23 Mats Lindberg .08 .25
24 Peter Johansson .08 .25
25 Patric Kjellberg .30 .75
26 Brynas IF .08 .25
27 Lars Eriksson .08 .25
28 Michael Sundlov .08 .25
29 Par Djoos .08 .25
30 Tommy Sjodin .08 .25
31 Nikolaj Davydkin .08 .25
32 Niklas Gallstedt .08 .25
33 Mikael Lindman .08 .25
34 Jan-Erik Stormqvist .08 .25
35 Tommy Melkersson .08 .25
36 Mikael Enander .08 .25
37 Anders Huss .08 .25
38 Anders Carlsson .08 .25
39 Willy Lindstrom .20 .50
40 Kyosti Karjalainen .08 .25
41 Jan Larsson .08 .25
42 Patrik Erickson .08 .25
43 Joakim Pehrson .08 .25
44 Johan Brummer .08 .25
45 Peter Eriksson .08 .25
46 Peter Gustafsson .08 .25
47 Tomas Olund .08 .25
48 Magnus Asberg .08 .25
49 Djurgardens IF .08 .25
50 Rolf Ridderwall .20 .50
51 Tommy Soderstrom .60 1.50
52 Thomas Eriksson .08 .25
53 Arto Blomsten .08 .25
54 Orvar Stambert .08 .25
55 Christian Due-Boje .08 .25
56 Kenneth Kennholt .08 .25
57 Mats Waltin .08 .25
58 Karl-Erik Lilja .08 .25
59 Marcus Ragnarsson .20 .50
60 Hakan Sodergren .08 .25
61 Mikael Johansson .08 .25
62 Jens Ohling .08 .25
63 Jan Viktorsson .08 .25
64 Peter Nilsson .08 .25
65 Charles Berglund .08 .25
66 Kent Johansson .08 .25
67 Johan Garpenlov .20 .50
68 Ola Andersson .08 .25
69 Anders Johnson .08 .25
70 Bengt Akerblom .08 .25
71 Ola Josefsson .08 .25
72 Mats Sundin 10.00 25.00
73 Farjestads BK .08 .25
74 Anders Bergman .08 .25
75 Jorgen Ryden .08 .25
76 Tommy Samuelsson .08 .25
77 Fredrik Olausson .30 .75
78 Peter Hasselblad .08 .25
79 Jesper Duus .08 .25
80 Anders Berglund .08 .25
81 Mattias Andersson .08 .25
82 Mattias Olsson .08 .25
83 Greger Artursson .08 .25
84 Jakob Karlsson .08 .25
85 Thomas Rundqvist .08 .25
86 Staffan Lundh .08 .25
87 Jan Ingman .08 .25
88 Kjell Dahlin .08 .25
89 Bengt-Ake Gustafsson .20 .50
90 Magnus Roupe .08 .25
91 Hakan Loob .40 1.00
92 Mikael Holmberg .08 .25
93 Daniel Rydmark .08 .25
94 Lars Karlsson .08 .25
95 Peter Ottosson .08 .25
96 HV 71 .08 .25
97 Kenneth Johansson .08 .25
98 Claes Heljemo .08 .25
99 Lars Ivarsson .08 .25
100 Arto Ruotanen .08 .25
101 Fredrik Stillman .08 .25
102 Klas Heed .08 .25
103 Nils-Gunnar Svensson .08 .25
104 Per Gustafsson .08 .25
105 Tommy Fritz .08 .25
106 Mats Nilsson .08 .25
107 Hasse Sjoo .08 .25
108 Mats Loov .08 .25
109 Ove Thornberg .08 .25
110 Eddy Ericsson .08 .25
111 Ivan Avdejev .08 .25
112 Stefan Persson .20 .50
113 Rick Erdall .08 .25
114 Stefan Nilsson .08 .25
115 Stefan Ornskog .08 .25
116 Patrik Ross .08 .25
117 Stefan Falk .08 .25
118 Claes Roupe .08 .25
119 Peter Ekelund .08 .25
120 Leksands IF .08 .25
121 Peter Aslin .30 .75
122 Olow Sundstrom .08 .25
123 Jonas Leven .08 .25
124 Tomas Jonsson .20 .50
125 Magnus Svensson .08 .25
126 Ricard Persson .20 .50
127 Per Lundell .08 .25
128 Tomas Nord .08 .25
129 Peter Wallin .08 .25
130 Orjan Lindmark .08 .25
131 Henric Bjorkman .08 .25
132 Anders Pettersson .08 .25
133 Per-Olof Carlsson .08 .25
134 Tomas Forslund .20 .50
135 Niklas Eriksson .08 .25
136 Richard Kromm .08 .25
137 Jarmo Makitalo .08 .25
138 Peter Lundmark .30 .75
139 Ronny Reichenberg .08 .25
140 Cenneth Soderlund .08 .25
141 Jens Nielsen .08 .25
142 Marcus Thuresson .08 .25
143 Anders Broms .08 .25
144 Joakim Backlund .08 .25
145 Lulea HF .08 .25
146 Robert Skoog .08 .25
147 Tomas Javeblad .08 .25
148 Lars Modig .08 .25
149 Jan-Ove Mettavainio .08 .25

150 Osmo Soutokorva .08 .25
151 Torbjorn Lindberg .08 .25
152 Timo Jutila .20 .50
153 Roger Akerstrom .08 .25
154 Per Ljusterang .08 .25
155 Tomas Lilja .08 .25
156 Johan Stromvall .08 .25
157 Lars-Gunnar Pettersson .08 .25
158 Lars Hurtig .08 .25
159 Morgan Samuelsson .08 .25
160 Stefan Nilsson .08 .25
161 Vesa Kangas .08 .25
162 Kari Jaako .08 .25
163 Juha Nurmi .08 .25
164 Jens Hellgren .08 .25
165 Tomas Berglund .08 .25
166 Lars Edstrom .08 .25
167 Petter Antti .08 .25
168 MoDo HK .08 .25
169 Fredrik Andersson .08 .25
170 Goran Arnmark .08 .25
171 Timo Blomqvist .08 .25
172 Hakan Stromqvist .08 .25
173 Robert Frestadius .08 .25
174 Lars Jansson .08 .25
175 Hans Lodin .08 .25
176 Ove Pettersson .08 .25
177 Tony Olofsson .08 .25
178 Jorgen Eriksson .08 .25
179 Ulf Sandstrom .08 .25
180 Michael Hjalm .08 .25
181 Urban Nordin .08 .25
182 Lars Bystrom .08 .25
183 Jens Ohman .08 .25
184 Ulf Odmark .08 .25
185 Mikael Stahl .08 .25
186 Per Nilsson .08 .25
187 Ingemar Strom .08 .25
188 Kent Lantz .08 .25
189 Kent Norberg .08 .25
190 Patrik Soderholm .08 .25
191 Skelleftea HC .08 .25
192 Sam Lindstahl .08 .25
193 Dick Andersson .08 .25
194 Kari Suoraniemi .08 .25
195 Robert Larsson .08 .25
196 Kari Yli-Maenpaa .08 .25
197 Ola Stenlund .08 .25
198 Tony Barthelson .08 .25
199 Lars Marklund .08 .25
200 Glenn Hedman .08 .25
201 Dick Burlin .08 .25
202 Michael Granstedt .08 .25
203 Pekka Jarvela .08 .25
204 Hans Hjalmar .08 .25
205 Mats Lundstrom .08 .25
206 Martin Pettersson .08 .25
207 Johnny Forsman .08 .25
208 Daniel Pettersson .08 .25
209 Niklas Mannberg .08 .25
210 Niklas Brannstrom .08 .25
211 Jan Johansson .08 .25
212 Jorgen Wannstrom .08 .25
213 Leif Johansson .08 .25
214 Par Mikaelsson .08 .25
215 Fredrik Andersson .08 .25
216 Sodertalje SK .08 .25
217 Reino Sundberg .08 .25
218 Jari Luoma .08 .25
219 Anders Eldebrink .08 .25
220 Mats Kilstrom .08 .25
221 Jonas Heed .08 .25
222 Hans Pettersson .08 .25
223 Jan Bergman .08 .25
224 Thomas Carlsson .08 .25
225 Stefan Jonsson .08 .25
226 Thom Eklund .08 .25
227 Ola Rosander .08 .25
228 Bjorn Carlsson .08 .25
229 Thomas Sjogren .08 .25
230 Thomas Ljungbergh .08 .25
231 Stefan Olsson .08 .25
232 Reine Landgren .08 .25
233 Anders Frykbo .08 .25
234 Conny Jansson .08 .25
235 Peter Larsson .08 .25
236 Tomaz Eriksson .08 .25
237 Erik Holmberg .08 .25
238 Patrik Lindh .08 .25
239 Vasteras IK .08 .25
240 Mats Ytter .08 .25
241 Par Hellenberg .08 .25
242 Jan Eriksson .08 .25
243 Peter Popovic .20 .50
244 Tore Lindgren .08 .25
245 Leif Rohlin .20 .50
246 Henrik Andersson .08 .25
247 Nicklas Lidstrom 40.00 100.00
248 Jan Karlsson .08 .25
249 Peter Jacobsson .08 .25
250 Patrik Juhlin .20 .50
251 Goran Sjoberg .08 .25
252 Fredrik Nilsson .08 .25
253 Stefan Hellkvist .08 .25
254 Tomas Strandberg .08 .25
255 Anders Berglund .08 .25
256 Claes Lindblom .08 .25
257 Magnus Wallin .08 .25
258 Bjorn Akerblom .08 .25
259 Joakim Lundholm .08 .25
260 Jorgen Holmberg .08 .25
261 Ronny Hansen .08 .25
262 Misjat Fachrutdinov .08 .25
263 Vastra Frolunda HC .08 .25
264 Hakan Algotsson .30 .75
265 Per Lundbergh .08 .25
266 Jan Karlsson .08 .25
267 Joacim Esbjors .08 .25
268 Leif Carlsson .08 .25
269 Stefan Axelsson .08 .25
270 Peter Ekroth .08 .25
271 Jorgen Palm .08 .25
272 Hakan Nordin .08 .25
273 Stefan Larsson .08 .25
274 Mikael Andersson .20 .50
275 Terho Koskela .08 .25
276 Patrik Carnback .20 .50
277 Serge Boisvert .08 .25
278 Arto Sirvio .08 .25
279 Peter Berndtsson .08 .25
280 Jorgen Pettersson .08 .25
281 Niklas Andersson .08 .25
282 Peter Gustavsson .08 .25
283 Paul Andersson .08 .25
284 Mats Graesen .08 .25
285 Kent Orrgren .08 .25

1990-91 Swedish Semic Elitserien Stickers

COMPLETE SET (294) 30.00 80.00
1 MoDo Hockey Team
Team Emblem .02 .10
2 MoDo Hockey
Team Picture .02 .10
3 Fredrik Andersson .08 .25
4 Goran Arnmark .08 .25
5 Ari Salo .02 .10
6 Anders Berglund .02 .10
7 Lars Jansson .02 .10
8 Hans Lodin .02 .10
9 Ove Pettersson .02 .10
10 Jorgen Eriksson .02 .10
11 Tony Olofsson .02 .10
12 Tomas Nanzen .02 .10
13 Michael Hjalm .02 .10
14 Erik Holmberg .02 .10
15 Urban Nordin .02 .10
16 Kent Lantz .02 .10
17 Lars Bystrom .02 .10
18 Jens Ohman .02 .10
19 Ulf Odmark .02 .10
20 Mikael Stahl .02 .10
21 Ingemar Strom .02 .10
22 Tommy Pettersson .02 .10
23 Markus Naslund 2.00 5.00
24 Per Wallin .05 .15
25 Vastra Frolunda HC
Team Emblem .02 .10
26 Vastra Frolunda HC
Team Picture .02 .10
27 Ake Lilljebjorn .20 .50
28 Hakan Algotsson .20 .50
29 Leif Carlsson .02 .10
30 Jonas Heed .02 .10
31 Hakan Nordin .02 .10
32 Joacim Esbjors .05 .15
33 Stefan Axelsson .15 .40
34 Stefan Larsson .05 .15
35 Jorgen Palm .02 .10
36 Oscar Ackerstrom .02 .10
37 Patrik Carnback .20 .50
38 Mats Lundstrom .02 .10
39 Niklas Andersson .08 .25
40 Serge Boisvert .07 .20
41 Arto Sirvio .02 .10
42 Terho Koskela .02 .10
43 Kari Jaako .02 .10
44 Peter Berndtsson .02 .10
45 Mikael Andersson .08 .25
46 Par Edlund .02 .10
47 Jonas Andersson .02 .10
48 Johan Witehall .20 .50
49 Sodertalje SK
Team Emblem .02 .10
50 Sodertalje SK
Team Picture .02 .10
51 Reino Sundberg .08 .25
52 Jari Luoma .08 .25
53 Mats Kilstrom .02 .10
54 Stefan Jonsson .02 .10
55 Peter Ekroth .02 .10
56 Mats Waltin .02 .10
57 Jan Bergman .02 .10
58 Hans Pettersson .02 .10
59 Stefan Nyman .02 .10
60 Conny Jansson .02 .10
61 Thom Eklund .02 .10
62 Otakar Hascak .07 .20
63 Morgan Samuelsson .05 .15
64 Reine Landgren .02 .10
65 Bjorn Carlsson .02 .10
66 Ola Andersson .02 .10
67 Tomaz Eriksson .02 .10
68 Bert-Olav Karlsson .02 .10
69 Ola Rosander .02 .10
70 Stefan Olsson .02 .10
71 Scott Moore .02 .10
72 Anders Frykbo .02 .10
73 AIK
Team Emblem .02 .10
74 AIK
Team Picture .02 .10
75 Thomas Ostlund .20 .50
76 Sam Lindstahl .08 .25
77 Borje Salming 1.25 3.00
78 Mats Thelin .08 .25
79 Petter Salsten .02 .10
80 Petri Liimatainen .02 .10
81 Rikard Franzen .05 .15
82 Stefan Claesson .02 .10
83 Torbjorn Mattsson .02 .10
84 Daniel Jardemyr .02 .10
85 Robert Burakovsky .07 .20
86 Peter Gradin .02 .10
87 Thomas Bjuhr .02 .10
88 Heinz Ehlers .02 .10
89 Tommy Lehmann .07 .20
90 Peter Hammarstrom .02 .10
91 Patric Kjellberg .40 1.00
92 Patric Englund .02 .10
93 Mats Lindberg .02 .10
94 Peter Johansson .02 .10
95 Kristian Gahn .07 .20
96 Niklas Sundblad .08 .25
97 Erik Andersson .02 .10
98 HV 71
Team Emblem .02 .10
99 HV 71
Team Picture .02 .10
100 Peter Aslin .20 .50
101 Kenneth Johansson .08 .25
102 Arto Ruotanen .02 .10
103 Fredrik Stillman .05 .15
104 Lars Ivarsson .02 .10
105 Klas Heed .02 .10
106 Per Gustafsson .20 .50
107 Mathias Svedberg .02 .10
108 Tommy Fritz .02 .10
109 Mats Nilsson .02 .10
110 Peter Eriksson .02 .10
111 Risto Kurkinen .02 .10
112 Thomas Ljungbergh .02 .10
113 Ove Thornberg .02 .10
114 Mats Loov .02 .10
115 Eddy Ericsson .02 .10
116 Stefan Ornskog .08 .25
117 Patrik Ross .02 .10
118 Stefan Persson .08 .25
119 Dennis Strom .02 .10
120 Peter Ekelund .02 .10
121 Jonas Jonsson .02 .10
122 Torbjorn Persson .02 .10
123 Malmo IF
Team Emblem .02 .10
124 Malmo IF
Team Picture .02 .10
125 Peter Lindmark .20 .50
126 Roger Nordstrom .08 .25
127 Timo Blomqvist .08 .25
128 Peter Andersson .08 .25
129 Mats Lusth .02 .10
130 Johan Salle .02 .10
131 Roger Ohman .05 .15
132 Anders Svensson .02 .10
133 Peter Imhauser .02 .10
134 Johan Norgren .02 .10
135 Raimo Helminen .20 .50
136 Peter Sundstrom .08 .25
137 Mats Hallin .02 .10
138 Matti Pauna .02 .10
139 Patrik Gustavsson .02 .10
140 Hakan Ahlund .02 .10
141 Daniel Rydmark .05 .15
142 Lennart Hermansson .02 .10
143 Carl-Erik Larsson .02 .10
144 Rick Erdall .02 .10
145 Bo Svanberg .02 .10
146 Fredrik Johansson .02 .10
147 Jens Hemstrom .02 .10
148 Vasteras IK
Team Emblem .02 .10
149 Vasteras IK
Team Picture .02 .10
150 Mats Ytter .08 .25
151 Par Hellenberg .08 .25
152 Nicklas Lidstrom 20.00 50.00
153 Leif Rohlin .15 .40
154 Peter Popovic .20 .50
155 Jan Karlsson .02 .10
156 Henrik Andersson .02 .10
157 Tore Lindgren .02 .10
158 Peter Jacobsson .02 .10
159 Pierre Ivarsson .02 .10
160 Jan Eriksson .02 .10
161 Goran Sjoberg .02 .10
162 Misjat Fachrutdinov .05 .15
163 Anders Berglund .02 .10
164 Claes Lindblom .02 .10
165 Jorgen Holmberg .02 .10
166 Stefan Hellkvist .02 .10
167 Tomas Strandberg .02 .10
168 Bjorn Akerblom .02 .10
169 Ronny Hansen .02 .10
170 Fredrik Nilsson .05 .15
171 Patrik Juhlin .20 .50
172 Henrik Nilsson .02 .10
173 Brynas IF
Team Emblem .02 .10
174 Brynas IF
Team Picture .02 .10
175 Michael Sundlov .20 .50
176 Lars Eriksson .08 .25
177 Tommy Sjodin .08 .25
178 Brad Berry .02 .10
179 Niklas Gallstedt .02 .10
180 Mikael Lindman .02 .10
181 Urban Molander .02 .10
182 Jan-Erik Stormqvist .02 .10
183 Stefan Klockare .07 .20
184 Tommy Melkersson .02 .10
185 Anders Carlsson .02 .10
186 Patrik Erickson .02 .10
187 Anders Huss .02 .10
188 Jan Larsson .02 .10
189 Peter Larsson .02 .10
190 Anders Gozzi .05 .15
191 Joakim Pehrson .05 .15
192 Peter Gustafsson .02 .10
193 Peter Eriksson .02 .10
194 Johan Brummer .02 .10
195 Tomas Olund .02 .10
196 Kenneth Andersson .02 .10
197 Leksands IF
Team Emblem .02 .10
198 Leksands IF
Team Picture .02 .10
199 Olow Sundstrom .08 .25
200 Lars-Erik Lord .08 .25
201 Jonas Leven .02 .10
202 Tomas Jonsson .08 .25
203 Ricard Persson .08 .25
204 Per Lundell .02 .10
205 Tomas Nord .02 .10
206 Mattias Andersson .02 .10
207 Henric Bjorkman .02 .10
208 Orjan Lindmark .02 .10
209 Tomas Forslund .08 .25
210 Niklas Eriksson .02 .10
211 Peter Lundmark .05 .15
212 Per-Olof Carlsson .02 .10
213 Marcus Thuresson .02 .10
214 Jens Nielsen .02 .10
215 Cenneth Soderlund .02 .10
216 Markus Akerblom .05 .15
217 Ronny Reichenberg .02 .10
218 Fredrik Olsson .02 .10
219 Niklas Hillblom .02 .10
220 Magnus Gustafsson .02 .10
221 Fredrik Jax .05 .15
222 Lulea HF
Team Emblem .02 .10
223 Lulea HF
Team Picture .02 .10
224 Robert Skoog .08 .25
225 Tomas Javeblad .08 .25
226 Timo Jutila .08 .25
227 Per Ljusterang .02 .10
228 Lars Modig .02 .10
229 Torbjorn Lindberg .02 .10
230 Tomas Lilja .20 .50
231 Osmo Soutukorva .02 .10
232 Jan-Ove Mettavainio .02 .10
233 Roger Akerstrom .02 .10
234 Johan Stromvall .02 .10
235 Ulf Sandstrom .02 .10
236 Lars-Gunnar Pettersson .02 .10
237 Pauli Jarvinen .02 .10
238 Lars Hurtig .02 .10
239 Tomas Berglund .02 .10
240 Stefan Nilsson .02 .10
241 Mikael Renberg .75 2.00
242 Hans Hjalmar .02 .10
243 Jens Hellgren .02 .10
244 Lars Edstrom .02 .10
245 Robert Nordberg .08 .25
246 Farjestads BK
Team Emblem .02 .10
247 Farjestads BK
Team Picture .02 .10
248 Anders Bergman .08 .25
249 Jorgen Ryden .08 .25
250 Patrik Haltia .20 .50
251 Tommy Samuelsson .02 .10
252 Jim Leavins .02 .10
253 Peter Hasselblad .02 .10
254 Jesper Duus .02 .10
255 Mattias Olsson .02 .10
256 Greger Artursson .02 .10
257 Jakob Karlsson .02 .10
258 Thomas Rhodin .02 .10
259 Bengt-Ake Gustafsson .15 .40
260 Hakan Loob .40 1.00
261 Thomas Rundqvist .08 .25
262 Kjell Dahlin .08 .25
263 Magnus Roupe .08 .25
264 Jan Ingman .02 .10
265 Lars Karlsson .02 .10
266 Mikael Holmberg .02 .10
267 Staffan Lundh .02 .10
268 Peter Ottosson .02 .10
269 Jonas Hoglund 1.25 3.00
270 Clas Eriksson .02 .10
271 Djurgardens IF
Team Emblem .02 .10
272 Djurgardens IF
Team Picture .02 .10
273 Tommy Soderstrom .40 1.00
274 Joakim Persson .20 .50
275 Thomas Eriksson .02 .10
276 Arto Blomsten .08 .25
277 Kenneth Kennholt .05 .15
278 Christian Due-Boje .07 .20
279 Orvar Stambert .02 .10
280 Per Nygards .02 .10
281 Marcus Ragnarsson .20 .50
282 Thomas Johansson .02 .10
283 Ronnie Pettersson .02 .10
284 Charles Berglund .02 .10
285 Jan Viktorsson .07 .20
286 Jens Ohling .05 .15
287 Ola Josefsson .02 .10
288 Peter Nilsson .02 .10
289 Andres Johnson .02 .10
290 Hakan Sodergren .02 .10
291 Stefan Gustavson .02 .10
292 Magnus Jansson .02 .10
293 Mikael Johansson .02 .10
294 Johan LIndstedt .02 .10

1991 Swedish Semic World Championship Stickers

COMPLETE SET (250) 125.00 300.00
1 Finnish Emblem .02 .10
2 Markus Ketterer .20 .50
3 Sakari Lindfors .08 .25
4 Jukka Tammi .08 .25
5 Timo Jutila .05 .15
6 Hannu Virta .05 .15
7 Simo Saarinen .02 .10
8 Jukka Marttila .02 .10
9 Ville Siren .05 .15
10 Pasi Huura .05 .15
11 Hannu Henriksson .02 .10
12 Arto Ruotanen .02 .10
13 Ari Haanpaa .02 .10
14 Pauli Jarvinen .02 .10
15 Teppo Kivela .02 .10
16 Risto Kurkinen .02 .10
17 Mika Nieminen .05 .15
18 Jari Kurri 4.00 10.00
19 Esa Keskinen .08 .25
20 Raimo Summanen .02 .10
21 Teemu Selanne 30.00 80.00
22 Jari Torkki .02 .10
23 Hannu Jarvenpaa .05 .15
24 Raimo Helminen .05 .15
25 Timo Peltomaa .05 .15
26 Swedish Emblem .02 .10
27 Peter Lindmark .08 .25
28 Rolf Ridderwall .05 .15
29 Tommy Soderstrom .20 .50
30 Thomas Eriksson .05 .15
31 Nicklas Lidstrom 10.00 25.00
32 Tomas Jonsson .05 .15
33 Tommy Samuelsson .02 .10
34 Fredrik Stillman .05 .15
35 Peter Andersson .05 .15
36 Peter Andersson .05 .15
37 Kenneth Kennholt .05 .15
38 Hakan Loob .08 .25
39 Thomas Rundqvist .05 .15
40 Hakan Ahlund .02 .10
41 Jan Viktorsson .02 .10
42 Charles Berglund .05 .15
43 Mikael Johansson .02 .10
44 Robert Burakovsky .02 .10
45 Bengt-Ake Gustafsson .05 .15
46 Patrik Carnback .02 .10
47 Patrik Erickson .02 .10
48 Anders Carlsson .02 .10
49 Mats Naslund .15 .40
50 Kent Nilsson .15 .40
51 Canadian Emblem .40 1.00
52 Patrick Roy 6.00 15.00
53 Ed Belfour 10.00 25.00
54 Daniel Berthiaume .05 .15
55 Ray Bourque 8.00 20.00
56 Scott Stevens .30 .75
57 Al MacInnis .60 1.50
58 Paul Coffey 4.00 10.00
59 Paul Cavallini .05 .15
60 Zarley Zalapski .05 .15
61 Steve Duchesne .05 .15
62 Dave Ellett .05 .15
63 Mark Messier 8.00 20.00
64 Wayne Gretzky 20.00 50.00
65 Steve Yzerman 6.00 15.00
66 Pierre Turgeon .60 1.50
67 Bernie Nicholls .20 .50
68 Cam Neely 1.50 4.00
69 Joe Nieuwendyk .30 .75
70 Luc Robitaille .60 1.50
71 Kevin Dineen .05 .15
72 John Cullen .05 .15
73 Steve Larmer .07 .20
74 Mark Recchi .60 1.50
75 Joe Sakic 2.00 5.00
76 Soviet Emblem .20 .50
77 Arturs Irbe 4.00 10.00
78 Alexei Marin .02 .10
79 Mikhail Shtalenkov .08 .25
80 Vladimir Malakhov .08 .25
81 Vladimir Konstantinov .40 1.00
82 Igor Kravchuk .05 .15
83 Ilya Byakin .05 .15
84 Dimitri Mironov .07 .20
85 Vladimir Turikov .02 .10
86 Vjatjeslav Uvajev .02 .10
87 Vladimir Fedosov .02 .10
88 Valeri Kamensky .20 .50
89 Pavel Bure 1.50 4.00
90 Vyacheslav Butsayev .05 .15
91 Igor Maslennikov .02 .10
92 Evgeny Davydov .05 .15
93 Andrei Kovalev .02 .10
94 Alexander Semak .05 .15
95 Alexei Zhamnov .15 .40
96 Sergei Nemchinov .05 .15
97 Viktor Gordijuk .02 .10
98 Vyacheslav Kozlov .30 .75
99 Andrei Khomotov .20 .50
100 Vyacheslav Bykov .15 .40
101 Czech Emblem .02 .10
102 Petr Briza .08 .25
103 Dominik Hasek 10.00 25.00
104 Eduard Hartmann .05 .15
105 Bedrich Scerban .05 .15
106 Jiri Slegr .07 .20
107 Josef Reznicek .02 .10
108 Petr Pavlas .02 .10
109 Peter Slanina .02 .10
110 Martin Maskarinec .02 .10
111 Antonin Stavjana .05 .15
112 Stanislav Medrik .02 .10
113 Dusan Pasek .07 .20
114 Jiri Lala .05 .15
115 Darius Rusnak .02 .10
116 Oto Hascak .05 .15
117 Radek Toupal .05 .15
118 Pavel Pycha .02 .10
119 Lubomir Kolnik .02 .10
120 Libor Dolana .02 .10
121 Ladislav Lubina .05 .15
122 Tomas Jelinek .02 .10
123 Petr Vlk .02 .10
124 Vladimir Petrovka .02 .10
125 Richard Zemlicka .05 .15
126 U.S.A. Emblem .20 .50
127 John Vanbiesbrouck .75 2.00
128 Mike Richter .75 2.00
129 Chris Terreri .08 .25
130 Chris Chelios .75 2.00
131 Brian Leetch 4.00 10.00
132 Gary Suter .07 .20
133 Phil Housley .08 .25
134 Mark Howe .05 .15
135 Al Iafrate .08 .25
136 Kevin Hatcher .08 .25
137 Mathieu Schneider .08 .25
138 Pat LaFontaine .30 .75
139 Darren Turcotte .05 .15
140 Neal Broten .07 .20
141 Mike Modano 10.00 25.00
142 Dave Christian .05 .15
143 Craig Janney .15 .40
144 Brett Hull 1.50 4.00
145 Kevin Stevens .15 .40
146 Joe Mullen .08 .25
147 Tony Granato .07 .20
148 Ed Olczyk .05 .15
149 Jeremy Roenick 1.50 4.00
150 Jimmy Carson .05 .15
151 West German Emblem .02 .10
152 Helmut De Raaf .02 .10
153 Josef Heiss .07 .20
154 Karl Friesen .07 .20
155 Uli Hiemer .05 .15
156 Harold Kreis .02 .10
157 Udo Kiessling .05 .15
158 Michael Schmidt .02 .10
159 Michael Heidt .05 .15
160 Andreas Pokorny .02 .10
161 Bernd Wagner .02 .10
162 Uwe Krupp .08 .25
163 Gerd Truntschka .05 .15
164 Bernd Truntschka .05 .15
165 Thomas Brandl .02 .10
166 Peter Draisaitl .02 .10
167 Andreas Brockmann .02 .10
168 Ulrich Liebsch .02 .10
169 Ralf Hantschke .02 .10
170 Thomas Schinko .02 .10
171 Anton Krinner .02 .10
172 Thomas Werner .02 .10
173 Dieter Hegen .05 .15
174 Helmut Steiger .02 .10
175 Georg Franz .02 .10
176 Swiss Emblem .02 .10
177 Renato Tosio .02 .10
178 Reto Pavoni .05 .15
179 Dino Stecher .02 .10
180 Sven Leuenberger .02 .10
181 Rick Tschumi .02 .10
182 Patrice Brasey .02 .10
183 Didier Massy .02 .10
184 Sandro Bertaggia .02 .10
185 Samuel Balmer .02 .10
186 Martin Rauch .02 .10
187 Marc Leuenberger .02 .10
188 Jorg Eberle .02 .10
189 Fredy Luthi .02 .10
190 Andy Ton .02 .10
191 Raymond Walder .02 .10
192 Manuele Celio .02 .10
193 Roman Wager .02 .10
194 Felix Hollenstein .02 .10
195 Andre Rotheli .02 .10
196 Christian Weber .02 .10
197 Peter Jaks .02 .10
198 Gil Montandon .02 .10
199 Oliver Hoffmann .02 .10
200 Thomas Vrabec .02 .10
201 Teppo Numminen .07 .20
202 Jyrki Lumme .05 .15
203 Esa Tikkanen .15 .40
204 Petri Skriko .05 .15
205 Christian Ruutu .07 .20
206 Ilkka Sinisalo .07 .20
207 Calle Johansson .07 .20
208 Tomas Sandstrom .07 .20
209 Thomas Steen .07 .20
210 Per-Erik Eklund .07 .20
211 Mats Sundin 8.00 20.00
212 Johan Garpenlov .07 .20
213 Slava Fetisov .40 1.00
214 Alexei Kasatonov .15 .40
215 Mikhail Tatarinov .02 .10
216 Sergei Makarov .20 .50
217 Igor Larionov .40 1.00
218 Alexander Mogilny .60 1.50
219 Sergei Fedorov 1.50 4.00
220 Petr Klima .05 .15
221 David Volek .07 .20
222 Michal Pivonka .08 .25
223 Robert Reichel .08 .25
224 Robert Holik .20 .50
225 Jaromir Jagr 2.00 5.00
226 Urpo Ylonen .02 .10
227 Ilpo Koskela .02 .10
228 Pekka Rautakallio .07 .20
229 Lasse Oksanen .02 .10
230 Veli-Pekka Ketola .07 .20
231 Leif Holmqvist .05 .15
232 Lennart Svedberg .04 .10
233 Sven Tumba Johansson .02 .10
234 Ulf Sterner .02 .10
235 Anders Hedberg .08 .25
236 Ken Dryden 2.00 5.00
237 Bobby Orr 6.00 15.00
238 Gordie Howe 2.00 5.00
239 Bobby Hull 1.25 3.00
240 Phil Esposito 1.50 4.00
241 Vladislav Tretiak 1.50 4.00
242 Alexander Ragulin .08 .25
243 Anatoli Firsov .08 .25
244 Valeri Kharlamov .40 1.00
245 Alexander Maltsev .20 .50
246 Jiri Holecek .07 .20
247 Jan Suchy .02 .10
248 Jozef Golonka .02 .10
249 Vaclav Nedomansky .07 .20
250 Ivan Hlinka .07 .20

1991-92 Swedish Semic Elitserien Stickers

COMPLETE SET (360) 60.00 150.00
1 AIK
Team Emblem .02 .10
2 Thomas Ostlund .08 .25
3 Sam Lindstahl .08 .25
4 Borje Salming .30 .75
5 Petri Liimatainen .02 .10
6 Mats Thelin .08 .25
7 Rikard Franzen .05 .15
8 Petter Sahlsten .02 .10
9 Daniel Jardemyr .02 .10
10 Thomas Nilsson .02 .10
11 Niclas Havelid .02 .10
12 Mattias Norstrom .08 .25
13 Peter Gradin .02 .10
14 Peter Hammarstrom .02 .10
15 Patrik Ericksson .05 .15
16 Thomas Bjuhr .02 .10
17 Thomas Strandberg .02 .10
18 Tommy Lehmann .07 .20
19 Mats Lindberg .02 .10
20 Patric Kjellberg .20 .50
21 Michael Nylander .40 1.00
22 Patric Englund .02 .10
23 Niclas Sundblad .20 .50
24 Kristian Gahn .08 .25
25 Erik Andersson .02 .10
26 Bjorn Ahlstrom .02 .10
27 Brynas
Team Emblem .02 .10
28 Michael Sundlov .08 .25
29 Lars Eriksson .08 .25
30 Lars Karlsson .02 .10
31 Tommy Sjodin .07 .20
32 Nikolaj Davydkin .02 .10
33 Niklas Gallstedt .02 .10
34 Mikael Lindman .02 .10
35 Tommy Melkersson .02 .10
36 Mikael Enander .02 .10
37 Urban Molander .02 .10
38 Stefan Klockare .05 .15
39 Anders Huss .05 .15
40 Mikael Lindholm .02 .10
41 Jan Larsson .02 .10
42 Anders Gozzi .05 .15
43 Peter Larsson .02 .10
44 Thomas Tallberg .05 .15
45 Peter Gustafsson .02 .10
46 Joakim Persson .20 .50
47 Peter Eriksson .02 .10
48 Ove Mohlin .05 .15
49 Jonas Johnsson .02 .10
50 Johan Schillgard .02 .10
51 Andreas Dackell .08 .25
52 Tom Bissett .05 .15
53 Djurgarden
Team Emblem .02 .10
54 Tommy Soderstrom .30 .75
55 Joakim Persson .20 .50
56 Petter Ronnqvist .08 .25
57 Thomas Eriksson .02 .10
58 Kenneth Kennholt .05 .15
59 Arto Blomsten .07 .20
60 Orvar Stambert .02 .10
61 Christian Due-Boje .05 .15
62 Marcus Ragnarsson .20 .50
63 Per Nygards .02 .10
64 Thomas Johansson .02 .10
65 Mikael Johansson .02 .10
66 Charles Berglund .05 .15
67 Jan Viktorsson .05 .15
68 Ola Josefsson .02 .10
69 Jens Ohling .05 .15
70 Magnus Jansson .02 .10
71 Peter Nilsson .02 .10
72 Fredrik Lindquist .08 .25
73 Mariusz Czerkawski .60 1.50
74 Johan Lindstedt .02 .10
75 Stefan Ketola .08 .25
76 Erik Huusko .05 .15
77 Anders Huusko .05 .15
78 Farjestad
Team Emblem .02 .10
79 Anders Bergman .08 .25
80 Jorgen Ryden .08 .25
81 Patrik Haltia .15 .40
82 Tommy Samuelsson .02 .10
83 Per Lundell .02 .10
84 Leif Carlsson .02 .10
85 Jesper Duus .02 .10
86 Mattias Olsson .02 .10
87 Thomas Rhodin .02 .10
88 Jakob Karlsson .02 .10
89 Greger Artursson .02 .10
90 Thomas Rundqvist .05 .15
91 Bengt-Ake Gustafsson .08 .25
92 Hakan Loob .40 1.00
93 Lars Karlsson .02 .10
94 Magnus Roupe .07 .20
95 Kjell Dahlin .08 .25
96 Staffan Lundh .02 .10
97 Peter Ottosson .02 .10
98 Niklas Brannstrom .02 .10
99 Jonas Hoglund .75 2.00
100 Clas Eriksson .02 .10
101 Andreas Johansson .20 .50
102 Mathias Johansson .02 .10
103 HV 71
Team Emblem .02 .10
104 Peter Aslin .15 .40
105 Boo Ahl .20 .50
106 Stefan Magnusson .02 .10
107 Fredrik Stillman .07 .20
108 Lars Ivarsson .02 .10
109 Klas Heed .02 .10
110 Arto Ruotanen .02 .10
111 Per Gustafsson .02 .10
112 Tommy Fritz .02 .10
113 Mathias Svedberg .02 .10
114 Kristian Pedersen .02 .10
115 Peter Eriksson .02 .10
116 Risto Kurkinen .02 .10
117 Ove Thornberg .02 .10
118 Stefan Ornskog .08 .25
119 Thomas Ljungberg .02 .10
120 Patrik Ross .02 .10
121 Eddy Ericsson .02 .10
122 Dennis Strom .02 .10
123 Torbjorn Persson .02 .10
124 Jonas Jonsson .02 .10
125 Peter Ekelund .02 .10
126 Stefan Falk .08 .25
127 Ronny Nilsson .02 .10
128 Leksand
Team Emblem .02 .10
129 Olow Sundstrom .08 .25
130 Jonas Leven .08 .25
131 Tomas Jonsson .08 .25
132 Ricard Persson .08 .25
133 Magnus Svensson .15 .40
134 Mattias Andersson .02 .10
135 Henric Bjorkman .02 .10
136 Orjan Lindmark .02 .10
137 Orjan Nilsson .02 .10
138 Tomas Ring .02 .10
139 Roger Johansson .02 .10
140 Marcus Thuresson .02 .10
141 Per-Olof Carlsson .02 .10
142 Jens Nielsen .02 .10
143 Cenneth Soderlund .02 .10
144 Markus Akerblom .07 .20
145 Fredrik Jax .07 .20
146 Reine Rauhala .05 .15
147 Niklas Eriksson .02 .10
148 Martin Wiita .02 .10
149 Jonas Bergqvist .07 .20
150 Hannu Jarvenpaa .08 .25
151 Lulea
Team Emblem .02 .10
152 Robert Skoog .08 .25
153 Erik Granqvist .08 .25
154 Timo Jutila .08 .25
155 Tomas Lilja .02 .10
156 Lars Modig .02 .10
157 Per Ljusterang .02 .10
158 Jari Gronstrand .02 .10
159 Torbjorn Lindberg .02 .10

160 Patrik Hoglund .07 .20
161 Petter Nilsson .02 .10
162 Daniel Behm .02 .10
163 Johan Stromvall .02 .10
164 Pauli Jarvinen .02 .10
165 Lars Edstrom .02 .10
166 Lars-Gunnar Pettersson .02 .10
167 Stefan Nilsson .02 .10
168 Lars Hurtig .02 .10
169 Tomas Berglund .02 .10
170 Robert Nordberg .08 .25
171 Mikael Renberg .75 2.00
172 Ulf Sandstrom .02 .10
173 Jens Hellgren .02 .10
174 Mikael Engstrom .02 .10
175 Malmo
Team Emblem .02 .10
176 Peter Lindmark .15 .40
177 Roger Nordstrom .15 .40
178 Johan Mansson .02 .10
179 Timo Blomqvist .15 .40
180 Peter Andersson .08 .25
181 Mats Lusth .02 .10
182 Roger Ohman .02 .10
183 Johan Salle .02 .10
184 Anders Svensson .02 .10
185 Johan Norgren .02 .10
186 Raimo Helminen .15 .40
187 Mats Hallin .08 .25
188 Mats Naslund .40 1.00
189 Robert Burakovsky .08 .25
190 Hakan Ahlund .02 .10
191 Peter Sundstrom .15 .40
192 Daniel Rydmark .07 .20
193 Matti Pauna .02 .10
194 Roger Hansson .02 .10
195 Patrik Gustavsson .02 .10
196 Rick Erdall .02 .10
197 Bo Svanberg .02 .10
198 Jesper Mattsson .20 .50
199 Jonas Hakansson .02 .10
200 MoDo
Team Emblem .02 .10
201 Fredrik Andersson .08 .25
202 Goran Arnmark .08 .25
203 Miloslav Horava .08 .25
204 Hans Lodin .02 .10
205 Lars Jansson .02 .10
206 Jorgen Eriksson .02 .10
207 Anders Berglund .02 .10
208 Osmo Soutokorva .02 .10
209 Tomas Nanzen .02 .10
210 Hans Jonsson .20 .50
211 Fredrik Bergqvist .02 .10
212 Erik Holmberg .02 .10
213 Peter Forsberg 4.00 10.00
214 Markus Naslund 1.25 3.00
215 Magnus Wernblom .02 .10
216 Lars Bystrom .02 .10
217 Kent Lantz .02 .10
218 Per Wallin .07 .20
219 Lennart Henriksson .02 .10
220 Ingemar Strom .02 .10
221 Ulf Odmark .02 .10
222 Jens Ohman .02 .10
223 Tommy Pettersson .02 .10
224 Andreas Salomonsson .05 .15
225 Sodertalje
Team Emblem .02 .10
226 Reino Sundberg .08 .25
227 Stefan Dernestal .08 .25
228 Mats Kihlstrom .02 .10
229 Stefan Jonsson .02 .10
230 Jan Bergman .02 .10
231 Peter Ekroth .02 .10
232 Stefan Nyman .02 .10
233 Thomas Carlsson .02 .10
234 Stefan Claesson .02 .10
235 Oto Hascak .07 .20
236 Morgan Samuelsson .02 .10
237 Tomaz Eriksson .02 .10
238 Thom Eklund .02 .10
239 Conny Jansson .02 .10
240 Bjorn Carlsson .02 .10
241 Scott Moore .02 .10
242 Reine Landgren .02 .10
243 Ola Rosander .02 .10
244 Stefan Olsson .02 .10
245 Anders Frykbo .02 .10
246 Ola Andersson .02 .10
247 Joe Tracy .02 .10
248 Christer Ljungberg .02 .10
249 Patrik Nyberg .02 .10
250 Joakim Skold .02 .10
251 Vasteras
Team Emblem .02 .10
252 Mats Ytter .08 .25
253 Par Hellenberg .08 .25
254 Tommy Salo 1.50 4.00
255 Nicklas Lidstrom 20.00 50.00
256 Robert Nordmark .08 .25
257 Leif Rohlin .15 .40
258 Roger Akerstrom .05 .15
259 Peter Popovic .08 .25
260 Jan Karlsson .02 .10
261 Tore Lindgren .02 .10
262 Peter Jacobsson .02 .10
263 Pierre Ivarsson .02 .10
264 Misjat Fachrutdinov .02 .10
265 Paul Andersson .02 .10
266 Patrik Juhlin .20 .50
267 Henrik Nilsson .02 .10
268 Anders Berglund .02 .10
269 Claes Lindblom .02 .10
270 Jorgen Holmberg .02 .10
271 Stefan Hellkvist .02 .10
272 Fredrik Nilsson .08 .25
273 Johan Brummer .02 .10
274 Micael Karlberg .02 .10
275 Niclas Lundberg .02 .10
276 Vastra Frolunda
Team Emblem .02 .10
277 Ake Lilljebjorn .08 .25
278 Hakan Algotsson .15 .40
279 Hakan Nordin .02 .10
280 Jonas Heed .02 .10
281 Joacim Esbjors .05 .15
282 Stefan Larsson .02 .10
283 Stefan Axelsson .08 .25
284 Oscar Ackestrom .02 .10
285 Jerk Hogstrom .02 .10
286 Patric Aberg .02 .10
287 Patrik Carnback .08 .25
288 Serge Boisvert .08 .25
289 Mats Lundstrom .02 .10
290 Mikael Andersson .20 .50
291 Kari Jaako .02 .10
292 Terho Koskela .02 .10
293 Lars Dahlstrom .02 .10
294 Jerry Persson .02 .10
295 Peter Berndtsson .02 .10
296 Thomas Sjogren .05 .15
297 Par Edlund .02 .10
298 Christian Lechtaler .02 .10
299 Jonas Esbjors .05 .15
300 Dennis Fredriksson .02 .10
301 Mats Hjalmarsson .02 .10
302 Leif Holmgren CO .02 .10
303 Tommy Sandlin CO .02 .10
304 Lars Falk CO .02 .10
305 Harald Luckner CO .02 .10
306 Lars-Erik Lundstrom CO .02 .10
307 Staffan Tholson CO .02 .10
308 Freddy Lindfors CO .02 .10
309 Timo Lahtinen CO .02 .10
310 Jan-Ake Andersson CO .02 .10
311 Claes-Goran Wallin CO .02 .10
312 Mikael Lundstrom CO .02 .10
313 Leif Boork CO .02 .10
314 Thomas Rundqvist .08 .25
315 Hakan Loob .40 1.00
316 Tommy Soderstrom .30 .75
317 Niklas Andersson .08 .25
318 Hakan Loob .40 1.00
319 Tomas Sandstrom .20 .50
320 Rolf Ridderwall .08 .25
321 Thomas Eriksson .02 .10
322 Nicklas Lidstrom 20.00 50.00
323 Mats Sundin 1.50 4.00
324 Thomas Rundqvist .08 .25
325 Hakan Loob .40 1.00
326 Marcus Karlsson .02 .10
327 Anders Eriksson .02 .10
328 Mats Lindgren .20 .50
329 Mikael Hakansson .08 .25
330 Mathias Johansson .02 .10
331 Niclas Sundstrom .40 1.00
332 Jesper Mattsson .20 .50
333 Anders Soderberg .20 .50
334 Swedish IHF Emblem .02 .10
335 1991 World Champions .02 .10
336 Rolf Ridderwall .08 .25
337 Peter Lindmark .15 .40
338 Tommy Soderstrom .30 .75
339 Kjell Samuelsson .08 .25
340 Calle Johansson .20 .50
341 Nicklas Lidstrom 1.50 4.00
342 Tomas Jonsson .08 .25
343 Peter Andersson .08 .25
344 Kenneth Kennholt .05 .15
345 Fredrik Stillman .07 .20
346 Thomas Rundqvist .08 .25
347 Hakan Loob .40 1.00
348 Bengt-Ake Gustafsson .08 .25
349 Mats Naslund .40 1.00
350 Mikael Johansson .02 .10
351 Charles Berglund .05 .15
352 Jan Viktorsson .05 .15
353 Johan Garpenlov .02 .10
354 Anders Carlsson .02 .10
355 Patrik Ericksson .05 .15
356 Jonas Bergqvist .07 .20
357 Mats Sundin 1.50 4.00
358 Per-Erik Eklund .02 .10
359 Conny Evensson .02 .10
360 Curt Lundmark .02 .10
NNO Sticker Album 4.00 10.00

1992-93 Swedish Semic Elitserien Stickers

COMPLETE SET (356) 30.00 75.00
1 AIK Team Picture .02 .10
2 AIK Team Picture .02 .10
3 Brynas Team Picture .02 .10
4 Brynas Team Picture .02 .10
5 Djurgarden Team Picture .02 .10
6 Djurgarden Team Picture .02 .10
7 Farjestad Team Picture .02 .10
8 Farjestad Team Picture .02 .10
9 HV 71 Team Picture .02 .10
10 HV 71 Team Picture .02 .10
11 Leksand Team Picture .02 .10
12 Leksand Team Picture .02 .10
13 Lulea Team Picture .02 .10
14 Lulea Team Picture .02 .10
15 Malmo Team Picture .02 .10
16 Malmo Team Picture .02 .10
17 MoDo Team Picture .02 .10
18 MoDo Team Picture .02 .10
19 Rogle Team Picture .02 .10
20 Rogle Team Picture .02 .10
21 Vasteras Team Picture .02 .10
22 Vasteras Team Picture .02 .10
23 Vastra Frolunda Team .02 .10
24 Vastra Frolunda Team .02 .10
25 AIK Team Emblem .02 .10
26 Rolf Ridderwall .08 .25
27 Sam Lindstahl .07 .20
28 Ronnie Karlsson .02 .10
29 Mats Thelin .08 .25
30 Mattias Norstrom .30 .75
31 Dick Tarnstrom .08 .25
32 Petri Liimatainen .02 .10
33 Rikard Franzen .05 .15
34 Daniel Jardemyr .02 .10
35 Niclas Havelid .40 1.00
36 Borje Salming .75 2.00
37 Thomas Bjuhr .02 .10
38 Peter Hammarstrom .02 .10
39 Thomas Strandberg .02 .10
40 Mats Lindberg .02 .10
41 Anders Bjork .02 .10
42 Anders Johnson .02 .10
43 Patrik Erickson .05 .15
44 Torbjorn Ohrlund .02 .10
45 Bjorn Ahlstrom .02 .10
46 Niclas Sundblad .05 .15
47 Patric Englund .02 .10
48 Kritian Gahn .02 .10
49 Morgan Samuelsson .05 .15
50 Brynas Team Emblem .02 .10
51 Michael Sundlov .20 .50
52 Lars Karlsson .08 .25
53 Bedrich Scerban .05 .15
54 Mikael Lindman .02 .10
55 Tommy Melkersson .02 .10
56 Stefan Klockare .05 .15
57 Mikael Enander .02 .10
58 Roger Karlsson .02 .10
59 Niklas Gallstedt .02 .10
60 Christer Olsson .20 .50
61 Anders Carlsson .02 .10
62 Thomas Tallberg .05 .15
63 Tom Bissett .05 .15
64 Andreas Dackell .40 1.00
65 Mikael Wahlberg .02 .10
66 Jan Larsson .02 .10
67 Anders Gozzi .02 .10
68 Ove Molin .02 .10
69 Anders Huss .05 .15
70 Peter Gustafsson .02 .10
71 Jonas Johnsson .02 .10
72 Peter Larsson .02 .10
73 Mikael Lindholm .02 .10
74 Djurgarden Team Emblem .02 .10
75 Thomas Ostlund .20 .50
76 Petter Ronnquist .07 .20
77 Christian Due-Boje .05 .15
78 Arto Blomsten .05 .15
79 Kenneth Kennholt .07 .20
80 Marcus Ragnarsson .20 .50
81 Thomas Johansson .02 .10
82 Joakim Lundberg .02 .10
83 Thomas Eriksson .02 .10
84 Bjorn Nord .08 .25
85 Mikael Magnusson .02 .10
86 Charles Berglund .02 .10
87 Erik Huusko .05 .15
88 Anders Huusko .02 .10
89 Tony Skopac .02 .10
90 Jens Ohling .07 .20
91 Peter Nilsson .02 .10
92 Magnus Jansson .02 .10
93 Kent Nilsson .30 .75
94 Mikael Hakansson .02 .10
95 Ola Josefsson .02 .10
96 Jerry Friman .02 .10
97 Fredrik Lindquist .15 .40
98 Mathias Hallback .02 .10
99 Jan Viktorsson .02 .10
100 Farjestad
Team Emblem .02 .10
101 Anders Bergman .08 .25
102 Jonas Eriksson .07 .20
103 Patrik Haltia .20 .50
104 Tommy Samuelsson .02 .10
105 Jesper Duus .02 .10
106 Leif Carlsson .02 .10
107 Per Lundell .02 .10
108 Jakob Karlsson .02 .10
109 Thomas Rhodin .02 .10
110 Mattias Olsson .02 .10
111 Hakan Loob .40 1.00
112 Thomas Rundqvist .02 .10
113 Andreas Johansson .20 .50
114 Staffan Lundh .02 .10
115 Jonas Hoglund .40 1.00
116 Bengt Ake Gustafsson .15 .40
117 Mattias Johansson .02 .10
118 Clas Eriksson .02 .10
119 Peter Ottosson .02 .10
120 Niklas Brannstrom .02 .10
121 Lars Karlsson .08 .25
122 Peter Hagstrom .02 .10
123 Kjell Dahlin .15 .40
124 HV 71
Team Emblem .02 .10
125 Peter Aslin .08 .25
126 Boo Ahl .20 .50
127 Antonin Stavjana .07 .20
128 Klas Heed .02 .10
129 Tommy Fritz .02 .10
130 Kristian Pedersen .02 .10
131 Per Gustafsson .20 .50
132 Mathias Svedberg .02 .10
133 Niclas Rahm .02 .10
134 Martin Danielsson .02 .10
135 Fredrik Stillman .02 .10
136 Lars Ivarsson .02 .10
137 Ove Thornberg .02 .10
138 Peter Ekelund .02 .10
139 Eddy Eriksson .02 .10
140 Stefan Ornskog .07 .20
141 Patrik Ross .02 .10
142 Torbjorn Persson .02 .10
143 Kamil Kastak .07 .20
144 Dennis Strom .02 .10
145 Peter Eriksson .02 .10
146 Magnus Axelsson .07 .20
147 Stefan Falk .07 .20
148 Thomas Ljungberg .02 .10
149 Leksand
Team Emblem .02 .10
150 Ake Lilljebjorn .08 .25
151 Jonas Leven .08 .25
152 Johan Hedberg 1.25 3.00
153 Tomas Jonsson .15 .40
154 Henric Bjorkman .02 .10
155 Mattias Andersson .02 .10
156 Rickard Persson .08 .25
157 Orjan Nilsson .02 .10
158 Magnus Svensson .08 .25
159 Orjan Lindmark .02 .10
160 Jan Huokko .02 .10
161 Reine Rauhala .02 .10
162 Emil Skoglund .02 .10
163 Jens Nielsen .02 .10
164 Marcus Thuresson .02 .10
165 Niklas Eriksson .02 .10
166 Tomas Srsen .05 .15
167 Jonas Bergqvist .08 .25
168 Per-Olof Carlsson .02 .10
169 Markus Akerblom .02 .10
170 Greg Parks .05 .15
171 Mattias Loof .02 .10
172 Cenneth Soderlund .02 .10
173 Jarmo Makitalo .02 .10
174 Lulea
Team Emblem .02 .10
175 Robert Skoog .07 .20
176 Erik Grankvist .07 .20
177 Lars Modig .02 .10
178 Patrik Hoglund .02 .10
179 Niklas Bjornfot .02 .10
180 Torbjorn Lindberg .02 .10
181 Ville Siren .08 .25
182 Petter Nilsson .02 .10
183 Joakim Gunler .02 .10
184 Tomas Lilja .02 .10
185 Stefan Jonsson .02 .10
186 Stefan Nilsson .07 .20
187 Johan Stromvall .02 .10
188 Robert Nordberg .05 .15
189 Tomas Berglund .05 .15
190 Mikael Renberg .75 2.00
191 Lars-Gunnar Pettersson .02 .10
192 Lars Edstrom .02 .10
193 Kyosti Karjalainen .07 .20
194 Lars Hurtig .02 .10
195 Fredrik Oberg .02 .10
196 Mikael Engstrom .02 .10
197 Mika Nieminen .20 .50
198 Malmo
Team Emblem .02 .10
199 Peter Lindmark .20 .50
200 Roger Nordstrom .08 .25
201 Johan Mansson .02 .10
202 Anders Svensson .02 .10
203 Timo Blomqvist .08 .25
204 Johan Norgren .02 .10
205 Mats Lusth .02 .10
206 Peter Hasselblad .02 .10
207 Robert Svehla .20 .50
208 Johan Salle .02 .10
209 Roger Ohman .02 .10
210 Raimo Helminen .20 .50
211 Roger Hansson .07 .20
212 Per Rosenqvist .02 .10
213 Bo Svanberg .02 .10
214 Daniel Rydmark .07 .20
215 Patrik Sylvegard .02 .10
216 Jonas Hakansson .02 .10
217 Jesper Mattsson .20 .50
218 Hakan Ahlund .02 .10
219 Peter Sundstrom .15 .40
220 Mats Naslund .75 2.00
221 Robert Burakovsky .05 .15
222 MoDo
Team Emblem .02 .10
223 Fredrik Andersson .07 .20
224 Anders Nasstrom .07 .20
225 Anders Berglund .02 .10
226 Miloslav Horava .05 .15
227 Hans Lodin .02 .10
228 Lars Jansson .02 .10
229 Jorgen Eriksson .02 .10
230 Anders Eriksson .40 1.00
231 Hans Jonsson .02 .10
232 Tomas Nanzen .02 .10
233 Mattias Timander .20 .50
234 Fredrik Bergqvist .02 .10
235 Magnus Wernblom .07 .20
236 Martin Hostak .05 .15
237 Mikael Pettersson .02 .10
238 Lennart Hermansson .02 .10
239 Tommy Lehmann .07 .20
240 Markus Naslund .40 1.00
241 Ulf Odmark .02 .10
242 Peter Forsberg 6.00 15.00
243 Andreas Salomonsson .02 .10
244 Niklas Sundstrom .40 1.00
245 Lars Bystrom .02 .10
246 Erik Holmberg .02 .10
247 Henrik Gradin .02 .10
248 Rogle
Team Emblem .02 .10
249 Kenneth Johansson .08 .25
250 Billy Nilsson .08 .25
251 Orjan Jacobsson .02 .10
252 Daniel Johansson .20 .50
253 Kenny Jonsson .60 1.50
254 Kari Eloranta .08 .25
255 Kari Suoraniemi .02 .10
256 Hakan Persson .02 .10
257 Rikard Gronborg .02 .10
258 Stefan Nilsson .02 .10
259 Per Ljusterang .02 .10
260 Igor Stelnov .02 .10
261 Peter Lundmark .08 .25
262 Heinz Ehlers .02 .10
263 Michael Hjalm .02 .10
264 Jan Ericson .02 .10
265 Pelle Svensson .02 .10
266 Mats Loov .05 .15
267 Stefan Elvenes .05 .15
268 Roger Elvenes .07 .20
269 Peter Wennberg .02 .10
270 Per Wallin .08 .25
271 Torgny Lowgren .02 .10
272 Jorgen Jonsson .02 .10
273 Vasteras
Team Emblem .02 .10
274 Mats Ytter .08 .25
275 Tommy Salo .75 2.00
276 Erik Bergstrom .02 .10
277 Pierre Ivarsson .02 .10
278 Peter Popovic .20 .50
279 Sergei Fokin .02 .10
280 Edvin Frylen .08 .25
281 Leif Rohlin .15 .40
282 Peter Karlsson .02 .10
283 Peter Jacobsson .02 .10
284 Roger Akerstrom .05 .15
285 Robert Nordmark .07 .20
286 Patrik Juhlin .20 .50
287 Misjat Fachrutdinov .05 .15
288 Henrik Nilsson .02 .10
289 Mikael Pettersson .02 .10
290 Fredrik Nilsson .05 .15
291 Stefan Hellkvist .02 .10
292 Henrik Pettersson .02 .10
293 Micael Karlberg .02 .10
294 Anders Berglund .02 .10
295 Claes Lindblom .05 .15
296 Johan Brummer .02 .10
297 Patrik Ulin .02 .10
298 Paul Andersson .02 .10
299 Vastra Frolunda
Team Emblem .02 .10
300 Hakan Algotsson .20 .50
301 Mikael Sandberg .08 .25
302 Patric Aberg .02 .10
303 Joacim Esbjors .05 .15
304 Oscar Ackestrom .02 .10
305 Jonas Heed .02 .10
306 Stefan Axelsson .08 .25
307 Ronnie Sundin .20 .50
308 Stefan Larsson .02 .10
309 Jonathan Hagrenius .02 .10
310 Serge Boisvert .05 .15
311 Jerry Persson .02 .10
312 Trond Magnussen .02 .10
313 Terho Koskela .02 .10
314 Peter Berndtsson .02 .10
315 Mikael Persson .02 .10
316 Mats Hjalmarsson .02 .10
317 Henrik Lundin .02 .10
318 Jonas Esbjors .02 .10
319 Daniel Alfredsson 1.00 2.50
320 Stefan Ketola .02 .10
321 Lars Dahlstrom .02 .10
322 Par Edlund .02 .10
323 Thomas Sjogren .05 .15
324 Leif Holmgren CO .02 .10
325 Tommy Sandlin CO .02 .10
326 Lars Falk CO .02 .10
327 Harald Luckner CO .02 .10
328 Lars-Erik Lundstrom CO .02 .10
329 Wayne Fleming CO .02 .10
330 Freddy Lindfors CO .02 .10
331 Timo Lahtinen CO .02 .10
332 Kent Forsberg CO .08 .25
333 Christer Abrahamsson CO .08 .25
334 Mikael Lundstrom CO .02 .10
335 Leif Boork CO .02 .10
336 Tommy Sjodin .08 .25
337 Hakan Loob .40 1.00
338 Michael Nylander .40 1.00
339 Michael Nylander .40 1.00
340 Hakan Loob .40 1.00
341 Calle Johansson .20 .50
342 Tommy Sandlin .02 .10
343 Tommy Soderstrom .40 1.00
344 Tommy Sjodin .08 .25
345 Peter Andersson .05 .15
346 Hakan Loob .40 1.00
347 Peter Forsberg 6.00 15.00
348 Mats Sundin 2.00 5.00
349 Jonas Forsberg .20 .50
350 Stefan Bjork .05 .15
351 Edvin Frylen .08 .25
352 Mikael Tjallden .05 .15
353 Johan Davidsson .20 .50
354 Markus Eriksson .05 .15
355 Fredrik Lindh .05 .15
356 Peter Nylander .05 .15

1993 Swedish Semic World Championships Stickers

COMPLETE SET (288) 24.00 60.00
1 Peter Aslin .08 .25
2 Hakan Algotsson .08 .25
3 Kenneth Kennholt .02 .10
4 Arto Blomsten .05 .15
5 Tomas Jonsson .02 .10
6 Fredrik Stillman .02 .10
7 Stefan Larsson .02 .10
8 Peter Popovic .08 .25
9 Hakan Loob .08 .25
10 Thomas Rudqvist .02 .10
11 Patrik Juhlin .08 .25
12 Mikael Renberg .20 .50
13 Peter Forsberg 2.00 5.00
14 Markus Naslund .60 1.50
15 Bengt-Ake Gustafsson .08 .25
16 Jan Larsson .02 .10
17 Fredrik Nilsson .02 .10
18 Roger Hansson .02 .10
19 Tommy Soderstrom .08 .25
20 Anders Eldebrink .05 .15
21 Ulf Samuelsson .02 .10
22 Kjell Samuelsson .08 .25
23 Nicklas Lidstrom 1.25 3.00
24 Tommy Sjodin .05 .15
25 Calle Johansson .08 .25
26 Fredrik Olausson .08 .25
27 Peter Andersson .05 .15
28 Tommy Albelin .05 .15
29 Roger Johansson .05 .15
30 Par Djoos .05 .15
31 Mikael Johansson .02 .10
32 Tomas Sandstrom .08 .25
33 Mats Sundin .60 1.50
34 Ulf Dahlen .08 .25
35 Jan Erixon .05 .15
36 Thomas Steen .08 .25
37 Mikael Andersson .05 .15
38 Johan Garpenlov .08 .25
39 Per-Erik Eklund .08 .25
40 Michael Nylander .08 .25
41 Tomas Forslund .02 .10
42 Patric Kjellberg .20 .50
43 Patrik Carnback .02 .10
44 Niclas Andersson .02 .10
45 Markus Ketterer .08 .25
46 Sakari Lindfors .08 .25
47 Jarmo Myllys .20 .50
48 Peter Ahola .05 .15
49 Mikko Haapakoski .02 .10
50 Kai Harila .02 .10
51 Pasi Huura .05 .15
52 Waltteri Immonen .05 .15
53 Timo Jutila .02 .10
54 Janne Laukkanen .08 .25
55 Harri Laurila .02 .10
56 Jyrki Lumme .08 .25
57 Teppo Numminen .08 25
58 Sami Nuutinen .02 .10
59 Ville Siren .05 .15
60 Pasi Sormunen .02 .10
61 Mika Stromberg .05 .15
62 Mika Alatalo .20 .50
63 Raimo Helminen .02 .10
64 Pauli Jarvinen .02 .10
65 Jarmo Kekalainen .05 .15
66 Jari Korpisalo .05 .15
67 Jari Kurri .40 1.00
68 Mikko Makela .08 .25
69 Mika Nieminen .08 .25
70 Timo Norppa .02 .10
71 Janne Ojanen .02 .10
72 Timo Peltomaa .02 .10
73 Rauli Raitanen .02 .10
74 Juha Riihijarvi .08 .25
75 Christian Ruuttu .08 .25
76 Timo Saarikoski .02 .10
77 Teemu Selanne 2.00 5.00
78 Jukka Seppo .05 .15
79 Petri Skriko .08 .25
80 Esa Tikkanen .20 .50
81 Pekka Tuomisto .02 .10
82 Petri Varis .08 .25
83 Jarkko Varvio .05 .15
84 Vesa Viitakoski .05 .15
85 Marko Virtanen .02 .10
86 Jali Wahlsten .02 .10
87 Sami Wahlsten .02 .10
88 Pentti Matikainen .02 .10
89 Petr Briza .08 .25
90 Roman Turek .40 1.00
91 Milos Holan .02 .10
92 Drahomir Kadlec .05 .15
93 Bedrick Scerban .05 .15
94 Frantisek Prochazka .02 .10
95 Richard Zemlicka .08 .25
96 Roman Horak .40 1.00
97 Lubos Rob .02 .10
98 Jiri Kucera .05 .15
99 Tomas Kapusta .02 .10
100 Roman Rysanek .02 .10
101 Roman Hamrlik .08 .25
102 Robert Svehla .08 .25
103 Tomas Jelinek .05 .15
104 Petr Klima .08 .25
105 Josef Beranek .07 .20
106 Robert Petrovicky .05 .15
107 Kamil Kastak .05 .15
108 David Volek .05 .15
109 Renato Tosio .02 .10
110 Patrick Schopf .02 .10
111 Samuel Balmer .02 .10
112 Andreas Beutler .02 .10
113 Patrice Brasey .02 .10
114 Rick Tschumi .02 .10
115 Sven Leuenberger .02 .10
116 Sandro Bertaggia .02 .10
117 Patrick Howald .02 .10
118 Andy Ton .02 .10
119 Keith Fair .02 .10
120 Mario Brodmann .02 .10
121 Fredy Luhti .02 .10
122 Jorg Eberle .05 .15
123 Roman Wager .02 .10
124 Manuele Celio .02 .10
125 Christian Weber .02 .10
126 Roger Thony .02 .10
127 Felix Hollenstein .02 .10
128 Gil Montandon .02 .10
129 Nikolai Khabibulin .60 1.50
130 Alexei Cherviakov .02 .10
131 Ilja Blakin .05 .15
132 Dmitri Filimonov .05 .15
133 Alexander Karpovtsev .08 .25
134 Sergei Sorokin .05 .15
135 Andrei Sapozhnikov .02 .10
136 Alexei Yashin .20 .50
137 Alexander Cherbayev .02 .10
138 Konstantin Astrakhantsev .05 .15
139 Sergei Petrenko .05 .15
140 Viktor Kozlov .08 .25
141 Roman Oksyuta .02 .10
142 Vladimir Malakhov .08 .25
143 Andrei Lomakin .05 .15
144 Dimitri Yushkevich .08 .25
145 Igor Korolev .02 .10
146 Darius Kasparaitis .08 .25
147 Vyacheslav Bykov .08 .25
148 Andrei Khomutov .08 .25
149 Helmut De Raaf .02 .10
150 Klaus Merk .08 .25
151 Michael Heidt .08 .25
152 Michael Schmidt .02 .10
153 Uli Hiemer .02 .10
154 Andreas Niederberger .02 .10
155 Rick Amann .02 .10
156 Andreas Brockmann .02 .10
157 Gerd Truntschka .05 .15
158 Dieter Hegen .05 .15
159 Stefan Ustorf .05 .15
160 Georg Holzmann .02 .10
161 Ernst Kopf Jr. .02 .10
162 Bernd Truntschka .05 .15
163 Raimund Hilger .02 .10
164 Wolfgang Kummer .02 .10
165 Georg Franz .02 .10
166 Thomas Brandl .02 .10
167 Michael Rumrich .02 .10
168 Uwe Krupp .08 .25
169 Tom Barrasso .20 .50
170 Mike Richter .60 1.50
171 Brian Leetch .60 1.50
172 Chris Chelios .60 1.50
173 Al Iafrate .08 .25
174 Phil Housley .08 .25
175 Kevin Hatcher .08 .25
176 Gary Suter .08 .25
177 Mathieu Schneider .08 .25
178 Joe Mullen .08 .25
179 Kevin Stevens .08 .25
180 Jeremy Roenick 1.50 4.00
181 Tony Granato .08 .25
182 Mike Modano 1.25 3.00
183 Pat LaFontaine .30 .75
184 Ed Olczyk .05 .15
185 Brett Hull 1.50 4.00
186 Craig Janney .08 .25
187 Jimmy Carson .05 .15
188 Tony Amonte .40 1.00
189 Patrick Roy 5.00 12.00
190 Kirk McLean .20 .50
191 Larry Murphy .20 .50
192 Ray Bourque 2.00 5.00
193 Al MacInnis .60 1.50
194 Steve Duchesne .08 .25
195 Eric Desjardins .20 .50
196 Scott Stevens .30 .75
197 Paul Coffey .60 1.50
198 Mario Lemieux 5.00 12.00
199 Wayne Gretzky 6.00 15.00
200 Rick Tocchet .20 .50
201 Eric Lindros 1.25 3.00
202 Mark Messier 1.25 3.00
203 Steve Yzerman 4.00 10.00
204 Luc Robitaille .60 1.50
205 Mark Recchi .60 1.50
206 Joe Sakic 2.00 5.00
207 Owen Nolan .40 1.00
208 Gary Roberts .20 .50
209 David Delfino .08 .25
210 Mike Rosati .08 .25
211 Robert Oberrauch .02 .10
212 Jim Camazzola .02 .10
213 Bill Stewart .02 .10
214 Mike DeAngelis .02 .10
215 Anthony Circelli .02 .10
216 Georg Comploy .02 .10
217 Frank DiMuzio .02 .10
218 Gates Orlando .05 .15
219 John Vecchiarelli .02 .10
220 Joe Foglietta .02 .10
221 Lucio Topatigh .02 .10
222 Carmine Vani .05 .15
223 Lino DeToni .02 .10
224 Mario Chitarron .02 .10
225 Bruno Zarrillo .02 .10
226 Maurizio Mansi .02 .10
227 Stefan Figliuzzi .02 .10
228 Santino Pellegrino .02 .10
229 Jim Marthinsen .08 .25
230 Rob Schistad .08 .25
231 Petter Salsten .02 .10
232 Cato Tom Andersen .02 .10
233 Tommy Jakobsen .02 .10
234 Svein E Norstebo .02 .10
235 Jon Magne Karlstad .02 .10
236 Kim Sogaard .02 .10
237 Geir Hoff .02 .10
238 Erik Kristiansen .02 .10
239 Petter Thoresen .02 .10
240 Ole Eskild Dahlstrom .02 .10
241 Espen Knutsen .20 .50
242 Oystein Olsen .02 .10
243 Roy Johansen .02 .10
244 Trond Magnussen .02 .10
245 Arne Billkvam .02 .10
246 Marius Rath .02 .10
247 Tom Erik Olsen .02 .10
248 Morten Finstad .02 .10
249 Petri Ylonen .08 .25
250 Michel Valliere .08 .25
251 Stephane Botteri .02 .10
252 Serge Poudrier .05 .15
253 Eric Durand .02 .10
254 Jean-Philippe Lemoine .05 .15
255 Denis Perez .05 .15
256 Sebastien Marquet .02 .10
257 Michael Babin .02 .10
258 Stephane Barin .02 .10
259 Arnaud Briand .02 .10
260 Yves Crettenand .02 .10
261 Laurent Deschaume .02 .10
262 Roger Dube .02 .10
263 Patrick Dunn .02 .10
264 Franck Pajonkowski .05 .15
265 Pierre Pousse .02 .10
266 Antoine Richer .02 .10
267 Christophe Ville .02 .10
268 Philippe Bozon .40 1.00
269 Brian Stankiewicz .02 .10
270 Claus Dalpiaz .08 .25
271 Michael Shea .08 .25
272 Robin Doyle .02 .10
273 Martin Ulrich .02 .10
274 Martin Krainz .02 .10
275 Erich Solderer .02 .10
276 Michael Guntner .02 .10
277 Friedrich Ganster .02 .10
278 Wayne Groulx .02 .10
279 Dieter Kalt .02 .10
280 Werner Kerth .02 .10
281 Arno Maier .02 .10
282 Richard Nasheim .02 .10
283 Christian Perthaler .02 .10
284 Andreas Puschnig .02 .10
285 Gerhard Puschnik .02 .10
286 Walter Putnik .02 .10
287 Reinhard Lampert .02 .10
288 Mario Schaden .02 .10

1993-94 Swedish Semic Elitserien

COMPLETE SET (320) 24.00 60.00
1 Bjorkloven Team Emblem .02 .10
2 Patrik Hofbauer .02 .10
3 Jorgen Wikstrom .02 .10
4 Mattias Hedlund .02 .10
5 Yuri Kuznetsov .07 .20
6 Ulf Odling .02 .10
7 Jorgen Eriksson .02 .10
8 Jorgen Hermansson .02 .10
9 Peter Andersson .02 .10
10 Joakim Lindgren .02 .10

11 Glenn Hedman .02 .10
12 Roger Kyro .02 .10
13 Niklas Norberg .02 .10
14 Alexander Belyavsky .05 .15
15 Anders Nejdsater .02 .10
16 Stefan Olofsson .02 .10
17 Mikael Andersson .08 .25
18 Ulf Andersson .02 .10
19 Patrik Sundstrom .08 .25
20 Hakan Hermansson .02 .10
21 Micael Karlberg .02 .10
22 Peder Bejegard .02 .10
23 Johan Boman .02 .10
24 Joakim Lindgren .02 .10
25 Brynas Team Emblem .02 .10
26 Michael Sundlov .07 .20
27 Lars Karlsson .07 .20
28 Bedrich Scerban .02 .10
29 Mikael Lindman .02 .10
30 Johan Tornberg .02 .10
31 Tommy Melkersson .02 .10
32 Stefan Klockare .05 .15
33 Mikael Enander .02 .10
34 Mikael Wiklander .02 .10
35 Christer Olsson .08 .25
36 Thomas Tallberg .05 .15
37 Andreas Dackell .40 1.00
38 Mikael Wahlberg .02 .10
39 Anders Gozzi .02 .10
40 Niklas Gallstedt .02 .10
41 Per-Johan Johansson .02 .10
42 Joakim Persson .08 .25
43 Branislav Janos .02 .10
44 Ove Molin .02 .10
45 Anders Huss .02 .10
46 Jonas Johnsson .02 .10
47 Peter Larsson .02 .10
48 Anders Carlsson .02 .10
49 Djurgarden Team Emblem .02 .10
50 Thomas Ostlund .08 .25
51 Petter Ronnquist .05 .15
52 Christian Due-Boje .05 .15
53 Marcus Ragnarsson .20 .50
54 Joakim Musakka .02 .10
55 Thomas Johansson .02 .10
56 Thomas Eriksson .02 .10
57 Bjorn Nord .08 .25
58 Mikael Magnusson .02 .10
59 Robert Nordmark .05 .15
60 Charles Berglund .02 .10
61 Erik Huusko .05 .15
62 Anders Huusko .02 .10
63 Jens Ohling .05 .15
64 Peter Nilsson .02 .10
65 Magnus Jansson .02 .10
66 Mikael Hakansson .02 .10
67 Ola Josefsson .02 .10
68 Jerry Friman .02 .10
69 Mariusz Czerkawski .40 1.00
70 Fredrik Lindquist .07 .20
71 Mattias Hallback .02 .10
72 Patrik Erickson .02 .10
73 Farjestad Team Emblem .02 .10
74 Anders Bergman .08 .25
75 Jonas Eriksson .07 .20
76 Tommy Samuelsson .02 .10
77 Jesper Duus .02 .10
78 Leif Carlsson .02 .10
79 Per Lundell .02 .10
80 Brian Tutt .05 .15
81 Jakob Karlsson .02 .10
82 Thomas Rhodin .02 .10
83 Mattias Olsson .02 .10
84 Hakan Loob .30 .75
85 Andreas Johansson .20 .50
86 Magnus Arvedsson .40 1.00
87 Anders Oberg .02 .10
88 Mattias Johansson .02 .10
89 Mats Lindgren .20 .50
90 Clas Eriksson .02 .10
91 Patrik Degerstedt .02 .10
92 Peter Ottosson .02 .10
93 Niklas Brannstrom .02 .10
94 Lars Karlsson .07 .20
95 Kjell Dahlin .08 .25
96 Jonas Hoglund .40 1.00
97 HV 71 Team Emblem .02 .10
98 Peter Aslin .08 .25
99 Boo Ahl .08 .25
100 Antonin Stavjana .07 .20
101 Kenneth Kennholt .05 .15
102 Hans Abrahamsson .02 .10
103 Andreas Schultz .02 .10
104 Per Gustafsson .08 .25
105 Mathias Svedberg .02 .10
106 Niklas Rahm .02 .10
107 Fredrik Stillman .02 .10
108 Owe Thornberg .02 .10
109 Thomas Gustavsson .02 .10
110 Stefan Ornskog .05 .15
111 Peter Hammarstrom .02 .10
112 Torbjorn Persson .02 .10
113 John Byce .05 .15
114 Peter Eriksson .02 .10
115 Magnus Axelsson .05 .15
116 Stefan Falk .05 .15
117 Patric Kjellberg .07 .20
118 Johan Davidsson .20 .50
119 Thomas Ljungberg .02 .10
120 Patrik Ross .02 .10
121 Leksand Team Emblem .02 .10
122 Johan Hedberg .75 2.00
123 Ake Lilljebjorn .05 .15
124 Tomas Jonsson .08 .25
125 Stefan Bergkvist .05 .15
126 Henric Bjorkman .02 .10
127 Hans Lodin .02 .10
128 Magnus Svensson .05 .15
129 Orjan Lindmark .02 .10
130 Jan Huokko .02 .10
131 Roger Johansson .02 .10
132 Per Widmark .02 .10
133 Marcus Thuresson .02 .10
134 Niklas Eriksson .02 .10
135 Peter Ciavaglia .05 .15
136 Jonas Bergkvist .08 .25
137 Martin Wiita .02 .10
138 Markus Akerblom .02 .10
139 Greg Parks .05 .15
140 Mattias Loof .02 .10
141 Andreas Karlsson .02 .10
142 Markus Eriksson .02 .10
143 Tomas Forslund .08 .25
144 Jarmo Makitalo .02 .10
145 Lulea Team Emblem .02 .10
146 Robert Skoog .05 .15
147 Erik Grankvist .07 .20
148 Lars Modig .02 .10
149 Patrik Hoglund .02 .10
150 Niklas Bjornfot .02 .10
151 Torbjorn Lindberg .02 .10
152 Ville Siren .07 .20
153 Petter Nilsson .02 .10
154 Tomas Lilja .02 .10
155 Stefan Jonsson .02 .10
156 Stefan Nilsson .02 .10
157 Joakim Gunler .02 .10
158 Johan Stromvall .02 .10
159 Kyosti Karjalainen .07 .20
160 Robert Nordberg .02 .10
161 Tomas Berglund .02 .10
162 Lars-Gunnar Pettersson .02 .10
163 Lars Edstrom .02 .10
164 Lars Hurtig .02 .10
165 Fredrik Oberg .02 .10
166 Mikael Engstrom .02 .10
167 Johan Rosen .02 .10
168 Mika Nieminen .08 .25
169 Malmo Team Emblem .02 .10
170 Peter Lindmark .08 .25
171 Roger Nordstrom .05 .15
172 Daniel Granqvist .05 .15
173 Johan Norgren .02 .10
174 Johan Salle .02 .10
175 Petri Liimatainen .02 .10
176 Peter Hasselblad .02 .10
177 Robert Svehla .08 .25
178 Ricard Persson .08 .25
179 Roger Ohman .02 .10
180 Raimo Helminen .08 .25
181 Marcus Magnertoft .02 .10
182 Mattias Bosson .02 .10
183 Roger Hansson .02 .10
184 Bo Svanberg .02 .10
185 Daniel Rydmark .07 .20
186 Patrik Sylvegard .02 .10
187 Jens Hemstrom .02 .10
188 Jesper Mattsson .08 .25
189 Hakan Ahlund .02 .10
190 Peter Sundstrom .08 .25
191 Mats Naslund .40 1.00
192 Mikko Makela .07 .20
193 MoDo Team Emblem .02 .10
194 Henrik Arvsell .02 .10
195 Fredrik Andersson .05 .15
196 Anders Berglund .02 .10
197 Mattias Timander .08 .25
198 Miloslav Horava .05 .15
199 Lars Jansson .02 .10
200 Anders Eriksson .20 .50
201 Hans Jonsson .20 .50
202 Tomas Nanzen .02 .10
203 Fredrik Bergqvist .02 .10
204 Magnus Wernblom .05 .15
205 Anders Soderberg .08 .25
206 Martin Hostak .05 .15
207 Lennart Hermansson .02 .10
208 Ulf Odmark .02 .10
209 Peter Forsberg 4.00 10.00
210 Per Svartvadet .20 .50
211 Andreas Salomonsson .02 .10
212 Niklas Sundstrom .40 1.00
213 Lars Bystrom .02 .10
214 Mats Lundstrom .02 .10
215 Erik Holmberg .02 .10
216 Henrik Gradin .02 .10
217 Rogle Team Emblem .02 .10
218 Kenneth Johansson .07 .20
219 Magnus Swardh .02 .10
220 Daniel Johansson .08 .25
221 Kari Suoraniemi .02 .10
222 Pierre Johnsson .02 .10
223 Kenny Jonsson .40 1.00
224 Per Ljusterang .02 .10
225 Arto Ruotanen .02 .10
226 Daniel Tjarnquist .08 .25
227 Kari Eloranta .05 .15
228 Per Wallin .08 .25
229 Peter Lundmark .05 .15
230 Roger Elvenes .05 .15
231 Michael Hjalm .02 .10
232 Mattias Olivestedt .02 .10
233 Jan Ericsson .02 .10
234 Tomas Srsen .02 .10
235 Pelle Svensson .02 .10
236 Jorgen Jonsson .02 .10
237 Stefan Elvenes .05 .15
238 Fredrik Moller .02 .10
239 Tord Elvenes .02 .10
240 Mats Loov .02 .10
241 Vasteras Team Emblem .02 .10
242 Mats Ytter .07 .20
243 Tommy Salo .40 1.00
244 Sergei Fokin .02 .10
245 Edvin Frylen .07 .20
246 Leif Rohlin .08 .25
247 Peter Karlsson .02 .10
248 Peter Jacobsson .02 .10
249 Thomas Carlsson .02 .10
250 Lars Ivarsson .02 .10
251 Roger Akerstrom .05 .15
252 Patrik Juhlin .08 .25
253 Alexei Salomatin .05 .15
254 Mishat Fahrutdinov .05 .15
255 Henrik Nilsson .02 .10
256 Mikael Pettersson .02 .10
257 Stefan Hellkvist .02 .10
258 Jens Nielsen .02 .10
259 Hans Huczkowski .02 .10
260 Claes Lindblom .02 .10
261 Johan Brummer .02 .10
262 Dejan Kostic .02 .10
263 Paul Andersson .02 .10
264 Henrik Nordfeldt .02 .10
265 Vastra Frolunda Team Emblem .02 .10
266 Hakan Algotsson .08 .25
267 Mikael Sandberg .07 .20
268 Stefan Nyman .02 .10
269 Joacim Esbjors .05 .15
270 Oscar Ackestrom .02 .10
271 Vladimir Kramskoy .02 .10
272 Richard Sohrman .02 .10
273 Stefan Axelsson .05 .15
274 Ronnie Sundin .08 .25
275 Stefan Larsson .02 .10
276 Thomas Sjogren .02 .10
277 Serge Boisvert .05 .15
278 Jerry Persson .02 .10
279 Terho Koskela .02 .10
280 Peter Strom .02 .10
281 Peter Berndtsson .02 .10
282 Henrik Lundin .02 .10
283 Jonas Esbjors .02 .10
284 Daniel Alfredsson 1.00 2.50
285 Stefan Ketola .02 .10
286 Lars Dahlstrom .02 .10
287 Par Edlund .02 .10
288 Oto Hascak .05 .15
289 Lars-Gunnar Jansson CO .02 .10
290 Tommy Sandlin CO .02 .10
291 Tommy Boustedt CO .02 .10
292 Jorgen Palm CO .02 .10
293 Hakan Nygren CO .02 .10
294 Wayne Fleming CO .02 .10
295 Sakari Pietila CO .02 .10
296 Timo Lahtinen CO .02 .10
297 Kent Forsberg CO .07 .20
298 Christer Abrahamsson CO .08 .25
299 Mikael Lundstrom CO .02 .10
300 Leif Boork CO .02 .10
301 Peter Forsberg 4.00 10.00
302 Peter Forsberg 4.00 10.00
303 Hakan Loob .30 .75
304 Kenny Jonsson .40 1.00
305 Peter Forsberg 4.00 10.00
306 Mats Sundin 1.50 4.00
307 Micheal Sundlov AS .07 .20
308 Roger Akerstrom AS .05 .15
309 Fredrik Stillman AS .02 .10
310 Mikael Renberg AS .40 1.00
311 Peter Forsberg AS 4.00 10.00
312 Ulf Dahlen AS .08 .25
313 Pal Grotnes FS .07 .20
314 Daniel Tjarnquist FS .08 .25
315 Henrik Rehnberg FS .05 .15
316 Mattias Ohlund FS .40 1.00
317 Jan Labraaten FS .08 .25
318 Patrik Wallenberg FS .07 .20
319 Niklas Wallin FS .07 .20
320 Tobias Thermell FS .07 .20

1994 Swedish Olympics Lillehammer

COMPLETE HOCKEY SET (56) 15.00 30.00
273 Ice Hockey Logo .02 .10
274 Russian Team Puzzle .07 .20
275 Russian Team Puzzle .07 .20
276 Russian Team Puzzle .07 .20
277 Russian Team Puzzle .07 .20
278 Russian Team Puzzle .07 .20
279 Russian Team Puzzle .07 .20
280 Konstantin Astrakhantsev .20 .50
281 Viacheslav Bykov .20 .50
282 Sergei Sorokin .20 .50
283 Alexander Smirnov .20 .50
284 Swedish Team Sticker .07 .20
285 Swedish Team Sticker .07 .20
286 Swedish Team Sticker .07 .20
287 Swedish Team Sticker .07 .20
288 Swedish Team Sticker .07 .20
289 Swedish Team Sticker .07 .20
290 Markus Naslund .75 2.00
291 Peter Forsberg 4.00 10.00
292 Mats Sundin 1.50 4.00
293 Mikael Renberg .20 .50
294 Tommy Soderstrom .20 .50
295 Finnish Team Puzzle .07 .20
296 Finnish Team Puzzle .07 .20
297 Finnish Team Puzzle .07 .20
298 Finnish Team Puzzle .07 .20
299 Finnish Team Puzzle .07 .20
300 Finnish Team Puzzle .07 .20
301 Markus Ketterer .20 .50
302 Vesa Viitakoski .07 .20
303 Esa Tikkanen .20 .50
304 Erik Hamalainen .07 .20
305 Norwegian Team Puzzle .07 .20
306 Norwegian Team Puzzle .07 .20
307 Norwegian Team Puzzle .07 .20
308 Norwegian Team Puzzle .07 .20
309 Norwegian Team Puzzle .07 .20
310 Norwegian Team Puzzle .07 .20
311 Jim Marthinsen .20 .50
312 Erik Kristiansen .07 .20
313 Petter Salsten .07 .20
314 Eric Lindros 1.50 4.00
315 Greg Johnson .20 .50
316 Allain Roy .20 .50
317 Hank Lammens .30 .75
318 Leo Gudas .20 .50
319 Petr Briza .30 .75
320 Petr Rosol .20 .50
321 Otakar Janecky .20 .50
322 Mike Richter .75 2.00
323 Brett Hull 2.00 5.00
324 Chris Chelios .75 2.00
325 Pat Lafontaine .75 2.00
326 Claus Dalpiaz .20 .50
327 Stephane Barin .07 .20
328 Gerd Truntschka .07 .20

1994-95 Swedish Leaf

COMPLETE SET (320) 26.00 65.00
COMPLETE SERIES 2 (161-320) 16.00 40.00
COMPLETE SERIES 1 (1-160) 10.00 25.00
1 Thomas Tallberg .02 .10
2 Hakan Algotsson .08 .25
3 Mikael Magnusson .02 .10
4 Per Lundell .02 .10
5 Kenneth Kennholt .02 .10
6 Jan Huokko .02 .10
7 Petter Nilsson .02 .10
8 Johan Norgren .02 .10
9 Anders Berglund .02 .10
10 Kari Eloranta .07 .20
11 Sam Lindstahl .02 .10
12 Johan Rosen .02 .10
13 Jonas Johnsson .02 .10
14 Erik Huusko .07 .20
15 Thomas Rhodin .02 .10
16 Patric Kjellberg .15 .40
17 Fredrik Andersson .02 .10
18 Stefan Nilsson .02 .10
19 Petri Liimatainen .02 .10
20 Lars Jansson .02 .10
21 Per Wallin .02 .10
22 Mika Nieminen .15 .40
23 Lars Ivarsson .02 .10
24 Ronnie Sundin .15 .40
25 Bedrich Scerban .02 .10
26 Anders Huusko .02 .10
27 Erik Grenkvist .02 .10
28 Stefan Ornskog .07 .20
29 Marcus Thuresson .02 .10
30 Johan Stromvall .02 .10
31 Peter Hasselblad .02 .10
32 Anders Eriksson .20 .50
33 Roger Elvenes .02 .10
34 Stefan Larsson .02 .10
35 Alexei Salomatin .02 .10
36 Niclas Havelid .40 1.00
37 Mikael Lindman .02 .10
38 Jens Ohling .02 .10
39 Hakan Loob .30 .75
40 Johan Hedberg .60 1.50
41 Niklas Eriksson .02 .10
42 Robert Nordberg .05 .15
43 Robert Svehla .40 1.00
44 Hans Jonsson .30 .75
45 Thomas Srsen .02 .10
46 Thomas Sjogren .02 .10
47 Mishat Fahrutdinov .02 .10
48 Thomas Strandberg .02 .10
49 Andreas Dackell .30 .75
50 Peter Nilsson .02 .10
51 Andreas Johansson .30 .75
52 Stefan Falk .02 .10
53 Marcus Akerblom .02 .10
54 Peter Aslin .08 .25
55 Ricard Persson .15 .40
56 Tomas Nanzen .02 .10
57 Per-Johan Svensson .02 .10
58 Terho Koskela .02 .10
59 Henrik Nilsson .02 .10
60 Mats Lindberg .02 .10
61 Anders Huss .02 .10
62 Magnus Jansson .02 .10
63 Mats Lindgren .20 .50
64 Thomas Ljungberg .02 .10
65 Tomas Forslund .08 .25
66 Thomas Ostlund .15 .40
67 Raimo Helminen .08 .25
68 Magnus Wernblom .02 .10
69 Jorgen Jonsson .02 .10
70 Peter Berndtsson .02 .10
71 Stefan Hellkvist .02 .10
72 Tommy Lehmann .07 .20
73 Stefan Klockare .02 .10
74 Ola Josefsson .02 .10
75 Peter Lindmark .08 .25
76 Owe Thornberg .02 .10
77 Jarmo Makitalo .02 .10
78 Tomas Berglund .02 .10
79 Bo Svanberg .02 .10
80 Lennart Hermansson .02 .10
81 Stefan Elvenes .02 .10
82 Daniel Alfredsson 1.50 4.00
83 Claes Lindblom .02 .10
84 Bjorn Ahlstrom .02 .10
85 Ove Molin .02 .10
86 Fredrik Lindquist .20 .50
87 Clas Eriksson .02 .10
88 Peter Hammarstrom .02 .10
89 Magnus Swardh .02 .10
90 Lars Hurtig .02 .10
91 Daniel Rydmark .02 .10
92 Lars Bystrom .02 .10
93 Mats Loov .02 .10
94 Lars Dahlstrom .02 .10
95 Johan Brummer .02 .10
96 Patric Englund .02 .10
97 Christer Olsson .15 .40
98 Patrik Erickson .02 .10
99 Peter Ottosson .02 .10
100 Tomas Jonsson .08 .25
101 Lars Modig .02 .10
102 Ake Lilljebjorn .02 .10
103 Patrik Sylvegard .02 .10
104 Daniel Johansson .20 .50
105 Edvin Frylen .08 .25
106 Par Edlund .02 .10
107 Paul Andersson .02 .10
108 Rikard Franzen .02 .10
109 Christian Due-Boje .08 .25
110 Tommy Samuelsson .02 .10
111 Mathias Svedberg .02 .10
112 Hans Lodin .02 .10
113 Jonas Eriksson .08 .25
114 Mikael Engstrom .02 .10
115 Hakan Ahlund .02 .10
116 Kari Suoraniemi .02 .10
117 Peter Jacobsson .02 .10
118 Kristian Gahn .02 .10
119 Tommy Melkersson .02 .10
120 Oscar Ackestrom .02 .10
121 Thomas Johansson .02 .10
122 Jesper Duus .02 .10
123 Hans Abrahamsson .02 .10
124 Orjan Lindmark .02 .10
125 Torbjorn Lindberg .02 .10
126 Michael Sundlov .08 .25
127 Peter Sundstrom .08 .25
128 Pierre Johnsson .02 .10
129 Thomas Carlsson .02 .10
130 Stefan Axelsson .02 .10
131 Robert Nordmark .07 .20
132 Torbjorn Persson .02 .10
133 Bjorn Nord .02 .10
134 Mats Ytter .02 .10
135 AIK
Team Statistics .02 .10
136 Brynas IF
Team Statistics .02 .10
137 Djurgardens IF
Team Statistics .02 .10
138 Vastra Frolunda
Team Statistics .02 .10
139 Farjestad BK
Team Statistics .02 .10
140 HV-71
Team Statistics .02 .10
141 Leksand IF
Team Statistics .02 .10
142 Lulea HF
Team Statistics .02 .10
143 Malmo IF
Team Statistics .02 .10
144 MoDo Hockey
Team Statistics .02 .10
145 Rogle BK
Team Statistics .02 .10
146 Varsteras IK
Team Statistics .02 .10
147 AIK Logo .02 .10
148 Brynas IF Logo .02 .10
149 Djurgardens IF .02 .10
150 Vastra Frolunda Logo .02 .10
151 Farjestads BK .02 .10
152 HV-71 Logo .02 .10
153 Leksands IF Logo .02 .10
154 Lulea HF .02 .10
155 Malmo IF .02 .10
156 MoDo Hockey .02 .10
157 Rogle BK .02 .10
158 Vasteras IK .02 .10
159 Checklist 1-80 .02 .10
160 Checklist 81-160 .02 .10
161 Kenneth Johansson .08 .25
162 Stefan Jonsson .02 .10
163 Mikael Wahlberg .02 .10
164 Per Djoos .08 .25
165 Andreas Schultz .02 .10
166 Sacha Molin .02 .10
167 Marcus Ramen .02 .10
168 Jergus Baca .02 .10
169 Erik Bergstrom .02 .10
170 Jonas Forsberg .15 .40
171 Olli Kaski .02 .10
172 Morgan Samuelsson .02 .10
173 Anders Burstrom .02 .10
174 Stanislav Meciar .02 .10
175 Leif Rohlin .15 .40
176 Lars Edstrom .02 .10
177 Esa Keskinen .08 .25
178 Daniel Casselstahl .02 .10
179 Mattias Timander .20 .50
180 Peter Nordstrom .02 .10
181 Patric Aberg .02 .10
182 Mikael Enander .02 .10
183 Charles Berglund .08 .25
184 Jonas Andersson-Junkka .15 .40
185 Sergei Fokin .02 .10
186 Boo Ahl .15 .40
187 Jiri Kucera .08 .25
188 Roger Nordstrom .02 .10
189 Peter Forsberg 6.00 15.00
190 Arto Ruotanen .02 .10
191 Mikael Wiklander .02 .10
192 Joakim Persson .08 .25
193 Peter Larsson .02 .10
194 Per Eklund .15 .40
195 Joacim Esbjors .02 .10
196 Magnus Arvedsson .60 1.50
197 Marko Palo .02 .10
198 Mikael Holmberg .02 .10
199 Mikael Renberg .75 2.00
200 Tero Lehtera .15 .40
201 Fredrik Lindh .02 .10
202 Joham Finnstrom .02 .10
203 Peter Popovic .08 .25
204 Tony Barthelson .02 .10
205 Stefan Polla .02 .10
206 Jonas Esbjors .02 .10
207 Roger Hansson .02 .10
208 Mikael Hakanson .02 .10
209 Daniel Tjarnqvist .15 .40
210 Anders Carlsson .08 .25
211 Dick Tarnstrom .15 .40
212 Johan Tornberg .02 .10
213 Joakim Lundberg .02 .10
214 Marko Jantunen .15 .40
215 Patrik Haltia .02 .10
216 Fredrik Stillman .02 .10
217 Andy Schneider .02 .10
218 Thomas Holmstrom ERC 2.00 5.00
219 Jens Hemstrom .02 .10
220 Anders Soderberg .20 .50
221 Peter Lundmark .02 .10
222 Patrik Juhlin .15 .40
223 Anders Gozzi .02 .10
224 Marcus Ragnarsson .30 .75
225 Mattias Olsson .02 .10
226 Andreas Karlsson .20 .50
227 Tomas Lilja .02 .10
228 Stefan Ohman .02 .10
229 Jarmo Kekalainen .08 .25
230 Tony Skopac .02 .10
231 Lars Karlsson .08 .25
232 Mats Sundin 1.00 2.50
233 Peter Strom .02 .10
234 Mattias Johansson .02 .10
235 Johan Lindbom .02 .10
236 Mats Lusth .02 .10
237 Marcus Magnertoft .02 .10
238 Martin Hostak .02 .10
239 Mikael Pettersson .02 .10
240 Johan Akerman .02 .10
241 Mathias Hallback .02 .10
242 Johan Davidsson .20 .50
243 Per-Erik Eklund .15 .40
244 Johan Salle .02 .10
245 Per Svartvadet .20 .50
246 Ville Siren .08 .25
247 Mattias Loof .02 .10
248 Per-Johan Axelsson .60 1.50
249 Peter Gerhardsson .02 .10
250 Jonas Bergqvist .08 .25
251 Per-Johan Johansson .40 1.00
252 Mattias Bosson .02 .10
253 Andreas Olsson .02 .10
254 Patrik Zetterberg .02 .10
255 Michael Johansson .02 .10
256 Stefan Gustavson .02 .10
257 Jerry Persson .02 .10
258 Stefan Nilsson .02 .10
259 Roger Johansson .02 .10
260 Jarmo Myllys .20 .50
261 Kyosti Karjalainen .02 .10
262 Thomas Eriksson .02 .10
263 Michael Hjalm .02 .10
264 Espen Knutsen .40 1.00
265 Andreas Salomonsson .02 .10
266 Patrik Hoglund .02 .10
267 Peter Andersson .02 .10
268 Brett Hauer .08 .25
269 Stefan Ketola .02 .10
270 Patrik Carnback .08 .25
271 Petter Ronnqvist .02 .10
272 Roger Ohman .02 .10
273 Fredrik Modin .75 2.00
274 Alexander Beliavski .02 .10
275 Niklas Brannstrom .02 .10
276 Per Gustafsson .15 .40
277 Nicklas Nordqvist .02 .10
278 Roger Akerstrom .02 .10
279 Jiri Vykoukal .08 .25
280 Jesper Mattsson .15 .40
281 Henrik Nordfeldt .02 .10
282 Joakim Musakka .02 .10
283 Anders Johnson .02 .10
284 Niklas Sundstrom .40 1.00
285 Nicklas Lidstrom 1.00 2.50
286 Tomas Sandstrom .40 1.00
287 Jens Nielsen .02 .10
288 Mattias Ohlund .75 2.00
289 Markus Eriksson .02 .10
290 Mikael Sandberg .08 .25
291 Sergeij Pushkov .02 .10
292 Jonas Hoglund .40 1.00
293 Peter Ekelund .02 .10
294 Fredrik Bergqvist .02 .10
295 Torgny Bendelin .02 .10
296 Tommy Sandlin .02 .10
297 Tommy Boustedt .02 .10
298 Conny Evensson .02 .10
299 Sune Bergman .02 .10
300 Wayne Fleming .02 .10
301 Lars Bergstrom .02 .10
302 Hannu Jortikka .02 .10
303 Leif Boork .02 .10
304 Christer Abrahamsson .08 .25
305 Randy Edmonds .02 .10
306 Ulf Labraaten .02 .10
307 AIK .02 .10
308 Brynas IF .02 .10
309 Djurgardens IF .02 .10
310 Farjestads BK .02 .10
311 HV 71 .02 .10
312 Leksands IF .02 .10
313 Lulea HF .02 .10
314 Malmo IF .02 .10
315 MoDo .02 .10
316 Rogle BK .02 .10
317 Vasteras IK .02 .10
318 Vastra Frolunda .02 .10
319 Checklist 161-240 .02 .10
320 Checklist 241-320 .02 .10
NNO1 Malmo IF SuperChase 10.00 25.00
NNO2 M.Lindgren SuperChase 6.00 15.00

1994-95 Swedish Leaf Clean Sweepers

COMPLETE SET (10) 10.00 25.00
1 Peter Lindmark 1.25 3.00
2 Michael Sundlov 1.25 3.00
3 Thomas Ostlund 1.25 3.00
4 Jonas Eriksson 1.25 3.00
5 Peter Aslin 1.25 3.00
6 Ake Lilljebjorn 1.25 3.00
7 Johan Hedberg 2.00 5.00
8 Henrik Arvsell 1.25 3.00
9 Fredrik Andersson 1.25 3.00
10 Hakan Algotsson 1.25 3.00

1994-95 Swedish Leaf Foreign Affairs

COMPLETE SET (10) 8.00 20.00
1 Espen Knutsen 2.00 5.00
2 Esa Keskinen .75 2.00
3 Marko Jantunen .75 2.00
4 Jarmo Myllys 1.25 3.00
5 Jiri Kucera .75 2.00
6 Jiri Vykoukal .75 2.00
7 Jarmo Kekalainen .75 2.00
8 Olli Kaski .75 2.00
9 Jergus Baca .75 2.00
10 Tero Lehtera .75 2.00

1994-95 Swedish Leaf Gold Cards

COMPLETE SET (24) 30.00 75.00
1 Title Card 2.00 5.00
2 Andreas Dackell 1.25 3.00
3 Charles Berglund .75 2.00
4 Christian Due-Boje .75 2.00
5 Daniel Rydmark .75 2.00
6 Fredrik Stillman .75 2.00
7 Hakan Algotsson 1.25 3.00
8 Hakan Loob 1.25 3.00
9 Jonas Bergqvist .75 2.00
10 Jorgen Jonsson .75 2.00
11 Kenny Jonsson 1.25 3.00
12 Leif Rohlin .75 2.00
13 Magnus Svensson .75 2.00
14 Mats Naslund 1.25 3.00
15 Michael Sundlov 1.25 3.00
16 Niklas Eriksson .75 2.00
17 Patric Kjellberg .75 2.00
18 Patrick Juhlin .75 2.00
19 Peter Forsberg 15.00 40.00
20 Roger Hansson .75 2.00
21 Roger Johansson .75 2.00
22 Stefan Ornskog .75 2.00
23 Tomas Jonsson .75 2.00
24 Tommy Salo 2.00 5.00

1994-95 Swedish Leaf Guest Special

COMPLETE SET (8) 16.00 40.00
1 Mats Sundin 4.00 10.00
2 Tomas Sandstrom .75 2.00
3 Peter Forsberg 10.00 25.00
4 Nicklas Lidstrom 4.00 10.00
5 Mikael Renberg 1.25 3.00
6 Roger Johansson .40 1.00
7 Peter Popovic .40 1.00
8 Patrick Juhlin .40 1.00

1994-95 Swedish Leaf NHL Draft

COMPLETE SET (10) 12.00 30.00
1 Mattias Ohlund 1.50 4.00
2 Johan Davidsson .40 1.00
3 Fredrik Modin 1.50 4.00
4 Johan Finnstrom .40 1.00
5 Edvin Frylen .40 1.00
6 Daniel Alfredsson 3.00 8.00
7 Patrik Haltia 1.25 3.00
8 Peter Strom .40 1.00
9 Thomas Holmstrom 4.00 10.00
10 Dick Tarnstrom .75 2.00

1994-95 Swedish Leaf Playmakers

COMPLETE SET (6) 2.00 5.00
1 Title Card .75 2.00
2 Stefan Nilsson .40 1.00
3 Mika Nieminen .40 1.00
4 Raimo Helminen .40 1.00
5 Peter Larsson .40 1.00
6 Hakan Loob .75 2.00

1994-95 Swedish Leaf Rookie Rockets

COMPLETE SET (10) 8.00 20.00
1 Fredrik Modin 1.25 3.00
2 Jonas Andersson-Junkka .75 2.00
3 Thomas Holmstrom 4.00 10.00
4 Mattias Ohlund 1.25 3.00
5 Per Eklund .40 1.00
6 Daniel Tjarnqvist .40 1.00
7 Joakim Persson .75 2.00
8 Patrik Haltia .75 2.00
9 Andreas Karlsson .40 1.00
10 Stefan Nilsson .40 1.00

1994-95 Swedish Leaf Studio Signatures

COMPLETE SET (12) 4.00 10.00
1 Rikard Franzen .40 1.00
2 Anders Huss .40 1.00
3 Jens Ohling .40 1.00
4 Tommy Samuelsson .40 1.00
5 Fredrik Stillman .40 1.00
6 Jonas Bergqvist .40 1.00
7 Johan Stromvall .40 1.00
8 Roger Nordstrom .40 1.00
9 Lars Bystrom .40 1.00
10 Roger Elvenes .40 1.00
11 Leif Rohlin .75 2.00
12 Tero Koskela .40 1.00

1994-95 Swedish Leaf Top Guns

COMPLETE SET (10) 4.80 12.00
1 Thomas Srsen .40 1.00
2 Hakan Loob 1.25 3.00
3 Lars Hurtig .40 1.00
4 Stefan Elvenes .40 1.00
5 Jorgen Jonsson .40 1.00
6 Robert Svehla 1.25 3.00
7 Daniel Rydmark .40 1.00
8 Owe Thornberg .40 1.00
9 Patric Kjellberg .75 2.00
10 Mats Loov .40 1.00

1995 Swedish Globe World Championships

COMPLETE SET (270) 20.00 50.00
1 Tommy Soderstrom .08 .25
2 Roger Nordstrom .02 .10
3 Tommy Salo .40 1.00
4 Hakan Algotsson .07 .20
5 Thomas Ostlund .08 .25
7 Ulf Samuelsson .05 .15
8 Calle Johansson .07 .20
9 Nicklas Lidstrom .60 1.50
10 Tommy Albelin .05 .15
11 Peter Andersson .02 .10
12 Magnus Svensson .05 .15
13 Mats Sundin .40 1.00
14 Tomas Jonsson .05 .15
15 Kenny Jonsson .08 .25
16 Tommy Sjodin .05 .15
17 Fredrik Stillman .02 .10
18 Marcus Ragnarsson .08 .25
19 Peter Popovic .05 .15
20 Arto Blomsten .02 .10
21 Peter Forsberg 1.25 3.00
22 Roger Johansson .02 .10
23 Leif Rohlin .05 .15
24 Bjorn Nord .02 .10
25 Stefan Larsson .02 .10
26 Fredrik Olausson .05 .15
27 Kjell Samuelsson .05 .15
28 Tomas Sandstrom .08 .25
29 Mikael Renberg .08 .25
30 Mikael Johansson .02 .10
31 Patrik Juhlin .05 .15
32 Roger Hansson .02 .10
33 Daniel Rydmark .05 .15
34 Jonas Bergqvist .05 .15
35 Michael Nylander .08 .25
36 Johan Garpenlov .05 .15
37 Charles Berglund .02 .10
38 Jorgen Jonsson .02 .10
39 Stefan Ornskog .02 .10
40 Thomas Steen .05 .15
41 Patrik Carnback .05 .15

42 Mikael Andersson .05 .15
43 Markus Naslund .30 .75
44 Andreas Dackell .08 .25
45 Erik Huusko .02 .10
46 Tomas Forslund .05 .15
47 Daniel Alfredsson .20 .50
48 Ulf Dahlen .08 .25
49 Anders Huusko .02 .10
50 Tomas Holmstrom .40 1.00
51 Niklas Andersson .02 .10
52 Hakan Loob .08 .25
53 Per-Erik Eklund .05 .15
54 Patrik Erickson .02 .10
55 Jonas Forsberg .08 .25
56 Daniel Johansson .05 .15
57 Mattias Ohlund .08 .25
58 Anders Eriksson .08 .25
59 Fredrik Modin .20 .50
60 Niklas Sundstrom .08 .25
61 Jesper Mattson .08 .25
62 Johan Davidsson .08 .25
63 Mats Lindgren .08 .25
64 Leif Holmqvist .02 .10
65 Pelle Lindbergh .40 1.00
66 Lennart Svedberg .02 .10
67 Borje Salming .08 .25
68 Sven Tumba Johansson .02 .10
69 Ulf Sterner .02 .10
70 Anders Hedberg .08 .25
71 Kent Nilsson .08 .25
72 Mats Naslund .08 .25
73 Patrick Roy 2.50 6.00
74 Ed Belfour .60 1.50
75 Bill Ranford .20 .50
76 Paul Coffey .40 1.00
77 Ray Bourque .75 2.00
78 Steve Smith .05 .15
79 Al MacInnis .30 .75
80 Mark Tinordi .05 .15
81 Scott Stevens .08 .25
82 Rob Blake .30 .75
83 Theo Fleury .40 1.00
84 Mark Messier .60 1.50
85 Mike Gartner UER
card n .20 .50
86 Brendan Shanahan .60 1.50
87 Mario Lemieux 2.50 6.00
88 Eric Lindros 1.25 3.00
89 Steve Yzerman 2.50 6.00
90 Adam Oates .20 .50
91 Paul Kariya 1.50 4.00
92 Rick Tocchet .20 .50
93 Doug Gilmour .40 1.00
94 Luc Robitaille .30 .75
95 Jason Arnott .20 .50
96 Adam Graves .20 .50
97 Petr Nedved .08 .25
98 Mark Recchi .30 .75
99 Wayne Gretzky 3.00 8.00
100 Mike Richter .60 1.50
101 John Vanbiesbrouck .40 1.00
102 Tom Barrasso .08 .25
103 Brian Leetch .30 .75
104 Gary Suter .08 .25
105 Kevin Hatcher .05 .15
106 Phil Housley .08 .25
107 Chris Chelios .40 1.00
108 Eric Weinrich .05 .15
109 Derian Hatcher .08 .25
110 Craig Wolanin .05 .15
111 Mike Modano .60 1.50
112 Joe Mullen .08 .25
113 Joel Otto .08 .25
114 Doug Brown .08 .25
115 Brett Hull .60 1.50
110 Pat LaFontaine .20 .50
117 Jeremy Roenick .60 1.50
118 Craig Janney .08 .25
119 Kevin Miller .05 .15
120 Tony Granato .08 .25
121 Tony Amonte .30 .75
122 Kevin Stevens .08 .25
123 Darren Turcotte .05 .15
124 Scott Young .20 .50
125 Doug Weight .30 .75
126 Phil Bourque .05 .15
127 Markus Ketterer .05 .15
128 Jarmo Myllys .20 .50
129 Jyrki Lumme .08 .25
130 Timo Jutila .05 .15
131 Marko Kiprusoff .05 .15
132 Hannu Virta .05 .15
133 Teppo Numminen .08 .25
134 Janne Laukkanen .08 .25
135 Mika Nieminen .08 .25
136 Janne Ojanen .05 .15
137 Jari Kurri .20 .50
138 Esa Tikkanen .08 .25
139 Saku Koivu .40 1.00
140 Teemu Selanne .75 2.00
141 Raimo Helminen .05 .15
142 Mikko Makela .05 .15
143 Christian Ruuttu .05 .15
144 Esa Keskinen .05 .15
145 Dominik Hasek .60 1.50
146 Petr Briza .08 .25
147 Richard Smehlik .05 .15
148 Leo Gudas .02 .10
149 Roman Hamrlik .08 .25
150 Antonin Stavjana .05 .15
151 Jiri Slegr .05 .15
152 Jiri Vykoukal .05 .15
153 Tomas Jelinek .05 .15
154 Richard Zemlicka .05 .15
155 Robert Lang .08 .25
156 Michal Pivonka .08 .25
157 Jaromir Jagr 1.25 3.00
158 Josef Beranek .05 .15
159 Robert Reichel .05 .15
160 Petr Hrbek .02 .10
161 Jiri Kucera .05 .15
162 Kamil Kastak .02 .10
163 Andrei Trefilov .08 .25
164 Mikhail Shtalenkov .08 .25
165 Sergei Zubov .08 .25
166 Vladimir Malakhov .05 .15
167 Igor Kravchuk .05 .15
168 Alexei Gusarov .05 .15
169 Alexei Zhitnik .08 .25
170 Alexander Smirnov .02 .10
171 Dimitri Yushkevich .08 .25
172 Alexei Yashin .15 .40
173 Alexei Zhamnov .08 .25
174 Pavel Bure .75 2.00
175 Sergei Fedorov .75 2.00
176 Andrei Kovalenko .08 .25
177 Alexei Kovalev .20 .50
178 Andrei Khomutov .05 .15
179 Valeri Kamensky .08 .25
180 Viacheslav Bykov .07 .20
181 Claus Dalpiaz .05 .15
182 Michael Puschacher .05 .15
183 Ken Strong .02 .10
184 Martin Ulrich .02 .10
185 Andreas Puschnig .02 .10
186 Herbert Hohenberger .08 .25
187 Marty Dallmann .02 .10
188 James Burton .02 .10
189 Michael Shea .02 .10
190 Jim Marthinsen .08 .25
191 Orjan Lovdal .02 .10
192 Cato Tom Andersen .02 .10
193 Geir Hoff .02 .10
194 Tommy Jakobsen .02 .10
195 Marius Rath .02 .10
196 Trond Magnussen .02 .10
197 Svein Enok Norstebo .02 .10
198 Espen Knutsen .20 .50
199 Petri Ylonen .05 .15
200 Michel Valliere .02 .10
201 Franck Pajonkowski .05 .15
202 Pierrick Maia .02 .10
203 Christophe Ville .02 .10
204 Serge Poudrier .02 .10
205 Philippe Bozon .05 .15
206 Gerald Guennelon .02 .10
207 Antoine Richer .02 .10
208 Reto Pavoni .05 .15
209 Renato Tosio .05 .15
210 Jorg Eberle .02 .10
211 Fredy Luthi .02 .10
212 Christian Weber .02 .10
213 Sandro Bertaggia .02 .10
214 Patrick Howald .02 .10
215 Gil Montandon .02 .10
216 Rick Tschumi .02 .10
217 Klaus Merk .07 .20
218 Josef Heiss .08 .25
219 Rick Amann .02 .10
220 Michael Rumrich .02 .10
221 Thomas Brandl .02 .10
222 Andreas Niederberger .02 .10
223 Leo Stefan .02 .10
224 Stefan Ustorf .05 .15
225 Dieter Hegen .05 .15
226 Michael Rosati .05 .15
227 Bruno Campese .05 .15
228 Roberto Oberrauch .02 .10
229 Anthony Circelli .02 .10
230 Bill Stewart .02 .10
231 Bruno Zarillo .02 .10
232 Gaetano Orlando .02 .10
233 Stefan Figliuzzi .02 .10
234 Jimmy Carnazzola .02 .10
235 Vladislav Tretiak .40 1.00
236 Slava Fetisov .20 .50
237 Alexei Kasatonov .08 .25
238 Sergei Makarov .08 .25
239 Igor Larionov .30 .75
240 Vladimir Krutov .08 .25
241 Valeri Kharlamov .08 .25
242 Vladimir Petrov .05 .15
243 Boris Mikhailov .08 .25
244 Sweden
Olympic Gold 94 .08 .25
245 Sweden
Olympic Gold 94 .08 .25
246 Sweden
Olympic Gold 94 .08 .25
247 Canada
World Champions .30 .75
248 Canada
World Champions .08 .25
249 Canada
World Champions .20 .50
250 Manon Rheaume 1.25 3.00
251 Sundin and Andersson .20 .50
252 Brolin and Knutsen .08 .25
253 Peter Forsberg Special 1.25 3.00
254 Peter Forsberg Special 1.25 3.00
255 Peter Forsberg Special 1.25 3.00
256 Mats Sundin Special .40 1.00
257 Mats Sundin Special .40 1.00
258 Mats Sundin Special .40 1.00
259 Mikael Renberg Special .08 .25
260 Mikael Renberg Special .08 .25
261 Mikael Renberg Special .08 .25
262 Eric Lindros Special 1.25 3.00
263 Eric Lindros Special 1.25 3.00
264 Eric Lindros Special 1.25 3.00
265 Wayne Gretzky Special 3.00 8.00
266 Wayne Gretzky Special 3.00 8.00
267 Wayne Gretzky Special 3.00 8.00
268 Checklist 1-90
(Renberg .08 .25
269 Checklist 91-180
(Sundi .40 1.00
270 Checklist 181-270
(Fors 1.25 3.00
XX Binder 2.00 5.00
NNO Peter Forsberg
Mats Sundin 10.00 20.00

1995 Swedish World Championships Stickers

1 Bill Ranford .02 .10
2 Stephane Fiset .20 .50
3 Steve Duchesne .08 .25
4 Brad Schlegel .02 .10
5 Luke Richardson .02 .10
6 Darryl Sydor .02 .10
7 Yves Racine .02 .10
8 Rob Blake .20 .50
9 Marc Bergevin .02 .10
10 Paul Coffey .60 1.50
11 Jason Arnott .20 .50
12 Geoff Sanderson .20 .50
13 Shayne Corson .20 .50
14 Mike Ricci .20 .50
15 Kelly Buchberger .20 .50
16 Brendan Shanahan .75 2.00
17 Patrick Verbeek .20 .50
18 Nelson Emerson .20 .50
19 Rod Brind'Amour .20 .50
20 Joe Sakic 2.00 5.00
21 Luc Robitaille .60 1.50
22 Stephen Thomas .08 .25
23 Paul Kariya 1.50 4.00
24 Theo Fleury .50 1.25
25 Dave Gagner .20 .50
26 Valeri Ivannikov .02 .10
27 Mikhail Shtalenkov .20 .50
28 Nikolai Tsulygin .02 .10
29 Dmitri Krasotkin .02 .10
30 Morat Davydov .02 .10
31 Andrei Sklopintsev .02 .10
32 Oleg Davydov .02 .10
33 Evgeni Gribko .02 .10
34 Andrei Yakhanov .02 .10
35 Igor Nikulin .02 .10
36 Valeri Kamensky .02 .10
37 Boris Timofeev .02 .10
38 Dmitri Denisov .02 .10
39 Rail Muftiev .02 .10
40 Andrei Tarasenko .02 .10
41 Oleg Belov .02 .10
42 Andrei Kovalenko .02 .10
43 Igor Varitski .02 .10
44 Ravil Yakubov .02 .10
45 Viacheslav Kozlov .20 .50
46 Alexander Vinogradov .02 .10
47 Yuri Tsyplakov .02 .10
48 Stanislav Romanov .02 .10
49 Slava Bykov .08 .25
50 Andrei Khomutov .08 .25
51 Joseph Heiss .02 .10
52 Klaus Merk .08 .25
53 Mirko Lüdemann .02 .10
54 Ulrich Hiemer .02 .10
55 Torsten Kienass .02 .10
56 Jayson Meyer .02 .10
57 Josef Lehner .02 .10
58 Ron Fischer .08 .25
59 Michael Bresagk .02 .10
60 Andreas Niederberger .02 .10
61 Peter Gulda .02 .10
62 Jan Benda .08 .25
63 Thomas Brandl .02 .10
64 Andreas Lupzig .02 .10
65 Michael Rumrich .02 .10
66 Benoit Doucet .08 .25
67 Raimond Hilger .02 .10
68 Georg Franz .02 .10
69 Jorg Handrick .02 .10
70 Dieter Hegen ..08 .25
71 Ernst Kopf .02 .10
72 Gunter Oswald .02 .10
73 Georg Holzmann .02 .10
74 Jürgen Rumrich .02 .10
75 Leo Stefan .02 .10
76 Bruno Campese .08 .25
77 Michael Rosati .20 .50
78 Giovanni Marchetti .02 .10
79 Georg Comploj .02 .10
80 Luigi da Corte .02 .10
81 Robert Oberrauch .02 .10
82 Anthony Circelli .02 .10
83 Alex Thaler .02 .10
84 Carlo Lorenzi .02 .10
85 Michael de Angelis .02 .10
86 Emilio Iovio .02 .10
87 Gaetano Orlando .08 .25
88 Lucio Topatigh .02 .10
89 Stefano Figliuzzi .02 .10
90 Bruno Zarrillo .02 .10
91 Mark Montanari .02 .10
92 Armando Chelodi .02 .10
93 Mirko Moroder .02 .10
94 Alex Gschliesser .02 .10
95 Maurizio Mansi .02 .10
96 Petri Ylönen .08 .25
97 Michel Valliere .08 .25
98 Serge Djelloul .02 .10
99 Christophe Moyon .02 .10
100 Gerald Guennelon .02 .10
101 Philippe Lemoine .02 .10
102 Denis Perez .08 .25
103 Serge Poudrier .08 .25
104 Steven Woodburn .02 .10
105 Michael Babin .02 .10
106 Benjamin Agnel .02 .10
107 Stephane Arcangeloni .02 .10
108 Laurent Deschaume .02 .10
109 Pierre Pousse .02 .10
110 Patrick Dunn .02 .10
111 Pierrick Maia .02 .10
112 Philippe Bozon .20 .50
113 Christian Pouget .02 .10
114 Antoine Richer .02 .10
115 Richard Aimonetto .02 .10
116 Reto Pavoni .02 .10
117 Renato Tosio .02 .10
118 Marco Bayer .02 .10
119 Sandro Bertaggia .02 .10
120 Fredy Bobillier .02 .10
121 Dino Kessler .02 .10
122 Sven Leuenberger .02 .10
123 Martin Steinegger .02 .10
124 Andreas Zehnder .02 .10
125 Misko Antisin .02 .10
126 Gian-Marco Crameri .08 .25
127 Jörg Eberle .08 .25
128 Patrick Fischer .02 .10
129 Patrick Howald .02 .10
130 Marcel Jenni .02 .10
131 Gil Montandon .02 .10
132 Pascal Schaller .02 .10
133 Andy Ton .02 .10
134 Roberto Triulzi .02 .10
135 Theo Wittman .02 .10
136 Roger Nordstrom .02 .10
137 Thomas Ostlund .08 .25
138 Magnus Svensson .02 .10
139 Tommy Sjodin .08 .25
140 Fredrik Stillman .02 .10
141 Tomas Jonsson .02 .10
142 Stefan Larsson .02 .10
143 Leif Rohlin .02 .10
144 Marcus Ragnarsson .02 .10
145 Christer Olsson .02 .10
146 Morgan Samuelsson .02 .10
147 Andreas Dackell .02 .10
148 Jonas Johnsson .02 .10
149 Charles Berglund .02 .10
150 Erik Huusko .02 .10
151 Daniel Rydmark .02 .10
152 Patrik Carnbäck .02 .10
153 Mats Lindgren .02 .10
154 Jonas Bergkvist .02 .10
155 Stefan Ornskog .02 .10
156 Per-Erik Eklund .08 .25
157 Thomas Forslund .02 .10
158 Roger Hansson .02 .10
159 Hakan Ahlund .02 .10
160 Daniel Alfredsson .20 .50
161 Jarmo Myllys .20 .50
162 Jukka Tammi .08 .25
163 Mika Stromberg .08 .25
164 Erik Hamalainen .02 .10
165 Karri Kivi .02 .10
166 Timo Jutila .02 .10
167 Petteri Nummelin .02 .10
168 Hannu Virta .02 .10
169 Marko Kiprusov .02 .10
170 Waltteri Immonen .08 .25
171 Janne Ojanen .02 .10
172 Esa Keskinen .02 .10
173 Marko Jantunen .02 .10
174 Saku Koivu .40 1.00
175 Marko Palo .02 .10
176 Tero Lehtera .02 .10
177 Mika Alatalo .20 .50
178 Ville Peltonen .08 .25
179 Raimo Helminen .02 .10
180 Petri Varis .08 .25
181 Jokke Heinänen .02 .10
182 Timo Saarikoski .02 .10
183 Sami Kapanen .20 .50
184 Tero Arkiomaa .02 .10
185 Mika Nieminen .08 .25
186 Peter Briza .20 .50
187 Roman Turek .20 .50
188 Milos Holan .02 .10
189 Drahomir Kadlec .08 .25
190 Frantisek Kaberle .02 .10
191 Bedrich Scerban .08 .25
192 Roman Hamrlik .08 .25
193 Jan Vopat .02 .10
194 Antonin Stavjana .02 .10
195 Jiri Vykoukal .02 .10
196 Jiri Veber .02 .10
197 Frantisek Musil .02 .10
198 Richard Zemlicka .08 .25
199 Kamil Kastak .08 .25
200 Jiri Kucera .08 .25
201 Roman Horak .02 .10
202 Martin Rucinsky .08 .25
203 Josef Beranek .08 .25
204 Bobby Holik .08 .25
205 Otakar Janecky .08 .25
206 Jiri Dolezal .02 .10
207 Martin Straka .08 .25
208 Martin Hostak .02 .10
209 Radek Toupal .02 .10
210 Tomas Kapusta .02 .10
211 Guy Hebert .40 1.00
212 Mike Richter .60 1.50
213 Shawn Chambers .02 .10
214 Sean Hill .02 .10
215 Don McSween .02 .10
216 Pat Neaton .02 .10
217 Barry Richter .02 .10
218 Craig Wolanin .02 .10
219 Gary Suter .08 .25
220 Robert Beers .08 .25
221 Brett Hauer .02 .10
222 Peter Ciavaglia .02 .10
223 Phil Bourque .02 .10
224 Shjon Podein .08 .25
225 John Lilley .08 .25
226 Tim Sweeney .08 .25
227 Scott Young .08 .25
228 Craig Janney .08 .25
229 Joe Sacco .08 .25
230 Jeffrey Lazaro .08 .25
231 Doug Weight .40 1.00
232 Thomas Bissott .20 .50
233 James Campbell .08 .25
234 Mark Beaufait .08 .25
235 Peter Ferraro .08 .25
236 Jim Marthinsen .08 .25
237 Robert Schistad .08 .25
238 Jan Roar Fagerli .02 .10
239 Petter Salsten .02 .10
240 Carl Oscar Boe Andersen .02 .10
241 Svein Enok Norstebo .02 .10
242 Tommie Eriksen .02 .10
243 Tom Erik Olsen .02 .10
244 Geir Hoff .02 .10
245 Bjorn Anders Dahl .02 .10
246 Trond Magnussen .02 .10
247 Orjan Lovdahl .02 .10
248 Espen Knutsen .20 .50
249 Rune Gulliksen .02 .10
250 Eirik Paulsen .02 .10
251 Sjur Robert Nilsen .02 .10
252 Petter Thoresen .02 .10
253 Rune Fjeldstad .02 .10
254 Erik Tveten .02 .10
255 Henrik Aaby .02 .10
256 Michael Puschacher .02 .10
257 Claus Dalpiaz .08 .25
258 Michael Guntner .02 .10
259 Martin Ulrich .02 .10
260 Peter Kasper .02 .10
261 Engelbert Linder .02 .10
262 Herbert Hohenberger .02 .10
263 Gerhard Unterluggauer .02 .10
264 Martin Krainz .02 .10
265 Helmut Karel .02 .10
266 Werner Kerth .02 .10
267 Dieter Kalt .02 .10
268 Patrick Pilloni .02 .10
269 Mario Schaden .02 .10
270 Wolfgang Kromp .02 .10
271 Gunter Lanzinger .02 .10
272 Manfred Muhr .02 .10
273 Gerald Ressman .02 .10
274 Siegfried Haberl .02 .10
275 Christoph Brandner .02 .10
276 Wayne Gretzky 6.00 15.00
277 Mario Lemieux 5.00 12.00
278 Eric Lindros 1.50 4.00
279 Mark Messier 1.25 3.00
280 Steve Yzerman 4.00 10.00
281 Pavel Bure 1.00 2.50
282 Sergei Fedorov 1.25 3.00
283 Igor Larionov .40 1.00
284 Sergei Makarov .40 1.00
285 Alexander Mogilny .40 1.00
286 Ulf Dahlen .08 .25
287 Peter Forsberg 2.00 5.00
288 Mikael Renberg .20 .50
289 Ulf Samuelsson .10 .25
290 Tomas Sandström .08 .25
291 Thomas Steen .08 .25
292 Mats Sundin .60 1.50
293 Jari Kurri .40 1.00
294 Teemu Selanne 2.00 5.00
295 Esa Tikkanen .20 .50
296 Dominik Hasek 1.25 3.00
297 Jaromir Jagr 1.50 4.00
298 Robert Reichel .10 .25
299 Brett Hull 1.50 4.00
300 Brian Leetch .60 1.50

1995-96 Swedish Leaf

COMPLETE SET (310) 16.00 40.00
COMPLETE SERIES 1 (150) 8.00 20.00
COMPLETE SERIES 2 (160) 8.00 20.00
1 Hakan Loob .20 .50
2 AIK .08 .25
3 AIK, Season Stats .05 .15
4 Joakim Persson .08 .25
5 Niclas Havelid .30 .75
6 Tony Barthelson .05 .15
7 Patric Aberg .05 .15
8 Johan Akerman .05 .15
9 Dick Tarnstrom .08 .25
10 Stefan Gustavson .05 .15
11 Anders Gozzi .05 .15
12 Morgan Samuelsson .08 .25
13 Brynas IF .05 .15
14 Brynas, Season Stats .05 .15
15 Michael Sundlov .08 .25
16 Stefan Klockare .08 .25
17 Bedrick Scerban .05 .15
18 Andreas Dackell .30 .75
19 Fredrik Modin .75 2.00
20 Ove Molin .05 .15
21 Mikael Wahlberg .05 .15
22 Thomas Tallberg .05 .15
23 Peter Larsson .05 .15
24 Stefan Ketola .08 .25
25 Djurgardens IF .08 .25
26 Djurgarden, Season Stats .05 .15
27 Jonas Forsberg .15 .40
28 Christian Due-Boje .08 .25
29 Mikael Magnusson .05 .15
30 Thomas Johansson .05 .15
31 Joakim Musakka .05 .15
32 Erik Hussko .08 .25
33 Jens Ohling .05 .15
34 Per Eklund .08 .25
35 Espen Knutsen .40 1.00
36 Patrik Erickson .05 .15
37 Farjestads BK .05 .15
38 Farjestad, Season Stats .05 .15
39 Patrik Haltia .08 .25
40 Sergei Fokin .05 .15
41 Thomas Rhodin .05 .15
42 Stefan Nilsson .05 .15
43 Magnus Arvedsson .30 .75
44 Mattias Johansson .05 .15
45 Clas Eriksson .05 .15
46 Peter Ottosson .05 .15
47 HV 71 .05 .15
48 HV 71, Season Stats .05 .15
49 Boo Ahl .15 .40
50 Kenneth Kennholt .05 .15
51 Hans Abrhamsson .05 .15
52 Peter Hammarstrom .05 .15
53 Johan Davidsson .20 .50
54 Stefan Falk .05 .15
55 Johan Lindbom .05 .15
56 Esa Keskinen .08 .25
57 Stefan Ornskog .08 .25
58 Peter Ekelund .05 .15
59 Leksands IF .05 .15
60 Leksand, Season Stats .05 .15
61 Johan Hedberg 1.50 4.00
62 Tomas Jonsson .08 .25
63 Hans Lodin .05 .15
64 Orjan Lindmark .05 .15
65 Jan Huokko .05 .15
66 Markus Eriksson .05 .15
67 Andreas Karlsson .05 .15
68 Mikael Holmberg .05 .15
69 Jonas Bergqvist .08 .25
70 Niklas Eriksson .05 .15
71 Per-Erik Eklund .08 .25
72 Lulea HF .05 .15
73 Lulea, Season Stats .05 .15
74 Jarmo Myllys .20 .50
75 Mattias Ohlund .40 1.00
76 Lars Modig .05 .15
77 Torbjorn Lindberg .05 .15
78 Roger Akerstrom .05 .15
79 Stefan Jonsson .05 .15
80 Johan Rosen .05 .15
81 Tomas Berglund .05 .15
82 Robert Nordberg .05 .15
83 Jiri Kucera .08 .25
84 Thomas Holmstrom .75 2.00
85 Malmo IF .05 .15
86 Malmo, Season Stats .05 .15
87 Peter Andersson .05 .15
88 Roger Ohman .05 .15
89 Marcus Magnertoft .05 .15
90 Patrik Sylvegard .05 .15
91 Hakan Ahlund .05 .15
92 Jesper Mattsson .08 .25
93 Roger Hansson .05 .15
94 Mattias Bosson .05 .15
95 Bo Svanberg .05 .15
96 Raimo Helminen .08 .25
97 MoDo Hockey .08 .25
98 MoDo, Season Stats .05 .15
99 Petter Ronnqvist .08 .25
100 Lars Jansson .05 .15
101 Mattias Timander .20 .50
102 Hans Jonsson .05 .15
103 Anders Soderberg .15 .40
104 Martin Hostak .05 .15
105 Kyosti Karjalainen .08 .25
106 Mikael Hakanson .05 .15
107 Per Svartvadet .15 .40
108 Andreas Salomonsson .40 1.00
109 Lars Bystrom .05 .15
110 Magnus Wernblom .05 .15
111 Rogle BK .05 .15
112 Rogle, Season Stats .05 .15
113 Magnus Swardh .08 .25
114 Arto Ruotanen .05 .15
115 Johan Finnstrom .08 .25
116 Daniel Tjarnqvist .20 .50
117 Pierre Johnsson .05 .15
118 Per Wallin .08 .25
119 Michael Johansson .05 .15
120 Per-Johan Svensson .05 .15
121 Roger Elvenes .05 .15
122 Mats Loov .05 .15
123 Michael Hjalm .08 .25
124 Vasteras IK .05 .15
125 Vasteras, Season Stats .05 .15
126 Mats Ytter .08 .25
127 Erik Bergstrom .08 .25
128 Lars Ivarsson .05 .15
129 Mishat Fahrutdinov .05 .15
130 Claes Lindblom .05 .15
131 Paul Andersson .05 .15
132 Henrik Nordfeldt .05 .15
133 Alexei Salomatin .05 .15
134 Mikael Pettersson .05 .15
135 Vastra Frolunda HC .05 .15
136 Frolunda, Season Stats .05 .15
137 Hakan Algotsson .08 .25
138 Jonas Andersson-Junkka .08 .25
139 Stefan Larsson .05 .15
140 Par Djoos .08 .25
141 Ronnie Sundin .08 .25
142 Par Edlund .08 .25
143 Peter Berndtsson .05 .15
144 Joacim Esbjors .05 .15
145 Alexander Beliavski .05 .15
146 Jonas Esbjors .05 .15
147 Marko Jantunen .08 .25
148 Peter Strom .05 .15
149 Checklist 1-75 .05 .15
150 Checklist 76-150 .05 .15
151 AIK .08 .25
152 AIK, Captains .05 .15
153 Mikael Nilsson .05 .15
154 Juha Jokiharju .08 .25
155 Stefan Andersson .05 .15
156 Thomas Strandberg .05 .15
157 Mats Lindberg .05 .15
158 Peter Gerhardsson .05 .15
159 Tommy Lehmann .08 .25
160 Tommy Hedlund .05 .15
161 Peter Wallin .08 .25
162 Bjorn Ahlstrom .05 .15
163 Erik Hamalainen .08 .25
164 Patric Englund .05 .15
165 Rikard Franzen .05 .15
166 BRYNAS IF .05 .15
167 Brynas, Captains .05 .15
168 Lars Karlsson .05 .15
169 Jonas Lofstrom .05 .15
170 Stefan Polla .05 .15
171 Mikael Lind .05 .15
172 Brian Rafalski .75 2.00
173 Roger Kyro .05 .15
174 Per-Johan Johansson .05 .15
175 Greg Parks .05 .15
176 Per Lofstrom .05 .15
177 Jonas Johnsson .05 .15
178 Mikael Lindman .05 .15
179 Mikael Wiklander .05 .15
180 Tommy Melkersson .05 .15
181 DJURGARDENS IF .08 .25
182 Djurgarden, Captains .05 .15
183 Thomas Ostlund .20 .50
184 Patrik Hofbauer .05 .15
185 Magnus Jansson .05 .15
186 Niklas Falk .05 .15
187 Ola Josefsson .05 .15
188 Joakim Lundberg .05 .15
189 Fredrik Lindquist .15 .40
190 Patrik Kjellberg .20 .50
191 Jan Viktorsson .08 .25
192 Bjorn Nord .05 .15
193 Tommy Jacobsen .05 .15
194 Anders Huusko .05 .15
195 Kristofer Ottosson .05 .15
196 VASTRA FROLUNDA HC .05 .15
197 Frolunda, Captains .05 .15
198 Mikael Sandberg .05 .15
199 Jerry Persson .05 .15
200 Peter Hogardh .05 .15
201 Stefan Axelsson .08 .25
202 Lars Edstrom .05 .15
203 Lars-Goran Wiklander .08 .25
204 Per-Johan Axelsson .40 1.00
205 Henrik Nilsson .05 .15
206 Petteri Nummelin .08 .25
207 Christian Ruuttu .20 .50
208 Oscar Ackestrom .05 .15
209 FARJESTADS BK .05 .15
210 Farjestad, Captains .05 .15
211 Markus Ketterer .08 .25
212 Bjorn Eriksson .05 .15
213 Jonas Hoglund .40 1.00
214 Peter Nordstrom .05 .15
215 Jorgen Jonsson .05 .15
216 Greger Artursson .05 .15
217 Jesper Duus .05 .15
218 Roger Johansson .05 .15
219 Leif Carlsson .05 .15
220 Per Lundell .05 .15
221 Vitali Prokhorov .08 .25
222 HV 71 .05 .15
223 HV 711, Captains .05 .15
224 Kenneth Johansson .05 .15
225 Thomas Gustavsson .05 .15
226 Marcus Thuresson .05 .15
227 Vesa Salo .08 .25
228 Kai Nurminen .20 .50
229 Johan Brummer .05 .15
230 Daniel Johansson .08 .25
231 Per Gustafsson .08 .25
232 Niklas Rahm .05 .15
233 LIKSANDS IF .05 .15
234 Leksand, Captains .05 .15
235 Per-Ragnar Bergkvist .08 .25
236 Anders Carlsson .05 .15
237 Micael Karlberg .05 .15
238 Torgny Lowgren .05 .15
239 Stefan Hellkvist .05 .15
240 Markus Akerblom .05 .15
241 Joakim Lidgren .05 .15
242 Tomas Froslund .08 .25
243 Torbjorn Johansson .05 .15
244 Nicklas Nordqvist .05 .15
245 LULEA HF .05 .15
246 Lulea, Captains .05 .15
247 Erik Grankvist .05 .15
248 Mikael Lindholm .05 .15
249 Johan Stromvall .05 .15
250 Anders Burstrom .05 .15
251 Lars Hurtig .05 .15
252 Stefan Nilsson .05 .15
253 Jan Mertzig .08 .25
254 Petter Nilsson .05 .15
255 Malmo IF .05 .15
256 Malmo IF, Captains .05 .15
257 Peter Lindmark .08 .25
258 Roger Nordstrom .08 .25
259 Andreas Lilja .05 .15
260 Brian McReynolds .05 .15
261 Ilja Byakin .08 .25
262 Robert Burakovsky .05 .15
263 Mikael Burakovsky .05 .15
264 Stefan Elvenes .08 .25
265 Johan Salle .05 .15
266 Kim Johnsson .05 .15
267 Peter Hasselblad .05 .15
268 Marko Palo .05 .15
269 MODO Hockey .08 .25
270 MoDo, Captains .08 .25
271 Fredrik Andersson .05 .15
272 Frantisek Kaberle .08 .25
273 Samuel Pahlsson .30 .75
274 Jan Larsson .05 .15
275 Per-Anton Lundstrom .08 .25
276 Tomas Nansen .05 .15
277 Marcus Karlsson .05 .15
278 Jan-Axel Alavaara .08 .25
279 Kristian Gahn .08 .25
280 ROGLE BK .05 .15
281 Rogle, Captains .05 .15
282 Patrik Backlund .05 .15
283 Peter Lundmark .05 .15
284 Anders Berglund .05 .15
285 Harijs Vitolins .05 .15
286 Jens Nielsen .05 .15
287 Greg Brown .08 .25
288 Bjorn Linden .05 .15
289 VASTERAS IK .05 .15
290 Vasteras, Captains .05 .15
291 Jakob Karlsson .05 .15
292 Patrik Zetterberg .05 .15
293 Mattias Loof .05 .15
294 Johan Tornberg .05 .15
295 Andrei Korolev .05 .15
296 Mattias Olsson .05 .15
297 Roger Rosen .05 .15
298 Andrei Lulin .05 .15
299 Edvin Fylen .08 .25
300 Mats Lusth .05 .15
301 Fredrik Oberg .05 .15
302 All Stars Myllys .20 .50
303 All Stars Jonsson .08 .25
304 All Stars Andersson .08 .25
305 All Stars Loob .20 .50
306 All Stars Keskinen .08 .25
307 All Stars Ruuttu .08 .25
308 Checklist 151-230 .05 .15
309 Checklist 231-310 .05 .15
310 Checklist Insert Cards .05 .15
NNO HV71, Svenska Mastare 4.00 10.00
NNO Per-Erik Eklund 4.00 10.00

1995-96 Swedish Leaf Champs

COMPLETE SET (15) 10.00 25.00
1 Tomas Jonsson .75 2.00
2 Patrik Kjellberg 1.25 3.00
3 Hakan Loob 1.25 3.00
4 Peter Lindmark 1.25 3.00
5 Anders Carlsson .75 2.00
6 Raimo Helminen 1.25 3.00
7 Esa Keskinen .75 2.00
8 Jan Larsson .75 2.00
9 Roger Johansson .75 2.00
10 Andreas Dackell 1.25 3.00
11 Stefan Ornskog .75 2.00
12 Michael Sundlov 1.25 3.00
13 Per-Erik Eklund .75 2.00
14 Kenneth Kennholt .75 2.00
15 Jan Viktorsson .75 2.00

1995-96 Swedish Leaf Face to Face

COMPLETE SET (15) 6.00 15.00
1 M.Samuelsson T.Strandberg .40 1.00
2 B.Scerban G.Parks .40 1.00
3 E.Huusko A.Hussko .40 1.00
4 S.Larsson M.Jantunen .40 1.00
5 H.Loob R.Johansson .75 2.00
6 K.Kennholt P.Gustafsson .40 1.00
7 Stefan Hellkvist T.Forslund .40 1.00
8 T.Holmstrom R.Akerstrom 2.00 5.00
9 S.Elvenes R.Burakovsky .40 1.00
10 M.Hostak M.Timander .40 1.00
11 M.Loov M.Hjalm .40 1.00
12 A.Salomatin F.Oberg .40 1.00
13 P.Erickson E.Knutsen 1.25 3.00
14 P.Andersson P.Hasselblad .40 1.00
15 T.Jonsson M.Akerblom .40 1.00

1995-96 Swedish Leaf Goldies

COMPLETE SET (10) 6.00 15.00
1 Morgan Samuelsson .75 2.00
2 Ove Molin .75 2.00
3 Fredrik Lindquist .75 2.00
4 Peter Strom .75 2.00
5 Mattias Johansson .75 2.00
6 Stefan Ornskog .75 2.00
7 Niklas Eriksson .75 2.00
8 Johan Rosen .75 2.00
9 Roger Ohman .75 2.00
10 Anders Soderberg .75 2.00

1995-96 Swedish Leaf Mega

COMPLETE SET (15) 12.00 30.00
1 Michael Sundlov 1.25 3.00
2 Jonas Bergqvist 1.25 3.00
3 Marko Jantunen .75 2.00
4 Thomas Ostlund 1.25 3.00
5 Tomas Jonsson .75 2.00
6 Esa Keskinen .75 2.00
7 Roger Nordstrom .75 2.00
8 Mattias Ohlund 1.50 4.00
9 Hakan Loob 1.25 3.00
10 Raimo Helminen .75 2.00
11 Per-Erik Eklund 1.25 3.00
12 Jarmo Myllys 1.50- 4.00
13 Rikard Franzen .75 2.00
14 Christer Olsson .75 2.00
15 Per Gustafsson .75 2.00

1995-96 Swedish Leaf Rookies

COMPLETE SET (9) 6.00 15.00
1 Peter Wallin .75 2.00
2 Jan-Axel Alavaara .75 2.00
3 Niklas Falk .75 2.00
4 Lars-Goran Wiklander .75 2.00
5 Torbjorn Johansson .75 2.00
6 Jan Mertzig .75 2.00
7 Mikael Burakovsky .75 2.00
8 Marcus Karlsson .75 2.00
9 Roger Rosen .75 2.00

1995-96 Swedish Leaf Spidermen

COMPLETE SET (14) 20.00 40.00
1 Joakim Persson 1.25 3.00
2 Michael Sundlov 1.25 3.00
3 Thomas Ostlund 1.50 4.00
4 Hakan Algotsson 1.25 3.00
5 Patrik Haltia 1.25 3.00
6 Boo Ahl 1.50 4.00
7 Johan Hedberg 2.00 5.00
8 Jarmo Myllys 1.50 4.00
9 Jonas Forsberg 1.50 4.00
10 Petter Ronnqvist 1.25 3.00
11 Magnus Swardh 1.25 3.00
12 Mats Ytter 1.25 3.00
13 Mikael Sandberg 1.25 3.00
14 Roger Nordstrom 1.25 3.00

1995-96 Swedish Upper Deck

COMPLETE SET (260) 16.00 40.00
1 Joakim Persson .08 .25
2 Erik Hamalainen .08 .25
3 Dick Tarnstrom .08 .25
4 Rikard Franzen .02 .10
5 Niclas Havelid .30 .75
6 Tony Barthelson .02 .10
7 Tommy Hedlund .02 .10
8 Patric Aberg .02 .10
9 Stefan Gustavson .02 .10
10 Anders Gozzi .02 .10
11 David Engblom .02 .10
12 Stefan Andersson .02 .10
13 Tomas Strandberg .02 .10
14 Mats Lindberg .02 .10
15 Tommy Lehmann .08 .25
16 Bjorn Ahlstrom .02 .10
17 Patrik Englund .02 .10
18 Morgan Samuelsson .08 .25
19 Michael Sundlov .20 .50
20 Bedrich Scerban .02 .10
21 Mikael Lindman .02 .10
22 Mikael Wiklander .02 .10
23 Tommy Melkersson .02 .10
24 Stefan Klockare .08 .25
25 Per Lofstrom .02 .10
26 Jonas Johnsson .02 .10
27 Roger Kyro .02 .10
28 Jonas Lofstrom .02 .10
29 Stefan Ketola .08 .25
30 Mikael Wahlberg .02 .10
31 Stefan Polla .02 .10
32 Greg Parks .02 .10
33 Ove Molin .02 .10
34 Peter Larsson .02 .10
35 Fredrik Modin .40 1.00
36 Andreas Dackell .30 .75
37 Thomas Ostlund .20 .50
38 Tommy Jakobsen .02 .10
39 Christian Due-Boje .08 .25
40 Thomas Johansson .02 .10
41 Joakim Lundberg .02 .10
42 Bjorn Nord .02 .10
43 Mikael Magnusson .02 .10
44 Erik Huusko .08 .25
45 Anders Huusko .02 .10
46 Kristofer Ottosson .02 .10
47 Magnus Jansson .02 .10
48 Niklas Falk .08 .25
49 Ola Josefsson .02 .10
50 Per Eklund .08 .25
51 Espen Knutsen .40 1.00
52 Jens Ohling .02 .10
53 Patric Kjellberg .30 .75
54 Patrik Erickson .02 .10
55 Jan Viktorsson .08 .25
56 Markus Ketterer .20 .50
57 Jesper Duus .02 .10
58 Sergei Fokin .02 .10
59 Per Lundell .02 .10
60 Thomas Rhodin .02 .10
61 Henrik Rehnberg .02 .10
62 Roger Johansson .02 .10
63 Leif Carlsson .02 .10
64 Hakan Loob .20 .50
65 Stefan Nilsson .02 .10
66 Vitali Prokhorov .08 .25
67 Magnus Arvedsson .02 .10
68 Jonas Hoglund .40 1.00
69 Mathias Johansson .02 .10
70 Patrik Wallenberg .02 .10
71 Claes Eriksson .02 .10
72 Jorgen Jonsson .02 .10
73 Peter Nordstrom .02 .10
74 Peter Ottosson .02 .10
75 Boo Ahl .15 .40
76 Per Gustafsson .08 .25
77 Niklas Rahm .02 .10
78 Hans Abrahamsson .02 .10
79 Kenneth Kennholt .02 .10
80 Daniel Johansson .08 .25
81 Vesa Salo .08 .25
82 Thomas Gustavsson .02 .10
83 Stefan Ornskog .08 .25
84 Stefan Falk .02 .10
85 Peter Hammarstrom .02 .10
86 Johan Davidsson .20 .50
87 Peter Ekelund .02 .10
88 Johan Lindbom .02 .10
89 Esa Keskinen .08 .25
90 Kai Nurminen .20 .50
91 Magnus Eliasson .02 .10
92 Marcus Thuresson .02 .10
93 Johan Brummer .02 .10
94 Johan Hedberg .40 1.00
95 Tomas Jonsson .08 .25
96 Torbjorn Johansson .02 .10
97 Hans Lodin .02 .10
98 Orjan Lindmark .02 .10
99 Jan Huokko .02 .10
100 Joakim Lidgren .02 .10
101 Per-Erik Eklund .08 .25
102 Anders Carlsson .02 .10
103 Niklas Eriksson .02 .10
104 Mikael Karlberg .02 .10
105 Jonas Bergqvist .08 .25
106 Torgny Lowgren .02 .10
107 Stefan Hellkvist .02 .10
108 Markus Akerblom .02 .10
109 Mikael Holmberg .02 .10
110 Andreas Karlsson .02 .10
111 Markus Akerblom .02 .10
112 Tomas Forslund .08 .25
113 Jarmo Myllys .20 .50
114 Lars Modig .02 .10
115 Patrik Hoglund .02 .10
116 Torbjorn Lindberg .02 .10
117 Jan Mertzig .08 .25
118 Petter Nilsson .02 .10
119 Mattias Ohlund .40 1.00
120 Roger Akerstrom .02 .10
121 Stefan Jonsson .02 .10
122 Stefan Nilsson .02 .10
123 Tomas Holmstrom .75 2.00
124 Mikael Lindholm .02 .10
125 Johan Stromvall .02 .10
126 Jiri Kucera .08 .25
127 Joakim Backlund .02 .10
128 Robert Nordberg .02 .10
129 Tomas Berglund .02 .10
130 Frederik Johansson .02 .10
131 Lars Hurtig .02 .10
132 Johan Rosen .02 .10
133 Roger Nordstrom .08 .25
134 Kim Johnsson .40 1.00
135 Peter Hasselblad .02 .10
136 Ilya Byakin .08 .25
137 Johan Salle .02 .10
138 Peter Andersson .02 .10
139 Roger Ohman .02 .10
140 Marko Palo .02 .10
141 Raimo Helminen .08 .25
142 Mattias Bosson .02 .10
143 Markus Magnertoft .02 .10
144 Roger Hansson .02 .10
145 Bo Svanberg .02 .10
146 Patrik Sylvegard .02 .10
147 Brian McReynolds .02 .10
148 Hakan Ahlund .02 .10
149 Robert Burakovsky .02 .10
150 Stefan Elvenes .08 .25
151 Patrik Boij .02 .10
152 Petter Ronnqvist .08 .25
153 Mattias Timander .20 .50
154 Lars Jansson .02 .10
155 Frantisek Kaberle .20 .50
156 Hans Jonsson .02 .10
157 Tomas Nansen .02 .10
158 Marcus Karlsson .02 .10
159 Kristian Gahn .08 .25
160 Magnus Wernblom .02 .10
161 Anders Soderberg .15 .40
162 Martin Hostak .02 .10
163 Kyosti Karjalainen .08 .25
164 Mikael Hakanson .02 .10
165 Jan Larsson .02 .10
166 Per Svartvadet .15 .40
167 Andreas Salomonsson .40 1.00
168 Samuel Pahlsson .60 1.50
169 Lars Bystrom .02 .10
170 Magnus Swardh .08 .25
171 Anders Berglund .02 .10
172 Pierre Johnsson .02 .10
173 Johan Finnstrom .08 .25
174 Arto Ruotanen .02 .10
175 Daniel Tjarnqvist .20 .50
176 Greg Brown .08 .25
177 Per Wallin .08 .25
178 Peter Lundmark .02 .10
179 Roger Elvenes .02 .10
180 Michael Hjalm .08 .25
181 Jens Hemstrom .02 .10
182 Pelle Svensson .02 .10
183 Harijs Vitolins .02 .10
184 Jens Nielsen .02 .10
185 Mats Loov .02 .10
186 Mats Ytter .08 .25
187 Lars Ivarsson .02 .10
188 Edvin Frylen .08 .25
189 Andrei Lyulin .02 .10
190 Johan Tornberg .02 .10
191 Mattias Olsson .02 .10
192 Mats Lusth .02 .10
193 Fredrik Oberg .02 .10
194 Alexei Salomatin .02 .10
195 Mishat Fahrutdinov .02 .10
196 Mikael Pettersson .02 .10
197 Andrei Korolev .02 .10
198 Mattias Loof .02 .10
199 Claes Lindblom .02 .10
200 Paul Andersson .02 .10
201 Roger Rosen .02 .10
202 Hakan Algotsson .08 .25
203 Par Djoos .08 .25
204 Mikael Sandberg .02 .10
205 Joachim Esbjors .02 .10
206 Stefan Axelsson .08 .25
207 Ronnie Sundin .15 .40
208 Stefan Larsson .02 .10
209 Petteri Nummelin .08 .25
210 Christian Ruuttu .20 .50
211 Marko Jantunen .08 .25
212 Peter Strom .02 .10
213 Peter Berndtsson .02 .10
214 Lars Edstrom .02 .10
215 Peter Hogardh .02 .10
216 Par Edlund .02 .10
217 Lars-Goran Wiklander .08 .25
218 Henrik Nilsson .02 .10
219 Rikard Franzen .02 .10
220 Fredrik Modin .30 .75
221 Anders Soderberg .15 .40
222 Per Eklund .08 .25
223 Hakan Loob .20 .50
224 Markus Ketterer .08 .25
225 Esa Keskinen .08 .25
226 Per Gustafsson .08 .25
227 Tomas Jonsson .08 .25
228 Per-Erik Eklund .08 .25
229 Mattias Ohlund .40 1.00
230 Jarmo Myllys .20 .50
231 Peter Andersson .02 .10
232 Raimo Helminen .08 .25
233 Christian Ruuttu .20 .50
234 Peter Forsberg 3.00 8.00
235 Mikael Renberg .20 .50
236 Mats Sundin 1.00 2.50
237 Michael Nylander .20 .50
238 Tommy Soderstrom .20 .50
239 Nicklas Lidstrom .75 2.00
240 Kenny Jonsson .30 .75
241 Patrik Carnback .08 .25
242 Johan Garpenlov .20 .50
243 Magnus Svensson .15 .40
244 Patrik Juhlin .15 .40
245 Markus Naslund .75 2.00
246 Tommy Salo .40 1.00
247 Fredrik Olausson .20 .50
248 Tommy Albelin .08 .25
249 Rikard Franzen .02 .10
250 Jonas Johnsson .02 .10
251 Thomas Ostlund .20 .50
252 Hakan Loob .20 .50
253 Per Gustafsson .08 .25
254 Per-Erik Eklund .08 .25
255 Tomas Jonsson .08 .25
256 Mattias Ohlund .40 1.00
257 Peter Andersson .02 .10
258 Christian Ruuttu .20 .50
259 Checklist .02 .10
260 Checklist .02 .10

1995-96 Swedish Upper Deck 1st Division Stars

COMPLETE SET (20) 6.00 15.00
DS1 Anders Huss .40 1.00
DS2 Igor Vlasov .40 1.00
DS3 Ulf Sandstrom .40 1.00
DS4 Hans Huczkowski .40 1.00
DS5 Johan Ramstedt .40 1.00
DS6 Anders Eldebrink .40 1.00
DS7 Niklas Brannstrom .40 1.00
DS8 Peter Nilsson .40 1.00
DS9 Sam Lindstahl .40 1.00
DS10 Tony Skopac .40 1.00
DS11 Jonas Eriksson .40 1.00
DS12 Anders Lonn .40 1.00
DS13 Peter Hagstrom .40 1.00
DS14 Magnus Roupe .40 1.00
DS15 Peter Pettersson .40 1.00
DS16 Peter Eriksson .40 1.00
DS17 Fredrik Bergqvist .40 1.00
DS18 Larry Pilut .40 1.00
DS19 Peter Olsson .40 1.00
DS20 Staffan Lundh .40 1.00

1995-96 Swedish Upper Deck Ticket to North America

COMPLETE SET (20) 12.00 30.00
NA1 Joakim Persson .75 2.00
NA2 Dick Tarnstrom .75 2.00
NA3 Andreas Dackell .75 2.00
NA4 Fredrik Modin 1.25 3.00
NA5 Per Eklund .40 1.00
NA6 Espen Knutsen 1.25 3.00
NA7 Fredrik Lindquist .40 1.00
NA8 Jonas Hoglund .75 2.00
NA9 Jorgen Jonsson .40 1.00
NA10 Johan Davidsson .75 2.00
NA11 Per Gustafsson .40 1.00
NA12 Johan Lindbom .40 1.00
NA13 Markus Akerblom .40 1.00
NA14 Jan Huokko .40 1.00
NA15 Tomas Holmstrom 4.00 10.00
NA16 Mattias Ohlund 1.25 3.00
NA17 Johan Rosen .40 1.00
NA18 Frantisek Kaberle .75 2.00
NA19 Mattias Timander .75 2.00
NA20 Magnus Wernblom .40 1.00

1996 Swedish Semic Wien

COMPLETE SET (240) 16.00 40.00
1 Jarmo Myllys .08 .25
2 Marko Kiprusoff .05 .15
3 Petteri Nummelin .02 .10
4 Erik Hamalainen .02 .10
5 Timo Jutila .05 .15
6 Janne Ninimaa .08 .25
7 Raimo Summanen .05 .15
8 Janne Ojanen .05 .15
9 Esa Keskinen .05 .15
10 Ari Sulander .08 .25
11 Saku Koivu .20 .50
12 Jukka Tammi .08 .25
13 Marko Palo .02 .10
14 Raimo Helminen .05 .15
15 Antti Tormanen .07 .20
16 Ville Peltonen .08 .25
17 Tero Lehtera .05 .15
18 Mika Stromberg .05 .15
19 Sami Kapanen .15 .40
20 Jere Lehtinen .15 .40
21 Juha Ylonen .07 .20
22 Mika Nieminen .07 .20
23 Hannu Virta .05 .15
24 Jari Kurri .15 .40
25 Christian Ruuttu .05 .15
26 Jyrki Lumme .05 .15
27 Teppo Numminen .08 .25
28 Esa Tikkanen .08 .25
29 Janne Laukkanen .07 .20
30 Aki Berg .08 .25
31 Teemu Selanne .60 1.50
32 Markus Ketterer .08 .25
33 Joni Lehto .02 .10
34 Juha Riihijarvi .05 .15
35 Sakari Lindfors .08 .25
36 Kai Nurminen .08 .25
37 Huey, Dewey, Louie .20 .50
38 Tommy Soderstrom .08 .25
39 Tommy Salo .20 .50
40 Thomas Ostlund .07 .20
41 Boo Ahl .07 .20
42 Calle Johansson .07 .20
43 Tommy Albelin .05 .15
44 Ulf Samuelsson .05 .15
45 Nicklas Lidstrom .40 1.00
46 Magnus Svensson .05 .15
47 Tomas Jonsson .05 .15
48 Tommy Sjodin .05 .15
49 Marcus Ragnarsson .08 .25
50 Christer Olsson .02 .10
51 Rikard Franzen .02 .10
52 Mattias Ohlund .08 .25
53 Kenny Jonsson .08 .25
54 Roger Johansson .02 .10
55 Anders Eriksson .08 .25
56 Mats Sundin .30 .75
57 Peter Forsberg .75 2.00
58 Mikael Renberg .08 .25
59 Tomas Sandstrom .07 .20
60 Ulf Dahlen .05 .15
61 Michael Nylander .05 .15
62 Patrik Juhlin .05 .15
63 Patrik Carnback .05 .15
64 Andreas Johansson .07 .20
65 Mikael Johansson .02 .10
66 Per-Erik Eklund .05 .15
67 Tomas Forslund .05 .15
68 Andreas Dackell .07 .20
69 Per Eklund .05 .15
70 Tomas Holmstrom .20 .50
71 Jonas Bergqvist .05 .15
72 Daniel Alfredsson .15 .40
73 Fredrik Modin .08 .25
74 Magic Moment .40 1.00
75 Ed Belfour .40 1.00
76 Bill Ranford .08 .25
77 Sean Burke .08 .25
78 Ray Bourque .60 1.50
79 Paul Coffey .20 .50
80 Scott Stevens .08 .25
81 Al MacInnis .20 .50
82 Larry Murphy .08 .25
83 Eric Desjardins .08 .25
84 Steve Duchesne .07 .20
85 Mario Lemieux 1.50 4.00
86 Mark Messier .40 1.00
87 Theo Fleury .30 .75
88 Eric Lindros .60 1.50
89 Rick Tocchet .15 .40
90 Brendan Shanahan .40 1.00
91 Claude Lemieux .15 .40
92 Joe Juneau .08 .25
93 Luc Robitaille .30 .75
94 Paul Kariya .75 2.00
95 Joe Sakic .75 2.00
96 Mark Recchi .20 .50
97 Jason Arnott .15 .40
98 Rod Brind'Amour .15 .40
99 Wayne Gretzky 2.00 5.00
100 Adam Oates .20 .50
101 Steve Yzerman 1.50 4.00
102 Roman Turek .20 .50
103 Dominik Hasek .40 1.00
104 Petr Briza .08 .25
105 Antonin Stavjana .05 .15
106 Frantisek Kaberle .07 .20
107 Jiri Vykoukal .05 .15
108 Jan Vopat .07 .20
109 Libor Prochazka .02 .10
110 Petr Kuchyna .05 .15
111 Frantisek Musil .05 .15
112 Leo Gudas .02 .10
113 Jiri Slegr .07 .20
114 Pavel Patera .08 .25
115 Otakar Vejvoda .08 .25
116 Martin Prochazka .08 .25
117 Jiri Kucera .02 .10
118 Pavel Janku .07 .20
119 Roman Meluzin .02 .10
120 Richard Zemlicka .02 .10
121 Martin Hostak .02 .10
122 Jiri Dopita .07 .20
123 Radek Belohlav .07 .20
124 Roman Horak .02 .10
125 Jaromir Jagr .60 1.50
126 Michal Pivonka .08 .25
127 Josef Beranek .05 .15
128 Robert Reichel .08 .25
129 Nikolai Khabibulin .20 .50
130 Sergei Abramov .07 .20
131 Yevgeny Tarasov .02 .10
132 Igor Kravchuk .07 .20
133 Dmitri Mironov .08 .25
134 Alexei Zhitnik .08 .25
135 Vladimir Malakhov .07 .20
136 Sergei Zubov .08 .25
137 Dimitri Yushkevich .08 .25
138 Ilya Byakin .02 .10
139 Alexander Smirnov .02 .10
140 Andrei Skopintsev .02 .10
141 Sergei Fedorov .60 1.50
142 Pavel Bure .75 2.00
143 Alexei Zhamnov .08 .25
144 Andrei Kovalenko .08 .25
145 Igor Korolev .05 .15
146 Vyacheslav Kozlov .15 .40
147 Viktor Kozlov .08 .25
148 Alexei Yashin .15 .40
149 Valeri Kamensky .08 .25
150 Stanislav Romanov .02 .10
151 Viacheslav Bykov .07 .20
152 Andrei Khomutov .08 .25
153 Sergei Berezin .15 .40
154 German Titov .08 .25
155 Dmitri Denisov .02 .10
156 John Vanbiesbrouck .20 .50
157 Jim Carey .08 .25
158 Mike Richter .30 .75
159 Chris Chelios .30 .75
160 Brian Leetch .30 .75
161 Phil Housley .08 .25
162 Gary Suter .07 .20
163 Kevin Hatcher .07 .20
164 Brett Hull .40 1.00
165 Pat LaFontaine .15 .40
166 Mike Modano .40 1.00
167 Jeremy Roenick .40 1.00
168 Keith Tkachuk .30 .75
169 Joe Mullen .07 .20
170 Craig Janney .08 .25
171 Joel Otto .07 .20
172 Doug Weight .20 .50
173 Scott Young .08 .25
174 Michael Rosati .05 .15
175 Bruno Campese .05 .15
176 Robert Oberrauch .02 .10
177 Robert Nardella .02 .10
178 Stefano Figfuzzi .02 .10
179 Maurizio Mansi .02 .10
180 Gaetano Orlando .02 .10
181 Mario Chitarroni .02 .10
182 Martin Pavlu .02 .10
183 Petri Ylonen .07 .20
184 Michel Valliere .02 .10
185 Serge Poudrier .02 .10
186 Denis Perez .02 .10
187 Antoine Richer .02 .10
188 Philippe Bozon .05 .15
189 Christian Pouget .02 .10
190 Franck Pajonkowski .05 .15
191 Stephane Barin .02 .10
192 Klaus Merk .07 .20
193 Marc Seliger .05 .15
194 Mirco Ludermann .02 .10
195 Jayson Meyer .02 .10
196 Benoit Doucet .05 .15
197 Thomas Brandl .02 .10
198 Dieter Hegen .05 .15
199 Martin Reichel .02 .10
200 Leo Stefan .02 .10
201 Robert Schistad .02 .10
202 Jim Marthinsen .07 .20
203 Tommy Jakobsen .02 .10
204 Petter Salsten .02 .10
205 Svein Norstebo .02 .10
206 Espen Knutsen .08 .25
207 Trond Magnussen .02 .10
208 Henrik Aaby .02 .10
209 Marius Rath .02 .10
210 Claus Dalpiaz .05 .15
211 Michael Puschacher .05 .15
212 Robin Doyle .02 .10
213 James Burton .02 .10
214 Herbert Hohenberger .02 .10
215 Andreas Pusnik .02 .10
216 Richard Nasheim .02 .10
217 Deiter Kalt .02 .10
218 Werner Kerth .02 .10
219 Eduard Hartmann .05 .15
220 Jaromir Dragan .08 .25
221 Robert Svehla .08 .25
222 Lubomir Sekeras .08 .25
223 Marian Smerciak .02 .10
224 Jergus Baca .05 .15
225 Stanslav Medrik .02 .10
226 Miroslav Marcinko .02 .10
227 Peter Stastny .08 .25
228 Peter Bondra .20 .50
229 Zdeno Ciger .08 .25
230 Jozef Stumpel .08 .25
231 Miroslav Satan .20 .50
232 Lubomir Kolnik .07 .20
233 Robert Petrovicky .05 .15
234 Zigmund Palffy .20 .50
235 Oto Hascak .05 .15
236 Jozef Dano .02 .10
237 Checklist .08 .25
238 Checklist .08 .25
239 Checklist .08 .25
240 Checklist .08 .25
NNO Super Chase Card 40.00 100.00

1996 Swedish Semic Wien All-Stars

COMPLETE SET (6) 3.00 8.00
AS1 Roman Turek Jarmo Myllys .75 2.00
AS2 Timo Jutila Christer Olsson .20 .50
AS3 Tommy Sjodin Marko Kiprusoff .20 .50
AS4 Jere Lehtinen Sergei Berezin .75 2.00
AS5 Saku Koivu Pelle Eklund 2.00 5.00
AS6 Ville Peltonen Andrew McKim .40 1.00

1996 Swedish Semic Wien Coca-Cola Dream Team

COMPLETE SET (12) 20.00 50.00
1 Tommy Soderstrom .75 2.00
2 Boo Ahl .75 2.00
3 Tomas Jonsson .40 1.00
4 Rikard Franzen .40 1.00
5 Mattias Ohlund 1.25 3.00
6 Roger Johansson .40 1.00
7 Mats Sundin 4.00 10.00
8 Peter Forsberg 12.00 30.00
9 Mikael Renberg 1.25 3.00
10 Per-Erik Eklund .40 1.00
11 Andreas Dackell 1.25 3.00
12 Jonas Bergqvist .75 2.00

1996 Swedish Semic Wien Hockey Legends

COMPLETE SET (18) 14.00 35.00
HL1 Ken Dryden 4.00 10.00
HL2 Guy Lafleur 2.00 5.00
HL3 Mike Bossy 1.50 4.00
HL4 Valeri Vasiliev .40 1.00
HL5 Anatoli Firosov .40 1.00
HL6 Alexander Maltsev .75 2.00
HL7 Tony Esposito 2.00 5.00
HL8 Rod Langway .40 1.00
HL9 Bryan Trottier 1.25 3.00
HL10 Lennart Haggroth .40 1.00
HL11 Ulf Nilsson .75 2.00
HL12 Lars-Gunnar Lundberg .40 1.00
HL13 Veli-Pekka Ketola .40 1.00
HL14 Lasse Oksanen .40 1.00
HL15 Pekka Rautakallio .40 1.00
HL16 Jiri Holecek .75 2.00
HL17 Jan Suchy .40 1.00
HL18 Vaclav Nedomansky .75 2.00

1996 Swedish Semic Wien Nordic Stars

COMPLETE SET (6) 10.00 25.00
NS1 Peter Forsberg 4.00 10.00
NS2 Teemu Selanne 2.50 6.00
NS3 Mats Sundin 2.00 5.00
NS4 Jari Kurri 2.00 5.00
NS5 Nicklas Lidstrom 2.00 5.00
NS6 Esa Tikkanen .75 2.00

1996 Swedish Semic Wien Super Goalies

COMPLETE SET (9) 15.00 30.00
SG1 Dominik Hasek 4.00 8.00
SG2 Ed Belfour 2.00 5.00
SG3 Jarmo Myllys .75 2.00
SG4 Tommy Soderstrom .75 2.00
SG5 Jim Carey .75 2.00
SG6 Roman Turek 1.25 3.00
SG7 Patrick Roy 8.00 20.00
SG8 Markus Ketterer .75 2.00
SG9 Tommy Salo .75 2.00

1997-98 Swedish Alfabilder Autographs

1 Sven Tumba Johansson 8.00 20.00
2 Roland Stoltz 4.00 10.00
3 Eilert Maatta 4.00 10.00
4 Lennart Haggroth 6.00 15.00
5 Nisse Nilsson 4.00 10.00
6 Ulf Sterner 8.00 20.00
7 Leif Holmqvist 8.00 20.00
8 Tord Lundstrom 4.00 10.00
9 Borje Salming 20.00 50.00
10 Anders Hedberg 12.00 30.00
11 Anders Kallur 6.00 15.00
12 Stefan Persson 6.00 15.00
13 Goran Hogosta 4.00 10.00
14 Bengt-Ake Gustafsson 8.00 20.00
15 Mats Naslund 12.00 30.00
16 Kent Nilsson 12.00 30.00
17 Hakan Loob 12.00 30.00
18 Peter Lindmark 10.00 25.00

1997-98 Swedish Collector's Choice

COMPLETE SET (225) 10.00 25.00
1 Miikka Kiprusoff 1.25 3.00
2 Karri Kivi .02 .10
3 Erik Hamalainen .07 .20
4 Libor Prochazka .02 .10
5 Dick Tarnstrom .20 .50
6 Niclas Havelid .20 .50
7 Tomas Strandberg .02 .10
8 Stefan Gustavsson .02 .10
9 Anders Gozzi .02 .10
10 Pavel Patera .15 .40
11 David Engblom .02 .10
12 Peter Hammarstrom .02 .10
13 Mats Lindberg .02 .10
14 Fredrik Krekula .02 .10
15 Otakar Vejvoda .02 .10
16 Bjorn Ahlstrom .02 .10
17 Michael Sundlov .08 .25
18 Pär Djoos .02 .10
19 Tommy Melkersson .02 .10
20 Stefan Klockare .02 .10
21 Johan Hansson .02 .10
22 Per Lofstrom .02 .10
23 Tommy Westlund .08 .25
24 Teppo Kivela .02 .10
25 Niclas Wallin .30 .75
26 Roger Kyro .02 .10
27 Ove Molin .02 .10
28 Mikko Luovi .02 .10
29 Evgenij Davydov .02 .10
30 Anders Huss .02 .10
31 Peter Nylander .02 .10
32 Jan Larsson .02 .10
33 Tommy Soderstrom .20 .50
34 Marcus Matthiasson .02 .10
35 Daniel Carlsson .02 .10
36 Ronnie Pettersson .02 .10
37 Kenneth Kennholt .02 .10
38 Bjorn Nord .07 .20
39 Mikael Hakansson .07 .20
40 Daniel Tjarnqvist .20 .50
41 Charles Berglund .02 .10
42 Mikael Johansson .02 .10
43 Marcus Nilsson .20 .50
44 Nichlas Falk .08 .25
45 Fredrik Lindqvist .08 .25
46 Patric Kjellberg .20 .50
47 Patrik Erickson .02 .10
48 Jan Viktorsson .02 .10
49 Niklas Anger .08 .25
50 Boris Rousson .08 .25
51 Peter Jakobsson .02 .10
52 Peter Nordstrom .08 .25
53 Sergei Fokin .02 .10
54 Niklas Sjokvist .02 .10
55 Jaroslav Spacek .08 .25
56 Greger Artursson .02 .10
57 Roger Johansson .02 .10
58 Stefan Nilsson .02 .10
59 Pelle Prestberg .02 .10
60 Kristian Huselius .75 2.00
61 Mathias Johansson .02 .10
62 Trond Magnussen .02 .10
63 Claes Eriksson .02 .10
64 Jorgen Jonsson .15 .40
65 Atle Olsen .02 .10
66 Patrik Wallenberg .02 .10
67 Lars-Goran Wiklander .02 .10
68 Mikael Sandberg .08 .25
69 Christer Olsson .02 .10
70 Joachim Esbjors .02 .10
71 Henrik Nilsson .02 .10
72 Arto Blomsten .02 .10
73 Magnus Johansson .02 .10
74 Stefan Larsson .02 .10
75 Par Edlund .02 .10
76 Marko Jantunen .02 .10
77 Joni Lius .02 .10
78 Patrik Carnback .07 .20
79 Ville Peltonen .20 .50
80 Peter Berndtsson .02 .10
81 Kai Nurminen .07 .20
82 Jonas Esbjors .02 .10
83 Peter Strom .02 .10
84 Kari Takko .08 .25
85 Johan Forsander .08 .25
86 Jouni Loponen .02 .10
87 David Petrasek .02 .10
88 Daniel Johansson .07 .20
89 Fredrik Stillman .02 .10
90 Anatoly Fedotov .02 .10
91 Stefan Ornskog .02 .10
92 Stefan Falk .02 .10
93 Peter Ekelund .02 .10
94 Esa Keskinen .02 .10
95 Patrik Lundback .02 .10
96 Anders Huusko .02 .10
97 Magnus Svensson .02 .10
98 Alexei Salomatin .02 .10
99 Patrik Englund .02 .10
100 Ake Lilljebjorn .08 .25
101 Tomas Jonsson .02 .10
102 Torbjorn Johansson .02 .10
103 Hans Lodin .02 .10
104 Magnus Svensson .02 .10
105 Andreas Karlsson .20 .50
106 Joakim Lidgren .02 .10
107 Fredrik Jonsson .02 .10
108 Per-Erik Eklund .02 .10
109 Anders Carlsson .02 .10
110 Johan Witehall .02 .10
111 Jens Nielsen .02 .10
112 Niklas Eriksson .02 .10
113 Jonas Bergqvist .07 .20
114 Stefan Hellkvist .02 .10
115 Markus Akerblom .07 .20
116 Anders Lonn .02 .10
117 Jarmo Myllys .08 .25
118 Johan Finnstrom .07 .20
119 Sergei Bautin .02 .10
120 Jan Mertzig .07 .20
121 Osmo Soutokorva .02 .10
122 Roger Akerstrom .02 .10
123 Stefan Jonsson .07 .20
124 Stefan Nilsson .02 .10
125 Jonas Ronnqvist .08 .25
126 Joakim Backlund .02 .10
127 Robert Nordberg .02 .10
128 Mikael Lovgren .02 .10
129 Anders Burstrom .02 .10
130 Fredrik Johansson .02 .10
131 Mika Alatalo .20 .50
132 Fredrik Nilsson .02 .10
133 Roger Nordstrom .08 .25
134 Andrew Verner .08 .25
135 Marko Kiprusoff .08 .25
136 Kim Johnsson .20 .50

137 Magnus Nilsson .02 .10
138 Jesper Damgaard .02 .10
139 Marek Malik .07 .20
140 Mats Lusth .02 .10
141 Janne Ojanen .07 .20
142 Mikko Peltola .02 .10
143 Mathias Bosson .02 .10
144 Daniel Rydmark .02 .10
145 Patrik Sylvegard .02 .10
146 Juha Riihijarvi .07 .20
147 Fredrik Oberg .02 .10
148 Mikael Burakovsky .02 .10
149 Petter Ronnqvist .08 .25
150 Pierre Hedin .15 .40
151 Jan-Axel Alavaara .02 .10
152 Frantisek Kaberle .20 .50
153 Hans Jonsson .20 .50
154 Jonas Junkka .07 .20
155 Marcus Karlsson .02 .10
156 Kristian Gahn .08 .25
157 Magnus Wernblom .08 .25
158 Anders Soderberg .08 .25
159 Daniel Sedin 1.25 3.00
160 Henrik Sedin 1.25 3.00
161 Samuel Pahlsson .30 .75
162 Per Svartvadet .15 .40
163 Andreas Salomonsson .20 .50
164 Ravil Yakubov .02 .10
165 David Vyborny .20 .50
166 Magnus Lindqvist .08 .25
167 Anders Eldebrink .02 .10
168 Johan Norgren .02 .10
169 Christian Due-Boje .02 .10
170 Jonas Heed .02 .10
171 Josef Boumedienne .15 .40
172 Marko Virtanen .02 .10
173 Kyosti Karjalainen .02 .10
174 Jorgen Bemstrom .02 .10
175 Joakim Ericsson .02 .10
176 Jens Ohling .02 .10
177 Martin Hostak .02 .10
178 Lars Dahlstrom .02 .10
179 Niklas Brannstrom .02 .10
180 Mikko Makela .02 .10
181 Petr Korinek .07 .20
182 Joakim Persson .08 .25
183 Tobias Lilja .02 .10
184 Edvin Frylen .07 .20
185 Jakob Karlsson .07 .20
186 Johan Tornberg .02 .10
187 Patrik Hoglund .02 .10
188 Mattias Loof .02 .10
189 Mikael Pettersson .02 .10
190 Johan Molin .02 .10
191 Fredrik Eriksson .02 .10
192 Henrik Nordfeldt .02 .10
193 Jonas Olsson .02 .10
194 Roger Jonsson .02 .10
195 Roger Rosen .02 .10
196 Henric Bjorkman .02 .10
197 Harri Sillgren .02 .10
198 Paul Andersson-Everberg .02 .10
199 Tommy Soderstrom .20 .50
200 Stefan Nilsson .02 .10
201 Tomas Jonsson .02 .10
202 Jonas Bergqvist .07 .20
203 Christer Olsson .02 .10
204 Per Svartvadet .15 .40
205 Anders Huss .02 .10
206 Roger Johansson .02 .10
207 Stefan Ornskog .02 .10
208 Anders Eldebrink .02 .10
209 Niclas Havelid .20 .50
210 Charles Berglund .02 .10
211 Kai Nurminen .07 .20
212 Stefan Nilsson .02 .10
213 Per-Erik Eklund .02 .10
214 Janne Ojanen .07 .20
215 Per Svartvadet .15 .40
216 Michael Sundlov .08 .25
217 Roger Johansson .02 .10
218 Stefan Ornskog .02 .10
219 Kyosti Karjalainen .02 .10
220 Roger Rosen .02 .10
221 Jonas Bergqvist .07 .20
222 Esa Keskinen .02 .10
223 Christer Olsson .02 .10
224 Checklist .05
225 Checklist .05

1997-98 Swedish Collector's Choice Crash the Game

COMPLETE SET (30) 8.00 20.00
*PRIZE CARDS: .3X TO .8X BASIC INSERTS
C1 Patric Kjellberg .60 1.50
C2 Mikael Johansson .25 .60
C3 Daniel Tjarnqvist .40 1.00
C4 Christer Olsson .25 .60
C5 Ville Peltonen .60 1.50
C6 Kai Nurminen .40 1.00
C7 Stefan Nilsson .25 .60
C8 Jan Mertzig .25 .60
C9 Anders Carlsson .25 .60
C10 Jonas Bergqvist .25 .60
C11 Magnus Svensson .25 .60
C12 Janne Ojanen .40 1.00
C13 Marko Kiprusoff .60 1.50
C14 Juha Riihijarvi .25 .60
C15 Daniel Sedin 1.50 4.00
C16 Henrik Sedin 1.50 4.00
C17 Evgenij Davydov .25 .60
C18 Anders Huss .25 .60
C19 Jan Larsson .25 .60
C20 Roger Johansson .25 .60
C21 Jorgen Jonsson .40 1.00
C22 Kristian Huselius 1.25 3.00
C23 Stefan Ornskog .25 .60
C24 Anders Huusko .25 .60
C25 Esa Keskinen .25 .60
C26 Joakim Eriksson .25 .60
C27 Anders Eldebrink .25 .60
C28 Mikko Makela .25 .60
C29 Henric Bjorkman .25 .60
C30 Roger Rosen .25 .60

1997-98 Swedish Collector's Choice Select

COMPLETE SET (15) 40.00 80.00
UD1 Peter Forsberg 12.00 30.00
UD2 Daniel Sedin 4.00 10.00
UD3 Nichlas Falk .75 2.00
UD4 Marko Jantunen .40 1.00
UD5 Ville Peltonen 1.25 3.00
UD6 Jorgen Jonsson .75 2.00
UD7 Roger Johansson .40 1.00
UD8 Stefan Ornskog .75 2.00
UD9 Henrik Sedin 4.80 10.00
UD10 Jonas Bergqvist .40 1.00
UD11 Tomas Jonsson .40 1.00
UD12 Stefan Nilsson .40 1.00
UD13 Janne Ojanen .40 1.00
UD14 Magnus Wernblom .40 1.00
UD15 Edvin Frylen .40 1.00
NNO Peter Forsberg Elite 20.00 50.00

1997-98 Swedish Collector's Choice Stick'Ums

COMPLETE SET (15) 4.00 10.00
S1 Miikka Kiprusoff 1.25 3.00
S2 Marcus Nilsson .40 1.00
S3 Christer Olsson .08 .25
S4 Jorgen Jonsson .20 .50
S5 Fredrik Stillman .08 .25
S6 Per-Erik Eklund .20 .50
S7 Jarmo Myllys .20 .50
S8 Daniel Rydmark .08 .25
S9 Henric Bjorkman .08 .25
S10 Henrik Sedin 1.00 2.50
S11 Daniel Sedin 1.00 2.50
S12 Anders Huss .08 .25
S13 Patrik Carnback .08 .25
S14 Daniel Tjarnqvist .20 .50
S15 Jonas Bergqvist .20 .50

1998-99 Swedish UD Choice

COMPLETE SET (225) 10.00 25.00
1 Jonas Forsberg .08 .25
2 Rikard Franzen .02 .10
3 Mathias Svedberg .02 .10
4 Dick Tarnstrom .20 .50
5 Jan Sandstrom .02 .10
6 Johan Silfwerplatz .02 .10
7 Henrik Tallinder .20 .50
8 Stefan Gustavson .02 .10
9 Kristian Gahn .20 .50
10 Bjorn Ahlstrom .02 .10
11 Peter Hammarstrom .02 .10
12 Anders Gozzi .02 .10
13 Fredrik Krekula .02 .10
14 Erik Norback .02 .10
15 Niklas Anger .20 .50
16 Mats Lindberg .02 .10
17 Jorgen Wikstrom .02 .10
18 Per-Anton Lundstrom .08 .25
19 Mattias Hedlund .02 .10
20 Jorgen Hermansson .02 .10
21 Fredrik Bergqvist .02 .10
22 Joakim Lidgren .02 .10
23 Robert Karlsson .02 .10
24 Christian Lechtaler .02 .10
25 Aleksandrs Beljavskis .02 .10
26 Jens Ohman .02 .10
27 Stefan Ohman .02 .10
28 Martin Wiita .02 .10
29 Johan Ramstedt .08 .25
30 Per Ledin .02 .10
31 Jukka Penttinen .02 .10
32 Aleksandrs Semjonovs .02 .10
33 Johan Holmqvist .60 1.50
34 Tommy Melkersson .02 .10
35 Marko Tuulola .02 .10
36 Johan Hansson .02 .10
37 Par Djoos .02 .10
38 Per Lofstrom .02 .10
39 Niclas Wallin .20 .50
40 Roger Kyro .02 .10
41 Ove Molin .02 .10
42 Stefan Lundqvist .02 .10
43 Peter Nylander .02 .10
44 Jan Larsson .02 .10
45 Teppo Kivela .02 .10
46 Tom Bissett .08 .25
47 Anders Huss .02 .10
48 Mikko Luovi .08 .25
49 Tommy Soderstrom .30 .75
50 Bjorn Nord .08 .25
51 Ronnie Pettersson .02 .10
52 Thomas Johansson .02 .10
53 Daniel Tjarnqvist .20 .50
54 Anders Myrvold .08 .25
55 Mikael Magnusson .02 .10
56 Mikael Johansson .02 .10
57 Nichlas Falk .08 .25
58 Mikael Hakanson .02 .10
59 Charles Berglund .08 .25
60 Lars-Goran Wiklander .02 .10
61 Per Eklund .07 .20
62 Jan Viktorsson .02 .10
63 Patrik Erickson .02 .10
64 Espen Knutsen .40 1.00
65 Jimmie Olvestad .20 .50
66 Mikael Sandberg .02 .10
67 Christer Olsson .02 .10
68 Petter Nilsson .02 .10
69 Magnus Johansson .02 .10
70 Ronnie Sundin .08 .25
71 Radek Hamr .02 .10
72 Stefan Larsson .02 .10
73 Mattias Nilimaa .02 .10
74 Linus Fagemo .02 .10
75 Marko Jantunen .02 .10
76 Patrik Carnback .02 .10
77 Peter Berndtsson .02 .10
78 Mikael Samuelsson .30 .75
79 Peter Strom .02 .10
80 Par Edlund .02 .10
81 Henrik Nilsson .20 .50
82 Jonas Johnson .02 .10
83 Kimmo Lecklin .02 .10
84 Roger Johansson .02 .10
85 Sergei Fokin .02 .10
86 Greger Artursson .02 .10
87 Jonas Elofsson .20 .50
88 Peter Jakobsson .02 .10
89 Dimitri Erofeev .02 .10
90 Patrik Zetterberg .02 .10
91 Niklas Sjokvist .02 .10
92 Trond Magnussen .02 .10
93 Peter Hagstrom .02 .10
94 Pelle Prestberg .02 .10
95 Mathias Johansson .08 .25
96 Michael Holmqvist .20 .50
97 Clas Eriksson .02 .10
98 Kristian Huselius 1.00 2.50
99 Jorgen Jonsson .20 .50
100 Kari Takko .08 .25
101 David Petrasek .02 .10
102 Daniel Johansson .20 .50
103 Per Gustafsson .02 .10
104 Fredrik Stillman .02 .10
105 Nicklas Rahm .02 .10
106 Mikael Lindman .02 .10
107 Jerry Persson .02 .10
108 Esa Keskinen .02 .10
109 Peter Ekelund .02 .10
110 Antti Tormanen .08 .25
111 Marcus Kristoffersson .20 .50
112 Anders Huusko .02 .10
113 Erik Huusko .02 .10
114 Johan Lindbom .08 .25
115 Jarkko Varvio .02 .10
116 Ulf Dahlen .08 .25
117 Johan Hedberg .40 1.00
118 Jan Huokko .02 .10
119 Torbjorn Johansson .02 .10
120 Hans Lodin .02 .10
121 Nicklas Nordqvist .02 .10
122 Stefan Bergqvist .02 .10
123 Magnus Svensson .02 .10
124 Andreas Karlsson .20 .50
125 Per-Erik Eklund .08 .25
126 Anders Carlsson .02 .10
127 Niklas Eriksson .02 .10
128 Stefan Hellkvist .02 .10
129 Jens Nielsen .02 .10
130 Anders Lonn .02 .10
131 Markus Akerblom .02 .10
132 Mikael Karlberg .02 .10
133 Jarmo Myllys .08 .25
134 Stefan Jonsson .02 .10
135 Osmo Soutokorva .02 .10
136 Johan Finnstrom .02 .10
137 Roger Akerstrom .08 .25
138 Igor Matushkin .02 .10
139 Jonas Ronnqvist .20 .50
140 Thomas Sjogren .02 .10
141 Tomas Berglund .02 .10
142 Mikael Lovgren .02 .10
143 Anders Burstrom .02 .10
144 Jorgen Bemstrom .02 .10
145 Martin Hostak .02 .10
146 Bert-Olav Karlsson .02 .10
147 Lars Edstrom .02 .10
148 Jiri Kucera .02 .10
149 Andrew Verner .08 .25
150 Kim Johnsson .08 .25
151 Kari Harila .02 .10
152 Niclas Havelid .40 1.00
153 Jesper Damgaard .02 .10
154 Johan Tornberg .02 .10
155 Mats Lusth .02 .10
156 Jan Hammar .02 .10
157 Marcus Magnertoft .02 .10
158 Marcus Thuresson .08 .25
159 Magnus Nilsson .02 .10
160 Mikael Lindholm .08 .25
161 Patrik Sylvegard .02 .10
162 Juha Riihijarvi .08 .25
163 Jesper Mattsson .08 .25
164 Niklas Sundblad .02 .10
165 Toivo Suursoo .02 .10
166 Petter Ronnqvist .08 .25
167 Pierre Hedin .20 .50
168 Per Hallberg .02 .10
169 Jan-Axel Alavaara .02 .10
170 Hans Jonsson .20 .50
171 Lars Jansson .02 .10
172 Frantisek Kaberle .20 .50
173 Andreas Salomonsson .08 .25
174 Magnus Wernblom .08 .25
175 Mikael Pettersson .02 .10
176 Per Svartvadet .20 .50
177 Daniel Sedin .75 2.00
178 Henrik Sedin .75 2.00
179 Jan Alinc .02 .10
180 Samuel Pahlsson .40 1.00
181 Anders Soderberg .02 .10
182 Magnus Eriksson .02 .10
183 Andrei Lulin .02 .10
184 Jakob Karlsson .08 .25
185 Patrik Huglund .02 .10
186 Joakim Lundberg .02 .10
187 Arto Blomsten .02 .10
188 Mattias Loof .02 .10
189 Mikael Pettersson .02 .10
190 Joakim Backlund .02 .10
191 Daniel Rydmark .02 .10
192 Johan Molin .02 .10
193 Paul Andersson-Everberg .02 .10
194 Henrik Nordfeldt .02 .10
195 Jonas Olsson .02 .10
196 Fredrik Oberg .02 .10
197 Roger Rosen .02 .10
198 Roland Stoltz .02 .10
199 Lars Bjorn .02 .10
200 Ulf Sterner .02 .10
201 Leif Holmqvist .08 .25
202 Hans Mild .02 .10
203 Bert-Ola Nordlander .02 .10
204 Eilert Maatta .02 .10
205 Ronald Pettersson .02 .10
206 Tord Lundstrom .02 .10
207 Lennart Svedberg .08 .25
208 Roland Stoltz .02 .10
209 Eilert Maatta .02 .10
210 Lennart Svedberg .08 .25
211 Tord Lundstrom .02 .10
212 Leif Holmqvist .08 .25
213 Magnus Nilsson .20 .50
214 Mikael Holmqvist .20 .50
215 Mattias Karlin .20 .50
216 Pierre Hedin .20 .50
217 Henrik Petre .20 .50
218 Johan Forsander .08 .25
219 Daniel Sedin .75 2.00
220 Henrik Sedin .75 2.00
221 Markus Nilsson .40 1.00
222 Checklist .02 .10
223 Checklist .02 .10
224 Checklist .02 .10
225 Checklist .02 .10
GJ1 D.Sedin
H.Sedin 20.00 50.00
GJA1 D.Sedin
H.Sedin 75.00 200.00

1998-99 Swedish UD Choice Day in the Life

COMPLETE SET (10) 4.00 10.00
1 Rikard Franzen .40 1.00
2 Par Djoos .40 1.00
3 Tommy Soderstrom .75 2.00
4 Pelle Prestberg .40 1.00
5 Esa Keskinen .40 1.00
6 Johan Hedberg .75 2.00
7 Jarmo Myllys .75 2.00
8 Marcus Thuresson .40 1.00
9 Samuel Pahlsson 1.00 2.50
10 Christer Olsson .40 1.00

1999-00 Swedish Upper Deck

COMPLETE SET (220) 10.00 25.00
1 Mattias Pettersson .07 .20
2 Rikard Franzen .08 .25
3 Mattias Svedberg .07 .20
4 Dick Tarnstrom .30 .75
5 Jan Sandstrom .07 .20
6 Anders Myrvold .08 .25
7 Henrik Tallinder .20 .50
8 Per-Anton Lundstrom .07 .20
9 Kristian Gahn .07 .20
10 Björn Ahlstrom .07 .20
11 Stefan Gustavsson .07 .20
12 Jarkko Varvio .08 .25
13 Fredrik Krekula .07 .20
14 Erik Norback .07 .20
15 Niklas Anger .15 .40
16 Mats Lindberg .07 .20
17 Erik Andersson .07 .20
18 Johan Holmqvist .60 1.50
19 Tommy Sjodin .07 .20
20 Marko Tuulola .07 .20
21 Henrik Petre .15 .40
22 Par Djoos .08 .25
23 Niclas Wallin .40 1.00
24 Roger Kyro .07 .20
25 Ove Molin .07 .20
26 Stefan Lundqvist .07 .20
27 Goran Hermansson .07 .20
28 Jan Larsson .07 .20
29 Daniel Rudslätt .07 .20
30 Tom Bisset .15 .40
31 Kenneth Bergqvist .07 .20
32 Mikko Luovi .07 .20
33 Johan Lindstrom .07 .20
34 Daniel Olsson .07 .20
35 Tommy Soderstrom .20 .50
36 Bjorn Nord .15 .40
37 Niklas Kronwall 1.00 2.50
38 Thomas Johansson .07 .20
39 Daniel Tjarnqvist .20 .50
40 Mikael Magnusson .07 .20
41 Mikael Johansson .08 .25
42 Niklas Falk .15 .40
43 Mikael Hakansson .15 .40
44 Charles Berglund .08 .25
45 Lars-Goran Wiklander .07 .20
46 Per Eklund .08 .25
47 Kristofer Johansson .07 .20
48 Mathias Tjarnqvist .15 .40
49 Espen Knutsen .40 1.00
50 Jimmie Olvestad .20 .50
51 Mikko Konttila .07 .20
52 Vesa Toskala .75 2.00
53 Roger Johansson .07 .20
54 Sergei Fokin .07 .20
55 Greger Artursson .07 .20
56 Jonas Elofsson .15 .40
57 Radek Hamr .07 .20
58 Henrik Rehnberg .07 .20
59 Peter Nordstrom .08 .25
60 Niklas Sjokvist .07 .20
61 Trond Magnussen .07 .20
62 Peter Hagstrom .07 .20
63 Pelle Prestberg .07 .20
64 Mathias Johansson .15 .40
65 Tore Vikingstad .07 .20
66 Clas Eriksson .07 .20
67 Marko Jantunen .07 .20
68 Christian Berglund .07 .20
69 Mario Brunetta .15 .40
70 Petter Nilsson .07 .20
71 Magnus Johansson .07 .20
72 Ronnie Sundin .15 .40
73 Stefan Larsson .07 .20
74 Christian Backman .15 .40
75 Par Edlund .08 .25
76 Reid Simonton .07 .20
77 Kristian Huselius .40 1.00
78 Pasi Saarela .07 .20
79 Juha Ikonen .07 .20
80 Linus Fagerno .07 .20
81 Patrik Carnback .08 .25
82 Peter Berndtsson .07 .20
83 Peter Strom .07 .20
84 Henrik Nilsson .07 .20
85 Jonas Johnson .07 .20
86 Kari Takko .15 .40
87 David Petrasek .07 .20
88 Joacim Esbjors .07 .20
89 Per Gustafsson .08 .25
90 Jani Nikko .07 .20
91 Mikael Lindman .07 .20
92 Oleg Belov .07 .20
93 Jonas Esbjors .07 .20
94 Jonas Forsander .15 .40
95 Peter Ekelund .07 .20
96 Antti Tormanen .08 .25
97 Anders Lonn .07 .20
98 Gabriel Karlsson .07 .20
99 Johan Hult .07 .20
100 Mattias Remstam .07 .20
101 Daniel Wallin .07 .20
102 Johan Lindbom .07 .20
103 Reinhard Divis .40 1.00
104 Jan Huokko .07 .20
105 Torbjorn Johansson .07 .20
106 Per Lundell .07 .20
107 David Ytfeldt .07 .20
108 Stefan Bergkvist .07 .20
109 Patrik Allvin .07 .20
110 Niklas Persson .07 .20
111 Martin Jansson .07 .20
112 Anders Carlsson .07 .20
113 Niklas Eriksson .07 .20
114 Stefan Hellkvist .07 .20
115 Jens Nielsen .07 .20
116 Morten Green .07 .20
117 Markus Akerblom .07 .20
118 Mikael Karlberg .07 .20
119 Mattias Elm .07 .20
120 Edvin Frylen .07 .20
121 Martin Knold .07 .20
122 Erkki Saramaa .07 .20
123 Nicklas Nordqvist .07 .20
124 Jesper Andersson .07 .20
125 Henrik Andersson .07 .20
126 Henrik Nordfeldt .07 .20
127 Ulf Soderstrom .07 .20
128 Ragnar Karlsson .07 .20
129 Fredrik Elmvall .07 .20
130 Peter Casparsson .07 .20
131 Dennis Ejdeholm .07 .20
132 Mattias Nilimaa .07 .20
133 Mike Helber .07 .20
134 Johan Bylow .07 .20
135 Jarmo Myllys .15 .40
136 Vaclav Burda .07 .20
137 Osmo Soutokorva .07 .20
138 Johan Finnstrom .08 .25
139 Roger Akerstrom .07 .20
140 Torbjorn Lindberg .07 .20
141 Jonas Ronnqvist .40 1.00
142 Jonathan Hedstrom .15 .40
143 Tomas Berglund .07 .20
144 Mikael Lovgren .07 .20
145 Anders Burstrom .07 .20
146 Jörgen Bemstrom .07 .20
147 Martin Hostak .07 .20
148 Hans Huczkowski .07 .20
149 Lars Edstrom .07 .20
150 Jiri Kucera .08 .25
151 Andreas Hadelov .07 .20
152 Johan Tornberg .07 .20
153 Mats Lusth .07 .20
154 Andreas Lilja .07 .20
155 Peter Jakobsson .07 .20
156 Henrik Malmstrom .07 .20
157 Tomas Sandstrom .20 .50
158 Kim Staal .07 .20
159 Jan Hammar .07 .20
160 Marcus Magnertoft .07 .20
161 Marcus Thuresson .07 .20
162 Magnus Nilsson .07 .20
163 Mikael Lindholm .07 .20
164 Juha Riihijarvi .07 .20
165 Jesper Mattsson .08 .25
166 Niklas Sundblad .08 .25
167 Toivo Suursoo .07 .20
168 Tobias Lundstrom .07 .20
169 Pierre Hedin .15 .40
170 Per Hallberg .07 .20
171 Jan-Axel Alavaara .07 .20
172 Jesper Duus .07 .20
173 Francois Bouchard .07 .20
174 Andreas Pihl .07 .20
175 Andreas Salomonsson .30 .75
176 Magnus Wernblom .07 .20
177 Mikael Pettersson .07 .20
178 Mattias Weinhandl .30 .75
179 Daniel Sedin .60 1.50
180 Henrik Sedin .60 1.50
181 Tommy Pettersson .07 .20
182 Samuel Pahlsson .40 1.00
183 Anders Soderberg .15 .40
184 Mattias Karlin .15 .40
185 Magnus Eriksson .07 .20
186 Andrei Lulin .07 .20
187 Denis Chervyakov .07 .20
188 Dimitri Chikin .07 .20
189 Joakim Lundberg .07 .20
190 Henric Bjorkman .07 .20
191 Roger Rosen .07 .20
192 Peter Nylander .07 .20
193 Mikael Pettersson .07 .20
194 Patrik Zetterberg .07 .20
195 Daniel Rydmark .08 .25
196 Johan Molin .07 .20
197 Paul Andersson-Everberg .07 .20
198 Jonas Finn-Olsson .07 .20
199 Fredrik Oberg .07 .20
200 Roger Rosen .07 .20
201 Henrik Tallinder .15 .40
202 Kenneth Bergqvist .07 .20
203 Mathias Tjarnqvist .15 .40
204 Jimmie Olvestad .30 .75
205 Jonas Elofsson .15 .40
206 Christian Berglund .30 .75
207 Johan Forsander .15 .40
208 David Ytfeldt .07 .20
209 Niklas Persson .07 .20
210 Henrik Andersson .07 .20
211 Jonathan Hedström .20 .50
212 Kim Staal .07 .20
213 Pierre Hedin .15 .40
214 Mattias Weinhandl .30 .75
215 Rikard Ekstrom .07 .20
216 Christian Backman .20 .50
217 Daniel Sedin CL .20 .50
218 Peter Ekelund CL .07 .20
219 Tommy Soderstrom CL .15 .40
220 Henrik Sedin CL .20 .50

1999-00 Swedish Upper Deck Hands of Gold

COMPLETE SET (15) 12.00 30.00
H1 Mats Lindberg .75 2.00
H2 Tom Bissett 1.25 3.00
H3 Jan Larsson .75 2.00
H4 Per Eklund 1.25 3.00
H5 Thomas Johansson .75 2.00
H6 Mathias Johansson .75 2.00
H7 Peter Ekelund .75 2.00
H8 Anders Carlsson .75 2.00
H9 Ulf Soderstrom .75 2.00
H10 Jonas Ronnqvist 1.25 3.00
H11 Marcus Thuresson 1.25 3.00
H12 Daniel Sedin 2.00 5.00
H13 Henrik Sedin 2.00 5.00
H14 Daniel Rydmark .75 2.00
H15 Kristian Huselius 2.00 5.00

1999-00 Swedish Upper Deck Lasting Impressions

COMPLETE SET (12) 12.00 30.00
1 Rikard Franzen 1.25 3.00
2 Par Djoos 1.25 3.00
3 Charles Berglund 1.25 3.00
4 Roger Johansson 1.25 3.00
5 Kari Takko 1.50 4.00
6 Anders Carlsson 1.25 3.00
7 Mike Helber 1.25 3.00
8 Jiri Kucera 1.25 3.00
9 Juha Riihijarvi 1.25 3.00
10 Samuel Pahlsson 2.00 5.00
11 Magnus Eriksson 1.25 3.00
12 Patrik Carnback 1.25 3.00

1999-00 Swedish Upper Deck PowerDeck

COMPLETE SET (2) 3.00 8.00
1 SHL 2.00 5.00
2 D.Sedin
H.Sedin 2.00 5.00

1999-00 Swedish Upper Deck SHL Signatures

COMPLETE SET (20) 70.00 150.00
1 Stefan Gustavsson 2.00 5.00
2 Rikard Franzen 2.00 5.00
3 Johan Holmqvist 6.00 12.00
4 Espen Knutsen 6.00 12.00
5 Peter Nordstrom 2.00 5.00
6 Marko Jantunen 2.00 5.00
7 Kristian Huselius 8.00 20.00
8 Jonas Johnson 2.00 5.00
9 Per Gustafsson 2.00 5.00
10 Johan Lindbom 4.00 10.00
11 Stefan Hellkvist 2.00 5.00
12 Ulf Soderstrom 2.00 5.00
13 Jarmo Myllys 4.00 10.00
14 Johan Tornberg 2.00 5.00
15 Daniel Sedin 10.00 20.00
16 Henrik Sedin 10.00 20.00
17 Magnus Eriksson 2.00 5.00
18 Tommy Sjodin 2.00 5.00
19 Tommy Soderstrom 4.00 10.00
20 Tomas Sandstrom 4.00 10.00

1999-00 Swedish Upper Deck Snapshots

COMPLETE SET (15) 12.00 30.00
1 Anders Myrvold .75 2.00
2 Johan Holmqvist 1.25 3.00
3 Ove Molin .40 1.00
4 Tommy Soderstrom 1.25 3.00
5 Espen Knutsen 1.50 4.00
6 Peter Nordstrom .40 1.00
7 Per Gustafsson .40 1.00
8 Stefan Bergkvist .40 1.00
9 Mattias Elm .40 1.00
10 Jarmo Myllys 1.50 4.00
11 Tomas Sandstrom 1.50 4.00
12 Magnus Wernblom .40 1.00
13 Mattias Weinhandl 1.50 4.00
14 Denis Chervyakov .40 1.00
15 Kristian Huselius 4.00 10.00

2000-01 Swedish Upper Deck

COMPLETE SET (220) 10.00 25.00
1 Tim Thomas .60 1.50
2 Per-Anton Lundstrom .15 .40
3 Dick Tarnstrom .20 .50
4 Rikard Franzen .04 .10
5 Rikard Ekstrom .04 .10
6 Jan Sandstrom .04 .10
7 Stefan Gustavson .04 .10
8 Anders Gozzi .04 .10
9 Stefan Hellkvist .04 .10
10 Mats Lindberg .04 .10
11 Bjorn Danielsson .04 .10
12 Erik Andersson .04 .10
13 Bjorn Ahlstrom .04 .10
14 Kristian Gahn .04 .10
15 Petter Sandstrom .04 .10
16 Mattias Hedlund .04 .10
17 Tommi Hamalainen .04 .10
18 Jorgen Hermansson .04 .10
19 Jesper Jager .04 .10
20 Christian Lechtaler .04 .10
21 Aleksanders Beliavskis .04 .10
22 Johan Ramstedt .04 .10
23 Lars Briell .04 .10
24 Johan Boman .04 .10
25 Aleksanders Semjonovs .04 .10
26 Mathias Bosson .04 .10
27 Niko Halttunen .04 .10
28 Fredrik Nasvall .04 .10
29 Johan Asplund .15 .40
30 Henrik Petre .04 .10
31 Par Djoos .04 .10
32 Tommy Sjodin .04 .10
33 Christer Olsson .04 .10
34 Marko Tuulola .04 .10
35 Johan Molin .04 .10
36 Tony Martensson .04 .10
37 Tom Bissett .15 .40
38 Roger Kyro .04 .10
39 Ove Molin .04 .10
40 Mikko Luovi .04 .10
41 Daniel Rudslatt .04 .10
42 Kenneth Bergqvist .04 .10
43 Jan Larsson .04 .10
44 Mikael Tellqvist .75 2.00
45 Niklas Kronwall 1.00 2.50
46 Francois Bouchard .04 .10
47 Edvin Frylen .04 .10
48 Mikael Magnusson .04 .10
49 Daniel Tjarnqvist .20 .50
50 Charles Berglund .04 .10
51 Kristofer Ottosson .04 .10
52 Kyosti Karjalainen .04 .10
53 Nichlas Falk .04 .10
54 Mathias Tjarnqvist .15 .40
55 Jimmie Olvestad .20 .50
56 Johan Garpenlov .04 .10
57 Andreas Salomonsson .20 .50
58 Mikael Johansson .04 .10
59 Vladimir Orszagh .15 .40
60 Henrik Lundqvist 8.00 20.00
61 Magnus Johansson .04 .10
62 Christian Backman .04 .10
63 Nicklas Rahm .04 .10
64 Ronnie Sundin .04 .10
65 Par Edlund .04 .10
66 Magnus Kahnberg .04 .10
67 Pelle Prestberg .04 .10
68 Patrik Carnback .04 .10
69 Juha Ikonen .04 .10
70 Jari Tolsa .04 .10
71 Kristian Huselius .40 1.00
72 Peter Strom .04 .10
73 Henrik Nilsson .04 .10
74 Jonas Johnsson .04 .10
75 Mikael Andersson .04 .10
76 Magnus Eriksson .04 .10
77 Sergei Fokin .04 .10
78 Jonas Frogren .04 .10
79 Thomas Rhodin .04 .10
80 Greger Artursson .04 .10
81 Radek Hamr .04 .10
82 Roger Johansson .04 .10
83 Marko Jantunen .04 .10
84 Ulf Soderstrom .04 .10
85 Christian Berglund .04 .10
86 Mathias Johansson .04 .10
87 Trond Magnussen .04 .10
88 Peter Nordstrom .15 .40
89 Clas Eriksson .04 .10
90 Jorgen Jonsson .04 .10
91 Marcel Jenni .04 .10
92 Stefan Liv .60 1.50
93 Joacim Esbjors .04 .10
94 Per Gustafsson .04 .10
95 Fredrik Stillman .04 .10
96 Mikael Lindman .04 .10
97 Peter Ottosson .04 .10
98 Oleg Belov .04 .10
99 Peter Ekelund .04 .10
100 Johan Hult .04 .10
101 Johan Lindbom .04 .10
102 Jonas Esbjors .04 .10
103 Johan Forsander .04 .10
104 Mattias Remstam .04 .10
105 Fredrik Oberg .04 .10
106 Reinhard Divis .40 1.00
107 Magnus Svensson .04 .10
108 Jan Huokko .04 .10
109 Stefan Bergkvist .04 .10
110 Lars Jonsson .20 .50
111 Per Lofstrom .04 .10
112 Jens Nielsen .04 .10
113 Niklas Eriksson .04 .10
114 Daniel Widing .04 .10
115 Niklas Persson .04 .10
116 Henrik Nordfeldt .04 .10
117 Tore Vikingstad .15 .40
118 Mikael Karlberg .04 .10
119 Robert Burakovsky .04 .10
120 Jarmo Myllys .20 .50
121 Torbjorn Lindberg .04 .10
122 Petter Nilsson .04 .10
123 Osmo Soutokorva .04 .10
124 Roger Akerstrom .04 .10
125 Johan Finnstrom .04 .10
126 Jiri Kucera .04 .10
127 Jonathan Hedstrom .20 .50
128 Tomas Berglund .04 .10
129 Mikael Renberg .20 .50
130 Anders Burstrom .04 .10
131 Hans Huczkowski .04 .10
132 Martin Hostak .04 .10
133 Lars Edstrom .04 .10
134 Sami Mettovaara .04 .10
135 Andreas Hadelov .04 .10
136 David Petrasek .04 .10
137 Peter Jakobsson .04 .10
138 Joakim Lundberg .04 .10
139 Christian Due-Boje .04 .10
140 Johan Tornberg .04 .10
141 Henrik Malmstrom .04 .10
142 Marcus Thuresson .04 .10
143 Daniel Rydmark .04 .10
144 Juha Riihijarvi .04 .10
145 Jesper Mattsson .04 .10
146 Fredrik Lindquist .04 .10
147 Tomas Sandstrom .04 .10
148 Kim Staal .04 .10
149 Jan Hammar .04 .10
150 Tobias Lundstrom .04 .10
151 Andreas Pihl .04 .10
152 Pierre Hedin .04 .10
153 Jan-Axel Alavaara .04 .10
154 Jan Larsson .04 .10
155 Per Hallberg .04 .10
156 Jesper Duus .04 .10
157 Magnus Wernblom .04 .10
158 Anders Soderberg .15 .40
159 Tommy Pettersson .04 .10
160 Mattias Weinhandl .40 1.00
161 Peter Hogardh .04 .10
162 Patrik Wallenberg .04 .10
163 Jorgen Bemstrom .04 .10
164 Stefan Ohman .04 .10
165 Boo Ahl .15 .40

Card	Low	High
166 Pasi Petrilainen	.15	.40
167 Stefan Klockare	.04	.10
168 Daniel Casselstahl	.04	.10
169 Marcus Karlsson	.04	.10
170 Robert Carlsson	.04	.10
171 Per Hallin	.04	.10
172 Nik Zupancic	.04	.10
173 Timo Peltomaa	.04	.10
174 Linus Fagemo	.04	.10
175 Henrik Zetterberg ERC	4.00	10.00
176 Mikael Lind	.04	.10
177 Anders Huss	.04	.10
178 Markus Matthiasson	.04	.10
179 Stefan Hellkvist SS	.04	.10
180 Kristian Gahn SS	.04	.10
181 Bjorn Ahlstrom SS	.04	.10
182 Aleksanders Beliavskis SS	.04	.10
183 Tom Bissett SS	.15	.40
184 Tommy Sjodin SS	.04	.10
185 Ove Molin SS	.04	.10
186 Mikael Tellqvist SS	.75	2.00
187 Mikael Johansson SS	.04	.10
188 Vladimir Orszagh SS	.15	.40
189 Johan Garpenlov SS	.04	.10
190 Christian Berglund SS	.04	.10
191 Jorgen Jonsson SS	.04	.10
192 Radek Hamr SS	.04	.10
193 Kristian Huselius SS	.40	1.00
194 Mikael Andersson SS	.04	.10
195 Patrik Carnback SS	.04	.10
196 Per Gustafsson SS	.04	.10
197 Johan Lindbom SS	.04	.10
198 Oleg Belov SS	.04	.10
199 Robert Burakovsky SS	.04	.10
200 Mikael Renberg SS	.20	.50
201 Petter Nilsson SS	.04	.10
202 Jarmo Myllys SS	.20	.50
203 Tomas Sandstrom SS	.15	.40
204 Marcus Thuresson SS	.04	.10
205 Fredrik Lindquist SS	.04	.10
206 Magnus Wernblom SS	.04	.10
207 Mattias Weinhandl SS	.20	.50
208 Henrik Zetterberg SS	4.00	10.00
209 Mats Lindberg CL	.04	.10
210 Jorgen Hermansson CL	.04	.10
211 Par Djoos CL	.04	.10
212 Jimmie Olvestad CL	.15	.40
213 Christian Backman CL	.04	.10
214 Radek Hamr CL	.04	.10
215 Peter Ekelund CL	.04	.10
216 Lars Jonsson CL	.20	.50
217 Mikael Renberg CL	.20	.50
218 Fredrik Lindquist CL	.04	.10
219 Mattias Weinhandl CL	.20	.50
220 Marcus Karlsson CL	.04	.10

2000-01 Swedish Upper Deck Game Jerseys

Card	Low	High
COMPLETE SET (2)	40.00	50.00
DS Daniel Sedin	20.00	30.00
HS Henrik Sedin	20.00	30.00

2000-01 Swedish Upper Deck Masked Men

Card	Low	High
COMPLETE SET (7)	20.00	40.00
M1 Tim Thomas	3.00	8.00
M2 Mikael Tellqvist	6.00	15.00
M3 Magnus Eriksson	2.50	6.00
M4 Reinhard Divis	4.00	10.00
M5 Jarmo Myllys	2.50	6.00
M6 Andreas Hadelov	2.00	5.00
M7 Boo Ahl	2.00	5.00

2000-01 Swedish Upper Deck SHL Excellence

Card	Low	High
COMPLETE SET (5)	15.00	30.00
S1 V.Orszagh / J.Garpenlov	2.00	5.00
S2 C.Berglund / J.Jonsson	2.00	5.00
S3 P.Carnback / K.Huselius	4.00	10.00
S4 M.Renberg / J.Myllys	2.50	6.00
S5 M.Weinhandl / M.Wernblom	3.00	8.00

2000-01 Swedish Upper Deck SHL Signatures

Card	Low	High
COMPLETE SET (42)	225.00	450.00
AB Alexander Beliavski	4.00	10.00
AG Anders Gozzi	4.00	10.00
AH Andreas Hadelov	4.00	10.00
AS Alexander Semjonovs	4.00	10.00
BA Boo Ahl	4.00	10.00
CB Christian Backman	4.00	10.00
CH Christian Berglund	4.00	10.00
DR Daniel Rydmark	4.00	10.00
FL Fredrik Lindquist	4.00	10.00
GA Greger Artursson	4.00	10.00
HZ Henrik Zetterberg	30.00	60.00
JE Jonas Esbjors	4.00	10.00
JG Johan Garpenlov	4.00	10.00
JH Jorgen Hermansson	4.00	10.00
JJ Jorgen Jonsson	4.00	10.00
JL Jan Larsson	4.00	10.00
JN Jens Nielsen	4.00	10.00
JO Jonathan Hedstrom	8.00	20.00
KG Kristian Gahn	4.00	10.00
KH Kristian Huselius	12.50	30.00
MA Mikael Andersson	4.00	10.00
ME Mikael Tellqvist	12.50	30.00
MH Martin Hostak	4.00	10.00
MI Mattias Weinhandl	8.00	20.00
MJ Mikael Johansson	4.00	10.00
ML Mats Lindberg	4.00	10.00
MN Mikael Renberg	8.00	20.00
MR Mattias Remstam	4.00	10.00
MS Magnus Svensson	4.00	10.00
MT Marcus Thuresson	4.00	10.00
MW Magnus Wernblom	4.00	10.00
NK Niklas Kronwall	20.00	50.00
OB Oleg Belov	4.00	10.00
OM Ove Molin	4.00	10.00
PC Patrik Carnback	4.00	10.00
PD Par Djoos	4.00	10.00
PN Petter Nilsson	4.00	10.00
RD Reinhard Divis	10.00	25.00
RJ Roger Johansson	4.00	10.00
SH Stefan Hellkvist	4.00	10.00
TB Tom Bissett	4.00	10.00
TL Tobias Lundstrom	4.00	10.00

2000-01 Swedish Upper Deck Top Draws

Card	Low	High
COMPLETE SET (11)	7.50	15.00
T1 Bjorn Ahlstrom	.40	1.00
T2 Ove Molin	.40	1.00
T3 Mikael Tellqvist	2.00	5.00
T4 Patrik Carnback	.40	1.00
T5 Roger Johansson	.40	1.00
T6 Oleg Belov	.40	1.00
T7 Jens Nielsen	.40	1.00
T8 Jonathan Hedstrom	.40	1.00
T9 Fredrik Lindquist	.40	1.00
T10 Mattias Weinhandl	.75	2.00
T11 Anders Huss	.40	1.00

2000-01 Swedish Upper Deck Top Playmakers

Card	Low	High
COMPLETE SET (8)	15.00	30.00
P1 Mats Lindberg	1.50	4.00
P2 Jan Larsson	1.50	4.00
P3 Mikael Johansson	1.50	4.00
P4 Jonas Johansson	1.50	4.00
P5 Jorgen Jonsson	1.50	4.00
P6 Martin Hostak	1.50	4.00
P7 Juha Riihijarvi	1.50	4.00
P8 Mattias Weinhandl	2.50	6.00

2001-02 Swedish Alfabilder

Card	Low	High
COMPLETE SET (18)	10.00	25.00
1 Sven Tumba Johansson	.40	1.00
2 Roland Rolle Stoltz	.40	1.00
3 Eilert Mattaa	.40	1.00
4 Lennart Klimpen Haggroth	.40	1.00
5 Nisse Nilsson	.40	1.00
6 Ulf Sterner	.40	1.00
7 Leif Honken Holmqvist	.75	2.00
8 Tord Lundstrom	.40	1.00
9 Borje Salming	2.00	5.00
10 Anders Hedberg	1.25	3.00
11 Anders Kallur	.75	2.00
12 Stefan Persson	.75	2.00
13 Goran Hogosta	.40	1.00
14 Bengt-Ake Gustavsson	.40	1.00
15 Mats Naslund	1.25	3.00
16 Kent Nilsson	1.25	3.00
17 Hakan Loob	1.25	3.00
18 Peter Lindmark	.75	2.00

2001-02 Swedish Brynas Tigers

Card	Low	High
COMPLETE SET (27)	10.00	25.00
1 Adam Andersson	.40	1.00
2 Johan Asplund	.75	2.00
3 Kenneth Bergqvist	.40	1.00
4 Tom Bissett	.60	1.50
5 Bjorn Danielsson	.40	1.00
6 Par Djoos	.40	1.00
7 Jonas Floberg	.40	1.00
8 Kristoffer Jobs	.40	1.00
9 Daniel Johansson	.40	1.00
10 Roger Kyro	.40	1.00
11 Jan Larsson	.40	1.00
12 Mikko Luovi	.40	1.00
13 Per Mars	.40	1.00
14 Tony Martensson	.40	1.00
15 Roger Melin	.40	1.00
16 Ove Molin	.40	1.00
17 Christer Olsson	.40	1.00
18 Jussi Pekkala	.40	1.00
19 Gunnar Persson	.40	1.00
20 Henrik Petre	.40	1.00
21 Mattias Pettersson	.40	1.00
22 Henrik Rehnberg	.40	1.00
23 Daniel Rudslatt	.40	1.00
24 Tommy Sjodin	.40	1.00
25 Jonas Soling	.40	1.00
26 Daniel Wagstrom	.40	1.00
27 Team Card	.40	1.00

2002-03 Swedish Malmo Red Hawks

Card	Low	High
1 Joakim Lundberg	.40	1.00
2 Johan Bjork	.40	1.00
3 Peter Hasselbald	.40	1.00
4 Henrik Malmstrom	.40	1.00
5 Jan Hammer	.40	1.00
6 Marcus Magnertoft	.40	1.00
7 Marcus Thuresson	.40	1.00
8 Frans Nielsen	.40	1.00
9 Daniel Rydmark	.40	1.00
10 Juha Riihijarvi	.40	1.00
11 Jesper Mattsson	.40	1.00
12 David Petrasek	.40	1.00
13 Mikael Wahlberg	.40	1.00
14 Toivo Suursoo	.40	1.00
15 Janos Vas	.40	1.00
16 Robert Borgqvist	.40	1.00
17 Petri Liimatainen	.40	1.00
18 Johan Norgren	.40	1.00
19 Andreas Valdix	.40	1.00
20 Peter Andersson	.40	1.00
21 Roger Ohman	.40	1.00

2002-03 Swedish SHL

Card	Low	High
COMPLETE SET (292)	20.00	50.00
1 Johan Asplund	.20	.50
2 Par Djoos	.08	.20
3 Tommy Sjodin	.08	.20
4 Henrik Rehnberg	.08	.20
5 Adam Andersson	.08	.20
6 Tony Martensson	.08	.20
7 Roger Kyro	.08	.20
8 Ove Molin	.08	.20
9 Bjorn Danielsson	.08	.20
10 Jan Larsson	.08	.20
11 Jonas Soling	.08	.20
12 Sergei Naumov	.20	.50
13 Ronnie Pettersson	.08	.20
14 Bjorn Nord	.08	.20
15 Mikael Magnusson	.08	.20
16 Tomas Strandberg	.08	.20
17 Peter Lindelof	.08	.20
18 Mikael Johansson	.08	.20
19 Christian Eklund	.08	.20
20 Johan Forsander	.08	.20
21 Mikael Hakanson	.08	.20
22 Nils Ekman	.20	.50
23 Martin Gerber	.40	1.00
24 Mats Trygg	.08	.20
25 Jonas Frogren	.08	.20
26 Thomas Rhodin	.08	.20
27 Greger Artursson	.08	.20
28 Marko Jantunen	.08	.20
29 Claes Eriksson	.08	.20
30 Rickard Wallin	.08	.20
31 Marcel Jenni	.08	.20
32 Mathias Johansson	.08	.20
33 Peter Hammarstrom	.08	.20
34 Boo Ahl	.20	.50
35 Daniel Ljungqvist	.08	.20
36 Per Gustafsson	.08	.20
37 Jouni Loponen	.08	.20
38 Richard Pavlikovsky	.08	.20
39 Peter Ekelund	.08	.20
40 Anders Huusko	.08	.20
41 Mattias Remstam	.08	.20
42 Johan Hult	.08	.20
43 Bjorn Melin	.08	.20
44 Kalle Sahlstedt	.08	.20
45 Fredrik Jensen	.08	.20
46 Mathias Ahxner	.08	.20
47 Martin Knold	.08	.20
48 Christoffer Norgren	.08	.20
49 Johan Bulow	.08	.20
50 Fredrik Johansson	.08	.20
51 Henrik Andersson	.08	.20
52 Fredrik Emvall	.08	.20
53 Per Eklund	.08	.20
54 Stefan Pettersson	.08	.20
55 Magnus Gastrin	.08	.20
56 Daniel Henriksson	.20	.50
57 Jonas Andersson-Junkka	.08	.20
58 Jan Sandstrom	.08	.20
59 Petter Nilsson	.08	.20
60 Roger Akerstrom	.08	.20
61 Stefan Nilsson	.08	.20
62 Jonathan Hedstrom	.08	.20
63 Per Ledin	.08	.20
64 Anders Burstrom	.08	.20
65 Hans Huczkowski	.08	.20
66 Emil Lundberg	.08	.20
67 Andreas Hadelov	.20	.50
68 Peter Hasselblad	.08	.20
69 Peter Andersson	.08	.20
70 Roger Ohman	.08	.20
71 Henrik Malmstrom	.08	.20
72 Marcus Thuresson	.08	.20
73 Daniel Rydmark	.08	.20
74 Juha Riihijarvi	.08	.20
75 Marcus Magnertoft	.08	.20
76 Mika Hannula	.08	.20
77 Jesper Mattsson	.08	.20
78 Peter Hirsch	.20	.50
79 Pierre Hedin	.08	.20
80 Jan Oberg	.08	.20
81 Magnus Wernblom	.08	.20
82 Tommy Pettersson	.08	.20
83 Peter Hogardh	.20	.50
84 Peter Oberg	.08	.20
85 Joakim Lindstrom	.08	.20
86 Magnus Hedlund	.08	.20
87 Mattias Wennerberg	.08	.20
88 Stefan Ohman	.08	.20
89 Rolf Wanhainen	.20	.50
90 Ola Mollerstedt	.08	.20
91 Stefan Bernstrom	.08	.20
92 Peter Popovic	.08	.20
93 Peter Ahola	.08	.20
94 Jesper Bjorck	.08	.20
95 Jukka Tiilikainen	.08	.20
96 Erik Norback	.08	.20
97 Juha Lind	.20	.50
98 Peter Gerhardsson	.08	.20
99 Jorgen Bernstrom	.08	.20
100 Fredrik Andersson	.08	.20
101 Tommi Rajamaki	.08	.20
102 David Halvardsson	.08	.20
103 Daniel Casselstahl	.08	.20
104 Niklas Nordgren	.08	.20
105 Markus Matthiasson	.20	.50
106 Robert Carlsson	.08	.20
107 Per Hallin	.08	.20
108 Henrik Zetterberg	1.00	2.50
109 Mikael Lind	.08	.20
110 Ed Ward	.08	.20
111 Henrik Lundqvist	2.00	5.00
112 Jan-Axel Alavaara	.08	.20
113 Christian Backman	.08	.20
114 Ronnie Sundin	.08	.20
115 Magnus Kahnberg	.08	.20
116 Jens Karlsson	.08	.20
117 Juha Ikonen	.08	.20
118 Jari Tolsa	.08	.20
119 Niklas Andersson	.08	.20
120 Jonas Johansson	.08	.20
121 Peter Strom	.08	.20
122 Brynas IF Logo	.08	.20
123 Djurgardens Logo	.08	.20
124 Farjestads Logo	.08	.20
125 HV 71 Logo	.08	.20
126 Leksands Logo	.08	.20
127 Linkopings Logo	.08	.20
128 Lulea Logo	.08	.20
129 Malmo Logo	.08	.20
130 MoDo Logo	.08	.20
131 Sodertalje Logo	.08	.20
132 Timra Logo	.08	.20
133 Vastra Frolunda Logo	.08	.20
134 Christer Olsson CL	.08	.20
135 Thomas Ostlund CL	.08	.20
136 Jorgen Jonsson CL	.08	.20
137 Johan Davidsson CL	.08	.20
138 Mikael Sandberg CL	.15	.40
139 Tomas Berglund CL	.08	.20
140 Tomas Sandstrom CL	.08	.20
141 Richard Lintner CL	.08	.20
142 Peter Larsson CL	.08	.20
143 Henrik Zetterberg CL	.75	2.00
144 Joel Lundqvist CL	.08	.20
145 Jamie Ram	.20	.50
146 Daniel Johansson	.08	.20
147 Jussi Pekkala	.08	.20
148 Veli-Pekka Laitinen	.08	.20
149 Kristoffer Jobs	.08	.20
150 Jonas Floberg	.08	.20
151 Simon Ostlund	.08	.20
152 Tommi Miettinen	.08	.20
153 Niklas Anger	.15	.40
154 Daniel Wagstrom	.08	.20
155 Joaquin Gage	.15	.40
156 Bjorn Bjurling	.08	.20
157 Niklas Kronwall	.40	1.00
158 Per-Anton Lundstrom	.20	.50
159 Kristofer Ottosson	.08	.20
160 Joakim Eriksson	.08	.20
161 Daniel Rudslatt	.08	.20
162 Nichlas Falk	.08	.20
163 Mathias Trattnig	.08	.20
164 Fredrik Lindqvist	.08	.20
165 Johan Lindstrom	.08	.20
166 Mikael Gerden	.08	.20
167 Sinuhe Wallinheimo	.08	.20
168 Per Lundell	.08	.20
169 Per Hallberg	.08	.20
170 Radek Hamr	.08	.20
171 Ulf Soderstrom	.08	.20
172 Marius Trygg	.08	.20
173 Peter Nordstrom	.08	.20
174 Jorgen Jonsson	.08	.20
175 Par Backer	.08	.20
176 Pelle Prestberg	.08	.20
177 Dieter Kalt	.08	.20
178 Stefan Liv	.60	1.50
179 Mika Niskanen	.08	.20
180 Timmy Pettersson	.08	.20
181 Daniel Josefsson	.08	.20
182 Jani Hassinen	.08	.20
183 Sebastian Meijer	.08	.20
184 Niklas Brannstrom	.08	.20
185 Par Arlbrandt	.08	.20
186 Pasi Maattanen	.08	.20
187 Johan Davidsson	.15	.40
188 Jonas Fransson	.08	.20
189 Sean Gauthier	.15	.40
190 Christer Olsson	.08	.20
191 Niklas Gallstedt	.08	.20
192 Hans Lodin	.08	.20
193 Per Lofstrom	.08	.20
194 Mike Stapleton	.08	.20
195 Jens Nielsen	.08	.20
196 Niklas Eriksson	.08	.20
197 Mikael Karlberg	.08	.20
198 Mikael Pettersson / Robert Nilsson	.08	.20
199 Tobias Holm	.08	.20
200 Niklas Persson	.08	.20
201 Goran Hermansson	.08	.20
202 Tomas Forslund	.08	.20
203 Henrik Nordfeldt	.08	.20
204 Johan Rosen	.08	.20
205 Joel Davis	.08	.20
206 Mikael Sandberg	.15	.40
207 Andreas Pihl	.08	.20
208 Jan Mertzig	.08	.20
209 Thomas Johansson	.08	.20
210 Andreas Holmqvist	.08	.20
211 Barry Richter	.15	.40
212 Stefan Gustavson	.08	.20
213 Brian Felsner	.15	.40
214 Johan Franzen ERC	1.00	2.50
215 Tim Eriksson	.08	.20
216 Mikael Hakanson	.08	.20
217 Gusten Tornqvist	.08	.20
218 Pavel Skrbek	.08	.20
219 Patrik Bjaarnhjelm	.08	.20
220 Johan Finnstrom	.20	.50
221 Fredrik Svensson	.08	.20
222 Linus Fagemo	.08	.20
223 Patrik Tano	.08	.20
224 Kamil Brabenec	.08	.20
225 Thomas Berglund	.08	.20
226 Jonas Hagerback	.08	.20
227 Magnus Nilsson	.08	.20
228 Robert Borgqvist	.08	.20
229 Joakim Lundberg	.08	.20
230 David Petrasek	.08	.20
231 Petri Liimatainen	.08	.20
232 Johan Norgren	.08	.20
233 Jan Hammar	.08	.20
234 Frans Nielsen	.08	.20
235 Mikael Wahlberg	.08	.20
236 Toivo Suursoo	.08	.20
237 Juuso Riksman	.08	.20
238 Tobias Enstrom	.08	.20
239 Jesper Damgaard	.08	.20
240 Erik Leverstrom	.08	.20
241 Dusan Milo	.08	.20
242 Martin Johansson	.08	.20
243 Anders Soderberg	.15	.40
244 Jonas Almtorp	.08	.20
245 Fredrik Warg	.08	.20
246 Joakim Lindstrom	.08	.20
247 Morten Green	.08	.20
248 Miroslav Hlinka	.08	.20
249 Magnus Lindquist	.08	.20
250 Alexander Blomqvist	.08	.20
251 Anders Back	.08	.20
252 Leif Rohlin	.08	.20
253 Robert Carlsson	.08	.20
254 Antti Tormanen	.08	.20
255 David Svee	.08	.20
256 Gabriel Karlsson	.08	.20
257 Mattias Carlsson	.08	.20
258 Peter Larsson	.08	.20
259 Patrik Zetterberg	.08	.20
260 Kristian Gahn	.08	.20
261 Kimmo Kapanen	.08	.20
262 Martin Lindman	.08	.20
263 Kalle Koskinen	.08	.20
264 Robert Jindrich	.08	.20
265 Par Styf	.08	.20
266 Patrik Wallenberg	.08	.20
267 Christian Soderstrom	.08	.20
268 Henrik Eriksson	.08	.20
269 Valeri Krykov	.08	.20
270 Toni Koivunen	.08	.20
271 Markus Akerblom	.08	.20
272 Fredrik Norrena	.40	1.00
273 Magnus Johansson	.08	.20
274 Kimmo Eronen	.08	.20
275 Oscar Ackestrom	.08	.20
276 Erik Kakko	.08	.20
277 Mattias Luukkonen	.08	.20
278 Patrik Carnback	.08	.20
279 Alexander Steen ERC	1.50	4.00
280 Joel Lundqvist	.08	.20
281 Jonas Esbjors	.08	.20
282 Mikael Andersson	.08	.20
283 Jamie Ram	.20	.50
284 Joaquin Gage	.20	.50
285 Sinuhe Wallinheimo	.20	.50
286 Stefan Liv	.60	1.50
287 Sean Gauthier	.15	.40
288 Mikael Sandberg	.08	.20
289 Daniel Henriksson	.08	.20
290 Andreas Hadelov	.08	.20
291 Peter Hirsch	.20	.50
292 Magnus Lindquist	.08	.20
293 Kimmo Kapanen	.08	.20
294 Fredrik Norrena	.40	1.00

2002-03 Swedish SHL Dynamic Duos

Card	Low	High
COMPLETE SET (9)	6.00	15.00
1 Par Djoos / Tommy Sjodin	.75	2.00
2 Mikael Johansson / Kristofer Ottosson	.75	2.00
3 Par Backer / Jorgen Jonsson	.75	2.00
4 Lars Jonsson / Daniel Widing	1.25	3.00
5 Petr Nilsson / Stefan Nilsson	.75	2.00
6 Mika Hannula / Juha Riihijarvi	.75	2.00
7 Juha Lind / Antti Tormanen	.75	2.00
8 Markus Matthiasson / Markus Akerblom	.75	2.00
9 Joel Lundqvist / Alexander Steen	2.00	5.00

2002-03 Swedish SHL Masks

Card	Low	High
COMPLETE SET (9)	25.00	50.00
1 Sinuhe Wallinheimo	3.00	8.00
2 Stefan Liv	4.00	10.00
3 Sean Gauthier	3.00	8.00
4 Mikael Sandberg	3.00	8.00
5 Andreas Hadelov	3.00	8.00
6 Peter Hirsch	3.00	8.00
7 Magnus Lindquist	3.00	8.00
8 Kimmo Kapanen	3.00	8.00
9 Fredrik Norrena	4.00	10.00

2002-03 Swedish SHL Netminders

Card	Low	High
COMPLETE SET (9)	15.00	20.00
NM1 Martin Gerber	2.00	5.00
NM2 Sergei Naumov	.75	2.00
NM3 Stefan Liv	2.00	5.00
NM4 Rolf Wanhainen	.75	2.00
NM5 Peter Hirsch	.75	2.00
NM6 Daniel Henriksson	.75	2.00
NM7 Mikael Sandberg	.75	2.00
NM8 Johan Asplund	.75	2.00
NM9 Andreas Hadelov	.75	2.00

2002-03 Swedish SHL Next Generation

Card	Low	High
COMPLETE SET (9)	15.00	30.00
NG1 Joel Lundqvist	1.50	4.00
NG2 Par Backer	1.50	4.00
NG3 Magnus Hedlund	1.50	4.00
NG4 Adam Andersson	1.50	4.00
NG5 Henrik Lundqvist	1.50	4.00
NG6 Joakim Lindstrom	1.50	4.00
NG7 Jonas Johansson	3.00	8.00
NG8 Bjorn Melin	1.50	4.00
NG9 Jens Karlsson	2.00	5.00

2002-03 Swedish SHL Parallel

*PARALLEL: 2X TO 5X BASIC CARDS

2002-03 Swedish SHL Promos

Card	Low	High
COMPLETE SET (11)	8.00	20.00
TCC1 Tommy Sjodin	.40	1.00
TCC2 Christian Eklund	.40	1.00
TCC3 Martin Gerber	.75	2.00
TCC4 Stefan Liv	.75	2.00
TCC5 Per Eklund	.40	1.00
TCC6 Jonas Andersson-Junkka	.40	1.00
TCC7 Mika Hannula	.40	1.00
TCC8 Mattias Weinhandl	.75	2.00
TCC9 Peter Popovic	.40	1.00
TCC10 Henrik Zetterberg	6.00	15.00
TCC11 Jan-Axel Alavaara	.40	1.00

2002-03 Swedish SHL Sharpshooters

Card	Low	High
COMPLETE SET (9)	20.00	40.00
SS1 Peter Hogardh	1.50	4.00
SS2 Jorgen Jonsson	1.50	4.00
SS3 Dieter Kalt	1.50	4.00
SS4 Per-Age Skroder	2.50	6.00
SS5 Juha Riihijarvi	1.50	4.00
SS6 Peter Larsson	1.50	4.00
SS7 Markus Matthiasson	1.50	4.00
SS8 Mattias Weinhandl	2.50	6.00
SS9 Nils Ekman	2.50	6.00

2002-03 Swedish SHL Signatures

Card	Low	High
1 Jonas Soling	4.00	10.00
2 Ove Molin	4.00	10.00
3 Nils Ekman	6.00	15.00
4 Kristofer Ottosson	4.00	10.00
5 Jorgen Jonsson	6.00	15.00
6 Rickard Wallin	6.00	15.00
7 Johan Davidsson	6.00	15.00
8 Mikael Sandberg	6.00	15.00
9 Stefan Nilsson	4.00	10.00
10 Andreas Hadelov	6.00	15.00
11 Jesper Mattsson	4.00	10.00
12 Peter Hogardh	6.00	15.00
13 Rolf Wanhainen	6.00	15.00
14 Juha Lind	6.00	15.00
15 Henrik Zetterberg	40.00	80.00
16 Per Hallin	4.00	10.00
17 Niklas Andersson	4.00	10.00
18 Alexander Steen	15.00	40.00

2002-03 Swedish SHL Signatures Series II

Card	Low	High
1 Stefan Pettersson	6.00	15.00
2 Daniel Henriksson	6.00	15.00
3 Erik Nordback	6.00	15.00
4 Bjorn Nord	6.00	15.00
5 Ulf Soderstrom	6.00	15.00
6 Stefan Liv	10.00	25.00
7 Mikael Hakansson	6.00	15.00
8 Joel Lundqvist	10.00	25.00
9 Robert Carlsson	6.00	15.00
10 Peter Popovic	6.00	15.00
11 Magnus Wernblom	6.00	15.00
12 Juha Riihijarvi	6.00	15.00
13 Jonathan Hedstrom	8.00	20.00
14 Marcus Thuresson	6.00	15.00
15 Per Eklund	6.00	15.00
16 Antti Tormanen	6.00	15.00
17 Fredrik Lindqvist	6.00	15.00
18 Jens Nielsen	6.00	15.00
19 Sean Gauthier	6.00	15.00
20 Niklas Eriksson	6.00	15.00
21 Leif Rohlin	6.00	15.00
22 Lars Jonsson	8.00	20.00
23 Kalle Sahlstedt SP	15.00	40.00
24 Per-Age Skroder SP	15.00	40.00
25 Dieter Kalt	6.00	15.00
26 Johan Asplund	8.00	20.00

2002-03 Swedish SHL Team Captains

Card	Low	High
COMPLETE SET (9)	6.00	15.00
1 Jan Larsson	.75	2.00
2 Nichlas Falk	.75	2.00
3 Jorgen Jonsson	.75	2.00
4 Johan Davidsson	.75	2.00
5 Christer Olsson	.75	2.00
6 Stefan Gustavson	.75	2.00
7 Roger Akerstrom	.75	2.00
8 Pierre Hedin	.75	2.00
9 Peter Popovic	.75	2.00

2003-04 Swedish Elite

Card	Low	High
COMPLETE SET (288)	20.00	40.00
COMMON CARD (1-144)	.02	.05
SEMISTARS	.08	.20
UNLISTED STARS	.20	.50
1 Joakim Lundstrom	.08	.20
2 Daniel Johansson	.08	.20
3 Tommy Sjodin	.08	.20
4 Adam Andersson	.08	.20
5 Veli-Pekka Laitinen	.08	.20
6 Jonas Soling	.08	.20
7 Simon Ostlund	.08	.20
8 Roger Kyro	.08	.20
9 Ove Molin	.08	.20
10 Bjorn Danielsson	.08	.20
11 Tommi Miettinen	.08	.20
12 Joaquin Gage	.20	.50
13 Ronnie Pettersson	.08	.20
14 Niklas Kronwall	.40	1.00
15 Bjorn Nord	.08	.20
16 Kristofer Ottosson	.08	.20
17 Daniel Rudslatt	.08	.20
18 Nichlas Falk	.20	.50
19 Mathias Tjarnqvist	.08	.20
20 Christian Eklund	.08	.20
21 Fredrik Lindqvist	.20	.50
22 Mikael Johansson	.08	.20
23 Fredrik Norrena	.20	.50
24 Kimmo Eronen	.08	.20
25 Ronnie Sundin	.08	.20
26 Erik Kakko	.08	.20
27 Mattias Luukkonen	.08	.20
28 Magnus Kahnberg	.08	.20
29 Jari Tolsa	.08	.20
30 Joel Lundqvist	.08	.20
31 Niklas Andersson	.08	.20
32 Peter Strom	.08	.20
33 Jens Karlsson	.08	.20
34 Sinuhe Wallinheimo	.20	.50
35 Per Hallberg	.08	.20
36 Mats Trygg	.08	.20
37 Greger Artursson	.08	.20
38 Radek Hamr	.08	.20
39 Peter Nordstrom	.08	.20
40 Claes Eriksson	.08	.20
41 Par Backer	.08	.20
42 Marcel Jenni	.08	.20
43 Peter Hammarstrom	.08	.20
44 Dieter Kalt	.08	.20
45 Boo Ahl	.20	.50
46 Daniel Ljungqvist	.08	.20
47 Ola Thorwalls	.08	.20
48 Timmy Pettersson	.08	.20
49 Jouni Loponen	.08	.20
50 Jani Hassinen	.08	.20
51 Peter Ekelund	.08	.20
52 Kalle Sahlstedt	.08	.20
53 Pasi Maattanen	.08	.20
54 Mattias Remstam	.08	.20
55 Johan Davidsson	.08	.20
56 Jonas Elofsson	.08	.20
57 Christer Olsson	.08	.20
58 Lars Jonsson	.30	.75
59 Hans Lodin	.08	.20
60 Jens Nielsen	.08	.20
61 Niklas Eriksson	.08	.20
62 Mikael Pettersson	.08	.20
63 Tobias Holm	.08	.20
64 Niklas Persson	.08	.20
65 Goran Hermansson	.08	.20
66 Henrik Nordfeldt	.08	.20
67 Andreas Pihl	.08	.20
68 Jan Mertzig	.08	.20
69 Martin Knold	.08	.20
70 Andreas Holmqvist	.08	.20
71 Barry Richter	.08	.20
72 Johan Bulow	.08	.20
73 Fredrik Johansson	.08	.20
74 Tim Eriksson	.08	.20
75 Fredrik Emvall	.08	.20
76 Mikael Hakanson	.08	.20
77 Per Eklund	.08	.20
78 Gusten Tornqvist	.08	.20
79 Jonas Andersson-Junkka	.08	.20
80 Petter Nilsson	.08	.20
81 Pavel Skrbek	.08	.20
82 Johan Finnstrom	.08	.20
83 Stefan Nilsson	.08	.20
84 Kamil Brabenec	.08	.20
85 Thomas Berglund	.08	.20
86 Hans Huczkowski	.08	.20
87 Per Ledin	.08	.20
88 Andreas Hadelov	.20	.50
89 Joakim Lundberg	.08	.20
90 David Petrasek	.08	.20
91 Petri Liimatainen	.08	.20
92 Peter Andersson	.08	.20
93 Frans Nielsen	.08	.20
94 Daniel Rydmark	.08	.20
95 Juha Riihijarvi	.08	.20
96 Jesper Mattsson	.08	.20
97 Toivo Suursoo	.08	.20
98 Mika Hannula	.08	.20
99 Juuso Riksman	.08	.20
100 Jan Oberg	.08	.20
101 Dusan Milo	.08	.20
102 Magnus Hedlund	.08	.20
103 Martin Wilde	.08	.20
104 Mika Lehtinen	.08	.20
105 Anders Soderberg	.08	.20
106 Tommy Pettersson	.08	.20
107 Peter Hogardh	.08	.20
108 Peter Oberg	.08	.20
109 Joakim Lindstrom	.08	.20
110 Mattias Wennerberg	.08	.20
111 Magnus Lindquist	.08	.20
112 Anders Back	.08	.20
113 Stefan Bernstrom	.08	.20
114 Peter Popovic	.08	.20
115 Peter Ahola	.08	.20
116 Robert Carlsson	.08	.20
117 Antti Tormanen	.08	.20
118 Gabriel Karlsson	.08	.20
119 Jorgen Bernstrom	.08	.20
120 Peter Larsson	.08	.20
121 Patrik Zetterberg	.08	.20
122 Kimmo Kapanen	.20	.50
123 David Halvardsson	.08	.20
124 Tommi Rajamaki	.08	.20
125 Kalle Koskinen	.08	.20
126 Par Styf	.08	.20
127 Christian Soderstrom	.08	.20
128 Niklas Nordgren	.08	.20
129 Valeri Krykov	.08	.20
130 Per Hallin	.08	.20
131 Christian Sjogren	.08	.20
132 Markus Matthiasson	.08	.20
133 Brynas IF	.04	.10
134 Djurgardens IF	.04	.10
135 Frolunda Indians	.04	.10
136 Farjestads BK	.04	.10
137 HV 71	.04	.10
138 Leksands IF	.04	.10
139 Linkopings HC	.04	.10
140 Lulea Hockey	.04	.10
141 MIF Redhawks	.04	.10
142 MoDo Hockey	.04	.10
143 Sodertalje SK	.04	.10
144 Timra IK	.04	.10
145 Markus Korhonen	.20	.50
146 Mikko Kuparinen	.08	.20
147 Jesper Bjorck	.08	.20
148 Daniel Casselstahl	.08	.20
149 Henrik Malmstrom	.08	.20
150 Nicklas Danielsson	.08	.20
151 Jacob Johansson	.08	.20
152 Patrik Ronnqvist	.08	.20
153 Peter Nylander	.08	.20
154 Niklas Anger	.08	.20
155 Mikael Lind	.08	.20
156 Bjorn Bjurling	.08	.20
157 Staffan Kronwall	.08	.20
158 Johnny Oduya	.08	.20
159 Mika Stromberg	.08	.20
160 Richard Lintner	.20	.50
161 Christopher Thorn	.08	.20
162 Jonathan Hedstrom	.20	.50
163 Tomas Kollar	.08	.20
164 Johannes Salmonsson	.08	.20
165 Fredrik Bremberg	.08	.20
166 Mikael Johansson	.08	.20
167 Marcus Kristoffersson	.20	.50
168 Stefan Pettersson	.08	.20
169 Kenneth Bergqvist	.08	.20
170 Henrik Lundqvist	.75	2.00
171 Jan-Axel Alavaara	.08	.20
172 Antti-Jussi Niemi	.08	.20
173 Oscar Ackestrom	.08	.20
174 Alexander Steen	2.00	5.00
175 Loui Eriksson	.40	1.00
176 Jonas Esbjors	.08	.20
177 Jonas Johnson	.40	1.00
178 Tomi Kallio	.20	.50
179 Robin Jonsson	.08	.20
180 Jonas Frogren	.08	.20
181 Janne Gronvall	.08	.20
182 Hannes Hyvonen	.08	.20
183 Pelle Prestberg	.08	.20
184 Ulf Soderstrom	.08	.20
185 Mathias Johansson	.08	.20
186 Jorgen Jonsson	.08	.20
187 Fredrik Eriksson	.08	.20
188 Calle Steen	.08	.20
189 Stefan Liv	.40	1.00
190 Fredrik Olausson	.20	.50
191 Simon Skoog	.08	.20
192 Mika Niskanen	.08	.20
193 Johan Halvardsson	.08	.20
194 Stefan Hellkvist	.08	.20
195 Per-age Skroder	.08	.20
196 Martin Thornberg	.08	.20
197 Anders Huusko	.08	.20
198 Bjorn Melin	.08	.20
199 Andreas Jamtin	.08	.20
200 Mike Bales	.08	.20
201 Johan Backlund	.08	.20
202 Richard Pavlikovsky	.08	.20

Card	Low	High
203 Tommy Westlund	.08	.20
204 Robert Nilsson	.08	.20
205 Johan Witehall	.08	.20
206 Christopher Lindholm	.08	.20
207 Joonas Jaaskelainen	.08	.20
208 Johan Rosén	.08	.20
209 Daniel Sperrle	.08	.20
210 Fredrik Norrena	.20	.50
211 Thomas Johansson	.08	.20
212 Peter Casparsson	.08	.20
213 Christoffer Norgren	.08	.20
214 Jyrki Valivaara	.08	.20
215 Johan Franzén	.40	1.00
216 Mikko Peltola	.08	.20
217 Ragnar Karlsson	.08	.20
218 Pekka Tirkkonen	.08	.20
219 Mikael von der Geest	.08	.20
220 Andreas Sundin	.08	.20
221 Jussi Tarvainen	.08	.20
222 Johan Lindstrom	.08	.20
223 Daniel Henriksson	.20	.50
224 Jonas Johansson	.08	.20
225 Johan Fransson	.40	1.00
226 Jan Sandstrom	.08	.20
227 Tuukka Mantyla	.08	.20
228 Roger Akerstrom	.08	.20
229 Jonas Ronnqvist	.08	.20
230 Linus Fagemo	.08	.20
231 Emil Lundberg	.08	.20
232 Jonas Nordquist	.08	.20
233 Jonas Hagerback	.08	.20
234 Magnus Nilsson	.08	.20
235 Johan Tellstrom	.08	.20
236 Pierre Berggren	.08	.20
237 Christopher Nilstorp	.20	.50
238 Johan Bjork	.08	.20
239 Magnus Osterby	.08	.20
240 Johan Norgren	.08	.20
241 Jens Olsson	.08	.20
242 Jan Hammar	.08	.20
243 Marcus Magnertoft	.08	.20
244 Niklas Sundblad	.08	.20
245 Mikael Wahlberg	.08	.20
246 Kim Staal	.08	.20
247 Andreas Valdix	.08	.20
248 Kimmo Vesa	.08	.20
249 Jesper Damgaard	.08	.20
250 Martin Johansson	.08	.20
251 Lars Jansson	.08	.20
252 Magnus Wernblom	.08	.20
253 Fredrik Warg	.08	.20
254 Morten Green	.08	.20
255 Per Svartvadet	.20	.50
256 Magnus Gastrin	.08	.20
257 Rolf Wanhainen	.20	.50
258 Johan Berggren	.08	.20
259 Bert Robertsson	.08	.20
260 Peter Messa	.08	.20
261 Jan Huokko	.08	.20
262 Joakim Eriksson	.08	.20
263 Urban Omark	.08	.20
264 Juha Lind	.08	.20
265 Bobbie Hagelin	.08	.20
266 Kristian Gahn	.08	.20
267 Mattias Ohrling	.08	.20
268 Jesper Jager	.08	.20
269 Jan Nemecek	.08	.20
270 Sanny Lindstrom	.08	.20
271 Mats Hansson	.08	.20
272 Robert Carlsson	.08	.20
273 Yared Hagos	.30	.75
274 Lee Jinman	.08	.20
275 Fredrik Sundin	.08	.20
276 Toni Koivunen	.08	.20
277 Brynas IF	.04	.10
278 Djurgardens IF	.04	.10
279 Frolunda Indians	.04	.10
280 Farjestads BK	.04	.10
281 HV 71	.04	.10
282 Leksands IF	.04	.10
283 Linkopings HC	.04	.10
284 Lulea Hockey	.04	.10
285 MIF Redhawks	.04	.10
286 MoDo Hockey	.04	.10
287 Sodertalje SK	.04	.10
288 Timra IK	.04	.10

2003-04 Swedish Elite Enforcers

Card	Low	High
COMPLETE SET (12)	5.00	10.00
F1 Hannes Hyvonen	.40	1.00
F2 Oscar Ackestrom	.40	1.00
F3 Thomas Berglund	.40	1.00
F4 Andreas Pihl	.40	1.00
F5 Joel Lundqvist	.75	2.00
F6 Par Styf	.40	1.00
F7 Bert Robertsson	.40	1.00
F8 Bjorn Nord	.40	1.00
F9 Henrik Nordfeldt	.40	1.00
F10 Christian Sjogren	.40	1.00
F11 Niklas Sundblad	.40	1.00
F12 Magnus Wernblom	.40	1.00

2003-04 Swedish Elite Global Impact

Card	Low	High
COMPLETE SET (12)	6.00	15.00
1 Markus Korhonen	.75	2.00
2 Richard Lintner	.40	1.00
3 Tomi Kallio	.75	2.00
4 Sinuhe Wallinheimo	.75	2.00
5 Per-age Skroder	.40	1.00
6 Mike Bales	1.25	3.00
7 Brian Felsner	1.00	2.50
8 Kamil Brabenec	.40	1.00
9 Toivo Suursoo	.40	1.00
10 Jesper Damgaard	.40	1.00
11 Juha Lind	.40	1.00
12 Jan Nemecek	.40	1.00

2003-04 Swedish Elite Hot Numbers

Card	Low	High
COMPLETE SET (12)	8.00	20.00
N1 Stefan Liv	1.50	4.00
N2 Robert Nilsson	.75	2.00
N3 Nicklas Falk	.40	1.00
N4 Alexander Steen	3.00	8.00
N5 Jorgen Jonsson	.40	1.00
N6 Rolf Wanhainen	.75	2.00
HN7 Markus Matthiasson	.40	1.00
HN8 Thomas Johansson	.40	1.00
HN9 Daniel Henriksson	.75	2.00
HN10 Mikael Lind	.40	1.00
HN11 Petri Liimatainen	.40	1.00
HN12 Per Svartvadet	.75	2.00

2003-04 Swedish Elite Jerseys

Card	Low	High
COMPLETE SET (5)	25.00	60.00
1 Kimmo Kapanen	4.00	10.00
2 Sinuhe Wallinheimo	8.00	20.00
3 Daniel Henriksson	4.00	10.00
4 Henrik Lundqvist	8.00	20.00
5 Magnus Johansson	4.00	10.00

2003-04 Swedish Elite Masks

Card	Low	High
COMPLETE SET (4)	15.00	30.00
1 Sinuhe Wallinheimo	4.00	10.00
2 Stefan Liv	5.00	12.00
3 Andreas Hadelov	4.00	10.00
4 Kimmo Kapanen	4.00	10.00

2003-04 Swedish Elite Masks II

Card	Low	High
COMPLETE SET (4)	15.00	30.00
1 Stefan Liv	5.00	12.00
2 Kimmo Kapanen	4.00	10.00
3 Andreas Hadelov	4.00	10.00
4 Sinuhe Wallinheimo	4.00	10.00

2003-04 Swedish Elite Rookies

Card	Low	High
COMPLETE SET (9)	6.00	15.00
1 Adam Andersson	.40	1.00
2 Joakim Lundstrom	.40	1.00
3 Nicklas Eckerblom	.40	1.00
4 Alexander Steen	3.00	8.00
5 Sebastian Meijer	.40	1.00
6 Robert Nilsson	1.00	2.50
7 Frans Nielsen	1.00	2.50
8 Tobias Enstrom	.40	1.00
9 Joakim Lindstrom	.40	1.00

2003-04 Swedish Elite Signatures

Card	Low	High
COMPLETE SET (16)	50.00	125.00
1 Antti Tormanen	4.00	10.00
2 Tommy Sjodin	4.00	10.00
3 Joel Lundqvist	8.00	20.00
4 Daniel Henriksson	4.00	10.00
5 Tobias Enstrom	4.00	10.00
6 Jonas Johnsson	4.00	10.00
7 Mika Lehtinen	4.00	10.00
8 Tommi Miettinen	4.00	10.00
9 Peter Popovic	4.00	10.00
10 Fredrik Norrena	8.00	20.00
11 Jonas Andersson-Junkka	4.00	10.00
12 Magnus Wernblom	4.00	10.00
13 Niklas Anger	4.00	10.00
14 Patrik Bjaarnhjelm	4.00	10.00
15 Mattias Wennerberg	4.00	10.00
16 Robert Nilsson SP	10.00	25.00

2003-04 Swedish Elite Signatures II

Card	Low	High
1 Sinuhe Wallinheimo	6.00	15.00
2 Per Hallberg	4.00	10.00
3 Par Backer	4.00	10.00
4 Jorgen Jonsson	4.00	10.00
5 Par Styf	4.00	10.00
6 Markus Matthiasson	4.00	10.00
7 Kimmo Kapanen	6.00	15.00
8 Niklas Kronwall	15.00	40.00
9 Bjorn Nord	4.00	10.00
10 Daniel Rudslatt	4.00	10.00
11 Per Eklund	4.00	10.00
12 Pasi Maatanen	4.00	10.00
13 Peter Ekelund	4.00	10.00
14 Stefan Liv	12.00	30.00
15 Johan Davidsson SP	20.00	50.00
16 Daniel Rydmark	4.00	10.00
17 Petri Liimatainen	4.00	10.00
18 Andreas Hadelov	6.00	15.00
19 Christer Olsson	4.00	10.00
20 Niklas Eriksson	4.00	10.00
21 Jens Nielsen	4.00	10.00

2003-04 Swedish Elite Stars of the Game

Card	Low	High
COMPLETE SET (9)	8.00	20.00
1 Kristofer Ottosson	1.25	3.00
2 Niklas Andersson	1.25	3.00
3 Jorgen Jonsson	1.25	3.00
4 Johan Davidsson	1.25	3.00
5 Per Eklund	1.25	3.00
6 Jonas Ronnqvist	1.25	3.00
7 Juha Riihijarvi	1.25	3.00
8 Antti Tormanen	1.25	3.00
9 Niklas Nordgren	1.25	3.00

2003-04 Swedish Elite Zero Hero

Card	Low	High
COMPLETE SET (9)	15.00	40.00
1 Henrik Lundqvist	5.00	12.00
2 Rolf Wanhainen	2.00	5.00
3 Andreas Hadelov	2.00	5.00
4 Joaquin Gage	2.00	5.00
5 Sinuhe Wallinheimo	2.00	5.00
6 Stefan Liv	2.50	6.00
7 Sean Gauthier	2.00	5.00
8 Juuso Riksman	2.00	5.00
9 Kimmo Kapanen	2.00	5.00

2004-05 Swedish Alfabilder Alfa Stars

Card	Low	High
COMPLETE SET (54)	10.00	25.00
1 Johan Hedberg	.20	.50
2 Mattias Ohlund	.20	.50
3 Kim Johnsson	.20	.50
4 Kenny Jonsson	.20	.50
5 Nicklas Lidstrom	.40	1.00
6 Mikael Renberg	.20	.50
7 Stefan Liv	.40	1.00
8 Christian Backman	.20	.50
9 Magnus Kahnberg	.20	.50
10 Andreas Johansson	.20	.50
11 Daniel Alfredsson	.40	1.00
12 Daniel Sedin	.40	1.00
13 Mats Sundin	.75	2.00
14 Mattias Norstrom	.20	.50
15 Johan Davidsson	.20	.50
16 Tomas Holmstrom	.40	1.00
17 Marcus Ragnarsson	.20	.50
18 Marcus Nilson	.20	.50
19 Markus Naslund	.75	2.00
20 Henrik Sedin	.40	1.00
21 Peter Forsberg	2.00	5.00
22 Per-Johan Axelsson	.20	.50
23 Kristian Huselius	.20	.50
24 Michael Nylander	.20	.50
25 Mattias Weinhandl	.20	.50
26 Samuel Pahlsson	.20	.50
27 Jorgen Jonsson	.20	.50
28 Dick Tarnstrom	.20	.50
29 Nils Ekman	.20	.50
30 Henrik Lundqvist	3.00	8.00
31 Fredrik Olausson	.20	.50
32 Mikael Tellqvist	.40	1.00
33 Fredrik Modin	.20	.50
34 Niklas Sundstrom	.20	.50
35 Tommy Salo	.20	.50
36 Daniel Tjarnqvist	.20	.50
37 Fredrik Sjostrom	.20	.50
38 Robert Nilsson	.20	.50
39 Alexander Steen	2.00	5.00
40 Henrik Zetterberg	.75	2.00
41 Tomas Sandstrom	.20	.50
42 Tomas Jonsson	.20	.50
43 Jonas Bergqvist	.20	.50
44 Magnus Svensson	.20	.50
45 Challe Berglund	.20	.50
46 Leif Holmqvist	.20	.50
47 Borje Salming	.40	1.00
48 Sven Tumba Johansson	.20	.50
49 Ulf Sterner	.20	.50
50 Anders Kallur	.20	.50
51 Mats Naslund	.20	.50
52 Hakan Loob	.20	.50
53 Kent Nilsson	.20	.50
54 Pekka Lindmark	.20	.50

2004-05 Swedish Alfabilder Alfa Stars Golden Ice

Card	Low	High
COMPLETE SET (12)	10.00	25.00
1 Jonas Bergqvist	.75	2.00
2 Sven Tumba	.75	2.00
3 Hakan Loob	.75	2.00
4 Peter Forsberg	4.00	10.00
5 Pekka Lindmark	.75	2.00
6 Tomas Jonsson	.75	2.00
7 Challe Berglund	.75	2.00
8 Tommy Salo	.75	2.00
9 Jorgen Jonsson	.75	2.00
10 M.Renberg N.Sundstrom	1.25	3.00
11 M.Norstrom M.Ohlund	1.25	3.00
12 F.Modin K.Johnsson	1.25	3.00

2004-05 Swedish Alfabilder Autographs

Card	Low	High
COMPLETE SET (28)	150.00	300.00
101 Markus Naslund	12.00	30.00
102 Henrik Zetterberg	12.00	30.00
103 Peter Forsberg	25.00	60.00
104 Per-Johan Axelsson	3.00	8.00
105 Henrik Sedin	5.00	12.00
106 Mikael Renberg	3.00	8.00
107 Nicklas Lidstrom	12.00	30.00
108 Tomas Sandstrom	4.00	10.00
109 Johan Hedberg	4.00	10.00
110 Tomas Jonsson	3.00	8.00
111 Michael Nylander	4.00	10.00
112 Mikael Tellqvist	10.00	25.00
113 Nils Ekman	4.00	10.00
114 Mattias Ohlund	3.00	8.00
115 Fredrik Modin	3.00	8.00
116 Jonas Bergqvist	3.00	8.00
117 Tommy Salo	4.00	10.00
118 Dick Tarnstrom	3.00	8.00
119 Niklas Sundstrom	3.00	8.00
120 Tomas Holmstrom	8.00	20.00
121 Charles Berglund	3.00	8.00
122 Christian Backman	3.00	8.00
123 Magnus Svensson	3.00	8.00
124 Marcus Nilson	4.00	10.00
125 Samuel Pahlsson	4.00	10.00
126 Daniel Tjarnqvist	3.00	8.00
127 Kristian Huselius	4.00	10.00
128 Mattias Weinhandl	3.00	8.00

2004-05 Swedish Alfabilder Limited Autographs

Card	Low	High
COMPLETE SET (28)	500.00	700.00
101 Markus Naslund	20.00	50.00
102 Henrik Zetterberg	20.00	50.00
103 Peter Forsberg	100.00	200.00
104 Per-Johan Axelsson	8.00	20.00
105 Henrik Sedin	10.00	25.00
106 Mikael Renberg	8.00	20.00
107 Nicklas Lidstrom	20.00	50.00
108 Tomas Sandstrom	8.00	20.00
109 Johan Hedberg	8.00	20.00
110 Tomas Jonsson	8.00	20.00
111 Michael Nylander	8.00	20.00
112 Mikael Tellqvist	15.00	40.00
113 Nils Ekman	8.00	20.00
114 Mattias Ohlund	8.00	20.00
115 Fredrik Modin	12.00	30.00
116 Jonas Bergqvist	8.00	20.00
117 Tommy Salo	8.00	20.00
118 Dick Tarnstrom	8.00	20.00
119 Niklas Sundstrom	8.00	20.00
120 Tomas Holmstrom	15.00	40.00
121 Charles Berglund	8.00	20.00
122 Christian Backman	8.00	20.00
123 Magnus Svensson	8.00	20.00
124 Marcus Nilson	8.00	20.00
125 Samuel Pahlsson	8.00	20.00
126 Daniel Tjarnqvist	8.00	20.00
127 Kristian Huselius	8.00	20.00
128 Mattias Weinhandl	8.00	20.00

2004-05 Swedish Alfabilder Next In Line

Card	Low	High
COMPLETE SET (6)	15.00	40.00
1 Leif Holmqvist Tommy Salo	2.00	5.00
2 Borje Salming Nick Lidstrom	4.00	10.00
3 Sven Johnasson Peter Forsberg	6.00	15.00
4 Ulf Sterner Henrik Zetterberg	4.00	10.00
5 Hakan Loob Mats Naslund	4.00	10.00
6 Kent Nilsson Robert Nilsson	2.00	5.00

2004-05 Swedish Alfabilder Proof Parallels

3X to 5X BASE CARD

2004-05 Swedish Djurgardens Postcards

Card	Low	High
COMPLETE SET		
1 Mariusz Czerkawski	.75	2.00
2 Daniel Fernholm	.75	2.00
3 Espen Knutsen	1.25	3.00
4 Marcus Kristofferson	.75	2.00
5 Staffan Kronwall	1.25	3.00
6 Robert Nilsson	1.25	3.00
7 Jimmie Olvestad	.75	2.00
8 Kristofer Ottosson	.75	2.00
9 Mika Stromberg	.75	2.00
10 Daniel Tjarnqvist	.75	2.00

2004-05 Swedish Elitset

Card	Low	High
COMPLETE SET (288)	15.00	40.00
1 Markus Korhonen	.08	.20
2 Daniel Johansson	.08	.20
3 Tommy Sjodin	.08	.20
4 Daniel Casselstahl	.08	.20
5 Henrik Malmstrom	.08	.20
6 Jakob Johansson	.08	.20
7 Patrik Ronnqvist	.08	.20
8 Roger Kyro	.08	.20
9 Ove Molin	.08	.20
10 Bjorn Danielsson	.08	.20
11 Tommi Miettinen	.08	.20
12 Bjorn Bjurling	.08	.20
13 Staffan Kronwall	.08	.20
14 Johnny Oduya	.20	.50
15 Daniel Rudslatt	.08	.20
16 Nichlas Falk	.08	.20
17 Tomas Kollar	.08	.20
18 Christian Eklund	.08	.20
19 Fredrik Bremberg	.08	.20
20 Mikael Johansson	.08	.20
21 Marcus Kristoffersson	.20	.50
22 Kenneth Bergqvist	.08	.20
23 Johan Jonfeldt	.08	.20
24 Jan-Axel Alavaara	.08	.20
25 Antti-Jussi Niemi	.08	.20
26 Ronnie Sundin	.08	.20
27 Magnus Kahnberg	.08	.20
28 Alexander Steen	1.50	4.00
29 Jari Tolsa	.08	.20
30 Jonas Esbjors	.08	.20
31 Niklas Andersson	.08	.20
32 Peter Strom	.08	.20
33 Jonas Johnson	.30	.75
34 Jens Karlsson	.08	.20
35 Fredrik Eriksson	.08	.20
36 Martin Lindman	.08	.20
37 Jonas Frogren	.08	.20
38 Greger Artursson	.08	.20
39 Radek Hamr	.08	.20
40 Janne Gronvall	.08	.20
41 Hannes Hyvonen	.08	.20
42 Peter Nordstrom	.08	.20
43 Par Backer	.08	.20
44 Marcel Jenni	.08	.20
45 Peter Hammarstrom	.08	.20
46 Dieter Kalt	.08	.20
47 Stefan Liv	.40	1.00
48 Fredrik Olausson	.08	.20
49 Ola Thorwalls	.08	.20
50 Jouni Loponen	.08	.20
51 Stefan Hellkvist	.08	.20
52 Per-Age Skroder	.08	.20
53 Peter Ekelund	.08	.20
54 Martin Thornberg	.08	.20
55 Anders Huusko	.08	.20
56 Kalle Sahlstedt	.08	.20
57 Pasi Maattanen	.08	.20
58 Mattias Remstam	.08	.20
59 Johan Davidsson	.08	.20
60 Fredrik Norrrena	.20	.50
61 Peter Casparsson	.08	.20
62 Martin Knold	.08	.20
63 Jyrki Valivaara	.08	.20
64 Mikko Peltola	.08	.20
65 Tim Eriksson	.08	.20
66 Fredrik Emvall	.08	.20
67 Jussi Tarvainen	.08	.20
68 Mikael Hakanson	.08	.20
69 Per Eklund	.08	.20
70 Gusten Tornqvist	.08	.20
71 Jonas Andersson-Junkka	.00	.20
72 Jan Sandstrom	.08	.20
73 Tuukka Mantyla	.08	.20
74 Stefan Nilsson	.08	.20
75 Linus Fagemo	.08	.20
76 Emil Lundberg	.08	.20
77 Thomas Berglund	.08	.20
78 Hans Huczkowski	.08	.20
79 Per Ledin	.08	.20
80 Johan Tellstrom	.08	.20
81 Pierre Berggren	.08	.20
82 Robert Borgqvist	.08	.20
83 David Petrasek	.08	.20
84 Magnus Osterby	.08	.20
85 Petri Liimatainen	.08	.20
86 Johan Norgren	.08	.20
87 Peter Andersson	.08	.20
88 Marcus Magnertoft	.08	.20
89 Frans Nielsen	.08	.20
90 Daniel Rydmark	.08	.20
91 Mikael Wahlberg	.08	.20
92 Kim Staal	.08	.20
93 Jan Oberg	.08	.20
94 Martin Johansson	.08	.20
95 Lars Jansson	.08	.20
96 Anders Soderberg	.08	.20
97 Tommy Pettersson	.08	.20
98 Fredrik Warg	.08	.20
99 Magnus Hedlund	.08	.20
100 Morten Green	.08	.20
101 Magnus Gastrin	.08	.20
102 Bengt Hoglund	.08	.20
103 Adam Andersson	.08	.20
104 Henrik Petre	.08	.20
105 Daniel Back	.08	.20
106 Hakan Bogg	.08	.20
107 Jonas Westerling	.08	.20
108 Magnus Sandberg	.08	.20
109 Magnus Lindquist	.08	.20
110 Bert Robertsson	.08	.20
111 Jonathan Ericsson ERC	.08	.20
112 Stefan Bemstrom	.08	.20
113 Erik Norback	.08	.20
114 Joakim Eriksson	.08	.20
115 Robert Dome	.08	.20
116 Robert Carlsson	.08	.20
117 Teemu Riihijarvi	.08	.20
118 Gabriel Karlsson	.08	.20
119 Jorgen Bemstrom	.08	.20
120 Peter Larsson	.08	.20
121 Kimmo Kapanen	.20	.50
122 Tommi Rajamaki	.08	.20
123 Jesper Jager	.08	.20
124 Sanny Lindstrom	.08	.20
125 Kalle Koskinen	.08	.20
126 Par Styf	.08	.20
127 Christian Soderstrom	.08	.20
128 Niklas Nordgren	.08	.20
129 Valeri Krykov	.08	.20
130 Per Hallin	.08	.20
131 Christian Sjogren	.08	.20
132 Fredrik Sundin	.08	.20
133 Peter Andersson	.08	.20
134 Ove Molin	.08	.20
135 Daniel Rydmark	.08	.20
136 Johan Davidsson	.08	.20
137 Thomas Berglund	.08	.20
138 Pelle Prestberg	.08	.20
139 Mathias Johansson	.08	.20
140 Roger Kyro	.08	.20
141 Kristofer Ottosson	.08	.20
142 Nichlas Falk	.08	.20
143 Dieter Kalt	.08	.20
144 Tomi Kallio	.20	.50
145 Johan Holmqvist	.20	.50
146 Niklas Andersson	.08	.20
147 Mikko Kuparinen	.08	.20
148 Mattias Karlsson	.08	.20
149 Sebastian Sulku	.08	.20
150 Jonas Soling	.08	.20
151 Nicklas Danielsson	.08	.20
152 Andreas Dackell	.20	.50
153 Mikko Luovi	.08	.20
154 Mikael Lind	.08	.20
155 Vesa Viitakoski	.08	.20
156 Rolf Wanhainen	.08	.20
157 Mika Stromberg	.08	.20
158 Daniel Fernholm	.08	.20
159 Daniel Tjarnqvist	.08	.20
160 Rikard Franzen	.08	.20
161 Nils Ekman	.20	.50
162 Kristofer Ottosson	.08	.20
163 Robert Nilsson	.08	.20
164 Johannes Salmonsson	.08	.20
165 Marcus Nilson	.30	.75
166 Jimmie Olvestad	.08	.20
167 Espen Knutsen	.30	.75
168 Mariusz Czerkawski	.20	.50
169 Henrik Lundqvist	2.00	5.00
170 Tom Koivisto	.08	.20
171 Arto Tukio	.08	.20
172 Christian Backman	.08	.20
173 Peter Hogardh	.08	.20
174 Joel Lundqvist	.08	.20
175 Loui Eriksson	.30	.75
176 Samuel Pahlsson	.20	.50
177 Martin Pluss	.08	.20
178 Per-Johan Axelsson	.20	.50
179 Tomi Kallio	.20	.50
180 Daniel Henriksson	.20	.50
181 Robin Jonsson	.08	.20
182 Per Hallberg	.08	.20
183 Mats Trygg	.08	.20
184 Pelle Prestberg	.08	.20
185 Jesper Mattsson	.08	.20
186 Christian Berglund	.08	.20
187 Jonas Hoglund	.20	.50
188 Mathias Johansson	.08	.20
189 Jorgen Jonsson	.08	.20
190 Fredrik Eriksson	.08	.20
191 Calle Steen	.08	.20
192 Boo Ahl	.20	.50
193 Daniel Ljungqvist	.08	.20
194 Per Gustafsson	.08	.20
195 Johan Halvardsson	.08	.20
196 Kimmo Peltonen	.08	.20
197 Mathias Tjarnqvist	.20	.50
198 Andreas Karlsson	.08	.20
199 Andreas Jamtin	.08	.20
200 Stefan Pettersson	.08	.20
201 Daniel Sperrle	.08	.20
202 Magnus Johansson	.08	.20
203 Henrik Tallinder	.20	.50
204 Christoffer Norgren	.08	.20
205 Jakob Karlsson	.08	.20
206 Johan Franzen	.40	1.00
207 Tony Martensson	.08	.20
208 Ulf Soderstrom	.08	.20
209 Brendan Morrison	.20	.50
210 Kristian Huselius	.20	.50
211 Mike Knuble	.20	.50
212 Johan Lindstrom	.08	.20
213 Kristian Antila	.08	.20
214 Johan Fransson	.20	.50
215 Niclas Wallin	.08	.20
216 Roger Akerstrom	.08	.20
217 Jaroslav Obsut	.08	.20
218 Jonas Ronnqvist	.08	.20
219 Thomas Koch	.08	.20
220 Justin Williams	.20	.50
221 Jonas Nordquist	.08	.20
222 Fredrik Hynning	.08	.20
223 Karl Fabritius	.08	.20
224 Tomas Holmstrom	.40	1.00
225 Andreas Hadelov	.20	.50
226 Christopher Nilstorp	.20	.50
227 Miska Kangasniemi	.08	.20
228 Bjorn Melin	.08	.20
229 Jan Hammar	.08	.20
230 Jason Deleurme	.08	.20
231 Carl Soderberg	.60	1.50
232 Andreas Valdix	.08	.20
233 Mika Hannula	.08	.20
234 Peter Hammarstrom	.08	.20
235 Markus Matthiasson	.08	.20
236 Tommy Salo	.20	.50
237 Mattias Timander	.08	.20
238 Hans Jonsson	.08	.20
239 Tobias Enstrom	.08	.20
240 Jesper Damgaard	.08	.20
241 Oscar Hedman	.08	.20
242 Pierre Hedin	.08	.20
243 Daniel Sedin	.40	1.00
244 Mattias Weinhandl	.20	.50
245 Andreas Salomonsson	.20	.50
246 Peter Oberg	.08	.20
247 Henrik Sedin	.40	1.00
248 Peter Forsberg	1.25	3.00
249 Alexander Steen	1.50	4.00
250 Per Svartvadet	.20	.50
251 Tero Leinonen	.08	.20
252 Andreas Lilja	.08	.20
253 Marko Kauppinen	.08	.20
254 Pavel Skrbek	.08	.20
255 Calle Bergstrom	.08	.20
256 Peter Nolander	.08	.20
257 Jonathan Granstrom	.08	.20
258 Marcus Eriksson	.08	.20
259 Shawn Horcoff	.20	.50
260 Kenneth Bergqvist	.08	.20
261 Anders Nilsson	.08	.20
262 Martin Jansson	.08	.20
263 Mikael Simons	.08	.20
264 Peter Nylander	.08	.20
265 Rastislav Stana	.30	.75
266 Niclas Havelid	.08	.20
267 Dick Tarnstrom	.20	.50
268 Peter Popovic	.08	.20
269 Petri Liimatainen	.08	.20
270 Timmy Pettersson	.08	.20
271 Jan Huokko	.08	.20
272 Anders Burstrom	.08	.20
273 Nicklas Bergfors	.40	1.00
274 Jonas Andersson	.08	.20
275 Peter Ferraro	.20	.50
276 Chris Ferraro	.20	.50
277 Miikka Kiprusoff	.75	2.00
278 Jimmy Danielsson	.08	.20
279 Johan Svedberg	.08	.20
280 Mats Hansson	.08	.20
281 Lars Jonsson	.20	.50
282 Teemu Aalto	.08	.20
283 Robert Carlsson	.08	.20
284 Kristian Gahn	.08	.20
285 Yared Hagos	.20	.50
286 Henrik Zetterberg	.75	2.00
287 Magnus Nilsson	.08	.20
288 Jonathan Hedstrom	.20	.50

2004-05 Swedish Elitset Dominators

Card	Low	High
COMPLETE SET (9)	25.00	50.00
1 Kahnberg Prestberg Eriksson	1.25	3.00
2 Forsberg Zetterberg Huselius	6.00	15.00
3 Kiprusoff Salo Holmqvist	6.00	15.00
4 Fransson Steen Lundqvist	4.00	10.00
5 Morrison Williams Horcoff	3.00	8.00
6 Tallinder Holmstrom Lilja	3.00	8.00
7 Knutsen Pluss Kallio	1.25	3.00
8 Tarnstrom Olausson Tjarnqvist	1.25	3.00
9 Sedin Sedin Forsberg	6.00	15.00

2004-05 Swedish Elitset Forsberg Tribute

Card	Low	High
COMPLETE SET (6)	10.00	25.00
1 Peter Forsberg	2.00	5.00
2 Peter Forsberg	2.00	5.00
3 Peter Forsberg	2.00	5.00
4 Peter Forsberg	2.00	5.00
5 Peter Forsberg	2.00	5.00
6 Peter Forsberg	2.00	5.00

2004-05 Swedish Elitset Future Stars

Card	Low	High
COMPLETE SET (12)	15.00	30.00
1 Carl Soderberg	1.50	4.00
2 Loui Eriksson	2.00	5.00
3 Linus Videll	.75	2.00
4 Johan Fransson	2.00	5.00
5 Robert Nilsson	2.00	5.00
6 Nicklas Danielsson	.75	2.00
7 Andreas Valdix	.75	2.00
8 Alexander Steen	4.00	10.00
9 Joakim Lundstrom	.75	2.00
10 Daniel Fernholm	.75	2.00
11 Joakim Lindstrom	.75	2.00
12 Mats Hansson	.75	2.00

2004-05 Swedish Elitset Gold

3X to 5X BASE CARD VALUE

2004-05 Swedish Elitset High Expectations

Card	Low	High
COMPLETE SET (10)	10.00	25.00
1 Jonas Soling	.75	2.00
2 Tomas Kollar	.75	2.00
3 Henrik Lundqvist	6.00	15.00
4 Mathias Johansson	.75	2.00
5 Bjorn Melin	.75	2.00
6 Tim Eriksson	.75	2.00
7 Jonas Ronnqvist	.75	2.00
8 Mattias Wennerberg	.75	2.00
9 Peter Popovic	.75	2.00
10 Yared Hagos	1.25	3.00

2004-05 Swedish Elitset In The Crease

Card	Low	High
COMPLETE SET (10)	15.00	40.00
1 Markus Korhonen	1.25	3.00
2 Bjorn Bjurling	1.25	3.00
3 Henrik Lundqvist	10.00	25.00
4 Sinuhe Wallinheimo	1.25	3.00
5 Stefan Liv	2.00	5.00
6 Fredrik Norrena	2.00	5.00
7 Daniel Henriksson	1.25	3.00
8 Andreas Hadelov	1.25	3.00
9 Rolf Wanhainen	1.25	3.00
10 Kimmo Kapanen	1.25	3.00

2004-05 Swedish Elitset Jerseys Series 1

Card	Low	High
1 Markus Korhonen	12.00	30.00
2 Kimmo Kapanen	12.00	30.00
3 Sinuhe Wallinheimo	12.00	30.00
4 Henrik Lundqvist	30.00	75.00
5 Per Gustavsson	12.00	30.00

2004-05 Swedish Elitset Jerseys Series 2

Card	Low	High
AH Andreas Hadelov	12.00	30.00
PP Peter Popovic	12.00	30.00
SL Stefan Liv	20.00	50.00
TJ Thomas Johansson	12.00	30.00

2004-05 Swedish Elitset Limited Signatures

Card	Low	High
1 Daniel Henriksson	10.00	25.00
2 Jorgen Jonsson	10.00	25.00
3 Per Gustavsson	10.00	25.00
4 Andreas Lilja	10.00	25.00
5 Niclas Havelid	10.00	25.00
6 Jonas Ronnqvist	10.00	25.00

2004-05 Swedish Elitset Masks

Card	Low	High
COMPLETE SET (8)	50.00	100.00
1 Johan Holmqvist	4.00	10.00
2 Bjorn Bjurling	4.00	10.00
3 Henrik Lundqvist	12.00	30.00
4 Stefan Liv	6.00	15.00
5 Andreas Hadelov	4.00	10.00
6 Gusten Tornqvist	4.00	10.00
7 Rastislav Stana	6.00	15.00
8 Miikka Kiprusoff	12.00	30.00

2004-05 Swedish Elitset Signatures

Card	Low	High
COMPLETE SET (15)	100.00	175.00
1 Andreas Hadelov	6.00	15.00
2 Andreas Valdix	6.00	15.00
3 Joakim Eriksson	6.00	15.00
4 Rolf Wanhainen	6.00	15.00
5 Jonas Ronnqvist	6.00	15.00
6 Johan Fransson	10.00	25.00
7 Per Svartvadet	6.00	15.00
8 Bjorn Bjurling	6.00	15.00
9 Niklas Falk	6.00	15.00
10 Robert Carlsson	6.00	15.00
11 Yared Hagos	6.00	15.00
12 Joakim Lundstrom	6.00	15.00
13 Mikael Lind	6.00	15.00
14 Pelle Prestberg	6.00	15.00
15 Hannes Hyvonen	6.00	15.00

2004-05 Swedish Elitset Signatures Series A

Card	Low	High
1 Frans Nielsen	4.00	10.00
2 Kim Staal	4.00	10.00
3 Per Eklund	4.00	10.00
4 Fredrik Norrena	6.00	15.00
5 Mikko Peltola	4.00	10.00
6 Tim Eriksson	4.00	10.00
7 Roger Akerstrom	4.00	10.00
8 Daniel Henriksson	4.00	10.00
9 Mats Hansson	4.00	10.00
10 Kimmo Kapanen	6.00	15.00
11 Tommi Miettinen	4.00	10.00
12 Bjorn Danielsson	4.00	10.00
13 Marcel Jenni	4.00	10.00
14 Henrik Lundqvist	20.00	50.00
15 Tomi Kallio	4.00	10.00
16 Niklas Andersson	4.00	10.00
17 Antti-Jussi Niemi	4.00	10.00

2004-05 Swedish Elitset Signatures Series B

Card	Low	High
1 Andreas Dackell	4.00	10.00
2 Johan Holmqvist	6.00	15.00
3 Daniel Henriksson	4.00	10.00
4 Jonas Hoglund	4.00	10.00
5 Jorgen Jonsson	4.00	10.00
6 Mathias Johansson	4.00	10.00
7 Kimmo Peltonen	4.00	10.00
8 Mathias Tjarnqvist	6.00	15.00
9 Stefan Pettersson	4.00	10.00
10 Andreas Lilja	6.00	15.00
11 Mikael Simons	4.00	10.00
12 Peter Nylander	4.00	10.00
13 Dick Tarnstrom	4.00	10.00
14 Niclas Havelid	6.00	15.00
15 Peter Forsberg	30.00	75.00
16 Tommy Salo	6.00	15.00
17 Tomas Holmstrom	10.00	25.00

2004-05 Swedish HV71 Postcards

Card	Low	High
COMPLETE SET		
1 Brian Boucher	1.25	3.00
2 Andreas Jamtin	.75	2.00
3 Simon Skoog	.75	2.00
4 David Fredriksson	.75	2.00
5 Fredrik Olausson	.75	2.00
6 Per Gustafsson	.75	2.00
7 Peter Ekelund	.75	2.00
8 Anders Huusko	.75	2.00

2004-05 Swedish MoDo Postcards

COMPLETE SET (30) 20.00 40.00
1 Peter Forsberg 4.00 10.00
2 Henrik Sedin 2.00 5.00
3 Daniel Sedin 2.00 5.00
4 Mattias Weinhandl .75 2.00
5 Adrian Aucoin .75 2.00
6 Mattias Timander .75 2.00
7 Per Svartvadet .75 2.00
8 Alexander Steen 4.00 10.00
9 Tommy Salo .75 2.00
10 Markus Naslund 2.00 5.00
11 Andreas Salomonsson .75 2.00
12 Frantisek Kaberle .75 2.00
13 Hans Jonsson .40 1.00
14 Joakim Lindstrom .40 1.00
15 Pierre Hedin .40 1.00
16 Dan Hinote .75 2.00
17 Lars Jansson .40 1.00
18 Magnus Gastrin .40 1.00
19 Mattias Hellstrom .40 1.00
20 Tobias Viklund .40 1.00
21 Michael Zajkowski .40 1.00
22 Morten Green .40 1.00
23 Mattias Wennerberg .40 1.00
24 Magnus Hedlund .40 1.00
25 Peter Oberg .40 1.00
26 Fredrik Warg .40 1.00
27 Oscar Hedman .40 1.00
28 Tobias Enstrom .40 1.00
29 Jan Oberg .40 1.00
30 Jesper Damgaard .40 1.00

2004-05 Swedish Pure Skills

COMPLETE SET (144) 20.00 50.00
1 Johan Holmqvist .20 .50
2 Chris Phillips .08 .20
3 Tommy Sjodin .08 .20
4 Andreas Dackell .08 .20
5 Tommi Miettinen .08 .20
6 Ronald Petrovicky .08 .20
7 Mikael Lind .08 .20
8 Jose Theodore 1.25 3.00
9 Daniel Tjarnqvist .08 .20
10 Dan Boyle .08 .20
11 Nils Ekman .08 .20
12 Marcus Nilson .08 .20
13 Espen Knutsen .08 .20
14 Mariusz Czerkawski .08 .20
15 Henrik Lundqvist 1.50 4.00
16 Tom Koivisto .08 .20
17 Sami Salo .08 .20
18 Christian Backman .08 .20
19 Daniel Alfredsson .40 1.00
20 Niklas Andersson .08 .20
21 Samuel Pahlsson .20 .50
22 Martin Pluss .08 .20
23 Jonas Johnson .08 .20
24 Tomi Kallio .08 .20
25 Martin Gerber .30 .75
26 Zdeno Chara .30 .75
27 Sheldon Souray .08 .20
28 Pelle Prestberg .08 .20
29 Christian Berglund .08 .20
30 Jonas Hoglund .08 .20
31 Peter Nordstrom .08 .20
32 Jorgen Jonsson .08 .20
33 Marian Gaborik 1.25 3.00
34 Stefan Liv .40 1.00
35 Anders Eriksson .08 .20
36 Per Gustafsson .08 .20
37 Manny Malhotra .08 .20
38 Andreas Karlsson .08 .20
39 Jonathan Cheechoo .60 1.50
40 Johan Davidsson .08 .20
41 Fredrik Norrena .40 1.00
42 Magnus Johansson .08 .20
43 Thomas Johansson .08 .20
44 Mikko Peltola .08 .20
45 Tony Martensson .08 .20
46 Brendan Morrison .20 .50
47 Michael Knuble .20 .50
48 Kristian Antila .20 .50
49 Niclas Wallin .08 .20
50 Roger Akerstrom .08 .20
51 Jaroslav Obsut .08 .20
52 Jonas Ronnqvist .08 .20
53 Justin Williams .20 .50
54 Per Ledin .08 .20
55 Tomas Holmstrom .40 1.00
56 Andreas Hadelov .20 .50
57 David Petrasek .08 .20
58 Peter Andersson .08 .20
59 Bjorn Melin .08 .20
60 Carl Soderberg .40 1.00
61 Mika Hannula .08 .20
62 Tommy Salo .20 .50
63 Mattias Timander .08 .20
64 Adrian Aucoin .20 .50
65 Daniel Sedin .30 .75
66 Mattias Weinhandl .20 .50
67 Markus Naslund .75 2.00
68 Henrik Sedin .30 .75
69 Peter Forsberg 2.00 5.00
70 Alexander Steen .75 2.00
71 Per Svartvadet .08 .20
72 Dan Hinote .20 .50
73 Tero Leinonen .20 .50
74 Pavel Skrbek .08 .20
75 Daniel Cleary .08 .20
76 Rastislav Pavlikovsky .20 .50
77 Marian Hossa .75 2.00
78 Shawn Horcoff .30 .75
79 Ladislav Nagy .30 .75
80 Marcel Hossa .30 .75
81 Rastislav Stana .30 .75
82 Dick Tarnstrom .20 .50
83 Peter Popovic .08 .20
84 Joakim Eriksson .08 .20
85 Kyle Calder .20 .50
86 Mikael Samuelsson .08 .20
87 Scott Thornton .20 .50
88 Dragan Umicevic .08 .20
89 Miikka Kiprusoff .75 2.00
90 Aki-Petteri Berg .08 .20
91 Teemu Aalto .08 .20
92 Niklas Nordgren .08 .20
93 Yared Hagos .20 .50
94 Henrik Zetterberg .75 2.00
95 Kent Manderville .08 .20
96 Jonathan Hedstrom .20 .50
97 Landon Wilson .20 .50
98 Ladislav Kohn .08 .20
99 Mike Ribeiro .20 .50
100 Tomas Vokoun .75 2.00
101 Marek Zidlicky .20 .50
102 Jere Karalahti .08 .20
103 Jarno Kultanen .08 .20
104 Lasse Pirjeta .20 .50
105 Jarkko Ruutu .20 .50
106 Timo Parssinen .08 .20
107 Brett Harkins .20 .50
108 Mika Noronen .20 .50
109 Josh Holden .20 .50
110 Riku Hahl .20 .50
111 Jani Rita .20 .50
112 Juuso Riksman .08 .20
113 Sami Helenius .08 .20
114 Steve Kariya .40 1.00
115 Patrik Stefan .20 .50
116 Hannes Hyvonen .08 .20
117 Tim Thomas .40 1.00
118 Ossi Vaananen .20 .50
119 Marko Jantunen .08 .20
120 Toni Dahlman .08 .20
121 Glen Metropolit .20 .50
122 Sinuhe Wallinheimo .20 .50
123 Steve Martins .20 .50
124 Jarkko Immonen .20 .50
125 Jody Shelley .40 1.00
126 Niklas Backstrom 1.00 2.50
127 Janne Niinimaa .20 .50
128 Josef Boumedienne .08 .20
129 Petr Tenkrat .08 .20
130 Michael Nylander .20 .50
131 Dwayne Roloson .75 2.00
132 Erik Hamalainen .08 .20
133 Esa Pirnes .08 .20
134 Pasi Nurminen .20 .50
135 Jarmo Myllys .20 .50
136 Andrew Raycroft 1.00 2.50
137 Ville Nieminen .20 .50
138 Stefan Ohman .08 .20
139 Teemu Lassila .08 .20
140 Craig Rivet .20 .50
141 Saku Koivu .60 1.50
142 Antti Aalto .08 .20
143 Scott Langkow .08 .20
144 Jason Williams .30 .75

2004-05 Swedish Pure Skills Jerseys

COMPLETE SET (4) 30.00 80.00
JR Jarkko Ruutu 10.00 25.00
PS Per Svartvadet 10.00 25.00
TS Tommy Salo 10.00 25.00
VN Ville Nieminen 10.00 25.00

2004-05 Swedish Pure Skills Parallel

5X to 8X BASE CARD VALUE

2004-05 Swedish Pure Skills Professional Power

COMPLETE SET (25) 30.00 75.00
AB Aki-Petteri Berg .75 2.00
CR Craig Rivet 1.25 3.00
DA Daniel Alfredsson 2.00 5.00
DS Daniel Sedin 1.25 3.00
DT Daniel Tjarnqvist .75 2.00
DT Dick Tarnstrom 1.25 3.00
HS Henrik Sedin 1.25 3.00
HZ Henrik Zetterberg 4.00 10.00
JN Janne Niinimaa .75 2.00
MC Mariusz Czerkawski .75 2.00
MG Marian Gaborik 6.00 15.00
MH Marian Hossa 4.00 10.00
MN Marcus Nilson .75 2.00
MN Markus Naslund 4.00 10.00
MN Michael Nylander 1.25 3.00
MZ Marek Zidlicky .75 2.00
OV Ossi Vaananen .75 2.00
PF Peter Forsberg 10.00 25.00
PS Patrik Stefan .75 2.00
RH Raimo Helminen .75 2.00
SK Saku Koivu 4.00 10.00
SP Samuel Pahlsson .75 2.00
SS Sami Salo .75 2.00
VN Ville Nieminen .75 2.00
ZC Zdeno Chara 1.25 3.00

2004-05 Swedish Pure Skills Signatures Limited

1 Andreas Dackell 10.00 25.00
2 Peter Forsberg 60.00 125.00
3 Henrik Zetterberg 20.00 50.00
4 Miikka Kiprusoff 20.00 50.00

2004-05 Swedish Pure Skills The Wall

COMPLETE SET (10) 40.00 100.00
AR Andrew Raycroft 8.00 20.00
FN Fredrik Norrena 2.00 5.00
HL Henrik Lundqvist 8.00 20.00
JT Jose Theodore 10.00 25.00
MG Martin Gerber 4.00 10.00
MK Miikka Kiprusoff 10.00 25.00
MN Mika Noronen 2.00 5.00
NB Niklas Backstrom 4.00 10.00
TS Tommy Salo 2.00 5.00
TT Tim Thomas 6.00 15.00

2005-06 Swedish SHL Elitset

COMPLETE SET (288) 25.00 60.00
1 Johan Holmqvist .40 1.00
2 Niklas Andersson .20 .50
3 Mikko Kuparinen .10 .25
4 Tommy Sjodin .10 .25
5 Sebastian Sulku .10 .25
6 Henrik Malmstrom .10 .25
7 Andreas Dackell .10 .25
8 Ove Molin .10 .25
9 Bjorn Danielsson .10 .25
10 Tommi Miettinen .10 .25
11 Mikael Lind .10 .25
12 Vesa Viitakoski .10 .25
13 Jose Theodore 1.25 3.00
14 Ronnie Pettersson .10 .25
15 Daniel Tjarnqvist .20 .50
16 Christopher Thorn .10 .25
17 Robert Nilsson .75 2.00
18 Daniel Rudslat .10 .25
19 Nichlas Falk .10 .25
20 Marcus Nilson .20 .50
21 Jimmie Olvestad .10 .25
22 Patrick Thoresen .40 1.00
23 Tom Koivisto .10 .25
24 Antti-Jussi Niemi .10 .25
25 Sami Salo .10 .25
26 Daniel Alfredsson .75 2.00
27 Magnus Kahnberg .10 .25
28 Peter Hogardh .10 .25
29 Jari Tolsa .10 .25
30 Joel Lundqvist .20 .50
31 Jonas Esbjors .10 .25
32 Niklas Andersson .10 .25
33 Samuel Pahlsson .20 .50
34 Martin Pluss .10 .25
35 Jonas Johnsson .10 .25
36 Tomi Kallio .10 .25
37 Martin Gerber .40 1.00
38 Daniel Henriksson .10 .25
39 Robin Jonsson .10 .25
40 Jonas Frogren .10 .25
41 Radek Hamr .10 .25
42 Zdeno Chara .75 2.00
43 Pelle Prestberg .10 .25
44 Jesper Mattsson .10 .25
45 Jonas Hoglund .10 .25
46 Mathias Johansson .10 .25
47 Peter Nordstrom .10 .25
48 Fredrik Eriksson .10 .25
49 Par Backer .10 .25
50 Stefan Liv .40 1.00
51 Anders Eriksson .10 .25
52 Daniel Ljungqvist .10 .25
53 Per Gustafsson .10 .25
54 Simon Skoog .10 .25
55 Ola Svanberg .10 .25
56 Johan Halvardsson .10 .25
57 Anders Huusko .10 .25
58 Andreas Karlsson .10 .25
59 Pasi Maattanen .10 .25
60 Stefan Pettersson .10 .25
61 Johan Davidsson .10 .25
62 Johan Backlund .10 .25
63 Stefan Bemstrom .10 .25
64 Örjan Lindmark .10 .25
65 Jens Bergenstrom .10 .25
66 Niklas Eriksson .10 .25
67 Niklas Persson .10 .25
68 Johan Rosen .10 .25
69 Fredrik Norrena .40 1.00
70 Magnus Johansson .10 .25
71 Thomas Johansson .10 .25
72 Christoffer Norgren .10 .25
73 Jyrki Välivaara .10 .25
74 Mikko Peltola .10 .25
75 Ulf Soderstrom .10 .25
76 Johan Andersson .10 .25
77 Tim Eriksson .10 .25
78 Michael Knuble .20 .50
79 Fredrik Emwall .10 .25
80 Jussi Tarvainen .10 .25
81 Mikael Hakanson .10 .25
82 Gusten Tornqvist .10 .25
83 Johan Fransson .10 .25
84 Jan Sandstrom .10 .25
85 Jaroslav Obsut .10 .25
86 Jonas Ronnqvist .10 .25
87 Thomas Koch .10 .25
88 Emil Lundberg .10 .25
89 Jonas Nordquist .10 .25
90 Fredrik Hynning .10 .25
91 Karl Fabricius .10 .25
92 Michael Zajkowski .10 .25
93 Hans Jonsson .10 .25
94 Tobias Enstrom .10 .25
95 Jesper Damgaard .10 .25
96 Oscar Hedman .10 .25
97 Daniel Sedin .40 1.00
98 Mattias Weinhandl .10 .25
99 Andreas Salomonsson .10 .25
100 Markus Naslund .75 2.00
101 Henrik Sedin .40 1.00
102 Peter Forsberg 2.00 5.00
103 Morten Green .10 .25
104 Per Svartvadet .10 .25
105 Magnus Gastrin .10 .25
106 Calle Bergström .10 .25
107 Peter Nolander .10 .25
108 Jonathan Granstrom .10 .25
109 Hakan Bogg .10 .25
110 Shawn Horcoff .40 1.00
111 Jonas Westerling .10 .25
112 Marian Hossa .75 2.00
113 Marcus Eriksson .10 .25
114 Magnus Sandberg .10 .25
115 Kenneth Bergkvist .10 .25
116 Anders Nilsson .10 .25
117 Mikael Simons .10 .25
118 Magnus Lindquist .10 .25
119 Bert Robertsson .10 .25
120 Nicklas Grossman .10 .25
121 Dick Tarnstrom .10 .25
122 Petri Liimatainen .10 .25
123 Timmy Pettersson .10 .25
124 Jan Huokko .10 .25
125 Anders Burstrom .10 .25
126 Robert Carlsson .10 .25
127 Nicklas Bergfors .40 1.00
128 Erik Norback .10 .25
129 Gabriel Karlsson .10 .25
130 Jorgen Bemstrom .10 .25
131 Miikka Kiprusoff 1.25 3.00
132 Johan Svedberg .10 .25
133 Sanny Lindstrom .10 .25
134 Kalle Koskinen .10 .25
135 Mats Hansson .10 .25
136 Teemu Aalto .10 .25
137 Christian Soderstrom .10 .25
138 Robert Carlsson .10 .25
139 Niklas Nordgren .20 .50
140 Per Hallin .10 .25
141 Kristian Gahn .10 .25
142 Henrik Zetterberg .75 2.00
143 Magnus Nilsson .10 .25
144 Jonathan Hedstrom .10 .25
145 Markus Korhonen .10 .25
146 Daniel Johansson .10 .25
147 Martin Ohrstedt .10 .25
148 Jorgen Sundqvist .10 .25
149 Daniel Casselstahl .10 .25
150 Rodrigo Lavins .10 .25
151 Antti Aarnio .10 .25
152 Jonas Almtorp .10 .25
153 Mathias Mansson .10 .25
154 Nicklas Backstom ERC 4.00 10.00
155 Lars-Erik Spets .10 .25
156 Mikael Wahlberg .10 .25
157 Petter Ronnquist .10 .25
158 Teemu Lassila .10 .25
159 Andre Mattsson .10 .25
160 Jonas Liwing .10 .25
161 Erik Ryman .10 .25
162 Adam Andersson .10 .25
163 Jesper Bjorck .10 .25
164 Henrik Nordfeldt .10 .25
165 Johan Eneqvist .10 .25
166 Christofer Lofberg .10 .25
167 Patric Hornqvist .10 .25
168 Fredrik Bremberg .10 .25
169 Marcus Kristoffersson .10 .25
170 Per Eklund .10 .25
171 Mikael Sandberg .10 .25
172 Tommy Salo .20 .50
173 Jan-Axel Alavaara .10 .25
174 Arto Tukio .10 .25
175 Richard Demen-Willaume .10 .25
176 Ronnie Sundin .10 .25
177 Johnny Oduya .20 .50
178 Sebastian Karlsson .10 .25
179 Kirill Starkov .10 .25
180 Johan Witehall .10 .25
181 Christopher Heino-Lindberg .10 .25
182 Rami Alanko .10 .25
183 Per Hallberg .10 .25
184 Thomas Rhodin .10 .25
185 Mikael Johansson .10 .25
186 Rickard Wallin .10 .25
187 Jorgen Jonsson .10 .25
188 Fredrik Eriksson .10 .25
189 Johan Olsson .10 .25
190 Emil Kaberg .10 .25
191 Per Ledin .10 .25
192 Erik Ersberg ERC 1.00 2.50
193 Fredrik Olausson .10 .25
194 Lars Jonsson .20 .50
195 Mika Niskanen .10 .25
196 David Petrasek .10 .25
197 Martin Thornberg .10 .25
198 David Fredriksson .10 .25
199 Bjorn Melin .10 .25
200 Jens Karlsson .10 .25
201 Mattias Remstam .10 .25
202 Mika Hannula .10 .25
203 Tomas Duba .10 .25
204 Elias Granat .10 .25
205 Magnus Osterby .10 .25
206 Yan Golubovsky .10 .25
207 Jan Srdinko .10 .25
208 Patrik Hucko .10 .25
209 Patrik Wallenberg .10 .25
210 Mike Watt .10 .25
211 Sebastian Meijer .10 .25
212 Jesper Ollas .10 .25
213 Niklas Broms .10 .25
214 Magnus Hedlund .10 .25
215 Oscar Steen .10 .25
216 Jimmie Ericsson .10 .25
217 Jukka Tiilikainen .10 .25
218 Jiri Bicek .10 .25
219 Jonas Fransson .10 .25
220 Andreas Pihl .10 .25
221 Mikko Luoma .10 .25
222 Victor Ringberg .10 .25
223 Tony Martensson .10 .25
224 Jonas Soling .10 .25
225 Sami Torkki .10 .25
226 Johan Lindstrom .10 .25
227 Patric Blomdahl .10 .25
228 David Rautio .10 .25
229 Mattias Modig .10 .25
230 Erik Lindberg .10 .25
231 Pekka Saravo .10 .25
232 Pavel Skrbek .10 .25
233 Per Savilahti-Nagander .10 .25
234 Johan Harju .10 .25
235 Mikael Renberg .20 .50
236 Ragnar Karlsson .10 .25
237 Vladimir Machulda .10 .25
238 Lubomir Bartecko .10 .25
239 Magnus Isaksson .10 .25
240 Christopher Konigsson .10 .25
241 Karol Krizan .10 .25
242 Mattias Timander .10 .25
243 Vladimir Sicak .10 .25
244 Tobias Viklund .10 .25
245 Mattias Hellstrom .10 .25
246 Pasi Tuominen .10 .25
247 Rastislav Pavlikovsky .10 .25
248 Peter Oberg .10 .25
249 Mikael Pettersson .10 .25
250 Miloslav Horava .10 .25
251 Jan Pardavy .10 .25
252 Daniel Sperrle .10 .25
253 Petri Vehanen .10 .25
254 Peter Smrek .10 .25
255 Atvars Tribuntsovs .10 .25
256 Ross Lupaschuk .10 .25
257 Pierre Johnsson .10 .25
258 Jarno Kultanen .10 .25
259 Thomas Skogs .10 .25
260 Jordan Krestanovich .10 .25
261 Marco Tuokko .10 .25
262 Eric Johansson .10 .25
263 Kalle Kerman .10 .25
264 Peter Fabus .10 .25
265 Teemu Elomo .10 .25
266 Martin Jansson .10 .25
267 Rastislav Stana .20 .50
268 Stanislav Neckar .10 .25
269 Henrik Petre .10 .25
270 Jonathan Ericsson .10 .25
271 Daniel Ljungqvist .10 .25
272 Pasi Petrilainen .10 .25
273 Per-Ake Skroder .10 .25
274 Christoph Brandner .10 .25
275 Anze Kopitar 6.00 15.00
276 Tomas Kollar .10 .25
277 Dragan Umicevic .10 .25
278 Petr Leska .10 .25
279 Johan Asplund .10 .25
280 Mika Oksa .10 .25
281 Par Styf .10 .25
282 Carl-Johan Johansson .10 .25
283 Peter Regin .10 .25
284 Frans Nielsen .40 1.00
285 Mattias Wennerberg .10 .25
286 Peter Strom .10 .25
287 Valeri Krykov .10 .25
288 Fredrik Warg .10 .25

2005-06 Swedish SHL Elitset Catchers

COMPLETE SET (12) 40.00 80.00
1 Johan Holmqvist 3.00 8.00
2 Teemu Lassila 3.00 8.00
3 Tommy Salo 3.00 8.00
4 Daniel Henriksson 3.00 8.00
5 Stefan Liv 4.00 10.00
6 Johan Backlund 3.00 8.00
7 Fredrik Norrena 4.00 10.00
8 David Rautio 3.00 8.00
9 Karol Krizan 3.00 8.00
10 Petri Vehanen 3.00 8.00
11 Rastislav Stana 4.00 10.00
12 Mika Oksa 3.00 8.00

2005-06 Swedish SHL Elitset Icons

COMPLETE SET (9) 15.00 30.00
1 Peter Hammarström 2.00 5.00
2 Jorgen Jonsson 2.00 5.00
3 Mathias Johansson 2.00 5.00
4 Thomas Johansson 2.00 5.00
5 Jonas Johnsson 2.00 5.00
6 Kristian Gahn 2.00 5.00
7 Ove Molin 2.00 5.00
8 Per Gustafsson 2.00 5.00
9 Fredrik Bremberg 2.00 5.00

2005-06 Swedish SHL Elitset Playmakers

COMPLETE SET (12) 25.00 60.00
1 Mikael Lind 2.00 5.00
2 Marcus Nilson 2.00 5.00
3 Niklas Andersson 2.00 5.00
4 Daniel Alfredsson 4.00 10.00
5 Jorgen Jonsson 2.00 5.00
6 Johan Davidsson 2.00 5.00
7 Brendan Morrison 2.00 5.00
8 Daniel Sedin 3.00 8.00
9 Henrik Sedin 3.00 8.00
10 Marian Hossa 6.00 15.00
11 Scott Thornton 2.00 5.00
12 Henrik Zetterberg 6.00 15.00

2005-06 Swedish SHL Elitset Rookies

COMPLETE SET (9) 12.00 30.00
1 Alexander Ribbenstrand 1.50 4.00
2 Anton Axelsson 1.50 4.00
3 Christopher Heino-Lindberg 1.50 4.00
4 Erik Andersson 1.50 4.00
5 Mattias Ritola 1.50 4.00
6 Robin Lindqvist 1.50 4.00
7 Tommy Enstrom 1.50 4.00
8 Jens Jakobs 1.50 4.00
9 Anton Stralman 2.50 6.00

2005-06 Swedish SHL Elitset Series One Signatures

COMPLETE SET (15) 100.00 200.00
1 Ulf Soderstrom 6.00 15.00
2 Tim Eriksson 6.00 15.00
3 Petri Liimatainen 6.00 15.00
4 Nicklas Grossman 6.00 15.00
5 Oscar Hedman 6.00 15.00
6 Tobias Viklund 6.00 15.00
7 Johan Davidsson 6.00 15.00
8 Ola Svanberg 6.00 15.00
9 Anders Huusko 6.00 15.00
10 Jonas Hoglund 6.00 15.00
11 Daniel Henriksson 6.00 15.00
12 Johan Fransson 6.00 15.00
13 Karl Fabricius 6.00 15.00
14 Gusten Tornqvist 6.00 15.00
15 Christopher Thorn 6.00 15.00

2005-06 Swedish SHL Elitset Series Two Signatures

3 Adam Andersson 6.00 15.00
4 Patrick Thoresen 8.00 20.00
5 Niklas Andersson 6.00 15.00
6 Magnus Kahnberg 6.00 15.00
7 Tomi Kallio 8.00 20.00
8 Mathias Johansson 6.00 15.00
9 Jesper Mattsson 6.00 15.00
10 Thomas Rhodin 6.00 15.00
11 Per Gustafsson 6.00 15.00
12 Stefan Liv 10.00 25.00
13 Stefan Pettersson 6.00 15.00
14 Tomas Duba 6.00 15.00
15 Örjan Lindmark 6.00 15.00
16 Niklas Persson 6.00 15.00
17 Fredrik Emwall 6.00 15.00
18 Tony Martensson 6.00 15.00
19 Fredrik Norrena 8.00 20.00
20 Lubomir Bartecko 6.00 15.00
21 David Rautio 6.00 15.00
22 Mikael Renberg 10.00 25.00
23 Christoph Brandner 6.00 15.00
24 Anze Kopitar 75.00 125.00
25 Jan Huokko 6.00 15.00
26 Peter Strom 6.00 15.00
27 Christian Soderstrom 6.00 15.00
28 Mattias Wennerberg 6.00 15.00

2005-06 Swedish SHL Elitset Star Potential

COMPLETE SET (18) 15.00 40.00
1 Niklas Andersson .75 2.00
2 Nicklas Backstrom 2.50 6.00
3 Robert Nilsson .75 2.00
4 Christopher Thorn 1.50 4.00
5 Loui Eriksson 1.50 4.00
6 Henrik Lundqvist 4.00 10.00
7 Robin Jonsson .75 2.00
8 Ola Svanberg .75 2.00
9 Tony Martensson .75 2.00
10 Johan Fransson .75 2.00
11 Tobias Enstrom .75 2.00
12 Oscar Hedman .75 2.00
13 Jonathan Granstrom .75 2.00
14 Nicklas Bergfors 1.50 4.00
15 Dragan Umisevic .75 2.00
16 Linus Videll .75 2.00
17 Yared Hagos .75 2.00
18 Mats Hansson .75 2.00

2005-06 Swedish SHL Elitset Stoppers

COMPLETE SET (12) 30.00 75.00
1 Johan Holmqvist 3.00 8.00
2 Jose Theodore 6.00 15.00
3 Rolf Wanhainen 2.00 5.00
4 Henrik Lundqvist 6.00 15.00
5 Martin Gerber 3.00 8.00
6 Daniel Henriksson 2.00 5.00
7 Stefan Liv 3.00 8.00
8 Fredrik Norrena 3.00 8.00
9 Tommy Salo 2.00 5.00
10 Tero Leinonen 2.00 5.00
11 Rastislav Stana 2.00 5.00
12 Miikka Kiprusoff 6.00 15.00

2005-06 Swedish SHL Elitset Teammates

COMPLETE SET (12) 8.00 20.00
1 Andreas Dackell / Mikael Lind .75 2.00
2 Nichlas Falk / Patrick Thoresen .75 2.00
3 Jonas Hoglund / Pelle Prestberg .75 2.00
4 Niklas Andersson / Tomi Kallio .75 2.00
5 Johan Davidsson / Mattias Remstam .75 2.00
6 Niklas Person / Patrik Wallenberg .75 2.00
7 Fredrik Emwall / Ulf Söderström .75 2.00
8 Karl Fabricius / Mikael Renberg 1.25 3.00
9 Andreas Salomonsson / Per Svartvadet .75 2.00
10 Anders Nilsson / Kalle Kerman .75 2.00
11 Jorgen Bemstrom / Timmy Pettersson .75 2.00
12 Robert Carlsson / Valeri Krykov .75 2.00

2006-07 Swedish SHL Elitset

COMPLETE SET (288) 25.00 50.00
1 Johan Holmqvist .40 1.00
2 Daniel Johansson .10 .25
3 Tommy Sodin .10 .25
4 Jorgen Sundqvist .10 .25
5 Rodrigo Lavins .10 .25
6 Henrik Malmstrom .10 .25
7 Jonas Almtorp .10 .25
8 Andreas Dackel .10 .25
9 Mathias Mansson .10 .25
10 Ove Molin .10 .25
11 Lars-Erik Spets .10 .25
12 Mikael Lind .10 .25
13 Petter Ronnquist .10 .25
14 Ronnie Pettersson .10 .25
15 Alexander Ribbenstrand .10 .25
16 Jonas Liwing .10 .25
17 Jesper Bjorck .10 .25
18 Henrik Nordfeldt .10 .25
19 Johan Eneqvist .10 .25
20 Nichlas Falk .10 .25
21 Christofer Lofberg .10 .25
22 Patric Hornqvist .10 .25
23 Jimmie Olvestad .10 .25
24 Patrick Thoresen .60 1.50
25 Per Eklund .10 .25
26 Mikael Sandberg .10 .25
27 Tom Koivisto .10 .25
28 Antti-Jussi Niemi .10 .25
29 Arto Tukio .10 .25
30 Richard Demen-Willaume .10 .25
31 Johnny Oduya .30 .75
32 Magnus Kahnberg .10 .25
33 Peter Hogardh .10 .25
34 Kirill Starkov .10 .25
35 Joel Lundqvist .60 1.50
36 Jonas Esbjors .10 .25
37 Niklas Andersson .10 .25
38 Martin Plass .10 .25
39 Tomi Kallio .10 .25
40 Daniel Henriksson .10 .25
41 Rami Alanko .10 .25
42 Robin Jonsson .10 .25
43 Jonas Frogren .10 .25
44 Thomas Rhodin .10 .25
45 Jesper Mattsson .10 .25
46 Jonas Hoglund .20 .50
47 Rickard Wallin .10 .25
48 Mathias Johansson .10 .25
49 Peter Nordstrom .10 .25
50 Jorgen Jonsson .10 .25
51 Per Ledin .10 .25
52 Pelle Prestberg .10 .25
53 Stefan Liv .40 1.00
54 Fredrik Olausson .10 .25
55 Per Gustafsson .10 .25
56 Ola Svanberg .10 .25
57 David Petrasek .10 .25
58 Johan Halvardsson .10 .25
59 Martin Thornberg .10 .25
60 Erik Andersson .10 .25
61 David Fredriksson .10 .25
62 Andreas Karlsson .10 .25
63 Bjorn Melin .10 .25
64 Mattias Remstam .10 .25
65 Johan Davidsson .10 .25
66 Stefan Pettersson .10 .25
67 Mika Hannula .10 .25
68 Jonas Fransson .10 .25
69 Mikko Luoma .10 .25
70 Magnus Johansson .10 .25
71 Christoffer Norgren .10 .25
72 Jyrki Valivaara .10 .25
73 Tony Martensson .10 .25
74 Jonas Soling .10 .25
75 Ulf Soderstrom .10 .25
76 Tim Eriksson .10 .25
77 Sami Torkki .10 .25
78 Fredrik Emwall .10 .25
79 Jussi Tarvainen .10 .25
80 Johan Lindstrom .10 .25
81 Mikael Hakansson .10 .25
82 David Rautio .10 .25
83 Johan Fransson .10 .25
84 Erik Lindberg .10 .25
85 Jan Sandstrom .10 .25
86 Pekka Saravo .10 .25
87 Thomas Koch .10 .25
88 Emil Lundberg .10 .25
89 Fredrik Hynning .10 .25
90 Mikael Renberg .20 .50
91 Ragnar Karlsson .10 .25
92 Vladimir Machulda .10 .25
93 Lubomir Bartecko .10 .25
94 Robin Lindqvist .10 .25
95 Gustaf Wesslau .10 .25
96 Edvin Frylen .10 .25
97 Jan oberg .10 .25
98 Juha Riihijarvi .10 .25
99 Mikael Wahlberg .10 .25
100 Robert Tomik .10 .25
101 Markus Matthiasson .10 .25
102 Karol Krizan .10 .25
103 Mattias Timander .10 .25
104 Hans Jonsson .10 .25
105 Tobias Enstrom .10 .25
106 Jesper Damgaard .10 .25
107 Oscar Hedman .10 .25
108 Tobias Viklund .10 .25
109 Pasi Tuominen .10 .25
110 Morten Green .10 .25
111 Andreas Salomonsson .10 .25
112 Peter Oberg .10 .25
113 Mikael Pettersson .10 .25
114 Per Svartvadet .10 .25
115 Magnus Gastrin .10 .25
116 Petri Vehanen .10 .25
117 Atvars Tribuntsovs .10 .25
118 Jarno Kultanen .10 .25
119 Thomas Skogs .10 .25
120 Calle Bergstrom .10 .25
121 Eric Johansson .10 .25
122 Kenneth Bergqvist .10 .25
123 Andreas Nilsson .10 .25
124 Teemu Elomo .10 .25
125 Martin Jansson .10 .25
126 Mikael Simons .10 .25
127 Andreas Hadelov .10 .25
128 Fredrik Bergqvist .10 .25
129 Libor Prochazka .10 .25
130 Johan Ramstedt .10 .25
131 Pontus Petterstrom .10 .25
132 Daniel Welser .10 .25
133 Brett Harkins .10 .25
134 Johan Asplund .10 .25
135 Anton Stralman .40 1.00
136 Carl-Johan Johansson .10 .25
137 Peter Regin .10 .25
138 Frans Nielsen .40 1.00
139 Per Hallin .10 .25
140 Kristian Gahn .10 .25
141 Magnus Nilsson .10 .25
142 Mattias Wennerberg .10 .25
143 Peter Strom .10 .25
144 Fredrik Warg .10 .25
145 Robert Kristan .10 .25
146 Daniel Sperrle .20 .50
147 Antti Hulkkonen .10 .25
148 Nicholas Angell .10 .25
149 Peter Nolander .10 .25
150 Daniel Casselstahl .10 .25
151 Daniel Hermansson .10 .25
152 Nicklas Backstrom 2.00 5.0
153 Johannes Salmonsson .10 .25
154 Bjorn Danielsson .10 .25
155 Mads Hansen .10 .25
156 Sebastian Karlsson .10 .25
157 Jiri Bicek .10 .25
158 Daniel Larsson .10 .25
159 Teemu Lassila .20 .5
160 Martin Lindman .10 .2
161 Thomas Johansson .10 .2
162 Timmy Pettersson .10 .2
163 Fredrik Ericson .10 .2
164 Kristofer Ottosson .10 .2
165 Christian Eklund .10 .2
166 Fredrik Bremberg .10 .2
167 Par Backer .10 .2
168 Morten Ask .10 .2
169 Nicklas Danielsson .10 .2
170 Dragan Umicevic .10 .2
171 Tommy Salo .20 .5
172 Jan-Axel Alavaara .10 .2
173 Markus Seikola .10 .2
174 Ronnie Sundin .10 .2
175 Tomi Pettinen .10 .2
176 Jonas Ahnelov .10 .2
177 Johan Fransson .10 .2
178 Fredrik Johansson .10 .2
179 Karl Fabricius .10 .2
180 Anton Axelsson .10 .2
181 Steve Kariya .40 1.0
182 Johan Ryno .10 .2

183 Christopher Heino-Lindberg .20 .50
184 Atte Pentikainen .10 .25
185 Janne Niskala .10 .25
186 Esa Pirnes .10 .25
187 Per Aslund .10 .25
188 Emil Kaberg .10 .25
189 Christian Soderstrom .10 .25
190 Mikael Johansson .10 .25
191 Erik Ersberg .10 .25
192 Scott Langkow .20 .50
193 Johan Akerman .10 .25
194 Daniel Grillfors .10 .25
195 Pasi Puistola .10 .25
196 Lance Ward .10 .25
197 Erik Andersson .10 .25
198 Andreas Falk .10 .25
199 Jari Kauppila .10 .25
200 Timo Vertala .10 .25
201 Jukka Voutilainen .10 .25
202 Andreas Jamtin .10 .25
203 Roman Cechmanek .20 .50
204 Christopher Kelleher .10 .25
205 Carl Gunnarsson .10 .25
206 Andreas Holmqvist .10 .25
207 Oscar Ackestrom .10 .25
208 Joakim Eriksson .10 .25
209 Martin Samuelsson .20 .50
210 Niklas Olausson .10 .25
211 Patric Blomdahl .10 .25
212 Tero Leinonen .10 .25
213 Pavel Skrbek .10 .25
214 Roger Akerstrom .10 .25
215 Per Savilahti-Nagander .10 .25
216 Jaroslav Obsut .10 .25
217 Tomas Wallgren .10 .25
218 Martin Chabada .10 .25
219 Jesse Niinimaki .10 .25
220 Anders Burstrom .10 .25
221 Kalle Kerman .10 .25
222 Johan Harju .10 .25
223 Viktor Lindgren .10 .25
224 Tomas Surovy .20 .50
225 Rastislav Stana .10 .25
226 Patrik Hersley .10 .25
227 Johan Bjork .10 .25
228 Ross Lupaschuk .10 .25
229 Simon Skoog .10 .25
230 Andreas Thuresson .10 .25
231 Lasse Pirjeta .10 .25
232 Milan Bartovic .10 .25
233 Nicklas Jadeland .10 .25
234 Marcus Paulsson .10 .25
235 Mikael Johansson .10 .25
236 David Moravec .10 .25
237 Linus Fagemo .10 .25
238 Michal Zajkowski .10 .25
239 Tommy Wargh .10 .25
240 Adam Andersson .10 .25
241 Mattias Hellstrom .10 .25
242 Per-Ake Skroder .10 .25
243 Oscar Steen .10 .25
244 Niklas Sundstrom .10 .25
245 Miloslav Horava .10 .25
246 Johan Nilsson .10 .25
247 Robert Dome .10 .25
248 Juha Pitkamaki .10 .25
249 Mikko Ramo .10 .25
250 Tomas Slovak .10 .25
251 Pierre Johnsson .10 .25
252 Anton Stralman .10 .25
253 Mikko Kurvinen .10 .25
254 Miroslav Blatek .10 .25
255 Hakan Bogg .10 .25
256 Anders Bastiansen .10 .25
257 Marco Tuokko .10 .25
258 Ryan Jardine .10 .25
259 Eric Beaudoin .10 .25
260 Pavel Brendl .20 .50
261 Dave Stathos .10 .25
262 Per Helmersson .10 .25
263 Per-Anton Lundstrom .10 .25
264 Fredrik Lindgren .10 .25
265 Daniel Sondell .10 .25
266 Kari Haakana .10 .25
267 Richard Lintner .10 .25
268 Magnus Wernblom .10 .25
269 Fredrik Krekula .10 .25
270 Jason King .10 .25
271 Jimmie Eriksson .10 .25
272 Anders Soderberg .10 .25
273 Marcus Kristoffersson .10 .25
274 Markku Tahtinen .10 .25
275 Fredrik Oberg .10 .25
276 Johan Backlund .10 .25
277 Sanny Lindstrom .10 .25
278 Kalle Koskinen .10 .25
279 Kimmo Lotvonen .10 .25
280 Petri Kokko .10 .25
281 Par Styf .10 .25
282 Oscar Sundh .10 .25
283 Peter Nordstrom .10 .25
284 Robert Carlsson .10 .25
285 Johan Andersson .10 .25
286 Timo Parssinen .10 .25
287 Riku Hahl .20 .50
288 Jonathan Hedstrom .10 .25

2006-07 Swedish SHL Elitset Goal Patrol

1 Johan Holmqvist 5.00 12.00
2 Markus Korhonen 4.00 10.00
3 Teemu Lassila 4.00 10.00
4 Tommy Salo 4.00 10.00
5 Mikael Sandberg 4.00 10.00
6 Christopher Heino-Lindberg 4.00 10.00
7 Daniel Henriksson 4.00 10.00
8 Stefan Liv 5.00 12.00
9 Tomas Duba 4.00 10.00
10 Jonas Fransson 4.00 10.00
11 Fredrik Norrena 6.00 15.00
12 Mattias Modig 4.00 10.00
13 David Rautio 4.00 10.00
14 Karol Krizan 4.00 10.00
15 Daniel Sperrle 4.00 10.00
16 Petri Vehanen 4.00 10.00
17 Magnus Lindquist 4.00 10.00
18 Mika Oksa 4.00 10.00

2006-07 Swedish SHL Elitset In The Crease

1 Johan Holmqvist 5.00 12.00
2 Teemu Lassila 4.00 10.00
3 Tommy Salo 4.00 10.00
4 Daniel Henriksson 4.00 10.00
5 Stefan Liv 5.00 12.00
6 Fredrik Norrena 6.00 15.00
7 Mattias Modig 4.00 10.00
8 Karol Krizan 4.00 10.00
9 Petri Vehanen 4.00 10.00

2006-07 Swedish SHL Elitset Performers

1 Nicklas Backstrom 6.00 15.00
2 Dragan Umicevic 1.50 4.00
3 Niklas Andersson 1.50 4.00
4 Tomi Kallio 1.50 4.00
5 Mathias Johansson 1.50 4.00
6 Mika Hannula 1.50 4.00
7 Johan Davidsson 1.50 4.00
8 Tony Martensson 1.50 4.00
9 Mikael Hakansson 1.50 4.00
10 Mikael Renberg 2.00 5.00
11 Lasse Pirjeta 1.50 4.00
12 Juha Riihijarvi 1.50 4.00
13 Per Svartvadet 1.50 4.00
14 Pavel Brendl 1.50 4.00
15 Magnus Wernblom 1.50 4.00
16 Anders Soderberg 1.50 4.00
17 Timo Parssinen 1.50 4.00
18 Jonathan Hedstrom 1.50 4.00

2006-07 Swedish SHL Elitset Playmakers

1 Mikael Lind 1.50 4.00
2 Fredrik Bremberg 1.50 4.00
3 Niklas Andersson 1.50 4.00
4 Joel Lundqvist 2.50 6.00
5 Jorgen Jonsson 1.50 4.00
6 Rickard Wallin 1.50 4.00
7 Andreas Karlsson 1.50 4.00
8 Tony Martensson 1.50 4.00
9 Lubomir Bartecko 1.50 4.00
10 Andreas Salomonsson 1.50 4.00
11 Hakan Bogg 1.50 4.00
12 Frans Nielsen 2.50 6.00

2007-08 Swedish Lulea Postcards

COMPLETE SET (21) 15.00 30.00
1 Robin Olsson .75 2.00
2 Mikko Pukka .75 2.00
3 Jan Sandstrom .75 2.00
4 Johan Ejdepalm .75 2.00
5 Tommi Miettinen .75 2.00
6 Pekka Saravo .75 2.00
7 Pavel Skrbek .75 2.00
8 Martin Chabada .75 2.00
9 Cory Larose .75 2.00
10 Anders Burstrom .75 2.00
11 Johan Harju .75 2.00
12 Lubos Bartecko .75 2.00
13 Mats Lavander .75 2.00
14 Robin Lindqvist .75 2.00
15 Viktor Lindgren .75 2.00
16 Linus Omark .75 2.00
17 Mikael Lidhammer .75 2.00
18 Per Savilahti-Nagander .75 2.00
19 Mattias Modig .75 2.00
20 Jaroslav Obsut .75 2.00
21 Gusten Tornqvist .75 2.00

2007-08 Swedish Malmo Red Hawks

COMPLETE SET (23) 15.00 30.00
1 Robin Woihagor .75 2.00
2 Johan Bjork .75 2.00
3 Daniel Casselstahl .75 2.00
4 Jonathan Sjolund .75 2.00
5 Jan Oberg .75 2.00
6 Robin Alvarez .75 2.00
7 Kim Johansson .75 2.00
8 Martin Samuelsson .75 2.00
9 Marcus Paulsson .75 2.00
10 Mikael Wahlberg .75 2.00
11 Carl Soderberg 1.25 3.00
12 Emil Lundgren .75 2.00
13 Antti Bruun .75 2.00
14 Jani Hurme 1.25 3.00
15 Jyrki Valivaara .75 2.00
16 Calle Steen .75 2.00
17 Mikko Eloranta .75 2.00
18 Andreas Bystrom .75 2.00
19 Ville Nieminen 1.25 3.00
20 Patrik Lundh .75 2.00
21 Jens Svensson .75 2.00
22 Fredrik Eriksson .75 2.00
23 Tomas Wallgren .75 2.00

2007-08 Swedish SHL Elitset

COMPLETE SET (288) 30.00 60.00
1 Daniel Sperrle .10 .25
2 Daniel Johansson .10 .25
3 Antti Hulkkonen .10 .25
4 Nicholas Angell .10 .25
5 Peter Nolander .10 .25
6 Mathias Mansson .10 .25
7 Daniel Hermansson .10 .25
8 Johannes Salmonsson .10 .25
9 Bjorn Danielsson .10 .25
10 Mads Hansen .10 .25
11 Sebastian Karlsson .10 .25
12 Daniel Larsson .10 .25
13 Ronnie Pettersson .10 .25
14 Dennis Persson .10 .25
15 Thomas Johansson .10 .25
16 Jonas Liwing .10 .25
17 Timmy Pettersson .10 .25
18 Fredrik Ericson .10 .25
19 Kristofer Ottosson .10 .25
20 Nichlas Falk .10 .25
21 Jimmie Olvestad .10 .25
22 Christian Eklund .10 .25
23 Par Backer .10 .25
24 Morten Ask .10 .25
25 Nicklas Danielsson .10 .25
26 Joel Gistedt .20 .50
27 Ronnie Sundin .10 .25
28 Fredrik Johansson .10 .25
29 Karl Fabricius .10 .25
30 Steve Kariya .40 1.00
31 Jonas Esbjörs .10 .25
32 Niklas Andersson .10 .25
33 Martin Pluss .10 .25
34 Johan Ryno .10 .25
35 Tomi Kallio .10 .25
36 Christopher Heino-Lindberg .10 .25
37 Jonas Frogren .10 .25
38 Thomas Rhodin .10 .25
39 Pelle Prestberg .10 .25
40 Jesper Mattsson .10 .25
41 Esa Pirnes .10 .25
42 Jonas Hoglund .10 .25
43 Peter Nordstrom .10 .25
44 Emil Kaberg .10 .25
45 Christian Soderström .10 .25
46 Mathias Johansson .10 .25
47 Mikael Johansson .10 .25
48 Erik Ersberg .10 .25
49 Johan Akerman .10 .25
50 Per Gustafsson .10 .25
51 Pasi Puistola .10 .25
52 David Petrasek .10 .25
53 Martin Thornberg .10 .25
54 Andreas Falk .10 .25
55 David Fredriksson .10 .25
56 Jari Kauppila .10 .25
57 Timo Vertala .10 .25
58 Jukka Voutilainen .10 .25
59 Andreas Jamtin .10 .25
60 Johan Davidsson .10 .25
61 Jonas Fransson .10 .25
62 Magnus Johansson .10 .25
63 Tony Martensson .10 .25
64 Ulf Soderstrom .10 .25
65 Joakim Eriksson .10 .25
66 Tim Eriksson .10 .25
67 Niklas Olausson .10 .25
68 Sami Torkki .10 .25
69 Fredrik Emvall .10 .25
70 Johan Lindstrom .10 .25
71 Mikael Hakansson .10 .25
72 Patric Blomdahl .10 .25
73 Jan Sandstrom .10 .25
74 Pekka Saravo .10 .25
75 Pavel Skrbek .10 .25
76 Jaroslav Obsut .10 .25
77 Tomas Wallgren .10 .25
78 Martin Chabada .10 .25
79 Jesse Niinimaki .10 .25
80 Andreas Burstrom .10 .25
81 Kalle Kerman .10 .25
82 Johan Harju .10 .25
83 Robin Lindqvist .10 .25
84 Viktor Lindgren .10 .25
85 Linus Omark .10 .25
86 Karol Krizan .10 .25
87 Mattias Timander .10 .25
88 Hans Jonsson .10 .25
89 Oscar Hedman .10 .25
90 Adam Andersson .10 .25
91 Mattias Hellstrom .10 .25
92 Per-Ake Skroder .10 .25
93 Andreas Salomonsson .10 .25
94 Peter Oberg .10 .25
95 Mikael Pettersson .10 .25
96 Niklas Sundstrom .10 .25
97 Miloslav Horava .10 .25
98 Magnus Gastrin .10 .25
99 Juha Pitkamaki .10 .25
100 Pierre Johnsson .10 .25
101 Jarno Kultanen .10 .25
102 Thomas Skogs .10 .25
103 Antti Bruun .10 .25
104 Anders Bastiansen .10 .25
105 Marco Tuokko .10 .25
106 Eric Beaudoin .10 .25
107 Kenneth Bergqvist .10 .25
108 Anders Nilsson .10 .25
109 Teemu Elomo .10 .25
110 Martin Jansson .10 .25
111 Andreas Hadelov .10 .25
112 Per-Anton Lundstrom .10 .25
113 Fredrik Lindgren .10 .25
114 Kari Haakana .10 .25
115 Fredrik Krekula .10 .25
116 Johan Ramstedt .10 .25
117 Pontus Pettersson .10 .25
118 Jimmie Eriksson .10 .25
119 Anders Soderberg .10 .25
120 Marcus Kristoffersson .10 .25
121 Fredrik Oberg .10 .25
122 Jhonas Enroth .40 1.00
123 Martin Thelander .10 .25
124 Daniel Josefsson .10 .25
125 Fredric Andersson .10 .25
126 Robert Carlsson .10 .25
127 Jorgen Bemstrom .10 .25
128 Tony Lagerstrom .10 .25
129 Ragnar Karlsson .10 .25
130 Tomas Kollar .10 .25
131 Johan Sjodell-Wiklander .10 .25
132 Andrée Persson .10 .25
133 Johan Backlund .10 .25
134 Anton Stralman .75 2.00
135 Sanny Lindstrom .10 .25
136 Kimmo Lotvonen .10 .25
137 Petri Kokko .10 .25
138 Par Styf .10 .25
139 Peter Regin .10 .25
140 Johan Andersson .10 .25
141 Bjorn Svensson .10 .25
142 Timo Parssinen .10 .25
143 Riku Hahl .10 .50
144 Jonathan Hedstrom .20 .50
145 Markus Korhonen .10 .25
146 Tommy Sjodin .10 .25
147 Niclas Andersen .10 .25
148 Pavel Brendl .20 .50
149 Andreas Dackell .10 .25
150 Daniel Widing .10 .25
151 Markus Kankaanpera .10 .25
152 Alexander Sundstrom .10 .25
153 Lars Erik Spets .10 .25
154 Jusso Hietanen .10 .25
155 Ove Molin .10 .25
156 Janne Hauhtonen .10 .25
157 Jorgen Sundqvist .10 .25
158 Daniel Larsson .10 .25
159 David Printz .20 .50
160 Fredrik Bremberg .10 .25
161 Patric Hornqvist .10 1.00
162 Dick Axelsson .10 .25
163 Andreas Engqvist .10 .25
164 Niklas Anger .10 .25
165 Edvin Frylen .10 .25
166 Oscar Eklund .10 .25
167 Mark Owuya .40 1.00
168 Jiri Marusak .10 .25
169 Ari Ahonen .40 1.00
170 Toni Soderholm .10 .25
171 Jonas Johnson .10 .25
172 Jonas Nordquist .10 .25
173 Philip Larsen .10 .25
174 Fredrik Pettersson .10 .25
175 Magnus Kahnberg .10 .25
176 Antti-Jussi Niemi .10 .25
177 Jonas Ahnelov .10 .25
178 Andreas Holmqvist .10 .25
179 Johan Andersson .10 .25
180 Tomi Kallio .10 .25
181 Oscar Ackestrom .10 .25
182 Michael Holmqvist .10 .25
183 Jonas Gustavsson .10 .25
184 Johan Motin .10 .25
185 Jens Skalberg .10 .25
186 Dominik Granak .10 .25
187 Rickard Wallin .10 .25
188 Per Aslund .10 .25
189 Jorgen Jonsson .10 .25
190 Martin Johansson .10 .25
191 Eero Somervuori .10 .25
192 Fabian Brunnstrom .10 2.50
193 Dave Cullen .10 .25
194 Stefan Liv .40 1.00
195 Mikko Luoma .10 .25
196 Daniel Grillfors .10 .25
197 Per Ledin .10 .25
198 Stefan Pettersson .10 .25
199 Jan Hrdina .10 .25
200 Jonas Johansson .10 .25
201 Andreas Jamtin .10 .25
202 Lance Ward .10 .25
203 Andreas Falk .10 .25
204 Andreas Andersson .10 .25
205 Rastislav Stana .10 .25
206 Fredrik Emvall .10 .25
207 Daniel Fernholm .10 .25
208 Calle Gunnarsson .10 .25
209 Mattias Weinhandl .10 .50
210 Ville Vahalahti .10 .25
211 Niklas Persson .10 .25
212 Patrik Zackrisson .10 .25
213 Kim Staal .10 .25
214 Tony Martensson .10 .25
215 Mattias Carlsson .10 .25
216 Andreas Pihl .10 .25
217 Mattias Modig .10 .25
218 Gusten Tornqvist .10 .25
219 Mikko Pukka .10 .25
220 Jan Sandstrom .10 .25
221 Jussi Tarvainen .10 .25
222 Tommi Miettinen .10 .25
223 Magnus Isaksson .10 .25
224 Mats Lavander .10 .25
225 Mikael Lidhammar .10 .25
226 Johan Ejdepalm .10 .25
227 Robin Olsson .10 .25
228 Michal Zajkowski .10 .25
229 Per Hallberg .10 .25
230 Victor Hedman .75 2.00
231 Tommy Wargh .10 .25
232 Pierre Hedin .10 .25
233 Magnus Wernblom .10 .25
234 Fredrik Warg .10 .25
235 Per Svartvadet .10 .25
236 Jari Tolsa .10 .25
237 Andreas Molinder .10 .25
238 Oscar Steen .10 .25
239 Lars Johansson .10 .25
240 Marco Tuokko .10 .25
241 Yared Hagos .20 .50
242 Ivan Huml .20 .50
243 Jonathan Granstrom .10 .25
244 Toni Dahlman .10 .25
245 Hakan Bogg .10 .25
246 Johan Lindstrom .10 .25
247 Tero Maatta .10 .25
248 Mikko Kurvinen .10 .25
249 Adam Andersson .10 .25
250 Martti Jarventie .10 .25
251 Nicklas Dahlberg .10 .25
252 Jan Novak .10 .25
253 Christoffer Norgren .10 .25
254 Tobias Viklund .10 .25
255 Pontus Petterström .10 .25
256 Lee Goren .40 1.00
257 Thomas Larsson .10 .25
258 Mikael Renberg .40 1.00
259 Kimmo Koskenkorva .10 .25
260 Kent McDonnell .20 .50
261 Erik Andersson .10 .25
262 Erik Forssell .10 .25
263 Jimmie Ericsson .10 .25
264 Bjorn Bjurling .10 .25
265 Linus Klasen .10 .25
266 Stefan Grahns .10 .25
267 Per Hallin .10 .25
268 Par Arlbrandt .10 .25
269 Linus Videll .10 .25
270 Petri Pakaslahti .10 .25
271 Martin Cibak .10 .25
272 Jens Olsson .10 .25
273 Kristian Kudroc .10 .25
274 Jarno Kultanen .10 .25
275 Stefan Bemstrom .10 .25
276 Duane Harmer .10 .25
277 Magnus Akerlund .10 .25
278 Par Styf .10 .25
279 Anton Axelsson .10 .25
280 Oscar Sundh .10 .25
281 Jonathan Hedstrom .10 .25
282 Erik Andersson .10 .25
283 Mika Pyorala .10 .25
284 Robert Carlsson .10 .25
285 Robin Jonsson .10 .25
286 Sanny Lindstrom .10 .25
287 Riku Hahl .10 .25
288 Kalle Koskinen Timra .10 .25

2007-08 Swedish SHL Elitset Complete Players

1 Nicklas Backstrom 4.00 10.00
2 Fredrik Bremberg 1.25 3.00
3 Steve Kariya 1.50 4.00
4 Martin Pluss 1.25 3.00
5 Peter Nordstrom 1.25 3.00
6 Andreas Jamtin 1.25 3.00
7 Johan Davidsson 1.25 3.00
8 Joakim Eriksson 1.25 3.00
9 Tony Martensson 1.25 3.00
10 Jaroslav Obsut 1.25 3.00
11 Tomas Surovy 1.25 3.00
12 Anders Bastiansen 1.25 3.00
13 Robert Dome 1.25 3.00
14 Per Svartvadet 1.25 3.00
15 Jimmie Eriksson 1.25 3.00
16 Linus Videll 1.25 3.00
17 Johan Backlund 1.25 3.00
18 Jonathan Hedstrom 2.00 5.00

2007-08 Swedish SHL Elitset Double Impact

COMPLETE SET (12) 12.00 30.00
1 P.Hornqvist/F.Bremberg 2.00 5.00
2 T.Sjodin/M.Mansson 1.25 3.00
3 A.Holmqvist/M.Holmqvist 1.25 3.00
4 P.Skroder/N.Sundstrom 1.25 3.00
5 T.Eriksson/F.Emwall 1.25 3.00
6 E.Somervuori/J.Jonsson 1.25 3.00
7 L.Omark/J.Harju 1.25 3.00
8 T.Dahlman/J.Pitkamaki 1.25 3.00
9 M.Renberg/J.Ericsson 1.50 4.00
10 J.Enroth/L.Klasen 2.00 5.00
11 J.Hedstrom/R.Hahl 2.00 5.00
12 A.Jamtin/P.Ledin 1.25 3.00

2007-08 Swedish SHL Elitset Future Watch

COMPLETE SET (12) 20.00 50.00
1 Niclas Andersen 2.50 6.00
2 Dick Axelsson 2.50 6.00
3 Philip Larsen 2.50 6.00
4 Johan Motin 2.50 6.00
5 Fredrik Pettersson 2.50 6.00
6 Patrik Zackrisson 2.50 6.00
7 Mattias Modig 2.50 6.00
8 Victor Hedman 6.00 15.00
9 Alexander Sundstrom 2.50 6.00
10 Thomas Larsson 2.50 6.00
11 Linus Klasen 2.50 6.00
12 Tobias Forsberg 2.50 6.00

2007-08 Swedish SHL Elitset Great Gloves

COMPLETE SET (9) 15.00 40.00
1 Daniel Sperrle 2.50 6.00
2 Daniel Larsson 2.50 6.00
3 Christopher Heino-Lindberg 2.50 6.00
4 Erik Ersberg 2.50 6.00
5 Jonas Fransson 2.50 6.00
6 Karol Krizan 2.50 6.00
7 Juha Pitkamaki 2.50 6.00
8 Andreas Hadelov 2.50 6.00
9 Johan Backlund 2.50 6.00

2007-08 Swedish SHL Elitset Jerseys

1 Kristofer Ottosson 10.00 25.00
2 Arto Tukio 10.00 25.00
3 Dennis Persson 10.00 25.00
4 Mathias Johansson 10.00 25.00
5 Stefan Liv 15.00 40.00

2007-08 Swedish SHL Elitset Signatures

1 Jimmie Olvestad 4.00 10.00
2 Dragan Umicevic 4.00 10.00
3 Peter Nordstrom 4.00 10.00
4 Tero Leinonen 4.00 10.00
5 Martin Chabada 4.00 10.00
6 Johan Harju 4.00 10.00
7 Rickard Lintner 4.00 10.00
8 Johan Backlund 4.00 10.00
9 Jonathan Hedstrom 8.00 20.00
10 Riku Hahl 4.00 10.00
11 Timo Parssinen 4.00 10.00
12 Mikael Johansson 4.00 10.00
13 Esa Pirnes 4.00 10.00
14 Johan Davidsson 4.00 10.00
15 Tony Martensson 4.00 10.00
16 Joakim Eriksson 4.00 10.00
17 Karol Krizan 4.00 10.00
18 Juha Pitkamaki 5.00 12.00
19 Mikael Simons 4.00 10.00
20 Tomas Skogs 4.00 10.00
21 Jhonas Enroth 8.00 20.00
22 Johan Sjodell-Wiklander 5.00 12.00
23 Fredrik Sonntag 4.00 10.00
24 Robert Carlsson 4.00 10.00
25 Jimmie Olvestad 4.00 10.00
26 Daniel Larsson 4.00 10.00
27 Patric Hornqvist 6.00 15.00
28 Nicklas Sundstrom 4.00 10.00
29 Tommy Wargh 4.00 10.00
30 Andreas Falk 4.00 10.00
31 Johan Akerman 4.00 10.00
32 Johan Backlund 4.00 10.00
33 Riku Hahl 6.00 15.00
34 Oscar Sundh 4.00 10.00
35 Timo Parssinen 4.00 10.00
36 Christian Soderstrom 4.00 10.00
37 Eric Beaudoin 4.00 10.00
38 Bjorn Danielsson 4.00 10.00
39 Mathias Mansson 4.00 10.00
40 Martin Chabada 4.00 10.00
41 Linus Omark 4.00 10.00
42 Johan Harju 4.00 10.00
43 Johan Ramstedt 4.00 10.00
44 Pontus Pettersson 4.00 10.00
45 Andreas Hadelov 4.00 10.00
46 Jimmie Eriksson 4.00 10.00

2007-08 Swedish SHL Elitset The Dominators

COMPLETE SET (18) 25.00 50.00
1 Pavel Brendl 2.00 5.00
2 Patric Hornqvist 2.00 5.00
3 Jimmie Olvestad 1.50 4.00
4 Jonas Nordquist 1.50 4.00
5 Rickard Wallin 1.50 4.00
6 Martin Thornberg 1.50 4.00
7 Jan Hrdina 1.50 4.00
8 Mattias Weinhandl 1.50 4.00
9 Jan Sandstrom 1.50 4.00
10 Jari Tolsa 1.50 4.00
11 Niklas Sundstrom 1.50 4.00
12 Juha Pitkamaki 2.00 5.00
13 Fredrik Lindgren 1.50 4.00
14 Sanny Lindstrom 1.50 4.00
15 Per Hallin 1.50 4.00
16 Riku Hahl 2.00 5.00
17 Esa Pirnes 1.50 4.00
18 Mathias Mansson 1.50 4.00

2007-08 Swedish SHL Elitset The Guardians

COMPLETE SET (12) 30.00 75.00
1 Markus Korhonen 3.00 8.00
2 Daniel Larsson 3.00 8.00
3 Joel Gistedt 3.00 8.00
4 Stefan Liv 3.00 8.00
5 Rastislav Stana 3.00 8.00
6 Mattias Modig 3.00 8.00
7 Karol Krizan 3.00 8.00
8 Juha Pitkamaki 3.00 8.00
9 Jhonas Enroth 3.00 8.00
10 Magnus Akerlund 3.00 8.00
11 Andreas Hadelov 3.00 8.00
12 Christopher Heino-Lindberg 3.00 8.00

2007-08 Swedish SHL Elitset The Specialists

COMPLETE SET (9) 20.00 40.00
1 Karol Krizan 2.00 5.00
2 Juha Pitkamaki 2.50 6.00
3 Janne Niskala 2.00 5.00
4 Johan Akerman 2.00 5.00
5 Fredrik Bremberg 2.00 5.00
6 Nicklas Backstrom 6.00 15.00
7 Fredrik Emvall 2.00 5.00
8 Tomi Kallio 2.00 5.00
9 Mikael Renberg 2.50 6.00

2007-08 Swedish SHL Elitset Wave of the Future

COMPLETE SET (9) 20.00 50.00
1 Patric Hornqvist 4.00 10.00
2 Joel Gistedt 2.50 6.00
3 Niklas Olausson 2.50 6.00
4 Linus Omark 2.50 6.00
5 Tommy Wargh 2.50 6.00
6 Lars Johansson 2.50 6.00
7 Jhonas Enroth 4.00 10.00
8 Oscar Sundh 2.50 6.00
9 Anton Stralman 5.00 12.00

2009-10 Swedish Upper Deck Victory

COMPLETE SET (250) 75.00 150.00
COMP.SET w/o SPS (200) 30.00 60.00
*SWEDISH: .6X TO 1.5X BASIC VICTORY
195 Nicklas Backstrom .40 1.00

2009-10 Swedish Upper Deck Victory Svenska Superstjarnor

COMPLETE SET (20) 12.00 30.00
SS1 Henrik Lundqvist 2.00 5.00
SS2 Loui Eriksson .50 1.25
SS3 Alexander Edler .50 1.25
SS4 P.J. Axelsson .50 1.25
SS5 Nicklas Lidstrom .50 1.25
SS6 Mattias Ohlund .50 1.25
SS7 Mikael Samuelsson .50 1.25
SS8 Henrik Zetterberg 1.00 2.50
SS9 Michael Nylander .50 1.25
SS10 Niklas Kronwall .60 1.50
SS11 Daniel Alfredsson .75 2.00
SS12 Kim Johnsson .50 1.25
SS13 Mats Sundin .75 2.00
SS14 Tomas Holmstrom .60 1.50
SS15 Fredrik Modin .50 1.25
SS16 Henrik Sedin 1.00 2.50
SS17 Daniel Sedin 1.00 2.50
SS18 Kristian Huselius .50 1.25
SS19 Nicklas Backstrom .75 2.00
SS20 Johan Franzen .60 1.50

1993-94 Swiss HNL

COMPLETE SET (510) 24.00 60.00
1 Title Card .05 .15
2 Title Card .05 .15
3 Title Card .05 .15
4 EHC-Kloten .05 .15
5 EHC-Kloten .05 .15
6 Conny Evensson CO .07 .20
7 Ernst Bruderer ACO .05 .15
8 Reto Pavoni .20 .50
9 Claudio Bayer .20 .50
10 Martin Bruderer .05 .15
11 Anders Eldebrink .08 .25
12 Marco Kloti .05 .15
13 Marco Knecht .05 .15
14 Martin Kout .05 .15
15 Fausto Mazzoleni .05 .15
16 Daniel Sigg .05 .15
17 Daniel Weber .05 .15
18 Manuele Celio .05 .15
19 Patric Della Rossa .20 .50
20 Michael Diener .05 .15
21 Bruno Erni .05 .15
22 Oliver Hoffmann .05 .15
23 Felix Hollenstein .08 .25
24 Mikael Johansson .08 .25
25 Daniel Knecht .05 .15
26 Roger Meier .05 .15
27 Sacha Ochsner .08 .25
28 Peter Schlagenhauf .05 .15
29 Roman Wager .08 .25
30 HC Fribourg-Gotteron .05 .15
31 HC Fribourg-Gotteron .05 .15
32 Paul-Andre Cadieux CO .05 .15
33 Francois Huppe ACO .05 .15
34 Dino Stecher .20 .50
35 Marc Gygli .20 .50
36 Patrice Brasey .05 .15
37 Fredy Bobillier .05 .15
38 Antoine Descloux .05 .15
39 Christian Hofstetter .05 .15
40 Douglas M. Honegger .05 .15
41 Olivier Keller .05 .15
42 David Leibzig .05 .15
43 Didier Princi .05 .15
44 Joel Aeschlimann .05 .15
45 Christophe Brown .05 .15
46 Slava Bykov .20 .50
47 Stefan Grogg .05 .15
48 Andrej Khomutov .20 .50
49 Marc Leuenberger .05 .15
50 Bruno Maurer .05 .15
51 Frank Monnier .05 .15
52 Alain Reymond .05 .15
53 Mario Rottaris .05 .15
54 Pascal Schaller .05 .15
55 Chad Silver .05 .15
56 SC Bern .05 .15
57 SC Bern .05 .15
58 Hannu Jortikka CO .05 .15
59 Jim Koleff ACO .05 .15
60 Renato Tosio .20 .50
61 Roland Meyer .20 .50
62 Raoul Baumgartner .05 .15
63 Andreas Beutler .05 .15
64 Martin Brich .05 .15
65 Mikko Haapakoski .05 .15
66 Martin Rauch .05 .15
67 Jorg Reber .05 .15
68 Daniel Rutschi .05 .15
69 Gaetan Voisard .08 .25
70 Peter Bartschi .05 .15
71 Michael Buhler .05 .15
72 Rene Friedli .05 .15
73 Regis Fuchs .05 .15
74 Gregor Horak .05 .15
75 Michael Meier .05 .15
76 Gil Montandon .05 .15
77 Dan Quinn .20 .50
78 Harry Rogenmoser .05 .15
79 Roberto Triulzi .05 .15
80 Thomas C. Vrabec .05 .15
81 HC Lugano .05 .15
82 HC Lugano .05 .15
83 John Slettvoll CO .05 .15
84 Bruno Rogger ACO .05 .15
85 Lars Weibel .20 .50
86 Christophe Wahl .20 .50
87 Samuel Balmer .05 .15
88 Sandro Bertaggia .20 .50
89 Per Djoos .08 .25
90 Claudio Ghillioni .05 .15
91 Davide Jelmini .05 .15
92 Sven Leuenberger .05 .15
93 Ruedi Niderost .05 .15
94 Patrick Sutter .05 .15
95 Jean-Jacques Aeschlimann .08 .25
96 Jorg Eberle .08 .25
97 Ruben Fontana .05 .15
98 Axel Heim .05 .15
99 Christian Hofstetter .05 .15
100 Patrick Howald .08 .25
101 Marcel Jenni .05 .15
102 Andreas Keller .05 .15
103 Jan Larccon .05 .15
104 Andre Rotheli .05 .15
105 Matthias Schenkel .05 .15
106 Raymond Walder .05 .15
107 EV Zug .05 .15
108 EV Zug .05 .15
109 Bjorn Kinding CO .05 .15
110 Sean Simpson ACO .05 .15
111 Patrick Schopf .20 .50
112 Tony Koller .20 .50
113 Jakub Horak .05 .15
114 Dino Kessler .08 .25
115 Andre Kunzi .05 .15
116 Thomas Kunzi .05 .15
117 Andreas Ritsch .05 .15
118 Bill Schafhauser .05 .15
119 Pat Schafhauser .05 .15
120 Misko Antisin .08 .25
121 Mario Brodmann .05 .15
122 Tom Fergus .20 .50
123 Andreas Fischer .05 .15
124 Patrick Fischer .05 .15
125 Daniel Giger .05 .15
126 Daniel Meier .05 .15
127 Colin Muller .05 .15
128 Neuenschwander Ph. .05 .15
129 Daniel Schaltegger .05 .15
130 Franz Steffen .05 .15
131 Ken Yaremchuk .20 .50
132 HC Ambri-Piotta .05 .15
133 HC Ambri-Piotta .05 .15
134 Perry Pearn CO .08 .25
135 Dale McCourt ACO .08 .25
136 Markus Bachschmied .20 .50
137 Marco Baron .20 .50
138 Mark Astley .08 .25
139 Brenno Celio .05 .15
140 Filippo Celio .05 .15
141 Ivan Gazzaroli .05 .15
142 Tiziano Gianini .08 .25
143 Blair Muller .05 .15
144 Luigi Riva .05 .15
145 Rick Tschumi .05 .15
146 Nicola Celio .08 .25
147 Keith Fair .05 .15
148 Igor Fedulov .05 .15
149 Mathias Holzer .05 .15
150 Peter Jaks .05 .15
151 Vincent Lechenne .05 .15
152 Juri Leonov .05 .15
153 Petr Malkov .05 .15

154 Markus Studer .05 .15
155 Stefano Togni .05 .15
156 Luca Vigano .05 .15
157 Theo Wittmann .05 .15
158 Zurcher SC .05 .15
159 Zurcher SC .05 .15
160 Arno Del Curto CO .05 .15
161 Ueli Hofmann ACO .05 .15
162 Daniel Riesen .20 .50
163 Rolf Simmen .20 .50
164 Marco Bayer .08 .25
165 Jiri Faic .05 .15
166 Yvan Griga .05 .15
167 Noel Guyaz .05 .15
168 Edgar Salis .05 .15
169 Christian Sigrist .05 .15
170 Bruno Vollmer .05 .15
171 Andreas Zehnder .05 .15
172 Matthias Baechler .05 .15
173 Vjeran Ivankovic .05 .15
174 Peter Kobel .05 .15
175 Ronnie Leuthold .05 .15
176 Claudio Micheli .05 .15
177 Patrizio Morger .05 .15
178 Sergei Priakhin .08 .25
179 Roger Thony .05 .15
180 Andy Ton .05 .15
181 Christian Weber .05 .15
182 Vladimir Yeremin .05 .15
183 Michel Zeiter .05 .15
184 EHC Biel-Bienne .05 .15
185 EHC Biel-Bienne .05 .15
186 Jakob Kolliker CO .05 .15
187 Lautenschlager ASST TR .05 .15
188 Oliver Anken .20 .50
189 Christian Cretin .20 .50
190 Beat Cattaruzza .05 .15
191 Jean-Michel Clavien .05 .15
192 Sven Dick .05 .15
193 Daniel Dubois .05 .15
194 Leo Gudas .08 .25
195 Bjorn Schneider .05 .15
196 Martin Steinegger .05 .15
197 Gaetan Boucher .05 .15
198 Thomas Burillo .05 .15
199 Reynald De Ritz .05 .15
200 Patrick Glanzmann .05 .15
201 Freddy Luthi .05 .15
202 Beat Nuspliger .05 .15
203 Cyrill Pasche .05 .15
204 Robert Yannick .05 .15
205 Andre Rufener .05 .15
206 Bernhard Schuemperli .08 .25
207 Marc Weber .08 .25
208 Ramil Yuldashev .05 .15
209 HC Davos .05 .15
210 HC Davos .05 .15
211 Mats Waltin CO .05 .15
212 Marcus Theus ACO .05 .15
213 Nando Wieser .20 .50
214 Marino Buriola .20 .50
215 Thomi Derungs .05 .15
216 Andy Egli .05 .15
217 Beat Equilino .05 .15
218 Marc Gianola .05 .15
219 Andrea Haller .05 .15
220 Didier Massy .05 .15
221 Roland Ruedi .05 .15
222 Roger Sigg .05 .15
223 Mica Blaha .08 .25
224 Gian Marco Crameri .05 .15
225 Remo Gross .05 .15
226 Martin Hanggi .05 .15
227 Markus Morf .05 .15
228 Rene Muller .05 .15
229 Andi Naser .05 .15
230 Oliver Roth .05 .15
231 Rato Schneider .05 .15
232 Serge Soguel .05 .15
233 Gilles Thibaudeau .20 .50
234 Steve Tsujiura .08 .25
235 EHC Olten .05 .15
236 EHC Olten .05 .15
237 Dick Decloe CO .05 .15
238 Beat Aebischer .20 .50
239 Sascha Friedli .20 .50
240 Matthias Aregger .05 .15
241 Eric Bourquin .05 .15
242 Fabian Gull .05 .15
243 Urs Hirschi .05 .15
244 Alessandro Reinhart .05 .15
245 Christian Schuster .05 .15
246 Christian Silling .05 .15
247 Richard Stucki .05 .15
248 Adrian Bachofner .05 .15
249 Markus Butler .05 .15
250 Ralph Donghi .05 .15
251 Guido Egli .05 .15
252 Paul Gagne .20 .50
253 Thomas Loosli .05 .15
254 Steve Metzger .05 .15
255 Viktor Muller .05 .15
256 Mike Richard .05 .15
257 Kevin Schlapfer .05 .15
258 Peter Trummer .05 .15
259 Andre Von Rohr .05 .15
260 HC Ajoie .05 .15
261 HC Ajoie .05 .15
262 Michael McNamara CO .05 .15
263 Claude Fugere ACO .05 .15
264 Nicola Fraschina .20 .50
265 Didier Tosi .20 .50
266 Dave Baechler .05 .15
267 Sandro Capaul .05 .15
268 Romain Fleury .05 .15
269 Carl Lapointe .05 .15
270 John Miner .05 .15
271 Daniel Rohrbach .05 .15
272 Ralph Tanner .05 .15
273 Yann Voillat .05 .15
274 Mauro Bornet .05 .15
275 Kalle Furer .05 .15
276 Thomas Griga .05 .15
277 Patrice Heiz .05 .15
278 Willy Kohler .05 .15
279 Daniel Lamminger .05 .15
280 Francois Marquis .05 .15
281 Marco Mozzini .05 .15
282 Giovanni Pestrin .05 .15
283 Ken Priestlay .08 .25
284 Frederic Rothen .05 .15
285 EHC Chur .05 .15
286 EHC Chur .05 .15
287 Bengt Ericsson CO .05 .15
288 Roberto Lavoie ACO .05 .15
289 Peter Martin .20 .50
290 Thomas Liesch .20 .50
291 Marco Capaul .05 .15
292 Marco Gazzola .05 .15
293 Bruno Habisreutinger .05 .15
294 Markus Knobel .05 .15
295 Thomas Locher .05 .15
296 Roger Schnoz .05 .15
297 Roland Simonet .05 .15
298 Ivo Stoffel .05 .15
299 Rene Ackermann .05 .15
300 Patrice Bosch .05 .15
301 Harry Derungs .05 .15
302 Marco Ferrari .05 .15
303 Miguel Fondado .05 .15
304 Claudio Kalser .05 .15
305 Claudio Krattli .05 .15
306 Zbysek Kurylowski .05 .15
307 Andrei Kwartalnov .05 .15
308 Albert Malgin .05 .15
309 Wayne Manley .05 .15
310 Riccardo Signorell .05 .15
311 HC Martigny .05 .15
312 HC Martigny .05 .15
313 Bob Mongrain CO .05 .15
314 Thierry Andrey .20 .50
315 Florian Garnier .20 .50
316 Thierry Evequoz .05 .15
317 Alexandre Formaz .05 .15
318 Tom Jaeggi .05 .15
319 Adrian Jezzone .05 .15
320 Jaques Mauron .05 .15
321 Patrick Neukom .05 .15
322 Brian Rueger .05 .15
323 Bruno Steck .05 .15
324 Steve Aebersold .05 .15
325 Nicolas Baumann .05 .15
326 Alain Bernard .05 .15
327 Jean-Daniel Bonito .05 .15
328 Olivier Ecoeur .05 .15
329 Kelly Glowa .05 .15
330 Thomas Heldner .05 .15
331 Thierry Moret .05 .15
332 Stefan Nussberger .05 .15
333 Petr Rosol .08 .25
334 Gabriel Taccoz .05 .15
335 SC Herisau .05 .15
336 SC Herisau .05 .15
337 Mike McParland CO .05 .15
338 Mark McGregor ACO .05 .15
339 Stephan Morf .20 .50
340 Stefan Allenspach .20 .50
341 Urs Balzarek .05 .15
342 Sascha Bleiker .05 .15
343 Damian Freitag .05 .15
344 Karl Knopf .05 .15
345 Andy Krapf .05 .15
346 Andreas Maag .05 .15
347 Paul Summermatter .05 .15
348 Markus Wetter .05 .15
349 Marco Beer .05 .15
350 Bernhard Blochliger .05 .15
351 Libor Dolana .05 .15
352 Philipp Egli .05 .15
353 Marco Fischer .05 .15
354 Reto Germann .05 .15
355 Urs Hartmann .05 .15
356 Markus Keller .05 .15
357 Trevor Meier .05 .15
358 Roger Nater .05 .15
359 Petr Vlk .08 .25
360 Gerd Zenhausern .05 .15
361 SC Rapperswil-Jona .05 .15
362 SC Rapperswil-Jona .05 .15
363 Pekka Rautakallio CO .20 .50
364 Ueli Scheidegger ACO .05 .15
365 Marius Boesch .05 .15
366 Michael Habig .08 .25
367 Armin Berchtold .05 .15
368 Daniel Bunzli .05 .15
369 Erich Frey .05 .15
370 Patrick Gotz .05 .15
371 Marc Haueter .05 .15
372 Christian Langer .05 .15
373 Markus Naef .05 .15
374 Daniel Aeschbacher .05 .15
375 Ray Allison .05 .15
376 Tom Bissett .20 .50
377 Warren Bruetsch .05 .15
378 Turi Camenzind .05 .15
379 Jean-Noel Honegger .05 .15
380 Roman Kessler .05 .15
381 Hans Kossman .05 .15
382 Marco Seeholzer .05 .15
383 Laurent Stehlin .05 .15
384 Marco Werder .05 .15
385 EHC Bulach .05 .15
386 EHC Bulach .05 .15
387 Lars-Erik Lundstrom CO .05 .15
388 Urs Liljequist ACO .05 .15
389 Ronnie Rueger .20 .50
390 Carlo Buriola .20 .50
391 Rolf Bunter .05 .15
392 David Erny .05 .15
393 Urs Gull .05 .15
394 Thomas Jaggli .05 .15
395 Stefan Meier .05 .15
396 Marco Schellenberg .05 .15
397 Marcel Schonhaar .05 .15
398 Robin Bauer .05 .15
399 Daniele Celio .05 .15
400 Peter Ekelund .05 .15
401 Urs Luthi .05 .15
402 Don McLaren .08 .25
403 Kim Pedersen .05 .15
404 Matthias Pittet .05 .15
405 Ercan Sahin .05 .15
406 Thomas Studer .05 .15
407 Markus Suter .05 .15
408 Martin Caretta .05 .15
409 Mike Tschumi .05 .15
410 Lausanne HC .05 .15
411 Lausanne HC .05 .15
412 Jean Lussier CO .05 .15
413 Beat Kindler .08 .25
414 Michel Pilet .05 .15
415 Urs Burkart .05 .15
416 Jean Gagnon .05 .15
417 Nicolas Goumaz .05 .15
418 Fabian Guignard .05 .15
419 Benedict Sapin .05 .15
420 Raymond Wyssen .05 .15
421 Laurent Bucher .05 .15
422 Olivier Chenuz .05 .15
423 Alain Comte .05 .15
424 Martin Desjardins .05 .15
425 Gaby Epiney .05 .15
426 Stephane Gasser .05 .15
427 Nicolas Gauch .05 .15
428 Gilles Guyaz .05 .15
429 Dan Hodgson .20 .50
430 Maxime Lapointe .05 .15
431 Laurent Pasquini .05 .15
432 Gilles Prince .05 .15
433 Yannick Theler .05 .15
434 HC Thurgau .05 .15
435 HC Thurgau .05 .15
436 Anders Sorensen CO .05 .15
437 Max Baumann .05 .15
438 Martin Studer .20 .50
439 Thomas Berger .20 .50
440 Andy Gasser .05 .15
441 Patrick Henry .05 .15
442 Reto Muller .05 .15
443 Ralph Ott .05 .15
444 Mike Posma .05 .15
445 Hadrian Rosenberg .05 .15
446 Marcel Stocker .05 .15
447 Robert Wiesmann .05 .15
448 Gianni Dalla Vecchia .05 .15
449 Dan Daoust .20 .50
450 Matthias Keller .05 .15
451 Roger Keller .05 .15
452 Peter Kostli .05 .15
453 Bernhard Lauber .05 .15
454 Benjamin Mueller .05 .15
455 Silvio Schai .05 .15
456 Rolf Schrepfer .05 .15
457 Robert Slehofer .05 .15
458 Thomas Steger .05 .15
459 Cuno Weisser .05 .15
460 Grasshoppers-Club Zurich .05 .15
461 Grasshoppers-Club Zurich .05 .15
462 Esa Siren CO .05 .15
463 Bruno Aegerter ACO .05 .15
464 Marcel Kohli .20 .50
465 Olivier Leuenberger .20 .50
466 Giorgio Giacomelli .05 .15
467 Roman Honegger .05 .15
468 Sandro Just .05 .15
469 Mats Lusth .05 .15
470 Marcel Wick .05 .15
471 Lukas Zehnder .05 .15
472 Rolf Ziegler .05 .15
473 Jerry Zuurmond .05 .15
474 Alain Ayer .05 .15
475 Leo Cadisch .05 .15
476 Pascal Fah .05 .15
477 Roman Furrer .05 .15
478 Marco Hagmann .05 .15
479 Peter Hofmann .05 .15
480 Adrian Hotz .05 .15
481 Patrick Looser .05 .15
482 Oliver Muffler .05 .15
483 Keith Osborne .08 .25
484 Thierry Paterlini .05 .15
485 Markus Schellenberg .05 .15
486 HC La Chaux-de-Fonds .05 .15
487 HC LaChaux-de-Fonds .05 .15
488 Ricardo Fuhrer CO .05 .15
489 Jean-Luc Schnegg .08 .25
490 Thierry Loup .08 .25
491 Thierry Baume .05 .15
492 Jean-Luc Christen .05 .15
493 Thierry Murisier .05 .15
494 Danny Ott .05 .15
495 Guido Pfosi .05 .15
496 Rene Raess .05 .15
497 Valeri Shirajev .08 .25
498 Frank Vuillemin .05 .15
499 Marco Dick .05 .15
500 Michael Ferrari .05 .15
501 Olivier Gazzaroli .05 .15
502 Sandy Jeannin .05 .15
503 Lane Lambert .08 .25
504 Guido Laczko .05 .15
505 Boris Leimgruber .05 .15
506 Claude Luthi .05 .15
507 Patrick Oppliger .05 .15
508 Jean-Luc Rod .05 .15
509 Gabriel Rohrbach .05 .15
510 Yvan Zimmermann .05 .15

1995-96 Swiss HNL

COMPLETE SET (545) 30.00 75.00
1 Kloten .02 .10
2 Kloten .02 .10
3 Alpo Suhonen CO .20 .50
4 Ernst Bruderer ACO .02 .10
5 Matthias Muller .08 .25
6 Reto Pavoni .20 .50
7 Marco Bayer .02 .10
8 Martin Bruderer .02 .10
9 Marco Kloti .02 .10
10 Michael Kress .02 .10
11 Marc Ochsner .02 .10
12 Bjorn Schneider .02 .10
13 Daniel Sigg .02 .10
14 Daniel Weber .02 .10
15 Charles Berglund .02 .10
16 Manuele Celio .02 .10
17 Patrik Della Rossa .02 .10
18 Michael Diener .02 .10
19 Bruno Erni .02 .10
20 Oliver Hoffmann .02 .10
21 Felix Hollenstein .02 .10
22 Mathias Holzer .02 .10
23 Mikael Johansson .02 .10
24 Roger Meier .02 .10
25 Sacha Oscsner .02 .10
26 Frederic Rothen .02 .10
27 Roman Wager .02 .10
28 ZSC .02 .10
29 ZSC .02 .10
30 Larry Huras TR .02 .10
31 Ted Snell ATR .02 .10
32 Thomas Papp .15 .40
33 Dino Stecher .15 .40
34 Patrick Hager .02 .10
35 Martin Kout .02 .10
36 Didier Princi .02 .10
37 Edgar Salis .02 .10
38 Bruno Steck .02 .10
39 Nicholas Steiger .02 .10
40 Andreas Zehnder .02 .10
41 Mario Brodmann .02 .10
42 Marc Fortier .08 .25
43 Nicholas Gauch .02 .10
44 Vjeran Ivankovic .02 .10
45 Sandy Jeannin .02 .10
46 Patrick Lebeau .20 .50
47 Phillipp Luber .02 .10
48 Don McLaren .08 .25
49 Claudio Micheli .02 .10
50 Patrizio Morger .02 .10
51 Marco Seeholzer .02 .10
52 Bruno Vollmer .02 .10
53 Michel Zeiter .02 .10
54 Fribourg .02 .10
55 Fribourg .02 .10
56 Kjell Larsson TR .02 .10
57 Ueli Hofmann ATR .02 .10
58 David Aebischer ERC 15.00 40.00
59 Thomas Berger .15 .40
60 Steve Meuwly .07 .20
61 Johan Bertholet .02 .10
62 Fredy Bobillier .02 .10
63 Patrice Brasey .02 .10
64 Antoine Descloux .02 .10
65 Andy Egli .02 .10
66 Christian Hofstetter .02 .10
67 Olivier Keller .02 .10
68 Andrei Lomakin .08 .25
69 Mark Streit .02 .10
70 Christophe Brown .02 .10
71 Slava Bykov .20 .50
72 Matthias Bachler .02 .10
73 Axel Heim .02 .10
74 Andrej Khomutov .20 .50
75 Marc Leuenberger .02 .10
76 Alfred Luthi .04 .10
77 Daniel Meier .02 .10
78 Mario Rottaris .02 .10
79 Pascal Schaller .02 .10
80 Sacha Schneider .02 .10
81 Joel Aeschlimann .02 .10
82 Bern .02 .10
83 Bern .02 .10
84 Brian Lefley CO .02 .10
85 Ueli Schwarz ATR .02 .10
86 Reto Schurch .15 .40
87 Renato Tosio .15 .40
88 Mikko Haapakoski .02 .10
89 Christian Langer .02 .10
90 Sven Leuenberger .02 .10
91 Phillippe Portner .02 .10
92 Martin Rauch .02 .10
93 Pascal Sommer .02 .10
94 Martin Steinegger .02 .10
95 Gaeton Voisard .02 .10
96 Rene Friedli .02 .10
97 Regis Fuchs .02 .10
98 Patrick Howald .02 .10
99 Andy Keller .02 .10
100 Vincent Lechenne .02 .10
101 Lars Leuenberger .02 .10
102 Trevor Meier .02 .10
103 Gilles Montandon .02 .10
104 Philippe Muller .02 .10
105 Gaetano Orlando .08 .25
106 Roberto Triuizi .02 .10
107 Thomas Vrabec .02 .10
108 Davos .02 .10
109 Davos .02 .10
110 Mats Waltin TR .02 .10
111 Evgeni Popichin ACO .02 .10
112 Ivo Kleeb .15 .40
113 Nando Wiesser .15 .40
114 Samuel Balmer .02 .10
115 Martin Brich .02 .10
116 Beat Equilino .02 .10
117 Ivan Gazzaroli .02 .10
118 Marc Gianola .02 .10
119 Andrea Haeller .02 .10
120 Doug Honegger .02 .10
121 Andrej Kovalev .02 .10
122 Jan Alston .02 .10
123 Gian-Marco Crameri .02 .10
124 Dan Hodgson .20 .50
125 Rene Muller .02 .10
126 Andy Naser .02 .10
127 Oliver Roth .02 .10
128 Ivo Ruthemann .02 .10
129 Reto Stirnimann .02 .10
130 Reto Von Arx .02 .10
131 Christian Weber .02 .10
132 Lugano .02 .10
133 Lugano .02 .10
134 John Slettvoll TR .02 .10
135 Nicola Fraschina .15 .40
136 Lars Weibel .30 .75
137 Sandro Bertaggia .07 .20
138 Francesco Bizzozero .02 .10
139 Michel Kamber .02 .10
140 Ruedi Niderost .02 .10
141 Pat Schafhauser .02 .10
142 Tommy Sjodin .08 .25
143 Patrick Sutter .02 .10
144 Rick Tschumi .02 .10
145 J. Jacques Aeschlimann .02 .10
146 Markus Butler .02 .10
147 Jorg Eberle .02 .10
148 Keith Fair .02 .10
149 Marcel Jenni .02 .10
150 Stephan Lebeau .40 1.00
151 Patrick Looser .02 .10
152 Stefano Togni .02 .10
153 Andy Ton .02 .10
154 Remo Walder .02 .10
155 EVZ .02 .10
156 EVZ .02 .10
157 Jim Koleff TR .02 .10
158 Bob Lesley ACO .02 .10
159 Sacha Friedli .15 .40
160 Patrick Schopf .15 .40
161 Livio Fazio .02 .10
162 Stefan Grauwiler .02 .10
163 Dino Kessler .02 .10
164 Andre Kunzi .02 .10
165 Thomas Kunzi .02 .10
166 Fausto Mazzoleni .02 .10
167 John Miner .02 .10
168 Bill Schafhauser .02 .10
169 Steve Aebersold .02 .10
170 Misko Antisin .02 .10
171 Patrick Fischer .02 .10
172 Daniel Giger .02 .10
173 Mathias Keller .02 .10
174 Marco Koppel .02 .10
175 Colin Muller .02 .10
176 Philipp Neuenschwander .02 .10
177 Andre Rotheli .02 .10
178 Chad Silver .02 .10
179 Franz Steffen .02 .10
180 Ken Yaremchuk .20 .50
181 Ambri Piotta .02 .10
182 Ambri Piotta .02 .10
183 Alexander Yakushev CO .08 .25
184 Petr Malkov ATR .02 .10
185 Markus Bachschmied .15 .40
186 Paolo Della Bella .15 .40
187 Pauli Jaks .20 .50
188 Brenno Celio .02 .10
189 Tiziano Gianini .07 .20
190 Fabian Gull .02 .10
191 Noel Guyaz .02 .10
192 Jakub Horak .02 .10
193 Alessandro Reinhart .02 .10
194 Luigi Riva .02 .10
195 Gianni Sanese .02 .10
196 Oskar Szczepaniec .02 .10
197 Mattia Baldi .02 .10
198 Nicola Celio .02 .10
199 Dmitri Denisov .02 .10
200 Gaby Epiney .02 .10
201 John Fritsche .02 .10
202 Patrick Glanzmann .02 .10
203 Thomas Heldner .02 .10
204 Paolo Imperatori .02 .10
205 Peter Jaks .02 .10
206 Dimitri Kvartalnov .20 .50
207 Omar Tognini .02 .10
208 Nicola Pini .02 .10
209 Luca Vigano .02 .10
210 Theo Wittmann .02 .10
211 Rapperswil .02 .10
212 Rapperswil .02 .10
213 Pekka Rautakallio TR .08 .25
214 Ueli Scheidegger ATR .02 .10
215 Claudio Bayer .15 .40
216 Christian Cretin .15 .40
217 Daniel Bunzli .02 .10
218 Marco Capaul .02 .10
219 Roland Kradolfer .02 .10
220 Blair Muller .02 .10
221 Andreas Ritsch .02 .10
222 Daniel Rutschi .02 .10
223 Roger Sigg .02 .10
224 Adrian Bachofner .02 .10
225 Arthur Camenzind .02 .10
226 Christian Hofstetter .02 .10
227 Michael Meier .02 .10
228 Mike Richard .07 .20
229 Harry Rogenmoser .02 .10
230 Andy Rufener .02 .10
231 Sergio Soguel .02 .10
232 Gilles Thibaudeau .08 .25
233 Roger Thony .02 .10
234 Marc Weber .02 .10
235 Marco Werder .02 .10
236 Lausanne HC .02 .10
237 Jean Lussier TR .02 .10
238 Thierry Andrey .15 .40
239 Beat Kindler .15 .40
240 Jean Gagnon .02 .10
241 Fabian Guignard .02 .10
242 Philippe Marquis .02 .10
243 Stephan Schneider .02 .10
244 Roland Simonet .02 .10
245 Ivo Stoffel .02 .10
246 Marcel Wick .02 .10
247 Raymond Wyssen .02 .10
248 Martin Desjardins .02 .10
249 Maxime Lapointe .02 .10
250 Bruno Maurer .02 .10
251 Frank Monnier .02 .10
252 Cyrill Pasche .02 .10
253 Laurent Pasquini .02 .10
254 Alain Reymond .02 .10
255 Yannick Robert .02 .10
256 Kevin Schlapfer .02 .10
257 Gabriel Taccoz .02 .10
258 Claude Verret .02 .10
259 Gerd Zenhausern .02 .10
260 Biel .02 .10
261 Biel .02 .10
262 Barry Jenkins TR .02 .10
263 Sacha Devaux .15 .40
264 Christoph Wahl .15 .40
265 Beat Cattaruzza .02 .10
266 Sven Dick .02 .10
267 Claudio Ghillioni .02 .10
268 Stefan Lutz .02 .10
269 Guido Pfosi .02 .10
270 Sven Schmid .02 .10
271 Daniel Schneider .02 .10
272 Frank Aeschlimann .02 .10
273 Thomas Burillo .02 .10
274 Stefan Choffat .02 .10
275 Reynald DeRitz .02 .10
276 Marco Dick .02 .10
277 Ralph Donghi .02 .10
278 Stefan Groff .02 .10
279 Andrej Kwartalnov .02 .10
280 Albert Malgin .02 .10
281 Oliver Muller .02 .10
282 Michel Riesen .75 2.00
283 Bernhard Schumperli .08 .25
284 Mike Tschumi .02 .10
285 Grasshoppers .02 .10
286 Grasshoppers .02 .10
287 Bruno Aegerter CO .02 .10
288 Matti Alatalo ATR .02 .10
289 Marcel Kohli .15 .40
290 Stephan Morf .15 .40
291 Michel Faeh .02 .10
292 Marc Haueter .02 .10
293 Roman Honegger .02 .10
294 Arne Ramholt .02 .10
295 Hannu Virta .08 .25
296 Rolf Ziegler .02 .10
297 Jerry Zuurmond .02 .10
298 Alain Ayer .02 .10
299 Andre Baumann .02 .10
300 Warren Bruetsch .02 .10
301 Pascal Faeh .02 .10
302 Roman Furrer .02 .10
303 Marco Hagmann .02 .10
304 Dominik Jenny .02 .10
305 Mika Nieminen .02 .10
306 Fabio Obrist .02 .10
307 Thierry Paterlini .02 .10
308 Marco Schellenberg .02 .10
309 Mathias Schenkel .02 .10
310 Peter Schlagenhauf .02 .10
311 Markus Studer .02 .10
312 Thomas Ziegler .02 .10
313 Thurgau .02 .10
314 Thurgau .02 .10
315 Mike McParland TR .02 .10
316 Fritz Lanz ATR .02 .10
317 Roger Hugentobler .15 .40
318 Peter Martin .15 .40
319 Dominik Schmid .02 .10
320 Andrea Baumgartner .02 .10
321 Nicolas Goumaz .02 .10
322 Martin Granicher .02 .10
323 Ralph Ott .02 .10
324 Henry Patrick .02 .10
325 Mike Posma .02 .10
326 Marcel Schmid .02 .10
327 Robert Wiesmann .02 .10
328 Dan Daoust .20 .50
329 Slaven Imhof .02 .10
330 Roger Keller .02 .10
331 Martin Knopfli .02 .10
332 Guido Laczko .02 .10
333 Bernhard Lauber .02 .10
334 Gery Othman .02 .10
335 Rolf Schrepfer .02 .10
336 Thomas Seitz .02 .10
337 Robert Slehofer .02 .10
338 Rene Stussi .02 .10
339 Cuno Weisser .02 .10
340 Benjamin Winkler .02 .10
341 Langnau .02 .10
342 Langnau .02 .10
343 Paul Andre Cadieux TR .02 .10
344 Jakob Kolliker ATR .02 .10
345 Thomas Dreier .15 .40
346 Toni Koller .15 .40
347 Daniel Aegerter .02 .10
348 Raoul Baumgartner .02 .10
349 Andreas Beutler .02 .10
350 Urs Hirschi .02 .10
351 Stefan Probst .02 .10
352 Raphael Schneider .02 .10
353 Pascal Stoller .02 .10
354 Rolf Badertscher .02 .10
355 Peter Bartschi .02 .10
356 Beat Friedrich .02 .10
357 Walter Gerber .02 .10
358 Kelly Glowa .02 .10
359 Alan Hirschi .02 .10
360 Markus Hirschi .02 .10
361 Gregor Horak .02 .10
362 Lane Lambert .08 .25
363 Beat Nuspliger .02 .10
364 Stefan Tschiemer .02 .10
365 Chaux De Fonds .02 .10
366 Chaux De Fonds .02 .10
367 Riccardo Fuhrer TR .02 .10
368 Roland Meyer .15 .40
369 Jean-Luc Schnegg .15 .40
370 Eric Bourquin .02 .10
371 Daniel Dubois .02 .10
372 Andres Egger .02 .10
373 Daniel Elsener .02 .10
374 Thierry Murisier .02 .10
375 Daniel Ott .02 .10
376 Jorg Reber .02 .10
377 Valeri Chiriaev .02 .10
378 Michele Bizzozero .02 .10
379 Philippe Bozon .40 1.00
380 Jean-Marc Brunner .02 .10
381 Florian Chappot .02 .10
382 Gilles Dubois .02 .10
383 Willy Kohler .02 .10
384 Boris Leimgruber .02 .10
385 Patrick Oppliger .02 .10
386 Benoit Pont .02 .10
387 Laurent Stehlin .02 .10
388 Olivier Wuthrich .02 .10
389 Herisau .02 .10
390 Herisau .02 .10
391 Mark McGregor TR .02 .10
392 Reto Roveda ATR .02 .10
393 Michael Habig .15 .40
394 Ronald Rueger .15 .40
395 Urs Balzarek .02 .10
396 Thomas Derungs .02 .10
397 Damian Freitag .02 .10
398 Roland Habisreutinger .02 .10
399 Marco Knecht .02 .10
400 Karl Knopf .02 .10
401 Andy Maag .02 .10
402 Krister Cantoni .02 .10
403 Rico Enzler .02 .10
404 John Fust .02 .10
405 Remo Gastaldo .02 .10
406 Reto German .02 .10
407 Frank Guay .02 .10
408 Daniel Knecht .02 .10
409 Andy Krapf .02 .10
410 Roger Nater .02 .10
411 Marco Tanner .02 .10
412 Claude Vilgrain .40 1.00
413 Chur .02 .10
414 Chur .02 .10
415 Juri Voshakov TR .02 .10
416 Thomas Liesch .15 .40
417 Reto Zuccolini .15 .40
418 Sacha Bleiker .02 .10
419 Patrick Fischer .02 .10
420 Bruno Habisreutinger .02 .10
421 Jurg Hardegger .02 .10
422 Dominic Meier .02 .10
423 Loris Papa .02 .10
424 Robert Papp .02 .10
425 Valery Belov .02 .10
426 Valery Cherny .02 .10
427 Miguel Fondado .02 .10
428 Oliver Gazzaroli .02 .10
429 Claudio Krattli .02 .10
430 Claudio Peer .02 .10
431 Michael Putzi .02 .10
432 Roger Rieder .02 .10
433 Riccardo Signorell .02 .10
434 Peter Thoma .02 .10
435 Patrick Werthan .02 .10
436 Olten .02 .10
437 Olten .02 .10
438 Milan Mrukvia ATR .02 .10
439 Beat Aebischer .15 .40
440 Thierry Loup .15 .40
441 Ralph Gugelmann .02 .10
442 Roland Ruedi .02 .10
443 Andre Schneeberger .02 .10
444 Richard Stucki .02 .10
445 Thomas Studer .02 .10
446 Ville Siren .08 .25
447 Pius Weber .02 .10
448 Rene Ackermann .02 .10
449 Lars Aebi .02 .10
450 Andreas Fischer .02 .10
451 Marcel Franzi .02 .10
452 Paul Gagne .20 .50
453 Stephane Gasser .02 .10
454 Pirmin Keller .02 .10
455 Claude Luthi .02 .10
456 Patrick Siegwart .02 .10
457 Patrik Traber .02 .10
458 Andre Van Rohr .02 .10
459 HCM .02 .10
460 Kent Ruhnke TR .02 .10
461 Patrick Grand .15 .40
462 Didier Tosi .15 .40
463 Pascal Avanthay .02 .10
464 Bernard Bauer .02 .10
465 Ayocholos Escher .02 .10
466 Thierry Evequoz .02 .10
467 David Jelmini .02 .10
468 Xavier Kappeler .02 .10
469 Patrik Neukom .02 .10
470 Pierre-Alain Ancay .02 .10
471 Florian Andenmatten .02 .10
472 J-Daniel Bonito .02 .10
473 Alain Darbellay .02 .10
474 Olivier Ecoeur .02 .10
475 Igor Fedulov .02 .10
476 Nicolas Gastaldo .02 .10
477 Thierry Moret .02 .10
478 Stephan Nussberger .02 .10
479 Achim Pleschberger .02 .10
480 Petr Rosol .02 .10
481 Fabrizio Silietti .02 .10
482 Yannick Theler .02 .10
483 Geneve .02 .10
484 Geneve .02 .10
485 Francois Huppe TR .02 .10
486 Gary Shennan ATR .02 .10
487 Jean-Philippe Challande .15 .40
488 Jerome Hagmann .15 .40
489 Claude Cienciala .02 .10
490 Chris Felix .02 .10
491 Romain Fleury .02 .10
492 Daniel Herlea .02 .10
493 Camille Meylan .02 .10
494 Toni Nelli .02 .10
495 Christian Serena .02 .10
496 David Leibzig .02 .10
497 Antoine Cloux .02 .10
498 Nicolas Corthay .02 .10
499 Marc Hinni .02 .10
500 Olivier Honsberger .02 .10
501 Gael Kertudo .02 .10
502 Jorg Ledermann .02 .10
503 Andrew McKim .20 .50
504 Benjamin Muller .02 .10
505 Martin Stastny .02 .10
506 Michel Wicky .02 .10
507 Schwiezer .08 .25
508 Christian Weber .20 .50
509 Jean-Jacques Aeschlimann .08 .25
510 Sandro Bertaggia .20 .50
511 Lars Weibel .20 .50
512 Tommy Sjodin .08 .25
513 Andrei Khomutov .20 .50
514 Lars Weibel .20 .50
515 Anders Eldebrink .08 .25
516 Ken Yaremchuk .20 .50
517 Reto Pavoni .20 .50
518 Dino Kessler .02 .10
519 Fausto Mazzoleni .02 .10
520 Andy Ton .02 .10
521 Dan Hodgson .20 .50
522 Roman Wager .02 .10
523 Reto Pavoni .20 .50

524 Reijo Ruotsalainen .20 .50
525 Tommy Sjodin .08 .25
526 Andrej Kwartalnov .02 .10
527 Mikael Johansson .02 .10
528 Ken Yaremchuk .40 1.00
529 Reto Pavoni .20 .50
530 Dino Kessler .02 .10
531 Marco Bayer .02 .10
532 Misko Antisin .02 .10
533 Sacha Ochsner .02 .10
534 Roman Wager .02 .10
535 Reto Pavoni .20 .50
536 Reijo Ruotsalainen .20 .50
537 Andreas Eldebrink .08 .25
538 Ken Yaremchuk .40 1.00
539 Mikael Johansson .02 .10
540 Tom Fergus .40 1.00
541 Dan Quinn .20 .50
542 Valeri Kamenski .40 1.00
543 Phil Housley .40 1.00
544 Chris Chelios 6.00 15.00
545 Doug Gilmour 6.00 15.00
NNO Beat Eichmann .02 .10
NNO Danny Kurmann .02 .10
NNO Reto Bertolotti .02 .10
NNO Roland Stadler .02 .10
NNO Beat Eichmann .02 .10

1996-97 Swiss HNL

COMPLETE SET (588) 40.00 80.00
1 EHC Kloten .02 .10
2 Fleming CO .02 .10
3 Schumacher .02 .10
4 Reto Pavoni .02 .10
5 Walter .02 .10
6 Marco Bayer .02 .10
7 Greg Brown .02 .10
8 Martin Bruderer .02 .10
9 Marco Kloti .02 .10
10 Marco Knecht .02 .10
11 Michael Kress .02 .10
12 Bjorn Schneider .02 .10
13 Daniel Weber .02 .10
14 Robin Bauer .02 .10
15 Charles Berglund .02 .10
16 Matthias Bachler .02 .10
17 Manuele Celio .02 .10
18 Patrick Della Rossa .02 .10
19 Jorg Eberle .02 .10
20 Felix Hollenstein .02 .10
21 Mathias Holzer .02 .10
22 Mikael Johansson .02 .10
23 Martin Pluss .02 .10
24 Frederic Rothen .02 .10
25 Roman Wager .02 .10
26 SC Bern .02 .10
27 Chuck Lefley CO .02 .10
28 Schwarz .02 .10
29 Renato Tosio .02 .10
30 Alex Reinhard .02 .10
31 Timo Jutila .02 .10
32 Christian Langer .02 .10
33 Sven Leuenberger .02 .10
34 Martin Rauch .02 .10
35 Ville Siren .02 .10
36 Martin Steinegger .02 .10
37 Gaetan Voisard .02 .10
38 Rene Friedli .02 .10
39 Regis Fuchs .02 .10
40 Patrick Howald .02 .10
41 Vincent Lechenne .02 .10
42 Stefan Moser .02 .10
43 Trevor Meier .02 .10
44 Gil Montandon .02 .10
45 Michael Mouther .02 .10
46 Laurent Muller .02 .10
47 Philippe Mueller .02 .10
48 Gates Orlando .20 .50
49 Thierry Paterlini .02 .10
50 Roberto Triulzi .02 .10
51 EV Zug .02 .10
52 Jim Kolett CO .02 .10
53 Simpson .02 .10
54 Patrick Schopf .02 .10
55 Ronnie Rueger .02 .10
56 Livio Fazio .02 .10
57 Stefan Grauwiler .02 .10
58 Dino Kessler .02 .10
59 Andre Kunzi .02 .10
60 Thomas Kunzi .02 .10
61 John Miner .02 .10
62 Patrick Sutter .02 .10
63 Steve Aebersold .02 .10
64 Misko Antisin .02 .10
65 Patrick Fischer .02 .10
66 Daniel Giger .02 .10
67 Stephen Grogg .02 .10
68 Bill McDougall .02 .10
69 Colin Muller .02 .10
70 Phil Neuenschwander .02 .10
71 Philipp Orlandi .02 .10
72 Andre Rotheli .02 .10
73 Chad Silver .02 .10
74 Franz Steffen .02 .10
75 Wes Walz .75 2.00
76 HC Ambri Piotta .02 .10
77 Alexander Jakushev CO .20 .50
78 Pauli Jaks .20 .50
79 Paolo Della Bella .02 .10
80 Brenno Celio .02 .10
81 Ivan Gazzaroli .02 .10
82 Tiziano Gianini .02 .10
83 Noel Guyaz .02 .10
84 Jakub Horak .02 .10
85 Alessandro Reinhart .02 .10
86 Oskar Szczepaniec .02 .10
87 Dmitri Tsygurov .02 .10
88 Mattia Baldi .02 .10
89 Nicola Celio .02 .10
90 John Fritsche .02 .10
91 Patrick Glanzmann .02 .10
92 Thomas Heldner .02 .10
93 Peter Jaks .02 .10
94 Dmitri Kvartalnov .20 .50
95 Oleg Petrov .02 .10
96 Omar Tognini .02 .10
97 Igor Chibirev .02 .10
98 Luca Vigano .02 .10
99 Theo Wittmann .02 .10
100 HC Davos .02 .10
101 Del Curto CO .02 .10
102 Evgeni Popichin ACO .02 .10
103 Nando Wieser .02 .10
104 Thomas Berger .02 .10
105 Samuel Balmer .02 .10
106 Beat Equilino .02 .10
107 Marc Gianola .02 .10
108 Malier .02 .10
109 Valeri Shiryaev .02 .10
110 Daniel Sigg .02 .10
111 Mark Streit .40 1.00
112 Jan Von Arx .02 .10
113 Dan Hodgson .02 .10
114 Philipp Luber .02 .10
115 Rene Mueller .02 .10
116 Andy Naser .02 .10
117 Sergei Petrenko .02 .10
118 Oliver Roth .02 .10
119 Ivo Ruthemann .02 .10
120 Mario Schocher .02 .10
121 Reto Stirnimann .02 .10
122 Reto Von Arx .20 .50
123 Christian Weber .02 .10
124 Ken Yaremchuk .20 .50
125 SC Rapperswil Jona .02 .10
126 Pekka Rautakallio CO .02 .10
127 Ueli Scheidegger .02 .10
128 Claudio Bayer .02 .10
129 Remo Wehrli .02 .10
130 Daniel Buenzli .02 .10
131 Marko Capaul .02 .10
132 Kari Martikainen .02 .10
133 Dominic Meier .02 .10
134 Blair Muller .02 .10
135 Mathias Seger .02 .10
136 Roger Sigg .02 .10
137 Adrian Bachofner .02 .10
138 Arthur Camenzind .02 .10
139 Oliver Hoffmann .02 .10
139 Daniel Bunzli .02 .10
140 Christian Hofstetter .02 .10
141 Michael Meier .02 .10
142 Mike Richard .02 .10
143 Harry Rogenmoser .02 .10
144 Sergio Soguel .02 .10
145 Gilles Thibaudeau .02 .10
146 Roger Thony .02 .10
147 Mark Weber .02 .10
148 Christian Wolhwend .02 .10
149 HC Lugano .02 .10
150 Mats Waltin CO .02 .10
151 Gunnar Leidborg .02 .10
152 Lars Weibel .20 .50
153 Davide Gislimberti .02 .10
154 Sandro Bertaggia .02 .10
155 Fabian Guignard .02 .10
156 David Jelmini .02 .10
157 Rudi Niderost .02 .10
158 Luigi Riva .02 .10
159 Tommy Sjodin .02 .10
160 Rick Tschumi .02 .10
161 Jerry Zuurmond .02 .10
162 J.-J. Aeschlimann .02 .10
163 Markus Butler .02 .10
164 Gian-Marco Crameri .02 .10
165 Bruno Erni .02 .10
166 Keith Fair .02 .10
167 Marcel Jenni .02 .10
168 Marcel Franzi .02 .10
169 Stephan Lebeau .20 .50
170 Stefano Togni .02 .10
171 Andy Ton .02 .10
172 Raymond Walder .02 .10
173 Marco Werder .02 .10
174 Michael Nylander .20 .50
175 Zurcher SC .02 .10
176 Alpo Suhonen CO .02 .10
177 Frutiger .02 .10
178 Thomas Papp .02 .10
179 M. Muller .02 .10
180 Patrick Hager .02 .10
181 Martin Kout .02 .10
182 Robert Nordmark .02 .10
183 Didier Princi .02 .10
184 Edgar Salis .02 .10
185 Bruno Sleck .02 .10
186 Nicolas Steiger .02 .10
187 Andreas Zehnder .02 .10
188 Mario Brodmann .02 .10
189 Marc Fortier .02 .10
190 Axel Heim .02 .10
191 Vjeran Ivankovic .02 .10
192 Sandy Jeannin .02 .10
193 Peter Kobel .02 .10
194 Patrick Lebeau .20 .50
195 Claudio Micheli .02 .10
196 Patrizio Morger .02 .10
197 Bruno Vollmer .02 .10
198 Michel Zeiter .02 .10
199 Gerd Zenhausern .02 .10
200 HC Fribourg .02 .10
201 Larsson CO .02 .10
202 Courvoisier .02 .10
203 Thomas Ostlund .02 .10
204 Steve Meuwly .02 .10
205 David Aebischer 4.00 10.00
206 Fredy Bobillier .02 .10
207 Patrice Brasey .02 .10
208 Antoine Descloux .02 .10
209 Andi Egli .02 .10
210 Christian Hofstetter .02 .10
211 Oliver Keller .02 .10
212 Philippe Marquis .02 .10
213 Marc Werlen .02 .10
214 Christophe Brown .02 .10
215 Slava Bykov .20 .50
216 David Dousse .02 .10
217 Stefan Choffat .02 .10
218 Andrei Khomutov .20 .50
219 Daniel Meier .02 .10
220 Patrick Oppliger .02 .10
221 Mario Rottaris .02 .10
222 Pascal Schaller .02 .10
223 Didier Schafer .02 .10
224 Al Raymond .02 .10
225 HC La Chaux De Fonds .02 .10
226 Ricardo Fuhrer CO .02 .10
227 Jean-Luc Schnegg .02 .10
228 Roland Meyer .02 .10
229 Eric Bourquin .02 .10
230 Rob Cowie .02 .10
231 Daniel Dubois .02 .10
232 Dan Eisener .02 .10
233 Thierry Murisier .02 .10
234 Dany Ott .02 .10
235 Jorg Reber .02 .10
236 Pascal Sommer .02 .10
237 Jan Alston .40 1.00
238 Florian Andenmatten .02 .10
239 Loic Burkhalter .02 .10
240 Christer Cantoni .02 .10
241 Florian Chappot .02 .10
242 Michael Diener .02 .10
243 Gilles Dubois .02 .10
244 Rob Gaudreau .02 .10
245 Boris Liemgruber .02 .10
246 Benoit Pont .02 .10
247 Bernhard Schumperli .02 .10
248 Michel Wicky .02 .10
249 HC Lausanne .02 .10
250 Johnston .02 .10
251 Beat Kindler .02 .10
252 Bernhard Lauber .02 .10
253 Sebastien De Allegri .02 .10
254 Thierry Evequoz .02 .10
255 Nicolas Goumaz .02 .10
256 Cull .02 .10
257 Ivo Stoffel .02 .10
258 Turcotte .02 .10
259 Philippe Bozon .40 1.00
260 Johan Bertholet .02 .10
261 Andre Doll .02 .10
262 Rolf Ziegler .02 .10
263 Horvath .02 .10
264 Bruno Maurer .02 .10
265 Alfie Michaud .20 .50
266 Frank Monnier .02 .10
267 Patrice Pellet .02 .10
268 Mario Seeholzer .02 .10
269 Robert Slehofer .02 .10
270 Laurent Stehlin .02 .10
271 Grasshoppers .02 .10
272 Bruno Aegerter .02 .10
273 Alatalo .02 .10
274 Marcel Kohli .02 .10
275 Olivier Wissmann .02 .10
276 Martin Brich .02 .10
277 Marc Haueter .02 .10
278 FahM. .02 .10
279 Roman Honegger .02 .10
280 Arne Ramholt .02 .10
281 Daniel Rutschi .02 .10
282 Alain Ayer .02 .10
283 Andre Baumann .02 .10
284 Warren Brutsch .02 .10
285 Roman Furrer .02 .10
286 Marco Hagmann .02 .10
287 Patrick Looser .02 .10
288 Lasse Nieminen .02 .10
289 Andy Rufener .02 .10
290 Christian Ruuttu .20 .50
291 Mathias Schenkel .02 .10
292 Peter Schlagenhauf .02 .10
293 HC Thurgau .02 .10
294 Mike McParland .02 .10
295 Peter Martin .02 .10
296 Sutter .02 .10
297 Martin Granicher .02 .10
298 Henry .02 .10
299 Ralph Ott .02 .10
300 Mike Posma .02 .10
301 Marcel Schmid .02 .10
302 Christian Schuster .02 .10
303 Robort Wiesmann .02 .10
304 Dan Daoust .02 .10
305 Slaven Imhof .02 .10
306 Matthias Keller .02 .10
307 Ronny Keller .02 .10
308 Guido Laczko .02 .10
309 Don McLaren .02 .10
310 Gery Othman .02 .10
311 Rolf Schrepfer .02 .10
312 Rene Stussi .02 .10
313 Cuno Weisser .02 .10
314 Benjamin Winkler .02 .10
315 SC Langnau .02 .10
316 Paul-Andre Cadieux .02 .10
317 Jakub Kolliker .02 .10
318 Martin Gerber ERC 4.00 10.00
319 Thomas Dreier .02 .10
320 Daniel Aegerter .02 .10
321 Raoul Baumgartner .02 .10
322 Andreas Beutler .02 .10
323 Mario Doyon .02 .10
324 Roland Kradolfer .02 .10
325 Raphael Schneider .02 .10
326 Pascal Stoller .02 .10
327 Rolf Badertscher .02 .10
328 Bruno Brechbuhl .02 .10
329 Peter Bartschi .02 .10
330 Walter Gerber .02 .10
331 Markus Hirschi .02 .10
332 Jakub Horak .02 .10
333 Andreas Keller .02 .10
334 Beat Nuspliger .02 .10
335 Greg Parks .02 .10
336 Kevin Schlapfer .02 .10
337 Stefan Tschiemer .02 .10
338 SC Herisau .02 .10
339 McGregor .02 .10
340 Markus Bachschmied .02 .10
341 Schiess .02 .10
342 Urs Balzarek .02 .10
343 Damien Freitag .02 .10
344 Fritz .02 .10
345 Thomas Jaggli .02 .10
346 Karl Knopf .02 .10
347 Andy Krapf .02 .10
348 Andy Maag .02 .10
349 Devin Edgerton .02 .10
350 Rico Enzler .02 .10
351 John Fust .02 .10
352 Martin Hanggi .02 .10
353 Francois Marquis .02 .10
354 Ludwig Marek .02 .10
355 Pinelli .02 .10
356 Ivo Ruthemann .02 .10
357 Scheiwiller .02 .10
358 Claude Vilgrain .40 1.00
359 Sacha Weibel .02 .10
360 HC Martigny .02 .10
361 Steve Pochon .02 .10
362 Patrick Grand .02 .10
363 Didier Tosi .02 .10
364 Pascal Avanthay .02 .10
365 Jean-Michel Clavien .02 .10
366 Ayocholos Escher .02 .10
367 Alan Hirschi .02 .10
368 Patrik Neukom .02 .10
369 Benedikt Sapin .02 .10
370 Marc Zurbriggen .02 .10
371 Jean-Daniel Bonito .02 .10
372 Igor Fedulov .02 .10
373 Nicolas Gastaldo .02 .10
374 Paolo Imperatori .02 .10
375 Thierry Moret .02 .10
376 Stephan Nussberger .02 .10
377 Petr Rosol .02 .10
378 Fabrizio Silietti .02 .10
379 Yannick Theler .02 .10
380 Natal Zurbriggen .02 .10
381 EHC Biel-Bienne .02 .10
382 Michael Zettel .02 .10
383 Christoph Wahl .02 .10
384 Devaux .02 .10
385 Sven Dick .02 .10
386 Romain Fleury .02 .10
387 Claudio Ghillioni .02 .10
388 Urs Hirschi .02 .10
389 Sven Schmid .02 .10
390 Daniel Schneider .02 .10
391 Alain Villard .02 .10
392 Thomas Burillo .02 .10
393 Reynald De Ritz .02 .10
394 Marco Dick .02 .10
395 Paul Gagne .02 .10
396 Gabriel Taccoz .02 .10
397 Shawn Heaphy .02 .10
398 Maxime Lapointe .02 .10
399 Luthi .02 .10
400 Serge Meyer .02 .10
401 Cyrill Pasche .02 .10
402 Michel Riesen .02 .10
403 HC Geneve-Servette .02 .10
404 Huppe .02 .10
405 Hagmann .02 .10
406 Michel Pilet .02 .10
407 Francesco Bizzozero .02 .10
408 Daniel Herlea .02 .10
409 Pascal Lamprecht .02 .10
410 Thevoz .02 .10
411 Daniel Zieri .02 .10
412 Christian Serena .02 .10
413 Nicolas Studer .02 .10
414 Joel Aeschlimann .02 .10
415 Antoine Cloux .02 .10
416 Claude Verret .02 .10
417 Martin Desjardins .02 .10
418 Olivier Ecoeur .02 .10
419 Gaby Epiney .02 .10
420 Laurent Faller .02 .10
421 Nicholas Gauch .02 .10
422 Olivier Honsberger .02 .10
423 Gael Kertudo .02 .10
424 Jorg Ledermann .02 .10
425 EHC Olten .02 .10
426 Hoffmann .02 .10
427 Beat Aebischer .02 .10
428 Thierry Loup .02 .10
429 Ralph Gugelmann .02 .10
430 Bruno Habisreutinger .02 .10
431 Phillippe Portner .02 .10
432 Gianni Sanese .02 .10
433 Schonauer .02 .10
434 Richard Stucki .02 .10
435 Thomas Studer .02 .10
436 Dobler .02 .10
437 Yanick Dube .02 .10
438 Mario Koppel .02 .10
439 Luthi .02 .10
440 Muller .02 .10
441 Nicola Pini .02 .10
442 Thomas Seitz .02 .10
443 Patrick Siegwart .02 .10
444 Pirmin Keller .02 .10
445 Andre Von Rohr .02 .10
446 Andre Von Rohr .02 .10
447 EHC Chur .02 .10
448 Voschakov .02 .10
449 Thomas Liesch .02 .10
450 Reto Zuccolini .02 .10
451 Armin Berchtold .02 .10
452 Sacha Bleiker .02 .10
453 Sandro Capaul .02 .10
454 Patrick Fischer .02 .10
455 Andreas Ritsch .02 .10
456 Stefan Schneider .02 .10
457 Roland Simonet .02 .10
458 Rene Ackermann .02 .10
459 Andreas Fischer .02 .10
460 Miguel Fondado .02 .10
461 Claudio Peer .02 .10
462 Reto Germann .02 .10
463 Albert Malgin .02 .10
464 Roger Rieder .02 .10
465 Michael Rosenast .02 .10
466 Riccardo Signorell .02 .10
467 Harijs Vitolinsh .02 .10
468 Patrick Werthan .02 .10
469 Nussle .02 .10
470 SC Luzern .02 .10
471 Hansson .02 .10
472 Beat Lautenschlager .02 .10
473 Patrice Bosch .02 .10
474 Rosset .02 .10
475 Alain Comte .02 .10
476 Dominik Jenny .02 .10
477 Samuelsson .02 .10
478 Ron Stillhardt .02 .10
479 Marco Tanner .02 .10
480 Markus Wetter .02 .10
481 Martin Bahnik .02 .10
482 Baiada .02 .10
483 Buchel .02 .10
484 Marco Fischer .02 .10
485 P. Giger .02 .10
486 Daniel Lamminger .02 .10
487 M. Ledermann .02 .10
488 Daniel Mares .02 .10
489 P. Mares .02 .10
490 Marco Mozzini .02 .10
491 Mario Schocher .02 .10
492 Ramil Yuldaschev .02 .10
493 Ron Stillhardt .02 .10
494 HC Ajoie .02 .10
495 Hans Kossmann .02 .10
496 Christian Cretin .02 .10
497 Rosado .02 .10
498 Rapheal Berger .02 .10
499 Matthias Bachler .02 .10
500 Erich Frey .02 .10
501 Heusler .02 .10
502 M. Reinhard .02 .10
503 Julien Vauclair ERC .40 1.00
504 Yann Voillat .02 .10
505 Patrick Adami .02 .10
506 Denis Chalifoux .02 .10
507 Guyaz .02 .10
508 Alexandre Von Arb .02 .10
509 Holmberg .02 .10
510 Honegger .02 .10
511 Herve Meyer .02 .10
512 Marc Fritsche .02 .10
513 Migy .02 .10
514 Giovanni Pestrin .02 .10
515 Geoffrey Vauclair .02 .10
516 Reto Pavoni .02 .10
517 Gaeten Voisard .02 .10
518 Martin Bruderer .02 .10
519 Felix Hollenstein .02 .10
520 Gil Montandon .02 .10
521 Patrick Howald .02 .10
522 National Team .02 .10
523 Schenk .02 .10
524 Paul-Andre Cadieux .02 .10
525 Jakub Kolliker .02 .10
526 Reto Pavoni .02 .10
527 Pauli Jaks .20 .50
528 Samuel Balmer .02 .10
529 Marco Bayer .02 .10
530 Sandro Bertaggia .02 .10
531 Martin Bruderer .02 .10
532 Tiziano Gianini .02 .10
533 Sven Leuenberger .02 .10
534 Gaetan Voisard .02 .10
535 Andreas Zehnder .02 .10
536 Manuele Celio .02 .10
537 Nicola Celio .02 .10
538 Patrick Fischer .02 .10
539 Felix Hollenstein .02 .10
540 Peter Jaks .02 .10
541 Sandy Jeannin .02 .10
542 Marcel Jenni .02 .10
543 Harry Rogenmoser .02 .10
544 Frederic Rothen .02 .10
545 Reto Von Arx .20 .50
546 Christian Weber .02 .10
547 Michel Zeiter .02 .10
548 SIHL .02 .10
549 Swiss National Inline Team .02 .10
550 Alan Wittwer .02 .10
551 Markus Dachschmied .02 .10
552 Waber .02 .10
553 Ochsner .02 .10
554 Mueller .02 .10
555 Bauer .02 .10
556 Ivo Ruthemann .02 .10
557 Sven Lindemann .02 .10
558 Alexandre Von Arb .02 .10
559 Ronnie Rueger .02 .10
561 Klaus .02 .10
562 Guido Lindemann .02 .10
563 Rico Enzler .02 .10
564 Andres Egger .02 .10
565 Kuendig .02 .10
566 Wild .02 .10
567 Johansson .02 .10
568 Patrick Howald .02 .10
569 Muller .02 .10
570 Tschibirev .02 .10
571 Jan Alston .40 1.00
572 Mike Richard .02 .10
573 Stephan Lebeau .20 .50
574 Marc Fortier .02 .10
575 Slava Bykov .20 .50
576 Frank Monnier .02 .10
577 Patrick Oppliger .02 .10
578 Lasse Nieminen .02 .10
579 Dan Daoust .20 .50
580 Glowa .02 .10
581 Claude Vilgrain .40 1.00
582 Petr Rosol .02 .10
583 Dmitri Kvartalnov .20 .50
584 Andrew McKim .20 .50
585 Rene Ackermann .02 .10
586 Valery Cherny .02 .10
587 Referees .02 .10
588 Referees .02 .10

1998-99 Swiss Power Play Stickers

COMPLETE SET (382) 40.00 80.00
1 Team Ambri Left .07 .20
2 Team Ambri Right .07 .20
3 Larry Hurras .07 .20
4 Pauli Jaks .07 .20
5 Peter Martin .07 .20
6 Fredy Bobillier .07 .20
7 Ivan Gazzaroli .07 .20
8 Tiziano Gianini .07 .20
9 Giordano Guidotti .07 .20
10 Leif Rohlin .07 .20
11 Edgar Salis .07 .20
12 Bruno Steck .07 .20
13 Oliver Tschanz .07 .20
14 Mattia Baldi .07 .20
15 Krister Cantoni .07 .20
16 Manuele Celio .07 .20
17 Nicola Celio .07 .20
18 Paul DiPietro .20 .50
19 John Fritsche .07 .20
20 Vjeran Ivankovic .07 .20
21 Oleg Petrov .07 .20
22 Franz Steffen .07 .20
23 Omar Tognini .07 .20
24 Theo Wittmann .07 .20
25 Thomas Ziegler .07 .20
26 Team Bern Left .07 .20
27 Team Bern Right .07 .20
28 Ueli Schwarz .07 .20
29 Renato Tosio .07 .20
30 Reto Schurch .07 .20
31 Alexander Godynyuk .07 .20
32 Sven Leuenberger .07 .20
33 Martin Rauch .07 .20
34 Bjorn Schneider .07 .20
35 Stefan Schneider .07 .20
36 Pascal Sommer .07 .20
37 Martin Steinegger .07 .20
38 Gregor Thommen .07 .20
39 Bjorn Christen .07 .20
40 David Jobin .07 .20
41 Patrick Howald .07 .20
42 Boris Leimgruber .07 .20
43 Lars Leuenberger .07 .20
44 Dave McLlwain .07 .20
45 Gil Montandon .07 .20
46 Daniel Marois .07 .20
47 Michel Mouther .07 .20
48 Thierry Paterlini .07 .20
49 Roberto Triulzi .07 .20
50 Marc Weber .07 .20
51 Team Davos Left .07 .20
52 Team Davos Right .07 .20
53 Arno Del Curto .07 .20
54 Stephane Beauregard .20 .50
55 Marco Wegmuller .07 .20
56 Beat Equilino .07 .20
57 Marc Gianola .07 .20
58 Andrea Haller .07 .20
59 Michael Kress .07 .20
60 Pettri Nummelin .07 .20
61 Mark Streit .40 1.00
62 Jan Von Arx .07 .20
63 Andre Baumann .07 .20
64 Sandy Jeannin .07 .20
65 Rene Muller .07 .20
66 Kai Nurminen .07 .20
67 Peter Kobel .07 .20
68 Sandro Rizzi .07 .20
69 Oliver Roth .07 .20
70 Ivo Ruthemann .07 .20
71 Mario Schocher .07 .20
72 Reto Stirnimann .07 .20
73 Reto Von Arx .20 .50
74 Beat Helbstab .07 .20
75 Timo Helbling .20 .50
76 Team Fribourg Left .07 .20
77 Team Fribourg Right .07 .20
78 Andre Peloffy .07 .20
79 David Aebischer 2.00 5.00
80 Thomas Ostlund .20 .50
81 Alain Sansonnens .07 .20
82 Patrice Brasey .07 .20
83 Antoine Descloux .07 .20
84 Livio Fazio .07 .20
85 Romain Fleury .07 .20
86 Olivier Keller .07 .20
87 Philippe Marquis .07 .20
88 Marc Werlen .07 .20
89 Igor Chibirev .07 .20
90 Flavien Conne .07 .20
91 David Dousse .07 .20
92 Rene Furler .07 .20
93 Daniel Giger .07 .20
94 Goran Bezina .07 .20
95 Philipp Orlandi .07 .20
96 Mario Rottaris .07 .20
97 Pascal Schaller .07 .20
98 Robert Slehofer .07 .20
99 Pavel Torgajev .07 .20
100 Gerd Zenhausern .07 .20
101 Team Kloten Left .07 .20
102 Team Kloten Right .07 .20
103 Reto Pavoni .07 .20
104 Marco Buhrer .07 .20
105 Samuel Balmer .07 .20
106 Marco Bayer .07 .20
107 Martin Bruderer .07 .20
108 Marco Kloti .07 .20
109 Beat Moicr .07 .20
110 Tommy Sjodin .07 .20
111 Daniel Weber .07 .20
112 Benjamin Winkler .07 .20
113 Philipp Folghera .07 .20
114 Thomas Heldner .07 .20
115 Felix Hollenstein .07 .20
116 Sven Lindemann .07 .20
117 Bill McDougall .07 .20
118 Martin Pluss .07 .20
119 Frederic Rothen .07 .20
120 Andy Rufener .07 .20
121 Matthias Schenkel .07 .20
122 Rene Stussi .07 .20
123 Chris Tancill .07 .20
124 Adrian Wichser .07 .20
125 Team Langnau Left .07 .20
126 Team Langnau Right .07 .20
127 Jakob Kolliker .07 .20
128 Martin Gerber 2.00 5.00
129 Ivo Kleeb .07 .20
130 Daniel Aegerter .07 .20
131 Mario Doyon .07 .20
132 Marco Knecht .07 .20
133 Pascal Muller .07 .20
134 Wesley Snell .07 .20
135 Oskar Szczepaniec .07 .20
136 Markus Wuthrich .07 .20
137 Alexis Vacheron .07 .20
138 Rolf Bradertscher .07 .20
139 Peter Bartschi .07 .20
140 Bruno Brechbuhl .07 .20
141 Marc Buhlmann .07 .20
142 Todd Elik .07 .20
143 Marco Fischer .07 .20
144 John Fust .07 .20
145 Andy Keller .07 .20
146 Michael Liniger .07 .20
147 Greg Parks .07 .20
148 Benoit Pont .07 .20
149 Stefan Tschiemer .07 .20
150 Team Lugano Left .07 .20
151 Team Lugano Right .07 .20
152 Jim Koleff CO .07 .20
153 Cristobal Huet 6.00 15.00
154 Lars Weibel .07 .20
155 Peter Andersson .07 .20
156 Mark Astley .07 .20
157 Sandro Bertaggia .07 .20
158 Fabian Guignard .07 .20
159 Rick Tschumi .07 .20
160 Julien Vauclair .20 .50
161 Gaetan Voisard .07 .20
162 Rolf Ziegler .07 .20
163 Jean Jacques Aeschlimann .07 .20
164 Misko Antisin .07 .20
165 Gian Marco Crameri .07 .20
166 Andre Doll .07 .20
167 Keith Fair .07 .20
168 Patrick Fischer .07 .20
169 Regis Fuchs .07 .20
170 Marcel Jenni .07 .20
171 Trevor Meier .07 .20
172 Andy Naser .07 .20
173 Gaetano Orlando .20 .50
174 Geoffrey Vauclair .07 .20
175 Team Rapperswil Left .07 .20
176 Team Rapperswil Right .07 .20
177 Mark McGregor .07 .20
178 Claudio Bayer .07 .20
179 Remo Wehrli .07 .20
180 Marco Capaul .07 .20
181 Christian Langer .07 .20
182 Dominic Meier .07 .20
183 Jorg Reber .07 .20
184 Matthias Seger .07 .20
185 Daniel Sigg .07 .20
186 Roger Sigg .07 .20
187 Adrian Bachofner .07 .20
188 Markus Butler .07 .20
189 Rene Friedli .07 .20
190 Oliver Hoffmann .07 .20
191 Christian Hofstetter .07 .20
192 Chris Lindberg .07 .20
193 Frank Monnier .07 .20
194 Mark Ouimet .07 .20
195 Mike Richard .07 .20
196 Harry Rogenmoser .07 .20
197 Bernhard Schumperli .07 .20
198 Ken Yaremchuk .07 .20
199 Team EVZ Left .07 .20
200 Team EVZ Right .07 .20
201 Sean Simpson .07 .20
202 Ronald Rueger .07 .20
203 Patrick Schopf .07 .20
204 Raphael Berger .07 .20
205 Matthias Holzer .07 .20
206 Jakub Horak .07 .20
207 Dino Kessler .07 .20
208 Reto Kobach .07 .20
209 Andre Kunzi .07 .20
210 Thomas Kunzi .07 .20
211 Patrick Sutter .07 .20
212 Christoph Brown .07 .20
213 Jorg Eberle .07 .20
214 Devin Edgerton .07 .20
215 Stefan Grogg .07 .20
216 Daniel Meier .07 .20
217 Colin Muller .07 .20
218 Patrick Oppliger .07 .20
219 Andre Rotheli .07 .20
220 Sacha Schneider .07 .20
221 Kevin Todd .07 .20
222 Samuel Villiger .07 .20
223 Wes Walz .40 1.00
224 Team ZSC Left .07 .20
225 Team ZSC Right .07 .20
226 Kent Ruhnke .07 .20
227 Thomas Papp .07 .20
228 Ari Sulander .20 .50
229 Martin Brich .07 .20
230 Marc Haueter .07 .20
231 Michel Kamber .07 .20
232 Martin Kout .07 .20
233 Kari Martikainen .07 .20
234 Adrien Plavsic .07 .20
235 Pascal Stoller .07 .20
236 Andreas Zehnder .07 .20
237 Patrik Della Rossa .07 .20
238 Axel Heim .07 .20
239 Dan Hodgson .07 .20
240 Peter Jaks .07 .20
241 Claudio Micheli .07 .20
242 Patrizio Morger .07 .20
243 Laurent Muller .07 .20
244 Rolf Schrepfer .07 .20
245 Chad Silver .07 .20
246 Christian Weber .07 .20
247 Michel Zeiter .07 .20
248 National Team Left .07 .20
249 National Team Right .07 .20
250 Raphael Kruger .07 .20
251 David Aebischer 2.00 5.00
252 Misko Antisin .07 .20
253 Mattia Baldi .07 .20
254 Gian Marco Crameri .07 .20
255 Patrick Fischer .07 .20
256 Peter Jaks .07 .20
257 Sandy Jeannin .07 .20
258 Marcel Jenni .07 .20
259 Dino Kessler .07 .20
260 Claudio Micheli .07 .20
261 Reto Pavoni .07 .20

262 Martin Pluss .07 .20
263 Martin Rauch .07 .20
264 Ivo Ruthemann .07 .20
265 Edgar Salis .07 .20
266 Matthias Seger .07 .20
267 Franz Steffen .07 .20
268 Martin Steinegger .07 .20
269 Mark Streit .20 .50
270 Patrick Sutter .07 .20
271 Reto Von Arx .20 .50
272 Michel Zeiter .07 .20
273 Bill Gilligan .07 .20
274 Marco Buhrer .07 .20
275 Ralph Bundi .07 .20
276 Alex Chatelain .07 .20
277 Bjorn Christen .07 .20
278 Flavien Conne .07 .20
279 Patrick Fischer .07 .20
280 Sven Lindemann .07 .20
281 Michel Mouther .07 .20
282 Laurent Muller .07 .20
283 Marc Reichert .07 .20
284 Alain Reist .07 .20
285 Michel Riesen .20 .50
286 Sandro Rizzi .07 .20
287 Mario Schocher .07 .20
288 Rene Stussi .07 .20
289 Julien Vauclair .20 .50
290 Jan Von Arx .07 .20
291 Marc Werlen .07 .20
292 Adrian Wichser .07 .20
293 Markus Wuthrich .07 .20
294 Thomas Ziegler .07 .20
295 Team Biel Left .07 .20
296 Team Biel Right .07 .20
297 Christian Cretin
Alain Reist .07 .20
298 Sven Schmid
Paul Gagne .07 .20
299 Paul-Andre Cadieux .07 .20
300 Shawn Heaphy
Cyrill Pasche .07 .20
301 Team La Chaux de Fonds Left .07 .20
302 Team La Chaux de Fonds Right .07 .20
303 Thomas Berger
Valeri Schirjaev .07 .20
304 Lugio Riva
Steve Aebersold .07 .20
305 Riccardo Fuhrer .07 .20
306 Stephan Lebeau
Stefano Togni .07 .20
307 Team Chur Left .07 .20
308 Team Chur Right .07 .20
309 Thomas Liesch
Patrick Fischer .07 .20
310 Mike Posma
Mario Brodmann .07 .20
311 Mike McParland .07 .20
312 Harijs Vitolinsh
Reymond Walder .07 .20
313 Team GC Left .07 .20
314 Team GC Right .07 .20
315 Olivier Wissmann
Arne Ramholt .07 .20
316 Marco Schellenberg
Domenic Amodeo .07 .20
317 Dave Tietzen .07 .20
318 Mark Kaufman
Riccardo Signorell .07 .20
319 Team Servette Left .07 .20
320 Team Servette Right .07 .20
321 Steve Meuwly
David Leibzig .07 .20
322 Maxime Lapointe
Christian Serena .07 .20
323 Jean Perron CO .07 .20
324 Mark Jorris
Sandy Smith .07 .20
325 Team Herisau Left .07 .20
326 Team Herisau Right .07 .20
327 Fabian Gull
Robert Burakowsky .07 .20
328 Markus Bachschmied
Urs Balzarek .07 .20
329 Evgeny Popichin .07 .20
330 Alain Fraser
Cuno Weisser .07 .20
331 Team Lausanne Left .07 .20
332 Team Lausannne Right .07 .20
333 Beat Kindler
Serge Poudrier .07 .20
334 Andy Krapf
Jorg Ledermann .07 .20
335 Benoit Laporte .07 .20
336 Slava Bykov
Daniel Nakaoka .07 .20
337 Team Martigny Left .07 .20
338 Team Martigny Right .07 .20
339 Didier Tosi
Jean-Michel Clavien .07 .20
340 Benedict Sapin
Jean-Daniel Bonito .07 .20
341 Petr Rosol .07 .20
342 Nicolas Gastaldo
Thierry Moret .07 .20
343 Team Olten Left .07 .20
344 Team Olten Right .07 .20
345 Beat Aebischer
Richard Stucki .07 .20
346 Igor Boriskov
Albert Malgin .07 .20
347 Markus Graf .07 .20
348 Luca Vigano
Andre Von Rohr .07 .20
349 Team Sierre Left .07 .20
350 Team Sierre Right .07 .20
351 Matthias Lauber
Michel Fah .07 .20
352 Philippe Faust
Bruno Erni .07 .20
353 Christian Wittwer .07 .20
354 Marco Poulsen
Gilles Thibaudeau .07 .20
355 Team Thurgau Left .07 .20
356 Team Thurgau Right .07 .20
357 Marius Bosch
Patrick Henry .07 .20
358 Ralph Ott
Scott Beattie .07 .20
359 Henryk Gruth .07 .20
360 Kevin Miehm
Roman Wager .07 .20
A SEHV
LSHG .07 .20
B HC Ambri Piotta .07 .20
C SC Bern .07 .20
D HC Davos .07 .20
E HC Fribourg Gotteron .07 .20
F EHC Kloten .07 .20
G SC Langnau .07 .20
H HC Lugano .07 .20
I SC Rapperswil-Jona .07 .20
J EV Zug .07 .20
K ZSC Lions .07 .20
L EHC Biel-Bienne .07 .20
M HC La Chaux De Fonds .07 .20
N EHC Chur .07 .20
O Grasshoppers .07 .20
P HC Geneve Servette .07 .20
Q SC Herisau .07 .20
R HC Lausanne .07 .20
S EHC Martigny .07 .20
T EHC Olten .07 .20
U HC Sierre .07 .20
V HC Thurgau .07 .20

1999-00 Swiss Panini Stickers

COMPLETE SET (380) 40.00 80.00
1 Team Ambri Left .07 .20
2 Team Ambri Right .07 .20
3 Larry Huras .07 .20
4 Pauli Jaks .07 .20
5 Peter Martin .07 .20
6 Fredy Bobillier .07 .20
7 Ivan Gazzaroli .07 .20
8 Tiziano Gianini .07 .20
9 John Gobbi .07 .20
10 Thomas Kunzi .07 .20
11 Leif Rohlin .07 .20
12 Bruno Steck .07 .20
13 Krister Cantoni .07 .20
14 Manuele Celio .07 .20
15 Nicola Celio .07 .20
16 Luca Cereda .20 .50
17 Alain Demuth .07 .20
18 Paolo Duca .07 .20
19 John Fritsche .07 .20
20 Ryan Gardner .07 .20
21 Vitaly Lakhmatov .07 .20
22 Stephan Lebeau .20 .50
23 Patrick Lebeau .20 .50
24 Franz Steffen .07 .20
25 Thomas Ziegler .07 .20
26 Team Bern Left .07 .20
27 Team Bern Right .07 .20
28 Pekka Rautakallio CO .07 .20
29 Martin Kilchor .07 .20
30 Renato Tosio .07 .20
31 David Jobin .07 .20
32 Sven Leuenberger .07 .20
33 Petri Liimatainen .07 .20
34 Martin Rauch .07 .20
35 Pascal Sommer .07 .20
36 Martin Steinegger .07 .20
37 Fabian Stephan .07 .20
38 Gregor Thommen .07 .20
39 Alex Chatelain .07 .20
40 Bjorn Christen .07 .20
41 Patrick Howald .07 .20
42 Roland Kaser .07 .20
43 Boris Leimgruber .07 .20
44 Lars Leuenberger .07 .20
45 Dave McLlwain .07 .20
46 Thierry Paterlini .07 .20
47 Jackson Penney .07 .20
48 Marc Reichert .07 .20
49 Ivo Ruthemann .07 .20
50 Marc Weber .07 .20
51 Team Davos Left .07 .20
52 Team Davos Right .07 .20
53 Arno Del Curto .07 .20
54 Petter Ronnqvist .07 .20
55 Marco Wegmuller .07 .20
56 Beat Equilino .07 .20
57 Marc Gianola .07 .20
58 Andreas Haller .07 .20
59 Timo Helbling .20 .50
60 Beat Heldstab .07 .20
61 Petteri Nummelin .07 .20
62 Jan Von Arx .07 .20
63 Andre Baumann .07 .20
64 Patrick Fischer .07 .20
65 Marc Heberlein .07 .20
66 Sandy Jeannin .07 .20
67 Michael Kress .07 .20
68 Fredrik Lindquist .07 .20
69 Rene Muller .07 .20
70 Claudio Neff .07 .20
71 Sandro Rizzi .07 .20
72 Oliver Roth .07 .20
73 Frederic Rothen .07 .20
74 Mario Schocher .07 .20
75 Reto Von Arx .20 .50
76 Team Fribourg Left .07 .20
77 Team Fribourg Right .07 .20
78 Ueli Schwarz .07 .20
79 Thomas Ostlund .20 .50
80 Alain Sansonnens .07 .20
81 Goran Bezina .07 .20
82 Livio Fazio .07 .20
83 Romain Fleury .07 .20
84 Fabian Guignard .07 .20
85 Philippe Marquis .07 .20
86 Mika Stromberg .07 .20
87 Marc Werlen .07 .20
88 Rolf Ziegler .07 .20
89 Robert Burakowski .07 .20
90 Flavien Conne .07 .20
91 Rene Furler .07 .20
92 Daniel Giger .07 .20
93 Gil Montandon .07 .20
94 Colin Muller .07 .20
95 Michael Neininger .07 .20
96 Real Raemy .07 .20
97 Mario Rottaris .07 .20
98 Pascal Schaller .07 .20
99 Robert Slehofer .07 .20
100 Gerd Zenhausern .07 .20
101 Team Kloten Left .07 .20
102 Team Kloten Right .07 .20
103 Vladimir Jursinov CO .07 .20
104 Reto Pavoni .07 .20
105 Samuel Balmer .07 .20
106 Andre Bielmann .07 .20
107 Martin Bruderer .07 .20
108 Martin Hohener .07 .20
109 Marco Klofi .07 .20
110 Arne Ramholt .07 .20
111 Oskar Szczepaniec .07 .20
112 Benjamin Winkler .07 .20
113 Mathias Wuest .07 .20
114 Thomas Heldner .07 .20
115 Felix Hollenstein .07 .20
116 Peter Kobel .07 .20
117 Sven Lindemann .07 .20
118 Andrew McKim .20 .50
119 Andreas Nauser .07 .20
120 Martin Pluss .07 .20
121 Sebastien Reuille .07 .20
122 Andy Rufener .07 .20
123 Matthias Schenkel .07 .20
124 Tomas Strandberg .07 .20
125 Adrian Wichser .07 .20
126 Team Langnau Left .07 .20
127 Team Langnau Right .07 .20
128 Bengt-Ake Gustafsson .07 .20
129 Alfred Bohren .07 .20
130 Martin Gerber 2.00 5.00
131 Adrian Hunziker .07 .20
132 Daniel Aegeter .07 .20
133 Antoine Descloux .07 .20
134 Steve Hirschi .07 .20
135 Erik Kakko .07 .20
136 Pascal Muller .07 .20
137 Markus Wuthrich .07 .20
138 Rolf Badertscher .07 .20
139 Daniel Bieri .07 .20
140 Bruno Brechbuhl .07 .20
141 Marc Buhlmann .07 .20
142 Todd Elik .07 .20
143 John Fust .07 .20
144 Daniel Gauthier .07 .20
145 Bjorn Guazzini .07 .20
146 Matthias Holzer .07 .20
147 Michael Liniger .07 .20
148 Benoit Pont .07 .20
149 Stefan Tschiemer .07 .20
150 Team Lugano Left .07 .20
151 Team Lugano Right .07 .20
152 Jim Koleff CO .07 .20
153 Cristobal Huet 4.00 10.00
154 Lars Weibel .20 .50
155 Peter Andersson .07 .20
156 Mark Astley .07 .20
157 Sandro Bertaggia .07 .20
158 Olivier Keller .07 .20
159 Rick Tschumi .07 .20
160 Julien Vauclair .20 .50
161 Gaetan Voisard .20 .50
162 J.Jacques Aeschlimann .07 .20
163 Misko Antisin .07 .20
164 Philippe Bozon .40 1.00
165 Gian Marco Crameri .07 .20
166 Andre Doll .07 .20
167 Christian Dube .07 .20
168 Keith Fair .07 .20
169 Igor Fedulov .07 .20
170 Regis Fuchs .07 .20
171 Marcel Jenni .07 .20
172 Trevor Meier .07 .20
173 Andy Naser .07 .20
174 Geoffrey Vauclair .07 .20
175 Team Rapperswil Left .07 .20
176 Team Rapperswil Right .07 .20
177 Evgeny Popichin .07 .20
178 Claudio Bayer .07 .20
179 Remo Wehrli .07 .20
180 Marco Capaul .07 .20
181 Dominic Meier .07 .20
182 Jorg Reber .07 .20
183 Alain Reist .07 .20
184 Daniel Sigg .07 .20
185 Roger Sigg .07 .20
186 Magnus Svensson .07 .20
187 Loic Burkhalter .07 .20
188 Markus Butler .07 .20
189 Rene Friedli .07 .20
190 Sandro Haberlin .07 .20
191 Axel Heim .07 .20
192 Oliver Hoffmann .07 .20
193 Vjeran Ivankovic .07 .20
194 Frank Monnier .07 .20
195 Mark Ouimet .07 .20
196 Mike Richard .07 .20
197 Bernhard Schumperli .07 .20
198 Marcel Sommer .07 .20
199 Paul Ysebaert .07 .20
200 Team EVZ Left .07 .20
201 Team EVZ Right .20 .50
202 Rauno Korpi .07 .20
203 Ronnie Rueger .07 .20
204 Patrick Schopf .07 .20
205 Marco Bayer .07 .20
206 Raphael Berger .07 .20
207 Patrick Fischer .07 .20
208 Jakub Horak .07 .20
209 Dino Kessler .07 .20
210 Reto Kobach .07 .20
211 Andre Kunzi .07 .20
212 Patrick Sutter .07 .20
213 Christophe Brown .07 .20
214 Paul Di Pietro .20 .50
215 Stefan Grogg .07 .20
216 Daniel Meier .07 .20
217 Stefan Niggli .07 .20
218 Patrick Oppliger .07 .20
219 Andre Rotheli .07 .20
220 Sascha Schneider .07 .20
221 Rene Stussi .07 .20
222 Chris Tancill .07 .20
223 Samuel Villiger .07 .20
224 Dave Roberts .07 .20
225 Team ZSC Left .07 .20
226 Team ZSC Right .07 .20
227 Kent Ruhnke .07 .20
228 Thomas Papp .07 .20
229 Ari Sulander .20 .50
230 Ronny Keller .07 .20
231 Martin Kout .07 .20
232 Kari Martikainen .07 .20
233 Adrien Plavsic .07 .20
234 Edgar Salis .07 .20
235 Mathias Seger .07 .20
236 Pascal Stoller .07 .20
237 Andreas Zehnder .07 .20
238 Mattia Baldi .07 .20
239 Robin Bauer .07 .20
240 Patric Della Rossa .07 .20
241 Dan Hodgson .07 .20
242 Peter Jaks .07 .20
243 Claudio Micheli .07 .20
244 Patrizio Morger .07 .20
245 Laurent Muller .07 .20
246 Rolf Schrepfer .07 .20
247 Reto Stirnimann .07 .20
248 Christian Weber .07 .20
249 Michel Zeiter .07 .20
250 Ralph Krueger .07 .20
251 National Team Left .07 .20
252 National Team Right .07 .20
253 David Aebischer 2.00 5.00
254 Pauli Jaks .20 .50
255 Reto Pavoni .07 .20
256 Olivier Keller .07 .20
257 Philippe Marquis .07 .20
258 Ivo Ruthemann .07 .20
259 Mathias Seger .07 .20
260 Martin Steinegger .07 .20
261 Mark Streit .20 .50
262 Patrick Sutter .07 .20
263 Benjamin Winkler .07 .20
264 Mattia Baldi .07 .20
265 Gian Marco Crameri .07 .20
266 Patric Della Rossa .07 .20
267 Patrick Fischer .07 .20
268 Sandy Jeannin .07 .20
269 Marcel Jenni .07 .20
270 Laurent Muller .07 .20
271 Martin Pluss .07 .20
272 Sandro Rizzi .07 .20
273 Geoffrey Vauclair .07 .20
274 Reto Von Arx .20 .50
275 Michel Zeiter .07 .20
276 John Slettvoll .07 .20
277 National U20 TeamLeft .07 .20
278 National U20 Team Right .07 .20
279 Marco Buhrer .07 .20
280 Oliver Wissmann .07 .20
281 Goran Bezina .07 .20
282 David Jobin .07 .20
283 Pascal Muller .07 .20
284 Alain Reist .07 .20
285 Gregor Thommen .07 .20
286 Alex Vacheron .20 .50
287 Julien Vauclair .20 .50
288 Fabio Beccarelli .07 .20
289 Luca Cereda .20 .50
290 Bjorn Christen .07 .20
291 Flavien Conne .07 .20
292 Alain Demuth .07 .20
293 Philipp Folghera .07 .20
294 Roland Kaser .07 .20
295 Cornel Prinz .07 .20
296 Marc Reichert .07 .20
297 Michel Riesen .20 .50
298 Sandro Tschour .07 .20
299 Adrian Wichser .07 .20
300 Team Biel Left .07 .20
301 Team Biel Right .07 .20
302 Paul Gagne .07 .20
303 Sebastien Kohler
Sven Schmid .07 .20
304 Gilles Dubois
Michel Mongeau .07 .20
305 Cyrill Pasche
Claude Vilgrain .20 .50
306 La Chaux De Fonds Left .07 .20
307 La Chaux De Fonds Right .07 .20
308 Jaroslav Jagr .07 .20
309 Thomas Berger
Ruedi Niderost .07 .20
310 Luigi Riva
Valeri Shiryaev .07 .20
311 Steve Aebersold
Christian Pouget .07 .20
312 Team Chur Left .07 .20
313 Team Chur Right .07 .20
314 Mike McParland .07 .20
315 Nando Wieser
Matthias Bachler .07 .20
316 Michael Meier
Roger Rieder .07 .20
317 Sandro Tschour
Theo Wittmann .07 .20
318 Team GC Left .07 .20
319 Team GC Right .07 .20
320 Riccardo Fuhrer .07 .20
321 Oliver Wissmann
Pascal Fah .07 .20
322 David Fehr
Oliver Kamber .07 .20
323 Patrick Looser
Riccardo Signorell .07 .20
324 Team Lausanne Left .07 .20
325 Team Lausanne Right .07 .20
326 Benoit Laporte .07 .20
327 Beat Kindler
Slava Bykov .07 .20
328 Patrick Giove
Maxime Lapointe .07 .20
329 Jorg Ledermann
Valentin Wirz .07 .20
330 Team Olten Left .07 .20
331 Team Olten Right .07 .20
332 Markus Graf .07 .20
333 Beat Aebischer
Andy Egli .07 .20
334 Richard Stucki
Evgeny Davydov .07 .20
335 Michel Mouther
Mikhail Volkov .07 .20
336 Team Servette Left .07 .20
337 Team Servette Right .07 .20
338 Francois Huppe .07 .20
339 David Bochy
Christian Serena .07 .20
340 Sott Beatti
Shawn Heaphy .07 .20
341 Paul Savary
Michel Wicky .07 .20
342 Team Sierre Left .07 .20
343 Team Sierre Right .07 .20
344 Kevin Primeau .07 .20
345 Matthias Lauber
Adrian Jezzone .07 .20
346 Patrick Neukom
Philipp Luber .07 .20
347 Dimitri Shamolin
Gilles Thibaudeau .07 .20
348 Team Thurgau Left .07 .20
349 Team Thurgau Right .07 .20
350 Robert Wiesmann .07 .20
351 Marco Buhrer
Stefan Grauwiler .07 .20
352 Domenic Amodeo
Matthias Keller .07 .20
353 Patrick Meier
Morgan Samuelsson .07 .20
354 Team Visp Left .07 .20
355 Team Visp Right .07 .20
356 Bruno Zenhausern .07 .20
357 Reiner Karlen
Wesley Snell .07 .20
358 Marc Zurbriggen
Franziskus Heinzmann .07 .20
359 Andy Egli
Gabriel Taccoz .07 .20
A SEHV/LSHG .07 .20
B HC Ambri Piotta .07 .20
C SC Bern .07 .20
D HC Davos .07 .20
E HC Fribourg Gotteron .07 .20
F EHC Kloten .07 .20
G SC Langnau .07 .20
H HC Lugano .07 .20
I SC Rapperswil-Jona .07 .20
J EV Zug .07 .20
K ZSC Lions .07 .20
L EHC Biel-Bienne .07 .20
M HC La Chaux De Fonds .07 .20
N EHC Chur .07 .20
O Grasshoppers .07 .20
P HC Lausanne .07 .20
Q EHC Olten .07 .20
R HC Geneve Servette .07 .20
S HC Sierre .07 .20
T HC Thurgau .07 .20
U Visp .07 .20

2000-01 Swiss Panini Stickers

COMPLETE SET (322) 20.00 50.00
1 Logo Swiss Hockey Federation .08 .20
2 Ambri Team Card .08 .20
3 Ambri Team Card .08 .20
4 Ambri Logo .08 .20
5 Pietre Page .08 .20
6 Pauli Jaks .08 .20
7 Gianluca Mona .08 .20
8 Fredy Bobillier .08 .20
9 Ivan Gazzaroli .08 .20
10 Tiziano Gianini .08 .20
11 Thomas Kunzi .08 .20
12 Leif Rohlin .08 .20
13 Krister Cantoni .08 .20
14 Manuele Celio .08 .20
15 Nicola Celio .08 .20
16 Alain Demuth .08 .20
17 Paolo Duca .08 .20
18 John Fritsche .08 .20
19 Ryan Gardner .08 .20
20 Paolo Imperatori .08 .20
21 Vitaly Lakhmatov .08 .20
22 Stephan Lebeau .08 .20
23 Dan Marois .08 .20
24 Omar Tognini .08 .20
25 Thomas Ziegler .08 .20
26 Logo SCB .08 .20
27 Team Card SCB .08 .20
28 Team Card SCB .08 .20
29 Pekka Rautakallio .08 .20
30 Renato Tosio .08 .20
31 David Jobin .08 .20
32 Marc Leuenberger .08 .20
33 Sven Leuenberger .08 .20
34 Dominic Meier .08 .20
35 Frederik Olausson .08 .20
36 Martin Steinegger .08 .20
37 Fabian Stephan .08 .20
38 Rolf Ziegler .08 .20
39 Alex Chatelain .08 .20
40 Bjorn Christen .08 .20
41 Patrick Howald .08 .20
42 Andreas Johansson .08 .20
43 Patrick Juhlin .08 .20
44 Rolan Kasar .08 .20
45 Boris Leimgruber .08 .20
46 Marc Reichert .08 .20
47 Ivo Ruthemann .08 .20
48 Franz Steffen .08 .20
49 Marc Weber .08 .20
50 La Chaux De Fonds Logo .08 .20
51 Chaux Fonds Team Card .08 .20
52 Chaux Fonds Team Card .08 .20
53 Dan Hober .08 .20
54 Thomas Berger .08 .20
55 Gilles Cattela .08 .20
56 Pascal Avanthay .08 .20
57 Raphael Brusa .08 .20
58 Fabian Guignard .08 .20
59 Ruedi Niderost .08 .20
60 Roger Ohmann .08 .20
61 Valery Schirjaev .08 .20
62 Alexis Vacheron .08 .20
63 Steve Aebersold .08 .20
64 Thomas Derungs .08 .20
65 Claude Luthi .08 .20
66 Fabrice Maillat .08 .20
67 Thibaut Monnet .08 .20
68 Daniel Nakaota .08 .20
69 Stefan Nilsson .08 .20
70 Steve Pochon .08 .20
71 Philippe Halmann .08 .20
72 Julien Turler .08 .20
73 Sami Villiger .08 .20
74 Chur Logo .08 .20
75 Chur Team Card .08 .20
76 Chur Team Card .08 .20
77 Mike McParland .08 .20
78 Marco Buhrer .08 .20
79 Nando Wieser .08 .20
80 Noel Guyaz .08 .20
81 Christian Langer .08 .20
82 Ivo Stoffel .08 .20
83 Pasi Sormunen .08 .20
84 Mika Stromberg .08 .20
85 Matthias Bachler .08 .20
86 Fabio Beccarelli .08 .20
87 Patrick Kruger .08 .20
88 Michael Meier .08 .20
89 Daniel Peer .08 .20
90 Roger Rieder .08 .20
91 Michael Rosenast .08 .20
92 Oliver Roth .08 .20
93 Rene Stussi .08 .20
94 Sandro Tschuor .08 .20
95 Harijs Vitolinsh .08 .20
96 Raymond Walder .08 .20
97 Theo Wittmann .08 .20
98 HC Davos Logo .08 .20
99 HC Davos Team Card .08 .20
100 HC Davos Team Card .08 .20
101 Arno Del Curto .08 .20
102 Petter Ronnquist .08 .20
103 Lars Weibel .08 .20
104 Beat Equilino .08 .20
105 Marc Gianola .08 .20
106 Andrea Haller .08 .20
107 Michael Kress .08 .20
108 Kevin Miller .08 .20
109 Ralph Ott .08 .20
110 Jan Von Arx .08 .20
111 Andre Baumann .08 .20
112 Lonny Bohonos .08 .20
113 Pat Falloon .08 .20
114 Patrick Fischer .08 .20
115 Marc Heberlein .08 .20
116 Rene Muller .08 .20
117 Claudio Neff .08 .20
118 Thierry Paterlini .08 .20
119 Sandro Rizzi .08 .20
120 Frederic Rothen .08 .20
121 Mario Schocher .08 .20
122 Gotteron Logo .08 .20
123 Gotteron Team Card .08 .20
124 Gotteron Team Card .08 .20
125 Serge Pelletier .08 .20
126 Thomas Ostlund .20 .50
127 Alain Sansonnens .08 .20
128 Raphael Berger .08 .20
129 Goran Bezina .08 .20
130 Christoph Decurtins .08 .20
131 Antoine Descloux .08 .20
132 Livio Fazio .08 .20
133 Philippe Marquis .08 .20
134 Martin Rauch .08 .20
135 Marc Werlen .08 .20
136 Craig Ferguson .08 .20
137 Lars Leuenberger .08 .20
138 Silvan Lussy .08 .20
139 Gil Montandon .08 .20
140 Michel Mouther .08 .20
141 Mario Rottaris .08 .20
142 Jean Yves Roy .08 .20
143 Pascal Schaller .08 .20
144 Robert Slehofer .08 .20
145 Gerd Zenhausern .08 .20
146 Kloten Logo .08 .20
147 Kloten Team Card .08 .20
148 Kloten Team Card .08 .20
149 Vladimir Yursinov CO .08 .20
150 Reto Pavoni .20 .50
151 Martin Hohener .08 .20
152 Ronny Keller .08 .20
153 Marko Kiprusoff .08 .20
154 Marco Kloti .08 .20
155 Dejan Lozanov .08 .20
156 Oskar Szczepaniec .08 .20
157 Beni Winkler .08 .20
158 Sven Hellenstein .08 .20
159 Felix Hollenstein .08 .20
160 Andy Keller .08 .20
161 Sven Lindemann .08 .20
162 Andreas Nauser .08 .20
163 Fredrik Nilsson .08 .20
164 Martin Pluss .08 .20
165 Sebastian Reuille .08 .20
166 Andy Rufener .08 .20
167 Adi Wichser .08 .20
168 Thomas Widmer .08 .20
169 Mathias Wust .08 .20
170 Langnau Logo .08 .20
171 Langnau Team Card .08 .20
172 Langnau Team Card .08 .20
173 Bengt Ake Gustafsson .08 .20
174 Martin Gerber .75 2.00
175 Martin Zerzuben .08 .20
176 Daniel Aegerter .08 .20
177 Samuel Balmer .08 .20
178 Steve Hirschi .08 .20
179 Erik Kakko .08 .20
180 Pascal Muller .08 .20
181 Pascal Stoller .08 .20
182 Florian Andenmatten .08 .20
183 Rolf Badertscher .08 .20
184 Bruno Brechbuhl .08 .20
185 John Fust .08 .20
186 Daniel Gauthier .08 .20
187 Thomas Heldner .08 .20
188 Matthias Holzer .08 .20
189 Michael Neininger .08 .20
190 Benoit Pont .08 .20
191 Vlastimil Plavucha .08 .20
192 Daniel Steiner .08 .20
193 Stefan Tschiemer .08 .20
194 Lugano Logo .08 .20
195 Lugano Team Card .08 .20
196 Lugano Team Card .08 .20
197 Jim Koleff .08 .20
198 Cristobal Huet .08 5.00
199 Peter Martin .08 .20
200 Peter Andersson .08 .20
201 Mark Astley .08 .20
202 Sandro Bertaggia .08 .20
203 Olivier Keller .08 .20
204 Rick Tschumi .08 .20
205 Gaetan Voisard .08 .20
206 Jean-Jacques Aeschlimann .08 .20
207 Misko Antisin .08 .20
208 Philippe Bozon .40 1.00
209 Flavien Conne .08 .20
210 Christian Dube .08 .20
211 Keith Fair .08 .20
212 Igor Fedulov .08 .20
213 Regis Fuchs .08 .20
214 Sandy Jeannin .08 .20
215 Trevor Meier .08 .20
216 Andy Naser .08 .20
217 Geoffrey Vauclair .08 .20
218 Rapperswil Logo .08 .20
219 Rapperswil Team Card .08 .20
220 Rapperswil Team Card .08 .20
221 Evgeny Popikhin .08 .20
222 Claudio Bayer .08 .20
223 Mathias Lauber .08 .20
224 Marco Capaul .08 .20
225 Jakub Horak .08 .20
226 Kari Martikainen .08 .20
227 Jorg Reber .08 .20
228 Alain Reist .08 .20
229 Roger Sigg .08 .20
230 Loic Burkhalter .08 .20
231 Markus Butler .08 .20
232 Rene Friedli .08 .20
233 Rene Furler .08 .20
234 Dani Giger .08 .20
235 Sandro Haberlin .08 .20
236 Axel Heim .08 .20
237 Philippe Luber .08 .20
238 Dale McTavish .08 .20
239 Patrick Morger .08 .20
240 Mike Richard .08 .20
241 Bernhard Schumperli .08 .20
242 EVZ Logo .08 .20
243 EVZ Team Card .08 .20
244 EVZ Team Card .08 .20
245 Andre Peloffy .08 .20
246 Ronnie Rueger .08 .20
247 Patrick Schopf .08 .20
248 Marco Bayer .08 .20
249 Ralph Bundi .08 .20
250 Patrick Fischer .08 .20
251 Dino Kessler .08 .20
252 Andre Kunzi .08 .20
253 Reto Kobach .08 .20
254 Patrick Sutter .08 .20
255 Christophe Brown .08 .20
256 Paul Di Pietro .20 .50
257 Todd Elik .08 .20
258 Stefan Grogg .08 .20
259 Vjeran Ivankovic .08 .20
260 Daniel Meier .08 .20
261 Stefan Niggli .08 .20
262 Patrick Oppliger .08 .20
263 Andre Rotheli .08 .20
264 Sascha Schneider .08 .20
265 Chris Tancill .08 .20
266 ZSC Logo .08 .20
267 ZSC Team Card .08 .20
268 ZSC Team Card .08 .20
269 Larry Hurras .08 .20
270 Thomas Papp .08 .20
271 Ari Sulander .20 .50
272 Martin Kout .08 .20
273 Adrien Plavsic .08 .20
274 Edgar Salis .08 .20
275 Mathias Seger .08 .20
276 Bruno Seck .08 .20
277 Andreas Zehnder .08 .20
278 Mattia Baldi .08 .20
279 Gian Marco Crameri .08 .20
280 Partric Della Rossa .08 .20
281 Daniel Hodgson .08 .20
282 Peter Jaks .08 .20
283 Andrew McKim .20 .50
284 Claudio Micheli .08 .20
285 Laurent Muller .08 .20
286 Mark Ouimet .08 .20
287 Rolf Schrepfer .08 .20
288 Reto Stirnimann .08 .20
289 Michel Zeiter .08 .20
290 HC Ajoie Logo .08 .20
291 Yann Voillat .08 .20
292 Chris Belanger .08 .20
293 EHC Basel Logo .08 .20
294 Todd Wetzel .08 .20
295 Patrice Girard .08 .20
296 EHC Biel Logo .08 .20
297 Sven Schmid .08 .20
298 Kevin Schlapfer .08 .20
299 GCK Lions Logo .08 .20
300 Patrick Looser .08 .20
301 Mikko Myllykoski .08 .20
302 HC Geneve Logo .08 .20
303 Patrice Brasey .08 .20
304 Scott Beattie .08 .20
305 SC Herisau Logo .08 .20
306 Andy Karpf .08 .20
307 Patrick Amann .08 .20
308 HC Lausanne Logo .08 .20
309 Beat Kindler .08 .20
310 Serge Poudrier .08 .20
311 EHC Olten Logo .08 .20
312 Beat Aebischer .08 .20
313 Richard Stucki .08 .20

314 HC Sierre Logo .08 .20
315 Jean Michel Clavien .08 .20
316 Gaby Epiney .08 .20
317 HC Thurgau Logo .08 .20
318 Martin Bruderer .08 .20
319 Morgan Samuelsson .08 .20
320 EHC Visp Logo .08 .20
321 Stefan Ketola .08 .20
322 Gabriel Taccoz .08 .20

2000-01 Swiss Panini Stickers National Team Insert

P1 Martin Gerber 1.00 2.50
P2 David Aebischer 1.00 2.50
P3 Relo Pavoni .40 1.00
P4 Patrick Fisher .40 1.00
P5 Olivier Keller .40 1.00
P6 Martin Steinegger .40 1.00
P7 Edgar Salis .40 1.00
P8 Mark Streit .40 1.00
P9 Julien Vavclair .40 1.00
P10 Patrick Sutter .40 1.00
P11 Mathias Seger .40 1.00
P12 Rolf Ziegler .40 1.00
P13 Flavien Conne .40 1.00
P14 Jean-Jaques Aeschlimann .40 1.00
P15 Mattia Baldi .40 1.00
P16 Patric Della Rossa .40 1.00
P17 Marcel Jenni .40 1.00
P18 Gian Marco Crameri .40 1.00
P19 Claudio Micheli .40 1.00
P20 Alain Demuth .40 1.00
P21 Thomas Ziegler .40 1.00
P22 Patrick Fischer .40 1.00
P23 Ivo Ruthemann .40 1.00
P24 Reto Von Arx .40 1.00
P25 Michel Zeiter .40 1.00
P26 Michel Riesen .40 1.00
P27 Sandy Jeannin .40 1.00
P28 Lurent Muller .40 1.00
P29 Martin Pluss .40 1.00
P30 Adi Wichser .40 1.00

2000-01 Swiss Slapshot Mini-Cards

COMPLETE SET (192) 20.00 40.00
LT1 Martin Gerber 2.00 5.00
LT2 Daniel Aegerter .10 .25
LT3 Samuel Balmer .10 .25
LT4 Beat Gerber .10 .25
LT5 Steve Hirschi .10 .25
LT6 Erik Kakko .10 .25
LT7 Pascal Muller .10 .25
LT8 Pascal Stoller .10 .25
LT9 Rolf Badertscher .10 .25
LT10 Bruno Brechbuhl .10 .25
LT11 John Fust .10 .25
LT12 Daniel Gauthier .10 .25
LT13 Thomas Heldner .10 .25
LT14 Matthias Holzer .10 .25
LT15 Vlastimil Plavucha .10 .25
LT16 Benoit Pont .10 .25
RJ1 Claudio Bayer .10 .25
RJ2 Marco Capaul .10 .25
RJ3 Kari Martikainen .10 .25
RJ4 Roger Sigg .10 .25
RJ5 Jorg Reber .10 .25
RJ6 Loic Burkhalter .10 .25
RJ7 Markus Butler .10 .25
RJ8 Rene Friedli .10 .25
RJ9 Rene Furler .10 .25
RJ10 Daniel Giger .10 .25
RJ11 Axel Heim .10 .25
RJ12 Philipp Luber .10 .25
RJ13 Dale McTavish .10 .25
RJ14 Patrizio Morger .10 .25
RJ15 Mike Richard .10 .25
RJ16 Bernhard Schumperli .10 .25
EVZ1 Ronnie Rueger .10 .25
EVZ2 Patrick Schopf .10 .25
EVZ3 Marco Bayer .10 .25
EVZ4 Patrick Fischer .10 .25
EVZ5 Dino Kessler .10 .25
EVZ6 Andre Kunzi .10 .25
EVZ7 Patrick Sutter .10 .25
EVZ8 Paul Di Pietro .20 .50
EVZ9 Todd Elik .20 .50
EVZ10 Stefan Grogg .10 .25
EVZ11 Vjeran Ivankovic .10 .25
EVZ12 Daniel Meier .10 .25
EVZ13 Patrick Oppliger .10 .25
EVZ14 Andre Rotheli .10 .25
EVZ15 Sascha Schneider .10 .25
EVZ16 Chris Tancill .10 .25
HCD1 Lars Weibel .20 .50
HCD2 Beat Equilino .10 .25
HCD3 Marc Gianola .10 .25
HCD4 Andreas Häller .10 .25
HCD5 Ralph Ott .10 .25
HCD6 Jan Von Arx .10 .25
HCD7 Andre Baumann .10 .25
HCD8 Lonny Bohonos .20 .50
HCD9 Patrick Fischer .10 .25
HCD10 Kevin Miller .20 .50
HCD11 Rene Muller .10 .25
HCD12 Thierry Paterlini .10 .25
HCD13 Sandro Rizzi .10 .25
HCD14 Frederic Rothen .10 .25
HCD15 Mario Schocher .10 .25
HCD16 Pat Falloon .20 .50
CL1 Cristobal Huet 2.00 5.00
CL2 Peter Anderson .10 .25
CL3 Igor Fedulov .10 .25
CL4 Sandro Bertaggia .10 .25
CL5 Olivier Keller .10 .25
CL6 Julien Vauclair .10 .25
CL7 Gaetan Voisard .10 .25
CL8 J.-Jacques Aeschlimann .10 .25
CL9 Misko Antisin .10 .25
CL10 Philippe Bozon .40 1.00
CL11 Jan-Philippe Cadieux .10 .25
CL12 Flavien Conne .10 .25
CL13 Christian Dube .10 .25
CL14 Regis Fuchs .10 .25
CL15 Sandy Jeannin .10 .25
CL16 Keith Fair .10 .25
SCB1 Renato Tosio .10 .25
SCB2 David Jobin .10 .25
SCB3 Sven Leuenberger .10 .25
SCB4 Dominic Meier .10 .25
SCB5 Frederik Olausson .10 .25
SCB6 Martin Steinegger .10 .25
SCB7 Rolf Ziegler .10 .25
SCB8 Bjorn Christen .10 .25
SCB9 Patrick Howald .10 .25
SCB10 Andreas Johansson .10 .25
SCB11 Patrick Juhlin .10 .25
SCB12 Alex Chatelain .10 .25
SCB13 Boris Leimgruber .10 .25
SCB14 Ivo Ruthemann .10 .25
SCB15 Franz Steffen .10 .25
SCB16 Marc Weber .10 .25
EHCC1 Nando Wieser .10 .25
EHCC2 Noel Guyaz .10 .25
EHCC3 Christian Langer .10 .25
EHCC4 Ivo Stoffel .10 .25
EHCC5 Mika Stromberg .10 .25
EHCC6 Pasi Sormunen .10 .25
EHCC7 Matthias Bachler .10 .25
EHCC8 Patrick Kruger .10 .25
EHCC9 Michael Meier .10 .25
EHCC10 Michael Rosenast .10 .25
EHCC11 Oliver Roth .10 .25
EHCC12 Marc Haueter .10 .25
EHCC13 Sandro Tschuor .10 .25
EHCC14 Raymond Walder .10 .25
EHCC15 Theo Wittmann .10 .25
EHCC16 UNKNOWN .10 .25
EHCK1 Reto Pavoni .10 .25
EHCK2 Martin Hohener .10 .25
EHCK3 Marko Kiprusoff .10 .25
EHCK4 Marco Kloti .10 .25
EHCK5 Oskar Szcepaniec .10 .25
EHCK6 UNKNOWN .10 .25
EHCK7 Fredrik Nilsson .10 .25
EHCK8 Sven Helfenstein .10 .25
EHCK9 Felix Hollenstein .10 .25
EHCK10 Andy Keller .10 .25
EHCK11 Sven Lindemann .10 .25
EHCK12 Martin Pluss .10 .25
EHCK13 Sebastien Reuille .10 .25
EHCK14 Andre Rufener .10 .25
EHCK15 Steve Washburn .10 .25
EHCK16 Adrian Wichser .10 .25
HCAP1 Pauli Jaks .10 .25
HCAP2 Fredy Bobillier .10 .25
HCAP3 Ivan Gazzaroli .10 .25
HCAP4 Tiziano Gianini .10 .25
HCAP5 Thomas Kunzi .10 .25
HCAP6 Leif Rohlin .10 .25
HCAP7 Krister Cantoni .10 .25
HCAP8 Manuele Celio .10 .25
HCAP9 Nicola Celio .10 .25
HCAP10 Alain Demuth .10 .25
HCAP11 Paolo Duca .10 .25
HCAP12 John Fritsche .10 .25
HCAP13 Ryan Gardner .10 .25
HCAP14 Paolo Imperatori .10 .25
HCAP15 Stephan Lebeau .20 .50
HCAP16 Daniel Marois .20 .50
HCCF1 Thomas Berger .10 .25
HCCF2 Raphael Brusa .10 .25
HCCF3 Fabian Guignard .10 .25
HCCF4 Valeri Shiryaev .10 .25
HCCF5 Ruedi Niderost .10 .25
HCCF6 Roger Ohmann .10 .25
HCCF7 Alexis Vacheron .10 .25
HCCF8 Steve Aebersold .10 .25
HCCF9 Thomas Derungs .10 .25
HCCF10 Claude Luthi .10 .25
HCCF11 Fabrice Maillat .10 .25
HCCF12 Daniel Nakaoka .10 .25
HCCF13 Stefan Nilsson .10 .25
HCCF14 Julien Turler .10 .25
HCCF15 Samuel Villiger .10 .25
HCCF16 Thibaut Monnet .10 .25
HCFG1 Thomas Ostlund .20 .50
HCFG2 Goran Bozina .10 .25
HCFG3 Antonie Descloux .10 .25
HCFG4 Livio Fazio .10 .25
HCFG5 Philippe Marquis .10 .25
HCFG6 Martin Rauch .10 .25
HCFG7 Marc Werlen .10 .25
HCFG8 Craig Ferguson .10 .25
HCFG9 Lars Leuenberger .10 .25
HCFG10 Gil Montandon .10 .25
HCFG11 Mario Rottaris .10 .25
HCFG12 Jean-Yves Roy .10 .25
HCFG13 Pascal Schaller .10 .25
HCFG14 Robert Slehofer .10 .25
HCFG15 Gerd Zenhäusern .10 .25
HCFG16 Michel Mouther .10 .25
ZSCL1 Ari Sulander .20 .50
ZSCL2 Adrien Plavsic .10 .25
ZSCL3 Edgar Salis .10 .25
ZSCL4 Matthias Seger .10 .25
ZSCL5 Mark Streit .20 .50
ZSCL6 Andreas Zehnder .10 .25
ZSCL7 Mattia Baldi .10 .25
ZSCL8 Gian Marco Crameri .10 .25
ZSCL9 Patric Della Rossa .10 .25
ZSCL10 Dan Hodgson .10 .25
ZSCL11 Peter Jaks .10 .25
ZSCL12 Andrew McKim .20 .50
ZSCL13 Claudio Micheli .10 .25
ZSCL14 Laurent Muller .10 .25
ZSCL15 Rolf Schrepfer .10 .25
ZSCL16 Michel Zeiter .10 .25

2001-02 Swiss EV Zug Postcards

COMPLETE SET (27) 10.00 25.00
1 Team photo .40 1.00
2 Doug Mason .40 1.00
3 Richmond Gosselin .40 1.00
4 Patrick Schopf .40 1.00
5 Ronnie Rueger .40 1.00
6 Ruedi Niderost .40 1.00
7 Ralf Bundi .40 1.00
8 Patrick Fischer .40 1.00
9 Fabio Schumacher .40 1.00
10 Pascal Muller .40 1.00
11 Arne Ramholt .40 1.00
12 Kevin Gloor .40 1.00
13 Andre Kunzi .40 1.00
14 Reto Kobach .40 1.00
15 Thomas Nussli .40 1.00
16 Stefan Voegele .40 1.00
17 Stefan Niggli .40 1.00
18 Duri Camichel .40 1.00
19 Vjeran Ivankovic .40 1.00
20 Patrick Oppliger .40 1.00
21 Frederic Rothen .40 1.00
22 Stefan Grogg .40 1.00
23 Christoph Brown .40 1.00
24 Chris Tancill .75 2.00
25 Todd Elik .75 2.00
26 Joel Savage .75 2.00
27 Paul DiPietro .75 2.00

2001-02 Swiss HNL

COMPLETE SET (480) 30.00 75.00
1 Larry Huras .10 .25
2 Thomas Papp .10 .25
3 Ari Sulander .40 1.00
4 Martin Kout .10 .25
5 Adrian Plavsic .10 .25
6 Tim Ramholt .60 1.50
7 Edgar Salis .10 .25
8 Mathias Seger .10 .25
9 Bruno Steck .10 .25
10 Mark Streit .10 .25
11 Jan Alston .20 .50
12 Mattia Baldi .10 .25
13 Gian-Marco Crameri .10 .25
14 Patric Della Rossa .10 .25
15 Paolo Duca .10 .25
16 Dan Hodgson .20 .50
17 Peter Jaks .10 .25
18 Claudio Micheli .10 .25
19 Mark Ouimet .20 .50
20 Morgan Samuelsson .10 .25
21 Stefan Schnyder .10 .25
22 Reto Stirnimann .10 .25
23 Petri Varis .20 .50
24 Michel Zeiter .10 .25
25 Zinetoula Bilyaletdinov .10 .25
26 Paolo Della Bella .10 .25
27 Cristobal Huet ERC 2.00 5.00
28 Mark Astley .20 .50
29 Sandro Bertaggia .10 .25
30 Olivier Keller .10 .25
31 Petteri Nummelin .10 .25
32 Patrick Sutter .10 .25
33 Rick Tschumi .10 .25
34 Gaetan Voisard .10 .25
35 Jean-Jacques Aeschlimann .10 .25
36 Jan Cadieux .10 .25
37 Gregory Christen .10 .25
38 Flavien Conne .10 .25
39 Christian Dube .10 .25
40 Keith Fair .10 .25
41 Regis Fuchs .10 .25
42 Ryan Gardner .20 .50
43 Sandy Jeannin .10 .25
44 Mike Maneluk .20 .50
45 Andy Naser .10 .25
46 Andre Rotheli .10 .25
47 Raffaele Sannitz .30 .75
48 Geoffrey Vauclair .10 .25
49 Kloten-Flyers .10 .25
50 Vladimir Jursinov .10 .25
51 Flavio Ludke .10 .25
52 Reto Pavoni .20 .50
53 Severin Blindenbacher .10 .25
54 Manuel Gossweiler .10 .25
55 Fabian Guignard .10 .25
56 Roman Hardmeier .10 .25
57 Martin Hohener .10 .25
58 Ronny Keller .10 .25
59 Chris O'Sullivan .20 .50
60 Gregor Thommen .10 .25
61 Mathias Wust .10 .25
62 Andre Bielmann .10 .25
63 Patrik Bartschi .10 .25
64 Andreas Cellar .10 .25
65 Felix Hollenstein .10 .25
66 Andy Keller .10 .25
67 Dario Kostovic .10 .25
68 Sven Lindemann .10 .25
69 Fredrik Nilsson .10 .25
70 Emanuel Peter .10 .25
71 Martin Pluss .10 .25
72 Kimmo Rintanen .10 .25
73 Adrian Wichser .30 .75
74 Thomas Widmer .10 .25
75 Riccardo Fuhrer .10 .25
76 Marco Buhrer .20 .50
77 Andreas Schweizer .10 .25
78 Rikard Franzen .10 .25
79 David Jobin .10 .25
80 Sven Leuenberger .10 .25
81 Marc Leuenberger .10 .25
82 Dominic Meier .10 .25
83 Martin Steinegger .10 .25
84 Rolf Ziegler .10 .25
85 Derek Armstrong .20 .50
86 Andre Baumann .10 .25
87 Alex Chatelain .10 .25
88 Sven Helfenstein .10 .25
89 Patrik Juhlin .20 .50
90 Laurent Muller .10 .25
91 Philippe Muller .10 .25
92 Marc Reichert .10 .25
93 Ivo Ruthemann .10 .25
94 Rolf Schrepfer .10 .25
95 Franz Steffen .10 .25
96 Fabian Sutter .10 .25
97 Marc Weber .10 .25
98 Arno Del Curto .10 .25
99 Jonas Hiller 1.00 2.50
100 Lars Weibel .20 .50
101 Beat Equilino .10 .25
102 Beat Forster .10 .25
103 Marc Gianola .10 .25
104 Andrea Haller .10 .25
105 Michael Kress .10 .25
106 Ralph Ott .10 .25
107 Jan von Arx .10 .25
108 Benjamin Winkler .10 .25
109 Andres Ambuhl .10 .25
110 Lonny Bohonos .20 .50
111 Andreas Camenzind .10 .25
112 Bjorn Christen .10 .25
113 Patrick Fischer .10 .25
114 Joel Frohlicher .10 .25
115 Stefan Gahler .10 .25
116 Marc Heberlein .10 .25
117 Josef Marha .10 .25
118 Kevin Miller .20 .50
119 Rene Muller .10 .25
120 Sandro Rizzi .10 .25
121 Serge Pelletier .10 .25
122 Matthias Lauber .20 .50
123 Gianluca Mona .20 .50
124 Raphael Berger .10 .25
125 Antoine Descloux .10 .25
126 Mike Gaul .20 .50
127 Lukas Gerber .10 .25
128 Philippe Marquis .10 .25
129 Martin Rauch .10 .25
130 Marc Werlen .10 .25
131 Craig Ferguson .20 .50
132 Gilbert Flueler .10 .25
133 Christof Hiltebrand .10 .25
134 Patrick Howald .10 .25
135 Lars Leuenberger .10 .25
136 Silvan Lussy .10 .25
137 David Maurer .10 .25
138 Thibaut Monnet .10 .25
139 Gil Montandon .10 .25
140 Michel Mouther .10 .25
141 Mario Rottaris .10 .25
142 Jean-Yves Roy .20 .50
143 Robert Slehofer .10 .25
144 Colin Muller .10 .25
145 Evgeni Popichin .10 .25
146 Thomas Berger .20 .50
147 Simon Zuger .20 .50
148 Marco Capaul .10 .25
149 Livio Fazio .10 .25
150 Jakub Horak .10 .25
151 Kari Martikainen .10 .25
152 Alain Reist .10 .25
153 Marc Schefer .10 .25
154 Fabian Stephan .10 .25
155 Markus Butler .10 .25
156 Rene Friedli .10 .25
157 Daniel Giger .10 .25
158 Axel Heim .10 .25
159 Philipp Luber .10 .25
160 Dale McTavish .20 .50
161 Claudio Moggi .10 .25
162 Sandro Moggi .10 .25
163 Patrizio Morger .10 .25
164 Sebastien Reuille .10 .25
165 Mike Richard .10 .25
166 Morgan Samuelsson .10 .25
167 Doug Mason .10 .25
168 Ronnie Rueger .20 .50
169 Patrick Schopf .20 .50
170 Ralf Bundi .10 .25
171 Patrick Fischer .10 .25
172 Reto Kobach .10 .25
173 Andre Kunzi .10 .25
174 Pascal Muller .10 .25
175 Ruedi Niderost .10 .25
176 Arne Ramholt .10 .25
177 Fabio Schumacher .10 .25
178 Christophe Brown .10 .25
179 Duri Camichel .10 .25
180 Paul Di Pietro .20 .50
181 Todd Elik .20 .50
182 Stefan Grogg .10 .25
183 Vjeran Ivankovic .10 .25
184 Stefan Niggli .10 .25
185 Thomas Nussli .10 .25
186 Patrick Oppliger .10 .25
187 Frederic Rothen .10 .25
188 Joel Savage .20 .50
189 Chris Tancill .20 .50
190 Vassily Tikhonov .10 .25
191 Claudio Bayer .20 .50
192 Marco Streit .20 .50
193 Daniel Aegerter .10 .25
194 Samuel Balmer .10 .25
195 Beat Gerber .10 .25
196 Steve Hirschi .10 .25
197 Erik Hamalainen .10 .25
198 Thomas Kunzi .10 .25
199 Pascal Stoller .10 .25
200 Rolf Badertscher .10 .25
201 Brian Bonin .20 .50
202 Bruno Brechbuhl .10 .25
203 John Fust .10 .25
204 Daniel Gauthier .10 .25
205 Thomas Heldner .10 .25
206 Matthias Holzer .10 .25
207 Benjamin Pluss .10 .25
208 Benoit Pont .10 .25
209 Bernhard Schumperli .10 .25
210 Daniel Steiner .10 .25
211 Rostislav Cada .10 .25
212 Lorenzo Barenco .10 .25
213 Pauli Jaks .20 .50
214 Marco Bayer .10 .25
215 Nicola Celio .10 .25
216 Ivan Gazzaroli .10 .25
217 Tiziano Gianini .10 .25
218 John Gobbi .10 .25
219 Andreas Hanni .10 .25
220 Martin Stepanek .10 .25
221 Loic Burkhalter .10 .25
222 Corsin Camichel .10 .25
223 Krister Cantoni .10 .25
224 Manuele Celio .10 .25
225 Alain Demuth .10 .25
226 John Fritsche .10 .25
227 Paolo Imperatori .10 .25
228 Roland Kaser .10 .25
229 Vitaly Lakhmatov .10 .25
230 Michel Liniger .10 .25
231 Robert Petrovicky .10 .25
232 Omar Tognini .10 .25
233 Tomas Vlasak .10 .25
234 Niklas Wikegard .10 .25
235 Tobias Stephan 1.25 3.00
236 Nando Wieser .10 .25
237 Rene Back .10 .25
238 Cyrill Geyer .10 .25
239 Noel Guyaz .10 .25
240 Marc Haueter .10 .25
241 Ivo Stoffel .10 .25
242 Mika Stromberg .10 .25
243 Andreas Zehnder .10 .25
244 Fabio Beccarelli .10 .25
245 Matthias Bachler .10 .25
246 Kristian Gahn .10 .25
247 Patrick Kruger .10 .25
248 Michael Meier .10 .25
249 Daniel Peer .10 .25
250 Roger Rieder .10 .25
251 Oliver Roth .10 .25
252 Ivo Simeon .10 .25
253 Rene Stussi .10 .25
254 Sandro Tschuor .10 .25
255 Johan Witehall .10 .25
256 Theo Wittmann .10 .25
257 HC Lausanne .10 .25
258 Mike McParland .10 .25
259 Beat Kindler .20 .50
260 Reto Schurch .20 .50
261 Malik Benturqui .10 .25
262 Michel Kamber .10 .25
263 Dejan Lozanov .10 .25
264 Michel N'Goy .10 .25
265 Serge Poudrier .10 .25
266 Roger Sigg .10 .25
267 Thomas Studer .10 .25
268 Oliver Tschanz .10 .25
269 Florian Andenmatten .10 .25
270 Andrei Bashkirov .20 .50
271 Daniel Bieri .10 .25
272 Thierry Bornand .10 .25
273 Sandro Haberlin .10 .25
274 Oliver Kamber .10 .25
275 Trevor Meier .10 .25
276 Philippe Orlandi .10 .25
277 Dmitri Shamolin .10 .25
278 Samuel Villiger .10 .25
279 Sacha Weibel .20 .50
280 Gerd Zenhausern .10 .25
281 Michel Lussier .10 .25
282 Gilles Cattela .10 .25
283 Thierry Noel .10 .25
284 Oliver Amadio .10 .25
285 Pascal Avanthay .10 .25
286 Nicolas Bernasconi .10 .25
287 Raphael Brusa .10 .25
288 Valeri Chiriaev .10 .25
289 Marc Tschudy .10 .25
290 Alexis Vacheron .10 .25
291 Steve Aebersold .10 .25
292 Jesse Belanger .20 .50
293 Thomas Deruns .10 .25
294 Jamie Heinrich .10 .25
295 Vincent Lechenne .10 .25
296 Claude Luethi .10 .25
297 Fabrice Maillat .10 .25
298 Daniel Nakaoka .10 .25
299 Michael Neininger .10 .25
300 Philippe Thalmann .10 .25
301 Markus Graf .10 .25
302 Marco Wegmuller .20 .50
303 Martin Zerzuben .10 .25
304 Sven Dick .10 .25
305 Serge Meyer .10 .25
306 Jorg Reber .10 .25
307 Sven Schmid .10 .25
308 Bjorn Schneider .10 .25
309 Pascal Sommer .10 .25
310 Mauro Beccarelli .10 .25
311 Philipp Folghera .10 .25
312 Rene Furler .10 .25
313 Stefan Moser .10 .25
314 Andreas Nauser .10 .25
315 Cyrill Pasche .10 .25
316 Reggie Savage .20 .50
317 Ryan Savoia .20 .50
318 Kevin Schlapfer .10 .25
319 Marco Signer .10 .25
320 Stefan Tschiemer .10 .25
321 Chris McSorley .10 .25
322 David Bochy .20 .50
323 Flavio Streit .10 .25
324 Fredy Bobillier .10 .25
325 Patrice Brasey .10 .25
326 Fabian Gull .10 .25
327 David Leibzig .10 .25
328 Todd Richards .20 .50
329 Nicolas Studer .10 .25
330 Misko Antisin .10 .25
331 Philippe Bozon .75 2.00
332 Igor Fedulov .10 .25
333 Marco Fischer .10 .25
334 Xavier Gattuso .10 .25
335 Maxime Lapointe .10 .25
336 Boris Leimgruber .10 .25
337 Paul Savary .10 .25
338 Didier Schafer .10 .25
339 Pascal Schaller .10 .25
340 Mario Schocher .10 .25
341 Bruno Aegerter .10 .25
342 Rainer Karlen .10 .25
343 Marc Zimmermann .20 .50
344 Beat Heldstab .10 .25
345 Karl Knopf .10 .25
346 Philipp Portner .10 .25
347 Francis Reichmuth .10 .25
348 Marco Schupbach .10 .25
349 Marc Zurbriggen .10 .25
350 Patrick Aeberli .10 .25
351 Sergio Biner .10 .25
352 Marc Buhlmann .10 .25
353 Nicolas Gastaldo .10 .25
354 Stefan Ketola .10 .25
355 Swen Kohler .10 .25
356 Richard Laplante .10 .25
357 Cedric Metrailler .10 .25
358 Detlef Prediger .10 .25
359 Gabriel Taccoz .10 .25
360 Ken Zurfluh .10 .25
361 Arnold Lortscher .10 .25
362 Beat Aebischer .10 .25
363 Rainer Kalin .10 .25
364 Francesco Bizzozero .10 .25
365 Christoph Decurtins .10 .25
366 Mark Emmenegger .10 .25
367 Ruedi Forster .10 .25
368 Jurg Hardegger .10 .25
369 Richard Stucki .10 .25
370 Stefan Wuthrich .10 .25
371 Alain Ayer .10 .25
372 Yanick Dube .10 .25
373 Reto Germann .10 .25
374 Patrick Giroud .10 .25
375 Bjorn Guazzini .10 .25
376 Albert Malgin .10 .25
377 Oliver Muller .10 .25
378 Patrick Siegwart .10 .25
379 Andre von Rohr .10 .25
380 Matti Alatalo .10 .25
381 Christian Weber .10 .25
382 Marc Eichmann .10 .25
383 Matthias Schoder .20 .50
384 Stefan Badrutt .10 .25
385 Chris Belanger .10 .25
386 Thomi Derungs .10 .25
387 Michael Hofer .10 .25
388 Andri Stoffel .10 .25
389 Andreas Furrer .10 .25
390 Lukas Grauwiler .10 .25
391 Rolf Hildebrand .10 .25
392 Alex Krstic .10 .25
393 Patrick Landolt .10 .25
394 Patrick Looser .10 .25
395 Dean Seymour .10 .25
396 Riccardo Signorell .10 .25
397 Pascal Tiegermann .10 .25
398 Thomas Walser .10 .25
399 Simon Wanner .10 .25
400 Merlin Malinowski .10 .25
401 Olivier Gigon .10 .25
402 Sebastien Kohler .20 .50
403 Ludovic Aubry .10 .25
404 Eric Bourquin .10 .25
405 Dany Ott .10 .25
406 Christian Schuster .10 .25
407 Wes Snell .10 .25
408 Markus Wuthrich .10 .25
409 Steven Barras .10 .25
410 Martin Bergeron .10 .25
411 Scott Biser .10 .25
412 Florian Conz .10 .25
413 Real Gerber .10 .25
414 Sacha Guerne .10 .25
415 Shawn Heaphy .10 .25
416 Jerome Kohler .10 .25
417 Jean-Charles Lapaire .10 .25
418 Boe Leslie .10 .25
419 Steve Pochon .10 .25
420 Yann Voillat .10 .25
421 Didier Massy .10 .25
422 Gregory Berclaz .10 .25
423 Roland Meyer .10 .25
424 Johan Bertholet .10 .25
425 Lionel D'Urso .10 .25
426 Cedric Favre .10 .25
427 Jonathan Lussier .10 .25
428 Pietro Ottini .10 .25
429 Emmanuel Tacchini .10 .25
430 Beat Brantschen .10 .25
431 Elvis Clavien .10 .25
432 Gaby Epiney .10 .25
433 Kelly Glowa .10 .25
434 Pietro Juri .10 .25
435 Daniel Mares .10 .25
436 Cedric Melly .10 .25
437 Thierry Metrailler .10 .25
438 Fabrizio Silietti .10 .25
439 Daniel Wobmann .10 .25
440 Raymond Zahnd .10 .25
441 Christian Ruegg .10 .25
442 Matthias Muller .10 .25
443 Pascal Sievert .10 .25
444 Claude Amstutz .10 .25
445 Roland Kradolfer .10 .25
446 Pascal Lamprecht .10 .25
447 Patrick Mader .10 .25
448 Michael Marki .10 .25
449 Alessandro Sellitto .10 .25
450 Daniel Sigg .10 .25
451 Rico Beltrame .10 .25
452 Marius Brugger .10 .25
453 Joel Camenzind .10 .25
454 Michael Diener .10 .25
455 Timmy Hoppe .10 .25
456 Roland Korsch .10 .25
457 Real Raemy .10 .25
458 Marco Seeholzer .10 .25
459 Harijs Vitolinsch .10 .25
460 Jacques Zimmermann .10 .25
461 Beat Lautenschlager .10 .25
462 Davide Gislimberti .10 .25
463 Peter Mettler .20 .50
464 Marc Gautschi .10 .25
465 Zbynek Hybler .10 .25
466 Stephane Julien .10 .25
467 Kim Scheidegger .10 .25
468 Olivier Schaublin .10 .25
469 Dominik Z'berg .10 .25
470 Philipp Dornbierer .10 .25
471 Patrick Girod .10 .25
472 Marco Graf .10 .25
473 Andreas Haner .10 .25
474 Michael Murer .10 .25
475 Robert Othmann .10 .25
476 Steve Potvin .10 .25
477 David Raissle .10 .25
478 Jarkko Schaublin .10 .25
479 Lovis Schonenberger .10 .25
480 Marcel Sommer .10 .25

2002-03 Swiss EV Zug Postcards

COMPLETE SET (26) 10.00 25.00
1 Team photo .40 1.00
2 Doug Mason .40 1.00
3 Chris Tancill .75 2.00
4 Paul DiPietro .75 2.00
5 Richmond Gosselin .40 1.00
6 Patrick Schopf .40 1.00
7 Peter Mettler .40 1.00
8 Ruedi Niderost .40 1.00
9 Ralf Bundi .40 1.00
10 Charles Simard .40 1.00
11 Patrick Fischer .40 1.00
12 Fabio Schumacher .40 1.00
13 Pascal Muller .40 1.00
14 Gaetan Voisard .40 1.00
15 Lovis Schonenberger .40 1.00
16 Stefan Voegele .40 1.00
17 Stefan Niggli .40 1.00
18 Duri Camichel .40 1.00
19 Patrick Oppliger .40 1.00
20 Paolo Duca .40 1.00
21 Andre Rufener .40 1.00
22 Alain Demuth .40 1.00
23 Oliver Kamber .40 1.00
24 Frederic Rothen .40 1.00
25 Joel Savage .75 2.00
26 Chris Armstrong .40 1.00

2002-03 Swiss HNL

COMPLETE SET (499) 30.00 75.00
1 Lars Weibel .20 .50
2 Andrea Haller .10 .25
3 Jonas Hiller 1.00 2.50
4 Jan von Arx .10 .25
5 Lonny Bohonos .20 .50
6 Marco Gruber .10 .25
7 Marc Gianola .10 .25
8 Josef Marha .10 .25
9 Michel Riesen .40 1.00
10 Reto von Arx .20 .50
11 Ralph Ott .10 .25
12 Ari Sulander .40 1.00
13 Martin Kout .10 .25
14 Edgar Salis .10 .25
15 Andres Ambuhl .10 .25
16 Jan Alston .20 .50
17 Gian-Carlo Hendry .10 .25
18 Peter Jaks .10 .25
19 Patrick Fischer .10 .25
20 Mark Ouimet .20 .50
21 Reto Stirnimann .10 .25
22 Davide Gislimberti .10 .25
23 Marc Heberlein .10 .25
24 Sandro Bertaggia .10 .25
25 Olivier Keller .10 .25
26 Jean-Jacques Aeschlimann .10 .25
27 Thierry Paterlini .10 .25
28 Flavien Conne .10 .25
29 Ryan Gardner .20 .50
30 Corey Millen .20 .50
31 Fabian Sutter .10 .25
32 Andre Rotheli .10 .25
33 Vladimir Jursinov .10 .25
34 Lukas Baumgartner .10 .25
35 Matthias Schoder .20 .50
36 Martin Hohener .10 .25
37 Alain Reist .10 .25
38 Deny Bartschi .10 .25
39 Jakub Horak .10 .25
40 Jaroslav Hlinka .10 .25
41 Sven Lindemann .10 .25
42 Marc Reichert .10 .25
43 Tim Ramholt .40 1.00
44 Thomas Widmer .10 .25
45 Gianluca Mona .20 .50
46 Mike Gaul .20 .50
47 Mark Streit .10 .25
48 Philippe Marquis .10 .25
49 Patrick Howald .10 .25
50 David Maurer .10 .25
51 Patric Della Rossa .10 .25
52 Michel Mouther .10 .25
53 Robert Slehofer .10 .25
54 Pauli Jaks .20 .50
55 Dan Hodgson .20 .50
56 Ivan Gazzaroli .10 .25
57 Martin Rauch .10 .25
58 Loic Burkhalter .10 .25
59 Claudio Micheli .10 .25
60 Nicola Celio .10 .25
61 Paolo Imperatori .10 .25
62 Robert Petrovicky .10 .25
63 Raeto Raffainer .10 .25
64 Doug Mason .10 .25
65 Chris Armstrong .10 .25
66 Ruedi Niderost .10 .25
67 Jim Koleff .10 .25
68 Duri Camichel .10 .25
69 Paolo Duca .10 .25
70 Patrick Oppliger .10 .25
71 Mark Astley .20 .50
72 Joel Savage .20 .50
73 Stefan Voegele .10 .25
74 Marc Eichmann .10 .25
75 Andreas Hanni .10 .25
76 Marc Leuenberger .10 .25
77 Martin Steinegger .10 .25
78 Alex Chatelain .10 .25
79 Patrick Sutter .10 .25
80 Patrik Juhlin .20 .50
81 Laurent Muller .10 .25
82 Rolf Schrepfer .10 .25
83 Krister Cantoni .10 .25
84 Beat Kindler .20 .50
85 Fredy Bobillier .10 .25
86 Serge Poudrier .10 .25
87 Regis Fuchs .10 .25
88 Florian Andenmatten .10 .25
89 Thierry Bornand .10 .25
90 Philipp Orlandi .10 .25
91 Mike Maneluk .20 .50
92 Sacha Weibel .20 .50
93 Kari Eloranta .20 .50
94 Livio Fazio .10 .25
95 Andy Naser .10 .25
96 Kari Martikainen .10 .25
97 Patrick Aeberli .10 .25
98 Axel Heim .10 .25
99 Adrian Wichser .20 .50
100 Patrizio Morger .10 .25
101 Jarno Peltonen .10 .25
102 Thomas Walser .10 .25
103 Tobias Stephan .75 2.00
104 Marco Streit .20 .50

105 Beat Gerber .10 .25
106 Pascal Stoller .10 .25
107 Fabian Guignard .10 .25
108 Bruno Brechbuhl .10 .25
109 Todd Elik .20 .50
110 Benjamin Pluss .10 .25
111 Marco Kloti .10 .25
112 Bernhard Schumperli .10 .25
113 Fabien Hecquet .10 .25
114 Brett Hauer .20 .50
115 Cyrill Buhler .10 .25
116 Wes Snell .10 .25
117 Misko Antisin .10 .25
118 Gian-Marco Crameri .10 .25
119 Andreas Camenzind .10 .25
120 Daniel Meier .10 .25
121 Paul Savary .10 .25
122 Dario Kostovic .10 .25
123 Michel Lussier .10 .25
124 Romano Lemm .10 .25
125 Oliver Amadio .10 .25
126 Dejan Lozanov .10 .25
127 Emanuel Peter .10 .25
128 Steve Aebersold .10 .25
129 Martin Pluss .10 .25
130 Boris Leimgruber .10 .25
131 Daniel Nakaoka .10 .25
132 Roger Rieder .10 .25
133 Julien Turler .10 .25
134 Kimmo Rintanen .10 .25
135 Martin Zerzuben .10 .25
136 Sven Dick .10 .25
137 Colin Muller .10 .25
138 Bjorn Schneider .10 .25
139 Matthias Lauber .20 .50
140 Mauro Beccarelli .10 .25
141 Stefan Moser .10 .25
142 Raphael Berger .10 .25
143 Kevin Schlapfer .10 .25
144 Alain Birbaum .10 .25
145 Thomas Papp .10 .25
146 Michael Hofer .10 .25
147 Lukas Gerber .10 .25
148 Andri Stoffel .10 .25
149 Tiziano Gianini .10 .25
150 Sandro Moggi .10 .25
151 Riccardo Signorell .10 .25
152 Oliver Tschanz .10 .25
153 Simon Wanner .10 .25
154 Craig Ferguson .20 .50
155 Rainer Karlen .10 .25
156 Beat Heldstab .10 .25
157 Vjeran Ivankovic .10 .25
158 Marco Schupbach .10 .25
159 Silvan Lussy .10 .25
160 Michael Gerber .10 .25
161 Cedric Metrailler .10 .25
162 Thibaut Monnet .10 .25
163 Stephane Roy .10 .25
164 Gil Montandon .10 .25
165 Merlin Malinowski .10 .25
166 Olivier Devaux .10 .25
167 Mario Rottaris .10 .25
168 Dany Ott .10 .25
169 Jean-Yves Roy .20 .50
170 Markus Wuthrich .10 .25
171 Florian Conz .10 .25
172 Valentin Wirz .10 .25
173 Jerome Kohler .10 .25
174 Rostislav Cada .10 .25
175 Yann Voillat .10 .25
176 Rainer Kalin .10 .25
177 Simon Zuger .20 .50
178 Jurg Hardegger .10 .25
179 Robin Breitbach .10 .25
180 Richard Stucki .10 .25
181 Reto Germann .10 .25
182 John Gobbi .10 .25
183 Claude Luethi .10 .25
184 Reto Kobach .10 .25
185 Robert Othmann .10 .25
186 Matthias Muller .10 .25
187 Martin Stepanek .10 .25
188 Pascal Lamprecht .10 .25
189 Alan Tallarini .10 .25
190 Andre Nussbaum .10 .25
191 Michael Diener .10 .25
192 Corsin Camichel .10 .25
193 Timmy Hoppe .10 .25
194 Manuele Celio .10 .25
195 Marco Signer .10 .25
196 Beat Lautenschlager .10 .25
197 John Fritsche .10 .25
198 Marco Knecht .10 .25
199 John Fust .10 .25
200 Alexis Vacheron .10 .25
201 Martin Bergeron .10 .25
202 Vitaly Lakhmatov .10 .25
203 Andreas Haner .10 .25
204 Michel Liniger .10 .25
205 Marco Seeholzer .10 .25
206 Samuel Villiger .10 .25
207 Zdenek Sedlak .10 .25
208 Roland Meyer .10 .25
209 Egor Shastin .10 .25
210 Cedric Favre .10 .25
211 Roland Kradolfer .10 .25
212 Peter Mettler .20 .50
213 Severin Cavegn .10 .25
214 Patrick Schopf .20 .50
215 Antoine Lussier .10 .25
216 Oleg Siritsa .10 .25
217 Patrick Fischer .10 .25
218 Sascha Friedli .10 .25
219 Pascal Muller .10 .25
220 Rolf Diethelm .10 .25
221 Alan Hirschi .10 .25
222 Charles Simard .10 .25
223 Mario Heiniger .10 .25
224 Gaetan Voisard .10 .25
225 Marco Pistolato .10 .25
226 Mischa von Gunten .10 .25
227 Alain Demuth .10 .25
228 Ralph Krueger .10 .25
229 Paul Di Pietro .20 .50
230 Flavien Conne .10 .25
231 Alain Demuth .10 .25
232 Oliver Kamber .10 .25
233 Martin Hohener .10 .25
234 Stefan Niggli .10 .25
235 David Jobin .10 .25
236 Marc Reichert .10 .25
237 Frederic Rothen .10 .25
238 Mathias Seger .10 .25
239 Andre Rufener .10 .25
240 Patrick Sutter .10 .25
241 Winners Pluss .10 .25
242 Lovis Schonenberger .10 .25
243 Lonny Bohonos .20 .50
244 Chris Tancill .20 .50
245 Mike Maneluk .20 .50
246 Martin Pluss .10 .25
247 Kent Ruhnke .10 .25
248 Arno Del Curto .10 .25
249 Marco Buhrer .20 .50
250 Florian Blatter .10 .25
251 Michael Kress .10 .25
252 Rikard Franzen .10 .25
253 Benjamin Winkler .10 .25
254 David Jobin .10 .25
255 Bjorn Christen .10 .25
256 Steivan Hasler .10 .25
257 Sven Leuenberger .10 .25
258 Kevin Miller .20 .50
259 Dominic Meier .10 .25
260 Sandro Rizzi .10 .25
261 Pekka Rautakallio .20 .50
262 Rolf Ziegler .10 .25
263 Rene Back .10 .25
264 Sebastien Bordeleau .20 .50
265 Arne Ramholt .10 .25
266 Mathias Seger .10 .25
267 Christian Dube .10 .25
268 Mattia Baldi .10 .25
269 Sven Helfenstein .10 .25
270 Rolf Hildebrand .10 .25
271 Christian Matte .20 .50
272 Andy Keller .10 .25
273 Derek Plante .20 .50
274 Lars Leuenberger .10 .25
275 Michel Zeiter .10 .25
276 Ronnie Rueger .20 .50
277 Philippe Muller .10 .25
278 Noel Guyaz .10 .25
279 Ivo Ruthemann .10 .25
280 Petteri Nummelin .10 .25
281 Jan Cadieux .10 .25
282 Thomas Ziegler .10 .25
283 Keith Fair .10 .25
284 Mike McParland .10 .25
285 Sandy Jeannin .10 .25
286 Mirko Murovic .20 .50
287 Reto Schurch .20 .50
288 Raffaele Sannitz .20 .50
289 Malik Benturqui .10 .25
290 Flavio Ludke .10 .25
291 Severin Blindenbacher .10 .25
292 Ronny Keller .10 .25
293 Marko Kiprusoff .10 .25
294 Michel N'Goy .10 .25
295 Gregor Thommen .10 .25
296 Patrik Bartschi .10 .25
297 Thomas Studer .10 .25
298 Marc Werlen .10 .25
299 Andrei Bashkirov .20 .50
300 Daniel Bieri .10 .25
301 Mathias Holzer .10 .25
302 Trevor Meier .10 .25
303 Dmitri Shamolin .10 .25
304 Jarrod Skalde .20 .50
305 Michel Wicky .10 .25
306 Gerd Zenhausern .10 .25
307 Thomas Berger .20 .50
308 Marco Capaul .10 .25
309 Cyrill Geyer .10 .25
310 Michel Kamber .10 .25
311 Marc Schefer .10 .25
312 Fabian Stephan .10 .25
313 Markus Butler .10 .25
314 Daniel Giger .10 .25
315 Philipp Luber .10 .25
316 Dale McTavish .20 .50
317 Thomas Nussli .10 .25
318 Mikko Peltola .10 .25
319 Sebastien Reuille .10 .25
320 Niki Siren .10 .25
321 Alfred Bohren .10 .25
322 Claudio Bayer .20 .50
323 Daniel Aegerter .10 .25
324 Samuel Balmer .10 .25
325 Steve Hirschi .10 .25
326 Thomas Kunzi .10 .25
327 Mathias Wust .10 .25
328 Brian Bonin .20 .50
329 Marc Buhlmann .10 .25
330 Mike Craig .20 .50
331 Stefan Grogg .10 .25
332 Thomas Heldner .10 .25
333 Benoit Pont .10 .25
334 Sascha Schneider .10 .25
335 Daniel Steiner .10 .25
336 Chris McSorley .10 .25
337 Reto Pavoni .20 .50
338 Patrice Brasey .10 .25
339 Jamie Heward .20 .50
340 Dino Kessler .10 .25
341 Nicolas Studer .10 .25
342 Pierre-Alain Ancay .10 .25
343 Yvan Benoit .10 .25
344 Philippe Bozon .40 1.00
345 Thomas Derungs .10 .25
346 Igor Fedulov .10 .25
347 Michael Neininger .10 .25
348 Kevin Romy .10 .25
349 Pascal Schaller .10 .25
350 Theo Wittmann .10 .25
351 Florien Bruegger .10 .25
352 Gilles Cattela .10 .25
353 Nicolas Bernasconi .10 .25
354 Valeri Chiriaev .10 .25
355 Jonathan Pan .10 .25
356 Marc Tschudy .10 .25
357 Philippe Fontana .10 .25
358 Jamie Heinrich .10 .25
359 Fabrice Maillat .10 .25
360 Damien Micheli .10 .25
361 Philippe Thalmann .10 .25
362 Omar Tognini .10 .25
363 Bror Hansson .10 .25
364 Simon Rytz .10 .25
365 Fabian Beck .10 .25
366 Chris Belanger .10 .25
367 Serge Meyer .10 .25
368 Jorg Reber .10 .25
369 Remo Altorfer .10 .25
370 Fabio Beccarelli .10 .25
371 Rene Furler .10 .25
372 Vincent Lechenne .10 .25
373 Steve Pochon .10 .25
374 Ryan Savoia .20 .50
375 Christian Weber .10 .25
376 Yves Burlimann .10 .25
377 Marco Baumann .10 .25
378 Andreas Furrer .10 .25
379 Patrick Meichtry .10 .25
380 Daniel Schnyder .10 .25
381 Lukas Grauwiler .10 .25
382 Claudio Moggi .10 .25
383 Andreas Nauser .10 .25
384 Mike Richard .10 .25
385 Pascal Tiegermann .10 .25
386 Petri Varis .20 .50
387 Alexis Weber .10 .25
388 Bruno Aegerter .10 .25
389 Marc Zimmermann .20 .50
390 Stefan Badrutt .10 .25
391 Philipp Portner .10 .25
392 Kim Scheidegger .10 .25
393 Marc Zurbriggen .10 .25
394 Nicolas Gastaldo .10 .25
395 Stefan Gahler .10 .25
396 Stefan Ketola .10 .25
397 Marcel Moser .10 .25
398 Detlef Prediger .10 .25
399 Adrian Witschi .10 .25
400 Ken Zurfluh .10 .25
401 Michael Fluckiger .10 .25
402 Ludovic Aubry .10 .25
403 John Miner .10 .25
404 Jonathan Miner .10 .25
405 Christian Schuster .10 .25
406 Martin Schupbach .10 .25
407 Steven Barras .10 .25
408 Elvis Clavien .10 .25
409 Gilbert Flueler .10 .25
410 Sacha Guerne .10 .25
411 Christoph Lindberg .10 .25
412 Cyrill Pasche .10 .25
413 Arnold Lortscher .10 .25
414 Beat Aebischer .10 .25
415 Francesco Bizzozero .10 .25
416 Ruedi Forster .10 .25
417 Karl Knopf .10 .25
418 Francis Reichmuth .10 .25
419 Stefan Wuthrich .10 .25
420 Martin Gendron .20 .50
421 Kevin Gloor .10 .25
422 Bjorn Guazzini .10 .25
423 Albert Malgin .10 .25
424 Oliver Muller .10 .25
425 Patrick Siegwart .10 .25
426 Christian Ruegg .10 .25
427 Pasqual Sievert .10 .25
428 Christoph Decurtins .10 .25
429 Patrick Mader .10 .25
430 Michael Marki .10 .25
431 Raphael Schoop .10 .25
432 Daniel Sigg .10 .25
433 Philipp Dornbierer .10 .25
434 Curdin Grischott .10 .25
435 Roland Korsch .10 .25
436 Mikko Liukonnen .10 .25
437 Christian Strasser .10 .25
438 Harijs Vitolinsch .10 .25
439 Flavio Streit .10 .25
440 Stephane Julien .10 .25
441 Roland Kaser .10 .25
442 Olivier Schaublin .10 .25
443 Andreas Zehnder .10 .25
444 Rolf Badertscher .10 .25
445 Marco Fischer .10 .25
446 Marco Graf .10 .25
447 Cornel Prinz .10 .25
448 David Raissle .10 .25
449 Marcel Sommer .10 .25
450 Rene Stussi .10 .25
451 Kim Collins .10 .25
452 Thomas Baumle .10 .25
453 Lionel D'Urso .10 .25
454 Philippe Faust .10 .25
455 Fabian Gull .10 .25
456 Terry Hollinger .10 .25
457 Andre Bielmann .10 .25
458 Joel Camenzind .10 .25
459 Derek Cormier .10 .25
460 Maxime Lapointe .10 .25
461 Thierry Metrailler .10 .25
462 Didier Schafer .10 .25
463 Daniel Wobmann .10 .25
464 Ernst Bruderer .10 .25
465 Andreas Schweizer .10 .25
466 Simon Born .10 .25
467 Bernhard Fankhauser .10 .25
468 Marcel Habisreutinger .10 .25
469 Reto Klay .10 .25
470 Lars Sommer .10 .25
471 Eric Lecompte .20 .50
472 Martin Meyer .10 .25
473 Tassilo Schwarz .10 .25
474 Zeno Schwarz .10 .25
475 Martin Wuthrich .10 .25
476 Bruno Zarrillo .20 .50
477 Jean-Jacques Aeschlimann .10 .25
478 Reto von Arx .20 .50
479 Gian-Marco Crameri .10 .25
480 Patric Della Rossa .10 .25
481 Patrick Fischer .10 .25
482 Martin Gerber 2.00 5.00
483 Sandy Jeannin .10 .25
484 Marcel Jenni .10 .25
485 Olivier Keller .10 .25
486 Martin Pluss .10 .25
487 Michel Riesen .40 1.00
488 Ivo Ruthemann .10 .25
489 Martin Steinegger .10 .25
490 Mark Streit .10 .25
491 Lars Weibel .20 .50
492 Rolf Ziegler .10 .25
493 Cristobal Huet 1.25 3.00
494 Mark Streit .10 .25
495 Charly Oppliger .10 .25
496 Fredy Pargatzi .10 .25
497 Lonny Bohonos .20 .50
498 Patrik Juhlin .20 .50
499 Felix Hollenstein .10 .25

2002-03 Swiss SCL Tigers

COMPLETE SET
1 Johan Fransson .75 2.00
2 Pavel Skrbek .75 2.00
3 Jonas Ronnqvist .75 2.00
4 Magnus Nilsson .75 2.00
5 Gusten Tornqvist .75 2.00
6 Daniel Henriksson .75 2.00
7 Todd Elik .75 2.00

2003-04 Swiss EV Zug Postcards

COMPLETE SET (27) 10.00 25.00
1 Team Photo .40 1.00
2 Silvan Anthamatten .40 1.00
3 Duri Camichel .40 1.00
4 Corsin Casutt .40 1.00
5 Alain Demuth .40 1.00
6 Rafael Diaz .40 1.00
7 Paul Dipietro .40 1.00
8 Thomas Dommen .40 1.00
9 Paolo Duca .40 1.00
10 Livio Fazio .40 1.00
11 Patrick Fischer .40 1.00
12 Patrick Fischer .40 1.00
13 Daniel Giger .40 1.00
14 Andreas Kung .40 1.00
15 Colin Muller .40 1.00
16 Pascal Muller .40 1.00
17 Patrick Oppliger .40 1.00
18 Barry Richter .40 1.00
19 Frederic Rothen .40 1.00
20 Joel Savage .40 1.00
21 Lovis Schonenberger .40 1.00
22 Patrick Schopf .40 1.00
23 Fabio Schumacher .40 1.00
24 Sean Simpson .40 1.00
25 Chris Tancill .40 1.00
26 Michael Tobler .40 1.00
27 Gaetan Voisard .40 1.00
28 Claude Lemieux 4.00 10.00

2004-05 Swiss Davos Postcards

COMPLETE SET (30) 40.00 80.00
1 Team photo .40 1.00
2 Team history .40 1.00
3 Andres Ambuhl 1.25 3.00
4 Thomas Baumle 1.25 3.00
5 Florian Blatter 1.25 3.00
6 Daniell Boss 1.25 3.00
7 Bjorn Christen 1.25 3.00
8 Franco Collenberg 1.25 3.00
9 Arno Del Curto 1.25 3.00
10 Beat Forster 1.25 3.00
11 Marc Gianola 1.25 3.00
12 Peter Guggisberg 1.25 3.00
13 Niklas Hagman 2.00 5.00
14 Andreas Haller 1.25 3.00
15 Stevan Hasler 1.25 3.00
16 Marc Heberlein 1.25 3.00
17 Jonas Hiller 2.00 5.00
18 Michael Kress 1.25 3.00
19 Josef Marha 1.25 3.00
20 Laurent Muller 1.25 3.00
21 Rick Nash 12.00 30.00
22 Claudio Neff 1.25 3.00
23 Arne Ramholt 1.25 3.00
24 Michel Riesen 1.25 3.00
25 Sandro Rizzi 1.25 3.00
26 Fabian Sutter 1.25 3.00
27 Joe Thornton 15.00 40.00
28 Jan Von Arx 1.25 3.00
29 Reto Von Arx 1.25 3.00
30 Benjamin Winkler 1.25 3.00

2004-05 Swiss EV Zug Postcards

COMPLETE SET (28) 10.00 25.00
1 Brett Hauer .75 2.00
2 Niko Kapanen .75 2.00
3 Mike Fisher 1.25 3.00
4 Barry Richter .40 1.00
5 Oleg Petrov .40 1.00
6 Lars Weibel .40 1.00
7 Rafael Walter .40 1.00
8 Jan Feldmann .40 1.00
9 Livio Fazio .40 1.00
10 Pascal Muller .40 1.00
11 Rafael Diaz .40 1.00
12 Rene Back .40 1.00
13 Gaetan Voisard .40 1.00
14 Silvan Anthamatten .40 1.00
15 Patric Della Rosa .40 1.00
16 Gian-Marco Crameri .40 1.00
17 Patrick Fisher .40 1.00
18 Duri Camichel .40 1.00
19 Patrick Oppliger .40 1.00
20 Duca Paolo .40 1.00
21 Fabian Schnyder .40 1.00
22 Corsin Casutt .40 1.00
23 Daniel Giger .40 1.00
24 Frederic Rothen .40 1.00
25 Beat Schuler .40 1.00
26 Sean Simpson CO .40 1.00
27 Colin Muller ACO .40 1.00
28 Team Photo .40 1.00

2004-05 Swiss Lausanne HC Postcards

COMPLETE SET (25) 10.00 25.00
1 Pascal Schaller .40 1.00
2 Robert Slehofer .40 1.00
3 Alain Reist .40 1.00
4 Bruno Steck .40 1.00
5 Andy Roach .75 2.00
6 Thomas Berger .40 1.00
7 Patrick Boileau .75 2.00
8 Florian Andenmatten .40 1.00
9 Sunshine Romerio .40 1.00
10 Julien Turler .40 1.00
11 Gerd Zenhausern .40 1.00
12 Loic Merz .40 1.00
13 Martin St. Louis 4.00 10.00
14 Christophe Brown .40 1.00
15 Michael Ngoy .40 1.00
16 Mathias Holzer .40 1.00
17 Laurent Emery .40 1.00
18 Florian Conz .40 1.00
19 Marko Tuomainen .40 1.00
20 Michael Kamber .40 1.00
21 Lovis Schonenberger .40 1.00
22 Sacha Weibel .40 1.00
23 Eric Landry .40 1.00
24 Bill Stewart CO .10 .25
25 Gary Sheehan ACO .10 .25

2007-08 Swiss HC Lugano

COMPLETE SET (27) 15.00 30.00
1 Krister Cantoni .60 1.50
2 Alessandro Chiesa .60 1.50
3 Flavien Conne .60 1.50
4 Fabrizio Conte .60 1.50
5 Andreas Hanni .60 1.50
6 Timo Helbling .60 1.50
7 Jukka Hentunen .60 1.50
8 Steve Hirschi .60 1.50
9 Sandy Jeannin .60 1.50
10 Mike Knoepfli .60 1.50
11 Dario Kostovic .60 1.50
12 Marty Murray .60 1.50
13 Andy Naser .60 1.50
14 Thierry Paterlini .60 1.50
15 Kevin Romy .60 1.50
16 Raffaele Sannitz .60 1.50
17 Yannick Tremblay .60 1.50
18 Julien Vauclair .60 1.50
19 Tristan Vauclair .60 1.50
20 Raffael Walter .60 1.50
21 Landon Wilson .60 1.50
22 Valentin Wirz .60 1.50
23 Simon Zuger .60 1.50
24 Ivano Zanatta HC .10 .25
25 Diego Scandella AC .10 .25
26 Dusan Sidor .60 1.50
27 Tiziano Muzio .60 1.50

2012-13 Swiss SNL

SNL001 Nolan Schaefer .40 1.00
SNL002 Lorenzo Croce .20 .50
SNL003 Julien Bonnet .20 .50
SNL004 Reto Kobach .20 .50
SNL005 Zdenek Kutlak .30 .75
SNL006 Maxim Noreau .40 1.00
SNL007 Marc Schulthess .20 .50
SNL008 Patrick Sidler .20 .50
SNL009 Adrian Trunz .20 .50
SNL010 Elias Bianchi .20 .50
SNL011 Mattia Bianchi .20 .50
SNL012 Paolo Duca .30 .75
SNL013 Daniele Grassi .20 .50
SNL014 Vitali Lakhmatov .20 .50
SNL015 Alain Mieville .20 .50
SNL016 Max Pacioretty .75 2.00
SNL017 Richard Park .40 1.00
SNL018 Marco Pedretti .30 .75
SNL019 Inti Pestoni .40 1.00
SNL020 Marc Reichert .20 .50
SNL021 Roman Schlagenhauf .20 .50
SNL022 Jason Williams .75 2.00
SNL023 Tim Weber .20 .50
SNL024 Serge Pelletier .20 .50
SNL025 Checklist Ambri-Piotta .20 .50
SNL026 Marco Buhrer .40 1.00
SNL027 Olivier Gigon .20 .50
SNL028 Franco Collenberg .20 .50
SNL029 Philippe Furrer .30 .75
SNL030 Beat Gerber .20 .50
SNL031 Andreas Hanni .20 .50
SNL032 Martin Hohener .20 .50
SNL033 David Jobin .20 .50
SNL034 Roman Josi 1.25 3.00
SNL035 Geoff Kinrade .40 1.00
SNL036 Travis Roche .40 1.00
SNL037 Mark Streit 1.25 3.00
SNL038 Pascal Berger .20 .50
SNL039 Christoph Bertschy .30 .75
SNL040 Nicklas Danielsson .30 .75
SNL041 Thomas Deruns .20 .50
SNL042 Ryan Gardner .40 1.00
SNL043 Caryl Neuenschwander .20 .50
SNL044 Martin Pluss .40 1.00
SNL045 Flurin Randegger .20 .50
SNL046 Byron Ritchie .40 1.00
SNL047 Daniel Rubin .20 .50
SNL048 Ivo Ruthemann .30 .75
SNL049 Tristan Scherwey .20 .50
SNL050 John Tavares 1.50 4.00
SNL051 Joel Vermin .40 1.00
SNL052 Antti Tormanen .40 1.00
SNL053 Lars Leuenberger .20 .50
SNL054 Checklist SC Bern .20 .50
SNL055 Reto Berra .60 1.50
SNL056 Marco Streit .20 .50
SNL057 Marc Schmid .20 .50
SNL058 Manuel Gossweiler .20 .50
SNL059 Marc Grieder .20 .50
SNL060 Anthony Huguenin .20 .50
SNL061 Clarence Kphargai .20 .50
SNL062 Dominic Meier .20 .50
SNL063 Dario Trutmann .30 .75
SNL064 Ramon Untersander .20 .50
SNL065 Thomas Wellinger .30 .75
SNL066 Eric Beaudoin .40 1.00
SNL067 Gianni Ehrensperger .20 .50
SNL068 Jeffrey Fuglister .20 .50
SNL069 Kevin Gloor .20 .50
SNL070 Gaetan Haas .30 .75
SNL071 Patrick Kane 1.50 4.00
SNL072 Steve Kellenberger .20 .50
SNL073 Adrien Lauper .20 .50
SNL074 Jacob Micflikier .40 1.00
SNL075 Emanuel Peter .20 .50
SNL076 Marc-Antoine Pouliot .40 1.00
SNL077 Tyler Seguin 1.50 4.00
SNL078 Ahren Spylo .40 1.00
SNL079 Mathieu Tschantre .30 .75
SNL080 Philipp Wetzel .20 .50
SNL081 Marc Wieser .20 .50
SNL082 Kevin Schlapfer .40 1.00
SNL083 Dino Stecher .20 .50
SNL084 Checklist Biel .20 .50
SNL085 Leonardo Genoni .40 1.00
SNL086 Janick Schwendener .20 .50
SNL087 Santeri Alatalo .30 .75
SNL088 Rene Back .20 .50
SNL089 Beat Forster .30 .75
SNL090 Robin Grossmann .30 .75
SNL091 Samuel Guerra .20 .50
SNL092 Mathias Joggi .20 .50
SNL093 Tim Ramholt .30 .75
SNL094 Noah Schneeberger .20 .50
SNL095 Jan Von Arx .20 .50
SNL096 Dario Burgler .40 1.00
SNL097 Corsin Camichel .20 .50
SNL098 Peter Guggisberg .20 .50
SNL099 Gregory Hofmann .30 .75
SNL100 Rick Nash 1.50 4.00
SNL101 Josef Marha .40 1.00
SNL102 Sandro Rizzi .20 .50
SNL103 Sven Ryser .20 .50
SNL104 Patrick Schommer .20 .50
SNL105 Gregory Sciaroni .20 .50
SNL106 Jannick Steinmann .20 .50
SNL107 Petr Sykora .40 1.00
SNL108 Petr Taticek .40 1.00
SNL109 Joe Thornton 1.50 4.00
SNL110 Reto Von Arx .40 1.00
SNL111 Dino Wieser .20 .50
SNL112 Arno Del Curto .40 1.00
SNL113 Checklist Davos .20 .50
SNL114 Benjamin Conz .40 1.00
SNL115 Simon Rytz .20 .50
SNL116 Marc Abplanalp .20 .50
SNL117 Alain Birbaum .20 .50
SNL118 Lukas Gerber .20 .50
SNL119 Shawn Heins .30 .75
SNL120 Joel Kwiatkowski .30 .75
SNL121 Romain Loeffel .20 .50
SNL122 Michael Ngoy .20 .50
SNL123 Sebastian Schilt .20 .50
SNL124 Cedric Botter .20 .50
SNL125 Andrey Bykov .40 1.00
SNL126 Jan Cadieux .20 .50
SNL127 David Desharnais 1.25 3.00
SNL128 Christian Dube .40 1.00
SNL129 Simon Gamache .40 1.00
SNL130 Adam Hasani .20 .50
SNL131 Sandy Jeannin .30 .75
SNL132 Mike Knoepfli .20 .50
SNL133 Greg Mauldin .40 1.00
SNL134 Melvin Merola .20 .50
SNL135 Benjamin Pluss .30 .75
SNL136 Pavel Rosa .40 1.00
SNL137 Julien Sprunger .40 1.00
SNL138 Tristan Vauclair .20 .50
SNL139 Hans Kossmann .40 1.00
SNL140 Rene Matte .20 .50
SNL141 Checklist Fribourg .20 .50
SNL142 Tobias Stephan .40 1.00
SNL143 Federico Tamo .20 .50
SNL144 Eliot Antonietti .20 .50
SNL145 Goran Bezina .30 .75
SNL146 Marc Gautschi .20 .50
SNL147 Kevin Hecquefeuille .30 .75
SNL148 Jonathan Mercier .20 .50
SNL149 Gian-Andrea Randegger .20 .50
SNL150 Daniel Vukovic .20 .50
SNL151 Yannick Weber 1.25 3.00
SNL152 Cody Almond .60 1.50
SNL153 Logan Couture 1.50 4.00
SNL154 Rico Fata .40 1.00
SNL155 Samuel Friedli .20 .50
SNL156 Dan Fritsche .60 1.50
SNL157 John Fritsche .20 .50
SNL158 Roland Gerber .20 .50
SNL159 Ryan Keller .40 1.00
SNL160 Alexandre Picard .60 1.50
SNL161 Christopher Rivera .20 .50
SNL162 Kevin Romy .30 .75
SNL163 Juraj Simek .30 .75
SNL164 Julian Walker .30 .75
SNL165 Chris McSorley .40 1.00
SNL166 Louis Matte .20 .50
SNL167 Checklist Servette Geneve .20 .50
SNL168 Lukas Meili .20 .50
SNL169 Ronnie Rueger .40 1.00
SNL170 Christopher Bagnoud .20 .50
SNL171 Eric Blum .30 .75
SNL172 Felicien Du Bois .20 .50
SNL173 Micki Dupont .60 1.50
SNL174 Philippe Schelling .20 .50
SNL175 Nicholas Steiner .20 .50
SNL176 Lukas Stoop .20 .50
SNL177 Patrick Von Gunten .40 1.00
SNL178 Matthias Bieber .30 .75
SNL179 Simon Bodenmann .30 .75
SNL180 Yannick Herren .20 .50
SNL181 Denis Hollenstein .40 1.00
SNL182 Marcel Jenni .40 1.00
SNL183 Kamil Kreps .30 .75
SNL184 Brooks Laich 1.50 4.00
SNL185 Romano Lemm .20 .50
SNL186 Robin Leone .20 .50
SNL187 Michael Liniger .20 .50
SNL188 Emil Lundberg .30 .75
SNL189 Lars Neher .20 .50
SNL190 Raffaele Sannitz .30 .75
SNL191 Tommi Santala .40 1.00
SNL192 Victor Stancescu .30 .75
SNL193 Samuel Walser .20 .50
SNL194 Tomas Tamfal .20 .50
SNL195 Frederic Rothen .20 .50
SNL196 Checklist Kloten .20 .50
SNL197 Thomas Baumle .40 1.00
SNL198 Remo Giovannini .20 .50
SNL199 Jaroslav Hubl .40 1.00
SNL200 Federico Lardi .20 .50
SNL201 Kim Lee Lindemann .20 .50
SNL202 Simon Luthi .20 .50
SNL203 Christian Moser .20 .50
SNL204 Mark Popovic .40 1.00
SNL205 Jorg Reber .20 .50
SNL206 Philippe Rytz .20 .50
SNL207 Jared Spurgeon .75 2.00
SNL208 Martin Stettler .20 .50
SNL209 Adrian Brunner .20 .50
SNL210 Tobias Bucher .20 .50
SNL211 Tyler Ennis 1.25 3.00
SNL212 Etienne Froidevaux .20 .50
SNL213 Joel Genazzi .20 .50
SNL214 Adrian Gerber .20 .50
SNL215 Lukas Haas .20 .50
SNL216 Arnaud Jacquemet .20 .50
SNL217 Robin Leblanc .20 .50
SNL218 Kurtis McLean .40 1.00
SNL219 Claudio Moggi .20 .50
SNL220 Sandro Moggi .20 .50
SNL221 Simon Moser .40 1.00
SNL222 Pascal Pelletier .40 1.00
SNL223 Alban Rexha .20 .50
SNL224 John Fust .20 .50
SNL225 Alex Reinhard .20 .50
SNL226 Checklist SCL Tigers .20 .50
SNL227 Michael Fluckiger .20 .50
SNL228 Daniel Manzato .30 .75
SNL229 Florian Blatter .20 .50
SNL230 Ilkka Heikkinen .60 1.50
SNL231 Steve Hirschi .20 .50
SNL232 Lorenz Kienzle .20 .50
SNL233 Johan Morant .20 .50
SNL234 Matteo Nodari .20 .50
SNL235 Petteri Nummelin .40 1.00
SNL236 Luca Sbisa 1.25 3.00
SNL237 Dominik Schlumpf .20 .50
SNL238 Stefan Ulmer .20 .50
SNL239 Julien Vauclair .40 1.00
SNL240 Patrice Bergeron 1.50 4.00
SNL241 Flavien Conne .20 .50
SNL242 Hnat Domenichelli .30 .75
SNL243 Luca Fazzini .20 .50
SNL244 Oliver Kamber .20 .50
SNL245 Diego Kostner .20 .50
SNL246 Brett McLean .40 1.00
SNL247 Glen Metropolit .60 1.50
SNL248 Brady Murray .30 .75
SNL249 Jordy Murray .30 .75
SNL250 Leandro Profico .20 .50
SNL251 Sebastien Reuille .20 .50
SNL252 Thomas Rufenacht .20 .50
SNL253 Dario Simion .20 .50
SNL254 Daniel Steiner .30 .75
SNL255 Larry Huras .40 1.00
SNL256 Patrick Fischer .30 .75
SNL257 Checklist Lugano .20 .50
SNL258 David Aebischer .40 1.00
SNL259 Jonas Muller .20 .50
SNL260 Sven Berger .20 .50
SNL261 Thomas Busser .20 .50
SNL262 Andreas Camenzind .20 .50
SNL263 Michael Del Zotto 1.25 3.00
SNL264 Cyrill Geyer .20 .50
SNL265 Sandro Gmur .20 .50
SNL266 Nicolas Marzan .20 .50
SNL267 Derrick Walser .40 1.00
SNL268 Marc Welti .20 .50
SNL269 Benjamin Winkler .20 .50
SNL270 Nils Berger .20 .50
SNL271 Loic Burkhalter .20 .50
SNL272 Duri Camichel .20 .50
SNL273 Robbie Earl .60 1.50
SNL274 Jeremy Gaillard .20 .50
SNL275 Lukas Grauwiler .20 .50
SNL276 Stefan Hurlimann .20 .50
SNL277 Mauro Jorg .30 .75
SNL278 Juraj Kolnik .40 1.00
SNL279 Benjamin Neukom .20 .50
SNL280 Michel Riesen .30 .75
SNL281 Antonio Rizzello .20 .50
SNL282 Peter Sejna .40 1.00
SNL283 Jason Spezza 1.50 4.00
SNL284 Nicholas Thibaudeau .20 .50
SNL285 Gian-Andrea Thony .20 .50
SNL286 Adrian Wichser .20 .50
SNL287 Harry Rogenmoser .20 .50
SNL288 Checklist Rapperswil .20 .50
SNL289 Lukas Flueler .40 1.00
SNL290 Tim Wolf .20 .50
SNL291 Severin Blindenbacher .40 1.00
SNL292 Luca Camperchioli .20 .50
SNL293 Patrick Geering .20 .50
SNL294 John Gobbi .20 .50
SNL295 Matt Lashoff .40 1.00
SNL296 Marco Maurer .20 .50
SNL297 Daniel Schnyder .20 .50
SNL298 Mathias Seger .40 1.00
SNL299 Andri Stoffel .20 .50
SNL300 Andres Ambuhl .40 1.00
SNL301 Chris Baltisberger .20 .50
SNL302 Mark Bastl .20 .50
SNL303 Dustin Brown 1.50 4.00
SNL304 Cyrill Buhler .20 .50
SNL305 Patrik Bartschi .20 .50
SNL306 Luca Cunti .40 1.00
SNL307 Ronalds Kenins .40 1.00
SNL308 Thibaut Monnet .40 1.00
SNL309 Reto Schappi .20 .50
SNL310 Ryan Shannon .40 1.00
SNL311 Jeff Tambellini .40 1.00
SNL312 Morris Trachsler .30 .75
SNL313 Roman Wick .40 1.00
SNL314 Sandro Zangger .20 .50
SNL315 Marc Crawford .40 1.00
SNL316 Rob Cookson .20 .50
SNL317 Checklist ZSC Lions .20 .50
SNL318 Jussi Markkanen .40 1.00
SNL319 Sandro Zurkirchen .20 .50
SNL320 Robin Kuonen .20 .50
SNL321 Yannick Blaser .20 .50
SNL322 Alessandro Chiesa .20 .50
SNL323 Raphael Diaz 1.25 3.00
SNL324 Patrick Fischer II .20 .50
SNL325 Andreas Furrer .20 .50

2002-03 Swiss SCL Tigers

SNL326 Timo Helbling .30 .75
SNL327 Andy Wozniewski .30 .75
SNL328 Patrick Zubler .20 .50
SNL329 Damien Brunner 1.25 3.00
SNL330 Corsin Casutt .20 .50
SNL331 Bjorn Christen .20 .50
SNL332 Josh Holden .60 1.50
SNL333 Dominic Lammer .20 .50
SNL334 Sven Lindemann .20 .50
SNL335 Fabian Luthi .20 .50
SNL336 Lino Martschini .30 .75
SNL337 Linus Omark .75 2.00
SNL338 Matthias Rossi .20 .50
SNL339 Cedric Schneuwly .20 .50
SNL340 Fabian Schnyder .30 .75
SNL341 Reto Suri .40 1.00
SNL342 Fabian Sutter .20 .50
SNL343 Henrik Zetterberg 1.50 4.00
SNL344 Doug Shedden .40 1.00
SNL345 Waltteri Immonen .20 .50
SNL346 Checklist EV Zug .20 .50
SNL347 Reto Berra .60 1.50
SNL348 Martin Gerber .60 1.50
SNL349 Alessandro Chiesa .20 .50
SNL350 Tim Ramholt .30 .75
SNL351 Patrick Von Gunten .40 1.00
SNL352 Clarence Kphargai .20 .50
SNL353 Robin Grossmann .30 .75
SNL354 Patrick Geering .20 .50
SNL355 Eric Blum .30 .75
SNL356 Romain Loeffel .30 .75
SNL357 Fabian Schnyder .20 .50
SNL358 Andres Ambuhl .40 1.00
SNL359 Simon Bodenmann .30 .75
SNL360 Inti Pestoni .30 .75
SNL361 Victor Stancescu .30 .75
SNL362 Reto Suri .40 1.00
SNL363 Daniel Rubin .20 .50
SNL364 Ryan Gardner .40 1.00
SNL365 Patrik Bartschi .20 .50
SNL366 Denis Hollenstein .40 1.00
SNL367 Dario Burgler .40 1.00
SNL368 Kevin Romy .30 .75
SNL369 Julian Walker .30 .75
SNL370 Roman Wick .40 1.00
SNL371 Sean Simpson .40 1.00
SNL372 Checklist Team Switzerland .20 .50
SNL373 Cory Schneider 1.50 4.00
SNL374 Matt Duchene 1.50 4.00
SNL375 Jaroslav Bednar .60 1.50
SNL376 Alain Berger .30 .75
SNL377 Petr Sykora .75 2.00
SNL378 Chris Campoli .75 2.00
SNL379 Nikolaj Ehlers .40 1.00
SNL380 Ryan MacMurchy .30 .75
SNL381 Sebastian Sutter .20 .50
SNL382 Martin Ulmer .20 .50
SNL383 Enzo Corvi .20 .50
SNL384 Radek Dvorak .75 2.00
SNL385 Loui Eriksson 1.50 4.00
SNL386 Lukas Sieber .20 .50
SNL387 Maxim Sushinsky .40 1.00
SNL388 Mathieu Carle .40 1.00
SNL389 Tony Salmelainen .40 1.00
SNL390 Paul Savary .30 .75
SNL391 Eric Walsky .30 .75
SNL392 Pascal Muller .20 .50
SNL393 Alexandre Giroux .40 1.00
SNL394 Felix Hollenstein .40 1.00
SNL395 Sami El-Assaoui .20 .50
SNL396 Bryce Lampman .40 1.00
SNL397 Thomas Nussli .20 .50
SNL398 Mark Bomersback .30 .75
SNL399 Charles Linglet .40 1.00
SNL400 Pierrick Pivron .20 .50
SNL401 Pavel Rosa .40 1.00
SNL402 Steve McCarthy .40 1.00
SNL403 Mikko Lehtonen .40 1.00
SNL404 Fabrice Herzog .20 .50
SNL405 Raphael Diaz 1.50 4.00
SNL406 Roman Josi 1.25 3.00
SNL407 Luca Sbisa 1.25 3.00
SNL408 Mark Streit 1.25 3.00
SNL409 Yannick Weber 1.25 3.00
SNL410 Damien Brunner 2.00 5.00

2012-13 Swiss SNL Captains

SNLCA01 Paolo Duca 2.00 5.00
SNLCA02 Martin Pluss 2.00 5.00
SNLCA03 Mathieu Tschantre 2.00 5.00
SNLCA04 Sandro Rizzi 2.00 5.00
SNLCA05 Sandy Jeannin 2.00 5.00
SNLCA06 Goran Bezina 2.00 5.00
SNLCA07 Victor Stancescu 2.00 5.00
SNLCA08 Simon Moser 2.00 5.00
SNLCA09 Julien Vauclair 2.00 5.00
SNLCA10 Cyrill Geyer 2.00 5.00
SNLCA11 Mathias Seger 2.00 5.00
SNLCA12 Fabian Schnyder 2.00 5.00

2012-13 Swiss SNL Global Impact

SNLGI01 Jason Williams 4.00 10.00
SNLGI02 Nicklas Danielsson 3.00 8.00
SNLGI03 Marc-Antoine Pouliot 3.00 8.00
SNLGI04 Petr Taticek 3.00 8.00
SNLGI05 Simon Gamache 3.00 8.00
SNLGI06 Cody Almond 3.00 8.00
SNLGI07 Micki Dupont 3.00 8.00
SNLGI08 Mark Popovic 3.00 8.00
SNLGI09 Ilkka Heikkinen 3.00 8.00
SNLGI10 Robbie Earl 3.00 8.00
SNLGI11 Ryan Shannon 3.00 8.00
SNLGI12 Linus Omark 4.00 10.00

2012-13 Swiss SNL Lockout Memories

SNLLM01 Matt Duchene 6.00 15.00
SNLLM02 John Tavares 6.00 15.00
SNLLM03 Patrick Kane 6.00 15.00
SNLLM04 Tyler Seguin 6.00 15.00
SNLLM05 Joe Thornton 6.00 15.00
SNLLM06 Rick Nash 6.00 15.00
SNLLM07 Logan Couture 6.00 15.00
SNLLM08 Brooks Laich 6.00 15.00
SNLLM09 Patrice Bergeron 6.00 15.00
SNLLM10 Jason Spezza 6.00 15.00
SNLLM11 Dustin Brown 6.00 15.00
SNLLM12 Henrik Zetterberg 6.00 15.00

2012-13 Swiss SNL Lockout Stars

SNLLS01 John Tavares 12.00 30.00
SNLLS02 Mark Streit 8.00 20.00
SNLLS03 Roman Josi 8.00 20.00
SNLLS04 Tyler Seguin 12.00 30.00
SNLLS05 Patrick Kane 12.00 30.00
SNLLS06 Joe Thornton 10.00 25.00
SNLLS07 Rick Nash 12.00 30.00
SNLLS08 Logan Couture 10.00 25.00
SNLLS09 Yannick Weber 8.00 20.00
SNLLS10 Brooks Laich 12.00 30.00
SNLLS11 Tyler Ennis 8.00 20.00
SNLLS12 Patrice Bergeron 12.00 30.00
SNLLS13 Luca Sbisa 8.00 20.00
SNLLS14 Jason Spezza 10.00 25.00
SNLLS15 Michael Del Zotto 10.00 25.00
SNLLS16 Dustin Brown 10.00 25.00
SNLLS17 Henrik Zetterberg 12.00 30.00
SNLLS18 Raphael Diaz 8.00 20.00

2012-13 Swiss SNL Masked Men

*BLACK/30: 1X TO 2.5X BASIC INSERT/600
SNLMM01 Nolan Schaefer 4.00 10.00
SNLMM02 Marco Buhrer 4.00 10.00
SNLMM03 Reto Berra 4.00 10.00
SNLMM04 Leonardo Genoni 4.00 10.00
SNLMM05 Benjamin Conz 4.00 10.00
SNLMM06 Tobias Stephan 4.00 10.00
SNLMM07 Ronnie Rueger 4.00 10.00
SNLMM08 Thomas Baumle 4.00 10.00
SNLMM09 Daniel Manzato 4.00 10.00
SNLMM10 David Aebischer 4.00 10.00
SNLMM11 Lukas Flueler 4.00 10.00
SNLMM12 Jussi Markkanen 4.00 10.00

2012-13 Swiss SNL Meisterkarte

*BLACK/30: 1X TO 2.5X BASIC INSERT/600
SNLMK01 ZSC Lions 5.00 12.00

2012-13 Swiss SNL Meisterpokal

SNLMP01 Meisterpokal 2.50 6.00

2012-13 Swiss SNL Playmakers

SNLPM01 Inti Pestoni 2.00 5.00
SNLPM02 John Tavares 5.00 12.00
SNLPM03 Tyler Seguin 5.00 12.00
SNLPM04 Joe Thornton 4.00 10.00
SNLPM05 Christian Dube 2.00 5.00
SNLPM06 Kevin Romy 2.00 5.00
SNLPM07 Denis Hollenstein 3.00 8.00
SNLPM08 Pascal Pelletier 2.00 5.00
SNLPM09 Glen Metropolit 3.00 8.00
SNLPM10 Jason Spezza 4.00 10.00
SNLPM11 Roman Wick 2.00 5.00
SNLPM12 Henrik Zetterberg 5.00 12.00

2012-13 Swiss SNL Scoring Kings

*PINK/30: 1X TO 2.5X BASIC INSERT/600
SNLSK01 Maxim Noreau 3.00 8.00
SNLSK02 Byron Ritchie 3.00 8.00
SNLSK03 Ahren Spylo 3.00 8.00
SNLSK04 Petr Sykora 3.00 8.00
SNLSK05 Julien Sprunger 3.00 8.00
SNLSK06 Rico Fata 3.00 8.00
SNLSK07 Tommi Santala 3.00 8.00
SNLSK08 Kurtis McLean 3.00 8.00
SNLSK09 Jaroslav Bednar 3.00 8.00
SNLSK10 Loic Burkhalter 3.00 8.00
SNLSK11 Jeff Tambellini 3.00 8.00
SNLSK12 Damien Brunner 6.00 15.00

2012-13 Swiss SNL Swiss Heroes

*PINK/30: 1X TO 2.5X BASIC INSERT/600
SNLSH01 Damien Brunner 6.00 15.00

2012-13 Swiss SNL Top Prospects

*BLACK/30: 1X TO 2.5X BASIC INSERT/600
SNLTP01 Daniele Grassi 3.00 8.00
SNLTP02 Christoph Bertschy 4.00 10.00
SNLTP03 Dario Trutmann 4.00 10.00
SNLTP04 Gregory Hofmann 4.00 10.00
SNLTP05 Melvin Merola 3.00 8.00
SNLTP06 Eliot Antonietti 3.00 8.00
SNLTP07 Lukas Meili 3.00 8.00
SNLTP08 Alban Rexha 3.00 8.00
SNLTP09 Luca Fazzini 3.00 8.00
SNLTP10 Tim Wolf 3.00 8.00
SNLTP11 Dominic Lammer 3.00 8.00
SNLTP12 Lino Martschini 4.00 10.00

1954 UK A and BC Chewing Gum

COMPLETE SET (?)
35 Chick Zamick 8.00 20.00
36 Cliff Ryan 8.00 20.00
37 Sonny Rost 8.00 20.00
38 Malcolm Davidson 8.00 20.00
39 Ray Gariepy 12.00 30.00
40 George Beach 8.00 20.00
41 Lefty Wilmot 8.00 20.00
74 Bill Johnson 8.00 20.00
75 Joe Shack 8.00 20.00
76 Tony Licari 8.00 20.00

1998-99 UK Basingstoke Bison

COMPLETE SET (24) 4.00 10.00
1 Rick Strachan .25 .60
2 Joe Baird .25 .60
3 Chris Crombie .25 .60
4 Steve Smillie .25 .60
5 Chris Bailey .25 .60
6 Bjarne Levison .25 .60
7 Mike Ellis .25 .60
8 Chris Chard .25 .60
9 Anthony Page .25 .60
10 Adam Cathcart .25 .60
11 Rick Fera .25 .60
12 Gary Clark .25 .60
13 Tony Redmond .25 .60
14 Alec Field .25 .60
15 Hakan Klys .25 .60
16 Mitch Grant .25 .60
17 Jake Armstrong .25 .60
18 Don Depoe CO .02 .10
19 Garfunkel's MASCOT .02 .10
20 The Puck .02 .10
21 The Goal .02 .10
22 Penalty Shots .02 .10
23 Team CL .02 .10
NNO Competition .02 .10

1999-00 UK Basingstoke Bison

COMPLETE SET (22) 4.00 10.00
1 Rick Strachan .20 .50
2 Dru Burgess .20 .50
3 Danny Meyers .20 .50
4 Gary Clark .20 .50
5 Peter Romeo .20 .50
6 Mike Ellis .20 .50
7 Joey Baird .20 .50
8 Charlie Colon .20 .50
9 Wayne Crawford .20 .50
10 Alec Field .20 .50
11 Tony Redmond .20 .50
12 Mitch Grant .20 .50
13 Duncan Paterson .20 .50
14 Dwayne Newman .20 .50
15 Mark Barrow .20 .50
16 Adam Greener .20 .50
17 Face Off .08 .25
18 Goal Mouth Scramble .08 .25
19 Joe Watkins .20 .50
20 Michael Knights .20 .50
21 Jeff Daniels .20 .50
22 Team CL .02 .10

2003-04 UK Basingstoke Bison

COMPLETE SET (21) 4.00 10.00
1 Curtis Cruickshank .30 .75
2 Dean Skinns .30 .75
3 David Geris .30 .75
4 James Hutchinson .20 .50
5 Phil Roy .20 .50
6 Doug Schueller .20 .50
7 Kim Vahanen .20 .50
8 Joe Ciccarello .20 .50
9 Martin Filip .20 .50
10 Richard Hargreaves .20 .50
11 Darren Hurley .20 .50
12 Jaromir Kverka .20 .50
13 Steve Moria .20 .50
14 Blake Sorensen .20 .50
15 Shaun Thompson .20 .50
16 Nicky Watt .30 .75
17 Christian Widauer .20 .50
18 Chris Slater .20 .50
19 Luc Chabot .20 .50
20 Matt Reid .20 .50
21 Checklist .04 .10

2001-02 UK Belfast Giants

COMPLETE SET (35) 8.00 20.00
1 Mike Bales .40 1.00
2 Terran Sandwith .30 .75
3 Dave Whistle CO .04 .10
4 Shane Johnson .30 .75
5 Colin Ward .30 .75
6 Kevin Riehl .30 .75
7 Rob Stewart .30 .75
8 Jason Ruff .30 .75
9 Sean Berens .30 .75
10 Jeff Hoad .30 .75
11 David Matsos .30 .75
12 Curtis Bowen .30 .75
14 Chad Allan .30 .75
15 Rod Stevens .30 .75
16 Paxton Schulte .40 1.00
17 Jason Bowen .40 1.00
18 Mark Cavallin .30 .75
19 Todd Kelman .30 .75
20 Checklist .04 .10
21 Tom Blatchford TR .04 .10
22 Redemption Card .04 .10
23 Shayne Toporowski .40 1.00
24 Derek Wilkinson .30 .75
25 Paul Ferone .30 .75
26 Todd Goodwin .30 .75
27 Kory Karlander .30 .75
28 Doug Searle .30 .75
29 Jerry Keefe .30 .75
30 Jason Wright .30 .75
31 Steve Roberts .30 .75
32 Mark Cavallin .30 .75
33 Mike Bales NM .40 1.00
34 Front Office .04 .10
35 Checklist .04 .10

2003-04 UK Belfast Giants

COMPLETE SET (19) 5.00 10.00
1 Sean Berens .20 .50
2 Curt Bowen .20 .50
3 Jason Bowen .20 .50
4 Mark Finney .20 .50
5 Leigh Jamieson .20 .50
6 Shane Johnson .20 .50
7 Todd Kelman .20 .50
8 Brad Kenny .20 .50
9 Gareth Martin .20 .50
10 Chris McGimpsey .20 .50
11 Mark Morrison .20 .50
12 Jason Ruff .20 .50
13 Colin Ryder .20 .50
14 Paul Sample .20 .50
15 Paxton Schulte .20 .50
16 Rob Stewart .20 .50
17 Grant Taylor .20 .50
18 Graeme Walton .20 .50
19 Colin Ward .20 .50

2004-05 UK Brent Bobyck Testimonial

COMPLETE SET (12) 2.00 5.00
COMMON CARD (1-12)
1 Brent Bobyck 1994-95 .20 .50
2 Brent Bobyck 1995-96 .20 .50
3 Brent Bobyck 1996-97 .20 .50
4 Brent Bobyck 1997-98 .20 .50
5 Brent Bobyck 1998-99 .20 .50
6 Brent Bobyck 1999-00 .20 .50
7 Brent Bobyck 2000-01 .20 .50
8 Brent Bobyck 2001-02 .20 .50
9 Brent Bobyck 2002-03 .20 .50
10 Brent Bobyck 2003-04 .20 .50
11 Brent Bobyck 2004-05 .20 .50
12 Brent Bobyck CL .04 .10

2000-01 UK Cardiff Devils

COMPLETE SET (14)
1 Derek Herlofsky .20 .50
2 Alan Schuler .20 .50
3 Vezio Sacratini .20 .50
4 Clayton Norris .20 .50
5 Rick Strachan .20 .50
6 John Parco .20 .50
7 Kip Noble .20 .50
8 Steve Thornton .20 .50
9 Denis Chasse .20 .50
10 Mike Ware .20 .50
11 Steve Moria .20 .50
12 Frank Evans .20 .50
13 Jonathan Phillips .20 .50
14 Ian McIntyre .20 .50

2001-02 UK Cardiff Devils

COMPLETE SET (19) 5.00 10.00
1 Clayton Norris .30 .75
2 Rick Strachan .20 .50
3 Alan Schuler .20 .50
4 Kim Ahlroos .20 .50
5 John Parco .20 .50
6 Frank Evans .20 .50
7 Denis Chasse .40 1.00
8 Steve Thornton .30 .75
9 Dwight Parrish .20 .50
10 Steve Moria .20 .50
11 Jonathan Phillips .20 .50
12 Ian McIntyre .20 .50
13 Ivan Matulik .20 .50
14 Mike Ware .30 .75
15 Vezio Sacratini .20 .50
16 Steve Lyle .30 .75
17 Derek Herlofsky .40 1.00
18 Kip Noble .20 .50
19 Checklist .04 .10

2002-03 UK Cardiff Devils

COMPLETE SET (19) 5.00 10.00
1 Clayton Norris .20 .50
2 Rick Strachan .20 .50
3 Alan Schuler .20 .50
4 Kim Ahlroos .20 .50
5 John Parco .20 .50
6 Frank Evans .30 .75
7 Denis Chasse .40 1.00
8 Steve Thornton .30 .75
9 Dwight Parrish .20 .50
10 Steve Moria .20 .50
11 Jonathan Phillips .20 .50
12 Ian McIntyre .20 .50
13 Ivan Matulik .20 .50
14 Mike Ware .30 .75
15 Vezio Sacratini .20 .50
16 Stevie Lyle .30 .75
17 Derek Herlofsky .30 .75
18 Kip Noble .20 .50
19 Checklist .04 .10

2003-04 UK Cardiff Devils

COMPLETE SET (21) 5.00 10.00
1 Jason Cugnet .30 .75
2 Jeff Burgoyne .20 .50
3 Matt Myers .20 .50
4 Jason Stone .20 .50
5 David James .20 .50
6 Phil Manny .20 .50
7 Russ Romaniuk .40 1.00
8 Phil Hill .20 .50
9 Jonathan Phillips .20 .50
10 Jeff Brown .20 .50
11 Ivan Matulik .20 .50
12 Ed Patterson .20 .50
13 Mike Ware .20 .50
14 Vezio Sacratini .20 .50
15 Neil Francis .20 .50
16 James Manson .20 .50
17 Jason Becker .20 .50
18 Dennis Maxwell .20 .50
19 Doug McEwen .20 .50
20 Dave Whistle CO .04 .10
21 Checklist .04 .10

2002-03 UK Coventry Blaze

COMPLETE SET (24) 5.00 12.00
1 Greg Rockman .20 .50
2 Jody Lehman .20 .50
3 Steve Carpenter .20 .50
4 Alan Levers .20 .50
5 James Pease .20 .50
6 Andreas Moborg .20 .50
7 Mathias Soderstrom .20 .50
8 Adam Radmall .20 .50
9 Ron Shudra .20 .50
10 Shaun Johnson .20 .50
11 Steve Chartrand .20 .50
12 Kurt Irvine .20 .50
13 Russ Cowley .20 .50
14 Tom Watkins .20 .50
15 Ashley Tait .20 .50
16 Gareth Owens .20 .50
17 Joel Poirier .20 .50
18 Hilton Ruggles .20 .50
19 Lee Richardson .20 .50
20 Michael Tasker .20 .50
21 Paul Thompson CO .04 .10
22 Steve Small
Phil Hadley
John Crook .04 .10
23 Blaze Dancers .20 .50
24 Checklist .04 .10

2003-04 UK Coventry Blaze

COMPLETE SET (18) 5.00 12.00
1 Alan Levers .25 .60
2 Mathias Soderstrom .25 .60
3 Steve Carpenter .30 .75
4 Jody Lehman .25 .60
5 Steve O'Brien .25 .60
6 Steve Gallace .25 .60
7 Adam Radmall .25 .60
8 Shaun Johnson .25 .60
9 Graham Schlender .25 .60
10 Steve Chartrand .25 .60
11 Russ Cowley .25 .60
12 Tom Watkins .25 .60
13 Ashley Tait .30 .75
14 Gareth Owen .25 .60
15 Joel Poirier .30 .75
16 Hilton Ruggles .25 .60
17 Lee Richardson .25 .60
18 Michael Tasker .25 .60

2003-04 UK Coventry Blaze Calendars

COMPLETE SET (12) 5.00 10.00
1 Mathias Soderstrom .40 1.00
2 Ashley Tait .40 1.00
3 Steve Carpenter .40 1.00
4 Steve Chartrand
Shaun Johnson .40 1.00
5 Russ Cowley
Tom Watkins .40 1.00
6 Graham Schlender .40 1.00
7 Jody Lehman .40 1.00
8 Michael Tasker
Hilton Ruggles .40 1.00
9 Lee Richardson
Alan Levers .40 1.00
10 Joel Poirier .40 1.00
11 Garth Owen
Adam Radmall .40 1.00
12 Steve Gallace
Steve O'Brien .40 1.00

2003-04 UK Coventry Blaze History

COMPLETE SET (18) 5.00 10.00
1 Steve Chartrand .20 .50
2 Kurt Irvine .20 .50
3 Mathias Soderstrom .20 .50
4 Michael Tasker .20 .50
5 A.J. Kelham .20 .50
6 Hilton Ruggles .20 .50
7 Luc Chabot .20 .50
8 Paul Thompson CO .20 .50
9 Steve Carpenter .30 .75
10 Shaun Johnson .20 .50
11 Andrew McNiven .20 .50
12 Jody Lehman .30 .75
13 Justin George .20 .50
14 Claude Dumas .20 .50
15 Craig Chapman .30 .75
16 Stephen Cooper .30 .75
17 Mike Shewan .20 .50
18 Ron Shudra .30 .75

2004-05 UK Coventry Blaze

COMPLETE SET (25) 5.00 10.00
1 Wade Belak .30 .75
2 Adam Brittle .20 .50
3 Adam Calder .20 .50
4 Tom Carlon .20 .50
5 Dan Carlson .20 .50
6 Luc Chabot ACO .04 .10
7 Russ Cowley .20 .50
8 Jody Lehman .20 .50
9 Neal Martin .20 .50
10 Chris McNamara .20 .50
11 Pavol Mihalik .20 .50
12 Andre Payette .20 .50
13 James Pease .20 .50
14 Joel Poirier .20 .50
15 Graham Schlender .20 .50
16 Doug Schueller .20 .50
17 Dan Shea .20 .50
18 Ashley Tait .20 .50
19 Paul Thompson CO .04 .10
20 Michal Vrabel .20 .50
21 Tom Watkins .20 .50
22 Nathanael Williams .20 .50
23 S.Small
A.Henry .20 .50
24 A.Buxton
M.Cowley .20 .50
25 Kix Kat MASCOT .04 .10

2004-05 UK Coventry Blaze Champions

COMPLETE SET (20) 5.00 10.00
1 Jody Lehman .30 .75
2 Dan Shea .20 .50
3 Wade Belak .40 1.00
4 Neal Martin .20 .50
5 Doug Schueller .20 .50
6 Pavol Mahalik .20 .50
7 Jozef Lukac .20 .50
8 James Pease .20 .50
9 Andre Payette .20 .50
10 Dan Carlson .20 .50
11 Graham Schlender .20 .50
12 Adam Calder .20 .50
13 Ashley Tait .30 .75
14 Joel Poirier .20 .50
15 Russ Cowley .20 .50
16 Chris McNamara .20 .50
17 Nathanael Williams .20 .50
18 Tom Watkins .20 .50
19 Card List .04 .10
20 Paul Thompson CO .20 .50

2006-07 UK Coventry Blaze

COMPLETE SET (20) 8.00 15.00
1 Neal Martin .30 .75
2 Joe Henry .30 .75
3 Reid Simonton .30 .75
4 Samy Nasreddine .30 .75
5 Tom Pease .30 .75
6 Barrie Moore .30 .75
7 Tom Watkins .30 .75
8 Ashley Tait .30 .75
9 James Pease .30 .75
10 Tom Carlon .30 .75
11 Adam Calder .30 .75
12 Dan Carlson .30 .75
13 Steve Fone .30 .75
14 Gareth Owen .30 .75
15 Trevor Koenig .30 .75
16 Danny Stewart .30 .75
17 Michael Wales .30 .75
18 Rumun Ndur .30 .75
19 Sylvain Cloutier .30 .75
20 Paul Thompson CO .30 .75

2007-08 UK Coventry Blaze

COMPLETE SET (43) 15.00 25.00
1 Hayden Laverick .30 .75
2 James Archer .30 .75
3 Josh Bruce .30 .75
4 Neal Martin .30 .75
5 Joe Henry .30 .75
6 Ryan Selwood .30 .75
7 James Cooke .30 .75
8 Tom Ledgard .30 .75
9 Scott Murray .30 .75
10 Ian Hunt .30 .75
11 Jonathan Weaver .30 .75
12 Russell Cowley .30 .75
13 Barrie Moore .30 .75
14 Tom Watkins .30 .75
15 James Pease .30 .75
16 Luke Curtis .30 .75
17 Chris Wilcox .30 .75
18 Adam Calder .30 .75
19 Dan Carlson .30 .75
20 Kieran Papps .30 .75
21 Steve Fone .30 .75
22 Stuart Dayton .30 .75
23 Dan Shea .30 .75
24 Trevor Koenig .30 .75
25 Aram Todd .30 .75
26 Danny Stewart .30 .75
27 Ollie Nabbs .30 .75
28 KC Timmons .30 .75
29 Matt Halford .30 .75
30 Tom Pease .30 .75
31 Scott Mulholland .30 .75
32 Rumun Ndur .30 .75
33 Tom Hooper .30 .75
34 Matt Soderstrom .30 .75
35 Michael Tasker .30 .75
36 Sylvain Cloutier .30 .75
37 Daniel Burgess .30 .75
38 Curtis Huppe .30 .75
39 David Vychodil .30 .75
40 Paul Thompson HC .02 .10
41 Luc Chabot AC .02 .10
42 Joel Poirier HC .02 .10
43 Reg Wilcox AC .02 .10

2001-02 UK Dundee Stars

COMPLETE SET (18) 5.00 10.00
1 Checklist .04 .10
2 Nate Leslie .25 .60
3 Scott Young .25 .60
4 Tony Hand .30 .75
5 Paul Berrington .25 .60
6 Gary Dowd .25 .60
7 Teeder Wynne .25 .60
8 Mikko Inkinen .25 .60
9 Andrew Finlay .25 .60
10 Jan Mikel .25 .60
11 Craig Nelson .25 .60
12 Dominic Hopkins .25 .60
13 Stewart Rugg .25 .60
14 Patrick Lochi .25 .60
15 Stephen Murphy .25 .60
16 Slava Koulikov .25 .60
17 Martin Wiita .25 .60
18 Scott Kirton .25 .60

2002-03 UK Dundee Stars

COMPLETE SET (18) 5.00 10.00
1 Checklist .04 .10
2 Nate Leslie .25 .60
3 Scott Young .25 .60
4 Tony Hand .30 .75
5 Paul Berrington .25 .60
6 Gary Dowd .25 .60
7 Teeder Wynne .25 .60
8 Mikko Inkinen .25 .60
9 Andy Finlay .25 .60
10 Jan Mikel .25 .60
11 Craig Nelson .25 .60
12 Dominic Hopkins .25 .60
13 Stewart Rugg .25 .60
14 Patric Lochi .25 .60
15 Stephen Murphy .25 .60
16 Viatcheslav Koulikov .25 .60
17 Martin Wiita .25 .60
18 Scott Kirton .25 .60

2004-05 UK Edinburgh Capitals

COMPLETE SET (18) 5.00 12.00
1 Jan Krajicek .30 .75
2 Mindraugas Kieras .40 1.00
3 Laurie Dunbar .30 .75
4 Steven Francey .30 .75
5 Marty Johnston .30 .75
6 Craig Wilson .30 .75
7 David Beatson .30 .75
8 Ross Hay .30 .75
9 Steven Lynch .30 .75
10 Daniel McIntyre .30 .75
11 Neil Hay .30 .75
12 Martin Cingel .30 .75
13 Dino Bauba .30 .75
14 David Trofimenkoff .40 1.00
15 Rastislav Bohme .30 .75
16 Miroslav Droppa .30 .75
17 Ryan Ford .40 1.00
18 Checklist .04 .10

2007-08 UK Edinburgh Capitals

COMPLETE SET (19) 7.00 15.00
1 Kyle Horne .40 1.00
2 Mark Garside .40 1.00
3 Jordan Steele .40 1.00
4 Ryan Crane .40 1.00
5 Colin Hemingway .40 1.00
6 Mark Wires .40 1.00
7 Neil Hay .40 1.00
8 Ross Dalgleish .40 1.00
9 Mike Stutzel .40 1.00
10 Adam Stefishen .40 1.00
11 Doug Christiansen .40 1.00
12 Martin Cingel .40 1.00
13 Dino Bauba .40 1.00
14 Mark Paterson .40 1.00
15 Iain Bowie .40 1.00
16 J.F. Perras .40 1.00
17 Ryan Ford .40 1.00
18 Patrik Luza .40 1.00
19 Ben O'Connor .40 1.00

2004-05 UK EIHL All-Stars

COMPLETE SET (18) 5.00 12.00
1 Jody Lehman .30 .75
2 Wade Belak .40 1.00
3 Neal Martin .20 .50
4 Tony Hand .40 1.00
5 Adam Calder .20 .50
6 Jon Cullen .20 .50
7 Martin Klempa .20 .50
8 Rob Davison .40 1.00
9 Dion Darling .20 .50
10 Dan Carlson .20 .50
11 George Awarda .20 .50
12 Vezio Sacratini .20 .50
13 Curtis Cruickshank .30 .75
14 Eric Cairns .40 1.00
15 Nick Boynton .40 1.00
16 Shawn Maltby .40 1.00
17 David Clarke .20 .50
18 Scott Nichol .40 1.00

1996-97 UK Fife Flyers

COMPLETE SET (20) 5.00 12.00
1 Gavin Fleming .30 .75
2 John Reid .30 .75
3 Russ Parent .30 .75
4 Derek E. King .30 .75
5 Colin Grubb .30 .75
6 Colin Hamilton .30 .75
7 Andy Finlay .30 .75
8 Richard Dingwall .30 .75
9 Andy Samuel .30 .75
10 Wayne Maxwell .30 .75
11 Craig Wilson .30 .75
12 Daryl Venters .30 .75
13 Gordon Latto .30 .75
14 Richard Danskin .30 .75
15 Martin McKay .30 .75
16 Kyle Horne .30 .75
17 Mark Morrison CO .20 .50
18 Frank Morris .30 .75
19 Steven E. King .30 .75
20 Lee Mercer .30 .75

1997-98 UK Fife Flyers

COMPLETE SET (20) 4.80 12.00
1 Team Photo .20 .50
2 Bernie McCrone .30 .75
3 Wayne Maxwell .30 .75
4 Derek E. King .30 .75
5 Mark Slater .30 .75
6 Bill Moody .30 .75
7 Lee Cowmedow .30 .75
8 Richard Charles .30 .75
9 Andy Finlay .30 .75
10 Daryl Venters .30 .75
11 Steven E. King .30 .75
12 Andy Samuel .30 .75
13 Gordon Latto .30 .75
14 Mark Morrison CO .30 .75
15 John Haig .30 .75
16 Lee Mercer .30 .75
17 Gary Wishart .30 .75
18 Colin Hamilton .30 .75
19 Frank Morris .30 .75
20 David Smith .30 .75

2001-02 UK Fife Flyers

COMPLETE SET (12) 4.00 10.00
1 Shawn Silver .40 1.00
2 Derek King .40 1.00
3 Kyle Horner .40 1.00
4 Todd Dutiaume .40 1.00
5 Steven King .40 1.00
6 Mark Morrison .40 1.00
7 Mark Dutiaume .40 1.00
8 Gary Wishart .40 1.00
9 Iain Robertson .40 1.00
10 Karry Biette .40 1.00
11 Russell Monteith .40 1.00
12 Frank Morris .40 1.00

1994-95 UK Guildford Flames

COMPLETE SET (25) 4.00 10.00
1 Ben Challice .20 .50
2 Wayne Trunchion .20 .50
3 Terry Kurtenbach .20 .50
4 Fred Perlini .20 .50
5 Andy Sparks .20 .50
6 Rob Friesen .20 .50
7 Drew Chapman .20 .50
8 Kevin Parish .20 .50
9 John Noctor .20 .50
10 Ron Charbonneau GM .02 .10
11 Peter Morley .20 .50
12 Andy Allan .20 .50
13 Ryan Campbell .20 .50
14 Ronnie Evans-Harvey .20 .50
15 Paul Thompson .20 .50
16 Bill Rawles .20 .50
17 Nicky Landoli .20 .50
18 Elliott Andrews .20 .50
19 Dean Russell-Samways .20 .50
20 Home Kit .02 .10
21 Away Kit .02 .10
22 5 Imports .20 .50
23 3 Letters .02 .10
24 Spectrum .02 .10
25 Checklist .02 .10

1995-96 UK Guildford Flames

COMPLETE SET (30) 6.00 15.00
1 Dave Gregory .20 .50
2 Wayne Trunchion .20 .50
3 Andy Allan .20 .50
4 Terry Kurtenbach .20 .50
5 Ryan Campbell .20 .50
6 Fred Perlini .20 .50
7 Ronnie Evans-Harvey .20 .50
8 Andy Sparks .20 .50
9 Paul Thompson .20 .50
10 Nick Rothwell .20 .50
11 Drew Chapman .20 .50
12 Troy Kennedy .20 .50
13 Barrie Aisbitt .20 .50
14 Elliott Andrews .20 .50

15 Darrin Zinger .20 .50
16 Dean Russell-Samways .20 .50
17 Dave Graham .20 .50
18 Ivan Brown .20 .50
19 Home Kit .20 .50
20 Away Kit .20 .50
21 Spectrum .20 .50
22 Checklist .20 .50
23 Home Action .20 .50
24 Away Action .20 .50
25 P.C. Jim Bennett .20 .50
26 Terry Kurtenbach GOLD .20 .50
27 Paul Thompson GOLD .20 .50
28 Fred Perlini GOLD .20 .50
29 Future GOLD .20 .50
30 Celebration GOLD .20 .50

1996-97 UK Guildford Flames

COMPLETE SET (30) 5.00 12.00
1 John Wolfe .20 .50
2 Rob Lamey .20 .50
3 Wayne Crawford .20 .50
4 Terry Kurtenbach .20 .50
5 Ryan Campbell .20 .50
6 Fred Parlini .20 .50
7 Paul Thompson .20 .50
8 Mike Bettens .20 .50
9 Mark Finney .20 .50
10 Ryan Ferster .20 .50
11 Nick Cross .20 .50
12 Damian Smith .20 .50
13 Mike Mowbray .20 .50
14 Elliott Andrews .20 .50
15 Darrin Zinger .20 .50
16 Brad Kirkwood .20 .50
17 Derek DeCosty .20 .50
18 Mark Hazelhurst .20 .50
19 Lee Saunders .20 .50
20 Barrie Aisbitt .20 .50
21 Paul McCallion .20 .50
22 Valeri Vasie .20 .50
23 Goalies .20 .50
24 Capt. & Ast.Capt. .20 .50
25 Celebration .08 .25
26 Pep Talk .08 .25
27 Home Kit .08 .25
28 Away Kit .08 .25
29 Spectrum .08 .25
30 Training Staff .08 .25

1997-98 UK Guildford Flames

COMPLETE SET (30) 4.80 12.00
1 Peter Morley .20 .50
2 Rob Larney .30 .75
3 Andrew Hannah .30 .75
4 Joe Johnson .30 .75
5 Terry Kurtenbach .30 .75
6 Ryan Campbell .20 .50
7 Scott Adair .20 .50
8 Paul Thompson .20 .50
9 Ricky Plant .20 .50
10 Pete Kasowski .20 .50
11 Andrew Einhorn .20 .50
12 Bobby Brown .20 .50
13 Anthony Page .20 .50
14 Nick Rothwell .20 .50
15 Mike Harding .20 .50
16 Darrin Zinger .30 .75
17 Jamie Organ .20 .50
18 Barcley Pearce .20 .50
19 Simon Smith .20 .50
20 Russ Plant .20 .50
21 Stan Marple CO .02 .10
22 Home Kit .02 .10
23 Away Kit .02 .10
24 Dressing Room .02 .10
25 Capt. & Ast. Capt. .20 .50
26 Celebration .02 .10
27 Checklist .02 .10
28 Spectrum .02 .10
29 Sizzler .02 .10
30 Training Staff .02 .10

1998-99 UK Guildford Flames

COMPLETE SET (30) 4.00 10.00
1 Team CL .02 .10
2 Ryan Campbell .20 .50
3 Robin Davison .20 .50
4 Derek DeCosty .20 .50
5 Dominic Hopkins .20 .50
6 Simon Howard .20 .50
7 Kirk Humphreys .20 .50
8 Andy Johnston .20 .50
9 Rob Johnston .20 .50
10 Peter Kasowski .20 .50
11 Terry Kurtenbach .20 .50
12 Rob Lamey .20 .50
13 Adrian Lomonaco .20 .50
14 Sam Mager .20 .50
15 Stan Marple CO .02 .10
16 Brian Mason .20 .50
17 Peter Morley .20 .50
18 Jamey Organ .20 .50
19 Barcley Pearce .20 .50
20 Andy Pickles .20 .50
21 Greg Randall .20 .50
22 Sizzler MASCOT .02 .10
23 Simon Smith .20 .50
24 Scott Stephenson .20 .50
25 Paul Thompson .20 .50
26 Captain & Assistants .02 .10
27 GB Uniform .02 .10
28 Trophies .02 .10
29 Home Kit .02 .10
30 Away Kit .02 .10

1999-00 UK Guildford Flames

COMPLETE SET (30) 4.00 10.00
1 Team CL .02 .10
2 Biette, Crombie, Dixon .20 .50
3 Team Photo (home) .20 .50
4 Team Photo (away) .20 .50
5 Celebration .02 .10
6 Karry Biette .20 .50
7 Tom Brown .20 .50
8 Ryan Campbell .20 .50
9 Gary Clark .20 .50
10 Chris Crombie .20 .50
11 Derek Decosty .20 .50
12 Paul Dixon .20 .50
13 GB Uniform .02 .10
14 Patrick Flanagan .20 .50
15 Dominic Hopkins .20 .50
16 Simon Howard .20 .50
17 Adrian Jenkinson TR .02 .10
18 Peter Kasowski .20 .50
19 Grant King .20 .50
20 Rob Lamey .20 .50
21 James Manson .20 .50
22 Stan Marple CO .02 .10
23 Stan Marple CO .02 .10
24 Jamey Organ .20 .50
25 Barcley Pearce .20 .50
26 Rick Plant .20 .50
27 Russ Plant .20 .50
28 Sizzlers MASCOT .02 .10
29 Jamie Thompson .20 .50
30 Mike Urquhart ACO .02 .10

2000-01 UK Guildford Flames

COMPLETE SET (30) 4.00 10.00
1 Karry Biette .14 .40
2 Tom Brown .14 .40
3 Ryan Campbell .14 .40
4 Scott Campbell .14 .40
5 Wayne Crawford .14 .40
6 Chris Crombie .14 .40
7 Derek DeCosty .14 .40
8 Paul Dixon .14 .40
9 John Haig .14 .40
10 Adrian Jenkinson TR .10 .25
11 Jason Jennings .14 .40
12 Grant King .14 .40
13 Rob Lamey .14 .40
14 Stan Marple CO .10 .25
15 Stan Marple CO .10 .25
16 Mark McArthur .20 .50
17 Tyrone Miller .14 .40
18 Jason Moses .14 .40
19 Barcley Pearce .14 .40
20 Ricky Plant .14 .40
21 Sizzler MASCOT .10 .25
22 Jason Stone .14 .40
23 David Smith .14 .40
24 Mike Urquhart .14 .40
25 Team Photo (home) .14 .40
26 Team Photo (away) .14 .40
27 Captain & Assistants .14 .40
28 Home Grown .14 .40
29 Celebration .10 .25
30 Logo Card .10 .25

2001-02 UK Guildford Flames

COMPLETE SET (30) 5.00 12.00
1 Checklist .04 .10
2 Mark McArthur .30 .75
3 Michael Plenty .20 .50
4 Stan Marple .20 .50
5 Regan Stocco .20 .50
6 Derek DeCosty .20 .50
7 Todd Wetzel .20 .50
8 Ricky Plant .20 .50
9 John Haig .20 .50
10 Tony Redmond .20 .50
11 Paul Dixon .20 .50
12 Grant King .30 .75
13 Greg Burke .20 .50
14 Scott Campbell .20 .50
15 Nicky Chinn .30 .75
16 Mark Galazzi .20 .50
17 David Smith .20 .50
18 Jason Dailey .20 .50
19 Michael Timms .20 .50
20 Mikko Koivunoro .20 .50
21 Stan Marple HCO .04 .10
22 Mike Urquhart ACO .04 .10
23 Adrian Jenkinson TR .04 .10
24 Paul Dixon
Derek DeCosty
Nicky Chinn .20 .50
25 Team Photo Home .20 .50
26 Team Photo Away .20 .50
27 Sizzler MASCOT .04 .10
28 Jason Dailey
Celebration .20 .50
29 Trophies .04 .10
30 Mark McArthur
Grant King .20 .50

2002-03 UK Guildford Flames

COMPLETE SET (30) 5.00 12.00
1 Ian Herbers .20 .50
2 Stan Marple HCO .20 .50
3 David Clarke .20 .50
4 Derek DeCosty .20 .50
5 Craig Lyons .20 .50
6 Ricky Plant .20 .50
7 Tony Redmond .20 .50
8 Paul Dixon .20 .50
9 Jason Lafreniere .30 .75
10 Jason Bowen .20 .50
11 Grant King .20 .50
12 Mike Torchia .30 .75
13 Corey Lyons .20 .50
14 Nicky Chinn .30 .75
15 Jeff White .20 .50
16 Mark Galazzi .20 .50
17 Ricky Skene .20 .50
18 Mike Urquhart ACO .04 .10
19 Stan Marple HCO .04 .10
20 Adrian Jenkinson TR .04 .10
21 Paul Dixon
Corey Lyons
Jason Lafreniere .20 .50
22 Team Photo
Home .20 .50
23 Team Photo
Away .20 .50
24 Team Photo
Alternate .20 .50
25 Sizzler MASCOT .04 .10
26 Grant King
Mike Torchia .30 .75
27 Ricky Plant GB .20 .50
28 David Clarke GB .20 .50
29 Andy Sparks
Fred Perlini
Ryan Campbell
Retired Numbers .20 .50
30 Checklist .04 .10

2003-04 UK Guildford Flames

COMPLETE SET (30) 5.00 12.00
1 Header Card .04 .10
2 Peter Michnac .20 .50
3 Stan Marple .20 .50
4 Marian Smerciak .20 .50
5 Neil Liddiard .20 .50
6 Ryan Vince .20 .50
7 Ricky Plant .30 .75
8 Michael Timms .20 .50
9 Tony Redmond .20 .50
10 Milos Melicherik .20 .50
11 Paul Dixon .20 .50
12 Rastislav Palov .20 .50
13 Jozef Kohut .20 .50
14 Joe Dollin .20 .50
15 Stevie Lyle .40 1.00
16 Peter Konder .20 .50
17 Mark Galazzi .20 .50
18 Nick Cross .20 .50
19 Paul Dixon ACO .04 .10
20 Stan Marple HCO .04 .10
21 Dave Wiggins AM .04 .10
22 Captains & Assistants .20 .50
23 Home Kit .04 .10
24 Away Kit .04 .10
25 Mascot .04 .10
26 Action Card .04 .10
27 Flames Goalies .30 .75
28 Flames Eastern Europeans .20 .50
29 British Line .30 .75
30 Ricky Plant
Leading British Points .20 .50

2004-05 UK Guildford Flames

COMPLETE SET (30) 5.00 12.00
1 Guildford Flames .04 .10
2 Peter Michnac .20 .50
3 Neil Liddiard .20 .50
4 Marian Smerciak .20 .50
5 David Savage .20 .50
6 Jason Reilly .20 .50
7 Stuart Potts .20 .50
8 Adam Walker .20 .50
9 Milos Melicherik .20 .50
10 Paul Dixon .20 .50
11 Andrew Hemmings .20 .50
12 Rastislav Palov .20 .50
13 Dusan Pohorelec .20 .50
14 Jozef Kohut .20 .50
15 Simon Lavis .20 .50
16 Miroslav Bielik .20 .50
17 Tom Annetts .20 .50
18 Peter Konder .20 .50
19 Nick Cross .20 .50
20 Paul Dixon .20 .50
21 Stan Marple CO .04 .10
22 Dave Wiggin ACO .04 .10
23 Captains and Assistants .20 .50
24 Home Jersey Team Photo .04 .10
25 Away Jersey Team Photo .04 .10
26 Sizzler MASCOT .04 .10
27 Celebration .04 .10
28 Netminders .30 .75
29 Playoff Trophy .04 .10
30 Terry Kurtenbach JSY RET .20 .50

2006-07 UK Guildford Flames

COMPLETE SET (24) 8.00 15.00
1 Neil Liddiard .25 .60
2 Marian Smerciak .25 .60
3 David Savage .25 .60
4 Ben Johnson .25 .60
5 Rob Lamey .25 .60
6 Stuart Potts .25 .60
7 Andrew Hemmings .25 .60
8 Rick Plant .25 .60
9 Robert Young .25 .60
10 Ben Duggan .25 .60
11 Milos Melicherik .25 .60
12 Paul Dixon .25 .60
13 Vaclav Zavoral .25 .60
14 Simon James .25 .60
15 Joe Watkins .40 1.00
16 Tom Annetts .40 1.00
17 Chris Wiggins .25 .60
18 Ben Austin .25 .60
19 Jozef Kohut .25 .60
20 Adam Hyman .25 .60
21 Rick Skene .25 .60
22 Ollie Bronniman .25 .60
23 Stan Marple .25 .60
24 Paul Dixon .25 .60

2007-08 UK Guildford Flames

COMPLETE SET (22) 7.00 15.00
1 Neil Liddiard .30 .75
2 David Savage .30 .75
3 Ben Johnson .30 .75
4 Rob Lamey .30 .75
5 Stuart Potts .30 .75
6 Rick Plant .30 .75
7 Ben Duggan .30 .75
8 Terry Miles .30 .75
9 Milos Melicherik .30 .75
10 Paul Dixon .30 .75
11 Vaclav Zavoral .30 .75
12 Dominic Hopkins .30 .75
13 Joe Watkins .60 1.50
14 Alexander Mettam .30 .75
15 Lukas Smital .30 .75
16 Ben Austin .30 .75
17 Jozef Kohut .30 .75
18 Nick Cross .30 .75
19 Rick Skene .30 .75
20 Taras Foremsky .30 .75
21 Ollie Bronnimann .30 .75
22 Paul Dixon HC .10 .25

1999-00 UK Hull Thunder

COMPLETE SET (20) 4.00 10.00
1 Team CL .02 .10
2 Don Depoe CO .08 .25
3 Ian Defty .20 .50
4 Simon Greaves .20 .50
5 Mark Florence .20 .50
6 Dan Carney .20 .50
7 Stephen Johnson .20 .50
8 Anthony Johnson .20 .50
9 Scott Stephenson .20 .50
10 Tam Watkins .20 .50
11 Paul Thompson .20 .50
12 Jason Tatarnic .20 .50
13 Mark Pallister .20 .50
14 Ron Shudra .20 .50
15 Pasi Raitanen .30 .75
16 Steve Morden .20 .50
17 Slava Koulikov .20 .50
18 Steve Brown .20 .50
19 Chris Douglas .20 .50
20 Chris Bailey .20 .50

2001-02 UK Hull Thunder

COMPLETE SET (25) 4.00 10.00
1 Checklist .04 .10
2 Mike Bishop CO .04 .10
3 Stephen Foster .20 .50
4 Andy Moffat .20 .50
5 Mike Bishop .20 .50
6 Corey Lyons .20 .50
7 Andy Munroe .20 .50
8 Mark Florence .20 .50
9 Stephen Johnson .20 .50
10 Anthony Johnson .20 .50
11 Anthony Payne .20 .50
12 Ryan Lake .20 .50
13 Karl Hopper UER .20 .50
14 Michael Bowman .20 .50
15 Stephen Wallace .20 .50
16 Ian Defty .20 .50
17 Oleg Synkov .20 .50
18 Steve Smillie .20 .50
19 Rob McCaig .20 .50
20 Darren Houghton .20 .50
21 Daryl Lavoie .20 .50
22 Eric Lavigne .20 .50
23 Mike O'Connor GM .04 .10
24 Terry Ward ACO .04 .10
25 Vanessa Brown TR .04 .10

2002-03 UK Hull Thunder

COMPLETE SET (25) 5.00 12.00
1 Checklist .04 .10
2 Mike Bishop HCO .04 .10
3 Stephen Foster .20 .50
4 Keith Leyland .20 .50
5 Anthony Payne .20 .50
6 Scott Young .20 .50
7 Nathan Hunt .20 .50
8 Paul Ferone .20 .50
9 Andy Munroe .20 .50
10 Mark Florence .20 .50
11 Paul Wallace .20 .50
12 Mike Morin .20 .50
13 Ryan Lake .20 .50
14 Karl Hopper .20 .50
15 Mark Bultje .20 .50
16 Jonathan Weaver .20 .50
17 Steve Smillie .20 .50
18 Dominic Parlatore .20 .50
19 Dan Currie .30 .75
20 Sam Roberts .20 .50
21 Eoin McInerney .40 1.00
22 Marc West .20 .50
23 Mike Bishop .20 .50
24 Eric Lavigne .30 .75
25 Mike O'Connor GM .04 .10

1993-94 UK Humberside Hawks

COMPLETE SET (18) 6.00 15.00
1 Kenny Johnson .40 1.00
2 Gavin De Jonge .40 1.00
3 Chris Hobson .40 1.00
4 Mike Bishop .40 1.00
6 Paul Simpson .40 1.00
7 Stewart Carvil .40 1.00
8 Shaun Johnson .40 1.00
9 Arren Burn .40 1.00
10 Stephen Johnson .40 1.00
12 Anthony Johnson .40 1.00
15 Anthony Payne .40 1.00
16 Andy Giles .40 1.00
17 Mike O'Conner .40 1.00
19 Andy Steel .40 1.00
20 Frank Killen .40 1.00
21 Dan Dorian .40 1.00
23 Alexander Koulikov .40 1.00
NNO Peter Johnson CO .40 1.00

1994-95 UK Humberside Hawks

COMPLETE SET (20) 8.00 20.00
2 Malcolm Bell .40 1.00
4 Mike Bishop .40 1.00
5 Scott Young .40 1.00
6 Paul Simpson .40 1.00
8 Shaun Johnson .40 1.00
9 Wayne Anchikoski .60 1.50
10 Stephen Johnson .40 1.00
12 Anthony Johnson .40 1.00
14 Tony Saxby .40 1.00
15 Darcy Cahill .40 1.00
16 Chris Hobson .40 1.00
17 Danny Parkin .40 1.00
19 Scott Morrison .40 1.00
20 Danny Thompson .40 1.00
21 Paul Cast .40 1.00
22 Andy Port .40 1.00
23 Dominik Love .40 1.00
NNO Peter Johnson CO .20 .50
NNO Gavin De Jonge .40 1.00
NNO David Standling .40 1.00

2002-03 UK Ivan Matulik Testimonial

COMPLETE SET (12) 2.00 5.00
1 Header .20 .50
2 Sheffield Steelers .20 .50
3 Murrayfield Racers .20 .50
4 Cardiff Devils .20 .50
5 Cardiff Devils .20 .50
6 Cardill Devils .20 .50
7 Cardiff Devils .20 .50
8 Cardiff Devils .20 .50
9 Cardiff Devils .20 .50
10 Manchester Storm .20 .50
11 Manchester Storm .20 .50
12 Cardiff Devils .20 .50

1998-99 UK Kingston Hawks

COMPLETE SET (25) 4.00 10.00
1 Dale Lambert CO .15 .40
2 Ian Defty .15 .40
3 Mikka Pynnonen .20 .50
4 Simon Greaves .15 .40
5 Kelly Reed .15 .40
6 Dominic Love .20 .50
7 Bjorn Widmark .20 .50
8 Steve Nemeth .20 .50
9 Christer Widmark .20 .50
10 Stephen Johnson .15 .40
11 Mark Florence .15 .40
12 Anthony Payne .15 .40
13 Chris Hobson .15 .40
14 Mark McCoy .20 .50
15 Andy Steel .15 .40
16 Paddy O'Conner .15 .40
17 Ashley Tait .15 .40
18 Matt Staunton .15 .40
19 Pasi Raitanen .20 .50
20 Jason Coles .15 .40
21 Simon Leach .15 .40
22 Lucas Miller .15 .40
23 Michael Tasker .15 .40
24 Keith Milhench GM .02 .10
25 Team CL .02 .10

1997-98 UK Kingston Hawks Stickers

COMPLETE SET (20) 4.80 12.00
1 Keith Milhench CO .08 .25
2 Bobby McEwen ACO .08 .25
3 Malcolm Bell .30 .75
4 Michael Knights .30 .75
5 Paul Simpson .30 .75
6 Kelly Reid .30 .75
7 Dominic Love .30 .75
8 Phil Brook .30 .75
9 Anthony Payne .30 .75
10 Chris Hobson .30 .75
11 Steve Smillie .30 .75
12 Andy Steel .30 .75
13 Ashley Tait .30 .75
14 Slava Koulikov .30 .75
15 Norman Pinnington .30 .75
16 Tony McAleavy .30 .75
17 Pasi Raitinen .30 .75
18 The Kingston Kid .08 .25
19 Ian Defty .30 .75
20 Michael Tasker .30 .75

2000-01 UK Kudos ISL

COMPLETE SET (169) 12.00 30.00
1 Ice Hockey Superleague .10 .30
2 Jim Lynch .10 .30
3 Paul Heavey .10 .30
4 Philippe Derouville .10 .30
5 Colin Ryder .10 .30
6 Trevor Doyle .10 .30
7 Derek Eberle .10 .30
8 Anders Hillstorm .10 .30
9 Jan Mikel .10 .30
10 Johan Silfwerplatz .10 .30
11 Scott Young .10 .30
12 Dainius Bauyba .10 .30
13 Cam Bristow .10 .30
14 Shawn Bryam .10 .30
15 Ed Courtenay .10 .30
16 Tony Hand .10 .30
17 Rhett Gordon .10 .30
18 Mike Harding .10 .30
19 Mark Montanari .10 .30
20 Jonathon Weaver .10 .30
21 Teeder Wynne .10 .30
22 Dave Whistle .10 .30
23 Mark Cavallin .10 .30
24 Todd Kelman .10 .30
25 Kevin Riehl .10 .30
26 Paxton Schulte .10 .30
27 Colin Ward .10 .30
28 Jeff Hoad .10 .30
29 Shane Johnson .10 .30
30 Enio Sacilotto .10 .30
31 Brian Greer .10 .30
32 Joe Watkins .10 .30
33 Matej Bukna .10 .30
34 Jimmy Drolet .10 .30
35 Jason Mansoff .10 .30
36 Mark Matier .10 .30
37 Steve O'Rourke .10 .30
38 Reid Simonton .10 .30
39 Brent Bobyck .10 .30
40 Chris Brant .10 .30
41 Mark Bultje .10 .30
42 Joe Cardarelli .10 .30
43 Dan Ceman .10 .30
44 Joe Ciccarello .10 .30
45 Darren Hurley .10 .30
46 Blaxe Knox .10 .30
47 Stephane Roy .10 .30
48 Bard Wingfield .10 .30
49 Doug McCarthy .10 .30
50 Troy Walkington .10 .30
51 Stevie Lyle .10 .30
52 Derek Herlofsky .10 .30
53 Frank Evans .10 .30
54 Kip Noble .10 .30
55 Claton Norris .10 .30
56 Dwight Parrish .10 .30
57 Alan Schuler .10 .30
58 Rick Strachan .10 .30
59 Denis Chasse .10 .30
60 James Hanlon .10 .30
61 Rick Kowalsky .10 .30
62 Ivan Matulik .10 .30
63 Ian Macintyre .10 .30
64 Steve Moria .10 .30
65 John Parco .10 .30
66 Vezio Sacratini .10 .30
67 Steve Thornton .10 .30
68 Mike Ware .10 .30
69 Chris McSorley .10 .30
70 Trevor Robins .10 .30
71 Shawn Silver .10 .30
72 Rich Bronilla .10 .30
73 Martin Neal .10 .30
74 Randy Perry .10 .30
75 Mikael Tjallden .10 .30
76 Nicky Chinn .10 .30
77 Pat Ferschweiler .10 .30
78 Claude Jutras .10 .30
79 Mikko Koivynoro .10 .30
80 Mark Kolesar .10 .30
81 Jay Neal .10 .30
82 Ryan Richardson .10 .30
83 Paul Rushforth .10 .30
84 David Vallieres .10 .30
85 Darby Walker .10 .30
86 Brendan Yarema .10 .30
87 Terry Cristensen .10 .30
88 Daryl Lipsey .10 .30
89 Frank Pietrangelo .10 .30
90 Dave Trofimenkoff .10 .30
91 Curtis Bowen .10 .30
92 Matt Eldred .10 .30
93 Perry Johnson .10 .30
94 Troy Neumeier .10 .30
95 Rob Robinson .10 .30
96 Blair Scott .10 .30
97 Pierre Allard .10 .30
98 Kevin Brown .10 .30
99 Greg Bullock .10 .30
100 Doug Doull .10 .30
101 Marty Flichel .10 .30
102 Trevor Gallant .10 .30
103 Jason Glover .10 .30
104 Mike Morin .10 .30
105 Corey Spring .10 .30
106 Shyne Stevenson .10 .30
107 Rob Trumbly .10 .30
108 Jukka Jalonen .10 .30
109 Jimmy Hibbert .10 .30
110 Tommi Satosaari .10 .30
111 Craig Binns .10 .30
112 Santeri Immonen .10 .30
113 Arttu Kaykho .10 .30
114 Miroslav Mosnar .10 .30
115 Darren Mcausland .10 .30
116 Rob Wilson .10 .30
117 Tero Arkiomaa .10 .30
118 Louis Bedard .10 .30
119 Tomas Kupka .10 .30
120 Matt Oates .10 .30
121 Joel Poirer .10 .30
122 Timo Salonen .10 .30
123 Tommi Sova .10 .30
124 Alex Dampier .10 .30
125 Edin Mcinerney .10 .30
126 Willis Jordan .10 .30
127 Greg Burke .10 .30
128 Ryan Gillis .10 .30
129 Eric Lavigne .10 .30
130 Daryl Lavoie .10 .30
131 Jim Paek .10 .30
132 Duncan Paterson .10 .30
133 Pierre Claude Drouin .10 .30
134 Graham Garden .10 .30
135 Greg Hadden .10 .30
136 Jamie Leach .10 .30
137 Daryl Moxam .10 .30
138 Barry Nieckar .10 .30
139 David Struch .10 .30
140 Ashley Tait .10 .30
141 Randall Weber .10 .30
142 Mike Blaisdell .10 .30
143 Mike O'Neill .10 .30
144 Steve Carpenter .10 .30
145 Shayne McCosh .10 .30
146 Jeff Sebastian .10 .30
147 Kayle Short .10 .30
148 Adam Smith .10 .30
149 Dennis Vial .10 .30
150 Scott Allison .10 .30
151 Paul Beraldo .10 .30
152 Rick Brebant .10 .30
153 Dale Craigwell .10 .30
154 David Longstaff .10 .30
155 Scott Metcalfe .10 .30
156 Warren Norris .10 .30
157 Steve Roberts .10 .30
158 Kent Simpson .10 .30
159 Jason Weaver .10 .30
160 Brent Bobyck .10 .30
161 Ayr Scottish Eagles .02 .10
162 Belfast Giants .02 .10
163 Bracknell Bees .02 .10
164 Bt Cardif Devils .02 .10
165 London Knights .02 .10
166 Manchester Storm .02 .10
167 Newcastle Jesters .02 .10
168 Nottingham Panthers .02 .10
169 Sheffield Steelers .02 .10

1999-00 UK London Knights

COMPLETE SET (17) 3.60 9.00
1 Tom Ashe .20 .50
2 Mark Bultje .20 .50
3 John Byce .30 .75
4 Scott Campbell .20 .50
5 Mark Cavallin .30 .75
6 Ryan Duthie .20 .50
7 Jeff Hoad .20 .50
8 Marc Hussey .30 .75
9 Guy Leveque .20 .50
10 Neal Martin .20 .50
11 Chris McSorley CO .20 .50
12 Tim Murray .20 .50
13 Scott Rex CO .08 .25
14 Paul Rushforth .20 .50
15 Claudio Scremin .30 .75
16 Mike Ware .30 .75
17 Todd Wetzel .20 .50

2001-02 UK London Knights

COMPLETE SET (34) 5.00 12.00
1 Logo and Checklist .04 .10
2 Doug Serle .20 .50
3 Gerald Adams .20 .50
4 Kim Ahlroos .20 .50
5 Sean Blanchard .20 .50
6 Trevor Roenick .30 .75
7 David Struch .20 .50
8 Dave Clark .20 .50
9 Nathan Leslie .20 .50
10 Maurizio Mansi .20 .50
11 Steve Thornton .20 .50
12 Mark Kolesar .20 .50
14 Mike Barrie .20 .50
15 Greg Burke .20 .50
16 Bob Leslie HCO .04 .10
17 Ian McIntyre .20 .50
18 Ritchie Bronilla .20 .50
19 Vezio Sacratini .20 .50
20 Trevor Robins .20 .50
21 Jason Ellery EQM .04 .10
22 Mike Ware .20 .50
23 Rob Donovan .20 .50
24 David Trofimenkoff .20 .50
25 Dominic Amodeo .30 .75
26 Scott Bailey .30 .75
27 Paul Rushforth .20 .50
28 Mighty Knight MASCOT .04 .10
29 Dave Struch
Mark Kolesar .20 .50
30 Vez
Mo
Dom .20 .50
31 London Knights Logo .04 .10
32 Mark Kolesar
Mike Barrie .20 .50
33 Rob Donovan
Mo Mansi .20 .50
34 Ian McIntyre
Dave Trofimenkoff .20 .50
35 Mo Mansi
Sue Chetham .20 .50

2002-03 UK London Knights

COMPLETE SET (24) 5.00 10.00
1 Checklist .04 .10
2 Ake Lilljebjorn .20 .50
3 Gerald Adams .20 .50
4 Kim Ahlroos .20 .50
5 Nathan Leslie .20 .50
6 Moe Mansi .20 .50
7 Mark Kolesar .30 .75
8 A.J. Kelham .20 .50
9 Jeff Hoad .20 .50
10 Chris Slater .20 .50
11 Ian McIntyre .20 .50
12 Greg Burke .20 .50
13 Steve Aronson .20 .50
14 Rich Bronilla .20 .50
15 Vezio Sacratini .20 .50
16 Dave Trofimenkoff .30 .75
17 Paul Rushforth .20 .50
18 Sean Blanchard .30 .75
19 Dennis Maxwell .30 .75
20 Ed Patterson .30 .75
21 Bob Leslie CO .04 .10
22 Mighty Knight .04 .10
23 Jim Brithen CO .04 .10
24 Jason Ellery EQM .04 .10

2003-04 UK London Racers

COMPLETE SET (20) 5.00 10.00
1 Chris Bailey .20 .50
2 Noel Burkitt .20 .50
3 Nick Burton .20 .50
4 Lukas Filip .20 .50
5 Kalle Konsti .20 .50
6 Zoran Kozic .20 .50
7 Evan Lindsay .30 .75
8 Marc Long .20 .50
9 Mike McKinnon .20 .50
10 Brian McLaughlin .20 .50
11 Sean Murdoch .20 .50
12 Mojmir Musil .20 .50
13 Oscar MASCOT .04 .10
14 Jason Robinson .20 .50
15 Mark Scott .20 .50
16 Jani Touminen .20 .50
17 Warren Tait .20 .50
18 Matt Van der Velden .30 .75
19 Erik Zachrisson .20 .50

2004-05 UK London Racers Playoffs

COMPLETE SET (18) 6.00 15.00
1 Eric Cairns .60 1.50
2 Joe Ciccarello .30 .75
3 Jeremy Cornish .30 .75
4 Adam Dobson .40 1.00
5 Matt Foord .30 .75
6 Mark Gouett .30 .75
7 Richard Hargreaves .30 .75
8 Jason Hewitt .30 .75
9 Denis Ladouceur .30 .75
10 Dennis Maxwell .30 .75
11 J.J. McGrath .30 .75
12 Ian McIntyre .30 .75
13 Steve Moria .30 .75
14 Scott Nichol .60 1.50
15 Jason Robinson .30 .75
16 Mark Thomas .30 .75
17 Jim Vickers .30 .75
18 Joe Watkins .30 .75

2003-04 UK Manchester Phoenix

COMPLETE SET (22) 5.00 10.00
1 Jayme Platt .30 .75
2 Rick Brebant .20 .50
3 Dave Clancy .30 .75
4 Dwight Parrish .20 .50
5 Mike Lankshear .20 .50
6 Mark Thomas .20 .50
7 Carl Greenhous .20 .50
8 Mark Bultje .20 .50
9 David Kozier .20 .50
10 Mike Morin .20 .50
11 Petteri Lotila .20 .50
12 Chad Brandimore .20 .50
13 George Awada .20 .50
14 Marc Lovell .20 .50
15 Jason Hewitt .20 .50
16 Aaron Davies .20 .50
17 Darcy Anderson .20 .50

18 Mika Skytta .20 .50
19 Jeff Sebastian .20 .50
20 Nick Poole .20 .50
21 Manace MASCOT .04 .10
NNO Checklist .04 .10
NNO Checklist .04 .10

2001-02 UK Manchester Storm

COMPLETE SET (24) 4.80 12.00
1 Paul Ferone .20 .50
2 Dan Preston .20 .50
3 Trevor Gallant .20 .50
4 Mike Morin .20 .50
5 Dwight Parrish .20 .50
6 Mark Bultje .20 .50
7 Joe Busillo .20 .50
8 Ivan Matulik .20 .50
9 Pierre Allard .20 .50
10 Russ Romaniuk .20 .50
11 Joe Cardarelli .20 .50
12 Stevie Lyle .30 .75
14 Mike Torchia .40 1.00
15 Kayle Short .20 .50
16 Justin Hocking .30 .75
17 Kris Miller .20 .50
18 Russ Richardson .20 .50
19 Daryl Lipsey HCO .04 .10
20 Mike Torchia .30 .75
21 Stevie Lyle .30 .75
22 Lightning Jack MASCOT .04 .10
23 Rob Wilson .04 .10
24 Redemption Card .04 .10
25 Checklist .04 .10

2001-02 UK Manchester Storm Retro

COMPLETE SET (21) 5.00 10.00
1 Dale Jago .20 .50
2 Craig Woodcroft .20 .50
3 Trevor Gallant .20 .50
4 Kelly Askew .20 .50
5 Jeff Tomlinson .20 .50
6 Daryl Lipsey .20 .50
7 Mike Morin .20 .50
8 Shawn Byram .20 .50
9 Pierre Allard .20 .50
10 Mark Bernard .20 .50
11 John Finnie .20 .50
12 Blair Scott .20 .50
13 Hilton Ruggles .20 .50
14 David Trofimenkoff .20 .50
15 Jim Hrivnak .30 .75
16 Frank Pietrangelo .30 .75
17 Brad Rubachuk .20 .50
18 Stefan Ketola .20 .50
19 Jeff Jablonski .20 .50
20 Kris Miller .20 .50
21 Logo Card .04 .10

2002-03 UK Manchester Storm

COMPLETE SET (21) 5.00 10.00
1 Colin Pepperall .20 .50
2 Dan Preston .20 .50
3 Shawn Maltby .20 .50
4 Geoff Peters .20 .50
5 Mike Perna .20 .50
6 Pasi Nielikainen .20 .50
7 Dwight Parrish .20 .50
8 Mark Bultje .20 .50
9 Rob Wilson .20 .50
10 Ivan Matulik .20 .50
11 Pierre Allard .20 .50
12 David Longstaff .20 .50
13 Ryan Stewart .20 .50
14 Joe Cardarelli .20 .50
15 Stevie Lyle .30 .75
16 Mike Torchia .30 .75
17 Dan Hodge .20 .50
18 Daryl Lipsey HCO .04 .10
19 Mike Torchia .30 .75
20 Stevie Lyle .30 .75
21 Checklist .04 .10

2000-01 UK Nottingham Panthers

COMPLETE SET (30) 4.80 12.00
1 Checklist .04 .10
2 Jordan Willis .30 .75
3 Paul Moran .16 .40
4 Duncan Paterson .16 .40
5 Kevin Hoffman .16 .40
6 David Struch .16 .40
7 Randall Weber .16 .40
8 Greg Hadden .16 .40
9 Daryl Lavoie .16 .40
10 P.C. Drouin .20 .50
11 Marc Levers .16 .40
12 Darryl Moxam .20 .50
14 Greg Burke .16 .40
15 Ashley Tait .16 .40
16 Ryan Gillis .16 .40
17 Jim Paek .20 .50
18 Chris Baxter .16 .40
19 Jamie Leach .30 .75
20 Eoin McInerney .30 .75
21 Robert Nordmark .16 .40
22 Graham Garden .16 .40
23 Casson Masters .16 .40
24 Barry Nieckar .20 .50
25 Eric Lavigne .20 .50
27 Peter Woods CO .04 .10
28 Redemption Voucher .02 .10
29 Alex Dampier DOH .04 .10
30 Gary Moran GM .04 .10
31 Team Photo .16 .40
32 Player Awards .16 .40
A Robert Nordmark .16 .40

2001-02 UK Nottingham Panthers

OMPLETE SET (31) 4.80 12.00
Team Logo .04 .10
Brent Pope .20 .50
Clayton Norris .20 .50
Patrick Wallenberg .20 .50
Randall Weber .20 .50
Greg Hadden .20 .50
Frank Evans .20 .50
8 Claude Savoie .20 .50
9 P.C. Drouin .30 .75
10 Steve Moira .20 .50
11 Ashley Tait .30 .75
12 Paul Adey CO .04 .10
14 Jimmy Drolet .30 .75
15 Danny Lorenz .30 .75
16 Joel Poirier .30 .75
17 Paul Moran .20 .50
18 Barry Nieckar .30 .75
19 Darren Maloney .20 .50
20 Calle Carlsson .20 .50
21 Pasi Hakkinen .20 .50
22 A.J. Kelham .20 .50
23 Alex Dampier CO .04 .10
24 Lee Jinman .30 .75
25 Gary Moran GM .04 .10
26 Paws MASCOT .04 .10
27 Equipment Managers .04 .10
28 Trainers .04 .10
29 Head Office .04 .10
30 Christian Sjogren .20 .50
31 Jim Paek .20 .50
32 Danny Lorenz .20 .50

2002-03 UK Nottingham Panthers

COMPLETE SET (22) 4.00 10.00
1 Mika Pietila .20 .50
2 Jim Paek .20 .50
3 Marc Hussey .20 .50
4 Eric Charron .20 .50
5 Greg Hadden .20 .50
6 Dody Wood .30 .75
7 Briane Thompson .20 .50
8 Jason Elders .20 .50
9 Kristian Taubert .20 .50
10 Scott Allison .20 .50
11 Mark Cadotte .20 .50
12 Petter Sandstrom .20 .50
13 John Purves .30 .75
14 Paul Moran .20 .50
15 Barry Nieckar .30 .75
16 Jason Clarke .20 .50
17 Lee Jinman .30 .75
18 Paul Adey .20 .50
19 Mascot .04 .10
20 Gary Moran GM .04 .10
21 Checklist .04 .10
22 Front Office .04 .10

2003-04 UK Nottingham Panthers

COMPLETE SET (18) 5.00 10.00
1 Niklas Sundberg .30 .75
2 David Clarke .20 .50
3 Kim Ahlroos .20 .50
4 James Morgan .20 .50
5 David Struch .20 .50
6 Robert Stancok .20 .50
7 Briane Thompson .20 .50
8 Marc Levers .20 .50
9 Kristian Taubert .20 .50
10 Mikko Koivunoro .20 .50
11 Geoff Woolhouse .30 .75
12 Joel Salonen .20 .50
13 Mark Cadotte .30 .75
14 Paul Moran .20 .50
15 Daniel Scott .20 .50
16 Calle Carlsson .20 .50
17 John Craighead .30 .75
18 Paul Addey CO .04 .10

2004-05 UK Nottingham Panthers

COMPLETE SET (20) 5.00 10.00
1 Paul Adey CO .04 .10
2 Kim Ahlroos .20 .50
3 Calle Carlsson .20 .50
4 David Clarke .20 .50
5 Mark Codotte .30 .75
6 John Craighead .20 .50
7 Curtis Cruickshank .20 .50
8 Marek Ivan .20 .50
9 Konstantin Kalmikov .20 .50
10 Jan Krulis .20 .50
11 Jan Magdosko .20 .50
12 Steve McKenna .40 1.00
13 Gary Moran GM .04 .10
14 Paul Moran .20 .50
15 Matt Myers .20 .50
16 Scott Ricci .20 .50
17 Daniel Scott .20 .50
18 Roman Tvrdon .20 .50
19 Richard Wojciak .20 .50
20 Geoff Woolhouse .20 .50

2006-07 UK Nottingham Panthers

COMPLETE SET (20) 8.00 15.00
1 Joe Cardarelli .30 .75
2 David Clarke .30 .75
3 James Cooke .30 .75
4 James Ferrara .30 .75
5 Jan Krajicek .30 .75
6 Sean McAslan .30 .75
7 Danny Meyers .30 .75
8 Paul Moran .30 .75
9 Matt Myers .30 .75
10 James Neil .30 .75
11 Corey Neilson .30 .75
12 Matus Petricko .30 .75
13 Mike Rees .30 .75
14 Rastislav Rovnianek .30 .75
15 Ryan Shmyr .30 .75
16 Steve Simoes .30 .75
17 Rod Stevens .30 .75
18 Geoff Woolhouse .60 1.50
19 Mike Ellis CO .02 .10
20 Calle Carlsson ACO .02 .10

2007-08 UK Nottingham Panthers

COMPLETE SET (19) 7.00 15.00
1 Tom Askey .40 1.00
2 Geoff Woolhouse .40 1.00
3 Patrik Wallenberg .30 .75
4 Matt Myers .30 .75
5 Jon Coleman .30 .75
6 James Neil .30 .75
7 Robert Stancok .30 .75
8 Johan Molin .30 .75
9 Marc Levers .30 .75
10 James Ferrara .30 .75
11 Danny Meyers .30 .75
12 Mark Richardson .30 .75
13 Kevin Bergin .30 .75
14 Ryan Shmyr .30 .75
15 Eric Nelson .30 .75
16 Steve Pelletier .30 .75
17 Sean McAslan .30 .75
18 Corey Neilson .30 .75
19 Mike Ellis .30 .75

2002-03 UK Peterborough Phantoms

COMPLETE SET (18) 5.00 10.00
1 Luc Chabot .30 .75
2 James Moore .25 .60
3 David Whitwell .25 .60
4 Craig Britton .25 .60
5 Jon Fone .25 .60
6 Pete Morley .25 .60
7 Jessie Hammill .25 .60
8 Jason Buckman .25 .60
9 Lewis Buckman .25 .60
10 Russell Coleman .25 .60
11 Duncan Cook .25 .60
12 Darren Cotton .25 .60
13 Jon Cotton .25 .60
14 James Ellwood .25 .60
15 Grant Hendry .25 .60
16 Doug McEwen .25 .60
17 Shaun Yardley .25 .60
18 Checklist .04 .10

2004-05 UK Ron Shudra Testimonial

COMPLETE SET (16) 3.00 8.00
1 Ron Shudra 1990-91 .20 .50
2 Ron Shudra 1991-92 .20 .50
3 Ron Shudra 1992-93 .20 .50
4 Ron Shudra 1993-94 .20 .50
5 Ron Shudra 1994-95 .20 .50
6 Ron Shudra 1995-96 .20 .50
7 Ron Shudra 1996-97 .20 .50
8 Ron Shudra 1997-98 .20 .50
9 Ron Shudra 1998-99 .20 .50
10 Ron Shudra 1999-00 .20 .50
11 Ron Shudra 2000-01 .20 .50
12 Ron Shudra 2001-02 .20 .50
13 Ron Shudra 2002-03 .20 .50
14 Ron Shudra 2003-04 .20 .50
15 Ron Shudra 2004-05 .20 .50
16 Ron Shudra CL .20 .50

2000-01 UK Sekonda Superleague

COMPLETE SET (170) 20.00 50.00
COMPLETE UPDATE SET (36) 4.00 10.00
1 Ice Hockey Superleague .10 .25
2 Jim Lynch CO .10 .25
3 Paul Heavey ACO .10 .25
4 Philippe DeRouville .40 1.00
5 Colin Ryder .30 .75
6 Trevor Doyle .20 .50
7 Derek Eberle .20 .50
8 Anders Hillstrom .20 .50
9 Jan Mikel .20 .50
10 Johan Silfwerplatz .20 .50
11 Scott Young .20 .50
12 Dainius Bauyba .20 .50
13 Cam Bristow .20 .50
14 Shawn Byram .20 .50
15 Ed Courtenay .30 .75
16 Tony Hand .30 .75
17 Rhett Gordon .20 .50
18 Mike Harding .20 .50
19 Mark Montanari .20 .50
20 Jonathan Weaver .20 .50
21 Teeder Wynne .20 .50
22 David Whistle CO .10 .25
23 Mark Cavallin .20 .50
24 Todd Kelman .20 .50
25 Kevin Riehl .20 .50
26 Paxton Schulte .20 .50
27 Colin Ward .20 .50
28 Jeff Hoad .20 .50
29 Shane Johnson .20 .50
30 Enio Sacilotto CO .10 .25
31 Brian Greer .20 .50
32 Joe Watkins .20 .50
33 Matej Bukna .20 .50
34 Jimmy Drolet .20 .50
35 Jason Mansoff .20 .50
36 Mark Matier .20 .50
37 Steve O'Rourke .20 .50
38 Reid Simonton .20 .50
39 Brent Bobyck .20 .50
40 Chris Brant .20 .50
41 Mark Bultje .20 .50
42 Joe Cardarelli .20 .50
43 Dan Ceman .20 .50
44 Joe Ciccarello .20 .50
45 Darren Hurley .20 .50
46 Blake Knox .20 .50
47 Stephane Roy .20 .50
48 Brad Wingfield .20 .50
49 Doug McCarthy CO .10 .25
50 Troy Walkington CO .10 .25
51 Stevie Lyle .80 2.00
52 Derek Herlofsky .40 1.00
53 Frank Evans .20 .50
54 Kip Noble .20 .50
55 Clayton Norris .10 .25
56 Dwight Parrish .20 .50
57 Alan Schuler .20 .50
58 Rick Strachan .20 .50
59 Denis Chasse .20 .50
60 James Hanlon .20 .50
61 Rick Kowalsky .20 .50
62 Ivan Matulik .20 .50
63 Ian McIntyre .20 .50
64 Steve Moria .20 .50
65 John Parco .20 .50
66 Vezio Sacratini .20 .50
67 Steve Thornton .20 .50
68 Mike Ware .20 .50
69 Chris McSorley CO .20 .50
70 Trevor Robins .20 .50
71 Shawn Silver .20 .50
72 Rich Bronilla .20 .50
73 Neal Martin .20 .50
74 Randy Perry .20 .50
75 Mikael Tjallden .20 .50
76 Nicky Chinn .30 .75
77 Pat Ferschweiler .20 .50
78 Claude Jutras .20 .50
79 Mikko Koivunoro .20 .50
80 Mark Kolesar .20 .50
81 Jay Neal .20 .50
82 Bryan Richardson .20 .50
83 Paul Rushforth .20 .50
84 David Vallieres .20 .50
85 Darby Walker .20 .50
86 Brendan Yarema .20 .50
87 Terry Cristensen CO .10 .25
88 Daryl Lipsey ACO .10 .25
89 Frank Pietrangelo .40 1.00
90 Dave Trofimenkoff .40 1.00
91 Curtis Bowen .20 .50
92 Matt Eldred .20 .50
93 Perry Johnson .20 .50
94 Troy Neumeier .20 .50
95 Rob Robinson .20 .50
96 Blair Scott .20 .50
97 Pierre Allard .20 .50
98 Kevin Brown .20 .50
99 Greg Bullock .20 .50
100 Doug Doull .20 .50
101 Marty Flichel .20 .50
102 Trevor Gallant .10 .25
103 Jason Glover .20 .50
104 Mike Morin .20 .50
105 Corey Spring .20 .50
106 Shayne Stevenson .20 .50
107 Rob Trumbley .20 .50
108 Jukka Jalonen CO .10 .25
109 Jim Hibbert .20 .50
110 Tommi Satosaari .20 .50
111 Craig Binns .20 .50
112 Santeri Immonen .20 .50
113 Arttu Kaykho .20 .50
114 Miroslav Mosnar .20 .50
115 Darren McAusland .20 .50
116 Rob Wilson .20 .50
117 Tero Arkiomaa .20 .50
118 Louis Bedard .20 .50
119 Tomas Kupka .20 .50
120 Matt Oates .20 .50
121 Joel Poirer .20 .50
122 Timo Salonen .20 .50
123 Tommi Sova .20 .50
124 Alex Dampier CO .10 .25
125 Eoin McInerney .40 1.00
126 Jordan Willis .40 1.00
127 Greg Burke .20 .50
128 Ryan Gillis .20 .50
129 Eric Lavigne .20 .50
130 Daryl Lavoie .20 .50
131 Jim Paek .20 .50
132 Duncan Paterson .20 .50
133 P. C. Drouin .20 .50
134 Graham Garden .20 .50
135 Greg Hadden .20 .50
136 Jamie Leach .20 .50
137 Daryl Moxam .20 .50
138 Barry Nieckar .20 .50
139 David Struch .20 .50
140 Ashley Tait .20 .50
141 Randall Weber .20 .50
142 Mike Blaisdell CO .20 .50
143 Mike O'Neill .40 1.00
144 Steve Carpenter .20 .50
145 Shayne McCosh .20 .50
146 Jeff Sebastian .20 .50
147 Kayle Short .20 .50
148 Adam Smith .20 .50
149 Dennis Vial .40 1.00
150 Scott Allison .20 .50
151 Paul Beraldo .20 .50
152 Rick Brebant .20 .50
153 Dale Craigwell .20 .50
154 David Longstaff .20 .50
155 Scott Metcalfe .20 .50
156 Warren Norris .20 .50
157 Steve Roberts .20 .50
158 Kent Simpson .20 .50
159 Jason Weaver .20 .50
160 Brent Bobyck .20 .50
161 Ayr Eagles .10 .25
162 Belfast Giants .10 .25
163 Bracknell Bees .10 .25
164 Cardiff Devils .10 .25
165 London Knights .10 .25
166 Manchester Storm .10 .25
167 Newcastle Jesters .10 .25
168 Nottingham Panthers .10 .25
169 Sheffield Steelers .10 .25
170 Lucky Card .40 1.00
171 Tony Hand .20 .50
172 Jason Bowen .10 .25
173 Paul Ferone .10 .25
174 Todd Goodwin .10 .25
175 Kory Karlander .10 .25
176 Jerry Keefe .10 .25
177 Steve Roberts .10 .25
178 Doug Searle .10 .25
179 Rod Stevens .10 .25
180 Rob Stewart .10 .25
181 Derek Wilkinson .40 1.00
182 Jason Wright .10 .25
183 Bob Maudie .10 .25
184 Jason Heywood .10 .25
185 Frank Defrenza .10 .25
186 J-F Tremblay .10 .25
187 Kim Ahlroos .10 .25
188 Aaron Boh .20 .50
189 Terry Marchant .10 .25
190 Grant Richison .10 .25
191 Mikael Tjallden .10 .25
192 Brendan Yarema .20 .50
193 Brent Bobyck .10 .25
194 Pat Mazzoli .10 .25
195 Barrie Moore .10 .25
196 Eric Fenton .20 .50
197 Daniel Lacroix .20 .50
198 Chris Baxter .10 .25
199 Casson Masters .10 .25
200 Robert Nordmark .10 .25
201 Paul Adey .10 .25
202 Kent Simpson .10 .25
203 Mike Torchia .40 1.00
204 Checklist .04 .10
205 Checklist .04 .10
206 Checklist .04 .10

1993-94 UK Sheffield Steelers

COMPLETE SET (19) 4.00 10.00
1 Andy Havenhand .20 .50
2 Alan Hague .20 .50
3 Tim Cranston .20 .50
4 Neil Abel .20 .50
5 Scott Neil .20 .50
6 Steve Nemeth .20 .50
7 Tommy Plommer .20 .50
8 Ivan Matulik .20 .50
9 Danny Boome .20 .50
10 Mark Wright .20 .50
11 Chris Kelland .20 .50
12 Les Millie .20 .50
13 Selmar Odeline .20 .50
14 Ron Shudra .20 .50
15 Martin McKay .20 .50
16 Dampier w
Tuyl .20 .50
17 Netminders .30 .75
18 Team Photo .30 .75
19 Sheffield Scimitars .20 .50

1994-95 UK Sheffield Steelers

COMPLETE SET (25) 4.00 10.00
1 Alex Dampier MGR .08 .25
2 Clyde Tuyl CO .08 .25
3 Paul Jackson .30 .75
4 Scott Neil .20 .50
5 Team Photo .20 .50
6 Ron Handy .20 .50
7 Patrick O'Conner .20 .50
8 Dean Smith .20 .50
9 Mike O'Conner .20 .50
10 Backroom Staff .08 .25
11 Tim Cranston .20 .50
12 Les Millie .20 .50
13 Alan Hague .20 .50
14 Perry Doyle .20 .50
15 Ron Shudra .20 .50
16 Mark Wright .20 .50
17 Tommy Plommer .20 .50
18 Scott Heaton .20 .50
19 Neil Abel .20 .50
20 Steeler Dan .08 .25
21 Rob Wilson .20 .50
22 Chris Kelland .20 .50
23 Andy Havenhand .20 .50
24 Martin McKay .20 .50
25 Steve Nemeth .30 .75

1995-96 UK Sheffield Steelers

COMPLETE SET (24) 4.00 10.00
1 Martin McKay .15 .40
2 Ron Shudra .15 .40
3 Ken Priestlay .20 .50
4 Steve Nemeth .20 .50
5 Tommy Plommer .15 .40
6 Nicky Chinn .40 1.00
7 Tony Hand .40 1.00
8 Mike O'Conner .15 .40
9 Mark Wright .15 .40
10 Chris Kelland .16 .40
11 Andre Malo .15 .40
12 Les Millie .15 .40
13 Sheffield Arena .08 .25
14 Team Photo .15 .40
15 Scott Heaton .15 .40
16 Tim Cranston .15 .40
17 Neil Abel .15 .40
18 Scott Neil .15 .40
19 Perry Doyle .15 .40
20 Backroom Staff .08 .25
21 Alex Dampier MGR .08 .25
22 Clyde Tuyl CO .08 .25
23 The Silverware .08 .25
24 Steeler Foggy Dan .08 .25

1997-98 UK Sheffield Steelers

COMPLETE SET (25) 4.80 12.00
1 James Hibbert .20 .50
2 Tim Cranston .20 .50
3 Rob Wilson .20 .50
4 Ken Priestlay .30 .75
5 Tommy Plommer .20 .50
6 Frank Kovacs .20 .50
7 Nicky Chinn .30 .75
8 David Longstaff .20 .50
9 Tony Hand .30 .75
10 Dion Del Monte .20 .50
11 Scott Allison .20 .50
12 Chris Kelland .20 .50
13 Sheffield Arena .08 .25
14 Team Photo .08 .25
15 Andre Malo .20 .50
16 Jamie Van Der Horst .20 .50
17 Andre Malo .20 .50
18 Mike Ware .20 .50
19 Ron Shudra .20 .50
20 Ed Courtenay .30 .75
21 Piero Greco .20 .50
22 Corey Beaulieu .20 .50
23 Steeler Foggy Dan .08 .25
24 Alex Dampier MGR .08 .25
25 Clyde Tuyl CO .08 .25

1999-00 UK Sheffield Steelers

COMPLETE SET (22) 4.80 12.00
1 Mike Blaisdell CO .20 .50
2 Dan Ceman .30 .75
3 Greg Clancy .20 .50
4 Ed Courtenay .40 1.00
5 Dale Craigwell .40 1.00
6 Matt Hoffman .20 .50
7 Dale Junkin .20 .50
8 Derek Laxdal .30 .75
9 David Longstaff .20 .50
10 Andre Malo .20 .50
11 Mark Matier .20 .50
12 Shayne McCosh .20 .50
13 Don McKee CO .02 .10
14 Kip Noble .20 .50
15 Thomas Plommer .20 .50
16 Kayle Short .20 .50
17 Shawn Silver .20 .50
18 Grant Sjerven .20 .50
19 Dennis Vial .40 1.00
20 Jason Weaver .20 .50
21 Rob Wilson .20 .50
22 Teeder Wynne .20 .50

2000-01 UK Sheffield Steelers

COMPLETE SET (27) 4.00 10.00
1 Logo Card .10 .25
2 Champions .14 .40
3 Team Photo .14 .40
4 Paul Adey .14 .40
5 Scott Allison .14 .40
6 Andy & Paul .04 .10
7 Paul Beraldo .20 .50
8 Mike Blaisdell .20 .50
9 Brent Bobyck .14 .40
10 Rick Brebant .14 .40
11 Steve Carpenter .14 .40
12 Dale Craigwell .30 .75
13 Steeler Dan MASCOT .10 .25
14 David Longstaff .14 .40
15 Shayne McCosh .20 .50
16 Scott Metcalfe .20 .50
17 Warren Norris .14 .40
18 Mike O'Neill .30 .75
19 Steve Roberts .14 .40
20 Jeff Sebastian .14 .40
21 Kayle Short .14 .40
22 David Simms CO .10 .25
23 Kent Simpson .14 .40
24 Adam Smith .14 .40
25 Mike Torchia .40 1.00
26 Dennis Vial .20 .50
27 Jason Weaver .14 .40

2000-01 UK Sheffield Steelers Centurions

COMPLETE SET (18) 4.00 10.00
1 Ed Courtenay .40 1.00
2 Tommy Plommer .20 .50
3 David Longstaff .20 .50
4 Rob Wilson .20 .50
5 Ron Shudra .20 .50
6 Tim Cranston .20 .50
7 Chris Kelland .20 .50
8 Andre Malo .20 .50
9 Ken Priestlay .30 .75
10 Scott Neil .20 .50
11 Tony Hand .40 1.00
12 Kayle Short .20 .50
13 Mike O'Connor .20 .50
14 Scott Allison .20 .50
15 Neil Abel .20 .50
16 Steve Nemeth .20 .50
17 Checklist .04 .10
18 Ron Shudra
Player of the Decade .20 .50

2001-02 UK Sheffield Steelers

COMPLETE SET (19) 5.00 10.00
1 Scott Allison .20 .50
2 Ryan Bach .30 .75
3 Cal Benazic .20 .50
4 Mike Blaisdell CO .20 .50
5 Brent Bobyck .20 .50
6 Chris Brant .20 .60
7 Rick Brebant .20 .50
8 Jeff Brown .20 .50
9 Mark Dutiaume .20 .50
10 Paul Kruse .30 .75
11 Mark Laniel .20 .50
12 Brad Lauer .20 .50
13 Peter Leboutillier .30 .75
14 Chris Lipsett .20 .50
15 Jason Mansoff .20 .50
16 Bob Maudie .20 .50
17 Kevin Miehm .20 .50
18 Jeff Sebastian .20 .50
19 Ron Shudra .20 .50

2002-03 UK Sheffield Steelers

COMPLETE SET (19) 5.00 10.00
1 Mike Blaisdell CO .20 .50
2 Brent Bobyck .20 .50
3 Rick Brebant .20 .50
4 Jeff Brown .20 .50
5 Calle Carlsson .20 .50
6 Dion Darling .20 .50
7 Mark Dutiaume .20 .50
8 Iain Fraser .20 .50
9 Rhett Gordon .20 .50
10 Joel Laing .30 .75
11 Marc Laniel .20 .50
12 Scott Levins .20 .50
13 Mike Morin .20 .50
14 Warren Norris .20 .50
15 Trevor Prior .30 .75
16 Jason Sessa .30 .75
17 Kent Simpson .20 .50
18 Chris Szysky .20 .50
19 Timo Willman .20 .50

2003-04 UK Sheffield Steelers

COMPLETE SET (21) 5.00 10.00
1 Gerald Adams .20 .50
2 Erik Anderson .20 .50
3 Mike Blaisdell CO .20 .50
4 Ben Bliss .20 .50
5 Brent Bobyck .20 .50
6 Kevin Bolibruck .20 .50
7 Christian Bronsard .30 .75
8 Dion Darling .20 .50
9 Kirk DeWaele .20 .50
10 Rob Dopson .30 .75
11 Steve Duncombe .20 .50
12 Mark Dutiaume .20 .50
13 Steve Ellis .20 .50
14 Gavin Farrand .20 .50
15 Joel Irving .20 .50
16 Ryan Lake .20 .50
17 David Lawrence .30 .75
18 Marc Lefebvre .30 .75
19 Mike Peron .20 .50
20 Pasi Raitanan UER .30 .75
21 Ron Shudra .30 .75

2003-04 UK Sheffield Steelers Stickers

COMPLETE SET (18) 3.00 6.00
1 Mark Dutiaume .20 .50
2 Gavin Farrand .20 .50
3 Mike Peron .20 .50
4 Ryan Lake .20 .50
5 Dion Darling .20 .50
6 Davey Lawrence .20 .50
7 Rob Dopson .30 .75
8 Steve Ellis .20 .50
9 Ron Shudra .30 .75
10 Brent Bobyck .20 .50
11 Erik Anderson .20 .50
12 Kirk DeWaele .20 .50
13 Joel Irving .20 .50
14 Steve Duncombe .20 .50
15 Dan Hughes .20 .50
16 Marc Lefebvre .30 .75
17 Ben Bliss .20 .50
18 Gerald Adams .20 .50

2004-05 UK Sheffield Steelers

COMPLETE SET (20) 5.00 10.00
1 Jayme Platt .20 .50
2 David Lawrence .20 .50
3 Daryl Andrews .20 .50
4 Gerad Adams .20 .50
5 Steve Duncombe .20 .50
6 Ron Shudra .30 .75
7 Dion Darling .30 .75
8 David Cousineau .30 .75
9 Marc Lefebvre .30 .75
10 Mike Peron .20 .50
11 Mark Dutiaume .20 .50
12 Rob Stewart .20 .50
13 Erik Anderson .20 .50
14 Gavin Ferrand .20 .50
15 Joe Ciccarello .20 .50
16 Ben Bliss .20 .50
17 Paul Sample .20 .50
18 Jeff Christian .20 .50
19 Brent Bobyck .20 .50
20 Checklist .04 .10

1994-95 UK Solihul Barons

COMPLETE SET (15) 5.00 10.00
1 Jake Armstrong .30 .75
2 Stephen Doyle .30 .75
3 Paul Frankum .30 .75
4 Justin George .30 .75
5 Andy Havenhand .30 .75
6 Nick Henry .30 .75
7 Richard Hillas .30 .75
8 Phil Lee .30 .75
9 Declan McNaughton .30 .75
10 Joel Pickering .30 .75
11 Dan Prachar .30 .75
12 Gareth Roddis .30 .75
13 Jamie Van der Horst .30 .75
14 Dave Wilkie .30 .75
15 Liam Young .30 .75

1995-96 UK Solihull Barons

COMPLETE SET (13) 2.00 5.00
1 Jamie Van Der Horst .20 .50
2 Nick Henry .20 .50
3 Gareth Roddis .20 .50
4 Jake Armstrong .20 .50
5 Andy Havenhand .20 .50
6 Paul Frankum .20 .50
7 David Wilkie .20 .50
8 Phil Lee .20 .50
9 Dan Pracher .20 .50
10 Alan Hague .20 .50
11 Justin George .20 .50
12 Liam Young .20 .50
13 Stephen Doyle .20 .50

2004-05 UK Steven Carpenter Testimonial

COMPLETE SET (10) 2.00 5.00
1 Steven Carpenter 1996-97 .20 .50
2 Steven Carpenter 1997-98 .20 .50
3 Steven Carpenter 1998-99 .20 .50
4 Steven Carpenter 1999-00 .20 .50
5 Steven Carpenter 2000-01 .20 .50
6 Steven Carpenter 2001-02 .20 .50
7 Steven Carpenter 2002-03 .20 .50
8 Steven Carpenter 2003-04 .20 .50
9 Steven Carpenter 2004-05 .20 .50
10 Steven Carpenter CL .20 .50

2004-05 UK Thommo's Top 10

COMPLETE SET (10) 5.00 10.00
1 Greg Hadden .40 1.00
2 Tony Hand .60 1.50
3 Claudio Scremin .40 1.00
4 Rick Brebant .40 1.00
5 Mike Blaisdell .40 1.00
6 Joel Laing .40 1.00
7 Darryl Olsen .40 1.00
8 Marty Dallman .40 1.00
9 Dennis Vial .60 1.50
10 Patrice Lefebvre .60 1.50

2004-05 UK U-20 Team

COMPLETE SET (23) 5.00 10.00
1 David Lawrence .20 .50
2 Kevin Phillips .20 .50
3 Simon Butterworth .20 .50
4 Shaun Thompson .20 .50
5 Kurt Reynolds .20 .50
6 Shane Moore .20 .50
7 Steven Duncombe .20 .50
8 Leigh Jamieson .20 .50
9 Adam Brittle .20 .50
10 Chad Reekie .20 .50
11 Chace Ferrand .20 .50
12 David Phillips .20 .50

Card	Low	High
13 Bari McKenzie	.20	.50
14 Lee Mitchell	.20	.50
15 Tom Carlon	.20	.50
16 Mark Richardson	.20	.50
17 Adam Walker	.20	.50
18 Euan Forsyth	.20	.50
19 Andrew Thornton	.20	.50
20 Luke Boothroyd	.20	.50
21 Lewis Day	.20	.50
22 Geoffrey Woolhouse	.20	.50
23 Checklist	.04	.10

1998-99 Abilene Aviators

Card	Low	High
COMPLETE SET (21)	8.00	20.00
1 Erik Noack	.40	1.00
2 Jeff Triano CO	.20	.50
3 Don Margettie	.40	1.00
4 Tony Martino	.40	1.00
5 Mathieu Raby	.60	1.50
6 Derek Booth	.40	1.00
7 Mario Dumoulin	.40	1.00
8 Charlie Lawson	.40	1.00
9 Jean-Francois Gregoire	.40	1.00
10 Craig Perrett	.40	1.00
11 Eric Naud	.60	1.50
12 Stephane Roy	.40	1.00
13 Charles Poulin	.40	1.00
14 Jayson Brunette	.40	1.00
15 Stephen Maltby	.40	1.00
16 Terho Koskela	.40	1.00
17 Francois Archambault	.40	1.00
18 Marty Dallman	.40	1.00
19 Mario Cormier	.40	1.00
20 Eric Brule	.40	1.00
21 Don Margettie PROMO	2.00	5.00

1995-96 Adirondack Red Wings

Card	Low	High
COMPLETE SET (25)	4.80	12.00
1 Jeff Bloemberg	.15	.40
2 Curtis Bowen	.15	.40
3 Dave Chyzowski	.15	.40
4 Sylvain Cloutier	.15	.40
5 Ryan Duthie	.15	.40
6 Anders Eriksson	.20	.50
7 Yan Golubovski	.30	.75
8 Ben Hankinson	.15	.40
9 Kevin Hodson	.40	1.00
10 Scott Hollis	.15	.40
11 Mike Knuble	.40	1.00
12 Jason MacDonald	.20	.50
13 Mark Major	.15	.40
14 Norm Maracle	.40	1.00
15 Kurt Miller	.15	.40
16 Mike Needham	.15	.40
17 Troy Neumeier	.15	.40
18 Mark Ouimet	.15	.40
19 Jamie Pushor	.20	.50
20 Stacy Roest	.40	1.00
21 Brandon Smith	.20	.50
22 Kerry Toporowski	.15	.40
23 Wes Walz	.40	1.00
24 Aaron Ward	.30	.75
25 Hockeye Mascot	.02	.10

1999-00 Adirondack IceHawks

Card	Low	High
COMPLETE SET (25)	4.00	10.00
1 Header Checklist	.08	.25
2 Stephan Brochu	.20	.50
3 Eric Boyte	.20	.50
4 David Dartsch	.20	.50
5 John Batten	.20	.50
6 Larry Empey	.20	.50
7 Chris Ross	.20	.50
8 Trent Schachle	.20	.50
9 Checklist	.08	.25
10 Shawn Yakimishyn	.20	.50
11 Francois Sasseville	.20	.50
12 Guillaume Rodrigue	.20	.50
13 Trevor Jobe	.20	.50
14 Tony Cimellaro	.20	.50
15 Cameron MacDonald	.20	.50
16 Bobby Cunningham	.20	.50
17 Checklist	.08	.25
18 Alexei Deev	.20	.50
19 Wade Welte	.20	.50
20 Alexei Yegorov	.30	.75
21 Chad Ford	.20	.50
22 Jack Greig	.20	.50
23 Ben Metzger	.20	.50
24 Robbie Nichols	.20	.50
25 Hawkeye	.08	.25

1999-00 AHL All-Stars

Card	Low	High
1 Martin Brochu	.60	1.50
2 Craig Ferguson	.40	1.00
3 Peter Ferraro	.40	1.00
4 Michael Gaul	.40	1.00
5 Miikka Kiprusoff	2.00	5.00
6 Christian Matte	.60	1.50
7 Chris O'Sullivan	.40	1.00
8 Martin St. Louis	2.00	5.00
9 Brad Tiley	.40	1.00
10 Daniel Trebil	.40	1.00
11 Alexandre Volchkov	.40	1.00
12 Bob Wren	.40	1.00

2004-05 AHL All-Stars

Card	Low	High
COMPLETE SET (49)	10.00	20.00
1 Keith Ballard	.10	.25
2 Nolan Baumgartner	.10	.25
3 Sean Bergenheim	.10	.25
4 Patrice Bergeron	1.25	3.00
5 Brandon Bochenski	.30	.75
6 Rene Bourque	.20	.50
7 Jay Bouwmeester	.40	1.00
8 Dustin Brown	.40	1.00
9 Mike Cammalleri	.40	1.00
10 Craig Darby	.10	.25
11 Christian Ehrhoff	.10	.25
12 Steve Eminger	.10	.25
13 Simon Gamache	.20	.50
14 Mathieu Garon	.30	.75
15 Denis Grebeshkov	.10	.25
16 Dan Hamhuis	.10	.25
17 Andy Hilbert	.10	.25
18 Michael Holmqvist	.10	.25
19 Andrew Hutchinson	.10	.25
20 Ryan Kesler	.10	.25
21 Jason King	.10	.25
22 Chuck Kobasew	.30	.75
23 Mikko Koivu	.40	1.00
24 Niklas Kronwall	.30	.75
25 Jason Labarbera	.20	.50
26 Kari Lehtonen	1.25	3.00
27 Joey MacDonald	.40	1.00
28 Ryan Miller	.60	1.50
29 Antero Niittymaki	.40	1.00
30 Lawrence Nycholat	.10	.25
31 Michel Ouellet	.10	.25
32 Zach Parise	1.25	3.00
33 Eric Perrin	.10	.25
34 Joni Pitkanen	.20	.50
35 Tomas Plekanec	.20	.50
36 Brian Pothier	.10	.25
37 Travis Roche	.10	.25
38 Tony Salmelainen	.10	.25
39 Patrick Sharp	.10	.25
40 Jason Spezza	.75	2.00
41 Eric Staal	.60	1.50
42 Alexander Svitov	.10	.25
43 Brad Tiley	.10	.25
44 Anton Volchenkov	.10	.25
45 Kyle Wellwood	.30	.75
46 Dennis Wideman	.10	.25
47 Finland Representatives	.20	.50
48 Manchester Monarchs	.10	.25
49 Checklist	.04	.10

2002-03 AHL Top Prospects

Card	Low	High
COMPLETE SET (45)	8.00	20.00
1 Ramzi Abid	.10	.25
2 Alex Auld	.30	.75
3 Jared Aulin	.20	.50
4 Jason Bacashihua	.20	.50
5 Kris Beech	.10	.25
6 Brad Boyes	.30	.75
7 Scott Clemmensen	.20	.50
8 Ty Conklin	.20	.50
9 Niko Dimitrakos	.10	.25
10 Rick DiPietro	.60	1.50
11 Micki Dupont	.10	.25
12 Ray Emery	.40	1.00
13 Shane Endicott	.10	.25
14 Garnet Exelby	.20	.50
15 Jim Fahey	.10	.25
16 Ron Hainsey	.20	.50
17 Darren Haydar	.20	.50
18 Jonathan Hedstrom	.10	.25
19 Jeff Heerema	.10	.25
20 Andy Hilbert	.10	.25
21 Trent Hunter	.20	.50
22 Mike Komisarek	.20	.50
23 Tomas Kopecky	.20	.50
24 Pascal Leclaire	.40	1.00
25 Guillaume Lefebvre	.10	.25
26 Michael Leighton	.20	.50
27 Roman Lyashenko	.10	.25
28 Tomas Malec	.10	.25
29 Ryan Miller	.75	2.00
30 Shaone Morrisonn	.20	.50
31 Filip Novak	.10	.25
32 Steve Ott	.40	1.00
33 Maxime Ouellet	.20	.50
34 Justin Papineau	.10	.25
35 John Pohl	.10	.25
36 Brandon Reid	.10	.25
37 Jani Rita	.10	.25
38 Phillippe Sauve	.20	.50
39 Jason Spezza	1.25	3.00
40 Charlie Stephens	.10	.25
41 Jeff Taffe	.10	.25
42 J.P. Vigier	.10	.25
43 Kyle Wanvig	.10	.25
44 Duvie Westcott	.10	.25
45 Tomas Zizka	.10	.25

2003-04 AHL Top Prospects

Card	Low	High
COMPLETE SET (46)	6.00	15.00
1 Anton Babchuk	.10	.25
2 Jason Bacashihua	.20	.50
3 Ryan Bayda	.10	.25
4 Brad Boyes	.20	.50
5 Ilja Bryzgalov	.20	.50
6 Peter Budaj	.20	.50
7 Carlo Colaiacovo	.10	.25
8 Ray Emery	.40	1.00
9 Kurtis Foster	.10	.25
10 Denis Grebeshkov	.10	.25
11 Chris Higgins	.40	1.00
12 Jiri Hudler	.40	1.00
13 Ryan Kesler	.20	.50
14 Mike Komisarek	.10	.25
15 Lukas Krajicek	.10	.25
16 Niklas Kronwall	.30	.75
17 Brooks Laich	.10	.25
18 Pascal Leclaire	.20	.50
19 Kari Lehtonen	.75	2.00
20 David LeNeveu	.20	.50
21 Ross Lupaschuk	.10	.25
22 Justin Mapletoft	.10	.25
23 Jay McClement	.10	.25
24 Ryan Miller	.40	1.00
25 Shaone Morrisonn	.10	.25
26 Maxime Ouellet	.20	.50
27 Johnny Pohl	.20	.50
28 Jason Pominville	.40	1.00
29 Mark Popovic	.10	.25
30 Jani Rita	.10	.25
31 Derek Roy	.40	1.00
32 Patrick Sharp	.10	.25
33 Charlie Stephens	.10	.25
34 Alexander Suglobov	.10	.25
35 Tomas Surovy	.10	.25
36 Jeff Taffe	.10	.25
37 Petr Taticek	.10	.25
38 Hannu Toivonen	.40	1.00
39 Fedor Tyutin	.10	.25
40 Scott Upshall	.20	.50
41 Stephane Veilleux	.10	.25
42 Kyle Wanvig	.10	.25
43 Stephen Weiss	.20	.50
44 Kyle Wellwood	.40	1.00
45 Jeff Woywitka	.10	.25
NNO Checklist	.04	.10

2004-05 AHL Top Prospects

Card	Low	High
COMPLETE SET (61)	10.00	25.00
1 Zach Parise	1.00	2.50
2 Alexander Suglobov	.10	.25
3 Jason Spezza	.60	1.50
4 Antoine Vermette	.20	.50
5 Anton Volchenkov	.10	.25
6 Sean Bergenheim	.10	.25
7 Kari Lehtonen	1.00	2.50
8 Karl Stewart	.10	.25
9 Joffrey Lupul	.30	.75
10 Stanislav Chistov	.10	.25
11 Marcel Goc	.10	.25
12 Brad Winchester	.10	.25
13 Doug Lynch	.10	.25
14 Niklas Kronwall	.30	.75
15 Nathan Robinson	.10	.25
16 Tomas Plekanec	.20	.50
17 Trevor Daley	.10	.25
18 Jozef Balej	.10	.25
19 Jason Labarbera	.20	.50
20 Peter Budaj	.20	.50
21 Pierre-Marc Bouchard	.30	.75
22 Brent Burns	.20	.50
23 Mikko Koivu	.40	1.00
24 Eric Staal	.60	1.50
25 Chuck Kobasew	.20	.50
26 Brent Krahn	.20	.50
27 Yanick Lehoux	.10	.25
28 Mike Cammalleri	.40	1.00
29 Dustin Brown	.20	.50
30 Denis Grebeshkov	.10	.25
31 Jason King	.10	.25
32 Ryan Kesler	.10	.25
33 Timofei Shishkanov	.10	.25
34 Scottie Upshall	.20	.50
35 Jordin Tootoo	.40	1.00
36 Mikhail Yakubov	.10	.25
37 Anton Babchuk	.10	.25
38 R.J. Umberger	.20	.50
39 Joni Pitkanen	.20	.50
40 Antero Niittymaki	.40	1.00
41 Steve Eminger	.10	.25
42 Jakub Klepis	.10	.25
43 Patrice Bergeron	1.00	2.50
44 Hannu Toivonen	.40	1.00
45 Derek Roy	.20	.50
46 Thomas Vanek	1.00	2.50
47 Stephen Weiss	.20	.50
48 Jay Bouwmeester	.30	.75
49 Nathan Horton	.30	.75
50 Adam Henrich	.10	.25
51 Kyle Wellwood	.30	.75
52 Matthew Stajan	.30	.75
53 Carlo Colaiacovo	.20	.50
54 Alexander Svitov	.10	.25
55 David LeNeveu	.20	.50
56 Michel Ouellet	.10	.25
57 Ryan Whitney	.30	.75
58 Marc-Andre Fleury	.60	1.50
59 Mike Glumac	.10	.25
60 Peter Sejna	.10	.25
NNO Checklist	.04	.10

2005-06 AHL All-Stars

Card	Low	High
COMPLETE SET (45)	10.00	25.00
1 Keith Aucoin	.20	.50
2 Sven Butenschon	.20	.50
3 Braydon Coburn	.20	.50
4 Yann Danis	.40	1.00
5 Andy Delmore	.20	.50
6 Eric Fehr	.20	.50
7 Valtteri Filppula	.50	1.25
8 Wade Flaherty	.40	1.00
9 Bruno Gervais	.20	.50
10 Denis Grebeshkov	.20	.50
11 Denis Hamel	.20	.50
12 Mark Hartigan	.20	.50
13 Eric Healey	.20	.50
14 Jiri Hudler	.40	1.00
15 Vitaly Kolesnik	.40	1.00
16 Kirby Law	.20	.50
17 Junior Lessard	.40	1.00
18 Corey Locke	.20	.50
19 Donald MacLean	.20	.50
20 Al Montoya	.75	2.00
21 Mike Mottau	.20	.50
22 Curtis Murphy	.20	.50
23 Filip Novak	.20	.50
24 Lawrence Nycholat	.20	.50
25 Patrick O'Sullivan	.40	1.00
26 Nathan Paetsch	.20	.50
27 Libor Pivko	.20	.50
28 Thomas Pock	.20	.50
29 Johnny Pohl	.20	.50
30 Richie Regehr	.20	.50
31 Pekka Rinne	.40	1.00
32 Pat Rissmiller	.20	.50
33 Jimmy Roy	.20	.50
34 Dany Sabourin	.40	1.00
35 Ryan Shannon	.20	.50
36 John Slaney	.20	.50
37 Martin St. Pierre	.20	.50
38 Alexander Suglobov	.20	.50
39 Jeff Tambellini	.20	.50
40 Layne Ulmer	.20	.50
41 Ryan Vesce	.20	.50
42 Noah Welch	.20	.50
43 Erik Westrum	.40	1.00
44 AHL All-Stars	.20	.50
NNO Checklist	.01	.01

2005-06 AHL Top Prospects

Card	Low	High
COMPLETE SET (50)	15.00	25.00
1 Nicklas Bergfors	.20	.50
2 Steve Bernier	.40	1.00
3 Kevin Bieksa	.20	.50
4 Chris Bourque	.40	1.00
5 Alexandre Burrows	.40	1.00
6 Braydon Coburn	.20	.50
7 Jeremy Colliton	.20	.50
8 Ryan Craig	.20	.50
9 Yann Danis	.40	1.00
10 Nigel Dawes	.20	.50
11 Patrick Eaves	.40	1.00
12 Dan Ellis	.40	1.00
13 Eric Fehr	.20	.50
14 Valtteri Filppula	.50	1.25
15 Tomas Fleischmann	.20	.50
16 Bruno Gervais	.20	.50
17 Mike Glumac	.20	.50
18 Josh Harding	.40	1.00
19 Jim Howard	.40	1.00
20 Jean-Francois Jacques	.20	.50
21 Matt Jones	.20	.50
22 Vitaly Kolesnik	.40	1.00
23 Staffan Kronwall	.20	.50
24 Ryan Lannon	.20	.50
25 Al Montoya	.75	2.00
26 Eric Nystrom	.20	.50
27 Patrick O'Sullivan	.40	1.00
28 Nathan Paetsch	.20	.50
29 Dustin Penner	.40	1.00
30 Alexandre Picard	.20	.50
31 Libor Pivko	.20	.50
32 Geoff Platt	.20	.50
33 Konstantin Pushkarev	.20	.50
34 Tyler Redenbach	.20	.50
35 Pekka Rinne	.40	1.00
36 Peter Sejna	.20	.50
37 Ryan Shannon	.20	.50
38 Brian Sipotz	.20	.50
39 Martin St. Pierre	.20	.50
40 Yan Stastny	.20	.50
41 Barry Tallackson	.20	.50
42 Jeff Tambellini	.20	.50
43 Chris Thorburn	.20	.50
44 Lauri Tukonen	.20	.50
45 Ryan Vesce	.20	.50
46 Roman Voloshenko	.20	.50
47 Ben Walter	.20	.50
48 Noah Welch	.20	.50
49 Jeremy Williams	.40	1.00
50 Checklist	.01	.01

2006-07 AHL Top Prospects

Card	Low	High
1 Kyle Cumiskey	.20	.50
2 Justin Peters	.20	.50
3 Andrew Ebbett	.20	.50
4 Josh Hennessy	.30	.75
5 Jeff Tambellini	.20	.50
6 Robert Nilsson	.20	.50
7 Blake Comeau	.20	.50
8 Brett Stirling	.30	.75
9 Nathan Oystrick	.20	.50
10 Boris Valabik	.20	.50
11 Jonathan Ericsson	.20	.50
12 Jimmy Howard	.40	1.00
13 Jaroslav Halak	.75	2.00
14 Ryan Callahan	.20	.50
15 Daniel Girardi	.30	.75
16 Jeff Schultz	.20	.50
17 Benoit Pouliot	.40	1.00
18 Joel Lundqvist	.40	1.00
19 Vojtech Polak	.20	.50
20 Andy Greene	.20	.50
21 Matt Moulson	.20	.50
22 Peter Harrold	.20	.50
23 Colby Genoway	.20	.50
24 Alex Edler	.30	.75
25 Rich Peverley	.20	.50
26 Cal O'Reilly	.20	.50
27 Troy Brouwer	.30	.75
28 Dustin Byfuglien	.20	.50
29 Corey Crawford	.30	.75
30 Dustin Boyd	.30	.75
31 Curtis McElhinney	.20	.50
32 Roman Polak	.20	.50
33 Marek Schwarz	.40	1.00
34 Stefan Ruzicka	.20	.50
35 Ryan Shannon	.20	.50
36 David Krejci	.30	.75
37 Matt Lashoff	.30	.75
38 Clarke MacArthur	.20	.50
39 Drew Stafford	.75	2.00
40 Bill Thomas	.20	.50
41 Blair Jones	.20	.50
42 Karri Ramo	.30	.75
43 Tomas Popperle	.20	.50
44 Colin Murphy	.20	.50
45 Justin Pogge	.75	2.00
46 Jon Filewich	.20	.50
47 Rob Schremp	.60	1.50
48 Jeff Drouin-Deslauriers	.30	.75
49 Joe Pavelski	.40	1.00
50 Thomas Greiss	.30	.75

2007-08 AHL Top Prospects

Card	Low	High
COMPLETE SET (50)	12.00	20.00
1 Bobby Hughes	.20	.50
2 Brian Lee	.20	.50
3 Nick Foligno	.20	.50
4 Frans Nielsen	.20	.50
5 Blake Comeau	.20	.50
6 Brett Sterling	.20	.50
7 Ondrej Pavelec	.30	.75
8 Jonathan Ericsson	.40	1.00
9 Jakub Kindl	.20	.50
10 Sergei Kostitsyn	.40	1.00
11 Ryan O'Byrne	.20	.50
12 Greg Moore	.20	.50
13 Brodie Dupont	.20	.50
14 Kyle Wilson	.20	.50
15 Daren Machesney	.20	.50
16 Petr Kalus	.20	.50
17 Cal Clutterbuck	.20	.50
18 Mark Fistric	.20	.50
19 T.J. Hensick	.20	.50
20 Chris Stewart	.20	.50
21 Mark Fraser	.20	.50
22 Teddy Purcell	.30	.75
23 Brian Boyle	.60	1.50
24 Luc Bourdon	.30	.75
25 Michael Grabner	.20	.50
26 Cal O'Reilly	.20	.50
27 Cody Franson	.20	.50
28 Vladimir Mihalik	.20	.50
29 Roman Polak	.20	.50
30 Marek Schwarz	.25	.60
31 Jonathan Matsumoto	.30	.75
32 Ryan Parent	.30	.75
33 Bobby Ryan	.30	.75
34 Brian Salcido	.20	.50
35 Matt Hunwick	.20	.50
36 Tuukka Rask	.30	.75
37 Kris Chucko	.20	.50
38 Matt Pelech	.20	.50
39 Stefan Meyer	.20	.50
40 Marek Zagrapan	.20	.50
41 Cam Barker	.20	.50
42 Jack Skille	.30	.75
43 Keith Yandle	.20	.50
44 Colin McDonald	.20	.50
45 Marc Pouliot	.20	.50
46 Derick Brassard	.20	.50
47 Justin Pogge	.40	1.00
48 Kristopher Letang	.20	.50
49 Mike Iggulden	.20	.50
50 Lukas Kaspar	.20	.50

2010-11 AHL Top Prospects

Card	Low	High
COMPLETE SET (50)	8.00	20.00
1 Luke Adam	.20	.50
2 Jake Allen	.40	1.00
3 Alexander Avtsin	.15	.40
4 Johan Backlund	.20	.50
5 Kyle Beach	.25	.60
6 Mikkel Boedker	.15	.40
7 Robert Bortuzzo	.20	.50
8 Zach Boychuk	.20	.50
9 Bobby Butler	.20	.50
10 Taylor Chorney	.20	.50
11 Joe Colborne	.25	.60
12 Ian Cole	.20	.50
13 Kaspars Daugavins	.25	.60
14 Corey Elkins	.15	.40
15 Benn Ferriero	.15	.40
16 Cameron Gaunce	.20	.50
17 Blake Geoffrion	.25	.60
18 Colton Gillies	.15	.40
19 Evgeny Grachev	.20	.50
20 Cody Hodgson	.50	1.25
21 Braden Holtby	.30	.75
22 Jesse Joensuu	.20	.50
23 Nick Johnson	.15	.40
24 Linus Klasen	.20	.50
25 Mikko Koskinen	.25	.60
26 Philip Larsen	.20	.50
27 Nick Leddy	.25	.60
28 Jacob Markstrom	.50	1.25
29 Alec Martinez	.20	.50
30 Thomas McCollum	.25	.60
31 John Moore	.20	.50
32 Greg Nemisz	.20	.50
33 Kyle Palmieri	.40	1.00
34 Aaron Palushaj	.25	.60
35 Mathieu Perreault	.15	.40
36 Alex Plante	.20	.50
37 Paul Postma	.25	.60
38 Kevin Quick	.15	.40
39 Michal Repik	.15	.40
40 Jussi Rynnas	.25	.60
41 Maxime Sauve	.25	.60
42 Marco Scandella	.20	.50
43 Jordan Schroeder	.25	.60
44 Zac Dalpe	.25	.60
45 Alex Stalock	.20	.50
46 Tomas Tatar	.50	1.25
47 Mattias Tedenby	.20	.50
48 Viktor Tikhonov	.20	.50
49 James Wright	.15	.40
50 Mats Zuccarello	.40	1.00

1995-96 AHCA

Card	Low	High
COMPLETE SET (10)	3.00	8.00
1 The Pioneers	.20	.50
2 The Inspiration Hobey Baker	.60	1.50
3 The Personalities John Mariucci	.20	.50
4 The Champions Michigan	.40	1.00
5 The Colleges Edward Jeremiah	.20	.50
6 The Coaches Ron Mason	.20	.50
7 The Records 1970 Cornell squad	.20	.50
8 The Moments Dean Talafous	.20	.50
9 The Traditions 1978 Boston University Champions	.20	.50
10 The Future Cammi Granato	.60	1.50

1991-92 Air Canada SJHL

Card	Low	High
COMPLETE SET (250)	14.00	35.00
A1 Dean Normand Humboldt Broncos	.10	.30
A2 Dan Meyers Estevan Brui	.08	.25
A3 Tyson Balog Weyburn Red Wings	.07	.20
A4 Tyler McMillan Weyburn Red Wings	.07	.20
A5 Jason Selkirk Saskatoon Titans	.07	.20
A6 Bryce Bohun	.07	.20
A7 Blaire Hornung Saskatoon Titans	.07	.20
A8 Craig McKechnie Melville Millionaires	.07	.20
A9 Rejean Stringer	.07	.20
A10 Corri Moffat Melville Millionaires	.07	.20
A11 Dion Johnson	.07	.20
A12 Rod Krushel Melville Millionaires	.07	.20
A13 Mike Langen Weyburn Red Wings	.07	.20
A14 Jeff Hassman Melville Millionaires	.07	.20
A15 Dean Moore Notre Dame Hounds	.07	.20
A16 Trevor Wathen Minot Americans	.07	.20
A17 Curtis Knight Humboldt Broncos	.07	.20
A18 Chris Morgan Minot Americans	.07	.20
A19 Trevor Thurstan Flin Flon Bombers	.07	.20
A20 Wayne Filipenko Minot Americans	.07	.20
A21 Jason Feiffer Weyburn Red Wings	.07	.20
A22 Layne Douglas Minot Americans	.07	.20
A23 Dave Gardner	.07	.20
A24 Ryan Sandholm Notre Dame Hounds	.07	.20
A25 Corey McKee Melfort Mustangs	.07	.20
A26 Trevor Schmiess Humboldt Broncos	.07	.20
A27 Todd Hollinger Saskatoon Titans	.20	.50
A28 Jay Dunn	.07	.20
A29 Jamie Ling Notre Dame Hounds	.10	.30
A30 Todd Small Saskatoon Titans	.07	.20
A31 Barret Kropf Melfort Mustangs	.07	.20
A32 Dean Gerard Melfort Mustangs	.07	.20
A33 Christian Dutil Yorkton Terriers	.07	.20
A34 Tyler Scheidt Aaron Campbell Melfort Mustangs	.07	.20
A35 Dean Sideroff Humboldt Broncos	.07	.20
A36 Dan Dufresne Notre Dame Hounds	.07	.20
A37 Cam Yager	.07	.20
A38 Richard Nagy Flin Flon	.08	.25
A39 Aaron Cain Flin Flon Bombers	.20	.50
A40 Rob Beck Flin Flon Bombers	.07	.20
A41 Blair Wagar Yorkton Terriers	.07	.20
A42 Kim Maier Estevan Bruins	.07	.20
A43 Brent Hoiness	.07	.20
A44 Troy Edwards Estevan Bruins	.07	.20
A45 Evan Anderson Estevan Bruins	.07	.20
A46 Carlin Nordstrom	.07	.20
A47 Dean Seymour Yorkton Terriers	.07	.20
A48 Scott Wotton Yorkton Terriers	.10	.30
A49 Curtis Joseph SJHL All Star	4.00	10.00
B1 Richard Boscher Saskatoon Titans	.07	.20
B2 James Schaeffler Saskatoon Titans	.07	.20
B3 Wes Rommel	.07	.20
B4 Corey Thompson	.07	.20
B5 Rob Phillips	.10	.30
B6 Jim McLean	.07	.20
B7 Trevor Warrener Saskatoon Titans	.20	.50
B8 Peter Boake Weyburn Red Wings	.07	.20
B9 Kevin Riffel Estevan Bruins	.07	.20
B10 Tom Perry Humboldt Broncos	.07	.20
B11 Mark Baird Humboldt Broncos	.07	.20
B12 Stacy Prevost Yorkton Terriers	.07	.20
B13 Taras Lendzyk Humboldt Broncos	.07	.20
B14 Shawn Reis Melfort Mustangs	.07	.20
B15 Shawn Thompson Future Prospect	.07	.20
B16 Curtis Kleisinger Notre Dame Hounds	.07	.20
B17 Kent Rogers Saskatoon Titans	.07	.20
B18 Scott Christion Notre Dame Hounds	.10	.30
B19 Gerald Tallaire Estevan Bruins	.10	.30
B20 Kelly Hollingshead Este	.10	.30
B21 Mike Savard	.07	.20
B22 Darren Maloney Melville Millionaires	.07	.20
B23 Jason Hynd	.07	.20
B24 Scott Stewart Flin Flon Bombers	.07	.20
B25 Scott Beattie SJHL All Star	.10	.30
B26 Dave McAmmond Flin Flon Bombers	.07	.20
B27 Myles Gibb	.07	.20
B28 Ryan Bach Notre Dame Hounds	.20	.50
B29 Martin Smith	.07	.20
B30 Leigh Brookbank Yorkton Terriers	.07	.20
B31 Todd Markus Melfort Mustangs	.07	.20
B32 The Boys From PA Dean Gerard Darryn Listwan Sco	.10	.30
B33 Randy Muise Weyburn Red Wings	.07	.20
B34 George Gervais Estevan Bruins	.07	.20
B35 Keith Harris Weyburn Red Wings	.07	.20
B36 Jamie Stelmak Melville Millionaires	.07	.20
B37 Bart Vanstaalduinen Notre Dame Hounds	.07	.20
B38 Scott Murray Minot Americans	.07	.20
B39 Danny Galarneau Yorkton Terriers	.07	.20
B40 Keith Murphy Melville Millionaires	.07	.20
B41 Jeff Kungle Melfort Mustangs	.10	.30
B42 Michel Cook Yorkton Terriers	.07	.20
B43 Daryl Krauss Weyburn Red Wings	.07	.20
B44 Derek Wynne Minot Americans	.07	.20
B45 Derek Crimin Minot Americans	.07	.20
B46 Jason Brown Flin Flon Bombers	.07	.20
B47 Bruce Matatall Minot Americans	.07	.20
B48 Chris Hatch Flin Flon Bombers	.07	.20
B49 Kurtise Souchotte Melville Millionaires	.07	.20
B50 Michael Brennan Humboldt Broncos	.07	.20
B51 Orrin Hergott Future Prospect	.07	.20
C1 Craig Matatall Notre Dame Hounds	.07	.20
C2 Brad Prefontaine Melville Millionaires	.07	.20
C3 Mike Evans Notre Dame Hounds	.07	.20
C4 Jody Reiter	.07	.20
C5 Jeremy Mylymok Notre Dame Hounds	.07	.20
C6 Dave Doucet Melville Mi	.10	.30
C7 Randy Kerr Melville Millionaires	.07	.20
C8 Gordon McCann Melville Millionaires	.07	.20
C9 Quinn Fair Notre Dame Hounds	.07	.20
C10 Kyle Niemegeers Estevan Bruins	.07	.20
C11 Ryan Smith North Battle	.10	.30
C12 Mike Hillock Minot Americans	.07	.20
C13 Vern Anderson	.07	.20
C14 Trent Hamm	.07	.20
C15 Curtis Folkett ACO Estevan Bruins	.07	.20
C16 Warren Pickford	.07	.20
C17 Craig Volstad	.07	.20
C18 Sean Tallaire Estevan B	.10	.30
C19 Jason Yaganiski Minot Americans	.07	.20
C20 Jim McLarty	.07	.20
C21 Jamie Fyfuglien Minot Americans	.07	.20
C22 Terry Metro Minot Americans	.07	.20
C23 Todd Kozak	.07	.20
C24 Jeff Huckle Saskatoon Titans	.07	.20
C25 Darren McLean Estevan Bruins	.07	.20
C26 Bret Mohninger Saskatoon Titans	.07	.20
C27 Tim Slukynsky Yorkton Terriers	.07	.20
C28 Roman Mrhalek Yorkton Terriers	.07	.20
C29 Joel Martinson Humboldt Broncos	.07	.20
C30 Ron Patterson Flin Flon Bombers	.07	.20
C31 Mark Gorgi Melfort Mustangs	.07	.20
C32 Tom Thomson Saskatoon Titans	.07	.20
C33 Greg Wahl Saskatoon Titans	.07	.20
C34 Craig Perrett Melfort Mustangs	.07	.20
C35 Mike Harder Weyburn Red Wings	.07	.20
C36 Jeff Cole Humboldt Broncos	.07	.20
C37 Justin Christoffer Humboldt Broncos	.07	.20
C38 Nolan Weir Flin Flon Bombers	.07	.20
C39 Jeff Knight Melfort Mustangs	.07	.20
C40 Lyle Vaughan Yorkton Terriers	.07	.20
C41 Scott Bellefontaine Yorkton Terriers	.07	.20
C42 Trevor Mathias Weyburn Red Wings	.07	.20
C43 Chris Schinkel Humboldt	.10	.30
C44 Scott Rogers Melfort Mustangs	.08	.20
C45 Shane Holunga Weyburn Red Wings	.07	.20
C46 Dwayne Rhinehart Flin Flon Bombers	.07	.20
C47 Eddy Marchant Flin Flon Bombers	.07	.20
C48 Travis Smith Weyburn Red Wings	.07	.20
C49 Not Known	.07	.20
C50 Mike Hidlebaugh Future Prospect	.07	.20
D1 Darcy Herlick Weyburn Red Wings	.07	.20
D2 Joel Appleton Humboldt Broncos	.07	.20
D3 Bobby Standish Melfort Mustangs	.07	.20
D4 Kory Karlander Saskatoon Titans	.10	.30
D5 Brett Kinaschuk Humboldt Broncos	.07	.20
D6 Kevin Messer	.07	.20
D7 Jason Martin Weyburn Red Wings	.07	.20
D8 Devin Zimmer		

Minot Americans .07 .20
D9 David Foster
Humboldt Broncos .07 .20
D10 Bob Schwark
Melfort Mustangs .07 .20
D11 Ted Grayling
Melville Millionaires .07 .20
D12 Travis Vantighem
Melvil .10 .30
D13 Darren Houghton
Melville Millionaires .07 .20
D14 Wade Welte
Melville Millionaires .07 .20
D15 1991 NB All Stars
Martin Smith
Ron Gunville
Der .20 .50
D16 Kevin Powell
Minot Americans .07 .20
D17 Returning Hounds
Dave Lovesin
Bernie Adlys
Bart .07 .20
D18 Dennis Budeau
Minot Americans .07 .20
D19 Darren Opp .07 .20
D20 Jeff Greenwood .07 .20
D21 Mark Daniels
Saskatoon Titans .20 .50
D22 Todd Murphy .07 .20
D23 Scott Weaver
Minot Americans .07 .20
D24 Robby Bear
Yorkton Terriers .07 .20
D25 Nigel Werenka
Yorkton Terriers .10 .30
D26 Sean Timmins
Notre Dame Hounds .07 .20
D27 Ken Malenfant
Saskatoon Titans .07 .20
D28 Greg Taylor
Melfort Mustangs .07 .20
D29 Sheldon Bylsma
Yorkton Terriers .07 .20
D30 Clint Hooge
Flin Flon Bombers .07 .20
D31 Bob McIntosh
Notre Dame Hounds .07 .20
D32 Dave Lovsin
Notre Dame Hounds .07 .20
D33 Jeremy Mathies .07 .20
D34 Blaine Fomradas
Weyburn Red Wings .07 .20
D35 Cory Borys
Yorkton Terriers .07 .20
D36 Brad Purdie
Weyburn Red Wings .07 .20
D37 J. Sotropa
Saskatoon Titans .07 .20
D38 Duane Vardale .07 .20
D39 Jim Nellis .07 .20
D40 Brent Sheppard
Humboldt Broncos .07 .20
D41 Cam Bristow
Melfort Mustangs .07 .20
D42 Steven Brent
Estevan Bruins .07 .20
D43 Mike Matteucci
Estevan Bruins .07 .20
D44 Bryan Cossette
Estevan Bruins .07 .20
D45 Tyler Kuhn
Flin Flon Bombers .07 .20
D46 Dave Debusschere
Esteva .07 .20
D47 Darryl Dickson
Flin Flon Bombers .07 .20
D48 Derek Meikle
Flin Flon Bombers .07 .20
D49 Parris Duffus
Ex SJHLer .20 .50
D50 Lance Wakefield
Future Prospect .10 .30
1 Brooke Battersby
Estevan Bruins .07 .20
2 Jay Dobrescu
Estevan Bruins .07 .20
3 Blair Allison
Estevan Bruins .07 .20
4 Shane Johnson
Estevan Bruins .07 .20
5 Carson Cardinal
Estevan Bruins .07 .20
6 Dean Pooyak
Flin Flon Bombers .07 .20
7 Mark Loeppky
Flin Flon Bombers .07 .20
8 Travis Cheyne
Flin Flon Bombers .07 .20
9 Karl Johnson
Flin Flon Bombers .07 .20
10 Jason Ahenakew
Flin Flon Bombers .07 .20
11 Darren Schmidt
Humboldt Broncos .10 .30
12 Larry Empey
Humboldt Broncos .07 .20
13 Colin Froese
Humboldt Broncos .07 .20
14 Darryn Listwan
Melfort Mustangs .07 .20
15 Todd MacMillan
Melfort Mustangs .07 .20
16 Ken Ruddock
Melfort Mustangs .07 .20
17 Derek Simonson
Melfort Mustangs .07 .20
18 Lyle Ehrmantraut
Minot Americans .07 .20
19 Jody Weller .07 .20
20 Danny Dennis
Melville Millionaires .07 .20
21 Trent Harper
Melville Millionaires .07 .20
22 Jason Prokopetz
Melvill .10 .30
E23 Tom Thomson
Saskatoon Titans .07 .20
E24 Trent Dumaine .07 .20
E25 Mike Wevers
Saskatoon Titans .07 .20
E26 Darren Duncalfe
Weyburn Red Wings .07 .20
E27 Regan Simpson .07 .20
E28 Jeff Bloski .07 .20
E29 Blake Sutton .07 .20
E30 Darcy Blair
North Battl .10 .30
E31 Marty Craigdallie
Notre Dame Hounds .07 .20
E32 Jason Krug
Notre Dame Hounds .07 .20
E33 Mark Hansen
Notre Dame Hounds .07 .20
E34 Bernie Adlys
Notre Dame Hounds .07 .20
E35 Brett Colborne
Notre Dame Hounds .07 .20
E36 Tony Bergin
Notre Dame Hounds .07 .20
E37 Ian Adamson .07 .20
E38 Darren MacMillan .07 .20
E39 Rob Neighbour .07 .20
E40 Jeff Lawson .07 .20
E41 Derrick Brucks
Saskatoon Titans .07 .20
E42 Todd Schoenroth
Saskatoon Titans .07 .20
E43 Jody Forseth
Weyburn Red Wings .07 .20
E44 Derek Beuselinck
Weyburn Red Wings .07 .20
E45 Clint Wensley
Weyburn Red Wings .07 .20
E46 Darren Donald
Weyburn Red Wings .07 .20
E47 Shane Stangby
Yorkton Terriers .07 .20
E48 Jamie Dunn
Yorkton Terriers .07 .20
E49 Steve Sabo
Yorkton Terriers .07 .20
E50 Anthony Toth
Yorkton Terriers .07 .20

1991-92 Air Canada SJHL All-Stars

COMPLETE SET (50) 4.80 12.00
1 Jeff Kungle .15 .40
2 Jay Dunn .08 .25
3 Kevin Dickie .08 .25
4 Martin Smith .08 .25
5 Jeff Cole .08 .25
6 Trent Hamm .08 .25
7 Kent Rogers .08 .25
8 Dean Gerard .08 .25
9 Jim McLarty .08 .25
10 Malcolm Kostuchenko .08 .25
11 Mark Scollan .08 .25
12 Brad Federenko .20 .50
13 Rob Beck .08 .25
14 Bryce Bohun .08 .25
15 Kory Karlander .15 .40
16 Scott Christion .15 .40
17 Tyler Kuhn .08 .25
18 Corri Moffatt .08 .25
19 Layne Douglas .08 .25
20 Shane Holunga .08 .25
21 Mike Matteucci .08 .25
22 Bart Vanstaalduinen .08 .25
23 Brad McEwen .08 .25
24 Kim Maier .08 .25
25 Jamie Ling .20 .50
26 Dean Seymour .08 .25
27 Derek Crimin .08 .25
28 Evan Anderson .08 .25
29 Craig Matatall .08 .25
30 Keith Murphy .08 .25
31 Jason Feiffer .08 .25
32 Michel Cook .08 .25
33 Rod Krushel .08 .25
34 Tyler Rice .15 .40
35 Gerald Tallaire .20 .50
36 Richard Nagy .08 .25
37 Taras Lendzyk .08 .25
38 Jeff Knight .08 .25
39 Darren Opp .08 .25
40 Dwayne Rhinehart .08 .25
41 Minot Americans
Layne Douglas
Derek Crimin .08 .25
42 Scott Bellefontaine .08 .25
43 Darren Maloney .08 .25
44 North Division
All-Star Team
Team Photo .20 .50
45 Yorkton Terriers
All Stars
Michel Cook
Dean Seymour
Scott Bellefontaine .20 .50
46 Melville Millionaires
All Stars
Team Photo .20 .50
47 Best 1992 All-Stars
Kevin Dickie CO
Mike Matteucci
Kory Karlander
Kim Maier
Darren Opp
Richard Nagy
Mark Scollan .20 .50
48 Estevan Bruins
All Stars
Gerald Tallaire
Kim Maier
Mike Matteucci
Evan Anderson .20 .50
49 Notre Dame Hounds
All Stars
Tyler Rice
Scott Christion
Bart Van Staalduinen
Jamie Ling
Craig Matatall .20 .50
50 Bob Robson CO .08 .25

2003-04 Alaska Aces

COMPLETE SET (16) 10.00 20.00
1 Jordan Cameron .50 1.25
2 Kimbi Daniels .50 1.25
3 Bret DeCecco .50 1.25
4 Wes Dorey .50 1.25
5 Jonathan Gauthier .50 1.25
6 Malcolm Hutt .50 1.25
7 Mike Jones .50 1.25
8 Charles Linglet .50 1.25
9 Chris Lipsett .50 1.25
10 Lance Mayes .75 2.00
11 Keith McCambridge .50 1.25
12 Ryan Moren .50 1.25
13 Dan Murphy .75 2.00
14 Shane Palahicky .50 1.25
15 Garrett Prosofsky .50 1.25
16 Mark Smith .50 1.25

2010-11 Alaska Aces

COMPLETE SET (20) 4.00 10.00
1 Scott Burt .30 .75
2 Wes Goldie .60 1.50
3 Bryan Miller .30 .75
4 Brian Swanson .60 1.50
5 Chad Anderson .30 .75
6 Ethan Cox .30 .75
7 Alex Dzielski .30 .75
8 Adam Courchaine .30 .75
9 Scott Howes .30 .75
10 Kory Falite .30 .75
11 Garry Nunn .30 .75
12 Maxime Tanguay .30 .75
13 Gerald Coleman .30 .75
14 Mark Isherwood .30 .75
15 Steve Ward .30 .75
16 Chris Langkow .30 .75
17 Jerad Stewart .30 .75
18 Zach Harrison .30 .75
19 Brandon Gentile .30 .75
20 Russ Sinkewich .30 .75

1995-96 Alaska Gold Kings

COMPLETE SET (19) 3.60 9.00
1 Title Card .08 .25
2 Derby Bognar .20 .50
3 Geoff Bumstead .30 .75
4 Chris Cahill .20 .50
5 Warren Carter .20 .50
6 John Haddad .20 .50
7 Todd Henderson .20 .50
8 Wade Klippenstein .20 .50
9 Matt Koleski .20 .50
10 Donald Lester .20 .50
11 Derek Linnell .20 .50
12 Jamie Loewen .20 .50
13 Travis MacMillan .20 .50
14 Kirk Patton .20 .50
15 Guy Prince .20 .50
16 Rob Proffitt .20 .50
17 Ryan Reynard .20 .50
18 Wayne Sawchuk CO .02 .10
19 Shawn Ulrich .20 .50

1996-97 Alaska Gold Kings

COMPLETE SET (14) 3.00 8.00
1 Mark Costea .30 .75
2 Shane Fisher .30 .75
3 Colin Foley .30 .75
4 Chris French .30 .75
5 Yoshifumi Fujtsawa .30 .75
6 Todd Henderson .30 .75
7 Kelly Hrycun .30 .75
8 Shawn Lofroth .30 .75
9 Brad McCaughey CO .02 .10
10 Billy McGuigan .30 .75
11 Jay Murphy .30 .75
12 Sergei Olympicv .30 .75
13 Orion The Lion
Mascot .02 .10
14 Shawn Ulrich .30 .75

1996-97 Albany River Rats

COMPLETE SET (26) 6.00 15.00
1 Eric Bertrand .20 .50
2 Brad Bombardir .20 .50
3 Steve Brule .20 .50
4 Mike Dunham .40 1.00
5 Patrik Elias .75 2.00
6 Bryan Helmer .20 .50
7 Bobby House .20 .50
8 Geordie Kinnear .20 .50
9 Chris McAlpine .20 .50
10 Krzysztof Oliwa .40 1.00
11 Jay Pandolfo .40 1.00
12 Denis Pederson .30 .75
13 Pascal Rheaume .30 .75
14 Vadim Sharifijanov .20 .50
15 Richard Shulmistra .30 .75
16 Peter Sidorkiewicz .30 .75
17 Zdenek Skorepa .20 .50
18 Sheldon Souray .20 .50
19 Mark Strobel .20 .50
20 Steve Sullivan .40 1.00
21 Sergei Vyshedkevich .20 .50
22 John Cunniff CO .02 .10
23 Dennis Gendron CO .02 .10
24 Rowdy MASCOT .02 .10
25 AHL Web Site .02 .10
26 PHPA Web Site .02 .10

1997-98 Albany River Rats

COMPLETE SET (26) 6.00 15.00
1 Eric Bertrand .15 .40
2 Jiri Bicek .40 1.00
3 Steve Brule .15 .40
4 Bryan Helmer .15 .40
5 Bobby House .15 .40
6 Geordie Kinnear .20 .50
7 Sasha Lakovic .20 .50
8 Judd Lambert .20 .50
9 John Madden .75 2.00
10 Brendan Morrison .75 2.00
11 Jay Pandolfo .20 .50
12 Richard Rochefort .15 .40
13 Vadim Sharifijanov .20 .50
14 Peter Sidorkiewicz .20 .50
15 Zdenek Skorepa .15 .40
16 Rob Skrlac .15 .40
17 Ken Sutton .15 .40
18 Paul Traynor .15 .40
19 Sergei Vyshedkevich .20 .50
20 Colin White .30 .75
21 Jeff Williams .15 .40
22 Peter Zezel .40 1.00
23 John Cunniff CO .10 .25
24 Dennis Gendron CO .10 .25
25 PHPA Web Site .02 .10
26 AHL Web Site .02 .10

1998-99 Albany River Rats

COMPLETE SET (25) 4.80 12.00
1 Eric Bertrand .15 .40
2 Jiri Bicek .30 .75
3 Steve Brule .20 .50
4 Mike Buzak .15 .40
5 David Cunniff .15 .40
6 Pierre Dagenais .30 .75
7 Josh DeWolf .15 .40
8 Sascha Goc .30 .75
9 Frederic Henry .15 .40
10 Geordie Kinnear .20 .50
11 John Madden .75 2.00
12 Rob Pattison .15 .40
13 Henrik Rehnberg .15 .40
14 Richard Rochefort .15 .40
15 Alexander Semak .15 .40
16 Rob Skrlac .15 .40
17 Ken Sutton .15 .40
18 Chris Thompson .15 .40
19 Sergei Vyshedkevich .15 .40
20 Colin White .30 .75
21 Jeff Williams .15 .40
22 Red Gendron CO .02 .10
23 John Cunniff CO .02 .10
24 Rowdy MASCOT .02 .10
25 AHL Web Site .02 .10

1999-00 Albany River Rats

COMPLETE SET (26) 4.80 12.00
1 George Awada .15 .40
2 Jiri Bicek .30 .75
3 Steve Brule .20 .50
4 Bobby Carpenter ACO .20 .50
5 Sylvain Cloutier .15 .40
6 David Cunniff .15 .40
7 John Cunniff CO .15 .40
8 Pierre Dagenais .30 .75
9 Jean-Francois Damphousse .60 1.50
10 Josh DeWolf .20 .50
11 Dennis Gendron ACO .15 .40
12 Sascha Goc .30 .75
13 Stanislav Gron .40 1.00
14 Frederic Henry .30 .75
15 Steve Kelly .20 .50
16 Andre Lakos .15 .40
17 Sasha Lakovic .20 .50
18 Carlyle Lewis .15 .40
19 David Maley .15 .40
20 Willie Mitchell .15 .40
21 Richard Rochefort .15 .40
22 Rob Skrlac .15 .40
23 Ken Sutton .15 .40
24 Rowdy MASCOT .02 .10
25 Colin White .30 .75
26 Jeff Williams .15 .40

2000-01 Albany River Rats

COMPLETE SET (27) 4.00 10.00
1 Daryl Andrews .15 .40
2 Jiri Bicek .30 .75
3 Max Birbraer .20 .50
4 Josef Boumedienne .15 .40
5 Sylvain Cloutier .15 .35
6 Mike Commodore .20 .50
7 Pierre Dagenais .30 .75
8 Chris Ferraro .15 .35
9 Sascha Goc .20 .50
10 Stanislav Gron .40 1.00
11 Mike Jefferson .20 .50
12 Andre Lakos .15 .35
13 Jason Lehoux .15 .35
14 Carlyle Lewis .15 .35
15 Willie Mitchell .20 .50
16 Lucas Nehrling .15 .35
17 Henrik Rehnberg .15 .35
18 Richard Rochefort .15 .35
19 Michael Rupp .40 1.00
20 Rob Skrlac .15 .35
21 Ed Ward .15 .35
22 Jean-Francois Damphousse .30 .75
23 Frederic Henry .20 .50
24 John Cunniff CO .04 .10
25 Bobby Carpenter ACO .10 .25
26 Alex Zinevych .15 .35
27 Team CL .04 .10

2001-02 Albany River Rats

COMPLETE SET (28) 6.00 12.00
1 Checklist .04 .10
2 Sylvain Cloutier .10 .25
3 Jean-Francois Damphousse .20 .50
4 Mike Commodore .10 .25
5 Daryl Andrews .10 .25
6 Andre Lakos .10 .25
7 Mikko Jokela .20 .50
8 Joel Dezainde .10 .25
9 Jiri Bicek .30 .75
10 Stanislav Gron .30 .75
11 Brian Gionta .40 1.00
12 Richard Rochefort .10 .25
13 Michael Rupp .30 .75
14 Ted Drury .10 .25
15 Max Birbraer .20 .50
16 Christian Berglund .10 .25
17 Scott Cameron .10 .25
18 Jason Lehoux .10 .25
19 Brett Clouthier .10 .25
20 Bruce Gardiner .10 .25
21 Stephen Guolla .20 .50
22 Victor Uchevatov .10 .25
23 Joel Bouchard .10 .25
24 Ari Ahonen 1.25 3.00
25 Scott Clemmensen .40 1.00
26 Bob Carpenter CO .04 .10
27 Geordie Kinnear ACO .04 .10
28 Rowdy .04 .10

2002-03 Albany River Rats

COMPLETE SET (28) 5.00 12.00
1 Ari Ahonen .40 1.00
2 Alex Brooks .20 .50
3 Brett Clouthier .20 .50
4 Christian Berglund .20 .50
5 Craig Darby .20 .50
6 Chris Hartsburg .20 .50
7 Daryl Andrews .20 .50
8 David Roche .20 .50
9 Eric Johansson .20 .50
10 Jiri Bicek .20 .50
11 Joe Hulbig .20 .50
12 Jason Lehoux .20 .50
13 Krisjanis Redlihs .20 .50
14 Ken Sutton .20 .50
15 Max Birbraer .40 1.00
16 Mikko Jokela .20 .50
17 Mike Matteucci .20 .50
18 Michael Rupp .40 1.00
19 Ray Giroux .20 .50
20 Rob Skrlac .20 .50
21 Scott Cameron .20 .50
22 Scott Clemmensen .40 1.00
23 Victor Uchevatov .20 .50
24 Greg Crozier .20 .50
25 Dennis Gendron HCO .04 .10
26 Geordie Kinnear ACO .04 .10
27 Gates Orlando ACO .04 .10
NNO Checklist .04 .10

2002-03 Albany River Rats AAP

COMPLETE SET (25) 8.00 20.00
1 Checklist card .04 .10
2 Ari Ahonen .50 1.25
3 Daryl Andrews .40 1.00
4 Max Birbraer .50 1.25
5 Alex Brooks .40 1.00
6 Scott Cameron .40 1.00
7 Scott Clemmensen .50 1.25
8 Brett Clouthier .40 1.00
9 Greg Crozier .40 1.00
10 Craig Darby .40 1.00
11 Ray Giroux .40 1.00
12 Red Gendron CO .04 .10
13 Chris Hartsburg .40 1.00
14 Joe Hulbig .40 1.00
15 Eric Johansson .40 1.00
16 Mikko Jokela .40 1.00
17 Jason Lehoux .40 1.00
18 Mike Matteucci .40 1.00
19 Krisjanis Redlihs .40 1.00
20 Dave Roche .40 1.00
21 Rowdy MASCOT .04 .10
22 Michael Rupp .50 1.25
23 Rob Skrlac .40 1.00
24 Ken Sutton .40 1.00
25 Victor Uchevatov .40 1.00

2003-04 Albany River Rats

COMPLETE SET (30) 5.00 12.00
1 Checklist .04 .10
2 Ari Ahonen .30 .75
3 Maxim Balmochnykh .15 .40
4 Jiri Bicek .15 .40
5 Alex Brooks .15 .40
6 Scott Clemmensen .30 .75
7 Brett Clouthier .15 .40
8 Greg Crozier .15 .40
9 Craig Darby .15 .40
10 Matt DeMarchi .15 .40
11 Adrian Foster .16 .40
12 Ray Giroux .15 .40
13 Tyler Hanchuck .15 .40
14 Chris Hartsburg .15 .40
15 Joe Hulbig .15 .40
16 Eric Johansson .15 .40
17 Steve Kariya .60 1.50
18 Matus Kostur .15 .40
19 Mike Matteucci .15 .40
20 Ryan Murphy .15 .40
21 Ahren Nittel .30 .75
22 Tuomas Pihlman .30 .75
23 Ilkka Pikkarainen .15 .40
24 Krisjanis Redlihs .15 .40
25 Rob Skrlac .15 .40
26 Alexander Suglobov .15 .40
27 Victor Uchevatov .15 .40
28 Dennis Gendron CO .04 .10
29 Gates Orlando ACO .04 .10
30 Geordie Kinnear ACO .04 .10

2003-04 Albany River Rats Kinko's

COMPLETE SET (26) 15.00 30.00
1 Ari Ahonen .60 1.50
2 Maxim Balmochnykh .40 1.00
3 Jiri Bicek .40 1.00
4 Alex Brooks .40 1.00
5 Scott Clemmensen .60 1.50
6 Brett Clouthier .40 1.00
7 Greg Crozier .40 1.00
8 Craig Darby .40 1.00
9 Matt DeMarchi .40 1.00
10 Adrian Foster .40 1.00
11 Ray Giroux .40 1.00
12 Tyler Hanchuck .40 1.00
13 Chris Hartsburg .40 1.00
14 Joe Hulbig .40 1.00
15 Eric Johansson .40 1.00
16 Steve Kariya 1.25 3.00
17 Matus Kostur .40 1.00
18 Mike Matteucci .40 1.00
19 Ryan Murphy .40 1.00
20 Ahren Nittel .75 2.00
21 Tuomas Pihlman .40 1.00
22 Ilkka Pikkarainen .40 1.00
23 Krisjanis Redlihs .40 1.00
24 Rob Skrlac .40 1.00
25 Alexander Suglobov .40 1.00
26 Victor Uchevatov .40 1.00

2004-05 Albany River Rats

COMPLETE SET (25) 6.00 15.00
1 Ari Ahonen .30 .75
2 Bobby Allen .15 .40
3 Alex Brooks .15 .40
4 Scott Clemmensen .30 .75
5 Brett Clouthier .15 .40
6 Matt DeMarchi .15 .40
7 Adrian Foster .15 .40
8 David Hale .40 1.00
9 Cam Janssen .40 1.00
10 Eric Johansson .15 .40
11 Teemu Kesa .15 .40
12 Ivan Khomutov .15 .40
13 Dean McAmmond .15 .40
14 Ryan Murphy .15 .40
15 Ahren Nittel .30 .75
16 Zach Parise 2.00 5.00
17 Tuomas Pihlman .15 .40
18 Ilkka Pikkarainen .15 .40
19 Krisjanis Redlihs .15 .40
20 Pascal Rheaume .15 .40
21 Ray Schultz .15 .40
22 Rob Skrlac .15 .40
23 Aaron Voros .15 .40
24 Aleksander Suglobov .15 .40
25 Robbie Ftorek CO .04 .10

2005-06 Albany River Rats

COMPLETE SET (28) 6.00 15.00
1 Ari Ahonen .40 1.00
2 Bobby Allen .20 .50
3 Nicklas Bergfors .20 .50
4 Alex Brooks .20 .50
5 Ben Carpentier .20 .50
6 David Clarkson .20 .50
7 Matt DeMarchi .20 .50
8 Frank Doyle .40 1.00
9 Adrian Foster .20 .50
10 David Hale .20 .50
11 Cam Janssen .40 1.00
12 Teemu Kesa .20 .50
13 Ivan Khomutov .20 .50
14 Bryan Miller .20 .50
15 Ryan Murphy .20 .50
16 Ahren Nittel .40 1.00
17 Tuomas Pihlman .20 .50
18 Ilkka Pikkarainen .20 .50
19 Krisjanis Redlihs .20 .50
20 Pascal Rheaume .20 .50
21 Jason Ryznar .20 .50
22 Ray Schultz .20 .50
23 Mike Sgroi .20 .50
24 Aleksander Suglobov .20 .50
25 Barry Tallackson .40 1.00
26 Aaron Voros .20 .50
27 Petr Vrana .20 .50
28 Robbie Ftorek .02 .10

2006-07 Albany River Rats

COMPLETE SET (27) 5.00 12.00
1 Kevin Estrada .20 .50
2 Keith Aucoin .20 .50
3 Ryan Bayda .20 .50
4 Joe Barnes .20 .50
5 Jesse Boulerice .20 .50
6 Johnny Boychuck .20 .50
7 Tim Conboy .20 .50
8 Kyle Cumiskey .20 .50
9 Dan DaSilva .20 .50
10 Pat Dwyer .20 .50
11 Jeff Finger .20 .50
12 Dave Gove .20 .50
13 Ben Guite .20 .50
14 Scott Kelman .20 .50
15 Mitch Love .20 .50
16 Cody McLeod .20 .50
17 Matt Murley .20 .50
18 Justin Peters .30 .75
19 Jakub Petruzalek .20 .50
20 Peter Tsimikalis .20 .50
21 Tyler Weiman .30 .75
22 Shane Willis .20 .50
23 Brett Carson .20 .50
24 Tom Rowe HC .02 .10
25 Joe Sacco CO .02 .10
NNO Rowdy MASCOT .02 .10
NNO Checklist .01 .01

2013-14 Alberni Valley Bulldogs

COMPLETE SET (22) 6.00 15.00
1 Hunter Stewart .30 .75
2 Nathan Warren .30 .75
3 Harlan Orr .30 .75
4 Craig Martin .30 .75
5 Robert Click .30 .75
6 Quinton Wunder .30 .75
7 Brett Stewart .30 .75
8 Ryan Buse .30 .75
9 Jake Kauppila .30 .75
10 Mitch Owsley .30 .75
11 Tryg Strand .30 .75
12 Darian Henry .30 .75
13 Zach Funk .30 .75
14 Scott Clark .30 .75
15 Mitch Makin .30 .75
16 Josh Adkins .30 .75
17 Justin Georgeson .30 .75
18 Zak Bowles .30 .75
19 Dylan Haugen .30 .75
20 Kurt Gosselin .30 .75
21 Garrett Halls .30 .75
22 Connor LaCouvee .30 .75

1999-00 Alexandria Warthogs

COMPLETE SET (23) 20.00 50.00
1 Mark Biesenthal .75 2.00
2 Jeff Blair .75 2.00
3 Jason Desloover .75 2.00
4 Josh Dobbyn .75 2.00
5 Valeri Ermolov .75 2.00
6 Dion Hagan .75 2.00
7 Daniel Korber .75 2.00
8 Chris Low .75 2.00
9 Jay Mazur .75 2.00
10 Jim Mroz .75 2.00
11 Matt Osiecki .75 2.00
12 Chris Peach .75 2.00
13 Marc Pethke .75 2.00
14 Robert Plante .75 2.00
15 Regan Stocco .75 2.00
16 Matt Turek .75 2.00
17 Colby Van Tassel .75 2.00
18 Miles Van Tassel .75 2.00
19 Mike Zruna CO .40 1.00
20 Jason Leveille 4.00 10.00
21 Marcus Adolfsson .75 2.00
22 Bill Weir .75 2.00
23 Chad Wilchynski .75 2.00

1998-99 Amarillo Rattlers

COMPLETE SET (21) 10.00 25.00
1 Matt Brenner .60 1.50
2 Chris Brooks .60 1.50
3 Stephen Douglas .60 1.50
4 Steve Ferranti .60 1.50
5 Bob Gohde .60 1.50
6 Brad Haelzle .60 1.50
7 Derek Innanen .60 1.50
8 Trevor Janicki .60 1.50
9 Brendan Kenny .60 1.50
10 Todd Laurin .60 1.50
11 Adam Lord .60 1.50
12 Cal McGowan .75 2.00
13 Jim McLean .60 1.50
14 David Rattray .60 1.50
15 Jaynen Rissling .60 1.50
16 Per Schlyter .60 1.50
17 Scott W. Stevens .60 1.50
18 Neil Gondek ACO .08 .25
19 Ken Karpuk CO .08 .25
20 Amarillo Rattlers .08 .25
21 Greg Sieg TR .08 .25

2000-01 Amarillo Rattlers

COMPLETE SET (20) 8.00 20.00
1 Eric Andersen .40 1.00
2 Chris Bell .40 1.00
3 Rodney Bowers .40 1.00
4 Jeff Cheeseman .40 1.00
5 Marc Dupuis .40 1.00
6 Larry Empey .40 1.00
7 Vincent Grant .40 1.00
8 Brad Haelzle .40 1.00
9 Toby Harris .40 1.00
10 Robert Holsinger .75 2.00
11 Todd MacDonald .75 2.00
12 Jeff Mancini .40 1.00
13 Jodi Murphy .75 2.00
14 Billy Newson .40 1.00
15 Jay Pecora .40 1.00
16 Doug Shepherd .40 1.00
17 Tony White .40 1.00
18 Chad Wilchynski .40 1.00
19 Kevin Abrams CO .08 .25
20 Team Card .08 .25

1993-94 Amos Les Forestiers

COMPLETE SET (26) 14.00 35.00
1 Jean-Francois Belley .40 1.00
2 Carl Benoit .40 1.00
3 Martin Biron 6.00 15.00
4 David Bolduc .40 1.00
5 Martin Bradette .40 1.00
6 Dave Fontaine .40 1.00
7 Paul-Sebastien Gagnon .40 1.00
8 Eric Germain .40 1.00
9 Eric Houle .40 1.00
10 Jacques Larrivee ACO .08 .25
11 Yannick Lavoie .40 1.00
12 Mathieu Letourneau .40 1.00
13 Vincent Levasseur .40 1.00
14 Jonathan Levesque .40 1.00
15 Eric Naud .40 1.00
16 Christian Neveu .40 1.00
17 Patrick Pelchat .40 1.00
18 John Pyliotic .40 1.00
19 Luc St-Germain .40 1.00
20 Frederick Servant .40 1.00
21 Philippe Tremblay .40 1.00
22 Serge Trepanier CO .08 .25
23 Dany Villeneuve .40 1.00
24 Les Veterans
Christian Neveu
Mathieu Letourneau .40 1.00
25 Team Photo
CL .40 1.00
26 Title card .08 .25

1992-93 Anaheim Bullfrogs RHI

COMPLETE SET (20) 4.00 10.00
1 Header Card .02 .10
2 Maury Silver .20 .50
3 Stuart Silver .20 .50
4 Marc Lyons .20 .50
5 Kevin Kerr .20 .50
6 Grant Sonier ACO .08 .25
7 Barry Potomski .30 .75
8 Bob McKillop .20 .50
9 Rob Laurie .30 .75
10 Bill Horn .20 .50
11 Savo Mitrovic .20 .50
12 Chris McSorley CO .20 .50
13 Victor Gervais .30 .75
14 Darren Perkins .20 .50
15 Christian LaLonde .20 .50
16 Joe Cook .20 .50
17 Ken Murchison .20 .50
18 Brad McCaghey .20 .50
19 Devin Edgerton .20 .50
20 Mike Butters .20 .50

1993-94 Anaheim Bullfrogs RHI

COMPLETE SET (21) 3.20 10.00
1 Shayne Arsenault .20 .50
2 Steve Beadle .20 .50
3 Jim Brown .20 .50
4 Joe Cook .20 .50
5 Victor Gervais .20 .50
6 Chris Gordon .20 .50
7 Kevin Kerr .30 .75
8 Yuri Krivokhija .20 .50
9 Christian Lalonde .20 .50
10 Darren Langdon .30 .75
11 Rob Laurie .30 .75
12 Brad McCaughey .20 .50
13 Bobby McKillop .30 .75

14 Savo Mitrovic .20 .50
15 Ken Murchison .20 .50
16 Darren Perkins .20 .50
17 Grant Sonier CO .08 .25
NNO The Mask .30 .75
NNO 1993 RHI World Champions .20 .50
NNO Header .02 .10
NNO Medallion Slammer .20 .50

1994-95 Anaheim Bullfrogs RHI

COMPLETE SET (20) 3.60 10.00
1 Darren Banks .30 .75
2 Jared Bednar .20 .50
3 Steve Cadieux .20 .50
4 Joe Cook .20 .50
5 Mark Deazeley .20 .50
6 Victor Gervais .30 .75
7 Chris Gordon .20 .50
8 Fredrik Jax .20 .50
9 Rick Judson .20 .50
10 Rob Laurie .30 .75
11 BJ MacPherson .20 .50
12 Brad McCaughey .20 .50
13 Savo Mitrovic .20 .50
14 Marc Ouimet .30 .75
15 Darren Perkins .20 .50
16 Daniel Shank .30 .75
17 Grant Sonier CO .02 .10
18 Brad Tiley .20 .50
19 Todd Wetzel .20 .50
20 Header/Checklist .02 .10

1995-96 Anaheim Bullfrogs RHI

COMPLETE SET (20) 3.00 8.00
1 Checklist .02 .10
2 Grant Sonier CO .02 .10
3 Brad McCaughey ACO .02 .10
4 Victor Gervais .15 .40
5 Darren Perkins .15 .40
6 Savo Mitrovic .15 .40
7 Joe Cook .15 .40
8 Todd Wetzel .15 .40
9 Scott Bell .15 .40
10 Rick Judson .15 .40
11 BJ MacPherson .15 .40
12 Rob Laurie .15 .40
13 Darren Banks .20 .50
14 Sean O'Brien .15 .40
15 Jakub Ficenec .15 .40
16 Mark Stitt .15 .40
17 Glenn Stewart .15 .40
18 Mark DeSantis .15 .40
19 Tom Menicci .15 .40
20 Eric Raymond .15 .40

1996-97 Anaheim Bullfrogs RHI

COMPLETE SET (21) 3.60 9.00
1 Bullfrogs Logo .02 .10
2 Zeus Mascot .02 .10
3 Rob Laurie .20 .50
4 Victor Gervais .20 .50
5 Doug McCarthy .20 .50
6 Kurt Seher .20 .50
7 Marty Yewchuk .20 .50
8 David Goverde .25 .60
9 BJ MacPherson .02 .10
10 Rick Judson .25 .60
11 Jakub Ficenec .20 .50
12 Tom Menicci .20 .50
13 Glenn Stewart .20 .50
14 Mark Stitt .20 .50
15 Jim Bermingham .20 .50
16 Todd Wetzel .20 .50
17 Joe Cook .20 .50
18 Ray Edwards .20 .50
19 Chris Newans .20 .50
20 Darren Perkins .20 .50
21 Brad McCaughey CO .02 .10

1994-95 Anchorage Aces

COMPLETE SET (27) 4.80 12.00
1 Kevin Fitzgerald .20 .50
2 Tony Link .20 .50
3 Zack Westin .20 .50
4 Kory Wright .20 .50
5 Kord Cernich .20 .50
6 Darrin Semeniuk .20 .50
7 Brian Kraft .20 .50
8 Raymond Blackadar .20 .50
9 Jim Tobin .20 .50
10 Tracy Link .20 .50
11 Michael Warde .20 .50
12 Garvin Federenko .20 .50
13 Jim Mayes .20 .50
14 Vern Hickel .20 .50
15 Derek Donald .20 .50
16 Brian Majeske .20 .50
17 Chad Meyhoff .20 .50
18 Doug Spooner .20 .50
19 Maurice Hall .20 .50
20 Pete McEnaney .20 .50
21 Keith Street .20 .50
22 Georg Thiele .20 .50
23 Tim Molle .20 .50
24 Brian Bethard .20 .50
25 Dean Trboyevich .20 .50
26 Logo Card .04 .10
27 Team Photo
Checklist .20 .50

1996-97 Anchorage Aces

COMPLETE SET (16) 3.00 8.00
1 Alaska's Morning Show .02 .10
2 Derek Donald .30 .75
3 Kiddie Fox .02 .10
4 Dean Larson .30 .75
5 Steve MacSwain .30 .75
6 Mark The Hitman .02 .10
7 J.J. Michaels .30 .75
8 Black Mike .02 .10
9 Craig Mittleholt .30 .75
10 Chris Newans .30 .75
11 Frank Ouellette .30 .75
12 Chad Richard .30 .75
13 Sean Rowe .30 .75
14 Keith Street .30 .75
15 Dean Trboyevich .30 .75
16 Free Q-Zar Game Card .02 .10

1997-98 Anchorage Aces

COMPLETE SET (25) 3.60 9.00
1 Title Card .02 .10
2 Walt Poddubny CO .20 .50
3 Kenny Huizenga .20 .50
4 Kord Cernich .20 .50
5 Bobby Cunningham .20 .50
6 Derek Donald .20 .50
7 Dallas Ferguson .20 .50
8 Derek Gauthier .20 .50
9 Jason Gibson .20 .50
10 Marc LaForge .20 .50
11 Dean Larson .20 .50
12 Dave Latta .20 .50
13 Steve MacSwain .20 .50
14 Chris Newans .20 .50
15 Hayden O'Rear .20 .50
16 Brian Renfrew .20 .50
17 Sean Rowe .20 .50
18 Jason Shmyr .20 .50
19 Keith Street .20 .50
20 Sergei Tkachenko .20 .50
21 George Wilcox .20 .50
22 Paul Williams .20 .50
23 Mascot .02 .10
24 Mascot .02 .10
25 Mascot .02 .10

1998-99 Anchorage Aces

COMPLETE SET (26) 4.00 10.00
1 Checklist
Team Photo .20 .50
2 Dean Trboyevich .20 .50
3 Kevin Epp .20 .50
4 Hayden O'Rear .20 .50
5 Richard Peacock .20 .50
6 Sean Rowe .20 .50
7 Boomer Mascot .02 .10
8 George Wilcox .20 .50
9 Sergei Tkachenko .20 .50
10 Frank Jury TR .02 .10
11 Walt Poddubny HCO .20 .50
12 Kent Baumbach .20 .50
13 Wade Brookbank .20 .50
14 Keith Street .20 .50
15 Bob Cunningham .20 .50
16 Kord Cernich .20 .50
17 Paul Williams .20 .50
18 Evgeny Kourilin .20 .50
19 Jason Gibson .20 .50
20 Steve MacSwain .20 .50
21 Dean Larson .20 .50
22 Dallas Ferguson .20 .50
23 Derek Gauthier .20 .50
24 Yvan Corbin .20 .50
25 Sponsor Card .02 .10
26 Fred Rannard BR .02 .10

1999-00 Anchorage Aces

COMPLETE SET (28) 4.00 10.00
1 Bob Wilkie HCO .08 .25
2 Fred Rannard .20 .50
3 Paul Williams .20 .50
4 Steve MacSwain .20 .50
5 Marc Charbonneau .20 .50
6 Chad Power .20 .50
7 Brian Elder .20 .50
8 Tim Lozinik .20 .50
9 Sponsor Card .02 .10
10 Sponsor Card .02 .10
11 Kord Cernich .20 .50
12 George Wilcox .20 .50
13 Keith Street .20 .50
14 Derek Gauthier .20 .50
15 Ruslan Batyrshin .30 .75
16 Sean Rowe .20 .50
17 Dean Larson .20 .50
18 Team Photo .20 .50
19 Sponsor Card .02 .10
20 Sponsor Card .02 .10
21 Walt Poddubny HCO .20 .50
22 Dallas Ferguson .20 .50
23 Chad Richard .20 .50
24 Denis Pigolitsyn .20 .50
25 Clayton Read .20 .50
26 Marc Delmore .20 .50
27 Lada Hampeis .20 .50
28 Sponsor Card .02 .10

2001-02 Anchorage Aces

COMPLETE SET (22) 8.00 20.00
1 Shane Calder .40 1.00
2 Bob Cunningham .40 1.00
3 Kimbi Daniels .40 1.00
4 Simon Duplessis .40 1.00
5 Yuri Krivokhija .40 1.00
6 Brian LaFleur .40 1.00
7 Dean Larson .40 1.00
8 Michael Marostega .40 1.00
9 Jamie McCaig .60 1.50
10 Chris Newans .40 1.00
11 Denis Pigolitsin .40 1.00
12 Tobin Praznik .40 1.00
13 Chad Richard .60 1.50
14 Olie Sundstrom .60 1.50
15 Paul Williams .40 1.00
16 J.J. Wrobel .40 1.00
17 Jami Yoder .40 1.00
18 B.J. Young .40 1.00
19 Walt Poddubny CO .10 .25
20 Boomer MASCOT .04 .10
21 ACS Wireless .04 .10
22 Team Photo .20 .50

1990-91 Arizona Icecats

COMPLETE SET (16) 3.00 8.00
1 Leo Golembiewski CO .30 .75
2 Icecat Leaders
Kevin Sheehan
John Allen
Leo Golembiewski CO
Kelly Walker
John Wegener .40 1.00
3 John Allen .30 .75
4 Don Carlson .20 .50
5 Dan Divjak .30 .75
6 Frank DeMaio .20 .50
7 Jeremy Goltz .30 .75
8 Aaron Joffe .20 .50
9 Dan O'Day .20 .50
10 Dan Olberg .20 .50
11 Cory Oleson .30 .75
12 Kevin Sheehan .30 .75
13 Dean Sives .20 .50
14 Kelly Walker .30 .75
15 John Wegener .30 .75
16 Logo Card
Checklist .20 .50

1991-92 Arizona Icecats

COMPLETE SET (20) 4.00 10.00
1 Leo Golembiewski CO .08 .25
2 Don Carlson .20 .50
3 Kelly Walker .30 .75
4 Cory Oleson .30 .75
5 Drew Sibr .20 .50
6 Dan Divjak .30 .75
7 Jeremy Goltz .20 .50
8 Aaron Joffe .20 .50
9 Tommy Smith .20 .50
10 Dan Anderson .20 .50
11 Dean Sives .20 .50
12 Steve Hutchings .20 .50
13 Shane Fausel .20 .50
14 Greg Mitchell .20 .50
15 Ricky Pope .20 .50
16 Nate Soules .20 .50
17 Flavio Gentile .20 .50
18 Icecats Leaders
Leo Golembiewski CO
Kelly Walker
Cory Oleson
Jeremy Goltz
Dan Divjak .20 .50
19 Glenn Hall
Honorary Captain 1.00 2.50
20 Logo Card
Checklist .08 .25

1992-93 Arizona Icecats

COMPLETE SET (20) 3.00 8.00
1 Leo Golembiewski CO .08 .25
2 Kelly Walker .25 .60
3 Cory Oleson .25 .60
4 Tommy Smith .20 .50
5 John Allen .20 .50
6 Dan Anderson .20 .50
7 Aaron Joffe .20 .50
8 Dan Divjak .25 .60
9 Jeremy Goltz .20 .50
10 Steve Hutchings .20 .50
11 Greg Mitchell .20 .50
12 Ricky Pope .20 .50
13 Nate Soules .20 .50
14 Matt Glines .20 .50
15 Mark Thawley .20 .50
16 Andre Zafrani .20 .50
17 Chris Noga .20 .50
18 Jim Kolbe
Honorary Captain .08 .25
19 Coach and Top Gun Line
Cory Oleson
Leo Golembiew .30 .75
20 Logo Card
Checklist .08 .25

1993-94 Arizona Icecats

COMPLETE SET (20) 3.00 8.00
1 Header Card .08 .25
2 Leo Golembiewski CO .08 .25
3 Greg Mitchell .20 .50
4 Ricky Pope .20 .50
5 Dan Divjak .25 .60
6 Brian Consolino .20 .50
7 Matt Gines .20 .50
8 Steve Hutchings .20 .50
9 Joel Nusbaum .20 .50
10 Sam Battaglia .20 .50
11 Kiva Gippo .20 .50
12 Jeremy Goltz .20 .50
13 Peter Scott .20 .50
14 Kevin Oztekin .20 .50
15 Nate Soules .20 .50
16 Chris Noga .20 .50
17 Dennis Hands .20 .50
18 Mark Thawley .20 .50
19 Leader Card .08 .25
20 Oliver North .30 .75

1994-95 Arizona Icecats

COMPLETE SET (24) 10.00 25.00
1 Title Card/CL .02 .10
2 Leo Golembiewski CO .40 1.00
3 Steve Hutchings .40 1.00
4 Nate Soules .40 1.00
5 Chris Noga .40 1.00
6 Kevin Oztekin .40 1.00
7 Greg Mitchell .40 1.00
8 Ricky Pope .40 1.00
9 Brian Consolino .40 1.00
10 John Muntz .40 1.00
11 Joel Nusbaum .40 1.00
12 Sam Battaglia .40 1.00
13 Kiva Gippo .40 1.00
14 Peter Scott .40 1.00
15 Dennis Hands .60 1.50
16 Mark Thawley .40 1.00
17 Ryan Rockabrand .40 1.00
18 Joe Joyce .40 1.00
19 Jeremy Walters .40 1.00
20 Ethan Kaulas .40 1.00
21 Reg Kerr#)Glen Hall .75 2.00
22 Leo Golembiewski
Keith Magnuson .60 1.50
23 Stan Mikita
Glen Hall
Keith Magnuson
Al Secord 2.00 5.00
24 Madhouse on Main Street .10 .25

1995-96 Arizona Icecats

COMPLETE SET (23) 25.00
1 Title Card/CL .02 .10
2 Leo Golembiewski CO .10 .25
3 Chris Noga .40 1.00
4 John Muntz .40 1.00
5 Kevin Oztekin .40 1.00
6 Mark Thawley .40 1.00
7 Sam Battaglia .40 1.00
8 Peter Scott .40 1.00
9 Joel Nusbaum .40 1.00
10 Ryan Rockabrand .40 1.00
11 Andy Knick .40 1.00
12 Brian Meehan .40 1.00
13 Bob Majka .40 1.00
14 Ben Ruston .40 1.00
15 Jeff Rice .40 1.00
16 Brian Consolino .40 1.00
17 Bryan Fork .40 1.00
18 Joel Hilshey .50 1.25
19 Joe Joyce .40 1.00
20 Jeremy Goltz ACO .10 .25
21 Icecat Leaders .20 .50
22 Scotty Bowman 2.00 5.00
23 Scotty Bowman Hon Capt. 2.00 5.00

1996-97 Arizona Icecats

COMPLETE SET (25) 4.00 25.00
1 Title Card/CL .02 .10
2 Leo Golembiewski HCO .10 .25
3 Kevin Baskel .40 1.00
4 Sam Battaglia .40 1.00
5 Brian Consolino .40 1.00
6 Josh Flett .40 1.00
7 Eric Holton .40 1.00
8 Paul Juran .40 1.00
9 Andy Knick .40 1.00
10 Eliot Komar .40 1.00
11 Beau Lemire .50 1.25
12 Joe McCaffrey .40 1.00
13 Brian Meehan .40 1.00
14 Joel Nusbaum .40 1.00
15 Ace Pascual .40 1.00
16 Rob Poupard .40 1.00
17 Ben Ruston .40 1.00
18 Peter Scott .40 1.00
19 Mike Tesi .40 1.00
20 Tom Thompson .40 1.00
21 Dave Weiss .40 1.00
22 Bob Majka .40 1.00
23 Leo Golembiewski HCO .10 .25
24 Jeremy Goltz ACO .10 .25
25 Stan Mikita Hon Capt. 2.00 5.00

1997-98 Arizona Icecats

COMPLETE SET (26) 10.00 25.00
1 Title Card/CL .02 .10
2 Leo Golembiewski HCO .20 .50
3 Benedictine HOF .10 .25
4 Kevin Baskel .40 1.00
5 Jordan Bolton .60 1.50
6 Tyler Brush .40 1.00
7 Ed Carfora .40 1.00
8 Paul Dorn .40 1.00
9 Chad Dyjak .40 1.00
10 Rodney Glassman .40 1.00
11 Mike Graves .40 1.00
12 Marc Harris .40 1.00
13 Joe McCaffrey .40 1.00
14 Charles McCarty .40 1.00
15 Bob Majka .40 1.00
16 Brian Meehan .40 1.00
17 Ace Pascual .40 1.00
18 Joe Peplinski .60 1.50
19 Ben Ruston .40 1.00
20 Mike Tesi .40 1.00
21 Tom Thompson .40 1.00
22 Kory Wagstaff .40 1.00
23 Max Wilkie .40 1.00
24 Jim Wilkey .40 1.00
25 Jeremy Goltz ACO .20 .50
26 Rex Allen, Jr. Hon Capt. .40 1.00

1998-99 Arizona Icecats

COMPLETE SET (27) 10.00 25.00
1 Tyler Brush .40 1.00
2 Ed Carfora .40 1.00
3 Quinn Carter .40 1.00
4 Hunter Cherenack .40 1.00
5 Paul Dorn .40 1.00
6 Andrew Edwards .40 1.00
7 Rodney Glassman .40 1.00
8 Leo Golembiewski CO .02 .10
9 Jeremy Goltz ACO .02 .10
10 Mike Graves .40 1.00
11 Marc Harris .40 1.00
12 Bobby Hull HON CPT 2.00 5.00
13 Pavel Jandura .40 1.00
14 Bob Majka .40 1.00
15 Joe McCaffrey .40 1.00
16 Kyle McNeilance .40 1.00
17 Brian Meehan .40 1.00
18 Kevin Meehan .40 1.00
19 Mark Meister .40 1.00
20 Eugene Mesh .40 1.00
21 Jason Morgan .40 1.00
22 Kyle Neary .40 1.00
23 Jason Royce .40 1.00
24 Mike Tesi .40 1.00
25 Tom Thompson .40 1.00
26 Team Leaders .40 1.00
27 Checklist .02 .10

1999-00 Arizona Icecats

COMPLETE SET (28) 8.00 20.00
1 Tyler Brush .40 1.00
2 Ed Carfora .40 1.00
3 Hunter Cherenack .40 1.00
4 Paul Dorn .40 1.00
5 Andrew Edwards .40 1.00
6 Dave Galardini .40 1.00
7 Leo Golembiewski CO .02 .10
8 Jeremy Goltz ACO .02 .10
9 Mike Graves .40 1.00
10 Marc Harris .40 1.00
11 Chase Hoyt .40 1.00
12 Pavel Jandura .40 1.00
13 Dave Loftus .40 1.00
14 Bob Majka .40 1.00
15 Joe McCaffrey .40 1.00
16 Kyle McNeilance .40 1.00
17 Brian Meehan .40 1.00
18 Kevin Meehan .40 1.00
19 Mark Meister .40 1.00
20 Jason Morgan .40 1.00
21 Kyle Neary .40 1.00
22 Ryan Roth .40 1.00
23 Jason Royce .40 1.00
24 Sgt. Slaughter HON CPT .75 2.00
25 Tom Thompson .40 1.00
26 Team Leaders .40 1.00
27 L. Golembiewski Golf Classic .02 .10
28 Checklist .02 .10

2000-01 Arizona Icecats

COMPLETE SET (30) 8.00 20.00
1 Header
Checklist .02 .10
2 Joe Boysen .40 1.00
3 Tyler Brush .40 1.00
4 Ed Carfora .40 1.00
5 Paul Dorn .40 1.00
6 Andrew Edwards .40 1.00
7 Andrew Fredericks .40 1.00
8 Dave Galardini .40 1.00
9 Mike Graves .40 1.00
10 Marc Harris .40 1.00
11 Pavel Jandura .40 1.00
12 Braden Koprivica .40 1.00
13 Wes Krisay .40 1.00
14 Dave Loftus .40 1.00
15 Kyle McNeilance .40 1.00
16 Kevin Meehan .40 1.00
17 Jason Morgan .40 1.00
18 Kyle Neary .40 1.00
19 Bill Pardue .40 1.00
20 Jason Royce .40 1.00
21 John Saunders .40 1.00
22 Stefan Thomasson .40 1.00
23 Bill Veasey .40 1.00
24 Tom Wood .40 1.00
25 Leo Golembiewski CO .02 .10
26 Brian Meehan ACO .02 .10
27 Bob Leoni ACO .02 .10
28 Team Leaders .20 .50
29 Golf Classic .02 .10
30 Joe Cristiani HON CAPT .02 .10

2001-02 Arizona Icecats

COMPLETE SET (26) 8.00 20.00
1 Bryan Aronchick .40 1.00
2 Shaun Brooks .40 1.00
3 Papa Joe Chevalier HON CPT .20 .50
4 Andrew Fredericks .40 1.00
5 Dave Galardini .40 1.00
6 Leo Golembiewski CO .04 .10
7 Pavel Jandura .40 1.00
8 Matt Johnson .40 1.00
9 Braden Koprivica .40 1.00
10 Wes Krisay .40 1.00
11 Dave Loftus .40 1.00
12 Brian Meehan ACO .04 .10
13 Kevin Meehan .40 1.00
15 Mickey Meehan .40 1.00
16 Matt Naylor .40 1.00
17 Kyle Neary .40 1.00
18 Bill Pardue .40 1.00
19 John Saunders .40 1.00
20 Mike Smith .40 1.00
21 Tom Wolf .40 1.00
22 Tom Wood .40 1.00
23 Nick Woods .40 1.00
24 Jerald Zivic .40 1.00
25 Team Leaders .20 .50
26 Checklist .04 .10

2002-03 Arizona Icecats

COMPLETE SET (32) 10.00 25.00
1 Bryan Aronchick .40 1.00
2 Matt Baumann .40 1.00
3 Shaun Brooks .40 1.00
4 Banks Concepcion .40 1.00
5 Cole Dunlop .40 1.00
6 Andrew Fredericks .40 1.00
7 Justin Guerra .40 1.00
8 Don Holtz .40 1.00
9 Matt Johnson .40 1.00
10 Rick Karasch .40 1.00
11 Braden Koprivica .40 1.00
12 Wes Krisay .40 1.00
13 Dave Loftus .40 1.00
14 Mickey Meehan .40 1.00
15 Keith Mitchell .40 1.00
16 Matt Muller .40 1.00
17 Matt Naylor .40 1.00
18 Eric Ormson .40 1.00
19 Bill Pardue .40 1.00
20 Mike Pelletier .40 1.00
21 Brian Pollock .40 1.00
22 Mike Smith .40 1.00
23 Dan Whitlock .40 1.00
24 Drew Williamson .40 1.00
25 Tim Wochok .40 1.00
26 Nick Woods .40 1.00
27 Leo Golembiewski CO .04 .10
28 Brian Meehan ACO .04 .10
29 Team Leaders .20 .50
30 Dwain Pipe MASCOT .04 .10
31 Don Rickles HON CPT .40 1.00
32 Checklist .04 .10

2003-04 Arizona Icecats

COMPLETE SET (31) 8.00 20.00
1 Bryan Aronchick .40 1.00
2 Shaun Brooks .40 1.00
3 Anthony Capone .40 1.00
4 Banks Concepion .40 1.00
5 Kevin Conners .40 1.00
6 Dave Cwik .40 1.00
7 Cole Dunlop .40 1.00
8 Andrew Fredericks .40 1.00
9 Don Holtz .40 1.00
10 Rick Karasch .40 1.00
11 Jerod Keene .40 1.00
12 Eric Kowalek .40 1.00
13 Casey Leyva .40 1.00
14 Bryan Meagher .40 1.00
15 Mickey Meehan .40 1.00
16 Jeff Merritt .40 1.00
17 Keith Mitchell .40 1.00
18 Josh Parry .40 1.00
19 D.J Pelletier .40 1.00
20 Brian Pollock .40 1.00
21 Mike Smith .40 1.00
22 Dan Whitlock .40 1.00
23 Drew Williamson .40 1.00
24 Tim Wochok .40 1.00
25 Leo Golembiewski CO .04 .10
26 Brian Meehan ACO .04 .10
27 Team Leaders .20 .50
28 Dwain Pipe MASCOT .04 .10
29 Don Rickles .40 1.00
30 John McCain HON CPT .40 1.00
31 Header Card .04 .10

2004-05 Arizona Icecats

COMPLETE SET (34) 6.00 15.00
1 Bryan Aronchick .30 .75
2 Anthony Capone .30 .75
3 Cole Dunlop .30 .75
4 Luke Edwall .30 .75
5 Leo Golembiewski CO .04 .10
6 Don Holtz .30 .75
7 Craig Irwin .30 .75
8 Eric Kowalek .30 .75
9 Dave Lawrence .30 .75
10 Casey Leyva .30 .75
11 Scott Marshall .30 .75
12 Brian Meehan ACO .04 .10
13 Mickey Meehan .30 .75
14 Keith Mitchell .30 .75
15 Josh Parry .30 .75
16 D.J. Pelletier .30 .75
17 Mike Pelletier .30 .75
18 Mark Perzi .30 .75
19 Jay Punsky .30 .75
20 Max Sliwinski .30 .75
21 Mike Smith .30 .75
22 Doug Wilson .30 .75
23 Tim Wochok .30 .75
24 Jerald Zivic .30 .75
25 Team Leaders .20 .50
26 Equipment Managers .04 .10
27 Sgt. Slaughter .40 1.00
28 L. Gombiewski Celebrity Golf .04 .10
29 Dwain Pipe MASCOT .04 .10
30 Sons of the Pioneers .04 .10
31 Team Picture .04 .10
32 Sen. John McCain .40 1.00
33 Willie Nelson HON CPT .40 1.00
34 Header Card .04 .10

2002-03 Arkansas Riverblades

COMPLETE SET (24) 10.00 25.00
1 Jason Bermingham .40 1.00
2 Mike Cirillo .40 1.00
3 Ryan Coole .40 1.00
4 Aaron Davis .40 1.00
5 Scott Fankhouser .75 2.00
6 Ernie Hartlieb .40 1.00
7 Maxim Linnik .40 1.00
8 Eric Long .40 1.00
9 Terry Marchant .40 1.00
10 Matt Pagnutti .40 1.00
11 Samuel Paquet .40 1.00
12 Mike Renzi .40 1.00
13 Jason Saal .75 2.00
14 Mike Sandbeck .40 1.00
15 Mark Scott .40 1.00
16 Bud Smith .40 1.00
17 Jimi St. John .40 1.00
18 Dean Stock .40 1.00
19 Dean Stork .40 1.00
20 Garry Toor .40 1.00
21 Damon Whitton .40 1.00
22 Chris Cichocki HCO .10 .25
23 RiverBabes .40 1.00
24 Rocky Bear-Boa Mascot .04 .10

1999-00 Asheville Smoke

COMPLETE SET (27) 30.00 75.00
1 Checklist .08 .25
2 Francois Bourdeau 1.25 3.00
3 Dan Brenzavich 1.25 3.00
4 Peter Cermak 1.25 3.00
5 Frank DeFrenza 1.25 3.00
6 Paul Giblin 1.25 3.00
7 Brent Gretzky 2.00 5.00
8 Francois Leroux 1.25 3.00
9 Dan McIntyre 1.25 3.00
10 Rob Milliken 1.25 3.00
11 Hayden O'Rear 1.25 3.00
12 Vaclav Pazourek 1.25 3.00
13 Cory Peterson 1.25 3.00
14 Jon Pirrong 2.00 5.00
15 Ken Plaquin 1.25 3.00
16 Ryan Prentice 1.25 3.00
17 Josh Tymchak 1.25 3.00
18 Shawn Ulrich 1.25 3.00
19 Lindsay Vallis 1.25 3.00
20 Richie Walcott 1.25 3.00
21 Bruce Watson 1.25 3.00
22 Cory Peterson
Josh Tymchak
Bruce Watson 1.25 3.00
23 Keith Gretzky HCO 1.25 3.00
24 Aaron Fackler EM .08 .25
25 Smoky Mascot .08 .25
26 Sponsor Card .01
27 Team Photo .40 1.00

2000-01 Asheville Smoke

COMPLETE SET (27) 6.00 15.00
1 Ryan Aikia .30 .75
2 Brent Belecki .30 .75
3 Blue Bennefield .30 .75
4 Derek Crimin .30 .75
5 Alexandre Fomitchev .40 1.00
6 John Hewitt .30 .75
7 Olaf Kjenstad .40 1.00
8 Dominic Maltais .40 1.00
9 Tyler Prosofsky .30 .75
10 Bobby Rapoza .30 .75
11 Bogdan Rudenko .30 .75
12 J.C. Ruid .30 .75
13 Lee Svangstu .30 .75
14 Shawn Ulrich .30 .75
15 Pat Bingham CO .20 .50
16 Smoky MASCOT .04 .10
17 Ingles Zamboni SPONSOR .04 .10
18 Manager TR .04 .10
19 Tom Wilson .30 .75
20 Brett Colborne .30 .75
21 Robert Marshall .30 .75
22 Alex Dumas .30 .75
23 Vitali Andreev .30 .75
24 Evan Lindsay .40 1.00
25 Bruce Watson .40 1.00
26 Asheville Smoke .04 .10
27 He Shoots Team Card .10 .25

2001-02 Asheville Smoke

COMPLETE SET (24) 8.00 20.00
1 Team Photo .20 .50
2 Kris Mallette .60 1.50
3 Tyler McMillan .40 1.00
4 Mike Payne .40 1.00
5 Chad Wagner .60 1.50
6 Forrest Gore .40 1.00
7 Tom Wilson .40 1.00
8 Todd Bisson .40 1.00
9 Geoff Derouin .60 1.50
10 Bobby Rapoza .40 1.00
11 Kamil Kuriplach .40 1.00
12 Todd MacIsaac .40 1.00
13 Sean Fitzgerald .40 1.00
14 Samuel Paquet .40 1.00
15 Kris Schultz .40 1.00
16 Bob Dalessio EQMG .04 .10
17 Smoky MASCOT .04 .10
18 Curtis Menzul .40 1.00
19 Cory Peterson .40 1.00
20 Jean-Francois Dufour .40 1.00
21 Jeff Petruic .40 1.00
22 J.C. Ruid .40 1.00
23 Blaine Russell .60 1.50
24 Shawn Ulrich CO .04 .10

1992-93 Atlanta Knights

COMPLETE SET (24) 4.80 12.00
1 Header Card .02 .10
2 Manon Rheaume 2.00 5.00
3 Jeff Buchanan .08 .25
4 Matt Hervey .08 .25
5 Rick Lanz .08 .25
6 Colin Miller .08 .25
7 Keith Osborne .08 .25
8 Jason Lafreniere .08 .25
9 Jock Callander .40 1.00
10 Brent Gretzky .20 .50
11 Steve Maltais .40 1.00
12 Serguei Ossipov .08 .25
13 Shayne Stevenson .20 .50
14 Scott Boston .08 .25
15 Jean Blouin .08 .25
16 Shawn Rivers .20 .50
17 Dan Vincelette .08 .25
18 Chris Lipuma .08 .25
19 Don Burke .08 .25
20 Christian Campeau .08 .25
21 Tim Bergland .08 .25
22 J.C. Bergeron .20 .50
23 David Littman .20 .50
24 Gene Ubriaco HCO .02 .10

1993-94 Atlanta Knights

COMPLETE SET (24) 6.00 15.00
1 Mike Greenlay .20 .50
2 Jeff Buchanan .15 .40
3 Eric Charron .15 .40
4 Colin Miller .15 .40
5 Brent Gretzky .30 .75
6 Steve LaRouche .15 .40
7 Marc Tardif .20 .50
8 Jeff Madill .15 .40
9 Devin Edgerton .15 .40
10 Bill McDougall .15 .40
11 Jason Ruff .15 .40
12 Eric Dubois .15 .40
13 Martin Tanguay .15 .40
14 Stan Drulia .30 .75
15 Normand Rochefort .15 .40
16 Shawn Rivers .20 .50
17 Chris Lipuma .15 .40
18 Cory Cross .15 .40
19 Christian Campeau .15 .40
20 Tim Bergland .15 .40
21 J.C. Bergeron .20 .50
22 Manon Rheaume 2.50 6.00
23 Gene Ubriaco HCO .02 .10
CL Header Card .02 .10

1994-95 Atlanta Knights

COMPLETE SET (27) 4.00 10.00
1 Header Card .02 .10
2 Mike Greenlay .30 .75
3 Chris Nelson .15 .40
4 Derek Mayer .15 .40
5 Drew Bannister .15 .40
6 Allen Pedersen .15 .40
7 Colin Miller .15 .40
8 Brent Gretzky .30 .75
9 Peter Ferraro .15 .40
10 Devin Edgerton .15 .40
11 Chris Ferraro .30 .75
12 Jason Ruff .15 .40
13 Eric Dubois .15 .40
14 Stan Drulia .30 .75
15 Allen Egeland .15 .40
16 Aaron Gavey .15 .40
17 Yves Heroux .15 .40
18 Brian Straub .15 .40
19 Jeff Toms .15 .40
20 Chris Lipuma .15 .40
21 Cory Cross .15 .40
22 Christian Campeau .15 .40
23 Derek Wilkinson .30 .75
24 Brantt Myhres .30 .75
25 John Paris Jr. HCO .02 .10
26 Scott Gordon ACO .02 .10
27 Sir Hat Trick Mascot .02 .10

1995-96 Atlanta Knights

COMPLETE SET (25) 5.00 12.00
1 Drew Bannister .20 .50
2 Doug Barrault .20 .50
3 Corey Beaulieu .20 .50
4 Ryan Brown .20 .50
5 Christian Campeau .20 .50
6 Stan Drulia .30 .75

7 Eric Dubois .20 .50
8 Allan Egeland .20 .50
9 Brantt Myhres .30 .75
10 Mark Greig .20 .50
11 Bob Halkidis .20 .50
12 Alexandre LaPorte .20 .50
13 Chris LiPuma .20 .50
14 Tyler Moss .30 .75
15 Brent Peterson .20 .50
16 Adrien Plavsic .20 .50
17 Jason Ruff .20 .50
18 Reggie Savage .20 .50
19 Corey Spring .20 .50
20 Jeff Toms .20 .50
21 Derek Wilkinson .30 .75
22 John Paris CO .08 .25
23 Scott Gordon CO .08 .25
24 Kurt Harvey TR .02 .10
25 Sir Hat Trick MAS .02 .10

2001-02 Atlantic City Boardwalk Bullies

COMPLETE SET (26) 10.00 20.00
1 Checklist .04 .10
2 Shane Belter .40 1.00
3 John Campbell .40 1.00
4 J.F. Caudron .40 1.00
5 Vratislav Cech .40 1.00
6 Kevin Colley .40 1.00
7 Sasha Cucuz .40 1.00
8 Luke Curtin .40 1.00
9 Shawn Degagne .60 1.50
10 Keith Dupee .40 1.00
11 Kirk Furey .40 1.00
12 Tyler Johnston .40 1.00
13 Jerry Keefe .40 1.00
14 Daniel Lacroix .40 1.00
15 Mark Loeding .40 1.00
16 Scott Matzka .40 1.00
17 Jamie O'Leary .40 1.00
18 Stefan Rivard .60 1.50
19 Rob Stanfield .40 1.00
20 Scott Stirling .60 1.50
21 Ian Walterson .40 1.00
22 Mike Haviland HCO .04 .10
23 Leigh Mendelson ACO .04 .10
24 Rick Bronwell EQM .04 .10
25 Woolly MASCOT .04 .10
26 Damien Hess TR .04 .10

2002-03 Atlantic City Boardwalk Bullies

COMPLETE SET (25) 10.00 20.00
1 Rick Bronwell EQM .04 .10
2 J. F. Caudron .40 1.00
3 Steve Cheredaryk .40 1.00
4 Kevin Colley .60 1.50
5 Luke Curtin .40 1.00
6 Kirk Furey .40 1.00
7 Jade Galbraith .75 2.00
8 Jerry Galway .40 1.00
9 Mike Haviland HCO .04 .10
10 Jimmy Henkel .40 1.00
11 Damien Hess TR .04 .10
12 Mark Loeding .40 1.00
13 Shawn Maltby .60 1.50
14 Scott Matzka .40 1.00
15 Leigh Mendelson ACO .04 .10
16 Ryan Mougenel .40 1.00
17 Steve Munn .40 1.00
18 Mike Nicholishen .40 1.00
19 Stefan Rivard .40 1.00
20 Paul Spadafora .40 1.00
21 Scott Stirling .60 1.50
22 Ian Walterson .40 1.00
23 Matthew Yeats .60 1.50
24 Wooly MASCOT .04 .10
25 Checklist .04 .10

2003-04 Atlantic City Boardwalk Bullies

COMPLETE SET (30) 10.00 25.00
1 Bujar Amidovski .75 2.00
2 Jon Cullen .40 1.00
3 Luke Curtin .40 1.00
4 Chad Dameworth .40 1.00
5 Danny Eberly .40 1.00
6 Brian Fahey .40 1.00
7 Aaron Foster .40 1.00
8 Kirk Furey .40 1.00
9 Jim Henkel .40 1.00
10 Scott Horvath .40 1.00
11 Matt Hubbauer .40 1.00
12 Jim Leger .40 1.00
13 John Longo .40 1.00
14 Preston Mizzi .40 1.00
15 Jake Moreland .40 1.00
16 Steve Munn .40 1.00
17 Sam Paolini .40 1.00
18 Joshua Prudden .40 1.00
19 Dave Reid .40 1.00
20 Stefan Rivard .40 1.00
21 John Sabo .40 1.00
22 Pierre-Luc Sleigher .40 1.00
23 Marc St. Jean .40 1.00
24 Scott Stirling .40 1.00
25 Ian Walterson .40 1.00
26 Kam White .40 1.00
27 Mike Haviland HCO .04 .10
28 Matt Thomas ACO .04 .10
29 Mascot .04 .10
30 Checklist .04 .10

2003-04 Atlantic City Boardwalk Bullies RBI Sports

COMPLETE SET (16) 3.00 8.00
17 Jon Cullen .20 .50
18 Luke Curtin .20 .50
19 Danny Eberly .20 .50
20 Brian Fahey .20 .50
21 Aaron Foster .20 .50
22 Scott Horvath .20 .50
23 Jake Moreland .20 .50
24 Steve Munn .20 .50
25 Sam Paolini .20 .50
26 Joshua Prudden .20 .50
27 Dave Reid .20 .50
28 Stefan Rivard .20 .50
29 Pierre-Luc Sleigher .20 .50
30 Scott Stirling .20 .50
31 Ian Walterson .20 .50
32 Kam White .20 .50

2004-05 Atlantic City Boardwalk Bullies

COMPLETE SET (30) 10.00 25.00
1 Dave Reid .40 1.00
2 Ian Walterson .40 1.00
3 Fraser Clair .40 1.00
4 Brad Both .40 1.00
5 Colin Shields .40 1.00
6 Scott Horvath .40 1.00
7 Kelsey Muench .40 1.00
8 Derek Edwardson .40 1.00
9 Jason Notermann .40 1.00
10 Dustan Heintz .40 1.00
11 Tom Reimann .40 1.00
12 Paul Caponigri .40 1.00
13 Luke Curtin .40 1.00
14 Eric Nelson .40 1.00
15 Trevor Koenig .60 1.50
16 Brian Maddox TR .04 .10
17 Matt Thomas CO .04 .10
18 Mark French ACO .04 .10
19 Chris Burke EQM .04 .10
20 Brian Fahey .40 1.00
21 Vincent Macri .40 1.00
22 Jake Moreland .60 1.50
23 Dan Peters .40 1.00
24 Brett Peterson .40 1.00
25 Peter Bournazakis .40 1.00
26 Shawn Mather .40 1.00
27 Brett Nowak .40 1.00
28 Jean-Francois Plourde .40 1.00
29 Ryan Reid .40 1.00
30 Woolly MASCOT .04 .10

2004-05 Atlantic City Boardwalk Bullies Kinko's

COMPLETE SET (30) 10.00 25.00
1 Kelly Cup CL .02 .10
2 Jake Moreland .40 1.00
3 Bujar Amidovski .75 2.00
4 Steve Munn .40 1.00
5 Brian Fahey .40 1.00
6 Kam Whie .40 1.00
7 Dave Reid .40 1.00
8 Ian Walterson .40 1.00
9 Pierre-Luc Sleigher .40 1.00
10 Danny Eberly .40 1.00
11 Jim Henkel .40 1.00
12 Scott Horvath .40 1.00
13 Sam Paolini .40 1.00
14 John Sabo .40 1.00
15 Josh Prudden .40 1.00
16 John Longo .40 1.00
17 Matt Hubbaer .40 1.00
18 Marc St.Jean .40 1.00
19 Stefan Rivard .40 1.00
20 Chad Dameworth .40 1.00
21 Preston Mizzi .40 1.00
22 Jim Leger .40 1.00
23 Kirk Furey .40 1.00
24 Aaron Foster .40 1.00
25 Luke Curtin .40 1.00
26 Jon Cullan .40 1.00
27 Scott Stirling .40 1.00
28 Mike Haviland .40 1.00
29 Matt Thomas .40 1.00
30 Wooly .02 .10

2001-02 Augusta Lynx

COMPLETE SET (8) 6.00 15.00
1 Patrick Yetman .75 2.00
2 Scott Morrow .75 2.00
3 Cris Classen .75 2.00
4 Tyler Willis 1.25 3.00
5 Jeff Bes 1.25 3.00
6 Wes Swinson .75 2.00
7 Guy Larose .75 2.00
8 John Whitwell .75 2.00

2002-03 Augusta Lynx

COMPLETE SET (18) 10.00 20.00
61 Ryan Crane .40 1.00
62 Curtis Cruickshank .60 1.50
63 Tom Draper .60 1.50
64 Chris Gustafson .40 1.00
65 Tyson Holly .40 1.00
66 Andrew Ianiero .40 1.00
67 Martin Lapointe .40 1.00
68 Ryan Lauzon .40 1.00
69 Jay Leach .40 1.00
70 Mike Legg .40 1.00
71 Vince Malts .40 1.00
72 Brad Ralph .40 1.00
73 Philippe Roy .40 1.00
74 Josh St. Louis .40 1.00
75 Jim Shepherd .40 1.00
76 Chris Thompson .40 1.00
77 Mark Thompson .40 1.00
78 Andrew Williamson .40 1.00

2003-04 Augusta Lynx

COMPLETE SET (16) 10.00 25.00
33 Todd Bennett .60 1.50
34 Scott Corbett .60 1.50
35 John Cronin .60 1.50
36 Brandon Doria .60 1.50
37 Matt Dzieduszycki .60 1.50
38 Paul Elliott .60 1.50
39 Jonathan Gagnon .60 1.50
40 Louis Goulet .60 1.50
41 Nick Greenough .60 1.50
42 Peter Hamerlik .75 2.00
43 Greg Jacina .60 1.50
44 Scott Kelman .60 1.50
45 Robert Liscak .60 1.50
46 Gregg Naumenko .75 2.00
47 Treavor Peterson .60 1.50
48 Shawn Weiman .60 1.50

2006-07 Augusta Lynx

COMPLETE SET (21) 15.00 30.00
1 Garrett Bembridge .75 2.00
2 Sean Blanchard .60 1.50
3 Mike Erickson .60 1.50
4 Louis Goulet .60 1.50
5 Shane Hynes .60 1.50
6 Jamie Johnson .60 1.50
7 Jason Kostadine .60 1.50
8 Nick Kuiper .60 1.50
9 Ryan Lang .60 1.50
10 Eric Lundberg .60 1.50
11 Roman Marakhovski .60 1.50
12 Nathan Marsters 1.25 3.00
13 David McKee 1.25 3.00
14 Brian Passmore .75 2.00
15 Joe Pereira .60 1.50
16 Jason Platt .60 1.50
17 Nathan Saunders .60 1.50
18 Ken Scuderi .60 1.50
19 Aaron Slattengren .60 1.50
20 Dirk Southern .60 1.50
21 Weston Tardy .60 1.50

2010-11 Augusta Riverhawks

COMPLETE SET (20) 4.00 10.00
1 Matt Auffrey .60 1.50
2 Adam Avramenko .30 .75
3 Drew Baker .30 .75
4 Nick Bydal .30 .75
5 Derek Fisher .30 .75
6 Kevin Fukala .30 .75
7 Jim Gehring .30 .75
8 Neil Graham .30 .75
9 Brandon Kosolofsky .30 .75
10 Lucas LaBelle .30 .75
11 Luke Lucyk .30 .75
12 Gus .30 .75
13 Aaron McGill .30 .75
14 Jordan McLaughlin .30 .75
15 Curtis Megginson .30 .75
16 Egor Mironov .30 .75
17 Ryan Olidis .30 .75
18 Jon Olthuis .30 .75
19 Jason Price .30 .75
20 Brad Ralph .30 .75

1997-98 Austin Ice Bats

COMPLETE SET (24) 5.00 10.00
1 Ryan Anderson .20 .50
2 Chad Erickson .30 .75
3 Tim Findlay .30 .75
4 Todd Harris .20 .50
5 Rob Hartnell .20 .50
6 Chris Haskett .20 .50
7 Kyle Haviland .20 .50
8 Mike Jackson .20 .50
9 Jeff Kungle .20 .50
10 Darrin MacKay .20 .50
11 Dean Mando .20 .50
12 Keith Moran .20 .50
13 Ryan Pawluk .20 .50
14 Derek Riley .20 .50
15 Jason Rose .20 .50
16 Andy Ross .20 .50
17 Brett Seguin .20 .50
18 Christian Soucy .30 .75
19 Jeremy Thompson .20 .50
20 Richard Uniacke .20 .50
21 Joe Van Volsen .20 .50
22 Paul Lawless CO .08 .25
23 Fang Mascot .02 .10
24 Ice Bats Hummer PROMO .02 .10

1999-00 Austin Ice Bats

COMPLETE SET (34) 12.00 30.00
1 Andy Ross .40 1.00
2 Shawn Legault .40 1.00
3 Craig Stahl .40 1.00
4 Ryan Pisiak .40 1.00
5 David Moore .40 1.00
6 David Brosseau .40 1.00
7 Jeff Greenlaw .40 1.00
8 Jeff Kungle .40 1.00
9 Bryan McMullen .40 1.00
10 Dan Price .40 1.00
11 Brent Hughes CO .08 .25
12 Glen Norman .40 1.00
13 Clint Shuman TR .08 .25
14 The IceBatmobile .08 .25
15 Rob Laurie .60 1.50
16 Brent Currie .40 1.00
17 Stu Kulak .40 1.00
18 Kelly Smart .40 1.00
19 Jim Shepherd .40 1.00
20 Ryan Anderson .40 1.00
21 Laird Lidster .40 1.00
22 Matt Sharuga .40 1.00
23 Derek Nicolson .40 1.00
24 Ryan Brindley .40 1.00
25 Tyler Perry .40 1.00
26 Fang MAS .08 .25
27 Ken McRae CO .08 .25
28 Gunner Garrett TR .08 .25
29 Ryan Pisiak 1.25 3.00
30 Ryan Anderson 1.25 3.00
31 Shawn Legault .40 1.00
32 Ryan Anderson .40 1.00
33 David Moore .40 1.00
34 Andy Ross .40 1.00

2000-01 Austin Ice Bats

COMPLETE SET (30) 8.00 30.00
1 Ryan Anderson .30 1.00
2 David Brosseau .30 1.00
3 Bobby Brown .30 1.00
4 Jonathan Forest .30 1.00
5 Mike Gaffney .40 1.50
6 Jeff Greenlaw .30 1.00
7 Daniel Kletke .30 1.00
8 Jeff Kungle .40 1.50
9 Eric Landry .30 1.00
10 Roger Lewis .30 1.00
11 Josh Maser .30 1.00
12 Bryan McMullen .30 1.00
13 Derek Nicolson .30 1.00
14 Erik Noack .30 1.00
15 Keith O'Brien .30 1.00
16 Tyler Perry .30 1.00
17 Philippe Plante .30 1.00
18 Dan Price .30 1.00
19 Brett Seguin .40 1.50
20 Kelly Smart .30 1.00
21 Troy Stonier .30 1.00
22 Daniel Tetrault .30 1.00
23 Brent Hughes CO .20 .50
24 Ken McRae CO .20 .50
25 Clint Shuman TR .10 .10
26 CC Comedy Club .01 .02
27 Hooters Hot Shot .20 .50
28 Fang MASCOT .04 .10
29 Redemption .04 .10
29R Spike & Fang MASCOTS .15 3.00
30 Redemption .04 .10
30R Ice Bats All Stars .15 3.00

2001-02 Austin Ice Bats

COMPLETE SET (25) 8.00 20.00
1 Ryan Anderson .40 1.00
2 Bobby Brown .40 1.00
3 Patrick Brownlee .40 1.00
4 Jeff Greenlaw .40 1.00
5 Ian LaRocque .40 1.00
6 Eric Labelle .40 1.00
7 Tab Lardner .40 1.00
8 Darryl McArthur .60 1.50
9 Dan McIntyre .40 1.00
10 Bryan McMullen .40 1.00
11 Dominic Periard .40 1.00
12 Ryan Pisiak .60 1.50
13 Dan Price .40 1.00
14 Brett Seguin .40 1.00
15 Kelly Smart .40 1.00
16 Gerald Tallaire .60 1.50
17 Daniel Tetrault .60 1.50
18 Greg Willers .40 1.00
19 Jeff Worlton .40 1.00
20 Brent Hughes CO .10 .25
21 Ken McRae ACO .10 .25
22 Fang MASCOT .04 .10
23 Glen Norman DB .04 .10
24 Gunner Garrett EQMG .04 .10
24 Clint Shuman TR .04 .10
25 Hootie Celebrates .04 .10

2002-03 Austin Ice Bats

COMPLETE SET (24) 10.00 20.00
1 Matt Barnes .60 1.50
2 Peter Brady .60 1.50
3 Patrick Brownlee .40 1.00
4 Mike Gaffney .40 1.00
5 Jeff Greenlaw .40 1.00
6 Doug Johnson .40 1.00
7 Tab Lardner .40 1.00
8 Shawn Legault .60 1.50
9 Darryl McArthur .40 1.00
10 Scott McCallum .40 1.00
11 Mike Olynyk .40 1.00
12 Randy Ponte .40 1.00
13 Dan Price .40 1.00
14 Mike Rees .40 1.00
15 Brett Seguin .40 1.00
16 Matt Sharuga .40 1.00
17 Kelly Smart .40 1.00
18 Gerald Tallaire .40 1.00
19 Brent Hughes HCO .10 .25
20 Jeff Kungle ACO .10 .25
21 Gunner Garrett EQM .04 .10
22 Fang Mascot .04 .10
23 Fang's Gang .04 .10
24 Clint Shuman TR .04 .10

2003-04 Austin Ice Bats

COMPLETE SET (24) 15.00 30.00
1 Peter Brady .60 1.50
2 Patrick Brownlee .60 1.50
3 Brandon Carper .60 1.50
4 Shawn Conschafter .60 1.50
5 Jonathan Forest .60 1.50
6 Brent Hughes .60 1.50
7 Tab Lardner .60 1.50
8 Shawn Legault .75 2.00
9 Chris Legg .60 1.50
10 Darryl McArthur .75 2.00
11 Scott McCallum .60 1.50
12 Mike Olynyk .60 1.50
13 Brett Seguin .60 1.50
14 Kelly Smart .60 1.50
15 Josh St. Louis .60 1.50
16 Derek Stone .60 1.50
17 Gerald Tallaire .60 1.50
18 Daniel Tetrault .60 1.50
19 Clint Way .60 1.50
20 Jeff Greenlaw HCO .10 .25
21 Gunner Garrett EQM .04 .10
22 Cheerleaders .10 .25
23 Mascot .04 .10
24 Clint Shuman TR .04 .10

2004-05 Austin Ice Bats

COMPLETE SET (23) 15.00 30.00
1 Peter-Emmanuel Brady .75 2.00
2 Brian Pasko .60 1.50
3 Kelly Smart .60 1.50
4 Ryan Leasa .60 1.50
5 Kris Knoblauch .60 1.50
6 Chris Richards .60 1.50
7 Dallas Anderson 1.25 3.00
8 John McNabb .75 2.00
9 Mike Olynyk .75 2.00
10 Sponsor Card .04 .10
11 Clint Shuman TR .04 .10
12 Fang MASCOT .04 .10
13 Matt Barnes .75 2.00
14 Benoit Genesse .60 1.50
15 Jonathan Jolette .60 1.50
16 Jeff Neufeld .60 1.50
17 Jared Dumba .60 1.50
18 Mike Mohr .60 1.50
19 Arturs Kupaks .60 1.50
20 Vinnie Jonasson .60 1.50
21 Greg Gatto CO .04 .10
22 Gunner Garrett EQM .04 .10
23 Bat Girls .20 .50

2006-07 Austin Ice Bats

1 Miguel Beaudry .60 1.50
2 Adam Holmgren .60 1.50
3 Chad McIver .60 1.50
4 Chris Murphy .60 1.50
5 Chris Ovington .60 1.50
6 Tony Quesada .60 1.50
7 John Ronan .60 1.50
8 Ray Smegal .60 1.50
9 Julian Smith .60 1.50
10 Mike Tucciarone .60 1.50
11 Terry Virtue .60 1.50
12 Logo Card .10 .25
13 Jordan Biachin .75 2.00
14 Kevin Couture .60 1.50
15 Aaron Davis .60 1.50
16 Britt Dougherty .60 1.50
17 Jason Kenyon .60 1.50
18 Henry Kuster .60 1.50
19 John McNabb .60 1.50
20 J.F. Picard .60 1.50
21 Mike Possin .60 1.50
22 Aaron Wilson .60 1.50
23 Fang MASCOT .10 .25
24 Logo Card .10 .25

1999-00 Baie-Comeau Drakkar

COMPLETE SET (28) 4.00 10.00
1 Daniel Bergeron .15 .40
2 Jerome Bergeron .15 .40
3 Eric Bleau .15 .40
4 Marco Charpentier .15 .40
5 Jean-Philippe Chartier .30 .75
6 Serge Crochetiere .15 .40
7 Sylvain Deschatelets .15 .40
8 Kevin Deslauriers .15 .40
9 Maxime Fortunus .15 .40
10 Jonathan Gautier .15 .40
11 Duilio Grande .15 .40
12 Evgeny Gusakov .15 .40
13 Paul Lavoie .15 .40
14 Robin Leblanc .15 .40
15 Yannick Lehoux .30 .75
16 Charles Linglet .15 .40
17 Andre Mercure .15 .40
18 Chris Page .15 .40
19 Dominic Periard .15 .40
20 Jerome Petit .15 .40
21 Ghyslain Rousseau .30 .75
22 Bruno St. Jacques .30 .75
23 Eric Tremblay .15 .40
24 Guy Turmel .15 .40
25 Patrick Daviault CO .02 .10
26 Richard Martel CO .02 .10
27 Michel Larocque TR .02 .10
28 Brian St.Louis TR .02 .10

2000-01 Baie-Comeau Drakkar

COMPLETE SET (26) 4.00 10.00
1 Jonathan Walsh .15 .40
2 Joel Perrault .15 .40
3 Pierre-Andre Leblanc .15 .40
4 Dominic Periard .15 .40
5 Maxime Fortunus .15 .40
6 Pascal Pelletier .15 .40
7 Robin Leblanc .15 .40
8 Luis Tremblay .15 .40
9 Thierry Douville .15 .40
10 Marco Charpentier .15 .40
11 Premysl Duben .15 .40
12 Yanick Lehoux .40 1.00
13 Duilio Grande .15 .40
14 Kevin Deslauriers .15 .40
15 Matthew Hyde .15 .40
16 Guy Turmel .15 .40
17 Evgeny Gusakov .15 .40
18 Ghyslain Rousseau .20 .50
19 David St. Germain .20 .50
20 Jonathan Jolette .15 .40
21 Martin Mandeville .15 .40
22 Daniel Bergeron .15 .40
23 Charles Linglet .15 .40
24 Jonathan Gautier .15 .40
25 Richard Martel CO CL .02 .10
NNO Snorri MASCOT .02 .10

2000-01 Baie-Comeau Drakkar Signed

COMPLETE SET (26) 20.00 50.00
1 Jonathan Walsh .80 2.00
2 Joel Perrault .80 2.00
3 Pierre-Andre Leblanc .80 2.00
4 Dominic Periard .80 2.00
5 Maxime Fortunus .80 2.00
6 Pascal Pelletier .80 2.00
7 Robin Leblanc .80 2.00
8 Luis Tremblay .80 2.00
9 Thierry Douville .80 2.00
10 Marco Charpentier .80 2.00
11 Premysl Duben .80 2.00
12 Yanick Lehoux 2.00 5.00
13 Duilio Grande .80 2.00
14 Kevin Deslauriers .80 2.00
15 Matthew Hyde .80 2.00
16 Guy Turmel .80 2.00
17 Evgeny Gusakov .80 2.00
18 Ghyslain Rousseau 2.00 5.00
19 David St. Germain 2.00 5.00
20 Jonathan Jolette .80 2.00
21 Martin Mandeville .80 2.00
22 Daniel Bergeron .80 2.00
23 Charles Linglet .80 2.00
24 Jonathan Gautier .80 2.00
25 Richard Martel CO CL .04 .10
NNO Snorri MASCOT .04 .10

2001-02 Baie-Comeau Drakkar

COMPLETE SET (25) 5.00 12.00
1 Joel Perrault .20 .50
2 Louis-Philippe Martin .20 .50
3 Jonathan Lachance .20 .50
4 Maxime Fortunus .20 .50
5 Pascal Pelletier .20 .50
6 Robin Leblanc .20 .50
7 Luis Tremblay .20 .50
8 Thierry Douville .20 .50
9 Martin Kuna .20 .50
10 Yanick Lehoux .30 .75
11 Duilio Grande .20 .50
12 Kevin Deslauriers .20 .50
13 Matthew Hyde .20 .50
14 Jean Junior Morin .20 .50
15 Ghyslain Rousseau .30 .75
16 Jonathan Dupras .20 .50
17 Caleb Moffat .20 .50
18 Marc-Andre Roy .20 .50
19 Martin Mandeville .20 .50
20 Daniel Bergeron .30 .75
21 Charles Linglet .20 .50
22 Jean-Francois Savage .20 .50
23 Benoit Mondou .30 .75
24 Jean-Francois Jacques .20 .50
NNO Richard Martel CO/CL .04 .10

2002-03 Baie-Comeau Drakkar

COMPLETE SET (26) 5.00 12.00
1 Maxime Belanger .20 .50
2 Joel Perrault .30 .75
3 Alexandre Lamarche .20 .50
4 Jean-Philippe Gauthier .20 .50
5 Louis-Philippe Martin .20 .50
6 Maxime Fortunus .20 .50
7 Pascal Pelletier .20 .50
8 Robin Leblanc .20 .50
9 Luis Tremblay .20 .50
10 Thierry Douville .20 .50
11 Jimmy Arsenault .20 .50
12 Travis Antler .20 .50
13 Kevin Deslauriers .20 .50
14 Patrick Lepage .30 .75
15 Sebastien Leonard .20 .50
16 Philip Lacroix .30 .75
17 Michel Bergevin-Robinson .30 .75
18 Caleb Moffat .20 .50
19 Marc-Andre Roy .20 .50
20 Patrick Thoresen .40 1.00
21 Martin Mandeville .20 .50
22 Charles Linglet .20 .50
23 Benoit Mondou .30 .75
24 Jean-Francois Jacques .20 .50
25 Richard Martel CO/CL .02 .10
26 Snorri MASCOT .02 .10

2003-04 Baie-Comeau Drakkar

COMPLETE SET (27) 5.00 12.00
1 Ryan-James Hand .20 .50
2 Patrick Simaro .20 .50
3 Ryan Lehr .20 .50
4 Maxime Belanger .20 .50
5 Martin Krayzel .20 .50
6 Alexandre Blais .20 .50
7 Jonathan Duchesneau .20 .50
8 Alexandre Lamarche Froelich .20 .50
9 Maxime Fortunas .20 .50
10 Robin Leblanc .20 .50
11 Luis Tremblay .20 .50
12 Frederic Gariepy .20 .50
13 Vitaly Lanochkin .20 .50
14 Olivier Furlong .20 .50
15 Simon Lepage .20 .50
16 Loic Lacasse .30 .75
17 Patrick Laurin .20 .50
18 Julien Walsh .30 .75
19 Pierre-Luc Leblond-Letourneau .20 .50
20 Martin Mandeville .20 .50
21 Nicolas Robillard .20 .50
22 Petr Preucil .20 .50
23 Philippe Cote .20 .50
24 Jean-Francois Jacques .30 .75
25 Alexandre Dulac Lemelin .20 .50
26 Maxime Fortunas TL .20 .50
27 Jean-Francois Jacques TL .30 .75

2004-05 Baie-Comeau Drakkar

COMPLETE SET (24) 4.00 10.00
1 Alexandre Blais .20 .50
2 Alexandre Dulac-Lemelin .20 .50
3 Alexandre Picard-Hooper .20 .50
4 Benjamin Breault .20 .50
5 Erick Lajoie .20 .50
6 Francois Bouchard .20 .50
7 Jean-Francois Jacques .20 .50
8 Joakim Jensen .20 .50
9 Jonathan Duchesneau .20 .50
10 Loic Lacasse .30 .75
11 Martin Aubin .20 .50
12 Martin Mandeville .20 .50
13 Mathieu Gravel .20 .50
14 Maxime Belanger .20 .50
15 Michael Dupont .30 .75
16 Nicolas Robillard .20 .50
17 Patrick Simard .20 .50
18 Philippe Cote .20 .50
19 Pierre-Luc Leblond-Letourneau .20 .50
20 Ryan Lehr .20 .50
21 Ryan-James Hand .20 .50
22 Sebastien Blouin .20 .50
23 Tomas Fendek .20 .50
24 Vitaly Lanochkin .20 .50

2005-06 Baie-Comeau Drakkar

COMPLETE SET (22) 5.00 10.00
1 Benjamin Breault .20 .50
2 Charles-Antoine Messier .20 .50
3 Patrick Simard .20 .50
4 Ryan Lehr .20 .50
5 Tomas Fendek .20 .50
6 Alexandre Blais .20 .50
7 Jonathan Duchesneau .20 .50
8 Christian Landry .20 .50
9 Francois Chabot .20 .50
10 Alexandre Picard-Hooper .20 .50
11 Francois Bouchard .20 .50
12 Jean-Sebastien Hogg .20 .50
13 Adam Bourque-Leblanc .20 .50
14 Joakim Jensen .20 .50
15 Alexandre Dulac-Lemelin .20 .50
16 Maxime D. Ouimet .20 .50
17 Oliver Donais .20 .50
18 Samuel Beland .20 .50
19 Francois Filion .20 .50
20 Loic Lacasse .20 .50
21 Michael Dupont .20 .50
22 Martin Aubin .20 .50

1998-99 Bakersfield Condors

COMPLETE SET (24) 4.00 10.00
1 Jamie Adams .30 .75
2 Kevin Barrett .30 .75
3 Brady Blain .30 .75
4 Marc Boxer .30 .75
5 Steve Chelios .40 1.00
6 Jamie Cooke .30 .75
7 Steve Dowhy .30 .75
8 Brad Guzda .30 .75
9 Nick Hriczov .30 .75
10 Kelly Hrycun .30 .75
11 Marcel Kuris .30 .75
12 Dan Marcotte .30 .75
13 Brian McCarthy .30 .75
14 Glen Mears .30 .75
15 Al Murphy .30 .75
16 Jay Neal .30 .75
17 Zbynek Neckar .30 .75
18 Dan Reja .30 .75
19 Stephane St. Amour .40 1.00
20 Briane Thompson .30 .75
21 Peter Zurba .30 .75
22 Bakersfield Centennial Arena .02 .10
23 Kevin MacDonald HCO .02 .10
24 Colonel Claw'd Mascot .02 .10

1999-00 Bakersfield Condors

COMPLETE SET (24) 8.00 20.00
1 Cory Banika .40 1.00
2 Philippe Bergeron .40 1.00
3 Kevin Boyd .40 1.00
4 Jamie Cooke .40 1.00
5 Dan Currie .60 1.50
6 Chris Dearden .40 1.00
7 Steve Dowhy .40 1.00
8 Chris Droeske .40 1.00
9 Brad Guzda .40 1.00
10 Paul McInnis .40 1.00
11 Glen Mears .40 1.00
12 Zbynek Neckar .40 1.00
13 Jani Ojala .40 1.00
14 Brad Phillips .40 1.00
15 Clark Polglase .40 1.00
16 Jason Reesor .40 1.00
17 Paul Rosebush .40 1.00
18 Briane Thompson .40 1.00
19 Rhett Trombley .40 1.00
20 Paul Willett .40 1.00
21 Kevin MacDonald CO .08 .25
22 Bakersfield Centennial .08 .25
23 Colonel Claw'd MAS .08 .25
24 Michael Ropchan TR .08 .25

2000-01 Bakersfield Condors

COMPLETE SET (24) 8.00 20.00
1 Trevor Amundrud .30 .75
2 Cory Banika .30 .75
3 Karel Betik .60 1.50
4 Kevin Boyd .30 .75
5 Jamie Cooke .30 .75
6 Dan Currie .60 1.50
7 Jean-Paul Davis .30 .75
8 Chris Dearden .30 .75
9 Quinn Fair .30 .75
10 Ben Gustavson .30 .75
11 Denis Ivanov .30 .75
12 Bryan Lachance .30 .75
13 Peter MacKellar .30 .75
14 Craig Martin .40 1.00
15 Glen Mears .30 .75
16 Pavel Mikulchik .30 .75
17 Matt Mullin .60 1.50
18 Jason Reesor .30 .75
19 Paul Rosebush .30 .75
20 Paul Willett .60 1.50
21 Paul Willett MVP .60 1.50
22 Kevin MacDonald CO .10 .25
23 Centenial Gardens ARENA .10 .25
24 Coloney
Cal MASCOTS .10 .25

2001-02 Bakersfield Condors

COMPLETE SET (24) 10.00 20.00
1 Ken Baker .40 1.00
2 Peter Brearley .40 1.00
3 Luciano Caravaggio .40 1.00
4 Jamie Cooke .40 1.00
5 Mark Edmundson .40 1.00
6 Todd Esselmont .40 1.00
7 Quinn Fair .40 1.00
8 Chris Felix .40 1.00
9 Jason Firth .40 1.00
10 Jeff Goldie .40 1.00
11 Ryan Hartung .40 1.00
12 Scott Hay .60 1.50
13 Sasha Lakovic .60 1.50
14 Josh Maser .40 1.00
15 Glen Mears .40 1.00
16 David Milek .40 1.00
17 Jason Ralph .40 1.00
18 Paul Rosebush .40 1.00
19 John Vary .40 1.00
20 Paul Willett .40 1.00
21 Paul Kelly HCO .04 .10
22 Condors in the Community .04 .10
23 Baby Cal MASCOT .04 .10
24 Colonel Claw MASCOT .04 .10

2002-03 Bakersfield Condors

COMPLETE SET (24) 10.00 20.00
1 Nate Anderson .40 1.00
2 David Bell .40 1.00
3 Shawn Byram .40 1.00
4 Jamie Cooke .40 1.00
5 Danielle Dube .40 1.00
6 Guy Dupuis .40 1.00
7 Quinn Fair .40 1.00
8 Jeff Goldie .40 1.00
9 Jason Jackman .40 1.00
10 Denis Ladouceur .40 1.00
11 Jonas Lennartsson .40 1.00
12 Christoffer Norgren .40 1.00
13 Jason Ralph .40 1.00
14 Jordan Roach .40 1.00
15 Paul Rosebush .40 1.00
16 Christian Skoryna .40 1.00
17 Jonathan Sorg .40 1.00
18 Kevin St. Pierre .60 1.50
19 Paul Willett .40 1.00
20 J.J. Wrobel .40 1.00
21 Paul Kelly HCO .10 .25
22 Martin Raymond ACO .10 .25
23 Colonel Claw'd
Baby Cal .04 .10

2003-04 Bakersfield Condors
COMPLETE SET (25) 10.00 25.00
1 Todd Alexander .40 1.00
2 Johan Astrom .40 1.00
3 Jamie Cooke .40 1.00
4 Paul Kelly CO .10 .25
5 Martin Raymond ACO .10 .25
6 Andrew Ianiero .40 1.00
7 Jason Jackman .40 1.00
8 Peter Hirsch .40 1.00
9 Devin Francon .40 1.00
10 Paul Rosebush .40 1.00
11 Kevin Riehl .40 1.00
12 Mascot .02 .10
13 Vince Malts .40 1.00
14 Quinn Fair .40 1.00
15 Jimmy Drolet .40 1.00
16 Glen Mears .40 1.00
17 Jon Mirasty .40 1.00
18 Darren Shakotko .40 1.00
19 Jani Virtanen .40 1.00
20 Joe Watkins .60 1.50
21 Paul Willett .40 1.00
22 Randy Perry .40 1.00
23 Jason Ralph .40 1.00
24 Denis Ladouceur .40 1.00
25 Jonas Lennartsson .40 1.00

2004-05 Bakersfield Condors
COMPLETE SET (24) 15.00 30.00
1 Ryan Coole .40 1.00
2 Guy Dupuis .40 1.00
3 Yutaka Fukufuji 4.00 10.00
4 Ryan Gillis .40 1.00
5 Ty Hennes .40 1.00
6 Mike Hofstrand .40 1.00
7 Connor James .40 1.00
8 David Kudelka .40 1.00
9 Ashlee Langdone .40 1.00
10 Tony Lawrence .40 1.00
11 Brett Lutes .40 1.00
12 Brad Mehalko .40 1.00
13 Dylan Mills .40 1.00
14 Lars Peder Nagel .40 1.00
15 Paul Rosebush .40 1.00
16 Vlad Serov .40 1.00
17 Dennis Shiryaev .40 1.00
18 Kevin St. Jacques .40 1.00
19 Luis Tremblay .40 1.00
20 ChrisTwerdun .40 1.00
21 Jason Wolfe .60 1.50
22 Marty Raymond CO .04 .10
23 Paul Willet ACO .04 .10
24 Mascots .04 .10

2005-06 Bakersfield Condors
COMPLETE SET (23) 8.00 20.00
1 Marty Raymond .40 1.00
2 Kevin Kotyluk .40 1.00
3 Brian Collins .40 1.00
4 Scott Balan .40 1.00
5 Paul Rosebush .40 1.00
6 Reagan Leslie .40 1.00
7 Scott Basiuk .40 1.00
8 Alexandre Bolduc .40 1.00
9 Nick Economakos .40 1.00
10 Oriel McHugh .40 1.00
11 Dennis Shiryaev .40 1.00
12 Kevin St.Jacques .40 1.00
13 Ryan Munce .40 1.00
14 Mike Hofstrand .40 1.00
15 Dave Bonk .40 1.00
16 Scott Borders .40 1.00
17 Andrew Ianiero .40 1.00
18 Eric Neilson .40 1.00
19 Kevin Truelson .40 1.00
20 Sean Venedam .40 1.00
21 Mark Pederson .40 1.00
22 Joel Irving .40 1.00
23 Mathieu Brunelle .40 1.00

2006-07 Bakersfield Condors
1 Sean Venedam .40 1.00
2 Rane Carnegie .60 1.50
3 Steve Rodberg .40 1.00
4 Brett Lutes .40 1.00
5 Coaches .10 .25
6 Kevin Truelson .40 1.00
7 David Kudelka .40 1.00
8 Andrew Oke .40 1.00
9 Andrew Ianiero .40 1.00
10 Alex Kim .40 1.00
11 Danny Taylor .40 1.00
12 Scott Borders .40 1.00
13 Mike Hofstrand .40 1.00
14 Josh Libenow .40 1.00
15 Alexandre Bolduc .40 1.00
16 Alec Rogosheske .40 1.00
17 Tyler Scott .40 1.00
18 Tyler Liebel .40 1.00
19 Jamie Hodson .75 2.00
20 Kevin St. Jacques .40 1.00
21 Scotty Balan .40 1.00
22 Kevin Asselin .40 1.00
23 Todd Griffith .40 1.00
24 Reagan Leslie .40 1.00

2013-14 Bakersfield Condors
COMPLETE SET () 6.00 15.00
1 Spencer Bennett .30 .75
2 Collin Bowman .30 .75
3 Joel Broda .30 .75
4 Laurent Brossoit .30 .75
5 Tyler Bunz .30 .75
6 Erik Burgdoerfer .30 .75
7 Andrew Carroll .30 .75
8 Chris Collins .30 .75
9 Wes Cunningham .30 .75
10 Travis Gawryletz .30 .75
11 George Hughes .30 .75
12 Jordan Knackstedt .30 .75
13 Joey Leach .30 .75
14 Ryan Little .30 .75
15 Troy Mann CO .30 .75
16 Joe Marciano .30 .75
17 Greg Miller .30 .75
18 Ryan Murphy Asst. CO .30 .75
19 Michael Neal .30 .75
20 Nick Pageau .30 .75
21 Chet Pickard .30 .75
22 Chase Schaber .30 .75
23 Gary Steffes .30 .75
24 Matt Thurber .30 .75
25 Ryan Watson .30 .75
26 Baby Cal MASCOT .30 .75

2014-15 Bakersfield Condors
COMPLETE SET (32) 8.00 20.00
1 Cameron Abney .30 .75
2 Akim Aliu .40 1.00
3 Kevin Barrett CA .30 .75
4 Scott Borders CA .30 .75
5 Jamie Cooke CA .30 .75
6 Graeme Craig .30 .75
7 Josh Currie .30 .75
8 Steve Dowhy CA .30 .75
9 Scott Hay CA .30 .75
10 Mike Hofstrand CA .30 .75
11 Andrew Ianiero CA .30 .75
12 Joel Irving CA .30 .75
13 Connor Jones .30 .75
14 Kellen Jones .30 .75
15 Jordan Kremyr .30 .75
16 Jonathan Lessard .30 .75
17 C.J. Ludwig .30 .75
18 Nick MacNeil .30 .75
19 Joe Marciano .30 .75
20 Brian McCarthy CA .30 .75
21 Glen Mears CA .30 .75
22 Brendon Nash .30 .75
23 Nick Pageau .30 .75
24 Paul Rosebush CA .30 .75
25 Chase Schaber .30 .75
26 Sebastien Sylvestre .30 .75
27 Kevin Truelson CA .30 .75
28 Gabriel Verpaelst .30 .75
29 Joe Watkins CA .30 .75
30 Ryan Watson .30 .75
31 Paul Willett CA .30 .75
32 Josh Winquist .30 .75

1997-98 Bakersfield Fog
COMPLETE SET (24) 5.00 12.00
1 John Devereaux .25 .60
2 Steve Dowhy .25 .60
3 Igor Galkin .40 1.00
4 Jeff Gorman .25 .60
5 Kelly Hrycun .25 .60
6 Jeff Jubenville .25 .60
7 Don Lester .25 .60
8 Brian McCarthy .25 .60
9 Glen Mears .25 .60
10 Rob Milliken .40 1.00
11 Jodi Murphy .40 1.00
12 Jay Neal .25 .60
13 Jeff Pierce .25 .60
14 Andrew Plumb .25 .60
15 Iannique Renaud .25 .60
16 Eddy Skazyk .40 1.00
17 Lindsay Vallis .25 .60
18 Wade Welte .40 1.00
19 Jason White .25 .60
20 Keith Gretzky HCO .40 1.00
21 Tule Fog Mascot .02 .10
22 Bakersfield Arena .02 .10
23 Sponsor Card .02 .10
24 Dick Earle TR .02 .10

1991-92 Baltimore Skipjacks
COMPLETE SET (15) 8.00 20.00
1 Tim Taylor .40 1.00
2 Brent Hughes .30 .75
3 Trevor Halverson .30 .75
4 Bobby Reynolds .30 .75
5 Ken Lovsin .30 .75
6 Olaf Kolzig 4.00 10.00
7 Reggie Savage .30 .75
8 Jim Mathieson .40 1.00
9 Todd Hlushko .40 1.00
10 Mark Ferner .30 .75
11 John Purves .30 .75
12 Steve Seftel .30 .75
13 Craig Duncanson .30 .75
14 Simon Wheeldon .40 1.00
15 Bob Babcock .30 .75

1995-96 Barrie Colts
COMPLETE SET (28) 4.80 12.00
1 Mauricio Alvarez .20 .50
2 Brian Barker .20 .50
3 Brock Boucher .20 .50
4 Jan Bulis .30 .75
5 Jason Cannon .20 .50
6 Jeff Cowan .30 .75
7 Shane Delaronde .30 .75
8 Robert DuBois .20 .50
9 Shawn Frappier .20 .50
10 Chris George .20 .50
11 In Action .02 .10
12 In Action .02 .10
13 In Action .02 .10
14 In Action .02 .10
15 Gerry Lanigan .20 .50
16 Quade Lightbody .20 .50
17 Jeremy Miculinic .20 .50
18 Andrew Morrison .20 .50
19 Luch Nasato .30 .75
20 Bert Templeton CO .08 .25
21 Jeff Tetzlaff .20 .50
22 Chris Thompson .30 .75
23 Justin Robinson .20 .50
24 Daniel Tkaczuk .30 .75
25 Alexander Volchkov .20 .50
26 Caleb Ward .20 .50
27 Mike White .20 .50
28 Darrell Woodley .20 .50

1996-97 Barrie Colts
COMPLETE SET (30) 6.00 15.00
1 Brian Barker .20 .50
2 Brock Boucher .20 .50
3 Casey Burnette .20 .50
4 Michael Christian .20 .50
5 Keith Delaney .20 .50
6 Adam Deleeuw .20 .50
7 Chris Feil .20 .50
8 Brian Finley .40 1.00
9 Michael Henrich .30 .75
10 John Hultberg .20 .50
11 Richard Kazda .20 .50
12 Darren Keily TR .02 .10
13 Cody Leibel .20 .50
14 Mihajlo Martinovich .20 .50
15 Kevin McClelland ACO .02 .10
16 Walker McDonald .20 .50
17 Jeff McKercher .20 .50
18 Luch Nasato .25 .60
19 Ryan O'Keefe .20 .50
20 Jason Pinizzotto .20 .50
21 Ryan Shaver .20 .50
22 Martin Skoula .40 1.00
23 Nick Smith .20 .50
24 Brandon Sugden .25 .60
25 Bert Templeton CO .20 .50
26 Jeff Tetzlaff .20 .50
27 Daniel Tkaczuk .30 .75
28 Charlie Horse(Mascot) .02 .10
29 Barrie Colts Team Picture .20 .50
30 Checklist .02 .10

1997-98 Barrie Colts
COMPLETE SET (27) 4.80 10.00
1 Brian Barker .15 .40
2 Brock Boucher .15 .40
3 Jan Bulis .30 .75
4 Casey Burnette .15 .40
5 Jason Cannon .15 .40
6 Keith Delaney .15 .40
7 Chris George .15 .40
8 Nick Grady .15 .40
9 Mike Henrich .30 .75
10 John Hultberg .20 .50
11 Marcel Kars .15 .40
12 Darren Keily TR .02 .10
13 Gerry Lanigan .15 .40
14 Kevin McClelland .02 .10
15 Walker McDonald .15 .40
16 Jeff McKercher .15 .40
17 Brad Morgan .15 .40
18 Luch Nasato .30 .75
19 Corey Neilson .15 .40
20 Nick Smith .15 .40
21 Bert Templeton CO .15 .40
22 Jeff Tetzlaff .15 .40
23 Chris Thompson .15 .40
24 Daniel Tkaczuk .30 .75
25 Alexandre Volchkov .20 .50
26 Darrell Woodley .15 .40
27 Charlie Horse MAS .02 .10

1998-99 Barrie Colts
COMPLETE SET (25) 7.20 15.00
1 Ryan O'Keefe .20 .50
2 Andre Lakos .20 .50
3 Shawn Cation .20 .50
4 Ed Hill .20 .50
5 Joel Dezainde .20 .50
6 Daniel Tkaczuk .30 .75
7 Martin Skoula .30 .75
8 Jerry Connell .20 .50
9 Tim Verbeek .20 .50
10 Rick Hwodeky .20 .50
11 Scott Cameron .30 .75
12 Ryan Barnes .20 .50
13 Sheldon Keefe .30 .75
14 Jeff Tetzlaff .20 .50
15 Chris Feil .20 .50
16 Michael Henrich .30 .75
17 Mike Christian .20 .50
18 Nick Smith .20 .50
19 Mike Jefferson .40 1.00
20 Denis Shvidki .30 .75
21 Brian Finley .30 .75
22 Ben Vanderklok .20 .50
23 Bert Templeton HCO .02 .10
24 D.Keily
G.Scott .02 .10
25 Charlie Horse MASCOT .02 .10

2000-01 Barrie Colts
COMPLETE SET (24) 4.00 10.00
1 Frantisek Bakrlik .14 .40
2 Tim Branham .20 .50
3 Jordan Brenner .14 .40
4 Dean Byvelds .14 .40
5 David Chant .40 1.00
6 Fraser Clair .14 .40
7 Mike D'Alessandro .30 .75
8 Blaine Down .14 .40
9 Matt Dzieduszycki .14 .40
10 Shayne Fryia .14 .40
11 Matt Grennier .14 .40
12 Bryan Hayes .14 .40
13 Tyler Hanchuck .20 .50
14 Mike Henderson .14 .40
15 Ed Hill .20 .35
16 Charlie Horse Mascot/CL .10 .10
17 Gregg Mizzi .14 .40
18 Stephen Morris .14 .40
19 Jan Platil .14 .40
20 Neil Posillico .14 .40
21 Aaron Power .14 .40
22 Erik Reitz .14 .40
23 Bud Stefanski CO .10 .10
24 Brent Sullivan .14 .40
25 Joey Tenute .14 .40

2001-02 Barrie Colts
COMPLETE SET (23) 5.00 10.00
1 David Chant .40 1.00
2 Ryan Stokes .20 .50
3 Rick Arnaldo .20 .50
4 Eric Reitz .30 .75
5 Aaron Powers .20 .50
6 Steven Morris .20 .50
7 Blaine Down .20 .50
8 Joey Tenute .20 .50
9 Nick Lees .20 .50
10 Tyler Hanchuck .20 .50
11 B.J. Crombeen .20 .50
12 Andrew Shennan .20 .50
13 Jeremy Swanson .20 .50
14 Simon Barq .20 .50
15 Frantisek Bakrlik .20 .50
16 Daniel Girardi .20 .50
17 Kevin Ambroski .20 .50
18 Steve Farquharson .20 .50
19 Jan Platil .20 .50
20 Shayne Fria .20 .50
21 Fraser Clair .20 .50
22 Mascot .04 .10
23 Arena Card .04 .10

2002-03 Barrie Colts
COMPLETE SET (24) 5.00 10.00
1 Evan Brophey .20 .50
2 Justin DaCosta .20 .50
3 Andrew Shennan .20 .50
4 Zach Tranmer .20 .50
5 Michael Tuomi .20 .50
6 Simon Barg .20 .50
7 Ryan Sharp .20 .50
8 Nick Lees .20 .50
9 Hunter Tremblay .20 .50
10 Riley Moher .20 .50
11 Eric Himelfarb .30 .75
12 Mark Langdon .20 .50
13 Luc Chiasson .20 .50
14 Jeremy Swanson .20 .50
15 Kenny Jung .20 .50
16 Tyler Lawson .20 .50
17 Daniel Girardi .20 .50
18 Michael Ouzas .30 .75
19 Paulo Colaiacovo .40 1.00
20 B.J. Crombeen .20 .50
21 Dan Speer .20 .50
22 Jan Platil .20 .50
23 Mascot .04 .10
24 Barrie Molson Centre .04 .10

2003-04 Barrie Colts
COMPLETE SET (24) 6.00 15.00
1 Thomas Lee .30 .75
2 Steve Spade .30 .75
3 Evan Brophey .30 .75
4 Ryan Hamilton .30 .75
5 Andrew Shennan .30 .75
6 Chad Thompson .30 .75
7 Chris Morrison .30 .75
8 Chad Robinson .30 .75
9 Hunter Tremblay .30 .75
10 Bryan Little 1.50 4.00
11 Scott Hotham .40 1.00
12 Mark Langdon .30 .75
13 Jeremy Swanson .30 .75
14 Michael Root .30 .75
15 Travis Fuller .30 .75
16 Paolo Colaiacovo .60 1.50
17 Lukas Bolf .30 .75
18 B.J. Crombeen .30 .75
19 Georgy Ryazantsev .30 .75
20 Dan Speer .30 .75
21 Cory Stillman .30 .75
22 Andrew Dennis .30 .75
23 Mascot
Checklist .04 .10
24 Barrie Molson Centre .04 .10

2004-05 Barrie Colts
COMPLETE SET (25) 5.00 10.00
1 Jeff Weber .20 .50
2 Nathan Martine .20 .50
3 Michael Lombardi .20 .50
4 Nicholas Plastino .20 .50
5 Ryan Hamilton .20 .50
6 Andrew Shennan .20 .50
7 Dan Speer .20 .50
8 Mike Roelofsen .20 .50
9 Chris Morrison .20 .50
10 Chad Robinson .20 .50
11 Hunter Tremblay .20 .50
12 Bryan Little .40 1.00
13 Scott Hotham .20 .50
14 Aaron Lewicki .20 .50
15 Michael Root .20 .50
16 Travis Fuller .20 .50
17 Michael Birner .20 .50
18 Francois Thuot .20 .50
19 Lukas Bolf .20 .50
20 B.J. Crombeen .30 .75
21 Andrew Marshall .20 .50
22 Jordan Shine .20 .50
23 Andrew Hotham .20 .50
24 Andrew Dennis .20 .50
25 Mascot
Checklist .04 .10

2004-05 Barrie Colts 10th Anniversary
COMPLETE SET (25) 5.00 12.00
1 Daniel Tkaczuk .20 .50
2 Bryan Little .40 1.00
3 Michael Henrich .20 .50
4 Martin Skoula .20 .50
5 Blaine Down .20 .50
6 Jan Bulis .20 .50
7 Erik Reitz .30 .75
8 Jeremy Swanson .20 .50
9 Luch Nasato .20 .50
10 B.J. Crombeen .30 .75
11 Jan Platil .20 .50
12 Denis Shvidki .20 .50
13 Joey Tenute .20 .50
14 Aaron Power .20 .50
15 Alexander Volchkov .20 .50
16 Mark Langdon .20 .50
17 Fraser Clair .20 .50
18 Nick Lees .20 .50
19 Cory Stillman .20 .50
20 Jeff Tetzlaff .20 .50
21 Tim Verbeek .20 .50
22 Matt Dzieduszycki .20 .50
23 Paulo Colaiacovo .30 .75
24 David Chant .30 .75
25 Brian Finley .30 .75

2006-07 Barrie Colts
1 Andrew Perugini .30 .75
2 Michael Hutchinson .20 .50
3 Kyle Van De Bospoort .20 .50
4 Brian Lashoff .20 .50
5 Thomas Marcinko .30 .75
6 Nicolas Plastino .20 .50
7 Shawn Franck .20 .50
8 Alex Hutchings .20 .50
9 Hunter Tremblay .20 .50
10 Bryan Little .60 1.50
11 Stefan Della Rovere .30 .75
12 Richard Clune .20 .50
13 Ryan Bellows .20 .50
14 Mike Webber .20 .50
15 Chris Purves .20 .50
16 Tyson Aitcheson .20 .50
17 Matthew Bragg .20 .50
18 Kris Sparre .20 .50
19 Ryan Gottschalk .20 .50
20 Andrew Marshall .20 .50
21 Cort McGillis .20 .50
22 Vladimir Nikiforov .20 .50
23 George Lovatsis .20 .50
24 Joe Pleckaitis .20 .50
25 Michael Lombardi .20 .50
26 T.J. Battani .20 .50
27 Checklist .02 .10
LE2 Andrew Perugini 2.00 5.00

2013-14 Barrie Colts
COMPLETE SET (24) 8.00 20.00
1 Liam Maaskant .30 .75
2 Jonathan Laser .30 .75
3 Jake Dotchin .30 .75
4 Aaron Ekblad 1.50 4.00
5 Josh Carrick .30 .75
6 Mac Clutsam .30 .75
7 C.J. Garcia .30 .75
8 Joseph Blandisi .30 .75
9 Not Issued .30 .75
10 Nick Pastorious .30 .75
11 Kevin Labanc .30 .75
12 Tyson Fawcett .30 .75
13 Matthew Kreis .30 .75
14 Justin Scott .30 .75
15 Brendan Lemieux 1.25 3.00
16 Andreas Athanasiou .60 1.50
17 Mitchell Theoret .30 .75
18 Michael Webster .30 .75
19 Garrett Hooey .30 .75
20 Andrew Mangiapane .30 .75
21 Cordell James .30 .75
22 Zach Hall .30 .75
23 Mackenzie Blackwood .30 .75
24 Daniel Gibl .30 .75

1951-52 Bas Du Fleuve
COMPLETE SET (58) 350.00 700.00
1 Gordon Poirier 12.50 25.00
2 Denis Brodeur 25.00 50.00
3 Conrad Poitras 7.50 15.00
4 Clement Tremblay 7.50 15.00
5 Raymond Leduc 7.50 15.00
6 Jacques Armstrong 7.50 15.00
7 Joe Schmidt 7.50 15.00
8 Gilles Laroche 7.50 15.00
9 Frank Pearce 7.50 15.00
10 Wayne Stephenson 7.50 15.00
11 Guy Lapointe 7.50 15.00
12 Guy Delisle 7.50 15.00
13 Ossie Carnegie 10.00 20.00
14 Gilbert Girouard 7.50 15.00
15 Jean-Paul Vandal 7.50 15.00
16 Guy Lalonde 7.50 15.00
17 Roland Bilodeau 7.50 15.00
18 Gaetan Laliberte 7.50 15.00
19 Maurice Benoit 7.50 15.00
20 Thomas McDougall 7.50 15.00
21 Roger Guay 7.50 15.00
22 Bob Brault 7.50 15.00
23 Edouard Theberge 7.50 15.00
24 Paul Lessard 7.50 15.00
25 Lucien Gilbert 7.50 15.00
26 Real Lafreniere 7.50 15.00
27 Ronald Limoges 7.50 15.00
28 Roger Ste. Marie 7.50 15.00
29 Arthur Leyte 7.50 15.00
30 Magella Laforest 7.50 15.00
31 Bill Leblanc 7.50 15.00
32 Pius Gaudet 7.50 15.00
33 Jean-Roch Bellavance 7.50 15.00
34 Gerard Lachance 7.50 15.00
35 Marcel St. Pierre 7.50 15.00
36 Pierre Brillant 7.50 15.00
37 Paul Provost 7.50 15.00
38 Maurice Lamirande 7.50 15.00
39 Roger Hayfield 7.50 15.00
40 Normand Bellavance 7.50 15.00
41 Marcel Houde 7.50 15.00
42 Dan Janelle 7.50 15.00
43 Roland Rossignol 7.50 15.00
44 Roger Gagne 7.50 15.00
45 Jacques Monette 7.50 15.00
46 Bernie Bernaquez 7.50 15.00
47 Paul Gagnon 7.50 15.00
48 Jean-Marie Fillion 7.50 15.00
49 Bert Scullion 7.50 15.00
50 Don Bellringer 7.50 15.00
51 Frank Cote 7.50 15.00
52 Eddy Bolan 7.50 15.00
53 Maurice Parr 7.50 15.00
54 Many McIntyre 7.50 15.00
55 Roger Jodoin 7.50 15.00
56 Mario Senecal 7.50 15.00
57 Denis Fillion 7.50 15.00
58 Marcel Fillion 12.50 25.00

1952-53 Bas Du Fleuve
COMPLETE SET (65) 400.00 800.00
1 Roger Gagner 12.50 25.00
2 Martial Pruneau 7.50 15.00
3 Fernand Gladu 7.50 15.00
4 Joseph Lacoursiere 7.50 15.00
5 Maurice Lamirande 7.50 15.00
6 Denis Smith 7.50 15.00
7 Real Jacques 7.50 15.00
8 Roland Landry 7.50 15.00
9 Dan Janelle 7.50 15.00
10 Pete Gaudette 7.50 15.00
11 Normand Bellavance 7.50 15.00
12 Roger Hayfield 7.50 15.00
13 Bill LeBlanc 7.50 15.00
14 Victor Corbin 7.50 15.00
15 Gerard Lachance 7.50 15.00
16 Guy Labrie 7.50 15.00
17 Denis Brodeur 15.00 30.00
18 Gerard Paquin 7.50 15.00
19 Irene St. Hilaire 10.00 . 20.00
20 Guy Gervais 7.50 15.00
21 Marcel Benoit 7.50 15.00
22 Roger Dumas 7.50 15.00
23 Gaston Gervais 7.50 15.00
24 Maurice St. Jean 7.50 15.00
25 Frank Pearce 7.50 15.00
26 Fernand Bernaquez 7.50 15.00
27 Henri-Paul Gagnon 7.50 15.00
28 Jean-Jacques Pichette 7.50 15.00
29 Jim Hayes 7.50 15.00
30 Fernand Rancourt 7.50 15.00
31 Nils Tremblay 7.50 15.00
32 Clement Tremblay 7.50 15.00
33 Jacques Lalancette 7.50 15.00
34 Marcel Fillion 10.00 20.00
35 Jacques Monette 7.50 15.00
36 Frank Cote 7.50 15.00
37 Bernie Lemonde 7.50 15.00
38 Guildor Levesque 7.50 15.00
39 Hector Legris 7.50 15.00
40 Jacques Gagnon 7.50 15.00
41 Donat Deschesnes 7.50 15.00
42 Bertrand LePage 7.50 15.00
43 Paul Lavoie 7.50 15.00
44 Denis Fillion 7.50 15.00
45 Floyd Crawford 12.50 25.00
46 Paul Duchesne 7.50 15.00
47 Rene Pronovost 7.50 15.00
48 Roger Jodoin 7.50 15.00
49 Mario Senecal 7.50 15.00
50 Garry Plamondon 12.50 25.00
51 Marcel Paille 7.50 15.00
52 Rene Pepin 7.50 15.00
53 Gilles Desrosiers 7.50 15.00
54 Edgard Gendron 7.50 15.00
55 Ronald Limoges 7.50 15.00
56 Roland Bilodeau 7.50 15.00
57 Leon Bouchard 7.50 15.00
58 Bob Leger 7.50 15.00
59 Conrad L'Heureux 7.50 15.00
60 Raymond Leduc 7.50 15.00
61 Bob Brault 7.50 15.00
62 Roger Ste. Marie 7.50 15.00
63 Real Lafreniere 7.50 15.00
64 Lucien Gilbert 7.50 15.00
65 Louis Desrosiers 12.50 25.00

1998-99 Baton Rouge Kingfish
COMPLETE SET (25) 8.00 20.00
1 Brett Abrahamson .40 1.00
2 Chris Aldous .40 1.00
3 Cam Brown .40 1.00
4 Jason Byrnes .40 1.00
5 Paul Croteau .40 1.00
6 Luke Curtin .40 1.00
7 Allan Hitchen .40 1.00
8 Scott Humeniuk .40 1.00
9 Trevor Jobe .40 1.00
10 Billy-Jay Johnston .40 1.00
11 Mike Josephson .40 1.00
12 Martin Laroche .40 1.00
13 Michel Massie .40 1.00
14 Eric Montreuil .40 1.00
15 Jon Rempel .40 1.00
16 Bryan Richardson .40 1.00
17 Dan Shermerhorn .40 1.00
18 Bob Westerby .40 1.00
19 Jordan Willis .60 1.50
20 Barry Smith CO .08 .25
21 Ron Hansis GM .02 .10
22 Bob McGill CO .08 .25
23 Huey P. Kingfish MAS .08 .25
24 Pat Loughlin TR .02 .10
25 Chris Kenyon .40 1.00

1998-99 BC Icemen
COMPLETE SET (22) 4.00 10.00
1 Mark Dutiaume .30 .75
2 Pete Vandermeer .20 .50
3 Patrice Robitaille .20 .50
4 Ales Dvorak .20 .50
5 Shane Dow .20 .50
6 Scott Ricci .20 .50
7 Doug Johnson .20 .50
8 Justin Kearns .30 .75
9 Justin Plamondon .30 .75
10 Jarno Mensonen .20 .50
11 Jamie Bird .20 .50
12 Greg Pajor .20 .50
13 Derek Knorr .20 .50
14 Chris Kavanagh .20 .50
15 Dallas Mann .20 .50
16 Jon Hillebrandt .30 .75
17 Dieter Kochan .75 2.00
18 Brad Jones HCO .08 .25
19 Brian Waselko TR .08 .25
20 Mike Thornton BR .08 .25
21 Phamtom Mascot .08 .25
22 Bamboni Mascot .08 .25

1998-99 BC Icemen II
COMPLETE SET (27) 8.00 20.00
1 Ales Dvorak .30 .75
2 Shane Dow .30 .75
3 Scott Ricci .30 .75
4 Pete Vandermeer .30 .75
5 Doug Johnson .30 .75
6 Mark Dutiaume .60 1.50
7 Justin Kearns .30 .75
8 Patrice Robitaille .30 .75
9 Justin Plamondon .40 1.00
10 Chris Greenville .30 .75
11 Jarno Mensonen .30 .75
12 Jamie Bird .30 .75
13 Greg Pajor .30 .75
14 Dmitri Deryabin .30 .75
15 Derek Knorr .30 .75
16 Peter Cermak .30 .75
17 Chris Kavanagh .30 .75
18 Jon Hillebrandt .75 2.00
19 Dieter Kochan 1.50 4.00
20 Brad Jones HCO .20 .50
21 Brian Weslro TR .08 .25
22 Dallas Mann .30 .75
23 Mike Thornton BR .08 .25
24 Phamton Mascot .08 .25
25 Bamboni Mascot .08 .25
NNO UHL Website .02 .10
NNO Checklist .08 .25

2001-02 BC Icemen
COMPLETE SET (29) 8.00 20.00
1 Chris Allen .30 .75
2 Eric Andersen .30 .75
3 Alex Andreyev .30 .75
4 Keith Aucoin .30 .75
5 Martin Belanger .30 .75
6 Karel Betik .40 1.00
7 Glendon Cominetti .30 .75
8 Ross Dufresne .30 .75
9 R.J. Gates .30 .75
10 Chris Grenville .30 .75
11 Eric Heffler .30 .75
12 David Jesiolowski .40 1.00
13 Marc Lauzon .30 .75
14 Jim Nagle .30 .75
15 Ryan Pepperall .30 .75
16 Larry Pierce .30 .75
17 Justin Plamondon .30 .75
18 Sean Rowe .60 1.50
19 Erasmo Saltarelli .30 .75
20 Bryan Schoen .40 1.00
21 Trevor Shoaf .30 .75
22 Marc Tropper .30 .75
23 Rob Voltera .30 .75
24 Derek Wood .30 .75
25 Brad Jones CO .10 .25
26 Pedro Trindade MGR .04 .10
27 Bamboni MASCOT .10 .25
28 Phantom MASCOT .10 .25
29 Jason Weinstein PR .04 .10

1983-84 Belleville Bulls
COMPLETE SET (30) 30.00 80.00
1 Belleville Bulls Logo .10 .25
2 Quinte Sports Centre .10 .25
3 Dan Quinn 1.00 2.50
4 Dave MacLean .20 .50
5 Scott Gardiner .20 .50
6 Mike Knuude .20 .50
7 Brian Martin .20 .50
8 R. Vaughan OWN .10 .25
9 John McDonald .30 .75
10 Brian Small .20 .50
11 Mike Savage .20 .50
12 Dunc MacIntyre .20 .50
13 Charlie Moore .20 .50
14 Jim Andanoff .20 .50
15 Mario Martini .20 .50
16 Rick Adolfi .20 .50
17 Mike Vellucci .20 .50
18 Scott McMichel .20 .50
19 Ali Butorac .20 .50
20 Al Iafrate 1.25 3.00
21 Rob Crocock .20 .50
22 Craig Coxe .60 1.50
23 Grant Robertson .20 .50
24 Craig Billington 1.25 3.00
25 Darren Gani .20 .50
26 Tim Bean .20 .50
27 Wayne Gretzky 30.00 75.00
28 Russ Soule TR .10 .25
29 Larry Mavety CO/GM .10 .25
30 Team Photo .20 .50

1984-85 Belleville Bulls
COMPLETE SET (31) 6.00 15.00
1 Team photo .20 .50
2 R. Vaughan OWN .02 .10
3 Larry Mavety CO/MG .02 .10
4 Dunc MacIntyre .20 .50
5 Belleville Bulls Logo .02 .10
6 Mike Knuude .20 .50
7 John Purves .40 1.00
8 Charlie Moore .20 .50
9 Stan Drulia .40 1.00
10 Craig Billington .75 2.00
11 Dave MacLean .20 .50
12 Darren Moxam .20 .50
13 Shane Doyle .20 .50
14 Larry VanHerzele .20 .50
15 Tim Bean .20 .50
16 Kent Brimmer .20 .50
17 Angelo Catenaro .20 .50
18 Steve Linesman .20 .50
19 Grant Robertson .20 .50
20 John Reid .20 .50
21 Dean Whyte .20 .50
22 Darren Gani .20 .50
23 Roger Robertson .20 .50
24 Gary Callaghan .20 .50
25 John Tamer .20 .50
26 Todd Hawkins .20 .50
27 Jim Andanoff .20 .50
28 Chris Rutledge TR .02 .10
29 Matt Taylor .20 .50
30 Mike Hartman .40 1.00
NNO Title Card .10 .25

2000-01 Belleville Bulls
COMPLETE SET (29) 5.00 12.00
1 Team Photo .20 .50
2 Paulo Colaiacovo .40 1.00
3 Nick Policelli .20 .50
4 Matt Coughlin .20 .50
5 Mike Jacobsen .20 .50
6 Malcolm Hutt .20 .50
7 Cody McCormick .20 .50
8 Mike Renzi .20 .50
9 Andrew Brown .20 .50
10 Andre Deveaux .20 .50
11 Matt Stajan .20 1.50
12 Alex White .20 .50
13 David Silverstone .20 .50
14 Randy Rowe .20 .50
15 Brad Efthimiou .20 .50
16 Dan Growden .20 .50
17 Adam Paiement .20 .50
18 Jan Chovan .30 .75
19 Branko Radivojevic .40 1.50
20 David Cornacchia .20 .50
21 Rob Dmytruk .20 .50
22 Nate Robinson .20 .50

23 Kyle Wellwood 1.00 2.50
24 In Action .20 .50
25 In Action .20 .50
26 In Action .20 .50
27 Jim Hulton CO .20 .50
28 Fan Pictures .02 .10
29 Directory .02 .10

2001-02 Belleville Bulls

COMPLETE SET (29) 5.00 12.00
1 Title card .04 .10
2 James Boyd ACO .04 .10
3 Andrew Brown .20 .50
4 Rane Carnegie .20 .50
5 Jan Chovan .30 .75
6 Paulo Colaiacovo .30 .75
7 Matt Coughlin .20 .50
8 Andre Deveaux .20 .50
9 Jake Gilmour .20 .50
10 Dan Growden .20 .50
11 Jim Hulton CO .20 .50
12 Malcolm Hutt .20 .50
13 Michael Knight .20 .50
14 Neill MacInnis .20 .50
15 Oliver Maron .20 .50
16 Cody McCormick .20 .50
17 Adam Paiement .20 .50
18 Marc Rancourt .20 .50
19 Michael Renzi .20 .50
20 Nathan Robinson .40 1.00
21 David Silverstone .20 .50
22 Matt Stajan .20 .50
23 Adam Sturgeon .20 .50
24 Kyle Wellwood .75 2.00
25 Alex White .20 .50
26 Celebration card .04 .10
27 Celebration card .04 .10
28 Michael Renzi Matt Coughlin#Cody McCormick(#Kyle .40 1.00
29 Bullie Mascot .04 .10

2001-02 Belleville Bulls Update

COMPLETE SET (9) 4.00 10.00
1 David Clarkson .10 .25
2 Steve Cooke .10 .25
3 Michael Mole .40 1.00
4 Neil Smith .10 .25
5 Jason Spezza 1.25 3.00
6 Jason Spezza 1.25 3.00
7 Jason Spezza 1.25 3.00
8 Glenn Ridler .10 .25
9 Lubos Velebny .10 .25

2002-03 Belleville Bulls

COMPLETE SET (30) 6.00 15.00
1 Blake Allan .20 .50
2 Andrew Brown .20 .50
3 Rane Carnegie .20 .50
4 Steve Cooke .20 .50
5 Andre Deveaux .20 .50
6 Jake Gilmour .20 .50
7 Todd Griffith .20 .50
8 Malcolm Hutt .20 .50
9 Mike Knight .20 .50
10 Josh Manning .20 .50
11 Oliver Maron .20 .50
12 Cody McCormick .30 .75
13 Michael Mole .30 .75
14 Adam Paiment .20 .50
15 Marc Rancourt .20 .50
16 Neil Smith .20 .50
17 Matt Stajan .60 1.50
18 Ivan Svarny .20 .50
19 Cody Thornton .20 .50
20 Eric Tobia .30 .75
21 Darcy Tuplin .20 .50
22 Patrick Turcotte .20 .50
23 Jordon Watson .20 .50
24 Coaches .04 .10
25 Michael Mole Eric Tobia .30 .75
26 Matt Stajan .60 1.50
27 Andre Deveaux .20 .50
28 Rookies .20 .50
29 Defencemen .04 .10
30 Team Captains .04 .10

2003-04 Belleville Bulls

COMPLETE SET (22) 5.00 10.00
1 Rane Carnegie .20 .50
2 Cody Thornton .20 .50
3 Matt Kelly .20 .50
4 Dan Rogers .20 .50
5 Marc Rancourt .20 .50
6 Eric Tobia .30 .75
7 Ryan Berard .20 .50
8 Josh Francis .20 .50
9 Andrew Brown .20 .50
10 Michael Knight .20 .50
11 Aaron Lewicki .20 .50
12 Geoff Patton .20 .50
13 Jake Gilmour .20 .50
14 Ivan Svarny .20 .50
15 Todd Griffith .20 .50
16 David Edgeworth .20 .50
17 Josh Manning .20 .50
18 Milan Hluchy .20 .50
19 Mike Roelofsen .20 .50
20 Shaun Clinton .20 .50
21 Andrew Brown TL .20 .50
22 Rane Carnegie TL .20 .50

2004-05 Belleville Bulls

OMPLETE SET (24) 5.00 12.00
Andrew Maksym .20 .50
Bobby Davey .20 .50
Cody Thornton .20 .50
Connor Cameron .20 .50
Jeff Leavitt .20 .50
Eric Tobia .20 .50
Evan Brophey .20 .50
Geoff Killing .20 .50
John Hughes .20 .50
0 Kevin Lalande .20 .50
1 Kyle Sonnenberg .20 .50
2 Lubomir Stach .20 .50
3 Mark Rancourt .20 .50
4 Marc Johnson .20 .50
15 Martin Novak .20 .50
16 Matt Beleskey .20 .50
17 Matt Kelly .20 .50
18 Pat Sutton .20 .50
19 Ryan Berard .20 .50
20 Ryan Rorabeck .20 .50
21 Scott Baker .20 .50
22 Shawn Matthias .40 1.00
23 Steve Spade .20 .50
NNO Marc Rancourt CAP .75 2.00

2005-06 Belleville Bulls

COMPLETE SET (24) 8.00 15.00
1 Matt Beleskey .30 .75
2 Ryan Rorabeck .30 .75
3 Sebastian Dahm .30 .75
4 Kyle Jukosky .30 .75
5 Matt Smyth .30 .75
6 P.K. Subban 2.00 5.00
7 Michael Neal .30 .75
8 Scott Baker .30 .75
9 Bryan Cameron .30 .75
10 Bobby Davey .30 .75
11 Bud Kelly .30 .75
12 Geoff Killing .30 .75
13 Nicholas Pageau .30 .75
14 John Hughes .30 .75
15 Bryan Cameron .30 .75
16 Steve Spade .30 .75
17 Kevin Lalande .30 .75
18 Ryan Berard .30 .75
19 Andrew Maksym .30 .75
20 Jeff Leavitt .30 .75
21 Shawn Matthias .40 1.00
22 Cory Tanaka .30 .75
23 Andrew Gibbons .30 .75
24 Andrew Self .30 .75

2006-07 Belleville Bulls

COMPLETE SET (23) 5.00 12.00
1 Matt Pelech .20 .50
2 Bryan Cameron .20 .50
3 Matt Beleskey .20 .50
4 Stephen Blunden .30 .75
5 Erik Caladi .20 .50
6 Tyler Donati .20 .50
7 Andrew Gibbons .20 .50
8 Jeff Leavitt .20 .50
9 Shawn Matthias .30 .75
10 Michael Neal .20 .50
11 Aaron Snow .20 .50
12 Cory Tanaka .20 .50
13 Eric Tangradi .20 .50
14 Matthew Tipoff .20 .50
15 Paul Cianfrini .20 .50
16 Geoff Killing .20 .50
17 Shawn Lalonde .20 .50
18 Nicholas Pageau .20 .50
19 P.K. Subban 1.00 2.50
20 Steven Whitely .20 .50
21 Kevin Lalande .20 .50
22 Mike Murphy .20 .50
LE2 Shawn Matthias 1.00 2.50

1981-82 Billings Bighorns

NNO Harry Mahood 4.00 10.00

1992-93 Binghamton Rangers

COMPLETE SET (24) 4.00 10.00
1 Team Card .15 .40
2 Mike Hurlbut .15 .40
3 Michael Stewart .15 .40
4 Craig Duncanson .15 .40
5 Rick Bennett .15 .40
6 Dave Thomlinson .15 .40
7 Mike Stevens .15 .40
8 Rob Kenny .15 .40
9 Chris Cichocki .15 .40
10 Sergei Zubov .40 1.00
11 Don Biggs .15 .40
12 Joby Messier .15 .40
13 Steven King .15 .40
14 Dave Archibald .15 .40
15 Brian McReynolds .15 .40
16 Dave Marcinyshyn .15 .40
17 Jean-Yves Roy .15 .40
18 Peter Fiorentino .15 .40
19 Daniel Lacroix .15 .40
20 Per Djoos .15 .40
21 Boris Rousson .30 .75
22 Corey Hirsch .30 .75
23 Rockey Ranger Mascot .08 .25
24 Ranger Victory .15 .40

1994-95 Binghamton Rangers

COMPLETE SET (22) 4.00 10.00
1 Eric Cairns .30 .75
2 Craig Duncanson .15 .40
3 Peter Fiorentino .15 .40
4 Ken Gernander .15 .40
5 Jim Hiller .15 .40
6 Corey Hirsch .30 .75
7 Rob Kenny .15 .40
8 Andrei Kudinov .15 .40
9 Darren Langdon .30 .75
10 Scott Malone .15 .40
11 Shawn McCosh .15 .40
12 Mike McLaughlin .15 .40
13 Joby Messier .15 .40
14 Jeff Nielsen .15 .40
15 Mattias Norstrom .30 .75
16 Jamie Ram .30 .75
17 Barry Richter .20 .50
18 Jean Yves Roy .15 .40
19 Brad Rubachuk .15 .40
20 Dave Smith .15 .40
21 Dmitri Starostenko .15 .40
22 Michael Stewart .15 .40
23 Darcy Werenka .15 .40

1995-96 Binghamton Rangers

COMPLETE SET (25) 4.00 10.00
1 Sylvain Blouin .20 .50
2 George Burnett CO .02 .10
3 Mike Busniuk ACO .02 .10
4 Eric Cairns .30 .75
5 Chris Ferraro .30 .75
6 Peter Ferraro .40 1.00
7 Maxim Galanov .20 .50
8 Ken Gernander .20 .50
9 Brad Jones .15 .40
10 Pavel Komarov .15 .40
11 Andrei Kudinov .15 .40
12 Daniel Lacroix .20 .50
13 Scott Baker .15 .40
14 Jon Hillebrandt .20 .50
15 Scott Malone .15 .40
16 Cal McGowan .15 .40
17 Jeff Nielsen .15 .40
18 Jamie Ram .20 .50
19 Shawn Reid .15 .40
20 Barry Richter .20 .50
21 Andy Silverman .15 .40
22 Lee Sorochan .20 .50
23 Dmitri Starostenko .15 .40
24 Ryan Vandenbussche .30 .75
25 Rick Willis .15 .40

1996-97 Binghamton Rangers

COMPLETE SET (24) 4.00 10.00
1 Micah Aivazoff .20 .50
2 Sylvain Blouin .15 .40
3 George Burnett .02 .10
4 Mike Busniuk .02 .10
5 Ed Campbell .15 .40
6 Dan Cloutier 1.00 2.50
7 Chris Ferraro .20 .50
8 Peter Ferraro .20 .50
9 Peter Fiorentino .15 .40
10 Eric Flinton .15 .40
11 Maxim Golanov .15 .40
12 Ken Gernander .15 .40
13 Mike Martin .15 .40
14 Bob Maudie .15 .40
15 Jeff Nielsen .15 .40
16 Rocky Raccoon .02 .10
17 Ken Shepard .15 .40
18 Andy Silverman .15 .40
19 Adam Smith .15 .40
20 Lee Sorochan .20 .50
21 Ryan VandenBussche .30 .75
22 Vladimir Vorobiev .15 .40
23 Rick Willis .15 .40
24 AHL Hockey Card .02 .10

2003-04 Binghamton Senators

COMPLETE SET (24) 6.00 15.00
1 Steve Bancroft .20 .50
2 Dennis Bonvie .40 1.00
3 Daniel Corso .20 .50
4 Ray Emery .40 1.00
5 Alexandre Giroux .20 .50
6 Denis Hamel .40 1.00
7 Andy Hedlund .20 .50
8 Jody Hull .20 .50
9 David Hymovitz .20 .50
10 Chris Kelly .40 1.00
11 Brooks Laich .20 .50
12 Josh Langfeld .20 .50
13 Chris Leinweber .20 .50
14 Brian McGrattan .40 1.00
15 Serge Payer .20 .50
16 Jan Platil .20 .50
17 Christoph Schubert .20 .50
18 Peter Smrek .20 .50
19 Billy Thompson .40 1.00
20 Tony Tuzzolino .20 .50
21 Julien Vauclair .20 .50
22 Antoine Vermette .40 1.00
23 Greg Watson .20 .50
24 Mascot .04 .10

2003-04 Binghamton Senators Postcards

COMPLETE SET (13) 15.00 30.00
1 Chris Kelly 1.25 3.00
2 Josh Langfeld .75 2.00
3 Julien Vauclair .75 2.00
4 Daniel Corso .75 2.00
5 Dennis Bonvie 1.25 3.00
6 David Hymovitz .75 2.00
7 Brooks Laich .75 2.00
8 Brian McGrattan 1.25 3.00
9 Alexandre Giroux .75 2.00
10 Denis Hamel 1.25 3.00
11 Antoine Vermette 1.25 3.00
12 Ray Emery 1.50 4.00
NNO Mascot .75 2.00

2004-05 Binghamton Senators

COMPLETE SET (26) 6.00 15.00
1 Brandon Bochenski .30 .75
2 Danny Bois .20 .50
3 Ray Emery .40 1.00
4 Jesse Fibiger .20 .50
5 Denis Hamel .40 1.00
6 Andy Hedlund .20 .50
7 Pat Kavanagh .20 .50
8 Chris Kelly .30 .75
9 Neil Komadoski .15 .40
10 Josh Langfeld .20 .50
11 Brian McGrattan .40 1.00
12 Arpad Mihaly .20 .50
13 Jan Platil .20 .50
14 Brian Pothier .20 .50
15 Grant Potulny .20 .50
16 Christoph Schubert .20 .50
17 Jason Spezza .75 2.00
18 Charlie Stephens .20 .50
19 Billy Thompson .30 .75
20 Antoine Vermette .30 .75
21 Anton Volchenkov .30 .75
22 Greg Watson .20 .50
23 David Cameron CO .04 .10
24 John Paddock CO .04 .10
25 Mike Busniuk ACO .04 .10
26 Max MASCOT .04 .10

2004-05 Binghamton Senators Hess

COMPLETE SET (14) 20.00 35.00
1 Chris Kelly 1.25 3.00
2 Denis Hamel 1.50 4.00
3 Brian Pothier .75 2.00
4 Christoph Schubert .75 2.00
5 Pat Kavanagh .75 2.00
6 Antoine Vermette 1.25 3.00
7 Brandon Bochenski 1.25 3.00
8 Andy Hedlund .75 2.00
9 Brian McGrattan 1.25 3.00
10 Josh Langfeld .75 2.00
11 Anton Volchenkov .75 2.00
12 Jason Spezza 4.00 10.00
13 Ray Emery 1.50 4.00
NNO Cover card .10 .25

2005-06 Binghamton Senators

COMPLETE SET (22) 10.00 25.00
1 Denis Hamel .75 2.00
2 Danny Bois .40 1.00
3 Jeff Heerema .40 1.00
5 Jan Platil .40 1.00
6 Charlie Stephens .40 1.00
7 Steve Martins .40 1.00
8 Brad Norton .40 1.00
9 Filip Novak .40 1.00
10 Billy Thompson .75 2.00
11 Grant Potulny .40 1.00
12 Patrick Eaves 1.25 3.00
13 Brett Clouthier .40 1.00
14 Tomas Malec .40 1.00
15 Kelly Guard .75 2.00
16 Neil Petruic .40 1.00
17 Brandon Bochenski .75 2.00
18 Brennan Evans .40 1.00
19 Gregg Johnson .40 1.00
20 Jeff Glass .75 2.00
21 Lance Ward .40 1.00
22 Sponsor Card .02 .10
23 Joe Cullen .40 1.00
24 Neil Komadoski .40 1.00
25 Billy Thompson .40 1.00
26 Greg Watson .40 1.00
27 Max The Mascot .20 .50
28 Dave Cameron .20 .50
29 Mike Busniuk .20 .50
30 Domenic Nicoletta .20 .50
31 Tom Severance .20 .50

2005-06 Binghamton Senators Quickway

COMPLETE SET (22) 10.00 25.00
1 Denis Hamel .40 1.00
2 Danny Bois .40 1.00
3 Jeff Heerema .40 1.00
4 Joe Cullen .40 1.00
5 Jan Platil .40 1.00
6 Charlie Stephens .40 1.00
7 Steve Martins .40 1.00
8 Brad Norton .40 1.00
9 Filip Novak .40 1.00
10 Billy Thompson .75 2.00
11 Grant Potulny .40 1.00
12 Patrick Eaves 1.25 3.00
13 Brett Clouthier .40 1.00
14 Tomas Malec .40 1.00
15 Kelly Guard .75 2.00
16 Neil Petruic .40 1.00
17 Brandon Bochenski .75 2.00
18 Brennan Evans .40 1.00
19 Gregg Johnson .40 1.00
20 Jeff Glass .75 2.00
21 Lance Ward .40 1.00
22 .04 .10

2006-07 Binghamton Senators

1 Jamie Allison .30 .75
2 Michal Barinka .30 .75
3 Danny Bois .30 .75
4 Charlie Cook .30 .75
5 Andrew Ebbett .30 .75
6 Chanse Fitzpatrick .30 .75
7 Jeff Glass .60 1.50
8 Kelly Guard .60 1.50
9 Andy Hedlund .30 .75
10 Jeff Heerema .30 .75
11 Josh Hennessy .60 1.50
12 Neil Komadoski .30 .75
13 Arttu Luttinen .30 .75
14 Tomas Malec .30 .75
15 Brian Maloney .30 .75
16 Serge Payer .30 .75
17 Cory Pecker .30 .75
18 Neil Petruic .30 .75
19 Grant Potulny .30 .75
20 Bobby Robins .30 .75
21 Ryan Vesce .30 .75
22 Mike Busniuk .30 .75
23 Dave Cameron CO .10 .25
24 Dom Nicoletta TR .02 .10
25 Tom Severance EQ .02 .10
26 Grady Whittenburg ANN .02 .10
27 Maximus MASCOT .02 .10

2006-07 Binghamton Senators 5th Anniversary

COMPLETE SET (35) 10.00 25.00
1 Steve Bancroft .30 .75
2 Cody Bass .30 .75
3 Brandon Bochenski .60 1.50
4 Danny Bois .30 .75
5 Dennis Bonvie .60 1.50
6 Patrick Eaves .60 1.50
7 Ray Emery .60 1.50
8 Alexandre Giroux .30 .75
9 Jeff Glass .40 1.00
10 Kelly Guard .40 1.00
11 Denis Hamel .40 1.00
12 Andy Hedlund .30 .75
13 Jeff Heerema .30 .75
14 David Hymovitz .30 .75
15 Chris Kelly .30 .75
16 Josh Langfeld .30 .75
17 Steve Martins .30 .75
18 Brian McGrattan .60 1.50
19 Joe Murphy .30 .75
20 Filip Novak .30 .75
21 Serge Payer .30 .75
22 Cory Pecker .30 .75
23 Jan Platil .30 .75
24 Brian Pothier .30 .75
25 Grant Potulny .30 .75
26 Bobby Robins .30 .75
27 Christoph Schubert .30 .75
28 Brad Smyth .30 .75
29 Jason Spezza .75 2.00
30 Charlie Stephens .30 .75
31 Billy Thompson .30 .75
32 Julien Vauclair .30 .75
33 Antoine Vermette .40 1.00
34 Anton Volchenkov .40 1.00
35 Max MASCOT .02 .10

2007-08 Binghamton Senators

COMPLETE SET (30) 10.00 20.00
1 Greg Amadio .30 .75
2 Cody Bass .30 .75
3 Danny Bois .30 .75
4 Matt Carkner .30 .75
5 Niko Dimitrakos .30 .75
6 Tyler Donati .30 .75
7 Brian Elliott .40 1.00
8 Ray Emery .40 1.00
9 Nick Foligno .40 1.00
10 Jeff Glass .40 1.00
11 Denis Hamel .30 .75
12 Josh Hennessy .30 .75
13 Matt Kinch .30 .75
14 Tomas Kudelka .30 .75
15 Brian Lee .60 1.50
16 Justin Mapletoft .30 .75
17 Greg Mauldin .30 .75
18 Scott May .30 .75
19 Alexander Nikulin .30 .75
20 Lawrence Nycholat .30 .75
21 Derek Smith .30 .75
22 Geoff Waugh .30 .75
23 Shawn Weller .40 1.00
24 Jeremy Yablonski .40 1.00
25 Ilya Zubov .40 1.00
26 Cory Clouston HC .02 .10
27 Mike Busniuk AC .02 .10
28 Tom Severance EQ .02 .10
29 Domenic Nicoletta TR .02 .10
NNO Max MASCOT Checklist .02 .10

2013-14 Binghamton Senators

COMPLETE SET (29) 10.00 25.00
1 Ben Blood .30 .75
2 Mark Borowiecki .30 .75
3 Cody Ceci .50 1.25
4 Fredrik Claesson .30 .75
5 Corey Cowick .30 .75
6 Jakub Culek .30 .75
7 Stephane Da Costa .30 .75
8 David Dziurzynski .30 .75
9 Tyler Eckford .30 .75
10 Derek Grant .30 .75
11 Wacey Hamilton .30 .75
12 Andrew Hammond .75 2.00
13 Mike Hoffman .75 2.00
14 Ludwig Karlsson .30 .75
15 Darren Kramer .30 .75
16 Nathan Lawson .30 .75
17 Jim O'Brien .30 .75
18 Jean-Gabriel Pageau .30 .75
19 Andre Petersson .30 .75
20 Shane Prince .30 .75
21 Matt Puempel .30 .75
22 Buddy Robinson .30 .75
23 Troy Rutkowski .30 .75
24 Cole Schneider .30 .75
25 Michael Sdao .30 .75
26 Steve Stirling Asst. CO Luke Richardson CO .30 .75
27 Mark Stone .75 2.00
28 Chris Wideman .30 .75
29 Mika Zibanejad .50 1.25

2014-15 Binghamton Senators

COMPLETE SET (30) 8.00 20.00
1 Fredrik Claesson .30 .75
2 Michael Sdao .30 .75
3 Chris Wideman .30 .75
4 Daniel New .30 .75
5 Matt Puempel .40 1.00
6 Buddy Robinson .30 .75
7 Carter Camper .30 .75
8 Danny Hobbs .30 .75
9 Patrick Mullen .30 .75
10 Cole Schneider .30 .75
11 Garrett Thompson .30 .75
12 Max McCormick .30 .75
13 Shane Prince .40 1.00
14 Brad Mills .30 .75
15 Alex Grant .30 .75
16 David Dziurzynski .40 1.00
17 Alex Guptill .30 .75
18 Darren Kramer .30 .75
19 Jakub Culek .30 .75
20 Ryan Dzingel .30 .75
21 Jean-Gabriel Pageau .40 1.00
22 Derek Grant .30 .75
23 Aaron Johnson .30 .75
24 Andrew Hammond 2.00 5.00
25 Chris Driedger .30 .75
26 Scott Greenham .30 .75
27 Luke Richardson CO .30 .75
28 Steve Stirling Asst. CO .30 .75
29 Tim Marks Video CO .30 .75
30 Tom Severance Equip. Mgr. .30 .75

1992-93 Birmingham Bulls

COMPLETE SET (23) 3.00 8.00
1 Logo Card .02 .10
2 Jim Larkin .15 .40
3 Brett Barnett .15 .40
4 Joe Flanagan .15 .40
5 Butch Kaebel .15 .40
6 Scott Matusovich .15 .40
7 Chuck Hughes .15 .40
8 Dave Craievich .15 .40
9 Alexander Khavanov .15 .40
10 Paul Marshall .15 .40
11 Jim Peters .15 .40
12 Chris Marshall .15 .40
13 Jerome Bechard .15 .40
14 Jean-Alain Schneider .15 .40
15 Kevin Kerr .15 .40
16 Rob Krauss .15 .40
17 Greg Burke .15 .40
18 Mark Romaine .15 .40
19 Bruce Garber CO .02 .10
20 Phil Roberto ASST CO .08 .25
21 Dave Cavaliere TR .02 .10
22 Tim Woodburn ANN .02 .10
NNO Team Logo/CL .02 .10

1993-94 Birmingham Bulls

COMPLETE SET (23) 4.00 10.00
1 Logo Card .02 .10
2 Jim Larkin .20 .50
3 Brett Barnett .20 .50
4 Joe Flanagan .20 .50
5 Butch Kaebel .20 .50
6 Scott Matusovich .20 .50
7 Chuck E. Hughes .20 .50
8 Dave Craievich .20 .50
9 Alexander Khavanov .75 2.00
10 Paul Marshall .20 .50
11 Jim Peters .20 .50
12 Chris Marshall .20 .50
13 Jerome Bechard .20 .50
14 Jean-Alain Schneider .20 .50
15 Kevin Kerr .20 .50
16 Rob Krauss .20 .50
17 Greg Burke .20 .50
18 Mark Romaine .20 .50
19 Bruce Garber CO .02 .10
20 Phil Roberto ACO .20 .50
21 Dave Cavaliere TR .02 .10
22 Tim Woodburn ANN .02 .10
NNO Title Card CL .02 .10

1993-94 Birmingham Bulls Birmingham News

COMPLETE SET (27) 4.80 12.00
1 Phil Roberto CO .07 .20
2 Phil Roberto CO .07 .20
3 Jerome Bechard .20 .50
4 Marc Beran .20 .50
5 Dave Craievich .20 .50
6 Murray Duval .20 .50
7 Dan Fournel .30 .75
8 Jon Duval .20 .50
9 Joe Flanagan .20 .50
10 Todd Harris .20 .50
11 Bill Kovacs .20 .50
12 Jim Larkin .20 .50
13 Paul Marshall .20 .50
14 Jim Mill .30 .75
15 Brad Mullahy .20 .50
16 Tom Neziol .20 .50
17 Darcy Norton .20 .50
18 Jay Schiavo .20 .50
19 J.A. Schneider .20 .50
20 Brad Smyth .30 .75
21 Rick Girhiny .20 .50
22 Sandy Galuppo .20 .50
23 Jamie Linden .30 .75
24 Ed Krayer ACO .02 .10
25 Joel Stern ANN .02 .10
26 Mark Mills EQM .02 .10
27 Header Card/CL .02 .10

1994-95 Birmingham Bulls

COMPLETE SET (22) 3.00 8.00
1 Greg Bailey .15 .40
2 Norm Bazin .15 .40
3 Jerome Bechard .15 .40
4 Dave Boyd .15 .40
5 David Craievich .15 .40
6 Rob Donovan .15 .40
7 Jon Duval .15 .40
8 Sandy Galuppo .20 .50
9 Todd Harris .15 .40
10 Ian Hebert .15 .40
11 Craig Johnson .15 .40
12 John Joyce .15 .40
13 Chris Kerber ANN .02 .10
14 Olaf Kjenstad .20 .50
15 Mike Krassner EQMG .02 .10
16 Jim Larkin .15 .40
17 Craig Lutes .15 .40
18 Mark Michaud .15 .40
19 Jean-Marc Plante .15 .40
20 Phil Roberto CO .15 .40
21 Brad Smyth .15 .40
22 Title Card CL .02 .10

1995-96 Birmingham Bulls

COMPLETE SET (29) 4.00 10.00
1 Toro the Bull .02 .10
2 Phil Roberto CO .08 .25
3 Lance Brady .20 .50
4 Jeff Wells .20 .50
5 Brad Prefontaine .20 .50
6 Mark Raiter .20 .50
7 Rob Donovan .20 .50
8 Chris Grenville .20 .50
9 Colin Gregor .20 .50
10 Mike Lafendresse .30 .75
11 John Morabito .20 .50
12 Brendan Creagh .20 .50
13 Chris Bergeron .20 .50
14 Jerome Bechard .20 .50
15 Craig Lutes .20 .50
16 Ian Hebert .20 .50
17 John Joyce .20 .50
18 Jeff Callinan .20 .50
19 Jason Dexter .20 .50
20 Olaf Kjenstad .20 .50
21 Chad Erickson .30 .75
22 Ray Pack EQMG .02 .10
23 Chris Kerber ANN .02 .10
24 M.Coulter S.Griffi DJs .02 .10
25 Doug Laxton DJ .02 .10
26 Randy Armstrong DJ .02 .10
27 Lee Davis DJ .02 .10
28 Herb Winches DJ .02 .10
29 Ben Cook DJ .02 .10

1982-83 Birmingham South Stars

COMPLETE SET (16) 24.00 60.00
1 Frank Beaton 1.25 3.00
2 Bob Bergloff 1.25 3.00
3 Bob Boileau 1.25 3.00
4 Rollie Boutin 1.25 3.00
5 Murray Brumwell 1.25 3.00
6 Steve Carlson 8.00 20.00
7 Dave Debol .75 2.00
8 Jim Dobson .75 2.00
9 Dave Richter 1.25 3.00
10 Keith Hanson .75 2.00
11 Peter Hayek .75 2.00
12 Glenn Hicks .75 2.00
13 Craig Homola .75 2.00
14 Wes Jarvis 1.25 3.00
15 Warren Young 2.00 5.00
16 Markus Mattsson 1.25 3.00

2013-14 Blainville-Boisbriand Armada

1 Aaron Hoyles .30 .75
2 Etienne Marcoux .30 .75
3 Marcus Hinds .30 .75
4 Frederic Bergeron .30 .75
5 Daniel Walcott .30 .75
6 Guillaume Beaudoin .30 .75
7 Nikita Jevpalovs .30 .75
8 Danick Martel .30 .75
9 Christopher Clapperton .30 .75
10 Samuel Montembeault .30 .75
11 Guillaume Decelles .30 .75
12 Samuel Tremblay .30 .75
13 Joseph Strong .30 .75
14 Antoine Dufort-Plante .30 .75
15 Ryan Tesink .30 .75
16 Julien Bahl .30 .75
17 Tyler Brown .30 .75
18 Philippe Sanche .30 .75
19 Marco Roy .30 .75
20 David Bedard .30 .75
21 Emil Aronsson .30 .75
22 Samuel Hodhod .30 .75
23 Nathanael Halbert .30 .75
24 Olivier Picard .30 .75

2015-16 Blainville-Boisbriand Armada

COMPLETE SET (23) 6.00 15.00
1 Morgan Adams-Moisan .30 .75
2 Guillaume Beaudoin .30 .75
3 Guillaume Bergeron-Charron .30 .75
4 Anthony Boucher .30 .75
5 Connor Bramwell .30 .75
6 Antoine Crete-Belzile .30 .75
7 Alexandre Delisle-Houde .30 .75
8 Mark Grametbauer .30 .75
9 Nathanael Halbert .30 .75
10 Brendan Hamelin .30 .75
11 Tyler Hylland .30 .75
12 Alexander Katerinakis .30 .75
13 T.J. Melancon .30 .75
14 Yvan-Gabriel Mongo .30 .75
15 Samuel Montembeault .30 .75
16 Miguel Picard .30 .75
17 Kristian Pospisil .30 .75
18 Charlie Roy .30 .75
19 Philippe Sanche .30 .75
20 Olivier Schingh-Gomez .30 .75
21 Joel Teasdale .30 .75
22 Matthew Thorpe .30 .75
23 Samuel Tremblay .30 .75

2006-07 Bloomington PrairieThunder

COMPLETE SET (24) 8.00 15.00
1 Mike Adamek .30 .75
2 Trevor Baker .30 .75
3 Jon Booras .30 .75
4 Jarad Bourassa .30 .75
5 Steffan Braunlich .30 .75
6 John Spoltore .30 .75
7 Mike Zbriger .30 .75
8 B.J. Gaustad .30 .75
9 Ryan Gillis .30 .75
10 Alex Goupil .30 .75
11 Dion Hyman .30 .75
12 Andrew Lackner .30 .75
13 Andre Niec .30 .75
14 Jason Payne .30 .75
15 Mark Phenow .30 .75
16 Tyler Rennette .30 .75
17 Jeff Reynaert .30 .75
18 Shawn Roed .30 .75
19 Tim Schneider .30 .75
20 Chip MASCOT .02 .10
21 Brad Thompson .30 .75
22 Derek Booth CO .10 .25
23 Clay Roffer EQ MGR .02 .10
24 Chris Walter TR .02 .10

2001-02 Bossier-Shreveport Mudbugs

COMPLETE SET (24) 4.00 10.00
1 Tony Bergin .20 .50
2 Trevor Buchanan .20 .50
3 Jason Campbell .20 .50
4 Bob Case TR .04 .10
5 Greg Foster .20 .50
6 Tim Hill .20 .50
7 Mike Johnson .20 .50
8 Derek Kups .20 .50
9 Bill Lang .20 .50
10 Chad Lang .30 .75
11 Dave Lemay .30 .75
12 Forbes MacPherson .20 .50
13 David Mills .20 .50
14 Scott Muscutt CO .04 .10
15 Pat Powers .20 .50
16 Ryan Rintoul .20 .50
17 Mark Rupnow .20 .50
18 Corey Smith .20 .50
19 Jim Sprott .20 .50
20 Brandon Walker BR .04 .10
21 Billy Welker EQMG .04 .10
22 Dan Wildfong .20 .50
23 Clawed MASCOT .04 .10
24 Team Photo .10 .25

2002-03 Bossier-Shreveport Mudbugs

COMPLETE SET (24) 6.00 15.00
1 Jason Basile .30 .75
2 Tony Bergin .30 .75
3 Chris Brassard .30 .75
4 Trevor Buchanan .30 .75

5 Dru Burgess .30 .75
6 Jason Campbell .30 .75
7 Ken Carroll .30 .75
8 Chris Chelios .30 .75
9 Jonathan Forest .30 .75
10 Jeff Glowa .30 .75
11 Willie Hubloo .30 .75
12 Forbes MacPherson .30 .75
13 Craig Minard .30 .75
14 David Oliver .30 .75
15 Mark Rupnow .30 .75
16 Jim Sprott .30 .75
17 Chad Spurr .30 .75
18 Luc Theoret .30 .75
19 Dan Wildfong .30 .75
20 Scott Muscutt CO .04 .10
21 George Bullock Jr. TR .04 .10
21 Billy Welker EQM .04 .10
23 Team Photo .20 .50
24 Steve Mears ANN .04 .10

2003-04 Bossier-Shreveport Mudbugs

COMPLETE SET (25) 6.00 15.00
1 Jason Basile .40 1.00
2 Travis Bell .30 .75
3 Jeff Blair .30 .75
4 Wes Blevins .30 .75
5 Chris Brassard .30 .75
6 Trevor Buchanan .30 .75
7 Jason Campbell .30 .75
8 Ken Carroll .30 .75
9 Colin Kendall .30 .75
10 Quade Lightbody .40 1.00
11 Forbes MacPherson .30 .75
12 Ryan Manitowich .30 .75
13 Craig Minard .40 1.00
14 David Oliver .30 .75
15 Craig Soke .30 .75
16 Jim Sprott .30 .75
17 Chad Spurr .30 .75
18 Dan Wildfong .30 .75
19 Scott Muscutt CO .04 .10
20 John Madden OWN .04 .10
21 George Bullock Jr. TR .04 .10
22 Billy Welker EQM .04 .10
23 Mascot .04 .10
24 Team photo .20 .50
25 Steve Mears ANN .04 .10

2005-06 Bossier-Shreveport Mudbugs

COMPLETE SET (26) 6.00 15.00
1 Jason Basile .30 .75
2 Chris Brassard .30 .75
3 David Cacciola .30 .75
4 Jason Campbell .30 .75
5 Ken Carroll .30 .75
6 Jeremy Downs .30 .75
7 Chad Kemp .30 .75
8 Quade Lightbody .40 1.00
9 Dale Lupul .30 .75
10 Ryan Manitowich .30 .75
11 Blair Manning .30 .75
12 Craig Minard .30 .75
13 Shane Palahicky .30 .75
14 Chris Shaw .30 .75
15 Scott Sheppard .30 .75
16 Brett Smith .30 .75
17 Chad Spurr .30 .75
18 Martin Stuchlik .30 .75
19 Milan Vodrazka .30 .75
20 Dan Wildfong .30 .75
21 Scott Muscutt HC .02 .10
22 Trevor Buchanan AC .02 .10
23 Billy Welker EM .02 .10
24 Clawed & Lil' Bugger MASCOTS .02 .10
25 George Bullock Jr. TR .02 .10
26 Steve Mears ANNCR .02 .10

2003-04 Boston College Eagles

COMPLETE SET (7) 5.00 10.00
1 Ben Eaves .75 2.00
2 Tony Voce .75 2.00
3 Brett Peterson .75 2.00
4 Ty Hennes .75 2.00
5 J.D. Forrest .75 2.00
6 Justin Dziama .75 2.00
7 Team Photo .40 1.00

2003-04 Boston University Terriers

COMPLETE SET (27) 10.00 25.00
1 Mark Mullen .40 1.00
2 Stephen Siwiec .40 1.00
3 Gregg Johnson .40 1.00
4 John Laliberte .40 1.00
5 Thomas Morrow .40 1.00
6 Jack Parker HCO .40 1.00
7 Stephen Greeley .40 1.00
8 Brian McConnell .40 1.00
9 E.J. Solimine .40 1.00
10 Sean Fields .40 1.00
11 Bryan Miller .40 1.00
12 Jakabs Redlihs .40 1.00
13 Kevin Schaeffer .40 1.00
14 Brad Zancanaro .40 1.00
15 Sean Sullivan .40 1.00
16 Ryan Whitney 1.25 3.00
17 David Van Der Gulik .40 1.00
18 Eric Thomassian .40 1.00
19 Ken Roche .40 1.00
20 David Klema .40 1.00
21 Dan Spang .40 1.00
22 Ken Magowan .40 1.00
23 Matt Radoslovich .40 1.00
24 Harry Agganis Arena .04 .10
25 John Curry .40 1.00
26 Frantisek Skladany .60 1.50
27 Mascot .04 .10

2009-10 Boston University Terriers

1 Eric Gryba .40 1.00
2 Kevin Shattenkirk .40 1.00
3 Ryan Ruikka .40 1.00
4 David Warsofsky .40 1.00
5 Joe Pereira .40 1.00
6 Max Nicastro .40 1.00
7 Ben Rosen .40 1.00
8 Alex Chiasson .40 1.00
9 Corey Trivino .40 1.00
10 Zach Cohen .40 1.00
11 Chris Connolly .40 1.00
12 Nick Bonino .40 1.00
13 Andrew Glass .40 1.00
14 Ryan Santana .40 1.00
15 Kevin Gilroy .40 1.00
16 Victor Saponari .40 1.00
17 Wade Megan .40 1.00
18 Justin Courtnall .40 1.00
19 Sean Escobedo .40 1.00
20 Ross Gaudet .40 1.00
21 Colby Cohen .40 1.00
22 Luke Popko .40 1.00
23 Vinny Saponari .40 1.00
24 Kieran Millan .40 1.00
25 Adam Kraus .40 1.00
26 Grant Rollheiser .40 1.00

2014-15 Boston University Terriers

COMPLETE SET (27) 25.00 50.00
1 Robbie Baillargeon .30 .75
2 J.D. Carrabino .30 .75
3 Brien Diffley .30 .75
4 Kevin Duane .30 .75
5 Jack Eichel 20.00 40.00
6 Brandon Fortunato .30 .75
7 A.J. Greer .30 .75
8 Matt Grzelcyk .30 .75
9 Brandon Hickey .30 .75
10 Cason Hohmann .30 .75
11 Tommy Kelley .30 .75
12 Connor LaCouvee .30 .75
13 Matthew Lane .30 .75
14 Dillon Lawrence .30 .75
15 Johnathan MacLeod .30 .75
16 Anthony Moccia .30 .75
17 Michael Moran .30 .75
18 Matt O'Connor .30 .75
19 Ahti Oksanen .30 .75
20 Nikolas Olsson .30 .75
21 Daniel O'Regan .30 .75
22 Chase Phelps .30 .75
23 J.J. Piccinich .30 .75
24 Nick Roberto .30 .75
25 Evan Rodrigues .30 .75
26 T.J. Ryan .30 .75
27 Doyle Somerby .30 .75

2003-04 Bowling Green Falcons

COMPLETE SET (18) 12.00 30.00
1 Brian Holzinger .75 2.00
2 Brian Escobedo .40 1.00
3 Alex Rogosheske .40 1.00
4 George McPhee .40 1.00
5 Garry Galley .75 2.00
6 D'Arcy McConvey .40 1.00
7 Rob Blake 2.00 5.00
8 Mark Wires .40 1.00
9 Jordan Sigalet 2.00 5.00
10 Steve Brudzewski .75 2.00
11 Erik Eaton .75 2.00
12 Dan Kane .75 2.00
13 Gary Kruzich .75 2.00
14 Dave Ellet .75 2.00
15 Kevin Bieksa .75 2.00
16 Ryan Minnabarriet .75 2.00
17 Gino Cavallini .75 2.00
18 John Samanski .75 2.00

1999-00 Brampton Battalion

COMPLETE SET (27) 10.00 25.00
1 Header Card .02 .10
2 Team Photo .08 .25
3 David Chant .60 1.50
4 Scott Della Vedova .08 .25
5 Tyler Hanchuck .08 .25
6 Jason Maleyko .08 .25
7 Paul Flache .08 .25
8 Cam McLaughlin .08 .25
9 Rostislav Klesla .60 1.50
10 Brad Woods .08 .25
11 Raffi Torres .75 2.00
12 Matt Reynolds .08 .25
13 Chris Rowan .08 .25
14 Lukas Havel .08 .25
15 Mike Rice .08 .25
16 Tyler Dukelow .08 .25
17 Jay McClement .20 .50
18 Matt Grennier .08 .25
19 Kurt MacSweyn .08 .25
21 Chris Cook .08 .25
21 Aaron Van Leusen .08 .25
22 Jay Harrison .40 1.00
23 Richard Kearns .08 .25
24 Jeff Bateman .20 .50
25 Scott Thompson .08 .25
26 Blair McLaughlin .08 .25
27 Jason Spezza 4.00 10.00
28 Stan Butler CO .08 .25
29 Bobby Jones .08 .25
30 Raffi Torres .75 2.00
31 Jason Maleyko .08 .25
32 Inaugural Season .02 .10

2000-01 Brampton Battalion

COMPLETE SET (32) 6.00 15.00
1 Logo .02 .10
2 Team Picture .02 .10
3 2001 WJC Banner .02 .10
4 Brian Finley .30 .75
5•Travis Parent .20 .50
6 Jason Maleyko .20 .50
7 Paul Flache .20 .50
8 Corey LeClair .20 .50
9 Rostislav Klesla .60 1.50
10 Adam Henrich .20 .50
11 Raffi Torres .60 1.50
12 Chris Clayton .20 .50
13 Chris Rowan .20 .50
14 Lukas Havel .20 .50
15 Jonah Leroux .20 .50
16 Jay McClement .20 .50
17 Kurt MacSweyn .20 .50
18 Aaron Van Leusen .20 .50
19 Jay Harrison .30 .75
20 Ryan Bowness .20 .50
21 Jeff Bateman .20 .50
22 Scott Thompson .20 .50
23 Alex MacDonell .20 .50
24 Anthony Marshall .20 .50
25 Brad Topping .20 .50
26 Stan Butler HCO .02 .10
27 Derrick Smith ACO .02 .10
28 Rostislav Klesla All-Star .60 1.50
29 Raffi Torres All-Star .60 1.50
30 Jay Harrison/1998 First Round .30 .75
31 Jay McClement/1999 First Round .20 .50
32 Adam Henrich/2000 First Round .20 .50

2003-04 Brampton Batallion

COMPLETE SET (24) 5.00 12.00
1 Ryan Bowness .20 .50
2 Chris Clayton .20 .50
3 Kevin Couture .30 .75
4 Nick Duff .20 .50
5 Jamie Fraser .20 .50
6 Tyler Harrison .20 .50
7 Robert Heickert .20 .50
8 Adam Henrich .20 .50
9 Kamil Kreps .60 1.50
10 Aaron Lobb .20 .50
11 Martin Lojek .20 .50
12 Howie Martin .20 .50
13 Eliott McCormick .20 .50
14 Brock McPherson .20 .50
15 Geordie Michie .20 .50
16 Phil Oreskovic .20 .50
17 Ryan Oulahen .20 .50
18 Erik Schwanz .20 .50
19 John Seymour .20 .50
20 Stuart Simmons .20 .50
21 Rob Smith .20 .50
22 Patrick Sweeney .20 .50
23 Brad Topping .30 .75
24 Wojtek Wolski .60 1.50
NNO Kamil Kreps LTD .20 .50

2004-05 Brampton Battalion

COMPLETE SET (25) 12.00
1 Wojtek Wolski .60 1.50
2 Daren Machesney .20 .50
3 Kevin Couture .20 .50
4 Michael Vernace .20 .50
5 Stuart Simmons .20 .50
6 Phil Oreskovic .30 .75
7 Nick Duff .20 .50
8 Martin Lojek .20 .50
9 Tomas Stryncl .20 .50
10 Danny McDonald .20 .50
11 Aaron Snow .20 .50
12 Brock McPherson .20 .50
13 John de Gray .20 .50
14 Howie Martin .20 .50
15 Luke Lynes .20 .50
16 Graham McNabb .20 .50
17 Luch Aquino .20 .50
18 John Seymour .20 .50
19 Patrick Sweeney .20 .50
20 Tyler Harrison .20 .50
21 J.F. Houle .20 .50
22 Scott Boomsma .20 .50
23 Jason Cassidy .20 .50
24 Ryan Oulahen .20 .50
25 Kyle Sonnenberg .20 .50

2005-06 Brampton Battalion

COMPLETE SET (25) 5.00 12.00
1 Wojtek Wolski .60 1.50
2 Phil Oreskovic .20 .50
3 Nick Duff .20 .50
4 John de Gray .20 .50
5 Daren Machesney .20 .50
6 Bryan Pitton .20 .50
7 Michael Vernace .20 .50
8 Tomas Stryncl .20 .50
9 Stephane Chabot .20 .50
10 Aaron Snow .20 .50
11 Matt Smyth .20 .50
12 Howie Martin .20 .50
13 Luke Lynes .20 .50
14 Graham McNabb .20 .50
15 Justin Levac .20 .50
16 Luch Aquino .20 .50
17 John Seymour .20 .50
18 Nolan Waker .20 .50
19 Taylor Raszka .20 .50
20 Cody Smith .20 .50
21 Jason Cassidy .20 .50
22 Michal Kljna .20 .50
23 Kyle Sonnenburg .20 .50
24 Corey George .20 .50
25 Brock McPherson .20 .50

2006-07 Brampton Battalion

COMPLETE SET (23) 6.00 15.00
1 Sarge's Checklist .02 .10
2 Patrick Killeen .30 .75
3 Bryan Pitton .30 .75
4 Ken Peroff .30 .75
5 Dalyn Flatt .30 .75
6 Brad Albert .30 .75
7 Tomas Stryncl .30 .75
8 Stephane Chabot .30 .75
9 John De Gray .30 .75
10 Kyle Sonnenburg .30 .75
11 Conor O'Donnell .30 .75
12 Matt Smyth .30 .75
13 Thomas Stajan .30 .75
14 Luke Lynes .30 .75
15 Graham McNabb .30 .75
16 Jason Dale .30 .75
17 Justin Levac .30 .75
18 Cody Hodgson .75 2.00
19 John Seymour .30 .75
20 Mike Lomas .30 .75
21 John Hughes .30 .75
22 Kyle Decoste .30 .75
23 Michal Klejna .30 .75

2009-10 Brampton Battalion

1 Patrick Killeen .40 1.00
2 Ken Peroff .40 1.00
3 Kyle Pereira .40 1.00
4 Ben Alavie .40 1.00
5 Matt Clark .40 1.00
6 Brad Albert .40 1.00
7 Zach Bell .40 1.00
8 Cameron Wind .40 1.00
9 Phil Lane .40 1.00
10 Scott Tanski .40 1.00
11 Craig Moore .40 1.00
12 Thomas Stajan .40 1.00
13 Sam Carrick .40 1.00
14 Sean Jones .40 1.00
15 Stephon Thorne .40 1.00
16 Cody Hodgson .40 1.00
17 Domenic Alberga .40 1.00
18 Shane Kinsella .40 1.00
19 Barclay Goodrow .40 1.00
20 Matt MacLeod .40 1.00
21 Alex O'Neil .40 1.00
22 Ian Watters .40 1.00
23 Jacob Riley .40 1.00

1982-83 Brandon Wheat Kings

COMPLETE SET (24) 12.00 30.00
1 Wheat Kings Logo .20 .50
2 Kevin Pylypow .30 .75
3 Dean Kennedy .40 1.00
4 Sonny Sodke .30 .75
5 Darren Schmidt .30 .75
6 Cam Plante .30 .75
7 Sid Cranston .30 .75
8 Bruce Thomson .30 .75
9 Dave McDowall CO .20 .50
10 Bill Vince .30 .75
11 Kelly Glowa .30 .75
12 Tom McMurchy .30 .75
13 Ed Palichuk .30 .75
14 Roy Caswell .30 .75
15 Allan Tarasuk .30 .75
16 Brent Jessiman .30 .75
17 Randy Slawson .30 .75
18 Gord Smith .30 .75
19 Mike Sturgeon .30 .75
20 Larry Bumstead .30 .75
21 Kirk Blomquist .30 .75
22 Ron Loustel .30 .75
23 Ron Hextall 6.00 15.00
24 Brandon Police Logo .08 .25

1983-84 Brandon Wheat Kings

COMPLETE SET (24) 10.00 25.00
1 Bryan Wells .20 .50
2 Jim Agnew .40 1.00
3 Gord Paddock .20 .50
4 John Dzikowski .20 .50
5 Kelly Kozack .20 .50
6 Byron Lomow .20 .50
7 Pat Loyer .20 .50
8 Rob Ordman .20 .50
9 Brad Wells .20 .50
10 Dave Thomlinson .30 .75
11 Cam Plante .20 .50
12 Jay Palmer .30 .75
13 Boyd Lomow .20 .50
14 Brent Jessiman .20 .50
15 Paul More .20 .50
16 Stacy Prtt .20 .50
17 Brandon City Police .08 .25
18 Jack Sangster CO .20 .50
19 Derek Laxdal .30 .75
20 Ray Ferraro 2.00 5.00
21 Allan Tarasuk .20 .50
22 Randy Cameron .20 .50
23 Dave Curry .20 .50
24 Ron Hextall 4.00 10.00

1984-85 Brandon Wheat Kings

COMPLETE SET (24) 4.80 12.00
1 Garnet Kazuik .20 .50
2 Brent Mireau .20 .50
3 Byron Lomow .20 .50
4 Dean Shaw .20 .50
5 Dean Sexsmith .20 .50
6 Brad Mueller .20 .50
7 John Dzikowski .20 .50
8 Artie Feher .20 .50
9 Pat Loyer .20 .50
10 Murray Rice .20 .50
11 Derek Laxdal .30 .75
12 Perry Fafard .20 .50
13 Lee Trim .20 .50
14 Dan Hart .20 .50
15 Trent Ciprick .20 .50
16 Jeff Waver .20 .50
17 Brandon Wheat Kings .20 .50
18 Jack Sangster CO .08 .25
19 Darwin McPherson .20 .50
20 Pokey Reddick .75 2.00
21 Boyd Lomow .20 .50
22 Dave Thomlinson .30 .75
23 Paul More .20 .50
24 Brent Severyn .40 1.00

1985-86 Brandon Wheat Kings

COMPLETE SET (24) 4.80 12.00
1 Kelly Hitchins .20 .50
2 Brent Mireau .20 .50
3 Byron Lomow .20 .50
4 Bob Heeney .20 .50
5 Dean Sexsmith .20 .50
6 Dave Curry .20 .50
7 John Dzikowski .20 .50
8 Artie Feher .20 .50
9 Kevin Mayo .20 .50
10 Murray Rice .20 .50
11 Derek Laxdal .40 1.00
12 Al Cherniwchan .20 .50
13 Lee Trim .20 .50
14 Terry Yake .40 1.00
15 Trent Ciprick .20 .50
16 Jeff Waver .20 .50
17 Team Photo .20 .50
18 Jack Sangster CO .20 .50
19 Mike Morin .20 .50
20 Jason Phillips .20 .50
21 Rod Williams .20 .50
22 Dave Thomlinson .40 1.00
23 Shane Eirickson .20 .50
24 Randy Hoffart .20 .50

1988-89 Brandon Wheat Kings

COMPLETE SET (24) 6.00 15.00
1 Kevin Cheveldayoff .20 .50
2 Bob Woods .20 .50
3 Dwayne Newman .20 .50
4 Mike Vandenberghe .20 .50
5 Brad Woods .20 .50
6 Gary Audette .20 .50
7 Mark Bassen .20 .50
8 Troy Frederick .20 .50
9 Troy Kennedy .20 .50
10 Barry Dreger .20 .50
11 Bill Whistle .20 .50
12 Jeff Odgers .40 1.00
13 Sheldon Kowalchuk .20 .50
14 Chris Robertson .20 .50
15 Don Laurin .20 .50
16 Curtis Folkett .20 .50
17 Team Photo .20 .50
18 Kelly McCrimmon ACO .20 .50
19 Doug Sauter CO .20 .50
20 Kelly Hitchins .20 .50
21 Trevor Kidd 1.25 3.00
22 Pryce Wood .20 .50
23 Cam Brown .20 .50
24 Greg Hutchings .20 .50

1989-90 Brandon Wheat Kings

COMPLETE SET (24) 4.80 12.00
1 Trevor Kidd 1.25 3.00
2 Troy Frederick .20 .50
3 Kelly Thiessen .30 .75
4 Pryce Wood .20 .50
5 Mike Vandenberghe .20 .50
6 Chris Constant .20 .50
7 Hardy Sauter .20 .50
8 Cam Brown .20 .50
9 Bart Cote .20 .50
10 Jeff Hoad .20 .50
11 Kevin Robertson .20 .50
12 Dwayne Newman .20 .50
13 Calvin Flint .20 .50
14 Glen Webster .20 .50
15 Greg Hutchings .30 .75
16 Rob Puchniak .20 .50
17 Gary Audette .20 .50
18 Kevin Schmalz .20 .50
19 Dwayne Gylywoychuk .20 .50
20 Jeff Odgers .30 .75
21 Brian Purdy .20 .50
22 Merv Priest .20 .50
23 Doug Sauter CO .08 .25
24 Team Photo .20 .50

1990-91 Brandon Wheat Kings

COMPLETE SET (24) 5.60 14.00
1 Jeff Hoad .20 .50
2 Merv Priest .20 .50
3 Mike Vandenberghe .20 .50
4 Bart Cote .20 .50
5 Hardy Sauter .20 .50
6 Mark Johnston ACO .08 .25
7 Kelly McCrimmon CO .08 .25
8 Team Photo .20 .50
9 Kevin Robertson .20 .50
10 Glen Webster .20 .50
11 Greg Hutchings .20 .50
12 Dan Kopec .20 .50
13 Dwayne Gylywoychuk .20 .50
14 Brian Purdy .20 .50
15 Trevor Kidd 1.25 3.00
16 Johan Skillgard .20 .50
17 Stu Scantlebury .20 .50
18 Byron Penstock .20 .50
19 Rob Puchniak .20 .50
20 Gary Audette .20 .50
21 Calvin Flint .20 .50
22 Jason White .20 .50
23 Chris Constant .20 .50
24 Glen Gulutzan .20 .50

1992-93 Brandon Wheat Kings

COMPLETE SET (24) 4.00 10.00
1 Aris Brimanis .15 .40
2 Colin Cloutier .20 .50
3 Chris Dingman .30 .75
4 Mike Dubinsky .20 .50
5 Todd Dutiaume .15 .40
6 Mark Franks .15 .40
7 Craig Geekie .15 .40
8 Dwayne Gylywoychuk .15 .40
9 Scott Hlady .15 .40
10 Jeff Hoad .15 .40
11 Bobby House .15 .40
12 Chris Johnston .15 .40
13 Mark Kolesar .20 .50
14 Scott Laluk .15 .40
15 Mike Maneluk .20 .50
16 Sean McFatridge .15 .40
17 Marty Murray .30 .75
18 Byron Penstock .20 .50
19 Darren Ritchie .15 .40
20 Trevor Robins .20 .50
21 Ryan Smith .15 .40
22 Jeff Staples .15 .40
23 Darcy Werenka .20 .50
24 Willie MASCOT .02 .10

1993-94 Brandon Wheat Kings

COMPLETE SET (24) 6.00 15.00
1 Byron Penstock .30 .75
2 Craig Hordal .30 .75
3 Jeff Staples .20 .50
4 Scott Laluk .20 .50
5 Wade Redden .75 2.00
6 Justin Kurtz .30 .75
7 Sven Butenschon .20 .50
8 Adam Magarrell .20 .50
9 Dwayne Gylywoychuk .20 .50
10 Scott Hlady .20 .50
11 Joel Korenko .20 .50
12 Chris Johnston .20 .50
13 Bobby Brown .20 .50
14 Mark Kolesar .20 .50
15 Chris Low .20 .50
16 Dean Kletzel .20 .50
17 Darren Ritchie .20 .50
18 Mark Dutiaume .20 .50
19 Mike Dubinsky .20 .50
20 Chris Dingman .30 .75
21 Mike Maneluk .30 .75
22 Colin Cloutier .20 .50
23 Paul Bailley .20 .50
24 Marty Murray .30 .75

1994-95 Brandon Wheat Kings

COMPELTE SET (24) 6.00 15.00
1 Bobby Brown .20 .50
2 Sven Butenschon .20 .50
3 Colin Cloutier .20 .50
4 Chris Dingman .30 .75
5 Mike Dubinsky .20 .50
6 Mark Dutiaume .20 .50
7 Brian Elder .20 .50
8 Dean Kletzel .20 .50
9 Joel Korenko .20 .50
10 Justin Kurtz .30 .75
11 Scott Laluk .20 .50
12 Chris Low .20 .50
13 Adam Magarrell .20 .50
14 Marty Murray .20 .50
15 Byron Penstock .20 .50
16 Kevin Pozzo .20 .50
17 Wade Redden .75 2.00
18 Darren Ritchie .20 .50
19 Peter Schaefer .30 .75
20 Kelly Smart .20 .50
21 Jeff Staples .20 .50
22 Oleg Tverdovsky .40 1.00
23 Darren Van Oene .20 .50
24 Ian Walterson .20 .50

1995-96 Brandon Wheat Kings

COMPLETE SET (24) 6.00 15.00
1 Bobby Brown .20 .50
2 Sven Butenschon .20 .50
3 Stefan Cherneski .20 .50
4 Cory Cyrenne .30 .75
5 David Draguzas .20 .50
6 Chris Dingman .30 .75
7 Mark Dutiaume .20 .50
8 Brian Elder .20 .50
9 Burke Henry .20 .50
10 Vincent Jonasson .20 .50
11 Dean Kletzel .20 .50
12 Justin Kurtz .30 .75
13 Mike LeClerc .40 1.00
14 Andrei Lupandin .20 .50
15 Wade Redden .75 2.00
16 Ryan Robson .20 .50
17 Peter Schaefer .30 .75
18 Jason Skilnick .20 .50
19 Kelly Smart .20 .50
20 Daryl Stockham .20 .50
21 Jeff Temple .20 .50
22 Daniel Tetrault .20 .50
23 Gerhard Unterluggauer .20 .50
24 Darren Van Oene .30 .75

1996-97 Brandon Wheat Kings

COMPLETE SET (24) 7.00 12.00
1 Les Borsheim .20 .50
2 Daniel Tetrault .20 .50
3 Burke Henry .40 1.00
4 Darryl Stockham .20 .50
5 Gerhard Unterluggauer .20 .50
6 Josh Woitas .20 .50
7 Mark Dutiaume .20 .50
8 Johnathan Aitken .30 .75
9 Dorian Anneck .20 .50
10 Brian Elder .20 .50
11 Andrei Lupandin .20 .50
12 Brad Twordik .20 .50
13 Jeff Katcher .20 .50
14 Kelly Smart .20 .50
15 Peter Schaefer .40 1.00
16 Ryan Robson .20 .50
17 Cory Cyrenne .40 1.00
18 Jason Boyd .20 .50
19 Darren Van Oene .20 .50
20 Stefan Cherneski .20 .50
21 Aaron Goldade .20 .50
22 Justin Kurtz .20 .50
23 David Haun .20 .50
24 Bobby Leavins .20 .50

1997-98 Brandon Wheat Kings

COMPLETE SET (26) 6.00 15.00
1 Alex Argyriou .20 .50
2 Johnathan Aitken .20 .50
3 Les Borsheim .20 .50
4 Stefan Cherneski .20 .50
5 Jomar Cruz .30 .75
6 Cory Cyrenne .30 .75
7 Brett Girard .20 .50
8 Aaron Goldade .20 .50
9 Bevin Guenther .20 .50
10 David Haun .20 .50
11 Burke Henry .20 .50
12 Jamie Hodson .40 1.00
13 Andrew Kaminsky .20 .50
14 Kirby Law .40 1.00
15 Bobby Leavins .20 .50
16 Andrei Lupandin .20 .50
17 Scott McCallum .20 .50
18 Brooks Paisley .20 .50
19 Randy Ponte .20 .50
20 Ryan Robson .20 .50
21 Wade Skolney .20 .50
22 Kelly Smart .20 .50
23 Daniel Tetrault .30 .75
24 Brent Twordik .20 .50
25 Darren Van Oene .20 .50
26 Josh Woitas .20 .50

1998-99 Brandon Wheat Kings

COMPLETE SET (24) 4.00 10.00
1 Alex Argyriou .20 .50
2 Ryan Craig .20 .50
3 Jomar Cruz .30 .75
4 Jan Fadrny .20 .50
5 Brett Girard .20 .50
6 Aaron Goldade .20 .50
7 Burke Henry .20 .50
8 Jamie Hodson .30 .75
9 Ryan Johnston .20 .50
10 J.D. Kehler .20 .50
11 Petr Kudrna .20 .50
12 Andrew Kaminsky .20 .50
13 Andrei Lupandin .20 .50
14 Scott McCallum .20 .50
15 Richard Mueller .20 .50
16 Randy Ponte .20 .50
17 Ryan Robson .20 .50
18 Wade Skolney .20 .50
19 Daniel Tetrault .20 .50
20 Brett Thurston .20 .50
21 Brad Twordik .20 .50
22 Cory Unser .20 .50
23 Mike Wirll .20 .50
24 Justin Yeoman .20 .50

1999-00 Brandon Wheat Kings

COMPLETE SET (24) 6.00 25.00
1 Mark Ardelan .20 .50
2 Milan Bartovic .20 .50
3 Les Borsheim .20 .50
4 Ryan Craig .20 .50
5 Brett Dickie .20 .50
6 Ryan Diduck .20 .50
7 Jan Fadrny .20 .50
8 Brett Girard .20 .50
9 Aaron Goldade .20 .50
10 Kevin Harris .20 .50
11 Jamie Hodson .30 .75
12 J.D. Kehler .20 .50
13 Colin McRae .20 .50
14 Robert McVicar .30 .75
15 Richard Mueller .20 .50
16 Randy Ponte .20 .50
17 Bart Rushmer .20 .50
18 Wade Skolney .20 .50
19 Daniel Tetrault .20 .50
20 Brett Thurston .20 .50
21 Jordin Tootoo 6.00 15.00
22 Brad Twordik .20 .50
23 Cory Unser .20 .50
24 Mike Wirll .20 .50

2000-01 Brandon Wheat Kings

COMPLETE SET (24) 10.00 25.00
1 Jordin Tootoo 4.00 10.00
2 Jamie Hodson .30 .75
3 Mark Ardelan .20 .50
4 Reagan Leslie .20 .50
5 Brett Thurston .20 .50
6 Travis Young .20 .50
7 Brett Dickie .20 .50
8 Richard Mueller .20 .50
9 Nolan Yonkman .30 .75
10 Brett Girard .20 .50
11 James Marquis .20 .50
12 Colin McRae .20 .50
13 Aaron Goldade .20 .50
14 Milan Bartovic .20 .50
15 J.D. Kehler .20 .50
16 Lance Monych .40 1.00
17 Tim Konsorada .20 .50
18 Caine Pearpoint .20 .50
19 Ryan Craig 1.25 3.00
20 Randy Ponte .40 1.00
21 Kevin Harris .20 .50
22 Wade Skolney .20 .50
23 Jiri Jakes .20 .50
24 Robert McVicar .30 .75

2001-02 Brandon Wheat Kings

COMPLETE SET (24) 10.00 25.00
1 Andre Blanchette .20 .50
2 Dustin Bru .20 .50
3 Ryan Craig .20 .50
4 Brett Dickie .20 .50
5 Travis Eagles .20 .50
6 Eric Fehr .20 .50
7 Adrian Foster .40 1.00
8 Josh Garbutt .30 .75
9 Kevin Harris .20 .50
10 Jiri Jakes .30 .75
11 Tim Konsorada .20 .50
12 Reagan Leslie .20 .50
13 Geoff McIntosh .20 .50
14 Colin McRae .20 .50
15 Robert McVicar .20 .50
16 Lance Monych .20 .50
17 Caine Pearpoint .20 .50
18 Randy Ponte .40 1.00
19 Wade Skolney .20 .50
20 Ryan Stone .20 .50
21 Brett Thurston .20 .50
22 Jordin Tootoo .75 2.00
23 Willie MASCOT .04 .10
24 Travis Young .20 .50

2002-03 Brandon Wheat Kings

COMPLETE SET (23) 10.00 25.00
1 Jonathan Webb .20 .50
2 Reagan Leslie .20 .50
3 Brett Thurston .20 .50
4 Bryan Nathe .20 .50
5 Brett Dickie .20 .50
6 Josh Garbutt .20 .50
7 Andre Blanchette .20 .50
8 Richard Jasovsky .20 .50
9 Tyler Dyck .20 .50
10 Derek Werenka .20 .50
11 Teegan Moore .20 .50
12 Eric Fehr 1.25 3.00
13 Ryan Stone .20 .50
14 Lance Monych .20 .50
15 Tim Konsorada .20 .50
16 Rick Kozak .20 .50
17 Jordin Tootoo 4.00 10.00
18 Greg Watson .40 1.00
19 Ryan Craig .20 .50
20 Ole-Kristian Tollefson .20 .50
21 Jeff Topilko .20 .50
22 Geoff McIntosh .30 .75
23 Robert McVicar .30 .75

2003-04 Brandon Wheat Kings

COMPLETE SET (24) 6.00 15.00
1 Josh Harding 1.25 3.00

2 Tyler Boldt .20 .50
3 Stephan Lenoski .20 .50
4 Erik Christensen .40 1.00
5 Lance Monych .40 1.00
6 Mark Derlago .20 .50
7 Corey Courchene .20 .50
8 Richard Jasovsky .20 .50
9 Tim Konsorada .20 .50
10 Codey Burki .20 .50
11 Teegan Moore .20 .50
12 Ryan Stone .40 1.00
13 Reagan Leslie .20 .50
14 Ole-Kristian Tollefsen .40 1.00
15 Steven Later .20 .50
16 Eric Fehr .75 2.00
17 Andre Blanchette .20 .50
18 Jeff Topilko .20 .50
19 Mark Louis .20 .50
20 Mark Shefchyk .20 .50
21 Jonathan Webb .20 .50
22 Tyler Dyck .20 .50
23 Derek LeBlanc .20 .50
24 Mike Nichol .20 .50

2004-05 Brandon Wheat Kings

COMPLETE SET (24) 8.00 20.00
1 Mike Nichol .30 .75
2 Jonathan Webb .30 .75
3 Corey Courchene .30 .75
4 Mike Cann .30 .75
5 Theran Yeo .30 .75
6 Steven Later .30 .75
7 Daryl Boyle .30 .75
8 Cole Hunter .30 .75
9 Sami Sandell .30 .75
10 Tyler Strautman .30 .75
11 Eric Fehr .75 2.00
12 Teegan Moore .30 .75
13 Ryan Stone .60 1.50
14 Lance Monych .40 1.00
15 Tim Konsorada .40 1.00
16 Jakub Sindel .30 .75
17 Riley Day .30 .75
18 Codey Burki .30 .75
19 Derek LeBlanc .30 .75
20 Ryan Reaves .30 .75
21 Jeff Topilko .30 .75
22 Mark Louis .30 .75
23 Stephan Lenoski .30 .75
24 Tyler Plante .30 .75

2005-06 Brandon Wheat Kings

COMPLETE SET (24) 10.00 18.00
1 Keith Aulie .30 .75
2 Daryl Boyle .30 .75
3 Codey Burki .30 .75
4 Andrew Clark .30 .75
5 Corey Courchene .30 .75
6 Riley Day .30 .75
7 Mark Derlago .30 .75
8 Tyler Dittmer .30 .75
9 Chad Erb .30 .75
10 Matt Hallick .30 .75
11 Cole Hunter .30 .75
12 Kurt Jory .30 .75
13 Bryan Kauk .30 .75
14 Dustin Kohn .30 .75
15 Stephan Lenoski .30 .75
16 Mark Louis .30 .75
17 Teegan Moore .30 .75
18 Tyler Plante .30 .75
19 Ryan Reaves .30 .75
20 Sami Sandell .30 .75
21 Tyler Strautman .30 .75
22 Jeff Topilko .30 .75
23 John Wikner .30 .75
24 Theran Yeo .30 .75

2009-10 Brandon Wheat Kings

1 Willie .40 1.00
2 Shayne Wiebe .40 1.00
3 Brenden Walker .40 1.00
4 Alexander Urbom .40 1.00
5 Mark Stone .40 1.00
6 Jesse Sinatynski .40 1.00
7 Mark Schneider .40 1.00
8 Brayden Schenn .40 1.00
9 Colby Robak .40 1.00
10 Toni Rajala .40 1.00
11 Brent Raedeke .40 1.00
12 Ryley Miller .40 1.00
13 Brodie Melnychuk .40 1.00
14 Aaron Lewadniuk .40 1.00
15 Andrew Hayes .40 1.00
16 Travis Hamonic .40 1.00
17 Jordan Hale .40 1.00
18 Scott Glennie .40 1.00
19 Michael Ferland .40 1.00
20 Jay Fehr .40 1.00
21 Jacob De Serres .40 1.00
22 Paul Ciarelli .40 1.00
23 Matt Calvert .40 1.00
24 Darren Bestland .40 1.00

2013-14 Brandon Wheat Kings

COMPLETE SET (24) 6.00 15.00
1 Rihards Bukarts .30 .75
2 Tyler Coulter .30 .75
3 Jesse Gabrielle .30 .75
4 Taylor Green .30 .75
5 Jayce Hawryluk .30 .75
6 Curtis Honey .30 .75
7 Rene Hunter .30 .75
8 Brett Kitt .30 .75
9 Ryley Lindgren .30 .75
10 Quintin Lisoway .30 .75
11 Tim McGauley .30 .75
12 Jens Meilleur .30 .75
13 Richard Nejezchleb .30 .75
14 Kord Pankewicz .30 .75
15 Jordan Papirny .30 .75
16 Ryan Pilon .30 .75
17 Ryan Pulock .30 .75
18 John Quenneville .30 .75
19 Peter Quenneville .30 .75
20 Chad Robinson .30 .75
21 Eric Roy .30 .75
22 Braylon Shmyr .30 .75
23 Colton Waltz .30 .75
24 Willie MASCOT .30 .75

1983-84 Brantford Alexanders

COMPLETE SET (30) 12.00 30.00
1 Ken Gratton ACO .20 .50
2 Shayne Corson 2.00 5.00
3 Bob Probert 4.00 10.00
4 Bruce Bell .60 1.50
5 Warren Bechard ACO .20 .50
6 Jason Lafreniere .40 1.00
7 Rob Moffat .30 .75
8 Jack Calbeck PR .20 .50
9 Marc West .30 .75
10 Larry Van Herzele .30 .75
11 Doug Stewart .30 .75
12 Brian MacDonald .30 .75
13 Dave Draper CO
GM .20 .50
14 Jeff Jackson .60 1.50
15 Steve Linseman .30 .75
16 Steve Short .30 .75
17 Allan Bester .75 2.00
18 John Weir COP .20 .50
19 Chris Pusey .30 .75
20 Mike Millar .30 .75
21 Chris Glover .30 .75
22 Bob Pierson .30 .75
23 Phil Priddle .30 .75
24 Grant Anderson .30 .75
25 Ken Gagner .30 .75
26 Andy Alway TR .20 .50
27 Todd Francis .30 .75
28 John Meulenbroeks .30 .75
29 Mike Chettleburgh .30 .75
30 Bill Dynes TR .20 .50

1994-95 Brantford Smoke

COMPLETE SET (26) 3.00 8.00
1 Checklist .02 .10
2 Bob Delorimiere .15 .40
3 Todd Francis .15 .40
4 Pete Liptrott .15 .40
5 Lorne Knauft .15 .40
6 Paul Polillo .15 .40
7 Rob Arabski .15 .40
8 Derek Gauthier .15 .40
9 Joe Simon .15 .40
10 Brad Barton .15 .40
11 Terry Chitaroni .20 .50
12 Paul Mitton .15 .40
13 Wayne MacPhee .15 .40
14 Brian Blad .20 .50
15 John Laan .15 .40
16 Shane MacEachern .15 .40
17 Wayne Muir .15 .40
18 Ted Miskolczi .15 .40
19 Marc Delorme .15 .40
20 Mike Speer .15 .40
21 Bob Baird TR
Ken Crabb .02 .10
22 Ken Gratton CO .02 .10
23 Team Photo .20 .50
24 Craig Newton .02 .10
25 Joe Lowes .02 .10
NNO Ad Card .02 .10

2003-04 Bridgeport Sound Tigers

COMPLETE SET (20) 15.00 40.00
1A Wade Dubielewicz 2.00 5.00
1B Ryan Kraft .60 1.50
2A Ben Guite .60 1.50
2B Kevin Colley .60 1.50
3A Cole Jarrett .60 1.50
3B Rob Collins .60 1.50
4A Alan Letang .60 1.50
4B Jeff Hamilton .60 1.50
5A Dieter Kochan 2.00 5.00
5B Cail MacLean .60 1.50
6A Eric Manlow .60 1.50
6B Justin Mapletoft 1.25 3.00
7A Graham Bolak .60 1.50
7B Alain Nasreddine .60 1.50
8A Martin Kariya 4.00 10.00
8B Tomi Pettinen .60 1.50
9 Brandon Smith .60 1.50
10 Derek Bekar .60 1.50
11 Blaine Down .60 1.50
12 Jody Robinson .60 1.50

2013-14 Bridgeport Sound Tigers

COMPLETE SET (8) 4.00 10.00
1 Johan Sundstrom .30 .75
2 Ryan Strome 1.00 2.50
3 Anders Lee 1.00 2.50
4 Mike Halmo .30 .75
5 Chris Bruton .30 .75
6 Scott Mayfield .30 .75
7 Aaron Ness .30 .75
8 Anders Nilsson 1.00 2.50

1991-92 British Columbia JHL

COMPLETE SET (173) 40.00 100.00
1 Vernon Lakers
Team Photo .08 .25
2 Scott Longstaff .05 .15
3 Rick Crowe .05 .15
4 Sheldon Wolitski .05 .15
5 Kevan Rilcof .05 .15
6 Greg Buchanan .05 .15
7 Vernon Lakers
Executives .05 .15
8 Murray Caton .05 .15
9 Adrian Bubola .05 .15
10 Troy Becker .05 .15
11 Shawn Potyok .05 .15
12 John Morabito .05 .15
13 Peter Zurba .05 .15
14 Chad Schraeder .05 .15
15 Shawn Bourgeois .05 .15
16 Michal Sup .05 .15
17 Rick Eremenko .05 .15
18 David Lemanowicz .05 .15
19 Daniel Blasko .05 .15
20 Gary Audette .20 .50
21 Graham Harder .05 .15
22 Ryan Nessman .05 .15
23 Jason Switzer .05 .15
24 Roland Ramoser .05 .15
25 Dusty McLellan .05 .15
26 Dustin Green .05 .15
27 Steve Roberts .05 .15
28 Jason Lowe .05 .15
29 Brad Knight .05 .15
30 Pavel Suchanek .05 .15
31 Ken Crockett .05 .15
32 Adam Smith .08 .25
33 Glen Pullishy .05 .15
34 Mike Zambon .05 .15
35 Scott Chartier .08 .25
36 Donny Hearn .05 .15
37 Jeff Denham .05 .15
38 Jamie Marriott .05 .15
39 Silverio Mirao .05 .15
40 Darren Tymchyshyn .05 .15
41 Mark Basanta .05 .15
42 Trevor Prest .05 .15
43 Jim Lessard .05 .15
44 Jade Kersey .05 .15
45 Geordie Young .05 .15
46 Darren Holmes .05 .15
47 Wade Dayley .05 .15
48 Dan Murphy .05 .15
49 Paul Taylor .05 .15
50 Sjon Wynia .05 .15
51 Ryan Loxam .05 .15
52 Andy Faulkner .05 .15
53 Scott Kowalski .05 .15
54 Mickey McGuire .05 .15
55 Jason Disiewich .05 .15
56 Jim Ingram .05 .15
57 Ryan Keller .05 .15
58 Brian Schiebel .05 .15
59 Shawn York .05 .15
60 Sean Krause .05 .15
61 Casey Hungle .05 .15
62 Chris Jones .05 .15
63 Doug Stewart .05 .15
64 Jason Sirota .08 .25
65 Dave Dunnigan .05 .15
66 Aaron Hoffman .05 .15
67 Jason Timewell .05 .15
68 Pat Meehan .05 .15
69 Mike Leduc .05 .15
70 Brad Koopmans .05 .15
71 Guy Prince .05 .15
72 Dorel Gecse .05 .15
73 Scott Salmond .05 .15
74 Brian Zakall .05 .15
75 Mike Josephson .05 .15
76 Derek Harper .05 .15
77 John Graham .05 .15
78 Dan Morrissey .08 .25
79 Glenn Calder .05 .15
80 Jason Northard .05 .15
81 Chris Kerr .05 .15
82 Bill Muckalt .40 1.00
83 Greg Hunt .05 .15
84 Paul Kariya
1990-91 AS 10.00 25.00
85 Dean Rowland .05 .15
86 Paul Kariya
Skating 10.00 25.00
87 David Kilduff .05 .15
88 Jeff Tory .05 .15
89 Mike Newman .05 .15
90 Tyler Boucher .05 .15
91 Paul Kariya
Skating with stick 10.00 25.00
92 Phil Valk .05 .15
93 Paul Kariya
Passing 10.00 25.00
94 Bob Lewis .05 .15
95 Steve Williams .05 .15
96 James Pelzer .05 .15
97 Shawn Carter .05 .15
98 Ryan Erasmas .08 .25
99 John Dehart .05 .15
100 David Green .05 .15
101 Derek Gecse .05 .15
102 Brian Barnes .05 .15
103 Jason Given .05 .15
104 Jason Podollan .20 .50
105 Brian Veale .05 .15
106 Rob Tallas .30 .75
107 Bob McBurnie .05 .15
108 Paul McMillan .05 .15
109 Ryan Donovan .05 .15
110 Kevin Robertson .05 .15
111 Milt Mastad .08 .25
112 Kees Roodbol .05 .15
113 Carey Causey .05 .15
114 Patrick O'Flaherty .05 .15
115 Chad Vestergaard .05 .15
116 Tyler Quiring .08 .25
117 Loui Mellios .05 .15
118 Bob Bell .05 .15
119 Rob Tallas .30 .75
120 Clint MacDonald .05 .15
121 Bart Taylor .05 .15
122 Mark Basanta .05 .15
123 Don McCusker .05 .15
124 Jason Howse .05 .15
125 Mike McKinlay .05 .15
126 Trevor Pennock .05 .15
127 Dean Shmyr .08 .25
128 Chris Kerr .05 .15
129 Erin Thornton .05 .15
130 Dennis Archibald .05 .15
131 Brian McDonald .05 .15
132 Bob Quinnell .05 .15
133 Clint Black .05 .15
134 Jason Peters .05 .15
135 Doug Ast .05 .15
136 Jason Bilous .08 .25
137 Lee Schill .05 .15
138 Jason Sanford .05 .15
139 Jeff Hokanson .05 .15
140 Marc Gagnon .05 .15
141 Gunnar Henrikson .05 .15
142 Jamie Lund .05 .15
143 Jason White .05 .15
144 Jag Bal .05 .15
145 Brad Loring .05 .15
146 Marc Gagnon .05 .15
147 Brian Veale .05 .15
148 Checklist 1 .05 .15
149 Checklist 2 .05 .15
150 The Centennial Cup .08 .25
151 Brian Law .05 .15
152 Al Radke .05 .15
153 Andy Faulkner
Jason Disiewich
Darren Holmes
Casey Hungle
Chris Jones .08 .25
154 1982 Coastal Division
Team Photo .08 .25
155 Dusty McLellan
Roland Ramoser
Rick Eremenko
Sheldon Wolitski
Shawn Potyok
Scott Longstaff .08 .25
156 Hendrikson
Anchikoski
Marc Gagnon
Jason White .08 .25
157 John Graham
Dave Dunnigan .08 .25
158 Scott Chartier
Mike Zambon
Paul Taylor
Jason Lowe .08 .25
159 Jeff Tory
Tyler Boucher
David Kilduff
Lee Davidson
John Dehart
Burns .08 .25
160 Didmon
Bentham
Marsh
Walsh .08 .25
161 Lipsett
McNeill
Klyn
Edgington .08 .25
162 1991 Interior
All-Stars Team
Photo .08 .25
163 Johnson
Meek
Welker
Fitzpatrick
Collins
Sofikitas
Hutson
Herman .08 .25
164 John Dehart .05 .15
165 John Craighead .08 .25
166 Mike Josephson .05 .15
167 Wayne Anchikoski .20 .50
168 Paul Kariya 10.00 25.00
169 Jim Lessard .05 .15
170 Tommi Virkgunen .05 .15
NNO Wayne Anchikoski .20 .50
NNO John Craighead .08 .25
NNO Tommi Virkgunen .08 .25

1992-93 British Columbia JHL

COMPLETE SET (246) 10.00 50.00
1 Tom Wittenberg .08 .25
2 Kendel Kelly .08 .25
3 Gus Rettschlag .08 .25
4 Don Barr .08 .25
5 Dave Kirkpatrick .08 .25
6 Josh Flett .08 .25
7 Paul McKenna .08 .25
8 Brad Wingfield .08 .25
9 Derek Gesce .08 .25
10 Garry Gulash .08 .25
11 Tim Bell .08 .25
12 Dean Stork .08 .25
13 Wes Reusse .08 .25
14 Jason Peipmann .08 .25
15 Tyler Johnston .08 .25
16 Jason Delesoy .08 .25
17 The Ice Man .08 .25
18 Don Barr .08 .25
19 Brad Swain .08 .25
20 Wes Rudy .08 .25
21 Michael Sigouin .08 .25
22 Kevan Rilcof .08 .25
23 Brian Preston .08 .25
24 Doug Ast .08 .25
25 Knut Engqvist .08 .25
26 Zac George .08 .25
27 Clint Black .08 .25
28 Cameron Campbell .08 .25
29 Dan Davies .08 .25
30 Bryce Munro .08 .25
31 Ryan Dayman .08 .25
32 Kevin Kimura .08 .25
33 Paul Nicolls .08 .25
34 Thomas Kraft .08 .25
35 Erin Thornton .08 .25
36 Brad Loring .08 .25
37 Jag Bal .08 .25
38 Jeff Grabinsky .08 .25
39 Johan Ahrgren .08 .25
40 The Lethal Weapon .08 .25
41 Two Unidentified
Players .08 .25
42 Judd Lambert .08 .25
43 Brian Schiebel .08 .25
44 Dennis Archibald .08 .25
45 David Longbroek .08 .25
46 Silverio Mirao .08 .25
47 Jason Haakstad .08 .25
48 Lee Grant .08 .25
49 Ryan Esselmont .08 .25
50 Steve Roberts .08 .25
51 Curtis Fry .08 .25
52 David Dollard .08 .25
53 Diano Zol .08 .25
54 Bob Needham .08 .25
55 Dustin Green .08 .25
56 Darren Tymchyshyn .08 .25
57 Peter Arvanitis .08 .25
58 Don Hearn .08 .25
59 Title Card
(Unnumbered) .10 .25
60 Martin Masa .08 .25
61 Steffon Walby .20 .50
62 Joel Irwin .08 .25
63 Brent Bradford .08 .25
64 Dieter Kochan 2.00 5.00
65 Brendan Kenny .08 .25
66 Marty Craigdallie .08 .25
67 Graeme Harder .08 .25
68 Pavel Suchanek .08 .25
69 Shane Johnson .08 .25
70 Burt Henderson .08 .25
71 Tyler Willis .08 .25
72 Mike Olaski .08 .25
73 David Green .08 .25
74 Tom Mix .08 .25
75 Walter(Guy) Prince .08 .25
76 Joseph Rybar .40 1.00
77 Bill Muckalt .75 2.00
78 Jason Mansoff .08 .25
79 Duane Puga .08 .25
80 Aaron Hoffman .08 .25
81 Dan Blasko .08 .25
82 Rob Szatmary .08 .25
83 Mike Minnis .08 .25
84 Pat Meehan .08 .25
85 Andre Robichaud .08 .25
86 The Terminator .02 .10
87 Derrek Harper .08 .25
88 Dan Morrissey .08 .25
89 Joey Kennedy .08 .25
90 Derrek Harper .08 .25
91 Lawrence Klyne .08 .25
92 Ryan Beamin .08 .25
93 Sjon Wynia .08 .25
94 Jason Disiewich .08 .25
95 Jason Sanford .08 .25
96 Casey Hungle .08 .25
97 Brent Murcheson .08 .25
98 Glenn Calder .08 .25
99 Jade Kersey .08 .25
100 Shawn York .08 .25
101 Bob Quinnell .08 .25
102 Geordie Dunstan .08 .25
103 Cory Crowther .08 .25
104 Jason Hodson .08 .25
105 Chris Jones .08 .25
106 Cory Green .08 .25
107 Chris Buie .08 .25
108 Shaun Peet .08 .25
109 Jason Wood .08 .25
110 Dan Murphy .08 .25
111 Jason Disiewich .08 .25
112 Cory Dayley .08 .25
113 Brian Veale .08 .25
114 Jason Northard .08 .25
115 Phil Valk .08 .25
116 Wade Dayley .08 .25
117 Brendan Morrison 4.00 10.00
118 Marcel Sakac .08 .25
119 Tyler Boucher .08 .25
120 Ray Guze .08 .25
121 Brian Barnes .08 .25
122 Jason Given .08 .25
123 Michael Dairon .08 .25
124 Mike Newman .08 .25
125 Craig Fletcher .08 .25
126 Ty Davidson .08 .25
127 Miki Antonik .08 .25
128 Rob Pennoyer .08 .25
129 Dave Whitworth .08 .25
130 Steve Williams .08 .25
131 Robbie Trampuh .08 .25
132 Mark Filipenko .08 .25
133 Clint MacDonald .08 .25
134 Colin Ryder .08 .25
135 David Kilduff .08 .25
136 Mickey McGuire .08 .25
137 Randy Polacik .08 .25
138 Jeff Tory .08 .25
139 Chris Duckman .08 .25
140 Bill Moody .08 .25
141 Rick McLarren .08 .25
142 The Phantom .02 .10
143 Jason Zaichkowski .08 .25
144 Tony Hrycuik .08 .25
145 Cameron Knox .08 .25
146 Mike Warriner .08 .25
147 Robb Gordon .08 .25
148 Mike Pawluk .08 .25
149 Tim Harris .08 .25
150 Mike Bzdel .08 .25
151 Chad Wilson .08 .25
152 Andrew Plumb .08 .25
153 Andy MacIntosh .08 .25
154 Stefan Brannare .08 .25
155 Matt Sharrers .08 .25
156 Brent Berry .08 .25
157 Ryan Douglas .08 .25
158 Heath Dennison .08 .25
159 Chad Vizzutti .08 .25
160 Adam Lord .08 .25
161 Brad Klyn .08 .25
162 Andrew Young .08 .25
163 Casey Lemanski .08 .25
164 Mike McKinlay .08 .25
165 Derek Robinson .08 .25
166 Kees Roodbol .08 .25
167 Scott Boucher .08 .25
168 Shawn Gervais .08 .25
169 Ryan Schaffer .08 .25
170 Kevin Robertson .08 .25
171 Ryan Donovan .08 .25
172 Bart Taylor .08 .25
173 Greg Hunt .08 .25
174 Darcy George .08 .25
175 Shane Tidsbury .08 .25
176 Rob Smillie .08 .25
177 Chad Vestergaard .08 .25
178 Al Kinisky .08 .25
179 Patrick O'Flaherty .08 .25
180 Loui Mellios .08 .25
181 Lorin Murdock
(Unnumbered) .08 .25
182 Jason Genik .08 .25
183 Rob Herrington .08 .25
184 Loui Mellios .08 .25
185 Cal Benazic .08 .25
186 Richard Kraus .08 .25
187 Geoff White .08 .25
188 Kirk Buchanan .08 .25
189 Peter Zurba .08 .25
190 John Morabito .08 .25
191 Corey Kruchkowski .08 .25
192 Spencer Ward .08 .25
193 Danny Shermerhorn .08 .25
194 Mark Davies .08 .25
195 Jason Rushton .08 .25
196 Chad Buckle .08 .25
197 Serge Beauchesne .08 .25
198 Todd Kelman .08 .25
199 Jason Switzer .08 .25
200 Eon MacFarlane .08 .25
201 Terry Ryan .20 .50
202 Shawn Bourgeois .08 .25
203 Chad Schraeder .08 .25
204 Dusty McLellan .08 .25
205 The Predator .08 .25
206 Danny Shermerhorn .08 .25
207 Chris Godard .08 .25
208 Jason Chipman .08 .25
209 Christian Twomey .08 .25
210 Ryan Loxam .08 .25
211 Greg Buchanan .08 .25
212 Kees Roodbol .08 .25
213 Ryan Keller .08 .25
214 Kevin Paschal .08 .25
215 David Hebky .08 .25
216 Vince Devlin .08 .25
217 Mike Cole .08 .25
218 Daljit Takhar .08 .25
219 Scott Hall .08 .25
220 Derek Lawrence .08 .25
221 Mark Basanta .08 .25
222 Jan Kloboucek .08 .25
223 Randy Barker .08 .25
224 Kris Gailloux .08 .25
225 Tyson Scheuer .08 .25
226 Brent Wormald .08 .25
227 Vince Devlin .08 .25
228 Gus Miller .08 .25
229 Todd McKave .08 .25
230 Lawrence Oliver .08 .25
231 Scott Garvin .08 .25
232 Rob Milliken .08 .25
233 Roman Kobrc .08 .25
234 Dan Skene .08 .25
235 Blair Marsh .08 .25
236 Maco Balkovec .08 .25
237 Scott Kirton .08 .25
238 Blaine Moore .08 .25
239 Nigel Creightney .08 .25
240 Bill Zapf .08 .25
241 Jason Elders .08 .25
242 BCJHL Officials
(Unidentified Referee) .02 .10
243 Masks of the BCJHL
The .40 1.00
244 Masks of the BCJHL
The .40 1.00
245 Mike Pawluk
BCJHL MVP .08 .25
246 Steffon Walby
Captains of the BCJHL .20 .50

1987-88 Brockville Braves

COMPLETE SET (25) 4.00 10.00
1 Title Card .08 .25
2 Steve Harper TR .08 .25
3 Peter Kelly TR .08 .25
4 Mac MacLean CO
MG .08 .25
5 Mike McCourt .20 .50
6 Paul MacLean .20 .50
7 Mark Michaud .20 .50
8 Alain Marchessault .20 .50
9 Tom Roman .20 .50
10 Darren Burns .20 .50
11 Scott Halpenny .20 .50
12 Ray Gallagher .20 .50
13 Bob Lindsay .20 .50
14 Brett Harkins .40 1.00
15 Dave Hyrsky .20 .50
16 Richard Marchessault .20 .50
17 Scott Boston .20 .50
18 Steve Hogg .30 .75
19 Chris Webster .20 .50
20 Stuart Birnie .20 .50
21 Brett Dunk .20 .50
22 Charles Cusson .20 .50
23 Pat Gooley .20 .50
24 Andy Rodman .20 .50
25 Peter Radlein .20 .50

1988-89 Brockville Braves

COMPLETE SET (25) 4.00 10.00
1 Ray Gallagher .20 .50
2 Peter Kelly TR .08 .25
3 Steve Harper TR .08 .25
4 Winston Jones ACO .08 .25
5 Mac MacLean CO/GM .08 .25
6 Kevin Doherty .20 .50
7 Stuart Birnie .20 .50
8 Charles Cusson .20 .50
9 Paul MacLean .20 .50
10 Bob Lindsay .20 .50
11 Darren Burns .20 .50
12 Rick Pracey .30 .75
13 Mike Malloy .20 .50
14 Dave Hyrsky .20 .50
15 Rob Percival .20 .50
16 Jarrett Eligh .20 .50
17 Pat Gooley .20 .50
18 Michael Bracco .30 .75
19 Ken Crook .20 .50
20 Brad Osborne .20 .50
21 Todd Reynolds .20 .50
22 Mike McCourt .20 .50
23 Chris Webster .20 .50
24 Kevin Lune .20 .50
25 Title Card .20 .50

1951-52 Buffalo Bison

COMPLETE SET (19) 50.00 100.00
1 Team Photo 5.00 10.00
2 Don Ashbee 5.00 10.00
3 Frankie Christy 2.50 5.00
4 Gerry Couture 4.00 8.00
5 Lou Crowdis 2.50 5.00
6 Harry Dick 2.50 5.00
7 Lloyd Finkbeiner 2.50 5.00
8 Ab Demarco 5.00 10.00
9 Leroy Goldsworthy 2.50 5.00
10 Les Hickey 5.00 10.00
11 Vern Kaiser 2.50 5.00
12 Sam Lavitt 2.50 5.00
13 Stan Long 2.50 5.00
14 Cal Mackay 5.00 10.00
15 Ed Mazur 2.50 5.00
16 Sid McNabney 2.50 5.00
17 George Pargeter 2.50 5.00
18 Gordie Pennell 2.50 5.00
19 Grant Warwick 2.50 5.00

1995 Buffalo Stampedes RHI

COMPLETE SET (21) 4.00 10.00
14 John Hendry .20 .50
16 Tom Nemeth .30 .75
19 John Vechiarelli .30 .75
19 John Vechiarelli IA .30 .75
20 Len Soccio .20 .50
24 Chris Bergeron .20 .50
32 Mark Major .20 .50
34 Jason Cirone .20 .50
36 Nick Vitucci .30 .75
37 Dave Lemay .20 .50
43 John Blessman .20 .50
44 Jay Neal .20 .50
61 Craig Martin .20 .50
72 Rick Corriveau .20 .50
94 Alex Hicks .30 .75
NNO1 Header Card .02 .10
NNO2 Title Card .02 .10
NNO3 Team Photo .02 .10
NNO4 Terry Buchwald .02 .10
NNO5 Stampede Cheerleaders .20 .50
NNO6 Claude the Trumpeter .08 .25

1998-99 Calgary Hitmen

COMPLETE SET (26) 8.00 20.00
1 Matt Kinch .30 .75
2 Ryan Shannon .20 .50
3 Jeff Feniak .20 .50
4 Kenton Smith .30 .75
5 Rod Sarich .20 .50
6 Pavel Brendl .60 1.50
7 Chris Nielsen .20 .50
8 Sean McAslan .20 .50
9 Jordan Krestanovich .60 1.50
10 Michael Bubnick .20 .50
11 Kris Beech .75 2.00
12 Ryan Geremia .20 .50
13 Wade Davis .20 .50
14 Brad Moran .30 .75
15 Lyle Steenbergen .20 .50
16 Curtis Rich .20 .50
17 Ryan Andres .20 .50
18 Brent Dodginghorse .20 .50
19 Jerred Smithson .20 .50
20 Peter Bergman .20 .50
21 Alexandre Fomitchev .30 .75
22 Eric Clark .20 .50
23 Donald Choukalos .30 .75
24 Dean Clark HCO .02 .10
25 Jeff Maher ACO .02 .10
26 Vulk MASCOT .02 .10

1998-99 Calgary Hitmen Autographs

COMPLETE SET (26) 40.00 80.00
1 Matt Kinch 1.25 3.00
2 Ryan Shannon 5.00 12.00
3 Jeff Feniak 1.25 3.00
4 Kenton Smith 1.25 3.00
5 Rod Sarich 1.25 3.00
6 Pavel Brendl 4.00 10.00
7 Chris Nielsen 1.25 3.00
8 Sean McAslan 1.25 3.00
9 Jordan Krestanovich 4.00 10.00
10 Michael Bubnick 1.25 3.00
11 Kris Beech 4.00 10.00
12 Ryan Geremia 1.25 3.00
13 Wade Davis 1.25 3.00
14 Brad Moran 1.25 3.00
15 Lyle Steenbergen 1.25 3.00
16 Curtis Rich 1.25 3.00
17 Ryan Andres 1.25 3.00
18 Brent Dodginghorse 1.25 3.00
19 Jerred Smithson 1.25 3.00
20 Peter Bergman 1.25 3.00
21 Alexandre Fomitchev
UNSIGNED .20 .50
22 Eric Clark 1.25 3.00
23 Donald Choukalos 1.25 3.00
24 Dean Clark HCO 2.00 5.00
25 Jeff Maher ACO 1.25 3.00
26 Vulk MASCOT .20 .50

1999-00 Calgary Hitmen

COMPLETE SET (25) 4.00 10.00
1 Kris Beech .60 1.50
2 Pavel Brendl .30 .75
3 Michael Bubnick .08 .25
4 Jared Carli .08 .25
5 Dean Clark CO .02 .10
6 Eric Clark .08 .25
7 Sean Connors .08 .25
8 Wade Davis .08 .25
9 Jeff Feniak .08 .25
10 Owen Fussey .08 .25
11 Robin Gomez .20 .50
12 Matt Kinch .30 .75
13 Brent Krahn .60 1.50
14 Jordan Krestanovich .40 1.00
15 Anders Lovdahl .15 .40
16 Jeff Maher ACO .08 .25
17 Sean McAslan .08 .25
18 Brad Moran .20 .50
19 Chris Nielsen .20 .50
20 Shaun Norrie .20 .50

21 Rod Sarich .08 .25
22 Brandon Segal .08 .25
23 Kenton Smith .15 .40
24 Jerred Smithson .08 .25
25 Vulk Mascot .02 .10
26 Calgary Herald .02 .10
27 Playstation Coupon .02 .10

1999-00 Calgary Hitmen Autographs

COMPLETE SET (27) 40.00 100.00
1 Kris Beech 4.00 10.00
2 Pavel Brendl 3.00 6.00
3 Michael Bubnick 1.25 3.00
4 Jared Carli 1.25 3.00
5 Dean Clark CO 1.25 3.00
6 Eric Clark DNS .08 .25
7 Sean Connors 1.25 3.00
8 Wade Davis 1.25 3.00
9 Jeff Feniak DNS .08 .25
10 Owen Fussey 1.25 3.00
11 Robin Gomez 2.00 5.00
12 Matt Kinch 3.00 6.00
13 Brent Krahn 4.00 8.00
14 Jordan Krestanovich 4.00 8.00
15 Anders Lovdahl 2.00 5.00
16 Jeff Maher ACO 1.25 3.00
17 Sean McAslan 1.25 3.00
18 Brad Moran 3.00 6.00
19 Chris Nielsen 3.00 6.00
20 Shaun Norrie 1.25 3.00
21 Rod Sarich 1.25 3.00
22 Brandon Segal 1.25 3.00
23 Kenton Smith 2.00 5.00
24 Jerred Smithson 1.25 3.00
25 Vulk Mascot .40 1.00
26 Calgary Herald .02 .10
27 Playstation Coupon .02 .10

2000-01 Calgary Hitmen

COMPLETE SET (28) 6.00 15.00
1 Toni Bader .20 .50
2 Kris Beech .50 1.25
3 Brady Block .20 .50
4 John Boychuk .40 1.00
5 Adam Breitkreuz .20 .50
6 Pavel Brendl .60 1.00
7 Michael Bubnick .20 .50
8 Jared Carli .20 .50
9 Dean Clark CO .10 .25
10 Wade Davis .20 .50
11 Mike Egener .20 .50
12 Dan Ehrman .20 .50
13 Owen Fussey .20 .50
14 Robin Gomez .20 .50
15 Matt Kinch .20 .50
16 Brent Krahn .40 1.00
17 Jordan Krestanovich .20 .50
18 Jeff Maher CO .10 .25
19 Sean McAslan .20 .50
20 Shaun Norrie .20 .50
21 Rod Sarich .20 .50
22 Brandon Segal .20 .50
23 Shaun Sutter .20 .50
24 David Vrbata .20 .50
25 The Vulk MASCOT .04 .10
26 Chad Wolkowski .20 .50
27 Calgary Herald .02 .10
28 Toys R Us .02 .10

2001-02 Calgary Hitmen

COMPLETE SET (26) 4.80 12.00
1 Paul Albers .20 .50
2 Kyle Annesley .20 .50
3 Tyler Beechey .30 .75
4 Johnny Boychuk .40 1.00
5 Adam Breitkreuz .20 .50
6 Michael Bubnick .20 .50
7 Jared Carli .20 .50
8 Wade Davis .20 .50
9 Mike Egener .20 .50
10 Dan Ehrman .20 .50
11 Owen Fussey .30 .75
12 Richard Kromm CO .10 .25
13 Sebastien LaPlante .20 .50
14 Jeff Maher ACO .10 .25
15 Ryan Martin .30 .75
16 Lance Morrison .20 .50
17 Ryan Papaioannou .20 .50
18 Wes Rypien .20 .50
19 Rod Sarich .20 .50
20 Brandon Segal .30 .75
21 Dennis Sergeyev .20 .50
22 Mark Shefchyk .20 .50
23 Fredrik Sjostrom .75 2.00
24 Rob Smith .20 .50
25 The Vulk MASCOT .10 .25
26 Chad Wolkowski .20 .50

2001-02 Calgary Hitmen Autographed

COMPLETE SET (26) 20.00 50.00
1 Paul Albers .75 2.00
2 Kyle Annesley .75 2.00
3 Tyler Beechey 1.25 3.00
4 Johnny Boychuk 1.60 5.00
5 Adam Breitkreuz .75 2.00
6 Michael Bubnick .75 2.00
7 Jared Carli .75 2.00
8 Wade Davis .75 2.00
9 Mike Egener .75 2.00
10 Dan Ehrman .75 2.00
11 Owen Fussey 1.50 4.00
12 Richard Kromm CO .40 1.00
13 Sebastien LaPlante .75 2.00
14 Jeff Maher ACO .40 1.00
15 Ryan Martin 1.25 3.00
16 Lance Morrison .75 2.00
17 Ryan Papaioannou .75 2.00
18 Wes Rypien .75 2.00
19 Rod Sarich .75 2.00
20 Brandon Segal 1.25 3.00
21 Dennis Sergeyev .75 2.00
22 Mark Shefchyk .75 2.00
23 Fredrik Sjostrom 4.00 10.00
24 Rob Smith .75 2.00
25 The Vulk MASCOT .04 .10
26 Chad Wolkowski .75 2.00

2002-03 Calgary Hitmen

COMPLETE SET (26) 8.00 18.00
1 Lance Morrison .20 .50
2 Michael Bubnick .20 .50
3 Gary Gladue .20 .50
4 Kris Deines .20 .50
5 Kyle Annesley .20 .50
6 Rob Smith .20 .50
7 Mark Shefchyk .20 .50
8 Bruno Campese ACO .04 .10
9 Richard Kromm HCO .04 .10
10 Mascot .04 .10
11 Fredrik Sjostrom .40 1.00
12 Wade Davis .20 .50
13 Paul Albers .20 .50
14 Patrick Wellar .20 .50
15 Marc Lesage .20 .50
16 Aaron Boogaard .20 .50
17 Jiri Cetkovsky .20 .50
18 Brandon Segal .20 .50
19 Owen Fussey .20 .50
20 Tyler Feakes .20 .50
21 Andy Rogers .20 .50
22 Steven Covington .20 .50
23 Johnny Boychuk .40 1.00
24 Michael Egener .40 1.00
25 Brent Krahn .40 1.00
26 Ryan Getzlaf 2.00 5.00

2003-04 Calgary Hitmen

COMPLETE SET (21) 6.00 15.00
1 Scott Bowles .30 .75
2 Brett Carson .20 .50
3 Dmitri Chupilkin .20 .50
4 Steve Covington .20 .50
5 Kris Deines .20 .50
6 Mike Egener .30 .75
7 Gerry Festa .30 .75
8 Paul Gentile .20 .50
9 Ryan Getzlaf 1.00 2.50
10 Dustin Kohn .20 .50
11 Andrew Ladd .75 2.00
12 Shaun Landolt .20 .50
13 Riley Merkley .20 .50
14 Andy Rogers .20 .50
15 Mark Rooneem .20 .50
16 Jeff Schultz .20 .50
17 Brandon Segal .20 .50
18 Tomas Troliga .20 .50
19 Patrick Wellar .20 .50
20 Darryl Yacboski .20 .50
21 Lee Zalasky .20 .50

2004-05 Calgary Hitmen

COMPLETE SET (25) 15.00 25.00
1 Karl Alzner .60 1.50
2 Brett Carlson .30 .75
3 Steven Covington .30 .75
4 Keegan Dansereau .30 .75
5 Brodie Dupont .30 .75
6 Ryan Getzlaf .75 2.00
7 Tyler Harder .30 .75
8 Dustin Kohn .30 .75
9 Andrew Ladd .60 1.50
10 Shaun Landolt .30 .75
11 Tyrel Lucas .30 .75
12 Riley Merkley .30 .75
13 Darryl Moscaluk .30 .75
14 Brett O'Malley .30 .75
15 Justin Pogge 2.00 5.00
16 Konstantin Pushkarev .40 1.00
17 Isaac Reid .30 .75
18 Jeff Schultz .40 1.00
19 Daniel Spence .30 .75
20 Ryan White .30 .75
21 Darryl Yacboski .30 .75
22 Dylan Yeo .30 .75
23 Dean Evason
Kelly Kisio CO .04 .10
24 Blaine Forsythe ACO
Farley MASCOT .04 .10
25 Ryan Getzlaf
Calgary Herald .60 1.50

2005-06 Calgary Hitmen

COMPLETE SET (28) 8.00 15.00
1 Karl Alzner .40 1.00
2 Brett Carson .30 .75
3 Steve Covington .30 .75
4 Keegan Dansereau .30 .75
5 Kris Deines .30 .75
6 Brodie Dupont .30 .75
7 Curtis Kelner .30 .75
8 Derek LeBlanc .30 .75
9 Ryan Letts .30 .75
10 Craig Lineker .30 .75
11 Carson McMillan .30 .75
12 Riley Merkley .30 .75
13 Shaden Moore .30 .75
14 Fredrik Pettersson .30 .75
15 Alexandre Plante .30 .75
16 Justin Pogge 1.25 3.00
17 Mike Reich .30 .75
18 Jeff Schultz .30 .75
19 Brett Sonne .40 1.00
20 Daniel Spence .30 .75
21 Lukas Vantuch .40 1.00
22 Ryan White .40 1.00
23 Dylan Yeo .30 .75
24 Kelly Kisio CO .04 .10
25 Blaine Forsythe ACO .10 .25
26 Dave Lowry ACO .10 .25
27 Farley the Fox MASCOT .10 .25
28 SPONSORS .01 .01

2009-10 Calgary Hitmen

1 Michael Snider .40 1.00
2 Ben Wilson .40 1.00
3 Matt Mackenzie .40 1.00
4 Peter Kosterman .40 1.00
5 Jaynen Rissling .40 1.00
6 Misha Fisenko .40 1.00
7 Zak Stebner .40 1.00
8 Justin Kirsch .40 1.00
9 Jimmy Bubnick .40 1.00
10 Brandon Kozun .40 1.00
11 Cody Sylvester .40 1.00
12 Giffen Nyren .40 1.00
13 Kris Foucault .40 1.00
14 Ian Schultz .40 1.00
15 MacKenzie Royer .40 1.00
16 Tyler Fiddler .40 1.00
17 Del Cowan .40 1.00
18 Rigby Burgart .40 1.00
19 Joel Broda .40 1.00
20 Kyle Aschim .40 1.00
21 Michael Stone .40 1.00
22 Tyler Shattock .40 1.00
23 Martin Jones .40 1.00
24 Cody Beach .40 1.00
25 Mike Williamson .40 1.00
26 Joel Otto ACO .40 1.00
27 Brent Kisio ACO .40 1.00
28 Farley the Fox .40 1.00

2013-14 Calgary Hitmen

COMPLETE SET (28) 8.00 20.00
1 Cal Babych .30 .75
2 Brady Brassart .30 .75
3 Greg Chase .30 .75
4 Terrell Draude .30 .75
5 Chris Driedger .30 .75
6 Radel Fazleev .30 .75
7 Colby Harmsworth .30 .75
8 Kenton Helgesen .30 .75
9 Brent Kisio Assoc. CO .30 .75
10 Chase Lang .30 .75
11 Joe Mahon .30 .75
12 Joel Otto Asst. CO .30 .75
13 Pavlo Padakin .30 .75
14 Linden Penner .30 .75
15 Elliot Peterson .30 .75
16 Connor Rankin .30 .75
17 Jaynen Rissling .30 .75
18 Alex Roach .30 .75
19 Travis Sanheim .50 1.25
20 Mack Shields .30 .75
21 Adam Tambellini .30 .75
22 Ben Thomas .30 .75
23 Jake Virtanen .30 .75
24 Landon Welykholowa .30 .75
25 Mike Williamson CO .30 .75
26 Mike Winther .30 .75
27 Michael Zipp .30 .75
28 Farley the Fox MASCOT .30 .75

2014-15 Calgary Hitmen

COMPLETE SET (28) 6.00 15.00
1 Jake Bean .30 .75
2 Layne Bensmiller .30 .75
3 Brendan Burke .30 .75
4 Terrell Draude .30 .75
5 Radel Fazleev .30 .75
6 Radel Fazleev TB Scorer .30 .75
7 Mark French CO .30 .75
8 Colby Harmsworth .30 .75
9 Kenton Helgesen .30 .75
10 Keegan Kanzig .30 .75
11 Pavel Karnaukhov .30 .75
12 Brent Kisio Asst. CO .30 .75
13 Chase Lang .30 .75
14 Beck Malenstyn .30 .75
15 Lochlan Morrison .30 .75
16 Joel Otto Asst. CO .30 .75
17 Elliot Peterson .30 .75
18 Connor Rankin .40 1.00
19 Taylor Sanheim .30 .75
20 Travis Sanheim .50 1.25
21 Mack Shields .30 .75
22 Jordan Stallard .30 .75
23 Adam Tambellini .30 .75
24 Ben Thomas .30 .75
25 Carsen Twarynski .30 .75
26 Jake Virtanen .75 2.00
27 Michael Zipp .30 .75
28 Farley the Fox MASCOT .30 .75

2007-08 Calgary Oval X-Treme

1 Lyndsay Baird .20 .50
2 Kelly Bechard .40 1.00
3 Delaney Collins .40 1.00
4 Meghan Corbett .20 .50
5 Gillian Ferrari .40 1.00
6 Kaley Hall .20 .50
7 Gina Kingsbury .40 1.00
8 Carla MacLeod .40 1.00
9 Stephanie Ramsay .20 .50
10 Rebecca Russell .20 .50
11 Colleen Sostorics .40 1.00
12 Laura St. Croix .20 .50
13 Amanda Tapp .20 .50
14 Meagan Walton .20 .50
15 Linuo Wang .20 .50
16 Samantha Watt .20 .50
17 Hayley Wickenheiser 1.00 2.50
18 Shi Yao .20 .50
19 Team Card .10 .25

2003-04 Camrose Kodiaks

COMPLETE SET (25) 6.00 15.00
1 Dan Bertram .40 1.00
2 Steve Bounds .30 .75
3 MacGregor Sharp .30 .75
4 Jared Veuger .30 .75
5 Jody Pederson .30 .75
6 Matt McKnight .30 .75
7 Travis Friedley .30 .75
8 Kyle Smith .30 .75
9 Rob MacIntyre .30 .75
10 Owen Langis .30 .75
11 Mason Raymond .40 1.00
12 Ryan Muspratt .30 .75
13 Ryan Antoniuk .30 .75
14 Chance Olsen .30 .75
15 Logan Gorsalitz .30 .75
16 Ryan Armstrong .30 .75
17 Lee Jubinville .30 .75
18 Justin Taylor .30 .75
19 Chris Wanchulak .30 .75
20 Justin Blacklock .30 .75
21 Todd Steil .30 .75
22 Bob Graham .30 .75
23 David Thompson .30 .75
24 Ryan Muth .30 .75
25 Coaches .04 .10

2004-05 Camrose Kodiaks

COMPLETE SET (16) 4.00 10.00
1 Jody Pederson .40 1.00
2 Kirk Irving .40 1.00
3 Clark Thompson .40 1.00
4 Ryan Mayko .40 1.00
5 Logan Gorsaltiz .40 1.00
6 Lee Jubinville .40 1.00
7 Todd Steil .40 1.00
8 Derek Wolbeck .40 1.00
9 Kyle Parkes .40 1.00
10 MacGregor Sharp .40 1.00
11 Chance Olsen .40 1.00
12 David Thompson .40 1.00
13 Mason Raymond .40 1.00
14 A.J. Nelson .40 1.00
15 Jason Roberts .40 1.00
16 Travis Friedley .40 1.00

2007-08 Camrose Kodiaks

COMPLETE SET (25) 6.00 15.00
1 David Anderson .30 .75
2 Jeremy Beirnes SP .30 .75
3 Scott Buchanan .30 .75
4 Nick Chartier .30 .75
5 Owen Chatwin .30 .75
6 Joe Colborne .75 2.00
7 Mike Connolly .30 .75
8 Nigel Dube .30 .75
9 Colin Dueck .30 .75
10 Wyatt Hamilton .30 .75
11 Jordan Heck .30 .75
12 Andre Herman SP .30 .75
13 David Jacobsen .30 .75
14 Clayton Jardine .30 .75
15 Mathieu Larochelle .30 .75
16 Alex Macleod SP .30 .75
17 Andrew MacWilliam .30 .75
18 Kyle Miller .30 .75
19 Dylan Olsen .30 .75
20 Shawn Ostrow .30 .75
21 Geoff Peet .30 .75
22 Dean Petiot .30 .75
23 Karl Stollery .30 .75
24 Jesse Todd .30 .75
25 Allen York .40 1.00

1994-95 Cape Breton Oilers

COMPLETE SET (23) 5.00 12.00
1 Scott Allison .15 .40
2 Martin Bakula .15 .40
3 Ladislav Benysek .15 .40
4 Dennis Bonvie .30 .75
5 Jozef Cierny .15 .40
6 Duane Dennis .15 .40
7 Greg DeVries .30 .75
8 Joaquin Gage .30 .75
9 Ian Herbers .15 .40
10 Ralph Intranuovo .15 .40
11 Claude Jutras .15 .40
12 Marc LaForge .15 .40
13 Todd Marchant .60 1.50
14 Darcy Martini .15 .40
15 Roman Oksiuta .15 .40
16 David Oliver .30 .75
17 Steve Passmore .40 1.00
18 Nick Stajduhar .15 .40
19 John Van Kessel .15 .40
20 David Vyborny .15 .40
21 Peter White .15 .40
22 Tyler Wright .30 .75
23 Brad Zavisha .15 .40

2001-02 Cape Breton Screaming Eagles

COMPLETE SET (23) 6.00 15.00
1 Steve Villeneuve .20 .50
2 Maxime Lessard .20 .50
3 Pierre-Luc Laprise .20 .50
4 David Cloutier .20 .50
5 Stuart MacRae .20 .50
6 Dominic Noel .20 .50
7 Jean-Philipe Cote .20 .50
8 Martin Kasik .20 .50
9 Steve Dixon .30 .75
10 Marc-Olivier Vary .20 .50
11 Justin Hawco .20 .50
12 Pierre-Luc Emond .20 .50
13 Guillaume Demers .20 .50
14 Rodrigue Boucher .20 .50
15 George Davis .20 .50
16 Andre Martineau .20 .50
17 Carl McLean .20 .50
18 Pascal Morency .20 .50
19 Mathieu Dumas .20 .50
20 Jean-Francois Dufort .20 .50
21 Marc-Andre Fleury 2.00 5.00
22 Jasen Awalt .20 .50
23 Kevin Asselin .20 .50

2002-03 Cape Breton Screaming Eagles

COMPLETE SET (25) 6.00 15.00
1 Marc-Andre Fleury 1.25 3.00
2 Martin Houle .60 1.50
3 Maxime Lessard .15 .40
4 Nathan Veinot .30 .75
5 Maxime Robert .15 .40
6 Jean-Claude Sawyer .15 .40
7 Vincent Zaore-Vanie .15 .40
8 Stephen Dixon .30 .75
9 Martin Slovak .15 .40
10 Joel Maas .15 .40
11 Pierre-Luc Emond .15 .40
12 Guillaume Demers .15 .40
13 Gregory Hoffe .15 .40
14 Jonathan Labelle .15 .40
15 Kevin Asselin .15 .40
16 Jared Vokey .15 .40
17 Michel Charette .15 .40
18 Samuel Beland .15 .40
19 Jean-Francois Dufort .30 .75
20 Patrick Gilbert .15 .40
21 Martin Trempe .15 .40
22 Steeve Villeneuve .15 .40
23 Stuart McRae .15 .40
24 Jean-Philippe Cote .15 .40
25 George Davis .15 .40
26 Marc-Andre Fleury CL 1.25 3.00

2003-04 Cape Breton Screaming Eagles

COMPLETE SET (24) 6.00 15.00
2 Adam Pardy .20 .50
4 Steve Villeneuve .20 .50
6 Tim Ramholt .20 .50
8 Nathan Veinot .20 .50
11 Francois-Pierre Guenette .20 .50
12 Jean-Claude Sawyer .20 .50
13 Vincent Zaore-Vanie .20 .50
14 Stephen Dixon .30 .75
15 Alexandre Picard .40 1.00
18 Guillaume Demers .20 .50
19 Gregory Hoffe .20 .50
20 Neil Smith .20 .50
21 Michael Tessier .20 .50
22 Kevin Asselin .20 .50
23 Jean-Francois Cyr .20 .50
24 Charles Fontaine .20 .50
26 Samuel Beland .20 .50
27 Philippe Bertrand .20 .50
28 Vincent Lambert .20 .50
29 Marc-Andre Fleury 1.25 3.00
30 Francois Proteau .30 .75
31 Martin Houle .40 1.00
41 Marc-Andre Bernier .40 1.00
84 Nicolas Corbeil .30 .75

2004-05 Cape Breton Screaming Eagles

COMPLETE SET (23) 5.00 12.00
1 Martin Houle .40 1.00
2 Kevin Asselin .20 .50
3 Stephen Dixon .30 .75
4 Samuel Beland .20 .50
5 Philippe Bertrand .20 .50
6 Chris Culligan .20 .50
7 Guillaume Demers .20 .50
8 Charles Fontaine .20 .50
9 Luke Gallant .20 .50
10 Vladimir Kubus .20 .50
11 Vincent Lambert .20 .50
12 Brendon MacDonald .20 .50
13 Dean Ouellet .20 .50
14 Adam Pardy .20 .50
15 Leonard Puterman .20 .50
16 Jean-Claude Sawyer .20 .50
17 James Sheppard .60 1.50
18 Neil Smith .20 .50
19 Francois Theriault .20 .50
20 David Victor .20 .50
21 Tyler Whitehead .20 .50
22 Vincent Zaore .20 .50
23 David Davenport .20 .50

2005-06 Cape Breton Screaming Eagles

COMPLETE SET (25) 5.00 12.00
1 James Sheppard .50 1.25
2 Ondrej Pavelec .30 .75
3 Jason Swit .20 .50
4 David Victor .20 .50
5 Darrell Simich .20 .50
6 Chris Culligan .20 .50
7 Robert Slaney .20 .50
8 Dean Ouellet .20 .50
9 Vladimir Kubus .20 .50
10 Brad Gallant .20 .50
11 Jean-Claude Sawyer .20 .50
12 Francois Gauthier .20 .50
13 Philippe Bertrand .20 .50
14 Scott Brannon .20 .50
15 Etienne Breton .20 .50
16 Jeff Grenier .20 .50
17 Brendon MacDonald .20 .50
18 Kevin Asselin .20 .50
19 Francois Theriault .20 .50
20 Charles Fontaine .20 .50
21 Vincent Zaore .20 .50
22 David Davenport .20 .50
23 Paul McIlveen .20 .50
24 Cam Fergus .20 .50
25 Alexandre Blais .20 .50

2006-07 Cape Breton Screaming Eagles

COMPLETE SET (25) 8.00 15.00
1 James Sheppard .60 1.50
2 Etienne Breton .30 .75
3 Jason Swit .30 .75
4 Daniel Fazzalari .30 .75
5 Chris Culligan .30 .75
6 Robert Sanley .30 .75
7 Dean Ouellet .30 .75
8 Scott Brannon .30 .75
9 Brad Gallant .30 .75
10 Jean-Claude Sawyer .30 .75
11 Cam Fergus .30 .75
12 Jean-Christophe Gauthier .30 .75
13 Oskars Bartulis .30 .75
14 Alexandre Quesnel .30 .75
15 Francois Gauthier .30 .75
16 Stephen Ceccanese .30 .75
17 Brendon Macdonald .30 .75
18 Charlie Pens .30 .75
19 Mark Barberio .30 .75
20 Mickey Macdonald .30 .75
21 Nick Macneil .30 .75
22 Paul McIlveen .30 .75
23 Ondrej Pavelec .40 1.00
24 David Davenport .30 .75
25 Screech MASCOT .02 .10

2009-10 Cape Breton Screaming Eagles

1 Luke Adam .40 1.00
2 Christopher Holden .40 1.00
3 Mathieu Brodeur .40 1.00
4 Morgan Ellis .40 1.00
5 Cory MacIntosh .40 1.00
6 Marc Bourgeois .40 1.00
7 Michael Ward .40 1.00
8 Logan Shaw .40 1.00
9 Nick MacNeil .40 1.00
10 Justin Chiasson .40 1.00
11 Maximilien Le Sieur .40 1.00
12 Taylor MacDougall .40 1.00
13 Brad Cuzner .40 1.00
14 Felix Bergeron .40 1.00
15 Stephen Horyl .40 1.00
16 Jean-Sebastien Fournier .40 1.00
17 Viktor Hertzberg .40 1.00
18 Myles Micallef .40 1.00
19 Jan Piskacek .40 1.00
20 Francis Meilleur .40 1.00
21 Patrick Lapostolle .40 1.00
22 Olivier Roy .40 1.00
23 Ashton Bernard .40 1.00

2003-04 Cape Fear Fire Antz

COMPLETE SET (17) 15.00 30.00
1 David Bagley .75 2.00
2 Mike Bournazakis .75 2.00
3 Kevin Fines .75 2.00
4 Ryan Kiley .75 2.00
5 Matt Kohanskey .75 2.00
6 Dave Leger .75 2.00
7 Mike Maurice .75 2.00
8 Darren McLean .75 2.00
9 Chris Migliore .75 2.00
10 Marc Milburn .75 2.00
11 Glenn Ridler 1.00 2.50
12 Tim Rink .75 2.00
13 Matt Shannon .75 2.00
14 Aaron Shrieves .75 2.00
15 Rob Vessio .75 2.00
16 Scott Young .75 2.00
17 Scott Rex CO .10 .25

1996-97 Carolina Monarchs

COMPLETE SET (30) 4.00 10.00
1 Checklist .02 .10
2 Chris Armstrong .15 .40
3 Drake Berehowsky .30 .75
4 Ashley Buckberger .15 .40
5 Chad Cabana .15 .40
6 Jon Christiano ACO .15 .40
7 Gilbert Dionne .30 .75
8 Trevor Doyle .15 .40
9 Ivan Droppa .15 .40
10 Craig Ferguson .20 .50
11 Craig Fisher .15 .40
12 Bob Halkidis .15 .40
13 Ryan Johnson .15 .40
14 Richard Kromm HCO .02 .10
15 Filip Kuba .15 .40
16 David Lemanowicz .08 .25
17 Craig Martin .20 .50
18 Eric Montreuil .15 .40
19 David Nemirovsky .15 .40
20 Jason Podollan .15 .40
21 Gaetan Poirier .15 .40
22 Garin Smith .15 .40
23 Geoff Smith .15 .40
24 Herbert Vasiljevs .15 .40
25 Steve Washburn .20 .50
26 Kevin Weekes .40 1.00
27 Dean Aayonce .15 .40
28 Monty MASCOT .02 .10
29 Prospect Card .15 .40
30 PHPA Web Site .01

2006-07 Cedar Rapids RoughRiders

COMPLETE SET (25) 10.00 20.00
1 Richard Bachman .40 1.00
2 Robin Bergman .40 1.00
3 David Boehm .40 1.00
4 Aaron Bogosian .40 1.00
5 Rob Bordson .40 1.00
6 Pat Cannone .40 1.00
7 Jacob Cepis .40 1.00
8 Brett Dickinson .40 1.00
9 Doug Jones .40 1.00
10 Sergei Kolosov .40 1.00
11 Scott Mathis .40 1.00
12 Kent Patterson .40 1.00
13 Mike Seidel .40 1.00
14 Ian Slater .40 1.00
15 Tomi Stahlhammer .40 1.00
16 Evan Stephens .40 1.00
17 Tyler Thompson .40 1.00
18 Matt Tomassoni .40 1.00
19 Kevin Wehrs .40 1.00
20 Casey Wellman .40 1.00
21 Scott Wietecha .40 1.00
22 Tommy Wingels .40 1.00
23 Mark Carlson CO .10 .25
24 Joe Exter ACO .10 .25
25 Ricochet MASCOT .02 .10

1994-95 Central Hockey League

COMPLETE SET (127) 15.00 40.00
1 Jamie Adams .15 .40
2 Wayne Anchikoski .20 .50
3 Jeff Beaudin .15 .40
4 Troy Binnie .20 .50
5 Don Burke .15 .40
6 Derek Crawford .15 .40
7 Ray Desouza .15 .40
8 Ron Flockhart CO .15 .40
9 Jon Gustafson .20 .50
10 Jason Heiland .15 .40
11 James Jensen .15 .40
12 Frank LaScala .15 .40
13 Ryan Leschasin .15 .40
14 Rob Madia .15 .40
15 Rob McCaig .15 .40
16 Jim McGeough .20 .50
17 Doug Roberts .15 .40
18 Jason Taylor .15 .40
19 Scott Allen .15 .40
20 Bruce Bell .20 .50
21 Francois Bourdeau .15 .40
22 Troy Frederick .15 .40
23 Steve Harrison CO .15 .40
24 Alex Kholomeyev .20 .50
25 Dominic Maltais .20 .50
26 Martin Masa .15 .40
27 Jeff Massey .15 .40
28 Mike McCormick .15 .40
29 Pat McGarry .20 .50
30 Dwight Mullins .15 .40
31 Eric Ricard .15 .40
32 Sean Rowe .15 .40
33 Bryan Schoen .15 .40
34 Darren Srochenski .15 .40
35 Andy Stewart .15 .40
36 Stephen Tepper .15 .40
37 Denis Beauchamp .15 .40
38 Herb Boxer CO .15 .40
39 Nicolas Brousseau .15 .40
40 Scott Brower .20 .50
41 Dan Brown .15 .40
42 Brian Cook .15 .40
43 Brent Fleetwood .15 .40
44 Francois Gagon .15 .40
45 Dominic Grand-Maison .15 .40
46 Kyle Haviland .15 .40
47 Jamie Hearn .15 .40
48 Mike Jackson .20 .50
49 Paul Krake .20 .50
50 Layne LeBel .15 .40
51 Steve Magnusson .15 .40
52 Mark McGinn .15 .40
53 Darren Miciak .15 .40
54 Bobby Wallwork .20 .50
55 Ron Aubrey .20 .50
56 Joe Burton .20 .50
57 George Dupont .20 .50
58 Tom Gomes .15 .40
59 Sean Gorman .15 .40
60 Viktor Ignatjev .20 .50
61 Chris Laganas .15 .40
62 Michael McEwen CO .20 .50
63 Chris McMurtry .15 .40
64 Derry Menard .15 .40
65 Sergei Naumov .20 .50
66 Trent Pankewicz .15 .40
67 Alan Perry .30 .75
68 Eric Plante .15 .40
69 Dave Slifka .15 .40
70 Steve Simoni .15 .40
71 Michel St. Jacques .15 .40
72 Tom Thornbury .15 .40
73 Trevor Buchanan .15 .40
74 Link Gaetz .30 .75
75 Sean Goldsworthy .15 .40
76 Fred Goltz .15 .40
77 Sheldon Gorski .15 .40
78 Ross Harris .15 .40
79 Dale Henry .20 .50
80 Paul Jackson .30 .75
81 Scott Kelsey .15 .40
82 John Klaers .15 .40
83 Stu Kulak .20 .50
84 Ken Plaquin .15 .40
85 Brian Shantz .20 .50
86 Dean Shmyr .20 .50
87 Adam Thompson .15 .40
88 John Torchetti .15 .40
89 Ken Venis .15 .40
90 Mike Williams .15 .40
91 Colin Baustad .15 .40
92 Luc Beausoleil .20 .50
93 Mike Berger .15 .40
94 Mark Cavallin .15 .40
95 Shaun Clouston .15 .40
96 Michel Couvrette .15 .40
97 Taylor Hall .15 .40
98 Ryan Harrison .15 .40
99 Sasha Lakovic .30 .75
100 Chuck Loreto .15 .40
101 Tony Martino .20 .50
102 David Moore .15 .40
103 Sylvain Naud .20 .50
104 Dan O'Rourke .15 .40
105 Jody Praznik .15 .40
106 Andy Ross .15 .40
107 Mike Shea .15 .40
108 Garry Unger CO .30 .75
109 Bob Berg .20 .50
110 John DePourcq .20 .50
111 Dave Doucette .20 .50
112 Ron Handy .20 .50
113 Mark Hilton .15 .40
114 Darcy Kaminski .15 .40
115 Mark Karpen .15 .40
116 Jim Latos .15 .40
117 George Maneluk .20 .50
118 Greg Neish .15 .40
119 Brent Sapergia .30 .75
120 Doug Shedden CO .15 .40
121 Greg Smith .15 .40
122 Conrade Thomas .15 .40
123 John Vary .15 .40
124 Rob Weingartner .15 .40
125 Bryan Wells .15 .40
126 Jack Williams .15 .40
127 Title Card CL .15 .40

1995-96 Central Hockey League

COMPLETE SET (90) 15.00 30.00
1 Scott Allen .15 .40
2 Trevor Burgess .15 .40
3 Brian Caruso .15 .40
4 Trevor Converse .15 .40
5 Steve Dykstra .30 .75
6 Troy Frederick .15 .40
7 Phil Groeneveld .15 .40
8 Mark Hilton .20 .50
9 Jeff Massey .15 .40
10 Dennis Miller .15 .40
11 Dwight Mullins .15 .40
12 Steve Plouffe .30 .75
13 Vern Ray .15 .40
14 Kyle Reeves .30 .75
15 Troy Stephens .15 .40
16 Sean Whyte .20 .50
17 Scorch .02 .10
18 Bill McDonald .15 .40
19 Scott Brower .20 .50
20 Dan Brown .15 .40
21 Jamie Cooke .15 .40
22 Kevin Evans .15 .40
23 Brent Fleetwood .15 .40
24 Ron Fogarty .15 .40
25 Trent Gleason .15 .40
26 Derek Grant .15 .40
27 Mike Jackson .30 .75

28 Scot Kelsey .15 .40
29 Steve Magnusson .15 .40
30 Carl Menard .30 .75
31 Chris Morque .20 .50
32 Rick Robus .15 .40
33 Andy Ross .15 .40
34 Stephane Roy .30 .75
35 Doug Stromback .15 .40
36 Herb Boxer .15 .40
37 Kevin Barrett .15 .40
38 Carl Boudreau .30 .75
39 Joe Burton .30 .75
40 George Dupont .20 .50
41 Dominic Fafard .15 .40
42 Jean-Ian Filiatrault .15 .40
43 Tom Gomes .15 .40
44 Todd Harris .15 .40
45 Mervin Kopeck .15 .40
46 Doug Lawrence .30 .75
47 Kevin Lune .15 .40
48 Steve Moore .15 .40
49 Simon Olivier .15 .40
50 Darren Pengelly .15 .40
51 Steve Simoni .15 .40
52 Barkley Swenson .15 .40
53 Serge Tkachenko .20 .50
54 Doug Sauter .15 .40
55 Colin Baustad .15 .40
56 Mike Berger .15 .40
57 Mike Chase .15 .40
58 Trevor Ellerman .15 .40
59 Bryan Forslund .15 .40
60 Taylor Hall .15 .40
61 Craig Hamelin .15 .40
62 Ryan Harrison .15 .40
63 John Laan .15 .40
64 Glen Lang .15 .40
65 Dave Larouche .15 .40
66 Tony Martino .30 .75
67 Sylvain Naud .30 .75
68 Jim Peters .15 .40
69 Cory Peterson .15 .40
70 Chris Robertson .15 .40
71 Kyuin Shim .15 .40
72 Garry Unger .30 .75
73 Clint Black .15 .40
74 Mike Chighisola .15 .40
75 Leonard Devuono .15 .40
76 Ty Eigner .30 .75
77 Anton Fedorov .20 .50
78 Paul Krake .30 .75
79 Antonin Necas .15 .40
80 Ryan Pisiak .15 .40
81 Richard Roesler .15 .40
82 Jason Rushton .15 .40
83 Art Saran .15 .40
84 Stefan Simoes .15 .40
85 Greg Smith .15 .40
86 Dale Turnbull .15 .40
87 Rob Weingartner .15 .40
88 Bryan Wells .15 .40
89 Jack Williams .15 .40
90 Don Jackson .30 .75

1997-98 Central Texas Stampede

COMPLETE SET (20) 3.00 8.00
1 Matt Brenner .20 .50
2 Mike Dick .20 .50
3 Darren Duncalfe .20 .50
4 Larry Dyck .20 .50
5 Dwayne Gylywoychuk .20 .50
6 Ricky Jacob .20 .50
7 Peter Jas .20 .50
8 Dean Kolstad .30 .75
9 Jacques Mailhot .30 .75
10 Don McGrath .20 .50
11 Derek Nicolson .20 .50
12 Jeff Rask .20 .50
13 Layne Roland .20 .50
14 Alex Rummo .20 .50
15 Doug Smith .20 .50
16 Greg Smith .20 .50
17 Joe Tassone .20 .50
18 Jason Taylor .20 .50
19 Peter Zurba .20 .50
20 Wild Thing Mascot .02 .10

1996-97 Charlotte Checkers

COMPLETE SET (20) 15.00 35.00
1 J.F. Aube .75 2.00
2 Eric Boulton 1.25 3.00
3 David Brosseau .75 2.00
4 Jeff Connolly .75 2.00
5 Kimbi Daniels .75 2.00
6 Mickey Elick .75 2.00
7 Eric Fenton .75 2.00
8 Mick Kempffer .75 2.00
9 Jay Kenney .75 2.00
10 Scott Kirton .75 2.00
11 Darcy Mitani .75 2.00
12 Darryl Norien .75 2.00
13 Kevin Rappana .75 2.00
14 Matt Robbins .75 2.00
15 Evgeni Ryabchikov .75 2.00
16 Kurt Seher .75 2.00
17 Nick Vitucci .75 2.00
18 Shawn Wheeler .75 2.00
19 John Marks HCO .75 2.00
20 Chubby Checker Mascot .02 .10

1997-98 Charlotte Checkers

COMPLETE SET (28) 15.00 30.00
1 Matt Alvey .40 1.00
2 Eric Boulton 1.25 3.00
3 David Brosseau .40 1.00
4 Paxton Schafer .60 1.50
5 Kurt Seher .40 1.00
6 Stephane Soulliere .40 1.00
7 Derek Crimin .40 1.00
8 Eric Flinton .40 1.00
9 Justin Gould .40 1.00
10 Jason Kelly .40 1.00
11 Mike Hartman .40 1.00
12 Jeff Heil .40 1.00
13 Jay Kenney .40 1.00
14 Milt Mastad .40 1.00
15 Dean Moore .40 1.00
16 Darryl Noren .40 1.00
17 Dale Purinton 1.25 3.00
18 Andre Roy 1.25 3.00
19 P.C. Drouin .60 1.50
20 Bill McCauley .40 1.00
21 Shawn Wheeler ACO .02 .10
22 John Marks HCO .02 .10
23 Chubby Checker Mascot .02 .10
24 Checklist .02 .10
25 Darryl Noren CAP .60 1.50
25 Eric Flinton CAP .60 1.50
25 Kurt Seher CAP .60 1.50
26 PHPA Web Site .02 .10

1998-99 Charlotte Checkers

COMPLETE SET (24) 10.00 25.00
1 J.F. Aube .60 1.50
2 Shannon Basaraba .40 1.00
3 Doug Battaglia .40 1.00
4 David Brosseau .40 1.00
5 Tom Brown .40 1.00
6 Pat Brownlee .40 1.00
7 Brooke Chateau .40 1.00
8 Jeff Heil .40 1.00
9 Boyd Kane .60 1.50
10 Kevin Kreutzer .40 1.00
11 Darryl Noren .60 1.50
12 Jason Norrie .40 1.00
13 Nikolai Pronin .40 1.00
14 Kurt Seher .60 1.50
15 Bob Sheehan .40 1.00
16 Ryan Sittler .40 1.00
17 Martin Sychra .40 1.00
18 Dean Zayonce .40 1.00
19 Shawn Wheeler CO .08 .25
20 Chubby Checker .08 .25
21 The Captains .40 1.00
22 Doug Battaglia
Pat Brownlee .40 1.00
23 J.F. Aube
Bob Sheehan .40 1.00
24 Checklist .02 .10

1999-00 Charlotte Checkers

COMPLETE SET (38) 8.00 20.00
1 Jason Dailey .20 .50
2 Brooke Chateau .20 .50
3 Rocky Welsing .20 .50
4 Kurt Seher .20 .50
5 Kevin Hilton .20 .50
6 Reggie Brezeault .20 .50
7 Lee Hamilton .20 .50
8 Dave Risk .20 .50
9 Taras Lendzyk .20 .50
10 Kurt Mallett .20 .50
11 Tyler Deis .20 .50
12 Mike Rucinski .30 .75
13 Derek Wilkinson .40 1.00
14 Richard Scott .40 1.00
15 David Beauregard .30 .75
16 Mike Jaros .20 .50
17 Darryl Noren .20 .50
18 Marc Tropper .20 .50
19 Scott Bailey .40 1.00
20 Jeff Brown .20 .50
21 Boyd Kane .40 1.00
22 Chubby Checker MASCOT .02 .10
23 The Carolina Cup .02 .10
24 Marc Tropper .30 .75
24 Brooke Chateau .20 .50
25 Mark Burgess TR .02 .10
26 Don MacAdam CO .02 .10
27 Scott Bailey .40 1.00
28 Dean Mando .30 .75
29 Kevin Pozzo .20 .50
30 Martin Cerven .20 .50
31 Marc Tropper AS .30 .75
32 Scott Bailey .40 1.00
33 Mike Rucinski .40 1.00
34 Tyler Deis .20 .50
34 David Beauregard .30 .75
35 Darryl Noren .20 .50
36 Checklist .02 .10

2000-01 Charlotte Checkers

COMPLETE SET (36) 10.00 25.00
1 Jason Labarbera .40 1.50
2 Scott Bailey .40 1.00
3 Scott King .40 1.00
4 Marc Tropper .30 .75
5 Boyd Kane .30 .75
6 Justin Harney .30 .75
7 Kurt Seher .30 .75
8 Brad Mehalko .30 .75
9 Kevin Hilton .30 .75
10 Mathieu Benoit .30 .75
11 David Oliver .30 .75
12 Lee Hamilton .30 .75
13 Wes Jarvis .30 .75
14 Josh MacNevin .30 .75
15 Kevin Pozzo .30 .75
16 Don MacAdam HCO .08 .25
17 Dave Baseggio CO .08 .25
18 Chubby Checker MASCOT .08 .25
19 Paul Giblin .30 .75
20 Tyler Deis .30 .75
21 Mark Spence .30 .75
22 Bob MacIsaac .30 .75
23 Steve Duke .30 .75
24 Andre Signoretti .30 .75
25 Brandon Dietrich .30 .75
26 Mike Derecola .30 .75
27 Chris Plumhoff .30 .75
28 Chubby Checker MASCOT .08 .25
29 Richard Scott .40 1.00
30 Vitali Yeremeyev .60 1.50
31 Benjamin Carpentier .30 .75
32 Francois Fortier .30 .75
33 Scott Wray .30 .75
34 Mark Moore .30 .75
35 Bryce Wandler .30 .75
36 Checklist .08 .10

2002-03 Charlotte Checkers

COMPLETE SET (18) 8.00 20.00
79 Nicholas Bilotto .40 1.00
80 Kevin Caulfield .40 1.00
81 Brandon Cullen .60 1.50
82 Allan Egeland .40 1.00
83 David Evans .40 1.00
84 David Inman .40 1.00
85 Dusty Jamieson .40 1.00
86 Vince Malts .40 1.00
87 Walker McDonald .40 1.00
88 Konrad McKay .60 1.50
89 Scott Meyer .60 1.50
90 Eduard Pershin .40 1.00
91 Kurt Seher .40 1.00
92 Takahito Suzuki .60 1.50
94 Craig Weller .40 1.00
95 Chad Wilchynski .40 1.00
96 Colin Zulianello .40 1.00

2003-04 Charlotte Checkers

COMPLETE SET (16) 6.00 15.00
65 Nicholas Bilotto .40 1.00
66 Kevin Caulfield .40 1.00
67 Doug Christiansen .40 1.00
68 Ryan Cuthbert .40 1.00
69 Allan Egeland .40 1.00
70 Blaz Emersic .40 1.00
71 Kengo Ito .40 1.00
72 Steven MacIntyre .40 1.00
73 Konrad McKay .40 1.00
74 Scott Meyer .60 1.50
75 Daisuke Obara .40 1.00
76 Rory Rawlyk .40 1.00
77 David St. Germain .60 1.50
78 Marc St. Jean .40 1.00
79 Jeff State .40 1.00
80 Mike Wirll .40 1.00

2013-14 Charlotte Checkers

COMPLETE SET () 6.00 15.00
1 Header Card .30 .75
2 Danny Biega .30 .75
3 Nicolas Blanchard .30 .75
4 Zach Boychuk .30 .75
5 Philippe Cornet .30 .75
6 Matt Corrente .30 .75
7 Sean Dolan .30 .75
8 Mark Flood .30 .75
9 A.J. Jenks .30 .75
10 Michal Jordan .30 .75
11 Austin Levi .30 .75
12 Keegan Lowe .30 .75
13 Matt Marquardt .30 .75
14 Mike Murphy .30 .75
15 John Muse .30 .75
16 Aaron Palushaj .30 .75
17 Victor Rask .30 .75
18 Rasmus Rissanen .30 .75
19 Beau Schmitz .30 .75
20 Justin Shugg .30 .75
21 Jared Staal .30 .75
22 Brett Sutter .30 .75
23 Brody Sutter .30 .75
24 Chris Terry .30 .75
25 Brendan Woods .30 .75

2002-03 Chicago Steel

COMPLETE SET (24) 8.00 20.00
1 Bill Bagron .40 1.00
2 Jordan Black .40 1.00
3 Dan Charleston .40 1.00
4 Adam D'Alba .60 1.50
5 Jeff Dunne .40 1.00
6 Josh Elzinga .40 1.00
7 Rene Gauthier .40 1.00
8 Ben Geelan .40 1.00
9 Brady Greco .60 1.50
10 Michael Grenzy .40 1.00
11 Eric Helstedt .40 1.00
12 Mike Kennedy .40 1.00
13 Vojtech Kloz .40 1.00
14 Justin Lewandowski .40 1.00
15 Travis Moran .40 1.00
16 Joseph Pearce 1.00 2.50
17 Topher Scott .40 1.00
18 Eric Slais .40 1.00
19 Chad Solberg .40 1.00
20 Alex Spezia .40 1.00
21 Lee Sweatt .40 1.00
22 Blake Williams .40 1.00
23 A.J. Toews CO .04 .10
24 Rusty Steel MASCOT .04 .10

2003-04 Chicago Steel

COMPLETE SET (18) 6.00 15.00
1 Matt McIlvane .60 1.50
2 Dan Marziani .40 1.00
3 Shane Connelly .60 1.50
4 Mike Van Wagner .40 1.00
5 Jay Sprague .40 1.00
6 Matt Clackson .40 1.00
7 Justin Lewandowski .40 1.00
8 Kevin Roeder .40 1.00
9 David Marshall .40 1.00
10 Chris Walsh .40 1.00
11 Jeff Dunne .40 1.00
12 Eric Lampe .40 1.00
13 Ryan Kim .40 1.00
14 John Kearns .40 1.00
15 Ryan Hawkins .40 1.00
16 T.J. Fox .40 1.00
17 Alex Spezia .40 1.00
18 Rene Gauthier .40 1.00
19 Rusty Steel MASCOT .04 .10

2004-05 Chicago Steel

COMPLETE SET (10) 4.00 10.00
1 Nathan Perkovich .40 1.00
2 T.J. Fox .40 1.00
3 Kevin Swallow .40 1.00
4 Eric Slais .40 1.00
5 Billy Sauer .40 1.00
6 Shane Connelly .40 1.00
7 Chris Clackson .40 1.00
8 Sami Liimainen .40 1.00
9 Ryan Oldis .40 1.00
10 Joe Loprieno .40 1.00

1998-99 Chicago Wolves

COMPLETE SET (25) 8.00 20.00
1 Brent Gretzky .40 1.00
2 Dan Plante .30 .75
3 Tim Bergland .30 .75
4 Steve Maltais .75 2.00
5 Steve Gosselin .40 1.00
6 Scott Pearson .30 .75
7 Niklas Andersson .40 1.00
8 Chris LiPuma .30 .75
9 Pat Jablonski .40 1.00
10 Skates MASCOT .02 .10
11 Tim Breslin .30 .75
12 Chris Marinucci .30 .75
13 Steve Larouche .30 .75
14 Wendell Young .75 2.00
15 Glen Featherstone .30 .75
16 Bob Nardella .30 .75
17 Guy Larose .30 .75
18 Dennis Vial .40 1.00
19 Kevin Dahl .30 .75
20 Jeremy Mylymok .30 .75
21 Paul Koch .30 .75
22 Tom Tilley .30 .75
23 John Anderson HCO .20 .50
24 Kevin Miller .40 1.00
25 PHPA Web Site .02 .10

1998-99 Chicago Wolves Turner Cup

COMPLETE SET (25) 10.00 25.00
1 Wendell Young .75 2.00
2 John Anderson .20 .50
3 Ray LeBlanc 1.25 3.00
3 Dave Craievich .20 .50
4 Paul Koch .20 .50
5 Kevin Dahl .20 .50
6 Jeremy Mylymok .20 .50
7 Bob Nardella .20 .50
8 Marc Rodgers 1.25 3.00
9 Marc Potvin .75 2.00
10 Steve Larouche .40 1.00
11 Steve Maltais 1.25 3.00
12 Doug Barrault .20 .50
13 Jamie Baker .20 .50
14 Chris Marinucci .20 .50
15 Tim Breslin .20 .50
16 Dennis Vial 1.25 3.00
17 Tom Tilley .20 .50
18 Scott Pearson .20 .50
19 Steve Martins .30 .75
20 Matt Martin .20 .50
21 Tim Bergland .20 .50
22 Alexander Semak .40 1.00
23 Ravil Gusmanov .20 .50
24 Stephane Beauregard .75 2.00

1999-00 Chicago Wolves

COMPLETE SET (25) 8.00 20.00
1 Header Card/PHPA .02 .10
2 Wendell Young .75 2.00
3 Kevin Dahl .30 .75
4 Dallas Eakins .30 .75
5 Bob Nardella .30 .75
6 Niklas Andersson .30 .75
7 Steve Larouche .75 2.00
8 Steve Maltais .75 2.00
9 Chris Marinucci .30 .75
10 Brian Noonan .40 1.00
11 Guy Larose .30 .75
12 Sean Berens .30 .75
13 Glen Featherstone .30 .75
14 Tom Tilley .30 .75
15 Scott Pearson .30 .75
16 Greg Andrusak .30 .75
17 Dean Malkoc .30 .75
18 David Mackey .30 .75
19 Dan Plante .30 .75
20 Chris LiPuma .30 .75
21 Andrei Trefilov .40 1.00
22 Daniel Lacroix .30 .75
23 John Anderson CO .08 .25
24 Marty Howe CO .30 .75
25 Skates MASCOT .08 .25

2000-01 Chicago Wolves

COMPLETE SET (25) 10.00 25.00
1 John Anderson .20 .50
2 Niklas Anderson .20 .50
3 Jesse Belanger .40 1.00
4 Rob Brown .40 1.00
5 Kevin Dahl .20 .50
6 Rick DiPietro 4.00 10.00
7 Ted Drury .20 .50
8 Dallas Eakins .20 .50
9 Glen Featherstone .20 .50
10 Eric Houde .20 .50
11 Paul Kruse .20 .50
12 Guy Larose .20 .50
13 Steve Larouche .40 1.00
14 Mark Lawrence .30 .75
15 Chris LiPuma .20 .50
16 Steve Maltais .80 2.00
17 Dean Melanson .20 .50
18 Bob Nardella .30 .75
19 Brian Noonan .40 1.00
20 Robert Petrovicky .30 .75
21 Dan Plante .20 .50
22 Tom Tilley .40 1.00
23 Wendell Young .40 1.00
24 Chicago Wolves .20 .25
25 Skates MASCOT .10 .25
NNO Header Card .02 .10

2001-02 Chicago Wolves

COMPLETE SET (25) 10.00 25.00
1 Bryan Adams .30 .75
2 Zdenek Blatny .40 1.00
3 Rob Brown .40 1.00
4 Frederic Cassivi .40 1.00
5 Jeff Dessner .30 .75
6 Dallas Eakins .30 .75
7 Garnet Exelby .60 1.50
8 Kurtis Foster .30 .75
9 Darcy Hordichuk .75 2.00
10 Derek MacKenzie .30 .75
11 Steve Maltais .40 1.00
12 Norm Maracle .40 1.00
13 Bob Nardella .30 .75
14 Pasi Nurminen 1.25 3.00
15 Kamil Piros .40 1.00
16 Dan Plante .30 .75
17 Brian Pothier .40 1.00
18 Luke Sellars .30 .75
19 Ben Simon .30 .75
20 Jarrod Skalde .40 1.00
21 Dan Snyder .40 1.00
22 Brad Tapper .40 1.00
23 J.P. Vigier .40 1.00
24 Mike Weaver .40 1.00
25 Skates MASCOT .10 .25

2002-03 Chicago Wolves

COMPLETE SET (25) 12.00 30.00
1 John Anderson CO .10 .25
2 Zdenek Blatny .60 1.50
3 Rob Brown .40 1.00
4 Frederic Cassivi .60 1.50
5 Joey DiPenta 1.25 3.00
6 Dallas Eakins .40 1.00
7 Garnet Exelby 1.25 3.00
8 Jeff Farkas .40 1.00
9 Kurtis Foster .40 1.00
10 Simon Gamache 1.25 3.00
11 Mark Hartigan .40 1.00
12 Milan Hnilicka 1.25 3.00
13 Andreas Karlsson .40 1.00
14 Francis Lessard .40 1.00
15 Derek MacKenzie .40 1.00
16 Steve Maltais 1.25 3.00
17 Norm Maracle 1.25 3.00
18 Kamil Piros .75 2.00
19 Kirill Safronov .40 1.00
20 Luke Sellars .40 1.00
21 Ben Simon .40 1.00
22 Skates MASCOT .04 .10
23 Ryan Tobler .40 1.00
24 Libor Ustrnul .40 1.00
25 J.P. Vigier .75 2.00

2003-04 Chicago Wolves

COMPLETE SET (25) 15.00 30.00
1 Stephen Baby .40 1.00
2 Zdenek Blatny .40 1.00
3 Jim Campbell .40 1.00
4 Frederic Cassivi .60 1.50
5 Daniel Corso .40 1.00
6 Joe DiPenta .60 1.50
7 Kurtis Foster .40 1.00
8 Michael Garnett .60 1.50
9 Greg Hawgood .40 1.00
10 Eric Healey .40 1.00
11 Shawn Heins .40 1.00
12 Kari Lehtonen 2.00 5.00
13 Derek MacKenzie .40 1.00
14 Brian Maloney .40 1.00
15 Steve Maltais .60 1.50
16 Kamil Piros .40 1.00
17 Tommi Santala .40 1.00
18 Luke Sellars .40 1.00
19 Karl Stewart .40 1.00
20 Brian Swanson .40 1.00
21 Libor Ustrnul .40 1.00
22 Mike Weaver .40 1.00
23 Brendan Yarema .40 1.00
24 John Anderson HCO .10 .25
25 Mascot .04 .10

2004-05 Chicago Wolves

COMPLETE SET (25) 40.00 75.00
1 Kari Lehtonen 4.00 10.00
2 Brad Larsen 1.00 2.50
3 Travis Roche 1.00 2.50
4 Michael Garnett 1.25 3.00
5 Greg Hawgood 1.00 2.50
6 Joe Corvo 1.00 2.50
7 Libor Ustrnul 1.00 2.50
8 Paul Flache 1.00 2.50
9 Colin Stuart 1.00 2.50
10 Kyle Rossiter 1.00 2.50
11 Brian Maloney 1.00 2.50
12 J.P. Vigier 1.50 4.00
13 Ben Simon 1.00 2.50
14 Brian Sipotz 1.00 2.50
15 Tim Wedderburn 1.00 2.50
16 Lonny Bohonos 1.50 4.00
17 Cory Larose 1.00 2.50
18 Kip Brennan 1.50 4.00
19 Stephen Baby 1.00 2.50
20 Kevin Doell 1.00 2.50
21 Karl Stewart 1.00 2.50
22 Steve Maltais 2.00 5.00
23 Derek MacKenzie 1.00 2.50
24 Tommi Santala 1.00 2.50
25 Skates MASCOT .40 1.00

2005-06 Chicago Wolves

COMPLETE SET (25) 10.00 25.00
1 Ramzi Abid .40 1.00
2 Stephen Baby .40 1.00
3 Scott Barney .40 1.00
4 Braydon Coburn .75 2.00
5 Kevin Doell .40 1.00
6 Pat Dwyer .40 1.00
7 Michael Garnett .75 2.00
8 Tomas Kloucek .40 1.00
9 Francis Lessard .40 1.00
10 Derek MacKenzie .40 1.00
11 Brian Maloney .40 1.00
12 Kip Miller .40 1.00
13 Justin Morrison .40 1.00
14 Nick Naumenko .40 1.00
15 Mark Popovic .40 1.00
16 Travis Roche .40 1.00
17 Jared Ross .40 1.00
18 Brian Sipotz .40 1.00
19 Karl Stewart .40 1.00
20 Colin Stuart .40 1.00
21 Tuomas Tarkki .40 1.00
22 Billy Tibbetts .40 1.00
23 Tim Wedderburn .40 1.00
24 John Anderson HC .02 .10
25 Skates MASCOT .02 .10

2007-08 Chicago Wolves

COMPLETE SET (27) 6.00 15.00
1 Joey Crabb .30 .75
2 Guillaume Desbiens .30 .75
3 Andre Deveaux .30 .75
4 Kevin Doell .30 .75
5 Brian Fahey .30 .75
6 Colton Fretter .30 .75
7 Robert Gherson .30 .75
8 Alexandre Giroux .30 .75
9 Darren Haydar .30 .75
10 Jason Krog .30 .75
11 Joel Kwiatkowski .30 .75
12 Jordan Lavallee .30 .75
13 Scott Lehman .30 .75
14 Grant Lewis .30 .75
15 Bryan Little .30 .75
16 Steve Martins .30 .75
17 Nathan Oystrick .30 .75
18 Chad Painchaud .30 .75
19 Ondrej Pavelec .75 2.00
20 Karel Pilar .30 .75
21 Jesse Schultz .30 .75
22 Brian Sipotz .30 .75
23 Brett Sterling .30 .75
24 Colin Stuart .30 .75
25 Boris Valabik .30 .75
26 John Anderson HC .30 .75
27 Skates MASCOT .30 .75

2009-10 Chicago Wolves

1 Paul Postma .40 1.00
2 Noah Welch .40 1.00
3 Reid Simpson .40 1.00
4 Brian Sipotz .40 1.00
5 Anthony Stewart .40 1.00
6 Chris Chelios .40 1.00
7 Spencer Machacek .40 1.00
8 Riley Holzapfel .40 1.00
9 Jason Krog .40 1.00
10 Mike Vernace .40 1.00
11 Patrick Galivan .40 1.00
12 Matt Anderson .40 1.00
13 Joey Crabb .40 1.00
14 Angelo Esposito .40 1.00
15 Rylan Kaip .40 1.00
16 Kevin Doell .40 1.00
17 Nathan Oystrick .40 1.00
18 Tim Stapleton .40 1.00
19 Jamie Hunt .40 1.00
20 Grant Lewis .40 1.00
21 Andrew Kozek .40 1.00
22 Johnny Pohl .40 1.00
23 Scott Lehman .40 1.00
24 Brett Sterling .40 1.00
25 Drew MacIntyre .40 1.00
26 Arturs Kulda .40 1.00
27 Peter Mannino .40 1.00
28 Steve McCarthy .40 1.00
29 Ivan Vishnevskiy .40 1.00
30 Don Granato CO .40 1.00
31 Ron Wilson ACO .40 1.00
32 Wendell Young GM .40 1.00
33 Skates .40 1.00

2013-14 Chicago Wolves

COMPLETE SET (31) 8.00 20.00
1 Cade Fairchild .30 .75
2 Joel Edmundson .30 .75
3 Taylor Chorney .30 .75
4 Jani Hakanpaa .30 .75
5 David Shields .30 .75
6 Ty Rattie .30 .75
7 Shane Harper .30 .75
8 Chris Porter .30 .75
9 Pat Cannone .30 .75
10 Michael Davies .30 .75
11 Mark Cundari .30 .75
12 Sergei Andronov .30 .75
13 Cody Beach .30 .75
14 Tyler Shattock .30 .75
15 Dmitrij Jaskin .30 .75
16 Adam Cracknell .30 .75
17 Mark Mancari .30 .75
18 Nathan Longpre .30 .75
19 Evan Oberg .30 .75
20 Brent Regner .30 .75
21 Keith Aucoin .30 .75
22 Christian Hanson .30 .75
23 Matt Climie .30 .75
24 Jake Allen .30 .75
25 Sebastian Wannstrom .30 .75
26 Alexandre Bolduc .30 .75
27 John Anderson CO .30 .75
28 Scott Allen Asst. CO .30 .75
29 Dave Allison Asst. CO .30 .75
30 Wendell Young GM .30 .75
31 Skates MASCOT .30 .75

2014-15 Chicago Wolves

COMPLETE SET (30) 8.00 20.00
1 John Anderson CO .30 .75
2 Cody Beach .30 .75
3 Jordon Binnington .30 .75
4 Rob Bordson .30 .75
5 Terry Broadhurst .30 .75
6 Mathieu Brodeur .40 1.00
7 Adam Burish .30 .75
8 Pat Cannone .30 .75
9 Jake Chelios .30 .75
10 Matt Climie .30 .75
11 Adam Cracknell .30 .75
12 Joel Edmundson .40 1.00
13 Benn Ferriero .30 .75
14 Colin Fraser .30 .75
15 Jani Hakanpaa .30 .75
16 Mark Hardy Asst. CO .30 .75
17 Shane Harper .30 .75
18 Petteri Lindbohm .30 .75
19 Nathan Longpre .30 .75
20 Phil McRae .30 .75
21 Magnus Paajarvi-Svensson .30 .75
22 Ty Rattie .75 2.00
23 Brent Regner .30 .75
24 David Shields .30 .75
25 Brad Tapper Asst. CO .30 .75
26 Yannick Veilleux .30 .75
27 Sebastian Wannstrom .30 .75
28 Jeremy Welsh .30 .75
29 Wendell Young GM .30 .75
30 Skates MASCOT .30 .75

1984-85 Chicoutimi Sagueneens

COMPLETE SET (24) 16.00 40.00
1 Mario Barbe .40 1.00
2 Mario Bazinet .40 1.00
3 Daniel Bedard
Michel Boivin
Guy Byatt
Jean-Marc Couture
Patrice Gosselin
Jean-Yves Laberge
Germain Munger
Reginald Riverin .40 1.00
4 Daniel Berthiaume 1.25 3.00
5 Francois Breault .60 1.50
6 Gregg Choules .40 1.00
7 Christian Duperron .40 1.00
8 Luc Dufour .40 1.00
9 Luc Duval .40 1.00
10 Patrick Emond .40 1.00
11 Marc Fortier .60 1.50
12 Steven Gauthier .40 1.00
13 Yves Heroux .60 1.50
14 Daniel Jomphe .40 1.00
15 Gilles Laberge .40 1.00
16 Claude Lajoie .40 1.00
17 Serge Lauzon .40 1.00
18 Roch Marinier .60 1.50
19 Pierre Millier .40 1.00
20 Marc Morin .40 1.00
21 Scott Rettew .40 1.00
22 Jean-Marc Richard .40 1.00
23 Stephane Richer 5.00 12.00
24 Pierre Sevigny .40 1.00

2000-01 Chicoutimi Sagueneens

COMPLETE SET (23) 4.80 15.00
1 Olivier Dannel .20 .50
2 Alex Turcotte .20 .50
3 Mathieu Betournay .20 .50
4 Michel Finn .20 .50
5 Eric Betournay .20 .50
6 Jonathan Francoeur .20 .50
7 Sebastien Laprise .20 .50
8 Sylvain Watt .20 .50
9 Sebastien Lucier .20 .50
10 Stanislav Hudec .20 .50
11 Christian Larrivee .20 .50
12 Francois Caron .20 .50
13 Eric Beaudin .20 .50
14 Alain Chenard .20 .50
15 Karl St-Pierre .20 .50
16 Michael Parent .20 .50
17 David Ouellet Beaudry .20 .50
18 Jean-Francois Demers .20 .50
19 Dave Verville .30 .75
20 Guillaume Karrer .20 .50
21 Martin Beauchesne .20 .50
22 Jean-Micheal Martin .20 .50
23 Pierre-Marc Bouchard 2.00 5.00

2000-01 Chicoutimi Sagueneens Signed

COMPLETE SET (23) 18.00 50.00
1 Olivier Dannel .80 2.00
2 Alex Turcotte .80 2.00
3 Mathieu Betournay .80 2.00
4 Michel Finn .80 2.00
5 Eric Betournay .80 2.00
6 Jonathan Francoeur .80 2.00
7 Sebastien Laprise .80 2.00
8 Sylvain Watt .80 2.00
9 Sebastien Lucier .80 2.00
10 Stanislav Hudec .80 2.00
11 Christian Larrivee .80 2.00
12 Francois Caron .80 2.00
13 Eric Beaudin .80 2.00
14 Alain Chenard .80 2.00
15 Karl St-Pierre .80 2.00
16 Michael Parent .80 2.00
17 David Ouellet Beaudry .80 2.00
18 Jean-Francois Demers .80 2.00
19 Dave Verville 2.00 5.00
20 Guillaume Karrer .80 2.00
21 Martin Beauchesne .80 2.00
22 Jean-Micheal Martin .80 2.00
23 Pierre-Marc Douchard 10.00 25.00

2001-02 Chicoutimi Sagueneens

COMPLETE SET (23) 6.00 15.00
1 Team Card .04 .10
2 Sebastien Lucier .20 .50
3 Eric Betournay .20 .50
4 Pierre-Alexandre Parenteau .30 .75
5 Stanislav Hudec .20 .50
6 Christian Larrivee .20 .50
7 Patrick Tessier .20 .50
8 Pierre-Luc Briere .20 .50
9 Yvan Busque .20 .50
10 Alexandre Blackburn .30 .75
11 Jean-Francois Demers .20 .50
12 Eric Tetrault .20 .50
13 Jeff Drouin Deslauriers .60 1.50
14 Eric Borbeau .20 .50
15 Michael Lanthier .20 .50
16 Nicolas Marcotte .20 .50
17 Hugues Verpaelst .20 .50
18 Francis Lemieux .20 .50
19 Jean-Vincent Lachance .20 .50
20 Martin Chabot .20 .50
21 Rosario Ruggeri .20 .50
22 Bruno Champagne .20 .50
23 Pierre-Marc Bouchard 1.25 3.00

2004-05 Chicoutimi Sagueneens

COMPLETE SET (24) 5.00 12.00
1 Alexandre Lamarche .20 .50
2 Alexandre Vincent .20 .50
3 Bernard Elhokayen .20 .50
4 Brandon Verge .20 .50
5 Brent Macsween .20 .50
6 David Desharnais .20 .50
7 Francis Lemieux .20 .50
8 Francis Verreault .20 .50
9 Gabriel Houde-Brisson .20 .50
10 Guillaume Lepine .20 .50
11 Julien Brouillette .20 .50
12 Louis-Etienne Leblanc .20 .50
13 Marc-Andre Roy .20 .50
14 Marek Zagrapan .60 1.50
15 Mathieu Bolduc .20 .50
16 Romy Elayoubi .30 .75
17 Stanislav Lascek .20 .50

18 Maxime Boisclair .40 1.00
19 Nicolas Blanchard .20 .50
20 Nicolas Marcotte .20 .50
21 Ryan Spaulding .20 .50
22 Shayne Tremblay .20 .50
23 Travis Coles .20 .50
24 Yan Gaudette .20 .50

2005-06 Chicoutimi Sagueneens

COMPLETE SET (31) 6.00 15.00
1 David Desharnais .20 .50
2 Stanislav Lascek .20 .50
3 Marek Zagrapan .40 1.00
4 Nicolas Blanchard .20 .50
5 Maxime Boisclair .40 1.00
6 Francis Verreault .20 .50
7 Shayne Tremblay .20 .50
8 Sylvain Michaud .20 .50
9 Alexandre Vincent .20 .50
10 Julien Brouillette .20 .50
11 Geoff Oliver .20 .50
12 Gabriel Carle .20 .50
13 Marc Myre .20 .50
14 Pierre-Luc Huot .20 .50
15 Maxime Tanguay .20 .50
16 Mathieu Bolduc .20 .50
17 Louis-Etienne Leblanc .20 .50
18 Jean-Claude Milot .20 .50
19 Brent MacSween .20 .50
20 Guillaume Lepine .20 .50
21 Oliver Lajeunesse .20 .50
22 Bruno-Pierre Gosselin .20 .50
23 Matthew Block .20 .50
24 Ryan Lehr .20 .50
25 Patrick Coulombe .20 .50
26 Jean-Sebastien Adam .20 .50
27 Gabriel Boies .20 .50
28 Nicolas Lafontaine .20 .50
29 Benoit Piche .20 .50
30 Jean-Sebastien Cote .20 .50
31 Sago MASCOT .02 .10

2006-07 Chicoutimi Sagueneens

COMPLETE SET (23) 8.00 15.00
1 David Desharnais .30 .75
2 Luc-Oliver Blain .30 .75
3 Nicolas Blanchard .30 .75
4 Mathieu Bolduc .30 .75
5 Julien Brouillette .30 .75
6 Patrick Campbell .30 .75
7 Francois Chabot .30 .75
8 Joel Champagne .30 .75
9 Derek Famulare .30 .75
10 Christopher Guay .30 .75
11 Alexandre Imbeault .30 .75
12 Dominic Jalbert .30 .75
13 Marc-Andre Julien .30 .75
14 Francois Levesque .30 .75
15 Jurai Mikus .30 .75
16 Bobby Nadeau .40 1.00
17 Olivier Painchaud .30 .75
18 Maxime Provencher .30 .75
19 Antoine Roussel .30 .75
20 Tommy Tremblay .30 .75
21 Kirill Tulupov .30 .75
22 Francois Verreault-Paul .30 .75
23 Joel Rechlicz .30 .75

2009-10 Chicoutimi Sagueneens

1 Robin Gusse .40 1.00
2 Jeremy Barriault .40 1.00
3 Michael Trudel .40 1.00
4 Steve Lebel .40 1.00
5 Emrick Guillemette .40 1.00
6 Mathieu Girard .40 1.00
7 Alexandre Roy .40 1.00
8 Marc-Andre Levasseur .40 1.00
9 Mathieu Populus .40 1.00
10 Adam Bourque-Leblanc .40 1.00
11 Gabriel Vermette .40 1.00
12 Maximilien Chevrier .40 1.00
13 Alexis Piette .40 1.00
14 Alexandre Lavoie .40 1.00
15 Christopher Tremblay .40 1.00
16 Julien Houle .40 1.00
17 Nicolas Therrien .40 1.00
18 Antoine Roussel .40 1.00
19 Michael Belanger .40 1.00
20 Christopher Gibson .40 1.00
21 Rock Regimbald .40 1.00
22 Dominic Jalbert .40 1.00
23 Eric Gelinas .40 1.00

2006-07 Chilliwack Bruins

COMPLETE SET (25) 15.00 25.00
1 Alex Archibald .60 1.50
2 Matt Esposito .60 1.50
3 Kevin Boutilier .40 1.00
4 Dylan Chapman .40 1.00
5 Cody Hobbs .40 1.00
6 Nick Holden .40 1.00
7 Craig Lineker .40 1.00
8 Scott Maetche .40 1.00
9 Cam Stevens .40 1.00
10 Matt McCue .40 1.00
11 Josh Aspenlind .40 1.00
12 Patrick Bhungal .40 1.00
13 Donnie Glennie .40 1.00
14 Colton Graf .40 1.00
15 Aki Kangasmaki .40 1.00
16 Colby Kulhanek .40 1.00
17 Matt Meropoulis .40 1.00
18 Dillon Johnstone .40 1.00
19 Oscar Moller .75 2.00
20 Special Edition Oscar Moller .75 2.00
21 Ken Petkau .40 1.00
22 Mark Santorelli .40 1.00
23 Cody Smuk .40 1.00
24 Mike Proudley .40 1.00
25 Bruiser MASCOT CL .02 .10

2009-10 Chilliwack Bruins

1 Chilliwack Bruins .40 1.00
2 Lucas Gore .40 1.00
3 Jesse Craige .40 1.00
4 Zach Habscheid .40 1.00
5 Matt Delahey .40 1.00
6 Jeff Einhorn .40 1.00
7 Tyler Stahl .40 1.00
8 Mitch Topping .40 1.00
9 Kevin Sundher .40 1.00
10 Roman Horak .40 1.00
11 Colton Grant .40 1.00
12 Chris Collins .40 1.00
13 Jamie Crooks .40 1.00
14 Travis Belohrad .40 1.00
15 Dylen McKinlay .40 1.00
16 Shayne Neigum .40 1.00
17 Ryan Howse .40 1.00
18 Blair Wentworth .40 1.00
19 Tim Traber .40 1.00
20 Brandon Manning .40 1.00
21 Alexander Wiklund .40 1.00
22 Braden Gamble .40 1.00
23 Marc Habscheid .40 1.00
24 Bruiser .40 1.00
25 The Bruinettes .40 1.00

1990-91 Cincinnati Cyclones

COMPLETE SET (23) 3.00 8.00
19 Steve McGrinder .15 .40
20 Steve Shaunessy .15 .40
21 Jay Rose .15 .40
22 Don Gagne .15 .40
23 Mike Williams .15 .40
24 Mike Chighisola .15 .40
25 Daryl Harpe .15 .40
26 Steve Cadieux .15 .40
27 Jeff Salzbrunn .15 .40
28 Rob Gador .15 .40
29 Chris Marshall .15 .40
30 Doug Melnyk .15 .40
31 Mark Turner .15 .40
32 Kevin Kerr .15 .40
33 Rob Krauss .15 .40
34 Mark Marentette .15 .40
35 Jamie Kompon .15 .40
36 Tom Neziol .15 .40
37 John Fletcher .15 .40
38 Dennis Desrosiers CO .08 .25
39 Todd Harrison TR .08 .25
40 Terry Ficorelli .15 .40
41 Craig Daly .15 .40

1991-92 Cincinnati Cyclones

COMPLETE SET (25) 3.00 8.00
1 Dan Beaudette .20 .50
2 Steve Benoit TR .02 .10
3 Steve Cadieux .15 .40
4 Craig Charron .15 .40
5 David Craievich .15 .40
6 Doug Dadswell .20 .50
7 Dennis Desrosiers CO .02 .10
8 Terry Ficorelli ANN .02 .10
9 Jeff Hogden .15 .40
10 Kevin Kerr .15 .40
11 Jaan Luik .15 .40
12 Scott Luik .15 .40
13 Chris Marshall .15 .40
14 Daryn McBride .15 .40
15 Doug Melnyk .15 .40
16 David Moore .15 .40
17 Tom Neziol .15 .40
18 Mark Romaine .15 .40
19 Jay Rose .15 .40
20 Martin St. Amour .20 .50
21 Kevin Scott .15 .40
22 Peter Schure .15 .40
23 Steve Shaunessy .15 .40
24 Blaine Stoughton CO .20 .50
25 Bobby Wallwork .15 .40

1992-93 Cincinnati Cyclones

COMPLETE SET (30) 3.00 8.00
1 Bill Armstrong .10 .30
2 Ralph Barahona .15 .40
3 Mike Bodnarchuk .15 .40
4 Craig Charron .15 .40
5 Todd Copeland .15 .40
6 Doug Dadswell .30 .75
7 Mike Dagenais .15 .40
8 Kevin Dean .15 .40
9 Chad Erickson .30 .75
10 Todd Flichel .15 .40
11 Alan Hepple .10 .30
12 Dennis Holland .15 .40
13 Sergei Kharin .15 .40
14 David Latta .15 .40
15 Jeff Madill .15 .40
16 Jon Morris .15 .40
17 Dean Morton .15 .40
18 Chris Nelson .15 .40
19 Darcy Norton .15 .40
20 Howie Rosenblatt .20 .50
21 Scott Shaunessy .15 .40
22 Mario Thyer .15 .40
23 Al Tuer .10 .30
24 Dennis Desrosiers HCO .02 .10
25 Blaine Stoughton ACO .02 .10
26 Alex Ochoa TR .10 .30
27 Mr. Cyclone Mascot .02 .10
28 Steve Benoit EM .02 .10
29 Terry Ficorelli ANN .02 .10
30 Wildman Walker ANN .08 .25

1993-94 Cincinnati Cyclones

COMPLETE SET (32) 4.00 10.00
1 Doug Barrault .15 .40
2 Len Barrie .30 .75
3 Don Biggs .15 .40
4 Chris Cichocki .10 .30
5 Jason Cirone .15 .40
6 Dallas Eakins .20 .50
7 Daniel Gauthier .15 .40
8 Jeff Greenlaw .15 .40
9 Rick Hayward .15 .40
10 Gord Hynes .15 .40
11 Ian Kidd .15 .40
12 Marc LaBelle .15 .40
13 Paul Lawless .15 .40
14 Jamie Leach .15 .40
15 Patrick Lebeau .20 .50
16 Ray LeBlanc .30 .75
17 Jamie Linden .15 .40
18 Jaroslav Nedved .15 .40
19 Darcy Norton .15 .40
20 Pokey Reddick .30 .75
21 Stephane Richer .15 .40
22 Jeff Serowik .15 .40
23 Scott Shaunessy .15 .40
24 Brad Smyth .10 .30
25 Dennis Desrosiers HCO .02 .10
26 Richard Kromm ACO .02 .10
27 Wildman Walker ANN .02 .10
28 Mr. Cyclone Mascot .02 .10
29 Mike Spilman TR .02 .10
30 Steve Benoit EQM .02 .10
31 Terry Ficorelli ANN .02 .10
NNO Header Checklist .02 .10

1995-96 Cincinnati Cyclones

COMPLETE SET (25) 4.00 10.00
1 Don Biggs .20 .50
2 Frederic Chabot .40 1.00
3 Chris Cichocki .20 .50
4 Chris Dahlquist .20 .50
5 Dale DeGray .20 .50
6 Brian Dobbin .20 .50
7 Len Esau .20 .50
8 Jeff Greenlaw .20 .50
9 Todd Hawkins .20 .50
10 Duane Joyce .20 .50
11 Chris Kontos .30 .75
12 Marc LaBelle .20 .50
13 Paul Lawless .30 .75
14 Danny Lorenz .30 .75
15 Doug MacDonald .20 .50
16 Dave Marcinyshyn .20 .50
17 Scott Thomas .20 .50
18 Dave Tomlinson .20 .50
19 Jeff Wells .20 .50
20 Bob Wilkie .20 .50
21 Nick Kenney TR .02 .10
22 Mark Mills TR .02 .10
23 Al Hill CO .02 .10
24 Ron Smith CO .02 .10
25 Snowbird MAS .02 .10

1996-97 Cincinnati Cyclones

COMPLETE SET (25) 4.00 10.00
1 Todd MacDonald .30 .75
3 Duane Joyce .20 .50
4 Ted Crowley .20 .50
5 Jeff Wells .20 .50
6 Myles O'Connor .20 .50
12 Todd Hawkins .20 .50
13 Paul Lawless .20 .50
17 Mike Casselman .20 .50
19 Scott Thomas .30 .75
22 Don Biggs .20 .50
24 Tony Horacek .20 .50
26 Marc Laniel .20 .50
27 Dave Marcinyshyn .20 .50
28 Scott Morrow .20 .50
29 Jeff Greenlaw .20 .50
31 Geoff Sarjeant .30 .75
33 Chris Cichocki .20 .50
37 Eric Dandenault .20 .50
44 Doug MacDonald .20 .50
51 Dale DeGray .20 .50
NNO Al Hill ASST CO .02 .10
NNO Snowbird (Mascot) .02 .10
NNO Nick Kenney TR .02 .10
NNO Mark Mills (Equip MG) .02 .10
NNO Ron Smith CO .02 .10

1997-98 Cincinnati Cyclones

COMPLETE SET (24) 4.80 12.00
1 Don Biggs .30 .75
2 Paul Broten .20 .50
3 Mike Casselman .20 .50
4 Eric Dandenault .20 .50
5 Gilbert Dionne .30 .75
6 Jeff Greenlaw .20 .50
7 Todd Hawkins .20 .50
8 Burt Henderson .20 .50
9 Steven King .20 .50
10 Marc LaBelle .20 .50
11 Doug MacDonald .20 .50
12 Todd MacDonald .20 .50
13 Pat MacLeod .20 .50
14 Scott Morrow .20 .50
15 Geoff Sarjeant .30 .75
16 Todd Simon .30 .75
17 Jeff Sirkka .20 .50
18 Jeff Wells .20 .50
19 David Williams .20 .50
20 Ron Smith CO .08 .25
21 Chris Cichocki CO .08 .25
22 Snowbird MAS .02 .10
23 Nick Kenney TR .02 .10
24 Mark Mills TR .02 .10

1998-99 Cincinnati Cyclones

COMPLETE SET (30) 6.00 10.00
1 Kaspars Astashenko .20 .50
2 Frederic Cassivi .30 .75
3 Phil Crowe .15 .40
4 Eric Dandenault .15 .40
5 Gilbert Dionne .30 .75
6 Todd Hawkins .15 .40
7 Jani Hurme .75 2.00
8 Burt Henderson .15 .40
9 Chris Joseph .15 .40
10 Ole Kjenstad .15 .40
11 Fred Knipscheer .15 .40
12 Doug Macdonald .15 .40
13 Pat Macleod .15 .40
14 Scott Morrow .15 .40
15 Tom Nemeth .15 .40
16 Kirk Nielsen .15 .40
17 Ed Patterson .15 .40
18 Rastislav Pavlikovsky .15 .40
19 Jeff Shevalier .15 .40
20 Todd Simon .15 .40
21 Geoff Smith .15 .40
22 Jeff Wells .15 .40
23 Snowbird Mascot .02 .10
24 Nick Kenney TR .02 .10
25 Mark Mills EQ .02 .10
26 Scott Macpherson ACO .02 .10
27 Chris Cichocki ACO .02 .10
28 Ron Smith CO .02 .10
29 Team Card .02 .10
30 Logo Card .02 .10

1998-99 Cincinnati Cyclones 2

COMPLETE SET (30) 10.00 25.00
1 Todd Hawkins .40 1.00
2 Kirk Nielsen .40 1.00
3 Ed Patterson .40 1.00
4 Fred Knipscheer .40 1.00
5 Doug Macdonald .40 1.00
6 Todd Simon .40 1.00
7 Phil Crowe .40 1.00
8 Gilbert Dionne .40 1.00
9 Scott Morrow .40 1.00
10 Rastislav Pavlikovsky .40 1.00
11 Jeff Shevalier .40 1.00
12 Kaspars Astashenko .40 1.00
13 Eric Dandenault .40 1.00
14 Burt Henderson .40 1.00
15 Chris Joseph .40 1.00
16 Pat MacLeod .40 1.00
17 Geoff Smith .40 1.00
18 Jeff Wells .40 1.00
19 Frederic Cassivi .75 2.00
20 Jani Hurme .75 2.00
21 Tom Nemeth .40 1.00
22 Olaf Kjenstad .40 1.00
23 Team Photo Card .20 .50
24 Ron Smith CO .20 .50
25 Chris Cichocki CO .20 .50
26 Scott MacPherson CO .20 .50
27 Mark Mills EM .20 .50
28 Nick Kenney TR .02 .10
29 Snowbird MASCOT .02 .10
30 PHPA Card .01 .05

1999-00 Cincinnati Cyclones

COMPLETE SET (27) 4.80 10.00
1 Team Logo .10 .25
2 Craig Adams .20 .50
3 Steve Bancroft .20 .50
4 Eric Dandenault .20 .50
5 Gilbert Dionne .30 .75
6 Gilbert Dionne MVP .30 .75
7 Mark Fitzpatrick .30 .75
8 Len Esau .20 .50
9 Todd Hawkins .20 .50
10 David Karpa .20 .50
11 Greg Koehler .20 .50
12 Greg Kuznik .20 .50
13 Craig McDonald .30 .75
14 Pat McLeod .20 .50
15 Ian McNeil .20 .50
16 Randy Petruk .30 .75
17 Mike Rucinski .20 .50
18 Todd Simon .30 .75
19 Nikos Tselios .30 .75
20 Stefan Ustorf .30 .75
21 Shane Willis .40 1.00
22 Chris Cichocki CO .20 .50
23 Nick Kenney TR .02 .10
24 Mark Mills EM .02 .10
25 Ron Smith HCO .20 .50
26 Snowbird MASCOT .02 .10
27 PHPA Logo .02 .10

2000-01 Cincinnati Cyclones

COMPLETE SET (30) 8.00 20.00
1 Nikos Tselios .30 .75
2 Jeremiah McCarthy .30 .75
3 Greg Kuznik .20 .50
4 Byron Ritchie .40 1.00
5 Craig MacDonald .30 .75
6 Greg Koehler .20 .50
7 Stefan Ustorf .30 .75
8 Jeff Heerema .40 1.00
9 Mike Rucinski .40 1.00
10 Ian MacNeil .20 .50
11 Gilbert Dionne .40 1.00
12 Erik Cole 1.50 4.00
13 Reggie Berg .30 .50
14 Jon Rohloff .20 .50
15 Len Esau .20 .50
16 Brian Felsner .30 .75
17 Brad DeFauw .20 .50
18 Harlan Pratt .20 .50
19 Jaroslav Svoboda .75 1.00
20 Jean-Marc Pelletier .40 1.00
21 Corey Hirsch .30 .75
22 Marc Magliarditi .30 .75
23 Ron Smith CO .20 .50
24 Mark Mills EM .04 .10
25 Nick Kenney TR .04 .10
26 Snowbird MASCOT .04 .10
27 GMC Zamboni SPONSOR .10 .25
28 Team Photo .20 .50
29 The Firstar Center .02 .10
30 PHPA Web Site .02 .10

1998-99 Cincinnati Mighty Ducks

COMPLETE SET (29) 8.00 20.00
1 Buster MASCOT .08 .25
2 Marc Andreozzi TR .02 .10
3 Gary Linquist EM .02 .10
4 John Walton .30 .75
5 Ed Johnstone ACO .08 .25
6 Moe Mantha HCO .08 .25
7 Frank Banham .40 1.00
8 Mike LeClerc 1.25 3.00
9 Byron Briske .30 .75
10 Eric Lecompte .30 .75
11 Terran Sandwith .30 .75
12 Jamie Ram .40 1.00
13 Craig Reichert .30 .75
14 Joel Kwiatkowski .30 .75
15 Mike Crowley .40 1.00
16 Matt Leon .30 .75
17 Jeremy Stevenson .30 .75
18 Dan Trebil .30 .75
19 Bob Wren .30 .75
20 Lloyd Shaw .30 .75
21 Igor Nikulin .30 .75
22 Jeff Winter .30 .75
23 Tony Mohagen .30 .75
24 Tony Tuzzolino .30 .75
25 Peter LeBoutillier .30 .75
26 Tom Askey .60 1.50
27 Marc Chouinard .40 1.00
28 Scott Ferguson .30 .75
29 PHPA Web Site .02 .10

1999-00 Cincinnati Mighty Ducks

COMPLETE SET (32) 12.00 30.00
1 Parent Clubs .08 .25
2 Moe Mantha CO .08 .25
3 Jason Payne .30 .75
4 Jeff Nielsen ALUM .30 .75
5 Antti Aalto ALUM .40 1.00
6 Ruslan Salei ALUM .30 .75
7 Joel Kwiatkowski .30 .75
8 Aren Miller .40 1.00
9 Dan Trebil .30 .75
10 Rastislav Pavlikovsky .30 .75
11 Frank Banham .40 1.00
12 Scott Ferguson .30 .75
13 Maxim Balmochnykh .60 1.50
14 Darryl Laplante .60 1.50
15 Johan Davidsson .60 1.50
16 Peter Leboutillier .30 .75
17 Jesse Wallin .40 1.00
18 Alexandre Jacques .40 1.00
19 B.J. Young .40 1.00
20 Ed Johnstone CO .08 .25
21 Ryan Hoople .20 .50
22 Matt Cullen ALUM .75 2.00
22 Mike LeClerc .75 2.00
22 Pavel Trnka ALUM .30 .75
23 Buster MASCOT .08 .25
24 Jeremy Stevenson .30 .75
25 Jay Legault .30 .75
26 Marc Chouinard .40 1.00
27 Torrey DiRoberto .40 1.00
28 Maxim Kuznetsov .40 1.00
29 Shane Hnidy .30 .75
30 Vitali Vishnevsky .40 1.00
31 Bob Wren .30 .75
32 Gregg Naumenko .60 1.50

2001-02 Cincinnati Mighty Ducks

COMPLETE SET (28) 10.00 25.00
1 Sean Avery 1.00 2.50
2 Maxim Balmochnykh .40 1.00
3 Drew Bannister .30 .75
4 Ryan Barnes .30 .75
5 Travis Brigley .30 .75
6 Aris Brimanis .30 .75
7 Steve Brule .30 .75
8 Ilja Bryzgalov 1.00 2.50
9 Garrett Burnett .40 1.00
10 Yuri Butsayev .30 .75
11 Josh DeWolf .30 .75
12 Jason Elliott .60 1.50
13 Ryan Gaucher .30 .75
14 Andy McDonald 1.00 2.50
15 Antti-Jussi Niemi .40 1.00
16 Timo Parssinen .40 1.00
17 Peter Podhradsky .30 .75
18 Bruce Richardson .30 .75
19 Bert Robertsson .30 .75
20 David Roche .30 .75
21 Jonas Ronnqvist .40 1.00
22 Jarrett Smith .30 .75
23 Brian White .30 .75
24 Jason Williams .30 .75
25 Dwayne Zinger .30 .75
26 Mike Babcock CO .10 .25
27 Kevin Kaminski ACO .10 .25
28 Buster the Duck MASCOT .04 .10

2002-03 Cincinnati Mighty Ducks

COMPLETE SET (28) 15.00 30.00
A1 Mike Commodore 1.25 3.00
A2 Samuel Pahlsson .75 2.00
A3 Jean-Francois Damphousse .75 2.00
A4 Todd Reirden .40 1.00
A5 Jonathan Hedstrom .75 2.00
A6 Chris O'Sullivan .40 1.00
A7 Jarrett Smith .40 1.00
A8 Travis Brigley .40 1.00
A9 Brian Gornick .40 1.00
A10 Tony Martensson .40 1.00
A11 Cory Pecker .75 2.00
A12 Nick Smith .40 1.00
A13 Cam Severson 1.25 3.00
A14 Pete Podrasky .40 1.00
B1 Ilja Bryzgalov 1.25 3.00
B2 Darryl Williams ACO .20 .50
B3 Brad Shaw CO .20 .50
B4 Buster MASCOT .04 .10
B5 Puck Boy .04 .10
B6 Jan Tabacek .40 1.00
B7 Mark Popovic .75 2.00
B8 Rob Valicevic .40 1.00
B9 Ben Guite .75 2.00
B10 Francis Belanger .40 1.00
B11 Team Photo .40 1.00
B12 Josh DeWolf .40 1.00
B13 Jason Krog .75 2.00
B14 Alexei Smirnov .40 1.00

2003-04 Cincinnati Mighty Ducks

COMPLETE SET (28) 10.00 25.00
A1 Keith Aucoin .40 1.00
A2 Eddie Ferhi .40 1.00
A3 Mike Mottau .40 1.00
A4 Pierre-Alexander Parenteau .40 1.00
A5 Cory Pecker .40 1.00
A6 Mark Popovic .40 1.00
A7 Todd Reirden .40 1.00
A8 Andy Reierson .40 1.00
A9 Cam Severson .40 1.00
A10 Alexei Smirnov .40 1.00
A11 Nick Smith .40 1.00
A12 Joel Stepp .40 1.00
A13 Darryl Williams ACO .10 .25
A14 Puck Boy .10 .25
B1 Juha Alen .40 1.00
B2 Chris Armstrong .40 1.00
B3 Sheldon Brookbank .40 1.00
B4 Ilja Bryzgalov .75 2.00
B5 Brian Gornick .40 1.00
B6 Casey Hankinson .40 1.00
B7 Mikael Holmqvist .40 1.00
B8 Chris Kunitz 1.00 2.50
B9 Tony Martensson .40 1.00
B10 Shane O'Brien .75 2.00
B11 Joel Perrault .40 1.00
B12 Igor Pohanka .40 1.00
B13 Brad Shaw CO .10 .25
B14 Mascot .04 .10

2004-05 Cincinnati Mighty Ducks

COMPLETE SET (30) 15.00 30.00
1 Brad Shaw CO .20 .50
2 Dan Bylsma ACO .20 .50
3 Aaron Rome .75 2.00
4 Juha Alen .40 1.00
5 Kurtis Foster .40 1.00
6 Shane O'Brien .75 2.00
7 Mark Popovic .40 1.00
8 Tim Brent .40 1.00
9 Buster MASCOT .04 .10
10 Joel Perrault .40 1.00
11 Zenon Konopka .40 1.00
12 Igor Pohanka .40 1.00
13 Sean O'Connor .40 1.00
14 Chris Kunitz .75 2.00
15 Joffrey Lupul 1.50 4.00
16 Joel Stepp .40 1.00
17 Sheldon Brookbank .40 1.00
18 Michael Holmqvist .40 1.00
19 Cory Pecker .40 1.00
20 Curtis Glencross .40 1.00
21 Sponsor card .04 .10
22 Alexei Smirnov .40 1.00
23 Stanislav Chistov .75 2.00
24 Dustin Penner 1.50 4.00
25 Pierre Parenteau .40 1.00
26 Checklist .04 .10
27 Tomas Malec .40 1.00
28 Eddie Ferhi .40 1.00
29 Ilja Bryzgalov .75 2.00
30 Frederic Cassivi .75 2.00

1992-93 Clarkson Knights

COMPLETE SET (24) 4.80 12.00
1 Josh Bartell .15 .40
2 Hugo Belanger .20 .50
3 Craig Conroy .60 1.50
4 Jason Currie .15 .40
5 Steve Dubinsky .20 .50
6 Shawn Fotheringham .15 .40
7 Dave Green .15 .40
8 Ed Henrich .15 .40
9 Chris Lipsett .15 .40
10 Todd Marchant .75 2.00
11 Brian Mueller .20 .50
12 Kevin Murphy .15 .40
13 Martin d'Orsonnens .15 .40
14 Steve Palmer .15 .40
15 Patrice Robitaille .15 .40
16 Chris Rogles .20 .50
17 Jerry Rosenheck .15 .40
18 Chris de Ruiter .15 .40
19 Guy Sanderson .15 .40
20 David Seitz .15 .40
21 Mikko Tavi .15 .40
22 Patrick Theriault .15 .40
23 Marko Tuomainen .20 .50
24 Men's Hockey 1992-93 Martin d'Orsonnens Steve Du .15 .40

1951-52 Cleveland Barons

COMPLETE SET (20) 75.00 150.00
1 Bun Cook CO 5.00 10.00
2 Fred Shero 10.00 20.00
3 Ed Reigle 3.00 6.00
4 Ike Hildebrand 3.00 6.00
5 Eddie Olson 3.00 6.00
6 Jerry Reid 3.00 6.00
7 Fred Thurier 3.00 6.00
8 Steve Wochy 3.00 6.00
9 Joe Carveth 4.00 8.00
10 Tom Williams 5.00 10.00
11 Johnny Bower 25.00 50.00
12 Jack Gordon 4.00 8.00
13 Ken Schultz 3.00 6.00
14 Fern Perreault 3.00 6.00
15 Ray Ceresino 3.00 6.00
16 Bob Bailey 3.00 6.00
17 Bob Chrystal 4.00 8.00
18 Phil Samis 3.00 6.00
19 Paul Gladu 3.00 6.00
20 Joe Lund 3.00 6.00

1960-61 Cleveland Barons

COMPLETE SET (19) 60.00 120.00
1 Ron Attwell 3.00 6.00
2 Les Binkley 5.00 10.00
3 Bill Dineen 4.00 8.00
4 John Ferguson 10.00 20.00
5 Cal Gardner 4.00 8.00
6 Fred Glover 4.00 8.00
7 Jack Gordon 4.00 8.00
8 Aldo Guidolin 4.00 8.00
9 Greg Hicks 3.00 6.00
10 Wayne Larkin 3.00 6.00
11 Moe Mantha 4.00 8.00
12 Gil Mayer 3.00 6.00
13 Eddie Mazur 3.00 6.00
14 Jim Mikol 3.00 6.00
15 Bill Needham 3.00 6.00
16 Cal Stearns 3.00 6.00
17 Bill Sutherland 5.00 10.00
18 Tom Williams 4.00 8.00
19 Team Photo 5.00 10.00

1992-93 Cleveland Lumberjacks

COMPLETE SET (25) 4.00 10.00
1 Title Card .02 .10
2 Larry Gordon GM .02 .10
3 Paul Laus .30 .75
4 Travis Thiessen .20 .50
5 Phil Russell CO .20 .50
6 Gilbert Delorme ACO .20 .50
7 Jamie Heward .20 .50
8 Greg Andrusak .20 .50
9 David Quinn .20 .50
10 Perry Ganchar .20 .50
11 George Zajankala UER Birthplace misspelled Reve .20 .50
12 Todd Nelson .20 .50
13 Dave Michayluk .20 .50
14 Bruce Racine .25 .60
15 Rob Dopson .25 .60
16 Bert Godin TR .02 .10
17 Ed Patterson .25 .60
18 Justin Duberman .20 .50
19 Sandy Smith .20 .50
20 Jason Smart .20 .50
21 Ken Priestlay .20 .50
22 Daniel Gauthier .20 .50
23 Robert Melanson .20 .50
24 Mark Major .20 .50
25 Paul Dyck .20 .50

1993-94 Cleveland Lumberjacks

COMPLETE SET (24) 4.00 10.00
1 Title Card .08 .25
2 Rick Paterson CO .08 .25
3 Gilbert Delorme ACO .08 .25
4 Paul Dyck .30 .75
5 Travis Thiessen .20 .50
6 Mike Dagenais .20 .50
7 Chris Tamer .20 .50
8 Greg Andrusak .20 .50
9 Todd Hawkins .20 .50
10 Jamie Black .20 .50
11 Justin Duberman .20 .50
13 Jock Callander UER (Misspelled Jack on front) .30 .75
14 Leonid Toropchenko .20 .50
15 Victor Gervais .20 .50
16 Perry Ganchar .20 .50
17 Ed Patterson .20 .50
18 Ladislav Karabin .20 .50
19 Dave Michayluk .20 .50
20 Jamie Heward .20 .50
21 Pat Neaton .20 .50
22 Rob Dopson .30 .75
23 Steve Bancroft .20 .50
24 Olie Sundstrom .20 .50
25 Grant Block .20 .50

1993-94 Cleveland Lumberjacks Postcards

COMPLETE SET (22) 4.00 10.00
1 Greg Andrusak .20 .50
2 Steve Bancroft .20 .50
3 Jamie Black .20 .50
4 Grant Block .20 .50
5 Jock Callander .30 .75
6 Mike Dagenais .20 .50
7 Gilbert Delorme ACO .08 .25
8 Rob Dopson .30 .75
9 Justin Duberman .20 .50
10 Paul Dyck .30 .75
11 Perry Ganchar .20 .50
12 Todd Hawkins .20 .50
13 Jamie Heward .20 .50
14 Ladislav Karabin .20 .50
15 Dave Michayluk .20 .50
16 Pat Neaton .20 .50
17 Rick Paterson CO .08 .25
18 Ed Patterson .20 .50
19 Olie Sundstrom .20 .50
20 Chris Tamer .20 .50
21 Travis Thiessen .20 .50
22 Leonid Toropchenko .20 .50

1994-95 Cleveland Lumberjacks

COMPLETE SET (25) 4.80 12.00
1 Rick Paterson HCO .08 .25
2 Philippe DeRouville .30 .75
3 Paul Dyck .25 .60
4 Rick Hayward .20 .50
5 Mike Dagenais .20 .50
6 Chris Tamer .30 .75
7 Len Barrie .30 .75
8 Eric Murano .20 .50
9 Brad Lauer .20 .50
10 Ian Moran .20 .50
11 Brian Farrell .20 .50
12 Jock Callander .30 .75
13 Jeff Christian .20 .50
14 Larry DePalma .20 .50
15 Joe Dziedzic .20 .50
16 Victor Gervais .20 .50
17 Dominic Pittis .20 .50
18 Perry Ganchar .20 .50
19 Ed Patterson .30 .75
20 Ladislav Karabin .20 .50
21 Dave Michayluk ACO .20 .50
22 Michal Straka .20 .50
23 Corey Beaulieu .20 .50
24 Olie Sundstrom .25 .60
25 Dale DeGray .20 .50

1995-96 Cleveland Lumberjacks

COMPLETE SET (24) 4.80 12.00
1 Peter Allen .15 .40
2 Bill Armstrong .15 .40
3 Len Barrie .30 .75
4 Dave Baseggio .15 .40
5 Oleg Belov .15 .40
6 Drake Berehowsky .15 .40
7 Stefan Bergkvist .15 .40
8 Jock Callander .30 .75
9 Jeff Christian .15 .40
10 Philippe DeRouville .30 .75
11 Rusty Fitzgerald .15 .40
12 Corey Foster .15 .40
13 Perry Ganchar ACO .02 .10
14 Victor Gervais .15 .40
15 Rick Hayward .15 .40
16 Patrick Lalime 1.25 3.00
17 Brad Lauer .15 .40
18 Dave McLlwain .20 .50
19 Dave Michayluk .15 .40
20 Mark Osborne .15 .40
21 Rick Paterson CO .02 .10
22 Dominic Pittis .15 .40
23 Ryan Savoia .15 .40

24 Mike Stevens .15 .40
25 Title Card .02 .10

1996-97 Cleveland Lumberjacks
COMPLETE SET (25) 10.00 20.00
1 Peter Allen .30 .75
2 Bill Armstrong .30 .75
3 Serge Aubin .40 1.00
4 Brian Bonin .40 1.00
5 Sven Butenschon .30 .75
6 Buzz MASCOT .08 .25
7 Jock Callendar .75 2.00
8 Jeff Christian .30 .75
9 Rusty Fitzgerald .30 .75
10 Corey Foster .30 .75
11 Rick Hayward .30 .75
12 Jan Hrdina .40 1.00
13 Petr Klima .40 1.00
14 Lane Lambert .30 .75
15 Brad Lauer .30 .75
16 Dave McLlwain .40 1.00
17 Dave Michayluk .40 1.00
18 Ian Moran .40 1.00
19 Mark Osborne .30 .75
20 Jim Paek .30 .75
21 Richard Park .30 .75
22 Rick Paterson CO .08 .25
23 Ed Patterson .30 .75
24 Mike Tamburro .30 .75
25 Derek Wilkinson .30 .75

1996-97 Cleveland Lumberjacks Multi-Ad
COMPLETE SET (30) 6.00 15.00
1 Checklist .02 .10
2 Peter Allen .15 .40
3 Bill Armstrong .15 .40
4 Serge Aubin .40 1.00
5 Stefan Bergkvist .15 .40
6 Brian Bonin .20 .50
7 Sven Butenschon .15 .40
8 Jock Callander .30 .75
9 Jeff Christian .15 .40
10 Rusty Fitzgerald .15 .40
11 Corey Foster .15 .40
12 Perry Ganchar CO .02 .10
13 Rick Hayward .15 .40
14 Jan Hrdina .40 1.00
15 Patrick Lalime 1.25 3.00
16 Lane Lambert .15 .40
17 Brad Lauer .15 .40
18 Dave McLlwain .30 .75
19 Dave Michayluk .30 .75
20 Ian Moran .20 .50
21 Mark Osborne .15 .40
22 Jim Paek .15 .40
23 Richard Park .15 .40
24 Rick Paterson CO .02 .10
25 Ed Patterson .15 .40
26 Mike Tamburro .15 .40
27 Derek Wilkinson .20 .50
28 Buzz MAS .02 .10
29 Heritage Night .02 .10
30 Logo Card .02 .10

1997-98 Cleveland Lumberjacks
COMPLETE SET (30) 4.00 20.00
1 Team Photo .02 .10
2 Perry Ganchar HCO .02 .10
3 Mark Osborne ACO .02 .10
4 Dave Baseggio .10 .30
5 Stefan Bergkvist .10 .30
6 Jock Callander .40 1.00
7 Mark Cornforth .10 .30
8 John Craighead .10 .30
9 Joe Dziedzic .10 .30
10 Vadim Epantchincov .10 .30
11 Rusty Fitzgerald .10 .30
12 Brett Harkins .10 .30
13 Rick Hayward .20 .50
14 Pat Jablonski .40 1.00
15 Alexei Krivchenkov .10 .30
16 Lane Lambert .10 .30
17 Brad Lauer .10 .30
18 Chris Longo .10 .30
19 Jason McBain .10 .30
20 Ryan Mougenel .10 .30
21 Jim Paek .10 .30
22 Rob Pearson .10 .30
23 Eric Perrin .75 2.00
24 Martin St. Louis 2.00 5.00
25 Mike Tamburro .10 .30
26 Darren Wetherill .10 .30
27 Derek Wilkinson .40 1.00
28 Martin St. Louis
Eric Perrin 2.00 5.00
29 Buzz Mascot .02 .10
30 PHPA Web site .02 .10

1997-98 Cleveland Lumberjacks Postcards
COMPLETE SET (25) 7.20 30.00
1 Perry Ganchar HCO .08 .25
2 Mark Osborne ACO .08 .25
3 Darren Wetherill .30 .75
4 Rick Hayward .30 .75
5 Jim Paek .30 .75
6 Dave Baseggio .30 .75
7 Martin St. Louis 4.00 10.00
8 John Craighead .30 .75
9 Eric Perrin 1.50 4.00
10 Rusty Fitzgerald .30 .75
11 Chris Longo .30 .75
12 Jock Callander .75 2.00
13 Joe Dziedzic .30 .75
14 Lane Lambert .30 .75
15 Mark Cornforth .30 .75
16 Vadim Epantchisev .30 .75
17 Rob Pearson .30 .75
18 Jason McBain .30 .75
19 Alexei Krivchenkov .30 .75
20 Derek Wilkinson .40 1.00
21 Brad Lauer .30 .75
22 Stefan Bergkvist .30 .75
23 Brett Harkins .30 .75
24 Mike Tamburro .30 .75
25 Buzz Mascot .08 .25

1998-99 Cleveland Lumberjacks
COMPLETE SET (24) 4.80 12.00
1 Header Card .02 .10
2 Perry Ganchar HCO .02 .10
3 Dave Baseggio .20 .50
4 Jesse Belanger .20 .50
5 Karel Betik .20 .50
6 Zac Bierk .75 2.00
7 Jason Bonsignore .20 .50
8 Jock Callander .40 1.00
9 John Cullen .40 1.00
10 Xavier Delisle .20 .50
11 Brett Harkins .20 .50
12 Lane Lambert .20 .50
13 Mario Larocque .20 .50
14 Eric Lavigne .15 .40
15 Chris Longo .20 .50
16 Jim Paek .20 .50
17 Eduard Pershin .15 .40
18 Brent Peterson .20 .50
19 Jason Ruff .20 .50
20 Corey Schwab .30 .75
21 Andrei Skopintsev .20 .50
22 Corey Spring .15 .40
23 Derek Wilkinson .30 .75
24 Buzz MASCOT .02 .10

1999-00 Cleveland Lumberjacks
COMPLETE SET (24) 4.80 12.00
1 Radim Bicanek .08 .25
2 Buzz MASCOT .02 .10
3 Kyle Calder .75 2.00
4 Jock Callander .40 1.00
5 Jeff Christian .08 .25
6 Ted Crowley .08 .25
7 Casey Hankinson .08 .25
8 Brett Harkins .20 .50
9 Chris Herperger .08 .25
10 Ty Jones .20 .50
11 Marc Lamothe .20 .50
12 Eric Lavigne .08 .25
13 Chris Longo .08 .25
14 Evgeni Nabokov 2.00 5.00
15 Jim Paek .08 .25
16 Jeff Paul .08 .25
17 Nathan Perrott .30 .75
18 Geoff Peters .08 .25
19 Todd Rohloff .08 .25
20 Remi Royer .20 .50
21 Reid Simpson .20 .50
22 Dmitri Tolkunov .20 .50
23 Todd White .20 .50
24 Header Card .01

2000-01 Cleveland Lumberjacks
COMPLETE SET (25) 8.00 20.00
1 Christian Matte .40 1.00
2 Brian Bonin .40 1.00
3 Mike Matteucci .40 1.00
4 Eric Charron .30 .75
5 Nick Naumenko .30 .75
6 Brett McLean .30 .75
7 Pavel Patera .40 .75
8 Chris Longo .40 .75
9 Ian Herbers .40 1.00
10 Pascal Dupuis .30 .75
11 Kai Nurminen .40 1.00
12 David Brumby .30 .75
13 Zac Bierk .60 2.00
14 Jonathon Shockey .30 .75
15 Darryl Laplante .40 1.00
16 J.J. Daigneault .30 .75
17 Garrett Burnett .30 .75
18 Chris Armstrong .30 .75
19 Richard Park .40 1.00
20 Todd McLellan CO .20 .50
21 Jock Callander CO .40 1.00
22 Ray Schultz .30 .75
23 Steve Aronson .40 1.00
24 Derek Gustafson .60 1.50
25 Buzz MASCOT .10 .25

2001-02 Cleveland Barons
COMPLETE SET (24) 10.00 25.00
1 Steve Bancroft .30 .75
2 Matt Carkner .30 .75
3 Jonathan Cheechoo 1.20 5.00
4 Adam Colagiacomo .40 1.00
5 Mike Craig .30 .75
6 Rob Davison .30 .75
7 Jesse Fibiger .30 .75
8 Hannes Hyvonen .30 .75
9 Jeff Jillson .75 2.00
10 Seamus Kotyk .75 2.00
11 Ryan Kraft .30 .75
12 Eric Laplante .30 .75
13 Lynn Loyns .40 1.00
14 Andy Lundbohm .30 .75
15 Graig Mischler .30 .75
16 Robert Mulick .30 .75
17 Adam Nittel .40 1.00
18 Joel Prpic .30 .75
19 Brandon Smith .30 .75
20 Vesa Toskala 1.25 3.00
21 Chad Wiseman .30 .75
22 Miroslav Zalesak .30 .75
23 Roy Sommer CO .10 .25
24 Nick Fotiu ACO .10 .25

2002-03 Cleveland Barons
COMPLETE SET (24) 10.00 25.00
1 Matt Carkner .40 1.00
2 David Cloutier .40 1.00
3 David Cunniff ACO .04 .10
4 Rob Davison .40 1.00
5 Niko Dimitrakos .60 1.50
6 Jesse Fibiger .40 1.00
7 Tavis Hansen .40 1.00
8 John Jakopin .40 1.00
9 Seamus Kotyk .60 1.50
10 Ryan Kraft .40 1.00
11 Eric Laplante .40 1.00
12 Willie Levesque .40 1.00
13 Lynn Loyns .40 1.00
14 Keith McCambridge .40 1.00
15 Graig Mischler .40 1.00
16 Yuri Moscevsky .40 1.00
17 Robert Mulick .40 1.00
18 Jeff Nelson .40 1.00
19 Pat Rissmiller .40 1.00
20 Roy Sommer CO .04 .10
21 Scott Thomas .40 1.00
22 Vesa Toskala 1.25 3.00
23 Chad Wiseman .40 1.00
24 Miroslav Zalesak .40 1.00

2003-04 Cleveland Barons
COMPLETE SET (25) 5.00 12.00
1 Brad Boyes .40 1.00
2 Matt Carkner .20 .50
3 David Cloutier .20 .50
4 Ryan Clowe .20 .50
5 Jon DiSalvatore .20 .50
6 Niko Dimitrakos .30 .75
7 Christian Ehrhoff .30 .75
8 Jesse Fibiger .20 .50
9 Marcel Goc .40 1.00
10 Tavis Hansen .20 .50
11 Todd Harvey .30 .75
12 Seamus Kotyk .30 .75
13 Lynn Loyns .20 .50
14 Yuri Moscevsky .20 .50
15 Robert Mulick .20 .50
16 Doug Murray .20 .50
17 Dmitri Patzold .40 1.00
18 Tomas Plihal .20 .50
19 Pat Rissmiller .20 .50
20 Grant Stevenson .20 .50
21 Craig Valette .20 .50
22 Miroslav Zalesak .20 .50
23 Roy Sommer HCO .04 .10
24 David Cunniff ACO .04 .10
25 Mascot .04 .10

2004-05 Cleveland Barons
COMPLETE SET (27) 6.00 15.00
1 Riley Armstrong .20 .50
2 Nick Bootland .30 .75
3 Matt Carkner .30 .75
4 Ryan Clowe .40 1.00
5 Tim Conboy .20 .50
6 Scott Dobben .20 .50
7 Christian Ehrhoff .30 .75
8 Jim Fahey .20 .50
9 Aaron Gill .20 .50
10 Marcel Goc .40 1.00
11 Josh Gorges .30 .75
12 Mike Hoffman .60 1.50
13 Shane Joseph .20 .50
14 Greg Labenski .20 .50
15 Doug Murray .20 .50
16 Glenn Olson .20 .50
17 Dimitri Patzold .30 .75
18 Tomas Plihal .20 .50
19 Josh Prudden .20 .50
20 Patrick Rissmiller .20 .50
21 Nolan Schaefer .30 .75
22 Garrett Stafford .20 .50
23 Grant Stevenson .20 .50
24 Craig Valette .20 .50
25 Roy Sommer CO .04 .10
26 David Cunniff ACO .04 .10
27 Slapshark MASCOT .04 .10

2005-06 Cleveland Barons
COMPLETE SET (28) 8.00 15.00
1 Riley Armstrong .20 .50
2 Steve Bernier .75 2.00
3 Matt Carkner .20 .50
4 Tom Cavanagh .20 .50
5 Ryan Clowe .30 .75
6 Tim Conboy .20 .50
7 Ray DiLauro .20 .50
8 Josh Gorges .20 .50
9 Josh Hennessy .20 .50
10 Jamie Holden .20 .50
11 Mike Iggulden .20 .50
12 Shane Joseph .20 .50
13 Lukas Kaspar .20 .50
14 Doug Murray .30 .75
15 Glenn Olson .20 .50
16 Dmitri Patzold .40 1.00
17 Tomas Plihal .20 .50
18 Joshua Prudden .20 .50
19 Pat Rissmiller .20 .50
20 Nolan Schaefer .40 1.00
21 Garrett Stafford .20 .50
22 Brad Staubitz .20 .50
23 Grant Stevenson .20 .50
24 Jonathan Tremblay .20 .50
25 Craig Valette .20 .50
26 Roy Sommer HC .02 .10
27 David Cunniff AC .02 .10
28 Jock Callander .02 .10

1998-99 Colorado Gold Kings
COMPLETE SET (24) 3.00 8.00
1 Nicholas Chabot .20 .50
2 Trevor Converse .20 .50
3 R.J. Enga .20 .50
4 Anton Federov .20 .50
5 Wade Fennig .20 .50
6 Mark Fox .20 .50
7 Jeff Grabinsky .20 .50
8 Shawn Harris .20 .50
9 Don Lester .20 .50
10 Kirk Llano .20 .50
11 Craig Lyons .20 .50
12 Rob McCaig .20 .50
13 Rusty McKie .20 .50
14 Kevin McKinnon .20 .50
15 Bryan McMullen .20 .50
16 Chad Penney .20 .50
17 Tom Perry .20 .50
18 Bob Revermann .20 .50
19 Bogdan Rudenko .20 .50
20 Jason Simon .20 .50
21 Jeff Sirkka .20 .50
22 Brad Toporowski .20 .50
23 Kirk Tomlinson CO .08 .25
24 King Midas Mascot .02 .10

1998-99 Colorado Gold Kings Postcards
COMPLETE SET (22) 8.00 20.00
1 Jason Simon .60 1.50
2 Brad Toporowski .60 1.50
3 Tom Perry .60 1.50
4 Jeff Sirkka .60 1.50
5 Chad Penney .60 1.50
6 Bryan McMullen .60 1.50
7 Bogdan Rudenko .60 1.50
8 Kevin McKinnon .60 1.50
9 Bob Revermann .60 1.50
10 Craig Lyons .60 1.50
11 Kirk Tomlinson HCO .20 .50
12 Trevor Converse .60 1.50
13 Jeff Grabinsky .60 1.50
14 R.J. Enga .60 1.50
15 Shawn Harris .60 1.50
16 Anton Fedorov .60 1.50
17 Hakan Jansson .60 1.50
18 Wade Fennig .60 1.50
19 Don Lester .60 1.50
20 Mark Fox .60 1.50
21 Kirk Llano .60 1.50
22 McDonald's Coupon .02 .10

1999-00 Colorado Gold Kings Taco Bell
COMPLETE SET (26) 5.00 12.00
1 Travis Thiessen .20 .50
2 R.J. Enga .20 .50
3 Tom Perry .20 .50
4 Corey Lyons .20 .50
5 Bogdan Rudenko .20 .50
6 Don Lester CO .08 .25
7 Stephane Madore .20 .50
8 Steve Dowhy .20 .50
9 Greg Eisler .20 .50
10 Jean-Francois Picard .20 .50
11 King Midas MAS .08 .25
12 Steve Vezina .30 .75
13 Kevin McKinnon .20 .50
14 Craig Lyons .20 .50
15 Aaron Schweitzer .20 .50
16 Carl LeBlanc .20 .50
17 Daniel Olers .20 .50
18 Dean Ewen .20 .50
19 Frederik Beaubien .30 .75
20 Kirk Tomlinson .20 .50
21 Wade Fennig .20 .50
22 Kristoffer Eriksson .20 .50
23 Rob McCaig .20 .50
24 Greg Gatto .20 .50
25 Colorado Gold Kings .08 .25
26 Taco Bell Logo .02 .10

1999-00 Colorado Gold Kings Wendy's
COMPLETE SET (22) 4.00 10.00
1 Jean-Francois Picard .20 .50
2 Corey Lyons .20 .50
3 Eric Long .20 .50
4 Wade Fennig .20 .50
5 R.J. Enga .20 .50
6 Travis Thiessen .20 .50
7 Daniel Olers .20 .50
8 Carl LeBlanc .20 .50
9 Greg Eisler .20 .50
10 Kevin McKinnon .20 .50
11 Dean Ewen .20 .50
12 Stephane Madore .20 .50
13 Darcy Anderson .20 .50
14 Tom Perry .20 .50
15 Rob McCaig .20 .50
16 Bogdan Rudenko .20 .50
17 Steve Vezina .30 .75
18 Aaron Schweitzer .20 .50
19 Craig Lyons .20 .50
20 Kirk Tomlinson CO .20 .50
21 Don Lester CO .08 .25
22 King Midas MAS .08 .25

2001-02 Colorado Gold Kings
COMPLETE SET (22) 10.00
1 Dwayne Blais .20 .50
2 Aaron Boh .20 .50
3 Zac Boyer .20 .50
4 Chad Cabana .20 .50
5 Colin Chaulk .20 .50
6 Kirk Daubenspeck .30 .75
7 R.J. Enga .20 .50
8 Mike Garrow .20 .50
9 Mark Gowan .20 .50
10 Brent Henley .20 .50
11 Darcy Johnson .20 .50
12 Jason Knox .20 .50
13 Cam Kryway .20 .50
14 Craig Lyons .20 .50
15 Mike Nicholishen .20 .50
16 Tom Perry .20 .50
17 Greg Schmidt .20 .50
18 Juraj Slovak .20 .50
19 Travis Thiessen .30 .75
20 Allen Pedersen HCO .04 .10
21 Kevin McKinnon ACO .04 .10
22 Mascot .04 .10

2003-04 Colorado Eagles
COMPLETE SET (25) 8.00 20.00
1 Lee Arnold .40 1.00
2 Ryan Bach .40 1.00
3 Gian Baldrica .40 1.00
4 Daniel Bohac .40 1.00
5 Igor Bonderev .40 1.00
6 Jesse Cook .40 1.00
7 Phil Crowe .60 1.50
8 Fraser Filipic .40 1.00
9 Aaron Grosul .40 1.00
10 Cam Kuzyk .40 1.00
11 Mike McGhan .40 1.00
12 Riley Nelson .40 1.00
13 Greg Pankewicz .40 1.00
14 Brad Patterson .40 1.00
15 Lee Ruff .40 1.00
16 Scott Swanson .40 1.00
17 Brent Thompson .60 1.50
18 Ryan Tobler .60 1.50
19 Brad Williamson .40 1.00
20 Karlis Zirnis .40 1.00
21 Chris Stewart CO .04 .10
22 Ralph Backstrom GM .04 .10
23 Mascot .04 .10
24 Team Photo .04 .10
25 Staff .04 .10

2004-05 Colorado Eagles
COMPLETE SET (24) 15.00
1 Team Card .04 .10
2 Ralph Backstrom .04 .10
3 Paulo Colaiacovo .40 1.00
4 Jesse Cook .30 .75
5 Matt Desrosiers .30 .75
6 Fraser Filipic .30 .75
7 Aaron Grosul .30 .75
8 Chris Hartsburg .30 .75
9 Mike Lephart .30 .75
10 Kris Mallette .30 .75
11 Kevin Marsh .30 .75
12 Kevin McDonald .30 .75
13 Riley Nelson .30 .75
14 Greg Pankewicz .30 .75
15 Sean Robertson .30 .75
16 Lee Ruff .30 .75
17 Chris Stewart CO .30 .75
18 David Svagrovsky .30 .75
19 Ryan Tobler .30 .75
20 Tyler Weiman .30 .75
21 Brad Williamson .30 .75
22 Karlis Zirnis .30 .75
23 Slapshot MASCOT .04 .10
24 Team Staff .04 .10

2005-06 Colorado Eagles
COMPLETE SET (26) 8.00 20.00
1 Erik Adams .40 1.00
2 Lee Arnold .40 1.00
3 Jeff Blair .40 1.00
4 Les Borsheim .40 1.00
5 Paulo Colaiacovo .60 1.50
6 Matt Desrosiers .40 1.00
7 Fraser Filipic .40 1.00
8 Aaron Grosul .40 1.00
9 Chris Hartsburg .40 1.00
10 Garrett Larson .40 1.00
11 Jason Lundmark .40 1.00
12 Ed McGrane .40 1.00
13 Riley Nelson .40 1.00
14 Greg Pankewicz .40 1.00
15 Nick Parillo .40 1.00
16 Scott Polaski .40 1.00
17 Sean Robertson .40 1.00
18 Ryan Tobler .40 1.00
19 Brad Williamson .40 1.00
20 Chris Stewart CO .02 .10
21 Phil Crowe AC .02 .10
22 Ralph Backstrom PRES
GM .10 .25
23 Team Staff .02 .10
24 Eagles Chicks DANCERS .40 1.00
25 Slapshot MASCOT .02 .10
26 Colorado Eagles .20 .50

2006-07 Colorado Eagles
COMPLETE SET (31) 6.00 15.00
1 Team Card .10 .25
2 Erik Adams .30 .75
3 Lee Arnold .30 .75
4 Jay Birnie .30 .75
5 Tim Boron .30 .75
6 Les Borsheim .30 .75
7 Paulo Colaiacovo .40 1.00
8 Marco Emond .30 .75
9 Fraser Filipic .30 .75
10 Steve Haddon .30 .75
11 Chris Hartsburg .30 .75
12 Brent Hughes .30 .75
13 Seth Leonard .30 .75
14 Ed McGrane .30 .75
15 Riley Nelson .30 .75
16 Greg Pankewicz .30 .75
17 Scott Polaski .30 .75
18 Sean Robertson .30 .75
19 Aaron Schneekloth .30 .75
20 Craig Strain .30 .75
21 Ryan Tobler .30 .75
22 Brad Williamson .30 .75
23 Slapshot MASCOT .10 .25
24 Chris Stewart CO .10 .25
25 Phil Crowe ACO .10 .25
26 Ryan Bach ACO .10 .25
27 Ralph Backstrom PRES .10 .25
28 Tony Deynzer EQ MGR .10 .25
29 Chris Porowski TR .10 .25
30 Tori Holt ANN .10 .25
31 Eagles Chicks DANCERS .20 .50

2007-08 Colorado Eagles
COMPLETE SET (30) 6.00 15.00
1 Team Picture .30 .75
2 Erik Adams .30 .75
3 Jason Beatty .30 .75
4 Jay Birnie .30 .75
5 Les Borsheim .30 .75
6 Bryan Bridges .30 .75
7 Fraser Filipic .30 .75
8 Steve Haddon .30 .75
9 Chris Hartsburg .30 .75
10 Dave Iannazzo .30 .75
11 Sebastien Laplante .30 .75
12 Seth Leonard .30 .75
13 Ed McGrane .30 .75
14 Riley Nelson .30 .75
15 Greg Pankewicz .30 .75
16 Scott Polaski .30 .75
17 Aaron Schneekloth .30 .75
18 Brett Thurston .30 .75
19 Ryan Tobler .30 .75
20 Kris Wiebe .30 .75
21 Brad Williamson .30 .75
22 Chris Stewart HC .30 .75
23 Ryan Bach AC .30 .75
24 Tony Deynzer EQ .30 .75
25 Chris Porowski .30 .75
26 Ralph Backstrom .30 .75
27 Phil Crowe .30 .75
28 Tori Holt .30 .75
29 Eagles Chicks .20 .50
30 Slapshot MASCOT .20 .50

2009-10 Colorado Eagles
1 Jason Beatty .40 1.00
2 Jay Birnie .40 1.00
3 Fraser Filipic .40 1.00
4 Steve Haddon .40 1.00
5 Adam Hogg .40 1.00
6 Jim Jackson .40 1.00
7 Felipe Larranaga .40 1.00
8 Jason Lundmark .40 1.00
9 Brett Lutes .40 1.00
10 Ed McGrane .40 1.00
11 Ryan McLeod .40 1.00
12 Mike Mole .40 1.00
13 Riley Nelson .40 1.00
14 Alex Penner .40 1.00
15 Andrew Penner .40 1.00
16 Aaron Schneekloth .40 1.00
17 Brett Thurston .40 1.00
18 Ryan Tobler .40 1.00
19 Kevin Ulanski .40 1.00
20 Kevin McClelland .40 1.00

2013-14 Colorado Eagles
COMPLETE SET (25) 6.00 15.00
A01 Marc Cheverie .30 .75
A02 Kyle Ostrow .30 .75
A03 A.J. Hau .30 .75
A04 Daniel Johnston .30 .75
A05 Trent Daavettila .30 .75
B01 Kevin Ulanski .30 .75
B02 John Ryder .30 .75
B03 Kevin Young .30 .75
B04 Ryan Bach Goal. CO .30 .75
B05 Greg Gardner .30 .75
C01 Adam Brown .30 .75
C02 Arthur Bidwill .30 .75
C03 Chris Stewart CO .30 .75
C04 Isaac Smeltzer .30 .75
C05 Jesse Mychan .30 .75
D01 Aaron Schneekloth Asst. CO .30 .75
D02 Mark Nemec .30 .75
D03 Riley Nelson .30 .75
D04 Dylan Hood .30 .75
D05 Alex Hudson .30 .75
E01 Ralph Backstrom .30 .75
E02 Paul Phillips .30 .75
E03 Jason Beatty .30 .75
E04 Luke Fulghum .30 .75
E05 Jonathan Parker .30 .75

2014-15 Colorado Eagles
COMPLETE SET (20) 6.00 15.00
A01 Clarke Saunders .30 .75
A02 Mark Nemec .30 .75
A03 Jordan Kwas .30 .75
A04 Sean Zimmerman .30 .75
A05 Brock Nixon .30 .75
B01 Darryl Bootland .30 .75
B02 Curtis Gedig .30 .75
B03 Greg Gardner .30 .75
B04 Vitali Pavlov .30 .75
B05 Jonathan Parker .30 .75
C01 Trent Daavettila .30 .75
C02 Teigan Zahn .30 .75
C03 Brett Kulak .30 .75
C04 Chris Knowlton .30 .75
C05 Derek Rodwell .30 .75
D01 Kyle Kraemer .30 .75
D02 Collin Bowman .30 .75
D03 Doug Carr .30 .75
D04 Chris Duszynski .30 .75
D05 Nathan Moon .30 .75

2002-03 Columbia Inferno
COMPLETE SET (18) 10.00 25.00
97 Josh Blackburn .75 2.00
98 Paul Cabana .50 1.25
99 Robin Carruthers .50 1.25
100 Trevor Demmans .50 1.25
101 Regan Darby .50 1.25
102 Corey Hessler .50 1.25
103 Eric Labelle .75 2.00
104 Denis Martynyuk .50 1.25
105 Barrie Moore .50 1.25
106 Justin Morrison .50 1.25
107 Sean Owens .50 1.25
108 Chris Pittman .50 1.25
109 Tim Smith .50 1.25
110 Chris St. Croix .50 1.25
111 Rejean Stringer .50 1.25
112 Matt Ulwelling .50 1.25
113 Dennis Vial 1.25 3.00
114 Shawn Wansborough .50 1.25

2003-04 Columbia Inferno
COMPLETE SET (16) 10.00 25.00
97 Greg Amadio .60 1.50
98 Josh Blackburn .75 2.00
99 Alexandre Burrows .60 1.50
100 Paul Cabana .60 1.50
101 Robin Carruthers .60 1.50
102 Derek Eastman .60 1.50
103 Terry Harrison .60 1.50
104 Corey Hessler .60 1.50
105 Eric Labelle .60 1.50
106 Robert McVicar .75 2.00
107 Barrie Moore .60 1.50
108 Brandon Nolan .60 1.50
109 Chris Pittman .60 1.50
110 Tim Smith .75 2.00
111 Chris St. Croix .60 1.50
112 Dennis Vial .75 2.00

2003-04 Columbia Inferno Update
COMPLETE SET (6) 2.00 5.00
50 Mike Hanson .40 1.00
51 Sean Owens .40 1.00
52 Mike Roemensky .40 1.00
53 Marc-Andre Roy .40 1.00
54 Jesse Schultz .40 1.00
55 Matt Ulwelling .40 1.00

1966-67 Columbus Checkers
COMPLETE SET (16) 35.00 70.00
1 John Bailey 2.50 5.00
2 Moe Bartoli 2.50 5.00
3 Kerry Bond 2.50 5.00
4 Andre Daoust 2.50 5.00
5 Bert Fizzell 2.50 5.00
6 Marcel Goudreau 2.50 5.00
7 Jim Graham 2.50 5.00
8 Paul Jackson 2.50 5.00
9 Ken Laidlaw 2.50 5.00
10 Noel Lirette 2.50 5.00
11 Gary Longman 2.50 5.00
12 Garry Macmillan 2.50 5.00
13 Gary Mork 2.50 5.00
14 Matt Thorpe 2.50 5.00
15 Jack Turner 2.50 5.00
16 Alton White 2.50 5.00

1967-68 Columbus Checkers
COMPLETE SET (16) 37.50 75.00
1 Team Photo 2.50 5.00
2 Moe Bartoli 2.50 10.00
3 Bill Bond 2.50 5.00
4 Serge Boudreault 2.50 5.00
5 Gord Dibley 2.50 10.00
6 Bert Fizzell 2.50 5.00
7 Chuck Kelly 2.50 5.00
8 Ken Saunders 2.50 5.00
9 Nelson Leclair 2.50 5.00
10 Real Paquette 2.50 5.00
11 Dick Proceviat 2.50 5.00
12 Hartley Estabrooks 2.50 5.00
13 Ken Sutyla 2.50 5.00
14 Nelson Tremblay 2.50 5.00
15 Jack Turner 2.50 5.00
16 Al White 2.50 5.00

1997-98 Columbus Cottonmouths
COMPLETE SET (24) 8.00 20.00
1 Jerome Bechard .40 1.00
2 Chris Bergeron .40 1.00
3 Claude Fillion .40 1.00
4 Eric Germain .40 1.00
5 Brian Idalski .40 1.00
6 Mick Kempffer .40 1.00
7 Olaf Kjenstadt .40 1.00
8 Doug Mann .40 1.00
9 Grady Manson .40 1.00
10 Derek Marchand .40 1.00
11 Bobby Marshall .40 1.00
12 Randy Murphy .40 1.00
13 Frankie Ouellette .60 1.50
14 Kevin Plager .40 1.00
15 Brad Prefontaine .40 1.00
16 Marcel Richard .40 1.00
17 John Sincinski .40 1.00
18 Greg Taylor .40 1.00
19 David Wainwright .40 1.00
20 Tom Wilson .40 1.00
21 Phil Roberto GM .08 .25
22 Bruce Garber HCO .08 .25
23 Charles B. Morrow .08 .25
24 Pete Carson .40 1.00

1998-99 Columbus Cottonmouths
COMPLETE SET (24) 3.60 9.00
1 Jerome Bechard .20 .50
2 Dan Brown .20 .50
3 Derek Crimin .20 .50
4 Claude Fillion .20 .50
5 Brian Idalski .20 .50
6 Mick Kempffer .20 .50
7 Grady Manson .20 .50
8 Roman Markhovski .20 .50
9 Mike Martens .20 .50
10 David Neilson .20 .50
11 Frankie Ouellette .20 .50
12 Kevin Plager .20 .50
13 Brad Prefontaine .20 .50
14 Marcel Richard .20 .50
15 Corwin Saurdiff .20 .50
16 Jean-Alain Schneider .20 .50
17 Robbie Sinclair .20 .50
18 Thomas Stewart .20 .50
19 Tom Wilson .20 .50
20 Derek Marchand ACO .02 .10
21 Phil Roberto GM .02 .10
22 Bruce Garber HCO .02 .10
23 Pete Carson HTR .02 .10
24 Martha Morrow .20 .50

1999-00 Columbus Cottonmouths
COMPLETE SET (28) 4.80 12.00
1 Aaron Vickar .20 .50
2 Kamil Kuriplach .20 .50
3 Mick Kempffer .20 .50
4 Kevin Plager .20 .50
5 Martha Morrow OWN .08 .25
6 Derek Crimin .20 .50
7 Jason Given .20 .50
8 Marcel Richard .20 .50
9 Ryan Aikia .20 .50
10 Phil Roberto GM .08 .25
11 Jerome Bechard .20 .50
12 Doug Mann .20 .50
13 Mark Martins .20 .50
14 Tommi Santala .30 .75
15 Bruce Garber HCO .08 .25
16 Mark Scott .20 .50
17 Kelly Van Hiltgen .20 .50
18 Frankie Ouellette .30 .75
19 Jaroslav Kerestes .20 .50
20 Brian Idalski ACO .08 .25
21 Per Fernhall .20 .50
22 Jackson Hegland .20 .50
23 Robert Frid .20 .50
24 Olaf Kjenstad .30 .75
25 Randy Scrimshire EQM .08 .25
26 Brodie Coffin .20 .50
27 Andy Powers .20 .50
28 Tonda Jackson AGM .08 .25

2000-01 Columbus Cottonmouths
COMPLETE SET (25) 8.00 20.00
1 Jerome Bechard .40 1.00
2 Ryan Brown .40 1.00
3 Kris Cantu .40 1.00
4 Mick Kempffer .40 1.00
5 Jaroslav Kerestes .40 1.00

6 Doug Mann .40 1.00
7 Bobby Marshall .40 1.00
8 Mike Martens .40 1.00
9 Martin Menard .40 1.00
10 Riley Nelson .40 1.00
11 Frankie Ouellette .40 1.00
12 Daniel Payette .40 1.00
13 Andy Powers .40 1.00
14 Greg Quebec .40 1.00
15 Blaine Russell .40 1.00
16 Drew Schoneck .40 1.00
17 Kris Schultz .40 1.00
18 Rob Schweyer .40 1.00
19 Blake Sheane .40 1.00
20 Craig Stahl .40 1.00
21 Bruce Garber CO .10 .25
22 Phil Roberto GM .10 .25
23 Randy Scrimpshire EM .10 .25
24 Boomer MASCOT .10 .25
25 Teri LaSalle TR .10 .25

2002-03 Columbus Cottonmouths

COMPLETE SET (24) 8.00 20.00
1 Jerome Bechard .40 1.00
2 Phil Cole .40 1.00
3 Randy Copley .60 1.50
4 Brent Cullaton .40 1.00
5 Mitch Fritz .40 1.00
6 Chad Hamilton .40 1.00
7 J.J.Hunter .40 1.00
8 Matus Kostur .60 1.50
9 Mike Lee .60 1.50
10 Carlyle Lewis .60 1.50
11 Andrew Long .40 1.00
12 Sean McAslan .40 1.00
13 Darren McAusland .40 1.00
14 John Morlang .40 1.00
15 Mike Morrison .60 1.50
16 Ryan Risidore .40 1.00
17 Bart Rushmer .40 1.00
18 Darren Tiemstra .40 1.00
19 Jeff Zehr .60 1.50
20 Phil Roberto GM/CO .10 .25
21 Larry Kish ACO .10 .25
22 Randy Scrimpshire EQM .10 .25
23 Boomer Mascot .02 .10
24 Owners .02 .10

2003-04 Columbus Cottonmouths

COMPLETE SET (30) 15.00 30.00
1 Salvador Diaz-Verson OWN .04 .10
2 Shelby Amos OWN .04 .10
3 Brian Curran CO .04 .10
4 Jerome Bechard ACO .04 .10
5 Heath Kaufman EQM .04 .10
6 Jason Stevens TR .04 .10
7 Rumun Ndur .75 2.00
8 Jason Tapp .75 2.00
9 Mitch Fritz .75 2.00
10 Marc-Andre Thinel .75 2.00
11 Ryan Davis .40 1.00
12 Joel Martin .75 2.00
13 Olivier Michaud .60 1.50
14 Tomas Micka .40 1.00
15 Mascot .04 .10
16 Brad Voth .40 1.00
17 Colin Pepperall .40 1.00
18 Dan Tudin .40 1.00
19 Matt Shasby .40 1.00
20 Mathieu Roy .75 2.00
21 Carlyle Lewis .40 1.00
22 John Morlang .40 1.00
23 Kenton Smith .40 1.00
24 Peter Hogan .40 1.00
25 Ryan Risidore .40 1.00
26 Christian Larrivee .75 2.00
27 Dan Tessier .75 2.00
28 Jean-Francois Plourde .40 1.00
29 Ray DiLauro .40 1.00
30 Matus Kostur .75 2.00

2004-05 Columbus Cottonmouths

COMPLETE SET

2009-10 Columbus Cottonmouths

1 Brent Clarke .40 1.00
2 Tim Green .40 1.00
3 Orrin Hergott .40 1.00
4 Tom McMonagle .40 1.00
5 Tyler Johnson .40 1.00
6 Levi Lind .40 1.00
7 Tim Hockley .40 1.00
8 Kyle Lundale .40 1.00
9 Andrew Dwyer .40 1.00
10 Ryan McCarthy .40 1.00
11 Jerome Bechard .40 1.00
12 Geoff Beauparlant .40 1.00
13 Boomer .40 1.00
14 Flag Ceremony .40 1.00
15 Goal Celebration .40 1.00
16 Team USA .40 1.00
17 Dan Leslie .40 1.00
18 Sam Bowles .40 1.00
19 Blake Miller .40 1.00
20 Jesse Cole .40 1.00
21 Craig Stahl .40 1.00
22 Chad Rycroft .40 1.00
23 Ian Vigier .40 1.00
24 Will Barlow .40 1.00

2003-04 Columbus Stars

COMPLETE SET (5)

2000-01 Connecticut Huskies

COMPLETE SET (18) 15.00 30.00
1 Mike Anderson .75 2.00
2 Bret Bostock .75 2.00
3 Mike Boylan .75 2.00
4 Scott Brown .75 2.00
5 Ron D'Angelo .75 2.00
6 Eric Goclowski .75 2.00
7 Michael Goldkind .75 2.00
8 Matt Herhal .75 2.00
9 Anders Johnson .75 2.00
10 Kurt Kamienski .75 2.00
11 Trent Landry .75 2.00
12 Ciro Longobardi .75 2.00
13 Charles Ridolf .75 2.00
14 Evan Schwarz .75 2.00
15 Travis Wood .75 2.00
16 Bruce Marshall CO .20 .50
17 UCONN Huskies .20 .50
18 UCONN SCHEDULE .04 .10

1992-93 Cornell Big Red

COMPLETE SET (30) 6.00 15.00
1 Andrew Bandurski .40 1.00
2 Etienne Belzile .20 .50
3 Geoff Bumstead .30 .75
4 Brad Chartrand .20 .50
5 Rick Davis .20 .50
6 John DeHart .20 .50
7 Andre Doll .20 .50
8 P.C. Drouin .40 1.00
9 Dan Dufresne .20 .50
10 Blair Ettles .20 .50
11 Christian Felli .20 .50
12 Russ Hammond .20 .50
13 Shaun Hannah .20 .50
14 Steve Hayden .20 .50
15 Bill Holowatiuk .20 .50
16 Ryan Hughes .20 .50
17 Jake Karam .20 .50
18 Jiri Kloboucek .20 .50
19 Geoff Lopatka .20 .50
20 Joel McArter .20 .50
21 Tyler McManus .20 .50
22 Devon Nielsen .20 .50
23 Geoff Raynak .20 .50
24 Mike Sancimino .20 .50
25 Mark Scollan .20 .50
26 Tim Shean .20 .50
27 Greg Swenson .20 .50
28 Alex Vershinin .20 .50
29 Jason Vogel .20 .50
30 Mark Taylor ACO .02 .10

1993-94 Cornell Big Red

COMPLETE SET (30) 4.80 12.00
1 Vincent Auger .15 .40
2 Andrew Bandurski .15 .40
3 Geoff Bumstead .15 .40
4 Brad Chartrand .15 .40
5 Matt Cooney .15 .40
6 John DeHart .15 .40
7 Andre Doll .15 .40
8 Dan Dufresne .15 .40
9 Blair Ettles .15 .40
10 Christian Felli .15 .40
11 Tony Fergin .15 .40
12 Shaun Hannah .15 .40
13 Bill Holowatiuk .15 .40
14 Jake Karam .15 .40
15 Jason Kendall .15 .40
16 Jiri Kloboucek .15 .40
17 Geoff Lopatka .15 .40
18 Joel McArter .15 .40
19 Tyler McManus .15 .40
20 Jamie Papp .15 .40
21 Mike Sancimino .15 .40
22 Mark Scollan .15 .40
23 Tim Shean .15 .40
24 Eddy Skazyk .15 .40
25 Alex Vershinin .15 .40
26 Jason Weber .15 .40
27 Steve Wilson .15 .40
28 Chad Wilson .15 .40
29 Jason Zubkus .15 .40
30 Mark Taylor ACO .02 .10

1991-92 Cornwall Royals

COMPLETE SET (29) 4.00 10.00
1 Jason Meloche .15 .40
2 Mark Desantis .15 .40
3 Richard Raymond .15 .40
4 Gord Pell .15 .40
5 Dave Lemay .15 .40
6 John Lovell CO .02 .10
7 Ryan Vandenbussche .40 1.00
8 David Babcock .15 .40
9 Sam Oliveira .15 .40
10 Jeremy Stevenson .20 .50
11 Todd Walker .15 .40
12 Jean-Alain Schneider .15 .40
13 Ilpo Kauhanen .20 .50
14 Guy Leveque .20 .50
15 Shayne Gaffar .15 .40
16 Rival Fullum .15 .40
17 Mike Prokopec .20 .50
18 Nathan LaFayette .20 .50
19 Larry Courville .20 .50
20 Chris Clancy .15 .40
21 Tom Nemeth .20 .50
22 Jeff Reid .15 .40
23 Paul Andrea .15 .40
24 John Slaney .40 1.00
25 Alan Letang .15 .40
26 Rob Dykeman .20 .50
27 Paul Fixter CO
Brian O'Leary CO .02 .10
28 Chief of Police .02 .10
29 Checklist .02 .10

1999-00 Cornwall Colts

COMPLETE SET

2003-04 Cornwall Colts

COMPLETE SET
1 Aaron Bogosian .40 1.00
2 Sean Flanagan .40 1.00

1999-00 Corpus Christi IceRays

COMPLETE SET (46) 8.00 20.00
1 Tyler Boucher .20 .50
2 Geoff Bumstead .30 .75
3 Paul Doherty .20 .50
4 Pat Dunn .20 .50
5 Jason Genik .20 .50
6 Regan Harper .20 .50
7 Brent Hoiness .20 .50
8 Trevor Janicki .20 .50
9 Cory Johnson .20 .50
10 Alex Kholomeyev .30 .75
11 Roger Lewis .20 .50
12 Dustin McArthur .20 .50
13 Darryl Olsen .20 .50
14 Jody Praznik .20 .50
15 Tobin Praznik .20 .50
16 Bob Quinnell .20 .50
17 Chris Robertson .20 .50
18 Layne Roland .20 .50
19 Andy Ross .20 .50
20 Dennis Shiryaev .20 .50
21 Eddy Skazyk .20 .50
22 Mike Tomlinson .20 .50
23 Phil Valk .20 .50
24 Quinten Van Horlick .20 .50
25 Mike Vandenberghe .20 .50
26 Kurt Wickenheiser .20 .50
27 Brad Wingfield .20 .50
28 Taylor Hall CO .20 .50
29 Jody Praznik .20 .50
30 Scott Brower .20 .50
31 Geoff Bumstead AS .30 .75
32 Jody Praznik .20 .50
32 Tobin Praznik .20 .50
33 Brad Wingfield .08 .25
33 Geoff Bumstead .30 .75
34 Kurt Wickenheiser .20 .50
34 Geoff Bumstead .30 .75
34 Tobin Praznik .08 .25
35 Radio Celebrities .02 .10
36 Home Opener .02 .10
37 Corpus Christi Icegirls .30 .75
38 Party Patrol .02 .10
39 SugarRay MASCOT .08 .25
40 Corpus Christi IceRays .20 .50
41 Best Fans in the WPHL .02 .10
42 ValueBank Texas .02 .10

1992-93 Dallas Freeze

COMPLETE SET (20) 3.00 8.00
1 Wayne Anchikoski .20 .50
2 Gary Audette .20 .50
3 Jeff Beaudin .20 .50
4 Troy Binnie .20 .50
5 Brian Bruininks .20 .50
6 Derek Crawford .20 .50
7 Dave Doucette .20 .50
8 Don Dwyer .20 .50
9 Joe Eagan .20 .50
10 Ron Flockhart CO .30 .75
11 Frank Lascala .20 .50
12 Robert Lewis .20 .50
13 Joey Mittelsteadt .20 .50
14 Rico Rossi .20 .50
15 Dean Shmyr .20 .50
16 Doug Sinclair .20 .50
17 Greg Smith .20 .50
18 Jason Taylor .20 .50
19 Mike Zanier .30 .75
20 Team Photo .20 .50

1993-94 Dallas Freeze

COMPLETE SET (18) 2.50 6.00
1 Wayne Anchikoski .20 .50
2 Jeff Beaudin .15 .40
3 Troy Binnie .20 .50
4 Brian Bruininks .15 .40
5 Derek Crawford .15 .40
6 Dave Doucette .20 .50
7 Don Dwyer .15 .40
8 Mark Holick .15 .40
9 Randy Jaycock .15 .40
10 Frank LaScala .15 .40
11 Robert Lewis .15 .40
12 Joey McTamney .15 .40
13 Joey Mittelsteadt .15 .40
14 Dean Shmyr .15 .40
15 Greg Smith .15 .40
16 Jason Taylor .15 .40
17 Jason White .15 .40
18 Ron Flockhart CO .20 .50

2005-06 Danbury Trashers

COMPLETE SET 5.00 12.00
1 Alex Goupil .20 .50
2 Donny Glover .20 .50
3 Eric Lind .20 .50
4 Drew Omicioli .20 .50
5 Danny Stewart .20 .50
6 Sergei Durden .20 .50
7 David Beauregard .20 .50
8 Frederic Belanger .20 .50
9 Jayme Platt .20 .50
10 Regan Kelly .20 .50
11 Sylvain Daigle .20 .50
12 Dave MacIsaac .20 .50
13 Mike Omicioli .20 .50
14 Luke Sellers .20 .50
15 Troy Smith .20 .50
16 Mario Larocque .20 .50
17 2005-06 UHL All-Stars .20 .50
18 Ryan Barnes .20 .50
19 Ed Campbell .20 .50
20 Jamie Thompson .20 .50
21 Jean-Michel Daoust .20 .50
22 Brad Wingfield .20 .50
23 Shawn Collymore .20 .50
24 Jeff Daw .20 .50
25 David Hymovitz .20 .50
26 Paul Gillis CO .04 .10
27 Paul Sacco .04 .10
28 A.J. Galante OWN .04 .10
29 Scrappy MASCOT .04 .10

1992-93 Dayton Bombers

COMPLETE SET (24) 4.00 10.00
1 John(B-Man) Beaulieu .02 .10
2 Steve Bogoyevac .20 .50
3 Christopher .02 .10
4 Darren Colbourne .20 .50
5 Derek Crawford .20 .50
6 Dan-O .02 .10
7 Derek Donald .20 .50
8 Ray Edwards .20 .50
9 Doug Evans .20 .50
10 Sandy Galuppo .30 .75
11 Shayne Green .20 .50
12 Rod Houk .20 .50
13 Peter Kasowski .20 .50
14 Steve Kerrigan .20 .50
15 Frank Kovacs .20 .50
16 Darren Langdon .30 .75
17 Denis Larocque .20 .50
18 Darwin McPherson .20 .50
19 Tom Nemeth .20 .50
20 Claude Noel CO .02 .10
21 Tony Peters .20 .50
22 Marshall Phillips .20 .50
23 Mike Reier .20 .50
24 Steve Wilson .20 .50

1993-94 Dayton Bombers

COMPLETE SET (28) 3.00 8.00
1 Title Card CL .02 .10
2 Jeff Levy .15 .40
3 Steve Wilson .15 .40
4 Jason Downey .15 .40
5 Jim Peters .15 .40
6 Ondrej Kriz .15 .40
7 Steve Bogoyevac .15 .40
8 Jason Disiewich .15 .40
9 Marc Savard .15 .40
10 Dan O'Shea .15 .40
11 Tom Nemeth .15 .40
12 Guy Prince .15 .40
13 Ray Edwards .15 .40
14 Sergei Kharin .15 .40
15 Derek Donald .15 .40
16 Darwin McPherson .15 .40
17 Jeff Stolp .15 .40
18 Adam Bomber (Mascot) .02 .10
19 Kim .02 .10
20 Robby .02 .10
21 Lisa .02 .10
22 Marshall Phillips .02 .10
23 Dan-O .02 .10
24 John(B-Man) Beaulieu .02 .10
25 Christopher .02 .10
26 Steve Kerrigan .15 .40
27 Tony Peters .15 .40
28 Shaun Higgins
Major Dic .02 .10

1994-95 Dayton Bombers

COMPLETE SET (24) 3.00 8.00
1 Title Card CL .02 .10
2 Paul Taylor .15 .40
3 Steve Wilson .15 .40
4 Jason Downey .15 .40
5 Craig Charron .15 .40
6 Jim Lessard .15 .40
7 Karson Kaebel .15 .40
8 Jamie Steer .15 .40
9 Rob Hartnell .15 .40
10 Mike Doers .15 .40
11 Sean Gagnon .20 .50
12 Kevin Brown .15 .40
13 John Brill .15 .40
14 Dean Fedorchuk .15 .40
15 Tony Gruba .15 .40
16 Steve Lingren .15 .40
17 Brandon Smith .15 .40
18 Jeff Stolp .20 .50
19 Mike Vandenberghe .15 .40
20 Jim Playfair .15 .40
21 Goal Celebration .15 .40
22 Jamie Steer AS .15 .40
23 Steve Wilson AW .15 .40
24 Jeff Stolp/1993-94 Top# .20 .50

1995-96 Dayton Bombers

COMPLETE SET (32) 10.00 25.00
1 Jim Playfair CO .30 .75
2 Sean Ortiz .30 .75
3 Derek Herlofsky .60 1.50
4 Paul Andrea .30 .75
5 Nick Poole .30 .75
6 Steve Lingren .40 1.00
7 Kevin Brown .30 .75
8 Jason Downey .30 .75
9 Sergei Kharin .40 1.00
10 Matt McElwee .30 .75
11 Mike Naylor .30 .75
12 Ted Russell .30 .75
13 Colin Miller .40 1.00
14 Brent Brekke .30 .75
15 John Brill .30 .75
16 Mike Murray .30 .75
17 Sean Gagnon .60 1.50
18 Brian Renfrew .40 1.00
19 Rob Peters .30 .75
20 Jeff Petruic .30 .75
21 Steve Roberts .30 .75
22 George Zajankala .30 .75
23 Adam Bomber MASCOT .20 .50
24 Steve Lingren AS .30 .75
25 Jim Playfair CO AS .30 .75
26 Jerry Buckley .40 1.00
27 Jeremy Stasiuk .30 .75
28 Greg Burke .30 .75
29 Chris Johnston .30 .75
30 Dwayne Gylywoychuk .30 .75
P1 Sean Gagnon .75 2.00
P2 Sergei Kharin .75 2.00

1996-97 Dayton Bombers

COMPLETE SET (24) 10.00 25.00
1 Steve Roberts .40 1.00
2 Chris Sullivan .40 1.00
3 Steve Lingren .40 1.00
4 Jordan Shields .40 1.00
5 Ildar Yubin .40 1.00
6 Dwight Parrish .40 1.00
7 Brian Ridolfi .40 1.00
8 Jordan Willis .75 2.00
9 Dale Hooper .40 1.00
10 Will Clarke .40 1.00
11 Tavis Morrison .40 1.00
12 Trent Schachle .40 1.00
13 John Emmons .60 1.50
14 Sam McKenney .40 1.00
15 Bryan Richardson .40 1.00
16 Ryan Gillis .40 1.00
17 Marty Flichel .60 1.50
18 Jason Downey .40 1.00
19 Troy Christensen .40 1.00
20 Derek Herlofsky .75 2.00
21 Sal Manganaro .40 1.00
22 Tom Nemeth .60 1.50
23 Evgeny Ryabchikov .75 2.00
24 Colin Miller .40 1.00

1998-99 Dayton Bombers

COMPLETE SET (25) 4.80 12.00
1 Frederic Bouchard .30 .75
2 Bobby Brown .20 .50
3 Norman Dezainde .30 .75
4 Travis Dillabough .20 .50
5 Ryan Furness .20 .50
6 Dan Hendrickson .20 .50
7 Trevor Koenig .20 .50
8 Justin Krall .20 .50
9 Aaron Kriss .20 .50
10 Jamie Ling .40 1.00
11 Jim Logan .20 .50
12 Colin Miller .20 .50
13 Tom Nemeth .30 .75
14 Brian Regan .20 .50
15 Brian Ridolfi .20 .50
16 Brian Secord .20 .50
17 Chris Wismer .20 .50
18 John Beaulieu ANN .02 .10
19 Dale Coulthard EQM .02 .10
20 Greg Ireland HCO .02 .10
21 Buddy Mascot .02 .10
22 Kerrigan & Christopher .02 .10
23 Team Photo .20 .50
24 Larry Thornton TR .02 .10
25 Lee Stieg .20 .50

1998-99 Dayton Bombers EBK

COMPLETE SET (22) 3.00 8.00
1 Frederic Bouchard .20 .50
2 Aaron Kriss .15 .40
3 Brian Secord .15 .40
4 Colin Miller .15 .40
5 Jamie Ling .30 .75
6 Bobby Brown .15 .40
7 Tom Nemeth .20 .50
8 Brian Ridolfi .15 .40
9 Travis Dillabough .15 .40
10 Justin Krall .15 .40
11 Dan Hendrickson .15 .40
12 Ed Gingher ACO .02 .10
13 Brian Regan .15 .40
14 Trevor Koenig .15 .40
15 Greg Ireland HCO .02 .10
16 Colin Miller
Tom Nemeth ACO .02 .10
17 Bucky Mascot .02 .10
18 Brandon Sugden .20 .50
19 Norman Dezainde .20 .50
20 Kiley Hill .15 .40
NNO Checklist .02 .10

2013-14 Dayton Demonz

COMPLETE SET (20) 5.00 12.00
1 Bonez MASCOT .30 .75
2 Trevor Karasiewicz CO .30 .75
3 Jack Collins Asst. CO .30 .75
4 Brandon Blair .30 .75
5 Brett Wall .30 .75
6 Jared Hicks .30 .75
7 August Aiken .30 .75
8 Casey Mignone .30 .75
9 Shaun Fisher .30 .75
10 Alex Norman .30 .75
11 Ahmed Mahfouz .30 .75
12 Jesse Felten .30 .75
13 Roger Tagoona .30 .75
14 Wehebe Darge .30 .75
15 Matt Kinsella .30 .75
16 Jeff Rose .30 .75
17 Len Pelletier .30 .75
18 Lee McClure .30 .75
19 Robert Vanwynsberghe .30 .75
20 Brian Marks .30 .75

2009-10 Dayton Gems

A1 Sam Bloom .40 1.00
A2 Preston Briggs .40 1.00
A3 A.J. MacLean .40 1.00
A4 Derek MacIntyre .40 1.00
A5 Nathan Oke .40 1.00
A6 John Snowden .40 1.00
B1 John Marks .40 1.00
B2 Mike Mullen .40 1.00
B3 Tim Hartung .40 1.00
B4 Corey Couturier .40 1.00
B5 Jonathan Ornelas .40 1.00
B6 Joe Van Culin .40 1.00
C1 Matt Szypura .40 1.00
C2 Greg Labenski .40 1.00
C3 Ryan Mior .40 1.00
C4 Pierce Norton .40 1.00
C5 Justin McCutcheon .40 1.00
C6 Mike Vaskivuo .40 1.00
D1 Todd Spencer .40 1.00
D2 Jeff Spencer .40 1.00
D3 Iain McPhee .40 1.00
D4 Greg McCauley .40 1.00
D5 Russell Smith .40 1.00
D6 Adam Maccarone .40 1.00
D7 Matt Smyth .40 1.00
D8 Brandon Weinert .40 1.00
D9 Matt Maccarone .40 1.00

1996-97 Dayton Ice Bandits

COMPLETE SET (29) 4.00 10.00
1 Checklist .02 .10
2 Jesse Austin .20 .50
3 Mike Bajurny .20 .50
4 Dan Belisle HCO .02 .10
5 Dan Carter .20 .50
6 Cosmo Clarke .20 .50
7 Bob Clouston .20 .50
8 Tom Colasanto .20 .50
9 Brad Cook .20 .50
10 Richard Fatrola .20 .50
11 Jack Greig .20 .50
12 Kelly Melton .20 .50
13 Andrew Plumb .20 .50
14 Brian Renfrew .20 .50
15 Bobby Rapoza .20 .50
16 Jacque Rodrigue .20 .50
17 Fred Scott .20 .50
18 Troy Stevens .20 .50
19 Larry Thornton TR .02 .10
20 Mike Thornton .20 .50
21 Scott Vettraino .20 .50
22 Marty Wells .20 .50
23 Kevin Young .20 .50
24 The Phantom Mascot .02 .10
25 The Famous Chicken .02 .10
26 WTUE Employees .02 .10
27 WTUE Employees .02 .10
28 WTUE Employees .02 .10
29 WTUE Employees .02 .10

1996-97 Denver University Pioneers

COMPLETE SET (10) 3.00 8.00
1 Travis Smith .40 1.00
2 Jim Mullin .30 .75
3 Mike Corbett .30 .75
4 Petri Gunther .30 .75
5 Garrett Buzan .30 .75
6 Antti Laaksonen .40 1.00
7 Charlie Host .30 .75
8 Erik Andersson .30 .75
9 Warren Smith .30 .75
10 Anders Bjork .30 .75

1999-00 Des Moines Buccaneers

COMPLETE SET (24) 4.00 12.00
1 Dominic Torretti .20 .50
2 Felipe Larranaga .20 .50
3 Paul Baumgartner .20 .50
4 Nathan Berry .20 .50
5 Matt Weber .20 .50
6 Troy Riddle .20 .50
7 Nick Dimella .20 .50
8 Jesse Lane .20 .50
9 Peter Sejna .75 2.00
10 Landon Bathe .20 .50
11 Travis Doan .20 .50
12 Mark Murphy .20 .50
13 Rob Novak .20 .50
14 Alex Kim .20 .50
15 Wade Chiodo .20 .50
16 Jerrid Reinholz .20 .50
17 Miroslav Durak .20 .50
18 Ryan Kirchhoff .20 .50
19 Mark Mullen .20 .50
20 Ryan Bennett .20 .50
21 Jeff Ronkoske .20 .50
22 Mike Mantua .20 .50
23 Paul Morrissey .20 .50
24 Winger MASCOT .02 .10

2007-08 Des Moines Buccaneers

COMPLETE SET (26) 5.00 12.00
1 Nielsson Arcibal .30 .75
2 Josh Balch .30 .75
3 Fredrik Bergman .30 .75
4 Brett Bruneteau .30 .75
5 Greg Burgdoerfer .30 .75
6 Rocco Carzo .30 .75
7 Alexander Denezhkin .30 .75
8 Nate Dewhurst .30 .75
9 Michael Dorr .30 .75
10 Derek Elliott .30 .75
11 Austin Handley .30 .75
12 Keith Kinkaid .30 .75
13 Chris Knowlton .30 .75
14 Cullen Lundholm .30 .75
15 J.P. Maley .30 .75
16 Taylor Matson .30 .75
17 Ryan McKiernan .30 .75
18 Andrew Panzarella .30 .75
19 Bobby Reiners .30 .75
20 Rody Selk .30 .75
21 Brad Walch .30 .75
22 Ryan Walters .30 .75
23 Matt White .30 .75
25 Todd Knott AC .30 .75
26 Rick Comley HC .30 .75
27 Bucky MASCOT .15 .40

1993-94 Detroit Jr. Red Wings

COMPLETE SET (26) 4.00 10.00
1 Todd Harvey .40 1.00
2 Jason Saal .20 .50
3 Aaron Ellis .15 .40
4 Chris Mailloux .15 .40
5 Robin Lacour .15 .40
6 Mike Rucinski .15 .40
7 Eric Cairns .20 .50
8 Matt Ball .15 .40
9 Dale Junkin .15 .40
10 Bill McCauley .15 .40
11 Jeremy Meehan .15 .40
12 Mike Harding .15 .40
13 Brad Cook .15 .40
14 Jeff Mitchell .15 .40
15 Jamie Allison .15 .40
16 Dan Pawlaczyk .15 .40
17 Kevin Brown .15 .40
18 Duane Harmer .15 .40
19 Gerry Skrypec .15 .40
20 Shayne McCosh .15 .40
21 Sean Haggerty .15 .40
22 Nic Beaudoin .15 .40
23 Paul Maurice CO .20 .50
24 Pete DeBoer ACO .20 .50
25 Bob Wren .15 .40
NNO Slapshot Ad Card .01

1994-95 Detroit Jr. Red Wings

COMPLETE SET (25) 4.00 10.00
1 Team Photo CL .15 .40
2 Darryl Foster .15 .40
3 Quade Lightbody .15 .40
4 Ryan MacDonald .15 .40
5 Mike Rucinski .15 .40
6 Murray Sheehan .15 .40
7 Matt Ball .15 .40
8 Gerry Lanigan .15 .40
9 Mike Morrone .15 .40
10 Tom Buckley .15 .40
11 Eric Manlow .30 .75
12 Bill McCauley .15 .40
13 Andrew Taylor .15 .40
14 Scott Blair .15 .40
15 Jeff Mitchell .15 .40
16 Jason Saal .25 .60
17 Jamie Allison .20 .50
18 Bryan Berard .40 1.00
19 Dan Pawlaczyk .15 .40
20 Milan Kostolny .15 .40
21 Duane Harmer .15 .40
22 Shayne McCosh .15 .40
23 Sean Haggerty .15 .40
24 Nic Beaudoin .15 .40
25 Paul Maurice CO
GM .15 .40

1994-95 Detroit Vipers Pogs

COMPLETE SET (6) .75 2.00
1 John Craighead .20 .50
2 Peter Ciavaglia .20 .50
3 Brad Tiley .20 .50
4 Al Conroy .20 .50
5 Daniel Shank .20 .50
6 Logo Pog .20 .50

1996-97 Detroit Vipers

COMPLETE SET (20) 30.00 75.00
1 Darren Banks .75 2.00
2 Peter Ciavaglia .75 2.00
3 Yvon Corriveau .75 2.00
4 Phil Crowe .60 1.50
5 Mike Donnelly .75 2.00
6 Stan Drulia 1.25 3.00
7 Len Esau .75 2.00
8 Ian Herbers .60 1.50
9 Bobby Jay .60 1.50
10 Dan Kesa .60 1.50
11 Rich Parent 1.25 3.00
12 Jeff Parrott .60 1.50
13 Wayne Presley .60 1.50
14 Jeff Reese 1.25 3.00
15 Sergei Samsonov 15.00 40.00
16 Brad Shaw 1.25 3.00
17 Todd Simon .75 2.00
18 Patrice Tardif .75 2.00
19 Phil Von Steffenelli .60 1.50
20 Steve Walker .60 1.50

1997-98 Detroit Vipers

COMPLETE SET (20) 16.00 30.00
1 Peter Ciavaglia .75 2.00
2 Phil Crowe .40 1.00
3 Dan Kesa .40 1.00
4 Stan Drulia .75 2.00
5 Bob Jay .40 1.00
6 Ian Herbers .40 1.00
7 Brad Shaw .75 2.00
8 Steve Walker .75 2.00
9 Trent McCleary .40 1.00
10 Scott Thomas .75 2.00
11 Johan Hedberg 2.00 5.00
12 Jimmy Carson .75 2.00
13 Clayton Beddoes .40 1.00
14 Tim Murray .40 1.00
15 John Gruden .40 1.00
16 Jeff Reese .75 2.00
17 Keith Aldridge .40 1.00
18 Brent Fedyk .40 1.00
19 Darren Banks .75 2.00
20 Vipe-Bear Mascot .40 1.00

1998-99 Detroit Vipers

COMPLETE SET (26) 6.00 15.00
1 Keith Aldridge .20 .50
2 Brad Shaw .40 1.00
3 Tim Murray .15 .40
4 Brian Felsner .15 .40
5 Peter Ciavaglia .30 .75
6 Andy Bezeau .15 .40
7 Mike Gaffney .15 .40
8 Phil Crowe .15 .40
9 John Emmons .15 .40
10 Kory Karlander .15 .40
11 Mike Prokopec .15 .40
12 Stan Drulia .40 1.00
13 Bob Jay .20 .50
14 Darren Banks .20 .50
15 Jeff Whittle .15 .40
16 Steve Walker .15 .40
17 Ian Herbers .15 .40
18 Jani Hurme 1.50 4.00
19 John Gruden .15 .40
20 Kevin Weekes .75 2.00
21 Vipe-Bear Mascot .02 .10
22 Steve Ludzik HCO .02 .10
23 John Blum ACO .02 .10
24 Dave Boyer TR .02 .10
25 Mike Astalos EQM .02 .10
26 Checklist .02 .10

1998-99 Detroit Vipers Freschetta

COMPLETE SET (16) 12.00 30.00
1 Kevin Weekes 1.50 4.00
2 Peter Ciavaglia .75 2.00
3 Bob Jay .60 1.50
4 Keith Aldridge .60 1.50
5 Andy Bezeau .60 1.50
6 Stan Drulia 1.25 3.00
7 Ian Herbers .60 1.50
8 John Emmons .60 1.50
9 Mike Prokopec .60 1.50
10 Tim Murray .60 1.50
11 Brad Shaw 1.25 3.00
12 Steve Walker .60 1.50
13 John Gruden .60 1.50
14 Darren Banks .75 2.00
15 Brian Felsner .60 1.50
16 Geoff Sarjeant .75 2.00

1999-00 Detroit Vipers

COMPLETE SET (15) 14.00 35.00
1 Andy Bezeau 1.25 3.00
2 Nils Ekman 1.25 3.00
3 Mario Larocque 1.25 3.00
4 Steve Walker .75 2.00
5 Matt Elich 1.25 3.00
6 Jeff Shevalier .75 2.00
7 Peter Ciavaglia 1.25 3.00
8 Alek Stojanov .75 2.00
9 Dave Baseggio .75 2.00
10 Zac Bierk 1.50 4.00
11 Kyle Kos .75 2.00
12 Tim Thomas 5.00 12.00

13 Dale Rominski .75 2.00
14 Kyle Freadrich .75 2.00
15 Samuel St. Pierre .75 2.00

1999-00 Detroit Vipers Kid's Club

COMPLETE SET (9) 10.00 25.00
1 Team Logo Card .40 1.00
2 Peter Ciavaglia 2.00 5.00
3 Andy Bezeau 2.00 5.00
4 Stan Drulia 2.00 5.00
5 Steve Walker 2.00 5.00
6 Ian Herbers 2.00 5.00
7 Paulin Bordeleau HCO 2.00 5.00
8 Vipe-Bear Mascot .40 1.00
9 Kid's Club Membership Card .40 1.00

1996-97 Detroit Whalers

COMPLETE SET (25) 4.00 10.00
1 Jessie Boulerice .30 .75
2 Mark Cadotte .20 .50
3 Chad Cavanagh .15 .40
4 Harold Druken .40 1.00
5 Steve Dumonski .20 .50
6 Robert Esche .75 2.00
7 Sergei Fedotov .20 .50
8 Randy Fitzgerald .20 .50
9 Eric Gooldy .15 .40
10 Kevin Holdridge .15 .40
11 John Paul Luciuk .15 .40
12 Mike Morrone .15 .40
13 Pat Parthenais .20 .50
14 Julian Smith .15 .40
15 Troy Smith .15 .40
16 Andrew Taylor .15 .40
17 Anthony Terzo .15 .40
18 Jan Vodrazka .15 .40
19 Steve Wasylko .20 .50
20 Nathan West .15 .40
21 Peter DeBoer .08 .25
22 Luc Rioux .15 .40
23 Slapshot .02 .10
24 Checklist .02 .10
25 Discount Card .02 .10

1993-94 Drummondville Voltigeurs

COMPLETE SET (28) 3.00 8.00
1 Title Card Checklist .02 .10
2 Stephane Routhier .15 .40
3 Yannick Gagnon .15 .40
4 Sebastien Bety .15 .40
5 Martin Latulippe .15 .40
6 Nicolas Savage .15 .40
7 Sylvain Ducharme .15 .40
8 Yan St. Pierre .15 .40
9 Emmanuel Labranche .15 .40
10 Ian Laperriere .30 .75
11 Louis Bernard .15 .40
12 Stephane St. Amour .15 .40
13 Vincent Tremblay .15 .40
14 Denis Gauthier Jr. .30 .75
15 Eric Plante .15 .40
16 Christian Marcoux .15 .40
17 Patrice Charbonneau .15 .40
18 Raymond Delarosbil .15 .40
19 Patrick Livernoche .15 .40
20 Luc Decelles .15 .40
21 Francois Sasseville .15 .40
22 Steve Tardif .15 .40
23 Mathieu Sunderland .15 .40
24 Alexandre Duchesne .15 .40
25 Jean Hamel CO GM .02 .10
26 Mario Carrier ACO .02 .10
27 Me Andre Lepage TR .02 .10
28 Slapshot Ad Card .02 .10

2001-02 Drummondville Voltigeurs

COMPLETE SET (23) 4.00 10.00
1 Jean-Francois Racine .30 .75
2 Patrick Turbide .20 .50
3 Evgueni Nourislamov .20 .50
4 Jean-Philippe Glaude .20 .50
5 Thierry Kaszap .20 .50
6 Eric Jean .20 .50
7 Louis-Philippe Lessard .20 .50
8 Andre Vincent .20 .50
9 Steve Proulx .20 .50
10 Oliver Proulx .20 .50
11 Martin Autotte .20 .50
12 Yanick Riendeau .20 .50
13 Michael Stacey .20 .50
14 Frederic Faucher .20 .50
15 Benoit Paris .20 .50
16 Vincent Tougas .20 .50
17 Kirill Alexeev .20 .50
18 Jean-Francois Cyr .20 .50
19 Carl Zacharie .20 .50
20 Kevin Rainville .20 .50
21 Sylvain Michaud .20 .50
22 Maxime Bouchard .20 .50
NNO Title Card/CL .04 .10

2002-03 Drummondville Voltigeurs

COMPLETE SET (25) 5.00 12.00
1 Francis Breault CO .04 .10
2 Evgueni Nourislamov .20 .50
3 Todd Paul .20 .50
4 Andre Joaniss .20 .50
5 Jules Melanson .20 .50
6 Andre Vincent .20 .50
7 Dominic Fiset .20 .50
8 Kevin Lacombe .20 .50
9 Alexandre Demers .20 .50
10 Laurent Lanoie .20 .50
11 Yannick Riendeau .20 .50
12 Patrick Levesque .20 .50
13 Sebastien Laprise .20 .50
14 Benoit Duhamel .20 .50
15 Jonathan Dick .20 .50
16 Kevin Mailhiot .20 .50
17 Jason D'Ascanio .20 .50
18 Thomas Bellemare .20 .50
19 Samuel Villeneuve .20 .50
20 Kevin Duchaine .20 .50
21 Eric Dagenais .20 .50
22 Sylvain Michaud .40 1.00
23 Pierre Olivier Girouard .30 .75
24 Pier Olivier Begin .30 .75
25 Checklist/Logo .04 .10

2003-04 Drummondville Voltigeurs

COMPLETE SET (22) 6.00 15.00
1 Thomas Bellemare .20 .50
2 David Bouchard .20 .50
3 Maxim Chamberland .20 .50
4 Michel Charrette .20 .50
5 Alexandre Demers .20 .50
6 Keven Gagne .20 .50
7 Samuel Gibbons .20 .50
8 Gabriel Houde-Brisson .20 .50
9 Andre Joanisse .20 .50
10 Kevin Lacombe .20 .50
11 Guillaume Latendresse 2.00 5.00
12 Kevin Mailhiot .20 .50
13 Louis-Philippe Martin .20 .50
14 Jamie McCabe .20 .50
15 Jules Melanson .20 .50
16 Sylvain Michaud .30 .75
17 Pierre Morvan .20 .50
18 Ervins Mustukovs .30 .75
19 Jean-Francois Parent .20 .50
20 Yannick Riendeau .20 .50
21 Frederic St. Denis .20 .50
22 Andre Vincent .20 .50

2004-05 Drummondville Voltigeurs

COMPLETE SET (30) 6.00 20.00
1 Guillaume Latendresse .75 2.00
2 Philippe Roberge .20 .50
3 Pier-Olivier Pelletier .60 1.50
4 Derick Brassard 1.25 3.00
5 Chaz Johnson .20 .50
6 Henrick Lavoie .20 .50
7 Mathieu Ste-Marie .20 .50
8 Alexandre Demers .20 .50
9 Keven Gagne .20 .50
10 Andre Vincent .20 .50
11 Frederic St-Denis .20 .50
12 Andre Joanisse .20 .50
13 Louis-Philippe Martin .20 .50
14 Dave Bouchard .20 .50
15 Jules Melanson .20 .50
16 Steve Cacciotti .20 .50
19 Romy Elayoubi .20 .50
20 Cedric Archambault .20 .50
21 Maxime Frechette .20 .50
22 Julien Beaulieu .20 .50
23 Maxime Aubut .20 .50
24 Jean-Philippe Cote .20 .50
25 Maxim Chamberland .20 .50
26 Kevin Mailhiot .20 .50
27 Gaby Roch .20 .50
28 Simon Archambault .20 .50
29 Sylvain Michaud .40 1.00
30 Jesse Arko .20 .50
NNO Derick Brassard 2.00 5.00
NNO Pier-Olivier Pelletier 2.00 5.00

2005-06 Drummondville Voltigeurs

COMPLETE SET (33) 6.00 15.00
1 Guillaume Latendresse .60 1.50
2 Derick Brassard .60 1.50
3 Pier-Olivier Pelletier .30 .75
4 Pierre-Alexandre Marion .15 .40
5 Jules Melanson .15 .40
6 Kevin Mailhiot .15 .40
7 Maxim Mallette .15 .40
8 Joey Pell .15 .40
9 Andre Joanisse .15 .40
10 Maxime Frechette .15 .40
11 Tomas Zohorna .15 .40
12 Dave Bouchard .15 .40
13 Nicolas Sigouin .15 .40
14 Steven Cacciotti .15 .40
15 Tomas Svoboda .15 .40
16 Gaby Roch .15 .40
17 Alexandre Demers .15 .40
18 Frederic St-Denis .15 .40
19 Vincent Beaulieu .15 .40
20 Keven Gagne .15 .40
21 Maxime Aubut .15 .40
22 Paul Yovanic .15 .40
23 Olivier Fortier .15 .40
24 Tirobut .02 .10
25 Bryan Wilson .15 .40
26 Olivier Legault .15 .40
27 Yanick Charron .15 .40
28 Nicolas D'Aoust .15 .40
29 Simon Bouchard .15 .40
30 Olivier Donovan .15 .40
31 Loic Lacasse .30 .75
32 Francis Charette .15 .40
33 Jean-Michel Bolduc .15 .40

2006-07 Drummondville Voltigeurs

COMPLETE SET (26) 8.00 15.00
1 Derick Brassard .75 2.00
2 Bryan Wilson .20 .50
3 Mackenzie Micks .20 .50
4 Drew Paris .20 .50
5 Simon Bouchard .20 .50
6 Benoit Levesque .20 .50
7 Jonathan Duchesneau .20 .50
8 Tomas Zohorna .20 .50
9 Eric Campeau-Charron .20 .50
10 Steven Cacciotti .20 .50
11 Olivier Jannard .20 .50
12 Corey Garland .20 .50
13 Tomas Svoboda .20 .50
14 Gaby Roch .20 .50
15 Alexandre Demers .20 .50
16 Frederic St. Denis .20 .50
17 Stephen Valente .20 .50
18 Sebastien Bernier .20 .50
19 Etienne Bellavance-Martin .20 .50
20 Marc-Olivier Vachon .20 .50
21 Scott Howes .20 .50
22 Maxime Frechette .20 .50
23 Francis Charette .20 .50
24 Pier-Olivier Pelletier .30 .75
25 Maxime Gougeon .30 .75
26 Pierre-Alexandre Marion .20 .50

2006-07 Drummondville Voltigeurs Edition Limitee

EL1 Derick Brassard 1.50 4.00
EL2 Pier-Olivier Pelletier .60 1.50

1994-95 Dubuque Fighting Saints

COMPLETE SET (29) 4.00 10.00
1 Title Card Season schedule .02 .10
2 Chris Addesa .20 .50
3 Matt Addesa .20 .50
4 Mark Allegrezza .15 .40
5 Todd Barclay .15 .40
6 Jay Boxer ACO .02 .10
7 Geoff Collard .15 .40
8 John Dwyer .15 .40
9 Jayme Filipowicz .20 .50
10 Zach Ham .15 .40
11 Mike Herrera .15 .40
12 Roger Holeczy .15 .40
13 Steve Holeczy .15 .40
14 John Hultberg .30 .75
15 Ryan Karasek .15 .40
16 Mike Kramer TR .02 .10
17 Chris Masters .15 .40
18 A.J. Melanson .15 .40
19 Mike Minichiello .15 .40
20 Berk Nelson .15 .40
21 Nik Patronas .15 .40
22 Andy Powers .15 .40
23 Matt Romaniski .15 .40
24 Tom Ryles .15 .40
25 John Sadowski .15 .40
26 Chris Showalter .15 .40
27 Dan Stepanek .15 .40
28 Trevor Tallackson .15 .40
29 Troy Ward GM CO .02 .10

1997-98 Dubuque Fighting Saints

COMPLETE SET (30) 4.00 10.00
1 Dubuque Fighting Saints .15 .40
2 Justin Aufmann .15 .40
3 Travis Rotariu .15 .40
4 Marty Rychley .15 .40
5 Mario LeBlanc .15 .40
6 David Patch .15 .40
7 Evan Stensrud .15 .40
8 Josh Kern .15 .40
9 Christian Fletcher .15 .40
10 Scott Deopere .15 .40
11 Jeff Tarala .15 .40
12 Phil Lewandowski .15 .40
13 Joe Dudek .15 .40
14 Trent Landry .15 .40
15 Tom Rouleau .15 .40
16 Kris Harris .15 .40
17 Anders Johnson .15 .40
18 Matt Herhal .15 .40
19 Josh Myers .15 .40
20 David Brien .15 .40
21 Carl Hanson .15 .40
22 Scott Brown .15 .40
23 Adam Pobiak .15 .40
24 Todd Sanden CO .02 .10
25 Tom Hasenzahl CO .02 .10
26 Corey Courtney TR .02 .10
27 Sebastian St. Bernard MAS .02 .10
28 USHL Team Directory .02 .10
29 Schedule .02 .10
30 Josh Blackburn .30 .75

1998-99 ECHL All-Star Northern Conference

COMPLETE SET (21) 15.00 40.00
1 Tom O'Connor .75 2.00
2 Duane Harmer 1.25 3.00
3 Jamie Ling 1.25 3.00
4 Darren Maloney .75 2.00
5 Bret Meyers .75 2.00
6 Jim Bermingham 1.25 3.00
7 Jamie Thompson .75 2.00
8 Andrew Williamson .75 2.00
9 Marc Tropper .75 2.00
10 Bobby Brown .75 2.00
11 Jakub Ficenec 1.25 3.00
12 Arturs Kupaks 1.25 3.00
13 Dru Burgess .75 2.00
14 Dan Ceman .75 2.00
15 Ryan Kraft 1.25 3.00
16 Joe Blaznek .75 2.00
17 Casey Kesselring .75 2.00
18 Matt Mullen 1.25 3.00
19 Maxime Gingras 1.50 4.00
20 Karl Infanger .75 2.00
21 Checklist .02 .10

1998-99 ECHL All-Star Southern Conference

COMPLETE SET (21) 15.00 40.00
1 Jaroslav Obsut 1.25 3.00
2 Terry Lindgren .75 2.00
3 Kelly Hurd .75 2.00
4 Dana Mulvihill .75 2.00
5 Jonas Soling .75 2.00
6 Jamey Hicks .75 2.00
7 Patrick Rochon .75 2.00
8 John Varga 1.25 3.00
9 Dave Seitz .75 2.00
10 Jason Elders .75 2.00
11 Cail MacLean .75 2.00
12 Allan Sirois .75 2.00
13 Shane Calder .75 2.00
14 Chris Valicevic 1.25 3.00
15 J.F. Aube .75 2.00
16 Luke Curtin .75 2.00
17 Jan Kobezda .75 2.00
18 Bujar Amidovski 1.50 4.00
19 Chris Hynnes .75 2.00
20 Chris Wickenheiser 1.50 4.00
21 Checklist .02 .10

1999-00 ECHL All-Star Northern Conference

COMPLETE SET (22) 8.00 20.00
1 Alexei Krovopuskov .30 .75
2 Andrew Williamson .30 .75
3 Blaine Fitzpatrick .30 .75
4 Bujar Amidovski .75 2.00
5 Calvin Elfring .30 .75
6 Chad Ackerman .30 .75
7 Chris Gignac .30 .75
8 Curtis Wilgosh .30 .75
9 Derek Walser .30 .75
10 Duane Harmer .30 .75
11 Jamie Ling .30 .75
12 Jan Lasak 1.00 2.50
13 Jason Lawmaster .30 .75
14 Jeff Mitchell .30 .75
15 Joel Irving .30 .75
16 Marc Tropper .30 .75
17 Mark Murphy .30 .75
18 Mike Perna .30 .75
19 Peter Vandermeer .75 2.00
20 Ryan Kraft .75 2.00
21 Sean Matile .75 2.00
22 EBK Sports .02 .10

1999-00 ECHL All-Star Southern Conference

COMPLETE SET (22) 8.00 20.00
1 Bobby Stewart .30 .75
2 Brad Dexter .30 .75
3 Buddy Smith .30 .75
4 Chris Valicevic .75 2.00
5 Dany Bousquet .40 1.00
6 David Brumby .30 .75
7 Eric Naud .30 .75
8 Greg Schmidt .30 .75
9 Jeff Lazaro .30 .75
10 Jeff Maund .75 2.00
11 John McNabb .30 .75
12 John Spoltore .75 2.00
13 Kelly Perrault .30 .75
14 Luke Curtin .30 .75
15 Marc Magliarditi .75 2.00
16 Neil Fewster .30 .75
17 Sean Venedam .60 1.50
18 Steve O'Brien .30 .75
19 Wes Mason .30 .75
20 Ryan Gaucher .30 .75
21 Olivier Morin .30 .75
22 EBK Sports .02 .10

2002-03 ECHL All-Star Northern

COMPLETE SET (20) 8.00 20.00
19 Kevin Colley .40 1.00
20 Pierre-Luc Courchesne .40 1.00
21 Ryan Gaucher .40 1.00
22 Jim Henkel .40 1.00
23 Jamie Herrington .40 1.00
24 Andrew Ianiero .40 1.00
25 Jason Jaffray .40 1.00
26 Zenon Konopka .60 1.50
27 Dan Lombard .40 1.00
28 Brian McCullough .40 1.00
29 Chris McNamara .40 1.00
30 Nick Parillo .40 1.00
31 Geno Parrish .40 1.00
32 Tyler Rennette .40 1.00
33 Brad Rooney .40 1.00
34 Mike Smith .40 1.00
35 Scott Stirling .40 1.00
36 Takahito Suzuki .60 1.50
37 Simon Tremblay .40 1.00
39 Dustin Wood .40 1.00
39 Jonathan Zion .40 1.00

2002-03 ECHL All-Star Southern

COMPLETE SET (21) 8.00 20.00
40 Jim Baxter .40 1.00
41 Kent Davyduke .40 1.00
42 Mike Glumac .40 1.00
43 Joe Guenther .40 1.00
44 Adam Hauser .75 2.00
45 Corey Hessler .40 1.00
46 J.J. Hunter .40 1.00
47 Marty Johnston .40 1.00
48 Judd Medak .40 1.00
49 Laurent Meunier .40 1.00
50 Justin Morrison .40 1.00
51 Ryan O'Keefe .40 1.00
52 Rod Sarich .40 1.00
53 Aaron Schneekloth .40 1.00
54 Bud Smith .40 1.00
55 Rejean Stringer .40 1.00
56 Matt Underhill .60 1.50
57 Steffon Walby .40 1.00
58 Brad Williamson .40 1.00
59 Patrick Yetman .40 1.00
60 Rob Zepp .75 2.00

2002-03 ECHL Update

COMPLETE SET (27) 8.00 20.00
U1 Rick Adduono HCO .10 .25
U2 Derrick Byfuglien .40 1.00
U3 Sebastien Centomo 1.25 3.00
U4 Jason Christie HCO .10 .25
U5 Pierre-Luc Courchesne .40 1.00
U6 Kent Davyduke .40 1.00
U7 Gord Dineen HCO .10 .25
U8 Gerry Fleming HCO .20 .50
U9 Joe Guenther .40 1.00
U10 Adam Hauser .60 1.50
U11 Jamie Hodson .60 1.50
U12 Zenon Konopka .60 1.50
U13 David Lohrei HCO .10 .25
U14 Don MacAdam HCO .10 .25
U15 Chris McNamara .40 1.00
U16 John Marks HCO .10 .25
U17 Ryan O'Keefe .40 1.00
U18 Mike Oliveira .40 1.00
U19 Davis Payne HCO .20 .50
U20 Bryan Richardson .40 1.00
U21 Rod Sarich .40 1.00
U22 Stefton Walby .40 1.00
U23 Niklas Sundberg .40 1.00
U24 Mark Turner .40 1.00
U25 Scott White HCO .10 .25
U26 Dustin Wood .40 1.00
U27 Patrick Yetman .40 1.00

2003-04 ECHL All-Stars

COMPLETE SET (42) 50.00 100.00
241 Morten Ask 1.25 3.00
242 Alexandre Burrows 1.25 3.00
243 Cory Campbell 1.25 3.00
244 Brian Fahey 1.25 3.00
245 Chris Houle .75 2.00
246 Jason Jaffray .75 2.00
247 Dusty Jamieson 1.25 3.00
248 Nate Kiser .75 2.00
249 Shawn Limpright .75 2.00
250 Chris Lynch .75 2.00
251 Jason Maleyko 1.25 3.00
252 David Masse .75 2.00
253 Brian McCullough .75 2.00
254 Mark McRae .75 2.00
255 Jason Notermann .75 2.00
256 Sam Paolini .75 2.00
257 Tom Reimann .75 2.00
258 Randy Rowe .75 2.00
259 Kevin Spiewak .75 2.00
260 Scott Stirling .75 2.00
261 Jonathan Zion .75 2.00
262 Greg Barber .75 2.00
263 Greg Chambers .75 2.00
264 Frederic Cloutier 1.25 3.00
265 David Cornacchia .75 2.00
266 David Cousineau .75 2.00
267 Dan Ellis 2.00 5.00
268 Nick Ganga .75 2.00
269 Michael Garnett 1.50 4.00
270 Brent Gauvreau .75 2.00
271 Andrew Ianiero .75 2.00
272 Greg Jacina 1.25 3.00
273 Justin Kelly .75 2.00
274 Charles Linglet .75 2.00
275 Troy Milam .75 2.00
276 Corey Neilson .75 2.00
277 Jean-Francois Plourde .75 2.00
278 John Snowden .75 2.00
279 Ben Storey .75 2.00
280 Joe Talbot .75 2.00
281 Kevin Truelson .75 2.00
282 Steffon Walby 1.25 3.00

2003-04 ECHL Update RBI Sports

COMPLETE SET (48) 30.00 60.00
49 Joe Talbot .40 1.00
56 Todd Alexander .40 1.00
57 Shane Bendera .75 2.00
58 Jon Mirasty .40 1.00
59 Joe Watkins .75 2.00
60 Lucas Lawson .40 1.00
61 Brett Clouthier .75 2.00
62 Phil Cole .40 1.00
63 Tyler Masters .40 1.00
64 Doug Teskey .40 1.00
113 Kristian Antila .40 1.00
114 Matus Kostur .75 2.00
115 Christian Larrivee .40 1.00
116 Olivier Michaud 1.50 4.00
117 Tomas Micka .40 1.00
118 Matt Shasby .40 1.00
119 Marc-Andre Thinel .75 2.00
120 Sean Connolly .40 1.00
121 Riley Cote .40 1.00
122 Jason Crain .40 1.00
123 Miguel Delisle .40 1.00
124 Janne Jokila .40 1.00
125 Andrew Penner .75 2.00
126 Olivier Proulx .40 1.00
127 Nicolas Corbeil .40 1.00
128 Daniel Boisclair .75 2.00
129 Mark Concannon .40 1.00
130 Brian Passmore .40 1.00
131 Michel Robinson .40 1.00
132 Russell Spence .40 1.00
133 Anthony Aquino .75 2.00
134 Wes Fox .40 1.00
135 Phil Lewandowski .40 1.00
136 Trevor Prior .75 2.00
137 Dan Ellis 1.50 4.00
138 Armands Berzins .40 1.00
139 Maxime Fortunus .40 1.00
140 Derek Gustafson .75 2.00
141 Jamie Johnson .40 1.00
142 Ed McGrane .40 1.00
143 Jean-Francois Soucy .75 2.00
144 Jeremy Van Hoof .40 1.00
283 Dustin Johner .40 1.00
284 Paul Ballantyne .40 1.00
285 Scott Kabotoff .40 1.00
286 Joe Exter 1.50 4.00
287 Tyler MacKay .40 1.00
288 Patrick Couture .75 2.00

1997-98 El Paso Buzzards

COMPLETE SET (32) 4.00 10.00
1 Jamie Thompson .20 .50
2 Brent Scott .20 .50
3 Mark Sakala .20 .50
4 Jason Rose .20 .50
5 Corri Moffat .20 .50
6 Chris MacKenzie .20 .50
7 Trent Eigner .20 .50
8 Rusty McKie .30 .75
9 Jason Welch .20 .50
10 Martin Balleux .20 .50
11 Corey Heon .20 .50
12 Derek Riley .20 .50
13 Chris Gordon .20 .50
14 Bill Trew .20 .50
15 Jason Carey .20 .50
16 Sandy Lamarre .20 .50
17 Dan Carter .20 .50
18 Robert Haddock .20 .50
19 Mark Hilton .20 .50
20 Todd Brost CO .02 .10
21 Swoop Mascot .02 .10
22 Teresa Fernandez RG .02 .10
23 Greg Sieg TR .02 .10
24 KLAQ Morning Show .02 .10
25 KISS Morning Show .02 .10
26 KROD Morning Show .02 .10
27 Paul Strelzin ANNC .02 .10
28 DJ Card .02 .10
29 TV-7 Anchors .02 .10
30 TV-7 Sports Team .02 .10
31 DJ Card .02 .10
32 TV-7 Reporters .02 .10

1998-99 El Paso Buzzards

COMPLETE SET (28) 20.00 40.00
1 Trent Eigner 1.25 3.00
2 Chris Gordon .75 2.00
3 Robert Haddock .75 2.00
4 Corey Heon .75 2.00
5 Alex Herbison .75 2.00
6 Bill Trew .75 2.00
7 Jeremy Vanin .75 2.00
8 Jason Welch .75 2.00
9 Deuce Wynes .75 2.00
10 Todd Brost CO .40 1.00
11 Steve Pottie .75 2.00
12 Mike Rees .75 2.00
13 Iannique Renaud .75 2.00
14 Jason Rushton .75 2.00
15 Blake Sheane .75 2.00
16 Mark Costea .75 2.00
17 Sandy Lamarre .75 2.00
18 Marc Labelle .75 2.00
19 Corri Moffat .75 2.00
20 Eric Peterson .75 2.00
21 McArthur/Palka .75 2.00
22 Warner/Casas .75 2.00
23 The Mike & Grace Show .02 .10
24 Cruz/Adams Keith/Steele .02 .10
25 Garcia/Medina/Kaplowitz .02 .10
26 Dodson/Romano .02 .10
27 Paul Strelzin ANN .02 .10
28 Checklist .02 .10

2001-02 El Paso Buzzards

COMPLETE SET (20) 6.00 15.00
1 Trent Eigner .40 1.00
2 Van Burgess .40 1.00
3 Clint Collins .40 1.00
4 Rhett Dudley .40 1.00
5 Kelly Riou .40 1.00
6 Chris Zaleski .40 1.00
7 Jeremy Vanin .40 1.00
8 Derrell Upton .40 1.00
9 Mike Rees .40 1.00
10 Justin Van Parys .40 1.00
11 Trevor Hammer .40 1.00
12 Jason Tessier .40 1.00
13 Dory Tisdale .40 1.00
14 Rob Laurie .60 1.50
15 Troy Linna .40 1.00
16 Jeff Levy .40 1.00
17 Aaron Phillips .40 1.00
18 Kory Baker .40 1.00
19 Corey Waring .40 1.00
20 John Hanson .40 1.00

2002-03 El Paso Buzzards

1 Jeff Levy .30 .75
2 Rhett Dudley .30 .75
3 Chris Zaleski .30 .75
4 John Hanson .30 .75
5 Aaron Phillips .30 .75
6 Rob Laurie .30 .75
7 Kory Baker .30 .75

2003-04 Elmira Jackals

COMPLETE SET (25) 12.00
1 Peter Aubry .30 .75
2 Cal Benazic .20 .50
3 J.F. Boutin .20 .50
4 Trevor Burgess .20 .50
5 Tom Clayton .20 .50
6 Carl Drakenojo .20 .50
7 Nathan Gillies .20 .50
8 Dean Jackson .20 .50
9 Greg Koehler Mike Thompson .20 .50
10 Ed Lowe .20 .50
11 Kris Mallette .30 .75
12 Ryan McIntosh .30 .75
13 Randy Murphy .20 .50
14 Geoff O'Leary .20 .50
15 Matt Osborne .20 .50
16 Neil Posillico .20 .50
17 Michael Prochazka .20 .50
18 Trevor Segstro .20 .50
19 James Sheehan .20 .50
20 Don Smith .20 .50
21 Jamie Thompson .20 .50
23 Todd Brost HCO .08 .20
24 Spud Hamilton EQM .04 .10
25 Brandon Dionne TR .04 .10
26 Team Photo .20 .50

2009-10 Elmira Jackals

1 Olivier Proulx .40 1.00
2 Yannick Tifu .40 1.00
3 Mat Robinson .40 1.00
4 Julien Ellis .40 1.00
5 Brendan Connolly .40 1.00
5 R.J. Anderson .40 1.00
6 Chaz Johnson .40 1.00
6 Brett Gallant .40 1.00
7 Tyler Donati .40 1.00
8 Maxime Gratchev .40 1.00
9 Andy Chiodo .40 1.00
9 Joe Grimaldi .40 1.00
10 Brennan Turner .40 1.00
11 Steve Martinson .40 1.00
12 Blade .40 1.00
13 Justin Donati .40 1.00
14 Chris Korchinski .40 1.00
15 Keegan Dansereau .40 1.00
15 Matt Lowry .40 1.00
16 Wes Cunningham .40 1.00
17 Guillaume Lepine .40 1.00
18 Checklist .40 1.00

2013-14 Elmira Jackals

COMPLETE SET () 5.00 12.00
1 Jakub Culek .30 .75
2 Jean Bourbeau .30 .75
3 Jordan Pietrus .30 .75
4 Kyle Bushee .30 .75
5 Ludwig Karlsson .30 .75
6 Maxim Lamarche .30 .75
7 Mike Vaskivuo .30 .75
8 Neil Conway .30 .75
9 Nik Pokulok .30 .75
10 Patch Alber .30 .75
11 Rob Bellamy .30 .75
12 Scott Greenham .30 .75
13 Artem Demkov .30 .75
14 Corey Bellamy .30 .75
15 Dane Walters .30 .75
16 Daniel Koger .30 .75
17 Danny Hobbs .30 .75
18 Harry Young .30 .75

2003-04 Erie Otters

COMPLETE SET (24) 6.00 15.00
1 Derrick Bagshaw .20 .50
2 Michael Blunden .40 1.00
3 Brad Bonello .20 .50
4 Chris Campoli .30 .75
5 Sean Courtney .20 .50
6 Josh Disher .30 .75
7 Tomas Galasek .20 .50
8 Bryan Hamm .20 .50
9 Jacob Heller .20 .50
10 David Herring .20 .50
11 Rob Hisey .20 .50
12 Alex Karaulchuk .20 .50
13 Brian Lee .20 .50
14 Chad Loikets .20 .50
15 Matthew Lynn .20 .50
16 Mike Melinko .20 .50
17 Derek Merlini .20 .50
18 Sean O'Connor .20 .50
19 Ryan O'Marra .40 1.00
20 Josh Patterson .20 .50
21 Geoff Platt .40 1.00
22 Vince Scott .20 .50
23 Jhase Sniderman .30 .75
24 Jason Speight .20 .50

2004-05 Erie Otters

COMPLETE SET (25) 5.00 12.00
1 Michael Blunden .30 .75
2 Tomas Galasek .20 .50
3 Derek Merlini .20 .50
4 Brett MacLean .20 .50
5 Jhase Sniderman .30 .75
6 Geoff Platt .30 .75
7 Chris Greene .20 .50
8 Sean O'Connor .20 .50
9 Vince Scott .20 .50
10 Jake Heller .20 .50
11 Derrick Bagshaw .20 .50
12 Andrew Hotham .20 .50
13 Brian Lee .20 .50
14 Chad Loikets .20 .50
15 Peter Sergeant .20 .50
16 Josh Kidd .20 .50
17 Ryan O'Marra .40 1.00
18 Eric Regan .20 .50
19 Andrew Shennan .20 .50
20 Jason Speight .20 .50
21 Josh Disher .30 .75
22 David Herring .20 .50
23 Dave MacQueen CO .04 .10
24 Peter Sidorkiewicz ACO .10 .25
25 Shooter MASCOT .04 .10
NNO Ryan O'Marra LTD 2.00 5.00
NNO Geoff Platt LTD 1.50 4.00

2005-06 Erie Otters

COMPLETE SET (23) 5.00 12.00
1 Ryan O'Marra .40 1.00
2 Derrick Bagshaw .20 .50
3 Michael Blunden .40 1.00
4 Chris Greene .20 .50
5 Justin Hodgman .20 .50
6 Patrick Lee .20 .50
7 Jordan Nolan .20 .50
8 Sean O'Connor .20 .50
9 Vince Scott .20 .50
10 Christian Seest Olsen .20 .50
11 Nick Palmieri .20 .50
12 Anthony Peluso .20 .50
13 Josh Vatri .20 .50
14 Jake Heller .20 .50
15 Andrew Hotham .20 .50
16 Josh Kidd .20 .50
17 Chad Loikets .20 .50
18 Josh Disher .20 .50
19 Ryan Ludzik .20 .50
20 Adam Berti .20 .50
21 Bret Nasby .20 .50
22 Jonathan Hull .20 .50
23 Tyler McKinley .20 .50

2006-07 Erie Otters

COMPLETE SET (24) 8.00 15.00
1 Nick Palmieri .20 .50
2 Sean O'Connor .20 .50
3 Patrick Lee .20 .50
4 Derrick Bagshaw .20 .50
5 Mitchell Forbes .20 .50
6 Stanislav Polodna .20 .50
7 Luke Gazdic .20 .50
8 Justin Hodgman .20 .50
9 Josh Vatri .20 .50
10 Shayne Taylor .20 .50
11 Kelly Geoffrey .20 .50
12 Kyle Ramsay .20 .50
13 Zack Torquato .60 1.50
14 Ronny Rogers .20 .50
15 Josh Kidd .20 .50
16 Mitch Gaulton .20 .50
17 Andrew Hotham .20 .50
18 Anthony Peluso .20 .50
19 Brian Shaw .20 .50
20 Michael Liambas .20 .50
21 Ryan Henry .20 .50
22 Jonathan Laniel .40 1.00
23 Justin Garay .40 1.00
24 Ryan Ludzik .40 1.00

2012-13 Erie Otters
COMPLETE SET (24) 20.00 40.00
1 Connor McDavid 15.00 30.00

2013-14 Erie Otters Choice
COMPLETE SET (25) 8.00 20.00
1 Spencer Abraham .30 .75
2 Nick Betz .30 .75
3 Connor Brown .40 1.00
4 Andre Burakovsky .30 .75
5 Michael Curtis .30 .75
6 Oscar Dansk .30 .75
7 Travis Dermott .30 .75
8 Troy Donnay .30 .75
9 Jake Evans .30 .75
10 Justin Felker .30 .75
11 Dane Fox .30 .75
12 Brendan Gaunce .30 .75
13 Cory Genovese .30 .75
14 Kurtis MacDermid .30 .75
15 Quentin Maksimovich .30 .75
16 Connor McDavid 2.00 5.00
17 Patrick Murphy .30 .75
18 Adam Pelech .40 1.00
19 Kyle Pettit .30 .75
20 Darren Raddysh .30 .75
21 Dylan Strome .40 1.00
22 Joel Wigle .30 .75
23 Devin Williams .30 .75
24 Travis Wood .30 .75
25 Shooter (Mascot) .30 .75

2014-15 Erie Otters Choice
COMPLETE SET (16) 8.00 20.00
1 Nick Betz .30 .75
2 Shaun Bily .30 .75
3 Alex DeBrincat .30 .75
4 Daniel Dekoning .30 .75
5 Troy Donnay .30 .75
6 Patrick Fellows .30 .75
7 T.J. Fergus .30 .75
8 Kurtis MacDermid .30 .75
9 Kyle Maksimovich .30 .75
10 Quentin Maksimovich .30 .75
11 Jake Marchment .30 .75
12 Mason Marchment .30 .75
13 Connor McDavid 3.00 8.00
14 Patrick Murphy .30 .75
15 Kyle Pettit .30 .75
16 Dylan Strome .75 2.00

1994-95 Erie Panthers
COMPLETE SET (20) 3.00 8.00
1 Title Card .02 .10
2 Ron Hansis CO .02 .10
3 Barry Smith ACO .02 .10
4 Patrick Laughlin TR .02 .10
5 Larry Empey .20 .50
6 Vassili Demin .20 .50
7 Sergei Stas .20 .50
8 Brad Harrison .20 .50
9 Cam Brown .20 .50
10 Kevin McKinnon .20 .50
11 Andrei Kozlov .20 .50
12 Chris Tschupp .20 .50
13 Jason Smith .20 .50
14 Justin Peca .20 .50
15 Francis Ouellette .20 .50
16 Vern Guetens .30 .75
17 Scott Burfoot .30 .75
18 Vyachaslav Polikarkin .20 .50
19 Stephane Charbonneau .20 .50
20 Ian Decorby .20 .50

2003-04 Everett Silvertips
COMPLETE SET (28) 5.00 12.00
1 Checklist .04 .10
2 Bryan Nathe .20 .50
3 Marc Desloges .20 .50
4 Jovan Matic .20 .50
5 Mike Wall .30 .75
6 Michael Wuchterl .20 .50
7 Mark Kress .20 .50
8 Devin Wilson .20 .50
9 Martin Ruzicka .20 .50
10 Curtis Billsten .20 .50
11 Barry Horman .20 .50
12 Shaun Heshka .20 .50
13 Jeff Schmidt .20 .50
14 Cody Thoring .20 .50
15 Ryan Blatchford .20 .50
16 Torrie Wheat .20 .50
17 Mitch Love .20 .50
18 Devin Welsh .20 .50
19 Riley Armstrong .20 .50
20 Tyler Dietrich .20 .50
21 John Dahl .20 .50
22 Jeff Harvey .30 .75
23 Ivan Baranka .20 .50
24 Chad Bassen .20 .50
25 Doug Soetaert GM .04 .10
26 Kevin Constantine CO .04 .10
27 John Becanic ACO .04 .10
28 Jay Varady ACO .04 .10

2004-05 Everett Silvertips
COMPLETE SET 10.00 20.00
1 Header Card .04 .10
2 Tyler Dietrich .20 .50
3 Alex Leavitt .20 .50
4 Mitch Love .20 .50
5 Doug Soetaert .04 .10
6 Mike Wuchterl .20 .50
7 Cody Thoring .20 .50
8 Karel Hromas .20 .50
9 Ryan Blatchford .20 .50
10 Zach Sim .20 .50
11 Mark Kress .20 .50
12 Brennan Zasitko .20 .50
13 Torrie Wheat .20 .50
14 Michael Wall .40 1.00
15 Graham Potuer .20 .50
16 Matt Sawa .20 .50
17 Randy King .20 .50
18 Leland Irving 1.25 3.00
19 Shaun Heshka .20 .50
20 Jonathan Harty .20 .50
21 Zach Hamill 1.25 3.00
22 Taylor Ellington .20 .50
23 Jeremy Creurer .20 .50
24 Brady Calla .30 .75
25 Curtis Billsten .20 .50
26 Ivan Baranka .20 .50
27 Kyle Annesley .20 .50
28 Jay Varady .20 .50
29 John Becanic .20 .50
30 Kevin Constantine .04 .10

2005-06 Everett Silvertips
COMPLETE SET (30) 10.00 20.00
1 Damir Alic .30 .75
2 Brady Calla .30 .75
3 Zack Dailey .30 .75
4 Eric Doyle .30 .75
5 Taylor Ellington .30 .75
6 Matt Esposito .30 .75
7 Ondrej Fiala .40 1.00
8 Jason Fransoo .30 .75
9 Zach Hamill .75 2.00
10 Shane Harper .30 .75
11 Jonathon Harty .30 .75
12 Shaun Heshka .30 .75
13 Karel Hromas .30 .75
14 Leland Irving .75 2.00
15 Mark Kress .30 .75
16 John Lammers .30 .75
17 Jonathan Milhouse .30 .75
18 Peter Mueller 2.00 5.00
19 Graham Potuer .30 .75
20 Ryan Sawka .30 .75
21 Zach Sim .30 .75
22 Jesse Smyke .30 .75
23 Brennan Sonne .30 .75
24 Cody Thoring .30 .75
25 Torrie Wheat .30 .75
26 Kevin Constantine HC .02 .10
27 John Becanic AC .02 .10
28 Jay Varady AC .02 .10
29 Scott Scoville DPP .02 .10
30 Zoran Rajcic DO .02 .10

2009-10 Everett Silvertips
1 Everett Silvertips .40 1.00
2 Zack Dailey .40 1.00
3 Radko Gudas .40 1.00
4 Daniel Iwanski .40 1.00
5 Clayton Cumiskey .40 1.00
6 Thomas Heemskerk .40 1.00
7 Rasmus Rissanen .40 1.00
8 Tyler Maxwell .40 1.00
9 Byron Froese .40 1.00
10 Shane Harper .40 1.00
11 Campbell Elynuik .40 1.00
12 Curtis Kulchar .40 1.00
13 Chris Langkow .40 1.00
14 Scott Macdonald .40 1.00
15 Kent Simpson .40 1.00
16 Chris de la Lande .40 1.00
17 Markus McCrea .40 1.00
18 D. Jay McGrath .40 1.00
19 Gabe Minville .40 1.00
20 Josh Winquist .40 1.00
21 Kellen Tochkin .40 1.00
22 Alex Theriau .40 1.00
23 Paul Sohor .40 1.00
24 Ryan Murray .40 1.00
25 Craig Hartsburg .40 1.00
26 Jay Varady .40 1.00
27 Chris Hartsburg .40 1.00

2013-14 Everett Silvertips
COMPLETE SET (28) 8.00 20.00
1 Logan Aasman .30 .75
2 Austin Adam .30 .75
3 Nik Amundrud .30 .75
4 Patrick Bajkov .30 .75
5 Kohl Bauml .30 .75
6 Ben Betker .30 .75
7 Kevin Constantine CO .30 .75
8 Kevin Davis .30 .75
9 Matt Fonteyne .30 .75
10 Manraj Hayer .30 .75
11 Zane Jones .30 .75
12 Noah Juulsen .30 .75
13 Jujhar Khaira .30 .75
14 Remi Laurencelle .30 .75
15 Dawson Leedahl .30 .75
16 Mark LeRose Asst. CO .30 .75
17 Austin Lotz .30 .75
18 Mitch Love Asst. CO .30 .75
19 Brayden Low .30 .75
20 Cole MacDonald .30 .75
21 Mirco Mueller .30 .75
22 Ivan Nikolishin .30 .75
23 Matthew Pufahl .30 .75
24 Tyler Sandhu .30 .75
25 Carson Stadnyk .30 .75
26 Jordan Wharrie .30 .75
27 Josh Winquist .30 .75
28 Header Card .30 .75

2005 Extreme Top Prospects Signature Edition
S1 Sidney Crosby 150.00 250.00
S2 Alex Bourret 6.00 15.00
S3 Guillaume Latendresse 12.00 30.00
S4 Marc-Antoine Pouliot 10.00 25.00
S5 Jean-Francois Jacques 6.00 15.00
S6 David Krejci 6.00 15.00
S7 Corey Perry 12.50 30.00
S7 Daren Machesney 6.00 15.00
S8 Rob Schremp 10.00 25.00
S9 Danny Syvret 6.00 15.00
S10 Petr Vrana 6.00 15.00
S11 Derick Brassard 10.00 25.00
S12 Stephen Dixon 6.00 15.00
S13 James Sheppard 8.00 20.00
S14 Marc Staal 8.00 20.00
S15 Benoit Pouliot 8.00 20.00
S16 Anthony Stewart 6.00 15.00
S17 Michael Ouzas 6.00 15.00
S18 Patrick O'Sullivan 8.00 20.00
S19 Lukas Kaspar 6.00 15.00
S20 Bobby Ryan 10.00 25.00
S21 Stanislav Lascek 6.00 15.00
S22 Marek Zagrapan 6.00 15.00
S23 Josh Hennessy 6.00 15.00
S24 Alexander Radulov 10.00 25.00
S25 Julien Ellis-Plante 8.00 20.00
S27 Wojtek Wolski 10.00 25.00
S28 Mike Richards 10.00 25.00
S29 Boris Valabik 6.00 15.00
S30 Ryan O'Marra 6.00 15.00
SS1 S.Crosby Stick AU/150 300.00 800.00

2013-14 Fargo Force
COMPLETE SET (26) 6.00 15.00
A01 Chris Buchanan .30 .75
A02 Andrew McDonald .30 .75
A03 C.J. Hayes .30 .75
A04 Michael Babcock .30 .75
A05 Hunter Warner .30 .75
A06 Butrus Ghafari .30 .75
B01 Christian Cakebread .30 .75
B02 Brendan Jensen .30 .75
B03 Alex Toscano .30 .75
B04 Garick Gray .30 .75
B05 Mason Morelli .30 .75
B06 Neal Goff .30 .75
C01 Tyler Hynes .30 .75
C02 Meirs Moore .30 .75
C03 Cody Longie .30 .75
C04 Tanner Jago .30 .75
C05 J.M. Piotrowski .30 .75
C06 Cam Ashley .30 .75
C07 Andrew Zerban .30 .75
C08 Mathias Israelsson .30 .75
D01 Kid Bobble MASCOT .30 .75
D02 Teemu Kivihalme .30 .75
D03 Cameron Johnson .30 .75
D04 John Baiocco .30 .75
D05 Alex Jackstadt .30 .75
D06 Mikey Eyssimont .30 .75

2014-15 Fargo Force
COMPLETE SET (21) 6.00 15.00
1 Colton Poolman .30 .75
2 Victor Bergstrom .30 .75
3 Brody Stevens .30 .75
4 Shane McMahan .30 .75
5 Christian Cakebread .30 .75
6 C.J. Hayes .30 .75
7 Zach Yon .30 .75
8 Denis Smirnov .30 .75
9 Michael Babcock .30 .75
10 Mikey Eyssimont .30 .75
11 Cole Bjugson .30 .75
12 Mason Morelli .30 .75
13 Mitch Slattery .30 .75
14 T.J. Roo .30 .75
15 Kyle Sylvester .30 .75
16 Chuck Bennis .30 .75
17 Mathias Israelsson .30 .75
18 Robbie Beydoun .30 .75
19 Justin Baudry .30 .75
20 Austin Pooley .30 .75
21 Matt McArdle .30 .75

1998-99 Fayetteville Force
COMPLETE SET (18) 3.60 9.00
1 David Lohrei HCO .20 .50
2 Darren McLean .20 .50
3 Rod Butler .20 .50
4 Steven Toll .20 .50
5 Justin Tomberlin .20 .50
6 Alexsandr Chunchukov .20 .50
7 Casey Hungle .20 .50
8 Jason Wright .20 .50
9 Roddy MacCormick .20 .50
10 Lon Hovland .20 .50
11 Chris Bernard .20 .50
12 Dan Dennis .20 .50
13 Chris Ford .20 .50
14 Ryan Guzior .20 .50
15 Chad Remackel .20 .50
16 Colin Muldoon .20 .50
17 Stephen Sangermano .20 .50
18 Tim Hill .20 .50

2006-07 Fayetteville FireAntz
COMPLETE SET (21) 20.00 40.00
1 Mike Clarke .75 2.00
2 Chad Collins 1.25 3.00
3 Bryan Dobek .75 2.00
4 Chris Furguson .75 2.00
5 Gavin Hodgson .75 2.00
6 Garrett Kindred 1.25 3.00
7 Nick Kormanyos .75 2.00
8 John Marks HC .20 .50
9 Rob Manchoff CO .20 .50
10 Adam Meyer .75 2.00
11 Marc Norrington .75 2.00
12 Josh Piro .75 2.00
13 Jarrett Robertson .75 2.00
14 Dylan Row .75 2.00
15 Pekka Saittakari .75 2.00
16 Rob Sich .75 2.00
17 B.J. Stephens .75 2.00
18 Josh Tataryn .75 2.00
19 Tim Velemirovich .75 2.00
20 Josh Welter .75 2.00
21 Chad Wilcox .75 2.00

1991-92 Ferris State Bulldogs
COMPLETE SET (30) 4.00 10.00
1 Aaron Asp .20 .50
2 Seth Appert .20 .50
3 J.J. Bamberger .20 .50
4 Kevin Beals ACO .02 .10
5 Scott Bell .20 .50
6 Brad Burnham .20 .50
7 Dan Chaput .20 .50
8 Tim Christian .20 .50
9 Bob Daniels .20 .50
10 Colin Dodunski .20 .50
11 Mick Dolan .20 .50
12 John Duff .20 .50
13 Daryl Filipek .20 .50
14 John Gruden .20 .50
15 Luke Harvey .20 .50
16 Jeff Jestadt .20 .50
17 Dave Karpa .30 .75
18 Gary Kitching .20 .50
19 Mike Kolenda .20 .50
20 Craig Lisko .20 .50
21 Mike May .20 .50
22 Pat Mazzoli .20 .50
23 Robb McIntyre .20 .50
24 Kevin Moore .20 .50
25 Greg Paine .20 .50
26 Dwight Parrish .20 .50
27 Val Passarelli .20 .50
28 Keith Sergott .20 .50
29 Doug Smith .20 .50
30 The Bulldog MASCOT .02 .10

1992-93 Ferris State Bulldogs
COMPLETE SET (30) 8.00 20.00
1 Seth Appert .30 .75
2 Aaron Asp .30 .75
3 J.J. Bamberger .30 .75
4 Kevin Beals .30 .75
5 Scot Bell .30 .75
6 Brad Burnham .30 .75
7 Daniel Chaput .30 .75
8 Tim Christian .30 .75
9 Bob Daniels CO .08 .25
10 Colin Dodunski .30 .75
11 Mick Dolan .30 .75
12 John Duff .30 .75
13 Daryl Filipek .30 .75
14 John Gruden .40 1.00
15 Luke Harvey .30 .75
16 Jeff Jestadt .30 .75
17 Dave Karpa .40 1.00
18 Gary Kitching .30 .75
19 Mike Kolenda .30 .75
20 Craig Lisko .30 .75
21 Mike May .30 .75
22 Pat Mazzoli .30 .75
23 Robb McIntyre .30 .75
24 Kevin Moore .30 .75
25 Greg Paine .30 .75
26 Dwight Parrish .30 .75
27 Val Passarelli .40 1.00
28 Keith Sergott .30 .75
29 Doug Smith .30 .75
30 The Bulldog MASCOT .02 .10

1993-94 Flint Generals
COMPLETE SET (20) 40.00 75.00
1 Header Card .40 1.00
2 Brent Stickney 1.50 4.00
3 Brett Strot 1.50 4.00
4 Brian Sakic 2.00 5.00
5 Chris O'Rourke 1.50 4.00
6 Dan Elsener 1.50 4.00
7 Darcy Austin 1.50 4.00
8 Dominic Niro 1.50 4.00
9 Jim Duhart 1.50 4.00
10 John Heasty 1.50 4.00
11 Keith Whitmore 1.50 4.00
12 Ken Spangler 1.50 4.00
13 Kevin Kerr 1.50 4.00
14 Larry Bernard 1.50 4.00
15 Lorne Knauft 1.50 4.00
16 Marc Vachon 1.50 4.00
17 Mark Gowens 2.00 5.00
18 Peter Horachek 1.50 4.00
19 Stephane Brochu 1.50 4.00
20 Todd Humphrey 2.00 5.00

1994-95 Flint Generals
COMPLETE SET (24) 20.00 50.00
1 Kevin Barrett .75 2.00
2 Larry Bernard .75 2.00
3 Ken Blum .75 2.00
4 Stephane Brochu .75 2.00
5 Keith Carney .75 2.00
6 Ryan Douglas .75 2.00
7 Jim Duhart .75 2.00
8 Ray Gallagher .75 2.00
9 Mark Gowens .75 2.00
10 Peter Horachek .75 2.00
11 Todd Humphrey .75 2.00
12 Fredrik Jax 1.00 2.50
13 Doug Jones .75 2.00
14 Kevin Kerr 1.00 2.50
15 Petr Leska .75 2.00
16 Stan Matwijiw 1.25 3.00
17 Glen Mears .75 2.00
18 Kyle Reeves 1.00 2.50
19 Brian Sakic 1.00 2.50
20 Stefan Simoes .75 2.00
21 Ken Spangler .75 2.00
22 Keith Whitmore .75 2.00
23 Jeff Whittle .75 2.00
24 Team Photo .75 2.00

1995-96 Flint Generals
COMPLETE SET (25) 4.80 12.00
1 Erin Whitten 1.00 2.50
2 Kevin Kerr .30 .75
3 Sverre Sears .15 .40
4 Scott Burfoot .20 .50
5 John Batten .15 .40
6 Chad Grills .15 .40
7 Lady Generals .30 .75
8 General Rally Mascot .02 .10
9 Rob Nichols GM CO .02 .10
10 Mikhail Nemirovsky .15 .40
11 Robin Bouchard .15 .40
12 Dominic Grandmaison .15 .40
13 Andrei Mezin .30 .75
14 Steve Beadle .15 .40
15 Darryl Lafrance .15 .40
16 Chris Gotziaman .15 .40
17 Gerry St. Cyr .30 .75
18 Derek Knorr .15 .40
19 Chris Gordon .20 .50
20 Brett MacDonald .15 .40
21 Brian Sakic .20 .50
22 Jamie Hearn .15 .40
23 Jeff Whittle .15 .40
24 Stephane Brochu .15 .40
25 Jim Duhart .15 .40

1996-97 Flint Generals
COMPLETE SET (28) 10.00 25.00
1 Steve Beadle .40 1.00
2 Pascal Belanger .40 1.00
3 Robin Bouchard .40 1.00
4 Stephane Brochu .40 1.00
5 Neil Eisenhut .40 1.00
6 Nick Forbes .40 1.00
7 Igor Galkin .40 1.00
8 Jason Glover .40 1.00
9 Chad Grills .40 1.00
10 John Heasty .40 1.00
11 Kevin Kerr .40 1.00
12 Lorne Knauft .40 1.00
13 Brett MacDonald .40 1.00
14 Andrei Mezin .60 1.50
15 Jason Payne .40 1.00
16 Jason Ralph .40 1.00
17 Dmitri Rodine .40 1.00
18 Zdenek Sikl .40 1.00
19 Ken Spangler .40 1.00
20 Matt Weder .40 1.00
21 Jeff Whittle .40 1.00
22 Ross Wilson .40 1.00
23 Rob Nichols HCO .20 .50
24 Karl Lawson .40 1.00
25 General Rally Mascot .20 .50
26 1996 Colonial Cup Champs .40 1.00
27 1996 Tarry Cup Champs .40 1.00
28 Checklist .20 .50

1997-98 Flint Generals
COMPLETE SET (30) 12.00 30.00
1 Steve Beadle .40 1.00
2 Stephane Brochu .60 1.50
3 Ian Crockford .40 1.00
4 Nick Forbes .40 1.00
5 Mark Giannetti .40 1.00
6 Jason Glover .40 1.00
7 Chad Grills .40 1.00
8 John Heasty .40 1.00
9 Raitis Ivanans .40 1.00
10 Kevin Kerr .60 1.50
11 Lorne Knauft .40 1.00
12 Ray LeBlanc .75 2.00
13 Brett MacDonald .40 1.00
14 Bryan McMullen .40 1.00
15 Andrei Mezin .75 2.00
16 Matt Mullin .60 1.50
17 Dmitri Rodine .40 1.00
18 Brian Sakic .60 1.50
19 Jeremy Sladovnik .40 1.00
20 Ken Spangler .40 1.00
21 Kahlil Thomas .40 1.00
22 Jeff Whittle .40 1.00
23 Ross Wilson .40 1.00
24 Rob Nichols CO .08 .25
25 General Rally MASCOT .08 .25
26 Mike Zanzarella TR .08 .25
27 Robert Roe STAFF .08 .25
28 Pam The Prize Lady .20 .50
29 Lady Generals .40 1.00
30 Flint Generals .40 1.00

1997-98 Flint Generals EBK
COMPLETE SET (23) 4.00 10.00
1 Checklist .02 .10
2 Kahlil Thomas .20 .50
3 Ken Spangler .20 .50
4 Stephane Brochu .30 .75
5 Lorne Knauft .20 .50
6 Janis Tomans .20 .50
7 Nick Forbes .20 .50
8 Trevor Jobe .20 .50
9 John Heasty .20 .50
10 Brian Sakic .30 .75
11 Kevin Kerr .30 .75
12 Chad Grills .20 .50
13 UHL All-Stars .20 .50
14 Jeremy Sladovnik .20 .50
15 Jeff Whittle .20 .50
16 Jason Glover .20 .50
17 Steve Beadle .20 .50
18 Bryan McMullen .20 .50
19 Emmanuel Labranche .20 .50
20 Brett MacDonald .20 .50
21 John Batten .20 .50
22 Ross Wilson .20 .50
23 Rob Nichols CO .08 .25

1998-99 Flint Generals
COMPLETE SET (22) 8.00 20.00
1 Logo Card .02 .10
2 Chad Grills .40 1.00
3 Jason Payne .40 1.00
4 Jeremy Sladovnik .40 1.00
5 Stephane Brochu .40 1.00
6 Jeff Whittle .40 1.00
7 Rob Nichols CO .08 .25
8 Brian Sakic .60 1.50
9 Checklist .02 .10
10 Nick Forbes .40 1.00
11 Mike Bondy .40 1.00
12 Peter Ambroziak .40 1.00
13 Luch Nasato .60 1.50
14 Mikhail Nemirovsky .40 1.00
15 Bobby Reynolds .40 1.00
16 Generals Staff .02 .10
17 Lorne Knauft .40 1.00
18 Rob Laurie .60 1.50
19 Ross Wilson .40 1.00
20 Jason Glover .40 1.00
21 Brett MacDonald .40 1.00
22 Kahlil Thomas .40 1.00

2001-02 Flint Generals
COMPLETE SET (24) 20.00
1 Joey Bastien .40 1.00
2 Sylvain Dufresne .40 1.00
3 Jim Duhart .40 1.00
4 Stu Dunn .60 1.50
5 Tim Findlay .40 1.00
6 Dale Greenwood .40 1.00
8 Lee Jelenic .40 1.00
9 Lorne Knauft .40 1.00
10 Corey Laniuk .40 1.00
11 Tom McKinnon .60 1.50
12 Frankie Nault .40 1.00
13 Eric Perricone .40 1.00
14 Jean-Francois Picard .40 1.00
15 Bobby Reynolds .40 1.00
16 Gary Roach .40 1.00
17 Mike Rutter .40 1.00
18 Jordan Trew .40 1.00
19 Mike Varhaug .60 1.50
20 Martin Woods .40 1.00
21 Vaclav Zavoral .40 1.00
22 Kirk Tomlinson HCO .20 .50
23 General Rally MASCOT .04 .10
24 The Lady Generals .04 .10

2007-08 Flint Generals
COMPLETE SET (21) 5.00 12.00
1 Team Checklist .15 .40
2 Jaroslav Cesky .30 .75
3 Eric Marvin .30 .75
4 Martin Ondrej .30 .75
5 Michel Beausoleil .30 .75
6 Greg Bullock .30 .75
7 Jared Dumba .30 .75
8 Brock Wilson .30 .75
9 Kris Mallette .30 .75
10 John DiPace .30 .75
11 Shaun Fisher .30 .75
12 Darren McCarty .30 .75
13 Ryan Jorde .30 .75
14 Josef Fojtik .30 .75
15 Mike Kinnie .30 .75
16 Jordan Fox .30 .75
17 Chad Alban .30 .75
18 Mike Alexiou .30 .75
19 Jonathan Duchesneau .30 .75
20 Nick Tuzzolino .30 .75
21 Justin Depretis .30 .75

1987-88 Flint Spirits
COMPLETE SET (20) 4.80 12.00
1 Mario Chitaroni .20 .50
2 John Cullen .40 1.00
3 Bob Fleming .20 .50
4 Keith Gretzky .40 1.00
5 Todd Hawkins .20 .50
6 Mike Hoffman .20 .50
7 Curtis Hunt .20 .50
8 Dwaine Hutton .20 .50
9 Trent Kaese .20 .50
10 Tom Karalis .20 .50
11 Ray LeBlanc .40 1.00
12 Darren Lowe .20 .50
13 Brett MacDonald .20 .50
14 Chris McSorley .40 1.00
15 Mike Mersch .20 .50
16 Victor Posa .20 .50
17 Kevin Schamehorn .20 .50
18 Ron Stern .40 1.00
19 Don Waddell .20 .50
20 Dan Woodley .20 .50

1988-89 Flint Spirits
COMPLETE SET (22) 4.00 10.00
1 Dean Anderson .20 .50
2 Rob Bryden .20 .50
3 John Devereaux .20 .50
4 Stephane Giguere .20 .50
5 Steve Harrison .20 .50
6 Yves Heroux .30 .75
7 Mike Hoffman .20 .50
8 Peter Horachek .20 .50
9 Guy Jacob .20 .50
10 Bob Kennedy .20 .50
11 Gary Kruzich .20 .50
12 Lonnie Loach .40 1.00
13 Brett MacDonald .20 .50
14 Mike MacWilliam .20 .50
15 Moe Mansi .20 .50
16 Mike Mersch .20 .50
17 Michel Mongeau .40 1.00
18 Ken Spangler .20 .50
19 Three Amigos
Steve Harrison
Mike Mersch
Mike Hoffman .30 .75
20 Mark Vichorek .20 .50
21 Troy Vollhoffer .20 .50
22 Don Waddell GM .20 .50

2003-04 Florence Pride
COMPLETE SET (16) 15.00
145 Jack Baker .40 1.00
146 Craig Brunel .40 1.00
147 Adam Elzinga .40 1.00
148 Ryan Gaucher .40 1.00
149 Wes Goldie .40 1.00
150 Vladimir Gusev .40 1.00
151 Kyle Kidney .40 1.00
152 Dan Lombard .40 1.00
153 Mark McRae .40 1.00
154 Matt Reid .40 1.00
155 Bobby Russell .40 1.00
156 Allan Sirois .40 1.00
157 Jeff Szwez .40 1.00
158 Shaun Sutter .40 1.00
159 Mike Torney .40 1.00
160 Matt Underhill .60 1.50

1998-99 Florida Everblades
COMPLETE SET (27) 7.20 50.00
1 Brett Bruininks .75 2.00
2 Matt Brush .75 2.00
3 Nick Checco .75 2.00
4 Matt Demarski .75 2.00
5 Sergei Fedotov .75 2.00
6 Tim Ferguson .75 2.00
7 Bob Ferguson CO .02 .10
8 Hugh Hamilton .75 2.00
9 Mike Jickling .75 2.00
10 Gary Koehler .75 2.00
11 Greg Kuznik .75 2.00
12 Dane Litke .75 2.00
13 Marc Magliarditi 2.00 5.00
14 Kevin McDonald .75 2.00
15 Pat Mikesch .75 2.00
16 P.K. O'Handley ACO .02 .10
17 Josh Penn EQ .02 .10
18 Randy Petruk 2.00 5.00
19 Jason Prokepetz .75 2.00
20 Dan Keimann .75 2.00
21 Eric Ricard .75 2.00
22 Eric Rud .75 2.00
23 Steve Tardif .75 2.00
24 Andrew Taylor .75 2.00
25 Todd Wisocki .75 2.00
26 Mascot .02 .10
27 Title Card .02 .10

1999-00 Florida Everblades
COMPLETE SET (26) 8.00 20.00
1 Jeff Maund .60 1.50
2 Hugh Hamilton .30 .75
3 Greg Kuznik .30 .75
4 Dane Litke .30 .75
5 Peter Kasper .30 .75
6 Tim Ferguson .30 .75
7 Brent Cullaton .30 .75
8 Reggie Berg .40 1.00
9 Steve Moffatt .30 .75
10 Tom Buckley .30 .75
11 Eric Rud .30 .75
12 Jason Prokopetz .30 .75
13 Terry Lindgren .40 1.00
14 Matt Demarski .30 .75
15 Marc Magliarditi .60 1.50
16 Ty Jones .40 1.00
17 Harlan Pratt .30 .75
18 John Varga .40 1.00
19 Joe Cardarelli .30 .75
20 Steve Tardif .30 .75
21 Andy MacIntyre .30 .75
22 Jason Morgan .30 .75
23 Bob Ferguson CO .08 .25
24 P.K. O'Handley CO .08 .25
25 Swampy MAS .08 .25
26 Celluar One .02 .10

2000-01 Florida Everblades
COMPLETE SET (26) 8.00 20.00
1 Bujar Amidovski .80 2.00
2 Reggie Berg .40 1.00
3 Sean Blanchard .40 1.00
4 Tom Buckley .40 1.00
5 Sandy Cohen .40 1.00
6 Randy Copley .40 1.00
7 Matt Demarski .30 .75
8 Bob Ferguson CO .20 .50
9 Hugh Hamilton .30 .75
10 Devin Hartnell .30 .75
11 Darrell Hay .40 1.00
12 Pete Hogan .30 .75
13 John Jennings EM .10 .25
14 Mike Jickling .30 .75
15 Terry Lindgren .40 1.00
16 Andy Macintyre .30 .75
17 Marc Magliarditi .60 1.50
18 Brent McDonald .30 .75
19 Jason Metcalfe .30 .75
20 Jason Morgan .30 .75
21 P.K. O'Handley CO .20 .50
22 Brent Pope .30 .75
23 Swampee MASCOT .20 .50
24 David Vallieres .30 .75
25 Todd Wisocki TR .10 .25
26 TTI Computers .01

2001-02 Florida Everblades
COMPLETE SET (21) 8.00 20.00
1 Checklist .20 .50
2 Gerry Fleming CO .20 .50
3 P.K. O'Handley ACO .20 .50
4 Vince Williams .40 1.00
5 Terry Lindgren .60 1.50
6 Duane Harmer .40 1.00
7 Andrew Long .40 1.00
8 Reggie Berg .40 1.00
9 Brent McDonald .40 1.00
10 Tom Buckley .40 1.00
11 Briane Thompson .40 1.00
12 Mike Cirillo .40 1.00
13 Don Smith .40 1.00
14 Joe Blaznek .40 1.00
15 Peter Reynolds .40 1.00
16 Paul Spadafora .60 1.50
17 Keith Anderson .40 1.00
18 Shaun Fisher .40 1.00
19 Randy Petruk .60 1.50
20 Ryan Murphy .40 1.00
21 Swampee .20 .50

2002-03 Florida Everblades
COMPLETE SET (26) 10.00 25.00
1 Keith Anderson .40 1.00
2 George Awada .40 1.00
3 Anthony Battaglia .40 1.00
4 Joe Blaznek .40 1.00
5 Kevin Brown .40 1.00
6 Tom Buckley .40 1.00
7 Sean Curry .40 1.00
8 Brian Goudie .40 1.00
9 Duane Harmer .40 1.00
10 Ed Hill .40 1.00
11 Marty Johnston .40 1.00
12 Cam McCormick .60 1.50
13 Laurent Meunier .40 1.00
14 Ryan Murphy .40 1.00
15 Tom Nelson .40 1.00
16 Peter Reynolds .40 1.00
17 Lee Ruff .40 1.00
18 Don Smith .40 1.00
19 Ryan Stewart .40 1.00
20 Jimmy Verdule .75 2.00
21 Jon Insana .40 1.00
22 Rob Zepp .75 2.00
23 Gerry Fleming CO .20 .50
24 Terry Lindgren ACO .04 .10
25 Swampee MASCOT .04 .10
26 Checklist .04 .10

2002-03 Florida Everblades RBI
COMPLETE SET (18) 20.00
115 Keith Anderson .40 1.00
116 George Awada .40 1.00
117 Anthony Battaglia .40 1.00
118 Joe Blaznek .40 1.00
119 Tom Buckley .40 1.00
120 Brian Goudie .40 1.00
121 Duane Harmer .40 1.00
122 Marty Johnston .40 1.00
123 Cam McCormick .60 1.50
124 Brent McDonald .40 1.00
125 Laurent Meunier .40 1.00
126 Ryan Murphy .40 1.00
127 Tom Nelson .40 1.00

128 Jared Newman .40 1.00
129 Peter Reynolds .40 1.00
130 Don Smith .40 1.00
131 Jimmy Verdule .75 2.00
132 Rob Zepp .75 2.00

2003-04 Florida Everblades

COMPLETE SET (25) 8.00 20.00
1 Keith Anderson .40 1.00
2 Reggie Berg .40 1.00
3 Jim Brown .40 1.00
4 Brandon Coalter .40 1.00
5 Paul Esdale .40 1.00
6 Gerry Fleming CO .08 .20
7 Ian Forbes .40 1.00
8 Chris Heisten .40 1.00
9 Tom Buckley .40 1.00
10 Jon Insana .40 1.00
11 Chad Larose .40 1.00
12 Jay Legault .40 1.00
13 Terry Lindgren ACO .08 .20
14 Tim O'Connell .40 1.00
15 Jeff Maund .60 1.50
16 Brian McCullough .40 1.00
17 Brent McDonald .40 1.00
18 Jared Newman .40 1.00
19 Matt Pagnutti .40 1.00
20 Paul Vincent .40 1.00
21 Gray Shaneberger .40 1.00
22 Mascot .08 .20
23 Chris Thompson .40 1.00
24 Ryan Van Buskirk .40 1.00
25 Rob Zepp .75 2.00

2003-04 Florida Everblades RBI Sports

COMPLETE SET (16) 10.00 18.00
161 Reggie Berg .40 1.00
162 Brandon Coalter .40 1.00
163 Paul Esdale .40 1.00
164 Kevin Holdridge .40 1.00
165 Jon Insana .40 1.00
166 Chad Larose .40 1.00
167 Carl Mallette .50 1.25
168 Jeff Maund .60 1.50
169 Brian McCullough .40 1.00
170 Jared Newman .40 1.00
171 Stuart Pietersma .40 1.00
172 Peter Reynolds .40 1.00
173 Gray Shaneberger .40 1.00
174 Damian Surma .50 1.25
175 Ryan Van Buskirk .40 1.00
176 Rob Zepp .75 2.00

2004-05 Florida Everblades

COMPLETE SET (30) 20.00
1 Tyler MacKay .30 .75
2 Jared Newman .30 .75
3 Matt Pagnutti .30 .75
4 Shane Hnidy .30 .75
5 Simon Tremblay .30 .75
6 Reggie Berg .30 .75
7 Brent MacDonald .30 .75
8 Steve Saviano .30 .75
9 Ryan Brindley .30 .75
10 Tim Branham .30 .75
11 Brandon Coalter .30 .75
12 Matt Hendricks .30 .75
13 David Lundbohm .30 .75
14 Tim O'Connell .30 .75
15 Bryce Charpentier .30 .75
16 Kris Vernarsky .40 1.00
17 Brad Church .40 1.00
18 Greg Hornby .30 .75
19 Keith Anderson .30 .75
20 Damian Surma .30 .75
21 Rob Zepp .40 1.00
22 Craig Kowalski .30 .75
23 Chris Lee .30 .75
24 Jason Nobili .30 .75
25 Gerry Fleming .04 .10
26 Todd Wisocki .04 .10
27 John Jennings .04 .10
28 Swampee MASCOT .04 .10
29 Sponsor card .04 .10
30 Checklist .04 .10

2005-06 Florida Everblades

COMPLETE SET (25) 6.00 15.00
1 Jonathan Lehun .30 .75
2 Martin Tuma .30 .75
3 Paul Cabana .30 .75
4 Reggie Berg .30 .75
5 Swampee MASCOT .02 .10
6 Phil Aucoin .30 .75
7 Brandon Coalter .30 .75
8 Ernie Hartlieb .30 .75
9 Phil Osaer .30 1.00
10 Steve Saviano .30 .75
11 Ryan Brindley .30 .75
12 Bryce Charpentier .30 .75
13 Craig Kowalski .30 .75
14 Daniel Sisca .30 .75
15 Anders Strome .30 .75
16 Sean Stefanski .30 .75
17 Corey Neilson .30 .75
18 Grant McNeill .30 .75
19 Chris Lee .30 .75
20 Kevin Bergin .30 .75
21 John Adams .30 .75
22 Vince Bellissimo .30 .75
23 John Ronan .30 .75
24 Jeremy Swanson .30 .75
25 Gerry Fleming HC .02 .10

2009-10 Florida Everblades Series 1

1 Peter Metcalf .40 1.00
2 Milan Gajic .40 1.00
3 Jacob Micflikier .40 1.00
4 Jordan Morrison .40 1.00
5 Rob Hennigar .40 1.00
6 Brandon Buck .40 1.00
7 Scott Hotham .40 1.00
8 Elgin Reid .40 1.00
9 Kevin Baker .40 1.00
10 Mike Morrison .40 1.00
11 Cornish
Zack Hill .40 1.00

2009-10 Florida Everblades Series 2

1 A.J. Thelen .40 1.00
2 Benn Olson .40 1.00
3 Brad Zanon .40 1.00
4 Chris Beckford-Tseu .40 1.00
5 Colin Nicholson .40 1.00
6 Ernie Hartlieb .40 1.00
7 Mathieu Roy .40 1.00
8 Matt Duffy .40 1.00
9 Ross Carlson .40 1.00
10 Ryan Lang .40 1.00
11 Swampee .40 1.00

1990-91 Fort Saskatchewan Traders

COMPLETE SET (24) 2.50 6.00
1 Michael Buzak .15 .40
2 Wade Fennig .15 .40
3 Mark Goodkey .15 .40
4 Richard Groten .15 .40
5 Brett Gullion .15 .40
6 Keith Hill .15 .40
7 Justin Hocking .30 .75
8 Ian Kallay .15 .40
9 Scott Lindsay .15 .40
10 Faron Luchkow .15 .40
11 Wayne MacDonald .15 .40
12 Ted Oloriz .15 .40
13 Jason Plandowski .15 .40
14 Dory Reich .15 .40
15 Shawn Reich .15 .40
16 Darren Smith .15 .40
17 Mark Souch .15 .40
18 Bryan Stewart .15 .40
19 Paul Strand .15 .40
20 Tim Wiwchar .15 .40
21 Paul Wozney .15 .40
22 Allen Young .15 .40
23 Jason Yuzda .15 .40
24 Team Photo .20 .50

1993-94 Fort Wayne Komets

COMPLETE SET (27) 6.00 15.00
1 Ian Boyce .30 .75
2 Colin Chin .30 .75
3 Lee Davidson .30 .75
4 Guy Dupuis .30 .75
5 Steve Fletcher .75 2.00
6 Sean Gauthier .30 .75
7 Darryl Gilmour .40 1.00
8 Kelly Hurd .30 .75
9 Carey Lucyk .30 .75
10 Kevin MacDonald .30 .75
11 Igor Malykhin .30 .75
12 Brian McKee .30 .75
13 Mitch Messier .40 1.00
14 Max Middendorf .40 1.00
15 John Purves .40 1.00
16 Grant Richison .30 .75
17 Darin Smith .30 .75
18 Dave Smith .30 .75
19 Shayne Stevenson .30 .75
20 David Tretowicz .30 .75
21 Vladimir Tsyplakov .30 .75
22 Doug Wickenheiser .40 1.00
23 Bruce Boudreau CO .20 .50
24 Derek Ray ACO .20 .50
25 Joe Franke TR .20 .50
26 Galen Head EQM .20 .50
27 Team Photo .20 .50

1995-96 Fort Wayne Komets

COMPLETE SET (25) 4.80 12.00
1 Andy Bezeau .20 .50
2 Colin Chin .20 .50
3 Shawn Cronin .20 .50
4 Guy Dupuis .20 .50
5 Pat Elynuik .20 .50
6 Bob Essensa .30 .75
7 Shawn Evans .20 .50
8 Steven Fletcher .20 .50
9 Peter Ing .20 .50
10 Andrew McBain .20 .50
11 Mitch Messier .20 .50
12 Rob Murphy .20 .50
13 Alex Nikolic .20 .50
14 Grant Richison .20 .50
15 Jeff Rohlicek .20 .50
16 Konstantin Shafronov .20 .50
17 Darin Smith .20 .50
18 Sergei Stas .20 .50
19 Brian Straub .20 .50
20 Chris Tok .20 .50
21 Paul Willett .20 .50
22 Kevin Wortman .20 .50
23 Oleg Yashin .20 .50
24 Derek Ray CO .08 .25
25 Icy MAS .02 .10

1997-98 Fort Wayne Komets

COMPLETE SET (21) 4.00 10.00
1 Guy Dupuis .20 .50
2 Ian Boyce .20 .50
3 Lee Davidson .20 .50
4 Bruce Racine .30 .75
5 Dan Currie .20 .50
6 Robin Bawa .20 .50
7 Tom Nemeth .20 .50
8 Ed Campbell .20 .50
9 Vyacheslav Butsayev .20 .50
10 Steffon Walby .20 .50
11 Derek Eberle .20 .50
12 Chris Armstrong .20 .50
13 Norm Batherson .20 .50
14 Konstantin Shafronov .20 .50
15 Tom Pederson .20 .50
16 Andrei Bashkirov .20 .50
17 Carlin Nordstrom .20 .50
18 Trevor Doyle .20 .50
19 Eric Boguniecki .30 .75
20 Kevin Weekes .60 1.50
21 Icy D. Eagle Mascot .02 .10

1998-99 Fort Wayne Komets

COMPLETE SET (29) 4.00 10.00
1 Ed Campbell .15 .40
2 Vyacheslav Butsayev .20 .50
3 Ian Boyce .15 .40
4 Eric Boguniecki .20 .50
5 Robin Bawa .15 .40
6 Gerard Gallant ACO .15 .40
7 Icy D. Eagle Mascot .02 .10
8 Guy Dupuis .15 .40
9 Dion Darling .15 .40
10 Bob Chase .15 .40
11 Brad Purdie .15 .40
12 Andrei Petrakov .15 .40
13 David Nemirovsky .20 .50
14 Mike Martin .15 .40
15 Tero Lehtera .20 .50
16 Oleg Shargorodsky .15 .40
17 Shawn Selmser .20 .50
18 Andre Roy .20 .50
19 Eldon Reddick .20 .50
20 Bruce Racine .20 .50
21 Memorial Coliseum .02 .10
22 Derek Wood .15 .40
23 Lee Sorochan .20 .50
24 Grant Sonier HCO .02 .10
25 Checklist .02 .10
26 Shawn Penn .15 .40
27 PHPA Web Site .02 .10
28 IHL Web Site .02 .10
29 Andrei Bashkirov .15 .40

1999-00 Fort Wayne Komets Points Leaders

COMPLETE SET (16) 6.00 15.00
1 Header Card .02 .10
2 Len Thornson .40 1.00
3 Eddie Long .40 1.00
4 Terry McDougall .40 1.00
5 Colin Chin .40 1.00
6 John Goodwin .40 1.00
7 Reg Primeau .40 1.00
8 Merv Dubchek .40 1.00
9 Barry Scully .40 1.00
10 Rob Laird .40 1.00
11 Jim Burton .60 1.50
12 Lionel Repka .40 1.00
13 Norman Waslowski .40 1.00
14 Ron Leef .40 1.00
15 Bobby Rivard .40 1.00
16 Dale Baldwin .40 1.00

1999-00 Fort Wayne Komets Penalty Leaders

COMPLETE SET (16) 8.00 35.00
1 Header Card .02 .10
2 Steven Fletcher 1.25 3.00
3 Dale Baldwin .75 2.00
4 Cal Purinton 1.25 3.00
5 Rob Laird .75 2.00
6 Dave Norris .75 2.00
7 Robin Bawa 1.25 3.00
8 Terry Pembroke .75 2.00
9 Andy Bezeau 1.25 3.00
10 Eddie Long .75 2.00
11 Craig Channell .75 2.00
12 Steve Salvucci .75 2.00
13 Carey Lucyk .75 2.00
14 Lionel Repka .75 2.00
15 Scott Gruhl 1.25 3.00
16 Guy Dupuis .75 2.00

2000-01 Fort Wayne Komets

COMPLETE SET (24) 4.80 12.00
1 Frederic Bouchard .20 .50
2 Dave Butler .20 .50
3 Keli Corpse .30 .75
4 Derek Gauthier .30 .75
5 Jason Goulet .20 .50
6 Brent Gretzky .30 .75
7 Kelly Hurd .20 .50
8 Rick Judson .20 .50
9 Dave Lemay .20 .50
10 Jim Logan .20 .50
11 Igor Malykhin .20 .50
12 Darren Mortono .20 .50
13 Mike McKay .20 .50
14 Geno Parrish .20 .50
15 Kevin Popp .20 .50
16 Sergei Radchenko .20 .50
17 Gary Ricciardi .20 .50
18 Dan Ronan .20 .50
19 Konstantin Simchuk .20 .50
20 Fred Slukynsky .20 .50
21 Doug Teskey .20 .50
22 Brad Twordik .20 .50
23 Greg Puhalski CO .10 .25
24 Ice Eagle MASCOT .04 .10

2000-01 Fort Wayne Komets Shoe Carnival

COMPLETE SET (16) 6.00 15.00
1 Rhett Trombley .40 1.00
2 Gary Ricciardi .40 1.00
3 Jason Goulet .40 1.00
4 Rick Judson .40 1.00
5 Igor Malykhin .40 1.00
6 Doug Teskey .40 1.00
7 Kelly Hurd .40 1.00
8 Mike McKay .40 1.00
9 Brent Gretzky .80 2.00
10 Geno Parrish .40 1.00
11 Dave Lemay .40 1.00
12 Jim Logan .40 1.00
13 Frederic Bouchard .40 1.00
14 Brad Twordik .40 1.00
15 Dan Ronan .40 1.00
16 Derek Gauthier .40 1.00

2001-02 Fort Wayne Komets

COMPLETE SET (22) 4.00 10.00
1 Doug Teskey .20 .50
2 Igor Bondarev .20 .50
3 Frederic Bouchard .30 .75
4 Christian Bragnalo .20 .50
5 Derek Gauthier .30 .75
6 Dustin Virag .20 .50
7 Chad Grills .20 .50
8 Kevin Holliday .20 .50
9 Icy D. Eagle Mascot .04 .10
10 Erik Landman .20 .50
11 Jim Logan .20 .50
12 Michael Massie .20 .50
13 David Mayes .20 .50
14 Mike McKay .20 .50
15 Kelly Miller .30 .75
16 Martin Fillion .20 .50
17 Kevin Schmidt .20 .50
18 Ryan Severson .20 .50
19 Matt Swain .20 .50
20 Kevin Bertram .20 .50
21 Steven Desjardins .20 .50
22 Brent Gretzky CO .30 .75

2001-02 Fort Wayne Komets Shoe Carnival

COMPLETE SET (16) 6.00 15.00
1 Dustin Virag .40 1.00
2 Reg Primeau .40 1.00
3 Kevin Holliday .40 1.00
4 Steven Fletcher .75 2.00
5 Brent Gretzky .40 1.00
6 Len Thornson .40 1.00
7 Derek Gauthier .40 1.00
8 Robin Bawa .40 1.00
9 Frederic Bouchard .40 1.00
10 Lionel Repka .40 1.00
11 Michel Masse .40 1.00
12 Eddie Long .40 1.00
13 Doug Teskey .40 1.00
14 Chuck Adamson .40 1.00
15 Jim Logan .40 1.00
16 Ian Boyce .40 1.00

2002-03 Fort Wayne Komets

COMPLETE SET (25) 4.00 10.00
1 Marc Barlow .20 .50
2 David Beauregard .20 .50
3 Kevin Bertram .20 .50
4 Ken Boone .20 .50
5 Colin Chaulk .20 .50
6 Parris Duffus .30 .75
7 Joe Franke .20 .50
8 Kevin Kotyluk .30 .75
9 Tom Lawson .30 .75
10 Adam Lewis .20 .50
11 Michel Massie .20 .50
12 Troy Neumeier .20 .50
13 Jake Ortmeyer .20 .50
14 Kelly Perrault .20 .50
15 Eldon Reddick .30 .75
16 Kevin Schmidt .20 .50
17 Jason Selleke .20 .50
18 Ryan Severson .20 .50
19 Bart Stevens .20 .50
20 Bobby Stewart .20 .50
21 Sean Venedam .20 .50
22 Dustin Virag .20 .50
23 Icy D. Eagle MASCOT .04 .10
24 Greg Puhalski HCO .04 .10
NNO Checklist .04 .10

2002-03 Fort Wayne Komets Shoe Carnival

COMPLETE SET (16) 12.00 30.00
1 Kelly Perrault .75 2.00
2 David Beauregard .75 2.00
3 Jake Ortmeyer .75 2.00
4 Michel Massie .75 2.00
5 Tom Lawson .75 2.00
6 Bobby Stewart .75 2.00
7 Ryan Severson .75 2.00
8 Eldon Reddick 1.25 3.00
9 Sean Venedam .75 2.00
10 Kevin Bertram .75 2.00
11 Marc Barlow .75 2.00
12 Dustin Virag .75 2.00
13 Icy D. Eagle MASCOT .04 .10
14 Kevin Schmidt .75 2.00
15 Colin Chaulk .75 2.00
16 Adam Lewis .75 2.00

2003-04 Fort Wayne Komets

COMPLETE SET (23) 4.00 10.00
1 Bobby Stewart .20 .50
2 Colin Chaulk .20 .50
3 David Beauregard .20 .50
4 Sean Venedam .20 .50
5 Dan Stewart .20 .50
6 Ryan Severson .20 .50
7 Michel Massie .20 .50
8 Dustin Virag .20 .50
9 Kevin Kotyluk .30 .75
10 Adam Lewis .20 .50
11 Dan Price .20 .50
12 Mascot .04 .10
13 Andy Townsend .20 .50
14 Kevin Schmidt .20 .50
15 Mark Cole .20 .50
16 Mike Perna .20 .50
17 Kelly Perrault .20 .50
18 Kevin Bertram .20 .50
19 Troy Neumeier .20 .50
20 Kelly Shields .30 .75
21 Kevin St. Pierre .30 .75
22 Ryan Coole .20 .50
23 Steve Rodberg .20 .50

2003-04 Fort Wayne Komets 2003 Champions

COMPLETE SET (21) 3.00 8.00
1 Colin Chaulk .20 .50
2 Kelly Perrault .20 .50
3 Dustin Virag .20 .50
4 Sean Venedam .20 .50
5 Tom Lawson .20 .50
6 Colin Chaulk .20 .50
7 Tom Lawson .20 .50
8 Parading the Cup .08 .20
9 Dustin Virag .20 .50
10 Kevin Bertram .20 .50
11 Greg Puhalski HCO .08 .20
12 Kelly Perrault .20 .50
13 Dustin Virag .20 .50
14 Michel Massie .20 .50
15 Marc Barlow .20 .50
16 Tom Lawson .20 .50
17 Team Photo .20 .50
17 Komets Fans .04 .10
18 Kelly Perrault .20 .50
19 Kevin Kotyluk .30 .75
20 Sponsor .04 .10

2003-04 Fort Wayne Komets Shoe Carnival

COMPLETE SET (16) 5.00 12.00
1 Kelly Perrault .40 1.00
2 Kevin Schmidt .40 1.00
3 Kevin Bertram .40 1.00
4 Adam Lewis .40 1.00
5 Troy Neumeier .40 1.00
6 Colin Chaulk .40 1.00
7 Kevin Kotyluk .60 1.50
8 Bobby Stewart .40 1.00
9 Kevin St. Pierre .60 1.50
10 David Beauregard .40 1.00
11 Michel Massie .40 1.00
12 Sean Venedam .40 1.00
13 Dan Price .40 1.00
14 Dan Stewart .40 1.00
15 Ryan Severson .40 1.00
16 Dustin Virag .40 1.00

2004-05 Fort Wayne Komets

COMPLETE SET (21) 3.00 8.00
1 Colin Chaulk .40 1.00
2 P.C. Drouin .30 .75
3 Jonathan Goodwin .20 .50
4 Chris Grenville .20 .50
5 Rob Guinn .20 .50
6 David Hukalo .20 .50
7 Jason Kean .20 .50
8 Shane Kenny .20 .50
9 Tyler Masters .30 .75
10 Tom Nelson .20 .50
11 Tom Nemeth .20 .50
12 Troy Nuemeier .20 .50
13 Steve Rodberg .20 .50
14 Kevin St. Pierre .30 .75
15 Danny Stewart .20 .50
16 Andy Townsend .20 .50
17 Sean Venedam .20 .50
18 Dustin Virag .20 .50
19 Jeff Worlton .20 .50
20 Team Checklist .04 .10
21 Mascot .04 .10
22 Sponsor Card .04 .10

2004-05 Fort Wayne Komets Shoe Carnival

COMPLETE SET (16) 10.00 25.00
1 Colin Chaulk 1.25 3.00
2 P.C. Drouin .75 2.00
3 Jonathan Goodwin .60 1.50
4 Chris Grenville .60 1.50
5 Rob Guinn .60 1.50
6 Jason Kean .60 1.50
7 Shane Kenny .60 1.50
8 Tim Krueckl .60 1.50
9 Corey Lucas .60 1.50
10 Tyler Masters .75 2.00
11 Troy Neumeier .60 1.50
12 Kevin St. Pierre .75 2.00
13 Dan Stewart .60 1.50
14 Sean Venedam .75 2.00
15 Dustin Virag .60 1.50
16 Jeff Worlton .60 1.50

2005-06 Fort Wayne Komets Choice

COMPLETE SET (25) 4.00 10.00
1 Kevin St. Pierre .20 .50
2 Jeff Worlton .20 .50
3 Jonathan Goodwin .20 .50
4 David Hukalo .20 .50
5 David Frawley .20 .50
6 David Carpentier .20 .50
7 Andrew Luciuk .20 .50
0 Drent Rumble .20 .50
9 Matt Hunter .20 .50
10 Kelly Miller .20 .50
11 Garrett Summerfield .20 .50
12 P.C. Drouin .20 .50
14 Lance Galbraith .20 .50
15 Mark Smith .20 .50
16 Kevin Kurk .20 .50
17 Guy Dupuis .20 .50
18 Jason Kean .20 .50
19 John Jarram .20 .50
20 A.J. Bozoian .20 .50
21 Rob Guinn .20 .50
22 Mark Lindsay .20 .50
23 Troy Neumeier .20 .50
24 Ryan Jorde .20 .50
25 Icy D. Eagle MASCOT .02 .10

2005-06 Fort Wayne Komets Sprint

COMPLETE SET (16) 8.00 20.00
1 A.J. Bozoian .60 1.50
2 David Carpentier .60 1.50
3 Colin Chaulk .60 1.50
4 P.C. Drouin .60 1.50
5 Guy Dupuis .60 1.50
6 Lance Galbraith .60 1.50
7 Lance Galbraith .60 1.50
8 Jonathan Goodwin .60 1.50
9 Rob Guinn .60 1.50
10 David Hukalo .60 1.50
11 John Jarram .60 1.50
12 Ryan Jorde .60 1.50
13 Mark Lindsay .60 1.50
14 Troy Neumeier .60 1.50
15 Brent Rumble .60 1.50
16 Kevin St. Pierre .60 1.50

2006-07 Fort Wayne Komets

COMPLETE SET (24) 10.00 20.00
1 A.J. Bozoian .40 1.00
2 Mike Dombkiewicz .40 1.00
3 Guy Dupuis .40 1.00
4 Martin Gascon .40 1.00
5 Daniel Goneau .40 1.00
6 Jonathan Goodwin .40 1.00
7 Kevin Hansen .40 1.00
8 Jani Honkanen .40 1.00
9 David Hukalo .40 1.00
10 Arthur Kiyaga .40 1.00
11 Jean-Francois Labarre .40 1.00
12 Mario Larocque .75 2.00
13 Dan McWhinney .60 1.50
14 Pascal Morency .40 1.00
15 Bruce Richardson .40 1.00
16 Bogdan Rudenko .40 1.00
17 J.C. Ruid .40 1.00
18 Kevin St. Pierre .60 1.50
19 Matt Syroczynski .40 1.00
20 Brent Henley .40 1.00
21 K.J. Voorhees .40 1.00
22 Pat Bingham .40 1.00
23 Icy D. Eagle MASCOT .02 .10
24 Nesquik SPONSOR .01 .01

2009-10 Fort Wayne Komets

1 Nick Boucher .40 1.00
2 Kevin Bertram .40 1.00
3 Colin Chaulk .40 1.00
4 Justin Chwedoruk .40 1.00
5 Frankie DeAngelis .40 1.00
6 P.C. Drouin .40 1.00
7 Guy Dupuis .40 1.00
8 Tim Haun .40 1.00
9 David Hukalo .40 1.00
10 Tomas Klempa .40 1.00
11 Brad MacMillan .40 1.00
12 Danko Mironovic .40 1.00
13 Sean O'Connor .40 1.00
14 Bobby Phillips .40 1.00
15 Keith Rodger .40 1.00
16 Kaleigh Schrock .40 1.00
17 Konstantin Shafronov .40 1.00
18 Blair Stayzer .40 1.00
19 Matt Syroczynski .40 1.00
20 Leo Thomas .40 1.00
21 Rick Varone .40 1.00
22 Brandon Warner .40 1.00
23 Matt Woodard .40 1.00
24 Icy D. Eagle .40 1.00

2013-14 Fort Wayne Komets

COMPLETE SET (4) 1.00 2.50
1 Andrey Makarov .30 .75
2 Mike Embach .30 .75
3 Jordon Southorn .30 .75
4 Mickey Lang .30 .75

2013-14 Fort Wayne Komets Choice

COMPLETE SET (28) 8.00 20.00
1 Brandon Marino .30 .75
2 Chris Auger .30 .75
3 Jace Coyle .30 .75
4 Simon Danis-Pepin .30 .75
5 Scott Fleming .30 .75
6 Joe Hartman .30 .75
7 Bobby Hughes .30 .75
8 Mike Embach .30 .75
9 Nathan Martine .30 .75
10 Mickey Lang .30 .75
11 Andrey Makarov .30 .75
12 Phil Mangan .30 .75
13 Kenton Miller .30 .75
14 Nik Pokulok .30 .75
15 Cody Reichard .30 .75
16 Jordon Southorn .30 .75
17 Shawn Szydlowski .30 .75
18 Mike Vaskivuo .30 .75
19 Gary Graham CO .30 .75
20 Kaleigh Schrock .30 .75
21 Matt Carter .30 .75
22 Jeremy Gates .30 .75
23 William Lacasse .30 .75
24 Ben Meisner .30 .75
25 Sy Nutkevitch .30 .75
26 Christian Ouellet .30 .75
27 Dean Ouellet .30 .75
28 Jason Dale .30 .75

2014-15 Fort Wayne Komets

COMPLETE SET (6) 7.50 15.00
1 Kyle Thomas 1.25 3.00
2 Jean-Michel Rizk 1.25 3.00
3 Matthew Pistilli 1.25 3.00
4 Cody Sol 1.25 3.00
5 Pat Nagle 1.25 3.00
6 Roman Will 1.25 3.00

2014-15 Fort Wayne Komets Choice

COMPLETE SET (22) 8.00 20.00
1 Pat Nagle .30 .75
2 Ian Barteaux .30 .75
3 Mikael Tam .30 .75
4 Paul Crowder .30 .75
5 Drew Daniels .30 .75
6 Mike Embach .30 .75
7 Eric Faille .75 2.00
8 Thomas Frazee .30 .75
9 Mitchell Heard .30 .75
10 Matt Krug .30 .75
11 William Lacasse .30 .75
12 Joey Leach .30 .75
13 James Martin .30 .75
14 Garrett Meurs .30 .75
15 Christian Ouellet .30 .75
16 Brett Perlini .30 .75
17 Reid Petryk .75 2.00
18 Matthew Pistilli .30 .75
19 Kaleigh Schrock .30 .75
20 C.J. Severyn .75 2.00
21 Cody Sol .30 .75
22 Shawn Szydlowski .30 .75

1997-98 Fort Worth Brahmas

COMPLETE SET (21) 4.00 10.00
1 Chris Albert .20 .50
2 Steve Carter .20 .50
3 Brian Caruso .20 .50
4 Cosmo DuPaul .20 .50
5 David Graff .20 .50
6 Craig Hayden .20 .50
7 Murray Hogg .20 .50
8 Alex Kholomeyev .30 .75
9 Stephane Larocque .30 .75
10 Rob Laurie .30 .75
11 Mike McCormick .20 .50
12 Nolan McDonald .20 .50
13 Terry Menard .20 .50
14 Max Middendorf .20 .50
15 Mark O'Donnell .20 .50
16 Adam Robbins .20 .50
17 Todd St. Louis .20 .50
18 Mark Strohack .20 .50
19 Gatis Tseplis .20 .50
20 Dwight Mullins ACO .20 .50
21 Bill McDonald CO .20 .50

1998-99 Fort Worth Brahmas

COMPLETE SET (20) 6.00 15.00
1 Terry Menard CO .20 .50
2 Steve Plouffe .60 1.50
3 Tim Green .40 1.00
4 Scott Shaunessy .40 1.00
5 Jim Dinneen .40 1.00
6 Martin Machacek .40 1.00
7 Francois Albert .40 1.00
8 Sean Brady .40 1.00
9 Murray Hogg .40 1.00
10 Ryan Black .40 1.00
11 Mark Strohack .40 1.00
12 Richie Walcott .40 1.00
13 Stephane Larocque .60 1.50
14 Barry Cummins .40 1.00
15 Phil Miaskowski .40 1.00
16 Martin Lamarche .40 1.00
17 Cosmo Dupaul .40 1.00
18 Jon Olofson .60 1.50
19 Craig Hayden .60 1.50
20 Steve Carter .40 1.00

1999-00 Fort Worth Brahmas

COMPLETE SET (20) 4.00 40.00
1 Louis Bernard .75 2.00
2 Bruiser MASCOT .02 .10
3 Jason Disher .75 2.00
4 Cosmo Dupaul .75 2.00
5 Cory Evans .75 2.00
6 Ross Harris .75 2.00
7 Murray Hogg .75 2.00
8 Alex Kholomeyev .75 2.00
9 Derek Kups .75 2.00
10 Martin Lamarche .75 2.00
11 Stephane Larocque .75 2.00
12 Terry Menard CO .20 .50
13 Jon Olofson 1.25 3.00
14 Steve Plouffe 2.00 5.00
15 Bobby Pochyly .75 2.00
16 Al Rooney .75 2.00
17 Mike Sanderson .75 2.00
18 Dennis Shiryaev .75 2.00
19 Mike Tilson .75 2.00
20 Gatis Tseplis .75 2.00

2000-01 Fort Worth Brahmas

COMPLETE SET (18) 4.80 12.00
1 Clint Cabana .30 .75
2 Justin Cardwell .30 .75
3 Jason Carey .30 .75
4 Steve Dowhy .30 .75
5 Ben Gorewich .30 .75
6 Jake Harney .30 .75
7 Ross Harris .30 1.00
8 Casey Hungle .30 .75
9 Craig Johnson .30 .75
10 Todd Lalonde CO .08 .25
11 Rob Laurie .30 1.00
12 Jason Pain .30 .75
13 Mike Rusk .30 .75
14 Ryan Shannon .30 .75
15 Mike Tilson .30 .75
16 Daniel Villeneuve .30 .75
17 Chad Woollard .30 .75
18 Mark Zacharias .30 .75

2001-02 Fort Worth Brahmas

COMPLETE SET (20) 8.00 20.00
1 Brady Austin .40 1.00
2 Jeff Bateman .60 1.50
3 Dave Bourque .40 1.00
4 Justin Cardwell .40 1.00
5 Jason Clarke .40 1.00
6 Kory Cooper .40 1.00
7 Dave Csumrik .40 1.00
8 Adam Davis .40 1.00
9 Sean Hughes .40 1.00
10 Craig Johnson .40 1.00
11 Chris Johnston .40 1.00
12 Cody Leibel .40 1.00
13 Todd Lalonde CO .20 .50
14 Cam MacDonald .40 1.00
15 Mike Tilson .60 1.50
16 Joe Van Volsen .60 1.50
17 Daniel Villeneuve .40 1.00
18 Chad Woollard .40 1.00
19 Scott Wray .40 1.00
20 Bruiser MASCOT .04 .10

2002-03 Fort Worth Brahmas

COMPLETE SET (20) 8.00 20.00
1 Adam Davis .40 1.00
2 Jason Fricker .60 1.50
3 David Fry .40 1.00
4 Rob Giffin .40 1.00
5 Chad Grills .40 1.00
6 Sean Hughes .40 1.00
7 Lee Jacobson .60 1.50
8 Lloyd Marks .40 1.00
9 Mike McKinnon .40 1.00
10 Jim Midgley .40 1.00
11 John Murphy .75 2.00
12 Jason Reesor .40 1.00
13 Mike Rusk .40 1.00
14 Joe Van Volsen .40 1.00
15 T.J. Warkus .40 1.00
16 Jeff Washbrook .40 1.00
17 Justin Williams .40 1.00
18 Chad Woollard .40 1.00
19 Bill Inglis CO .04 .10
20 Bruiser MASCOT .04 .10

2003-04 Fort Worth Brahmas

COMPLETE SET (20) 6.00 15.00
1 Gary Baronick .40 1.00
2 Joey Bastien .40 1.00
3 Aaron Davis .40 1.00
4 Adam Davis .40 1.00
5 Scott English .60 1.50

6 Taras Foremsky .40 1.00
7 Chad Grills .40 1.00
8 Jan Jas .40 1.00
9 Jay McGee .40 1.00
10 Tyler Nilsson .60 1.50
11 Jason Reesor .40 1.00
12 Erasmo Saltarelli .60 1.50
13 Jeff Scharf .40 1.00
14 Peter Trumbley .40 1.00
15 Derrell Upton .40 1.00
16 Jeremy Vanin .40 1.00
17 Justin Williams .40 1.00
18 Chad Woollard .40 1.00
19 Al Sims HCO .20 .50
20 Mascot .04 .10

2004-05 Fort Worth Brahmas

COMPLETE SET (20) 12.00 30.00
1 Jay Banach .60 1.50
2 Brian Basner 1.00 2.50
3 Brandon Carper .60 1.50
4 Dave Csumrik .60 1.50
5 Aaron Davis .60 1.50
6 Adam Davis .60 1.50
7A Mark Hynes ERR
Adam Davis back .60 1.50
7B Mark Hynes COR .60 1.50
8A Jan Jas ERR
Mark Hynes back .60 1.50
8B Jan Jas COR .60 1.50
9 Brad Lukowich .75 2.00
10 Bryan Lundbohm .60 1.50
11 Dan Murphy .75 2.00
12 Sheldon Nedjelski .60 1.50
13 Martin Paquet .60 1.50
14 Larry Sterling .75 2.00
15 Nick Udovicic .60 1.50
16 Derrell Upton .60 1.50
17 Jorin Welsh .60 1.50
18 Chad Woollard .60 1.50
19 Al Sims CO .20 .50
20 Bruiser MASCOT .04 .10

1992-93 Fort Worth Fire

COMPLETE SET (18) 4.00 10.00
1 Ron Aubrey .20 .50
2 Roch Belley .40 1.00
3 Jason Brousseau .20 .50
4 Eric Brule .20 .50
5 Todd Drevitch .20 .50
6 Trevor Duhaime .20 .50
7 Steve Harrison ACO .08 .25
8 Ernest Hornak .20 .50
9 Alex Kholomeyev .30 .75
10 Curt Krolak .20 .50
11 Ryan Leschasin .20 .50
12 Peter Mahovlich CO .75 2.00
13 Mike McCormick .20 .50
14 Mike O'Hara .20 .50
15 Pat Penner .20 .50
16 Paolo Racicot .20 .50
17 Dan Rolfe .20 .50
18 Mike Sanderson .20 .50

1993-94 Fort Worth Fire

COMPLETE SET (18) 2.40 75.00
1 Ron Aubrey 2.00 5.00
2 Derby Bognar 2.00 5.00
3 Reggie Brezeault 2.00 5.00
4 Jason Brousseau 2.00 5.00
5 Ty Eigner 2.00 5.00
6 Todd Huyber 2.00 5.00
7 Chris Jensen 2.00 5.00
8 Chad Johnson 2.00 5.00
9 Ryan Leschasin 2.00 5.00
10 Dominic Maltais 2.00 5.00
11 Mike McCormick 2.00 5.00
12 Patrick McGarry 2.00 5.00
13 Mike O'Hara 2.00 5.00
14 Sean Rowe 2.00 5.00
15 Mike Sanderson 2.50 6.00
16 Rob Striar 2.00 5.00
17 Scott Zygulski 2.00 5.00
18 Steve Harrison CO .75 2.00

1995-96 Fort Worth Fire

COMPLETE SET (18) 4.00 10.00
1 Team Photo .30 .75
2 Bill McDonald CO .08 .25
3 Phil Groeneveld .20 .50
4 Vern Ray .20 .50
5 Steve Dykstra .30 .75
6 Trevor Burgess .20 .50
7 Scott Allen .20 .50
8 Sean Whyte .20 .50
9 Troy Frederick .20 .50
10 Troy Stephens .20 .50
11 Jeff Massey .20 .50
12 Dwight Mullins .20 .50
13 Kyle Reeves .40 1.00
14 Mike Gruttaduria .20 .50
15 Mark Hilton .20 .50
16 Brian Caruso .20 .50
17 Dennis Miller .20 .50
18 Steve Plouffe .30 .75

1996-97 Fort Worth Fire

COMPLETE SET (18) 3.00 8.00
1 Malcolm Cameron .20 .50
2 Steve Carter .20 .50
3 Mike Sanderson .20 .50
4 Stephane Larocque .20 .50
5 Murray Hogg .20 .50
6 Bob Delorimiere .30 .75
7 Steve Plouffe .40 1.00
8 Glenn Painter .20 .50
9 Mark Strohack .20 .50
10 Brian Caruso .20 .50
11 Dwight Mullins .20 .50
12 Terry Menard .20 .50
13 Vern Ray .20 .50
14 Adam Robbins .20 .50
15 Mark O'Donnell .20 .50
16 Mike McCourt .20 .50
17 Ryan Black .20 .50
18 Bill McDonald CO .02 .10

1981-82 Fredericton Express

COMPLETE SET (26) 8.00 20.00
1 Team Photo .20 .50
2 B.J. MacDonald .30 .75
3 Sylvain Cote .20 .50
4 Michel Bolduc .20 .50
5 Gary Lupul .20 .50
6 Clint Malarchuk .75 2.00
7 Tony Currie .20 .50
8 Tim Tookey .20 .50
9 Anders Eldebrink .40 1.00
10 Basil McRae .75 2.00
11 Kelly Elcombe .20 .50
12 Jacques Demers 1.25 3.00
13 Frank Caprice .40 1.00
14 Terry Johnson .20 .50
15 Grant Martin .20 .50
16 Andre Chartrain .20 .50
17 Marc Crawford 1.25 3.00
18 Gaston Therrien .20 .50
19 Andy Schliebener .20 .50
20 Christian Tanguay .20 .50
21 Art Rutland .20 .50
22 Jean MarcGaulin .20 .50
23 Neil Belland .20 .50
24 Andre Cote .20 .50
25 Jim MacRae .20 .50
26 Scott Beckingham
Marty Flynn .08 .25

1982-83 Fredericton Express

COMPLETE SET (26) 8.00 20.00
1 Team Photo .40 1.00
2 B.J. MacDonald .30 .75
3 Sylvain Cote .30 .75
4 Michel Bolduc .20 .50
5 Gary Lupul .20 .50
6 Clint Malarchuk .75 2.00
7 Tony Currie .20 .50
8 Tim Tookey .20 .50
9 Anders Eldebrink .20 .50
10 Basil McRae 1.25 3.00
11 Kelly Elcombe .20 .50
12 Jacques Demers .75 2.00
13 Frank Caprice .60 1.50
14 Terry Johnson .20 .50
15 Grant Martin .20 .50
16 Andre Chartrain .20 .50
17 Marc Crawford .75 2.00
18 Gaston Therrien .20 .50
19 Andy Schliebener .20 .50
20 Christian Tanguay .20 .50
21 Art Rutland .20 .50
22 Jean-Marc Gaulin .20 .50
23 Neil Belland .20 .50
24 Andre Cote .20 .50
25 Jim MacRae .20 .50
26 Scott Beckingham TR
Marty Flynn TR .08 .25

1983-84 Fredericton Express

COMPLETE SET (27) 6.00 15.00
1 Team Photo .40 1.00
2 Frank Caprice .60 1.50
3 Michel Dufour .30 .75
4 Brian Ford .30 .75
5 Jean-Marc Lanthier .20 .50
6 Jim Dobson .20 .50
7 Mike Hough .40 1.00
8 Rick Lapointe .30 .75
9 Michel Bolduc .20 .50
10 Christian Tanguay .20 .50
11 Tony Currie .20 .50
12 Moe Lemay .40 1.00
13 Bruce Holloway .20 .50
14 Neil Belland .20 .50
15 Richard Turmel .20 .50
16 Claude Julien .30 .75
17 Andre Chartrain .20 .50
18 Grant Martin .20 .50
19 Rejean Vignola .20 .50
20 Andre Cote .20 .50
21 Jean-Marc Gaulin .20 .50
22 Andy Schliebener .20 .50
23 Stu Kulak .30 .75
24 Mike Eagles .60 1.50
25 Earl Jessiman CO
GM .08 .25
26 Marty Flynn TR
Scott Beckingham TR .08 .25
NNO Checklist .20 .50

1984-85 Fredericton Express

COMPLETE SET (28) 6.00 15.00
1 Dave Morrison .20 .50
2 Dave Shaw .40 1.00
3 Bruce Holloway .20 .50
4 Roger Haegglund .20 .50
5 Neil Belland .20 .50
6 Gord Donnelly .40 1.00
7 David Bruce .20 .50
8 Claude Julien .20 .50
9 Dan Wood .20 .50
10 Clint Malarchuk .75 2.00
11 Jere Gillis .20 .50
12 Mike Hough .40 1.00
13 Michel Bolduc .20 .50
14 Peter Loob .20 .50
15 Steve Driscoll .20 .50
16 Newell Brown .20 .50
17 Jim Dobson .20 .50
18 Wendell Young .75 2.00
19 Mark Kumpel .30 .75
20 Mike Eagles .40 1.00
21 Tom Thornbury .20 .50
22 Grant Martin .20 .50
23 Marc Crawford .40 1.00
24 Andy Schliebener .20 .50
25 Earl Jessiman CO/GM .08 .25
26 Yvon Vautour .20 .50
27 Craig Coxe .40 1.00
28 Blake Wesley .20 .50

1985-86 Fredericton Express

COMPLETE SET (28) 4.80 12.00
1 Scott Tottle .20 .50
2 David Bruce .20 .50
3 Team Photo .30 .75
4 Marc Crawford .40 1.00
5 Mike Stevens .20 .50
6 Gary Lupul .20 .50
7 Alain Lemieux .30 .75
8 Mike Hough .40 1.00
9 Tony Currie .20 .50
10 Dunc MacIntyre .20 .50
11 Jere Gillis .20 .50
12 Wendell Young .60 1.50
13 Jean-Marc Lanthier .20 .50
14 Ken Quinney .30 .75
15 Claude Julien .20 .50
16 Michel Petit .40 1.00
17 Luc Guenette .20 .50
18 Andy Schliebener .20 .50
19 Mark Kirton .20 .50
20 Gord Donnelly .30 .75
21 Tom Karalis .20 .50
22 Daniel Poudrier .20 .50
23 Neil Belland .20 .50
24 Dale Dunbar .20 .50
25 Marty Flynn TR
Scott Beckingham TR .08 .25
26 Jean-Marc Gaulin .20 .50
27 Al MacAdam .30 .75
28 Andre Savard CO
GM .20 .50

1986-87 Fredericton Express

COMPLETE SET (26) 4.00 10.00
1 Jim Agnew .20 .50
2 Brian Bertuzzi .20 .50
3 David Bruce .20 .50
4 Frank Caprice .30 .75
5 Marc Crawford .30 .75
6 Steven Finn .30 .75
7 Marty Flynn TR
Scott Beckingham TR .08 .25
8 Jean-Marc Gaulin .20 .50
9 Scott Gordon .30 .75
10 Taylor Hall .20 .50
11 Yves Heroux .20 .50
12 Mike Hough .30 .75
13 Tom Karalis .20 .50
14 Mark Kirton .20 .50
15 Jean-Marc Lanthier .20 .50
16 Jean LeBlanc .20 .50
17 Brett MacDonald .20 .50
18 Duncan MacIntyre .20 .50
19 Greg Malone .20 .50
20 Terry Perkins .20 .50
21 Daniel Poudrier .20 .50
22 Jeff Rohlicek .20 .50
23 Andre Savard CO .20 .50
24 Mike Stevens .20 .50
25 Trevor Stienburg .20 .50
26 Team Photo .30 .75

1992-93 Fredericton Canadiens

COMPLETE SET (28) 4.80 12.00
1 Jesse Belanger .30 .75
2 Paulin Bordeleau CO .20 .50
3 Donald Brashear .30 .75
4 Patrik Carnback .20 .50
5 Eric Charron .20 .50
6 Frederic Chabot .40 1.00
7 Alain Cote .20 .50
8 Paul DiPietro .30 .75
9 Craig Ferguson .20 .50
10 Gerry Fleming .20 .50
11 Luc Gauthier .20 .50
12 Robert Guillet .20 .50
13 Patric Kjellberg .30 .75
14 Les Kuntar .30 .75
15 Ryan Kuwabara .20 .50
16 Patrick Langlois TR .02 .10
17 Steve Larouche .20 .50
18 Jacques Parent TR .02 .10
19 Charles Poulin .20 .50
20 Oleg Petrov .20 .50
21 Yves Sarault .20 .50
22 Pierre Sevigny .20 .50
23 Darcy Simon .20 .50
24 Turner Stevenson .30 .75
25 Tricolo (Mascot) .02 .10
26 Lindsay Vallis .20 .50
27 Steve Veilleux .20 .50
28 Title card .08 .25

1993-94 Fredericton Canadiens

COMPLETE SET (29) 4.80 12.00
1 Brent Bilodeau .20 .50
2 Paulin Bordeleau CO .08 .25
3 Donald Brashear .30 .75
4 Martin Brochu .40 1.00
5 Craig Darby .20 .50
6 Kevin Darby .20 .50
7 Mario Doyon .20 .50
8 Craig Ferguson .20 .50
9 Craig Fiander .20 .50
10 Gerry Fleming .20 .50
11 Luc Gauthier ACO .02 .10
12 Robert Guillet .20 .50
13 Les Kuntar .25 .60
14 Ryan Kuwabara .20 .50
15 Patrick Langlois .20 .50
16 Marc Laniel .20 .50
17 Christian Lariviere .20 .50
18 Kevin O'Sullivan .20 .50
19 Denis Ouellete .20 .50
20 Jacques Parent THER .02 .10
21 Oleg Petrov .30 .75
22 Charles Poulin .20 .50
23 Christian Proulx .20 .50
24 Tony Prpic .20 .50
25 Yves Sarault .20 .50
26 Turner Stevenson .30 .75
27 Tricolo (Mascot) .02 .10
28 Lindsay Vallis .20 .50
29 Title Card .02 .10

1994-95 Fredericton Canadiens

COMPLETE SET (30) 4.80 12.00
1 Louis Bernard .15 .40
2 Brent Bilodeau .20 .50
3 Paulin Bordeleau CO .15 .40
4 Donald Brashear .40 1.00
5 Martin Brochu .40 1.00
6 Valeri Bure .60 1.50
7 Jim Campbell .20 .50
8 Paul Chagnon .15 .40
9 Craig Conroy .30 .75
10 Craig Darby .20 .50
11 Dion Darling .15 .40
12 Craig Ferguson .15 .40
13 Scott Fraser .15 .40
14 Luc Gauthier ACO .02 .10
15 Patrick Labrecque .20 .50
16 Marc Lamothe .30 .75
17 Patrick Langlois .15 .40
18 Brad Layzelle .15 .40
19 Derek Maguire .15 .40
20 Chris Murray .20 .50
21 Kevin O'Sullivan .15 .40
22 Jacques Parent THER .02 .10
23 Christian Proulx .15 .40
24 Craig Rivet .20 .50
25 Yves Sarault .15 .40
26 Turner Stevenson .20 .50
27 Martin Sychra .15 .40
28 Tim Tisdale .15 .40
29 Tricolo (Mascot) .02 .10
30 David Wilkie .15 .40

1995-96 Fredericton Canadiens

COMPLETE SET (29) 4.80 12.00
1 Louis Bernard .15 .40
2 Paulin Bordeleau CO .08 .25
3 Sebastien Bordeleau .20 .50
4 Martin Brochu .40 1.00
5 Jim Campbell .20 .50
6 Paul Chagnon .15 .40
7 Craig Conroy .30 .75
8 Keli Corpse .15 .40
9 Dion Darling .15 .40
10 Rory Fitzpatrick .15 .40
11 Scott Fraser .15 .40
12 Gaston Gingras .20 .50
13 David Grenier .15 .40
14 Harold Hersh .20 .50
15 Patrick Labrecque .30 .75
16 Marc Lamothe .30 .75
17 Patrick Langlois .15 .40
18 Alan Letang .20 .50
19 Alexei Lojkin .15 .40
20 Xavier Majic .15 .40
21 Chris Murray .20 .50
22 Jacques Parent .15 .40
23 Craig Rivet .20 .50
24 Mario Roberge .15 .40
25 Pierre Sevigny .20 .50
26 Tricolo (Mascot) .02 .10
27 Darcy Tucker .40 1.00
28 Adam Wiesel .15 .40
29 Luc Gauthier ACO .02 .10

1996-97 Fredericton Canadiens

COMPLETE SET (30) 30.00 80.00
1 Sebastien Bordeleau .15 .40
2 Brad Brown .40 1.00
3 Earl Cronan .15 .40
4 Dion Darling .15 .40
5 Jimmy Drolet .15 .40
6 Gerry Fleming .40 1.00
7 Scott Fraser .15 .40
8 Francois Groleau .15 .40
9 Miloslav Guren .15 .40
10 Harold Hersh .40 1.00
11 Eric Houde .15 .40
12 Alan Letang .15 .40
13 David Ling .20 .50
14 Alexei Lojkin .15 .40
15 Boyd Olson .15 .40
16 Tony Prpic .15 .40
17 Jesse Rezansoff .15 .40
18 Craig Rivet .40 1.00
19 Pierre Sevigny .20 .50
20 Todd Sparks .15 .40
21 Jose Theodore 20.00 40.00
22 Tomas Vokoun 8.00 20.00
23 Adam Wiesel .15 .40
24 Paulin Bordeleau CO .10 .25
25 Luc Gauthier CO .10 .25
26 Patrick Langlois TR .10 .25
27 Paul Chagnon TR .10 .25
28 Jacques Parent TR .10 .25
29 Tricolo MAS .02 .10
30 Jolly Rancher .02 .10

2000-01 Fresno Falcons

COMPLETE SET (30) 8.00 20.00
1 Chris Albert .30 .75
2 Matt Alvey .40 1.00
3 Brad Both .30 .75
4 Brodie Coffin .30 .75
5 Kirk DeWaele .30 .75
6 Sheldon Flaman .40 1.00
7 Terry Friesen .40 1.00
8 Glen Gulutzan .30 .75
9 Don Malko .30 .75
10 Mike Mathers .30 .75
11 Mike McCourt .30 .75
12 David Mitchell .30 .75
13 Kory Mullin .40 1.00
14 Cory Murphy .30 .75
15 Kris Porter .30 .75
16 Chris Skoryna .30 .75
17 Adrian Smith .40 1.00
18 Greg Spenrath .30 .75
19 Rejean Stringer .30 .75
20 Darren Wetherill .30 .75
21 Terry Friesen SO .40 1.00
22 Blaine Moore CO .10 .25
23 Freddie Falcon MASCOT .04 .10
24 Mike Carey TR .04 .10
25 Fresno Falcons Celebration .20 .50
26 TV-47 ANCHORS .01 .05
27 Star-101 DJ's SPONSOR .01 .05
28 Mark Kuntz EM .04 .10
29 Brian Clark .30 .75
30 Team Photo .20 .50

2001-02 Fresno Falcons

COMPLETE SET (30) 8.00 20.00
1 Brad Both .40 1.00
2 Brodie Coffin .40 1.00
3 Kirk DeWaele .40 1.00
4 Joe Frederick .40 1.00
5 Terry Friesen .60 1.50
6 Glen Gulutzan .40 1.00
7 Dale Junkin .40 1.00
8 Dan Kerluke .40 1.00
9 Mike Mathers .40 1.00
10 Mike McCourt .40 1.00
11 David Mitchell .40 1.00
12 Kory Mullin .40 1.00
13 Cory Murphy .40 1.00
14 Kris Porter .40 1.00
15 Chris Skoryna .40 1.00
16 Adrian Smith .20 .50
17 Greg Spenrath .40 1.00
18 Ryan Tocher .40 1.00
19 Alex Todd .40 1.00
20 Jason Weaver .40 1.00
21 Darren Wetherill .40 1.00
22 Blaine Moore CO .10 .25
23 Game Winner Action Photo .10 .25
24 Mike Carey TR .04 .10
25 Mark Kuntz EQMG .04 .10
26 Freddie Falcon MASCOT .04 .10
27 Team Photo .20 .50
28 Carls Jr. .04 .10
29 Fresno Bee .04 .10
30 KRZR 103.7 .04 .10

2002-03 Fresno Falcons

COMPLETE SET (25) 8.00 20.00
1 Checklist .04 .10
2 Kevin Haupt .40 1.00
3 Chris Kenady .40 1.00
4 Cory Murphy .40 1.00
5 Mike Mathers .40 1.00
6 Alex Todd .40 1.00
7 Brad Both .60 1.50
8 Steve Lowe .40 1.00
9 Scott Borders .40 1.00
10 Jordan Landry .40 1.00
11 Colin Embley .40 1.00
12 Glen Gulutzan .40 1.00
13 Kirk DeWaele .40 1.00
14 Jason Weaver .40 1.00
15 Drew Schoneck .40 1.00
16 Mark Gowan .60 1.50
17 Terry Friesen .60 1.50
18 Joe Frederick .40 1.00
19 Kayle Short .40 1.00
20 Jason McBain .40 1.00
21 Kris Porter .40 1.00
22 Blaine Moore HCO .04 .10
23 Greg Spenrath ACO .04 .10
24 Happy Star .04 .10
25 KRZR-103.7 .04 .10

2003-04 Fresno Falcons

COMPLETE SET (25) 10.00
1 Scott Borders .20 .50
2 Mike Brusseau .30 .75
3 Blair Clarance .20 .50
4 Terry Friesen .30 .75
5 Nathan Horne .20 .50
6 Mark Jackson .20 .50
7 Michael Kiesman .20 .50
8 Jordan Landry .20 .50
9 Mike Mathers .20 .50
10 Blaine Moore CO .20 .50
11 Kory Mullin .20 .50
12 Dominic Periard .20 .50
13 Kris Porter .20 .50
14 Boris Protsenko .20 .50
15 Riku Rahikainen .20 .50
16 Tapio Sammalkangas .20 .50
17 Mike Sandbeck .20 .50
18 Nolan Schaefer .30 .75
19 Drew Schoneck .20 .50
20 Greg Spenrath CO .20 .50
21 Adam Stefishen .20 .50
22 Kevin Truelson .20 .50
23 Jason Weaver .20 .50
24 John Wroblewski .20 .50
25 Mascot .04 .10
NNO Checklist .04 .10

2004-05 Fresno Falcons

COMPLETE SET (TBD) 10.00 25.00
1 David Brisson .40 1.00
2 Clint Cabana .40 1.00
3 John Dahl .40 1.00
4 Thierry Douville .40 1.00
5 Lanny Gare .40 1.00
6 Shawn Heaphy .40 1.00
7 Brett Jaegar .75 2.00
8 Tomas Jasko .40 1.00
9 Mike Kiesman .40 1.00
10 Derek Krestanovich .40 1.00
11 Simon Lajeunesse .75 2.00
12 Jim Lorentz .40 1.00
13 Matt O'Dette .40 1.00
14 Wes Rypien .40 1.00
15 Curtis Sheptak .40 1.00
16 Charles Simard .40 1.00
17 Greg Spenrath .40 1.00
18 Shaun Sutter .40 1.00
19 Dan Tessier .40 1.00
20 Kevin Truelson .40 1.00
21 Dustin VanBallegooie .40 1.00
22 Jason Weaver .40 1.00
23 John Wroblewski .40 1.00

2005-06 Fresno Falcons

COMPLETE SET (26) 6.00 15.00
1 P.O. Beaulieu .30 .75
2 Brad Both .30 .75
3 Fraser Clair .30 .75
4 Luke Curtin .30 .75
5 Matt Deschamps .30 .75
6 Peter Fregoe .30 .75
7 Brett Hammond .30 .75
8 Jamie Holden .30 .75
9 Brett Jaeger .30 .75
10 Derek Krestanovich .30 .75
11 Shawn Mather .30 .75
12 Rob McFeeters .30 .75
13 Kelsey Muench .30 .75
14 Cory Murphy .30 .75
15 Matt O'Dette .30 .75
16 Glenn Olson .30 .75
17 J.F. Plourde .30 .75
18 Dustin Vanballegooie .30 .75
19 Shawn Weiman .30 .75
20 John Wroblewski .30 .75
21 Ryan Mougenel .30 .75
22 Chris Burke .30 .75
23 Brian Clark .30 .75
24 Brad Jellis .30 .75
25 Matt Thomas .30 .75

2003-04 Gatineau Olympiques

COMPLETE SET (27) 5.00 12.00
1 Gabriel Bouthillette .30 .75
2 Scott Brophy .20 .50
3 Bruno Champagne .20 .50
4 Yanick Charron .20 .50
5 Dominic D'Amour .20 .50
6 Jean-Michel Daoust .20 .50
7 Philippe Dupuis .20 .50
8 Vincent Duriau .20 .50
9 Guillaume Fournier .20 .50
10 Martin Frechette .20 .50
11 Nick Fugere .20 .50
12 Derrick Kent .20 .50
13 Olivier Labelle .20 .50
14 Guillaume Labrecque .20 .50
15 Christian Laroche .20 .50
16 Doug O'Brien .20 .50
17 Keven Petit .20 .50
18 Petr Pohl .20 .50
19 Nicolas Ranger .20 .50
20 Maxime Robert .20 .50
21 Sam Roberts .20 .50
22 Maxime Rousseau .20 .50
23 Maxime Talbot .20 .50
24 David Tremblay .30 .75
25 Martin Vagner .30 .75
26 Francis Wathier .20 .50
27 Lance Woodman .20 .50

2004-05 Gatineau Olympiques

COMPLETE SET (24) 5.00 12.00
1 David Tremblay .30 .75
2 Martin Frechette .20 .50
3 Sam Roberts .20 .50
4 Scott Brophy .20 .50
5 Olivier Laliberte .30 .75
6 Francis Wathier .20 .50
7 Nicolas Ranger .20 .50
8 Keven Petit .20 .50
9 Jonathan Carrier .20 .50
10 Nick Fugere .20 .50
11 Olivier Labelle .20 .50
12 Maxime Rousseau .20 .50
13 Pierre-Luc Lessard .20 .50
14 Brett Morrison .20 .50
15 David Krejci .40 1.00
16 Petr Pohl .20 .50
17 Ryan Graham .20 .50
18 Guillaume Labrecque .20 .50
19 Cam Fergus .20 .50
20 Dave Starenky .20 .50
21 Bryan Wilson .20 .50
22 Geoffrey Walker .20 .50
23 Francis Gagnon .20 .50
24 Luke Pelham .20 .50

2005-06 Gatineau Olympiques

COMPLETE SET (28) 5.00 12.00
1 David Tremblay .20 .50
2 Olivier Laliberte .20 .50
3 Guillaume Labrecque .20 .50
4 Nick Fugere .20 .50
5 Keven Petit .20 .50
6 Maxime Rousseau .20 .50
7 Claude Giroux .50 1.25
8 David Krejci .40 1.00
9 Bryan Wilson .20 .50
10 Martin Frechette .20 .50
11 Jonathan Carrier .20 .50
12 Pierre-Luc Lessard .20 .50
13 Brad Tesink .20 .50
14 Michael Stinziani .20 .50
15 Colin Escott .20 .50
16 Benoit Gervais .20 .50
17 Maxime Malette .20 .50
18 Michel Champagne .20 .50
19 Maxime Langelier-Parent .20 .50
20 Brett Morrison .20 .50
21 Mathieu Curadeau .20 .50
22 Alexandre Boivin .20 .50
23 Bryan Main .20 .50
24 Darryl Smith .20 .50
25 Antonin Manavian .20 .50
26 Matthew Pistilli .20 .50
27 Philippi Cote .20 .50
28 Mascot .02 .10

2006-07 Gatineau Olympiques

COMPLETE SET (28) 8.00 15.00
1 Martin Frechette .20 .50
2 Olivier Laliberte .30 .75
3 Maxime Mallette .20 .50
4 Jonathan Carrier .20 .50
5 Viatcheslav Trukhno .20 .50
6 Steven Delisle .20 .50
7 Daniel Sauve .20 .50
8 Brad Tesink .20 .50
9 Keven Petit .20 .50
10 Brett Morrison .20 .50
11 Jean-Philipp Chabot .20 .50
12 Alexandre Boivin .20 .50
13 Claude Giroux .50 1.25
14 Bryan Main .20 .50
15 Paul Byron .20 .50
16 Benoit Gervais .20 .50
17 Matthew Pistilli .20 .50
18 Darryl Smith .20 .50
19 Travis Stacey .20 .50
20 Michael Stinziani .20 .50
21 Pierre-Marc Guilbault .20 .50
22 Alexandre Touchette .20 .50
23 Ken Dufresne .20 .50
24 Dave Bertrand-Duclos .20 .50
25 Chad Loikets .20 .50
26 David Kveton .20 .50
27 Ryan Mior .30 .75
28 Tyler Pugh .20 .50

2009-10 Gatineau Olympiques

1 Mathieu Gagnon .40 1.00
2 Adam Janosik .40 1.00
3 Vincent Barnard .40 1.00
4 Jason Seed .40 1.00
5 Hugo Laporte .40 1.00
6 Denis Kindl .40 1.00
7 Yoan Pinette .40 1.00
8 Jean-Gabriel Pageau .40 1.00
9 Mitchell Porowski .40 1.00
10 Hubert Labrie .40 1.00
11 Philippe Halley .40 1.00
12 Mathieu Talbot .40 1.00
13 Josh Domingues .40 1.00
14 Ben Miller .40 1.00
15 Benjamin Laliberte .40 1.00
16 Christian Ouellet-Martel .40 1.00
17 Alexander Beaton .40 1.00
18 Olivier Croteau .40 1.00
19 Tye McGinn .40 1.00
20 Dereck Tait .40 1.00
21 Jacob Conrad .40 1.00
22 Maxime Clermont .40 1.00
23 Alex Noel .40 1.00

1977-78 Granby Vics

COMPLETE SET (20) 17.50 35.00
1 Mario Beauregard 1.00 2.00
2 Luc Breton 1.00 2.00
3 Daniel Caron 1.50 3.00
4 Mario Casavant 1.00 2.00
5 Marc Courtemanche 1.00 2.00
6 Yves Courtemanche 1.00 2.00
7 Sylvain d'Amour 1.00 2.00
8 Rene Delorme 1.00 2.00
9 Denis Dumas Jr. 1.00 2.00
10 Pierre Grondin 1.00 2.00
11 Andre Hebert 1.00 2.00
12 Marcel Lachance 1.00 2.00
13 Andre Lemieux 1.00 2.00
14 Pierre Lepage 1.00 2.00
15 Daniel Menard 1.00 2.00
16 Jacques Pomerleau 1.00 2.00
17 Mario Roy 1.00 2.00
18 Alain Tetrault 1.00 2.00
19 Paul Thibert 1.00 2.00
20 Luc Turgeon 1.00 2.00

1996-97 Grand Rapids Griffins

COMPLETE SET (30) 20.00 50.00
1 Kevyn Adams 1.25 3.00
2 Dave Allison CO .40 1.00
3 Danton Cole .75 2.00
4 Keli Corpse .75 2.00
5 Pavol Demitra 4.00 10.00
6 Griff/Mascot .20 .50
7 Ben Hankinson .75 2.00
8 Stanislav Jasecko .75 2.00
10 Sean McCann .75 2.00
11 Cory Johnson .75 2.00
12 Jamie Linden .75 2.00
13 Don McSween .75 2.00
14 Tyler Moss 1.50 4.00
15 Jeff Nelson .75 2.00
16 Todd Nelson .75 2.00
17 Michel Picard .75 2.00
18 Bruce Ramsay .75 2.00
19 Pokey Reddick 1.50 4.00
20 Chad Remackel .75 2.00
21 Travis Richards .75 2.00
22 Matt Ruchty .75 2.00
23 Darcy Simon .75 2.00
24 1996 Inaugural Face-Off .20 .50
25 1996-97 Inaugural Team .75 2.00
26 Van Andel Arena .20 .50
NNO Title card 1 .08 .20
NNO Title card 2 .08 .20
NNO Title card 3 .08 .20
NNO Title card 4 .08 .20
NNO Title card 5 .08 .20

1997-98 Grand Rapids Griffins

COMPLETE SET (24) 4.00 10.00
1 Michel Picard .30 .75
2 Tom Ashe .20 .50
3 Greg Clancy .20 .50
4 Danton Cole .20 .50
5 Ian Gordon .20 .50
6 Mark Greig .20 .50
7 Shane Hnidy .30 .75
8 Kerry Huffman .20 .50
9 Glen Metropolit .40 1.00
10 Todd Nelson .20 .50
11 Ed Patterson .20 .50
12 Bruce Ramsay .20 .50
13 Eldon Reddick .40 1.00
14 Travis Richards .20 .50
15 Matt Ruchty .20 .50
16 Darcy Simon .20 .50
17 Brian Sullivan .20 .50
18 Sean Tallaire .20 .50
19 Dean Trboyevich .20 .50
20 Jason Weaver .20 .50
21 Dave Allison HCO .10 .25
22 Curtis Hunt ACO .10 .25
23 Griff Mascot .02 .10
24 PHPA Web Site .02 .10

1998-99 Grand Rapids Griffins

COMPLETE SET (25) 5.00 12.00
1 Tom Ashe .20 .50
2 Jared Bednar .20 .50
3 Radim Bicanek .30 .75
4 Anders Bjork .20 .50
5 Aris Brimanis .20 .50
6 Danton Cole .20 .50
7 Jed Fiebelkorn .20 .50
8 Ian Gordon .20 .50
9 Todd Hlushko .20 .50
10 Kerry Huffman .20 .50
11 Neil Little .75 2.00
12 Glen Metropolit .40 1.00
13 Vaclav Nedomansky .20 .50
14 Robert Petrovicky .30 .75
15 Bruce Ramsay .20 .50
16 Travis Richards .20 .50
17 Gaetan Royer .20 .50
18 Darren Rumble .20 .50

19 Maxim Spiridonov .20 .50
20 Andrei Vasilyev .20 .50
21 Curtis Hunt ACO .10 .25
22 Guy Charron HCO .10 .25
23 Griff Mascot .02 .10
24 The Zone .02 .10
25 PHPA Web Site .02 .10

1999-00 Grand Rapids Griffins
COMPLETE SET (25) 6.00 15.00
1 Viacheslav Butsayev .20 .50
2 Guy Charron CO .08 .25
3 Ivan Ciernik .20 .50
4 Danton Cole CO .08 .25
5 John Emmons .20 .50
6 Mike Fountain .30 .75
7 Rick Goldman .20 .50
8 Konstantin Gorovikov .20 .50
9 John Gruden .20 .50
10 Curtis Hunt CO .08 .25
11 Jani Hurme 1.25 3.00
12 Derek King .20 .50
13 Kevin Miller .20 .50
14 Chris Neil .40 1.00
15 Todd Nelson .20 .50
16 Ed Patterson .20 .50
17 Michel Picard .20 .50
18 Phillippe Plante .20 .50
19 Karel Rachunek .30 .75
20 Travis Richards .20 .50
21 Yves Sarault .20 .50
22 Petr Schastlivy .60 1.50
23 Andrei Sryubko .20 .50
24 Chris Szysky .20 .50
25 Dave Van Drunen .20 .50

2000-01 Grand Rapids Griffins
COMPLETE SET (25) 4.00 10.00
1 Keith Aldridge .14 .35
2 Sean Berens .14 .35
3 Vyacheslav Butsayev .14 .40
4 Mathieu Chouinard .40 1.00
5 Ivan Ciernik .14 .40
6 Ilja Demidov .14 .40
7 Mike Fountain .20 .50
8 Sean Gagnon .14 .40
9 Konstantin Gorovikov .14 .35
10 John Gruden .14 .35
11 Derek King .20 .50
12 Joel Kwiatkowski .14 .35
13 Marty McSorley .40 1.00
14 Kip Miller .20 .50
15 Chris Neil .40 1.00
16 David Oliver .15 .40
17 Ed Patterson .14 .40
18 Travis Richards .14 .40
19 David Roberts .14 .35
20 Petr Schastlivy .40 1.00
21 Chris Szysky .14 .35
22 Todd White .20 .50
23 Bruce Cassidy CO .10 .25
24 Danton Cole CO .10 .25
25 Griff MASCOT .04 .10

2001-02 Grand Rapids Griffins
COMPLETE SET (24) 4.80 12.00
1 Julien Vauclair .20 .50
2 John Gruden .20 .50
3 Wade Brookbank .20 .50
4 Kip Miller .20 .50
5 Alexandre Giroux .20 .50
6 Hugo Boisvert .20 .50
7 James Black .20 .50
8 Steve Martins .20 .50
9 David Hymovitz .20 .50
10 Chris Szysky .20 .50
11 Petr Schastlivy .40 1.00
12 Jeff Ulmer .20 .50
13 Josh Langfeld .20 .50
14 Chris Kelly .20 .50
15 Joe Murphy .20 .50
16 Travis Richards .20 .50
17 Martin Prusek .60 1.50
18 Chris Bala .20 .50
19 Dave Van Drunen .20 .50
20 Jason Doig .20 .50
21 Joel Kwiatkowski .20 .50
22 Mathieu Chouinard .60 1.50
23 Toni Dahlman .20 .50
24 Bruce Cassidy CO .04 .10
25 Gene Reilly ACO .04 .10
26 Griff MASCOT .04 .10

2002-03 Grand Rapids Griffins
COMPLETE SET (27) 5.00 12.00
1 Bryan Adams .30 .75
2 Sean Avery .75 2.00
3 Paul Ballantyne .30 .75
4 Ryan Barnes .30 .75
5 Gregor Baumgartner .30 .75
6 Patrick Boileau .30 .75
7 Hugo Boisvert .30 .75
8 Sheldon Brookbank .30 .75
9 Ed Campbell .30 .75
10 Danton Cole CO .04 .10
11 Rob Collins .30 .75
12 Nick Greenough .30 .75
13 Griff MASCOT .04 .10
14 Danny Groulx .30 .75
15 Derek King .30 .75
16 Tomas Kopecky .30 .75
17 Marc Lamothe .30 .75
18 Joey MacDonald .40 1.00
19 Mark Mowers .30 .75
20 Todd Nelson .30 .75
21 Michel Picard .30 .75
22 Travis Richards .30 .75
23 Nathan Robinson .30 .75
24 Stacy Roest .30 .75
25 Tim Skarperud .30 .75
26 Dave Van Drunen .30 .75
27 Shoe Carnival Ad .04 .10

2003-04 Grand Rapids Griffins
COMPLETE SET (29) 20.00 30.40
1 Ryan Barnes .60 1.50
2 Hugo Boisvert .60 1.50
3 Darryl Bootland .75 2.00
4 David Brisson .60 1.50
5 Matt Ellis .60 1.50
6 Danny Groulx .60 1.50
7 Jiri Hudler 2.00 5.00
8 Derek King .60 1.50
9 Tomas Kopecky 1.25 3.00
10 Niklas Kronwall 2.00 5.00
11 Marc Lamothe .75 2.00
12 Joey MacDonald 1.25 3.00
13 Kevin Miller .75 2.00
14 Mark Mowers .75 2.00
15 Anders Myrvold .60 1.50
16 Michel Picard .60 1.50
17 Travis Richards .60 1.50
18 Nathan Robinson .75 2.00
19 Aaron Schneekloth .60 1.50
20 Tim Skarperud .60 1.50
21 David Van Drunen .60 1.50
22 Danton Cole CO .10 .25
23 Greg Ireland ACO .04 .10
24 Brad Thompson EQM .04 .10
25 Jiri Hudler 2.00 5.00
26 Kory Karlander .60 1.50
27 Jeff Nelson .60 1.50
28 Rob Snitzer TR .04 .10
29 Shoe Carnival Ad .04 .10

2013-14 Grand Rapids Griffins
COMPLETE SET (25) 6.00 15.00
1 Adam Almquist .30 .75
2 Mitch Callahan .30 .75
3 Patrick Eaves .30 .75
4 Cory Emmerton .30 .75
5 Brennan Evans .30 .75
6 Landon Ferraro .30 .75
7 Gleason Fournier .30 .75
8 Martin Frk .30 .75
9 Luke Glendening .30 .75
10 Triston Grant .30 .75
11 Jeff Hoggan .30 .75
12 Calle Jarnkrok .30 .75
13 Nick Jensen .30 .75
14 Tomas Jurco .30 .75
15 Alexey Marchenko .30 .75
16 Thomas McCollum .30 .75
17 David Mcintyre .30 .75
18 Petr Mrazek .30 .75
19 Andrej Nestrasil .30 .75
20 Xavier Ouellet .30 .75
21 Nathan Paetsch .30 .75
22 Teemu Pulkkinen .30 .75
23 Riley Sheahan .30 .75
24 Ryan Sproul .30 .75
25 Jordin Tootoo .30 .75

2004-05 Green Bay Gamblers
COMPLETE SET (28) 10.00 25.00
1 Jeff Carlson .40 1.00
2 Corey Couturier .40 1.00
3 Derek Danowski .40 1.00
4 Jeremy Dehner .40 1.00
5 Spencer Dillon .40 1.00
6 Justin Johnson .40 1.00
7 Carl Lackey ACO .04 .10
8 Tyler Lehrke .40 1.00
9 Joe Long .40 1.00
10 Mark Magnowski .40 1.00
11 Mark Mazzoleni CO .04 .10
12 Andrew Meyer .40 1.00
13 Brad Miller .40 1.00
14 Ryan Peterson .40 1.00
15 Garren Reisweber .40 1.00
16 Daniel Rosen .40 1.00
17 Billy Smith .40 1.00
18 Chris Stansik .40 1.00
19 Mark Stockdale .40 1.00
20 Luke Strand ACO .04 .10
21 Dan Sturges .40 1.00
22 Garrett Suter .40 1.00
23 Blake Wheeler 1.25 3.00
24 Michael Zacharias .40 1.00
25 Suter
Dehner
Sturges .40 1.00
26 Missconducts .40 1.00
27 Mask Card .40 1.00
28 Mini Plan .04 .10

1991-92 Greensboro Monarchs
COMPLETE SET (19) 3.00 8.00
1 Rob Bateman .25 .60
2 Phil Berger .20 .50
3 Mike Butters .20 .50
4 John Devereaux .20 .50
5 Eric Dubois .20 .50
6 Todd Gordon .20 .50
7 Chris Laganas .20 .50
8 Eric LeMarque .20 .50
9 Timo Makela .20 .50
10 Greg Menges .20 .50
11 Daryl Noren .20 .50
12 Peter Sentner .20 .50
13 Boyd Sutton .20 .50
14 Nick Vitucci .25 .60
15 Shawn Wheeler .20 .50
16 Scott White .20 .50
17 Chris Wolanin .20 .50
18 Dean Zayonce .20 .50
19 Team Photo .20 .50

1992-93 Greensboro Monarchs
COMPLETE SET (19) 3.00 8.00
1 Team Photo .30 .75
2 Chris Wolanin .20 .50
3 Bill Horn .20 .50
4 Brock Woods .20 .50
5 Phil Berger .20 .50
6 Dan Bylsma .20 .50
7 Davis Payne .30 .75
8 Wayne Muir .20 .50
9 Andrei Iakovenko .20 .50
10 Roger Larche .20 .50
11 Jamie Nicolls .20 .50
12 Darryl Noren .20 .50
13 Todd Gordon .20 .50
14 Claude Maillet .20 .50
15 Dave Burke .20 .50
16 Jamie Steer .25 .60
17 Greg Capson .20 .50
18 Chris Lappin .20 .50
19 Greg Menges .20 .50

1993-94 Greensboro Monarchs
COMPLETE SET (16) 2.00 5.00
1 Phil Berger .20 .50
2 Trevor Burgess .15 .40
3 Dan Bylsma .20 .50
4 Greg Capson .15 .40
5 Brendan Creagh .15 .40
6 Dan Gravelle .15 .40
7 Sebastien LaPlante .15 .40
8 Savo Mitrovic .15 .40
9 Tom Newman .15 .40
10 Jamie Nicolls .15 .40
11 Davis Payne .20 .50
12 Stig Salomonsson .15 .40
13 Sverre Sears .15 .40
14 Chris Valicevic .15 .40
15 John Young .15 .40
16 Dean Zayonce .15 .40

1994-95 Greensboro Monarchs
COMPLETE SET (20) 4.00 10.00
1 Dean Zayonce .20 .50
2 Jeremy Stevenson .20 .50
3 Glenn Stewart .20 .50
4 Peter Skudra .40 1.00
5 Chad Seibel .20 .50
6 Sverre Sears .20 .50
7 Howie Rosenblatt .40 1.00
8 Hugo Proulx .20 .50
9 Davis Payne .20 .50
10 Ron Pasco .20 .50
11 Monte MASCOT .02 .10
12 Scott McKay .20 .50
13 Arturs Kupaks .20 .50
14 Bill Horn .20 .50
15 Dwayne Gylywoychuk .20 .50
16 Jeff Gabriel .20 .50
17 Doug Evans .20 .50
18 Mark DeSantis .20 .50
19 Brendan Creagh .20 .50
20 Phil Berger .20 .50

1999-00 Greensboro Generals
COMPLETE SET (26) 4.00 10.00
1 Ian Walterson .15 .40
2 Clay Awe .15 .40
3 Sal Manganaro .15 .40
4 Oleg Timchenko .15 .40
5 David Whitworth .15 .40
6 T.J. Tanberg .15 .40
7 Keith O'Connell .15 .40
8 Tracy Egeland .15 .40
9 Igor Boiko .15 .40
10 Martin Galik .15 .40
11 Dean Shmyr .15 .40
12 Juraj Slovak .15 .40
13 Aniket Dhadphale .15 .40
14 Dean Zayonce .15 .40
15 Alexei Krovopuskov .15 .40
16 Van Burgess .15 .40
17 Matt Eisler .15 .40
18 Justin Cardwell .15 .40
19 Joel Irwin .15 .40
20 Wes Swinson .15 .40
21 Francis Larivee .30 .75
22 40th Anniversary Puck Drop .15 .40
23 Group Celebrates .15 .40
24 Settling Differences .75 2.00
25 Bill Flynn .15 .40
26 Greensboro Generals CL .08 .25

2001-02 Greensboro Generals
COMPLETE SET (20) 16.00 40.00
1 Daniel Passero .75 2.00
2 Rob Sandrock 1.25 3.00
3 Sal Manganaro .75 2.00
4 Vladislav Serov .75 2.00
5 Jarrett Thompson .75 2.00
6 Ryan Kummu .75 2.00
7 David Whitworth .75 2.00
8 Brian Loney .75 2.00
9 Chris Bell .75 2.00
10 Casey Kesselring .75 2.00
11 Shaun Peet .75 2.00
12 Jason Metcalfe .75 2.00
13 Chris Brassard .75 2.00
14 Dion Lassu .75 2.00
15 Jason Robinson .75 2.00
16 Jonathan Forest .75 2.00
17 Craig Stahl .75 2.00
18 Bujar Amidovski 1.25 3.00
19 Graeme Townshend CO .40 1.00
20 Sarge MASCOT .40 1.00

2002-03 Greensboro Generals RBI
COMPLETE SET (18) 6.00 15.00
1 Rod Aldoff .40 1.00
2 Chris Allen .40 1.00
3 Alex Andreyev .40 1.00
4 Chris Bell .40 1.00
5 Daniel Berthiaume .60 1.50
6 Shane Campbell .40 1.00
7 Matt Chandler .40 1.00
8 Kurt Drummond .40 1.00
9 Sam Ftorek .40 1.00
10 Pete Gardiner .40 1.00
11 Kevin Grimes .40 1.00
12 Olaf Kjenstad .40 1.00
13 Roman Marakhovski .40 1.00
14 Jay Murphy .40 1.00
15 Geno Parrish .40 1.00
16 Juraj Slovak .40 1.00
17 Matt Turek .40 1.00
18 David Whitworth .40 1.00

2003-04 Greensboro Generals
COMPLETE SET (16) 6.00 15.00
177 Alex Andreyev .40 1.00
178 Mike Bayrack .40 1.00
179 Daniel Berthiaume .60 1.50
180 Matt Chandler .40 1.00
181 Kurt Drummond .40 1.00
182 Matt Elich .40 1.00
183 Eric Fortier .40 1.00
184 Pete Gardiner .40 1.00
185 Joe Gerbe .40 1.00
186 Kevin Grimes .40 1.00
187 Jamie Hodson .60 1.50
188 Geno Parrish .40 1.00
189 Tom Reimann .40 1.00
190 Dean Shmyr .40 1.00
191 Matt Turek .40 1.00
192 Mark Turner .40 1.00

2001-02 Greenville Grrrowl
COMPLETE SET (24) 10.00 20.00
1 John Marks CO .20 .50
2 Nick Vitucci ACO .20 .50
3 Eric Lind .40 1.00
4 Judd Stauss .40 1.00
5 Eric Van Acker .40 1.00
6 Roger Trudeau .40 1.00
7 Jason Windle .40 1.00
8 Sean Venedam .75 2.00
9 Jay Langager .40 1.00
10 Steve Rymsha .40 1.00
11 Jonathan Roy .75 2.00
12 Colin Pepperall .40 1.00
13 Kevin Bergin .40 1.00
14 David Bell .40 1.00
15 Damon Whitten .40 1.00
16 Ryan Stewart .40 1.00
17 Martin Masa .40 1.00
18 David Kaczowka .40 1.00
19 Simon Gamache .75 2.00
20 Tyrone Garner .75 2.00
21 Jayme Platt .40 1.00
22 Chad Nelson .40 1.00
23 Grrruff MASCOT .10 .25
24 Greenville Grrrowl CL .10 .25

2002-03 Greenville Grrrowl
COMPLETE SET (23) 6.00 15.00
1 Michael Garnett .75 2.00
2 Paul Flache 1.00
3 Rico Fatticci .40 1.00
4 Matt Demarski .40 1.00
5 Tyler Deis .40 1.00
6 Alexandre Burrows .40 1.00
7 Josh Legge .40 1.00
8 David Kaczowka .40 1.00
9 Mike Henderson .40 1.00
10 Grrruff MASCOT .04 .10
11 Mark Gouett .40 1.00
12 Jonathan Gauthier .40 1.00
13 Judd Medak .40 1.00
14 Dan McIntyre .40 1.00
15 Martin Masa .40 1.00
16 John Marks HCO .04 .10
17 Chris Lynch .40 1.00
18 Eric Lind .40 1.00
19 Krzysztof Wieckowski .40 1.00
20 Nick Vitucci ACO .04 .10
21 Eric Van Acker .40 1.00
22 John Nail .40 1.00
23 Checklist .04 .10

2003-04 Greenville Grrrowl
COMPLETE SET (24) 10.00 25.00
1 Stacey Bauman .40 1.00
2 Daniel Boisclair 1.25 3.00
3 Steve Burgess .40 1.00
4 Michael Chin .40 1.00
5 Bob Cunningham .40 1.00
6 Randy Dagenais .40 1.00
7 Robin Delacoure .40 1.00
8 Matt Demarski .40 1.00
9 Mike Henderson .40 1.00
10 Troy Ilijow .40 1.00
11 Han-Sung Kim .75 2.00
12 Scott Kirton .40 1.00
13 Jeremy Kyte .40 1.00
14 Bryan Lachapelle .40 1.00
15 David Lizotte .40 1.00
16 Jason Metcalfe .40 1.00
17 Mike Nelson .40 1.00
18 Michel Robinson .75 2.00
19 Russell Spence .40 1.00
20 Ryan Stewart .40 1.00
21 Jonathan Zion .60 1.50
22 John Marks CO .20 .50
23 Team Photo .20 .50
24 John Nail .40 1.00

1993-94 Guelph Storm
COMPLETE SET (31) 5.00 12.00
1 Title Card .15 .40
2 Jeff O'Neill .60 1.50
3 Mark McArthur .20 .50
4 Kayle Short .15 .40
5 Ryan Risidore .15 .40
6 Mike Rusk .15 .40
7 Regan Stocco .15 .40
8 Duane Harmer .15 .40
9 Sylvain Cloutier .15 .40
10 Eric Landry .15 .40
11 Jamie Wright .20 .50
12 Todd Norman .15 .40
13 Mike Pittman .15 .40
14 Ken Belanger .30 .75
15 Viktor Reuta .15 .40
16 Mike Prokopec .15 .40
17 Jeff Williams .20 .50
18 Chris Skoryna .15 .40
19 Stephane Lefebvre .15 .40
20 Jeff Cowan .20 .50
21 Murray Hogg .15 .40
22 Andy Adams .15 .40
23 Todd Bertuzzi 1.25 3.00
24 Grant Pritchett .15 .40
25 Rumun Ndur .20 .50
26 Jeff O'Neill .60 1.50
27 Paul Brydges ACO .10 .25
28 John Lovell CO .10 .25
29 Team Photo/CL .02 .10
30 Domino's Pizza .02 .10
NNO Slapshot Ad Card .02 .10

1994-95 Guelph Storm
COMPLETE SET (31) 5.00 12.00
1 Team Photo/CL .15 .40
2 Mark McArthur .20 .50
3 Andy Adams .15 .40
4 Bryan McKinney .15 .40
5 Ryan Risidore .20 .50
6 Joel Cort .15 .40
7 Chris Hajt .20 .50
8 Regan Stocco .15 .40
9 Dwayne Hay .20 .50
10 Andrew Clark .15 .40
11 Neil Fewster .15 .40
12 Jamie Wright .20 .50
13 Jason Jackman .15 .40
14 Pat Barton .15 .40
15 Tom Johnson .15 .40
16 Brian Wesenberg .20 .50
17 Mike Pittman .15 .40
18 Jeff Williams .15 .40
19 Todd Norman .20 .50
20 Mike Rusk .15 .40
21 David Lylyk .15 .40
22 Todd Bertuzzi 1.00 2.50
23 Jeff Cowan .20 .50
24 Rumun Ndur .20 .50
25 Jeff O'Neill .40 1.00
26 Andrew Long .15 .40
27 Craig Hartsburg CO .20 .50
28 Paul Brydges ACO .10 .25
29 Sponsor Card/Burger King .02 .10
30 Sponsor Card/Domino's .02 .10
NNO Ad Card .02 .10

1995-96 Guelph Storm
COMPLETE SET (30) 4.00 10.00
1 Checklist .15 .40
2 Andrew Clark .15 .40
3 Dwayne Hay .20 .50
4 Jason Jackman .15 .40
5 Burger King Ad .02 .10
6 Nick Bootland .15 .40
7 Andrew Long .15 .40
8 Todd Norman .20 .50
9 Michael Pittman .15 .40
10 Herbert Vasilijevs .20 .50
11 Jeff Williams .15 .40
12 Joel Cort .20 .50
13 Chris Hajt .20 .50
14 Brian Willsie .20 .50
15 Brian Wesenberg .20 .50
16 Mike Lankshear .15 .40
17 Darryl McArthur .20 .50
18 Bryan McKinney .15 .40
19 Regan Stocco .15 .40
20 Ryan Risidore .20 .50
21 Mike Vellinga .15 .40
22 Dan Cloutier .40 1.00
23 Bryan McMullen .20 .50
24 Brett Thompson .20 .50
25 Ryan Robichaud .15 .40
26 Kid's Club .02 .10
27 Jamie Wright .20 .50
28 Guelph Police .02 .10
29 Mike Galati .15 .40
30 Domino's Pizza Ad .02 .10

1996-97 Guelph Storm
COMPLETE SET (36) 5.00 12.00
1 Checklist .02 .10
2 Brett Thompson .15 .40
3 David MacDonald .15 .40
4 John Zubyck .15 .40
5 Denis Ivanov .15 .40
6 Joel Cort .15 .40
7 Chris Hajt .20 .50
8 Manny Malhotra .30 .75
9 Mike Dombkiewicz .15 .40
10 Ryan Robichaud .15 .40
11 Kent McDonell .20 .50
12 Joe Gerbe .15 .40
13 Mike Christian .15 .40
14 Brian Wesenberg .15 .40
15 Todd Norman .15 .40
16 Darryl McArthur .15 .40
17 Richard Irwin .15 .40
18 Brian Willsie .15 .40
19 Mike Vellinga .15 .40
20 Jason Jackman .15 .40
21 Chris Madden .30 .75
22 Dwayne Hay .20 .50
23 Joey Bartley .15 .40
24 Mike Lankshear .20 .50
25 Andrew Long .15 .40
26 Matt Bell .15 .40
27 Nick Bootland .20 .50
28 E.J. McGuire .20 .50
29 Rick Allain .02 .10
30 Burger King Ad .02 .10
31 Burger King Kid's Club .02 .10
32 Guelph Police .15 .40
33 Domino's Pizza Ad .02 .10
34 Domino's Pizza Ad .02 .10
35 Chris Hajt
Dwayne Hay .15 .40
36 96-97 Team Picture .15 .40

1996-97 Guelph Storm Premier Collection
COMPLETE SET (12) 4.80 10.00
1 Todd Norman .40 1.00
2 Brian Wesenberg .40 1.00
3 Mike Vellinga .40 1.00
4 Brett Thompson .40 1.00
5 Joel Cort .40 1.00
6 Jason Jackman .40 1.00
7 Brian Willsie .40 1.00
8 Mike Lankshear .40 1.00
9 Dwayne Hay .40 1.00
10 Manny Malhotra .75 2.00
11 Chris Hajt .40 1.00
12 Nick Bootland .40 1.00

1997-98 Guelph Storm
COMPLETE SET (34) 5.00 12.00
1 Header Card .02 .10
2 Chris Thompson .15 .40
3 Daniel Jacques .15 .40
4 Chris Madden .30 .75
5 Kevin Mitchell .15 .40
6 Joey Bartley .15 .40
7 Chris Hajt .20 .50
8 Manny Malhotra .30 .75
9 Mike Dombkiewicz .15 .40
10 Ian Forbes .15 .40
11 Joe Gerbe .15 .40
12 Mike Vellinga .15 .40
13 Lindsay Plunkett .15 .40
14 Kent McDonell .15 .40
15 Matt Lahey .15 .40
16 Bohuslav Subr .15 .40
17 Bob Crummer .15 .40
18 Andrew Long .15 .40
19 Brian McGrattan .15 .40
20 Darryl McArthur .30 .75
21 Brian Willsie .20 .50
22 John Zubyck .15 .40
23 Dusty Jamieson .30 .75
24 Eric Beaudoin .15 .40
25 Jason Jackman .15 .40
26 Nick Bootland .15 .40
27 George Burnett CO .15 .40
28 Rick Allain ACO .02 .10
29 Spyke .02 .10
30 Guelph Police .02 .10
31 Burger King .02 .10
32 Burger King .02 .10
33 Domino's .02 .10
34 Domino's .02 .10

1998-99 Guelph Storm
COMPLETE SET (36) 5.00 12.00
1 Title Card/CL .02 .10
2 Mike D'Alessandro .30 .75
3 Chris Madden .40 1.00
4 Kevin Mitchell .20 .50
5 Jean Sebastien Larocque .20 .50
6 Kevin Dallman .30 .75
7 Matt Rock .20 .50
8 Ian Forbes .20 .50
9 Joe Gerbe .20 .50
10 Bo Subr .30 .75
11 Lindsay Plunkett .20 .50
12 Kent McDonell .20 .50
13 Garrett McAiney .20 .50
14 Nathan Herrington .20 .50
15 Bob Crummer .20 .50
16 Charlie Stephens .30 .75
17 Darryl Knight .20 .50
18 Darryl McArthur .30 .75
19 Ryan Davis .20 .50
20 Joey Bartley .20 .50
21 Frank Jolette .20 .50
22 Eric Beaudoin .20 .50
23 Lucas Nehrling .20 .50
24 Geoff Ward ACO .10 .25
25 Bart Crashley ACO .10 .25
26 Shane Mabey TR .02 .10
27 Russ Hammond ATR .02 .10
28 Spyke MASCOT .02 .10
29 Guelph Police .02 .10
30 1997-98 OHL Champs .20 .50
31 Robertson Cup .20 .50
32 Memorial Cup AS .08 .25
33 Burge King Ad .02 .10
34 Burger King Ad .02 .10
35 Domino's Ad .02 .10
36 Domino's Ad .02 .10

1999-00 Guelph Storm
COMPLETE SET (36) 4.00 10.00
1 Header Card/CL .02 .10
2 Craig Andersson .60 1.50
3 Chris Madden .40 1.00
4 Kevin Mitchell .15 .40
5 Kevin Dallman .15 .40
6 Matt Rock .15 .40
7 Jon Hedberg .15 .40
8 Radek Matalik .15 .40
9 Joe Gerbe .15 .40
10 Bo Suba .15 .40
11 Lindsay Plunkett .15 .40
12 Kent McDonell .30 .75
13 Peter Flache .15 .40
14 Charlie Stephens .30 .75
15 Colt King .30 .75
16 Nick Jones .15 .40
17 Brent Kelly .15 .40
18 Jon Peters .15 .40
19 Derek Hennessey .15 .40
20 Andrew Brown .15 .40
21 Aran Myers .15 .40
22 Matt House .15 .40
23 Eric Beaudoin .15 .40
24 Ian Forbes .15 .40
25 Morgan McCormick .15 .40
26 Paul Gillis .15 .40
27 Bart Crashley .15 .40
28 Shane Mabey .15 .40
29 Russ Hammond .15 .40
30 Spyke Mascot .02 .10
31 Team Photo .15 .40
32 Guelph Police .02 .10
33 Burger King Coupon .02 .10
34 Burger King Coupon .02 .10
35 Domino's Coupon .02 .10
36 Domino's Coupon .02 .10

2000-01 Guelph Storm
1 Craig Anderson 1.50 4.00
2 Andrew Archer .40 1.00
3 Dustin Brown 1.50 4.00
4 Kevin Dallman .40 1.00

2001-02 Guelph Storm
COMPLETE SET (35) 8.00 20.00
1 Fedor Tyutin .40 1.00
2 Frank Burgio .20 .50
3 Kevin Dallman .30 .75
4 Leonid Zvachkin .20 .50
5 Tim Branham .20 .50
6 George Bradley .20 .50
7 Martin St. Pierre .20 .50
8 Malcolm MacMillan .20 .50
9 Michael Krelove .20 .50
10 Colin Power .20 .50
11 Aaron Lobb .20 .50
12 Daniel Paille .75 2.00
13 Alex Butkus .20 .50
14 Ryan Thompson .20 .50
15 Luc Chiasson .20 .50
16 Derek Hennessey .20 .50
17 Evan Kotsopoulos .20 .50
18 Matt Puntureri .20 .50
19 Andrew Archer .20 .50
20 Morgan McCormick .20 .50
21 Chris Beckford-Tseu 1.25 3.00
22 Andrew Penner .30 .75
23 Dustin Brown 1.50 4.00
24 Dwight LaBrosse .20 .50
25 Jeff Jackson CO .08 .20
26 Shawn Camp ACO .20 .50
27 Spyke MASCOT .04 .10
28 Shane Mabey TR .20 .50
29 Russ Hammond ATR .20 .50
30 Police Services .04 .10
31 Dominos .04 .10
32 Guelph Dominators .04 .10
33 Guelph Dominators .04 .10
34 M&T Printing Group .04 .10
35 Checklist .04 .10

2001-02 Guelph Storm Memorial Cup
COMPLETE SET (35) 8.00 20.00
1 Fedor Tyutin .60 1.50
2 Kevin Dallman .60 1.50
3 Leonid Zvachkin .30 .75
4 Tim Branham .30 .75
5 Eric Larochelle .30 .75
6 George Bradley .30 .75
7 Martin St. Pierre .30 .75
8 Malcolm MacMillan .30 .75
9 Michael Krelove .30 .75
10 Colin Power .30 .75
11 Aaron Lobb .30 .75
12 Daniel Paille 1.00 2.50
13 Alex Butkus .30 .75
14 Ryan Thompson .30 .75
15 Luc Chiasson .30 .75
16 Derek Hennessey .30 .75
17 Lou Dickenson .30 .75
18 Matt Puntureri .30 .75
19 Scott Rozendal .30 .75
20 Andrew Archer .30 .75
21 Morgan McCormick .30 .75
22 Andrew Penner .40 1.00
23 Dustin Brown 1.50 4.00
24 Dwight LaBrosse .30 .75
25 Jeff Jackson CO .04 .10
26 Shawn Camp ACO .04 .10
27 Spyke MASCOT .04 .10
28 Shane Mabey TR .04 .10
29 Russ Hammond ATR .04 .10
30 Sponsor .04 .10
31 Memorial Cup Card .04 .10
32 Team Photo .04 .10
33 Community .04 .10
34 Community .04 .10
35 Checklist .04 .10

2002-03 Guelph Storm
COMPLETE SET (36) 6.00 15.00
1 Andrew Penner .30 .75
2 Martin St. Pierre .20 .50
3 Andrew Archer .20 .50
4 Ryan Thompson .20 .50
5 Daniel Paille .60 1.50
6 Adam Dennis .30 .75
7 Dustin Brown .60 1.50
8 Eric Larochelle .20 .50
9 George Bradley .20 .50
10 Corey LeClair .20 .50
11 Geoff Patton .20 .50
12 Lou Dickenson .20 .50
13 Matt Ryan .20 .50
14 Colin Power .20 .50
15 Ryan Garlock .40 1.00
16 Steve Zmudczynski .20 .50
17 Leonid Zvachkin .20 .50
18 Brett Trudell .20 .50
19 Michael Okrzesik .20 .50
20 Ryan Callahan .40 1.00
21 Emil Rucic .20 .50
22 Aaron Lobb .20 .50
23 Tyler Haskins .20 .50
24 Malcolm MacMillan .20 .50
25 Matt Puntureri .20 .50
26 Jeff Jackson CO .10 .25
27 Shawn Camp ACO .10 .25
28 Jason Brooks ACO .10 .25
29 Shawn Mabey AT .10 .25
30 Russ Hammond ATR .04 .10
31 Spyke MASCOT .04 .10
32 Ad card .04 .10
33 Junior Storm .04 .10
34 Home Ice .04 .10
35 Guelph Police .04 .10
36 Team Photo/CL .04 .10

2003-04 Guelph Storm
COMPLETE SET (30) 6.00 15.00
1 Header Card .04 .10
2 Danny Taylor .20 .50
3 Mick Okrzesik .20 .50
4 Dan Girardi .40 1.00
5 Kevin Klein .40 1.00
6 Ryan Parent .75 2.00
7 George Bradley .20 .50
8 Marty St. Pierre .20 .50
9 Niko Tuomi .20 .50
10 Mark Lytwyn .20 .50
11 Nathan Spaling .20 .50
12 Steve Zmudczynski .20 .50
13 Daniel Paille .40 1.00
14 Brett Trudell .20 .50
15 Shane Hart .20 .50
16 Ryan Garlock .40 1.00
17 Ryan Card .20 .50
18 Matt Ryan .20 .50
19 Ryan Callahan .30 .75
20 Kyle Spurr .20 .50
21 Adam Dennis .40 1.00
22 Jakub Koreis .40 1.00
23 Dustin Brown 1.00 2.50
24 Shawn Camp CO .10 .25
25 Jason Brooks ACO .10 .25
26 Paul Brydges ACO .10 .25
27 Sponsor Card .04 .10
28 Sponsor Card .04 .10

29 Guelph Police .04 .10
30 Team Photo/CL .04 .10

2004-05 Guelph Storm

COMPLETE SET (31) 8.00 20.00
1 Danny Taylor .30 .75
2 Michael Caruso .30 .75
3 Shawn Haviland .30 .75
4 Michael Okrzesik .30 .75
5 Daniel Girardi .40 1.00
6 Josh Godfrey .30 .75
7 Ryan Parent .40 1.00
8 Brent Mackie .30 .75
9 Andy Hyvarinen .30 .75
10 Jaromir Florian .30 .75
11 Mark Versteeg-Lytwyn .40 1.00
12 Mark O'Leary .30 .75
13 Steve Zmudczynski .30 .75
14 Scot Zimmerman .30 .75
15 Ryan Kitchen .30 .75
16 Mike McLean .30 .75
17 Kyle Paige .30 .75
18 Matt Lyall .30 .75
19 Matt D'Agostini .30 .75
20 Ryan Card .30 .75
21 Darryl Smith .30 .75
22 Ryan Callahan .40 1.00
23 Kyle Spurr .30 .75
24 Tyler Doig .30 .75
25 Adam Dennis .40 1.00
26 Dave Barr CO .04 .10
27 Jason Brooks ACO .04 .10
28 Trent Cull ACO .04 .10
29 Spyke MASCOT .04 .10
30 Team Photo/CL .04 .10
31 Guelph Police .04 .10

2005-06 Guelph Storm

COMPLETE SET (32) 10.00 25.00
A01 Josh Godfrey .40 1.00
A02 Jamie Arniel .40 1.00
A03 Mark O'Leary .40 1.00
A04 Tyler Doig .40 1.00
A05 Ryan MacDonald .40 1.00
A06 Jason Brooks ACO .20 .50
A07 Guelph Police .02 .10
A08 Guelph Storm CL1 .10 .25
B01 Ryan Pottruff .40 1.00
B02 Ryan Parent 1.00 2.50
B03 Andy Hyvarinen .40 1.00
B04 Kelsey Wilson .40 1.00
B05 Matt D'Agostini .40 1.00
B06 Domino's Pizza SPONSOR .02 .10
B07 Dave Barr CO .20 .50
B08 Guelph Storm CL2 .02 .10
C01 Michael Caruso .40 1.00
C02 Drew Doughty 2.00 5.00
C03 Brandon Biggers .40 1.00
C04 Leigh Salters .40 1.00
C05 Rafael Rotter .40 1.00
C06 M&T Printing SPONSOR .02 .10
C07 Trent Cull ACO .10 .25
C08 Guelph Storm CL3 .02 .10
D01 Shawn Haviland .40 1.00
D02 Kyle Wharton .40 1.00
D03 Jason Pitton .40 1.00
D04 Mike McLean .40 1.00
D05 Harry Young .40 1.00
D06 Ryan Callahan .75 2.00
D07 Jason Guy .40 1.00
D08 Guelph Storm CL4 .02 .10

2006-07 Guelph Storm

COMPLETE SET (25) 6.00 15.00
1 Thomas McCollum .40 1.00
2 Ryan Pottruff .20 .50
3 Joe Underwood .20 .50
4 Brandon Buck .20 .50
5 Drew Doughty 1.25 3.00
6 Matt Kennedy .20 .50
7 Leigh Salters .20 .50
8 Anthony Nigro .20 .50
9 Jeff Hayes .20 .50
10 Tyler Melancon .20 .50
11 Tyler Doig .20 .50
12 Mike McLean .20 .50
13 Patrick Moran .20 .50
14 Anton Hedman .20 .50
15 Luke Pither .20 .50
16 Grant McGee .20 .50
17 Rafael Rotter .20 .50
18 Tim Priamo .20 .50
19 Jamie Arniel .20 .50
20 Ryan Parent .60 1.50
21 Corey Syvret .20 .50
22 Michael Caruso .20 .50
23 Cody St Jacques .20 .50
24 Dave Barr CO .10 .25
25 Rusty Hammond TR .02 .10

2013-14 Guelph Storm

COMPLETE SET (33) 8.00 20.00
A01 Series 1 Header .30 .75
A02 Justin Auger .30 .75
A03 Hunter Garlent .30 .75
A04 Tyler Bertuzzi .30 .75
A05 Ryan Horvat .30 .75
A06 Brody Milne .30 .75
A07 Jason Dickinson .30 .75
A08 Ben Harpur .30 .75
A09 Pius Suter .30 .75
A10 Zack Mitchell .30 .75
A11 Scott Kosmachuk .30 .75
A12 Chadd Bauman .30 .75
A13 Justin Nichols .30 .75
A14 Guelph Police Services .30 .75
A15 RBC Bank .30 .75
A16 M & T Printing Group .30 .75
B01 Series 2 Header .30 .75
B02 Steven Trojanovic .30 .75
B03 Matt Finn .30 .75
B04 Phil Baltisberger .30 .75
B05 Zac Leslie .30 .75
B06 Robby Fabbri .30 .75
B07 Nick Ebert .30 .75
B08 Adam Craievich .30 .75
B09 Marc Stevens .30 .75
B10 Kerby Rychel .30 .75
B11 Stephen Pierog .30 .75
B12 Brock McGinn .30 .75
B13 Garrett McFadden .30 .75
B14 Matthew Mancina .30 .75
B15 RBC Bank .30 .75
B16 Speedvale Dental Centre .30 .75
B17 Guelph Police Services .30 .75

2014-15 Guelph Storm

COMPLETE SET (33) 8.00 20.00
A01 Series 1 Header .30 .75
A02 Kyle Rhodes .30 .75
A03 Ben Harpur .30 .75
A04 Zac Leslie .30 .75
A05 Robby Fabbri .50 1.25
A06 Jason Dickinson .30 .75
A07 Adam Craievich .30 .75
A08 Marc Stevens .30 .75
A09 James McEwan .30 .75
A10 Pius Suter .30 .75
A11 Matthew Hotchkiss .30 .75
A12 Garrett McFadden .30 .75
A14 Bradley Van Schubert .30 .75
A15 Guelph Police Services .30 .75
A16 Royal Bank of Canada .30 .75
A17 M&T Printing Group .30 .75
B01 Series 2 Header .30 .75
B02 Noah Carroll .30 .75
B03 C.J. Garcia .30 .75
B04 Phil Baltisberger .30 .75
B05 Austin Hall .30 .75
B06 Tyler Hill .30 .75
B07 Tyler Boston .30 .75
B08 Ryan Foss .30 .75
B09 Tyler Bertuzzi .40 1.00
B10 Chris Marchese .30 .75
B11 Luke Cairns .30 .75
B12 Givani Smith .30 .75
B13 Luke Burghardt .30 .75
B14 Justin Nichols .30 .75
B15 Guelph Police Services .30 .75
B16 Royal Bank of Canada .30 .75
B17 Speedvale Dental .30 .75

2003-04 Gwinnett Gladiators

COMPLETE SET (36) 12.00 30.00
1 Checklist .04 .10
2 Kevin Doell .40 1.00
3 Brad Peddle .40 1.00
4 Brandon Dietrich .40 1.00
5 Chris Durno .40 1.00
6 Rick Emmett .40 1.00
7 Anthony Aquino .60 1.50
8 Steve Slonina .40 1.00
9 Cam Brown .40 1.00
10 Wes Fox .40 1.00
11 Mike Buckley .60 1.50
12 Paul Flache .40 1.00
13 Joe Bourne .40 1.00
14 Blue Bennefield .60 1.50
15 Michael Garnett .60 1.50
16 Evan Nielsen .40 1.00
17 Jim Jackson .40 1.00
18 Troy Milam .40 1.00
19 Adam Munro .60 1.50
20 Kris Goodjohn .40 1.00
21 Mike Vigilante .40 1.00
22 Phil Lewandowski .40 1.00
23 J.P. O'Connor .40 1.00
24 Jeff Pyle CO .10 .25
25 Megan Guthrie TR .10 .25
26 Patrick Houlihan EQM .10 .25
27 Steve Chapman GM .10 .25
28 Dustin Bixby ANN .10 .25
29 Celebration Photo .20 .50
30 Mascot .10 .25
31 Gladiators first ever goal .20 .50
32 Gladiators win first game .20 .50
33 Opening Night .20 .50
34 Scramble in the crease .20 .50
35 Team Photo .20 .50
36 The Zamboni .10 .25

2003-04 Gwinnett Gladiators RBI Sports

COMPLETE SET (16) 6.00 15.00
193 Blue Bennefield .60 1.50
194 Joe Bourne .40 1.00
195 Cam Brown .40 1.00
196 Brandon Dietrich .40 1.00
197 Kevin Doell .40 1.00
198 Chris Durno .40 1.00
199 Rick Emmett .40 1.00
200 Paul Flache .40 1.00
201 Michael Garnett .60 1.50
202 Kris Goodjohn .40 1.00
203 Jim Jackson .40 1.00
204 Troy Milam .40 1.00
205 Adam Munro .60 1.50
206 Evan Nielsen .40 1.00
207 Steve Slonina .40 1.00
208 Mike Vigilante .40 1.00

2004-05 Gwinnett Gladiators

COMPLETE SET (30) 8.00 20.00
1 T.J. Aceti .60 1.50
2 Adam Berkhoel .75 2.00
3 Dustin Bixby .30 .75
4 Joe Bourne .30 .75
5 Cam Brown .30 .75
6 Jeff Campbell .30 .75
7 Steve Champman GM .04 .10
8 Chris Durno .30 .75
9 Rick Emmett .30 .75
10 Brett Engelhardt .30 .75
11 Sean Fields .30 .75
12 Peter Flache .30 .75
13 Kris Goodjohn .30 .75
14 Megan Guthrie TR .04 .10
15 Patrick Houlihan EQMG .04 .10
16 Jim Jackson .30 .75
17 Lane Manson .30 .75
18 Dave McCullough .30 .75
19 Dr. Brian Morgan .04 .10
20 Chris Peterson .30 .75
21 Jeff Pyle CO .04 .10
22 Brad Schell .30 .75
23 Adam Smyth .30 .75
24 Mike Stathopoulos .30 .75
25 Kevin Truelson .30 .75
26 Ryan Van Buskirk .30 .75
27 Mike Vigilante .30 .75
28 Maximus MASCOT .04 .10
29 Team Picture .04 .10
30 Checklist .04 .10

1989-90 Halifax Citadels

COMPLETE SET (26) 4.80 12.00
1 Joel Baillargeon .20 .50
2 Jamie Baker .25 .60
3 Mario Brunetta .30 .75
4 Gerald Bzdel .20 .50
5 David Espe .20 .50
6 Bryan Fogarty .20 .50
7 Robbie Ftorek GM .20 .50
8 Scott Gordon .30 .75
9 Dean Hopkins .20 .50
10 Miroslav Ihnacak .20 .50
11 Claude Julien .20 .50
12 Kevin Kaminski .30 .75
13 Claude Lapointe .30 .75
14 Chris McQuaid EQ
Brent Smith TR .08 .25
15 Max Middendorf .20 .50
16 Stephane Morin .30 .75
17 Dave Pichette .20 .50
18 Ken Quinney .20 .50
19 Jean-Marc Richard .20 .50
20 Jean Marc Routhier .20 .50
21 Jaroslav Sevcik .20 .50
22 Brent Severyn .30 .75
23 Greg Smyth .20 .50
24 Trevor Steinburg .20 .50
25 Mark Vermette .20 .50
26 Ladislav Tresl .20 .50

1990-91 Halifax Citadels

COMPLETE SET (28) 4.80 12.00
1 Jamie Baker .20 .50
2 Mike Bishop .15 .40
3 Gerald Bzdel .15 .40
4 Daniel Dore .15 .40
5 Mario Doyon .15 .40
6 Dave Espe .15 .40
7 Stephane Fiset 1.25 3.00
8 Scott Gordon .30 .75
9 Stephane Guerard .15 .40
10 Dean Hopkins ACO .08 .25
11 Miroslav Ihnacak .20 .50
12 Jeff Jackson .20 .50
13 Clement Jodoin CO/MG .08 .25
14 Claude Lapointe .20 .50
15 Dave Latta .15 .40
16 Chris McQuaid EQ MG .08 .25
17 Kip Miller .20 .50
18 Stephane Morin .20 .50
19 Ken Quinney .15 .40
20 Jean-Marc Richard .15 .40
21 Serge Roberge .15 .40
22 Jaroslav Sevcik .15 .40
23 Brent Severyn .30 .75
24 Mike Shuman TR .08 .25
25 Greg Smyth .15 .40
26 Jim Sprott .15 .40
27 Trevor Stienburg .15 .40
28 Mark Vermette .15 .40

1995-96 Halifax Mooseheads

COMPLETE SET (25) 8.00 25.00
1 Harlin Hayes .20 .50
2 Jean-Sebastien Giguere 4.00 10.00
3 Patrick Lafleur .20 .50
4 Jamie Brown .20 .50
5 Elias Abrahamsson .20 .50
6 Didier Tremblay .20 .50
7 Chris Halverson .20 .50
8 Chris Peyton .20 .50
9 Frederic Belanger .20 .50
10 Joel Theriault .20 .50
11 Mark Lynk .20 .50
12 Derrick Pyke .20 .50
13 Steve Mongrain .20 .50
14 David Carson .20 .50
15 Jody Shelley 2.00 5.00
16 Daniel Payette .20 .50
17 Brian Surette .20 .50
18 Etienne Drapeau .30 .75
19 Billy Manley .20 .50
20 Jan Melichercik .20 .50
21 Nicolas Maheux .20 .50
22 Eric Houde .30 .75
23 Shawn MacKenzie CO .08 .25
24 Clement Jodoin CO .08 .25
25 Chris McQuaid TR .02 .10

1996-97 Halifax Mooseheads I

COMPLETE SET (27) 12.00 30.00
1 Elias Abrahamsson .30 .75
2 Frederic Belanger .20 .50
3 Martin Bilodeau .20 .50
4 Jamie Brown .20 .50
5 Marc Chouinard .40 1.00
6 Benoit Dusablon .60 1.50
7 Jean-Sebastien Giguere 2.50 6.00
8 Andrew Gilby .20 .50
9 Alex Johnstone .20 .50
10 Eric Laplante .30 .75
11 Jean-Simon Lemay .20 .50
12 Mark Lynk .20 .50
13 Billy Manley .20 .50
14 Alexander Mathieu .20 .50
15 Todd Row .20 .50
16 Ryan Rowell .20 .50
17 Francois Sasseville .20 .50
18 Jody Shelley 1.50 4.00
19 Jeffrey Sullivan .20 .50
20 Alex Tanguay 4.00 10.00
21 Didier Tremblay .30 .75
22 Jason Troini .20 .50
23 Clark Udle .20 .50
24 Clement Jodoin HCO .02 .10
25 Shawn MacKenzie ACO .02 .10
26 Chris McQuaid TR .02 .10
27 Team Photo .20 .50

1996-97 Halifax Mooseheads II

COMPLETE SET (27) 14.22 35.56
1 Elias Abrahamsson .40 1.00
2 Frederic Belanger .30 .75
3 Martin Bilodeau .30 .75
4 Jamie Brown .30 .75
5 Marc Chouinard .50 1.25
6 Benoit Dusablon .75 2.00
7 Jean-Sebastien Giguere 4.00 10.00
8 Andrew Gilby .30 .75
9 Alex Johnstone .30 .75
10 Eric Laplante .40 1.00
11 Jean-Simon Lemay .30 .75
12 Mark Lynk .30 .75
13 Billy Manley .30 .75
14 Alexander Mathieu .30 .75
15 Todd Row .30 .75
16 Ryan Rowell .30 .75
17 Francois Sasseville .30 .75
18 Jody Shelley 2.00 5.00
19 Jeffrey Sullivan .30 .75
20 Alex Tanguay 5.00 12.00
21 Didier Tremblay .40 1.00
22 Jason Troini .30 .75
23 Clark Udle .30 .75
24 Clement Jodoin HCO .02 .10
25 Shawn MacKenzie ACO .02 .10
26 Chris McQuaid TR .02 .10
27 Team Photo .20 .50

1997-98 Halifax Mooseheads I

COMPLETE SET (27) 8.00 20.00
1 Frederic Belanger .20 .50
2 Martin Bilodeau .20 .50
3 Marc-Andre Binette .20 .50
4 Alexandre Couture .20 .50
5 Andrew Gilby .20 .50
6 Alex Johnstone .20 .50
7 Eric Laplante .30 .75
8 P.J. Lynch .20 .50
9 Mark Lynk .20 .50
10 Joey MacDonald .50 1.25
11 Ali MacEachern .20 .50
12 Billy Manley .20 .50
13 Alexander Mathieu .20 .50
14 Steve Mongrain .20 .50
15 Ryan Power .20 .50
16 Brandon Reid 1.25 3.00
17 Todd Row .20 .50
18 Dean Stock .20 .50
19 Jeffrey Sullivan .20 .50
20 Alex Tanguay 3.00 8.00
21 Didier Tremblay .30 .75
22 Jason Troini .20 .50
23 Dwight Wolfe .20 .50
24 Danny Grant HCO .20 .50
25 Shawn MacKenzie ACO .02 .10
26 Chris McQuaid TR .02 .10
27 Team Photo .20 .50

1997-98 Halifax Mooseheads II

COMPLETE SET (27) 12.00 30.00
1 Checklist .02 .10
2 Frederic Belanger .30 .75
3 Martin Bilodeau .30 .75
4 Marc-Andre Binette .30 .75
5 Alexandre Couture .30 .75
6 Mauro DiPaolo .30 .75
7 Alex Johnstone .30 .75
8 P.J. Lynch .30 .75
9 Joey MacDonald .40 1.00
10 Ali MacEachern .30 .75
11 Boris Majesky .30 .75
12 Billy Manley .30 .75
13 Alexander Mathieu .30 .75
14 Ryan Power .30 .75
15 Stephen Quirk .30 .75
16 Brandon Reid 1.50 4.00
17 A.J.Rivers .30 .75
18 Dean Stock .30 .75
19 Jeffrey Sullivan .30 .75
20 Alex Tanguay 4.00 10.00
21 Jason Troini .30 .75
22 Andrew Warr .30 .75
23 Dwight Wolfe .30 .75
24 Shawn MacKenzie ACO .10 .25
25 Danny Grant HCO .30 .75
26 Hal Mascot .02 .10
27 Alex Tanguay CAN 4.00 10.00
28 Chris McQuad TR .02 .10

1998-99 Halifax Mooseheads

COMPLETE SET (23) 12.00 20.00
1 Alexei Volkov .30 .75
2 Pascal Leclaire .75 2.00
3 Mathieu Paul .20 .50
4 Samuel Seguin .20 .50
5 Billy Manley .20 .50
6 Ladislav Nagy 1.25 3.00
7 Alex Tanguay 1.25 3.00
8 Mike Bray .20 .50
9 Carlyle Lewis .20 .50
10 Frederic Belanger .20 .50
11 David McCutcheon .20 .50
12 Jeff Sullivan .20 .50
13 Alexandre Mathieu .20 .50
14 Jason Troini .20 .50
15 Alex Johnstone .20 .50
16 Ali MacEachern .20 .50
17 Brandon Benedict .20 .50
18 Tyler Reid .20 .50
19 Jasmin Gelinas .20 .50
20 P.J. Lynch .20 .50
21 Mauro DiPaolo .20 .50
22 Brandon Reid .60 1.50
23 Marc-Andre Binette .20 .50
24 Jeff Towriss .20 .50
25 Rocco Anoia .20 .50
26 Daniel Villeneuve .20 .50
27 Alex Tanguay CL .75 2.00

1998-99 Halifax Mooseheads Second Edition

COMPLETE SET (27) 8.00 20.00
1 Tyler Reid .20 .50
2 Jasmin Gelinas .20 .50
3 Hal MASCOT .02 .10
4 Brandon Reid .40 1.00
5 Jeff Sullivan .20 .50
6 Alex Johnstone .20 .50
7 P.J. Lynch .20 .50
8 Mauro Dipaolo .20 .50
9 Marc-andre Binette .20 .50
10 Carlyle Lewis .20 .50
11 David McCutcheon .20 .50
12 Mike Bray .20 .50
13 Samuel Seguin .20 .50
14 Brandon Benedict .20 .50
15 Jason Troini .20 .50
16 Ali MacEachern .20 .50
17 Mathieu Paul .20 .50
18 Alexei Volkov .30 .75
19 Billy Manley .20 .50
20 Frederic Belanger .20 .50
21 Alex Tanguay 1.25 3.00
22 Pascal Leclaire .75 2.00
23 Ladislav Nagy 1.25 3.00
24 Alexandre Mathieu .30 .75
25 World Junior .40 1.00
26 Halifax Radio Team .02 .10
27 Team Card .02 .10

1999-00 Halifax Mooseheads

COMPLETE SET (29) 7.20 18.00
1 Alexei Volkov .40 1.00
2 Pascal Leclaire 2.00 5.00
3 Carlos Sayde .08 .25
4 Joey Dipenta 1.25 3.00
5 Joe Groleau .08 .25
6 Jonathan Boone .08 .25
7 Nick Greenough .08 .25
8 Jason King .08 .25
9 Shawn Lewis .08 .25
10 Ramzi Abid .40 1.00
11 Jonathan St. Louis .08 .25
12 Darrell Jarrett .08 .25
13 Ryan Flinn .60 1.50
14 Robbie Sutherland .08 .25
15 Ali MacEachern .08 .25
16 Brandon Benedict .08 .25
17 Jules-Edy Laraque .40 1.00
18 Jasmin Gelinas .08 .25
19 Hugo Lehoux .08 .25
20 Gary Zinck .08 .25
21 Brandon Reid .75 2.00
22 Benoit Dusablon .40 1.00
23 Hal MASCOT .02 .10
24 Team Photo .08 .25
25 Cover Card 1 .02 .10
26 Cover Card 2 .02 .10
27 Cover Card 3 .02 .10
28 Cover Card 4 .02 .10
29 Cover Card 5 .02 .10

2000-01 Halifax Mooseheads

COMPLETE SET (26) 4.80 12.00
1 Brandon Benedict .15 .40
2 Jonathan Boone .15 .40
3 Michael Couch .15 .40
4 Dany Dallaire .30 .75
5 Bruce Gillis .15 .40
6 Nick Greenough .15 .40
7 Milan Jurcina .40 1.00
8 Derrick Kent .15 .40
9 Jason King .15 .40
10 Sergei Klyazmin .30 .75
11 Sebastien Laprise .15 .40
12 Jules-Edy Laraque .30 .75
13 Pascal Leclaire 1.25 3.00
14 Hugo Lehoux .15 .40
15 Ali MacEachern .15 .40
16 A.J. Maclean .15 .40
17 Ryan MacPherson .15 .40
18 Louis Mandeville .15 .40
19 Conor McGuire .15 .40
20 Jules Saulnier .15 .40
21 Giulio Scandella .15 .40
22 Robbie Sutherland .15 .40
23 Randy Upshall .15 .40
24 Ryan White .15 .40
25 Gary Zinck .15 .40
26 Team CL .01 .05

2001-02 Halifax Mooseheads

COMPLETE SET (26) 6.00 15.00
1 Dany Dallaire .40 1.00
2 Jonathan Boutin .30 .75
3 Milan Jurcina .40 1.00
4 Bobby Clarke .30 .75
5 Sergei Klyazmin .30 .75
6 Francois-Pierre Guenette .30 .75
7 A.J. MacLean .30 .75
8 Bruce Gillis .30 .75
9 Jason King .50 1.25
10 Derrick Kent .30 .75
11 Giulio Scandella .30 .75
12 Jean-Francois Cyr .30 .75
13 Michael Couch .30 .75
14 Robbie Sutherland .30 .75
15 Ryan White .30 .75
16 Randy Upshall .30 .75
17 Patrick Gilbert .30 .75
18 Brandon Benedict .30 .75
19 Marc-Andre Bernier .40 1.00
20 Louis-Philippe Lessard .30 .75
21 Alexandre Picard .30 .75
22 Louis Mandeville .30 .75
23 Action Shot 1 .10 .25
24 Action Shot 2 .10 .25
25 Action Shot 3 .10 .25
26 Checklist .04 .10

2002-03 Halifax Mooseheads

COMPLETE SET (22) 5.00 10.00
1 Chesklist .04 .10
2 Guillaume Lavallee .20 .50
3 Jonathan Boutin .20 .50
4 Milan Jurcina .40 1.00
5 Stuart McRae .20 .50
6 Francois-Pierre Guenette .20 .50
7 A.J. MacLean .20 .50
8 Kyle Doucet .20 .50
9 Thatcher Bell .20 .50
10 Derrick Kent .20 .50
11 Petr Vrana .60 1.50
12 Frederik Cabana .20 .50
13 Jean-Francois Cyr .20 .50
14 Jordie Preston .20 .50
15 George Davis .20 .50
16 Randy Upshall .20 .50
17 Brandon Benedict .20 .50
18 Marc-Andre Bernier .40 1.00
19 Colby MacIntyre .20 .50
20 Jimmy Sharrow .20 .50
21 Alexandre Picard .75 2.00
22 Steve Villeneuve .20 .50

2003-04 Halifax Mooseheads

COMPLETE SET (26) 6.00 15.00
1 Jimmy Sharrow .30 .75
2 Bobby Clarke .30 .75
3 James Pouliot .20 .50
4 Justin Munden .20 .50
5 Evan Jones .20 .50
6 Daniel Sparre .20 .50
7 Petr Vrana .40 1.00
8 George Davis .20 .50
9 Frederik Cabana .20 .50
10 Jared Vokey .20 .50
11 Jan Steber .20 .50
12 Justin Saulnier .20 .50
13 Jason Churchill .30 .75
14 Ryan Moore .20 .50
15 Randy Upshall .20 .50
16 Sebastien Nolet .30 .75
17 Federick Sonier .20 .50
18 Jean-Francois Brault .20 .50
19 Colby MacIntyre .20 .50
20 Franklin MacDonald .20 .50
21 David Brine .20 .50
22 Pierre-Olivier Beaulieu .20 .50
23 Luciano Lomanno .20 .50
24 Kenzie Sheppard .20 .50
NNO Petr Vrana TL .40 1.00
NNO Jimmy Sharrow TL .30 .75

2004-05 Halifax Mooseheads

COMPLETE SET (26) 6.00 15.00
1 Alexandre Picard .40 1.00
2 Bryce Swan .20 .50
3 Daniel Sparre .20 .50
4A David Brine
full cage, X 8.00 20.00
4B David Brine
common version .20 .50
5 Francois-Pierre Guenette .20 .50
6 Franklin MacDonald .20 .50
7 Frederik Cabana .20 .50
8 James Pouliot .20 .50
9 Jan Steber .20 .50
10 Jason Churchill .40 1.00
11 Jean-Francois Brault .20 .50
12 Jeff MacAuley .20 .50
13 Jimmy Sharrow .20 .50
14 Ryan Moore .20 .50
15 Justin Saulnier .20 .50
16 Kenzie Sheppard .20 .50
17 Kevin Cormier .20 .50
18 Luciano Lomanno .20 .50
19 Marc-Andre Bernier .40 1.00
20 Petr Vrana .40 1.00
21 Pierre-Olivier Beaulieu .20 .50
22 Rane Carnegie .30 .75
23 Roger Kennedy .40 1.00
24 Ryan Hillier .20 .50
25 Austin Corredato .20 .50
26 Jeremy Duchesne .40 1.00

2005-06 Halifax Mooseheads

COMPLETE SET (25) 8.00 20.00
1 Jeremy Duchesne .30 .75
2 Roger Kennedy .30 .75
3 Andrew Bodnarchuk .60 1.50
4 Jiri Suchy .30 .75
5 Luciano Lomanno .30 .75
6 Rane Carnegie .30 .75
7 James Pouliot .30 .75
8 Garrett Peters .30 .75
9 Kirk Forrest .30 .75
10 Bryce Swan .30 .75
11 Ryan Hillier .30 .75
12 Justin Saulnier .30 .75
13 Philippe Poirier .30 .75
14 Logan MacMillan .30 .75
15 Daniel Smith .30 .75
16 Ben Macaskill .30 .75
17 Kevin Cormier .30 .75
18 Brent Lynch .30 .75
19 Justin Pender .30 .75
20 Jean-Francois Brault .30 .75
21 Mikhail Aseev .30 .75
22 Franklin MacDonald .30 .75
23 David Brine .30 .75
24 Yuri Cheremetiev .30 .75
25 Frederik Cabana .30 .75

2006-07 Halifax Mooseheads

COMPLETE SET (21) 10.00 18.00
1 Jeremy Duchesne .40 1.00
2 Andrew Bodnarchuk .40 1.00
3 Roger Kennedy .40 1.00
4 Jiri Suchy .30 .75
5 Luciano Lomanno .30 .75
6 Ryan Seymour .30 .75
7 James Pouliot .30 .75
8 Garrett Peters .30 .75
9 Logan Macmillan .30 .75
10 Benjamin Chaisson .30 .75
11 Daniel Smith .30 .75
12 Bryce Swan .30 .75
13 Ryan Hillier .30 .75
14 Jakub Voracek 1.25 3.00
15 Andrew White .30 .75
16 Justin Pender .30 .75
17 Ben Macaskill .30 .75
18 Gabriel O'Connor .30 .75
19 Colby Pridham .30 .75
20 Yuri Cheremetiev .30 .75
21 Eric Louis-Seize .30 .75

2015-16 Halifax Mooseheads

COMPLETE SET (24) 6.00 15.00
1 Domenico Argento .30 .75
2 Kelly Bent .30 .75
3 Joel Bishop .30 .75
4 Dominik Blain-Dupuis .30 .75
5 Eric Brassard .30 .75
6 Brett Crossley .30 .75
7 Barrett Dachyshyn .30 .75
8 Cody Donaghey .30 .75
9 Arnaud Durandeau .30 .75
10 Cavan Fitzgerald .30 .75
11 Walter Flower .30 .75
12 Taylor Ford .30 .75
13 Maxime Fortier .30 .75
14 Cooper Jones .30 .75
15 Timo Meier .30 .75
16 Connor Moynihan .30 .75
17 Danny Moynihan .30 .75
18 Morgan Nauss .30 .75
19 Ilya Putintsev .30 .75
20 Kevin Resop .30 .75
21 Andrew Shewfelt .30 .75
22 Otto Somppi .30 .75
23 Jean-Sebastien Taillefer .30 .75
24 Vincent Watt .30 .75

1975-76 Hamilton Fincups

COMPLETE SET (18) 15.00 30.00
1 Jack Anderson .75 1.50
2 Mike Clarke .75 1.50
3 Greg Clause .75 1.50
4 Joe Contini .75 1.50
5 Mike Fedorko .75 1.50
6 Paul Foley .75 1.50
7 Greg Hickey .75 1.50
8 Tony Horvath .75 1.50
9 Mike Keating .75 1.50
10 Archie King .75 1.50
11 Ted Long .75 1.50
12 Dale McCourt 2.50 5.00
13 Dave Norris .75 1.50
14 Greg Redquest .75 1.50
15 Glen Richardson .75 1.50
16 Ron Roscoe .75 1.50
17 Ric Seiling 1.25 2.50
18 Danny Shearer .75 1.50

1999-00 Hamilton Bulldogs

COMPLETE SET (25) 4.00 10.00
1 Mike Minard .30 .75
2 Chris Hajt .15 .40
3 Brad Norton .15 .40
4 Walt Kyle CO .08 .25
5 Eric Houde .15 .40
6 Kevin Bolibruck .15 .40
7 Daniel Cleary .20 .50
8 Vladimir Vorobiev .20 .50
9 Dan LaCouture .20 .50
10 Brian Swanson .20 .50
11 Martin Laitre .15 .40
12 Peter Sarno .40 1.00
13 Alex Zhurik .15 .40
14 Chad Hinz .15 .40
15 Kevin Brown .15 .40
16 Matthieu Descoteaux .15 .40
17 Jason Chimera .40 1.00
18 Alex Henry .30 .75
19 Sean Selmser .20 .50
20 Ryan Risidore .15 .40
21 Michel Riesen .30 .75
22 Sergei Yerkovich .15 .40
23 Elias Abrahamsson .15 .40
24 Eric Heffler .15 .40
25 Bruiser MASCOT .08 .25

2000-01 Hamilton Bulldogs

COMPLETE SET (28) 5.00 12.00
1 Chris Madden .30 .75
2 Terran Sandwith .15 .40
3 Ryan Risidore .15 .40
4 Kurt Drummond .15 .40
5 Chris Hajt .15 .40
6 Brad Norton .15 .40
7 Maxim Spiridonov .15 .40
8 Patrick Cote .30 .75
9 Alex Henry .30 .75
10 Paul Healey .15 .40
11 Jason Chimera .40 1.00
12 Peter Sarno .30 .75
13 Brian Urick .15 .40
14 Michael Henrich .30 .75
15 Brian Swanson .20 .50
16 Martin Laitre .15 .40
17 Chris Albert .15 .40
18 Fernando Pisani .40 1.00
19 Lloyd Shaw .15 .40
20 Scott Ferguson .15 .40
21 Michel Riesen .20 .50
22 Alain Nasreddine .15 .40
23 Chad Hinz .15 .40
24 Joaquin Gage .30 .75
25 Claude Julien CO .10 .25
26 Morey Gare CO .10 .25
27 Bruiser MASCOT .04 .10
28 Team CL .01 .05

2001-02 Hamilton Bulldogs

COMPLETE SET (26) 4.80 12.00
1 Ales Pisa .20 .50
2 Chris Hajt .20 .50
3 Alex Henry .30 .75
4 Jan Horacek .20 .50
5 Kevin Brown .20 .50
6 Jason Chimera .40 1.00
7 Peter Sarno .20 .50
8 Craig Reichert .20 .50
9 Greg Leeb .20 .50
10 Marc-Andre Bergeron .20 .50
11 Brian Swanson .20 .50
12 Jani Rita .40 1.00
13 Fernando Pisani .20 .50
14 Michael Henrich .20 .50
15 Sean Selmser .20 .50
16 Ty Conklin .40 1.00
17 Alain Nasreddine .20 .50
18 Alexei Semenov .30 .75
19 Adam Dewan .20 .50
20 Marc Lamothe .30 .75
21 Sven Butenschon .20 .50
22 Chad Hinz .20 .50
23 Claude Julien CO .04 .10
24 Geoff Ward ACO .04 .10

25 Bruiser Mascot .04 .10
NNO Title Card
CL .04 .10

2002-03 Hamilton Bulldogs

COMPLETE SET (28) 8.00 20.00
1 Bobby Allen .20 .50
2 Ben Carpentier .20 .50
3 Ron Hainsey .40 1.00
4 Tony Salmelainen .20 .50
5 Chad Hinz .20 .50
6 Nate DiCasmirro .20 .50
7 Tomas Plekanec .40 1.00
8 Jason Ward .30 .75
9 Jarret Stoll .40 1.00
10 Matt O'Dette .20 .50
11 Marc-Andre Bergeron .20 .50
12 Jani Rita .30 .75
13 Francois Beauchemin .40 1.00
14 Fernando Pisani .30 .75
15 Michael Ryder 1.25 3.00
16 Michael Henrich .20 .50
17 Ty Conklin .30 .75
18 Eric Fichaud .30 .75
19 Alexei Semenov .20 .50
20 Adam Dewan .20 .50
21 Mathieu Garon .40 1.00
22 Benoit Gratton .20 .50
23 Francois Bouillon .30 .75
24 Mike Komisarek .30 .75
25 Jozef Balej .40 1.00
26 Marcel Hossa .40 1.00
27 Bruiser MASCOT .04 .10
28 Checklist .04 .10

2004-05 Hamilton Bulldogs

COMPLETE SET (30) 8.00 20.00
1 Andrew Archer .20 .50
2 Ben Carpentier .20 .50
3 JP Cote .20 .50
4 Trevor Daley .20 .50
5 Yann Danis .60 1.50
6 Benoit Dusablon .20 .50
7 Dan Ellis .60 1.50
8 Jonathan Ferland .20 .50
9 Dan Focht .20 .50
10 Ron Hainsey .40 1.00
11 Chris Higgins .40 1.00
12 Raitis Ivanans .20 .50
13 Dan Jancevski .20 .50
14 Doug Jarvis CO .20 .50
15 Andrei Kostitsyn 1.00 2.50
16 Michael Lambert .20 .50
17 Christian Larrivee .20 .50
18 Corey Locke .20 .50
19 Antti Miettinen .40 1.00
20 Duncan Milroy .20 .50
21 Gavin Morgan .20 .50
22 Steve Ott .60 1.50
23 Tomas Plekanec .40 1.00
24 Philippe Plante .20 .50
25 James Sanford .20 .50
26 Matt Shasby .20 .50
27 Marc-Andre Thinel .30 .75
28 Jason Ward .30 .75
29 Ron Wilson ACO .20 .50
30 Bruiser MASCOT .04 .10

2005-06 Hamilton Bulldogs

COMPLETE SET 6.00 15.00
1 Jonathan Aitken .20 .50
2 Andrew Archer .20 .50
3 Ryan Barnes .20 .50
4 Andre Benoit .20 .50
5 Jean-Philippe Cote .20 .50
6 Yann Danis .40 1.00
7 Jeff Drouin-Deslauriers .40 1.00
8 Jonathan Ferland .20 .50
9 Ron Hainsey .20 .50
10 Raitis Ivanans .40 1.00
11 Jean-Francois Jacques .20 .50
12 Andrei Kostitsyn .40 1.00
13 Michael Lambert .20 .50
14 Maxim Lapierre .20 .50
15 Francis Lemieux .20 .50
16 Corey Locke .20 .50
17 Olivier Michaud .40 1.00
18 Duncan Milroy .20 .50
19 Garth Murray .20 .50
20 Jeff Paul .20 .50
21 Marc-Antoine Pouliot .40 1.00
22 Mathieu Roy .75 2.00
23 James Sanford .20 .50
24 Dan Smith .20 .50
25 Danny Syvret .20 .50
26 Peter Vandermeer .40 1.00
27 Brad Winchester .20 .50
28 Don Lever .02 .10
9 Ron Wilson .02 .10
0 Bruiser .02 .10

2006-07 Hamilton Bulldogs

COMPLETE SET (26) 8.00 15.00
Andrew Archer .20 .50
Mathieu Aubin .20 .50
Ajay Baines .20 .50
Andre Benoit .20 .50
Kyle Chipchura .30 .75
Jean-Philippe Cote .20 .50
Matt D'Agostini .20 .50
Yann Danis .30 .75
Eric Manlow .20 .50
Jonathan Ferland .20 .50
Jon Gleed .20 .50
Mikhail Grabovsky .20 .50
Danny Groulx .20 .50
Jaroslav Halak .75 2.00
Dan Jancevski .20 .50
Andrei Kostitsyn .40 1.00
Michael Lambert .20 .50
Maxim Lapierre .30 .75
Francis Lemieux .20 .50
Corey Locke .20 .50
Duncan Milroy .20 .50
Ryan O'Byrne .20 .50
Mathieu Roy .40 1.00

24 Zach Stortini .40 1.00
25 Patrick Traverse .20 .50
26 Cory Urquhart .20 .50

2013-14 Hamilton Bulldogs

COMPLETE SET () 6.00 15.00
1 Greg Pateryn .30 .75
2 Jarred Tinordi .30 .75
3 Darren Dietz .30 .75
4 Nathan Beaulieu .30 .75
5 Justin Courtnall .30 .75
6 Nathan McIver .30 .75
7 Maxime Macenauer .30 .75
8 Mike Blunden .30 .75
9 Louis Leblanc .30 .75
10 Drew Schiestel .30 .75
11 Joonas Nattinen .30 .75
12 Jordan Owens .30 .75
13 Sven Andrighetto .30 .75
14 Robert Mayer .30 .75
15 Dustin Tokarski .30 .75
16 Patrick Holland .30 .75
17 Gabriel Dumont .30 .75
18 Morgan Ellis .30 .75
19 Stefan Fournier .30 .75
20 Joel Chouinard .30 .75
21 Nick Tarnasky .30 .75
22 Christian Thomas .30 .75
23 Martin St. Pierre .30 .75

2014-15 Hamilton Bulldogs

COMPLETE SET (25) 8.00 20.00
1 Gabriel Dumont .40 1.00
2 Joey MacDonald .30 .75
3 Magnus Nygren .30 .75
4 Michael Bournival .40 1.00
5 Sven Andrighetto .40 1.00
6 Joe Finley .30 .75
7 Eric Tangradi .40 1.00
8 Jack Nevins .30 .75
9 Connor Crisp .30 .75
10 Nick Sorkin .30 .75
11 Jacob De La Rose .75 2.00
12 Christian Thomas .30 .75
13 Jake Dowell .30 .75
14 T.J. Hensick .30 .75
15 Drayson Bowman .30 .75
16 Maxime Macenauer .30 .75
17 Daniel Carr .30 .75
18 Charles Hudon .30 .75
19 Mac Bennett .30 .75
20 Nathan Beaulieu .50 1.25
21 Darren Dietz .30 .75
22 Jarred Tinordi .40 1.00
23 Davis Drewiske .30 .75
24 Greg Pateryn .30 .75
25 Mike Condon .40 1.00

1992-93 Hamilton Canucks

COMPLETE SET (30) 4.00 10.00
1 Shawn Antoski .30 .75
2 Robin Bawa .15 .40
3 Jamie Carlson TR .02 .10
4 Jassen Cullimore .20 .50
5 Alain Deeks .15 .40
6 Neil Eisenhut .15 .40
7 Mike Fountain .30 .75
8 Troy Gamble .30 .75
9 Jason Herter .15 .40
10 Pat Hickey PR .02 .10
11 Dane Jackson .15 .40
12 Dan Kesa .15 .40
13 Jeff Lumby ANN .02 .10
14 Mario Marois UER
Last name misspelled
Marios on back .20 .50
15 Bob Mason .30 .75
16 Mike Maurice .15 .40
17 Jay Mazur .15 .40
18 Jack McIlhargey CO .02 .10
19 Sandy Moger .30 .75
20 Stephane Morin .15 .40
21 Eric Murano .15 .40
22 Troy Neumeier .15 .40
23 Matt Newsom GM .02 .10
24 Libor Polasek .15 .40
25 Phil von Stefenelli .15 .40
26 Doug Torrel .15 .40
27 Doug Tretiak TR .02 .10
28 Rick Vaive CO .15 .40
29 Opening Night
Puck-Drop
Mario Marois
Pat Hickey .15 .40
30 Team Photo
(Checklist) .20 .50

1961-62 Hamilton Red Wings

COMPLETE SET (21) 37.50 75.00
1 Bud Blom 1.50 3.00
2 Eddie Bush 2.00 4.00
3 Bob Dean 1.50 3.00
4 John Gofton 1.50 3.00
5 Bob Hamilton 1.50 3.00
6 Bob Hamilton 1.50 3.00
7 Ron Harris 2.00 4.00
8 Earl Heiskala 2.00 4.00
9 Paul Henderson 7.50 15.00
10 Roger Lafreniere 1.50 3.00
11 Lowell Macdonald 4.00 8.00
12 Pit Martin 5.00 10.00
13 Jim Mclellan 1.50 3.00
14 Harvey Meisenheimer 1.50 3.00
15 Howie Menard 1.50 3.00
16 Wayne Rivers 4.00 8.00
17 Jim Peters 2.00 4.00
18 Bob Wall 1.50 3.00
19 Jack Wildfong 1.50 3.00
20 Terry Urkewicz 1.50 3.00
21 Larry Zilliotto 1.50 3.00

1989-90 Hampton Roads Admirals

COMPLETE SET (21) 4.00 400.00
1A Mike Black 8.00 20.00
1H Mike Black 8.00 20.00
2 John Brophy CO 10.00 25.00
3A David Buckley 8.00 20.00
3H David Buckley 8.00 20.00
4A Pat Cavanagh 8.00 20.00
4H Pat Cavanagh 8.00 20.00
5A Mike Flanagan 8.00 20.00
5H Mike Flanagan 8.00 20.00
6A Frank Furlan 8.00 20.00
6H Frank Furlan 8.00 20.00
7A Don Gagne 8.00 20.00
7H Don Gagne 8.00 20.00
8A Steve Greenberg 8.00 20.00
8H Steve Greenberg 8.00 20.00
9A Murray Hood 8.00 20.00
9H Murray Hood 8.00 20.00
10A Trevor Jobe 8.00 20.00
10H Trevor Jobe 8.00 20.00
11A Trevor Kruger 8.00 20.00
11H Trevor Kruger 8.00 20.00
12A Chris Lukey 8.00 20.00
12H Chris Lukey 8.00 20.00
13A Brian Martin 8.00 20.00
13H Brian Martin 8.00 20.00
14A Dennis McEwen 8.00 20.00
14H Dennis McEwen 8.00 20.00
15A Bobby McGrath 8.00 20.00
15H Bobby McGrath 8.00 20.00
16A Darren Miciak 8.00 20.00
16H Darren Miciak 8.00 20.00
17A Al Murphy 8.00 20.00
17H Al Murphy 8.00 20.00
18A Jody Praznik 8.00 20.00
18H Jody Praznik 8.00 20.00
19A Alain Raymond 8.00 20.00
19H Alain Raymond 8.00 20.00
20A Wayne Stripp 8.00 20.00
20H Wayne Stripp 8.00 20.00
21 Scott Taylor 8.00 20.00

1990-91 Hampton Roads Admirals

COMPLETE SET (20) 3.00 8.00
41 Scott King .20 .50
42 Greg Bignell .15 .40
43 David Buckley .15 .40
44 Jody Praznik .15 .40
45 John East .15 .40
46 Steve Greenberg .15 .40
47 Darcy Kaminski .15 .40
48 Glen Kehrer .15 .40
49 Murray Hood .15 .40
50 Dennis McEwen .15 .40
51 Billy Nolan .15 .40
52 Bill Thomas .15 .40
53 Pat Cavanagh .15 .40
54 Cory Banika .20 .50
55 Al Murphy .15 .40
56 Harry Mews .15 .40
57 Mark Bernard .15 .40
58 Brian Martin .15 .40
59 Curt Brackenbury ACO .08 .25
60 John Brophy CO .15 .40

1991-92 Hampton Roads Admirals

COMPLETE SET (20) 4.00 50.00
1 Mark Bernard 1.25 3.00
2 Mike Chighisola .75 2.00
3 John East .75 2.00
4 Victor Gervais .75 2.00
5 Murray Hood .75 2.00
6 Scott Johnson .75 2.00
7 Olaf Kolzig 6.00 15.00
8 Paul Krepelka .75 2.00
9 Al MacIsaac .75 2.00
10 Brian Martin .75 2.00
11 Dennis McEwen .75 2.00
12 Dave Morissette .75 2.00
13 Billy Nolan .75 2.00
14 Randy Pearce .75 2.00
15 Steve Poapst 1.25 3.00
16 Pete Siciliano .75 2.00
17 Shawn Snesar .75 2.00
18 Keith Whitmore .75 2.00
19 John Brophy CO .40 1.00
20 Darcy Kaminski ACO .02 .10

1992-93 Hampton Roads Admirals

COMPLETE SET (20) 3.00 8.00
1 Shawn Snesar .20 .50
2 Paul Krepelka .20 .50
3 Claude Barthe .20 .50
4 Steve Poapst .30 .75
5 Kelly Sorenson .20 .50
6 Trevor Duhaime .20 .50
7 Steve Mirabile .20 .50
8 Kurt Kabat .20 .50
9 Victor Gervais .25 .60
10 Jason Rathbone .20 .50
11 Rod Taylor .20 .50
12 Al MacIsaac CO .08 .25
13 Brian Martin .20 .50
14 Dave Morissette .20 .50
15 Harry Mews .20 .50
16 Mark Bernard .20 .50
17 Nick Vitucci .30 .75
18 Steve Martell .20 .50
19 Chris Scarlata TR .02 .10
20 John Brophy CO .20 .50

1993-94 Hampton Roads Admirals

COMPLETE SET (20) 3.00 8.00
1 John Brophy CO .20 .50
2 Rick Burrill TR .02 .10
3 Daniel Chaput .20 .50
4 Brendan Curley .20 .50
5 Victor Gervais .20 .50
6 Brian Goudie .20 .50
7 Shamus Gregga .20 .50
8 Jason MacIntyre .20 .50
9 Al MacIsaac ACO .02 .10
10 Kevin Malgunas .20 .50
11 Dennis McEwen .20 .50
12 Mark Michaud .20 .50
13 Ron Pascucci .20 .50
14 Darren Perkins .20 .50
15 Steven Perkovic .20 .50
16 Shawn Snesar .20 .50
17 Kelly Sorenson .20 .50
18 Rod Taylor .20 .50
19 Richie Walcott .20 .50
20 Shawn Wheeler .20 .50

1994-95 Hampton Roads Admirals

COMPLETE SET (23) 4.80 12.00
1 John Brophy CO .20 .50
2 Al MacIsaac ACO .02 .10
3 Patrick Lalime 2.00 5.00
4 Colin Gregor .15 .40
5 Ron Pascucci .15 .40
6 John Porco .15 .40
7 Trevor Halverson .20 .50
8 Rod Taylor .15 .40
9 Brian Goudie .15 .40
10 Chris Phelps .15 .40
11 Tom Menicci .15 .40
12 Anthony MacAulay .15 .40
13 Rick Kowalsky .15 .40
14 Dennis McEwen .15 .40
15 Kelly Sorenson .15 .40
16 Brendan Curley .15 .40
17 Jason MacIntyre .15 .40
18 Jim Brown .15 .40
19 Matt Mallgrave .15 .40
20 Ron Majic .15 .40
21 Corwin Saurdiff .15 .40
22 Rick Burrill TR .02 .10
23 Team Photo CL .15 .40
NNO Logo Card .02 .10

1995-96 Hampton Roads Admirals

COMPLETE SET (25) 4.00 10.00
1 Team Photo .15 .40
2 John Brophy CO .15 .40
3 Al MacIsaac ACO .02 .10
4 Darryl Paquette .20 .50
5 Mark Bernard .15 .40
6 Ron Pascucci .15 .40
7 Dominic Maltais .15 .40
8 Jason MacIntyre .15 .40
9 Serge Aubin .40 1.00
10 Rick Kowalsky .08 .25
11 Claude Fillion .20 .50
12 Rod Taylor .15 .40
13 Alexei Krivchenkov .15 .40
14 David St. Pierre .15 .40
15 Steve Richards .15 .40
16 Trevor Halverson .30 .75
17 Chris Phelps .15 .40
18 Jeff Kostuch .15 .40
19 Sean Selmser .30 .75
20 Aaron Downey .40 1.00
21 Bob Woods .15 .40
22 Sergei Voronov .15 .40
23 Corwin Saurdiff .20 .50
24 Rick Burrell TR .02 .10
25 Gary Mansfield EQMG .02 .10

1997-98 Hampton Roads Admirals

COMPLETE SET (24) 7.20 18.00
1 Chad Ackerman .30 .75
2 Alexander Alexeev .30 .75
3 Rob Bonneau .30 .75
4 Dan Carney .30 .75
5 Dan Ceman .40 1.00
6 Sebastien Charpentier .40 1.00
7 Marty Clapton .30 .75
8 Victor Gervais .30 .75
9 Alexander Kharlamov .40 1.00
10 Rick Kowalsky .30 .75
11 Mike Larkin .30 .75
12 Bill Lincoln .30 .75
13 Ron Majic .30 .75
14 Jason Mansoff .30 .75
15 Chris Phelps .30 .75
16 Joel Poirier .30 .75
17 Jason Saal .60 1.50
18 Kayle Short .30 .75
19 Rod Taylor .30 .75
20 Joel Theriault .30 .75
21 Yuri Yuresko .30 .75
22 John Brophy HCO .20 .50
23 Al MacIsaac ACO .02 .10
24 Trainers .02 .10

1996-97 Hampton Roads Admirals

COMPLETE SET (25) 4.00 10.00
HRA1 Darryl Paquette .20 .50
HRA2 Mike Larkin .15 .40
HRA3 Chris Phelps .15 .40
HRA4 Alex Alexeev .15 .40
HRA5 Joel Theriault .15 .40
HRA6 Neal Martin .15 .40
HRA7 Ryan Mulhern .15 .40
HRA8 Darryl Shedden .15 .40
HRA9 Victor Gervais .15 .40
HRA10 Rod Taylor .15 .40
HRA11 Andy Weidenbach .15 .40
HRA12 Alain Savage .15 .40
HRA13 Randy Pearce .15 .40
HRA14 Chad Ackerman .15 .40
HRA15 Alexei Krivchenkov .15 .40
HRA16 Rick Kowalsky .15 .40
HRA17 Dominic Maltais .15 .40
HRA18 Joel Poirier .20 .50
HRA19 Marc Seliger .30 .75
HRA20 Aaron Downey .30 .75
HRA21 John Brophy CO .20 .50
HRA22 Al MacIsaac ACO .02 .10
HRA23 G.Mansfield EQMG
K.Bender TR .02 .10
HRA24 Salty (Mascot) .02 .10
NNO Team Photo .15 .40

1998-99 Hampton Roads Admirals

COMPLETE SET (26) 6.00 15.00
1 Mascot
Checklist .08 .25
2 John Brophy .20 .50
3 Al MacIsaac ACO .08 .25
4 Chris Phelps .20 .50
5 Trevor Johnson .20 .50
6 Jami Yoder .20 .50
7 Joel Poirier .30 .75
8 Alexander Kharlamov .30 .75
9 Bobby Russell .20 .50
10 Trever Fraser .20 .50
11 Jason Deleurme .20 .50
12 Henry Higdon .20 .50
13 Rod Taylor .20 .50
14 Jeff Corbett .20 .50
15 Derek Ernest .20 .50
16 Charlie Retter .20 .50
17 Chad Ackerman .20 .50
18 Boris Zelenko .20 .50
19 Dan Ceman .30 .75
20 Marty Clapton .20 .50
21 Milt Mastad .20 .50
22 Dominic Maltais .30 .75
23 Stephen Valiquette .75 2.00
24 Jason Saal .40 1.00
25 Stu Bender TR .08 .25
25 Scott Boggs EM .08 .25

1998-99 Hampton Roads Admirals 10th Anniversary

COMPLETE SET (30) 10.00 25.00
1 John Brophy HCO .20 .50
2 Rod Taylor .20 .50
3 Victor Gervais .20 .50
4 Brian Martin .20 .50
5 Dennis McEwen .20 .50
6 Chris Phelps .20 .50
7 Randy Pearce .20 .50
8 Murray Hood .20 .50
9 Olaf Kolzig 2.00 5.00
10 Kelly Sorenson .20 .50
11 Mark Bernard .20 .50
12 Andrew Brunette .40 1.00
13 Trevor Halverson .20 .50
14 Rick Kowalsky .20 .50
15 Aaron Downey .75 2.00
16 Patrick Lalime 1.50 4.00
17 Steve Poapst .30 .75
18 Alexander Alexeev .20 .50
19 Harry Mews .20 .50
20 Al MacIsaac .20 .50
21 John Parco .20 .50
22 Kent Hawley .20 .50
23 Dave Flanagan .20 .50
24 Billy Nolan .20 .50
25 Brendan Curley .20 .50
26 Ron Pascucci .20 .50
27 Mark Michaud .20 .50
28 Shawn Snesar .20 .50
29 Byron Dafoe 1.25 3.00
30 Sebastien Charpentier .40 1.00

1999-00 Hampton Roads Admirals

COMPLETE SET (25) 8.00 20.00
1 Chad Ackerman .30 .75
2 Gerad Adams .30 .75
3 Louis Bedard .40 1.00
4 Brad Church .40 1.00
5 Marty Clapton .30 .75
6 Curtis Cruickshank .40 1.00
7 Derek Ernest .30 .75
8 Ryan Gillis .30 .75
9 Trevor Johnson .30 .75
10 Rick Kowalsky .30 .75
11 Jan Lasak 1.25 3.00
12 Dominic Maltais .40 1.00
13 Mike Omicioli .30 .75
14 John Parco .30 .75
15 Dwight Parrish .30 .75
16 Colin Pepperall .30 .75
17 Richard Pitirri .30 .75
18 Bobby Russell .30 .75
19 Mike Siklenka .30 .75
20 Dean Stork .30 .75
21 Rod Taylor .30 .75
22 John Brophy CO .08 .25
23 Al MacIsaac CO .08 .25
24 Stu Bender
Scott Boggs TR .08 .25
NNO Checklist .08 .25

1997-98 Hartford Wolf Pack

COMPLETE SET (29) 12.00 35.00
1 Derek Armstrong .40 1.00
2 Sylvain Blouin .60 1.50
3 Eric Cairns .60 1.50
4 Dan Cloutier 1.50 4.00
5 Christian Dube .40 1.00
6 Peter Ferraro .60 1.50
7 Maxim Galanov .40 1.00
8 Ken Gernander .40 1.00
9 Daniel Goneau .40 1.00
10 Todd Hall .40 1.00
11 Johan Lindbom .40 1.00
12 Mike Martin .40 1.00
13 Jason Muzzatti .60 1.50
14 Dale Purinton .75 2.00
15 Marc Savard .75 2.00
16 Pierre Sevigny .40 1.00
17 Adam Smith .40 1.00
18 Geoff Smith .40 1.00
19 Brad Smyth .40 1.00
20 Lee Sorochan .40 1.00
21 Robb Stauber .60 1.50
22 P.J. Stock 1.50 4.00
23 Ronnie Sundin .40 1.00
24 Tim Sweeney .40 1.00
25 Brent Thompson .40 1.00
26 Ryan VandenBussche .75 2.00
27 Vladimir Vorobiev .40 1.00
28 Chris Winnes .40 1.00
29 Sonar MASCOT .08 .25

1998-99 Hartford Wolf Pack

COMPLETE SET (28) 14.00 35.00
1 Derek Armstrong .40 1.00
2 Jeff Brown .40 1.00
3 Ed Campbell .40 1.00
4 Ben Carpentier .40 1.00
5 Christian Dube .40 1.00
6 Bob Errey .40 1.00
7 Jeff Finley .40 1.00
8 Ken Gernander .40 1.00
9 Daniel Goneau .40 1.00
10 Todd Hall .40 1.00
11 Boyd Kane .75 2.00
12 Jean-Francois Labbe .75 2.00
13 Mike Martin .40 1.00
14 Dale Purinton .60 1.50
15 Ryan Risidore .40 1.00
16 Marc Savard .75 2.00
17 Adam Smith .40 1.00
18 Lee Sorochan .60 1.50
19 P.J. Stock 3.00 8.00
20 Brent Thompson .40 1.00
21 Alexei Vasiliev .40 1.00
22 Vladimir Vorobiev .40 1.00
23 Kay Whitmore .60 1.50
24 Chris Winnes .40 1.00
25 Johan Witehall .40 1.00
26 Sonar MASCOT .08 .25
27 Rich Brennan .40 1.00
28 Stefan Cherneski .40 1.00

1999-00 Hartford Wolf Pack

COMPLETE SET (23) 12.00 30.00
1 Derek Armstrong .40 1.00
2 Drew Bannister .40 1.00
3 Ben Carpentier .40 1.00
4 Stefan Cherneski .40 1.00
5 Jason Doig .60 1.50
6 Francois Fortier .40 1.00
7 Ken Gernander .40 1.00
8 Daniel Goneau .40 1.00
9 Todd Hall .40 1.00
10 Mike Harder .40 1.00
11 Burke Henry .40 1.00
12 Milan Hnilicka 1.50 4.00
13 Chris Kenady .40 1.00
14 Tomas Kloucek .75 2.00
15 Alexander Korobolin .40 1.00
16 Jean-Francois Labbe .75 2.00
17 Dale Purinton .75 2.00
18 Brad Smyth .60 1.50
19 P.J. Stock 1.25 3.00
20 Tony Tuzzolino .60 1.50
21 Alexei Vasiliev .40 1.00
22 Terry Virtue .60 1.50
23 Johan Witehall .60 1.50

2000-01 Hartford Wolf Pack

COMPLETE SET (29) 10.00 25.00
1 Derek Armstrong .30 .75
2 Drew Bannister .30 .75
3 Ryan Bast .30 .75
4 Ben Carpentier .30 .75
5 Jason Dawe .30 .75
6 Brandon Dietrich .30 .75
7 Jason Doig .30 .75
8 Dave Duerden .30 .75
9 Ken Gernander .30 .75
10 Michal Grosek .30 1.00
11 Todd Hall .30 .75
12 Burke Henry .30 .75
13 Johan Holmqvist .80 2.00
14 Boyd Kane .40 1.00
15 Chris Kenady .30 .75
16 Tomas Kloucek .80 2.00
17 Jason Labarbera .80 2.00
18 Manny Malhotra .60 1.00
19 Brad Mehalko .30 .75
20 Mike Mottau .60 1.50
21 Dale Purinton .40 1.00
22 Bert Robertsson .30 .75
23 Richard Scott .40 1.00
24 Brad Smyth .30 .75
25 Tony Tuzzolino .30 .75
26 Jeff Ulmer .30 .75
27 Terry Virtue .40 1.00
28 Vitali Yeremeyev .60 1.50
29 Sonar MASCOT .10 .25

2001-02 Hartford Wolf Pack

COMPLETE SET (26) 20.00 40.00
1 Benoit Dusablon .75 2.00
2 Jason Dawe .75 2.00
3 Rico Fata .75 2.00
4 Sean Gagnon .75 2.00
5 Ken Gernander .40 1.00
6 Christian Gosselin .40 1.00
7 Michal Grosek .40 1.00
8 Barrett Heisten .75 2.00
9 Johan Holmqvist .75 2.00
10 Wes Jarvis .40 1.00
11 Boyd Kane .75 2.00
12 Matt Kinch .40 1.00
13 Jason Labarbera .75 2.00
14 Jamie Lundmark 3.00 8.00
15 Dave MacIsaac .40 1.00
16 Brad Mehalko .40 1.00
17 Scott Meyer .40 1.00
18 Mike Mottau 1.25 3.00
19 Cam Severson .40 1.00
20 Peter Smrek .75 2.00
21 Brad Smyth .40 1.00
22 Chris St. Croix .40 1.00
23 John Tripp .40 1.00
24 Igor Ulanov 3.00 8.00
25 Terry Virtue .75 2.00
26 Sonar MASCOT .20 .50

2002-03 Hartford Wolf Pack

COMPLETE SET (30) 12.00 30.00
1 Bobby Andrews .40 1.00
2 Dean Arsene .40 1.00
3 Patrick Aufiero .40 1.00
4 Ryan Bast .40 1.00
5 Garrett Burnett .40 1.00
6 Ted Donato .40 1.00
7 Benoit Dusablon .75 2.00
8 Nils Ekman .40 1.00
9 Ken Gernander .40 1.00
10 Johan Holmqvist .75 2.00
11 Dave Karpa .40 1.00
12 Matt Kinch .40 1.00
13 Jason Labarbera .75 2.00
14 Bryce Lampman .40 1.00
15 Cory Larose .40 1.00
16 Janne Laukkanen .40 1.00
17 Roman Lyashenko .40 1.00
18 Garth Murray .40 1.00
19 Chris Pittman .40 1.00
20 Richard Scott .40 1.00
21 Billy Tibbetts 1.25 3.00
22 John Tripp .40 1.00
23 Layne Ulmer .40 1.00
24 Dixon Ward .40 1.00
25 Mike Wilson .40 1.00
26 Patrick Yetman .40 1.00
27 Damon Scott ANN .04 .10
28 Nick Fotiu ACO .20 .50
29 Ryan McGill HCO .20 .50
30 Sonar Mascot .04 .10

2003-04 Hartford Wolf Pack

COMPLETE SET (27) 25.00 50.00
1 Bobby Andrews .40 1.00
2 Brandon Cullen .40 1.00
3 Ryan Cuthbert .40 1.00
4 Benoit Dusablon .75 2.00
5 Jayme Filipowicz .40 1.00
6 Ken Gernander .40 1.00
7 Paul Healey .40 1.00
8 Jeff Heerema .75 2.00
9 John Jakopin .40 1.00
10 Matt Kinch .40 1.00
11 Jason Labarbera 1.25 3.00
12 Bryce Lampman .40 1.00
13 Cory Larose .40 1.00
14 Lucas Lawson .40 1.00
15 Jason MacDonald .40 1.00
16 Dominic Moore SP 4.00 10.00
17 Garth Murray .60 1.50
18 Lawrence Nycholat .40 1.00
19 Phil Osaer .40 1.00
20 Jamie Pushor SP 4.00 10.00
21 Richard Scott .75 2.00
22 Juris Stals .40 1.00
23 Jeff State .40 1.00
24 Fedor Tyutin 1.25 3.00
25 Layne Ulmer .60 1.50
26 Craig Weller .40 1.00
27 Chad Wiseman .40 1.00

2004-05 Hartford Wolf Pack

COMPLETE SET (26) 30.00 60.00
1 Jozef Balej 1.25 3.00
2 Blair Betts .75 2.00
3 Ken Gernander .75 2.00
4 Trevor Gillies 1.25 3.00
5 Alexandre Giroux 1.25 3.00
6 Martin Grenier .75 2.00
7 Jeff Hamilton .75 2.00
8 Dwight Helminen .75 2.00
9 Ryan Hollweg 1.25 3.00
10 Jason Labarbera 1.25 3.00
11 Bryce Lampman .75 2.00
12 Lucas Lofton .75 2.00
13 Dave Liffiton .75 2.00
14 Jamie Lundmark 1.25 3.00
15 Steven MacIntyre .75 2.00
16 Jeff MacMillan .75 2.00
17 Dominic Moore .75 2.00
18 Garth Murray .75 2.00
19 Lawrence Nycholat .75 2.00
20 Jed Ortmeyer 1.25 3.00
21 Thomas Pock 1.25 3.00
22 Jake Taylor .75 2.00
23 Layne Ulmer .75 2.00
24 Stephen Valiquette 1.25 3.00
25 Craig Weller .75 2.00
26 Chad Wiseman .75 2.00

2005-06 Hartford Wolf Pack

COMPLETE SET (28) 15.00 30.00
1 Ivan Baranka .40 1.00
2 Nigel Dawes .75 2.00
3 Lee Falardeau .40 1.00
4 Fedor Fedorov .40 1.00
5 Colby Genoway .40 1.00
6 Robert Gherson .40 1.00
7 Daniel Girardi .75 2.00
8 Alexandre Giroux .40 1.00
9 Bruce Graham .40 1.00
10 Martin Grenier .40 1.00
11 Dwight Helminen .40 1.00
12 Jarkko Immonen .40 1.00
13 Hugh Jessiman .40 1.00
14 Bryce Lampman .40 1.00
15 Dave Liffiton .40 1.00
16 Al Montoya .50 4.00
17 Thomas Pock .40 1.00
18 Dale Purinton .75 2.00
19 Joe Rullier .40 1.00
20 Martin Sonnenberg .40 1.00
21 Daniel Sparre .40 1.00
22 Jake Taylor .40 1.00
23 Craig Weller .40 1.00
24 Chad Wiseman .40 1.00
25 Jim Schoenfeld HC .02 .10
26 Ken Gernander AC .02 .10
27 Ulf Samuelsson AC .02 .10
28 Sonar & Torpedo MASCOTS .01 .01

2006-07 Hartford Wolf Pack

COMPLETE SET (28) 25.00 50.00
1 Ryan Constant .60 1.50
2 Hugh Jessiman .60 1.50
3 Mark Lee .60 1.50
4 Bryce Lampman .60 1.50
5 Corey Potter .60 1.50
6 Bruce Graham .60 1.50
7 Zdenek Bahensky .60 1.50
8 Lee Falardeau .60 1.50
9 Daniel Girardi 1.25 3.00
10 Darius Kasparaitis .60 1.50
11 Steve Valiquette .75 2.00
12 Brad Isbister .60 1.50
13 Jarkko Immonen 1.25 3.00
14 Marvin Degon .60 1.50
15 Lauri Korpikoski 1.25 3.00
16 Jake Taylor .60 1.50
17 Nigel Dawes 1.25 3.00
18 Dale Purinton .60 1.50
19 Dane Byers 1.25 3.00
20 Dwight Helminen .60 1.50
21 Greg Moore .60 1.50
22 Martin Richter .60 1.50
23 Craig Weller .60 1.50

24 Ryan Callahan 1.25 3.00
25 Dave Liffiton .60 1.50
26 Al Montoya 1.25 3.00
27 Francis Lessard .60 1.50
28 Brandon Dubinsky .60 1.50

2014-15 Hartford Wolf Pack

COMPLETE SET (30) 8.00 20.00
1 Dylan McIlrath .40 1.00
2 Mathew Bodie .30 .75
3 Ryan Bourque .40 1.00
4 Chris Bourque .40 1.00
5 Joey Crabb .30 .75
6 Cedrick Desjardins .30 .75
7 Jesper Fast .40 1.00
8 Ryan Haggerty .30 .75
9 Marek Hrivik .30 .75
10 Tommy Hughes .30 .75
11 Dallas Jackson .30 .75
12 Josh Nicholls .30 .75
13 Danny Kristo .30 .75
14 Oscar Lindberg 1.50 4.00
15 J.T. Miller .40 1.00
16 Chris Mueller .30 .75
17 Shawn O'Donnell .30 .75
18 Ryan Potulny .30 .75
19 Mackenzie Skapski .30 .75
20 Steve Spinell .30 .75
21 Mike Kostka .30 .75
22 Nick Tarnasky .30 .75
23 Justin Vaive .30 .75
24 Conor Allen .30 .75
25 Ryan Malone .30 .75
26 Ken Gernander CO .30 .75
27 Jeff Beukeboom Asst. CO .30 .75
28 Pat Boller Asst. CO .30 .75
29 Sonar MASCOT .30 .75
CL Header Card CL .30 .75

1992-93 Harvard Crimson

COMPLETE SET (31) 8.00 20.00
1 Brian Adams .30 .75
2 Chris Baird .30 .75
3 Lou Body .30 .75
4 Michel Breistroff .30 .75
5 Perry Cohagen .30 .75
6 Ben Coughlin .30 .75
7 Ted Drury .40 1.00
8 Brian Farrell .30 .75
9 Steven Flomenhoft .30 .75
10 Eric Grahling .30 .75
11 Cory Gustafson .30 .75
12 Kevin Hampe ACO .02 .10
13 Steve Hermsdorf .30 .75
14 Tom Holmes .30 .75
15 Aaron Israel .30 .75
16 Jason Karmanos .30 .75
17 Ian Kennish .30 .75
18 Brad Konik .30 .75
19 Bryan Lonsinger .30 .75
20 Derek Maguire .40 1.00
21 Matt Mallgrave .30 .75
22 Geb Marett .30 .75
23 Steve Martins .40 1.00
24 Sean McCann .40 1.00
25 Peter McLaughlin .30 .75
26 Keith McLean .30 .75
27 Kirk Nielsen .40 1.00
28 Jerry Pawloski ACO .02 .10
29 Ronn Tomassoni CO .02 .10
30 Tripp Tracy .60 1.50
31 Header Card .02 .10

1994-95 Hershey Bears

COMPLETE SET (24) 8.00 20.00
1 Vladislav Boulin .40 1.00
2 Aris Brimanis .40 1.00
3 Bruce Coles .40 1.00
4 Yanick Dupre .40 1.00
5 Tracy Egeland .40 1.00
6 Andre Faust .40 1.00
7 Jeff Finley .40 1.00
8 Milos Holan .40 1.00
9 Paul Jerrard .40 1.00
10 Dan Kordic .40 1.00
11 Les Kuntar .60 1.50
12 Mitch Lamoureux .60 1.50
13 Neil Little 1.25 3.00
14 Mike McHugh .40 1.00
15 Clayton Norris .40 1.00
16 Vaclav Prospal .75 2.00
17 Terran Sandwith .40 1.00
18 Ryan Sittler .40 1.00
19 Bob Wilkie .40 1.00
20 Chris Winnes .40 1.00
21 Mike Stothers ACO .02 .10
22 Brad Dibeler ATR .02 .10
23 Jay Leach HCO .02 .10

1998-99 Hershey Bears

COMPLETE SET (40) 12.00 30.00
1 Evgeny Lazarev
Mitch Lamoureux .30 .75
2 Marc Denis 1.50 4.00
3 Jeff Buchanan .15 .40
4 Ted Crowley .15 .40
5 Yuri Babenko .15 .40
6 Evgeny Lazarev .30 .75
7 Scott Parker 1.25 3.00
8 Mike Foligno CO .20 .50
9 Rob Shearer .20 .50
10 Brad Larsen .15 .40
11 1946-47 Team Photo .20 .50
12 Rick Berry .20 .50
13 Troy Crowder .15 .40
14 Dan Hinote .40 1.00
15 Serge Aubin .40 1.00
16 1957-58 Team Photo .20 .50
17 1958-59 Team Photo .20 .50
18 1968-69 Team Photo .20 .50
19 David Aebischer 2.00 5.00
20 Mitch Lamoureux .30 .75
21 Christian Matte .20 .50
22 Dan Smith .15 .40
23 Jay Wells CO .15 .40
24 1973-74 Team Photo .15 .40
25 Ville Nieminen .75 2.00
26 Nick Bootland .15 .40
27 1979-80 Team Photo .20 .50
28 Bruce Richardson .15 .40
29 Brian Willsie .15 .40
30 Hershey Park Arena .08 .25
31 Brian White .15 .40
32 1980-81 Team Photo .20 .50
33 1987-88 Team Photo .20 .50
34 Dan Stuck TR .08 .25
35 1996-97 Team Photo .20 .50
36 Frank Mathers .20 .50
37 Arnie Kullman .15 .40
38 Mike Nykoluk .15 .40
39 Tim Tookey .30 .75
40 Team Logo .08 .25

2000-01 Hershey Bears

COMPLETE SET (20) 5.00 25.00
1 Yuri Babenko .20 1.00
2 Rick Berry .20 1.50
3 Nick Bootland .20 1.00
4 Frederic Cassivi .30 2.00
5 Mike Craig .20 1.00
6 Kelly Fairchild .20 1.00
7 Brad Larsen .20 1.00
8 Yevgeny Lazarev .20 1.50
9 Stewart Malgunas .20 1.00
10 Ville Nieminen .15 3.00
11 Joel Prpic .20 1.00
12 Alex Ryazantsev .30 1.50
13 Philippe Sauve .15 4.00
14 Matthew Scorsune .20 1.00
15 Rob Shearer .20 1.50
16 Dan Smith .20 1.00
17 Ben Storey .20 1.00
18 K.C. Timmons .20 1.00
19 Steffon Walby .20 1.00
20 Brian White .20 1.00

2001-02 Hershey Bears

COMPLETE SET (28) 20.00 40.00
1 Yuri Babenko .60 1.50
2 Frederic Cassivi .60 1.50
3 Mike Cirillo .60 1.50
4 Coco MASCOT .50 1.25
5 Larry Courville .60 1.50
6 Jeff Daw .60 1.50
7 Kelly Fairchild .60 1.50
8 Paul Fixter ACO .50 1.25
9 Mike Foligno CO .50 1.25
10 Riku Hahl .75 2.00
11 Matt Herr .60 1.50
12 Jordan Krestanovich .60 1.50
13 Mikhail Kuleshov .60 1.50
14 Yevgeny Lazarev .60 1.50
15 Dave MacIsaac .60 1.50
16 Steve Moore .60 1.50
17 Bryan Muir .60 1.50
18 Vaclav Nedorost .60 1.50
19 Brad Norton .60 1.50
20 Jaroslav Obsut .60 1.50
21 Jeff Paul .60 1.50
22 Alex Riazantsev .60 1.50
23 Phil Sauve .75 2.00
24 Matt Scorsune .60 1.50
25 Brent Thompson .60 1.50
26 Rocky Thompson .60 1.50
27 K.C. Timmons .60 1.50
28 Radim Vrbata .75 2.00

2002-03 Hershey Bears

COMPLETE SET (30) 12.00 30.00
1 Eric Bertrand .40 1.00
2 Nick Bootland .40 1.00
3 Steve Brule .40 1.00
4 Peter Budaj .75 2.00
5 Marc Busenburg .40 1.00
6 Brett Clark .40 1.00
7 Dale Clarke .40 1.00
8 Pierre-Luc Emond .40 1.00
9 Mark Freer .40 1.00
10 Riku Hahl .75 2.00
11 Jordan Krestanovich .40 1.00
12 Mikhail Kuleshov .40 1.00
13 Cail MacLean .40 1.00
14 Steve Moore .40 1.00
15 Bryan Muir .40 1.00
16 Jeff Paul .40 1.00
17 Alexander Ryazantsev .40 1.00
18 Philippe Sauve 1.25 3.00
19 Agris Saviels .40 1.00
20 Charlie Stephens .40 1.00
21 Marek Svatos 1.25 3.00
22 Brent Thompson .40 1.00
23 K.C.Timmons .40 1.00
24 Rob Voltera .40 1.00
25 Tim Wedderburn .40 1.00
26 Brian Willsie .40 1.00
27 Mike Foligno HCO .10 .25
28 Paul Fixter ACO .10 .25
29 Coco Mascot .04 .10
30 Giant Center Arena .04 .10

2003-04 Hershey Bears

COMPLETE SET (24) 4.00 10.00
1 Peter Budaj .40 1.00
2 Jeff Finger .20 .50
3 D.J. Smith .20 .50
4 Brett Clark .20 .50
5 Tomas Slovak .20 .50
6 Pascal Trepanier .20 .50
7 Jordan Krestanovich .20 .50
8 Gavin Morgan .20 .50
9 Eric Perrin .40 1.00
10 Ryan Craig .20 .50
11 Mikhail Kuleshov .20 .50
12 Shane Willis .20 .50
13 Rob Voltera .20 .50
14 Steve Brule .20 .50
15 Bruce Richardson .20 .50
16 Sheldon Keefe .20 .50
17 Agris Saviels .20 .50
18 Charlie Stephens .20 .50
19 Marc Busenburg .20 .50
20 Mark Jerant .20 .50
21 Evgeny Artyukhin .30 .75
22 Tom Lawson .20 .50
23 Paul Fixter HCO .10 .25
24 Paul Jerrard ACO .10 .25

2003-04 Hershey Bears Patriot News

COMPLETE SET (30) 15.00 40.00
1 Evgeny Artyukhin .60 1.50
2 Dennis Bonvie .75 2.00
3 Steve Brule .60 1.50
4 Peter Budaj .75 2.00
5 Marc Busenburg .60 1.50
6 Brett Clark .60 1.50
7 Ryan Craig .60 1.50
8 Jeff Finger .60 1.50
9 Mark Jerant .60 1.50
10 Sheldon Keefe .60 1.50
11 Jordan Krestanovich .60 1.50
12 Mikhail Kuleshov .60 1.50
13 Brad Larsen .60 1.50
14 Tom Lawson .75 2.00
15 Steve Moore .60 1.50
16 Gavin Morgan .60 1.50
17 Eric Perrin 1.25 3.00
18 Bruce Richardson .60 1.50
19 Darren Rumble .60 1.50
20 Agris Saviels .60 1.50
21 Tomas Slovak .60 1.50
22 D.J. Smith .60 1.50
23 Charlie Stephens .60 1.50
24 Pascal Trepanier .60 1.50
25 Mikko Viitanen .60 1.50
26 Rob Voltera .60 1.50
27 Shane Willis .60 1.50
28 Paul Fixter HCO .10 .25
29 Paul Jerrard ACO .10 .25
30 Mascot .10 .25

2004-05 Hershey Bears Patriot News

COMPLETE SET (31) 15.00 40.00
1 Dean Arsene .40 1.00
2 Chris Bala .40 1.00
3 Greg Barber .40 1.00
4 Dennis Bonvie 1.50 4.00
5 Johnny Boychuk .40 1.00
6 Peter Budaj .75 2.00
7 Brett Clark .40 1.00
8 Carl Corrazzini .75 2.00
9 Mathieu Darche .75 2.00
10 Jeff Finger .40 1.00
11 Paul Fixter CO .20 .50
12 Martin Hlinka .40 1.00
13 Paul Jerrard ACO .20 .50
14 Sergei Klyazmin .40 1.00
15 Tom Lawson .75 2.00
16 David Masse .40 1.00
17 Frank Mathers .75 2.00
18 Frank Mathers .75 2.00
19 Cody McCormick .75 2.00
20 Cail MacLean .40 1.00
21 Eric Perrin 1.25 3.00
22 Jamie Rivers .40 1.00
23 Agris Saviels .40 1.00
24 Frantisek Skladany .40 1.00
25 Mike Souza .40 1.00
26 Ryan Steeves .40 1.00
27 Marek Svatos 1.25 3.00
28 Jeff Ulmer .40 1.00
29 Mikko Viitanen .75 2.00
30 Martin Wilde .75 2.00
31 Coco MASCOT .04 .10

2005-06 Hershey Bears

COMPLETE SET (28) 8.00 20.00
1 Dean Arsene .30 .75
2 Jared Aulin .30 .75
3 Chris Bourque .60 1.50
4 Frederic Cassivi .60 1.50
5 Jakub Cutta .30 .75
6 Eric Fehr .30 .75
7 Tomas Fleischmann .30 .75
8 Owen Fussey .30 .75
9 Mike Green .30 .75
10 Jonas Johansson .30 .75
11 Boyd Kane .30 .75
12 Jakub Klepis .30 .75
13 Graham Mink .60 1.50
14 Lawrence Nycholat .30 .75
15 Dave Steckel .30 .75
16 Joey Tenute .30 .75
17 Martin Wilde .30 .75
18 Bruce Boudreau HC .02 .10
19 Bob Woods AC .02 .10
20 Coco the Bear MASCOT .02 .10
21 Kirk Daubenspeck .40 1.00
22 Deryk Engelland .30 .75
23 Colin Forbes .30 .75
24 J.F. Fortin .30 .75
25 Brooks Laich .30 .75
26 Louis Robitaille .75 2.00
27 Mark Wotton .30 .75
28 Dwayne Zinger .30 .75

2013-14 Hershey Bears

COMPLETE SET () 8.00 20.00
1 Team Photo .30 .75
2 Patrick Wellar .30 .75
3 Steven Oleksy .30 .75
4 Tomas Kundratek .30 .75
5 Nate Schmidt .30 .75
6 Coco the Bear MASCOT .30 .75
7 Peter Leblanc .30 .75
8 Dustin Gazley .30 .75
9 Chay Genoway .30 .75
10 Grant Potulny .30 .75
11 David Kolomatis .30 .75
12 Nicolas Deschamps .30 .75
13 Patrick Wey .30 .75
14 Tyson Strachan .30 .75
15 Matt Watkins .30 .75
16 Nathan Walker .30 .75
17 Jeff Taffe .30 .75
18 Josh Brittain .30 .75
19 Casey Wellman .30 .75
20 Julien Brouillette .30 .75
21 Cameron Schilling .30 .75
22 Ryan Stoa .30 .75
23 Michael Latta .30 .75
24 Joel Rechlicz .30 .75
25 Philipp Grubauer .30 .75
26 Brandon Segal .30 .75
27 Dane Byers .30 .75
28 Garrett Mitchell .30 .75
29 Dmitri Orlov .30 .75
30 Derek Whitmore .30 .75

2014-15 Hershey Bears

COMPLETE SET (30) 8.00 20.00
1 Joel Broda .30 .75
2 Chris Brown .30 .75
3 Erik Burgdoerfer .30 .75
4 Dane Byers .30 .75
5 Michal Cajkovsky .30 .75
6 Connor Carrick .40 1.00
7 Chris Conner .30 .75
8 Pheonix Copley .30 .75
9 Philippe Cornet .40 1.00
10 Stanislav Galiev .40 1.00
11 Dustin Gazley .30 .75
12 Philipp Grubauer .30 .75
13 Bryan Helmer .30 .75
14 Tim Kennedy .30 .75
15 Tomas Kundratek .30 .75
16 Jon Landry .30 .75
17 Troy Mann CO .30 .75
18 Garrett Mitchell .30 .75
19 Mike Moore .30 .75
20 Kris Newbury .30 .75
21 Jim O'Brien .30 .75
22 Liam O'Brien .30 .75
23 Steven Oleksy .30 .75
24 Cameron Schilling .30 .75
25 Tim Spencer .30 .75
26 Chandler Stephenson .30 .75
27 Nathan Walker .30 .75
28 Casey Wellman .40 1.00
29 Coco the Bear MASCOT .30 .75
30 Team Photo .30 .75

1995-96 Houston Aeros

COMPLETE SET (25) 4.80 12.00
1 Scott Arniel .30 .75
2 Al Conroy .20 .50
3 Paul DiPietro .20 .50
4 Gord Donnelly .20 .50
5 Rob Dopson .30 .75
6 Mark Freer .20 .50
7 Troy Gamble .30 .75
8 Kevin Grant .20 .50
9 Curtis Hunt .20 .50
10 Steve Jaques .20 .50
11 Gord Kruppke .20 .50
12 Mark Lamb .30 .75
13 Marc Laniel .30 .75
14 Kevin Malgunas .20 .50
15 Mike Maurice .20 .50
16 Scott McCrory .20 .50
17 Myles O'Connor .20 .50
18 Jim Paek .20 .50
19 Vadim Slivchenko .20 .50
20 Graeme Townshend .20 .50
21 Sylvain Turgeon .20 .50
22 Carl Valimont .20 .50
23 Mike Yeo .20 .50
24 Dave Tippett .20 .50
25 Terry Ruskowski CO .20 .50

1999-00 Houston Aeros

COMPLETE SET (29) 10.00 25.00
1 Paul Dyck .40 1.00
2 Marty Wilford .40 1.00
3 Matt Swanson .40 1.00
4 Mark Lamb .60 1.50
5 Jeff Daw .40 1.00
6 Brian Wiseman .60 1.50
7 Lane Lambert .60 1.50
8 Brian Felsner .40 1.00
9 Terry Marchant .40 1.00
10 Lee Jinman .40 1.00
11 Rudy Poeschek .60 1.50
12 David Oliver .40 1.00
13 Brad Williamson .40 1.00
14 Mark Major .40 1.00
15 David Wilkie .40 1.00
16 Maxime Gingras .75 2.00
17 Greg Pankewicz .40 1.00
18 Gregg Walters .40 1.00
19 Sandy Moger .60 1.50
20 Frederic Chabot 1.25 3.00
21 Ron Low CO .40 1.00
22 Dave Barr ACO .20 .50
25 Mascot .08 .25
NNO Steve Sumner EQ .02 .10
NNO Jerry Meins TR .02 .10
NNO Checklist .08 .25
NNO Header Card .02 .10

2003-04 Houston Aeros

COMPLETE SET (20) 10.00
1 Chris Bala .20 .50
2 Jason Beckett .20 .50
3 Dan Cavanaugh .20 .50
4 Marc Cavosie .20 .50
5 Mark Cullen .20 .50
6 Josh DeWolf .20 .50
7 Chris Dyment .20 .50
8 Matthew Foy .20 .50
9 Mika Hannula .20 .50
10 Chris Heid .20 .50
11 Jeff Hoggan .20 .50
12 Johan Holmqvist .30 .75
13 Jason Marshall .20 .50
14 Zbynek Michalek .20 .50
15 Kevin Mitchell .20 .50
16 Bill Muckalt .20 .50
17 Eric Reitz .20 .50
18 Stephane Veilleux .20 .50
19 Rickard Wallin .20 .50
20 Kyle Wanvig .20 .50

2004-05 Houston Aeros

COMPLETE SET (20) 12.00 30.00
1 Derek Boogaard .75 2.00
2 Pierre-Marc Bouchard 1.25 3.00
3 Brent Burns 1.25 3.00
4 Dan Cavanaugh .40 1.00
5 Mark Cullen .40 1.00
6 John Erskine .60 1.50
7 Matt Foy .40 1.00
8 Ray Giroux .40 1.00
9 Josh Harding 1.25 3.00
10 Mikko Koivu 1.25 3.00
11 Kirby Law .40 1.00
12 Junior Lessard .75 2.00
13 Zbynek Michalek .40 1.00
14 Todd Reirden .40 1.00
15 Eric Reitz .40 1.00
16 Mike Smith .75 2.00
17 Patrick Traverse .75 2.00
18 Stephane Veilleux .40 1.00
19 Rickard Wallin .40 1.00
20 Kyle Wanvig .40 1.00

2006-07 Houston Aeros Retro

COMPLETE SET (10) 5.00 10.00
1 Frederic Chabot .75 2.00
2 Mark Freer .30 .75
3 Cam Stewart .30 .75
4 Brian Wiseman .30 .75
5 Derek Boogaard 1.25 3.00
6 Jeff Christian .30 .75
7 Manny Fernandez .40 1.00
8 Curtis Murphy .30 .75
9 Todd McLellan .30 .75
10 Dave Tippett CO .30 .75

1987-88 Hull Olympiques

COMPLETE SET (24) 35.00 75.00
1 Header Card .08 .25
2 Joe Aloi .40 1.00
3 Joel Blain .40 1.00
4 Christian Breton .40 1.00
5 Benoit Brunet .75 2.00
6 Guy Dupuis .40 1.00
7 Martin Gelinas 1.25 3.00
8 Jason Glickman .60 1.50
9 Wayne Gretzky OWN 25.00 60.00
10 Herbert Hohenberger .60 1.50
11 Ken MacDermid .40 1.00
12 Craig Martin .75 2.00
13 Mark McLane .40 1.00
14 Stephane Matteau .75 2.00
15 Kelly Nester .40 1.00
16 Marc Saumier .40 1.00
17 Claude-Charles Sauriol .40 1.00
18 Daniel Shank 1.00 2.50
19 Joe Suk .40 1.00
20 Alain Vigneault .40 1.00
21 George Wilcox .40 1.00
22 Team Card .20 .50
23 Team Card .20 .50
24 Team Card .20 .50

1999-00 Hull Olympiques

COMPLETE SET (24) 5.00 12.00
1 Erich Paroshy .15 .40
2 Andrew Carver .15 .40
3 Bobby Clarke .15 .40
4 Donald Johnstone .15 .40
5 Bruno Lemire .15 .40
6 Derrick Martin .15 .40
7 Alexandre Giroux .30 .75
8 Dustin Russell .15 .40
9 Daniel Hudgin .15 .40
10 Roberto Bissonnette .15 .40
11 Daniel Clermont .15 .40
12 Radim Vrbata .40 1.00
13 Mario Joly .15 .40
14 Jason Lehoux .15 .40
15 Brock Boucher .15 .40
16 Philippe Lacasse .15 .40
17 Paul Spadafora .15 .40
18 Ryan Lauzon .15 .40
19 Michael Ryder 1.25 3.00
20 Adam Rivet .15 .40
21 Patrick Lafreniere .15 .40
22 Eric Lafrance .20 .50
23 Philippe Sauve .40 1.00
24 Team Photo/CL .15 .40
NNO Luc Robitaille .60 1.50

1999-00 Hull Olympiques Signed

COMPLETE SET (24) 30.00 80.00
1 Erich Paroshy .75 2.00
2 Andrew Carver .75 2.00
3 Bobby Clarke .75 2.00
4 Donald Johnstone .75 2.00
5 Bruno Lemire .75 2.00
6 Derrick Martin .75 2.00
7 Alexandre Giroux 2.00 5.00
8 Dustin Russell .75 2.00
9 Daniel Hudgin .75 2.00
10 Roberto Bissonnette .75 2.00
11 Daniel Clermont .75 2.00
12 Radim Vrbata 6.00 15.00
13 Mario Joly .75 2.00
14 Jason Lehoux .75 2.00
15 Brock Boucher .75 2.00
16 Philippe Lacasse .75 2.00
17 Paul Spadafora .75 2.00
18 Ryan Lauzon .75 2.00
19 Michael Ryder 15.00 30.00
20 Adam Rivet .75 2.00
21 Patrick Lafreniere .75 2.00
22 Eric Lafrance 1.25 3.00
23 Philippe Sauve 6.00 15.00
24 Team Photo/CL .08 .25
NNO Luc Robitaille 6.00 15.00

2000-01 Hull Olympiques

COMPLETE SET (24) 6.00 20.00
1 Chris Moher .20 .50
2 Andrew Carver .20 .50
3 Bobby Clarke .20 .50
4 Doug O'Brien .20 .50
5 Bruno Lemire .20 .50
6 John Cilladi .20 .50
7 Derrick Martin .20 .50
8 Roberto Bissonnette .20 .50
9 Ales Hemsky 4.00 10.00
10 Phillippe Chainlere .20 .50
11 Jonathan Labelle .20 .50
12 Mario Joly .20 .50
13 Jason Kostadine .20 .50
14 Carl Rochon .20 .50
15 Philippe Lacasse .20 .50
16 Maxime Talbot .75 2.00
17 Jean-Michel Daoust .20 .50
18 Brent G. Roach .20 .50
19 Dale Sullivan .20 .50
20 Adam Rivet .30 .75
21 Eric Lafrance .20 .50
22 Olivier Dannel .30 .75
23 Ian Courville .20 .50
NNO Team CL .01 .05

2000-01 Hull Olympiques Signed

COMPLETE SET (24) 24.00 60.00
1 Chris Moher .80 2.00
2 Andrew Carver .80 2.00
3 Bobby Clarke .80 2.00
4 Doug O'Brien .80 2.00
5 Bruno Lemire .80 2.00
6 John Cilladi .80 2.00
7 Derrick Martin 1.20 3.00
8 Roberto Bissonnette .80 2.00
9 Ales Hemsky 6.00 30.00
10 Phillippe Chainlere .80 2.00
11 Jonathan Labelle .80 2.00
12 Mario Joly .80 2.00
13 Jason Kostadine .80 2.00
14 Carle Rochon .80 2.00
15 Philippe Lacasse .75 2.00
16 Maxime Talbot .80 2.00
17 Jean-Michel Daoust .80 2.00
18 Brent G. Roach .80 2.00
19 Dale Sullivan .80 2.00
20 Adam Rivet 2.00 5.00
21 Eric Lafrance .80 2.00
22 Olivier Dannel 2.00 5.00
23 Ian Courville .80 2.00
NNO Team CL .10 .25

2001-02 Hull Olympiques

COMPLETE SET (23) 4.80 12.00
1 Chris Moher .20 .50
2 Bryan Riddell .20 .50
3 Charles Fontaine .20 .50
4 Dominic D'Amour .20 .50
5 Doug O'Brien .20 .50
6 Francis Wathier .20 .50
7 Derrick Martin .20 .50
8 Philippe Dupuis .20 .50
9 Scott Gibson .20 .50
10 Ales Hemsky 2.00 5.00
11 Nick Fugere .20 .50
12 Jonathan Labelle .20 .50
13 Martin Vagner .40 1.00
14 Jason Kostadine .20 .50
15 Jesse Lane .20 .50
16 Philippe Lacasse .20 .50
17 Brent Roach .20 .50
18 Maxime Talbot .20 .50
19 Jean-Michel Daoust .20 .50
20 Dale Sullivan .20 .50
21 Eric Lafrance .30 .75
22 Michael Dilorenzo .20 .50
23 Jean-Junior Morin .20 .50

2002-03 Hull Olympiques

COMPLETE SET (24) 5.00 12.00
1 Christopher Pottie .20 .50
2 Jeff Smith .20 .50
3 Charles Fontaine .20 .50
4 Dominic D'Amour .20 .50
5 Doug O'Brien .20 .50
6 Sam Roberts .20 .50
7 Francis Wathier .20 .50
8 Jonathan Bellemare .20 .50
9 Philippe Dupuis .20 .50
10 Guillaume Labrecque .20 .50
11 Nick Fugere .20 .50
12 Olivier Labelle .20 .50
13 Martin Vagner .30 .75
14 Renaud des Alliers .20 .50
15 Andrew Hayes .20 .50
16 Brent Roach .20 .50
17 Maxime Talbot .30 .75
18 Jean Michel Daoust .20 .50
19 Dale Sullivan .20 .50
20 Mathieu Brunelle .20 .50
21 Eric Lafrance .30 .75
22 David Tremblay .30 .75
23 Tyler Reid .20 .50
24 Checklist/Logo .04 .10

2003 Hull Olympiques Memorial Cup

COMPLETE SET (20) 15.00
1 Jonathan Bellemare .30 .75
2 Mathieu Brunelle .30 .75
3 Dominic D'Amour .30 .75
4 Jean-Michel D'Aoust .30 .75
5 Renaud DesAlliers .30 .75
6 Philippe Dupuis .30 .75
7 Nick Fugere .30 .75
8 Olivier Labelle .30 .75
9 Guillaume Labrecque .30 .75
10 Eric Lafrance .40 1.00
11 Doug O'Brien .30 .75
12 Tyler Reid .30 .75
13 Sam Roberts .30 .75
14 Brent Roach .30 .75
15 Jeff Smith .30 .75
16 Dale Sullivan .30 .75
17 Maxime Talbot .30 .75
18 David Tremblay .40 1.00
19 Martin Vagner .40 1.00
20 Francis Wathier .30 .75

1993-94 Huntington Blizzard

COMPLETE SET (27) 3.00 8.00
1 Ray Alcindor .15 .40
2 Shayne Antoski .15 .40
3 Greg Bailey .15 .40
4 Jared Bednar .15 .40
5 Andy Borggaard .15 .40
6 Malcolm Cameron .15 .40
7 Dave Dimitri .15 .40
8 Mark Franks .15 .40
9 Ray Gallagher .15 .40
10 Murray Garbutt .15 .40
11 Brad Harrison .15 .40
12 Henry's Blizzard Babes .20 .50
13 Todd Huyber .15 .40
14 Klondike The Bear
(Masc .02 .10
15 Ron Majic .15 .40
16 Bob May .15 .40
17 Jim Mill .15 .40
18 Jim Mirabello ANN .02 .10
19 Dan Persiegh ANN .02 .10
20 Paul Pickard CO .02 .10
21 Scott Roberts
(TV ancho .02 .10
22 Greg Scott .15 .40
23 Geoff Simpson .15 .40
24 Doug Stromback .15 .40
25 Dave Weekley
(TV Sports .02 .10
26 Misty Zambito .20 .50
27 Title Card .02 .10

1994-95 Huntington Blizzard

COMPLETE SET (32) 4.00 10.00
1 Title Card CL .02 .10
2 Steve Barnes .20 .50
3 Jared Bednar .20 .50
4 Jim Bermingham .20 .50
5 Todd Brost .30 .75
6 Alan Brown .20 .50
7 Ray Edwards .20 .50
8 Trent Eigner .20 .50
9 Dan Fournel .20 .50
10 Mark Franks .20 .50
11 Gord Frantti .20 .50
12 Chris Gordon .20 .50
13 Kelly Harper .20 .50
14 J.C. Ihrig TR
EQMG .02 .10
15 Mitch Kean .20 .50
16 Jeff Levy .20 .50
17 Chris Morque .20 .50
18 Derek Schooley .20 .50
19 Jim Solly .20 .50
20 Mike Stone .20 .50
21 Jason Weinrich .20 .50
22 Mark Woolf .20 .50
23 Paul Pickard CO .02 .10
24 Klondike MASCOT .02 .10
25 Blizzard Babes .30 .75
26 Jim Mirabello ANN .02 .10
27 Dan Persiegh ANN .02 .10
28 Jeff Crawford DJ
Van Ma .02 .10
29 Russell T. Hill DJ
Sara .02 .10
30 Jeff Ramsey DJ
Teresa N .02 .10
31 Melanie Shafer
(TV anch .02 .10
32 Title Card .02 .10

1998-99 Huntington Blizzard

COMPLETE SET (27) 3.20 50.00
1 Bill Baaki .75 2.00
2 Mike Perna .75 2.00
3 Chad Lang 1.50 4.00
4 Jamie Sokolsky .75 2.00
5 D.J. Harding .75 2.00
6 Jan Slavik .75 2.00
7 Karson Kaebel 1.50 4.00
8 Jason Bermingham .75 2.00
9 Kelly Harper .75 2.00
10 Derek Smith .75 2.00
11 Jim Bermingham 1.50 4.00
12 Tracy Egeland .75 2.00
13 Brodie Coffin 1.50 4.00
14 Rob Stanfield .75 2.00
15 Kevin Paden .75 2.00
16 Mike Schultz .75 2.00
17 Rich Bronilla .75 2.00
18 Jake Deadmarsh 1.50 4.00
19 Butch Kaebel .75 2.00
20 Blaine Russell .75 2.00
21 Ray Edwards HCO .02 .10
22 Chris Plumhoff EM .02 .10
23 Dave Allen .02 .10
24 Klondike Mascot .02 .10
25 Checklist .02 .10
26 Blizzard Pro Shop .02 .10
27 PHPA
ECHL .02 .10

1999-00 Huntington Blizzard

COMPLETE SET (24) 30.00 50.00
1 Anthony Cappelletti 1.25 3.00
2 Mike Perna 1.25 3.00
3 Jamie Pegg 1.25 3.00
4 Jamie Sokolsky 1.25 3.00
5 Andrew Pearsall 1.25 3.00
6 Jason Bermingham 1.25 3.00
7 Peter Brearley 1.25 3.00
8 Jim Bermingham 1.25 3.00
9 Jim Moss 1.25 3.00
10 Bill Baaki 1.25 3.00
11 Anthony Terzo 1.25 3.00
12 David Oliver 1.25 3.00
13 Keith Cassidy 1.25 3.00
14 Mark Spence 1.25 3.00
15 Ryan Hoople 1.50 4.00
16 Butch Kaebel 1.25 3.00
17 Blaine Russell 1.50 4.00
18 WRVC AM390 .02 .10
19 Huntington Blizzard .15 .40
20 Klondike MAS .02 .10
21 Ray Edwards CO .40 1.00
22 Dave Allen .02 .10
23 Kelly Harper .02 .10
24 Curtis Bois .02 .10

1998-99 Huntsville Channel Cat

COMPLETE SET (22) 6.00 15.00
1 Chris Stewart HCO .02 .10
2 John Gibson .40 1.00
3 Igor Bonderev .40 1.00
4 Jonathan Dubois .40 1.00
5 Phil Daigle .40 1.00
6 Pat Bingham ACO .02 .10
7 Mike Degurse .40 1.00
8 Ryan Wood .40 1.00
9 Tyler Quiring .40 1.00
10 Greg Lakovic .40 1.00
11 Wade Gibson .40 1.00
12 Josh Erdman .40 1.00

13 Ken Richardson .40 1.00
14 Todd Dougherty .40 1.00
15 Finnley Mascot .02 .10
16 Clint Collins .40 1.00
17 Mike Gamble .40 1.00
18 Marc Vachon .40 1.00
19 Chris George .40 1.00
20 Derek Puppa .40 1.00
21 Schedule Card .02 .10
22 Message Card .02 .10

2003-04 Huntsville Channel Cats

COMPLETE SET (18) 5.00 12.00
1 Claude Amstutz .30 .75
2 Joel Bresciani .30 .75
3 Dan Buccella .30 .75
4 Dave Cadarette .30 .75
5 Matt Carmichael .40 1.00
6 Allan Carr .30 .75
7 Jason Deguehery .30 .75
8 Mike Degurse .40 1.00
9 Scott Graham .40 1.00
10 Daniel Kletke .30 .75
11 Shawn Martin .30 .75
12 Jessi Otis .30 .75
13 James Patterson .30 .75
14 Luke Phillips .40 1.00
15 Greg Snitowsky .30 .75
16 Joe Urbanik .30 .75
17 John Gibson CO .20 .50
18 Finnley MASCOT .04 .10

2004-05 Huntsville Havoc

COMPLETE SET (27) 8.00 20.00
1 Chaos MASCOT .04 .10
2 John Gibson CO .20 .50
3 Adam MacLean .60 1.50
4 Steve Howard .40 1.00
5 Jason Deguehery .60 1.50
6 Tim Plett .40 1.00
7 Aaron Lewis .40 1.00
8 Jeremy Law .40 1.00
9 Jeff Dams .40 1.00
10 Brandon Doria .40 1.00
11 James Patterson .40 1.00
12 Josh Liebenow .40 1.00
13 Brad McDonald .40 1.00
14 Mark Cole .40 1.00
15 Jason Simon .40 1.00
16 Doug Merrill .40 1.00
17 Matt Carmichael .75 2.00
18 Mike Degurse .40 1.00
19 Derek McKinlay .40 1.00
20 Luke Phillips .40 1.00
21 Dan Bucella .40 1.00
22 DeWayne Manning TR .04 .10
23 Chad Daniels TR .04 .10
24 John Markushewski DR .04 .10
25 Brian Carter DR .04 .10
26 John Greco DR .04 .10
27 Stanton Davis DR .04 .10

1997-98 Idaho Steelheads

COMPLETE SET (22) 12.00 30.00
1 Rob Dumas .60 1.50
2 Frederik Beaubien .75 2.00
3 Patrick Moreau .60 1.50
4 Bill McGuigan .60 1.50
5 Alain Savage .60 1.50
6 Mario Therrien .60 1.50
7 Kevin Deschambeault .60 1.50
8 Sean Farmer .60 1.50
9 Scott Davis .60 1.50
10 Lee Svangstu .60 1.50
11 Troy Edwards .60 1.50
12 Andreas Sjolund .60 1.50
13 Pat O'Connell .60 1.50
14 Patrick Gallagher .60 1.50
15 Sam Fields .60 1.50
16 Marco Pietroniro .60 1.50
17 Dmitri Leonov .75 2.00
18 Jamie Cooke .60 1.50
19 Todd Dougherty .60 1.50
20 Carl Menard .60 1.50
21 Bart Hull .75 2.00
22 Dave Langevin HCO .60 1.50

1998-99 Idaho Steelheads

COMPLETE SET (23) 10.00 25.00
1 Alex Alepin .40 1.00
2 Frederik Beaubien .60 1.50
3 Francois Bourdeau .40 1.00
4 Scott Davis .40 1.00
5 Rob Dumas .40 1.00
6 Troy Edwards .40 1.00
7 Christian Friberg .40 1.00
8 Marc Genest .40 1.00
9 Cal Ingraham .75 2.00
10 Jason Lammers .40 1.00
11 Dmitri Leonov .60 1.50
12 Sebastian Parent .40 1.00
13 Marco Pietroniro .40 1.00
14 Tony Prpic .40 1.00
15 Bryan Randall .40 1.00
16 Alain Savage .40 1.00
17 Jonathon Shockey .40 1.00
18 Andreas Sjolund .40 1.00
19 Mario Thierren .40 1.00
20 Jeff Trigg .40 1.00
21 All-Star Trio .60 1.50
22 Clint Malarchuk HCO .60 1.50
23 Bonk Mascot .08 .25

1999-00 Idaho Steelheads

COMPLETE SET (22) 4.00 10.00
1 Cal Ingraham .30 .75
2 Nicolas Chabot .30 .75
3 Troy Edwards .20 .50
4 Todd Robinson .20 .50
5 Dan Marcotte .20 .50
6 Bryan Randall .20 .50
7 Tom Menicci .20 .50
8 Roy Mitchell .20 .50
9 Scott Davis .20 .50
10 Andrei Lupandin .20 .50
11 Gavin Morgan .20 .50
12 Jeff Petruic .20 .50
13 Clint Malarchuk CO .20 .50
14 Marc Genest .20 .50
15 Darcy Loewen .20 .50
16 Rob Dumas .20 .50
17 Rob Hartnell .20 .50
18 Ryan Johnston .20 .50
19 Matt Garver .20 .50
20 Andreas Sjolund .30 .75
21 Kory Cooper .30 .75
22 Bonk MAS .08 .25

2000-01 Idaho Steelheads

COMPLETE SET (25) 6.00 20.00
1 Chad Alban .40 1.00
2 Colin Anderson .24 .75
3 Adam Borzecki .24 .75
4 Scott Burt .24 .75
5 Rob Concannon .24 .75
6 Thom Cullen .24 .75
7 Bobby Hayes .24 .75
8 Cal Ingraham .40 1.50
9 Kevin Knopp .24 .75
10 Arturs Kupaks .24 .75
11 Mike Legg .24 .75
12 Darcy Loewen .24 .75
13 Matt Martin .24 .75
14 Roy Mitchell .24 .75
15 Jeremy Mylymok .40 1.00
16 Vladimir Nemec .24 .75
17 Barry Potomski .40 1.50
18 Eric Rud .24 .75
19 Dan Shermerhorn .24 .75
20 Kendall Sidoruk .24 .75
21 Shawn Wansborough .24 .75
22 Cal Ingraham AS .40 1.00
23 Jeremy Mylymok AS .40 1.00
24 Todd Hine TR .04 .10
25 Khris Bestel EQM .04 .10

2001-02 Idaho Steelheads

COMPLETE SET (24) 10.00 25.00
1 Blair Allison .60 1.50
2 Scott Burt .40 1.00
3 Adam Copeland .40 1.00
4 Jason Cugnet .60 1.50
5 Thom Cullen .40 1.00
6 Wes Dorey .40 1.00
7 Cal Ingraham .60 1.50
8 Dan Kerluke .40 1.00
9 Jeremy Mylymok .40 1.00
10 Matt Oates .40 1.00
11 Zdenek Ondrej .40 1.00
12 Derek Paget .40 1.00
13 Eric Rud .40 1.00
14 Terry Ryan .40 1.00
15 Dan Shermerhorn .40 1.00
16 Jeff Shevalier .40 1.00
17 Kevin Smyth .40 1.00
18 Bobby Stewart .40 1.00
19 Petr Suchanek .40 1.00
20 Scott Swanson .40 1.00
21 Garry Toor .40 1.00
22 Jeremy Yablonski .60 1.50
23 Edgars Zaltkovskis .40 1.00
24 John Oliver HCO .10 .25

2004-05 Idaho Steelheads

COMPLETE SET (25) 6.00 15.00
1 Mascot .04 .10
2 John Oliver CO .10 .25
3 Blair Allison ACO .10 .25
4 Frank Doyle .40 1.00
5 Jeremy Mylymok .20 .50
6 Petr Suchanek .20 .50
7 Billy Tibbetts .60 1.50
8 Ben Keup .20 .50
9 Scott Burt .20 .50
10 Darren McLachlan .40 1.00
11 Jim Leger .20 .50
12 Dan Vandermeer .20 .50
13 David Morrisett .40 1.00
14 Frank Lukes .20 .50
15 Jonathan Zion .20 .50
16 Bobby Russell .20 .50
17 Peter Metcalf .20 .50
18 Warren Peters .20 .50
19 Matt Elich .20 .50
20 Landon Bathe .20 .50
21 Colin Zulianello .40 1.00
22 Tim Verbeek .20 .50
23 Brett Draney .20 .50
24 David Cornacchia .20 .50
25 Darrell Hay .20 .50
26 Marty Flichel .20 .50
27 Lance Galbraith .40 1.00

2005-06 Idaho Steelheads

COMPLETE SET (26) 10.00 25.00
1 David Bararuk .60 1.50
2 Garrett Bembridge .60 1.50
3 Jarad Bourassa .40 1.00
4 Scott Burt .40 1.00
5 Justin Cox .40 1.00
6 Brian Fahey .40 1.00
7 Marty Flichel .40 1.00
8 Blake Forsyth .40 1.00
9 Mike Gabinet .40 1.00
10 Kevin Gardner .40 1.00
11 Dan Hacker .40 1.00
12 Jim Hakewill .40 1.00
13 Greg Hornby .40 1.00
14 Kurt MacSweyn .40 1.00
15 D'Arcy McConvey .40 1.00
16 Tyrell Moulton .40 1.00
17 Jeremy Mylymok .60 1.50
18 Matt Reid .40 1.00
19 Steve Silverthorn .40 1.00
20 Mike Stutzel .40 1.00
21 Brad Thompson .40 1.00
22 Janos Vas .40 1.00
23 Matthew Yeats .40 1.00
24 Jonathan Zion .40 1.00
25 Derek Laxdal HC .02 .10
26 Bonk MASCOT .02 .10

2006-07 Idaho Steelheads

COMPLETE SET (27) 10.00 20.00
1 Idaho Steelheads .02 .10
2 Kyle Bruce .40 1.00
3 Scott Burt .40 1.00
4 Taggart Desmet .40 1.00
5 Marty Flichel .40 1.00
6 Lance Galbraith .75 2.00
7 Charlie Johnson .40 1.00
8 D'Arcy McConvey .40 1.00
9 Tuomas Mikkonen .40 1.00
10 Derek Nesbitt .40 1.00
11 Greg Rallo .40 1.00
12 Francis Wathier .40 1.00
13 Jeremy Yablonski .75 2.00
14 Cody Blanshan .40 1.00
15 Blake Forsyth .40 1.00
16 Mike Gabinet .40 1.00
17 Darrell Hay .40 1.00
18 Jared Nightingale .40 1.00
19 Colin Peters .40 1.00
20 Kory Scoran .40 1.00
21 Travis Wight .40 1.00
22 John Daigneau .60 1.50
23 Steve Silverthorn .40 1.00
24 Derek Laxdal CO .10 .25
25 Khris Bestel EQ MGR .02 .10
26 Dennis Brogna TR .02 .10
27 Blue MASCOT .02 .10

2013-14 Idaho Steelheads

COMPLETE SET (20) 6.00 15.00
1 Dmitri Leonov .30 .75
2 Frederik Beaubien .30 .75
3 Bill McGuigan .30 .75
4 Kendall Sidoruk .30 .75
5 Cal Ingraham .30 .75
6 Bobby Stewart .30 .75
7 Jim Gattolliat .30 .75
8 Andrei Vasilyev .30 .75
9 Tyler Kindle .30 .75
10 Lance Galbraith .30 .75
11 Dan Ellis .30 .75
12 Steve Silverthorn .30 .75
13 Greg Rallo .30 .75
14 John-Scott Dickson .30 .75
15 Dustin Friesen .30 .75
16 Jerry Kuhn .30 .75
17 Andrew Carroll .30 .75
18 David de Kastrozza .30 .75
19 Josh Robinson .30 .75
CL Header Card CL .30 .75

2013-14 Idaho Steelheads Choice

COMPLETE SET (21) 6.00 15.00
1 Blair Allison .30 .75
2 Richard Bachman .30 .75
3 Scott Burt .30 .75
4 Matt Case .30 .75
5 Mark Derlago .30 .75
6 Rob Dumas .30 .75
7 Dan Ellis .30 .75
8 Marty Flichel .30 .75
9 Lance Galbraith .30 .75
10 Darrell Hay .30 .75
11 Cal Ingraham .30 .75
12 Zenon Konopka .30 .75
13 Jerry Kuhn .30 .75
14 Kael Mouillierat .30 .75
15 Jeremy Mylymok .30 .75
16 Alain Savage .30 .75
17 Kory Scoran .30 .75
18 Dan Shermerhorn .30 .75
19 Steve Silverthorn .30 .75
20 Jeremy Yablonski .30 .75
NNO Header Card .30 .75

1998-99 IHL All-Star Eastern Conference

COMPLETE SET (25) 14.00 35.00
1 Guy Dupuis .20 .50
2 Viacheslav Butsayev .20 .50
3 Zac Bierk .40 1.00
4 Brian Noonan .20 .50
5 Dave Hymovitz .20 .50
6 Marty Turco 8.00 20.00
7 Jon Sim .60 1.50
8 Brad Shaw .75 2.00
9 Pat Neaton .20 .50
10 Peter Ciavaglia .40 1.00
11 Mike Prokopec .20 .50
12 Stan Drulia .40 1.00
13 Steve Walker .75 2.00
14 Todd Richards .20 .50
15 Maxim Spiridonov .20 .50
16 Robert Petrovicky .20 .50
17 Curtis Murphy .20 .50
18 Mark Beaufait .40 1.00
19 Gilbert Dionne .40 1.00
20 Brad Lukowich .40 1.00
21 Bruce Cassidy ACO .08 .25
22 Steve Ludzik HCO .20 .50
23 Keith Aldridge .30 .75
24 IHL Logo .02 .10
25 Checklist .02 .10

1998-99 IHL All-Star Western Conference

COMPLETE SET (24) 8.00 20.00
1 Richard Shulmistra .40 1.00
2 Brett Hauer .20 .50
3 Bill Bowler .60 1.50
4 Pat Jablonski .60 1.50
5 Niklas Andersson .20 .50
6 Steve Maltais .75 2.00
7 Tom Tilley .20 .50
8 Dan Ratushny .20 .50
9 Andy Roach .20 .50
10 Rob Valicevic .75 2.00
11 Jeff Tory .20 .50
12 Patrik Augusta .20 .50
13 Kimmo Timonen .75 2.00
14 Mark Mowers .60 1.50
15 Patrice Lefebvre .60 1.50
16 Cam Stewart .20 .50
17 Brian Wiseman .40 1.00
18 Greg Hawgood .40 1.00
19 John Purves .75 2.00
20 Scott Thomas .75 2.00
21 Randy Carlyle ACO .08 .25
22 Dave Tippett HCO .08 .25
23 IHL Logo .02 .10
24 Checklist .02 .10

1999-00 IHL All-Stars

COMPLETE SET (24) 16.00 50.00
1 Mike Crowley .75 2.00
2 Nils Ekman .60 1.50
3 Rich Parent .75 2.00
4 Shane Willis 1.25 3.00
5 John Purves .75 2.00
6 Kevin Miller .75 2.00
7 Mike Prokopec .40 1.00
8 Petr Schastlivy 1.25 3.00
9 Marty Turco 10.00 25.00
10 Stewart Malgunas .40 1.00
11 Curtis Murphy .40 1.00
12 Todd White .60 1.50
13 Brett Hauer .40 1.00
14 David Gosselin .40 1.00
15 David Ling .60 1.50
16 Gilbert Dionne .75 2.00
17 Jeff Sharples .40 1.00
18 John Gruden .40 1.00
19 Jarrod Skalde .75 2.00
20 Steve Maltais .75 2.00
21 Bob Bourne .40 1.00
22 Al Sims .40 1.00
NNO Checklist Card .08 .25
NNO Header Card .08 .25

1981-82 Indianapolis Checkers

COMPLETE SET (20) 12.00 30.00
1 Bruce Andres .40 1.00
2 Frank Beaton .40 1.00
3 Kelly Davis .40 1.00
4 Kevin Devine .40 1.00
5 Glen Duncan .40 1.00
6 Mats Hallin .60 1.50
7 Neil Hawryliw .40 1.00
8 Bob Holland .40 1.00
9 Mike Hordy .40 1.00
10 Kelly Hrudey 4.00 10.00
11 Randy Johnston .40 1.00
12 Red Laurence .40 1.00
13 Tim Lockridge .40 1.00
14 Garth MacGuigan .40 1.00
15 John Marks .60 1.50
16 Darcey Regier .75 2.00
17 Charlie Skjodt .40 1.00
18 Lorne Stamler .40 1.00
19 Steve Stoyanovich .40 1.00
20 Monty Trottier .40 1.00

1982-83 Indianapolis Checkers

COMPLETE SET (21) 16.00 40.00
1 Kelly Davis .40 1.00
2 Kevin Devine .40 1.00
3 Gord Dineen .60 1.50
4 Glen Duncan .40 1.00
5 Greg Gilbert .75 2.00
6 Mike Gredder .40 1.00
7 Mats Hallin .75 2.00
8 Dave Hanson 4.00 10.00
9 Rob Holland .40 1.00
10 Scott Howson .40 1.00
11 Kelly Hrudey 3.00 8.00
12 Randy Johnston .40 1.00
13 Red Laurence .40 1.00
14 Tim Lockridge .40 1.00
15 Garth MacGuigan .40 1.00
16 Darcey Regier .60 1.50
17 Dan Revell .40 1.00
18 Dave Simpson .40 1.00
19 Lorne Stamler .40 1.00
20 Steve Stoyanovich .40 1.00
21 Monty Trottier .40 1.00

1992-93 Indianapolis Ice

COMPLETE SET (26) 4.00 10.00
1 Alexandr Andrievski .15 .40
2 Steve Bancroft .15 .40
3 Zac Boyer .15 .40
4 Rod Buskas .20 .50
5 Shawn Byram .15 .40
6 Jim Cummins .30 .75
7 Joe Cleary .15 .40
8 Joe Crowley .15 .40
9 Trevor Dam .15 .40
10 Ivan Droppa .15 .40
11 Tracy Egeland .15 .40
12 Dave Hakstol .15 .40
13 Kevin Hodson .30 .75
14 Tony Horacek .15 .40
15 Tony Hrkac .30 .75
16 Sergei Krivokrasov .30 .75
17 Brad Lauer .20 .50
18 Ray LeBlanc .30 .75
19 Owen Lessard .15 .40
20 Jim Playfair ACO John M .02 .10
21 Kevin St. Jacques .15 .40
22 Michael Speer .15 .40
23 Milan Tichy .15 .40
24 Kerry Toporowski .15 .40
25 Sean Williams .15 .40
26 Craig Woodcroft .15 .40

1993-94 Indianapolis Ice

COMPLETE SET (25) 6.00 15.00
1 Hugo Belanger .30 .75
2 Zac Boyer .30 .75
3 Shawn Byram .30 .75
4 Rob Cimetta .30 .75
5 Rob Conn .30 .75
6 Joe Crowley .30 .75
7 Ivan Droppa .30 .75
8 Steve Dubinsky .30 .75
9 Karl Dykhuis .30 .75
10 Dino Grossi .30 .75
11 Dave Hakstol .30 .75
13 Bobby House .30 .75
14 Tony Horacek .30 .75
15 Bob Kellogg .30 .75
16 Jeff Ricciardi .30 .75
17 Sergei Krivokrasov .30 .75
18 Chris Rogles .60 1.50
19 Kevin St. Jacques .30 .75
20 Christian Soucy .60 1.50
21 Yves Heroux .30 .75
21 Michael Speer .30 .75
22 Kerry Toporowski .60 1.50
23 Duane Sutter CO .40 1.00
24 Gene Parfet TR .02 .10
25 Polar Bear MASCOT .02 .10

1994-95 Indianapolis Ice

COMPLETE SET (26) 4.00 10.00
1 Hugo Belanger .15 .40
2 Bruce Cassidy .15 .40
3 Rob Conn .20 .50
4 Ivan Droppa .15 .40
5 Steve Dubinsky .20 .50
6 Karl Dykhuis .20 .50
7 Craig Fisher .15 .40
8 Daniel Gauthier .15 .40
9 Tony Horacek .15 .40
10 Bobby House .15 .40
11 Bob Kellogg .15 .40
12 Sergei Klimovich .15 .40
13 Sergei Krivokrasov .30 .75
14 Andy MacIntyre .15 .40
15 Dean Malkoc .20 .50
16 Matt Oates .15 .40
17 Mike Pomichter .15 .40
18 Mike Prokopec .15 .40
19 Jeff Ricciardi .15 .40
20 Chris Rogles .30 .75
21 Bogdan Savenko .15 .40
22 Jeff Shantz .30 .75
23 Christian Soucy .30 .75
24 Duane Sutter CO .20 .50
25 Travis Thiessen .15 .40
26 Team Photo .15 .40

1995-96 Indianapolis Ice

COMPLETE SET (23) 4.00 10.00
1 Bill Armstrong .15 .40
2 James Black .15 .40
3 Jeff Buchanan .15 .40
4 Bruce Cassidy .15 .40
5 Ivan Droppa .15 .40
6 Steve Dubinsky .15 .40
7 Dmitri Filimonov .15 .40
8 Daniel Gauthier .15 .40
9 Ryan Huska .15 .40
10 Sergei Klimovich .15 .40
11 Eric Lecompte .20 .50
12 Andy MacIntyre .15 .40
13 Eric Manlow .15 .40
14 Steve McLaren .15 .40
15 Kip Miller .30 .75
16 Ethan Moreau .30 .75
17 Mike Prokopec .20 .50
18 Andre Racicot .30 .75
19 Jeff Serowik .20 .50
20 Christian Soucy .30 .75
21 Jimmy Waite .30 .75
22 Brad Werenka .20 .50
23 Bob Ferguson .15 .40

1997-98 Indianapolis Ice

COMPLETE SET (30) 6.00 15.00
1 Bob Ferguson HCO .02 .10
2 Chris Mizer HTR .02 .10
3 Jim Stuckey EM .02 .10
4 Kory Cooper .20 .50
5 Kirk Daubenspeck .30 .75
6 Glen Featherstone .20 .50
7 Brian Felsner .20 .50
8 Martin Gendron .20 .50
9 Jani Hurme 1.25 3.00
10 Ryan Huska .20 .50
11 Marc Hussey .20 .50
12 David Hymovitz .20 .50
13 Marc Lamothe .40 1.00
14 Eric Lecompte .20 .50
15 Eric Manlow .20 .50
16 Steve McLaren .20 .50
17 Kevin Miller .20 .50
18 Craig Mills .20 .50
19 Frank Musil .20 .50
20 Dmitri Nabokov .20 .50
21 Alain Nasreddine .20 .50
22 Ryan Risidore .20 .50
23 Michal Sykora .20 .50
24 Steve Tardif .20 .50
25 Alfie Turcotte .20 .50
26 Petri Varis .20 .50
27 Todd White .20 .50
28 Marty Wilford .20 .50
29 M.J.'s Collectibles .02 .10
30 PHPA Web Site .02 .10

1998-99 Indianapolis Ice

COMPLETE SET (29) 4.00 10.00
1 Brian Noonan .20 .50
2 Matt Cooney .15 .40
3 Ryan VandenBussche .30 .75
4 Marty Wilford .15 .40
5 Nathan Perrott .40 1.00
6 Mike Vukonich .15 .40
7 Remi Royer .20 .50
8 Marc Dupuis .15 .40
9 Mike Hall .15 .40
10 Sylvain Cloutier .15 .40
11 Andrei Trefilov .20 .50
12 Andrei Kozyrev .15 .40
13 Chris Herperger .15 .40
14 Marc Lamothe .30 .75
15 Erik Andersson .15 .40
16 Bryan Fogarty .15 .40
17 Slapshot MASCOT .02 .10
18 Bob Lachance .15 .40
19 Kirk Daubenspeck .30 .75
20 Barrie Moore .15 .40
21 Bruce Cassidy HCO .15 .40
22 David Hymovitz .15 .40
23 Justin Hocking .15 .40
24 King Team .02 .10
25 Dale DeGray .15 .40
26 Jeff Paul .15 .40
27 IHL Web Site .02 .10
28 MJ Collectibles .02 .10
29 PHPA Web Site .02 .10

1999-00 Indianapolis Ice

COMPLETE SET (21) 90.00 150.00
1 Mike Berger 3.00 8.00
2 Ken Boone 4.00 10.00
3 Jason Carriere 3.00 8.00
4 Yvan Corbin 3.00 8.00
5 Dan Cousineau 3.00 8.00
6 Robert Davidson 3.00 8.00
7 Jay Hern 3.00 8.00
8 Peter Jas 3.00 8.00
9 Bernie John 3.00 8.00
10 Lubos Krajcovic 3.00 8.00
11 Eric Landry 3.00 8.00
12 Chris MacKenzie 3.00 8.00
13 Jason Mansoff 3.00 8.00
14 Jamie Morris 4.00 10.00
15 Sebastian Pajerski 3.00 8.00
16 Tom Stewart 3.00 8.00
17 Benoit Thibert 4.00 10.00
18 Steven Toll 3.00 8.00
19 M.J. Collectibles .40 1.00
20 Rod Davidson CO 2.00 5.00
21 Joe Trotta CO 2.00 5.00
22 Slapshot MAS 2.00 5.00

2000-01 Indianapolis Ice

COMPLETE SET (23) 4.00 10.00
COMPLETE MJ SET (24) 8.00 20.00
1 Ray Aho .20 .50
2 Dan Back .20 .50
3 Ken Boone .20 .50
4 Brandon Christian .20 .50
5 Yvan Corbin .20 .50
5GJ Yvan Corbin 4.00 10.00
6 Dan Cousineau .20 .50
7 Robert Davidson .20 .50
8 Casey Harris .20 .50
9 Jan Jas .20 .50
10 Peter Jas .20 .50
11 David Jesiolowski .20 .50
12 Bernie John .20 .50
13 Lubos Krajcovic .20 .50
14 Marc Laforge .20 .50
15 Chris MacKenzie .20 .50
16 Aigars Mironovics .20 .50
17 Jamie Morris .20 .50
18 Chris Richards .20 .50
19 Kevin Schmidt .20 .50
20 Jason Selleke .20 .50
21 Rod Davidson CO .10 .25
22 Slapshot MASCOT .04 .10
23 MJ's Collectibles .04 .10

2001-02 Indianapolis Ice

COMPLETE SET (23) 8.00 20.00
1 Ryan Aikia .20 .50
2 Mike Berger ACO .04 .10
3 Peter Bournazakis .20 .50
4 Dan Cousineau .20 .50
5 Robert Davidson .20 .50
6 Rod Davidson CO .04 .10
7 Charlie Elezi .20 .50
8 Chris George .20 .50
9 Casey Harris .20 .50
10 Jay Hern .20 .50
11 Bernie John .20 .50
12 Bernie John GJ 4.00 10.00
13 Justin Kearns .30 .75
14 Chris MacKenzie .20 .50
15 Don Malko .20 .50
16 Jamie Morris .20 .50
17 Kevin Popp .20 .50
18 Jason Selleke .20 .50
19 Jonathan Sorg .20 .50
20 Dylan Taylor .20 .50
21 J.C. Wells .20 .50
22 Slapshot MASCOT .10 .25
23 MJs Collectibles .04 .10

2002-03 Indianapolis Ice

COMPLETE SET (23) 4.00 10.00
1 Ryan Aikia .20 .50
2 Jason Baird .20 .50
3 Ryan Carter .20 .50
4 Bryce Classen .20 .50
5 Jared Dumba .20 .50
6 Nate Elliott .20 .50
7 Randy Holmes .20 .50
8 Bernie John .20 .50
9 Justin Kearns .30 .75
10 Scott Lewis .20 .50
11 Etienne Morin .20 .50
12 Jamie Morris .20 .50
13 Greg Olsen .20 .50
14 Byron Pool .20 .50
15 Kevin Popp .20 .50
16 Shawn Silver .30 .75
17 Kevin St. Jacques .20 .50
18 Kevin St. Jacques .20 .50
19 Andrew Taylor .20 .50
20 Ken McRae CO .10 .25
21 Darrin Flinchem EQM .04 .10
22 Mascot .04 .10
23 Todd Champlin TR .04 .10

2003-04 Indianapolis Ice

COMPLETE SET (24) 10.00
1 Ryan Aikia .20 .50
2 Jason Baird .20 .50
3 Ken Boone .20 .50
4 Ryan Carter .20 .50
5 Philippe Choiniere .20 .50
6 Mario Doyon .20 .50
7 Jared Dumba .20 .50
8 Nate Elliott .20 .50
9 Dave Gilmore .20 .50
10 Joe Guenther .20 .50
11 Russ Guzior .20 .50
12 Bernie John .20 .50
13 Steve Lecuyer .20 .50
14 Chad McIver .20 .50
15 Adam Redmond .20 .50
16 Remi Royer .20 .50
17 Jeff Sanger .30 .75
18 Jason Selleke .20 .50
19 Mike Zeibaq .20 .50
20 Brent Zelenewich .30 .75
21 Ken McRae CO .10 .25
22 Darren Flinchem EQM .04 .10
23 Mascot .04 .10
24 Marc Schlichtenmyer TR .04 .10

2014-15 Indy Fuel

COMPLETE SET (26) 6.00 15.00
1 Anders Franzon .30 .75
2 Nick Bruneteau .30 .75
3 Nick Jones .30 .75
4 Dean Chelios .30 .75
5 Rhett Bly .30 .75
6 Dan Ford .30 .75
7 Kyle Stroh .30 .75
8 Evan Vossen .30 .75
9 Mike Duco .30 .75
10 Saverio Posa .30 .75
11 Pete Massar .30 .75
12 Jamie Wise .30 .75
13 Nicklas Lindberg .30 .75
14 Matt White .30 .75
15 Johnny McGuire .30 .75
16 Dillon Fournier .30 .75
17 Kirill Gotovets .30 .75
18 Justin Holl .30 .75
19 Vincent Arseneau .30 .75
20 Chris DeSousa .30 .75
21 Mac Carruth .30 .75
22 Garett Bembridge .30 .75
23 Shane Owen .30 .75
24 Garrett Klotz .30 .75
25 Scott Hillman CO .30 .75
26 Header Card CL .30 .75

2006-07 Iowa Stars

COMPLETE SET (27) 8.00 15.00
1 Greg Amadio .20 .50
2 Mark Ardelan .20 .50
3 Krys Barch .30 .75
4 Chris Conner .40 1.00
5 Dan Ellis .30 .75
6 Loui Eriksson .60 1.50
7 Mark Fistric .30 .75
8 Mike Green .20 .50
9 Nicklas Grossman .20 .50
10 Dan Hacker .20 .50
11 Yared Hagos .20 .50
12 Marius Holtet .20 .50
13 John Lammers .20 .50
14 Junior Lessard .40 1.00
15 Joel Lundqvist .40 1.00
16 Matt Nickerson .40 1.00
17 Toby Petersen .20 .50
18 Vojtech Polak .20 .50
19 Mario Scalzo .20 .50
20 Marty Sertich .40 1.00
21 Tobias Stephan .40 1.00
22 Janos Vas .20 .50
23 Francis Wathier .20 .50
24 Marty Wilford .20 .50
25 Dave Allison CO .02 .10
26 Paul Jerrard ACO .02 .10
27 Shooter MASCOT .02 .10

2000-01 Jackson Bandits

COMPLETE SET (25) 4.80 12.00
1 Mike Tamburro .20 .50
2 Jeff Helperl .20 .50
3 Derek Gustafson .30 .75
4 Randy Fitzgerald .20 .50
5 Milt Mastad .20 .50
6 Jonathon Shockey .20 .50
7 Chris Wismer .20 .50
8 J.P. O'Connor .20 .50
9 Bobby Russell .20 .50
10 Cory Larose .20 .50
11 Brendan Walsh .20 .50
12 Ryan Mougenel .20 .50
13 Chris Peyton .20 .50
14 Brian Callahan .20 .50
15 Jim Bermingham .20 .50
16 Dan Carney .20 .50
17 Dave Stewart .20 .50
18 Brad Peddle .20 .50
19 Denny Felsner .20 .50
20 Steve Wilson .20 .50
21 Quintin Laing .20 .50
22 J.P. Tessier .20 .50
23 Lee Jinman .30 .75
24 Derek Clancey .20 .50
25 Tim Green .20 .50

2000-01 Jackson Bandits Promos

COMPLETE SET (8) 3.20 8.00
1 David Brumby .40 1.00
2 Derek Gustafson .60 1.50
3 Denny Felsner .60 1.50
4 Brian Callahan .40 1.00
5 Bobby Russell .40 1.00
6 Dave Stewart .40 1.00
7 Mike Tamburro .40 1.00
8 Brendan Walsh .40 1.00

1999-00 Jacksonville Lizard Kings

COMPLETE SET (15) 4.80 12.00
1 Jean-Philippe Soucy .40 1.00
2 Alex Podalinski .30 .75
3 Rich Bronilla .30 .75
4 Brad Federenko .30 .75
5 Dan Reja .40 1.00
6 Ray LeBlanc .60 1.50
7 Mark Giannetti .30 .75
8 Patrick Gingras .30 .75
9 Derek Eberle .40 1.00
10 Eric Naud .40 1.00
11 Bryan Forslund .30 .75
12 Ryan Cirillo .30 .75
13 Lenny the Lizard MAS .20 .50
14 Alain Lemieux CO .20 .50
15 Jacksonville Lizard Kings .20 .50

1989-90 Johnstown Chiefs

COMPLETE SET (18) 6.00 50.00
19 Rick Burchill 1.25 3.00
20 Bob Goulet .75 2.00
21 John Messuri .75 2.00
22 Darren Servatius .75 2.00
23 Rick Boyd .75 2.00
24 Bob Kennedy .75 2.00
25 Mike Rossetti .75 2.00
26 Dan Williams .75 2.00

27 Mark Bogoslowski .75 2.00
28 Dean Hall .75 2.00
29 Mitch Molloy .75 2.00
30 Darren Schwartz 1.25 3.00
31 Doug Weiss .75 2.00
32 Marc Vachon .75 2.00
33 Mike Jeffrey 1.25 3.00
34 Frank Dell ANN .08 .25
35 Sean Finn .75 2.00
36 Steve Carlson CO 6.00 15.00

1991-92 Johnstown Chiefs

COMPLETE SET (20) 4.00 10.00
1 Steve Carlson CO .75 2.00
2 Dana Heinze TR .02 .10
3 John Fletcher .20 .50
4 Mark Krys .20 .50
5 Doug Sinclair .20 .50
6 Bruce Coles .20 .50
7 Doug Weiss .20 .50
8 Dave MacIntyre .20 .50
9 Bob Woods .20 .50
10 Mike Roberts .20 .50
11 Jeff Beaudin .20 .50
12 Brian Ferreira .20 .50
13 Christian Lariviere .20 .50
14 Ted Miskolczi .20 .50
15 Rob Hrytsak .20 .50
16 Mark Green .20 .50
17 Matt Glennon .20 .50
18 Mike Rossetti .30 .75
19 Stan Reddick .30 .75
20 Perry Florio .20 .50

1993-94 Johnstown Chiefs

COMPLETE SET (22) 3.00 8.00
1 John Bradley .15 .40
2 Campbell Blair .15 .40
3 Francois Bourdeau .15 .40
4 Bob Woods .15 .40
5 Ted Dent .15 .40
6 Matt Hoffman .15 .40
7 Gord Christian .15 .40
8 Tim Hanus .15 .40
9 Phil Soukoroff .15 .40
10 Jason Jennings .15 .40
11 Dusty McLellan .15 .40
12 Dennis Purdie .20 .50
13 Chuck Wiegand .15 .40
14 Jamie Adams .15 .40
15 Jan Beran .15 .40
16 Rob Laurie .20 .50
17 Cory Banika .15 .40
18 Perry Florio .15 .40
19 Rob Leask .15 .40
20 Ed Johnstone CO .08 .25
21 John Daley GM .02 .10
22 Matt Koeck TR .02 .10
NNO Header Card .02 .10

1994-95 Johnstown Chiefs

COMPLETE SET (24) 3.00 8.00
1 Cover Card CL .02 .10
2 Jason Brousseau .15 .40
3 Brandon Christian .15 .40
4 Gord Christian .15 .40
5 Bruce Coles .15 .40
6 Ted Dent .15 .40
7 Martin D'Orsonnens .15 .40
8 Perry Florio .15 .40
9 Rod Hinks .15 .40
10 Matt Hoffman .15 .40
11 Aaron Israel .15 .40
12 Jason Jennings .15 .40
13 Rob Laurie .15 .40
14 Rob Leask .15 .40
15 Dennis Purdie .40 1.00
16 Kevin Quinn .15 .40
17 Jason Richard .15 .40
18 Dan Sawyer .15 .40
19 Ben Wyzansky .15 .40
20 Matt Yingst .15 .40
21 Training Staff .02 .10
22 Ed Johnstone .02 .10
23 WMTZ-FM Personalities .02 .10
24 WMTZ-FM Personalities .02 .10

1996-97 Johnstown Chiefs

COMPLETE SET (31) 15.00 40.00
1 Greg Callahan .75 2.00
2 Brandon Christian .75 2.00
3 Alexandr Chunchukov .75 2.00
4 Trevor Converse .75 2.00
5 Chad Dameworth .75 2.00
6 Carl Fleury 1.25 3.00
7 Dan Harrison .75 2.00
8 Jim Krayer .75 2.00
9 Denis Lamoureux .75 2.00
10 Kelly Leroux .75 2.00
11 Martin Masa .75 2.00
12 Klemen Mohoric .75 2.00
13 Sean Perry .75 2.00
14 Ryan Petz .75 2.00
15 Dan Reimann .75 2.00
16 Beau Riedel .75 2.00
17 Ted Russell .75 2.00
18 Ryan Savoia .75 2.00
19 Marc Siegel .75 2.00
20 Lukas Smital .75 2.00
21 Olie Sundstrom .75 2.00
22 Kam White .75 2.00
23 Martin Woods .75 2.00
24 Nick Fotiu HCO .40 1.00
25 Scott Allen ACO .20 .50
26 Mic Midderhoff EM .08 .25
26 Dana Heinze TR .08 .25
27 Chief's Office Staff .08 .25
28 The Iron Dog Mascot .08 .25
29 Home Schedule .08 .25
30 Logo Card .02 .10

1997-98 Johnstown Chiefs

COMPLETE SET (29) 30.00 60.00
1 Schedule Card .02 .10
2 Logo Card .02 .10
3 10th Anniversary Logo Card .02 .10
4 The Iron Dog Mascot .02 .10
5 Staff .10 .25
6 Scott Allen ACO .40 1.00
7 Nick Fotiu HCO .75 2.00
8 Martin Masa 1.50 4.00
9 Harold Hersh 1.50 4.00
10 Lukas Smital 1.50 4.00
11 Steve Plouffe 3.00 8.00
12 Jonathan Sorg 1.00 2.50
13 Dan Harrison 1.00 2.50
14 Carl Fleury 3.00 8.00
15 Martin Woods 1.00 2.50
16 Mark Yannetti 1.00 2.50
17 Garrett Burnett 1.00 2.50
18 Greg Callahan 1.00 2.50
19 Ivo Jan 1.00 2.50
20 Kelly Leroux 1.00 2.50
21 Brian Scott 1.00 2.50
22 Scott Stephens 1.00 2.50
23 Marcus Draxler 1.00 2.50
24 Brian Callahan 1.00 2.50
25 Francois Archambault 1.00 2.50
26 Dan Dennis 1.00 2.50
27 Reg Cardinal 1.00 2.50
28 Ian Smith 1.00 2.50
29 Yuri Krivokhija 1.00 2.50

1998-99 Johnstown Chiefs

COMPLETE SET (23) 8.00 20.00
1 Schedule Card .02 .10
2 Logo Card .02 .10
3 Iron Dog Mascot .02 .10
4 Scott Allen HCO .02 .10
5 Galen Head ACO .02 .10
6 Training Staff .02 .10
7 Office Staff .02 .10
8 Etienne Drapeau .40 1.00
9 Jody Shelley 2.00 5.00
10 Jeremy Thompson .40 1.00
11 Carl Fleury .60 1.50
12 Lukas Smital .40 1.00
13 Jonathan Sorg .40 1.00
14 Matt Eisler .40 1.00
15 Martin Masa .40 1.00
16 Shawn Frappier .40 1.00
17 E.J. Bradley .40 1.00
18 Joel Irving .40 1.00
19 Pavel Nestak .40 1.00
20 Kent Simpson .40 1.00
21 Steve Duke .40 1.00
22 Brad Englehart .40 1.00
23 Eric Normandin .40 1.00

1999-00 Johnstown Chiefs

COMPLETE SET (28) 10.00 25.00
1 Johnstown Chiefs Schedule .08 .25
2 Johnstown Chiefs .40 1.00
3 Iron Dog MASCOT .08 .25
4 Staff Card .08 .25
5 Scott Allen HCO .08 .25
6 Jason Spence .40 1.00
7 Ryan Chaytors .40 1.00
8 Jeffrey Sullivan .40 1.00
9 Andrew Dale .40 1.00
10 Derrick Walser .40 1.00
11 Dmitri Tarabrin .40 1.00
12 Carl Fleury .60 1.50
13 Joel Irving .40 1.00
14 Shawn Frappier .40 1.00
15 John Tripp .40 1.00
16 Chuck Mindel .40 1.00
17 Andrew Clark .40 1.00
18 Jody Shelley 2.00 5.00
19 Brent Bilodeau .40 1.00
20 Mike Vellinga .40 1.00
21 E.J. Bradley .40 1.00
22 Bryan McKinney .40 1.00
23 Mike Thompson .40 1.00
24 Frederic Deschenes .60 1.50
25 Kevin Kellett .40 1.00
26 Tyrone Garner .60 1.50
27 Training Staff .08 .25
28 Frank Cislo DRVR .08 .25

2000-01 Johnstown Chiefs

COMPLETE SET (28) 12.00 30.00
1 Schedule Card .04 .10
2 Johnstown Chiefs .40 1.00
3 Scott Allen HCO .10 .25
4 Galen Head ACO .10 .25
5 Toby O'Brien .60 1.50
6 Training Staff .04 .10
7 Radio Guys .04 .10
8 Frank Cislo DRVR .04 .10
9 Front Office Staff .04 .10
10 Iron Dog MASCOT .04 .10
11 Frederic Deschenes .80 2.00
12 Dorian Anneck .60 1.50
13 Maxim Potapov .60 1.50
14 Eric Schneider .60 1.50
15 Jason Spence .60 1.50
16 Michael Kiesman .60 1.50
17 Mikko Kuparinen .60 1.50
18 Brent Bilodeau .80 2.00
19 Mike Vellinga .60 1.50
20 Jeffrey Sullivan .60 1.50
21 Andrew Clark .60 1.50
22 Jan Sulc .60 1.50
23 Dany Sabourin .80 2.00
24 Ryan Tocher .60 1.50
25 Dmitri Tarabrin .60 1.50
26 Mike Rodrigues .60 1.50
27 Mark Thompson .60 1.50
28 Andrew Dale .60 1.50

2001-02 Johnstown Chiefs

COMPLETE SET (29) 20.00 50.00
1 Header Card .04 .10
2 Home Schedule .10 .25
3 Toby & James PRES/GM .20 .50
4 Brent Bilodeau 1.25 3.00
5 Jeffrey Sullivan .75 2.00
6 Kevin Baker .75 2.00
7 Dan Carlson .75 2.00
8 Kevin Clauson .75 2.00
9 Frank Cislo DR .20 .50
10 Staff .10 .25
11 Jim Leger .75 2.00
12 Dany Sabourin 1.25 3.00
13 Lukas Smital .75 2.00
14 J.F. Boutin .75 2.00
15 David Gove 1.25 3.00
16 Frederic Deschenes 1.25 3.00
17 Jason Spence .75 2.00
18 Andrew Clark 1.25 3.00
19 Blair Stayzer 1.25 3.00
20 Mike Rodrigues .75 2.00
21 Philippe Roy .75 2.00
22 Eric Schneider .75 2.00
23 Jim Shepherd .75 2.00
24 Ryan Townsend .75 2.00
25 Chad Onufrechuk .75 2.00
26 Vladimir Nemec .75 2.00
27 Mark White .75 2.00
28 Training Staff .10 .25
29 Mascots .20 .50

2002-03 Johnstown Chiefs

COMPLETE SET (23) 20.00 40.00
1 Peter Aubry .75 2.00
2 Brent Bilodeau 1.00 2.50
3 J.F. Boutin .75 2.00
4 Pierre-Luc Courchesne .75 2.00
5 Andy Doktorchik .75 2.00
6 Dominic Forget .75 2.00
7 Steve Hildenbrand .75 2.00
8 Jay Langager .75 2.00
9 Jim Leger .75 2.00
10 Vladimir Nemec .75 2.00
11 Toby O'Brien .75 2.00
12 Mike Rodrigues .75 2.00
13 Philippe Roy .75 2.00
14 Mark Scally .75 2.00
15 Lukas Smital .75 2.00
16 Jason Spence .75 2.00
17 Sam St. Pierre .75 2.00
18 Jeff Sullivan .75 2.00
19 Dmitri Tarabrin .75 2.00
20 Ryan Townsend .75 2.00
21 Anniversary Logo .04 .10
22 Mascots .10 .25
23 Training Staff .04 .10

2003-04 Johnstown Chiefs

COMPLETE SET (19)

2003-04 Johnstown Chiefs RBI Sports

COMPLETE SET (16) 6.00 15.00
209 Brent Bilodeau .40 1.00
210 Chad Cavanagh .40 1.00
211 Pierre-Luc Courchesne .40 1.00
212 Larry Courville .40 1.00
213 David Currie .60 1.50
214 Dominic Forget .40 1.00
215 Steve Hildenbrand .40 1.00
216 Mike James .40 1.00
217 Brent Kelly .40 1.00
218 Jay Langager .40 1.00
219 Chris Leinweber .40 1.00
220 Ian Manzano .40 1.00
221 Shawn Mather .40 1.00
222 Jason Notermann .40 1.00
223 Dmitri Patzold .60 1.50
224 Dmitri Tarabrin .40 1.00

2004-05 Johnstown Chiefs

COMPLETE SET (21) 6.00 15.00
1 Brent Bilodeau .40 1.00
2 David Bowman .30 .75
3 David Cann .40 1.00
4 Chad Cavanagh .30 .75
5 P.L. Courchesne .30 .75
6 David Currie .40 1.00
7 Jean Desrochers .30 .75
8 Steve Hildenbrand .30 .75
9 Mike James .60 1.50
10 Brent Kelly .30 .75
11 Chris Leinweber .30 .75
12 Ian Manzano .30 .75
13 Shawn Mather .30 .75
14 Dennis Packard .30 .75
15 Matt J. Reid .30 .75
16 Jeff Sullivan .30 .75
17 Joe Tallari .30 .75
18 Dmitri Tarabrin .30 .75
19 Johnathan Tremblay .30 .75
20 Jeremy Van Hoof .30 .75
21 Toby O'Brien CO .04 .10

2005-06 Johnstown Chiefs

COMPLETE SET (20) 6.00 15.00
1 Doug Andress .30 .75
2 J.B. Bittner .30 .75
3 Jonathan Boutin .30 .75
4 Morgan Cey .30 .75
5 Steve Cygan .30 .75
6 Jean Desrochers .30 .75
7 Gerard Dicaire .30 .75
8 Mike Egener .30 .75
9 Brandon Elliott .30 .75
10 Brady Greco .30 .75
11 Adam Henrich .30 .75
12 Justin Kelly .30 .75
13 Ian Manzano .30 .75
14 Brett Peterson .30 .75
15 Randy Rowe .30 .75
16 Jason Spence .30 .75
17 Joe Tallari .30 .75
18 Dmitri Tarabrin .30 .75
19 John Toffey .30 .75
20 Ben Wallace .30 .75

1971-72 Johnstown Jets Acme

COMPLETE SET (16) 40.00 80.00
1 Dave Birch 2.00 5.00
2 Vern Campigatto 2.00 5.00
3 Len Cunning 2.00 5.00
4 Guy Delparte 2.00 5.00
5 Wynne Dempster 2.00 5.00
6 Ron Docken 2.00 5.00
7 Galen Head 2.00 5.00
8 Eddie Kachur 2.00 5.00
9 Reg Kent(Taschuk) 2.00 5.00
10 Jerry MacDonald 2.00 5.00
11 Gene Peacosh 2.50 6.00
12 Dick Roberge 2.00 5.00
13 Jim Trewin 2.00 5.00
14 Brian Vescio 2.00 5.00
15 Bob Vroman 2.50 6.00
16 Gary Wood 2.00 5.00

1972-73 Johnstown Jets

COMPLETE SET (18) 50.00 100.00
1 Ron Docken 2.50 6.00
2 Brian Coughlin 2.00 5.00
3 Tony McCarthy 2.00 5.00
4 Tom Steeves 2.00 5.00
5 Kevin Collins 2.00 5.00
6 Jerry MacDonald 2.00 5.00
7 Wynne Dempster 2.00 5.00
8 Ted Lanyon 2.00 5.00
9 Brian Vescio 2.00 5.00
10 Denis Erickson 2.50 6.00
11 Vern Campigatto 2.00 5.00
12 Gary Wood 2.00 5.00
13 Dave Birch 2.00 5.00
14 Galen Head 2.50 6.00
15 Reg Kent(Taschuk) 2.00 5.00
16 Tom McVie 2.50 6.00
17 Bill McEwan 2.00 5.00
18 Doug Anderson 2.00 5.00

2014-15 Johnstown Tomahawks

COMPLETE SET (24) 6.00 15.00
1 Mike Letizia (Head Coach) .30 .75
2 Jacob Gwillim .30 .75
3 Jake Houston .30 .75
4 Ian Spencer .30 .75
5 Steven Quagliata .30 .75
6 Logan Hudson .30 .75
7 Collin Montgomery .30 .75
8 Lane Valimont .30 .75
9 Joe Drabin .30 .75
10 Andrew Romano .30 .75
11 Joe Delandro .30 .75
12 Brady Bender .30 .75
13 Zac Robbins .30 .75
14 Dalton Hunter .30 .75
15 Alex Alger .30 .75
16 Nick Le Sage .30 .75
17 Tanner Barnes .30 .75
18 Josh Bowes .30 .75
19 Casey Linkenheld .30 .75
20 Filips Buncis .30 .75
21 Alex Jaeckle .30 .75
22 Trevor Recktenwald .30 .75
23 Luke Lynch .30 .75
24 Ryan Bednard .30 .75

1952-53 Juniors Blue Tint

COMPLETE SET (182) 1250.00 2500.00
1 Dennis Riggin 8.00 20.00
2 Joe Zorica 5.00 10.00
3 Larry Hillman 10.00 25.00
4 Edward(Ted) Reid 5.00 10.00
5 Al Arbour 35.00 75.00
6 Marlin McAlendin 5.00 10.00
7 Ross Graham 5.00 10.00
8 Cumming Burton 5.00 10.00
9 Ed Palamar 5.00 10.00
10 Elmer Skov 6.00 15.00
11 Eddie Louttit 5.00 10.00
12 Gerry Price 5.00 10.00
13 Lou Dietrich 5.00 10.00
14 Gaston Marcotte 5.00 10.00
15 Bob Brown 5.00 10.00
16 Archie Burton 5.00 10.00
17 Marv Edwards 15.00 40.00
18 Norman Defelice 6.00 15.00
19 Pete Kamula 5.00 10.00
20 Charles Marshall 5.00 10.00
21 Alex Leslie 5.00 10.00
22 Minpy Roberts 5.00 10.00
23 Danny Poliziani 5.00 10.00
24 Allen Kellogg 5.00 10.00
25 Brian Cullen 15.00 40.00
26 Ken Schinkel 6.00 15.00
27 W. Hass 5.00 10.00
28 Don Nash 5.00 10.00
29 Robert Maxwell 5.00 10.00
30 Eddie Mateka 5.00 10.00
31 Joe Kastelic 5.00 10.00
32 Hank Ciesla 6.00 15.00
33 Hugh Barlow 5.00 10.00
34 Claude Roy 5.00 10.00
35 Jean-Guy Gamache 5.00 10.00
36 Leon Michelin 5.00 10.00
37 Gerard Bergeron 5.00 10.00
38 Herve Lalonde 5.00 10.00
39 J.M. Cossette 5.00 10.00
40 Jean-Guy Gendron 10.00 25.00
41 Gamill Bedard 5.00 10.00
42 Alfred Soucy 5.00 10.00
43 Jean Leclerc 5.00 10.00
44 Raymond St.Cyr 6.00 15.00
45 Lester Lahaye 5.00 10.00
46 Yvan Houle 5.00 10.00
47 Louis Desrosiers 5.00 10.00
48 Douglas Lessor 5.00 10.00
49 Irvin Scott 5.00 10.00
50 Danny Blair 5.00 10.00
51 Jim Connelly 6.00 15.00
52 William Chalmers 5.00 10.00
53 Frank Bettiol 5.00 10.00
54 James Holmes 5.00 10.00
55 Birley Dimme 5.00 10.00
56 Donald Beattie 5.00 10.00
57 Terrance Chattington 5.00 10.00
58 Bruce Wallace 5.00 10.00
59 William McCreary 6.00 15.00
60 Fred Brady 5.00 10.00
61 Ronald Murphy 6.00 15.00
62 Lavi Purola 5.00 10.00
63 George Whyte 5.00 10.00
64 Marcel Paille 25.00 50.00
65 Maurice Collins 5.00 10.00
66 Gerard(Butch) Houle 6.00 15.00
67 Gilles Laperriere 5.00 10.00
68 Robert Chevalier 5.00 10.00
69 Bertrand Lepage 5.00 10.00
70 Michel Labadie 5.00 10.00
71 Gabriel Alain 5.00 10.00
72 Jean-Jacques Pichette 6.00 15.00
73A Camille Henry (Citadelles) 12.00 30.00
73B Camille Henry (New York 100.00 200.00
74 Jean-Guy Gignac 5.00 10.00
75 Leo Amadio 6.00 15.00
76 Gilles Thibault 6.00 15.00
77 Gaston Pelletier 6.00 15.00
78 Adolph Kukulowicz 6.00 15.00
79 Roland Leclerc 5.00 10.00
80 Phil Watson CO 20.00 40.00
81 Raymond Cyr 6.00 15.00
82 Jacques Marcotte 5.00 10.00
83 Floyd Hillman 6.00 15.00
84 Bob Attersley 5.00 10.00
85 Harry Sinden 35.00 75.00
86 Stan Parker 5.00 10.00
87 Bob Mader 5.00 10.00
88 Roger Maisonneuve 5.00 10.00
89 Phil Chapman 5.00 10.00
90 Don McIntosh 5.00 10.00
91 Jack Armstrong 5.00 10.00
92 Carlo Montemurro 5.00 10.00
93 Ken Courtney 5.00 10.00
94 Bill Stewart 6.00 15.00
95 Gerald Casey 5.00 10.00
96 Fred Etcher 5.00 10.00
97 Orrin Carver 5.00 10.00
98 Ralph Willis 5.00 10.00
99 Kenneth Robertson 5.00 10.00
100 Don Cherry 175.00 350.00
101 Fred Pletsch 5.00 10.00
102 Larry Thibault 5.00 10.00
103 James Robertson 5.00 10.00
104 Orval Tessier 10.00 25.00
105 Jack Higgins 5.00 10.00
106 Robert White 5.00 10.00
107 Doug Mohns 15.00 40.00
108 William Sexton 5.00 10.00
109 John Martan 5.00 10.00
110 Tony Poeta 6.00 15.00
111 Don McKenney 10.00 25.00
112 Bill Harrington 5.00 10.00
113 Allen Peal 5.00 10.00
114 John Ford 5.00 10.00
115 Kenneth Collins 6.00 15.00
116 Marc Boileau 6.00 15.00
117 Doug Vaughan 5.00 10.00
118 Gilles Boisvert 5.00 10.00
119 Buddy Horne 5.00 10.00
120 Graham Joyce 5.00 10.00
121 Gary Collins 5.00 10.00
122 Roy Greenan 5.00 10.00
123 Beryl Klynck 5.00 10.00
124 Grieg Hicks 5.00 10.00
125 Jack Novak 5.00 10.00
126 Ken Tennant 5.00 10.00
127 Glen Cressman 5.00 10.00
128 Curly Davies 5.00 10.00
129 Charlie Hodge 37.50 75.00
130 Bob McCord 6.00 15.00
131 Gordie Hollinworth 5.00 10.00
132 Ronald Pilon 5.00 10.00
133 Brian Mackay 5.00 10.00
134 Yvon Chasle 5.00 10.00
135 Denis Boucher 6.00 15.00
136 Claude Boileau 5.00 10.00
137 Claude Vinet 5.00 10.00
138 Claude Provost 20.00 40.00
139 Henri Richard 150.00 300.00
140 Les Lilley 5.00 10.00
141 Phil Goyette 15.00 40.00
142 Guy Rousseau 5.00 10.00
143 Paul Knox 5.00 10.00
144 Bill Lee 5.00 10.00
145 Ted Topazzini 6.00 15.00
146 Marc Reaume 6.00 15.00
147 Bill Dineen 15.00 40.00
148 Ed Plata 5.00 10.00
149 Noel Price 6.00 15.00
150 Mike Ratchford 5.00 10.00
151 Jim Logan 5.00 10.00
152 Art Clune 5.00 10.00
153 Jerry MacNamara 5.00 10.00
154 Jack Caffery 6.00 15.00
155 Les Duff 5.00 10.00
156 Murray Costello 6.00 15.00
157 Ed Chadwick 40.00 80.00
158 Mike Desilets 5.00 10.00
159 Ross Watson 5.00 10.00
160 Roger Landry 5.00 10.00
161 Terry O'Connor 5.00 10.00
162 Ovila Gagnon 5.00 10.00
163 Dave Broadbelt 5.00 10.00
164 Sandy Morrisson 5.00 10.00
165 John McGillvray 5.00 10.00
166 Claude Beaupre 5.00 10.00
167 Eddie Eustache 5.00 10.00
168 Stan Rodek 5.00 10.00
169 Maurice Mantha 6.00 15.00
170 Hector Lalande 8.00 20.00
171 Bob Wilson 5.00 10.00
172 Frank Bonello 5.00 10.00
173 Peter Kowalchuch 5.00 10.00
174 Les Binkley 25.00 50.00
175 John Muckler 20.00 40.00
176 Ken Wharram 15.00 40.00
177 John Sleaver 5.00 10.00
178 Ralph Markarian 5.00 10.00
179 Ken McMeekin 5.00 10.00
180 Ron Boomer 5.00 10.00
181 Kenneth (Red) Crawford 5.00 10.00
182 Jim McBurney 8.00 20.00

2001-02 Kalamazoo K-Wings

COMPLETE SET (24) 4.00 10.00
1 Andrew Huggett .20 .50
2 Michael Goldkind .20 .50
3 Sergei Deshevyy .20 .50
4 Randy Holmes .20 .50
5 Michael Ford .20 .50
6 Jeff Scharf .20 .50
7 Mathieu Paul .20 .50
8 Jim Brown .20 .50
9 Darcy Anderson .20 .50
10 Harry Schwefel .20 .50
11 Greg Dupre .20 .50
12 Benoit Beausoleil .20 .50
13 Craig Patterson .20 .50
14 Jeff Foster .20 .50
15 Mark Lawrence .30 .75
16 Steve Moore .20 .50
17 Tim Knudsen .30 .75
18 Scott Langkow .30 .75
19 Brad Cook .20 .50
20 Sandy Lamarre .20 .50
21 Ted Laviolette .20 .50
22 Dennis Desrosiers CO .04 .10
23 Scott Allison TR .04 .10
24 Slappy MASCOT .04 .10
NNO Team CL .04 .10

1977-78 Kalamazoo Wings

COMPLETE (15) 15.00 30.00
1 George Kisons 1.00 2.00
2 Ron Wilson 1.00 2.00
3 Bob Lemieux 1.00 2.00
4 Len Ircandia 1.00 2.00
5 Ron Kennedy 1.00 2.00
6 Daniel Poulin 1.00 2.00
7 Terry Evans 1.00 2.00
8 Yvon Douris 1.00 2.00
9 Tom Milani 1.00 2.00
10 Mike Wanchuk 1.00 2.00
11 Steve Lee 1.00 2.00
12 Yves Guilmette 1.00 2.00
13 Al Genovy 1.00 2.00
15 Jim Baxter 1.00 2.00
18 Alvin White 1.00 2.00

2002-03 Kalamazoo Wings

COMPLETE SET (29) 8.00 20.00
1 Checklist .04 .10
2 Kirill Alexeev .40 1.00
3 Tyson Turgeon .40 1.00
4 Eric Lawson .40 1.00
5 Quade Lightbody .40 1.00
6 Herman Hultgren .40 1.00
7 Bryan Farquhar .40 1.00
8 Mike Ford .40 1.00
9 Peter Roed .40 1.00
10 Joe Pecoraro .40 1.00
11 Jordan Trew .40 1.00
12 Glendon Cominetti .40 1.00
13 Pete Pierman .40 1.00
14 Kurt Miller .40 1.00
15 Mark Phenow .40 1.00
16 Craig Bilick .40 1.00
17 Mark Lawrence .40 1.00
18 Justin Cardwell .40 1.00
19 Richard Keyes .40 1.00
20 Chad Dameworth .40 1.00
21 Chad Alban .60 1.50
22 Brian Rogers .40 1.00
23 Jeff Reynaert .40 1.00
24 Mark Kaufman CO .04 .10
25 Mike Modugno ANN .04 .10
26 Scott Allison TR .04 .10
27 Slappy Mascot .04 .10
28 Shoe Carnival .04 .10
29 Burger King .04 .10

2003-04 Kalamazoo Wings

COMPLETE SET (32) 4.00 10.00
1 Checklist .04 .10
2 Mark Reeds CO .04 .10
3 Mark Vilneff .15 .40
4 Guy Dupuis .15 .40
5 Tyson Turgeon .15 .40
6 Jim Dube .15 .40
7 Kevin Caudill .15 .40
8 Daniel Carriere .15 .40
9 Steve Doherty .15 .40
10 Tyler Willis .30 .75
11 Jeff Turner .15 .40
12 Kurt Miller .15 .40
13 Marty Flichel .15 .40
14 Tim Turner .15 .40
15 David Hukalo .15 .40
16 Yannick Carpentier .15 .40
17 Pat O'Leary .15 .40
18 Josh Akright .15 .40
19 Andrew Luciuk .15 .40
20 Dan Watson .15 .40
21 Chad Alban .30 .75
22 Brock McGillis .30 .75
23 Brent Rumble .15 .40
24 Nick Bootland .30 .75
25 Joe Ritson .15 .40
26 Team Staff .04 .10
27 Mike Modugno ANN .04 .10
28 Mascot .04 .10
29 Ad Card .04 .10
30 Ad Card .04 .10
31 Ad Card .04 .10
32 Ad Card .04 .10

2004-05 Kalamazoo Wings

COMPLETE SET (30) 5.00 12.00
1 Checklist .04 .10
2 Mark Reeds CO .04 .10
3 Josh Elzinga .20 .50
4 Mark Vilneff .20 .50
5 Kevin Holdridge .20 .50
6 Tyson Turgeon .20 .50
7 Shaun Fisher .20 .50
8 Daniel Carriere .20 .50
9 Greg Labenski .20 .50
10 Tyler Willis .20 .50
11 Tom Ditzer .20 .50
12 Steve Doherty .20 .50
13 Tim Turner .20 .50
14 Matt Noga .20 .50
15 Tim Krueckl .20 .50
16 Yannick Carpentier .20 .50
17 Ryan Crane .20 .50
18 Gray Shaneberger .20 .50
19 Andrew Luciuk .20 .50
20 Sean Starke .20 .50
21 Kevin Kotyluk .20 .50
22 Chad Alban .40 1.00
23 Joel Martin .20 .50
24 Mike Manley .20 .50
25 Daniel Carriere AS
Greg Labenski AS .20 .50
26 Trainers .04 .10
27 Slappy MASCOT .04 .10
28 Announcer .04 .10
29 Rocker Morning Show .04 .10
30 WKFR Morning Show .04 .10

2005-06 Kalamazoo Wings

COMPLETE SET (30) 8.00 20.00
1 Kalamazoo Wings CL .02 .10
2 Mark Reeds HC .02 .10
3 Josh Elzinga .40 1.00
4 Mark Vilneff .40 1.00
5 Mike Dombkiewicz .40 1.00
6 Jason Deitsch .40 1.00
7 Daniel Carriere .40 1.00
8 Tyler Willis .40 1.00
9 Damian Surma .40 1.00
10 Tim Turner .40 1.00
11 Lucas Drake .40 1.00
12 Tyler Rennette .40 1.00
13 Dustin Virag .40 1.00
14 Adam Elzinga .40 1.00
15 Lee Ruff .40 1.00
16 Brad Church .40 1.00
17 Greg Labenski .40 1.00
18 Kory Karlander .40 1.00
19 Jeff Reynaert .40 1.00
20 Mike Manley .40 1.00
21 Joel Martin .40 1.00
22 Nick Bootland .40 1.00
23 K-Wings Alumni .40 1.00
24 Mike Plandowski TR .02 .10
25 Eric Bechtol EQM .02 .10
26 Slappy MASCOT .02 .10
27 Mike Modugno ANN .02 .10
28 The Rocker Morning Show .02 .10
29 The KFR Morning Show .02 .10
30 Scoopie MASCOT .02 .10

1984-85 Kamloops Blazers

COMPLETE SET (24) 8.00 20.00
1 Will Anderson .30 .75
2 Brian Benning .30 .75
3 Brian Bertuzzi .30 .75
4 Rob Brown .60 1.50
5 Todd Carnelley .30 .75
6 Dean Clark .40 1.00
7 Rob Dimaio .75 2.00
8 Greg Evtushevski .30 .75
9 Mark Ferner .30 .75
10 Greg Hawgood .60 1.50
11 Ken Hitchcock CO .75 2.00
12 Mark Kachowski .30 .75
13 Bob Labrier ACO .08 .25
14 Pat Mangold .30 .75
15 Gord Mark .30 .75
16 Len Mark .30 .75
17 Rob McKinley .40 1.00
18 Mike Nottingham .30 .75
19 Neil Pilon .30 .75
20 Rudy Poeschek .75 2.00
21 Daryl Reaugh .75 2.00
22 Ryan Stewart .30 .75
23 Mark Thietke .30 .75
24 Gord Walker .30 .75

1985-86 Kamloops Blazers

COMPLETE SET (26) 12.00 30.00
1 Robin Bawa .75 2.00
2 Craig Berube 2.00 5.00
3 Pat Bingham .40 1.00
4 Rob Brown .75 2.00
5 Todd Carnelly .40 1.00
6 Randy Hansch .75 2.00
7 Greg Hawgood .75 2.00
8 Ken Hitchcock CO 2.00 5.00
9 Mark Kachowski .40 1.00
10 Troy Kennedy .40 1.00
11 R.T. Labrier ACO .20 .50
12 Dave Marcinyshyn .40 1.00
13 Len Mark .40 1.00
14 Rob McKinley .40 1.00
15 Ken Morrison .40 1.00
16 Pat Nogier .40 1.00
17 Mike Nottingham .40 1.00
18 Doug Pickell .40 1.00
19 Rudy Poeschek 2.00 5.00
20 Mike Ragot .40 1.00
21 Don Schmidt .40 1.00
22 Ron Shudra .40 1.00
23 Peter Soberlak .40 1.00
24 Lonnie Spink .40 1.00
25 Chris Tarnowski .40 1.00
26 Greg Wallace TR .07 .20

1986-87 Kamloops Blazers

COMPLETE SET (24) 12.00 30.00
1 Warren Babe .20 .50
2 Robin Bawa .20 .50
3 Rob Brown .60 1.50
4 Dean Cook .40 1.00
5 Scott Daniels .20 .50
6 Mario Desjardines .20 .50
7 Bill Harrington .20 .50
8 Greg Hawgood .40 1.00
9 Serge Lajoie .20 .50
10 Dave Marcinyshyn .20 .50
11 Len Mark .20 .50
12 Rob McKinley .40 1.00
13 Casey McMillan .20 .50
14 Darcy Norton .20 .50
15 Kelly Para .20 .50
16 Doug Pickell .20 .50
17 Rudy Poeschek .60 1.50
18 Mark Recchi 6.00 15.00
19 Don Schmidt .20 .50
20 Ron Shudra .20 .50
21 Chris Tarnowski .20 .50
22 Steve Wienke .20 .50
23 Rich Wiest .20 .50
24 Team Photo .20 .50

1987-88 Kamloops Blazers

COMPLETE SET (24) 12.00 30.00
1 Warren Babe .30 .75
2 Paul Checknita .30 .75
3 Dave Chyzowski .40 1.00
4 Dean Cook .30 .75
5 Greg Davies .30 .75
6 Kim Deck .30 .75
7 Todd Decker .30 .75
8 Bill Harrington .30 .75

9 Phil Huber	.30	.75
10 Steve Kloepzig	.30	.75
11 Willie MacDonald	.40	1.00
12 Pat MacLeod	.30	.75
13 Glenn Mulvenna	.40	1.00
14 Mike Needham	.30	.75
15 Darcy Norton	.30	.75
16 Devon Oleniuk	.30	.75
17 Doug Pickell	.30	.75
18 Garth Premak	.30	.75
19 Mark Recchi	6.00	15.00
20 Don Schmidt	.30	.75
21 Alec Sheflo	.30	.75
22 Team Photo	.20	.50
23 Logo Card	.08	.25
24 Logo Card	.08	.25

1988-89 Kamloops Blazers

COMPLETE SET (36)	8.00	20.00
COMMON AD CARD (25-36)	.02	.10
1 Cory Anderson	.20	.50
2 Pat Bingham	.20	.50
3 Ed Bertuzzi	.20	.50
4 Zac Boyer	.20	.50
5 Trevor Buchanan	.20	.50
6 Dave Chyzowski	.30	.75
7 Dean Cook	.30	.75
8 Cory Crichton	.20	.50
9 Kim Deck	.20	.50
10 Ryan Harrison	.20	.50
11 Brad Heschuk	.20	.50
12 Corey Hirsch	1.25	3.00
13 Phil Huber	.20	.50
14 Len Jorgenson	.20	.50
15 Paul Kruse	.30	.75
16 Dave Linford	.20	.50
17 Pat MacLeod	.20	.50
18 Darwin McClelland	.20	.50
19 Cal McGowan	.20	.50
20 Mike Needham	.20	.50
21 Don Schmidt	.20	.50
22 Brian Shantz	.20	.50
23 Darryl Sydor	1.50	3.50
24 Steve Yule	.20	.50
25 Hasty Market Ad	.02	.10
26 McDonalds Ad	.02	.10
27 Mr. Mike's Ad	.02	.10
28 Yellow Submarine Ad	.02	.10
29 Blazers Logo	.02	.10
30 Blazers Logo	.02	.10
31 Blazers Logo	.02	.10
32 Blazers Logo	.02	.10
33 Blazers Logo	.02	.10
34 Blazers Logo	.02	.10
35 Blazers Logo	.02	.10
36 Blazers Logo	.02	.10

1989-90 Kamloops Blazers

COMPLETE SET (24)	6.00	15.00
1 Len Barrie	.20	.50
2 Craig Bonner	.20	.50
3 Jarrett Bousquet	.20	.50
4 Zac Boyer	.25	.60
5 Murray Duval	.20	.50
6 Shea Essolmont	.20	.50
7 Todd Esselmont	.20	.50
8 Todd Harris	.20	.50
9 Corey Hirsch	.60	1.50
10 Phil Huber	.20	.50
11 Lance Johnson	.20	.50
12 Paul Kruse	.25	.60
13 Dean Malkoc	.20	.50
14 Dale Mason	.20	.50
15 Cal McGowan	.20	.50
16 Joey Mittelsteadt	.20	.50
17 Mike Needham	.25	.60
18 Scott Niedermayer	1.50	4.00
19 Brian Shantz	.20	.50
20 Trevor Sim	.20	.50
21 Darryl Sydor	.75	2.00
22 Jeff Waalchom	.20	.50
23 Clayton Young	.20	.50
24 Steve Yule	.20	.50

1993-94 Kamloops Blazers

COMPLETE SET (24)	12.00	35.00
1 Nolan Baumgartner	.30	.75
2 Rod Branch	.20	.50
3 Jarrett Deuling	.20	.50
4 Shane Doan	2.00	5.00
5 Hnat Domenichelli	.30	.75
6 Scott Ferguson	.20	.50
7 Greg Hart	.20	.50
8 Jason Holland	.20	.50
9 Ryan Huska	.20	.50
10 Jarome Iginla	6.00	15.00
11 Mike Josephson	.20	.50
12 Aaron Keller	.20	.50
13 Mike Krooshoop	.20	.50
14 Scott Loucks	.20	.50
15 Brad Lukowich	.40	1.00
16 Bob Maudie	.20	.50
17 Chris Murray	.20	.50
18 Tyson Nash	1.25	3.00
19 Steve Passmore	.60	1.50
20 Rod Stevens	.20	.50
21 Jason Strudwick	.30	.75
22 Darcy Tucker	1.50	4.00
23 Bob Westerby	.20	.50
24 David Wilkie	.20	.50

1994-95 Kamloops Blazers

COMPLETE SET (24)	12.00	30.00
1 Darcy Tucker	.75	2.00
2 Jarome Iginla	4.00	10.00
3 Nolan Baumgartner	.40	1.00
4 Jeff Oldenborger	.20	.50
5 Ivan Vologjaninov	.20	.50
6 Shawn McNeil	.20	.50
7 Donnie Kinney	.20	.50
8 Bob Maudie	.20	.50
9 Jason Holland	.20	.50
10 Greg Hart	.20	.50
11 Shane Doan	1.25	3.00
12 Brad Lukowich	.40	1.00
13 Randy Petruk	.40	1.00
14 Jason Strudwick	.40	1.00
15 Jeff Ainsworth	.20	.50
16 Aaron Keller	.20	.50
17 Rod Branch	.20	.50
18 Bob Westerby	.20	.50
19 Tyson Nash	1.25	3.00
20 Hnat Domenichelli	.40	1.00
21 Ryan Huska	.20	.50
22 Jeff Henkelman	.20	.50
23 Cam Severson	.20	.50
24 Kamloops Arena	.04	.10

1995-96 Kamloops Blazers

COMPLETE SET (31)	8.00	20.00
1 Jarome Iginla	2.00	5.00
2 Nolan Baumgartner	.20	.50
3 Jake Deadmarsh	.20	.50
4 Scott Reid	.20	.50
5 Randy Petruk	.30	.75
6 Brad Lukowich	.40	1.00
7 Shawn McNeil	.30	.75
8 Ed Dempsey CO	.08	.25
9 Peter Bergman	.20	.50
10 Greg Hart	.20	.50
11 Hnat Domenichelli	.40	1.00
12 Al Glendenning CO	.08	.25
13 Digger MAS	.02	.10
14 Rob Skrlac	.20	.50
15 Donnie Kinney	.20	.50
16 Chris St. Croix	.20	.50
17 Jeff Oldenborger	.20	.50
18 Steve Albrecht	.20	.50
19 Bob Maudie	.20	.50
20 Blair Rota	.20	.50
21 Brian Henderson CO	.08	.25
22 Aaron Keller	.20	.50
23 Ryan Rishaug	.20	.50
24 Steve Gainey	.40	1.00
25 Jeff Ainsworth	.20	.50
26 Ajay Baines	.20	.50
27 Jordan Landry	.20	.50
28 Jason Holland	.20	.50
29 Kamloops Arena	.08	.25
30 Cadrin Smart	.20	.50
31 Konrad Brand	.20	.50

1996-97 Kamloops Blazers

COMPLETE SET (28)	8.00	20.00
1 Jeff Ainsworth	.30	.75
2 Steve Albrecht	.30	.75
3 Nils Antons	.30	.75
4 Ajay Baines	.30	.75
5 Konrad Brand	.30	.75
6 Wade Burt	.30	.75
7 Jake Deadmarsh	.30	.75
8 Ed Dempsey CO	.08	.25
9 Digger MAS	.02	.10
10 Micki DuPont	.40	1.00
11 Steve Gainey	.40	1.00
12 Jonathan Hobson	.30	.75
13 Drew Kehler	.30	.75
14 Donnie Kinney	.30	.75
15 Alan Manness	.30	.75
16 Shawn McNeil	.30	.75
17 Randy Petruk	.40	1.00
18 Clayton Pool	.40	1.00
19 Gennady Razin	.30	.75
20 Robyn Regehr	.60	1.50
21 Blair Rota	.30	.75
22 Thomas Scantlebury	.30	.75
23 Steve Shrum	.30	.75
24 Rob Skrlac	.30	.75
25 Darcy Smith	.30	.75
26 Chris St. Croix	.30	.75
27 Spike Wallace	.08	.25
28 Darren Wright	.30	.75

1998-99 Kamloops Blazers

COMPLETE SET (24)	12.00	20.00
1 Jared Aulin	.40	1.00
2 Ajay Baines	.40	1.00
3 Anton Borodkin	.30	.75
4 Mike Brown	.30	.75
5 Paul Deniset	.30	.75
6 Adam Dombrowski	.30	.75
7 Brett Draney	.30	.75
8 Micki Dupont	.40	1.00
9 Kenric Exner	.40	1.00
10 Jordon Flodell	.30	.75
11 Steve Gainey	.40	1.00
12 Aaron Gionet	.30	.75
13 Gable Gross	.30	.75
14 Jonathan Hobson	.30	.75
15 Donnie Kinney	.30	.75
16 David Klatt	.30	.75
17 Kevin MacKie	.30	.75
18 Alan Manness	.30	.75
19 Konstantin Panov	.30	.75
20 Robyn Regehr	.75	2.00
21 Steve Shrum	.30	.75
22 Chris St. Croix	.30	.75
23 Chad Starling	.30	.75
24 Ryan Thorpe	.30	.75

1999-00 Kamloops Blazers

COMPLETE SET (24)	6.00	15.00
1 Jared Aulin	.75	2.00
2 Jason Bone	.30	.75
3 Anton Borodkin	.20	.50
4 Erik Christensen	.20	.50
5 Paul Deniset	.20	.50
6 Blaine Depper	.20	.50
7 Brett Draney	.20	.50
8 Micki DuPont	.40	1.00
9 Aaron Gionet	.30	.75
10 Gable Gross	.20	.50
11 Jonathan Hobson	.20	.50
12 Kyle Ladobruk	.20	.50
13 Kevin Mackie	.20	.50
14 Grant McCune	.30	.75
15 Shaone Morrisonn	.60	1.50
16 Mike Munro	.20	.50
17 Konstantin Panov	.30	.75
18 Davis Parley	.30	.75
19 Mark Rooneem	.20	.50
20 Chad Schockenmaier	.20	.50
21 Steve Shrum	.20	.50
22 Chad Starling	.20	.50
23 Jordan Walker	.20	.50
24 Digger MASCOT	.08	.25

2000-01 Kamloops Blazers

COMPLETE SET (24)	6.00	15.00
1 Ryan Cuthbert	.20	.50
2 Steve Belanger	.40	1.00
3 Tyler Boldt	.20	.50
4 Josh Bonar	.20	.50
5 Pat Brandreth	.20	.50
6 Erik Christensen	.40	1.00
7 Paul Elliott	.20	.50
8 Aaron Gionet	.40	1.00
9 Gable Gross	.20	.50
10 Jonathan Hobson	.20	.50
11 Nikita Korovkin	.20	.50
12 Derek Krestanovich	.20	.50
13 Kyle Ladobruk	.20	.50
14 Jarret Lukin	.20	.50
15 Shaone Morrisonn	.40	1.00
16 Colton Orr	1.25	3.00
17 Konstantin Panov	.20	.50
18 Davis Parley	.40	1.00
19 Mark Rooneem	.20	.50
20 Chad Shockenmaier	.20	.50
21 Conlan Seder	.20	.50
22 Tyler Sloan	.20	.50
23 Scottie Upshall	.75	2.00
24 Digger MASCOT	.02	.10

2002-03 Kamloops Blazers

1 The Coaches	.10	.25
2 Mascot	.04	.10
3 Devan Dubnyk	1.25	3.00
4 Paul Brown	.30	.75
5 Wade Davis	.30	.75
6 Reid Jorgensen	.30	.75
7 Jason Lloyd	.30	.75
8 Moises Gutierrez	.30	.75
9 Cam Cunning	.30	.75
10 Grant Jacobsen	.30	.75
11 Josh Morrow	.30	.75
12 Davis Parley	.60	1.50
13 Jonas Johansson	.60	1.50
14 Nikita Korovkin	.30	.75
15 Tyler Boldt	.30	.75
16 Scottie Upshall	.60	1.50
17 Erik Christensen	.60	1.50
18 Aaron Gionet	.30	.75
19 Kris Hogg	.30	.75

2003-04 Kamloops Blazers

COMPLETE SET (24)	8.00	20.00
1 Geoff McIntosh	.30	.75
2 Roman Tesliuk	.30	.75
3 Kalvin Sagert	.30	.75
4 Max Gordichuk	.30	.75
5 Josh Garbutt	.30	.75
6 Grant Jacobsen	.30	.75
7 Jonas Johansson	.60	1.50
8 Nathan Grochmal	.30	.75
9 Cam Cunning	.30	.75
10 Kris Hogg	.30	.75
11 Kyle Sheen	.30	.75
12 Brock Nixon	.30	.75
13 Rick Kozak	.30	.75
14 Paul Brown	.40	1.00
15 Conlan Seder	.30	.75
16 Codey Becker	.30	.75
17 Ryan Bender	.30	.75
18 Ray Macias	.30	.75
19 Moises Gutierrez	.30	.75
20 Devan Dubnyk	1.00	2.50
21 Jarret Lukin	.30	.75
22 Reid Jorgensen	.30	.75
23 Derek Werenka	.30	.75
24 Checklist	.04	.10

2005-06 Kamloops Blazers

COMPLETE SET (25)	6.00	15.00
1 Checklist	.02	.10
2 Michael Maniago	.30	.75
3 Roman Tesliuk	.30	.75
4 Garrett Thiessen	.30	.75
5 Keaton Ellerby	.30	.75
6 Ryan White	.40	1.00
7 Victor Bartley	.30	.75
8 Ashton Rome	.40	1.00
9 Janick Steinmann	.30	.75
10 C.J. Stretch	.30	.75
11 Travis Dunstall	.30	.75
12 Scott Skrudland	.30	.75
13 T.J. Mulock	.30	.75
14 Brady Mason	.30	.75
15 Brock Nixon	.30	.75
16 Matt Kassian	.30	.75
17 Kevin Hayman	.30	.75
18 Terrance Delaronde	.30	.75
19 Ryan Bender	.30	.75
20 Ray Macias	.30	.75
21 Moises Gutierrez	.30	.75
22 Devan Dubnyk	.60	1.50
23 Joel Eisenkirch	.30	.75
24 Reid Jorgensen	.30	.75
25 911 Digger MASCOT	.02	.10

2006-07 Kamloops Blazers

COMPLETE SET (25)	10.00	18.00
1 Victor Bartley	.30	.75
2 Ryan Bender	.30	.75
3 Dustin Butler	.40	1.00
4 Terrance Delaronde	.30	.75
5 Brenden Dowd	.30	.75
6 Travis Dunstall	.30	.75
7 Keaton Ellerby	.30	1.25
8 Dalyn Flette	.40	1.00
9 Sasha Golin	.30	.75
10 Mark Hall	.30	.75
11 Reid Jorgensen	.30	.75
12 Matt Kassian	.30	.75
13 Kevin Kraus	.30	.75
14 Raymond Macias	.30	.75
15 Brady Mason	.30	.75
16 Brock Nixon	.30	.75
17 Juuso Puustinen	.30	.75
18 Alex Rodgers	.30	.75
19 Ivan Rohac	.30	.75
20 Jordan Rowley	.30	.75
21 Tyler Shattock	.30	.75
22 C.J. Stretch	.30	.75
23 Ryan White	.30	.75
24 Kamloops Blazers CL	.01	.05
25 Digger MASCOT	.02	.10

2007-08 Kamloops Blazers

COMPLETE SET (25)	5.00	12.00
1 Kurt Torbohm	.25	.60
2 Spencer Fraipont	.25	.60
3 Ivan Rohac	.25	.60
4 Mark Hall	.25	.60
5 Brady Calla	.25	.60
6 CJ Stretch	.25	.60
7 Scott Wasden	.25	.60
8 Kenton Dulle	.25	.60
9 Tyler Shattock	.25	.60
10 Juuso Puustinen	.25	.60
11 Matt Wray	.25	.60
12 Devon Kalinski	.25	.60
13 Jimmy Bubnick	.25	.60
14 Alex Rodgers	.25	.60
15 Sasha Golin	.25	.60
16 Jordan Rowley	.25	.60
17 Darcy Huisman	.25	.60
18 Nick Ross	.25	.60
19 Mark Schneider	.25	.60
20 James Priestner	.25	.60
21 Justin Leclerc	.25	.60
22 Mike Gauthier	.25	.60
23 Shayne Wiebe	.25	.60
24 Digger	.15	.40
25 Kamloops Blazers Checklist	.15	.40

2014-15 Kamloops Blazers

COMPLETE SET (25)	6.00	15.00
1 Quinn Benjafield	.30	.75
2 Matthew Campese	.30	.75
3 Nick Chyzowski	.30	.75
4 Dawson Davidson	.30	.75
5 Michael Fora	.30	.75
6 Brady Gaudet	.30	.75
7 Joel Hamilton	.30	.75
8 Luke Harrison	.30	.75
9 Connor Ingram	.30	.75
10 Cole Kehler	.30	.75
11 Jake Kryski	.30	.75
12 Jermaine Loewen	.30	.75
13 Patrik Maier	.30	.75
14 Marc McNulty	.30	.75
15 Logan McVeigh	.30	.75
16 Matt Needham	.30	.75
17 Cam Reagan	.30	.75
18 Ryan Rehill	.30	.75
19 Matt Revel	.30	.75
20 Collin Shirley	.30	.75
21 Deven Sideroff	.30	.75
22 Cole Ully	.30	.75
23 Travis Verveda	.30	.75
24 Jesse Zaharichuk	.30	.75
25 Header Card	.30	.75

1990-91 Kansas City Blades

COMPLETE SET (20)	4.00	10.00
1 Claudio Scremin	.20	.50
2 Jeff Odgers	.30	.75
3 Wade Flaherty	.30	.75
4 Rick Barkovich	.20	.50
5 Ron Handy	.20	.50
6 Kevin Sullivan	.20	.50
7 Randy Exelby	.30	.75
8 Darin Smith	.20	.50
9 Stu Kulak	.20	.50
10 Andrew Akervik	.20	.50
11 Scott White	.20	.50
12 Claude Julien	.20	.50
13 Mike Hiltner	.20	.50
14 Michael Colman	.20	.50
15 Kurt Semandel	.20	.50
16 Mike Kelter	.20	.50
17 Mark Karpen	.20	.50
18 Lee Giffin	.20	.50
19 Cam Plante	.20	.50
20 Jim Latos	.30	.75

1991-92 Kansas City Blades

COMPLETE SET (20)	4.80	12.00
1 Pat McLeod	.20	.50
2 Rick Lessard	.20	.50
3 Duane Joyce	.20	.50
4 David Williams	.20	.50
5 Arturs Irbe	1.25	3.00
6 Murray Garbutt	.20	.50
7 Gary Emmons	.20	.50
8 Jeff Madill	.20	.50
9 Ron Handy	.20	.50
10 Peter Lappin	.20	.50
11 Mike Colman	.20	.50
12 Ed Courtenay	.20	.50
13 Mikhail Kravets	.20	.50
14 Claudio Scremin	.20	.50
15 Dale Craigwell	.20	.50
16 Wade Flaherty	.30	.75
17 Kevin Evans	.20	.50
18 Larry DePalma	.20	.50
19 Dean Kolstad	.20	.50
20 Gord Frantti	.20	.50

1992-93 Kansas City Blades

COMPLETE SET (20)	4.00	10.00
1 Wade Flaherty	.30	.75
2 David Williams	.20	.50
3 Duane Joyce	.20	.50
4 Jeff Sharples	.20	.50
5 Victor Ignatjev	.20	.50
6 Jeff McLean	.20	.50
7 Brian Lawton	.20	.50
8 Troy Frederick	.20	.50
9 Jaroslav Otevrel	.20	.50
10 Gary Emmons	.20	.50
11 Dody Wood	.20	.50
12 Ed Courtenay	.20	.50
13 Mark Beaufait	.20	.50
14 J.F. Quintin	.20	.50
15 Dale Craigwell	.20	.50
16 Mikhail Kravets	.20	.50
17 John Weisbrod	.20	.50
18 Mike Colman	.20	.50
19 Claudio Scremin	.20	.50
20 Dean Kolstad	.20	.50

1993-94 Kansas City Blades

COMPLETE SET (20)	4.00	10.00
1 Duane Joyce	.20	.50
2 Sean Gorman	.20	.50
3 Victor Ignatjev	.20	.50
4 Jeff McLean	.20	.50
5 Kip Miller	.30	.75
6 Jaroslav Otevrel	.20	.50
7 David Bruce	.20	.50
8 Gary Emmons	.20	.50
9 Dody Wood	.20	.50
10 Lee Leslie	.20	.50
11 Alexander Cherbayev	.20	.50
12 J.F. Quintin	.20	.50
13 Ed Courtenay	.20	.50
14 Andrei Nazarov	.30	.75
15 Mikhail Kravets	.20	.50
16 Mike Colman	.20	.50
17 Vlastimil Kroupa	.20	.50
18 Andrei Buschan	.20	.50
19 Trevor Robins	.20	.50
20 Wade Flaherty	.30	.75

1994-95 Kansas City Blades

COMPLETE SET (20)	4.00	10.00
1 Duane Joyce	.20	.50
2 Ken Hammond	.20	.50
3 Michal Sykora	.20	.50
4 Kevin Wortman	.20	.50
5 Andrei Buschan	.20	.50
6 Chris Tancill	.20	.50
7 Ken Hodge	.20	.50
8 David Bruce	.20	.50
9 Jan Caloun	.30	.75
10 Gary Emmons	.20	.50
11 Dody Wood	.20	.50
12 Lee Leslie	.20	.50
13 Alexander Cherbayev	.20	.50
14 J.F. Quintin	.20	.50
15 Claudio Scremin	.20	.50
16 Dean Grillo	.20	.50
17 Andrei Nazarov	.30	.75
18 Todd Holt	.20	.50
19 Vlastimil Kroupa	.20	.50
20 Trevor Robins	.20	.50

1995-96 Kansas City Blades

COMPLETE SET (25)	4.00	10.00
1 Larry Dyck	.15	.40
2 Paul Dyck	.15	.40
3 Jeff Batters	.15	.40
4 David Bruce	.15	.40
5 Jan Caloun	.30	.75
6 Alexander Cherbayev	.20	.50
7 Gary Emmons	.15	.40
8 Dean Ewens	.15	.40
9 Pat Ferschweiler	.15	.40
10 Dean Grillo	.15	.40
11 Ken Hammond	.15	.40
12 Alexander Osadchy	.15	.40
13 Jeff McLean	.15	.40
14 Fredrik Nilsson	.20	.50
15 Fredrik Oduya	.15	.40
16 J.F. Quintin	.15	.40
17 Geoff Sarjeant	.20	.50
18 Claudio Scremin	.15	.40
19 Chris Tancill	.20	.50
20 Alexi Yegorov	.20	.50
21 Viktor Kozlov	.40	1.00
22 Sergei Bautin	.15	.40
23 Vasily Tikhonov HCO	.02	.10
24 Drew Remenda ACO	.02	.10
25 Chilly MASCOT	.02	.10

1996-97 Kansas City Blades

COMPLETE SET (25)	4.80	12.00
1 Ian Boyce	.20	.50
2 David Bruce	.30	.75
3 Jason Cirone	.20	.50
4 Dale Craigwell	.30	.75
5 Brent Cullaton	.20	.50
6 Philippe DeRouville	.30	.75
7 Larry Dyck	.20	.50
8 Paul Dyck	.20	.50
9 Gary Emmons	.20	.50
10 Dean Ewen	.20	.50
11 Bryan Fogarty	.20	.50
12 Jason Herter	.20	.50
13 Jim Kyte	.20	.50
14 Jeff Madill	.20	.50
15 Jeff McLean	.20	.50
16 John Purves	.30	.75
17 J.F. Quintin	.20	.50
18 Normand Rochefort	.20	.50
19 Claudio Scremin	.20	.50
20 Brian Stacey	.20	.50
21 Dean Sylvester	.30	.75
22 Don Jackson HCO	.02	.10
23 Lucien DeBlois ACO	.20	.50
24 KC Blades	.02	.10
25 PHPA Web Site	.02	.10

1997-98 Kansas City Blades Magnets

COMPLETE SET (5)	4.00	10.00
1 Claudio Scremin	.75	2.00
2 Gary Emmons	.75	2.00
3 David Bruce	.75	2.00
4 Jan Caloun	.75	2.00
5 Dean Grillo	.75	2.00

1998-99 Kansas City Blades

COMPLETE SET (30)	6.00	15.00
1 Title Card	.02	.10
2 Brian Leitza	.20	.50
3 Dan Ratushny	.20	.50
4 Trevor Sherban	.20	.50
5 Eric Rud	.20	.50
6 Tuomas Gronman	.20	.50
7 Eric Perrin	.20	.50
8 Brendan Yarema	.20	.50
9 Brian Bonin	.20	.50
10 Pat Ferschweiler	.20	.50
11 Dody Wood	.40	1.00
12 David Ling	.40	1.00
13 Rocky Weising	.20	.50
14 Jean-Guy Trudel	.30	.75
15 Vlastimil Kroupa	.20	.50
16 Steven Low	.20	.50
17 Ryan Mulhern	.20	.50
18 Brent Bilodeau	.20	.50
19 Grant Richison	.20	.50
20 Dave Chyzowski	.20	.50
21 David Vallieres	.20	.50
22 Patrick Lalime	.75	2.00
23 Jean Sebastien Aubin	.75	2.00
24 Jason Cirone	.20	.50
25 Paul MacLean CO	.02	.10
26 Gary Emmons ACO	.02	.10
27 John Doolan EQ	.02	.10
28 Jeff Kreuser TR	.02	.10
29 Scrapper Mascot	.02	.10
30 Logo Card	.02	.10

1999-00 Kansas City Blades

COMPLETE SET (2)	.75	2.00
1 Gary Emmons	.40	1.00
2 Wade Flaherty	.40	1.00

1999-00 Kansas City Blades Supercuts

COMPLETE SET	6.00	15.00
1 Tom Askey	.40	1.00
2 Joe Blaznek	.20	.50
3 Aris Brimanis	.20	.50
4 Dave Chyzowski	.20	.50
5 Jason Cirone	.20	.50
6 Pat Ferschweiler	.20	.50
7 Forrest Gore	.20	.50
8 Sean Haggerty	.20	.50
9 David Ling	.40	1.00
10 Steve Lingren	.20	.50
11 Tyler Moss	.40	1.00
12 Nick Naumenko	.20	.50
13 Eric Perrin	.20	.50
14 Michal Pivonka	.40	1.00
15 Bruce Racine	.40	1.00
16 Grant Richison	.20	.50
17 Jon Rohloff	.20	.50
18 Ray Schultz	.20	.50
19 David Valliers	.20	.50
20 Jan Vodrazka	.20	.50
21 Dody Wood	.40	1.00
22 Brendan Yarema	.20	.50
23 Scrapper MASCOT	.08	.25
24 Jeff Kreuser TR	.08	.25
25 John Doolan MGR	.08	.25
26 Gary Emmons CO	.08	.25
27 Paul MacLean HCO	.08	.25
28 PHPA Logo		.01
29 Supercuts Coupon		.01

2000-01 Kansas City Blades

COMPLETE SET (27)	6.00	15.00
1 Ryan Bonni	.30	.75
2 Jan Vodrazka	.20	.50
3 Bryan Allen	.30	.75
4 Zenith Komarniski	.20	.50
5 Sean Tallaire	.20	.50
6 Ryan Ready	.20	.50
7 Regan Darby	.20	.50
8 Dody Wood	.30	.75
9 Harold Druken	.30	.75
10 Darrell Hay	.20	.50
11 Vadim Sharifijanov	.30	.75
12 Steve Lingren	.20	.50
13 Josh Holden	.40	1.00
14 Mike Brown	.30	.75
15 Jeff Scissons	.20	.50
16 Jarkko Ruutu	.30	.75
17 Pat Kavanagh	.20	.50
18 Brad Leeb	.20	.50
19 Bryan Helmer	.20	.50
20 Artem Chubarov	.30	.50
21 Corey Schwab	.30	.75
22 Alfie Michaud	.30	.75
23 Stan Smyl CO	.20	.60
24 Barry Smith CO	.20	.50
25 Ryno SPONSOR	.02	.10
26 Dick's SPONSOR	.02	.10
27 PHPA SPONSOR	.02	.10

1998-99 Kelowna Rockets

COMPLETE SET (28)	6.00	15.00
1 Ryan Cuthbert	.20	.50
2 Jan Dusanek	.20	.50
3 B.J. Fehr	.20	.50
4 Vernon Fiddler	.30	.75
5 Mitch Fritz	.20	.50
6 Carsen Germyn	.20	.50
7 Scott Hannan	.40	1.00
8 Bruce Harrison	.20	.50
9 Trevor Hitchings	.20	.50
10 J.J. Hunter	.20	.50
11 Justin Jack	.20	.50
12 Clint Keichinger	.20	.50
13 Kevin Korol	.20	.50
14 Corey Koski	.20	.50
15 Quintin Laing	.20	.50
16 Lindsey Materi	.20	.50
17 Rory McDade	.20	.50
18 Brett McLean	.30	.75
19 Gavin McLeod	.20	.50
20 Kiel Mcleod	.40	1.00
21 Lubomir Pistek	.20	.50
22 Robby Sandrock	.20	.50
23 David Selthun	.20	.50
24 Joe Suderman	.20	.50
25 Kevin Swanson	.20	.50
26 Ryan Wade	.20	.50
27 Nolan Yonkman	.30	.75
28 Rocky Racoon MASCOT	.02	.10

2000-01 Kelowna Rockets

COMPLETE SET (22)	6.00	15.00
1 Kiel McLeod	.40	1.00
2 Rory McDade	.30	.75
3 Tomas Oravec	.30	.75
4 Carsen Germyn	.40	1.00
5 Chris Di Ubaldo	.30	.75
6 Ryan Cuthbert	.30	.75
7 Randall Gelech	.30	.75
8 Blaine Depper	.30	.75
9 Gavin McLeod	.30	.75
10 Bart Rushmer	.30	.75
11 Tyler Mosienko	.30	.75
12 Josh Gorges	.30	.75
13 Jason Stone	.30	.75
14 Brett Palin	.30	.75
15 Richie Regehr	.40	1.00
16 David Selthun	.30	.75
17 Seth Leonard	.30	.75
18 Jan Fadrny	.30	.75
19 Joe Suderman	.30	.75
20 Kevin Swanson	.30	.75
21 Rocky Raccoon MASCOT	.02	.10
22 Marc Habscheid CO	.10	.25
23 Paul Hurd	.20	.50
24 Cam Paddock	.20	.50
25 Richard Kelly	.20	.50
26 Travis Moen	.40	1.00

2001-02 Kelowna Rockets

COMPLETE SET (28)	8.00	20.00
1 Shane Bendera	.40	1.00
2 Jeff Coulter	.30	.75
3 Ryan Cuthbert	.30	.75
4 Jesse Ferguson	.30	.75
5 Randall Gelech	.30	.75
6 Josh Gorges	.40	1.00
7 Richard Kelly	.30	.75
8 Chuck Kobasew	1.25	3.00
9 Seth Leonard	.30	.75
10 Josh Lepp	.30	.75
11 Nick Marach	.30	.75
12 Ryan Mayko	.30	.75
13 Kiel McLeod	.40	1.00
14 Travis Moen	.40	1.00
15 Tyler Mosienko	.30	.75
16 Tomas Oravec	.30	.75
17 Cam Paddock	.30	.75
18 Brett Palin	.30	.75
19 Bart Rushmer	.30	.75
20 Tomas Slovak	.30	.75
21 Stephen Sunderman	.30	.75
22 Kevin Young	.30	.75
23 Marc Habscheid HCO	.08	.20
24 Larry Keating ACO	.04	.10
25 Jeff Truitt ACO	.04	.10
26 Scott Hoyer TR	.04	.10
27 Regan Bartel PA	.04	.10
28 Mascot	.04	.10

2002-03 Kelowna Rockets

COMPLETE SET (28)	6.00	15.00
1 Josh Lepp	.30	.75
2 Cam Paddock	.20	.50
3 Kiel McLeod	.40	1.00
4 Joel Henituik	.20	.50
5 Brett Palin	.20	.50
6 Richard Kelly	.20	.50
7 Stephen Sunderman	.20	.50
8 Tyler Spurgeon	.20	.50
9 Joni Lindolf	.20	.50
10 Darren Deschamps	.20	.50
11 Shea Weber	1.50	4.00
12 Randall Gelech	.20	.50
13 David Jacobson	.20	.50
14 Jesse Schultz	.20	.50
15 Blake Comeau	.20	.50
16 Ryan Mayko	.20	.50
17 Mike Card	.20	.50
18 Josh Gorges	.40	1.00
19 Tomas Slovak	.30	.75
20 Kelly Guard	.40	1.00
21 Troy Bodie	.20	.50
22 Ryan Cuthbert	.20	.50
23 Tyler Mosienko	.20	.50
24 Mark Olafson	.20	.50
25 Nick Tarnasky	.20	.50
26 Marc Habscheid HCO	.20	.50
27 Jeff Truitt ACO	.10	.25
28 Mascot	.04	.10

2003 Kelowna Rockets Memorial Cup

COMPLETE SET (20)	6.00	15.00
1 Troy Brodie	.30	.75
2 Mike Card	.30	.75
3 Blako Comoau	.30	.75
4 Ryan Cuthbert	.30	.75
5 Simon Ferguson	.30	.75
6 Randall Gelech	.30	.75
7 Josh Gorges	.40	1.00
8 Kelly Guard	.30	1.50
9 Duncan Keith	1.00	2.50
10 Josh Lepp	.40	1.00
11 Joni Lindolf	.30	.75
12 Kiel McLeod	.40	1.00
13 Tyler Mosienko	.30	.75
14 Mark Olafson	.30	.75
15 Cam Paddock	.30	.75
16 Brett Palin	.30	.75
17 Jesse Schultz	.40	1.00
18 Tomas Slovak	.40	1.00
19 Tyler Spurgeon	.30	.75
20 Shea Weber	1.00	2.50

2003-04 Kelowna Rockets

COMPLETE SET (28)	10.00	25.00
1 Michael Blanar	.40	1.00
2 Troy Bodie	.40	1.00
3 Mike Card	.40	1.00
4 Blake Comeau	.75	2.00
5 Kyle Cumiskey	.40	1.00
6 Darren Deschamps	.40	1.00
7 Simon Ferguson	.40	1.00
8 Randall Gelech	.40	1.00
9 Josh Gorges	.75	2.00
10 Kelly Guard	.75	2.00
11 Brent Howarth	.40	1.00
12 Justin Keller	.40	1.00
13 Joni Lindlof	.40	1.00
14 Tyler Mosienko	.40	1.00
15 Mark Olafson	.40	1.00
16 Cam Paddock	.40	1.00
17 Brett Palin	.40	1.00
18 Chris Ray	.40	1.00
19 Kevin Reinholt	.40	1.00
20 Tyler Spurgeon	.40	1.00
21 Nolan Waker	.40	1.00
22 Shea Weber	1.25	3.00
23 Derek Yeomans	.40	1.00
24 Marc Habscheid CO	.04	.10
25 Jeff Truitt ACO	.04	.10
26 Regan Bartel ANN	.04	.10

27 Scott Hoyer TR .04 .10
28 Rocky Raccoon MASCOT .04 .10

2004-05 Kelowna Rockets

COMPLETE SET (28) 8.00 20.00
1 Troy Bodie .30 .75
2 Shea Weber 1.25 3.00
3 Justin Keller .30 .75
4 Craig Cuthbert .30 .75
5 Darren Deschamps .30 .75
6 Kristofer Westblom .30 .75
7 Brett Palin .30 .75
8 Kyle Cumiskey .30 .75
9 Chris Ray .30 .75
10 Lauris Darzins .30 .75
11 Rockey Raccoon .04 .10
12 Jeff Truitt .30 .75
13 Colin Joe .30 .75
14 Tyler Mosienko .30 .75
15 Blake Comeau .50 1.25
16 Tyler Spurgeon .30 .75
17 Derek Yeomans .30 .75
18 Ryan Huska .30 .75
19 Scott Hoyer .30 .75
20 Regan Bartel .30 .75
21 Gary Sylvester .30 .75
22 Troy Ofukany .30 .75
23 Kirt Hill .30 .75
24 Brent Howarth .30 .75
25 Clayton Bauer .30 .75
26 Michal Blanar .30 .75
27 Mike Card .30 .75
28 Kevin Reinholt .30 .75

2005-06 Kelowna Rockets

COMPLETE SET (28) 8.00 20.00
1 Cody Almond .30 .75
2 Josiah Anderson .30 .75
3 Clayton Bauer .30 .75
4 Troy Bodie .30 .75
5 Mike Card .30 .75
6 Blake Comeau .60 1.50
7 Liam Couture .30 .75
8 Kyle Cumiskey .30 .75
9 Craig Cuthbert .30 .75
10 Lauris Darzins .30 .75
11 Tysen Dowzak .30 .75
12 Alexander Edler .30 .75
13 Kirt Hill .30 .75
14 Brent Howarth .30 .75
15 Colin Joe .30 .75
16 Justin Keller .30 .75
17 Colin Long .30 .75
18 Myles MacRae .30 .75
19 Troy Ofukany .30 .75
20 Chris Ray .30 .75
21 Kevin Reinholt .30 .75
22 Rob Roteliuk .30 .75
23 Luke Schenn .30 .75
24 Tyler Spurgeon .30 .75
25 Kristofer Westblom .30 .75
26 Derek Yeomans .30 .75
27 Jeff Truitt HC .02 .10
28 Rocky Raccoon MASCOT .02 .10

2014-15 Kelowna Rockets

COMPLETE SET (32) 8.00 20.00
1 Header Card CL .30 .75
2 Riley Stadel .30 .75
3 Madison Bowey .30 .75
4 Mitch Wheaton .30 .75
5 Lucas Johansen .30 .75
6 Cole Martin .30 .75
7 Tanner Wishnowski .30 .75
8 Nick Merkley .30 .75
9 Tyrell Goulbourne .30 .75
10 Rourke Chartier .30 .75
11 Tomas Soustal .30 .75
12 Rodney Southam .30 .75
13 Tate Coughlin .30 .75
14 Dillon Dube .30 .75
15 Gage Quinney .30 .75
16 Devante Stephens .30 .75
17 Chance Braid .30 .75
18 Justin Kirkland .30 .75
19 Tyson Baillie .50 1.25
20 Cole Linaker .30 .75
21 Josh Morrissey .30 .75
22 Joe Gatenby .30 .75
23 Leon Draisaitl 3.00 8.00
24 Jackson Whistle .30 .75
25 Michael Herringer .30 .75
26 Jake Morrissey .30 .75
27 Dan Lambert CO .30 .75
28 Kim Gellert Skills Ins. .30 .75
29 Travis Crickard Goalie CO .30 .75
30 Kris Mallette Asst. CO .30 .75
31 Scott Hoyer Trainer .30 .75
32 Rocky MASCOT .30 .75

1984-85 Kelowna Wings

COMPLETE SET (56) 32.00 80.00
1 Checklist .20 .50
2 Darcy Wakaluk .60 1.50
3 Stacey Nickel .20 .50
4 Jeff Sharples .30 .75
5 Greg Zuk .20 .50
6 Daryn Sivertson .20 .50
7 Randy Cameron .20 .50
8 Mark Fioretti .20 .50
9 Ron Viglasi .20 .50
10 Ian Herbers .20 .50
11 Mike Wegleitner .20 .50
12 Terry Zaporzan .20 .50
13 Dwaine Hutton .20 .50
14 Rod Williams .20 .50
15 Jeff Rohlicek .20 .50
16 Brent Gilchrist .60 1.50
17 Rocky Dundas .20 .50
18 Grant Delcourt .20 .50
19 Cam Laronuk .20 .50
20 Tony Horacek .20 .50
21 Mark Wingerter .20 .50
22 Mick Vukota .30 .75
23 Danny Gare .60 1.50
24 Rich Sutter .40 1.00
25 Alfie Turcotte .20 .50
26 Bryan Trottier 4.00 10.00
27 Bill Derlago .40 1.00
28 Stan Smyl .75 2.00
29 Brent Sutter .75 2.00
30 Mel Bridgman .40 1.00
31 Paul Cyr .30 .75
32 Gary Lupul .20 .50
33 Ray Neufeld .30 .75
34 Brian Propp .75 2.00
35 Bob Nystrom .75 2.00
36 Ryan Walter .40 1.00
37 Russ Courtnall .75 2.00
38 Larry Playfair .20 .50
39 Ron Delorme .20 .50
40 Ron Sutter .40 1.00
41 Bobby Clarke 4.00 10.00
42 Bob Bourne .40 1.00
43 Cam Neely 15.00 40.00
44 Murray Craven .40 1.00
45 Clark Gillies 1.25 3.00
46 Ron Flockhart .40 1.00
47 Harold Snepsts 1.25 3.00
48 Duane Sutter .40 1.00
49 Garth Butcher .40 1.00
50 Bill Hajt .20 .50
51 Jim Benning .20 .50
52 Ray Allison .20 .50
53 Ken Wregget .75 2.00
54 Phil Russell .30 .75
55 Brad McCrimmon .60 1.50
56 Dan Hodgson .20 .50

1996-97 Kentucky Thoroughblades

COMPLETE SET (26) 5.00 12.00
1 Ken Belanger .30 .75
2 Alexandre Boikov .20 .50
3 Jan Caloun .30 .75
4 Denis Chervyakov .20 .50
5 Jarrett Deuling .20 .50
6 Iain Fraser .20 .50
7 Dean Grillo .20 .50
8 Steve Guolla .30 .75
9 Sean Haggerty .20 .50
10 Jason Holland .20 .50
11 Lance Leslie .20 .50
12 Chris Lipuma .20 .50
13 Pat Mikesch .20 .50
14 Fredrik Oduya .20 .50
15 Jamie Ram .30 .75
16 Chris Tancill .30 .75
17 Jason Strudwick .30 .75
18 Steve Webb .30 .75
19 Jason Widmer .20 .50
20 Jim Wiley .20 .50
21 Alexei Yegorov .30 .75
NNO Ad Card-In Your Face .02 .10
NNO Ad Card-PHPA .02 .10
NNO Lucky the Mascot .02 .10
NNO Rupp Arena .20 .50
NNO Team Photo .08 .25

1997-98 Kentucky Thoroughblades

COMPLETE SET (25) 8.00 20.00
1 Team Photo .10 .25
2 Peter Allen .20 .50
3 Niklas Andersson .20 .50
4 Alexandre Boikov .20 .50
5 Zdeno Chara 1.25 3.00
6 Steve Guolla .25 .60
7 Sean Haggerty .20 .50
8 Jason Holland .20 .50
9 Alexander Korolyuk .30 .75
10 Evgeni Nabokov 4.00 10.00
11 Fredrik Oduya .20 .50
12 Chad Penney .20 .50
13 Jamie Ram .30 .75
14 Peter Roed .20 .50
15 Jason Strudwick .20 .50
16 Tony Tuzzolino .30 .75
17 Steve Webb .30 .75
18 Jason Widmer .20 .50
19 Brendan Yarema .20 .50
20 Alexei Yegorov .25 .60
21 Andrei Zyuzin .30 .75
22 Jim Wiley HCO .10 .25
23 Lucky Mascot .02 .10
24 PHPA Web Site .02 .10
25 AHL Web Site .02 .10

1998-99 Kentucky Thoroughblades

COMPLETE SET (25) 8.00 20.00
1 Peter Allen .15 .40
2 Eric Boulton .75 2.00
3 Dan Boyle .30 .75
4 Matt Bradley .20 .50
5 Mike Craig .15 .40
6 Jarrett Deuling .15 .40
7 Curtis Doell .15 .40
8 Dave Duerden .15 .40
9 Sean Gauthier .15 .40
10 Christian Gosselin .15 .40
11 Steve Guolla .20 .50
12 Harold Hersh .20 .50
13 Alexander Korolyuk .20 .50
14 Filip Kuba .20 .50
15 Steve Lingren .15 .40
16 Andy MacIntyre .10 .30
17 Evgeni Nabokov
Nickname John on card front 4.00 10.00
18 Jarrod Skalde .30 .75
19 Mark Smith .60 1.50
20 Herbert Vasiljevs .15 .40
21 Eric Veilleux .15 .40
22 Andrei Zyuzin .30 .75
23 Roy Sommer HCO .10 .25
24 Lucky Mascot .02 .10
25 AHL Web Site .02 .10

1999-00 Kentucky Thoroughblades

COMPLETE SET (25) 8.00 20.00
1 Kentucky Thoroughblades .08 .25
2 Coaching Staff .08 .25
3 Chris Armstrong .20 .50
4 Matt Bradley .20 .50
5 Garrett Burnett .20 .50
6 Adam Colagiacomo .30 .75
7 Jon Coleman .20 .50
8 Larry Courville .20 .50
9 Mike Craig .20 .50
10 Jarrett Deuling .20 .50
11 Doug Friedman .20 .50
12 Christian Gosselin .20 .50
13 Scott Hannan .30 .75
14 Johan Hedberg 2.00 5.00
15 Shawn Heins .30 .75
16 Robert Jindrich .20 .50
17 Miikka Kiprusoff 2.00 5.00
18 Eric Landry .20 .50
19 Chris Lipsett .20 .50
20 Andy Lundbohm .20 .50
21 Robert Mulick .20 .50
22 Adam Nittel .40 1.00
23 Peter Roed .20 .50
24 Mark Smith .30 .75
25 Lucky MASCOT .08 .25

2000-01 Kentucky Thoroughblades

COMPLETE SET (30) 30.00 80.00
1 Greg Andrusak .14 .35
2 Steve Bancroft .14 .40
3 Zoltan Batovsky .14 .40
4 Matt Bradley .14 .40
5 Jonathan Cheechoo 4.00 10.00
6 Adam Colagiacomo .20 .50
7 Larry Courville .20 .50
8 Rob Davison .20 .50
9 Jarrett Deuling .14 .35
10 Christian Gosselin .14 .40
11 Robert Jindrich .20 .50
12 Miikka Kiprusoff 4.00 10.00
13 Ryan Kraft .14 .50
14 Eric Laplante .14 .40
15 Chris Lipsett .14 .35
16 Andy Lundbohm .14 .35
17 Dave MacIsaac .14 .35
18 Jim Montgomery .20 .50
19 Robert Mulick .14 .40
20 Adam Nittel .40 1.00
21 Mikael Samuelsson .20 .50
22 Mark Smith .30 .75
23 Vesa Toskala 2.00 5.00
24 Miroslav Zalesak .10 .25
25 Roy Sommer CO
Nick Fotiu CO .10 .25
L1 Kentucky Thoroughblades .40 1.00
P1 Adam Nittel 1.00 2.50
P2 Jonathan Cheechoo 10.00 25.00
SP1 Ryan Kraft .60 2.00
SP2 Evgeni Nabokov 10.00 25.00

1981-82 Kingston Canadians

COMPLETE SET (25) 12.00 30.00
1 Canadians Logo .20 .50
2 Scott MacLellan .20 .50
3 Dave Courtemanche .20 .50
4 Mark Reade .20 .50
5 Shawn Babcock .20 .50
6 Phil Bourque .40 1.00
7 Ian MacInnis .20 .50
8 Neil Trineer .20 .50
9 Syl Grandmaitre .20 .50
10 Carmine Vani .30 .75
11 Chuck Brimmer .20 .50
12 Mike Linseman .20 .50
13 Steve Seguin .20 .50
14 Dan Wood .20 .50
15 Kirk Muller 6.00 15.00
16 Jim Aldred .20 .50
17 Rick Wilson .60 1.50
18 Mike Siltala .20 .50
19 Howie Scruton .20 .50
20 Mike Stothers .40 1.00
21 Dennis Smith .20 .50
22 Steve Richey .20 .50
23 Mike Moffat .75 2.00
24 Jim Morrison CO/MG .20 .50
25 Randy Plumb .20 .50

1982-83 Kingston Canadians

COMPLETE SET (27) 6.00 15.00
1 Jim Morrison MG .08 .25
2 Dennis Smith .20 .50
3 Curtis Collin .30 .75
4 Joel Brown .30 .75
5 Ron Handy .30 .75
6 Carmine Vani .30 .75
7 Al Andrews .40 1.00
8 Mike Siltala .30 .75
9 Syl Grandmaitre .30 .75
10 Steve Seguin .30 .75
11 Brian Dobbin .40 1.00
12 Mark Reade .30 .75
13 John Kemp .40 1.00
14 Dan Mahon .30 .75
15 Keith Knight .30 .75
16 Ron Sanko .30 .75
17 John Landry .30 .75
18 Chris Brant .30 .75
19 Dave Simurda .30 .75
20 Mike Lafoy .30 .75
21 Scott MacLellan .30 .75
22 Brad Walcot .30 .75
23 Steve Richey .30 .75
24 Rod Graham CO .08 .25
25 Ben Levesque .30 .75
26 Canadians Logo .08 .25
27 International Hockey
Hall of Fame .20 .50

1983-84 Kingston Canadians

COMPLETE SET (30) 6.00 15.00
1 Kingston Police Crest .08 .25
2 Dennis Smith .20 .50
3 Ben Levesque .20 .50
4 Const. Arie Moraal .08 .25
5 Tom Allen .20 .50
6 Mike Plesh .20 .50
7 Roger Belanger .20 .50
8 Jeff Chychrun .40 1.00
9 Mike King .20 .50
10 Scott Metcalfe .30 .75
11 David Lundmark .20 .50
12 Tim Salmon .20 .50
13 Ted Linesman .20 .50
14 Chris Clifford .30 .75
15 Todd Elik .40 1.00
16 Kevin Conway .20 .50
17 Barry Burkholder .20 .50
18 Joel Brown .20 .50
19 Steve King .20 .50
20 Craig Kales .20 .50
21 John Humphries TR .08 .25
22 David James .20 .50
23 Dave Simurda .20 .50
24 Allen Bishop .20 .50
25 Jeff Hogg .30 .75
26 Rick Cornacchia CO .30 .75
27 Ken Slater .08 .25
28 Bill Dextater .08 .25
29 Canadians Crest .08 .25
30 IHHOF logo .08 .25

1984-85 Kingston Canadians

COMPLETE SET (30) 6.00 15.00
1 Kingston Police Force .08 .25
2 Rick Cornacchia CO .20 .50
3 Const. Arie Moraal .08 .25
4 Ken Slater/DPP .08 .25
5 Kingston Crest .08 .25
6 Scott Metcalfe .30 .75
7 Chris Clifford .30 .75
8 Todd Elik .30 .75
9 Len Spratt .30 .75
10 Mike Plesh .20 .50
11 Marc Lyons .20 .50
12 Barry Burkholder .20 .50
13 Rick Fera .20 .50
14 David Hoover .20 .50
15 Andy Rivers .20 .50
16 Marc Laforge .30 .75
17 Peter Viscovich .20 .50
18 Jeff Chychrun .30 .75
19 Wayne Erskine .20 .50
20 Todd Clarke .20 .50
21 Darren Wright .20 .50
22 Tony Rocca .20 .50
23 Brian Verbeek .20 .50
24 Herb Raglan .30 .75
25 Daril Holmes .20 .50
26 Len Coyle TR .08 .25
27 Ted Linesman .20 .50
28 IHHOF logo .08 .25
29 Troy MacNevin .20 .50
30 Peter Campbell TR .08 .25

1985-86 Kingston Canadians

COMPLETE SET (30) 5.00 12.00
1 Kingston Police Crest .08 .25
2 Dale Sandles ACO .08 .25
3 Const. Arie Moraal .08 .25
4 Fred O'Donnell GM/CO .08 .25
5 Kingston Crest .08 .25
6 Scott Metcalfe .20 .50
7 Chris Clifford .30 .75
8 Steve Seftel .20 .50
9 Andy Pearson .20 .50
10 Jeff Cornelius .20 .50
11 Marc Lyons .20 .50
12 Barry Burkholder .20 .50
13 Bryan Fogarty .30 .75
14 Jeff Sirkka .20 .50
15 Scott Pearson .30 .75
16 Marc Laforge .20 .50
17 Peter Viscovich .20 .50
18 Jeff Chychrun UER
Name misspelled Chycren .30 .75
19 Wayne Erskine .20 .50
20 Todd Clarke .20 .50
21 Darren Wright .20 .50
22 Mike Maurice .20 .50
23 Brian Verbeek .20 .50
24 Mike Fiset .20 .50
25 Daril Holmes .20 .50
26 Len Coyle TR .08 .25
27 Ted Linesman .20 .50
28 IHHOF logo .08 .25
29 Troy MacNevin .20 .50
30 Peter Campbell TR .08 .25

1986-87 Kingston Canadians

COMPLETE SET (30) 4.00 10.00
1 Kingston Crest .08 .25
2 Fred O'Donnell GM/CO .02 .10
3 Arie Moraal COP .02 .10
4 Dale Sandles CO .02 .10
5 Kingston Police Crest .02 .10
6 Brian Tessier .30 .75
7 Franco Giammarco .20 .50
8 Peter Liptrott .20 .50
9 Chris Clifford .30 .75
10 Scott Metcalfe .20 .50
11 Scott Pearson .30 .75
12 Bryan Fogarty .30 .75
13 Daril Holmes .20 .50
14 Andy Rivers .20 .50
15 Troy MacNevin .20 .50
16 Marc Laforge .20 .50
17 Wayne Erskine .20 .50
18 Peter Viskovich .20 .50
19 Mike Maurice .20 .50
20 Steve Seftel .20 .50
21 Chad Badaway .20 .50
22 Marc Lyons .20 .50
23 Jeff Sirkka .20 .50
24 Mike Fiset .20 .50
25 John Battice .20 .50
26 Len Coyle TR .02 .10
27 Sloan Torti .20 .50
28 Alain Laforge .20 .50
29 Ted Linesman .20 .50
30 Peter Campbell TR .02 .10

1987-88 Kingston Canadians

COMPLETE SET (30) 4.80 12.00
1 Arie Moraal COP .02 .10
2 Gord Wood GM .02 .10
3 Kingston Police Crest .08 .25
4 Jacques Tremblay CO .08 .25
5 Rhonda Sheridan PR .02 .10
6 Jeff Wilson .30 .75
7 Franco Giammarco .30 .75
8 Peter Liptrott .20 .50
9 David Weiss .30 .75
10 Joel Morin .20 .50
11 Mark Turner .20 .50
12 Jeff Sirkka .20 .50
13 James Henckle .20 .50
14 Mike Bodnarchuk .20 .50
15 Mike Cavanaugh .20 .50
16 Darcy Cahill .20 .50
17 Kevin Falesy .20 .50
18 Dean Pella .20 .50
19 Brad Gratton .20 .50
20 Steve Seftel .30 .75
21 Bryan Fogarty .30 .75
22 Scott Pearson .20 .50
23 Tyler Pella .20 .50
24 Mike Fiset .20 .50
25 John Battice .20 .50
26 Len Coyle TR .02 .10
27 Geoff Schneider .20 .50
28 Chris Lukey .20 .50
29 Trevor Smith .20 .50
30 Peter Campbell TR .02 .10

1993-94 Kingston Frontenacs

COMPLETE SET (25) 4.00 10.00
1 Greg Lovell .15 .40
2 Marc Lamothe .15 .40
3 Tyler Moss .20 .50
4 Marc Moro .15 .40
5 Trevor Doyle .15 .40
6 Jeff Dacosta .15 .40
7 Gord Walsh .15 .40
8 Brian Scott .15 .40
9 Jason Disher .15 .40
10 Alexander Zhurik .15 .40
11 Ken Boone .30 .75
12 Cail MacLean .15 .40
13 Bill Maranduik .15 .40
14 Martin Sychra .15 .40
15 Duncan Fader .15 .40
16 David Ling .30 .75
17 Chad Kilger .30 .75
18 Greg Kraemer .15 .40
19 Trent Cull .15 .40
20 Steve Parson .15 .40
21 Craig Rivet .15 .40
22 Keli Corpse .15 .40
23 Brett Lindros .30 .75
24 David Allison CO
Michae .02 .10
NNO Slapshot Ad Card .02 .10

1998-99 Kingston Frontenacs

COMPLETE SET (25) 4.80 12.00
1 Eric Braff .20 .50
2 Brett Clouthier .20 .50
3 Curtis Cruickshank .20 .50
4 Matt Elich .30 .75
5 Aaron Fransen .20 .50
6 Sean Griffin .30 .75
7 Kevin Grimes .20 .50
8 Andrew Ianiero .20 .50
9 Chad Lynch .20 .50
10 D.J. Maracle .20 .50
11 Larry Mavety HCO .08 .25
12 Morgan McCormick .30 .75
13 Walker McDonald .30 .75
14 Matt Price .20 .50
15 Mike Oliveira .20 .50
16 Brett Ormond .20 .50
17 Ryan Rivard .20 .50
18 Jonathan Schill .20 .50
19 Colin Scotland .20 .50
20 Nathan Tennant .20 .50
21 Darryl Thomson .20 .50
22 Ian Turner .20 .50
23 Jamie Young .20 .50
24 Mike Zigomanis .40 1.00
25 Checklist .02 .10

1999-00 Kingston Frontenacs

COMPLETE SET (23) 6.00 15.00
1 Checklist .02 .10
2 Sean Avery .60 1.50
3 Eric Braff .20 .50
4 Brett Clouthier .30 .75
5 Chris Cook .20 .50
6 Sean Griffin .20 .50
7 Brad Horan .20 .50
8 Andrew Ianiero .20 .50
9 Matt Junkins .20 .50
10 Darryl Knight .20 .50
11 Travis Lisabeth .30 .75
12 Doug MacIver .20 .50
13 Shaun Peet .20 .50
14 Jason Polera .20 .50
15 Andrew Raycroft 1.00 2.50
16 Johnathan Schill .20 .50
17 J-F Seguin .20 .50
18 Tomas Skvaridlo .20 .50
19 Mike Smith .20 .50
20 Cory Stillman .40 1.00
21 Nathan Tennant .30 .75
22 Darryl Thomson .20 .50
23 Michael Zigomanis .40 1.00

2000-01 Kingston Frontenacs

COMPLETE SET (23) 4.80 10.00
1 Eric Braff .15 .40
2 Derek Campbell .15 .40
3 Brett Clouthier .30 .75
4 Chris Cook .15 .40
5 Count Frontenac MASCOT .04 .10
6 Peter Hamerlik .40 1.00
7 Brad Horan .15 .40
8 Andrew Ianiero .15 .40
9 Travis Lisabeth .15 .40
10 Doug MacIver .15 .40
11 The Coaches .04 .10
12 Justin McCutcheon .15 .40
13 Sean McMorrow .20 .50
14 Shane O'Brien .60 1.50
15 Glenn Ridler .30 .75
16 Corey Sabourin .15 .40
17 J.F. Seguin .15 .40
18 Tomas Skvaridlo .15 .40
19 Cory Stillman .30 .75
20 Nathan Tennant .15 .40
21 Darryl Thomson .15 .40
22 Brody Todd .15 .40
23 Mike Zigomanis .40 1.00
NNO Coca Cola .01 .05
NNO Title Card .01 .05

2001-02 Kingston Frontenacs

COMPLETE SET (25) 5.00 12.00
1 Header Card .04 .10
2 Chris Cook .20 .50
3 Lou Dickenson .30 .75
4 Josh Gratton .20 .50
5 Peter Hamerlik .40 1.00
6 Chris Hardill .20 .50
7 Brad Horan .20 .50
8 Andrew Ianiero .30 .75
9 Drew Kivell .20 .50
10 Sean Langdon .20 .50
11 Doug MacIver .20 .50
12 Brandon McBride .20 .50
13 Justin McCutcheon .20 .50
14 Kyle Neufeld .20 .50
15 Shane O'Brien .20 .50
16 Scott Sheppard .20 .50
17 Mike Smith .20 .50
18 Sean Stefanski .20 .50
19 Anthony Stewart 1.25 3.00
20 Cory Stillman .30 .75
21 Justin Suda .20 .50
22 Nathan Tennant .30 .75
23 Ed Van Herpt .20 .50
24 Nick Van Herpt .20 .50
25 Coca-Cola Ad .04 .10

2002-03 Kingston Frontenacs

COMPLETE SET (25) 5.00 12.00
1 Header Card .04 .10
2 Chris Cook .20 .50
3 Austin Corredato .20 .50
4 Miguel Delisle .20 .50
5 Drew Fata .20 .50
6 Peter Hamerlik .30 .75
7 Brad Horan .20 .50
8 Bill Kinkel .20 .50
9 Drew Kivell .20 .50
10 Dwight LaBrosse .20 .50
11 Scott Maher .20 .50
12 Brandon McBride .20 .50
13 Justin McCutcheon .20 .50
14 Danny McDonald .20 .50
15 Clay McFadden .20 .50
16 Richard Power .20 .50
17 Bryan Rodney .20 .50
18 Ryan Stephenson .20 .50
19 Anthony Stewart .75 2.00
20 Cory Stillman .20 .50
21 Justin Suda .20 .50
22 Dan Turple .20 .50
23 Nick Van Herpt .20 .50
24 The Count MASCOT .04 .10
25 Ad card .04 .10

2004-05 Kingston Frontenacs

COMPLETE SET (24) 5.00 12.00
1 Evan Kotsopoulos .20 .50
2 Anthony Stewart .40 1.00
3 Bobby Bolt .20 .50
4 Chris Stewart .20 .50
5 Dayne Davis .20 .50
6 David Edgeworth .20 .50
7 Cory Emmerton .20 .50
8 Shawn Futers .20 .50
9 Todd Griffith .20 .50
10 Bobby Hughes .20 .50
11 Michael Kolarz .20 .50
12 Derek Lyons .20 .50
13 Phil Mangan .20 .50
14 Adam Nemeth .20 .50
15 Chris Petrow .20 .50
16 Blake Pronk .20 .50
17 Dany Revelle .20 .50
18 Ben Shutron .20 .50
19 Radek Smolenak .40 1.00
20 Justin Suda .20 .50
21 Justin Wallingford .20 .50
22 Tony Rizzi .20 .50
23 Greg Williams .20 .50
24 Brady Morrison .20 .50

2005-06 Kingston Frontenacs

COMPLETE SET (23) 12.00 30.00
1 Cory Emmerton 1.00 2.50
2 Chris Stewart 1.00 2.50
3 Ben Shutron .50 1.25
4 Shawn Connors .50 1.25
5 Adam Nemeth .50 1.25
6 Matt Reis .50 1.25
7 Blake Pronk .50 1.25
8 Radek Smolenak 1.00 2.50
9 Luke Pither .50 1.25
10 Andrew Kizito .50 1.25
11 Tony Rizzi .50 1.25
12 Andrew Wilson .50 1.25
13 Bobby Hughes .50 1.25
14 Justin Wallingford .50 1.25
15 Todd Griffith .50 1.25
16 Michael Kolarz .50 1.25
17 Bobby Bolt .50 1.25
18 Connor Cameron .50 1.25
19 Mike Looby .50 1.25
20 Peder Skinner .50 1.25
21 J.F. Houle .50 1.25
22 Danny Taylor .60 1.50
23 Daryl Borden .60 1.50

2006-07 Kingston Frontenacs

COMPLETE SET (23) 8.00 15.00
1 Chris Stewart .40 1.00
2 Kyle Bochek .30 .75
3 Bobby Mignardi .30 .75
4 Nathan Moon .30 .75
5 Peder Skinner .30 .75
6 Matt Auffrey .30 .75
7 Matthew Kang .30 .75
8 Bobby Nyholm .30 .75
9 Jesse Biduke .30 .75
10 Bobby Hughes .30 .75
11 Josh Brittain .30 .75
12 Bobby Bolt .30 .75
13 Cory Emmerton .40 1.00
14 Peter Stevens .30 .75
15 Michael Kolarz .30 .75
16 Ben Shutron .40 1.00
17 Kevin Mole .40 1.00
18 Adam Nemeth .30 .75
19 Jonathan Sciacca .30 .75
20 Andrew Kizito .30 .75
21 Justin Wallingford .30 .75
22 Daryl Borden .30 .75
23 Jason Guy .30 .75

1982-83 Kitchener Rangers

COMPLETE SET (30) 16.00 40.00
1 Waterloo Regional
Police Crest .08 .25
2 Harold Basse
Chief of Police .08 .25
3 Sponsors' Card .08 .25
4 Joe Crozier GM .20 .50
5 Checklist .08 .25
6 Kerry Kerch .30 .75
7 Tom St. James .20 .50
8 Wendell Young .75 2.00
9 David Shaw .60 1.50
10 Darryl Boudreau .30 .75
11 David Bruce .40 1.00
12 Wayne Presley .60 1.50
13 Garnet McKechney .20 .50
14 Kevin Petendra .20 .50
15 Brian Wilks .20 .50
16 Jim Quinn .20 .50
17 Al MacInnis 8.00 20.00
18 Dave Nicholls .20 .50
19 Mike Eagles .60 1.50
20 Mike Hough .60 1.50
21 Greg Puhalski .20 .50
22 Darren Wright .20 .50
23 Todd Steffen .20 .50
24 John Tucker .60 1.50
25 Kent Paynter .20 .50
26 Andy O'Brien .20 .50
27 Les Bradley TR .08 .25
28 Scott Biggs .20 .50
29 Chris Martin TR .08 .25
30 Dave Webster .20 .50

1983-84 Kitchener Rangers

COMPLETE SET (30) 6.00 15.00
1 Joe Mantione .40 1.00
2 Jim Quinn .20 .50
3 Kitchener Rangers logo
Checklist .08 .25
4 Rob MacInnis .20 .50
5 Louie Berardicurti .20 .50
6 Neil Sandilands .20 .50
7 Darren Wright .20 .50
8 Tom Barrett CO
GM .08 .25
9 Brian Wilks .20 .50
10 Garnet McKechney .20 .50
11 David Bruce .40 1.00
12 Kent Paynter .20 .50
13 Sponsor's card
P.L.A.Y. .08 .25
14 Scott Kerr .20 .50
15 Greg Puhalski .20 .50
16 Wayne Presley .40 1.00
17 Carmine Vani .20 .50
18 Shawn Burr .75 2.00
19 Dave Latta .30 .75
20 John Tucker .60 1.50
21 Mike Stevens .20 .50
22 Harold Basse
Chief of Police .08 .25
23 Waterloo Regional
Police .08 .25
24 Peter Bakovic .20 .50
25 Brian Ross .20 .50
26 Brad Balshin .20 .50
27 David Shaw .40 1.00
28 Chris Trainer TR .08 .25
29 Les Bradley TR .08 .25
30 Ray LeBlanc .75 2.00

1984-85 Kitchener Rangers

COMPLETE SET (30) 4.80 12.00
1 Waterloo Regional
Police Crest .08 .25
2 Harold Basse
Chief of Police .08 .25
3 Garnet McKechney .20 .50
4 Tom Barrett GM/CO .08 .25
5 Kitchener Rangers logo .08 .25
6 Mike Bishop .30 .75
7 Craig Wolanin .40 1.00
8 Steve Marcolini .20 .50
9 Peter Langlois .20 .50
10 Dave Weiss .30 .75
11 Ken Alexander .20 .50
12 Ian Pound .20 .50
13 Doug Stromback .20 .50
14 Joel Brown .20 .50
15 Brian Wilks .20 .50
16 Robin Rubic .20 .50
17 Kent Paynter .20 .5
18 Jon Helinski .20 .5
19 Greg Puhalski .20 .5
20 Wayne Presley .40 1.0
21 Dave McLlwain .40 1.0
22 Shawn Burr .40 1.0
23 Dave Latta .25 .6
24 John Keller .20 .5
25 Mike Stevens .20 .5
26 Sponsors' Card .08
27 Richard Adolfi .20
28 Grant Sanders .20
29 Les Bradley TR .08
30 Sponsors' Card .08

1985-86 Kitchener Rangers

COMPLETE SET (30) 5.00 12.0
1 Waterloo Regional Police .08
2 Harold Basse
Chief of Police .08
3 Sponsors' Card .08

4 Tom Barrett GM/CO	.08	.25
5 Kitchener Rangers logo Checklist	.20	.50
6 Dave Weiss	.30	.75
7 Steve Marcolini	.20	.50
8 Kevin Gant	.20	.50
9 Ken Alexander	.20	.50
10 Mike Volpe	.30	.75
11 Ian Pound	.20	.50
12 Brett MacDonald	.20	.50
13 Scott Taylor	.20	.50
14 Greg Hankkio	.20	.50
15 Mike Morrison	.20	.50
16 Mike Wolak	.20	.50
17 Craig Booker	.20	.50
18 Jeff Noble	.20	.50
19 Shawn Tyers	.20	.50
20 Peter Lisy	.20	.50
21 Shawn Burr	.40	1.00
22 David Latta	.20	.50
23 Ron Sanko	.20	.50
24 Doug Jones	.20	.50
25 Paul Penelton	.20	.50
26 Blair MacPherson	.20	.50
27 Richard Hawkins	.20	.50
28 Brad Sparkes	.20	.50
29 Ron Goodall	.20	.50
30 Kevin Duguay TR	.08	.25

1986-87 Kitchener Rangers

COMPLETE SET (30)	4.00	10.00
1 Waterloo Police Crest	.02	.10
2 Harold Basse COP	.02	.10
3 Sponsor's Card	.02	.10
4 Tom Barrett GM/CO	.02	.10
5 Checklist	.08	.25
6 Dave Weiss	.30	.75
7 Darren Rumble	.20	.50
8 Kevin Grant	.20	.50
9 Len Fawcett	.20	.50
10 Darren Beals	.30	.75
11 Ed Kister	.20	.50
12 Scott Taylor	.20	.50
13 Darren Moxam	.20	.50
14 Paul Epoch	.20	.50
15 Richard Borgo	.20	.50
16 Allan Lake	.20	.50
17 Jeff Noble	.20	.50
18 Mark Montanari	.20	.50
19 Jim Hulton	.20	.50
20 Kelly Cain	.20	.50
21 Craig Booker	.20	.50
22 David Latta	.20	.50
23 Doug Jones	.20	.50
24 Gary Callahan	.20	.50
25 Bruno Lapensee	.20	.50
26 Scott Montgomery TR	.02	.10
27 Ron Goodall	.20	.50
28 Discount Card	.02	.10
29 Steve Ewing	.20	.50
30 Joe McDonnell ACO	.08	.25

1987-88 Kitchener Rangers

COMPLETE SET (30)	4.00	10.00
1 Waterloo Regional Police	.02	.10
2 Harold Basse Chief of Police	.02	.10
3 Children's Bonus Card	.02	.10
4 Joe McDonnell GM/CO	.02	.10
5 Kitchener Ranger logo	.08	.25
6 Gus Morschauser	.30	.75
7 Rick Allain	.20	.50
8 Kevin Grant	.20	.50
9 Rob Thiel	.20	.50
10 Darren Beals	.30	.75
11 Cory Keenan	.20	.50
12 Rival Fullum	.20	.50
13 Tony Crisp	.20	.50
14 Tyler Ertel	.20	.50
15 Richard Borgo	.20	.50
16 Steven Rice	.20	.50
17 Rob Sangster	.20	.50
18 Jeff Noble	.20	.50
19 Mark Montanari	.20	.50
20 Jim Hulton	.20	.50
21 Craig Booker	.20	.50
22 Doug Jones	.20	.50
23 Randy Pearce	.20	.50
24 Darren Rumble	.20	.50
25 Joe Ranger	.20	.50
26 Optimist's Sponsor Card	.02	.10
27 Ron Goodall	.20	.50
28 Allan Lake	.20	.50
29 Scott Montgomery TR	.02	.10
30 Optimist's Sponsor Card	.02	.10

1988-89 Kitchener Rangers

COMPLETE SET (30)	4.00	10.00
1 Waterloo Regional Police Crest	.02	.10
2 Harold Basse Chief of Police	.02	.10
3 Children's Bonus Card	.02	.10
4 Joe McDonnell GM/CO	.02	.10
5 Kitchener Rangers logo Checklist	.20	.50
6 Mike Torchia	.30	.75
7 Rick Allain	.20	.50
8 John Uniac	.20	.50
9 Rob Thiel	.20	.50
10 Gus Morschauser	.30	.75
11 Cory Keenan	.20	.50
12 Rival Fullum	.20	.50
13 Jason Firth	.20	.50
14 Joey St. Aubin	.20	.50
15 Richard Borgo	.20	.50
16 Steven Rice	.20	.50
17 Rob Sangster	.20	.50
18 Gilbert Dionne	.30	.75
19 Mark Montanari	.20	.50
20 Shayne Stevenson	.30	.75
21 Pierre Gagnon	.20	.50
22 Kirk Tomlinson	.20	.50
23 Randy Pearce	.20	.50
24 Brad Barton	.20	.50
25 Chris LiPuma	.20	.50
26 Optimist's Sponsor's Card A-K	.02	.10
27 Steve Herniman	.20	.50
28 Darren Rumble	.20	.50
29 Rick Chambers TR	.02	.10
30 Optimist's Sponsor's Card L-W	.02	.10

1989-90 Kitchener Rangers

COMPLETE SET (30)	4.80	12.00
1 Waterloo Police Crest	.02	.10
2 Harold Basse COP	.02	.10
3 Children's Bonus Card	.02	.10
4 Joe McDonnell GM/CO	.02	.10
5 Logo/Checklist	.08	.25
6 Mike Torchia	.30	.75
7 Rick Allain	.20	.50
8 John Uniac	.20	.50
9 Jack Williams	.20	.50
10 Dave Schill	.30	.75
11 John Copley	.20	.50
12 Cory Keenan	.20	.50
13 Rival Fullum	.20	.50
14 Jason Firth	.20	.50
15 Joey St. Aubin	.20	.50
16 Richard Borgo	.20	.50
17 Steven Rice	.20	.50
18 Rob Sangster	.20	.50
19 Gilbert Dionne	.30	.75
20 Jamie Israel	.20	.50
21 Shayne Stevenson	.30	.75
22 Gib Tucker	.20	.50
23 Randy Pearce	.20	.50
24 Brad Barton	.20	.50
25 Chris Li Puma	.20	.50
26 Optimist's Sponsors Card A-L	.02	.10
27 Kevin Falesy	.20	.50
28 Steve Smith	.20	.50
29 Rick Chambers TR	.02	.10
30 Optimist's Sponsors Card M-W	.02	.10

1990-91 Kitchener Rangers

COMPLETE SET (30)	3.00	8.00
1 Waterloo Regional Police Crest	.02	.10
2 Harold Basse Chief of Police	.02	.10
3 Joe McDonnell GM/CO	.02	.10
4 Rick Chambers TR	.02	.10
5 Kitchener Rangers logo Checklist	.08	.25
6 Mike Torchia	.20	.50
7 Len DeVuono	.10	.30
8 John Uniac	.10	.30
9 Steve Smith	.10	.30
10 Rob Stopar	.10	.30
11 Tony McCabe	.10	.30
12 Jason Firth	.10	.30
13 Joey St. Aubin	.10	.30
14 Richard Borgo	.10	.30
15 Norm Dezainde	.10	.30
16 Jeff Szeryk	.10	.30
17 Derek Gauthier	.10	.30
18 Jamie Israel	.10	.30
19 Shayne McCosh	.10	.30
20 Gib Tucker	.10	.30
21 Paul McCallion	.10	.30
22 Mike Allen	.10	.30
23 Brad Barton	.10	.30
24 Chris LiPuma	.15	.40
25 Justin Cullen	.10	.30
26 Optimist's Sponsors Card (A-K)	.02	.10
27 Rod Saarinen	.10	.30
20 Jack Williams	.10	.30
29 Steven Rice	.20	.50
30 Optimist's Sponsors Card (K-W)	.02	.10

1993-94 Kitchener Rangers

COMPLETE SET (31)	3.60	9.00
1 Eric Manlow Jason Gladney Tim Spitig Checklist	.15	.40
2 David Belitski	.20	.50
3 Darryl Whyte	.20	.50
4 Greg McLean	.15	.40
5 Jason Hughes	.15	.40
6 Gord Dickie	.15	.40
7 Travis Riggin	.15	.40
8 Norm Dezainde	.15	.40
9 Tim Spitzig	.15	.40
10 Trevor Gallant	.15	.40
11 Chris Pittman	.15	.40
12 Ryan Pawluk UER (Name m	.15	.40
13 Jason Morgan	.15	.40
14 James Boyd	.15	.40
15 Todd Warriner	.30	.75
16 Mark Donahue	.15	.40
17 Peter Brearley	.15	.40
18 Andrew Taylor	.15	.40
19 Jason Gladney	.15	.40
20 Wes Swinson	.15	.40
21 Matt O'Dette	.15	.40
22 Darren Schmidt	.15	.40
23 Jason Johnson	.15	.40
24 Eric Manlow	.15	.40
25 Jeff Lillie	.15	.40
26 Sergei Olympiev	.15	.40
27 Joe McDonnell CO	.02	.10
28 Rick Chambers TR	.02	.10
29 Andrew Taylor Travis Riggin David Belitski Top	.15	.40
30 Sponsor Card Domino's P	.02	.10
NNO Slapshot Ad Card	.02	.10

1994-95 Kitchener Rangers

COMPLETE SET (31)	3.00	8.00
1 Checklist	.02	.10
2 David Belitski	.20	.50
3 Darryl Whyte	.20	.50
4 Daniel Godbout	.15	.40
5 Greg McLean	.15	.40
6 Jason Hughes	.15	.40
7 Jason Byrnes	.15	.40
8 Paul Traynor	.15	.40
9 Travis Riggin	.15	.40
10 Tim Spitzig	.15	.40
11 Trevor Gallant	.15	.40
12 Chris Pittman	.20	.50
13 Rick Emmett	.15	.40
14 Jason Morgan	.15	.40
15 Luch Nasato	.30	.75
16 Ryan Pepperall	.20	.50
17 Keith Welsh	.15	.40
18 Bill McGuigen	.15	.40
19 Chris Brassard	.15	.40
20 Andrew Taylor	.15	.40
21 Rob Deciantis	.15	.40
22 Wes Swinson	.20	.50
23 Lucas Miller	.15	.40
24 Sergei Olympiev	.15	.40
25 Rob Maric	.15	.40
26 Eric Manlow	.20	.50
27 Geoff Ward CO	.02	.10
28 Bob Ertel GM	.02	.10
29 Rick Chambers TR Dave N	.02	.10
30 Sponsor Card Domino's P	.02	.10
NNO Ad Card	.02	.10

1994-95 Kitchener Rangers Update

COMPLETE SET (7)	.75	2.00
31 Brian Scott	.20	.50
32 Robin LaCour	.15	.40
33 Jim Ensom	.20	.50
34 Dylan Seca	.15	.40
35 Garrett Burnett	.15	.40
NNO Craig Bignell ACO Mike Wright ACO	.15	.40
NNO Ad Card	.02	.10

1996-97 Kitchener Rangers

COMPLETE SET (30)	4.00	15.00
1 Jeff Ambrosio	.20	.50
2 David Belitski	.40	1.00
3 Jason Byrnes	.20	.50
4 Peter Bureaux	.20	.50
5 Vratislav Cech	.20	.50
6 Rob DeCiantis	.20	.50
7 Shawn Degagne	.20	.50
8 Boyd Devereaux	.60	1.50
9 Boyd Devereaux	.60	1.50
10 Bryan Duce	.20	.50
11 Michal Dvorak	.20	.50
12 Darcy Harris	.20	.50
13 Bryan Hayton ACO	.02	.10
14 Wes Jarvis	.20	.50
15 Dan Lebold TR	.02	.10
16 Adam Lewis	.20	.50
17 Rob Marc	.20	.50
18 Mark McMahon	.20	.50
19 Ryan Milanovic	.30	.75
20 Ryan Mougenel	.20	.50
21 Serge Payer	.20	.50
22 Ryan Pepperall	.20	.50
23 Alan Rourke	.20	.50
24 Rob Stanfield	.20	.50
25 Paul Traynor	.20	.50
26 Tim Verbeek	.20	.50
27 Geoff Ward CO	.02	.10
28 Keith Welsh	.20	.50
29 Header Card	.02	.10
30 Checklist	.02	.10

1999-00 Kitchener Rangers

COMPLETE SET (30)	4.00	10.00
1 John Eminger	.15	.40
2 Matt Armstrong	.15	.40
3 Serge Payer	.20	.50
4 Steve Eminger	.60	1.50
5 Andrew Peters	.40	1.00
6 Mike Amodeo	.15	.40
7 Bill Browne	.15	.40
8 Maxim Sharifijanov	.20	.50
9 Tex Mascot	.02	.10
10 Dan Lebold	.15	.40
11 Michael Wehrstedt	.15	.40
12 Jeff Snyder	.15	.40
13 Ryan Held	.20	.50
14 John Dunphy	.15	.40
15 Rusian Akhmadulin	.15	.40
16 Bobby Naylor	.15	.40
17 Jimmy Gagnon	.15	.40
18 Brandon Merli	.15	.40
19 Chris Brannen	.15	.40
20 Alan Rourke	.15	.40
21 Sean McMorrow	.30	.75
22 Mike Mazzuca	.15	.40
23 Reg Bourcier	.20	.50
24 Scott Dickie	.20	.50
25 Kevin Bloch	.15	.40
26 Jeff McGee	.15	.40
27 Derek Roy	.75	2.00
28 Header Card/CL	.02	.10
29 Kinsmen Club	.02	.10
30 Kinsmen Club	.02	.10

2000-01 Kitchener Rangers

COMPLETE SET (30)	4.80	10.00
1 Team CL	.15	.40
2 Matt Armstrong	.15	.40
3 Josh Bennett	.15	.40
4 Andre Benoit	.15	.40
5 Vasily Bizyayev	.15	.40
6 Kevin Bloch CO	.04	.10
7 Chris Brannen	.15	.40
8 Chris Cava	.20	.50
9 Travis Chapman	.15	.40
10 Scott Dickie	.30	.75
11 John Dunphy	.15	.40
12 Steve Eminger	.40	1.00
13 Jimmy Gagnon	.15	.40
14 Mike Hough	.20	.50
15 Jeff Johnston	.30	.75
16 Brad Larter	.15	.40
17 Dan Lebold TR	.02	.10
18 Jamie Minchella	.15	.40
19 Steve Richards	.15	.40
20 Matt Rock	.15	.40
21 Derek Roy	.60	1.50
22 Derrick Shultz	.30	.75
23 Scott Sheppard	.15	.40
24 Sam Skwarchuk	.15	.40
25 Marcus Smith	.15	.40
26 Jeff Snyder CO	.02	.10
27 Tex MASCOT	.02	.10
28 Brock Yates	.15	.40
29 Kinsmen Club	.02	.10
30 Kinsmen Club 2	.02	.10

2001-02 Kitchener Rangers

COMPLETE SET (22)		12.00
1 Scott Dickie	.30	.75
2 Nick Policelli	.20	.50
3 Thomas Harrison	.20	.50
4 Ryan Ramsay	.20	.50
5 Steve Eminger	.30	.75
6 Peter Kanko	.40	1.00
7 Mike Amodeo	.20	.50
8 Matt Grennier	.20	.50
9 Derek Roy	.30	.75
10 Andre Benoit	.20	.50
11 Mike Richards	.60	1.50
12 Petr Hemsky	.20	.50
13 John Osborne	.20	.50
14 Rafal Martynowski	.20	.50
15 Marcus Smith	.20	.50
16 T.J. Eason	.20	.50
17 Adam Keefe	.20	.50
18 Matt Harpwood	.30	.75
19 Bill Kinkel	.20	.50
20 Jeff Szwez	.20	.50
21 Chad McCaffrey	.20	.50
22 Checklist	.04	.10

2002-03 Kitchener Rangers

COMPLETE SET(19)		12.00
1 Andre Benoit	.20	.50
2 Jesse Boucher	.20	.50
3 Greg Campbell	.40	1.00
4 David Clarkson	.20	.50
5 Carlo DiRienzo	.20	.50
6 Scott Dickie	.30	.75
7 T.J. Eason	.20	.50
8 Steve Eminger	.40	1.00
9 Matt Grennier	.20	.50
10 George Halkidis	.20	.50
11 Peter Kanko	.40	1.00
12 Adam Keefe	.20	.50
13 Rafal Martynowski	.20	.50
14 Chad McCaffrey	.20	.50
15 Evan McGrath	.20	.50
16 Nathan O'Nabigon	.20	.50
17 Mike Richards	.60	1.50
18 Derek Roy	.40	1.00
19 Marcus Smith	.20	.50

2002-03 Kitchener Rangers Postcards

COMPLETE SET		
1 Steve Eminger	.75	2.00
2 Petr Kanko	.75	2.00
3 Mike Richards	.75	2.00
4 Derek Roy	.75	2.00
5 Evan McGrath	.75	2.00

2003-04 Kitchener Rangers

COMPLETE SET (24)		12.00
1 Andre Benoit	.20	.50
2 Jesse Boucher	.20	.50
3 Mike Chmielewski	.20	.50
4 David Clarkson	.20	.50
5 Patrick Davis	.20	.50
6 Carlo DiRienzo	.30	.75
7 Nick Duff	.20	.50
8 Cam Fergus	.20	.50
9 Peter Franchin	.20	.50
10 Chris Gravelding	.20	.50
11 Thomas Harrison	.20	.50
12 Devereaux Heshmatpour	.20	.50
13 Petr Kanko	.30	.75
14 Adam Keefe	.20	.50
15 Tyson Kellerman	.30	.75
16 Matt Lashoff	.20	.50
17 Rafal Martynowski	.20	.50
18 Paul McFarland	.20	.50
19 Evan McGrath	.20	.50
20 Nathan O'Nabigon	.20	.50
21 Anthony Pototschnik	.20	.50
22 Mike Richards	.40	1.00
23 Marcus Smith	.20	.50
24 Boris Valabik	.30	.75

2003 Kitchener Rangers Memorial Cup

COMPLETE SET (19)	6.00	15.00
1 Andre Benoit	.30	.75
2 Jesse Boucher	.30	.75
3 Gregory Campbell	.40	1.00
4 David Clarkson	.30	.75
5 Scott Dickie	.40	1.00
6 Carlo Dirienzo	.40	1.00
7 T.J. Eason	.30	.75
8 Steve Eminger	.30	1.50
9 Matt Grennier	.30	.75
10 George Halkidis	.30	.75
11 Petr Kanko	.40	1.00
12 Adam Keefe	.30	.75
13 Rafal Martynowski	.30	.75
14 Chad McCaffrey	.30	.75
15 Evan McGrath	.30	.75
16 Nathan O'Nabigon	.30	.75
17 Mike Richards	1.00	2.50
18 Derek Roy	.60	1.50
19 Marcus Smith	.30	.75

2004-05 Kitchener Rangers

COMPLETE SET (24)	6.00	15.00
2 Andre Benoit	.20	.50
2 Mike Richards	.60	1.50
3 Boris Valabik	.30	.75
4 Mark Packwood	.20	.50
5 Craig Voakes	.20	.50
6 Dan Turple	.20	.50
7 Dan Cyenes	.20	.50
8 David Clarkson	.20	.50
9 Eric Pfligler	.20	.50
10 Evan McGrath	.40	1.00
11 Jack Combs	.20	.50
12 Jakub Kindl	.30	.75
13 Joe McCann	.20	.50
14 Justin Azevedo	.20	.50
15 Justin Piquette	.20	.50
16 Kevin Henderson	.20	.50
17 Mark Fraser	.20	.50
18 Matt Lashoff	.40	1.00
19 Matt Pepe	.20	.50
20 Adam Keefe	.20	.50
21 Michael Duco	.20	.50
22 Myles Applebaum	.20	.50
23 Patrick Davis	.20	.50
24 Paul McFarland	.20	.50

2005-06 Kitchener Rangers

COMPLETE SET (27)	6.00	15.00
1 Dan Turple	.40	1.00
2 Julien Machabee	.30	.75
3 Mark Packwood	.40	1.00
4 Matt Lashoff	.40	1.00
5 Patrick Davis	.30	.75
6 Justin Azevedo	.30	.75
7 Evan McGrath	.40	1.00
8 Sean Smyth	.30	.75
9 Dan Gyenes	.30	.75
10 Boris Valabik	.40	1.00
11 Kevin Henderson	.30	.75
12 Matt Thomson	.30	.75
13 Mark Fraser	.30	.75
14 Jakub Kindl	.30	.75
15 Nick Spaling	.30	.75
16 Mike Duco	.30	.75
17 Yves Bastien	.30	.75
18 Matt Pepe	.30	.75
19 Craig Voakes	.30	.75
20 Michael Pelech	.30	.75
21 Jean-Michel Rizk	.30	.75
22 Ryan Donally	.30	.75
23 Myles Applebaum	.30	.75
24 Matt Auffrey	.30	.75
25 Cory Konecny	.30	.75
26 David Lomas	.30	.75
27 Victor Oreskovich	.30	.75

2006-07 Kitchener Rangers

COMPLETE SET (25)	8.00	15.00
1 Jakub Kindl	.30	.75
2 Steve Tarasuk	.30	.75
3 Nick Spaling	.30	.75
4 Scott Timmins	.30	.75
5 Mike Duco	.30	.75
6 Justin Azevedo	.30	.75
7 Yves Bastien	.30	.75
8 Mike Mascioli	.30	.75
9 Matt Halischuk	.30	.75
10 Nazem Kadri	.50	1.25
11 Matt Pepe	.30	.75
12 Robert Bortuzzo	.30	.75
13 Dan Gyenes	.30	.75
14 Denver Manderson	.30	.75
15 Mark Packwood	.40	1.00
16 John Murray	.40	1.00
17 Jean-Michel Rizk	.30	.75
18 Adam Zamec	.30	.75
19 Kevin Henderson	.30	.75
20 Victor Oreskovich	.30	.75
21 Yannick Weber	.30	.75
22 Brian Soso	.30	.75
23 Phil Varone	.30	.75
24 Dan Kelly	.30	.75
LE1 Justin Azevedo	1.25	3.00

2007-08 Kitchener Rangers

COMPLETE SET (24)	5.00	12.00
1 Josh Unice	.25	.60
2 Mavric Parks	.25	.60
3 Alex Dzielski	.25	.60
4 Yannick Weber	.25	.60
5 Steve Jensen	.25	.60
6 Phil Varone	.25	.60
7 Dan Kelly	.25	.60
8 Steve Tarasuk	.25	.60
9 Nick Spaling	.25	.60
10 Myles Barbieri	.25	.60
11 Scott Timmins	.25	.60
12 Mike Duco	.25	.60
13 Justin Azevedo	.25	.60
14 Mike Mascioli	.25	.60
15 Matt Halischuk	.25	.60
16 Nazem Kadri	.40	1.00
17 Matt Pepe	.25	.60
18 Robert Bortuzzo	.25	.60
19 Brandon Mashinter	.25	.60
20 Spencer Anderson	.25	.60
21 T.J. Battani	.25	.60
22 Doug Clarkson	.25	.60
23 Alexei Dostoinov	.25	.60
24 Mikkel Boedker	.25	.60

2014-15 Kitchener Rangers

COMPLETE SET ()	6.00	15.00
1 Justin Bailey	.30	.75
2 Doug Blaisdell	.30	.75
3 Connor Bunnaman	.30	.75
4 Mark Bzowey	.30	.75
5 Dawson Carty	.30	.75
6 Mike Davies	.30	.75
7 Dylan DiPerna	.30	.75
8 Gustaf Franzen	.30	.75
9 Matthew Greenfield	.30	.75
10 Frank Hora	.30	.75
11 Max Iafrate	.30	.75
12 Mason Kohn	.30	.75
13 Darby Llewellyn	.30	.75
14 Liam Maaskant	.30	.75
15 Ryan MacInnis	.40	1.00
16 Nick Magyar	.30	.75
17 Adam Mascherin	.40	1.00
18 Curtis Meighan	.30	.75
19 Brent Pedersen	.30	.75
20 Brandon Robinson	.30	.75
21 Logan Schmidt	.30	.75
22 Dmitrii Sergeev	.30	.75

2015-16 Kitchener Rangers

COMPLETE SET (23)	6.00	15.00
1 Doug Blaisdell	.30	.75
2 Jeremy Bracco	.30	.75
3 Brian Brosnan	.30	.75
4 Connor Bunnaman	.30	.75
5 Dawson Carty	.30	.75
6 Dylan Di Perna	.30	.75
7 Gustaf Franzen	.30	.75
8 Joseph Garreffa	.30	.75
9 Connor Hall	.30	.75
10 Jake Henderson	.30	.75
11 Frank Hora	.30	.75
12 Mason Kohn	.30	.75
13 Darby Llewellyn	.30	.75
14 Ryan MacInnis	.30	.75
15 Nick Magyar	.30	.75
16 Adam Mascherin	.30	.75
17 Nick McHugh	.30	.75
18 David Miller	.30	.75
19 Luke Opilka	.30	.75
20 Luke Richardson	.30	.75
21 Elijah Roberts	.30	.75
22 Brandon Robinson	.30	.75
23 Dmitrii Sergeev	.30	.75

1990-91 Knoxville Cherokees

COMPLETE SET (19)	3.60	9.00
101 David Williams	.25	.60
102 Paul Laus	.40	1.00
103 Don Jackson CO	.08	.25
104 Steve Ryding	.20	.50
105 Jeff Lindsay	.20	.50
106 Daniel Gauthier	.20	.50
107 Stan Drulia	.25	.60
108 Mike Murray	.20	.50
109 Tom Sasso	.20	.50
110 Butch Kaebel	.20	.50
111 Don McClennan	.20	.50
112 Jamie Hanlon	.20	.50
113 Troy Mick	.20	.50
114 Brett Strot	.20	.50
115 Dean Anderson	.20	.50
116 Quinton Brickley	.20	.50
117 Greg Batters	.20	.50
118 Alex Daviault	.20	.50
119 Mike Greenlay	.30	.75

1991-92 Knoxville Cherokees

COMPLETE SET (20)	3.60	9.00
1 Bill Nyrop CO	.20	.50
2 Galen Head TR	.02	.10
3 Mike Greenlay	.30	.75
4 Karl Clauss	.30	.75
5 Steve Ryding	.20	.50
6 Mike Gober	.20	.50
7 Chad Thompson	.20	.50
8 Trevor Forsythe	.20	.50
9 Greg Pankewicz	.20	.50
10 David Shute	.20	.50
11 Jamie Dabanovich	.20	.50
12 Shawn Lillie	.20	.50
13 Joel Gardner	.20	.50
14 Roman Hubalek	.20	.50
15 Bruno Villeneuve	.20	.50
16 Troy Mick	.20	.50
17 Dean McDonald	.20	.50
18 Brett Lawrence	.20	.50
19 Dean Anderson	.20	.50
20 Robert Melanson	.20	.50

1993-94 Knoxville Cherokees

COMPLETE SET (20)	6.00	15.00
NNO Scott Boston	.15	.40
NNO Cory Cadden	.15	.40
NNO Tim Chase	.15	.40
NNO Steven Flomenhoft	.15	.40
NNO Scott Gordon	.20	.50
NNO Jon Larson	.15	.40
NNO Carl LeBlanc	.15	.40
NNO Kim Maier	.15	.40
NNO Wes McCauley	.15	.40
NNO Scott Metcalfe	.15	.40
NNO Mike Murray	.15	.40
NNO Hayden O'Rear	.15	.40
NNO Jeff Reid	.15	.40
NNO Manon Rheaume	3.00	8.00
NNO Marc Rodgers	.15	.40
NNO Doug Searle	.15	.40
NNO Barry Smith CO	.08	.25
NNO Martin Tanguay	.15	.40
NNO Nicholas Vachon	.20	.50
NNO Bruno Villeneuve	.15	.40

1994-95 Knoxville Cherokees

COMPLETE SET (24)	3.00	8.00
1 Checklist	.02	.10
2 Barry Smith CO	.08	.25
3 Aaron Fackler TR	.02	.10
4 Andy Davis Broadcaster	.02	.10
5 Stephane Menard	.15	.40
6 Doug Searle	.15	.40
7 Hayden O'Rear	.15	.40
8 Sean Brown	.15	.40
9 Mike Murray	.15	.40
10 Jon Jenkins	.15	.40
11 Sean Pronger	.30	.75
12 Steven Flomenhoft	.15	.40
13 David Neilson	.15	.40
14 Jack Callahan	.15	.40
15 Carl LeBlanc	.15	.40
16 Alain Deeks	.20	.50
17 George Zajankala	.15	.40
18 Chris Fess	.15	.40
19 Michel Gaul	.15	.40
20 Pat Murray	.15	.40
21 Robb McIntyre	.15	.40
22 Vaclav Nedomansky	.15	.40
23 Cory Cadden	.15	.40
24 Michael Burman	.15	.40

1996-97 Knoxville Cherokees

COMPLETE SET (20)	4.00	10.00
1 Knoxville Cherokees	.20	.50
2 Barry Smith HCO	.20	.50
3 Sean Halifax	.20	.50
4 Daniel Chaput	.20	.50
5 Jamie Bird	.20	.50
6 Matt Turek	.20	.50
7 Chris Fees	.20	.50
8 Kelly Hollingshead	.20	.50
9 Darren Johnson	.20	.50
10 Vaclav Nedomansky	.20	.50
11 Kent Fearns	.20	.50
12 Martin Tanguay	.20	.50
13 Wayne Anchikoski	.20	.50
14 Jim Brown	.20	.50
15 Garrett Burnett	.40	1.00
16 Stephane Soulliere	.20	.50
17 Dean Moore	.20	.50
18 David Neilson	.20	.50
19 Mike Vandenberghe	.20	.50
20 Brad Guzda	.40	1.00
21 Olaf Kjenstad	.20	.50
22 PHPA Web Site	.02	.10
P1 Brad Guzda LL	2.00	5.00
P2 Jim Brown LL	2.00	5.00

2004-05 Knoxville Ice Bears

COMPLETE SET (24)	10.00	20.00
1 K.C. Caudill	.25	.60
2 Chris Bodnar	.25	.60
3 Kevin Swider	.25	.60
4 Todd MacIsaac	.25	.60
5 Marcus Forsberg	.25	.60
6 Civic Colisseum	.20	.50
7 Chilly MASCOT	.20	.50
8 TCS card	.25	.60
9 Doug Serle	.25	.60
10 Craig Desjarlais	.25	.60
11 Mike Cragen	.25	.60
12 Darren Caine	.25	.60
13 Curtis Menzul	.25	.60
14 Terry Dunbar	.25	.60
15 Free Kid's Ticket	.20	.50
16 David Bagley	.25	.60
17 Matt Moore	.25	.60
18 Jeff Hansen	.25	.60
19 James Ronayne	.25	.60
20 Miss Icebear	.25	.60
21 Liam McCarthy	.25	.60
22 Jim Bermingham	.25	.60
23 Rob Miller	.25	.60
24 K.J. Voorhees	.25	.60

2005-06 Knoxville Ice Bears

COMPLETE SET (24)	6.00	15.00
1 Jason Bermingham	.30	.75
2 Patrick Carriere	.30	.75
3 Kevin Caudill	.30	.75
4 Mike Craigen	.30	.75
5 Nathan Daly	.30	.75
6 Marcus Forsberg	.30	.75
7 Aaron Lewis	.30	.75
8 Ben Manny	.30	.75
9 Liam McCarthy	.30	.75
10 Curtis Menzul	.30	.75
11 Rob Miller	.30	.75
12 Matt Moore	.30	.75
13 Ryan Person	.30	.75
14 Bob Rangus	.30	.75
15 Jamie Ronayne	.30	.75
16 Doug Searle	.30	.75
17 Kevin Swider	.30	.75
18 K.J. Voorhees	.30	.75
19 Jim Bermingham HC	.02	.10
20 Dance Team	.02	.10
21 Drew Kitts EM	.02	.10
22 Chilly MASCOT	.02	.10
23 Tim Douglas TP	.02	.10
24 Knoxville Ice Bears	.20	.50

1999-00 Knoxville Speed

COMPLETE SET (29)	6.00	15.00
1 Sponsor Card	.02	.05
2 Sponsor Card	.02	.05
3 Bradley Denis	.30	.75
4 Hockey History	.02	.05
5 UHL History	.02	.05
6 Trevor Jobe	.40	1.00
7 Cam Law	.30	.75
8 Rusty McKie	.40	1.00
9 Eric Mohntreuil	.30	.75
10 Mike Murray	.30	.75
11 Dan Myre	.30	.75
12 Sergei Radchenko	.30	.75
13 Bill Russell	.30	.75
14 Eric Schneider	.30	.75
15 Mike Schultz	.30	.75
16 Doug Searle	.30	.75
17 Jordan Shaw	.30	.75
18 Konstantin Simchuk	.40	1.00
19 Jeff Suggitt	.30	.75
20 Jeremy Thompson	.30	.75
21 Andrew Tortorella	.30	.75
22 Dmitry Ustyuzhanin	.30	.75
23 Team on the Bench	.20	.50
24 Mike Wilhelm EM	.02	.10
25 Torry Ruskowski CO	.30	.75
26 Tim Douglas TR	.02	.10
27 Hersheys Pilot	.02	.05
28 Hersheys Pilot	.02	.05
29 Eyewitness Sports	.02	.05

2000-01 Knoxville Speed

COMPLETE SET (29)	10.00	30.00
1 Alex Alepin	.30	1.00
2 Bradley Denis	.60	1.50
3 Craig Desjarlais	.60	1.50
4 Brad Guzda	.40	1.50
5 Tom Lawson	.30	1.00
6 David Mayes	.30	1.00
7 Alain Savage	.30	1.00
8 Mike Schultz	.30	1.00
9 Dean Shmyr	.40	1.50
10 Mike Vandenberghe	.30	1.00
11 Mike Wilhelm EM	.04	.10
12 Nick Paranjape (Fox 43)	.04	.10
13 Brad Domonsky	.80	2.00
14 Dmitry Ustyuzhanin	.30	1.00
15 Yannick Latour	.30	1.00
16 Sergei Petrov	.60	1.50
17 Iannique Renaud	.30	1.00
18 Mikko Sivonen	.40	1.50
19 Mike Henderson	.80	2.00
20 Geno Parrish	.30	1.00

21 Andrew Tortorella .60 1.50
22 Mark Karpen .30 1.00
23 Dan Myre .30 1.00
24 Mike Murray .30 1.00
25 Mike Green .30 1.00
26 Oleg Kuzmin .30 1.00
27 Terry Ruskowski CO .20 .50
28 Tim Douglas TR .04 .10
29 JBG SPONSOR .04 .10

1998-99 Kootenay Ice

COMPLETE SET (24) 6.00 15.00
1 Clayton Pool .20 .50
2 Scott Roles .20 .50
3 Dean Arsene .20 .50
4 Jesse Ferguson .20 .50
5 Dion Lassu .20 .50
6 Mark Thompson .20 .50
7 Steve McCarthy .75 2.00
8 Rod Leroux .20 .50
9 Mike Green .20 .50
10 Wade Burt .20 .50
11 Nick Marach .20 .50
12 Jaroslav Svoboda .40 1.00
13 Trevor Wasyluk .40 1.00
14 Jarret Stoll 1.25 3.00
15 Jason Jaffray .20 .50
16 Trevor Johnson .20 .50
17 Kyle Wanvig .75 2.00
18 Tyler Beechey .20 .50
19 Stanislav Gron .40 1.00
20 Colin Sinclair .20 .50
21 Jeremy Yablonski .20 .50
22 Graham Belak .20 .50
23 B.J. Boxma .20 .50
24 Brad Tutschek .20 .50

2000-01 Kootenay Ice

COMPLETE SET (24) 8.00 20.00
1 Dean Arsene .20 .50
2 Tyler Beechey .20 .50
3 Dan Blackburn .75 2.00
4 Zdenek Blatny .80 1.00
5 Eric Bowen .20 .50
6 Bret DeCecco .40 1.00
7 Brennan Evans .20 .50
8 Cole Fischer .20 .50
9 Richard Hamula .20 .50
10 Jeff Harvey .20 .50
11 Pat Iannone .20 .50
12 Jason Jaffray .20 .50
13 Trevor Johnson .20 .50
14 Mike Lee .20 .50
15 Steve Makway .20 .50
16 Lance Morrison .20 .50
17 Aaron Rome .20 .50
18 Mascot Shivers .04 .10
19 Colin Sinclair .20 .50
20 Jarret Stoll 1.25 3.00
21 Marek Svatos 2.00 5.00
22 Adam Taylor .20 .50
23 Andy Thompson .20 .50
24 Craig Weller .20 .50

2002-03 Kootenay Ice

1 Gerard Dicaire .30 .75
2 Duncan Milroy .30 .75
3 Tomas Plihal .30 .75
4 Adam Taylor .30 .75

2003-04 Kootenay Ice

COMPLETE SET (25) 8.00 20.00
1 Taylor Dakers .30 .75
2 Jeff Glass 2.00 5.00
3 Derek Price .30 .75
4 Donny Lloyd .30 .75
5 James Cherewyk .30 .75
6 Brad Zanon .30 .75
7 Brad Cole .30 .75
8 Travis Featherstone .30 .75
9 Nigel Dawes .75 2.00
10 Mike Boxma .30 .75
11 Glenn Olson .30 .75
12 Josh Morrow .30 .75
13 Adam Taylor .30 .75
14 Igor Agarunov .30 .75
15 Adam Cracknell .30 .75
16 Jeremy Schenderling .30 .75
17 Dale Mahovsky .30 .75
18 Ryan Russell .30 .75
19 Aaron Bader .30 .75
20 Sean Affleck .30 .75
21 Martin Sagat .30 .75
22 Brett Sutter .60 1.50
23 Checklist .04 .10
24 Shivers MASCOT .04 .10
25 Sponsor .04 .10

2004-05 Kootenay Ice

COMPLETE SET (25) 8.00 20.00
1 Laine Allen .30 .75
2 Andy Bossence .30 .75
3 Michael Busto .30 .75
4 James Cherewyk .30 .75
5 Brad Cole .30 .75
6 Adam Cracknell .30 .75
7 Steven DaSilva .30 .75
8 Taylor Dakers .30 .75
9 Nigel Dawes .60 1.50
10 Joshua Fauth .30 .75
11 Jeff Glass 1.25 3.00
12 Chad Greenan .30 .75
13 Casey Lee .30 .75
14 Dale Mahovsky .30 .75
15 Ben Maxwell .30 .75
16 Roman Polak .30 .75
17 Derek Price .30 .75
18 Ryan Russell .30 .75
19 Martin Sagat .30 .75
20 Josh Saywell .30 .75
21 Brett Sutter .40 1.00
22 Adam Taylor .30 .75
23 Devin Welsh .30 .75
24 Commitment .04 .10
25 Sponsor Card .04 .10

2005-06 Kootenay Ice

COMPLETE SET (25) 6.00 15.00
1 Andrew Bailey .30 .75
2 Curtis Billsten .30 .75
3 Lukas Bohunicky .30 .75
4 Michael Busto .30 .75
5 Adam Cracknell .30 .75
6 Steven DaSilva .30 .75
7 Taylor Dakers .30 .75
8 Dalyn Flatt .30 .75
9 Trent Fussi .30 .75
10 Chad Greenan .30 .75
11 Paul Kurceba .30 .75
12 Kris Lazaruk .30 .75
13 Casey Lee .30 .75
14 Paul MacDonald .30 .75
15 Dale Mahovsky .30 .75
16 Ben Maxwell .30 .75
17 John Negrin .30 .75
18 Michal Psurny .30 .75
19 Ryan Russell .30 .75
20 Dustin Sylvester .30 .75
21 Devin Welsh .30 .75
22 Luke Wiens .30 .75
23 Shivers MASCOT .02 .10
24 Concord Pacific SPONSOR .01 .01
25 Kootenay Ice .20 .50

1991-92 Lake Superior State Lakers

COMPLETE SET (28) 8.00 20.00
1 1991 CCHA Champs .08 .25
2 Dan Angelelli .30 .75
3 Mark Astley .30 .75
4 Mike Bachusz .30 .75
5 Steve Barnes .30 .75
6 Clayton Beddoes .30 .75
7 Paul Constantin .30 .75
8 Vincent Faucher .30 .75
9 David Gartshore .30 .75
10 Tim Hanley .30 .75
11 John Hendry .30 .75
12 Dean Hulett .30 .75
13 Jeff Jackson CO .20 .50
14 Blaine Lacher .40 1.00
15 Darrin Madeley .40 1.00
16 Kurt Miller .30 .75
17 Sandy Moger .40 1.00
18 Mike Morin .30 .75
19 Jay Ness .30 .75
20 Jim Peters .30 .75
21 Brian Rolston .75 2.00
22 Michael Smith .30 .75
23 Wayne Strachan .30 .75
24 Jason Trzcinski .30 .75
25 Rob Valicevic .60 1.50
26 Darren Wetherill .30 .75
27 Brad Willner .30 .75
28 Jason Welch .30 .75

1992-93 Lake Superior State Lakers

COMPLETE SET (33) 6.00 15.00
1 Team Photo/1992 NCAA Ch .20 .50
2 Team Photo/1992 CCHA Champions .20 .50
3 Keith Aldridge .20 .50
4 Dan Angelelli .15 .40
5 Mark Astley .20 .50
6 Mike Bachusz .15 .40
7 Steven Barnes .15 .40
8 Clayton Beddoes .15 .40
9 David Gartshore .15 .40
10 Tim Hanley .15 .40
11 Matt Hansen .15 .40
12 John Hendry .15 .40
13 Dean Hulett .15 .40
14 Jeff Jackson .20 .50
15 Blaine Lacher .40 1.00
16 Darrin Madeley .20 .50
17 Mike Matteucci .15 .40
18 Scott McCabe .15 .40
19 Kurt Miller .15 .40
20 Mike Morin .15 .40
21 Jay Ness .15 .40
22 Gino Pulente .15 .40
23 Brian Rolston .75 2.00
24 Paul Sass .15 .40
25 Michael Smith .15 .40
26 Wayne Strachan .15 .40
27 Sean Tallaire .15 .40
28 Adam Thompson .15 .40
29 Jason Trzcinski .15 .40
30 Rob Valicevic .60 1.50
31 Jason Welch .15 .40
32 Darren Wetherill .15 .40
33 Brad Willner .15 .40

2004-05 Lakehead University Thunderwolves

COMPLETE SET (27) 8.00 20.00
1 Joel Scherban .30 .75
2 Chris Shaffer .30 .75
3 Jeff Richards .30 .75
4 Erik Lodge .30 .75
5 Murray Magill .30 .75
6 Jason Lange .30 .75
7 Robert Hillier .30 .75
8 Francis Walker .30 .75
9 Andrew Brown .30 .75
10 Kris Callaway .30 .75
11 Jouni Kuokkanen .30 .75
12 Leon Cooper .30 .75
13 Hugo Lehoux .30 .75
14 Michael Wehrstedt .30 .75
15 Mike Self .30 .75
16 Austin Wycisk .30 .75
17 Steve Rawski .30 .75
18 Grant McCune .30 .75
19 Sean Stefanski .30 .75
20 Drew Kivell .30 .75
21 Jesse Baraniuk .30 .75
22 Dene Poulin .30 .75
23 Tobias Whelan .30 .75
24 Chris Whitley .30 .75
25 Peter Cava .40 1.00
26 Mark Robinson .30 .75
27 Brad Priestlay .30 .75

1993-94 Lakeland Ice Warriors

COMPLETE SET (25) 10.00 25.00
1 Lakeland Ice Warriors .75 2.00
2 Chief Mascot .40 1.00
3 Chris Babkirk .40 1.00
4 Chris Baxter .40 1.00
5 Pat Bingham .40 1.00
6 Ian Collins .40 1.00
7 Ian Collins .40 1.00
8 Eric Daoust .40 1.00
9 Eric Daoust .40 1.00
10 Derek Edgerly .40 1.00
11 Andrew Ernst .40 1.00
12 John Finnie .40 1.00
13 John Finnie .40 1.00
14 Sean Gabriele .40 1.00
15 John Grand .40 1.00
16 Manny Hawkins .40 1.00
17 Jules Jardine .40 1.00
18 John Labenski .40 1.00
19 Francois Michaud .40 1.00
20 Bob Nicholls .40 1.00
21 Ed Sabo .40 1.00
22 Brent Selman .40 1.00
23 Gary Thomas .40 1.00
24 Dean Turgeon .40 1.00
25 Dave Wright .40 1.00

2004-05 Langley Hornets

COMPLETE SET (22) 10.00 25.00
1 Matt Allen .40 1.00
2 Aaron Berman .40 1.00
3 Justin Binab .40 1.00
4 Tyler Boice .40 1.00
5 Marcel Bruinsma .40 1.00
6 Gary Butler .40 1.00
7 Tyson Chernask .40 1.00
8 Steve Christie .75 2.00
9 Tyson Daniels .60 1.50
10 Gord Edmondson .40 1.00
11 Brian Harris .40 1.00
12 Steve Matic .40 1.00
13 Taylor Moore .75 2.00
14 Robert Pritchard .40 1.00
15 Graham Sheppard .40 1.00
16 Luke Shier .75 2.00
17 Justin Taylor .40 1.00
18 Chris Vassos .40 1.00
19 Nathan Westover .40 1.00
20 Mike Wilson .40 1.00
21 Jason Wright .40 1.00
22 Robert Pritchard#}Brian Harris AS .40 1.00

2003-04 Laredo Bucks

COMPLETE SET (23) 30.00 60.00
1 Mike Amodeo 1.50 4.00
2 Jeff Bes 1.25 3.00
3 Max Birbraer 1.50 4.00
4 Brent Cullaton 1.25 3.00
5 Jean-Francois David 1.25 3.00
6 Serge Dube 1.25 3.00
7 Marco Emond 1.50 4.00
8 Chris Grenville 1.25 3.00
9 David Guerrera 1.50 4.00
10 James Hiebert 1.25 3.00
11 Dion Hyman 1.25 3.00
12 Mark Matier 1.25 3.00
13 Bobby-Chad Mitchell 1.25 3.00
14 Patrik Nilson 1.25 3.00
15 Adam Paiement 1.25 3.00
16 Gabriel Proulx 1.25 3.00
17 Steve Simoes 1.25 3.00
18 Jason Spence 1.25 3.00
19 Mike Vellinga 1.25 3.00
20 Steve Weidlich 1.25 3.00
21 Terry Ruskowski CO .40 1.00
22 Derek Craft EQM .20 .50
23 Bobby Moore TR .20 .50

1998-99 Las Vegas Coyotes RHI

COMPLETE SET (20) 3.00 8.00
1 Konstantin Simchuk .20 .50
2 Jay Neal .20 .50
3 Mike Ciolli .20 .50
4 Jakub Ficenec .20 .50
5 Blake Knox .20 .50
6 Darren Meek .20 .50
7 Mike Jorgensen .20 .50
8 Kirk Llano .20 .50
9 Jamie Cooke .20 .50
10 Tom Perry .20 .50
11 Don Parsons .20 .50
12 Rich Bronilla .20 .50
13 Gerry St. Cyr .30 .75
14 Brad Guzda .20 .50
15 Rob Pallin .20 .50
16 Dan Reja .20 .50
17 Chris McSorley CO .20 .50
18 Howl N. Coyote Mascot .02 .10
19 KOMP Morning Crew .02 .10
20 1999 Las Vegas Coyotes .02 .10

1993-94 Las Vegas Thunder

COMPLETE SET (32) 3.00 8.00
1 Brent Ashton .15 .40
2 Boom Boom (Mascot) .02 .10
3 Bob Bourne CO .15 .40
4 Rod Buskas .08 .25
5 Lyndon Byers .30 .75
6 Rich Campbell TR .02 .10
7 Colin Cowherd ANN .02 .10
8 Butch Goring CO .15 .40
9 Steve Gotaas .08 .25
10 Marc Habscheid .08 .25
11 Brett Hauer .08 .25
12 Shawn Heaphy .08 .25
13 Scott Hollis .08 .25
14 Peter Ing .20 .50
15 Steve Jaques .08 .25
16 Bob Joyce .08 .25
17 Jim Kyte .08 .25
18 Patrice Lefebvre .30 .75
19 Clint Malarchuk .20 .50
20 Ken Quinney .08 .25
21 Jean-Marc Richard .08 .25
22 Todd Richards .08 .25
23 Marc Rodgers .08 .25
24 Jeff Sharples .08 .25
25 Randy Smith .08 .25
26 Greg Spenrath .08 .25
27 Bob Strumm GM .02 .10
28 Kirk Tomlinson .08 .25
29 Kerry Toporowski .15 .40
30 Mark Vermette .08 .25
31 Steve Wissman EQMG .02 .10
32 Title Card .02 .10

1994-95 Las Vegas Thunder

COMPLETE SET (29) 4.80 12.00
1 James Black .08 .25
2 Radek Bonk .40 1.00
3 Boom Boom MASCOT .02 .10
4 Rich Campbell Athletic .02 .10
5 Frank Evans .08 .25
6 Marc Habscheid .20 .50
7 Alex Hicks .20 .50
8 Bob Joyce .20 .50
9 Jim Kyte .08 .25
10 Lark & Craig Morning Ra .02 .10
11 Patrice Lefebvre .40 1.00
12 Darcy Loewen .20 .50
13 Sal Lombardi EQMG .02 .10
14 Clint Malarchuk .20 .50
15 Andrew McBain .20 .50
16 Chris McSorley CO .20 .50
17 David Neilson .08 .25
18 Jerry Olenyn .08 .25
19 Ken Quinney .20 .50
20 Pokey Reddick .20 .50
21 Jeff Reid .08 .25
22 Manon Rheaume 2.00 5.00
23 Jean-Marc Richard .20 .50
24 Todd Richards .08 .25
25 Marc Rodgers .08 .25
26 Jeff Sharples .08 .25
27 Jarrod Skalde .20 .50
28 Bob Strumm GM CO .02 .10
29 Kerry Toporowski .20 .50

1995-96 Las Vegas Thunder

COMPLETE SET (26) 4.80 12.00
1 Bill Bowler .30 .75
2 Peter Fiorentino .15 .40
3 Greg Hawgood .30 .75
4 Sasha Lakovic .15 .40
5 Patrice Lefebvre .40 1.00
6 Darcy Loewen .15 .40
7 Gord Marx .15 .40
8 Blaine Moore .15 .40
9 Vaclav Nedomansky .15 .40
10 Pokey Reddick .30 .75
11 Jeff Ricciardi .15 .40
12 Jean-Marc Richard .15 .40
13 Marc Rodgers .40 1.00
14 Chris Rogles .30 .75
15 Ken Quinney .20 .50
16 Ruslan Salei .20 .50
17 Jeff Sharples .20 .50
18 Daniel Shank .20 .50
19 Todd Simon .20 .50
20 Rhett Trombley .15 .40
21 Vladimir Tsyplakov .20 .50
22 Sergei Zholtok .30 .75
23 Chris McSorley CO .08 .25
24 Clint Malarchuk AGM .20 .50
25 Bob Strumm GM .02 .10
26 BoomBoom .02 .10

1996-97 Las Vegas Thunder

COMPLETE SET (24) 4.80 12.00
1 Egor Bashkatov .20 .50
2 Boom Boom (Mascot) .02 .10
3 Kevin Dahl .20 .50
4 Chris Dahlquist .20 .50
5 Pavol Demitra .60 1.50
6 Parris Duffus .30 .75
7 Martin Gendron .20 .50
8 Brent Gretzky .20 .50
9 Kerry Huffman .20 .50
10 Igor Karpenko .30 .75
11 Don Larner .20 .50
12 Patrice Lefebvre .40 1.00
13 Darcy Loewen .20 .50
14 Clint Malarchuk AGM .20 .50
15 Chris McSorley CO .02 .10
16 Blaine Moore .20 .50
17 Ken Quinney .30 .75
18 Jeff Serowik .20 .50
19 Jason Simon .20 .50
20 Bob Strumm GM .02 .10
21 Rhett Trombley .20 .50
22 Sergei Yerkovich .20 .50
23 Sergei Zholtok .30 .75
24 Logo Card .02 .10

1997-98 Las Vegas Thunder

COMPLETE SET (28) 4.80 12.00
1 Ken Quinney .30 .75
2 Manny Legace .60 1.50
3 Jesse Belanger .20 .50
4 Joe Day .20 .50
5 Darcy Loewan .20 .50
6 Trevor Roenick .20 .50
7 Steve Bancroft .20 .50
8 Thom Cullen .20 .50
9 John Slaney .20 .50
10 Sergei Yerkovich .20 .50
11 Bob Strumm GM .02 .10
12 Chris McSorley HCO .08 .25
13 Doug Tretiak EQM .02 .10
14 KKLZ .02 .10
15 Patrice Lefebvre .40 1.00
16 Tim Cheveldae .40 1.00
17 Jeff Christian .20 .50
18 Sergei Klimovich .20 .50
19 Rob Pattison .20 .50
20 Dan Shermerhorn .20 .50
21 Ilya Byakin .20 .50
22 Justin Kurtz .20 .50
23 Radoslav Suchy .20 .50
24 Boom Boom MASCOT .02 .10
25 Clint Malarchuk AGM .20 .50
26 Van Parfet TR .02 .10
27 Dave McCann TV .02 .10
28 PHPA Web Site .02 .10

1998-99 Las Vegas Thunder

COMPLETE SET (30) 4.00 10.00
1 Drew Bannister .15 .40
2 Sean Berens .15 .40
3 Dampy Brar .15 .40
4 Dean Ewen .15 .40
5 Petr Franek .15 .40
6 Brad Guzda .15 .40
7 Sami Helenius .30 .75
8 Bryan Helmer .20 .50
9 Scott Hollis .15 .40
10 Kevin Kaminski .30 .75
11 Patrice Lefebvre .30 .75
12 Jason McBain .15 .40
13 Taj Melson .15 .40
14 Brad Miller .15 .40
15 Nick Naumenko .20 .50
16 Petr Nedved .30 .75
17 Trevor Roenick .20 .50
18 Russ Romaniuk .20 .50
19 Konstantin Simchuk .15 .40
20 Andrei Sryubko .15 .40
21 Stefan Ustorf .20 .50
22 Shawn Wansborough .15 .40
23 Mike Wilson .15 .40
24 Bob Strumm GM .02 .10
25 Bob Bourne CO .02 .10
26 Rod Buskas ACO .02 .10
27 Van Parfet TR .02 .10
28 Bubba Kennedy Richard Krouse EQ .02 .10
29 BoomBoom Mascot .02 .10
30 Logo Card .02 .10

2003-04 Las Vegas Wranglers

COMPLETE SET (24) 4.00 10.00
1 Jeff Attard .20 .50
2 Blaine Bablitz .20 .50
3 Cam Bristow .20 .50
4 Ryan Christie .20 .50
5 David Cousineau .20 .50
6 Greg Day .20 .50
7 Deryk Engelland .20 .50
8 Justin Kelly .20 .50
9 Chris Kenady .20 .50
10 Brent Krahn .40 1.00
11 Marc Magliarditi .30 .75
12 Jason McBain .20 .50
13 Mike McBain .20 .50
14 Tom Nelson .20 .50
15 Kevin O'Flaherty .20 .50
16 Eric Schneider .20 .50
17 Jonathon Shockey .20 .50
18 Kayle Short .20 .50
19 Riku Varjamo .20 .50
20 Chris Wheaton .20 .50
21 Doug Wright .20 .50
22 Glen Gulutzan GM CO .20 .50
23 Mascot .04 .10
24 Checklist .04 .10

2003-04 Las Vegas Wranglers RBI

COMPLETE SET (16) 6.00 15.00
225 Jeff Attard .40 1.00
226 Cam Bristow .40 1.00
227 Ryan Christie .40 1.00
228 David Cousineau .40 1.00
229 Greg Day .40 1.00
230 Deryk Engelland .40 1.00
231 Chris Kenady .40 1.00
232 Brent Krahn .75 2.00
233 Marc Magliarditi .60 1.50
234 Jason McBain .40 1.00
235 Mike McBain .40 1.00
236 Tom Nelson .40 1.00
237 Kevin O'Flaherty .40 1.00
238 Eric Schneider .40 1.00
239 Jonathon Shockey .40 1.00
240 Doug Wright .40 1.00

2004-05 Las Vegas Wranglers

COMPLETE SET (24) 8.00 20.00
1 Mike McBain .40 1.00
2 Jon Krall .40 1.00
3 Deryk Engelland .40 1.00
4 Jason McBain .40 1.00
5 Dustin Johner .40 1.00
6 Christian Chartier .40 1.00
7 Chris Stanley .40 1.00
8 Adam Huxley .40 1.00
9 Dana Lattery .40 1.00
10 Dan Tudin .40 1.00
11 Jeff Attard .40 1.00
12 Marc Magliarditi .60 1.50
13 Regan Darby .40 1.00
14 Shawn Limpright .40 1.00
15 Darren Lynch .40 1.00
16 Doug Wright .40 1.00
17 Jason Spence .40 1.00
18 Sebastien Centomo .75 2.00
19 Ryan Gaucher .40 1.00
20 Glen Gulutzan CO .04 .10
21 Drew Schoneck ACO .04 .10
22 Joe Frederick ACO .04 .10
23 Jeff Sharples ACO .04 .10
24 The Duke MASCOT .04 .10

2005-06 Las Vegas Wranglers

COMPLETE SET (25) 6.00 15.00
1 Todd Alexander .30 .75
2 Nick Anderson .30 .75
3 Thomas Bellemare .30 .75
4 Christian Chartier .30 .75
5 Steven Crampton .30 .75
6 Matt Dzieduszycki .30 .75
7 Derek Edwardson .30 .75
8 Lee Green .30 .75
9 Tim Hambly .30 .75
10 Shawn Limpright .30 .75
11 Darren Lynch .30 .75
12 Marc Magliarditi .40 1.00
13 Mike McBain .30 .75
14 Mike McKenna .30 .75
15 Chris Neiszner .30 .75
16 Sean O'Connor .30 .75
17 Adam Pardy .30 .75
18 Marco Peluso .30 .75
19 Scott Schoneck .30 .75
20 Tyler Sloan .30 .75
21 Chris Stanley .30 .75
22 Dan Tudin .30 .75
23 Glen Gulutzan CO .02 .10
24 Brent Bilodeau ACO .02 .10
25 The Duke MASCOT .02 .10

2006-07 Las Vegas Wranglers

COMPLETE SET (25) 10.00 20.00
1 Nick Anderson .30 .75
2 Ryan Bonni .30 .75
3 Adam Cracknell .30 .75
4 Steve Crampton .60 1.50
5 Kelly Czuy .30 .75
6 Ryan Donally .30 .75
7 Derek Edwardson .30 .75
8 Jason Jozsa .30 .75
9 Jason Krischuk .30 .75
10 Shawn Limpright .30 .75
11 Marc Magliarditi .60 1.50
12 Mike McBain .30 .75
13 Mike McKenna .30 .75
14 Arpad Mihaly .30 .75
15 Tyler Mosienko .30 .75
16 Kevin Nastiuk .60 1.50
17 Chris Neiszner .30 .75
18 Marco Peluso .30 .75
19 Aaron Power .30 .75
20 Scott Schoneck .30 .75
21 Aki Seitsonen .30 .75
22 Joe Tallari .30 .75
23 Bryce Thoma .30 .75
24 Brent Bilodeau ACO .10 .25
25 Glen Gulutzan CO .10 .25

1951-52 Laval Dairy Lac St. Jean

COMPLETE SET (59) 750.00 1500.00
1 Eddy Daoust 25.00 50.00
2 Guy Gareau 20.00 40.00
3 Gilles Desrosiers 20.00 40.00
4 Robert Desbiens 20.00 40.00
5 James Hayes 20.00 40.00
6 Paul Gagnon 20.00 40.00
7 Gerry Perreault 20.00 40.00
8 Marcel Dufour 20.00 40.00
9 Armand Bourdon 20.00 40.00
10 Jean-Marc Pichette 25.00 50.00
11 Gerry Gagnon 20.00 40.00
12 Jules Racette 20.00 40.00
13 Real Marcotte 20.00 40.00
14 Gerry Theberge 20.00 40.00
15 Rene Harvey 20.00 40.00
16 Joseph Lacoursiere 20.00 40.00
17 Fernand Benaquez 20.00 40.00
18 Andre Boisvert 20.00 40.00
19 Claude Chretien 20.00 40.00
20 Norbert Clark 20.00 40.00
21 Sylvio Lambert 20.00 40.00
22 Lucien Roy 20.00 40.00
23 Gerard Audet 20.00 40.00
24 Jacques Lalancette 20.00 40.00
25 Maurice St.Jean 20.00 40.00
26 Camille Lupien 20.00 40.00
27 Rodrigue Pelchat 20.00 40.00
28 Conrad L'Heureux 20.00 40.00
29 Paul Tremblay 20.00 40.00
30 Robert Vincent 20.00 40.00
31 Charles Lamirande 20.00 40.00
32 Leon Gaudreault 20.00 40.00
33 Maurice Thiffault 20.00 40.00
34 Marc-Aurele Tremblay 20.00 40.00
35 Rene Pronovost 20.00 40.00
36 Victor Corbin 20.00 40.00
37 Tiny Tamminen 25.00 50.00
38 Guildor Levesque 20.00 40.00
39 Gaston Lamirande 20.00 40.00
40 Guy Gervais 20.00 40.00
41 Rayner Makila 25.00 50.00
42 Jules Tremblay 20.00 40.00
43 Roland Girard 20.00 40.00
44 Germain Bergeron 20.00 40.00
45 Paul Duchesne 20.00 40.00
46 Roger Beaudoin 20.00 40.00
47 Georges Archibal 20.00 40.00
48 Claude Basque 20.00 40.00
49 Roger Sarda 20.00 40.00
50 Edgard Gendron 20.00 40.00
51 Gaston Labossiere 20.00 40.00
52 Roland Clantara 20.00 40.00
53 Florian Gravel 20.00 40.00
54 Jean-Guy Thompson 20.00 40.00
55 Yvan Forton 20.00 40.00
56 Yves Laporte 20.00 40.00
57 Claude Germain 20.00 40.00
58 Gerry Brunet 20.00 40.00
59 Maurice Courteau 25.00 50.00

1951-52 Laval Dairy QSHL

COMPLETE SET (109) 1000.00 2000.00
1 Jean Beliveau 375.00 750.00
2 Jean Marois 5.00 10.00
3 Joe Crozier 12.50 25.00
4 Jack Gelineau 5.00 10.00
5 Murdo McKay 6.00 12.00
6 Arthur Leyte 5.00 10.00
7 Bill LeBlanc 5.00 10.00
8 Robert Hayes 5.00 10.00
9 Yogi Kraiger 6.00 12.00
10 Frank King 5.00 10.00
11 Ludger Tremblay 6.00 12.00
12 Jackie Leclair 20.00 40.00
13 Martial Pruneau 5.00 10.00
14 Armand Gaudreault 5.00 10.00
15 Marcel Bonin 20.00 40.00
16 Herbie Carnegie 37.50 75.00
17 Claude Robert 5.00 10.00
18 Phil Renaud 5.00 10.00
19 Roland Hebert 5.00 10.00
20 Donat Duschene 5.00 10.00
21 Jacques Gagnon 5.00 10.00
22 Normand Dussault 6.00 12.00
23 Stan Smrke 10.00 20.00
24 Louis Smrke 6.00 12.00
25 Floyd Crawford 5.00 10.00
26 Germain Leger 5.00 10.00
27 Delphis Franche 5.00 10.00
28 Dick Wray 5.00 10.00
29 Guildor Levesque 7.50 15.00
30 Georges Roy 5.00 10.00
31 J.P. Lamirande 5.00 10.00
32 Gerard Glaude 5.00 10.00
33 Marcel Pelletier 10.00 20.00
34 Pete Tkachuck 5.00 10.00
35 Sherman White 5.00 10.00
36 Jimmy Moore 5.00 10.00
37 Punch Imlach 50.00 100.00
38 Alex Sandalax 5.00 10.00
39 William Kyle 5.00 10.00
40 Kenneth Biggs 5.00 10.00
41 Peter Wright 5.00 10.00
42 Rene Pepin 5.00 10.00
43 Tod Campeau 6.00 12.00
44 John Smith 5.00 10.00
45 Thomas McDougall 5.00 10.00
46 Jos. Lepine 5.00 10.00
47 Guy Labrie 5.00 10.00
48 Roger Bessette 5.00 10.00
49 Yvan Dugre 6.00 12.00
50 James Planche 5.00 10.00
51 Nils Tremblay 5.00 10.00
52 Bill MacDonagh 5.00 10.00
53 Georges Ouellet 5.00 10.00
54 Billy Arcand 5.00 10.00
55 Johnny Mahaffy 6.00 12.00
56 Bucky Buchanan 10.00 20.00
57 Al Miller 5.00 10.00
58 Don Penniston 5.00 10.00
59 Spike Laliberte 5.00 10.00
60 Ernie Oakley 5.00 10.00
61 Jack Bownass 5.00 10.00
62 Ted Hodgson 5.00 10.00
63 Lyall Wiseman 5.00 10.00
64 Erwin Grosse 5.00 10.00
65 Mel Read 5.00 10.00
66 Lloyd Henchberger 5.00 10.00
67 Jack Taylor 5.00 10.00
68 Marcel Bessette 5.00 10.00
69 Jack Schmidt 5.00 10.00
70 Paul Saindon 5.00 10.00
71 J.P. Bisaillon 5.00 10.00
72 Eddie Redmond 5.00 10.00
73 Larry Kwong 10.00 20.00
74 Andre Corriveau 5.00 10.00
75 Kitoute Joanette 5.00 10.00
76 Toe Blake 75.00 150.00
77 Georges Bougie 5.00 10.00
78 Jack Irvine 5.00 10.00
79 Paul Larivee 5.00 10.00
80 Paul Leclerc 5.00 10.00
81 Bertrand Bourassa 5.00 10.00
82 Jacques Deslauriers 5.00 10.00
83 Bingo Ernst 5.00 10.00
84 Gaston Gervais 5.00 10.00
85 Gerry Plamondon 6.00 12.00
86 Glen Harmon 5.00 10.00
87 Bob Friday 5.00 10.00
88 Rolland Rousseau 5.00 10.00
89 Billy Goold 5.00 10.00
90 Lloyd Finkbeiner 5.00 10.00
91 Cliff Malone 5.00 10.00
92 Jacques Plante 375.00 750.00
93 Gerard Desaulniers 6.00 12.00
94 Arthur Rose 5.00 10.00
95 Jacques Locas 5.00 10.00
96 Walter Clune 5.00 10.00
97 Louis Denis 5.00 10.00
98 Fernand Perreault 5.00 10.00
99 Douglas McNeil 6.00 12.00
100 Les Douglas 5.00 10.00
101 Howard Riopelle 10.00 20.00
102 Vic Grigg 5.00 10.00
103 Bobby Roberts 5.00 10.00
104 Legs Fraser 5.00 10.00
105 Butch Stahan 5.00 10.00
106 Fritz Frazer 5.00 10.00
107 Bill Robinson 5.00 10.00
108 Eddie Emberg 5.00 10.00
109 Leo Gravelle 12.50 25.00

1951-52 Laval Dairy Subset

COMPLETE SET (66) 750.00 1500.00
4 Jack Gelineau SP 25.00 50.00
7 Al Miller 10.00 20.00
8 Walter Pawlyshyn 10.00 20.00
9 Yogi Kraiger SP 25.00 50.00
10 Al Baccari 10.00 20.00
12 Denis Smith 10.00 20.00
13 Pierre Brillant 10.00 20.00
14 Frank Mario 10.00 20.00
15 Danny Nixon 10.00 20.00
25 Leon Bouchard 10.00 20.00
26 Pete Taillefer 10.00 20.00
29 Bucky Buchanan 12.50 25.00
36 Marius Groleau 10.00 20.00
38 Fernand Perreault 10.00 20.00
39 Robert Drainville 10.00 20.00
40 Ronnie Matthews 10.00 20.00
44 Roger Roberge 10.00 20.00
46 Pete Wywrot 10.00 20.00
50 Gilles Dube 10.00 20.00
51 Nils Tremblay SP 25.00 50.00
52 Bob Pepin 10.00 20.00
53 Dewar Thompson 10.00 20.00
55 Irene St.Hilaire 10.00 20.00
56 Martial Pruneau 10.00 20.00
57 Jacques Locas 10.00 20.00
59 Nelson Podolsky 10.00 20.00
60 Bert Giesebrecht 10.00 20.00
61 Steve Brklaicich 10.00 20.00
65 Jack Hamilton 10.00 20.00
66 Dave Gatherum 10.00 20.00
67 Jean-Marie Plante 10.00 20.00
68 Gordie Haworth 12.50 25.00
69 Jack Schmidt SP 25.00 50.00
70 Bruce Cline 12.50 25.00
72 Phil Vitale 10.00 20.00
81 Carl Smelle 10.00 20.00
84 Tom Smelle 10.00 20.00
85 Gerry Plamondon 12.50 25.00
86 Glen Harmon 10.00 20.00
89 Frank Bathgate 10.00 20.00
90 Bernie Lemonde 10.00 20.00
92 Jacques Plante 375.00 750.00

93 Gerard Desaulniers 10.00 20.00
94 J.C. Lebrun 10.00 20.00
95 Bob Leger 10.00 20.00
96 Walter Clune 10.00 20.00
97 Louis Denis 10.00 20.00
98 Jackie Leclair 15.00 30.00
99 John Arundel 10.00 20.00
100 Les Douglas 10.00 20.00
103 Bobby Robertson 10.00 20.00
104 Ray Fredericks 10.00 20.00
106 Emile Dagenais 10.00 20.00
108 Al Kuntz 10.00 20.00
110 Red Johnson 10.00 20.00
111 John O'Flaherty 10.00 20.00
112 Jack Giesebrecht 12.50 25.00
113 Bill Richardson 10.00 20.00
114 Bep Guidolin 20.00 40.00
115 Roger Bedard 10.00 20.00
116 Renald Lacroix 10.00 20.00
117 Gordie Hudson 10.00 20.00
118 Dick Wray 10.00 20.00
119 Ronnie Hurst 10.00 20.00
120 Eddie Joss 10.00 20.00
121 Lyall Wiseman 10.00 20.00

2014-15 Laval Predateurs
COMPLETE SET (25) 6.00 15.00
1 Steve Bosse .30 .75
2 Mathieu Brisson .30 .75
3 Mathieu Brunelle .30 .75
4 Mathieu Corbeil-Theriault .30 .75
5 Frederick Cote .30 .75
6 Nicolas D'Aoust .30 .75
7 Joshua Desmarais .30 .75
8 Chris Doyle .30 .75
9 Manuel Frechette .30 .75
10 Francis Gourdeau .30 .75
11 Alexandre Imbeault .30 .75
12 Jeremi Janneteau .30 .75
13 Juraj Kolnik .30 .75
14 Jean-Francois LaPlante .30 .75
15 David Lacroix .30 .75
16 Louis-Philip Lacroix .30 .75
17 Eric Lajeunesse .30 .75
18 Dannick Lessard Asst. CO .30 .75
19 David Masse .30 .75
20 Pierre-Luc O'Brien .30 .75
21 Jonathan Oligny .30 .75
22 Steven Oligny .30 .75
23 Vincent Richer .30 .75
24 Joe Rullier .30 .75
25 Curtis Tidball .30 .75

1988-89 Lethbridge Hurricanes
COMPLETE SET (24) 4.80 12.00
1 Mark Bassen .20 .50
2 Pete Berthelsen .20 .50
3 Bryan Bosch .20 .50
4 Paul Checknita .20 .50
5 Kelly Ens .20 .50
6 Jeff Ferguson .20 .50
7 Scott Fukami .20 .50
8 Colin Gregor .20 .50
9 Mark Greig .30 .75
10 Rob Hale .20 .50
11 Ted Hutchings .20 .50
12 Dusty Imoo .30 .75
13 Ivan Jessey .20 .50
14 Mark Kuntz .20 .50
15 Corey Lyons .20 .50
16 Shane Mazutinec .20 .50
17 Casey McMillan .20 .50
18 Pat Pylypuik .20 .50
19 Brad Rubachuk .20 .50
20 Jason Ruff .20 .50
21 Chad Seibel .20 .50
22 Wes Walz .60 1.50
23 Jim Wheatcroft .20 .50
24 Team Picture .20 .50

1989-90 Lethbridge Hurricanes
COMPLETE SET (24) 8.00 20.00
1 Doug Barrault .30 .75
2 Peter Berthelsen .30 .75
3 Bryan Bosch .30 .75
4 Kelly Ens .30 .75
5 Mark Greig .30 .75
6 Ron Gunville .30 .75
7 Rob Hale .30 .75
8 Neil Hawryluk .30 .75
9 David Holzer .30 .75
10 Dusty Imoo .60 1.50
11 Darcy Kaminski ACO .08 .25
12 Bob Loucks CO .08 .25
13 Corey Lyons .30 .75
14 Duane Maruschak .30 .75
15 Jamie McLennan 1.25 3.00
16 Shane Peacock .30 .75
17 Pat Pylypuik .30 .75
18 Gary Reilly .30 .75
19 Brad Rubachuk .30 .75
20 Jason Ruff .30 .75
21 Kevin St. Jacques .30 .75
22 Wes Walz .60 1.50
23 Darcy Werenka .40 1.00
24 Brad Zimmer .30 .75

1993-94 Lethbridge Hurricanes
COMPLETE SET (24) 4.80 12.00
1 Rob Daum CO .08 .25
2 Kirk DeWaele .20 .50
3 Derek Diener .20 .50
4 Scott Grieco .20 .50
5 David Jesiolowski .20 .50
6 Todd MacIsaac .20 .50
7 Stan Matwijiw .40 1.00
8 Larry McMorran .20 .50
9 Brad Mehalko .20 .50
10 Shane Peacock .20 .50
11 Randy Perry .20 .50
12 Domenic Pittis .30 .75
13 Byron Ritchie .25 .60
14 Bryce Salvador .40 1.00
15 Ryan Smith .20 .50
16 Lee Sorochan .30 .75
17 Mark Szoke .20 .50
18 Scott Townsend .20 .50
19 David Trofimenkoff .20 .50
20 Twister (Mascot) .02 .10
21 Ivan Vologjaninov .20 .50
22 Jason Widmer .20 .50
23 Derek Wood .20 .50
24 Aaron Zarowny .20 .50

1995-96 Lethbridge Hurricanes
COMPLETE SET (25) 8.00 20.00
1 Mike Bayrack .40 1.00
2 John Bradley .40 1.00
3 Travis Brigley .40 1.00
4 David Brumby .40 1.00
5 Derek Diener .40 1.00
6 Scott Grieco .40 1.00
7 Lee Hamilton .40 1.00
8 Trevor Hanas .40 1.00
9 Ryan Hoople .40 1.00
10 Mike Josephson .40 1.00
11 Kirby Law .40 1.00
12 Bryan Maxwell CO .02 .10
13 Doyle McMorris .40 1.00
14 Brad Mehalko .40 1.00
15 Dennis Mullen .40 1.00
16 Jiri Novotny .40 1.00
17 Mike O'Grady .40 1.00
18 Randy Perry .40 1.00
19 Byron Ritchie .40 1.00
20 Bryce Salvador .60 1.50
21 Darren Shakotko .40 1.00
22 Mark Smith .40 1.00
23 Dave Taylor .40 1.00
24 Luc Theoret .40 1.00
25 Windy MASCOT .02 .10

1996-97 Lethbridge Hurricanes
COMPLETE SET (24) 4.80 12.00
1 Travis Brigley .20 .50
2 David Cameron .20 .50
3 Matt Demarski .20 .50
4 Paul Elliott .20 .50
5 Jason Hegberg .20 .50
6 Martin Hohenberger .20 .50
7 Ryan Hoople .20 .50
8 Mark Ivan .20 .50
9 Mike Josephson .20 .50
10 Kirby Law .30 .75
11 Mike O'Grady .20 .50
12 Dale Purinton .75 2.00
13 Byron Ritchie .30 .75
14 Bryce Salvador .30 .75
15 Richard Seeley .20 .50
16 Cam Severson .20 .50
17 Darren Shakotko .20 .50
18 Wes Schneider .20 .50
19 Parry Shockey CO
Bryan Maxwell GM .08 .25
20 Mark Smith .20 .50
21 Dave Taylor .20 .50
22 Luc Theoret .20 .50
23 Evgeni Tsybouk .25 .60
24 Shane Yellowhorn .20 .50

1997-98 Lethbridge Hurricanes
COMPLETE SET (25) 4.80 12.00
1 Derrick Atkinson .20 .50
2 Brady Block .20 .50
3 Scott Borders .20 .50
4 Jeff Church .20 .50
5 Jason Hegberg .20 .50
6 Derek Holland .20 .50
7 Curtis Huppe .20 .50
8 Dustin Kazak .20 .50
9 Chad Kletzel .20 .50
10 Vladislav Klochkov .20 .50
11 Charlie Mattersdorfer .20 .50
12 Jason McLean .20 .50
13 Sean Robertson .20 .50
14 Bart Hushmer .20 .50
15 Thomas Scantlebury .20 .50
16 Darren Shakotko .20 .50
17 Mark Smith .40 1.00
18 Shaun Sutter .20 .50
19 Luc Theoret .20 .50
20 Kaleb Toth .20 .50
21 Evgeni Tsybouk .30 .75
22 Mike Varhaug .20 .50
23 Trevor Wasyluk .20 .50
24 Shane Willis .40 1.00
25 Lethbridge Power .02 .10

1999-00 Lethbridge Hurricanes
COMPLETE SET (25) 4.80 12.00
1 Derek Atkinson .20 .50
2 Brian Ballman .20 .50
3 Nathan Barrett .20 .50
4 Brady Block .30 .75
5 Scott Borders .20 .50
6 Phil Cole .20 .50
7 Radek Duda .30 .75
8 Simon Ferguson .20 .50
9 Jordon Flodell .20 .50
10 Eric Godard .30 .75
11 Jason Hegberg .20 .50
12 Brandon Janes .20 .50
13 Ryan Jorde .20 .50
14 Dustin Kazak .20 .50
15 Angel Krstev .20 .50
16 Petr Kudrna .20 .50
17 Darren Lynch .20 .50
18 Warren McCutheon .20 .50
19 Justin Ossachuk .20 .50
20 Derek Parker .02 .10
21 Brian Patterson .20 .50
22 Derrick Ruck .20 .50
23 Thomas Scantlebury .20 .50
24 Eric Sonnenberg .20 .50
25 Chad Yaremko .20 .50

2000-01 Lethbridge Hurricanes
COMPLETE SET (25) 4.80 40.00
1 Brian Ballman .60 1.50
2 Nathan Barrett 2.00 5.00
3 Scott Borders .60 1.50
4 Phil Cole .60 1.50
5 Simon Ferguson .60 1.50
6 Matt Fetzner .60 1.50
7 Mark Forth .60 1.50
8 Tim Green .60 1.50
9 Matt Jacques .60 1.50
10 Adam Johnson .60 1.50
11 Andrew Jungwirth .60 1.50
12 Tomas Kopecky 2.00 5.00
13 Ryley Layden .60 1.50
14 Darren Lynch .60 1.50
15 Joel Martin .75 2.00
16 Warren McCutcheon .60 1.50
17 Brett O'Malley .60 1.50
18 Brian Patterson .60 1.50
19 Martin Podlesak .75 2.00
20 Derek Ruck .60 1.50
21 Thomas Scantlebury .60 1.50
22 Blake Ward .75 2.00
23 Twister MASCOT .02 .10
24 Header Card .02 .10
25 Sponsor Card .02 .10

2001-02 Lethbridge Hurricanes
COMPLETE SET (23) 5.00 12.00
1 Matthew Berger .20 .50
2 Simon Ferguson .20 .50
3 Stewart Thiessen .20 .50
4 Tim Green .20 .50
5 Braden Appleby .20 .50
6 Tomas Kopecky .30 .75
7 Paul McBrien .20 .50
8 Nathan Barrett .30 .75
9 Martin Podlesak .30 .75
10 Kris Callaway .20 .50
11 Brian Patterson .20 .50
12 Ryley Layden .20 .50
13 D.J. King .20 .50
14 Logan Koopmans .30 .75
15 Brett O'Malley .20 .50
16 Scott Borders .20 .50
17 David Selthun .20 .50
18 Clay Plume .20 .50
19 Blake Ward .30 .75
20 Brent Seabrook .20 .50
21 Jeremy Jackson .20 .50
22 Nick Chibi .20 .50
23 Tyrell Moulton .20 .50

2003-04 Lethbridge Hurricanes
1 Joel Andresen .75 2.00
2 John Lammers .75 2.00
3 Jake Riddle .75 2.00
4 Brent Seabrook 1.50 4.00
5 Nick Tarnasky .75 2.00
6 Kris Versteeg 2.00 5.00

2004-05 Lethbridge Hurricanes
COMPLETE SET (24) 10.00 25.00
1 Mark Ashton .40 1.00
2 Shawn Mezei .40 1.00
3 Brennan Chapman .40 1.00
4 Brent Seabrook .40 1.00
5 Tyler Redenbach .40 1.00
6 Kris Versteeg 2.00 5.00
7 Mark Olafson .40 1.00
8 John Lammers .40 1.00
9 Martin Ruzicka .40 1.00
10 Colton Yellow Horn .60 1.50
11 Kyle Pess .40 1.00
12 Michael Kaye .40 1.00
13 Kenny Petkau .40 1.00
14 Jon Flewich .40 1.00
15 Chase Hentuik .40 1.00
16 Neil Kodman .40 1.00
17 Rob Klinkhammer .40 1.00
18 Michal Gulasi .40 1.00
19 Mike Ulrich .40 1.00
20 Lenny Thunderchild .40 1.00
21 Jesse Dudas .40 1.00
22 Aaron Sorochan .60 1.50
23 Scott Bolland .60 1.50
24 MASCOT .04 .10

2005-06 Lethbridge Hurricanes
COMPLETE SET (24) 8.00 20.00
1 Mark Ashton .40 1.00
2 Andrew Bentz .40 1.00
3 Zach Boychuk .40 1.00
4 Ryan Bryce .40 1.00
5 Mike Cann .40 1.00
6 Jacob Dietrich .40 1.00
7 Mitch Fadden .40 1.00
8 Yashar Farmanara .40 1.00
9 Kris Hogg .40 1.00
10 Michael Kaye .40 1.00
11 Ryan Kerr .40 1.00
12 Dwight King .40 1.00
13 Randy King .40 1.00
14 Tomas Kudelka .40 1.00
15 Justin Leclerc .40 1.00
16 Gavin McHale .40 1.00
17 Mark Olafson .40 1.00
18 Isaac Reid .40 1.00
19 Brad Riege .40 1.00
20 Roman Wick .40 1.00
21 Ben Wright .40 1.00
22 Michael Wuchterl .40 1.00
23 Colton Yellowhorn .75 2.00
24 Twister MASCOT .02 .10

2014-15 Lethbridge Hurricanes
COMPLETE SET (22) 6.00 15.00
1 Scott Allan .30 .75
2 Carter Amson .30 .75
3 Florian Baltram .30 .75
4 Brayden Burke .30 .75
5 Giorgio Estephan .30 .75
6 Devan Fafard .30 .75
7 Carter Folk .30 .75
8 Kade Jensen .30 .75
9 Brandon Kennedy .30 .75
10 Ryley Lindgren .30 .75
11 Andrew Nielsen .30 .75
12 Kord Pankewicz .30 .75
13 Brady Reagan .30 .75
14 Jayden Sittler .30 .75
15 Stuart Skinner .30 .75
16 Pavel Skumatov .30 .75
17 Nick Walters .30 .75
18 Jamal Watson .30 .75
19 John Wesley .30 .75
20 Jaeger White .30 .75
21 Mike Winther .30 .75
22 Tyler Wong .30 .75

2003-04 Lewiston Maineiacs
COMPLETE SET (28) 12.00 20.00
1 Mathieu Aubin .30 .75
2 Gabriel Balasescu .30 .75
3 Vladislav Balaz .30 .75
4 Alex Bourret .60 1.50
5 Marc-Andre Cliché .60 1.50
6 Nicolas Cowan .30 .75
7 Matthew Davis .30 .75
8 Chad Denny .30 .75
9 Pierre-Luc Faubert .30 .75
10 Karl Fournier .30 .75
11 Bobby Gates .30 .75
12 Olivier Legault .30 .75
13 Travis Mealey .30 .75
14 Ryan Murphy .30 .75
15 Jonathan Paiement .30 .75
16 Alexandre Picard .75 2.00
17 Brandon Roach .30 .75
18 Maxime Robert .30 .75
19 Richard Stehlik .30 .75
20 Francis Trudel .30 .75
21 Kevin Turgeon .30 .75
22 Brandon Verge .30 .75
23 Sheldon Wenzel .30 .75
24 Mario Durocher CO .04 .10
25 Jeff Guay ACO .04 .10
26 Ed Harding ACO .04 .10
27 Lewy MASCOT .04 .10
28 Team Photo CL .10 .25

2002-03 Lexington Men O'War
COMPLETE SET (26) 8.00 20.00
1 Team Photo .20 .50
2 Jim Wiley .30 .75
3 Justin Van Parys .30 .75
4 Mike Smith .30 .75
5 Marc-Andre Thinel .30 .75
6 Jared Smyth .30 .75
7 Jesse Cook .30 .75
8 Ben Storey .30 .75
9 Mark Smith .60 1.50
10 Dan Murphy .60 1.50
11 Daryl Moor .30 .75
12 Alexander Mathieu .30 .75
13 Dominic Periard .30 .75
14 Chris Dirkes .30 .75
15 Van Burgess .30 .75
16 Fraser Clair .30 .75
17 Terry Craven .30 .75
18 Brett Draney .30 .75
19 Joe Vandermeer .30 .75
20 Aaron Miskovich .30 .75
21 Jay Banach .30 .75
22 Ryan Fultz .30 .75
23 Mike Sgroi .30 .75
24 Josh Mizerek .30 .75
25 Kevin Knopp .30 .75
26 Mow MASCOT .04 .10

2000-01 Lincoln Stars
COMPLETE SET (28)
1 Nick Fouts .30 .75
2 Ken Scruderi .15 .40
3 Tom Watkins .15 .40
4 Andy Schneider .15 .40
5 Matt Wavra .15 .40
6 Chris Fournier .15 .40
7 Mike Fournier .15 .40
8 John Snowden .15 .40
9 Nick Fuher .15 .40
10 Preston Callander .15 .40
11 Bobby John Byfuglien .15 .40
12 Josh Magnuson .15 .40
13 Brandon Polich .15 .40
14 Chad Hontvet .15 .40
16 Billy Hengen .15 .40
16 Ryan Young .15 .40
17 Matthew Trojovsky .15 .40
18 Lee Marvin .15 .40
19 Brandon Bochenski .15 .40
20 Trevor Frischmon .15 .40
21 Marco Peluso .15 .40
22 Jake Brandt .30 .75
23 Justin Johnson .30 .75
24 Beau Fritz .30 .75
25 Steve Johnson HCO .10 .25
26 Steve Ross ACO .10 .25
27 Corey Courtney TR .10 .25
28 Mascot .10 .25

2001-02 Lincoln Stars
COMPLETE SET (28) 5.00 12.00
1 Ben Assenmacher .20 .50
2 David Backes .40 1.00
3 Josh Budish .20 .50
4 Jamie Dowhatko .20 .50
5 Mike Eickman .20 .50
6 Luke Erickson .20 .50
7 Matt Erickson .20 .50
8 Mike Fournier .20 .50
9 Trevor Frischmon .20 .50
10 Beau Fritz .30 .75
11 Ethan Graham .20 .50
12 Billy Hengen .20 .50
13 Chad Hontvet .20 .50
14 Dan Irmen .20 .50
15 Patrick Knutson .20 .50
16 Philippe Lamoureux .20 .50
17 Lee Marvin .20 .50
18 T.J. McElroy .20 .50
19 Ryan Potulny .20 .50
20 John Snowden .20 .50
21 Dirk Southern .20 .50
22 Ryan Swanson .20 .50
23 Matt Wavra .20 .50
24 Nate Ziegelmann .20 .50
25 Steve Johnson HCO .04 .10
26 Mark Pivetz ACO .04 .10
27 Corey Courtney TR .04 .10
28 Mascot .04 .10

2002-03 Lincoln Stars
COMPLETE SET (48) 8.00 20.00
1 Philippe Lamoureux .20 .50
2 Ethan Graham .20 .50
3 David Backes .40 1.00
4 Mike Eickman .20 .50
5 Chris Porter .20 .50
6 Ryan Potulny .20 .50
7 Danny Irmen .20 .50
8 Mike Fournier .20 .50
9 Tyler Magura .20 .50
10 John Snowden .20 .50
11 Ben Gordon .20 .50
12 Jamison Orr .20 .50
13 Mick Berge .20 .50
14 Mike Nesdill .20 .50
15 Brent Borgen .20 .50
16 Matt Hayek .20 .50
17 David Carlisle .20 .50
18 Luke Erickson .20 .50
19 Jesse Lindenberg .20 .50
20 Keith Rodger .20 .50
21 Robbie Bina .20 .50
22 Joel Gasper .20 .50
23 Ross Cherry .20 .50
24 Nate Ziegelmann .20 .50
25 Steve Johnson .20 .50
26 Mark Pivetz .20 .50
27 Rob Facca .20 .50
28 Corey Courtney .20 .50
29 Starzan MASCOT .04 .10
30 Checklist .04 .10
31 Mark Schwamberger .20 .50
32 Jeff McFarland .20 .50
33 Per Mars .20 .50
34 David Backes AS .40 1.00
35 Chris Porter AS .20 .50
36 Ryan Potulny AS .20 .50
37 Dan Irmen AS .20 .50
38 John Snowden AS .20 .50
39 Nate Ziegelmann AS .20 .50
40 Philippe Lamoureux .20 .50
41 Ethan Graham .20 .50
42 David Backes .40 1.00
43 Mike Eickman .20 .50
44 Ryan Potulny .20 .50
45 Dan Irmen .20 .50
46 John Snowden .20 .50
47 Nate Ziegelmann .20 .50
48 Update Checklist .04 .10

2003-04 Lincoln Stars
COMPLETE SET (29) 12.00
1 Philippe Lamoureux .20 .50
2 Morgan Simonson .20 .50
3 Kaj Kallarsson .20 .50
4 Jared Boll .20 .50
5 Evan Rankin .20 .50
6 Nick Tuzzolino .20 .50
7 Garrett Raboin .20 .50
8 Tyler Magura .20 .50
9 Ben Gordon .20 .50
10 Mick Berge .20 .50
11 Michael Nesdill .20 .50
12 Brent Borgen .20 .50
13 Alexei McAvoy .20 .50
14 Matt Hayek .20 .50
15 David Carlisle .20 .50
16 Andrew Guyer .20 .50
17 Jesse Lindenberg .20 .50
18 Chris Tarkir .20 .50
19 Keith Rodger .20 .50
20 Adam Bartholomay .20 .50
21 Michael Waidlich .20 .50
22 Dan Cormie .20 .50
23 Aaron Walski .20 .50
24 Aaron McCloy .20 .50
25 Steve Johnson CO .04 .10
26 Rob Facca ACO .04 .10
27 Corey Courtney TR .04 .10
28 Mascot .04 .10
29 Checklist .04 .10

2003-04 Lincoln Stars Update
COMPLETE SET (18) 3.00 8.00
30 Checklist .04 .10
31 John Vadnais .20 .50
32 Dan Riedel .20 .50
33 Derek Whitmore .20 .50
34 Jered Bye .20 .50
35 Chris Robinson .20 .50
36 John Swanson .20 .50
37 Matt Weir .20 .50
38 Checklist .04 .10
39 Philippe Lamoureux
Tyler Magura .20 .50
40 Ben Gordon
Mick Berge .20 .50
41 Mike Nesdill
Brent Borgen .20 .50
42 Matt Hayek
David Carlisle .20 .50
43 Philippe Lamoureux RB .20 .50
44 Philippe Lamoureux RB .20 .50
45 Evan Rankin AS .20 .50
46 Nick Tuzzolino AS .20 .50
47 David Carlisle AS .20 .50

2004-05 Lincoln Stars
COMPLETE SET (30) 5.00 12.00
1 Jordan Pearce .40 1.00
2 Brian Bina .20 .50
3 John Vadnais .20 .50
4 Jared Boll .40 1.00
5 Dillon Duncan .20 .50
6 Dan Riedel .20 .50
7 Garrett Raboin .20 .50
8 Erik Condra .20 .50
9 Eli Vlaisavljevich .20 .50
10 J.J. Koehler .20 .50
11 Ryan Hohl .20 .50
12 Shawn Gawrys .20 .50
13 Chris Nugent .20 .50
14 David Carlisle .20 .50
15 Mike Kramer .20 .50
16 Mick Berge .20 .50
17 Tom Sawatske .20 .50
18 Brock Trotter .20 .50
19 Chris Robinson .20 .50
20 John Swanson .20 .50
21 Steve Jakiel .20 .50
22 Patrik Valcak .20 .50
23 Linus Klasen .20 .50
24 Steve Johnson CO .04 .10
25 Ryan Bencurik ACO .04 .10
26 Derek Reynolds ACO .04 .10
27 Corey Courtney TR .04 .10
28 Starzan MASCOT .04 .10
29 Checklist .04 .10
30 contest card .04 1.00

2004-05 Lincoln Stars Update
COMPLETE SET (18) 5.00 12.00
31 Brian Lee 1.50 4.00
32 Kyle Hardwick .20 .50
33 Chris Vande Velde .40 1.00
34 Russ Sinkewich .20 .50
35 Ryan Salvis .20 .50
36 Chris Murphy .20 .50
37 Ryan Kelly .20 .50
38 Taylor Raszka .20 .50
39 Jared Boll .40 1.00
40 Dan Riedel .20 .50
41 Garrett Raboin .20 .50
42 David Carlisle .20 .50
43 Mick Berge .20 .50
44 Chris Robinson .20 .50
45 Jordan Pearce AS .40 1.00
46 Jared Boll AS .40 1.00
47 Dan Riedel AS .20 .50
48 Tom Sawatske AS .20 .50

2006-07 Lincoln Stars
COMPLETE SET (29) 10.00 18.00
1 Lincoln Stars .10 .25
2 David Brack .30 .75
3 Chad Langlais .30 .75
4 Rick Carden .30 .75
5 Eric Lake .30 .75
6 Chris Stansik .30 .75
7 Jared Brown .30 .75
8 Matt Bartkowski .30 .75
9 Stephen Schultz .30 .75
10 Ryan Ruikka .30 .75
11 Jason Gregoire .40 1.00
12 Brandon Bollig .30 .75
13 Danny Baco .30 .75
14 Ross Henry .30 .75
15 Mike Kramer .30 .75
16 Ryan Lowery .30 .75
17 Colby Cohen .30 .75
18 Kyle O'Kane .30 .75
19 Pat McAuley .30 .75
20 Jon Morrow .40 1.00
21 Kyle Follmer .30 .75
22 Bryan Hogan .40 1.00
23 Anthony Principato .30 .75
24 Carter Camper .30 .75
25 Steve Johnson CO .10 .25
26 Ryan Bencurik ACO .02 .10
27 Jim McGroarty ACO .02 .10
28 Corey Courtney TR .02 .10
29 Starzan MASCOT .02 .10

2006-07 Lincoln Stars Traded
COMPLETE SET (18) 5.00 12.00
1T Checklist .02 .10
2T Patrick Johnson .30 .75
3T Joey Miller .30 .75
4T J.J. Crew .30 .75
5T Mike Hull .30 .75
6T Dan Lawson .30 .75
7T Bryce Christianson .30 .75
8T Chad Langlais .30 .75
9T Chris Stansik .30 .75
10T Jared Brown .30 .75
11T Brandon Bollig .30 .75
12T Danny Baco .30 .75
13T Mike Kramer .30 .75
14T Bryan Hogan .30 .75
15T Chad Langlais .30 .75
16T Stephen Schultz .30 .75
17T Colby Cohen .30 .75
18T Carter Camper .40 1.00

2006-07 Lincoln Stars Upper Deck Signature Series
1 Danny Baco 20.00 50.00
2 Matt Bartowski 20.00 50.00
3 Brandon Bollig 25.00 60.00
4 David Brack 20.00 50.00
5 Jared Brown 20.00 50.00
6 Carter Camper 20.00 50.00
7 Rick Carden 20.00 50.00
8 Bryce Christianson 20.00 50.00
9 Colby Cohen 20.00 50.00
10 J.J. Crew 20.00 50.00
11 Kyle Follmer 20.00 50.00
12 Jason Gregoire 25.00 60.00
13 Ross Henry 20.00 50.00
14 Bryan Hogan 25.00 60.00
15 Mike Hull 20.00 50.00
16 Patrick Johnson 20.00 50.00
17 Mike Kramer 20.00 50.00
18 Eric Lake 20.00 50.00
19 Chad Langlais 20.00 50.00
20 Dan Lawson 20.00 50.00
21 Pat McAuley 4.00 10.00
22 Joey Miller 20.00 50.00
23 Kyle O'Kane 4.00 10.00
24 Stephen Schultz 20.00 50.00
25 Chris Stansik 20.00 50.00

2007-08 Lincoln Stars
COMPLETE SET (57) 10.00 25.00
1 Kevin Murdock .25 .60
2 Mike Dalhuisen .25 .60
3 Jake Newton .25 .60
4 Dennis Brown .25 .60
5 Michael Sdao .25 .60
6 Rick Carden .25 .60
7 Mike Henderson .25 .60
8 Kyle Follmer .25 .60
9 Jared Festler .25 .60
10 Matt Bartkowski .25 .60
11 Ryan Kretzer .25 .60
12 Kyle Verbeek .25 .60
13 Jason Gregoire .25 .60
14 Brandon Bollig .25 .60
15 Danny Baco .25 .60
16 Ross Henry .25 .60
17 P.J. Tatum .25 .60
18 Travis Erstad .25 .60
19 J.J. Crew .25 .60
20 Kyle Delaurell .25 .60
21 Tyler Brickler .25 .60
22 Tyler Kieffer .25 .60
23 Nick Hopper .25 .60
24 Jimmy McGroarty .25 .60
25 Nick Fuher .25 .60
26 Nick Fouts .25 .60
27 Corey Courtney .25 .60
28 I.C. Starz (Mascot) .15 .40
29 Lincoln Stars CL .15 .40
30 Checklist .15 .40
31 Kevin Murdock .25 .60
32 Mike Dalhuisen .25 .60
33 Lyon Messier .25 .60
34 Jake Newton .25 .60
35 Taylor Kuypers .25 .60
36 Michael Sdao .25 .60
37 Rick Carden .25 .60
38 Kyle Follmer .25 .60
39 Jared Festler .25 .60
40 Matt Bartkowski .25 .60
41 Ryan Kretzer .25 .60
42 Jimmy Hayes .25 .60
43 Jason Gregoire .25 .60
44 Brandon Bollig .25 .60
45 Danny Baco .25 .60
46 Ross Henry .25 .60
47 Chris Forfar .25 .60
48 Travis Erstad .25 .60
49 J.J. Crew .25 .60
50 Eric Meland .25 .60
51 Josh Myers .25 .60
52 Tyler Brickler .25 .60
53 David Reekie .25 .60
54 Jared Festler .25 .60
55 Matt Bartkowski .25 .60
56 Jason Gregoire .25 .60
57 Ross Henry .25 .60

2014-15 Lincoln Stars
COMPLETE SET (36) 10.00 25.00
1 Header Card CL .30 .75
2 Cam Hackett .30 .75
3 Connor Frantti .30 .75
4 James LaDouce .30 .75
5 Dylan Woolf .30 .75
6 Ryan Cook .30 .75
7 Chris Klack .30 .75
8 Dominick Sacco .30 .75
9 Miguel Fidler .30 .75
10 Christopher Dodero .30 .75
11 Max Humitz .30 .75
12 Joe Lappin .30 .75
13 August Von Ungern-Sternberg .30 .75
14 Michael Gillespie .30 .75
15 Ludvig Hoff .30 .75
16 Wyatt Kalynuk .30 .75
17 Angus Scott .30 .75
18 Tye Ausmus .30 .75
19 Ryan Jones .30 .75
20 Cam Lee .30 .75
21 Grant Jozefek .30 .75
22 Biagio Lerario .30 .75
23 Patrick Polino .30 .75
24 Blake Christensen .30 .75
25 Peyton Jones .30 .75
26 Chris Hartsburg CO .30 .75
27 Mick Berge Asst. CO .30 .75
28 Corey Courtney Trainer .30 .75
29 John Hull GM .30 .75
30 Southside Auto Tech Ad .30 .75
1T Luke Jaycox .30 .75
2T Ethan Price .30 .75
3T Waltteri Hopponen .30 .75
4T Jack Badini .30 .75
5T Chris Gambardella .30 .75
6T Sean MacTavish .30 .75

2015-16 Lincoln Stars
COMPLETE SET (30) 6.00 15.00
1 Checklist .30 .75
2 Dylan Woolf .30 .75
3 Christian Hausinger .30 .75
4 Luke Jaycox .30 .75
5 Liam Schioler .30 .75
6 Anthony Wyse .30 .75
7 Will D'Orsi .30 .75
8 Carson Gicewicz .30 .75
9 Joachim Weber .30 .75
10 Henry Bowlby .30 .75
11 Christian Evers .30 .75
12 Sam Kauppila .30 .75
13 Ludvig Hoff .30 .75
14 Nate Pionk .30 .75
15 Adam Brady .30 .75
16 Tye Ausmus .30 .75
17 Jack Badini .30 .75
18 Ryan Jones .30 .75
19 Grant Jozefek .30 .75
20 Biagio Lerario .30 .75
21 Patrick Polino .30 .75
22 Dominick Mersch .30 .75
23 Peyton Jones .30 .75
24 Patrik Virtanen .30 .75
25 Ethen Frank .30 .75
26 Chris Hartsburg CO .30 .75
27 Mick Berge Asst. CO .30 .75
28 Clay Adams .30 .75
29 Corey Courtney .30 .75
30 Cayden Primeau UCS .30 .75

1985-86 London Knights
COMPLETE SET (30) 20.00 50.00
1 LaVerne Shipley CoP .08 .25
2 Joe Ranger .20 .50
3 Kellogg's Ad CL .08 .25
4 Don Boyd GM/CO .08 .25
5 Harry E. Sparling COP .08 .25
6 Murray Nystrom .20 .50
7 Bob Halkidis .30 .75
8 Morgan Watts .20 .50
9 Brendan Shanahan 15.00 40.00
10 Brian Dobbin .30 .75
11 Ed Kister .20 .50
12 Darin Smith .20 .50
13 Greg Puhalski .20 .50
14 Dave Haas .20 .50

15 Pete McLeod .20 .50
16 Frank Tremblay .20 .50
17 Matthew Smyth .20 .50
18 Glen Leslie .20 .50
19 Mike Zombo .20 .50
20 Jamie Groke .20 .50
21 Brad Schlegel .30 .75
22 Kelly Cain .20 .50
23 Tom Allen .20 .50
24 Rod Gerow .20 .50
25 Pat Vachon .20 .50
26 Paul Cook ACO .08 .25
27 Jeff Reese .60 1.50
28 Fred Kean PR .08 .25
29 Scott Cumming .30 .75
30 John Williams ACO .08 .25

1986-87 London Knights

COMPLETE SET (30) 14.00 35.00
1 LaVerne Shipley CoP .08 .25
2 Tom Gosnell Mayor .08 .25
3 Kellogg's Ad CL .08 .25
4 Wayne Maxner CO/GM .20 .50
5 Harry E. Sparling COP .08 .25
6 Brendan Shanahan 10.00 25.00
7 Pat Vachon .20 .50
8 Brad Schlegel .20 .50
9 Barry Earhart .20 .50
10 Jean Marc MacKenzie .20 .50
11 Jason Simon .20 .50
12 Jim Sprott .20 .50
13 Bill Long VP .08 .25
14 Murray Nystrom .20 .50
15 Shayne Stevenson .30 .75
16 Don Martin .20 .50
17 Ian Pound .20 .50
18 Peter Lisy .20 .50
19 Steve Marcolini .20 .50
20 Craig Majaury .20 .50
21 Trevor Dam .20 .50
22 Dave Akey .20 .50
23 Dennis McEwen .20 .50
24 Shane Whelan .20 .50
25 Greg Hankkio .20 .50
26 Pat Kelly TR .08 .25
27 Stephen Titus .30 .75
28 Fred Kean PR .08 .25
29 Chris Somers .30 .75
30 Gord Clark MD .08 .25

1993-94 London Knights

COMPLETE SET (29) 4.80 12.00
1 Jason Allison 2.00 5.00
2 Ryan Appel .15 .40
3 Tim Bacik .08 .25
4 Ryan Black .08 .25
5 Chris Brassard .08 .25
6 Ryan Burgoyne .08 .25
7 Brodie Coffin .08 .25
8 Rob Frid .08 .25
9 David Gilmore .08 .25
10 Roy Gray .08 .25
11 John Guirestante .08 .25
12 Brent Holdsworth .08 .25
13 Don Margettie .08 .25
14 Dan Reja .08 .25
15 Daryl Rivers .08 .25
16 Gord Ross .08 .25
17 Kevin Slota .08 .25
18 Brian Stacey .08 .25
19 Nick Stajduhar .08 .25
20 Bill Tibbetts .40 1.00
21 Ben Walker .08 .25
22 Jordan Willis .15 .40
23 Chris Zanutto .08 .25
24 Knights Top Picks
Ryan Appel
Ben Walker
Den Reja
Roy Gray .08 .25
25 Knights Future Stars
Nick Stajduhar
Jason Allison
John Guirestante
Ryan Black
Jordan Willis .40 1.00
26 Gary Agnew CO .02 .10
27 Steve Stoyanovich ACO
Tom Hedican CO .02 .10
28 Murray Nystrom ACO .02 .10
29 Title Card .02 .10

2000-01 London Knights

COMPLETE SET (35) 25.00 50.00
1 Mark Hunter
Dale Hunter .20 .50
2 Bobby Turner .20 .50
3 Matt Cooper .20 .50
4 Aaron Lobb .20 .50
5 Lou Dickenson .20 .50
6 Lindsay Hofford ACO .02 .10
7 Kyle Neufeld .20 .50
8 Petr Hemsky .20 .50
9 Rick Nash 8.00 20.00
10 Brent Varty .20 .50
11 Danny Bois .30 .75
12 Joel Scherban .20 .50
13 Brian Dobbin .20 .50
14 Aaron Molnar .30 .75
15 Mike Clarke .20 .50
16 Ian Turner .20 .50
17 John Eminger .20 .50
18 Dan Jancevski .40 1.00
19 Jason Davies .20 .50
20 Logan Hunter .40 1.00
21 Checklist card .01 .01
22 Don Brankley TR .01 .01
23 Josh Chambers .20 .50
24 Chris Kelly .20 .50
25 Matt Albiani .20 .50
26 Matt Junkins .20 .50
27 Mike Stathopoulos .20 .50
U1 Chris Kelly .40 1.00
U2 Mark Hunter ACO .10 .25
U3 Dan Jancevski .40 1.00
U4 Logan Hunter .40 1.00
U5 Dale Hunter CO .20 .50
U6 Danny Bois .40 1.00
U7 Scorch MASCOT .02 .10
U8 Rick Nash 10.00 25.00

2001-02 London Knights

COMPLETE SET (30) 10.00 25.00
1 Title Card CL .04 .10
2 Sean Dixon .20 .50
3 Dennis Wideman .30 .75
4 Patrick Barbieri .20 .50
5 Bryan Thompson .20 .50
6 Chris Bain .20 .50
7 Mike Stathopoulos .20 .50
8 Danny Bois .20 .50
9 Matt Iannetta .20 .50
10 Charlie Stephens .30 .75
11 Dylan Hunter .20 .50
12 Logan Hunter .20 .50
13 Sean McMorrow .30 .75
14 Chad Thompson .20 .50
15 Rick Steadman .20 .50
16 Matt Junkins .20 .50
17 Dan Buccella .20 .50
18 Rick Nash 6.00 15.00
19 Robbie Colangelo .20 .50
20 Matt Iorianni .20 .50
21 Ian Turner .20 .50
22 Corey Perry 1.50 4.00
23 Jan Chovan .30 .75
24 Matt Weir .20 .50
25 Alex White .20 .50
26 Jacques Beaulieu ACO .04 .10
27 Lindsay Hofford ACO .04 .10
28 Dale Hunter CO .20 .50
29 Don Brankley TR .04 .10
NNO Mission Hockey AD .04 .10

2002-03 London Knights

COMPLETE CHECKLIST 8.00 20.00
1 Team Picture
CL .04 .10
2 Dennis Wideman .30 .75
3 Logan Hunter .30 .75
4 Corey Perry .75 2.00
5 Mike Stathopoulos .20 .50
6 Danny Bois .30 .75
7 Ryan Hare .20 .50
8 Dylan Hunter .40 1.00
9 Rick Steadman .20 .50
10 Matt Weir .20 .50
11 David Bolland .75 2.00
12 Kyle Piwowarczyk .20 .50
13 Brandon Prust .30 .75
14 Chris Bain .20 .50
15 Adam Nemeth .20 .50
16 Zach Trammer .20 .50
17 Danny Syvret .30 .75
18 Jimmy Ball .20 .50
19 Kyle Quincey .40 1.00
20 Marc Methot .30 .75
21 Gerald Coleman .40 1.00
22 Chris Houle .20 .50
23 Jayme Helmer .20 .50
24 Robbie Drummond .20 .50
25 Tomas Linhart .20 .50
26 Matt Iorianni .20 .50
27 Dale Hunter CO .20 .50
28 Don Brankley TR .04 .10
29 Jacques Beaulieu ACO .04 .10
30 Opening Night .04 .10

2003-04 London Knights

COMPLETE SET (26) 10.00 20.00
1 Rob Schremp 1.25 3.00
2 Corey Perry .60 1.50
3 Adam Nemeth .30 .75
4 Danny Syvret .30 .75
5 Ivan Khomutov .20 .50
6 Jacques Beaulieu ACO .04 .10
7 Don Brankley TR .04 .10
8 Trevor Kell .20 .50
9 Dennis Wideman .30 .75
10 Marc Methot .20 .50
11 Vadim Karaga .20 .50
12 Scott Sheppard .20 .50
13 Dale Hunter CO .20 .50
14 Logan Hunter .30 .75
15 Rick Steadman .20 .50
16 Ryan MacDonald .40 1.00
17 Danny Bois .20 .50
18 David Bolland .40 1.00
19 Tommy Mannino .20 .50
20 Gerald Coleman .40 1.00
21 Dylan Hunter .40 1.00
22 Josh Beaulieu .20 .50
23 Robbie Drummond .20 .50
24 Ryan Pottruff .20 .50
25 Brandon Prust .30 .75
26 Danny Richmond .40 1.00
27 Corey Perry TL 2.50 6.00

2004-05 London Knights

COMPLETE SET (26) 15.00
1 Ryan MacDonald .30 .75
2 Rick Steadman .20 .50
3 Steve Ferry .20 .50
4 Rob Schremp .40 1.00
5 Trevor Kell .20 .50
6 Robbie Drummond .20 .50
7 Bryan Rodney .20 .50
8 Brandon Prust .20 .50
9 Corey Perry .75 2.00
10 Frank Rediker .20 .50
11 Danny Syvret .30 .75
12 Gerald Coleman .30 .75
13 David Bolland .40 1.00
14 Josh Beaulieu .20 .50
15 Dylan Hunter .40 1.00
16 Drew Larman .20 .50
17 Jordan Foreman .20 .50
18 Ryan Pottruff .20 .50
19 Kelly Thomson .20 .50
20 Shawn Futers .20 .50
21 Marc Methot .30 .75
22 Jeff Whitfield .20 .50
23 Dale Hunter CO .20 .50
25 Don Brankley TR .04 .10
25 Jacques Beaulieu ACO .04 .10
NNO Re
Max Sponsor Card .04 .10

2005-06 London Knights

COMPLETE SET (26) 5.00 12.00
1 Rob Schremp .60 1.50
2 Dylan Hunter .40 1.00
3 Trevor Kell .20 .50
4 Kris Belan .20 .50
5 Matt Clarke .20 .50
6 Jamie Vanderveeken .20 .50
7 Sergei Kostitsyn .40 1.00
8 Jordan Foreman .20 .50
9 Adam Perry .20 .50
10 David Bolland .40 1.00
11 Frank Rediker .20 .50
12 Matt McCready .20 .50
13 Scott Aarssen .20 .50
14 Steve Ferry .20 .50
15 Robbie Drummond .20 .50
16 Andrew Wilkins .20 .50
17 Ryan Martinelli .20 .50
18 Corey Syvret .20 .50
19 Josh Beaulieu .20 .50
20 Adam Dennis .40 1.00
21 Steve Mason .60 1.50
22 Dale Hunter CO .02 .10
23 Jaques Beaulieu ACO .02 .10
24 Jeff Perry ACO .02 .10
25 Don Brankley WATERBOY .01 .01
26 Chris Maton .02 .10

2006-07 London Knights

COMPLETE SET (26) 12.00 20.00
1 Sam Gagner 1.25 4.00
2 Patrick Kane 5.00 12.00
3 Steve Mason .40 1.00
4 Todd Perry .30 .75
5 Kevin Bodker .20 .50
6 Scott Aarssen .20 .50
7 David Jarram .20 .50
8 Josh Beaulieu .20 .50
9 Matt Clarke .20 .50
10 Philip Mcrae .20 .50
11 Robbie Drummond .20 .50
12 Tony Dehart .20 .50
13 Sergei Kostitsyn .40 1.00
14 Andrew Wilkins .20 .50
15 Ryan Martinelli .20 .50
16 Jordan Shine .20 .50
17 Adam Hasani .20 .50
18 Stephane Cesar .20 .50
19 Luke Vanmoerkerke .20 .50
20 David Meckler .20 .50
21 Jordan Foreman .20 .50
22 Corey Syvret .20 .50
23 Adam Perry .20 .50
24 Dale Hunter .20 .50
25 Dave Gagner .20 .50
26 Todd Bidner .10 .25

2007-08 London Knights

COMPLETE SET (26) 5.00 12.00
1 Steve Mason .25 .60
2 Stephen Heming .25 .60
3 Michael Zador .25 .60
4 Scott Aarssen .25 .60
5 Matt Ashmann .25 .60
6 Jadran Beljo .25 .60
7 Matt Clarke .25 .60
8 Tucker Hunter .25 .60
9 Garett Hunter .25 .60
10 Tony DeHart .25 .60
11 Kevin Montgomery .25 .60
12 Vladimir Roth .25 .60
13 Andrew Wilkins .25 .60
14 Kale Kerbashian .25 .60
15 Jordan Shine .25 .60
16 Patrick Maroon .25 .60
17 Akim Aliu .25 .60
18 Adam Perry .25 .60
19 Philip McRae .25 .60
20 Tony Romano .25 .60
21 Justin Taylor .25 .60
22 Sean O'Connor .25 .60
23 Dale Hunter .25 .60
24 Dave Gagne .25 .60
25 Pat Curcio .25 .60
26 Don Brankley .25 .60

2015-16 London Knights

COMPLETE SET (25) 6.00 15.00
1 Aaron Berisha .30 .75
2 Evan Bouchard .30 .75
3 Brandon Crawley .30 .75
4 Christian Dvorak .30 .75
5 Eric Henderson .30 .75
6 Jack Hidi .30 .75
7 Aiden Jamieson .30 .75
8 Max Jones .30 .75
9 Olli Juolevi .30 .75
10 Owen MacDonald .30 .75
11 Mitchell Marner 1.25 3.00
12 Chris Martenet .30 .75
13 Nicolas Mattinen .30 .75
14 Victor Mete .30 .75
15 Sam Miletic .30 .75
16 Tyler Parsons .30 .75
17 J.J. Piccinich .30 .75
18 Cliff Pu .40 1.00
19 Kole Sherwood .30 .75
20 Robert Thomas .30 .75
21 Matthew Tkachuk .30 .75
22 Ryan Valentini .30 .75
23 Emanuel Vella .30 .75
24 C.J. Yakimowicz .30 .75
25 Header Card CL .30 .75

1997-98 Long Beach Ice Dogs

COMPLETE SET (20) 4.00 10.00
1 Doug Ast .20 .50
2 Patrik Augusta .20 .50
3 Collin Bauer .20 .50
4 Mike Buzak .20 .50
5 John Byce .20 .50
6 Brian Chapman .20 .50
7 Mark Ferner .20 .50
8 Victor Ignatjev .20 .50
9 Rob Kenny .20 .50
10 Dan Lambert .40 1.00
11 Mike Matteucci .20 .50
12 Joby Messier .20 .50
13 Stephane Morin .20 .50
14 Shawn Penn .20 .50
15 Russ Romaniuk .20 .50
16 Nicholas Vachon .20 .50
17 Andrei Vasilyev .20 .50
18 Kay Whitmore .40 1.00
19 Darryl Williams .20 .50
20 Spike MASCOT .02 .10

1998-99 Long Beach Ice Dogs

COMPLETE SET (20) 6.00 15.00
1 Doug Ast .20 .50
2 Patrik Augusta .20 .50
3 John Byce .20 .50
4 Dan Bylsma .20 .50
5 Mark Ferner .20 .50
6 Mike Jickling .20 .50
7 Frederick Jobin .20 .50
8 Claude Jutras .20 .50
9 Dan Lambert .30 .75
10 Manny Legace .60 1.50
11 Jocelyn Lemieux .20 .50
12 Mike Matteucci .20 .50
13 Sacha Molin .20 .50
14 Jan Nemecek .20 .50
15 Andy Roach .20 .50
16 Pavel Rosa .20 .50
17 Patrik Stefan 2.00 5.00
18 Darryl Williams .20 .50
19 John Van Boxmeer HCO .08 .25
20 Spike MASCOT .02 .10

1998-99 Long Beach Ice Dogs Promo

NNO Patrik Stefan 2.00 5.00

1999-00 Long Beach Ice Dogs

COMPLETE SET (10) 6.00 15.00
1 Rene Chapdelaine .75 2.00
2 Pavel Rosa .75 2.00
3 Mike Crowley .75 2.00
4 Mike O'Neill .75 2.00
5 Len Barrie .75 2.00
6 Mike Matteucci .40 1.00
7 Scott Thomas .75 2.00
8 Doug Ast .40 1.00
9 Spike Mascot .40 1.00
10 John Van Boxmeer HCO .40 1.00

1994-95 Los Angeles Blades RHI

COMPLETE SET (20) 3.00 8.00
1 Checklist .02 .10
2 Chris Nelson .20 .50
3 Mike Burman .20 .50
4 Steve Wilson .20 .50
5 Vaclav Nedomansky, Jr. .20 .50
6 Rob Hartnell .20 .50
7 Kraig Nienhuis .30 .75
8 Eric LeMarque .20 .50
9 Peter Kasowski .20 .50
10 Brett Kurtz .20 .50
11 Terran Sandwith .20 .50
12 Brad Sholl .20 .50
13 Mike Doers .20 .50
14 Steve Bogoyevac .20 .50
15 Sean Gauthier .20 .50
16 Eric Lavigne .20 .50
17 Mike Callahan .20 .50
18 Bobby Hull Jr. CO .20 .50
19 Jeanie Buss .02 .10
20 Los Angeles Blades Logo .02 .10

1995-96 Louisiana Ice Gators

COMPLETE SET (21) 4.80 12.00
1 Bob Berg .20 .50
2 John Depourcq .20 .50
3 Wade Fournier .20 .50
4 Fred Goltz .20 .50
5 Ron Handy .20 .50
6 Mike Heany .20 .50
7 Dean Hulett .20 .50
8 Jim Latos .20 .50
9 George Maneluk .30 .75
10 Rob McCaig .20 .50
11 Jason McQuat .20 .50
12 Rod Pasma .30 .75
13 Sean Rowe .20 .50
14 Bryan Schoen .30 .75
15 Darryl Shedden .20 .50
16 Doug Shedden CO .20 .50
17 Fred Spoltore .20 .50
18 Chris Valicevic .20 .50
19 Rob Valicevic .75 2.00
20 John Vary .20 .50
21 Marty Yewchuk .20 .50

1995-96 Louisiana Ice Gators Playoffs

COMPLETE SET (21) 4.00 10.00
1 Bob Berg .20 .50
2 Aaron Boh .20 .50
3 Eric Cloutier .20 .50
4 John DePourcq .20 .50
5 Wade Fournier .20 .50
6 Ron Handy .25 .60
7 Mike Heaney .20 .50
8 Dean Hulett .20 .50
9 Jim Latos .20 .50
10 George Maneluk .25 .60
11 Rob McCaig .20 .50
12 Jason McQuat .20 .50
13 Chad Nelson .20 .50
14 Dan O'Rourke .20 .50
15 Rod Pasma .30 .75
16 Darryl Shedden .20 .50
17 Doug Shedden CO .25 .60
18 John Spoltore .25 .60
19 Chuck Thuss .25 .60
20 Rob Valicevic
Chris Valicevic .40 1.00
21 John Vary .20 .50

1995 Louisiana Ice Gators Glossy

COMPLETE SET (?)
1 Aaron Boh 4.00 10.00
2 Eric Cloutier 4.00 10.00
3 Chad Nelson 4.00 10.00
4 Dan O'Rourke 4.00 10.00
5 Chuck Thuss 5.00 12.00

1996-97 Louisiana Ice Gators

COMPLETE SET (23) 4.80 12.00
1 Bujar Amidovski .40 1.00
2 Doug Bonner .30 .75
3 Eric Cloutier .20 .50
4 Mark DeSantis .20 .50
5 Louis Dumont .20 .50
6 Blair Manning .20 .50
7 Roger Maxwell .20 .50
8 Jason McQuat .20 .50
9 Stan Melanson .20 .50
10 Jay Murphy .20 .50
11 Michael Murray .20 .50
12 Matt Pagnutti .20 .50
13 Don Parsons .20 .50
14 Team Photo .20 .50
15 Gary Roach .20 .50
16 Ryan Shanahan .20 .50
17 John Spoltore .30 .75
18 Chris Valicevic .30 .75
19 John Varga .30 .75
20 Rob Weingartner .20 .50
21 Billy Thurlow
Bruce Livin .20 .50
22 Doug Shedden HCO .08 .25
23 Alphonse MAS .02 .10

1996-97 Louisiana Ice Gators II

COMPLETE SET (22) 4.00 10.00
1 Aaron Boh .20 .50
2 John DePourcq .20 .50
3 Mark Delmore .20 .50
4 Louis Dumont .20 .50
5 Ron Handy .20 .50
6 Mikhail Kravets .20 .50
7 James Latos .20 .50
8 Rob McCaig .20 .50
9 Jason McQuat .20 .50
10 Stan Melanson .20 .50
11 Joey Mittelsteadt .30 .75
12 Chad Nelson .20 .50
13 Dan O'Rourke .20 .50
14 Ken Ruddick .20 .50
15 Dean Seymour .20 .50
16 Ryan Shanahan .20 .50
17 Darryl Shedden .20 .50
18 Sergei Tkachenko .20 .50
19 Chris Valicevic .30 .75
20 Rob Weingartner .20 .50
21 Jack Williams .20 .50
22 Doug Shedden HCO .08 .25

1997-98 Louisiana Ice Gators

COMPLETE SET (22) 4.00 10.00
1 Louis Dumont .20 .50
2 Jason McQuat .20 .50
3 Alphonse MAS .02 .10
4 Matt Pagnutti .20 .50
5 Richard Smit .20 .50
6 John Varga .30 .75
7 Jay Murphy .20 .50
8 Darrel Woodley .20 .50
9 Scott McKay .20 .50
10 Jack Williams .20 .50
11 Stan Melanson .20 .50
12 Brad Toporowski .20 .50
13 John Jennings EM .02 .10
14 Eric Cloutier .20 .50
15 Ryan Pisiak .20 .50
16 John Spoltore .30 .75
17 Mikhail Kravets .20 .50
18 Paul Rushforth .20 .50
19 Doug Bonner .30 .75
20 Chad Nelson .20 .50
21 Doug Shedden HCO .08 .25
22 Don Parsons .20 .50

1998-99 Louisiana Ice Gators

COMPLETE SET (26) 4.00 10.00
1 Mascot .15 .40
2 Bujar Amidovski .30 .75
3 Doug Bonner .30 .75
4 Eric Cloutier .15 .40
5 Mark Desantis .15 .40
6 Louis Dumont .15 .40
7 Blair Manning .15 .40
8 Roger Maxwell .15 .40
9 Jason McQuat .15 .40
10 Stan Melanson .15 .40
11 Jay Murphy .30 .75
12 Mike P. Murray .20 .50
13 Matthew Pagnutti .15 .40
14 Don Parsons .15 .40
15 Gary Roach .15 .40
16 Ryan Shanahan .30 .75
17 Doug Shedden CO .15 .40
18 John Spoltore .02 .10
19 Billy Thurlow
Bruce Livin CO .30 .75
20 Chris Valicevic .30 .75
21 John Varga .20 .50
22 Rob Weingartner .15 .40
23 Team Card .02 .10

1999-00 Louisiana Ice Gators

COMPLETE SET (25) 4.80 12.00
1 Vaclav Nedomansky .20 .50
1 Sean Gauthier .20 .50
2 Michael Murray .20 .50
2 Mike Oliveira .20 .50
3 Matt Pagnutti .20 .50
4 Jesse Rezansoff .20 .50
5 Mike Kucsulain .20 .50
6 Stan Melanson .20 .50
7 Shawn McNeil .20 .50
8 Ryan Shanahan .20 .50
9 John DePourcq .30 .75
10 Hugo Marchand .20 .50
11 Corey Neilson .20 .50
12 Chris Bogas .20 .50
13 Jason McQuat .30 .75
14 John Spoltore .30 .75
15 Dave Arsenault .20 .50
16 Chris Valicevic .30 .75
17 Jason Sessa .20 .50
18 Mark Cadotte .20 .50
19 Jay Murphy .20 .50
20 John Jennings TR .02 .10
24 Dennis Holland CO .02 .10
25 Don Murdoch CO .02 .10
26 Claw'd MAS .08 .25

2000-01 Louisiana Ice Gators

COMPLETE SET (25) 4.00 10.00
1 Stan Melanson .16 .40
2 Jay Murphy .16 .40
3 Nathan Borega .16 .40
4 Shawn McNeil .16 .40
5 Ryan Shanahan .16 .40
6 Roman Marakhovski .16 .40
7 Mike Kucsulain .16 .40
8 Dalen Hrooshkin .16 .40
9 Kevin Karlander .16 .40
10 Corey Neilson .16 .40
11 Bruce Richardson .16 .40
12 Jason Saal .30 .75
13 Michael Murray .16 .40
14 Jason McQuat .16 .40
15 John Spoltore .30 .75
16 Mike Valley .16 .40
17 Magnus Nilsson .30 .75
18 Dan Tessier .30 .75
19 Matt Pagnutti .16 .40
20 Roger Maxwell .16 .40
21 Dave Farrish HCO .10 .25
22 John DePourcq ACO .10 .25
23 Johnny Gomez TR .04 .10
24 Greg Sieg EM .04 .10
25 Andy Davis DOB .04 .10

2001-02 Louisiana Ice Gators

COMPLETE SET (26) 4.00 10.00
1 Header Card .04 .10
2 Steve Aronson .20 .50
3 Frederic Cloutier .20 .50
4 Cory Cyrenne .30 .75
5 Andy Davis DBR .04 .10
6 John DePourcq ACO .04 .10
7 Dave Farrish CO .10 .25
8 Dominic Forget .30 .75
9 Russell Hewson .20 .50
10 Konstantin Kalmikov .30 .75
11 Branislav Kvetan .20 .50
12 Greg Labenski .20 .50
13 Marc Magliarditi .30 .75
14 Ryan Marsh .20 .50
15 Shawn McNeil .20 .50
16 Kevin Mitchell .20 .50
17 Jay Murphy .20 .50
18 Corey Neilson .20 .50
19 Dennis Shiryaev .20 .50
20 Randy Perry .20 .50
21 Nathan Rempel .20 .50
22 Ryan Shanahan .20 .50
23 Ricky Casataneda TR
Greg Sieg EQMG .04 .10
24 Chris Valicevic .30 .75
25 Alphonse MASCOT .04 .10

2002-03 Louisiana Ice Gators

COMPLETE SET (25) 5.00 12.00
1 Header Card .04 .10
2 Semir Ben-Amor .20 .50
3 Cal Benazic .20 .50
4 Bobby Brown .20 .50
5 Frederic Cloutier .30 .75
6 Kenny Corupe .20 .50
7 John DePourcq .30 .75
8 Daniel Goneau .30 .75
9 Kyle Kettles .20 .50
10 Branislav Kvetan .20 .50
11 Louis Mass .20 .50
12 Shawn McNeil .20 .50
13 Kevin Mitchell .20 .50
14 J.P. Morin .20 .50
15 Nathan Rempel .20 .50
16 Bruce Richardson .20 .50
17 Rod Sarich .20 .50
18 Dennis Shiryaev .20 .50
19 Shawn Skiehar .20 .50
20 Chris Taliercio .20 .50
21 Tony Tuzzolino .20 .50
22 Jeff Worlton .20 .50
23 Dave Farrish HCO .04 .10
24 Andy Davis ANN .04 .10
25 Greg Sieg EQM .04 .10

2003-04 Louisiana Ice Gators

COMPLETE SET (25) 5.00 12.00
1 Armands Berzins .20 .50
2 Bobby Brown .20 .50
3 Frederic Cloutier .30 .75
4 Kenny Corupe .20 .50
5 Maxime Fortunus .20 .50
6 Derek Gustafson .30 .75
7 Jason Hamilton .30 .75
8 Brian Herbert .20 .50
9 Jamie Johnson .20 .50
10 Konstantin Kalmikov .20 .50
11 Ben Kilgour .20 .50
12 Martin Masa .20 .50
13 Milt Mastad .20 .50
14 Alex Materukhin .20 .50
15 Ed McGrane .20 .50
16 Kevin Mitchell .20 .50
17 Josh Mizerek .20 .50
18 Rod Sarich .20 .50
19 Dennis Shiryaev .30 .75
20 Ben Storey .20 .50
21 Jim Vickers .20 .50
22 Dave Farrish CO .04 .10
23 Team Photo .20 .50
24 Checklist .04 .10
25 Mascot .04 .10

2004-05 Louisiana Ice Gators

COMPLETE SET (26) 6.00 15.00
1 David Bararuk .75 2.00
2 Josh Barker .40 1.00
3 Ricky Castaneda TR .04 .10
4 Randy Dagenais .30 .75
5 John Evangelista .30 .75
6 Maxime Fortunus .40 1.00
7 Jody Green EQMG .04 .10
8 Todd Gordon CO .04 .10
9 Kyle Kettles .30 .75
10 Roger Leonard .30 .75
11 Doug Maciver .30 .75
12 Nathan Marsters .30 .75
13 Wes Mason .30 .75
14 Alex Materukhin .30 .75
15 Mike Omicioli .30 .75
16 Jake Ortmeyer .40 1.00
17 Pascal Pelletier .30 .75
18 Bryan Perez .30 .75
19 Mark Rooneem .30 .75
20 Shawn Skiehar .30 .75
21 Troy Smith .30 .75
22 Chris Thompson .30 .75
23 Gator Girls .10 .25
24 Gator Girls .10 .25
25 Mascots .04 .10
26 Announcers .04 .10

1999-00 Louisville Panthers

COMPLETE SET (33) 8.00 20.00
1 Craig Ferguson .30 .75
2 Brent Thompson .30 .75
3 Craig Reichert .30 .75
4 Eric Boguniecki .60 1.50
5 Dan Boyle .40 1.00
6 Ivan Novoseltsev .40 1.00
7 Dave Duerden .30 .75
8 Curtis Doell .30 .75
9 Sean Gauthier .40 1.00
10 Peter Ratchuk .30 .75
11 John Jakopin .30 .75
12 Marcus Nilson .40 1.00
13 Paws MASCOT .08 .25
14 Chris Wells .30 .75
15 Kirby Law .40 1.00
16 Chris Allen .30 .75
17 Chad Cabana .30 .75
18 Richard Shulmistra .40 1.00
19 Dwayne Hay .30 .75
20 Joey Tetarenko .60 1.50
21 Paul Brousseau .30 .75
22 Nick Smith .40 1.00
23 Brad Ference .40 1.00
24 Lance Ward .30 .75
25 Jeff Ware .30 .75
26 Paul Harvey .08 .25
27 Andrew Long .30 .75
28 Joe Paterson CO .08 .25
29 Gerard Gallant CO .08 .25
30 Tamer Afr PRES .08 .25
31 Chuck Fletcher GM .08 .25
32 UPS Zamboni .08 .25
33 Indiana Casino Zamboni .08 .25

2000-01 Louisville Panthers

COMPLETE SET (24) 7.20 18.00
1 Team CL .10 .25
2 Brent Thompson .40 1.00
3 Paul Brousseau .30 .75
4 David Emma .30 .75
5 Joey Tetarenko .40 1.00
6 Peter Ratchuk .40 .75
7 Dave Duerden .30 .75
8 Sean Gauthier .30 .75
9 Kyle Rossiter .30 .75
10 Rocky Thompson .30 .75
11 Denis Shvidki .60 1.00
12 Brad Ference .40 1.00
13 Joe Paterson CO .20 .50
14 Gord Dineen ACO .20 .50
15 Travis Brigley .40 1.00
16 Ryan Bach .40 1.00
17 Andrei Podkonicky .40 .75
18 Mike Harder .40 1.00
19 Evgeny Korolev .30 .75
20 Eric Godard .30 .75
21 Mike Cirillo .30 .75
22 Eric Beaudoin .30 .75
23 Paul Harvey .30 .75
24 Paws Mascot .10 .25

1996-97 Louisville Riverfrogs

COMPLETE SET (30) 4.00 20.00
1 Checklist .02 .10
2 Sandy Allan .60 1.50
3 Gino Santerre .30 .75
4 Pete Liptrott .30 .75
5 Jason Hanchuk .30 .75
6 Adam Young .30 .75
7 Dan Reja .30 .75
8 Terry Lindgren .30 .75
9 Sheldon Gorski .30 .75
10 Jeff Kostuch .30 .75
11 Randy Stevens .30 .75
12 Chris Rowland .30 .75
13 Chris DeProfio .30 .75
14 Mike Sancimino .30 .75
15 Dean Seymour .30 .75
16 Stephane Madore .30 .75
17 Chet Cullic .30 .75
18 Tim Chase .30 .75
19 Jack Kowal .30 .75
20 Tom MacDonald .30 .75
21 Jimmy Provencher .30 .75
22 Lance Leslie .30 .75
23 Warren Young CO .08 .25
24 R.J. Romero TR .02 .10
25 Mark Shepherd EQMG .02 .10
26 David Wilson ANN .02 .10
27 Rowdy the Riverfrog .02 .10
28 Sandy Allan AS .60 1.50
29 Warren Young
Future Riverfrog Brett Young .08 .25
30 Team Photo .30 .75

1997-98 Louisville Riverfrogs

COMPLETE SET (29) 4.00 10.00
1 Title Card .02 .10
2 Craig Nelson .15 .40
3 P.J. Lepler .15 .40
4 Jason Pain .15 .40
5 Terry Lindgren .15 .40
6 Michael Flynn .15 .40
7 Sheldon Gorski .15 .40

8 Jeff Kostuch .15 .40
9 Steve Ferranti .15 .40
10 Bob Gohde .15 .40
11 Marko Makinen .15 .40
12 Mike Sancimino .15 .40
13 Tobias Ablad .15 .40
14 Jeff Kikesch .15 .40
15 Stephane Madore .15 .40
16 Chris DeProfio .15 .40
17 Danny Reja .15 .40
18 Jack Kowal .15 .40
19 Dan Reimann .15 .40
20 Rob Frid .15 .40
21 Deiter Kochan .60 1.50
22 Lance Leslie .15 .40
23 Warren Young CO .15 .40
24 R.J. Romeiro TR .02 .10
25 Mark Miller EQ .02 .10
26 Matt Gorsky BR .02 .10
27 Rowdy Mascot .02 .10
28 Sheldon Gorski .15 .40
29 Team Photo .15 .40

1999-00 Lowell Lock Monsters

COMPLETE SET (27) 6.00 15.00
1 Ray Giroux .30 .75
2 Dave MacIsaac .20 .50
3 Richard Seeley .20 .50
4 Nathan LaFayette .20 .50
5 Rich Brennan .30 .75
6 Petr Mika .20 .50
7 Donald MacLean .20 .50
8 Cody Bowtell .20 .50
9 Vladimir Chebaturkin .20 .50
10 David Hymovitz .20 .50
11 Sean Blanchard .20 .50
12 Eric Belanger .20 .50
13 Dmitri Nabokov .20 .50
14 Vladimir Orszagh .40 1.00
15 Greg Phillips .20 .50
16 Jason Krog .40 1.00
17 Eric Brewer .75 2.00
18 Travis Scott .40 1.00
19 Evgeny Korolev .20 .50
20 Stephen Valiquette .60 1.50
21 Jason Podollan .20 .50
22 Jack Baldwin .20 .50
23 Lowell Lock Monsters .08 .25
24 Louie MASCOT .02 .10
25 Bruce Boudreau CO .08 .25
26 Steve Stirling CO .08 .25
27 Tom Rowe GM .08 .25

2000-01 Lowell Lock Monsters

COMPLETE SET (30) 7.20 20.00
1 Joe Corvo .30 .75
2 Andreas Lilja .30 .75
3 Joe Rullier .30 .75
4 Jeff Daw .20 .50
5 Petr Mika .30 .75
6 Rich Brennan .20 .50
7 Brad Chartrand .20 .50
8 Marko Tuomainen .30 .75
9 Eric Veilleux .20 .50
10 Eric Belanger .40 1.00
11 Peter Leboutillier .20 .50
12 David Hymovitz .20 .50
13 Juraj Kolnik .40 1.00
14 Chris Schmidt .20 .50
15 Kevin Baker .20 .50
16 Steve Passmore .40 1.00
17 Richard Seeley .20 .50
18 Jason Krog .30 1.00
19 Travis Scott .30 1.00
20 Marcel Cousineau .30 1.00
21 Nate Miller .20 .50
22 Braniclav Mezei .40 1.00
23 Mathieu Biron .30 .75
24 Kip Brennan .40 1.00
25 Greg Phillips .20 .50
26 Louie MAS .04 .10
27 Mike Pudlick .20 .50
28 Bruce Boudreau CO .10 .25
29 Steve Stirling CO .10 .25
30 Tom Rowe GM .04 .10

2002-03 Lowell Lock Monsters

COMPLETE SET (25) 8.00 20.00
1 Igor Knyazev .40 1.00
2 Nikos Tselios .40 1.00
3 Sean Curry .40 1.00
Ed Hill .40 1.00
Mike Zigomanis .40 1.00
6 Ryan Bayda .40 1.00
Craig MacDonald .40 1.00
Jeff Daw .40 1.00
Steve Halko .40 1.00
0 Jeff Heerema .40 1.00
1 Brent McDonald .40 1.00
2 Mike Watt .40 1.00
3 Tomas Kurka .40 1.00
Damian Surma .40 1.00
5 Kaspars Astashenko .40 1.00
6 Greg Kuznik .40 1.00
Tommy Westlund .40 1.00
3 Randy Petruk .60 1.50
Brett Lysak .40 1.00
Ryan Bast .40 1.00
Jean-Marc Pelletier .60 1.50
2 Brad DeFauw .40 1.00
3 Tomas Malec .40 1.00
Lowell Lock Monsters AU .04 .10
5 Lowell Lock Monsters AU .04 .10

2003-04 Lowell Lock Monsters

COMPLETE SET (25) 4.00 10.00
Alan Rourke .15 .40
Brad DeFauw .15 .40
Brad Fast .15 .40
Brennan Evans .15 .40
Brent Krahn .30 .75
Brett Lysak .15 .40
Damian Surma .15 .40
Dany Sabourin .30 .75
Dan Sullivan .15 .40
Jason Morgan .15 .40
Jesse Wallin .15 .40
Joey Tetarenko .15 .40
13 Josh Green .15 .40
14 Martin Sonnenberg .15 .40
15 Matt Davidson .15 .40
16 Mike Commodore .15 .40
17 Mike Zigomanis .15 .40
18 Patrick DesRochers .30 .75
19 Pavel Brendl .15 .40
20 Robert Dome .15 .40
21 Ryan Bayda .15 .40
22 Sean Curry .15 .40
23 Tomas Kurka .15 .40
24 Tomas Malec .15 .40
25 Checklist .04 .10

2003-04 Lowell Lock Monsters Photo Album

COMPLETE SET (25) 8.00 20.00
1 Mike Commodore .30 .75
2 Jesse Wallin .30 .75
3 Sean Curry .30 .75
4 Ryan Bayda .30 .75
5 Jason Morgan .30 .75
6 Mike Zigomanis .30 .75
7 Tomas Kurka .30 .75
8 Damian Surma .30 .75
9 Brad Fast .30 .75
10 Martin Sonnenberg .30 .75
11 Allan Rourke .30 .75
12 Josh Green .30 .75
13 Autograph Card .04 .10
14 Dan Sullivan .30 .75
15 Brett Lysak .30 .75
16 Joey Tetarenko .40 1.00
17 Robert Dome .30 .75
18 Brad DeFauw .30 .75
19 Pavel Brendl .30 .75
20 Matt Davidson .30 .75
21 Brennan Evans .30 .75
22 Tomas Malec .30 .75
23 Autograph Card .04 .10
24 Dany Sabourin .60 1.50
25 Patrick DesRochers .60 1.50

2004-05 Lowell Lock Monsters

COMPLETE SET (24) 6.00 15.00
1 Ryan Bayda .20 .50
2 Mike Commodore .20 .50
3 Sean Curry .20 .50
4 Gordie Dwyer .40 1.00
5 Brennan Evans .20 .50
6 Brad Fast .30 .75
7 Colin Forbes .20 .50
8 Carsen Germyn .20 .50
9 Mark Giordano .20 .50
10 Jim Henkel .20 .50
11 Chuck Kobasew .40 1.00
12 Brent Krahn .40 1.00
13 Chad Larose .20 .50
14 Lynn Loyns .20 .50
15 Craig MacDonald .20 .50
16 Brantt Myhres .60 1.50
17 Richie Regehr .20 .50
18 Danny Richmond .20 .50
19 Allan Rourke .20 .50
20 Eric Staal .75 2.00
21 Bruno St. Jacques .40 1.00
22 Justin Taylor .20 .50
23 Cam Ward .40 1.00
24 Mike Zigomanis .20 .50

2004-05 Lowell Lock Monsters Photo Album

COMPLETE SET (25) 12.00 30.00
1 Ryan Bayda .40 1.00
2 Mike Commodore .40 1.00
3 Sean Curry .40 1.00
4 Gordie Dwyer .75 2.00
5 Brennan Evans .40 1.00
6 Brad Fast .60 1.50
7 Colin Forbes .40 1.00
8 Carsen Germyn .40 1.00
9 Mark Giordano .40 1.00
10 Jim Henkel .40 1.00
11 Chuck Kobasew .75 2.00
12 Brent Krahn .75 2.00
13 Chad Larose .40 1.00
14 Lynn Loyns .40 1.00
15 Craig MacDonald .40 1.00
16 Brantt Myhres 1.25 3.00
17 Richie Regehr .40 1.00
18 Danny Richmond .40 1.00
19 Allan Rourke .40 1.00
20 Bruno St. Jacques .75 2.00
21 Eric Staal 1.50 4.00
22 Justin Taylor .40 1.00
23 Cam Ward .75 2.00
24 Mike Zigomanis .40 1.00
25 Logo Card .04 .10

2000-01 Lubbock Cotton Kings

COMPLETE SET (20) 4.00 10.00
1 Kyle Reeves .30 .75
2 Tracy Egeland .20 .50
3 Jan Melichercik .20 .50
4 Peter Cava .20 .50
5 Dave MacIntyre .20 .50
6 Patrick Brownlee .20 .50
7 Chris Rowland .20 .50
8 Bill McDonald HCO .10 .25
9 Neil Savary .30 .75
10 Lance Leslie .20 .50
11 Mike Hiebert .20 .50
12 Ryan Shmyr .20 .50
13 Brandon Carper .20 .50
14 Trevor Burgess .20 .50
15 Tom Menicci .20 .50
16 Derek Holland .20 .50
17 Walker McDonald .20 .50
18 Cosmo DuPaul .30 .75
19 Adam Robbins .20 .50
20 Lubbock Cotton Kings .10 .25

2003-04 Lubbock Cotton Kings

COMPLETE SET (20) 3.00 8.00
1 Checklist .04 .10
2 Craig Binns .20 .50
3 Steve Birch .20 .50
4 Joe Blaznek .20 .50
5 Mike Brusseau .30 .75
6 Jeff Dewar .20 .50
7 Chris Duggan .20 .50
8 Kevin Fines .30 .75
9 Paul Fioroni .20 .50
10 Derek Holland .20 .50
11 Jean-Francois Labarre .20 .50
12 Dave MacIntyre .20 .50
13 Jan Melichercik .20 .50
14 Mathieu Paul .20 .50
15 Sebastien Roy .20 .50
16 Jim Shepherd .20 .50
17 Jeremy Symington .30 .75
18 Rob Vessio .20 .50
19 Kirk Tomlinson HCO .04 .10
20 Mascot .04 .10
NNO Sponsor .04 .10
NNO Sponsor .04 .10

2002-03 Macon Trax

COMPLETE SET (20) 3.00 8.00
1 Corey Smith .20 .50
2 Dan Welch .20 .50
3 David Deeves .20 .50
4 Landon Bathe .20 .50
5 Tom Stewart .20 .50
6 Corey Lucas .20 .50
7 Rick Emmett .20 .50
8 Jeremy Kyte .20 .50
9 Brad Rice .20 .50
10 Nolan Weir .20 .50
11 Brad Bourhis .20 .50
12 Stephane Desjardins .20 .50
13 Luke Murphy .20 .50
14 Steve Howard .20 .50
15 Geoff Faulkner .20 .50
16 Dennis Brogna TR .04 .10
17 Brian Curran HCO .04 .10
18 Dave Monteiro ACO .04 .10
19 Todd MacGowan EM .04 .10
20 Mascot .04 .10
NNO Checklist .04 .10

1997-98 Macon Whoopee

COMPLETE SET (18) 3.60 9.00
1 Steve Vezina .30 .75
2 Martin Belanger .20 .50
3 John Paris HCO .02 .10
4 Sebastien Parent .20 .50
5 Gary Golczewski .20 .50
6 Jocelyn Langlois .20 .50
7 Joe Letendre .20 .50
8 Martin LaChaine .20 .50
9 Todd MacIsaac .20 .50
10 Patrice Charbonneau .30 .75
11 Marc Genest .20 .50
12 Claude Fillion .20 .50
13 Craig Willard .20 .50
14 Raymond Delarosbil .20 .50
15 Francois Leroux .20 .50
16 Trent Cavicchi .20 .50
17 Alexei Deev .30 .75
18 Alain Cote .20 .50

1997-98 Macon Whoopee Autographs

COMPLETE SET (18) 14.00 35.00
1 Steve Vezina 1.50 4.00
2 Martin Belanger .75 2.00
3 John Paris HCO .75 2.00
4 Sebastien Parent 1.50 4.00
5 Gary Golczewski .75 2.00
6 Jocelyn Langlois .75 2.00
7 Joe Letendre .75 2.00
8 Martin LaChaine .75 2.00
9 Todd MacIsaac .75 2.00
10 Patrice Charbonneau 1.25 3.00
11 Marc Genest .75 2.00
12 Claude Fillion .75 2.00
13 Craig Willard .75 2.00
14 Raymond Delarosbil .75 2.00
15 Francois Leroux .75 2.00
16 Trent Cavicchi .75 2.00
17 Alexei Deev 1.25 3.00
18 Alain Cote .75 2.00

2001-02 Macon Whoopee

COMPLETE SET (21) 8.00 20.00
1 Checklist .40 1.00
2 Andrew Allen .75 2.00
3 Krikor Arman .40 1.00
4 Nic Beaudoin .40 1.00
5 David Brosseau .40 1.00
6 Travis Dillabough .40 1.00
7 Gord Dineen CO .40 1.00
8 Rick Emmett .40 1.00
9 Paul Giblin .40 1.00
10 Mike Green .40 1.00
11 Mike Josefowicz .40 1.00
12 Chris Madden .75 2.00
13 Milt Mastad .40 1.00
14 Luke Murphy .40 1.00
15 Johan Olsson .40 1.00
16 Michel Periard .40 1.00
17 Doug Schueller .40 1.00
18 Kris Waltze .60 1.50
19 Alex Zinevych .40 1.00
20 Casey Kesselring .40 1.00
21 Header Card CL .04 .10

1995-96 Madison Monsters

COMPLETE SET (24) 8.00 25.00
1 Duane Derksen .75 2.00
2 Brian Downey .40 1.00
3 Dmitri Alekhin .40 1.00
4 Monster MASCOT .02 .10
5 Sean Wilmert .40 1.00
6 Corey Grassel .40 1.00
7 Dan Ruoho .40 1.00
8 Billy Brown TR .02 .10
9 Kent Hawley .40 1.00
10 Dan Laughlin .40 1.00
11 Vyacheslav Polikarkin .40 1.00
12 Todd Dvorak .40 1.00
13 Brian Idalski .40 1.00
14 Gunnar Kroseberg .40 1.00
15 Brett Larson .40 1.00
16 Paul Clatney .40 1.00
17 Matt Loen .40 1.00
18 Stanislav Tkach .60 1.50
19 Glenn Painter .40 1.00
20 Joe Bonvie .60 1.50
21 Mark Johnson CO .60 1.50
22 Justin Morrison .60 1.50
23 Marcel Richard .60 1.50
24 Sponsor card .01 .05

1996-97 Madison Monsters

COMPLETE SET (24) 8.00 20.00
1 Electroalarm Services .02 .10
2 Dave Schultz HCO .60 1.50
3 Kent Hawley .40 1.00
4 Alexander Galchenyuk .40 1.00
5 Jeremie Legault .40 1.00
6 Randy Holmes .40 1.00
7 Fran Reed .40 1.00
8 Chris Markstrom .40 1.00
9 Team Photo .40 1.00
10 Duane Derksen .60 1.50
11 Brian Downey .40 1.00
12 Matt Loen .40 1.00
13 Justin Morrison .40 1.00
14 Dave Rowe .40 1.00
15 Colby Van Tassel .40 1.00
16 Dan Ruoho .40 1.00
17 ElectroAlarm Security Sys .02 .10
18 Brian Idalski .40 1.00
19 Brian LaVack .40 1.00
20 Todd Passini .40 1.00
21 Stas Tkatch .40 1.00
22 Joakin Wiberg .40 1.00
23 Jeff Winter .40 1.00
24 Jose Ortiz TR .20 .50

1998-99 Madison Monsters

COMPLETE SET (16) 8.00 20.00
1 Kent Hawley CO .08 .25
2 Andrew Wilhelm OWN .08 .25
3 Dana Doll TR .08 .25
4 Jason Disher .60 1.50
5 Kelly Stephens .60 1.50
6 Derek Beuselinck .60 1.50
7 Cory Holland .60 1.50
8 Mike Maurice .60 1.50
9 Luke Strand .60 1.50
10 Brian Downey .60 1.50
11 David Fletcher .60 1.50
12 Andy Faulkner .60 1.50
13 Jim Duhart .60 1.50
14 Jay Wilson .60 1.50
15 Ed Corwin .60 1.50
16 Monster Madness .40 1.00

1992-93 Maine Black Bears

COMPLETE SET (36) 20.00 50.00
1 Title Card .10 .25
2 Mike Dunham 1.25 3.00
3 Andy Silverman .20 .50
4 Matt Martin .20 .50
5 Chris Imes .20 .50
6 Jason Weinrich .20 .50
7 Scott Pellerin .30 .75
8 Dan Murphy .20 .50
9 Dave LaCouture .20 .50
10 Patrice Tardif .40 1.00
11 Eric Fenton .20 .50
12 Jim Montgomery .40 1.00
13 Kent Salfi .20 .50
14 Jean-Yves Roy .40 1.00
15 Garth Snow .40 1.00
16 Cal Ingraham .20 .50
17 Title Card .10 .25
18 Mike Dunham 1.25 3.00
19 Chris Imes .20 .50
20 Paul Kariya 15.00 40.00
21 Mike Latendresse .20 .50
22 Dan Murphy .20 .50
23 Dave MacIsaac .20 .50
24 Dave LaCouture .20 .50
25 Chris Ferraro .40 1.00
26 Peter Ferraro .40 1.00
27 Jim Montgomery .40 1.00
28 Brad Purdie .20 .50
29 Lee Saunders .20 .50
30 Justin Tomberlin .20 .50
31 Chuck Texeira .20 .50
32 Martin Mercier .20 .50
33 Garth Snow .40 1.00
34 Cal Ingraham .40 1.00
35 Greg Hirsch .20 .50
36 Jamie Thompson .20 .50

1993-94 Maine Black Bears

COMPLETE SET (25) 24.00 60.00
37 Paul Kariya
Leo Wlasow# 4.00 10.00
38 Andy Silverman .20 .50
39 Jason Weinrich .20 .50
40 Jason Mansoff .20 .50
41 Paul Kariya 8.00 20.00
42 Mike Latendresse .20 .50
43 Barry Clukey .20 .50
44 Wayne Conlan .20 .50
45 Dave MacIsaac .20 .50
46 Patrice Tardif .30 .75
47 Brad Purdie .20 .50
48 Dan Shermerhorn .20 .50
49 Lee Saunders .20 .50
50 Justin Tomberlin .20 .50
51 Chuck Texeira .20 .50
52 Tim Lovell .20 .50
53 Cal Ingraham .20 .50
54 Leo Wlasow .20 .50
55 Blair Allison .20 .50
56 Blair Marsh .20 .50
57 Marcel Pineau .20 .50
58 Trevor Roenick .20 .50
59 Reg Cardinal .20 .50
60 Paul Kariya 8.00 20.00
61 Jim Montgomery
Paul Kar 4.00 10.00

2004-05 Maine Black Bears

COMPLETE SET (32) 25.00 50.00
1 Mike Lundin .75 2.00
2 Tom Zabkowicz .75 2.00
3 Steve Mullin .75 2.00
4 Travis Wight .75 2.00
5 Troy Barnes .75 2.00
6 Matt Deschamps .75 2.00
7 John Ronan .75 2.00
8 Michel Leveille .75 2.00
9 Keith Johnson .75 2.00
10 Keenan Hopson .75 2.00
11 Billy Ryan .75 2.00
12 Greg Moore .75 2.00
13 Robert Bellamy .75 2.00
14 Ben Murphy .75 2.00
15 Josh Soares .75 2.00
16 Tim Maxwell .75 2.00
17 Mike Hamilton .75 2.00
18 Jon Jankus .75 2.00
19 Wes Clark .75 2.00
20 Travis Ramsey .75 2.00
21 Derek Damon .75 2.00
22 Brent Shepheard .75 2.00
23 Matt Lundin .75 2.00
24 Jim Howard 1.25 3.00
25 Matt Greyeyes .75 2.00
26 Ryan Shelley .75 2.00
27 Bret Tyler .75 2.00
28 Jeff Mushaluk .75 2.00
29 Staff .04 .10
30 Erik Soltys ACO .04 .10
31 Tim Whitehead CO .04 .10
32 Team Picture .20 .50

2005-06 Maine Black Bears

COMPLETE SET (32) 10.00 25.00
1 Rob Bellamy .30 .75
2 Ben Bishop .75 2.00
3 Wes Clark .30 .75
4 Derek Damon .30 .75
5 Simon Danis-Pepin .60 1.50
6 Matt Duffy .30 .75
7 Chris Hahn .30 .75
8 Mike Hamilton .30 .75
9 John Hopson .30 .75
10 Keenan Hopson .30 .75
11 Jon Jankus .30 .75
12 Keith Johnson .30 .75
13 Vince Laise .30 .75
14 Michel Leveille .30 .75
15 Matt Lundin .40 1.00
16 Mike Lundin .30 .75
17 Jeff Marshall .30 .75
18 Greg Moore .30 .75
19 Steve Mullin .30 .75
20 Brian Plasszcz .30 .75
21 Travis Ramsey .30 .75
22 Billy Ryan .30 .75
23 Ryan Shelley .30 .75
24 Brent Shepheard .30 .75
25 Josh Soares .30 .75
26 Bret Tyler .30 .75
27 Travis Wight .30 .75
28 Tim Whitehead HC .20 .50
29 Campbell Blair AC .20 .50
30 Dan Kerluke AC .20 .50
31 Grant Standbrook AC .20 .50
32 Maine Black Bears .20 .50

2007-08 Maine Black Bears

COMPLETE SET (32) 6.00 15.00
1 Mike Banwell .25 .60
2 Rob Bellamy .25 .60
3 Glenn Belmore .25 .60
4 Ben Bishop .75 2.00
5 Nolan Boike .25 .60
6 Brett Carriere .25 .60
7 Wes Clark .25 .60
8 Simon Danis-Pepin .25 .60
9 David de Kastrozza .25 .60
10 Robby Dee .25 .60
11 Jeff Dimmen .25 .60
12 Matt Duffy .25 .60
13 Shane Foley .25 .60
14 Chris Hahn .25 .60
15 Keenan Hopson .25 .60
16 Tanner House .25 .60
17 Vince Laise .25 .60
18 Jeff Marshall .25 .60
19 Keif Orsini .25 .60
20 Nick Payson .25 .60
21 Travis Ramsey .25 .60
22 Lem Randall .25 .60
23 Billy Ryan .25 .60
24 Kevin Swallow .25 .60
25 Andrew Sweetland .25 .60
26 Bret Tyler .25 .60
27 Josh Van Dyk .25 .60
28 Dave Wilson .25 .60
29 Tim Whitehead HC .15 .40
30 Guy Perron AHC .15 .40
31 Dan Kerluke AC .10 .25
32 Grant Standbrook AC .10 .25

2001-02 Manchester Monarchs

COMPLETE SET (30) 8.00 20.00
1A Randy Robitaille .25 .60
1B Dane Jackson .25 .60
2A Derek Bekar .25 .60
2B Travis Scott .30 .75
3A Brad Chartrand .25 .60
3B Ted Donato .25 .60
4A Nate Miller .25 .60
4B Joe Rullier .25 .60
5A Andre Payette .25 .60
5B Rich Brennan .25 .60
6A Brett Hauer .25 .60
6B Eric Healey .25 .60
7A Chris Schmidt .25 .60
7B Jason Holland .25 .60
8A Mike Pudlick .25 .60
8B Richard Seeley .25 .60
9A Kip Brennan .30 .75
9B Jaroslav Bednar .40 1.00
10A Tomas Zizka .25 .60
10B Ryan Flinn .60 1.50
11A Jerred Smithson .25 .60
11B Rob Valicevic .60 1.50
12A Joe Corvo .25 .60
12B Steve Kelly .25 .60
13A Stephane Fiset .60 1.50
13B Dan Riva .25 .60
14A Marcel Cousineau .25 .60
14B Scott Thomas .25 .60
15A Bruce Boudreau CO .04 .10
15B Maximillian MASCOT .04 .10

2002-03 Manchester Monarchs

COMPLETE SET (30) 10.00 25.00
1 Chris Aldous .20 .50
2 Scott Barney .20 .50
3 Bruce Boudreau HCO .30 .75
4 Kip Brennan .30 .75
5 Mike Cammalleri 1.00 2.50
6 Joe Corvo .20 .50
7 Eric Healey .20 .50
8 Steve Heinze .20 .50
9 Dane Jackson .20 .50
10 Steve Kelly .30 .75
11 Yanick Lehoux .30 .75
12 Mike Pudlick .20 .50
13 Joe Rullier .20 .50
14 Travis Scott .30 .75
15 Richard Seeley .20 .50
16 Derek Armstrong .20 .50
17 Jared Aulin .60 1.50
18 Derek Bekar .20 .50
19 Chris Bogas .20 .50
20 Ryan Flinn .40 1.00
21 Jeff Giuliano .20 .50
22 Jason Holland .20 .50
23 Cristobal Huet .75 2.00
24 Maximillian MASCOT .04 .10
25 Dan Riva .20 .50
26 Pavel Rosa .20 .50
27 Chris Schmidt .20 .50
28 Jerred Smithson .20 .50
29 Mat Snesrud .20 .50
30 Tomas Zizka .30 .75

2003-04 Manchester Monarchs

COMPLETE SET (25) 6.00 15.00
1 Scott Barney .20 .50
2 Noah Clarke .30 .75
3 Ryan Flinn .30 .75
4 Jeff Giuliano .20 .50
5 Denis Grebeshkov .20 .50
6 Adam Hauser .30 .75
7 Leon Hayward .20 .50
8 Steve Kelly .20 .50
9 Yanick Lehoux .20 .50
10 Bryan Muir .20 .50
11 Doug Nolan .20 .50
12 George Parros .20 .50
13 Pavel Rosa .20 .50
14 Joe Rullier .20 .50
15 Chris Schmidt .20 .50
16 Richard Seeley .20 .50
17 Jerred Smithson .20 .50
18 John Tripp .20 .50
19 Dan Welch .20 .50
20 Tomas Zizka .20 .50
21 Mascot .04 .10
22 Bruce Boudreau HCO .20 .50
23 Jim Hughes ACO .04 .10
24 Verizon Wireless Arena .04 .10
25 Checklist .04 .10

2003-04 Manchester Monarchs Team Issue

COMPLETE SET (20) 8.00 20.00
1 Scott Barney .40 1.00
2 Mathieu Chouinard .60 1.50
3 Noah Clarke .60 1.50
4 Ryan Flinn .60 1.50
5 Jeff Giuliano .40 1.00
6 Denis Grebeshkov .40 1.00
7 Milan Hnilicka .60 1.50
8 Steve Kelly .40 1.00
9 Yanick Lehoux .40 1.00
10 Bryan Muir .40 1.00
11 Doug Nolan .40 1.00
12 George Parros .40 1.00
13 Pavel Rosa .40 1.00
14 Joe Rullier .40 1.00
15 Chris Schmidt .40 1.00
16 Richard Seeley .40 1.00
17 Jerred Smithson .40 1.00
18 John Tripp .40 1.00
19 Dan Welch .40 1.00
20 Tomas Zizka .40 1.00

2004-05 Manchester Monarchs

COMPLETE SET (26) 6.00 15.00
1 Adam Hauser .40 1.00
2 Brad Smyth .40 1.00
3 Chris Schmidt .15 .40
4 Dan Welch .15 .40
5 Dave Steckel .30 .75
6 Denis Grebeshkov .15 .40
7 Doug Nolan .15 .40
8 Dustin Brown .40 1.00
9 George Parros .15 .40
10 Greg Hogeboom .15 .40
11 Jeff Giuliano .15 .40
12 Joe Rullier .30 .75
13 Mathieu Garon .60 1.50
14 Matt Ryan .15 .40
15 Michael Cammalleri .40 1.00
16 Mike Weaver .15 .40
17 Noah Clarke .40 1.00
18 Petr Kanko .40 1.00
19 Ryan Flinn .40 1.00
20 Scott Barney .15 .40
21 Tim Gleason .30 .75
22 Tom Kostopoulos .30 .75
23 Troy Milam .15 .40
24 Yanick Lehoux .30 .75
25 Maximillian MASCOT .04 .10
NNO Checklist .04 .10

2004-05 Manchester Monarchs Tobacco

COMPLETE SET (25) 12.00 30.00
1 Mathieu Garon 1.25 3.00
2 Adam Hauser .75 2.00
3 Brad Smyth .75 2.00
4 Chris Schmidt .30 .75
5 Dan Welch .30 .75
6 Dave Steckel .60 1.50
7 Denis Grebeshkov .30 .75
8 Doug Nolan .30 .75
9 Dustin Brown .75 2.00
10 George Parros .30 .75
11 Greg Hogeboom .30 .75
12 Jeff Giuliano .30 .75
13 Joe Rullier .60 1.50
14 Matt Ryan .30 .75
15 Mike Cammalleri .75 2.00
16 Mike Weaver .30 .75
17 Noah Clarke .75 2.00
18 Petr Kanko .75 2.00
19 Ryan Flinn .75 2.00
20 Scott Barney .30 .75
21 Tim Gleason .60 1.50
22 Tom Kostopoulos .60 1.50
23 Troy Milam .30 .75
24 Yanick Lehoux .60 1.50
25 Mascot .04 .10

2005-06 Manchester Monarchs

COMPLETE SET (48) 12.00 30.00
COMPLETE SER. 2 (24) 6.00 15.00
COMPLETE SER. 1 (24) 6.00 15.00
1 Barry Brust .40 1.00
2 Noah Clarke .25 .60
3 Brad Fast .25 .60
4 Ryan Flinn .40 1.00
5 Jeff Giuliano .25 .60
6 Denis Grebeshkov .25 .60
7 Adam Hauser .40 1.00
8 Connor James .25 .60
9 Petr Kanko .25 .60
10 Joey Mormina .25 .60
11 Ryan Murphy .25 .60
12 Doug Nolan .25 .60
13 Richard Petiot .25 .60
14 Konstantin Pushkarev .25 .60
15 Dany Roussin .25 .60
16 Matt Ryan .25 .60
17 Richard Seeley .25 .60
18 Brad Smyth .25 .60
19 Jeff Tambellini .40 1.00
20 Lauri Tukonen .60 1.50
21 Marty Wilford .40 1.00
22 Derek Clancey AC .02 .10
23 Jim Hughes HC .02 .10
24 Maximillian MASCOT .10 .25
25 Brendan Bernakevitch .25 .60
26 Dustin Brown .75 2.00
27 Michael Cammalleri .40 1.00
28 Noah Clarke .25 .60
29 Ryan Flinn .40 1.00
30 Yutaka Fukufuji 1.25 3.00
31 Mathieu Garon .40 1.00
32 Jeff Giuliano .25 .60
33 Tim Gleason .25 .60
34 Denis Grebeshkov .25 .60
35 Adam Hauser .40 1.00
36 Greg Hogeboom .25 .60
37 Connor James .25 .60
38 Petr Kanko .25 .60
39 Tom Kostopoulos .25 .60
40 Yanick Lehoux .25 .60
41 George Parros .60 1.50
42 Richard Petiot .25 .60
43 Reagan Rome .25 .60
44 Dany Roussin .25 .60
45 Matt Ryan .25 .60
46 Jeff Tambellini .40 1.00
47 Mike Weaver .25 .60
48 Eric Werner .25 .60

2006-07 Manchester Monarchs

COMPLETE SET (24) 7.00 12.00
1 Barry Brust .30 .75
2 Brendan Buckley .20 .50
3 Bryan Schmidt .20 .50
4 Dany Roussin .30 .75
5 Doug Nolan .20 .50
6 Eric Werner .20 .50
7 Jason Labarbera .30 .75
8 Jeff Giuliano .30 .75
9 Joey Mormina .20 .50
10 John Zeiler .20 .50
11 Konstantin Pushkarev .20 .50
12 Lauri Tukonen .40 1.00
13 Matt Moulson .20 .50
14 Matt Ryan .20 .50
15 Ned Lukacevic .20 .50
16 Noah Clarke .20 .50
17 Peter Harrold .20 .50
18 Petr Kanko .20 .50
19 Ryan Murphy .20 .50
20 Shay Stephenson .20 .50
21 Tim Jackman .20 .50
22 Mark Morris CO .02 .10
23 Scott Pellerin ACO .02 .10
24 Max MASCOT .02 .10

2014-15 Manchester Monarchs

COMPLETE SET (25) 6.00 15.00
1 Justin Auger .30 .75
2 Sean Backman .30 .75
3 Patrik Bartosak .30 .75
4 Jean-Francois Berube .50 1.25
5 Andrew Bodnarchuk .30 .75
6 Andrew Crescenzi .30 .75
7 Nic Dowd .30 .75
8 Nick Ebert .30 .75
9 Derek Forbort .30 .75
10 Josh Gratton .30 .75
11 Kevin Gravel .30 .75
12 Ryan Horvat .30 .75
13 Vincent LoVerde .30 .75
14 Michael Mersch .40 1.00
15 Colin Miller .40 1.00
16 Zach O'Brien .40 1.00
17 Brian O'Neill .30 .75
18 Kevin Raine .30 .75
19 Scott Sabourin .30 .75
20 Jeff Schultz .30 .75
21 Nick Shore .30 .75
22 David Van Der Gulik .30 .75
23 Jordan Weal .50 1.25
24 Max MASCOT .30 .75
25 Header Card CL .30 .75

1992-93 Manitoba Junior League

COMPLETE SET (?)

1997-98 Manitoba Moose

COMPLETE SET (16)	15.00	40.00
A1 Ralph Intranuovo	.75	2.00
A2 Russ Romaniuk	.75	2.00
A3 Randy Gilhen	.75	2.00
A4 Dave Thomlinson	.75	2.00
A5 Fred Brathwaite	2.00	5.00
A6 Mick E. Moose Mascot	.40	1.00
A7 Scott Arniel	2.00	5.00
A8 Randy Carlyle HCO	2.00	5.00
B1 Brian Chapman	.75	2.00
B2 Radim Bicanek	.75	2.00
B3 Michael Stewart	.75	2.00
B4 Jason Christie	.75	2.00
B5 Greg Pankewicz	.75	2.00
B6 Brad Purdie	.75	2.00
B7 Kent Fearns	2.00	5.00
B8 Mike Ruark	2.00	5.00

1998-99 Manitoba Moose

COMPLETE SET (16)	16.00	40.00
C1 Scott Arniel	1.25	3.00
C2 Bill Bowler	1.25	3.00
C3 Kent Fearns	.75	2.00
C4 Brett Hauer	.75	2.00
C5 Ralph Intranuovo	.75	2.00
C6 Mike Ruark	.75	2.00
C7 Michael Stewart	2.00	5.00
C8 Scott Thomas	2.00	5.00
D1 Jason MacDonald	1.25	3.00
D2 Christian Bronsard	1.25	3.00
D3 Jeff Parrott	.75	2.00
D4 Brian Chapman	.75	2.00
D5 Richard Shulmistra	1.25	3.00
D6 Jimmy Roy	.75	2.00
D7 Rhett Gordon	2.00	5.00
D8 Patrice Tardif	2.00	5.00

1999-00 Manitoba Moose

COMPLETE SET (22)	10.00	25.00
1 Manny Legace	1.25	3.00
2 Michael Stewart	.40	1.00
3 Vladislav Serov	.40	1.00
4 Lonny Bohonos	.75	2.00
5 Mike Prokopec	.75	2.00
6 Jeff Parrott	.40	1.00
7 Bill Bowler	.75	2.00
8 Mike Ruark	.40	1.00
9 Eric Veilleux	.40	1.00
10 Brett Hauer	.40	1.00
11 Jason Elliott	.75	2.00
12 Cory Cyrenne	.60	1.50
13 Justin Kurtz	.40	1.00
14 Patrice Tardif	.75	2.00
15 Jimmy Roy	.40	1.00
16 Jason MacDonald	.40	1.00
17 Larry Shapley	.40	1.00
18 Brian Chapman	.40	1.00
19 Marc Rodgers	.75	2.00
20 Jim Montgomery	.40	1.00
21 M2K Header Card	.20	.50
22 Checklist	.20	.50

2000-01 Manitoba Moose

COMPLETE SET	6.00	12.00
1 Mel Angelstad	.30	.75
2 Doug Ast	.20	.50
3 Cal Benazic	.20	.50
4 Philippe Boucher	.20	.50
5 Steve Brule	.20	.50
6 Brian Chapman	.20	.50
7 Dion Darling	.20	.50
8 Bobby Dollas	.20	.50
9 Rusty Fitzgerald	.20	.50
10 Daniel Goneau	.20	.50
11 Brett Hauer	.20	.50
12 Johan Hedberg	2.00	3.00
13 Dan Kesa	.20	.50
14 Justin Kurtz	.20	.75
15 Dmitri Leonov	.20	.50
16 John MacLean	.30	.75
17 Sean Pronger	.20	.50
18 Bruce Richardson	.20	.50
19 Jimmy Roy	.20	.75
20 Mike Ruark	.20	.50
21 Scott Thomas	.20	.50
22 Ken Wregget	.30	.75
23 Mick E. Moose MASCOT	.02	.10

2001-02 Manitoba Moose

COMPLETE SET (23)	6.00	15.00
1 Header Card	.04	.10
2 Bryan Allen	.30	.75
3 Ryan Bonni	.30	.75
4 Brian Chapman	.30	.75
5 Artem Chubarov	.30	.75
6 Jason Cipolla	.30	.75
7 Regan Darby	.30	.75
8 Fedor Fedorov	.30	.75
9 Darrell Hay	.30	.75
10 Bryan Helmer	.30	.75
11 Josh Holden	.30	.75
12 Steve Kariya	.40	1.00
13 Pat Kavanagh	.30	.75
14 Zenith Komarniski	.30	.75
15 Justin Kurtz	.30	.75
16 Brad Leeb	.30	.75
17 Alfie Michaud	.40	1.00
18 Justin Morrison	.30	.75
19 Ryan Ready	.30	.75
20 Brandon Reid	.40	1.00
21 Jimmy Roy	.30	.75
22 Andre Savage	.30	.75
23 Mick E. Moose MASCOT	.10	.25

2002-03 Manitoba Moose

COMPLETE SET (26)	6.00	15.00
1 Header Card	.04	.10
2 Mick E. Moose Mascot	.04	.10
3 Zenith Komarniski	.20	.50
4 Bryan Helmer	.20	.50
5 Ryan Ready	.20	.50
6 Steve Kariya	.60	1.50
7 Nolan Baumgartner	.20	.50
8 Regan Darby	.20	.50
9 Jimmy Roy	.20	.50
10 Fedor Fedorov	.40	1.00
11 Jaroslav Obsut	.20	.50
12 Jason King	.20	.50
13 Darrell Hay	.20	.50
14 Tyler Moss	.30	.75
15 Herbert Vasilijevs	.20	.50
16 Nathan Smith	.20	.50
17 Alex Auld	.40	1.00
18 Bryan Allen	.20	.50
19 Brandon Reid	.60	1.50
20 Jason Goulet	.20	.50
21 Justin Kurtz	.20	.50
22 Brian Chapman	.20	.50
23 Pat Kavanagh	.20	.50
24 Rene Vydareny	.20	.50
25 Tyler Bouck	.20	.50
26 Jason Shmyr	.20	.50

2003-04 Manitoba Moose

COMPLETE SET (24)	6.00	15.00
1 Checklist	.04	.10
2 Autograph Card	.04	.10
3 Mascot	.04	.10
4 Tomas Mojzis	.25	.60
5 Mikko Jokela	.25	.60
6 Nolan Baumgartner	.25	.60
7 Chris Nielsen	.25	.60
8 Tyler Bouck	.25	.60
9 Nathan Smith	.25	.60
10 Ryan Ready	.25	.60
11 Pat Kavanagh	.25	.60
12 Ryan Kesler	.75	2.00
13 Sean Pronger	.25	.60
14 Rene Vydareny	.25	.60
15 Jimmy Roy	.25	.60
16 Justin Morrison	.25	.60
17 Martin Grenier	.25	.60
18 Tyler Moss	.40	1.00
19 Alex Auld	.40	1.00
20 Dallas Eakins	.25	.60
21 Jaroslav Obsut	.25	.60
22 Kirill Koltsov	.25	.60
23 Brandon Reid	.40	1.00
24 Fedor Fedorov	.40	1.00

2004-05 Manitoba Moose

COMPLETE SET (24)	8.00	20.00
1 Kevin Bieksa	.40	1.00
2 Tomas Mojzis	.40	1.00
3 Joey DiPenta	.60	1.50
4 Kent Huskins	.40	1.00
5 Nolan Baumgartner	.40	1.00
6 Justin Morrison	.40	1.00
7 Jeff Heerema	.40	1.00
8 Ryan Kesler	.60	1.50
9 Peter Sarno	.60	1.50
10 Nathan Smith	.40	1.00
11 Jimmy Roy	.40	1.00
12 Jesse Schultz	.40	1.00
13 Brandon Nolan	.40	1.00
14 Jason King	.60	1.50
15 Wade Flaherty	.60	1.50
16 Alex Auld	.60	1.50
17 Josh Green	.40	1.00
18 Lee Goren	.60	1.50
19 Wade Brookbank	.40	1.00
20 Johnathan Aitken	.40	1.00
21 Autograph Card	.04	.10
22 MTS Centre 1st Goal	.04	.10
23 Inaugural Season	.04	.10
24 Mick E. Moose MASCOT	.04	.10

2005-06 Manitoba Moose

COMPLETE SET (27)	5.00	12.00
1 Jozef Balej	.20	.50
2 Ryan Bayda	.20	.50
3 Kevin Bieksa	.20	.50
4 Mike Brown	.20	.50
5 Alexandre Burrows	.40	1.00
6 Sven Butenschon	.20	.50
7 Craig Darby	.20	.50
8 Wade Flaherty	.40	1.00
9 Maxime Fortunus	.20	.50
10 Josh Green	.20	.50
11 Jason Jaffray	.20	.50
12 Mike Keane	.20	.50
13 Nathan McIver	.20	.50
14 Tomas Mojzis	.20	.50
15 Yuri Moscevsky	.20	.50
16 Maxime Ouellet	.60	1.50
17 Jimmy Roy	.20	.50
18 Prestin Ryan	.20	.50
19 Rick Rypien	.20	.50
20 Jesse Schultz	.40	1.00
21 Brett Skinner	.20	.50
22 Nathan Smith	.20	.50
23 AHL All-Star Classic	.02	.10
24 Autograph Card	.02	.10
25 The Home of Hockey	.02	.10
26 Manitoba Moose CL	.02	.10
27 Mick E. Moose MASCOT	.02	.10

2006-07 Manitoba Moose

COMPLETE SET (27)	12.00	20.00
1 Mick E. Moose MASCOT	.10	.25
2 Drew McIntyre	.40	1.00
3 Alexander Edler	.30	.75
4 Prestin Ryan	.30	.75
5 Joe Rullier	.30	.75
6 Nathan McIver	.30	.75
7 Brandon Reid	.40	1.00
8 Mike Keane	.30	.75
9 Mike Brown	.30	.75
10 Jason Jaffray	.30	.75
11 Jannik Hansen	.60	1.50
12 J.J. Hunter	.30	.75
13 Nathan Smith	.30	.75
14 Brad Moran	.30	.75
15 Jesse Schultz	.30	.75
16 Dustin Wood	.30	.75
17 Adam Keefe	.30	.75
18 Maxime Fortunus	.30	.75
19 Marc-Andre Bernier	.30	.75
20 Tyler Bouck	.30	.75
21 Wade Flaherty	.40	1.00
22 Julien Ellis	.40	1.00
23 Lee Goren	.40	1.00
24 Yannick Tremblay	.30	.75
25 Patrick Coulombe	.30	.75
26 Shaun Heshka	.30	.75
27 Alexandre Bolduc	.30	.75

2007-08 Manitoba Moose

COMPLETE SET (29)	6.00	15.00
1 Mike E. Moose MASCOT	.15	.40
2 Drew MacIntyre	.50	1.25
3 Luc Bourdon	.50	1.25
4 Mason Raymond	.50	1.25
5 Nathan McIver	.20	.50
6 Jozef Balej	.20	.50
7 Rick Rypien	.20	.50
8 Mike Keane	.20	.50
9 Mike Brown	.20	.50
10 Jason Jaffray	.20	.50
11 Jannik Hansen	.50	1.25
12 Zack Fitzgerald	.20	.50
13 Greg Classen	.20	.50
14 Brad Moran	.20	.50
15 Ryan Shannon	.20	.50
16 Juraj Simek	.20	.50
17 Shaun Heshka	.20	.50
18 Maxime Fortunis	.20	.50
19 Colby Genoway	.20	.50
20 Pierre-Cedric Labrie	.20	.50
21 Cory Schneider	.50	1.25
22 Michael Grabner	.20	.50
23 Jimmy Sharrow	.20	.50
24 Danny Groulx	.20	.50
25 Alexandre Bolduc	.20	.50
26 Team Checklist	.10	.25
27 Scott Arniel HC	.15	.40
28 Brad Berry AC	.10	.25
29 Autograph Card	.10	.25

1982-83 Medicine Hat Tigers

COMPLETE SET (21)	8.00	20.00
1 Al Conroy	.60	1.50
2 Murray Craven	.75	2.00
3 Mark Frank	.40	1.00
4 Kevan Guy	.40	1.00
5 Jim Hougen	.40	1.00
6 Ken Jorgenson	.40	1.00
7 Matt Kabayama	.40	1.00
8 Brent Kisilivich	.40	1.00
9 Mark Lamb	1.25	3.00
10 Mike Lay	.40	1.00
11 Dean McArthur	.40	1.00
12 Brent Meckling	.40	1.00
13 Shawn Nagurny	.40	1.00
14 Kodie Nelson	.40	1.00
15 Al Pedersen	.60	1.50
16 Todd Pederson	.40	1.00
17 Jay Reid	.40	1.00
18 Gord Shmyrko	.40	1.00
19 Brent Steblyk	.40	1.00
20 Rocky Trottier	.40	1.00
21 Dan Turner	.40	1.00

1983-84 Medicine Hat Tigers

COMPLETE SET (23)	12.00	40.00
1 Murray Craven	.75	2.00
2 Shane Churla	2.00	5.00
3 Don Herczeg	.60	1.50
4 Gary Johnson	.60	1.50
5 Brent Kisilivich	.60	1.50
6 Blair MacGregor	.60	1.50
7 Terry Knight	.60	1.50
8 Mark Lamb	1.25	3.00
9 Al Pedersen	.75	2.00
10 Trevor Semeniuk	.60	1.50
11 Dan Turner	.60	1.50
12 Brent Steblyk	.60	1.50
13 Rocky Trottier	.75	2.00
14 Kevan Guy	.75	2.00
15 Bobby Bassen	.75	2.00
16 Brent Meckling	.60	1.50
17 Matt Kabayama	.60	1.50
18 Gord Hynes	.75	2.00
19 Daryl Henry	.60	1.50
20 Jim Kambeitz	.60	1.50
21 Mike Lay	.75	2.00
22 Gord Shmyrko	.60	1.50
23 Al Conroy	.75	2.00

1985-86 Medicine Hat Tigers

COMPLETE SET (24)	8.00	20.00
1 Mike Claringbull	.30	.75
2 Doug Houda	.40	1.00
3 Mark Kuntz	.30	.75
4 Guy Phillips	.30	.75
5 Rob DiMaio	.75	2.00
6 Al Conroy	.40	1.00
7 Craig Berube	.75	2.00
8 Doug Sauter CO	.20	.50
9 Dean Chynoweth	.40	1.00
10 Scott McCrady	.30	.75
11 Neil Brady	.30	.75
12 Dale Kushner	.30	.75
13 Jeff Wenaas	.30	.75
14 Wayne Hynes	.30	.75
15 Troy Gamble	.75	2.00
16 Bryan Maxwell ACO	.20	.50
17 Gord Hynes	.30	.75
18 Wayne McBean	.40	1.00
19 Mark Pederson	.40	1.00
20 Darren Cota	.30	.75
21 Randy Siska	.30	.75
22 Dave Mackey	.30	.75
23 Mark Fitzpatrick	1.25	3.00
24 Doug Ball TR	.08	.25

1995-96 Medicine Hat Tigers

COMPLETE SET (21)	6.00	15.00
1 Johnathan Aitken	.30	.75
2 Brady Austin	.30	.75
3 Cal Benazic	.30	.75
4 Scott Buhler	.30	.75
5 Clint Cabana	.30	.75
6 Mike Eley	.30	.75
7 Josh Green	.40	1.00
8 Curtis Huppe	.30	.75
9 Henry Kuster	.30	.75
10 Aaron Millar	.30	.75
11 Mark Polak	.30	.75
12 Bryan Randall	.30	.75
13 Chad Reich	.30	.75
14 Kyle Ronan	.30	.75
15 Rroary MASCOT	.02	.10
16 Blair St. Martin	.30	.75
17 Paxton Schafer	.30	.75
18 Derek Senkow	.30	.75
19 Darcy Smith	.30	.75
20 Rocky Thompson	.40	1.00
21 Trevor Wasyluk	.40	1.00

1996-97 Medicine Hat Tigers

COMPLETE SET (25)	6.00	15.00
1 Berkeley Buchko	.30	.75
2 Scott Buhler	.30	.75
3 Jason Chimera	.60	1.50
4 Michael Dyck ACO	.02	.10
5 Mike Eley	.30	.75
6 Josh Green	.30	.75
7 Derek Holland	.30	.75
8 Curtis Huppe	.30	.75
9 Henry Kuster	.30	.75
10 Kurt Lackten CO	.02	.10
11 Kevin McDonald	.30	.75
12 Aaron Millar	.30	.75
13 Doug Mosher GM	.02	.10
14 Jaroslav Obsut	.30	.75
15 Colin O'Hara	.30	.75
16 Mark Polak	.30	.75
17 Rroary MASCOT	.02	.10
18 Blair St. Martin	.30	.75
19 Rob Sandrock	.30	.75
20 Dustin Schwartz	.30	.75
21 Lee Svangstu	.30	.75
22 Jeff Temple	.30	.75
23 Rocky Thompson	.30	.75
24 Trevor Wasyluk	.30	.75
25 Chad Wilchynski	.30	.75

1997-98 Medicine Hat Tigers

COMPLETE SET (25)	4.80	12.00
1 Steve Albrecht	.20	.50
2 James Boyd	.20	.50
3 Konrad Brand	.20	.50
4 Berkeley Buchko	.20	.50
5 Scott Buhler	.40	1.00
6 Rick Carriere CO	.04	.10
7 Jason Chimera	.75	2.00
8 Randall Dyck	.20	.50
9 Shaun Hill	.20	.50
10 Derek Holland	.20	.50
11 Henry Kuster	.20	.50
12 Kevin McDonald	.20	.50
13 Aaron Millar	.20	.50
14 Derek Rupprecht	.20	.50
15 Rob Sandrock	.20	.50
16 Brett Scheffelmaier	.30	.75
17 Justin Schwartz	.30	.75
18 Blair Simpson	.20	.50
19 Blair St. Martin	.20	.50
20 Jeff Temple	.20	.50
21 Brad Voth	.20	.50
22 Trevor Wasyluk	.20	.50
23 Travis Willie	.20	.50
24 Randy Wong ACO	.02	.10
25 Rroary MASCOT	.02	.10

1998-99 Medicine Hat Tigers

COMPLETE SET (25)	4.80	12.00
1 Brady Austin	.20	.50
2 James Boyd	.20	.50
3 Konrad Brand	.20	.50
4 Berkeley Buchko	.20	.50
5 Scott Buhler	.30	.75
6 Rick Carriere CO	.02	.10
7 Jason Chimera	.60	1.50
8 Martin Cibak	.40	1.00
9 Frazer Donahue	.20	.50
10 Paul Elliott	.20	.50
11 Kris Graf	.20	.50
12 Shaun Hill	.20	.50
13 Denny Johnston	.20	.50
14 Tyson Kentel	.20	.50
15 Cody Lyseng	.20	.50
16 Aaron Millar	.20	.50
17 Derek Rupprecht	.20	.50
18 Brett Scheffelmaier	.30	.75
19 Justin Schwartz	.30	.75
20 Blair Simpson	.20	.50
21 Ben Thompson	.20	.50
22 Brad Voth	.20	.50
23 Kevin Young	.20	.50
24 Randy Wong ACO	.02	.10
25 Rroary MASCOT	.02	.10

1999-00 Medicine Hat Tigers

COMPLETE SET (25)	10.00	25.00
1 Header Card	.02	.10
2 Chris Ferguson	.20	.50
3 Jay Bouwmeester	6.00	15.00
4 Josh Morrow	.20	.50
5 Paul Elliott	.20	.50
6 Tyson Mulock	.20	.50
7 Kevin Labbe	.20	.50
8 Ryan Hollweg	.30	.75
9 Berkeley Buchko	.20	.50
10 Chris St. Jacques	.20	.50
11 Cody Jensen	.20	.50
12 Ben Thompson	.20	.50
13 Brad Voth	.20	.50
14 Martin Cibak	.20	.50
15 Denny Johnston	.20	.50
16 Konrad Brand	.20	.50
17 Shaun Sutter	.30	.75
18 Ken Davis	.20	.50
19 Ryan Kinasewich	.20	.50
20 Brett Scheffelmaier	.30	.75
21 Justin Taylor	.20	.50
22 Vladimir Sicak	.20	.50
23 Ben McMullin	.30	.75
24 Kyle Kettles	.30	.75
25 Josh Maser	.20	.50
27 Brett Scheffelmaier	.20	.50
28 Justin Taylor	.20	.50
29 Vladimir Sicak	.20	.50
30 Ben McMullin	.20	.50
31 Kyle Kettles	.20	.50
32 Jash Maser	.20	.50

2000-01 Medicine Hat Tigers

COMPLETE SET (26)	8.00	25.00
1 Jay Bouwmeester	4.00	8.00
2 Ryan Chieduch	.16	.40
3 Petr Chivojka	.16	.40
4 Ken Davis	.16	.40
5 Brett Draney	.16	.40
6 Bryan Ellerman ACO	.04	.10
7 B.J. Fehr	.16	.40
8 Vernon Fiddler	.16	.40
9 Jeremy Goetzinger	.16	.40
10 Ryan Hollweg	.30	.75
11 Denny Johnston	.16	.40
12 Kyle Kettles	.16	.40
13 Ryan Kinasewich	.16	.40
14 Bob Loucks HCO	.04	.10
15 Joffrey Lupul	2.00	10.00
16 Ben McMullin	.20	.50
17 Josh Morrow	.16	.40
18 Tyson Mulock	.16	.40
19 Ryan Olynyk	.16	.40
20 Brett Scheffelmaier	.30	.75
21 Chris St. Jacques	.16	.40
22 Ben Thompson	.16	.40
23 David Ullmann	.16	.40
24 Brad Voth	.16	.40
26 Mascot	.04	.10
26 Randy Wong ACO	.04	.10

2002-03 Medicine Hat Tigers

COMPLETE SET (25)	8.00	20.00
1 Curtis Austring	.20	.50
2 Cam Barker	.60	1.50
3 Chad Bassen	.20	.50
4 Kieran Block	.20	.50
5 Brenden Cuthbert	.20	.50
6 Riley Day	.20	.50
7 Tyler Dietrich	.20	.50
8 Nick Harsulla	.20	.50
9 Ryan Hollweg	.30	.75
10 Daniel Idema	.20	.50
11 Martin Kubaliak	.20	.50
12 Joffrey Lupul	2.00	5.00
13 Steve Marr	.20	.50
14 Tommy Maxwell	.20	.50
15 Stefan Meyer	.20	.50
16 Clarke MacArthur	.40	1.00
17 Kevin Nastiuk	.60	1.50
18 Kyle Pess	.20	.50
19 Adam Redmond	.20	.50
20 Steven Regier	.20	.50
21 Darren Reid	.20	.50
22 Mark Vodden	.20	.50
23 Chris St. Jacques	.20	.50
24 Ryan Stempfle	.20	.50
25 Ben Thomson	.20	.50

2003-04 Medicine Hat Tigers

COMPLETE SET		

2004-05 Medicine Hat Tigers

COMPLETE SET (25)	8.00	20.00
1 Gord Baldwin	.30	.75
2 Cam Barker	.60	1.50
3 Jordan Bendfeld	.30	.75
4 Cody Blanshan	.30	.75
5 Kieran Block	.30	.75
6 Derek Dorsett	.30	.75
7 Nathan Exner	.30	.75
8 Trevor Glass	.30	.75
9 Darren Helm	.30	.75
10 Matt Keetley	.30	.75
11 Jarret Lukin	.30	.75
12 Clarke MacArthur	.40	1.00
13 Steve Marr	.30	.75
14 Tommy Maxwell	.30	.75
15 Stefan Meyer	.30	.75
16 Kevin Nastiuk	.60	1.50
17 Roman Psurny	.30	.75
18 Brett Robertson	.30	.75
19 Kris Russell	.30	.75
20 David Schlemko	.30	.75
21 Daine Todd	.30	.75
22 Devyn Tremblay	.30	.75
23 Kevin Undershute	.30	.75
24 Willie Desjardins CO	.04	.10
25 Shaun Clouston ACO	.04	.10

2005-06 Medicine Hat Tigers

COMPLETE SET (25)	8.00	20.00
1 Gord Baldwin	.30	.75
2 Cam Barker	.60	1.50
3 Jason Battershill	.30	.75
4 Jordan Bendfeld	.30	.75
5 Kieran Block	.30	.75
6 Brennan Bosch	.30	.75
7 Shayne Brown	.30	.75
8 Marek Curilla	.30	.75
9 Derek Dorsett	.30	.75
10 Tyler Ennis	.50	1.25
11 Trevor Glass	.30	.75
12 Darren Helm	.30	.75
13 Matt Keetley	.30	.75
14 Tommy Maxwell	.30	.75
15 Blaine Neufeld	.30	.75
16 Roman Psurny	.30	.75
17 Brett Robertson	.30	.75
18 Kris Russell	.30	.75
19 Jerrid Sauer	.30	.75
20 David Schlemko	.30	.75
21 Matt Sokol	.30	.75
22 Chris Stevens	.30	.75
23 Daine Todd	.30	.75
24 Kevin Undershute	.30	.75
25 Scott Wasden	.30	.75

2006-07 Medicine Hat Tigers

COMPLETE SET (25)	12.00	20.00
1 Gord Baldwin	.30	.75
2 Jordan Bendfeld	.30	.75
3 Brennan Bosch	.30	.75
4 Shayne Brown	.30	.75
5 Derek Dorsett	.30	.75
6 Tyler Ennis	.50	1.25
7 Trevor Glass	.30	.75
8 Colton Grant	.30	.75
9 Darren Helm	.30	.75
10 Jordan Hickmott	.30	.75
11 Ryan Holfeld	.40	1.00
12 Mark Isherwood	.30	.75
13 Matt Keetley	.40	1.00
14 Matt Lowry	.30	.75
15 Jakub Rumpel	.30	.75
16 Kris Russell	.75	2.00
17 Jerrid Sauer	.30	.75
18 Michael Sauer	.30	.75
19 David Schlemko	.30	.75
20 Chris Stevens	.30	.75
21 Tyler Swystun	.30	.75
22 Daine Todd	.30	.75
23 Kevin Undershute	.30	.75
24 Scott Wasden	.30	.75
25 Willie Desjardins CO	.10	.25

1993-94 Memphis RiverKings

COMPLETE SET (18)	3.60	9.00
1 Rocco Amonte	.20	.50
2 Peter D'Amario	.20	.50
3 Roydon Gunn	.20	.50
4 Kyle Haviland	.20	.50
5 Mike Jackson	.20	.50
6 Scot Johnston	.20	.50
7 Robert Kelley	.20	.50
8 Mark McGinn	.20	.50
9 Antoine Mindjimba	.30	.75
10 David Moore	.20	.50
11 Glenn Painter	.20	.50
12 Scott Phillips	.20	.50
13 Mike Roberts	.20	.50
14 Andy Ross	.20	.50
15 Steve Shaunessy	.20	.50
16 Ken Venis	.20	.50
17 Bobby Wallwork	.20	.50
18 Randy Boyd CO	.08	.25

1994-95 Memphis RiverKings

COMPLETE SET (18)	3.00	8.00
1 Denis Beauchamp	.20	.50
2 Nicolas Brousseau	.20	.50
3 Scott Bower	.30	.75
4 Dan Brown	.20	.50
5 Brian Cook	.20	.50
6 Brent Fleetwood	.20	.50
7 Francois Gagnon	.20	.50
8 Dominic Grand'maison	.20	.50
9 Kyle Haviland	.20	.50
10 Jamie Hearn	.20	.50
11 Mike Jackson	.30	.75
12 Paul Krake	.30	.75
13 Layne LeBel	.20	.50
14 Steve Magnusson	.20	.50
15 Darren Miciak	.20	.50
16 Mark McGinn	.20	.50
17 Bobby Wallwork	.20	.50
18 Herb Boxer CO	.08	.25

1999-00 Memphis RiverKings All-Time

COMPLETE SET (20)	4.00	10.00
1 Tom Mutch	.20	.50
2 Doug Stromback	.20	.50
3 Mike Jackson	.30	.75
4 Mark McGinn	.20	.50
5 Antoine Mindjimba	.30	.75
6 Andrew Miller	.20	.50
7 Dan Brown	.20	.50
8 Hugo Hamelin	.20	.50
9 Derek Grant	.20	.50
10 Steve Thorpe	.20	.50
11 Bobby Wallwork	.20	.50
12 Peter D'Amario	.20	.50
13 John Batten	.20	.50
14 Andy Ross	.20	.50
15 Kyle Haviland	.20	.50
16 Scot Kelsey	.20	.50
17 Scott Brower	.20	.50
18 Jamie Cooke	.30	.75
19 Craig Lindsay	.20	.50
20 Riverthing MAS	.08	.25

2001-02 Memphis RiverKings

COMPLETE SET (21)	6.00	15.00
1 Team CL Centomo	.30	.75
2 Kahlil Thomas	.20	.50
3 Brad Mueller	.20	.50
4 Kevin Fricke	.20	.50
5 Anthony DiPalma	.20	.50
6 Michal Stastny	.30	.75
7 Jean-Francois Picard	.20	.50
8 Jay Neal	.20	.50
9 Jacques Lariviere	.30	.75
10 Rob Palahnuk	.20	.50
11 Kevin Ryan	.20	.50
12 Sebastien Centomo	2.00	5.00
13 Don Parsons	.20	.50
14 Luch Nasato	.30	.75
15 Mark Richards	.20	.50
16 Brian Tucker	.20	.50
17 Don Martin	.20	.50
18 Ben Gorewich	.20	.50
19 A.J. Aitken	.20	.50
20 Jonathan Gagnon	.20	.50
21 Doug Shedden CO	.20	.50

2003-04 Memphis RiverKings

COMPLETE SET	6.00	15.00
1 Jeremy Cornish	.40	1.00
2 Trent Dickson	.30	.75
3 Juraj Durco	.30	.75
4 Jonathan Gagnon	.30	.75
5 Jasmin Gelinas	.30	.75
6 Jerry Gernander	.30	.75
7 Jeremy Goetzinger	.30	.75
8 Chad Grills	.30	.75
9 Derek Landmesser	.40	1.00
10 Stephen Margeson	.30	.75
11 Alexandre Mathieu	.40	1.00
12 Mike Minard	.40	1.00
13 Brad Mueller	.30	.75
14 Jay Neal	.30	.75
15 Brent Ozarowski	.30	.75
16 Don Parsons	.40	1.00
17 Jean-Francois Racine	.60	1.50
18 Mark Richards	.30	.75
19 Tim Schneider	.30	.75
20 Brian Tucker	.30	.75
21 David Turon	.30	.75

2004-05 Memphis RiverKings

COMPLETE SET (22)	6.00	15.00
1 Header Card	.04	.10
2 Aaron Lewis	.20	.50
3 Allan Carr	.20	.50
4 Brad Mueller	.20	.50
5 David Lemanowicz	.60	1.50
6 Derek Landmesser	.20	.50
7 Don Parsons	.30	.75
8 J.F. Racine	.60	1.50
9 Jeremy Goetzinger	.20	.50
10 Jeremy Wray	.20	.50
11 Ken Goetz	.60	1.50
12 Mark Richards	.20	.50
13 Peter Robertson	.20	.50
14 Phil Aucoin	.20	.50
15 Ryan Rome	.20	.50
16 Scott English	.75	2.00
17 Stephen Margeson	.20	.50
18 Ted Crowley	.20	.50
19 Tim Plett	.20	.50
20 Travis Banga	.20	.50
21 Tyson Gajda	.20	.50
22 Wayne Hall	.20	.50

1991-92 Michigan Falcons

COMPLETE SET (21)	8.00	20.00
1 Christian LaLonde	.40	1.00
2 Victor Posa	.40	1.00
3 Al Murphy	.40	1.00
4 Bill Horn	.40	1.00
5 Rich Sewell	.40	1.00
6 Dan Fowler	.40	1.00
7 Kip Noble	.40	1.00
8 Ange Guzzo	.40	1.00
9 Dean Morton	.40	1.00
10 Jeff Lindsay	.40	1.00
11 Mike Vellucci	.60	1.50
12 Brett Strot	.40	1.00
13 Rick Berens	.40	1.00
14 Kevin Clayton	.40	1.00
15 Todd Humphrey	.40	1.00
16 Ray De Grendel ACO	.08	.25
16 Terry Christensen CO	.08	.25
16 Tom Viggiano ACO	.08	.25
17 Bill Gutenberg	.40	1.00
18 Jamie Stewart	.40	1.00
19 Bob McKillop	.40	1.00
20 Clayton Young	.40	1.00
21 Steve Beadle	.40	1.00

1996-97 Michigan K-Wings

COMPLETE SET (27)	4.80	10.00
1 Dan Keczmer	.15	.40
2 Dennis Smith	.15	.40
3 Brad Berry	.15	.40
4 Shane Peacock	.15	.40
5 Jason Lafreniere	.15	.40
6 Collin Bauer	.15	.40
7 Sergei Gusev	.15	.40
8 Igor Korolev	.15	.40
9 Brent Fedyk	.15	.40
10 Pat Elynuik	.15	.40
11 Jamie Wright	.15	.40
12 Lee Jinman	.15	.40
13 Jeff Mitchell	.15	.40
14 Brad Lukowich	.20	.50
15 Derrick Smith	.15	.40
16 Petr Buzek	.15	.40
17 Patrick Cote	.20	.50
18 Mark Lawrence	.15	.40
19 Jim Storm	.15	.40
20 Roman Turek	.40	1.00
21 Neil Brady	.15	.40
22 Manny Fernandez	.75	2.00
23 Claude Noel CO	.02	.10
24 Jim Playfair CO	.02	.10
25 Checklist	.01	.05
26 PHPA Web Site	.01	.05
27 BJ Sports	.01	.05

1998-99 Michigan K-Wings

COMPLETE SET (21)	8.00	25.00
1 Mel Angelstad	.40	1.00
2 Jason Botterill	.15	.40
3 Ryan Christie	.15	.40
4 Doug Doull	.75	2.00
5 Kelly Fairchild	.15	.40
6 Marty Flichel	.15	.40
7 Aaron Gavey	.30	.75
8 Greg Leeb	.15	.40
9 Jeff Mitchell	.15	.40
10 Dave Roberts	.15	.40
11 Jon Sim	.30	.75
12 Brad Berry	.15	.40
13 Petr Buzek	.30	.75
14 Richard Jackman	.30	.75
15 Brad Lukowich	.30	.75
16 Matt Martin	.15	.40
17 Evgueni Tsybouk	.15	.40
18 Mike Bales	.30	.75
19 Marty Turco	6.00	15.00
20 IHL Logo card	.02	.10
21 Header Checklist	.02	.10

1999-00 Michigan K-Wings

COMPLETE SET (21)	14.00	40.0
1 Jamie Wright	.30	.75
2 Keith Aldridge	.30	.75
3 Steve Gainey	.30	.75
4 Jonathan Sim	.40	1.0
5 Mike Martin	.20	.5
6 Gaetan Royer	.20	.5
7 Jeff MacMillan	.20	.5
8 Aaron Gavey	.20	.5
9 Evgeny Tsybouk	.20	.5
10 Marty Turco	8.00	20.0
11 Matt Martin	.20	.5
12 Ryan Christie	.20	.5
13 Greg Leeb	.20	.5
14 Mark Wotton	.20	.5
15 Kelly Fairchild	.20	.5
16 Gregor Baumgartner	.20	.5
17 Brenden Morrow	4.00	10.0
18 Mel Angelstad	.75	2.0
19 Mike Bales	.30	.7
20 Richard Jackman	.30	.7
21 Roman Lyashenko	.40	1.0

1990-91 Michigan Tech Huskie

COMPLETE SET (31)	6.00	15.0
1 Jim Bonner	.20	.5
2 Newell Brown CO	.08	.2
3 Dwight DeGiacomo	.20	.5

Card	Low	High
4 Rod Ewacha	.20	.50
5 Peter Grant	.20	.50
6 Tim Hartnett	.20	.50
7 Mike Hauswirth	.20	.50
8 Kelly Hurd	.20	.50
9 Kelly Hurd Red Wings	.20	.50
10 Layne Lebel Jeff Hill	.20	.50
11 Randy Lewis	.20	.50
12 Jay Luknowsky	.20	.50
13 Ken Martel CO Mark Leach CO	.08	.25
14 Darcy Martini	.20	.50
15 Reid McDonald	.20	.50
16 Hugh McEwen Jim Storm Kevin Manninen	.30	.75
17 Don Osborne	.20	.50
18 Greg Parnell	.20	.50
19 Davis Payne	.20	.50
20 Kirby Perrault Darren Brkic	.20	.50
21 Ken Plaquin	.20	.50
22 Damian Rhodes	.75	2.00
23 Geoff Sarjeant	.30	.75
24 Jamie Steer	.20	.50
25 Rob Tustian	.20	.50
26 Scott Vettraino Jamie Ram	.30	.75
27 Tim Watters b/w	.20	.50
28 John Young	.20	.50
29 John Young Kelly Hurd	.20	.50
30 1991 MacInnes Cup	.20	.50
31 1975 NCAA Champions	.20	.50

1991-92 Michigan Tech Huskies

Card	Low	High
COMPLETE SET (36)	6.00	15.00
1 Jim Bonner	.20	.50
2 Darren Brkic	.20	.50
3 Rod Ewacha	.20	.50
4 Tim Hartnett	.20	.50
5 Mike Hauswirth	.20	.50
6 Jeff Hill	.20	.50
7 Layne LeBel	.20	.50
8 Randy Lewis	.20	.50
9 Randy Lewis Hit Squad	.20	.50
10 John MacInnes CO	.02	.10
11 Darcy Martini	.20	.50
12 Darcy Martini Rink Blaster	.20	.50
13 Reid McDonald	.20	.50
14 Hugh McEwen	.20	.50
15 Bob Olson ANN	.02	.10
16 Don Osborne	.20	.50
17 Greg Parnell	.20	.50
18 Davis Payne	.20	.50
19 Kirby Perrault	.20	.50
20 Ken Plaquin	.20	.50
21 Jamie Ram	.30	.75
22 Geoff Sarjeant	.30	.75
23 Geoff Sarjeant WCHA Student-Athlete	.30	.75
24 Jamie Steer	.20	.50
25 Jamie Steer Blade Runner	.20	.50
26 Jim Storm	.20	.50
27 Scott Vettraino	.20	.50
28 John Young	.20	.50
29 Credits (Team huddling on ice)	.20	.50
30 Freshman Justin Peca Liam Garvey Randy Stevens Brent Peterson Travis Seale	.20	.50
31 Great Lakes Invitational	.02	.10
32 Home Ice MacInnes Student Ice Arena	.02	.10
33 Team Photo	.20	.50
34 NHL Draft Darcy Martini Davis Payne Geoff Sarjeant Ken Plaquin Jim Storm Jamie Ram Jamie Steer Jim Bonner	.20	.50
35 Pep Band	.02	.10
36 Michigan Tech Univ.	.02	.10

1993-94 Michigan Tech Huskies

Card	Low	High
COMPLETE SET (25)	4.80	12.00
1 Pat Mikesch	.20	.50
2 Eric Jensen	.20	.50
3 Kyle Peterson	.20	.50
4 Jay Storm	.20	.50
5 Jason Hanchuk	.20	.50
6 Mike Figliomeni	.20	.50
7 Randy Stevens	.20	.50
8 Brent Peterson	.20	.50
9 Kirby Perrault	.20	.50
10 Brian Hunter	.20	.50
11 Travis Seale	.20	.50
12 Jamie Ram	.30	.75
13 Jeff Hill	.20	.50
14 Justin Peca	.20	.50
15 Layne LeBel	.20	.50
16 Jeff Mikesch	.20	.50
17 John Kisil	.20	.50
18 Liam Garvey	.20	.50
19 Kyle Ferguson	.20	.50
20 Jason Wright	.20	.50
21 Luciano Caravaggio	.20	.50
22 Mitch Lane	.20	.50
23 Randy Wakeham	.20	.50
24 Martin Machacek	.20	.50
25 Winter Carnival	.02	.10

2001-02 Michigan Tech Huskies

Card	Low	High
COMPLETE SET (33)	8.00	20.00
1 Greg Amadio	.30	.75
2 Justin Brown	.30	.75
3 Paul Cabana	.30	.75
4 Tony DeLorenzo	.30	.75
5 Jaron Doetzel	.30	.75
6 Chris Durno	.30	.75
7 Cam Ellsworth	.40	1.00
8 Brett Engelhardt	.30	.75
9 Chuck Fabry	.30	.75
10 Brady Greco	.30	.75
11 John Hartman	.30	.75
12 Blizzard T. Husky	.04	.10
13 Tom Kaiman	.30	.75
14 Bryan Konkel	.30	.75
15 Tim Laurila	.40	1.00
16 Ryan Lenton	.30	.75
17 MacInnes Arena	.04	.10
18 Ryan Markham	.30	.75
19 Pep Band	.04	.10
20 Colin Murphy	.30	.75
21 Bob Olson ANN	.04	.10
22 Brad Patterson	.30	.75
23 Bryan Perez	.30	.75
24 Phil Pietila	.30	.75
25 Jon Pittis	.30	.75
26 Bob Rangus	.30	.75
27 Rob Rankin	.30	.75
28 Brian Rogers	.40	1.00
29 Mike Sertich CO	.10	.25
30 Josh Singer	.30	.75
31 Brad Sullivan	.30	.75
32 Frank Werner	.30	.75
33 Clay Wilson	.30	.75

1991-92 Michigan Wolverines

Card	Low	High
COMPLETE SET (25)	6.00	15.00
1 Doug Evans	.20	.50
2 Denny Felsner	.20	.50
3 Anton Fedorov	.20	.50
4 Chris Gordon	.20	.50
5 David Harlock	.20	.50
6 Mike Helber	.20	.50
7 Tim Hogan	.20	.50
8 Mike Knuble	.30	.75
9 Ted Kramer	.20	.50
10 Pat Neaton	.20	.50
11 David Oliver	.30	.75
12 David Roberts	.20	.50
13 Mark Ouimet	.20	.50
14 Ron Sacka	.20	.50
15 Mark Sakala	.20	.50
16 Steve Shields	1.25	3.00
17 Alan Sinclair	.20	.50
18 Cam Stewart	.30	.75
19 Dan Stiver	.20	.50
20 Mike Stone	.20	.50
21 Chris Tamer	.25	.60
22 Aaron Ward	.30	.75
23 Rick Willis	.20	.50
24 Brian Wiseman	.20	.50
25 Team Card	.02	.10

1993-94 Michigan Wolverines

Card	Low	High
COMPLETE SET (28)	8.00	20.00
1 John Arnold	.20	.50
2 Jason Botterill	.30	.75
3 Peter Bourke	.20	.50
4 Drew Denzin	.20	.50
5 Anton Fedorov	.20	.50
6 Chris Frescoln	.20	.50
7 Chris Gordon	.20	.50
8 Steve Halko	.20	.50
9 Kevin Hilton	.20	.50
10 Tim Hogan	.20	.50
11 Mike Knuble	.30	.75
12 Mike Legg	.20	.50
13 Al Loges	.20	.50
14 Warren Luhning	.20	.50
15 John Madden	1.50	4.00
16 Brendan Morrison	.75	2.00
17 David Oliver	.20	.50
18 Ron Sacka	.20	.50
19 Mark Sakala	.20	.50
20 Harold Schock	.20	.50
21 Steve Shields	.60	1.50
22 Alan Sinclair	.20	.50
23 Ryan Sittler	.20	.50
24 Blake Sloan	.40	1.00
25 Mike Stone	.20	.50
26 Rick Willis	.20	.50
27 Brian Wiseman	.20	.50
28 Team Photo	.20	.50

2002-03 Michigan Wolverines

Card	Low	High
COMPLETE SET (30)	15.00	35.00
1 Billy Powers ACO	.04	.10
2 Danny Richmond	.75	2.00
3 Mike Roemensky	.40	1.00
4 David Wyzgowski	.40	1.00
5 Charlie Henderson	.40	1.00
6 Jed Ortmeyer	.75	2.00
7 Jeff Tambellini	1.25	3.00
8 David Moss	.40	1.00
9 Gordon Berenson HCO	.40	1.00
10 NCAA Frozen Four	.10	.25
11 Eric Nystrom	1.25	3.00
12 John Shouneyia	.40	1.00
13 Andrew Ebbett	.40	1.00
14 Michael Woodford	.40	1.00
15 Mel Pearson ACO	.10	.25
16 Brandon Rogers	.40	1.00
17 Joe Kautz	.40	1.00
18 Mark Mink	.40	1.00
19 Nick Martens	.40	1.00
20 2002 CCHA Champions	.10	.25
21 Jason Ryznar	.40	1.00
22 Andy Burnes	.40	1.00
23 Dwight Helminen	.40	1.00
24 Milan Gajic	.40	1.00
25 Yost Arena	.04	.10
26 2002 CCHA Tournament Champs.	.10	.25
27 J.J. Swistak	.40	1.00
28 Al Montoya	3.00	8.00
29 Brandon Kaleniecki	.40	1.00
30 Eric Werner	.40	1.00

2003-04 Michigan Wolverines

Card	Low	High
COMPLETE SET (30)	20.00	40.00
1 Jeff Tambellini	1.25	3.00
2 Mike Mayhew	.40	1.00
3 David Moss	.75	2.00
4 Red Berenson CO	.40	1.00
5 Endowed Scholarships	.04	.10
6 Jason Ryznar	.40	1.00
7 Andy Burnes	.40	1.00
8 Dwight Helminen	.40	1.00
9 Milan Gajic	.40	1.00
10 Reilly Olson	.40	1.00
11 Brandon Rogers	.40	1.00
12 Joe Kautz	.40	1.00
13 Tim Cook	.40	1.00
14 Nick Martens	.40	1.00
15 T.J. Hensick	.75	2.00
16 Eric Werner	.40	1.00
17 Brandon Kaleniecki	.40	1.00
18 Al Montoya	3.00	8.00
19 Mike Brown	.40	1.00
20 Noah Ruden	.40	1.00
21 David Rohlfs	.40	1.00
22 Eric Nystrom	1.25	3.00
23 Andrew Ebbett	.40	1.00
24 Michael Woodford	.40	1.00
25 Mel Pearson ACO	.04	.10
26 Charlie Henderson	.40	1.00
27 David Wyzgowski	.40	1.00
28 Jason Dest	.40	1.00
29 Matt Hunwick	.75	2.00
30 Billy Powers ACO	.04	.10

2004-05 Michigan Wolverines

Card	Low	High
COMPLETE SET (25)	12.00	30.00
1 David Rohlfs	.40	1.00
2 Andrew Ebbett	.40	1.00
3 Brandon Kaleniecki	.40	1.00
4 Al Montoya	2.00	5.00
5 Gameday	.04	.10
6 Chad Kolarik	.40	1.00
7 Kevin Porter	.40	1.00
8 Mike Brown	.60	1.50
9 Tim Cook	.40	1.00
10 Yost Arena	.04	.10
11 Jason Dest	.40	1.00
12 Matt Hunwick	.60	1.50
13 T.J. Hensick	.75	2.00
14 Mike Mayhew	.40	1.00
15 Endowed Scholarships	.04	.10
16 Nick Martens	.40	1.00
17 David Moss	1.25	3.00
18 Eric Nystrom	1.25	3.00
19 Reilly Olson	.40	1.00
20 Mel Pearson ACO	.04	.10
21 Noah Ruden	.40	1.00
22 Jeff Tambellini	1.25	3.00
23 Milan Gajic	.40	1.00
24 Charlie Henderson	.40	1.00
25 Billy Powers	.40	1.00

2007-08 Michigan Wolverines

Card	Low	High
COMPLETE SET (28)	4.00	10.00
1 Louie Caporusso	.15	.40
2 Anthony Ciraulo	.15	.40
3 Eric Elmblad	.15	.40
4 Danny Fardig	.15	.40
5 Chris Fragner	.15	.40
6 Carl Hagelin	.15	.40
7 Bryan Hogan	.15	.40
8 Shawn Hunwick	.15	.40
9 Steve Kampfer	.15	.40
10 Chad Kolarik	.15	.40
11 Chad Langlais	.15	.40
12 Brian Lebler	.15	.40
13 Tristin Llewellyn	.15	.40
14 Tim Miller	.15	.40
15 Mark Mitera	.15	.40
16 Brandon Naurato	.15	.40
17 Max Pacioretty	.15	.40
18 Aaron Palushaj	.15	.40
19 Kevin Porter	.15	.40
20 Kevin Quick	.15	.40
21 Matt Rust	.15	.40
22 Billy Sauer	.15	.40
23 Chris Summers	.15	.40
24 Travis Turnbull	.15	.40
25 Scooter Vaughn	.15	.40
26 Ben Winnett	.15	.40
27 Red Berenson HC	.10	.25
28 Yost Arena	.15	.40

1992-93 Michigan State Spartans

Card	Low	High
COMPLETE SET (30)	15.00	40.00
1 Team Photo	.60	1.50
2 Ron Mason HCO	.60	1.50
3 Matt Albers	.60	1.50
4 Michael Burkett	.60	1.50
5 Mike Buzak	.60	1.50
6 Anson Carter	2.50	6.00
7 Brian Clifford	.60	1.50
8 Scott Dean	.60	1.50
9 Ryan Fleming	.60	1.50
10 Ryan Folkening	.60	1.50
11 Steve Guolla	1.25	3.00
12 Kelly Harper	.60	1.50
13 Eric Kruse	.60	1.50
14 James Lambros	.60	1.50
15 Mike Mattis	.60	1.50
16 Wes McCauley	.60	1.50
17 Rem Murray	1.25	3.00
18 Steve Norton	.60	1.50
19 Nicolas Perreault	.60	1.50
20 Bill Shalawylo	.60	1.50
21 Chris Smith	.60	1.50
22 Bryan Smolinski	1.25	3.00
23 Steve Suk	.60	1.50
24 Chris Sullivan	.60	1.50
25 Bart Turner	.60	1.50
26 Bart Vanstaalduinen	.60	1.50
27 Mike Ware	.60	1.50
28 John Weidenbach	.60	1.50
29 Rob Woodward	.60	1.50
30 Scott Worden	.60	1.50

1993-94 Michigan State Spartans

Card	Low	High
COMPLETE SET (32)	15.00	40.00
1 Matt Albers	.40	1.00
2 Michael Burkett	.40	1.00
3 Mike Buzak	.40	1.00
4 Anson Carter	2.00	5.00
5 Brian Clifford	.75	2.00
6 Brian Crane	.40	1.00
7 Steve Ferranti	.40	1.00
8 Ryan Fleming	.40	1.00
9 Steve Guolla	.75	2.00
10 Kelly Harper	.40	1.00
11 Eric Kruse	.40	1.00
12 Ron Mason CO	.40	1.00
13 Mike Mattis	.40	1.00
14 Rem Murray	.75	2.00
15 Steve Norton	.40	1.00
16 Nicolas Perreault	.40	1.00
17 Tom Ross Spartan Great	.75	2.00
18 Chris Slater	.40	1.00
19 Chris Smith	.40	1.00
20 Bryan Smolinski	1.25	3.00
21 Sparty (Mascot)	.02	.10
22 Chris Sullivan	.40	1.00
23 Steve Suk	.40	1.00
24 Bart Turner	.40	1.00
25 Tony Tuzzolino	1.25	3.00
26 Bart Vanstaalduinen	.40	1.00
27 Mike Ware	.40	1.00
28 John Weidenbach	.40	1.00
29 Josh Wiegand	.40	1.00
30 Scott Worden	.40	1.00
31 Munn Arena	.02	.10
32 Title Card	.02	.10

2000-01 Michigan State Spartans

Card	Low	High
COMPLETE SET (21)	10.00	35.00
1 Joe Blackburn	.75	2.00
2 Andrew Bogle	.40	1.00
3 Steve Clark	.40	1.00
4 Rustyn Dolyny	.40	1.00
5 Brad Fast	.40	1.00
6 Troy Ferguson	.40	1.00
7 Joe Goodenow	.40	1.00
8 Adam Hall	2.00	5.00
9 Andrew Hutchinson	.75	2.00
10 Jon Insana	.40	1.00
11 Steve Jackson	.40	1.00
12 Kris Koski	.40	1.00
13 John-Michael Liles	2.00	5.00
14 Brian Maloney	.40	1.00
15 Ryan Miller	6.00	15.00
16 John Nail	.40	1.00
17 Sean Patchell	.40	1.00
18 Damon Whitten	.40	1.00
19 Ron Mason CO	.40	1.00
20 White Out Game 3/2/01	.10	.25
21 Chevy Fans.Com	.02	.10

1981-82 Milwaukee Admirals

Card	Low	High
COMPLETE SET (15)	6.00	15.00
1 Pat Rabbitt	.40	1.00
2 Real Paiement	.40	1.00
3 Fred Berry	.40	1.00
4 Blaine Peerless	.40	1.00
5 John Flesch	.40	1.00
6 Yves Preston	.40	1.00
7 Bruce McKay	.40	1.00
8 Dale Yakiwchuk	.40	1.00
9 Lorne Bokshowan	.40	1.00
10 Danny Lecours	.40	1.00
11 Sheldon Currie	.40	1.00
12 Doug Robb	.40	1.00
13 Rob Polman Tuin	.60	1.50
14 Bob Collyard	.40	1.00
15 Tim Ringler TR	.20	.50

1994-95 Milwaukee Admirals

Card	Low	High
COMPLETE SET (28)	3.00	8.00
1 Doug Agnew TR	.02	.10
2 Peter Bakovic ACO	.02	.10
3 Matt Block	.08	.25
4 Gino Cavallini	.15	.40
5 Sylvain Couturier	.15	.40
6 Brian Dobbin	.15	.40
7 Shawn Evans	.08	.25
8 Fabulous Fritz	.02	.10
9 Chris Govedaris	.20	.50
10 Jim Hrivnak	.30	.75
11 Tony Hrkac	.20	.50
12 Fabian Joseph	.20	.50
13 Mark Laforest	.20	.50
14 Don MacAdam ACO	.02	.10
15 Dave Mackey	.08	.25
16 Pat MacLeod	.08	.25
17 Dave Marcinyshyn	.08	.25
18 Bob Mason	.20	.50
19 Mike McNeill	.08	.25
20 Kent Paynter	.08	.25
21 Ken Sabourin	.08	.25
22 Trevor Sim	.08	.25
23 Martin Simard	.08	.25
24 Mike Tomlak	.08	.25
25 Steve Tuttle	.08	.25
26 Randy Velischek	.15	.40
27 Brad Werenka	.15	.40
28 Phil Wittliff CO	.02	.10

1995-96 Milwaukee Admirals

Card	Low	High
COMPLETE SET (25)	4.00	10.00
1 Shawn Anderson	.20	.50
2 Jergus Baca	.20	.50
3 Gino Cavallini	.30	.75
4 Joe Cirella	.20	.50
5 Sylvain Couturier	.20	.50
6 Tom Draper	.30	.75
7 Robert Guillet	.20	.50
8 Tony Hrkac	.30	.75
9 Fabian Joseph	.20	.50
10 Mark LaForest	.30	.75
11 Dave MacIsaac	.20	.50
12 Mike McNeill	.20	.50
13 Dave Mackey	.20	.50
14 Kent Paynter	.20	.50
15 Ken Sabourin	.20	.50
16 Andrew Shier	.20	.50
17 Tom Tilley	.20	.50
18 Mike Tomlak	.20	.50
19 Steve Tuttle	.20	.50
20 Terry Yake	.30	.75
21 Phil Wittliff CO	.02	.10
22 Peter Bakovic ASST CO	.02	.10
23 Rob Irsch ASST CO	.02	.10
24 Doug Agnew TR	.02	.10
25 Dream Ride	.02	.10

1995-96 Milwaukee Admirals Postcards

Card	Low	High
COMPLETE SET (21)	10.00	25.00
1 Dave MacIsaac	.40	1.00
2 Kent Paynter	.40	1.00
3 Garry Gulash	.40	1.00
4 Jergus Baca	.40	1.00
5 Fabian Joseph	.40	1.00
6 Sylvain Couturier	.40	1.00
7 Mike McNeill	.40	1.00
8 Terry Yake	.40	1.00
9 David Mackey	.40	1.00
10 Bruce Ramsay	.40	1.00
11 Tony Hrkac	.75	2.00
12 Robert Guillet	.40	1.00
13 Shawn Anderson	.40	1.00
14 Andrew Shier	.40	1.00
15 Steve Tuttle	.40	1.00
16 Mike Tomlak	.40	1.00
17 Tom Draper	.75	2.00
18 Mark Laforest	.75	2.00
19 Mikhail Kravets	.40	1.00
20 Gino Cavallini	.75	2.00
21 Ken Sabourin	.40	1.00

1996-97 Milwaukee Admirals

Card	Low	High
COMPLETE SET (27)	4.00	10.00
1 Doug Agnew TR	.02	.10
2 Peter Bakovic ACO	.02	.10
3 Sylvain Couturier	.15	.40
4 Larry DePalma	.15	.40
5 Peter Douris	.15	.40
6 Denny Felsner	.15	.40
7 Eric Fenton	.15	.40
8 Shannon Finn	.15	.40
9 Tony Hrkac	.30	.75
10 Fabian Joseph ASST CO	.15	.40
11 Jacques Joubert	.15	.40
12 Rick Knickle	.30	.75
13 Brad Layzell	.15	.40
14 Danny Lorenz	.30	.75
15 Chris Luongo	.15	.40
16 Dave Mackey	.15	.40
17 Mike McNeill	.15	.40
18 Michel Mongeau	.30	.75
19 Kent Paynter	.15	.40
20 Christian Proulx	.15	.40
21 Patrice Robitaille	.15	.40
22 Ken Sabourin	.15	.40
23 Steve Strunk	.15	.40
24 Tom Tilley	.15	.40
25 Mike Tomlak	.15	.40
26 Steve Tuttle	.15	.40
27 Phil Wittliff CO	.02	.10

1997-98 Milwaukee Admirals

Card	Low	High
COMPLETE SET (25)	4.00	10.00
1 Jason Cipolla	.15	.40
2 Kerry Clark	.15	.40
3 Jarrett Deuling	.15	.40
4 Kelly Fairchild	.20	.50
5 Eric Fenton	.15	.40
6 Shannon Finn	.15	.40
7 Martin Gendron	.30	.75
8 Mike Harder	.15	.40
9 Marc Hussey	.15	.40
10 Danny Lorenz	.30	.75
11 Dave MacIntyre	.15	.40
12 Mike McNeill	.15	.40
13 Don McSween	.15	.40
14 Jeff Nelson	.15	.40
15 Brent Peterson	.15	.40
16 Christian Proulx	.15	.40
17 Ken Sabourin	.15	.40
18 Mike Tomlak	.15	.40
19 Mike Torchia	.20	.50
20 Steve Tuttle	.15	.40
21 Mark Visheau	.15	.40
22 Al Sims HCO	.02	.10
23 Peter Bakovic ACO	.02	.10
24 Fabian Joseph ACO	.02	.10
25 Doug Agnew TR	.02	.10

1998-99 Milwaukee Admirals

Card	Low	High
COMPLETE SET (24)	4.00	10.00
1 Al Sims CO	.02	.10
2 Jeff Daniels	.15	.40
3 Sergei Klimentiev	.15	.40
4 Chris Mason	.20	.50
5 Eric Fenton	.15	.40
6 Shannon Finn	.15	.40
7 Jason Cipolla	.15	.40
8 Jeff Kealty	.15	.40
9 Bobby Russell	.15	.40
10 David Gosselin	.30	.75
11 Richard Lintner	.30	.75
12 Jeff Nelson	.20	.50
13 Kay Whitmore	.25	.60
14 Claude Noel ACO	.02	.10
15 Karlis Skrastins	.20	.50
16 Mark Mowers	.20	.50
17 Craig Darby	.20	.50
18 Roscoe MASCOT	.02	.10
19 Doug Friedman	.15	.40
20 Matt Henderson	.15	.40
21 Marc Moro	.30	.75
22 Petr Sykora	.30	.75
23 Jeff Staples	.15	.40
24 Marian Cisar	.40	1.00

1998-99 Milwaukee Admirals Postcards

Card	Low	High
COMPLETE SET (11)	4.00	10.00
1 Doug Friedman	.20	.50
2 Brad Smyth	.20	.50
3 Jeff Staples	.20	.50
4 Matt Henderson	.20	.50
5 Petr Sykora	.40	1.00
6 Jeff Kealty	.20	.50
7 Jason Cipolla	.20	.50
8 Richard Lintner	.30	.75
9 Kimmo Timonen	.30	.75
10 Vitali Yachmenev	.30	.75
11 Tomas Vokoun	1.25	3.00

1999-00 Milwaukee Admirals Keebler

Card	Low	High
COMPLETE SET (20)	6.00	15.00
1 Corey Hirsch	.40	1.00
2 Marian Cisar	.40	1.00
3 Chris Mason	.40	1.00
4 Jayme Filipowicz	.40	1.00
5 Bubba Berenzweig	.40	1.00
6 Mark Mowers	.40	1.00
7 Brent Peterson	.40	1.00
8 Phil Crowe	.40	1.00
9 Dan Keczmer	.40	1.00
10 Jason Dawe	.40	1.00
11 Eric Fenton	.40	1.00
12 Matt Eldred	.40	1.00
13 Alexandre Boikov	.40	1.00
14 Marc Moro	.40	1.00
15 Paul Healey	.40	1.00
16 Daniel Riva	.40	1.00
17 Ryan Tobler	.40	1.00
18 David Gosselin	.40	1.00
19 Al Sims CO	.40	1.00
20 Claude Noel ACO	.40	1.00

2000-01 Milwaukee Admirals Keebler

Card	Low	High
COMMON CARD (20)	8.00	20.00
1 Jonas Andersson	.60	1.50
2 Denis Arkhipov	.60	2.00
3 Bubba Berenzweig	.30	.75
4 Greg Classen	.30	1.00
5 Mark Eaton	.30	.75
6 Jayme Filipowicz	.30	.75
7 Sean Haggerty	.30	.75
8 Jan Lasak	.40	2.00
9 Chris Mason	.40	1.00
10 Marc Moro	.40	1.00
11 Mark Mowers	.30	1.00
12 John Namestnikov	.30	.75
13 Ville Peltonen	.40	1.00
14 Daniel Riva	.30	.75
15 Petr Sachl	.30	.75
16 Pavel Skrbek	.30	1.00
17 Jeremy Stevenson	.30	1.00
18 Ryan Tobler	.30	.75
19 Alexei Vasiliev	.30	.75
20 Mike Watt	.30	.75

2000-01 Milwaukee Admirals Postcards

Card	Low	High
COMPLETE SET (18)	6.00	15.00
1 Jonas Andersson	.60	1.50
2 Andrew Berenzweig	.30	.75
3 Alexandre Boikov	.30	.75
4 Jayme Filipowicz	.30	.75
5 David Gosselin	.60	1.50
6 Jason Goulet	.30	.75
7 Sean Haggerty	.30	.75
8 Jan Lasak	.80	2.00
9 Chris Mason	.40	1.00
10 Mark Mowers	.40	1.00
11 Ville Peltonen	.40	1.00
12 Dan Riva	.30	.75
13 Petr Sachl	.30	.75
14 Pavel Skrbek	.40	1.00
15 Ryan Tobler	.30	.75
16 Alexei Vasiliev	.30	.75
17 Mike Watt	.30	.75
18 Alex Westlund	.30	.75

2001-02 Milwaukee Admirals

Card	Low	High
COMPLETE SET (25)	8.00	20.00
1 Erik Anderson	.30	.75
2 Jonas Andersson	.30	.75
3 Martin Bartek	.30	.75
4 Bubba Berenzweig	.30	.75
5 Alexandre Boikov	.30	.75
6 Frederic Bouchard	.30	.75
7 Marian Cisar	.40	1.00
8 Kevin Dean	.30	.75
9 Steve Dubinsky	.30	.75
10 David Gosselin	.40	1.00
11 Jason Goulet	.30	.75
12 Chris Mason	.40	1.00
13 Brett Hauer	.30	.75
14 Timo Helbling	.30	.75
15 Jan Lasak	.75	2.00
16 Jay Legault	.30	.75
17 Bryan Lundbohm	.30	.75
18 Marc Moro	.60	1.50
19 Mark Mowers	.40	1.00
20 Konstantin Panov	.30	.75
21 Nathan Perrott	.60	1.50
22 Petr Sachl	.30	.75
23 Yves Sarault	.30	.75
24 Robert Schnabel	.30	.75
25 Jeremy Stevenson	.30	.75

2001-02 Milwaukee Admirals Postcards

Card	Low	High
COMPLETE SET (11)	2.00	5.00
1 Robert Schnabel	.20	.50
2 Bryan Lundbohm	.20	.50
3 Yves Sarault	.20	.50
4 Timo Helbling	.20	.50
5 Martin Bartek	.20	.50
6 Kevin Dean	.20	.50
7 David Gosselin	.30	.75
8 Marc Moro	.40	1.00
9 Jason Goulet	.20	.50
10 Jonas Andersson	.20	.50
11 Roscoe MASCOT	.10	.25

2002-03 Milwaukee Admirals

Card	Low	High
COMPLETE SET (25)	15.00	40.00
1 Tomas Kloucek	1.25	3.00
2 Chris Madden	1.25	3.00
3 Wyatt Smith	.40	1.00
4 Brian Finley	1.25	3.00
5 Dan Hamhuis	1.25	3.00
6 Andrew Hutchinson	.75	2.00
7 Robert Schnabel	.40	1.00
8 Bob Wren	.40	1.00
9 Reid Simpson	.40	1.00
10 Jan Lasak	1.25	3.00
11 Cameron Mann	.75	2.00
12 Domenic Pittis	.75	2.00
13 Martin Erat	.75	2.00
14 Jonas Andersson	.40	1.00
15 Greg Koehler	.40	1.00
16 Bubba Berenzweig	.40	1.00
17 Konstantin Panov	.40	1.00
18 Peter Smrek	.40	1.00
19 Vernon Fiddler	.40	1.00
20 Jason Beckett	.40	1.00
21 Greg Classen	.40	1.00
22 Timo Helbling	.40	1.00
23 Darren Haydar	.75	2.00
24 Pascal Trepanier	.40	1.00
25 Bryan Lundbohm	.40	1.00

2002-03 Milwaukee Admirals Postcards

Card	Low	High
COMPLETE SET (15)	6.00	15.00
1 Jonas Andersson	.30	.75
2 Jason Beckett	.30	.75
3 Bubba Berenzweig	.30	.75
4 Greg Classen	.30	.75
5 Martin Erat	.60	1.50
6 Vern Fiddler	.30	.75
7 Dan Hamhuis	.75	2.00
8 Darren Haydar	.40	1.00
9 Tomas Kloucek	.75	2.00
10 Jan Lasak	.75	2.00
11 Chris Madden	.75	2.00
12 Cameron Mann	.40	1.00
13 Konstantin Panov	.20	.50
14 Robert Schnabel	.20	.50
15 Pascal Trepanier	.20	.50

2003-04 Milwaukee Admirals

Card	Low	High
COMPLETE SET (30)	6.00	15.00
1 Kirill Safronov	.20	.50
2 Jay Henderson	.20	.50
3 Brian Finley	.30	.75
4 Timo Helbling	.20	.50
5 Cheerleaders	.04	.10
6 Darren Haydar	.30	.75
7 Curtis Murphy	.20	.50
8 Tony Hrkac	.20	.50
9 Andrew Hutchinson	.30	.75
10 Mascot	.04	.10
11 Brad Tiley	.20	.50
12 Timofei Shishkanov	.20	.50
13 Vernon Fiddler	.20	.50
14 Scott Upshall	.75	2.00
15 Claude Noel CO	.04	.10
16 Raitis Ivanans	.20	.50
17 Mathieu Darche	.20	.50
18 Wade Flaherty	.30	.75
19 Brandon Segal	.20	.50
20 Arena	.04	.10
21 Greg Zanon	.20	.50
22 Simon Gamache	.40	1.00
23 Greg Classen	.20	.50
24 Wyatt Smith	.20	.50
25 Team Photo	.10	.25
26 Ray Schultz	.20	.50
27 Mike Farrell	.20	.50
28 Bryan Lundbohm	.20	.50
29 Libor Pivko	.20	.50
30 Todd Richards ACO	.04	.10

2003-04 Milwaukee Admirals Postcards

Card	Low	High
COMPLETE SET (23)	8.00	20.00
1 Greg Classen	.30	.75
2 Mathieu Darche	.30	.75
3 Mike Farrell	.30	.75
4 Vernon Fiddler	.30	.75
5 Brian Finley	.40	1.00
6 Wade Flaherty	.40	1.00
7 Simon Gamache	.60	1.50
8 Darren Haydar	.40	1.00
9 Timo Helbling	.30	.75
10 Jay Henderson	.30	.75
11 Tony Hrkac	.30	.75
12 Andrew Hutchinson	.40	1.00
13 Raitis Ivanans	.30	.75
14 Bryan Lundbohm	.30	.75
15 Curtis Murphy	.30	.75
16 Libor Pivko	.30	.75
17 Kirill Safronov	.30	.75
18 Ray Schultz	.30	.75
19 Timofei Shishkanov	.30	.75
20 Wyatt Smith	.30	.75
21 Brad Tiley	.30	.75
22 Scott Upshall	1.00	2.50
23 Greg Zanon	.30	.75

2004-05 Milwaukee Admirals

Card	Low	High
COMPLETE SET (30)	20.00	50.00
1 Brian Finley	1.25	3.00
2 Jeremy Yablonski	.40	1.00
3 Brad Tiley	.40	1.00
4 Cam Severson	.75	2.00
5 Roscoe MASCOT	.04	.10
6 Seamus Kotyk	.75	2.00
7 Paul Brown	.40	1.00
8 Burke Henry	.40	1.00
9 Libor Pivko	.40	1.00
10 Brendan Yarema	.40	1.00
11 Jerred Smithson	.40	1.00
12 Bryan Lundbohm	.75	2.00
13 Ryan Suter	1.25	3.00
14 Brandon Segal	.40	1.00
15 Calder Cup Winners	.40	1.00
16 Jordin Tootoo	4.00	10.00
17 Scottie Upshall	1.25	3.00
18 Dan Hamhuis	.75	2.00
19 Andrew Hutchinson	.75	2.00
20 Admirals Ice Angels	.40	1.00
21 Greg Zanon	.40	1.00
22 Simon Gamache	.75	2.00
23 Kevin Klein	.40	1.00
24 Wyatt Smith	.40	1.00
25 Todd Richards	.40	1.00
26 Darren Haydar	.40	1.00
27 Timofei Shishkanov	.40	1.00
28 Vernon Fiddler	.40	1.00
29 Tony Hrkac	.40	1.00
30 Claude Noel	.40	1.00

2005-06 Milwaukee Admirals Choice

COMPLETE SET (19) 4.00 10.00
1 Kris Beech .20 .50
2 Sheldon Brookbank .20 .50
3 Paul Brown .20 .50
4 Greg Classen .20 .50
5 Vern Fiddler .20 .50
6 Brian Finley .30 .75
7 Darren Haydar .20 .50
8 Kevin Klein .20 .50
9 Libor Pivko .20 .50
10 T.J. Reynolds .20 .50
11 Pekka Rinne .60 1.50
12 Marco Rosa .20 .50
13 Brandon Segal .20 .50
14 Timofei Shishkanov .20 .50
15 Jordin Tootoo .75 2.00
16 Shea Weber .20 .50
17 Jeremy Yablonski .20 .50
18 Greg Zanon .20 .50
19 Claude Noel HC .02 .10

2005-06 Milwaukee Admirals Pepsi

COMPLETE SET (26) 10.00 25.00
1 Kris Beech .40 1.00
2 Rick Berry .40 1.00
3 Sheldon Brookbank .40 1.00
4 Paul Brown .40 1.00
5 Greg Classen .40 1.00
6 Chris Durno .40 1.00
7 Brian Finley .60 1.50
8 Simon Gamache .40 1.00
9 Darren Haydar .40 1.00
10 Kevin Klein .40 1.00
11 Nathan Lutz .40 1.00
12 Scott May .40 1.00
13 Rich Peverley .40 1.00
14 Libor Pivko .40 1.00
15 T.J. Reynolds .40 1.00
16 Pekka Rinne 1.25 3.00
17 Brandon Segal .40 1.00
18 Zach Stortini .40 1.00
19 Jordin Tootoo 1.25 3.00
20 Scottie Upshall .75 2.00
21 Shea Weber .40 1.00
22 Jeremy Yablonski .40 1.00
23 Greg Zanon .40 1.00
24 Claude Noel HC .02 .10
25 Todd Richards AC .02 .10
26 Roscoe MASCOT .02 .10

2006-07 Milwaukee Admirals

COMPLETE SET (24) 8.00 20.00
1 Ramzi Abid .30 .75
2 Sheldon Brookbank .40 1.00
3 Chris Durno .30 .75
4 Karl Goehring .40 1.00
5 Jason Guerriero .30 .75
6 Alex Henry .30 .75
7 Bracken Kearns .30 .75
8 Kevin Klein .30 .75
9 Ville Koistinen .30 .75
10 John Laliberte .30 .75
11 Patrick Leahy .30 .75
12 Cal O'Reilly .30 .75
13 Rich Peverley .30 .75
14 T.J. Reynolds .30 .75
15 Pekka Rinne .40 1.00
16 Brandon Segal .30 .75
17 Kim Staal .30 .75
18 Victor Uchevatov .30 .75
19 John Vigilante .30 .75
20 Kelsey Wilson .60 1.50
21 Nolan Yonkman .30 .75
22 Claude Noel CO .10 .25
23 Lane Lambert ACO .10 .25
24 Roscoe MASCOT .02 .10

2007-08 Milwaukee Admirals

COMPLETE SET (24) 4.00 10.00
1 Dov Grumet-Morris .50 1.25
2 Bryan Schmidt .15 .40
3 Cody Franson .50 1.25
4 Ryan Maki .15 .40
5 Mike Santorelli .15 .40
6 John Vigilanti .15 .40
7 Andreas Thuresson .15 .40
8 Jason Guerriero .15 .40
9 John Laliberti .15 .40
10 Cal O'reilly .15 .40
11 Kelsey Wilson .15 .40
12 Mark Matheson .15 .40
13 Matt Ellison .15 .40
14 Josh Langfeld .15 .40
15 Kevin Ulanski .15 .40
16 Janne Niskala .15 .40
17 Alex Henry .15 .40
18 Pekka Rinne .15 .40
19 Rich Peverley .15 .40
20 Antti Pihlstrom .15 .40
21 Nolan Yonkman .15 .40
22 Alexander Sulzer .15 .40
23 Lane Lambert .15 .40
24 Brad Lauer .15 .40

2014-15 Milwaukee Admirals

COMPLETE SET (25) 6.00 15.00
1 Pontus Aberg .30 .75
2 Johan Alm .30 .75
3 Taylor Aronson .30 .75
4 Viktor Arvidsson .30 .75
5 Anthony Bitetto .30 .75
6 Zach Budish .30 .75
7 Patrick Cehlin .30 .75
8 Richard Clune .30 .75
9 Jonathan-Ismael Diaby .30 .75
10 Frederick Gaudreau .30 .75
11 Felix Girard .30 .75
12 Triston Grant .30 .75
13 Magnus Hellberg .30 .75
14 Brendan Leipsic .30 .75
15 Michael Liambas .30 .75
16 Marek Mazanec .40 1.00
17 Garrett Noonan .30 .75
18 Jimmy Oligny .30 .75
19 Joseph Pendenza .30 .75
20 Joe Piskula .30 .75
21 Miikka Salomaki .30 .75
22 Josh Shalla .30 .75
23 Colton Sissons .30 .75
24 Mark Van Guilder .30 .75
25 Austin Watson .30 .75

1984-85 Minnesota-Duluth Bulldogs

COMPLETE SET (33) 35.00 75.00
1 Ben Duffey .40 1.00
2 Brett Hull 25.00 50.00
3 Danny May .40 1.00
4 Dave Morrow .40 1.00
5 Joe Delisle .40 1.00
6 Brian Nelson .40 1.00
7 Jon Downing .40 1.00
8 Brian Nelson .40 1.00
9 Sean Toomey .40 1.00
10 Brian Durand .40 1.00
11 Jim Plankers .40 1.00
12 Mark Odnokon .40 1.00
13 Jim Sprenger .40 1.00
14 Tom Lorentz .40 1.00
15 Darin Illikainen .40 1.00
16 Rick Kosti .40 1.00
17 Norm Maciver .75 2.00
18 Guy Gosselin .40 1.00
19 Matt Christensen .40 1.00
20 Jim Johnson .75 2.00
21 Mark Baron .40 1.00
22 Bill Watson .40 1.00
23 Bruce Fishback .40 1.00
24 Dave Cowan .40 1.00
25 Mike Cortes .40 1.00
26 Jim Toninato .40 1.00
27 Skeeter Moore .40 1.00
28 Mike DeAngelis .40 1.00
29 Tom Herzig .40 1.00
30 Mike Sertich CO .08 .25
31 Bulldog Cheerleaders .40 1.00
32 Bulldogs Assistants .08 .25
33 Team Photo .08 .25

1985-86 Minnesota-Duluth Bulldogs

COMPLETE SET (36) 12.00 30.00
1 Skeeter Moore .30 .75
2 Terry Shold .20 .50
3 Mike DeAngelis .20 .50
4 Rob Pallin .20 .50
5 Norm Maciver .30 .75
6 Wayne Smith .20 .50
7 Dave Cowan .20 .50
8 Darin Illikainen .20 .50
9 Rick Hayko .20 .50
10 Guy Gosselin .30 .75
11 Paul Roff .20 .50
12 Jim Toninato .20 .50
13 Tom Hanson .20 .50
14 Mike Cortes .20 .50
15 Matt Christensen .20 .50
16 Bruce Fishback .20 .50
17 Mark Odnokon .20 .50
18 Brian Johnson .20 .50
19 Bob Alexander .20 .50
20 Tom Lorentz .20 .50
21 Roman Sindelar .20 .50
22 Jim Sprenger .20 .50
23 Dan Tousignant .20 .50
24 Sean Toomey .20 .50
25 Brian Durand .20 .50
26 John Hyduke .20 .50
27 Brian Nelson .20 .50
28 Brett Hull 8.00 20.00
29 Joe DeLisle .20 .50
30 Pat Janostin .20 .50
31 Ben Duffy .20 .50
32 Sean Krakiwsky .20 .50
33 Mike Sertich .20 .50
34 Coaching Staff
Jim Knapp ACO
Glenn Kulyk ACO
Tim McDonald ACO
Mike Valesano ACO
Rick Menz EQUIP
Dale Hoganson EQUIP
Betty Fleissner TR .08 .25
35 Cheerleaders .40 1.00
36 Jay Jackson (Mascot) .08 .25

1993-94 Minnesota-Duluth Bulldogs

COMPLETE SET (30) 4.00 10.00
1 Rod Aldoff .15 .40
2 Niklas Axelson .15 .40
3 David Buck .15 .40
4 Jerome Butler .15 .40
5 Brian Caruso .20 .50
6 Matt Christian
Chet Culic .20 .50
7 Marc Christian .15 .40
8 Joe Ciccarello .15 .40
9 Kyle Erickson
Adam Roy .15 .40
10 Brad Federenko .20 .50
11 Rusty Fitzgerald .20 .50
12 Jason Garatti .15 .40
13 Greg Hanson .20 .50
14 Don Jablonic .15 .40
15 Kraig Karakas .15 .40
16 Brett Larson .20 .50
17 Taras Lendzyk .15 .40
18 Derek Locker .15 .40
19 Chris Marinucci .20 .50
20 Todd Mickolajak
Chris Snell .20 .50
21 Rod Miller .15 .40
22 Rick Mrozik .20 .50
23 Aaron Novak .15 .40
24 Corey Osmak .15 .40
25 Sergei Petrov .15 .40
26 Jeff Romfo .15 .40
27 Mike Sertich CO .02 .10
28 Chris Sittlow .15 .40
29 Joe Tamminen .15 .40
30 Title Card
Roster .08 .25

1993-94 Minnesota-Duluth Commemorative

COMPLETE SET (4) 1.50 4.00
1 Chris Marinucci .40 1.00
2 Derek Plante .75 2.00
3 Brett Hauer .40 1.00
4 Jon Rohloff .40 1.00

2004-05 Minnesota-Duluth Bulldogs

COMPLETE SET (33) 12.00 30.00
1 Nick Anderson .40 1.00
2 Tyler Brosz .40 1.00
3 T. J. Caig .40 1.00
4 Dan Carlson .40 1.00
5 Mike Curry .40 1.00
6 Steve Czech .40 1.00
7 Travis Gawryletz .40 1.00
8 Ryan Garis .40 1.00
9 Tim Hambly .40 1.00
10 Brett Hammond .40 1.00
11 Josh Johnson .60 1.50
12 Blair Lefebvre .40 1.00
13 Jeff McFarland .40 1.00
14 Bryan McGregor .40 1.00
15 Matt McKnight .60 1.50
16 Josh Miskovich .40 1.00
17 Marco Peluso .40 1.00
18 Neil Petruic .40 1.00
19 Isaac Reichmuth .60 1.50
20 Jay Rosehill .40 1.00
21 Evan Schwabe .60 1.50
22 Todd Smith .40 1.00
23 Tim Stapleton .40 1.00
24 Luke Stauffacher .40 1.00
25 Ryan Swanson .40 1.00
26 Justin Williams .40 1.00
27 Lee Davidson ACO
Scott Sandelin CO
Steve Rohlik .04 .10
28 Tom Kurvers .40 1.00
29 Junior Lessard .75 2.00
30 Chris Marinucci .75 2.00
31 Bill Watson .40 1.00
32 Mascots .04 .10
33 Sponsor .04 .10

1991-92 Minnesota Golden Gophers

COMPLETE SET (26) 6.00 15.00
1 Scott Bell .20 .50
2 Tony Bianchi .20 .50
3 John Brill .20 .50
4 Jeff Callinan .20 .50
5 Joe Dziedzic .30 .75
6 Sean Fabian .20 .50
7 Jed Fiebelkorn .20 .50
8 Nick Gerebi .20 .50
9 Darby Hendrickson .30 .75
10 Craig Johnson .30 .75
11 Trent Klatt .40 1.00
12 Cory Laylin .20 .50
13 Steve Magnusson .30 .75
14 Chris McAlpine .30 .75
15 Justin McHugh .20 .50
16 Eric Means .20 .50
17 Mike Muller .20 .50
18 Tom Newman .20 .50
19 Jeff Nielsen .20 .50
20 John O'Connell .20 .50
21 Larry Olimb .20 .50
22 Travis Richards .20 .50
23 Brandon Steege .20 .50
24 Jeff Stolp .20 .50
25 Todd Westlund .20 .50
26 Doug Zmolek .30 .75

1992-93 Minnesota Golden Gophers

COMPLETE SET (25) 4.00 10.00
1 Scott Bell .15 .40
2 Jesse Bertogliat
Brian Bonin .40 1.00
3 Tony Bianchi .15 .40
4 John Brill .15 .40
5 Jeff Callinan .15 .40
6 Bobby Dustin
Dave Larson .15 .40
7 Joe Dziedzic .20 .50
8 Jed Fiebelkorn .15 .40
9 Darby Hendrickson .20 .50
10 Craig Johnson .15 .40
11 Steve Magnusson .20 .50
12 Chris McAlpine .20 .50
13 Justin McHugh .15 .40
14 Eric Means .15 .40
15 Jeff Moen .15 .40
16 Tom Newman .15 .40
17 Jeff Nielsen .20 .50
18 Travis Richards .15 .40
19 Brandon Steege .15 .40
20 Matt Stelljes
Ryan Alstead .15 .40
21 Dan Trebil
Greg Zwakman .02 .10
22 Charlie Wasley
Mike McAlpine .15 .40
23 Todd Westlund .15 .40
24 Dan Woog
Jim Hillman .08 .25
25 Doug Woog CO .08 .25

1993-94 Minnesota Golden Gophers

COMPLETE SET (30) 6.00 100.00
1 Brett Abrahamson 1.50 4.00
2 Jesse Bertogliat 1.50 4.00
3 Tony Bianchi 1.50 4.00
4 Brian Bonin 2.00 5.00
5 Andy Brink 1.50 4.00
6 Jeff Callinan 1.50 4.00
7 Nick Checco 1.50 4.00
8 Bobby Dustin 1.50 4.00
9 Joe Dziedzic 2.00 5.00
10 Jed Fiebelkorn 1.50 4.00
11 Brent Godbout 1.50 4.00
12 Dan Hendrickson 1.50 4.00
13 Jim Hillman 1.50 4.00
14 John Hillman 1.50 4.00
15 Brian LaFleur 1.50 4.00
16 Dave Larson 1.50 4.00
17 Steve Magnusson 1.50 4.00
18 Chris McAlpine 2.00 5.00
19 Mike McAlpine 1.50 4.00
20 Justin McHugh 1.50 4.00
21 Eric Means 1.50 4.00
22 Jeff Moen 1.50 4.00
23 Jeff Nielsen 2.00 5.00
24 Brandon Steege 1.50 4.00
25 Dan Trebil 1.50 4.00
26 Charlie Wasley 1.50 4.00
27 Dan Woog ACO .40 1.00
28 Doug Woog CO .75 2.00
29 Greg Zwakman 1.50 4.00
30 Title Card .02 .10

1994-95 Minnesota Golden Gophers

COMPLETE SET (31) 10.00 25.00
1 Will Anderson .30 .75
2 Scott Bell .30 .75
3 Jesse Bertogliat .30 .75
4 Brian Bonin .40 1.00
5 Andy Brink .30 .75
6 Aaron Broten
Neal Brote .75 2.00
7 Jeff Callinan .30 .75
8 Nick Checco .30 .75
9 Mike Crowley .75 2.00
10 Steve DeBus .30 .75
11 Bobby Dustin .30 .75
12 Jed Fiebelkorn .30 .75
13 Brent Godbout .30 .75
14 Jason Godbout .30 .75
15 Casey Hankinson .30 .75
16 Dan Hendrickson .30 .75
17 Ryan Kraft .30 .75
18 Brian LaFleur .30 .75
19 Dave Larson .30 .75
20 Justin McHugh .30 .75
21 Jeff Moen .30 .75
22 Jay Moser .30 .75
23 Lou Nanne .40 1.00
24 Joe Pankratz .30 .75
25 Jason Seils .30 .75
26 Brandon Steege .30 .75
27 Dan Trebil .40 1.00
28 Charlie Wasley .30 .75
29 Dan Woog .08 .25
30 Doug Woog CO .08 .25
31 Greg Zwakman .30 .75

1995-96 Minnesota Golden Gophers

COMPLETE SET (30) 100.00 175.00
1 Checklist .40 1.00
2 Doug Woog CO .75 2.00
3 Brett Abrahamson 3.00 6.00
4 Mike Anderson 3.00 6.00
5 Reggie Berg 3.00 6.00
6 Jesse Bertogliat 3.00 6.00
7 Brian Bonin 5.00 10.00
8 Andy Brink 3.00 6.00
9 Nick Checco 3.00 6.00
10 Nick Crowley 3.00 6.00
11 Steve Debus 3.00 6.00
12 Bobby Dustin 3.00 6.00
13 Jason Godbout 3.00 6.00
14 Casey Hankinson 3.00 6.00
15 Dan Hendrickson 3.00 6.00
16 Clint Johnson 3.00 6.00
17 Bill Kohn 3.00 6.00
18 Ryan Kraft 3.00 6.00
19 Brian LaFleur 3.00 6.00
20 Dave Larson 3.00 6.00
21 Jeff Moen 3.00 6.00
22 Jay Moser 3.00 6.00
23 Tom Nevers 3.00 6.00
24 Erik Rasmussen 5.00 10.00
25 Jason Seils 3.00 6.00
26 Wyatt Smith 3.00 6.00
27 Dan Trebil 3.00 6.00
28 Charlie Wasley 3.00 6.00
29 Dan Woog ACO .75 2.00
30 Greg Zwakman 3.00 6.00

1996-97 Minnesota Golden Gophers

COMPLETE SET (27) 25.00 50.00
1 Checklist .02 .10
2 Doug Woog CO .02 .10
3 Brett Abrahamson .60 1.50
4 Mike Anderson .60 1.50
5 Reggie Berg 1.25 3.00
6 Nick Checco 1.25 3.00
7 Ben Clymer 1.25 3.00
8 Mike Crowley 1.25 3.00
9 Eric Day .60 1.50
10 Steve DeBus .60 1.50
11 Brent Godbout .60 1.50
12 Jason Godbout .60 1.50
13 Casey Hankinson 1.25 3.00
14 Dan Hendrickson 1.25 3.00
15 Bill Kohn .60 1.50
16 Ryan Kraft 1.25 3.00
17 Brian LaFleur .60 1.50
18 Mike Lyons .60 1.50
19 Willy Marvin .60 1.50
20 Cory Miller .60 1.50
21 Nate Miller .60 1.50
22 Rico Pagel .60 1.50
23 Erik Rasmussen 1.25 3.00
24 Wyatt Smith 1.25 3.00
25 Dave Spehar .60 1.50
26 Ryan Trebil .60 1.50
27 Dan Woog .02 .10

1997-98 Minnesota Golden Gophers

COMPLETE SET (26) 15.00 30.00
1 Checklist .08 .25
2 Doug Woog HCO .20 .50
3 Mike Anderson .40 1.00
4 Stev Debus .40 1.00
5 Ryan Kraft .60 1.50
6 Nate Miller .40 1.00
7 Brett Abrahamson .40 1.00
8 Erik Day .40 1.00
9 Bill Kohn .40 1.00
10 Cory Miller .40 1.00
11 Ben Clymer .75 2.00
12 Casey Hankinson .40 1.00
13 Willy Marvin .40 1.00
14 Reggie Berg .40 1.00
15 Jason Godbout .40 1.00
16 Mike Lyons .40 1.00
17 Ryan Trebil .40 1.00
18 Dylan Mills .40 1.00
19 Dave Spehar .40 1.00
20 Erik Westrum .75 2.00
21 Wyatt Smith .60 1.50
22 Aaron Miskovich .40 1.00
23 Rico Pagel .40 1.00
24 Matt Leimbeck .40 1.00
25 Stuart Senden .40 1.00
26 Goldy Gopher Mascot .20 .50

1998-99 Minnesota Golden Gophers

COMPLETE SET (30) 20.00 35.00
1 Header Card .02 .10
2 Doug Woog HCO .20 .50
3 Mark Nenovich .40 1.00
4 Erik Wendell .75 2.00
5 Dylan Mills .40 1.00
6 Nate Miller .40 1.00
7 Rob LaRue .40 1.00
8 Reggie Berg .40 1.00
9 Bill Kohn .40 1.00
10 Mike Lyons .40 1.00
11 Cory Miller .40 1.00
12 Mike Anderson .40 1.00
13 Jordon Leopold 1.50 4.00
14 Ryan Westrum .40 1.00
15 Doug Meyer .40 1.00
16 Rico Pagel .40 1.00
17 Stuart Senden .40 1.00
18 Nick Angell .40 1.00
19 Dave Spehar .40 1.00
20 Pat O'Leary .40 1.00
21 Ryan Trebil .40 1.00
22 Adam Hauser .75 2.00
23 Wyatt Smith .75 2.00
24 Brad Timmons .40 1.00
25 Matt Leimbeck .40 1.00
26 Aaron Miskovich .40 1.00
27 Erik Daly .40 1.00
28 Erik Westrum .75 2.00
29 John Pohl .75 2.00
30 Goldy Gopher Mascot .08 .25

1998-99 Minnesota Golden Gophers Women

COMPLETE SET (25) 10.00 25.00
1 Angela Borek .40 1.00
2 Winny Brodt .40 1.00
3 Emily Buchholz .40 1.00
4 Tracy Donaghue .40 1.00
5 Tracy Engstrom .40 1.00
6 Lacey Franzmeier .40 1.00
7 Laura Halldorson CO .08 .25
8 Amber Hegland .40 1.00
9 David Horn ACO .08 .25
10 Courtney Kennedy .40 1.00
11 Shannon Kennedy .40 1.00
12 Erica Killewald .40 1.00
13 Betsey Kukowski .40 1.00
14 Megan Milbert .40 1.00
15 Nadine Muzerall .40 1.00
16 Crystal Nicholas .40 1.00
17 Kelly Olson .40 1.00
18 Sarma Pone .40 1.00
19 Brittny Ralph .40 1.00
20 Jenny Schmidgall 1.25 3.00
21 Kris Scholz .40 1.00
22 Laura Slominski .40 1.00
23 Ambria Thomas .40 1.00
24 Tai Thorsheim .40 1.00
25 Libby Witchger ACO .08 .25

1999-00 Minnesota Golden Gophers

COMPLETE SET (30) 8.00 20.00
1 Nick Angell .20 .50
2 Nick Anthony .20 .50
3 Matt DeMarchi .20 .50
4 Goldy Gopher MAS .08 .25
6 Ben Hamilton .20 .50
7 Adam Hauser .75 2.00
8 Matt Leimbeck .20 .50
9 Jordan Leopold 1.25 3.00
10 Don Lucia CO .08 .25
11 Mike Lyons .20 .50
12 Doug Meyer .20 .50
13 Nate Miller .20 .50
14 Dylan Mills .20 .50
15 Aaron Miskovich .20 .50
16 Mark Nenovich .20 .50
17 Pat O'Leary .20 .50
18 Rico Pagel .20 .50
19 John Pohl 1.25 3.00
20 Chad Roberge .20 .50
21 Pete Samargia .20 .50
22 Stuart Senden .20 .50
23 Dave Spehar .20 .50
24 Jeff Taffe 2.00 5.00
25 Ben Tharp .20 .50
26 Ryan Trebil .20 .50
27 University of Minnesota .08 .25
28 Dan Welch .20 .50
29 Erik Wendell .30 .75
29 Erik Young .20 .50
30 Erik Westrum .40 1.00

2000-01 Minnesota Golden Gophers

COMPLETE SET (28) 15.00 25.00
1 Header Card .02 .10
2 Nick Angell .30 .75
3 Nick Anthony .30 .75
4 Matt DeMarchi .30 .75
5 Goldy Gopher MASCOT .04 .10
6 Adam Hauser .75 2.00
7 Rod Johnson FOOTBALL .30 .75
8 Matt Koalska .30 .75
9 Matt Leimbeck .30 .75
10 Jordan Leopold 1.25 3.00
11 Don Lucia CO .10 .25
12 Joey Martin .30 .75
13 Paul Martin .30 .75
14 Dylan Mills .30 .75
15 Aaron Miskovich .30 .75
16 Mark Nenovich .30 .75
17 Pat O'Leary .30 .75
18 John Pohl .75 2.00
19 Grant Potulny .40 1.00
20 Troy Riddle .30 .75
21 Chad Roberge .30 .75
22 Pete Samargia .30 .75
23 Stuart Senden .30 .75
24 Jeff Taffe 1.25 3.00
25 Ben Tharp .30 .75
26 Jon Waibel .30 .75
27 Erik Wendell .30 .75
28 Erik Westrum .75 2.00

2001-02 Minnesota Golden Gophers

COMPLETE SET (29) 12.00 30.00
1 Header Card .10 .25
2 Don Lucia CO .10 .25
3 Goldy Gopher MASCOT .04 .10
4 Nick Anthony .40 1.00
5 Mike Erickson .40 1.00
6 Chad Roberg .60 1.50
7 Keith Ballard .60 1.50
8 Erik Wendell .60 1.50
9 Paul Martin .40 1.00
10 John Pohl .60 1.50
11 Judd Stevens .40 1.00
12 Jon Waibel .40 1.00
13 Jordan Leopold 1.25 3.00
14 Mark Nenovich .40 1.00
15 Adam Hauser .40 1.00
16 Garrett Smaagaard .40 1.00
17 Grant Potulny .40 1.00
18 Matt DeMarchi .40 1.00
19 Joey Martin .40 1.00
20 Troy Riddle .40 1.00
21 Jeff Taffe 1.25 3.00
22 Matt Koalska .40 1.00
23 Pat O'Leary .40 1.00
24 Nick Angell .40 1.00
25 Barry Tallackson .40 1.00
26 Brett MacKinnon .40 1.00
27 Jake Fleming .40 1.00
28 Travis Weber .40 1.00
29 Justin Johnson .40 1.00

2002-03 Minnesota Golden Gophers

COMPLETE SET (31) 20.00 40.00
1 Nick Anthony .40 1.00
2 P.J. Atherton .40 1.00
3 Keith Ballard 1.00 2.50
4 Matt DeMarchi .40 1.00
5 Mike Erickson .40 1.00
6 Jake Fleming .40 1.00
7 Gino Guyer .60 1.50
8 Chris Harrington .40 1.00
9 Tyler Hirsch .40 1.00
10 Justin Johnson .40 1.00
11 Peter Kennedy .40 1.00
12 Matt Koalska .40 1.00
13 Brett MacKinnon .40 1.00
14 Joey Martin .40 1.00
15 Paul Martin .75 2.00
16 Grant Potulny .60 1.50
17 Jerrid Reinholz .40 1.00
18 Troy Riddle .40 1.00
19 Chad Roberg .40 1.00
20 Andrew Sertich .40 1.00
21 Garrett Smaagaard .40 1.00
22 Dustin Smieja .40 1.00
23 Judd Stevens .40 1.00
24 Barry Tallackson .75 2.00
25 Thomas Vanek 6.00 15.00
26 Jon Waibel .40 1.00
27 Travis Weber .40 1.00
28 Dan Welch .40 1.00
29 Don Lucia HCO .10 .25
30 Goldy Gopher Mascot .04 .10
31 NCAA Champs .20 .50

2003-04 Minnesota Golden Gophers

COMPLETE SET (28) 20.00 40.00
1 Barry Tallackson .75 2.00
2 Jake Taylor .50 1.25
3 Thomas Vanek 3.00 8.00
4 Mike Vannelli .50 1.25
5 Jon Waibel .50 1.25
6 Dustin Smieja .50 1.25
7 Championship Team Photo .10 .25
8 Don Lucia CO .04 .10
9 P.J. Atherton .50 1.25
10 Keith Ballard 1.00 2.50
11 Kellen Briggs .75 2.00
12 Jake Fleming .50 1.25
13 Gino Guyer 1.00 2.50
14 Chris Harrington .50 1.25
15 Tyler Hirsch .50 1.25
16 Dan Irmen .75 2.00
17 Justin Johnson .75 2.00
18 Peter Kennedy .50 1.25
19 Matt Koalska .60 1.50
20 Brett MacKinnon .50 1.25
21 Joey Martin .50 1.25
22 Grant Potulny .50 1.25
23 Ryan Potulny 1.25 3.00
24 Jerrid Reinholz .50 1.25
25 Troy Riddle .50 1.25
26 Andy Sertich .60 1.50
27 Garrett Smaagaard .50 1.25
28 Judd Stevens .50 1.25

2004-05 Minnesota Golden Gophers

COMPLETE SET (27) 10.00 25.00
1 PJ Atherton .40 1.00
2 Brent Borgen .40 1.00
3 Kellen Briggs .60 1.50
4 Kris Chucko .75 2.00
5 Jake Fleming .40 1.00
6 Alex Goligoski 1.25 3.00
7 Ben Gordon .40 1.00
8 Gino Guyer .40 1.00
9 Nate Hagemo .40 1.00
10 Chris Harrington .40 1.00
11 Tyler Hirsch .40 1.00
12 Mike Howe .40 1.00
13 Danny Irmen .40 1.00
14 Justin Johnson .60 1.50
15 Evan Kaufman .40 1.00
16 Peter Kennedy .40 1.00
17 Don Lucia .40 1.00
18 Derek Peltier .40 1.00
19 Tom Pohl .40 1.00
20 Ryan Potulny .40 1.00
21 Jerrid Reinholz .40 1.00
22 Andy Sertich .75 2.00
23 Garrett Smaagaard .40 1.00
24 Brent Solei .40 1.00
25 Judd Stevens .40 1.00
26 Barry Tallackson .40 1.00
27 Mike Vannelli .40 1.00

2004-05 Minnesota Golden Gophers Women

COMPLETE SET (14) 6.00 15.00
1 Natalie Darwitz 1.00 2.50
2 Krissy Wendell 1.00 2.50
3 Anya Miller .40 1.00
4 Erica McKenzie .40 1.00
5 Natalie Lamme .40 1.00
6 Krista Johnson .40 1.00
7 Jody Horak .40 1.00
8 Stacy Troumbly .40 1.00
9 Becky Wacker .40 1.00
10 Lyndsay Wall .40 1.00
11 Whitney Graft .40 1.00
12 Chelsey Brodt .40 1.00
13 Ashley Albrecht .40 1.00
14 Laura Halldorson CO .04 .10

2005-06 Minnesota Golden Gophers

COMPLETE SET (27) 15.00 30.00
1 R.J. Anderson .30 .75
2 P.J. Atherton .30 .75
3 Brent Borgen .30 .75
4 Justin Bostrom .30 .75
5 Kellen Briggs .30 .75
6 Kris Chucko .60 1.50
7 Jeff Frazee 1.25 3.00
8 Alex Goligoski .75 2.00
9 Ben Gordon .30 .75
10 Gino Guyer .40 1.00
11 Nate Hagemo .40 1.00
12 Chris Harrington .30 .75
13 Mike Howe .30 .75
14 Danny Irmen .40 1.00
15 Evan Kaufmann .30 .75
16 Peter Kennedy .30 .75
17 Phil Kessel 4.00 10.00
18 Derek Peltier .30 .75
19 Tom Pohl .30 .75
20 Ryan Potulny 1.25 3.00
21 Andy Sertich .30 .75
22 Brent Solei .30 .75
23 Ryan Stoa .60 1.50
24 Mike Vannelli .30 .75
25 Blake Wheeler .75 2.00
26 Don Lucia HC .02 .10
27 Goldy Gopher MASCOT .02 .10

2006-07 Minnesota Golden Gophers

COMPLETE SET (25) 25.00 35.00
1 R.J. Anderson .40 1.00
2 Jay Barriball .60 1.50
3 Justin Bostrom .40 1.00
4 Kellen Briggs .40 1.00
5 Mike Carman .40 1.00
6 David Fischer .40 1.00
7 Ryan Flynn .40 1.00
8 Jeff Frazee .75 2.00
9 Alex Goligoski .75 2.00
10 Ben Gordon .40 1.00
11 Mike Howe .40 1.00
12 Erik Johnson 2.00 5.00
13 Evan Kaufmann .40 1.00
14 Tony Lucia .40 1.00
15 Jim O'Brien .75 2.00
16 Kyle Okposo 2.00 5.00
17 Derek Peltier .40 1.00
18 Tom Pohl .40 1.00
19 Brian Schack .40 1.00
20 Brent Solei .40 1.00
21 Ryan Stoa .75 2.00
22 Mike Vannelli .40 1.00
23 Blake Wheeler .75 2.00
24 Don Lucia CO .10 .25
25 Goldy Gopher MASCOT .10 .25

2007-08 Minnesota Golden Gophers

COMPLETE SET (25) 4.00 10.00
1 R.J. Anderson .15 .40
2 Jay Barriball .15 .40
3 Stu Bickel .30 .75
4 Justin Bostrom .15 .40
5 Mike Carman .15 .40
6 Cade Fairchild .15 .40
7 David Fischer .15 .40
8 Drew Fisher .15 .40
9 Ryan Flynn .15 .40
10 Jeff Frazee .15 .40
11 Ben Gordon .15 .40
12 Mike Hoeffel .15 .40
13 Mike Howe .15 .40
14 Alex Kangas .15 .40
15 Evan Kaufmann .15 .40

16 Tony Lucia .15 .40
17 Derek Peltier .15 .40
18 Tom Pohl .15 .40
19 Brian Schack .15 .40
20 Brent Solei .15 .40
21 Ryan Stor .15 .40
22 Kevin Wehrs .15 .40
23 Blake Wheeler .15 .40
24 Patrick White .15 .40
25 Don Lucia HC .10 .40

1994-95 Minnesota Moose
COMPLETE SET (16) 8.00 20.00
1 Dave Christian .60 1.50
2 Kris Miller .60 1.50
3 John Young .60 1.50
4 Tom Draper .75 2.00
5 Daniel Shank .60 1.50
6 Dean Kolstad .60 1.50
7 Yvon Corriveau .60 1.50
8 Frank Serratore CO .20 .50
9 Dave Snuggerud .60 1.50
10 Mark Osiecki .60 1.50
11 Brad Miller .60 1.50
12 Frank Pietrangelo .75 2.00
13 Stephane Morin .60 1.50
14 Sean Williams .60 1.50
15 Dave Hakstol .60 1.50
16 Mick E. Moose MAS .20 .50

1995-96 Minnesota Moose
COMPLETE SET (16) 6.00 15.00
1 Dave Christian .40 1.00
2 Chris Jensen .40 1.00
3 Sandy Smith .60 1.50
4 Stephane Morin .60 1.50
5 Dave Gagnon .60 1.50
6 Sean Williams .40 1.00
7 Yvon Corriveau .40 1.00
8 Chris Govedaris .40 1.00
9 Mike Hurlbut .40 1.00
10 Dave Hakstol .40 1.00
11 Bryan Fogarty .40 1.00
12 Dave Morissette .40 1.00
13 Brad Miller .40 1.00
14 Kris Miller .40 1.00
15 Frank Serratore CO .20 .50
16 Mick E. Moose,MASCOT .20 .50

2003-04 Minnesota State Mavericks
COMPLETE SET (20) 8.00 20.00
1 Cole Bassett .40 1.00
2 Brock Becker .40 1.00
3 Jake Brenk .40 1.00
4 Chad Clower .40 1.00
5 Jon Dubel .40 1.00
6 Aaron Forsythe .40 1.00
7 Adam Gerlach .40 1.00
8 Jon Hart .40 1.00
9 Steven Johns .50 1.25
10 Shane Joseph .40 1.00
11 Rick Kisskeys .40 1.00
12 Jeff Marler .40 1.00
13 Ryan McKelvie .40 1.00
14 Nate Metcalf .40 1.00
15 Kyle Nixon .60 1.50
16 Matt Paluczak .40 1.00
17 Dana Sorensen .40 1.00
18 Brad Thompson .40 1.00
19 Christian Toll .40 1.00
20 Jon Volp .60 1.50

2000-01 Mississauga Ice Dogs
COMPLETE SET (28) 8.00 20.00
Team CL .04 .10
Brett Angel .20 .50
Bluo and Baby Bluo MASCOT .10 .25
Grant Buckley .15 .40
Don Cherry OWN .75 2.00
Steve Cherry CO .04 .10
Fraser Clair .15 .40
Mark Cranley .15 .40
David Dalliday .15 .40
Andrew Davis .15 .40
Justin Dumont .15 .40
Omar Ennaffati .15 .40
John Jarram .15 .40
Patrick Jarrett .40 1.00
Brent Labre .15 .40
Brian McGrattan .15 .40
Sean McMorrow .40 1.00
Michael Mole .40 1.00
Chris Osborne .15 .40
Jeff Paisley .15 .40
Brandon Robinson .15 .40
Adam Solnik .15 .40
Jason Spezza 4.00 10.00
Dan Sullivan .15 .40
Chris Thaler .15 .40
Rick Vaive CO .10 .25
Mike Wehrstedt .15 .40
Chad Wiseman .15 .40

2001-02 Mississauga Ice Dogs
COMPLETE SET (26) 5.00 12.00
Team card .04 .10
Matt Tanel .15 .40
J. Reynolds .15 .40
Travis Parent .15 .40
Nathan O'Nabigon .15 .40
Patrick O'Sullivan .60 1.50
Chris Churran .15 .40
Dan Rudisuela .15 .40
Mike Wehrstedt .15 .40
Tyler Eady .15 .40
John Kozoriz .15 .40
Adam Sturgeon .15 .40
Chris Hawley .15 .40
Alexander Skorohod .15 .40
Miguel Beaudry .15 .40
Andrew Smale .15 .40
Bobby Turner .15 .40
John Eminger .15 .40
Igor Radulov .75 2.00
Greg Jacina .15 .40
Mike Barrett .15 .40
Daniel Sisca .15 .40
Don Cherry OWN .75 2.00
24 Steve Cherry GM .04 .10
25 Joel Washkurak ACO .04 .10
26 Blue MASCOT .04 .10

2002-03 Mississauga Ice Dogs
COMPLETE SET (31) 6.00 15.00
1 Checklist .04 .10
2 Travis Parent .20 .50
3 Ian Maracle .20 .50
4 Scott Hotham .20 .50
5 Derek Lyons .20 .50
6 Chris Curran .20 .50
7 Dan Rudisuela .20 .50
8 Tyler Eady .20 .50
9 Tomas Linhart .30 .75
10 Chris Hawley .20 .50
11 Pavel Voroshin .30 .75
12 Wes Rypien .20 .50
13 Miguel Beaudry .30 .75
14 Matt Harpwood .30 .75
15 Daniel Buccella .20 .50
16 Rob Schremp 1.25 3.00
17 Salvatore Malandrino .20 .50
18 Greg Jacina .20 .50
19 Ryan Stokes .20 .50
20 Patrick O'Sullivan .60 1.50
21 Dany Revelle .20 .50
22 Blair Jarrett .20 .50
23 Daniel Sisca .20 .50
25 Matt Harpwood .20 .50
26 Steve Ludzik .20 .50
27 Mark Osborne .20 .50
28 Wayne Crawford .20 .50
29 Dave Sweetman .20 .50
30 Kevin Elliot .20 .50
31 Blue the mascot .10 .25

2003-04 Mississauga Ice Dogs
COMPLETE SET (24) 5.00 12.00
1 Adam Abraham .20 .50
2 Chris Bain .30 .75
3 Cody Bass .20 .50
4 Anthony Butera .20 .50
5 Rick Caughell .20 .50
6 Chris Chimienti .20 .50
7 Chris Curran .20 .50
8 Brad Efthimiou .20 .50
9 Brandon Elliott .20 .50
10 Lukas Grauwiler .20 .50
11 Doug Groenestege .30 .75
12 Blair Jarrett .20 .50
13 Daryl Knowles .20 .50
14 Mark O'Leary .20 .50
15 Patrick O'Sullivan .30 .75
16 Chad Painchaud .20 .50
17 Kyle Quincey .20 .50
18 Dany Revelle .20 .50
19 Dan Rudisuela .20 .50
20 David Shantz .60 1.50
21 Ryan Stokes .20 .50
22 Nick Van Herpt .20 .50
23 Tom Zanoski .20 .50
24 Scott Zimmerman .20 .50

2004-05 Mississauga Ice Dogs
COMPLETE SET (24) 6.00 15.00
1 Anthony Butera .30 .75
2 Bradley Snetsinger .20 .50
3 Adam Abraham .20 .50
4 Cody Bass .20 .50
5 David Shantz .60 1.50
6 Dustin Jeffrey .20 .50
7 Kyle Quincey .30 .75
8 Michael Swift .30 .75
9 Gianluc Caputi .20 .50
10 Craig Cescon .20 .50
11 Tom Zanoski .20 .50
12 Vladimir Svacina .20 .50
13 Patrick O'Sullivan .60 1.50
14 Daniel Carcillo .20 .50
15 John Hecimovic .20 .50
16 Paul Merchese .20 .50
17 Michael Ouzas .20 .50
18 David Pszenyczny .20 .50
19 Frankie Santini .20 .50
20 Justin DaCosta .40 1.00
21 Stefan Legein .20 .50
22 Nathan Hooper .20 .50
23 Jordan Owens .20 .50
24 Aaron Barton .20 .50

2005-06 Mississauga Ice Dogs
COMPLETE SET (24) 6.00 15.00
1 Cody Bass .30 .75
2 Vladimir Svacina .30 .75
3 Jordan Owens .30 .75
4 Drew Schiestel .30 .75
5 Michael Smith .30 .75
6 Keith Wynn .30 .75
7 Lucas Lobsinger .40 1.00
8 Luca Caputi .30 .75
9 Kyle Lamb .30 .75
10 Justin Gvora .30 .75
11 Jordan Skellett .30 .75
12 Andrew Marcoux .30 .75
13 Andrew Merrett .30 .75
14 Oskar Osala .30 .75
15 Brett Oliphante .30 .75
16 Justin Dacosta .30 .75
17 Kyle Knechtel .30 .75
18 Joshua Day .30 .75
19 Franck Santini .30 .75
20 Nathan Martine .30 .75
21 Drew McAvoy .30 .75
22 Stefan Legein .30 .75
23 Jadran Beljo .30 .75
24 Chris Lawrence .30 .75

2006-07 Mississauga Ice Dogs
COMPLETE SET (23) 8.00 15.00
1 Cody Bass .25 .60
2 Alex Pietrangelo .25 .60
3 Stephan Legein .25 .60
4 Jadran Beljo .25 .60
5 Chris Lawrence .25 .60
6 Jordan Owens .25 .60
7 Brett Oliphant .25 .60
8 Michael Swift .25 .60
9 Luca Caputi .25 .60
10 Barry Sanderson .25 .60
11 Jordan Skellett .25 .60
12 Andrew Merrett .25 .60
13 Travis Fuller .25 .60
14 Oskar Osala .25 .60
15 Steven Manojlovic .25 .60
16 Josh Day .25 .60
17 Franck Santini .25 .60
18 Nathan Martine .25 .60
19 Drew Mcavoy .25 .60
20 Drew Schiestel .25 .60
21 Kyle Lamb .25 .60
22 Lucas Lobsinger .40 1.00
23 Andrew Loverrock .40 1.00

2014-15 Mississauga Steelheads
COMPLETE SET (25) 6.00 15.00
1 Sam Babintsev .30 .75
2 Nathan Bastian .30 .75
3 Justin Bean .30 .75
4 Damian Bourne .30 .75
5 Jacob Brennan .30 .75
6 Josh Burnside .30 .75
7 Bryson Cianfrone .30 .75
8 Everett Clark .30 .75
9 Sean Day .30 .75
10 Brandon Devlin .30 .75
11 Marcus Dickerson .30 .75
12 Adam Donnelly .30 .75
13 Austin Gerhart .30 .75
14 Stephen Gibson .30 .75
15 Leif Hertz .30 .75
16 Stefan Leblanc .30 .75
17 Jimmy Lodge .30 .75
18 Bobby MacIntyre .30 .75
19 Spencer Martin .30 .75
20 Michael McLeod .30 .75
21 Jason Smith .30 .75
22 Cody Thompson .30 .75
23 Jared Walsh .30 .75
24 Cameron Zanussi .30 .75
25 Nick Zottl .30 .75

1996-97 Mississippi Sea Wolves
COMPLETE SET (22) 4.00 10.00
1 Frederik Beaubien .30 .75
2 Alexei Budayev .20 .50
3 Sylvain Daigle .20 .50
4 Kevin Evans .20 .50
5 Quinn Fair .20 .50
6 Shawn Frappier .20 .50
7 Kevin Hilton .20 .50
8 Kelly Hurd .20 .50
9 Derek Innanen .20 .50
10 Yanick Jean .20 .50
11 John Kosobud .20 .50
12 Troy Mann .20 .50
13 Roger Maxwell .20 .50
14 Mike Muller .30 .75
15 Simon Oliver .20 .50
16 Patrick Rochon .20 .50
17 Jeff Rohlicek .30 .75
18 Mark Rupnow .20 .50
19 Joaikin Wassberger .20 .50
20 Steven Yule .20 .50
21 Bruce Boudreau HCO .08 .25
22 Hook Mascot .02 .10

1997-98 Mississippi Sea Wolves
COMPLETE SET (22) 4.00 10.00
1 Sinuhe Wallinheimo .40 1.00
2 Neal Martin .20 .50
3 Don Chase .20 .50
4 John Kosobud .20 .50
5 Jeff Rohlicek .20 .50
6 Kelly Hurd .20 .50
7 Chad Dameworth .20 .50
8 Bruce Boudreau HCO .02 .10
9 Teemu Numminen .20 .50
10 Dan Back .20 .50
11 Dean Hulett .20 .50
12 Mark Rupnow .20 .50
13 Hook Mascot .02 .10
14 Patrick Rochon .20 .50
15 Troy Mann .20 .50
16 Quinn Fair .20 .50
17 Shawn Frappier .20 .50
18 Brian Farrell .20 .50
19 Steve Yule .20 .50
20 Kevin Evans .20 .50
21 Brad Guzda .20 .50
22 Forbes MacPherson .20 .50

1999-00 Mississippi Sea Wolves
COMPLETE SET (25) 20.00 50.00
1 Rob Flahiff EQM .02 .10
2 Marc Potvin HCO .75 2.00
3 Hook MAS .02 .10
4 Team Photo .75 2.00
5 Cynthia Dedeaux TR .02 .10
6 Trevor Gillies .75 2.00
7 Steve Duke .75 2.00
8 Sean Gillam .75 2.00
9 Bob Woods .75 2.00
10 Cody Bowtell .75 2.00
11 Patrick Rochon .75 2.00
12 Jonathan Weaver .75 2.00
13 John Kosobud .75 2.00
14 Brad Essex 1.25 3.00
15 Scott King .75 2.00
16 Ryan Gaucher .75 2.00
17 Brad Goulet .75 2.00
18 Mike Martone .75 2.00
19 J.F. Aube .75 2.00
20 Dave Paradise .75 2.00
21 John Evangelista .75 2.00
22 Mikhail Kravets .75 2.00
23 Chuck Thuss 1.25 3.00
24 Sylvain Daigle 1.25 3.00
25 Mark Rupnow .75 2.00

1999-00 Mississippi Sea Wolves Kelly Cup
COMPLETE SET (25) 4.00 10.00
1 Bruce Boudreau CO .20 .50
2 Hook MAS .02 .10
3 James Carey TR .02 .10
4 Cynthia Dedeaux TR .02 .10
5 Karl Infanger .20 .50
6 Sean Blanchard .20 .50
7 Bob Woods .20 .50
8 Cody Bowtell .20 .50
9 Vaclav Nedomansky .20 .50
10 Patrick Rochon .20 .50
11 John Kosobud .20 .50
12 Brad Essex .30 .75
13 Andrew Dale .20 .50
14 Dean Mando .20 .50
15 Kevin Hilton .20 .50
16 Quinn Fair .20 .50
17 Chris Schmidt .20 .50
18 Mike Martone .20 .50
19 Kelly Hurd .20 .50
20 Mikhail Kravets .20 .50
21 Travis Scott .30 .75
22 Mark Rupnow .20 .50
23 Troy Mann .20 .50
24 Chuck Thuss .30 .75
25 Mississippi Sea Wolves .20 .50

2003-04 Mississippi Sea Wolves
COMPLETE SET (17)

1999-00 Missouri River Otters
COMPLETE SET (29) 4.00 10.00
1 Team Photo .20 .50
2 Tomas Baluch .15 .40
3 Chris Bernard .15 .40
4 Charles Blyth .15 .40
5 Colin Chaulk .15 .40
6 Randy Gallatin .15 .40
7 Forrest Gore .15 .40
8 Ben Gorewich .15 .40
9 Jay Hebert .15 .40
10 Kiley Hill .15 .40
11 Jan Kobezda .15 .40
12 Lonnie Loach .30 .75
13 Jeremiah McCarthy .20 .50
14 Jeremy Rebek .15 .40
15 Brian Regan .15 .40
16 Allan Roulette .15 .40
17 Alain St. Hilaire .15 .40
18 Curtis Sayler .15 .40
19 Trevor Sherban .15 .40
20 Marty Standish .15 .40
21 Michal Stastny .30 .75
22 Chris Tok .15 .40
23 Dan Tompkins .15 .40
24 Mark Reeds HCO .15 .40
25 Scott Bell CO .15 .40
26 Oscar MASCOT .08 .25
27 Otter Mobile .08 .25
28 Checklist .08 .25
29 Cover Card .08 .25

2000-01 Missouri River Otters
COMPLETE SET (27) 7.20 18.00
1 Team CL #1 .04 .10
2 Lonnie Loach .40 1.00
3 Chris Tok .30 .75
4 Colin Chaulk .40 1.00
5 Kiley Hill .40 1.00
6 Jeremy Rebek .30 .75
7 Trevor Sherban .30 .75
8 Jay Hebert .30 .75
9 Randy Gallatin .30 .75
10 Team CL #2 .04 .10
11 Darin Kimble .40 1.00
12 Troy Michalski .30 .75
13 Benoit Thibert .30 .75
14 Eric Murano .40 1.00
15 Lee Cole .30 .75
16 Robert Starke .30 .75
17 Ryan Johnston .30 .75
18 Mark Reeds CO .10 .25
19 Team CL #3 .04 .10
20 Kevin Plager .30 .75
21 Mike Bayrack .30 .75
22 Jay Woodcroft .30 .75
23 Jared Reigstad .30 .75
24 Anthony Cappelletti .30 .75
25 Kiley Hill AS .30 .75
26 Colin Chaulk AS .30 .75
27 Jim Jeans EM .04 .10
27 John Sheehan TR .04 .10

1999-00 Missouri River Otters Sheet
COMPLETE SET (25) 7.20 18.00
1 Tomas Baluch .30 .75
2 Charlie Blythe .30 .75
3 Colin Chaulk .30 .75
4 Randy Gallatin .30 .75
5 Yuri Gerasimov .30 .75
6 Ben Gorewich .30 .75
7 Jay Hebert .30 .75
8 Kiley Hill .30 .75
9 Jan Kobezda .30 .75
10 Lonnie Loach .40 1.00
11 Jeremiah McCarthy .30 .75
12 Jeremy Rebek .30 .75
13 Brian Regan .30 .75
14 Alan Roulette .30 .75
15 Alain St. Hilaire .30 .75
16 Curtis Sayler .30 .75
17 Trevor Sherban .30 .75
18 Marty Standish .30 .75
19 Michal Stastny .40 1.00
20 Jason Stewart .30 .75
21 Chris Tok .30 .75
22 Dan Tompkins .30 .75
23 Mark Reeds CO .08 .25
24 Scott Bell .30 .75
25 Oscar the Otter MASCOT .02 .10

2001-02 Missouri River Otters
COMPLETE SET (30) 8.00 20.00
1 Missouri River Otters Logo .04 .10
2 Aaron Vickar .30 .75
3 Lonnie Loach .40 1.00
4 Dustin Whitecotton .30 .75
5 Troy Mann .30 .75
6 Anthony Cappelletti .30 .75
7 Casey VanSchagen .30 .75
8 Ben White .30 .75
9 Curtis Sayler .40 1.00
10 Charlie Blyth .30 .75
11 Scott Perry .30 .75
12 Kelvin Solari .30 .75
13 Mark Reeds CO .30 .75
14 Oscar the River Otter MASCOT .04 .10
15 Checklist I .04 .10
16 Missouri River Otters .30 .75
17 Brian Regan .30 .75
18 Darin Kimble .60 1.50
19 Eric Murano .40 1.00
20 Jason Gudmundson .30 .75
21 Mike Jaros .30 .75
22 Joe Ritson .30 .75
23 Tony White .30 .75
24 Simon Poirier .30 .75
25 Vaclav Pazourek .30 .75
26 Joe Pecoraro .30 .75
27 Kevin Chabbert .30 .75
28 John Sheehan TR .04 .10
29 Team Photo .30 .75
30 Checklist 2 .04 .10

2003-04 Missouri River Otters
COMPLETE SET (24) 8.00 20.00
1 Checklist .04 .10
2 Anthony Cappelletti .40 1.00
3 Charlie Blyth .40 1.00
4 Jesse Heerema .40 1.00
5 Jeff Cameron .40 1.00
6 Jeff Petruic .40 1.00
7 Colin Embley .40 1.00
8 Bobby Rapoza .40 1.00
9 Troy Mann .40 1.00
10 Tony White .40 1.00
11 Chad Moore .40 1.00
12 Team Photo .10 .25
13 Checklist .04 .10
14 Ben White .40 1.00
15 Kevin Chabbert .40 1.00
16 Forrest Gore .40 1.00
17 Joe Ritson .40 1.00
18 Brian Regan .60 1.50
19 George Cantrall .60 1.50
20 River Otters Kids Club .04 .10
21 Ryan Gillis .40 1.00
22 Tim Knudsen .60 1.50
23 Rob Davidson .40 1.00
24 Lonnie Loach HCO .10 .25

2004-05 Missouri River Otters
COMPLETE SET (32) 5.00 12.00
1 Header .04 .10
2 Charlie Blyth .20 .50
3 Jason Tapp .20 .50
4 B.J. Heckendorn .20 .50
5 Barrie Moore .20 .50
6 Mike Dombkiewicz .20 .50
7 Cole Bassett .20 .50
8 Ryan Johnson .30 .75
9 Riku Varjamo .20 .50
10 Mat Snesrud .20 .50
11 Quinten Van Horlick .30 .75
12 Jim Montgomery .30 .75
13 Kevin Kaminski CO .20 .50
14 Ice Zone .04 .10
15 Prize Card .04 .10
16 Checklist Series 1 .04 .10
17 Header .04 .10
18 Bob Rapoza .20 .50
19 Josh Legge .20 .50
20 Kevin Reiter .20 .50
21 Lars Pettersen .20 .50
22 Mark Odut .20 .50
23 George Cantrall .20 .50
24 Justin Quenneville .20 .50
25 Glen Detulleo .20 .50
26 Rod Sundquist .20 .50
27 Brad MacMillan .20 .50
28 Barret Jackman .60 1.50
29 Team Photo .20 .50
30 Sponsor Card .04 .10
31 Prize Card .04 .10
32 Checklist Series 2 .04 .10

2005-06 Missouri River Otters
COMPLETE SET (24) 8.00 20.00
1 Missouri River Otters .04 .10
2 Kevin Kaminski HC .04 .10
3 Richard Paul .40 1.00
4 Dave Stewart .40 1.00
5 Martin Vasut .40 1.00
6 Jim Murphy .40 1.00
7 J.P. Beilsten .40 1.00
8 Lars Pettersen .40 1.00
9 B.J. Heckendorn .40 1.00
10 Tyler Butler .40 1.00
11 Mark Lindsay .40 1.00
12 Brenden Cuthbert .40 1.00
13 Missouri River Otters .04 .10
14 Brad Church .40 1.00
15 Tim O'Connell .40 1.00
16 Jimmy Callahan .40 1.00
17 Frank Littlejohn .40 1.00
18 Mark Odut .40 1.00
19 Brad MacMillan .40 1.00
20 Kevin Reiter .40 1.00
21 Damian Surma .40 1.00
22 Oscar (Mascot) .04 .10
23 Matt Suderman .40 1.00
24 Scott Horvath .40 1.00

1997-98 Mobile Mysticks
COMPLETE SET (21) 4.00 10.00
1 Chuck Thuss .20 .50
2 Mike Mayhew .20 .50
3 Matt Shaw CO .08 .25
4 Dave Craievich .20 .50
5 Jim Jensen .20 .50
6 Anton Fedorov .20 .50
7 Russell Monteith .20 .50
8 Yanick Jean .20 .50
9 Dave Larson .20 .50
10 Chris Brooks .20 .50
11 Brandon Carper .20 .50
12 Phil Valk .20 .50
13 Patrice Paquin .20 .50
14 Kevin Hilton .20 .50
15 Fredrick Nasvall .20 .50
16 Andrew Will .20 .50
17 Steve Suk .20 .50
18 Mike Lenarduzzi .30 .75
19 Neil Donovan .20 .50
20 Hugues Gervais .20 .50
21 Chad Remackel .20 .50

1997-98 Mobile Mysticks Kellogg's
COMPLETE SET (21) 6.00 15.00
1 Andrew Will .40 1.00
3 Neil Donovan .40 1.00
5 Dave Larson .40 1.00
6 Jim Jensen .40 1.00
7 Mike Mayhew .40 1.00
8 Matt Shaw HCO .15 .40
9 Yanick Jean .40 1.00
10 Steve Suk .40 1.00
11 Chad Remackel .40 1.00
12 Tom Neziol ACO .08 .25
13 Dave Craievich .40 1.00
14 Chris Brooks .40 1.00
15 Fredrick Nasvall .40 1.00
16 Puck MAS .08 .25
17 Anton Fedorov .40 1.00
18 Hugues Gervais .40 1.00
19 Phil Valk .40 1.00
20 Mike Lenarduzzi .60 1.50
21 Russell Monteith .40 1.00

1998-99 Mobile Mysticks
COMPLETE SET (22) 6.00 15.00
1 Russell Monteith .40 1.00
2 Slapshot Mascot .02 .10
3 Tom Neziol ACO .02 .10
4 Kevin Kerr .40 1.00
5 Steve Debus .40 1.00
6 Steve Chapman GM .02 .10
7 Puck Mascot .02 .10
8 Yanick Jean .40 1.00
9 Dave Craievich .40 1.00
10 Jason Elders .40 1.00
11 Alain Savage .40 1.00
12 Joel Theriault .40 1.00
13 Chad Alban .60 1.50
14 John McCabe .40 1.00
15 Simmons
Jeffreys
Young .20 .50
16 Hughes Gervais .40 1.00
17 Brandon Carper .40 1.00
18 Craig Binns .40 1.00
19 Jeff Pyle HCO .08 .25
20 Jim Shepherd .40 1.00
21 Andrew Will .40 1.00
22 Francois Page .40 1.00

1999-00 Mobile Mysticks
COMPLETE SET (23) 6.00 50.00
1 Dave Craievich 1.00 2.50
2 David Van Drunen 1.00 2.50
3 Mitch Vig 1.00 2.50
4 Benoit Cotnoir 1.00 2.50
5 Bobby Stewart 1.00 2.50
6 John McCabe 1.00 2.50
7 Hugues Gervais 1.00 2.50
8 Tom Nolan 1.00 2.50
9 Chad Onufrechuk 1.00 2.50
10 Jason Elders 1.00 2.50
11 B.J. Kilbourne 1.00 2.50
12 Mark Turner 1.00 2.50
13 Jeff Kozakowski 1.00 2.50
14 Josh Harrold 1.00 2.50
15 Russ Guzior 1.00 2.50
16 Anders Sorensen 1.00 2.50
17 Jason Clarke 1.00 2.50
18 Chad Alban 2.00 5.00
19 Steve Debus 2.00 5.00
20 Scott Cherrey 1.00 2.50
21 Jeff Pyle CO 1.00 2.50
22 Tom Neziol CO .08 .25
23 Southern Ford Dealers .01

1983-84 Moncton Alpines
COMPLETE SET (28) 6.00 15.00
1 Doug Messier CO .20 .50
2 Chris Smith .20 .50
3 Marco Baron .40 1.00
4 Mike Zanier .40 1.00
5 Dwayne Boettger .20 .50
6 Lowell Loveday .20 .50
7 Joe McDonnell .20 .50
8 Peter Dineen .20 .50
9 John Blum .30 .75
10 Steve Smith .75 2.00
11 Reg Kerr .20 .50
12 Tom Rowe .20 .50
13 Ross Lambert .20 .50
14 Pat Conacher .40 1.00
15 Paul Miller .20 .50
16 Bert Yachimel .20 .50
17 Tom Gorence .30 .75
18 Jeff Crawford .20 .50
19 Serge Bolsvert .20 .50
20 Todd Strueby .30 .75
21 Todd Bidner .20 .50
22 Dean Dachyshyn .20 .50
23 Ray Cote .20 .50
24 Shawn Babcock .20 .50
25 Shawn Dineen .20 .50
26 Marc Habscheid .40 1.00
27 Charlie Lavalee TR
Kevin Ferris TR .08 .25
NNO Checklist Card .20 .50

1984-85 Moncton Golden Flames
COMPLETE SET (26) 10.00 25.00
1 Brian Patafie TR .08 .25
2 Mike Bianni TR .08 .25
3 Pierre Page CO .20 .50
4 Neil Sheehy .40 1.00
5 George White .20 .50
6 Mark Lamb .40 1.00
7 Dan Kane .20 .50
8 Dan Bolduc .40 1.00
9 Lou Kiriakou .20 .50
10 Joel Otto .75 2.00
11 Dale Degray .40 1.00
12 Mike Clayton .20 .50
13 Mickey Volcan .20 .50
14 Ted Pearson .20 .50
15 Mario Simioni .20 .50
16 Keith Hanson .20 .50
17 Yves Courteau .20 .50
18 Dan Cormier .20 .50
19 Todd Hooey .20 .50
20 Mike Vernon 4.00 10.00
21 Dave Meszaros .20 .50
22 Bruce Eakin .20 .50
23 Ed Kastelic .40 1.00
24 Tony Stiles .20 .50
25 Pierre Rioux .20 .50
26 Gino Cavallini .40 1.00

1985-86 Moncton Golden Flames
COMPLETE SET (28) 8.00 20.00
1 Terry Crisp GM/CO .40 1.00
2 Dan Bolduc ACO .08 .25
3 Terry Crisp GM/CO
Dan Bolduc ACO .40 1.00
4 Al Pedersen .30 .75
5 Dave Meszaros .20 .50
6 George White .20 .50
7 Mark Lamb .60 1.50
8 Doug Kostynski .20 .50
9 Brian Bradley .75 2.00
10 Rob Kivell .20 .50
11 Geoff Courtnall 1.25 3.00
12 Tony Stiles .20 .50
13 Jim Buettgen .20 .50
14 Cleon Daskalakis .40 1.00
15 Rick Kosti .20 .50
16 Kevan Guy .20 .50
17 John Blum .20 .50
18 Brian Patafie
Mike Baiani
Jamie Druet .08 .25
19 Greg Johnston .30 .75
20 Dale Degray .20 .50
21 John Meulenbroeks .20 .50
22 Dave Reid .40 1.00
23 Jay Miller 1.25 3.00
24 Yves Courteau .20 .50
25 Robin Bartel .20 .50
26 Benoit Doucet .20 .50
27 Pete Bakovic .20 .50
28 Team Photo .40 1.00

1986-87 Moncton Golden Flames
COMPLETE SET (28) 30.00 75.00
1 Terry Crisp CO/GM .40 1.00
2 Danny Bolduc ACO .08 .25
3 Doug Dadswell .40 1.00
4 Doug Kostynski .20 .50
5 Bill Ranford 6.00 15.00
6 Brian Patafie TR .08 .25
7 Dave Pasin .30 .75
8 Darwin McCutcheon .20 .50
9 Team Photo .40 1.00
10 Kevan Guy .20 .50
11 Kraig Nienhuis .30 .75
12 Gary Roberts 2.00 5.00
13 Ken Sabourin .30 .75
14 Marc D'Amour .40 1.00
15 Don Mercier .20 .50
16 Wade Campbell .20 .50
17 Mark Paterson .20 .50
18 Cleon Daskalakis .40 1.00
19 Lyndon Byers 2.00 5.00
20 Brett Hull 15.00 40.00
21 Bob Sweeney .40 1.00
22 Gord Hynes .20 .50
23 Peter Bakovic .20 .50
24 Dave Reid .40 1.00
25 Mike Rucinski .20 .50
26 Ray Podloski .20 .50
27 Bob Bodak .20 .50
28 John Carter .30 .75

1987-88 Moncton Hawks
COMPLETE SET (25) 4.80 12.00
1 Joel Baillargeon .20 .50
2 Rick Bowness CO .20 .50
3 Rick Carrano TR
Wayne Fleming EQ .08 .25
4 Bobby Dollas .30 .75
5 Peter Douris .30 .75
6 Iain Duncan .20 .50
7 Bob Essensa .75 2.00
8 Todd Flichel .20 .50
9 Rob Fowler .20 .50
10 Randy Gilhen .30 .75
11 Matt Hervey .20 .50
12 Brent Hughes .30 .75
13 Jamie Husgen .20 .50
14 Mike Jeffrey .20 .50
15 Guy Larose .20 .50
16 Chris Levasseur .20 .50
17 Len Nielson .20 .50
18 Roger Ohman .20 .50
19 Dave Quigley .20 .50
20 Ron Pesetti .20 .50
21 Steve Penney .40 1.00
22 Scott Schneider .20 .50
23 Ryan Stewart .20 .50
24 Gord Whitaker .20 .50
25 Team Photo .40 1.00

1990-91 Moncton Hawks
COMPLETE SET (25) 4.00 10.00
1 Larry Bernard .15 .40
2 Lee Davidson .15 .40
3 Iain Duncan .15 .40
4 Craig Duncanson .15 .40
5 Dallas Eakins .20 .50
6 Dave Farrish CO/GM .02 .10
7 Wayne Flemming EQMG .02 .10
8 Todd Flichel .15 .40
9 Peter Hankinson .15 .40
10 Matt Hervey .15 .40
11 Brent Hughes .20 .50
12 Anthony Joseph .15 .40
13 Sergei Kharin .15 .40
14 Denis Larocque .15 .40
15 Guy Larose .20 .50
16 Scott Levins .20 .50
17 Bryan Marchment .40 1.00
18 Chris Norton .15 .40
19 Mike O'Neill .30 .75

20 Grant Richison .15 .40
21 Scott Schneider .15 .40
22 Rob Snitzer TR .02 .10
23 Rick Tabaracci .40 1.00
24 Simon Wheeldon .20 .50
25 Team Card .20 .50

1991-92 Moncton Hawks

COMPLETE SET (28) 4.00 10.00
1 Luciano Borsato .15 .40
2 Jason Cirone .15 .40
3 Rob Cowie .15 .40
4 Lee Davidson .15 .40
5 Kris Draper .40 1.00
6 Dallas Eakins .20 .50
7 Dave Farrish GM/CO .02 .10
8 Wayne Flemming EQMG .02 .10
9 Sean Gauthier .20 .50
10 Ken Gernander .20 .50
11 Tod Hartje .15 .40
12 Bob Joyce .20 .50
13 Claude Julien .15 .40
14 Chris Kiene .15 .40
15 Mark Kumpel P/ACO .15 .40
16 Derek Langille .15 .40
17 Tyler Larter .15 .40
18 John LeBlanc .15 .40
19 Scott Levins .15 .40
20 Rob Murray .15 .40
21 Kent Paynter .15 .40
22 Rudy Poeschek .20 .50
23 Dave Prior CO .02 .10
24 Warren Rychel .20 .50
25 Rob Snitzer TR .02 .10
26 Rick Tabaracci .40 1.00
27 The Hawk (Mascot) .02 .10
28 Darren Veitch .20 .50

2001-02 Moncton Wildcats

COMPLETE SET (26) 6.00 15.00
1 Bill Ruggiero .30 .75
2 Andrew Carver .20 .50
3 James Sanford .20 .50
4 Kyle Murnaghan .20 .50
5 Daniel Hudgin .20 .50
6 Mathieu Betournay .20 .50
7 Karl Gagne .20 .50
8 Ian Seguin .20 .50
9 Michel Dube .20 .50
10 Francois Caron .20 .50
11 Nathan Saunders .20 .50
12 Brad Larter .20 .50
13 Teddy Kyres .20 .50
14 Kevin Glode .20 .50
15 David Philpott .20 .50
16 Ryan Salvis .20 .50
17 Collin Circelli .20 .50
18 Corey Crawford .30 .75
19 Matt Davis .30 .75
20 Patrick Thoreson .75 2.00
21 Maxime Desruisseaux .20 .50
22 Julien Lavoie .20 .50
23 Scott English .20 .50
24 Luke Pelham .20 .50
25 Steve Bernier 1.00 2.50
NNO Title Card
CL .04 .10

2002-03 Moncton Wildcats

COMPLETE SET (26) 8.00 15.00
1 Nathan Saunders .20 .50
2 Matt Davis .20 .50
3 Francois Caron .20 .50
4 Evgeni Artukhin .30 .75
5•Evgeni Artukhin WJC .30 .75
6 Corey Crawford .40 1.00
7 Bruce Graham .30 .75
8 James Sanford .30 .75
9 Patrick Sampson .20 .50
10 Mathieu Betournay .20 .50
11 Ryan Salvis .20 .50
12 Kevin Glode .20 .50
13 Luke Pelham .20 .50
14 Maxime Desruisseaux .20 .50
15 Kevin Hamel .20 .50
16 Josh Hepditch .20 .50
17 Jonathan Favreau .20 .50
18 Kyle Murnaghan .20 .50
19 Daniel Hudgin .20 .50
20 Michel Dube .20 .50
21 Sebastien Strozynski .20 .50
22 Yannick Searles .20 .50
23 Carl McLean .20 .50
24 Karl Gagne .20 .50
25 Steve Bernier 1.25 3.00
26 Team Picture .10 .25

2003-04 Moncton Wildcats

COMPLETE SET (25) 5.00 12.00
1 James Sanford .15 .40
2 Yan Ouimet .15 .40
3 Bruce Graham .40 1.00
4 Mathieu Betournay .15 .40
5 Karl Gagne .15 .40
6 Christian Gaudet .15 .40
7 Martin Karsums .40 1.00
8 Francois Caron .15 .40
9 Kevin Hamel .15 .40
10 Nathan Saunders .15 .40
11 Kevin Glode .15 .40
12 Thierry Douville .15 .40
13 Cody Doucette .15 .40
14 Joshua Hepditch .15 .40
15 Mathieu Wathier .15 .40
16 Ryan Salvis .15 .40
17 Bobby Mazerolle .15 .40
18 Konstantin Zakharov .15 .40
19 Corey Crawford .30 .75
20 Ryan Papaioannou .30 .75
21 Luke Pelham .15 .40
22 Maxime Desruisseaux .15 .40
23 Steve Bernier .40 1.00
NNO Steve Bernier TL .40 1.00
NNO James Sanford TL .15 .40

2004-05 Moncton Wildcats

COMPLETE SET (25) 5.00 12.00
1 Wesley Welcher .20 .50
2 Oskars Bartulis .20 .50
3 Corey Crawford .40 1.00
4 Charles Bergeron .20 .50
5 Kevin Glode .20 .50
6 Brad Marchand .20 .50
7 Adam Blanchette .20 .50
8 Charles Tanguay .20 .50
9 Luke Pelham .20 .50
10 Christian Gaudet .20 .50
11 Jean-Sebastien Adam .20 .50
12 Stephane Goulet .20 .50
13 Jason Demers .20 .50
14 Ryan Salvis .20 .50
15 Adam Pineault .20 .50
16 Yan Ouimet .20 .50
17 Jean-Christophe Blanchard .40 1.00
18 Stanson Donovan .20 .50
19 Martins Karsums .40 1.00
20 Bruce Graham .30 .75
21 Steve Bernier .40 1.00
22 Jerome Samson .20 .50
23 Josh Hepditch .20 .50
24 Guillaume Veilleux .20 .50
25 Nathan Saunders .20 .50

2005-06 Moncton Wildcats

COMPLETE SET (30) 8.00 20.00
1 Adam Pineault .40 1.00
2 Stephane Goulet .30 .75
3 Jean Christophe Blanchard .30 .75
4 Matt Eagles .30 .75
5 Brad Marchand .30 .75
6 Christian Gaudet .30 .75
7 Guillaume Blouin .30 .75
8 Oskars Bartulis .30 .75
9 Keith Yandle .30 .75
10 Josh Hepditch .30 .75
11 Maxime Belanger .30 .75
12 Tim Spencer .30 .75
13 Martins Karsums .60 1.50
14 Jerome Samson .30 .75
15 Jean Sebastien Adam .30 .75
16 Andrew MacDonald .30 .75
17 Philippe Dupuis .30 .75
18 Nathan Welton .30 .75
19 Nick Emanuele .30 .75
20 Jason Demers .30 .75
21 Ian-Mathieu Girard .30 .75
22 Jean-Philip Chabot .30 .75
23 Matt Marquardt .30 .75
24 Chris Morehouse .30 .75
25 Brad Ouskun .30 .75
26 Brad Smith .30 .75
27 Jhase Sniderman .30 .75
28 Josh Tordjman .60 1.50
29 Luc Bourdon .60 1.50
30 David MacDonald .30 .75

2006-07 Moncton Wildcats

COMPLETE SET (24) 8.00 15.00
1 Nicola Riopel .40 1.00
2 Andrew Macdonald .25 .60
3 Roopertti Martikainen .25 .60
4 Matthew Brenton .25 .60
5 Randy Cameron .25 .60
6 Jason Lepage .25 .60
7 Jerome Samson .25 .60
8 Pierre-Marc Lessard .25 .60
9 Matt Marquardt .25 .60
10 Matt Eagles .25 .60
11 Nathan Welton .25 .60
12 Murdock Maclellan .25 .60
13 Jhase Sniderman .40 1.00
14 Nick Emanuele .25 .60
15 Alexi Pianosi .25 .60
16 Brad Smith .25 .60
17 Marc-Andre Labelle .25 .60
18 Chris Morehouse .25 .60
19 Brad Ouskun .25 .60
20 Patrick Campbell .25 .60
21 Igor Voroshilov .25 .60
22 Matt Boyle .25 .60
23 Kelan Herr .25 .60
24 Christian Gaudet .25 .60

2015-16 Moncton Wildcats

COMPLETE SET (23) 6.00 15.00
1 Cameron Askew .30 .75
2 William Bower .30 .75
3 Lane Cormier .30 .75
4 Noah Corson .30 .75
5 Ethan Crossman .30 .75
6 Sebastien Dupre .30 .75
7 Conor Garland .30 .75
8 Maximilian Glaessl .30 .75
9 Adam Holwell .30 .75
10 Stephen Johnson .30 .75
11 Matthew Klebanskyj .30 .75
12 Kevin Klima .30 .75
13 Kelly Klima .30 .75
14 Austin Kosack .30 .75
15 Eric Leger .30 .75
16 Zack MacEwen .30 .75
17 Zachary Malatesta .30 .75
18 Blade Mann-Dixon .30 .75
19 Liam Murphy .30 .75
20 Will Smith .30 .75
21 Jacob Sweeney .30 .75
22 Marcus Tesink .30 .75
23 Mauel Wiederer .30 .75

1997-98 Moose Jaw Warriors

COMPLETE SET (19) 5.00 12.00
1 Jay Ewasiuk .40 1.00
2 Jordon Flodell .30 .75
3 Justin Hansen .30 .75
4 Cory Hintz .30 .75
5 Chad Hinz .30 .75
6 Brent Hobday .30 .75
7 Marek Ivan .30 .75
8 Trevor Johnson .30 .75
9 Tim McEachen .30 .75
10 Donavan Nunweiler .40 1.00
11 Dustin Paul .30 .75
12 Nathan Read .30 .75
13 Scott Schoneck .30 .75
14 Shawn Skolney .30 .75
15 Dave Taylor .30 .75
16 Chris Twerdun .30 .75
17 Dreu Volk .30 .75
18 Jason Weitzel .30 .75
19 Dayle Wilcox .30 .75

2001-02 Moose Jaw Warriors

COMPLETE SET (22) 4.80 12.00
1 Ryan Jorde .20 .50
2 Jarad Bourassa .20 .50
3 Deryk Engelland .20 .50
4 Nathan Paetsch .40 1.00
5 Bobby-Chad Mitchell .20 .50
6 Kyle Brodziak .20 .50
7 Derek Krestanovich .40 1.00
8 Steve Crampton .20 .50
9 Sean O'Connor .20 .50
10 Brian Sutherby .60 1.50
11 Tim Plett .20 .50
12 Shawn Limpright .20 .50
13 Lee Zalasky .20 .50
14 Harlan Anderson .20 .50
15 Tyler Johnson .20 .50
16 David Bararuk .20 .50
17 Mark Kitts .20 .50
18 Craig Olynick .30 .75
19 Lane Manson .20 .50
20 Shaun Landolt .20 .50
21 Kyle Kettles .20 .50
22 Blake Grenier .20 .50

2002-03 Moose Jaw Warriors

COMPLETE SET (22) 5.00 12.00
1 John Boychuk .40 1.00
2 Jarad Bourassa .20 .50
3 Deryk Engelland .20 .50
4 Nathan Paetsch .40 1.00
5 Michael Busto .20 .50
6 Kyle Brodziak .20 .50
7 Tomas Fleischmann .75 2.00
8 Derek Krestanovich .30 .75
9 Owen Fussey .30 .75
10 Petr Jelinek .20 .50
11 Jon Kress .20 .50
12 Harlan Anderson .20 .50
13 Tyler Johnson .20 .50
14 David Bararuk .20 .50
15 Troy Brouwer .20 .50
16 Ashton Rome .20 .50
17 Lane Manson .20 .50
18 Dustin Boyd .20 .50
19 Cam Lilley .20 .50
20 Blake Grenier .30 .75
21 Steve Belanger .30 .75
22 Checklist Logo .04 .10

2004-05 Moose Jaw Warriors

COMPLETE SET (24) 8.00 20.00
1 Greg Park .30 .75
2 Jordan Henry .30 .75
3 Cole Simpson .30 .75
4 Cole Butterfield .30 .75
5 Dan Ehrman .30 .75
6 Dylan Chapman .30 .75
7 Jacob Dietrich .30 .75
8 Justin Scott .30 .75
9 Kenndal McArdle 1.25 3.00
10 Blair Jones .30 .75
11 Garrett Robinson .30 .75
12 Dustin Boyd .30 .75
13 Andre Hermanson .30 .75
14 Brennen Wray .30 .75
15 Masi Marjamaki .40 1.00
16 Stuart Kerr .30 .75
17 Riley Holzapfel .30 .75
18 Troy Brouwer .30 .75
19 Steven Gillen .30 .75
20 Ian McKenzie .30 .75
21 Carter Smith .30 .75
22 Joey Perricone .30 .75
23 Josh Lepp .40 1.00
24 Checklist .04 .10

2005-06 Moose Jaw Warriors

COMPLETE SET (25) 6.00 15.00
1 Jason Bast .25 .60
2 Dustin Boyd .60 1.50
3 Troy Brouwer .25 .60
4 Dylan Chapman .25 .60
5 Travis Ehrhardt .25 .60
6 Kyle Fecho .25 .60
7 Steven Gillen .25 .60
8 Martin Grundling .25 .60
9 Matthew Hansen .25 .60
10 Andre Herman .25 .60
11 Riley Holzapfel .25 .60
12 Blair Jones .25 .60
13 Andrew Leslie .20 .50
14 Kendall McArdle .60 1.50
15 Ian McKenzie .25 .60
16 Joey Perricone .40 1.00
17 Garrett Robinson .25 .60
18 Cole Simpson .25 .60
19 Carter Smith .25 .60
20 Bjorn Svensson .25 .60
21 Brennen Wray .25 .60
22 Jesse Zetariuk .25 .60
23 Old Dutch Foods SPONSOR .04 .10
24 Boston Pizza SPONSOR .04 .10
25 Air Waves SPONSOR .04 .10

2006-07 Moose Jaw Warriors

COMPLETE SET (24) 10.00 18.00
1 Jock Sutter .30 .75
2 Travis Hamonic .30 .75
3 Ryan Stanton .30 .75
4 Chad Suer .30 .75
5 Travis Ehrhardt .30 .75
6 Martin Grundling .30 .75
7 Keith Voytechek .30 .75
8 Neal Prokop .30 .75
9 Brady Calla .30 .75
10 Matt Isbister .30 .75
11 Garrett Robinson .30 .75
12 Brad Riege .30 .75
13 Ryley Grantham .30 .75
14 Jordan Knackstedt .30 .75
15 Jason Bast .30 .75
16 Riley Holzaphel .40 1.00
17 Michael Hengen .30 .75
18 Steven Gillen .30 .75
19 Jason Reese .30 .75
20 Cody Thoring .30 .75
21 Jason Grecica .30 .75
22 Joey Perricone .40 1.00
23 Kurt Jory .40 1.00
24 Giffen Nyren .30 .75

1990-91 Montreal-Bourassa AAA

COMPLETE SET (25) 2.00 5.00
1 Team Card .02 .10
2 Police Card .02 .10
3 Coach Card .02 .10
4 Coach Card .02 .10
5 Coach Card .02 .10
6 Peter Arvanitis .08 .25
7 Luc Bilodeau .08 .25
8 Luc Corriveau .08 .25
9 David Desnoyers .08 .25
10 Alexandre Duchesne .08 .25
11 Dominic Gagne .08 .25
12 Benoit Goyer .08 .25
13 Serge Kiopini .08 .25
14 Ted Laviolette .08 .25
15 Ian McIntyre .08 .25
16 Nathan Morin .08 .25
17 Valentino Passarelli .08 .25
18 Jean-Sebastien Perras .08 .25
19 Sylvain Pinel .08 .25
20 Sebastien Plouffe .15 .40
21 Simon Roy .08 .25
22 Erasmo Saltarelli .15 .40
23 Alain Savage .08 .25
24 Christian Sbrocca .08 .25
25 Patrick Traverse .30 .75

1979-80 Montreal Juniors

1 Jeff Barratt 2.00 5.00
2 Andre Begin 2.00 5.00
3 Dennis Champagne 2.00 5.00
4 Denis Cyr 2.00 5.00
5 Ghyslain Cyr 2.00 5.00
6 Roland Diotte 2.00 5.00
7 Pierre Dubois 2.00 5.00
8 Sylvain Gagne 2.00 5.00
9 Guy Jacob 2.00 5.00
10 Mike Krushelnyski 2.00 5.00
11 Ron Lapointe 2.00 6.00
12 Richard Lavallee 2.00 5.00
13 Daniel Laxton 2.00 5.00
14 Francois Laxton 2.00 5.00
15 Francois Lecompte 2.00 5.00
16 Eikke Leime 2.00 5.00
17 Pierre Martin 2.00 5.00
18 Bill Mulcahey 2.00 5.00
19 Gates Orlando 2.00 5.00
20 Patrice Pare 2.00 5.00
21 Mario Patry 2.00 5.00
22 Fabian Pavlin 2.00 5.00
23 Roger Poitras 2.00 5.00
24 Constant Prindolo 2.00 5.00
25 Denis Savard 5.00 10.00
26 Eric Taylor 2.00 5.00
27 Denis Tremblay 2.50 6.00
28 J.J. Vezina 2.00 5.00
29 Taras Zytynsky 2.00 5.00

1955-56 Montreal Royals

COMPLETE SET (6) 50.00 350.00
1 Walter Cline 6.00 50.00
2 Andre Corriveau 6.00 50.00
3 Jacques Deslauriers 6.00 50.00
4 Cec Hoekstra 10.00 60.00
5 Gerry McNeil 20.00 100.00
6 Guy Rousseau 10.00 60.00

1993-94 Muskegon Fury

COMPLETE SET (20) 10.00 25.00
1 Header Card .08 .25
2 Steve Ludzik CO .50 1.25
3 Bob Jones .50 1.25
4 Darrel Newman .50 1.25
5 Brett Seguin .50 1.25
6 Dan Woodley .75 2.00
7 Jodi Murphy .50 1.25
8 Mark Karpen .50 1.25
9 Robert Melanson .50 1.25
10 Paul Kelly .50 1.25
11 Joey Simon .50 1.25
12 Scott Feasby .50 1.25
13 Scott Campbell .50 1.25
14 Joe Hawley .50 1.25
15 Justin Morrison .50 1.25
16 Roch Belley 1.25 3.00
17 Todd Charlesworth .75 2.00
18 Kevin Barrett .50 1.25
19 Mark Turner .50 1.25
20 Steve Herniman .50 1.25

1994-95 Muskegon Fury

COMPLETE SET (18) 3.00 8.00
1 Header Card .02 .10
2 Rich Parent .40 1.00
3 Grant Block .20 .50
4 Justin Morrison .20 .50
5 Scott Feasby .20 .50
6 Scott Campbell .20 .50
7 Mark Vilneff .20 .50
8 Brett Seguin .20 .50
9 Todd Charlesworth .20 .50
10 Marc Saumier .20 .50
11 Norm Krumpschmid .20 .50
12 Darryl Gilmour .30 .75
13 Paul Kelly .20 .50
14 Steve Walker .20 .50
15 Wes McCauley .20 .50
16 Steve Herniman .20 .50
17 Andy Bezeau .20 .50
18 Jamie Black .20 .50

1995-96 Muskegon Fury

COMPLETE SET (20) 4.00 10.00
1 Team Photo .20 .50
2 Mark Vilneff .20 .50
3 Kyle Haviland .20 .50
4 Brett Seguin .20 .50
5 Rick Girhiny .20 .50
6 Cory Johnson .20 .50
7 Paul Kelly .20 .50
8 Mark Turner .20 .50
9 Scott Feasby .20 .50
10 Stephen Webb .30 .75
11 Bobby Wallwork .20 .50
12 Richard Fatrola .20 .50
13 Steve Walker .20 .50
14 Robert Melanson .20 .50
15 Rich Parent .60 1.50
16 Jamie Hearn .20 .50
17 Brian Greer .20 .50
18 Steve Herniman .20 .50
19 Terry Ficorelli ANN .02 .10
20 McDonald's
Sponsor .02 .10

1998-99 Muskegon Fury

COMPLETE SET (30) 12.00 30.00
1 Terry Ficorelli ANN .02 .10
2 Jason Pain .60 1.50
3 Furious Fred MAS .02 .10
4 Lubos Krajcovic .60 1.50
5 Chris Maillet .60 1.50
6 Robin Bouchard .60 1.50
7 Randy Cantu TR .02 .10
8 Francis Nault .60 1.50
9 Checklist .02 .10
10 Richard Kromm CO .02 .10
11 Joe Dimaline .60 1.50
12 Richard Kromm CO .02 .10
13 David Bouskill .60 1.50
14 Cory Banika .75 2.00
15 Rob Melanson .60 1.50
16 John Vary .60 1.50
17 Ginman Tire AD .01 .05
18 Andy Bezeau .75 2.00
18 Steve Webb .75 2.00
19 Paul Willett .60 1.50
20 Mike Feasby .60 1.50
21 Sergei Kharin .75 2.00
22 Denis Khlopotnov .75 2.00
23 David Beauregard .75 2.00
24 Dmitri Emilyantsev .60 1.50
25 Mark Vilneff .60 1.50
26 Scott Feasby .60 1.50
27 Andrei Petrunin .75 2.00
28 Vadim Podrezov .60 1.50
29 Grant Richison .60 1.50
30 Tony Lisman GM .02 .10

1999-00 Muskegon Fury

COMPLETE SET (36) 8.00 20.00
1 Sergei Kharin .30 .75
2 Vadim Podrezov .30 .75
3 Andrei Petrunin .40 1.00
4 Scott Feasby .30 .75
5 Joe Dimaline .40 1.00
6 Rob Melanson .30 .75
7 Robin Bouchard .30 .75
8 Muskegon Fury .30 .75
9 Quinn Hancock .30 .75
10 Francis Nault .30 .75
11 Alex Vasilevski .30 .75
12 Mark Vilneff .30 .75
13 Andrew Luciuk .30 .75
14 Bob Janosz .40 1.00
15 Chris Maillet .30 .75
16 Tomas Kapusta .30 .75
17 Mike McCourt .30 .75
18 Brian Tucker .30 .75
19 Aaron Porter .30 .75
20 Jason Rose .30 .75
21 Alain LaPlante .30 .75
22 Mike Feasby .08 .25
23 Terry Ficorelli .08 .25
24 Furious Fred MAS .08 .25
25 Richard Kromm CO .08 .25
26 Phil Kopinski TR .08 .25
27 Mikhail Nemirovsky .30 .75
28 Don McSween .30 .75
29 Dalen Hrooshkin .30 .75
30 Lucas Nehrling .30 .75
31 1999-00 Fury AS .30 .75
32 Tony Lisman GM .08 .25
33 Checklist .08 .25
34 Rob Hutson .30 .75
35 Joel Gardner .30 .75
36 Muskegon Fury .20 .50

2000-01 Muskegon Fury

COMPLETE SET (30) 15.00 30.00
1 Robin Bouchard .40 1.00
2 Philippe Roy .60 1.50
3 Alain O'Driscoll .40 1.00
4 Todd Robinson .60 1.50
5 J.F. Tremblay .40 1.00
6 Ed Kowalski .40 1.00
7 Dean Mayrand .40 1.00
8 Glenn Crawford .60 1.50
9 Sergei Kharin .40 1.00
10 Andrew Luciuk .40 1.00
11 Sylvain Daigle .60 1.50
12 Maxim Linnik .60 1.50
13 Andrew Merrick .40 1.00
14 Mark Vilneff .40 1.00
15 Rob Melanson .40 1.00
16 Scott Feasby .60 1.50
17 Quinn Hancock .40 1.00
18 Francis Nault .40 1.00
19 Krikor Arman .40 1.00
20 Richard Kromm CO .40 1.00
21 Joe Dimaline .40 1.00
22 Justin Martin .40 1.00
23 Alexei Krovopuskov .40 1.00
24 Rob Hutson .40 1.00
25 Furious Fred MAS .04 .10
26 Scott Hlady .40 1.00
27 Phil Kopinski TR .04 .10
28 Rick Emmett .40 1.00
29 Scott Myers .40 1.00
30 Terry Ficorelli ANN .04 .10

2002-03 Muskegon Fury

COMPLETE SET (27) 4.00 10.00
1 Brant Blackned .20 .50
2 Robin Bouchard .20 .50
3 Josh Burk .20 .50
4 Mike Busniuk HCO .04 .10
5 Sylvain Daigle .30 .75
6 Rustyn Dolyny .20 .50
7 Terry Ficorelli ANN .04 .10
8 John Glavota .20 .50
9 Shane Glover .20 .50
10 Scott Hollis .20 .50
11 Rob Kennedy EQM .04 .10
12 Jeff Kozakowski .20 .50
13 Tony Lisman OWNER .04 .10
14 Andrew Luciuk .20 .50
15 Jeff Lukasak .20 .50
16 Mike Feasby ACO .04 .10
17 Steven MacIntyre .20 .50
18 Philippe Plante .20 .50
19 Chris Porowski TR .04 .10
20 Billy Pugliese .20 .50
21 Gary Ricciardi .20 .50
22 Todd Robinson .20 .50
23 Scott Feasby .20 .50
24 Brandon Snee .20 .50
25 Travis Thiessen .20 .50
26 Furious Fred Mascot .04 .10
NNO Checklist .04 .10

2003-04 Muskegon Fury

COMPLETE SET (23) 4.00 10.00
1 David Ambler .20 .50
2 Brant Blackned .20 .50
3 Robin Bouchard .20 .50
4 Sylvain Daigle .30 .75
5 Rustyn Dolyny .20 .50
6 Scott Feasby .20 .50
7 B.J. Gaustad .20 .50
8 Brian Haaland .30 .75
9 Scott Hollis .20 .50
10 Jason Jaworski .20 .50
11 Trevor Johnson .20 .50
12 Jason Lawmaster .30 .75
13 Jeff Nelson .20 .50
14 Dave Noel-Bernier .20 .50
15 Tyler Palmer .20 .50
16 Michal Pinc .20 .50
17 Billy Pugliese .20 .50
18 Todd Robinson .20 .50
19 Petr Suchanek .20 .50
20 Garry Toor .20 .50
21 Todd Nelson CO .04 .10
22 Chris Davidson-Adams EQM .04 .10
23 Brad Chavis TR .04 .10

2005-06 Muskegon Fury

COMPLETE SET (24) 6.00 15.00
1 Brett Angel .40 1.00
2 Robin Bouchard .30 .75
3 Bill Collins .30 .75
4 Rustyn Dolyny .30 .75
5 Ken Fels .40 1.00
6 Nigel Hawryliw .30 .75
7 Jon Insana .30 .75
8 Trevor Johnson .30 .75
9 Ryan Keller .30 .75
10 Kevin LaPointe .40 1.00
11 Jason Lawmaster .40 1.00
12 Jeff Nelson .30 .75
13 Steve O'Rourke .30 .75
14 Jeff Petruic .30 .75
15 Joe Pomaranski .30 .75
16 Clayton Pool .40 1.00
17 Todd Robinson .30 .75
18 David Van Drunen .30 .75
19 Clay Wilson .30 .75
20 David Wrigley .30 .75
21 Bill Zalba .30 .75
22 Todd Nelson CO .04 .10
23 Furious Fred MASCOT .04 .10
24 Terry Ficorelli VPC .04 .10

1984-85 Nanaimo Clippers

COMPLETE SET (22) 8.00 20.00
1 Team Picture .20 .50
2 Jay Barner .40 1.00
3 Dale Brisco .40 1.00
4 Chris Calverley .40 1.00
5 Jamie Cayford .40 1.00
6 Carey Coroy .40 1.00
7 Brian Deleeuw .40 1.00
8 Frank Furlan .60 1.50
9 Bill Hardy .40 1.00
10 Rick Hunt .40 1.00
11 Rob Jack .60 1.50
12 Al Johnson .40 1.00
13 Gery Keremidschieff .40 1.00
14 Wade Michalenko .40 1.00
15 Mitch Poulin .40 1.00
16 Kevin Rabbitt .40 1.00
17 Rob Schmidt .40 1.00
18 Ron Sparks .40 1.00
19 Joe Stanley .40 1.00
20 Rod Summers .40 1.00
21 Kevin Thorlakson .40 1.00
22 Darren Wourns .60 1.50

1991-92 Nanaimo Clippers

COMPLETE SET (22) 3.00 8.00
1 Glenn Calder .15 .40
2 Wade Dayley .15 .40
3 Jason Disiewich .15 .40
4 Andy Faulkner .15 .40
5 Darren Holme .15 .40
6 Casey Hungle .15 .40
7 Jim Ingram .15 .40
8 Chris Jones .15 .40
9 Ryan Keller .15 .40
10 Jade Kersey .15 .40
11 Scott Kowalski .15 .40
12 Sean Krause .15 .40
13 Jim Lessard .15 .40
14 Ryan Loxam .15 .40
15 Mickey McGuire .15 .40
16 Dan Murphy .15 .40
17 Jason Northand .15 .40
18 Trevor Post .15 .40
19 Brian Schiebel .15 .40
20 Sjon Wynia .15 .40
21 Shawn York .15 .40
22 Geordie Young .15 .40

1989-90 Nashville Knights

COMPLETE SET (23) 3.00 8.00
1 Pat Bingham .15 .40
2 Andre Brassard .15 .40
3 Mike Bukta .15 .40
4 Chris Cambio .15 .40
5 Chick-E-Lee (Mascot) .08 .25
6 Glen Engevik .15 .40
7 Matt Gallagher
Dir. Player Development
Scott Greer AGM .08 .25
8 Archie Henderson CO .20 .50
9 Billy Huard .30 .75
10 Craig Jenkins ANN
Dave Cavaliere TR .08 .25
11 Todd Jenkins .15 .40
12 Brock Kelly .15 .40
13 Paul Krayer .15 .40
14 Garth Lamb .15 .40
15 Rob Levasseur .15 .40
16 Dan O'Brien .15 .40
17 Bob Polk OWN
Ron Fuller .08 .25
18 John Reid (In action) .15 .40
19 John Reid (Portrait) .15 .40
20 Jeff Salzbrunn .15 .40
21 Mike Schwalb .20 .50
22 Ron Servatius .15 .40
23 Jason Simon .20 .50

1991-92 Nashville Knights

COMPLETE SET (25) 2.80 50.00
1 Header Card .02 .10
2 San Jose Sharks .40 1.00
3 Chris Harvey 1.25 3.00
4 Chris Grassie .75 2.00
5 Daryll Mitchell .75 2.00
6 Ron Majic .75 2.00
7 Daniel Rolfe .75 2.00
8 Mark Hilton .75 2.00
9 Angelo Russo .75 2.00
10 Jeff Jablonski .75 2.00
11 Rob Dumas .75 2.00
12 Chuck Wiegand .75 2.00
13 Steve Chelios .75 2.00
14 Kevin Sullivan .75 2.00
15 Mike Hiltner .75 2.00
16 Brock Kelly 1.25 3.00
17 Paul Cohen 1.25 3.00
18 Scott Taylor .75 2.00
19 Mike DeCarle .75 2.00
20 Jim Ritchie .75 2.00
21 Michael Seaton .75 2.00
22 Frank Anzalone CO .08 .25
23 Dave Cavaliere TR .02 .10
24 Mike Eruzione
Part Owner 2.00 5.00
25 Sean Tomalty .75 2.00

1992-93 Nashville Knights

COMPLETE SET (25) 3.00 8.00
1 Header Card .08 .25
2 Nick Fotiu CO .20 .50
3 George Kozak ACO .02 .10
4 Tom Cole .15 .40
5 Scott Matusovich .15 .40
6 Chris Grassie .15 .40
7 Bob Creamer .15 .40
8 Ray DeSouza .20 .50
9 Stanislav Tkach .15 .40
10 Don Parsons .15 .40
11 Steve Sullivan .15 .40
12 Brian Ferreira .15 .40
13 Rob Dumas .15 .40
14 Michael Seaton .15 .40
15 Mike DeCarle .15 .40
16 Trevor Jobe .15 .40
17 Brian Horan .15 .40
18 Andrey Dylevsky .15 .40
19 Rob Pallante .15 .40
20 Bryan Krygier .15 .40
21 Troy Mick .20 .50
22 Darcy Kaminski .15 .40
23 Olie Sundstrom .20 .50
24 Dale King TR .02 .10
25 Kevin Krueger
Sports Medicine .02 .10

1995-96 Neepewa Natives

COMPLETE SET (24) 4.00 10.0
1 Ryan Anderson .20 .5
2 Ryan Brunel .20 .5
3 Jeff Hudson .20 .5
4 Darren Kirk .20 .5
5 Dwayne Ripley .20 .5
6 Trevor Angus .20 .5
7 Mike Baranyk .20 .5
8 Duane Hoey .20 .5
9 Spencer Platt .20 .5
10 Jeremy Robinson .20 .5
11 Ryan Ogilvie .20 .5
12 Angelo Kokanas .20 .5
13 Craig Anderson .20 .5
14 Dale Isfeld .20 .5
15 Derek Henkelman .20 .5
16 Darcy Pengelly .20 .5
17 Kori Pearson .20 .5
18 Brett Hagberg .20 .5
19 Keith Carson .20 .5
20 Todd Barth .20 .5
21 Craig Martin .20 .5
22 Jason Glover .20 .5
23 Danny Senff .20
24 Billy Joe Stasiuk HCO .08

1996-97 New Hampshire Wildcats

COMPLETE SET (10) 10.00 25.0
21 Derek Bekar .75 2.0
22 Eric Boguniecki 2.00 5.0
23 Christian Bragnalo .75 2.
24 Eric Fitzgerald .75 2.
25 Jason Krog 1.50 4.
26 Mark Mowers 1.50 4.
27 Eric Nickulas 1.50 4.
28 Tim Murray .75 2.
29 Tom Nolan .75 2.
30 Steve O'Brien .75 2.

1997-98 New Hampshire Wildcats

13 Steve O'Brien .40 1.
14 Dan Enders .40 1.

15 Jason Krog 1.25 3.00
16 Dylan Dellezay .40 1.00
17 Sean Matile .60 1.50
18 Chad Onufrechuk .40 1.00
19 Tim Walsh .40 1.00
20 Tom Nolan .40 1.00
21 Derek Bekar .60 1.50
22 Erik Johnson .40 1.00
23 Ryan Harris .40 1.00
24 Christian Bragnalo .40 1.00

1998-99 New Hampshire Wildcats

COMPLETE SET (18) 10.00 25.00
1 John Sadowski .40 1.00
2 Chad Onufrechuk .40 1.00
3 Dan Enders .40 1.00
4 Jason Krog 1.25 3.00
5 Sean Matile .60 1.50
6 Michelle Thornton .75 2.00
7 Kim Knox .75 2.00
8 Tina Carrabba .75 2.00
9 Megan Hales .75 2.00
10 Allicia Roberts .75 2.00
11 Samantha Holmes .75 2.00
12 Steve O'Brien .40 1.00
13 Ryan Harris .40 1.00
14 Jay Shipulski .40 1.00
15 Tim Walsh .40 1.00
16 Jayme Filipowicz .75 2.00
17 Mike Souza .40 1.00
18 Christian Bragnalo .40 1.00

1998-99 New Haven Beast

COMPLETE SET(20) 4.00 8.00
1 Craig Ferguson .15 .40
2 Ian MacNeil .15 .40
3 Marek Malik .15 .40
4 Craig MacDonald .15 .40
5 Byron Ritchie .15 .40
6 Steve Halko .15 .40
7 Shane Willis .40 1.00
8 Todd MacDonald .15 .40
9 Scott Levins .15 .40
10 Dwayne Hay .15 .40
11 Chad Cabana .15 .40
12 Tom Buckley .15 .40
13 Ryan Johnson .15 .40
14 Mike Fountain .30 .75
15 Ashlin Halfnight .15 .40
16 John Jakopin .15 .40
17 Chris Allen
Peter Ratchuk .15 .40
18 Lance Ward
Joey Tetarenko .40 1.00
19 Greg Koehler
Andrw Long .15 .40
20 Marcus Nilsson
Tommy Westlund .30 .75

1989-90 New Haven Nighthawks

COMPLETE SET (15) 4.80 12.00
1 Ken Baumgartner .75 2.00
2 John Bednarski .20 .50
3 Tom Colley .20 .50
4 Daryl Evans .30 .75
5 Ed Johnstone .30 .75
6 Alain Langlais .20 .50
7 Mark Lofthouse .30 .75
8 Hubie McDonough .60 1.50
9 Bill Plager .75 2.00
10 Ron Scott .30 .75
11 Bobby Sheehan .40 1.00
12 Doug Soetaert .60 1.50
13 Jim Wiemer .30 .75
14 Rick Dudley CO .40 1.00
15 Parker McDonald GM/CO .30 .75

1990-91 Newmarket Saints

COMPLETE SET (26) 4.00 10.00
1 Frank Anzalone CO .08 .25
2 Tim Bean .15 .40
3 Brian Blad .15 .40
4 Bryan Cousineau COP .02 .10
5 Alan Hepple .15 .40
6 Donald Hillock COP .02 .10
7 Robert Horyna .15 .40
8 Kent Hulst .15 .40
9 Mike Jackson .15 .40
10 Greg Johnston .20 .50
11 Eldred King MAYOR .02 .10
12 Frank Kovacs COP .02 .10
13 Derek Langille .15 .40
14 Lanny the dog .02 .10
15 Mike Millar .15 .40
16 Mike Moes .15 .40
17 Bill Purcell ACO .02 .10
18 Bobby Reynolds .15 .40
19 Damian Rhodes .60 1.50
20 Bill Root .20 .50
21 Joe Sacco .30 .75
22 Darryl Shannon .30 .75
23 Doug Shedden .30 .75
24 Mike Stevens .20 .50
25 Darren Veitch .20 .50
26 Greg Walters .15 .40

1997-98 New Mexico Scorpions

COMPLETE SET (30) 4.80 12.00
1 Team Photo .15 .40
2 Regan Harper .15 .40
3 Eric Ricard .15 .40
4 Darren Wright .15 .40
5 Derek Crawford .15 .40
6 Sylvain Naud .30 .75
7 Mike Sanderson .15 .40
8 Brian Barnes .15 .40
9 Craig Hamelin .15 .40
10 Darcy Pengelly .15 .40
11 Todd Marcellus .15 .40
12 George Dupont .15 .40
13 Jordan Shields .15 .40
14 Francois Chaput .15 .40
15 Nick Hriczov .15 .40
16 Frederik Beaubien .30 .75
17 David Lessard .15 .40
18 Hugh Bertrand .15 .40
19 Kelly Morel .15 .40
20 Derek Shybunka .15 .40
21 Tony Martino .20 .50
22 Marc Sigel .15 .40
23 Brad Wingfield .15 .40
24 Tyler Boucher .15 .40
25 Carl Paradis .15 .40
26 Aldo Iaquinta .15 .40
27 Garry Unger CO .20 .50
28 Spencer MAS .02 .10
29 Team shot .15 .40
30 New Year's Celebration .02 .10

1997-98 New Mexico Scorpions II

COMPLETE SET (12) 2.50 6.00
1 Center Ice .08 .25
2 Eric Ricard .20 .50
3 Sylvain Naud .30 .75
4 Sylvain Naud .30 .75
5 Tony Martino .30 .75
6 Tony Martino .30 .75
7 Tyler Boucher .20 .50
8 Tyler Boucher .20 .50
9 Tyler Boucher .20 .50
10 George Dupont .20 .50
11 Aldo Iaquinta .20 .50
12 Spencer the Scorpion .08 .25

2001-02 New Mexico Scorpions

COMPLETE SET (23) 40.00 80.00
1 Sergei Radchenko .60 1.50
2 Trevor Hammer .60 1.50
3 Jay Banach .60 1.50
4 Shaun Fairweather .60 1.50
5 Mike O'Malley .60 1.50
6 Peter Ambroziak 2.00 5.00
7 Chris Richards .60 1.50
8 Yann Joseph .60 1.50
9 Jonathan St. Louis .60 1.50
10 Tyler Baines .60 1.50
11 Alek Stojanov 2.00 5.00
12 Jonathan Delisle .60 1.50
13 Scott Myers .60 1.50
14 Travis Van Tighem .60 1.50
15 Arturs Kupaks 1.50 4.00
16 David Cornacchia .60 1.50
17 Donald Choukalos 2.00 5.00
18 Steve Zoryk .60 1.50
19 Gatis Tseplis .60 1.50
20 Tony Martino CO .60 1.50
21 Robert Haddock ACO .20 .50
22 The Scorpion MASCOT .20 .50
NNO Header Card .04 .10

2002-03 New Mexico Scorpions

COMPLETE SET (23) 8.00 20.00
1 Peter Ambroziak .40 1.00
2 Tyler Baines .40 1.00
3 Peter Brearley .40 1.00
4 Luciano Caravaggio .60 1.50
5 Leigh Dean .40 1.00
6 Mario Dumoulin .40 1.00
7 Arturs Kupaks .40 1.00
8 Stephen Margeson .40 1.00
9 Nate Mauer .40 1.00
10 Scott Myers .60 1.50
11 Mike O'Malley .40 1.00
12 Shaun Peet .40 1.00
13 Neil Breen .40 1.00
14 Tobin Praznik .40 1.00
15 Chris Richards .40 1.00
16 Craig Stahl .40 1.00
17 Dave Bourque .40 1.00
18 Bill McDonald HCO .04 .10
19 Mike Payne .40 1.00
21 Travis Van Tighem ACO .04 .10
22 Stanley the Scorpion Mascot .04 .10
NNO Checklist .04 .10

2003-04 New Mexico Scorpions

COMPLETE SET (22) 4.00 10.00
1 Checklist .04 .10
2 Erik Adams .20 .50
3 Jeff Alcombrack .20 .50
4 Ben Gorewich .20 .50
5 Brian Barker .20 .50
6 Chris Richards .20 .50
7 Clint Wensley .20 .50
8 Danny Lorenz .30 .75
9 Vladimir Hartinger .20 .50
10 Jaroslav Kerestes .20 .50
11 Kevin Edgar .20 .50
12 Arturs Kupaks .20 .50
13 Matt Mathias .20 .50
14 Miguel Beaudry .30 .75
15 Mike Oliveira .20 .50
16 Mike Possin .20 .50
17 Shaun Peet .20 .50
18 Peter Ambroziak .20 .50
19 Craig Stahl .20 .50
20 Walker McDonald .20 .50
21 Bill McDonald HCO .04 .10
22 Mascot .04 .10

2004-05 New Mexico Scorpions

COMPLETE SET (25) 12.00 30.00
1 Peter Ambroziak .40 1.00
2 Miguel Beaudry .75 2.00
3 Jordan Bianchin .40 1.00
4 Vladimir Hartinger .40 1.00
5 Mike Possin .40 1.00
6 Ladislav Kouba .40 1.00
7 Alexandre Piche .40 1.00
8 Aaron Schneekloth .40 1.00
9 Guy St. Vincent .40 1.00
10 Matt Weber .40 1.00
11 Erik Adams .40 1.00
12 Trevor Hammer .40 1.00
13 Andrew Katzburg .75 2.00
14 Konrad McKay .40 1.00
15 Ivan Svarny .40 1.00
16 Shawn Legault 1.00 2.50
17 Daryl Moor .40 1.00
18 Randy Murphy .40 1.00
19 Mike Oliveira .40 1.00
20 Daniel Tetrault .40 1.00
21 Ladislav Kouba .40 1.00
22 Alexandre Piche .40 1.00
23 Aaron Schneekloth .40 1.00
24 Guy St. Vincent .75 2.00
25 Matt Weber .40 1.00

2006-07 New Mexico Scorpions

COMPLETE SET (21) 20.00 35.00
1 Ray Edwards CO .10 .25
2 Randy Murphy ACO .10 .25
3 Stanley The Scorpion MASCOT .02 .10
4 Chris Robertson .60 1.50
5 Mike Falk .60 1.50
6 Scott Reid .75 2.00
7 Dave Cacciola .75 2.00
8 Andrew Smale .60 1.50
9 Ryan McLeod .60 1.50
10 Rob Guinn .60 1.50
11 Konrad Reeder .60 1.50
12 Mike Prpich .75 2.00
13 Kevin Harvey .60 1.50
14 Craig MacDonald .60 1.50
15 Jamie Herrington .60 1.50
16 Lance Herauf .60 1.50
17 Josh Garbutt .60 1.50
18 Matt Frick .60 1.50
19 Peter Kennedy .60 1.50
20 Aaron MacInnis .60 1.50
21 Vladimir Hartinger .60 1.50

1997-98 New Orleans Brass

COMPLETE SET (21) 4.00 10.00
1 Jeff Lazaro .30 .75
2 Darryl LaFrance .20 .50
3 Eric Montreuil .20 .50
4 Steve Cheredaryk .30 .75
5 Brad Symes .20 .50
6 Bill McKay .20 .50
7 Martin Villeneuve .20 .50
8 Martin Woods .20 .50
9 Joe Seroski .20 .50
10 Russ Guzior .20 .50
11 Scratch Mo Mascot .02 .10
12 Kevin Pozzo .20 .50
13 Pierre Gendron .20 .50
14 Mike Minard .30 .75
15 Scott Allegrino TR .02 .10
16 Mikhail Nemirovsky .20 .50
17 Kyle Peterson .20 .50
18 Ted Sator HCO .02 .10
19 Scott King .30 .75
20 Jason Downey .20 .50
21 Eric Brule .30 .75

1988-89 Niagara Falls Thunder

COMPLETE SET (25) 8.00 20.00
1 Title Card .08 .25
2 Brad May .75 2.00
3 Paul Wolanski .20 .50
4 Keith Primeau 3.00 8.00
5 Mark Lawrence .20 .50
6 Mike Rosati .40 1.00
7 Dennis Vial .30 .75
8 Shawn McCosh .20 .50
9 Jason Soules .20 .50
10 Rob Fournier .20 .50
11 Scott Pearson .20 .50
12 Jamie Leach .20 .50
13 Colin Miller .20 .50
14 Bryan Fogarty .20 .50
15 Keith Osborne .20 .50
16 Stan Drulia .40 1.00
17 Paul Laus .40 1.00
18 Adrian Van Der Sloot .20 .50
19 Greg Allen .20 .50
20 Don Pancoe .20 .50
21 Alain LaForge .20 .50
22 Bill LaForge GM
CO .08 .25
23 Steve Locke .20 .50
24 Benny Rogano ACO .08 .25
25 Heavy Evason ACO .08 .25

1989-90 Niagara Falls Thunder

COMPLETE SET (25) 6.00 15.00
1 Greg Allen .20 .50
2 Roch Belley .20 .50
3 David Benn .20 .50
4 Andy Bezeau .20 .50
5 George Burnett CO .20 .50
6 Todd Coopman .20 .50
7 Randy Hall ACO .08 .25
8 John Johnson .20 .50
9 Paul Laus .40 1.00
10 Mark Lawrence .20 .50
11 Brad May .40 1.00
12 Don McConnell .20 .50
13 Brian Mueggler .20 .50
14 Don Pancoe .20 .50
15 Keith Primeau 2.00 5.00
16 Geoff Rawson .20 .50
17 Ken Ruddick .20 .50
18 Greg Suchan .20 .50
19 Trainers
Paul Bruneau
Dennis Scott .08 .25
20 Steve Udvari .30 .75
21 Jeff Walker .20 .50
22 Jason Winch .20 .50
23 Paul Wolanski .20 .50
24 Title Card .08 .25
25 Checklist Card .20 .50

1993-94 Niagara Falls Thunder

COMPLETE SET (29) 4.00 10.00
1 Title Card
Checklist .02 .10
2 Jimmy Hibbert .15 .40
3 Darryl Foster .15 .40
4 Gerry Skrypec .15 .40
5 Greg de Vries .30 .75
6 Tim Thompson .15 .40
7 Joel Yates .15 .40
8 Yianni Ioannou .15 .40
9 Steve Nimigon .15 .40
10 Jeff Johnstone .15 .40
11 Brandon Convery .15 .40
12 Dale Junkin .15 .40
13 Ethan Moreau .30 .75
14 Derek Grant .15 .40
15 Neil Fewster .15 .40
16 Jason Reesor .15 .40
17 Tom Moores .15 .40
18 Matthew Mayo .15 .40
19 Bogdan Savenko .15 .40
20 Corey Bricknell .15 .40
21 Derek Sylvester .15 .40
22 Anatoli Filatov .15 .40
23 Jason Bonsignore .15 .40
24 Mike Perna .15 .40
25 Manny Legace .40 1.00
26 Randy Hall CO GM .02 .10
27 Chris Johnstone CO .02 .10
28 Jason Bonsignore
Ethan Moreau
Brandon Convery
Towering Prospects .20 .50
NNO Slapshot Ad Card .01 .05

2001-02 Norfolk Admirals

COMPLETE SET (27) 4.80 12.00
1 Ajay Baines .20 .50
2 Bill Bowler .30 .75
3 Bobby Russell .15 .35
4 Casey Hankinson .30 .75
5 Chris McAlpine .15 .35
6 Craig Anderson .60 1.50
7 Dmitri Tolkunov .14 .35
8 Jean-Yves Leroux .15 .35
9 Jeff Helperl .15 .35
10 Jim Campbell .15 .35
11 Kent Huskins .15 .35
12 Matt Henderson .15 .35
13 Michael Leighton .75 2.00
14 Mike Peluso .30 .75
15 Mike Souza .15 .35
16 Nolan Baumgartner .15 .35
17 Peter White .15 .35
18 Quintin Laing .15 .35
19 Rumun Ndur .15 .35
20 Shawn Thornton .15 .35
21 Steve McCarthy .20 .50
22 Ty Jones .20 .50
23 Tyler Arnason .30 .75
24 Valeri Zelepukin .15 .35
25 Vladimir Chebaturkin .15 .35
26 Trent Yawney CO .04 .10
NNO Team CL .04 .10

2002-03 Norfolk Admirals

COMPLETE SET (26) 15.00
1 Johnathan Aitken .20 .50
2 Craig Andersson .40 1.00
3 Ajay Baines .20 .50
4 Scotty Balan .20 .50
5 Cam Bristow .20 .50
6 Brandin Cote .20 .50
7 Louie DeBrusk .20 .50
8 Casey Hankinson .20 .50
9 Jeff Helperl .20 .50
10 Matt Henderson .20 .50
11 Burke Henry .20 .50
12 Kent Huskins .20 .50
13 Quintin Laing .20 .50
14 Mike Leighton .60 1.50
15 Steve McCarthy .30 .75
16 Brett McLean .20 .50
17 Travis Moen .30 .75
18 Mike Peluso .30 .75
19 Igor Radulov .75 2.00
20 Shawn Thornton .40 1.00
21 Dmitri Tolkunov .20 .50
22 Yorick Treille .20 .50
23 Marty Wilford .20 .50
24 Mikhail Yakubov .40 1.00
25 Trent Yawney CO .04 .10
NNO Checklist .04 .10

2003-04 Norfolk Admirals

COMPLETE SET (24) 5.00 12.00
1 Johnathan Aitken .30 .75
2 Craig Andersson .40 1.00
3 Anton Babchuk .20 .50
4 Ajay Baines .20 .50
5 Michal Barinka .20 .50
6 Blake Bellefeuille .30 .75
7 Brandin Cote .20 .50
8 Matt Ellison .20 .50
9 Carsen Germyn .30 .75
10 Burke Henry .20 .50
11 Duncan Keith .30 .75
12 Matt Keith .20 .50
13 Lasse Kukkonen .20 .50
14 Quintin Laing .40 1.00
15 Adam Munro .40 1.00
16 Steve Passmore .40 1.00
17 Bobby Russell .20 .50
18 Shawn Thornton .20 .50
19 Yorick Treille .20 .50
20 Pavel Vorobiev .20 .50
21 Marty Wilford .20 .50
22 Mikhail Yakubov .20 .50
23 Trent Yawney CO .04 .10
24 Checklist .04 .10

2004-05 Norfolk Admirals

COMPLETE SET (26) 6.00 15.00
1 Craig Anderson .40 1.00
2 Anton Babchuk .20 .50
3 Ajay Baines .20 .50
4 Michal Barinka .20 .50
5 Rene Bourque .40 1.00
6 Mike Brown .20 .50
7 Brandin Cote .20 .50
8 Matt Ellison .20 .50
9 Duncan Keith .20 .50
10 Matt Keith .20 .50
11 Nick Kuiper .20 .50
12 Quintin Laing .30 .75
13 Michael Leighton .40 1.00
14 Travis Moen .20 .50
15 Jason Morgan .20 .50
16 Eric Nickulas .30 .75
17 Igor Radulov .30 .75
18 Shawn Thornton .40 1.00
19 Jim Vandermeer .40 1.00
20 Pavel Vorobiev .20 .50
21 Marty Wilford .20 .50
22 James Wisniewski .20 .50
23 Mikhail Yakubov .20 .50
24 Trent Yawney CO .04 .10
25 Training Staff .04 .10
NNO Checklist .04 .10

2005-06 Norfolk Admirals

COMPLETE SET (30) 6.00 15.00
1 Norfolk Admirals .04 .10
2 Steve Munn .20 .50
3 Michal Barinka .20 .50
4 Brian Lee .20 .50
5 Carl Corazzini .20 .50
6 Anton Babchuk .20 .50
7 Martin St. Pierre .20 .50
8 Milan Bartovic .20 .50
9 Mark Cullen .20 .50
10 Colin Fraser .30 .75
11 Dustin Byfuglien 2.00 5.00
12 Jason Morgan .20 .50
13 Nathan Barrett .20 .50
14 James Wisniewski .20 .50
15 Mike Brown .20 .50
16 Matt Keith .20 .50
17 Nick Kuiper .20 .50
18 Eric Meloche .20 .50
19 Quintin Laing .20 .50
20 Corey Crawford .40 1.00
21 Ajay Baines .20 .50
22 Adam Munro .40 1.00
23 Mikhail Yakubov .20 .50
24 Shawn Thornton .40 1.00
25 Mike Haviland HC .04 .10
26 Rick Kowalsky AC .04 .10
27 McClung
Bender TR .04 .10
28 Cinq-Mars
Holden EQM .04 .10
29 Al MacIsaac GM .04 .10
30 Pascal Bedard .20 .50

2006-07 Norfolk Admirals

COMPLETE SET (28) 6.00 15.00
1 Patrick Lalime .30 .75
2 Corey Crawford .30 .75
3 Steve Munn .20 .50
4 David Koci .20 .50
5 Brandon Rogers .20 .50
6 Cam Barker .20 .50
7 Jordan Hendry .20 .50
8 Carl Corazzini .20 .50
9 Bruno St. Jacques .20 .50
10 Martin St. Pierre .20 .50
11 Craig MacDonald .20 .50
12 Troy Brouwer .30 .75
13 David Bolland 1.25 3.00
14 Colin Fraser .20 .50
15 Dustin Byfuglien 2.00 5.00
16 Bryan Bickell .20 .50
17 Adam Burish .20 .50
18 Jonas Nordqvist .20 .50
19 Michael Blunden .30 .75
20 Pierre Parenteau .20 .50
21 Reed Low .30 .75
22 Adam Berti .20 .50
23 Brandon Bochenski .20 .50
24 Danny Richmond .20 .50
25 Al MacIsaac GM .05 .10
26 Mike Haviland CO .10 .25
27 Ted Dent ACO .05 .10
28 Trainers .05 .10

2007-08 Norfolk Admirals

COMPLETE SET (30) 6.00 15.00
1 Jonathan Boutin .40 1.00
2 Marc Denis .40 1.00
3 Karri Ramo .40 1.00
4 Jay Leach .20 .50
5 Matt Smaby .20 .50
6 Mario Scalzo .20 .50
7 David Schneider .20 .50
8 Vladimir Mihalik .20 .50
9 Jay Rosehill .20 .50
10 Andy Rogers .20 .50
11 Justin Keller .20 .50
12 Adam Henrich .20 .50
13 Kyle Wanvig .20 .50
14 Norm Milley .20 .50
15 Chris Lawrence .20 .50
16 Junior Lessard .20 .50
17 Paul Szczechura .20 .50
18 Karl Stewart .20 .50
19 Radek Smolenak .40 1.00
20 Rob Klinkhammer .20 .50
21 Bracken Kearns .20 .50
22 Blair Jones .20 .50
23 Justin Fletcher .20 .50
24 Zbynek Hrdel .20 .50
25 Marek Kvapil .20 .50
26 Stanislav Lascek .20 .50
27 Shawn Collymore .20 .50
28 Steve Stirling HC .04 .10
29 Darren Rumble AC .04 .10
30 T.Alva/P.Henderson TR .04 .10

2014-15 Norfolk Admirals

COMPLETE SET (33) 8.00 20.00
1 Yann Danis .50 1.25
2 Josh Manson .30 .75
3 Kevin Gagne .30 .75
4 Nathan McIver .30 .75
5 Matt Bailey .30 .75
6 Brandon Yip .40 1.00
7 Louis Leblanc .50 1.25
8 Antoine Laganiere .30 .75
9 Steve MacIntyre .30 .75
10 Jarrod Skalde CO .30 .75
11 John Gibson .75 2.00
12 Matt Clark .30 .75
13 Nicolas Kerdiles .30 .75
14 Emerson Etem .50 1.25
15 Charles Sarault .30 .75
16 Joseph Cramarossa .30 .75
17 William Karlsson .50 1.25
18 Andrew O'Brien .30 .75
19 Dave Steckel .30 .75
20 Eric Veilleux Asst. CO .30 .75
21 Jason Labarbera .30 .75
22 Mark Fistric .30 .75
23 Brendan Bell .30 .75
24 Stefan Noesen .30 .75
25 John Kurtz .30 .75
26 Max Friberg .50 1.25
27 Brad Winchester .40 1.00
28 Chris Wagner .30 .75
29 Colby Robak .30 .75
30 Jaycob Megna .30 .75
31 Shea Theodore .40 1.00
32 Dany Heatley .50 1.25
33 Marty Wilford Asst. CO .30 .75

1982-83 North Bay Centennials

COMPLETE SET (24) 8.00 20.00
1 Allen Bishop .30 .75
2 John Capel .30 .75
3 Rob Degagne .30 .75
4 Phil Drouillard .30 .75
5 Jeff Eatough .30 .75
6 Tony Gilliard .30 .75
7 Paul Gillis .60 1.50
8 Pete Handley .30 .75
9 Mark Hatcher .30 .75
10 Tim Helmer .30 .75
11 Craig Kales .30 .75
12 Bob LaForest .30 .75
13 Mark LaForest .75 2.00
14 Bill Maguire .30 .75
15 Andrew McBain .60 1.50
16 Ron Meighan .30 .75
17 Rick Morocco .30 .75
18 Alain Raymond .30 .75
19 Joe Reekie .75 2.00
20 Joel Smith .40 1.00
21 Bert Templeton CO .30 .75
22 Kevin Vescio .30 .75
23 Peter Woodgate .30 .75
24 Don Young .30 .75

1983-84 North Bay Centennials

COMPLETE SET (25) 8.00 20.00
1 Sponsor's Card .08 .25
2 Peter Abric .30 .75
3 Richard Benoit .30 .75
4 Scott Birnie .30 .75
5 John Capel .30 .75
6 Curtis Collin .30 .75
7 Rob Degagne .30 .75
8 Kevin Hatcher 1.25 3.00
9 Mark Hatcher .30 .75
10 Tim Helmer .30 .75
11 Jim Hunter .30 .75
12 Kevin Kerr .30 .75
13 Nick Kypreos .60 1.50
14 Mike Larouche .30 .75
15 Greg Larsen .30 .75
16 Mark Lavarre .30 .75
17 Brett MacDonald .30 .75
18 Wayne Macphee .30 .75
19 Peter McGrath .30 .75
20 Rob Nichols .30 .75
21 Ron Sanko .30 .75
22 Kevin Vescio .30 .75
23 Mike Webber .30 .75
24 Peter Woodgate .30 .75
25 Bert Templeton CO/GM .30 .75

1993-94 North Bay Centennials

COMPLETE SET (26) 4.00 10.00
1 Brad Brown .20 .50
2 Sandy Allan .20 .50
3 Rob Lave .15 .40
4 Steve McLaren .15 .40
5 Andy Delmore .40 1.00
6 Corey Neilson .15 .40
7 Jason Campeau .15 .40
8 Jim Ensom .15 .40
9 Bill Lang .15 .40
10 Ryan Gillis .15 .40
11 Michael Burman .15 .40
12 Stefan Rivard .15 .40
13 D.J. MacPherson .15 .40
14 Lee Jinman .15 .40
15 Scott Cherrey .15 .40
16 Damien Bloye .15 .40
17 Denis Gaudet .15 .40
18 Bob Thornton .15 .40
19 John Guirestante .15 .40
20 Jeff Shevalier .15 .40
21 Scott Roche .20 .50
22 Vitali Yachmenev .30 .75
23 Bert Templeton CO .15 .40
24 Rob Kirsch ACO .02 .10
25 Brad Brown
Vitali Yachmenev
Top Prospects .15 .40
NNO Slapshot Ad Card .01 .05

1994-95 North Bay Centennials

COMPLETE SET (26) 4.00 10.00
1 Joel Gagnon .15 .40
2 Scott Roche .20 .50
3 Derek Lahnalampi .15 .40
4 Brad Brown .20 .50
5 Steve McLaren .15 .40
6 Kam White .15 .40
7 Corey Neilson .15 .40
8 Jason Campeau .15 .40
9 Stephen Carpenter .15 .40
10 Trevor Gallant .15 .40
11 Alex Matvichuk .15 .40
12 Ryan Gillis .15 .40
13 Kris Cantu .15 .40
14 Stefan Rivard .15 .40
15 Brian Whitley .15 .40
16 Dustin Virag .15 .40
17 Lee Jinman .20 .50
18 Scott Cherrey .15 .40
19 Damien Bloye .15 .40
20 Justin Robinson .15 .40
21 Kody Grigg .15 .40
22 John Guirestante .15 .40
23 Gary Roach .15 .40
24 Vitali Yachmenev .30 .75
25 Shane Parker CO/GM
Tom .02 .10
NNO Ad Card .01 .05

1992-93 North Dakota Fighting Sioux

COMPLETE SET (32) 8.00 20.00
1 Akil Adams .30 .75
2 Darren Bear .30 .75
3 Sean Beswick .30 .75
4 Brad Bombardir .40 1.00
5 Joby Bond .30 .75
6 Troy Davis .30 .75
7 Chris Gotziaman .30 .75
8 Dean Grillo .30 .75
9 Corey Howe .30 .75
10 Brett Hryniuk .30 .75
11 Greg Johnson .75 2.00
12 Chad Johnson .30 .75
13 Corey Johnson .30 .75
14 Todd Jones .30 .75
15 Scott Kirton .30 .75
16 Page Klostreich .30 .75
17 Jon Larson .30 .75
18 Jeff Lembke .30 .75
19 John McCoy .30 .75
20 Kevin McKinnon .30 .75
21 Darcy Mitani .30 .75
22 Keith Murphy .30 .75
23 Nick Naumenko .40 1.00
24 Jarrod Olson .30 .75
25 Lars Oxholm .30 .75
26 Kevin Powell .30 .75
27 Kevin Rappana .30 .75

2003-04 North Dakota Fighting Sioux

COMPLETE SET (30) 20.00 50.00
1 Brandon Bochenski 1.25 3.00
2 Nate Ziegelmann .40 1.00
3 James Massen .40 1.00
4 Quinn Fylling .40 1.00
5 Mike Prpich .40 1.00
6 Ryan Hale .40 1.00
7 Tyler Palmiscno .40 1.00
8 Matt Jones .75 2.00
9 Brad Berry ACO .20 .50
10 Chris Porter .40 1.00
11 Zach Parise 8.00 20.00
12 Drew Stafford 2.00 5.00
13 Colby Genoway .75 2.00
14 Lee Marvin .40 1.00
15 Team Logo .04 .10
16 Andy Schneider .40 1.00
17 Brady Murray 1.25 3.00
18 Engelstad Arena .04 .10
19 Rory McMahon .40 1.00
20 Matt Smaby 1.25 3.00
21 Jordan Parise 1.25 3.00
22 Brian Canady .40 1.00
23 Robbie Bina .40 1.00
24 Jake Brandt .40 1.00
25 Dean Blais CO .40 1.00
26 Matt Greene 1.25 3.00
27 Erik Fabian .40 1.00
28 David Lundholm .40 1.00
29 Dave Hakstol .75 2.00
30 Nick Fuher .40 1.00

2004-05 North Dakota Fighting Sioux

COMPLETE SET (30) 15.00 40.00
1 Header Card .04 .10
2 Robbie Bina .40 1.00
3 Jake Brandt .75 2.00
4 Brian Canady .40 1.00
5 Erik Fabian .40 1.00
6 Scott Foyt .40 1.00
7 Nick Fuher .40 1.00
8 Quinn Fylling .40 1.00
9 Colby Genoway .40 1.00
10 Matt Greene 1.25 3.00
11 Matt Jones .75 2.00
12 Rylan Kaip .40 1.00
13 Philippe Lamoureux .75 2.00
14 Lee Marvin .40 1.00
15 James Massen .40 1.00
16 Rory McMahon .40 1.00
17 Brady Murray .75 2.00
18 Jordan Parise 1.25 3.00
19 Chris Porter .40 1.00
20 Mike Prpich .40 1.00
21 Kyle Radke .40 1.00
22 Andy Schneider .40 1.00
23 Matt Smaby .75 2.00
24 Rastislav Smirko .75 2.00
25 Drew Stafford 1.25 3.00
26 Travis Zajac 1.25 3.00
27 Brad Berry ACO .20 .50
28 Carey Eades ACO .20 .50
29 Dave Hakstol CO .20 .50
30 Team Photo .20 .50

1995-96 North Iowa Huskies

COMPLETE SET (34) 20.00 50.00
1 Dave Boehm .75 2.00
2 Mike Cerniglia .75 2.00
3 Lionel Crump .75 2.00
4 Peter Cullen .75 2.00
5 Nate Dicasmirro .75 2.00
6 D.J. Drayna .75 2.00
7 Andy Fermoyle .75 2.00
8 Matt Fetterman .75 2.00
9 Mike Fryar 1.25 3.00
10 Shane Fukushima .75 2.00
11 Bucky Gruber .75 2.00
12 Jason Helgeson TR .02 .10
13 Mark Hicks ACO .02 .10
14 Huskies CL .02 .10
15 Furlin Husky (Mascot) .02 .10
16 Ryan James .75 2.00
17 Tom Lund .75 2.00
18 Kevin Mackey .75 2.00
19 Erik Macy .75 2.00
20 Josh Mizerek .75 2.00
21 Joe Mussey ACO .02 .10
22 Gregg Naumenko 2.00 5.00
23 Matt Noga .75 2.00
24 P.K. O'Handley CO .02 .10
25 Mark Pannitto 1.25 3.00
26 Matt Romaniski .75 2.00

27 Mike Romano .75 2.00
28 Mike Rucinski 1.25 3.00
29 R.J. Schriefer .75 2.00
30 Mike Skogland .75 2.00
31 Matt Snesrud .75 2.00
32 Team Media/ .02 .10
33 Season Schedule .02 .10
34 Title Card .02 .10

1992-93 Northern Michigan Wildcats

COMPLETE SET (32) 4.80 12.00
1 Brian Barker .20 .50
2 Steve Carpenter .20 .50
3 Chad Dameworth .20 .50
4 Dustin Fahl .20 .50
5 Joe Frederick .20 .50
6 Bryan Ganz .20 .50
7 Scott Green .20 .50
8 Greg Hadden .20 .50
9 Steve Hamilton .20 .50
10 Mike Harding .20 .50
11 Jason Hehr .20 .50
12 Dave Huettl .20 .50
13 Troy Johnson .20 .50
14 Karson Kaebel .20 .50
15 Kory Karlander .20 .50
16 Rob Kruhlak .20 .50
17 Garett MacDonald .20 .50
18 Bill MacGillivray .20 .50
19 Don McCusker .20 .50
20 Brent Riplinger .20 .50
21 Dan Ruoho .20 .50
22 Corwin Saurdiff .20 .50
23 Kyuin Shim .20 .50
24 Geoff Simpson .20 .50
25 Scott Smith .20 .50
26 Paul Taylor .20 .50
27 Steve Woog .20 .50
28 Rick Comley CO .02 .10
29 Pat Ford ACO .02 .10
30 Morey Gare ACO .02 .10
31 Dave Shyiak .02 .10
32 Wildcat Willy .02 .10

1993-94 Northern Michigan Wildcats

COMPLETE SET (32) 6.00 15.00
1 Brian Barker .20 .50
2 Keith Bartholomaus .20 .50
3 Steve Carpenter .20 .50
4 Darcy Dallas .20 .50
5 Chad Dameworth .20 .50
6 Bryan Ganz .20 .50
7 Justin George .20 .50
8 Scott Green .20 .50
9 Greg Hadden .20 .50
10 Steve Hamilton .20 .50
11 Patrick Hansson .20 .50
12 Mike Harding .20 .50
13 Jason Hehr .20 .50
14 Mike Hillock .20 .50
15 Trevor Janicki .20 .50
16 Karson Kaebel .20 .50
17 Kory Karlander .20 .50
18 Dieter Kochan .40 1.00
19 Roger Lewis .20 .50
20 Garett MacDonald .20 .50
21 Bill MacGillivray .20 .50
22 Don McCusker .20 .50
23 Brent Riplinger .20 .50
24 Dean Seymour .20 .50
25 Scott Smith .20 .50
26 Paul Taylor .20 .50
27 Shayne Tomlinson .20 .50
28 Jason Welch .20 .50
29 Steve Woog .20 .50
30 Pat Ford ACO .02 .10
31 Morey Gare ACO .02 .10
32 Rick Comley CO .02 .10

2004-05 Northern Michigan Wildcats

COMPLETE SET (27) 12.00 30.00
1 Pat Bateman .40 1.00
2 Matt Ciancio .40 1.00
3 Dusty Collins .40 1.00
4 Andrew Contois .40 1.00
5 Blake Cosgrove .40 1.00
6 Kevin Gardner .40 1.00
7 Tim Hartung .40 1.00
8 Josh Hatinger .40 1.00
9 Bob Helminen .40 1.00
10 Clayton Lainsbury .40 1.00
11 Rob Lehtinen .40 1.00
12 Matt Maunu .40 1.00
13 Jamie Milam .40 1.00
14 John Miller .40 1.00
15 Patrick Murphy .40 1.00
16 Dan Olver .75 2.00
17 Nathan Oystrick .40 1.00
18 Mike Santorelli .40 1.00
19 Andrew Sarauer .40 1.00
20 Bobby Selden .40 1.00
21 Matt Siddall .40 1.00
22 Dirk Southern .40 1.00
23 Alan Swanson .40 1.00
24 Zach Tarkir .40 1.00
25 Tuomas Tarkki .75 2.00
26 Geoff Waugh .40 1.00
27 Bill Zaniboni .75 2.00

2001-02 Notre Dame Fighting Irish

COMPLETE SET 15.00 30.00
1 Jeremiah Kimento .75 2.00
2 David Inman .75 2.00
3 Jon Maruk .75 2.00
4 Sam Cornelius .75 2.00
5 Rob Globke 1.25 3.00
6 Neil Komadoski .75 2.00
7 Brett Lebda .75 2.00
8 Connor Dunlop 1.25 3.00
9 Evan Neilsen .75 2.00
10 T.J. Mathieson .75 2.00
11 Brad Wanchulak .75 2.00
12 Ryan Mundt .75 2.00
13 Paul Harris .75 2.00
14 Aaron Gill .75 2.00
15 John Wroblewski .75 2.00
16 Derek Smith .75 2.00
17 Cory McLean .75 2.00
18 Michael Chin .75 2.00

2002-03 Notre Dame Fighting Irish

COMPLETE SET (16) 8.00 20.00
1 Jake Wiegand .60 1.50
2 Connor Dunlop .75 2.00
3 Michael Chin .60 1.50
4 Tony Zasowski .60 1.50
5 John Wroblewski .60 1.50
6 Ad card .04 .10
7 Evan Nielsen .60 1.50
8 team card .04 .10
9 Ad card .04 .10
10 Kyle Dolder .60 1.50
11 Tom Galvin .60 1.50
12 Neil Komadoski .60 1.50
13 Brett Lebda 1.25 3.00
14 Rob Globke .75 2.00
15 Aaron Gill .60 1.50
16 T.J. Mathieson .75 2.00

2003-04 Notre Dame Fighting Irish

1 Joe Zurenko .40 1.00
2 Derek Smith .40 1.00
3 Cory McLean .40 1.00
4 Brad Wanchulak .40 1.00
5 Morgan Cey .60 1.50
6 T.J. Mathieson .40 1.00
7 Brett Lebda .40 1.00
8 Rob Globke 1.25 3.00
9 Neil Komadoski .40 1.00
10 Tom Galvin .40 1.00
11 Aaron Gill .60 1.50

2004-05 Notre Dame Fighting Irish

COMPLETE SET (25) 10.00 25.00
1 Wes O'Neill .75 2.00
2 David Brown .75 2.00
3 Bryan D'Arcy .40 1.00
4 Mark Van Guilder .40 1.00
5 Victor Oreskovich .40 1.00
6 Evan Rankin .40 1.00
7 Brock Sheahan .40 1.00
8 Andrew Eggert .40 1.00
9 Luke Lucyk .40 1.00
10 Dave Venard .40 1.00
11 Michael Bartlett .40 1.00
12 T.J. Jindra .40 1.00
13 Matt Williams-Kovacs .40 1.00
14 Josh Sciba .40 1.00
15 Noah Babin .40 1.00
16 Jason Paige .40 1.00
17 Rory Walsh .75 2.00
18 Tim Wallace .40 1.00
19 Tony Gill .40 1.00
20 Mike Walsh .40 1.00
21 Matt Amado .40 1.00
22 Chris Trick .40 1.00
23 Joe Zurenko .40 1.00
24 Cory McLean .40 1.00
25 Morgan Cey .75 2.00

2005-06 Notre Dame Freshmen

COMPLETE SET (5) 2.00 5.00
1 Eric Condra .40 1.00
2 Justin White .40 1.00
3 Garrett Regan .40 1.00
4 Jordan Pierce .40 1.00
5 Christian Hanson .40 1.00

2014-15 Notre Dame Fighting Irish

COMPLETE SET () 6.00 15.00
1 Joe Aiken .30 .75
2 Anders Bjork .30 .75
3 Bo Brauer .30 .75
4 Tony Bretzman .30 .75
5 Dawson Cook .30 .75
6 Thomas DiPauli .30 .75
7 Jake Evans .30 .75
8 Steven Fogarty .30 .75
9 Jordan Gross .30 .75
10 Sam Herr .30 .75
11 Vince Hinostroza .30 .75
12 Connor Hurley .30 .75
13 Eric Johnson .30 .75
14 Chad Katunar .30 .75
15 Mario Lucia .30 .75
16 Ben Ostlie .30 .75
17 Cal Petersen .30 .75
18 Luke Ripley .30 .75
19 Robbie Russo .30 .75
20 Andy Ryan .30 .75
21 Peter Schneider .30 .75
22 Nick Stasack .30 .75
23 Ali Thomas .30 .75
24 Justin Wade .30 .75
25 Austin Wuthrich .30 .75

1984-85 Nova Scotia Oilers

COMPLETE SET (26) 6.00 15.00
1 Mark Holden .30 .75
2 Dave Allison .20 .50
3 Dwayne Boettger .20 .50
4 Lowell Loveday .20 .50
5 Rejean Cloutier .20 .50
6 Ray Cote .20 .50
7 Pat Conacher .40 1.00
8 Ken Berry .40 1.00
9 Steve Graves .20 .50
10 Todd Strueby .40 1.00
11 Steve Smith .75 2.00
12 Archie Henderson .30 .75
13 Dean Dachyshyn .20 .50
14 Marc Habscheid .40 1.00
15 Larry Melnyk .30 .75
16 Raimo Summanen .40 1.00
17 Jim Playfair .20 .50
18 Mike Zanier .40 1.00
19 Ian Wood .20 .50
20 Dean Hopkins .20 .50
21 Norm Aubin .20 .50
22 Tony Currie .20 .50
23 Ross Lambert .20 .50
24 Terry Martin .20 .50
25 Ed Chadwick CO
Larry Kish CO
Bob Boucher CO .40 1.00
26 Lou Christian TR
Kevin Farris TR .08 .25

1985-86 Nova Scotia Oilers

COMPLETE SET (28) 6.00 15.00
1 Dean Hopkins .20 .50
2 Jeff Larmer .20 .50
3 Mike Moller .20 .50
4 Dean Dachyshyn .20 .50
5 Bruce Boudreau .30 .75
6 Ken Solheim .20 .50
7 Jeff Beukeboom .30 .75
8 Mark Lavarre .20 .50
9 John Ollson .20 .50
10 Lou Crawford .20 .50
11 Warren Skorodenski .40 1.00
12 Dwayne Boettger .20 .50
13 Daryl Reaugh 1.25 3.00
14 John Miner .20 .50
15 Jim Ralph 1.25 3.00
16 Wayne Presley .30 .75
17 Steve Graves .20 .50
18 Tom McMurchy .20 .50
19 Darin Sceviour .20 .50
20 Kent Paynter .20 .50
21 Larry Kish GM/CO .08 .25
22 Jim Playfair .20 .50
23 Kevin Farris TR
Ralph Mosher TR .08 .25
24 Mickey Volcan .20 .50
25 Ron Low ACO .40 1.00
26 Don Biggs .20 .50
27 Bruce Eakin .20 .50
28 Team Photo .30 .75

1976-77 Nova Scotia Voyageurs

COMPLETE SET (?)

1977-78 Nova Scotia Voyageurs

COMPLETE SET (24) 15.00 30.00
1 Bruce Baker .50 1.00
2 Maurice Barrette .50 1.00
3 Barry Borrett .50 1.00
4 Tim Burke .50 1.00
5 Jim Cahoon .50 1.00
6 Norm Dupont .75 1.50
7 Greg Fox .75 1.50
8 Mike Hobin .50 1.00
9 Bob Holland .50 1.00
10 Don Howse .50 1.00
11 Pat Hughes 1.00 2.00
12 Chuck Luksa .50 1.00
13 Dave Lumley 1.00 2.00
14 Al MacNeil CO .75 1.50
15 Gord McTavish .50 1.00
16 Rick Meagher 1.50 3.00
17 Mike Pollich .50 1.00
18 Moe Robinson .50 1.00
19 Gaeton Rochette .50 1.00
20 Pierre Roy .50 1.00
21 Frank St.Marseille 1.00 2.00
22 Derrick St.Marseille TR .25 .50
23 Rod Schutt .50 1.00
24 Ron Wilson 1.00 2.00

1983-84 Nova Scotia Voyageurs

COMPLETE SET (24) 6.00 15.00
1 Mark Holden .40 1.00
2 Bill Kitchen .20 .50
3 Dave Allison .20 .50
4 Stephane Lefebvre .20 .50
5 Stan Hennigar .20 .50
6 Steve Marengere .20 .50
7 John Goodwin .20 .50
8 John Newberry .20 .50
9 Bill Riley .30 .75
10 Norman Baron .30 .75
11 Brian Skrudland .75 2.00
12 Mike Lalor .40 1.00
13 Blair Barnes .20 .50
14 Remi Gagne .20 .50
15 Steve Penney .75 2.00
16 Michel Therrien .30 .75
17 Dave Stoyanovich .20 .50
18 Brian Patafie TR
Lou Christian TR .08 .25
19 Mike McPhee .75 2.00
20 Wayne Thompson .20 .50
21 Ted Fauss .20 .50
22 Jeff Teal .20 .50
23 Larry Landon .20 .50
24 Greg Moffett .20 .50

1996-97 OCN Blizzard

COMPLETE SET (25) 4.00 10.00
1 Rick Gregory .20 .50
2 Reynold Monias .20 .50
3 Dave Patenaude .20 .50
4 Clint Miller .20 .50
5 Alec Durocher .20 .50
6 Peter Bird .20 .50
7 Steve Ford .20 .50
8 Devin Salisbury .20 .50
9 John Brass .20 .50
10 Barrett Labossiere .20 .50
11 Cliff Duchesne .20 .50
12 Mike Stevenson .20 .50
13 Wally Wuttunee .20 .50
14 Don Boyer .20 .50
15 Jay Seymour .20 .50
16 Darren Kirk .20 .50
17 Tobias Hall .20 .50
18 John O'Toole .20 .50
19 Chad Ramsay .20 .50
20 Clayton Debray .20 .50
21 Konrad Mckay .20 .50
22 Ryan Belbas .20 .50
23 John McCusker .20 .50
24 Ryan Person .20 .50
25 Patrick Herman .20 .50

1997-98 OCN Blizzard

COMPLETE SET (24) 20.00
1 Team Picture .20 .50
2 Tucker Madder .20 .50
3 Kevin Wilson .20 .50
4 Larry Willerton .20 .50
5 Terence Tootoo 4.00 10.00
6 Clayton Quinn .20 .50
7 Shaun Rose .20 .50
8 Brad Hicks .20 .50
9 Barrett Labossiere .20 .50
10 Curtis Baldwin .20 .50
11 Jimmie Ronnback .20 .50
12 Wally Wuttunee .20 .50
13 Don Boyer .20 .50
14 Aaron Porter .20 .50
15 Alec Durocher .20 .50
16 Cliff Duchesne .20 .50
17 Devin Salisbury .20 .50
18 Cory Dittmer .20 .50
19 Derek Ernest .20 .50
20 Konrad Mckay .20 .50
21 Ryan Belbas .20 .50
22 John McCusker .20 .50
23 Ryan Person .20 .50
24 Tyler Love .20 .50

1998-99 OCN Blizzard

COMPLETE SET (24) 20.00 40.00
1 Team Picture .40 1.00
2 Terence Tootoo 4.00 10.00
3 Kevin Wilson .20 .50
4 Larry Willerton .20 .50
5 Morris Elderkin .20 .50
6 Darcy Johnson .20 .50
7 Shaun Rose .20 .50
8 Brad Hicks .20 .50
9 Barrett Labossiere .20 .50
10 Kevin Stoneman .20 .50
11 Jamie Vossen .20 .50
12 Jordin Tootoo 10.00 25.00
13 Aaron Porter .20 .50
14 Chad Ryan .20 .50
15 Cliff Duchesne .20 .50
16 Devin Salisbury .20 .50
17 Jimmie Ronnback .20 .50
18 Tom Herman .20 .50
19 Konrad Mckay .20 .50
20 Ryan Belbas .20 .50
21 John McCusker .20 .50
22 Ryan Person .20 .50
23 Preston McKay .20 .50
24 Brian Tucker .20 .50

1999-00 OCN Blizzard

COMPLETE SET (24)
1 Team Picture .20 .50
2 Rob Hrabec .20 .50
3 Justin Relland .20 .50
4 Cory Sawatzky .20 .50
5 Justin Seaborg .20 .50
6 Gary Lafreniere .20 .50
7 Darcy Johnson .20 .50
8 Darryl Crumb .20 .50
9 Kirk Zieffle .20 .50
10 Jamie Muswagon .20 .50
11 Michael Young .20 .50
12 Ryan Braun .20 .50
13 Mike Glover .20 .50
14 Dustin Rogers .20 .50
15 Phillip Albert .20 .50
16 Justin Williams .20 .50
17 Dave Splawinski .20 .50
18 Steve Reid .20 .50
19 Clifford Scatch .20 .50
20 Tom Herman .20 .50
21 Terence Tootoo 4.00 10.00
22 Dwayne Twerdin .20 .50
23 Jeff Grandfield .20 .50
24 Preston McKay .20 .50

2000-01 OCN Blizzard

COMPLETE SET (25) 8.00 20.00
1 Team Picture .20 .50
2 Marc-Andre Leclerc .20 .50
3 Garrett Hildebrandt .20 .50
4 Matko Malbasa .20 .50
5 Jared Lang .20 .50
6 Darcy Johnson .20 .50
7 Alton Jackson .20 .50
8 Kirk Zieffle .20 .50
9 Jamie Muswagon .20 .50
10 Michael Young .20 .50
11 Ryan Braun .20 .50
12 Shayne Emmons .20 .50
13 Derek Sharp .20 .50
14 Phillip Albert .20 .50
15 Justin Williams .20 .50
16 Curtis Campbell .20 .50
17 Clifford Scatch .20 .50
18 Trevor Len .20 .50
19 Terence Tootoo 4.00 10.00
20 Justin Tetrault .20 .50
21 Jeff Grandfield .20 .50
22 Dan Joyal .20 .50
23 Steve Macintyre .20 .50
24 Tim Haun .20 .50
25 Dave Splawinski .20 .50

2001-02 OCN Blizzard

COMPLETE SET (27) 5.00 12.00
1 Header Card .04 .10
2 Team Picture .10 .25
3 Louis Chabot .20 .50
4 Mike Gooch .20 .50
5 Garrett Hildebrandt .20 .50
6 Jeff Froese .20 .50
7 Cody Reynolds .20 .50
8 Andy Coates .20 .50
9 Aaron Starr .20 .50
10 Alton Jackson .20 .50
11 Kirk Zieffle .20 .50
12 Jamie Muswagon .20 .50
13 Michael Young .20 .50
14 Ryan Braun .20 .50
15 Russell Spence .20 .50
16 Phillip Albert .20 .50
17 Justin Williams .20 .50
18 Justin Seaborg .20 .50
19 Leighton Alexson .20 .50
20 Trevor Len .20 .50
21 Mark Wallmann .20 .50
22 Justin Tetrault .20 .50
23 Mike Ouellet .20 .50
24 Everett Bear .20 .50
25 Dylan Rochon .20 .50
26 Marc-Andre Leclerc .20 .50
27 Dave Splawinski .20 .50

2002-03 OCN Blizzard

COMPLETE SET (27) 5.00 12.00
1 Team Picture .10 .25
2 Andrew Gallant .20 .50
3 Mike Gooch .20 .50
4 Garrett Hildebrandt .20 .50
5 Dallas Jackson .20 .50
6 Paul Wallmann .20 .50
7 Andy Coates .20 .50
8 Aaron Starr .20 .50
9 Alton Jackson .20 .50
10 Jared Lang .20 .50
11 Michael Young .20 .50
12 Ryan Braun .20 .50
13 Kiel Wilgosh .20 .50
14 Daniel Mayer .20 .50
15 Jason Kowalski .20 .50
16 Mike Kaluzny .20 .50
17 Ryan Weistche .20 .50
18 Trevor Len .20 .50
19 Tyler Rhyorchuk .20 .50
20 Jason Marin .20 .50
21 Everett Bear .20 .50
22 Chop Melnyk .20 .50
23 Dylan Rochon .20 .50
24 Ryan Constant .20 .50
25 Jonathon Meyer .20 .50
26 Mark Wallmann .20 .50
27 League Champs .04 .10

2003-04 OCN Blizzard

COMPLETE SET (27) 4.00 10.00
1 Header Card .04 .10
2 Everett Bear .20 .50
3 Jason Butler .20 .50
4 Ryan Constant .20 .50
5 Pierre-Olivier Girouard .20 .50
6 Mike Gooch .20 .50
7 Tim Hammell .20 .50
8 Cole Hunter .20 .50
9 Dallas Jackson .20 .50
10 Travis Kotyk .20 .50
11 Jared Lang .20 .50
12 Daniel Mayer .20 .50
13 Lyle McKay .20 .50
14 Don Melnyk .20 .50
15 Jonathon Meyer .20 .50
16 Brett Needham .20 .50
17 Lem Randell .20 .50
18 Jonathon Romic .20 .50
19 Aaron Starr .20 .50
20 Matt Summers .20 .50
21 Stephen Sunderman .20 .50
22 David Victor .20 .50
23 Mark Wallmann .20 .50
24 Paul Wallmann .20 .50
25 Kiel Wilgosh .20 .50
26 Michael Young .20 .50
27 Team Photo .04 .10

1998-99 Odessa Jackalopes

COMPLETE SET (22) 10.00 25.00
1 Jacque Rodrigue .40 1.00
2 Rob Lukacs .75 2.00
3 Ryan Equale .40 1.00
4 Rick Girhiny .75 2.00
5 Terry Flynn .40 1.00
6 Paul Fioroni .40 1.00
7 Mike Ross .60 1.50
8 Johan Hagman .40 1.00
9 Sami Laine .60 1.50
10 Anders Lindberg .75 2.00
11 Dan Lavergne .40 1.00
12 Bo Anderson .40 1.00
13 Shayne LeBreton .40 1.00
14 Michael Tornquist .60 1.50
15 Christian Wibner .75 2.00
16 Chris Morque .40 1.00
17 Bill Pye .75 2.00
18 Martin Ohestedt .75 2.00
19 Joe Clark CO .02 .10
20 Pat Kerin EM .02 .10
21 Greg Andis TR .02 .10
22 Golden Corral .02 .10

1999-00 Odessa Jackalopes

COMPLETE SET (21) 5.60 20.00
1 Michael Tornquist .40 1.00
2 Paul Vincent .40 1.00
3 Chris Morque .40 1.00
4 Fredrick Lindh .40 1.00
5 Bill Pye .75 2.00
6 Sami Laine .75 2.00
7 Jason Pellerin .40 1.00
8 Eric Pericone .40 1.00
9 Karson Kaebel .40 1.00
10 Roy Gray .40 1.00
11 Rick Girhiny .40 1.00
12 Mark Smith .40 1.00
13 John Bossio .40 1.00
14 Mike Vandenberghe .40 1.00
15 Gary Coupal .75 2.00
16 Jacque Rodrigue .40 1.00
17 Savo Mitrovic .40 1.00
18 George Umunna .40 1.00
19 Greg Andis TR .02 .10
20 Joe Harrell EQM .02 .10
21 Kentucky Fried Chicken .02 .10

2001-02 Odessa Jackalopes

COMPLETE SET (21) 12.00 30.00
1 Trevor Allman .60 1.50
2 Jeffrey Ambrosio .75 2.00
3 John Bossio .60 1.50
4 Kenny Corupe .75 2.00
5 Matt Cressman .60 1.50
6 Adam Doyle .60 1.50
7 Robert Frid .60 1.50
8 Mike Gorman .60 1.50
9 Joe Harris .60 1.50
10 Jeff Haydar .60 1.50
11 Scott Hillman .60 1.50
12 Doug Johnson .60 1.50
13 Derek Laxdal ACO .10 .25
14 Alexander Lyubimov .60 1.50
15 Don Margettie .60 1.50
16 Don McKee CO .10 .25
17 Jacque Rodrigue .60 1.50
18 Mike Sanderson .75 2.00
19 Mark Smith .60 1.50
20 Tim Stay .60 1.50
21 Team Photo .20 .50

2002-03 Odessa Jackalopes

COMPLETE SET (24) 8.00 20.00
1 John Bossio .40 1.00
2 Matt Carney .60 1.50
3 Matt Cressman .40 1.00
4 Jerry Cunningham .40 1.00
5 Denis Desmarais .40 1.00
6 Adam Doyle .40 1.00
7 Ryan Edwards .40 1.00
8 David Francis .40 1.00
9 Robert Frid .40 1.00
10 Greg Gatto .40 1.00
11 Mike Gorman .60 1.50
12 Scott Green .40 1.00
13 Kevin Hansen .40 1.00
14 Scott Hillman .40 1.00
15 Don Margettie .40 1.00
16 Mike Rutter .40 1.00
17 Sebastien Thinel .40 1.00
18 Greg Willers .40 1.00
19 Jami Yoder .40 1.00
20 Don McKee HCO .10 .25
21 Derek Laxdal ACO .10 .25
22 Joe Harrell EQM .04 .10
23 Greg Andis TR .04 .10
24 Sonic Ad .04 .10

2003-04 Odessa Jackalopes

COMPLETE SET (22) 4.00 10.00
1 Header Card .04 .10
2 John Bossio .20 .50
3 Mark Cairns .30 .75
4 Matt Cressman .20 .50
5 Adam Doyle .20 .50
6 Shaun Fairweather .20 .50
7 Jeff Goldie .20 .50
8 Mike Gorman .30 .75
9 Scott Green .20 .50
10 Wayne Hall .20 .50
11 Scott Hillman .20 .50
12 Jaroslav Kerestes .20 .50
13 Sal Lettieri .20 .50
14 Joel Martin .30 .75
15 Matt Price .20 .50
16 Mike Rutter .20 .50
17 Pat Stachniak .30 .75
18 Sebastien Thinel .30 .75
19 Danny Williams .20 .50
20 Jami Yoder .20 .50
21 Don McKee HCO .04 .10
22 Greg Gatto ACO .04 .10

2004-05 Odessa Jackalopes

COMPLETE SET (21) 8.00 20.00
1 B.J. Adams .40 1.00
2 Pascal Bedard .40 1.00
3 Matt Cressman .40 1.00
4 Paul Davies .40 1.00
5 Derek Dolson .75 2.00
6 Adam Doyle .60 1.50
7 Mike Gorman .75 2.00
8 Mike Hanson .40 1.00
9 Scott Hillman .40 1.00
10 Joel Irving .40 1.00
11 Tom Kotsopolous .75 2.00
12 John Kozoriz .40 1.00
13 R.C. Lyke .40 1.00
14 Don Margettie .40 1.00
15 Chris Paradise .40 1.00
16 Mike Rutter .75 2.00
17 Sebastien Thinel .75 2.00
18 Ben Wallace .40 1.00
19 Don McKee CO .20 .50
20 Slappy MASCOT .04 .10
21 Midland Memorial Hospital .04 .10

2005-06 Odessa Jackalopes

COMPLETE SET (19) 6.00 15.00
1 Pascal Bedard .30 .75
2 Chris Brannen .30 .75
3 Mike Carter .30 .75
4 Matt Cressman .30 .75
5 Paul Davies .30 .75
6 Andrew Davis .30 .75
7 Derek Dolson .60 1.50
8 Jeff Ewasko .30 .75
9 Mike Gorman .60 1.50
10 Scott Hillman .30 .75
11 John Kozoriz .30 .75
12 Josh Legge .30 .75
13 Dominic Leveille .30 .75
14 Adam Loncan .60 1.50
15 Jamie Lovell .30 .75
16 Don Margettie .30 .75
17 Mike Rutter .30 .75
18 Sebastien Thinel .30 .75
19 Don McKee HC .10 .25

2006-07 Odessa Jackalopes

COMPLETE SET (21) 15.00 30.00
1 Blaine Bablitz .60 1.50
2 Pascal Bedard .60 1.50
3 Chris Brannen .60 1.50
4 Matt Cressman .60 1.50
5 Andrew Davis .60 1.50
6 Derek Dolson 1.00 2.50
7 Alex Dunn .60 1.50
8 Jeff Ewasko 1.25 3.00
9 Mike Gorman 1.00 2.50
10 Scott Hillman .60 1.50
11 John Kozoriz .60 1.50
12 Jay Latulippe .60 1.50
13 Josh Legge .60 1.50
14 Don Margettie .60 1.50
15 Mike Ramsay .60 1.50
16 Mike Rutter .60 1.50
17 Steve Shrum .60 1.50
18 Brian Swiniarski .60 1.50
19 Nathan Ward .60 1.50
20 Don McKee CO .20 .50
21 Doug Johnson ACO .20 .50

1999-00 Ohio State Buckeyes

COMPLETE SET (20) 6.00 20.00
1 Ray Aho .60 1.50
2 Peter Broccoli .40 1.00
3 Louie Colsant .40 1.00
4 Jason Crain .40 1.00
5 Yan DesGagne .40 1.00
6 Jean-Francois Dufour .40 1.00
7 Jaisen Freeman .40 1.00
8 Nick Ganga .40 1.00
9 Ryan Jestadt .40 1.00
10 Miguel LaFleche .40 1.00
11 Mike McCormick .40 1.00
12 Eric Meloche .40 1.00
13 Luke Pavlas .60 1.50
14 Jason Selleke .40 1.00
15 Andre Signoretti .40 1.00
16 Ryan Skaleski .40 1.00
17 Ryan Smith .40 1.00
18 Scott Titus .40 1.00
19 Benji Wolke .40 1.00
20 Brutus Buckeye MASCOT .08 .25

2000-01 Ohio State Buckeyes

COMPLETE SET (20) 8.00 20.00
1 Andre Signoretti .30 .75
2 Jean-Francois Dufour .30 .75
3 Jaisen Freeman .30 .75
4 Jason Crain .30 .75
5 Mike McCormick .30 .75
6 Scott Titus .30 .75
7 Nick Ganga .30 .75
8 Yan DesGagne .30 .75
9 Miguel LaFleche .30 .75
10 Ryan Smith .30 .75
11 Peter Broccoli .30 .75
12 Luke Pavlas .40 1.00
13 Peter Wishloff .30 .75
14 Mike Betz .30 .75
15 R.J. Umberger 2.00 5.00
16 Dave Steckel 1.20 3.00
17 Scott May .30 .75
18 Doug Andress .30 .75
19 Brutus Buckeye MASCOT .10 .25
20 John Markell CO .10 .25

2001-02 Ohio State Buckeyes

COMPLETE SET (20) 12.00 30.00
1 Doug Andress .60 1.50
2 Daymen Bencharski .60 1.50
3 Mike Betz .60 1.50
4 Peter Broccoli .60 1.50
5 Paul Caponigri .60 1.50
6 Jason Crain .60 1.50
7 Yan DesGagne .60 1.50
8 Miguel LaFleche .60 1.50
9 T.J. Latorre .60 1.50
10 Scott May .60 1.50
11 Mike McCormick .60 1.50
12 Chris Olsgard .60 1.50
13 Luke Pavlas .75 2.00
14 Eric Skaug .60 1.50
15 Ryan Smith .60 1.50
16 Dave Steckel 1.25 3.00
17 Scott Titus .60 1.50
18 R.J. Umberger 1.25 3.00
19 Reed Whiting .60 1.50
20 Brutus Buckeye MASCOT .10 .25

2002-03 Ohio State Buckeyes

COMPLETE SET (20) 8.00 20.00
1 Doug Andress .40 1.00
2 Daymen Bencharski .40 1.00
3 Mike Betz .60 1.50
4 J.B. Bittner .40 1.00
5 Peter Broccoli .40 1.00
6 Paul Caponigri .40 1.00
7 Miguel LaFleche .40 1.00
8 Scott May .40 1.00
9 Chris Olsgard .40 1.00
10 Luke Pavlas .40 1.00
11 Eric Skaug .40 1.00
12 Lee Spector .40 1.00
13 Dave Steckel .60 1.50
14 Scott Titus .40 1.00
15 R.J. Umberger 1.00 2.50
16 Thomas Welsh .40 1.00
17 Reed Whiting .40 1.00
18 John Markell HCO .10 .25
19 Brutus Buckeye .04 .10
20 Nathan Guenin
Ryan Kesler
Dan Knapp{#Rod Pelley# .20 .50

2003-04 Ohio State Buckeyes

COMPLETE SET (20) 8.00 20.00
1 Doug Andress .40 1.00
2 Daymen Bencharski .40 1.00
3 Mike Betz .60 1.50
4 J.B. Bittner .40 1.00
5 Paul Caponigri .40 1.00
6 Dave Caruso .60 1.50
7 Nathan Guenin .40 1.00
8 Kelly Holoway .40 1.00
9 Dan Knapp .40 1.00
10 Scott May .40 1.00
11 Chris Olsgard .40 1.00
12 Rod Pelley .40 1.00
13 Lee Spector .40 1.00
14 Dave Steckel .75 2.00
15 Thomas Welsh .40 1.00
16 Reed Whiting .40 1.00
17 Sean Collins
Andrew Schembri .40 1.00
18 Matt Beaudoin
Kenny Bernard
Matt Waddell .40 1.00
19 Bryce Anderson
Tyson Strachan
Dave Barton .40 1.00
20 Mascot .10 .25

2004-05 Ohio State Buckeyes
COMPLETE SET (20) 10.00 25.00
1 Bryce Anderson .40 1.00
2 Dave Barton .40 1.00
3 Matt Beaudoin .40 1.00
4 Kenny Bernard .40 1.00
5 J.B. Bittner .40 1.00
6 Dave Carusa .75 2.00
7 Sean Collins .40 1.00
8 Nate Guenin .75 2.00
9 Dan Knapp .40 1.00
10 Rod Pelley .40 1.00
11 Andrew Schembri .40 1.00
12 Lee Spector .40 1.00
13 Tyson Strachan .40 1.00
14 Matt Waddell .40 1.00
15 Thomas Welsh .40 1.00
16 Ian Keserich
Johan Krull .75 2.00
17 Matt McIlvane
Domenic Maiani .40 1.00
18 Tom Fritsche
Kyle Hood .75 2.00
19 John Dingle
Jason DeSantis .40 1.00
20 Sam Campbell
Phil Lauderdale
Zach Pelletier .40 1.00

2004-05 Ohio State Buckeyes Women
COMPLETE SET (20) 8.00 20.00
1 Melissa Glasser .75 2.00
2 Jennifer Desson .40 1.00
3 Jeni Creary .40 1.00
4 Jaclyn Haines .40 1.00
5 Meaghan Mulvaney .40 1.00
6 Jana Harrigan .40 1.00
7 Crystal Sayther .40 1.00
8 Katie Sershen .40 1.00
9 Tessa Bonhomme .40 1.00
10 Amber Bowman .40 1.00
11 Katie Maroney .40 1.00
12 Lacey Schultz .40 1.00
13 Krysta Skarda .40 1.00
14 Erika Vanderweer .75 2.00
15 Shelby Aldous
Lisa Chesson .75 2.00
16 Jody Heywood
Erin Keyes .40 1.00
17 Jill Mauch
Pamela Patterson .75 2.00
18 Mallory Peckels
Rachel Vanscoy .40 1.00
19 Jackie Barto CO .04 .10
20 Buckeye MASCOT .04 .10

2005-06 Ohio State Buckeyes
COMPLETE SET (25) 8.00 20.00
1 Bryce Anderson .30 .75
2 Dave Barton .30 .75
3 Matt Beaudoin .30 .75
4 Kenny Bernard .30 .75
5 Dave Caruso .60 1.50
6 Sean Collins .30 .75
7 Tom Fritsche .60 1.50
8 Nate Guenin .30 .75
9 Kyle Hood .30 .75
10 Dan Knapp .30 .75
11 Domenic Maiani .30 .75
12 Rod Pelley .60 1.50
13 Andrew Schembri .30 .75
14 Tyson Strachan .30 .75
15 Matt Waddell .30 .75
16 Ian Keserich SO .60 1.50
17 Zach Pelletier SO .30 .75
18 Jason DeSantis SO .30 .75
19 Phil Lauderdale SO .30 .75
20 Johann Kroll SO .30 .75
21 Sam Campbell SO .30 .75
22 Matt McIlvane SO .30 .75
23 John Dingle SO .30 .75
24 Corey Elkins FR .30 .75
25 Nick Biondo FR .30 .75

2006-07 Ohio State Buckeyes
COMPLETE SET (25) 15.00 25.00
1 Bryce Anderson .40 1.00
2 Dave Barton .40 1.00
3 Matt Beaudoin .40 1.00
4 Kenny Bernard .40 1.00
5 Sean Collins .40 1.00
6 Jason DeSantis .40 1.00
7 John Dingle .40 1.00
8 Tommy Goebel .40 1.00
9 Johann Kroll .40 1.00
10 Domenic Maiani .40 1.00
11 Matt McIlvane .40 1.00
12 Andrew Schembri .40 1.00
13 Tyson Strachan .40 1.00
14 Matt Waddell .40 1.00
15 Phil Lauderdale .40 1.00
16 Nick Filion .60 1.50
17 Corey Elkins .40 1.00
18 Nick Biondo .40 1.00
19 Tom Fritsche .60 1.50
20 Zach Pelletier .40 1.00
21 Kyle Hood .40 1.00
22 Sam Campbell .40 1.00
23 Joe Palmer .60 1.50
24 Mathieu Picard .40 1.00
25 Brutus Buckeye MASCOT .10 .25

2006-07 Ohio State Buckeyes Women
COMPLETE SET (20) 15.00 25.00
Mallory Peckels .50 1.25
Katie Maroney .50 1.25
Jody Heywood .50 1.25
Tessa Bonhomme .50 1.25
Erika Vanderveer .50 1.25
Whitney Miller .50 1.25
Hayley Klassen .50 1.25
Lisa Chesson .50 1.25
Liana Bonanno .50 1.25
0 Krysta Skarda .50 1.25
1 Jill Mauch .50 1.25
2 Erin Keys .50 1.25
13 Kelly Cahill .50 1.25
14 Olivia Antognoli .50 1.25
15 Lacey Schultz .50 1.25
16 Morgan Marziali .50 1.25
17 Megan Hostasek .50 1.25
18 Amber Bowman .50 1.25
19 Shelby Aldous .50 1.25
20 The Freshmen .50 1.25

2007-08 Ohio State Buckeyes
1 Nick Biondo .15 .40
2 Jason DeSantis .15 .40
3 John Dingle .15 .40
4 Corey Elkins .15 .40
5 Nick Filion .15 .40
6 Tom Fritsche .15 .40
7 Tommy Goebel .15 .40
8 Kyle Hood .15 .40
9 Johann Kroll .15 .40
10 Phil Lauderdale .15 .40
11 Matt McIlvane .15 .40
12 Joseph Palmer .15 .40
13 Zach Pelletier .15 .40
14 Mathieu Picard .15 .40
15 J.Albert/E.Belanger .15 .40
16 Boyd/Carlson/Gorham .15 .40
17 Markell/Reed/Reed .15 .40
18 Rudasill/Schafer/Severyn .15 .40
19 Sims/Somma/Toy .15 .40
20 Brutus Buckeye MASCOT .10 .40

2005-06 OHL Bell All-Star Classic
COMPLETE SET (38) 8.00 20.00
1 Kevin Lalande .20 .50
2 David Bolland .20 .50
3 Wojtek Wolski .40 1.00
4 Bobby Ryan .40 1.00
5 Matt Lashoff .20 .50
6 John Vigilante .20 .50
7 Cory Emmerton .20 .50
8 Derek Joslin .20 .50
9 Andrej Sekera .20 .50
10 Marc Staal .20 .50
11 Chris Stewart .20 .50
12 Jonathan D'Aversa .20 .50
13 Ryan Parent .20 .50
14 Peter Aston .20 .50
15 Benoit Pouliot .40 1.00
16 Dan Lacosta .20 .50
17 Jordan Owens .40 1.00
18 Patrick McNeill .20 .50
19 Peter Tsimikalis .20 .50
20 Andrew Marshall .20 .50
21 Bobby Sanguinetti .20 .50
22 Michael Blunden .40 1.00
23 Ryan Callahan .20 .50
24 Adam Dennis .40 1.00
25 Justin Donati .20 .50
26 Steve Downie .75 2.00
27 Tyler Haskins .20 .50
28 Dylan Hunter .20 .50
29 Tyler Kennedy .20 .50
30 Scott Lehman .20 .50
31 Bryan Little .40 1.00
32 Ryan MacDonald .20 .50
33 Evan McGrath .40 1.00
34 Ryan O'Marra .40 1.00
35 Chad Painchaud .20 .50
36 Tommy Pyatt .20 .50
37 Robbie Schremp .40 1.00
38 Jordan Staal 1.25 3.00
39 Matt Kelly .20 .50
40 Jamie Tardif .20 .50

2007-08 OHL All-Stars
1 Justin Azevedo .20 .50
2 Joshua Dailey .20 .50
3 Matt Beleskey .20 .50
4 Zach Bogosian .50 1.25
5 Luca Caputi .30 .75
6 Michael Caruso .20 .50
7 Jack Combs .20 .50
8 Logan Couture .30 .75
9 Tyler Cuma .20 .50
10 Wes Cunningham .20 .50
11 Kaspars Daugavins .20 .50
12 Justin DiBenedetto .20 .50
13 Drew Doughty .60 1.50
14 Josh Godfrey .20 .50
15 Justin Hodgman .20 .50
16 Cody Hodgson .60 1.50
17 Alex Hutchings .20 .50
18 Dustin Jeffrey .20 .50
19 David Kolomatis .20 .50
20 Stefan Legein .20 .50
21 Brett MacLean .20 .50
22 Patrick Maroon .30 .75
23 Steve Mason .60 1.50
24 Shawn Matthias .20 .50
25 Ryan McGinnis .20 .50
26 Nathan Moon .20 .50
27 Mike Murphy .30 .75
28 Alex Pietrangelo .50 1.25
29 Bryan Pitton .20 .50
30 Bob Sanguinetti .20 .50
31 Cal Simmonds .30 .75
32 Jeremy Smith .30 .75
33 Bradley Snetsinger .20 .50
34 Nick Spaling .20 .50
35 Jared Staal .30 .75
36 Steven Stamkos 1.25 3.00
37 P.K. Subban 1.50 4.00
38 John Tavares 1.25 3.00
39 Chris Terry .20 .50
40 Yannick Weber .20 .50

1992-93 Oklahoma City Blazers
COMPLETE SET (18) 3.00 8.00
1 Title Card .08 .25
2 Carl Boudreau .20 .50
3 Joe Burton .20 .50
4 Sylvain Fleury .20 .50
5 Brendan Garvey .20 .50
6 Guy Girouard .20 .50
7 Sean Gorman .20 .50
8 Jamie Hearn .20 .50
9 Craig Johnson .20 .50
10 Paul Krake .30 .75
11 Chris Laganas .20 .50
12 Daniel Larin .20 .50
13 Mark McGinn .20 .50
14 Alan Perry .30 .75
15 Steve Simoni .20 .50
16 Jim Solly .20 .50
17 Boyd Sutton .20 .50
18 Team Photo .20 .50

1993-94 Oklahoma City Blazers
COMPLETE SET (18) 3.00 8.00
1 Kent Anderson .20 .50
2 Carl Boudreau .20 .50
3 Joe Burton .20 .50
4 Mike Ciolli .20 .50
5 Guy Girouard .20 .50
6 Jules Jardine .20 .50
7 Craig Johnson .20 .50
8 Chris Laganas .20 .50
9 Jeff Massey .20 .50
10 Derry Menard .20 .50
11 Trent Pankewicz .20 .50
12 Alan Perry .30 .75
13 James Richmond .20 .50
14 Bruce Shoebottom .20 .50
15 Steve Simoni .20 .50
16 Jim Solly .20 .50
17 Mike Williams .20 .50
18 Mike McEwen CO .07 .20

1998-99 Oklahoma City Blazers
COMPLETE SET (23) 4.00 10.00
1 Peter Arvanitis .20 .50
2 Dan Fournel .20 .50
3 Dominic Fafard .20 .50
4 Craig Willard .20 .50
5 Simon Olivier .20 .50
6 Joe Burton .30 .75
7 Craig Johnson .20 .50
8 Tom Gomes .20 .50
9 Steve Moore .20 .50
10 Jim Jensen .20 .50
11 Brad Preston .20 .50
12 Rod Butler .20 .50
13 Michael Pozzo .20 .50
14 Chris Johnston .20 .50
15 Hardy Sauter .20 .50
16 Jean-Ian Filiatrault .30 .75
17 Mike Williams .20 .50
18 Doug Sauter HCO .02 .10
19 Corey MacIntyre .20 .50
20 Daniel Larin .20 .50
21 Brandon Rose TR .02 .10
22 Team Photo .20 .50
23 Checklist .02 .10

2003-04 Oklahoma City Blazers
COMPLETE SET (24) 4.00 10.00
1 Header Card .04 .10
2 Peter Arvanitis .20 .50
3 Boyd Ballard .30 .75
4 Les Borsheim .20 .50
5 Ryan Campbell .20 .50
6 Sean Connors .30 .75
7 Qamil Charlie Elezi .30 .75
8 Tyler Fleck .20 .50
9 Bryan Forslund .20 .50
10 Brad Herauf .20 .50
11 Stefan Katalina .20 .50
12 Justin Kot .20 .50
13 Tim Laurila .20 .50
14 Mike Lucci .20 .50
15 Blair Manning .20 .50
16 Peter Robertson .20 .50
17 Jesse Saltmarsh .20 .50
18 Hardy Sauter .20 .50
19 Doug Sheppard .20 .50
20 Marty Standish .30 .75
21 Ryan Watson .20 .50
22 Doug Sauter HCO .04 .10
23 Sponsor .04 .10
24 Sponsor .04 .10

2004-05 Oklahoma City Blazers
COMPLETE SET (24) 10.00 25.00
1 B.J. Ballas .40 1.00
2 Jarad Bourassa .40 1.00
3 Michel Beausoleil .60 1.50
4 Brenden Morrow 4.00 10.00
5 Hardy Sauter .60 1.50
6 Pat Hallett .40 1.00
7 Tyler Fleck .40 1.00
8 Brad Herauf .40 1.00
9 Scott Selig .40 1.00
10 Cody Loughlean .40 1.00
11 Bryan Forslund .40 1.00
12 Garrett Prosofsky .60 1.50
13 Boyd Ballard .60 1.50
14 Jason Goulet .60 1.50
15 Sean Connors .60 1.50
16 Kevin Harris .40 1.00
17 Kahlil Thomas .40 1.00
18 Shawn Weiman .40 1.00
19 Doug Sauter CO .04 .10
20 Team Photo .04 .10
21 Clyde S. Dale MASCOT .04 .10
22 Crash Test Dummies .04 .10
23 Sponsor .04 .10
NNO Header Card .04 .10

1995-96 Oklahoma Coyotes RHI
COMPLETE SET (18) 6.00 15.00
1 Kevin Barrett .30 .75
2 Joe Burton .40 1.00
3 Scott Drevitch .30 .75
4 George Dupont .30 .75
5 Jason Elders .30 .75
6 Jean-Ian Filiatrault .40 1.00
7 Johan Finnstrom .30 .75
8 Tom Gomes .30 .75
9 Radek Hamr .30 .75
10 Ross Harris .40 1.00
11 Jason Knox .30 .75
12 Perry Neufeld .30 .75
13 Darcy Pengelly .30 .75
14 Trevor Sherban .30 .75
15 Peter Skudra .75 2.00
16 Darren Stolk .30 .75
17 Rob Weingartner .30 .75
18 Guy Gadowsky CO .08 .25

2006-07 Okotoks Oilers
COMPLETE SET (24) 12.00 20.00
1 Nathan Brummit .40 1.00
2 Jesse Budkins .40 1.00
3 Derrick Burnett .40 1.00
4 David Civitarese .40 1.00
5 Dan Conacher .40 1.00
6 Justin Daigle .40 1.00
7 Bradley Eidsness .40 1.00
8 Mark Jensen .40 1.00
9 Curtis Leinweber .40 1.00
10 Zack MacKinnon .40 1.00
11 Spencer Mcelhinney .40 1.00
12 Carter Madsen .40 1.00
13 Jeff Matheson .40 1.00
14 Andrew Owsiak .40 1.00
15 Jesse Perrin .40 1.00
16 Jeff Sapisha .40 1.00
17 Brian Schmautz .40 1.00
18 Kyle Schussler .40 1.00
19 Elliott Sheen .40 1.00
20 Everett Sheen .40 1.00
21 Devin Welsh .40 1.00
22 Garry Vanherewghe CO .10 .25
23 Trevor McFarlane ACO .10 .25
24 Jeff Totz ACO .10 .25

2007-08 Okotoks Oilers
COMPLETE SET (20) 4.00 10.00
1 James Bannister .25 .60
2 David Civitarese .25 .60
3 Dan Conacher .25 .60
4 Mason Conway .25 .60
5 Justin Daigle .25 .60
6 Brian Doust .25 .60
7 Chris Duszynsky .25 .60
8 Brad Eidsness .25 .60
9 Corbin Gavin .25 .60
10 Brandon Hoogenboom .25 .60
11 Jesse Hudkins .25 .60
12 Curtis Leinweber .25 .60
13 Zak MacKinnon .25 .60
14 Carter Madsen .25 .60
15 Amory Mudrewich .25 .60
16 Jesse Perrin .25 .60
17 Derek Rodwell .25 .60
18 Kyle Schussler .25 .60
19 Elliot Sheen .25 .60
20 Braely Torris .25 .60

1993-94 Omaha Lancers
COMPLETE SET (28) 4.00 10.00
1 Ryan Bencurik .15 .40
2 Jeff Borders .15 .40
3 Sean Bowman .15 .40
4 Doc Del Castillo ACO .02 .10
5 Jeff Edwards .15 .40
6 Tony Gasparini .15 .40
7 Mike Guentzel CO .02 .10
8 Scott Haig .15 .40
9 Ken Hemenway .15 .40
10 Bill Hubbard .15 .40
11 Klage Kaebel .15 .40
12 Rob Klasnick .15 .40
13 Tony Kolozsy .15 .40
14 Tom Kowal .15 .40
15 Charlie Lentz .15 .40
16 Justin Lyle .15 .40
17 Chris Marvel .15 .40
18 Mike Peluso .15 .40
19 Scott Pionk ACO .02 .10
20 Dan Riva .15 .40
21 Nathan Rocheleau .15 .40
22 Eric Runyan .15 .40
23 Joe Russo .15 .40
24 Brian Swanson .40 1.00
25 Scott Swanson .15 .40
26 Justin Theel .15 .40
27 Jamie Thompson .15 .40
28 Brendan Walsh .15 .40

2002-03 Orlando Seals
COMPLETE SET 6.00 15.00
1 B.J. Stephens .40 1.00
2 Mike Correia .40 1.00
3 Stan Drulia HCO .40 1.00
4 Mascot .04 .10
5 Todd Bennett .40 1.00
6 Chris LiPuma .40 1.00
7 Louis Goulet .40 1.00
8 Zac Boyer .40 1.00
9 David Goverde .60 1.50
10 Mark White .40 1.00
11 Jad Ramsay .40 1.00
12 Joe Spencer .40 1.00
13 Sponsor Card .04 .10
14 Ethan Burnes .40 1.00
15 Ryan Anderson .40 1.00
16 Mascot .04 .10
17 Chris Cerrella .40 1.00
18 Todd Nowicki .40 1.00
19 Joe Seroski .40 1.00

1998-99 Orlando Solar Bears
COMPLETE SET (19) 4.00 10.00
1 Checklist
Logo card .02 .10
2 Patrick Neaton .20 .50
3 Sean McCann .20 .50
4 Clayton Norris .20 .50
5 Hubie McDonough .30 .75
6 Shawn Carter .20 .50
7 Grigori Panteleyev .30 .75
8 Todd Richards .30 .75
9 Shawn Wansborough .20 .50
10 Mark Beaufait .40 1.00
11 Scott Hollis .20 .50
12 David Mackey .20 .50
13 David Littman .30 .75
14 Grigori Panteleyev AS .30 .75
15 Mark Beaufait AS .40 1.00
16 Curt Fraser CO .20 .50
17 Peter Horachek ACO .20 .50
18 Orlando Arena .20 .50
19 Shades MASCOT .20 .50

1998-99 Orlando Solar Bears II
COMPLETE SET (22) 10.00 25.00
1 David Littman .60 1.50
2 Mark Beaufait .75 2.00
3 Shawn Carter .40 1.00
4 David Mackey .40 1.00
5 Sean McCann .40 1.00
6 Hubie McDonough .60 1.50
7 Patrick Neaton .40 1.00
8 Clayton Norris .40 1.00
9 Grigori Panteleyev .60 1.50
10 Todd Richards .60 1.50
11 Curt Fraser HCO .40 1.00
12 Scott Bailey .60 1.50
13 Rob Bonneau .40 1.00
14 Allan Egeland .40 1.00
15 Todd Krygier .40 1.00
16 Kirby Law .40 1.00
17 Curtis Murphy .40 1.00
18 Mike Nicholishen .40 1.00
19 Frederik Oduya .40 1.00
20 Ken Sabourin .40 1.00
21 Pierre Sevigny .40 1.00
22 Peter Horachek ACO .40 1.00

1980-81 Oshawa Generals
COMPLETE SET (25) 62.50 125.00
1 Generals Logo .40 1.00
2 Ray Flaherty .40 1.00
3 Craig Kitchener .40 1.00
4 Dan Revell .40 1.00
5 Bob Kucheran .40 1.00
6 Pat Poulin .40 1.00
7 Dave Andreychuk 7.50 15.00
8 Barry Tabobondung .40 1.00
9 Steve Konroyd 1.25 3.00
10 Paul Edwards .40 1.00
11 Dale Degray 1.25 3.00
12 Joe Cirella 1.25 3.00
13 Norm Schmidt .40 1.00
14 Markus Lehto .60 1.50
15 Mitch Lamoureux .60 1.50
16 Tony Tanti 1.50 4.00
17 Bill Laforge .40 1.00
18 Greg Gravel .40 1.00
19 Mike Lekun .40 1.00
20 Chris Smith .40 1.00
21 Peter Sidorkiewicz 1.50 4.00
22 Greg Stefan 1.50 4.00
23 Tom McCarthy 1.50 4.00
24 Rick Lanz 1.50 4.00
25 Bobby Orr 40.00 80.00

1981-82 Oshawa Generals
COMPLETE SET (25) 24.00 60.00
1 Generals Logo .40 1.00
2 Chris Smith .60 1.50
3 Peter Sidorkiewicz 1.50 4.00
4 Ali Butorac .60 1.50
5 Dan Revell .60 1.50
6 Mitch Lamoureux .75 2.00
7 Norm Schmidt .60 1.50
8 Paul Edwards .60 1.50
9 Dan Nicholson .60 1.50
10 John Hutchings .60 1.50
11 Dave Gans .60 1.50
12 Dave Andreychuk 6.00 15.00
13 Mike Stern .60 1.50
14 Dale Degray .75 2.00
15 Mike Lekun .60 1.50
16 Greg Gravel .60 1.50
17 Dave MacLean .60 1.50
18 Tony Tanti 1.25 3.00
19 John MacLean 6.00 15.00
20 Jim Uens .60 1.50
21 Guy Jacob .60 1.50
22 Jeff Steffan .60 1.50
23 Paul Theriault .60 1.50
24 Sherry Bassin .60 1.50
25 Durham Regional
Police Logo .20 .50

1982-83 Oshawa Generals
COMPLETE SET (25) 14.00 35.00
1 Generals Logo .20 .50
2 Jeff Hogg .60 1.50
3 Peter Sidorkiewicz 1.25 3.00
4 Dale Degray .60 1.50
5 Joe Cirella .60 1.50
6 Todd Smith .40 1.00
7 Scott Brydges .40 1.00
8 Jeff Steffen .40 1.00
9 Don Biggs .40 1.00
10 Todd Hooey .40 1.00
11 Tony Tanti .75 2.00
12 Danny Gratton .40 1.00
13 Steve King .40 1.00
14 Dan Defazio .40 1.00
15 John MacLean 3.00 8.00
16 Tim Burgess .40 1.00
17 Mike Stern .40 1.00
18 Dan Nicholson .40 1.00
19 David Gans .40 1.00
20 John Hutchings .40 1.00
21 Norm Schmidt .40 1.00
22 Todd Charlesworth .40 1.00
23 Paul Theriault CO .30 .75
24 Sherry Bassin GM .40 1.00
25 Durham Regional
Police Logo .20 .50

1983-84 Oshawa Generals
COMPLETE SET (30) 12.00 30.00
1 Peter Sidorkiewicz .75 2.00
2 Kirk McLean 4.00 10.00
3 Todd Charlesworth .40 1.00
4 Ian Ferguson .30 .75
5 John Hutchings .30 .75
6 Generals Logo .08 .25
7 Mark Haarmann .30 .75
8 Joel Curtis .30 .75
9 Dan Gratton .30 .75
10 Steve Hedington .30 .75
11 Scott Brydges .30 .75
12 CKAR Radio .08 .25
13 Brad Walcot .30 .75
14 Paul Theriault CO .30 .75
15 Jon Jenkins
Chief of Police .08 .25
16 Sherry Bassin GM .40 1.00
17 Craig Morrison .30 .75
18 Bolahood's .08 .25
19 Bruce Melanson .30 .75
20 Mike Stern .30 .75
21 Gary McColgan .30 .75
22 Lee Giffin .40 1.00
23 Brent Maki .30 .75
24 Ronald McDonald .20 .50
25 Jeff Steffen .30 .75
26 John Stevens .30 .75
27 David Gans .30 .75
28 Don Biggs .40 1.00
29 Chip Crandall .30 .75
30 Durham Police Logo .08 .25

1989-90 Oshawa Generals
COMPLETE SET (35) 10.00 25.00
1 Corey Banika .20 .50
2 David Craievich .20 .50
3 Scott Hollis .20 .50
4 Mike Decoff .20 .50
5 Joe Busillo .20 .50
6 Matt Hoffman .20 .50
7 Craig Donaldson .20 .50
8 Jason Denomme .20 .50
9 Brian Grieve .20 .50
10 Wade Simpson .20 .50
11 Dale Craigwell .40 1.00
12 Mike Lenarduzzi .20 .50
13 Rick Cornacchia CO .04 .10
14 David Edwards .20 .50
15 Kevin Butt .40 1.00
16 Team Photo .08 .20
17 Clair Cornish .20 .50
18 Jarrod Skalde .40 1.00
19 Mark Deazeley .20 .50
20 Jean Paul Davis .20 .50
21 Todd Coopman .04 .10
22 Trevor McIvor .20 .50
23 Mike Craig .40 1.00
24 Paul O'Hagan .20 .50
25 Iain Fraser .20 .50
26 Brent Grieve .20 .50
27 Lions International .04 .10
28 National Sports Centre .04 .10
29 Durham Regional Police .04 .10
30 Oshawa Generals .04 .10
31 Eric Lindros 6.00 15.00
32 Bill Armstrong .20 .50
33 Chris Vanclief .20 .50
34 Scott Luik .20 .50
35 Fred Brathwaite 1.25 3.00

1989-90 Oshawa Generals 7th Inning Sketch
COMPLETE SET (23) 6.00 15.00
1 Eric Lindros 2.00 5.00
2 Jarrod Skalde .30 .75
3 Joe Busillo .20 .50
4 Dale Craigwell .30 .75
5 Clair Cornish .20 .50
6 Jean-Paul Davis .20 .50
7 Craig Donaldson .20 .50
8 Wade Simpson .20 .50
9 Mike Craig .20 .50
10 Mark Deazeley .20 .50
11 Scott Hollis .20 .50
12 Brian Grieve .20 .50
13 Dave Craievich .20 .50
14 Paul O'Hagan .20 .50
15 Matt Hoffman .20 .50
16 Trevor McIvor .20 .50
17 Cory Banika .20 .50
18 Kevin Butt .30 .75
19 Iain Fraser .20 .50
20 Bill Armotrong .20 .50
21 Scott Luik .20 .50
22 Brent Grieve .20 .50
23 Fred Brathwaite .60 1.50

1991-92 Oshawa Generals
COMPLETE SET (32) 8.00 20.00
1 Mike Fountain .30 .75
2 Brian Grieve .15 .40
3 Trevor Burgess .15 .40
4 Wade Simpson .15 .40
5 Ken Shepard .15 .40
6 Stephane Yelle .30 .75
7 Matt Hoffman .15 .40
8 Neil Iserhoff .15 .40
9 Rob Leask .15 .40
10 Kevin Spero .15 .40
11 Scott Hollis .15 .40
12 Sean Brown .20 .50
13 Todd Bradley .15 .40
14 Darryl LaFrance .15 .40
15 Markus Brunner .20 .50
16 B.J. MacPherson .15 .40
17 Jason Campeau .15 .40
18 Jason Weaver .15 .40
19 Jan Benda .20 .50
20 Jason Arnott 1.50 4.00
21 Eric Lindros 3.00 8.00
22 Wayne Daniels
Dir. of Operations .02 .10
23 Joe Cook .15 .40
24 Can't Beat the Real
Thing (Coke Ad) .02 .10
25 Experience the
Domino's Effect/(Pizza Ad) .02 .10
26 Mark Deazeley .15 .40
27 Jean-Paul Davis .15 .40
28 Brian Grieve .15 .40
29 Oshawa Generals
Team Photo .40 1.00
30 Ian Young CO
Larry Marson CO5
Rick Cornacchia CO .02 .10
31 Sponsor Ads
Checklist .02 .10
32 Prosport's Action .02 .10

1991-92 Oshawa Generals Sheet
COMPLETE SHEET (26) 8.00 20.00
1 Scott Hollis .15 .40
2 Jan Benda .20 .50
3 Joe Cook .15 .40
4 Wade Simpson .15 .40
5 B.J. MacPherson .15 .40
6 David Anderson .15 .40
7 Stephane Yelle .30 .75
8 Troy Sweet .15 .40
9 Matt Hoffman .15 .40
10 Trevor Burgess .15 .40
11 Jason Weaver .15 .40
12 Craig Lutes .15 .40
13 Darryl LaFrance .15 .40
14 Jason Arnott 1.50 4.00
15 Eric Lindros 3.00 8.00
16 Brian Grieve .15 .40
17 Mark Deazeley .15 .40
18 Mike Cote .15 .40
19 Markus Brunner .20 .50
20 Kevin Spero .15 .40
21 Todd Bradley .15 .40
22 Mike Fountain .30 .75
23 Fred Brathwaite .30 .75
24 Jean-Paul Davis .15 .40
25 Jason Campeau .15 .40
26 Neil Iserhoff .15 .40

1992-93 Oshawa Generals Sheet
COMPLETE SHEET (26) 6.00 15.00
1 Wade Simpson .20 .50
2 Jamie Kress .20 .50
3 Sean Brown .25 .60
4 Jason Arnott 1.25 3.00
5 Mark Brooks .20 .50
6 Rob McQuat .20 .50
7 Joe Cook .20 .50
8 Chris Hall .20 .50
9 Jason McQuat .20 .50
10 Jason Julian .20 .50
11 Kevin Spero .20 .50
12 Steve Haight .20 .50
13 B.J. MacPherson .20 .50
14 Billy-Jay Johnston .20 .50
15 Stephane Soulliere .20 .50
16 Todd Bradley .20 .50
17 Darryl Lafrance .20 .50
18 Aaron Albright .20 .50
19 Trevor Burgess .20 .50
20 Scott Hollis .20 .50
21 Serge Dunphy .20 .50
22 Joel Gagnon .30 .75
23 Brian Kent .30 .75
24 Stephane Yelle .40 1.00
25 Jason Campeau .20 .50
26 Neil Iserhoff .20 .50

1993-94 Oshawa Generals
COMPLETE SET (27) 4.00 10.00
1 Title Card
Checklist .02 .10
2 Joel Gagnon .20 .50
3 Ken Shepard .20 .50
4 Jan Snopek .20 .50
5 David Froh .15 .40
6 Brandon Gray .15 .40
7 Damon Hardy .15 .40
8 Sean Brown .25 .60
9 Jeff Andrews .15 .40
10 Stephane Yelle .30 .75
11 Stephane Soulliere .15 .40
12 Andrew Power .15 .40
13 Todd Bradley .15 .40
14 Darryl Lafrance .20 .50
15 Darryl Moxam .15 .40
16 Robert Dubois .15 .40
17 Kevin Vaughan .15 .40
18 Rob McQuat .20 .50
19 B.J. Johnston .15 .40
20 Paul Doherty .15 .40
21 Eric Boulton .40 1.00
22 Marc Savard .40 1.00
23 Chris Hall .15 .40
24 Jason McQuat .15 .40
25 Ryan Lindsay .15 .40
26 Rick Cornacchia CO
Wayne Daniels DIR
Brian Drumm .02 .10
NNO Slapshot Ad Card .02 .10

2003-04 Oshawa Generals
COMPLETE SET (26) 5.00 12.00
1 Dan Turple .30 .75
3 John Neal .20 .50
4 Chris Petrow .20 .50
6 Bret Nasby .20 .50
7 Clay McFadden .20 .50
8 Fred Hatziioannou .20 .50
10 Tyler Donati .20 .50
11 Andrew Gibbons .20 .50
12 Justin Donati .20 .50
14 Andy Reiss .20 .50
15 Aaron Lobb .20 .50
16 Mike McLean .20 .50
17 Chris Hulit .20 .50
19 Jordan Beirnes .20 .50
20 Justin Wallingford .20 .50
21 Adam Berti .20 .50
22 Mike Kavanagh .20 .50
23 Brandon McBride .20 .50
24 Ryan Kitchen .20 .50
25 Ben Eager .40 1.00
26 Paul Ranger .20 .50
27 Gary Friesen .20 .50
28 Tobias Whelan .20 .50
31 Ryan Gibb .30 .75
NNO Paul Ranger TL .75 2.00
NNO Ben Eager TL .75 2.00

2004-05 Oshawa Generals
COMPLETE SET (22) 5.00 12.00
1 Carlo Di Rienzo .40 1.00
2 Ryan Gibb .40 1.00
3 John Neal .60 1.50
4 Trevor Waddell .20 .50
5 Bret Nasby .20 .50
6 Brett Trudell .20 .50
7 Justin Allen .20 .50
8 Peter Tsimikalis .20 .50
9 Tom Jefferson .20 .50
10 Cal Clutterbuck .40 1.00

11 Matt Piva .20 .50
12 Matt Puntureri .20 .50
13 Jesse Biduke .20 .50
14 Devereaux Heshmatpour .30 .75
15 Adam Berti .40 1.00
16 Mike Kavanaugh .20 .50
17 Brandon McBride .20 .50
18 Chad Thompson .20 .50
19 James DeLory .20 .50
20 David Halasz .20 .50
21 Gary Friesen .20 .50
22 Checklist .04 .10

2006-07 Oshawa Generals

COMPLETE SET (24) 12.00 20.00
1 John Tavares 3.00 8.00
2 Dale Mitchell .40 1.00
3 Tyler Taylor .20 .50
4 Igor Gongalsky .20 .50
5 Cal Clutterbuck .20 .50
6 Dean Howard .20 .50
7 Kory Nagy .20 .50
8 Brett Maclean .40 1.00
9 Corey Cowick .20 .50
10 Kyle Paige .20 .50
11 Kody Musselman .20 .50
12 Shea Kewin .20 .50
13 Brett Parnham .20 .50
14 Ziga Pance .20 .50
15 Trevor Koverko .20 .50
16 Michael Del Zotto .60 1.50
17 Matt Seegmiller .20 .50
18 Peter Aston .20 .50
19 Eric Regan .20 .50
20 Billy Siekris .20 .50
21 James Delory .20 .50
22 Loic Lacasse .30 .75
23 Mark Packwood .30 .75
24 Oshawa Generals .10 .25

2014-15 Oshawa Generals

COMPLETE SET (24) 6.00 15.00
1 Ken Appleby .30 .75
2 Jeremy Brodeur .30 .75
3 Josh Brown .30 .75
4 Chris Carlisle .30 .75
5 Cole Cassels .30 .75
6 Anthony Cirelli .30 .75
7 Michael Dal Colle .30 .75
8 Stephen Desrocher .30 .75
9 Sam Harding .30 .75
10 Sonny Hertzberg .30 .75
11 Kenny Huether .30 .75
12 Bradley Latour .30 .75
13 Tobias Lindberg .30 .75
14 Joe Manchurek .30 .75
15 Will Petschenig .30 .75
16 Cliff Pu .40 1.00
17 Daniel Robertson .30 .75
18 Hunter Smith .30 .75
19 Josh Sterk .30 .75
20 Stephen Templeton .30 .75
21 Michael Turner .30 .75
22 Mitchell Vande-Sompel .30 .75
23 Aidan Wallace .30 .75
24 Header Card CL .30 .75

1981-82 Ottawa 67's

COMPLETE SET (25) 12.00 30.00
1 James Allison .30 .75
2 John Boland .30 .75
3 Randy Boyd .30 .75
4 Adam Creighton 1.25 3.00
5 Bill Dowd .30 .75
6 Dwayne Davison .30 .75
7 Alan Hepple .30 .75
8 Mike James .30 .75
9 Brian Kilrea CO .75 2.00
10 Moe Lemay .60 1.50
11 Benny Longe .30 .75
12 Paul Louttit .30 .75
12 Doug Stewart .30 .75
13 Fraser Wood .30 .75
13 Don McLaren .30 .75
14 John Ollson .30 .75
15 Brian Patafie TR .20 .50
16 Mark Paterson .40 1.00
17 Phil Patterson .30 .75
18 Larry Power .30 .75
19 Jim Ralph 2.00 5.00
20 Darcy Roy .40 1.00
21 Brad Shaw 1.25 3.00
22 Brian Small .30 .75
23 Doug Stewart .30 .75
24 Jeff Vaive .30 .75
25 Fraser Wood .30 .75

1982-83 Ottawa 67's

COMPLETE SET (25) 12.00 30.00
1 Bruce Cassidy .30 .75
2 Greg Coram .30 .75
3 Adam Creighton .75 2.00
4 Bill Dowd .30 .75
5 Gord Hamilton ACO .20 .50
6 Scott Hammond .30 .75
7 Alan Hepple .30 .75
8 Alan Hepple .30 .75
9 Jim Jackson TR .20 .50
10 Mike James .30 .75
11 Brian Kilrea CO .75 2.00
12 Paul Louttit .30 .75
13 Brian McKinnon .30 .75
14 Don McLaren .30 .75
15 John Ollson .30 .75
16 Darren Pang 2.00 5.00
17 Mark Paterson .30 .75
18 Phil Patterson .30 .75
19 Larry Power .30 .75
20 Gary Roberts 3.00 8.00
21 Brian Rome .30 .75
22 Darcy T. Roy .30 .75
23 Brad Shaw 1.00 2.50
24 Doug Stewart .30 .75
25 Jeff Vaive .30 .75
26 Larry MacAndrew .30 .75
27 Gord Hamilton Jr. .30 .75

1983-84 Ottawa 67's

COMPLETE SET (27) 10.00 25.00
1 Richard Adolfi .20 .50
2 Bill Bennett .20 .50
3 Bruce Cassidy .30 .75
4 Todd Clarke .20 .50
5 Greg Coram .30 .75
6 Adam Creighton .75 2.00
7 Bob Giffin .20 .50
8 Gord Hamilton ACO .08 .25
9 Gord Hamilton Jr. TR .08 .25
10 Scott Hammond .20 .50
11 John Hanna .20 .50
12 Tim Helmer .20 .50
13 Steve Hrynewich .20 .50
14 Jim Jackson TR .08 .25
15 Mike James .20 .50
16 Brian Kilrea CO/MG .40 1.00
17 Larry MacAndrew TR .08 .25
18 Brian McKinnon .20 .50
19 Don McLaren .30 .75
20 Roy Myllari .20 .50
21 Darren Pang 1.50 4.00
22 Mark Paterson .30 .75
23 Phil Patterson .20 .50
24 Gary Roberts 2.00 5.00
25 Darcy Roy .20 .50
26 Brad Shaw .75 2.00
27 Steve Simoni .20 .50

1984-85 Ottawa 67's

COMPLETE SET (28) 8.00 20.00
1 Tom Allen .30 .75
2 Graydon Almstedt .30 .75
3 Bill Bennett .30 .75
4 Bruce Cassidy .30 .75
5 Greg Coram .40 1.00
6 Bob Ellett CO .08 .25
7 Tony Geesink .30 .75
8 Bob Giffin .30 .75
9 John Hanna .30 .75
10 Tim Helmer .30 .75
11 Andy Helmuth .30 .75
12 Steve Hrynewich .30 .75
13 Rob Hudson .30 .75
14 Jim Jackson TR .08 .25
15 Steve Kayser .30 .75
16 Bill Kuchma .30 .75
17 Mike Larouche .30 .75
18 Tom Lawson MG .08 .25
19 Richard Lessard .30 .75
20 Gary Roberts 1.50 4.00
21 Jerry Scott .30 .75
22 John Shepherd PR .08 .25
23 Steve Simoni .30 .75
24 Greg Sliz .30 .75
25 Gord Thomas TR .08 .25
26 Chris Vickers .30 .75
27 Bert Weir .30 .75
28 Dennis Wigle .30 .75

1992-93 Ottawa 67's

COMPLETE SET (24) 4.80 12.00
1 Ken Belanger .30 .75
2 Curt Bowen .20 .50
3 Rich Bronilla .20 .50
4 Mathew Burnett .20 .50
5 Shawn Caplice .20 .50
6 Mike Carr .20 .50
7 Chris Coveny .20 .50
8 Howard Darwin (Founder) .08 .25
9 Shean Donovan .40 1.00
10 Mark Edmundson .20 .50
11 Billy Hall .20 .50
12 Mike Johnson .20 .50
13 Brian Kilrea GM CO .20 .50
14 Grayson Lafoley .20 .50
15 Grant Marshall .40 1.00
16 Cory Murphy .20 .50
17 Mike Peca 1.25 3.00
18 Greg Ryan .20 .50
19 Jeff Salajko .20 .50
20 Gerry Skrypec .20 .50
21 Sean Spencer .20 .50
22 Steven Washburn .25 .60
23 Mark Yakabuski .20 .50
24 Title Card .08 .25

1999-00 Ottawa 67's

COMPLETE SET (30) 4.80 12.00
1 Mark Bell .60 1.50
2 Matt Zultek .20 .50
3 Adam Chapman .08 .25
4 Miguel Delisle .30 .75
5 Randy Davidson .08 .25
6 Lance Galbraith .20 .50
7 Ian Jacobs .08 .25
8 Mike James .08 .25
9 Zenon Konopka .20 .50
10 Marc Lefebvre .08 .25
11 Joe Talbot .08 .25
12 Josh Tataryn .08 .25
13 Dan Tessier .20 .50
14 Vincent Grant .20 .50
15 Brendan Bell .08 .25
16 Chris Cava .08 .25
17 Kevin Malcolm .08 .25
18 Mike Gresdal .08 .25
19 Russ Moyer .08 .25
20 Luke Sellars .20 .50
21 Jeremy Van Hoof .20 .50
22 Jon Zion .30 .75
23 Seamus Kotyk .40 1.00
24 Lavente Szuper .40 1.00
25 Jeff Hunt .08 .25
26 Brian Kilrea HCO .20 .50
27 Bert O'Brien ACO .02 .10
28 Vince Mallette ACO .02 .10
29 Jeff Keech TR .02 .10
30 Checklist .02 .10

2000-01 Ottawa 67's

COMPLETE SET (30) 4.80 12.00
1 Joe Talbot .20 .50
2 Lance Galbraith .20 .50
3 Jeremy Van Hoof .20 .50
4 Jon Zion .20 .50
5 Russ Moyer .15 .40
6 Pierre Mitsou .15 .40
7 Brendan Bell .20 .50
8 Adam Smyth .15 .40
9 Marc Lefebvre .15 .40
10 Sean Scully .15 .40
11 Brett McGrath .15 .40
12 Zenon Konopka .20 .50
13 Rodney Bauman .15 .40
14 Luke Sellars .20 .50
15 Miguel Delisle .20 .50
16 Vadim Sozinov .20 .50
17 Adam Chapman .15 .40
18 Bryan Rodney .15 .40
19 Sebastien Savage .15 .40
20 Seamus Kotyk .30 .75
21 John Ceci .15 .40
22 Vince Mallette CO .10 .25
23 Bert O'Brien CO .10 .25
24 Brian Kilrea CO .20 .50
25 Jeff Hunt OWN .04 .10
26 Riley & Killer Puck MASCOT .04 .10
27 Brian Kilrea 900 .20 .50
28 Doug Wilson .20 .50
29 Team Photo .10 .25
30 Team CL .10 .25

2001-02 Ottawa 67's

COMPLETE SET (30) 4.80 12.00
1 J.F. Perras .30 .75
2 Jon Ceci .20 .50
3 Karol Sloboda .20 .50
4 Carter Trevisani .20 .50
5 Jon Zion .30 .75
6 Russ Moyer .20 .50
7 Pierre Mitsou .20 .50
8 Adam Smyth .20 .50
9 Brendan Bell .30 .75
10 Matthew Albiani .20 .50
11 Lane Moodie .20 .50
12 Sean Scully .20 .50
13 Brett McGrath .20 .50
14 Zenon Konopka .30 .75
15 Rodney Bauman .20 .50
16 Miguel Delisle .20 .50
17 Jeremy Akeson .20 .50
18 Mark Mancari .20 .50
19 Adam Chapman .20 .50
20 Bryan Rodney .20 .50
21 Corey Locke .20 .50
22 Vince Malette ACO .04 .10
23 Bert O'Brien ACO .04 .10
24 Brian Kilrea CO .20 .50
25 Jeff Hunt OWN .04 .10
26 Banner Ceremony .04 .10
27 Brad Marsh .20 .50
28 Riley and Riley Jr. .04 .10
29 Killer Puck .04 .10
30 Dance Team CL .20 .50

2002-03 Ottawa 67's

COMPLETE SET 5.00 12.00
1 Chris Hardill .30 .75
2 Karol Sloboda .20 .50
3 Carter Trevisani .20 .50
4 Will Colbert .20 .50
5 Russ Moyer .20 .50
6 Pierre Mitsou .20 .50
7 Adam Smyth .20 .50
8 Brendan Bell .30 .75
9 Matthew Albiani .20 .50
10 Lou Dickenson .20 .50
11 Scott Sheppard .20 .50
12 Bryan Bickell .20 .50
13 Sean Scully .20 .50
14 Peter Tsimikalis .20 .50
15 Rodney Bauman .20 .50
16 Kyle Wharton .20 .50
17 Jeremy Akeson .20 .50
18 Mark Mancari .20 .50
19 Julian Talbot .20 .50
20 Lukas Mensator .40 1.00
21 Matthew Foy .30 .75
22 Corey Locke .60 1.50
23 Jeff Hunt Owner .04 .10
24 Brian Kilrea HCO .10 .25
25 Bert O'Brien ACO .04 .10
26 Vince Malette ACO .04 .10
27 Mascot .04 .10
28 XFM Girls .10 .25
29 Mike Peca Brian Kilrea .20 .50
30 Girl Guides of Canada .04 .10

2003-04 Ottawa 67's

COMPLETE SET (25) 6.00 15.00
1 Tyson Aitcheson .20 .50
2 Jeremy Akeson .20 .50
3 Matthew Albiani .20 .50
4 Danny Battochio .30 .75
5 Rodney Bauman .20 .50
6 Brodie Beard .20 .50
7 Bryan Bickell .20 .50
8 Will Colbert .20 .50
9 Greg Goodnough .20 .50
10 David Halasz .20 .50
11 Brad Hartley .20 .50
12 Robbie Lawrance .20 .50
13 Corey Locke .40 1.00
14 Mark Mancari .20 .50
15 Phil Mangan .20 .50
16 Lukas Mensator .40 1.00
17 Pierre Mitsou .20 .50
18 Elgin Reid .20 .50
19 Julian Talbot .20 .50
20 Brody Todd .20 .50
21 Peter Tsimikalis .20 .50
22 Kyle Wharton .20 .50
NNO Lukas Mensator TL .75 2.00
NNO Brian Kilrea CO .04 .10
NNO Corey Locke TL .75 2.00

2004-05 Ottawa 67's

COMPLETE (23) 5.00 12.00
1 Lukas Kaspar .20 .50
2 Anthony Guadagnolo .40 1.00
3 Bryan Bickell .20 .50
4 Brodie Beard .20 .50
5 Pat Ouellette .20 .50
6 Robbie Lawrance .20 .50
7 Jeremy Akeson .20 .50
8 Mark Mancari .20 .50
9 Julian Talbot .20 .50
10 Brad Bonello .20 .50
11 Nick Van Herpt .20 .50
12 Danny Battochio .60 1.50
13 Will Colbert .20 .50
14 David Jarram .20 .50
15 Brad Staubitz .40 1.00
16 Jamie Vanderveeken .20 .50
17 Arron Alphonso .20 .50
18 Derek Joslin .20 .50
19 Elgin Reid .20 .50
20 Jamie McGinn .20 .50
21 Chris Hulit .40 1.00
22 Jakub Petruzalek .20 .50
23 Matt Lahey .20 .50

2005-06 Ottawa 67's

COMPLETE SET (25) 8.00 15.00
1 Julian Talbot .20 .50
2 Brodie Beard .20 .50
3 Bryan Bickell .20 .50
4 Pat Campbell .20 .50
5 Shea Kewin .20 .50
6 Thomas Kiriakou .20 .50
7 Robbie Lawrence .20 .50
8 Pat Ouellette .20 .50
9 Sean Ryan .20 .50
10 Jakub Vojta .20 .50
11 Brent Mackie .20 .50
12 Danny Battochio .40 1.00
13 Arron Alphonso .20 .50
14 Logan Couture 1.00 2.50
15 Pat Daley .20 .50
16 Chris Hulit .20 .50
17 Brady Morrison .40 1.00
18 Derek Joslin .20 .50
19 Matt Lahey .20 .50
20 Jamie McGinn .30 .75
21 Joe Pleckaitis .20 .50
22 Tibor Radulay .20 .50
23 Elgin Reid .20 .50
24 Joe Grimaldi .20 .50
25 Brett Liscomb .20 .50

2006-07 Ottawa 67's

COMPLETE SET (22) 8.00 15.00
1 Logan Couture .60 1.50
2 Scott Cowie .25 .60
3 Thomas Kiriakou .25 .60
4 Matt Lahey .25 .60
5 Cody Lindsay .25 .60
6 Brett Liscomb .40 1.00
7 Jamie Mcginn .40 1.00
8 Matthieu Methot .25 .60
9 Thomas Nesbitt .25 .60
10 Matt Ribeiro .25 .60
11 Brodie Beard .25 .60
12 Tyler Cuma .25 .60
13 Julien Demers .25 .60
14 Joe Grimaldi .25 .60
15 Derek Joslin .25 .60
16 Sean Ryan .25 .60
17 Jakub Vojta .25 .60
18 Arron Alphonso .25 .60
19 Jason Bailey .25 .60
20 Julian Cimadamore .25 .60
21 Lukas Flueler .40 1.00
22 Brady Morrison .40 1.00

2000-01 Owen Sound Attack

COMPLETE SET (26) 4.80 12.00
1 Michael Barrett .20 .50
2 Trevor Blanchard .20 .50
3 Luc Chiasson .20 .50
4 Richard Colwill .20 .50
5 Justin Day .30 .75
6 Kris Fraser .20 .50
7 Justin Hodgins .20 .50
8 Greg Jacina .20 .50
9 Bryan Kazarian .30 .75
10 Josh Legge .20 .50
11 Paul MacDermid CO .10 .25
12 Jason Nobili CO .10 .25
13 Brian O'Leary CO .10 .25
14 Dene Poulin .20 .50
15 Richard Power .20 .50
16 Corey Roberts .30 .75
17 Agris Saviels .30 .75
18 Ryan Sharp .20 .50
19 Daniel Sisca .20 .50
20 Shawn Snider .20 .50
21 Dan Sullivan .20 .50
22 Brandon Verner .20 .50
23 Nick Vukovic .30 .75
24 Joel Ward .20 .50
25 Bill Zalba .20 .50
26 Team Photo .20 .25

2001-02 Owen Sound Attack

COMPLETE SET (24) 4.80 12.00
1 Robert Chapman .20 .50
2 Richard Colwill .20 .50
3 Ryan Courtney .20 .50
4 David Dalliday .20 .50
5 Justin Day .30 .75
6 Jesse Gimblett .20 .50
7 Fred Hatziioannou .20 .50
8 Greg Jacina .30 .75
9 Michael Jacobsen .20 .50
10 Ladislav Kolda .20 .50
11 Jeff MacDermid .20 .50
12 Kyle McAllister .30 .75
13 Richard Power .20 .50
14 Justin Renner .30 .75
15 Brad Richardson .20 .50
16 Cory Roberts .30 .75
17 Dan Rogers .20 .50
18 Agris Saviels .30 .75
19 Ryan Sharp .20 .50
20 Daniel Sisca .20 .50
21 Sean Stefanski .20 .50
22 Dan Sullivan .20 .50
23 John Wheaton .20 .50
24 Tom Zanoski .20 .50

2002-03 Owen Sound Attack

COMPLETE SET (26) 5.00 12.00
1 Mascot .04 .10
2 Brett Howden .20 .50
3 Pat Sutton .20 .50
4 Jiri Paska .20 .50
5 Mark Giordano .20 .50
6 Patrick Jarrett .40 1.00
7 Dan Rogers .20 .50
8 Matt Passfield .40 1.00
9 Tom Zanoski .20 .50
10 Jesse Gimblett .20 .50
11 Michael Gough .20 .50
12 Brad Richardson .20 .50
13 Andrew Maksym .20 .50
14 Steve Henwood .20 .50
15 Brett McGrath .20 .50
16 Justin Renner .20 .50
17 Ladislav Kolda .20 .50
18 John Weathon .20 .50
19 Fred Hatziioannou .20 .50
20 Jeff McDermid .20 .50
21 Miguel Delisle .20 .50
22 David Edgeworth .20 .50
23 Mike Angelidis .20 .50
24 Dan LaCosta .30 .75
25 Marty Magers .30 .75
26 Checklist .04 .10

2003-04 Owen Sound Attack

COMPLETE SET (25) 6.00 15.00
1 The Bear Cubby .04 .10
2 Matt Smyth .20 .50
3 Wes Cunningham .20 .50
4 Pat Sutton .20 .50
5 Justin Dacosta .20 .50
6 Mark Giordano .20 .50
7 Patrick Jarrett .30 .75
8 Bobby Ryan 1.50 4.00
9 Andrew Maksym .20 .50
10 Richard Hornseth .20 .50
11 Brad Richardson .20 .50
12 Kevin Baker .20 .50
13 Kevin Harvey .20 .50
14 Jonathan Lehun .20 .50
15 Pavel Voroshnin .30 .75
16 Andre Deveaux .20 .50
17 Jim Kehoe .20 .50
18 Stefan Ruzicka .40 1.00
19 Jeff MacDermid .20 .50
20 John Wires .20 .50
21 Adam Smyth .20 .50
22 Mike Angelidis .20 .50
23 Dan LaCosta .30 .75
24 Robert Gherson .30 .75
25 Checklist .04 .10

2004-05 Owen Sound Attack

COMPLETE SET (24) 6.00 15.00
1 Mike Angelidis .20 .50
2 Neil Conway .40 1.00
3 Igor Gongalsky .20 .50
4 Derek Brochu .20 .50
5 Brad Richardson .20 .50
6 Kevin Baker .20 .50
7 Matthew Kang .20 .50
8 Colin Hanley .20 .50
9 Jonathan Lehun .20 .50
10 Matt Smyth .20 .50
11 Bob Sanguinetti .40 1.00
12 Stefan Ruzicka .40 1.00
13 Theo Peckham .20 .50
14 Payton Liske .20 .50
15 Robin Big Snake .60 1.50
16 Andrej Sekera .20 .50
17 Dan Lacosta .20 .50
18 Wes Cunningham .20 .50
19 Trevor Koverko .40 1.00
20 Justin Dacosta .20 .50
21 Scott Giles .20 .50
22 Patrick Jarrett .30 .75
23 Bobby Ryan 1.50 4.00
24 Cubby MASCOT .04 .10

2005-06 Owen Sound Attack

COMPLETE SET (24) 8.00 15.00
1 Bobby Ryan .75 2.00
2 Neil Conway .40 1.00
3 Andrej Sekera .20 .50
4 Kyle Lamb .20 .50
5 Trevor Koverko .20 .50
6 Jeff Moor .20 .50
7 Scott Giles .20 .50
8 Igor Gongalsky .20 .50
9 Derek Brochu .20 .50
10 Scott Tregunna .20 .50
11 Josh Catto .20 .50
12 Jeff Kyrzakos .20 .50
13 Matthew Kang .20 .50
14 Zach McCullough .20 .50
15 Joshua Bailey .20 .50
16 Marcus Carroll .20 .50
17 Bob Sanguinetti .40 1.00
18 Theo Peckham .40 1.00
19 Marek Bartanus .20 .50
20 Payton Liske .20 .50
21 Mike Angelidis .20 .50
22 Miles Cope .20 .50
23 Justin Allen .20 .50
24 Kyle Knechtel .40 1.00

2006-07 Owen Sound Attack

COMPLETE SET (22) 8.00 15.00
1 Theo Peckham .20 .50
2 Michael D'orazio .20 .50
3 Neil Conway .40 1.00
4 Dalyn Flatt .20 .50
5 Andrew Shorkey .20 .50
6 David Kolomatis .20 .50
7 Guy Carteciano .20 .50
8 Bobby Ryan .75 2.00
9 Derek Brochu .20 .50
10 Scott Tregunna .20 .50
11 Lane Macdermid .20 .50
12 Thomas Stajan .20 .50
13 Wayne Simmonds .20 .50
14 Zach Mccullough .20 .50
15 Josh Bailey .20 .50
16 Michael Farrell .20 .50
17 Marcus Carroll .20 .50
18 Bobby Sanguinetti .40 1.00
19 Marek Bartanus .20 .50
20 Anton Hedman .20 .50
21 Trevor Lewis .60 1.50
22 Scott Bowles .40 1.00

1993-94 Owen Sound Platers

COMPLETE SET (36) 8.00 20.00
1 Craig Binns .15 .40
2 Jim Brown .15 .40
3 Andrew Brunette .60 1.50
4 Luigi Calce .15 .40
5 Jason Campbell .15 .40
6 Draft Veterans Rod Hinks Jason MacDonald Kevin .15 .40
7 Paddy Flynn ACO .02 .10
8 Kirk Furey .15 .40
9 Jerry Harrigan CO .02 .10
10 Joe Harris .15 .40
11 Rod Hinks .15 .40
12 Marian Kacir .15 .40
13 Shane Kenny .15 .40
14 Jeff Kostuch .15 .40
15 Dave Lemay .15 .40
16 Jason MacDonald .20 .50
17 Rick Mancini TR .02 .10
18 Kirk Maltby .40 1.00
19 Brian Medeiros .15 .40
20 Mike Morrone .15 .40
21 Ryan Mougenel .15 .40
22 Scott Penton .15 .40
23 Wayne Primeau .40 1.00
24 Jeremy Rebek .15 .40
25 Rob Schweyer .15 .40
26 Willie Skilliter .15 .40
27 Jamie Storr .60 1.50
28 Jamie Storr Pure Gold .60 1.50
29 Jamie Storr's Mask .60 1.50
30 Jamie Storr Wayne Prime .60 1.50
31 Scott Walker .40 1.00
32 Kevin Weekes .60 1.50
33 Kevin Weekes' Mask .40 1.00
34 Shayne Wright .15 .40
35 Title Card Domino's Ad .02 .10
36 Title Card Eastwood Ad .02 .10

1994-95 Owen Sound Platers

COMPLETE SET (36) 6.00 15.00
1 Shawn Silver .20 .50
2 Shane Kenny .15 .40
3 Kevin Young .15 .40
4 Kirk Furey .15 .40
5 Peter MacKellar .15 .40
6 Willie Skilliter .15 .40
7 Joe Harris .15 .40
8 Brian Medeiros .15 .40
9 David Zunic .15 .40
10 Jeff Kostuch .15 .40
11 Jason Campbell .15 .40
12 Scott Smith .15 .40
13 Rob Schweyer .15 .40
14 Shayne Wright .15 .40
15 Scott Seiling .15 .40
16 Jeremy Rebek .15 .40
17 Rob Fitzgerald .15 .40
18 Ryan Mougenel .15 .40
19 John Argiropoulos .15 .40
20 Wayne Primeau .20 .50
21 Chris Wismer .15 .40
22 Matt Osborne .15 .40
23 Murray Hogg .15 .40
24 Brent Johnson 2.00 5.00
25 Jamie Storr (Jersey #31) .40 1.00
26 Jamie Storr (Jersey #92 .40 1.00
27 Jamie Storr (King Tut Mask) .40 1.00
28 Jamie Storr Draft .40 1.00
28 Wayne Primeau Draft .20 .50
28 Shayne Wright Draft .15 .40
29 Wayne Primeau Prime Time .20 .50
30 Coaching Staff .04 .10
31 Larry Gibson SB .04 .10
32 Joel Traplin TR .04 .10
33 Broadcast Team .04 .10
34 Ed Schambers Bus Dr. .04 .10
35 Domino's Pizza .01 .02
36 Jim Gardhouse Motors .01 .02

1995-96 Owen Sound Platers

COMPLETE SET (36) 4.80 12.00
1 Team Photo Card .15 .40
2 Ric Seiling CO .02 .10
3 Gus Eyers CO .02 .10
4 Brian Warrilow CO .02 .10
5 Rick Mancini TR .02 .10
6 Wayne Primeau .20 .50
7 Shawn Gallant .15 .40
8 Shane Kenny .15 .40
9 Chris Biagini .15 .40
10 Marek Babic .15 .40
11 Oleg Tsirkounov .15 .40
12 Peter MacKellar .15 .40
13 Ryan Davis .15 .40
14 John Argiropoulos .15 .40
15 Jason Campbell .15 .40
16 Dan Snyder .40 1.00
17 Steve Gallace .15 .40
18 Scott Seiling .15 .40
19 Jeremy Rebek .15 .40
20 Adam Mair .20 .50
21 Ryan Christie .20 .50
22 Larry Paleczny .20 .50
23 Wayne Primeau .20 .50
24 Chris Wismer .15 .40
25 Matt Osborne .15 .40
26 Mike Loach .15 .40
27 Brent Johnson .75 2.00
28 Jim Ensom .15 .40
29 Brent Johnson .75 2.00
30 Mike Loach .15 .40
31 Jim Ensom .15 .40
32 Wayne Primeau .20 .50
33 Shane Kenny .15 .40
34 Sun Times News .01 .05
35 Jim Gardhouse Motors .01 .05
36 Domino's Pizza .01 .05

1996-97 Owen Sound Platers

COMPLETE SET (27) 6.00 15.00
1 John Lovell CO .02 .10
2 Brian O'Leary CO .02 .10
3 Curtis Sanford .60 1.50
4 Shawn Gallant .15 .40
5 Brent Johnson .75 2.00
6 Joel Dezainde .15 .40
7 Kyle Dafoe .15 .40
8 Kyle Flaxey .15 .40
9 Matt Osborne .15 .40
10 Jamie Sokolsky .15 .40
11 Kurt Walsh .15 .40
12 Andrew Williamson .15 .40
13 Ryan Davis .15 .40
14 Sean Avery .75 2.00
15 Pascal Daze .15 .40
16 Dan Snyder .40 1.00
17 Steve Gallace .15 .40
18 Scott Wray .15 .40
19 Adam Mair .30 .75
20 Larry Paleczny .20 .50
21 Ryan Christie .15 .40
22 Chris Wismer .15 .40
23 Todd Miller .15 .40
24 Adam Campbell .15 .40
25 Jason Doyle .30 .75
26 Wes Goldie .15 .40
27 Owen Sound Platers .15 .40

1997-98 Owen Sound Platers

COMPLETE SET (26) 4.80 12.00
1 Owen Sound Platers .20 .50
2 Curtis Sanford .30 .75
3 Adam Campbell .20 .50
4 Kyle Dafoe .20 .50
5 Kyle Flaxey .20 .50
6 Chris Hopiavuori .20 .50
7 Jamie Sokolsky .20 .50
8 Colin Beardsmore .20 .50
9 Dave Stephenson .20 .50
10 Ryan Davis .20 .50
11 Ryan Rivard .20 .50
12 Sean Avery .75 2.00
13 Dan Snyder .40 1.00
14 Wes Goldie .20 .50
15 Adam Mair .30 .75
16 Larry Paleczny .20 .50
17 Ryan Christie .20 .50
18 Randy Davidson .20 .50
19 Joel Ward .20 .50
20 Chris Wismer .20 .50
21 Jason Doyle .30 .75
22 Brendan Brooks .20 .50
23 Adam Collins .20 .50
24 Eoin McInerney .40 1.00
25 Brian O'Leary CO .08 .25
26 Kirk Maltby .30 .75

1998-99 Owen Sound Platers

COMPLETE SET (28) 4.80 12.00
1 Owen Sound Platers .08 .25
2 Curtis Sanford .40 1.00
3 Mike Barrett .15 .40
4 Kyle Flaxey .15 .40
5 Chris Hopiavuori .20 .50
6 Mike Dombkiewicz .15 .40
7 Jeff Kaufman .15 .40
8 Dave Stephenson .15 .40
9 Chris Minard .30 .75
10 Stephane Savage .15 .40
11 Sean Avery .40 1.00
12 Peter Campbell .15 .40
13 Dan Snyder .40 1.00
14 Jan Sulc .15 .40
15 Wes Goldie .30 .75
16 Adam Mair .30 .75
17 Chad Woollard .20 .50
18 Stephen Lafleur .20 .50
19 Randy Davidson .20 .50
20 Joel Ward .20 .50
21 Juri Golicic .20 .50
22 Bryan Kazarian .20 .50
23 Nick Vukovic .30 .75
24 Brent Sullivan .15 .40
25 Adam Campbell .15 .40
26 Corey Roberts .15 .40
27 Adam Mair .30 .75
28 Coaches .02 .10

1999-00 Owen Sound Platers

COMPLETE SET (31) 4.00 10.00
1 Brian O'Leary ACO .02 .10
2 Dave Siciliano HCO .02 .10
3 Michael Barrett .15 .40
4 Kenny Corupe .20 .50
5 Tim Hamel .15 .40
6 Curtis Sanford .40 1.00
7 Agris Saviels .20 .50
8 Joel Ward .15 .40
9 Bill Zalba .15 .40
10 Matt Rock .15 .40
11 Mike Lymer .15 .40
12 Adam Campbell .15 .40
13 Chris Hopiavuori .15 .40
14 Mike Dombkiewicz .15 .40
15 Cory Roberts .20 .50
16 Greg Jacina .15 .40
17 Wes Goldie .20 .50
18 Dave Stephenson .15 .40
19 Daniel Sisca .15 .40
20 Bryan Kazarian .30 .75
21 Kyle McAllister .30 .75
22 Shawn Snider .15 .40
23 Trevor Blanchard .15 .40
24 Derek Campbell .15 .40
25 Jason Kowalski .15 .40
26 Brent Sullivan .15 .40
27 Alexei Salaschenko .15 .40
28 Nick Vukovic .15 .40
29 Kris Fraser .15 .40
30 Chris Minard .15 .40
31 Team Photo .02 .10

2003-04 Pacific AHL Prospects
COMPLETE SET (100) 15.00 40.00
1 Ari Ahonen .40 1.00
2 Adrian Foster .20 .50
3 Tuomas Pihlman .20 .50
4 Aleksander Suglobov .20 .50
5 Ray Emery .75 2.00
6 Alexandre Giroux .20 .50
7 Chris Kelly .20 .50
8 Julien Vauclair .20 .50
9 Wade Dubielewicz .40 1.00
10 Jeff Hamilton .20 .50
11 Justin Mapletoft .20 .50
12 Mattias Weinhandl .20 .50
13 Kari Lehtonen 2.00 5.00
14 Tommi Santala .20 .50
15 Karl Stewart .20 .50
16 Ilja Bryzgalov .40 1.00
17 Chris Kunitz .75 2.00
18 Tony Martensson .20 .50
19 Brad Boyes .40 1.00
20 Marcel Goc .30 .75
21 Seamus Kotyk .40 1.00
22 Garrett Stafford .20 .50
23 Miroslav Zalesak .30 .75
24 Jiri Hudler .75 2.00
25 Niklas Kronwall .75 2.00
26 Marc Lamothe .40 1.00
27 Nathan Robinson .20 .50
28 Benoit Gratton .20 .50
29 Alexander Perezhogin .40 1.00
30 Tomas Plekanec .40 1.00
31 Eero Somervuori .20 .50
32 Jozef Balej .40 1.00
33 Jason LaBarbera .60 1.50
34 Dominic Moore .30 .75
35 Fedor Tyutin .30 .75
36 Layne Ulmer .20 .50
37 Chad Wiseman .20 .50
38 Peter Budaj .60 1.50
39 Eric Perrin .40 1.00
40 Dan Cavanaugh .20 .50
41 Kyle Wanvig .40 1.00
42 Patrick DesRochers .30 .75
43 Dany Sabourin .40 1.00
44 Mike Zigomanis .20 .50
45 Scott Barney .20 .50
46 Mathieu Chouinard .40 1.00
47 Noah Clarke .20 .50
48 Denis Grebeshkov .20 .50
49 Adam Hauser .75 2.00
50 Steve Kelly .20 .50
51 Yanick Lehoux .20 .50
52 Pavel Rosa .20 .50
53 Fedor Fedorov .40 1.00
54 Kirill Koltsov .20 .50
55 Brandon Reid .40 1.00
56 Simon Gamache .40 1.00
57 Darren Haydar .40 1.00
58 Andrew Hutchinson .20 .50
9 Timofei Shishkanov .20 .50
0 Scottie Upshall SP 6.00 15.00
1 Anton Babchuk .20 .50
2 Matt Ellison .20 .50
3 Kirby Law .20 .50
4 Antero Niittymaki .40 1.00
5 Graham Mink .20 .50
6 Maxime Ouellet .40 1.00
7 Pat Leahy .20 .50
8 Colton Orr .75 2.00
9 Hannu Toivonen .75 2.00
0 Ryan Miller 1.25 3.00
1 Jason Pominville .75 2.00
2 Eric Beaudoin .20 .50
3 Mike Green .40 1.00
4 Lukas Krajicek .20 .50
5 Denis Shvidki .20 .50
6 Petr Taticek .20 .50
7 David LeNeveu .40 1.00
8 Fredrik Sjostrom .20 .50
9 Jeff Taffe .20 .50
0 Brendan Bell .20 .50
Sebastien Centomo .40 1.00
Mikael Tellqvist .60 1.50
Kyle Wellwood .40 1.00
Tim Jackman .20 .50
Aaron Johnson .20 .50
Pascal Leclaire .40 1.00
Brad Moran .20 .50
Doug Lynch .20 .50
Mike Morrison .40 1.00
Jani Rita .20 .50
Steve Valiquette .40 1.00
Jason Bacashihua .40 1.00
Dan Jancevski .20 .50
Colby Armstrong .40 1.00
Andy Chiodo .40 1.00
Michel Ouellet .40 1.00
Michal Sivek .20 .50
Jay McClement .20 .50
Johnny Pohl .20 .50
0 Peter Sejna .20 .50

2003-04 Pacific AHL Prospects Gold
OLD/925: 2X TO 5X BASIC CARDS

2003-04 Pacific AHL Prospects Autographs
ari Lehtonen 15.00 40.00
yan Miller 12.50 30.00
Vade Dubielewicz 12.50 30.00
avid LeNeveu 12.50 30.00
ri Ahonen 15.00 40.00
ascal Leclaire 12.50 30.00

2003-04 Pacific AHL Prospects Crease Lightning
ri Ahonen 1.50 4.00
ari Lehtonen 3.00 8.00
hil Sauve 1.50 4.00
lex Auld 1.50 4.00
astislav Stana 2.50 6.00
ndrew Raycroft 3.00 8.00
yan Miller 2.50 6.00
ascal Leclaire 2.00 5.00

2003-04 Pacific AHL Prospects Destined for Greatness
COMMON CARD (1-10) 1.25 3.00
1 Jason Spezza 3.00 8.00
2 Antoine Vermette 1.25 3.00
3 Rick DiPietro 1.25 3.00
4 Trent Hunter 2.50 6.00
5 Jonathan Cheechoo 3.00 8.00
6 Jiri Hudler 1.50 4.00
7 Michael Ryder 2.00 5.00
8 Jason King 1.25 3.00
9 Carlo Colaiacovo 1.25 3.00
10 Peter Sejna 1.25 3.00

2003-04 Pacific AHL Prospects Jerseys
1 Wade Dubielewicz 10.00 25.00
2 Jeff Hamilton 6.00 15.00
3 Tomas Plekanec 5.00 12.00
4 Denis Shvidki 5.00 12.00
5 David LeNeveu 8.00 20.00
6 Matt Murley 8.00 20.00

1995-96 PEI Senators
COMPLETE SET (24) 6.00 15.00
1 Scott Allison .20 .50
2 Radim Bicanek .20 .50
3 Patrick Charbonneau .20 .50
4 Pavol Demitra 1.25 3.00
5 Cosmo Dupaul .20 .50
6 Daniel Guerard .20 .50
7 Steve Guolla .30 .75
8 Shawn Heaphy .20 .50
9 Justin Hocking .20 .50
10 Martin Lamarche .20 .50
11 Eric Lavigne .20 .50
12 Kaj Linna .30 .75
13 Darrin Madeley .30 .75
14 Chad Penney .20 .50
15 Michel Picard .20 .50
16 Lance Pitlick .30 .75
17 Jean-Yves Roy .30 .75
18 Claude Savoie .20 .50
19 Darcy Simon .20 .50
20 Steve Strunk .20 .50
21 Patrick Traverse .20 .50
22 Jason Zent .20 .50
23 Coaching Staff .08 .25
24 Brutus MAS .02 .10

2003-04 P.E.I. Rocket
COMPLETE SET (24) 5.00 12.00
1 Julien Beaulieu .20 .50
2 Jimmy Bonneru .20 .50
3 Jonathan Boutin .30 .75
4 Pierre-Andre Bureau .20 .50
5 Yanick Charron .20 .50
6 Marc-Andre Gragnani .20 .50
7 Tyler Hawes .20 .50
8 Milan Hruska .20 .50
9 David Laliberte .20 .50
10 Michael Lambert .20 .50
11 Mark Lee .20 .50
12 Fabien Laniel .20 .50
13 Maxim Lapierre .20 .50
14 Jeff Macauley .20 .50
15 Tyler Noye .20 .50
16 Brent Maclellan .20 .50
17 Ryan Mior .30 .75
18 Sebastien Nolet .30 .75
19 Steve Pelletier .20 .50
20 Jonathan Persson .20 .50
21 Jean-Francois Roux .20 .50
22 Dominic Soucy .20 .50
23 Steve Tilley .20 .50
24 Cory Urquhart .20 .50

2004-05 P.E.I. Rocket
COMPLETE SET (30) 5.00 12.00
1 Alexandre Boivin .15 .40
2 Anthony Pototschnik .15 .40
3 Billy Bezeau .15 .40
4 Connor MacDonald .15 .40
5 David Laliberte .15 .40
6 David MacDonald .15 .40
7 Dominic Soucy .15 .40
8 Greg O'Brien .15 .40
9 Jimmy Bonneau .15 .40
10 Jonathan Boutin .40 1.00
11 Julien Beaulieu .15 .40
12 Kris MacDonald .15 .40
13 Marc-Andre Gragnani .15 .40
14 Maxim Lapierre .15 .40
15 Michael Dubuc .15 .40
16 Michel Charette .15 .40
17 Pierre-Andre Bureau .15 .40
18 Riku Korpinen .15 .40
19 Ryan Mior .40 1.00
20 Tyler Hawes .15 .40
21 Viatcheslav Trukhno .30 .75
22 Yanick Charron .15 .40
24 Kevin Hamel .15 .40
25 Alexander Ennaffati .15 .40
26 Pierre Bergeron .15 .40
27 Jean-Francois Boucher .15 .40
28 Jean-Francois Bernard .40 1.00
29 Fabien Laniel .15 .40
30 Louis-Philippe Lachance .15 .40
31 Alain Vigneault CO .15 .40

2005-06 P.E.I. Rocket
COMPLETE SET (29) 6.00 15.00
1 Ryan Mior .40 1.00
2 Stephen Lund .20 .50
3 Louis-Phillippe LaChance .20 .50
4 Travis Mealy .20 .50
5 Nathan Snowie .20 .50
6 Alexandre Boivin .20 .50
7 Geoff Walker .20 .50
8 Slava Trukhno .40 1.00
9 Greg O'Brien .20 .50
10 Stanson Donovan .20 .50
11 David Laliberte .20 .50
12 Devan Praught .20 .50
13 Olivier Gauthier .20 .50
14 Tyler Hawes .20 .50
15 Anton Skorykh .20 .50
16 Lucasz Steciuk .20 .50
17 Nicolas Leduc .20 .50
18 Jean-Claude Milot .20 .50
19 Joseph Haddad .20 .50
20 Michael Dubuc .20 .50
21 Chad Locke .20 .50
22 Steve Natywary .20 .50
23 Matthew LaChaine .20 .50
24 Antoine Lafleur .40 1.00
25 Simon Bolduc .20 .50
26 David MacDonald .20 .50
27 Pascal Lebel .20 .50
28 Marc-Andre Gragnani .20 .50
29 Danny Stewart .20 .50

2006-07 P.E.I. Rocket
COMPLETE SET (23) 8.00 15.00
1 David Laliberte .25 .60
2 Geoff Walker .25 .60
3 Ryan Mior .30 .75
4 Antoine Lafleur .50 1.25
5 Stephen Lund .25 .60
6 Pierre-Marc Guilbault .25 .60
7 Jordon Southorn .25 .60
8 Pierre-Luc Lessard .25 .60
9 Marc-Andre Gragnani .40 1.00
10 Pascal Boutin .25 .60
11 Chris Doyle .25 .60
12 Martin Latal .25 .60
13 Guillaume Doucet .25 .60
14 Lucas Mckinley .25 .60
15 Devan Praught .25 .60
16 Benoit Levesque .25 .60
17 Tyles Hawes .25 .60
18 Peter Cmorej .25 .60
19 Matthew Lachaine .25 .60
20 Maxim Cliché .25 .60
21 Joey Haddad .25 .60
22 Chad Locke .25 .60
23 Gregory Paynter .25 .60

2002-03 Pee Dee Pride RBI
COMPLETE SET (18) 8.00 20.00
133 B.J. Adams .40 1.00
134 Daniel Carriere .40 1.00
135 Aaron Gates .40 1.00
136 Mike Glumac .60 1.50
137 Wes Goldie .40 1.00
138 Derek Halldorson .40 1.00
139 Kyle Kidney .40 1.00
140 Gregor Krajnc .40 1.00
141 Ryan Knox .40 1.00
142 Eric Naud .40 1.00
143 Jason Metcalfe .40 1.00
144 Matt Reid .40 1.00
145 Jason Robinson .40 1.00
146 Greg Schmidt .40 1.00
147 Allan Sirois .40 1.00
148 Mike Torney .40 1.00
149 Matt Underhill .40 1.00
150 Ron Vogel .75 2.00

1996-97 Pensacola Ice Pilots
COMPLETE SET (24) 4.00 10.00
1 Craig Brown .15 .40
2 Stephane Julien .15 .40
3 David Borrozino .15 .40
4 Jeremy Mylymok .15 .40
5 Patrik Alvin .15 .40
6 Rostislav Saglo .15 .40
7 Glen Metropolit .40 1.00
8 Chad Quenneville .15 .40
9 Trevor Buchanan .15 .40
10 Brandon Gray .15 .40
11 Jon Pirrong .30 .75
12 Brent Gretzky .30 .75
13 Martin LaChaine .15 .40
14 Brian Secord .15 .40
15 Hugo Belanger .15 .40
16 Christian Sbrocca .15 .40
17 Tony Prpic .15 .40
18 Shane Calder .15 .40
19 Nick Stajduhar .15 .40
20 Brendan Concannon .15 .40
21 Sean Gauthier .20 .50
22 Al Pederson CO .15 .40
23 George Kozak .15 .40
NNO Header Card .02 .10

1997-98 Pensacola Ice Pilots
COMPLETE SET (25) 5.00 10.00
1 Team Photo .20 .50
2 J.F. Aube .30 .75
3 Craig Brown .20 .50
4 Michael Burkett .20 .50
5 Shane Calder .20 .50
6 Martin Chouinard .20 .50
7 Brendan Concannon .20 .50
8 Jon Dunmar .20 .50
9 Sean Gauthier .20 .50
10 Christian Gosselin .20 .50
11 Brian LaFleur .20 .50
12 Steven Low .20 .50
13 Scott Malone .20 .50
14 Mike Mayhew .20 .50
15 Keith O'Connell .20 .50
16 Val Passarelli .30 .75
17 Mark Polak .20 .50
18 Chad Quenneville .20 .50
19 Andrew Rodgers .20 .50
20 Nick Stajduhar .20 .50
21 Mike Sullivan .20 .50
22 Kelly Hultgren .20 .50
23 George Kozak ACO .20 .50
24 Allen Pedersen HCO .20 .50
25 D-Lux Printing .20 .50

1998-99 Pensacola Ice Pilots
1 Shane Calder 2.00 5.00
2 Nick Stajduhar 2.00 5.00
3 Etienne Beaudry 2.00 5.00
4 Bob Wilkie 2.00 5.00
5 Don Chase 2.00 5.00
6 Stephen Naughton 2.00 5.00
7 Chad Quenneville 2.00 5.00
8 Keith O'Connell 2.00 5.00
9 Brendan Concannon 2.00 5.00
10 Keli Corpse 2.00 5.00
11 Andrew Rodgers 2.00 5.00
12 Dave Ivaska 2.00 5.00
13 Rob Phillips 2.00 5.00
14 Mark Polak 2.00 5.00
15 Craig Brown 2.00 5.00
16 Tom Noble 2.00 5.00
17 Eon MacFarlane 2.00 5.00
18 Allen Pedersen CO 2.00 5.00
19 George Kosak CO 2.00 5.00
20 Iceman MAS 2.00 5.00
21 Pensacola Ice Pilots 2.00 5.00
22 The Hangar 2.00 5.00
23 Pensacola Ice Pilots 2.00 5.00
24 Kelly Hultgren 2.00 5.00
25 Mike Sullivan 2.00 5.00
26 Pensacola Ice Pilots CL 2.00 5.00
27 PHPA Web Site 2.00 5.00

2003-04 Pensacola Ice Pilots
COMPLETE SET (16) 8.00 20.00
337 Tyler Beechey .40 1.00
338 Greg Chambers .40 1.00
339 Brian Collins .40 1.00
340 Brad Cruikshank .40 1.00
341 Brian Eklund .75 2.00
342 Brandon Fleenor .40 1.00
343 Brett Gibson .40 1.00
344 Jade Galbraith .40 1.00
345 Aaron Gionet .40 1.00
346 Dwayne Hay .40 1.00
347 Andreas Holmqvist .40 1.00
348 Evgeny Konstantinov .75 2.00
349 Wes Mason .40 1.00
350 Corey Neilson .75 2.00
351 Aaron Phillips .40 1.00
352 Kent Sauer .40 1.00

2004-05 Penticton Vees
COMPLETE SET (25) 6.00 15.00
1 History Card .04 .10
2 Checklist .04 .10
3 Josh Brown .30 .75
4 Aaron Agnew .30 .75
5 Ben Robinson .30 .75
6 Brian Lebler .30 .75
7 Shaun MacDonald .30 .75
8 Ryan Coghlan .60 1.50
9 Jon Cara .30 .75
10 Colin Williams .30 .75
11 Mike Towns .30 .75
12 Jason Harding .30 .75
13 Kevin Borba .60 1.50
14 Cody Collins .30 .75
15 Alex MacLeod .30 .75
16 Chris Rengert .30 .75
17 Peter Farrell .30 .75
18 Justin Coutu .30 .75
19 John Kopp .30 .75
20 Adrian Jack .30 .75
21 Brad Thiessen .75 2.00
22 Corey Milan .60 1.50
23 Bruno Campese CO .04 .10
24 Ken Law ACO .04 .10
25 Dan Marshall ANN .04 .10

2005-06 Penticton Vees
COMPLETE SET (24) 10.00 20.00
1 Brennan Barker .40 1.00
2 Jordan Cheveldave .40 1.00
3 Ryan Costanzo .40 1.00
4 Deron Cousens .40 1.00
5 Peter Farrell .40 1.00
6 Tanner House .40 1.00
7 John Kopp .40 1.00
8 Justin Krueger .40 1.00
9 Brian Lebler .40 1.00
10 Alex MacLeod .40 1.00
11 Corey Milan .40 1.00
12 T.J. Miller .40 1.00
13 Ivo Musa .40 1.00
14 Lee Pagee .40 1.00
15 Ben Robinson .40 1.00
16 Robert Skinner .40 1.00
17 Gary Sylvester .40 1.00
18 Mike Towns .40 1.00
19 Evan Trupp .40 1.00
20 Ryan Wagner .40 1.00
21 Mark Walters .40 1.00
22 Jordan White .40 1.00
23 Bruno Campese CO .10 .25
24 1986 Penticton Knights .10 .25

2006-07 Penticton Vees
COMPLETE SET (25) 12.00 20.00
1 Jeremy Beller .30 .75
2 Travis Briard .30 .75
3 Steve Cameron .30 .75
4 Deron Cousens .30 .75
5 Brad Davis .30 .75
6 Dustin Donaghy .30 .75
7 Nigel Dube .30 .75
8 Joel Eisenkirch .30 .75
9 Jordan Funk .30 .75
10 Elias Grossmann .30 .75
11 Michael Guzzo .30 .75
12 Brett Hextall .30 .75
13 Tanner House .30 .75
14 Alex MacLeod .30 .75
15 Kyle McMurphy .30 .75
16 Corey Milan .30 .75
17 Bryant Molle .40 1.00
18 Robert Skinner .30 .75
19 Evan Smith .30 .75
20 Gary Sylvester .30 .75
21 Mike Towns .30 .75
22 Evan Trupp .30 .75
23 Ryan Wagner .30 .75
24 Bruno Campese HC .30 .75
25 72-73 Penticton Broncos Team Photo .30 .75

2007-08 Penticton Vees
COMPLETE SET (21) 5.00 12.00
1 James Bettauer .25 .60
2 Zak Dalpe .25 .60
3 Alex Evin .25 .60
4 Elias Grossmann .25 .60
5 Michael Guzzo .25 .60
6 Michael Hengen .25 .60
7 Brett Hextall .25 .60
8 Zack Josepher .25 .60
9 Nic Knudsen .25 .60
10 Devon Krogh .25 .60
11 Eric Kroshus .25 .60
12 Mitch Labreche .25 .60
13 Denver Manderson .25 .60
14 Kyle McMurphy .25 .60
15 Bryan Mountain .25 .60
16 Trevor Nill .25 .60
17 Cory Schneider .50 1.25
18 Austin Smith .25 .60
19 Ryan Wagner .25 .60
20 Nathan Westover .25 .60
21 Fred Harbinson HC .15 .40

1992-93 Peoria Rivermen
COMPLETE SET (30) 4.00 10.00
1 Jeff Batters .15 .40
2 Parris Duffus .20 .50
3 Greg Eberle TR .02 .10
4 John Faginkrantz MG .02 .10
5 Denny Felsner .15 .40
6 Derek Frenette .15 .40
7 Ron Handy .15 .40
8 Joe Hawley .15 .40
9 Terry Hollinger .15 .40
10 Ron Hoover .15 .40
11 Daniel Laperriere .20 .50
12 Lee J. Leslie .15 .40
13 Dave Mackey .15 .40
14 Jason Marshall .20 .50
15 Brian McKee .15 .40
16 Rick Meagher CO .15 .40
17 Kevin Miehm .15 .40
18 Brian Pellerin ACO .02 .10
19 Mark Reeds .15 .40
20 Kyle Reeves .15 .40
21 Rob Robinson .15 .40
22 Jason Ruff .15 .40
23 Geoff Sarjeant .30 .75
24 Richard Pion .15 .40
25 Darren Veitch .15 .40
26 Doug Wickenheiser .15 .40
27 Shawn Wheeler .15 .40
28 Checklist .02 .10
29 Coca Cola Coupon .02 .10
30 Title Card .02 .10

1993-94 Peoria Rivermen
COMPLETE SET (31) 4.00 10.00
1 Mark Bassen .15 .40
2 Jeff Batters .15 .40
3 Rene Chapdelaine .15 .40
4 Doug Crossman .20 .50
5 Parris Duffus .30 .75
6 Greg Eberle TR .02 .10
7 Doug Evans .15 .40
8 Kevin Evans .15 .40
9 John Faginkrantz EQ MG .02 .10
10 Denny Felsner .15 .40
11 Derek Frenette .15 .40
12 Terry Hollinger .15 .40
13 Ron Hoover .15 .40
14 Butch Kaebel .15 .40
15 Nathan Lafayette .15 .40
16 Dan Laperriere .20 .50
17 Dave Mackey .15 .40
18 Paul MacLean CO .15 .40
19 Michel Mongeau .20 .50
20 Brian Pellerin .15 .40
21 Rick Pion .15 .40
22 Vitali Prokhorov .15 .40
23 Mark Reeds ACO .02 .10
24 John Roderick .15 .40
25 Geoff Sarjeant .30 .75
26 Steve Staios .20 .50
27 Darren Veitch .15 .40
28 Nick Vitucci .30 .75
29 Title card (Team history on back) .02 .10
30 Checklist .02 .10
31 Alcohol is its own puni .02 .10

1995-96 Peoria Rivermen
COMPLETE SET (24) 4.00 10.00
1 Jon Casey .30 .75
2 Rene Chapdelaine .20 .50
3 Doug Evans .20 .50
4 Eric Fenton .20 .50
5 Shannon Finn .15 .40
6 Martin Hamrlik .15 .40
7 Ron Hoover .15 .40
8 Jacques Joubert .15 .40
9 Lee J. Leslie .20 .50
10 Dave MacIntyre .20 .50
11 Jason Miller .15 .40
12 Michel Mongeau .30 .75
13 Glenn Mulvenna .20 .50
14 Eric Murano .15 .40
15 Keith Osborne .20 .50
16 Greg Paslawski .20 .50
17 Jon Pratt .15 .40
18 Dan Ratushny .20 .50
19 Patrice Robitaille .20 .50
20 Paul Taylor .15 .40
21 Travis Thiessen .15 .40
22 Steve Thornton .15 .40
23 Kirk Tomlinson .20 .50
24 Steve Wilson .15 .40

1996-97 Peoria Rivermen
COMPLETE SET (25) 4.00 10.00
1 Mike Barrie .20 .50
2 Doug Bonner .30 .75
3 Greg Eberle John Krouse .02 .10
4 Brad Essex .15 .40
5 Doug Evans ASST CO .02 .10
6 Liam Garvey .15 .40
7 Trevor Hanas .15 .40
8 Jon Hillebrandt .30 .75
9 Dan Hodge .20 .50
10 Butch Kaebel .15 .40
11 Karson Kaebel .15 .40
12 Justin Krall .15 .40
13 Jeff Kungle .15 .40
14 Kevin Lune .15 .40
15 Darren Maloney .15 .40
16 Dustin McArthur .15 .40
17 Jon Pratt .15 .40
18 Brad Purdie .15 .40
19 Mark Reeds CO .02 .10
20 Jason Saal .30 .75
21 Jan Slavik .15 .40
22 Marc Terris .15 .40
23 Jean-Guy Trudel .20 .50
24 Paul Vincent .20 .50
25 Title Card .02 .10

1996-97 Peoria Rivermen Photo Album
COMPLETE SET (24) 8.00 20.00
1 Mike Barrie .30 .75
2 Doug Bonner .60 1.50
3 Greg Eberle TR .20 .50
4 Brad Essex .30 .75
5 Doug Evans ASST CO .20 .50
6 Liam Garvey .30 .75
7 Trevor Hanas .30 .75
8 Jon Hillebrandt .60 1.50
9 Dan Hodge .30 .75
10 Butch Kaebel .30 .75
11 Karson Kaebel .30 .75
12 Justin Krall .30 .75
13 John Krouse EQUIP .20 .50
14 Jeff Kungle .30 .75
15 Kevin Lune .30 .75
16 Darren Maloney .30 .75
17 Dustin McArthur .30 .75
18 Jon Pratt .30 .75
19 Brad Purdie .30 .75
20 Jason Saal .60 1.50
21 Jan Slavik .30 .75
22 Marc Terris .30 .75
23 Jean-Guy Trudel .40 1.00
24 Paul Vincent .30 .75

1997-98 Peoria Rivermen
COMPLETE SET (29) 4.00 10.00
1 Garry Gruber .15 .40
2 Derek Diener .15 .40
3 Samy Nasreddine .20 .50
4 Doug Evans .15 .40
5 Darren Maloney .15 .40
6 Joe Craigen .20 .50
7 Rob Phillips .15 .40
8 Brian Clifford .15 .40
9 Darcy Smith .15 .40
10 Butch Kaebel .20 .50
11 Jean Guy Trudel .20 .50
12 Brad Essex .15 .40
13 Justin Krall .15 .40
14 John Dance .15 .40
15 Marc Terris .15 .40
16 Trevor Hanas .15 .40
17 Dave Paradise .15 .40
18 David Vallieres .15 .40
19 Scott Roche .30 .75
20 Marcel Kuris .15 .40
21 Jon Pratt .15 .40
22 Rob Giffin .20 .50
23 Mark Reeds .20 .50
24 Greg Eberle .15 .40
25 John Krouse EQ .02 .10
26 Mascot .02 .10
27 Title Card .02 .10
28 Header Card .02 .10

1998-99 Peoria Rivermen
COMPLETE SET (27) 4.80 12.00
1 Darren Maloney .15 .40
2 Dan Hodge .15 .40
3 Doug Evans .15 .40
4 Dan Carney .15 .40
5 Chris Coveny .15 .40
6 Alexandre Couture .15 .40
7 Jamie Thompson .15 .40
8 Jay Kenney .15 .40
9 J.F. Boutin .15 .40
10 Joe Craigen .30 .75
11 Darcy Smith .15 .40
12 Dan Murphy .15 .40
13 Quinn Hancock .15 .40
14 Mark Reeds CO .02 .10
15 Marek Ivan .15 .40
16 Kory Karlander .15 .40
17 Ken Boone .15 .40
18 Jeff Trembecky .15 .40
19 Steve MacKinnon .15 .40
20 Joe Rybar .30 .75
21 Peoria Rivermen .15 .40
22 Scott Roche .30 .75
23 Chad Lang .30 .75
24 Kevin Paden .20 .50
25 Blaine Fitzpatrick .15 .40
26 Mike Schultz .15 .40
27 Darren Maloney AS .02 .10
28 Jamie Thompson AS .15 .40

1999-00 Peoria Rivermen
COMPLETE SET (36) 40.00 80.00
1 Rocky MAS .08 .25
2 Don Granato CO .40 1.00
3 Greg Eberle TR .02 .10
4 Jamie Healy TR .02 .10
5 Trevor Baker 1.50 4.00
6 Duane Derksen 2.00 5.00
7 Darren Clark 1.50 4.00
8 Jason Christie 1.50 4.00
9 Blaine Fitzpatrick 1.50 4.00
10 John Gurskis 1.50 4.00
11 Alexandre Couture 1.50 4.00
12 Darren Maloney 1.50 4.00
13 Blaz Emersic 1.50 4.00
14 Cody Rudkowsky 2.00 5.00
15 J.F. Boutin 1.50 4.00
16 Joe Rybar 2.00 5.00
17 Matt Smith 1.50 4.00
18 Tomaz Razinger 1.50 4.00
19 Craig Anderson 1.50 4.00
20 Jason Lawmaster 1.50 4.00
21 Bret Meyers 1.50 4.00
22 Sean Farmer 1.50 4.00
23 Darin Kimble 3.00 8.00
24 Dan Hodge 1.50 4.00
25 Luke Gruden 1.50 4.00
26 Tyler McMillan 1.50 4.00
27 Kenzie Homer 1.50 4.00
28 James Desmarais 1.50 4.00
29 John Butler PRES .02 .10
30 Mike Nelson VP .02 .10
31 Bart Rogers GM .02 .10
32 Michael Sauers GM .02 .10
33 Jim Small GM .02 .10
34 Norm Ulrich DOB .02 .10
35 Manda Girard SALES .02 .10
36 B.J. Stone SALES .02 .10

2001-02 Peoria Rivermen
COMPLETE SET (24) 8.00 20.00
1 Checklist .04 .10
2 Jason Christie CO .04 .10
3 Curtis Sanford .75 2.00
4 Bob Gassoff Jr. .40 1.00
5 Chad Starling .40 1.00
6 Blake Evans .40 1.00
7 Kevin Tucker .40 1.00
8 Trevor Baker .40 1.00
9 Jonathan Fauteux .40 1.00
10 Randy Rowe .40 1.00
11 Dustin Kuk .40 1.00
12 Bret Meyers .40 1.00
13 Kevin Granato .40 1.00
14 Dan Hodge .40 1.00
15 Tyler Rennette .40 1.00
16 Ryan Finnerty .40 1.00
17 Brad Voth .40 1.00
18 Joe Rybar .60 1.50
19 Darren Clark .40 1.00
20 Matt Golden .40 1.00
21 Phil Osaer .40 1.00
22 Jason Lawmaster .40 1.00
23 Arvid Rekis .40 1.00
24 Kevin Cloutier .40 1.00

2000-01 Peoria Rivermen
COMPLETE SET (21) 4.00 10.00
1 Curtis Sanford .30 2.00
2 Didier Tremblay .20 .50
3 Luke Gruden .20 .50
4 J.F. Boutin .20 .50
5 Lauri Kinos .20 .50
6 Darren Maloney .20 .50
7 Trevor Baker .20 .50
8 Tyler Willis .20 .50
9 Bret Meyers .20 .50
10 Dustin Kuk .20 .50
11 Dan Hodge .20 .50
12 Joe Rybar .20 .50
13 Blaine Fitzpatrick .20 .50
14 Darren Clark .20 .50
15 Matt Golden .20 .50
16 Kenric Exner .40 1.00
17 Jason Lawmaster .20 .50
18 Arvid Rekis .20 .50
19 Tomaz Razinger .20 .50
20 Joe Trotta ACO .10 .25
21 Jason Christie HCO .10 .25

2002-03 Peoria Rivermen
COMPLETE SET (25) 5.00 12.00
1 Jason Christie HCO .10 .25
2 Simon Lajeunesse .40 1.00
3 Trevor Gillies .20 .50
4 Lauri Kinos .20 .50
5 Darren Clark .20 .50
6 Trevor Baker .20 .50
7 Greg Day .20 .50
8 Brett DeCecco .20 .50
9 Randy Rowe .20 .50
10 Randy Copley .20 .50
11 Duane Derksen .40 1.00
12 Kevin Granato .20 .50
13 Tyler Rennette .20 .50
14 Ryan Finnerty .20 .50
15 Brad Voth .20 .50
16 Brendan Brooks .20 .50
17 Derek Booth .20 .50
18 Scott Crawford .20 .50
19 Jeremy Yablonski .20 .50
20 Jason Lawmaster .20 .50
21 Josh Kern .20 .50
22 Arvid Rekis .20 .50
23 Anthony Belza .20 .50
24 Alfie Michaud .40 1.00
NNO Checklist .04 .10

2002-03 Peoria Rivermen Photo Pack
COMPLETE SET (8) 25.00 50.00
1 Trevor Baker 2.50 6.00
2 Brendan Brooks 2.50 6.00
3 Darren Clark 2.50 6.00
4 Duane Derksen 4.00 10.00
5 Ryan Finnerty 2.50 6.00
6 Jason Lawmaster 2.50 6.00
7 Alfie Michaud 4.00 10.00
8 Tyler Rennette 2.50 6.00

2002-03 Peoria Rivermen RBI Sports
COMPLETE SET (18) 8.00 20.00
151 Trevor Baker .40 1.00
152 Anthony Belza .40 1.00
153 Derek Booth .40 1.00
154 Brendan Brooks .40 1.00
155 Darren Clark .40 1.00
156 Randy Copley .40 1.00
157 Scott Crawford .40 1.00
158 Greg Day .40 1.00
159 Duane Derksen .75 2.00
160 Trevor Gillies .40 1.00
161 Josh Kern .40 1.00
162 Jason Lawmaster .75 2.00
163 Alfie Michaud .75 2.00
164 Arvid Rekis .40 1.00
165 Tyler Rennette .40 1.00
166 Randy Rowe .40 1.00
167 Rod Taylor .40 1.00
168 Brad Voth .40 1.00

2003-04 Peoria Rivermen
COMPLETE SET (24) 4.00 10.00
1 Adam Edinger .15 .40
2 Brendan Brooks .15 .40

3 Bret DeCecco .15 .40
4 Brett Scheffelmaier .15 .40
5 Chad Starling .15 .40
6 Colin Hemingway .15 .40
7 Craig Olynick .15 .40
8 Doug MacIver .15 .40
9 George Halkidis .15 .40
10 Greg Black .15 .40
11 Joe Pereira .15 .40
12 Joe Vandermeer .15 .40
13 Ken Goetz .30 .75
14 Levente Szuper .40 1.00
15 Malcolm Hutt .15 .40
16 Malcolm MacMillan .15 .40
17 Marty Johnston .15 .40
18 Mike Valley .30 .75
19 Randy Rowe .15 .40
20 Scott Crawford .15 .40
21 Scott Turner .15 .40
22 Trevor Baker .30 .75
23 Tyler Rennette .15 .40
24 Jason Christie HCO .04 .10
NNO Checklist .04 .10

2004-05 Peoria Rivermen

COMPLETE SET (25) 5.00 12.00
1 Chad Starling .20 .50
2 Warren Toews .20 .50
3 Mark Jarant .20 .50
4 Chris Bogas .20 .50
5 Brian McCullough .20 .50
6 Randy Rowe .20 .50
7 Trevor Baker .20 .50
8 Justin Maiser .20 .50
9 Travis Rycroft .20 .50
10 Scott Turner .20 .50
11 Alfie Michaud .40 1.00
12 Chris Beckford-Tseu .40 1.00
13 Kris Kasper .40 1.00
14 Ed Hill .20 .50
15 Jake Riddle .20 .50
16 James Sanford .20 .50
17 Patrick Wellar .20 .50
18 David Kaczowka .20 .50
19 Tyler Rennette .20 .50
20 Joe Pereira .20 .50
21 Rejean Stringer .04 .10
22 Stringer MASCOT .04 .10
23 Colin Hemingway .20 .50
24 Trevor Byrne .20 .50
25 Jason Christie CO .04 .10

2005-06 Peoria Rivermen

1 Curtis Sanford .40 1.00
2 Mike Mottau .30 .75
3 Rocky Thompson .20 .50
4 Trevor Byrne .20 .50
5 Brendan Buckley .20 .50
6 Gavin Morgan .20 .50
7 Colin Hemingway .20 .50
8 Jon DiSalvatore .20 .50
9 Mike Stuart .20 .50
10 Blake Evans .20 .50
11 Mike Glumac .20 .50
12 D.J. King .20 .50
13 Aaron MacKenzie .20 .50
14 Troy Riddle .20 .50
15 Trent Whitfield .20 .50
16 Peter Sejna .20 .50
17 Brendan Brooks .20 .50
18 Ryan Ramsay .20 .50
19 Chris Beckford-Tseu .75 2.00
20 Doug Lynch .20 .50
21 Jason Bacashihua .40 1.00
22 Patrick Lalime .40 1.00
23 Jeff Woywitka .20 .50
24 Steve Pleau CO .02 .10

2006-07 Peoria Rivermen

COMPLETE SET (25) 8.00 15.00
1 Chris Beckford-Tseu .60 1.50
2 Michal Birner .20 .50
3 Jon DiSalvatore .20 .50
4 Zack Fitzgerald .20 .50
5 Mike Glumac .30 .75
6 Cam Keith .20 .50
7 D.J. King .20 .50
8 Charles Linglet .20 .50
9 Doug Lynch .20 .50
10 Aaron MacKenzie .20 .50
11 Ryan MacMurchy .20 .50
12 Tomas Mojzis .20 .50
13 Gavin Morgan .20 .50
14 Roman Polak .20 .50
15 Ryan Ramsay .30 .75
16 Marek Schwarz .60 1.50
17 Peter Sejna .20 .50
18 Mike Stuart .20 .50
19 Rocky Thompson .20 .50
20 Trent Whitfield .20 .50
21 Stephen Wood .20 .50
22 Jeff Woywitka .20 .50
23 Konstantin Zakharov .20 .50
24 Dave Baseggio .20 .50
25 Checklist .02 .10

2007-08 Peoria Rivermen

COMPLETE SET (26) 5.00 12.00
1 Dave Baseggio HC .15 .40
2 Chris Beckford-Tseu .25 .60
3 Hans Benson .25 .60
4 Alex Brooks .25 .60
5 Nicholas Drazenovic .25 .60
6 Micki DuPont .25 .60
7 Ryan Glenn .25 .60
8 Mike Glumac .25 .60
9 Alexander Hellstrom .25 .60
10 Martin Kariya .25 .60
11 Cam Keith .25 .60
12 Neil Komadoski .25 .60
13 Nikolay Lemtyugov .25 .60
14 Charles Linglet .25 .60
15 Aaron MacKenzie .25 .60
16 Roman Polak .25 .60
17 Chris Porter .25 .60
18 Ryan Reaves .25 .60
19 Marek Schwarz .25 .60
20 Yan Stastny .25 .60
21 Julian Talbot .25 .60
22 Jean-Guy Trudel .25 .60
23 Steve Wagner .25 .60
24 Trent Whitfield .25 .60
25 Jeff Woywitka .25 .60
NNO Checklist .10 .25

1989-90 Peterborough Petes

COMPLETE SET (26) 10.00 25.00
98 Troy Stephens .40 1.00
99 Dan Brown .40 1.00
100 Mike Ricci 1.25 3.00
101 Brent Pope .40 1.00
102 Mike Dagenais .40 1.00
103 Scott Campbell .40 1.00
104 Jamie Pegg .40 1.00
105 Joe Hawley .40 1.00
106 Jason Dawe .40 1.00
107 Paul Mitton .40 1.00
108 Mike Tomlinson .40 1.00
109 Dave Lorentz .40 1.00
110 Dale McTavish .40 1.00
111 Willie McGarvey .40 1.00
112 Don O'Neill .40 1.00
113 Mark Myles .40 1.00
114 Chris Longo .40 1.00
115 Tom Hopkins .40 1.00
116 Jassen Cullimore .40 1.00
117 Geoff Ingram .40 1.00
118 Twohey
Bovair TR .40 1.00
119 Doug Searle .40 1.00
120 Bryan Gendron .40 1.00
121 Andrew Verner .60 1.50
122 Todd Bocjun .60 1.50
123 Dick Todd CO .20 .50

1991-92 Peterborough Petes

COMPLETE SET (30) 8.00 20.00
1 Jason Dawe .30 .75
2 Chris Pronger 3.00 8.00
3 Scott Turner .20 .50
4 Chad Grills .20 .50
5 Brent Tully .20 .50
6 Mike Harding .20 .50
7 Chris Longo .20 .50
8 Slapshot MASCOT .02 .10
9 Doug Searle .20 .50
10 Mike Tomlinson .20 .50
11 Bryan Gendron .20 .50
12 Andrew Verner .30 .75
13 Ryan Black .20 .50
14 Don O'Neill .20 .50
15 Jeff Twohey MG
CO .02 .10
16 Dale McTavish .20 .50
17 Jeff Walker .20 .50
18 Matt St. Germain .20 .50
19 Dave Roche .20 .50
20 Colin Wilson .20 .50
21 Jassen Cullimore .20 .50
22 Chad Lang .30 .75
23 Dick Todd MG
CO .20 .50
24 Geordie Kinnear .20 .50
25 Shawn Heins .25 .60
26 John Johnson .20 .50
27 Kelly Vipond .20 .50
NNO Police Crest .02 .10
NNO Kiwanis Sponsor Card .02 .10
NNO Quaker Sponsor Card .02 .10

1993-94 Peterborough Petes

COMPLETE SET (31) 6.00 15.00
1 1992-93 OHL Champions .15 .40
2 Jonathan Murphy .15 .40
3 Dave Roche .15 .40
4 Rob Giffin .15 .40
5 Mike Harding .15 .40
6 Tim Hill .15 .40
7 Darryl Moxam .15 .40
8 Pat Paone .15 .40
9 Brent Tully .15 .40
10 Zac Bierk .30 .75
11 Chad Grills .15 .40
12 Matt St. Germain .15 .40
13 Henrik Eppers .15 .40
14 Rick Emmett .15 .40
15 Chad Lang .20 .50
16 Cameron Mann .40 1.00
17 Steve Hogg .15 .40
18 Mike Williams .15 .40
19 Ryan Nauss .15 .40
20 Jamie Langenbrunner .40 1.00
21 Ryan Douglas .15 .40
22 Matt Johnson .30 .75
23 Kelvin Solari .15 .40
24 Dan Delmonte .15 .40
25 Quayde Lightbody .15 .40
26 Adrian Murray .15 .40
27 Jason Dawe .15 .40
28 Mike Harding .15 .40
29 Chris Pronger 2.00 5.00
30 Sponsor Card
Cardboard .02 .10
NNO Slapshot Ad Card .02 .10

2001-02 Peterborough Petes

COMPLETE SET (20) 8.00 20.00
1 Cody Spicer .60 1.50
2 Dustin Wood .40 1.00
3 Bryan Hamm .40 1.00
4 Mark Flood .40 1.00
5 Trevor Hendrix .40 1.00
6 James Edgar .40 1.00
7 Jason Penner .40 1.00
8 Jon Howse .40 1.00
9 Ryan Card .40 1.00
10 Eric Staal 4.00 10.00
11 Josh Patterson .40 1.00
12 Jim Gagnon .40 1.00
13 Brad Self .40 1.00
14 Matt Herneisen .40 1.00
15 Adam Elzinga .40 1.00
16 Greg Chambers .40 1.00
17 Jamie Tardif .40 1.00
18 Matt Armstrong .40 1.00
19 David Currie .60 1.50
20 Lukas Krajicek .75 2.00

2002-03 Peterborough Petes

COMPLETE SET (24) 6.00 15.00
1 Rick Allain CO .04 .10
2 Steve Smith ACO .04 .10
3 Aaron Dawson .20 .50
4 Mark Flood .20 .50
5 Shawn Futers .20 .50
6 Trevor Hendrix .20 .50
7 Jordan Morrison .20 .50
8 Jon Howse .20 .50
9 Ryan Card .20 .50
10 Eric Staal 2.00 5.00
11 Evgeny Kadatskiy .20 .50
12 Josh Patterson .20 .50
13 Jason Penner .20 .50
14 Greg Williams .20 .50
15 Chad Robinson .20 .50
16 Mike Ramsay .20 .50
17 Patrick Kaleta .20 .50
18 Adam Elzinga .20 .50
19 Greg Chambers .20 .50
20 Jamie Tardif .20 .50
21 Mike McKeown .20 .50
22 Jeff MacDougald .20 .50
23 David Currie .20 .50
24 Lukas Krajicek .40 1.00

2004-05 Peterborough Petes Postcards

COMPLETE SET (25) 10.00 25.00
1 Jordan Staal 1.25 3.00
2 Liam Reddox .40 1.00
3 Daniel Ryder .40 1.00
4 Jamie Tardif .40 1.00
5 Eero Kilpelainen .75 2.00
6 Patrick Kaleta .40 1.00
7 Jordan Morrison .40 1.00
8 Trevor Henrikx .40 1.00
9 Mark Flood .40 1.00
10 Niko Vainio .40 1.00
11 Justin Carauna .40 1.00
12 Mike Montgomery .40 1.00
13 Aaron Barton .40 1.00
14 Patrick Kaleta .40 1.00
15 Aaron Dawson .40 1.00
16 Scott Cowie .40 1.00
17 Justin Soryal .40 1.00
18 Darryl Flowers .40 1.00
19 Bryan Young .40 1.00
20 Peter Aston .40 1.00
21 Jadran Baljo .40 1.00
22 Greg Stewart .40 1.00
23 Greg Williams .40 1.00
24 Corey Gault .40 1.00
25 Jeff MacDougald .40 1.00

2002-03 Philadelphia Phantoms

COMPLETE SET (26) 6.00 15.00
1 Antero Niittymaki .75 2.00
2 Bruno St. Jacques .20 .50
3 Dan Peters .20 .50
4 Mark Greig .20 .50
5 Kirby Law .30 .75
6 Peter White .30 .75
7 Eric Betournay .20 .50
8 Jack Baker .20 .50
9 Patrick Sharp .30 .75
10 Guillaume Lefebvre .30 .75
11 Pete Vandermeer .30 .75
12 Andre Savage .20 .50
13 Jim Vandermeer .30 .75
14 Mike Siklenka .30 .75
15 Ian MacNeil .20 .50
16 Ben Stafford .20 .50
17 John Slaney .20 .50
18 Mike Lephart .20 .50
19 Brad Tiley .20 .50
20 Wade Skolney .20 .50
21 Neil Little .40 1.00
22 David Harlock .20 .50
23 John Stevens CO .04 .10
24 Phlex Mascot .04 .10
25 Subway Coupon .04 .10
NNO Checklist .04 .10

2003-04 Philadelphia Phantoms

COMPLETE SET (26) 5.00 12.00
1 Checklist .04 .10
2 Antero Niittymaki .60 1.50
3 Ben Stafford .15 .40
4 Boyd Kane .15 .40
5 Craig Berube .15 .40
6 Dennis Seidenberg .15 .40
7 Freddy Meyer .15 .40
8 Ian MacNeil .15 .40
9 Jeff Woywitka .20 .50
10 Joey Hope .15 .40
11 John Slaney .15 .40
12 Kirby Law .30 .75
13 Mark Murphy .15 .40
14 Mike Peluso .15 .40
15 Mike Siklenka .15 .40
16 Neil Little .40 1.00
17 Nick Deschenes .15 .40
18 P.J. Stock .40 1.00
19 Patrick Sharp .15 .40
20 Pete Vandermeer .30 .75
21 Peter White .15 .40
22 Randy Jones .15 .40
23 Wade Skolney .15 .40
24 John Stevens .15 .40
25 Mascot .04 .10
26 Sponsor .04 .10

2004-05 Philadelphia Phantoms

COMPLETE SET (25) 6.00 15.00
1 Riley Cote .20 .50
2 Ben Eager .30 .75
3 Todd Fedoruk .40 1.00
4 Josh Gratton .60 1.50
5 Joey Hope .20 .50
6 Randy Jones .20 .50
7 Boyd Kane .30 .75
8 Neil Little .40 1.00
9 Eric Meloche .20 .50
10 Freddy Meyer .30 .75
11 Mark Murphy .20 .50
12 Antero Niittymaki .75 2.00
13 Joni Pitkanen .40 1.00
14 David Printz .20 .50
15 Ryan Ready .20 .50
16 Dennis Seidenberg .20 .50
17 Patrick Sharp .30 .75
18 Jon Sim .30 .75
19 Wade Skolney .20 .50
20 John Slaney .20 .50
21 Jeff Smith .20 .50
22 Ben Stafford .20 .50
23 R.J. Umberger .60 1.50
24 Tony Voce .20 .50
NNO Checklist .04 .10

2005-06 Philadelphia Phantoms

COMPLETE SET (26) 5.00 12.00
1 Philadelphia Phantoms CL .01 .01
2 B.J. Abel .20 .50
3 Rejean Beauchemin .40 1.00
4 Marc Cavosie .20 .50
5 Eric Chouinard .20 .50
6 Charlie Cook .20 .50
7 Riley Cote .20 .50
8 Ben Eager .20 .50
9 Triston Grant .20 .50
10 Josh Gratton .40 1.00
11 Joey Hope .20 .50
12 Randy Jones .20 .50
13 Pat Kavanagh .20 .50
14 Eric Meloche .20 .50
15 Freddy Meyer .20 .50
16 Alexandre Picard .20 .50
17 David Printz .20 .50
18 Ryan Ready .20 .50
19 Stefan Ruzicka .20 .50
20 Wade Skolney .20 .50
21 John Slaney .20 .50
22 Jamie Storr .30 .75
23 R.J. Umberger .40 1.00
24 Tony Voce .20 .50
25 John Stevens HC .02 .10
26 Phlex MASCOT .02 .10

2005-06 Philadelphia Phantoms All-Decade Team

COMPLETE SET (12) 8.00 15.00
1 Patrick Sharp .40 1.00
2 Frank Bialowas .75 2.00
3 Mark Greig .40 1.00
4 John Slaney .40 1.00
5 John Stevens .40 1.00
6 Neil Little .75 2.00
7 Peter White .40 1.00
8 Mike Maneluk .40 1.00
9 Kirby Law .40 1.00
10 Freddy Meyer .40 1.00
11 Dennis Seidenberg .40 1.00
12 Antero Niittymaki .75 2.00

2006-07 Philadelphia Phantoms

COMPLETE SET (30) 10.00 18.00
1 Joe Mullen ACO .10 .25
2 Kjell Samuelsson CO .10 .25
3 Ryan Potulny .60 1.50
4 Niko Dimitrakos .30 .75
5 Lars Jonsson .20 .50
6 Denis Tolpeko .20 .50
7 Eric Meloche .20 .50
8 John Slaney .20 .50
9 Martin Houle .40 1.00
10 Rejean Beauchemin .40 1.00
11 Scott Munroe .20 .50
12 Tony Voce .20 .50
13 Triston Grant .40 1.00
14 David Printz .30 .75
15 Nate Guenin .30 .75
16 Ben Eager .30 .75
17 Martin Grenier .20 .50
18 Riley Cote .20 .50
19 Matt Ellison .40 1.00
20 Alexandre Picard .20 .50
21 Nolan Baumgartner .20 .50
22 Stefan Ruzicka .30 .75
23 Mark Cullen .20 .50
24 Matt Davis .20 .50
25 Don Morrison .20 .50
26 Jussi Timonen .20 .50
27 Darren Reid .20 .50
28 Frederik Cabana .20 .50
29 Peter Zingoni .20 .50
30 Gino Pisellini .20 .50

1993-94 Phoenix Cobras RHI

COMPLETE SET (20) 3.00 8.00
1 Header Card .02 .10
2 Lee Kasper .20 .50
3 Stuart Silver .20 .50
4 Lou Franceschetti HCO .02 .10
5 Aaron Boh .20 .50
6 Todd Brost .30 .75
7 Michel Couvrette .20 .50
8 Wade Gibson .20 .50
9 Rickard Gronborg .20 .50
10 Hugo Hamelin .20 .50
11 Daniel Larin .20 .50
12 Mike O'Hara .20 .50
13 Sergei Olympiev .20 .50
14 John Redinger .20 .50
15 Brent Sapergia .30 .75
16 Daniel Shank .30 .75
17 Troy Stephens .20 .50
18 Boyd Sutton .20 .50
19 Mike Vukonich .20 .50
20 Alex Zhurik .20 .50

1992-93 Phoenix Roadrunners

COMPLETE SET (28) 4.00 10.00
1 Tim Bothwell CO .15 .40
2 Frank Breault .15 .40
3 Tim Breslin .15 .40
4 Rene Chapdelaine .15 .40
5 Sylvain Couturier .20 .50
6 Phil Crowe .20 .50
7 Darryl Gilmour .20 .50
8 David Goverde .20 .50
9 Ed Kastelic .15 .40
10 Rick Kozuback ACO .02 .10
11 Ted Kramer .15 .40
12 Robert Lang .30 .75
13 Guy Leveque .15 .40
14 Jim Maher .15 .40
15 Brad McCaughey .15 .40
16 Shawn McCosh .15 .40
17 John Mokosak .15 .40
18 Keith Redmond .15 .40
19 Mike Ruark .15 .40
20 Brandy Semchuk .15 .40
21 Dave Stewart .15 .40
22 Brad Tiley .15 .40
23 Dave Tretowicz .15 .40
24 Mike Vukonich .15 .40
25 Tim Watters .20 .50
26 Sean Whyte .15 .40
27 Darryl Williams .15 .40
28 Rocky Roadrunner
(Masco .02 .10

1993-94 Phoenix Roadrunners

COMPLETE SET (25) 4.00 10.00
1 Tim Breslin .15 .40
2 Brian Chapman .15 .40
3 Stephane Charbonneau .15 .40
4 Dan Currie .20 .50
5 Rick Dudley CO .20 .50
6 Marc Fortier .20 .50
7 David Goverde .20 .50
8 Kevin Grant .15 .40
9 Mark Hardy Player/Coach .15 .40
10 Dean Hulett .15 .40
11 Pauli Jaks .20 .50
12 Bob Jay .15 .40
13 Rick Knickle .30 .75
14 Guy Leveque .20 .50
15 Eric Lavigne .20 .50
16 Dominic Lavoie .15 .40
17 Jim Maher .15 .40
18 Brian McReynolds .15 .40
19 Rob Murphy .15 .40
20 Keith Redmond .15 .40
21 Dave Stewart .15 .40
22 Dave Thomlinson .15 .40
23 Brad Tiley .15 .40
24 Jim Vesey .15 .40
25 Darryl Williams .15 .40

1995-96 Phoenix Roadrunners

COMPLETE SET (24) 4.80 12.00
1 Ruslan Batyrshin .15 .40
2 Frederik Beaubien .30 .75
3 John Blue .30 .75
4 Mike Boback .15 .40
5 Kevin Brown .20 .50
6 Jim Burton .15 .40
7 Dan Bylsma .20 .50
8 Brian Chapman .15 .40
9 Rob Cowie .15 .40
10 Devin Edgerton .15 .40
11 Ken McRae .15 .40
12 Barry Potomski .30 .75
13 Daniel Rydmark .15 .40
14 Jeff Shevalier .20 .50
15 Gary Shuchuk .20 .50
16 Chris Snell .20 .50
17 Jamie Storr .75 2.00
18 Dave Thomlinson .15 .40
19 Nicholas Vachon .15 .40
20 Jan Vopat .20 .50
21 Steve Wilson .15 .40
22 S.Green
S.Wissman
J.Adams .02 .10
23 Rob Laird CO .02 .10
24 Rocky Roadrunner .02 .10

1998-99 Phoenix Mustangs

COMPLETE SET (25) 60.00 150.00
1 Hugo Belanger 3.00 8.00
2 David Goverde 3.00 8.00
3 Dana G. Seltzer MD .08 .25
4 Iannique Renaud 2.50 6.00
5 Mark Spence 2.50 6.00
6 Daniel Shank 8.00 20.00
7 Stu Kulak 3.00 8.00
8 Rusty McKie 2.50 6.00
9 Gene Bono 2.50 6.00
10 Jamie Allan 2.50 6.00
11 Michel Couvrette 2.50 6.00
12 Sebastien Fortier 2.50 6.00
13 Corey Laniuk 2.50 6.00
14 Doug McCarthy 2.50 6.00
15 Tom Menicci 2.50 6.00
16 Savo Mitrovic 2.50 6.00
17 Matt Oliver 2.50 6.00
18 Teemu Numminen 3.00 8.00
19 Bobby Rapoza 2.50 6.00
20 Jason Rose 2.50 6.00
21 Darren Veitch 2.50 6.00
22 Sean Whyte 2.50 6.00
23 Brad McCaughey HCO .08 .25
24 Dick Earle TR .08 .25
25 Rusty the Wrangler Mascot .08 .25

1983-84 Pinebridge Bucks

COMPLETE SET (12) 6.00 15.00
1 Dave Burke .60 1.50
2 Dan Burrows .60 1.50
3 Kim Collins .60 1.50
4 Bob Fleming .60 1.50
5 Rick Harris .60 1.50
6 Steve Heittola .60 1.50
7 Ken Latta .60 1.50
8 Tom Madsen .60 1.50
9 Larry Mollard .60 1.50
10 Kelly Rissling .60 1.50
11 Frank Perkins CO .20 .50
12 Frank Juror TR .20 .50

2001-02 Plymouth Whalers

COMPLETE SET (33) 15.00 30.00
1 Libor Ustrnul .30 .75
2 Jared Newman .30 .75
3 Stephen Weiss 1.25 3.00
4 Nathan Tennant .30 .75
5 Damian Surma .30 .75
6 Chad LaRose .60 1.50
7 Jeff Phillips .30 .75
8 Kyle Neufeld .30 .75
9 Brad Yeo .30 .75
10 Paul Drew .30 .75
11 Cole Jarrett .30 .75
12 Nate Kiser .30 .75
13 Karl Stewart .60 1.50
14 John Mitchell .30 .75
15 Greg Campbell .60 1.50
16 George Nistas .30 .75
17 Tim Sestito .30 .75
18 Kris Vernarsky .30 .75
19 James Wisniewski .30 .75
20 Danny McDonald .30 .75
21 Jason Bacashihua 1.25 3.00
22 Jonas Fiedler .30 .75
23 David Liffiton .60 1.50
24 Roberts ACO .04 .10
25 Mike Vellucci CO .04 .10
26 Dan Reed .30 .75
27 Bryan Thompson .30 .75
28 Stephen Weiss AS 1.25 3.00
29 Jason Bacashihua AS 1.25 3.00
30 Chad LaRose AS .60 1.50
31 Greg Campbell TP .40 1.00
32 James Wisniewski TP .30 .75

2002-03 Plymouth Whalers

COMPLETE SET (30) 5.00 12.00
1 Cole Jarrett .15 .40
2 Nate Kiser .15 .40
3 Karl Stewart .30 .75
4 John Mitchell .15 .40
5 Jimmy Gagnon .15 .40
6 Sean Thompson .15 .40
7 Chad LaRose .40 1.00
8 John Vigilante .15 .40
9 Taylor Raszka .15 .40
10 Ryan Ramsay .15 .40
11 Mike Letizia .15 .40
12 Steve Phillips .15 .40
13 Paul Drew .30 .75
14 Jonas Fielder .15 .40
15 Brent Mahon .15 .40
16 Cole Jarrett AS .15 .40
17 Tim Sestito .15 .40
18 Martin Cizek .15 .40
19 Chad LaRose AS .40 1.00
20 Chris Thorburn .30 .75
21 James Wisniewski .30 .75
22 Mike Nelson .15 .40
23 Nick Vernelli .15 .40
24 Jeff Weber .30 .75
25 Erik Lundmark .15 .40
26 David Liffiton .30 .75
27 David Liffiton
Top Prospect .30 .75
28 Mascot .04 .10
29 Pat Peake RET .10 .25
30 Team Photo .10 .25

2003-04 Plymouth Whalers

COMPLETE SET (28) 6.00 15.00
1 Rane Carnegie .30 .75
2 Dan Collins .20 .50
3 Jonas Fiedler .20 .50
4 Jordan Grant .20 .50
5 Brent Mahon .20 .50
6 Mike Martinelli .20 .50
7 Vaclav Meidl .20 .50
8 John Mitchell .20 .50
9 Gino Pisellini .20 .50
10 Ryan Ramsay .20 .50
11 Tim Sestito .20 .50
12 Sean Thompson .20 .50
13 Nick Vernelli .20 .50
14 John Vigilante .20 .50
15 Craig Cescon .20 .50
16 Mike Knight .20 .50
17 David Liffiton .30 .75
18 Erik Lundmark .20 .50
19 Ryan McGinnis .20 .50
20 Richard Power .20 .50
21 James Wisniewski .30 .75
22 Paul Drew .20 .50
23 Dan Miller .20 .50
24 Ryan Nie .20 .50
25 Michael Vellucci CO .04 .10
26 Coaching Staff .04 .10
27 Alex Roberts .20 .50
28 Mascot .04 .10

2005-06 Plymouth Whalers

COMPLETE SET (29) 8.00 15.00
A01 John Vigilante .20 .50
A02 John Armstrong .20 .50
A03 Jared Boll .30 .75
A04 Steve Ward .20 .50
A05 Cory Tanaka .20 .50
A06 Tom Sestito .20 .50
A07 Gino Pisellini .30 .75
A08 Ryan Nie .20 .50
A09 James Neal .50 1.25
A10 Vaclav Meidl .30 .75
A11 Ryan McGinnis .20 .50
A12 Mike Letizia .20 .50
A13 Andrew Fournier .20 .50
A14 Dan Collins .20 .50
B01 Justin Peters .30 .75
B02 Justin Garay .20 .50
B03 Jeremy Smith .60 1.50
B04 Ondrej Otcenas .20 .50
B05 Wes Cunningham .20 .50
B06 Derek Merlini .20 .50
B07 Zack Shepley .20 .50
B08 Joe McCann .20 .50
B09 Brett Bellemore .20 .50
B10 Leo Jenner .20 .50
B11 Chris Terry .20 .50
B12 Joe Gaynor .20 .50
B13 Ryan Stephenson .20 .50
B14 Evan Brophey .20 .50
B15 Plymouth Whalers CL .01 .01

2006-07 Plymouth Whalers

COMPLETE SET (29) 12.00 20.00
1 John Armstrong .20 .50
2 Brett Bellemore .20 .50
3 Jared Boll .20 .50
4 Evan Brophey .20 .50
5 Dan Collins .20 .50
6 Vern Cooper .30 .75
7 Wes Cunningham .20 .50
8 Andrew Fournier .20 .50
9 Joe Gaynor .20 .50
10 Kaine Geldart .20 .50
11 A.J. Jenks .20 .50
12 Leo Jenner .20 .50
13 Joe McCann .20 .50
14 Ryan McGinnis .20 .50
15 James Neal 1.00 2.50
16 Michal Neuvirth .60 1.50
17 Sean O'Connor .20 .50
18 Dan Ryder .40 1.00
19 Tom Sestito .40 1.00
20 Zack Shepley .20 .50
21 Jozef Sladok .20 .50
22 Jeremy Smith .60 1.50
23 Chris Terry .40 1.00
24 Brett Valliquette .20 .50
25 Steve Ward .20 .50
26 Steven Whitely .20 .50
27 James Neal 1.00 2.50
28 Plymouth Whalers .10 .25
29 Shooter MASCOT .02 .10

2014-15 Plymouth Whalers

COMPLETE SET (32) 8.00 20.00
1 Header Card .30 .75
2 Alex Peters .30 .75
3 Alex DiCarlo .30 .75
4 Sean Callaghan .30 .75
5 Tyler Sensky .30 .75
6 Mitch Jones .30 .75
7 Frankie Vilardi .30 .75
8 Nicholas Caamano .30 .75
9 Connor Chatham .30 .75
10 Viktor Crus-Rydberg .30 .75
11 Bryce Yetman .30 .75
12 Danny Vanderwiel .30 .75
13 Cullen Mercer .30 .75
14 Joshua Wesley .30 .75
15 Ryan Moore .40 1.00
16 Connor Sills .30 .75
17 Mathieu Henderson .30 .75
18 Yannick Rathgeb .30 .75
19 Zach Bowman .30 .75
20 Gianluca Curcuruto .30 .75
21 Vincent Scognamiglio .30 .75
22 Alex Nedeljkovic .30 .75
23 William Bitten .30 .75
24 Jacob Collins .30 .75
25 Sonny Milano .30 .75
26 Mathew Campagna .40 1.00
27 Overage Players .30 .75
28 Shooter MASCOT .30 .75
29 Tyler Seguin AL .50 1.25
30 James Neal AL .40 1.00
31 David Legwand AL .40 1.00
32 Team Photo .30 .75

2003-04 Port Huron Beacons

COMPLETE SET (23) 10.00 25.00
1 Michel Beausoleil .40 1.00
2 David Bell .40 1.00
3 Aaron Brand .40 1.00
4 Kory Cooper .60 1.50
5 Mike Corneau .40 1.00
6 Adam Dewan .40 1.00
7 Stu Dunn .60 1.50
8 Ken Fels .40 1.00
9 Jason Firth .60 1.50
10 Benoit Genesse .40 1.00
11 Matt Goody .40 1.00
12 Brent Gretzky .40 1.00
13 Casey Harris .40 1.00
14 Ian Jacobs .40 1.00
15 Trevor Karasiewicz .40 1.00
16 Barry McKinlay .40 1.00
17 Sam Miller .40 1.00
18 Simon Poirier .40 1.00
19 Michael Prochazka .40 1.00
20 Joey Sewell .40 1.0
21 Josh Tataryn .40 1.0
22 John Vary .40 1.0
23 Wade Winkler .40 1.0

1998-99 Port Huron Border Cats

COMPLETE SET (26) 4.80 12.0
1 Wayne Muir .30 .7
2 Mike O'Grady .20 .5
3 Adam Robbins .20 .5
4 Curtis Sayler .20 .5
5 Olie Sundstrom .20 .5
6 Bob McKillop .20 .5
7 Chris Bergeron .20 .5
8 Lee Cole .20 .5
9 Chad Dameworth .20 .5
10 Mike Zanzarella TR .02 .1
11 Bernie John .20
12 Matt Carmichael .20
13 Kevin Brown .20
14 Kevin Boyd .20
15 Jeff Blum .20
16 Bruce Watson .20
17 Andrei Sryubko .20
18 Paul Polillo .20
19 Kraig Nienhuis .30
20 Brock Myles EM .02
21 Nikolai Syrtsov .20
22 Greg Puhalski CO .08
23 Bridges MASCOT .02
24 Fedor Fedorov .75 2.
25 Konstantin Simchuk .30
26 Team CL .02

2006-07 Port Huron Flags

COMPLETE SET (25) 12.00 20.
1 Team Photo .10
2 Craig Mahon .30
3 Pat Sutton .30
4 Mike Olynyk .30
5 Bobby Kukulka .30
6 Kris Vernarsky .30
7 Robert Snowball .75 2
8 Jeremy Tucker .30
9 Mike James .30

10 B.J. Adams .30 .75
11 Mark Cadotte .30 .75
12 Ben Gustovson .30 .75
13 Greg Bullock .30 .75
14 Ryan Markham .30 .75
15 Scott Wray .30 .75
16 Trevor Edwards .30 .75
17 John Doherty .30 .75
18 Dustin Traylen .40 1.00
19 Noah Ruden .40 1.00
20 Shayne Tomlinson .30 .75
21 Steve Hildebrand .30 .75
22 Chris Bogas .30 .75
23 Colt King .75 2.00
24 Garett Cameron .30 .75
25 Slapshot MASCOT .02 .10

1993-94 Portland Pirates

COMPLETE SET (24) 4.80 12.00
1 Randy Pearce .15 .40
2 Crackers MASCOT .02 .10
3 Barry Trotz CO .08 .25
4 Paul Gardner ASST CO .02 .10
5 Chris Jensen .08 .25
6 Ken Klee .20 .50
7 Steve Poapst .15 .40
8 Jason Woolley .20 .50
9 Jim Mathieson .15 .40
10 Michel Picard .15 .40
11 Jeff Nelson .15 .40
12 Kent Hulst .15 .40
13 Eric Fenton .15 .40
14 Martin Jiranek .15 .40
15 Mike Boback .15 .40
16 Darren McAusland .15 .40
17 Chris Longo .15 .40
18 Kerry Clark .15 .40
19 Jeff Sirkka .15 .40
20 John Slaney .20 .50
21 Kevin Kaminski .20 .50
22 Byron Dafoe .75 2.00
23 Olaf Kolzig 1.25 3.00
24 Todd Nelson .15 .40
NNO Header Card .02 .10

1994-95 Portland Pirates

COMPLETE SET (23) 4.00 10.00
1 Norm Batherson .15 .40
2 Mike Boback .15 .40
3 Andrew Brunette .40 1.00
4 Jim Carey .30 .75
5 Jason Christie .15 .40
6 Kerry Clark .15 .40
7 Brian Curran .15 .40
8 Martin Gendron .30 .75
9 Sergei Gonchar .40 1.00
10 Kent Hulst .15 .40
11 Chris Jensen .15 .40
12 Kevin Kaminski .20 .50
13 Ken Klee .15 .40
14 Chris Longo .15 .40
15 Jim Mathieson .15 .40
16 Darren McAusland .15 .40
17 Jeff Nelson .20 .50
18 Todd Nelson .15 .40
19 Mike Parson .20 .50
20 Steve Poapst .15 .40
21 Andre Racicot .20 .50
22 Sergei Tertyshny .15 .40
23 Stefan Ustorf .20 .50

1995-96 Portland Pirates

COMPLETE SET (24) 6.00 15.00
1 Alexander Alexeev .15 .40
2 Jason Allison .75 2.00
3 Norm Batherson .15 .40
4 Frank Bialowas .40 1.00
5 Patrick Boileau .15 .40
6 Andrew Brunette .60 1.50
7 Stephane Charbonneau .15 .40
8 Jason Christie .15 .40
9 Crackers MASCOT .02 .10
10 Brian Curran .08 .25
11 Martin Gendron .20 .50
12 Kent Hulst .15 .40
13 Alexander Kharlamov .15 .40
14 Jim Mathieson .20 .50
15 Darren McAusland .15 .40
16 Jeff Nelson .15 .40
17 Darryl Paquette .20 .50
18 Rob Pearson .20 .50
19 Steve Poapst .15 .40
20 Joel Poirier .15 .40
21 Sergei Tertyshny .15 .40
22 Barry Trotz CO .08 .25
23 Ron Tugnutt .60 1.50
24 Stefan Ustorf .20 .50

1996-97 Portland Pirates

COMPLETE SET (25) 5.00 12.00
1 Robb Stauber .30 .75
3 Steve Poapst .20 .50
4 Stewart Malgunas .20 .50
5 Nolan Baumgartner .20 .50
6 Ron Pascucci .20 .50
7 Norm Batherson .20 .50
9 Marc Potvin .30 .75
10 Kent Hulst .20 .50
12 Brad Church .20 .50
14 Richard Zednik .40 1.00
15 Jaroslav Svejkovsky .30 .75
16 Darren McAusland .20 .50
19 Andrew Brunette .40 1.00
20 Miika Elomo .20 .50
21 Jason Christie .20 .50
22 Alexander Kharlamov .20 .50
24 Daniel Laperriere .20 .50
25 Benoit Gratton .20 .50
27 Patrick Boileau .20 .50
28 Trevor Halverson .20 .50
30 Martin Brochu .40 1.00
33 Anson Carter .60 1.50
NNO Paul Gardner ACO .10 .25
NNO AHL Hockey Card .01 .05
NNO Barry Trotz CO .20 .50

1996-97 Portland Pirates Shop N' Save

COMPLETE SET (10) 4.00 10.00
1 Robb Stauber .50 1.25
2 Steve Poapst .40 1.00
3 Nolan Baumgartner .40 1.00
4 Norm Batherson .40 1.00
5 Kent Hulst .40 1.00
6 Jaroslav Svejkovsky .40 1.00
7 Andrew Brunette .75 2.00
8 Miika Elomo .75 2.00
9 Jason Christie .40 1.00
10 Benoit Gratton .40 1.00

1997-98 Portland Pirates

COMPLETE SET (26) 5.00 12.00
1 Nolan Baumgartner .20 .50
2 Jan Benda .15 .40
3 Patrick Boileau .15 .40
4 Martin Brochu .40 1.00
5 Andrew Brunette .40 1.00
6 Sebastien Charpentier .30 .75
7 Jason Christie .15 .40
8 Brad Church .15 .40
9 Miika Elomo .20 .50
10 Benoit Gratton .30 .75
11 David Harlock .20 .50
12 Dwayne Hay .20 .50
13 Kent Hulst .15 .40
14 Kevin Kaminski .30 .75
15 Mark Major .15 .40
16 Stewart Malgunas .15 .40
17 Rick Mrozik .15 .40
18 Ryan Mulhern .15 .40
19 Mike O'Neill .30 .75
20 Steve Poapst .20 .50
21 Kayle Short .15 .40
22 Alexandre Volchkov .20 .50
23 Jay Wells ACO .15 .40
24 Bryan Trottier HCO .40 1.00
25 PHPA Web Site .01 .05
26 AHL Web Site .01 .05

1998-99 Portland Pirates

COMPLETE SET (26) 5.00 12.00
1 J-P Dumont .75 2.00
2 Patrick Boileau .15 .40
3 Martin Brochu .30 .75
4 Trevor Halverson .15 .40
5 Matt Herr .20 .50
6 Benoit Gratton .20 .50
7 Nolan Baumgartner .15 .40
8 Casey Hankinson .15 .40
9 Kent Hulst .15 .40
10 Rick Kowalsky .15 .40
11 Daniel Cleary .30 .75
12 Todd Rohloff .15 .40
13 Jeff Toms .15 .40
14 Steve Poapst .15 .40
15 Mike Peluso .30 .75
16 Young/Soutuyo .15 .40
17 Mike Rosati .30 .75
18 Trent Whitfield .30 .75
19 Mark Kumpel HCO .02 .10
19 Neil Belland ACO .02 .10
20 Craig Mills .20 .50
21 Stewart Malgunas .15 .40
22 Rick Mrozik .15 .40
23 Dwight Parrish .15 .40
24 Mark Major .15 .40
25 AHL Web Site .01 .05

1999-00 Portland Pirates

COMPLETE SET (25) 4.00 10.00
1 Nolan Baumgartner .20 .50
2 Alexei Tezikov .30 .75
3 Patrick Boileau .15 .40
4 Martin Brochu .40 1.00
5 Sebastien Charpentier .40 1.00
6 Miika Elomo .20 .50
7 Jakub Ficenec .15 .40
8 J.F. Fortin .20 .50
9 Matt Herr .20 .50
10 Kent Hulst .15 .40
11 Jamie Huscroft .15 .40
12 M.Kumpel/G.Hanlon .15 .40
13 Mascot .02 .10
14 Glen Metropolit .30 .75
15 Barrie Moore .15 .40
16 Ryan Mulhern .15 .40
17 Jeff Nelson .15 .40
18 Mike Peluso .20 .50
19 Steve Poapst .15 .40
20 Steve Shirreffs .15 .40
21 Jason Shmyr .15 .40
22 Trainer Card .02 .10
23 Alexandre Volchkov .15 .40
24 Trent Whitfield .30 .75
25 Rob Zettler .15 .40

2000-01 Portland Pirates

COMPLETE SET (20) 5.00 12.00
1 Kent Hulst .20 .50
2 Jeff Nelson .20 .50
3 Krys Barch .30 .75
4 Mark Murphy .20 .50
5 Patrick Boileau .20 .50
6 Todd Rohloff .20 .50
7 Jean-Francois Fortin .20 .50
8 Sebastien Charpentier .40 1.00
9 Glen Metropolit .30 .75
10 Remi Royer .20 .75
11 Derek Bekar .20 .50
12 Martin Hlinka .20 .50
13 Corey Hirsch .40 1.00
14 Alexei Tezikov .40 1.00
15 Rob Zettler .20 .50
16 Mike Farrell .20 .50
17 Jakub Ficenec .20 .50
18 Matt Pettinger .40 1.00
19 Jason Shmyr .20 .50
20 Brad Church .30 .75

2004-05 Portland Pirates

COMPLETE SET (12) 12.00
1 Steve Eminger .20 .50
2 Brian Sutherby .30 .75
3 Boyd Gordon .20 .50
4 Owen Fussey .20 .50
5 Jason Ulmer .20 .50
6 Justin Eddy .20 .50
7 Jeff Paul .20 .50
8 Jared Aulin .30 .75
9 Michel Periard .20 .50
10 Graham Mink .40 1.00
11 Chris Hajt
Mike Amodeo .20 .50
12 Cam McCaffrey
Jonas Johansson .20 .50
13 Jakub Cutta .20 .50
14 Brooks Laich .30 .75
15 Carlyle Lewis .20 .50
16 Shaone Morrisonn .20 .50
17 Maxime Ouellet .40 1.00
18 Louis Robitaille .20 .50
19 Garrett Stroshein .40 1.00
20 Darcy Verot .40 1.00
21 Trent Whitfield .40 1.00
22 Nolan Yonkman .20 .50
23 Dwayne Zinger .20 .50
24 Jakub Klepis
Tomas Fleischmann .40 1.00

2005-06 Portland Pirates

COMPLETE SET (24) 8.00 15.00
1 Geoff Peters .20 .50
2 Aaron Rome .40 1.00
3 Shane O'Brien .20 .50
4 Tim Brent .20 .50
5 Aaron Gavey .20 .50
6 Pierre Parenteau .20 .50
7 Corey Perry .60 1.50
8 Curtis Glencross .20 .50
9 Jordan Smith .20 .50
10 Kenny Smith .20 .50
11 Dieter Kochan .60 1.50
12 Ryan Shannon .20 .50
13 Joel Perrault .20 .50
14 Nathan Saunders .20 .50
15 Ryan Getzlaf .60 1.50
16 Ladislav Smid .40 1.00
17 Igor Pohanka .20 .50
18 Kent Huskins .20 .50
19 Bruno St. Jaques .20 .50
20 Dustin Penner .40 1.00
21 Simon Ferguson .20 .50
22 Nathan Marsters .40 1.00
23 Shane Hynes .20 .50
24 Trevor Gillies .60 1.50

2006-07 Portland Pirates

COMPLETE SET (24) 10.00 18.00
1 Bruce Crowder ACO .10 .25
2 Eric Weinrich ACO .10 .25
3 Zenon Konopka .30 .75
4 Aaron Rome .30 .75
5 Nathan Marsters .30 .75
6 Tim Brent .30 .75
7 Clay Wilson .30 .75
8 Brian Salcido .30 .75
9 Curtis Glencross .30 .75
10 Chris Durno .30 .75
11 Colby Genoway .30 .75
12 Simon Ferguson .30 .75
13 Geoff Peters .30 .75
14 Brett Skinner .30 .75
15 Drew Miller .60 1.50
16 Matt Keith .30 .75
17 Shawn Thornton .40 1.00
18 Petteri Wirtanen .30 .75
19 Bjorn Melin .30 .75
20 Trevor Gillies .40 1.00
21 Ryan Carter .40 1.00
22 Kent Huskins .30 .75
23 Mike Wall .40 1.00
24 Kevin Dineen CO .10 .25

2007-08 Portland Pirates

COMPLETE SET (24) 6.00 15.00
1 Crackers and Salty Pete MASCOTS .30 .75
2 Brendan Mikkelson .30 .75
3 Stephen Dixon .30 .75
4 Darryl Bootland .30 .75
5 Tyler Bouck .30 .75
6 Simon Ferguson .30 .75
7 Brandon Segal .30 .75
8 Joe Callahan .30 .75
9 Bobby Ryan .30 .75
10 Mike McKenna .30 .75
11 Matt Christie .30 .75
12 Drew Miller 1.00 2.50
13 Eric Weinrich .30 .75
14 Jason King .30 .75
15 Bruno St. Jacques .30 .75
16 Mike Hoffman .50 1.25
17 Geoff Platt .30 .75
18 Andrew Ebbett .30 .75
19 Brian Salcido .30 .75
20 Michal Birner .30 .75
21 Petteri Wirtanen .30 .75
22 Gerald Coleman .30 .75
23 Brett Festerling .30 .75
24 Andy Schneider .30 .75

1986-87 Portland Winter Hawks

COMPLETE SET (24) 15.00 40.00
1 Dave Archibald 1.00 2.50
2 Bruce Basken .60 1.50
3 Thomas Bjuhr .60 1.50
4 Shaun Clouston .60 1.50
5 Jeff Finley .60 1.50
6 Bob Foglietta .60 1.50
7 Brian Gerrits .60 1.50
8 Darryl Gilmour 1.00 2.50
9 Dennis Holland .60 1.50
10 Steve Kloepzig .60 1.50
11 Jim Latos .60 1.50
12 Dave McLay .60 1.50
13 Scott Melnyk .60 1.50
14 Troy Mick .60 1.50
15 Roy Mitchell .60 1.50
16 Jamie Nicolls .60 1.50
17 Trevor Pohl .60 1.50
18 Troy Pohl .60 1.50
19 Glen Seymour 1.00 2.50
20 Jeff Sharples .60 1.50
21 Jay Stark .60 1.50
22 Jim Swan .60 1.50
23 Glen Wesley 2.00 5.00
24 Dan Woodley .60 1.50

1987-88 Portland Winter Hawks

COMPLETE SET (21) 4.80 12.00
1 Wayne Anchikoski .20 .50
2 Eric Badzgon .30 .75
3 Chad Biafore .20 .50
4 James(Hamish) Black .20 .50
5 Terry Black .20 .50
6 Shaun Clouston .20 .50
7 Byron Dafoe 1.25 3.00
8 Brent Fleetwood .20 .50
9 Rob Flintoft .20 .50
10 Bryan Gourlie .20 .50
11 Mark Greyeyes .20 .50
12 Dennis Holland .20 .50
13 Kevin Jorgenson .20 .50
14 Greg Leahy .20 .50
15 Troy Mick .20 .50
16 Roy Mitchell .20 .50
17 Joey Mittelsteadt .20 .50
18 Mike Moore .20 .50
19 Scott Mydan .20 .50
20 Calvin Thudiun .20 .50
21 Pepsi Ad Card .02 .10

1988-89 Portland Winter Hawks

COMPLETE SET (21) 4.80 12.00
1 Wayne Anchikoski .20 .50
2 Eric Badzgon .30 .75
3 Chad Biafore .20 .50
4 James(Hamish) Black .20 .50
5 Terry Black .20 .50
6 Shaun Clouston .20 .50
7 Byron Dafoe 1.25 3.00
8 Brent Fleetwood .20 .50
9 Rob Flintoft .20 .50
10 Bryan Gourlie .20 .50
11 Mark Greyeyes .20 .50
12 Dennis Holland .20 .50
13 Kevin Jorgenson .20 .50
14 Greg Leahy .20 .50
15 Troy Mick .20 .50
16 Roy Mitchell .20 .50
17 Joey Mittelsteadt .20 .50
18 Mike Moore .20 .50
19 Scott Mydan .20 .50
20 Calvin Thudiun .20 .50
21 Pepsi Coupon .02 .10

1989-90 Portland Winter Hawks

COMPLETE SET (21) 4.80 12.00
1 Jamie Black .20 .50
2 Vince Cocciolo .20 .50
3 Byron Dafoe .75 2.00
4 Cam Danyluk .20 .50
5 Kim Deck .20 .50
6 Dean Dorchak .20 .50
7 Brent Fleetwood .20 .50
8 Rick Fry .20 .50
9 Bryan Gourlie .20 .50
10 Brad Harrison .20 .50
11 Judson Innes .20 .50
12 Dean Intwert .30 .75
13 Kevin Jorgenson .20 .50
14 Todd Kinniburgh .20 .50
15 Greg Leahy .20 .50
16 Jamie Linden .20 .50
17 Scott Mydan .20 .50
18 Mike Ruark .20 .50
19 Jeff Sebastian .20 .50
20 Brandon Smith .25 .60
21 Steve Young .20 .50

1993-94 Portland Winter Hawks

COMPLETE SET (27) 8.00 15.00
1 Mike Arbulic .10 .30
2 Lonny Bohonos .20 .50
3 Shannon Briske .10 .30
4 Dave Cammock .10 .30
5 Shawn Collins .10 .30
6 Matt Davidson .10 .30
7 Adam Deadmarsh 1.25 3.00
8 Adam Deadmarsh GM 1.25 3.00
9 Jake Deadmarsh .10 .30
10 Brett Fizzell .10 .30
11 Colin Foley .10 .30
12 Brad Isbister .60 1.50
13 Scott Langkow .40 1.00
14 Mike Little .10 .30
15 Dmitri Markovsky .10 .30
16 Jason McBain .10 .30
17 Scott Nichol .10 .30
18 Brent Peterson .10 .30
19 Nolan Pratt .20 .50
20 Scott Rideout .10 .30
21 Layne Roland .10 .30
22 Dave Scatchard .30 .75
23 Brandon Smith .20 .50
24 Brad Swanson .10 .30
25 Brad Symes .10 .30
26 Jason Wiemer .75 2.00
27 Mike Williamson .10 .30

1997-98 Portland Winter Hawks

COMPLETE SET (27) 16.00 40.00
1 Checklist .02 .10
2 Brent Belecki .15 .40
3 Mike Muzechka .15 .40
4 Marian Hossa 6.00 15.00
5 Ken Davis .15 .40
6 Jerad Smith .15 .40
7 Josh Green .40 1.00
8 Bobby Russell .15 .40
9 Kyle Chant .15 .40
10 Brenden Morrow 4.00 10.00
11 Derek MacLean .40 1.00
12 Todd Hornung .15 .40
13 Andrej Podkonicky .30 .75
14 Bobby Duncan .15 .40
15 Todd Robinson .15 .40
16 Chris Jacobson .15 .40
17 Shon Jones-Parry .15 .40
18 Kevin Haupt .15 .40
19 Ryan Thrussell .15 .40
20 Marty Standish .15 .40
21 Jason Labarbera .75 2.00
22 Matt Walker .15 .40
23 Andrew Ference .40 1.00
24 Joey Tetarenko 1.25 3.00
25 Brent Peterson HCO .08 .25
26 Mike Williamson ACO .02 .10
27 Julius Supler ACO .02 .10

2003-04 Portland Winter Hawks

COMPLETE SET (29) 5.00 12.00
1 Dustin Butler .30 .75
2 Tomas Fojtik .15 .40
3 Taylor Sutherlin .15 .40
4 Michael Funk .15 .40
5 Richie Regehr .30 .75
6 Brendan Mikkelson .15 .40
7 Cody McLeod .15 .40
8 Aaron Roberge .15 .40
9 Brian Woolger .15 .40
10 C.J. Jackson .15 .40
11 Chad Wolkowski .15 .40
12 Shane Halifax .15 .40
13 Robin Big Snake .30 .75
14 Alex Aldred .15 .40
15 Brandon Dubinsky 1.25 3.00
16 Ivan Dornic .15 .40
17 Dan Da Silva .15 .40
18 Braydon Coburn .15 .40
19 Frazer McLaren .15 .40
20 Derek Poplawski .15 .40
21 Kyle Bailey .15 .40
22 Kevin Opsahl .30 .75
23 Krister Toews .30 .75
24 Ivan Dornic Draft .15 .40
25 Braydon Coburn Draft .60 1.50
26 Mike Williamson HCO .10 .25
27 Blake Wesley ACO .10 .25
28 Mascot .04 .10
29 Checklist .04 .10

2004-05 Portland Winter Hawks

COMPLETE SET (25) 4.00 10.00
1 Dustin Butler .20 .50
2 Cameron Cepek .20 .50
3 Braydon Coburn .50 1.25
4 Dan DaSilva .20 .50
5 Brandon Dubinsky .75 2.00
6 Michael Funk .20 .50
7 Frazer McLaren .75 2.00
8 Mike Sauer .75 2.00
9 Brian Woolger .20 .50
10 Paul Gaustad .20 .50
11 Richie Regehr .20 .50
12 Cody McLeod .20 .50
13 Robin Big Snake .20 .50
NNO Braydon Coburn MCT .40 1.00
NNO R. Regehr/P. Gaustad .10 .25
NNO C. McLeod/R. Big Snake .10 .25

1984-85 Prince Albert Raiders Stickers

COMPLETE SET (22) 10.00 25.00
1 Ken Baumgartner 1.25 3.00
2 Brad Bennett .40 1.00
3 Dean Braham .40 1.00
4 Rod Dallman .40 1.00
5 Neil Davey .40 1.00
6 Pat Elynuik .60 1.50
7 Collin Feser .40 1.00
8 Dave Goertz .40 1.00
9 Steve Gotaas .40 1.00
10 Tony Grenier .40 1.00
11 Roydon Gunn .40 1.00
12 Doug Hobson .40 1.00
13 Dan Hodgson .60 1.50
14 Curtis Hunt .40 1.00
15 Kim Issel .40 1.00
16 Ward Komonosky .40 1.00
17 David Manson .40 1.00
18 Dale McFee .40 1.00
19 Ken Morrison .40 1.00
20 Dave Pasin .60 1.50
21 Don Schmidt .40 1.00
22 Emanuel Viveiros .40 1.00

1990-91 Prince Albert Raiders

COMPLETE SET (25) 4.00 10.00
1 Scott Allison .15 .40
2 Laurie Billeck .15 .40
3 Jeff Gorman .15 .40
4 Donevan Hextall .20 .50
5 Troy Hjertaas .15 .40
6 Dan Kesa .20 .50
7 Jason Kwiatkowski .15 .40
8 Travis Laycock .15 .40
9 Lee J. Leslie .20 .50
10 Jamie Linden .15 .40
11 Dean McAmmond .30 .75
12 Dave Neilson .15 .40
13 Jeff Nelson .20 .50
14 Troy Neumeier .15 .40
15 Pat Odnokon .15 .40
16 Brian Pellerin .15 .40
17 Darren Perkins .15 .40
18 Curt Regnier .20 .50
19 Chad Seibel .15 .40
20 Mark Stowe .15 .40
21 Darren Van Impe .30 .75
22 Shane Zulyniak .15 .40
23 Title Card .02 .10
24 Info Card (Strangers) .02 .10
25 Info Card (Vandalism) .02 .10

1991-92 Prince Albert Raiders

COMPLETE SET (24) 3.00 8.00
1 Mike Fedorko CO .02 .10
2 Jeff Gorman .15 .40
3 Merv Haney .15 .40
4 Donevan Hextall .20 .50
5 Troy Hjertaas .15 .40
6 Dan Kesa .20 .50
7 Jason Klassen .15 .40
8 Jason Kwiatkowski .15 .40
9 Jeff Lank .15 .40
10 Travis Laycock .15 .40
11 Lee J. Leslie .15 .40
12 Stan Matwijiw .20 .50
13 Dean McAmmond .20 .50
14 David Neilson .15 .40
15 Jeff Nelson .15 .40
16 Mark Odnokon ACO .02 .10
17 Darren Perkins .15 .40
18 Ryan Pisiak .15 .40
19 Nick Polychronopoulos .15 .40
20 Curt Regnier .20 .50
21 Jason Renard .15 .40
22 Barkley Swenson .15 .40
23 Darren Van Impe .20 .50
24 Shane Zulyniak .15 .40

1993-94 Prince Albert Raiders

COMPLETE SET (22) 4.00 10.00
1 Ryan Bast .15 .40
2 Rodney Bowers .15 .40
3 Van Burgess .15 .40
4 Brad Church .30 .75
5 Joaquin Gage .30 .75
6 Jeff Gorman .15 .40
7 Merv Haney .15 .40
8 Greg Harvey .15 .40
9 Paul Healey .15 .40
10 Shane Hnidy .30 .75
11 Russell Hogue .15 .40
12 Jason Issel .15 .40
13 Steve Kelly .30 .75
14 Jeff Lank .15 .40
15 Mike McGhan .15 .40
16 Denis Pederson .30 .75
17 Mitch Shawara .15 .40
18 Shayne Toporowski .15 .40
19 David Van Drunen .15 .40
20 Dean Whitney .15 .40
21 Darren Wright .15 .40
22 Shane Zulyniak .15 .40

1994-95 Prince Albert Raiders

COMPLETE SET (23) 4.80 12.00
1 Sandy Allan .20 .50
2 Ryan Bast .20 .50
3 Brad Church .30 .75
4 Kris Fizzell .15 .40
5 Paul Healey .15 .40
6 Rob Hegberg .15 .40
7 Shane Hnidy .30 .75
8 Russell Hogue .15 .40
9 Craig Hordal .20 .50
10 Jason Issel .15 .40
11 Neil Johnston .15 .40
12 Steve Kelly .30 .75
13 Jeff Lank .15 .40
14 Mike McGhan .15 .40
15 Denis Pederson .60 1.50
16 Sean Robertson .15 .40
17 Mitch Shawara .15 .40
18 Shayne Toporowski .20 .50
19 Kaleb Toth .15 .40
20 Dave Van Drunen .20 .50
21 Shane Willis .60 1.50
22 Darren Wright .15 .40
23 Shane Zulyniak .15 .40

1995-96 Prince Albert Raiders

COMPLETE SET (22) 4.80 25.00
1 Rod Branch .40 1.00
2 Curtis Brown .75 2.00
3 Brad Church .40 1.00
4 Kris Fizzell .40 1.00
5 Dallas Flaman .40 1.00
6 Don Halverson .40 1.00
7 Shane Hnidy .40 1.00
8 Russell Hogue .40 1.00
9 Jason Issel .40 1.00
10 Garnet Jacobson .40 1.00
11 Kevin Kellett .40 1.00
12 Steve Kelly .60 1.50
13 Dylan Kemp .40 1.00
14 Michael McGhan .40 1.00
15 Marian Menhart .40 1.00
16 Chris Phillips .75 2.00
17 Blaine Russell .40 1.00
18 Mitch Shawara .40 1.00
19 Dave Van Drunen .40 1.00
20 Roman Vopat .40 1.00
21 Shane Willis .60 1.50
22 Darren Wright .40 1.00

1996-97 Prince Albert Raiders

COMPLETE SET (23) 4.80 12.00
1 Trevor Baker .20 .50
2 Scott Botterill .20 .50
3 Craig Brunel .20 .50
4 Marco Cefalo .20 .50
5 Dallas Flaman .20 .50
6 Jeremy Goetzinger .20 .50
7 Don Halverson .20 .50
8 Russell Hogue .20 .50
9 Jason Issel .20 .50
10 Garnet Jacobson .20 .50
11 Kevin Kellett .20 .50
12 Dylan Kemp .20 .50
13 Evan Lindsay .30 .75
14 Marian Menhart .20 .50
15 Cory Morgan .20 .50
16 Derek Paget .20 .50
17 Chris Phillips .60 1.50
18 Harlan Pratt .20 .50
19 Blaine Russell .15 .40
20 Adam Stewart .20 .50
21 Dave Van Drunen .30 .75
22 Steve Wilejto .20 .50
23 Shane Willis .40 1.00

1997-98 Prince Albert Raiders

COMPLETE SET (21) 4.00 10.00
1 Scott Botterill .20 .50
2 Derek Brandon .20 .50
3 Craig Brunel .20 .50
4 David Cameron .20 .50
5 Clayton Chartrand .20 .50
6 Dallas Flaman .20 .50
7 Jeremy Goetzinger .20 .50
8 Don Halverson .20 .50
9 Trevor Hitchings .20 .50
10 Kevin Kellett .20 .50
11 Evan Lindsay .30 .75
12 Ross Lupaschuk .40 1.00
13 Brady Magneson .20 .50
14 Grant McCune .30 .75
15 Cory Morgan .20 .50
16 Derek Paget .20 .50
17 Harlan Pratt .30 .75
18 Richard Seeley .20 .50
19 Cam Severson .20 .50
20 Brad Swanson .20 .50
21 Steve Wilejto .20 .50

1998-99 Prince Albert Raiders

COMPLETE SET (22) 12.00 20.00
1 Derek Brandon .20 .50
2 Marc Brown .20 .50
3 Craig Brunel .20 .50
4 Clayton Chartrand .20 .50
5 Riley Cote .20 .50
6 Todd Fedoruk .75 2.00
7 Dallas Flaman .20 .50
8 Jeremy Goetzinger .20 .50
9 Scott Hartnell 2.00 5.00
10 Shaun Hill .20 .50
11 Cody Jensen .20 .50
12 Kevin Kellet .20 .50
13 Milan Kraft .75 2.00
14 Evan Lindsay .30 .75
15 Ross Lupachuk .40 1.00
16 Grant McCune .20 .50
17 Cory Morgan .20 .50
18 Kerry Nice .20 .50
19 Derek Paget .20 .50
20 Garrett Prosofsky .20 .50
21 Nick Schultz .75 2.00
22 Richard Seeley .20 .50

2000-01 Prince Albert Raiders

COMPLETE SET (25) 4.80 12.00
1 Jay Batchelor .20 .50
2 Anton Borodkin .20 .50
3 Kyle Bruce .20 .50
4 Jordan Clarke .20 .50
5 Riley Cote .20 .50
6 Cary Grant TR .04 .11
7 Ryan Haggarty .20 .50
8 J.J. Hunter .20 .50
9 Dustin Kazak .20 .50
10 Jon Kress .20 .50
11 Landon Lillejord .20 .50
12 Connor Lowe .20 .50
13 Grant McCune .31 .78
14 Grant McNeill .20 .50
15 Scott McQueen .20 .50
16 Jon Mirasty .20 .50
17 Chris Harper .20 .50
18 Igor Pohanka .20 .50
19 Garett Prosofsky .31 .78
20 Riley MASCOT .04 .11
21 Jeff Schmidt .20 .50
22 Nick Schultz .80 2.00
23 Aaron Sorochan .31 .78
24 Blain Stowards .20 .50
25 Greg Watson .31 .78

2001-02 Prince Albert Raiders

COMPLETE SET (24) 6.00 15.00
1 Jay Batchelor .30 .75
2 Kyle Bruce .30 .75
3 Jeremy Colliton .60 1.50
4 Riley Cote .30 .75
5 Justin Cruse .30 .75
6 James Demone .30 .75
7 Paul Deniset .30 .75
8 Perry Faul .30 .75
9 Luke Fritshaw .30 .75
10 Jon Kress .30 .75
11 Wade Klippenstein CO .10 .25
12 Landon Lillejord .30 .75
13 Rastislav Lipka .30 .75
14 Grant McNeill .30 .75
15 Brett Novak .30 .75
16 Igor Pohanka .30 .75
17 Jeff Schmidt .30 .75
18 Drew Schoneck ACO .10 .25
19 Jesse Schultz .30 .75
20 Aaron Sorochan .40 1.00
21 Joe Suderman .30 .75
22 Thomas Vicars .40 1.00
23 Greg Watson .40 1.00
24 Mike Wirll .30 .75

2002-03 Prince Albert Raiders

COMPLETE SET (23) 8.00 20.00
1 Rejean Beauchemin 1.25 3.00
2 Kyle Bruce .30 .75
3 Dane Byers .60 1.50
4 Kyle Chipchura .75 2.00
5 Jeremy Colliton .75 2.00
6 Mark Cress .30 .75
7 Justin Cruse .30 .75
8 Chris Di Ubaldo .30 .75
9 Perry Faul .30 .75
10 Luke Fritshaw .30 .75
11 Kevin Harris .30 .75
12 Jon Kress .30 .75
13 Colin Lafreniere .30 .75
14 Seth Leonard .30 .75
15 Rastislav Lipka .30 .75
16 Grant McNeill .30 .75
17 Brett Novak .30 .75
18 Igor Pohanka .30 .75
19 Rory Rawlyk .30 .75
20 Evan Schafer .30 .75
21 Aaron Sorochan .30 .75
22 Greg Watson .30 .75
23 Andy Zulyniak .30 .75

2003-04 Prince Albert Raiders

COMPLETE SET (25) 6.00 15.00
1 Aki Seitsonen .30 .75
2 Brandon Peet .20 .50
3 Brant Hilton .20 .50
4 Brett Novak .20 .50
5 Caine Pearpoint .20 .50
6 Colin Lafreniere .20 .50
7 Dane Byers .60 1.50
8 Dave Manson .20 .50
9 Evan Schafer .20 .50
10 Garth Collins .20 .50
11 Jeff May .20 .50
12 Jeremy Colliton .60 1.50
13 Jordan Morgan .20 .50
14 Justin Cruse .20 .50

15 Kyle Chipchura .60 1.50
16 Luke Fritshaw .20 .50
17 Mark Ardelan .20 .50
18 Michal Polak .20 .50
19 Mike Gauthier .20 .50
20 Mike Hellyer .20 .50
21 Perry Faul .20 .50
22 Peter Anholt .20 .50
23 Rejean Beauchemin .60 1.50
24 Seth Leonard .20 .50
25 Travis Young .20 .50

2004-05 Prince Albert Raiders

COMPLETE SET (24) 8.00 20.00
1 Alex Archibald .30 .75
2 Mike Gauthier .30 .75
3 Jeff May .30 .75
4 Evan Schafer .30 .75
5 Luke Fritshaw .40 1.00
6 Landon Jones .30 .75
7 Scott Doucet .30 .75
8 Mike Hellyer .30 .75
9 Brandon Peet .30 .75
10 Brad Erickson .30 .75
11 Brett Ottmann .30 .75
12 Nolan Waker .30 .75
13 Kyle Chipchura .60 1.50
14 Aki Seitsonen .40 1.00
15 Ryan Depape .30 .75
16 Brett Novak .30 .75
17 Jeremy Colliton .60 1.50
18 Josh Elder .30 .75
19 Caine Pearpoint .30 .75
20 Chris Schlenker .30 .75
21 Dane Byers .60 1.50
22 Garth Collins .30 .75
23 Rejean Beauchemin .75 2.00
24 Peter Anholt CO .04 .10

2005-06 Prince Albert Raiders

COMPLETE SET (26) 8.00 20.00
1 Alex Archibald .40 1.00
2 Dane Byers .60 1.50
3 Kyle Chipchura .60 1.50
4 Peter Cmorej .30 .75
5 Ryan DePape .30 .75
6 Jesse Deckert .40 1.00
7 Scott Doucet .30 .75
8 Jarrid Dowhay .30 .75
9 Josh Elder .30 .75
10 Brad Erickson .30 .75
11 Mike Gauthier .30 .75
12 Mike Hellyer .30 .75
13 Ashton Hewson .30 .75
14 Kyle Howarth .30 .75
15 Jeff May .30 .75
16 Brett Novak .30 .75
17 Brent Ottmann .30 .75
18 Justin Palazzo .30 .75
19 Evan Schafer .30 .75
20 Aki Seitsonen .40 1.00
21 A.J. Thelen .60 1.50
22 Kevin Tipper .30 .75
23 Peter Anholt CO .02 .10
24 Dave Manson ACO .20 .50
25 Mark Odnokon ACO .02 .10
26 Duane Bartley AT .02 .10

2006-07 Prince Albert Raiders

COMPLETE SET (26) 12.00 20.00
1 David Aime .40 1.00
2 Jesse Deckert .40 1.00
3 Mike Gauthier .40 1.00
4 Jeff May .30 .75
5 A.J. Thelen .60 1.50
6 Blaine Tendler .30 .75
7 Cody Vann .30 .75
8 Scott Doucet .30 .75
9 Mike Hellyer .30 .75
10 Jarrid Dowhay .30 .75
11 Matthew Robertson .30 .75
12 Brent Ottmann .30 .75
13 Milan Jurik .30 .75
14 Lukas Zeliska .30 .75
15 Jordan Trach .30 .75
16 Ryan DePape .30 .75
17 Cody Gross .30 .75
18 Andy Smith .40 1.00
19 Josh Elder .30 .75
20 Ashton Hewson .30 .75
21 Justin Palazzo .30 .75
22 Bryce Lamb .30 .75
23 Shane Malone .30 .75
24 Peter Anholt CO .10 .25
25 Dave Manson ACO .20 .50
26 Kris Knoblauch ACO .10 .25

1998-99 Prince George Cougars

COMPLETE SET (27) 15.00 40.00
1 Header card .02 .10
2 Mike Bayrack .40 1.00
3 Blair Betts .75 2.00
4 Tyler Bouck .75 2.00
5 Eric Brewer 4.00 10.00
6 Tyler Brough .40 1.00
7 Justin Cox .40 1.00
8 Travis Eagles .40 1.00
9 Dan Hamhuis 4.00 10.00
10 Trent Hunter 4.00 10.00
11 Michael Kiesman .40 1.00
12 Petr Kubos .40 1.00
13 Adam Loncan .40 1.00
14 Jozef Mrena .40 1.00
15 Scott Myers .75 2.00
16 Mike Olynyk .40 1.00
17 Jonathan Parker .40 1.00
18 Owen Richey .40 1.00
19 Jarrett Smith .75 2.00
20 Kevin Swanson .75 2.00
21 Curtis Tipler .75 2.00
22 Gary Toor .40 1.00
23 Jordan Walker .40 1.00
24 Ian Walterson .40 1.00
25 Tim Wedderburn .40 1.00
26 Jeff Zorn .40 1.00
27 Cougar Coaches .02 .10

1999-00 Prince George Cougars

COMPLETE SET (25) 6.00 15.00
1 Scott Meyers .20 .50
2 Tim Wedderburn .20 .50
3 Ryan Chieduch .20 .50
4 Jeff Zorn .20 .50
5 Dan Hamhuis .75 2.00
6 Kevin Seibel .20 .50
7 Gary Toor .20 .50
8 Devin Wilson .20 .50
9 Jozef Mrena .20 .50
10 Aaron Foster .20 .50
11 Tyler Bouck .30 .75
12 Jonathan Parker .20 .50
13 Shon Jones-Parry .20 .50
14 Roman Takac .20 .50
15 Chris Falloon .20 .50
16 Justin Hansen .20 .50
17 Trent Hunter .75 2.00
18 Blair Betts .40 1.00
19 Travis Eagles .20 .50
20 Ed Dempsey CO .02 .10
21 Dallas Thompson CO .02 .10
22 Paul Valaitis .20 .50
23 Billy Thompson .20 .50
24 Justin Cox .30 .75
25 Dan Baum .20 .50

2000-01 Prince George Cougars

COMPLETE SET (25) 4.80 12.00
1 Team Card .10 .25
2 Billy Thompson .16 .75
3 Tim Wedderburn .16 .40
4 David Koci .16 .40
5 Dan Hamhuis 1.20 2.00
6 Gary Gladue .16 .40
7 Joey Hope .16 .40
8 Devin Wilson .16 .40
9 Chris Falloon .16 .40
10 Nathan Brice .16 .40
11 Christian Chartier .30 .75
12 Berkeley Buchko .30 .75
13 Scott Lynch .16 .40
14 Aaron Foster .16 .40
15 Jon Filewich .16 .40
16 Tomas Tesarek .16 .40
17 Dan Baum .16 .40
18 Adam Stefishen .16 .40
19 Mark Kitts .16 .40
20 Willy Glover .16 .40
21 Brett Allan .16 .40
22 Travis Eagles .16 .40
23 Justin Cox .16 .40
24 Duane Perillat .16 .40
25 Derek Boogaard .16 .50

2001-02 Prince George Cougars

COMPLETE SET

2003-04 Prince George Cougars

COMPLETE SET (25) 10.00 25.00
1 Header Card .04 .10
2 Justin Pogge 3.00 8.00
3 Devin Featherstone .20 .50
4 Curtis Cooper .20 .50
5 Dustin Byfuglien 4.00 10.00
6 Brett Dickie .20 .50
7 Mike Fogolin .20 .50
8 Dennis Rehak .20 .50
9 Chris Falloon .20 .50
10 Nicholas Drazenovic .20 .50
11 Stanislav Bolshakov .20 .50
12 Dylan Yeo .30 .75
13 Brad Priestlay .20 .50
14 Jon Filewich .20 .50
15 Joshua Aspenlind .20 .50
16 Eric Hunter .20 .50
17 Greg Gardiner .20 .50
18 Danny Lapointe .20 .50
19 Myles Zimmer .30 .75
20 Steven Later .20 .50
21 Colin Patterson .20 .50
22 Tyrell Moulton .30 .75
23 Brett Parker .20 .50
24 Todd Ford .20 .50
25 Team Photo .20 .50

1988-89 ProCards AHL

COMPLETE SET (348) 32.00 80.00
1 Rob Nichols .07 .20
2 Bill Dineen CO .08 .25
3 Tim Paris Asst.TR .01 .05
4 Glenn Merkosky .05 .15
5 Mike Gober .07 .20
6 Dave Casey TR .01 .05
7 Sam St.Laurent .30 .75
8 Mark Reimer .08 .25
9 Dennis Smith .07 .20
10 Lou Crawford .07 .20
11 John Mokosak .07 .20
12 Murray Eaves .07 .20
13 Dave Korol .07 .20
14 Miroslav Ihnacak .20 .50
15 Dale Krentz .07 .20
16 Brent Fedyk .20 .50
17 Dean Morton .07 .20
18 Jeff Brubaker .15 .40
19 Tim Cheveldae .60 1.50
20 Randy McKay .40 1.00
21 Peter Dineen .07 .20
22 Rob Doyle .07 .20
23 Daniel Shank .40 1.00
24 Joe Ferras .07 .20
25 John Blum .08 .25
26 Tim Bergland .07 .20
27 Robin Bawa .07 .20
28 Shawn Simpson .07 .20
29 Chris Felix .08 .25
30 Jeff Greenlaw .07 .20
31 Frank Dimuzio .07 .20
32 Tyler Larter .07 .20
33 Rob Whistle .07 .20
34 Dallas Eakins .07 .20
35 Mark Hatcher .07 .20
36 Dave Farrish .08 .25
37 Bill Houlder .20 .50
38 Doug Keans .30 .75
39 Lou Franceschetti .08 .25
40 Rob Murray .05 .15
41 Terry Murray GM/CO .20 .50
42 Steve Seftel .07 .20
43 J.P. Mattingly TR .01 .05
44 Mike Richard .07 .20
45 Shawn Cronin .20 .50
46 Scott McCrory .07 .20
47 Mike Millar .07 .20
48 Dave Sherrid TR .01 .05
49 Marc Laforge .07 .20
50 David O'Brien .07 .20
51 Dave Rowbotham .07 .20
52 Kay Whitmore .40 1.00
53 Richard Brodeur .20 .50
54 Mike Vellucci .07 .20
55 Terry Yake .20 .50
56 Roger Kortko .07 .20
57 Jon Smith TR .01 .05
58 Lindsay Carson UER
Misspelled Lindsy .07 .20
59 Chris Brant .07 .20
60 Claude Larose CO .08 .25
61 Dallas Gaume .07 .20
62 Charlie Bourgeois .07 .20
63 Todd Krygier .20 .50
64 Gary Callahan .07 .20
65 Mark Reeds .07 .20
66 Al Tuer .07 .20
67 Brian Chapman .07 .20
68 Mark Lavarre .07 .20
69 Mark Dumas .07 .20
70 Jim Culhane .07 .20
71 Larry Trader .07 .20
72 Tom Mitchell GM .01 .05
73 Rob MacInnis .07 .20
74 John B. Hanna .07 .20
75 Dan Currie .20 .50
76 Dave Roach .07 .20
77 Jamie Nicolls .07 .20
78 Alan May .08 .25
79 David Haas .07 .20
80 Daryl Reaugh .60 1.50
81 Mike Ware .07 .20
82 Mike Glover .07 .20
83 Nick Beaulieu .07 .20
84 Mario Barbe .07 .20
85 Darren Beals .07 .20
86 Kim Issel .07 .20
87 Shaun Van Allen .20 .50
88 Jim Ennis .07 .20
89 Mark Lamb .40 1.00
90 Larry Floyd .07 .20
91 Ron Shudra .07 .20
92 Fabian Joseph .08 .25
93 Selmar Odelein .08 .25
94 Don Martin .07 .20
95 Jim Wiemer .08 .25
96 Brad MacGregor .07 .20
97 Gerald Bzdel .07 .20
98 Mike Hough .20 .50
99 Ken McRae .08 .25
100 Bobby Dollas .08 .25
101 Joel Baillargeon .07 .20
102 Ladislav Tresl .05 .15
103 Jacques Mailhot .20 .50
104 Dean Hopkins .07 .20
105 Claude Julien .07 .20
106 Brent Severyn .30 .75
107 Keith Miller .07 .20
108 Scott Shaunessy .07 .20
109 Jaroslav Sevcik .07 .20
110 Darin Kimble .20 .50
111 Jean-Marc Routhier .07 .20
112 Ken Quinney .07 .20
113 Max Middendorf .07 .20
114 Marc Fortier .15 .40
115 Jean-Marc Richard .07 .20
116 Mike Natyshak .07 .20
117 Ron Tugnutt 1.25 3.00
118 Scott Gordon .20 .50
119 Doug Carpenter CO/GM .02 .10
120 Jeff Harding .07 .20
121 Jocelyn Perrault .07 .20
122 Darryl Gilmour .20 .50
123 John Stevens .07 .20
124 Warren Harper .07 .20
125 Chris Jensen .07 .20
126 Mark Freer .08 .25
127 Gordon Paddock .07 .20
128 Bruce Randall .07 .20
129 Glen Seabrooke .07 .20
130 Mike Stothers .07 .20
131 Dave Fenyves .08 .25
132 Mark Lofthouse .07 .20
133 Marc D'Amour .20 .50
134 Shaun Sabol .07 .20
135 Craig Kitteringham .07 .20
136 J.J. Daigneault .20 .50
137 Don Biggs .08 .25
138 Kent Hawley .07 .20
139 Tony Horacek .07 .20
140 Al Hill .08 .25
141 Don Nachbaur .07 .20
142 John Paddock CO .07 .20
143 Kevin McCarthy CO .07 .20
144 Dan Stuck TR .01 .05
145 Doug Yingst .07 .20
146 Frank Mathers PR/GM .07 .20
147 Brian Bucciarelli TR .01 .05
148 Terry Taillefer .07 .20
149 Paul Beraldo .07 .20
150 Jeff Lamb .07 .20
151 Mitch Molloy .07 .20
152 Darren Lowe .07 .20
153 Stephane Quintal .40 1.00
154 Norm Foster .08 .25
155 Jean-Marc Lanthier .07 .20
156 Carl Mokosak .07 .20
157 Mike Neill .07 .20
158 Mike Jeffrey .07 .20
159 Steve Tsujiura .07 .20
160 Scott Drevitch .07 .20
161 Paul Guay .08 .25
162 Scott Wykoff ANN .01 .05
163 John Carter .08 .25
164 Phil Degaetano .07 .20
165 Doug Foerster PB .01 .05
166 Bruce Shoebottom .08 .25
167 Ray Podloski .07 .20
168 Greg Hawgood .20 .50
169 Joe Flaherty .07 .20
170 Todd Flichel .07 .20
171 Steven Fletcher .08 .25
172 Len Nielson .07 .20
173 Neil Meadmore .07 .20
174 Gilles Hamel .08 .25
175 Ron Wilson .20 .50
176 Stu Kulak .08 .25
177 Scott Schneider .07 .20
178 Mike Warus .07 .20
179 Jamie Husgen .07 .20
180 Tom Draper .20 .50
181 Guy Gosselin .07 .20
182 Guy Larose .08 .25
183 Stephane Beauregard .30 .75
184 Brent Hughes .15 .40
185 Sean Clement .07 .20
186 Matt Hervey .05 .15
187 Chris Norton .07 .20
188 Rob Snitzer THER .01 .05
189 Rick Bowness CO .20 .50
190 Wayne Flemming MG .01 .05
191 Tim Tookey .08 .25
192 Ken Baumgartner .40 1.00
193 John English .07 .20
194 Darryl Williams .07 .20
195 Hubie McDonough .20 .50
196 Brad Hyatt .07 .20
197 Phil Sykes .05 .15
198 Mario Chitaroni .07 .20
199 Tom Pratt .07 .20
200 Sal Lombardi TR .01 .05
201 Rick Dudley CO .08 .25
202 John Tortorella CO .01 .05
203 Chris Panek .07 .20
204 Scott Green TR .01 .05
205 Eric Germain .07 .20
206 Bob Kudelski .20 .50
207 Joe Paterson .07 .20
208 Al Loring .07 .20
209 Mark Fitzpatrick 1.25 3.00
210 Dan Gratton .07 .20
211 Sylvain Couturier .07 .20
212 Pat Hickey DIR .01 .05
213 Petr Prajsler .05 .15
214 Lyle Phair .07 .20
215 Bob Logan .07 .20
216 Francois Breault .07 .20
217 Paul Kelly .07 .20
218 Steve Richmond .07 .20
219 Denis Larocque .07 .20
220 Brian Wilks .07 .20
221 Dave Pasin .08 .25
222 Gordie Walker .07 .20
223 Marty Dallman .07 .20
224 Jim Ralph .60 1.50
225 Mike Blaisdell .20 .50
226 Sean McKenna .07 .20
227 Mark Kirton .08 .25
228 Greg Hotham .07 .20
229 Bill Root .08 .25
230 Wes Jarvis .07 .20
231 Daryl Evans .07 .20
232 Jack Capuano .07 .20
233 Tim Armstrong .07 .20
234 Alan Hepple .07 .20
235 Brian Blad .07 .20
236 Ken Yaremchuk .08 .25
237 Paul Gagne .15 .40
238 Doug Shedden .20 .50
239 Brian Hoard .07 .20
240 Greg Terrion .15 .40
241 Trevor Jobe .01 .05
242 Jeff Reese .40 1.00
243 Darryl Shannon .20 .50
244 Tim Bernhardt .30 .75
245 The Moose Mascot .02 .10
246 Paul Brydges .07 .20
247 Ken Priestlay .08 .25
248 Jacques Cloutier .20 .50
249 Steve Smith .07 .20
250 Jim Jackson .08 .25
251 Grant Tkachuk .07 .20
252 Kevin Kerr .07 .20
253 Mark Ferner .08 .25
254 Jeff Parker .07 .20
255 Don McSween .08 .25
256 Jim Hofford .07 .20
257 Darcy Wakaluk .60 1.50
258 Scott Metcalfe .07 .20
259 Richie Dunn .07 .20
260 Wayne Van Dorp .15 .40
261 Shawn Anderson .08 .25
262 Jeff Capello .07 .20
263 Mike Donnelly .20 .50
264 Mikael Anderson .20 .50
265 Robert Ray 1.50 4.00
266 Jody Gage .30 .75
267 Francois Guay .05 .15
268 John Van Boxmeer CO .08 .25
269 Jim Nesich .07 .20
271 J.J. Daigneault .20 .50
272 Randy Exelby .08 .25
273 Jyrki Lumme .60 1.50
275 Francois Gravel .07 .20
276 Jacques Parent THER .01 .05
277 Bobby Boulanger MG .01 .05
278 Benoit Brunet .40 1.00
279 Martin Nicoletti .07 .20
280 Mark Pederson .08 .25
281 Stephan Lebeau .40 1.00
282 Claude Larose CO .08 .25
283 Steve Bisson .07 .20
284 Scott Sandelin .07 .20
285 Rocky Dundas .07 .20
286 Serge Roberge .07 .20
287 Rob Bryden .07 .20
288 Marc Saumier .07 .20
289 Jean Hamel CO .07 .20
290 Mario Roberge .08 .25
291 Jocelyn Lemieux .20 .50
292 Ron Chyzowski .07 .20
293 Martin Desjardins .07 .20
294 Steven Martinson .07 .20
295 Jose Charbonneau .08 .25
296 Stephane J.G. Richer .05 .15
297 Sylvain Lefebvre .30 .75
298 Donald Dufresne .08 .25
299 Luc Gauthier .07 .20
300 Shawn Evans .05 .15
301 Mike Stevens .07 .20
302 Bruce Boudreau .20 .50
303 Todd McLellan .07 .20
304 Jeff Hackett 1.50 4.00
305 Bill Berg .20 .50
306 Stu Burnie .07 .20
307 Duncan McPherson .07 .20
308 Jeff Finley .08 .25
309 Ralph Calvanese MG .01 .05
310 Rob DiMaio .40 1.00
311 Chris Pryor .07 .20
312 Jim Roberts CO .07 .20
313 Vern Smith .07 .20
314 Mike Walsh .07 .20
315 Ed Tyburski TR .01 .05
316 Rod Dallman .07 .20
317 George Maneluk .08 .25
318 Richard Kromm .08 .25
319 Kerry Clark .07 .20
320 Hank Lammens .08 .25
321 Tom Fitzgerald .20 .50
322 Dale Henry .07 .20
323 Shawn Byram .07 .20
324 Doug Weiss .07 .20
325 John Walker .07 .20
326 Paul Ysebaert .30 .75
327 Chris Cichocki .07 .20
328 Marc Laniel .07 .20
329 Kevin Todd .20 .50
330 Dan Delianedls .07 .20
331 Robert Bill TR .01 .05
332 Jeff Croop TR .01 .05
333 Craig Billington .75 2.00
334 Alan Stewart .07 .20
335 Jeff Madill .08 .25
336 Scott Moon TR .01 .05
337 Neil Brady .08 .25
338 Murray Brumwell .07 .20
339 Anders Carlsson .07 .20
340 Dan Dorion .07 .20
341 Tom McVie CO .08 .25
342 David Marcinyshyn .07 .20
343 John Blessman .07 .20
344 Chris Terreri .75 2.00
345 Eric Weinrich .30 .75
346 Janne Ojanen .20 .50
347 Tim Lenardon .07 .20
348 Jamie Huscroft .20 .50

1988-89 ProCards IHL

COMPLETE SET (119) 20.00 50.00
1 Bob Lakso .07 .20
2 Rick Boyd .07 .20
3 Alan Perry .20 .50
4 Mark Teevens .07 .20
5 Gary Stewart .07 .20
6 Randy Taylor .07 .20
7 Scott Clements .07 .20
8 Chris McSorley .20 .50
9 Dave Allison .07 .20
10 Shane Doyle .07 .20
11 Darwin McCutcheon .07 .20
12 Geoff Benic .07 .20
13 Rich Oberlin TR .01 .05
14 Glen Johannesen .07 .20
15 Graeme Bonar .07 .20
16 Ron Handy .07 .20
17 Archie Henderson .08 .25
18 Brent Sapergia .07 .20
19 Brad Beck .07 .20
20 Paul Houck .07 .20
21 Jimmy Mann .20 .50
22 Rick Barkovich .07 .20
23 Scott McCrady .07 .20
24 Andy Akervik .07 .20
25 Rob Zettler .20 .50
26 Jarmo Myllys .40 1.00
27 D'Arcy Norton .07 .20
28 Ken Hodge Jr. .20 .50
29 Emanuel Viveiros .07 .20
30 Scott Bjugstad .07 .20
31 Mike Berger .07 .20
32 Joe Lockwood .07 .20
33 Stephane Roy .08 .25
34 Randy Smith .08 .25
35 Mike McHugh .07 .20
36 Warren Babe .07 .20
37 Gary McColgan .07 .20
38 Darin Baker .07 .20
39 Neil Wilkinson .20 .50
40 Kirk Tomlinson .07 .20
41 Larry Dyck .15 .40
42 Dave Schofield .07 .20
43 Brad Aitken .07 .20
44 Jock Callander .40 1.00
45 Todd Charlesworth .07 .20
46 Jeff Cooper .07 .20
47 Jeff Daniels .20 .50
48 Greg Davies .07 .20
49 Lee Giffin .07 .20
50 Dave Goertz .07 .20
51 Steve Gotaas .07 .20
52 Scott Gruhl .40 1.00
53 Doug Hobson .07 .20
54 Kevin MacDonald .07 .20
55 Pat Mayer .07 .20
56 Dave McLlwain .20 .50
57 Dave Michayluk .07 .20
58 Glenn Mulvenna .07 .20
59 Jim Paek .20 .50
60 Frank Pietrangelo .30 .75
61 Bruce Racine .20 .50
62 Mark Recchi 3.00 8.00
63 Troy Vollhoffer .07 .20
64 Jeff Waver .07 .20
65 Mitch Wilson .07 .20
66 Mitch Messier .08 .25
67 Dave Lowry .20 .50
68 Tim Bothwell .08 .25
69 Sheryl Reeves ADM .01 .05
70 Shane MacEachern .08 .25
71 Glen Featherstone .20 .50
72 Charlie Thompson MGR .01 .05
73 Wayne Thomas CO .08 .25
74 Dominic Lavoie .08 .25
75 Team Photo
Peoria Rivermen .20 .50
76 Scott Paluch .07 .20
77 Wayne Gagne .07 .20
78 Dave Thomlinson .20 .50
79 Tony Twist 2.00 5.00
80 Brad McCaughey .07 .20
81 Kelly Chase 1.25 3.00
82 Scott Harlow .07 .20
83 Peter Douris .20 .50
84 Cliff Ronning 1.00 2.50
85 Lyle Odelein .40 1.00
86 Terry MacLean .07 .20
87 Darin Smith .07 .20
88 Skip Probst .07 .20
89 Ed McMurray MGR .01 .05
90 Greg Eberle TR .01 .05
91 Jim Vesey .07 .20
92 Toby Ducolon .07 .20
93 Pat Jablonski .60 1.50
94 Darrell May .07 .20
95 Ed Belfour 10.00 25.00
96 Bruce Cassidy .08 .25
97 Chris Clifford .20 .50
98 Mario Doyon .07 .20
99 Bill Gardner .07 .20
100 Mark Kurzawski .07 .20
101 Lonnie Loach .20 .50
102 Steve Ludzik .08 .25
103 David Mackey .07 .20
104 Dale Marquette .07 .20
105 Gary Moscaluk .07 .20
106 Marty Nanne .07 .20
107 Brian Noonan .40 1.00
108 Mark Paterson .07 .20
109 Kent Paynter .07 .20
110 Guy Phillips .07 .20
111 John Reid .07 .20
112 Mike Rucinski .07 .20
113 Warren Rychel .30 .75
114 Everett Sanipass .20 .50
115 Mike Stapleton .08 .25
116 Darryl Sutter .40 1.00
117 Jari Torkki .07 .20
118 Bill Watson .08 .25
119 Sean Williams .08 .25

1989-90 ProCards AHL

COMPLETE SET (360) 36.00 90.00
1 New Haven Checklist .01 .05
2 Francois Breault .08 .25
3 Paul Kelly .08 .25
4 Phil Sykes .15 .40
5 Ron Scott .15 .40
6 Micah Aivazoff .15 .40
7 Sylvain Couturier .08 .25
8 Carl Repp .08 .25
9 Murray Brumwell .08 .25
10 Todd Elik .20 .50
11 Darwin Bozek .08 .25
12 Eric Germain .08 .25
13 Scott Young .40 1.00
14 Chris Kontos .20 .50
15 Scott Bjugstad .15 .40
16 Eric Ricard .08 .25
17 Ross Wilson .08 .25
18 Graham Stanley .08 .25
19 Chris Panek .10 .25
20 Nick Fotiu .40 1.00
21 Rene Chapdelaine .08 .25
22 Gordie Walker .08 .25
23 Tim Bothwell .15 .40
24 Kevin MacDonald .08 .25
25 Darryl Williams .08 .25
26 John Van Kessel .08 .25
27 Paul Brydges .08 .25
28 Moncton Checklist .01 .05
29 Guy Larose .15 .40
30 Danton Cole .15 .40
31 Brent Hughes .15 .40
32 Larry Bernard .08 .25
33 Stu Kulak .08 .25
34 Bob Essensa .75 2.00
35 Luciano Borsato .15 .40
36 Guy Gosselin .08 .25
37 Todd Flichel .08 .25
38 Brian Hunt .08 .25
39 Neil Meadmore .08 .25
40 Matt Hervey .08 .25
41 Dallas Eakins .08 .25
42 Brad Jones .08 .25
43 Chris Norton .08 .25
44 Bryan Marchment .40 1.00
45 Rick Tabaracci .60 1.50
46 Grant Richison .08 .25
47 Brian McReynolds .08 .25
48 Tony Joseph .08 .25
49 Dave Farrish .15 .40
50 Rob Snitzer .01 .05
51 Ron Wilson .15 .40
52 Scott Schneider .08 .25
53 Maine Checklist .01 .05
54 Dave Buda .08 .25
55 Paul Beraldo .08 .25
56 Lou Crawford .08 .25
57 Mark Montanari .08 .25
58 Don Sweeney .40 1.00
59 Jeff Sirkka .08 .25
60 Norm Foster .20 .50
61 Greg Poss .08 .25
62 Gord Cruickshank .08 .25
63 Bruce Shoebottom .08 .25
64 Mark Ziliotto .08 .25
65 Ron Hoover .08 .25
66 Scott Harlow .08 .25
67 Mike Millar .08 .25
68 Bob Beers .20 .50
69 Ray Neufeld .15 .40
70 Graeme Townshend .20 .50
71 Billy O'Dwyer .08 .25
72 Frank Caprice .20 .50
73 John Blum .08 .25
74 Jerry Foster .08 .25
75 Bill Sutherland
Rick Bowness .08 .25
76 Scott Drevitch .08 .25
77 Baltimore Checklist .01 .05
78 John Purves .08 .25
79 Jeff Greenlaw .08 .25
80 Jim Taylor .08 .25
81 Alfie Turcotte .08 .25
82 Dan Redmond .01 .05
83 Chris Felix .08 .25
84 Bobby Babcock .08 .25
85 Steve Maltais .08 .25
86 Mike Richard .08 .25
87 Team Picture .08 .25
88 Bob Mason .30 .75
89 Mark Ferner .15 .40
90 Steve Seftel .08 .25
91 Brian Tutt .08 .25
92 Terry Murray .15 .40
93 Jim Hrivnak .20 .50
94 Tyler Larter .08 .25
95 Tim Bergland .08 .25
96 Dennis Smith .08 .25
97 Steve Hollett .08 .25
98 Shawn Simpson .08 .25
99 Robin Bawa .08 .25
100 John Druce .20 .50
101 Kent Paynter .08 .25
102 Alain Cote .15 .40
103 J.P. Mattingly .01 .05
104 Newmarket Checklist .01 .05
105 Dean Anderson .08 .25
106 Wes Jarvis .08 .25
107 Brian Blad .08 .25
108 Derek Laxdal .08 .25
109 Kent Hulst .08 .25
110 Tim Bernhardt .20 .50
111 Brian Hoard .08 .25
112 Bill Root .15 .40
113 Paul Gardner .08 .25
114 Tim Armstrong .08 .25
115 Sean McKenna .08 .25
116 Tim Bean .08 .25
117 Alan Hepple .08 .25
118 Greg Hotham .08 .25
119 Scott Pearson .20 .50
120 Peter Ihnacak .15 .40
121 John McIntyre .08 .25
122 Paul Gagne .08 .25
123 Darren Veitch .15 .40
124 Mark LaForest .15 .40
125 Doug Shedden .15 .40
126 Bobby Reynolds .08 .25
127 Tie Domi 3.00 8.00
128 Ken Hammond .15 .40
129 Cape Breton Checklist .01 .05
130 Wade Campbell .08 .25
131 Chris Joseph .15 .40
132 Mario Barbe .08 .25
133 Mike Greenlay .20 .50
134 Peter Soberlak .08 .25
135 Bruce Bell .15 .40
136 Dan Currie .08 .25
137 Fabian Joseph .15 .40
138 Stan Drulia .20 .50
139 Todd Charlesworth .08 .25
140 Norm Maciver .20 .50
141 David Haas .08 .25
142 Tim Tisdale .08 .25
143 Eldon Reddick .20 .50
144 Alexander Tyznych .08 .25
145 Kim Issel .08 .25
146 Corey Foster .08 .25
147 Tomas Kapusta .08 .25
148 Brian Wilks .08 .25
149 John LeBlanc .08 .25
150 Ivan Matulik .08 .25
151 Shaun Van Allen .30 .75
152 Halifax Checklist .01 .05
153 Scott Gordon .20 .50
154 Trevor Steinburg .08 .25
155 Miroslav Ihnacak .15 .40
156 Jamie Baker .15 .40
157 Robbie Ftorek .20 .50
158 C. McQuaid
B.Smith .01 .05
159 Mario Brunetta .20 .50
160 Jean-Marc Routhier .08 .25
161 David Espe .08 .25
162 Ken Quinney .08 .25
163 Mark Vermette .08 .25
164 Dean Hopkins .08 .25
165 Claude Julien .08 .25
166 Claude Lapointe .20 .50
167 Stephane Morin .20 .50
168 Bryan Fogarty .20 .50
169 Dave Pichette .08 .25
170 Kevin Kaminski .15 .40
171 Brent Severyn .40 1.00
172 Max Middendorf .08 .25
173 Jean-Marc Richard .08 .25
174 Gerald Bzdel .08 .25
175 Ladislav Tresl .08 .25
176 Jaroslav Sevcik .08 .25
177 Greg Smyth .15 .40
178 Joel Baillargeon .08 .25
179 Sherbrooke Checklist .01 .05
180 Andre Racicot .20 .50
181 Jean-Claude Bergeron .20 .50
182 Jim Nesich .08 .25
183 Todd Richards .08 .25
184 Francois Gravel .08 .25
185 Lyle Odelein .40 1.00
186 Benoit Brunet .30 .75
187 Mario Roberge .15 .40
188 Marc Saumier .08 .25
189 Norman Desjardins .08 .25
190 Dan Woodley .08 .25
191 Andrew Cassels .30 .75
192 Roy Mitchell .08 .25
193 Guy Darveau .08 .25
194 Ed Cristofoli .08 .25
195 Stephane J.G. Richer .08 .25
196 Jacques Parent .01 .05

197 Luc Gauthier .08 .25
198 John Ferguson .08 .25
199 Mathieu Schneider .40 1.00
200 Serge Roberge .08 .25
201 Jean Hamel .08 .25
202 Utica Checklist .01 .05
203 Jason Simon .08 .25
204 Jeff Madill .08 .25
205 Kevin Todd .20 .50
206 Myles O'Connor .08 .25
207 Jon Morris .15 .40
208 Bob Hoffmeyer .08 .25
209 Paul Ysebaert .30 .75
210 Steve Rooney .15 .40
211 Claude Vilgrain .20 .50
212 Paul Guay .08 .25
213 Roland Melanson .30 .75
214 Tom McVie .15 .40
215 David Marcinyshyn .08 .25
216 Perry Anderson .08 .25
217 Jamie Huscroft .20 .50
218 Bob Woods .08 .25
219 Pat Conacher .20 .50
220 Jean-Marc Lanthier .08 .25
221 Chris Kiene .08 .25
222 Eric Weinrich .20 .50
223 Brian Fitzgerald .01 .05
224 Craig Billington .60 1.50
225 Jim Thomson .15 .40
226 Tim Budy .08 .25
227 Marc Laniel .08 .25
228 Robert Bill .01 .05
229 Springfield Checklist .01 .05
230 Mike Walsh .08 .25
231 Dale Henry .08 .25
232 Bill Berg .20 .50
233 Hank Lammens .08 .25
234 Rob DiMaio .40 1.00
235 Shawn Byram .08 .25
236 Jeff Hackett .75 2.00
237 Wayne McBean .15 .40
238 Tim Hanley .08 .25
239 Tom Fitzgerald .15 .40
240 Mike Stevens .08 .25
241 George Maneluk .08 .25
242 Dean Ewen .08 .25
243 Dale Kushner .08 .25
244 Shawn Evans .08 .25
245 Rod Dallman .08 .25
246 Mike Kelfer .08 .25
247 Sean LeBrun .08 .25
248 Kerry Clark .08 .25
249 Ed Tyburski .01 .05
250 Derek King .40 1.00
251 Marc Bergevin .20 .50
252 Jeff Finley .15 .40
253 Jim Roberts .08 .25
254 Chris Pryor .08 .25
255 Rochester Checklist .01 .05
256 Robert Ray 2.00 5.00
257 Ken Priestlay .15 .40
258 Darcy Wakaluk .30 .75
259 Richie Dunn .08 .25
260 Ken Sutton .20 .50
261 Terry Martin .08 .25
262 Scott Metcalfe .08 .25
263 Joel Savage .08 .25
264 Brad Miller .08 .25
265 Donald Audette .75 2.00
266 John Van Boxmeer .08 .25
267 The Moose .01 .05
268 Brian Ford .08 .25
269 Darcy Loewen .08 .25
270 Bob Halkidis .15 .40
271 Steve Ludzik .15 .40
272 Steve Smith .08 .25
273 Francois Guay .08 .25
274 Mike Donnelly .20 .50
275 Darrin Shannon .30 .75
276 Jody Gage .40 1.00
277 Dave Baseggio .00 .25
278 Bob Corkum .30 .75
279 Jim Jackson .08 .25
280 Don McSween .08 .25
281 Jim Hofford .08 .25
282 Scott McCrory .08 .25
283 Binghamton Checklist .01 .05
284 Raymond Saumier .08 .25
285 Mike Berger .08 .25
286 Corey Beaulieu .08 .25
287 Doug McKay .08 .25
288 Blair Atcheynum .08 .25
289 Al Tuer .08 .25
290 Chris Lindberg .15 .40
291 Daryl Reaugh .75 2.00
292 James Black .08 .25
293 Vern Smith .08 .25
294 Todd Krygier .20 .50
295 Bob Bodak .08 .25
296 Jon Smith .01 .05
297 Michel Picard .15 .40
298 Jim Culhane .08 .25
299 Brian Chapman .08 .25
300 Jim Ennis .08 .25
301 Jacques Caron .08 .25
302 Jim McKenzie .15 .40
303 Kay Whitmore .40 1.00
304 Terry Yake .15 .40
305 Mike Moller .08 .25
306 Adirondack Checklist .01 .05
307 Bob Wilkie .08 .25
308 Chris McRae .08 .25
309 Chris Kotsopoulos .15 .40
310 Steve Sumner .01 .05
311 Timothy Abbott .01 .05
312 Gord Kruppke .08 .25
313 Mike Gober .08 .25
314 Al Conroy .08 .25
315 Sam St.Laurent .15 .40
316 Dave Casey .01 .05
317 Yves Racine .20 .50
318 Randy McKay .20 .50
319 Dale Krentz .08 .25
320 Sheldon Kennedy .30 .75
321 Barry Melrose 1.25 3.00
322 Dennis Holland .08 .25
323 Glenn Merkosky .08 .25
324 Murray Eaves .08 .25
325 Mark Reimer .15 .40
326 Tim Cheveldae .40 1.00
327 Peter Dineen .08 .25
328 Dean Morton .08 .25
329 Derek Mayer .15 .40
330 Hershey Checklist .01 .05
331 Don Biggs .08 .25
332 Scott Sandelin .08 .25
333 Shaun Sabol .08 .25
334 Murray Baron .15 .40
335 Dave Fenyves .08 .25
336 Glen Seabrooke .08 .25
337 Mark Freer .15 .40
338 Ray Allison .08 .25
339 Chris Jensen .08 .25
340 Ross Fitzpatrick .08 .25
341 Brian Dobbin .08 .25
342 Darren Rumble .08 .25
343 Mike Stothers .08 .25
344 Jiri Latal .08 .25
345 Don Nachbaur .08 .25
346 John Stevens .08 .25
347 Steven Fletcher .08 .25
348 Kent Hawley .08 .25
349 Bill Armstrong .08 .25
350 Bruce Hoffort .15 .40
351 Gordon Paddock .08 .25
352 Marc D'Amour .20 .50
353 Tim Tookey .08 .25
354 Reid Simpson .08 .25
355 Mark Bassen .08 .25
356 Rocky Trottier .08 .25
357 Harry Bricker .01 .05
358 Dan Stuck .01 .05
359 Al Hill .08 .25
360 Kevin McCarthy .08 .25

1989-90 ProCards IHL

COMPLETE SET (208) 28.00 70.00
1 Peoria Checklist .01 .05
2 Darwin McPherson .08 .25
3 Pat Jablonski .30 .75
4 Scott Paluch .08 .25
5 Guy Hebert 2.00 5.00
6 Rich Pilon .15 .40
7 Curtis Joseph 8.00 20.00
8 Robert Dirk .20 .50
9 Darin Smith .08 .25
10 Terry McLean .08 .25
11 Kevin Miehm .15 .40
12 Toby Ducolon .08 .25
13 Mike Wolak .08 .25
14 Adrien Plavsic .20 .50
15 Dave Thomlinson .15 .40
16 Jim Vesey .08 .25
17 Michel Mongeau .20 .50
18 Tom Nash .01 .05
19 David O'Brien .08 .25
20 Dominic Lavoie .20 .50
21 Keith Osborne .08 .25
22 Rob Robinson .08 .25
23 Wayne Thomas .15 .40
24 Flint Checklist .01 .05
25 Jason Lafreniere .15 .40
26 Rick Knickle .30 .75
27 Jerry Tarrant .08 .25
28 Paul Broten .20 .50
29 Kevin Miller .40 1.00
30 Jim Latos .08 .25
31 Daniel Lacroix .15 .40
32 Dennis Vial .40 1.00
33 Denis Larocque .08 .25
34 Mike Golden .08 .25
35 Mike Hurlbut .08 .25
36 Scott Brower .08 .25
37 Lee Giffin .08 .25
38 Jeff Bloemberg .08 .25
39 Simon Wheeldon .20 .50
40 Rob Zamuner .40 1.00
41 Joe Paterson .08 .25
42 Barry Chyzowski .08 .25
43 Peter Laviolette .08 .25
44 Corey Millen .20 .50
45 Darren Lowe .08 .25
46 Peter Fiorentino .08 .25
47 Soren True .08 .25
48 Mike Richter 4.00 10.00
49 Ice Checklist .01 .05
50 Sean Williams .08 .25
51 Bruce Cassidy .08 .25
52 Mark Kurawski .08 .25
53 Bob Bassen .20 .50
54 Marty Nanne .08 .25
55 Jari Torkki .08 .25
56 Ryan McGill .15 .40
57 Mike Peluso .60 1.50
58 Darryl Sutter .40 1.00
59 Dan Vincelette .08 .25
60 Lonnie Loach .15 .40
61 Mike Rucinski .08 .25
62 Jim Playfair .08 .25
63 Everett Sanipass .08 .25
64 Dale Marquette .08 .25
65 Gary Moscaluk .08 .25
66 Mario Doyon .08 .25
67 Ray LeBlanc .40 1.00
68 Mike Eagles .15 .40
69 Warren Rychel .20 .50
70 Jim Johannson .15 .40
71 Cam Russell .20 .50
72 Mike McNeil .08 .25
73 Jimmy Waite .30 .75
74 Kalamazoo Checklist .01 .05
75 Kevin Schamehorn .08 .25
76 Kevin Evans .08 .25
77 D'Arcy Norton .08 .25
78 Scott Robinson .08 .25
79 Larry DePalma .08 .25
80 Ed Courtenay .15 .40
81 Rob Zettler .20 .50
82 Dusan Pasek .08 .25
83 Gary Emmons .08 .25
84 Peter Lappin .08 .25
85 Mario Thyer .08 .25
86 Mike McHugh .08 .25
87 Randy Smith .15 .40
88 Link Gaetz .40 1.00
89 Ken Hodge Jr. .15 .40
90 Pat MacLeod .20 .50
91 Neil Wilkinson .20 .50
92 Brett Barnett .08 .25
93 Larry Dyck .15 .40
94 Dean Kolstad .08 .25
95 Jarmo Myllys .30 .75
96 Paul Jerrard .08 .25
97 Jean-Francois Quintin .15 .40
98 Mitch Messier .08 .25
99 Phoenix Checklist UER
110 Jeff Lamb not listed .01 .05
100 Bryant Perrier .08 .25
101 Keith Gretzky .40 1.00
102 Don Martin .08 .25
103 David Littman .15 .40
104 Mike DeCarle .08 .25
105 Grant Tkachuk .08 .25
106 Richard Novak .08 .25
107 Chris Luongo .08 .25
108 Bruce Boudreau .15 .40
109 Nick Beaulieu .08 .25
110 Jeff Lamb .08 .25
111 Rob Nichols .08 .25
112 Garry Unger .20 .50
113 Larry Floyd .08 .25
114 Brent Sapergia .08 .25
115 Randy Exelby .20 .50
116 Jim McGeough .08 .25
117 Tom Karalis .08 .25
118 Ken Spangler .08 .25
119 Jacques Mailhot .08 .25
120 Shawn Dineen .08 .25
121 Dave Korol .08 .25
122 Fort Wayne Checklist .01 .05
123 Colin Chin .08 .25
124 Scott Shaunessy .08 .25
125 Bob Lakso .08 .25
126 Duane Joyce .08 .25
127 Joe Stephan .08 .25
128 Ron Shudra .08 .25
129 Bob Fowler .08 .25
130 Steve Bisson .08 .25
131 Craig Endean .08 .25
132 Carl Mokosak .08 .25
133 Carey Lucyk .08 .25
134 Craig Channell .08 .25
135 Frederic Chabot .75 2.00
136 Brian Hannon .08 .25
137 Keith Miller .08 .25
138 Al Sims .20 .50
139 Stephane Beauregard .30 .75
140 Ron Handy .08 .25
141 Byron Lomow .08 .25
142 Muskegon Checklist .01 .05
143 Jamie Leach .08 .25
144 Chris Clifford .08 .25
145 Dave Capuano .15 .40
146 Jeff Daniels .08 .25
147 Dave Goertz .08 .25
148 Perry Ganchar .08 .25
149 Mitch Wilson .08 .25
150 Scott Gruhl .30 .75
151 Randy Taylor .08 .25
152 Bruce Racine .20 .50
153 Dave Michayluk .15 .40
154 Richard Zemlak .15 .40
155 Brad Aitken .08 .25
156 Paul Stanton .15 .40
157 Darren Stolk .08 .25
158 Jim Paek .15 .40
159 Mark Kachowski .08 .25
160 Dan Frawley .08 .25
161 Mike Mersch .08 .25
162 Glenn Mulvenna .08 .25
163 Phil Russell .15 .40
164 Blair McDonald .08 .25
165 Milwaukee Checklist .01 .05
166 Shaun Clouston .08 .25
167 Steve Veilleux .08 .25
168 Peter Bakovic .08 .25
169 Peter DeBoer .20 .50
170 Ernie Vargas .08 .25
171 Keith Street .08 .25
172 Rob Murphy .15 .40
173 David Bruce .20 .50
174 Shannon Travis .08 .25
175 Jeff Rohlicek .08 .25
176 Jay Mazur .08 .25
177 Kevan Guy .08 .25
178 Troy Gamble .40 1.00
179 Ronnie Stern .20 .50
180 Jim Revenberg .08 .25
181 Jose Charbonneau .08 .25
182 Ian Kidd .08 .25
183 Todd Hawkins .08 .25
184 Carl Valimont .08 .25
185 Jim Agnew .08 .25
186 Curtis Hunt .08 .25
187 Dean Cook .08 .25
188 Ron Wilson .15 .40
189 Ron Lapointe .08 .25
190 Salt Lake City
Checklist .01 .05
191 Brian Glynn .15 .40
192 Stephane Matteau .30 .75
193 Rick Barkovich .08 .25
194 Jeff Wenaas .08 .25
195 Darryl Olsen .08 .25
196 Rick Lessard .08 .25
197 Kevin Grant .08 .25
198 Rich Chernomaz .08 .25
199 Stu Grimson 1.25 3.00
200 Jamie Hislop
Bob Francis .08 .25
201 Doug Pickell .08 .25
202 Chris Biotti .08 .25
203 Tim Sweeney .20 .50
204 Ken Sabourin .15 .40
205 Randy Bucyk .08 .25
206 Wayne Cowley .15 .40
207 Rick Hayward .08 .25
208 Marc Bureau .20 .50

1990-91 ProCards AHL/IHL

COMPLETE SET (632) 40.00 100.00
1 Rob Zamuner .30 .75
2 Todd Charlesworth .05 .15
3 Bob Bodak .05 .15
4 Len Hachborn .08 .25
5 Peter Fiorentino .05 .15
6 Kord Cernich .05 .15
7 Daniel Lacroix .20 .50
8 Joe Paterson .05 .15
9 Sam St.Laurent .20 .50
10 Jeff Bloemberg .05 .15
11 Mike Golden .05 .15
12 Mike Hurlbut .08 .25
13 Mark LaForest .20 .50
14 Chris Cichocki .05 .15
15 John Paddock .08 .25
16 Peter Laviolette .20 .50
17 Martin Bergeron .05 .15
18 Rudy Poeschek .40 1.00
19 Eric Germain .05 .15
20 Al Hill ACO .05 .15
21 Rick Bennett .08 .25
22 Tie Domi 2.00 5.00
23 Ross Fitzpatrick .05 .15
24 Brian McReynolds .08 .25
25 Binghampton Rangers CL .01 .05
26 Mike Eaves CO .05 .15
27 Lance Pitlick .15 .40
28 Dale Kushner .05 .15
29 Reid Simpson .05 .15
30 Craig Fisher .08 .25
31 Dominic Roussel .30 .75
32 Dave Fenyves .05 .15
33 Brian Dobbin .05 .15
34 Darren Rumble .15 .40
35 Murray Baron .15 .40
36 Bruce Hoffort .08 .25
37 Steve Beadle .05 .15
38 Chris Jensen .05 .15
39 Mike Stothers .05 .15
40 Kent Hawley .05 .15
41 Scott Sandelin .05 .15
42 Guy Phillips .05 .15
43 Mark Bassen .05 .15
44 Steve Scheifele .05 .15
45 Bill Armstrong .05 .15
46 Shaun Sabol .05 .15
47 Mark Freer .05 .15
48 Claude Boivin .08 .25
49 Len Barrie .08 .25
50 Bill Armstrong .05 .15
51 Tim Tookey .08 .25
52 Harry Bricker ACO .01 .05
53 Hershey Bears TC .01 .05
54 Alain Cote .08 .25
55 Luc Gauthier .05 .15
56 Eric Charron .05 .15
57 Mario Roberge .05 .15
58 Tom Sagissor .05 .15
59 Brent Bobyck .05 .15
60 John Ferguson .05 .15
61 Jim Nesich .05 .15
62 Gilbert Dionne .15 .40
63 Herbert Hohenberger .05 .15
64 Dan Woodley .05 .15
65 Roy Mitchell .05 .15
66 Frederic Chabot .60 1.50
67 Andre Racicot .20 .50
68 Paul DiPietro .20 .50
69 Norman Desjardins .05 .15
70 Martin St.Amour .05 .15
71 Jesse Belanger .20 .50
72 Ed Cristofoli .05 .15
73 Patrick Lebeau .08 .25
74 Paulin Bordeleau CO .05 .15
75 Fredericton Canadiens TC .01 .05
76 Keith Osborne .05 .15
77 Rich Pilon .15 .40
78 Alain Raymond .05 .15
79 Rob Robinson .05 .15
80 Andy Rymsha .05 .15
81 Randy Skarda .08 .25
82 Dave Thomlinson .08 .25
83 Tom Tilley .15 .40
84 Steve Tuttle .05 .15
85 Tony Twist 1.50 4.00
86 David Bruce .08 .25
87 Kelly Chase .40 1.00
88 Nelson Emerson .75 2.00
89 Guy Hebert 1.25 3.00
90 Tony Hejna .05 .15
91 Michel Mongeau .15 .40
92 David O'Brien .05 .15
93 Kevin Miehm .08 .25
94 Darwin McPherson .05 .15
95 Dominic Lavoie .05 .15
96 Yves Heroux .05 .15
97 Pat Jablonski .30 .75
98 Bob Plager CO .20 .50
99A Peoria Rivermen TC .01 .05
99B Jayson More .08 .25
100 Kevin Evans .05 .15
101 Warren Babe .05 .15
102 Mitch Messier .05 .15
103 John Blue .20 .50
104 Larry Dyck .08 .25
105 Duane Joyce .05 .15
106 Kari Takko .15 .40
107 Brett Barnett .05 .15
108 Pat MacLeod .08 .25
109 Peter Lappin .05 .15
110 Link Gaetz .40 1.00
111 Larry DePalma .05 .15
112 Steve Gotaas .05 .15
113 Mike McHugh .05 .15
114 Dan Keczmer .08 .25
115 Jackson Penney .05 .15
116 Ed Courtenay .15 .40
117 Jean-Francois Quintin .05 .15
118 Scott Robinson .05 .15
119 Mario Thyer .05 .15
120 Enrico Ciccone .30 .75
121 Kevin Constantine
John Marks .15 .40
122 Kalamazoo Wings TC .01 .05
123 Shayne Stevenson .20 .50
124 Jeff Lazaro .08 .25
125 Matt DelGuidice .20 .50
126 Ron Hoover .05 .15
127 John Mokosak .05 .15
128 John Blum .05 .15
129 Mike Parson .20 .50
130 Bruce Shoebottom .05 .15
131 Dave Donnelly .05 .15
132 Ralph Barahona .05 .15
133 Graeme Townshend .40 1.00
134 Ken Hodge Jr. .15 .40
135 Norm Foster .20 .50
136 Greg Poss .05 .15
137 Brad James .05 .15
138 Lou Crawford .05 .15
139 Rick Allain .05 .15
140 Bob Beers .15 .40
141 Ken Hammond .08 .25
142 Mark Montanari .05 .15
143 Rick Bowness CO .08 .25
144 Bob Gould PLAYER/COACH .05 .15
145 Maine Mariners TC .01 .05
146 Mike Stevens .05 .15
147 Greg Walters .05 .15
148 Mike Moes .05 .15
149 Kent Hulst .05 .15
150 Len Esau .05 .15
151 Darryl Shannon .15 .40
152 Bobby Reynolds .05 .15
153 Derek Langille .05 .15
154 Jeff Serowik .08 .25
155 Darren Veitch .15 .40
156 Joe Sacco .15 .40
157 Alan Hepple .05 .15
158 Doug Shedden .15 .40
159 Steve Bancroft .05 .15
160 Greg Johnston .15 .40
161 Trevor Jobe .05 .15
162 Bill Root .15 .40
163 Tim Bean .05 .15
164 Brian Blad .05 .15
165 Robert Hornya .05 .15
166 Dean Anderson .05 .15
167 Damian Rhodes .75 2.00
168 Mike Millar .05 .15
169 Mike Jackson .05 .15
170 Newmarket Saints .01 .05
171 Cal Brown .05 .15
172 Michel Picard .15 .40
173 Cam Brauer .05 .15
174 Jim Burke .05 .15
175 Jim McKenzie .15 .40
176 Mike Tomlak .05 .15
177 Ross McKay .05 .15
178 Blair Atcheynum .20 .50
179 Chris Tancill .08 .25
180 Mark Greig .08 .25
181 Joe Day .05 .15
182 Jim Roberts CO .05 .15
183 Emanuel Viveiros .05 .15
184 Daryl Reaugh .75 2.00
185 Tommie Eriksen .05 .15
186 Terry Yake .15 .40
187 Chris Govedaris .05 .15
188 Chris Bright .05 .15
189 John Stevens .05 .15
190 Brian Chapman .05 .15
191 James Black .08 .25
192 Scott Daniels .05 .15
193 Kelly Ens .05 .15
194 Springfield Indians TC .01 .05
195 Ken Lovsin .05 .15
196 Kent Paynter .05 .15
197 Jim Mathieson .20 .50
198 Bob Mendel .05 .15
199 Reggie Savage .08 .25
200 Alfie Turcotte .05 .15
201 Victor Gervais .05 .15
202 Todd Hlushko .20 .50
203 Steve Seftel .05 .15
204 Thomas Sjogren .05 .15
205 Steve Maltais .08 .25
206 Bob Joyce .15 .40
207 Tyler Larter .05 .15
208 Mark Ferner .08 .25
209 Bobby Babcock .05 .15
210 Jeff Greenlaw .05 .15
211 Tim Taylor .30 .75
212 John Purves .05 .15
213 Chris Felix .15 .40
214 Jiri Vykoukal .05 .15
215 Shawn Simpson .05 .15
216 Jim Hrivnak .20 .50
217 Rob Laird CO/GM .01 .05
218 Barry Trotz Asst.CO .20 .50
219 Baltimore Skipjacks TC .01 .05
220 David Haas .05 .15
221 Wade Campbell .05 .15
222 Dan Currie .05 .15
223 Shaun Van Allen .15 .40
224 Norm Maciver .20 .50
225 Mike Greenlay .20 .50
226 Peter Soberlak .05 .15
227 Tim Tisdale .05 .15
228 Mario Barbe .05 .15
229 Shjon Podein .40 1.00
230 Trevor Sim .05 .15
231 Corey Foster .08 .25
232 Mike Ware .05 .15
233 Marc Laforge .05 .15
234 Bruce Bell .08 .25
235 Tomas Kapusta .05 .15
236 Alexander Tyjynch .05 .15
237 Tomas Srsen .05 .15
238 Collin Bauer .05 .15
239 Francois Leroux .20 .50
240 Don MacAdam CO .01 .05
241 Norm Ferguson ACO .01 .05
242 Cape Breton Oilers TC .01 .05
243 Tony Joseph .05 .15
244 Brent Hughes .15 .40
245 Larry Bernard .05 .15
246 Simon Wheeldon .05 .15
247 Todd Flichel .05 .15
248 Craig Duncanson .05 .15
249 Iain Duncan .05 .15
250 Bryan Marchment .20 .50
251 Matt Hervey .05 .15
252 Chris Norton .05 .15
253 Dallas Eakins .05 .15
254 Peter Hankinson .05 .15
255 Grant Richison .05 .15
256 Lee Davidson .05 .15
257 Denis Larocque .05 .15
258 Scott Levins .15 .40
259 Guy Larose .08 .25
260 Scott Schneider .05 .15
261 Sergei Kharin .05 .15
262 Hawk .01 .05
263 Dave Farrish CO .05 .15
264 Moncton Hawks TC .01 .05
265 Kevin Haller .20 .50
266 Joel Savage .05 .15
267 Scott Metcalfe .05 .15
268 Ian Boyce .05 .15
269 David Littman .20 .50
270 Dave Baseggio .05 .15
271 Ken Sutton .15 .40
272 Brad Miller .05 .15
273 Bill Houlder .20 .50
274 Dan Frawley .15 .40
275 Scott McCrory .05 .15
276 Steve Ludzik .15 .40
277 Robert Ray 1.50 4.00
278 Darrin Shannon .20 .50
279 Dale Degray .05 .15
280 Bob Corkum .30 .75
281 Grant Tkachuk .05 .15
282 Kevin Kerr .05 .15
283 Mitch Molloy .05 .15
284 Darcy Loewen .08 .25
285 Jody Gage .20 .50
286 Jiri Sejba .05 .15
287 Steve Smith .05 .15
288 Darcy Wakaluk .20 .50
289 Donald Audette .60 1.50
290 Don McSween .08 .25
291 Francois Guay .05 .15
292 Terry Martin ACO .01 .05
293 Don Lever CO .05 .15
294 The Moose .01 .05
295 Rochester Americans TC .01 .05
296 Mike O'Connell CO .15 .40
297 Paul Marshall .05 .15
298 Darin Bannister .05 .15
299 Rob Nichols .05 .15
300 Charlie Simmer P/CO .20 .50
301 Bob Jones .05 .15
302 Scott Brower .05 .15
303 Taylor Hall .05 .15
304 Carl Mokosak .05 .15
305 Glen Hanlon .20 .50
306 Peter Dineen .05 .15
307 Mike Sullivan .20 .50
308 Steven Martinson .05 .15
309 Dave Korol .05 .15
310 Darren Lowe .05 .15
311 Mark Reimer .08 .25
312 Mike Gober .05 .15
313 Al Tuer .05 .15
314 Dean Morton .05 .15
315 Jim McGeough .05 .15
316 Clark Donatelli .05 .15
317 Steven Dykstra .05 .15
318 Brent Sapergia .05 .15
319 Lloyd Floyd .05 .15
320 D'Arcy Norton .05 .15
321 San Diego Gulls TC .01 .05
322 Garry Valk .20 .50
323 Ian Kidd .05 .15
324 Todd Hawkins .05 .15
325 Carl Valimont .05 .15
326 Peter DeBoer .05 .15
327 Curt Fraser ACO .15 .40
328 David Mackey .05 .15
329 Jim Benning .20 .50
330 Peter Bakovic .08 .25
331 Steve Weeks .20 .50
332 Steve Veilleux .05 .15
333 Shaun Clouston .05 .15
334 Gino Odjick .75 2.00
335 Mike Murphy CO .08 .25
336 Cam Brown .05 .15
337 Patrice LeFebvre .08 .25
338 Eric Murano .05 .15
339 Jim Revenberg .05 .15
340 Don Gibson .05 .15
341 Steve McKichan .05 .15
342 Milwaukee Admirals TC .01 .05
343 Rick Tabaracci .30 .75
344 Mike O'Neill .20 .50
345 Rick Hayward .05 .15
346 Sean Whyte .05 .15
347 Petr Prajsler .05 .15
348 John Van Kessel .05 .15
349 Mario Gosselin .20 .50
350 Kyosti Karjalainen .05 .15
351 Mikael Lindholm .05 .15
352 David Goverde .08 .25
353 Graham Stanley .05 .15
354 Stephane J.G. Richer .05 .15
355 Brian Lawton .15 .40
356 Jerome Bechard .05 .15
357 Jeff Rohlicek .05 .15
358 Steve Jacques .06 .15
359 Chris Kontos .20 .50
360 Sylvain Couturier .05 .15
361 Peter Sentner .05 .15
362 Steve Graves .05 .15
363 Daryn McBride .05 .15
364 Steve Rooney .15 .40
365 Mickey Volcan .05 .15
366 Kevin MacDonald .05 .15
367 Ralph Backstrom CO .20 .50
368 Garry Unger ACO .20 .50
369 Phoenix Roadrunners TC .01 .05
370 Rob Dopson .20 .50
371 Jock Callander .40 1.00
372 Chris Clifford .20 .50
373 Sandy Smith .05 .15
374 Jim Kyte .15 .40
375 Mike Needham .15 .40
376 Mitch Wilson .05 .15
377 Dave Goertz .05 .15
378 Mark Kachowski .05 .15
379 Perry Ganchar .05 .15
380 Mark Major .08 .25
381 Joel Gardner .05 .15
382 Scott Gruhl .30 .75
383 Todd Nelson .05 .15
384 Darren Stolk .05 .15
385 Scott Shaunessy .05 .15
386 Mike Mersch .05 .15
387 Glenn Mulvenna .05 .15
388 Brad Aitken .05 .15
389 Dave Michayluk .05 .15
390 Blair MacDonald CO .05 .15
391 Phil Russell ACO .08 .25
392 Muskegon
Lumberjacks TC .01 .05
393 Sean Williams .05 .15
394 Ryan McGill .05 .15
395 Mike Eagles .15 .40
396 Jim Johannson .15 .40
397 Marty Nanne .05 .15
398 Jim Playfair .05 .15
399 Warren Rychel .30 .75
400 Cam Russell .20 .50
401 Jimmy Waite .20 .50
402 Mike Stapleton .05 .15
403 Trevor Dam .05 .15
404 Tracy Egeland .05 .15
405 Owen Lessard .05 .15
406 Jeff Sirkka .05 .15
407 Mike Dagenais .05 .15
408 Alex Roberts .05 .15
409 Dominik Hasek 10.00 25.00
410 Martin Desjardins .05 .15
411 Frantisek Kucera .15 .40
412 Carl Mokosak .05 .15
413 Dave McDowell .05 .15
414 Indianapolis Ice TC .01 .05
415 Paul Saundercock .05 .15
416 Darryl Williams .05 .15
417 Micah Aivazoff .05 .15
418 Robb Stauber .20 .50
419 Tom Martin .05 .15
420 Billy O'Dwyer .05 .15
421 Scott Harlow .05 .15
422 Jim Thomson .05 .15
423 Jim Pavese .05 .15
424 Ron Scott .05 .15
425 Dave Pasin .05 .15
426 Serge Roy .05 .15
427 Darryl Gilmour .15 .40
428 Mike Donnelly .20 .50
429 Rene Chapdelaine .05 .15
430 Brandy Semchuk .05 .15
431 Paul Holden .05 .15
432 Bob Berg .05 .15
433 Ladislav Tresl .05 .15
434 Eric Ricard .05 .15
435 Murray Brumwell .05 .15
436 Shawn McCosh .05 .15
437 Ross Wilson .05 .15
438 Scott Young .40 1.00
439 David Moylan .05 .15
440 Marcel Comeau CO .05 .15
441 New Haven
Nighthawks TC .01 .05
442 David Espe .05 .15
443 Mario Doyon .05 .15
444 Gerald Bzdel .05 .15
445 Claude Lapointe .20 .50
446 Dean Hopkins .05 .15
447 Clement Jodoin .05 .15
448 Kevin Kaminski .40 1.00
449 Jamie Raker .15 .40
450 Mark Vermette .05 .15
451 Iiro Jarvi .15 .40
452 Kip Miller .40 1.00
453 Greg Smyth .08 .25
454 Serge Roberge .05 .15
455 Stephane Morin .20 .50
456 Brent Severyn .40 1.00
457 Jean-Marc Richard .05 .15
458 Ken Quinney .05 .15
459 Jeff Jackson .15 .40
460 Jaroslav Sevcik .05 .15
461 David Latta .05 .15
462 Trevor Steinburg .05 .15
463 Miroslav Ihnacak .05 .15
464 Jim Sprott .05 .15
465 Mike Bishop .05 .15
466 Stephane Fiset .75 2.00
467 Scott Gordon .20 .50
468 Halifax Citadels TC .01 .05
469 Gord Kruppke .05 .15
470 Glenn Merkosky .15 .40
471 Dennis Holland .05 .15
472 Chris McRae .05 .15
473 Al Conroy .05 .15
474 Yves Racine .20 .50
475 Jim Nill P/CO .05 .15
476 Barry Melrose CO .75 2.00
477 Bob Wilkie .05 .15
478 Guy Dupuis .05 .15
479 Doug Houda .15 .40
480 Tom Bissett .05 .15
481 Bill McDougall .08 .25
482 Glen Goodall .05 .15
483 Kory Kocur .05 .15
484 Chris Luongo .05 .15
485 Serge Anglehart .05 .15
486 Marc Potvin .40 1.00
487 Stewart Malgunas .05 .15
488 John Chabot .20 .50
489 Daniel Shank .20 .50
490 Randy Hansch .20 .50
491 Dave Gagnon .08 .25
492 Scott King .05 .15
493 Adirondack
Red Wings TC .01 .05
494 Derek Laxdal .05 .15
495 Sean LeBrun .05 .15
496 Shawn Bryan .05 .15
497 Wayne Doucet .05 .15

498 Rich Kromm .05 .15
499 Chris Pryor P/CO .05 .15
500 George Maneluk .05 .15
501 Brad Lauer .08 .25
502 Wayne McBean .08 .25
503 Jeff Finley .15 .40
504 Jim Culhane .05 .15
505 Paul Cohen .05 .15
506 Brent Grieve .08 .25
507 Kevin Cheveldayoff .05 .15
508 Dennis Vaske .08 .25
509 Dave Chyzowski .05 .15
510 Travis Green .75 2.00
511 Dean Chynoweth .20 .50
512 Rob DiMaio .30 .75
513 Paul Guay .05 .15
514 Capital District Islanders TC .01 .05
515 Rick Knickle .20 .50
516 Curtis Hunt .05 .15
517 Bruce Racine .20 .50
518 Yves Heroux .05 .15
519 Joe Stefan .05 .15
520 Torrie Robertson .20 .50
521 Nick Beaulieu .05 .15
522 Dave Richter .08 .25
523 Jeff Waver .05 .15
524 Gordon Paddock .05 .15
525 Darryl Noren .05 .15
526 Byron Lomow .05 .15
527 Ivan Matulik .05 .15
528 Dan Woodley .05 .15
529 Dale Henry .05 .15
530 Soren True .05 .15
531 Stuart True .05 .15
532 Rob MacInnis .05 .15
533 Vern Smith .05 .15
534 Paul Laus .40 1.00
535 Albany Choppers TC .01 .05
536 Robin Bawa .05 .15
537 Steven Fletcher .05 .15
538 Lonnie Loach .08 .25
539 Al Sims CO .08 .25
540 Colin Chin .05 .15
541 Bruce Boudreau P/CO .05 .15
542 Bob Lakso .05 .15
543 John Anderson .15 .40
544 Kevin Kaminski .40 1.00
545 Bruce Major .05 .15
546 Stephane Brochu .05 .15
547 Peter Hankinson .05 .15
548 Carey Lucyk .05 .15
549 Tom Karalis .05 .15
550 Bob Jay .05 .15
551 Mike Butters .05 .15
552 Brian McKee .05 .15
553 Ray LeBlanc .30 .75
554 Tom Draper .15 .40
555 Steve Laurin .05 .15
556 Fort Wayne Komets TC .01 .05
557 Sergei Starikov .05 .15
558 Claude Vilgrain .15 .40
559 Jeff Sharples .08 .25
560 Bob Woods .05 .15
561 Perry Anderson .08 .25
562 Brennan Maley .05 .15
563 Mike Posma .05 .15
564 Tom McVie GM/CO .05 .15
565 Chris Palmer .05 .15
566 Bill Huard .15 .40
567 Marc Laniel .05 .15
568 Neil Brady .05 .15
569 Jason Simon .08 .25
570 Kevin Todd .20 .50
571 Jeff Madill .08 .25
572 Jeff Christian .05 .15
573 Todd Copeland .05 .15
574 Mike Bodnarchuk .05 .15
575 Chris Kiene .05 .15
576 Myles O'Connor .08 .25
577 Jamie Huscroft .15 .40
578 Mark Romaine .05 .15
579 Rollie Melanson .20 .50
580 Utica Devils Team .08 .25
581 Utica Devils TC .01 .05
582 Ron Handy .05 .15
583 Cam Plante .05 .15
584 Lee Giffin .08 .25
585 Jim Latos .05 .15
586 Stu Kulak .08 .25
587 Claude Julien .05 .15
588 Rick Barkovich .05 .15
589 Randy Exelby .20 .50
590 Mark Vichorek .05 .15
591 Darin Smith .05 .15
592 Mike Kelfer .05 .15
593 Andy Akervik .05 .15
594 Mike Hiltner .05 .15
595 Kevin Sullivan .05 .15
596 Troy Frederick .05 .15
597 Claudio Scremin .05 .15
598 Kurt Semandel .05 .15
599 Mike Colman .05 .15
600 Jeff Odgers .40 1.00
601 Wade Flaherty .20 .50
602 Kansas City Blades TC .01 .05
603 Marc Bureau .20 .50
604 Darryl Olsen .05 .15
605 Rick Lessard .05 .15
606 Kevin Grant .05 .15
607 Rich Chernomaz .05 .15
608 Randy Bucyk .05 .15
609 Wayne Crowley .05 .15
610 Ken Sabourin .05 .15
611 Bob Francis CO .01 .05
612 Jamie Hislop CO .05 .15
613 Kevan Melrose .05 .15
614 Scott McCrady .05 .15
615 Corey Lyons .05 .15
616 Martin Simard .05 .15
617 C.J. Young .08 .25
618 Mark Osiecki .08 .25
619 Bryan Deasley .05 .15
620 Kerry Clark .05 .15
621 Paul Kruse .15 .40
622 Darren Banks .40 1.00
623 Richard Zemlak .08 .25
624 Todd Harkins .05 .15
625 Warren Sharples .05 .15
626 Andrew McKim .15 .40
627 Steve Guenette .08 .25
628 Salt Lake City
Golden Eagles TC .01 .05
NNO Bobby Boulanger .05 .15
NNO Ray Dudley Mariners mascot .05 .15
NNO Jerry Foster Mariners TR .05 .15
NNO Patrick Langlois .05 .15
NNO Jacques Parent .05 .15

1991-92 ProCards

COMPLETE SET (620) 40.00 100.00
1 Bill Houlder .15 .40
2 Brian Curran .08 .25
3 Dan Frawley .08 .25
4 Darcy Loewen .08 .25
5 Jiri Sejba .08 .25
6 Lindy Ruff .08 .25
7 Chris Snell .08 .25
8 Bob Corkum .20 .50
9 Dave Baseggio .05 .15
10 Sean O'Donnell .05 .15
11 Brad Rubachuk .05 .15
12 Peter Ciavaglia .08 .25
13 Joel Savage .05 .15
14 Jason Winch .05 .15
15 Steve Ludzik .08 .25
16 Don McSween .08 .25
17 David DaVita .05 .15
18 Greg Brown .08 .25
19 David Littman .20 .50
20 Tom Draper .20 .50
21 Jody Gage .40 1.00
22 Terry Martin .07 .20
23 Don Lever .08 .25
24 Rochester Checklist .01 .05
25 Jason Marshall .08 .25
26 Michel Mongeau .08 .25
27 Derek Frenette .05 .15
28 Kevin Miehm .08 .25
29 Guy Hebert .75 2.00
30 Greg Poss .05 .15
31 Dave Mackey .08 .25
32 Dan Fowler .05 .15
33 Mark Bassen .07 .20
34 Yves Heroux .08 .25
35 Harold Snepsts .40 1.00
36 Bruce Shoebottom .07 .20
37 Jaan Luik .05 .15
38 Alain Raymond .05 .15
39 Kyle Reeves .05 .15
40 Brian McKee .05 .15
41 Steve Tuttle .08 .25
42 Rob Tustian .05 .15
43 Richard Pion .08 .25
44 Joe Hawley .05 .15
45 Brian Pellerin .05 .15
46 Jason Ruff .08 .25
47 Rivermen Checklist .01 .05
48 Wes Walz .30 .75
49 Steve Bancroft .05 .15
50 John Blue .20 .50
51 Rick Allain .05 .15
52 Mike Walsh .08 .25
53 Dave Thomlinson .08 .25
54 Dennis Smith .05 .15
55 Jack Capuano .08 .25
56 Mike Rossetti .05 .15
57 Petr Prajsler .08 .25
58 Matt Glennon .05 .15
59 John Byce .08 .25
60 Howie Rosenblatt .08 .25
61 Brad Tiley .05 .15
62 Lou Crawford .05 .15
63 Matt Hervey .08 .25
64 Peter Douris .08 .25
65 Jeff Lazaro .08 .25
66 David Reid .20 .50
67 E.J. McGuire .05 .15
68 Frank Bathe .07 .20
69 Maine Checklist .01 .05
70 Paul DiPietro .08 .25
71 Darcy Simon .05 .15
72 Patrick Lebeau .20 .50
73 Gilbert Dionne .20 .50
74 John Ferguson .08 .25
75 Norman Desjardins .05 .15
76 Luc Gauthier .07 .20
77 Jean-Claude Bergeron .20 .50
78 Andre Racicot .15 .40
79 Steve Veilleux .05 .15
80 Patrice Brisebois .20 .50
81 Tom Sagissor .05 .15
82 Lindsay Vallis .05 .15
83 Steve Larouche .08 .25
84 Sean Hill .20 .50
85 Jesse Belanger .20 .50
86 Stephane J.G. Richer .08 .25
87 Marc Labelle .05 .15
88 Pierre Sevigny .08 .25
89 Eric Charron .08 .25
90 Ed Ronan .08 .25
91 Paulin Bordeleau .08 .25
92 Fredericton Checklist .01 .05
93 Daryl Reaugh .75 2.00
94 Jergus Baca .08 .25
95 Karl Johnston .05 .15
96 Shawn Evans .05 .15
97 Scott Humeniuk .05 .15
98 Cam Brauer .05 .15
99 Scott Eichstadt .05 .15
100 Paul Cyr .08 .25
101 James Black .08 .25
102 Chris Govedaris .08 .25
103 Joe Day .08 .25
104 Chris Tancill .08 .25
105 Kerry Russell .07 .20
106 Denis Chalifoux .05 .15
107 Blair Atcheynum .08 .25
108 John Stevens .05 .15
109 Brian Chapman .05 .15
110 Chris Bright .05 .15
111 Jim Burke .05 .15
112 Scott Daniels .08 .25
113 Kelly Ens .05 .15
114 Mike Tomlak .08 .25
115 Mario Gosselin .20 .50
116 Jay Leach .05 .15
117 Springfield Checklist .01 .05
118 Allan Bester .20 .50
119 Daniel Shank .20 .50
120 Lonnie Loach .08 .25
121 Mark Reimer .08 .25
122 Kirk Tomlinson .05 .15
123 Stewart Malgunas .08 .25
124 Serge Anglehart .05 .15
125 Chris Luongo .08 .25
126 Keith Primeau 1.25 3.00
127 Ken Quinney .08 .25
128 Dave Flanagan .05 .15
129 Pete Stauber .05 .15
130 Mike Sillinger .20 .50
131 Micah Aivazoff .08 .25
132 Gary Schuchuk .08 .25
133 Bill McDougall .08 .25
134 Sheldon Kennedy .20 .50
135 Derek Mayer .05 .15
136 Darin Bannister .05 .15
137 Guy Dupuis .05 .15
138 Gord Kruppke .05 .15
139 Jason York .20 .50
140 Barry Melrose .40 1.00
141 Glenn Merkosky .08 .25
142 Adirondack Checklist .01 .05
143 Larry Dyck .08 .25
144 Roy Mitchell .05 .15
145 Greg Spenrath .05 .15
146 Steve Herniman .05 .15
147 Brad Berry .08 .25
148 Jim Nesich .05 .15
149 Tim Lenardon .05 .15
150 Steve Guenette .08 .25
151 Paul Jerrard .05 .15
152 Cal McGowan .08 .25
153 Scott Robinson .05 .15
154 Mitch Messier .08 .25
155 Tony Joseph .05 .15
156 Steve Maltais .40 1.00
157 Steve Gotaas .05 .15
158 Doug Barrault .08 .25
159 Dave Moylan .05 .15
160 Mario Thyer .08 .25
161 Bob Hoffmeyer .05 .15
162 Wade Dawson .05 .15
163 Wings Checklist .01 .05
164 Rob Murray .07 .20
165 Chris Kiene .05 .15
166 Lee Davidson .05 .15
167 Rudy Poeschek .40 1.00
168 Kent Paynter .05 .15
169 John LeBlanc .07 .20
170 Dallas Eakins .05 .15
171 Claude Julien .05 .15
172 Bob Joyce .08 .25
173 Derek Langille .05 .15
174 Rob Cowie .08 .25
175 Warren Rychel .40 1.00
176 Tom Karalis .05 .15
177 Kris Draper .40 1.00
178 Ken Gernander .05 .15
179 Tod Hartje .08 .25
180 Sean Gauthier .05 .15
181 Tyler Larter .05 .15
182 Scott Levins .08 .25
183 Jason Cirone .05 .15
184 Mark Kumpel .08 .25
185 Rick Tabaracci .40 1.00
186 Luciano Borsato .08 .25
187 Dave Farrish .08 .25
188 Dave Prior .05 .15
189 Moncton Checklist .01 .05
190 Peter Fiorentino .05 .15
191 Glen Goodall .05 .15
192 John Mokosak .05 .15
193 Sam St.Laurent .20 .50
194 Daniel Lacroix .20 .50
195 Guy Larose .08 .25
196 Mike Hurlbut .08 .25
197 Peter Laviolette .08 .25
198 Eric Bennett .05 .15
199 Steven King .08 .25
200 Boris Rousson .40 1.00
201 Jody Hull .15 .40
202 Shaun Sabol .05 .15
203 Joe Paterson .05 .15
204 Rob Zamuner .30 .75
205 Don Biggs .08 .25
206 Chris Cichocki .07 .20
207 Ross Fitzpatrick .05 .15
208 Mark LaForest .08 .25
209 Brian McReynolds .07 .20
210 Jeff Bloemberg .08 .25
211 Kord Cernich .05 .15
212 Ron Smith .05 .15
213 Al Hill .08 .25
214 Binghamton Checklist .01 .05
215 Francois Leroux .15 .40
216 Marc Laforge .05 .15
217 Max Middendorf .07 .20
218 Shjon Podein .30 .75
219 Jason Soules .07 .20
220 Collin Bauer .05 .15
221 Shaun Van Allen .15 .40
222 Eldon Reddick .20 .50
223 Eygeny Belosheiken .20 .50
224 David Haas .05 .15
225 Norm Foster .20 .50
226 Greg Hawgood .20 .50
227 Steven Rice .15 .40
228 Dan Currie .08 .25
229 Peter Soberlak .05 .15
230 Martin Rucinsky .40 1.00
231 Tomas Kapusta .08 .25
232 Dean Antos .05 .15
233 Craig Fisher .07 .20
234 Tomas Srsen .05 .15
235 Don McAdam .05 .15
236 Norm Ferguson .05 .15
237 Coaching Staff .01 .05
238 Cape Breton Checklist .01 .05
239 Peter Hankinson .05 .15
240 Chris McRae .05 .15
241 Craig Martin .08 .25
242 Carey Lucyk .05 .15
243 Jean-Marc Richard .05 .15
244 Grant Richison .05 .15
245 Mark Turner .05 .15
246 Todd Flichel .05 .15
247 Scott Shaunessy .05 .15
248 Darin Smith .05 .15
249 Ian Boyce .05 .15
250 Colin Chin .07 .20
251 Bob Jones .05 .15
252 Bob Jay .07 .20
253 Kelly Hurd .05 .15
254 Scott Gruhl - .40 1.00
255 Kory Kocur .07 .20
256 Steven Fletcher .05 .15
257 Bob Lakso .07 .20
258 Dusty Imoo .20 .50
259 Mike O'Neill .20 .50
260 Bruce Boudreau .08 .25
261 Al Sims .15 .40
262 Komets Checklist .01 .05
263 Ray Letourneau .05 .15
264 Marc D'Amour .20 .50
265 Dominic Roussel .30 .75
266 Bill Armstrong (LW) .07 .20
267 Al Conroy .08 .25
268 Dale Kushner .08 .25
269 Toni Porkka .05 .15
270 Mike Stothers .05 .15
271 Darren Rumble .08 .25
272 Reid Simpson .05 .15
273 Claude Boivin .08 .25
274 Len Barrie .08 .25
275 Chris Jensen .08 .25
276 Pat Murray .08 .25
277 Eric Dandenault .05 .15
278 Rod Dallman .05 .15
279 Mark Freer .08 .25
280 Bill Armstrong (D) .08 .25
281 Tim Tookey .08 .25
282 Jamie Cooke .05 .15
283 Dave Fenyves .08 .25
284 Steve Morrow .05 .15
285 Martin Hostak .08 .25
286 Mike Eaves .08 .25
287 Hershey Checklist .01 .05
288 Dave Michayluk .20 .50
289 Glenn Mulvenna .07 .20
290 Jean Blouin .05 .15
291 Jock Callander .40 1.00
292 Perry Ganchar .05 .15
293 Paul Laus .30 .75
294 Mark Major .05 .15
295 Bruce Racine .20 .50
296 Daniel Gauthier .05 .15
297 Mike Needham .08 .25
298 Jeff Daniels .08 .25
299 Sandy Smith .05 .15
300 Gilbert Delorme .08 .25
301 Rob Dopson .20 .50
302 Eric Brule .05 .15
303 Alain Morissette .05 .15
304 Paul Dyck .05 .15
305 Jason Smart .05 .15
306 Gord Dineen .08 .25
307 Todd Nelson .08 .25
308 Jamie Heward .05 .15
309 Paul Russell .05 .15
310 Lumberjack Checklist .01 .05
311 Soren True .05 .15
312 Murray Duval .05 .15
313 Dmitri Kvartalnov .15 .40
314 Larry Floyd .05 .15
315 Alan Legett .05 .15
316 Alan Hepple .05 .15
317 Ron Duguay .20 .50
318 Len Hachborn .08 .25
319 Steve Martinson .08 .25
320 Rick Knickle .30 .75
321 Darcy Norton .05 .15
322 Keith Gretzky .20 .50
323 Brian Straub .05 .15
324 Denny Lambert .08 .25
325 Jason Prosofsky .08 .25
326 Bruce Hoffort .08 .25
327 Sergei Starikov .07 .20
328 Dave Korol .05 .15
329 Robbie Nichols .05 .15
330 Kord Cernich .05 .15
331 Brent Sapergia .08 .25
332 Don Waddell .05 .15
333 Charlie Simmer .20 .50
334 San Diego Checklist .01 .05
335 Rob Mendel .05 .15
336 Curtis Hunt .05 .15
337 Jeff Serowik .08 .25
338 Bruce Bell .08 .25
339 Yanic Perreault .30 .75
340 Brad Aitken .05 .15
341 Keith Osborne .05 .15
342 Todd Hawkins .05 .15
343 Andrew McKim .08 .25
344 Kevin McClelland .08 .25
345 Mike Stevens .08 .25
346 Dave Tomlinson .08 .25
347 Kevin Maguire .08 .25
348 Mike MacWilliams .05 .15
349 Greg Walters .05 .15
350 Guy Lehoux .05 .15
351 Todd Gillingham .05 .15
352 Len Esau .05 .15
353 Greg Johnston .08 .25
354 Felix Potvin 2.00 5.00
355 Damian Rhodes .40 1.00
356 Joel Quenneville .05 .15
357 Marc Crawford .30 .75
358 Mike Eastwood .08 .25
359 St.Johns Checklist .01 .05
360 Lou Franceschetti .08 .25
361 John Murray Anderson .05 .15
362 Scott Schneider .05 .15
363 Jerome Bechard .05 .15
364 Mario Doyon .07 .20
365 Jeff Jackson .08 .25
366 John Tanner .08 .25
367 Al Tuer .05 .15
368 Paul Willett .05 .15
369 Darryl Williams .05 .15
370 George Maneluk .08 .25
371 Eric Ricard .05 .15
372 Trevor Stienburg .05 .15
373 Jerry Tarrant .05 .15
374 Michael McEwen .08 .25
375 Brian Dobbin .08 .25
376 David Latta .05 .15
377 Jim Sprott .05 .15
378 Trevor Pochipinski .05 .15
379 Stan Drulia .20 .50
380 Kent Hulst .05 .15
381 Brad Turner .05 .15
382 Doug Carpenter .08 .25
383 New Haven Checklist .01 .05
384 Bob Berg .05 .15
385 Steve Jaques .05 .15
386 Chris Norton .05 .15
387 Vern Smith .05 .15
388 Kevin MacDonald .05 .15
389 Ross Wilson .05 .15
390 Shawn McCosh .05 .15
391 Mike Vukonich .05 .15
392 Marc Saumier .05 .15
393 Mike Ruark .05 .15
394 Kris Miller .05 .15
395 Tim Breslin .05 .15
396 Paul Holden .05 .15
397 Jeff Rohlicek .05 .15
398 Kyosti Karjalainen .08 .25
399 David Goverde .20 .50
400 John Van Kessel .05 .15
401 Sean Whyte .05 .15
402 Brent Thompson .08 .25
403 Darryl Gilmour .20 .50
404 Scott Bjugstad .07 .20
405 Ralph Backstrom .15 .40
406 Rick Kozuback .05 .15
407 Roadrunner Checklist .01 .05
408 Brent Severyn .40 1.00
409 Dean Malkoc .08 .25
410 Matt Ruchty .05 .15
411 Jarrod Skalde .20 .50
412 Brian Sullivan .05 .15
413 Ben Hankinson .08 .25
414 Bill Huard .15 .40
415 Jeff Christian .05 .15
416 Corey Schwab .20 .50
417 Kevin Dean .05 .15
418 Todd Copeland .05 .15
419 Mike Bodnarchuk .05 .15
420 Jason Miller .05 .15
421 Chad Erickson .20 .50
422 David Craievich .05 .15
423 Jim Dowd .20 .50
424 Jamie Huscroft .15 .40
425 Myles O'Connor .08 .25
426 Jon Morris .08 .25
427 Valeri Zelepukin .20 .50
428 Utica Checklist .01 .05
429 Brad Beck .05 .15
430 Brett MacDonald .05 .15
431 Jacques Mailhot .08 .25
432 Francois Ouellette .05 .15
433 Ron Kinghorn .05 .15
434 Dennis Miller .05 .15
435 Darren Miciak .05 .15
436 Tom Sasso .05 .15
437 Peter Corbett .05 .15
438 Brian Horan .05 .15
439 John Messuri .05 .15
440 E.J. Sauer .05 .15
441 Tom Mutch .05 .15
442 Jason Simon .05 .15
443 Steve Sullivan .05 .15
444 Scott Allen .05 .15
445 Stephane Brochu .08 .25
446 Ken Spangler .08 .25
447 Lee Odelein .05 .15
448 Antti Autere .05 .15
449 John Reid .05 .15
450 Skip Probst CO .01 .05
451 Flint Checklist .05 .15
452 Dean Ewen .05 .15
453 Brent Grieve .15 .40
454 Jim Culhane .05 .15
455 Joni Lehto .05 .15
456 Graeme Townshend .08 .25
457 Danny Lorenz .08 .25
458 Phil Huber .05 .15
459 Kevin Cheveldayoff .07 .20
460 Dennis Vaske .15 .40
461 Wayne Doucet .05 .15
462 Greg Parks .07 .20
463 Dean Chynoweth .05 .15
464 Lee Giffin .08 .25
465 Richard Kromm .08 .25
466 Derek Laxdal .08 .25
467 Travis Green .40 1.00
468 Iain Fraser .08 .25
469 Rick Hayward .08 .25
470 Jeff Finley .08 .25
471 Dave Chyzowski .07 .20
472 Mark Fitzpatrick .40 1.00
473 Hubie McDonough .08 .25
474 Sean LeBrun .05 .15
475 Chris Pryor .05 .15
476 Capital District CL .01 .05
477 Jeff Sirkka .05 .15
478 Owen Lessard .05 .15
479 Jim Playfair .05 .15
480 Dan Vincelette .07 .20
481 Tracey Egeland .05 .15
482 Shawn Byram .05 .15
483 Trevor Dam .05 .15
484 Martin Desjardins .05 .15
485 Milan Tichy .08 .25
486 Cam Russell .15 .40
487 Mike Speer .05 .15
488 Sean Williams .05 .15
489 Paul Gillis .08 .25
490 Brad Lauer .08 .25
491 Trent Yawney .15 .40
492 Craig Woodcroft .08 .25
493 Justin LaFayette .05 .15
494 Rob Conn .08 .25
495 Frantisek Kucera .08 .25
496 Mike Peluso .40 1.00
497 Roch Belley .20 .50
498 Ryan McGill .07 .20
499 Kerry Toporowski .08 .25
500 Dominik Hasek 4.00 8.00
501 Adam Bennett .07 .20
502 Ray LeBlanc .20 .50
503 John Marks .07 .20
504 Ice Checklist .01 .05
505 Mikhail Kravets .07 .20
506 Gary Emmons .05 .15
507 Ed Courtenay .08 .25
508 Claudio Scremin .05 .15
509 Jarmo Myllys .40 1.00
510 Mike Colman .05 .15
511 Kevin Evans .08 .25
512 Troy Frederick .05 .15
513 Ron Handy .05 .15
514 Murray Garbutt .05 .15
515 Gordon Frantti .05 .15
516 Dale Craigwell .20 .50
517 Wade Flaherty .30 .75
518 Dean Kolstad .08 .25
519 Rick Lessard .08 .25
520 Craig Coxe .40 1.00
521 Jeff Madill .08 .25
522 Peter Lappin .08 .25
523 Duane Joyce .05 .15
524 Larry DePalma .08 .25
525 Pat MacLeod .08 .25
526 Andy Akervik .05 .15
527 Blades Checklist .01 .05
528 Mike Dagenais .05 .15
529 Gerald Bzdel .05 .15
530 Stephane Fiset .40 1.00
531 David Espe .05 .15
532 Patrick Labrecque .20 .50
533 Niclas Andersson .08 .25
534 Jon Klemm .30 .75
535 Denis Chasse .20 .50
536 Stephane Charbonneau .05 .15
537 Ivan Matulik .05 .15
538 Serge Roberge .05 .15
539 Daniel Dore .05 .15
540 Sergei Kharin .08 .25
541 Jamie Baker .08 .25
542 Ken McRae .08 .25
543 David Marcinyshyn .07 .20
544 Clement Jodoin .05 .15
545 Dean Hopkins .05 .15
546 Checklist .01 .05
547 Jeff Greenlaw .07 .20
548 Byron Dafoe .40 1.00
549 Jim Hrivnak .20 .50
550 Olaf Kolzig 1.25 3.00
551 John Purves .07 .20
552 Bobby Reynolds .05 .15
553 Simon Wheeldon .20 .50
554 Jim Mathieson .20 .50
555 Trevor Halverson .08 .25
556 Steve Seftel .05 .15
557 Ken Lovsin .08 .25
558 Victor Gervais .05 .15
559 Steve Martell .08 .25
560 Chris Clarke .05 .15
561 Brent Hughes .08 .25
562 Jiri Vykoukal .05 .15
563 Tim Taylor .20 .50
564 Richie Walcott .05 .15
565 Harry Mews .05 .15
566 Craig Duncanson .08 .25
567 Todd Hlushko .08 .25
568 Mark Ferner .08 .25
569 Bobby Babcock .07 .20
570 Reggie Savage .08 .25
571 Rob Laird .05 .15
572 Barry Trotz .01 .05
573 Baltimore Checklist .01 .05
574 Kevan Melrose .05 .15
575 Kevin Grant .05 .15
576 Kevan Guy .08 .25
577 Darryl Olsen .05 .15
578 Kevin Worthman .05 .15
579 Darren Stolk .05 .15
580 Bryan Deasley .05 .15
581 Paul Kruse .08 .25
582 Darren Banks .40 1.00
583 Corey Lyons .05 .15
584 Kenny Clark .05 .15
585 Todd Strueby .08 .25
586 Rich Chernomaz .05 .15
587 Tim Harris .05 .15
588 Shawn Heaphy .05 .15
589 Todd Harkins .08 .25
590 Richard Zemlak .08 .25
591 Warren Sharples .08 .25
592 Jason Muzzatti .20 .50
593 Dennis Holland .05 .15
594 Salt Lake City CL .01 .05
595 Shawn Antoski .15 .40
596 Peter Bakovic .05 .15
597 Robin Bawa .07 .20
598 Cam Brown .05 .15
599 Neil Eisenhut .08 .25
600 Jason Herter .07 .20
601 Ian Kidd .05 .15
602 Troy Neumeier .05 .15
603 Carl Valimont .05 .15
604 Phil Von Stefenelli .08 .25
605 Andrew McBain .08 .25
606 Eric Murano .08 .25
607 Rob Murphy .08 .25
608 Brian Blad .05 .15
609 Randy Boyd .05 .15
610 Don Gibson .05 .15
611 Paul Guay .08 .25
612 Jay Mazur .08 .25
613 Jeff Larmer .08 .25
614 Ladislav Tresl .08 .25
615 Dennis Snedden .05 .15
616 Corrie D'Alessio .08 .25
617 Bob Mason .20 .50
618 Jack McIlhargey .08 .25
619 Curt Fraser .08 .25
620 Admirals Checklist .01 .05

1996-97 Providence Bruins

COMPLETE SET (25) 4.00 10.00
2 Mark Cornforth .15 .40
3 Charles Paquette .15 .40
4 John Gruden .15 .40
6 Peter Laviolette .20 .50
8 Jean-Yves Roy .15 .40
9 Justin Gould .15 .40
10 David Emma .15 .40
11 Davis Payne .20 .50
13 Martin Simard .20 .50
14 Kirk Nielsen .15 .40
17 P.C. Drouin .20 .50
18 Jay Moser .15 .40
19 Bill McCauley .15 .40
21 Tim Sweeney LL .15 .40
22 Mitch Lamoureux .20 .50
23 Yevgeny Shaldybin .15 .40
25 Kevin Sawyer .30 .75
27 Brad Konik .15 .40
28 Milt Mastad .15 .40
29 Rob Tallas .30 .75
34 Bob Beers .20 .50
44 Brett Harkins .15 .40
49 Andre Roy .20 .50
NNO Bob Francis CO .10 .25
NNO AHL Web Site .01 .05

1997-98 Providence Bruins

COMPLETE SET (26) 5.00 12.00
1 Rob Tallas .30 .75
2 Elias Abrahamsson .15 .40
3 Bill Armstrong .15 .40
4 Dean Chynoweth .15 .40
5 Aaron Downey .60 1.50
6 Hal Gill .30 .75
7 John Grahame .60 1.50
8 Antti Laaksonen .20 .50
9 Cameron Mann .20 .50
10 Anders Myrvold .20 .50
11 Eric Naud .15 .40
12 Kirk Nielsen .15 .40
13 Charles Paquette .15 .40
14 Joel Prpic .15 .40
15 Barry Richter .20 .50
16 Randy Robitaille .30 .75
17 Jon Rohloff .15 .40
18 Andre Roy .30 .75
19 Jean-Yves Roy .15 .40
20 Yevgeny Shaldybin .15 .40
21 Landon Wilson .20 .50
22 Andrei Yakhanov .15 .40
23 Tom McVie HCO .02 .10
24 Rod Langway ACO .02 .10
25 PHPA Web Site .01 .05
26 AHL Web Site .01 .05

1998-99 Providence Bruins

COMPLETE SET (25) 5.00 10.00
1 Peter Laviolette .25 .60
2 Elias Abrahamsson .15 .40
3 Johnathan Aitken .15 .40
4 Bill Armstrong .15 .40
5 Steve Bancroft .15 .40
6 Shawn Bates .30 .75
7 Jim Carey .30 .75
8 Aaron Downey .60 1.50
9 John Grahame .60 1.50
10 Joe Harney .15 .40
11 Jay Henderson .20 .50
12 Antti Laaksonen .30 .75
13 Cameron Mann .20 .50
14 Marquis Mathieu .20 .50
15 Eric Nickulas .20 .50
16 Peter Nordstrom .15 .40
17 Joel Prpic .15 .40
18 Randy Robitaille .20 .50
19 Andre Savage .30 .75
20 Brandon Smith .20 .50
21 Mattias Timander .15 .40
22 Joel Trottier .15 .40
23 Terry Virtue .20 .50
24 Landon Wilson .20 .50
25 AHL Web Site .01 .05

1999-00 Providence Bruins

COMPLETE SET (25) 5.00 12.00
1 Elias Abrahamsson .15 .40
2 Johnathan Aitken .15 .40
3 Shane Belter .15 .40
4 Nick Boynton .40 1.00
5 Jeremy Brown .15 .40
6 Vratislav Cech .15 .40
7 Jassen Cullimore .15 .40
8 Aaron Downey .60 1.50
9 Peter Ferraro .15 .40
10 Maxime Gingras .30 .75
11 John Grahame .60 1.50
12 Jay Henderson .30 .75
13 Joe Hulbig .15 .40
14 Antti Laaksonen .15 .40
15 Tim Lovell .15 .40
16 Cameron Mann .30 .75
17 Marquis Mathieu .20 .50
18 Keith McCambridge .15 .40
19 Eric Nickulas .30 .75
20 Joel Prpic .15 .40
21 Andre Savage .20 .50
22 Brandon Smith .20 .50
23 Denis Timofeev .15 .40
24 Jeff Wells .15 .40
25 Kay Whitmore .20 .5

2000-01 Providence Bruins

COMPLETE SET (22) 6.00 10.0
1 Kay Whitmore .30 .7
2 Keith McCambridge .20 .5
3 Nick Boynton .40 1.0
4 Eric Manlow .20 .5
5 Zdenek Kutlak .20 .5
6 Cameron Mann .30 .7
7 Eric Nickulas .30 .5
8 Pavel Kolarik .20 .5
9 Jay Henderson .20 .5
10 Lee Goren .40 .7

- 11 Peter Vandermeer .20 .75
- 12 Marquis Mathieu .30 .50
- 13 Ivan Huml .60 1.00
- 14 Terry Hollinger .20 .50
- 15 Elias Abrahamsson .20 .50
- 16 Jeremy Brown .20 .50
- 17 Brandon Smith .20 .50
- 18 Mattias Karlin .20 .50
- 19 Jon Coleman .20 .50
- 20 Jonathan Girard .40 1.00
- 21 Peter Ferraro .20 .50
- 22 Kay Whitmore .30 .75
- NNO Team CL .10 .25

2001-02 Providence Bruins

- COMPLETE SET (21) 5.00 12.00
- 1 Andrew Raycroft .75 2.00
- 2 Jeff Maund .20 .50
- 3 Keith McCambridge .15 .35
- 4 Bobby Allen .15 .35
- 5 Chris Kelleher .15 .35
- 6 Eric Manlow .15 .35
- 7 Zdenek Kutlak .20 .50
- 8 Tony Tuzzolino .20 .50
- 9 Pavel Kolarik .15 .35
- 10 Lee Goren .40 1.00
- 11 John Emmons .15 .35
- 12 Andy Hilbert .40 1.00
- 13 Joe Hulbig .15 .35
- 14 Carl Corazzini .15 .35
- 15 Ivan Huml .40 1.00
- 16 Sean Haggerty .15 .35
- 17 Dennis Bonvie .20 .50
- 18 Mattias Karlin .20 .50
- 19 Martin Wilde .15 .35
- 20 Greg Crozier .20 .50
- 21 Jonathan Girard .40 1.00
- NNO Title Card/CL .02 .10

2002-03 Providence Bruins

- COMPLETE SET (21) 5.00 12.00
- 1 Andrew Raycroft .75 2.00
- 2 Kevin Dallman .20 .50
- 3 Chris Kelleher .20 .50
- 4 Keith Aucoin .20 .50
- 5 Rich Brennan .20 .50
- 6 Zdenek Kutlak .20 .50
- 7 Matt Herr .20 .50
- 8 Martin Samuelsson .40 1.00
- 9 Kris Vernarsky .30 .75
- 10 Jay Henderson .20 .50
- 11 Chris Paradise .20 .50
- 12 Andy Hilbert .30 .75
- 13 Shaone Morrisonn .40 1.00
- 14 Darren Van Oene .20 .50
- 15 Peter Metcalf .20 .50
- 16 Lee Goren .30 .75
- 17 Mike Gellard .20 .50
- 18 Brantt Myhres .20 .50
- 19 Pat Leahy .30 .75
- 20 Tim Thomas .75 2.00
- NNO Checklist .04 .10

2003-04 Providence Bruins

- COMPLETE SET (24) 5.00 12.00
- 1 Rich Brennan .15 .40
- 2 Ed Campbell .15 .40
- 3 Carl Corazzini .15 .40
- 4 Kevin Dallman .15 .40
- 5 Mike Gellard .15 .40
- 6 Matt Herr .15 .40
- 7 Andy Hilbert .30 .75
- 8 Ivan Huml .15 .40
- 9 Milan Jurcina .30 .75
- 10 Zdenek Kutlak .15 .40
- 11 Pat Leahy .30 .75
- 12 Robert Liscak .15 .40
- 13 Peter Metcalf .15 .40
- 14 Brett Nowak .15 .40
- 15 Colton Orr .40 1.00
- 16 Martin Samuelsson .15 .40
- 17 Andre Savage .15 .40
- 18 Tim Thomas .60 1.50
- 19 Hannu Toivonen 1.25 3.00
- 20 Darren Van Oene .15 .40
- 21 Kris Vernarsky .15 .40
- 22 Brendan Walsh .15 .40
- 23 Brian White .15 .40
- 24 Martin Wilde .15 .40
- NNO Checklist .04 .10

2004-05 Providence Bruins

- COMPLETE SET (25) 5.00 12.00
- 1 Pat Aufiero .20 .50
- 2 Patrice Bergeron .60 1.50
- 3 Brad Boyes .40 1.00
- 4 Carl Corazzini .20 .50
- 5 Kevin Dallman .20 .50
- 6 Chris Dyment .20 .50
- 7 Jayme Filipowicz .20 .50
- 8 David Gove .20 .50
- 9 Ben Guite .20 .50
- 10 Jay Henderson .20 .50
- 11 Andy Hilbert .20 .50
- 12 Milan Jurcina .20 .50
- 13 Pat Leahy .20 .50
- 14 Steve Munn .20 .50
- 15 Colton Orr .40 1.00
- 16 Martin Samuelsson .20 .50
- 17 Brent Thompson .20 .50
- 18 Yorick Treille .20 .50
- 19 Kris Vernarsky .20 .50
- 20 Brendan Walsh .20 .50
- 21 Peter Hamerlik .30 .75
- 22 Hannu Toivonen .75 2.00
- 23 Scott Gordon CO .04 .10
- 24 Rob Murray ACO .04 .10
- 25 Checklist .04 .10

2005-06 Providence Bruins

- COMPLETE SET (25) 6.00 15.00
- Zdenek Blatny .20 .50
- Sean Curry .20 .50
- Chris Dyment .20 .50
- Scott Ford .30 .75
- Ben Guite .20 .50
- Eric Healey .20 .50
- Jay Leach .20 .50
- David Lundbohm .20 .50
- 9 Jason MacDonald .20 .50
- 10 Eric Nickulas .20 .50
- 11 Pascal Pelletier .30 .75
- 12 Tyler Redenbach .20 .50
- 13 Jeremy Reich .20 .50
- 14 Nathan Robinson .40 1.00
- 15 Michael Schutte .20 .50
- 16 Jonathan Sigalet .40 1.00
- 17 Jordan Sigalet .75 2.00
- 18 Garret Stroshein .40 1.00
- 19 Mark Stuart .40 1.00
- 20 Tim Thomas .60 1.50
- 21 Nate Thompson .20 .50
- 22 Ben Walter .20 .50
- 23 Scott Gordon HC .02 .10
- 24 Rob Murray AC .02 .10
- NNO Providence Bruins CL .02 .10

2006-07 Providence Bruins

- COMPLETE SET (25) 8.00 15.00
- 1 Bobby Allen .20 .50
- 2 Chris Collins .30 .75
- 3 Sean Curry .20 .50
- 4 Nathan Dempsey .20 .50
- 5 Nate DiCasmirro .20 .50
- 6 Brian Finley .30 .75
- 7 Petr Kalus .30 .75
- 8 Martin Karsums .20 .50
- 9 David Krejci .30 .75
- 10 Matt Lashoff .30 .75
- 11 Jay Leach .20 .50
- 12 Dennis Packard .20 .50
- 13 Pascal Pelletier .20 .50
- 14 Wacey Rabbit .60 1.50
- 15 Jeremy Reich .30 .75
- 16 Jonathan Sigalet .40 1.00
- 17 Jordan Sigalet .75 2.00
- 18 Yan Stastny .20 .50
- 19 Mark Stuart .40 1.00
- 20 Philippe Sauve .30 .75
- 21 Nate Thompson .30 .75
- 22 T.J. Trevelyan .40 1.00
- 23 Kris Versteeg 2.00 5.00
- 24 Ben Walter .20 .50
- 25 Dwayne Zinger .20 .50

2014-15 Providence Bruins

- COMPLETE SET (28) 8.00 20.00
- 1 Christopher Breen .30 .75
- 2 Anthony Camara .30 .75
- 3 Chris Casto .30 .75
- 4 Andrew Cherniwchan .30 .75
- 5 Tommy Cross .30 .75
- 6 Steve Eminger .40 1.00
- 7 Brian Ferlin .30 .75
- 8 Rob Flick .30 .75
- 9 Justin Florek .30 .75
- 10 Seth Griffith .40 1.00
- 11 Cory Kane .30 .75
- 12 Alexander Khokhlachev .30 .75
- 13 Jared Knight .30 .75
- 14 Matt Lindblad .40 1.00
- 15 Joseph Morrow .30 .75
- 16 Tyler Randell .30 .75
- 17 Bobby Robins .30 .75
- 18 Ben Sexton .30 .75
- 19 Jeremy Smith .30 .75
- 20 Ryan Spooner .50 1.25
- 21 Colin Stuart .40 1.00
- 22 Malcolm Subban .75 2.00
- 23 Niklas Svedberg .40 1.00
- 24 Zach Trotman .30 .75
- 25 David Warsofsky .30 .75
- 26 Ethan Werek .30 .75
- 27 Ben Youds .30 .75
- 28 Header Card CL .30 .75

1936-37 Providence Reds

- COMPLETE SET (10) 200.00 400.00
- 1 Bobby Bauer 37.50 75.00
- 2 Paddy Byrne 12.50 25.00
- 3 Woody Dumart 37.50 75.00
- 4 Jackie Keating 12.50 25.00
- 5 Art Lesieur 12.50 25.00
- 6 Bert McInenly 12.50 25.00
- 7 Gus Rivers 12.50 25.00
- 8 Milt Schmidt 75.00 150.00
- 9 Jerry Shannon 12.50 25.00
- 10 Player Unidentified 12.50 25.00

2000 QMJHL All-Star Program Inserts

- COMPLETE SET (46) 20.00 50.00
- 1 Guy Chouinard CO .20 .50
- 2 Maxime Ouellet .60 1.50
- 3 Sebastien Caron .75 2.00
- 4 Joe Rullier .40 1.00
- 5 Marc-Andre Bergeron .75 2.00
- 6 Chris Lyness .40 1.00
- 7 Jonathan Gautier .40 1.00
- 8 Francois Beauchemin 1.25 3.00
- 9 Michel Periard .40 1.00
- 10 Mike Ribeiro .75 2.00
- 11 Wesley Scanzano .40 1.00
- 12 Jonathan Roy .40 1.00
- 13 Carl Malette .40 1.00
- 14 Ramzi Abid .40 1.00
- 15 Simon Gamache .40 1.00
- 16 Marco Charpentier .40 1.00
- 17 Marc-Andre Thinel .40 1.00
- 18 Jerome Tremblay .40 1.00
- 19 Brandon Reid .75 2.00
- 20 Benoit Dusablon .40 1.00
- 21 Eric Chouinard .40 1.00
- 22 Claude Julien CO .40 1.00
- 23 Alexei Volkov .40 1.00
- 24 Drew MacIntyre .40 1.00
- 25 Joey DiPenta .75 2.00
- 26 Kirill Safronov .40 1.00
- 27 Alexander Riazantsev .40 1.00
- 28 Daniel MacLeod .40 1.00
- 29 Roustam Bakhriddinov .40 1.00
- 30 Adam Rivet .40 1.00
- 31 Miroslav Zalesak .40 1.00
- 32 Edo Terglav .40 1.00
- 33 Maxim Potapov .40 1.00
- 34 Thatcher Bell .40 1.00
- 35 Radim Vrbata 1.25 3.00
- 36 Jan-Philippe Cadieux .40 1.00
- 37 Dmitri Afanassenkov .40 1.00
- 38 Michael Ryder 2.00 5.00
- 39 Artem Rybin .40 1.00
- 40 Andrei Shefer .40 1.00
- 41 Brad Richards 4.00 10.00
- 42 Juraj Kolnik .40 1.00
- 43 Danny Bowie .40 1.00
- 44 All-Star Game Logo .02 .10
- 45 Team World Logo .02 .10
- 46 Team Quebec Logo .02 .10

1996-97 Quad-City Mallards

- COMPLETE SET (22) 8.00 20.00
- 1 Todd Newton .40 1.00
- 2 Brad Barton .40 1.00
- 3 Travis Tucker .40 1.00
- 4 Stephen Sangermano .40 1.00
- 5 Dave Larson .40 1.00
- 6 Jim Ensom .40 1.00
- 7 Justin McHugh .40 1.00
- 8 Fredrick Nasvall .40 1.00
- 9 Hugo Proulx .40 1.00
- 10 Carl LeBlanc .40 1.00
- 11 Glenn Stewart .40 1.00
- 12 Brett Strot .40 1.00
- 13 Andy Faulkner .40 1.00
- 14 Mark McFarlane .40 1.00
- 15 Howie Rosenblatt .60 1.50
- 16 Rick Emmett .40 1.00
- 17 Sergei Zvyagin .40 1.00
- 18 David Fletcher .40 1.00
- 19 John Batten .40 1.00
- 20 John Anderson HCO .40 1.00
- 21 Matt Shaw ACO .40 1.00
- 22 Mo Mallard Mascot .20 .50

1997-98 Quad-City Mallards

- COMPLETE SET (23) 4.80 12.00
- 1 Glenn Stewart .20 .50
- 2 Rick Emmett .20 .50
- 3 Sergei Zvyagin .20 .50
- 4 Howie Rosenblatt .30 .75
- 5 Brad Barton .20 .50
- 6 Kirk Llano .20 .50
- 7 Wayne Muir .30 .75
- 8 Hugo Proulx .20 .50
- 9 Mark McFarlane .20 .50
- 10 Steve Chelios .30 .75
- 11 Travis Tucker .20 .50
- 12 Carl LeBlanc .20 .50
- 13 Stas Tkatch .20 .50
- 14 Andy Faulkner .20 .50
- 15 Steve Gibson .20 .50
- 16 Tom Perry .20 .50
- 17 Matt Mullin .30 .75
- 18 Bogdan Rudenko .30 .75
- 19 Ryan Gelinas .30 .75
- 20 Jim Brown .20 .50
- 21 Kerry Toporowski .30 .75
- 22 Corey Neilson .20 .50
- 23 Quad City Mallards CL .02 .10

1998-99 Quad-City Mallards

- COMPLETE SET (24) 4.00 10.00
- 1 Sergei Zvyagin .20 .50
- 2 Brendan Brooks .20 .50
- 3 Scott Burfoot .02 .10
- 4 Matt Carey .20 .50
- 5 Rick Emmett .20 .50
- 6 Martin Fillion .20 .50
- 7 Rusty Fitzgerald .20 .50
- 8 Chad Ford .20 .50
- 9 Robert Frid .20 .50
- 10 Steve Gibson .20 .50
- 11 Garry Gulash .20 .50
- 12 Kevin Kerr .30 .75
- 13 Brian LaFleur .20 .50
- 14 Carl LeBlanc .30 .75
- 15 Mark McFarlane .20 .50
- 16 Stephanie Madore .20 .50
- 17 Miko Molas .20 .50
- 18 Hugo Proulx .20 .50
- 19 Bruce Richardson .20 .50
- 20 Howie Rosenblatt .30 .75
- 21 Scott Thompson .20 .50
- 22 Bill Weir .20 .50
- 23 Glenn Stewart .20 .50
- 24 Team CL .02 .10

1999-00 Quad-City Mallards

- COMPLETE SET (24) 4.00 10.00
- 1 Iannique Renaud .20 .50
- 1 Moe Mallard MAS .02 .10
- 2 Yannick Latour .20 .50
- 3 Steve Gibson .20 .50
- 4 Garry Gulash .20 .50
- 5 Mike Melas .20 .50
- 6 Rick Emmett .20 .50
- 7 Ryan Lindsay .20 .50
- 8 Patrick Nadeau .20 .50
- 9 Hugo Proulx .20 .50
- 10 Paul Johnson .20 .50
- 11 Brendan Buckley .20 .50
- 12 Martin Hlinka .20 .50
- 13 Brendan Brooks .20 .50
- 14 Rusty Fitzgerald .20 .50
- 15 Kelly Hultgren .20 .50
- 16 Mark McFarlane .20 .50
- 17 Glenn Stewart .20 .50
- 18 Martin Villeneuve .30 .75
- 19 Brian LaFleur .20 .50
- 20 Robert DeCiantis .20 .50
- 21 Kevin Kerr .30 .75
- 22 Scott Buhler .30 .75
- 24 Quad City Mallards CL .02 .10

2000-01 Quad-City Mallards

- COMPLETE SET (27) 4.00 10.00
- 1 Team CL .04 .10
- 2 Andy Fermoyle .15 .40
- 3 Garry Gulash .15 .40
- 4 Frederick Jobin .15 .40
- 5 Vlad Serov .15 .40
- 6 Dan Bjornlie .15 .40
- 7 Peter Armbrust .15 .40
- 8 Patrick Nadeau .15 .40
- 9 Ryan Lindsay .15 .40
- 10 Jason Ulmer .15 .40
- 11 Hugo Proulx .15 .40
- 12 Mike Sim .15 .40
- 13 Chad Power .15 .40
- 14 Paul Johnson .15 .40
- 15 Kelly Perrault .15 .40
- 16 Mark McFarlane .15 .40
- 17 Etienne Drapeau .20 .50
- 18 Martin Hlinka .15 .40
- 19 Rick Emmett .20 .50
- 20 Martin Villeneuve .15 .40
- 21 Scott Myers .15 .40
- 22 Cam Severson .15 .40
- 23 Steve Gibson .15 .40
- 24 Kerry Toporowski .20 .50
- 25 Paul MacLean CO .10 .25
- 26 Mo Mallard MASCOT .04 .10
- 27 Ima Duck MASCOT .04 .10

2001-02 Quad-City Mallards

- COMPLETE SET (24) 4.80 12.00
- 1 Peter Armbrust .20 .50
- 2 Dan Bjornlie .20 .50
- 3 Keli Corpse .30 .75
- 4 Joe Dimaline .20 .50
- 5 Andy Fermoyle .20 .50
- 6 Nick Ganga .20 .50
- 7 Steve Gibson .30 .75
- 8 Garry Gulash .20 .50
- 9 Frederick Jobin .20 .50
- 10 Kyle Kidney .20 .50
- 11 Sanny Lindstrom .20 .50
- 12 Brian McCullough .20 .50
- 13 Mark McFarlane .20 .50
- 14 Paul MacLean CO .20 .50
- 15 Dylan Mills .20 .50
- 16 Aaron Miskovich .30 .75
- 17 Patrick Nadeau .20 .50
- 18 Brant Nicklin .20 .50
- 19 Hugo Proulx .30 .75
- 20 Jesse Rooney .20 .50
- 21 Brandon Sampair .20 .50
- 22 Kerry Toporowski .30 .75
- 23 Jason Ulmer .30 .75
- 24 Mo and Ima MASCOTS .04 .10

2005-06 Quad City Mallards

- COMPLETE SET (25) 6.00 12.00
- 1 Anthony Blumer .20 .50
- 2 Tom Clayton .20 .50
- 3 Glenn Detulleo .20 .50
- 4 Terry Friesen .40 1.00
- 5 Tom Galvin .20 .50
- 6 Jason Jaworski .20 .50
- 7 Andrei Lupandin .20 .50
- 8 Rafal Martynowski .20 .50
- 9 Patrick Nadeau .20 .50
- 10 Samy Nasreddine .40 1.00
- 11 Mike Olynyk .20 .50
- 12 Joe Pace .20 .50
- 13 Joel Pullman .20 .50
- 14 Matt Radoslovich .20 .50
- 15 Jesse Rycroft .20 .50
- 16 Jason Tapp .40 1.00
- 17 Jonathan Tremblay .20 .50
- 18 Noah Whyte .20 .50
- 19 Chad Wollard .20 .50
- 20 J. J. Wrobel .20 .50
- 21 Jami Yoder .20 .50
- 22 Brian Curran CO .04 .10
- 23 Larry Easter TR .04 .10
- 24 Jason Rivera TR .04 .10
- 25 Aaron Roof ANN .04 .10

2006-07 Quad City Mallards

- COMPLETE SET (20) 12.00 20.00
- 1 Justin Chwedoruk .40 1.00
- 2 Brian Curran CO .20 .50
- 3 Bront Currio .75 2.00
- 4 Sergei Durdin .20 .50
- 5 Travis Granbois .20 .50
- 6 Nick Harloff .40 1.00
- 7 Andrei Lupandin .40 1.00
- 8 Patrick Nadeau .40 1.00
- 9 Don Parsons .40 1.00
- 10 Jeff Petruic .40 1.00
- 11 Brett Pilkington .40 1.00
- 12 Matt Radoslovich .40 1.00
- 13 Zach Sikich .60 1.50
- 14 Sean Starke .40 1.00
- 15 Luke Stauffacher .75 2.00
- 16 Blake Stewart .40 1.00
- 17 Jason Tapp .75 2.00
- 18 Mathieu Wathier .40 1.00
- 19 Chad Woollard .40 1.00
- 20 Jami Yoder .40 1.00

2007-08 Quad City Flames

- COMPLETE SET (25) 5.00 12.00
- 1 Ryan McGill HC .15 .40
- 2 David van der Gulik .25 .60
- 3 Brett Sutter .25 .60
- 4 Grant Stevenson .25 .60
- 5 Brandon Prust .25 .60
- 6 Warren Peters .25 .60
- 7 Matt Pelech .25 .60
- 8 Eric Nystrom .25 .60
- 9 Dustin Boyd .25 .60
- 10 Brent Krahn .25 .60
- 11 Adam Pardy .25 .60
- 12 Brett Palin .25 .60
- 13 Tomi Maki .25 .60
- 14 Krys Kolanos .25 .60
- 15 Matt Keetley .25 .60
- 16 Tim Hambly .25 .60
- 17 Carsen Germyn .25 .60
- 18 Cam Cunning .25 .60
- 19 Derek Couture .25 .60
- 20 Kris Chucko .25 .60
- 21 Gord Baldwin .25 .60
- 22 Curtis McElhinney .25 .60
- 23 Kevin Lalande .25 .60
- 24 Tim Ramholt .25 .60
- 25 Team Card .10 .25

2007-08 Quad City Flames Franchise Firsts

- COMPLETE SET (5) 2.00 5.00
- A Dustin Boyd .40 1.00
- B Matt Keetley .40 1.00
- C Grant Stevenson .40 1.00
- D Eric Nystrom .40 1.00
- E Curtis McElhinney .40 1.00

1956-57 Quebec Aces

- COMPLETE SET (16) 75.00 150.00
- 1 Gene Achtymichuk 3.00 6.00
- 2 Bob Beckett 6.00 12.00
- 3 Marcel Bonin 7.50 15.00
- 4 Joe Crozier 10.00 20.00
- 5 Jacque Gagne 3.00 6.00
- 6 Dick Gamelle 3.00 6.00
- 7 Floyd Hillman 6.00 12.00
- 8 Jean Paul Lamonde 3.00 6.00
- 9 Jean-Marie Loisette 3.00 6.00
- 10 Brent MacNab 3.00 6.00
- 11 Al Millar 3.00 6.00
- 12 Willie O'Ree 15.00 30.00
- 13 Nick Tabuchie 3.00 6.00
- 14 Skip Teal 3.00 6.00
- 15 Orval Tessier 7.50 15.00
- 16 Judges Tremblay 5.00 10.00

1962-63 Quebec Aces

- COMPLETE SET (21) 50.00 100.00
- 1 Ronald Attwell 2.00 4.00
- 2 Serge Aubry 3.00 6.00
- 3 Guy Black 2.00 4.00
- 4 Skippy Burchell 2.00 4.00
- 5 Jean Marie Cossette 2.00 4.00
- 6 Robert Courcy 2.00 4.00
- 7A Bill Dineen UER (Misspelled Dinenn 6.00 12.00
- 7B Bill Dineen COR 7.50 15.00
- 8 Terry Gray 5.00 10.00
- 9 Reggie Grigg 2.00 4.00
- 10 John Hanna 2.00 4.00
- 11 Michel Harvey 2.00 4.00
- 12 Charlie Hodge 12.50 25.00
- 13 Ed Hoekstra 3.00 6.00
- 14 Michel Labadie 2.00 4.00
- 15 Claude Labrosse 2.00 4.00
- 16 Danny Lewicki 4.00 8.00
- 17 Frank Martin 2.00 4.00
- 18 Jim Morrison 3.00 6.00
- 19 Guy Rousseau 2.00 4.00
- 20 Dollard St. Laurent 5.00 10.00
- 21 Bill Sutherland 4.00 8.00

1963-64 Quebec Aces

- COMPLETE SET (23) 75.00 150.00
- 1 Gilles Banville 1.50 3.00
- 2 Don Blackburn 1.50 3.00
- 3 Skippy Burchell 1.50 3.00
- 4 Billy Carter 1.50 3.00
- 5 Floyd Curry CO 5.00 10.00
- 6 Bill Dineen 5.00 10.00
- 7 Wayne Freitag 1.50 3.00
- 8 Jean Gauthier 1.50 3.00
- 9 Terry Gray 2.50 5.00
- 10 John Hanna 1.50 3.00
- 11 Doug Harvey 15.00 30.00
- 12 Wayne Hicks 1.50 3.00
- 13 Charlie Hodge 7.50 15.00
- 14 Charlie Hodge 7.50 15.00
- 15 Ed Hoekstra 2.50 5.00
- 16 Frank Martin 1.50 3.00
- 17 Rene LaCasse 1.50 3.00
- 18 Cleland Mortson 1.50 3.00
- 19 Gerry O'Drowski 2.50 5.00
- 20 Rino Robazzo 2.50 5.00
- 21 Leon Rochefort 1.50 3.00
- 22 Cliff Pennington 2.50 5.00
- 23 Lorne Worsley 17.50 35.00

1964-65 Quebec Aces

- COMPLETE SET (19) 62.50 125.00
- 1 Gilles Banville 1.50 3.00
- 2 Red Berenson 5.00 10.00
- 3 Don Blackburn 1.50 3.00
- 4 Jean Guy Gendron 4.00 8.00
- 5 Bernard Geoffrion 15.00 30.00
- 6 Terry Gray 4.00 8.00
- 7 John Hanna 1.50 3.00
- 8 Doug Harvey 12.50 25.00
- 9 Wayne Hicks 1.50 3.00
- 10 Edward Hoekstra 2.50 5.00
- 11 Rene Lacasse 1.50 3.00
- 12 Raymond Larose 1.50 3.00
- 13 Jimmy Morrison 2.50 5.00
- 14 Cleland Mortson 1.50 3.00
- 15 Leon Rochefort 4.00 8.00
- 16 Guy Rousseau 1.50 3.00
- 17 Bill Sutherland 2.00 4.00
- 18 Brian Watson 2.00 4.00
- 19 Lorne Worsley 12.50 25.00

1965-66 Quebec Aces

- COMPLETE SET (19) 37.50 75.00
- 1 Gilles Banville 1.50 3.00
- 2 Gary Bauman 1.50 3.00
- 3 Don Blackburn 1.50 3.00
- 4 Jean-Guy Gendron 2.50 5.00
- 5 Bernard Geoffrion CO 12.50 25.00
- 6 Terry Gray 2.50 5.00
- 7 John Hanna 1.50 3.00
- 8 Wayne Hicks 1.50 3.00
- 9 Ed Hoekstra 2.50 5.00
- 10 Don Johns 1.50 3.00
- 11 Gordon Labossiere 2.50 5.00
- 12 Yvon Lacoste 1.50 3.00
- 13 Jimmy Morrison 2.50 5.00
- 14 Cleland Mortson 1.50 3.00
- 15 Simon Nolet 4.00 8.00
- 16 Noel Price 2.50 5.00
- 17 Rino Robazzo 2.50 5.00
- 18 Leon Rochefort 2.50 5.00
- 19 Bill Sutherland 2.50 5.00

1950 Quebec Citadelles

- COMPLETE SET (20) 200.00 400.00
- 1 Neil Amadio 5.00 10.00
- 2 Jean Beliveau 125.00 250.00
- 3 Georges Bergeron CO 4.00 8.00
- 4 Bruce Cline 6.00 12.00
- 5 Norm Diviney 4.00 8.00
- 6 Guy Gervais 4.00 8.00
- 7 Bernard Guay 4.00 8.00
- 8 Gord Haworth 5.00 10.00
- 9 Camille Henry 12.50 25.00
- 10 Gordie Hudson 4.00 8.00
- 11 Claude Larochelle 6.00 12.00
- 12 Bernie Lemonde 4.00 8.00
- 13 Paul-Emile Legault 4.00 8.00
- 14 Copper Leyte 4.00 8.00
- 15 Rainer Makila 5.00 10.00
- 16 Marcel Paille 12.50 25.00
- 17 Jean-Marie Plante 4.00 8.00
- 18 Claude Senechal 4.00 8.00
- 19 Jean Tremblay 12.50 25.00
- 20 Alphonses Gagnon CO 4.00 8.00

1999-00 Quebec Citadelles

- COMPLETE SET (26) 4.80 12.00
- 1 Mike McBain .15 .40
- 2 Gennady Razin .15 .40
- 3 Chris Albert .15 .40
- 4 Xavier Delisle .15 .40
- 5 Darcy Harris .15 .40
- 6 Marc Beaucage .15 .40
- 7 Stephane Robidas .15 .40
- 8 Jason Ward .30 .75
- 9 Francois Groleau .15 .40
- 10 Jonathan Delisle .15 .40
- 11 Stephane Roy .15 .40
- 12 Patrice Tardif .30 .75
- 13 Pierre Sevigny .30 .75
- 14 Jesse Belanger .15 .40
- 15 Eric Fichaud .30 .75
- 16 Andre Bashkirov .15 .40
- 17 Mathieu Garon .60 1.50
- 18 Dave Morissette .15 .40
- 19 Miloslav Guren .15 .40
- 20 Matthieu Descoteaux .15 .40
- 21 Jeff Shevalier .15 .40
- 22 Josh DeWolf .15 .40
- 23 Boyd Olson .15 .40
- 24 Matt Higgins .15 .40
- 25 Arron Asham .20 .50
- NNO Quebec Citadelles .08 .25

2000-01 Quebec Citadelles

- COMPLETE SET (24) 6.00 15.00
- 1 Gennady Razin .20 .50
- 2 Eric Chouinard .40 1.00
- 3 Francois Beauchemin .20 .50
- 4 Xavier Delisle .20 .50
- 5 Marc Beaucage .20 .50
- 6 Jason Ward .30 .75
- 7 Matt Higgins .20 .50
- 8 Mike McBain .20 .50
- 9 Miloslav Guren .20 .50
- 10 Pierre Sevigny .20 .50
- 11 Michael Ryder .75 2.00
- 12 Jonathan Delisle .20 .50
- 13 Eric Fichaud .30 .75
- 14 Andrei Bashkirov .30 .75
- 15 Mathieu Garon .60 1.50
- 16 Matt O'Dette .20 .50
- 17 Mathieu Raby .20 .50
- 18 Barry Richter .20 .50
- 19 Matthieu Descoteaux .20 .50
- 20 Josh DeWolf .20 .50
- 21 Eric Bertrand .20 .50
- 22 Arron Asham .30 .75
- 23 Mike Ribeiro .40 1.00
- NNO Team CL .10 .25

2000-01 Quebec Citadelles Signed

- COMPLETE SET (24) 30.00 75.00
- 1 Gennady Razin 1.20 3.00
- 2 Eric Chouinard 4.00 10.00
- 3 Francois Beauchemin 1.20 3.00
- 4 Xavier Delisle 1.20 3.00
- 5 Marc Beaucage 1.20 3.00
- 6 Jason Ward 2.00 5.00
- 7 Matt Higgins 1.20 3.00
- 8 Mike McBain 1.20 3.00
- 9 Miloslav Guren 1.20 3.00
- 10 Pierre Sevigny 1.20 3.00
- 11 Michael Ryder 8.00 20.00
- 12 Jonathan Delisle 1.20 3.00
- 13 Eric Fichaud 1.20 3.00
- 14 Andrei Bashkirov 1.20 3.00
- 15 Mathieu Garon 6.00 15.00
- 16 Matt O'Dette 1.20 3.00
- 17 Mathieu Raby 1.20 3.00
- 18 Barry Richter 1.20 3.00
- 19 Matthieu Descoteaux 1.20 3.00
- 20 Josh DeWolf 1.25 3.00
- 21 Eric Bertrand 1.20 3.00
- 22 Arron Asham 1.20 3.00
- 23 Mike Ribeiro 4.00 10.00
- NNO Team CL .10 .25

2001-02 Quebec Citadelles

- COMPLETE SET (28) 8.00 20.00
- 1 Gennady Razin .20 .50
- 2 Eric Chouinard .30 .75
- 3 Eric Landry .20 .50
- 4 Ron Hainsey .40 1.00
- 5 Jason Ward .20 .50
- 6 Craig Darby .20 .50
- 7 Marc-Andre Thinel .30 .75
- 8 Martti Jarventie .20 .50
- 9 Francois Bouillon .30 .75
- 10 Francis Belanger .20 .50
- 11 Francois Beauchemin .20 .50
- 12 Pierre Sevigny .20 .50
- 13 Michael Ryder .40 1.00
- 14 Jonathan Delisle .20 .50
- 15 Vadim Tarasov .40 1.00
- 16 Mathieu Garon .40 1.00
- 17 Matt O'Dette .20 .50
- 18 Luc Belanger .30 .75
- 19 Jayme Filipowicz .20 .50
- 20 Mathieu Descoteaux .20 .50
- 21 Benoit Gratton .20 .50
- 22 Timo Vertala .20 .50
- 23 Arron Asham .20 .50
- 24 Andrei Markov .20 .50
- 25 Xavier Delisle .20 .50
- 26 Mike Ribeiro .30 .75
- 27 Marcel Hossa 1.50 4.00
- 28 Title Card/CL .04 .10

1992 Quebec Pee-Wee Tournament

- COMPLETE SET (1903) 50.00 125.00
- 495 Daniel Tkaczuk .75 2.00
- 560 J-P Dumont 1.25 3.00
- 777 J.F. Damphousse .75 2.00
- 836 Steve Begin .75 2.00
- 1002 Bobby Allen .75 2.00
- 1120 Chris Bala .75 2.00
- 1403 David Aebischer 2.00 5.00
- 1464 Dainius Zubrus .40 1.00
- 1576 Mike York 1.25 3.00
- 1741 Robert Dome .40 1.00
- 1776 Sergei Samsonov 4.00 10.00

1993 Quebec Pee-Wee Tournament

- COMPLETE SET (1808) 80.00 200.00
- COMMON CARD (1-1808) .02 .10
- 15 Sebastien Caron 1.25 3.00
- 116 Eric Chouinard .60 1.50
- 301 Frederic Brindamour .40 1.00
- 342 Simon Gagne 10.00 25.00
- 348 Jean-Francois Damphousse 1.25 3.00
- 432 Sebastien Caron 1.25 3.00
- 523 Alex Tanguay 8.00 20.00
- 562 Daniel Tkaczuk .75 2.00
- 565 Peter Sarno .40 1.00
- 597 Paul Mara 1.25 3.00
- 664 Tim Connolly 2.00 5.00
- 704 Niklos Tselios .30 .75
- 877 Brian Gionta 3.00 8.00
- 903 Jonathan Girard .40 1.00
- 911 Eric Bertrand .20 .50
- 1053 Philippe Sauve 2.50 6.00
- 1152 Mike Comrie 2.00 5.00
- 1227 Jason Labarbera .75 2.00
- 1391 Mike Ribeiro 2.50 6.00
- 1398 Patrick Desrosiers .75 2.00
- 1408 Adam Colagiacomo .75 2.00
- 1417 Michael Ryder 2.00 5.00
- 1529 Gregor Baumgartner .20 .50
- 1554 Marian Hossa 12.00 30.00
- 1560 Robert Dome .40 1.00
- 1704 Ladislav Nagy 2.00 5.00
- 1717 Jan Lasak .75 2.00
- 1775 Sascha Goc 2.00 5.00
- NNO Manon Rheaume 2.00 5.00

1993 Quebec Pee-Wee Tournament Gold

- COMPLETE SET (3) 4.80 12.00
- 1 Brad Park .75 2.00
- 2 Manon Rheaume 4.00 10.00
- NNO Guy Chouinard .40 1.00

1994 Quebec Pee Wee Tournament

- COMPLETE SET (1853) 60.00 150.00
- COMMON CARD (1-1853) .01 .05
- 11 Vincent Lecavalier 10.00 25.00
- 246 John-Michael Liles 1.50 4.00
- 345 Eric Chouinard .40 1.00
- 418 Ramzi Abid .40 1.00
- 497 Mathieu Chouinard .40 1.00
- 512 Phillipe Sauve 1.25 3.00
- 565 Seamus Kotyk .40 1.00
- 573 Rico Fata .40 1.00
- 617 Jonathan Girard .40 1.00
- 628 Martin Grenier .40 1.00
- 649 Tim Connolly .75 2.00
- 806 Justin Papineau .60 1.50
- 888 David Legwand 1.25 3.00
- 902 Junior Lessard 1.50 4.00
- 934 Marcel Rodman .40 1.00
- 1025 Norm Milley .75 2.00
- 1077 Simon Gagne 4.00 10.00
- 1148 Maxime Ouellet 1.25 3.00
- 1169 Jordan Krestanovich .40 1.00
- 1182 Brian Eklund .75 2.00
- 1202 Freddy Meyer .75 2.00
- 1211 Rick DiPietro 4.00 10.00
- 1256 Michael Ryan .40 1.00
- 1607 Dominic Moore .75 2.00
- 1717 Sheldon Keefe .40 1.00
- 1752 Mathieu Biron .40 1.00

1995 Quebec Pee Wee Tournament

- COMPLETE SET (1825) 50.00 125.00
- COMMON CARD (1-1825) .01 .05
- 1 Jozef Balej .40 1.00
- 109 Brandon Reid 1.25 3.00
- 234 Simon Gamache .75 2.00
- 278 Antoine Vermette 2.00 5.00
- 378 Maxime Ouellet .75 2.00
- 448 Marc-Andre Thinel .75 2.00
- 516 Tim Connolly .75 2.00
- 552 Zenon Konopka .40 1.00
- 607 Dusty Jamieson .40 1.00
- 608 Michael Leighton 1.25 3.00
- 617 Jamie Chamberlain .40 1.00
- 692 Justin Williams 1.50 4.00
- 762 Andy Hilbert .75 2.00
- 764 Damian Surma .40 1.00
- 834 Luke Sellars .40 1.00
- 1054 Craig Andersson .75 2.00
- 1153 Alexandre Giroux .40 1.00
- 1205 Luca Cereda .40 1.00
- 1243 Ron Hainsey 1.25 3.00
- 1318 Jason Pominville 2.00 5.00
- 1438 Jamie Lundmark .75 2.00

1996 Quebec Pee Wee Tournament

- COMPLETE SET (1474) 50.00 125.00
- COMMON CARD (1-1474) .01 .05
- 1 Jozef Balej .40 1.00
- 2 Michal Barinka .40 1.00
- 16 Daniel Boisclair .75 2.00
- 23 Bobby Goeppert 1.50 4.00
- 32 Ryan Shannon .75 2.00
- 166 Brett Lebda .75 2.00
- 245 Jared Aulin 1.25 3.00
- 328 Pascal Leclaire 2.00 5.00
- 333 Yanick Lehoux .75 2.00
- 335 Jason Pominville 1.50 4.00

531 Rob Globke 1.00 2.50
560 J-F Racine 1.25 3.00
578 Gregory Campbell 1.25 3.00
668 Tim Gleason 1.50 4.00
678 Jim Slater .75 2.00
680 Kris Vernarsky .75 2.00
720 Jay Bouwmeester 6.00 15.00
899 Michael Komisarek 2.00 5.00
975 Sean McMorrow .75 2.00
992 Alexandre Vermette 1.50 4.00
1174 Michael Cammalleri 2.00 5.00
1227 M-A Pouliot 2.00 5.00
1288 Charline Labonte 2.00 5.00
1406 Scottie Upshall 2.00 5.00

1997 Quebec Pee Wee Tournament

COMMON CARD .05
284 Stephen Werner .40 1.00
290 Scottie Upshall 1.50 4.00
820 Eric Nystrom 2.00 5.00
831 Chris Higgins 2.00 5.00
835 Bobby Goeppert 1.00 2.50
1113 Oliver Setzinger .40 1.00
1118 Thomas Vanek 10.00 25.00
1126 Tobias Stephan 1.50 4.00
1165 Ryan Whitney 2.00 5.00
1234 Sean Collins .40 1.00
1384 Marcel Goc 1.25 3.00

1998 Quebec Pee Wee Tournament

157 Ryan Kesler 3.00 10.00
544 Danny Richmond .40 1.00
1032 Igor Mirnov .40 1.00
1225 Christopher Campoli 1.50 4.00

1999 Quebec Pee Wee Tournament Collection Souvenir

COMPLETE SET (30) 16.00 40.00
1 Brad Park .40 1.00
2 Guy Chouinard .08 .25
3 Manon Rheaume 1.25 3.00
4 Patrick Roy 4.00 10.00
5 Joe Juneau .20 .50
6 Sergei Samsonov 1.25 3.00
7 Dainius Zubrus .20 .50
8 Robert Dome .08 .25
9 Daniel Tkaczuk .20 .50
10 Alex Tanguay 1.25 3.00
11 Jean-Marc Pelletier .40 1.00
12 Oleg Kvasha .20 .50
13 Steve Begin .08 .25
14 Daniel Corso .20 .50
15 Sacha Goc .20 .50
16 Marian Hossa 2.00 5.00
17 Paul Mara .40 1.00
18 J-F Damphousse .40 1.00
19 Philippe Sauve .75 2.00
20 Gregor Baumgartner .08 .25
21 Ladislav Nagy .75 2.00
22 Vincent Lecavalier 2.00 5.00
23 David Legwand .75 2.00
24 Rico Fata .40 1.00
25 Mathieu Chouinard .40 1.00
26 Eric Chouinard .40 1.00
27 Mathieu Biron .20 .50
28 Simon Gagne 1.50 4.00
29 Mike Ribeiro .40 1.00
30 Jonathan Girard .40 1.00

2000 Quebec Pee Wee Tournament

COMPLETE SET
1276 Evan McGrath .75 2.00
1347 Robbie Schremp 4.00 10.00

1980-81 Quebec Remparts

COMPLETE SET (22) 10.00 20.00
1 Marc Bertrand .30 .75
2 Jacques Chouinard .30 .75
3 Roger Cote .30 .75
4 Gaston Drapeau CO .20 .50
5 Claude Drouin .30 .75
6 Gaetan Duchesne .75 2.00
7 Scott Fraser .40 1.00
8 Jean-Marc Lanthier .40 1.00
9 Jean Paul Lariviere .30 .75
10 Andre Larocque .30 .75
11 Roberto Lavoie .30 .75
12 Marc Lemay .30 .75
13 Stephane Lessard .30 .75
14 Paul Levesque .30 .75
15 Richard Linteau .30 .75
16 Patrice Masse .30 .75
17 David Pretty .30 .75
18 Guy Riel .30 .75
19 Daniel Rioux .30 .75
20 Roberto Romano .75 2.00
21 Michel Therrien .75 2.00
22 Gilles Tremblay .60 1.50

1998-99 Quebec Remparts

COMPLETE SET (25) 16.00 40.00
1 David Archambault .20 .50
2 David Bernier .20 .50
3 Nicholas Bilotto .20 .50
4 Tommy Bolduc .20 .50
5 Eric Chouinard .75 2.00
6 Ray Dalton .20 .50
7 Joey Fetta .20 .50
8 Simon Gagne 6.00 15.00
9 Martin Grenier .40 1.00
10 Eric Laplante .20 .50
11 Jeff Leblanc .20 .50
12 Pierre Loiselle .20 .50
13 Jerome Marois .20 .50
14 Andre Martineau .20 .50
15 Martin Moise .20 .50
16 Alexandre Morel .20 .50
17 Maxime Ouellet 4.00 10.00
18 Sylvain Plamondon .20 .50
19 Wesley Scanzano .20 .50
20 Simon Tremblay .20 .50
21 Dmitri Tolkunov .75 2.00
22 Antoine Vermette 1.25 3.00
23 Jonathan Wilhelmy .20 .50
24 Travis Zachary .20 .50
25 Title Card .02 .10

1998-99 Quebec Remparts Signed

COMPLETE SET (25) 40.00 100.00
1 David Archambault 1.25 3.00
2 David Bernier 1.25 3.00
3 Nicholas Bilotto 1.25 3.00
4 Tommy Bolduc 1.25 3.00
5 Eric Chouinard 4.80 10.00
6 Ray Dalton 1.25 3.00
7 Joey Fetta 1.25 3.00
8 Simon Gagne 15.00 40.00
9 Martin Grenier 2.00 5.00
10 Eric Laplante 1.25 3.00
11 Jeff Leblanc 1.25 3.00
12 Pierre Loiselle 1.25 3.00
13 Jerome Marois 1.25 3.00
14 Andre Martineau 1.25 3.00
15 Martin Moise 1.25 3.00
16 Alexandre Morel 1.25 3.00
17 Maxime Ouellet 10.00 25.00
18 Sylvain Plamondon 1.25 3.00
19 Wesley Scanzano 1.25 3.00
20 Simon Tremblay 1.25 3.00
21 Dmitri Tolkunov 2.00 5.00
22 Antoine Vermette 4.00 10.00
23 Jonathan Wilhelmy 1.25 3.00
24 Travis Zachary 1.25 3.00
25 Title Card .08 .25

1999-00 Quebec Remparts

COMPLETE SET (25) 5.00 12.00
1 Jean Mallette .15 .40
2 Patrick Chouinard .15 .40
3 Kirill Safronov .30 .75
4 Eric Chouinard .40 1.00
5 Patrick Grandmaitre .15 .40
6 Eric Laplante .15 .40
7 Wesley Scanzano .15 .40
8 Chris Lyness .15 .40
9 Tommy Bolduc .15 .40
10 Jean-Francois Touchette .15 .40
11 Philippe Paris .15 .40
12 Karl Morin .15 .40
13 Andre Martineau .15 .40
14 Sylvain Plamondon .15 .40
15 Martin Moise .15 .40
16 Martin Grenier .30 .75
17 Andre Hart .15 .40
18 Maxime Ouellet 1.25 3.00
19 Martin Pare .15 .40
20 Eric Cloutier .15 .40
21 Kristian Kudroc .30 .75
22 Casey Leggett .15 .40
23 Shawn Collymore .20 .50
24 Mike Ribeiro .75 2.00
25 Header Card/CL .02 .10

1999-00 Quebec Remparts Signed

COMPLETE SET (25) 30.00 75.00
1 Jean Mallette .75 2.00
2 Patrick Chouinard .75 2.00
3 Kirill Safronov 2.00 5.00
4 Eric Chouinard 4.00 10.00
5 Patrick Grandmaitre .75 2.00
6 Eric Laplante .75 2.00
7 Wesley Scanzano .75 2.00
8 Chris Lyness .75 2.00
9 Tommy Bolduc .75 2.00
10 Jean-Francois Touchette .75 2.00
11 Philippe Paris .75 2.00
12 Karl Morin .75 2.00
13 Andre Martineau .75 2.00
14 Sylvain Plamondon .75 2.00
15 Martin Moise .75 2.00
16 Martin Grenier 2.00 5.00
17 Andre Hart .75 2.00
18 Maxime Ouellet 8.00 20.00
19 Martin Pare .75 2.00
20 Eric Cloutier .75 2.00
21 Kristian Kudroc 2.00 5.00
22 Casey Leggett .75 2.00
23 Shawn Collymore 1.25 3.00
24 Mike Ribeiro 6.00 15.00
25 Header Card/CL .08 .25

2000-01 Quebec Remparts

COMPLETE SET (24) 4.80 12.00
1 Jean Mallette .20 .50
2 Sebastian Bourgon .20 .50
3 Richard Paul .20 .50
4 David Boilard .20 .50
5 Jeff Hadley .20 .50
6 Remi Bergeron .20 .50
7 Sebastian Morissette .20 .50
8 Philippe Paris .20 .50
9 Justin Stewart .20 .50
10 Yannick Searles .20 .50
11 Mike Bray .20 .50
12 Guillaume Fournier .20 .50
13 Robert Pearce .20 .50
14 Petr Preucil .20 .50
15 Philippe Parent .20 .50
16 Didier Bochatay .20 .50
17 Scott Della Vedova .30 .75
18 Alexandre Reuben .20 .50
19 David Masse .20 .50
20 Shawn Collymore .20 .75
21 Guillaume Berube .20 .50
22 Kevin Lachance .30 .75
23 Cory Urquhart .20 .50
NNO Team CL .04 .10

2000-01 Quebec Remparts Signed

COMPLETE SET (24) 14.00 35.00
2 Sebastian Bourgon .80 2.00
3 Richard Paul .80 2.00
5 Jeff Hadley .80 2.00
6 Remi Bergeron .80 2.00
7 Sebastian Morissette .80 2.00
8 Philippe Paris .80 2.00
9 Justin Stewart .80 2.00
10 Yannick Searles .80 2.00
11 Mike Bray .80 2.00
12 Guillaume Fournier .80 2.00
13 Robert Pearce .80 2.00
14 Petr Preucil .80 2.00
15 Philippe Parent .80 2.00
17 Scott Della Vedova 2.00 5.00
20 Shawn Collymore .80 5.00
21 Guillaume Berube .80 2.00
22 Kevin Lachance 2.00 5.00
NNO Team CL .04 .25

2001-02 Quebec Remparts

COMPLETE SET (24) 5.00 12.00
1 Jean-Michel Bolduc .20 .50
2 Sebastien Bourgon .20 .50
3 Yan Turcotte .20 .50
4 Jeff Hadley .20 .50
5 Josh Hennessy .20 .50
6 Mark Hurtubise .20 .50
7 Mathieu Dery .20 .50
8 Robert Pearce .20 .50
9 Yannick Searles .20 .50
10 Mike Bray .20 .50
11 Tomas Spila .20 .50
12 Samuel Duplain .20 .50
13 Petr Preucil .20 .50
14 Daniel Houle .20 .50
15 Didier Bochatay .20 .50
16 Denis Berube .20 .50
17 Jeff MacAulay .20 .50
18 Mario Joly .20 .50
19 David Masse .20 .50
20 Shawn Collymore .20 .50
21 Guillaume Berube .20 .50
22 Kevin Lachance .20 .50
23 Sebastien Thinel .20 .50
24 Cory Urquhart .20 .50

2002-03 Quebec Remparts

COMPLETE SET (23) 8.00 20.00
1 Jean-Michel Bolduc .30 .75
2 Sebastien Bourgon .20 .50
3 Colin Ledaire .20 .50
4 Josh Hennessy .20 .50
5 Mark Hurtubise .20 .50
6 Vladimir Kutny .20 .50
7 Robert Pearce .20 .50
8 Jordan LaVallee .20 .50
9 Timofei Shishkanov .40 1.00
10 Jason Kostadine .20 .50
11 Curtis Tidball .20 .50
12 Frederic Faucher .20 .50
13 Karl St. Pierre .20 .50
14 Didier Bochatay .20 .50
15 Ben McMullin .30 .75
16 David Masse .20 .50
17 Shawn Collymore .30 .75
18 Guillaume Berube .20 .50
19 Steve Pelletier .20 .50
20 Kevin Lachance .30 .75
21 Pierre-Olivier Beaulieu .20 .50
22 Chris Montgomery .20 .50
U12 Evan Shaw .20 .50
U14 Jean-Michel Filiatrault .75 2.00
U15 Alexandre Rouleau .30 .75
U16 Aaron Johnson .20 .50
U17 Pierre Morvan .20 .50
U20 Benoit Beauchemin .20 .50
U21 Remy Tremblay .20 .50
U22 Checklist/Logo .04 .10
U23 Jamie McCabe .20 .50
NNO Checklist .04 .10

2003 Quebec Remparts Memorial Cup

COMPLETE SET (21) 6.00 15.00
1 Guillaume Berube .30 .75
2 Jean-Michel Bolduc .40 1.00
3 Sebastien Bourgon .30 .75
4 Frederic Faucher .30 .75
5 Jean-Michel Filiatrault 1.00 2.50
6 Josh Hennessy .30 .75
7 Aaron Johnson .30 .75
8 Jason Kostadine .30 .75
9 Vladimir Kutny .30 .75
10 Kevin Lachance .40 1.00
11 Jordan Lavallee .30 .75
12 David Masse .30 .75
13 Jamie McCabe .30 .75
14 Chris Montgomery .30 .75
15 Pierre Morvan .30 .75
16 Robert Pearce .30 .75
17 Alexandre Rouleau .40 1.00
18 Evan Shaw .30 .75
19 Timofei Shishkanov .30 1.25
20 Karl St.Pierre .30 .75
21 Curtis Tidball .30 .75

2003-04 Quebec Remparts

COMPLETE SET (28) 5.00 12.00
1 Andrew Andricopoulos .20 .50
2 Adam Blanchette .20 .50
3 Christian Brideau .20 .50
4 Tyler Chambers .20 .50
5 Jean-Michel Cote .30 .75
6 Kevin Coughlin .20 .50
7 Simon Courcelles .20 .50
8 Jean-Michel Filiatrault .40 1.00
9 Ian Girard .20 .50
10 Stephane Goulet .20 .50
11 Josh Hennessy .30 .75
12 Alexandre Imbeault .20 .50
13 Alexandre Kojevnikov .20 .50
14 Louis-Phillipe Lachance .20 .50
15 Jordan LaVallee .20 .50
16 Justin Laverdiere .20 .50
17 Maxime Lincourt .20 .50
18 Eric L'Italien .20 .50
19 Mathieu Melanson .20 .50
20 Corey Pastershank .20 .50
21 Robert Pearce .20 .50
22 Joey Ryan .20 .50
23 Evan Shaw .20 .50
24 Alexei Shkotov .20 .50
25 Brandon Tidball .20 .50
26 Marc-Edouard Vlasic .60 1.50
27 Nathan Welton .20 .50
28 Checklist
Title Card .04 .10

2004-05 Quebec Remparts

COMPLETE SET (25) 6.00 15.00
1 Gennady Churilov .20 .50
2 Jordan LaVallee .20 .50
3 Karl Gagne .20 .50
4 Maxime Lacroix .20 .50
5 Maxime Lincourt .20 .50
6 Simon Courcelles .20 .50
7 Andrew Andricopoulos .20 .50
8 Ian Girard .20 .50
9 Maxime Joyal .20 .50
10 Alexander Radulov 1.50 4.00
11 Brandon Tidball .40 1.00
12 Marc-Edouard Vlasic 1.25 3.00
13 Max Gratchev .20 .50
14 Josh Hennessy .40 1.00
15 Mathieu Melanson .20 .50
16 Drew Paris .20 .50
17 Jonathan Alain-Rochette .20 .50
18 Joey Ryan .20 .50
19 Sebastien Bernier .20 .50
20 Kevin Coughlin .20 .50
21 Jonathan Boutin .30 .75
22 Alexandre Mineault .20 .50
23 Michael Tessier .20 .50
24 Guillaume Veilleux .20 .50
25 Evan Shaw .20 .50

2005-06 Quebec Remparts

COMPLETE SET (25) 10.00 18.00
1 Angelo Esposito 2.00 5.00
2 Alexander Radulov .75 2.00
3 Stephen Valente .20 .50
4 Joey Ryan .20 .50
5 Drew Paris .20 .50
6 Michal Sersen .20 .50
7 Simon Coucelles .20 .50
8 Felix Petit .20 .50
9 Maxime Lacroix .20 .50
10 Alexandre Mineault .20 .50
11 Max Gratchev .20 .50
12 Andrew Andricopoulos .20 .50
13 Jordan Lavallee .20 .50
14 Cedrick Desjardins .30 .75
15 Kevin Desfosses .20 .50
16 Kenzie Sheppard .20 .50
17 Nicolas Robillard .20 .50
18 Pierre Bergeron .20 .50
19 Brent Aubin .20 .50
20 Christophe Poirier .20 .50
21 Guillaume Veilleux .20 .50
22 Marc-Edouard Vlasic .20 .50
23 Todd Chinova .20 .50
24 Yan Ouimet .20 .50
25 Mathieu Melanson .20 .50

2006-07 Quebec Remparts

COMPLETE SET (27) 12.00 20.00
1 Angelo Esposito 2.00 5.00
2 Andrew Andricopoulos .20 .50
3 Joey Ryan .20 .50
4 Pierre Bergeron .20 .50
5 Kelsey Tessier .40 1.00
6 Roman Bashkirov .40 1.00
7 Hubert Genest .20 .50
8 Felix Petit .20 .50
9 Brent Aubin .40 1.00
10 Maxime Sauve .20 .50
11 Loic Lacasse .20 .50
12 Alexandre Mineault .20 .50
13 Ruslan Bashkirov .40 1.00
14 Billy Bezeau .20 .50
15 Kevin Desfosses .40 1.00
16 Boby Fugere .20 .50
17 Maxime Lacroix .20 .50
18 Christophe Poirier .20 .50
19 Philippe Poirier .20 .50
20 Joel Roch .20 .50
21 Benjamin Rubin .20 .50
22 Kenzie Sheppard .20 .50
23 Matthew Smith .40 1.00
24 Marc-Olivier Vallerand .20 .50
25 Guillaume Veilleux .20 .50
26 Mathieu Lavoie .20 .50
EL2 Brent Aubin .20 .50

2015-16 Quebec Remparts

COMPLETE SET (26) 6.00 15.00
1 Bronson Beaton .30 .75
2 Callum Booth .30 .75
3 Matthew Boucher .30 .75
4 Nikolas Brouillard .30 .75
5 Massimo Carozza .30 .75
6 Alexandre Drapeau .30 .75
7 Aaron Dutra .30 .75
8 Julian Galloway .30 .75
9 Olivier Garneau .30 .75
10 Derek Gentile .30 .75
11 Charley Graaskamp .30 .75
12 Christian Huntley .30 .75
13 Auguste Impase .30 .75
14 Ross MacDougall .30 .75
15 Raphael Maheux .30 .75
16 Austin McEneny .30 .75
17 Ryan McReynolds .30 .75
18 Zachery Moody .30 .75
19 Matt Murphy .30 .75
20 Sean O'Brien .30 .75
21 Mikael Robidoux .30 .75
22 Jesse Sutton .30 .75
23 Lucas Thierus .30 .75
24 Dmytro Timashov .30 .75
25 Yanick Turcotte .30 .75
26 Dakotah Woods .30 .75

1992-93 Raleigh Icecaps

COMPLETE SET (38) 6.00 15.00
1 Cappy Bear (Mascot) .02 .10
2 Sean Cowan .20 .50
3 Joel Gardner .20 .50
4 Bill Kovacs .20 .50
5 Alan Leggett .20 .50
6 Kirby Lindal .20 .50
7 Derek Linnell .20 .50
8 Jim Mill .20 .50
9 Kris Miller .20 .50
10 Todd Person .20 .50
11 Chic Pojar .20 .50
12 Jim Powers .20 .50
13 Stan(Smokey) Reddick .30 .75
14 Doug Roberts .20 .50
15 Jeff Robison .20 .50
16 Jeff Tomlinson .20 .50
17 Brian Tulik .20 .50
18 Bruno Villeneuve .20 .50
19 Lyle Wildgoose .20 .50
20 Team Photo DP .15 .40
21 Bruno Villeneuve .20 .50
22 Jeff Robison .20 .50
23 Jim Powers .20 .50
24 Derek Linnell .20 .50
25 Chris Marshall .20 .50
26 Kris Miller .20 .50
27 Joel Gardner .20 .50
28 Stan(Smokey) Reddick .30 .75
29 Jim Mill .20 .50
30 Alan Leggett .20 .50
31 Brian Tulik .20 .50
32 Kirby Lindal .20 .50
33 Sean Cowan .20 .50
34 Lyle Wildgoose .20 .50
35 Todd Person .20 .50
36 Chic Pojar .20 .50
37 Mike Lappin .20 .50
38 Doug Bacon .20 .50

1993-94 Raleigh Icecaps

COMPLETE SET (20) 3.00 8.00
1 Ralph Barahona .15 .40
2 Rick Barkovich .15 .40
3 Matt Delguidice .20 .50
4 Martin D'Orsonnens .15 .40
5 Jamie Erb .15 .40
6 Chad Erickson .20 .50
7 Donevan Hextall .20 .50
8 Shaun Kane .15 .40
9 Al Leggett .15 .40
10 Derek Linnell .15 .40
11 Joe McCarthy .15 .40
12 Chris Nelson .15 .40
13 Barry Nieckar .15 .40
14 Jim Powers .15 .40
15 Stan Reddick .20 .50
16 Kevin Riehl .15 .40
17 Jeff Robison .15 .40
18 David Shute .15 .40
19 Lyle Wildgoose .15 .40
20 Kurt Kleinendorst CO .08 .25

1994-95 Raleigh Icecaps

COMPLETE SET (19) 3.00 8.00
1 John Blessman .20 .50
2 Rick Barkovich CO .08 .25
3 Alexsandr Chunchukov .20 .50
4 Frank Cirone .20 .50
5 Brett Duncan .20 .50
6 Anton Fedorov .20 .50
7 Todd Hunter .20 .50
8 Rodrigo Lavinsh .30 .75
9 Derek Linnell .20 .50
10 Eric Long UER .20 .50
11 Scott MacNair .20 .50
13 Brad Mullahy .20 .50
14 Lenny Pereira .20 .50
15 Jimmy Powers .20 .50
16 Chic Pojar .20 .50
17 Kevin Riehl .20 .50
18 Todd Reirden .30 .75
19 Justin Tomberlin UER .20 .50
20 Lyle Wildgoose .20 .50

1989-90 Rayside-Balfour Jr. Canadians

COMPLETE SET (20) 3.00 8.00
1 Team Photo .40 1.00
2 Dave Barrett .20 .50
3 Dan Baston .20 .50
4 Rick Chartrand .20 .50
5 Simon Chartrand .20 .50
6 Ron Clark .20 .50
7 Brian Dickinson .20 .50
8 Trevor Duncan .20 .50
9 Don Gauthier .20 .50
10 Shawn Hawkins .20 .50
11 Roy Hildebrandt .20 .50
12 Al Laginski .20 .50
13 Eric Lanteigne .20 .50
14 Mike Leblanc .20 .50
15 Kevin MacDonald .20 .50
16 Mike Mooney .20 .50
17 Rick Potvin .20 .50
18 Rick Poulin .20 .50
19 Steve Prior .20 .50
20 Scott Sutton .20 .50

1990-91 Rayside-Balfour Jr. Canadians

COMPLETE SET (23) 3.00 8.00
1 Dan Baston .15 .40
2 Jon Boeve .15 .40
3 Jordan Boyle .15 .40
4 Serge Coulombe .15 .40
5 Mike Dore .15 .40
6 Denis Gosselin .15 .40
7 Mike Gratton .15 .40
8 Jason Hall .15 .40
9 Grant Healey .15 .40
10 Marc Lafreniere .15 .40
11 Alain Leclair .15 .40
12 Mike Longo .15 .40
13 Troy Mallette
1985-86 rookie photo .30 .75
14 Matthew Mooney .15 .40
15 Virgil Nose .15 .40
16 Trevor Oystrick .15 .40
17 Steve Proceviat .15 .40
18 Chris Puskas .15 .40
19 Yvon Quenneville .15 .40
20 Michael Sullivan .20 .50
21 Trevor Tremblay .15 .40
22 Sean Van Amburg .15 .40
23 Title Card .02 .10

1991-92 Rayside-Balfour Jr. Canadians

COMPLETE SET (23) 3.00 8.00
1 Dan Baston .20 .50
2 Don Cucksey .20 .50
3 Dean Cull .20 .50
4 Mike Dore .20 .50
5 Denis Gosselin .20 .50
6 Jason Hall .20 .50
7 Grant Healey .20 .50
8 Marc Lafreniere .20 .50
9 Mike Longo .20 .50
10 Scott Maclellan .20 .50
11 Matt Mooney .20 .50
12 Rob Moxness .20 .50
13 Virgil Nose .20 .50
14 Trent Oystrick .20 .50
15 Jon Stewart .20 .50
16 Jon Stos .20 .50
17 Dave Sutton .20 .50
18 Scott Sutton .20 .50
19 Trevor Tremblay .20 .50
20 Jaak Valiots .20 .50
21 Sean Van Amburg .20 .50
22 Jason Young
Stickboy .02 .10
23 Title Card .02 .10

2002-03 Reading Royals

COMPLETE SET (32) 10.00 25.00
1 Series 1 Header Card .04 .10
2 Francois Drainville .40 1.00
3 David Lohrei CO .20 .50
4 Matt Snesrud .40 1.00
5 Ray DiLauro .40 1.00
6 Chris Bogas .40 1.00
7 Simon Tremblay .40 1.00
8 Jim Dube .40 1.00
9 Series 2 Header Card .04 .10
10 Jonathon Shockey .40 1.00
11 Colin Pepperall .40 1.00
12 Brad Rooney .40 1.00
13 Brandon Dietrich .40 1.00
14 Kris Waltze .40 1.00
15 Hunter Lahache .40 1.00
16 Jeff Giuliano .40 1.00
17 Series 3 Header Card .20 .50
18 Sean Gauthier .40 1.00
19 Steve Rymsha .40 1.00
20 Tom Rouleau .40 1.00
21 Geoff Peters .40 1.00
22 Duilio Grande .40 1.00
23 Keegan McAvoy .40 1.00
24 Brian McCullough .40 1.00
25 Series 4 Header Card .04 .10
26 Steve Shirreffs .40 1.00
27 Ryan Flinn .60 1.50
28 Scott Fankhouser .60 1.50
29 Jeff Sanger .40 1.00
30 Antoine Bergeron .40 1.00
31 Alex Kim .40 1.00
32 Dan Riva .40 1.00

2002-03 Reading Royals RBI Sports

COMPLETE SET (18) 8.00 20.00
169 Antoine Bergeron .40 1.00
170 Craig Brunel .40 1.00
171 Brandon Dietrich .40 1.00
172 Ray DiLauro .40 1.00
173 Jim Dube .40 1.00
174 Jeff Giuliano .40 1.00
175 Duilio Grande .40 1.00
176 Alex Kim .40 1.00
177 Brian McCullough .40 1.00
178 Colin Pepperall .40 1.00
179 Dan Riva .40 1.00
180 Brad Rooney .40 1.00
181 Remi Royer .75 2.00
182 Tom Rouleau .40 1.00
183 Steve Rymsha .40 1.00
184 Jeff Sanger .75 2.00
185 Mat Snesrud .40 1.00
186 Simon Tremblay .40 1.00

2003-04 Reading Royals

COMPLETE SET (30) 12.00 30.00
1 Header Card Series One .04 .10
2 Derek Clancey .40 1.00
3 Adam Hauser 1.25 3.00
4 Mat Snesrud .40 1.00
5 Jason Maleyko .40 1.00
6 Tomas Slovak .40 1.00
7 Jonathan Zion .40 1.00
8 Leon Hayward .40 1.00
9 Header Card Series Two .04 .10
10 Judd Medak .40 1.00
11 David Masse .40 1.00
12 Nick Lent .40 1.00
13 Jeff Finger .40 1.00
14 Francis Nault .40 1.00
15 Graig Mischler .40 1.00
16 Header Card Series Three .04 .10
17 Peter Hay .40 1.00
18 Ian Turner .40 1.00
19 Kent Davyduke .40 1.00
20 Dean Arsene .40 1.00
21 Darryl Laplante .40 1.00
22 Dave Stewart .75 2.00
23 Header Card Series Four .04 .10
24 Mascot .04 .10
25 Reading Royals .04 .10
26 Brad Church .40 1.00
27 Cody Rudkowsky .75 2.00
28 Terry Denike .75 2.00
29 Matt Passfield .40 1.00
30 Doug Nolan .40 1.00

2003-04 Reading Royals RBI Sports

COMPLETE SET (18) 6.00 15.00
289 Brad Church .40 1.00
290 Kent Davyduke .40 1.00
291 Peter Hay .40 1.00
292 Leon Hayward .40 1.00
293 Nick Lent .40 1.00
294 Jason Maleyko .40 1.00
295 Judd Medak .40 1.00
296 Graig Mischler .40 1.00
297 Francis Nault .40 1.00
298 Doug Nolan .40 1.00
299 Matt Passfield .40 1.00
300 Cody Rudkowsky .60 1.50
301 Tomas Slovak .40 1.00
302 Scooter Smith .40 1.00
303 Mat Snesrud .40 1.00
304 Ian Turner .40 1.00
305 David Belitski .60 1.50
306 Josh Barker .40 1.00

2005-06 Reading Royals

COMPLETE SET (19) 8.00 15.00
1 Chris Bala .30 .75
2 Doug Christiansen .30 .75
3 Larry Courville .30 .75
4 Jon Francisco .30 .75
5 Yutaka Fukufuji .75 2.00
6 Tyler Hanchuck .30 .75
7 T.J. Kemp .30 .75
8 Mike Kompon .30 .75
9 Malcolm MacMillan .30 .75
10 John Morlang .30 .75
11 Reagan Rome .30 .75
12 Dany Roussin .60 1.50
13 Cody Rudkowsky .60 1.50
14 Jeff State .30 .75
15 Shay Stephenson .30 .75
16 Eric Werner .30 .75
17 Karl Taylor HC .02 .10
18 Slapshot MASCOT .02 .10
19 Reading Royals .02 .10

2006-07 Reading Royals

COMPLETE SET (18) 15.00 30.00
1 Rob Lalonde .75 2.00
2 Shawn German .60 1.50
3 Taylor Christie .60 1.50
4 Reagan Rome .60 1.50
5 Jason Becker .60 1.50
6 Malcolm Macmillan 1.00 2.50
7 Shawn Collymore .60 1.50
8 Joe Zappala .60 1.50
9 John Snowden .60 1.50
10 Jon Francisco .60 1.50
11 Dany Roussin .60 1.50
12 Ned Lukacevic .60 1.50
13 Kevin Saurette .60 1.50
14 Greg Hogeboom .60 1.50
15 Chris Bala .60 1.50
16 Jeff Pietrasiak .75 2.00
17 Yutaka Fukufuji 2.00 5.00
18 Karl Taylor CO .20 .50

2007-08 Reading Royals

COMPLETE SET (22) 4.00 10.00
1 Terry Denike .25 .60
2 Rob LaLonde .25 .60
3 Patrik Hersley .25 .60
4 Shawn Germain .25 .60
5 Victor Uchevatov .25 .60
6 Steven Later .25 .60
7 Ned Lukacevic .25 .60
8 Malcolm MacMillan .25 .60
9 Joe Zappala .25 .60
10 Chris Blight .25 .60
11 Patrick Jarrett .25 .60
12 Dany Roussin .25 .60
13 Brock Hooton .25 .60
14 Mike Salekin .25 .60
15 Kevin Saurette .25 .60
16 Matt Herneisen .25 .60
17 Marc Cavosie .25 .60
18 Brian Boulay .25 .60
19 Charlie Kronschnabel .25 .60
20 Jon Quick .25 .60
21 PJ Atherton .25 .60
22 Karl Taylor .25 .60

2014-15 Reading Royals

COMPLETE SET (27) 8.00 20.00
1 Brandon Alderson .30 .75
2 Michael Caruso .40 1.00
3 Willie Coetzee .30 .75
4 Adam Comrie .30 .75
5 Larry Courville CO .30 .75
6 Ryan Cruthers .30 .75
7 Zach Davies .30 .75
8 Brett Flemming .30 .75
9 Matt Hatch .30 .75
10 Jordan Heywood .30 .75
11 Adam Hughesman .30 .75
12 Andrew Johnston .30 .75
13 Connor Knapp .30 .75
14 Olivier Labelle .30 .75
15 Maxim Lamarche .30 .75
16 Mike Marcou .30 .75
17 David Marshall .30 .75
18 Derek Mathers .30 .75
19 Bryant Molle .30 .75
20 Pat Mullane .30 .75
21 Martin Ouellette .30 .75
22 Cam Reid .30 .75
23 Kevin Walrod .30 .75
24 Ian Watters .30 .75
25 Sean Wiles .30 .75
26 Slapshot MASCOT .30 .75
27 Tiara MASCOT .30 .75

1993-94 Red Deer Rebels

COMPLETE SET (30) 4.00 10.00
1 Peter Anholt CO .02 .10
2 Byron Briske .15 .40
3 Curtis Cardinal .15 .40
4 Jason Clague .15 .40
5 Dale Donaldson .15 .40
6 Dave Greenway .15 .40
7 Scott Grimwood TR .02 .10
8 Sean Halifax .15 .40
9 Chris Kibermanis .15 .40
10 Pete LeBoutillier .15 .40
11 Pete LeBoutillier
In Ac .15 .40
12 Terry Lindgren .15 .40
13 Chris Maillet .15 .40
14 Eddy Marchant .15 .40
15 Mike McBain .15 .40
16 Mike Moller ACO .02 .10
17 Andy Nowicki ACO .02 .10
18 Berkley Pennock .15 .40
19 Tyler Quiring .15 .40
20 Craig Reichert .15 .40
21 Ken Richardson .15 .40
22 Sean Selmser .15 .40

23 Vaclav Slansky .15 .40
24 Mark Toljanich .15 .40
25 Darren Van Impe .20 .50
26 Pete Vandermeer .30 .75
27 Chris Wickenheiser .20 .50
28 Brad Zimmer .15 .40
29 Jonathan Zukiwsky .15 .40
30 The Centrum .02 .10

1995-96 Red Deer Rebels

COMPLETE SET (24) 4.00 10.00
1 Arron Asham .15 .40
2 Bryan Boorman .15 .40
3 Aleksei Boudaev .15 .40
4 Mike Broda .15 .40
5 Mike Brown .20 .50
6 Jay Henderson .30 .75
7 David Hruska .15 .40
8 Chris Kibermanis .15 .40
9 Brad Leeb .30 .75
10 Terry Lindgren .15 .40
11 Mike McBain .20 .50
12 Brent McDonald .15 .40
13 Ken McKay .15 .40
14 Harlan Pratt .15 .40
15 Greg Schmidt .15 .40
16 Pete Vandermeer .30 .75
17 Jesse Wallin .20 .50
18 Lance Ward .20 .50
19 Mike Whitney .15 .40
20 Chris Wickenheiser .30 .75
21 B.J. Young .15 .40
22 Jonathan Zukiwsky .20 .50
23 Drug Awareness Team .02 .10
24 Team Picture .15 .40

1996-97 Red Deer Rebels

COMPLETE SET (29) 6.00 15.00
1 Collector Series Card .01 .05
2 Team Photo .08 .25
3 Mike McBain .20 .50
4 Jesse Wallin .20 .50
5 Arron Asham .40 1.00
6 Kyle Kos .20 .50
7 Jonathan Zukiwsky .20 .50
8 Stephen Peat .75 2.00
9 Brent McDonald .20 .50
10 Greg Schmidt .20 .50
11 Chris Ovington .20 .50
12 Martin Tomasek .20 .50
13 Brad Rohrig .20 .50
14 Devin Francon .20 .50
15 B.J. Young .20 .50
16 Mike Broda .20 .50
17 Matt Van Horlick .20 .50
18 Mike Brown .20 .50
19 Lance Ward .20 .50
20 Kris Knoblauch .20 .50
21 Brad Leeb .20 .50
22 Garnet Stevenson .20 .50
23 Lloyd Shaw .20 .50
24 Mike Whitney .20 .50
25 Jesse Wallin .20 .50
26 Lance Ward .20 .50
27 The Centrum .02 .10
28 Drug Awareness .02 .10
29 Rowdy MASCOT .02 .10

1997-98 Red Deer Rebels

COMPLETE SET (25) 5.00 12.00
1 Team photo .15 .40
2 Arron Asham .30 .75
3 Andrew Bergen .15 .40
4 Joel Boschman .15 .40
5 Chris Cederstrand .15 .40
6 Devin Francon .15 .40
7 John Kachur .15 .40
8 Kyle Kos .15 .40
9 Brad Leeb .15 .40
10 Justin Mapletoft .60 1.50
11 Brent McDonald .15 .40
12 Shawn McNeil .15 .40
13 Scott McQueen .15 .40
14 Frank Mrazek .20 .50
15 Cam Ondrik .15 .40
16 Chris Ovington .15 .40
17 Stephen Peat .60 1.50
18 Brad Rohrig .15 .40
19 Robert Schnabel .20 .50
20 Jesse Wallin .30 .75
21 Lance Ward .30 .75
22 Mike Whitney .15 .40
23 Jon Zukiwsky .20 .50
24 Woolly Bully MASCOT .02 .10
25 Drug Awareness .01 .05

1998-99 Red Deer Rebels

COMPLETE SET (24) 5.00 12.00
1 Jay Batchelor .20 .50
2 Lukas Bednarik .20 .50
3 Andrew Bergen .20 .50
4 Michael Clague .30 .75
5 Andrew Coates .20 .50
6 Devin Francon .20 .50
7 Kyle Kos .20 .50
8 Brad Leeb .20 .50
9 Justin Mapletoft .60 1.50
10 Kevin Marsh .20 .50
11 Brett McDonald .20 .50
12 Shawn McNeil .20 .50
13 Scott McQueen .20 .50
14 Frank Mrazek .20 .50
15 Rhett Nevill .20 .50
16 Chris Ovington .20 .50
17 Stephen Peat .60 1.50
18 Dustin Schwartz .30 .75
19 Jeff Smith .20 .50
20 Jim Vandermeer .20 .50
21 Justin Wallin .20 .50
22 Jordan Watt .30 .75
23 Wooly Bully MASCOT .02 .10
24 Drug Awareness Card .01 .05

2000-01 Red Deer Rebels

COMPLETE SET (24) 4.80 15.00
1 Checklist .04 .10
2 Colby Armstrong .40 1.50
3 Shane Bendera .40 1.00
4 Andrew Bergen .16 .40
5 Devin Francon .16 .40
6 Michael Garnett .16 .40
7 Boyd Gordon .16 .40
8 Shane Grypiuk .16 .40
9 Diarmuid Kelly .16 .40
10 Ladislav Kouba .16 .40
11 Ross Lupaschuk .30 .75
12 Doug Lynch .30 .75
13 Justin Mapletoft .60 1.50
14 Derek Meech .16 .40
15 Donovan Rattray .16 .40
16 Jeff Smith .16 .40
17 Shay Stephenson .16 .40
18 Joel Stepp .16 .40
19 Bryce Thoma .16 .40
20 Jim Vandermeer .16 .75
21 Martin Vymazal .16 .40
22 Justin Wallin .16 .40
23 Kyle Wanvig .60 1.50
24 Jeff Woywitka .40 1.50

2000-01 Red Deer Rebels Signed

COMPLETE SET (24) 24.00 60.00
1 Checklist .04 .10
2 Colby Armstrong 3.00 8.00
3 Shane Bendera 2.00 5.00
4 Andrew Bergen .80 2.00
5 Devin Francon .80 2.00
6 Michael Garnett .80 2.00
7 Boyd Gordon .80 2.00
8 Shane Grypiuk .80 2.00
9 Diarmuid Kelly .80 2.00
10 Ladislav Kouba .80 2.00
11 Ross Lupaschuk 2.00 5.00
12 Doug Lynch 2.00 5.00
13 Justin Mapletoft 3.00 7.50
14 Derek Meech .80 2.00
15 Donovan Rattray .80 2.00
16 Jeff Smith .80 2.00
17 Shay Stephenson .80 2.00
18 Joel Stepp .80 2.00
19 Bryce Thoma .80 2.00
20 Jim Vandermeer .80 3.00
21 Martin Vymazal .80 2.00
22 Justin Wallin .80 2.00
23 Kyle Wanvig 3.00 7.50
24 Jeff Woywitka 2.00 8.00

2001-02 Red Deer Rebels

COMPLETE SET (21) 6.00 15.00
1 Cover Card .04 .10
2 Colby Armstrong .40 1.00
3 Shane Bendera .40 1.00
4 Andrew Bergen .20 .50
5 Derek Endicott .20 .50
6 Jason Ertl .20 .50
7 Colin Fraser .20 .50
8 Boyd Gordon .40 1.00
9 Diarmuid Kelly .20 .50
10 Ladislav Kouba .20 .50
11 Doug Lynch .30 .75
12 Derek Meech .30 .75
13 Chris Neiszner .20 .50
14 Joel Rupprecht .20 .50
15 Jeff Smith .20 .50
16 Shay Stephenson .20 .50
17 Joel Stepp .20 .50
18 Bryce Thoma .20 .50
19 Cam Ward 4.00 10.00
20 Mikhail Yakubov .40 1.00
21 Woolly Bully MAS .04 .10

2002-03 Red Deer Rebels

COMPLETE SET (26) 15.00 40.00
1 Cam Ward
CL 2.00 5.00
2 Derek Meech .40 1.00
3 Dion Phaneuf 6.00 15.00
4 Bryce Thoma .20 .50
5 Jeff Woywitka .40 1.00
6 Cody Holzapfel .20 .50
7 Masi Marjamaki .40 1.00
8 Matt Ellison .20 .50
9 Joel Stepp .20 .50
10 Colin Fraser .30 .75
11 Blair Jones .20 .50
12 Jason Ertl .20 .50
13 Jared Walker .20 .50
14 Derek Endicott .20 .50
15 Carsen Germyn .20 .50
16 Boyd Gordon .40 1.00
17 Stuart Kerr .20 .50
18 Ladislav Kouba .20 .50
19 Matt Keith .20 .50
20 Diarmuid Kelly .20 .50
21 Shay Stephenson .20 .50
22 Nathan Brice .20 .50
23 Jesse Zetariuk .20 .50
24 Chris Neiszner .20 .50
25 Cam Ward 2.00 5.00
26 Adam Jennings .30 .75

2003-04 Red Deer Rebels

COMPLETE SET (24) 10.00 25.00
1 Derek Meech .30 .75
2 Dion Phaneuf 6.00 15.00
3 Paul Kurceba .20 .50
4 Dan Mercer .20 .50
5 Mikko Kuukka .20 .50
6 Andre Herman .20 .50
7 Colin Fraser .30 .75
8 Kyle Ross .20 .50
9 Jason Ertl .20 .50
10 Jared Walker .20 .50
11 Derek Endicott .20 .50
12 Justin Taylor .20 .50
13 Ted Vandermeer .20 .50
14 Stuart Kerr .30 .75
15 Blair Jones .20 .50
16 Shay Stephenson .20 .50
17 Nathan Brice .20 .50
18 Jesse Zetariuk .20 .50
19 Chris Neiszner .20 .50
20 Cam Ward 1.50 4.00
21 Trevor Peeters .30 .75
22 Wooly Bully MASCOT .04 .10
23 Brent Sutter CO .20 .50
24 Team Photo .20 .50

2005-06 Red Deer Rebels

COMPLETE SET (25) 8.00 15.00
1 Brennan Chapman .20 .50
2 Matthew Cline .20 .50
3 Luke Egener .20 .50
4 Eric Frere .20 .50
5 Tanner Gillies .20 .50
6 Matthew Hansen .20 .50
7 Garrett Klotz .20 .50
8 Jordan Knackstedt .20 .50
9 Pierre-Paul Lamoureux .20 .50
10 Devon LeBlanc .20 .50
11 Andrew Leslie .40 1.00
12 Vladimir Mihalik .20 .50
13 Karey Pieper .20 .50
14 Alex Poulter .20 .50
15 James Reimer .20 .50
16 Justin Scott .20 .50
17 Jonathon Smith .20 .50
18 Brandon Sutter 1.00 2.50
19 Brett Sutter .40 1.00
20 Ted Vandermeer .20 .50
21 Kris Versteeg 2.00 5.00
22 Roman Wick .20 .50
23 Mike Berube .20 .50
24 Josh Bray .20 .50
25 Red Deer Rebels CL .01 .01

2014-15 Red Deer Rebels

1 Conner Bleackley .30 .75
2 Brayden Burke .30 .75
3 Taz Burman .30 .75
4 Nick Charif .30 .75
5 Brett Cote .30 .75
6 Kolton Dixon .30 .75
7 Kayle Doetzel .30 .75
8 Devan Fafard .30 .75
9 Scott Feser .30 .75
10 Haydn Fleury .50 1.25
11 Mario Grman .30 .75
12 Wyatt Johnson .30 .75
13 Presten Kopeck .30 .75
14 Josh Mahura .30 .75
15 Brooks Maxwell .30 .75
16 Mason McCarty .30 .75
17 Adam Musil .30 .75
18 Meyer Nell .30 .75
19 Grayson Pawlenchuk .30 .75
20 Evan Polei .30 .75
21 Tyler Sandhu .30 .75
22 Austin Shmoorkoff .30 .75
23 Austin Strand .30 .75
24 Rylan Toth .30 .75
25 Jeff de Wit .30 .75
26 Header Card .30 .75

1981-82 Regina Pats

COMPLETE SET (25) 12.00 30.00
1 Pats Logo .20 .50
2 Garth Butcher .75 2.00
3 Lyndon Byers 2.00 5.00
4 Jock Callander 1.50 4.00
5 Marc Centrone .40 1.00
6 Dave Goertz .40 1.00
7 Evans Dobni .40 1.00
8 Dale Derkatch .40 1.00
9 Jeff Crawford .40 1.00
10 Jim Clarke .40 1.00
11 Jayson Meyer .40 1.00
12 Gary Leeman .75 2.00
13 Bruce Holloway .40 1.00
14 Ken Heppner .40 1.00
15 Taylor Hall .40 1.00
16 Wally Schreiber .60 1.50
17 Kevin Pylypow .40 1.00
18 Ray Plamondon .40 1.00
19 Brent Pascal .40 1.00
20 Dave Michayluk .60 1.50
21 Barry Trotz .40 1.00
22 Al Tuer .60 1.50
23 Tony Vogel .40 1.00
24 Martin Wood .40 1.00
25 Regina Police Logo .20 .50

1982-83 Regina Pats

COMPLETE SET (25) 10.00 25.00
1 Regina Pats and
Police Logo .08 .25
2 Todd Lumbard .40 1.00
3 Jamie Reeve .40 1.00
4 Dave Goertz .30 .75
5 John Miner .30 .75
6 Doug Trapp .30 .75
7 R.J. Dundas .30 .75
8 Stu Grimson 1.50 4.00
9 Al Tuer .30 .75
10 Rick Herbert .30 .75
11 Tony Vogel .30 .75
12 John Bekkers .30 .75
13 Dale Derkatch .60 1.50
14 Gary Leeman .75 2.00
15 Nevin Markwart .40 1.00
16 Kurt Wickenheiser .30 .75
17 Jeff Frank .30 .75
18 Marc Centrone .30 .75
19 Taylor Hall .30 .75
20 Lyndon Byers 1.50 4.00
21 Jayson Meyer .30 .75
22 Jeff Crawford .30 .75
23 Don Boyd CO .20 .50
24 Barry Trapp ACO .20 .50
25 K-9 Big Blue (Mascot) .08 .25

1983-84 Regina Pats

COMPLETE SET (25) 8.00 20.00
1 Title Card .08 .25
2 Todd Lumbard .40 1.00
3 Jamie Reeve .40 1.00
4 Dave Goertz .30 .75
5 John Miner .30 .75
6 Doug Trapp .30 .75
7 R.J. Dundas .30 .75
8 Stu Grimson 1.25 3.00
9 Al Tuer .30 .75
10 Rick Herbert .30 .75
11 Tony Vogel .30 .75
12 John Bekkers .30 .75
13 Dale Derkatch .40 1.00
14 Gary Leeman .60 1.50
15 Nevin Markwart .40 1.00
16 Kurt Wickenheiser .30 .75
17 Jeff Frank .30 .75
18 Marc Centrone .30 .75
19 Taylor Hall .30 .75
20 Lyndon Byers 1.25 3.00
21 Jayson Meyer .30 .75
22 Jeff Crawford .30 .75
23 Don Boyd CO .20 .50
24 Barry Trapp ACO .20 .50
25 K-9 Big Blue (Mascot) .08 .25

1986-87 Regina Pats

COMPLETE SET (30) 6.00 15.00
1 Troy Bakogeorge .20 .50
2 Grant Chorney .20 .50
3 Gary Dickie .20 .50
4 Milan Dragicevic .20 .50
5 Mike Dyck .20 .50
6 Craig Endean .20 .50
7 Mike Gibson .20 .50
8 Erin Ginnell .20 .50
9 Brad Hornung .20 .50
10 Mark Janssens .30 .75
11 K-9 (Mascot) .08 .25
12 Trent Kachur .20 .50
13 Craig Kalawsky .20 .50
14 Dan Logan .20 .50
15 Jim Mathieson .20 .50
16 Darin McInnes .20 .50
17 Darrin McKechnie .20 .50
18 Rob McKinley .30 .75
19 Brad Miller .20 .50
20 Stacy Nickel .20 .50
21 Cregg Nicol .20 .50
22 Len Nielsen .20 .50
23 Darren Parsons .20 .50
24 Doug Sauter .20 .50
25 Ray Savard .20 .50
26 Dennis Sobchuk .30 .75
27 Chris Tarnowski .20 .50
28 Mike Van Slooten .20 .50
29 Brian Wilkie .20 .50
30 Rod Williams .20 .50

1987-88 Regina Pats

COMPLETE SET (28) 4.80 12.00
1 Kevin Clemens .20 .50
2 Gary Dickie .20 .50
3 Milan Dragicevic .20 .50
4 Mike Dyck .20 .50
5 Craig Endean .20 .50
6 Kevin Gallant PR .08 .25
7 Jamie Heward .20 .50
8 Rod Houk .30 .75
9 Mark Janssens .30 .75
10 Trent Kachur .20 .50
11 Craig Kalawsky .20 .50
12 K-9 (Mascot) .08 .25
13 Frank Kovacs .20 .50
14 Darren Kwiatkowski .20 .50
15 Brian Leibel .20 .50
16 Tim Logan .20 .50
17 Jim Mathieson .20 .50
18 Darrin McKechnie .20 .50
19 Rob McKinley .20 .50
20 Brad Miller .20 .50
21 Cregg Nicol .20 .50
22 Doug Sauter CO .08 .25
23 Dan Sexton .20 .50
24 Mike Sillinger .40 1.00
25 Dennis Sobchuk .30 .75
26 Stanley Szumlak TR .08 .25
27 Mike Van Slooten .20 .50
28 Team Photo .20 .50

1988-89 Regina Pats

COMPLETE SET (24) 4.80 12.00
1 Shane Bogden .20 .50
2 Cam Brauer .20 .50
3 Scott Daniels .25 .60
4 Gary Dickle .20 .50
5 Mike Dyck .20 .50
6 Dave Gerse .20 .50
7 Kevin Haller .25 .60
8 Jamie Heward .20 .50
9 Terry Hollinger .20 .50
10 Rod Houk .20 .50
11 Frank Kovacs .20 .50
12 Brian Leibel .20 .50
13 Bernie Lynch CO .20 .50
14 Kelly Markwart .20 .50
15 Jim Mathieson .30 .75
16 Brad Mcginnis .20 .50
17 Brad Miller .20 .50
18 Dwayne Montieth TR .08 .25
19 Curtis Nykyforuk .20 .50
20 Darren Parsons .20 .50
21 Cory Paterson .20 .50
22 Jeff Sebastian .20 .50
23 Mike Sillinger .30 .75
24 Chad Silver .20 .50
25 Jamie Splett .20 .50

1989-90 Regina Pats

COMPLETE SET (21) 4.00 10.00
1 Kelly Chotowetz .20 .50
2 Hal Christiansen .20 .50
3 Scott Daniels .25 .60
4 Wade Fennig .20 .50
5 Jason Glickman .20 .50
6 Kevin Haller .30 .75
7 Jamie Heward .30 .75
8 Terry Hollinger .20 .50
9 Frank Kovacs .20 .50
10 Mike Kirby .20 .50
11 Kelly Markwart .20 .50
12 Jim Mathieson .30 .75
13 Cam McLellan .20 .50
14 Troy Mick .20 .50
15 Greg Pankewicz .20 .50
16 Cory Paterson .20 .50
17 Garry Pearce .20 .50
18 Mike Risdale .20 .50
19 Colin Ruck .20 .50
20 Mike Sillinger .30 .75
21 Jamie Splett .20 .50
22 Heath Weenk .20 .50

1996-97 Regina Pats

COMPLETE SET (25) 7.20 15.00
1 Josh Holden .30 .75
2 Curtis Tipler .15 .40
3 Shane Lanigan .15 .40
4 Brad Stuart 1.25 3.00
5 David Maruca .15 .40
6 Perry Johnson .15 .40
7 Chad Mercier .15 .40
8 Kyle Calder .40 1.00
9 Josh Dobbyn .15 .40
10 Aaron Mori .15 .40
11 Gerad Adams .15 .40
12 Boyd Kane .20 .50
13 Lars Pattersen .15 .40
14 Dean Arsene .15 .40
15 Andy Adams .15 .40
16 Derek Morris .75 2.00
17 Kyle Freadrich .20 .50
18 Bryan Randall .15 .40
19 Clint Orr .15 .40
20 Brett Lysak .30 .75
21 Joey Bouvier .15 .40
22 Cody Jensen .15 .40
23 Rich Preston CO .08 .25
24 Team Photo .15 .40
25 Dmitri Nabokov .15 .40

1997-98 Regina Pats

COMPLETE SET (25) 7.20 20.00
1 Gerad Adams .20 .50
2 Kyle Calder .75 2.00
3 Boyd Kane .30 .75
4 Brett Lysak .30 .75
5 Kevin Saurette .20 .50
6 Travis Churchman .20 .50
7 Dean Arsene .20 .50
8 Barret Jackman 2.00 5.00
9 Scott Roles .20 .50
10 John Cirjak .20 .50
11 Ronald Petrovicky .30 .75
12 Kyle Freadrich .30 .75
13 David Maruca .20 .50
14 Drew Kehler .20 .50
15 Bryan Randall .20 .50
16 Joey Bouvier .20 .50
17 Cody Jensen .20 .50
18 Shane Lanigan .20 .50
19 Mark Thompson .20 .50
20 Dennis Bassett .20 .50
21 Chris Kwas .20 .50
22 Derek Morris .75 2.00
23 Aaron Mori .20 .50
24 Brad Stuart 1.25 3.00
25 Josh Holden .40 1.00

2001-02 Regina Pats

COMPLETE SET (24) 10.00 25.00
1 Curtis Austring .40 1.00
2 Chad Bassen .40 1.00
3 Corey Becker .40 1.00
4 Dean Beuker .40 1.00
5 Drew Callender ACO .04 .10
6 Brennan Chapman .40 1.00
7 Chad Davidson .75 2.00
8 Jeff Feniak .40 1.00
9 Josh Harding .75 2.00
10 Grant Jacobsen .40 1.00
11 Kevin Korol .40 1.00
12 Kyle Ladobruk .40 1.00
13 Bob Lowes CO .10 .25
14 David McDonald .40 1.00
15 Chad Mercier ACO .04 .10
16 Tyson Moulton .40 1.00
17 Garth Murray .75 2.00
18 Filip Novak .75 2.00
19 Zach Roe .40 1.00
20 Chris Schlenker .40 1.00
21 Eric Sonnenberg .40 1.00
22 Matej Trojovsky .40 1.00
23 Daniel Waschuk .40 1.00
24 Darryl Yacboski .40 1.00

2002-03 Regina Pats

COMPLETE SET (23) 8.00 20.00
1 Grant Jacobsen .30 .75
2 Matt Trojovsky .30 .75
3 Petr Dvorak .30 .75
4 Matt Hubbauer .30 .75
5 •Darryl Yacboski .30 .75
6 Jesse Deckert .30 .75
7 Todd Davison .30 .75
8 Rick Rypien .40 1.00
9 David Graden .30 .75
10 Wade Davis .30 .75
11 Britt Dougherty .30 .75
12 Curtis Austring .30 .75
13 Kyle Ladobruk .30 .75
14 Codey Becker .30 .75
15 Chris Schlenker .30 .75
16 Tyson Mulock .30 .75
17 Daniel Waschuk .30 .75
18 David McDonald .30 .75
19 Jordan McGillivary .30 .75
20 Brennan Chapman .30 .75
21 Tyson Moulton .40 1.00
22 Kyle Fecho .30 .75
23 Josh Harding 1.25 3.00

2003-04 Regina Pats

COMPLETE SET (24) 5.00 12.00
1 Paul Albers .20 .50
2 Craig Lineker .20 .50
3 Kyle Deck .20 .50
4 Derek Reinhart .20 .50
5 Landon Jones .20 .50
6 Tanner Stockwell .20 .50
7 Lance Morrison .20 .50
8 Rick Rypien .30 .75
9 David McDonald .20 .50
10 Kyle Lamb .20 .50
11 Dan Waschuk .20 .50
12 Ivo Kratena .20 .50
13 Kamil Vavra .20 .50
14 Kyle Nason .20 .50
15 Chris Schlenker .20 .50
16 Codey Becker .20 .50
17 Jonathan Bubnick .20 .50
18 Mike O'Dwyer .20 .50
19 Jordan McGillivray .20 .50
20 Andrew DeSousa .20 .50
21 Nick Olynyk .20 .50
22 Jesse Deckert .20 .50
23 Josh Harding .75 2.00
24 Britt Dougherty .20 .50

2004-05 Regina Pats

COMPLETE SET (24) 5.00 12.00
1 Regina Pats CL .04 .10
2 Paul Albers .20 .50
3 Craig Lineker .20 .50
4 Kyle Deck .20 .50
5 Derek Reinhart .20 .50
6 Logan Pyett .20 .50
7 Rick Rypien .30 .75
8 Kyle Ross .20 .50
9 Justin Bernhardt .20 .50
10 Braden Appleby .20 .50
11 Dan Waschuk .20 .50
12 Ryan McDonald .20 .50
13 Ian Duval .20 .50
14 Kyle Nason .20 .50
15 Terrance Delaronde .20 .50
16 Brent Hill .20 .50
17 Jonathan Bubnick .20 .50
18 Jordan McGillivray .20 .50
19 Jan Zapletal .20 .50
20 David Reekie .20 .50
21 Jordan Fuder .20 .50
22 Dustin Slade .20 .50
23 Craig Schira .20 .50
24 Preston Mosewich .20 .50

2005-06 Regina Pats

COMPLETE SET (28) 8.00 15.00
1 Justin Bernhardt .20 .50
2 Kyle Deck .20 .50
3 Ian Duval .20 .50
4 Garrett Festerling .20 .50
5 Spencer Fraipont .20 .50
6 Jordan Fuder .20 .50
7 Shane Halifax .20 .50
8 Petr Kalus .60 1.50
9 Brett Leffler .20 .50
10 Levi Lind .20 .50
11 Jason MacDonald .20 .50
12 Jordan McGillivray .20 .50
13 Curtis Patterson .20 .50
14 Logan Pyett .20 .50
15 David Reekie .40 1.00
16 Derek Reinhart .20 .50
17 Matt Robinson .20 .50
18 Kyle Ross .20 .50
19 Nick Ross .20 .50
20 Linden Rowatt .40 1.00
21 Andy Schenn .20 .50
22 Craig Schira .20 .50
23 Michael Senseman .20 .50
24 Tyson Sievert .20 .50
25 Denis Tolpeko .20 .50
26 Ryan McDonald .20 .50
27 Matt MacDermott .20 .50
28 Joshua Fauth .20 .50

2006-07 Regina Pats

COMPLETE SET (23) 12.00 20.00
1 Justin Bernhardt .40 1.00
2 Scott Brownlee .40 1.00
3 Kyle Deck .40 1.00
4 Matt Delahey .40 1.00
5 Ian Duval .40 1.00
6 Jordan Eberle .75 2.00
7 Garrett Festerling .40 1.00
8 Derek Hulak .40 1.00
9 Jared Jagow .40 1.00
10 Brett Leffler .40 1.00
11 Levi Lind .40 1.00
12 Jason MacDonald .40 1.00
13 Ryan McDonald .40 1.00
14 Logan Pyett .40 1.00
15 Derek Reinhart .40 1.00
16 Kyle Ross .40 1.00
17 Nick Ross .40 1.00
18 Linden Rowatt .60 1.50
19 Craig Schira .40 1.00
20 Justin Scott .40 1.00
21 Niko Snellman .40 1.00
22 Colten Teubert .40 1.00
23 Regina Pats .10 .25

2014-15 Regina Pats

COMPLETE SET (22) 6.00 15.00
1 Adam Brooks .30 .75
2 Tyler Brown .30 .75
3 Braden Christoffer .30 .75
4 Rykr Cole .30 .75
5 Taylor Cooper .30 .75
6 Patrick D'Amico .30 .75
7 Jesse Gabrielle .30 .75
8 Carter Hansen .30 .75
9 Chase Harrison .30 .75
10 James Hilsendager .30 .75
11 Connor Hobbs .40 1.00
12 Colton Kroeker .30 .75
13 Ryan Krushen .30 .75
14 Jared McAmmond .30 .75
15 Nathyn Mortlock .30 .75
16 Pavlo Padakin .30 .75
17 Luc Smith .30 .75
18 Sam Steel .30 .75
19 Austin Wagner .30 .75
20 Daniel Wapple .30 .75
21 Colby Williams .30 .75
22 Sergey Zborovskiy .30 .75

1996 RHI Inaugural Edition

COMPLETE SET (19) 1.25 3.00
1 Los Angeles Blades .08 .25
2 Long Island Jaws .08 .25
3 Empire State Cobras .08 .25
4 Denver DareDevils .08 .25
5 Anaheim Bullfrogs .08 .25
6 Orlando Jackals .08 .25
7 Ottawa Loggers .08 .25
8 Oklahoma Coyotes .08 .25
9 Oakland Skates .08 .25
10 New Jersey Rockin Rollers .08 .25
11 Montreal Roadrunners .08 .25
12 Minnesota Arctic Blast .08 .25
13 Vancouver VooDoo .08 .25
14 St. Louis Vipers .08 .25
15 San Jose Rhinos .08 .25
16 San Diego Barracudas .08 .25
17 Sacramento River Rats .08 .25
18 Philadelphia Bulldogs .08 .25
NNO Checklist .02 .10

1984-85 Richelieu Riverains

COMPLETE SET (19) 4.80 12.00
1 Miguel Baldris .30 .75
2 Nicolas Beaulieu .30 .75
3 Martin Cote .30 .75
4 Sylvain Coutourier .40 1.00
5 Dominic Edmond .30 .75
6 Yues Gaucher .30 .75
7 Eric Gobel .30 .75
8 Carl Lemieux .30 .75
9 Michel Levesque .30 .75
10 Brad Loi .30 .75
11 Eric Primeau .30 .75
12 Stephane Quintal .60 1.50
13 Jean-Michel Ray .30 .75
14 Serge Richard .30 .75
15 Stephane Robinson .30 .75
16 Danny Rochefort .30 .75
17 Martin Savaria .30 .75
18 Sylvain Senecal .30 .75
19 Eric Sharron .30 .75

1988-89 Richelieu Riverains

COMPLETE SET (30) 4.80 12.00
1 Header Card .07 .20
2 Marc Beaurivage .20 .50
3 Denis Benoit .20 .50
4 Jonathan Black .20 .50
5 Richard Boisvert .20 .50
6 Hugues Bouchard .20 .50
7 Francois Bourdeau .20 .50
8 Guy Caplette .20 .50
9 Bertrand Cournoyer .20 .50
10 Yves Cournoyer .20 .50
11 Michel Deguise .20 .50
12 Patrick Grise .20 .50
13 Robert Guillet .20 .50
14 Jimmy Lachance .20 .50
15 Roger Laporte .20 .50
16 Frederic Lefebvre .20 .50
17 Frederic Maltais .20 .50
18 Andre Kid Millette .20 .50
19 Joseph Napolitano .20 .50
20 Remy Patoine .20 .50
21 Jean Plamondon .20 .50
22 Steve Plasse .20 .50
23 Jean Francois Poirier .20 .50
24 Jacques Provencal .20 .50
25 Alain Rancourt .20 .50
26 Francois St.Germain .20 .50
27 Frederic Savard .20 .50
28 Martin Tanguay .20 .50
29 Richard Valois .20 .50
30 Stephane Valois .20 .50

1990-91 Richmond Renegades

COMPLETE SET (18) 3.00 8.00
1 Brad Turner .20 .50
2 Victor Posa .20 .50
3 Antti Autere .20 .50
4 Phil Huber .20 .50
5 Steve Spott .20 .50
6 Kelly Mills .20 .50
7 Paul Cain .20 .50
8 Shawn Lillie .20 .50
9 Kirby Lindal .20 .50
10 Dave Aiken .20 .50
11 Terry McCutcheon .20 .50
12 Jordan Fois .20 .50
13 Brad Beck .20 .50
14 Doug Pickell .20 .50
15 Frank Lascala .20 .50
16 John Haley .20 .50
17 Peter Harris .20 .50
18 Chris McSorley CO .30 .75

1991-92 Richmond Renegades

COMPLETE SET (20) 3.60 9.00
1 Rob Vanderydt .20 .50
2 Larry Rooney .15 .40
3 Brendan Flynn .15 .40
4 Scott Drevitch .15 .40
5 Joni Lehto .15 .40
6 Todd Drevitch .15 .40
7 Paul Rutherford .15 .40
8 Dave Aiken .15 .40
9 Pat Bingham .15 .40
10 Trevor Jobe .15 .40
11 Bob Berg .15 .40
12 Mark Kuntz .15 .40
13 Joe Capprini .15 .40
14 Trevor Converse .15 .40
15 Steve Scheifele .15 .40
16 Jon Gustafson .20 .50
17 Marco Fuster .15 .40
18 Guy Gadowsky .15 .40
19 Dave Allison CO .08 .25
20 Jamie McLennan .40 1.00
NNO Large Team Photo .75 2.00

1992-93 Richmond Renegades

COMPLETE SET (20) 3.00 8.00
1 Will Averill .15 .40
2 Frank Bialowas .20 .50
3 Scott Drevitch .15 .40
4 Brendan Flynn .15 .40
5 Guy Gadowsky ACO .02 .10
6 Jon Gustafson .20 .50
7 Phil Huber .15 .40
8 Mike James .15 .40
9 Jeffery Kampersal .15 .40
10 Mark Kuntz .15 .40
11 Sean LeBrun .15 .40
12 Kevin Malgunas .15 .40
13 Jim McGeough .20 .50
14 Ed Sabo .15 .40
15 Jeff Saterdalen .15 .40
16 Alan Schuler .15 .40
17 Martin Smith .15 .40

18 Roy Sommer CO .02 .10
19 Jeff Torrey .15 .40
20 Ben Wyzansky .15 .40
NNO Large Team Photo 1.00 2.50

1993-94 Richmond Renegades
COMPLETE SET (20) 3.00 8.00
1 Ken Weiss .15 .40
2 Guy Phillips .15 .40
3 Alexander Zhdan .15 .40
4 Alan Schuler .15 .40
5 John Craighead .15 .40
6 Colin Gregor .15 .40
7 Rob MacInnis .15 .40
8 Devin Derksen .20 .50
9 Jason Renard .15 .40
10 Peter Allen .15 .40
11 Roy Sommer CO .08 .25
12 Milan Hnilicka .60 1.50
13 Oleg Santurian .15 .40
14 Brendan Flynn .15 .40
15 Ken Blum .15 .40
16 Steve Bogoyevac .15 .40
17 Eric Germain .15 .40
18 Chris Foy .15 .40
19 Darren Colbourne .15 .40
20 Jon Gustafson .20 .50

1994-95 Richmond Renegades
COMPLETE SET (20) 4.00 10.00
1 Andrew Shier .20 .50
2 Shane Henry .20 .50
3 Shawn Snesar .20 .50
4 Steve Bogoyevac .20 .50
5 Chris Foy .20 .50
6 Scott Gruhl .30 .75
7 Blaine Moore .20 .50
8 Don Lester .20 .50
9 Kurt Mallett .20 .50
10 Garett MacDonald .20 .50
11 Jay Murphy .20 .50
12 Darren Wetherill .20 .50
13 Grant Sjerven .20 .50
14 Jan Benda .30 .75
15 Lou Body .20 .50
16 Mike Taylor .20 .50
17 Sean O'Brien .20 .50
18 Chris Tucker .20 .50
19 Jason Currie .20 .50
20 Roy Sommer CO .08 .25

1995-96 Richmond Renegades
COMPLETE SET (25) 3.60 9.00
1 Greg Hadden .15 .40
2 Mike Taylor .15 .40
3 Jay Murphy .15 .40
4 Todd Sparks .15 .40
5 Lou Body .15 .40
6 Sandy Allan .30 .75
7 Darren Wetherill .15 .40
8 Brian Goudie .15 .40
9 Brendan Flynn .15 .40
10 Kurt Mallett .15 .40
11 Dmitri Pankov .15 .40
12 Steve Carpenter .15 .40
13 Jason Mallon .15 .40
14 Scott Gruhl .40 1.00
15 Trevor Senn .15 .40
16 Garett MacDonald .15 .40
17 Martin Roy .15 .40
18 Michael Burman .15 .40
19 Grant Sjerven .15 .40
20 Mike Morin .15 .40
21 Andy Davis Broadcaster .02 .10
22 The Gade Mascot .02 .10
23 Rob Jones TR .02 .10
24 Roy Sommer CO .02 .10
25 C.Laughlin GM H.Feuerstein CEO .02 .10

1996-97 Richmond Renegades
COMPLETE SET (25) 3.00 8.00
1 Scott Burfoot .20 .50
2 Taylor Clarke .15 .40
3 David Dartsch .15 .40
4 Freezer .02 .10
5 Gade .02 .10
6 Matt Garzone .15 .40
7 Brian Goudie .15 .40
8 Scott Gruhl CO .20 .50
9 Garry Gulash .15 .40
10 Mike Harding .15 .40
11 Tommy Holmes .15 .40
12 Rod Langway ACO .20 .50
13 Paul Lepler .15 .40
14 Jay McNeill .15 .40
15 Craig Paterson .15 .40
16 Chris Pittman .15 .40
17 Mike Rucinski .15 .40
18 Brian Secord .15 .40
19 Trevor Senn .15 .40
20 Grant Sjerven .15 .40
21 Andrew Shier .15 .40
22 Mike Taylor .15 .40
23 Tripp Tracy .30 .75
24 Jason Wright .15 .40
25 Title Card .02 .10

2000-01 Richmond Renegades
COMPLETE SET (19) 8.00 20.00
1 Gerad Adams .40 1.00
2 Brian Goudie .40 1.00
3 Nathan Forster .40 1.00
4 Joe Blaznek .40 1.00
5 Bob Thornton .40 1.00
6 Forrest Gore .40 1.00
7 Dan Vandermeer .40 1.00
8 Joe Vandermeer .40 1.00
9 Rod Taylor .40 1.00
10 Richard Pitirri .40 1.00
11 George Awada .40 1.00
12 Ryan Skaleski .40 1.00
13 Derek Schutz .40 1.00
14 Frank Novock .40 1.00
15 Matt Noga .40 1.00
16 Mike Siklenka .40 1.00
17 Sean Matile .60 1.50
18 Rastislav Stana .80 2.00
19 Brian McCullough .40 1.00

2006-07 Richmond Renegades
COMPLETE SET (20) 8.00 15.00
1 Jay Chrapala .40 1.00
2 Scott Corbett .30 .75
3 Brett Cross .30 .75
4 Andre Gill .30 .75
5 Mat Goody .75 2.00
6 Brian Goudie .30 .75
7 Doug Groenestege .40 1.00
8 Dean Jackson .30 .75
9 Don Melnyk .30 .75
10 David Mitchell .30 .75
11 Mike Owens .30 .75
12 Joe Pace .30 .75
13 Richard Reichenbach .30 .75
14 Tyler Schremp .30 .75
15 Danny White .30 .75
16 Duane Whitehead .30 .75
17 J.J. Wrobel .30 .75
18 Phil Youngclaus .30 .75
19 John Brophy CO .10 .25
20 Graffiti Ink Gallery SPONSOR .01 .01

2004-05 Richmond Riverdogs
COMPLETE SET (28) 5.00 12.00
1 Checklist .04 .10
2 Donny Martin CO .04 .10
3 Glenn Morelli OWN .04 .10
4 Jim Duhart .40 1.00
5 Simo Pulkki .20 .50
6 Brian Goudie .20 .50
7 Ivan Curic .40 1.00
8 Francis Belanger .40 1.00
9 Ryan Prentice .20 .50
10 David Hymovitz .40 1.00
11 Mark Turner .20 .50
12 Mark Langdon .20 .50
13 David Brosseau .20 .50
14 Luch Nasato .20 .50
15 Trevor Senn .20 .50
16 Brian Herbert .20 .50
17 J.J. Wrobel .20 .50
18 Dennis Vial .40 1.00
19 Derek Shutz .20 .50
20 Brett Cross .20 .50
21 Anthony Dipalma .20 .50
22 Brent Belecki .20 .50
23 Dan McIntyre .20 .50
24 Semir Ben-Amor .20 .50
25 Razz MASCOT .04 .10
26 Team Photo .04 .10
27 Zamboni .04 .10
28 Richmond Coliseum .04 .10

1996-97 Rimouski Oceanic
COMPLETE SET (28) 12.00 25.00
1 Jonathan Beaulieu .15 .40
2 Martin Bedard .15 .40
3 Eric Belzile .15 .40
4 Denis Boily .15 .40
5 Dave Bolduc .15 .40
6 Yan Bouchard .20 .50
7 Nicolas Chabot .20 .50
8 Eryc Collin .15 .40
9 Eric Drouin .15 .40
10 Yannick Dupont .15 .40
11 Frederic Girard .15 .40
12 Jimmy Grondin .15 .40
13 Bobby Lebel .08 .25
14 Vincent Lecavalier 7.50 15.00
15 Frederic Levac .15 .40
16 Francois Levesque .15 .40
17 Philippe Lord .15 .40
18 Dave Malenfant .15 .40
19 Eric Normandin .20 .50
20 Mathieu Normandin .15 .40
21 Philippe Plante .15 .40
22 Martin Poitras .20 .50
23 Saison 1996-1997 .08 .25
24 Philippe Sauve 1.25 3.00
25 Sebastien Simard .15 .40
26 David St-Onge .15 .40
27 Mathieu Sunderland .20 .50
28 Gaston Therrien CO .08 .25

1996-97 Rimouski Oceanic Quebec Provincial Police
COMPLETE SET (26) 16.00 40.00
1 Jonathan Beaulieu .20 .50
2 Martin Bedard .20 .50
3 Eric Belzile .20 .50
4 Maxime Blouin .20 .50
5 Denis Boily .20 .50
6 Yan Bouchard .20 .50
7 Nicolas Chabot .20 .50
8 Eryc Collin .20 .50
9 Eric Drouin .20 .50
10 Yannick Dupont .20 .50
11 Frederic Girard .20 .50
12 Jimmy Grondin .20 .50
13 Vincent Lecavalier 12.00 25.00
14 Frederic Levac .20 .50
15 Francois Levesque .20 .50
16 Philipe Lord .20 .50
17 Dave Malenfant .20 .50
18 Eric Normandin .20 .50
19 Mathieu Normandin .20 .50
20 Philippe Plante .20 .50
21 Martin Poitras .20 .50
22 Philippe Sauve 2.00 5.00
23 Nicola Spaccucci .20 .50
24 David St-Onge .20 .50
25 Sebastien Tremblay .20 .50
26 Title Card .02 .10

1996-97 Rimouski Oceanic Update
COMPLETE SET (10) 2.50 6.00
1 Eric Belanger (LW) .20 .50
2 Eric Belanger (C) .60 1.50
3 Philippe Grondin .20 .50
4 Jason Lehoux .20 .50
5 Jonathan Levesque .20 .50
6 Louki MASCOT .08 .25
7 Guillaume Rodrigue .20 .50
8 Joe Rullier .40 1.00
9 Russell Smith .20 .50
10 Derrick Walser .30 .75

1997-98 Rimouski Oceanic
COMPLETE SET (25) 10.00 25.00
4 Vincent Lecavalier 4.00 10.00
7 Joe Rullier .30 .75
9 Jonathan Beaulieu .15 .40
10 David Bilodeau .15 .40
11 Jimmy Grondin .15 .40
14 Dave Malenfant .15 .40
17 Kevin Bolduc .15 .40
19 Eric Normandin .15 .40
20 Francois Drainville .15 .40
21 Eric Belanger .30 .75
22 Eric Drouin .15 .40
24 Julien Desrosiers .15 .40
25 David St-Onge .15 .40
27 Phillippe Grondin .15 .40
33 Phillippe Sauve 1.25 3.00
35 Jean-Marc Pelletier .60 1.50
36 Jonathan St-Louis .15 .40
39 Brad Richards 5.00 12.00
44 Guillaume Couture .15 .40
45 Chad Gagnon .15 .40
55 Casey Leggett .15 .40
79 Denis Boily .15 .40
91 Derrick Walser .30 .75
98 Adam Borzecki .15 .40
NNO Team Card .15 .40

1999-00 Rimouski Oceanic
COMPLETE SET (24) 6.00 15.00
1 Nicolas Pilote .15 .40
2 Joe Rullier .30 .75
3 Jonathan Beaulieu .15 .40
4 Nicolas Poirier .15 .40
5 Thatcher Bell .20 .50
6 Brent Maclellan .15 .40
7 Alexandre Tremblay .15 .40
8 Jean-Francois Babin .15 .40
9 Benoit Martin .15 .40
10 Jan Philippe Cadieux .15 .40
11 Jean-Philippe Briere .15 .40
12 Alexis Castonguay .15 .40
13 Rene Vydareny .15 .40
14 Ronnie Decontie .15 .40
15 Shawn Scanzano .15 .40
16 Michel Ouellet .15 .40
17 Jacques Lariviere .15 .40
18 Eric Salvail .15 .40
19 Sebastien Caron .40 1.00
20 Brad Richards 2.00 5.00
21 Aaron Johnson .15 .40
22 Juraj Kolnik .60 1.50
23 Michel Periard .30 .75
24 Header Card/CL .02 .10

1999-00 Rimouski Oceanic Signed
COMPLETE SET (24) 30.00 75.00
1 Nicolas Pilote .75 2.00
2 Joe Rullier 1.50 4.00
3 Jonathan Beaulieu .75 2.00
4 Nicolas Poirier .75 2.00
5 Thatcher Bell 1.50 4.00
6 Brent Maclellan .75 2.00
7 Alexandre Tremblay .75 2.00
8 Jean-Francois Babin .75 2.00
9 Benoit Martin .75 2.00
10 Jan Philippe Cadieux .75 2.00
11 Jean-Philippe Briere .75 2.00
12 Alexis Castonguay .75 2.00
13 Rene Vydareny .75 2.00
14 Ronnie Decontie .75 2.00
15 Shawn Scanzano .75 2.00
16 Michel Ouellet .75 2.00
17 Jacques Lariviere .75 2.00
18 Eric Salvail .75 2.00
19 Sebastien Caron 2.00 5.00
20 Brad Richards 10.00 25.00
21 Aaron Johnson .75 2.00
22 Juraj Kolnik 3.00 8.00
23 Michel Periard 1.50 4.00
24 Header Card/CL .08 .25

2000-01 Rimouski Oceanic
COMPLETE SET (26) 5.00 12.00
1 Phillippe Lauze .20 .75
2 Tim Sinasac .20 .50
3 Jonathan Beaulieu .20 .50
4 Nichola Pilote .20 .50
5 Nicolas Poirier .20 .50
6 Thatcher Bell .20 .50
7 Tomas Malec .20 .50
8 Brent MacLellan .20 .50
9 Jean-Francois Plourde .20 .50
10 Jean-Francois Babin .20 .50
11 Benoit Martin .20 .50
12 Daniel Petiguay .30 .75
13 Jean-Phillippe Briere .20 .50
14 Ryan Clowe .75 2.00
15 Mathieu Fournier .20 .50
16 Gabriel Balasescu .20 .50
17 Mathieu Simard .20 .50
18 Samuel Gibbons .20 .50
19 Michel Ouellet .20 .50
20 Jonathan Pelletier .30 .75
21 Eric Salvail .30 .75
22 Aaron Johnson .20 .50
23 Sebastien Bolduc .30 .75
24 Louky MASCOT .04 .10
25 Doris Labonte CO .04 .10
NNO Team CL .04 .10

2000-01 Rimouski Oceanic Signed
COMPLETE SET (26) 15.00 40.00
1 Phillippe Lauze .80 4.00
2 Tim Sinasac .80 2.00
3 Jonathan Beaulieu .80 2.00
4 Nichola Pilote .80 2.00
5 Nicolas Poirier .80 2.00
6 Thatcher Bell 1.20 3.00
7 Tomas Malec .80 2.00
8 Brent MacLellan .80 2.00
9 Jean-Francois Plourde .80 2.00
10 Jean-Francois Babin .80 2.00
11 Benoit Martin .80 2.00
12 Daniel Petiguay .80 4.00
13 Jean-Phillippe Briere .80 2.00
14 Ryan Clowe 4.00 10.00
15 Mathieu Fournier .80 2.00
16 Gabriel Balasescu .80 2.00
17 Mathieu Simard .80 2.00
18 Samuel Gibbons .80 2.00
19 Michel Ouellet .80 2.00
20 Jonathan Pelletier 1.20 4.00
21 Eric Salvail 1.20 4.00
22 Aaron Johnson .80 2.00
23 Sebastien Bolduc .80 4.00
24 Louky MASCOT .04 .10
25 Doris Labonte CO .04 .10
NNO Team CL .04 .10

2001-02 Rimouski Oceanic
COMPLETE SET (23) 5.00 12.00
1 Chaz Johnson .20 .50
2 Philippe Lauze .20 .50
3 Dany Stewart .20 .50
4 Michael Gavalier .20 .50
5 Nicolas Poirier .40 1.00
6 Thatcher Bell .30 .75
7 Thomas Malec .30 .75
8 Brent Maclellan .20 .50
9 Jean-Francois Plourde .20 .50
10 Benoit Martin .20 .50
11 Daniel Petiquay .20 .50
12 Jean-Philippe Briere .20 .50
13 Ryan Clowe .30 .75
14 Mathieu Fournier .20 .50
15 Gabriel Balasescu .20 .50
16 Samuel Gibbons .20 .50
17 Michel Ouellet .20 .50
18 Eric Neilson .20 .50
19 Patrick Lepage .40 1.00
20 Eric Salvail .40 1.00
21 Aaron Johnson .40 1.00
22 Sebastien Bolduc .40 1.00
23 Marc-Antoine Pouliot 1.25 3.00

2002-03 Rimouski Oceanic
COMPLETE SET (22) 5.00 12.00
1 Guillaume Chicoine .20 .50
2 Patrick Coulombe .20 .50
3 Jason D'Ascanio .20 .50
4 Francois Gauthier .20 .50
5 Michel Gavalier .20 .50
6 Zbynek Hrdel .20 .50
7 Danick Jasmin-Riel .20 .50
8 Philippe Lauze .20 .50
9 Mattews Lemaire .20 .50
10 Eric Neilson .20 .50
11 Sebastien Nolet .20 .50
12 Daniel Petiquay .20 .50
13 Marc-Antoine Pouliot .75 2.00
14 Jonathan Robert .20 .50
15 Dany Roussin .40 1.00
16 Eric Salvail .20 .50
17 Christopher Sorensen .20 .50
18 Dany Stewart .20 .50
19 Mark Tobin .20 .50
20 Erick Tremblay .20 .50
21 Jeremy Turgeon .20 .50
22 Alexander Vachon .40 1.00

2003-04 Rimouski Oceanic
COMPLETE SET (26) 30.00 60.00
1 Benoit Arsenault .20 .50
2 Charles Bergeron .20 .50
3 Francois Bolduc .20 .50
4 Jean-Michael Bolduc .20 .50
5 Jean-Sebastien Cote .20 .50
6 Patrick Coulombe .20 .50
7 Sidney Crosby 8.00 20.00
8 Cedrick Desjardins .40 1.00
9 Olivier Didier .20 .50
10 Zbynek Hrdel .20 .50
11 Danick Jasmin-Riel .20 .50
12 Philippe Lauze .30 .75
13 Guillaume Lavallee .20 .50
14 Mattews Lemaire .20 .50
15 Eric Neilson .20 .50
16 Marc-Antoine Pouliot .40 1.00
17 Dany Roussin .20 .50
18 Michal Sersen .20 .50
19 Danny Stewart .20 .50
20 Mark Tobin .20 .50
21 Erick Tremblay .20 .50
22 Alexandre Vachon .20 .50
23 Guillaume Veilleux .20 .50
24 Hubert Veilleux .20 .50
25 Sidney Crosby TL SP 12.00 30.00
26 Marc-Antoine Pouliot TL SP .75 2.00

2003-04 Rimouski Oceanic Sheets
COMPLETE SET (5) 20.00 40.00
1 Mattews Lemaire
Charles Bergeron
Eric Nelson
Olivier Didier
Danick Jasmin Riel 2.00 5.00
2 Erick Tremblay
Dany Roussin
Philippe Lauze
Jean-Sebastien Cote
Michal Sersen 2.00 5.00
3 Mark Tobin
Patrick Coulombe
Marc-Antone Pouliot
Francois Bolduc
Cedrick Desjardins 2.00 5.00
4 Guillame Veilleux
Sidney Crosby
Guillame Lavallee
Alexandre Vachon 10.00 25.00
5 Jean-Michal Bolduc
Hubert Veilleux
Zbynek Hrdel
Dany Stewart
Benoit Arsenault 2.00 5.00

2004-05 Rimouski Oceanic
COMPLETE SET (23) 10.00 25.00
1 Sidney Crosby 4.00 10.00
2 Alexandre Vachon .40 1.00
3 Dany Roussin .40 1.00
4 Graham Bona .20 .50
5 Sebastien Aspirot .20 .50
6 Nicolas Bachand .20 .50
7 Jamie Blom .20 .50
8 Francois Bolduc .20 .50
9 Francis Charette .20 .50
10 Jean-Sebastien Cote .20 .50
11 Patrick Coulombe .20 .50
12 Cedrick Desjardins .40 1.00
13 Maxime Desruisseaux .20 .50
14 Zbynek Hrdel .20 .50
15 Sebastien Laferriere .20 .50
16 Eric Neilson .40 1.00
17 Marc-Antoine Pouliot .40 1.00
18 Michal Sersen .20 .50
19 Danny Stewart .20 .50
20 Mark Tobin .20 .50
21 Erick Tremblay .20 .50
22 Jean-Michel Filiatrault .75 2.00
23 Jean-Michel Bolduc .20 .50
LE1 Sidney Crosby LTD/300 15.00 40.00
LE2 Marc-Antoine Pouliot LTD/300 4.00 10.00

2004-05 Rimouski Oceanic Season Ticket
COMPLETE SET (6) 25.00 60.00
1 Jonathan Beaulieu .75 2.00
2 Sebastien Caron 1.50 4.00
3 Sidney Crosby 15.00 40.00
4 Vincent Lecavalier 4.00 10.00
5 Brad Richards 4.00 10.00
6 Allan Sirois .75 2.00

2005-06 Rimouski Oceanic
COMPLETE SET (30) 6.00 15.00
1 Patrick Coulombe .20 .50
2 Erick Tremblay .20 .50
3 Jean-Michel Bolduc .20 .50
4 Jamie Blom .20 .50
5 Mark Tobin .20 .50
6 Sebastien Aspirot .20 .50
7 Francois Bolduc .20 .50
8 Jean-Sebastien Cote .20 .50
9 Sebastien Laferriere .20 .50
10 Graham Bona .20 .50
11 Francis Charette .20 .50
12 Maxime Lincourt .20 .50
13 Philippe Roberge .40 1.00
14 David Skokan .40 1.00
15 Pierre-Alexandre Joncas .20 .50
16 Maxime Macenauer .20 .50
17 David Bouchard .40 1.00
18 Jason Caron .20 .50
19 Nicholas Goyens .20 .50
20 Guillaume Mailloux .20 .50
21 Dave Plante .20 .50
22 Michael Chiasson .20 .50
23 Marc-Andre Laroche .20 .50
24 Guillaume Letourneau .20 .50
25 Olivier Fortier .20 .50
26 Philippe Garnier .20 .50
27 Drew Paris .20 .50
28 Max Gratchev .20 .50
29 Maxime Tanguay .20 .50
30 Tommy Legault .20 .50

2006-07 Rimouski Oceanic
COMPLETE SET (24) 8.00 15.00
1 Olivier Fortier .25 .60
2 Maxime Tanguay .40 1.00
3 Philippe Garnier .25 .60
4 Maxime Gratchev .40 1.00
5 François Bolduc .25 .60
6 Graham Bona .25 .60
7 David Skokan .25 .60
8 Pierre-Alexandre Joncas .25 .60
9 David Bouchard .25 .60
10 Nicholas Goyens .25 .60
11 Dave Plante .25 .60
12 Marc-André Laroche .25 .60
13 Philippe Cornet .25 .60
14 Patrice Cormier .25 .60
15 Alexandre Néron .25 .60
16 Jordan Caron .25 .60
17 Alexandre Brunet .25 .60
18 Louis-Philippe Lachance .25 .60
19 Christopher Stevens .25 .60
20 Frédéric Desrochers .25 .60
21 Michal Frolik .60 1.50
22 Kevin Cormier .25 .60
23 Tommy Legault .40 1.00
24 Michael Chiasson .40 1.00

1993-94 Roanoke Express
COMPLETE SET (25) 3.00 8.00
1 Frank Anzalone CO .08 .25
2 Will Averill .15 .40
3 Claude Barthe .15 .40
4 Lev Berdichevsky .15 .40
5 Hughes Bouchard .15 .40
6 Reggie Brezeault .15 .40
7 Ilja Dubkov .15 .40
8 Pat Ferschweiler .15 .40
9 Kyle Galloway .15 .40
10 Jeff Jestadt .15 .40
11 Roger Larche .15 .40
12 Dana McGuane TR .02 .10
13 Jim Mill .15 .40
14 Dave Morissette .15 .40
15 Chris Potter .15 .40
16 Dan Ryder .15 .40
17 Gairin Smith .15 .40
18 Michael Smith .15 .40
19 Tony Szabo .15 .40
20 Stephen Tepper .15 .40
21 Oleg Yashin .15 .40
22 Team Photo .15 .40
23 Dave Morissette First F .02 .10
24 Sponsor Card Advance Au .02 .10
25 Sponsor Card First Virg .02 .10

1994-95 Roanoke Express
COMPLETE SET (24) 4.00 10.00
1 Team Photo .20 .50
2 Dave Gagnon .30 .75
3 Chris Potter .20 .50
4 Dave Stewart .20 .50
5 Michael Smith .20 .50
6 Jon Larson .20 .50
7 Carl Fleury .20 .50
8 Jeff Jestadt .20 .50
9 Marty Schriner .20 .50
10 Rouslan Toujikov .20 .50
11 Jason Clarke .20 .50
12 Stephane Desjardins .20 .50
13 Robin Bouchard .20 .50
14 Oleg Yashin .20 .50
15 Ilja Dubkov .20 .50
16 Derek Laxdal .30 .75
17 Mark Luger .20 .50
18 Pat Ferschweiler .20 .50
19 Dan Ryder .20 .50
20 Frank Anzalone CO .08 .25
21 Dana McGuane TR .02 .10
22 Loco/Mascot .02 .10
23 Board of Directors .02 .10
24 Fan Card .01 .05

1995-96 Roanoke Express
COMPLETE SET (25) 6.00 15.00
1 Jeff Jestadt .15 .40
2 Dave Stewart .15 .40
3 Matt DelGuidice .30 .75
4 Dave Holum .15 .40
5 Mike Stacchi .15 .40
6 Paul Croteau .15 .40
7 Marty Schriner .15 .40
8 L.P. Charbonneau .15 .40
9 Michael Smith .15 .40
10 Ilja Dubkov .20 .50
11 Tim Christian .15 .40
12 Brian Gallentine .15 .40
13 Jeff Jablonski .15 .40
14 Daniel Berthiaume .40 1.00
15 Duane Harmer .15 .40
16 Jason Clarke .15 .40
17 Tim Hanley .15 .40
18 Jon Larson .15 .40
19 Nick Jones .15 .40
20 Chris Potter .15 .40
21 Craig Herr .15 .40
22 Frank Anzalone CO .08 .25
23 Chris Pollack TR .02 .10
24 Loco Mascot .02 .10
25 Team Photo .02 .10

1996-97 Roanoke Express
COMPLETE SET (24) 8.00 20.00
1 Dave Gagnon .20 .50
2 Dave Stewart .15 .40
3 Eric Landry .15 .40
5 Michael Smith .15 .40
7 Jeff Loder .15 .40
8 Duane Harmer .15 .40
10 Bobby Brown .15 .40
11 J.F. Tremblay .15 .40
12 Ryan Equale .15 .40
14 Doug Searle .15 .40
15 Jeff Jablonski .15 .40
17 Jeff Cowan .20 .50
18 Sean Brown .20 .50
21 Ilya Dubkov .15 .40
22 Matt O'Dette .15 .40
23 Chris Lipsett .15 .40
24 Tim Christian .15 .40
35 Larry Moberg .20 .50
NNO Mike Holden TR .02 .10
NNO Checklist .02 .10
NNO Frank Anzalone CO .02 .10
NNO Loco the Railyard Dog .02 .10
NNO Team Photo .15 .40
NNO Elmer the Engine .02 .10

1998-99 Roanoke Express
COMPLETE SET (26) 10.00 25.00
1 Tony Mancuso GM .20 .50
2 Scott Gordon HCO .20 .50
3 Perry Florio ACO .20 .50
4 Darren Abbott DOB .20 .50
5 Dave Gagnon .60 1.50
6 Daniel Berthiaume .75 2.00
7 Unknown .40 1.00
8 Doug Searle .40 1.00
9 Jason Dailey .40 1.00
10 Duane Harmer .40 1.00
11 Mike Peron .40 1.00
12 Kris Cantu .40 1.00
13 Travis Smith .40 1.00
14 J.C. Ruid .40 1.00
15 Ben Schust .40 1.00
16 Jeremy Schaefer .40 1.00
17 J.F. Tremblay .40 1.00
18 Mike Mader .40 1.00
19 Nicholas Windsor .40 1.00
20 Peter Brearley .40 1.00
21 Nic Beaudoin .40 1.00
22 Chris Lipsett .40 1.00
23 Tim Christian .40 1.00
24 Dru Burgess .40 1.00
25 Chris Wismer .40 1.00
26 Loco Mascot .20 .50

2000-01 Roanoke Express
COMPLETE SET (22) 8.00 20.00
1 Roanoke Express .20 .50
2 Mike Peron .40 1.00
3 Joe Dusbabek .40 1.00
4 Troy Lake .40 1.00
5 Jeff Burgoyne .40 1.00
6 Ben Schust .40 1.00
7 Dave Gagnon .60 1.50
8 Calvin Elfring .40 1.00
9 Colin Anderson .40 1.00
10 Todd Compeau .40 1.00
11 Daniel Berthiaume .60 1.50
12 Loco MASCOT .10 .25
13 Aaron Gates .40 1.00
14 Travis Smith .40 1.00
15 John Sadowski .40 1.00
16 Perry Florio CO .10 .25
17 Nate Handrahan .40 1.00
18 Jeff Sproat .40 1.00
19 Jay Shipulski .40 1.00
20 Doug Sheppard .40 1.00
21 George McMillan SHERIFF .04 .10
22 Adam Dewan .40 1.00

2001-02 Roanoke Express
COMPLETE SET (24) 20.00 50.00
1 Daniel Berthiaume 1.25 3.00
2 Chris Cava .75 2.00
3 Steve Chabbert .75 2.00
4 Duncan Dalmao .75 2.00
5 Brett DeCecco 1.25 3.00
6 Joe Dusbabek .75 2.00
7 Brad Essex .75 2.00
8 Vernon Fiddler .75 2.00
9 Pete Gardiner .75 2.00
10 Jeff Helperl .75 2.00
11 Marty Hughes .75 2.00
12 Rick Kowalsky .75 2.00
13 Troy Lake .75 2.00
14 Frank Novock .75 2.00
15 Mike Omicioli 1.25 3.00
16 Mike Peron .75 2.00
17 Gary Ricciardi 1.25 3.00
18 Travis Smith .75 2.00
19 Jeff Sproat .75 2.00
20 Terence Tootoo 2.00 5.00
21 Jordan Willis 1.50 4.00
22 Perry Florio CO .20 .50
23 Mark Bernard ACO .20 .50
24 George McMillan .75 2.00

2002-03 Roanoke Express
COMPLETE SET (25) 15.00 40.00
1 Sebastien Laplante .75 2.00
2 Sheriff McMillan .10 .25
3 Dan Sullivan .75 2.00
4 Loco Mascot .10 .25
5 Cole Fischer .75 2.00
6 Perry Florio HCO .10 .25
7 Tony MacAulay ACO .10 .25
8 Scotty Balan .75 2.00
9 Josh Barker .75 2.00
10 Dan Carlson .75 2.00
11 Adam Colagiacomo .75 2.00
12 Duncan Dalmao .75 2.00
13 Joe Dusbabek .75 2.00
14 Brad Essex .75 2.00
15 Dylan Gyori 1.25 3.00
16 Jason Jaffray .75 2.00
17 Rick Kowalsky .75 2.00
18 Shawn Limpright .75 2.00
19 Evan Lindsay .75 2.00
20 Chad Mazurak .75 2.00
21 Frank Novock .75 2.00
22 Mike Peron .75 2.00
23 Doug Schueller .75 2.00
24 David Silverstone .75 2.00
25 Tim O'Connell .75 2.00

2002-03 Roanoke Express RBI Sports
COMPLETE SET (18) 10.00 18.00
187 Josh Barker .40 1.00
188 Scotty Balan .40 1.00
189 Cam Bristow .40 1.00
190 Dan Carlson .40 1.00
191 Duncan Dalmao .40 1.00
192 Joe Dusbabek .40 1.00
193 Brad Essex .40 1.00
194 Cole Fisher .40 1.00
195 Dylan Gyori .60 1.50
196 Jason Jaffray .40 1.00
197 Rick Kowalsky .40 1.00
198 Sebastien Laplante .60 1.50
199 Chad Mazurak .40 1.00
200 Frank Novock .40 1.00
201 Tim O'Connell .40 1.00
202 Mike Peron .40 1.00
203 Doug Schueller .40 1.00
204 David Silverstone .40 1.00

2003-04 Roanoke Express
COMPLETE SET (16) 6.00 15.00
305 Josh Barker .40 1.00
306 David Belitski .60 1.50
307 Kevin Bergin .40 1.00
308 Dan Carlson .40 1.00
309 Dan Carney .40 1.00
310 Duncan Dalmao .40 1.00
311 Joe Dusbabek .40 1.00
312 Rick Kowalsky .40 1.00
313 Shawn Limpright .40 1.00
314 Andrew McPherson .40 1.00
315 Andrew Oke .40 1.00
316 Bryan Perez .40 1.00
317 Doug Scatchard .40 1.00
318 Robert Snowball .40 1.00
319 Blair Stayzer .40 1.00
320 Jason Wolfe .60 1.50

1963-64 Rochester Americans
COMPLETE SET (20) 100.00 200.00
1 Lou Angotti 4.00 8.00
2 Al Arbour 10.00 20.00
3 Norm Armstrong 2.50 5.00
4 Ed Babiuk 2.50 5.00
5 Wally Boyer 4.00 8.00
6 Arnie Brown 4.00 8.00
7 Gerry Cheevers UER 25.00 50.00
8 Don Cherry 30.00 60.00
9 Mike Corbett 2.50 5.00
10 Joe Crozier CO 2.50 5.00
11 Jack Curran TR 2.50 5.00
12 Les Duff 2.50 5.00
13 Gerry Ehman 2.50 5.00
14 Dick Gamble 4.00 8.00
15 Larry Hillman 2.50 5.00
16 Bronco Horvath 7.50 15.00
17 Eddie Lawson 2.50 5.00
18 Jim Pappin 4.00 8.00
19 Darryl Sly 2.50 5.00
20 Stan Smrke 3.00 6.00

1971-72 Rochester Americans
COMPLETE SET (18) 30.00 80.00
1 Red Armstrong 2.00 5.00
2 Guy Burrowes 2.00 5.00
3 Gaye Cooley 2.00 5.00
4 Bob Craig 2.00 5.00

5 Bob Ellett 2.00 5.00
6 Ron Fogal 2.00 5.00
7 Rod Graham 2.00 5.00
8 Dave Hrechkosy 2.50 6.00
9 Herman Karp 2.00 5.00
10 Bob Kelly 4.00 10.00
11 Larry McKillop 2.00 5.00
12 Bob Malcolm 2.00 5.00
13 Barry Merrell 2.00 5.00
14 Wayne Morusyk 2.00 5.00
15 Rick Pagnutti 2.00 5.00
16 Gerry Sillers 2.00 5.00
17 Gene Sobchuk 2.00 5.00
18 Lynn Zimmerman 2.00 5.00

1977-78 Rochester Americans

COMPLETE SET (24) 12.50 25.00
1 Team Photo .50 1.00
2 Duane Rupp .75 1.50
3 Nate Angelo TR .25 .50
4 Earl Anderson .75 1.50
5 Bill Bennett .50 1.00
6 Daryl Drader .50 1.00
7 Rene Drolet .50 1.00
8 Rene Drolet .50 1.00
9 Darryl Edestrand .75 1.50
10 Ron Garwasiuk .50 1.00
11 Rod Graham .50 1.00
12 Rod Graham .50 1.00
13 Doug Halward .75 1.50
14 Bjorn Johansson .50 1.00
15 Steve Langdon .50 1.00
16 Ray Maluta .50 1.00
17 Brian McGregor .50 1.00
18 Clayton Pachal .50 1.00
19 Dave Parro .75 1.50
20 Jim Pettie .50 1.00
21 Sean Shanahan .50 1.00
22 Al Sims 1.00 2.00
23 Barry Smith .75 1.50

1979-80 Rochester Americans

1 Mike Boland 2.00 5.00
2 Mike Breen 2.00 5.00
3 Paul Crowley 2.00 5.00
4 Daryl Drader 2.00 5.00
5 Ron Garwasiuk 2.00 5.00
6 Chris Halyk 2.00 5.00
7 Bill Inglis CO 1.50 4.00
8 Randy Ireland 2.00 5.00
9 Joe Kowal 2.00 5.00
10 Normand Lefebvre 2.00 5.00
11 Bob Mongrain 2.00 5.00
12 Wayne Ramsey 2.00 5.00
13 Jacques Richard 3.00 8.00
14 Geordie Robertson 2.00 5.00
15 Andre Savard 3.00 10.00
16 Ron Schock 3.00 8.00
17 Dave Schultz 12.00 30.00
18 Barry Smith 2.00 5.00
19 Bill Stewart 2.00 5.00
20 Richard Suwek 2.00 5.00
21 Mark Toffolo 2.00 5.00
22 Jim Turkiewicz 2.00 5.00
23 Ed Walsh 2.00 5.00
24 Jim Walsh 2.00 5.00

1991-92 Rochester Americans Dunkin' Donuts

OMPLETE SET (20) 4.00 10.00
Greg Brown .20 .50
Peter Ciavaglia .30 .75
Bob Corkum .30 .75
Brian Curran .20 .50
David DiVita .20 .50
Tom Draper .30 .75
Jody Gage .40 1.00
Dan Frawley .20 .50
Dave Littman .30 .75
0 Darcy Loewen .20 .50
1 Don McSween .20 .50
2 Brad Rubachuk .20 .50
3 Lindy Ruff .40 1.00
4 Joel Savage .20 .50
5 Jiri Sejba .20 .50
6 Chris Snell .20 .50
7 Coupon Dunkin' Donuts .01 .05
8 Coupon Dunkin' Donuts .01 .05
9 Coupon Dunkin' Donuts .01 .05
0 Coupon Dunkin' Donuts .01 .05

1991-92 Rochester Americans Kodak

OMPLETE SET (26) 5.00 12.00
Don Lever CO .20 .50
Terry Martin ACO .08 .25
an Boyce .20 .50
John Bradley .20 .50
Greg Brown .20 .50
Keith Carney .20 .50
Peter Ciavaglia .30 .75
Bob Corkum .30 .75
Brian Curran .20 .50
David DiVita .20 .50
Lou Franceschetti .30 .75
Dan Frawley .20 .50
Jody Gage .40 1.00
Kevin Haller .30 .75
Dave Littman .25 .60
Darcy Loewen .20 .50
Steve Ludzik .20 .50
Don McSween .20 .50
Brad Miller .20 .50
Sean O'Donnell .30 .75
Brad Rubachuk .20 .50
Lindy Ruff .40 1.00
Joel Savage .20 .50
Jiri Sejba .20 .50
Chris Snell .20 .50
Jason Winch .20 .50

1991-92 Rochester Americans Postcards

MPLETE SET (21) 4.00 10.00
ave Baseggio .20 .50
ohn Bradley .20 .50
Greg Brown .20 .50
Keith Carney .20 .50
5 Peter Ciavaglia .20 .50
6 Bob Corkum .30 .75
7 David DiVita .20 .50
8 Tom Draper .30 .75
9 Lou Franceschetti .30 .75
10 Dan Frawley .20 .50
11 Bill Houlder .30 .75
12 Don Lever CO .08 .25
13 David Littman .30 .75
14 Terry Martin ACO .08 .25
15 Don McSween .20 .50
16 Sean O'Donnell .30 .75
17 Lindy Ruff .20 .50
18 Joel Savage .20 .50
19 Jiri Sejba .20 .50
20 Chris Snell .20 .50
21 Ed Zawatsky .20 .50

1992-93 Rochester Americans Dunkin' Donuts

COMPLETE SET (20) 6.00 15.00
1 Peter Ambroziak .20 .50
2 Greg Brown .20 .50
3 Peter Ciavaglia .25 .60
4 Jozef Cierny .20 .50
5 David DiVita .20 .50
6 Dan Frawley .20 .50
7 Jody Gage .30 .75
8 Andrei Jakovenko .20 .50
9 Olaf Kolzig 2.00 5.00
10 Doug Macdonald .20 .50
11 Mike McLaughlin .20 .50
12 Sean O'Donnell .30 .75
13 Bill Pye .30 .75
14 Brad Rubachuk .20 .50
15 Bruce Shoebottom .20 .50
16 Todd Simon .20 .50
17 Jeff Sirkka .20 .50
18 Chris Snell .20 .50
19 Scott Thomas .30 .75
20 Jason Young .20 .50

1992-93 Rochester Americans Kodak

COMPLETE SET (26) 15.00 40.00
1 John Van Boxmeer CO .40 1.00
2 Terry Martin ACO .08 .25
3 Peter Ambroziak .40 1.00
4 Greg Brown .40 1.00
5 Peter Ciavaglia .40 1.00
6 Jozef Cierny .40 1.00
7 David DiVita .40 1.00
8 Dan Frawley .40 1.00
9 Jody Gage 1.00 2.50
10 The Moose (mascot) .08 .25
11 Tony Iob .40 1.00
12 Olaf Kolzig 4.00 10.00
13 Doug MacDonald .40 1.00
14 Mike McLaughlin .40 1.00
15 Sean O'Donnell 1.00 2.50
16 Brad Pascall 1.00 2.50
17 Bill Pye 1.00 2.50
18 Brad Rubachuk .40 1.00
19 Joel Savage .40 1.00
20 Bruce Shoebottom .75 2.00
21 Todd Simon .40 1.00
22 Jeff Sirkka .40 1.00
23 Chris Snell .40 1.00
24 Scott Thomas 1.00 2.50
25 Jason Winch .40 1.00
26 Jason Young .40 1.00

1993-94 Rochester Americans Kodak

COMPLETE SET (25) 4.80 12.00
1 John Van Boxmeer CO .20 .50
2 Terry Martin ASST CO .08 .25
3 Peter Ambroziak .25 .60
4 Mike Bavis .25 .60
5 James Black .25 .60
6 Derek Booth .25 .60
7 Philippe Boucher .25 .60
8 David Cooper .25 .60
9 Todd Flichel .25 .60
10 Jody Gage .40 1.00
11 Viktor Gordiouk .25 .60
12 Bill Horn .25 .60
13 Markus Ketterer .30 .75
14 Mark Krys .25 .60
15 Doug MacDonald .25 .60
16 Dean Melanson .25 .60
17 Moose Mascot .08 .25
18 Sean O'Donnell .30 .75
19 Brad Pascall .25 .60
20 Sergei Petrenko .25 .60
21 Brad Rubachuk .25 .60
22 Todd Simon .25 .60
23 Scott Thomas .30 .75
24 Mikhail Volkov .25 .60
25 Jason Young .25 .60

1995-96 Rochester Americans

COMPLETE SET (25) 6.00 15.00
1 Craig Charron .20 .50
2 David Cooper .20 .50
3 Dan Frawley .20 .50
4 Jody Gage .40 1.00
5 Terry Hollinger .25 .60
6 Dane Jackson .20 .50
7 Ladislav Karabin .20 .50
8 Sergei Klimentiev .20 .50
9 Jamie Leach .20 .50
10 Jay Mazur .20 .50
11 Dean Melanson .20 .50
12 Scott Metcalfe .20 .50
13 Barrie Moore .20 .50
14 Scott Nichol .20 .50
15 Rumun Ndur .25 .60
16 Scott Pearson .20 .50
17 Serge Roberge .20 .50
18 Steve Shields .75 2.00
19 Robb Stauber .30 .75
20 Mikhail Volkov .20 .50
21 Dixon Ward .30 .75
22 Bob Westerby .20 .50
23 Mike Wilson .20 .50
24 Shayne Wright .20 .50
25 John Tortorella CO .08 .25

1996-97 Rochester Americans

COMPLETE SET (26) 4.00 10.00
1 Rochester Americans .15 .40
2 Sergei Klimentiev .15 .40
3 Craig Charron .15 .40
4 Craig Millar .15 .40
5 Scott Metcalfe .15 .40
6 Ed Ronan .15 .40
7 Terry Hollinger .15 .40
8 Shayne Wright .15 .40
9 Barrie Moore .15 .40
10 Scott Nichol .15 .40
11 Charlie Huddy .15 .40
12 Vaclav Varada .20 .50
13 Wayne Primeau .30 .75
14 Terry Yake .15 .40
15 Dan Frawley .15 .40
16 Frederic Deschenes .15 .40
17 Steve Shields .40 1.00
18 Paul Rushforth .15 .40
19 Dane Jackson .15 .40
20 Rumun Ndur .20 .50
21 Greg Walters .15 .40
22 Eric Lavigne .15 .40
23 John Tortorella CO .40 1.00
24 Moose MAS .02 .10
25 AHL Web Site .01 .05
26 PHPA Web Site .01 .05

1997-98 Rochester Americans

COMPLETE SET (25) 8.00 20.00
1-1 Dane Jackson .30 .75
1-2 Scott Metcalfe .30 .75
1-3 Denis Hamel .30 .75
1-4 Mark Dutiaume .30 .75
1-5 Daniel Bienvenue .30 .75
2-1 Craig Charron .30 .75
2-2 Scott Nichol .30 .75
2-3 Martin Menard .30 .75
2-4 Erik Rasmussen .40 1.00
2-5 Mike Zanutto .30 .75
3-1 Vaclav Varada .40 1.00
3-2 Dan Frawley .30 .75
3-3 Patrice Tardif .40 1.00
3-4 Greg Walters .30 .75
3-5 Matt Davidson .30 .75
4-1 Mike Hurlbut .30 .75
4-2 Shayne Wright .30 .75
4-3 Jay McKee .30 .75
4-4 Dean Melanson .30 .75
4-5 Eric Lavigne .30 .75
5-1 Martin Biron 2.00 5.00
5-2 Sergei Klimentiev .30 .75
5-3 Mike Bales .40 1.00
5-4 Rumun Ndur .30 .75
5-5 Jean-Luc Grand-Pierre .30 .75

1998-99 Rochester Americans

COMPLETE SET (25) 6.00 15.00
1 Craig Fisher .20 .50
2 Greg Walters .20 .50
3 Matt Davidson .20 .50
4 Randy Cunneyworth .20 .50
5 Martin Biron 1.25 3.00
6 Mike Hurlbut .20 .50
7 Tom Draper .30 .75
8 Mike Harder .20 .50
9 Denis Hamel .20 .50
10 Jean-Luc Grand-Pierre .20 .50
11 Scott Nichol .20 .50
12 Francois Methot .20 .50
13 Dean Melanson .20 .50
14 Jason Mansoff .20 .50
15 Jason Holland .20 .50
16 Darren Van Oene .20 .50
17 Dean Sylvester .30 .75
18 Cory Sarich .20 .50
19 Erik Rasmussen .30 .75
20 Dominic Pittis .20 .50
21 The Moose MAS .02 .10
22 Darwin McCutcheon CO .02 .10
23 Jody Gage .30 .75
24 Shane Kenny .20 .50
25 Steffon Walby .20 .50

2000-01 Rochester Americans

COMPLETE SET (29) 4.80 12.00
1 Jeremy Adduono .15 .40
2 Tom Askey .20 .50
3 Martin Biron .75 2.00
4 Kevin Bolibruck .15 .40
5 Craig Brunel .15 .40
6 Brian Campbell .20 .50
7 Craig Charron .15 .40
8 Jason Cipolla .15 .40
9 Jason Holland .15 .40
10 Doug Houda .15 .40
11 Mike Hurlbut .15 .40
12 Dane Jackson .15 .40
13 Jaroslav Kristek .20 .50
14 Mike Mader .15 .40
15 Francois Methot .15 .40
16 Norm Milley .30 .75
17 Joe Murphy .15 .40
18 Todd Nelson .15 .40
19 Mika Noronen .60 1.50
20 Andrew Peters .40 1.00
21 Chris Taylor .15 .40
22 Paul Traynor .15 .40
23 Darren Van Oene .15 .40
24 Randy Cunneyworth CO .10 .25
25 Jon Christiano CO .04 .10
26 Dave A. Williams EM .04 .10
27 Kent Weisbeck TR .04 .10
28 The Moose MASCOT .04 .10
NNO Team CL .04 .10

2002-03 Rochester Americans

COMPLETE SET (26) 8.00 20.00
1 Tom Askey .30 .75
2 Milan Bartovic .20 .50
3 Jason Botterill .20 .50
4 Rory Fitzpatrick .20 .50
5 Paul Gaustad .30 .75
6 Denis Hamel .20 .50
7 Radoslav Hecl .20 .50
8 Doug Houda .20 .50
9 Doug Janik .20 .50
10 Ryan Jorde .20 .50
11 Jaroslav Kristek .30 .75
12 Sean McMorrow .30 .75
13 Francois Methot .20 .50
14 Ryan Miller 2.00 5.00
15 Norm Milley .20 .50
16 Karel Mosovsky .20 .50
17 Jiri Novotny .30 .75
18 Andrew Peters .60 1.50
19 Jason Pominville .60 1.50
20 Peter Ratchuk .20 .50
21 Chris Taylor .20 .50
22 Ryan Miller 2.00 5.00
23 Randy Cunneyworth HCO .04 .10
24 Jon Christiano ACO .04 .10
25 The Moose Mascot .04 .10
NNO Checklist .04 .10

2003-04 Rochester Americans

COMPLETE SET (29) 6.00 15.00
1 Doug Houda ACO .04 .10
2 Tom Askey .30 .75
3 Milan Bartovic .12 .30
4 Jason Botterill .12 .30
5 Brian Chapman .12 .30
6 David Cullen .12 .30
7 Randy Cunneyworth .12 .30
8 Pete Gardiner .12 .30
9 Paul Gaustad .20 .50
10 Doug Janik .12 .30
11 Ryan Jorde .12 .30
12 Steve Lingren .12 .30
13 Sean McMorrow .30 .75
14 Ryan Miller 1.25 3.00
15 Jason Dawe .12 .30
16 Norm Milley .30 .75
17 Karel Mosovsky .12 .30
18 Rick Mrozik .12 .30
19 Jiri Novotny .30 .75
20 Nathan Paetsch .30 .75
21 Geoff Peters .30 .75
22 Domenic Pittis .20 .50
23 Jason Pominville .75 2.00
24 Scott Ricci .12 .30
25 Derek Roy .75 2.00
26 Derek Roy .75 2.00
27 Michael Ryan .20 .50
28 Mascot .04 .10
29 Chris Thorburn .20 .50
NNO Checklist .04 .10

2004-05 Rochester Americans

COMPLETE SET (30) 8.00 20.00
1 Checklist .04 .10
2 Tom Askey .30 .75
3 Milan Bartovic .20 .50
4 Jason Botterill .20 .50
5 David Cullen .20 .50
6 Paul Gaustad .20 .50
7 Doug Janik .20 .50
8 Jeff Jillson .20 .50
9 Ryan Jorde .20 .50
10 Steve Lingren .20 .50
11 Sean McMorrow .30 .75
12 Ryan Miller .75 2.00
13 Norm Milley .20 .50
14 Jiri Novotny .20 .50
15 Nathan Paetsch .20 .50
16 Daniel Paille .40 1.00
17 Geoff Peters .60 1.50
18 Jason Pominville .40 1.00
19 Todd Rohloff .20 .50
20 Derek Roy .40 1.00
21 Michael Ryan .20 .50
22 Brandon Smith .20 .50
23 Chris Taylor .20 .60
24 Chris Thorburn .20 .50
25 Thomas Vanek .75 2.00
26 The Moose MASCOT .04 .10
27 Ryan Miller .75 2.00
28 Derek Roy .40 1.00
29 Thomas Vanek .75 2.00
30 Randy Cunneyworth CO Doug Houda CO .04 .10

2014-15 Rochester Americans

COMPLETE SET (25) 6.00 15.00
1 Joel Armia .30 .75
2 Brady Austin .30 .75
3 Drew Bagnall .30 .75
4 William Carrier .30 .75
5 Chadd Cassidy CO .30 .75
6 Daniel Catenacci .30 .75
7 Jerry D'Amigo .40 1.00
8 Zac Dalpe .30 .75
9 Matt Ellis .30 .75
10 Mikhail Grigorenko .50 1.25
11 Brayden Irwin .30 .75
12 Justin Kea .30 .75
13 Johan Larsson .30 .75
14 Jerome Gauthier-Leduc .30 .75
15 Nathan Lieuwen .30 .75
16 Matt Mackenzie .30 .75
17 Andrey Makarov .30 .75
18 Jake McCabe .40 1.00
19 Nick Petrecki .30 .75
20 Mark Pysyk .40 1.00
21 Chad Ruhwedel .30 .75
22 Jordan Samuels-Thomas .30 .75
23 Tim Schaller .30 .75
24 Kevin Sundher .30 .75
25 Philip Varone .30 .75

1999-00 Rockford IceHogs

COMPLETE SET (26) 20.00 40.00
1 Brant Blackned .75 2.00
2 Peter Cava 1.25 3.00
3 Patrice Charbonneau .75 2.00
4 Mike Correia .75 2.00
5 Dan Davies .75 2.00
6 Raymond Delarosbil .75 2.00
7 Mike Figliomeni 1.25 3.00
8 Jason Firth 1.25 3.00
9 Sheldon Gorski 1.25 3.00
10 Jeff Kostuch .75 2.00
11 Evgeny Krivomaz .75 2.00
12 Derek Landmesser .75 2.00
13 Alexandre Makombo 1.25 3.00
14 Barry McKinley .75 2.00
15 Normand Paquet .75 2.00
16 Jean-Francois Rivard .75 2.00
17 Shawn Smith .75 2.00
18 Carlos Soke .75 2.00
19 Wayne Strachan .75 2.00
20 Curtis Tipler .75 2.00
21 Jesse Welling .75 2.00
22 Scott Burfoot CO .08 .25
23 Dale DeGray CO .08 .25
24 Hamilton E. Hog MASCOT .02 .10
25 Mike Figliomeni AS 1.25 3.00
26 Jason Firth AS 1.25 3.00

2000-01 Rockford IceHogs

COMPLETE SET (25) 4.00 10.00
1 Curtis Bois .20 .50
2 Patrice Charbonneau .20 .50
3 Nick Checco .20 .50
4 Curtis Cruickshank .30 .75
5 Jeff DaCosta .20 .50
6 Dan Davies .20 .50
7 Steve Dumonski .20 .50
8 Chris Fattey .20 .50
9 Mike Figliomeni .20 .50
10 Justin Kearns .30 .75
11 Evgeny Krivomaz .20 .50
12 Jocelyn Langlois .20 .50
13 Michel Periard .20 .50
14 Jean-Francois Rivard .20 .50
15 David Runge .20 .50
16 Francois Sasseville .20 .50
17 Shawn Smith .20 .50
18 Mike Tobin .20 .50
19 Yan Turgeon .20 .50
20 Eduard Zankovets .20 .50
21 Dale DeGray CO .10 .25
22 Scott Burfoot CO .10 .25
23 Hamilton E. Hog MASCOT .10 .25
24 Logo Card .04 .10
25 Header Card .04 .10

2001-02 Rockford IceHogs

COMPLETE SET (25) 8.00 20.00
1 Ben Christopherson .40 1.00
2 Clint Wensley .40 1.00
3 Dan Davies .40 1.00
4 Darwin Murray .40 1.00
5 David Hoogsteen .40 1.00
6 Ernie Thorp .40 1.00
7 Forrest Gore .40 1.00
8 Hamilton E. Hog .40 1.00
9 Harold Hersh .10 .25
10 J.F. Rivard .40 1.00
11 Jared Reigstad .40 1.00
12 Jeff Antonovich .40 1.00
13 Jeff Dacosta .40 1.00
14 Jeremy Vokes .40 1.00
15 Joe Statkus .40 1.00
16 Mike Sgroi .40 1.00
17 Nick Checco .40 1.00
18 Oak Hewer .40 1.00
19 Quinten Van Horlick .40 1.00
20 Scott Bell CO .10 .25
21 Sergei Petrov .40 1.00
22 Steve Debus .40 1.00
23 T.J. Guidarelli .40 1.00
24 Wes Blevins .40 1.00
NNO Team CL .40 1.00

2002-03 Rockford IceHogs

COMPLETE SET (25) 8.00 20.00
1 Scott Bell CO .04 .10
2 Darwin Murray .40 1.00
3 Raitis Ivanans .40 1.00
4 Kenzie Homer .40 1.00
5 Alexander Alexeev .40 1.00
6 Oak Hewer .40 1.00
7 Erik Wendell .40 1.00
8 Jeff Antonovich .40 1.00
9 Matt Loen .40 1.00
10 Jeremy Rebek .40 1.00
11 Steve Cygan .40 1.00
12 Clint Wensley .40 1.00
13 Quinten Van Horlick .40 1.00
14 Steve Dumonski .40 1.00
15 Nick Angell .40 1.00
16 Joe Statkus .40 1.00
17 Jay Hebert .40 1.00
18 Dan Davies .40 1.00
19 Brad Olsen .40 1.00
20 Jeff Dacosta .40 1.00
21 Brant Nicklin .40 1.00
22 Ryan McIntosh .40 1.00
23 Mascot .04 .10
24 Mascot .04 .10
25 Team card/CL .04 .10

2003-04 Rockford IceHogs

COMPLETE SET (20) 6.00 15.00
1 B.J. Adams .30 .75
2 Justin Cardwell .30 .75
3 Steve Cygan .30 .75
4 Dan Davies .30 .75
5 Jeff Ewasko .40 1.00
6 John Glavota .30 .75
7 Kenzie Homer .30 .75
8 Dale Junkin .30 .75
9 Nathan Lutz .30 .75
10 Don Margettie .40 1.00
11 Kelly Miller .30 .75
12 Bob Nardella .30 .75
13 Dave Paradise .30 .75
14 Gary Ricciardi .30 .75
15 Paul Schonfelder .40 1.00
16 Adam Solnik .30 .75
17 Ron Vogel .40 1.00
18 Owen Walter .30 .75
19 Maris Zledins .30 .75
20 Mark Bernard HCO .10 .25

2005-06 Rockford IceHogs

COMPLETE SET (27) 8.00 15.00
1 Greg Barber .20 .50
2 Robin Big Snake .75 2.00
3 Dan Boeser .20 .50
4 Ryan Carrigan .20 .50
5 Matt Gens .20 .50
6 Corey Hessler .20 .50
7 Chaz Johnson .40 1.00
8 Nathan Lutz .20 .50
9 Preston Mizzi .20 .50
10 Bob Nardella .20 .50
11 Jason Notermann .40 1.00
12 Steve Pelletier .20 .50
13 Olivier Proulx .20 .50
14 Jason Ralph .40 1.00
15 Billy Tibbetts .40 1.00
16 Yannick Tifu .20 .50
17 Rob Voltera .20 .50
18 Bruce Watson .40 1.00
19 Steve Yetman .20 .50
20 Tom Zabkowicz .20 .50
21 Josh Mizerek .20 .50
22 Ron Vogel .40 1.00
23 Michel Robinson .20 .50
24 Steve Martinson .20 .50
25 Hammer Hog MASCOT .02 .10
26 Hamilton E. Hog MASCOT .02 .10
NNO Rockford Ice Hogs CL .02 .10

2006-07 Rockford IceHogs

COMPLETE SET (27) 12.00 20.00
1 Jesse Bennefield .30 .75
2 Kaleb Betts .40 1.00
3 Robin Big Snake .75 2.00
4 Dan Boeser .30 .75
5 Paul Brown .30 .75
6 Frederic Cloutier .60 1.50
7 Bryce Cockburn .30 .75
8 Nicolas Corbeil .30 .75
9 Mike Doyle .30 .75
10 Luke Fritshaw .30 .75
11 Matt Gens .30 .75
12 Corey Hessler .30 .75
13 Chaz Johnson .30 .75
14 Mike Letizia .30 .75
15 Erik Lizon .30 .75
16 Nathan Lutz .30 .75
17 Preston Mizzi .40 1.00
18 Jake Moreland .40 1.00
19 Jason Notermann .30 .75
20 Jason Ralph .30 .75
21 Kevin Ulanski .30 .75
22 Bruce Watson .30 .75
23 Tim Wedderburn .30 .75
24 Steve Martinson CO .20 .50
25 Hammer Hog MASCOT .02 .10
26 Hamilton E. Hog MASCOT .02 .10
27 Team Card .10 .25

2014-15 Rockford IceHogs

COMPLETE SET () 10.00 25.00
1 Header Card .30 .75
2 Ted Dent CO .30 .75
3 Adam Clendening .50 1.25
4 Zach Miskovic .30 .75
5 Stephen Johns .30 .75
6 T.J. Brennan .40 1.00
7 Viktor Svedberg .50 1.25
8 Klas Dahlbeck .30 .75
9 Peter Regin .30 .75
10 Dennis Rasmussen .30 .75
11 Drew LeBlanc .30 .75
12 Kyle Cumiskey .30 .75
13 Cody Bass .40 1.00
14 Phillip Danault .30 .75
15 Teuvo Teravainen 1.25 3.00
16 Pierre-Cedric Labrie .30 .75
17 Joakim Nordstrom .50 1.25
18 Ryan Hartman .40 1.00
19 Alex Broadhurst .30 .75
20 Garret Ross .30 .75
21 Matt Carey .30 .75
22 Mark McNeill .30 .75
23 Ville Pokka .30 .75
24 Scott Darling .40 1.00
25 Mac Carruth .30 .75
26 Ryan Schnell .30 .75
27 Mike Leighton .30 .75
28 Brandon Mashinter .30 .75

1995-96 Roller Hockey Magazine RHI

COMPLETE SET (6) 2.00 5.00
1 Oleg Yashin .40 1.00
2 Frankie Ouellette .40 1.00
3 Nick Vitucci .60 1.50
4 Mike Martens .40 1.00
5 Alain Morissette .40 1.00
6 Simon Roy .40 1.00

1999-00 Rouyn-Noranda Huskies

COMPLETE SET (26) 4.80 12.00
1 Kyrill Alexeev .15 .40
2 Marc-Andre Binette .15 .40
3 Maxime Bouchard .15 .40
4 Bruno Cadieux .15 .40
5 Sebastien Centomo .60 1.50
6 Kevin Cloutier .15 .40
7 Jonathan Gauthier .15 .40
8 Patrick Gilbert .15 .40
9 Andre Hart .15 .40
10 Robert Horak .15 .40
11 Eric L'Italien .15 .40
12 Mathieu Leclerc .15 .40
13 Jason Lehoux .15 .40
14 Jonathan Pelletier .15 .40
15 Bertrand-Pierre Plouffe .15 .40
16 Matthew Quinn .15 .40
17 Mike Ribeiro .60 1.50
18 Shawn Scanzano .15 .40
19 Jason Tessier .15 .40
20 Jerome Tremblay .15 .40
21 Alain Turcotte .15 .40
22 Steve Vandal .15 .40
23 Guy Boucher CO .02 .10
24 Andre Parke CO .02 .10
25 Jean Pronovost CO .02 .10
26 Michel Maroux TR .02 .10

2000-01 Rouyn-Noranda Huskies

COMPLETE SET (26) 6.00 15.00
1 Dominic D'Amour .20 .50
2 Jonathan Gauthier .20 .50
3 Matthew Quinn .20 .50
4 Kirill Alexeev .20 .50
5 Sebastian Strozynski .20 .50
6 Bertrand Pierre Plouffe .20 .50
7 Maxime Talbot .20 .50
8 Guillaume Lefebvre .40 1.00
9 Alexandre Morel .20 .50
10 Michal Pinc .20 .50
12 Mathieu Leclerc .20 .50
13 Jerome Marois .20 .50
14 Patrice Theriault .20 .50
15 Patrick Gilbert .20 .50
16 Maxime Ouellet .75 2.00
17 Louis Mandeville .20 .50
18 Wesley Scanzano .30 .75
19 Sebastien Centomo .40 1.00
20 Maxime Bouchard .20 .50
21 Bruno Cadieux .20 .50
22 Jean-Philippe Hamel .20 .50
23 Shawn Scanzano .20 .50
24 Jonathan Gagnon .20 .50
25 Marc-Andre Binette .20 .50
26 Jean Pronovost CO .10 .25
NNO Lappy MASCOT .04 .10

2000-01 Rouyn-Noranda Huskies Signed

COMPLETE SET (26) 24.00 60.00
1 Dominic D'Amour .80 2.00
2 Jonathan Gauthier .80 2.00
3 Matthew Quinn .80 2.00
4 Kirill Alexeev .80 2.00
5 Sebastian Strozynski .80 2.00
6 Bertrand Pierre Plouffe .80 2.00
7 Maxime Talbot .80 2.00
8 Guillaume Lefebvre 2.00 5.00
9 Alexandre Morel .75 2.00
10 Michal Pinc .80 2.00
12 Mathieu Leclerc .80 2.00
13 Jerome Marois .80 2.00
14 Patrice Theriault .80 2.00
15 Patrick Gilbert .80 2.00
16 Maxime Ouellet 4.00 10.00
17 Louis Mandeville .80 2.00
18 Wesley Scanzano 1.20 3.00
19 Sebastien Centomo 6.00 8.00
20 Maxime Bouchard .80 2.00
21 Bruno Cadieux .80 2.00
22 Jean-Philippe Hamel .75 2.00
23 Shawn Scanzano .80 2.00
24 Jonathan Gagnon .80 2.00
25 Marc-Andre Binette .80 2.00
26 Jean Pronovost CO .80 2.00
NNO Lappy MASCOT .04 .10

1993-94 RPI Engineers

COMPLETE SET (31) 4.00 10.00
1 Kelly Askew .15 .40
2 Adam Bartell .15 .40
3 Kobie Boykins .15 .40
4 Jeff Brick .15 .40
5 Tim Carvel .15 .40
6 Wayne Clarke .15 .40
7 Cam Cuthbert .15 .40
8 Steve Duncan ACO .02 .10
9 Dan Fridgen ACO .02 .10
10 Jeff Gabriel .15 .40
11 Craig Hamelin .15 .40
12 Chris Kiley .15 .40
13 Ken Kwasniewski .15 .40
14 Brad Layzell .15 .40
15 Neil Little .30 .75
16 Xavier Majic .20 .50
17 Jeff Matthews .15 .40
18 Chris Maye .15 .40
19 Jeff O'Connor .15 .40
20 Ron Pasco .15 .40
21 Eric Perardi .15 .40
22 Jon Pirrong .15 .40
23 Buddy Powers CO .02 .10
24 Tim Regan .15 .40
25 Bryan Richardson .15 .40
26 Patrick Rochon .15 .40
27 Mike Rolanti .15 .40
28 Tim Spadafore .15 .40
29 Mike Tamburro .15 .40
30 1993-94 Team .15 .40
31 Checklist .02 .10

1976-77 Saginaw Gears

COMPLETE SET (13) 17.50 35.00
1 Rick Chinnick 1.50 3.00
2 Marcel Comeau 1.50 3.00
3 Michel DeGuise 1.50 3.00
4 Marc Gaudreault 1.50 3.00
5 Greg Hotham 1.50 3.00
6 Stu Irving 1.50 3.00
7 Kevin Kemp 1.50 3.00
8 Mario Lessard 1.50 3.00
9 Gord Malinoski 1.50 3.00
10 Mike Ruest 1.50 3.00
11 D'Arcy Ryan 1.50 3.00
12 Dave Westner 1.50 3.00
13 Wayne Zuk 1.50 3.00

1978-79 Saginaw Gears

COMPLETE SET (20) 175.00 300.00
1 Wren Blair 6.00 15.00
2 Marcel Comeau 6.00 15.00
3 Dennis Desrosiers 6.00 15.00
4 Jon Fontas 6.00 15.00
5 Bob Froese 12.50 25.00
6 Gunnar Garrett TR 4.00 10.00
7 Bob Gladney 6.00 15.00
8 Warren Holmes 6.00 15.00
9 Stu Irving 6.00 15.00
10 Larry Hopkins 6.00 15.00
11 Scott Jessee 6.00 15.00
12 Lynn Jorgenson 6.00 15.00
13 Doug Keans 12.50 25.00
14 Claude Larochelle 7.50 15.00
15 Paul McIntosh 6.00 15.00
16 Don Perry 6.00 15.00
17 Greg Steel 6.00 15.00
18 Mark Suzor 6.00 15.00
19 Mark Toffolo 6.00 15.00
20 Dave Westner 6.00 15.00

1999-00 Saginaw Gears
COMPLETE SET (4) 2.00 5.00
1 Brian Mueller .40 1.00
2 Derek Pinfold .40 1.00
3 Jeff Loder .75 2.00
4 Keith Osborne .40 1.00

2003-04 Saginaw Spirit
COMPLETE SET (28) 5.00 12.00
1 Patrick Asselin .20 .50
2 Paul Bissonnette .20 .50
3 Daniel Borges .20 .50
4 Mike Brown .30 .75
5 Chase Crowder .20 .50
6 Steve Dix .20 .50
7 Adam Gibson .20 .50
8 Jesse Gimblett .20 .50
9 Jesse Jenish .20 .50
10 Phil Kozak .20 .50
11 Nick Lees .20 .50
12 Justin McCutcheon .20 .50
13 Patrick McNeill .20 .50
14 Georgi Misharin .20 .50
15 Mike Pain .20 .50
16 Eric Pfligler .20 .50
17 Geoff Platt .20 .50
18 Tom Pyatt .30 .75
19 Taylor Raszka .20 .50
20 Jean-Michel Rizk .30 .75
21 Marc-Andre Rizk .20 .50
22 Adam Sturgeon .20 .50
23 Mike Suggs .20 .50
24 Stephen Sunderman .20 .50
25 Team Card .04 .10
26 Rizk Brothers .20 .50
27 Moe Mantha CO .04 .10
28 Bryan and Jose .04 .10

2004-05 Saginaw Spirit
COMPLETE SET (24) 5.00 12.00
1 Patrick McNeill .20 .50
2 Marek Kvapil .20 .50
3 Jean-Michel Rizk .20 .50
4 Paul Bissonnette .20 .50
5 Patrick Asselin .20 .50
6 Peter Franchin .20 .50
7 Rick Caughell .20 .50
8 Kevin Tuckey .20 .50
9 Gary Klapkowski .20 .50
10 Scott Fletcher .20 .50
11 Daniel Borges .20 .50
12 Jamie Klie .20 .50
13 Chris Ferguson .20 .50
14 Taylor Raszka .20 .50
15 Dan Idema .20 .50
16 Chase Crowder .20 .50
17 Tom Pyatt .30 .75
18 Thomas Harrison .20 .50
19 Sean Courtney .20 .50
20 Aaron Rock .20 .50
21 Jesse Gimblett .20 .50
22 Matt Corrente .40 1.00
23 Mike Brown .30 .75
24 Mascot .04 .10

2005-06 Saginaw Spirit
COMPLETE SET (24) 6.00 12.00
1 Patrick Asselin .20 .50
2 Michal Birner .20 .50
3 Chris Chappell .20 .50
4 Jack Combs .20 .50
5 Matt Corrente .40 1.00
6 Tom Craig .20 .50
7 Ryan Daniels .20 .50
8 Chris Ferguson .20 .50
9 Scott Fletcher .20 .50
10 Jesse Gimblett .20 .50
11 Tyson Gimblett .20 .50
12 Jamie Klie .20 .50
13 Erik Lundmark .20 .50
14 Tom Mannino .20 .50
15 Joe McCann .20 .50
16 Ryan McDonough .20 .50
17 Patrick McNeill .20 .50
18 Tim Priamo .20 .50
19 Tom Pyatt .40 1.00
20 Garrett Sinfield .20 .50
21 Anthony Soboczynski .20 .50
22 Francois Thuot .40 1.00
23 Zack Torquato .20 .50
24 Steven Whitely .20 .50

2006-07 Saginaw Spirit
COMPLETE SET (25) 8.00 15.00
1 Tom Pyatt .40 1.00
2 Patrick Mcneill .30 .75
3 Garrett Sinfield .20 .50
4 Curtis Cooper .20 .50
5 Nick Crawford .20 .50
6 Tommy Mannino .20 .50
7 Christopher Breen .20 .50
8 Tomas Zaborsky .20 .50
9 Jan Mursak .20 .50
10 Matt Corrente .30 .75
11 Tyler Haskins .20 .50
12 Andrew Cloutier .20 .50
13 Tom Craig .20 .50
14 Chris Chappell .20 .50
15 Ryan Daniels .40 1.00
16 Jack Combs .20 .50
17 Zack Torquato .40 1.00
18 Patrick Asselin .20 .50
19 Jovica Zelenbaba .20 .50
20 T.J. Brodie .20 .50
21 Ryan Berard .20 .50
22 Ryan McDonough .20 .50
23 Sammy Spirit MASCOT .10 .25
24 Steagle Colbeagle MASCOT .40 1.00
LE1 Patrick Mcneill .75 2.00

2014-15 Saginaw Spirit
COMPLETE SET (24) 6.00 15.00
1 Nick Moutrey .30 .75
2 Artem Artemov .30 .75
3 Jacob Ringuette .30 .75
4 Blake Clarke .30 .75
5 Tye Felhaber .30 .75
6 Jake Paterson .30 .75
7 Keaton Middleton .30 .75
8 Luke Cairns .30 .75
9 David Ovsjannikov .30 .75
10 Nikita Serebryakov .30 .75
11 Mitchell Stephens .30 .75
12 Jack Webb .30 .75
13 Jimmy Lodge .30 .75
14 Connor Brown .30 .75
15 Adam McPhail .30 .75
16 Devon Paliani .30 .75
17 Mitchell Webb .30 .75
18 Michael Holmes .30 .75
19 Kris Bennett .30 .75
20 Dylan Sadowy .30 .75
21 Ryan Orban .30 .75
22 Marcus Crawford .30 .75
23 Sean Callaghan .30 .75
CL Header Card CL .30 .75

1994-95 Saint John Flames
COMPLETE SET (26) 3.00 8.00
1 Joel Bouchard .20 .50
2 Rick Carriere ACO .02 .10
3 Ryan Duthie .08 .25
4 Neil Eisenhut .08 .25
5 Leonard Esau .08 .25
6 Bob Francis CO .02 .10
7 Mark Greig .08 .25
8 Francois Groleau .08 .25
9 Sami Helenius .30 .75
10 Todd Hlushko .20 .50
11 Dale Kushner .08 .25
12 Bobby Marshall .08 .25
13 Scott Morrow .08 .25
14 Michael Murray .08 .25
15 Jason Muzzatti .30 .75
16 Barry Nieckar .08 .25
17 Nicolas Perreault .08 .25
18 Jeff Perry .08 .25
19 Dwayne Roloson .30 .75
20 Todd Simpson .08 .25
21 Harbour Station .02 .10
22 Cory Stillman .30 .75
23 David Struch .08 .25
24 Niklas Sundblad .08 .25
25 Andrei Trefilov .20 .50
26 Vesa Viitakoski .08 .25

1996-97 Saint John Flames
COMPLETE SET (26) 4.00 10.00
1 Jamie Allison .15 .40
2 Chris Dingman .20 .50
3 Scott Fraser .15 .40
4 Denis Gauthier .15 .40
5 Ian Gordon .15 .40
6 Patrik Haltia .20 .50
7 Sami Helenius .30 .75
8 Marc Hussey .15 .40
9 Marko Jantunen .20 .50
10 Ladislav Kohn .15 .40
11 Martin Lamarche .15 .40
12 Jesper Mattsson .20 .50
13 Keith McCambridge .15 .40
14 Dale McTavish .15 .40
15 Burke Murphy .15 .40
16 Marty Murray .30 .75
17 Paxton Schulte .15 .40
18 Jarrod Skalde .30 .75
19 Jason Smith .30 .75
20 Clarke Wilm .20 .50
21 Ravil Yakubov .15 .40
22 Paul Baxter CO .08 .25
23 Jeff Perry CO .08 .25
24 Fleaburn MAS .02 .10
25 AHL Web Site .01 .05
26 PHPA Web Site .01 .05

1995-96 Saint John Flames
COMPLETE SET (25) 15.00 40.00
1 Jamie Allison .60 1.50
2 Paul Baxter CO .60 1.50
3 Joel Bouchard .60 1.50
4 Tom Coolen CO .60 1.50
5 Brett Duncan .60 1.50
6 Ian Gordon .60 1.50
7 Sami Helenius 1.25 3.00
8 Todd Hlushko .60 1.50
9 Marc Hussey .60 1.50
10 Ladislav Kohn .60 1.50
11 Frank Kovacs .60 1.50
12 David Ling .75 2.00
13 Jesper Mattsson .60 1.50
14 Keith McCambridge .60 1.50
15 Marty Murray .75 2.00
16 Michael Murray .60 1.50
17 David Neilson .60 1.50
18 Jeff Perry .60 1.50
19 Darren Ritchie .60 1.50
20 Dwayne Roloson 6.00 15.00
21 Todd Simpson .60 1.50
22 Jarrod Skalde .75 2.00
23 David Struch .60 1.50
24 Niklas Sundblad .75 2.00
25 Vesa Viitakoski .60 1.50

1997-98 Saint John Flames
COMPLETE SET (25) 8.00 15.00
1 Jamie Allison .15 .40
2 Erik Andersson .15 .40
3 Ryan Bast .15 .40
4 Travis Brigley .15 .40
5 Eric Charron .15 .40
6 Jeff Cowan .30 .75
7 Hnat Domenichelli .20 .50
8 Jim Dowd .20 .50
9 Denis Gauthier .30 .75
10 Jean-Sebastien Giguere 2.00 5.00
11 Sami Helenius .30 .75
12 Ladislav Kohn .15 .40
13 Eric Landry .15 .40
14 Jesper Mattsson .15 .40
15 Keith McCambridge .15 .40
16 Tyler Moss .20 .50
17 Burke Murphy .15 .40
18 Marty Murray .20 .50
19 Chris O'Sullivan .15 .40
20 Paxton Schulte .20 .50
21 Rocky Thompson .15 .40
22 John Tripp .20 .50
23 Clarke Wilm .15 .40
24 Bill Stewart HCO .08 .25
25 Jeff Perry CO .08 .25

2005-06 Saint John Sea Dogs
COMPLETE SET (24) 6.00 12.00
1 Jason Churchill .40 1.00
2 Alex Grant .20 .50
3 Alexandre Monahan .20 .50
4 Alexandre Labonte .20 .50
5 Brett Gallant .20 .50
6 Cedric Archambault .20 .50
7 Charles Bergeron .40 1.00
8 Felix Schutz .40 1.00
9 Jean-Philippe Cote .20 .50
10 Jeff Caron .20 .50
11 Jevin Maclellan .20 .50
12 Jonathan Laberge .20 .50
13 Kevin Coughlin .20 .50
14 Martin Bartos .20 .50
15 Maxime Dubuc .20 .50
16 Mike Neil .20 .50
17 Patrick Leask .20 .50
18 Riley Whitlock .40 1.00
19 Ryan Moore .20 .50
20 Ryan Sparling .20 .50
21 Sebastien Rioux .20 .50
22 Vincent Lambert .20 .50
23 Matthew Block .20 .50
24 Luc Melanson .20 .50

2006-07 Saint John Sea Dogs
COMPLETE SET (25) 8.00 15.00
1 Alex Grant .40 1.00
2 Mike Noyers .25 .60
3 Ryan Sparling .25 .60
4 Felix Schutz .40 1.00
5 David Macdonald .25 .60
6 Dave Bouchard .25 .60
7 Bruce Crawford .25 .60
8 Sebastien Rioux .25 .60
9 Jonathan Laberge .25 .60
10 Mike Thomas .25 .60
11 Charles Bergeron .25 .60
12 Shayne Tremblay .25 .60
13 Maxime Dubuc .25 .60
14 Alexandre Labonte .25 .60
15 Olivier Painchaud .25 .60
16 David Stich .25 .60
17 Chris Didomenico .25 .60
18 Alexandre Monohan .25 .60
19 Anthony Bergin .25 .60
20 Maxime Joyal .40 1.00
21 Aaron Barton .40 1.00
22 Pascal Amyot .25 .60
23 Brett Gallant .25 .60
24 Yann Sauve .25 .60
LE1 Alex Grant .75 2.00

2015-16 Saint John Sea Dogs
COMPLETE SET (25) 6.00 15.00
1 Adam Bateman .30 .75
2 Jason Bell .30 .75
3 Alex Bishop .30 .75
4 Thomas Chabot .30 .75
5 Austin Clapman .30 .75
6 Daniel Del Paggio .30 .75
7 Samuel Dove-Mcfalls .30 .75
8 Oliver Felixson .30 .75
9 Matt Green .30 .75
10 Luke Green .30 .75
11 Matthew Highmore .30 .75
12 Bokondji Imana .30 .75
13 Mathieu Joseph .30 .75
14 Adam Marsh .30 .75
15 Nathan Noel .30 .75
16 Sam Povorozniouk .30 .75
17 Spencer Smallman .30 .75
18 Julien Tessier .30 .75
19 Dawson Theede .30 .75
20 Marc-Antoine Turcotte .30 .75
21 Joe Veleno .30 .75
22 Joe Veleno FG .30 .75
23 Kyle Ward .30 .75
24 Bailey Webster .30 .75
25 Jakub Zboril .30 .75

2003-04 Salmon Arm Silverbacks
COMPLETE SET (25) 8.00 20.00
1 Evan Barlow .20 .50
2 Jay Birnie .40 1.00
3 Steve Christie .40 1.00
4 Kris Chucko 1.25 3.00
5 Rick Cleaver .20 .50
6 Spencer Dillon .20 .50
7 Bryn Gagnon .20 .50
8 Trevor Geiger .20 .50
9 Blaine Jarvis .20 .50
10 Jaye Judd .20 .50
11 Patrick Lepage .40 1.00
12 Julian Marcuzzi .20 .50
13 Tyrell Mason .20 .50
14 Ryan McLeod .20 .50
15 Jason Miller .20 .50
16 Travis Ramsey .20 .50
17 Chris Shudo .20 .50
18 Kiel Sonne .40 1.00
19 Ben Street .20 .50
20 Craig Switzer .20 .50
21 Travis Zajac 2.00 5.00
22 Header Card .04 .10
23 Award Winners .40 1.00
24 Header Card .04 .10
25 Team Photo .20 .50

2004-05 Salmon Arm Silverbacks
COMPLETE SET (24) 5.00 12.00
1 Jamie Silverson .30 .75
2 Brendon Nash .30 .75
3 Dustin Degagne .30 .75
4 Robbie Rodgers .30 .75
5 Mark Santorelli .30 .75
6 Brodie Sheahan .30 .75
7 Ben Street .30 .75
8 Tyrell Mason .30 .75
9 Darcy Zajac .40 1.00
10 Bryn Gagnon .30 .75
11 Trevor Geiger .30 .75
12 Luke Cain .30 .75
13 Ryan Duncan .30 .75
14 Ernie Stewart .30 .75
15 Kiel Sonne .30 .75
16 Jesse Deckert .30 .75
17 Brad Atkinson .30 .75
18 Evan Barlow .30 .75
19 Julian Marcuzzi .30 .75
20 Jesse Griffith .30 .75
21 Kong MASCOT .04 .10
22 Team Card .04 .10
23 Logo Card .04 .10
24 Logo Card .30 .75

2005-06 Salmon Arm Silverbacks
COMPLETE SET (25) 10.00 20.00
1 Logo .01 .01
2 Logo .01 .01
3 August Aiken .40 1.00
4 Billy Blase .40 1.00
5 Luke Cain .40 1.00
6 Dustin Degagne .40 1.00
7 Matt Dyck .40 1.00
8 Jesse Griffith .40 1.00
9 Travis Holloway .40 1.00
10 Damon Kipp .40 1.00
11 Josh Lund .40 1.00
12 Cam Macintyre .40 1.00
13 Brendon Nash .40 1.00
14 Evan Pighin .40 1.00
15 Chris Rawlings .40 1.00
16 Rob Rodgers .40 1.00
17 Brodie Sheahan .40 1.00
18 Erik Spady .40 1.00
19 Ernie Stewart .40 1.00
20 Justin Taylor .40 1.00
21 Ben Winnet .40 1.00
22 Shaun Witschen .40 1.00
23 Darcy Zajac .40 1.00
24 Kong MASCOT .01 .01
25 Ad Card .01 .01

2014-15 Salmon Arm Silverbacks
COMPLETE SET (20) 5.00 12.00
1 Angus Redmond .30 .75
2 Phillip Middleton .30 .75
3 Andrew Farny .30 .75
4 Chase Priskie .30 .75
5 Ryley Booth .30 .75
6 Damian Chrcek .30 .75
7 Logan Mick .30 .75
8 Nick Hutchison .30 .75
9 Carson Bolduc .30 .75
10 Thomas Plese .30 .75
11 Josh Blanchard .30 .75
12 Taro Hirose .30 .75
13 Jack Berezan .30 .75
14 Colton Thibault .30 .75
15 Shane Danyluk .30 .75
16 Ross Heidt .30 .75
17 Bryden Marsh .30 .75
18 Taylor Maruya .30 .75
19 Josh Laframboise .30 .75
20 Zach Dyment .30 .75

1988-89 Salt Lake Golden Eagles
COMPLETE SET (24) 12.00 30.00
1 Rick Barkovich .20 .50
2 Michael Dark .20 .50
3 Terry Perkins .20 .50
4 Peter Lappin .20 .50
5 Wayne Cowley .20 .50
6 Rich Chernomaz .20 .50
7 Steve Smith .40 1.00
8 Theo Fleury 8.00 20.00
9 Dave Reierson .20 .50
10 Not Issued .20 .50
11 Martin Simard .20 .50
12 Stu Grimson 1.25 3.00
13 Darwin McCutcheon .20 .50
14 Doug Clarke .20 .50
15 Doug Pickell .20 .50
16 Randy Bucyk .20 .50
17 Jim Johannson .20 .50
18 Rick Lessard .20 .50
19 Ken Sabourin .20 .50
20 Chris Biotti .20 .50
21 Jeff Wenaas .20 .50
22 Mark Holmes .20 .50
23 Bob Bodak .20 .50
24 Marc Bureau .40 1.00
NNO Smokey the Bear .20 .50

1992-93 Salt Lake Golden Eagles
COMPLETE SET (26) 4.00 10.00
1 Todd Brost .15 .40
2 Rod Buskas .15 .40
3 Rich Chernomaz .15 .40
4 Kerry Clark .15 .40
5 Tomas Forslund .15 .40
6 Todd Gillingham .15 .40
7 Todd Harkins .15 .40
8 Tim Harris .15 .40
9 Shawn Heaphy .15 .40
10 Paul Holden .15 .40
11 Trevor Kidd .40 1.00
12 Paul Kruse .20 .50
13 Patrick Lebeau .20 .50
14 Sandy McCarthy .30 .75
15 Kris Miller .15 .40
16 Jason Muzzatti .20 .50
17 Alex Nikolic .15 .40
18 Ken Sabourin .15 .40
19 David St. Pierre .15 .40
20 Darren Stolk .15 .40
21 David Sturch .15 .40
22 Andrei Trefilov .20 .50
23 Kevin Wortman .15 .40
24 Bob Francis CO .08 .25
25 Brian Patafie TR .02 .10
26 Team card .15 .40

1998-99 San Angelo Outlaws
COMPLETE SET (27) 7.20 18.00
1 Jason Abel .30 .75
2 Jean Blouin .30 .75
3 Carl Boudreau .40 1.00
4 Daniel Chaput .30 .75
5 Ryan Connolly .30 .75
6 Brad Cook .30 .75
7 Marty Diamond .30 .75
8 Chad Erickson .40 1.00
9 Sandis Girvitch .30 .75
10 Ross Harris .40 1.00
11 Kevin McKinnon .30 .75
12 Aigars Mironovics .30 .75
13 Skeeter Moore .30 .75
14 Carl Paradis .40 1.00
15 Ryan Reid .30 .75
16 Al Rooney .30 .75
17 Shayne Stevenson .40 1.00
18 Mike Vandenberghe .30 .75
19 Kris Waltze .30 .75
20 Tom Nurre .30 .75
21 Rich Van Patten EM .08 .25
22 Shaun Clouston CO .08 .25
23 Ransom Mascot .08 .25
24 Rusty Mascot .08 .25
25 Jay Willman ANNC .08 .25
26 Jonathan Luce .30 .75
27 Joe Briley TR .08 .25

1999-00 San Angelo Outlaws
COMPLETE SET (31) 30.00 75.00
1 Mike Bajurny 1.50 4.00
2 Scott Chartier 1.25 3.00
3 Jamie Garrick 1.25 3.00
4 Sandis Girvitch 1.25 3.00
5 Corey Isen 1.25 3.00
6 Ed Kowalski 1.25 3.00
7 Kevin Kreutzer 1.50 4.00
8 Adam Lord 1.50 4.00
9 Dave Lylyk 1.25 3.00
10 Kevin McKinnon 1.25 3.00
11 Skeeter Moore 1.25 3.00
12 Erik Noack 1.25 3.00
13 Carl Paradis 1.50 4.00
14 Pavel Evstigneev 1.25 3.00
15 Robby Sandrock 1.25 3.00
17 Kris Waltze 1.50 4.00
18 Dion Wandler 1.25 3.00
19 Darren Wright 1.25 3.00
21 San Angelo Coliseum .40 1.00
22 Frank Froio EQM .40 1.00
23 Jeff Smith 1.25 3.00
24 Harvard
Henry .40 1.00
26 Mike Collins CO .40 1.00
27 Off-Ice Officials .40 1.00
28 Ransom Mascot .40 1.00
29 Rusty Mascot .40 1.00
31 Inflatable Rusty .40 1.00
32 Side Rink Action .40 1.00
33 Team Photo .40 1.00
34 Jay Willman 1.25 3.00
35 Booster Club .40 1.00

1998-99 San Antonio Iguanas
COMPLETE SET (21) 4.80 12.00
1 Ken Shepard .20 .50
2 John Hultberg .40 1.00
3 Brian Shantz .40 1.00
4 Paul Jackson .40 1.00
5 Iggy Mascot .02 .10
6 Jason MacIntyre .75 2.00
7 Pat Caron .20 .50
8 Mike Tobin .20 .50
9 Dave Doucette .20 .50
10 Marc Laforge .20 .50
11 Kevin Lune .20 .50
12 Jay Pylypuik .20 .50
13 Johnny Brdarovic .20 .50
14 Roy Gray .20 .50
15 Ricky Jacob .20 .50
16 Blair Rota .20 .50
17 Cheyne Lazar .20 .50
18 Trevor Matschke .20 .50
19 Fred Goltz .20 .50
20 Todd Gordon HCO .02 .10
21 Iguanas Cheerleaders .40 1.00

1999-00 San Antonio Iguanas
COMPLETE SET (25) 4.00 10.00
1 San Antonio Iguanas .20 .50
2 Church's Chicken .10 .25
3 Jason MacIntyre .20 .50
4 Trevor Matschke .20 .50
5 Johnny Brdarovich .20 .50
6 Scott Green .20 .50
7 Brian Shantz .30 .75
8 Henry Kuster .30 .75
9 Bob Westerby .30 .75
10 Blair Rota .20 .50
11 Garnet Jacobson .20 .50
12 Ricky Jacob .20 .50
13 Jeff Boettger .20 .50
14 Wade Gibson .20 .50
15 Sam Fields .20 .50
16 Marc Laforge .30 .75
17 Trevor Anderson .20 .50
18 Corwin Saurdiff .30 .75
19 Mitch Shawara .20 .50
20 Chris Stewart CO .08 .25
21 Craig Coxe CO .30 .75
22 Manny Sanchez TR .02 .10
23 Chad Daniels TR .02 .10
24 Iggy MAS .02 .10
25 San Antonio Iguanas CL .02 .10

2003-04 San Antonio Rampage
COMPLETE SET (24) 5.00 12.00
1 Scott Allen HCO .04 .10
2 Ian Herbers ACO .04 .10
3 Lukas Krajicek .30 .75
4 Daryl Andrews .30 .75
5 Mascot .04 .10
6 Kent Huskins .20 .50
7 Paul Elliott .20 .50
8 Grant McNeill .20 .50
9 Vaclav Nedorost .20 .50
10 Greg Campbell .30 .75
11 Sean O'Connor .20 .50
12 Ryan Jardine .20 .50
13 Brent Cullaton .20 .50
14 Denis Shvidki .20 .50
15 Josh Olson .20 .50
16 Eric Beaudoin .20 .50
17 Matt Dzieduszycki .20 .50
18 Petr Taticek .40 1.00
19 Michel Periard .20 .50
20 Simon Lajeunesse .40 1.00
21 Kristian Kudroc .20 .50
22 Lee Goren .30 .75
23 Travis Scott .30 .75
24 Sponsor .04 .10

2004-05 San Antonio Rampage
COMPLETE SET (22) 10.00 25.00
1 Mascot .04 .10
2 Lukas Krajicek .40 1.00
3 T.J. Reynolds .40 1.00
4 Jay Bouwmeester .75 2.00
5 Filip Novak .40 1.00
6 Joel Kwiatkowski .40 1.00
7 Serge Payer .40 1.00
8 Stephen Weiss .75 2.00
9 Chris Nielsen .40 1.00
10 Gregory Campbell .75 2.00
11 Joe Cullen .40 1.00
12 Ryan Jardine .40 1.00
13 Rob Globke .75 2.00
14 Nathan Horton .75 2.00
15 Juraj Kolnik .40 1.00
16 Jeff Brown .40 1.00
17 Petr Taticek .40 1.00
18 Kamil Kreps .40 1.00
19 Patrick DesRochers .75 2.00
20 Victor Uchevatov .40 1.00
21 Travis Scott .40 1.00
22 Greg Jacina .40 1.00

1995-96 San Diego Barracudas RHI
COMPLETE SET (14) 2.00 5.00
1 Dan Elsener .20 .50
2 Sandy Gasseau .20 .50
3 Brad Belland .20 .50
4 Stephen Grogg .20 .50
5 Frankie Ouellette .30 .75
6 Alan Leggett .20 .50
7 Soren True .20 .50
8 John Spoltore .30 .75
9 Ralph Barahona .20 .50
10 Oleg Yashin .20 .50
11 Stephane St. Amour .20 .50
12 Max Middendorf .30 .75
13 Clark Polgase .20 .50
14 Steve Martinson HCO .08 .25

1992-93 San Diego Gulls
COMPLETE SET (24) 4.00 10.00
1 John Anderson .20 .50
2 Perry Anderson .15 .40
3 Scott Arniel .20 .50
4 Michael Brewer .15 .40
5 Dale DeGray .15 .40
6 Gord Dineen .15 .40
7 Rick Dudley CO .15 .40
8 Larry Floyd .15 .40
9 Keith Gretzky .20 .50
10 Peter Hankinson .15 .40
11 Bill Houlder .20 .50
12 Andrei Iakovenko .15 .40
13 Rick Knickle .30 .75
14 Denny Lambert .20 .50
15 Mitch Lamoureux .20 .50
16 Clint Malarchuk .30 .75
17 Steve Martinson .15 .40
18 Hubie McDonough .20 .50
19 Don McSween .15 .40
20 Mitch Molloy .15 .40
21 Robbie Nichols .15 .40
22 Lindy Ruff .20 .50
23 Daniel Shank .30 .75
24 Sergei Starikov .15 .40

1999-00 San Diego Gulls
COMPLETE SET (20) 6.00 15.00
1 Rod Aldoff .20 .50
2 Brad Belland .20 .50
3 Jamie Black .30 .75
4 Frederick Jobin .20 .50
5 Olaf Kjenstadt .30 .75
6 Brett Larson .20 .50
7 Steven Low .20 .50
8 B.J. MacPherson .20 .50
9 Petr Marek .20 .50
10 Taj Melson .20 .50
11 Sergei Naumov .60 1.50
12 Barry Potomski .60 1.50
13 Dennis Purdie .60 1.50
14 Martin St. Amour .30 .75
15 Stephane St. Amour .30 .75
16 Mark Woolf .30 .75
17 Steve Martinson HCO .30 .75
18 Gulls Win .20 .50
19 Goal Celebration .20 .50
20 Gulls Girls Cheerleaders .40 1.00

2000-01 San Diego Gulls
COMPLETE SET (22) 3.60 10.00
1 Jamie Black .16 .40
2 Cris Classen .16 .75
3 Serge Crochetiere .16 .40
4 Dan Gravelle .16 .40
5 Trevor Koenig .16 .75
6 Ashley Langdone .16 1.00
7 Brett Larson .16 .40
8 Cory Laylin .16 .40
9 B.J. MacPherson .16 .40
10 Kevin Mackie .16 .40
11 Petr Marek .16 .40
12 Taj Melson .16 .40
13 Brian Morrison .16 .40
14 Samy Nasreddine .16 .40
15 Jeff Petruic .16 .40
16 Dennis Purdie .30 .75
17 Mark Stitt .16 .40
18 Mike Taylor .16 .40
19 Chad Wagner .16 .40
20 Mark Woolf .16 .40
21 Gulls Score! .10 .25
22 San Diego Gulls Bench .16 .40

2001-02 San Diego Gulls
COMPLETE SET (24) 10.00 25.00
1 Boyd Ballard .40 1.00
2 Jamie Black .40 1.00
3 Clint Cabana .40 1.00
4 Serge Crochetiere .40 1.00
5 Jaisen Freeman .40 1.00
6 Dan Gravelle .40 1.00
7 Trevor Koenig .40 1.00
8 Ashley Langdone .40 1.00
9 Shawn Mansoff .40 1.00
10 Petr Marek .40 1.00
11 Taj Melson .40 1.00
12 Brian Morrison .40 1.00
13 Samy Nasreddine .60 1.50
14 Billy Pugliese .40 1.00
15 Dennis Purdie .75 2.00
16 Trevor Sherban .40 1.00
17 John Spoltore .75 2.00
18 Mark Stitt .40 1.00
19 Mark Woolf .75 2.00
20 B.J. MacPherson .60 1.50
21 Gulls Girls .75 2.00
22 Sandy MASCOT .04 .10
23 Gulls Bench .04 .10
24 Gulls Score! .20 .50

1994-95 San Jose Rhinos RHI
COMPLETE SET (16) 3.00 8.00
1 Rocky Mascot .08 .25
2 Ken Blum .20 .50
3 Steve Carpenter .20 .50
4 Will Clarke .20 .50
5 Darren Colbourne .20 .50
6 Bart Cote .20 .50
7 Brian Goudie .20 .50
8 Jon Gustafson .30 .75
9 Greg Hadden .20 .50
10 Blaine Moore .20 .50
11 Jay Murphy .20 .50
12 Dennis Purdie .40 1.00
13 Roy Sommer CO .08 .25
14 Mike Taylor .20 .50
15 Darren Wetherill .20 .50
16 Mark Woolf .30 .75

1994-95 Sarnia Sting
COMPLETE SET (31) 4.00 10.00
1 Checklist .02 .10
2 Ken Carroll .10 .30
3 Scott Hay .10 .30
4 Kam White .10 .30
5 Joe Doyle .10 .30
6 Tom Brown .10 .30
7 Jeremy Miculinic .10 .30
8 Darren Mortier .10 .30
9 Aaron Brand .20 .50
10 Chris George .10 .30
11 Stephane Soulliere .10 .30
12 Paul McInnes .10 .30
13 Trevor Letowski .40 1.00
14 Dustin McArthur .10 .30
15 Rob Massa .10 .30
16 Brendan Yarema .10 .30
17 Dan DelMonte .10 .30
18 B.J. Johnston .10 .30
19 Wes Mason .10 .30
20 Rob Guinn .10 .30
21 Jeff Brown .10 .30
22 Dennis Maxwell .10 .30
23 Damon Hardy .10 .30
24 Alan Letang .20 .50
25 Matt Hogan .10 .30
26 Sasha Cucuz .10 .30
27 Rich Brown CO .02 .10
28 Gord Hamilton TR .02 .10
29 Dino Ciccarelli
Shawn Burr .20 .50
30 Buzz MASCOT .02 .10
NNO Ad Card .02 .10

1995-96 Sarnia Sting
COMPLETE SET (25) 5.00 12.00
1 Jeff Salajko .20 .5
2 Patrick DesRochers .30 .7
3 Gerald Moriarity .20 .5
4 Allan Carr .20 .5
5 Tom Brown .20 .5
6 Andy Delmore .30 .7
7 Darren Mortier .20 .5
8 Aaron Brand .20 .5
9 Eric Boulton .60 1.5
10 Jonathan Sim .30 .7
11 Trevor Letowski .30 .7
12 Mike Hanson .20 .5
13 Todd Miller .20 .5
14 Brendan Yarema .20 .5
15 Brad Simms .20 .5
16 David Nemirovsky .20 .5
17 Jeff Brown .20 .5
18 Andrew Proskurnicki .20 .5
19 Wes Mason .20 .5
20 Scott Corbett .20 .5
21 Dave Bourque .20 .5
22 Sean Brown .20 .5
23 Marcin Snita .20 .5
24 Rich Brown ACO .02 .1
25 Mark Hunter HCO .08 .2

1996-97 Sarnia Sting
COMPLETE SET (31) 6.00 10.0
1 Bill Abercrombie ACO .10 .2
2 Louie Blackbird .15 .4
3 Bryan Blair .15 .4
4 Dave Bourque .15 .4
5 Joe Canale CO .10 .2
6 Scott Corbett .15 .4
7 Andy Delmore .30 .7
8 Patrick DesRochers .30 .7
9 Michael Hanson .15 .4
10 Abe Herbst .20 .5
11 Shane Kenny .15 .4
12 Darryl Knight .15 .4
13 Trevor Letowski .40 1.0
14 Trevor Letowski .40 1.
15 Wes Mason .20 .5
16 Darren Mortier .15 .4
17 Kevin Mota .15 .4
18 Eoin McInerney .30 .7
19 Lucas Nehrling .15 .4
20 Dan Pawlaczyk .15 .4

21 Andrew Proskurnicki .15 .40
22 Richard Rochefort .15 .40
23 Bogdan Rudenko .15 .40
24 Jon Sim .40 1.00
25 Brad Simms .15 .40
26 Marcin Snita .15 .40
27 Casey Wolak .15 .40
28 Season Line-Up .02 .10
29 Title Card .10 .25
30 Team Logo .10 .25
31 Calendar Card .02 .10

2000-01 Sarnia Sting

COMPLETE SET (24) 4.80 12.00
1 Header Card .04 .10
2 Larry Bernard CO .10 .25
3 Chris Berti .20 .50
4 Cory Brekelmans .20 .50
5 Rick Brown CO .10 .25
6 Alex Buturlin .20 .50
7 Adam Campbell .20 .50
8 Tyler Coleman .20 .50
9 Ryan Fraser .20 .50
10 Robert Gherson .40 1.00
11 Julius Halfkenny .20 .50
12 Ryan Hare .20 .50
13 John Hecimovic .20 .50
14 Scott Heffernan .20 .50
15 Eric Himelfarb .40 1.00
16 Dusty Jamieson .30 .75
17 Jeff Luckovitch .20 .50
18 Preston Mizzi .20 .50
19 Kris Newbury .30 .75
20 Robb Palahnuk .20 .50
21 Jason Penner .30 .75
22 Tom Rogerson .20 .50
23 Maxim Rybin .30 .75
24 Reg Thomas .20 .50

2003-04 Sarnia Sting

COMPLETE SET (23) 5.00 12.00
1 Charles Amodeo .20 .50
2 John Barrow .30 .75
3 Marco Caprara .30 .75
4 Daniel Carcillo .75 2.00
5 Marek Chvatal .20 .50
6 Richard Clune .20 .50
7 Craig Foster .20 .50
8 Dan Fritsche .75 2.00
9 Micheal Haley .20 .50
10 John Hecimovic .20 .50
11 Anton Kadeykin .20 .50
12 Colt King .30 .75
13 Drew Larman .20 .50
14 Matt Manias .20 .50
15 Ryan Munce .60 1.50
16 Matt Pelech .20 .50
17 David Pszenyczny .20 .50
18 Daniel Sisca .20 .50
19 Trevor Solomon .20 .50
20 Joey Tenute .30 .75
21 Steve Ward .20 .50
22 Jeff Whitfield .20 .50
23 Kelsey Wilson .20 .50

2006-07 Sarnia Sting

COMPLETE SET (22) 12.00 20.00
1 Steven Stamkos 4.00 10.00
2 Trevor Kell .30 .75
3 Tomas Pospisil .30 .75
4 Steven Reese .30 .75
5 Steve Ferry .30 .75
6 Sebastian Dahm .40 1.00
7 Ryan Wilson .30 .75
8 Parker Van Buskirk .40 1.00
9 Mike Roelofsen .30 .75
10 Matt Martin .30 .75
11 Mark Katic .50 1.25
12 Kyle Tront .30 .75
13 Justin Dibenedetto .30 .75
14 Jared Gomes .30 .75
15 Harrison Rood .30 .75
16 Danny Anger .30 .75
17 Daniel Lombardi .30 .75
18 Dalton Prout .30 .75
19 Christian Steingraber .30 .75
20 Chris Mifflen .30 .75
21 Brandon Mashinter .30 .75
22 Bobby Davey .30 .75

2007-08 Sarnia Sting

COMPLETE SET (25) 5.00 12.00
1 Tomi Karhunen .15 .40
2 Peter DiSalvo .15 .40
3 Ryan Berard .15 .40
4 Justin DiBenedetto .15 .40
5 Devin Didiomete .15 .40
6 Steve Ferry .15 .40
7 Jared Gomes .15 .40
8 Jordan Hill .15 .40
9 Marek Indra .15 .40
10 Mark Katic .15 .40
11 Colt Kennedy .15 .40
12 Dan Lombardi .15 .40
13 Matt Martin .15 .40
14 Brett Oliphant .15 .40
15 Ben O'Quinn .15 .40
16 Dalton Prout .15 .40
17 Harrison Reed .15 .40
18 Steve Reese .15 .40
19 Joe Rogalski .15 .40
20 Matt Smyth .15 .40
21 Steven Stamkos 1.00 2.50
22 Steve Whitely .15 .40
23 Ryan Wilson .15 .40
24 Aaron Snow .15 .40
25 Jamie Arniel .15 .40

1992-93 Saskatchewan JHL

COMPLETE SET (168) 8.00 20.00
1 Troy Edwards .05 .15
2 Simon Oliver .05 .15
3 Gerald Tallaire .05 .15
4 Blair Allison .05 .15
5 Mads True .05 .15
6 Steve Brent .05 .15
7 Jay Dobrescu .05 .15
8 Dave Debusschere .05 .15
9 Bryan Cossette .05 .15
10 Brooke Battersby .05 .15
11 Kyle Niemegeers .05 .15
12 Darren McLean .05 .15
13 Carson Cardinal .05 .15
14 Bill McKay .05 .15
15 Chris Hatch .05 .15
16 Nolan Weir .05 .15
17 Karl Johnson .05 .15
18 Jason Brown .05 .15
19 Tyler Kuhn .05 .15
20 Daniel Dennis .05 .15
21 Wally Spence .05 .15
22 Rob Beck .05 .15
23 Aaron Cain .20 .50
24 Darryl Dickson .05 .15
25 Travis Cheyne .05 .15
26 Mark Leoppky .05 .15
27 Jason Ahenakew .05 .15
28 Kyle Paul .05 .15
29 Dean Normand .05 .15
30 Brett Kinaschuk .05 .15
31 Darren Schmidt .05 .15
32 Chris Schinkel .05 .15
33 David Foster .05 .15
34 Jason Zimmerman .05 .15
35 Tom Perry .05 .15
36 Kent Kinaschuk .05 .15
37 Colin Froese .05 .15
38 Shawn Zimmerman .05 .15
39 Larry Empey .05 .15
40 Curtis Knight .05 .15
41 Blake Shipley .05 .15
42 Cory Heon .05 .15
43 Steve Pashulka .05 .15
44 Rob Kinch .05 .15
45 Dean Gerard .05 .15
46 Matt Desmarais .05 .15
47 Chad Rusnak .05 .15
48 Brad Bagu .05 .15
49 Cam Bristow .05 .15
50 Derek Simonson .05 .15
51 Ken Ruddock .05 .15
52 Tyler Deis .05 .15
53 Steve Tansowny .05 .15
54 Bill Stait .05 .15
55 Garfield Henderson .05 .15
56 Lonny Deobald .05 .15
57 Lyle Ehrmantraut .05 .15
58 Layne Humenny .05 .15
59 Darren Balcombe .05 .15
60 Jeff McCutheon .05 .15
61 Trevor Wathen .05 .15
62 Derek Wynne .05 .15
63 Matt Russo .05 .15
64 Bruce Matatall .05 .15
65 Derek Crimin .05 .15
66 Chad Crumley .05 .15
67 Mike Hillock .05 .15
68 Art Houghton .05 .15
69 Lee Materi .05 .15
70 Nick Dyhr .05 .15
71 Darren Maloney .05 .15
72 Kurtise Souchotte .05 .15
73 Noel Kamel .05 .15
74 Trent Harper .05 .15
75 Ted Grayling .05 .15
76 Keith Harris .05 .15
77 Corri Moffat .05 .15
78 Travis Vantighem .05 .15
79 Darren Houghton .05 .15
80 Wade Welte .05 .15
81 Dave Doucet .05 .15
82 Jason Prokopetz .05 .15
83 Gordon McCann .05 .15
84 Clint Hooge .05 .15
85 Glen McGillvary .05 .15
86 Regan Simpson .05 .15
87 Mike Masse .05 .15
88 Jeremy Procyshyn .05 .15
89 Jim Nellis .05 .15
90 Todd Kozak .05 .15
91 Brent Hoiness .05 .15
92 Josh Welter
Jason Welter .05 .15
93 Eldon Barker .05 .15
94 Duane Vandale .05 .15
95 Brad McEwen .05 .15
96 Trent Tibbatts .05 .15
97 Jody Reiter .05 .15
98 Greg Moore .05 .15
99 Jon Rowe .05 .15
100 Mike Evans .05 .15
101 Jason Krug .05 .15
102 Jon Bracco .05 .15
103 Ryan Sandholm .05 .15
104 Darryl Sangster .05 .15
105 Brett Colborne .05 .15
106 Dean Moore .05 .15
107 Chris Dochaine .05 .15
108 Steve McKenna .05 .15
109 Tony Bergin .05 .15
110 Tim Murray .05 .15
111 Casey Kesselring .05 .15
112 Todd Barth .05 .15
113 Ryan McConnell .05 .15
114 Ian Adamson .05 .15
115 Warren Pickford .05 .15
116 Todd Murphy .05 .15
117 Rob Phillips .05 .15
118 Trevor Demmans .05 .15
119 Jeff Greenwood .05 .15
120 Kevin Messer .05 .15
121 Dion Johnson .05 .15
122 Rejean Stringer .05 .15
123 Scott Mead .05 .15
124 Jeff Lawson .05 .15
125 Scot Newberry .05 .15
126 Bill Reid .05 .15
127 Chris Winkler .05 .15
128 Kyle Girgan .05 .15
129 Trevor Warrener .05 .15
130 Richard Boscher .05 .15
131 Tom Thomson .05 .15
132 Mike Wevers .05 .15
133 Barton Holt .05 .15
134 Kent Rogers .05 .15
135 Richard Gibbs .05 .15
136 Jared Witt .05 .15
137 Jamie Stelmak .05 .15
138 Greg Wahl .05 .15
139 J. Sotropa .05 .15
140 Mark Pivetz .05 .15
141 Travis Kirby .05 .15
142 Jason Scanzano .05 .15
143 Tyson Balog .05 .15
144 Daryl Krauss .05 .15
145 Mike Harder .05 .15
146 Tyler McMillan .05 .15
147 Darcy Herlick .05 .15
148 Dave Zwyer .05 .15
149 Craig McKechnie .05 .15
150 Cam Cook .05 .15
151 Derek Bruselinck .05 .15
152 Travis Smith .05 .15
153 Daryl Jones .05 .15
154 Mike Savard .05 .15
155 Jeremy Matthies .05 .15
156 Michel Cook .05 .15
157 Leigh Brookbank .05 .15
158 Christian Dutil .05 .15
159 Scott Heshka .05 .15
160 Danny Galarneau .05 .15
161 Jamie Dunn .05 .15
162 Nigel Werenka .05 .15
163 Steve Sabo .05 .15
164 Tony Toth .05 .15
165 Sebastien Moreau .05 .15
166 Tim Slukynsky .05 .15
167 Sheldon Bylsma .05 .15
168 Stacy Prevost .10 .30

1981-82 Saskatoon Blades

COMPLETE SET (25) 10.00 25.00
1 Blades Team Photo .75 2.00
2 Daryl Stanley .30 .75
3 Leroy Gorski .30 .75
4 Donn Clark .30 .75
5 Brad Duggan .30 .75
6 Dave Chartier .30 .75
7 Dave Brown 1.25 3.00
8 Adam Thompson .30 .75
9 Bruce Eakin .30 .75
10 Brian Skrudland 1.25 3.00
11 Roger Kortko .30 .75
12 Ron Dreger .30 .75
13 Daryl Lubiniecki .30 .75
14 Marc Habscheid .75 2.00
15 Saskatoon Police Logo .20 .50
16 Todd Strueby .40 1.00
17 Craig Hurley .30 .75
18 Bill Hlynsky .30 .75
19 Lane Lambert .75 2.00
20 Mike Bloski .30 .75
21 Bruce Gordon .30 .75
22 Perry Ganchar .40 1.00
23 Ron Loustel .30 .75
24 Blades Logo .20 .50
25 Checklist Card .20 .50

1983-84 Saskatoon Blades

COMPLETE SET (24) 12.00 30.00
1 Team Photo .40 1.00
2 Trent Yawney .40 1.00
3 Grant Jennings .40 1.00
4 Duncan MacPherson .20 .50
5 Greg Holtby .20 .50
6 Dan Leier .20 .50
7 Dwaine Hutton .20 .50
8 Wendel Clark 6.00 15.00
9 Kerry Laviolette .20 .50
10 Dave Chartier .20 .50
11 Dale Henry .20 .50
12 Randy Smith .20 .50
13 Kevin Kowalchuk .20 .50
14 Todd McLellan .20 .50
15 Title Card
Saskatoon Police .08 .25
16 Larry Korchinski .20 .60
17 Curtis Chamberlain .20 .50
18 Greg Josak .20 .50
19 Ron Dreger .20 .50
20 Doug Kyle .20 .50
21 Rick Smith .20 .50
22 Joey Kocur 2.00 5.00
23 Allan Larochelle .20 .50
24 Mark Thietke .20 .50

1984-85 Saskatoon Blades Stickers

COMPLETE SET (20) 10.00 25.00
1 Jack Bowkus .30 .75
2 Curtis Chamberlain .30 .75
3 Wendel Clark 6.00 15.00
4 Ron Dreger .30 .75
5 Randy Hoffart .30 .75
6 Mark Holick .30 .75
7 Greg Holtby .30 .75
8 Grant Jennings .40 1.00
9 Kevin Kowalchuk .30 .75
10 Bryan Larkin .30 .75
11 James Latos .30 .75
12 Duncan MacPherson .30 .75
13 Rod Matechuk .30 .75
14 Todd McLellan .30 .75
15 Darren Moren .30 .75
16 Mike Morin .30 .75
17 Devon Oleniuk .30 .75
18 Grant Tkachuk .30 .75
19 Troy Vollhoffer .30 .75
20 Trent Yawney .40 1.00

1986-87 Saskatoon Blades Photos

COMPLETE SET (24) 14.00 35.00
1 Blair Atcheynum .75 2.00
2 Colin Bauer .40 1.00
3 Jack Bowkus .40 1.00
4 Mike Butkas .40 1.00
5 Kelly Chase 2.00 5.00
6 Tim Cheveldae .75 2.00
7 Blaine Chrest .40 1.00
8 Kerry Clark .40 1.00
9 Brian Glynn .40 1.00
10 Mark Holick .40 1.00
11 Kevin Kaminski .75 2.00
12 Tracey Katelnikoff .40 1.00
13 Kory Kocur .40 1.00
14 Bryan Larkin .40 1.00
15 Curtis Leschyshyn .75 2.00
16 Dan Logan .40 1.00
17 Todd MacLellan .40 1.00
18 Devon Oleniuk .40 1.00
19 Marty Prazma .40 1.00
20 Marty Weimer .40 1.00
21 Walter Shutter .40 1.00
22 Grant Tkachuk .40 1.00
23 Tony Twist 2.00 5.00
24 Shaun Van Allen .75 2.00

1988-89 Saskatoon Blades

COMPLETE SET (25) 4.00 10.00
1 Joe Penkala .20 .50
2 Saskatoon Police Emblem .07 .20
3 Marcel Comeau .20 .50
4 Dean Kuntz .20 .50
5 Mike Greenlay .20 .50
6 Jody Praznik .20 .50
7 Ken Sutton .20 .50
8 Sawn Snesar .20 .50
9 Shane Langager .20 .50
10 Dean Holdien .20 .50
11 Rob Lelacheur .20 .50
12 David Struch .20 .50
13 Collin Bauer .20 .50
14 Kevin Yellowaga .20 .50
15 Drew Sawtell .20 .50
16 Brian Gerrits .20 .50
17 Kirk Roworth .20 .50
18 Tracey Katelnikoff .20 .50
19 Scott Scissons .20 .50
20 Jason Smart .20 .50
21 Jason Christie .20 .50
22 Daren Bader .20 .50
23 Kevin Kaminski .20 .50
24 Kory Kocur .20 .50
25 Darwin McPherson .20 .50

1989-90 Saskatoon Blades

COMPLETE SET (25) 6.00 15.00
1 Terry Ruskowski .30 .75
2 Cam Moon .20 .50
3 Damon Kustra .20 .50
4 Trevor Robins .20 .50
5 Mark Raiter .20 .50
6 Mark Wotton .30 .75
7 Shawn Snesar .20 .50
8 Trevor Sherban .20 .50
9 Shane Langager .20 .50
10 Dean Holdien .20 .50
11 Rob Lelacheur .20 .50
12 David Struch .20 .50
13 Derek Tibbatts .20 .50
14 Drew Sawtell .20 .50
15 Richard Matvichuk .60 1.50
16 Trent Coghill .20 .50
17 Jeff Buchanan .20 .50
18 Grant Chorney .20 .50
19 Shawn Yakimishyn .20 .50
20 Scott Scissons .20 .50
21 Jason Smart .20 .50
22 Jason Christie .20 .50
23 Darin Bader .20 .50
24 Dean Rambo .20 .50
25 Collin Bauer .20 .50

1990-91 Saskatoon Blades

COMPLETE SET (27) 4.80 12.00
1 Terry Ruskowski CO .25 .60
2 Trevor Robins .20 .50
3 Cam Moon .20 .50
4 Jeff Buchanan .20 .50
5 Mark Raiter .20 .50
6 Trevor Sherban .20 .50
7 Jason Knox .20 .50
8 Dean Rambo .20 .50
9 Rob LeLacheur .20 .50
10 David Struch .20 .50
11 Greg Leahy .20 .50
12 Derek Tibbatts .20 .50
13 Shane Calder .20 .50
14 Richard Matvichuk .40 1.00
15 Trent Coghill .20 .50
16 Mark Wotton .25 .60
17 Kelly Markwart .20 .50
18 Mark Franks .20 .50
19 Scott Scissons .20 .50
20 Tim Cox .20 .50
21 Gaetan Blouin .20 .50
22 Darin Bader .20 .50
23 Shawn Yakimishyn .20 .50
24 Ryan Strain .20 .50
25 Jason Peters .20 .50
26 Team Card .20 .50
27 Title Card .20 .50

1991-92 Saskatoon Blades

COMPLETE SET (25) 4.80 12.00
1 Lorne Molleken CO .08 .25
2 Trevor Robins .20 .50
3 Norm Maracle .40 1.00
4 Jeff Buchanan .20 .50
5 Mark Raiter .20 .50
6 Bryce Goebel .20 .50
7 Rhett Trombley .20 .50
8 Chad Rusnak .20 .50
9 Jason Knight .20 .50
10 David Struch .20 .50
11 Shane Calder .20 .50
12 Derek Tibbatts .20 .50
13 Glen Gulutzan .20 .50
14 Richard Matvichuk .60 1.50
15 Chad Michalchuk .20 .50
16 Mark Wotton .30 .75
17 Mark Franks .20 .50
18 Andy MacIntyre .20 .50
19 Ryan Fujita .20 .50
20 Sean McFatridge .20 .50
21 Jason Becker .20 .50
22 Shawn Yakimishyn .20 .50
23 James Startup .20 .50
24 Paul Buczkowski .20 .50
NNO McGruff .02 .10

1993-94 Saskatoon Blades

COMPLETE SET (24) 4.80 12.00
1 Chad Allan .20 .50
2 Frank Banham .25 .60
3 Frank Banham
Mark Deyel .25 .60
4 Wade Belak .20 .50
5 Paul Buczkowski .20 .50
6 Shane Calder .25 .60
7 Mark Deyell .30 .75
8 Jason Duda .20 .50
9 Trevor Ethier .20 .50
10 Mike Gray .20 .50
11 Trevor Hanas .20 .50
12 Devon Hanson .20 .50
13 Andrew Kemper .20 .50
14 Kirby Law .20 .50
15 Andy MacIntyre .20 .50
16 Norm Maracle .40 1.00
17 Ivan Salon .20 .50
18 Todd Simpson .20 .50
19 Derek Tibbatts .20 .50
20 Derek Tibbatts
Clarke W .20 .50
21 Rhett Warrener .30 .75
22 Clarke Wilm .30 .75
23 Mark Wotton .25 .60
24 Team Photo .20 .50

1995-96 Saskatoon Blades

COMPLETE SET (27) 4.80 12.00
1 Chad Allan .20 .50
2 Frank Banham .30 .75
3 Dennis Bassett .20 .50
4 Wade Belak .30 .75
5 Ryan Bonni .30 .75
6 Paul Buczkowski .20 .50
7 Don Clark CO .20 .50
8 Mattieu Cusson .20 .50
9 Mark Deyell .30 .75
10 Pavel Kriz .20 .50
11 Jeromie Kufflick .20 .50
12 Laird Laluk .20 .50
13 Erik Leefe .20 .50
14 Richard Peacock .20 .50
15 Greg Phillips .20 .50
16 Garrett Prosofsky .30 .75
17 Nathan Rempel .20 .50
18 Cory Sarich .40 1.00
19 Jeremy Schaefer .20 .50
20 Mark Smith .20 .50
21 Martin Sonnenberg .20 .50
22 Randy Weinberger .20 .50
23 Clark Wilm .30 .75
24 Team Logo CL .02 .10
25 Crime Stoppers Logo .02 .10
26 Celebration 30 Years .02 .10
27 Assistant Coaches
Chartier
Engele
Federke .02 .10

1996-97 Saskatoon Blades

COMPLETE SET (28) 5.00 12.00
1 Stewart Bacharuk .20 .50
2 Jon Barkman .20 .50
3 Justin Bekkering .20 .50
4 Derek Bjornson .20 .50
5 Ryan Bonni .20 .50
6 Christian Chartier .30 .75
7 Matt Cockell .20 .50
8 Mathieu Cusson .20 .50
9 Jared Dumba .20 .50
10 Ryan Gaucher .20 .50
11 Ryan Henderson .20 .50
12 Ryan Johnston .20 .50
13 Vladislav Klochkov .20 .50
14 Laird Laluk .20 .50
15 Tyler Love .20 .50
16 Sheldon Nedielski .20 .50
17 Greg Phillips .20 .50
18 Garrett Prosofsky .20 .50
19 Nathan Rempel .20 .50
20 Cory Sarich .20 .50
21 Brian Skrudland .20 .50
22 Martin Sonnenberg .20 .50
23 Lyle Steenbergen .20 .50
24 Rhett Warrener .30 .75
25 Kyle Werner .20 .50
26 Team Logo CL .08 .25
27 Action/Goal .08 .25
28 Team(Reebok) .08 .25

1997-98 Saskatoon Blades

COMPLETE SET (27) 5.00 12.00
1 Jon Barkman .20 .50
2 Garett Bembridge .20 .50
3 Derek Bjornson .20 .50
4 Ryan Bonni .30 .75
5 Christian Chartier .30 .75
6 Matt Cockell .20 .50
7 Mathieu Cusson .20 .50
8 Chad Elmy .20 .50
9 Ryan Gaucher .20 .50
10 Derek Halldorson .20 .50
11 Ryan Johnston .20 .50
12 Dylan Kemp .20 .50
13 Tyler Mackay .20 .50
14 Kevin McKay .20 .50
15 Matt Miller .20 .50
16 Dennis Mullen .20 .50
17 Greg Phillips .20 .50
18 Petja Pietilainen .20 .50
19 Garrett Prosofsky .20 .50
20 Nathan Rempel .20 .50
21 Darcy Robinson .20 .50
22 Cory Sarich .30 .75
23 Martin Sonnenberg .20 .50
24 Header Card .08 .25
25 Mascot - Hermutt .08 .25
26 Price Watchers .08 .25
27 Team Photo .20 .50

2000-01 Saskatoon Blades

COMPLETE SET (32) 4.80 12.00
1 Logo Card .04 .11
2 Team Photo .16 .40
3 Kevin Dickie CO .10 .25
4 Bruno Baseotto ACO .10 .25
5 Tim Cheveldae ACO .16 .40
6 Jason Goulet .16 .40
7 Matt Suderman .16 .40
8 Scotty Balan .16 .40
9 Ryan Stempfle .16 .40
10 Kane Ludwar .16 .40
11 Adrian Foster .40 1.00
12 Martin Erat .40 1.00
13 Garrett Bembridge .16 .40
14 Davin Heintz .16 .40
15 Justin Wallin .16 .40
16 Trent Adamus .16 .40
17 Jeff Coulter .16 .40
18 Chris Manchakowski .16 .40
19 Justin Kanigan .16 .40
20 David Cameron .16 .40
21 Derek Halldorson .16 .40
22 Aaron Starr .16 .40
23 Ryan Kehrig .16 .40
24 Rob Woods .16 .40
25 Warren Peters .16 .40
26 Petr Prochazka .16 .40
27 Justin Kelly .16 .40
28 Michael Garnett .16 .40
29 Tony Kolewaski .16 .40
30 Martin Vymazal .16 .40
31 Helmutt MASCOT .04 .11
32 Jay Richards DJ .04 .11

2001-02 Saskatoon Blades

COMPLETE SET (32) 6.00 15.00
1 Header .04 .10
2 Derek Couture .20 .50
3 Paul Gentile .20 .50
4 Willy Glover .20 .50
5 Kyle Harris .20 .50
6 Davin Heintz .20 .50
7 Adam Huxley .30 .75
8 Justin Keller .30 .75
9 Ryan Keller .75 2.00
10 Justin Kelly .20 .50
11 Richard Mueller .20 .50
12 Warren Peters .20 .50
13 Tim Preston .20 .50
14 Daniel Volrab .20 .50
15 Trent Adamus .20 .50
16 Tiger Williams
Kelly Hrudey .40 1.00
17 Scotty Balan .20 .50
18 Mike Green .60 1.50
19 Kane Ludwar .20 .50
20 Stephen Mann .20 .50
21 Sean Moir .20 .50
22 Ryan Stempfle .20 .50
23 Matt Suderman .20 .50
24 Rob Woods .20 .50
25 Michael Garnett .40 1.00
26 Ryan Senft .20 .50
27 Helmutt .04 .10
28 Steve Hildebrand TR .04 .10
29 Kevin Dickie CO .04 .10
30 Bruno Baseotto .04 .10
31 Wendel Clark Night .40 1.00
32 Team Photo .20 .50

2002-03 Saskatoon Blades

COMPLETE SET (30) 4.00 10.00
1 Evan Haw .20 .50
2 Sean Moir .20 .50
3 Matt Suderman .20 .50
4 Matt Bergen .20 .50
5 Steven Later .20 .50
6 Denny Johnston .20 .50
7 Trent Adamus .20 .50
8 Michael Bubnick .20 .50
9 Marcus Paulsson .20 .50
10 Adam Houle .20 .50
11 Daniel Volrab .20 .50
12 Wacey Rabbit .20 .50
13 Derek Couture .20 .50
14 Joe Barnes .20 .50
15 Rob Woods .20 .50
16 Warren Peters .20 .50
17 Adam Huxley .30 .75
18 Mike Green .40 1.00
19 John Dahl .20 .50
20 Stephen Mann .20 .50
21 Adam Ward .30 .75
22 Brett Jaeger .30 .75
23 Ryan Keller .30 .75
24 Tanner Shultz .20 .50
25 Jack Brodsky PRES .04 .10
26 Brent McEwan GM .04 .10
27 Kevin Dickie CO .04 .10
28 Bruno Baseotto ACO .04 .10
29 Stev Hildebrand TR .04 .10
30 Team Photo
CL .04 .10

2003-04 Saskatoon Blades

COMPLETE SET (23) 6.00 15.00
1 Mascot .04 .10
2 Team Photo .04 .10
3 Boris Lekovic .30 .75
4 Adam Ward .30 .75
5 Joel Eisenkirch .30 .75
6 Dane Crowley .30 .75
7 Evan Haw .30 .75
8 Nicolaus Knudsen .30 .75
9 Ben Van Lare .30 .75
10 Richard Kelly .30 .75
11 Rob Woods .30 .75
12 Matt Fetzner .30 .75
13 Mike Green .40 1.00
14 Bjorn Svensson .30 .75
15 Ryan Cyr .30 .75
16 Dayln Flatt .30 .75
17 Joe Barnes .30 .75
18 Trent Adamus .30 .75
19 Derek Couture .30 .75
20 Tanner Shultz .30 .75
21 Wacey Rabbit .75 2.00
22 Devin Setoguchi .75 2.00
23 Ryan Keller .30 .75

2004-05 Saskatoon Blades

COMPLETE SET (22) 8.00 20.00
1 Nicolaus Knudsen .30 .75
2 Joel Eisenkirch .30 .75
3 Justin McCrae .30 .75
4 Russell Monette .30 .75
5 Tyson Sievert .30 .75
6 Aaron Bader .30 .75
7 Daniel Waschuk .30 .75
8 Chris Cloud .30 .75
9 Ben Van Lare .30 .75
10 Tyler Boldt .30 .75
11 Mike Green .40 1.00
12 Zdenek Bahensky .40 1.00
13 Ryan Cyr .30 .75
14 Ryan Keller .30 .75
15 Devin Setoguchi .75 2.00
16 Joe Barnes .30 .75
17 Dayln Flatt .40 1.00
18 Dane Crowley .30 .75
19 Evan Haw .30 .75
20 Wacey Rabbit .75 2.00
21 Ryan Menei .30 .75
22 Bjorn Svensson .30 .75

2005-06 Saskatoon Blades

COMPLETE SET (24) 10.00 20.00
1 Aaron Bader .30 .75
2 Zdenek Bahensky .30 .75
3 Joe Barnes .30 .75
4 Chris Cloud .30 .75
5 Brad Cole .30 .75
6 Ryan Funk .30 .75
7 Adam Geric .30 .75
8 Colton Gillies .30 .75
9 Michael Hengen .30 .75
10 Anton Khudobin .40 1.00
11 Chad Klassen .30 .75
12 Joe Logan .30 .75
13 Michael MacAngus .30 .75
14 Blair MacAulay .30 .75
15 Justin McCrae .30 .75
16 Ryan Menei .30 .75
17 Todd Panchyson .30 .75
18 Derek Price .30 .75
19 Wacey Rabbit .60 1.50
20 David Schulz .30 .75
21 Devin Setoguchi .60 1.50
22 Brett Ward .30 .75
23 Jim Watt .40 1.00
24 Brennan Zasitko .30 .75

2006-07 Saskatoon Blades

COMPLETE SET (24) 8.00 15.00
1 Dustin Cameron .25 .60
2 Chris Cloud .25 .60
3 Brad Cole .25 .60
4 Troy Crowley .25 .60
5 Craig Cuthbert .25 .60
6 Kenton Dulle .25 .60
7 Ryan Funk .25 .60
8 Adam Geric .25 .60
9 Colton Gillies .75 2.00
10 Braden Holtby .25 .60
11 Derek Hulak .25 .60
12 Sam Klassen .25 .60
13 Garrett Klotz .25 .60
14 Rastislav Konecny .25 .60
15 Joe Logan .25 .60
16 Blair MacAulay .25 .60
17 Justin McCrae .25 .60
18 Ryan Menei .25 .60
19 Gaelan Patterson .25 .60
20 Bohdan Visnak .25 .60
21 Brett Ward .25 .60
22 Walker Wintoneak .25 .60
23 Teigan Zahn .25 .60
24 Garrett Zemlak .25 .60

1980-81 Sault Ste. Marie Greyhounds

COMPLETE SET (25) 37.50 75.00
1 Ken Porteous .30 .75
2 Brian Petterle .30 .75
3 Gord Dineen .40 1.00
4 Tony Cella .30 .75
5 Doug Shedden .60 1.50
6 Terry Tait .30 .75
7 Greyhounds Logo .20 .50
8 Steve Smith .30 .75
9 Huey Larkin .30 .75
10 Steve Gatzos .30 .75
11 Tim Zwijack .30 .75
12 Vic Morin .30 .75
13 John Vanbiesbrouck 12.50 25.00
14 Ron Francis 10.00 25.00
15 Tony Butorac .30 .75
16 John Goodwin .30 .75
17 Ron Handy .30 .75
18 Jim Pavese .40 1.00
19 Sault Ste. Marie
Police Logo .20 .50
20 Rick Morocco .30 .75
21 Ken Latta .30 .75
22 Kirk Rueter .30 .75
23 OMJHL Logo .20 .50
24 Terry Crisp 1.00 2.50
25 Marc D'Amour .75 2.00

1981-82 Sault Ste. Marie Greyhounds

COMPLETE SET (28) 32.00 80.00
1 Jim Aldreda .30 .75
2 Dave Andreoli .30 .75
3 Richard Beaulne .30 .75
4 Bruce Bell .30 .75
5 Chuck Brimmer .30 .75
6 Tony Cella .30 .75
7 Kevin Conway .30 .75
8 Terry Crisp CO .75 2.00
9 Marc D'Amour .60 1.50
10 Gord Dineen .40 1.00
11 Chris Felix .40 1.00
12 Ron Francis 10.00 25.00
13 Steve Graves .30 .75
14 Wayne Groulx .30 .75
15 Huey Larkin .30 .75
16 Ken Latta .30 .75

17 Mike Lococo .30 .75
18 Jim Pavese .40 1.00
19 Dirk Rueter .30 .75
20 Steve Smith .30 .75
21 Terry Tait .30 .75
22 Rick Tocchet 8.00 20.00
23 John Vanbiesbrouck 10.00 25.00
24 Harry Wolfe ANN .20 .50
25 J.D. Yari .02 .10
26 Bluebird Bakery
Limited Logo .02 .10
27 Canadian Tire Logo .02 .10
28 Coca-Cola Ad .02 .10

1982-83 Sault Ste. Marie Greyhounds

COMPLETE SET (25) 16.00 40.00
1 Jim Aldred .30 .75
2 John Armelin .30 .75
3 Richard Beaulne .30 .75
4 Jeff Beukeboom .60 1.50
5 Tony Cella .30 .75
6 Kevin Conway .30 .75
7 Terry Crisp .60 1.50
8 Chris Felix .40 1.00
9 Steve Graves .30 .75
10 Gus Greco .30 .75
11 Wayne Groulx .30 .75
12 Sam Haidy .30 .75
13 Tim Hoover .30 .75
14 Pat Lahey .30 .75
15 Huey Larkin .30 .75
16 Mike Lococo .30 .75
17 Mike Neill .30 .75
18 Ken Sabourin .30 .75
19 Steve Smith .30 .75
20 Terry Tait .30 .75
21 Rick Tocchet 4.00 10.00
22 John Vanbiesbrouck 6.00 15.00
23 Harry Wolfe ANN .20 .50
24 Station Mall Sponsor .02 .10
25 Bluebird Bakery Ltd. .02 .10

1983-84 Sault Ste. Marie Greyhounds

COMPLETE SET (25) 8.00 20.00
1 Jeff Beukeboom .40 1.00
2 Graeme Bonar .20 .50
3 Chris Brant .20 .50
4 John English .20 .50
5 Chris Felix .40 1.00
6 Rick Fera .20 .50
7 Marc Tournier .20 .50
8 Steve Graves .20 .50
9 Gus Greco .20 .50
11 Wayne Groulx .20 .50
11 Sam Haidy .20 .50
12 Tim Hoover .20 .50
13 Jerry Iuliano .20 .50
14 Pat Lahey .20 .50
15 Mike Lococo .20 .50
16 Jean-Marc MacKenzie .20 .50
17 Mike Oliverio .20 .50
18 Brit Peer .20 .50
19 Joey Rampton .20 .50
20 Ken Sabourin .40 1.00
21 Jim Samec .20 .50
22 Rick Tocchet 3.00 8.00
23 Harry Wolfe ANN .20 .50
24 IGA Sponsor Card .02 .10
25 Coke Sponsor Card .02 .10

1984-85 Sault Ste. Marie Greyhounds

COMPLETE SET (25) 8.00 20.00
1 Marty Abrams .20 .50
2 Jeff Beukeboom .30 .75
3 Graeme Bonar .20 .50
4 Chris Brant .20 .50
5 Terry Crisp CO .40 1.00
6 Chris Felix .40 1.00
7 Scott Green .20 .50
8 Wayne Groulx .20 .50
9 Steve Hollett .20 .50
10 Tim Hoover .20 .50
11 Derek King .60 1.50
12 Tyler Larter .20 .50
13 Jean-Marc MacKenzie .20 .50
14 Scott Mosey .20 .50
15 Mike Oliverio .20 .50
16 Brit Peer .20 .50
17 Wayne Presley .40 1.00
18 Bob Probert 3.00 8.00
19 Brian Rome .20 .50
20 Ken Sabourin .30 .75
21 Rob Veccia .20 .50
22 Harry Wolfe ANN .08 .25
23 Rob Zettler .40 1.00
24 IGA Ad .08 .25
25 Coca-Cola Ad .08 .25

1987-88 Sault Ste. Marie Greyhounds

COMPLETE SET (35) 50.00 125.00
1 Barry King
Chief of Police .08 .25
2 Dan Currie .20 .50
3 Mike Glover .20 .50
4 Tyler Larter .20 .50
5 Bob Jones .20 .50
6 Lyndon Slewidge
Anthem Singer .08 .25
7 Brad Jones .20 .50
8 Ron Francis 3.00 8.00
9 Dale Turnbull .20 .50
10 Don McConnell .20 .50
11 Chris Felix .30 .75
12 Steve Udvari .20 .50
13 Shawn Simpson .20 .50
14 Rob Zettler .40 1.00
15 Phil Esposito
Co-owner 6.00 15.00
16 John Vanbiesbrouck 6.00 15.00
17 Mike Oliverio .20 .50
18 Colin Ford .20 .50
19 Steve Herniman .20 .50
20 Troy Mallette .40 1.00
21 Craig Hartsburg .40 1.00
22 Don Boyd CO
GM .08 .25
23 Peter Fiorentino .20 .50
24 Jeff Columbus .20 .50
25 Brad Stepan .20 .50
26 Rick Tocchet 2.00 5.00
27 Shane Sargant .20 .50
28 Wayne Muir .20 .50
29 Wayne Gretzky 40.00 100.00
30 Gary Luther .20 .50
31 Harry Wolfe ANN .08 .25
32 Rod Thacker .20 .50
33 Coaches Card
Terry Tait
Ted Nolan
Mark Pavoni .08 .25
34 Brian Hoard .20 .50
35 Glen Johnston .20 .50

1989-90 Sault Ste. Marie Greyhounds

COMPLETE SET (30) 8.00 20.00
1 Barry King CL
Chief of Police .08 .25
2 Sault Ste. Marie
Police Logo .08 .25
3 Ted Nolan CO .30 .75
4 Team Logo .20 .50
5 Sherry Bassin GM .20 .50
6 Jim Ritchie .20 .50
7 Bob Boughner .30 .75
8 Denny Lambert .40 1.00
9 Doug Minor .20 .50
10 Rick Pracey .20 .50
11 Colin Miller .20 .50
12 Kevin King .20 .50
13 Ron Francis 2.00 5.00
14 Rick Kowalsky .20 .50
15 Adam Foote .75 2.00
16 Wade Whitten .20 .50
17 Dale Turnbull .20 .50
18 Bob Jones .20 .50
19 David Carrie .20 .50
20 Brad Tiley .20 .50
21 Wayne Muir .20 .50
22 Dave Babcock .20 .50
23 David Matsos .20 .50
24 Dan Ferguson .20 .50
25 Jeff Szeryk .20 .50
26 Mike Zuke ACO .08 .25
27 Dave Doucette .20 .50
28 John Campbell
Constable .08 .25
29 Graeme Harvey .20 .50
30 John Fuselli ACO .08 .25

1993-94 Sault Ste. Marie Greyhounds

COMPLETE SET (30) 4.80 10.00
1 Andrea Carpano .15 .40
2 Ryan Douglas .15 .40
3 Dan Cloutier .75 2.00
4 Oliver Pastinsky .15 .40
5 Scott King .25 .60
6 Drew Bannister .25 .60
7 Sean Gagnon .15 .40
8 Andre Payette .15 .40
9 Peter MacKellar
UER Name spelled
Mackellar on fr .15 .40
10 Richard Uniacke .15 .40
11 Steve Zoryk .15 .40
12 Brad Baber .15 .40
13 Gary Roach .15 .40
14 Jeff Gies .15 .40
15 Tom MacDonald .15 .40
16 Rhett Trombley .15 .40
17 Joe VanVolsen .15 .40
18 Andrew Clark .15 .40
19 Briane Thompson .15 .40
20 Aaron Gavey .25 .60
21 Wade Gibson .15 .40
22 Chad Grills .15 .40
23 Jeff Toms .15 .40
24 Steve Sullivan .60 1.50
25 Jeremy Stevenson .15 .40
26 Corey Moylan .15 .40
27 Steve Spina .15 .40
28 Dave Mayville GM .02 .10
29 Ted Nolan CO .30 .75
30 Dan Flynn ACO
Mike Zuke ACO .02 .10

1993-94 Sault Ste. Marie Greyhounds Memorial Cup

COMPLETE SET (32) 6.00 15.00
1 Memorial Cup .40 1.00
2 Dan Tanevski .15 .40
3 Mark Matier .15 .40
4 Oliver Pastinsky .15 .40
5 Peter MacKellar .15 .40
6 Drew Bannister .20 .50
7 Sean Gagnon .20 .50
8 Joe Clarke .15 .40
9 Chad Penney .15 .40
10 Neal Martin .15 .40
11 Perry Pappas .15 .40
12 David Matsos .15 .40
13 Rick Kowalsky .15 .40
14 Gary Roach .15 .40
15 Jarret Reid .15 .40
16 Steve Sullivan .60 1.50
17 Tom MacDonald .15 .40
18 Jodie Murphy .15 .40
19 Ralph Intranuovo .15 .40
20 Brad Baber .15 .40
21 Briane Thompson .15 .40
22 Aaron Gavey .20 .50
23 Wade Gibson .15 .40
24 Kiley Hill .15 .40
25 Jeff Toms .15 .40
26 Joe Van Volsen .15 .40
27 Dan Cloutier .75 2.00
28 Kevin Hodson .60 1.50
29 David Mayville DIR
Sher .02 .10
30 Ted Nolan CO
Danny Flyn .20 .50
31 Executive and Office
St .02 .10
32 Mike Zuke ACO
Forrest V .02 .10

1995-96 Sault Ste. Marie Greyhounds

COMPLETE SET (30) 10.00 25.00
1 Peter Cava .15 .40
2 Scott Cherrey .15 .40
3 Dan Cloutier .60 1.50
4 Lee Cole .15 .40
5 Jason Doyle .20 .50
6 Rico Fata .30 .75
7 Blaine Fitzpatrick .15 .40
8 Jeff Gies .15 .40
9 Richard Jackman .30 .75
10 Steve Lowe .15 .40
11 Dave Mayville Director of Oper. .02 .10
12 Robert Mulick .15 .40
13 Kevin Murnaghan .15 .40
14 Cory Murphy .15 .40
15 Joe Paterson
Head Coach .02 .10
16 Andre Payette .15 .40
17 Michal Podolka .30 .75
18 Ben Schust .15 .40
19 Brian Stacey .15 .40
20 Brian Stewart .15 .40
21 Joe Thornton 6.00 15.00
22 Trevor Tokarczyk .15 .40
23 Richard Uniacke .20 .50
24 Joe Vanvolsen .15 .40
25 Jamie Wentzell .15 .40
26 M.Zuke
B.Jones ACO .02 .10
27 Greyhounds Staff .02 .10
28 Toronto Bank and Trust .02 .10
29 Greyhounds and Toronto
School of Business .02 .10
30 Team Photo .02 .10

1996-97 Sault Ste. Marie Greyhounds

COMPLETE SET (30) 10.00 25.00
1 Wes Booker .15 .40
2 Bill Browne .15 .40
3 Peter Cava .15 .40
4 Justin Davis .15 .40
5 J.J. Dickie .15 .40
6 Oak Hewer .15 .40
7 Richard Jackman .20 .50
8 Richard Jackman
Team Canada 1997 .20 .50
9 Matt Lahey .15 .40
10 David Mayville
Director of Operations .02 .10
11 Jake McCracken .30 .75
12 Marc Moro .30 .75
13 Robert Mulick .15 .40
14 Joe Paterson CO .02 .10
15 Daniel Passero .15 .40
16 Nathan Perrott .30 .75
17 Michael Podolka .30 .75
18 Nick Robinson .15 .40
19 Ben Schust .15 .40
20 Joe Seroski .15 .40
21 Chad Spurr .15 .40
22 Brian Stewart .15 .40
23 Joe Thornton 4.00 10.00
24 Joe Thornton
Team Canada 1997 4.00 10.00
25 Trevor Tokarczyk .15 .40
26 Richard Uniacke .15 .40
27 David Wight .15 .40
28 Chad Woollard .15 .40
29 Mike Zuke ACO
B.Jones ACO .02 .10
30 Team Photo .02 .10

1996-97 Sault Ste. Marie Greyhounds Autographed

COMPLETE SET (24) 40.00 100.00
1 Wes Booker .75 2.00
2 Bill Browne .75 2.00
3 Peter Cava .75 2.00
4 Justin Davis .75 2.00
5 J.J. Dickie .75 2.00
6 Oak Hewer .75 2.00
7 Richard Jackman 1.25 3.00
8 Richard Jackman
Team Canada 1997 1.25 3.00
9 Matt Lahey .75 2.00
11 Jake McCracken 1.50 4.00
12 Marc Moro 2.00 5.00
13 Robert Mulick .75 2.00
14 Joe Paterson CO .75 2.00
15 Daniel Passero .75 2.00
16 Nathan Perrott 2.00 5.00
17 Michael Podolka 1.50 4.00
18 Nick Robinson .75 2.00
19 Ben Schust .75 2.00
20 Joe Seroski 1.25 3.00
21 Chad Spurr .75 2.00
22 Brian Stewart .75 2.00
23 Joe Thornton 15.00 40.00
24 Joe Thornton
Team Canada 1997 15.00 40.00
25 Trevor Tokarczyk .75 2.00
26 Richard Uniacke 1.25 3.00
27 David Wight .75 2.00
28 Chad Woollard .75 2.00
29 Mike Zuke ACO
B.Jones ACO .75 2.00

2002-03 Sault Ste. Marie Greyhounds

COMPLETE SET (23) 8.00 20.00
1 Adam Munro .40 1.00
2 Joey Biasucci .30 .75
3 Trevor Daley .40 1.00
4 Jeff Carter 3.00 8.00
5 Michael Krelove .20 .50
6 Matt Herneisen .20 .50
7 Jeff Doyle .20 .50
8 Mike Moher .20 .50
9 Tyler Kennedy .20 .50
10 Tyler Dutchyshen .20 .50
11 Brian Rempel .20 .50
12 Petr Taticek .40 1.00
13 Jeff Larsh .20 .50
14 Sean Stefanski .20 .50
15 Jordan Smith .20 .50
16 Mike Amodeo .20 .50
17 Jiri Drtina .20 .50
18 Niko Tuomi .20 .50
19 Ryan Kitchen .20 .50
20 Scott Dobben .20 .50
21 Brad Staubitz .20 .50
22 Jordan Kennedy .20 .50
23 Ryan McKay .20 .50

2003-04 Sault Ste. Marie Greyhounds

COMPLETE SET (32) 6.00 15.00
1 Jakub Cechs .30 .75
2 Travis Chapman .20 .50
3 Brett Connolly .20 .50
4 Andrew Desjardins .20 .50
5 Scott Dobben .20 .50
6 Jeffrey Doyle .20 .50
7 Kevin Druce .30 .75
8 Brad Good .20 .50
9 Jeff Carter 1.50 4.00
10 David Jarram .20 .50
11 Tyler Kennedy .20 .50
12 Jacob King .20 .50
13 Jeff Larsh .20 .50
14 Chris Lawrence .20 .50
15 Matt Leszczynski .20 .50
16 Aaron Lewicki .20 .50
17 Mike Looby .20 .50
18 Jason Pitton .20 .50
19 Matt Puntureri .20 .50
20 Jordan Smith .20 .50
21 Brad Staubitz .20 .50
22 Reg Thomas .20 .50
23 Martin Tuma .20 .50
24 Marty Abrams CO .04 .10
25 Denny Lambert ACO .04 .10
26 Terry Barbeau ACO .04 .10
27 Andy Martin EQM .04 .10
28 Dave Torrie GM .04 .10
29 Rod Bogart TR .04 .10
30 Header Card .04 .10
31 Header Card .04 .10
32 Checklist .04 .10

2004-05 Sault Ste. Marie Greyhounds

COMPLETE SET (25) 6.00 15.00
1 Jakub Cech .20 .50
2 Kyle Gajewski .20 .50
3 Brad Good .20 .50
4 David Jarram .20 .50
5 Joshua Day .20 .50
6 Jeff Carter 1.25 3.00
7 Tyler Cuthbert .20 .50
8 Chris Lawrence .20 .50
9 Ryan McInerny .20 .50
10 Brandon MacLean .20 .50
11 Tyler Kennedy .20 .50
12 Tyler McKinley .20 .50
13 Jason Pitton .20 .50
14 Jeff Larsh .20 .50
15 Jordan Smith .20 .50
16 Jacob King .20 .50
17 Andrew Desjardins .20 .50
18 Matt Puntureri .30 .75
19 Matthew Leszczynski .20 .50
20 Blair Jarrett .20 .50
21 Brad Staubitz .20 .50
22 Martin Tuma .20 .50
23 Jacob Lalonde .20 .50
24 Reg Thomas .20 .50
25 Checklist .04 .10

1993-94 Seattle Thunderbirds

COMPLETE SET (30) 4.80 12.00
1 Mike Barrie .20 .50
2 Doug Bonner .20 .50
3 Davie Carson .20 .50
4 Jeff Dewar .20 .50
5 Brett Duncan .20 .50
6 Shawn Gervais .20 .50
7 Chris Herperger .30 .75
8 Troy Hyatt .20 .50
9 Curt Kamp TR .02 .10
10 Olaf Kjenstadt .20 .50
11 Walt Kyle CO .02 .10
12 Milt Mastad .20 .50
13 Larry McMorran .20 .50
14 Jim McTaggart ACO .02 .10
15 Regan Mueller .20 .50
16 Kevin Mylander .20 .50
17 Drew Palmer .20 .50
18 Jeff Peddigrew .20 .50
19 Darryl Plandowski ACO .02 .10
20 Deron Quint .30 .75
21 Darrell Sandback .20 .50
22 Chris Schmidt .20 .50
23 Lloyd Shaw .20 .50
24 Alexandre Matvichuk .20 .50
25 Darcy Smith .20 .50
26 Rob Tallas .30 .75
27 Paul Vincent .20 .50
28 Chris Wells .20 .50
29 Brendan Witt .30 .75
30 Team photo .20 .50

1995-96 Seattle Thunderbirds

COMPLETE SET (32) 10.00 30.00
1 Perry Andrusiak ACO .02 .10
2 Shane Belter .20 .50
3 Rick Berry .30 .75
4 Jeff Blair .20 .50
5 Doug Bonner .30 .75
6 Kevin Borris .15 .40
7 Torrey DiRoberto .20 .50
8 Michal Divisek .15 .40
9 Paul Ferone .15 .40
10 Shawn Gervais .15 .40
11 Jan Hrdina .75 2.00
12 Curt Kamp TR .02 .10
13 Greg Kuznik .15 .40
14 Blair Manning .15 .40
15 Patrick Marleau 8.00 20.00
16 Jim McTaggart ACO .02 .10
17 Tony Mohagen .15 .40
18 Don Nachbaur CO .02 .10
19 Jason Norrie .15 .40
20 Drew Palmer .15 .40
21 Tyler Perry .15 .40
22 Jame Pollock .15 .40
23 Kevin Popp .15 .40
24 Jeremy Reich .20 .50
25 Cody Rudkowsky .40 1.00
26 Chris Schmidt .15 .40
27 Lloyd Shaw .15 .40
28 Chris Thompson .15 .40
29 Dan Tompkins .15 .40
30 Cool Bird MASCOT .02 .10
32 Seattle Key Arena .02 .10
NNO Title Card .02 .10

1996-97 Seattle Thunderbirds

COMPLETE SET (28) 8.00 20.00
1 Jeff Blair .20 .50
3 Rod LeRoux .20 .50
4 Nathan Forster .20 .50
5 Brad Swanson .20 .50
6 Rick Berry .30 .75
7 Paul Ferone .20 .50
8 Jame Pollock .20 .50
9 Tyler Willis .20 .50
11 Chris Thompson .20 .50
12 Patrick Marleau 12.00 30.00
13 Jouni Kuokkanen .20 .50
14 Martin Cerven .20 .50
15 Jeremy Reich .30 .75
16 Bret DeCecco .40 1.00
17 Tony Mohagen .20 .50
18 Torrey DiRoberto .20 .50
19 Nick Szadkowski .20 .50
21 Brian Ballman .20 .50
22 Greg Kuznik .20 .50
23 Randy Perry .20 .50
24 Shawn Skolney .20 .50
30 Cody Rudkowsky .40 1.00
31 Kris Cantu .20 .50
32 Shane Belter .20 .50
NNO Rob Sumner ASST CO .02 .10
NNO Thunderbirds
Through the Years .02 .10
NNO Don Nachbaur CO .02 .10
NNO Cool Bird MASCOT .02 .10

1997-98 Seattle Thunderbirds

COMPLETE SET (1-27) 7.20 15.00
1 Header Card .02 .10
2 Cool Bird Mascot .02 .10
3 Rod Leroux .20 .50
4 Nathan Forster .20 .50
5 Jason Beckett .20 .50
6 Rick Berry .30 .75
7 Chris Thompson .20 .50
8 Jame Pollock .20 .50
9 David Morisset .30 .75
10 Jeff Blair .20 .50
11 Jouni Kuokkanen .20 .50
12 Scott Kelman .30 .75
13 Jeremy Reich .30 .75
14 Brett DeCecco .30 .75
15 Tim Preston .20 .50
16 Torrey DiRoberto .30 .75
17 Petr Vala .20 .50
18 Ryan Tresk .20 .50
19 Greg Kuznik .20 .50
20 Matt Demarski .20 .50
21 Mark Parrish .75 2.00
22 Stanislav Gron .60 1.50
23 Cody Rudkowsky .40 1.00
24 A.J. Van Bruggen .20 .50
25 Don Nachbaur HCO .08 .25
26 Rob Sumner ACO .04 .10
27 Curt Kamp TR .02 .10

2014-15 Seattle Thunderbirds

COMPLETE SET (30) 8.00 20.00
1 Header Card .30 .75
2 Danny Mumaugh .30 .75
3 Jerret Smith .30 .75
4 Turner Ottenbreit .30 .75
5 Sahvan Khaira .30 .75
6 Scott Eansor .30 .75
7 Justin Hickman .30 .75
8 Kaden Elder .30 .75
9 Ryan Gropp .50 1.25
10 Mathew Barzal .75 2.00
11 Lane Pederson .30 .75
12 Alexander True .30 .75
13 Shea Theodore .40 1.00
14 Donovan Neuls .30 .75
15 Cory Millette .30 .75
16 Florian Baltram .30 .75
17 Calvin Spencer .30 .75
18 Ethan Bear .30 .75
19 Nolan Volcan .30 .75
20 Evan Wardley .30 .75
21 Keegan Kolesar .30 .75
22 Roberts Lipsbergs .30 .75
23 Logan Flodell .30 .75
24 Jared Hauf .30 .75
25 Luke Osterman .30 .75
26 Taran Kozun .30 .75
27 Nick Holowko .30 .75
28 Steve Konowalchuk CO .30 .75
29 Cool Bird MASCOT .30 .75
30 Header Card .30 .75

1969-70 Seattle Totems

COMPLETE SET (20) 60.00 150.00
1 Don Head 8.00 20.00
2 Chuck Holmes 3.00 8.00
3 Bob Courcy 3.00 8.00
4 Marc Boileau 3.00 8.00
5 Gerry Leonard 3.00 8.00
6 Art Stratton 3.00 8.00
7 Gary Kilpatrick 3.00 8.00
8 Don Ward 3.00 8.00
9 Jack Michie 3.00 8.00
10 Ronald Ingram 3.00 8.00
11 John Hanna 3.00 8.00
12 Ray Larose 3.00 8.00
13 Jack Dale 3.00 8.00
14 Tom McVie 3.00 8.00
15 Gerry Meehan 6.00 15.00
16 Chris Worthy 3.00 8.00
17 Bobby Schmautz 8.00 20.00
18 Dwight Carruthers 3.00 8.00
19 Patrick Dunn TR .75 2.00
20 Bill MacFarland CO .75 2.00

1989-90 7th Inning Sketch OHL

COMPLETE SET (200) 12.00 30.00
COMPLETE FACT.SET (167) 12.00 30.00
1 Eric Lindros
(Beware counterfeits) 1.50 4.00
2 Jarrod Skalde .20 .50
3 Joe Busillo .02 .10
4 Dale Craigwell .08 .25
5 Clair Cornish .02 .10
6 Jean-Paul Davis .02 .10
7 Craig Donaldson .02 .10
8 Wade Simpson .02 .10
9 Mike Craig .08 .25
10 Mark Deazeley .02 .10
11 Scott Hollis .02 .10
12 Brian Grieve .02 .10
13 Dave Craievich .02 .10
14 Paul O'Hagan .02 .10
15 Matt Hoffman .02 .10
16 Trevor McIvor .02 .10
17 Cory Banika .02 .10
18 Kevin Butt .07 .20
19 Iain Fraser .02 .10
20 Bill Armstrong .07 .20
21 Scott Luik .02 .10
22 Brent Grieve .02 .10
23 Fred Brathwaite .40 1.00
24 Paul Holden .02 .10
25 Trevor Dam .02 .10
26 Chris Taylor .02 .10
27 Mark Guy .02 .10
28 Louie DeBrusk .30 .75
29 John Battice .02 .10
30 Chris Crombie .02 .10
31 Sean Basilio .07 .20
32 Aaron Nagy .02 .10
33 Greg Ryan .02 .10
34 Steve Martell .02 .10
35 Scott MacKay .02 .10
36 Dennis Purdie .30 .75
37 Steve Boyd .02 .10
38 John Tanner .08 .25
39 David Anderson .02 .10
40 Rick Corriveau .02 .10
41 Todd Hlushko .08 .25
42 Doug Synish .02 .10
43 Dan LeBlanc .07 .20
44 Dave Noseworthy .02 .10
45 Karl Taylor .02 .10
46 Jeff Hodgen .02 .10
47 Mike Kelly
Gary Agnew .01 .05
48 Wayne Maxner .02 .10
49 Brett Seguin .02 .10
50 Greg Walters .02 .10
51 Chris Snell .02 .10
52 Troy Binnie .02 .10
53 Joni Lehto .02 .10
54 Steve Kluczkowski .02 .10
55 Ryan Kuwabara .07 .20
56 Chris Simon .40 1.00
57 Jerrett DeFazio .07 .20
58 Rob Sangster .02 .10
59 Greg Clancy .02 .10
60 Peter Ambroziak .02 .10
61 Jeff Ricciardi .02 .10
62 John East .02 .10
63 Joey McTamney .02 .10
64 Dan Poirier .02 .10
65 Gairin Smith .02 .10
66 Wade Gibson .02 .10
67 Checklist Card .01 .05
68 Andrew Brodie .02 .10
69 Craig Wilson .02 .10
70 Peter McGlynn .02 .10
71 George Dourian .02 .10
72 Bob Berg .07 .20
73 Richard Fatrola .02 .10
74 Craig Fraser .02 .10
75 Brent Gretzky .20 .50
76 Jake Grimes .02 .10
77 Darren McCarty .75 2.00
78 Ted Miskolczi .02 .10
79 Rob Pearson .08 .25
80 Gordon Pell .02 .10
81 John Porco .02 .10
82 Ken Rowbotham .02 .10
83 Scott Thornton .20 .50
84 Shawn Way .02 .10
85 Steve Bancroft .02 .10
86 Greg Bignell .02 .10
87 Scott Boston .02 .10
88 Scott Feasby .02 .10
89 Derek Morin .07 .20
90 Sean O'Reilly .07 .20
91 Jason Skelet .02 .10
92 Greg Dreveny .02 .10
93 Jeff Fife .02 .10
94 Rob Stopar .02 .10
95 Joe Desrosiers .01 .05
96 Danny Flynn .02 .10
97 Dr. R.L. Vaughan .01 .05
98 Troy Stephens .02 .10
99 Dan Brown .02 .10
100 Mike Ricci .40 1.00
101 Brent Pope .02 .10
102 Mike Dagenais .07 .20
103 Scott Campbell .02 .10
104 Jamie Pegg .02 .10
105 Joe Hawley .02 .10
106 Jason Dawe .08 .25
107 Paul Mitton .02 .10
108 Mike Tomlinson .02 .10
109 Dave Lorentz .02 .10
110 Dale McTavish .02 .10
111 Willie McGarvey .02 .10
112 Don O'Neill .02 .10
113 Mark Myles .02 .10
114 Chris Longo .07 .20
115 Tom Hopkins .02 .10
116 Jassen Cullimore .02 .10
117 Geoff Ingram .02 .10
118 Twohey
Bovair TR .01 .05
119 Doug Searle .02 .10
120 Bryan Gendron .02 .10
121 Andrew Verner .08 .25
122 Todd Bocjun .07 .20
123 Dick Todd .02 .10
124 George Burnett .02 .10
125 Brad May .30 .75
126 David Benn .02 .10
127 Brian Mueggler .02 .10
128 Todd Coopman .02 .10
129 Geoff Rawson .02 .10
130 Keith Primeau .75 2.00
131 Mark Lawrence .07 .20
132 Randy Hall .02 .10
133 Greg Suchan .02 .10
134 Ken Ruddick .02 .10
135 Jason Winch .07 .20
136 Paul Wolanski .02 .10
137 Dennis Scott .01 .05
138 Steve Udvari .02 .10
139 Rich Beley .07 .20
140 Don Pancoe .02 .10
141 Paul Bruneau .01 .05
142 Paul Laus .20 .50
143 Mike St. John .02 .10
144 John Johnson .02 .10
145 Greg Allen .02 .10
146 Don McConnell .02 .10
147 Andy Bezeau .02 .10
148 Jeff Walker .02 .10
149 John Spoltore .02 .10
150 Derek Switzer .07 .20
151 Tyler Ertel .02 .10
152 Shawn Antoski .08 .25
153 Jason Corrigan .02 .10
154 Derian Hatcher .30 .75
155 John Vary .02 .10
156 Jamie Caruso .02 .10
157 Trevor Halverson .02 .10
158 Robert Deschamps .02 .10
159 Jeff Gardiner .07 .20
160 Gary Miller .02 .10
161 Shayne Antoski .08 .25
162 John Van Kessel .02 .10
163 Colin Austin .02 .10
164 Tom Purcell .02 .10
165 Joel Morin .02 .10
166 Tim Favot .02 .10
167 Checklist Card .01 .05
168 Jason Beaton .02 .10
169 Chris Ottmann .02 .10
170 Mike Matuszek .02 .10
171 Rob Fournier .02 .10
172 Ron Bertrand .07 .20
173 Bert Templeton .02 .10
174 Casey Jones .01 .05
175 Robert Frayn .02 .10
176 Claude Noel .02 .10
177 Sean Basilio Award .02 .10
178 Chris Longo Rookie .02 .10
179 Cory Keenan AS .02 .10
180 Owen Nolan Award .40 1.00
181 Steven Rice AS .08 .25
182 Shayne Stevenson
Scorer .08 .25
183 Mike Ricci Award .20 .50
184 Jason Firth Award .02 .10
185 John Slaney Award .02 .10
186 Iain Fraser Award .02 .10
187 Steven Rice Star .08 .25
188 Eric Lindros Scorer 1.25 3.00
189 Keith Primeau Scorer .40 1.00
190 Mike Ricci Award .20 .50
191 Mike Torchia AS .08 .25
192 Mike Torchia Star .07 .20
193 Jarrod Skalde Champs .08 .25
194 Paul O'Hagan Award .02 .10
195 Eric Lindros
(Where in 1991) 1.25 3.00
196 Eric Lindros AS 1.25 3.00
197 Jeff Fife Award .02 .10
198 Iain Fraser MVP .02 .10
199 Bill Armstrong Winner .02 .10
200 Checklist Card .01 .05

1990-91 7th Inning Sketch OHL

COMPLETE SET (400) 8.00 20.00
COMPLETE FACT.SET (400) 10.00 25.00
1 Eric Lindros 1.50 4.00
2 Greg Dreveny .02 .10
3 Belleville Checklist UER .01 .05
4 Richard Fatrola .02 .10
5 Craig Fraser .02 .10
6 Robert Frayn .02 .10
7 Brent Gretzky .15 .40
8 Jake Grimes .02 .10
9 Darren Hurley .02 .10
10 Rick Marshall .02 .10
11 Checklist UER .01 .05
12 Darren McCarty .75 2.00
13 Derek Morin .02 .10
14 Sean O'Reilly .02 .10
15 Rob Pearson UER .08 .25
16 John Porco .02 .10
17 Ken Rowbotham .02 .10
18 Ken Ruddick .02 .10
19 Jim Sonmez .02 .10
20 Brad Teichmann .02 .10
21 Chris Varga .02 .10
22 Checklist Card .01 .05
23 Larry Mavety CO .01 .05
24 Rival Fullum .02 .10
25 Nathan Lafayette .02 .10
26 Darren Bell .02 .10
27 Craig Brocklehurst .02 .10
28 Shawn Caplice .02 .10
29 Mike Cavanaugh .02 .10
30 Jason Cirone .02 .10
31 Chris Clancy .02 .10
32 Mark DeSantis .02 .10

33 Rob Dykeman .02 .10
34 Shayne Gaffar .02 .10
35 Ilpo Kauhanen .02 .10
36 Rob Kinghan .02 .10
37 Dave Lemay .02 .10
38 Guy Leveque .02 .10
39 Matt McGuffin .02 .10
40 Marcus Middleton .02 .10
41 Thomas Nemeth .02 .10
42 Rod Pasma .02 .10
43 Richard Raymond .02 .10
44 Jeff Reid .02 .10
45 Jerry Ribble .02 .10
46 Jean-Alain Schneider .02 .10
47 John Slaney .02 .10
48 Jeremy Stevenson .02 .10
49 Ryan VandenBussche .40 1.00
50 Marc Crawford CO .20 .50
51 Tony Bella .02 .10
52 Drake Berehowsky .20 .50
53 Jason Chipman .02 .10
54 Tony Cimellaro .02 .10
55 Keli Corpse .02 .10
56 Mike Dawson .02 .10
57 Sean Gauthier UER .02 .10
58 Fred Goltz .02 .10
59 Gord Harris .02 .10
60 Tony Iob .02 .10
61 John Bernie .02 .10
62 Dale Junkin .02 .10
63 Nathan Lafayette .02 .10
64 Blake Martin .02 .10
65 Mark McCague .02 .10
66 Bob McKillop .02 .10
67 Justin Morrison .02 .10
68 Bill Robinson .02 .10
69 Joel Sandie .02 .10
70 Kevin King .02 .10
71 Dave Stewart .02 .10
72 Joel Washkurak .02 .10
73 Brock Woods .02 .10
74 Randy Hall CO .02 .10
75 John Vary .02 .10
76 Peter Ambroziak .02 .10
77 Troy Binnie .02 .10
78 Curt Bowen .02 .10
79 Andrew Brodie .02 .10
80 Ottawa Checklist .02 .10
81 Greg Clancy .02 .10
82 Jerrett DeFazio .02 .10
83 Kris Draper .40 1.00
84 Wade Gibson .02 .10
85 Ryan Kuwabara .02 .10
86 Joni Lehto .02 .10
87 Donald MacPherson .02 .10
88 Grant Marshall .20 .50
89 Peter McGlynn .02 .10
90 Maurice O'Brien .02 .10
91 Jeff Ricciardi .02 .10
92 Brett Seguin .02 .10
93 Len DeVuono .02 .10
94 Gerry Skrypec .02 .10
95 Chris Snell .02 .10
96 Jason Snow .02 .10
97 Sean Spencer .02 .10
98 Brad Spry .02 .10
99 Matt Stone .02 .10
100 Brian Kilrea CO .02 .10
101 Kevin Butt .08 .25
102 Glen Craig .02 .10
103 Paul Doherty .02 .10
104 Mark Donahue .02 .10
105 Jeff Gardiner .02 .10
106 Trent Gleason .02 .10
107 Troy Gleason .02 .10
108 Mark Lawrence .08 .25
109 Trevor McIvor .02 .10
110 Paul Mitton .02 .10
111 David Myles .02 .10
112 Jeffory Nolan .02 .10
113 Rob Papineau .02 .10
114 Pat Peake .02 .10
115 Chris Phelps .02 .10
116 John Pinches .02 .10
117 James Shea .02 .10
118 James Sheehan .02 .10
119 John Stos .02 .10
120 Tom Sullivan .02 .10
121 John Wynne .02 .10
122 Robert Thorpe .02 .10
123 David Benn .02 .10
124 Andy Weidenbach CO UER .01 .05
125 Detroit Checklist .01 .05
126 David Anderson .02 .10
127 Sean Basilio .08 .25
128 Brent Brownlee .02 .10
129 Rick Corriveau .02 .10
130 Derrick Crane .02 .10
131 Chris Crombie .02 .10
132 Louie DeBrusk .40 1.00
133 Mark Guy .02 .10
134 Brett Marrietti .02 .10
135 Steve Martell .02 .10
136 Scott McKay .02 .10
137 Aaron Nagy .02 .10
138 Brett Nicol .02 .10
139 Barry Potomski .40 1.00
140 Dennis Purdie .40 1.00
141 Kelly Reed .02 .10
142 Gregory Ryan .02 .10
143 Brad Smyth .02 .10
144 Nick Stajduhar .02 .10
145 John Tanner .08 .25
146 Chris Taylor .02 .10
147 Mark Visheau .02 .10
148 Gary Agnew CO .08 .25
149 London Checklist .02 .10
150 Sault Ste. Marie Checklist .02 .10
151 David Babcock .02 .10
152 Drew Bannister .02 .10
153 Bob Boughner .30 .75
154 Joe Busillo .02 .10
155 Mike DeCoff .02 .10
156 Jason Denomme .02 .10
157 Adam Foote .75 2.00
158 Kevin Hodson .30 .75
159 Shaun Imber .02 .10
160 Ralph Intranuovo .02 .10
161 Kevin King .02 .10
162 Rick Kowalsky .02 .10
163 Chris Kraemer .02 .10
164 Dan Lambert .08 .25
165 Mike Lenarduzzi .08 .25
166 Tom MacDonald .02 .10
167 Mark Matier .02 .10
168 David Matsos .02 .10
169 Colin Miller .02 .10
170 Perry Pappas .02 .10
171 Jarrett Reid .02 .10
172 Kevin Reid .02 .10
173 Brad Tiley UER .02 .10
174 Windsor Checklist .01 .05
175 Wade Whitten .02 .10
176 Ted Nolan CO .20 .50
177 Sean Burns .02 .10
178 Jason Cirone .02 .10
179 John Copley .02 .10
180 Tyler Ertel .02 .10
181 Brian Forestell .02 .10
182 Rival Fullum .02 .10
183 Steve Gibson .02 .10
184 Leonard MacDonald .02 .10
185 Mike Speer .02 .10
186 Kevin MacKay .02 .10
187 Ryan Merritt .02 .10
188 Doug Minor .02 .10
189 Rick Morton .02 .10
190 Sean O'Hagan .08 .25
191 Mike Polano .02 .10
192 Cory Stillman .20 .50
193 Jason Stos .02 .10
194 Trevor Walsh .02 .10
195 Todd Warriner .20 .50
196 Jeff Wilson .02 .10
197 Jason York .20 .50
198 Jason Zohil .02 .10
199 Steve Smith .02 .10
200 Brad Smith CO .02 .10
201 Jeff Bes .02 .10
202 Mike Blum .02 .10
203 Sean Brown .02 .10
204 Darcy Cahill .02 .10
205 Dale Chokan .02 .10
206 Chris Code .02 .10
207 George Dourion .02 .10
208 Todd Gleason .02 .10
209 Hamilton Checklist UER .01 .05
210 Michael Hartwick .02 .10
211 Scott Jenkins .02 .10
212 Rob Leask .02 .10
213 Gordon Pell .02 .10
214 Michael Reier .02 .10
215 Kayle Short .02 .10
216 Jason Skellett .02 .10
217 Gairin Smith .02 .10
218 Jeff Smith .02 .10
219 Jason Soules .02 .10
220 Alex Stojanov .02 .10
221 Dan Tanevski .02 .10
222 Gary Taylor .02 .10
223 Brent Watson .02 .10
224 Steve Woods .02 .10
225 Jay Johnston CO UER .01 .05
226 Mike Allen .02 .10
227 Brad Barton .02 .10
228 Richard Borgo .02 .10
229 Justin Cullen .02 .10
230 Lenny DeVuono .02 .10
231 Norman Dezainde .02 .10
232 Jason Firth .02 .10
233 Derek Gauthier .02 .10
234 Jamie Israel .02 .10
235 Chris LiPuma .02 .10
236 Tony McCabe .02 .10
237 Paul McCallion .02 .10
238 Shayne McCosh .02 .10
239 Rod Saarinen .02 .10
240 Steve Smith .02 .10
241 Joey St.Aubin .02 .10
242 Rob Stopar .02 .10
243 Jason Zohil UER .02 .10
244 Mike Torchia .08 .25
245 Gib Tucker .02 .10
246 John Uniac .02 .10
247 Jack Williams .02 .10
248 Joe McDonnell CO .02 .10
249 Steven Rice .02 .10
250 Mike Polano .02 .10
251 Greg Allen .02 .10
252 Roch Belley .08 .25
253 Andy Bezeau .02 .10
254 Derek Booth .02 .10
255 Kevin Brown .02 .10
256 Mark Cardiff .02 .10
257 Jason Coles .02 .10
258 Todd Coopman .02 .10
259 Richard Girhiny .02 .10
260 Brian Holk .02 .10
261 John Johnson .02 .10
262 Dan Krisko .02 .10
263 Manny Legace .75 2.00
264 Brad May .30 .75
265 Don McConnell .02 .10
266 Niagara Falls CL .01 .05
267 Aaron Morrison .02 .10
268 Cory Pageau .02 .10
269 Geoff Rawson .02 .10
270 Todd Simon .02 .10
271 Steve Staios .08 .25
272 Jeff Walker .02 .10
273 Todd Wetzel .02 .10
274 Jason Winch .02 .10
275 Paul Wolanski .02 .10
276 Owen Sound Checklist .01 .05
277 Andrew Brunette .40 1.00
278 Wyatt Buckland .02 .10
279 Jason Buetow .02 .10
280 Jason Castellan .02 .10
281 Trent Cull .02 .10
282 Robert Deschamps .02 .10
283 Chris Driscoll .02 .10
284 Bryan Drury .02 .10
285 Todd Hunter .02 .10
286 Troy Hutchinson .02 .10
287 Kirk Maltby .30 .75
288 Geordie Maynard .02 .10
289 Kevin McDougall .02 .10
290 Ted Miskolczi .02 .10
291 Steve Parson .02 .10
292 Jeff Perry .02 .10
293 Grayden Reid .02 .10
294 Mike Speer .02 .10
295 Mark Strohack .02 .10
296 Mark Vilneff .02 .10
297 Keith Whitmore .02 .10
298 Jim Brown .02 .10
299 Len McNamara CO .01 .05
300 David Branch COMM .02 .10
301 Shayne Antoski .02 .10
302 Jason Beaton .02 .10
303 Ron Bertrand .02 .10
304 Michael Burman .02 .10
305 Jamie Caruso .02 .10
306 Allan Cox .02 .10
307 Tim Favot .02 .10
308 Trevor Halverson .02 .10
309 Derian Hatcher .40 1.00
310 Bill Lang .02 .10
311 Jason MacDonald .02 .10
312 Gary Miller .02 .10
313 Chris Ottmann .02 .10
314 Chad Penney .02 .10
315 Rick Pollard .02 .10
316 Bradley Shepard .02 .10
317 John Spoltore .08 .25
318 Derek Switzer .02 .10
319 Karl Taylor .02 .10
320 John Vary .02 .10
321 Kevin White .02 .10
322 Billy Wright .02 .10
323 Bert Templeton CO .02 .10
324 North Bay Checklist .01 .05
325 Oshawa Checklist UER .01 .05
326 Jan Benda .02 .10
327 Fred Brathwaite .40 1.00
328 Markus Brunner .02 .10
329 Trevor Burgess .02 .10
330 Clair Cornish .02 .10
331 Mike Cote .02 .10
332 Dave Craievich .02 .10
333 Dale Craigwell .20 .50
334 Jean-Paul Davis .02 .10
335 Mark Deazeley .02 .10
336 Mike Fountain .08 .25
337 Brian Grieve .02 .10
338 Matt Hoffman .02 .10
339 Scott Hollis .02 .10
340 Scott Boston .02 .10
341 Scott Luik .02 .10
342 Craig Lutes .02 .10
343 William MacPherson .02 .10
344 Paul O'Hagan .02 .10
345 Wade Simpson .02 .10
346 Jarrod Skalde UER .20 .50
347 Troy Sweet .02 .10
348 Jason Weaver .02 .10
349 Rick Cornacchia CO .02 .10
350 The Trophy .02 .10
351 Greg Bailey .02 .10
352 Ryan Black .02 .10
353 Todd Bocjun UER .08 .25
354 Toby Burkitt .02 .10
355 Scott Campbell .02 .10
356 Jassen Cullimore .02 .10
357 Jason Dawe .08 .25
358 Dan Ferguson .02 .10
359 Bryan Gendron .02 .10
360 Michael Harding .02 .10
361 Joe Hawley .02 .10
362 Peterborough CL .01 .05
363 Geordie Kinnear .02 .10
364 Chris Longo UER .02 .10
365 Dale McTavish .02 .10
366 Mark Myles .02 .10
367 Don O'Neill .02 .10
368 Jamie Pegg .02 .10
369 Brent Pope .02 .10
370 Kitchener CL .01 .05
371 Doug Searle .02 .10
372 Troy Stephens .02 .10
373 Mike Tomlinson .02 .10
374 Brent Tully .02 .10
375 Andrew Verner .08 .25
376 Dick Todd CO .02 .10
377 John Tanner .08 .25
378 Adam Bennett .02 .10
379 Kyle Blacklock .02 .10
380 Terry Chitaroni .02 .10
381 Brandon Convery .02 .10
382 J.D. Eaton .02 .10
383 Derek Etches .02 .10
384 Rod Hinks .02 .10
385 Bill Kovacs .02 .10
386 Alain Laforge .02 .10
387 Jamie Matthews .02 .10
388 Glen Murray .75 2.00
389 Dean Cull .02 .10
390 Sean O'Donnell .20 .50
391 Sudbury Checklist UER .01 .05
392 Mike Peca .75 2.00
393 Shawn Rivers .02 .10
394 Dan Ryder .02 .10
395 Alastair Still .02 .10
396 Michael Yeo .02 .10
397 Barry Young .02 .10
398 Jason Young .02 .10
399 Ken MacKenzie CO .02 .10
400 Bob Berg UER .02 .10
NNO Eric Lindros promo 2.00 5.00

1990-91 7th Inning Sketch QMJHL

COMPLETE SET (268) 8.00 20.00
COMPLETE FACT.SET (268) 10.00 25.00
1 Patrick Poulin .08 .25
2 Steve Lupien .08 .25
3 Pierre Gagnon .08 .25
4 Eric Plante .02 .10
5 Stephane Desjardins .02 .10
6 Peter Valenta .02 .10
7 Alexander Legault .02 .10
8 Patrice Brisebois .20 .50
9 Martin Charrois .02 .10
10 Eric Dandenault .02 .10
11 Claude Juiras Jr. .02 .10
12 David Pekarek .02 .10
13 Denis Chasse .08 .25
14 Ian Laperriere .08 .25
15 Roger Larche .02 .10
16 Dave Paquet .02 .10
17 Pascal Lebrasseur .02 .10
18 Eric Meloche .02 .10
19 The Face Off .01 .05
20 Sylvain Rodrigue .08 .25
21 Dary Giarard .02 .10
22 Eric Rochette .02 .10
23 Steve Gosselin .02 .10
24 Martin Lavalle .02 .10
25 Martin Lapointe .75 2.00
26 Eric Brule .02 .10
27 Richard Boivin .02 .10
28 Patrice Martineau .02 .10
29 Dave Tremblay .02 .10
30 Steve Larouche .02 .10
31 Danny Beauregard .02 .10
32 Francois Belanger .02 .10
33 Michel St.Jacques .02 .10
34 Patric Sissillan .02 .10
35 Felix Potvin 1.50 4.00
36 Sebastien Parent .02 .10
37 Eric Duchesne .02 .10
38 Gilles Bouchard .02 .10
39 Martin Gagne .02 .10
40 Stephane Charbonneau .02 .10
41 Martin Beaupre .02 .10
42 Daniel Paradis .02 .10
43 Joe Canale .02 .10
44 Georges Vezina Arena .02 .10
45 Francois Leblanc .08 .25
46 Martin Chaput .02 .10
47 Marc Beaucage .02 .10
48 Carl Mantha .02 .10
49 Jim Bermingham .02 .10
50 Philippe Boucher .08 .25
51 Denis Chalifoux .02 .10
52 Sylvain Naud .02 .10
53 Jean Roberge .02 .10
54 Sandy McCarthy .40 1.00
55 Eric Dubois .02 .10
56 Jean Blouin .08 .25
57 Jason Brousseau .02 .10
58 Pierre Sandke .02 .10
59 Benoit Larose .02 .10
60 Yanick Frechette .02 .10
61 Pierre Calder .02 .10
62 Patric Grise .02 .10
63 Martin Balleux .02 .10
64 Boris Rousson .40 1.00
65 Martin Trudeli .02 .10
66 Carl Leblanc .02 .10
67 Martin Brochu .40 1.00
68 Benoit Terrien .02 .10
69 QMJHL Action .02 .10
70 Pascal Vincent .02 .10
71 Christian Tardi .02 .10
72 Christian Campeau .02 .10
73 Eric Raymond .08 .25
74 John Kovacs .02 .10
75 Steve Areas .02 .10
76 Pascal Dufalt .02 .10
77 Greg MacEachern .02 .10
78 Remi Belliveau .02 .10
79 Jocelyn Langlois .02 .10
80 Carl Menard .02 .10
81 Sebastein Foneir .02 .10
82 Jean-Franco Gregoire .02 .10
83 Normand Demers .02 .10
84 Nicolas Lefebvre .02 .10
85 Dominic Maltais .02 .10
86 Mario Therrien .02 .10
87 Daniel Thibault .02 .10
88 Jean-Francois Labbe .40 1.00
89 Alain Cote .02 .10
90 Eric Prillo .02 .10
91 Patrick Nadeau .02 .10
92 Claude Poner .02 .10
93 Stephane Julier .02 .10
94 Patrice Rene .02 .10
95 Francis Coutineir .02 .10
96 Guy Lefebvre .02 .10
97 Carl Boudreau .02 .10
98 Jacques Parent .02 .10
99 Stephane Bouquet .02 .10
100 Yanic Perreault .20 .50
101 Yvan Bergeron .02 .10
102 Jean-Francois Rivard .08 .25
103 Daniel Laflamme .02 .10
104 Francois Bourdeau .02 .10
105 Yvan Charrois .02 .10
106 Patric Genest .02 .10
107 Herve Lapointe .02 .10
108 Jean-Francois Jomphe .08 .25
109 Marc Tardif .02 .10
110 Eric Cardinal .02 .10
111 Denis Cloutier .02 .10
112 QMJHL Action .02 .10
113 Alain Samscartier .01 .05
114 Marquis Mathieu .08 .25
115 Stephan Tartari .02 .10
116 QMJHL Action .02 .10
117 QMJHL Action .02 .10
118 Martin Ray .02 .10
119 David Boudreault .02 .10
120 Mario Durroulin .02 .10
121 Jean-Francis Dieard .02 .10
122 QMJHL Action .02 .10
123 QMJHL Action .02 .10
124 Maxime Gagne .02 .10
125 Stephane Guellet .02 .10
126 Steven Paiement .02 .10
127 Francois Olympique .02 .10
128 Eric Coci .02 .10
129 Simon Toupin .02 .10
130 Shane Doirrin .02 .10
131 Todd Sparks .02 .10
132 Bruno Lajeunesse .02 .10
133 Marcel Cousineau .20 .50
134 Claude-Charl Sauirol .02 .10
135 Eric Bellerose .02 .10
136 QMJHL Action .02 .10
137 QMJHL Action .02 .10
138 Martin Lepage .02 .10
139 Michael Langauer .02 .10
140 Fredric Boivin .02 .10
141 Steven Dion .02 .10
142 QMJHL Action .02 .10
143 QMJHL Action .02 .10
144 Dan Paolucci .02 .10
145 Bruno Villeneuve .02 .10
146 Yanic Perreault CL .08 .25
147 Checklist Card .01 .05
148 Stefan Simoes .02 .10
149 Joel Blain .02 .10
150 Eric Lavigne .02 .10
151 Checklist Card .01 .05
152 Patrick Poulin CL .02 .10
153 Robert Melanson .02 .10
154 Brian Rogger .02 .10
155 Checklist Card .01 .05
156 Checklist Card .01 .05
157 Francois Ouellette .08 .25
158 QMJHL Action .02 .10
159 Felix Potvin CL .75 2.00
160 Checklist Card .01 .05
161 Checklist Card .01 .05
162 Checklist Card .01 .05
163 QMJHL Action .02 .10
164 QMJHL Action .02 .10
165 Checklist Card .01 .05
166 Checklist Card .01 .05
167 QMJHL Action .02 .10
168 QMJHL Action .02 .10
169 Pierre Fillon .02 .10
170 Yanick Degrace .08 .25
171 Paul Daigneault .02 .10
172 Stacy Dellaire .02 .10
173 Steve Searles .02 .10
174 Todd Gillingham .02 .10
175 Yves Sarault .02 .10
176 Jason Downey .02 .10
177 Paul Brousseau .02 .10
178 Raymond Delarosbi .02 .10
179 Yvan Corbin .02 .10
180 Gaston Drapeau .02 .10
181 Celebration .02 .10
182 Reginald Brezeault .02 .10
183 Eric Lafrance .02 .10
184 Martin Lavalle .08 .25
185 Sebastein Lavallere .02 .10
186 Martin Lefebvre .02 .10
187 Richard Hamelin .02 .10
188 Eric Beauvois .02 .10
189 Hughes Mongeon .02 .10
190 Alaine Cole .40 1.00
191 Eric Desrochers .08 .25
192 Eric Joyal .02 .10
193 Steve Dortigny .40 1.00
194 Fredrick Lefebvre .02 .10
195 Patrick Hebert .02 .10
196 Johnny Lorenzo .08 .25
197 Sylvain Cornier .02 .10
198 QMJHL Action .02 .10
199 Dave Morissette .08 .25
200 Yanick Dupre .02 .10
201 Eric Marcoux .02 .10
202 Bruno Ducharme .02 .10
203 Martin Caron .02 .10
204 Yves Meunier .02 .10
205 Eric Bissonette .02 .10
206 Jason Underhill .02 .10
207 Dave Belliveau .02 .10
208 Steve Lapointe .02 .10
209 Dean Melanson .02 .10
210 Trevor Dehaime .02 .10
211 Jacques Leblanc .02 .10
212 Normand Pacquet .02 .10
213 Huges Laliberte .02 .10
214 Craig Prior .02 .10
215 Patrick Labrecque .08 .25
216 Patrick Cloutier .02 .10
217 Michael Bazinet .02 .10
218 Christian Proulx .02 .10
219 QMJHL Action .02 .10
220 Charles Poulin .02 .10
221 Christian Lariviere .02 .10
222 Martin Brodeur 3.00 8.00
223 Yanick Lemay .02 .10
224 Dennis Leblanc .02 .10
225 Francis Groleau .02 .10
226 Pierre Sevigny .02 .10
227 Pierre Allard .02 .10
228 Craig Martin .02 .10
229 Karl Dykhuis .08 .25
230 Etienne Lavoie .02 .10
231 Stan Melanson .02 .10
232 Dominic Rheaume .02 .10
233 Mario Nobili .02 .10
234 Martin Gendron .08 .25
235 Stephane Menard .02 .10
236 David St.Pierre .02 .10
237 Yan Arsenault .02 .10
238 Norman Flynn .01 .05
239 QMJHL Action .02 .10
240 David Chouinard .02 .10
241 Robert Guilliet .02 .10
242 Martin Lajeunesse .02 .10
243 Nichol Cloutier .02 .10
244 Joel Brouchard .08 .25
245 Donald Brashear .40 1.00
246 Sebastien Tremblay .02 .10
247 Dominique Grandmaison .02 .10
248 Nicolas Lefebvre .02 .10
249 Joseph Napolitano .02 .10
250 Marc Savard .02 .10
251 Alain Gauthier .02 .10
252 Patrick Cole .02 .10
253 Richard Aimonette .02 .10
254 Martin Laitre .02 .10
255 Carl Lamonthe .02 .10
256 QMJHL Action .02 .10
257 Andre Durocher .02 .10
258 Jocelyn Martel .02 .10
259 Jeanot Ferlard .20 .50
260 Claude Savoie .02 .10
262 Denis Beauchamp .02 .10
263 Jean-Francois Gagnon .02 .10
264 Andre Boulaine .02 .10
265 Paul-Emile Exantus .02 .10
266 Danny Nolet .02 .10
267 Jean Lebreau .02 .10
268 Claude Barthe .02 .10

1990-91 7th Inning Sketch WHL

COMPLETE SET (347) 7.20 18.00
COMPLETE FACT.SET (347) 8.00 20.00
1 Brent Bilodeau .08 .25
2 Craig Chapman .02 .10
3 Jeff Jubenville .02 .10
4 Al Kinisky .02 .10
5 Kevin Malgunas .02 .10
6 Andy MacIntyre .02 .10
7 Darren McAusland .02 .10
8 Mike Seaton .02 .10
9 Turner Stevenson .20 .50
10 Lindsay Vallis .02 .10
11 Dave Wilkie .08 .25
12 Jesse Wilson .02 .10
13 Dody Wood .02 .10
14 Bradley Zavisha .02 .10
15 Vince Boe .02 .10
16 Scott Davis .02 .10
17 Troy Hyatt .02 .10
18 Trevor Pennock .02 .10
19 Corey Schwab .20 .50
20 Scott Bellefontaine .08 .25
21 Travis Kelln .02 .10
22 Peter Anholt CO/GM .01 .05
23 Sonny Mignacca UER .08 .25
24 Chris Osgood .75 2.00
25 Murray Garbutt .02 .10
26 Kalvin Knibbs .02 .10
27 Jason Krywulak .02 .10
28 Jason Miller .02 .10
29 Rob Niedermayer .30 .75
30 Clayton Norris .02 .10
31 Jason Prosofsky .02 .10
32 Dana Rieder .02 .10
33 Kevin Riehl .02 .10
34 Tyler Romanchuk .02 .10
35 Dave Shute .02 .10
36 Lorne Toews .02 .10
37 Scott Townsend .02 .10
38 David Cooper .02 .10
39 Jon Duval .02 .10
40 Dan Kordic .08 .25
41 Mike Rathje .20 .50
42 Tim Bothwell CO .02 .10
43 Brent Thompson .08 .25
44 Jeff Knight .02 .10
45 Van Burgess .02 .10
46 Kimbi Daniels .08 .25
47 Curtis Friesen .02 .10
48 Todd Holt .02 .10
49 Blake Knox .02 .10
50 Trent McCleary .02 .10
51 Mark McFarlane .02 .10
52 Eddie Patterson .02 .10
53 Lloyd Pellitier .02 .10
54 Geoff Sanderson .30 .75
55 Adam Schneider .02 .10
56 Tyler Wright .08 .25
57 Joel Dyck .02 .10
58 Len MacAusland .02 .10
59 Evan Marble .02 .10
60 David Podlubny .02 .10
61 Kurt Seher .02 .10
62 Jason Smith .02 .10
63 Justin Burke .08 .25
64 Kelly Thiessen .08 .25
65 Todd Esselmont .02 .10
66 Graham James CO/GM .01
67 Chris Herperger .02 .10
68 Mark McCoy .02 .10
69 Dean Malkoc .08 .25
70 Dennis Sproxton .08 .25
71 Centennial Civic Center .02 .10
72 Kimbi Daniels .08 .25
73 Shane Calder .02 .10
74 Mark Franks .02 .10
75 Greg Leahy .02 .10
76 Dean Rambo .02 .10
77 Scott Scissons .02 .10
78 David Struch .02 .10
79 Derek Tibbatts .02 .10
80 Shawn Yakimishyn .02 .10
81 Trent Coghill .02 .10
82 Robert Lelacheur .02 .10
83 Richard Matvichuk .30 .75
84 Mark Raiter .02 .10
85 Trevor Sherban .02 .10
86 Mark Wotton .08 .25
87 Cam Moon .08 .25
88 Trevor Robins .08 .25
89 Jeff Buchanan .02 .10
90 Ryan Strain .02 .10
91 Tim Cox .02 .10
92 Terry Ruskowski CO .02 .10
93 Saskatchewan Place .02 .10
94 Darin Bader .02 .10
95 Gaetan Blouin .02 .10
96 Rick Kozuback CO/GM .01 .05
97 Jason Bowen .02 .10
98 Fran Deferenza .02 .10
99 Terry Degner .02 .10
100 Devin Derksen .02 .10
101 Martin Svetlik .02 .10
102 Jeremy Warring .08 .25
103 Corey Jones .08 .25
104 Dean Tiltgen UER .02 .10
105 Ryan Fujita .02 .10
106 Jeff Fancy .02 .10
107 Terry Virtue .20 .50
108 Dennis Pinfold .02 .10
109 Kyle Reeves .02 .10
110 Steve McNutt UER .02 .10
111 Todd Klassen .02 .10
112 Darren Hastman .02 .10
113 Bill Lindsay .20 .50
114A Brian Sakic ERR .02 .10
114B Brian Sakic COR .02 .10
115 Dan Sherstenka .02 .10
116 Don Blishen .08 .25
117 Jason Marshall .02 .10
118 Dean Zayonce .02 .10
119 Brad Loring .02 .10
121 Darcy Austin UER .08 .25
122 Darcy Werenka .02 .10
123 Shane Peacock .02 .10
124 Rob Hartnell UER .02 .10
125 Brad Zimmer .02 .10
126 Allan Egeland .02 .10
127 Brad Rubachuk .02 .10
128 Jamie Pushor .20 .50
129 Jamie McLennan UER .30 .75
130 Lance Burns .02 .10
131 Ryan Smith .02 .10
132 Jason McBain .02 .10
133 Duane Maruschak UER .02 .10
134 Kevin St.Jacques .02 .10
135 Jason Sorochan .02 .10
136 Jason Widmer .02 .10
137 Bob Loucks CO .02 .10
138 Jason Ruff .02 .10
139 Pat Pylypuik .02 .10
140 Scott Adair .02 .10
141 Radek Sip .02 .10
142 Russ West .02 .10
143 Scott Thomas .02 .10
144 Kent Staniforth .02 .10
145 Travis Thiessen .02 .10
146 Mark Hussey .02 .10
147 Kevin Masters .02 .10
148 Todd Johnson .02 .10
149 Bob Loucks .02 .10
150A Rob Reimer ERR .02 .10
150B Rob Reimer COR .02 .10
151 Jeff Petruic .02 .10
152 Chris Schmidt .02 .10
153 Scott Barnstable .02 .10
154 Ian Layton .02 .10
155 Kevin Smyth .02 .10
156 Kim Deck .02 .10
157 Jason White .02 .10
158 Peter Cox .02 .10
159 Jeff Calvert UER .08 .25
160 Paul Dyck UER .02 .10
161 Derek Kletzel .02 .10
162 Jason Fitzsimmons UER .08 .25
163 Darcy Jerome .02 .10
164 Hal Christiansen .02 .10
165 Terry Hollinger .02 .10
166 Mike Risdale .08 .25
167 Jamie Heward .02 .10
168 Louis Dumont .02 .10
169 Cory Dosdall .02 .10
170 Terry Bendera .02 .10
171 Jamie Hayden .02 .10
172 Kelly Chotowetz .02 .10
173 Brad Scott .02 .10
174 Jeff Shantz .30 .75
175 Kelly Markwart .02 .10
176 Gary Pearce .02 .10
177 Kerry Biette .02 .10
178 Jamie Splett .02 .10
179 Frank Kovacs .02 .10
180 Greg Pankewicz .02 .10
181 Colin Ruck .02 .10
182 Brad Tippett CO .02 .10
183 Dusty Imoo .08 .25
184 Derek Eberle .02 .10
185 Heath Weenk .02 .10
186 Mike Sillinger .20 .50
187 Erin Thornton .02 .10
188 Mike Chrun .02 .10
189 Pat Falloon .20 .50
190 Bobby House UER .02 .10
191 Mike Jickling .02 .10
192 Trevor Tovall UER .02 .10
193 Steve Junker .02 .10
194 Shane Maitland .02 .10
195 Chris Lafreniere .02 .10
196 Frank Evans .02 .10
197 Jon Klemm .30 .75
198 Shawn Dietrich UER .08 .25
199 Dennis Saharchuk UER .02 .10
200 Mark Woolf .02 .10
201 Ray Whitney .20 .50
202 Scott Bailey .08 .25
203 Mark Ruark .02 .10
204 Brent Thurston .02 .10
205 Dan Faassen .02 .10
206 Kerry Toporowski .02 .10
207 Des Christopher .08 .25
208 Geoff Grandberg .02 .10
209 Bryan Maxwell CO .02 .10
210 Cam Danyluk .02 .10
211 Bram Vanderkracht .02 .10
212 Calvin Thudium .02 .10
213 Mark Szoke UER .02 .10
214 Kelly McCrimmon CO/GM .02 .10
215 Kevin Robertson UER .02 .10
216A Brian Purdy ERR .02 .10
216B Brian Purdy COR .02 .10
217 Hardy Sauter .02 .10
218 Dwayne Gylywoychuk .02 .10
219 Bart Cote .02 .10
220 Merv Priest .02 .10
221 Jeff Hoad .02 .10
222 Glen Gulutzan .02 .10
223 Johan Skillgard .02 .10
224 Byron Penstock .08 .25
225A Mike Vadenberghe ERR .02 .10
225B Mike Vadenberghe COR .02 .10
226 Trevor Kidd .40 1.00
227 Dan Kopec .02 .10
228 Greg Hutchings .02 .10
229 Chris Constant .02 .10
230 Glen Webster .02 .10
231 Rob Puchniak .02 .10
232 Calvin Flint .02 .10
233 Stuart Scantlebury .02 .10
234 Jason White .02 .10

235 Gary Audette .02 .10
236 Kevin Schmalz .02 .10
237 Dwayne Newman .02 .10
238 Chris Catellier .02 .10
239 Todd Harris .02 .10
240 Mike Shemko .02 .10
241 John Badduke .02 .10
242 Mark Cipriano .02 .10
243 Brad Bagu .02 .10
244 Ross Harris .02 .10
245 Dino Caputo .02 .10
246 Cam Bristow .02 .10
247 Jarret Zukiwsky UER .02 .10
248 Jason Knox .02 .10
249 Gerry St.Cyr .02 .10
250 Larry Woo .02 .10
251 Jason Peters .02 .10
252 Shane Stangby .02 .10
253 Dave McMillen .02 .10
254 Colin Gregor UER .02 .10
255 Steve Passmore .40 1.00
256 Shayne Green UER .02 .10
257 Kevin Koopman .08 .25
258 Larry Watkins UER .02 .10
259 Scott Fukami UER .02 .10
260 Rick Hopper CO .01 .05
261 Laurie Billeck .02 .10
262 Rob Daum CO/GM UER .01 .05
263 Mark Stowe .02 .10
264 Curtis Regnier .02 .10
265 David Neilson .02 .10
266 Brian Pellerin .02 .10
267 Dean McAmmond .20 .50
268 Darren Van Impe .15 .40
269 Troy Neumeier .02 .10
270 Mike Langen .08 .25
271 Dan Kesa .02 .10
272 Travis Laycock .08 .25
273 Scott Allison .02 .10
274 Jeff Gorman .02 .10
275 Lee J. Leslie .02 .10
276 Jason Kwiatkowski .02 .10
277 Donevan Hextall UER .02 .10
278 Shane Zulyniak .02 .10
279 Darren Perkins .02 .10
280 Chad Seibel .02 .10
281 Jeff Nelson .02 .10
282 Troy Hjertas .02 .10
283 Jamie Linden .02 .10
284 Zac Boyer .02 .10
285 Jarret Bousquet .02 .10
286 Steven Yule .02 .10
287 Tommy Renney CO UER .08 .25
288 Lance Johnson .02 .10
289 Scott Niedermayer .75 2.00
290 Ryan Harrison .02 .10
291 Ed Patterson .08 .25
292 Jeff Watchorn .02 .10
293 Cal McGowan .02 .10
294 Dale Masson .08 .25
295 Joey Mittelsteadt UER .02 .10
296 Scott Loucks .02 .10
297 Shea Esselmont .02 .10
298 Craig Bonner .02 .10
299 Mike Mathers .02 .10
300 Fred Hettle .02 .10
301 Craig Lyons .02 .10
302 Murray Duval .02 .10
303 Jamie Barnes .02 .10
304 Bryan Gourlie .02 .10
305 Chad Berezniuk .02 .10
306 Corey Hirsch .20 .50
307 Darryl Sydor .30 .75
308 Jarrett Deuling .02 .10
309 Cory Stock .02 .10
310 Chris Rowland .02 .10
311 Mike Ruark .02 .10
312 Steve Konowalchuk .30 .75
313 Jeff Sebastian .02 .10
314 Brandon Smith .08 .25
315 Greg Gatto .02 .10
316 Brad Harrison .02 .10
317 Brantt Myhres .40 1.00
318 Jamie Black .02 .10
319 Colin Foley .02 .10
320 Cam Danyluk .02 .10
321 Dean Dorchak .02 .10
322 Ryan Slemko .02 .10
323 Kim Deck .02 .10
324 Kelly Harris .02 .10
325 Murray Bokenfohr .02 .10
326 Dean Intwert .08 .25
327 Dennis Saharchuk UER .02 .10
328 Shane Seiker UER .02 .10
329 Terry Virtue .20 .50
330 Josh Erdman .02 .10
331 Layne Roland .02 .10
332 Michel Michon .02 .10
333 Scott Mydan UER .02 .10
334 Brandon Wheat Kings .01 .05
335 Moose Jaw Warriors .01 .05
336 Swift Current Broncos .01 .05
337 Regina Pats UER .01 .05
338 Saskatoon Blades .01 .05
339 Medicine Hat Tigers .01 .05
340 The Goalmouth .01 .05
341 Portland Winter Hawks .01 .05
342 Kamloops Blazers UER .01 .05
343 Victoria Cougars .01 .05
344 Tri City Americans .01 .05
345 Spokane Chiefs .01 .05
346 Seattle Thunderbirds .01 .05
347 Lethbridge Hurricanes .01 .05
348 Prince Albert Raiders .01 .05

1990 7th Inning Sketch Memorial Cup

COMPLETE SET (100) 30.00 50.00
1 Len Barrie .20 .50
2 Zac Boyer .20 .50
3 Dave Chyzowski .20 .50
4 Shea Esselmont .20 .50
5 Todd Esselmont .20 .50
6 Phil Huber .20 .50
7 Lance Johnson .20 .50
8 Paul Kruse .20 .50
9 Cal McGowan .20 .50
10 Mike Needham .20 .50
11 Brian Shantz .20 .50
12 Darryl Sydor .75 2.00
13 Jeff Watchorn .20 .50
14 Jarrett Bousquet .20 .50
15 Todd Harris .20 .50
16 Deen Malkoc .20 .50
17 Joey Mittelstadt .20 .50
18 Scott Niedermayer 1.25 3.00
19 Clayton Young .20 .50
20 Trevor Sim .20 .50
21 Murray Duval .20 .50
22 Steve Yule .20 .50
23 Craig Bonner .20 .50
24 Dale Masson .20 .50
25 Corey Hirsch .40 1.00
26 Joe McDonnell .20 .50
27 Rick Chambers .20 .50
28 John Finnie .20 .50
29 Randy Pearce .20 .50
30 Mark Montanari .20 .50
31 Mike Torchia .20 .50
32 Jason York .30 .75
33 Jason Firth .20 .50
34 Jamie Israel .20 .50
35 Richard Borgo .20 .50
36 John Uniac .20 .50
37 Steve Smith .20 .50
38 Steven Rice .20 .50
39 Gilbert Dionne .30 .75
40 Cory Keenan .20 .50
41 Rick Allain .20 .50
42 John Copley .20 .50
43 Gib Tucker .20 .50
44 Chris LiPuma .20 .50
45 Brad Barton .20 .50
46 Rival Fullum .20 .50
47 Joey St.Aubin .20 .50
48 Jack Williams .20 .50
49 Shayne Stevenson .20 .50
50 Pierre Creamer .20 .50
51 Carl Mantha .20 .50
52 Julien Cameron .20 .50
53 Sandy McCarthy .75 2.00
54 Gino Odjick .40 1.00
55 Eric Raymond .20 .50
56 Carl Boudreau .20 .50
57 Greg MacEachern .20 .50
58 Allen Kerr .20 .50
59 Patrice Brisebois .30 .75
60 Eric Bissonette .20 .50
61 Martin Lapointe 1.25 3.00
62 Michel Gingras .20 .50
63 Sylvain Naud .20 .50
64 Pat Caron .20 .50
65 Regis Tremblay .20 .50
66 Francois Pelletier .20 .50
67 Jason Brousseau .20 .50
68 Eric Dubois .20 .50
69 Claude Boivin .20 .50
70 Denis Chalifoux .20 .50
71 Jim Bermingham .20 .50
72 Daniel Arsenault .20 .50
73 Normand Demers .20 .50
74 Serge Anglehart .20 .50
75 Rick Cornacchia .20 .50
76 Kevin Butt .20 .50
77 Fred Brathwaite 1.25 3.00
78 Paul O'Hagan .20 .50
79 Craig Donaldson .20 .50
80 Jean-Paul Davis .20 .50
81 Brian Grieve .20 .50
82 Bill Armstrong .20 .50
83 Wade Simpson .20 .50
84 Dave Craievich .20 .50
85 Dale Craigwell .30 .75
86 Joe Busillo .20 .50
87 Cory Banika .20 .50
88 Eric Lindros 10.00 20.00
89 Iain Fraser .20 .50
90 Mike Craig .20 .50
91 Jarrod Skalde .30 .75
92 Brent Grieve .20 .50
93 Scott Luik .20 .50
94 Matt Hoffman .20 .50
95 Trevor McIvor .20 .50
96 Scott Hollis .20 .50
97 Mark Deazeley .20 .50
98 Clair Cornish .20 .50
99 Oshawa Wins (Eric Lindros w/Memorial Cup 2.00 5.00
100 Checklist Card .02 .10

1991-92 7th Inning Sketch OHL

COMPLETE SET (384) 8.00 20.00
1 John Slaney .07 .20
2 Jason Meloche .02 .10
3 Mark DeSantis .02 .10
4 Richard Raymond .02 .10
5 Dave Lemay .02 .10
6 Matt McGuffin .02 .10
7 Sam Oliveira .02 .10
8 Jeremy Stevenson .05 .15
9 Todd Walker .02 .10
10 Jean-Alain Schneider .02 .10
11 Guy Leveque .05 .15
12 Shayne Gaffar .02 .10
13 Mike Prokopec .05 .15
14 Nathan LaFayette .07 .20
15 Larry Courville .08 .25
16 Chris Clancy .02 .10
17 Tom Nemeth .05 .15
18 Jeff Reid .02 .10
19 Ilpo Kauhanen .08 .25
20 Rob Dykeman .08 .25
21 Rival Fullum .05 .15
22 Ryan VandenBussche .08 .25
23 Gordon Pell .05 .15
24 Paul Andrea UER Team affiliation says Generals .02 .10
25 John Lovell CO UER Team affiliation says Generals .01 .05
26 Alan Letang .02 .10
27 Chris Phelps .02 .10
28 John Wynne .02 .10
29 Rob Kinghan .02 .10
30 Glen Craig .02 .10
31 Eric Cairns .40 1.00
32 John Pinches .02 .10
33 Todd Harvey .20 .50
34 Craig Fraser .02 .10
35 Pat Peake .08 .25
36 Chris Skoryna .02 .10
37 Bob Wren .05 .15
38 Chris Varga .02 .10
39 David Benn .02 .10
40 Mark Lawrence .05 .15
41 Jeff Kostuch .02 .10
42 J.D. Eaton .02 .10
43 Derek Etches .02 .10
44 Jeff Gardiner .02 .10
45 James Shea .08 .25
46 Brad Teichmann .08 .25
47 Jim Rutherford CO .05 .15
48 Derek Wilkinson .05 .15
49 OHL Action .02 .10
50 OHL Action .02 .10
51 Sandy Allan .08 .25
52 Ron Bertrand .08 .25
53 Brad Brown .08 .25
54 Dennis Bonvie .40 1.00
55 Bradley Shepard .02 .10
56 Allan Cox .02 .10
57 Jack Williams .05 .15
58 Chad Penney .02 .10
59 Jason Firth .02 .10
60 Bill Lang .02 .10
61 Ryan Merritt .02 .10
62 Michael Burman .02 .10
63 Billy Wright .02 .10
64 Dave Szabo .02 .10
65 James Sheehan .02 .10
66 John Spoltore .02 .10
67 Paul Rushforth .02 .10
68 Jeff Shevalier .07 .20
69 Robert Thorpe .02 .10
70 Drake Berehowsky .08 .25
71 Patrick Barton .02 .10
72 Bert Templeton CO .05 .15
73 Wade Gibson .02 .10
74 C.J. Denomme UER Name spelled C. Jay on back .08 .25
75 Mike Torchia .08 .25
76 Mike Polano .02 .10
77 Tony McCabe .02 .10
78 Chris Kraemer .02 .10
79 Tim Spitzig .02 .10
80 Trevor Gallant .02 .10
81 Yvan Corbin .02 .10
82 Norman Dezainde .05 .15
83 Marc Robillard .02 .10
84 Derek Gauthier .02 .10
85 Gib Tucker .02 .10
86 Paul McCallion .02 .10
87 Eric Manlow .05 .15
88 Jamie Caruso .05 .15
89 Gary Miller .02 .10
90 Jason Stevenson .02 .10
91 Shayne McCosh .02 .10
92 Jason Gladney .02 .10
93 Brad Barton .02 .10
94 Chris LiPuma .07 .20
95 Justin Cullen .02 .10
96 Bill Smith SCOUT .01 .05
97 Joe McDonnell CO .01 .05
99 Brent Gretzky .08 .25
100 Gairin Smith .02 .10
101 Blair Scott .02 .10
102 Daniel Godbout .02 .10
103 Dan Preston .02 .10
104 Ian Keiller .02 .10
105 Rick Marshall .02 .10
106 Aaron Morrison .02 .10
107 Dominic Belanger .02 .10
108 Kevin Brown .05 .15
109 Tony Cimellaro .02 .10
110 Larry Mavety CO .01 .05
111 Jake Grimes .05 .15
112 Greg Dreveny .08 .25
113 Darren McCarty .75 2.00
114 Doug Doull .02 .10
115 Scott Boston .05 .15
116 Dale Chokan .02 .10
117 Darren Hurley .02 .10
118 Brian Mielko UER Card misnumbered 61 .02 .10
119 Richard Gallace UER Card misnumbered 65 .02 .10
120 Shayne Antoski .08 .25
121 Greg Bailey .02 .10
122 Keith Redmond .02 .10
123 Dick Todd CO .05 .15
124 Scott Turner .02 .10
125 Colin Wilson .02 .10
126 Mike Tomlinson .02 .10
127 Dale McTavish .02 .10
128 Chris Longo .02 .10
129 Chad Lang .08 .25
130 Brent Tully .05 .15
131 Shawn Heins .05 .15
132 Geordie Kinnear .05 .15
133 Jeff Walker .02 .10
134 Chris Pronger 1.25 3.00
135 Chad Grills .02 .10
136 Michael Harding .02 .10
137 Matt St.Germain .02 .10
138 Don O'Neill .02 .10
139 Dave Roche .08 .25
140 Doug Searle .02 .10
141 Bryan Gendron .02 .10
142 Kelly Vipond .05 .15
143 Andrew Verner .08 .25
144 Ryan Black .05 .15
145 Jason Dawe .08 .25
146 Jassen Cullimore .08 .25
148 Jason Arnott .40 1.00
149 Jan Benda .05 .15
150 Todd Bradley .02 .10
151 Markus Brunner .05 .15
152 Jason Campeau .02 .10
153 Mark Deazeley .02 .10
154 Matt Hoffman .02 .10
155 Scott Hollis .02 .10
156 Neil Iserhoff .02 .10
157 Darryl Lafrance .02 .10
158 B.J. MacPherson .05 .15
159 Troy Sweet .02 .10
160 Jason Weaver .02 .10
161 Stephane Yelle .20 .50
162 Trevor Burgess .02 .10
163 Joe Cook .02 .10
164 Jean-Paul Davis .02 .10
165 Brian Grieve .02 .10
166 Rob Leask .07 .20
167 Wade Simpson .02 .10
168 Kevin Spero .02 .10
169 Fred Brathwaite .40 1.00
170 Mike Fountain .08 .25
171 Rick Cornacchia .05 .15
172 Checklist 1-98 .01 .05
173 Todd Warriner .08 .25
174 Reuben Castella .02 .10
175 Cory Stillman .20 .50
176 Steve Gibson .02 .10
177 Trent Cull .02 .10
178 John Copley .02 .10
179 Craig Binns .02 .10
180 Ryan O'Neill .02 .10
181 Matthew Mullin .08 .25
182 Todd Hunter .02 .10
183 Jason Stos .02 .10
184 Robert Frayn .02 .10
185 Leonard MacDonald .02 .10
186 Tom Sullivan .02 .10
187 Steve Smith .02 .10
188 Bill Bowler .08 .25
189 James Allison .02 .10
190 Kevin MacKay .02 .10
191 David Myles .02 .10
192 Wayne Maxner GM CO .02 .10
193 Dave Prpich CO UER Windsor on front .01 .05
194 Brady Blain .02 .10
195 Eric Stamp UER Windsor on front .02 .10
196 OHL Action .02 .10
197 David Babcock .02 .10
198 Brad Love .02 .10
199 Dale Junkin .02 .10
200 Rick Corriveau .02 .10
201 Scott Campbell .02 .10
202 Jason Clarke .02 .10
203 George Burnett .02 .10
204 Ryan Tocher .02 .10
205 Dennis Maxwell .08 .25
206 Greg Scott .02 .10
207 Mark Tardiff .02 .10
208 Neil Fewster .02 .10
209 Jason Coles .02 .10
210 Randy Hall CO .01 .05
211 Todd Simon .05 .15
212 Ethan Moreau .30 .75
213 Todd Wetzel .02 .10
214 Tom Moores .02 .10
215 Geoff Rawson .02 .10
216 Dan Krisko .02 .10
217 Manny Legace .40 1.00
218 Kevin Brown .05 .15
219 Steve Staios .07 .20
220 Checklist 99-196 .01 .05
221 Checklist 197-290 .01 .05
222 Tony Bella .02 .10
223 Shawn Caplice .02 .10
224 Keli Corpse .05 .15
225 Chris Gratton .40 1.00
226 Gord Harris .02 .10
227 Cory Johnson .02 .10
228 Kevin King .02 .10
229 Justin Morrison .05 .15
230 Alastair Still .02 .10
231 Chris Scharf .02 .10
232 Brian Stagg .02 .10
233 Mike Dawson .02 .10
234 Rod Pasma .02 .10
235 Craig Rivet .08 .25
236 Dave Stewart .02 .10
237 John Vary .02 .10
238 Jason Wadel .02 .10
239 Joel Yates .02 .10
240 Marc Lamothe .08 .25
241 Pete McGlynn .08 .25
242 OHL Action .02 .10
243 Checklist 291-383 .01 .05
244 Joel Sandie .02 .10
245 Glen Murray .40 1.00
246 Derek Armstrong .02 .10
247 Michael Peca .40 1.00
248 Barry Young .02 .10
249 Bernie John .02 .10
250 Terry Chitaroni .05 .15
251 Jason Young .02 .10
252 Rod Hinks .02 .10
253 Michael Yeo .02 .10
254 Kyle Blacklock .02 .10
255 Dan Ryder .08 .25
256 Doug Mason CO .01 .05
257 Jamie Rivers .08 .25
258 Brandon Convery .07 .20
259 Barrie Moore .02 .10
260 Shawn Rivers .05 .15
261 Jamie Matthews .07 .20
262 Tim Favot .02 .10
263 Bob MacIsaac .02 .10
264 Sean Gagnon .02 .10
265 Ken MacKenzie GM CO .01 .05
266 George Dourion .02 .10
267 Brian MacKenzie .02 .10
268 Jason Zohil .02 .10
269 Rick Tarasuk .02 .10
270 Jamie Storr .30 .75
271 Sean Basilio .08 .25
272 Rick Morton .02 .10
273 Jason Hughes .02 .10
274 Scott Walker .40 1.00
275 Willie Skilliter .02 .10
276 Shawn Krueger .02 .10
277 Jason MacDonald .02 .10
278 Kirk Maltby .20 .50
279 Brock Woods .02 .10
280 Troy Hutchinson .02 .10
281 Geordie Maynard .02 .10
282 Luigi Calce .02 .10
283 Steven Parson .02 .10
284 Andrew Brunette .20 .50
285 Robert MacKenzie .02 .10
286 Jason Buetow .02 .10
287 Wyatt Buckland .02 .10
288 Jim Brown .02 .10
289 Gord Dickie .02 .10
290 Jeff Smith .02 .10
291 Peter Ambroziak .05 .15
292 Mark O'Donnell UER Name spelled O'donnell on back .02 .10
294 Grayden Reid .05 .15
295 Sean Spencer .08 .25
296 Gerry Skrypec .02 .10
297 Billy Hall .02 .10
298 Sean Gawley .02 .10
299 Grant Marshall .08 .25
300 Michael Johnson .02 .10
301 Brett Seguin .02 .10
302 Chris Coveny .02 .10
303 Ryan Kuwabara .05 .15
304 Jeff Ricciardi .02 .10
305 Curt Bowen .05 .15
306 Zbynek Kukacka .02 .10
307 Chris Gignac .02 .10
308 Steve Washburn .08 .25
309 Brian Kilrea CO .05 .15
310 Mike Lenarduzzi .08 .25
311 Matt Stone .02 .10
312 Ken Belanger .02 .10
313 Chris Simon .20 .50
314 Kiley Hill .02 .10
315 Chris Grenville .02 .10
316 Aaron Gavey .08 .25
317 Briane Thompson .02 .10
318 Ted Nolan CO .08 .25
319 Perry Pappas .02 .10
320 Kevin Hodson .20 .50
321 Colin Miller .02 .10
322 Tom MacDonald .02 .10
323 Shaun Imber .02 .10
324 Jarret Reid .02 .10
325 Tony Iob .02 .10
326 Mark Matier .02 .10
327 Drew Bannister .07 .20
328 Jason Denomme .02 .10
329 David Matsos .02 .10
330 Rick Kowalsky .02 .10
331 Tim Bacik .08 .25
332 Ralph Intranuovo .07 .20
333 Jonas Rudberg .02 .10
334 Jeff Toms .02 .10
335 Jason Julian .02 .10
336 Brian Goudie .02 .10
337 Gary Roach .02 .10
338 Brad Baber .02 .10
339 Todd Gleason UER Team affiliation says Greyhound .05 .15
340 Chris McMurtry .02 .10
341 Matt Turek .02 .10
342 Shane Johnson .02 .10
343 Grant Pritchett .02 .10
344 Mike Cote .02 .10
345 Duane Harmer .02 .10
346 Jeff Bes .05 .15
347A Wade Whitten .02 .10
347B Dan Tanevski UER (Should be number 360) .02 .10
348 Bill Kovacs .05 .15
349 Kayle Short .02 .10
350 Sylvain Cloutier .07 .20
351 Brent Watson .02 .10
352 Brent Pope .02 .10
353 Craig Lutes .02 .10
354 Michael Hartwick .02 .10
355 Kevin Reid .02 .10
356 Toby Burkitt .02 .10
357 Todd Bertuzzi .75 2.00
358 Angelo Amore .08 .25
359 Jeff Pawluk .02 .10
361 Gordon Ross .02 .10
362 Dennis Purdie .30 .75
363 Dave Gilmore .02 .10
364 Brent Brownlee .08 .25
365 Aaron Nagy .02 .10
366 Barry Potomski .40 1.00
367 Steve Smillie .02 .10
368 Kelly Reed .02 .10
369 Gary Agnew CO .01 .05
370 Chris Taylor .05 .15
371 Brett Marietti .02 .10
372 Cory Evans .02 .10
373 Brian Stacey .02 .10
374 Chris Crombie .02 .10
375 Derrick Crane .02 .10
376 Scott McKay .05 .15
377 Gregory Ryan .02 .10
378 Mark Visheau .02 .10
379 Gerry Arcella .02 .10
380 Nick Stajduhar .05 .15
381 Jason Allison .75 2.00
382 Sean O'Reilly .02 .10
383 Paul Wolanski .02 .10
XXX Chris Schushack .05 .15

1991-92 7th Inning Sketch QMJHL

COMPLETE SET (297) 6.00 15.00
1 Martin Brodeur 1.50 4.00
2 Normand Paquet .02 .10
3 David Desnoyers .02 .10
4 Carlo Colombi .02 .10
5 Stephane Menard .08 .25
6 Sebastien Berube .02 .10
7 Marc Desgagne .02 .10
8 Mil Sukovic .02 .10
9 Patrick Belisle .02 .10
10 Patrick Poulin .08 .25
11 Martin Trudel .02 .10
12 Charles Poulin .05 .15
13 Etienne Thibault .02 .10
14 Pierre Allard .02 .10
15 Francois Gagnon .02 .10
16 Stephane Huard .02 .10
17 Yannik Lemay .02 .10
18 Dany Fortin .02 .10
19 Carl Menard .02 .10
20 Serge Labelle .02 .10
21 Dean Melanson .02 .10
22 Yves Meunier .02 .10
23 Pierre Petroni CO .01 .05
24 Mario Pouliot CO .01 .05
25 Alain Cote .05 .15
26 Hugues Laliberte .02 .10
27 Martin Gendron .08 .25
28 Stan Melanson .02 .10
29 Carl Leblanc .02 .10
30 Patrick Grise .02 .10
31 Yves Charron .02 .10
32 Hughes Mongeon .02 .10
33 Christian Tardif .02 .10
34 Patrick Tessier .02 .10
35 Christian Campeau .02 .10
36 Mario Therrien .02 .10
37 Martin Balleux .02 .10
38 Joel Brassard .02 .10
39 Sebastien Fortier .02 .10
40 Jocelyn Langlois .02 .10
41 Giuseppe Argentos .02 .10
42 Sylvain Brisson .02 .10
43 Philippe Boucher .08 .25
44 Martin Brochu .40 1.00
45 Marc Rodgers .02 .10
46 Pascal Gagnon .02 .10
47 Benoit Therrien .02 .10
48 Robin Bouchard .02 .10
49 Michel Savoie .02 .10
50 Jean-Sebastien Boiteau .02 .10
51 Patrick Lamoureux .02 .10
52 Stephane Giard .08 .25
53 Maxime Jean .02 .10
54 Alain Cote .05 .15
55 Francois Groleau .05 .15
56 Richard Hamelin .05 .15
57 Eric Beauvis UER (Name misspelled Beavis on back .05 .15
58 Steve Laplante .02 .10
59 Yves Meunier .02 .10
60 Steve Dontigny .02 .10
61 Simon Roy .02 .10
62 Jean-Francois Laroche .02 .10
63 Patrick Traverse .08 .25
64 Eric Joyal .02 .10
65 Jean-Francois Gregoire UER/(Name misspelled Jean-Fracois on front) .02 .10
66 Jocelyn Charbonneau .05 .15
67 Jean Imbeau .05 .15
68 Francois Bourdeau .02 .10
69 Alain Savage Jr. .02 .10
70 Johnny Lorenzo .08 .25
71 Patrick Lalime .75 2.00
72 Patrick Melfi .02 .10
73 Marc Tardif .02 .10
74 Marc Savard .02 .10
75 Alain Sanscartier CO .01 .05
76 Pascal Lebrasseur .05 .15
77 Checklist 1-101 .01 .05
78 Dany Girard .02 .10
79 Eddy Gervais .02 .10
80 Dave Tremblay .02 .10
81 Dany Larochelle .02 .10
82 Michel St.Jacques .02 .10
83 Rodney Petawabano .02 .10
84 Eric Duchesne .02 .10
85 Patrick Clement .02 .10
86 Steve Gosselin .02 .10
87 Patrick Lacombe .02 .10
88 Patrice Martineau .02 .10
89 Danny Beauregard .02 .10
90 Martin Lamarche .02 .10
91 Sebastien Parent .02 .10
92 Christian Caron .02 .10
93 Sylvain Careau .08 .25
94 Martin Beaupre .02 .10
95 Daniel Paradis .02 .10
96 Sylvain Rodrigue .08 .25
97 Joe Canale CO .01 .05
98 Patrick Lampron .02 .10
99 Carl Blondin .02 .10
100 Carl Wiseman .02 .10
101 Hugo Hamelin .08 .25
102 Claude Poirier .02 .10
103 Charles Paquette .02 .10
104 Carl Fleury UER (Name spelled FLeury on front) .05 .15
105 Paolo Racicot .02 .10
106 Sebastien Moreau .02 .10
107 Pascal Trepanier .02 .10
108 Dominic Maltais .05 .15
109 Steve Ares .02 .10
110 Daniel Thibault .02 .10
111 Eric Messier .20 .50
112 Stephane Julien .02 .10
113 Dave Paquet .02 .10
114 Nicolas Turmel .02 .10
115 Pascal Rheaume .20 .50
116 Carl Boudreau .02 .10
117 Dave Boudreault .02 .10
118 Eric Bellerose .05 .15
119 Steve Searles .02 .10
120 Patrick Nadeau .05 .15
121 Stephan Viens .02 .10
122 Jean-Francois Labbe .40 1.00
123 Jocelyn Thibault 1.25 3.00
124 Gaston Drapeau CO .01 .05
125 Checklist 102-198 .01 .05
126 Martin Lajeunesse .02 .10
127 Etienne Lavoie .02 .10
128 Dominic Rheaume .02 .10
129 Robert Guillet .02 .10
130 Francois Rivard .02 .10
131 Phillippe DeRouville .15 .40
132 Andrej Dobrota .02 .10
133 Pierre Gendron .02 .10
134 Dave Chouinard .02 .10
135 Martin Tanguay .05 .15
136 Jacques Blouin .02 .10
137 Martin Larochelle .02 .10
138 Jean-Martin Morin .02 .10
139 Donald Brashear .40 1.00
140 Stephane Paradis .02 .10
141 Jan Simcik .02 .10
142 Yan Arsenault .02 .10
143 Joel Bouchard .08 .25
144 Jean-Sebastien Lefebvre .02 .10
145 David St. Pierre UER (Name misspelled St-Pierre on front) .05 .15
146 Mario Nobili .02 .10
147 Stacy Dallaire .02 .10
148 Carl Lamothe .05 .15
149 Andre Bouliane .08 .25
150 Simon Arial .02 .10
151 Stephane Madore .02 .10
152 Hughes Bouchard .02 .10
153 Steve Decaen .02 .10
154 Jason Downey .02 .10
155 Raymond Delarosbil .02 .10
156 Lino Salvo .02 .10
157 Reginald Brezeault .02 .10
158 Nathan Morin .02 .10
159 Samuel Groleau .05 .15
160 Patrick Carignan .02 .10
161 Stephane St-Amour .02 .10
162 Marquis Mathieu .05 .15
163 Yves Sarault .05 .15
164 Dave Belliveau .02 .10
165 Trevor Duhaime .02 .10
166 Eric O'Connor .02 .10
167 Christian Proulx .05 .15
168 Martin Lavallee .08 .25
169 Jean-Francois Gagnon .08 .25
170 Eric Lafrance .02 .10
171 Enrico Scardocchio .02 .10
172 David Bergeron .02 .10
173 Guillaume Morin .08 .25
174 Charlie Boucher .02 .10
175 Martin Rozon .02 .10
176 Brandon Piccarreto .02 .10
177 Simon Toupin .05 .15
178 Jamie Bird .02 .10
179 Herve Lapointe .02 .10
180 Ian MacIntyre .02 .10
181 Jean-Francois Rivard .08 .25
182 Alain Chainey CO .02 .10
183 Daniel Laflamme .02 .10
184 Patrice Paquin .02 .10
185 Patrick Deraspe .02 .10
186 Martin Roy .02 .10
187 Jeannot Ferland .02 .10
188 Patrick Genest .02 .10
189 Matthew Barnaby .40 1.00
190 Jean-Guy Trudel .02 .10
191 Eric Moreau .02 .10
192 Eric Cool .05 .15
193 Alexandre Legault .02 .10
194 Gregg Pineo .02 .10
195 LHJMQ Action .02 .10
196 Radoslav Balaz .02 .10
197 Stefan Simoes .02 .10
198 LHJMQ Action .02 .10
199 Francois Paquette .02 .10
200 Paul Macdonald .02 .10
201 Shane Doiron .02 .10
202 Michal Longauer .02 .10
203 Joe Crowley .02 .10
204 Joey Deliva .02 .10
205 Pierre-Francois Lalonde .02 .10
206 Paul Brousseau .05 .15
207 Martin Lepage .02 .10
208 Yanick DeGrace .08 .25
209 Jim Campbell .08 .25
210 Sebastien Bordeleau .02 .10
211 Marc Legault .08 .25
212 Joel Blain .02 .10
213 Claude Jutras .02 .10
214 Eric Lavigne .05 .15
215 Todd Sparks .02 .10
216 Sylvain Lapointe .02 .10
217 Eric Lecompte .08 .25
218 Thierry Mayer .02 .10
219A Harold Hersh ERR (Jim Campbell photo on back) .08 .25
219B Harold Hersh COR .02 .10
220 Frederic Boivin .02 .10
221 Steven Dion .02 .10
222 Alain Vigneault .15 .40
223 Checklist 199-298 .01 .05
224 Petr Valenta .02 .10
225 LHJMQ Action .02 .10
226 Jim Bermingham .02 .10
227 Yanick Dube .08 .25
228 Sandy McCarthy .40 1.00
229 Dany Michaud .02 .10
230 Jason Brousseau .02 .10
231 Marc Beaucage .02 .10
232 Eric Cardinal .02 .10
233 Martin Chaput .02 .10
234 Jean Roberge .02 .10
235 Philip Gathercole .02 .10
236 Michael Gaul .02 .10
237 Yannick Frechette .02 .10
238 Sylvain Blouin .02 .10
239 David Pekarek .02 .10
240 John Kovacs .02 .10
241 Eric Raymond .08 .25
242 Emmanuel Fernandez 1.25 3.00
243 Yan St. Pierre .02 .10
244 Brant Blackned .02 .10
245 Eric Veilleux .02 .10
246 Pascal Vincent .02 .10
247 Benoit Larose .02 .10
248 Olivier Guillaume .02 .10
249 Alain Gauthier .08 .25
250 Bruno Ducharme .08 .25

Card	Low	High
251 Patrick Charbonneau	.08	.25
252 Daniel Germain	.02	.10
253 Pascal Chiasson	.02	.10
254 Marc Thibeault	.02	.10
255 Martin Woods	.02	.10
257 Dominic Grand'maison	.02	.10
258 Carl Poirer	.02	.10
259 Stephane Larocque	.02	.10
260 Mario Dumoulin	.02	.10
261 Yan Laterreur	.02	.10
262 Claude Savoie	.05	.15
263 Denis Beauchamp	.02	.10
264 Patrick Bisaillon	.02	.10
265 Pascal Bernier	.02	.10
266 Nicolas Lefebvre	.02	.10
267 LHJMQ Action	.02	.10
268 Joseph Napolitano	.02	.10
269 Sebastien Tremblay	.02	.10
270 Alexandre Daigle	.20	.50
271 Pierre Pillion	.02	.10
272 Yves Lambert	.02	.10
273 Pierre Aubry CO	.01	.05
274 Yves Loubier	.08	.25
275 Pierre Sandke UER (First name Peter on back)	.02	.10
276 Louis Bernard	.02	.10
277 Alain Nasreddine	.05	.15
278 Sylvain Ducharme	.02	.10
279 Jeremy Caissie	.02	.10
280 Eric Meloche	.02	.10
281 Ian Laperriere	.20	.50
282 Hugo Proulx	.07	.20
283 Dave Whittom	.02	.10
284 Yanick Dupre	.05	.15
285 Eric Plante	.02	.10
286 Stephane Desjardins	.02	.10
287 Rene Corbet	.20	.50
288 David Lessard	.02	.10
289 Eric Marcoux	.02	.10
290 Alexandre Duchesne	.02	.10
291 Maxime Petitclerc UER (Name misspelled Peticlerc on front)	.02	.10
292 Pierre Gagnon	.08	.25
293 Roger Larche UER (Name misspelled Larache on front)	.02	.10
294 Jean Hamel	.02	.10
295 Alexandre Gaumond	.02	.10
296 Paul-Emile Exentus	.02	.10
297 LHJMQ Action	.02	.10
298 LHJMQ Action	.02	.10

1991-92 7th Inning Sketch WHL

Card	Low	High
COMPLETE SET (361)	6.00	15.00
1 Valeri Bure	.30	.75
2 Hardy Sauter	.02	.10
3 Bryan Maxwell CO	.02	.10
4 Scott Bailey	.08	.25
5 Mike Gray	.02	.10
6 Mark Szoke	.02	.10
7 Mike Jickling	.02	.10
8 Frank Evans	.02	.10
9 Steve Junker	.07	.20
10 Greg Gatto	.02	.10
11 Jared Bednar	.02	.10
12 Justin Hocking	.07	.20
13 Paxton Schulte	.07	.20
14 Brad Toporowski	.02	.10
15 Shane Maitland	.02	.10
16 Aaron Boh	.02	.10
17 Ryan Duthie	.05	.15
18 Craig Reichert	.05	.15
19 Danny Faassen	.02	.10
20 Randy Toye	.02	.10
21 Geoff Grandberg	.02	.10
22 Jeremy Warring	.08	.25
23 Tyler Romanchuck	.02	.10
24 Jamie Linden	.05	.15
25 1990-91 Champs	.02	.10
26 Corey Jones	.08	.25
27 Brandon Smith	.02	.10
28 Mike Williamson	.02	.10
29 Adam Murray	.02	.10
30 Steve Konowalchuk	.20	.50
31 Shawn Stone	.02	.10
32 Adam Deadmarsh	.40	1.00
33 Rick Mearns	.02	.10
34 Chris Rowland	.02	.10
35 Brandon Coates	.02	.10
36 Dave Cammock	.02	.10
37 Colin Foley	.02	.10
38 Dennis Saharchuk	.02	.10
39 Jiri Beranek	.02	.10
40 Chad Seibel	.02	.10
41 Kelly Harris	.02	.10
42 Layne Roland	.02	.10
43 Cale Hulse	.05	.15
44 Ken Hodge CO	.02	.10
45 Peter Cox	.02	.10
46 Joaquin Gage	.20	.50
47 Brent Peterson CO	.02	.10
48 Jason McBain	.02	.10
49 John Badduke	.02	.10
50 Rick Hopper	.01	.05
51 Dave Hamilton	.08	.25
52 Dwayne Newman	.02	.10
53 Chris Catellier	.02	.10
54 Fran Defrenza	.02	.10
55 Randy Chadney	.02	.10
56 David Hebky	.02	.10
57 Craig Fletcher	.02	.10
58 Kane Chaloner	.02	.10
59 Ross Harris	.02	.10
60 Mike Barrie	.02	.10
61 Steve Lingren	.02	.10
62 Shea Esselmont	.02	.10
63 Matt Smith	.02	.10
64 Gerry St.Cyr	.05	.15
65 Andrew Laming	.02	.10
66 Jeff Fancy	.02	.10
67 Ryan Pellaers	.02	.10
68 Steve Passmore	.40	1.00
69 Scott Fukami	.02	.10
70 Darcy Mattersdorfer	.02	.10
71 Chris Hawes	.02	.10
72 The Goalies I	.05	.15
73 Checklist 1-97	.01	.05
74 Riverside Coliseum	.02	.10
75 Tom Renney	.07	.20
76 Corey Hirsch	.20	.50
77 Scott Ferguson	.02	.10
78 Steve Yule	.02	.10
79A Todd Johnson Warriors	.02	.10
79B Todd Johnson Blazers	.02	.10
80 Jarrett Bousquet	.02	.10
81 Mike Mathers	.02	.10
82 Rod Stevens	.02	.10
83 Lance Johnson	.02	.10
84 Zac Boyer	.02	.10
85 Craig Lyons	.05	.15
86 Dale Masson	.08	.25
87 Scott Loucks	.05	.15
88 Darcy Tucker	.20	.50
89 Shayne Green	.05	.15
90 Michal Sup	.02	.10
91 Craig Bonner	.02	.10
92 Jeff Watchorn	.02	.10
93 Jarrett Dueling	.05	.15
94 Ed Patterson	.07	.20
95 David Wilkie	.08	.25
96 The Goalies III	.05	.15
97 A Goal	.02	.10
98 Andy MacIntyre	.02	.10
99 Rhett Trombley	.07	.20
100 Lorne Molleken CO	.01	.05
101 Trevor Robins	.08	.25
102 Jeff Buchanan	.02	.10
103 Mark Raiter	.02	.10
104 Bryce Goebel	.02	.10
105 Paul Buczkowski	.02	.10
106 James Startup	.02	.10
107 Chad Rusnak	.02	.10
108 Sean McFatridge	.02	.10
109 Shane Calder	.05	.15
110 Ryan Fujita	.02	.10
111 Derek Tibbatts	.02	.10
112 Glen Gulutzan	.02	.10
113 Richard Matvichuk	.20	.50
114 Chad Michalchuk	.02	.10
115 Mark Wotton	.07	.20
116 Mark Franks	.02	.10
117 Norm Maracle	.20	.50
118 Jason Becker	.02	.10
119 Shawn Yakimishyn	.02	.10
120 Ed Chynoweth PRES	.05	.15
121 Checklist 98-195	.01	.05
122 Craig Chapman	.02	.10
123 Jeff Jubenville	.02	.10
124 George Zajankala	.02	.10
125 Turner Stevenson	.20	.50
126 Rob Tallas	.20	.50
127 Ryan Brown	.02	.10
128 Andrew Kemper	.02	.10
129 Brendan Witt	.20	.50
130 Troy Hyatt	.02	.10
131 Mike Kennedy	.08	.25
132 Jesse Wilson	.02	.10
133 Kurt Seher	.05	.15
134 Dody Wood	.05	.15
135 Darren McAusland	.02	.10
136 Jeff Sebastian	.02	.10
137 Eric Bouchard	.02	.10
138 Joel Dyck	.02	.10
139 Blake Knox	.02	.10
140 Peter Anholt CO	.01	.05
141 Chris Wells	.08	.25
142 Andrew Reimer	.07	.20
143 Along the Boards	.02	.10
144 Which Way Is Up	.01	.05
145 Checklist 196-287	.01	.05
146 Tacoma Dome	.02	.10
147 Opening Ceremonies	.02	.10
148 Marcel Comeau CO	.02	.10
149 Donn Clark CO	.01	.05
150 John Varga	.05	.15
151 Joey Young	.02	.10
152 Laurie Billeck	.02	.10
153 Jeff Calvert	.08	.25
154 Tuomas Gronman	.08	.25
155 Jason Knox	.02	.10
156 Kevin Malgunas	.02	.10
157 Dave McMillen	.02	.10
158 Darryl Onofrychuk	.08	.25
159 Mike Piersol	.02	.10
160 Lasse Pirjeta	.02	.10
161 Drew Schoneck	.02	.10
162 Corey Stock	.02	.10
163 Ryan Strain	.02	.10
164 Michal Sykora	.05	.15
165 Scott Thomas	.05	.15
166 Toby Weishaar	.02	.10
167 Jeff Whittle	.05	.15
168 The Rockettes	.02	.10
169 Allan Egeland	.05	.15
170 Van Burgess	.02	.10
171 Trever Fraser	.02	.10
172 Jamie Black	.05	.15
173 WHL Action	.02	.10
174 Andy Schneider	.05	.15
175 John McMulkin	.02	.10
176 Rick Girard	.05	.15
177 Shane Hnidy	.02	.10
178 Jason Krywulak	.05	.15
179 Jeremy Riehl	.05	.15
180 Brent Bilodeau	.08	.25
181 Mark McCoy	.02	.10
182 Matt Young	.02	.10
183 Dan Sherstenka	.02	.10
184 Jarrod Daniel	.08	.25
185 Lennie MacAusland	.02	.10
186 Keith McCambridge	.02	.10
187 Jason Horvath	.02	.10
188 Kevin Koopman	.08	.25
189 Chris Herperger	.05	.15
190 Trent McCleary	.08	.25
191 Tyler Wright	.08	.25
192 Todd Holt	.05	.15
193 Ashley Buckberger	.05	.15
194 Bram Vanderkracht	.02	.10
195 Ken Zilka	.02	.10
196 Chris Osgood	.75	2.00
197 Rob Puchniak	.02	.10
198 Todd Dutiaume	.02	.10
199 Mike Maneluk	.07	.20
200 Shawn Dietrich	.08	.25
201 Chris Johnston	.02	.10
202 Brian Purdy	.05	.15
203 Mike Chrun	.02	.10
204 Dan Kopec	.02	.10
205 Ryan Smith	.05	.15
206 Marty Murray	.08	.25
207 Merv Priest	.02	.10
208 Bobby House	.05	.15
209 Chris Constant	.02	.10
210 Dwayne Gylywoychuk	.02	.10
211 Stu Scantlebury	.02	.10
212 Mark Kolesar	.07	.20
213 Craig Geekie	.02	.10
214 Terran Sandwith	.02	.10
215 Jeff Hoad	.02	.10
216 Kelly McCrimmon	.02	.10
217 Carlos Bye	.02	.10
218 Trevor Hanas	.02	.10
219 Jeff Shantz	.20	.50
220 Heath Weenk	.02	.10
221 Nathan Dempsey	.02	.10
222 Louis Dumont	.02	.10
223 Garry Pearce	.02	.10
224 Terry Bendera	.02	.10
225 Hal Christiansen	.02	.10
226 Jason Smith	.20	.50
227 Kerry Biette	.02	.10
228 Barry Becker	.08	.25
229 Derek Eberle	.02	.10
230 Ken Richardson	.02	.10
231 Niklas Barklund	.02	.10
232 Frank Kovacs	.02	.10
233 Not Issued	.01	.05
234 Not Issued	.01	.05
235 Lloyd Pelletier	.08	.25
236 Dale Vossen	.01	.05
237 A.J. Kelham	.02	.10
238 Mike Risdale	.08	.25
239 Brad Bagu	.02	.10
240 Niko Ovaska	.02	.10
241 Brad Tippett CO	.01	.05
242 The Goalies II	.05	.15
243 Lee J. Leslie	.05	.15
244 Darren Perkins	.02	.10
245 Jason Kwiatkowski	.05	.15
246 Jason Renard	.02	.10
247 Dan Kesa	.07	.20
248 Jason Klassen	.02	.10
249 Nick Polychronopoulus	.02	.10
250 David Neilson	.02	.10
251 Merv Haney	.02	.10
252 Troy Hjertaas	.02	.10
253 Curt Regnier	.07	.20
254 Dean McAmmond	.20	.50
255 Travis Laycock	.08	.25
256 Jeff Lank	.02	.10
257 Barkley Swenson	.02	.10
258 Darren Van Impe	.08	.25
259 Ryan Pisiak	.02	.10
260 Jeff Gorman	.02	.10
261 Stan Matwijiw	.08	.25
262 Mike Fedorko	.02	.10
263 Mark Odnokon	.01	.05
264 Shane Zulyniak	.02	.10
265 Jeff Nelson	.07	.20
266 Donevan Hextall	.07	.20
267 Kevin Masters	.02	.10
268 Chris Schmidt	.02	.10
269 Jeff Budai	.02	.10
270 Bill Hooson	.02	.10
271 Fred Hettle	.02	.10
272 Kent Staniforth	.02	.10
273 Travis Stevenson	.02	.10
274 David Jesiolowksi	.02	.10
275 Mike Babcock CO	.01	.05
276 Scott Allison	.02	.10
277 Travis Thiessen	.02	.10
278 Marc Hussey	.02	.10
279 Kevin Smyth	.05	.15
280 Jason Fitzsimmons	.08	.25
281 Jeff Petruic	.02	.10
282 Russ West	.02	.10
283 Derek Kletzel	.05	.15
284 Jarret Zukiwsky	.02	.10
285 Jason Carey	.02	.10
286 Close Checking	.02	.10
287 Checklist 288-360	.01	.05
288 Jason Bowen	.05	.15
289 Dean Tiltgen	.05	.15
290 Terry Degner	.07	.20
291 Jodie Murphy	.02	.10
292 Brian Sakic	.05	.15
293 Jamie Barnes	.02	.10
294 Darren Hastman	.02	.10
295 Todd Klassen	.05	.15
296 Mirsad Mujcin	.02	.10
297 Trevor Sherban	.02	.10
298 Chadden Cabana	.02	.10
299 Adam Rettschlag	.02	.10
300 Mark Toljanich	.02	.10
301 Kory Mullin	.02	.10
302 Byron Penstock	.08	.25
303 Vladimir Vujtek	.07	.20
304 Bill Lindsay	.08	.25
305 Jeff Cej	.02	.10
306 Mike Busniak CO	.02	.10
307 Todd Harris	.02	.10
308 Cory Dosdall	.02	.10
309 Jason Smith	.20	.50
310 Mark Dawkins	.08	.25
311 Dan O'Rourke	.02	.10
312 Darby Walker	.02	.10
313 Olaf Kjenstadt	.05	.15
314 Sonny Mignacca	.08	.25
315 Jon Duval	.02	.10
316 Lorne Toews	.02	.10
317 Dana Rieder	.02	.10
318 Clayton Norris	.05	.15
319 David Cooper	.07	.20
320 Larry Watkins	.02	.10
321 Evan Marble	.02	.10
322 Scott Lindsay	.05	.15
323 Ryan Petz	.02	.10
324 Jeramie Heistad	.02	.10
325 Scott Townsend	.02	.10
326 Stacy Roest	.20	.50
327 Rob Niedermayer	.30	.75
328 Tim Bothwell CO	.05	.15
329 Kevin Riehl	.07	.20
330 Mike Rathje	.08	.25
331 Bryan McCabe	.20	.50
332 MHT Tiger MASCOT	.02	.10
333 Dean Intwert	.08	.25
334 Mike Vandenberghe	.02	.10
335 Cam Danyluk	.02	.10
336 Darcy Austin	.08	.25
337 Jason Knight	.02	.10
338 Lee Sorochan	.08	.25
339 Al Kinisky	.02	.10
340 Rob Hartnell	.02	.10
341 Radek Sip	.02	.10
342 Jamie Pushor	.08	.25
343 Shane Peacock	.02	.10
344 Cadrin Smart	.02	.10
345 Maurice Meagher	.02	.10
346 Lance Burns	.02	.10
347 Dominic Pittis	.20	.50
348 Todd MacIsaac	.02	.10
349 Brad Zimmer	.02	.10
350 Jason Sorochan	.02	.10
351 Darcy Werenka	.07	.20
352 Kevin St.Jacques	.05	.15
353 David Trofimenkoff	.02	.10
354 Terry Hollinger	.05	.15
355 Travis Munday	.02	.10
356 Slade Stephenson	.02	.10
357 Jason Widmer	.07	.20
358 Brad Zavisha	.05	.15
359 Bob Loucks CO	.01	.05
360 Brantt Myhres	.40	1.00
0 Garfield Henderson	.05	.15

1991 7th Inning Sketch CHL Award Winners

Card	Low	High
COMPLETE SET (30)	4.00	10.00
1 Eric Lindros	.75	2.00
2 Dale Craigwell	.08	.25
3 Nathan Lafayette	.07	.20
4 Chris Snell	.08	.25
5 Cory Stillman	.20	.50
6 Mike Torchia	.20	.50
7 George Burnett	.07	.20
8 Eric Lindros	.75	2.00
9 Sherwood Bassin	.07	.20
10 Eric Lindros	.75	2.00
11 Scott Niedermayer	.20	.50
12 Pat Falloon	.08	.25
13 Scott Niedermayer	.20	.50
14 Darryl Sydor	.20	.50
15 Donevan Hextall	.07	.20
16 Jamie McLennan	.15	.40
17 Tom Renney	.08	.25
18 Frank Evans	.07	.20
19 Bob Brown	.07	.20
20 Ray Whitney	.20	.50
21 Philippe Boucher	.07	.20
22 Yanic Perreault	.15	.40
23 Benoit Larose	.07	.20
24 Patrice Brisebois	.08	.25
25 Philippe Boucher	.07	.20
26 Felix Potvin	.40	1.00
27 Joe Canale	.07	.20
28 Christian Lariviere	.07	.20
29 Roland Janelle	.07	.20
30 Yanic Perreault	.15	.40

1991 7th Inning Sketch Memorial Cup

Card	Low	High
COMPLETE SET (130)	50.00	100.00
COMPLETE SHORT SET (113)	6.00	15.00
1 Mike Lenarduzzi	.10	.25
2 Kevin Hodson	.20	.50
3 OHL Action Sault Ste. Marie vs. Oshawa	.05	.15
4 Bob Boughner	.20	.50
5 Adam Foote	.30	.75
6 Brad Tiley	.05	.15
7 Brian Goudie	.05	.15
8 Wade Whitten	.05	.15
9 Jason Denomme	.05	.15
10 David Matsos	.05	.15
11 Rick Kowalsky	.05	.15
12 Jarret Reid	.05	.15
13 Perry Pappas	.05	.15
14 Tom MacDonald	.05	.15
15 Mike DeCoff	.05	.15
16 Joe Busillo	.05	.15
17 Denny Lambert	.10	.30
18 Mark Matier	.05	.15
19 Shaun Imber	.05	.15
20 Ralph Intranuovo	.08	.25
21 Chris Snell SP	.75	2.00
22 Tony Iob	.05	.15
23 Colin Miller	.05	.15
24 Ted Nolan	.20	.50
25 Sylvain Rodrigue	.05	.15
26 Felix Potvin	1.50	4.00
27 Martin Lavallee	.05	.15
28 Eric Brule	.05	.15
29 Steve Larouche	.05	.15
30 Michel St-Jacques	.05	.15
31 Patrick Clement	.05	.15
32 Patrick Bisaillon	.05	.15
33A Checklist 62-131 SP	.75	2.00
33B Checklist 62-131 (Withdrawn numbers omitted)	.08	.25
34 Gilles Bouchard	.05	.15
35 Eric Rochette	.05	.15
36 Rob Dykeman SP	.75	2.00
37A Checklist 1-61 SP	.75	2.00
37B Checklist 1-61 (Withdrawn numbers omitted)	.08	.25
38 Patrice Martineau	.05	.15
39 Danny Beauregard	.05	.15
40 Francois Belanger	.05	.15
41 Sebastien Parent	.08	.25
42 Martin Gagne	.05	.15
43 Stephane Charbonneau	.05	.15
44 Martin Beaupre	.05	.15
45 Daniel Paradis	.05	.15
46 Joe Canale	.05	.15
47 OHL Action Sault Ste. Marie vs. Oshawa	.05	.15
48 Jubilation	.05	.15
49 Steve Lupien	.05	.15
50 Pierre Gagnon	.05	.15
51 Alexandre Legault	.05	.15
52 Martin Charrois	.05	.15
53 Eric Dandenault	.05	.15
54 Denis Chasse	.08	.25
55 Guy Lehoux	.05	.15
56 Ian Laperriere	.20	.50
57 Hugo Proulx	.05	.15
58 Dave Whittom	.05	.15
59 Yanick Dupre UER	.08	.25
60 Eric Plante	.05	.15
61 Stephane Desjardins	.08	.25
62 Patrice Brisebois	.08	.25
63 Rene Corbet	.20	.50
64 Marc Savard	.05	.15
65 Claude Jutras Jr.	.05	.15
66 David Pekarek	.05	.15
67 Roger Larche UER (Name misspelled Larohe on front)	.05	.15
68 Dave Paquet	.08	.25
69 Eric Meloche	.05	.15
70 CHL Action Spokane vs. Lethbridge	.05	.15
71 Celebration Ed Chynoweth PRES Jon Klemm	.15	.40
72 Felix Potvin MVP	1.50	4.00
73 Scott Bailey	.20	.50
74 Trevor Kidd	.30	.75
75 Chris Lafreniere	.05	.15
76 Frank Evans	.05	.15
77 Jon Klemm	.20	.50
78 Brent Thurston	.05	.15
79 Jamie McLennan	.20	.50
80 Steve Junker	.05	.15
81 Mark Szoke	.05	.15
82 Ray Whitney	.40	1.00
83 Geoff Grandberg	.05	.15
84 Cam Danyluk	.05	.15
85 Kerry Toporowski	.05	.15
86 Trevor Tovell	.05	.15
87 Pat Falloon	.20	.50
88 Bram Vanderkracht	.05	.15
89 Mike Jickling	.05	.15
90 Murray Garbutt	.05	.15
91 Calvin Thudium	.05	.15
92 Mark Woolf	.05	.15
93 Shane Maitland	.05	.15
94 Bart Cote	.05	.15
95 Bryan Maxwell	.05	.15
96 Eric Lindros SP	12.00	25.00
97 Scott Niedermayer	.40	1.00
98 Patrick Poulin	.08	.25
99 Brent Bilodeau	.08	.25
100 Pat Falloon	.20	.50
101 Darcy Werenka	.08	.25
102 Martin Lapointe	.60	1.50
103 Philippe Boucher	.08	.25
104 Jeff Nelson	.08	.25
105 Rene Corbet	.20	.50
106 Pat Peake SP	.75	2.00
107 Steve Staios SP	.75	2.00
108 Richard Matvichuk	.20	.50
109 Dean McAmmond	.20	.50
110 Alex Stojanov SP	.75	2.00
111 Glen Murray SP	1.50	4.00
112 Tyler Wright	.08	.25
113 Jason Dawe SP	1.25	3.00
114 Nathan Lafayette SP	.75	2.00
115 Yanic Perreault	.20	.50
116 Guy Leveque SP	.75	2.00
117 Darren Van Impe	.08	.25
118 Shawn Antoski SP	.75	2.00
119 Eric Lindros SP	12.00	25.00
120 Dennis Purdie SP	.75	2.00
121 Terry Chitaroni SP	.75	2.00
122 Jamie Pushor	.08	.25
123 Chris Osgood	1.50	4.00
124 Jamie Matthews SP	.75	2.00
125 Yves Sarault	.05	.15
126 Yanic Dupre UER	.08	.25
127 Brad Zimmer	.05	.15
128 Copps Coliseum	.05	.15
129 Jason Widmer	.08	.25
130 Marc Savard	.05	.15
131 Mike Torchia	.08	.15
132 Andrew Verner	.10	.25

1999-00 Shawinigan Cataractes

Card	Low	High
COMPLETE SET (24)	4.00	10.00
1 Jonathan Lessard	.15	.40
2 Philippe Gelinas	.15	.40
3 Jonathan Bellemare	.15	.40
4 Anthony Quessy	.20	.50
5 Alexandre Blackburn	.15	.40
6 Pascal Dupuis	.15	.40
7 Marc-Andre Bergeron	.20	.50
8 Francis Desaluriers	.15	.40
9 Jean-Sebastien Trudelle	.15	.40
10 Jean-Philippe Pare	.20	.50
11 Jean-Francois David	.15	.40
12 Philippe Deblois	.15	.40
13 Dave Verville	.15	.40
14 Mathieu Chouinard	.60	1.50
15 Gilbert Lefrancois	.15	.40
16 Denis Desmarais	.15	.40
17 Yannick Noiseux	.15	.40
18 Dominic Forget	.15	.40
19 Conor McGuire	.15	.40
20 Jean-Francois Dufort	.15	.40
21 Andre Landry	.15	.40
22 David Chicoine	.15	.40
23 Jason Pominville	.60	1.50
24 Header Card/CL	.02	.10

1999-00 Shawinigan Cataractes Signed

Card	Low	High
COMPLETE SET (24)	20.00	50.00
1 Jonathan Lessard	.75	2.00
2 Philippe Gelinas	.75	2.00
3 Jonathan Bellemare	.75	2.00
4 Anthony Quessy	.75	2.00
5 Alexandre Blackburn	.75	2.00
6 Pascal Dupuis	.75	2.00
7 Marc-Andre Bergeron	1.50	4.00
8 Francis Desaluriers	.75	2.00
9 Jean-Sebastien Trudelle	.75	2.00
10 Jean-Philippe Pare	1.50	4.00
11 Jean-Francois David	.75	2.00
12 Philippe Deblois	.75	2.00
13 Dave Verville	.75	2.00
14 Mathieu Chouinard	4.00	10.00
15 Gilbert Lefrancois	.75	2.00
16 Denis Desmarais	.75	2.00
17 Yannick Noiseux	.75	2.00
18 Dominic Forget	.75	2.00
19 Conor McGuire	.75	2.00
20 Jean-Francois Dufort	.75	2.00
21 Andre Landry	.75	2.00
22 David Chicoine	.75	2.00
23 Jason Pominville	4.00	10.00
24 Header Card/CL	.20	.50

2000-01 Shawinigan Cataractes

Card	Low	High
COMPLETE SET (24)	6.00	15.00
1 Denis Desmarais	.16	.40
2 Zbynek Michalek	.16	.40
3 Jonathan Beaulieu	.16	.40
4 Jonathan Lessard	.16	.40
5 Jonathan Bellemare	.16	.40
6 Patrick Bolduc	.16	.40
7 Anthony Quessy	.16	.40
8 David Chicoine	.16	.40
9 Gilbert Lefrancois	.16	.40
10 Radim Vrbata	.60	1.00
11 Yannick Noiseux	.16	.40
12 Marc-Andre Bergeron	.16	.50
13 Jimmy Cuddihy	.20	1.00
14 Kevin Bergin	.16	.40
15 Francois Gagnon	.16	.40
16 Olivier Michaud	2.00	3.00
17 Frederic Cloutier	.16	1.00
18 Jean-Francois David	.16	.40
19 Alexandre Menard Burrows	.16	.40
20 Jason Pominville	.40	1.50
21 Dominic Forget	.16	.40
22 Trevor Ettinger	.16	.40
23 Jean-Francois Dufort	.16	.40
NNO Coaches	.10	.25

2000-01 Shawinigan Cataractes Signed

Card	Low	High
COMPLETE SET (24)	24.00	60.00
1 Denis Desmarais	.80	2.00
2 Zbynek Michalek	.80	2.00
3 Jonathan Beaulieu	.80	2.00
4 Jonathan Lessard	.80	2.00
5 Jonathan Bellemare	.80	2.00
6 Patrick Bolduc	.80	2.00
7 Anthony Quessy	.80	2.00
8 David Chicoine	.80	2.00
9 Gilbert Lefrancois	.80	2.00
10 Radim Vrbata	3.20	8.00
11 Yannick Noiseux	.80	2.00
12 Marc-Andre Bergeron	.80	4.00
13 Jimmy Cuddihy	1.20	5.00
14 Kevin Bergin	.80	2.00
15 Francois Gagnon	.80	2.00
16 Olivier Michaud	4.00	10.00
17 Frederic Cloutier	.80	5.00
18 Jean-Francois David	.80	2.00
19 Alexandre Menard Burrows	.80	2.00
20 Jason Pominville	2.00	10.00
21 Dominic Forget	.80	2.00
22 Trevor Ettinger	.75	2.00
23 Jean-Francois Dufort	.80	2.00
NNO Coaches	.10	.25

2001-02 Shawinigan Cataractes

Card	Low	High
COMPLETE SET (24)	6.00	15.00
1 Denis Desmarais	.20	.50
2 Zbynek Michalek	.20	.50
3 Paul-Andre Bourgoin	.20	.50
4 Jimmy Fillion	.30	.75
5 Jonathan Lessard	.20	.50
6 Jonathan Bellemore	.20	.50
7 Mathieu Gravel	.20	.50
8 Jonathan Villeneuve	.20	.50
9 David Chicoine	.20	.50
10 Armands Berzins	.20	.50
11 Philippe Bastarache	.20	.50
12 Jimmy Cuddihy	.40	1.00
13 Chris Hodgson	.20	.50
14 Thiery Poudrier	.20	.50
15 Olivier Michaud	2.00	5.00
16 Guillaume Lavallee	.20	.50
17 David Leroux	.20	.50
18 Jean-Francois David	.20	.50
19 Jonathan Boutin	.20	.50
20 Alexandre Burrows	.20	.50
21 Mathieu Payette	.20	.50
22 Jason Pominville	.30	.75
23 Jean-Francois Dufort	.20	.50
NNO Title Card/CL	.04	.10

2002-03 Shawinigan Cataractes

Card	Low	High
COMPLETE SET (25)	5.00	12.00
1 Julien Ellis	.30	.75
2 Dave Grenier	.20	.50
3 Paul-Andre Bourgouin	.20	.50
4 Frederic Gariepy	.20	.50
5 Mathieu Gravel	.20	.50
6 Karl Morin	.20	.50
7 Armands Berzins	.20	.50
8 Danick Bouchard	.20	.50
9 Jimmy Cuddihy	.30	.75
10 Mathieu Fournier	.20	.50
11 Kevin Deslauriers	.20	.50
12 Thiery Poudrier	.20	.50
13 David Leroux	.20	.50
14 Sebastien Gauthier	.20	.50
15 Jonathan Villeneuve	.20	.50
16 Michel Bergevin-Robinson	.30	.75
17 Jonathan Boutin	.20	.50
18 Justin Vienneau	.20	.50
19 Marek Hascak	.20	.50
20 Simon-Pierre Sauve	.20	.50
21 Dominic Plante	.20	.50
22 Benoit Mondou	.30	.75
23 Nicolas Desilets	.20	.50
24 Charles Gauthier	.20	.50
25 Checklist	.04	.10

2003-04 Shawinigan Cataractes

Card	Low	High
COMPLETE SET (23)	5.00	12.00
1 Eric Begin	.20	.50
2 Steve Bellefleur	.20	.50
3 Danick Bouchard	.20	.50
4 Jonathan Boutin	.20	.50
5 Ben Chaisson	.20	.50
6 Jimmy Cuddihy	.30	.75
7 Marty Doyle	.30	.75
8 Nicolas Desilets	.20	.50
9 Julien Ellis	.30	.75
10 Charles Gauthier	.20	.50
11 Sebastien Gauthier	.20	.50
12 Michal Gavalier	.20	.50
13 Marc-Olivier Gignac	.30	.75
14 Mathieu Gravel	.20	.50
15 Pierre-Marc Guilbault	.20	.50
16 Marek Hascak	.20	.50
17 Jonathan Jolette	.20	.50
18 Benoit Mondou	.30	.75
19 Jean-Philippe Paquet	.20	.50
20 Pascal Pelletier	.30	.75
21 Thiery Poudrier	.20	.50
22 Simon-Pierre Sauve	.20	.50
23 Justin Vienneau	.20	.50

2005-06 Shawinigan Cataractes

Card	Low	High
COMPLETE SET (23)	6.00	12.00
1 Julien Ellis	.30	.75
2 Ben MacFarlane	.20	.50
3 Alex Bourret	.40	1.00
4 Benoit Mondou	.30	.75
5 Jean-Philippe Paquet	.20	.50
6 Justin Vienneau	.20	.50
7 Eric Begin	.20	.50
8 Steve Bellefleur	.20	.50
9 Patrick Bernier	.20	.50
10 Danick Bouchard	.20	.50
11 Nicolas Desilets	.20	.50
12 Guillaume Durand	.20	.50
13 Pierre-Marc Guilbault	.20	.50
14 Kyell Henegan	.20	.50
15 Cedric Lalonde-McNicoll	.20	.50
16 Triston Manson	.20	.50
17 Francis Pare	.20	.50
18 Mathieu Petrin	.20	.50
19 Egor Egorov	.20	.50
20 Charles Milette	.20	.50
21 Guillaume Labreque	.20	.50
22 Jan Danecek	.20	.50
23 Sean Smyth	.20	.50

1986-87 Sherbrooke Canadiens

Card	Low	High
COMPLETE SET (30)	4.00	10.00
1 Entraineurs 1986-87	.02	.10
2 Soigneurs 1986-87	.02	.10
3 Coupe Stanley 1986	.20	.50
4 Joel Baillargeon	.15	.40
5 Daniel Berthiaume	.30	.75
6 Serge Boisvert	.15	.40
7 Graeme Bonar	.15	.40
8 Randy Bucyk	.15	.40
9 Bill Campbell	.15	.40
10 Jose Charbonneau	.15	.40
11 Rejean Cloutier	.15	.40
12 Bobby Dollas	.15	.40
13 Peter Douris	.15	.40
14 Steven Fletcher	.15	.40
15 Perry Ganchar	.15	.40
16 Luc Gauthier	.15	.40
17 Randy Gilhen	.15	.40
18 Scott Harlow	.15	.40
19 Rick Hayward	.15	.40
20 Kevin Houle	.15	.40
21 Rick Knickle	.30	.75
22 Vincent Riendeau	.30	.75
23 Guy Rouleau	.15	.40
24 Scott Sandelin	.15	.40
25 Karel Svoboda	.15	.40
26 Peter Taglianetti	.15	.40
27 Gilles Thibaudeau	.15	.40
28 Ernie Vargas	.15	.40
29 Andre Villeneuve	.15	.40
30 Brian Williams	.15	.40

2000-01 Sherbrooke Castors

Card	Low	High
COMPLETE SET (19)	3.60	10.00
1 Drew MacIntyre	.20	.75
2 Sebastien Courcelles	.20	.50
3 Simon Tremblay	.20	.50
4 Eric Lavigne	.20	.50
5 Patrick Gosselin	.20	.50
6 Steve Morency	.20	.50
7 Francis Trudel	.20	.50
9 Jonathan Robert	.20	.50
11 Eric Dagenais	.20	.50
12 Louis-Philip Lemay	.20	.75
13 Artem Trmavski	.20	.50
14 Joey Neale	.20	.50
15 Benoit Genesse	.20	.50
16 Pierre-Luc Courchesne	.20	.50
17 Mathieu Thibodeau	.20	.50
18 Nicolas Corbeil	.40	1.00
21 Francois Belanger	.20	.50
22 Cajou MAS	.04	.10
23 Jos Canale CO	.20	.50

2000-01 Sherbrooke Castors Signed

Card	Low	High
COMPLETE SET (19)	16.00	40.00
1 Drew MacIntyre	1.00	5.00
2 Sebastien Courcelles	1.00	2.50
3 Simon Tremblay	1.00	2.50
4 Eric Lavigne	1.00	2.50
5 Patrick Gosselin	1.00	2.50
6 Steve Morency	1.00	2.50
7 Francis Trudel	1.00	2.50
9 Jonathan Robert	1.00	2.50
11 Eric Dagenais	1.00	2.50

12 Louis-Philip Lemay 1.00 5.00
13 Artem Trmavski 1.00 2.50
14 Joey Neale 1.00 2.50
15 Benoit Genesse 1.00 2.50
16 Pierre-Luc Courchesne 1.00 2.50
17 Mathieu Thibodeau 1.00 2.50
18 Nicolas Corbeil 2.00 5.00
21 Francois Belanger 1.00 2.50
22 Cajou MAS .04 .10
23 Jos Canale CO 1.00 2.50

2001-02 Sherbrooke Castors

COMPLETE SET (21) 4.80 12.00
1 Drew MacIntyre .30 .75
2 Eric Dagenais .20 .50
3 Dany Roussin .20 .50
4 Juha-Pekka Ketola .20 .50
5 Patrik Levesque .20 .50
6 David Chicoine .20 .50
7 Jonathan Paiement .20 .50
8 Cedrick Duhamel .20 .50
9 Yan Gaudette .20 .50
10 Francis Trudel .20 .50
11 Maxime Boisclair .30 .75
12 Jonathan Robert .20 .50
13 Mathieu Wathier .20 .50
14 Louis-Philip Lemay .30 .75
15 Bertrand-Pierre Plouffe .30 .75
16 Sebastien Courcelles .20 .50
17 Patrick Mbaraga .20 .50
18 Pierre-Luc Courchesne .20 .50
19 Nicolas Corbeil .40 1.00
20 Bruno D'Amico .20 .50
21 Francois Belanger .20 .50

1993-94 Sherbrooke Faucons

COMPLETE SET 6.00 15.00
1 Jocelyn Thibault 2.00 5.00
2 Mathieu Dandenault .40 1.00
3 Christian Dube .20 .50
4 Luc Belanger .20 .50
5 Dany Larochelle .20 .50
6 Charles Paquette .20 .50
7 Daniel Villeneuve .20 .50
8 Etienne Beaudry .20 .50
9 Jean-Francois Boutin .20 .50
10 Lachlan Coombe .20 .50
11 Pascal Trepanier .30 .75
12 Dave Douville .20 .50
13 Stephane Larocque .20 .50
14 Eric Messier .30 .75
15 Francois Archambault .20 .50
16 Stephane Julien .20 .50
17 Dave Belliveau .20 .50
18 Hugo Turcotte .20 .50
19 Rocco Anoia .20 .50
20 Carl Fleury .30 .75
21 Mirko Langlois .20 .50
22 Hugo Hamelin .20 .50
23 Steven Low .20 .50
24 Atoucou MASCOT .02 .10
25 Guy Chouinard HCO .08 .25
26 Mario Durocher ACO .02 .10

1974-75 Sioux City Musketeers

COMPLETE SET (20) 50.00 100.00
1 Steve Boyle 2.50 5.00
2 Dave Davies 2.50 5.00
3 Steve Desloges 2.50 5.00
4 Greg Gilbert 2.50 5.00
5 Barry Head 2.50 5.00
6 Steve Heathwood 2.50 5.00
7 Dave Kartio 2.50 5.00
8 Ralph Kloiber 2.50 5.00
9 Pete Maxwell 2.50 5.00
10 Randy McDonald 2.50 5.00
11 Terry Mulroy 2.50 5.00
12 Sam Nelligan 2.50 5.00
13 Julian Nixon 2.50 5.00
14 Mike Noel 2.50 5.00
15 Jim Peck 2.50 5.00
16 Bogdan Podwysocki 2.50 5.00
17 John Saville P/CO 2.50 5.00
18 Alex Shibicky Jr. 5.00 10.00
19 Bob Thomerson 2.50 5.00
20 Jim White 5.00 10.00

1998-99 Sioux City Musketeers

COMPLETE SET (25) 8.00 15.00
1 Lee Arnold .20 .50
2 Michael Betz .20 .50
3 Mark Bry .20 .50
4 Chad Dahlen .20 .50
5 Ruslan Fedotenko .75 2.00
6 Cullen Flaherty .20 .50
7 David Hale .40 1.00
8 Tim Judy .20 .50
9 Rostislav Klesla 2.00 5.00
10 Nathan Kotewa .20 .50
11 A.J. Kratofil .20 .50
12 Jordan Lashmett .20 .50
13 Brendan McCartin .20 .50
14 Jake Moreland .20 .50
15 Trent Mozak .20 .50
16 Chad Nordhagen .20 .50
17 Pat O'Leary .20 .50
18 Chris Olsgard .20 .50
19 Tyler Palmiscno .20 .50
20 Luke Pavlas .30 .75
21 Morgan Roach .20 .50
22 Tim Skarperud .20 .50
23 Jeff Van Dyke .20 .50
24 Adam Wallace .20 .50
25 B.J. Willis .20 .50

1999-00 Sioux City Musketeers

COMPLETE SET (21) 4.00 10.00
1 Mike Betz .20 .50
2 Max Bull .20 .50
3 Matt Ciancio .20 .50
4 Chad Dahlen .20 .50
5 Henry Dryden .20 .50
6 Lukas Fiala .20 .50
7 David Hale .40 1.00
8 Eric Helstedt .20 .50
9 Justin Hillier .20 .50
10 Steve Jones .20 .50
11 Tim Judy .20 .50
12 A.J. Kratofil .20 .50
13 Brendan McCartin .20 .50
14 John Miller .20 .50
15 Trent Mozak .20 .50
16 Chad Nordhagen .20 .50
17 Chris Olsgard .20 .50
18 Tyler Palmiscno .20 .50
19 Scott Palaski .20 .50
20 Brandon Schmitt .20 .50
21 Jeff Van Dyke .20 .50

2000-01 Sioux City Musketeers

COMPLETE SET (30) 8.00 20.00
1 Cover Card .04 .10
2 Casey Beauvais .30 .75
3 Matt Ciancio .30 .75
4 Dan Cohen .30 .75
5 Jeff Van Dyke .30 .75
6 Dan Fallon .30 .75
7 Arthur Femenella .30 .75
8 Matt Fetzer .30 .75
9 Justin Fletcher .30 .75
10 Ryan Geris .30 .75
11 Brent Halverson .30 .75
12 Fred Harbinson CO .10 .25
13 Tim Judy .30 .75
14 Erik Johnson .30 .75
15 Brian Kerr .30 .75
16 Zechariah Klann .30 .75
17 Patrick Knutson .30 .75
18 Jack Kowal CO .10 .25
19 Brendan McCartin .30 .75
20 Trent Mozak .30 .75
21 Brian Panik .30 .75
22 Scott Polaski .30 .75
23 Brandon Schmitt .30 .75
24 Brandon Schwartz .30 .75
25 Dave Siciliano CO .10 .25
26 Bryan Smith .30 .75
27 Mitch Thortsen .30 .75
28 Aaron Venasky .30 .75
29 David Vychodil .30 .75
30 John Zeiler .30 .75

2004-05 Sioux City Musketeers

COMPLETE SET (30) 8.00 20.00
1 Brian Bales .30 .75
2 Justin Bostrom .30 .75
3 Kent Bostrom .30 .75
4 Chris Butler .30 .75
5 John Cartera .30 .75
6 Joe Charlebois .30 .75
7 Adam Davis .30 .75
8 Phil DeSimone .30 .75
9 Corey Elkins .30 .75
10 Steve Kampfer .30 .75
11 Nick Kemp .30 .75
12 Tim Kennedy .30 .75
13 Peter Lenes .30 .75
14 Louis Liotti .30 .75
15 Blake Martin .30 .75
16 Dennis McCauley .60 1.50
17 Josh Meyers .30 .75
18 Christian Minella UER .30 .75
19 Jon Ralph .30 .75
20 Chris Spicer .30 .75
21 Jimmy Spratt .60 1.50
22 Travis Turnbull .30 .75
23 Jeff Zatkoff .60 1.50
24 Team Picture .30 .75
25 Schedule .04 .10
26 Mascot .04 .10
27 Dave Siciliano CO .04 .10
28 Marty Quarters ACO .04 .10
29 Chris Brandenberger TR .04 .10
30 Bill Danderand EQM .04 .10

2000-01 Sioux Falls Stampede

COMPLETE SET (21) 10.00 25.00
1 Robbie Barker .30 .75
2 J.B. Bittner .30 .75
3 Jon Booras .30 .75
4 Kellen Briggs .30 .75
5 Jeff Corey .30 .75
6 Donny DeMars .30 .75
7 Mike Doyle .30 .75
8 Jon Dubel .30 .75
9 John Funk .30 .75
10 Dave Iannazzo .30 .75
11 Joe Jensen .30 .75
12 Josh Grahn .30 .75
13 Dustan Lick .30 .75
14 James Massen .30 .75
15 Jamie Mattie .30 .75
16 Zach Sikich .30 .75
17 Dinos Stamoulis .30 .75
18 Thomas Vanek 4.00 10.00
19 Eric Werner .30 .75
20 Tom Zaleski .30 .75
21 Stomp MASCOT .02 .10

2001-02 Sioux Falls Stampede

COMPLETE SET (19) 10.00 25.00
1 Cody Blanshan .30 .75
2 Kellen Briggs .75 2.00
3 Mike Forconi .30 .75
4 Alex Foster .30 .75
5 Quinn Fylling .60 1.50
6 Joe Jensen .30 .75
7 Jacob Micflikier .30 .75
8 Jason Moul .30 .75
9 Eric Przepiorka .30 .75
10 Layne Sedevie .40 1.00
11 Marty Sertich 1.50 4.00
12 Jeremy Smith .30 .75
13 Jesse Stokke .30 .75
14 Kelly Sullivan .30 .75
15 Thomas Vanek 3.00 8.00
16 Mike Vannelli .30 .75
17 Merit Waldrop .30 .75
18 Jake Wilkens .30 .75
19 Chris Wothe .30 .75

2004-05 Sioux Falls Stampede

COMPLETE SET (24) 15.00 30.00
1-1 Andrew Carroll .40 1.00
1-2 Tom Gorowsky .40 1.00
1-3 Nate Prosser .40 1.00
1-4 Greg Barrett .75 2.00
1-5 Ryan Thang .40 1.00
1-6 T.J. Oshie 2.00 5.00
2-1 Chris Peluso .40 1.00
2-2 Stewart Carlin .40 1.00
2-3 Aleksanders Jerofejevs .40 1.00
2-4 Joe Vitale .40 1.00
2-5 Justin White .40 1.00
2-6 Andreas Nodl .40 1.00
3-1 Evan Stephens .40 1.00
3-2 Warren Byrne .40 1.00
3-3 Joe Finley .75 2.00
3-4 John Murray .75 2.00
3-5 Ben Holmstrom .40 1.00
3-6 Blake Friesen .40 1.00
4-1 Justin Milo .40 1.00
4-2 Jacob Hipp .40 1.00
4-3 Jon Globke .40 1.00
4-4 Patrick Mullen .75 2.00
4-5 Buffalo Wild Wings ad .04 .10
4-6 Brandon Harrington .40 1.00

2006-07 Sioux Falls Stampede

COMPLETE SET (24) 12.00 20.00
1 Brad Malone .40 1.00
2 Patrick Tiesling .40 1.00
3 Drew Fisher .40 1.00
4 Ryan Guentzel .40 1.00
5 David Grun .40 1.00
6 Matt Lundin .75 2.00
7 Joey Miller .40 1.00
8 David Solway .40 1.00
9 Eric Peterson .40 1.00
10 Robbie Vrolyk .40 1.00
11 Doug Schueller ACO .10 .25
12 Nick Dineen .40 1.00
13 Stu Bickel .40 1.00
14 Jake Bauer .40 1.00
15 Sam Zabkowicz .40 1.00
16 Zach Redmond .40 1.00
17 Chris Huxley .40 1.00
18 Zach Hansen .40 1.00
19 Dan Sexton .40 1.00
20 Stomp Mascot .02 .10
21 Alexi Dostoinov .40 1.00
22 Jake Drewiske .40 1.00
23 Kevin Hartzell CO .10 .25
24 Corey Tropp .75 2.00

2001-02 Sorel Royaux

COMPLETE SET (28) 4.80 12.00
1 Daniel Archambault .20 .50
2 Francois Bourdeau .20 .50
3 Michel Caron .20 .50
4 L.P. Charbonneau .20 .50
5 Georges-Etienne Cote .20 .50
6 Dany Couette .20 .50
7 Christian Deschenes .20 .50
8 Stephane Groleau .20 .50
9 Eric Joyal .20 .50
10 Patrick Labrecque .40 1.00
11 Martin Lacroix .20 .50
12 Stephane Larocque .20 .50
13 Jamie Leinhos .20 .50
14 Justin Leinhos .20 .50
15 Yanick Levesque GM .04 .10
16 Dominic Maltais .40 1.00
17 Francois Paquette .20 .50
18 Guillaume Rodrigue .20 .50
19 Patrick Roy .20 .50
20 Carl St. Germain .20 .50
21 Yannick Theriault .20 .50
22 Dan Tice .20 .50
23 Steve Vincent .20 .50
24 Sponsor Card .04 .10
25 Coaching Staff .04 .10
26 Rink Staff .04 .10
27 Team Photo .20 .50
28 History Card .20 .50

1995-96 South Carolina Stingrays

COMPLETE SET (24) 3.60 9.00
1 Rick Vaive CO .20 .50
2 Dan Wiebe ASST CO .02 .10
3 Joseph Cramp TR .02 .10
4 Aaron Fackler
Equipment Manager .02 .10
5 Mikhail Volkov .15 .40
6 Jason Cipolla .15 .40
7 Mike Ross .15 .40
8 Rob Concannon .15 .40
9 Dan Fournel .15 .40
10 Mark Bavis .15 .40
11 Darren Ritchie .15 .40
12 Mike Barrie .15 .40
13 Marc Tardif .15 .40
14 Chris Foy .15 .40
15 Scott Boston .20 .50
16 Carl LeBlanc .15 .40
17 Brett Marietti .15 .40
18 Jared Bednar .15 .40
19 Paul Rushforth .15 .40
20 Kevin Knopp .15 .40
21 Todd Sullivan .20 .50
22 Justin Duberman .15 .40
23 Sean Gauthier .20 .50
24 Mark Rupnow .15 .40
NNO Header Card .02 .10

1996-97 South Carolina Stingrays

COMPLETE SET (28) 4.00 10.00
9 Mike Ross .15 .40
10 Marc Genest .15 .40
11 Dan Fournel .40 1.00
12 David Mayes .15 .40
14 David Seitz .15 .40
15 Jeff Romfo .15 .40
16 Kyle Ferguson .15 .40
17 Marc Tardif .15 .40
18 Steve Parson .15 .40
19 Doug Wood .15 .40
20 Scott Boston .30 .75
21 Rob Concannon .15 .40
22 Rob Butler .15 .40
24 Brett Marietti .15 .40
25 Jared Bednar .15 .40
27 Ed Courtenay .20 .50
28 Kevin Knopp .15 .40
29 Jay Moser .15 .40
30 Corey Cadden .15 .40
31 Jason Fitzsimmons .15 .40
33 Chris Hynnes .15 .40
35 Taras Lendzyk .15 .40
NNO Kevin Snider(Medical Trainer) .02 .10
NNO Rick Vaive CO .20 .50
NNO Aaron Fackler
(Equipment Manager) .02 .10
NNO Rick Adduono ASST CO .02 .10
NNO Randy Page(Radio Broadcaster) .02 .10

2001-02 South Carolina Stingrays

COMPLETE SET (20) 12.00 30.00
1 Rick Adduono CO .20 .50
2 Jared Bednar .75 2.00
3 Ryan Brindley .60 1.50
4 Adam Calder .60 1.50
5 Marty Clapton .60 1.50
6 Jason Fitzsimmons ACO .20 .50
7 Alan Fyfe .60 1.50
8 Zach Ham .60 1.50
9 Jamie Hodson .75 2.00
10 Joel Irving .60 1.50
11 Trevor Johnson .60 1.50
12 Jody Lehman .60 1.50
13 Hugo Marchand .60 1.50
14 Brett Marietti .60 1.50
15 David Seitz .60 1.50
16 Jason Sessa .75 2.00
17 Paul Traynor .75 2.00
18 Buddy Wallace .60 1.50
19 Chris Wheaton .60 1.50
20 Brad Williamson .60 1.50

2002-03 South Carolina Stingrays

COMPLETE SET (24) 8.00 20.00
1 Peter Armbrust .40 1.00
2 Jeff Boulanger .40 1.00
3 Ryan Brindley .40 1.00
4 Adam Calder .40 1.00
5 Marty Clapton .40 1.00
6 Kirk Daubenspeck .60 1.50
7 Matt Desrosiers .40 1.00
8 Robin Gomez .60 1.50
9 Brent Henley .60 1.50
10 Curtis Huppe .40 1.00
11 Joel Irving .40 1.00
12 Mike Jickling .40 1.00
13 Trevor Johnson .40 1.00
14 Brett Marietti .40 1.00
15 Andy Powers .40 1.00
16 Aaron Schneekloth .40 1.00
17 David Seitz .40 1.00
18 Rod Taylor .40 1.00
19 Dean Weasler .40 1.00
20 Brad Williamson .40 1.00
21 Jason Fitzsimmons CO .10 .25
22 Jared Bednar ACO .10 .25
23 DJ Church TR .04 .10
24 Jocko Cayer EQM .10 .25

2002-03 South Carolina Stingrays RBI

COMPLETE SET (18) 8.00 20.00
205 Ryan Brinkley .40 1.00
206 David Brumby .60 1.50
207 Adam Calder .40 1.00
208 Marty Clapton .40 1.00
209 Matt Desrosiers .40 1.00
210 Kirk Daubenspeck .60 1.50
211 Robin Gomez .60 1.50
212 Brent Henley .60 1.50
213 Curtis Huppe .40 1.00
214 Joel Irving .40 1.00
215 Mike Jickling .40 1.00
216 Trevor Johnson .40 1.00
217 Brett Marietti .40 1.00
218 Andy Powers .40 1.00
219 Aaron Schneekloth .40 1.00
220 David Seitz .40 1.00
221 Rod Taylor .40 1.00
222 Brad Williamson .40 1.00

2003-04 South Carolina Stingrays

COMPLETE SET (16) 6.00 15.00
321 Chris Allen .40 1.00
322 Jeff Boulanger .40 1.00
323 David Brumby .60 1.50
324 Ed Courtenay .40 1.00
325 Kirk Daubenspeck .60 1.50
326 Robin Gomez .60 1.50
327 Curtis Huppe .40 1.00
328 Mike Jickling .40 1.00
329 Colin Johnson .40 1.00
330 Trevor Johnson .60 1.50
331 Jim Lorentz .40 1.00
332 Aaron Power .40 1.00
333 David Seitz .40 1.00
334 Shawn Skiehar .40 1.00
335 Steven Spencer .40 1.00
336 Kevin Spiewak .40 1.00

2005-06 South Carolina Stingrays

COMPLETE SET (16) 10.00 20.00
1 Matt Reid .75 2.00
2 Jeff Legue .75 2.00
3 Chick-Fil-A Cow .01 .01
4 Ticket Voucher Card .01 .01
5 Trevor Johnson .75 2.00
6 Robin Gomez .75 2.00
7 Maxime Daigneault 1.50 4.00
8 Ticket Voucher Card .01 .01
9 Cail McLean .75 2.00
10 Marty Clapton .75 2.00
11 Steve Spencer .75 2.00
12 Ticket Voucher Card .01 .01
13 Brad Parsons .75 2.00
14 Nate Kiser .75 2.00
15 Aaron Power .75 2.00
16 Ticket Voucher Card .01 .01

1989-90 Spokane Chiefs

COMPLETE SET (20) 6.00 15.00
1 Mike Chrun .20 .50
2 John Colvin .20 .50
3 Shawn Dietrich .20 .50
4 Milan Dragicevic .20 .50
5 Frank Evans .20 .50
6 Pat Falloon .40 1.00
7 Scott Farrell .20 .50
8 Jeff Ferguson .20 .50
9 Travis Green 1.25 3.00
10 Mike Hawes .20 .50
11 Bobby House .20 .50
12 Mike Jickling .20 .50
13 Steve Junker .20 .50
14 Jon Klemm .40 1.00
15 Chris Rowland .20 .50
16 Dennis Saharchuk .20 .50
17 Kerry Toporowski .20 .50
18 Trevor Tovell .20 .50
19 Bram Vanderkracht .20 .50
20 Ray Whitney 1.25 3.00

1993-94 Spokane Chiefs

COMPLETE SET (30) 6.00 15.00
1 Barry Becker .30 .75
2 Maxim Bets .20 .50
3 Valeri Bure .75 2.00
4 Shaun Byrne .20 .50
5 Joe Cardarelli .20 .50
6 John Cirjak .20 .50
7 Dion Darling .20 .50
8 Derek Descoteau .20 .50
9 Ryan Duthie .20 .50
10 Randy Favaro .20 .50
11 Craig Geekie .20 .50
12 Sean Gillam .20 .50
13 Hugh Hamilton .20 .50
14 David Jesiolowski .20 .50
15 Dmitri Leonov .20 .50
16 Bryan Maxwell CO .02 .10
17 Bryan McCabe .40 1.00
18 Memorial Cup Champs .20 .50
19 Rick More TR .02 .10
20 Jason Podollan .20 .50
21 Kevin Popp .20 .50
22 Kevin Sawyer .75 2.00
23 Trevor Shoaf .20 .50
24 Darren Sinclair .20 .50
25 Darren Smadis .30 .75
26 Jeremy Stasiuk .20 .50
27 Scott Townsend .20 .50
28 Spokane Coliseum .02 .10
29 Checklist .02 .10
30 Clover Club Cheerleaders .20 .50

1994-95 Spokane Chiefs

COMPLETE SET (32) 6.00 15.00
1 Randy Favaro .20 .50
2 Jarrod Daniel .20 .50
3 Jason Podollan .40 1.00
4 Trent Whitfield .40 1.00
5 Greg Leeb .20 .50
6 Jay Bertsch .20 .50
7 Joe Cardarelli .20 .50
8 Robby Sandrock .20 .50
9 Kevin Sawyer .40 1.00
10 Sean Gillam .20 .50
11 Ryan Berry .20 .50
12 Mike Haley .20 .50
13 John Cirjak .20 .50
14 Jared Hope .20 .50
15 Joel Boschman .20 .50
16 Derek Descoteau .20 .50
17 Jeremy Stasiuk .20 .50
18 Tomas Pisa .20 .50
19 Darren Sinclair .20 .50
20 Paul Bailley .20 .50
21 Dmitri Leonov .20 .50
22 Bryan McCabe .40 1.00
23 Hugh Hamilton .20 .50
24 Scott Fletcher .20 .50
25 David Lemanowicz .40 1.00
26 Mike Babcock CO .04 .10
27 Parry Shockey CO .04 .10
28 T.D. Forbes EQMG .04 .10
29 Ted Schott EQMG .04 .10
30 Veterans Memorial .04 .10
31 Veterans Memorial .04 .10
32 Veterans Memorial .04 .10

1995-96 Spokane Chiefs

COMPLETE SET (30) 4.80 12.00
1 David Lemanowicz .30 .75
2 Scott Fletcher .20 .50
3 Hugh Hamilton .20 .50
4 Chris Lane .20 .50
5 Dmitri Leonov .20 .50
6 Darren Sinclair .20 .50
7 Ty Jones .30 .75
8 Kris Graf .20 .50
9 Trent Whitfield .30 .75
10 Martin Cerven .20 .50
11 Randy Favaro .20 .50
12 Jason Podollan .30 .75
13 Joel Boschman .20 .50
14 Jared Hope .20 .50
15 Greg Leeb .20 .50
16 John Cirjak .20 .50
17 Mike Haley .20 .50
18 Ryan Berry .20 .50
19 Sean Gillam .20 .50
20 Derek Schutz .20 .50
21 Joe Cardarelli .20 .50
22 Adam Magarrell .20 .50
23 Jay Bertsch .20 .50
24 John Shockey .20 .50
25 Mike Babcock CO .15 .40
26 Parry Shockey ACO .02 .10
27 T.D. Forss EQMG .02 .10
28 Ted Schott AEQMG .02 .10
29 Dan Mitchell .02 .10
30 Aren Miller .30 .75

1996-97 Spokane Chiefs

COMPLETE SET (30) 6.00 15.00
1 Aren Miller .30 .75
2 Brad Ference .40 1.00
3 Hugh Hamilton .20 .50
4 Chris Lane .20 .50
5 Yegor Mikhailov .20 .50
6 Ty Jones .30 .75
7 Kris Graf .20 .50
8 Trent Whitfield .30 .75
9 Blake Evans .20 .50
10 Jared Smyth .20 .50
11 Joel Boschman .20 .50
12 Greg Leeb .30 .75
13 John Cirjak .20 .50
14 Mike Haley .20 .50
15 Kyle Rossiter .30 .75
16 Derek Schutz .40 1.00
17 Marian Cisar .40 1.00
18 Joe Cardarelli .20 .50
19 Adam Magarrell .20 .50
20 Jay Bertsch .20 .50
21 Curtis Suter .20 .50
22 Marc Brown .20 .50
23 Marc Magliarditi .30 .75
24 Boomer Mascot .02 .10
25 Mike Babcock HCO .30 .75
26 Brett Cox ACO .02 .10
27 T.D. Forss TR .02 .10
28 Ted Schott EM .02 .10
29 Dan Mitchell DRM .02 .10
30 Spokane All-Star Game .02 .10

1997-98 Spokane Chiefs

COMPLETE SET (30) 6.00 15.00
1 Aren Miller .30 .75
2 Brad Ference .40 1.00
3 Perry Johnson .20 .50
4 Mark Forth .20 .50
5 Zenith Komarniski .30 .75
6 Justin Ossachuk .20 .50
7 Cole Fischer .20 .50
8 Brandin Cote .20 .50
9 Ty Jones .30 .75
10 Kris Graf .20 .50
11 Trent Whitfield .30 .75
12 Jared Smyth .20 .50
13 Marc Brown .20 .50
14 Greg Leeb .30 .75
15 Justin Kelly .20 .50
16 Ben Johnson .20 .50
17 Kyle Rossiter .30 .75
18 Derek Schutz .30 .75
19 Marian Cisar .40 1.00
20 Lynn Loyns .40 1.00
21 Kris Waltze .20 .50
22 Curtis Suter .20 .50
23 Josh Maser .20 .50
24 Ron Grimard .20 .50
25 Dan Vandermeer .20 .50
26 Shaun Fleming .20 .50
27 Mike Babcock HCO .02 .10
28 Mike Pelino ACO .02 .10
29 T.D. Forss TR .02 .10
30 Dan Mitchell DRM .02 .10

1998-99 Spokane Chiefs

COMPLETE SET (28) 6.00 15.00
1 Mike Babcock CO .20 .50
2 Daniel Bohac .20 .50
3 Kris Callaway .20 .50
4 Brandin Cote .20 .50
5 Jeremy Farr .20 .50
6 Brad Ference .30 .75
7 Cole Fischer .20 .50
8 Mark Forth .20 .50
9 David Hajek .20 .50
10 Chris Harper .20 .50
11 David Haun .20 .50
12 Simon Jones .20 .50
13 Ty Jones .20 .50
14 Tim Krymusa .20 .50
15 Bobby Leavins .20 .50
16 Mike Lencucha .20 .50
17 Lynn Loyns .30 .75
18 Josh Maser .20 .50
19 Mike Pelino .20 .50
20 Kyle Rossiter .20 .50
21 Derek Schutz .20 .50
22 Cam Severson .40 1.00
23 Tim Smith .20 .50
24 Jared Smyth .20 .50
25 Curtis Suter .20 .50
26 Shawn Thompson .20 .50
27 Dan Vandermeer .20 .50
28 Mason Wallin .20 .50

1999-00 Spokane Chiefs

COMPLETE SET (30) 5.00 12.00
1 Mike Babcock CO .40 1.00
2 Chris Barr .20 .50
3 Daniel Bohac .20 .50
4 David Boychuk .20 .50
5 Kris Callaway .20 .50
6 Brandin Cote .20 .50
7 Jeremy Farr .20 .50
8 T.D. Forss EQMG .02 .10
9 Chris Heid .20 .50
10 Matt Keith .20 .50
11 Tim Krymusa .20 .50
12 Mike Lencucha .30 .75
13 Lynn Loyns .20 .50
14 Jeff Lucky .20 .50
15 Tyler MacKay .20 .50
16 Brent McDonald .20 .50
17 Dan Mitchell STAFF .02 .10
18 Bill Peters ACO .02 .10
19 Scott Roles .20 .50
20 Kyle Rossiter .40 1.00
21 Kurt Sauer .20 .50
22 Beau Schott EQMG .02 .10
23 Derek Schutz .20 .50
24 Tim Smith .20 .50
25 Shawn Thompson .20 .50
26 Ryan Thorpe .20 .50
27 Roman Tvrdon .20 .50
28 Mason Wallin .20 .50
29 Boomer MASCOT .02 .10
30 Spokane Arena .02 .10

2000-01 Spokane Chiefs

COMPLETE SET (30) 4.80 12.00
1 Chris Barr .20 .50
2 David Boychuk .20 .50
3 Barry Brust .30 .75
4 Brandin Cote .20 .50
5 Jevon Desautels .20 .50
6 T.D. Forss EQMG .04 .10
7 Perry Ganchar CO .04 .10
8 Chris Heid .20 .50
9 Barry Horman .20 .50
10 Joff Kehler .20 .50
11 Matt Keith .20 .50
12 Justin Keller .20 .50
13 Tim Krymusa .20 .50
14 Ratislav Lipka .20 .50
15 Lynn Loyns .20 1.00
16 Jeff Lucky .20 .50
17 Tyler MacKay .30 .75
18 Stephen Mann .20 .50
19 Dan Mitchell STAFF .04 .10
20 Chris Ovington .20 .50
21 Craig Perry .20 .50
22 Bill Peters ACO .04 .10
23 Kurt Sauer .20 .75
24 Brad Schell .20 .50
25 Tim Smith .20 .50
26 Shawn Thompson .20 .50
27 Ryan Thorpe .20 .50
28 Roman Tvrdon .20 .50
29 Mason Wallin .20 .50
30 Boomer MASCOT .04 .10

2001-02 Spokane Chiefs

COMPLETE SET (28) 5.00 12.00
1 Header Card .04 .10
2 Chris Barr .20 .50
3 David Boychuk .20 .50
4 Barry Brust .40 1.00
5 Jordan Clarke .20 .50
6 Brandin Cote .20 .50
7 Curtis Darling .40 1.00
8 Jevon Desautels .20 .50
9 Ivan Garcia .20 .50
10 Chris Heid .20 .50
11 Barry Horman .20 .50
12 Joff Kehler .20 .50
13 Matt Keith .30 .75
14 Stuart Kerr .20 .50
15 Chad Klassen .20 .50
16 Tim Krymusa .20 .50
17 Jeff Lucky .20 .50
18 Jeff Lynch .20 .50
19 Kurt Sauer .30 .75
20 Brad Schell .20 .50
21 Scott Scherger .20 .50
22 Mason Wallin .20 .50
23 Perry Ganchar CO .04 .10
24 Bill Peters ACO .04 .10
25 Dan Mitchell TR .04 .10
26 Darcy Bishop TR .04 .10
27 Boomer MASCOT .04 .10
28 Overagers .20 .50

2002-03 Spokane Chiefs

COMPLETE SET (30) 5.00 12.00
1 Chris Barr .20 .50
2 Ryan Blatchford .20 .50
3 Barry Brust .40 1.00
4 Liam Couture .20 .50
5 Andrew DeSousa .20 .50
6 Jevon Desautels .20 .50
7 Chris Heid .20 .50
8 Barry Horman .20 .50
9 Joff Kehler .20 .50
10 Chad Klassen .20 .50
11 Tim Krymusa .20 .50
12 Jakub Langhammer .20 .50
13 Darren Lefebvre .20 .50
14 Jeff Lucky .20 .50
15 Ned Lukacevic .20 .50
16 Doug Lynch .30 .75
17 Jeff Lynch .20 .50
18 Joel Rupprecht .20 .50
19 Brad Schell .20 .50
20 Andy Schenn .20 .50
21 Scott Scherger .20 .50
22 Miroslav Stolc .20 .50
23 Mason Wallin .20 .50
24 Jim Watt .20 .50
25 Colby Zavisha .20 .50
26 Al Conroy CO .04 .10
27 Jamie Huscroft ACO .04 .10
28 Dan Mitchell TR .04 .10
29 Boomer MASCOT .04 .10
30 Darcy Bishop TR .04 .10

2004-05 Spokane Chiefs Magnets

1 Gary Gladue .75 2.00
2 Jevon Desautels .75 2.00
3 Scott Lynch .75 2.00
4 Chad Klassen .75 2.00
5 Jim Watt .75 2.00
6 Ned Lukacevic .75 2.00
7 Gustav Engman .75 2.00
8 Jeff Lynch .75 2.00

1996-97 Springfield Falcons

COMPLETE SET (21) 4.00 10.00
3 Brent Thompson .30 .75
4 Deron Quint .30 .75
5 Steve Cheredaryk .15 .40
10 Kent Manderville .15 .40
11 Hnat Domenichelli .30 .75
12 Steve Martins .30 .75
14 Tom Buckley .15 .40
15 Juha Ylonen .30 .75
16 Chris Longo .15 .40
17 Rhett Gordon .15 .40
19 Tavis Hansen .15 .40
20 Steve Halko .15 .40
22 Scott Levins .15 .40
23 Rob Murray .15 .40
25 Jason McBain .15 .40
27 Jeff Daniels .15 .40
28 Ryan Risidore .20 .50
30 Manny Legace .60 1.50
33 Reggie Savage .15 .40
34 Nolan Pratt .20 .50
35 Scott Langkow .30 .75
44 Kevin Brown .15 .40
NNO AHL Hockey Card .02 .10

1997-98 Springfield Falcons
COMPLETE SET (26) 5.00 15.00
1 Daniel Briere 1.00 2.50
2 Ruslan Batyrshin .15 .40
3 Ted Crowley .15 .40
4 Sylvain Daigle .15 .40
5 Andrew Dale .15 .40
6 Shane Doan 1.00 2.50
7 Jason Doig .20 .50
8 Dan Focht .15 .40
9 Sean Gagnon .15 .40
10 Rhett Gordon .15 .40
11 Tavis Hansen .15 .40
12 Chad Kilger .30 .75
13 Scott Langkow .30 .75
14 Trevor Letowski .40 1.00
15 Scott Levins .20 .50
16 Richard Lintner .20 .50
17 Jason Morgan .15 .40
18 Rob Murray .15 .40
19 Mike Pomichter .15 .40
20 Jeff Shevalier .15 .40
21 Martin Simard .15 .40
22 Brad Tiley .15 .40
23 Dave Farrish CO .08 .25
24 Ron Wilson CO .08 .25
25 PHPA Web Site .01 .05
26 AHL Web Site .01 .05

2002-03 Springfield Falcons
COMPLETE SET (24) 6.00 15.00
1 Ramzi Abid .30 .75
2 Dmitry Atanasenkov .30 .75
3 Nikita Alexeev .40 1.00
4 Frank Banham .20 .50
5 Goran Bezina .20 .50
6 Zac Bierk .40 1.00
7 Jason Bonsignore .20 .50
8 Martin Cibak .20 .50
9 Dan Focht .20 .50
10 Corey Foster .20 .50
11 Martin Grenier .30 .75
12 Jason Jaspers .20 .50
13 Boyd Kane .40 1.00
14 Evgeny Konstantinov .30 .75
15 Kristian Kudroc .20 .50
16 Norm Maciver ACO .04 .10
17 Marty McSorley HCO .20 .50
18 Rob Murray .20 .50
19 Darren Rumble .20 .50
20 Michael Schutte .20 .50
21 Dan Smith .20 .50
22 Jeff Taffe .40 1.00
23 Erik Westrum .40 1.00
24 Shane Willis .20 .50

2003-04 Springfield Falcons Postcards
COMPLETE SET (28) 15.00 30.00
1 Goran Bezina .40 1.00
2 Trevor Gillies .40 1.00
3 Kiel McLeod .40 1.00
4 Erik Westrum .75 2.00
5 Dustin Wood .40 1.00
6 Igor Knyazev .40 1.00
7 Nikos Tselios .40 1.00
8 Martin Podlesak .40 1.00
9 Darren McLachlin .40 1.00
10 Frederik Sjostrom .40 1.00
11 Jason Jaspers .40 1.00
12 Bryan Helmer .40 1.00
13 Mike Stutzel .40 1.00
14 Peter Ferraro .40 1.00
15 Gary Shuchuk .40 1.00
16 Frank Lukes .40 1.00
17 Chris Ferraro .40 1.00
18 Chris Dyment .40 1.00
19 Frank Banham .75 2.00
20 Jean-Marc Pelletier .75 2.00
21 Miko Wilson .40 1.00
22 Ladislav Kouba .40 1.00
23 Jeremiah McCarthy .40 1.00
24 David LeNeveu .75 2.00
25 Michael Schutte .40 1.00
26 Marty McSorley CO .40 1.00
27 Gord Dineen ACO .20 .50
28 MASCOT .04 .10

2004-05 Springfield Falcons
COMPLETE SET (27) 6.00 15.00
1 Adam Henrich .20 .50
2 Andre Deveaux .20 .50
3 Andreas Holmqvist .20 .50
4 Brian Chapman .20 .50
5 Brian Eklund .30 .75
6 Craig Darby .20 .50
7 Darren Reid .20 .50
8 Dennis Packard .20 .50
9 Derek Bekar .20 .50
10 Doug O'Brien .20 .50
11 Evgeny Artukhin .20 .50
12 Gerard DiCaire .20 .50
13 Harlan Pratt .20 .50
14 Jamie Storr .30 .75
15 Jason Jaspers .20 .50
16 Marc Busenburg .20 .50
17 Mike Egener .20 .50
18 Mitch Fritz .40 1.00
19 Nick Tarnasky .40 1.00
20 Nikita Alexeev .20 .50
21 Nikos Tselios .20 .50
22 Paul Ranger .20 .50
23 Ryan Craig .75 2.00
24 Shane Willis .20 .50
25 Steve McLaren .20 .50
26 Phil Russell ACO .04 .10
27 Dirk Graham CO .04 .10

2005-06 Springfield Falcons
COMPLETE SET (27) 8.00 15.00
1 Adam Henrich .20 .50
2 Andre Deveaux .20 .50
3 Brad Tiley .20 .50
4 Brian Eklund .30 .75
5 Darren Reid .20 .50
6 Dennis Packard .20 .50
7 Doug O'Brien .20 .50
8 Evgeny Artyukhin .20 .50
9 Gerald Coleman .40 1.00
10 Gerard Dicaire .20 .50
11 Harlan Pratt .20 .50
12 Jason Jaspers .20 .50
13 Jim Campbell .20 .50
14 Marek Kvapil .20 .50
15 Mike Egener .40 1.00
16 Mitch Fritz .40 1.00
17 Nick Tarnasky .30 .75
18 Norm Milley .20 .50
19 Paul Ranger .20 .50
20 Steve McLaren .20 .50
21 Ryan Craig .40 1.00
22 Ryan Vesce .20 .50
23 Timo Helbling .20 .50
24 Todd Rohloff .20 .50
25 Dirk Graham HC .02 .10
26 Phil Russell ACO .02 .10
27 Darren Rumble ACO .02 .10

2006-07 Springfield Falcons
COMPLETE SET (28) 8.00 15.00
1 Sean Burke .40 1.00
2 Doug O'Brien .20 .50
3 Dan Cavanaugh .20 .50
4 Andy Delmore .20 .50
5 Eric Healey .20 .50
6 Blair Jones .20 .50
7 Sylvain Dufresne .20 .50
8 Mitch Fritz .30 .75
9 Jay Rosehill .20 .50
10 Karri Ramo .40 1.00
11 Zdenek Blatny .20 .50
12 Justin Keller .20 .50
13 Mike Egener .30 .75
14 Darren Reid .20 .50
15 David Spina .20 .50
16 Marek Kvapil .20 .50
17 Norm Milley .20 .50
18 Andy Rogers .20 .50
19 Matt Smaby .40 1.00
20 Jonathan Boutin .40 1.00
21 Zbynek Hrdel .20 .50
22 Steve Stirling HC .10 .25
23 Darren Rumble CO .10 .25
24 Jared Aulin .20 .50
25 Andre Deveaux .20 .50
26 Adam Henrich .20 .50
27 Geoff Waugh .20 .50
28 Screech MASCOT .02 .10

2014-15 Springfield Falcons
COMPLETE SET (25) 6.00 15.00
1 Anton Forsberg .30 .75
2 Hubert Labrie .30 .75
3 Will Weber .30 .75
4 Austin Madaisky .30 .75
5 Dennis Urban .30 .75
6 Marko Dano .50 1.25
7 Mike Hoeffel .30 .75
8 Ryan Craig .30 .75
9 Trent Vogelhuber .30 .75
10 Dana Tyrell .40 1.00
11 Kerby Rychel .30 .75
12 Sean Collins .30 .75
13 T.J. Tynan .30 .75
14 Nathan Oystrick .30 .75
15 Lukas Sedlak .30 .75
16 Brett Ponich .30 .75
17 Mathieu Gagnon .30 .75
18 Jaime Sifers .30 .75
19 Oscar Dansk .40 1.00
20 Frederic St. Denis .30 .75
21 Corey Cowick .30 .75
22 Thomas Larkin .30 .75
23 Domenic Monardo .30 .75
24 Josh Anderson .30 .75
25 Jared Bednar CO .30 .75

1983-84 Springfield Indians
COMPLETE SET (25) 7.20 18.00
1 Gil Hudon .30 .75
2 Jim Ralph 1.25 3.00
3 Todd Bergen .30 .75
4 Len Hachborn .40 1.00
5 John Ollson .20 .50
6 Steve Tsujiura .40 1.00
7 Gordie Williams .20 .50
8 Dave Brown 1.25 3.00
9 Dan Frawley .20 .50
10 Tom McMurchy .20 .50
11 Dave Michayluk .30 .75
12 Bob Mormina .20 .50
13 Perry Pelensky .20 .50
14 Andy Brickley .40 1.00
15 Ross Fitzpatrick .20 .50
16 Florent Robidoux .20 .50
17 Jeff Smith .20 .50
18 Rod Willard .20 .50
19 Darrell Anholt .20 .50
20 Steve Blyth .20 .50
21 Don Dietrich .20 .50
22 Steve Smith .20 .50
23 Daryl Stanley .40 1.00
24 Taras Zytynsky .20 .50
25 Doug Sauter CO .20 .50

1984-85 Springfield Indians
COMPLETE SET (25) 6.00 15.00
1 Mike Sands .40 1.00
2 Lorne Molleken .20 .50
3 Todd Lumbard .20 .50
4 Randy Velischek .30 .75
5 David Jensen .30 .75
6 Ken Leiter .20 .50
7 Vern Smith .20 .50
8 Alan Kerr .30 .75
9 Scott Howson .20 .50
10 Tim Coulis .20 .50
11 Terry Tait .20 .50
12 Tim Trimper .20 .50
13 Rob Flockhart .30 .75
14 Ron Handy .20 .50
15 Jiri Poner .20 .50
16 Chris Pryor .20 .50
17 Dale Henry .20 .50
18 Mark Hamway .20 .50
19 Monty Trottier .20 .50
20 Miroslav Maly .20 .50
21 Dirk Graham 1.25 3.00
22 Roger Kortko .20 .50
23 Bob Bodak .20 .50
24 Lorne Henning CO .30 .75
25 Checklist Card .20 .50

1957-58 St. Catharines Tee Pees Murray's Chips
1 Bob Corupe 18 25.00 50.00
2 Don Cosburn 25.00 50.00
3 Roy Edwards 1 40.00 80.00
4 Don Grosso 17 25.00 50.00
5 Ed Hoekstra 30.00 60.00
6 Chico Maki 16 40.00 80.00
7 John McKenzie 50.00 100.00
8 Stan Mikita 200.00 400.00
9 Matt Ravlich 30.00 60.00

1993-94 St. Cloud State Huskies
COMPLETE SHEET (30) 6.00 15.00
1 Randy Best .20 .50
2 Chad Brennan .20 .50
3 Neil Cooper .20 .50
4 Chris Dopp .20 .50
5 Marc Gagnon .20 .50
6 Sandy Gasseau .20 .50
7 Jay Geisbaur .20 .50
8 Tony Gruba .20 .50
9 Dave Holum .20 .50
10 Kelly Hultgren .20 .50
11 Jason Jiskra .20 .50
12 Eric Johnson .20 .50
13 P.J. Lepler .20 .50
14 Brett Lievers .20 .50
15 Billy Lund .20 .50
16 Mike Maristuen .20 .50
17 Chris Markstrom .20 .50
18 Taj Melson .20 .50
19 Brad Nelson .20 .50
20 Mike O'Connell .20 .50
21 Dave Paradise .20 .50
22 Dan Reimann .20 .50
23 Kelly Rieder .20 .50
24 Adam Rodak .20 .50
25 Gino Santerre .20 .50
26 Jeff Schmidt .20 .50
27 Grant Sjerven .20 .50
28 Coaching Staff .20 .50
29 Marc Gagnon IA .20 .50
30 Kelly Rieder IA .20 .50

2000-01 St. Cloud State Huskies
COMPLETE SET (31) 4.00 10.00
1 Keith Anderson .15 .40
2 Tyler Arnason .30 .75
3 Lee Brooks .15 .40
4 Jon Cullen .15 .40
5 Nate DiCasmirro .15 .40
6 Derek Eastman .15 .40
7 Jeff Finger .15 .40
8 Brian Gaffaney .15 .40
9 Mark Hartigan .15 .40
10 Matt Hendricks .15 .40
11 Ryan Johnson .15 .40
12 Ryan LaMere .15 .40
13 Ritchie Larson .15 .40
14 Andy Lundbohm .15 .40
15 Ryan Malone .15 .40
16 Jim McNamara .15 .40
17 Scott Meyer .15 .40
18 Jake Moreland .15 .40
19 Joe Motzko .15 .40
20 Joel Peterson .15 .40
21 Chris Purslow .15 .40
22 Brandon Sampair .15 .40
23 Brian Schuette .15 .40
24 Mike Walsh .15 .40
25 Dean Weasler .15 .40
26 Duvie Westcott .15 .40
27 Craig Dahl .15 .40
28 Doc DelCastillo .15 .40
29 Brad Willner .15 .40
30 Dog Pound .15 .40
31 Chuck Clausen .15 .40

2003-04 St. Cloud State Huskies
COMPLETE SET (31) 8.00 20.00
1 Casey Borer .30 .75
2 Tim Boron .40 1.00
3 Grant Clafton .30 .75
4 Tim Conboy .30 .75
5 Adam Coole .40 1.00
6 Mike Doyle .30 .75
7 Justin Fletcher .30 .75
8 Matt Gens .30 .75
9 Matt Hendricks .30 .75
10 Billy Hengen .30 .75
11 Brock Hooton .30 .75
12 Gary Houseman .30 .75
13 Dave Iannazzo .30 .75
14 Joe Jensen .30 .75
15 Ryan LaMere .30 .75
16 Garrett Larson .30 .75
17 Bille Luger .30 .75
18 Andy Lundbohm .30 .75
19 Brian McCormack .30 .75
20 T.J. McElroy .30 .75
21 Jason Montgomery .40 1.00
22 Colin Peters .30 .75
23 Nate Raduns .30 .75
24 Konrad Reeder .30 .75
25 Peter Szabo .30 .75
26 Nate Wright .30 .75
27 Craig Dahl CO .04 .10
28 Brad Willner ACO .04 .10
29 Fred Harbinson ACO .04 .10
30 Mascot .04 .10
31 Team Photo .20 .50

2004-05 St. Cloud State Huskies
COMPLETE SET (32) 10.00 25.00
1 Chris Anderson .40 1.00
2 Casey Borer .40 1.00
3 Tim Boron .40 1.00
4 Aaron Brocklehurst .40 1.00
5 Grant Clafton .40 1.00
6 Nate Dey .40 1.00
7 Mike Doyle .40 1.00
8 Justin Fletcher .40 1.00
9 Matt Francis .40 1.00
10 Sean Garrity .40 1.00
11 Matt Gens .40 1.00
12 Andrew Gordon .40 1.00
13 Matt Hartman .40 1.00
14 Billy Hengen .40 1.00
15 Brock Hooton .40 1.00
16 Gary Houseman .40 1.00
17 Dave Iannazzo .40 1.00
18 Joe Jensen .40 1.00
19 Ethan Lyerly .40 1.00
20 T.J. McElroy .40 1.00
21 Marty Mjelleli .40 1.00
22 Jason Montgomery .40 1.00
23 Nate Raduns .40 1.00
24 Konrad Reeder .40 1.00
25 Josh Singer .40 1.00
26 Matt Stephenson .40 1.00
27 Peter Szabo .40 1.00
28 Craig Dahl CO .10 .25
29 Fred Harbinson ACO .10 .25
30 Brad Willner ACO .10 .25
31 Sean Donley TR .10 .25
32 Jeremiah Minkel EQM .10 .25

2005-06 St. Cloud State Huskies
COMPLETE SET (33) 10.00 20.00
1 Chris Anderson .30 .75
2 Casey Borer .30 .75
3 Tim Boron .30 .75
4 Aaron Brocklehurst .30 .75
5 David Carlisle .30 .75
6 Grant Clafton .30 .75
7 Nate Dey .30 .75
8 Justin Fletcher .30 .75
9 Matt Francis .30 .75
10 Sean Garrity .30 .75
11 Bobby Goepfert .60 1.50
12 Andrew Gordon .30 .75
13 Matt Hartman .30 .75
14 Billy Hengen .30 .75
15 Brock Hooton .30 .75
16 Gary Houseman .30 .75
17 Joe Jensen .30 .75
18 Dan Kronick .30 .75
19 T.J. McElroy .30 .75
20 Marty Mjelleli .30 .75
21 Jason Montgomery .30 .75
22 Michael Olson .30 .75
23 Nate Raduns .30 .75
24 Konrad Reeder .30 .75
25 Josh Singer .30 .75
26 Matt Stephenson .30 .75
27 John Swanson .30 .75
28 Bob Motzko CO .02 .10
29 Fred Harbinson ACO .02 .10
30 Eric Rud ACO .02 .10
31 Bryan Demaine TR .02 .10
32 Jeremiah Minkel EQM .02 .10
33 Blizzard MASCOT .02 .10

2003-04 St. Francis Xavier X-Men
COMPLETE SET (30) 5.00 12.00
1 Ryan White .20 .50
2 Ryan Armstrong .20 .50
3 Stuart MacRae .20 .50
4 Wes Jarvis .20 .50
5 Mike Martone .20 .50
6 Bobby Reed .20 .50
7 Blake Robson .20 .50
8 Ben Berthiaume .20 .50
9 Troy Smith .20 .50
10 Mike Smith .20 .50
11 Danny White .20 .50
12 Graham Power .20 .50
13 Patrick Grandmaitre .20 .50
14 Dustin Russell .20 .50
15 Darren MacMillan .20 .50
16 Alan Dwyor .20 .50
17 Colin Circelli .20 .50
18 Dwayne Bateman .20 .50
19 Ryan Walsh .20 .50
20 Omar Ennaffati .20 .50
21 Eric Braff .20 .50
22 Mike Mole .20 .50
23 Shawn Snider .20 .50
24 Chris Brannen .20 .50
25 Dallas Flaman .20 .50
26 Todd Norman .20 .50
27 Danny Flynn CO .04 .10
28 Greg MacDonald ACO .04 .10
29 John Kibyuk ACO .04 .10
30 Kyle MacIsaac ACO .04 .10

2004-05 St. Francis Xavier X-Men
COMPLETE SET (24) 5.00 12.00
1 Ryan Armstrong .20 .50
2 Eric Braff .20 .50
3 Collin Circelli .20 .50
4 Alan Dwyer .20 .50
5 Tyler Dyck .20 .50
6 Omar Ennaffati .20 .50
7 Patrick Grandmaitre .20 .50
8 Wes Jarvis .20 .50
9 Jim Kehoe .20 .50
10 Tyson Kellerman .20 .50
11 Matthew Lynn .20 .50
12 Ryan MacKay .20 .50
13 Stuart MacRae .20 .50
14 Darren McMillan .20 .50
15 Michael Mole .40 1.00
16 Graham Power .20 .50
17 Bobby Reed .20 .50
18 Blake Robson .20 .50
19 Mike Smith .20 .50
20 Shawn Snider .20 .50
21 Niko Tuomi .20 .50
22 Ryan Walsh .20 .50
23 Danny White .20 .50
24 Ryan White .20 .50

2003-04 St. Georges de Beauce Garaga
COMPLETE SET (20) 4.00 10.00
1 Philippe Audet .20 .50
2 Kevin Cloutier .20 .50
3 Philippe Deblois .20 .50
4 Raymond Delarosbil .20 .50
5 Jonathan Delisle .20 .50
6 Carl Fleury .20 .50
7 Francois Garand .20 .50
8 Steve Gosselin .20 .50
9 Jason Groleau .20 .50
10 Jean-Francois Labbe .20 .50
11 Daniel Laflamme .20 .50
12 Jean-Yves Leroux .20 .50
13 Dannick Lessard .20 .50
14 Claude Morin .20 .50
15 Normand Rochefort .20 .50
16 Paul Shantz UER .20 .50
17 Steve Tardif .20 .50
18 Hugo Turcotte .20 .50
19 Mathieu Vachon .20 .50
20 Frederic Vermette .20 .50

2004-05 St. Georges de Beauce Garaga
COMPLETE SET (24) 6.00 15.00
1 Steve Tardif .30 .75
2 Jonathan Forest .30 .75
3 Paul Shantz .30 .75
4 Nicolas Poirier .30 .75
5 Claude Morin .30 .75
6 Raymond Delarosbil .30 .75
7 Martin Fillion .30 .75
8 Eric Bertrand .30 .75
9 David Lessard .30 .75
10 Jonathan Delisle .30 .75
11 Mathieu Vachon .30 .75
12 Tommy Bolduc .30 .75
13 Daniel Laflamme .30 .75
14 Kevin Cloutier .30 .75
15 Jean-Philippe Soucy .40 1.00
16 Mike Bajurny .60 1.50
17 Carl Paradis .30 .75
18 John Murphy .30 .75
19 Hugo Levesque .30 .75
20 Jason Rushton .30 .75
21 Didier Tremblay .30 .75
22 Rejean Dufour .30 .75
23 Brandon Christian .30 .75
24 Randy Copley .30 .75

2014-15 St. Georges Cool 103.5FM
COMPLETE SET (25) 7.50 15.00
1 David Starenky .30 .75
2 Robin Lemay .30 .75
3 Jean-Philippe Pare .30 .75
4 Mike Novosad .30 .75
5 Michel Leveille .30 .75
6 Keven Dupont .30 .75
7 Dany Roussin .30 .75
8 Alex Gagne .30 .75
9 Mikael Bedard .30 .75
10 Pascal Lariviere .30 .75
11 Martin Nolet .30 .75
12 Charles Bety .30 .75
13 Jean-Philipp Paquet .30 .75
14 Jeremy Duchesne .30 .75
15 Michel Robinson .30 .75
16 Tommy Gauthier .30 .75
17 Hubert Morin .30 .75
18 Stephane Goulet .30 .75
19 Jean-Francois St. Laurent .30 .75
20 Maxime Levesque .30 .75
21 Philippe Lauze .30 .75
22 Samuel Grenache .30 .75
23 Hubert Poulin .30 .75
24 Guillaume Parenteau .30 .75
25 Mario Boilard .30 .75

2003-04 St. Jean Mission
COMPLETE SET (28) 6.00 15.00
1 Luc Bilodeau .20 .50
2 Murray Cobb .20 .50
3 Alain Cote .20 .50
4 Greg Davis .20 .50
5 Mario DeBenedictis .20 .50
6 Martin Dicaire .20 .50
7 Bobby Dollas .20 .50
8 Corey Foster .20 .50
9 Link Gaetz .75 2.00
10 Pierre Gendron .20 .50
11 Victor Gervais .20 .50
12 Daniel Guerard .20 .50
13 Hugo Hamelin .20 .50
14 Eric Lachapelle .20 .50
15 Steven Low .20 .50
16 Dominique Maltais .20 .50
17 Eric McIntyre .20 .50
18 Rob Murphy .20 .50
19 Charles Paquette .30 .75
20 Pierre Pelletier .20 .50
21 Jean-Francois Piche .20 .50
22 Guillaume Richard .20 .50
23 Sebastien Roger .20 .50
24 Christian Sbrocca .20 .50
25 Dan Tice .20 .50
26 Ronny Valenti .20 .50
27 Steve Vezina .30 .75
28 Dan Zimmerman .20 .50

2015-16 St. John's IceCaps
COMPLETE SET (28) 8.00 20.00
1 Josiah Didier .30 .75
2 Morgan Ellis .30 .75
3 Dalton Thrower .30 .75
4 Darren Dietz .30 .75
5 Mark Barberio .30 .75
6 Mac Bennett .30 .75
7 Charles Hudson .30 .75
8 Daniel Carr .30 .75
9 Ryan Johnston .30 .75
10 Brett Lernout .30 .75
11 Joel Hanley .30 .75
12 Mark MacMillan .30 .75
13 Nikita Scherbak .30 .75
14 Christian Thomas .30 .75
15 Jacob de la Rose .50 1.25
16 Bud Holloway .30 .75
17 Connor Crisp .30 .75
18 Brandon McNally .30 .75
19 Michael McCarron .60 1.50
20 Eric Neilson .30 .75
21 Sven Andrighetto .40 1.00
22 Tim Bozon .30 .75
23 Zachary Fucale .75 2.00
24 Dustin Tokarski .40 1.00
25 Jeremy Gregoire .30 .75
26 Markus Eisenschmid .30 .75
27 Gabriel Dumont .30 .75
NNO Header Card CL .30 .75

1992-93 St. John's Maple Leafs
COMPLETE SET (25) 4.00 10.00
1 Patrik Augusta .15 .40
2 Drake Berehowsky .20 .50
3 Robert Cimetta .15 .40
4 Marc Crawford CO .20 .50
5 Ted Crowley .15 .40
6 Mike Eastwood .30 .75
7 Todd Hawkins .15 .40
8 Curtis Hunt .15 .40
9 Eric Lacroix .20 .50
10 Guy Lehoux .15 .40
11 Kent Manderville .20 .50
12 Kevin McClelland .15 .40
13 Ken McRae .15 .40
14 Brad Miller .15 .40
15 Yanic Perreault .40 1.00
16 Rudy Poeschek .30 .75
17 Joel Quenneville ACO .08 .25
18 Damian Rhodes .40 1.00
19 Joe Sacco .15 .40
20 Jeff Serowik .15 .40
21 Scott Sharples .15 .40
22 Dave Tomlinson .15 .40
23 Nick Wohlers .15 .40
24 Team Photo .15 .40
25 Buddy (Mascot) .02 .10

1993-94 St. John's Maple Leafs
COMPLETE SET (25) 4.00 10.00
1 Patrick Augusta .15 .40
2 Frank Bialowas .20 .50
3 Buddy (Mascot) .02 .10
4 Rich Chernomaz .15 .40
5 Terry Chitaroni .15 .40
6 Marcel Cousineau .20 .50
7 Marc Crawford CO .20 .50
8 Todd Gillingham .15 .40
9 Chris Govedaris .15 .40
10 Paul Holden .15 .40
11 Curtis Hunt .15 .40
12 Alexei Kudashov .15 .40
13 Eric Lacroix .40 1.00
14 Guy Lehoux .15 .40
15 Matt Mallgrave .15 .40
16 Grant Marshall .20 .50
17 Ken McRae .15 .40
18 Yanic Perreault .30 .75
19 Bruce Racine .20 .50
20 Damian Rhodes .40 1.00
21 Chris Snell .15 .40
22 Dan Stiver .15 .40
23 Andy Sullivan .15 .40
24 Ryan Vandenbussche .20 .50
25 Steffon Walby .15 .40

1994-95 St. John's Maple Leafs
COMPLETE SET (24) 3.60 9.00
1 Patrick Augusta .08 .25
2 Ken Belanger .20 .50
3 Frank Bialowis .40 1.00
4 Rich Chernomaz .08 .25
5 Brandon Convery .08 .25
6 Marcel Cousineau .08 .25
7 Trent Cull .08 .25
8 Nathan Dempsey .20 .50
9 Kelly Fairchild .20 .50
10 Janne Gronvall .08 .25
11 David Harlock .08 .25
12 Darby Hendrickson .20 .50
13 Marc Hussey .08 .25
14 Kenny Jonsson .40 1.00
15 Mark Kolesar .08 .25
16 Alexei Kudashov .08 .25
17 Guy Lehoux .08 .25
18 Guy Leveque .08 .25
19 Matt Martin .08 .25
20 Robb McIntyre .08 .25
21 Bruce Racine .20 .50
22 Ryan Vandenbussche .30 .75
23 Steffon Walby .08 .25
24 Todd Warriner .20 .50

1995-96 St. John's Maple Leafs
COMPLETE SET (25) 4.00 10.00
1 Team Photo .15 .40
2 Ken Belanger .30 .75
3 Rob Butz .15 .40
4 Brandon Convery .20 .50
5 Marcel Cousineau .20 .50
6 Trent Cull .15 .40
7 Nathan Dempsey .15 .40
8 Kelly Fairchild .15 .40
9 Brent Gretzky .20 .50
10 Janne Gronvall .15 .40
11 David Harlock .20 .50
12 Jamie Heward .15 .40
13 Mark Kolesar .15 .40
14 Guy Lehoux .15 .40
15 Kent Manderville .30 .75
16 Kory Mullin .15 .40
17 Jason Saal .20 .50
18 Shayne Toporowski .15 .40
19 Paul Vincent .15 .40
20 Steffon Walby .15 .40
21 Mike Ware .15 .40
22 Todd Warriner .30 .75
23 Tom Watt CO .02 .10
24 Mike Foligno CO .08 .25
25 Buddy Mascot .02 .10

1996-97 St. John's Maple Leafs
COMPLETE SET (25) 4.00 10.00
1 Don Beaupre .30 .75
2 Jared Bednar .15 .40
3 Aaron Brand .20 .50
4 Rich Brown CO .15 .40
5 Buddy MAS .02 .10
6 Greg Bullock .15 .40
7 Rob Butz .15 .40
8 Shawn Carter .15 .40
9 Jason Cipolla .15 .40
10 Brandon Convery .20 .50
11 David Cooper .15 .40
12 John Craighead .30 .75
13 Trent Cull .15 .40
14 Nathan Dempsey .20 .50
15 Mark Deyell .20 .50
16 Jamie Heward .15 .40
17 Mark Hunter CO .15 .40
18 Mark Kolesar .20 .50
19 Guy Lehoux .20 .50
20 Sgt. Randy Mercer .15 .40
21 Jason Saal .30 .75
22 Greg Smyth .15 .40
23 Shayne Toporowski .15 .40
24 Yannick Tremblay .20 .50
25 Brian Wiseman .15 .40

1997-98 St. John's Maple Leafs
COMPLETE SET (25) 4.00 10.00
1 Kevyn Adams .30 .75
2 Lonny Bohonos .20 .50
3 Aaron Brand .15 .40
4 Rich Brown ACO .02 .10
5 Buddy .02 .10
6 Shawn Carter .15 .40
7 David Cooper .15 .40
8 Marcel Cousineau .30 .75
9 Nathan Dempsey .15 .40
10 Mark Deyell .20 .50
11 Todd Gillingham .15 .40
12 Per Gustafsson .15 .40
13 Mike Kennedy .15 .40
14 Francis Larivee .15 .40
15 Al MacAdam CO .02 .10
16 Daniil Markov .30 .75
17 Zdenek Markov .15 .40
18 Clayton Norris .15 .40
19 Warren Norris .15 .40
20 Ryan Pepperall .15 .40
21 Jason Podoll .15 .40
22 D.J. Smith .20 .50
23 Greg Smyth .15 .40
24 Shawn Thornton .15 .40
25 Jeff Ware .15 .40

1999-00 St. John's Maple Leafs
COMPLETE SET (25) 4.00 10.00
1 Kevyn Adams .30 .75
2 Vladimir Antipov .15 .40
3 Syl Apps .15 .40
4 Jason Bonsignore .20 .50
5 Aaron Brand .15 .40
6 Craig Charron .15 .40
7 Nathan Dempsey .30 .75
8 Tyler Harlton .15 .40
9 Justin Hocking .15 .40
10 Bobby House .15 .40
11 Konstantin Kalmikov .20 .50
12 Alan MacAdam CO .08 .25
13 Dennis Maxwell .15 .40
14 David Nemirovsky .20 .50
15 Adam Mair .20 .50
16 Ryan Pepperall .15 .40
17 Marek Posmyk .20 .50
18 Marc Robitaille .15 .40
19 Terry Ryan .20 .50
20 Terran Sandwith .15 .40
21 Darrin Shannon .15 .40
22 D.J. Smith .20 .50
23 Shawn Thornton .15 .40
24 Jimmy Waite .30 .75
25 Dimitri Yakushin .15 .40

2000-01 St. John's Maple Leafs
COMPLETE SET (30) 4.80 12.00
1 Chad Allan .14 .40
2 Syl Apps .14 .40
3 Patrik Augusta .20 .50
4 Buddy The Puffin MASCOT .04 .10
5 Rich Chernomaz .20 .50
6 David Cooper .14 .40
7 Lou Crawford CO .10 .25
8 Nathan Dempsey .30 .75
9 Jeff Farkas .30 .75
10 Mikael Hakanson .14 .40
11 Tyler Harlton .14 .40
12 Bobby House .14 .40
13 Konstantin Kalmikov .30 .75
14 Jacques Lariviere .14 .35
15 Don MacLean .20 .50
16 Adam Mair .20 .50
17 Kevin McClelland CO .10 .25
18 Mike Minard .20 .50
19 Frank Mrazek .14 .35
20 Yanic Perreault .30 .75
21 Alexei Ponikarovsky .30 .75
22 Felix Potvin .40 1.00
23 Alan Rourke .14 .35
24 D.J. Smith .20 .75
25 Chris Snell .14 .35
26 Shawn Thornton .14 .35
27 Michal Travnicek .14 .35
28 Jimmy Waite .20 .50
29 Morgan Warren .14 .40
30 Dmitri Yakushin .14 .35

2001-02 St. John's Maple Leafs
COMPLETE SET (30) 7.20 18.00
1 Russ Adam ACO .04 .10
2 Nikolai Antropov .40 1.00
3 Francois Bouchard .20 .50
4 Luca Cereda .40 1.00
5 Christian Chartier .20 .50
6 Lou Crawford CO .10 .25
7 Nathan Dempsey .30 .75
8 Doug Doull .20 .50
9 Jeff Farkas .40 1.00
10 Paul Healey .20 .50
11 Bobby House .20 .50
12 Jacques Lariviere .20 .50
13 Donald MacLean .20 .50
14 Kevin McClelland ACO .10 .25
15 Craig Mills .20 .50

16 Mike Minard .30 .75
17 Frank Mrazek .20 .50
18 Karel Pilar .40 1.00
19 Alexei Ponikarovsky .40 1.00
20 Alan Rourke .20 .50
21 D.J. Smith .40 1.00
22 Petr Svoboda .20 .50
23 Mikael Tellqvist 1.25 3.00
24 Michal Travnicek .30 .75
25 Morgan Warren .20 .50
26 Marty Wilford .30 .75
27 Bob Wren .30 .75
28 Mile One Stadium .04 .10
29 Buddy the Puffin MASCOT .04 .10
30 All-Star Game PROMO .04 .10

2001-02 St. John's Maple Leafs Police

COMPLETE SET (16) 15.00 30.00
1 Luca Cereda .75 2.00
2 Christian Chartier .75 2.00
3 Nathan Dempsey 1.25 3.00
4 Doug Doull 2.00 5.00
5 Jeff Farkas .75 2.00
6 Paul Healey .75 2.00
7 Bobby House .75 2.00
8 Donald MacLean .75 2.00
9 Craig Mills .75 2.00
10 Mike Minard .75 2.00
11 Alexei Ponikarovsky 1.25 3.00
12 Allan Rourke .75 2.00
13 D.J.Smith 1.25 3.00
14 Petr Svoboda .75 2.00
15 Morgan Warren .75 2.00
16 Marty Wilford .75 2.00

2002-03 St. John's Maple Leafs Aliant

COMPLETE SET (6) 4.00 10.00
1 Doug Doull .75 2.00
2 Aaron Gavey .40 1.00
3 Mikael Tellqvist UER
Misspelled Mikeal 2.00 5.00
4 Brad Boyes .75 2.00
5 Josh Holden .40 1.00
6 Craig Mills .40 1.00

1996-97 St. Louis Vipers RHI

COMPLETE SET (16) 75.00 125.00
1 Frank LaScala 4.00 10.00
2 Russ Parent 4.00 10.00
3 Jeff Beaudin 4.00 10.00
4 Perry Turnbull HCO 2.00 5.00
5 Chris Skoryna 4.00 10.00
6 Chris Rogles 6.00 15.00
7 Kevin Plager 4.00 10.00
8 Wayne Anchikoski 6.00 15.00
9 Vipers Record Holders 4.00 10.00
10 Frank Cirone 4.00 10.00
11 C.J. Yoder 4.00 10.00
12 Victor Viper Mascot 2.00 5.00
13 Series 1 Checklist 2.00 5.00
14 Series 2 Checklist 2.00 5.00
15 Series 1 Header 2.00 5.00
16 Series 2 Header 2.00 5.00

1952-53 St. Lawrence Sales

COMPLETE SET (108) 700.00 1400.00
1 Jacques Plante 175.00 350.00
2 Glen Harmon 5.00 10.00
3 Jimmy Moore 5.00 10.00
4 Gerard Desaulniers 5.00 10.00
5 Les Douglas 5.00 10.00
6 Fred Burchell 6.00 12.00
7 Ed Litzenberger 7.50 15.00
8 Rollie Rousseau 5.00 10.00
9 Roger Leger 5.00 10.00
10 Phil Samis 5.00 10.00
11 Paul Masnick 6.00 12.00
12 Walter Clune 5.00 10.00
13 Louis Denis 5.00 10.00
14 Gerry Plamondon 6.00 12.00
15 Cliff Malone 5.00 10.00
16 Pete Morin 6.00 12.00
17A Jack Schmidt 6.00 12.00
17B Aldo Guidolin 10.00 20.00
18 Paul Leclerc 5.00 10.00
19 Larry Kwong 6.00 12.00
20 Rosario Joanette 5.00 10.00
21 Tom Smelle 5.00 10.00
22 Gordie Haworth 6.00 12.00
23 Bruce Cline 6.00 12.00
24 Andre Corriveau 5.00 10.00
25 Jacques Deslauriers 5.00 10.00
26 Bingo Ernst 5.00 10.00
27 Jacques Chartrand 5.00 10.00
28 Phil Vitale 5.00 10.00
29 Renald Lacroix 5.00 10.00
30 J.P. Bisaillon 5.00 10.00
31 Jack Irvine 5.00 10.00
32 Georges Bougie 5.00 10.00
33 Paul Larivee 5.00 10.00
34 Carl Smelle 5.00 10.00
35 Walter Pawlyschyn 5.00 10.00
36 Jean Marois 5.00 10.00
37 Jack Gelineau 5.00 10.00
38 Danny Nixon 5.00 10.00
39 Jean Beliveau 200.00 400.00
40 Phil Renaud 5.00 10.00
41 Leon Bouchard 5.00 10.00
42 Dennis Smith 5.00 10.00
43 Joe Crozier 7.50 15.00
44 Al Bacari 5.00 10.00
45 Murdo MacKay 6.00 12.00
46 Gordie Hudson 5.00 10.00
47 Claude Robert 5.00 10.00
48 Yogi Kraiger 6.00 12.00
49 Ludger Tremblay 6.00 12.00
50 Pierre Brillant 5.00 10.00
51 Frank Mario 5.00 10.00
52 Copper Leyth 5.00 10.00
53 Herbie Carnegie 20.00 50.00
54 Punch Imlach 20.00 40.00
55 Howard Riopelle 5.00 10.00
56 Ken Laufman 5.00 10.00
57 Jackie Leclair 7.50 15.00
58 Bill Robinson 5.00 10.00
59 George Ford 5.00 10.00
60 Bill Johnson 5.00 10.00
61 Leo Gravelle 5.00 10.00
62 Jack Giesebrecht 5.00 10.00
63 John Arundel 5.00 10.00
64 Vic Gregg 5.00 10.00
65 Bep Guidolin 7.50 15.00
66 Al Kuntz 5.00 10.00
67 Emile Dagenais 5.00 10.00
68 Bill Richardson 5.00 10.00
69 Bob Robertson 5.00 10.00
70 Ray Fredericks 5.00 10.00
71 James O'Flaherty 5.00 10.00
72 Butch Stahan 5.00 10.00
73 Roger Roberge 5.00 10.00
74 Guy Labrie 5.00 10.00
75 Gilles Dube 5.00 10.00
76 Pete Wywrot 5.00 10.00
77 Tod Campeau 6.00 12.00
78 Roger Bessette 5.00 10.00
79 Martial Pruneau 5.00 10.00
80 Nils Tremblay 5.00 10.00
81 Jacques Locas 5.00 10.00
82 Rene Pepin 5.00 10.00
83 Bob Pepin 5.00 10.00
84 Tom McDougall 5.00 10.00
85 Peter Wright 5.00 10.00
86 Ronnie Matthews 5.00 10.00
87 Irene St-Hilaire 5.00 10.00
88 Dewar Thompson 5.00 10.00
89 Bob Dainville 5.00 10.00
90 Marcel Pelletier 5.00 10.00
91 Delphis Franche 5.00 10.00
92 Georges Roy 5.00 10.00
93 Andy McCallum 5.00 10.00
94 Lou Smrke 5.00 10.00
95 J.P. Lamirande 5.00 10.00
96 Normand Dussault 5.00 10.00
97 Stan Smrke 6.00 12.00
98 Jack Bownass 5.00 10.00
99 Billy Arcand 5.00 10.00
100 Lyall Wiseman 5.00 10.00
101 Jack Hamilton 5.00 10.00
102 Bob Leger 5.00 10.00
103 Larry Regan 6.00 12.00
104 Erwin Grosse 5.00 10.00
105 Roger Bedard 5.00 10.00
106 Ted Hodgson 5.00 10.00
107 Dave Gatherum 7.50 15.00

2000-01 St. Michaels Majors

COMPLETE SET (27) 4.80 12.00
1 Team CL .04 .10
2 Team Photo .16 .40
3 Majors Review .10 .25
4 Matt Bacon .16 .40
5 Matt Bannan .16 .40
6 Darryl Bootland .16 .75
7 Chris Boucher .16 .40
8 Tim Brent .30 .75
9 Peter Budaj .60 1.50
10 Dave Cameron CO .10 .25
11 Andy Chiodo .40 2.00
12 Tyler Cook .16 .40
13 Adam Deleeuw .30 .75
14 Matt Ellis .16 .40
15 Steve Farquharson .16 .40
16 Drew Fata .30 .75
17 Michael Gough .16 .40
18 Bob Jones CO .04 .10
19 Kevin Klein .16 1.00
20 Frantisek Lukes .16 .40
21 Lorne Misita .16 .40
22 Lindsay Plunkett .16 .40
23 Mark Popovic .40 1.00
24 T.J. Reynolds .16 .40
25 Ryan Robert .16 .40
26 Mike Sellan .16 .40
27 Ryan Walsh .16 .40

2001-02 St. Michaels Majors

COMPLETE SET (28) 6.00 15.00
1 Logo Checklist .04 .10
2 Team Photo .04 .10
3 Geoff Patton .20 .50
4 Scott Heffernan .20 .50
5 Tyson Gimblett .20 .50
6 Steven Rawski .20 .50
7 Kevin Klein .30 .75
8 Mark Popovic .30 .75
9 Tim Brent .40 1.00
10 Drew Fata .20 .50
11 Jordan Freeland .20 .50
12 Jerrod Smith .20 .50
13 Michael Gouch .20 .50
14 Kyle Spurr .20 .50
15 Ryan Rorabeck .20 .50
16 Matt Bacon .20 .50
17 Frantisek Lukes .20 .50
18 Matt Ellis .20 .50
19 Darryl Boyce .20 .50
20 Daryl Knowles .20 .50
21 Matt Seymour .20 .50
22 Joe Guenther .20 .50
23 Darryl Bootland .30 .75
24 Peter Budaj .60 1.50
25 Andy Chiodo .75 2.00
26 Dave Cameron .20 .50
27 Bob Jones .20 .50
28 Mascot .04 .10

2002-03 St. Michaels Majors

COMPLETE SET (28) 5.00 12.00
1 Justin Peters .30 .75
2 Ted Perry .15 .40
3 Martin Karafiat .15 .40
4 Tyson Gimblett .15 .40
5 Steven Rawski .15 .40
6 Kevin Klein .40 1.00
7 Nathan McIver .15 .40
8 Tim Brent .40 1.00
9 Drew Fata .40 1.00
10 Scott Lehman .15 .40
11 Scott Horvath .15 .40
12 Chris Rebernik .15 .40
13 Kyle Spurr .15 .40
14 Ryan Rorabeck .15 .40
15 Matt Bacon .15 .40
16 Frantisek Lukes .15 .40
17 Connor Cameron .15 .40
18 Darryl Boyce .15 .40
19 Alan Nolan .15 .40
20 Matt Seymour .15 .40
21 Cory Vitarelli .15 .40
22 Darryl Knowles .15 .40
23 Sal Peralta .15 .40
24 Andy Chiodo .75 2.00
25 Dave Cameron CO .04 .10
26 Bob Jones CO .04 .10
27 Mascot .04 .10
28 Logo/CL .04 .10

2003-04 St. Michael's Majors

COMPLETE SET (27) 5.00 12.00
1 Justin Peters .30 .75
2 Ted Perry .20 .50
3 Jamie Vanderveeken .20 .50
4 Ryan Wilson .20 .50
5 Nathan McIver .20 .50
6 Tim Brent .30 .75
7 Ryan Rorabeck .20 .50
8 Chris Cunningham .20 .50
9 Scott Lehman .20 .50
10 Cal Clutterbuck .40 1.00
11 Colin Power .30 .75
12 Tyler Haskins .20 .50
13 Brent Small .20 .50
14 Ian Maracle .20 .50
15 Conner Cameron .20 .50
16 Richard Kelly .20 .50
17 Thomas Waugh .20 .50
18 Darryl Boyce .20 .50
19 Joe Rand .20 .50
20 Cory Vitarelli .20 .50
21 Dustin Vanballegooie .20 .50
22 Sal Peralta .20 .50
23 Michael Ouzas .30 .75
24 Dave Cameron CO .04 .10
25 Bob Jones ACO .04 .10
26 Mikey MASCOT .04 .10
27 Checklist .04 .10

2004-05 St. Michael's Majors

COMPLETE SET (24) 5.00 12.00
1 Justin Peters .30 .75
2 Steve Whitely .20 .50
3 Jamie Vanderveeken .20 .50
4 Ryan Wilson .20 .50
5 Dale Good .20 .50
6 Nathan McIver .20 .50
7 Matt Halischuk .20 .50
8 John Adamsa .20 .50
9 Chris Cunningham .20 .50
10 Scott Lehman .20 .50
11 Cal Clutterbuck .30 .75
12 Colin Power .20 .50
13 Tyler Haskins .20 .50
14 Cassidy Preston .20 .50
15 Justin DiBenedetto .20 .50
16 Alexei Ivanov .20 .50
17 Scott Levigne .20 .50
18 Travis Elder .20 .50
19 Darryl Boyce .20 .50
20 Joe Rand .20 .50
21 Cory Vitarelli .20 .50
22 Jaroslav Mrazek .20 .50
23 Wayne Savage .20 .50
24 Checklist .04 .10

2005-06 Stockton Thunder

COMPLETE SET (25) 6.00 15.00
1 Likit Andersson .30 .75
2 Casey Bartzen .30 .75
3 Landon Bathe .30 .75
4 Derek Campbell .30 .75
5 Aaron Foster .30 .75
6 Nick Greenough .30 .75
7 Joel Irwin .30 .75
8 Tony Johnson .30 .75
9 Jason Kostadine .30 .75
10 Mike Lalonde .30 .75
11 Aaron MacInnis .30 .75
12 Nathan Martz .30 .75
13 Dave McCulloch .30 .75
14 Jason Metcalfe .30 .75
15 Jake Moreland .30 .75
16 Geno Parrish .30 .75
17 Steve Slonina .30 .75
18 Dean Stork .30 .75
19 Jeff Weber .30 .75
20 Maris Ziedins .30 .75
21 Opening Night .10
22 Chris Cichocki HC .02 .10
23 Stockton Arena .02 .10
24 Thor MASCOT .02 .10
NNO Stockton Thunder CL .02 .10

2006-07 Stockton Thunder

COMPLETE SET (25) 15.00 30.00
1 Jason Beckett .75 2.00
2 Devan Dubnyk .75 2.00
3 Stephane Goulet .40 1.00
4 Jeff Lang .40 1.00
5 Fans Tribute Card .02 .10
6 Beau Geisler .40 1.00
7 Mike Lalonde .40 1.00
8 Tim Sestito .40 1.00
9 Tyler Spurgeon .40 1.00
10 Thor MASCOT .02 .10
16 Tim Verbeek .75 2.00
17 Eric Main .40 1.00
18 Bryan Young .40 1.00
19 Jim Dahl .40 1.00
20 Adam Huxley .40 1.00
11a Troy Bodie .40 1.00
11b Stephen Slonina .40 1.00
12a Cam Ellsworth .40 1.00
12b Liam Reddox .40 1.00
13a Brendon Hodge .40 1.00
13b Mark Adamek .40 1.00
14a Nathan Martz .40 1.00
14b Frank Rediker .40 1.00
15a Chris Cichoki CO .40 1.00
15b Tim O'Connell .02 .10

2014-15 Stockton Thunder

COMPLETE SET (15) 4.00 10.00
1 Ryan Constant .30 .75
2 Ryan Hayes .30 .75
3 James Henry .30 .75
4 Garet Hunt .30 .75
5 Loic Leduc .30 .75
6 Jack MacLellan .30 .75
7 Tyler Maxwell .30 .75
8 Michael Pereira .30 .75
9 Shane Owen .30 .75
10 Adam Phillips .30 .75
11 Peter Sivak .30 .75
12 Brad Stebner .30 .75
13 Lukas Sutter .30 .75
14 Shane Owen .30 .75
15 Garet Hunt .30 .75

1962-63 Sudbury Wolves

COMPLETE SET (22) 40.00 100.00
1 Paul Andrea 2.50 5.00
2 Norm Armstrong 1.50 3.00
3 Ed Babiuk 2.00 5.00
4 Hub Beaudry ANN .75 1.50
5 Vern Buffey REF 1.50 3.00
6 Murph Chamberlain CO 1.50 3.00
7 Gerry Cheevers UER 20.00 50.00
8 Wally Chevrier 1.50 3.00
9 Marc Dufour 2.00 4.00
10 Edgar Ehrenverth 1.50 3.00
11 Bill Friday REF 2.50 5.00
12 Jim Johnson 1.50 3.00
13 Chico Kozurok TR .75 1.50
14 Gord Labossiere 2.00 4.00
15 Dunc McCallum 4.00 8.00
16 Dave McComb 1.50 3.00
17 Hugh McLean REF 1.50 3.00
18 Mike McMahon 1.50 3.00
19 Dave Richardson 1.50 3.00
20 Joe Spence ANN .75 1.50
21 Ted Taylor 1.50 3.00
22 Bob Woytowich 4.00 8.00

1984-85 Sudbury Wolves

COMPLETE SET (16) 6.00 15.00
1 Andy Spruce CO .20 .50
2 Sean Evoy .60 1.50
3 Mario Martini .40 1.00
4 Brent Daugherty .40 1.00
5 Mario Chitaroni .40 1.00
6 Dan Chiasson .40 1.00
7 Jeff Brown .75 2.00
8 Todd Sepkowski .40 1.00
9 Brad Belland .40 1.00
10 Glenn Greenough .40 1.00
11 John Landry .40 1.00
12 Max Middendorf .40 1.00
13 David Moylan .40 1.00
14 Jamie Nadjiwan .40 1.00
15 Warren Rychel .75 2.00
16 Ed Smith .40 1.00

1985-86 Sudbury Wolves

COMPLETE SET (26) 4.80 12.00
1 Sudbury Police Crest .10 .25
2 Sponsor Card .10 .25
3 Logo Checklist .20 .50
4 R. Zanibbi
Chief of Police .02 .10
5 Wayne Maxner CO .20 .50
6 Sean Evoy .20 .50
7 Todd Lalonde .20 .50
8 Costa Papista .20 .50
9 Robin Rubic .20 .50
10 Dave Moylan .20 .50
11 Brent Daugherty .20 .50
12 Glenn Greenough .20 .50
13 Mario Chitaroni .30 .75
14 Ken McRae .30 .75
15 Mike Hudson .40 1.00
16 Andy Paquette .20 .50
17 Ed Lemaire .20 .50
18 Mark Turner .20 .50
19 Craig Duncanson .20 .50
20 Jeff Brown .40 1.00
21 Team Photo .40 1.00
22 Max Middendorf .20 .50
23 Keith Van Rooyen .20 .50
24 Brad Walcot .20 .50
25 Rob Wilson .20 .50
26 Bill White .20 .50

1986-87 Sudbury Wolves

COMPLETE SET (33) 4.80 12.00
1 Ted Mielczarek .30 .75
2 Todd Lalonde .20 .50
3 Costa Papista .20 .50
4 Justin Corbeil .20 .50
5 Dave Moylan .20 .50
6 Brent Daugherty .20 .50
8 Mario Chitaroni .30 .75
9 Jim Way .20 .50
10 Dean Jalbert .20 .50
11 Joe Dragon .20 .50
12 Ken McRae .20 .50
14 Steve Hedington .20 .50
15 Mike Hudson .30 .75
16 Pierre Gagnon .20 .50
17 Peter Hughes .20 .50
18 Mark Turner .20 .50
19 Sudbury Police Logo .08 .25
20 Wayne Doucet .20 .50
21 Paul Dipietro .25 .60
22 Max Middendorf .30 .75
23 Phil Paquette .20 .50
25 Rob Wilson .20 .50
26 Checklist .08 .25
27 Chief of Police .08 .25
28 Claude D'Amour .20 .50
29 Guy Blanchard .20 .50
30 Joe Desrosiers .20 .50
31 Jake Disschops .20 .50
33 Bill White .30 .75
34 Anders Hogberg .20 .50

1987-88 Sudbury Wolves

COMPLETE SET (26) 4.00 10.00
1 Checklist Card .08 .25
2 Ted Mielczarek .30 .75
3 Dan Gatenby .20 .50
4 Todd Lalonde .20 .50
5 Justin Corbeil .20 .50
6 Jordan Fois .20 .50
7 Rodney Lapointe .20 .50
8 Dave Akey .20 .50
9 Jim Smith .20 .50
10 Fred Pennell .20 .50
11 Joey Simon .20 .50
12 Luciano Fagioli .20 .50
13 Robb Graham .20 .50
14 John Uniac .20 .50
15 Dave Carrie .20 .50
16 Pierre Gagnon .20 .50
17 Peter Hughes .20 .50
18 Scott McCullough .20 .50
19 Dean Guitard .20 .50
20 Pat Holley .20 .50
21 Chad Badaway .20 .50
22 Paul DiPietro .20 .50
23 Derek Thompson .20 .50
24 Scott Luce .20 .50
25 Rob Wilson .20 .50
26 R. Zanibbi
Chief of Police .02 .10

1988-89 Sudbury Wolves

COMPLETE SET (26) 4.00 10.00
1 Checklist .08 .25
2 David Goverde .30 .75
3 Ted Mielczarek .30 .75
4 Adam Bennett .20 .50
5 Kevin Grant .20 .50
6 Jordan Fois .20 .50
7 Sean O'Donnell .30 .75
8 Kevin Meisner .20 .50
9 Jim Smith .20 .50
10 Red Pennell .20 .50
11 Tyler Pella .20 .50
12 Dean Pella .20 .50
13 Darren Bell .20 .50
14 Derek Thompson .20 .50
15 Terry Chitaroni .20 .50
16 Sean Stansfield .20 .50
17 Alastair Still .20 .50
18 Jim Sonmez .20 .50
19 Shannon Bolton .20 .50
20 Andy Paquette .20 .50
21 Mark Turner .20 .50
22 Paul DiPietro .20 .50
23 Robert Knesaurek .20 .50
24 Todd Lalonde .20 .50
25 Scott Herniman .20 .50
26 R. Zanibbi
Chief of Police .08 .25

1989-90 Sudbury Wolves

COMPLETE SET (25) 4.80 12.00
1 Checklist NNO .08 .25
2 Alastair Still .20 .50
3 Bill Kovacs .20 .50
4 Darren Bell .20 .50
5 Scott Mahoney .20 .50
6 Glen Murray .75 2.00
7 Alain Laforge .20 .50
8 Jamie Matthews .20 .50
9 Jon Boeve .30 .75
10 Adam Bennett .20 .50
11 Derek Etches .20 .50
12 Marcus Middleton .20 .50
13 Jim Sonmez .20 .50
14 Leonard MacDonald .20 .50
15 Paul DiPietro .30 .75
16 Neil Ethier .20 .50
17 Sean O'Donnell .20 .50
18 Andy MacVicar .20 .50
19 David Goverde .30 .75
20 Jason Young .20 .50
21 Wade Bartley .20 .50
22 Barry Young .20 .50
23 R. Zanibbi
Chief of Police .08 .25
24 Terry Chitaroni .20 .50
25 Rob Knesaurek .20 .50

1990-91 Sudbury Wolves

COMPLETE SET (25) 4.80 12.00
1 Darryl Paquette .25 .60
2 Adam Bennett .20 .50
3 Barry Young .20 .50
4 Jon Boeve .20 .50
5 Kyle Blacklock .20 .50
6 Sean O'Donnell .25 .60
7 Dan Ryder .25 .60
8 Wade Bartley .20 .50
9 Jamie Matthews .20 .50
10 Rod Hinks .20 .50
11 Derek Etches .20 .50
12 Brandon Convery .20 .50
13 Glen Murray .75 2.00
14 Bill Kovacs .20 .50
15 Terry Chitaroni .20 .50
16 Jason Young .20 .50
17 Alastair Still .20 .50
18 Shawn Rivers .20 .50
19 Alain Laforge .20 .50
20 J.D. Eaton .20 .50
21 Mike Peca .75 2.00
22 Howler (Mascot) .02 .10
23 Mike Yeo .20 .50
24 L'il Rookie
Checklist .02 .10
25 R. Zanibbi
Chief of Police .02 .10

1991-92 Sudbury Wolves

COMPLETE SET (25) 4.80 12.00
1 R. Zanibbi
Chief of Police .02 .10
2 Howler (Mascot) .02 .10
3 Team Photo .20 .50
4 Kyle Blacklock .15 .40
5 Sean Gagnon .20 .50
6 Bernie John .15 .40
7 Bob MacIsaac .15 .40
8 Jamie Rivers .20 .50
9 Shawn Rivers .15 .40
10 Joel Sandie .15 .40
11 Barry Young .15 .40
12 George Dourian .15 .40
13 Dan Ryder .30 .75
14 Derek Armstrong .15 .40
15 Terry Chitaroni .15 .40
16 Brandon Convery .20 .50
17 Tim Favot .15 .40
18 Rod Hinks .15 .40
19 Jamie Matthews .20 .50
20 Barrie Moore .20 .50
21 Glen Murray .40 1.00
22 Michael Peca .75 2.00
23 Michael Yeo .15 .40
24 Jason Young .15 .40
25 Jason Zohil .15 .40

1992-93 Sudbury Wolves

COMPLETE SET (27) 4.80 12.00
1 Howler and Lil Rookie .02 .10
2 Sudbury Regional Police .02 .10
3 Bob MacIsaac .20 .50
4 Joel Sandie .20 .50
5 Rory Fitzpatrick .20 .50
6 Mike Wilson .20 .50
7 Shawn Frappier .20 .50
8 Bernie John .20 .50
9 Jamie Rivers .30 .75
10 Jamie Matthews .20 .50
11 Zdenek Nedved .20 .50
12 Ryan Shanahan .20 .50
13 Corey Crane .20 .50
14 Matt Kiereck .20 .50
15 Rick Bodkin .20 .50
16 Derek Armstrong .20 .50
17 Barrie Moore .20 .50
18 Rod Hinks .20 .50
19 Kayle Short .20 .50
20 Michael Yeo .20 .50
21 Gary Coupal .20 .50
22 Dennis Maxwell .20 .50
23 Steve Potvin .20 .50
24 Joel Poirier .20 .50
25 Greg Dreveny .20 .50
26 Mark Gowan .30 .75
27 Steve Staios .25 .60

1993-94 Sudbury Wolves

COMPLETE SET (25) 4.00 10.00
1 Shawn Silver .20 .50
2 Jeff Melnechuk .15 .40
3 Jay McKee .30 .75
4 Chris McMurtry .15 .40
5 Rory Fitzpatrick .20 .50
6 Mike Wilson .20 .50
7 Shawn Frappier .15 .40
8 Jamie Rivers .30 .75
9 Zdenek Nedved .20 .50
10 Ryan Shanahan .20 .50
11 Sean Venedam .20 .50
12 Andrew Dale .15 .40
13 Mark Giannetti .15 .40
14 Rick Bodkin .20 .50
15 Barrie Moore .20 .50
16 Jamie Matthews .20 .50
17 Gary Coupal .15 .40
18 Ilya Lysenko .15 .40
19 Simon Sherry .15 .40
20 Steve Potvin .15 .40
21 Joel Poirier .20 .50
22 Mike Yeo .15 .40
23 Bob MacIsaac .15 .40
24 Paul DiPietro .20 .50
NNO Slapshot Ad Card .02 .10

1993-94 Sudbury Wolves Police

COMPLETE SET (26) 4.00 10.00
1 Chief of Police .07 .20
2 The Howler .07 .20
3 Jay McKee .30 .75
4 Chris McMurtry .15 .40
5 Rory Fitzpatrick .20 .50
6 Mike Wilson .20 .50
7 Shawn Frappier .15 .40
8 Jamie Rivers .30 .75
9 Jamie Matthews .20 .50
10 Zdenek Nedved .20 .50
11 Ryan Shanahan .20 .50
12 Andrew Dale .15 .40
13 Mark Giannetti .15 .40
14 Rick Bodkin .20 .50
15 Barrie Moore .20 .50
16 Gary Coupal .15 .40
17 Ilya Lysenko .15 .40
18 Simon Sherry .15 .40
19 Steve Potvin .15 .40
20 Joel Poirier .20 .50
21 Shawn Silver .20 .50
22 Micheal Yeo .15 .40
23 Jeff Melnechuk .15 .40
24 Sean Venedam .20 .50
25 Bob Macisaac .15 .40
26 Sudbury Police .07 .20

1994-95 Sudbury Wolves

COMPLETE SET (26) 4.00 10.00
1 Checklist .02 .10
2 Dave MacDonald .15 .40
3 Rory Fitzpatrick .15 .40
4 Mike Wilson .15 .40
5 Neal Martin .15 .40
6 Shawn Frappier .15 .40
7 Jamie Rivers .20 .50
8 Zdenek Nedved .15 .40
9 Ryan Shanahan .15 .40
10 Sean Venedam .20 .50
11 Andrew Dale .15 .40
12 Rick Bodkin .15 .40
13 Luc Gagne .15 .40
14 Barrie Moore .15 .40
15 Richard Rochefort .15 .40
16 Krystof Secemski .15 .40
17 Jason Bonsignore .15 .40
18 Liam MacEachern .15 .40
19 Simon Sherry .15 .40
20 Ethan Moreau .30 .75
21 Matt Mullin .20 .50
22 Aaron Starnyski .15 .40
23 Ron Newhook .30 .75
24 Glenn Merkosky CO/GM/To .02 .10
25 Dan Lebold TR/Jason All .02 .10
NNO Ad Card .02 .10

1994-95 Sudbury Wolves Police

COMPLETE SET (27) 4.80 12.00
1 Chief of Police .02 .10
2 The Howler .02 .10
3 Rick Bodkin .15 .40
4 Gary Coupal .15 .40
5 Andrew Dale .15 .40
6 Luc Gagne .15 .40
7 Chester Gallant .02 .10
8 Kiley Hill .15 .40
9 Liam MacEachern .15 .40
10 Barrie Moore .15 .40
11 Zdenek Nedved .20 .50
12 Ron Newhook .40 1.00
13 Richard Rochefort .15 .40
14 Krysztof Secemski .15 .40
15 Ryan Shanahan .15 .40
16 Simon Sherry .15 .40
17 Sean Venedam .40 1.00
18 Rory Fitzpatrick .15 .40
19 Shawn Frappier .15 .40
20 Gregg Lalonde .15 .40
21 Neal Martin .15 .40
22 Jay McKee .40 1.00
23 Jamie Rivers .20 .50
24 Mike Wilson .20 .50
25 Dave Macdonald .15 .40
26 Matt Mullin .30 .75
27 Steve Valiquette .40 1.00

1995-96 Sudbury Wolves

COMPLETE SET (25) 4.00 10.00
1 Sean Venedam .20 .50
2 Brad Domonsky .20 .50
3 Joe Lombardo .15 .40
4 Tyson Flinn .15 .40
5 Luc Gagne .15 .40
6 Ryan Shanahan .15 .40
7 Simon Sherry .15 .40
8 Kevin Hansen .15 .40
9 Gregg Lalonde .15 .40
10 Liam MacEachern .15 .40
11 Jeremy Adduono .20 .50
12 Ron Newhook .30 .75
13 Noel Burkitt .15 .40
14 Neal Martin .15 .40
15 Tim Swartz .15 .40
16 Rob Butler .15 .40
17 Darryl Moxam .15 .40
18 Steve Valiquette .30 .75
19 Ryan Sly .15 .40
20 Dave MacDonald .20 .50
21 Andrew Dale .15 .40
22 Belanger's All-Star Team .02 .10
23 Four Star Sports .02 .10
24 Richard Rochefort .15 .40
25 Title Card .02 .10

1995-96 Sudbury Wolves Police

COMPLETE SET (24) 4.00 10.00
1 Chief Alex McCauley .02 .10
2 The Howler
Mascot .02 .10
3 Jeremy Adduono .20 .50
4 Noel Burkitt .15 .40
5 Rob Butler .15 .40
6 Andrew Dale .15 .40
7 Brad Domonsky .20 .50
8 Tyson Flinn .15 .40
9 Luc Gagne .15 .40
10 Kevin Hansen .15 .40
11 Gregg Lalonde .15 .40
12 Joe Lombardo .15 .40
13 Dave MacDonald .20 .50
14 Liam MacEachern .15 .40
15 Neal Martin .15 .40
16 Darryl Moxam .15 .40
17 Ron Newhook .30 .75
18 Richard Rochefort .15 .40
19 Ryan Shanahan .15 .40
20 Simon Sherry .15 .40
21 Ryan Sly .15 .40
22 Shawn Sobush .15 .40
23 Stephen Valiquette .30 .75
24 Sean Venedam .20 .50

1996-97 Sudbury Wolves

COMPLETE SET (27) 4.80 12.00
1 Title card .08 .25
2 Jeremy Adduono .20 .50
3 Louie Blackbird .15 .40
4 Tom Brown .20 .50
5 Peter Campbell .15 .40
6 Brad Domonsky .15 .40
7 Jason Gaggi .20 .50
8 Luc Gagne .15 .40
9 Kevin Hansen .15 .40
10 Jason Hurlbut .15 .40
11 Konstantin Kalmikov .20 .50
12 Robin LaCour .15 .40
13 Paul Mara .40 1.00
14 Norm Milley .60 1.50
15 Gerald Moriarty .15 .40
16 Scott Page .15 .40
17 Steve Reid .15 .40
18 Richard Rochefort .15 .40
19 Brian Scott .15 .40
20 Chris Shanahan .15 .40
21 Ryan Sly .15 .40
22 Jonas Soling .15 .40
23 Steve Valiquette .60 1.50
24 Sean Venedam .20 .50
25 Great Canadian Card Co. .02 .10
26 LaSalle Court Plaza .02 .10
27 Derek Chartrand .08 .25

1996-97 Sudbury Wolves Police

COMPLETE SET (26) 4.80 12.00
1 Chief Alex McCauley .02 .10
2 The Howler MASCOT .02 .10
3 Sudbury Wolves 25th .02 .10
4 Jeremy Adduono .20 .50
5 Louie Blackbird .15 .40
6 Tom Brown .20 .50
7 Peter Campbell .15 .40
8 Brad Domonsky .15 .40
9 Tyson Flinn .15 .40
10 Jason Gaggi .15 .40

11 Luc Gagne .15 .40
12 Kevin Hansen .15 .40
13 Konstantin Kalmikov .20 .50
14 Robin Lacour .15 .40
15 Joe Lombardo .15 .40
16 Paul Mara .40 1.00
17 Norm Milley .60 1.50
18 Scott Page .15 .40
19 Richard Rochefort .15 .40
20 Brian Scott .15 .40
21 Chris Shanahan .15 .40
22 Ryan Sly .15 .40
23 Jonas Soling .15 .40
24 Tim Swartz .15 .40
25 Steve Valiquette .60 1.50
26 Sean Venedam .15 .40

1997-98 Sudbury Wolves Police

COMPLETE SET (25) 8.00 20.00
1 Chief of Police .02 .10
2 Jeremy Adduono .15 .40
3 Ryan Barnes .15 .40
4 Peter Campbell .15 .40
5 Konstantin Kalmikov .20 .50
6 Tom Watt .15 .40
7 Norm Milley .60 1.50
8 Scott Page .15 .40
9 Jonas Soling .15 .40
10 Mike Fisher .75 2.00
11 Taylor Pyatt .40 1.00
12 Derek MacKenzie .40 1.00
13 Nevin Patterson .15 .40
14 Jason Sands .15 .40
15 Colin Scotland .15 .40
16 Paul Mara .40 1.00
17 David Cornacchia .15 .40
18 Ryan McKie .15 .40
19 Michael Tilson .15 .40
20 Brad Morgan .15 .40
21 Matthew Hodges .15 .40
22 Brad Simms .15 .40
23 Steve Valiquette .60 1.50
24 Andrew Raycroft 1.50 4.00
25 The Howler .02 .10

1998-99 Sudbury Wolves

COMPLETE SET (25) 7.20 18.00
1 Alex McCauley POLICE .02 .10
2 Ken MacKenzie CO .02 .10
3 Alexei Salashchenko .20 .50
4 Kevin Beaumont .20 .50
5 Norm Milley .40 1.00
6 Derek MacKenzie .40 1.00
7 Reg Higgs CO .02 .10
8 Matt Barnhardt .20 .50
9 Mike Fisher .60 1.50
10 Tom Kotsopoulos .40 1.00
11 Marc Long .20 .50
12 Kyle Dafoe .20 .50
13 Jason Jaspers .40 1.00
14 Glenn Crawford .20 .50
15 Ryan McKie .20 .50
16 Corey Sabourin .20 .50
17 Kip Brennan .75 2.00
18 Serge Dube .20 .50
19 Brad Morgan .20 .50
20 Brian McGrattan .20 .50
21 Taylor Pyatt .40 1.00
22 Abe Herbst .20 .50
23 Kevin Mota .20 .50
24 Mark Aggio .20 .50
25 Andrew Raycroft 1.25 3.00

1999-00 Sudbury Wolves

COMPLETE SET (26) 4.80 12.00
1 Chief Alex McCauley .02 .10
2 Bert Templeton CO .08 .25
3 Darren Keily ACO .02 .10
4 Corey Sabourin .15 .40
5 Kyle Dafoe .15 .40
6 Abe Herbst .15 .40
7 Dennis Wideman .15 .40
8 Kevin Mota .15 .40
9 Norm Milley .40 1.00
10 Taylor Pyatt .40 1.00
11 Mike Fisher .60 1.50
12 Alexei Semenov .40 1.00
13 Alexei Salashcenko .15 .40
14 Derek MacKenzie .40 1.00
15 Steve Ellis .15 .40
16 Warren Hefford .15 .40
17 Jason Jaspers .40 1.00
18 Brian Mcgrattan .15 .40
19 Drew Kivell .15 .40
20B Tom Kotsopoulos .40 1.00
21 Brad Morgan .15 .40
22 Scott Smith .15 .40
23 R.A. Mobile .02 .10
24 Mike Vaillancourt .15 .40
25 Mike Gorman .15 .40
26 Miguel Beaudry .15 .40

2000-01 Sudbury Wolves

COMPLETE SET (26) 8.00 20.00
1 Chief Alex McCauley .04 .10
2 Bert Templeton CO .20 .50
3 Darren Keily CO .10 .25
4 T.J. Warkus .30 .75
5 Dave Csumrik .30 .75
6 Jason Hicks .30 .75
7 Wally Prawdzik .30 .75
8 Dennis Wideman .30 .75
9 Mike Vaillancourt .30 .75
10 Troy Duncan .30 .75
11 Ladislav Reznicek .30 .75
12 Alexei Semenov .60 1.50
13 Chad Starling .30 .75
14 Nathan Harrington .30 .75
15 Derek MacKenzie .40 1.00
16 Jerry Connell .30 .75
17 Steve Ellis .30 .75
18 Adam Keefe .30 .75
19 Jason Jaspers .40 1.00
20 Jason Bone .30 .75
21 Drew Kivell .30 .75
22 Tom Kotsopoulos .40 1.00
23 Fedor Fedorov .60 1.50
24 Mike Smith .30 .75
25 Miguel Beaudry .30 .75
26 Howler MASCOT .04 .10

2001-02 Sudbury Wolves

COMPLETE SET (30) 6.00 15.00
1 Shandor Alphonso .25 .60
2 Trevor Blanchard .25 .60
3 Travis Chapman .25 .60
4 Bob Chaumont .25 .60
5 Jerry Connell .25 .60
6 Ryan Hastings .25 .60
7 Jim Kehoe .25 .60
8 Darren Keily ACO .04 .10
9 Josh Legge .25 .60
10 Tyler Leggo .25 .60
11 Andrei Mikhnov .60 1.50
12 Dene Poulin .25 .60
13 Jean-Francois Seguin .25 .60
14 Jeff Shaw .25 .60
15 Rob Shilton .25 .60
16 Sam Skwarchuk .25 .60
17 Mike Smith .40 1.00
18 Shawn Snider .25 .60
19 Dan Speer .25 .60
20 Zach Stortini .25 .60
21 Bert Templeton CO .20 .50
22 Brody Todd .25 .60
23 Joel Whitmarsh .40 1.00
24 John Winstanley .25 .60
25 Sudbury Wolves Card .10 .25
26 Wolves Season Line-Up .10 .25
27 Randy Carlyle No. Retired .20 .50
28 Sudbury Carpetland .04 .10
29 Sudbury City Centre .04 .10
30 Sudbury King Sportswear .04 .10

2001-02 Sudbury Wolves Police

COMPLETE SET (26) 6.00 15.00
1 Chief Alex McCauley .04 .10
2 Bert Templeton CO .04 .10
3 Darren Keily ACO .04 .10
4 Brody Todd .30 .75
5 Travis Chapman .30 .75
6 Jim Kehoe .30 .75
7 Josh Legge .30 .75
8 J.F. Seguin .30 .75
9 Andrei Mikhnov .40 1.00
10 John Winstanley .30 .75
11 Shawn Snider .30 .75
12 Jeff Shaw .30 .75
13 Bobby Chaumont .30 .75
14 Rob Shilton .30 .75
15 Tyler Leggo .30 .75
16 Shandor Alphonso .30 .75
17 Jerry Connell .30 .75
18 Zack Stortini .30 .75
19 Dan Speer .30 .75
20 Trevor Blanchard .30 .75
21 Sam Skwarchuk .30 .75
22 Dene Poulin .30 .75
23 Ryan Hastings .30 .75
24 Mike Smith .40 1.00
25 Joel Whitmarsh .40 1.00
26 Howler MASCOT .04 .10

2003-04 Sudbury Wolves

COMPLETE SET (25) 6.00 15.00
1 Header Card .04 .10
2 Shandor Alphonso .25 .60
3 Kevin Beech .40 1.00
4 Stefan Blaho .25 .60
5 Bobby Chaumont .25 .60
6 Jonathan D'Aversa .25 .60
7 Luke Dubbin .25 .60
8 Alexander Eaton .30 .75
9 Patrick Ehelechner .60 1.50
10 Chanse Fitzpatrick .25 .60
11 Ryan Hastings .25 .60
12 Kyle Lamb .25 .60
13 Sean Langdon .25 .60
14 Eric Larochelle .25 .60
15 Matt Maccarone .25 .60
16 Rafal Martynowski .25 .60
17 Adam McQuaid .25 .60
18 Mike Mills .25 .60
19 Dene Poulin .25 .60
20 Jordan Prevost .25 .60
21 Chris Robertson .25 .60
22 Marc Staal .75 2.00
23 Sean Stefanski .25 .60
24 Zach Stortini .25 .60
25 Mike Foligno HCO .10 .25

2004-05 Sudbury Wolves

COMPLETE SET (26) 8.00 20.00
1 Luke Dubbin .30 .75
2 Bobby Chaumont .40 1.00
3 Tomas Sample .30 .75
4 Marc Staal .75 2.00
5 Nick Foligno .75 2.00
6 Kevin Beech .30 .75
7 Zach Stortini .30 .75
8 Stefan Blaho .30 .75
9 Devin Didiomete .30 .75
10 Kyle Musselman .30 .75
11 Patrick Ehelechner .60 1.50
12 Alexander Eaton .30 .75
13 Stephen Miller .30 .75
14 Ryan Hastings .30 .75
15 Adam McQuaid .30 .75
16 Ryan McDonough .30 .75
17 Benoit Pouliot 1.25 3.00
18 Mike Mills .30 .75
19 Jonathan D'Aversa .30 .75
20 Rafal Martynowski .30 .75
21 Troy Murray .30 .75
22 Kevin Baker .30 .75
23 Mike Foligno CO .04 .10
24 Bob Jones ACO .04 .10
25 Bryan Verrault ACO .04 .10
26 Howler MASCOT .04 .10

2005-06 Sudbury Wolves

COMPLETE SET (26) 8.00 15.00
1 Marc Staal .60 1.50
2 Kevin Beech .20 .50
3 Chris Abbey .20 .50
4 Ryan Hastings .20 .50
5 Adam McQuaid .20 .50
6 Troy Murray .20 .50
7 Jonathan D'Aversa .20 .50
8 Ryan Crouch .20 .50
9 Kevin Baker .20 .50
10 Matt Dias .20 .50
11 Nick Foligno .60 1.50
12 Devin Didiomete .20 .50
13 Anton Hedman .20 .50
14 Akim Aliu .20 .50
15 Mike Mills .20 .50
16 Mark Versteeg-Lytwyn .20 .50
17 Gary Friesen .20 .50
18 Ryan Donally .20 .50
19 Nicholas Tuzzolino .20 .50
20 Justin Allen .20 .50
21 Gerome Giudice .20 .50
22 Mike Foligno .10 .25
23 Bob Jones .20 .50
24 Bryan Verreault .20 .50
25 Howler .02 .10
26 Benoit Pouliot .60 1.50

2006-07 Sudbury Wolves

COMPLETE SET (27) 8.00 20.00
1 Marc Staal .60 1.50
2 Andrew Self .20 .50
3 J.K. Gill .20 .50
4 Matt Dias .20 .50
5 Nick Foligno .60 1.50
6 Gerome Giudice .20 .50
7 Kyle Tarini .20 .50
8 Gary Friesen .20 .50
9 Geoff Guimond .20 .50
10 Devin Didiomete .20 .50
11 Jared Staal 2.00 5.00
12 Patrik Lusnak .20 .50
13 Justin Larson .20 .50
14 Akim Aliu .60 1.50
15 Justin Donati .20 .50
16 Kevin Baker .20 .50
17 Ryan Crouch .20 .50
18 Stephen Miller .20 .50
19 Zach Mccullough .20 .50
20 Adam Mcquaid .40 1.00
21 Tyler Arps .20 .50
22 Jonathan D'Aversa .20 .50
23 Sebastien Dahm .40 1.00
24 Michael Swick .40 1.00
25 Mike Foligno CO .20 .50
26 Bob Jones .10 .25
27 Bryan Verreault .10 .25

1995-96 Swift Current Broncos

COMPLETE SET (20) 3.00 8.00
1 Derek Arbez .15 .40
2 Chad Beagle .15 .40
3 Kurt Drummond .15 .40
4 Terry Friesen .30 .75
5 Ryan Geremia .15 .40
6 Jeff Henkelman .15 .40
7 Jeff Kirwan .15 .40
8 Brad Larsen .30 .75
9 Aaron MacDonald .20 .50
10 Craig Millar .15 .40
11 Jaroslav Obsut .20 .50
12 Colin O'Hara .15 .40
13 Jeff Schaeffer .15 .40
14 Brent Sopel .30 .75
15 Josh St. Louis .15 .40
16 Chris Szysky .15 .40
17 Jesse Rezansoff .15 .40
18 Jeremy Rondeau .15 .40
19 Sergei Varlamov .30 .75
20 Tyler Willis .15 .40

1996-97 Swift Current Broncos

COMPLETE SET (24) 4.00 10.00
1 Terry Friesen .30 .75
2 Lindsey Materi .20 .50
3 Kevin Mackie .15 .40
4 Jeff Henkelman .15 .40
5 Michal Rozsival .30 .75
6 Brent Sopel .30 .75
7 Lawrence Nycholat .15 .40
8 Chad Beagle .15 .40
9 Jeff Schaeffer .15 .40
10 Tyler Shybunka .15 .40
11 Josh St. Louis .15 .40
12 Chris Szysky .20 .50
13 Tyler Perry .15 .40
14 Dreu Volk .15 .40
15 Nathan Strueby .15 .40
16 Kurt Drummond .15 .40
17 Brad Larsen .30 .75
18 Ryan Tobler .30 .75
19 Jeremy Rondeau .15 .40
20 Jeff Kirwan .15 .40
21 Brett Allan .15 .40
22 Andrew Milne .15 .40
23 Sergei Varlamov .30 .75
24 Derek Arbez .20 .50

1997-98 Swift Current Broncos

COMPLETE SET (22) 4.80 12.00
1 Terry Friesen .30 .75
2 Lindsey Materi .20 .50
3 Tyson Motz .20 .50
4 Jeffrey Beatch .20 .50
5 Jeff Henkelman .20 .50
6 Michal Rozsival .30 .75
7 Dan Hulak .20 .50
8 Lawrence Nycholat .20 .50
9 Toni Bader .20 .50
10 Chad Beagle .20 .50
11 Jeff Schaeffer .20 .50
12 Tyler Shybunka .20 .50
13 Tyler Murray .20 .50
14 Tony Mohagen .20 .50
15 Layne Ulmer .30 .75
16 Dean Serdachny .20 .50
17 Brent Twordik .20 .50
18 Quinn Sherdahl .20 .50
19 Jeff Kirwan .20 .50
21 Brett Allan .20 .50
22 Sergei Varlamov .30 .75

1998-99 Swift Current Broncos

COMPLETE SET (24) 4.80 12.00
1 Chad Beagle .20 .50
2 Brett Allan .20 .50
3 Quinn Sherdahl .20 .50
4 Bryce Wandler .20 .50
5 Dean Serdachny .20 .50
6 Danis Zaripov .20 .50
7 Kurt Drummond .20 .50
8 Tyler Murray .20 .50
9 Toni Bader .20 .50
10 Brent Twordik .20 .50
11 Nathan Smith .20 .50
12 Jakub Cutta .40 1.00
13 Lawrence Nycholat .20 .50
14 Ben Ondrus .20 .50
15 Tyson Motz .20 .50
16 Jay Langager .20 .50
17 Brad Rohrig .20 .50
18 Jeremy Reich .30 .75
19 Layne Ulmer .40 1.00
20 Chris Sotiropolous .20 .50
21 Josh Maser .20 .50
22 Dan Hulak .20 .50
23 Dustan Heintz .20 .50
24 Jeremy Rondeau .20 .50

1999-00 Swift Current Broncos

COMPLETE SET (25) 6.00 15.00
1 Brett Allan .20 .50
2 Jay Batchelor .20 .50
3 Jakub Cutta .30 .75
4 Houston Hair .20 .50
5 Scott Henkelman .20 .50
6 James Hiebert .20 .50
7 Todd Hornung .20 .50
8 Dan Hulak .20 .50
9 Jay Langager .20 .50
10 Duncan Milroy .40 1.00
11 Tyson Motz .40 1.00
12 Lawrence Nycholat .20 .50
13 Ben Ondrus .20 .50
14 Colton Orr .40 1.00
15 Craig Priestlay .20 .50
16 Jeremy Reich .20 .50
17 Dean Serdachny .20 .50
18 Nathan Smith .30 .75
19 Matt Sommerfield .20 .50
20 Clay Thoring .20 .50
21 Brent Twordik .20 .50
22 Layne Ulmer .40 1.00
23 Igor Valeev .20 .50
24 Brendan Vanthuyne .20 .50
25 Bryce Wandler .30 .75

2000-01 Swift Current Broncos

COMPLETE SET (24) 4.80 15.00
1 B.J. Boxma .40 1.00
2 Ales Cerny .20 .50
3 Jakub Cutta .40 1.00
4 John Dahl .20 .50
5 Paul Deniset .20 .50
6 Adam Dumbrowski .20 .50
7 Todd Ford .40 1.00
8 Dustin Friesen .30 .75
9 Scott Henkelman .20 .50
10 James Hiebert .20 .50
11 Jay Langager .20 .50
12 Duncan Milroy .60 1.50
13 Tyson Motz .40 1.00
14 Ben Ondrus .20 .50
15 Craig Priestlay .20 .50
16 Kevin Seibel .20 .50
17 Dean Serdachny .20 .50
18 Nathan Smith .30 .75
19 Mat Sommerfeld .20 .50
20 Clay Thoring .20 .50
21 Ian White .20 2.00
22 Header Card .04 .10
23 Checklist .04 .10
24 Charlie MASCOT .04 .10

2001-02 Swift Current Broncos

COMPLETE SET (24) 5.00 12.00
1 Steven Spencer .20 .50
2 Ales Cerny .20 .50
3 Kevin Seibel .20 .50
4 Travis Friedley .20 .50
5 Ian White .40 1.00
6 Aaron Richards .20 .50
7 James Hiebert .20 .50
8 Nathan Smith .20 .50
9 Tim Smith .20 .50
10 Dustin Friesen .20 .50
11 Jason Roberts .20 .50
12 Ben Ondrus .40 1.00
13 John Dahl .20 .50
14 Luke Hunter .20 .50
15 Mitch Love .20 .50
16 Brent Twordik .20 .50
17 Torrie Wheat .20 .50
18 Colin Slobodian .20 .50
19 Ivan Usenko .20 .50
20 Duncan Milroy .40 1.00
21 Mat Sommerfeld .20 .50
22 Todd Ford .20 .50
23 B.J. Boxma .20 .50
24 Mascot .04 .10

2002-03 Swift Current Broncos

COMPLETE SET (24) 5.00 12.00
1 John Dahl .20 .50
2 Todd Ford .20 .50
3 Travis Friedlay .20 .50
4 Dustin Friesen .20 .50
5 Jeff Harvey .20 .50
6 Marian Havel .20 .50
7 James Hiebert .20 .50
8 Luke Hunter .20 .50
9 Alex Lentowich .20 .50
10 Mitch Love .20 .50
11 Darryl Moscaluk .20 .50
12 Ben Ondrus .20 .50
13 Derek Poplawski .20 .50
14 Aaron Richards .20 .50
15 Jason Roberts .20 .50
16 Aaron Rome .40 1.00
17 David Schulz .20 .50
18 Dennis Sergeyev .20 .50
19 Steven Spencer .20 .50
20 Colin Stone .20 .50
21 Torrie Wheat .20 .50
22 Ian White .40 1.00
23 Jeremy Williams .40 1.00
24 Charlie Horse MASCOT .04 .10

2003-04 Swift Current Broncos

COMPLETE SET (24) 6.00 15.00
1 Bryn Brucks .20 .50
2 Jason Fransoo .20 .50
3 Dustin Friesen .20 .50
4 Davin Heintz .20 .50
5 Michael Hengen .20 .50
6 Luke Hunter .20 .50
7 Alex Leavitt .20 .50
8 Alex Lentowich .20 .50
9 Kyle Moir .30 .75
10 Ty Morris .20 .50
11 Darryl Moscaluk .20 .50
12 Tyler Redenbach .30 .75
13 Aaron Richards .20 .50
14 Aaron Rome .30 .75
15 Myles Rumsey .20 .50
16 Jerrid Sauer .20 .50
17 David Schulz .20 .50
18 Colin Stone .20 .50
19 Michael Szczachor .20 .50
20 Matej Trojovsky .30 .75
21 Brent Walker .30 .75
22 Ian White .40 1.00
23 Bobby Williams .20 .50
24 Jeremy Williams .40 1.00

2004-05 Swift Current Broncos

COMPLETE SET (24) 8.00 15.00
1 Travis Brisebois .30 .75
2 Marc Defoe .30 .75
3 Marc Desloges .30 .75
4 Tyler Feakes .30 .75
5 Jason Fransoo .30 .75
6 Michael Hengen .30 .75
7 Barry Horman .30 .75
8 Luke Hughson .30 .75
9 Luke Hunter .30 .75
10 Marek Knebl .30 .75
11 Brady Leavold .30 .75
12 Andrew Leslie .30 .75
13 Don Lloyd .30 .75
14 Kyle Moir .40 1.00
15 Tyler Redenbach .40 1.00
16 Myles Rumsey .30 .75
17 Jerrid Sauer .30 .75
18 Jeremy Schenderling .30 .75
19 David Schulz .30 .75
20 Blair Stengler .30 .75
21 Colin Stone .30 .75
22 Michael Szczachor .30 .75
23 Matej Trojovsky .40 1.00
24 Andrew Wasmuth .30 .75

2005-06 Swift Current Broncos

COMPLETE SET (24) 8.00 15.00
1 Karl Benke .30 .75
2 Michael Hengen .30 .75
3 Derek Price .30 .75
4 Thomas Raffl .30 .75
5 Andrew Wasmuth .30 .75
6 Daniel Rakos .30 .75
7 R.J. Larochelle .30 .75
8 Travis Yonkman .30 .75
9 Kyle Bortis .30 .75
10 Kyle Moir .30 .75
11 Luke Hunter .30 .75
12 Spencer McAvoy .30 .75
13 Donny Lloyd .30 .75
14 Josh Aspenlind .30 .75
15 Levi Nelson .40 1.00
16 Grant Toulmin .30 .75
17 Dale Weise .30 .75
18 Charlie Horse .02 .10
19 Paul Postma .30 .75
20 Jeremy Schenderling .30 .75
21 Myles Rumsey .30 .75
22 Ned Lukacevic .30 .75
23 Marc Desloges .30 .75
24 Zack Smith .30 .75

2006-07 Swift Current Broncos

COMPLETE SET (24) 12.00 20.00
1 Travis Yonkman .60 1.50
2 Kyle Moir .60 1.50
3 David Stieler .30 .75
4 Grant Toulmin .30 .75
5 R.J Larochelle .30 .75
6 Ryan Molle .30 .75
7 Levi Nelson .60 1.50
8 Geordie Wudrick .30 .75
9 Dale Weise .30 .75
10 Kyle Bortis .30 .75
11 Phil Gervais .30 .75
12 Michael Wilson .30 .75
13 Daniel Rakos .30 .75
14 Brady Leavold .30 .75
15 Spencer Mcavoy .30 .75
16 Matt Tassone .30 .75
17 Paul Postma .30 .75
18 Derek Claffey .30 .75
19 Zack Smith .30 .75
20 Myles Rumsey .30 .75
21 Dane Crowley .30 .75
22 Jeremy Schenderling .30 .75
23 L.Nelson
D.Crowley .60 1.50
24 Charlie Horse .10 .25

2007-08 Swift Current Broncos

COMPLETE SET (24) 12.00 20.00
1 Mike Brown .30 .75
2 Derek Claffey .30 .75
3 Ian Curtis .60 1.50
4 Jan Dalecky .30 .75
5 Keegan Dansereau .30 .75
6 Justin Dowling .30 .75
7 Eric Doyle .30 .75
8 Cody Eakin .30 .75
9 Erik Felde .30 .75
10 Brad Hoban .30 .75
11 R.J. LaRochelle .30 .75
12 Spencer McAvoy .30 .75
13 Ryan Molle .30 .75
14 Levi Nelson .60 1.50
15 Joel Rogers .30 .75
16 Zack Smith .30 .75
17 Dave Stieler .30 .75
18 Matt Tassone .30 .75
19 Dale Weise .30 .75
20 Michael Wilson .30 .75
21 George Wudrick .30 .75
22 Travis Younkman .60 1.50
23 Charlie Horse MASCOT .02 .10
24 Team Checklist .02 .10

2014-15 Swift Current Broncos

COMPLETE SET (24) 6.00 15.00
1 Header Card .35 .75
2 Colby Cave .35 .75
3 Jay Merkley .35 .75
4 Cavin Leth .35 .75
5 Kristian Ferletak .35 .75
6 Glenn Gawdin .35 .75
7 Tyler Steenbergen .35 .75
8 Cole Johnson .35 .75
9 Jake DeBrusk .35 .75
10 Carter Rigby .35 .75
11 Zac MacKay .35 .75
12 Andreas Schumacher .35 .75
13 Coda Gordon .35 .75
14 Tanner Lesann .35 .75
15 Dillon Heatherington .35 .75
16 Jordan Harris .35 .75
17 Brett Lernout .35 .75
18 Brycen Martin .35 .75
19 Ayrton Nikkel .35 .75
20 Max Lajoie .35 .75
21 Jaydan Gordon .35 .75
22 Landon Bow .35 .75
23 Travis Child .35 .75
24 Charlie Horse MASCOT .35 .75

1996-97 Syracuse Crunch

COMPLETE SET (25) 4.80 12.00
1 Mike Fountain .30 .75
4 Mark Wotton .15 .40
5 Mark Krys .15 .40
9 Robb Gordon .30 .75
10 Darren Sinclair .15 .40
11 Ian McIntyre .15 .40
14 John Badduke .15 .40
16 Doug Ast .15 .40
17 Brian Loney .15 .40
18 Tyson Nash .60 1.50
19 Lonny Bohonos .20 .50
21 Dave Scatchard .30 .75
23 Chad Allan .15 .40
25 Bogdan Savenko .15 .40
26 John Namestnikov .15 .40
27 Bert Robertsson .20 .50
28 Chris McAllister .20 .50
30 Frederic Cassivi .30 .75
35 Larry Courville .20 .50
37 Rick Girard .15 .40
38 Rod Stevens .15 .40
44 Brent Tully .15 .40
NNO AHL Ad Card .02 .10
NNO Jack McIlhargey CO .02 .10
NNO Crunchman (Mascot) .02 .10

1999-00 Syracuse Crunch

COMPLETE SET (25) 10.00 25.00
1 Harold Druken .40 1.00
2 Matt Cooke .75 2.00
3 Brian Bonin .40 1.00
4 Zenith Komarniski .40 1.00
5 Chad Allan .40 1.00
6 Crunchman MASCOT .08 .25
7 Ryan Ready .40 1.00
8 Brad Leeb .40 1.00
9 Reggie Savage .40 1.00
10 Trent Klatt .40 1.00
11 Martin Gendron .40 1.00
12 Lubomir Vaic .40 1.00
13 Ryan Bonni .40 1.00
14 Brent Sopel .60 1.50
15 Christian Bronsard .60 1.50
16 Barry Smith CO .20 .50
17 Stan Smyl CO .40 1.00
18 Alfie Michaud .60 1.50
19 Trevor Doyle .40 1.00
20 Jarkko Ruutu .40 1.00
21 Chris O'Sullivan .40 1.00
22 Ryan Shannon .40 1.00
23 Pat Kavanagh .40 1.00
24 Mike Brown .40 1.00
25 Tully's Restaurant .02 .10

2000-01 Syracuse Crunch

COMPLETE SET (24) 10.00 25.00
1 Marc Lamothe .80 1.50
2 Jean-Francois Labbe .60 1.50
3 Andrei Sryubko .40 1.00
4 Jonas Junkka-Andersson .40 1.00
5 Mike Gaul .40 1.00
6 Dan Watson .40 1.00
7 Bill Bowler .60 1.50
8 Chris Nielsen .40 1.00
9 Jody Shelley 2.00 5.00
10 Mathieu Darche .80 1.50
11 Blake Bellefeuille .60 1.50
12 Jeremy Reich .40 1.00
13 Jeff Williams .40 1.00
14 Martin Spanhel .60 1.50
15 Brad Moran .40 1.00
16 Scott Hollis .40 1.00
17 Jeff Ware .40 1.00
18 Matt Davidson .40 1.00
19 Sean Selmser .40 1.00
20 Radim Bicanek .40 1.00
21 Reggie Savage .40 1.00
22 Gary Agnew CO .10 .25
23 Ross Yates CO .10 .25
24,Al MASCOT .04 .10

2001-02 Syracuse Crunch

COMPLETE SET (25) 6.00 15.00
1 Jean-Francois Labbe .30 .75
2 Andrei Sryubko .20 .50
3 Dan Watson .20 .50
4 Paul Manning .20 .50
5 Matt Davidson .30 .75
6 Duvie Westcott .30 .75
7 Jody Shelley .60 1.50
8 Mathieu Darche .30 .75
9 Blake Bellefeuille .30 .75
10 Jeremy Reich .20 .50
11 Martin Spanhel .30 .75
12 David Ling .30 .75
13 Sean Pronger .20 .50
14 Brad Moran .30 .75
15 Derrick Walser .30 .75
16 Jeff Ware .20 .50
17 Martin Paroulek .20 .50
18 Darrel Scoville .20 .50
19 Kent McDonell .20 .50
20 Adam Borzecki .20 .50
21 Andrej Nedorost .30 .75
22 Brett Harkins .20 .50
23 Jonathan Schill .20 .50
24 Tully's Ad Card .04 .10
25 Al MASCOT .04 .10

2002-03 Syracuse Crunch

COMPLETE SET (25) 12.00
1 Karl Goehring .30 .75
2 Pascal Leclaire .60 1.50
3 Tyler Sloan .20 .50
4 Dan Watson .20 .50
5 Paul Manning .20 .50
6 Matt Davidson .20 .50
7 Mathieu Darche .30 .75
8 Blake Bellefeuille .20 .50
9 Jeremy Reich .20 .50
10 Tim Jackman .20 .50
11 David Ling .20 .50
12 Jonathan Schill .20 .50
13 Brad Moran .20 .50
14 Pauli Levokari .20 .50
15 Darrel Scoville .20 .50
16 Kent McDonell .20 .50
17 Adam Borzecki .20 .50
18 Andrej Nedorost .20 .50
19 Radim Bicanek .20 .50
20 Trevor Ettinger .20 .50
21 Matt Dzieduszycki .20 .50
22 Mike Pandolfo .20 .50
23 Trent Cull .20 .50
24 Al the Gorilla Mascot .04 .10
NNO Quickway Ad .04 .10

2003-04 Syracuse Crunch

COMPLETE SET (24) 4.00 10.00
1 Karl Goehring .30 .75
2 Jamie Pushor .15 .40
3 Mark Hartigan .20 .50
4 Darrel Scoville .15 .40
5 Zenith Komarniski .15 .40
6 Ben Knopp .15 .40
7 Todd Rohloff .15 .40
8 Paul Traynor .15 .40
9 Donald MacLean .15 .40
10 Jeremy Reich .20 .50
11 Tim Jackman .15 .40
12 Joe Motzko .15 .40
13 Brad Moran .15 .40
14 Derrick Walser .15 .40
15 Pauli Levokari .15 .40
16 Aaron Johnson .15 .40
17 Kent McDonell .15 .40
18 Tyler Sloan .15 .40
19 Brandon Sugden .30 .75
20 Pascal Leclaire .40 1.00
21 Anders Eriksson .15 .40
22 Mike Pandolfo .15 .40
23 Trent Cull .15 .40
24 Mascot .04 .10

2004-05 Syracuse Crunch

COMPLETE SET (25) 5.00 12.00
1 Header
Checklist .04 .10
2 Karl Goehring .30 .75
3 Jamie Pushor .20 .50
4 Mark Hartigan .20 .50
5 Zenith Komarniski .20 .50
6 Ole-Kristian Tollefsen .20 .50
7 Prestin Ryan .20 .50
8 Matthias Trattnig .20 .50
9 Jeremy Reich .20 .50
10 Tim Jackman .20 .50
11 Steven Goertzen .20 .50
12 Alexander Svitov .20 .50
13 Joe Motzko .20 .50
14 Brad Moran .20 .50
15 Andre Lakos .20 .50
16 Aaron Johnson .20 .50
17 Francois Beauchemin .30 .75
18 Brandon Sugden .40 1.00
19 Raffaele Sannitz .20 .50
20 Pascal Leclaire .40 1.00
21 Greg Mauldin .20 .50
22 Jeff Panzer .20 .50
23 Mike Pandolfo .20 .50
24 Al MASCOT .04 .10
25 Sponsor card .04 .10

2005-06 Syracuse Crunch

COMPLETE SET (26) 8.00 15.00
1 Mike Ayers .20 .50
2 Marc Methot .30 .75
3 Mark Hartigan .20 .50
4 Darcy Verot .20 .50
5 Ben Simon .20 .50
6 Geoff Platt .30 .75
7 Andrew Murray .20 .50
8 Tyler Kolarik .20 .50
9 Steven Goertzen .20 .50
10 Peter Sarno .30 .75
11 Joe Motzko .20 .50
12 Brett Nowak .20 .50
13 Alexandre Picard .60 1.50
14 Jeff MacMillan .20 .50
15 Jamie Pushor .20 .50
16 Andy Canzanello .20 .50
17 Ole-Kristian Tollefsen .20 .50
18 Brandon Sugden .40 1.00
19 Martin Prusek .30 .75
20 Tim Konsorada .20 .50
21 Andrew Penner .40 1.00

22 Joakim Lindstrom .30 .75
23 Greg Mauldin .20 .50
24 Aaron Johnson .20 .50
25 Andy Delmore .20 .50
26 Al MASCOT .02 .10

2006-07 Syracuse Crunch

COMPLETE SET (26) 8.00 15.00
1 Tomas Popperle .30 .75
2 Marc Methot .20 .50
3 Mark Hartigan .20 .50
4 Filip Novak .20 .50
5 Darcy Verot .30 .75
6 Ben Simon .20 .50
7 Geoff Platt .30 .75
8 Andrew Murray .20 .50
9 Adam Pineault .30 .75
10 Philippe Dupuis .20 .50
11 Steven Goertzen .20 .50
12 Janne Hauhtonen .20 .50
13 Joe Motzko .20 .50
14 Alexandre Picard .30 .75
15 Tomas Kloucek .20 .50
16 Jeff Szwez .20 .50
17 Ryan Caldwell .20 .50
18 Jamie Pushor .20 .50
19 Andy Canzanello .20 .50
20 Derrick Walser .20 .50
21 Dan LaCosta .20 .50
22 Jekabs Redlihs .20 .50
23 Ty Conklin .30 .75
24 Joakim Lindstrom .30 .75
25 Olivier Labelle .20 .50
26 Al MASCOT .02 .10

1992-93 Tacoma Rockets

COMPLETE SET (30) 4.00 10.00
1 Alexander Alexeev .15 .40
2 Jamie Black .20 .50
3 Jamie Butt .20 .50
4 Jeff Calvert .15 .40
5 Don Clark ACO .02 .10
6 Marcel Comeau CO .15 .40
7 Duane Crouse TR .02 .10
8 Allan Egeland .15 .40
9 Marty Flichel .15 .40
10 Trever Fraser .15 .40
11 Jason Kwiatkowski .15 .40
12 Todd MacDonald .15 .40
13 Dave McMillen .15 .40
14 Tony Pechthalt TR .02 .10
15 Ryan Phillips .15 .40
16 Mike Piersol .15 .40
17 Dennis Pinfold .15 .40
18 Kevin Powell .15 .40
19 Tyler Prosofsky .15 .40
20 Stu Scantlebury .15 .40
21 Drew Schoneck .15 .40
22 Adam Smith .15 .40
23 Corey Stock .15 .40
24 Barkley Swenson .15 .40
25 Michal Sykora .20 .50
26 Dallas Thompson .15 .40
27 John Varga .15 .40
28 Toby Weishaar .15 .40
29 Michal Sykora IA .20 .50
30 Cover Card (Team Logo) .08 .25

1993-94 Tacoma Rockets

COMPLETE SET (30) 4.80 12.00
1 Alexander Alexeev .20 .50
2 Jamie Butt .20 .50
3 Trevor Cairns .15 .40
4 Jeff Calvert .15 .40
5 Marcel Comeau CO .15 .40
6 Jason Deleurme .15 .40
7 Allan Egeland .20 .50
8 Marty Flichel .15 .40
9 Trever Fraser .15 .40
10 Michal Grosek .40 1.00
11 Lada Hampeis .15 .40
12 Tavis Hansen .20 .50
13 Burt Henderson .15 .40
14 Jeff Jubenville .15 .40
15 Todd MacDonald .20 .50
16 Kyle McLaren .60 1.50
17 Kory Mullin .15 .40
18 Steve Oviatt TR .02 .10
19 Ryan Phillips .15 .40
20 Mike Piersol .15 .40
21 Dennis Pinfold .15 .40
22 Tyler Prosofsky .20 .50
23 Jamie Reeve ACO .02 .10
24 Adam Smith .15 .40
25 Corey Stock .15 .40
26 Dallas Thompson .15 .40
27 John Varga .20 .50
28 Team Photo .20 .50
29 The Tacoma Dome .02 .10
30 The Tacoma Rockets In Action Marty Flichel .15 .40

1998-99 Tacoma Sabercats

COMPLETE SET (25) 8.00 20.00
1 Blair Allison .30 .75
2 Jergis Bertins .30 .75
3 Scott Boston .60 1.50
4 Dampy Brar .30 .75
5 Jamie Butt .60 1.50
6 Scott Drevitch .60 1.50
7 Brett Duncan .30 .75
8 Jim Gattolliat .30 .75
9 Scott Green .30 .75
10 Casey Hungle .30 .75
11 Tim Lovell .60 1.50
12 Kim Maier .30 .75
13 Trevor Matter .30 .75
14 Brad Mehalko .40 1.00
15 Alex Mukhanov .40 1.00
16 Chris Nelson .30 .75
17 Alex Podalinski .30 .75
18 Chad Richard .30 .75
19 Kevin Smyth .30 .75
20 Paul Taylor .30 .75
21 Edgar Zalitkovskis .30 .75
22 John Oliver HCO .20 .50
23 Sponsor Card .02 .10
24 Mike Carey TR .08 .25
25 Sponsor Card .02 .10

1999-00 Tacoma Sabercats

COMPLETE SET (25) 6.00 15.00
1 Scott Boston .40 1.00
2 Alexander Alexeev .40 1.00
3 Pavel Mikulchik .30 .75
4 Trever Fraser .30 .75
5 Chad Richard .30 .75
6 Cory Morgan .30 .75
7 Brian Leitza .30 .75
8 Alexander Kharlamov .40 1.00
9 Craig Chapman .30 .75
10 Ashley Buckberger .30 .75
11 Trevor Roenick .30 .75
12 Scott Drevitch .30 .75
13 Jim Gattolliat .30 .75
14 Dampy Brar .30 .75
15 Blair Allison .30 .75
16 Brandon Fleenor .30 .75
17 Kim Maier .30 .75
18 Edgars Zaltkovskis .30 .75
19 Shayne Green .30 .75
20 Brett Duncan .30 .75
21 Local Electrician .02 .10
22 Local Electrician .02 .10
23 Local Electrician .02 .10
24 John Olver CO .08 .25
25 Mike Carey TR .08 .25

2000-01 Tacoma Sabercats

COMPLETE SET (24) 8.00 20.00
1 Cory Morgan .40 1.00
2 Scott Boston .50 1.25
3 Trever Fraser .40 1.00
4 Jarrett Whidden .40 1.00
5 Charlie Blyth .40 1.00
6 Rob Dumas .40 1.00
7 Alexei Deev .50 1.25
8 Danny Lorenz .50 1.25
9 Alexander Alexeev .40 1.00
10 Ashley Buckberger .50 1.25
11 Brandon Fleenor .40 1.00
12 Luke Curtin .40 1.00
13 Gavin Hodgson .40 1.00
14 Dampy Brar .40 1.00
15 Steve Lowe .40 1.00
16 Dennis Pinfold .40 1.00
17 Scott Drevitch .40 1.00
18 Curtis Menzul .40 1.00
19 Phil Husak .40 1.00
20 Robert Dirk CO .10 .25
21 Jason Kirkman TR .04 .10
22 Sponsor .04 .10
23 Sponsor .04 .10
24 Sponsor .04 .10

2001-02 Tacoma Sabercats

COMPLETE SET (24) 8.00 20.00
1 Alexander Alexeev .40 1.00
2 Eric Bowen .40 1.00
3 Dampy Brar .60 1.50
4 Mike Brusseau .40 1.00
5 Etienne Drapeau .40 1.00
6 Scott Drevitch .60 1.50
7 Marty Flichel .60 1.50
8 Trever Fraser .40 1.00
9 David Goverde .60 1.50
10 Nathan Horne .40 1.00
11 Yannick Latour .40 1.00
12 Matt Loen .40 1.00
13 Casson Masters .40 1.00
14 Dennis Pinfold .40 1.00
15 Clayton Read .40 1.00
16 Francois Sasseville .40 1.00
17 Brian Stacey .40 1.00
18 Jarrett Whidden .40 1.00
19 Jeff Winter .40 1.00
20 Dampy Brar .60 1.50
21 Scott Drevitch .60 1.50
22 Robert Dirk CO .10 .25
23 Fang MASCOT .10 .25
24 Saberkitty MASCOT .10 .25

1995-96 Tallahassee Tiger Sharks

COMPLETE SET (27) 3.00 8.00
1 Rodrigo Lavinsh .15 .40
2 Jon Engler .15 .40
3 Rod Aldoff .15 .40
4 Aaron Kriss .15 .40
5 Ron Pasco .15 .40
6 Mark Deazley .20 .50
7 Sean O'Brien .20 .50
8 Kevin Paden .15 .40
9 Darren Schwartz .15 .40
10 Jim Paradise .15 .40
11 John Uniac .15 .40
12 Cal Ingraham .15 .40
13 Matt Osiecki .15 .40
14 Greg Geldart .15 .40
15 Alexander Savchenkov .15 .40
16 Casey Hungle .15 .40
17 Mark Richards .20 .50
18 Bob Bell .20 .50
19 Frenzy (Mascot) .02 .10
20 Jim Mirabello ANN .02 .10
21 Mark Richards Bob Bell .20 .50
22 Terry Christensen CO .02 .10
23 Jack Capuano ACO .02 .10
24 Jerry Hilker TR .02 .10
25 Walter Edwards VP GM .02 .10
26 Tony Mancuso AGM .02 .10
27 John Summers ANN .02 .10

1999-00 Tallahassee Tiger Sharks

COMPLETE SET (26) 6.00 15.00
1 Kevin Kellett .25 .60
2 Derek Paget .25 .60
3 Jason Reid .25 .60
4 Darren McAusland .25 .60
5 Adam Copeland .25 .60
6 David Thibeault .25 .60
7 Matt Oates .25 .60
8 Paul Buczkowski .25 .60
9 Alexandre LaPorte .25 .60
10 Mike Thompson .25 .60
11 Kimbi Daniels .25 .60
12 Ian Perkins .25 .60
13 Chris Wickenheiser .40 1.00
14 Larry Shapley .25 .60
15 Chad Hinz .30 .75
16 Brent Cullaton .25 .60
17 Jean-Francois Houle .25 .60
18 Jason Weinrich .25 .60
19 Maxim Spiridonov .30 .75
20 Pavel Smirnov .25 .60
21 Marc-Andre Gaudet .25 .60
22 Terry Christensen CO .08 .25
23 Jim Paradise CO .08 .25
24 Kyle Schultz .25 .60
24 Cory Paterson .25 .60
25 Frenzy MAS .08 .25

1994 Tampa Bay Tritons RHI

COMPLETE SET (21) 7.20 25.00
1 Paul Messier HCO .08 .25
2 Mark Messier 6.00 15.00
3 Mike Jickling .15 .40
4 John Spoltore .40 1.00
5 Todd Goodwin .15 .40
6 Craig Streu .15 .40
7 Dennis Sproxton .15 .40
8 Norman Dezainde .40 1.00
9 Peter Esdale ACO .08 .25
10 Trevor Sherban .15 .40
11 Duane Dennis .15 .40
12 Jarret Zukiwsky .15 .40
13 Dion Darling .40 1.00
14 Sean Basilio .40 1.00
15 Jeff MacLeod .15 .40
16 Cheerleaders .20 .50
17 Sean Rowe .20 .50
18 George Dupont .15 .40
19 Team Photo .15 .40
20 Doug Messier ACO .08 .25
21 Brad Woods .15 .40

2009-10 Texas Stars

COMPLETE SET (24) 4.00 8.00
1 Landon Wilson .20 .50
2 Dan Jancevski .20 .50
3 Maxime Fortunus .20 .50
4 Garrett Stafford .20 .50
5 Francis Wathier .20 .50
6 Aaron Gagnon .20 .50
7 Perttu Lindgren .20 .50
8 Sergei Korostin .20 .50
9 Matt Beaudoin .20 .50
10 Luke Gazdic .20 .50
11 Trevor Ludwig .20 .50
12 Scott McCulloch .20 .50
13 Colton Sceviour .20 .50
14 Matt Stephenson .20 .50
15 Mathieu Tousignant .20 .50
16 Warren Peters .20 .50
17 Matt Climie .20 .50
18 Brent Krahn .20 .50
19 Raymond Sawada .20 .50
20 Greg Rallo .20 .50
21 Travis Morin .20 .50
22 Andrew Hutchinson .20 .50
23 Glen Gulutzan .20 .50
NNO Checklist .20 .50

2010-11 Texas Stars

COMPLETE SET (28) 4.00 8.00
1 Tyler Beskorowany .20 .50
2 Dan Spang .20 .50
3 Severin Blindenbacher .20 .50
4 Colton Sceviour .20 .50
5 Jordie Benn .30 .75
6 Aaron Gagnon .20 .50
7 Scott McCulloch .20 .50
8 Raymond Sawada .20 .50
9 Sean Backman .20 .50
10 Tomas Vincour .30 .75
11 Maxime Fortunus .20 .50
12 Ondrej Roman .20 .50
13 Travis Morin .20 .50
14 Trevor Ludwig .20 .50
15 Matt Stephenson .20 .50
16 Cody Chupp .20 .50
17 Greg Rallo .20 .50
18 Fabian Brunnstrom .20 .50
19 Richard Bachman .20 .50
20 Luke Gazdic .20 .50
21 Philip Larsen .20 .50
22 Brad Lukowich .20 .50
23 Francis Wathier .20 .50
24 Mathieu Tousignant .20 .50
25 Brent Krahn .20 .50
26 Glen Gulutzan .20 .50
27 Paul Jerrard .20 .50
NNO Checklist .20 .50

2014-15 Texas Stars

COMPLETE SET (27) 8.00 20.00
1 Jack Campbell .40 1.00
2 William Wrenn .30 .75
3 Jamie Oleksiak .40 1.00
4 Julius Honka .30 .75
5 Kevin Henderson .30 .75
6 Derek Meech .30 .75
7 Justin Dowling .30 .75
8 Branden Troock .30 .75
9 Gemel Smith .30 .75
10 Scott Glennie .30 .75
11 Curtis McKenzie .40 1.00
12 Maxime Fortunus .30 .75
13 Brendan Ranford .30 .75
14 Brett Ritchie .40 1.00
15 Scott Valentine .30 .75
16 Travis Morin .30 .75
17 Cameron Gaunce .30 .75
18 Taylor Peters .30 .75
19 Matt Mangene .30 .75
20 Greg Rallo .30 .75
21 Matej Stransky .30 .75
22 Radek Faksa .40 1.00
23 Derek Hulak .30 .75
24 Jussi Rynnas .40 1.00
25 Karl Taylor Asst. CO .30 .75
26 Derek Laxdal CO .30 .75
27 Header Card CL .30 .75

2006-07 Texas Tornados

COMPLETE SET (25) 15.00 25.00
1 Thomas Murphy .40 1.00
2 Lyon Messier 2.00 5.00
3 Troy Puente .40 1.00
4 Jake Newton .40 1.00
5 Nielsson Arcibal .40 1.00
6 Dylan Cooper .40 1.00
7 Justin King .40 1.00
8 Julian Mikola .40 1.00
9 Ryan Fuller .40 1.00
10 Colin Long .40 1.00
11 Tom Brooks .40 1.00
12 Sean Roadhouse .40 1.00
13 Adam Flink .40 1.00
14 John Bullis .40 1.00
15 Brendan Brickley .40 1.00
16 Ben Miller .40 1.00
17 Rob Blanchette .40 1.00
18 Brian Reagan .40 1.00
19 Stephane Da Costa .40 1.00
20 Paul Yovanic .40 1.00
21 Mike Cifelli .40 1.00
22 Corson Cramer .40 1.00
23 Thomas Tragust .60 1.50
24 Tony Curtale CO .02 .10
25 Tom Murphy ACO .02 .10

1998-99 Thetford Mines Coyotes

COMPLETE SET (23) 4.00 10.00
1 Steven Paiement .20 .50
2 Marco Sevigny .20 .50
3 Stephane Nepveu .20 .50
4 Jean-Pierre Tardif .20 .50
5 Eric Roy .20 .50
6 Eric Deblois .20 .50
7 Nick Perreault .20 .50
8 Sebastian Vallee .20 .50
9 Yohan Bedard .20 .50
10 Francois Allaire .20 .50
11 Bernard Bouffard .20 .50
12 Philippe Morin .20 .50
13 Pierre Perron .20 .50
14 Michel Dodier .20 .50
15 Frederic Barbeau .20 .50
16 Yves Loubier .20 .50
17 Michel Bisson .20 .50
18 David Desnoyers .20 .50
19 Dominic Cote .20 .50
20 Jean Roberge .20 .50
21 Pierre Marcoux .20 .50
22 Nathan Morin .20 .50
23 Marc Rodrigue .20 .50

2001-02 Thetford Mines Coyotes

COMPLETE SET (25) 10.00 25.00
1 Sebastien Bety .60 1.50
2 Louis Bernard .40 1.00
3 Terry Bartlett .40 1.00
4 Stephane Thivierge .40 1.00
5 Mathieu Gagne .40 1.00
6 Frederic Barbeau .40 1.00
7 Jean-Francois Brunelle .40 1.00
8 Martin Fillion .40 1.00
9 Pierre Perron .40 1.00
10 Eric Roy .40 1.00
11 Francois Page .40 1.00
12 Eric Drouin .40 1.00
13 Jean Roberge .40 1.00
14 Daniel Payette .40 1.00
15 Marc-Andre Gaudet .40 1.00
16 Denis Desbiens .40 1.00
17 Yves Loubier .40 1.00
18 Daniel Poudrier .40 1.00
19 Pierre Marcoux .40 1.00
20 Hugo Poulin .40 1.00
21 Patrice Tardif .75 2.00
22 Bryan Faucher .40 1.00
23 David Thibeault .40 1.00
24 Martin Lamarche .40 1.00
NNO Checklist .10 .25

2002-03 Thetford Mines Coyotes

COMPLETE SET (23) 5.00 12.00
1 Benoit Beausoleil .20 .50
2 Louis Bernard .20 .50
3 Sebastien Bety .30 .75
4 Jean-Francois Brunelle .20 .50
5 Christian Caron .20 .50
6 Denis Desbiens .20 .50
7 Frederic Deschenes .20 .50
8 Jason Disher .20 .50
9 Eric Drouin .20 .50
10 Martin Fillion .20 .50
11 Marc-Andre Gaudet .20 .50
12 Guy Loranger .20 .50
13 Pierre Marcoux .20 .50
14 Andre Martineau .20 .50
15 Francois Page .20 .50
16 Daniel Payette .20 .50
17 Daniel Poudrier .20 .50
18 Hugo Poulin .20 .50
19 Jean Roberge .20 .50
20 Eric Roy .20 .50
21 Claude Savoie .20 .50
22 Patrice Tardif .30 .75
23 David Thibeault .20 .50

2003-04 Thetford Mines Prolab

COMPLETE SET (24) 4.00 10.00
1 Benoit Beausoleil .20 .50
2 Louis Bernard .20 .50
3 Eric Betournay .20 .50
4 Sebastien Bety .20 .50
5 Patrick Bolduc .20 .50
6 Denis Desbiens .20 .50
7 Frederic Deschenes .20 .50
8 Martin Fillion .20 .50
9 Marc-Andre Gaudet .20 .50
10 Eric Lavigne .20 .50
11 David Lessard .20 .50
12 Pierre Marcoux .20 .50
13 Andre Martineau .20 .50
14 Simon Olivier .20 .50
15 Francois Page .20 .50
16 Daniel Poudrier .20 .50
17 Hugo Poulin .20 .50
18 Christian Proulx .20 .50
19 Jean Roberge .20 .50
20 Eric Roy .20 .50
21 Claude Savoie .20 .50
22 Pierre Sevigny .20 .50
23 Patrice Tardif .20 .50
24 David Thibeault .20 .50

2004-05 Thetford Mines Prolab

COMPLETE SET (24) 6.00 15.00
1 David Thibeault .20 .50
2 Benoit Deschamps .20 .50
3 Marc-Andre Gaudet .20 .50
4 Dany Lavoie .20 .50
5 Patrice Tardif .20 .50
6 Michel Picard .30 .75
7 Frederic Deschenes .30 .75
8 Andre Martineau .20 .50
9 Serge Poudrier .20 .50
10 Marquis Mathieu .40 1.00
11 Francois Page .20 .50
12 Eric Lavigne .20 .50
13 Samuel Groleau .20 .50
14 Yves Racine .20 .50
15 Hugo Poulin .20 .50
16 Glen Kjernisted .20 .50
17 Frederic Henry .20 .50
18 Jean-Francois Beliveau .20 .50
19 Samuel Gagnon .20 .50
20 Simon Olivier .20 .50
21 Mathieu Biron .20 .50
22 Matt Holmes .20 .50
23 Dennis Leblanc .20 .50
24 Benoit Beausoleil .20 .50
25 Ryan Pisiak .20 .50
26 Link Gaetz .75 2.00
27 Gaetan Royer .20 .50
28 Frederic Deschenes .30 .75

2014-15 Thetford Mines Isothermic

COMPLETE SET (24) 6.00 15.00
1 Sylvain Dufresne .30 .75
2 Guillaume Letourneau .40 1.00
3 Matthew Medley .30 .75
4 Sebastien Courcelles .30 .75
5 Gabriel Lemieux .30 .75
6 Alexandre Neron .30 .75
8 Philippe Pepin .30 .75
9 Tommy Bolduc .30 .75
10 Isothermic 2012 Champs .30 .75
11 Joel Theriault .40 1.00
12 Jean-Philippe Levasseur .30 .75
13 Kevin Bolduc .30 .75
14 Gabriel Girard .30 .75
15 Eric Fortier .30 .75
16 Simon Courcelles .30 .75
17 Andrzej Sandrzyk .30 .75
18 Michel Ouellet .40 1.00
19 Keven Veilleux .30 .75
20 Martin Lariviere .30 .75
21 Maxime Villemaire .30 .75
22 Simon Gamache .30 .75
23 Marc-Antoine Desnoyers .30 .75
24 Pierre-Luc Sleigher .30 .75
25 Bobby Baril CO .30 .75

1993-94 Thunder Bay Senators

COMPLETE SET (19) 4.00 10.00
1 Jean-Francois Labbe .40 1.00
2 Jamie Hayden .20 .50
3 Llew NcWana .20 .50
4 Chris Hynnes .20 .50
5 Trent McCleary .40 1.00
6 Richard Borgo .20 .50
7 Bryan Wells .20 .50
8 Don Osborne .20 .50
9 Todd Howarth .20 .50
10 Bruce Ramsay .20 .50
11 Brian Downey .20 .50
12 Barry McKinley .20 .50
13 Ron Talakowski .20 .50
14 Tom Warden .20 .50
15 Mel Angelstad .30 .75
16 Tommi Hietala .20 .50
17 Vern Ray .20 .50
18 Gerry St. Cyr .20 .50
19 Terry Menard .20 .50

1994-95 Thunder Bay Senators

COMPLETE SET (20) 3.00 8.00
1 Todd Howarth .15 .40
2 Darren Perkins .15 .40
3 Derek Scanlan .15 .40
4 Pat Szturm .20 .50
5 Barry McKinley .15 .40
6 Jake Grimes .15 .40
7 Alain Cote .15 .40
8 Rival Fullum .15 .40
9 Terry Menard .20 .50
10 Mike McCourt .15 .40
11 Mel Angelstad .40 1.00
12 Jason Firth .15 .40
13 Llew NcWana .15 .40
14 Lance Leslie .15 .40
15 Neal Purdon .15 .40
16 Steve Parson .15 .40
17 Chris Rowland .15 .40
18 Bruce Ramsay .15 .40
19 Don Osborne .15 .40
20 Jean Blouin .15 .40

1995-96 Thunder Bay Senators

COMPLETE SET (20) 6.00 15.00
1 Team Photo .30 .75
2 Mel Angelstad .40 1.00
3 Omer Belisle .30 .75
4 Frederic Cassivi .60 1.50
5 Brandon Christian .30 .75
6 Jason Disher .30 .75
7 Jason Firth .30 .75
8 Rival Fullum .30 .75
9 Todd Howarth .30 .75
10 Chris Hynnes .30 .75
11 Barry McKinley .30 .75
12 Terry Menard .30 .75
13 Derek Nicolson .30 .75
14 Llew NcWana .30 .75
15 Steve Parson .30 .75
16 Darren Perkins .30 .75
17 Dan Poirier .30 .75
18 Neal Purdon .30 .75
19 Bruce Ramsay .30 .75
20 Pat Szturm .40 1.00

1998-99 Thunder Bay Thunder Cats

COMPLETE SET (21) 4.00 10.00
1 Jason Lehman .20 .50
2 Barry McKinlay .20 .50
3 David Mayes .20 .50
4 Darrin Szczygiel .20 .50
5 Allan Roulette .20 .50
6 Normand Paquet .20 .50
7 Wayne Strachan .20 .50
8 Kevin Holliday .20 .50
9 Dan Brenzavich .20 .50
10 Mike Henderson .20 .50
11 Neal Purdon .20 .50
12 Nikolai Pronin .20 .50
13 Dan Myre .20 .50
14 Derek Landmesser .30 .75
15 Jason Firth .30 .75
16 Shawn Smith .20 .50
17 Jean-Francois Rivard .20 .50
18 Brant Blackned .20 .50
19 Darrell Clarke TR .02 .10
20 Tom Warden CO .02 .10
21 Sean McEachran .20 .50

1992-93 Thunder Bay Thunder Hawks

COMPLETE SET (30) 6.00 15.00
1 Checklist .02 .10
2 Bill McDonald CO .02 .10
3 Larry Wintoneak ACO .02 .10
4 Mark Michaud .20 .50
5 Marc Lyons .20 .50
6 Jamie Hayden .20 .50
7 Llew Ncwana .20 .50
8 Marc LaBelle .20 .50
9 Gary Callaghan .20 .50
10 Jason Firth .30 .75
11 Mike Martens .30 .75
12 Gerry St. Cyr .20 .50
13 Everton Blackwin .20 .50
14 Bryan Wells .20 .50
15 Brian Downey .20 .50
16 Todd Howarth .20 .50
17 Bruce Rendall .20 .50
18 Vern Ray .20 .50
19 Bruce Ramsay .20 .50
20 Chris Rowland .20 .50
21 Barry McKinlay .20 .50
22 Vincent Faucher .20 .50
23 Tom Warden .20 .50
24 Brock Shyiak .20 .50
25 Mel Angelstad .40 1.00
26 Harijs Vitolinsh .20 .50
27 Steve Hogg .30 .75
28 Terry Menard .30 .75
29 Mark Woolf .30 .75
30 Darrell Clarke TR .02 .10

1992-93 Toledo Storm

COMPLETE SET (25) 3.00 8.00
1 Checklist .02 .10
2 Chris McSorley CO .20 .50
3 Scott Luhrmann EQMG .02 .10
4 Barry Soskin GM .02 .10
5 Tim Mouser PR .02 .10
6 Jeff Gibbons PR .02 .10
7 Claude Scott The Happy Trumpeter .02 .10
8 Scott King .20 .50
9 Andy Suhy .15 .40
10 Pat Pylypuik .15 .40
11 Alex Roberts .15 .40
12 Mark Deazley .15 .40
13 John Johnson .15 .40
14 Jeff Rohlicek .15 .40
15 Dan Wiebe .15 .40
16 Jeff Jablonski .15 .40
17 Greg Puhalski .15 .40
18 Bruce MacDonald .15 .40
19 Iain Duncan .15 .40
20 Rick Judson .15 .40
21 Alex Hicks .20 .50
22 Barry Potomski .20 .50
23 Derek Booth .15 .40
24 Rick Corriveau .15 .40
25 Mark Richards .15 .40

1992-93 Toledo Storm Team Issue

COMPLETE SET (30) 3.00 8.00
1 Logo Card .02 .10
2 Chris McSorley CO .20 .50
3 Scott Luhrmann EQMG .02 .10
4 Barry Soskin GM .02 .50
5 Tim Mouser PR .02 .10
6 Jeff Gibbons PR .15 .40
7 Mike Williams .15 .40
8 Scott King .20 .50
9 Alex Hicks .20 .50
10 Rick Judson .15 .40
11 Brent Sapergia .08 .25
12 Iain Duncan .15 .40
13 Mark Deazley .15 .40
14 Jeff Jablonski .15 .40
15 Bruce MacDonald .15 .40
16 Rick Corriveau .15 .40
17 Pat Pylypuik .15 .40
18 Alex Roberts .15 .40
19 Derek Booth .15 .40
20 Andy Suhy .15 .40
21 Jason Stos .15 .40
22 Greg Puhalski .15 .40
23 Wade Bartley .08 .25
24 Distillery Crew .02 .10
25 The Dawnbusters .02 .10
26 Becky Shock .02 .10
27 Don Davis .02 .10
28 Beth Daniels .02 .10
29 Dennis O'Brien .02 .10
30 Will Worster .02 .10

1993-94 Toledo Storm

COMPLETE SET (29) 4.00 10.00
1 Checklist Card .02 .10
2 Chris McSorley CO .20 .50
3 Barry Soskin PRES .02 .10
4 Tim Mouser MG .02 .10
5 Jeff Gibbons ANN .02 .10
6 Scott Luhrmann TR .02 .10
7 Nick Vitucci .20 .50
8 Andy Suhy .08 .25
9 Pat Pylypuik .08 .25
10 Chris Belanger .08 .25
11 Mike Markovich .08 .25
12 Darren Perkins .08 .25
13 Dennis Snedden .08 .25
14 Mark Deazley .20 .50
15 Mark McCreary .08 .25
16 Jeff Rohlicek .08 .25
17 Chris Bergeron .08 .25
18 John Hendry .08 .25
19 Greg Puhalski .08 .25
20 Bruce MacDonald .08 .25
21 Marc Lyons .08 .25
22 Rick Judson .08 .25
23 Alex Hicks .20 .50
24 Barry Potomski .30 .75
25 Rick Corriveau .20 .50
26 Kyle Reeves .20 .50
27 Erin Whitten 1.25 3.00
28 Brian Schoen .08 .25
29 Riley Cup Champions .08 .25
30 Erin Whitten First Win 1.25 3.00

1994-95 Toledo Storm

COMPLETE SET (24) 3.00 8.00
1 Dave Bankoske .15 .40
2 Wyatt Buckland .15 .40
3 Rick Corriveau .15 .40
4 Norm Dezainde .20 .50
5 Iain Duncan .15 .40
6 Jeff Gibbons .15 .40
7 Alain Harvey .20 .50
8 John Hendry .15 .40
9 Ed Henrich .15 .40
10 Rick Judson .15 .40
11 Mike Latendresse .15 .40
12 Scott Luhrmann TR .02 .10
13 B.J. MacPherson .15 .40
14 Jim Maher .15 .40
15 Jay Neal .15 .40
16 Marquis Mathieu .15 .40
17 Shawn Penn .15 .40
18 Darren Perkins .15 .40
19 Greg Puhalski CO .02 .10
20 Barry Soskin PR/GM .02 .10
21 Gerry St. Cyr .15 .40
22 Rhett Trombley .20 .50
23 Nick Vitucci .20 .50
24 1993-94 Riley Cup Champ .20 .50

1995-96 Toledo Storm

COMPLETE SET (26) 3.00 8.00
1 Rob Laurie .15 .40
2 Nicolas Perreault .20 .50
3 Brandon Carper .15 .40
4 Paul Koch .15 .40
5 Glen Mears .15 .40
6 Dan Carter .15 .40
7 Patrick Gladu .15 .40
8 Todd Wetzel .15 .40
9 B.J. MacPherson .15 .40
10 Mark Stitt .15 .40
11 Dennis Purdie .20 .50
12 Rick Judson .15 .40
13 Mike Whitton .15 .40
14 Norman Dezainde .15 .40
15 Jason Gladney .15 .40
16 Wade Bartley .15 .40
17 Jason Smart .15 .40
18 Mike Kolenda .15 .40
19 Shawn Penn .15 .40
20 David Goverde .20 .50
21 Barry Soskin Owner .02 .10
22 Greg Puhalski CO .02 .10
23 Chuck Imburgia Director of Players .02 .10
24 Scott Luhrmann Equipment Manager .02 .10
25 Mark Kelly Broadcaster .02 .10
26 Raging Color Classics Sponsor .02 .10

1996-97 Toledo Storm

COMPLETE SET (24) 3.00 8.00
1 Ryan Bach .30 .75
5 Paul Koch .15 .40
6 Ryan Bast .15 .40
8 Andrei Srubko .15 .40
11 Brian Clifford .15 .40
14 Mike Sullivan .15 .40
17 Alex Matvichuk .15 .40
18 Arturs Kupaks .15 .40
19 Dennis Purdie .20 .50
20 Rick Judson .15 .40
22 Norm Dezainde .15 .40
23 Jason Gladney .15 .40
24 Chris Bergeron .15 .40
25 Mike Whitton .15 .40
27 Mike Kolenda .15 .40
28 Dan Pawlaczyk .15 .40
29 Jeremy Mylymok .15 .40
32 Don Larner .15 .40
33 Rob Thorpe .15 .40
35 David Goverde .30 .75
NNO Mark Kelly ANN .02 .10
NNO Scott Luhrmann TR .02 .10
NNO Greg Puhalski CO .02 .10
NNO Barry Soskin PRES .02 .10

1997-98 Toledo Storm

COMPLETE SET (30) 3.00 8.00
1 Louis Bernard .10 .30
2 Robert Thorpe .10 .30
3 Greg Lakovic .10 .30
4 Alexandre Jacques .10 .30
5 Gordy Hunt .10 .30

2006-07 Syracuse Crunch

6 Andrei Sryubko .10 .30
7 Sean Venedam .10 .30
8 Jeremy Rebek .10 .30
9 Sean Ortiz .10 .30
10 Tony Prpic .10 .30
11 Brian Blad .10 .30
12 Ron Newhook .20 .50
13 Nick Vitucci .20 .50
14 Dennis Holland .10 .30
15 Mark Deazeley .10 .30
16 Rick Judson .10 .30
17 Lee Cole .10 .30
18 Mike Kolenda .10 .30
19 Dave Arsenault .10 .30
20 Jason Gladney .10 .30
21 Bruce MacDonald .10 .30
22 Kevin Brown .10 .30
23 Andrew Williamson .10 .30
24 Shawn Maltby .10 .30
25 Mike Loach .10 .30
26 Greg Puhalski HCO .02 .10
27 Barry Soskin PR .02 .10
28 Team Staff .02 .10
29 Mark Kelly .02 .10
30 Matt Bresnan EM .02 .10

2003-04 Toledo Storm

COMPLETE SET (12) 4.00 10.00
1 Toledo Storm .04 .10
2 Doug Teskey .60 1.50
3 Mike Nelson .40 1.00
4 Josh Legge .40 1.00
5 Morten Ask .40 1.00
6 Nick Parillo .40 1.00
7 Tom Nemeth .40 1.00
8 Alexandre Jacques .40 1.00
9 Rick Judson .40 1.00
10 Landon Bathe .40 1.00
11 Kris Waltze .40 1.00
12 Jim Abbott .40 1.00

2006-07 Toledo Storm

COMPLETE SET (26) 8.00 15.00
1 Andrew Martin .30 .75
2 Jamie Tardif .30 .75
3 Jason Maleyko .30 .75
4 Tim Songin .30 .75
5 P.J. Martin .30 .75
6 Paul Crosty .40 1.00
7 Jon Sitko .30 .75
8 Jason Schweinsberg EQ MGR .02 .10
9 Mike Brodeur .40 1.00
10 Dominic Vicari .40 1.00
11 Scooter Smith .30 .75
12 Chris Blight .30 .75
13 Logan Koopmans .40 1.00
14 Mike James .30 .75
15 Taylor Raszka .30 .75
16 Ken Magowan .30 .75
17 Nick Parillo .30 .75
18 Jeff Attard .30 .75
19 Gerry Burke .30 .75
20 Dan Watson .30 .75
21 Mike Walsh .30 .75
22 Matt Zultek .30 .75
23 Nick Vitucci CO .10 .25
24 Rick Judson CO .02 .10
25 Barry Soskin PRES .02 .10
26 Dukes MASCOT .02 .10

2014-15 Toledo Walleye

COMPLETE SET (24) 6.00 15.00
1 Tyler Barnes .30 .75
2 Shane Berschbach .30 .75
3 Kyle Bonis .30 .75
4 Joel Chouinard .30 .75
5 Kevin Clare .30 .75
6 Jared Coreau .30 .75
7 Scott Czarnowczan .30 .75
8 Tyler Elbrecht .30 .75
9 A.J. Jenks .30 .75
10 Derek Lalonde CO .30 .75
11 Cody Lampl .30 .75
12 Jeff Lerg .30 .75
13 Anthony Luciani .30 .75
14 Justin Mercier .30 .75
15 Jared Nightingale .30 .75
16 Kyle Rogers .30 .75
17 Troy Schwab .30 .75
18 Shane Sims .30 .75
19 Marek Tvrdon .30 .75
20 Dane Walters .30 .75
21 Dan Watson Asst. CO .30 .75
22 Cattrick MASCOT .30 .75
23 Spike MASCOT .30 .75
24 Header Card CL .30 .75

1998-99 Topeka Scarecrows

COMPLETE SET (23) 4.00 10.00
1 Topeka Scarecrows CL .02 .10
2 Michal Podolka .30 .75
3 Shawn Randall .20 .50
4 Mike Rusk .20 .50
5 Brett Seguin .20 .50
6 Tom Stewart .20 .50
7 Andy Adams .20 .50
8 Chad Antonishyn .20 .50
9 Chris Bowen .20 .50
10 Joe Coombs .20 .50
11 Scott Dickson .20 .50
12 Troy Frederick .20 .50
13 Dave Gregory .20 .50
14 Trevor Hanas .20 .50
15 Kyle Haviland .20 .50
16 Haywire Mascot .02 .10
17 Kevin Lune .20 .50
18 Sergei Olympiev .20 .50
19 Ryan Phillips .20 .50
20 Paul Kelly HCO .02 .10
21 Michael Podolka NM .40 1.00
21 Andy Adams NM .40 1.00
22 Team Photo .20 .50

1999-00 Topeka Scarecrows

COMPLETE SET (21) 4.00 10.00
1 Topeka Scarecrows .20 .50
2 John Vary .20 .50
3 Oleg Tsirkounov .20 .50
4 Bill Monkman .20 .50
5 Sergei Deschevvy .20 .50
6 Randy Best .20 .50
7 Blair Manning .20 .50
8 Steve Moore .20 .50
9 Kirk Llano .20 .50
10 Joey Beaudry .20 .50
11 Trevor Hanas .20 .50
12 David Bouskill .20 .50
13 Rod Branch .20 .50
14 Joe Coombs .20 .50
15 Mike Rusk .20 .50
16 Scot Bell .20 .50
17 Michal Podolka .30 .75
18 Brett Seguin .30 .75
19 Haywire MAS .08 .25
20 Paul Kelly CO .08 .25
21 Topeka Scarecrows .20 .50

2002-03 Topeka Scarecrows

COMPLETE SET (30) 10.00 25.00
1 Layne Sedevie .40 1.00
2 Slavomir Tomko .40 1.00
3 Tony Gliniany .40 1.00
4 Phil Angell .40 1.00
5 Jeff Balvin .40 1.00
6 Ryan Peterson .40 1.00
7 Nick Pernula .40 1.00
8 J.P. Platisha .40 1.00
9 Justin White .40 1.00
10 Luke Erickson .40 1.00
11 Wade Harstad .40 1.00
12 James Unger .40 1.00
13 Steve Eastman .40 1.00
14 Ryan Miller .40 1.00
15 Erik Fabian .40 1.00
16 Eric Vesely .40 1.00
17 Brent Cummings .40 1.00
18 Nick Miller .40 1.00
19 Rob Rankin .40 1.00
20 Mark Buchholz .40 1.00
21 Adam Bartholomay .40 1.00
22 Michael Zacharias .40 1.00
23 Mascots .04 .10
24 Zambeauty-Taumi .20 .50
25 Zambeauty-Janea .20 .50
26 Zambeauty-Audrey .20 .50
27 Zambeauty-Tara .20 .50
28 Zambeauty-Melissa .20 .50
29 Zambeauty-Amanda .20 .50
30 Scarecrows logo .04 .10

2006-07 Toronto Marlies

COMPLETE SET (34) 12.00 20.00
1 J.S. Aubin .30 .75
2 Bates Battaglia .20 .50
3 Brendan Bell .20 .50
4 Brad Brown .20 .50
5 Carlo Colaiacovo .20 .50
6 Jeff Corey .20 .50
7 Dominic D'Amour .20 .50
8 Duke The Dog MASCOT .02 .10
9 Robbie Earl .40 1.00
10 Brett Engelhardt .20 .50
11 Alex Foster .20 .50
12 Owen Fussey .20 .50
13 Greg Gilbert CO .02 .10
14 Jay Harrison .20 .50
15 Staffan Kronwall .20 .50
16 Brad Leeb .20 .50
17 John Mitchell .20 .50
18 Marc Moro .30 .75
19 Colin Murphy .20 .50
20 Kris Newbury .20 .50
21 Ben Ondrus .20 .50
22 Justin Pogge .75 2.00
23 John Pohl .30 .75
24 J.F. Racine .30 .75
25 Martin Sagat .20 .50
26 Justin Sawyer .20 .50
27 Jamie Sifers .20 .50
28 Chris St. Jacques .20 .50
29 Alexander Suglobov .20 .50
30 Jiri Tlusty .40 1.00
31 Erik Westrum .40 1.00
32 Ian White .20 .50
33 Jeremy Williams .20 .50
34 Andy Wozniewski .20 .50

2007-08 Toronto Marlies

COMPLETE SET (23) 15.00 25.00
1 Justin Pogge 2.00 5.00
2 Bryan Muir .75 2.00
3 Chris Harrington .40 1.00
4 Anton Stralman .60 1.50
5 Simon Gamache .40 1.00
6 Robbie Earl .60 1.50
7 Kris Newbury .40 1.00
8 David Ling .75 2.00
9 Brent Aubin .40 1.00
10 Jeremy Williams .40 1.00
11 Jay Harrison .40 1.00
12 Alex Foster .40 1.00
13 Ben Ondrus .40 1.00
14 Jaime Siffers .40 1.00
15 Scott Clemmensen .60 1.50
16 Michel Leveille .40 1.00
17 Derrick Walser .40 1.00
18 Colin Murphy .40 1.00
19 Darryl Boyce .40 1.00
20 John Mitchell .10 .25
21 Greg Gilbert .10 .25
22 Dance Park .02 .10
23 Duke The Dog MASCOT .02 .10

2003-04 ITG Toronto Star

COMPLETE SET (100) 10.00 25.00
1 Jean-Sebastien Giguere .20 .50
2 Petr Sykora .08 .20
3 Stanislav Chistov .08 .20
4 Dany Heatley .30 .75
5 Ilya Kovalchuk .40 1.00
6 Glen Murray .08 .20
7 Joe Thornton .40 1.00
8 Sergei Samsonov .20 .50
9 Martin Biron .20 .50
10 Miroslav Satan .08 .20
11 Ryan Miller .40 1.00
12 Rod Brind'Amour .08 .20
13 Jeff O'Neill .08 .20
14 Ron Francis .08 .20
15 Rick Nash .40 1.00
16 Rostislav Klesla .08 .20
17 Jarome Iginla .40 1.00
18 Eric Daze .08 .20
19 Jocelyn Thibault .20 .50
20 Alex Tanguay .20 .50
21 Joe Sakic .50 1.25
22 Milan Hejduk .20 .50
23 Patrick Roy 1.50 4.00
24 Peter Forsberg .60 1.50
25 Rob Blake .08 .20
26 Bill Guerin .08 .20
27 Marty Turco .20 .50
28 Mike Modano .25 .60
29 Brendan Shanahan .25 .60
30 Brett Hull .30 .75
31 Chris Chelios .20 .50
32 Dominik Hasek .40 1.00
33 Henrik Zetterberg .20 .50
34 Nicklas Lidstrom .20 .50
35 Pavel Datsyuk .20 .50
36 Steve Yzerman 1.25 3.00
37 Mike Comrie .08 .20
38 Ryan Smyth .20 .50
39 Jay Bouwmeester .08 .20
40 Kristian Huselius .08 .20
41 Roberto Luongo .25 .60
42 Olli Jokinen .08 .20
43 Alexander Frolov .08 .20
44 Jason Allison .08 .20
45 Zigmund Palffy .08 .20
46 Marian Gaborik .40 1.00
47 Manny Fernandez .20 .50
48 Jose Theodore .25 .60
49 Saku Koivu .20 .50
50 Jeff Friesen .08 .20
51 Martin Brodeur 1.00 2.50
52 Patrik Elias .08 .20
53 Scott Niedermayer .08 .20
54 Scott Stevens .08 .20
55 Jamie Langenbrunner .08 .20
56 Alexei Yashin .08 .20
57 Rick DiPietro .20 .50
58 Alexei Kovalev .08 .20
59 Anson Carter .08 .20
60 Eric Lindros .25 .60
61 Mark Messier .25 .60
62 Mike Dunham .20 .50
63 Pavel Bure .25 .60
64 Daniel Alfredsson .08 .20
65 Jason Spezza .25 .60
66 Marian Hossa .20 .50
67 Martin Havlat .20 .50
68 Patrick Lalime .20 .50
69 Jeremy Roenick .25 .60
70 John LeClair .08 .20
71 Simon Gagne .08 .20
72 Tony Amonte .08 .20
73 Sean Burke .20 .50
74 Mario Lemieux 1.50 4.00
75 Evgeni Nabokov .25 .60
76 Pavol Demitra .08 .20
77 Al MacInnis .08 .20
78 Barret Jackman .08 .20
79 Chris Pronger .08 .20
80 Doug Weight .08 .20
81 Keith Tkachuk .20 .50
82 Brad Richards .25 .60
83 Nikolai Khabibulin .25 .60
84 Vincent Lecavalier .25 .60
85 Martin St.Louis .25 .60
86 Owen Nolan .08 .20
87 Alexander Mogilny .08 .20
88 Carlo Colaiacovo .08 .20
89 Nikolai Antropov .08 .20
90 Ed Belfour .25 .60
91 Gary Roberts .08 .20
92 Mats Sundin .25 .60
93 Tie Domi .08 .20
94 Tomas Kaberle .08 .20
95 Ed Jovanovski .08 .20
96 Markus Naslund .08 .20
97 Todd Bertuzzi .08 .20
98 Jaromir Jagr .40 1.00
99 Olaf Kolzig .20 .50
100 Peter Bondra .08 .20

2003-04 ITG Toronto Star Foil

1 Mario Lemieux 2.00 5.00
2 Steve Yzerman 1.50 4.00
3 Peter Forsberg 1.25 3.00
4 Marian Gaborik .75 2.00
5 Dominik Hasek .75 2.00
6 Joe Thornton .75 2.00
7 Henrik Zetterberg .40 1.00
8 Mike Modano .75 2.00
9 Ed Belfour .40 1.00
10 Marian Hossa .40 1.00
11 Owen Nolan .40 1.00
12 Pavel Bure .75 2.00
13 Jose Theodore .75 2.00
14 Mike Comrie .40 1.00
15 Tie Domi .40 1.00
16 Roberto Luongo .75 2.00
17 Saku Koivu .40 1.00
18 Jarome Iginla .75 2.00
19 Brett Hull .75 2.00
20 Markus Naslund .40 1.00
21 Jaromir Jagr 1.25 3.00
22 Jason Spezza .75 2.00
23 Rick Nash 1.25 3.00
24 Jean-Sebastien Giguere .40 1.00
25 Mats Sundin .75 2.00
26 Ilya Kovalchuk 1.25 3.00
27 Dany Heatley .75 2.00
28 Joe Sakic 1.25 3.00
29 Martin Brodeur 1.50 4.00
30 Patrick Roy 2.00 5.00

2000-01 Trenton Titans

COMPLETE SET (24) 12.00 30.00
1 Scott Bertoli .60 1.50
2 Sandy Cohen .80 2.00
3 Aniket Dhadphale .60 1.50
4 Mike Hall .60 1.50
5 Cail MacLean .60 1.50
6 Steve O'Brien .60 1.50
7 Alain St. Hilaire .60 1.50
8 Scott Stirling .60 1.50
9 Jed Whitchurch .60 1.50
10 Vince Williams .60 1.50
11 Mike Haviland ACO .10 .25
12 Troy Ward HCO .10 .25
13 Dennis Bassett .60 1.50
14 Shane Belter .60 1.50
15 Sasha Cucuz .60 1.50
16 Ian Forbes .60 1.50
17 Butch Kaebel .60 1.50
18 Sean Molina .60 1.50
19 Benoit Morin .60 1.50
20 Jeff Potter .60 1.50
21 Paul Spadafora .60 1.50
22 Kam White .60 1.50
23 David Whitworth .60 1.50
24 Clash MASCOT .10 .25

2001-02 Trenton Titans

COMPLETE SET (24) 12.00 30.00
1-1 Syl Apps .75 2.00
1-2 Marco Charpentier .60 1.50
1-3 Aniket Dhadphale .60 1.50
1-4 Kirk Lamb .60 1.50
1-5 Matt Libby .60 1.50
1-6 Cail MacLean .60 1.50
1-7 John Nail .60 1.50
1-8 Geoff Peters .60 1.50
1-9 Scott Ricci .60 1.50
1-10 David St. Germain .60 1.50
1-11 Chuck Weber ACO .10 .25
1-12 Matt Zultek .75 2.00
2-1 Graham Belak .75 2.00
2-2 Scott Bertoli .60 1.50
2-3 Ian Forbes .60 1.50
2-4 Peter Horachek CO .20 .50
2-5 Pat Leahy .60 1.50
2-6 Andreas Moborg .60 1.50
2-7 Dan Murphy .60 1.50
2-8 Steve O'Brien .60 1.50
2-9 Alain St. Hilaire .75 2.00
2-10 Ben Stafford .60 1.50
2-11 Kam White .60 1.50
2-12 Rivet MASCOT .10 .25

2002-03 Trenton Titans

COMPLETE SET (24) 20.00
A1 Scott Bertoli .40 1.00
A2 Adam Edinger .40 1.00
A3 Andy Hedlund .40 1.00
A4 Yann Joseph .40 1.00
A5 B.J. Kilbourne .40 1.00
A6 John Nail .40 1.00
A7 Cody Rudkowsky 1.25 3.00
A8 Kam White .40 1.00
A9 Dustin Wood .40 1.00
A10 Matt Zultek .60 1.50
A11 Bill Armstrong CO .04 .10
A12 Rivet MASCOT .04 .10
B1 Syl Apps .40 1.00
B2 Tyler Beechey .40 1.00
B3 Sean Connolly .40 1.00
B4 Shaun Fisher .40 1.00
B5 Ian Forbes .40 1.00
B6 Mike Hurley .40 1.00
B7 Steve O'Brien .40 1.00
B8 David St. Germain .40 1.00
B9 Jeff Smith .40 1.00
B10 Daniel Tetrault .40 1.00
B11 Vince Williams .40 1.00
B12 Clash MASCOT .04 .10

2003-04 Trenton Titans

COMPLETE SET (16) 6.00 15.00
353 B.J. Abel .40 1.00
354 Andrew Allen .50 1.25
355 Scott Bertoli .40 1.00
356 Mathieu Brunelle .40 1.00
357 Bill Cass .40 1.00
358 Bryce Cockburn .40 1.00
359 Nick Deschenes .40 1.00
360 Peter Fregoe .40 1.00
361 Jay Leach .40 1.00
362 P.J. Martin .40 1.00
363 Devin Rask .40 1.00
364 Dan Riva .40 1.00
365 Jeff Smith .50 1.25
366 Pete Summerfelt .40 1.00
367 Vince Williams .40 1.00
368 Matt Zultek .60 1.50

1994-95 Tri-City Americans

COMPLETE SET (8) 10.00 25.00
1 Dorian Anneck .40 1.00
2 Brent Ascroft .20 .50
3 Brian Boucher 6.00 15.00
4 Rob Butz .20 .50
5 Chad Cabana .30 .75
6 Daymond Langkow 2.00 5.00
7 Ryan Marsh .20 .50
8 Terry Ryan .75 2.00

1995-96 Tri-City Americans

COMPLETE SET (31) 8.00 20.00
1 Chris Anderson .15 .40
2 Dorian Anneck .20 .50
3 Brent Ascroft .15 .40
4 Aaron Baker .20 .50
5 Alexandre Boikov .15 .40
6 Brian Boucher 2.00 5.00
7 Byron Briske .20 .50
8 Bob Brown GM .02 .10
9 Jerry Fredericksen TR .02 .10
10 Dan Focht .20 .50
11 Dylan Gyori .30 .75
12 Mark Hurley .15 .40
13 Mike Hurley .15 .40
14 Zenith Komarniski .20 .50
15 Daymond Langkow .75 2.00
16 Jody Lapeyre .15 .40
17 Bob Loucks CO .02 .10
18 Scott McCallum .15 .40
19 Boyd Olson .15 .40
20 Warren Renden ACO .02 .10
21 Terry Ryan .30 .75
22 Eric Schneider .15 .40
23 Dan Smith .15 .40
24 Craig Stahl .15 .40
25 Jaroslav Svejkovsky .30 .75
26 Jeremy Thompson .15 .40
27 Gary Toor .15 .40
28 Tom Zavediuk .15 .40
29 Eddie the Eagle (Mascot) .02 .10
30 Brian Boucher
Daymond Langkow
Terry Ryan 1.25 3.00
31 Logo Card .02 .10

1998-99 Tri-City Americans

COMPLETE SET (28) 8.00 20.00
1 Jeff Blair .20 .50
2 Josef Melichar .40 1.00
3 Andrew DeSousa .30 .75
4 Darrell Hay .40 1.00
5 Jeff Katcher .20 .50
6 Toni Bader .20 .50
7 Jaroslav Kristek .40 1.00
8 Ken McKay .20 .50
9 Eric Johannson .20 .50
10 Scott Gomez 1.25 3.00
11 Ryley Layden .20 .50
12 Tim Green .20 .50
13 Blake Evans .20 .50
14 K.C. Timmons .20 .50
15 Jordan Landry .20 .50
16 Dylan Gyori .40 1.00
17 Brad Ference .60 1.50
18 Mike Muzechka .20 .50
19 Stephen Peat .60 1.50
20 Curtis Huppe .30 .75
21 Mike Lee .20 .50
22 Jody Lapeyre .20 .50
23 Andrew Guindon .20 .50
24 Blake Ward .30 .75
25 Terry Bangen ACO
AGM .02 .10
26 Training Staff .02 .10
27 Don Hay HCO
GM .20 .50
28 Craig West BR .02 .10

2002-03 Tri-City Stormfront

COMPLETE SET (25) 20.00 40.00
1 Cover Card .10 .25
2 Stormy MASCOT .10 .25
3 Brian Kilburg .75 2.00
4 Nick Klaren .75 2.00
5 Luke Lucyk 1.25 3.00
6 Mark Agnew .75 2.00
7 Tim Madsen .75 2.00
8 Geoff Paukovich .75 2.00
9 Chris Nathe .75 2.00
10 Ryan Dingle .75 2.00
11 Josh Leddy .75 2.00
12 Matt Scherer .75 2.00
13 Bill Thomas .75 2.00
14 Scott Parse .75 2.00
15 Steve Wagner .75 2.00
16 Tom Pohl .75 2.00
17 David Boguslawski .75 2.00
18 James Martin .75 2.00
19 Chad Anderson .75 2.00
20 Mark Van Guilder .75 2.00
21 T.J. Dahl .75 2.00
22 Casey Mapes .75 2.00
23 Eric Aarnio .75 2.00
24 Tom Kowal .75 2.00
25 Regg Simon .75 2.00

2014-15 Trois-Rivieres Blizzard

COMPLETE SET () 6.00 15.00
1 Etienne Archambault .30 .75
2 Pierre-Olivier Beaulieu .30 .75
3 Michael Belanger .30 .75
4 Thomas Bellemare .30 .75
5 Jonathan Bellemarre .30 .75
6 Stephane Boileau .30 .75
7 Gabriel Boulin-Gagnon .30 .75
8 Marco Cousineau .30 .75
9 Marco Cousineau .30 .75
10 Marc-Andre Daneau .30 .75
11 Jean-Francois David .30 .75
12 Nicolas Dumoulin .30 .75
13 Nicolas Dumoulin .30 .75
14 Boby Fugere .30 .75
15 Carl Gelinas .30 .75
16 Marc-Antoine Gelinas .30 .75
17 Mathieu Guertin .30 .75
18 Marc-Andre Huot .30 .75
19 Yann Joseph .30 .75
20 Tommy Lafontaine .30 .75
21 Benjamin Lecomte .30 .75
22 Marc-Antoine Moisan .30 .75
23 Francois Ouimet .30 .75
24 Hubert Poulin .30 .75
25 Christophe Rodrigue .30 .75

1997-98 Tucson Gila Monsters

COMPLETE SET (10) 4.00 10.00
1 Jon Rowe .40 1.00
2 Dan Marcotte .40 1.00
3 David Piirto .40 1.00
4 Peter Romeo .40 1.00
5 Patrick Bisaillon .40 1.00
6 Jason Crane .40 1.00
7 Chris Everett .40 1.00
8 Sam Fields .40 1.00
9 Pierre Gagnon .40 1.00
10 Aigars Mironovics .40 1.00

1966-67 Tulsa Oilers

COMPLETE SET (12) 25.00 50.00
1 Ken Campbell 1.50 3.00
2 Andrew Champagne 1.50 3.00
3 Doug Dunville 1.50 3.00
4 Bill Flett 5.00 10.00
5 Nick Harbaruk 1.50 3.00
6 Lowell MacDonald 5.00 10.00
7 Jim McKenny 2.50 5.00
8 Al Millar 1.50 3.00
9 Marc Reaume 2.00 4.00
10 Harry Shaw 1.50 3.00
11 Gary Venneruzzo 2.50 5.00
12 Ron Ward 2.00 4.00

1992-93 Tulsa Oilers

COMPLETE SET (18) 3.00 8.00
1 Mike Berger .20 .50
2 Pat Cavanagh .20 .50
3 Shaun Clouston .20 .50
4 Brian Fiatt
Tony Martin .20 .50
5 Tony Fiore .20 .50
6 Taylor Hall .30 .75
7 Tom Karalis .20 .50
8 Greg MacEachern .20 .50
9 Terry MacLean .20 .50
10 Al Murphy .20 .50
11 Sylvain Naud .30 .75
12 Mario Nobili .20 .50
13 Jody Praznik .20 .50
14 E.J. Sauer .20 .50
15 Craig Shepherd .20 .50
16 Garry Unger .40 1.00
17 Team Photo .20 .50
18 Title Card .20 .50

1993-94 Tulsa Oilers

COMPLETE SET (18) 3.00 8.00
1 Luc Beausoleil .30 .75
2 Mike Berger .20 .50
3 Shaun Clouston .20 .50
4 Craig Coxe .30 .75
5 Brian Flatt .20 .50
6 Taylor Hall .20 .50
7 Tom Karalis .20 .50
8 Doug Lawrence .30 .75
9 Jamie Loewen .20 .50
10 Mike MacWilliam .20 .50
11 Al Murphy .20 .50
12 Sylvain Naud .30 .75
13 Jody Praznik .20 .50
14 Chad Seibel .20 .50
15 Brian Shantz .20 .50
16 Sean Whyte .20 .50
17 Garry Unger CO .30 .75
18 Crown Auto World
Sponsor .02 .10

2003-04 Tulsa Oilers

COMPLETE SET (24) 4.00 10.00
1 Header Card .04 .10
2 Jason Bermingham .20 .50
3 Rod Branch .30 .75
4 Anthony D'Arpino .20 .50
5 Jordon Flodell .20 .50
6 Dan Gravelle .20 .50
7 Regan Harper .20 .50
8 Tim Kelleher .30 .75
9 Cam Kuzyk .20 .50
10 Branislav Kvetan .20 .50
11 Todd Marcellus .20 .50
12 Rob Meanchoff .20 .50
13 Aaron Millar .20 .50
14 Chris Page .20 .50
15 Derek Reynolds .20 .50
16 Jordan Roach .20 .50
17 Shawn Scanzano .20 .50
18 Wes Scanzano .20 .50
19 Lukas Sedlacek .20 .50
20 Butch Kaebel CO .04 .10
21 Steve Enlow EQM .04 .10
22 Ad card .04 .10
23 Ad card .04 .10
24 Stuart Nichols TR .04 .10

2004-05 Tulsa Oilers

COMPLETE SET (24) 6.00 15.00
1 Cover Card .04 .10
2 Jason Birmingham .30 .75
3 Cameron Breitkreuz .30 .75
4 Mike Brusseau .30 .75
5 Jeff Cameron .30 .75
6 Jaroslav Cesky .30 .75
7 Lucas Dora .30 .75
8 Steve Enlow .30 .75
9 John Glavota .30 .75
10 Dan Gravelle .30 .75
11 Malcolm Hutt .30 .75
12 Mario Joly .30 .75
13 Butch Kaebel CO .04 .10
14 Klage Kaebel .30 .75
15 Justin Laird .30 .75
16 Todd Marcellus .30 .75
17 Justin Ossachuk .30 .75
18 Todd Paul .30 .75
19 Chris Pelletier .30 .75
20 Doug Pirnak .30 .75
21 Angela Ruggiero 1.25 3.00
22 Bill Ruggiero .40 1.00
23 Dallas Steward .30 .75
24 Oklahoma Trooper .04 .10

1999-00 Tupelo T-Rex

COMPLETE SET (19) 12.00 30.00
1 Brent Scott 1.25 3.00
2 Trevor Amundrud 1.25 3.00
3 Bob Brandon 1.25 3.00
4 Jay Pecora .75 2.00
5 Marc Vachon .75 2.00
6 Dave Szabo .75 2.00
7 Joe Van Volsen .75 2.00
8 Regan Harper .75 2.00
9 Jeff Mercer .75 2.00
10 Dave Wilejto .75 2.00
11 Clint Black .75 2.00
12 Pat Powers .75 2.00
13 Roby Gropp 1.25 3.00
14 Casey Hungle .75 2.00
15 Mike Mayhew .75 2.00
16 Jason Dexter .75 2.00
17 Kevin Evans .75 2.00
18 Martin Belanger .75 2.00
19 Ryan Rintoul .75 2.00

1998-99 UHL All-Stars

COMPLETE SET (22) 16.00 40.00
1 Ross Wilson .75 2.00
2 Stephane Brochu .75 2.00
3 Brian Downey .75 2.00
4 Mark Bultje .75 2.00
5 David Beauregard .75 2.00
6 Joe Dimaline .75 2.00
7 John Vary .75 2.00
8 Paul Willett .75 2.00
9 Vadim Podrezov .75 2.00
10 Wayne Muir .75 2.00
11 Brian Mueller .75 2.00
12 Alexei Deev .75 2.00
13 Lindsay Vallis .75 2.00
14 Patrice Robitaille .75 2.00
15 Jean-Francois Rivard .75 2.00
16 Jason Firth .75 2.00
17 Wayne Strachan .75 2.00
18 Brian LaFleur .75 2.00
19 Kevin Kerr .75 2.00
20 Garry Gulash .75 2.00
21 Mike Melas .75 2.00
22 Glenn Stewart .75 2.00

1999-00 UHL All-Stars East

COMPLETE SET (22) 4.80 12.00
1T Yevgeny Shaldybin .20 .50
2T Stephan Brochu .20 .50
3T Nick Stajduhar .20 .50
4T Sam Myre .20 .50
5T Mike Maurice .20 .50
6T Chris Palmer .20 .50
7T Chris Grenville .20 .50
8T Gary Roach .20 .50
9T David Mayes .20 .50
10T John Vecchiarelli .40 1.00
11T Nic Beaudoin .20 .50
12T Peter Cermak .20 .50
13T Jay Neal .20 .50
14T Alexei Deev .20 .50
15T Chad Grills .20 .50
16T Dieter Kochan .75 2.00
17T Mark Richards .20 .50
18T Lindsay Vallis .20 .50
19T Ross Wilson .20 .50
20T Doug Searle .20 .50
21T Brent Gretzky .40 1.00
22T Header
Checklist .08 .25

1999-00 UHL All-Stars West

COMPLETE SET (22) 4.80 12.00
1T Kelly Hurd .20 .50
2T Frederic Bouchard .20 .50
3T Jim Durhart .20 .50
4T Jeff Winter .20 .50
5T Lonnie Loach .40 1.00
6T Brian Regan .30 .75
7T Ryan Lindsay .20 .50
8T Jeremy Rebek .20 .50
9T Colin Chaulk .20 .50
10T Scott Feasby .20 .50
11T Joe Dimaline .20 .50
12T Quinn Hancock .20 .50
13T Mike McCourt .20 .50
14T Keith Osborne .30 .75
15T Jeff Loder .20 .50
16T Garry Gulash .20 .50
17T Hugo Proulx .20 .50
18T Glenn Stewart .20 .50
19T Kevin Kerr .40 1.00
20T Jason Firth .30 .75
21T Mike Figliomeni .20 .50
22T Header
Checklist .08 .25

1990 UMD Hull Collection

COMPLETE SET (12) 6.00 15.00
COMMON CARD (1-12) .60 1.50
1 Hull Portrait 1.25 3.00

1999-00 Utah Grizzlies

COMPLETE SET (36) 8.00 20.00
1 Volkswagon Golf .04 .10
2 Rich Parent .75 2.00
3 Richard Park .30 .75
4 John Purves .75 2.00
5 Jarrod Skalde .75 2.00
6 Bob Bourne CO .20 .50
7 Checklist .04 .10
8 Volkswagon Jetta .04 .10
9 Gord Dineen .08 .25
10 Sean Tallaire .30 .75
11 Micah Aivazoff .75 2.00
12 Shawn Penn .30 .75
13 Larry Ness TR .08 .25
14 Utah Grizzlies .08 .25
15 Volkswagon New Beetle .04 .10
16 Joe Frederick .30 .75
17 Stewart Malgunas .30 .75
18 Mick Vukota .30 .75
19 Patrick Neaton .30 .75
20 Dean Chynoweth .30 .75
21 Micah Aivazoff .75 2.00
21 Gord Dineen .08 .25
22 Volkswagon Passat .04 .10
23 Rob Bonneau .30 .75
24 Ian Gordon .30 .75
25 Brad Lauer .30 .75
26 Neil Brady .30 .75
27 Grizbee MAS .08 .25
28 Mick Vukota .30 .75
29 Volkswagon GTI .04 .10
30 Brad Miller .30 .75
31 Jeff Sharples .30 .75
32 Darcy Werenka .30 .75
33 Zarley Zalapski .30 .75
34 Greg Payette TR .08 .25
35 Utah Freezz Indoor Soccer .04 .10

2000-01 Utah Grizzlies

COMPLETE SET (37) 10.00 25.00
1 Volkswagon GTI SPONSOR .04 .10
2 Mike Bales .40 1.50
3 Steve Gainey .80 1.50
4 Brad Lauer .30 1.00
5 Jeff MacMillan .30 1.00
6 Bob Bourne CO .20 .50
7 Utah Grizzlies CL .04 .10
8 Passat SPONSOR .04 .10
9 Patrick Neaton .30 1.00
10 John Erskine .80 2.00
11 John Purves .40 1.50
12 Greg Leeb .40 1.00
13 Jason Taylor CO .10 .25
14 Team Photo .30 1.00
15 New Beetle SPONSOR .04 .10

16 Rick Tabaracci .40 1.50
17 Chris Wells .30 1.00
18 Ryan Christie .60 1.00
19 Alan Letang .30 1.00
20 Craig Ludwig CO .30 1.00
21 1997-98 Team Photo .10 .25
22 Jetta SPONSOR .04 .10
23 Evgeny Tsybouk .40 1.00
24 Eric Houde .40 1.00
25 David Ling .40 1.50
26 Gavin Morgan .30 1.00
27 Payette
Ness
Lund STAFF .04 .10
28 1996-97 Team Photo .10 .25
29 Golf SPONSOR .04 .10
30 Richard Jackman .40 1.00
31 Gregor Baumgartner .40 1.00
32 Jamie Wright .40 1.00
33 Mark Wotton .30 1.00
34 Grizzbee MASCOT .04 .10
35 1995-96 Team Photo .10 .25
36 1998-99 Team Photo .04 .10
37 1999-00 Team Photo .04 .10

2001-02 Utah Grizzlies

COMPLETE SET (35) 14.22 35.56
1 Paul Elliott .40 1.00
2 John Erskine .75 2.00
3 Gregor Baumgartner .40 1.00
4 Jon Sim .60 1.50
5 Tommy Salo 1.25 3.00
6 Mascot .04 .10
7 The New Beetle .04 .10
8 Greg Hawgood .40 1.00
9 John Purves .75 2.00
10 Steve Gainey .75 2.00
11 Serge Payer .40 1.00
12 Zigmund Palffy 1.25 3.00
13 Equipment Assistants .04 .10
14 The Cabrino GL .04 .10
15 Mark Wotton .40 1.00
16 Marc Kristoffersson .60 1.50
17 Eric Beaudoin .40 1.00
18 Roman Lyashenko .60 1.50
19 Vladimir Orszagh .40 1.00
20 Bob Bassen ACO .04 .10
21 The GTI .04 .10
22 Jeff MacMillan .40 1.00
23 Cameron Mann .60 1.50
24 Ryan Jardine .60 1.50
25 Jim Montgomery .60 1.50
26 Chad Alban .75 2.00
27 EQMG and TR .04 .10
28 The New Passat .04 .10
29 Dan Jancevski .60 1.50
30 Justin Cox .40 1.00
31 Kyle Rossiter .60 1.50
32 Gavin Morgan .40 1.00
33 Wade Flaherty .60 1.50
34 Don Hay CO .04 .10
35 The Jetta Wagon .04 .10

2002-03 Utah Grizzlies

COMPLETE SET (30) 15.00 40.00
1 Jonathan Sim .60 1.50
2 Steve Ott 3.00 8.00
3 Dan Jancevski .40 1.00
4 Eric Chouinard .40 1.00
5 Justin Cox .40 1.00
6 Checklist .04 .10
7 John Erskine .40 1.00
8 Corey Hirsch .60 1.50
9 Barrett Heisten .40 1.00
10 David Gosselin .40 1.00
11 Jim Montgomery .40 1.00
12 Don Hay HCO .04 .10
13 Steve Gainey .40 1.00
14 Marc-Andre Thinel .40 1.00
15 Jeff Bateman .40 1.00
16 Greg Hawgood .40 1.00
17 David Oliver .40 1.00
18 Bob Bassen ACO .04 .10
19 Jason Bacashihua 2.00 5.00
20 Marc Kristoffersson .60 1.50
21 Jeff MacMillan .40 1.00
22 Alexei Komarov .40 1.00
23 Matthieu Descoteaux .40 1.00
24 Richard Krouse EM .04 .10
25 Gavin Morgan .40 1.00
26 Mark Wotton .40 1.00
27 Mike Smith .40 1.00
28 Eric Landry .40 1.00
29 Mascot .04 .10
30 Greg Payette .40 1.00

1998-99 Val d'Or Foreurs

COMPLETE SET (29) 16.00 40.00
1 Christian Daigle .40 1.00
2 Benoit Dusablon 1.25 3.00
3 Guillaume Lamoureux .40 1.00
4 Danny Groulx .40 1.00
5 Alain Charbonneau .40 1.00
6 Jonathan Fauteux .40 1.00
7 Didier Tremblay .40 1.00
8 Dynamit MASCOT .40 1.00
9 Roberto Luongo 6.00 15.00
10 Nick Greenough .40 1.00
11 Lucio DeMartinis .40 1.00
12 Gaston Therien .40 1.00
13 Francois Hardy .40 1.00
14 David St.Germain .40 1.00
15 Sebastien Laprise .40 1.00
16 Luc Girard .40 1.00
17 Simon Gamache 1.50 4.00
18 Steve Morency .40 1.00
19 Seneque Hyacinthe .40 1.00
20 Dave Verville .40 1.00
21 Alexandre Page .40 1.00
22 Denis Boily .40 1.00
23 Dwight Wolfe .40 1.00
24 Jerome Petit .40 1.00
25 Eric Dubois .40 1.00
26 Jonathan Charron .40 1.00
S1 Anthony Quessy .40 1.00
S2 Mathieau Lendick .40 1.00
S3 Philippe Ouellette .40 1.00

2000-01 Val d'Or Foreurs

COMPLETE SET (25) 6.00 15.00
1 Mathieu Roy .15 .40
2 Yan Hallee .15 .40
3 Chris Lyness .15 .40
4 Hugo Levesque .15 .40
5 Luc Girard .15 .40
6 David Cloutier .15 .40
7 Tomas Psenka .15 .40
8 Nicolas Pelletier .30 .75
9 Kory Baker .15 .40
10 Steve Pelletier .15 .40
11 Alex Turcotte .15 .40
12 Simon Gamache 1.25 3.00
13 Simon Lajeunesse .75 2.00
14 Alexandre Rouleau .15 .40
15 Samuel Duplain .15 .40
16 Pierre Morvan .15 .40
17 Brandon Reid 1.25 3.00
18 Mathieu Bastien .15 .40
19 Maxime Daigneault .75 2.00
20 Jerome Bergeron .15 .40
21 Frederic Bedard .15 .40
22 Eric Fortier .15 .40
23 Stephane Veilleux .15 .40
24 Seneque Hyacinthe .15 .40
NNO Team CL .04 .10

2000-01 Val d'Or Foreurs Signed

COMPLETE SET (25) 30.00 75.00
1 Mathieu Roy .80 2.00
2 Yan Hallee .80 2.00
3 Chris Lyness .80 2.00
4 Hugo Levesque .80 2.00
5 Luc Girard .80 2.00
6 David Cloutier .80 2.00
7 Tomas Psenka .80 2.00
8 Nicolas Pelletier 1.60 4.00
9 Kory Baker .80 2.00
10 Steve Pelletier .80 2.00
11 Alex Turcotte .80 2.00
12 Simon Gamache 4.00 15.00
13 Simon Lajeunesse 4.00 10.00
14 Alexandre Rouleau .80 2.00
15 Samuel Duplain .80 2.00
16 Pierre Morvan .80 2.00
17 Brandon Reid 4.00 15.00
18 Mathieu Bastien .80 2.00
19 Maxime Daigneault 6.00 10.00
20 Jerome Bergeron .80 2.00
21 Frederic Bedard .80 2.00
22 Eric Fortier .80 2.00
23 Stephane Veilleux .80 2.00
24 Seneque Hyacinthe .80 2.00
NNO Team CL .04 .25

2001-02 Val d'Or Foreurs

COMPLETE SET (24) 4.80 12.00
1 Philippe Seguin .20 .50
2 Hugo Levesque .20 .50
3 Chaz Johnson .20 .50
4 Remy Tremblay .20 .50
5 Steve Richards .20 .50
6 Jonathan Gautier .20 .50
7 Vincent Duriau .20 .50
8 Jeff Cotton .20 .50
9 Patrice Bilodeau .20 .50
10 Frederic Bedard .20 .50
11 Nicolas Pelletier .20 .50
12 Francois Gagnon .20 .50
13 Alexandre Rouleau .20 .50
14 Pierre Morvan .20 .50
15 Mathieu Roy .20 .50
16 Samuel Gibbons .20 .50
17 Jonathan Charette .20 .50
18 Kyle Schutte .20 .50
19 Steve Pelletier .20 .50
20 Maxime Daigneault .40 1.00
21 Eric Fortier .30 .75
22 Mathieu Simard .20 .50
23 Adam Morneau .20 .50
24 David Rodman .20 .50

2002-03 Val d'Or Foreurs

COMPLETE SET (24) 5.00 12.00
1 Eric Glaude .20 .50
2 Pierre-Luc Laprise .20 .50
3 Patrice Bilodeau .20 .50
4 Vincent Duriau .20 .50
5 Mark Hurtubise .20 .50
6 Frederic Bedard .20 .50
7 Artem Kozitsyn .20 .50
8 Mathieu Curadeau .20 .50
9 Francois Gagnon .20 .50
10 Erik Lajoie .20 .50
11 Mathieu Dumas .20 .50
12 Denis Berube .30 .75
13 Olivier Latendresse .30 .75
14 Mathieu Roy .60 1.50
15 Benoit Genesse .20 .50
16 Jonathan Charette .20 .50
17 Shawn Collymore .30 .75
18 Didier Bochatay .20 .50
19 Maxime Daigneault .30 .75
20 Jeff Cotton .20 .50
21 Dominic Lachaine .20 .50
22 David Rodman .20 .50
23 Chaz Johnson .20 .50
24 Checklist .04 .10

2003-04 Val d'Or Foreurs

COMPLETE SET (23) 5.00 12.00
1 Benoit Lessard .20 .50
2 Etienne Grandmont .20 .50
3 Dominic Lachaine .20 .50
4 Patrice Bilodeau .20 .50
5 Mark Hurtubise .20 .50
6 Luc Bourdon .75 2.00
7 Vladimir Kutny .20 .50
8 Artem Kozitsyn .20 .50
9 Jonathan Charette .20 .50
10 Francois Gagnon .20 .50
11 Erik Lajoie .20 .50
12 Mathieu Dumas .20 .50
13 Francois Thuot .30 .75
14 Olivier Latendresse .20 .50
15 Benoit Piche .20 .50
16 Shawn Collymore .20 .50
17 Guillaume Chicoine .20 .50
18 Maxime Daigneault .40 1.00
19 Jeff Cotton .20 .50
20 Patrick Bordeleau .20 .50
21 Mathieu Curadeau .20 .50
22 Sebastien Bisaillon .20 .50
23 Chaz Johnson .20 .50

1973-74 Vancouver Blazers

COMPLETE SET (21) 25.00 50.00
1 Jim Adair 1.50 3.00
2 Yves Archambault 1.50 3.00
3 Don Burgess 2.00 4.00
4 Bryan Campbell 2.00 4.00
5 Colin Campbell 2.50 6.00
6 Jim Cardiff 1.50 3.00
7 Mike Chernoff 1.50 3.00
8 Peter Donnelly 1.50 3.00
9 George Gardner 1.50 3.00
10 Sam Gellard 1.50 3.00
11 Ed Hatoum 1.50 3.00
12 Dave Hutchison 2.00 4.00
13 Danny Lawton 1.50 3.00
14 Ralph MacSweyn 1.50 3.00
15 Denis Meloche 1.50 3.00
16 John Migneault 1.50 3.00
17 Murray Myers 1.50 3.00
18 Michel Plante 1.50 3.00
19 Ron Plumb 2.00 4.00
20 Claude St. Sauveur 1.50 3.00
21 Irv Spencer 2.00 4.00

2001-02 Vancouver Giants

COMPLETE SET (25) 4.80 12.00
1 Title Card .10 .25
2 Mark Ardelan .20 .50
3 Mark Ashton .20 .50
4 Chad Bassen .20 .50
5 Jeff Beatch .20 .50
6 Robin Big Snake .40 1.00
7 Josh Bonar .20 .50
8 Pat Brandreth .20 .50
9 Jeff Coulter .20 .50
10 Don Choukalos .30 .75
11 Andrew Davidson .20 .50
12 Andrew DeSousa .20 .50
13 Marian Havel .30 .75
14 Jeremy Jackson .20 .50
15 Brett Jaeger .20 .50
16 Robin Kovar .20 .50
17 Darren Lynch .30 .75
18 Nick Marach .20 .50
19 Tyson Marsh .20 .50
20 T.J. Mulock .20 .50
21 Jack Redlick .20 .50
22 Dave Selthun .20 .50
23 Chris Stubel .20 .50
24 Ryan Thomas .20 .50
25 Clay Thoring .20 .50

2003-04 Vancouver Giants

COMPLETE SET (25) 10.00 25.00
1 Title Card .04 .10
2 Jordan McLaughlin .20 .50
3 Aaron Sorochan .20 .50
4 Ryan Mayko .20 .50
5 Chad Scharff .20 .50
6 Mark Fistric .30 .75
7 Brennan Chapman .20 .50
8 Joe Logan .20 .50
9 Marcin Kolusz .20 .50
10 Adam Courchaine .20 .50
11 Triston Grant .20 .50
12 Kyle Bruce .20 .50
13 Darrell May .20 .50
14 Gilbert Brule 6.00 15.00
15 Kevin Hayman .20 .50
16 Mitch Bartley .20 .50
17 Braden Appleby .20 .50
18 Matt Kassian .20 .50
19 Tyson Marsh .30 .75
20 Darren Lynch .20 .50
21 Tim Kraus .20 .50
22 Ty Morris .20 .50
23 Lukas Pulpan .20 .50
24 Dean Evason HCO .04 .10
25 Team Photo .20 .50

2004-05 Vancouver Giants

COMPLETE SET 8.00 20.00
1 Luke Egener .20 .50
2 Mark Fistric .30 .75
3 Cody Franson .20 .50
4 Stewart Thiessen .20 .50
5 Jason Reese .20 .50
6 Matt Robinson .20 .50
7 J.D. Watt .20 .50
8 Adam Courchaine .20 .50
9 Triston Grant .20 .50
10 Keith Voytechek .20 .50
11 Shaun Vey .20 .50
12 Andrej Meszaros .40 1.00
13 Gilbert Brule 2.00 5.00
14 Mitch Bartley .20 .50
15 Matt Kassian .20 .50
16 Max Gordichuk .20 .50
17 Garet Hunt .20 .50
18 Paul Albers .20 .50
19 Kyle Lamb .20 .50
20 Tim Kraus .20 .50
21 Chad Scharff .20 .50
22 Marek Schwarz .75 2.00
23 Conlan Seder .20 .50
24 Adam Jennings .20 .50

2005-06 Vancouver Giants

COMPLETE SET (25) 8.00 20.00
1 Paul Albers .30 .75
2 Mitchell Bartley .30 .75
3 Mario Bliznak .30 .75
4 Jonathon Blum .30 .75
5 Gilbert Brule 2.00 4.00
6 Mitch Czibere .30 .75
7 Brett Festerling .30 .75
8 Mark Fistric .50 1.25
9 John Flatters .30 .75
10 Cody Franson .30 .75
11 Garet Hunt .30 .75
12 Tim Kraus .30 .75
13 Kyle Lamb .30 .75
14 Milan Lucic 2.00 5.00
15 Spencer Machacek .30 .75
16 Brendan Mikkelson .40 1.00
17 Jason Reese .30 .75
18 Michal Repik .30 .75
19 David Rutherford .30 .75
20 Chad Scharff .30 .75
21 Tyson Sexsmith .30 .75
22 Dustin Slade .30 .75
23 Tommy Tartaglione .30 .75
24 J.D. Watt .30 .75
25 Vancouver Giants .04 .10

1995 Vancouver VooDoo RHI

COMPLETE SET (25) 3.00 8.00
1 Title Card CL .02 .10
2 Tiger Williams .40 1.00
3 James Jenson .20 .50
4 Laurie Billeck .15 .40
5 Doug McCarthy .15 .40
6 Jason Knox .15 .40
7 Brent Thurston .15 .40
8 Dave Cairns CO .02 .10
9 Jason Jennings .15 .40
10 Shayne Green .15 .40
11 Rob Dumas .15 .40
12 Ivan Matulik .15 .40
13 Rob Stewart .15 .40
14 Doug Ast .20 .50
15 Chris Morrison .15 .40
17 Kevin Hoffman .15 .40
17 Ryan Harrison .15 .40
18 Ken Kinney .20 .50
19 Merv Priest .15 .40
20 Steve Brown .15 .40
21 Ryan Harrison/1994 All Star Card .15 .40
22 VooDoo Dolls .15 .40
23 1995 Season Schedules .02 .10
24 VooDoo Merchandise Card .02 .10
25 Titan (Mascot) .02 .10

2003-04 Vernon Vipers

COMPLETE SET (22) 4.00 10.00
1 Checklist .04 .10
2 Steve Belanger .20 .50
3 David Boudreau .20 .50
4 Cole Byers .20 .50
5 Dustin Claffey .20 .50
6 Dallas Costanzo .20 .50
7 Scott Dafoe .20 .50
8 Ryan Kindret .20 .50
9 Reed Kipp .20 .50
10 Andrew Lord .20 .50
11 Mark Nelson .20 .50
12 Luke Pierce .20 .50
13 Les Reaney .20 .50
14 Mike Santorelli .20 .50
15 Mark Sibbald .20 .50
16 Aaron Volpatti .20 .50
17 Jake Wilkens .20 .50
18 Mark Wilson .20 .50
19 Andy Zulyniak .20 .50
20 Mike Vandekamp CO .04 .10
21 Bob Dever ACO .04 .10
22 Shawn Bourgeois ACO .04 .10

2004-05 Vernon Vipers

COMPLETE SET (25) 6.00 15.00
1 Checklist Card .04 .10
2 Mark Nelson .30 .75
3 Mark Sibbald .30 .75
4 Dean Strong .30 .75
5 Matt Watkins .30 .75
6 History Card .04 .10
7 Sssniper MASCOT .04 .10
8 Andy Zulyniak .30 .75
9 Ryan Whitfield .30 .75
10 Scott Wallace .30 .75
11 Aaron Volpatti .30 .75
12 Mike Ullrich .30 .75
13 Rob Turville .30 .75
14 Lyle Tassone .30 .75
15 Matt Swerhone .30 .75
16 Aaron Schepers .30 .75
17 Mick McCrimmon .30 .75
18 Reed Kipp .30 .75
19 Corey Gannon .30 .75
20 Jeff Fedyk .30 .75
21 Wade Davison .30 .75
22 Dallas Costanzo .30 .75
23 Kurtis Colling .30 .75
24 Troy Cherwinski .30 .75
25 Matt Bourdreau .30 .75

2005-06 Vernon Vipers

COMPLETE SET (25) 6.00 15.00
1 Vernon Vipers CL .02 .10
2 David Arduin .30 .75
3 Hunter Bishop .30 .75
4 Travis Brisebois .30 .75
5 Patrick Cey .30 .75
6 Troy Cherwinski .30 .75
7 Andrew Coburn .30 .75
8 Chris Crowell .30 .75
9 Wade Davison .30 .75
10 Korey Gannon .30 .75
11 Chay Genoway .30 .75
12 Jerry Holden .30 .75
13 Kevyn Kirbyson .30 .75
14 Mickey McCrimmon .30 .75
15 Cody McMullin .30 .75
16 Mike Nichol .30 .75
17 Jon Olthuis .30 .75
18 Shawn Overton .30 .75
19 Matt Swerhone .30 .75
20 Mike Ullrich .30 .75
21 Aaron Volpatti .30 .75
22 Chad Wren .30 .75
23 Andy Zulyniak .30 .75
24 Viper History .02 .10
25 Sniper MASCOT .02 .10

2007-08 Vernon Vipers

COMPLETE SET (25) 10.00 20.00
1 History Card .02 .10
2 Kyle Bigos .40 1.00
3 Hunter Bishop .40 1.00
4 Travis Brisebois .40 1.00
5 Bryce Christianson .40 1.00
6 Chris Crowell .40 1.00
7 Matt Cumming .40 1.00
8 John Digness .40 1.00
9 Trent Dorais .40 1.00
10 Dallas Goodrunning .40 1.00
11 Lucas Gore .40 1.00
12 Cody Ikkala .40 1.00
13 Conner Jones .40 1.00
14 Kellen Jones .40 1.00
15 Ryan Kakoske .40 1.00
16 Brock Palasty .40 1.00
17 Braden Pimm .40 1.00
18 Eliot Raibl .40 1.00
19 Patrick Raley .40 1.00
20 Patrick Rogan .40 1.00
21 Rob Short .40 1.00
22 Evan Witt .40 1.00
23 Scott Zurevinski .40 1.00
24 SS Sniper MASCOT .02 .10
25 Checklist .02 .10

2014-15 Vernon Vipers

COMPLETE SET (22) 6.00 15.00
1 Thomas Aldworth .30 .75
2 Mackenzie Bauer .30 .75
3 Riley Brandt .30 .75
4 Blaine Caton .30 .75
5 Ken Citron .30 .75
6 Johny Coughlin .30 .75
7 Liam Coughlin .30 .75
8 T.J. Dumonceaux .30 .75
9 Brandon Egli .30 .75
10 Liam Finlay .30 .75
11 Riley Guenther .30 .75
12 Linden Hora .30 .75
13 Anthony Latina .30 .75
14 Colton McCarthy .30 .75
15 Mitch Meek .30 .75
16 Mitchell Oliver .30 .75
17 Nicholas Rasovic .30 .75
18 Jarrod Schamerhorn .30 .75
19 Luke Shiplo .30 .75
20 Danny Todosychuk .30 .75
21 Luke Voltin .30 .75
22 Jagger Williamson .30 .75

1981-82 Victoria Cougars

COMPLETE SET (16) 8.00 20.00
1 Bob Bales .40 1.00
2 Greg Barber .40 1.00
3 Ray Benik .40 1.00
4 Rich Chernomaz .60 1.50
5 Daryl Coldwell .40 1.00
6 Geoff Courtnall 3.00 8.00
7 Paul Cyr .75 2.00
8 Wade Jenson .40 1.00
9 Stu Kulak .60 1.50
10 Peter Martin .40 1.00
11 John Mokosak .40 1.00
12 Mark Morrison .40 1.00
13 Bryant Seaton .40 1.00
14 Jack Shupe .40 1.00
15 Eric Thurston .40 1.00
16 Randy Wickware .40 1.00

1982-83 Victoria Cougars

COMPLETE SET (23) 25.00 50.00
1 Steve Bayliss .20 .50
2 Ray Benik .20 .50
3 Rich Chernomaz .40 1.00
4 Geoff Courtnall 1.50 4.00
5 Russ Courtnall 2.50 6.00
6 Paul Cyr .40 1.00
7 Curt Fraser .60 1.50
8 Grant Fuhr 10.00 25.00
9 Shawn Green .20 .50
10 Fabian Joseph .40 1.00
11 Stu Kulak .40 1.00
12 Brenn Leach .20 .50
13 Gary Lupul .20 .50
14 Jack MacKeigan .20 .50
15 Dave Mackey .40 1.00
16 Mark McLeary .20 .50
17 Dan Moberg .20 .50
18 John Mokosak .20 .50
19 Mark Morrison .20 .50
20 Brad Palmer .40 1.00
21 Barry Pederson .75 2.00
22 Eric Thurston .20 .50
23 Ron Viglasi .20 .50
24 Doug Hannesson 10.00 25.00

1983-84 Victoria Cougars

COMPLETE SET (24) 8.00 20.00
1 Misko Antisin .40 1.00
2 Murray Bannerman .75 2.00
3 Steve Baylis .20 .50
4 Paul Bifano .20 .50
5 Russ Courtnall 2.00 5.00
6 Greg Davies .20 .50
7 Dean Drozdiak .20 .50
8 Jim Gunn .20 .50
9 Richard Hajdu .20 .50
10 Randy Hansch .40 1.00
11 Matt Hervey .20 .50
12 Fabian Joseph .40 1.00
13 Rob Kivell .20 .50
14 Brenn Leach .20 .50
15 Jack Mackeigan .20 .50
16 Dave Mackey .20 .50
17 Tom Martin .20 .50
18 Darren Moren .30 .75
19 Adam Morrison .20 .50
20 Gord Roberts .20 .50
21 Dan Sexton .20 .50
22 Randy Siska .20 .50
23 Eric Thurston .20 .50
24 Simon Wheeldon .40 1.00

1984-85 Victoria Cougars

COMPLETE SET (24) 6.00 15.00
1 Misko Antisin .30 .75
2 Greg Batters .20 .50
3 Mel Bridgman .60 1.50
4 Chris Calverley .20 .50
5 Darin Choquette .20 .50
6 Geoff Courtnall .75 2.00
7 Russ Courtnall 1.25 3.00
8 Rick Davidson .20 .50
9 Bill Gregoire .20 .50
10 Richard Hajdu .30 .75
11 Randy Hansch .30 .75
12 Rob Kivell .20 .50
13 Brad Melin .20 .50
14 Jim Mentis .20 .50
15 Adam Morrison .20 .50
16 Mark Morrison .20 .50
17 Kodie Nelson .20 .50
18 Ken Priestlay .30 .75
19 Bruce Pritchard .20 .50
20 Torrie Robertson .40 1.00
21 Trevor Semeniuk .20 .50
22 Dan Sexton .20 .50
23 Randy Siska .20 .50
24 Chris Tarnowski .20 .50

1989-90 Victoria Cougars

COMPLETE SET (21) 4.00 10.00
1 John Badduke .20 .50
2 Terry Bendera .20 .50
3 Trevor Buchanan .20 .50
4 Jaret Burgoyne .30 .75
5 Dino Caputo .20 .50
6 Chris Catellier .20 .50
7 Mark Cipriano .20 .50
8 Milan Drag .20 .50
9 Dean Dyer .20 .50
10 Shayne Green .20 .50
11 Ryan Harrison .20 .50
12 Corey Jones .30 .75
13 Terry Klapstein .20 .50
14 Jason Knox .20 .50
15 Curtis Nykyforuk .20 .50
16 Jason Peters .20 .50
17 Blair Scott .20 .50
18 Mike Seaton .20 .50
19 Rob Sumner .20 .50
20 Larry Woo .20 .50
21 Jarret Zukiwsky .20 .50

2014-15 Victoria Royals

COMPLETE SET () 6.00 15.00
1 Axel Blomqvist .30 .75
2 Travis Brown .30 .75
3 Austin Carroll .30 .75
4 Greg Chase .30 .75
5 Taylor Crunk .30 .75
6 Jared Dmytriw .30 .75
7 Logan Fisher .30 .75
8 Brandon Fushimi .30 .75
9 Ryan Gagnon .30 .75
10 Dante Hannoun .30 .75
11 Joe Hicketts .30 .75
12 Marsel Ibragimov .30 .75
13 Ralph Jarratt .30 .75
14 Brandon Magee .30 .75
15 Regan Nagy .30 .75
16 Jack Palmer .30 .75
17 Chaz Reddekopp .30 .75
18 Jayden Sittler .30 .75
19 Mitch Skapski .30 .75
20 Evan Smith .30 .75
21 Tyler Soy .30 .75
22 Coleman Vollrath .30 .75
23 Jack Walker .30 .75
24 Marty the Marmot MASCOT .30 .75

2015-16 Victoria Royals

COMPLETE SET (24) 6.00 15.00
1 Keith Anderson .30 .75
2 Vladimir Bobylev .30 .75
3 Jared Dmytriw .30 .75
4 Matt Dykstra .30 .75
5 Logan Fisher .30 .75
6 Alex Forsberg .40 1.00
7 Ryan Gagnon .30 .75
8 Dante Hannoun .30 .75
9 Joe Hicketts .30 .75
10 Marsel Ibragimov .30 .75
11 Ralph Jarratt .30 .75
12 Regan Nagy .30 .75
13 Griffen Outhouse .30 .75
14 Brayden Pachel .30 .75
15 Ryan Peckford .30 .75
16 Matthew Phillips .30 .75
17 Ethan Price .30 .75
18 Chaz Reddekopp .30 .75
19 Tyler Soy .30 .75
20 Tyler Thompson .30 .75
21 Coleman Vollrath .30 .75
22 Scott Walford .30 .75
23 Jack Walker .30 .75
24 Jordan Wharrie .30 .75

2000-01 Victoriaville Tigres

COMPLETE SET (24) 4.80 12.00
1 James Sanford .20 .50
2 Carl Mallette .30 .75
3 Matthew Lombardi .20 .50
4 Teddy Kyres .20 .50
5 Martin Autotte .20 .50
6 Simon St-Pierre .20 .50
7 Pierre-Luc Daneau .20 .50
8 Antoine Vermette .40 1.00
9 Marc-Andre Thinel .40 1.00
10 Mathieu Wathier .20 .50
11 Pierre-Luc Sleigher .20 .50
12 Sandro Sbrocca .20 .50
13 Jonathan Fauteux .20 .50
14 Sergei Kaltygen .20 .50
15 Adam Wojcik .20 .50
16 Jean-Francois Nogues .30 .75
17 Richard Paul .20 .50
18 David Masse .20 .50
19 Luc Levesque .20 .50
20 Mathieu Brunelle .20 .50
21 Sebastien Morissette .20 .50
22 Sebastien Thinel .20 .50
23 Danny Groulx .20 .50
24 Mario Durocher CO .10 .25

2000-01 Victoriaville Tigres Signed

COMPLETE SET (24) 20.00 50.00
1 James Sanford .80 2.00
2 Carl Mallette 1.20 3.00
3 Matthew Lombardi .80 2.00
4 Teddy Kyres .80 2.00
5 Martin Autotte .80 2.00
6 Simon St-Pierre .80 2.00
7 Pierre-Luc Daneau .80 2.00
8 Antoine Vermette 2.00 5.00
9 Marc-Andre Thinel 2.00 5.00
10 Mathieu Wathier .80 2.00
11 Pierre-Luc Sleigher .80 2.00
12 Sandro Sbrocca .80 2.00
13 Jonathan Fauteux .80 2.00
14 Sergei Kaltygen .80 2.00
15 Adam Wojcik .80 2.00
16 Jean-Francois Nogues 1.20 3.00
17 Richard Paul .80 2.00
18 David Masse .80 2.00
19 Luc Levesque .80 2.00
20 Mathieu Brunelle .80 2.00
21 Sebastien Morissette .80 2.00
22 Sebastien Thinel .80 2.00
23 Danny Groulx .80 2.00
24 Mario Durocher CO .80 2.00

2003-04 Victoriaville Tigres

COMPLETE SET (29) 6.00 15.00
1 Matthew Augustine .20 .50
2 Justin Belanger .20 .50
3 Gabriel Boies .20 .50
4 Francis Charland .20 .50
5 Renaud Des Alliers .20 .50
6 Benoit Doucet .20 .50
7 Kyle Doucet .20 .50
8 Jeremy Duchesne .30 .75
9 Cole Fetzner .20 .50
10 Benoit Fournier .20 .50
11 Guillaume Fournier .20 .50
12 Scott Gibson .20 .50
13 Ryan Jenner .20 .50
14 Martin Kasik .20 .50
15 Arthur Kiyaga .20 .50
16 Tommy Lafontaine .20 .50
17 Christian Laroche .20 .50
18 Daniel Manzato .30 .75
19 Olivier Plouffe .20 .50
20 Michael Ramsay .20 .50
21 Robin Richards .20 .50
22 Jonathan Ryan .20 .50
23 Mario Scalzo .40 1.00
24 Daniel Sparre .20 .50
25 Simon St-Pierre .20 .50
26 Josh Tordjman .60 1.50
27 Guillaume Trudel .20 .50
NNO Francis Charland TL .20 .50
NNO Mario Scalzo TL .20 .50

2004-05 Victoriaville Tigres

COMPLETE SET (30) 6.00 15.00
1 Maxim Noreau .20 .50
2 Jeremy Duchesne .20 .50
3 Justin Belanger .20 .50
4 Jan Danecek .20 .50
5 Gabriel Boies .20 .50
6 Pierre-Olivier Dupere .20 .50
7 Danny Hollet .20 .50
8 Alexandre Imbeault .20 .50
9 Josh Tordjman .60 1.50
10 Jason Legault .20 .50
11 Tommy Lafontaine .20 .50
12 Bruce Noivo .20 .50
13 Mike Ramsay .20 .50
14 Arthur Kiyaga .20 .50
15 Matt Nickerson .40 1.00
16 Renaud Des Alliers .20 .50
17 Mario Scalzo Jr .40 1.00
18 Samuel Hounsell .20 .50
19 Benoit Doucet .20 .50
20 Francis Guerette-Charland .20 .50
21 Kyle Doucet .20 .50
22 Trevor Mock .20 .50
23 Erick Lizon .20 .50
24 Ryan Jenner .20 .50
25 Maxime Desruisseaux .20 .50
26 Brant Miller .20 .50
27 Nicolas Laplante .20 .50
28 Gabriel Houde-Brisson .20 .50
29 Toby Lafrance .20 .50
30 Alexandre Vachon .20 .50

2005-06 Victoriaville Tigres

COMPLETE SET (22) 6.00 15.00
1 Keven Guerette-Charland .30 .75
2 Jason Legault .30 .75
3 Ryan Jenner .30 .75
4 Benoit Doucet .30 .75
5 Josh Tordjman .60 1.50
6 Benoit Massicotte .30 .75
7 Toby Lafrance .30 .75
8 Gabriel Boies .30 .75
9 Jan Danecek .30 .75
10 Renaud Des Alliers .30 .75
11 Philippe Brisebois .30 .75
12 Alexandre Imbeault .30 .75
13 Maxim Noreau .30 .75
14 Brant Miller .60 1.50
15 Carl Chamberland .30 .75
16 Pierre-Olivier Duperre .30 .75
17 Matthew David .30 .75
18 Erick Lizon .30 .75
19 Trevor Mock .30 .75
20 Francis Guerette-Charland .30 .75
21 Adam Ross .30 .75
22 Stephan Lebeau .30 .75

2006-07 Victoriaville Tigres

COMPLETE SET (24) 5.00 12.00
1 Morten Madsen .40 1.00
2 Keven Veilleux .40 1.00
3 Jean-Christophe Blanchard .20 .50
4 Kevin Poulin .20 .50
5 Maxim Noreau .20 .50
6 Carl Chamberland .20 .50
7 Erick Tremblay .20 .50
8 Jan Kolarik .20 .50
9 Sansdrick Lavoie .20 .50
10 Dave Nolin .20 .50
11 Maxime Robichaud .20 .50
12 Jason Demers .20 .50
13 Jason Legault .20 .50
14 David Foucher .20 .50

15 Keven Guerette-Charland .20 .50
16 Dany Roch .20 .50
17 Adam Ross .20 .50
18 Vincent Zaore-Vanie .20 .50
19 Philippe-Michael Devos .20 .50
20 Kyle Kelly .20 .50
21 Kyle Mcneil .20 .50
22 Benoit Doucet .20 .50
23 Francis Guerette-Charland .20 .50
24 Toby Lafrance .20 .50

1993-94 Waterloo Black Hawks

COMPLETE SET (27) 3.60 9.00
1 Brent Bessey .15 .40
2 Jason Blake .30 .75
3 Scott Brand GM .02 .10
4 Eric Brown .15 .40
5 Rod Butler .15 .40
6 Chris Coakley .15 .40
7 Austin Crawford .15 .40
8 Doug Dietz ACO .02 .10
9 Jon Garver .15 .40
10 Brian Folden .15 .40
11 Bobby Hayes .15 .40
12 Jake Jacoby .15 .40
13 Terry Jarkowsky .15 .40
14 Jeff Kozakowski UER
(Misspelled
Kozakowskl on fr .15 .40
15 Josh Lampman .15 .40
16 Marty Laurila .15 .40
17 Steve McCall ANN .02 .10
18 Bill McNelis .15 .40
19 Rich Metro .15 .40
20 Scott Mikesch CO .02 .10
21 Barry Soskin PR .02 .10
22 Ben Stadey .15 .40
23 Ed Stanek .15 .40
24 Todd Steinmetz .15 .40
25 Scott Swanjord .20 .50
26 Miles Van Tassel .15 .40
27 Supporting Staff
Dave Christians
Mike Christians .02 .10

1995-96 Waterloo Black Hawks

COMPLETE SET (26) 25.00 50.00
1 Jayme Adduono 1.00 2.50
2 Chris Cerrella 1.00 2.50
3 Mark Eaton 1.25 3.00
4 Jason Furness 1.00 2.50
5 Joe Gray UER .08 .25
6 Zach Ham 1.00 2.50
7 Trevor Hanger 1.00 2.50
8 Kris Harris 1.00 2.50
9 Steve Holeczy 1.00 2.50
10 Lubos Krajcovic 1.00 2.50
11 Jeff Melnechuk 1.00 2.50
12 Jimmy Mroz 1.00 2.50
13 Bobby Owen 1.00 2.50
14 Anthony Perardi 1.00 2.50
15 Chad Poliquin 1.00 2.50
16 Dan Ragusett 1.00 2.50
17 Ryan Rentz 1.00 2.50
18 Ryan Sarazin 1.00 2.50
19 Doug Schmidt 1.00 2.50
20 Andrew Tortorella 1.00 2.50
21 Roger Trudeau 1.00 2.50
22 Mark Wilkinson 1.00 2.50
23 Scott Mikesch CO .08 .25
24 Barry Soskin Owner .08 .25
25 Scott Brand GM .08 .25
26 Jason Shaver PR .08 .25

2003-04 Waterloo Black Hawks

COMPLETE SET (21) 8.00 20.00
1 Joel Hanson .40 1.00
2 Joe Pavelski 4.00 10.00
3 Matt Fornataro .40 1.00
4 Kevin Regan .75 2.00
5 Garrett Regan .40 1.00
6 Zach Bearson .40 1.00
7 Dan Sturges .40 1.00
8 Tim Filangieri .40 1.00
9 Mike Radja .40 1.00
10 Michael Annett .40 1.00
11 Andrew Thomas .40 1.00
12 Aaron Johnson .75 2.00
13 John Vadnais .40 1.00
14 Jesse Vesel .40 1.00
15 Jake Schwan .40 1.00
16 Josh Duncan .40 1.00
17 Jon-Paul Testwuide .40 1.00
18 Mike Dagenais .40 1.00
19 Dustin Molle .40 1.00
20 David Meckler .40 1.00
21 Peter MacArthur .40 1.00

2005-06 Waterloo Black Hawks

COMPLETE SET (30) 6.00 15.00
1 Ricky Akkerman .20 .50
2 Matt Arhontas .20 .50
3 Zach Bearson .20 .50
4 Eric Bennett .20 .50
5 Andy Bohmbach .20 .50
6 Mike Borisnok .20 .50
7 Cody Chupp .20 .50
8 Kurt Davis .20 .50
9 Drew Dobson .20 .50
10 Tim Gilbert .20 .50
11 Joe Grossman .20 .50
12 Brad Hoelzer .20 .50
13 Christian Jensen .20 .50
14 Vincent LeVerde .20 .50
15 James Marcou .20 .50
16 Clark Oliver .20 .50
17 Kyle Reeds .20 .50
18 Mitch Ryan .40 1.00
19 Pasko Skarica .20 .50
20 Joe Sova .20 .50
21 Jeremy Tejchma .20 .50
22 Mike Testwuide .20 .50
23 Isak Tranvik .20 .50
24 Kenny Wochele .40 1.00
25 P K O'Handley CO .20 .50
26 Chris Tok ACO .20 .50
27 Zac Headrick ACO .20 .50
28 Derrick Johnson ACO .20 .50
29 Dave Graham EQM .20 .50
30 Todd Klein TR .20 .50

2014-15 Waterloo Black Hawks

COMPLETE SET (25) 6.00 15.00
1 Philip Beaulieu .30 .75
2 Kris Carlson .30 .75
3 Max Coatta .30 .75
4 Jeremy Davies .30 .75
5 Marcel Godbout .30 .75
6 Niko Hildenbrand .30 .75
7 Steve Howard Asst. CO .30 .75
8 Larry Jungwirth .30 .75
9 Craig Laue Announ. .30 .75
10 Hayden Lavigne .30 .75
11 Sean MacTavish .30 .75
12 Alec McCrea .30 .75
13 Tyson McLellan .30 .75
14 George Mika .30 .75
15 P.K. O'Handley CO .30 .75
16 Nick Olczyk .30 .75
17 Rem Pitlick .30 .75
18 Alex Robert .30 .75
19 Henrik Rommel .30 .75
20 Sam Rossini .30 .75
21 Brendan Shane .30 .75
22 Hayden Shaw .30 .75
23 Tyler Sheehy .30 .75
24 John Wiitala .30 .75
25 Waterloo Black Hawks Champs .30 .75

1992-93 Western Michigan Broncos

COMPLETE SET (30) 4.80 12.00
1 Chris Belanger .20 .50
2 Joe Bonnett .15 .40
3 Brent Brekke .20 .50
4 Chris Brooks .15 .40
5 Craig Brown .15 .40
6 Jeremy Brown .15 .40
7 Tom Carriere .15 .40
8 Scott Chartier .20 .50
9 Ryan D'Arcy .15 .40
10 Pat Ferschweiler .15 .40
11 Brian Gallentine .15 .40
12 Jim Holman .15 .40
13 Derek Innanen .15 .40
14 Jason Jennings .20 .50
15 Mikhail Lapin .20 .50
16 Francois Leroux .20 .50
17 Jamal Mayers .60 1.50
18 Kevin McCaffrey ACO .02 .10
19 Dave Mitchell .15 .40
20 Brian Renfrew .15 .40
21 Mike Schafer ACO .02 .10
22 Derek Schooley .15 .40
23 Neil Smith
WMU Hall of Fame .20 .50
24 Colin Ward .15 .40
25 Dave Weaver .15 .40
26 Mike Whitton .15 .40
27 Bill Wilkinson CO .02 .10
28 Peter Wilkinson .15 .40
29 Byron Witkowski .15 .40
30 Lawson Arena .02 .10

1993-94 Western Michigan Broncos

COMPLETE SET (30) 6.00 15.00
1 David Agnew .20 .50
2 Brent Brekke .30 .75
3 Chris Brooks .20 .50
4 Craig Brown .20 .50
5 Jeremy Brown .20 .50
6 Justin Cardwell .20 .50
7 Tom Carriere .20 .50
8 Tony Codo .20 .50
9 Matt Cressman .20 .50
10 Jim Culhane ACO .02 .10
11 Ryan D'Arcy .20 .50
12 Brian Gallentine .20 .50
13 Matt Greene .20 .50
14 Rob Hodge
WMU Hall of Fame .20 .50
15 Jim Holman .20 .50
16 Derek Innanen .20 .50
17 Mark Jodoin .20 .50
18 Brendan Kenny .20 .50
19 Misha Lapin .20 .50
20 Darren Maloney .20 .50
21 Jamal Mayers .75 2.00
22 Dave Mitchell .20 .50
23 Brian Renfrew .20 .50
24 Mike Schafer ACO .02 .10
25 Derek Schooley .20 .50
26 Colin Ward .20 .50
27 Mike Whitton .20 .50
28 Bill Wilkinson CO .02 .10
29 Peter Wilkinson .20 .50
30 Shawn Zimmerman .20 .50

2001-02 Western Michigan Broncos

COMPLETE SET (10) 4.00 10.00
1 Anthony Battaglia .40 1.00
2 Mike Bishai .40 1.00
3 Ryan Crane .40 1.00
4 Bryan Farquhar .40 1.00
5 Chad Kline .40 1.00
6 Austin Miller .40 1.00
7 Jeff Reynaert .40 1.00
8 Wayne Gagne ATG .40 1.00
9 Harry Lawson CO .40 1.00
10 Team Photo .40 1.00

2006-07 Westside Warriors

COMPLETE SET (21) 6.00 15.00
1 The General MASCOT .02 .10
2 Mark Howell CO .02 .10
3 Stephen Caple .30 .75
4 Eric Fraser .30 .75
5 Brock Meadows .30 .75
6 Joel Woznikoski .30 .75
7 Chris Santiago .30 .75
8 Denis Semenov .30 .75
9 Craig Eisenhut .30 .75
10 Kevin Walrod .30 .75
11 Tommy Grant .30 .75
12 Micah Anderson .30 .75
13 Chris Vassos .30 .75
14 Ron Kelly .30 .75
15 Brad Plumton .30 .75
16 Trevor Bailey .30 .75
17 Brendan Ellis .30 .75
18 August Aiken .30 .75
19 Konrad Becker .30 .75
20 Bryce Kakoske .30 .75
21 Sam Huston .30 .75
22 Milrod Kos .30 .75
23 Marcel Bruinsma .30 .75
24 Mark Howell CO .02 .10

1996-97 Wheeling Nailers

COMPLETE SET (23) 3.00 8.00
1 Scotty Allegrino TR .02 .10
2 John Badduke .20 .50
3 Frederic Barbeau .15 .40
4 John Blessman .15 .40
5 Francois Bouillon .15 .40
6 Greg Callahan .15 .40
7 Don Chase .15 .40
8 Jason Clark .15 .40
9 Keli Corpse .15 .40
10 Chad Dameworth .15 .40
11 Ryan Haggerty .20 .50
12 Martin LePage .15 .40
13 Ian McIntyre .15 .40
14 Greg McLean .15 .40
15 Mike Minard .20 .50
16 Perry Pappas .15 .40
17 Eric Royal .15 .40
18 Brad Symes .15 .40
19 John Tanner .20 .50
20 Rob Trumbley .15 .40
21 John Varga .30 .75
22 Tom McVie CO .15 .40
23 Spike Mascot .02 .10

1997-98 Wheeling Nailers

COMPLETE SET (25) 3.00 8.00
1 J.F. Boutin .15 .40
2 Chris Jensen .15 .40
3 Dan Jablonic .15 .40
4 Dmitri Tarabrin .15 .40
5 Matt Garzone .15 .40
6 Jeremy Brown .15 .40
7 Joe Harney .15 .40
8 Scott Kirton .15 .40
9 Patrick Charbonneau .15 .40
10 Matt Van Horlick .15 .40
11 Mike Latendresse .20 .50
12 Karl Infanger .15 .40
13 Olie Sundstrom .20 .50
14 Stefan Brannare .15 .40
15 Fredrik Svensson .15 .40
16 Marquis Mathieu .30 .75
17 Sergei Radchenko .20 .50
18 Alex Matvichuk .15 .40
19 Kurt Brown .15 .40
20 Quinten Van Horlick .15 .40
21 Nailers Logo .02 .10
22 Swaze Armstrong TR .02 .10
23 Vinny Ferraiuolo EM .02 .10
24 Spike Mascot .02 .10
25 Peter Laviolette HCO .20 .50

1997-98 Wheeling Nailers Photo Pack

COMPLETE SET (25) 4.80 12.00
1 J.F. Boutin .20 .50
2 Chris Jensen .20 .50
3 Dan Jablonic .20 .50
4 Dimitri Tarabrin .30 .75
5 Matt Garzone .20 .50
6 Jeremy Brown .20 .50
7 Joe Harney .20 .50
8 Scott Kirton .20 .50
9 Patrick Charbonneau .20 .50
10 Matt Van Horlick .20 .50
11 Mike Latendresse .30 .75
12 Karl Infanger .20 .50
13 Olie Sundstrom .30 .75
14 Stefane Brannare .20 .50
15 Fredrik Svensson .20 .50
16 Marquis Mathieu .40 1.00
17 Sergei Radchenko .30 .75
18 Alex Matvichuk .20 .50
19 Kurt Brown .20 .50
20 Quinten Van Horlick .20 .50
21 Nailers History Card .02 .10
22 Swaze Armstrong TR .02 .10
23 Vinny Ferraiuolo MGR .02 .10
24 Spike Mascot .02 .10
25 Peter Laviolette HCO .20 .50

2003-04 Wheeling Nailers

COMPLETE SET (16) 8.00 20.00
81 Nick Boucher .75 2.00
82 Steven Crampton .50 1.25
83 Jean-Francois Dufour .50 1.25
84 Drew Fata .60 1.50
85 Brendon Hodge .50 1.25
86 Jason Jaffray .50 1.25
87 Mark Kosick .50 1.25
88 Kamil Kuriplach .50 1.25
89 Mario Larocque .50 1.25
90 Brad Mehalko .50 1.25
91 Jake Ortmeyer .50 1.25
92 Eduard Pershin .50 1.25
93 T.J. Reynolds .75 2.00
94 Alexandre Rouleau .50 1.25
95 Bogdan Rudenko .50 1.25
96 J.C. Ruid .50 1.25

2004-05 Wheeling Nailers Riesbeck's

COMPLETE SET (20) 8.00 20.00
1 Team Card .20 .50
2 Alexandre Rouleau .40 1.00
3 Armands Berzins .40 1.00
4 Team Staff .20 .50
5 Cam Paddock .40 1.00
6 Cliff Loya .40 1.00
7 Curtiss Patrick .40 1.00
8 Dany Sabourin 1.25 3.00
9 Ed McGrane .40 1.00
10 Evgeny Lazarev .40 1.00
11 Brendon Hodge .40 1.00
12 James Laux .40 1.00
13 Joe Exter .40 1.00
14 Kenny Corupe .75 2.00
15 Pascal Morency .40 1.00
16 Randy Perry .40 1.00
17 Ray DiLauro .40 1.00
18 Steve Crampton .40 1.00
19 Kraft Sponsor .04 .10
20 FritoLay Sponsor .04 .10

2014-15 Wheeling Nailers

COMPLETE SET (23) 6.00 15.00
1 Derek Army .30 .75
2 Shane Bakker .30 .75
3 Riley Brace .30 .75
4 Jarrett Burton .30 .75
5 Paul Cianfrini .30 .75
6 Morgan Ellis .30 .75
7 Tyler Fernandez .30 .75
8 Stefan Fournier .30 .75
9 David Gilbert .30 .75
10 Sahir Gill .30 .75
11 Eric Hartzell .30 .75
12 Chaz Johnson .30 .75
13 Nicholas Kugali .30 .75
14 Tristin Llewellyn .30 .75
15 David Makowski .30 .75
16 Patrick McGrath .30 .75
17 Frank Palazzese .30 .75
18 Mike Ratchuk .30 .75
19 Harrison Ruopp .30 .75
20 Clark Seymour .30 .75
21 Bobby Shea .30 .75
22 Shawn Skelly .30 .75
23 Zack Torquato .30 .75

1992-93 Wheeling Thunderbirds

COMPLETE SET (24) 3.00 8.00
1 Title Card .02 .10
2 Claude Barthe .15 .40
3 Joel Blain .15 .40
4 Derek DeCosty .15 .40
5 Marc Deschamps .15 .40
6 Tom Dion .15 .40
7 Devin Edgerton .15 .40
8 Pete Heine .15 .40
9 Kim Maier .15 .40
10 Mike Millham .20 .50
11 Cory Paterson .15 .40
12 Trevor Pochipinski .15 .40
13 Tim Roberts .15 .40
14 Mark Rodgers .15 .40
15 Darren Schwartz .15 .40
16 Trevor Senn .15 .40
17 Tim Tisdale .15 .40
18 John Uniac .20 .50
19 Denny Magruder MG .02 .10
20 Chuck Greenwood
Jim Smi .02 .10
21 Larry Kish VP/MG .02 .10
22 Doug Sauter CO .02 .10
23 T-Bird (Mascot) .02 .10
24 Doug Bacon .15 .40

1993-94 Wheeling Thunderbirds

COMPLETE SET (21) 10.00 25.00
1 Header Card CL .02 .10
2 Darren Schwartz .15 .40
3 Cory Paterson .15 .40
4 Derek DeCosty .15 .40
5 Jim Bermingham .15 .40
6 Brock Woods .15 .40
7 Tim Roberts .15 .40
8 Eric Raymond .15 .40
9 Brett Abel .15 .40
10 Sebastien Fortier .15 .40
11 John Johnson .15 .40
12 Brent Pope .15 .40
13 Marquis Mathieu .30 .75
14 Terry Virtue .20 .50
15 Vadim Slivchenko .20 .50
16 Clayton Gainer .15 .40
17 Sylvain LaPointe .15 .40
18 Doug Sauter CO .02 .10
19 Larry Kish VP GM .02 .10
20 Denny Magruder GM .02 .10
21 Bill Cordery ASST TR .02 .10
PC1 Wheeling Thunderbirds 2.00 5.00
PC2 Darren Schwartz 2.00 5.00
PC3 Tim Tisdale 2.00 5.00
PC4 Cory Paterson 2.00 5.00
UD1 Update Checklist .02 .10
UD2 Tim Tisdale .40 1.00
UD3 John Van Kessel .40 1.00
UD4 Rival Fullum .40 1.00
UD5 Steve Gibson .40 1.00
UD6 Dave Goucher
Director of Communication .02 .10
UD7 Gary Zearott
Photographer .02 .10
UD8 Darren Schwartz
T-Bird Leader .02 .10
UD9 Vadim Slivchenko
T-Bird Leader .40 1.00
UD10 Brock Woods
T-Bird Leader .40 1.00

1994-95 Wheeling Thunderbirds

COMPLETE SET (25) 2.00 5.00
1 Checklist .08 .25
2 Tim Tisdale .20 .50
3 Brock Woods .20 .50
4 Vadim Slivchenko .20 .50
5 Tim Roberts .20 .50
6 Derek DeCosty .20 .50
7 Steve Gibson .20 .50
8 Xavier Majic .25 .60
9 Peter Marek .20 .50
10 Greg Louder .20 .50
11 Gairin Smith .20 .50
12 Darren McAusland .20 .50
13 Brent Pope .08 .25
14 Dominic Fafard .08 .25
15 Pat Barton .08 .25
16 Patrick Labrecque .08 .25
17 Lorne Toews .08 .25
18 Scott Matusovich .08 .25
19 Louis Bernard .08 .25
20 Doug Sutter .08 .25
21 Scott Allegrino TR .08 .25
22 Bill Cordery .08 .25
23 Mark Landini .08 .25
PC1 Xavier Majic .30 .75
PC2 Vadim Slivchenko .30 .75

1995-96 Wheeling Thunderbirds

COMPLETE SET (24) 4.00 10.00
1 Rob Trumbley .15 .40
2 Geoff Finch .15 .40
3 Samuel Groleau .15 .40
4 Keli Corpse .15 .40
5 Tomas Vokoun .60 1.50
6 Steve Gibson .15 .40
7 Eric Royal .15 .40
8 Brock Woods .15 .40
9 Derek Decosty .15 .40
10 Lorne Toews .15 .40
11 Gairin Smith .15 .40
12 Tony Prpic .20 .50
13 Brent Pope .15 .40
14 Martin Sychra .15 .40
15 Martin LePage .15 .40
16 John Blessman .15 .40
17 Louis Dumont .15 .40
18 Pat Barton .15 .40
19 Ron Wilson .15 .40
20 Martin Brochu .40 1.00
21 Tim Tisdale .15 .40
22 Larry Kish HCO .02 .10
23 Scott Allegrino TR .02 .10
24 T Bird Mascot .02 .10

1995-96 Wheeling Thunderbirds Series II

COMPLETE SET (20) 3.00 8.00
1 John Badduke .20 .50
2 Pat Barton .15 .40
3 John Blessman .15 .40
4 Keli Corpse .15 .40
5 Louis Dumont .15 .40
6 Geoff Finch .30 .75
7 Steve Gibson .15 .40
8 Samuel Groleau .15 .40
9 Martin LePage .15 .40
10 Kevin Lune .15 .40
11 Brent Pope .15 .40
12 Tim Roberts .15 .40
13 Eric Royal .15 .40
14 Gairin Smith .15 .40
15 Lorne Toews .15 .40
16 Tim Tisdale .15 .40
17 Rob Trumbley .15 .40
18 Tomas Vokoun .60 1.50
19 Ron Wilson .15 .40
20 Brock Woods .15 .40

1993-94 Wichita Thunder

COMPLETE SET (18) 3.00 8.00
1 Bob Berg .20 .50
2 Mark Bourgeois .20 .50
3 Steve Chelios .20 .50
4 Robert Desjardins .20 .50
5 Paul Dukovac .20 .50
6 Yannick Gosselin .20 .50
7 Ron Handy .20 .50
8 Jamie Hearn .20 .50
9 Roger Hunt .20 .50
10 Paul Jackson .20 .50
11 James Latos .20 .50
12 Greg Neish .20 .50
13 Brent Sapergia .20 .50
14 Darren Srochenski .20 .50
15 Stephane Venne .20 .50
16 Rob Weingartner .20 .50
17 Jack Williams .20 .50
18 Doug Shedden CO .07 .20

1998-99 Wichita Thunder

COMPLETE SET (25) 4.80 12.00
1 Checklist .02 .10
2 Vernon Beardy .20 .50
3 Travis Clayton .20 .50
4 Chris Dashney .20 .50
5 Mike Donaghue .20 .50
6 Jason Duda .20 .50
7 Rhett Dudley .20 .50
8 Trevor Folk .20 .50
9 Todd Howarth .20 .50
10 John Kachur .20 .50
11 Mark Karpen .20 .50
12 Lance Leslie .30 .75
13 Brad Link .20 .50
14 Mark Macera .30 .75
15 Walker McDonald .20 .50
16 John McGeough .20 .50
17 Thomas Migdal .20 .50
18 Aaron Novak .20 .50
19 Sean O'Reilly .30 .75
20 Kevin Powell .20 .50
21 Greg Smith .30 .75
22 Travis Tipler .20 .50
23 Troy Yarosh .20 .50
24 Bryan Wells HCO .04 .10
25 Goodwrench Dealer Logo .04 .10

1999-00 Wichita Thunder

COMPLETE SET (25) 4.00 10.00
1 Vern Beardy .15 .40
2 Travis Clayton .30 .75
3 Chris Dashney .15 .40
4 Mike Donaghue .15 .40
5 Jason Duda .15 .40
6 Rhett Dudley .15 .40
7 Trevor Folk .15 .40
8 Todd Howarth .15 .40
9 John Kachur .15 .40
10 Mark Karpen .15 .40
11 Lance Leslie .30 .75
12 Brad Link .15 .40
13 Mark Macera .15 .40
14 Walker McDonald .15 .40
15 Jim McGeough .15 .40
16 Thomas Migdal .15 .40
17 Aaron Novak .15 .40
18 Sean O'Reilly .15 .40
19 Kevin Powell .15 .40
20 Greg Smith .30 .75
21 Travis Tipler .15 .40
22 Troy Yarosh .15 .40
23 Bryan Wells .15 .40
24 Title Card .02 .10
25 Dealer Logo Card .02 .10

2000-01 Wichita Thunder

COMPLETE SET (22) 6.00 15.00
1 Jerod Bina .30 .75
2 Troy Caley .30 .75
3 Travis Clayton .30 .75
4 Trevor Converse .30 .75
5 Mike Donaghue .30 .75
6 Jason Duda .30 .75
7 Rhett Dudley .30 .75
8 Rocky Florio .30 .75
9 Trevor Folk .30 .75
10 Dwayne Gylywoychuk .30 .75
11 Derrek Harper .30 .75
12 Mike Hiebert .30 .75
13 Mark Karpen .30 .75
14 Lance Leslie .30 .75
15 Jim McGeough .30 .75
16 Aaron Novak .30 .75
17 Sean O'Reiley .30 .75
18 Kevin Powell .30 .75
19 Kris Schultz .30 .75
20 Greg Smith .30 .75
21 Mark Strohack .30 .75
22 Checklist .02 .10

2000-01 Wilkes-Barre Scranton Penguins

COMPLETE SET (28) 5.00 20.00
1 Dennis Bonvie .60 1.50
2 Brendan Buckley .30 .75
3 Sven Butenschon .30 .75
4 Sebastien Caron .60 1.50
5 Greg Crozier .40 1.00
6 Trent Cull .30 .75
7 Andrew Ference .40 1.00
8 Dylan Gyori .40 1.00
9 Chris Kelleher .30 .75
10 Tom Kostopoulos .40 1.00
11 Joel Laing .30 .75
12 Jim Leger .30 .75
13 Jason MacDonald .30 .75
14 Alexandre Mathieu .30 .75
15 Josef Melichar .30 .75
16 Eric Meloche .30 .75
17 Rich Parent .40 1.00
18 Glenn Patrick HCO .10 .25
19 Toby Petersen .40 1.00
20 John Slaney .30 .75
21 Martin Sonnenberg .30 .75
22 Jean-Philippe Soucy .40 1.00
23 Billy Tibbetts .60 1.50
24 Darcy Verot .30 .75
25 Mike Yeo ACO .02 .10
26 Alexander Zevakhin .30 .75
27 Tux MASCOT .02 .10
28 Checklist .02 .10

2001-02 Wilkes-Barre Scranton Penguins

COMPLETE SET (26) 4.80 12.00
1 Robbie Tallas .30 .75
2 Robert Scuderi .20 .50
3 David Koci .20 .50
4 Brooks Orpik .30 .75
5 Darcy Robinson .20 .50
6 Mike Wilson .20 .50
7 Darcy Verot .20 .50
8 Ross Lupaschuk .20 .50
9 Martin Sonnenberg .20 .50
10 Jan Fadrny .20 .50
11 Alexander Zevakhin .20 .50
12 Shane Endicott .40 1.00
13 Brendan Buckley .20 .50
14 Jason MacDonald .20 .50
15 Tomas Surovy .20 .50
16 Tom Kostopoulos .30 .75
17 Alexandre Mathieu .20 .50
18 Peter Ratchuk .20 .50
19 Sebastien Caron .30 .75
20 Steve Parsons .30 .75
21 Robert Dome .30 .75
22 Eric Meloche .30 .75
23 Glenn Patrick CO .04 .10
24 Mike Yeo ACO .04 .10
25 Tux MASCOT .04 .10
NNO Checklist .04 .10

2002-03 Wilkes-Barre Scranton Penguins

COMPLETE SET (27) 5.00 12.00
1 Rob Scuderi .40 1.00
2 Brooks Orpik .40 1.00
3 Darcy Robinson .20 .50
4 Mike Wilson .20 .50
5 Michel Ouellet .20 .50
6 Ross Lupaschuk .20 .50
7 Matt Hussey .20 .50
8 Milan Kraft .30 .75
9 Alexander Zevakhin .20 .50
10 Kris Beech .30 .75
11 Shane Endicott .30 .75
12 Toby Petersen .20 .50
13 Colby Armstrong .30 .75
14 Michal Sivek .30 .75
15 Matt Murley .20 .50
16 Brendan Buckley .20 .50
17 Jason MacDonald .20 .50
18 Tomas Surovy .30 .75
19 Francois Leroux .20 .50
20 Konstantin Koltsov .30 .75
21 Tom Kostopoulos .20 .50
22 Rob Tallas .30 .75
23 Sebastien Caron .30 .75
24 Eric Meloche .20 .50
25 Glen Patrick HCO .04 .10
26 Mike Yeo ACO .04 .10
NNO Checklist .04 .10

2003-04 Wilkes-Barre Scranton Penguins

COMPLETE SET (30) 4.00 10.00
1 Checklist .04 .10
2 Colby Armstrong .30 .75
3 Jean-Sebastien Aubin .30 .75
4 Kris Beech .30 .75
5 Patrick Boileau .15 .40
6 Martin Brochu .30 .75
7 Brendan Buckley .15 .40
8 Andy Chiodo .60 1.50
9 Shane Endicott .15 .40
10 Drew Fata .15 .40
11 Matt Hussey .15 .40
12 David Koci .30 .75
13 Tom Kostopoulos .15 .40
14 Guillaume Lefebvre .15 .40
15 Ross Lupaschuk .15 .40
16 Marquis Mathieu .15 .40
17 Eric Meloche .15 .40
18 Matt Murley .15 .40
19 Michel Ouellet .15 .40
20 Toby Petersen .15 .40
21 Darcy Robinson .15 .40
22 Alexandre Rouleau .15 .40
23 Rob Scuderi .30 .75
24 Reid Simpson .15 .40
25 Michal Sivek .15 .40
26 Tomas Surovy .15 .40
27 Steve Webb .15 .40
28 Michel Therrien CO .04 .10
29 Mike Yeo ACO .04 .10
30 Mascot .04 .10

2004-05 Wilkes-Barre Scranton Penguins

COMPLETE SET (30) 6.00 15.00
1 Checklist .04 .10
2 Rob Scuderi .20 .50
3 David Koci .20 .50
4 Chris Kelleher .20 .50
5 Darcy Robinson .20 .50
6 Ryan Whitney .30 .75
7 Michel Ouellet .20 .50
8 Ross Lupaschuk .20 .50
9 Colby Armstrong .30 .75
10 Kris Beech .20 .50
11 Ben Eaves .30 .75
12 Shane Endicott .20 .50
13 Cam Paddock .20 .50
14 Erik Christensen .30 .75
15 Guillaume Lefebvre .20 .50
16 Ramzi Abid .20 .50
17 Mike Sgroi .20 .50
18 Maxime Talbot .20 .50
19 Matt Murley .20 .50
20 Tomas Surovy .20 .50
21 Drew Fata .20 .50
22 Matt Hussey .20 .50
23 Marc-Andre Fleury 1.00 2.50
24 Alain Nasreddine .20 .50
25 Dany Sabourin .40 1.00
26 Andy Chiodo .40 1.00
27 Tux MASCOT .04 .10
28 Michel Therrien CO .04 .10
29 Mike Yeo ACO .04 .10
30 Wachovia Arena .04 .10

2005-06 Wilkes-Barre Scranton Penguins

COMPLETE SET (29) 6.00 15.00
1 Colby Armstrong .40 1.00
2 Dennis Bonvie .40 1.00
3 Daniel Carcillo .20 .50
4 Sebastien Caron .40 1.00
5 Erik Christensen .40 1.00
6 Kenny Corupe .20 .50
7 Stephen Dixon .20 .50
8 Ben Eaves .20 .50
9 Rico Fata .20 .50
10 Daniel Fernholm .20 .50
11 Jon Filewich .20 .50
12 Marc-Andre Fleury .75 2.00
13 Matt Hussey .20 .50
14 Chris Kelleher .20 .50
15 David Koci .20 .50
16 Konstantin Koltsov .20 .50
17 Ryan Lannon .20 .50
18 Guillaume Lefebvre .30 .75
19 Arpad Mihaly .20 .50
20 Alain Nasredinne .20 .50
21 Michel Ouellet .40 1.00
22 Dany Sabourin .40 1.00
23 Andy Schneider .20 .50
24 Ryan Stone .20 .50
25 Tomas Surovy .20 .50
26 Noah Welch .30 .75
27 Ryan Whitney .40 1.00
28 Joe Mullen ACO .20 .50
29 Al Sims CO .07 .20

2006-07 Wilkes-Barre Scranton Penguins

COMPLETE SET (25) 5.00 12.00
1 Alain Nasreddine .30 .75
2 Alexei Mikhnov .20 .50
3 Andrew Penner .30 .75
4 Connor James .20 .50
5 Daniel Carcillo .30 .75
6 Dennis Bonvie .40 1.00
7 Erik Christensen .30 .75
8 Jeff Deslauriers .30 .75
9 Jon Filewich .30 .75
10 Kyle Brodziak .20 .50
11 Marc-Antoine Pouliot .30 .75
12 Matt Carkner .20 .50
13 Maxime Talbot .30 .75
14 Micki DuPont .20 .50
15 Noah Welch .20 .50
16 Rob Schremp .40 1.00
17 Ryan Lannon .30 .75
18 Ryan Stone .40 1.00
19 Stephen Dixon .20 .50
20 Tom Gilbert .20 .50
21 Tyler Kennedy .20 .50
22 Wade Skolney .20 .50
23 Dan Bylsma ACO .02 .10
24 Todd Richards CO .02 .10
NNO Checklist .01 .01

2006-07 Wilkes-Barre Scranton Penguins Jerseys
COMPLETE SET (22) 125.00 300.00
1 Jeff Deslauriers 8.00 20.00
2 Andrew Penner 8.00 20.00
3 Micki DuPont 6.00 15.00
4 Kyle Brodziak 6.00 15.00
5 Jon Filewich 6.00 15.00
6 Ryan Lannon 6.00 15.00
7 Connor James 6.00 15.00
8 Noah Welch 6.00 15.00
9 Tom Gilbert 6.00 15.00
10 Stephen Dixon 6.00 15.00
11 Tyler Kennedy 6.00 15.00
12 Daniel Carcillo 8.00 20.00
13 Dennis Bonvie 10.00 25.00
14 Tim Sesito 6.00 15.00
15 Erik Christensen 10.00 25.00
16 Maxime Talbot 10.00 25.00
17 Matt Carkner 6.00 15.00
18 Ryan Stone 10.00 25.00
19 Marc Antoine Pouliot 10.00 25.00
20 Wade Skolney 6.00 15.00
21 Alain Nasreddine 6.00 15.00
22 Rob Schremp 10.00 25.00

2007-08 Wilkes-Barre Scranton Penguins
COMPLETE SET (29) 10.00 20.00
1 Mark Ardelan .30 .75
2 Dennis Bonvie .60 1.50
3 Aaron Boogaard .40 1.00
4 Tim Brent .30 .75
5 Ty Conklin .40 1.00
6 John Curry .30 .75
7 Jon D'Aversa .30 .75
8 Deryk Engelland .30 .75
9 Jon Filewich .30 .75
10 Alex Goligoski .60 1.50
11 Ned Havern .40 1.00
12 Connor James .30 .75
13 Joe Jensen .30 .75
14 Tyler Kennedy .30 .75
15 Ryan Lannon .30 .75
16 Kris Letang .30 .75
17 Mark Letestu .30 .75
18 Ben Lovejoy .30 .75
19 Kurtis McLean .30 .75
20 Chris Minard .30 .75
21 Alain Nasreddine .30 .75
22 Nathan Smith .30 .75
23 Ryan Stone .30 .75
24 Jeff Taffe .30 .75
25 Tim Wallace .30 .75
26 Dan Bylsma ACO .02 .10
27 Todd Richards CO .02 .10
28 Tux MASCOT .02 .10
29 Team Photo .02 .10

2007-08 Wilkes-Barre Scranton Penguins Jersey Edition
1 Ryan Lannon 3.00 8.00
2 Deryk Engelland 3.00 8.00
3 Ben Lovejoy 3.00 8.00
4 Nathan Smith 3.00 8.00
5 Tim Brent 3.00 8.00
6 Connor James 3.00 8.00
7 Tyler Kennedy 4.00 10.00
8 Mark Ardelan 3.00 8.00
9 Alex Goligoski 5.00 12.00
10 Chris Minard 3.00 8.00
11 Joe Jensen 3.00 8.00
12 Kurtis McLean 3.00 8.00
13 Jon Filewich 3.00 8.00
14 Jeff Taffe 3.00 8.00
15 Ryan Stone 3.00 8.00
16 Tim Wallace 3.00 8.00
17 Dennis Bonvie 6.00 15.00
18 Alain Nasreddine 3.00 8.00
19 Ty Conklin 5.00 12.00
20 Karl Goehring 5.00 12.00
21 Kris Letang 5.00 12.00
27 Dennis Bonvie LE 8.00 20.00

2014-15 Wilkes-Barre Scranton Penguins
COMPLETE SET (25) 6.00 15.00
1 Josh Archibald .30 .75
2 Taylor Chorney .30 .75
3 Jean-Sebastien Dea .30 .75
4 Nick Drazenovic .30 .75
5 Brian Dumoulin .30 .75
6 Andrew Ebbett .30 .75
7 Bobby Farnham .30 .75
8 Barry Goers .30 .75
9 Scott Harrington .30 .75
10 Jayson Megna .30 .75
11 Tom Kostopoulos .30 .75
12 Tom Kuhnhackl .30 .75
13 Pierre-Luc Letourneau-Leblond .40 1.00
14 Reid McNeill .30 .75
15 Matt Murray .50 1.25
16 Adam Payerl .30 .75
17 Derrick Pouliot .40 1.00
18 Carter Rowney .30 .75
19 Bryan Rust .30 .75
20 Conor Sheary 2.00 5.00
21 Dominik Uher .30 .75
22 Scott Wilson .30 .75
23 Jeff Zatkoff .30 .75
24 Tux MASCOT .30 .75
CL Header Card CL .30 .75

2004-05 Williams Lake Timberwolves
COMPLETE SET (28) 8.00 20.00
1 Andrew Braithwaite .40 1.00
2 Cody Brookwell .30 .75
3 Matt Crowell .30 .75
4 Bryce Dale .30 .75
5 Mark Ehl .30 .75
6 Kevin Galan .30 .75
7 Zach Gieszler .30 .75
8 Alex Greenlay .30 .75
9 Dustin Honing .30 .75
10 Dave Krisky .30 .75
11 Mike Leidl .30 .75
12 Fabio Luongo 1.25 3.00
13 Trent Manchur .30 .75
14 Tyler Mazzei .30 .75
15 Josh Murray .30 .75
16 Brad Reaney .30 .75
17 Les Reaney .40 1.00
18 Trever Turner .30 .75
19 Steve Van Oosten .30 .75
20 Duane Whitehead .30 .75
21 Shaun Witschen .30 .75
22 Josh Murray .30 .75
23 Dave Krisky .30 .75
24 Rick Pitta CO .04 .10
25 Peter Martin ACO .04 .10
26 Zamboni .04 .10
27 Action photo .04 .10
28 T.H. Wolf MASCOT .04 .10

1989-90 Windsor Spitfires
COMPLETE SET (22) 4.00 10.00
1 Sean Burns .20 .50
2 Glen Craig .20 .50
3 Brian Forestell .20 .50
4 Chris Fraser .20 .50
5 Trent Gleason .20 .50
6 Jon Hartley .20 .50
7 Ron Jones .20 .50
8 Bob Leeming .20 .50
9 Kevin MacKay .20 .50
10 Kevin McDougall .20 .50
11 Ryan Merritt .20 .50
12 David Myles .20 .50
13 Sean O'Hagan .30 .75
14 Mike Polano .20 .50
15 Jason Snow .20 .50
16 Brad Smith CO .30 .75
17 Jason Stos .20 .50
18 Jon Stos .20 .50
19 Jamie Vargo .20 .50
20 Trevor Walsh .20 .50
21 K.J. White .20 .50
22 Jason Zohl .20 .50

1992-93 Windsor Spitfires
COMPLETE SET (31) 4.80 12.00
1 Team Card Checklist .08 .25
2 Mike Martin .15 .40
3 Luke Clowes .15 .40
4 Jason Haelzle .15 .40
5 Adam Graves 1.25 3.00
6 Craig Lutes .15 .40
7 David Pluck .15 .40
8 Colin Wilson .15 .40
9 Bill Bowler .30 .75
10 Ryan O'Neill .15 .40
11 Adam Young .15 .40
12 Gerrard Masse .15 .40
13 Daryl Lavoie .15 .40
14 Peter Allison .15 .40
15 Ernie Godden RET .15 .40
16 Brady Blain .15 .40
17 Todd Warriner .30 .75
18 Rick Marshall .15 .40
19 Craig Johnson .15 .40
20 Kelly Vipond .15 .40
21 Devy Bear MASCOT .02 .10
22 Stephen Webb .20 .50
23 Scott Miller RET .15 .40
24 Dennis Purdie .20 .50
25 Steve Gibson .15 .40
26 Mike Hartwick .15 .40
27 Shawn Heins .30 .75
28 David Benn .15 .40
29 Matt Mullin .20 .50
30 David Mitchell .15 .40
31 The Dynamic Duo Todd Wa .20 .50

1993-94 Windsor Spitfires
COMPLETE SET (27) 4.80 12.00
1 Ed Jovanovski .75 2.00
2 Shawn Silver .20 .50
3 Travis Scott .20 .50
4 Mike Martin .20 .50
5 Daryl Lavoie .15 .40
6 Craig Lutes .15 .40
7 David Pluck .15 .40
8 Bill Bowler .20 .50
9 David Green .15 .40
10 Adam Young .15 .40
11 Mike Loach .15 .40
12 Brady Blain .15 .40
13 Shayne McCosh .15 .40
14 Rob Shearer .20 .50
15 Joel Poirier .15 .40
16 Cory Evans .15 .40
17 Vladimir Kretchine .15 .40
18 Dave Roche .20 .50
19 Ryan Stewart .15 .40
20 Dave Geris .15 .40
21 Dan West .15 .40
22 Luke Clowes .15 .40
23 John Cooper .15 .40
24 Akil Adams .15 .40
25 Sponsor Card Pizza Hut .02 .10
26 Sponsor Card Steve Bell .02 .10
NNO Slapshot Ad Card .02 .10

1994-95 Windsor Spitfires
COMPLETE SET (29) 6.00 15.00
1 Checklist .04 .10
2 Jamie Storr .30 .75
3 Travis Scott .20 .50
4 Paul Beazley .15 .40
5 Mike Martin .15 .40
6 Chris Van Dyk .15 .40
7 Denis Smith .20 .50
8 Glenn Crawford .15 .40
9 David Pluck .15 .40
10 Bill Bowler .30 .75
11 David Green .15 .40
12 Adam Young .15 .40
13 Wes Ward .15 .40
14 Ed Jovanovski 1.25 3.00
15 Kevin Paden .15 .40
16 Rob Shearer .20 .50
17 Joel Poirier .15 .40
18 Cory Evans .15 .40
19 Vladimir Kretchine .15 .40
20 David Roche .20 .50
21 Rick Emmett .15 .40
22 David Geris .15 .40
23 Caleb Ward .15 .40
24 Luke Clowes .15 .40
25 John Cooper .15 .40
26 Tim Findlay .20 .50
27 Pizza Hut .10
28 Sponsor Card Steve Bell .04 .10
NNO Ad Card .04 .10

1998-99 Windsor Spitfires
COMPLETE SET (9) 3.00 8.00
1 Fire Chief .04 .10
2 Coaches .04 .10
3 Duke MASCOT .04 .10
4 Michael Hanson .40 1.00
5 Jeff Kapitanchuk .40 1.00
6 Michael Leighton 1.25 3.00
7 Jason Polera .40 1.00
8 Blair Stayzer .75 2.00
9 Curtis Watson .40 1.00

2002-03 Windsor Spitfires
COMPLETE SET (30) 8.00 20.00
1 Title Card Checklist .04 .10
2 Ryan Aschaber .40 1.00
3 Frank Rediker .40 1.00
4 David Lomas .15 .40
5 Iain McPhee .15 .40
6 Mitchell Maunu .60 1.50
7 Tim Gleason .75 2.00
8 Mike James .15 .40
9 David Bowman .15 .40
10 Chief of Police .04 .10
11 Jason Dixon .15 .40
12 Rob Hennigar .30 .75
13 Craig Kennedy .30 .75
14 Elmer Mascot .04 .10
15 Ahren Nittel .20 .50
17 Phil Gibson .15 .40
18 Ryan Donnally .30 .75
19 Paul Giallonardo .15 .40
20 Josh Gratton .15 .40
21 Alexander Shevchenko .15 .40
22 Darryl Lloyd .15 .40
23 Jeff Leavitt .15 .40
24 Duke Mascot .04 .10
25 Ryan Dickie .15 .40
26 Matt Anthony .15 .40
27 John-Scott Dickson .15 .40
28 Denis Khudyakov .40 1.00
29 Mike Self .15 .40
30 Kyle Wellwood .60 1.50
116 Cam Janssen .75 2.00

2007-08 Windsor Spitfires
COMPLETE SET (30) 3.00 10.00
1 Team Checklist .02 .10
2 Joshua Bailey 1.25 3.00
3 Ryan Baldwin .40 1.00
4 Marek Biro .40 1.00
5 Jesse Blacker .40 1.00
6 Matthew Bragg .40 1.00
7 Mark Cundari .40 1.00
8 Ryan Ellis .40 1.00
9 Andrew Engelage .60 1.50
10 Richard Greenop .40 1.00
11 Taylor Hall 1.50 4.00
12 Adam Henrique .40 1.00
13 Tom Kane .40 1.00
14 Greg Nemisz .60 1.50
15 Michal Neuvirth .75 2.00
16 Jordan Nolan .60 1.50
17 Blake Parlett .40 1.00
18 Elgin Reid .40 1.00
19 Mickey Renaud .75 2.00
20 Bradley Snetsinger .40 1.00
21 Eric Wellwood .40 1.00
22 Andrew Yogan .40 1.00
23 Harry Young .40 1.00
24 Bob Boughner PRES .10 .25
25 Warren Rychel VP/GM .10 .25
26 Bob Jones AC .02 .10
27 D.J. Smith AC .02 .10
28 Bomber Spitfire MASCOT .02 .10
29 Glenn Stannard CHIEF OF POLICE.02 .10
30 Elmer Windsor POLICE MASCOT.02 .10

2003-04 Wisconsin Badgers
COMPLETE SET (30) 20.00 40.00
1 Dan Boeser .30 .75
2 Rene Bourque 1.50 4.00
3 Andy Brandt .75 2.00
4 Bernd Bruckler .60 1.50
5 Adam Burish .75 2.00
6 A.J. Degenhardt .30 .75
7 Jake Dowell .30 .75
8 Robbie Earl 1.25 3.00
9 John Eichelberger .30 .75
10 Brian Elliott .60 1.50
11 John Funk .30 .75
12 Brent Gibson .30 .75
13 Tom Gilbert 1.25 3.00
14 Mark Heatley .75 2.00
15 Andrew Joudrey .30 .75
16 Chris Julka .30 .75
17 Luke Kohtala .60 1.50
18 Jon Krall .30 .75
19 Nick Licari .30 .75
20 Jeff Likens .30 .75
21 Ryan MacMurchy .30 .75
22 Joey McElroy .30 .75
23 Matt Olinger .30 .75
24 Ken Rowe .30 .75
25 Tom Sawatske .30 .75
26 Ryan Suter 1.50 4.00
27 Pete Talafous .30 .75
28 Andy Wozniewski .60 1.50
29 Mike Eaves HCO .20 .50
30 Mascot .04 .10

2004-05 Wisconsin Badgers
COMPLETE SET (28) 15.00 30.00
1 Brian Elliott .40 1.00
2 Matt Olinger .40 1.00
3 Matt Auffrey .40 1.00
4 Robbie Earl 1.25 3.00
5 Pete Talafous .40 1.00
6 Matt Ford .75 2.00
7 Davis Drewiske .40 1.00
8 Bernd Bruckler .75 2.00
9 Ken Rowe .40 1.00
10 Jeff Likens .40 1.00
11 John Funk .40 1.00
12 Andy Brandt .40 1.00
13 Jake Dowell .40 1.00
14 Kyle Klubertanz .40 1.00
15 Joe Pavelski .40 1.00
16 Mike Eaves CO .20 .50
17 Joe Piskula .40 1.00
18 Ryan MacMurchy .40 1.00
19 Ross Carlson .40 1.00
20 A.J. Degenhardt .40 1.00
21 Josh Engel .40 1.00
22 Tom Gilbert 1.25 3.00
23 Andrew Joudrey .40 1.00
24 Nick Licari .40 1.00
25 Jeff Slinde .40 1.00
26 Luke Kohtala .75 2.00
27 Mark Heatley .75 2.00
28 Adam Burish .75 2.00

2004-05 Wisconsin Badgers Women
COMPLETE SET (24) 10.00 25.00
1 Sara Bauer .40 1.00
2 Nikki Burish .40 1.00
3 Sharon Cole .40 1.00
4 Vicki Davis .40 1.00
5 Christine Dufour .40 1.00
6 Molly Engstrom .40 1.00
7 Jackie Friesen .40 1.00
8 Meghan Horras .40 1.00
9 Grace Hutchins .40 1.00
10 Mark Johnson CO .40 1.00
11 Cyndy Kenyon .40 1.00
12 Heidi Kletzien .40 1.00
13 Carla MacLeod .75 2.00
14 Lindsay Macy .40 1.00
15 Meaghan Mikkelson .40 1.00
16 Phoebe Monteleone .40 1.00
17 Emily Morris .40 1.00
18 Mikka Nordby .40 1.00
19 Bobbi-Jo Slusar .40 1.00
20 Nicole Uliasz .40 1.00
21 Amy Vermeulen .40 1.00
22 Jesse Vetter .40 1.00
23 Kristen Witting .40 1.00
24 Jinelle Zaugg .40 1.00

2005-06 Wisconsin Badgers
COMPLETE SET (27) 15.00 30.00
1 Andy Brandt .40 1.00
2 Adam Burish .40 1.00
3 Ross Carlson .40 1.00
4 Shane Connelly .75 2.00
5 A.J. Degenhardt .40 1.00
6 Jake Dowell .40 1.00
7 Davis Drewiske .40 1.00
8 Robbie Earl .75 2.00
9 Brian Elliott .75 2.00
10 Josh Engel .40 1.00
11 Matthew Ford .40 1.00
12 Tom Gilbert .40 1.00
13 Tom Gorowsky .40 1.00
14 Ryan Jeffery .40 1.00
15 Andrew Joudrey .40 1.00
16 Kyle Klubertanz .40 1.00
17 Nick Licari .40 1.00
18 Jeff Likens .40 1.00
19 Ryan MacMurchy .40 1.00
20 Matt Olinger .40 1.00
21 Joe Pavelski .40 1.00
22 Joe Piskula .40 1.00
23 Jack Skille 2.00 5.00
24 Jeff Slinde .40 1.00
25 Ben Street .40 1.00
26 Mike Eaves HC .20 .50
27 Bucky Badger MASCOT .02 .10

2007-08 Wisconsin Badgers
COMPLETE SET (27) 25.00 40.00
1 Tom Bardis .60 1.50
2 Zach Bearson .60 1.50
3 Aaron Bendickson .60 1.50
4 Andy Bohmbach .60 1.50
5 Shane Connelly .60 1.50
6 Michael Davies .60 1.50
7 Sean Dolan .60 1.50
8 Davis Drewiske .60 1.50
9 Josh Engel .60 1.50
10 Matthew Ford .60 1.50
11 Blake Geoffrion 1.00 2.50
12 Cody Goloubef .60 1.50
13 Tom Gorowsky .60 1.50
14 Ben Grotting .60 1.50
15 Scott Gudmandson .60 1.50
16 Jeff Henderson .60 1.50
17 Ryan Jeffery .60 1.50
18 Craig Johnson .60 1.50
19 Patrick Johnson .60 1.50
20 Kyle Klubertanz .60 1.50
21 Jamie McBain .75 2.00
22 Ryan McDonagh 1.00 2.50
23 John Mitchell .60 1.50
24 Brendan Smith .60 1.50
25 Podge Turnbull .60 1.50
26 Kyle Turris 4.00 10.00
27 Mike Eaves HC .60 1.50

2014-15 Wisconsin Badgers
COMPLETE SET (28) 7.50 15.00
1 Grant Besse .30 .75
2 Jake Bunz .30 .75
3 Aiden Cavallini .30 .75
4 Tim Davison .30 .75
5 Jack Dougherty .30 .75
6 Chase Drake .30 .75
7 Mike Eaves CO .30 .75
8 Jason Ford .30 .75
9 Gabe Grunwald .30 .75
10 Cameron Hughes .30 .75
11 Cullen Hurley .30 .75
12 Joseph Labate .30 .75
13 Jake Linhart .30 .75
14 Corbin McGuire .30 .75
15 Adam Miller .30 .75
16 Brad Navin .30 .75
17 Matt Paape .30 .75
18 Landon Peterson .30 .75
19 Adam Rockwood .30 .75
20 Joel Rumpel .30 .75
21 Kevin Schulze .30 .75
22 Alex Shuchuk .30 .75
23 Jedd Soleway .30 .75
24 Matt Ustaski .30 .75
25 Ryan Wagner .30 .75
26 Eddie Wittchow .30 .75
27 Morgan Zulinick .30 .75
28 Bucky Badger MASCOT .30 .75

2000-01 Worcester IceCats
COMPLETE SET (30) 8.00 20.00
1 Ed Campbell .20 .50
2 Daniel Corso .40 1.00
3 Justin Papineau .40 1.00
4 Jaroslav Obsut .20 .50
5 Ladislav Nagy .75 2.00
6 Marc Brown .20 .50
7 Pascal Rheaume .20 .50
8 Mike Van Ryn .40 1.00
9 Cody Rudkowsky .60 1.50
10 Andrei Troschinsky .20 .50
11 Mark Rycroft .40 1.00
12 Matt Walker .20 .50
13 Jamie Thompson .20 .50
14 Darren Rumble .30 .75
15 Scratch MASCOT .04 .10
16 Team CL .04 .10
17 Dwayne Roloson .75 2.00
18 Jame Pollock .20 .50
19 Eric Boguniecki .60 1.50
20 Chris Murray .40 1.00
21 Tyler Rennette .20 .50
22 Marty Reasoner .40 1.00
23 Dale Clarke .30 .75
24 Tyler Willis .30 .75
25 Jan Horacek .30 .75
26 Peter Smrek .30 .75
27 Mike Peluso .30 .75
28 Doug Friedman .20 .50
29 Shawn Mamane .20 .50
30 Don Granato CO .10 .25

2001-02 Worcester IceCats
COMPLETE SET (15) 10.00 25.00
1 Darren Rumble .30 .75
2 Marc Brown .30 .75
3 Ed Campbell .30 .75
4 Jeff Panzer .30 .75
5 Cody Rudkowsky .40 1.00
6 Igor Valeev .30 .75
7 Dale Clarke .30 .75
8 Mike Van Ryn .40 1.00
9 Barret Jackman .75 2.00
10 Jame Pollock .30 .75
11 Daniel Tkaczuk .30 .75
12 Greg Davis .30 .75
13 Jamie Thompson .30 .75
14 Tyson Nash .60 1.50
15 Scratch MASCOT .04 .10
16 Team Photo/CL .10 .25
17 Reinhard Divis .60 1.50
18 Andrei Troschinsky .30 .75
19 Steve Halko .30 .75
20 Matt Walker .30 .75
21 Eric Boguniecki .40 1.00
22 Justin Papineau .40 1.00
23 Christian Laflamme .30 .75
24 Brad Voth .30 .75
25 Mark Rycroft .30 .75
26 Steve McLaren .30 .75
27 Eric Nickulas .30 .75
28 Justin Papineau {# Jeff Panzer {# Eric Boguniecki .30 .75
29 Brent Johnson .75 2.00
30 Don Granato CO .10 .25

2002-03 Worcester IceCats
COMPLET SET (28) 6.00 15.00
1 Checklist .04 .10
2 Terry Virtue .20 .50
3 Steve Bancroft .20 .50
4 Aris Brimanis .20 .50
5 John Pohl .75 2.00
6 Jame Pollock .20 .50
7 Eric Nickulas .20 .50
8 Jason Dawe .20 .50
9 Blake Evans .20 .50
10 Greg Davis .20 .50
11 Marc Brown .20 .50
12 Steve Dubinsky .20 .50
13 Steve McLaren .20 .50
14 Brett Scheffelmaier .20 .50
15 Mark Rycroft .20 .50
16 Christian Laflamme .20 .50
17 Justin Papineau .20 .50
18 Igor Valeev .20 .50
19 Matt Walker .20 .50
20 Jeff Panzer .20 .50
21 Sergei Varlamov .20 .50
22 Christian Backman .20 .50
23 Curtis Sanford .60 1.50
24 Phil Osaer .20 .50
25 Reinhard Divis .40 1.00
26 Eric Boguniecki MVP .20 .50
27 Don Granato HCO .04 .10
28 Scratch Mascot .04 .10

2003-04 Worcester IceCats
COMPLETE SET (28) 4.00 10.00
1 Checklist .04 .10
2 Curtis Sanford .40 1.00
3 Joe Vandermeer .15 .40
4 Terry Virtue .15 .40
5 Jon Coleman .15 .40
6 Trevor Byrne .15 .40
7 Aris Brimanis .15 .40
8 Johnny Pohl .40 1.00
9 Tom Koivisto .15 .40
10 Jame Pollock .15 .40
11 Greg Black .15 .40
12 Mike Stuart .15 .40
13 Blake Evans .15 .40
14 Mike Glumac .15 .40
15 Chris Corrinet .15 .40
16 Marc Brown .15 .40
17 Jay McClement .15 .40
18 Steve McLaren .30 .75
19 Aaron MacKenzie .15 .40
20 Colin Hemingway .15 .40
21 Ernie Hartlieb .15 .40
22 Steve Martins .15 .40
23 Brett Scheffelmaier .15 .40
24 Jeff Panzer .15 .40
25 Sergei Varlamov .15 .40
26 Reinhard Divis .30 .75
27 Don Granato CO .04 .10
28 Steve Pleau ACO .04 .10

2003-04 Worcester IceCats 10th Anniversary
COMPLETE SET (20) 4.00 10.00
1 Checklist .04 .10
2 Dwayne Roloson .40 1.00
3 Brent Johnson .40 1.00
4 Barret Jackman .30 .75
5 Bryce Salvador .15 .40
6 Terry Virtue .30 .75
7 Matt Walker .15 .40
8 Ed Campbell .15 .40
9 Rory Fitzpatrick .15 .40
10 Ricard Persson .15 .40
11 Eric Boguniecki .15 .40
12 Justin Papineau .15 .40
13 Marty Reasoner .15 .40
14 Ladislav Nagy .30 .75
15 Jeff Panzer .15 .40
16 Stephane Roy .15 .40
17 Jochen Hecht .15 .40
18 Johnny Pohl .30 .75
19 Michal Handzus .15 .40
20 Reed Low .15 .40

2004-05 Worcester IceCats
COMPLETE SET (26) 5.00 12.00
1 Curtis Sanford .40 1.00
2 Mike Mottau .20 .50
3 Trevor Byrne .20 .50
4 Aris Brimanis .20 .50
5 Brendan Buckley .20 .50
6 Johnny Pohl .40 1.00
7 Jon DiSalvatore .20 .50
8 Mike Stuart .20 .50
9 Blake Evans .20 .50
10 Mike Glumac .20 .50
11 Erkki Rajamaki .20 .50
12 Jay McClement .20 .50
13 D.J. King .20 .50
14 Aaron MacKenzie .20 .50
15 Alexei Shkotov .20 .50
16 Peter Sejna .20 .50
17 Dennis Wideman .20 .50
18 Brendan Brooks .20 .50
19 Jason Bacashihua .60 1.50
20 Jeff Hoggan .40 1.00
21 Ryan Ramsay .20 .50
22 Robin Gomez .20 .50
23 Don Granato CO .04 .10
24 Steve Pleau ACO .04 .10
25 Mascots .04 .10
NNO Checklist .04 .10

2007-08 Worcester Sharks
COMPLETE SET (27) 12.00 20.00
1 Riley Armstrong .30 .75
2 Marc Busenburg .30 .75
3 Tom Cavanagh .30 .75
4 Taylor Dakers .60 1.50
5 Brennan Evans .30 .75
6 T.J. Fox .30 .75
7 Thomas Greiss .60 1.50
8 Mike Iggulden .30 .75
9 Derek Joslin .30 .75
10 Lukas Kaspar .30 .75
11 Graham Mink .60 1.50
12 Mike Morris .30 .75
13 Dennis Packard .30 .75
14 Dimitri Patzold .60 1.50
15 Tomas Plihal .30 .75
16 Nate Raduns .30 .75
17 Ashton Rome .30 .75
18 Devin Setoguchi .75 2.00
19 Dan Spang .30 .75
20 Brad Staubitz .30 .75
21 Patrick Traverse .30 .75
22 Jonathan Tremblay .30 .75
23 Craig Valette .30 .75
24 Tom Walsh .30 .75
25 Roy Sommer HC .02 .10
26 David Cunniff AC .02 .10
27 Finz MASCOT .02 .10

2003-04 Yarmouth Mariners
COMPLETE SET (31) 4.00 10.00
1 Checklist .04 .10
2 Travis Antler .20 .50
3 Todd Ballah .20 .50
4 Jamie Barbour .20 .50
5 Brent Boardman .20 .50
6 Jarrett Bottomley .20 .50
7 Tim Clayton .20 .50
8 Georges d'Entremont .20 .50
9 Justin d'Entremont .20 .50
10 Jason Hedges .20 .50
11 Steve Holland .20 .50
12 Grant Kenny .20 .50
13 Brad Larter .20 .50
14 Jordan McMullen .20 .50
15 Jody Mosher .20 .50
16 Matt Oxtoby .20 .50
17 David Philpott .20 .50
18 Mark Plenzich .20 .50
19 Jason Robichaud .20 .50
20 Curtis Thorne .20 .50
21 Michael Dilorenzo .20 .50
22 Josh Vanderbreggen .20 .50
23 Sean Wadden .20 .50
24 Steve Yetman .20 .50
25 Paul Currie CO .04 .10
26 Laurie Barron ACO .04 .10
27 Mark Muise EQM .04 .10
28 Mark Wheeler TR .04 .10
29 One Team One Goal .04 .10
30 Mariner Pressure .04 .10
31 Hard to the Net .04 .10

1991 Arena Draft Picks
COMPLETE SET (33) 1.25 3.00
1 Pat Falloon .02 .10
2 Scott Niedermayer .08 .25
3 Scott Lachance .01 .05
4 Peter Forsberg UER .40 1.00
5 Alek Stojanov .01 .05
6 Richard Matvichuk .02 .10
7 Patrick Poulin .01 .05
8 Martin Lapointe .20 .50
9 Tyler Wright .01 .05
10 Philippe Boucher .01 .05
11 Pat Peake .01 .05
12 Markus Naslund UER .20 .50
13 Brent Bilodeau .01 .05
14 Glen Murray .20 .50
15 Niklas Sundblad .01 .05
16 Trevor Halverson .01 .05
17 Dean McAmmond .02 .10
18 Rene Corbet .01 .05
19 Eric Lavigne .01 .05
20 Steve Staios .01 .05
21 Jim Campbell .02 .10
22 Jassen Cullimore .01 .05
23 Jamie Pushor .02 .10
24 Donevan Hextall .01 .05
25 Andrew Verner .02 .10
26 Jason Dawe .01 .05
27 Jeff Nelson .01 .05
28 Darcy Werenka .01 .05
29 Francois Groleau .01 .05
30 Guy Leveque .01 .05
31 Yanic Perreault .05 .15
32 Pat Falloon Scott Lachance .02 .10
NNO Checklist Card .02 .10
HOLO Pat Falloon Hologram .08 .25

1991 Arena Draft Picks Autographs
COMPLETE SET (33) 75.00 125.00
1 Pat Falloon 2.00 5.00
2 Scott Niedermayer 6.00 15.00
3 Scott Lachance 1.25 3.00
4 Peter Forsberg UER 25.00 60.00
5 Alek Stojanov 1.25 3.00
6 Richard Matvichuk 2.00 5.00
7 Patrick Poulin 1.25 3.00
8 Martin Lapointe 6.00 15.00
9 Tyler Wright 1.25 3.00
10 Philippe Boucher 1.25 3.00
11 Pat Peake 1.25 3.00
12 Markus Naslund UER 6.00 15.00
13 Brent Bilodeau 1.25 3.00
14 Glen Murray 6.00 15.00
15 Niklas Sundblad 1.25 3.00
16 Trevor Halverson 1.25 3.00
17 Dean McAmmond 2.00 5.00
18 Rene Corbet 2.00 5.00
19 Eric Lavigne 1.25 3.00
20 Steve Staios 1.25 3.00
21 Jim Campbell 1.25 3.00
22 Jassen Cullimore 1.25 3.00
23 Jamie Pushor 1.25 3.00
24 Donevan Hextall 1.25 3.00
25 Andrew Verner 2.00 5.00
26 Jason Dawe 1.25 3.00
27 Jeff Nelson 1.25 3.00
28 Darcy Werenka 1.25 3.00
29 Francois Groleau 1.25 3.00
30 Guy Leveque 1.25 3.00
31 Yanic Perreault 2.00 5.00

1997 Bowman CHL
COMPLETE SET (160) 10.00 25.00
1 Jan Bulis .15 .40
2 Daniel Cleary .15 .40
3 Dave Duerden .07 .20
4 Cameron Mann .07 .20
5 Alyn McCauley .15 .40
6 Tyler Rennette .07 .20
7 Marc Savard .20 .50
8 Daniel Tkaczuk .15 .40
9 John Tripp .07 .20
10 Joel Trottier .07 .20
11 Sean Yenedam .07 .20
12 Alexander Volchkov .07 .20
13 Sean Blanchard .07 .20
14 Kevin Bolibruck .07 .20
15 Nick Boynton .20 .50
16 Paul Mara .15 .40
17 Marc Moro .07 .20
18 Marty Wilford .07 .20
19 Zac Bierk .20 .50
20 Kory Cooper .07 .20
21 Richard Rochefort .07 .20
22 Matt Cooke .20 .50
23 Boyd Devereaux .20 .50
24 Rico Fata .15 .40
25 Dwayne Hay .07 .20
26 Trevor Letowski .07 .20
27 Ryan Mougenel .07 .20
28 Todd Norman .07 .20
29 Larry Paleczny .07 .20
30 Colin Pepperall .07 .20
31 Jonathan Sim .07 .20
32 Joe Thornton 1.50 4.00
33 Brian Wesenberg .07 .20
34 Andy Delmore .07 .20
35 Chris Hajt .07 .20
36 Richard Jackman .07 .20
37 Denis Smith .07 .20
38 Jamie Sokolsky .07 .20
39 Paul Traynor .07 .20
40 Patrick DesRochers .15 .40

41 Robert Esche .40 1.00
42 Roberto Luongo 1.50 4.00
43 Frederic Henry .07 .20
44 Marc Oliver Roy .07 .20
45 Samy Nasreddine .07 .20
46 Jean-Francois Fortin .07 .20
47 Martin Ethier .07 .20
48 Jason Doig .07 .20
49 Dominic Perna .07 .20
50 Daniel Briere .30 .75
51 Pavel Rosa .07 .20
52 Philippe Audet .07 .20
53 Gordie Dwyer .07 .20
54 Martin Menard .07 .20
55 Jonathan Delisle .07 .20
56 Peter Worrell .20 .50
57 Francois Methot .07 .20
58 Steve Begin .07 .20
59 Karol Bartanus .07 .20
60 J-P Dumont .40 1.00
61 Marc Denis .40 1.00
62 Jean-Sebastien Giguere .75 2.00
63 Jason Gorleau .07 .20
64 Radoslav Suchy .07 .20
65 Stephane Robidas .07 .20
66 Marc-Andre Gaudet .07 .20
67 Eric Drouin .07 .20
68 Derrick Walser .07 .20
69 Vincent Lecavalier 1.25 3.00
70 Denis Hamel .07 .20
71 Daniel Corso .07 .20
72 Martin Moise .07 .20
73 Eric Belanger .07 .20
74 Olivier Morin .07 .20
75 Jerome Tremblay .07 .20
76 Jody Shelley .30 .75
77 Eric Normandin .07 .20
78 David Thibeault .07 .20
79 Christian Daigle .15 .40
80 Alexandre Jacques .07 .20
81 Brian Boucher .40 1.00
82 Randy Petruk .15 .40
83 Hugh Hamilton .07 .20
84 Joel Kwiatkowski .07 .20
85 Zenith Komarniski .07 .20
86 Joey Tetarenko .20 .50
87 Tyler Willis .07 .20
88 Patrick Marleau 1.00 2.50
89 Trent Whitfield .07 .20
90 Martin Cerven .07 .20
91 Donnie Kinney .07 .20
92 Brad Isbister .15 .40
93 Todd Robinson .07 .20
94 Greg Leeb .07 .20
95 John Cirjak .07 .20
96 Randy Perry .07 .20
97 Derek Schutz .07 .20
98 Brenden Morrow .40 1.00
99 Shawn McNeil .07 .20
100 Brad Ference .07 .20
101 Ryan Hoople .07 .20
102 Brian Elder .07 .20
103 Mike McBain .07 .20
104 Jesse Wallin .07 .20
105 Chris Phillips .20 .50
106 Kelly Smart .07 .20
107 Arron Asham .07 .20
108 Byron Ritchie .07 .20
109 Derek Morris .20 .50
110 Travis Brigley .07 .20
111 Justin Kurtz .07 .20
112 B.J. Young .07 .20
113 Shane Willis .07 .20
114 Josh Holden .07 .20
115 Cory Sarich .07 .20
116 Brad Larsen .07 .20
117 Stefan Cherneski .07 .20
118 Peter Schaefer .07 .20
119 Dmitri Nabokov .07 .20
120 Sergei Varlamov .20 .50
121 Daniel Cleary TP .07 .20
122 Jarrett Smith TP .07 .20
123 Alexandre Mathieu TP .07 .20
124 Matt Elich TP .07 .20
125 Joe Thornton TP .75 2.00
126 Mike Brown TP .07 .20
127 Derek Schutz TP .07 .20
128 Benoit Cote TP .07 .20
129 Jason Ward TP .07 .20
130 Karol Bartanus TP .07 .20
131 Tyler Rennette TP .07 .20
132 Matt Zultek TP .15 .40
133 Brad Ference TP .15 .40
134 Daniel Tetrault TP .07 .20
135 Ray Bonni TP .07 .20
136 Kevin Grimes TP .07 .20
137 Paul Mara TP .15 .40
138 Nikos Tselios TP .07 .20
139 Curtis Cruickshank TP .07 .20
140 Pierre-Luc Therrien TP .07 .20
141 Patrick Marleau TP .50 1.50
142 Ty Jones TP .07 .20
143 Jeremy Reich TP .07 .20
144 Adam Mair TP .15 .40
145 Adam Colagiacomo TP .07 .20
146 Harold Druken TP .15 .40
147 Brenden Morrow TP .30 .75
148 Jay Legault TP .07 .20
149 Jeff Zehr TP .07 .20
150 Scott Barney TP .07 .20
151 Gregor Baumgartner TP .07 .20
152 Daniel Tkaczuk TP .20 .50
153 Eric Brewer TP .20 .50
154 Nick Boynton TP .20 .50
155 Vratislav Cech TP .07 .20
156 Kyle Kos TP .07 .20
157 Jean-Francois Fortin TP .07 .20
158 Wes Jarvis TP .07 .20
159 Roberto Luongo TP .75 2.00
160 Jean-Francois Damphousse TP .07 .20
NNO B.B.Redempt. .40 1.00
NNO Ref.Redempt. .40 1.00
NNO Ato.Ref.Redempt. .40 1.00
NNO Auto.Redempt. .40 1.00

1997 Bowman CHL OPC

COMPLETE SET (160) 300.00 600.00
*STARS: 4X TO 10X BASIC CARDS

1997 Bowman CHL Autographs

COMPLETE SET (40) 150.00 200.00
2 Jarrett Smith 2.00 5.00
3 Alexandre Mathieu 2.00 5.00
4 Matt Elich 2.00 5.00
10 Karol Bartanus 2.00 5.00
11 Tyler Rennette 2.00 5.00
13 Brad Ference 2.00 5.00
14 Daniel Tetrault 2.00 5.00
15 Ray Bonni 2.00 5.00
16 Kevin Grimes 2.00 5.00
18 Nikos Tselios 2.00 5.00
19 Curtis Cruickshank 2.00 5.00
20 Pierre-Luc Therrien 2.00 5.00
22 Ty Jones 2.00 5.00
23 Jeremy Reich 2.00 5.00
24 Adam Mair 2.00 5.00
25 Adam Colagiacomo 2.00 5.00
26 Harold Druken 2.00 5.00
28 Jay Legault 2.00 5.00
29 Jeff Zehr 4.00 10.00
30 Scott Barney 2.00 5.00
31 Jonathan Sim 2.00 5.00
33 Eric Brewer 5.00 12.00
34 Nick Boynton 5.00 12.00
35 Vratislav Cech 2.00 5.00
36 Kyle Kos 2.00 5.00
37 Jean Francois Fortin 2.00 5.00
38 Wes Jarvis 2.00 5.00
39 Roberto Luongo 8.00 20.00
121 Daniel Cleary 2.00 5.00
125 Joe Thornton 20.00 40.00
126 Mike Brown 2.00 5.00
127 Derek Schutz 2.00 5.00
128 Benoit Cote 2.00 5.00
129 Jason Ward 4.00 10.00
132 Matt Zultek 2.00 5.00
147 Brenden Morrow 10.00 20.00
160 Jean-Francois Damphousse 5.00 12.00
149 Jeff Zehr 2.00 5.00
151 Gregor Baumgartner 2.00 5.00
152 Daniel Tkaczuk 2.00 5.00

1997 Bowman CHL Bowman's Best

COMPLETE SET (20) 25.00 35.00
*REF.STARS: 1.5X TO 3X BASIC BOWMAN'S BEST
*ATOMIC REF: 2.5X TO 5X BASIC BOWMAN'S BEST
1 Joe Thornton 4.00 10.00
2 Patrick Marleau 2.00 5.00
3 Paul Mara .60 1.50
4 Daniel Tkaczuk .60 1.50
5 Jason Ward .60 1.50
6 Nick Boynton .75 2.00
7 Daniel Cleary .60 1.50
8 Eric Brewer .75 2.00
9 Brad Ference .60 1.50
10 Stefan Cherneski .60 1.50
11 Ryan Bonni .60 1.50
12 Adam Colagiacomo .60 1.50
13 Mike Brown .60 1.50
14 Scott Barney .60 1.50
15 Jarrett Smith .60 1.50
16 Brenden Morrow 1.25 3.00
17 Jean-Francois Fortin .60 1.50
18 Roberto Luongo 4.00 10.00
19 Curtis Cruickshank .60 1.50
20 Pierre-Luc Therrien .60 1.50

1998 Bowman CHL

COMPLETE SET (165) 20.00 60.00
1 Robert Esche .20 .50
2 Chris Hajt .07 .20
3 Mark McMahon .07 .20
4 Jeff Brown .07 .20
5 Richard Jackman .07 .20
6 Greg Labenski .07 .20
7 Marek Posmyk .07 .20
8 Brian Willsie .07 .20
9 Jason Ward .07 .20
10 Manny Malhotra .07 .20
11 Matt Cooke .40 1.00
12 Mike Gorman .07 .20
13 Rodney Richard .07 .20
14 David Legwand .40 1.00
15 Jon Sim .07 .20
16 Peter Sarno .07 .20
17 Andrew Long .07 .20
18 Peter Cava .07 .20
19 Colin Pepperall .07 .20
20 Jay Legault .07 .20
21 Brian Finley .15 .40
22 Martin Skoula .07 .20
23 Brian Campbell .07 .20
24 Sean Blanchard .07 .20
25 Bryan Allen .07 .20
26 Peter Hogan .07 .20
27 Nick Boynton .30 .75
28 Matt Bradley .07 .20
29 Jeremy Adduono .07 .20
30 Mike Henrich .07 .20
31 Justin Papineau .20 .50
32 Bujar Amidovski .30 .75
33 Robert Mailloux .07 .20
34 Daniel Tkaczuk .07 .20
35 Sean Avery .40 1.00
36 Mark Bell .20 .50
37 Kevin Colley .07 .20
38 Norm Milley .30 .75
39 Scott Barney .07 .20
40 Joel Trottier .07 .20
41 Brent Belecki .07 .20
42 Randy Petruk .20 .50
43 Brad Ference .07 .20
44 Perry Johnson .07 .20
45 Joel Kwiatkowski .07 .20
46 Zenith Komarniski .07 .20
47 Greg Kuznik .07 .20
48 Andrew Ference .07 .20
49 Jason Deleurme .07 .20
50 Trent Whitfield .07 .20
51 Dylan Gyori .07 .20
52 Todd Robinson .07 .20
53 Marian Hossa .40 1.00
54 Mike Hurley .07 .20
55 Greg Leeb .07 .20
56 Andrej Podkonicky .20 .50
57 Quinn Hancock .07 .20
58 Marian Cisar .07 .20
59 Bret DeCecco .07 .20
60 Brenden Morrow .20 .50
61 Evan Lindsay .20 .50
62 Terry Friesen .20 .50
63 Ryan Shannon .07 .20
64 Michal Rozsival .07 .20
65 Luc Theoret .07 .20
66 Brad Stuart .40 1.00
67 Burke Henry .07 .20
68 Cory Sarich .07 .20
69 Martin Sonnenberg .07 .20
70 Mark Smith .20 .50
71 Shawn McNeil .07 .20
72 Brad Moran .07 .20
73 Josh Holden .07 .20
74 Cory Cyrenne .07 .20
75 Shane Willis .07 .20
76 Stefan Cherneski .07 .20
77 Jay Henderson .07 .20
78 Ronald Petrovicky .07 .20
79 Sergei Varlamov .07 .20
80 Chad Hinz .07 .20
81 Mathieu Garon .20 .50
82 Mathieu Chouinard .20 .50
83 Dominic Perna .07 .20
84 Didier Tremblay .07 .20
85 Mike Ribeiro .20 .50
86 Marty Johnston .07 .20
87 Remi Royer .07 .20
88 Patrick Pelchat .07 .20
89 Daniel Corso .07 .20
90 Francois Fortier .07 .20
91 Marc-Andre Gaudet .07 .20
92 Francois Beauchemin .07 .20
93 Michel Tremblay .07 .20
94 Jean-Philippe Pare .07 .20
95 Francois Methot .07 .20
96 David Thibeault .07 .20
97 Jonathan Girard Jr. .20 .50
98 Karol Bartanus .07 .20
99 Peter Ratchuk .07 .20
100 Pierre Dagenais .20 .50
101 Philippe Sauve .40 1.00
102 Remi Bergeron .07 .20
103 Vincent Lecavalier .20 .50
104 Eric Chouinard .40 1.00
105 Oleg Timchenko .07 .20
106 Sebastien Roger .07 .20
107 Simon Gagne .40 1.00
108 Alex Tanguay .40 1.00
109 David Gosselin .07 .20
110 Ramzi Abid .20 .50
111 Eric Drouin .07 .20
112 Dominic Auger .07 .20
113 Martin Moise .07 .20
114 Randy Copley .07 .20
115 Alexandre Mathieu .07 .20
116 Brad Richards .20 .50
117 Dmitri Tolkunov .07 .20
118 Alexei Tezikov .07 .20
119 Derrick Walser .07 .20
120 Adam Borzecki .07 .20
121 Ramzi Abid .20 .50
122 Brett Allan .07 .20
123 Mark Bell .20 .50
124 Blair Betts .07 .20
125 Randy Copley .07 .20
126 Simon Gagne .40 1.00
127 Mike Henrich .07 .20
128 Vincent Lecavalier .20 .50
129 Norm Milley .40 1.00
130 Chris Neilsen .07 .20
131 Rico Fata .20 .50
132 Mike Ribeiro .20 .50
133 Bryan Allen .07 .20
134 John Erskine .20 .50
135 Jonathan Girard Jr. .20 .50
136 Stephen Peat .40 1.00
137 Robyn Regehr .30 .75
138 Brad Stuart .40 1.00
139 Patrick Desrochers .20 .50
140 Jason Labarbera .20 .50
141 David Cameron .07 .20
142 Jonathan Cheechoo .40 1.00
143 Eric Chouinard .40 1.00
144 Brent Gauvreau .07 .20
145 Scott Gomez .20 .50
146 Jeff Heerema .07 .20
147 David Legwand .40 1.00
148 Manny Malhotra .20 .50
149 Justin Papineau .07 .20
150 Andrew Peters .07 .20
151 Michael Rupp .40 1.00
152 Alex Tanguay .40 1.00
153 Francois Beauchemin .07 .20
154 Mathieu Biron .07 .20
155 Jiri Fischer .40 1.00
156A Alex Henry ERR Jer #26 .20 .50
156B Alex Henry COR Jer #68 .20 .50
157 Kyle Rossiter .07 .20
158 Martin Skoula .07 .20
159 Mathieu Chouinard .20 .50
160 Philippe Sauve .40 1.00
161 Brian Finley .15 .40
162 Brent Belecki .07 .20
163A Dominic Perna ERR IHMQ .07 .20
163B Dominic Perna COR MVP .07 .20
164 Jonathan Cheechoo .40 1.00
165 Checklist .07 .20

1998 Bowman CHL Golden Anniversary

*STARS: 12.5X TO 30X BASIC CARDS

1998 Bowman CHL OPC International

*STARS: .75X TO 2X BASIC CARDS

1998 Bowman CHL Autographs Blue

*SILVER AU's: .75X TO 2X BASIC AU
*GOLD AU's: 2X TO 5X BASIC AU
A1 Justin Papineau 2.50 6.00
A2 Jason Labarbera 4.00 10.00
A3 Michael Rupp 8.00 8.00
A4 Stephen Peat 3.00 8.00
A5 Manny Malhotra 2.50 6.00
A6 Michael Henrich 2.50 6.00
A7 Kyle Rossiter 2.50 6.00
A8 Mark Bell 3.00 8.00
A9 Mathieu Chouinard 4.00 10.00
A10 Vincent Lecavalier 10.00 25.00
A11 David Legwand 4.00 10.00
A12 Bryan Allen 2.50 6.00
A13 Francois Beauchemin 2.50 6.00
A14 Robyn Regehr 5.00 12.00
A15 Eric Chouinard 8.00 8.00
A16 Norman Milley 8.00 8.00
A17 Alex Henry 2.50 6.00
A18 Ramzi Abid 3.00 8.00
A19 Jiri Fischer 5.00 12.00
A20 Patrick Desrochers 8.00 8.00
A21 Mathieu Biron 2.50 6.00
A22 Brad Stuart 5.00 12.00
A23 Philippe Sauve 8.00 20.00
A24 John Erskine 8.00 8.00
A25 Jonathan Cheechoo 10.00 25.00
A26 Brett Allan 2.50 6.00
A27 Scott Gomez 6.00 15.00
A28 Chris Neilsen 2.50 6.00
A29 David Cameron 2.50 6.00
A30 Jonathan Girard Jr. 4.00 10.00
A31 Jeff Heerema 2.50 6.00
A32 Blair Betts 2.50 6.00
A33 Andrew Peters 2.50 6.00
A34 Randy Copley 8.00 8.00
A35 Alex Tanguay 6.00 15.00
A36 Simon Gagne 8.00 20.00
A37 Brent Gauvreau 2.50 6.00
A38 Mike Ribeiro 5.00 12.00
A39 Martin Skoula 2.50 6.00
A40 Rico Fata 4.00 10.00

1998 Bowman CHL Scout's Choice

COMPLETE SET (21) 8.00 20.00
SC1 Bryan Allen .40 1.00
SC2 Manny Malhotra .40 1.00
SC3 Daniel Tkaczuk .40 1.00
SC4 Bujar Amidovski .40 1.00
SC5 Patrick Desrochers .40 1.00
SC6 Brad Ference .40 1.00
SC7 Marian Hossa .60 1.50
SC8 Brad Stuart .40 1.00
SC9 Sergei Varlamov .40 1.00
SC10 Randy Petruk .40 1.00
SC11 Karol Bartanus .40 1.00
SC12 Vincent Lecavalier .50 1.25
SC13 Jonathan Girard .40 1.00
SC14 Peter Ratchuk .40 1.00
SC15 Alex Tanguay .60 1.50
SC16 Rico Fata .40 1.00
SC17 Brian Finley .50 1.25
SC18 Jonathan Cheechoo .40 1.00
SC19 Scott Gomez .40 1.00
SC20 Michal Rozsival .40 1.00
SC21 Mathieu Garon .40 1.00

1998 Bowman Chrome CHL

COMPLETE SET (165) 30.00 60.00
1 Robert Esche .60 1.50
2 Chris Hajt .15 .40
3 Mark McMahon .15 .40
4 Jeff Brown .15 .40
5 Richard Jackman .15 .40
6 Greg Labenski .15 .40
7 Marek Posmyk .15 .40
8 Brian Willsie .15 .40
9 Jason Ward .15 .40
10 Manny Malhotra .15 .40
11 Matt Cooke .75 2.00
12 Mike Gorman .15 .40
13 Rodney Richard .15 .40
14 David Legwand .75 2.00
15 Jon Sim .15 .40
16 Peter Sarno .60 1.50
17 Andrew Long .15 .40
18 Peter Cava .15 .40
19 Colin Pepperall .15 .40
20 Jay Legault .15 .40
21 Brian Finley .60 1.50
22 Martin Skoula .15 .40
23 Brian Campbell .15 .40
24 Sean Blanchard .15 .40
25 Bryan Allen .15 .40
26 Peter Hogan .15 .40
27 Nick Boynton .75 2.00
28 Matt Bradley .15 .40
29 Jeremy Adduono .15 .40
30 Mike Henrich .15 .40
31 Justin Papineau .15 .40
32 Bujar Amidovski .60 1.50
33 Robert Mailloux .15 .40
34 Daniel Tkaczuk .15 .40
35 Sean Avery .75 2.00
36 Mark Bell .75 2.00
37 Kevin Colley .15 .40
38 Norm Milley .60 1.50
39 Scott Barney .15 .40
40 Joel Trottier .15 .40
41 Brent Belecki .15 .40
42 Randy Petruk .60 1.50
43 Brad Ference .15 .40
44 Perry Johnson .15 .40
45 Joel Kwiatkowski .15 .40
46 Zenith Komarniski .15 .40
47 Greg Kuznik .15 .40
48 Andrew Ference .60 1.50
49 Jason Deleurme .15 .40
50 Trent Whitfield .15 .40
51 Dylan Gyori .15 .40
52 Todd Robinson .15 .40
53 Marian Hossa .75 2.00
54 Mike Hurley .15 .40
55 Greg Leeb .15 .40
56 Andrej Podkonicky .15 .40
57 Quinn Hancock .15 .40
58 Marian Cisar .15 .40
59 Bret DeCecco .15 .40
60 Brenden Morrow .60 1.50
61 Evan Lindsay .60 1.50
62 Terry Friesen .60 1.50
63 Ryan Shannon .15 .40
64 Michal Rozsival .15 .40
65 Luc Theoret .15 .40
66 Brad Stuart .75 2.00
67 Burke Henry .15 .40
68 Cory Sarich .15 .40
69 Martin Sonnenberg .15 .40
70 Mark Smith .60 1.50
71 Shawn McNeil .15 .40
72 Brad Moran .15 .40
73 Josh Holden .15 .40
74 Cory Cyrenne .15 .40
75 Shane Willis .15 .40
76 Stefan Cherneski .15 .40
77 Jay Henderson .15 .40
78 Ronald Petrovicky .15 .40
79 Sergei Varlamov .15 .40
80 Chad Hinz .15 .40
81 Mathieu Garon .40 1.00
82 Mathieu Chouinard .60 1.50
83 Dominic Perna .15 .40
84 Didier Tremblay .15 .40
85 Mike Ribeiro .40 1.00
86 Marty Johnston .15 .40
87 Remi Royer .15 .40
88 Patrick Pelchat .15 .40
89 Daniel Corso .15 .40
90 Francois Fortier .15 .40
91 Marc-Andre Gaudet .15 .40
92 Francois Beauchemin .15 .40
93 Michel Tremblay .15 .40
94 Jean-Philippe Pare .15 .40
95 Francois Methot .15 .40
96 David Thibeault .15 .40
97 Jonathan Girard Jr. .60 1.50
98 Karol Bartanus .15 .40
99 Peter Ratchuk .15 .40
100 Pierre Dagenais .60 1.50
101 Philippe Sauve .75 2.00
102 Remi Bergeron .15 .40
103 Vincent Lecavalier .60 1.50
104 Eric Chouinard .60 1.50
105 Oleg Timchenko .15 .40
106 Sebastien Roger .15 .40
107 Simon Gagne .75 2.00
108 Alex Tanguay .75 2.00
109 David Gosselin .15 .40
110 Ramzi Abid .15 .40
111 Eric Drouin .15 .40
112 Dominic Auger .15 .40
113 Martin Moise .15 .40
114 Randy Copley .15 .40
115 Alexandre Mathieu .15 .40
116 Brad Richards .60 1.50
117 Dmitri Tolkunov .15 .40
118 Alexei Tezikov .15 .40
119 Derrick Walser .15 .40
120 Adam Borzecki .15 .40
121 Ramzi Abid .15 .40
122 Brett Allan .15 .40
123 Mark Bell .40 1.00
124 Blair Betts .15 .40
125 Randy Copley .60 1.50
126 Simon Gagne .75 2.00
127 Mike Henrich .15 .40
128 Vincent Lecavalier .60 1.50
129 Norm Milley .60 1.50
130 Chris Nielsen .15 .40
131 Rico Fata .60 1.50
132 Mike Ribeiro .40 1.00
133 Bryan Allen .15 .40
134 John Erskine .60 1.50
135 Jonathan Girard Jr. .60 1.50
136 Stephen Peat .75 2.00
137 Robyn Regehr .60 1.50
138 Brad Stuart .75 2.00
139 Patrick Desrochers .60 1.50
140 Jason Labarbera .60 1.50
141 David Cameron .15 .40
142 Jonathan Cheechoo 1.25 3.00
143 Eric Chouinard .60 1.50
144 Brent Gauvreau .15 .40
145 Scott Gomez .40 1.00
146 Jeff Heerema .15 .40
147 David Legwand .75 2.00
148 Manny Malhotra .15 .40
149 Justin Papineau .15 .40
150 Andrew Peters .15 .40
151 Michael Rupp .60 1.50
152 Alex Tanguay .75 2.00
153 Francois Beauchemin .15 .40
154 Mathieu Biron .15 .40
155 Jiri Fischer .75 2.00
156 Alex Henry .15 .40
157 Kyle Rossiter .15 .40
158 Martin Skoula .15 .40
159 Mathieu Chouinard .60 1.50
160 Philippe Sauve .75 2.00
161 Brian Finley .60 1.50
162 Brent Belecki .15 .40
163 Dominic Perna .15 .40
164 Jonathan Cheechoo .75 2.00
165 Checklist .15 .40
NNO Puck Redemption .15 .40

1998 Bowman Chrome CHL Golden Anniversary

*STARS: 10X TO 25X BASIC CARDS

1998 Bowman Chrome CHL OPC International

*STARS: 2.5X TO 5X BASIC CARD
*REF.STARS: 8X TO 20X BASIC CARDS

1998 Bowman Chrome CHL Refractors

REF.STARS: 4X TO 10X BASIC CARD

1999 Bowman CHL

COMPLETE SET (165) 20.00 50.00
1 Alex Auld .30 .75
2 Maxime Ouellet .40 1.00
3 Nolan Yonkman .07 .20
4 Jeff Beatch .07 .20
5 Pavel Brendl .20 .50
6 Jamie Chamberlain .07 .20
7 Kyle Wanvig .07 .20
8 Chris Kelly .07 .20
9 Scott Kelman .07 .20
10 Derek MacKenzie .07 .20
11 Tim Connolly .20 .50
12 Alexandre Giroux .07 .20
13 Oleg Saprykin .20 .50
14 Sheldon Keefe .20 .50
15 Branislav Mezei .20 .50
16 Brett Lysak .07 .20
17 Peter Reynolds .07 .20
18 Ross Lupaschuk .07 .20
19 Mirko Murovic .07 .20
20 Steve McCarthy .20 .50
21 Radim Vrbata .20 .50
22 Dusty Jamieson .07 .20
23 Matt Carkner .07 .20
24 Denis Shvidki .20 .50
25 Jonathan Fauteux .07 .20
26 Martin Grenier .07 .20
27 Marc-Andre Thinel .20 .50
28 Luke Sellars .07 .20
29 Brad Ralph .07 .20
30 Scott Cameron .07 .20
31 Charlie Stephens .07 .20
32 Jamie Lundmark .20 .50
33 Justin Mapletoft .20 .50
34 Kristopher Beech .20 .50
35 Taylor Pyatt .20 .50
36 Michael Zigomanis .20 .50
37 Edward Hill .07 .20
38 Barret Jackman .40 1.00
39 Simon LaJeunesse .30 .75
40 Brian Finley .30 .75
41 Maxime Ouellet .40 1.00
42 Alexei Volkov .30 .75
43 Roberto Luongo .60 1.50
44 Chris Lyness .07 .20
45 Simon Tremblay .07 .20
46 Eric Tremblay .07 .20
47 Jonathan Girard .20 .50
48 Dimitri Tolkunov .07 .20
49 Philippe Plante .07 .20
50 Eric Chouninard .20 .50
51 Wesley Scanzano .07 .20
52 Vincent Dionne .07 .20
53 Sebastien Roger .07 .20
54 Ladislav Nagy .40 1.00
55 Alex Tanguay .40 1.00
56 Martin Moise .07 .20
57 Brad Richards .40 1.00
58 Juraj Kolnik .20 .50
59 Simon Gagne .40 1.00
60 Gregor Baumgartner .07 .20
61 Mathieu Benoit .07 .20
62 Pierre-Luc Therrien .07 .20
63 Danny LaVoie .07 .20
64 Mathieu Chouinard .07 .20
65 Andrew Carver .07 .20
66 Jiri Fischer .20 .50
67 Alexander Ryazantsev .07 .20
68 Didier Tremblay .07 .20
69 Mathieu Biron .07 .20
70 Michel Periard .07 .20
71 Mike Ribeiro .30 .75
72 Francois Fortier .07 .20
73 Benoit Dusablon .07 .20
74 Jerome Tremblay .07 .20
75 Samuel St.Pierre .07 .20
76 Marc-Andre Thinel .20 .50
77 Alexandre Tremblay .07 .20
78 Patrick Grandmaitre .07 .20
79 Christian Daigle .07 .20
80 David Thibeault .07 .20
81 Dominic Forget .07 .20
82 James Desmarais .07 .20
83 Pavel Brendl .20 .50
84 Kyle Calder .20 .50
85 Jason Chimera .20 .50
86 Chad Hinz .07 .20
87 Curtis Huppe .07 .20
88 Milan Kraft .20 .50
89 Brad Leeb .07 .20
90 Jamie Lundmark .20 .50
91 Brett Lysak .07 .20
92 Brad Moran .20 .50
93 Frantisek Mrazek .07 .20
94 Brad Twordik .07 .20
95 Kurt Drummond .07 .20
96 Burke Henry .07 .20
97 Steve McCarthy .20 .50
98 Richard Seeley .07 .20
99 Brad Stuart .30 .75
100 Luc Theoret .07 .20
101 Alexandre Fomitchev .07 .20
102 Brady Block .07 .20
103 Ajay Baines .07 .20
104 Blair Betts .20 .50
105 Tyler Bouck .20 .50
106 Mike Brown .07 .20
107 Bret DeCecco .07 .20
108 Scott Gomez .30 .75
109 Dylan Gyori .07 .20
110 Donnie Kinney .07 .20
111 Ken McKay .07 .20
112 Brett McLean .07 .20
113 Brenden Morrow .30 .75
114 Marty Standish .07 .20
115 Andrew Ference .20 .50
116 Brad Ference .07 .20
117 Scott Hannan .30 .75
118 Darrell Hay .07 .20
119 Robyn Regehr .30 .75
120 Chris St. Croix .07 .20
121 Kenric Exner .20 .50
122 Cody Rudkowsky .20 .50
123 Scott Barney .07 .20
124 Kevin Colley .07 .20
125 Sheldon Keefe .20 .50
126 Norman Milley .20 .50
127 Scott Page .07 .20
128 Justin Papineau .20 .50
129 Ryan Ready .07 .20
130 Denis Shvidki .20 .50
131 Chris Stanley .07 .20
132 Dan Tessier .07 .20
133 Daniel Tkaczuk .07 .20
134 Michael Zigomanis .20 .50
135 Jim Baxter .07 .20
136 Branislav Mezei .20 .50
137 Brian Campbell .07 .20
138 Greg Labenski .07 .20
139 Jeff McKercher .07 .20
140 Martin Skoula .20 .50
141 Brian Finley .20 .50
142 Seamus Kotyk .20 .50
143 Adam Colagiacomo .07 .20
144 Tim Connolly .30 .75
145 Harold Druken .20 .50
146 Rico Fata .20 .50
147 David Legwand .30 .75
148 Adam Mair .07 .20
149 Kent McDonell .07 .20
150 Ivan Novoseltsev .20 .50
151 Peter Sarno .20 .50
152 Dan Snyder .40 1.00
153 Jason Spezza 1.50 4.00
154 Jason Ward .07 .20
155 Alex Henry .07 .20
156 Wes Jarvis .07 .20
157 Paul Mara .20 .50
158 Kevin Mitchell .07 .20
159 Dan Passero .07 .20
160 Dan Watson .07 .20
161 Gene Chiarello .07 .20
162 Chris Madden .30 .75
163 Maxime Ouellet
B.DeCecco .30 .75
164 S.Barney
M.Thinel .07 .20
165 Checklist .07 .20

1999 Bowman CHL Gold

*STARS: 6X TO 15X BASIC CARDS

1999 Bowman CHL OPC International

COMPLETE SET (165) 50.00 100.00
*STARS: .75X TO 2X BASIC CARDS

1999 Bowman CHL Autographs

*SILVER: 1X TO 2X BASIC CARDS
*GOLD: 2.5X TO 5X BASIC CARDS
BA1 Brian Finley 2.50 6.00
BA2 Simon Lajeunesse 3.00 8.00
BA3 Barret Jackman 4.00 10.00
BA4 Edward Hill 2.00 5.00
BA5 Michael Zigomanis 2.50 6.00
BA6 Taylor Pyatt 4.00 10.00
BA7 Kristopher Beech 4.00 10.00
BA8 Justin Mapletoft 3.00 8.00
BA9 Jamie Lundmark 4.00 10.00
BA10 Charlie Stephens 2.00 5.00
BA11 Scott Cameron 2.00 5.00
BA12 Brad Ralph 2.00 5.00
BA13 Luke Sellars 2.00 5.00
BA14 Marc-Andre Thinel 2.50 6.00
BA15 Martin Grenier 3.00 8.00
BA16 Jonathan Fauteux 2.00 5.00
BA17 Denis Shvidki 2.00 5.00
BA18 Matt Carkner 2.00 5.00
BA19 Dusty Jamieson 2.00 5.00
BA20 Radim Vrbata 4.00 10.00
BA21 Alex Auld 5.00 12.00
BA22 Maxime Ouellet 6.00 15.00
BA23 Nolan Yonkman 2.00 5.00
BA24 Jeff Beatch 2.00 5.00
BA25 Pavel Brendl 3.00 8.00
BA26 Jamie Chamberlain 2.00 5.00
BA27 Kyle Wanvig 4.00 10.00
BA28 Chris Kelly 2.00 5.00
BA29 Scott Kelman 2.00 5.00
BA30 Derek MacKenzie 2.00 5.00
BA31 Tim Connolly 4.00 10.00
BA32 Alexandre Giroux 2.00 5.00
BA33 Oleg Saprykin 3.00 8.00
BA34 Sheldon Keefe 2.00 5.00
BA35 Branislav Mezei 2.00 5.00
BA36 Brett Lysak 3.00 8.00
BA37 Peter Reynolds 2.50 6.00
BA38 Ross Lupaschuk 2.00 5.00
BA39 Mirko Murovic 2.00 5.00
BA40 Steve McCarthy 2.00 5.00

1999 Bowman CHL Scout's Choice

SC1 Tim Connolly 1.25 3.00
SC2 Scott Kelman .75 2.00
SC3 Pavel Brendl .75 2.00
SC4 Maxime Ouellet 1.25 3.00
SC5 Brian Finley 1.25 3.00
SC6 Denis Shvidki .75 2.00
SC7 Michael Zigomanis .75 2.00
SC8 Taylor Pyatt .75 2.00
SC9 Kris Beech .75 2.00
SC10 Jamie Lundmark .75 2.00
SC11 Jason Spezza 2.00 5.00
SC12 Rico Fata .75 2.00
SC13 David Legwand 1.25 3.00
SC14 Daniel Tkaczuk .75 2.00
SC15 Brad Stuart .75 2.00
SC16 Jiri Fischer .75 2.00
SC17 Simon Gagne 1.50 4.00
SC18 Alex Tanguay 1.25 3.00
SC19 Scott Gomez .75 2.00
SC20 Ladislav Nagy .75 2.00
SC21 Roberto Luongo 1.50 4.00

1991 Classic

COMPLETE SET (50) 1.25 3.00
*FRENCH: SAME VALUE
1 Eric Lindros .60 1.50
2 Pat Falloon .02 .10
3 Scott Niedermayer .30 .75
4 Scott Lachance .02 .10
5 Peter Forsberg .75 2.00
6 Alek Stojanov .02 .10
7 Richard Matvichuk .02 .10
8 Patrick Poulin .02 .10
9 Martin Lapointe .08 .25

10 Tyler Wright .02 .10
11 Philippe Boucher .02 .10
12 Pat Peake .02 .10
13 Markus Naslund .30 .75
14 Brent Bilodeau .02 .10
15 Glen Murray .15 .40
16 Niklas Sundblad .02 .10
17 Martin Rucinsky .08 .25
18 Trevor Halverson .02 .10
19 Dean McAmmond .02 .10
20 Ray Whitney .08 .25
21 Rene Corbet .02 .10
22 Eric Lavigne .02 .10
23 Zigmund Palffy .15 .40
24 Steve Staios .02 .10
25 Jim Campbell .02 .10
26 Jassen Cullimore .02 .10
27 Martin Hamrlik .02 .10
28 Jamie Pushor .02 .10
29 Donevan Hextall .02 .10
30 Andrew Verner .02 .10
31 Jason Dawe .02 .10
32 Jeff Nelson .02 .10
33 Darcy Werenka .02 .10
34 Jozef Stumpel .08 .25
35 Francois Groleau .02 .10
36 Guy Leveque .02 .10
37 Jamie Matthews .02 .10
38 Dody Wood .02 .10
39 Yanic Perreault .08 .25
40 Jamie McLennan .08 .25
41 Yanic Dupre UER .02 .10
42 Sandy McCarthy .08 .25
43 Chris Osgood .30 .75
44 Fredrik Lindquist .02 .10
45 Jason Young .02 .10
46 Steve Konowalchuk .08 .25
47 Michael Nylander UER .08 .25
48 Shane Peacock .02 .10
49 Yves Sarault .02 .10
50 Marcel Cousineau .08 .25
NNO Patrick Poulin AU/1100 .75 2.00
NNO Rocket Ismail .08 .25

1991 Classic Promos

COMPLETE SET (2) 1.20 3.00
1 Eric Lindros 1.25 3.00
2 Pat Falloon .08 .25

1992 Classic

COMPLETE SET (120) 5.00 10.00
1 Roman Hamrlik .02 .10
2 Alexei Yashin .02 .10
3 Mike Rathje .02 .10
4 Darius Kasparaitis .02 .10
5 Cory Stillman .02 .10
6 Robert Petrovicky .02 .10
7 Andrei Nazarov .02 .10
8 Cory Stillman CL .02 .10
9 Jason Bowen .02 .10
10 Jason Smith .02 .10
11 David Wilkie .02 .10
12 Curtis Bowen .02 .10
13 Grant Marshall .02 .10
14 Valeri Bure .10 .30
15 Jeff Shantz .02 .10
16 Justin Hocking .02 .10
17 Mike Peca .20 .50
18 Marc Hussey .02 .10
19 Sandy Allan .10 .30
20 Kirk Maltby .10 .30
21 Cale Hulse .02 .10
22 Sylvain Cloutier .10 .30
23 Martin Gendron .02 .10
24 Kevin Smyth .02 .10
25 Jason McBain .02 .10
26 Lee J. Leslie .02 .10
27 Ralph Intranuovo .02 .10
28 Martin Reichel .02 .10
29 Stefan Ustorf .02 .10
30 Jarkko Varvio .02 .10
31 Jere Lehtinen .15 .40
32 Janne Gronvall .02 .10
33 Martin Straka .15 .40
34 Libor Polasek .02 .10
35 Jozef Cierny .02 .10
36 Jan Vopat .02 .10
37 Ondrej Steiner .02 .10
38 Jan Caloun .02 .10
39 Petr Hrbek .02 .10
40 Richard Smehlik .02 .10
41 Sergei Gonchar CL .02 .10
42 Sergei Krivokrasov .02 .10
43 Sergei Gonchar .10 .30
44 Boris Mironov .02 .10
45 Denis Metlyuk .02 .10
46 Sergei Klimovich .02 .10
47 Sergei Brylin .02 .10
48 Andrei Nikolishin .02 .10
49 Alexander Cherbayev .02 .10
50 Sergei Zholtok .02 .10
51 Vitali Prokhorov .02 .10
52 Nikolai Borschevsky .02 .10
53 Vitali Tomilin .02 .10
54 Alexander Alexeyev .02 .10
55 Roman Zolotov .02 .10
56 Konstantin Korotkov .02 .10
57 Laperriere Family .02 .10
58 Lacroix Family .02 .10
59 Manon Rheaume 1.50 4.00
60 Hamrlik
Yashin
Rathje CL .02 .10
61 Viktor Kozlov CL .02 .10
62 Viktor Kozlov .10 .30
63 Denny Felsner CL .02 .10
64 Denny Felsner .02 .10
65 Darrin Madeley .02 .10
66 Mario Lemieux FLB .60 1.50
67 Sandy Moger .02 .10
68 Dave Karpa .02 .10
69 Martin Jiranek .02 .10
70 Dwayne Norris .02 .10
71 Michael Stewart .02 .10
72 Joby Messier .02 .10
73 Mike Bales .10 .30
74 Scott Thomas .02 .10
75 Dan Laperriere .02 .10
76 Mike Lappin .02 .10
77 Eric Lacroix .02 .10
78 Martin Lacroix .02 .10
79 Scott LaGrand .02 .10
80 Jean-Yves Roy .02 .10
81 Scott Pellerin .02 .10
82 Rob Gaudreau .02 .10
83 Mike Boback .02 .10
84 Dixon Ward .02 .10
85 Jeff McLean .02 .10
86 Dallas Drake .02 .10
87 Bret Hedican .02 .10
88 Doug Zmolek .02 .10
89 Trent Klatt .02 .10
90 Larry Olimb .02 .10
91 Duane Derksen .10 .30
92 Doug MacDonald .02 .10
93 Dmitri Kvartalnov CL .02 .10
94 Jim Cummins .02 .10
95 Lonnie Loach .02 .10
96 Keith Jones .02 .10
97 Jason Woolley .02 .10
98 Rob Zamuner .10 .30
99 Brad Werenka .02 .10
100 Brent Grieve .02 .10
101 Sean Hill .10 .30
102 Keith Carney .02 .10
103 Peter Ciavaglia .02 .10
104 David Littman .10 .30
105 Bill Guerin .25 .60
106 Mikhail Kravets .02 .10
107 J.F. Quintin .02 .10
108 Mike Needham .02 .10
109 Jason Ruff .02 .10
110 Mike Vukonich .02 .10
111 Shawn McCosh .02 .10
112 Dave Tretowicz .02 .10
113 Todd Harkins .02 .10
114 Jason Muzzatti .02 .10
115 Paul Kruse .02 .10
116 Kevin Wortman .02 .10
117 Sean Burke .10 .30
118 Keith Gretzky .02 .10
119 Ray Whitney .10 .30
120 Dmitri Kvartalnov .02 .10
SP1 Mario Lemieux FLB 2.00 5.00
AU1 M.Lemieux AU/2000 40.00 80.00
AU2 Bure Brothers AU/6000 10.00 20.00

1992 Classic Gold

*GOLD STARS: 1.5X TO 4X BASIC CARDS

1992 Classic Autographs

COMPLETE SET
NNO Mike Peca 3.00 8.00
NNO Petr Hrbek 2.50 6.00
NNO Eric Lacroix 2.50 6.00
NNO Jeff McLean 2.50 6.00
NNO David Wilkie 2.50 6.00

1992 Classic Gold Promo

NNO Mario Lemieux 3.00 8.00

1992 Classic LPs

COMPLETE SET (10) 2.50 6.00
LP1 Roman Hamrlik .20 .50
LP2 Alexei Yashin .20 .50
LP3 Mike Rathje .20 .50
LP4 Darius Kasparaitis .20 .50
LP5 Cory Stillman .20 .50
LP6 Dmitri Kvartalnov .20 .50
LP7 David Wilkie .20 .50
LP8 Curtis Bowen .20 .50
LP9 Valeri Bure .40 1.00
LP10 Joby Messier .20 .50

1992 Classic Promos

COMPLETE SET (3) 3.00 8.00
1 Roman Hamrlik 1.25 3.00
2 Mario Lemieux
(Flash Back 92) 2.00 5.00
3 Ray Whitney .40 1.00

1992-93 Classic Manon Rheaume C3 Presidential

1 Manon Rheaume 4.00 10.00

1992-93 Classic Manon Rheaume Promo

NNO Manon Rheaume 3.00 8.00

1993 Classic

COMPLETE SET (150) 4.00 10.00
1 Alexandre Daigle .02 .10
2 Chris Pronger .20 .50
3 Chris Gratton .08 .25
4 Paul Kariya .40 1.00
5 Rob Niedermayer .02 .10
6 Viktor Kozlov .08 .25
7 Jason Arnott .20 .50
8 Niklas Sundstrom .02 .10
9 Todd Harvey .02 .10
10 Jocelyn Thibault .20 .50
11 Checklist 1
Top Draft Picks .02 .10
12 Pat Peake
1993 CHL POY .02 .10
13 Jason Allison .25 .60
14 Todd Bertuzzi .20 .50
15 Maxim Bets .02 .10
16 Curtis Bowen .02 .10
17 Kevin Brown .02 .10
18 Valeri Bure .08 .25
19 Jason Dawe .02 .10
20 Adam Deadmarsh .02 .10
21 Aaron Gavey .02 .10
22 Nathan Lafayette .02 .10
23 Eric Lecompte .02 .10
24 Manny Legace .20 .50
25 Mike Peca .20 .50
26 Denis Pederson .02 .10
27 Jeff Shantz .02 .10
28 Nick Stadjuhar .02 .10
29 Cory Stillman .02 .10
30 Michal Sykora .02 .10
31 Brent Tully .02 .10
32 Mike Wilson .02 .10
33 K.Brown
P.Peake
B.Wren .02 .10
34 Daigle/Yashin .02 .10
35 Antti Aalto .02 .10
36 Radim Bicanek .02 .10
37 Vladimir Chebaturkin .02 .10
38 Alexander Cherbayev .02 .10
39 Markus Ketterer .02 .10
40 Saku Koivu .20 .50
41 Vladimir Kretchine .02 .10
42 Alexei Kudashov .02 .10
43 Janne Laukkanen .02 .10
44 Janne Niinimaa .02 .10
45 Juha Riihijarvi .02 .10
46 Nikolai Tsulygin .02 .10
47 Vesa Viitakoski .02 .10
48 David Vyborny .02 .10
49 Nikolai Zavarukhin .02 .10
50 Alexandre Daigle .02 .10
51 Alexandre Daigle .02 .10
52 Alexandre Daigle .02 .10
53 Alexandre Daigle .02 .10
54 Alexandre Daigle .02 .10
55 Jim Montgomery .02 .10
56 Mike Dunham .02 .10
57 Matt Martin .02 .10
58 Garth Snow .08 .25
59 Shawn Walsh .02 .10
60 Mark Bavis
Mike Bavis .02 .10
61 Scott Chartier .02 .10
62 Craig Darby .02 .10
63 Ted Drury .02 .10
64 Steve Dubinsky .02 .10
65 Joe Frederick .02 .10
66 Cammi Granato .20 .50
67 Brett Hauer .02 .10
68 Jon Hillebrandt .02 .10
69 Ryan Hughes .02 .10
70 Dean Hulett .02 .10
71 Kevin O'Sullivan .02 .10
72 Dan Plante .02 .10
73 Derek Plante .02 .10
74 Travis Richards .02 .10
75 Barry Richter .02 .10
76 David Roberts .02 .10
77 Chris Rogles .02 .10
78 Jon Rohloff .02 .10
79 Brian Rolston .02 .10
80 David Sacco .02 .10
81 Brian Savage .08 .25
82 Mike Smith .02 .10
83 Chris Tamer .02 .10
84 Chris Therien .02 .10
85 Aaron Ward .02 .10
86 Russian Celebration .02 .10
87 Vyacheslav Butsayev .02 .10
88 Jan Kaminsky .02 .10
89 Alexander Karpovtsev .02 .10
90 Valeri Karpov .02 .10
91 Sergei Petrenko .02 .10
92 Andrei Sapozhnikov .02 .10
93 Sergei Sorokin .02 .10
94 German Titov .02 .10
95 Andrei Trefilov .02 .10
96 Alexei Yashin .02 .10
97 Dimitri Yushkevich .02 .10
98 Radek Bonk .02 .10
99 Jason Bonsignore .02 .10
100 Brad Brown .02 .10
101 Chris Drury .40 1.00
102 Jeff Friesen .02 .10
103 Sean Haggerty .02 .10
104 Jeff Kealty .02 .10
105 Alexander Kharlamov .02 .10
106 Stanislav Neckar .02 .10
107 Tom O'Connor .02 .10
108 Jeff O'Neill .20 .50
109 Deron Quint .02 .10
110 Vadim Sharifianov .02 .10
111 Oleg Tverdovsky .08 .25
112 Manon Rheaume COMIC .30 .75
113 Paul Kariya COMIC .20 .50
114 Alexandre Daigle COMIC .02 .10
115 Jeff O'Neill COMIC .02 .10
116 Mike Bossy .20 .50
117 Pavel Bure .20 .50
118 Chris Chelios .20 .50
119 Doug Gilmour .08 .25
120 Roman Hamrlik .08 .25
121 Jari Kurri .20 .50
122 Alexander Mogilny .08 .25
123 Felix Potvin .20 .50
124 Teemu Selanne .40 1.00
125 Tommy Soderstrom .08 .25
126 Mike Bales .02 .10
127 Jozef Cierny .02 .10
128 Ivan Droppa .02 .10
129 Anders Eriksson .02 .10
130 Anatoli Fedotov .02 .10
131 Martin Gendron .02 .10
132 Daniel Guerard .02 .10
133 Corey Hirsch .02 .10
134 Milos Holan .02 .10
135 Kenny Jonsson .02 .10
136 Steven King .02 .10
137 Alexei Kovalev .20 .50
138 Sergei Krivokrasov .02 .10
139 Mats Lindgren .02 .10
140 Grant Marshall .02 .10
141 Jesper Mattsson .02 .10
142 Sandy McCarthy .02 .10
143 Dean Melanson .02 .10
144 Robert Petrovicky .02 .10
145 Mike Rathje .02 .10
146 Manon Rheaume .40 1.00
147 Claude Savoie .02 .10
148 Mikhail Shtalenkov .08 .25
149 Manon Rheaume .40 1.00
150 Manon Rheaume .40 1.00
MR1 M.Rheaume Acetate 10.00 25.00

1993 Classic Autographs

AU1 M.Bossy AU/975 12.50 30.00
AU2 P.Bure AU/900 20.00 50.00
AU3 C.Chelios AU/1800 15.00 40.00
AU4 D.Gilmour AU/1850 15.00 40.00
AU5 A.Mogilny/950 12.50 30.00
AU6 J.Montgomery AU/1800 2.00 5.00
AU7 R.Niedermayer AU/2500 12.50 30.00
AU8 J.O'Neill AU/2225 8.00 20.00
AU9 P.Peake AU/790 2.00 5.00
AU10 M.Recchi AU/1725 12.00 30.00
AU11 M.Rheaume AU/1500 15.00 40.00
AU12 G.Sanderson AU/875 2.00 5.00

1993 Classic Class of '94

COMPLETE SET (7) 3.00 8.00
CL1 Jeff O'Neill .60 1.50
CL2 Jason Bonsignore .40 1.00
CL3 Jeff Friesen .40 1.00
CL4 Radek Bonk .40 1.00
CL5 Deron Quint .40 1.00
CL6 Vadim Sharifianov .40 1.00
CL7 Tom O'Connor .40 1.00

1993 Classic Crash Numbered

COMPLETE SET (10) 30.00 80.00
N1 Alexandre Daigle 2.00 5.00
N2 Paul Kariya 6.00 15.00
N3 Jeff O'Neill 1.25 3.00
N4 Jason Bonsignore 2.00 5.00
N5 Teemu Selanne 6.00 15.00
N6 Pavel Bure 2.00 5.00
N7 Alexander Mogilny 2.00 5.00
N8 Manon Rheaume 5.00 12.00
N9 Felix Potvin 2.00 5.00
N10 Radek Bonk 1.25 3.00

1993 Classic Manon Rheaume Promo

NNO Manon Rheaume
Up Close 2.00 5.00

1993 Classic Previews

COMPLETE SET (5) 2.00 5.00
HK1 Alexandre Daigle .20 .50
HK2 Manon Rheaume 1.50 4.00
HK3 Barry Richter .20 .50
HK4 Teemu Selanne .75 2.00
HK5 Alexei Yashin .20 .50

1993 Classic Promos

COMPLETE SET (4) 8.00 20.00
1 Alexandre Daigle 2.00 5.00
2 Jeff O'Neill
Jason Bonsignore
Jeff Friesen
The 2.00 5.00
3 Pavel Bure 2.00 5.00
NNO Paul Kariya 2.00 5.00

1993 Classic Team Canada

COMPLETE SET (7) 7.50 15.00
TC1 Greg Johnson .75 2.00
TC2 Paul Kariya 2.00 5.00
TC3 Brian Savage .75 2.00
TC4 Bill Ranford .75 2.00
TC5 Mark Recchi .75 2.00
TC6 Geoff Sanderson .75 2.00
TC7 Adam Graves .75 2.00

1993 Classic Top Ten

COMPLETE SET (10) 10.00 20.00
DP1 Alexandre Daigle .40 1.00
DP2 Chris Pronger 1.00 2.50
DP3 Chris Gratton .40 1.00
DP4 Paul Kariya 2.00 5.00
DP5 Rob Niedermayer .40 1.00
DP6 Viktor Kozlov .40 1.00
DP7 Jason Arnott .40 1.00
DP8 Niklas Sundstrom .40 1.00
DP9 Todd Harvey .40 1.00
DP10 Jocelyn Thibault 1.00 2.50

1993 Classic Superheroes

COMPLETE SET (3) 8.00 20.00
SS2 Manon Rheaume 2.00 5.00

1994 Classic

COMPLETE SET (120) 4.00 10.00
1 Ed Jovanovski .02 .10
2 Oleg Tverdovsky .01 .05
3 Radek Bonk .01 .05
4 Jason Bonsignore .01 .05
5 Jeff O'Neill .01 .05
6 Ryan Smyth .08 .25
7 Jamie Storr .02 .10
8 Jason Wiemer .01 .05
9 Nolan Baumgartner .01 .05
10 Jeff Friesen .01 .05
11 Wade Belak .01 .05
12 Ethan Moreau .02 .10
13 Alexander Kharlamov .01 .05
14 Eric Fichaud .02 .10
15 Wayne Primeau .01 .05
16 Brad Brown .01 .05
17 Chris Dingman .01 .05
18 Evgeni Ryabchikov .01 .05
19 Yan Golubovsky .01 .05
20 Chris Wells .01 .05
21 Vadim Sharifjanov .01 .05
22 Dan Cloutier .08 .25
23 Checklist .01 .05
24 Jamie Langenbrunner .01 .05
25 Kenny Jonsson .01 .05
26 Curtis Bowen .01 .05
27 Sergei Gonchar .02 .10
28 Stefan Bergqvist .01 .05
29 Vaclav Prospal .01 .05
30 Valeri Bure .01 .05
31 Richard Shulmistra .01 .05
32 Chris Armstrong .01 .05
33 Brian Farrell .01 .05
34 Brian Savage .02 .10
35 Blaine Lacher .01 .05
36 Kevin Brown .01 .05
37 Joe Dziedzic .01 .05
38 Peter Ferraro .01 .05
39 Chris Ferraro .01 .05
40 Todd Harvey .02 .10
41 Eric Lecompte .01 .05
42 Dean Grillo .01 .05
43 Valeri Karpov .01 .05
44 Andrew Shier .01 .05
45 Vesa Viitakoski .01 .05
46 Xavier Majic .01 .05
47 Kevin Smyth .01 .05
48 Jeff Nelson .01 .05
49 Cory Stillman .01 .05
50 Clayton Beddoes .01 .05
51 Craig Conroy .01 .05
52 Dean Fedorchuk .01 .05
53 John Gruden .01 .05
54 Chris McAlpine .01 .05
55 Sean McCann .01 .05
56 Derek Maguire .01 .05
57 David Oliver .01 .05
58 Mike Pomichter .01 .05
59 Jamie Ram .01 .05
60 Shawn Reid .01 .05
61 Dwayne Roloson .01 .05
62 Steve Shields .08 .25
63 Brian Wiseman .01 .05
64 Drew Bannister .01 .05
65 Matt Johnson .01 .05
66 Scott Malone .01 .05
67 Sergei Berezin .01 .05
68 Chad Penney .01 .05
69 Ian Laperriere .01 .05
70 Andrei Nikolishin .01 .05
71 Kelly Fairchild .01 .05
72 Jere Lehtinen .08 .25
73 Ravil Gusmanov .01 .05
74 Checklist .01 .05
75 Neil Little .01 .05
76 Brian Rolston .02 .10
77 David Vyborny .01 .05
78 Nikolai Tsulygin .01 .05
79 Niklas Sundstrom .01 .05
80 Patrik Juhlin .01 .05
81 Dan Plante .01 .05
82 Brandon Convery .01 .05
83 Nick Stajduhar .01 .05
84 Garth Snow .02 .10
85 Corey Hirsch .02 .10
86 Craig Darby .01 .05
87 Andrei Nazarov .01 .05
88 Todd Marchant .01 .05
89 Jeff Neilson .01 .05
90 Brendan Witt .01 .05
91 Denis Metlyuk .01 .05
92 Maxim Bets .01 .05
93 Sean Pronger .01 .05
94 Chris Tamer .01 .05
95 Saku Koivu .08 .25
96 Mattias Norstrom .02 .10
97 Ville Peltonen .02 .10
98 Rene Corbet .01 .05
99 Brent Gretzky .01 .05
100 Chris Marinucci .01 .05
101 Ian Moran .01 .05
102 Janne Laukkanen .01 .05
103 Todd Bertuzzi .08 .25
104 Darby Hendrickson .01 .05
105 Janne Niinimaa .01 .05
106 David Roberts .01 .05
107 Pat Neaton .01 .05
108 Mats Lindgren .01 .05
109 Todd Warriner .01 .05
110 Jason Allison .08 .25
111 Radim Bicanek .01 .05
112 Denis Pederson .02 .10
113 Viktor Kozlov .02 .10
114 Mike Murray .01 .05
115 Aaron Gavey .01 .05
116 Mike Peca .08 .25
117 Jason Zent .01 .05
118 Jason MacDonald .01 .05
119 Aaron Israel .01 .05
120 Manon Rheaume .60 1.50
TC1 Jason Arnott CWC .75 2.00
AU1 Doug Gilmour AU 8.00 20.00
AU2 Cam Neely AU 12.50 30.00
AU3 Manon Rheaume AU 12.50 30.00

1994 Classic Gold

*STARS: 1.25X TO 3X BASIC CARDS

1994 Classic All-Americans

COMPLETE SET (10) 3.00 8.00
AA1 Craig Conroy .40 1.00
AA2 John Gruden .40 1.00
AA3 Chris Marinucci .40 1.00
AA4 Chris McAlpine .40 1.00
AA5 Sean McCann .40 1.00
AA6 David Oliver .40 1.00
AA7 Mike Pomichter .40 1.00
AA8 Jamie Ram .40 1.00
AA9 Shawn Reid .40 1.00
AA10 Dwayne Roloson .75 2.00

1994 Classic All-Rookie Team

COMPLETE SET (6) 4.00 10.00
AR1 Martin Brodeur 4.00 10.00
AR2 Jason Arnott .20 .50
AR3 Alexei Yashin .20 .50
AR4 Oleg Petrov .08 .25
AR5 Chris Pronger .75 2.00
AR6 Alexander Karpovtsev .08 .25

1994 Classic Autographs

3 Radek Bonk/4940 1.50 4.00
4 Jason Bonsignore/4300 .75 2.00
5 Jeff O'Neill/5380 1.50 4.00
10 Jeff Friesen/6145 4.00 10.00
34 Brian Savage/4930 1.50 4.00
38 Peter Ferraro/4875 .75 2.00
39 Chris Ferraro/4770 .75 2.00
76 Brian Rolston/2400 1.50 4.00
86 Craig Darby/1915 .75 2.00
94 Chris Tamer/1900 .75 2.00
106 David Roberts/1970 .75 2.00
NNO Rob Niedermayer/950 8.00 20.00
NNO Mike Dunham/1955 4.00 10.00
NNO Chris Marinucci .75 2.00
NNO Doug Gilmour/1950 15.00 30.00
120 Manon Rheaume/2280 15.00 40.00
NNO Chris Gratton/2000 6.00 15.00
NNO Dan Plante .75 2.00
NNO Dallas Drake/960 .75 2.00
NNO Dean Hulett/1955 .75 2.00
NNO Aaron Ward/1965 .75 2.00
NNO Jon Rohloff/2010 .75 2.00
NNO Mike Bavis/1955 4.00 10.00
NNO Ryan Hughes/1940 .75 2.00
NNO Brett Hauer/1930 .75 2.00
NNO Travis Richards/1950 .75 2.00
NNO Jim Storm/1950 .75 2.00
NNO Scott Chartier/1930 .75 2.00
NNO Ted Drury/1920 .75 2.00
NNO Brett Harkins/1885 .75 2.00
NNO Fred Knipscheer/1945 .75 2.00
NNO Stanislav Neckar/4645 .75 2.00
NNO Chris Rogles/1920 .75 2.00
NNO Jon Hillebrandt/1570 .75 2.00
NNO Cam Stewart/970 .75 2.00
NNO Barry Richter/1935 .75 2.00
NNO David Sacco/1975 .75 2.00
NNO Eric Fenton/1845 .75 2.00
NNO John Lilley/2460 .75 2.00
NNO Derek Plante/1970 1.50 4.00

1994 Classic CHL All-Stars

COMPLETE SET (10) 7.50 20.00
C1 Jason Allison 1.25 3.00
C2 Yanick Dube .40 1.00
C3 Eric Fichaud .75 2.00
C4 Jeff Friesen .40 1.00
C5 Aaron Gavey .40 1.00
C6 Ed Jovanovski .75 2.00
C7 Jeff O'Neill 1.25 3.00
C8 Ryan Smyth 1.25 3.00
C9 Jamie Storr .75 2.00
C10 Brendan Witt .40 1.00

1994 Classic CHL Previews

COMPLETE SET (6) 15.00 25.00
CP1 Wayne Primeau 1.25 3.00
CP2 Eric Fichaud 2.50 6.00
CP3 Wade Redden 2.50 5.00
CP4 Jason Doig 1.25 3.00
CP5 Vitali Yachmenev 1.25 3.00
CP6 Nolan Baumgartner 1.25 3.00

1994 Classic Draft Day

COMPLETE SET (10) 12.50 30.00
1 Radek Bonk 1.50 4.00
2 Radek Bonk 1.50 4.00
3 Radek Bonk 1.50 4.00
4 Jason Bonsignore 1.50 4.00
5 Ed Jovanovski 1.50 4.00
6 Ed Jovanovski 1.50 4.00
7 Ed Jovanovski 1.50 4.00
8 Jeff O'Neill 1.50 4.00
9 Jeff O'Neill 1.50 4.00
10 Jeff O'Neill 1.50 4.00

1994 Classic Draft Prospects

COMPLETE SET (10) 5.00 12.00
DP1 Bubba Berenzweig .40 1.00
DP2 Aki Berg .40 1.00
DP3 Chad Kilger .40 1.00
DP4 Daymond Langkow .75 2.00
DP5 Alyn McCauley .75 2.00
DP6 Igor Melyakov .40 1.00
DP7 Erik Rasmussen .40 1.00
DP8 Marty Reasoner .75 2.00
DP9 Scott Roche .75 2.00
DP10 Petr Sykora 2.00 5.00

1994 Classic Enforcers

COMPLETE SET (10) 7.50 15.00
E1 Donald Brashear 1.25 3.00
E2 Daniel Lacroix .60 1.50
E3 Dale Henry .60 1.50
E4 John Badduke .60 1.50
E5 Corey Schwab 1.25 3.00
E6 Craig Martin .60 1.50
E7 Kerry Clark .60 1.50
E8 Kevin Kaminski .60 1.50
E9 Jim Kyte .60 1.50
E10 Mark DeSantis .60 1.50

1994 Classic Enforcers Promo

PR1 Richard Zemlak .40 1.00

1994 Classic Picks

COMPLETE SET (5) 6.00 15.00
CP11 Ed Jovanovski 2.00 5.00
CP12 Oleg Tverdovsky .75 2.00
CP13 Radek Bonk .75 2.00
CP14 Jason Allison 2.00 5.00
CP15 Manon Rheaume 2.00 5.00

1994 Classic Previews

COMPLETE SET (5) 10.00 20.00
HK1 Jason Allison 1.50 4.00
HK2 Radek Bonk .75 2.00
HK3 Xavier Majic .75 2.00
HK4 Manon Rheaume 7.50 15.00
HK5 Oleg Tverdovsky 1.50 4.00

1994 Classic ROY Sweepstakes

COMPLETE SET (20) 4.00 10.00
R1 Jason Allison .60 1.50
R2 Radek Bonk .20 .50
R3 Jason Bonsignore .08 .25
R4 Valeri Bure .20 .50
R5 Jeff Friesen .20 .50
R6 Aaron Gavey .08 .25
R7 Todd Harvey .20 .50
R8 Kenny Jonsson .20 .50
R9 Ed Jovanovski .60 1.50
R10 Patrik Juhlin .08 .25
R11 Valeri Karpov .08 .25
R12 Viktor Kozlov .20 .50
R13 Blaine Lacher .20 .50
R14 Andrei Nikolishin .08 .25
R15 Jeff O'Neill .40 1.00
R16 David Oliver .08 .25
R17 Garth Snow .20 .50
R18 Jamie Storr .20 .50
R19 Oleg Tverdovsky .20 .50
R20 Field Card WIN G .08 .25

1994 Classic Tri-Cards

COMPLETE SET (26) 30.00 60.00
T1 Karpov/2 Tsul/3 Tverdovsky 1.25 3.00
T4 Knip/5 Lacher/6 Ryabchikov 1.25 3.00
T7 David CooperT8
Wayne Primeau
T9Steve Shields .75 2.00
T10 Chris Dingman
T11Cory Stillman
T12Vesa Vii .75 2.00
T13 Eric Lecompte
T14Ethan Moreau
T15Mike Pomichter .75 2.00
T16 Harvey/17 Langen/18 Lehtin 1.25 3.00
T19 Curtis Bowen
T20Yan Golubovsky
T21Kevin Hodson .75 2.00
T22 Bonsignore/23 Lind/24 Oliver 1.25 3.00
T25 Arms/26 Jovanovski/27 Podo 1.50 4.00
T28 Andrei Nikolishin
T29}Jeff O'Neill
T30}Kevin Smyth .75 2.00
T31 Brown/32 Johnson/33 Storr 1.25 3.00
T34 Bure/35 Koivu/36 Savage 3.00 8.00
T37 Denis Pederson
T38}Brian Rolston
T39}Vadim .75 2.00
T40 Todd Bertuzzi
T41} Chris Marinucci
T42}Dan .75 2.00
T43 Corey Hirsch
T44Niklas Sundstrom
T45Scott Malone .75 2.00
T46 Bicanek/47 Bonk/48 Penney 1.25 3.00
T49 Patrik Juhlin
50Denis Metlyuk
T51Janne Niinimaa .75 2.00
T52 Greg Andrusak
T53Pat Neaton
T54Chris Wells .75 2.00
T55 Rene Corbet
T56Adam Deadmarsh
T57Garth Snow .75 2.00
T58 David Roberts
T59Ian Laperriere
T60Patrice Tardiff .75 2.00
T61 Friesen/62 Kozlov/63 Pelton 1.50 4.00
T64 Aaron Gavey
T65Brent Gretzky
T66Jason Weimer .75 2.00
T67 Conv/68 Fichaud/69 Jonsson 1.50 4.00
T70 Mike Fountain
T71Rick Girard
T72Mike Peca .75 2.00
T73 Jason Allison
T74Alexander Kharlamov
T75Brendan Witt .75 2.00
T76 Mika Alatalo
T77Ravil Gusmanov
T78Deron Quint .75 2.00

1994 Classic Women of Hockey

COMPLETE SET (40) 8.00 20.00
W1 Manon Rheaume 1.25 3.00
W2 France St. Louis .20 .50
W3 Cheryl Pounder .20 .50
W4 Therese Brisson .20 .50
W5 Cassie Campbell .75 2.00
W6 Angela James .20 .50
W7 Danielle Goyette .40 1.00
W8 Jane Robinson .20 .50
W9 Stacy Wilson .20 .50
W10 Margot Page .20 .50
W11 Laura Leslie .20 .50
W12 Judy Diduck .20 .50
W13 Hayley Wickenheiser 2.00 5.00
W14 Nathalie Picard .20 .50
W15 Leslie Reddon .20 .50
W16 Marianne Grnak .20 .50
W17 Andria Hunter .20 .50
W18 Nancy Drolet .40 1.00
W19 Geraldine Heaney .20 .50
W20 Karen Nystrom .20 .50
W21 Manon Rheaume CL .40 1.00
W22 Kelly Dyer .20 .50
W23 Vicki Movsessian .20 .50
W24 Lisa Brown .20 .50
W25 Shawna Davidson .20 .50
W26 Colleen Coyne .20 .50
W27 Karyn Bye .75 2.00
W28 Suzanne Merz .20 .50
W29 Gretchen Ulion .20 .50
W30 Sandra Whyte .20 .50
W31 Cindy Curley .20 .50
W32 Michele DiFronzo .20 .50
W33 Stephanie Boyd .20 .50
W34 Shelley Looney .20 .50
W35 Jeanine Sobek .20 .50
W36 Beth Beagan .20 .50
W37 Cammi Granato .75 2.00
W38 Christina Bailey .20 .50
W39 Kelly O'Leary .20 .50
W40 Erin Whitten .30 .75

1995 Classic

COMPLETE SET (100) 3.00 8.00
1 Bryan Berard .05 .15
2 Wade Redden .01 .05
3 Aki Berg .01 .05
4 Chad Kilger .01 .05
5 Daymond Langkow .05 .15
6 Steve Kelly .01 .05
7 Shane Doan .08 .25
8 Terry Ryan .01 .05
9 Mike Martin .01 .05
10 Radek Dvorak .08 .25
11 Jarome Iginla .08 .25
12 Teemu Riihijarvi .01 .05
13 Jean-Sebastien Giguere .08 .25
14 Peter Schaefer .01 .05
15 Jeff Ware .01 .05
16 Martin Biron .60 1.50
17 Brad Church .01 .05
18 Petr Sykora .08 .25
19 Denis Gauthier .01 .05
20 Sean Brown .01 .05
21 Brad Isbister .20 .50
22 Miikka Elomo .01 .05
23 Mathieu Sunderland .01 .05
24 Marc Moro .01 .05
25 Jan Hlavac .08 .25
26 Brian Wesenberg .01 .05
27 Mike McBain .01 .05
28 Georges Laraque .08 .25
29 Marc Chouinard .08 .25
30 Donald MacLean .01 .05
31 Jason Doig .01 .05
32 Aaron MacDonald .01 .05
33 Patrick Cote .01 .05
34 Christian Dube .01 .05

35 Chris McAllister .01 .05
36 Denis Smith .01 .05
37 Mark Dutiaume .01 .05
38 Dwayne Hay .01 .05
39 Nathan Perrott .01 .05
40 Christian Laflamme .01 .05
41 Paxton Schafer .01 .05
42 Shane Kenny .01 .05
43 Nic Beaudoin .01 .05
44 Philippe Audet .01 .05
45 Brad Larsen .01 .05
46 Ryan Pepperall .01 .05
47 Mike Leclerc .05 .15
48 Shane Willis .10 .30
49 Darryl Laplante .01 .05
50 Larry Courville .01 .05
51 Mike O'Grady .01 .05
52 Petr Buzek .01 .05
53 Alyn McCauley .01 .05
54 Scott Roche .01 .05
55 John Tripp .01 .05
56 Johnathan Aitken .01 .05
57 Blake Bellefeuille .01 .05
58 Daniel Briere .20 .50
59 Josh DeWolf .01 .05
60 Josh Green .01 .05
61 Chris Hajt .01 .05
62 Josh Holden .01 .05
63 Henry Kuster .01 .05
64 Dan Lacouture .01 .05
65 Oleg Orekhovsky .01 .05
66 Andrei Petrunin .01 .05
67 Tom Poti .01 .05
68 Peter Ratchuk .01 .05
69 Andrei Zyuzin .01 .05
70 George Breen .01 .05
71 Greg Bullock .01 .05
72 Kent Fearns .01 .05
73 Eric Flinton .01 .05
74 Brian Holzinger .01 .05
75 Chris Kenady .01 .05
76 Kaj Linna .01 .05
77 Brian Mueller .01 .05
78 Brent Peterson .01 .05
79 Chad Quenneville .01 .05
80 Randy Stevens .01 .05
81 Adam Wiesel .01 .05
82 Barrie Colts .01 .05
83 Belleville Bulls .01 .05
84 Detroit Jr. Whalers .01 .05
85 Guelph Storm .01 .05
86 Kingston Frontenacs .01 .05
87 Kitchener Rangers .01 .05
88 London Knights .01 .05
89 Niagara Falls Thunder .01 .05
90 North Bay Centennials .01 .05
91 Oshawa Generals .08 .25
92 Ottawa 67's .01 .05
93 Owen Sound Platers .01 .05
94 Peterborough Petes .01 .05
95 S.S. Marie Greyhounds .50 1.25
96 Sarnia Sting .01 .05
97 Sudbury Wolves .01 .05
98 Windsor Spitfires .01 .05
99 Bryan Berard CL .01 .05
100 Wade Redden CL .01 .05

1995 Classic Gold

COMPLETE SET (100) 20.00 40.00
*GOLD: 1.2X TO 3X BASIC CARDS

1995 Classic Printer's Proofs

COMPLETE SET (100) 150.00 300.00
*PRINT.PROOF/749: 8X TO 20X BASIC CARDS

1995 Classic Printer's Proofs Gold

GOLD/249. 12X TO 30X BASIC CARDS

1995 Classic Silver

COMPLETE SET (100) 20.00 40.00
*SILVER: .6X TO 1.5X BASIC CARDS

1995 Classic Autographs

1 George Breen/2400 .75 2.00
2 Greg Bullock/2485 .75 2.00
3 Petr Buzek/3978 1.50 4.00
4 Radek Dvorak/4022 2.00 5.00
5 Kent Fearns/4034 .75 2.00
6 Eric Flinton/2495 .75 2.00
7 Josh Green/4293 .75 2.00
8 Josh Holden/4994 .75 2.00
9 B.Holzinger/2599 .75 2.00
10 Ed Jovanovski/2584 1.50 4.00
11 Chris Kenady/2500 .75 2.00
12 Henry Kuster/2490 .75 2.00
13 Josef Marha/2584 .75 2.00
14 Brian Mueller/2488 .75 2.00
15 Angel Nikolov/2500 .75 2.00
16 Oleg Orekhovsky/5090 .75 2.00
17 Brent Peterson/2468 .75 2.00
18 A.Petrunin/4764 .75 2.00
19 Chad Quenneville/2500 .75 2.00
20 M.Satan/2487 12.50 30.00
21 Randy Stevens/2591 .75 2.00
22 Petr Sykora/792 12.50 30.00
23 Adam Wiesel/2511 .75 2.00
24 Andrei Zyuzin/5076 .75 2.00
NNO Manon Rheaume/6300 12.50 30.00

1995 Classic CHL All-Stars

COMPLETE SET (18) 25.00 50.00
AS1 Nolan Baumgartner .75 2.00
AS2 Wade Redden 1.50 4.00
AS3 Henry Kuster .75 2.00
AS4 Daymond Langkow 1.50 4.00
AS5 Shane Doan 2.00 5.00
AS6 Steve Kelly .75 2.00
AS7 Tyler Moss .75 2.00
AS8 Bryan Berard 1.50 4.00
AS9 Ed Jovanovski 1.50 4.00
AS10 Chad Kilger .75 2.00
AS11 Daniel Cleary .75 2.00
AS12 Ethan Moreau .75 2.00
AS13 Jean-Sebastien Giguere 1.50 4.00
AS14 Denis Gauthier .75 2.00
AS15 Jason Doig .75 2.00
AS16 Etienne Drapeau .75 2.00
AS17 Daniel Briere 1.50 4.00
AS18 Mark Chouinard .75 2.00

1995 Classic Ice Breakers

COMPLETE SET (20) 15.00 40.00
*DIE CUT/495: 1X TO 2.5X BASIC INSERT
BK1 Bryan Berard 1.25 3.00
BK2 Wade Redden 1.25 3.00
BK3 Aki Berg 1.00 2.50
BK4 Chad Kilger 1.00 2.50
BK5 Daymond Langkow 1.25 3.00
BK6 Steve Kelly 1.00 2.50
BK7 Shane Doan 1.50 4.00
BK8 Terry Ryan 1.00 2.50
BK9 Radek Dvorak 1.50 4.00
BK10 Miikka Elomo 1.00 2.50
BK11 Teemu Riihijarvi 1.00 2.50
BK12 Jean-Sebastien Giguere 1.25 3.00
BK13 Martin Biron 1.50 4.00
BK14 Jeff Ware 1.00 2.50
BK15 Brad Church 1.00 2.50
BK16 Petr Sykora 1.50 4.00
BK17 Jason Bonsignore 1.00 2.50
BK18 Brian Holzinger 1.00 2.50
BK19 Ed Jovanovski 1.25 3.00
BK20 Nolan Baumgartner 1.00 2.50

1993 Classic Pro Prospects

COMPLETE SET (150) 4.00 10.00
1 Manon Rheaume .40 1.00
2 Manon Rheaume .40 1.00
3 Manon Rheaume .40 1.00
4 Manon Rheaume .40 1.00
5 Manon Rheaume .40 1.00
6 Manon Rheaume .40 1.00
7 Manon Rheaume .40 1.00
8 Oleg Petrov .01 .05
9 Shjon Podein .01 .05
10 Alexei Kovalev AS .08 .25
11 Roman Oksiuta .01 .05
12 Dave Tomlinson .01 .05
13 Jason Miller .01 .05
14 Andrew McKim .01 .05
15 Dallas Drake .01 .05
16 Rob Gaudreau .01 .05
17 Darrin Madeley .01 .05
18 Scott Pellerin .01 .05
19 Scott Thomas .01 .05
20 Chris Tancill AS .01 .05
21 Patrick Kjellberg .01 .05
22 Jim Dowd .01 .05
23 Daniel Gauthier .01 .05
24 Mark Beaufait .01 .05
25 Milan Tichy AS .01 .05
26 Chris Osgood .50 1.25
27 Charles Poulin .01 .05
28 Patrick Lebeau .01 .05
29 Chris Govedaris .01 .05
30 Andrei Trefilov AS .01 .05
31 Kevin Stevens MLG .08 .25
32 Dmitri Kvartalnov MLG .01 .05
33 Patrick Roy MLG .60 1.50
34 Mark Recchi MLG .20 .50
35 Adam Oates MLG .20 .50
36 Patrick Augusta .01 .05
37 Gerry Fleming .01 .05
38 Sergei Krivokrasov .01 .05
39 Mike O'Neill .01 .05
40 Darrin Madeley AS .01 .05
41 Lindsay Vallis .01 .05
42 Todd Nelson .01 .05
43 Keith Jones .01 .05
44 Howie Rosenblatt .01 .05
45 Jason Ruff AS .01 .05
46 Robert Lang .01 .05
47 Andre Faust .01 .05
48 Steve Bancroft .01 .05
49 Iain Fraser .01 .05
50 Roman Hamrlik AS .01 .05
51 Pierre Sevigny .01 .05
52 Jeff Levy .01 .05
53 Len Barrie .01 .05
54 David Goverde .01 .05
55 Vladimir Malakhov AS .01 .05
56 Scott White .01 .05
57 Dmitri Motkov .01 .05
58 Jason Herter .01 .05
59 Drake Berehowsky .01 .05
60 Steve King AS .01 .05
61 Doug Barrault .01 .05
62 Martin Hamrlik .01 .05
63 Kevin Miehm .01 .05
64 Shaun Van Allen .01 .05
65 Corey Hirsch AS .01 .05
66 Dwayne Norris .01 .05
67 Petr Hrbek .01 .05
68 Philippe Boucher .01 .05
69 Denis Chervyakov .01 .05
70 Sergei Zubov AS .01 .05
71 Geoff Sarjeant .01 .05
72 Les Kuntar .01 .05
73 Byron Dafoe .20 .50
74 Checklist
Alexei Kovalev
Sergei Zubov
Steve King
Corey Hirsch .01 .05
75 Alexander Andrievski AS .01 .05
76 Checklist
Joby Messier
Mitch Messier .01 .05
77 Brian Sullivan .01 .05
78 Steve Larouche .01 .05
79 Denis Chasse .01 .05
80 Felix Potvin AS .20 .50
81 Josef Beranek .01 .05
82 Ken Klee .01 .05
83 Jozef Stumpel .08 .25
84 Andrew Verner .01 .05
85 Keith Osborne AS .01 .05
86 Igor Malykhin .01 .05
87 Gilbert Dionne .01 .05
88 Viktor Gordiouk .01 .05
89 Glen Murray .01 .05
90 Scott Pellerin AS .01 .05
91 Tommy Soderstrom .08 .25
92 Terry Chitaroni .01 .05
93 Viktor Kozlov .08 .25
94 Mikhail Shtalenkov .08 .25
95 Leonid Toropchenko .01 .05
96 Alexander Galchenyuk .01 .05
97 Anatoli Fedotov .01 .05
98 Igor Chibirev .01 .05
99 Keith Gretzky .01 .05
100 Manon Rheaume .60 1.50
101 Sean Whyte .01 .05
102 Steve Konowalchuk .08 .25
103 Richard Borgo .01 .05
104 Paul DiPietro .01 .05
105 Patrik Carnback AS .01 .05
106 Mike Fountain .01 .05
107 Jamie Heward .01 .05
108 David St. Pierre .01 .05
109 Sean O'Donnell .01 .05
110 Greg Andrusak AS .01 .05
111 Damian Rhodes .08 .25
112 Ted Crowley .01 .05
113 Chris Taylor .01 .05
114 Terran Sandwith .01 .05
115 Jesse Belanger AS .01 .05
116 Justin Duberman .01 .05
117 Arturs Irbe .20 .50
118 Chris LiPuma .01 .05
119 Mike Torchia .01 .05
120 Niclas Andersson AS .01 .05
121 Rick Knickle .01 .05
122 Scott Gruhl .01 .05
123 Dave Michayluk .01 .05
124 Guy Leveque .01 .05
125 Scott Thomas AS .01 .05
126 Travis Green .01 .05
127 Joby Messier .01 .05
128 Victor Ignatjev .01 .05
129 Brad Tiley .01 .05
130 Grigori Panteleyev AS .01 .05
131 Vyatcheslav Butsayev .01 .05
132 Danny Lorenz .01 .05
133 Marty McInnis .01 .05
134 Ed Ronan .01 .05
135 Slava Kozlov AS .20 .50
136 Kevin St. Jacques .01 .05
137 Pavel Kostichkin .01 .05
138 Mike Hurlbut .01 .05
139 Tomas Forslund .01 .05
140 Rob Gaudreau AS .01 .05
141 Shawn Heaphy .01 .05
142 Radek Hamr .01 .05
143 Jaroslav Otevrel .01 .05
144 Keith Redmond .01 .05
145 Tom Pederson AS .01 .05
146 Jaroslav Modry .01 .05
147 Darren McCarty .01 .05
148 Terry Yake .01 .05
149 Ivan Droppa .01 .05
150 S.Van Allen
D.Currie
S.Rice .01 .05
AU1 D.Kvartalnov AU/4000 2.00 5.00
AU2 M.Rheaume AU/6500 20.00 40.00

1993 Classic Pro Prospects BCs

COMPLETE SET (20) 15.00 30.00
BC1 Alexei Kovalev .40 1.00
BC2 Andrei Trefilov .20 .50
BC3 Roman Hamrlik .20 .50
BC4 Vladimir Malakhov .20 .50
BC5 Corey Hirsch .30 .75
BC6 Sergei Zubov .20 .50
BC7 Felix Potvin .40 1.00
BC8 Tommy Soderstrom .30 .75
BC9 Viktor Kozlov .30 .75
BC10 Manon Rheaume 1.50 4.00
BC11 Jesse Belanger .20 .50
BC12 Rick Knickle .20 .50
BC13 Joby Messier .20 .50
BC14 Vyacheslav Butsayev .20 .50
BC15 Tomas Forslund .20 .50
BC16 Jozef Stumpel .30 .75
BC17 Dmitri Kvartalnov MLG .20 .50
BC18 Adam Oates MLG .40 1.00
BC19 Dallas Drake .20 .50
BC20 Mark Recchi MLG .40 1.00

1993 Classic Pro Prospects LPs

COMPLETE SET (5) 12.50 25.00
LP1 Manon Rheaume 6.00 15.00
LP2 Alexei Kovalev 1.25 3.00
LP3 Rob Gaudreau .75 2.00
LP4 Viktor Kozlov 1.25 3.00
LP5 Dallas Drake .75 2.00

1993 Classic Pro Prospects Prototypes

COMPLETE SET (3) 3.00 8.00
PR1 Steve King .60 1.50
PR2 Manon Rheaume 2.50 6.00
PR3 Rob Gaudreau .60 1.50

1994 Classic Pro Prospects

COMPLETE SET (250) 3.00 8.00
1 Radek Bonk .01 .05
2 Radek Bonk .01 .05
3 Radek Bonk .01 .05
4 Vlastimil Kroupa .01 .05
5 Mattias Norstrom .01 .05
6 Jaroslav Nedved .01 .05
7 Steve Dubinsky .01 .05
8 Christian Proulx .01 .05
9 Michal Grosek .01 .05
10 Pat Neaton .01 .05
11 Jason Arnott .01 .05
12 Martin Brodeur .40 1.00
13 Alexandre Daigle .01 .05
14 Ted Drury .01 .05
15 Iain Fraser .01 .05
16 Chris Gratton .08 .25
17 Greg Johnson .01 .05
18 Paul Kariya .40 1.00
19 Alexander Karpovtsev .01 .05
20 Chris Lipuma .01 .05
21 Kirk Maltby .01 .05
22 Sandy McCarthy .01 .05
23 Darren McCarty .01 .05
24 Jaroslav Modry .01 .05
25 Jim Montgomery .01 .05
26 Markus Naslund .20 .50
27 Rob Niedermayer .08 .25
28 Chris Osgood .30 .75
29 Pat Peake .01 .05
30 Derek Plante .01 .05
31 Chris Pronger .20 .50
32 Mike Rathje .01 .05
33 Mikael Renberg .08 .25
34 Damian Rhodes .08 .25
35 Garth Snow .08 .25
36 Cam Stewart .01 .05
37 Jim Storm .01 .05
38 Michal Sykora .01 .05
39 Jocelyn Thibault .20 .50
40 Alexei Yashin .01 .05
41 Checklist 1 .01 .05
42 Vesa Viitakoski .01 .05
43 Jake Grimes .01 .05
44 Jim Dowd .01 .05
45 Craig Ferguson .01 .05
46 Mike Boback .01 .05
47 Francois Groleau .01 .05
48 Juha Riihijarvi .01 .05
49 Mikhail Shtalenkov .08 .25
50 Zigmund Palffy .08 .25
51 Felix Potvin .20 .50
52 Alexei Kovalev .08 .25
53 Larry Robinson .08 .25
54 John LeClair .30 .75
55 Dominic Roussel .08 .25
56 Geoff Sanderson .08 .25
57 Greg Pankewicz .01 .05
58 Brent Bilodeau .01 .05
59 Brandon Convery .01 .05
60 Fred Knipscheer .01 .05
61 Igor Chibirev .01 .05
62 Anatoli Fedotov .01 .05
63 Bob Kellogg .01 .05
64 Mike Maurice .01 .05
65 Chad Penney .01 .05
66 Mike Bavis .01 .05
67 Eric Veilleux .01 .05
68 Parris Duffus .01 .05
69 Daniel Lacroix .01 .05
70 Milos Holan .01 .05
71 Mike Muller .01 .05
72 Micah Aivazoff .01 .05
73 Krzysztof Oliwa .01 .05
74 Ryan Hughes .01 .05
75 Christian Soucy .01 .05
76 Keith Redmond .01 .05
77 Mark De Santis .01 .05
78 Craig Martin .01 .05
79 Mike Kennedy .01 .05
80 Pauli Jaks .01 .05
81 Colin Chin .01 .05
82 Jody Gage .01 .05
83 Don Biggs .01 .05
84 Tim Tookey .01 .05
85 Clint Malarchuk .08 .25
86 Jozef Cierny .01 .05
87 Radek Hamr .01 .05
88 Jason Dawe .01 .05
89 Chris Longo .01 .05
90 Brian Rolston .08 .25
91 Mike McKee .01 .05
92 Vitali Prokhorov .01 .05
93 Chris Snell .01 .05
94 Martin Brochu .08 .25
95 Dan Plante .01 .05
96 Darcy Werenka .01 .05
97 Steffon Walby .01 .05
98 David Emma .01 .05
99 Dan Stiver .01 .05
100 Radek Bonk .01 .05
101 Mark Visheau .01 .05
102 Dean Melanson .01 .05
103 Vladimir Tsyplakov .01 .05
104 Mikhail Volkov .01 .05
105 Aaron Miller .01 .05
106 Alexei Kudashov .01 .05
107 Shawn Rivers .01 .05
108 Ladislav Karabin .01 .05
109 Matt Mallgrave .01 .05
110 Craig Darby .01 .05
111 Marcel Cousineau .01 .05
112 Jamie McLennan .08 .25
113 Yanic Perreault .08 .25
114 Zac Boyer .01 .05
115 Sergei Zubov .01 .05
116 Dan Kesa .01 .05
117 Jim Hiller .01 .05
118 Dmitri Starostenko .01 .05
119 Chris Tamer .01 .05
120 Aaron Ward .01 .05
121 Claude Savoie .01 .05
122 Jamie Black .01 .05
123 Jean-Francois Jomphe .01 .05
124 Paxton Schulte .01 .05
125 Jarkko Varvio .01 .05
126 Jaroslav Otevrel .01 .05
127 Dane Jackson .01 .05
128 Brent Grieve .01 .05
129 Rheaumes CL .30 .75
130 Rene Corbet .01 .05
131 Joe Frederick .01 .05
132 Martin Tanguay .01 .05
133 Fredrik Jax .01 .05
134 Jamie Linden .01 .05
135 Jason Smith .01 .05
136 Rick Kowalsky .01 .05
137 Dino Grossi .01 .05
138 Aris Brimanis .01 .05
139 Jeff McLean .01 .05
140 Tyler Wright .01 .05
141 Roman Gorev .01 .05
142 Dean Hulett .01 .05
143 Niklas Sundblad .01 .05
144 Jeff Bes .01 .05
145 Pascal Rheaume .01 .05
146 Donald Brashear .01 .05
147 Hugo Belanger .01 .05
148 Blair Scott .01 .05
149 Steve Staios .01 .05
150 Matt Martin .01 .05
151 Richard Matvichuk .01 .05
152 Paul Brousseau .01 .05
153 Evgeny Namestnikov .01 .05
154 Mike Peca .20 .50
155 Jeff Nelson .01 .05
156 Greg Andrusak .01 .05
157 Norm Batherson .01 .05
158 Martin Bakula .01 .05
159 Ed Patterson .01 .05
160 Steve Larouche .01 .05
161 Libor Polasek .01 .05
162 Jon Hillebrandt .01 .05
163 Guy Leveque .01 .05
164 Eric Lacroix .01 .05
165 Scott Walker .01 .05
166 Robert Burakovsky .01 .05
167 Markus Ketterer .01 .05
168 Mike Speer .01 .05
169 Martin Jiranek .01 .05
170 Andy Schneider .01 .05
171 Terry Hollinger .01 .05
172 Mark Lawrence .01 .05
173 Martin Lapointe .20 .50
174 Vaclav Prospal .01 .05
175 Mike Fountain .01 .05
176 Alexander Kerch .01 .05
177 Oleg Petrov .01 .05
178 Derek Armstrong .01 .05
179 Matthew Barnaby .01 .05
180 Andrei Nazarov .01 .05
181 Andrei Trefilov .01 .05
182 Jean-Yves Roy .01 .05
183 Boris Rousson .01 .05
184 Dan Laperriere .01 .05
185 Yan Kaminsky .01 .05
186 Ralph Intranuovo .01 .05
187 Sandy Moger .01 .05
188 Grant Marshall .01 .05
189 Denny Felsner .01 .05
190 Cory Stillman .01 .05
191 Eric Lavigne .01 .05
192 Jarrod Skalde .01 .05
193 Steve Junker .01 .05
194 Alexander Cherbayev .01 .05
195 Nathan Lafayette .01 .05
196 Ed Ward .01 .05
197 Harijs Vitolinsh .01 .05
198 Jarmo Kekalainen .01 .05
199 Neil Eisenhut .01 .05
200 Radek Bonk .01 .05
201 Jason Bonsignore .01 .05
202 Jeff Friesen .01 .05
203 Ed Jovanovski .08 .25
204 Brett Lindros .01 .05
205 Jeff O'Neill .20 .50
206 Deron Quint .01 .05
207 Vadim Sharifjanov .01 .05
208 Oleg Tverdovsky .01 .05
209 Friesen
O'Neill CL .01 .05
210 David Cooper .01 .05
211 Doug McDonald .01 .05
212 Leonid Toropchenko .01 .05
213 Chris Rogles .01 .05
214 Slava Kozlov .08 .25
215 Denis Metlyuk .01 .05
216 Scott McKay .01 .05
217 Brian Loney .01 .05
218 Kevin Hodson .01 .05
219 Bobby House .01 .05
220 Sergei Krivokrasov .01 .05
221 Brett Harkins .01 .05
222 Cale Hulse .01 .05
223 Marc Tardif .01 .05
224 Jon Rohloff .01 .05
225 Kevin Smyth .01 .05
226 Jason Young .01 .05
227 Sergei Zholtok .01 .05
228 Todd Simon .01 .05
229 Jerome Bechard .01 .05
230 Matt Robbins .01 .05
231 Joe Cook .01 .05
232 John Brill .01 .05
233 Dan Goldie .01 .05
234 Dan Gravelle .01 .05
235 Shawn Wheeler .01 .05
236 Brad Harrison .01 .05
237 Joe Dragon .01 .05
238 Jason Jennings .01 .05
239 Manon Rheaume .75 2.00
240 Jamie Steer .01 .05
241 Scott Rogers .01 .05
242 Lyle Wildgoose .01 .05
243 Darren Colbourne .01 .05
244 Mike Smith .01 .05
245 Chris Bright .01 .05
246 Chris Belanger .01 .05
247 Darren Schwartz .01 .05
248 Cammi Granato .60 1.50
249 Erin Whitten .20 .50
250 Manon Rheaume .75 2.00
NNO Arnott
Yashin ROY .40 1.00

1994 Classic Pro Prospects Autographs

AU1 R.Bonk AU/2400 5.00 10.00
AU2 J.Bonsignore AU/2450 5.00 10.00
AU3 J.Friesen AU/2450 10.00 25.00
AU4 J.Juneau AU/1370 8.00 20.00
AU5 A.Kovalev AU/1900 5.00 10.00
AU6 C.Pronger AU/1400 12.50 30.00
AU7 M.Rheaume AU/1900 30.00 80.00
AU8 E.Whitten AU/1800 12.50 30.00
AU9 A.Yashin AU/1400 6.00 15.00

1994 Classic Pro Prospects Ice Ambassadors

COMPLETE SET (20) 3.00 8.00
IA1 Adrian Aucoin .08 .25
IA2 Corey Hirsch .15 .40
IA3 Paul Kariya 1.00 2.50
IA4 David Harlock .08 .25
IA5 Manny Legace .30 .75
IA6 Chris Therien .08 .25
IA7 Todd Warriner .08 .25
IA8 Todd Marchant .08 .25
IA9 Matt Martin .08 .25
IA10 Peter Ferraro .08 .25
IA11 Brian Rolston .15 .40
IA12 Jim Campbell .08 .25
IA13 Mike Dunham .30 .75
IA14 Craig Johnson .08 .25
IA15 Saku Koivu 1.00 2.50
IA16 Jere Lehtinen .30 .75
IA17 Viktor Kozlov .15 .40
IA18 Andrei Nikolishin .08 .25
IA19 Sergei Gonchar .15 .40
IA20 Valeri Karpov .08 .25

1994 Classic Pro Prospects International Heroes

COMPLETE SET (25) 20.00 40.00
LP1 Jim Campbell .75 2.00
LP2 Ted Drury .75 2.00
LP3 Mike Dunham 1.25 3.00
LP4 Chris Ferraro .75 2.00
LP5 Peter Ferraro .75 2.00
LP6 Darby Hendrickson .75 2.00
LP7 Craig Johnson .75 2.00
LP8 Todd Marchant .75 2.00
LP9 Matt Martin .75 2.00
LP10 Brian Rolston .75 2.00
LP11 Adrian Aucoin .75 2.00
LP12 Martin Gendron .75 2.00
LP13 David Harlock .75 2.00
LP14 Corey Hirsch .75 2.00
LP15 Paul Kariya 3.00 8.00
LP16 Manny Legace 1.25 3.00
LP17 Brett Lindros .75 2.00
LP18 Brian Savage .75 2.00
LP19 Chris Therien .75 2.00
LP20 Todd Warriner .75 2.00
LP21 Radek Bonk .75 2.00
LP22 Pavel Bure 1.25 3.00
LP23 Teemu Selanne 3.00 8.00
LP24 Mark Recchi 1.50 4.00
LP25 Alexei Yashin 1.50 4.00

1994 Classic Pro Prospects Promo

NNO Radek Bonk PROMO 1.50 4.00

1994 Classic Pro Prospects Prototype

NNO Jason Arnott 2.00 5.00

1996 Collector's Edge Future Legends

COMPLETE SET (50) 6.00 15.00
1 Brad Bombardir .07 .20
2 Niklas Andersson .07 .20
3 Mike Dunham .20 .50
4 Anders Eriksson .07 .20
5 Kelly Fairchild .07 .20
6 Chris Ferraro .07 .20
7 Peter Ferraro .07 .20
8 Eric Fichaud .15 .40
9 Manny Legace .20 .50
10 David Ling .07 .20
11 Jim Montgomery .07 .20
12 Chris Murray .07 .20
13 Rob Brown .07 .20
14 Rem Murray .07 .20
15 Rob Murray .07 .20
16 Jan Caloun .07 .20
17 Frederic Chabot .15 .40
18 Craig Fisher .07 .20
19 Dwayne Roloson .15 .40
20 Brad Smyth .07 .20
21 Steve Sullivan .20 .50
22 Petr Sykora .07 .20
23 Darcy Tucker .15 .40
24 Landon Wilson .15 .40
25 Greg Hawgood .07 .20
26 Stephane Beauregard .15 .40
27 Aki Berg .07 .20
28 Matt Johnson .07 .20
29 Curtis Joseph .20 .50
30 Dan Lambert .07 .20
31 Eric LeCompte .07 .20
32 Brett Lievers .07 .20
33 Mark McArthur .15 .40
34 Ethan Moreau .15 .40
35 Marty Murray .07 .20
36 Wayne Primeau .07 .20
37 John Purves .07 .20
38 Manon Rheaume 1.00 2.50
39 Barry Richter .07 .20
40 Jamie Rivers .07 .20
41 Tommy Salo .20 .50
42 Jamie Storr .20 .50
43 Tom Tilley .07 .20
44 Derek Wilkinson .15 .40
45 Mike Wilson .07 .20
46 Sandis Ozolinsh .07 .20
47 Andrew Brunette .15 .40
48 James Black .07 .20
49 Terry Yake .07 .20
50 Mike Prokopec .07 .20

1996 Collector's Edge Future Legends Autographed Hot Picks

COMPLETE SET (4) 10.00 20.00
1 Chris Phillips/6000 2.00 5.00
2 Boyd Devereaux/6000 2.00 5.00
3 Richard Jackman/5000 2.00 5.00
4 Marcus Nilsson/6000 2.00 5.00

1996 Collector's Edge Ice

COMPLETE SET (200) 15.00 30.00
1 Curtis Bowen .02 .10
2 Anders Eriksson .02 .10
3 Kevin Hodson .08 .25
4 Martin Lapointe .20 .50
5 Aaron Ward .02 .10
6 Mike Dunham .20 .50
7 Chris McAlpine .02 .10
8 Brian Rolston .20 .50
9 Corey Schwab .08 .25
10 Steve Sullivan .20 .50
11 Petr Sykora .20 .50
12 Darren Van Impe .02 .10
13 Mike Maneluk .02 .10
14 David Sacco .02 .10
15 Jarrod Skalde .08 .25
16 Nikolai Tsulygin .02 .10
17 Peter Ferraro .02 .10
18 Chris Ferraro .02 .10
19 Corey Hirsch .08 .25
20 Mattias Norstrom .08 .25
21 Jamie Ram .08 .25
22 Chris Armstrong .02 .10
23 Alexei Kudashov .02 .10
24 Todd MacDonald .02 .10
25 Steve Washburn .02 .10
26 Kevin Weekes .20 .50
27 Rene Corbet .02 .10
28 Janne Laukkanen .02 .10
29 Aaron Miller .02 .10
30 Landon Wilson .08 .25
31 Fred Brathwaite .20 .50
32 Ryan Haggerty .02 .10
33 Ralph Intranuovo .02 .10
34 Todd Marchant .20 .50
35 David Oliver .02 .10
36 Marko Tuomainen .02 .10
37 Peter White .02 .10
38 Sebastien Bordeleau .02 .10
39 Martin Brochu .08 .25
40 Valeri Bure .08 .25
41 Craig Conroy .08 .25
42 Darcy Tucker .20 .50
43 David Wilkie .02 .10
44 Paul Healey .02 .10
45 Chris Herperger .02 .10
46 Jim Montgomery .02 .10
47 Chris Therien .02 .10
48 Pavol Demitra .20 .50
49 Michel Picard .02 .10
50 Jason Zent .02 .10
51 Patrick Boileau .02 .10
52 Jim Carey .08 .25
53 Sergei Gonchar .08 .25
54 Jeff Nelson .02 .10
55 Stefan Ustorf .02 .10
56 Alexander Kharlamov .02 .10
57 Ron Tugnutt .20 .50
58 Scott Bailey .08 .25
59 Clayton Beddoes .02 .10
60 Andre Roy .08 .25
61 Evgeny Ryabchikov .08 .25
62 Mark Astley .02 .10
63 Jody Gage .08 .25
64 Sergei Klimentiev .02 .10
65 Barrie Moore .02 .10
66 Mike Wilson .02 .10
67 Shayne Wright .02 .10
68 Michal Grosek .08 .25
69 Tavis Hansen .02 .10
70 Nikolai Khabibulin .30 .75
71 Scott Langkow .08 .25
72 Jason McBain .02 .10
73 Dwayne Roloson .08 .25
74 Cory Stillman .08 .25
75 Jamie Allison .02 .10
76 Jesper Mattson .02 .10
77 David Ling .02 .10
78 Brandon Convery .02 .10
79 Darby Hendrickson .02 .10
80 Janne Gronvall .02 .10
81 Jason Saal .02 .10
82 Brent Gretzky .02 .10
83 Kent Manderville .02 .10
84 Shayne Toporowski .02 .10
85 Paul Vincent .02 .10
86 Mark Kolesar .02 .10
87 Lonny Bohonos .02 .10
88 Larry Courville .02 .10
89 Jassen Cullimore .02 .10
90 Scott Walker .08 .25
91 Mike Buzak .02 .10
92 Craig Darby .02 .10
93 Eric Fichaud .08 .25
94 Andreas Johansson .02 .10
95 Jamie Rivers .02 .10
96 Jason Strudwick .02 .10
97 Patrice Tardif .02 .10
98 Alex Vasilevskii .02 .10
99 Drew Bannister .02 .10
100 Stan Drulia .08 .25
101 Aaron Gavey .02 .10
102 Reggie Savage .02 .10
103 Derek Wilkinson .08 .25
104 Rob Brown .02 .10
105 Dan Currie .02 .10
106 Kevin MacDonald .02 .10
107 Steve Maltais .08 .25
108 Shawn Rivers .02 .10
109 Wendell Young .08 .25
110 Don Biggs .02 .10
111 Dale DeGray .02 .10
112 Paul Lawless .02 .10
113 Danny Lorenz .02 .10
114 Dave Tomlinson .02 .10
115 Jock Callander .08 .25
116 Phillipe DeRouville .02 .10
117 Ryan Savoia .02 .10
118 Mike Stevens .02 .10
119 Chris Tamer .08 .25
120 Peter Bondra .20 .50
121 Peter Ciavaglia .02 .10
122 Rick Knickle .02 .10
123 Lonnie Loach .02 .10
124 Michal Pivonka .02 .10
125 Andy Bezeau .02 .10
126 Bob Essensa .08 .25
127 Andrew McBain .02 .10
128 Kevin Miehm .02 .10
129 Scott Arniel .02 .10
130 Kevin Dineen .08 .25
131 Rob Dopson .08 .25
132 Mark Freer .02 .10
133 Troy Gamble .08 .25
134 Ethan Moreau .08 .25
135 Sergei Klimovich .02 .10
136 Eric Lecompte .02 .10
137 Eric Manlow .02 .10
138 Kip Miller .02 .10
139 Manny Fernandez .20 .50
140 Mike Kennedy .02 .10
141 Jamie Langenbrunner .20 .50
142 Derrick Smith .02 .10
143 Jordan Willis .08 .25
144 Jan Caloun .02 .10

145 Viktor Kozlov .08 .25
146 Andrei Nazarov .02 .10
147 Geoff Sarjeant .02 .10
148 Patrik Augusta .02 .10
149 Viktor Gordiouk .02 .10
150 Dave Littman .08 .25
151 Todd Gillingham .02 .10
152 Greg Hawgood .02 .10
153 Patrice Lefebvre .02 .10
154 Pokey Reddick .08 .25
155 Manon Rheaume .75 2.00
156 Jeff Sharples .02 .10
157 Todd Simon .02 .10
158 Radek Bonk .20 .50
159 Gino Cavallini .02 .10
160 Tom Draper .08 .25
161 Tony Hrkac .08 .25
162 Fabian Joseph .02 .10
163 Mark Laforest .02 .10
164 Dave Christian .02 .10
165 Bryan Fogarty .02 .10
166 Chris Govedaris .02 .10
167 Mike Hurlbut .02 .10
168 Chris Imes .02 .10
169 Stephane Morin .02 .10
170 Allan Bester .08 .25
171 Kerry Clark .02 .10
172 Neil Eisenhut .02 .10
173 Craig Fisher .02 .10
174 Patrick Neaton .02 .10
175 Todd Richards .02 .10
176 Jon Casey .08 .25
177 Doug Evans .02 .10
178 Michel Mongeau .02 .10
179 Greg Paslawski .02 .10
180 Darren Veitch .02 .10
181 Frederick Beaubien .02 .10
182 Kevin Brown .02 .10
183 Rob Cowie .02 .10
184 Yanic Perreault .08 .25
185 Chris Snell .02 .10
186 Jan Vopat .02 .10
187 Robin Bawa .02 .10
188 Stephane Beauregard .08 .25
189 Dale Craigwell .02 .10
190 John Purves .08 .25
191 Jeff Madill .02 .10
192 Gord Dineen .02 .10
193 Chris Marinucci .08 .25
194 Mark McArthur .02 .10
195 Zigmund Palffy .20 .50
196 Tommy Salo .20 .50
197 Checklist .02 .10
198 Checklist .02 .10
199 Checklist .02 .10
200 Checklist .02 .10

1996 Collector's Edge Ice Crucibles

COMPLETE SET (25) 15.00 30.00
C1 David Roberts .40 1.00
C2 Ian Laperriere .40 1.00
C3 Kevin Dineen .40 1.00
C4 Kenny Jonsson .40 1.00
C5 Jim Carey .75 2.00
C6 Todd Marchant .40 1.00
C7 David Oliver .40 1.00
C8 Yanic Perreault .75 2.00
C9 Chris Therien .40 1.00
C10 Viktor Kozlov .75 2.00
C11 Valeri Bure .40 1.00
C12 Nikolai Khabibulin 1.00 2.50
C13 Steven Rice .40 1.00
C14 Mike Kennedy .40 1.00
C15 Peter Bondra .75 2.00
C16 Sergei Zubov .40 1.00
C17 Slava Kozlov .75 2.00
C18 Chris Osgood .75 2.00
C19 Darren McCarty .40 1.00
C20 Jason Dawe .40 1.00
C21 Trevor Kidd 1.00 2.50
C22 Tommy Salo 1.00 2.50
C23 Michal Pivonka .40 1.00
C24 Zigmund Palffy .75 2.00
NNO Checklist .40 1.00

1996 Collector's Edge Ice Livin' Large

COMPLETE SET (11) 20.00 40.00
L1 Adam Graves .75 2.00
L2 Marty McSorley .75 2.00
L3 Adam Oates 1.25 3.00
L4 Keith Primeau .75 2.00
L5 Bill Ranford 1.25 3.00
L6 Curtis Joseph 1.50 4.00
L7 Felix Potvin 1.50 4.00
L8 Mike Vernon 1.25 3.00
L9 Theo Fleury .75 2.00
L10 Kevin Stevens .75 2.00
L11 Martin Brodeur 8.00 20.00
NNO Checklist .75 2.00

1996 Collector's Edge Ice Future Legends Hot Picks Autographs

1 Chris Phillips/6000 1.25 3.00
3 Richard Jackman/5000 1.25 3.00

1996 Collector's Edge Ice Future Legends Platinum Club

COMPLETE SET (8) 10.00 25.00
1 Mike Dunham 2.00 5.00
2 Eric Fichaud .75 2.00
3 Manny Legace 2.00 5.00
4 Steve Sullivan .75 2.00
5 Darcy Tucker .75 2.00
6 Jamie Langenbrunner .75 2.00
7 Ethan Moreau .75 2.00
8 Jamie Storr .75 2.00

1996 Collector's Edge Ice Prism

*PRISM CARDS: 2X to 5X BASIC CARDS

1996 Collector's Edge Ice Promos

COMPLETE SET (7) .75 2.00
PR1 Todd Marchant .08 .25
PR2 Tommy Salo .20 .50
PR3 Michael Dunham .20 .50
PR4 Viktor Kozlov .15 .40
PR5 Dwayne Roloson .15 .40
PR6 Tony Hrkac .08 .25
NNO Title Card .20 .50

1996 Collector's Edge Ice Quantum Motion

COMPLETE SET (13) 15.00 30.00
1 Manny Fernandez 1.50 4.00
2 Pokey Reddick .75 2.00
3 Yanic Perreault .75 2.00
4 Rob Brown .75 2.00
5 Hubie McDonough .75 2.00
6 Stan Drulia .75 2.00
7 Michel Picard .75 2.00
8 Jim Carey 1.25 3.00
9 Martin Lapointe 1.25 3.00
10 Valeri Bure .75 2.00
11 Martin Brochu 1.25 3.00
12 Corey Schwab 1.25 3.00

1996 Collector's Edge Ice Future Legends Signed, Sealed and Delivered

COMPLETE SET (8) 8.00 20.00
1 Alexandre Volchkov/5000 1.25 3.00
2 Chris Allen/4000 1.25 3.00
3 Brian Bonin 1.25 3.00
4 Josh Green/6000 1.25 3.00
5 Chris Hajt/4000 1.25 3.00
6 Josh Holden 1.25 3.00
8 Andrei Zyuzin/6000 1.25 3.00
P1 Alexandre Volchkov Proto Unsigned 1.00 2.50

1996 Collector's Edge Ice The Wall

COMPLETE SET (12) 6.00 12.00
TW1 Ray LeBlanc .40 1.00
TW2 Manny Fernandez .75 2.00
TW3 Rick Knickle .40 1.00
TW4 Troy Gamble .40 1.00
TW5 Pokey Reddick .40 1.00
TW6 Wendell Young .40 1.00
TW7 Jim Carey .40 1.00
TW8 Dwayne Roloson .40 1.00
TW9 Les Kuntar .40 1.00
TW10 Mike Dunham .75 2.00
TW11 Eric Fichaud .40 1.00
TW12 Kevin Hodson .40 1.00

1995 Images

COMPLETE SET (100) 5.00 12.00
1 Bryan Berard .07 .20
2 Jeff Friesen .02 .10
3 Tommy Salo .25 .60
4 Jim Carey .07 .20
5 Wade Redden .07 .20
6 Jocelyn Thibault .15 .40
7 Ian Laperriere .02 .10
8 Todd Marchant .02 .10
9 Blaine Lacher .02 .10
10 Pavel Bure .15 .40
11 Alex Vasilevskii .02 .10
12 Jason Doig .02 .10
13 Eric Fichaud .07 .20
14 Eric Daze .07 .20
15 Ed Jovanovski .07 .20
16 Alexander Selivanov .02 .10
17 Brent Gretzky .02 .10
18 Terry Ryan .02 .10
19 Chris Wells .02 .10
20 Wade Belak .02 .10
21 Kevin Dineen .02 .10
22 Craig Fisher .02 .10
23 Jan Caloun .02 .10
24 Manny Fernandez .15 .40
25 Radek Bonk .02 .10
26 Dave Christian .02 .10
27 Patrice Tardif .02 .10
28 Kevin Brown .02 .10
29 Hubie McDonough .02 .10
30 Yan Golubovsky .02 .10
31 Steve Larouche .02 .10
32 Chris Therien .02 .10
33 Craig Darby .02 .10
34 Dwayne Norris .02 .10
35 Roman Oksiuta .02 .10
36 Steve Washburn .02 .10
37 Todd Bertuzzi .15 .40
38 Cory Stillman .07 .20
39 Steve Kelly .02 .10
40 Nathan LaFayette .02 .10
41 Dwayne Roloson .07 .20
42 Nikolai Khabibulin .15 .40
43 Radim Bicanek .02 .10
44 Jeff O'Neill .02 .10
45 Jason Bonsignore .02 .10
46 Shean Donovan .02 .10
47 Wayne Primeau .02 .10
48 Jamie Langenbrunner .02 .10
49 Dan Cloutier .15 .40
50 Ethan Moreau .07 .20
51 Brad Bombardir .02 .10
52 Jason Muzzatti .02 .10
53 Jassen Cullimore .02 .10
54 Jason Zent .02 .10
55 Sergei Gonchar .07 .20
56 Steve Rucchin .02 .10
57 Rob Cowie .02 .10
58 Miroslav Satan .40 1.00
59 Kenny Jonsson .07 .20
60 Adam Deadmarsh .02 .10
61 Mike Dunham .15 .40
62 Corey Hirsch .02 .10
63 Janne Laukkanen .02 .10
64 Craig Conroy .02 .10
65 Ryan Sittler .02 .10
66 Jeff Nelson .02 .10
67 Michel Picard .02 .10
68 Mark Astley .02 .10
69 Lonny Bohonos .02 .10
70 Evgeny Ryabchikov .02 .10
71 Chris Osgood .07 .20
72 Manon Rheaume 1.00 2.50
73 Mike Kennedy .02 .10
74 Deron Quint .02 .10
75 Jamie Storr .07 .20
76 Aris Brimanis .02 .10
77 Valeri Bure .02 .10
78 Rene Corbet .02 .10
79 David Oliver .02 .10
80 Chris McAlpine .02 .10
81 Petr Sykora .15 .40
82 Brad Church .07 .20
83 Daymond Langkow .15 .40
84 Chad Kilger .02 .10
85 Shane Doan .20 .50
86 Jeff Ware .02 .10
87 Christian Laflamme .02 .10
88 Cory Cross .02 .10
89 Al Secord .02 .10
90 Jason Woolley .02 .10
91 Bryan McCabe .02 .10
92 Travis Richards .02 .10
93 Andrei Nazarov .02 .10
94 Mike Pomichter .02 .10
95 Chris Marinucci .02 .10
96 Jean-Yves Roy .02 .10
97 Brian Rolston .07 .20
98 Aaron Ward .02 .10
99 Jim Carey CL .02 .10
100 Pavel Bure CL .07 .20

1995 Images Gold

*STARS: 1.25X TO 2.5X BASIC CARDS

1995 Images Autographs

2A J.Friesen/1500 4.00 10.00
6A J.Thibault/1185 4.00 10.00
9A B.Lacher/1500 2.00 5.00
25A R.Bonk/970 3.00 8.00
30A Yan Golubovsky/1500 .75 2.00
36A Steve Washburn/1500 .75 2.00
41A Dwayne Roloson/1115 .75 2.00
45A Jason Bonsignore/1500 2.00 5.00
46A Shean Donovan/1500 .75 2.00
48A J.Langenbrunner/1500 5.00 12.00
54A Jason Zent/1125 .75 2.00
59A K.Jonsson/1180 2.00 5.00
60A A.Deadmarsh/1500 6.00 15.00
64A Craig Conroy/1170 .75 2.00
74A D.Quint/1500 .75 2.00
76A Aris Brimanis/1500 .75 2.00
79A David Oliver/1500 .75 2.00
80A Chris McAlpine/1185 .75 2.00
81A P.Sykora/1500 3.00 8.00
94A Mike Pomichter/1175 .75 2.00
95A Chris Marinucci/1500 .75 2.00
98A Aaron Ward/1190 .75 2.00

1995 Images Clear Excitement

COMPLETE SET (20) 75.00 150.00
CE1 Bryan Berard 2.50 6.00
CE2 Jeff Friesen 2.00 5.00
CE3 Tommy Salo 3.00 8.00
CE4 Jim Carey 2.50 6.00
CE5 Wade Redden 2.50 6.00
CE6 Jocelyn Thibault 3.00 8.00
CE7 Ian Laperriere 2.00 5.00
CE8 Todd Marchant 2.00 5.00
CE9 Blaine Lacher 2.00 5.00
CE10 Pavel Bure 3.00 8.00
CE11 Petr Sykora 3.00 8.00
CE12 Daymond Langkow 2.50 6.00
CE13 Radek Bonk 2.00 5.00
CE14 Patrice Tardif 2.00 5.00
CE15 Jeff Nelson 2.00 5.00
CE16 Jeff O'Neill 2.00 5.00
CE17 Ed Jovanovski 2.50 6.00
CE18 Jason Doig 2.00 5.00
CE19 Chris Marinucci 2.00 5.00
CE20 Manon Rheaume 12.50 30.00

1995 Images Platinum Players

COMPLETE SET (10) 10.00 20.00
PL1 Pavel Bure 1.50 4.00
PL2 Tony Granato .40 1.00
PL3 Kevin Dineen .40 1.00
PL4 Ron Hextall 1.25 3.00
PL5 Claude Lemieux .40 1.00
PL6 Mark Recchi 1.50 4.00
PL7 Benoit Hogue .40 1.00
PL8 Tim Cheveldae .40 1.00
PL9 Darcy Wakaluk .40 1.00
PL10 Todd Gill .40 1.00

1995 Images Premier Draft Choice

COMPLETE SET (10) 10.00 20.00
PD1 Bryan Berard 1.00 2.50
PD2 Wade Redden 1.00 2.50
PD3 Steve Kelly .40 1.00
PD4 Petr Sykora 3.00 8.00
PD5 Brad Church .40 1.00
PD6 Daymond Langkow 1.50 4.00
PD7 Chad Kilger .40 1.00
PD8 Terry Ryan .40 1.00
PD9 Jason Doig .40 1.00
PD10 Field Card .40 1.00

1995 Images Platinum Prospects

COMPLETE SET (10) 10.00 20.00
PR1 Jeff Nelson .40 1.00
PR2 Jim Carey 1.25 3.00
PR3 Ian Laperriere .40 1.00
PR4 Chris Osgood 1.25 3.00
PR5 Todd Marchant .40 1.00
PR6 Radek Bonk .40 1.00
PR7 Chris Marinucci .40 1.00
PR8 Tommy Salo 2.50 5.00
PR9 Manny Fernandez 1.50 4.00
PR10 Jan Caloun .40 1.00

2015 ITG CHL Draft

COMPLETE SET (30) 10.00 25.00
*BLACK/50: .6X TO 1.5X BASIC CARDS
*BLUE/25: 1X TO 2.5X BASIC CARDS
*GOLD/100: .5X TO 1.2X BASIC CARDS
*PINK/200: .5X TO 1.2X BASIC CARDS
*RED/10: 1.2X TO 3X BASIC CARDS
*SILVER/500: .4X TO 1X BASIC CARDS
1 Connor McDavid 1.50 4.00
2 Mathew Barzal .75 2.00
3 Dylan Strome .60 1.50
4 Jeremy Roy .20 .50
5 Travis Konecny .60 1.50
6 Mitchell Marner 1.00 2.50
7 Daniel Sprong .40 1.00
8 Lawson Crouse .30 .75
9 Nick Merkley .50 1.25
10 Pavel Zacha .50 1.25
11 Connor McDavid CB 1.50 4.00
12 Mathew Barzal CB .75 2.00
13 Dylan Strome CB .60 1.50
14 Jeremy Roy CB .20 .50
15 Travis Konecny CB .60 1.50
16 Mitchell Marner CB 1.00 2.50
17 Daniel Sprong CB .40 1.00
18 Lawson Crouse CB .30 .75
19 Nick Merkley CB .50 1.25
20 Pavel Zacha CB .50 1.25
21 Connor McDavid YS 1.50 4.00
22 Mathew Barzal YS .75 2.00
23 Dylan Strome YS .60 1.50
24 Jeremy Roy YS .20 .50
25 Travis Konecny YS .60 1.50
26 Mitchell Marner YS 1.00 2.50
27 Daniel Sprong YS .40 1.00
28 Lawson Crouse YS .30 .75
29 Nick Merkley YS .50 1.25
30 Pavel Zacha YS .50 1.25

1995 Signature Rookies

COMPLETE SET (70) 5.00 12.00
1 Vaclav Varada .02 .10
2 Roman Vopat .02 .10
3 Yanick Dube UER .02 .10
4 Colin Cloutier .02 .10
5 Scott Cherrey .02 .10
6 Johan Finnstrom .02 .10
7 Fredrik Modin .20 .50
8 Stephane Roy .02 .10
9 Yevgeni Ryabchikov .02 .10
10 Jose Theodore .50 1.25
11 Jason Holland .02 .10
12 Richard Park .02 .10
13 Jason Podollan .02 .10
14 Mattias Ohlund .20 .50
15 Chris Wells .02 .10
16 Hugh Hamilton .02 .10
17 Edvin Frylen .02 .10
18 Wade Belak .02 .10
19 Sebastien Bety .02 .10
20 Chris Dingham .02 .10
21 Peter Nylander .02 .10
22 Daymond Langkow .40 1.00
23 Kelly Fairchild .02 .10
24 Norm Dezainde .02 .10
25 Nolan Baumgartner .02 .10
26 Deron Quint .02 .10
27 Sheldon Souray .02 .10
28 Stefan Ustorf .02 .10
29 Juha Vuorivirta UER .02 .10
30 Mark Seliger .02 .10
31 Ryan Smyth .50 1.25
32 Dimitri Tabarin .02 .10
33 Nikolai Tsulygin .02 .10
34 Paul Vincent .02 .10
35 Rhett Warrener .02 .10
36 Jamie Rivers .02 .10
37 Rumun Ndur .02 .10
38 Phil Huber .02 .10
39 Radek Dvorak .20 .50
40 Mike Barrie .02 .10
41 Chris Hynnes .02 .10
42 Mike Dubinsky .02 .10
43 Steve Cheredaryk .02 .10
44 Jim Carey .08 .25
45A Dorian Anneck ERR .02 .10
45B Dorian Anneck COR .02 .10
46 Jorgen Jonsson .02 .10
47 Alyn McCauley .02 .10
48 Corey Nielson .02 .10
49 Daniel Tjarnqvist .08 .25
50 Vadim Yepanchintsev .02 .10
51 Sean Haggerty .02 .10
52A Milan Hejduk ERR 1.00 2.50
52B Milan Hejduk COR 1.00 2.50
53 Adam Magarrell .02 .10
54 Dave Scatchard .08 .25
55 Sebastien Vallee .02 .10
56 Milos Guren .02 .10
57 Johan Davidsson .02 .10
58 Byron Briske .02 .10
59 Sylvain Blouin .02 .10
60 Bryan Berard UER .60 1.50
61 Tim Findlay .02 .10
62 Doug Bonner .02 .10
63 Curtis Brown .08 .25
64A Brad Symes ERR .02 .10
64B Brad Symes COR .02 .10
65 Andrew Taylor .02 .10
66 Brad Bombardir .02 .10
67 Joe Dziedzic .02 .10
68 Valentin Morozov .02 .10
69A Mark McArthur ERR .02 .10
69B Mark McArthur COR .02 .10
70 Checklist .02 .10

1995 Signature Rookies Auto-Phonex

COMPLETE SET (41) 2.00 5.00
1 Mika Alatalo .02 .10
2 Chad Allan UER .02 .10
3 J. Andersson-Junkka .02 .10
4 Serge Aubin .08 .25
5 David Belitski .05 .15
6 Aki Berg .02 .10
7 Zac Bierk .08 .25
8 Lou Body .02 .10
9 Kevin Bolibruck .02 .10
10 Brian Boucher .30 .75
11 Jack Callahan .02 .10
12 Jake Deadmarsh .02 .10
13 Andy Delmore .02 .10
14 Shane Doan .30 .75
15 Daniel Cleary .02 .10
16 Ian Gordon .02 .10
17 Jochen Hecht .08 .25
18 Martin Hohenberger .02 .10
19 Thomas Holmstrom .30 .75
20 Cory Keenan .02 .10
21 Shane Kenny .02 .10
22 Pavel Kriz .02 .10
23 Justin Kurtz .02 .10
24 Jan Labraaten .02 .10
25 Brad Larsen .02 .10
26 Donald MacLean .02 .10
27 Tavis MacMillan .02 .10
28 Mike Martin .02 .10
29 Bryan Berard .08 .25
30 Dmitri Nabokov .02 .10
31 Todd Norman .02 .10
32 Cory Peterson .02 .10
33 Johan Ramstedt .02 .10
34 Wade Redden .08 .25
35 Kevin Riehl .02 .10
36 David Roberts .02 .10
37 Terry Ryan .02 .10
38 Brian Scott .02 .10
39 Alexander Selivanov .08 .25
40 Peter Wallin .02 .10
NNO Checklist .02 .10

1995 Signature Rookies Auto-Phonex Beyond 2000

COMPLETE SET (5) 2.00 5.00
B1 Jamie Rivers .20 .50
B2 Terry Ryan .20 .50
B3 Ryan Smyth .75 2.00
B4 Nolan Baumgartner .20 .50
B5 Jose Theodore 1.25 3.00

1995 Signature Rookies Auto-Phonex Jaromir Jagr

COMPLETE SET (5) 3.00 8.00
COMMON JAGR (JJ1-JJ5) .75 2.00
JAGR SIGNATURE (JJ1-JJ5) 40.00 100.00

1995 Signature Rookies Auto-Phonex Phone Cards

COMPLETE SET (40) 60.00 120.00
1 Mika Alatalo 1.50 4.00
2 Chad Allan .75 2.00
3 Jonas Andersson-Junkka .75 2.00
4 Serge Aubin 1.50 4.00
5 David Belitski .75 2.00
6 Aki Berg 1.25 3.00
7 Zac Bierk 1.25 3.00
8 Lou Body .75 2.00
9 Kevin Bolibruck .75 2.00
10 Brian Boucher 8.00 20.00
11 Jack Callahan .75 2.00
12 Jake Deadmarsh .75 2.00
13 Andy Delmore 1.25 3.00
14 Shane Doan 2.00 5.00
15 Daniel Cleary 1.25 3.00
16 Ian Gordon .75 2.00
17 Jochen Hecht 3.00 8.00
18 Martin Hohenberger .75 2.00
19 Thomas Holmstrom 2.00 5.00
20 Cory Keenan .75 2.00
21 Shane Kenny .75 2.00
22 Pavel Kriz .75 2.00
23 Justin Kurtz .75 2.00
24 Jan Labraaten .75 2.00
25 Brad Larsen .75 2.00
26 Donald MacLean .75 2.00
27 Tavis MacMillan .75 2.00
28 Mike Martin .75 2.00
29 Bryan Berard 1.50 4.00
30 Dmitri Nabokov .75 2.00
31 Todd Norman .75 2.00
32 Cory Peterson .75 2.00
33 Johan Ramstedt .75 2.00
34 Wade Redden 1.25 3.00
35 Kevin Riehl .75 2.00
36 David Roberts .75 2.00
37 Terry Ryan .75 2.00
38 Brian Scott .75 2.00
39 Alexander Selivanov .75 2.00
40 Peter Wallin .75 2.00
NNO Nolan Baumgartner $6 1.50 4.00
NNO Daymond Langkow $30 1.50 4.00
NNO Wade Redden $6 1.50 4.00
NNO Terry Ryan $6 1.50 4.00

1995 Signature Rookies Auto-Phonex Prodigies

COMPLETE SET (5) 2.00 5.00
P1 Bryan Berard UER .40 1.00
P2 Daymond Langkow .75 2.00
P3 Daniel Cleary .40 1.00
P4 Aki Berg .40 1.00
P5 Wade Redden .75 2.00

1995 Signature Rookies Club Promos

COMPLETE SET (5) 20.00 20.00
1 Sergei Luchinkin 2.00 5.00
2 Stefan Ustorf 2.00 5.00
3 Brad Brown 2.00 5.00
4 Yanick Dube 2.00 5.00
5 Vitali Yachmenev 2.00 5.00

1995 Signature Rookies Cool Five

COMPLETE SET (5) 10.00 10.00
CF1 Radek Bonk .20 .50
CF2 Brad Park .75 2.00
CF3 Brian Leetch .75 2.00
CF4 Maurice Richard 2.00 5.00
CF5 Henri Richard .75 2.00

1995 Signature Rookies Cool Five Signatures

CF1 Radek Bonk 2.00 5.00
CF2 Brad Park 6.00 15.00
CF3 Brian Leetch 5.00 10.00
CF4 Maurice Richard 40.00 80.00
CF5 Henri Richard 10.00 25.00

1995 Signature Rookies Future Flash

COMPLETE SET (10) 2.00 5.00
FF1 Jeff Ambrosio .40 1.00
FF2 Brad Brown .40 1.00
FF3 Patrick Juhlin .40 1.00
FF4 Sergei Gorbachev .40 1.00
FF5 Vasili Kamenev 1.50 4.00
FF6 Oleg Orekhovski .40 1.00
FF7 Maxim Kuznetsov .40 1.00
FF8 Sergei Luchinkin .40 1.00
FF9 Scott Roche .75 2.00
FF10 Alexei Morozov .75 2.00

1995 Signature Rookies Future Flash Signatures

COMPLETE SET (10) 60.00 120.00
FF1 Jeff Ambrosio 6.00 15.00
FF2 Brad Brown 6.00 15.00
FF3 Patrick Juhlin 6.00 15.00
FF4 Sergei Gorbachev 6.00 15.00
FF5 Vasili Kamenev 6.00 15.00
FF6 Oleg Orekhovski 6.00 15.00
FF7 Maxim Kuznetsov 8.00 20.00
FF8 Sergei Luchinkin 6.00 15.00
FF9 Scott Roche 8.00 20.00
FF10 Alexei Morozov 8.00 20.00

1995 Signature Rookies Miracle on Ice

COMPLETE SET (50) 10.00 20.00
1 Bill Baker .07 .20
2 Bill Baker .07 .20
3 Neal Broten .30 .75
4 Neal Broten .30 .75
5 Dave Christian .20 .50
6 Dave Christian .20 .50
7 Steve Christoff .07 .20
8 Steve Christoff .07 .20
9 Jim Craig .60 1.50
10 Jim Craig .60 1.50
11 Mike Eruzione .60 1.50
12 Mike Eruzione .60 1.50
13 John Harrington .07 .20
14 John Harrington .07 .20
15 Steve Janaszak .07 .20
16 Steve Janaszak .07 .20
17 Mark Johnson .07 .20
18 Mark Johnson .07 .20
19 Rob McClanahan .07 .20
20 Rob McClanahan .07 .20
21 Ken Morrow .20 .50
22 Ken Morrow .20 .50
23 Jack O'Callahan .07 .20
24 Jack O'Callahan .07 .20
25 Mark Pavelich .07 .20
26 Mark Pavelich .07 .20
27 Mike Ramsey .08 .25
28 Mike Ramsey .08 .25
29 Buzz Schneider .07 .20
30 Buzz Schneider .07 .20
31 Dave Silk .07 .20
32 Dave Silk .07 .20
33 Bob Suter .07 .20
34 Bob Suter .07 .20
35 Eric Strobel .07 .20
36 Eric Strobel .07 .20
37 Phil Verchota .07 .20
38 Phil Verchota .07 .20
39 Marc Wells .07 .20
40 Marc Wells .07 .20
41 Herb Brooks CO .60 1.50
42 Herb Brooks CO .60 1.50
43 Craig Patrick ACO .20 .50
44 Craig Patrick ACO .20 .50
45 Clinching The Gold .20 .50
46 Do You Believe In Miracles .20 .50
47 Eruzione Decides It .20 .50
48 Celebration .20 .50
49 A Dream Becomes Reality .20 .50
50 Checklist .07 .20
P1 Jim Craig Promo 1.00 2.50

1995 Signature Rookies Miracle on Ice Signatures

COMPLETE SET (43) 175.00 350.00
1 Bill Baker 5.00 12.00
2 Bill Baker 5.00 12.00
3 Neal Broten 5.00 12.00
4 Neal Broten 5.00 12.00
5 Dave Christian 5.00 12.00
6 Dave Christian 5.00 12.00
7 Steve Christoff 5.00 12.00
8 Steve Christoff 5.00 12.00
9 Jim Craig 12.00 30.00
10 Jim Craig 12.00 30.00
11 Mike Eruzione 20.00 50.00
12 Mike Eruzione 20.00 50.00
13 John Harrington 5.00 12.00
14 John Harrington 5.00 12.00
15 Steve Janaszak 5.00 12.00
16 Steve Janaszak 5.00 12.00
17 Mark Johnson 10.00 25.00
18 Mark Johnson 10.00 25.00
19 Rob McClanahan 5.00 12.00
20 Rob McClanahan 5.00 12.00
21 Ken Morrow 4.00 10.00
22 Ken Morrow 4.00 10.00
23 Jack O'Callahan 12.50 30.00
24 Jack O'Callahan 12.50 30.00
25 Mark Pavelich 5.00 12.00
26 Mark Pavelich 5.00 12.00
27 Mike Ramsey 5.00 12.00
28 Mike Ramsey 5.00 12.00
29 Buzz Schneider 10.00 25.00
30 Buzz Schneider 10.00 25.00
31 Dave Silk 4.00 10.00
32 Dave Silk 4.00 10.00
33 Bob Suter 6.00 15.00
34 Bob Suter 6.00 15.00
35 Eric Strobel 10.00 25.00
36 Eric Strobel 10.00 25.00
37 Phil Verchota 5.00 12.00
38 Phil Verchota 6.00 15.00
39 Marc Wells 5.00 12.00
40 Marc Wells 5.00 12.00
42 Herb Brooks CO 90.00 150.00
43 Craig Patrick ACO 4.00 10.00
44 Craig Patrick ACO 4.00 10.00
P1 Celebration Promo Herb Brooks/7500 30.00 80.00

1995 Signature Rookies Signatures

COMPLETE SET (69) 75.00 150.00
1 Vaclav Varada 1.25 3.00
2 Roman Vopat 1.25 3.00
3 Yanick Dube 1.25 3.00
4 Colin Cloutier 1.25 3.00
5 Scott Cherrey 1.25 3.00
6 Johan Finnstrom 1.25 3.00
7 Fredrik Modin 2.00 5.00
8 Stephane Roy 1.25 3.00
9 Evgeni Ryabchikov 1.25 3.00
10 Jose Theodore 6.00 15.00
11 Jason Holland 1.25 3.00
12 Richard Park 1.25 3.00
13 Jason Podollan 1.25 3.00
14 Mattias Ohlund 2.00 5.00
15 Chris Wells 1.25 3.00
16 Hugh Hamilton 1.25 3.00
17 Edvin Frylen 1.25 3.00
18 Wade Belak 5.00 12.00
19 Sebastien Bety 1.25 3.00
20 Chris Dingman 1.25 3.00
21 Peter Nylander 1.25 3.00
22 Daymond Langkow 2.00 5.00
23 Kelly Fairchild 1.25 3.00
24 Norm Dezainde 1.25 3.00
25 Nolan Baumgartner 1.25 3.00
26 Deron Quint 1.25 3.00
27 Sheldon Souray 1.25 3.00
28 Stefan Ustorf 1.25 3.00
29 Juha Vuorivirta UER 1.25 3.00
30 Marc Seliger 1.50 4.00
31 Ryan Smyth 4.00 10.00
32 Dimitri Tabarin 1.25 3.00
33 Nikolai Tsulygin 1.25 3.00
34 Paul Vincent 1.25 3.00
35 Rhett Warrener 1.25 3.00
36 Jamie Rivers 1.25 3.00
37 Rumun Ndur 1.50 4.00
38 Phil Huber 1.25 3.00
39 Radek Dvorak 2.00 5.00
40 Mike Barrie 1.25 3.00
41 Chris Hynnes 1.25 3.00
42 Mike Dubinsky 1.25 3.00
43 Steve Cheredaryk 1.25 3.00
44 Jim Carey 2.00 5.00
45 Brad Symes 1.25 3.00
46 Jorgen Jonsson 1.25 3.00
47 Alyn McCauley 1.25 3.00
48 Corey Nielson 1.25 3.00
49 Daniel Tjarnqvist 1.50 4.00
50 Vadim Epanchintsev 1.25 3.00
51 Sean Haggerty 1.25 3.00
52 Mark McArthur 1.25 3.00
53 Adam Magarrell 1.25 3.00
54 Dave Scatchard 1.50 4.00
55 Sebastien Vallee 1.25 3.00
56 Milos Guren 1.25 3.00
57 Johan Davidsson 1.25 3.00
58 Byron Briske 1.25 3.00
59 Sylvain Blouin 1.25 3.00
60 Bryan Berard UER 1.50 4.00
61 Tim Findlay 1.25 3.00
62 Doug Bonner 1.50 4.00
63 Curtis Brown 1.25 3.00
64 Dorian Anneck 1.25 3.00
65 Andrew Taylor 1.25 3.00
66 Brad Bombardir 1.25 3.00
67 Joe Dziedzic 1.25 3.00
68 Valentin Morozhov 1.25 3.00
69 Milan Hejduk 6.00 15.00

1994 Signature Rookies Gold Standard Legends

COMPLETE SET (5) 3.00 8.00
L5 Brian Leetch .40 1.00

1995 Slapshot Memorial Cup

COMPLETE SET (110) 12.00 30.00
1 Rod Branch .07 .20
2 Jeff Oldenborger .07 .20
3 Jason Holland .07 .20
4 Nolan Baumgartner .15 .40
5 Keith McCambridge .07 .20
6 Ivan Vologjaninov .07 .20
7 Aaron Keller .07 .20
8 Greg Hart .07 .20
9 Jarome Iginla 2.00 5.00
10 Ryan Huska .07 .20
11 Jeff Ainsworth .07 .20
12 Darcy Tucker .40 1.00
13 Hnat Domenichelli .15 .40
14 Tyson Nash .75 2.00
15 Shane Doan 1.25 3.00
16 Jeff Antonovich .07 .20
17 Bonnie Kinney .07 .20
18 Ashley Buckberger .07 .20
19 Brad Lukowich .30 .75
20 Bob Westerby .07 .20
21 Jason Strudwick .15 .40
22 Bob Maudie .07 .20
23 Randy Petruk .20 .50
24 Shawn McNeil .07 .20
25 Don Hay CO .07 .20
26 Bryon Penstock .07 .20
27 Brian Elder .07 .20
28 Jeff Staples .07 .20
29 Scott Laluk .07 .20
30 Kevin Pozzo .07 .20
31 Wade Redden .40 1.00
32 Justin Kurtz .15 .40
33 Sven Butenschon .07 .20
34 Bryan McCabe .20 .50
35 Kelly Smart .07 .20
36 Bobby Brown .07 .20
37 Mike Dubinsky .07 .20
38 Mike LeClerc .30 .75
39 Dean Kletzel .07 .20
40 Darren Ritchie .07 .20
41 Mark Dutiaume .07 .20
42 Ryan Robson .07 .20
43 Chris Dingman .15 .40
44 Darren Van Oene .07 .20
45 Colin Cloutier .07 .20
46 Darryl Stockham .07 .20
47 Peter Schaefer .20 .50
48 Marty Murray .20 .50
49 Alex Vasilevski .07 .20
50 Bob Lowes CO .07 .20
51 Michael Coveny .07 .20
52 Jan Nemecek .15 .40
53 Chris Hall .07 .20

54 Jason Groleau .07 .20
55 Alex Rodrigue .07 .20
56 Jamie Bird .07 .20
57 Harold Hersh .07 .20
58 Carl Prud'Homme .07 .20
59 Sean Farmer .07 .20
60 Carl Beaudoin .07 .20
61 Gordie Dwyer .07 .20
62 Richard Safarik .07 .20
63 Carl Charland .07 .20
64 Jean-Guy Trudel .15 .40
65 Francois Cloutier .07 .20
66 Roddie MacKenzie .07 .20
67 Colin White .30 .75
68 Martin Menard .07 .20
69 Sebastien Bordeleau .07 .20
70 Jonathan Delisle .07 .20
71 Peter Worrell .40 1.00
72 Louis-Philippe Charbonn .15 .40
73 Jose Theodore 2.00 5.00
74 Neil Savary .15 .40
75 Michael McKay .15 .40
76 Darryl Foster .07 .20
77 Quade Lightbody .07 .20
78 Ryan MacDonald .07 .20
79 Mike Rucinski .07 .20
80 Murray Sheehan .07 .20
81 Matt Ball .07 .20
82 Gerry Lanigan .07 .20
83 Mike Morrone .07 .20
84 Tom Buckley .07 .20
85 Eric Manlow .07 .20
86 Bill McCauley .07 .20
87 Andrew Taylor .07 .20
88 Scott Blair .07 .20
89 Jeff Mitchell .07 .20
90 Jason Saal .15 .40
91 Jamie Allison .15 .40
92 Bryan Berard .20 .50
93 Dan Pawlaczyk .07 .20
94 Milan Kostolny .07 .20
95 Duane Harmer .07 .20
96 Shayne McCosh .07 .20
97 Sean Haggerty .07 .20
98 Nic Beaudoin .07 .20
99 Paul Maurice CO/GM .07 .20
100 Pete Deboer ACO .07 .20
101 Kamloops Checklist .07 .20
102 Brandon Checklist .07 .20
103 Hull Checklist .07 .20
104 Detroit Checklist .07 .20
105 OHL Champions Detroit J .07 .20
106 WHL Champions Kamloops .07 .20
107 LHJMQ Champions Hull Ol .07 .20
NNO OHL Playoff Summary .07 .20
NNO LHJMQ Playoff Summary .07 .20
NNO WHL Playoff Summary .07 .20

2019-20 SP Game Used CHL

2 Matthew Robertson/21* 6.00 15.00
4 Cole Perfetti/90* 12.00 30.00
5 Justin Barron/19* 8.00 20.00
7 Brandt Clarke/54* 8.00 20.00
8 Bowen Byram/43* 8.00 20.00
9 Mavrik Bourque/21* 8.00 20.00
11 Hunter Jones/28* 5.00 12.00
12 Cedric Pare/19 5.00 12.00
13 Connor McClennon/93* 5.00 12.00
14 Graeme Clarke/91* 5.00 12.00
16 Dylan Cozens/23* 10.00 25.00
17 Justin Sourdif/41* 5.00 12.00
18 Mason McTavish/23 6.00 15.00
19 Antonio Stranges/39* 5.00 12.00
20 Jamieson Rees/38* 5.00 12.00
21 Mads Sogaard/30 5.00 12.00
22 Jack Quinn/21* 10.00 25.00
23 Samuel Poulin/28* 6.00 15.00
24 Kevin Bahl/88 5.00 12.00
25 Quinton Byfield/54* 15.00 40.00
26 Trent Miner/30* 5.00 12.00
27 Serron Noel/17* 5.00 12.00
28 Thomas Harley/47* 8.00 20.00
29 Arthur Kaliyev/34 5.00 12.00
30 Connor Zary/17* 8.00 20.00
31 Olivier Rodrigue/32* 5.00 12.00
32 Matthew Welsh/73 5.00 12.00
34 Cole Sillinger/43* 6.00 15.00
35 Dawson Mercer/18* 10.00 25.00
36 Peyton Krebs/18* 8.00 20.00
37 Sasha Mutala/33* 5.00 12.00
38 Hendrix Lapierre/91* 8.00 20.00
39 Ozzy Wiesblatt/18* 6.00 15.00
41 Thimo Nickl/77* 5.00 12.00
42 Theo Rochette/18* 5.00 12.00
44 Philip Tomasino/25* 6.00 15.00
45 Zane Franklin/16 5.00 12.00
46 Cole Fonstad/23* 5.00 12.00
47 Nolan Foote/28* 5.00 12.00
50 Aliaksei Protas/21 5.00 12.00
51 Aidan Dudas/26* 5.00 12.00
52 Samuel Hlavaj/31 5.00 12.00
53 Jacob Ingham/67* 5.00 12.00
54 Jacob Perreault/43* 8.00 20.00
56 Zachary L'Heureux/25* 10.00 25.00
57 Jeremie Poirier/53* 5.00 12.00
59 Oliver Suni/18* 6.00 15.00
60 Felix Bibeau/20* 5.00 12.00
61 Luka Burzan/26* 5.00 12.00
63 Joel Hofer/30 8.00 20.00
65 Ryan Merkley/27* 5.00 12.00
66 Benoit-Olivier Groulx/18* 6.00 15.00
67 Shane Wright/50* 15.00 40.00
68 Vasily Ponomarev/91* 5.00 12.00
69 Jean-Luc Foudy/92* 5.00 12.00
70 Akil Thomas/43* 5.00 12.00
71 Seth Jarvis/23* 12.00 30.00
72 Marco Rossi/22* 12.00 30.00
73 Isaac Belliveau/57* 5.00 12.00
74 Jake Neighbours/20* 8.00 20.00
75 Dustin Wolf/31* 15.00 40.00

2021-22 SP Game Used CHL

1 Shane Wright/50* 12.00 30.00
2 Connor Bedard/97* 300.00 800.00
3 Danil Gushchin/65* 6.00 15.00
7 Ryder Korczak/37* 6.00 15.00
8 Tristan Lennox/29* 8.00 20.00
11 Oskar Olausson/82* 6.00 15.00
13 Connor McClennon/93* 5.00 12.00
14 Benjamin Gaudreau/69* 6.00 15.00
15 Sebastian Cossa/32* 10.00 25.00
17 Ty Nelson/23* 6.00 15.00
19 Calum Ritchie/20* 6.00 15.00
20 Chase Stillman/20* 6.00 15.00
22 Riley Heidt/26* 8.00 20.00
23 Tyler Tullio/70* 6.00 15.00
24 Olivier Nadeau/19* 5.00 12.00
25 Justin Sourdif/41* 6.00 15.00
26 Wyatt Johnston/54* 15.00 40.00
27 Olen Zellweger/47* 6.00 15.00
28 Tyler Peddle/90* 6.00 15.00
30 Dylan Garand/30* 5.00 12.00
31 Nate Danielson/28* 8.00 20.00
32 Jack Beck/18* 5.00 12.00
34 Elliot Desnoyers/90* 5.00 12.00
38 Francesco Pinelli/70* 5.00 12.00
39 Mavrik Bourque/21* 6.00 15.00
40 Brandon Coe/20* 5.00 12.00
42 Xavier Bourgault/97* 6.00 15.00
43 Owen Outwater/17* 8.00 20.00
44 Brandt Clarke/54* 6.00 15.00
45 Ozzy Wiesblatt/18* 5.00 12.00
46 Colton Dach/16* 6.00 15.00
47 Brennan Othmann/77* 6.00 15.00
49 Conor Geekie/27* 8.00 20.00
50 Tucker Robertson/21* 5.00 12.00
51 Justin Robidas/18* 5.00 12.00
52 Jack Matier/26* 5.00 12.00
53 Danny Zhilkin/16* 6.00 15.00
55 Matthew Savoie/92* 8.00 20.00
56 Jan Mysak/18* 6.00 15.00
57 Jeremie Poirier/53* 6.00 15.00
59 Lukas Cormier/50* 6.00 15.00
60 Josh Pillar/71* 5.00 12.00
61 Evan Vierling/40* 5.00 12.00
62 Robert Orr/87* 8.00 20.00
63 Conner Roulette/33* 6.00 15.00
64 Jacob Melanson/22* 5.00 12.00
65 Brayden Yager/28* 8.00 20.00
67 William Dufour/27* 5.00 12.00
69 Cole Huckins/41* 6.00 15.00
70 Trevor Wong/37* 5.00 12.00

2021-22 SP Game Used CHL Orange

1 Shane Wright 5.00 12.00
2 Connor Bedard 80.00 200.00
3 Danil Gushchin 2.50 6.00
4 Zachary Dean 2.00 5.00
5 Kaiden Guhle 2.50 6.00
6 Riley Kidney 2.00 5.00
7 Ryder Korczak 2.50 6.00
8 Tristan Lennox 3.00 8.00
9 Ridly Greig 2.50 6.00
10 Nolan Allan 2.50 6.00
11 Oskar Olausson 2.50 6.00
12 Markus Vidicek 3.00 8.00
13 Connor McClennon 2.00 5.00
14 Benjamin Gaudreau 2.50 6.00
15 Sebastian Cossa 4.00 10.00
16 Maxime Coursol 2.50 6.00
17 Ty Nelson 2.50 6.00
18 Dylan Guenther 3.00 8.00
19 Calum Ritchie 2.50 6.00
20 Chase Stillman 2.50 6.00
21 Tristen Robins 2.50 6.00
22 Riley Heidt 3.00 8.00
23 Tyler Tullio 2.50 6.00
24 Olivier Nadeau 2.00 5.00
25 Justin Sourdif 2.50 6.00
26 Wyatt Johnston 6.00 15.00
27 Olen Zellweger 2.50 6.00
28 Tyler Peddle 2.50 6.00
29 Will Cuylle 2.50 6.00
30 Dylan Garand 2.00 5.00
31 Nate Danielson 3.00 8.00
32 Jack Beck 2.00 5.00
33 Logan Stankoven 5.00 12.00
34 Elliot Desnoyers 2.00 5.00
35 Joshua Roy 2.50 6.00
36 Manix Landry 2.00 5.00
37 Zack Stringer 2.00 5.00
38 Francesco Pinelli 2.00 5.00
39 Mavrik Bourque 2.50 6.00
40 Brandon Coe 2.00 5.00
41 Luke Evangelista 2.50 6.00
42 Xavier Bourgault 2.50 6.00
43 Owen Outwater 3.00 8.00
44 Brandt Clarke 2.50 6.00
45 Ozzy Wiesblatt 2.00 5.00
46 Colton Dach 2.50 6.00
47 Brennan Othmann 2.50 6.00
48 Zachary Bolduc 2.50 6.00
49 Conor Geekie 3.00 8.00
50 Tucker Robertson 2.00 5.00
51 Justin Robidas 2.00 5.00
52 Jack Matier 2.00 5.00
53 Danny Zhilkin 2.50 6.00
54 Brady Burns 2.00 5.00
55 Matthew Savoie 3.00 8.00
56 Jan Mysak 2.50 6.00
57 Jeremie Poirier 2.50 6.00
58 Zach Benson 8.00 20.00
59 Lukas Cormier 2.50 6.00
60 Josh Pillar 2.00 5.00
61 Evan Vierling 2.00 5.00
62 Robert Orr 3.00 8.00
63 Conner Roulette 2.50 6.00
64 Jacob Melanson 2.00 5.00
65 Brayden Yager 3.00 8.00
66 Sasha Pastujov 2.50 6.00
67 William Dufour 2.00 5.00
68 Carson Lambos 2.50 6.00
69 Cole Huckins 2.50 6.00
70 Trevor Wong 2.00 5.00

2021-22 SP Game Used CHL Silver

*SILVER: .6X TO 1.5X ORANGE

2021-22 SP Game Used CHL Autographs Blue

1 Shane Wright A 25.00 60.00
2 Connor Bedard C 800.00 2000.00
3 Danil Gushchin D 8.00 20.00
4 Zachary Dean D 6.00 15.00
5 Kaiden Guhle A 8.00 20.00
6 Riley Kidney D 6.00 15.00
7 Ryder Korczak D 8.00 20.00
8 Tristan Lennox D 10.00 25.00
9 Ridly Greig B 8.00 20.00
11 Oskar Olausson D 8.00 20.00
12 Markus Vidicek D 10.00 25.00
13 Connor McClennon D 6.00 15.00
14 Benjamin Gaudreau D 8.00 20.00
15 Sebastian Cossa B 12.00 30.00
16 Maxime Coursol D 8.00 20.00
17 Ty Nelson D 8.00 20.00
18 Dylan Guenther B 10.00 25.00
19 Calum Ritchie C 8.00 20.00
20 Chase Stillman B 8.00 20.00
22 Riley Heidt D 10.00 25.00
23 Tyler Tullio D 8.00 20.00
24 Olivier Nadeau D 6.00 15.00
25 Justin Sourdif D 8.00 20.00
27 Olen Zellweger C 8.00 20.00
28 Tyler Peddle D 8.00 20.00
30 Dylan Garand D 6.00 15.00
33 Logan Stankoven D 15.00 40.00
34 Elliot Desnoyers D 6.00 15.00
35 Joshua Roy D 8.00 20.00
36 Manix Landry D 6.00 15.00
37 Zack Stringer D 6.00 15.00
39 Mavrik Bourque B 8.00 20.00
40 Brandon Coe A 6.00 15.00
41 Luke Evangelista D 8.00 20.00
42 Xavier Bourgault B 8.00 20.00
43 Owen Outwater D 10.00 25.00
44 Brandt Clarke B 8.00 20.00
45 Ozzy Wiesblatt C 6.00 15.00
46 Colton Dach D 8.00 20.00
47 Brennan Othmann B 8.00 20.00
48 Zachary Bolduc B 8.00 20.00
49 Conor Geekie B 10.00 25.00
50 Tucker Robertson D 6.00 15.00
51 Justin Robidas D 6.00 15.00
54 Brady Burns D 6.00 15.00
55 Matthew Savoie B 10.00 25.00
56 Jan Mysak D 8.00 20.00
57 Jeremie Poirier D 8.00 20.00
58 Zach Benson D 40.00 100.00
59 Lukas Cormier D 8.00 20.00
60 Josh Pillar D 6.00 15.00
61 Evan Vierling D 6.00 15.00
63 Conner Roulette D 8.00 20.00
64 Jacob Melanson D 6.00 15.00
65 Brayden Yager C 10.00 25.00
67 William Dufour D 6.00 15.00
68 Carson Lambos B 8.00 20.00
69 Cole Huckins D 8.00 20.00

2021-22 SP Game Used CHL Jerseys Red

1 Shane Wright 5.00 12.00
2 Connor Bedard 100.00 250.00
3 Danil Gushchin 2.50 6.00
5 Kaiden Guhle 2.50 6.00
6 Riley Kidney 2.00 5.00
7 Ryder Korczak 2.50 6.00
8 Tristan Lennox 3.00 8.00
13 Connor McClennon 2.00 5.00
14 Benjamin Gaudreau 2.50 6.00
15 Sebastian Cossa 4.00 10.00
16 Maxime Coursol 2.50 6.00
18 Dylan Guenther 3.00 8.00
20 Chase Stillman 2.50 6.00
21 Tristen Robins 2.50 6.00
23 Tyler Tullio 2.50 6.00
24 Olivier Nadeau 2.00 5.00
25 Justin Sourdif 2.50 6.00
26 Wyatt Johnston 8.00 20.00
27 Olen Zellweger 2.50 6.00
29 Will Cuylle 2.50 6.00
30 Dylan Garand 2.00 5.00
33 Logan Stankoven 5.00 12.00
34 Elliot Desnoyers 2.00 5.00
35 Joshua Roy 2.50 6.00
37 Zack Stringer 2.00 5.00
38 Francesco Pinelli 2.00 5.00
39 Mavrik Bourque 2.50 6.00
41 Luke Evangelista 2.50 6.00
42 Xavier Bourgault 2.50 6.00
43 Owen Outwater 3.00 8.00
44 Brandt Clarke 2.50 6.00
46 Colton Dach 2.50 6.00
47 Brennan Othmann 2.50 6.00
48 Zachary Bolduc 2.50 6.00
49 Conor Geekie 3.00 8.00
51 Justin Robidas 2.00 5.00
52 Jack Matier 2.00 5.00
53 Danny Zhilkin 2.50 6.00
54 Brady Burns 2.00 5.00
55 Matthew Savoie 3.00 8.00
56 Jan Mysak 2.50 6.00
57 Jeremie Poirier 2.50 6.00
59 Lukas Cormier 2.50 6.00
60 Josh Pillar 2.00 5.00
61 Evan Vierling 2.00 5.00
63 Conner Roulette 2.50 6.00
64 Jacob Melanson 2.00 5.00
65 Brayden Yager 3.00 8.00
66 Sasha Pastujov 2.50 6.00
68 Carson Lambos 2.50 6.00
69 Cole Huckins 2.50 6.00
70 Trevor Wong 2.00 5.00

2021-22 SP Game Used CHL Jerseys Patch Gold

*PATCH: .75X TO 2X BASIC
2 Connor Bedard 150.00 400.00
26 Wyatt Johnston 20.00 50.00

2021-22 SP Game Used CHL New Style Autographs Blue

NSBC Brandt Clarke C 10.00 25.00
NSBG Benjamin Gaudreau C 10.00 25.00
NSBO Brennan Othmann C 10.00 25.00
NSBY Brayden Yager C 12.00 30.00
NSCG Conor Geekie C 12.00 30.00
NSCL Carson Lambos C 10.00 25.00
NSCR Conner Roulette C 10.00 25.00
NSDG Dylan Guenther C 12.00 30.00
NSJP Jeremie Poirier C 10.00 25.00
NSKG Kaiden Guhle C 10.00 25.00
NSKI Riley Kidney C 8.00 20.00
NSLC Lukas Cormier C 10.00 25.00
NSLE Luke Evangelista C 10.00 25.00
NSLS Logan Stankoven C 20.00 50.00
NSMB Mavrik Bourque C 10.00 25.00
NSMS Matthew Savoie C 12.00 30.00
NSRG Ridly Greig C 10.00 25.00
NSRK Ryder Korczak C 10.00 25.00
NSSC Sebastian Cossa C 15.00 40.00
NSTN Ty Nelson C 10.00 25.00
NSTT Tyler Tullio C 10.00 25.00
NSZD Zachary Dean C 8.00 20.00

2021-22 SP Game Used CHL New Style Orange

NSBC Brandt Clarke 1.50 4.00
NSBG Benjamin Gaudreau 1.50 4.00
NSBO Brennan Othmann 1.50 4.00
NSBY Brayden Yager 2.00 5.00
NSCB Connor Bedard 125.00 300.00
NSCG Conor Geekie 2.00 5.00
NSCL Carson Lambos 1.50 4.00
NSCR Conner Roulette 1.50 4.00
NSDG Dylan Guenther 2.00 5.00
NSDZ Danny Zhilkin 1.50 4.00
NSFP Francesco Pinelli 1.25 3.00
NSJP Jeremie Poirier 1.50 4.00
NSKG Kaiden Guhle 1.50 4.00
NSKI Riley Kidney 1.25 3.00
NSLC Lukas Cormier 1.50 4.00
NSLE Luke Evangelista 1.50 4.00
NSLS Logan Stankoven 3.00 8.00
NSMB Mavrik Bourque 1.50 4.00
NSMS Matthew Savoie 2.00 5.00
NSRG Ridly Greig 1.50 4.00
NSRK Ryder Korczak 1.50 4.00
NSSC Sebastian Cossa 2.50 6.00
NSSP Sasha Pastujov 1.50 4.00
NSSW Shane Wright 3.00 8.00
NSTN Ty Nelson 1.50 4.00
NSTT Tyler Tullio 1.50 4.00
NSWC Will Cuylle 1.50 4.00
NSZD Zachary Dean 1.25 3.00

2021-22 SP Game Used CHL New Style Jersey Autographs

NSBC Brandt Clarke 20.00 50.00
NSBG Benjamin Gaudreau 20.00 50.00
NSBO Brennan Othmann 20.00 50.00
NSBY Brayden Yager 25.00 60.00
NSCG Conor Geekie 25.00 60.00
NSCL Carson Lambos 20.00 50.00
NSCR Conner Roulette 20.00 50.00
NSDG Dylan Guenther 25.00 60.00
NSJP Jeremie Poirier 20.00 50.00
NSKG Kaiden Guhle 20.00 50.00
NSKI Riley Kidney 15.00 40.00
NSLC Lukas Cormier 20.00 50.00
NSLE Luke Evangelista 20.00 50.00
NSLS Logan Stankoven 40.00 100.00
NSMB Mavrik Bourque 20.00 50.00
NSMS Matthew Savoie 25.00 60.00
NSRK Ryder Korczak 20.00 50.00
NSTT Tyler Tullio 20.00 50.00
NSWC Will Cuylle 20.00 50.00

2021-22 SP Game Used CHL New Style Patches Gold

NSBC Brandt Clarke 5.00 12.00
NSBG Benjamin Gaudreau 5.00 12.00
NSBO Brennan Othmann 5.00 12.00
NSBY Brayden Yager 6.00 15.00
NSCG Conor Geekie 6.00 15.00
NSCL Carson Lambos 5.00 12.00
NSCR Conner Roulette 5.00 12.00
NSDG Dylan Guenther 6.00 15.00
NSDZ Danny Zhilkin 5.00 12.00
NSFP Francesco Pinelli 4.00 10.00
NSJP Jeremie Poirier 5.00 12.00
NSKG Kaiden Guhle 5.00 12.00
NSKI Riley Kidney 4.00 10.00
NSLC Lukas Cormier 5.00 12.00
NSLE Luke Evangelista 5.00 12.00
NSLS Logan Stankoven 10.00 25.00
NSMB Mavrik Bourque 5.00 12.00
NSMS Matthew Savoie 6.00 15.00
NSRK Ryder Korczak 5.00 12.00
NSSC Sebastian Cossa 8.00 20.00
NSSW Shane Wright 10.00 25.00
NSTT Tyler Tullio 5.00 12.00
NSWC Will Cuylle 5.00 12.00

2021-22 SP Game Used CHL Patch Autographs Gold

1 Shane Wright/25 25.00 60.00
2 Connor Bedard/49 1500.00 4000.00
3 Danil Gushchin/49 12.00 30.00
6 Riley Kidney/49 10.00 25.00
7 Ryder Korczak/49 12.00 30.00
8 Tristan Lennox/49 15.00 40.00
13 Connor McClennon/49 10.00 25.00
14 Benjamin Gaudreau/49 12.00 30.00
15 Sebastian Cossa/49 20.00 50.00
16 Maxime Coursol/49 12.00 30.00
18 Dylan Guenther/49 15.00 40.00
23 Tyler Tullio/49 12.00 30.00
24 Olivier Nadeau/49 10.00 25.00
25 Justin Sourdif/49 12.00 30.00
27 Olen Zellweger/49 12.00 30.00
30 Dylan Garand/49 10.00 25.00
33 Logan Stankoven/49 25.00 60.00
34 Elliot Desnoyers/49 10.00 25.00
37 Zack Stringer/49 10.00 25.00
39 Mavrik Bourque/49 12.00 30.00
41 Luke Evangelista/49 12.00 30.00
42 Xavier Bourgault/49 12.00 30.00
43 Owen Outwater/49 15.00 40.00
44 Brandt Clarke/49 12.00 30.00
46 Colton Dach/49 12.00 30.00
47 Brennan Othmann/49 12.00 30.00
48 Zachary Bolduc/25 12.00 30.00
49 Conor Geekie/49 15.00 40.00
51 Justin Robidas/49 10.00 25.00
54 Brady Burns/49 10.00 25.00
55 Matthew Savoie/25 15.00 40.00
56 Jan Mysak/49 12.00 30.00
57 Jeremie Poirier/49 12.00 30.00
59 Lukas Cormier/49 12.00 30.00
60 Josh Pillar/49 10.00 25.00
61 Evan Vierling/49 10.00 25.00
63 Conner Roulette/49 12.00 30.00
64 Jacob Melanson/49 10.00 25.00
65 Brayden Yager/25 15.00 40.00
68 Carson Lambos/49 12.00 30.00
69 Cole Huckins/49 12.00 30.00

2023-24 SP Game Used CHL Orange

1 Michael Misa 6.00 15.00
2 Andrew Cristall 2.50 6.00
3 Conor Geekie 3.00 8.00
4 Eduard Sale 2.00 5.00
5 Gavin Hayes 2.50 6.00
7 Koehn Ziemmer 2.50 6.00
8 Colby Barlow 2.00 5.00
9 Ethan Gauthier 2.50 6.00
10 Nick Lardis 2.00 5.00
11 Jakub Chromiak 2.50 6.00
12 Carey Terrance 2.00 5.00
13 Etienne Morin 2.00 5.00
14 David Goyette 2.50 6.00
15 Ty Nelson 2.50 6.00
16 Riley Heidt 3.00 8.00
17 Nate Danielson 3.00 8.00
18 Lukas Dragicevic 3.00 8.00
19 Quentin Musty 2.50 6.00
20 Owen Beck 3.00 8.00
21 Pano Fimis 2.50 6.00
22 Brayden Yager 3.00 8.00
23 Berkly Catton 5.00 12.00
24 Nico Myatovic 1.50 4.00
25 Cam Squires 2.00 5.00
26 Justin Gill 2.00 5.00
27 Teague Patton 2.00 5.00
28 Coulson Pitre 2.00 5.00
29 Connor Levis 3.00 8.00
30 Luca Pinelli 2.00 5.00
31 Luca Cagnoni 2.00 5.00
32 Riley Patterson 2.00 5.00
33 Owen Griffin 2.00 5.00
34 Matyas Sapovaliv 2.50 6.00
35 Noah Chadwick 1.50 4.00
36 Tanner Howe 2.50 6.00
37 Malcolm Spence 2.50 6.00
38 Tij Iginla 4.00 10.00
39 Caden Taylor 2.00 5.00
40 Cameron Reid 2.00 5.00
41 Jeremy Langlois 2.00 5.00
42 Emmitt Finnie 1.50 4.00
43 Quentin Miller 1.50 4.00
44 Gavin McKenna 40.00 100.00
45 Scott Ratzlaff 2.00 5.00
46 Vincent Collard 2.00 5.00
47 Matthew Butler 1.50 4.00
48 Ollie Josephson 1.50 4.00
49 Ryder Ritchie 2.50 6.00
50 Spencer Sova 2.50 6.00
51 Beau Akey 2.00 5.00
52 Gabriel D'Aigle 5.00 12.00
53 Maxim Masse 3.00 8.00
54 Maveric Lamoureux 3.00 8.00
55 Caden Price 2.00 5.00
56 Andrew Basha 2.00 5.00
57 Cameron MacDonald 3.00 8.00
58 Cole Huckins 2.50 6.00
59 Tanner Molendyk 3.00 8.00
60 Zach Pelletier 1.50 4.00
61 Michael Buchinger 3.00 8.00
62 Mathieu Cataford 2.00 5.00
63 Cameron Schmidt 1.50 4.00
64 Easton Cowan 5.00 12.00
65 Kalan Lind 3.00 8.00
66 Tyler Peddle 2.50 6.00
67 Oliver Bonk 2.00 5.00
68 Jake Karabela 2.00 5.00
69 Jagger Firkus 4.00 10.00
70 Samuel Honzek 2.00 5.00

2023-24 SP Game Used CHL Teal

*TEAL/249: .6X TO 1.5X ORANGE

2023-24 SP Game Used CHL Autographs Blue

1 Michael Misa 80.00 200.00
2 Andrew Cristall 8.00 20.00
3 Conor Geekie 10.00 25.00
4 Eduard Sale 6.00 15.00
5 Gavin Hayes 8.00 20.00
7 Koehn Ziemmer 8.00 20.00
9 Ethan Gauthier SP 8.00 20.00
10 Nick Lardis SP 6.00 15.00
11 Jakub Chromiak 8.00 20.00
12 Carey Terrance 6.00 15.00
15 Ty Nelson 8.00 20.00
16 Riley Heidt 10.00 25.00
18 Lukas Dragicevic 10.00 25.00
19 Quentin Musty 8.00 20.00
20 Owen Beck SP 10.00 25.00
21 Pano Fimis 8.00 20.00
22 Brayden Yager SP 10.00 25.00
23 Berkly Catton 25.00 60.00
24 Nico Myatovic 5.00 12.00
25 Cam Squires 6.00 15.00
28 Coulson Pitre 6.00 15.00
29 Connor Levis 10.00 25.00
31 Luca Cagnoni 6.00 15.00
34 Matyas Sapovaliv 8.00 20.00
35 Noah Chadwick 5.00 12.00
36 Tanner Howe 8.00 20.00
38 Tij Iginla 20.00 50.00
41 Jeremy Langlois 6.00 15.00
42 Emmitt Finnie 5.00 12.00
45 Scott Ratzlaff 6.00 15.00
46 Vincent Collard 6.00 15.00
48 Ollie Josephson 5.00 12.00
49 Ryder Ritchie 8.00 20.00
50 Spencer Sova 8.00 20.00
51 Beau Akey 6.00 15.00
52 Gabriel D'Aigle 25.00 60.00
53 Maxim Masse 10.00 25.00
54 Maveric Lamoureux 10.00 25.00
55 Caden Price 6.00 15.00
56 Andrew Basha 6.00 15.00
57 Cameron MacDonald 10.00 25.00
58 Cole Huckins 8.00 20.00
59 Tanner Molendyk 10.00 25.00
60 Zach Pelletier 5.00 12.00
61 Michael Buchinger 10.00 25.00
62 Mathieu Cataford 6.00 15.00
64 Easton Cowan 25.00 60.00
65 Kalan Lind 10.00 25.00
66 Tyler Peddle 8.00 20.00
67 Oliver Bonk 6.00 15.00
68 Jake Karabela 6.00 15.00
69 Jagger Firkus 40.00 100.00
70 Samuel Honzek 6.00 15.00

2023-24 SP Game Used CHL Jerseys Red

*PATCH/49: .8X TO 2X BASIC
2 Andrew Cristall 3.00 8.00
4 Eduard Sale 2.50 6.00
5 Gavin Hayes 3.00 8.00
7 Koehn Ziemmer 3.00 8.00
9 Ethan Gauthier 3.00 8.00
10 Nick Lardis 2.50 6.00
11 Jakub Chromiak 3.00 8.00
14 David Goyette 3.00 8.00
15 Ty Nelson 3.00 8.00
16 Riley Heidt 4.00 10.00
17 Nate Danielson 4.00 10.00
18 Lukas Dragicevic 4.00 10.00
19 Quentin Musty 3.00 8.00
21 Pano Fimis 3.00 8.00
22 Brayden Yager 4.00 10.00
23 Berkly Catton 6.00 15.00
25 Cam Squires 2.50 6.00
26 Justin Gill 2.50 6.00
27 Teague Patton 2.50 6.00
28 Coulson Pitre 2.50 6.00
29 Connor Levis 4.00 10.00
30 Luca Pinelli 2.50 6.00
31 Luca Cagnoni 2.50 6.00
32 Riley Patterson 2.50 6.00
34 Matyas Sapovaliv 3.00 8.00
36 Tanner Howe 3.00 8.00
37 Malcolm Spence 3.00 8.00
38 Tij Iginla 10.00 25.00
39 Caden Taylor 2.50 6.00
40 Cameron Reid 2.50 6.00
45 Scott Ratzlaff 2.50 6.00
52 Gabriel D'Aigle 8.00 20.00
53 Maxim Masse 4.00 10.00
54 Maveric Lamoureux 4.00 10.00
56 Andrew Basha 2.50 6.00

2023-24 SP Game Used CHL Patch Autographs

2 Andrew Cristall 20.00 50.00
4 Eduard Sale 15.00 40.00
5 Gavin Hayes 20.00 50.00
7 Koehn Ziemmer 20.00 50.00
9 Ethan Gauthier 20.00 50.00
11 Jakub Chromiak 20.00 50.00
14 David Goyette 20.00 50.00
15 Ty Nelson 20.00 50.00
16 Riley Heidt 25.00 60.00
18 Lukas Dragicevic 25.00 60.00
19 Quentin Musty 20.00 50.00
21 Pano Fimis 20.00 50.00
22 Brayden Yager 25.00 60.00
23 Berkly Catton 40.00 100.00
25 Cam Squires 15.00 40.00
28 Coulson Pitre 15.00 40.00
29 Connor Levis 25.00 60.00
31 Luca Cagnoni 15.00 40.00
34 Matyas Sapovaliv 20.00 50.00
36 Tanner Howe 20.00 50.00
38 Tij Iginla 30.00 80.00
45 Scott Ratzlaff 15.00 40.00
52 Gabriel D'Aigle 40.00 100.00
53 Maxim Masse 25.00 60.00
54 Maveric Lamoureux 25.00 60.00
56 Andrew Basha 15.00 40.00

2023-24 SP Game Used CHL Stardom Awaits Orange

*TEAL/49: .8X TO 2X BASIC
SAAC Andrew Cristall 4.00 10.00
SABY Brayden Yager 5.00 12.00
SACB Colby Barlow 3.00 8.00
SACL Connor Levis 5.00 12.00
SACP Coulson Pitre 3.00 8.00
SACR Calum Ritchie 4.00 10.00
SADG David Goyette 4.00 10.00
SAEC Easton Cowan 8.00 20.00
SAEG Ethan Gauthier 4.00 10.00
SAEM Etienne Morin 3.00 8.00
SAES Eduard Sale 3.00 8.00
SAGH Gavin Hayes 4.00 10.00
SAJG Justin Gill 3.00 8.00
SAKZ Koehn Ziemmer 4.00 10.00
SALC Luca Cagnoni 3.00 8.00
SALD Lukas Dragicevic 5.00 12.00
SALP Luca Pinelli 3.00 8.00
SAMM Michael Misa 10.00 25.00
SAND Nate Danielson 5.00 12.00
SANL Nick Lardis 3.00 8.00
SANM Nico Myatovic 2.50 6.00
SAOB Oliver Bonk 3.00 8.00
SAQM Quentin Musty 4.00 10.00
SARH Riley Heidt 5.00 12.00
SARP Riley Patterson 3.00 8.00
SASH Samuel Honzek 3.00 8.00
SATM Tanner Molendyk 5.00 12.00
SATN Ty Nelson 4.00 10.00
SAYS Yegor Sidorov 3.00 8.00

2023-24 SP Game Used CHL Stardom Awaits Autographs Blue

SAAC Andrew Cristall 12.00 30.00
SABY Brayden Yager SP 15.00 40.00
SACL Connor Levis 15.00 40.00
SACP Coulson Pitre 10.00 25.00
SACR Calum Ritchie 12.00 30.00
SADG David Goyette SP 12.00 30.00
SAEC Easton Cowan SP 25.00 60.00
SAEG Ethan Gauthier SP 12.00 30.00
SAES Eduard Sale SP 10.00 25.00
SAGH Gavin Hayes 12.00 30.00
SAKZ Koehn Ziemmer 12.00 30.00
SALC Luca Cagnoni 10.00 25.00
SALD Lukas Dragicevic 15.00 40.00
SAMM Michael Misa SP 30.00 80.00
SANL Nick Lardis 10.00 25.00
SANM Nico Myatovic 8.00 20.00
SAOB Oliver Bonk SP 10.00 25.00
SAQM Quentin Musty SP 12.00 30.00
SARH Riley Heidt 15.00 40.00
SASH Samuel Honzek 10.00 25.00
SATM Tanner Molendyk 15.00 40.00
SATN Ty Nelson 12.00 30.00
SAYS Yegor Sidorov 10.00 25.00

2023-24 SP Game Used CHL Stardom Awaits Patches

SAAC Andrew Cristall 10.00 25.00
SABY Brayden Yager 12.00 30.00
SACB Colby Barlow 8.00 20.00
SACL Connor Levis 12.00 30.00
SACP Coulson Pitre 8.00 20.00
SACR Calum Ritchie 10.00 25.00
SADG David Goyette 10.00 25.00
SAEC Easton Cowan 20.00 50.00
SAEG Ethan Gauthier 10.00 25.00
SAEM Etienne Morin 8.00 20.00
SAGH Gavin Hayes 10.00 25.00
SAKZ Koehn Ziemmer 10.00 25.00
SALD Lukas Dragicevic 12.00 30.00
SALP Luca Pinelli 8.00 20.00
SAMM Michael Misa 25.00 60.00
SAND Nate Danielson 12.00 30.00
SANL Nick Lardis 8.00 20.00
SANM Nico Myatovic 6.00 15.00
SAOB Oliver Bonk 8.00 20.00
SAQM Quentin Musty 10.00 25.00
SARH Riley Heidt 12.00 30.00
SARP Riley Patterson 8.00 20.00
SATN Ty Nelson 10.00 25.00
SAYS Yegor Sidorov 8.00 20.00

1991 Star Pics

SEALED SET (72) 2.00 10.00
1 Al Morganti .02 .10
2 Pat Falloon .02 .10
3 Jamie Pushor .02 .10
4 Jean Beliveau FLB .08 .25
5 Martin Lapointe .20 .50
6 Jamie Matthews .02 .10
7 Rod Gilbert FLB .08 .25
8 Niklas Sundblad .02 .10
9 Steve Konowalchuk .02 .10
10 Alex Delvecchio FLB .08 .25
11 Donevan Hextall .02 .10
12 Dody Wood .02 .10
13 Scott Niedermayer .20 .50
14 Trevor Halverson .02 .10
15 Terry Chitaroni .02 .10
16 Tyler Wright .02 .10
17 Andrei Lomakin UER .02 .10
18 Martin Hamrlik .02 .10
19 Dimitri Filimonov UER .02 .10
20 Ed Belfour FLB .20 .50
21 Andrew Verner .02 .10
22 Yanic Perreault .02 .10
23 Michael Nylander .02 .10
24 Scott Lachance .02 .10
25 Pavel Bure .60 1.50
26 Mike Torchia .02 .10
27 Frank Mahovlich FLB .08 .25
28 Philippe Boucher .02 .10
29 Jiri Slegr .02 .10
30 Sergei Fedorov FLB .30 .75
31 Rene Corbet .02 .10
32 Jamie McLennan .02 .10
33 Shane Peacock .02 .10
34 Mario Nobili .02 .10
35 Peter Forsberg .75 2.00
36 All-Rookie Team Pat Falloon Tyler Wright Philippe Boucher Andrew Verner Scott Lachance .02 .10
37 Arturs Irbe .20 .50
38 Alexei Zhitnik .02 .10
39 Pat Peake .02 .10
40 Adam Oates FLB .08 .25
41 Markus Naslund .20 .50
42 Eric Lavigne .02 .10
43 Jeff Nelson .02 .10
44 Yanic Dupre UER .02 .10
45 Justin Morrison .02 .10
46 Alek Stojanov .02 .10
47 Marcel Cousineau .02 .10
48 Alexei Kovalev .08 .25
49 Andrei Trefilov .02 .10
50 Mats Sundin FLB .20 .50
51 Steve Staios .02 .10
52 Glenn Hall FLB .08 .25
53 Brent Bilodeau .02 .10
54 Darcy Werenka .02 .10
55 Chris Osgood .40 1.00
56 Nathan Lafayette .02 .10
57 Richard Matvichuk .02 .10
58 Dimitri Mironov UER .02 .10
59 Jason Dawe .02 .10
60 Mike Ricci FLB .02 .10
61 Gerry Cheevers FLB .08 .25
62 Jim Campbell .02 .10
63 Francois Groleau .02 .10
64 Glen Murray .20 .50
65 Jason Young .02 .10
66 Dean McAmmond .02 .10
67 Guy Leveque .02 .10

68 Patrick Poulin .02 .10
69 Bobby House .02 .10
70 Jaromir Jagr FLB .40 1.00
71 Jassen Cullimore .02 .10
72 Checklist Card .02 .10

2000-01 UD CHL Prospects

COMPLETE SET (100) 10.00 25.00
1 Jay Harrison .25 .60
2 Jay McClement .20 .50
3 Adam Henrich .25 .60
4 Carlo Colaiacovo .30 .75
5 Nikita Alexeev .20 .50
6 Brad Boyes .40 1.00
7 Peter Hamrlik .25 .60
8 Cory Stillman .20 .50
9 Derek Roy .30 .75
10 Michael Zigomanis .25 .60
11 Jason Spezza 1.00 2.50
12 Chad Wiseman .20 .50
13 Patrick Jarrett .25 .60
14 Chris Thornburn .25 .60
15 John Kozoriz .20 .50
16 Brandon Cullen .20 .50
17 Jonathan Zion .20 .50
18 Miguel Delisle .20 .50
19 Ryan Ramsay .20 .50
20 Marcel Rodman .20 .50
21 Stephen Weiss .40 1.00
22 Libor Ustrnul .20 .50
23 Rob Zepp .25 .60
24 Kris Vernarsky .25 .60
25 Jason Penner .20 .50
26 Trevor Daley .25 .60
27 Alexei Semenov .25 .60
28 Mark Popovic .20 .50
29 Tim Gleason .30 .75
30 Craig Kennedy .20 .50
31 Steve Ott .20 .50
32 Brian Finley .25 .60
33 Kyle Wellwood .30 .75
34 Raffi Torres .30 .75
35 Chris Kelly .20 .50
36 Scott Cameron .20 .50
37 Cole Jarrett .20 .50
38 Maxim Rybin .20 .50
39 Derek MacKenzie .20 .50
40 Ryan Held .20 .50
41 Colt King .20 .50
42 Rick Nash 1.25 3.00
43 Greg Jacina .20 .50
44 Branko Radivojevic .25 .60
45 Jordin Tootoo .60 1.50
46 Pavel Brendl .20 .50
47 Ryan Craig .20 .50
48 Owen Fussey .20 .50
49 Brent Krahn .25 .60
50 Erik Christensen .20 .50
51 Jared Aulin .25 .60
52 Kiel McLeod .20 .50
53 Dan Blackburn .25 .60
54 Jeff Woywitka .25 .60
55 Ryan Hollweg .25 .60
56 Jay Bouwmeester .50 1.25
57 Ben Knopp .20 .50
58 Marcel Hossa .25 .60
59 Greg Watson .20 .50
60 Justin Mapletoft .25 .60
61 Matt Hubbauer .20 .50
62 Garth Murray .20 .50
63 Matthew Spiller .25 .60
64 Barrett Heisten .30 .75
65 Gerard Dicaire .20 .50
66 Jamie Lundmark .30 .75
67 Duncan Milroy .20 .50
68 Nathan Smith .20 .50
69 Konstantin Panov .20 .50
70 Mike Comrie .50 1.25
71 Tomas Kopecky .30 .75
72 Jozef Balej .30 .75
73 Shane Bendera .25 .60
74 Blake Evans .20 .50
75 Igor Pohanka .20 .50
76 Robin LeBlanc .20 .50
77 Yanick Lehoux .25 .60
78 Jean-Francois Racine .25 .60
79 Pascal LeClaire .30 .75
80 Chris Montgomery .20 .50
81 Brent MacLellan .20 .50
82 Thatcher Bell .20 .50
83 Antoine Vermette .30 .75
84 Carl Mallette .20 .50
85 Nicolas Poirier .20 .50
86 Radim Vrbata .20 .50
87 Maxime Ouellet .30 .75
88 Brandon Reid .30 .75
89 Jason Spezza 1.00 2.50
90 Pascal LeClaire .30 .75
91 Dan Blackburn .25 .60
92 Stephen Weiss .40 1.00
93 Tim Gleason .30 .75
94 Duncan Milroy .20 .50
95 Kiel McLeod .20 .50
96 Jay McClement .20 .50
97 Jay Harrison .25 .60
98 Greg Watson .20 .50
99 Jason Spezza 1.00 2.50
100 Jay Bouwmeester .50 1.25

2000-01 UD CHL Prospects Autographs

ABK Brent Krahn 4.00 10.00
ABO Bobby Orr 100.00 200.00
ADB Dan Blackburn 5.00 12.00
AJB Jay Bouwmeester 10.00 25.00
AJS Jason Spezza 12.50 30.00
APB Pavel Brendl 4.00 10.00
APL Pascal LeClaire 5.00 12.00
ART Raffi Torres 5.00 12.00
ARZ Rob Zepp 6.00 15.00

2000-01 UD CHL Prospects CHL Class

COMPLETE SET (10) 12.50 25.00
CC1 Brian Finley .75 2.00
CC2 Michael Zigomanis .40 1.00
CC3 Jason Spezza 3.00 8.00
CC4 Jay Bouwmeester 2.00 5.00
CC5 Rob Zepp .75 2.00
CC6 Pavel Brendl .40 1.00
CC7 Dan Blackburn 1.25 3.00
CC8 Mike Comrie .75 2.00
CC9 Pascal LeClaire .75 2.00
CC10 Maxime Ouellet .75 2.00

2000-01 UD CHL Prospects Destination the Show

COMPLETE SET (6) 8.00 20.00
D1 Jason Spezza 4.00 8.00
D2 Dan Blackburn 1.50 3.00
D3 Pavel Brendl .50 1.00
D4 Jay Bouwmeester 2.50 5.00
D5 Zdenek Blatny .50 1.00
D6 Pascal LeClaire 1.00 2.00

2000-01 UD CHL Prospects Future Leaders

COMPLETE SET (10) 6.00 15.00
FL1 Jason Spezza 3.00 5.00
FL2 Raffi Torres .75 2.00
FL3 Brad Boyes .75 2.00
FL4 Stephen Weiss .75 2.00
FL5 Michael Zigomanis .40 1.00
FL6 Jamie Lundmark .60 1.50
FL7 Mike Comrie .75 2.00
FL8 Nathan Smith .40 1.00
FL9 Radim Vrbata .40 1.00
FL10 Brandon Reid .40 1.00

2000-01 UD CHL Prospects Game Jerseys

BK Brent Krahn 6.00 15.00
DB Dan Blackburn 8.00 20.00
JA Jason Spezza Win 8.00 20.00
JB Jay Bouwmeester 6.00 15.00
JL Jamie Lundmark 5.00 12.00
JS Jason Spezza Mis 8.00 20.00
NE Nikita Alexeev 4.00 10.00
PB Pavel Brendl 5.00 12.00
RT Raffi Torres 6.00 15.00
RZ Rob Zepp 5.00 12.00
BB D.Blackburn B.Krahn 10.00 25.00
BZ D.Blackburn R.Zepp 8.00 20.00
LB J.Lundmark D.Blackburn 10.00 25.00
LK J.Lundmark B.Krahn 6.00 15.00
SB J.Spezza J.Bouwmeester 20.00 50.00
SL J.Spezza J.Lundmark 15.00 40.00
SS J.Spezza J.Spezza 20.00 50.00
ST J.Spezza R.Torres 15.00 40.00
SZ J.Spezza R.Zepp 12.50 30.00
TZ R.Torres R.Zepp 6.00 15.00

2000-01 UD CHL Prospects Great Desire

COMPLETE SET (6) 10.00 25.00
GD1 Jason Spezza 4.00 8.00
GD2 Jay Bouwmeester 2.50 5.00
GD3 Mike Comrie 1.25 3.00
GD4 Raffi Torres .75 2.00
GD5 Brandon Reid .75 2.00
GD6 Pascal LeClaire 1.25 3.00

2000-01 UD CHL Prospects Supremacy

COMPLETE SET (10) 10.00 25.00
CS1 Jason Spezza 3.00 8.00
CS2 Brian Finley .75 2.00
CS3 Raffi Torres 1.00 2.50
CS4 Rob Zepp .75 2.00
CS5 Pavel Brendl .60 1.50
CS6 Justin Mapletoft .75 2.00
CS7 Barrett Heisten 1.00 2.50
CS8 Mike Comrie 1.50 4.00
CS9 Jay Bouwmeester 1.50 4.00
CS10 Pascal LeClaire 1.00 2.50

1999-00 UD Prospects

COMPLETE SET (90) 12.50 30.00
1 Wayne Gretzky 1.25 3.00
2 Jason Spezza 1.25 3.00
3 Sheldon Keefe .08 .25
4 Mark Bell .20 .50
5 Justin Papineau .15 .40
6 Denis Shvidki .15 .40
7 Darryl Bootland .20 .50
8 Michael Zigomanis .15 .40
9 Chris Eade .08 .25
10 Brad Boyes .60 1.50
11 Michael Henrich .08 .25
12 Nikita Alexeev .08 .25
13 Libor Ustrnul .08 .25
14 Brian Finley .15 .40
15 Chris Berti .08 .25
16 Agris Saviels .08 .25
17 Kris Newbury .08 .25
18 Jared Newman .08 .25
19 Samu Isosalo .08 .25
20 Mike Van Ryn .15 .40
21 Miguel Delisle .08 .25
22 Rostislav Klesla .20 .50
23 Raffi Torres .20 .50
24 Kurtis Foster .08 .25
25 Lou Dickenson .08 .25
26 Milan Kraft .15 .40
27 Jamie Lundmark .20 .50
28 Scott Hartnell .50 1.25
29 Ben Knopp .08 .25
30 Mike Wirll .08 .25
31 Ryan Craig .08 .25
32 Kris Beech .15 .40
33 Pavel Brendl .15 .40
34 Blake Robson .08 .25
35 Jarret Stoll .15 .40
36 Oleg Saprykin .15 .40
37 Eric Johannson .08 .25
38 Warren Peters .08 .25
39 Marcel Hossa .30 .75
40 Shane Endicott .08 .25
41 Craig Olynick .08 .25
42 Brent Krahn .30 .75
43 Matt Pettinger .15 .40
44 Jaroslav Kristek .08 .25
45 Milan Bartovic .08 .25
46 Jared Aulin .15 .40
47 Jakub Cutta .15 .40
48 Blake Ward .08 .25
49 Lynn Lyons .15 .40
50 Jay Bouwmeester .75 2.00
51 Nick Schultz .15 .40
52 Filip Novak .08 .25
53 Michael Bubnick .08 .25
54 Charline Labonte .75 2.00
55 Thatcher Bell .08 .25
56 Yanick Lehoux .08 .25
57 Antoine Vermette .20 .50
58 Alexei Volkov .15 .40
59 Michal Sivek .15 .40
60 Carl Mallette .08 .25
61 Maxime Ouellet .30 .75
62 Simon Lagace-Daigle .08 .25
63 Andrei Shefer .08 .25
64 Mathieu Chouinard .15 .40
65 Philippe Sauve .20 .50
66 Daniel Sedin .30 .75
67 Henrik Sedin .30 .75
68 Thatcher Bell .08 .25
69 Brad Boyes .60 1.50
70 Jared Aulin .15 .40
71 Dany Heatley 1.25 3.00
72 Ryan Hare .08 .25
73 Scott Hartnell .75 2.00
74 Jay Bouwmeester .75 2.00
75 Kiel McLeod .08 .25
76 Kris Newbury .08 .25
77 Blake Robson .08 .25
78 Jarret Stoll .15 .40
79 Antoine Vermette .20 .50
80 Mike Wirll .08 .25
81 Jason Spezza 1.25 3.00
82 Jay Harrison .08 .25
83 Brandon Janes .08 .25
84 Craig Olynick .08 .25
85 Mark Popovic .08 .25
86 Nick Schultz .15 .40
87 Karl St. Pierre .08 .25
88 Pascal Leclaire .30 .75
89 Blake Ward .08 .25
90 Checklist .08 .25

1999-00 UD Prospects CHL Class

COMPLETE SET (10) 6.00 15.00
C1 Jason Spezza 2.00 5.00
C2 Justin Papineau .60 1.50
C3 Mark Bell .60 1.50
C4 Kris Beech .60 1.50
C5 Jay Bouwmeester 1.25 3.00
C6 Denis Shvidki .60 1.50
C7 Pavel Brendl .60 1.50
C8 Brian Finley .60 1.50
C9 Jamie Lundmark .75 2.00
C10 Thatcher Bell .60 1.50

1999-00 UD Prospects Destination the Show

COMPLETE SET (10) 20.00 35.00
DS1 Jason Spezza 4.00 10.00
DS2 Pavel Brendl 1.25 3.00
DS3 Henrik Sedin 1.50 4.00
DS4 Daniel Sedin 1.50 4.00
DS5 Jamie Lundmark 1.50 4.00
DS6 Taylor Pyatt 1.25 3.00
DS7 Brian Finley 1.50 4.00
DS8 Kris Beech 1.50 4.00
DS9 Denis Shvidki 1.25 3.00
DS10 Jay Bouwmeester 2.00 5.00

1999-00 UD Prospects Game Jerseys

CL Charline Labonte 25.00 60.00
HS Henrik Sedin 15.00 30.00
JB Jay Bouwmeester 40.00 50.00
JS Jason Spezza 60.00 100.00
KB Kris Beech 15.00 30.00
LD Lou Dickenson 10.00 20.00
PB Pavel Brendl 10.00 20.00
TB Thatcher Bell 10.00 20.00
DSD Daniel Sedin 15.00 30.00

1999-00 UD Prospects International Stars

COMPLETE SET (10) 20.00 40.00
IN1 Daniel Sedin .75 2.00
IN2 Henrik Sedin .75 2.00
IN3 Pavel Brendl .60 1.50
IN4 Alexei Volkov .75 2.00
IN5 Denis Shvidki .60 1.50
IN6 Milan Kraft .75 2.00
IN7 Nikita Alexeev .60 1.50
IN8 Oleg Saprykin .75 2.00
IN9 Jaroslav Kristek .60 1.50
IN10 Marcel Hossa .75 2.00

1999-00 UD Prospects Signatures of Tradition

AV Alexei Volkov 6.00 15.00
BF Brian Finley 6.00 15.00
BM Branislav Mezei 4.00 10.00
CL Charline Labonte 8.00 20.00
DS Daniel Sedin 10.00 25.00
HS Henrik Sedin 6.00 15.00
JB Jay Bouwmeester 8.00 20.00
JL Jamie Lundmark 6.00 15.00
JS Jason Spezza 6.00 15.00
KB Kris Beech 6.00 15.00
MB Mark Bell 6.00 15.00
MC Mathieu Chouinard 6.00 15.00
MO Maxime Ouellet 6.00 15.00
MV Mike Van Ryn 4.00 10.00
PB Pavel Brendl 4.00 10.00
TP Taylor Pyatt 4.00 10.00
WG Wayne Gretzky 300.00 800.00
DSH Denis Shvidki 4.00 10.00

2001-02 UD Prospects

COMPLETE SET (45) 12.50 30.00
1 Jason Spezza 1.25 3.00
2 Dan Blackburn .30 .75
3 Daniel Boisclair .30 .75
4 Jeff Woywitka .30 .75
5 Matthew Spiller .25 .60
6 Nathan Paetsch .25 .60
7 Mark Popovic .25 .60
8 Jay McClement .25 .60
9 Garth Murray .25 .60
10 Aaron Lobb .25 .60
11 Derek Roy .40 1.00
12 Jean-Francois Soucy .30 .75
13 Nicolas Corbeil .25 .60
14 Colt King .25 .60
15 Robin Leblanc .25 .60
16 Jay Harrison .25 .60
17 Jiri Jakes .25 .60
18 Lukas Krajicek .25 .60
19 Jason Pominville .60 1.50
20 Shawn Collymore .25 .60
21 Michael Garnett .30 .75
22 Adam Munro .40 1.00
23 Dan Hamhuis .30 .75
24 Doug Lynch .25 .60
25 Shaone Morrisonn .30 .75
26 Carlo Colaiacovo .40 1.00
27 Stephen Weiss .60 1.50
28 Joel Stepp .25 .60
29 Jeff Lucky .25 .60
30 Cory Stillman .25 .60
31 Chris Thorburn .25 .60
32 Colby Armstrong .30 .75
33 Brent Maclellan .25 .60
34 Jordin Tootoo .75 2.00
35 Greg Watson .25 .60
36 Martin Podlesak .25 .60
37 Duncan Milroy .25 .60
38 Frantisek Bakrlik .25 .60
39 Brendan Bell .25 .60
40 Kiel McLeod .25 .60
41 Jason Spezza 1.25 3.00
42 Jason Spezza 1.25 3.00
43 Jason Spezza 1.25 3.00
44 Jason Spezza 1.25 3.00
45 2001 Top Prospects Summary .25 .50

2001-02 UD Prospects Autographs

AAM Adam Munro 8.00 20.00
ABK Brent Krahn 6.00 15.00
ABO Bobby Orr 125.00 250.00
ACK Colt King 4.00 10.00
ACS Cory Stillman 4.00 10.00
ACT Chris Thorburn 4.00 10.00
ADB Dan Blackburn 6.00 15.00
ADH Dan Hamhuis 8.00 20.00
ADM Duncan Milroy 4.00 10.00
AGW Greg Watson 4.00 10.00
AJB Jay Bouwmeester 12.50 25.00
AJH Jay Harrison 4.00 10.00
AJL Jamie Lundmark 6.00 15.00
AJM Jay McClement 4.00 10.00
AJS Jason Spezza 12.50 30.00
AKM Kiel McLeod 4.00 10.00
AMG Michael Garnett 6.00 15.00
AMP Mark Popovic 4.00 10.00
APL Pascal Leclaire 6.00 15.00
ARK Rostislav Klesla 6.00 15.00
ART Raffi Torres 8.00 20.00
ASW Stephen Weiss 8.00 20.00
AWG Wayne Gretzky 250.00 600.00

2001-02 UD Prospects Jersey Autographs

SAM Adam Munro 20.00 50.00
SCK Colt King 15.00 40.00
SCS Cory Stillman 15.00 40.00
SCT Chris Thorburn 15.00 40.00
SDB Dan Blackburn 15.00 40.00
SDH Dan Hamhuis 30.00 80.00
SDM Duncan Milroy 15.00 40.00
SGW Greg Watson 15.00 40.00
SJH Jay Harrison 15.00 40.00
SJM Jay McClement 15.00 40.00
SJS Jason Spezza 60.00 150.00
SKM Kiel McLeod 15.00 40.00
SMG Michael Garnett 20.00 50.00
SMP Mark Popovic 15.00 40.00
SSW Stephen Weiss 25.00 60.00
SWA Jason Spezza 60.00 150.00
SWH Jason Spezza 60.00 150.00

2001-02 UD Prospects Jerseys

JAL Aaron Lobb 4.00 10.00
JAM Adam Munro 5.00 12.00
JBB Brendan Bell 4.00 10.00
JBM Brent Maclellan 4.00 10.00
JBO Daniel Boisclair 5.00 12.00
JCA Colby Armstrong 4.00 10.00
JCK Colt King 4.00 10.00
JCS Cory Stillman 4.00 10.00
JCT Chris Thorburn 4.00 10.00
JDB Dan Blackburn 6.00 15.00
JDH Dan Hamhuis 5.00 12.00
JDL Doug Lynch 4.00 10.00
JDM Duncan Milroy 4.00 10.00
JDR Derek Roy 5.00 12.00
JFB Frantisek Bakrlik 4.00 10.00
JGM Garth Murray 4.00 10.00
JGW Greg Watson 4.00 10.00
JJF Jean-Francois Soucy 5.00 12.00
JJH Jay Harrison 4.00 10.00
JJJ Jiri Jakes 4.00 10.00
JJL Jeff Lucky 4.00 10.00
JJM Jay McClement 4.00 10.00
JJP Jason Pominville 8.00 20.00
JJS Jason Spezza 8.00 20.00
JJT Jordin Tootoo 15.00 40.00
JJW Jeff Woywitka 5.00 12.00
JKM Kiel McLeod 4.00 10.00
JLK Lukas Krajicek 5.00 12.00
JMG Michael Garnett 4.00 10.00
JMP Mark Popovic 4.00 10.00
JMS Matthew Spiller 4.00 10.00
JNC Nicolas Corbeil 4.00 10.00
JNP Nathan Paetsch 4.00 10.00
JPO Martin Podlesak 4.00 10.00
JRL Robin Leblanc 4.00 10.00
JSC Shawn Collymore 4.00 10.00
JSM Shaone Morrisonn 5.00 12.00
JST Joel Stepp 4.00 10.00
JSW Stephen Weiss 4.00 10.00
JWA Jason Spezza 8.00 20.00
JWH Jason Spezza 8.00 20.00
CBD D.Blackburn/D.Milroy 8.00 20.00
CBG D.Boisclair/M.Garnett 8.00 20.00
CBM D.Blackburn/A.Munro 8.00 20.00
CBS D.Blackburn/J.Spezza 15.00 40.00
CBW D.Blackburn/S.Weiss 10.00 25.00
CHM J.Harrison/K.McLeod 8.00 20.00
CHW D.Hamhuis/S.Weiss 8.00 20.00
CKP L.Krajicek/M.Podlesak 6.00 15.00
CKW C.King/G.Watson 8.00 20.00
CMS J.McClement/C.Stillman 8.00 20.00
CMT G.Murray/C.Thorburn 8.00 20.00
CPM M.Popovic/D.Milroy 8.00 20.00
CRT D.Roy/J.Tootoo 50.00 125.00
CSA Jason Spezza Dual 15.00 40.00
CSB Jason Spezza Dual 15.00 40.00
CSH J.Spezza/D.Hamhuis 12.50 30.00
CSM J.Spezza/D.Milroy 10.00 25.00
CSS Jason Spezza Dual 15.00 40.00
CSW J.Spezza/S.Weiss 15.00 40.00
CWA J.Woywitka/C.Armstrong 8.00 20.00
CWM S.Weiss/D.Milroy 10.00 25.00

1991 Ultimate Draft

COMPLETE SET (90) 3.00 8.00
*FRENCH: .4X TO 1X BASIC CARDS
1 Ultimate Preview .01 .05
2 Pat Falloon .02 .10
3 Scott Niedermayer .02 .10
4 Scott Lachance .01 .05
5 Peter Forsberg .40 1.00
6 Alek Stojanov .01 .05
7 Richard Matvichuk .02 .10
8 Patrick Poulin .01 .05
9 Martin Lapointe .08 .25
10 Tyler Wright .01 .05
11 Philippe Boucher .01 .05
12 Pat Peake .01 .05
13 Markus Naslund .08 .25
14 Brent Bilodeau .01 .05
15 Glen Murray .08 .25
16 Niklas Sundblad .01 .05
17 Trevor Halverson .01 .05
18 Dean McAmmond UER .01 .05
19 Jim Campbell .01 .05
20 Rene Corbet .01 .05
21 Eric Lavigne .01 .05
22 Steve Staios .01 .05
23 Jassen Cullimore .01 .05
24 Jamie Pushor .01 .05
25 Donevan Hextall .01 .05
26 Andrew Verner .02 .10
27 Jason Dawe .01 .05
28 Jeff Nelson .01 .05
29 Darcy Werenka .01 .05
30 Francois Groleau .01 .05
31 Guy Leveque .01 .05
32 Jamie Matthews .01 .05
33 Dody Wood .02 .10
34 Yanic Perreault .01 .05
35 Jamie McLennan UER .02 .10
36 Yanic Dupre .01 .05
37 1st Round Checklist .01 .05
38 Chris Osgood .40 1.00
39 Fredrik Lindquist .01 .05
40 Jason Young .01 .05
41 Steve Konowalchuk .02 .10
42 Michael Nylander .02 .10
43 Shane Peacock .01 .05
44 Yves Sarault .01 .05
45 Marcel Cousineau .02 .10
46 Nathan Lafayette .01 .05
47 Bobby House .01 .05
48 Kerry Toporowski .01 .05
49 Terry Chitaroni .01 .05
50 Mike Torchia .02 .10
51 Mario Nobili .01 .05
52 Justin Morrison .01 .05
53 Grayden Reid .01 .05
54 Yanic Perreault Underdog .01 .05
55 2nd Round Checklist .01 .05
56 Scott Niedermayer Pat Falloon Scott Lachance .02 .10
57 The Goalies .02 .10
58 Pat Falloon FDP .02 .10
59 Scott Niedermayer FDP .02 .10
60 Scott Lachance FDP .01 .05
61 Peter Forsberg FDP .40 1.00
62 Alek Stojanov FDP .01 .05
63 Richard Matvichuk FDP .02 .10
64 Patrick Poulin FDP .01 .05
65 Martin Lapointe FDP .08 .25
66 Tyler Wright FDP .01 .05
67 Philippe Boucher FDP .01 .05
68 Pat Peake FDP .01 .05
69 Markus Naslund FDP .08 .25
70 Brent Bilodeau FDP .01 .05
71 Glen Murray FDP .08 .25
72 Niklas Sundblad FDP .01 .05
73 Trevor Halverson FDP .01 .05
74 Dean McCammond FDP .01 .05
75 Award Winners Philippe Boucher Jeff Nelson Scott Niedermayer .01 .05
76 The Swedes Markus Naslund Peter Forsberg .08 .25
77 3rd and 4th Round Checklist .01 .05
78 Pat Falloon BW .02 .10
79 Scott Niedermayer BW .02 .10
80 Falloon/Niedermayer BW .02 .10
81 Scott Lachance BW .01 .05
82 Philippe Boucher BW .01 .05
83 Markus Naslund BW .08 .25
84 Glen Murray BW .08 .25
85 Niklas Sundblad BW .01 .05
86 Jason Dawe BW .01 .05
87 Yanic Perreault BW .02 .10
88 Offensive Threats Yanic Dupre Mikael Nylander .01 .05
89 Group Shot/Overview .01 .05
90 Face the Future .01 .05

1991 Ultimate Draft Promos

COMPLETE SET (3) .40 1.00
1 Pat Falloon .20 .50
2 Alex Stojanov .08 .25
3 Mike Torchia .08 .25

2014-15 Upper Deck AHL

COMPLETE SET (150) 40.00 80.00
COMP.SET w/o SPs (100) 15.00 40.00
1 J.C. Lipon .30 .75
2 Seth Griffith .50 1.25
3 Igor Bobkov .30 .75
4 Alex Petrovic .25 .60
5 Troy Bourke .40 1.00
6 Brody Sutter .25 .60
7 Markus Granlund .60 1.50
8 Ryan Haggerty .30 .75
9 Andreas Athanasiou .50 1.25
10 Derek Forbort .30 .75
11 Philipp Grubauer .40 1.00
12 Jujhar Khaira .50 1.25
13 Phil Varone .30 .75
14 Michael Chaput .25 .60
15 Tyler Pitlick .25 .60
16 T.J. Tynan .40 1.00
17 Johan Gustafsson .30 .75
18 Taylor Leier .40 1.00
19 Landon Ferraro .25 .60
20 Sven Baertschi .25 .60
21 Nick Cousins .25 .60
22 Gabriel Dumont .30 .75
23 Sebastian Collberg .40 1.00
24 Cedrick Desjardins .25 .60
25 David Pastrnak 2.00 5.00
26 Mark McNeill .30 .75
27 Slater Koekkoek .25 .60
28 Connor Hellebuyck .75 2.00
29 Connor Brown .40 1.00
30 Radek Faksa .50 1.25
31 Jeff Zatkoff .30 .75
32 Freddie Hamilton .25 .60
33 Christopher Gibson .60 1.50
34 Mike Zalewski .30 .75
35 Brendan Leipsic .30 .75
36 Nic Dowd .40 1.00
37 Kris Newbury .25 .60
38 Anthony Stolarz .50 1.25
39 Trevor Carrick .25 .60
40 Keegan Lowe .25 .60
41 Michael Sgarbossa .30 .75
42 Joey MacDonald .50 1.25
43 Joni Ortio .50 1.25
44 Jared Staal .30 .75
45 Max Reinhart .30 .75
46 Chris Bourque .30 .75
47 Zack Mitchell .50 1.25
48 Marek Mazanec .30 .75
49 Anton Lander .25 .60
50 Jean-Francois Berube .40 1.00
51 Calvin Pickard .40 1.00
52 Ryan Bourque .30 .75
53 Rocco Grimaldi .40 1.00
54 T.J. Brennan .25 .60
55 Ryan Dzingel .25 .60
56 Daniil Tarasov .30 .75
57 Jacob Markstrom .40 1.00
58 Sean Collins .25 .60
59 Nick Petrecki .25 .60
60 Phoenix Copley .50 1.25
61 Jacob de la Rose .30 .75
62 Keith Kinkaid .25 .60
63 Ryan Sproul .40 1.00
64 Pat Cannone .40 1.00
65 Gustav Olofsson .30 .75
66 Pontus Aberg .25 .60
67 Greg McKegg .30 .75
68 Michael Leighton .40 1.00
69 Brenden Kichton .25 .60
70 Brendan Gaunce .50 1.25
71 Troy Grosenick .40 1.00
72 Curtis McKenzie .30 .75
73 Eric O'Dell .25 .60
74 Joe Morrow .50 1.25
75 Chris Wagner .40 1.00
76 Cameron Schilling .25 .60
77 Yannick Veilleux .25 .60
78 Corban Knight .40 1.00
79 David Shields .25 .60
80 Michael Mersch .30 .75
81 Andrey Makarov .40 1.00
82 Max Friberg .30 .75
83 Cedric Paquette .40 1.00
84 Petter Granberg .30 .75
85 Philip Samuelsson .25 .60
86 Adam Clendening .40 1.00
87 Anton Zlobin .30 .75
88 Joe Whitney .25 .60
89 Drew MacIntyre .40 1.00
90 Michael Houser .30 .75
91 Travis Morin .25 .60
92 Ryan Spooner .30 .75
93 Kevin Poulin .30 .75
94 Jordan Szwarz .25 .60
95 Andrew Agozzino .30 .75
96 Austin Watson .25 .60
97 Carl Klingberg .25 .60
98 Brian Dumoulin .25 .60
99 Martin Marincin .30 .75
100 Andrew Hammond .60 1.50
101 Joel Armia .75 2.00
102 Ty Rattie .75 2.00
103 Joey Hishon 1.00 2.50
104 Nicolas Kerdiles .75 2.00
105 Reid Boucher .50 1.25
106 Alexander Khokhlachev .75 2.00
107 Jack Campbell .75 2.00
108 Zack Phillips .50 1.25
109 Kerby Rychel .60 1.50
110 Jean-Gabriel Pageau .50 1.25
111 Josh Leivo .50 1.25
112 Jordan Weal .50 1.25
113 Teemu Pulkkinen 1.00 2.50
114 Chandler Stephenson .50 1.25
115 Laurent Brossoit .75 2.00
116 Stefan Matteau .50 1.25
117 Josh Archibald .50 1.25
118 Quinton Howden .50 1.25
119 Henrik Samuelsson .60 1.50
120 Shayne Gostisbehere 1.50 4.00
121 Ryan Pulock .60 1.50
122 Mitchell Moroz .50 1.25
123 Colton Sissons .75 2.00
124 Oscar Lindberg 2.00 5.00
125 Matt Puempel .50 1.25
126 Brandon Gormley .75 2.00
127 Jordan Binnington 2.50 6.00
128 Stefan Noesen .50 1.25
129 Anders Lee .75 2.00
130 Scott Kosmachuk .50 1.25
131 Ryan Hartman .75 2.00
132 Scott Laughton .50 1.25
133 Nick Shore .75 2.00
134 Sven Andrighetto 1.00 2.50
135 Hunter Shinkaruk 1.25 3.00
136 Konrad Abeltshauser .50 1.25
137 Malcolm Subban 1.25 3.00
138 Charles Hudon .75 2.00
139 Brock McGinn .60 1.50
140 Mikhail Grigorenko .50 1.25
141 Anthony Mantha 1.25 3.00
142 Oscar Dansk 1.00 2.50
143 Teuvo Teravainen 1.25 3.00
144 Andrei Vasilevskiy 8.00 20.00
145 Duncan Siemens .50 1.25
146 Danny Kristo .60 1.50
147 Nicklas Jensen .50 1.25
148 William Nylander 2.50 6.00
149 Vincent Trocheck 1.50 4.00
150 Brett Ritchie .75 2.00

2014-15 Upper Deck AHL Autographs

1 J.C. Lipon 2.50 6.00
2 Seth Griffith 4.00 10.00
11 Philipp Grubauer 3.00 8.00
13 Phil Varone 2.50 6.00
14 Michael Chaput 2.00 5.00
17 Johan Gustafsson 2.50 6.00
21 Nick Cousins 2.00 5.00
22 Gabriel Dumont 2.50 6.00
24 Cedrick Desjardins 2.00 5.00
27 Slater Koekkoek 2.00 5.00
28 Connor Hellebuyck 6.00 15.00
30 Radek Faksa 4.00 10.00
31 Jeff Zatkoff 2.50 6.00
32 Freddie Hamilton 2.00 5.00
33 Christopher Gibson 5.00 12.00
35 Brendan Leipsic 2.50 6.00
37 Kris Newbury 2.00 5.00
38 Anthony Stolarz 4.00 10.00
39 Trevor Carrick 2.00 5.00
40 Keegan Lowe 2.00 5.00
41 Michael Sgarbossa 2.50 6.00
42 Joey MacDonald 4.00 10.00
43 Joni Ortio 4.00 10.00
44 Jared Staal 2.50 6.00
45 Max Reinhart 2.50 6.00
47 Zack Mitchell 4.00 10.00
48 Marek Mazanec 2.50 6.00
49 Anton Lander 2.00 5.00
50 Jean-Francois Berube 3.00 8.00
53 Rocco Grimaldi 3.00 8.00
54 T.J. Brennan 2.00 5.00
55 Ryan Dzingel 2.00 5.00
58 Sean Collins 2.00 5.00
59 Nick Petrecki 2.00 5.00
60 Phoenix Copley 4.00 10.00
61 Jacob de la Rose 2.50 6.00
62 Keith Kinkaid 2.00 5.00
63 Ryan Sproul 3.00 8.00
64 Pat Cannone 3.00 8.00
65 Gustav Olofsson 2.50 6.00
66 Pontus Aberg 2.00 5.00
67 Greg McKegg 2.50 6.00
69 Brenden Kichton 2.00 5.00
70 Brendan Gaunce 4.00 10.00
71 Troy Grosenick 3.00 8.00
72 Curtis McKenzie 2.50 6.00
73 Eric O'Dell 2.00 5.00
74 Joe Morrow 4.00 10.00
75 Chris Wagner 3.00 8.00
76 Cameron Schilling 2.00 5.00
77 Yannick Veilleux 2.00 5.00
78 David Shields 2.00 5.00
83 Cedric Paquette 3.00 8.00
84 Petter Granberg 2.50 6.00
85 Philip Samuelsson 2.00 5.00
86 Adam Clendening 3.00 8.00
89 Drew MacIntyre 3.00 8.00
91 Travis Morin 2.00 5.00
92 Ryan Spooner 2.50 6.00
94 Jordan Szwarz 2.00 5.00
100 Andrew Hammond 25.00 50.00
102 Ty Rattie 3.00 8.00
103 Joey Hishon 4.00 10.00
104 Nicolas Kerdiles 3.00 8.00
106 Alexander Khokhlachev 3.00 8.00
108 Zack Phillips 2.00 5.00
109 Kerby Rychel 2.50 6.00
110 Jean-Gabriel Pageau 2.00 5.00
111 Josh Leivo 2.00 5.00
113 Teemu Pulkkinen 4.00 10.00
114 Chandler Stephenson 2.00 5.00
116 Stefan Matteau 2.00 5.00
117 Josh Archibald 2.00 5.00
118 Quinton Howden 2.00 5.00
119 Henrik Samuelsson 2.50 6.00
120 Shayne Gostisbehere 6.00 15.00

121 Ryan Pulock 2.50 6.00
122 Mitchell Moroz 2.00 5.00
123 Colton Sissons 3.00 8.00
124 Oscar Lindberg 8.00 20.00
125 Matt Puempel 2.00 5.00
127 Jordan Binnington 10.00 25.00
128 Stefan Noesen 2.00 5.00
129 Anders Lee 3.00 8.00
130 Scott Kosmachuk 2.00 5.00
132 Scott Laughton 2.00 5.00
134 Sven Andrighetto 4.00 10.00
135 Hunter Shinkaruk 5.00 12.00
136 Konrad Abeltshauser 2.00 5.00
137 Malcolm Subban 5.00 12.00
138 Charles Hudon 3.00 8.00
139 Brock McGinn 2.50 6.00
141 Anthony Mantha 10.00 25.00
142 Oscar Dansk 4.00 10.00
144 Andrei Vasilevskiy 30.00 80.00
146 Danny Kristo 2.50 6.00
147 Nicklas Jensen 2.00 5.00
150 Brett Ritchie 3.00 8.00

2014-15 Upper Deck AHL Logo Patches

1 Adirondack Flames 8.00 20.00
2 Albany Devils 8.00 20.00
3 Binghamton Senators 8.00 20.00
4 Bridgeport Sound Tigers 8.00 20.00
5 Charlotte Checkers 8.00 20.00
6 Chicago Wolves 8.00 20.00
7 Grand Rapids Griffins 8.00 20.00
8 Hamilton Bulldogs 8.00 20.00
9 Hartford Wolf Pack 8.00 20.00
10 Hershey Bears 8.00 20.00
11 Iowa Wild 8.00 20.00
12 Lake Erie Monsters 8.00 20.00
13 Lehigh Valley Phantoms 8.00 20.00
14 Manchester Monarchs 8.00 20.00
15 Milwaukee Admirals 8.00 20.00
16 Norfolk Admirals 8.00 20.00
17 Oklahoma City Barons 8.00 20.00
18 Portland Pirates 8.00 20.00
19 Providence Bruins 8.00 20.00
20 Rochester Americans 8.00 20.00
21 Rockford IceHogs 8.00 20.00
22 San Antonio Rampage 8.00 20.00
23 Springfield Falcons 8.00 20.00
24 St. John's IceCaps 8.00 20.00
25 Syracuse Crunch 8.00 20.00
26 Texas Stars 8.00 20.00
27 Toronto Marlies 8.00 20.00
28 Utica Comets 8.00 20.00
29 Wilkes-Barre/Scranton 8.00 20.00
30 Worcester Sharks 8.00 20.00
31 Adirondack Flames Alt. 10.00 25.00
32 Albany Devils Alt. 10.00 25.00
33 Binghamton Senators Alt. 10.00 25.00
34 Bridgeport Sound Tigers Alt. 10.00 25.00
35 Charlotte Checkers Alt. 10.00 25.00
36 Chicago Wolves Alt. 10.00 25.00
37 Grand Rapids Griffins Alt. 10.00 25.00
38 Hamilton Bulldogs Alt. 10.00 25.00
39 Hartford Wolf Pack Alt. 10.00 25.00
40 Hershey Bears Alt. 10.00 25.00
41 Iowa Wild Alt. 10.00 25.00
42 Lake Erie Monsters Alt. 10.00 25.00
43 Lehigh Valley Phantoms Alt. 10.00 25.00
44 Manchester Monarchs Alt. 10.00 25.00
45 Milwaukee Admirals Alt. 10.00 25.00
46 Norfolk Admirals Alt. 10.00 25.00
47 Oklahoma City Barons Alt. 10.00 25.00
48 Portland Pirates Alt. 10.00 25.00
49 Providence Bruins Alt. 10.00 25.00
50 Rochester Americans Alt. 10.00 25.00
51 Rockford IceHogs Alt. 10.00 25.00
52 San Antonio Rampage Alt. 10.00 25.00
53 Springfield Falcons Alt. 10.00 25.00
54 St. John's IceCaps Alt. 10.00 25.00
55 Syracuse Crunch Alt. 10.00 25.00
56 Texas Stars Alt. 10.00 25.00
57 Toronto Marlies Alt. 10.00 25.00
58 Utica Comets Alt. 10.00 25.00
59 Wilkes-Barre/Scrntn Alt. 10.00 25.00
60 Worcester Sharks Alt. 10.00 25.00

2014-15 Upper Deck AHL Logo Stickers

Adirondack Flames Primary 1.25 3.00
Albany Devils Primary 1.25 3.00
Binghamton Senators Primary 1.25 3.00
Bridgeport Sound Tigers Primary 1.25 3.00
Charlotte Checkers Primary 1.25 3.00
Chicago Wolves Primary 1.25 3.00
Grand Rapids Griffins Primary 1.25 3.00
Hamilton Bulldogs Primary 1.25 3.00
Hartford Wolf Pack Primary 1.25 3.00
0 Hershey Bears Primary 1.25 3.00
1 Iowa Wild Primary 1.25 3.00
2 Lake Erie Monsters Primary 1.25 3.00
3 Lehigh Valley Phantoms Primary 1.25 3.00
4 Manchester Monarchs Primary 1.25 3.00
5 Milwaukee Admirals Primary 1.25 3.00
6 Norfolk Admirals Primary 1.25 3.00
7 Oklahoma City Barons Primary 1.25 3.00
8 Portland Pirates Primary 1.25 3.00
9 Providence Bruins Primary 1.25 3.00
0 Rochester Americans Primary 1.25 3.00
1 Rockford IceHogs Primary 1.25 3.00
2 San Antonio Rampage Primary 1.25 3.00
3 Springfield Falcons Primary 1.25 3.00
4 St. John's IceCaps Primary 1.25 3.00
5 Syracuse Crunch Primary 1.25 3.00
6 Texas Stars Primary 1.25 3.00
7 Toronto Marlies Primary 1.25 3.00
8 Utica Comets Primary 1.25 3.00
9 Wilkes-Barre/Scranton Penguins Primary 1.25 3.00
Worcester Sharks Primary 1.25 3.00
Adirondack Flames Alternate 2.00 5.00
Albany Devils Alternate 2.00 5.00
Binghamton Senators Alternate 2.00 5.00
Bridgeport Sound Tigers Alternate 2.00 5.00
Charlotte Checkers Alternate 2.00 5.00
Chicago Wolves Alternate 2.00 5.00
Grand Rapids Griffins Alternate 2.00 5.00
Hamilton Bulldogs Alternate 2.00 5.00
39 Hartford Wolf Pack Alternate 2.00 5.00
40 Hershey Bears Alternate 2.00 5.00
41 Iowa Wild Alternate 2.00 5.00
42 Lake Erie Monsters Alternate 2.00 5.00
43 Lehigh Valley Phantoms Alternate 2.00 5.00
44 Manchester Monarchs Alternate 2.00 5.00
45 Milwaukee Admirals Alternate 2.00 5.00
46 Norfolk Admirals Alternate 2.00 5.00
47 Oklahoma City Barons Alternate 2.00 5.00
48 Portland Pirates Alternate 2.00 5.00
49 Providence Bruins Alternate 2.00 5.00
50 Rochester Americans Alternate 2.00 5.00
51 Rockford IceHogs Alternate 2.00 5.00
52 San Antonio Rampage Alternate 2.00 5.00
53 Springfield Falcons Alternate 2.00 5.00
54 St. John's IceCaps Alternate 2.00 5.00
55 Syracuse Crunch Alternate 2.00 5.00
56 Texas Stars Alternate 2.00 5.00
57 Toronto Marlies Alternate 2.00 5.00
58 Utica Comets Alternate 2.00 5.00
59 Wilk-Bre/Scrntn Pegns Alt 2.00 5.00
60 Worcester Sharks Alternate 2.00 5.00
61 New Haven Nighthawks Vintage 3.00 8.00
62 Iowa Chops Vintage 3.00 8.00
63 Kentucky Thoroughblades Vintage 3.00 8.00
64 Lowell Monsters Vintage 3.00 8.00
65 Manitoba Moose Vintage 3.00 8.00
66 St. John's Maple Leafs Vintage 3.00 8.00
67 Nova Scotia Voyagers Vintage 3.00 8.00
68 Quebec Aces Vintage 3.00 8.00
69 Saint John Flames Vintage 3.00 8.00
70 Springfield Kings Vintage 3.00 8.00

2014-15 Upper Deck AHL Box Set

COMP.FACT.SET (105) 35.00 50.00
COMPLETE SET (100) 4.00 10.00
1 Sven Baertschi .12 .30
2 Max Reinhart .15 .40
3 Markus Granlund .30 .75
4 Corban Knight .20 .50
5 Joni Ortio .25 .60
6 Jason Akeson .12 .30
7 Nick Cousins .12 .30
8 Tye McGinn .12 .30
9 Stefan Matteau .12 .30
10 Keith Kinkaid .12 .30
11 Scott Wedgewood .15 .40
12 David Wohlberg .15 .40
13 Joe Whitney .12 .30
14 Mike Hoffman .12 .30
15 Shane Prince .12 .30
16 Anders Lee .20 .50
17 Scott Mayfield .15 .40
18 Zach Boychuk .12 .30
19 Brett Sutter .12 .30
20 Aaron Palushaj .25 .60
21 Victor Rask .20 .50
22 Jake Allen .20 .50
23 Dmitrij Jaskin .15 .40
24 Ty Rattie .20 .50
25 Cory Emmerton .12 .30
26 Tomas Jurco .12 .30
27 Tom McCollum .15 .40
28 Alexey Marchenko .12 .30
29 Dustin Tokarski .12 .30
30 Nathan Beaulieu .12 .30
31 Louis Leblanc .12 .30
32 Oscar Lindberg .50 1.25
33 Jesper Fast .12 .30
34 Danny Kristo .15 .40
35 Philipp Grubauer .20 .50
36 Nate Schmidt .12 .30
37 Ryan Stoa .12 .30
38 Patrick Wey .12 .30
39 Johan Gustafsson .15 .40
40 Josh Caron .12 .30
41 Calvin Pickard .20 .50
42 Michael Sgarbossa .15 .40
43 Jordan Weal .12 .30
44 Martin Jones .15 .40
45 Linden Vey .15 .40
46 Derek Forbort .15 .40
47 Maxim Kitsyn .12 .30
48 Calle Jarnkrok .20 .50
49 Austin Watson .12 .30
50 Magnus Hellberg .20 .50
51 Colton Sissons .20 .50
52 Emerson Etem .15 .40
53 John Gibson .20 .50
54 Rickard Rakell .15 .40
55 Max Friberg .15 .40
56 Will Acton .12 .30
57 Oscar Klefbom .40 1.00
58 David Musil .12 .30
59 Chet Pickard .12 .30
60 Andy Miele .12 .30
61 Brandon Yip .12 .30
62 Mark Visentin .20 .50
63 Matt Fraser .12 .30
64 Alexander Khokhlachev .20 .50
65 Andrey Makarov .20 .50
66 Phil Varone .15 .40
67 Jeremy Morin .12 .30
68 Brandon Pirri .12 .30
69 Adam Clendening .20 .50
70 Quinton Howden .12 .30
71 Jacob Markstrom .20 .50
72 Michael Houser .15 .40
73 Frederic St. Denis .12 .30
74 Cody Goloubef .12 .30
75 Mike McKenna .12 .30
76 Jonathan Marchessault .25 .60
77 Kael Mouillierat .12 .30
78 Patrice Cormier .12 .30
79 Brenden Kichton .12 .30
80 Edward Pasquale .12 .30
81 Brett Connolly .12 .30
82 Kristers Gudlevskis .20 .50
83 Cedric Paquette .20 .50
84 Jack Campbell .20 .50
85 Travis Morin .12 .30
86 Curtis McKenzie .15 .40
87 Colton Sceviour .12 .30
88 T.J. Brennan .12 .30
89 Josh Leivo .12 .30
90 Greg McKegg .15 .40
91 Benn Ferriero .12 .30
92 Pascal Pelletier .12 .30
93 Joe Cannata .12 .30
94 Nicklas Jensen .12 .30
95 Brian Gibbons .12 .30
96 Eric Hartzell .12 .30
97 Harry Zolnierczyk .12 .30
98 Freddie Hamilton .12 .30
99 Konrad Abeltshauser .12 .30
100 Brodie Reid .12 .30

2014-15 Upper Deck AHL Box Set Autographs

1 Sven Baertschi 5.00 12.00
2 Max Reinhart 3.00 8.00
3 Markus Granlund 6.00 15.00
4 Corban Knight 4.00 10.00
5 Joni Ortio 5.00 12.00
6 Jason Akeson 2.50 6.00
7 Nick Cousins 2.50 6.00
8 Tye McGinn 2.50 6.00
9 Stefan Matteau 2.50 6.00
10 Keith Kinkaid 2.50 6.00
11 Scott Wedgewood 3.00 8.00
12 David Wohlberg 3.00 8.00
13 Joe Whitney 2.50 6.00
14 Mike Hoffman 2.50 6.00
15 Shane Prince 2.50 6.00
16 Anders Lee 4.00 10.00
17 Scott Mayfield 3.00 8.00
18 Zach Boychuk 2.50 6.00
19 Brett Sutter 2.50 6.00
20 Aaron Palushaj 5.00 12.00
21 Victor Rask 4.00 10.00
22 Jake Allen 4.00 10.00
23 Dmitrij Jaskin 3.00 8.00
24 Ty Rattie 4.00 10.00
25 Cory Emmerton 2.50 6.00
26 Tomas Jurco 2.50 6.00
27 Tom McCollum 3.00 8.00
28 Alexey Marchenko 2.50 6.00
29 Dustin Tokarski 2.50 6.00
30 Nathan Beaulieu 2.50 6.00
31 Louis Leblanc 2.50 6.00
32 Oscar Lindberg 10.00 25.00
33 Jesper Fast 2.50 6.00
34 Danny Kristo 3.00 8.00
35 Philipp Grubauer 4.00 10.00
36 Nate Schmidt 2.50 6.00
37 Ryan Stoa 2.50 6.00
38 Patrick Wey 2.50 6.00
39 Johan Gustafsson 3.00 8.00
40 Josh Caron 2.50 6.00
41 Calvin Pickard 4.00 10.00
42 Michael Sgarbossa 3.00 8.00
43 Jordan Weal 2.50 6.00
44 Martin Jones 6.00 15.00
45 Linden Vey 3.00 8.00
46 Derek Forbort 3.00 8.00
47 Maxim Kitsyn 2.50 6.00
48 Calle Jarnkrok 4.00 10.00
49 Austin Watson 2.50 6.00
50 Magnus Hellberg 4.00 10.00
51 Colton Sissons 4.00 10.00
52 Emerson Etem 3.00 8.00
53 John Gibson 4.00 10.00
54 Rickard Rakell 3.00 8.00
55 Max Friberg 3.00 8.00
56 Will Acton 2.50 6.00
57 Oscar Klefbom 8.00 20.00
58 David Musil 2.50 6.00
59 Chet Pickard 2.50 6.00
60 Andy Miele 2.50 6.00
61 Brandon Yip 2.50 6.00
62 Mark Visentin 4.00 10.00
63 Matt Fraser 2.50 6.00
04 Alexander Khokhlachev 4.00 10.00
65 Andrey Makarov 4.00 10.00
66 Phil Varone 3.00 8.00
67 Jeremy Morin 2.50 6.00
68 Brandon Pirri 2.50 6.00
69 Adam Clendening 4.00 10.00
70 Quinton Howden 2.50 6.00
71 Jacob Markstrom 4.00 10.00
72 Michael Houser 3.00 8.00
73 Frederic St. Denis 2.50 6.00
74 Cody Goloubef 2.50 6.00
75 Mike McKenna 4.00 10.00
76 Jonathan Marchessault 5.00 12.00
77 Kael Mouillierat 2.50 6.00
78 Patrice Cormier 2.50 6.00
79 Brenden Kichton 2.50 6.00
80 Edward Pasquale 2.50 6.00
81 Brett Connolly 2.50 6.00
82 Kristers Gudlevskis 4.00 10.00
83 Cedric Paquette 4.00 10.00
84 Jack Campbell 4.00 10.00
85 Travis Morin 2.50 6.00
86 Curtis McKenzie 3.00 8.00
87 Colton Sceviour 2.50 6.00
88 T.J. Brennan 2.50 6.00
89 Josh Leivo 2.50 6.00
90 Greg McKegg 3.00 8.00
91 Benn Ferriero 2.50 6.00
92 Pascal Pelletier 2.50 6.00
93 Joe Cannata 2.50 6.00
94 Nicklas Jensen 2.50 6.00
95 Brian Gibbons 2.50 6.00
96 Eric Hartzell 2.50 6.00
97 Harry Zolnierczyk 4.00 10.00
98 Freddie Hamilton 2.50 6.00
99 Konrad Abeltshauser 2.50 6.00
100 Brodie Reid 2.50 6.00

2015-16 Upper Deck AHL

1 Stefan Noesen .25 .60
2 Petteri Lindbohm .25 .60
3 Blake Coleman .25 .60
4 Jeremy Langlois .25 .60
5 Connor Hellebuyck 1.50 4.00
6 Michael Keranen .30 .75
7 Zack Mitchell .25 .60
8 Marek Hrivik .25 .60
9 Nick Baptiste .25 .60
10 Michael Mersch .40 1.00
11 Rocco Grimaldi .25 .60
12 Chad Ruhwedel .25 .60
13 Devin Shore .40 1.00
14 Riley Barber .30 .75
15 Adam Erne .25 .60
16 Andrew Miller .30 .75
17 Justin Shugg .25 .60
18 Stephon Williams .25 .60
19 Brady Skjei .30 .75
20 Chris Driedger .30 .75
21 Nikita Scherbak .25 .60
22 Yanni Gourde .60 1.50
23 Christopher Gibson .25 .60
24 Calvin Pickard .40 1.00
25 Antoine Bibeau .40 1.00
26 Bryan Rust .40 1.00
27 Zachary Fucale .30 .75
28 Jordan Schmaltz .25 .60
29 Oliver Bjorkstrand .30 .75
30 Kevin Fiala .50 1.25
31 Joe Cannata .25 .60
32 Hunter Shinkaruk .40 1.00
33 Byron Froese .30 .75
34 Julius Honka .25 .60
35 Brendan Ranford .30 .75
36 Anthony DeAngelo .30 .75
37 Scott Wilson .25 .60
38 Chris Bigras .25 .60
39 Markus Hannikainen .30 .75
40 Brock McGinn .40 1.00
41 Ryan Graves .25 .60
42 Ivan Barbashev .25 .60
43 Markus Granlund .30 .75
44 Mattias Plachta .25 .60
45 Alexandre Grenier .30 .75
46 Kasperi Kapanen .60 1.50
47 Brendan Gaunce .50 1.25
48 Garnet Hathaway .25 .60
49 Tanner Richard .25 .60
50 Curtis McKenzie .25 .60
51 Jean-Sebastien Dea .40 1.00
52 Josh Leivo .25 .60
53 Kenny Agostino .25 .60
54 Colin Smith .25 .60
55 Max Friberg .25 .60
56 Mirco Mueller .25 .60
57 Bill Arnold .25 .60
58 Jacob de la Rose .40 1.00
59 Louis Domingue .40 1.00
60 Ryan Hartman .50 1.25
61 Garrett Wilson .25 .60
62 Tim Schaller .25 .60
63 Phil Varone .25 .60
64 Garret Sparks .40 1.00
65 Adrian Kempe .40 1.00
66 Joel Armia .25 .60
67 Anthony Stolarz 1.00 2.50
68 T.J. Tynan .25 .60
69 Greg McKegg .25 .60
70 Ryan Sproul .30 .75
71 Trevor Carrick .25 .60
72 Frank Vatrano .50 1.25
73 Jordan Schroeder .25 .60
74 Raman Hrabarenka .30 .75
75 Leon Draisaitl 1.25 3.00
76 Matt O'Connor .30 .75
77 Jon Gillies .25 .60
78 Mitch Callahan .25 .60
79 Paul Thompson .50 1.25
80 Brad Hunt .25 .60
81 Aaron Ness .25 .60
82 Brody Sutter .25 .60
83 Anthony Mantha .60 1.50
84 Magnus Hellberg .25 .60
85 Connor Carrick .25 .60
86 Colton Sissons .25 .60
87 Taylor Leier .40 1.00
88 Chandler Stephenson .50 1.25
89 John Albert .25 .00
90 Max Reinhart .25 .60
91 Reid Boucher .25 .60
92 Henrik Samuelsson .25 .60
93 Remi Elie .25 .60
94 Gabriel Dumont .25 .60
95 Joey Hishon .25 .60
96 Tyler Bertuzzi .40 1.00
97 Daniel Carr .30 .75
98 Troy Grosenick .25 .60
99 Nick Ritchie .40 1.00
100 Marek Mazanec .25 .60
101 Brendan Shinnimin .50 1.25
102 Cole Cassels .50 1.25
103 Kristers Gudlevskis .60 1.50
104 Cole Ully .50 1.25
105 Conor Sheary 2.00 5.00
106 Matt Puempel .60 1.50
107 Charles Hudon .75 2.00
108 John Gibson .75 2.00
109 Madison Bowey .50 1.25
110 Tobias Lindberg .50 1.25
111 Petr Straka .50 1.25
112 Morgan Klimchuk .50 1.25
113 Jonathan Marchessault 1.00 2.50
114 Jordan Binnington 1.25 3.00
115 Mike Reilly .50 1.25
116 Nicolas Kerdiles .50 1.25
117 Shane Harper .50 1.25
118 Anton Forsberg .50 1.25
119 Ryan Pulock .50 1.25
120 Alexander Khokhlachev .50 1.25
121 Darnell Nurse .60 1.50
122 Sonny Milano .75 2.00
123 Sergey Tolchinsky .50 1.25
124 Cole Schneider .50 1.25
125 Andrew Agozzino .50 1.25
126 Mark McNeill .50 1.25
127 Jason Dickinson .60 1.50
128 Nikolay Goldobin .75 2.00
129 Adam Tambellini .50 1.25
130 Derrick Pouliot .50 1.25
131 Matt Murray 3.00 8.00
132 Connor Brown .75 2.00
133 Garret Ross .50 1.25
134 Shea Theodore 1.25 3.00
135 Marko Dano .50 1.25
136 Sven Andrighetto .50 1.25
137 Kerby Rychel .50 1.25
138 Emile Poirier .60 1.50
139 Ryan Bourque .60 1.50
140 Linden Vey .50 1.25
141 Brendan Leipsic .50 1.25
142 Alan Quine .50 1.25
143 Ty Rattie .50 1.25
144 Laurent Brossoit .50 1.25
145 Jared Coreau .50 1.25
146 Valentin Zykov .50 1.25
147 Malcolm Subban 1.25 3.00
148 Nick Cousins .75 2.00
149 Josh Morrissey .75 2.00
150 William Nylander 2.50 6.00

2015-16 Upper Deck AHL Autographs

1 Stefan Noesen 2.50 6.00
2 Petteri Lindbohm 2.50 6.00
3 Blake Coleman 2.50 6.00
4 Jeremy Langlois 2.50 6.00
5 Connor Hellebuyck 15.00 40.00
6 Michael Keranen 3.00 8.00
8 Marek Hrivik 2.50 6.00
11 Rocco Grimaldi 2.50 6.00
13 Devin Shore 4.00 10.00
15 Adam Erne 2.50 6.00
16 Andrew Miller 3.00 8.00
17 Justin Shugg 2.50 6.00
18 Stephon Williams 2.50 6.00
20 Chris Driedger 3.00 8.00
21 Nikita Scherbak 2.50 6.00
22 Yanni Gourde 6.00 15.00
23 Christopher Gibson 2.50 6.00
25 Antoine Bibeau 4.00 10.00
27 Zachary Fucale 3.00 8.00
31 Joe Cannata 2.50 6.00
32 Hunter Shinkaruk 4.00 10.00
33 Byron Froese 3.00 8.00
34 Julius Honka 2.50 6.00
35 Brendan Ranford 3.00 8.00
36 Anthony DeAngelo 3.00 8.00
37 Scott Wilson 2.50 6.00
39 Markus Hannikainen 3.00 8.00
41 Ryan Graves 2.50 6.00
43 Markus Granlund 3.00 8.00
44 Mattias Plachta 2.50 6.00
45 Alexandre Grenier 3.00 8.00
47 Brendan Gaunce 5.00 12.00
48 Garnet Hathaway 2.50 6.00
50 Curtis McKenzie 2.50 6.00
51 Jean-Sebastien Dea 4.00 10.00
52 Josh Leivo 2.50 6.00
56 Mirco Mueller 2.50 6.00
57 Bill Arnold 2.50 6.00
61 Garrett Wilson 2.50 6.00
67 Anthony Stolarz 10.00 25.00
69 Greg McKegg 2.50 6.00
70 Ryan Sproul 3.00 8.00
73 Jordan Schroeder 2.50 6.00
76 Matt O'Connor 3.00 8.00
81 Aaron Ness 2.50 6.00
82 Brody Sutter 2.50 6.00
83 Anthony Mantha 6.00 15.00
85 Connor Carrick 2.50 6.00
86 Colton Sissons 2.50 6.00
87 Taylor Leier 4.00 10.00
88 Chandler Stephenson 5.00 12.00
93 Remi Elie 2.50 6.00
94 Gabriel Dumont 2.50 6.00
95 Joey Hishon 2.50 6.00
96 Tyler Bertuzzi 4.00 10.00
101 Brendan Shinnimin 2.50 6.00
104 Cole Ully 2.50 6.00
106 Matt Puempel 3.00 8.00
107 Charles Hudon 4.00 10.00
110 Tobias Lindberg 2.50 6.00
112 Morgan Klimchuk 2.50 6.00
113 Jonathan Marchessault 5.00 12.00
114 Jordan Binnington 6.00 15.00
116 Nicolas Kerdiles 2.50 6.00
119 Ryan Pulock 2.50 6.00
120 Alexander Khokhlachev 2.50 6.00
122 Sonny Milano 5.00 12.00
123 Sergey Tolchinsky 2.50 6.00
124 Cole Schneider 2.50 6.00
125 Andrew Agozzino 2.50 6.00
127 Jason Dickinson 3.00 8.00
128 Nikolay Goldobin 4.00 10.00
129 Adam Tambellini 2.50 6.00
130 Derrick Pouliot 2.50 6.00
134 Shea Theodore 6.00 15.00
135 Marko Dano 2.50 6.00
136 Sven Andrighetto 2.50 6.00
137 Kerby Rychel 2.50 6.00
139 Ryan Bourque 3.00 8.00
142 Alan Quine 2.50 6.00
143 Ty Rattie 2.50 6.00
144 Laurent Brossoit 2.50 6.00
145 Jared Coreau 2.50 6.00
147 Malcolm Subban 6.00 15.00
148 Nick Cousins 4.00 10.00
149 Josh Morrissey 4.00 10.00

2015-16 Upper Deck AHL Logo Stickers

1 Albany Devils 1.25 3.00
2 Bakersfield Condors 1.25 3.00
3 Binghamton Senators 1.25 3.00
4 Bridgeport Sound Tigers 1.25 3.00
5 Charlotte Checkers 1.25 3.00
6 Chicago Wolves 1.25 3.00
7 Grand Rapids Griffins 1.25 3.00
8 Hartford Wolf Pack 1.25 3.00
9 Hershey Bears 1.25 3.00
10 Iowa Wild 1.25 3.00
11 Lake Erie Monsters 1.25 3.00
12 Lehigh Valley Phantoms 1.25 3.00
13 Manitoba Moose 1.25 3.00
14 Milwaukee Admirals 1.25 3.00
15 Ontario Reign 1.25 3.00
16 Portland Pirates 1.25 3.00
17 Providence Bruins 1.25 3.00
18 Rochester Americans 1.25 3.00
19 Rockford IceHogs 1.25 3.00
20 San Antonio Rampage 1.25 3.00
21 San Diego Gulls 1.25 3.00
22 San Jose Barracuda 1.25 3.00
23 Springfield Falcons 1.25 3.00
24 St. John's IceCaps 1.25 3.00
25 Stockton Heat 1.25 3.00
26 Syracuse Crunch 1.25 3.00
27 Texas Stars 1.25 3.00
28 Toronto Marlies 1.25 3.00
29 Utica Comets 1.25 3.00
30 Wilkes-Barre/Scranton Penguins 1.25 3.00

2015-16 Upper Deck AHL Logo Tattoos

1 Albany Devils 1.25 3.00
2 Bakersfield Condors 1.25 3.00
3 Binghamton Senators 1.25 3.00
4 Bridgeport Sound Tigers 1.25 3.00
5 Charlotte Checkers 1.25 3.00
6 Chicago Wolves 1.25 3.00
7 Grand Rapids Griffins 1.25 3.00
8 Hartford Wolf Pack 1.25 3.00
9 Hershey Bears 1.25 3.00
10 Iowa Wild 1.25 3.00
11 Lake Erie Monsters 1.25 3.00
12 Lehigh Valley Phantoms 1.25 3.00
13 Manitoba Moose 1.25 3.00
14 Milwaukee Admirals 1.25 3.00
15 Ontario Reign 1.25 3.00
16 Portland Pirates 1.25 3.00
17 Providence Bruins 1.25 3.00
18 Rochester Americans 1.25 3.00
19 Rockford IceHogs 1.25 3.00
20 San Antonio Rampage 1.25 3.00
21 San Diego Gulls 1.25 3.00
22 San Jose Barracuda 1.25 3.00
23 Springfield Falcons 1.25 3.00
24 St. John's IceCaps 1.25 3.00
25 Stockton Heat 1.25 3.00
26 Syracuse Crunch 1.25 3.00
27 Texas Stars 1.25 3.00
28 Toronto Marlies 1.25 3.00
29 Utica Comets 1.25 3.00
30 Wilkes-Barre/Scranton Penguins 1.25 3.00

2015-16 Upper Deck AHL Upper Deck Logo Stickers

UD1 Upper Deck Logo 1.25 3.00
UD2 Upper Deck Logo 1.25 3.00
UD3 Upper Deck Logo 1.25 3.00
UD4 Upper Deck Logo 1.25 3.00
UD5 Upper Deck Logo 1.25 3.00

2015-16 Upper Deck AHL Upper Deck Logo Tattoos

UD1 Upper Deck Logo 1.25 3.00
UD2 Upper Deck Logo 1.25 3.00
UD3 Upper Deck Logo 1.25 3.00
UD4 Upper Deck Logo 1.25 3.00
UD5 Upper Deck Logo 1.25 3.00

2016-17 Upper Deck AHL

1 Chris Bourque .40 1.00
2 Scott Wedgewood .60 1.50
3 Danny Kristo .40 1.00
4 Cole Schneider .40 1.00
5 Taylor Beck .40 1.00
6 Trevor Carrick .40 1.00
7 Matthew Lorito .40 1.00
8 Bracken Kearns .40 1.00
9 Justin Dowling .25 .60
10 Mac Carruth .30 .75
11 JC Lipon .40 1.00
12 Jake Guentzel 1.25 3.00
13 Jordan Schmaltz .30 .75
14 Matthew Ford .30 .75
15 Jordan Binnington .60 1.50
16 T.J. Tynan .30 .75
17 Daniel Zaar .30 .75
18 Casey Bailey .25 .60
19 Jared Coreau .50 1.25
20 Mathew Bodie .40 1.00
21 Eric Tangradi .30 .75
22 Stanislav Galiev .25 .60
23 Mackenzie Skapski .40 1.00
24 Vitek Vanacek .40 1.00
25 Derek Ryan .30 .75
26 Zack Mitchell .40 1.00
27 Taylor Leier .30 .75
28 Nick Baptiste .40 1.00
29 Quinton Howden .40 1.00
30 Vincent Loverde .30 .75
31 Justin Bailey .40 1.00
32 Tanner Kero .25 .60
33 Evan Rodrigues .60 1.50
34 Greg Carey .30 .75
35 Pat Cannone .30 .75
36 Chris Conner .30 .75
37 Marko Dano .25 .60
38 Eric Comrie .30 .75
39 Yanni Gourde .30 .75
40 Malcolm Subban .30 .75
41 Sean Backman .40 1.00
42 Cal O'Reilly .25 .60
43 Griffin Reinhart .25 .60
44 Barclay Goodrow .25 .60
45 Cameron Schilling .40 1.00
46 Max Friberg .30 .75
47 Emile Poirier .25 .60
48 Brett Sterling .30 .75
49 Brad Hunt .25 .60
50 Matt Hackett .30 .75
51 Tom Kostopoulos .30 .75
52 T.J. Hensick .30 .75
53 Tanner Richard .30 .75
54 Mike McKenna .30 .75
55 Mark McNeill .40 1.00
56 Mike Zalewski .30 .75
57 Andy Miele .30 .75
58 Brendan Ranford .30 .75
59 Michael Bournival .30 .75
60 Jakub Vrana .50 1.25
61 Ville Pokka .40 1.00
62 Jordan Weal .25 .60
63 Maxime Lagace .30 .75
64 Mike Sislo .30 .75
65 Ryan Hamilton .30 .75
66 Andrew Copp .25 .60
67 Colton Hargrove .40 1.00
68 Curtis Lazar .25 .60
69 Mirco Mueller .25 .60
70 Aaron Palushaj .30 .75
71 Craig Cunningham .30 .75
72 Sven Andrighetto .30 .75
73 Linden Vey .40 1.00
74 Brandon Defazio .40 1.00
75 Michael Sgarbossa .30 .75
76 Connor Brickley .25 .60
77 Jack Campbell .40 1.00
78 Kenny Agostino .30 .75
79 Carter Rowney .30 .75
80 Michael Leighton .40 1.00
81 Anton Forsberg .25 .60
82 Alexandre Grenier .30 .75
83 Jeremy Smith .30 .75
84 Colin Smith .30 .75
85 Colin Greening .30 .75
86 Mike Kostka .30 .75
87 Juuse Saros .50 1.25
88 Chris Mueller .30 .75
89 Travis Morin .40 1.00
90 Adam Erne .50 1.25
91 Corey Tropp .30 .75
92 Austin Watson .30 .75
93 Justin Peters .30 .75
94 Antoine Bibeau .25 .60
95 Tanner Glass .30 .75
96 Michael Latta .30 .75
97 Landon Ferraro .25 .60
98 Danick Martel .30 .75
99 Erik Condra .30 .75
100 Tobias Lindberg 1.25 3.00
101 Michael Dal Colle .75 2.00
102 Sergey Tolchinsky .60 1.50
103 Thatcher Demko 2.00 5.00
104 Jordan Subban .75 2.00
105 Nicolas Petan .50 1.25
106 Chase De Leo .75 2.00
107 Cristoval Nieves 1.00 2.50
108 Zachary Fucale .60 1.50
109 Rourke Chartier .75 2.00
110 Brandon Montour 2.00 5.00
111 Anthony Mantha 1.50 4.00
112 Charles Hudon .60 1.50
113 Timo Meier 1.50 4.00
114 Jon Gillies .60 1.50
115 Oliver Kylington .60 1.50
116 Mike McCarron .75 2.00
117 Jack Roslovic .75 2.00
118 Chris Bigras .60 1.50
119 John Quenneville .75 2.00
120 Anthony DeAngelo .60 1.50
121 Kasperi Kapanen 1.25 3.00
122 Christian Fischer .75 2.00
123 Alex Tuch .75 2.00
124 Brendan Leipsic .60 1.50
125 Alexander Nylander .75 2.00
126 Nick Paul 1.00 2.50
127 Nikita Scherbak .75 2.00
128 Tyler Bertuzzi 1.25 3.00
129 Vladislav Kamenev .60 1.50
130 Brendan Lemieux .60 1.50
131 Christian Djoos .75 2.00
132 Joel Eriksson Ek 1.25 3.00
133 Tristan Jarry 1.50 4.00
134 Kevin Labanc .75 2.00
135 Madison Bowey .50 1.25
136 Joe Hicketts .50 1.25
137 Evgeny Svechnikov .75 2.00
138 Sonny Milano 1.00 2.50
139 Travis Sanheim .75 2.00
140 Oskar Sundqvist .75 2.00
141 Hunter Shinkaruk .75 2.00
142 Adrian Kempe .75 2.00
143 Joseph Blandisi .60 1.50
144 Ivan Barbashev .75 2.00
145 Haydn Fleury .75 2.00
146 Nikita Soshnikov .50 1.25
147 Kyle Wood .60 1.50
148 Riley Barber .60 1.50
149 Shea Theodore 1.00 2.50
150 Pontus Aberg 1.00 2.50

2016-17 Upper Deck AHL Autographs

1 Chris Bourque 4.00 10.00
2 Scott Wedgewood 6.00 15.00
3 Danny Kristo 4.00 10.00
6 Trevor Carrick 4.00 10.00
7 Matthew Lorito 4.00 10.00
8 Bracken Kearns 4.00 10.00
9 Justin Dowling 2.50 6.00
10 Mac Carruth 3.00 8.00
11 JC Lipon 4.00 10.00
14 Matthew Ford 3.00 8.00
18 Casey Bailey 2.50 6.00
19 Jared Coreau 5.00 12.00
20 Mathew Bodie 4.00 10.00
21 Eric Tangradi 3.00 8.00
22 Stanislav Galiev 2.50 6.00
23 Mackenzie Skapski 4.00 10.00
24 Vitek Vanacek 4.00 10.00
25 Derek Ryan 3.00 8.00
27 Taylor Leier 3.00 8.00
28 Nick Baptiste 4.00 10.00
30 Vincent Loverde 3.00 8.00
32 Tanner Kero 2.50 6.00
33 Evan Rodrigues 6.00 15.00
34 Greg Carey 3.00 8.00
36 Chris Conner 3.00 8.00
37 Marko Dano 2.50 6.00
38 Eric Comrie 3.00 8.00
39 Yanni Gourde 3.00 8.00
41 Sean Backman 4.00 10.00
43 Griffin Reinhart 2.50 6.00
44 Barclay Goodrow 2.50 6.00
45 Cameron Schilling 4.00 10.00
47 Emile Poirier 2.50 6.00
48 Brett Sterling 3.00 8.00
49 Brad Hunt 2.50 6.00
50 Matt Hackett 3.00 8.00
51 Tom Kostopoulos 3.00 8.00
52 T.J. Hensick 3.00 8.00
53 Tanner Richard 3.00 8.00
54 Mike McKenna 3.00 8.00
55 Mark McNeill 4.00 10.00
56 Mike Zalewski 3.00 8.00
57 Andy Miele 3.00 8.00
60 Jakub Vrana 5.00 12.00

61 Ville Pokka 4.00 10.00
63 Maxime Lagace 3.00 8.00
64 Mike Sislo 3.00 8.00
65 Ryan Hamilton 3.00 8.00
67 Colton Hargrove 4.00 10.00
69 Mirco Mueller 2.50 6.00
70 Aaron Palushaj 3.00 8.00
74 Brandon Defazio 4.00 10.00
75 Michael Sgarbossa 3.00 8.00
78 Kenny Agostino 3.00 8.00
79 Carter Rowney 3.00 8.00
80 Michael Leighton 4.00 10.00
81 Anton Forsberg 2.50 6.00
82 Alexandre Grenier 3.00 8.00
83 Jeremy Smith 3.00 8.00
84 Colin Smith 3.00 8.00
87 Juuse Saros 5.00 12.00
88 Chris Mueller 3.00 8.00
89 Travis Morin 4.00 10.00
90 Adam Erne 5.00 12.00
91 Corey Tropp 3.00 8.00
94 Antoine Bibeau 2.50 6.00
103 Thatcher Demko 10.00 25.00
106 Chase De Leo 4.00 10.00
108 Zachary Fucale 3.00 8.00
109 Rourke Chartier 4.00 10.00
112 Charles Hudon 3.00 8.00
116 Mike McCarron 4.00 10.00
119 John Quenneville 4.00 10.00
122 Christian Fischer 4.00 10.00
123 Alex Tuch 4.00 10.00
124 Brendan Leipsic 3.00 8.00
128 Tyler Bertuzzi 6.00 15.00
129 Vladislav Kamenev 3.00 8.00
131 Christian Djoos 4.00 10.00
133 Tristan Jarry 8.00 20.00
134 Kevin Labanc 4.00 10.00
136 Joe Hicketts 2.50 6.00
137 Evgeny Svechnikov 4.00 10.00
138 Sonny Milano 5.00 12.00
139 Travis Sanheim 4.00 10.00
140 Oskar Sundqvist 4.00 10.00
141 Hunter Shinkaruk 4.00 10.00
143 Joseph Blandisi 3.00 8.00
145 Haydn Fleury 4.00 10.00
148 Riley Barber 3.00 8.00

2016-17 Upper Deck AHL Team Mascots

TM1 Devil Dawg 1.00 2.50
TM2 Coloniel Claw'd 1.00 2.50
TM3 Max 1.00 2.50
TM4 Storm 1.00 2.50
TM5 Chubby 1.00 2.50
TM6 Skates The Grey Wolf 1.00 2.50
TM7 Sully 1.00 2.50
TM8 Griff 1.00 2.50
TM9 Crash 1.00 2.50
TM10 Sonar The Wolf 1.00 2.50
TM11 Coco The Bear 1.00 2.50
TM12 meLVin 1.00 2.50
TM13 Mick E. Moose 1.00 2.50
TM14 Roscoe 1.00 2.50
TM15 Kingston 1.00 2.50
TM16 Samboni 1.00 2.50
TM17 Moose 1.00 2.50
TM18 Hammy Hog 1.00 2.50
TM19 T-Bone 1.00 2.50
TM20 Gulliver 1.00 2.50
TM21 Frenzy 1.00 2.50
TM22 Boomer 1.00 2.50
TM23 Frankie The Firebird 1.00 2.50
TM24 Buddy The Puffin 1.00 2.50
TM25 Crunchman 1.00 2.50
TM26 Dusty The Roadrunner 1.00 2.50
TM27 Duke The Dog 1.00 2.50
TM28 Audie 1.00 2.50
TM29 Tux The Penguin 1.00 2.50
TM30 Mulllet Brothers 1.00 2.50

2016-17 Upper Deck AHL Wordmark Logo Window Cling

1 Albany Devils 1.50 4.00
2 Bakersfield Condors 1.50 4.00
3 Binghamton Senators 1.50 4.00
4 Bridgeport Sound Tigers 1.50 4.00
5 Charlotte Checkers 1.50 4.00
6 Chicago Wolves 1.50 4.00
7 Cleveland Monsters 1.50 4.00
8 Grand Rapids Griffins 1.50 4.00
9 Iowa Wild 1.50 4.00
10 Hartford Wolf Pack 1.50 4.00
11 Hershey Bears 1.50 4.00
12 Lehigh Valley Phantoms 1.50 4.00
13 Manitoba Moose 1.50 4.00
14 Milwaukee Admirals 1.50 4.00
15 Ontario Reign 1.50 4.00
16 Providence Bruins 1.50 4.00
17 Rochester Americans 1.50 4.00
18 Rockford IceHogs 1.50 4.00
19 San Antonio Rampage 1.50 4.00
20 San Diego Gulls 1.50 4.00
21 San Jose Barracuda 1.50 4.00
22 Springfield Thunderbirds 1.50 4.00
23 Stockton Heat 1.50 4.00
24 St. John's IceCaps 1.50 4.00
25 Syracuse Crunch 1.50 4.00
26 Texas Stars 1.50 4.00
27 Tucson Roadrunners 1.50 4.00
28 Toronto Marlies 1.50 4.00
29 Utica Comets 1.50 4.00
30 Wilkes-Barre/Scranton Penguins 1.50 4.00

2017-18 Upper Deck AHL

1 Cameron Schilling .40 1.00
2 Ville Husso .50 1.25
3 Nick Paul .25 .60
4 Joey LaLeggia .30 .75
5 Nick Lappin .30 .75
6 Colin White .50 1.25
7 Jordan Schmaltz .50 1.25
8 Travis Boyd .30 .75
9 Gage Quinney .30 .75
10 Samuel Blais .40 1.00
11 Adin Hill .75 2.00
12 Roope Hintz .50 1.25
13 Linus Ullmark .40 1.00
14 Adam Erne .25 .60
15 Noah Juulsen .40 1.00
16 Anders Lindback .30 .75
17 Rudolfs Balcers .30 .75
18 Ryan Graves .30 .75
19 Ville Pokka .30 .75
20 Daniel Audette .30 .75
21 Ken Appleby .30 .75
22 Matiss Kivlenieks .40 1.00
23 Nick Ellis .30 .75
24 Lawson Crouse .25 .60
25 Alex Nedeljkovic .60 1.50
26 Michael Bournival .30 .75
27 Brendan Guhle .30 .75
28 Matt Lorito .40 1.00
29 Mike McKenna .30 .75
30 Connor Ingram .40 1.00
31 Paul LaDue .30 .75
32 Andreas Johnsson .30 .75
33 Cal Petersen .30 .75
34 Hunter Miska .30 .75
35 Jeremy Bracco .30 .75
36 Ivan Barbashev .50 1.25
37 Darren Raddysh .30 .75
38 Reid Boucher .25 .60
39 Samuel Montembeault .60 1.50
40 Peter Cehlarik .40 1.00
41 Dean Kukan .30 .75
42 Kevin Roy .40 1.00
43 Chris Nell .30 .75
44 Niklas Svedberg .30 .75
45 Mason Appleton .30 .75
46 Morgan Klimchuk .30 .75
47 Oskar Lindblom .30 .75
48 Charlie Lindgren .30 .75
49 Spencer Foo .30 .75
50 Mike Vecchione .30 .75
51 Teemu Pulkkinen .30 .75
52 Carter Bancks .30 .75
53 Julien Gauthier .40 1.00
54 Tyler Moy .30 .75
55 Mike Reilly .25 .60
56 Devon Toews .40 1.00
57 Andy Welinski .30 .75
58 T.J. Tynan .30 .75
59 Brendan Lemieux .40 1.00
60 Tommy Cross .30 .75
61 Scott Eansor .30 .75
62 Dominic Turgeon .30 .75
63 Eric Comrie .30 .75
64 Ty Rattie .25 .60
65 Adam Helewka .30 .75
66 Austin Ortega .30 .75
67 Adam Carlson .30 .75
68 Nikita Soshnikov .25 .60
69 Sergey Tolchinsky .30 .75
70 Lane Pederson .30 .75
71 Maxime Lagace .40 1.00
72 Jean-Francois Berube .30 .75
73 Casey DeSmith .60 1.50
74 Jared Coreau .30 .75
75 Emil Pettersson .30 .75
76 Kevin Boyle .30 .75
77 Mark Jankowski .25 .60
78 Chris Bourque .30 .75
79 Tom Kostopoulos .30 .75
80 Juho Lammikko .30 .75
81 Alex Broadhurst .30 .75
82 Lucas Johansen .30 .75
83 Michael Amadio .40 1.00
84 Travis Morin .30 .75
85 Andrew Hammond .30 .75
86 Nicolas Aube-Kubel .30 .75
87 Austin Czarnik .40 1.00
88 Christopher Gibson .30 .75
89 Kyle Rau .30 .75
90 Axel Holmstrom .30 .75
91 Maxim Mamin .30 .75
92 Kyle Baun .25 .60
93 Adam Tambellini .30 .75
94 Kevin Porter .30 .75
95 Garret Sparks .25 .60
96 Antoine Bibeau .25 .60
97 Guillaume Brisebois .40 1.00
98 Alex Lyon .40 1.00
99 Garnet Hathaway .30 .75
100 Nathan Bastian .30 .75
101 Mitchell Stephens SP .50 1.25
102 Daniel O'Regan SP 1.25 3.00
103 Michael Dal Colle SP .75 2.00
104 Michael Mersch SP .75 2.00
105 Thatcher Demko SP 1.00 2.50
106 Daniel Sprong SP .50 1.25
107 Denis Gurianov SP 2.00 5.00
108 Filip Chytil SP .75 2.00
109 Jon Gillies SP .75 2.00
110 Klim Kostin SP .75 2.00
111 Chandler Stephenson SP .60 1.50
112 Luke Kunin SP .75 2.00
113 Philippe Myers SP .60 1.50
114 Anthony Cirelli SP .75 2.00
115 Tage Thompson SP 2.00 5.00
116 Laurent Dauphin SP 1.25 3.00
117 Jesse Puljujarvi SP .75 2.00
118 Josh Ho-Sang SP 1.00 2.50
119 Vladislav Kamenev SP .75 2.00
120 Kasperi Kapanen SP .75 2.00
121 Shea Theodore SP 1.00 2.50
122 Nikita Scherbak SP 1.00 2.50
123 Ethan Bear SP .75 2.00
124 Alex Tuch SP 2.00 5.00
125 Lucas Wallmark SP .75 2.00
126 Jayce Hawryluk SP .75 2.00
127 Nick Merkley SP .75 2.00
128 Filip Chlapik SP .60 1.50
129 Timothy Liljegren SP .75 2.00
130 Nikolay Goldobin SP .75 2.00
131 Jack Roslovic SP 1.00 2.50
132 Zane Mcintyre SP .75 2.00
133 Andrew Mangiapane SP 1.25 3.00
134 Tyler Motte SP .50 1.25
135 Mike McCarron SP .75 2.00
136 Jason Dickinson SP .50 1.25
137 Evgeny Svechnikov SP 1.50 4.00
138 Kyle Connor SP 1.25 3.00
139 Jacob Larsson SP .75 2.00
140 Matthew Highmore SP .75 2.00
141 Dylan Strome SP 1.00 2.50
142 Thomas Chabot SP .75 2.00
143 Nick Baptiste SP .75 2.00
144 Nicolas Kerdiles SP .75 2.00
145 Valentin Zykov SP .75 2.00
146 C.J. Smith SP .60 1.50
147 Danick Martel SP .75 2.00
148 John Quenneville SP .60 1.50
149 Danton Heinen SP .75 2.00
150 Dominik Simon SP .50 1.25

2017-18 Upper Deck AHL Autographs

1 Cameron Schilling A 4.00 10.00
2 Ville Husso A 5.00 12.00
3 Nick Paul A 2.50 6.00
4 Joey LaLeggia B 3.00 8.00
7 Jordan Schmaltz B 5.00 12.00
8 Travis Boyd A 3.00 8.00
11 Adin Hill A 8.00 20.00
12 Roope Hintz A 5.00 12.00
13 Linus Ullmark B 4.00 10.00
14 Adam Erne B 2.50 6.00
17 Rudolfs Balcers B 3.00 8.00
18 Ryan Graves B 3.00 8.00
19 Ville Pokka A 3.00 8.00
21 Ken Appleby A 3.00 8.00
22 Matiss Kivlenieks A 4.00 10.00
23 Nick Ellis A 3.00 8.00
25 Alex Nedeljkovic A 6.00 15.00
26 Michael Bournival B 3.00 8.00
27 Brendan Guhle B 3.00 8.00
28 Matt Lorito B 4.00 10.00
29 Mike McKenna B 3.00 8.00
33 Cal Petersen A 3.00 8.00
35 Jeremy Bracco A 3.00 8.00
36 Ivan Barbashev A 5.00 12.00
37 Darren Raddysh A 3.00 8.00
40 Peter Cehlarik A 4.00 10.00
41 Dean Kukan A 3.00 8.00
43 Chris Nell B 3.00 8.00
44 Niklas Svedberg B 3.00 8.00
46 Morgan Klimchuk B 3.00 8.00
47 Oskar Lindblom A 3.00 8.00
48 Charlie Lindgren A 3.00 8.00
51 Teemu Pulkkinen A 3.00 8.00
52 Carter Bancks A 3.00 8.00
53 Julien Gauthier A 4.00 10.00
54 Tyler Moy A 3.00 8.00
55 Mike Reilly A 2.50 6.00
56 Devon Toews A 4.00 10.00
60 Tommy Cross A 3.00 8.00
61 Scott Eansor B 3.00 8.00
62 Dominic Turgeon A 3.00 8.00
63 Eric Comrie A 3.00 8.00
64 Ty Rattie B 2.50 6.00
66 Austin Ortega A 3.00 8.00
67 Adam Carlson B 3.00 8.00
70 Lane Pederson B 3.00 8.00
71 Maxime Lagace A 4.00 10.00
72 Jean-Francois Berube B 3.00 8.00
73 Casey DeSmith A 6.00 15.00
74 Jared Coreau A 3.00 8.00
76 Kevin Boyle A 3.00 8.00
78 Chris Bourque A 3.00 8.00
79 Tom Kostopoulos B 3.00 8.00
80 Juho Lammikko B 3.00 8.00
81 Alex Broadhurst B 3.00 8.00
82 Lucas Johansen A 3.00 8.00
83 Michael Amadio A 4.00 10.00
84 Travis Morin B 3.00 8.00
86 Nicolas Aube-Kubel A 3.00 8.00
87 Austin Czarnik A 4.00 10.00
88 Christopher Gibson B 3.00 8.00
89 Kyle Rau B 3.00 8.00
92 Kyle Baun A 2.50 6.00
93 Adam Tambellini B 3.00 8.00
94 Kevin Porter B 3.00 8.00
95 Garret Sparks A 2.50 6.00
96 Antoine Bibeau A 2.50 6.00
97 Guillaume Brisebois A 4.00 10.00
98 Alex Lyon B 4.00 10.00
100 Nathan Bastian A 3.00 8.00
103 Michael Dal Colle SP 6.00 15.00
104 Michael Mersch SP 6.00 15.00
107 Denis Gurianov SP 15.00 40.00
110 Klim Kostin SP 6.00 15.00
111 Chandler Stephenson SP 5.00 12.00
112 Luke Kunin SP 6.00 15.00
113 Philippe Myers SP 5.00 12.00
114 Anthony Cirelli SP 5.00 12.00
115 Tage Thompson SP 15.00 40.00
119 Vladislav Kamenev SP 6.00 15.00
123 Ethan Bear SP 6.00 15.00
126 Jayce Hawryluk SP 6.00 15.00
127 Nick Merkley SP 6.00 15.00
129 Timothy Liljegren SP 6.00 15.00
132 Zane Mcintyre SP 6.00 15.00
135 Mike McCarron SP 6.00 15.00
137 Evgeny Svechnikov SP 12.00 30.00
139 Jacob Larsson SP 6.00 15.00
140 Matthew Highmore SP 6.00 15.00
144 Nicolas Kerdiles SP 6.00 15.00
145 Valentin Zykov SP 6.00 15.00
147 Danick Martel SP 6.00 15.00
149 Danton Heinen SP 6.00 15.00

2017-18 Upper Deck AHL Team Logo Mini Posters

1 Bakersfield Condors 1.25 3.00
2 Belleville Senators 1.25 3.00
3 Binghamton Devils 1.25 3.00
4 Bridgeport Sound Tigers 1.25 3.00
5 Charlotte Checkers 1.25 3.00
6 Chicago Wolves 1.25 3.00
7 Cleveland Monsters 1.25 3.00
8 Grand Rapids Griffins 1.25 3.00
9 Hartford Wolf Pack 1.25 3.00
10 Hershey Bears 1.25 3.00
11 Iowa Wild 1.25 3.00
12 Laval Rocket 1.25 3.00
13 Lehigh Valley Phantoms 1.25 3.00
14 Manitoba Moose 1.25 3.00
15 Milwaukee Admirals 1.25 3.00
16 Ontario Reign 1.25 3.00
17 Providence Bruins 1.25 3.00
18 Rochester Americans 1.25 3.00
19 Rockford IceHogs 1.25 3.00
20 San Antonio Rampage 1.25 3.00
21 San Diego Gulls 1.25 3.00
22 San Jose Barracuda 1.25 3.00
23 Springfield Thunderbirds 1.25 3.00
24 Stockton Heat 1.25 3.00
25 Syracuse Crunch 1.25 3.00
26 Texas Stars 1.25 3.00
27 Toronto Marlies 1.25 3.00
28 Tucson Roadrunners 1.25 3.00
29 Utica Comets 1.25 3.00
30 Wilkes-Barre/Scranton Penguins 1.25 3.00

2017-18 Upper Deck AHL Team Standouts

TS1 Ty Rattie .40 1.00
TS2 Colin White .75 2.00
TS3 Nick Lappin .50 1.25
TS4 Christopher Gibson .50 1.25
TS5 Lucas Wallmark .60 1.50
TS6 Teemu Pulkkinen .50 1.25
TS7 Tyler Motte .40 1.00
TS8 Matt Puempel .40 1.00
TS9 Cole Schneider .40 1.00
TS10 Chris Bourque .50 1.25
TS11 Zack Mitchell .50 1.25
TS12 Daniel Carr .40 1.00
TS13 Danick Martel .60 1.50
TS14 Jack Roslovic .75 2.00
TS15 Emil Pettersson .50 1.25
TS16 Cal Petersen .50 1.25
TS17 Jakob Forsbacka-Karlsson .60 1.50
TS18 C.J. Smith .50 1.25
TS19 Vincent Hinostroza .40 1.00
TS20 Klim Kostin .60 1.50
TS21 Giovanni Fiore .60 1.50
TS22 Rudolfs Balcers .50 1.25
TS23 Alexandre Grenier .50 1.25
TS24 Andrew Mangiapane 1.00 2.50
TS25 Anthony Cirelli .50 1.25
TS26 Jason Dickinson .40 1.00
TS27 Garret Sparks .40 1.00
TS28 Dylan Strome .75 2.00
TS29 Nikolay Goldobin .60 1.50
TS30 Casey DeSmith 1.00 2.50

2018-19 Upper Deck AHL

1 Thatcher Demko .50 1.25
2 Max Jones .40 1.00
3 Brandon Pirri .30 .75
4 Cory Conacher .30 .75
5 Erik Condra .30 .75
6 Carter Verhaeghe .50 1.25
7 Kaapo Kahkonen .40 1.00
8 Josef Korenar .30 .75
9 Victor Olofsson .40 1.00
10 Rudolfs Balcers .30 .75
11 Christopher Gibson .30 .75
12 Alex Nedeljkovic .30 .75
13 Joel L'Esperance .30 .75
14 Josh Ho-Sang .30 .75
15 Kerby Rychel .30 .75
16 Jacob Larsson .30 .75
17 Eric Robinson .30 .75
18 Laurent Dauphin .30 .75
19 Al Montoya .30 .75
20 Alexandre Carrier .30 .75
21 Francis Perron .30 .75
22 Charlie Lindgren .30 .75
23 Curtis Lazar .25 .60
24 Tim Gettinger .30 .75
25 Julien Gauthier .30 .75
26 Taylor Raddysh .30 .75
27 Lawrence Pilut .30 .75
28 Cooper Marody .40 1.00
29 Victor Ejdsell .30 .75
30 Oscar Dansk .25 .60
31 Anthony Greco .30 .75
32 Andrew Agozzino .30 .75
33 Zac Dalpe .25 .60
34 Kevin Boyle .30 .75
35 Tyler Sikura .30 .75
36 Matt Puempel .25 .60
37 Samuel Montembeault .75 2.00
38 Ville Husso .25 .60
39 Jayden Halbgewachs .30 .75
40 Rocco Grimaldi .25 .60
41 Chris Bigras .30 .75
42 Harri Sateri .30 .75
43 Curtis McKenzie .25 .60
44 Joey Anderson .40 1.00
45 Jake Walman .30 .75
46 Alexandre Alain .30 .75
47 Greg Carey .30 .75
48 Michael Sgarbossa .30 .75
49 Adin Hill .40 1.00
50 Brett Seney .30 .75
51 Alexander Nylander .30 .75
52 Nicolas Meloche .30 .75
53 Jeremy Bracco .30 .75
54 Tomas Hyka .40 1.00
55 Jonah Gadjovich .30 .75
56 Eric Comrie .25 .60
57 Filip Gustavsson .60 1.50
58 Urho Vaakanainen .75 2.00
59 Cale Fleury .30 .75
60 Anthony Peters .40 1.00
61 Liam O'Brien .25 .60
62 Roope Hintz 1.00 2.50
63 Riley Barber .30 .75
64 Anthony Angello .30 .75
65 Linus Olund .30 .75
66 Brett Sutter .25 .60
67 Ville Meskanen .30 .75
68 Jack Rodewald .30 .75
69 Andrew Poturalski .25 .60
70 Mackenzie Blackwood .75 2.00
71 Troy Grosenick .30 .75
72 Brendan Guhle .30 .75
73 Seth Griffith .25 .60
74 Jonathan Dahlen .30 .75
75 Sheldon Rempal .30 .75
76 Michael Bournival .30 .75
77 Cameron Schilling .30 .75
78 Josh Mahura .30 .75
79 Chris Mueller .30 .75
80 Pavel Francouz .40 1.00
81 Nicolas Aube-Kubel .30 .75
82 Boston Leier .30 .75
83 Tyler Steenbergen .30 .75
84 Michael McLeod .30 .75
85 Trevor Murphy .30 .75
86 Alex Barre-Boulet .30 .75
87 Matthew Highmore .40 1.00
88 Timothy Liljegren .30 .75
89 Jean-Francois Berube .30 .75
90 Kale Clague .30 .75
91 Reid Boucher .25 .60
92 Mark McNeill .30 .75
93 Adam Mascherin .30 .75
94 Ryan Murphy .25 .60
95 Jeremy Roy .25 .60
96 Dmitry Sokolov .30 .75
97 Cameron Hebig .30 .75
98 Trevor Moore .30 .75
99 Jayce Hawryluk .30 .75
100 Calle Rosen .30 .75
101 Carter Hart SP 1.50 4.00
102 Michael Dal Colle SP .75 2.00
103 Klim Kostin SP .60 1.50
104 Andrew Hammond SP .60 1.50
105 Antoine Bibeau SP .60 1.50
106 Jake Evans SP .60 1.50
107 Lias Andersson SP 1.25 3.00
108 Spencer Foo SP .60 1.50
109 Sam Carrick SP .60 1.50
110 Dan Vladar SP 1.00 2.50
111 Rasmus Asplund SP .60 1.50
112 Adam Helewka SP .60 1.50
113 Martin Kaut SP .60 1.50
114 Landon Bow SP .60 1.50
115 Janne Kuokkanen SP .50 1.25
116 Drake Batherson SP 1.50 4.00
117 Dylan Gambrell SP .75 2.00
118 Cal Petersen SP .60 1.50
119 Filip Zadina SP .60 1.50
120 Mason Appleton SP .60 1.50
121 Kieffer Bellows SP .75 2.00
122 Zach Aston-Reese SP 1.25 3.00
123 Nick Lappin SP .60 1.50
124 Logan Stanley SP .75 2.00
125 Jakob Forsbacka-Karlsson SP .60 1.50
126 Tyler Benson SP .60 1.50
127 Luke Kunin SP .50 1.25
128 Erik Brannstrom SP .60 1.50
129 Nicolas Roy SP .50 1.25
130 Eeli Tolvanen SP 1.50 4.00
131 Chris Terry SP .75 2.00
132 Vitaly Abramov SP .75 2.00
133 Sam Gagner SP .50 1.25
134 Cal Foote SP .60 1.50
135 Dylan Sikura SP 1.00 2.50
136 Michael Mersch SP .75 2.00
137 Adam Gaudette SP 1.25 3.00
138 Phil Varone SP .75 2.00
139 Henrik Borgstrom SP 1.25 3.00
140 Ilya Samsonov SP 1.50 4.00

2018-19 Upper Deck AHL Autographs

1 Thatcher Demko A 5.00 12.00
2 Max Jones A 4.00 10.00
5 Erik Condra B 3.00 8.00
6 Carter Verhaeghe B 5.00 12.00
9 Victor Olofsson A 4.00 10.00
10 Rudolfs Balcers A 3.00 8.00
11 Christopher Gibson B 3.00 8.00
12 Alex Nedeljkovic B 3.00 8.00
15 Kerby Rychel B 3.00 8.00
16 Jacob Larsson A 3.00 8.00
17 Eric Robinson A 3.00 8.00
18 Laurent Dauphin A 3.00 8.00
21 Francis Perron A 3.00 8.00
23 Curtis Lazar B 2.50 6.00
24 Tim Gettinger A 3.00 8.00
25 Julien Gauthier A 3.00 8.00
28 Cooper Marody A 4.00 10.00
32 Andrew Agozzino B 3.00 8.00
33 Zac Dalpe B 2.50 6.00
34 Kevin Boyle A 3.00 8.00
38 Ville Husso A 2.50 6.00
43 Curtis McKenzie B 2.50 6.00
46 Alexandre Alain B 3.00 8.00
48 Michael Sgarbossa B 3.00 8.00
49 Adin Hill B 4.00 10.00
50 Brett Seney A 3.00 8.00
52 Nicolas Meloche B 3.00 8.00
53 Jeremy Bracco A 3.00 8.00
56 Eric Comrie A 2.50 6.00
57 Filip Gustavsson A 6.00 15.00
60 Anthony Peters B 4.00 10.00
63 Riley Barber A 3.00 8.00
64 Anthony Angello B 3.00 8.00
68 Jack Rodewald A 3.00 8.00
72 Brendan Guhle A 3.00 8.00
75 Sheldon Rempal A 3.00 8.00
77 Cameron Schilling A 3.00 8.00
79 Chris Mueller B 3.00 8.00
81 Nicolas Aube-Kubel A 3.00 8.00
82 Boston Leier A 3.00 8.00
87 Matthew Highmore A 4.00 10.00
88 Timothy Liljegren A 3.00 8.00
90 Kale Clague A 3.00 8.00
91 Reid Boucher A 2.50 6.00
93 Adam Mascherin B 3.00 8.00
97 Cameron Hebig B 3.00 8.00
99 Jayce Hawryluk A 3.00 8.00
105 Antoine Bibeau SP A 2.50 6.00
114 Landon Bow SP B 3.00 8.00
118 Cal Petersen SP B 3.00 8.00
119 Filip Zadina SP A 3.00 8.00
125 Jakob Forsbacka-Karlsson SP B 3.00 8.00
127 Luke Kunin SP A 2.50 6.00
128 Erik Brannstrom SP A 3.00 8.00
129 Nicolas Roy SP B 3.00 8.00
136 Michael Mersch SP A 4.00 10.00

2018-19 Upper Deck AHL Team Leaders

TL1 Brandon Pirri .50 1.25
TL2 Cory Conacher .50 1.25
TL3 Collin Delia .60 1.50
TL4 Henrik Borgstrom 1.00 2.50
TL5 Alex Nedeljkovic .50 1.25
TL6 Eeli Tolvanen 1.25 3.00
TL7 Greg Carey .50 1.25
TL8 Sam Gagner .40 1.00
TL9 Zac Dalpe .40 1.00
TL10 Michael Dal Colle .60 1.50
TL11 Anthony Peters .60 1.50
TL12 Lias Andersson 1.00 2.50
TL13 Brett Sutter .40 1.00
TL14 Andrew Hammond .50 1.25
TL15 Nick Lappin .50 1.25
TL16 Reid Boucher .40 1.00
TL17 Drake Batherson 1.25 3.00
TL18 Victor Olofsson .60 1.50
TL19 Al Montoya .50 1.25
TL20 Antoine Bibeau .40 1.00

2018-19 Upper Deck AHL Team Leaders Autographs

TL3 Collin Delia 8.00 20.00
TL5 Alex Nedeljkovic 6.00 15.00
TL9 Zac Dalpe 5.00 12.00
TL10 Michael Dal Colle 8.00 20.00
TL11 Anthony Peters 8.00 20.00
TL16 Reid Boucher 5.00 12.00
TL18 Victor Olofsson 8.00 20.00
TL20 Antoine Bibeau 5.00 12.00

2019-20 Upper Deck AHL

1 Drake Batherson .30 .75
2 Kieffer Bellows .30 .75
3 Lucas Elvenes .25 .60
4 Alexander Chmelevski .25 .60
5 Isaac Ratcliffe .25 .60
6 Ivan Chekhovich .25 .60
7 Shane Starrett .25 .60
8 Josh Norris .30 .75
9 Veini Vehvilainen .25 .60
10 Evan Bouchard .40 1.00
11 Nick Merkley .25 .60
12 Aleksi Heponiemi .25 .60
13 Rem Pitlick .30 .75
14 Pheonix Copley .20 .50
15 Rasmus Kupari .25 .60
16 Stefan Noesen .20 .50
17 Evan Cormier .20 .50
18 Vinni Lettieri .25 .60
19 Trey Fix-Wolansky .20 .50
20 Michael McLeod .20 .50
21 Pierre-Olivier Joseph .25 .60
22 Jake Oettinger .30 .75
23 Vitaly Abramov .20 .50
24 Igor Shesterkin 1.25 3.00
25 Kyle Capobianco .25 .60
26 German Rubtsov .25 .60
27 Joseph Veleno .25 .60
28 Riley Tufte .20 .50
29 Alex Nedeljkovic .25 .60
30 Ben Street .20 .50
31 Gabe Vilardi .30 .75
32 Louie Belpedio .20 .50
33 Filip Zadina .50 1.25
34 Alex Barre-Boulet .30 .75
35 Adin Hill .30 .75
36 Morgan Geekie .25 .60
37 Casey DeSmith .25 .60
38 Matthew Phillips .25 .60
39 Jack Studnicka .30 .75
40 Conor Timmins .25 .60
41 Moritz Seider .30 .75
42 Andrew Peeke .20 .50
43 Michael DiPietro .30 .75
44 Owen Tippett .25 .60
45 Joachim Blichfeld .30 .75
46 Philipp Kurashev .25 .60
47 Jansen Harkins .20 .50
48 Glenn Gawdin .25 .60
49 Chris Terry .20 .50
50 Brandon Gignac .25 .60
51 Tage Thompson .40 1.00
52 Zack MacEwen .25 .60
53 Shane Bowers .30 .75
54 Seth Griffith .20 .50
55 Antoine Morand .25 .60
56 Troy Grosenick .25 .60
57 Rasmus Asplund .20 .50
58 Alex Formenton .25 .60
59 Cameron Gaunce .20 .50
60 Kaapo Kahkonen .75 2.00
61 Jake Leschyshyn .25 .60
62 Kenny Agostino .20 .50
63 Lane Pederson .20 .50
64 Jordan Kyrou .25 .60
65 Cameron Schilling .25 .60
66 Kiefer Sherwood .20 .50
67 Cal Foote .25 .60
68 Dan Vladar .25 .60
69 Jake Evans .25 .60
70 Julien Gauthier .25 .60
71 Sebastian Aho .20 .50
72 Reid Boucher .20 .50
73 Cal Petersen .25 .60
74 Calle Rosen .20 .50
75 Mitch Reinke .20 .50
76 Andrew Poturalski .20 .50
77 Tyler Benson .30 .75
78 Adam Boqvist .30 .75
79 Jake Bean .25 .60
80 Jeremy Bracco .25 .60
81 Urho Vaakanainen .25 .60
82 Klim Kostin .30 .75
83 Eeli Tolvanen .30 .75
84 Logan Stanley .20 .50
85 Michael Sgarbossa .20 .50
86 Jonas Johansson .25 .60
87 Kristian Vesalainen .20 .50
88 Chris Mueller .20 .50
89 Josh Brook .30 .75
90 Sam Carrick .25 .60

2019-20 Upper Deck AHL Autographs

1 Drake Batherson C 4.00 10.00
2 Kieffer Bellows B 4.00 10.00
3 Lucas Elvenes C 3.00 8.00
5 Isaac Ratcliffe D 3.00 8.00
8 Josh Norris D 4.00 10.00
11 Nick Merkley C 3.00 8.00
12 Aleksi Heponiemi C 3.00 8.00
13 Rem Pitlick C 4.00 10.00
14 Pheonix Copley D 2.50 6.00
15 Rasmus Kupari B 3.00 8.00
18 Vinni Lettieri C 3.00 8.00
19 Trey Fix-Wolansky C 2.50 6.00
23 Vitaly Abramov C 4.00 10.00
24 Igor Shesterkin A 60.00 150.00
25 Kyle Capobianco D 3.00 8.00
26 German Rubtsov C 3.00 8.00
29 Alex Nedeljkovic D 3.00 8.00
30 Ben Street C 2.50 6.00
32 Louie Belpedio D 2.50 6.00
34 Alex Barre-Boulet C 4.00 10.00
35 Adin Hill D 4.00 10.00
36 Morgan Geekie D 3.00 8.00
37 Casey DeSmith C 3.00 8.00
39 Jack Studnicka B 10.00 25.00
43 Michael DiPietro C 4.00 10.00
44 Owen Tippett C 3.00 8.00
45 Joachim Blichfeld C 4.00 10.00
47 Jansen Harkins D 3.00 8.00
48 Glenn Gawdin D 3.00 8.00
49 Chris Terry D 3.00 8.00
53 Shane Bowers C 4.00 10.00
61 Jake Leschyshyn B 3.00 8.00
65 Cameron Schilling D 3.00 8.00
67 Cal Foote C 3.00 8.00
68 Dan Vladar C 3.00 8.00
69 Jake Evans B 6.00 15.00
70 Julien Gauthier D 4.00 10.00
71 Sebastian Aho D 2.50 6.00
72 Reid Boucher D 2.50 6.00
73 Cal Petersen C 2.50 6.00
77 Tyler Benson B 3.00 8.00
79 Jake Bean B 3.00 8.00
84 Logan Stanley C 4.00 10.00
85 Michael Sgarbossa D 3.00 8.00
88 Chris Mueller D 3.00 8.00
90 Sam Carrick D 3.00 8.00

2019-20 Upper Deck AHL Impact

I1 Cal Petersen .40 1.00
I2 Drake Batherson .60 1.50
I3 Jeremy Bracco .50 1.25
I4 Alex Barre-Boulet .60 1.50
I5 Lucas Elvenes .50 1.25
I6 Igor Shesterkin 2.50 6.00
I7 Chris Terry .50 1.25
I8 Jansen Harkins .50 1.25
I9 Tyler Benson .50 1.25
I10 Michael Sgarbossa .50 1.25

2019-20 Upper Deck AHL Impact Autographs

I1 Cal Petersen C 5.00 12.00
I2 Drake Batherson B 8.00 20.00
I3 Jeremy Bracco C 6.00 15.00
I4 Alex Barre-Boulet D 8.00 20.00
I5 Lucas Elvenes C 6.00 15.00
I6 Igor Shesterkin A 60.00 150.00
I7 Chris Terry D 6.00 15.00
I8 Jansen Harkins D 6.00 15.00
I9 Tyler Benson D 6.00 15.00
I10 Michael Sgarbossa D 6.00 15.00

2020-21 Upper Deck AHL

1 Cooper Marody .40 1.00
2 Nathan Todd .30 .75
3 Tyler Benson .60 1.50
4 Lane Pederson .40 1.00
5 Andrew Poturalski .30 .75
6 Matthew Phillips .40 1.00
7 Riley Barber .40 1.00
8 Cole Schneider .30 .75
9 Josef Korenar .50 1.25
10 Ryan McLeod .50 1.25
11 Riley Tufte .30 .75
12 Ryan Murphy .30 .75
13 Alex Petrovic .30 .75
14 Antoine Bibeau .30 .75
15 Jonny Brodzinski .50 1.25
16 Adam Brooks .30 .75
17 Charlie Lindgren .40 1.00
18 Paul Carey .30 .75
19 Lukas Vejdemo .50 1.25
20 Andrew Agozzino .30 .75
21 Gage Quinney .40 1.00
22 Chase De Leo .30 .75
23 Timothy Liljegren .60 1.50
24 Michael Sgarbossa .30 .75
25 Trey Fix-Wolansky .30 .75
26 Dmitry Sokolov .30 .75
27 Louie Belpedio .30 .75
28 Ben Street .30 .75
29 Glenn Gawdin .50 1.25
30 Cameron Gaunce .30 .75
31 Landon Bow .30 .75
32 Seth Griffith .30 .75
33 Kevin Roy .30 .75
34 Tanner Jeannot .50 1.25
35 Trevor Carrick .30 .75
36 Joachim Blichfeld .40 1.00
37 Tyler Gaudet .30 .75
38 Nick Baptiste .30 .75
39 Ryan Poehling .50 1.25
40 Brett Seney .30 .75
41 Joey Keane .40 1.00
42 Yannick Veilleux .30 .75
43 Brett Leason .30 .75
44 Curtis McKenzie .30 .75
45 David Cotton .40 1.00
46 Brandon Gignac .30 .75
47 Connor Zary .75 2.00
48 Ryan Fitzgerald .30 .75
49 Vitaly Abramov .40 1.00
50 Fredrik Handemark .30 .75
51 Otto Leskinen .30 .75
52 Collin Delia .30 .75
53 Robbie Russo .30 .75
54 Sean Durzi .40 1.00
55 Rem Pitlick .30 .75
56 Tye Felhaber .30 .75
57 Logan Shaw .30 .75
58 Stefan Noesen .30 .75
59 Patrick Brown .30 .75
60 Anthony Louis .30 .75

61 Mike Vecchione .30 .75
62 Lucas Elvenes .30 .75
63 Josh Brook .30 .75
64 Brett Sutter .30 .75
65 Brad Malone .30 .75
66 Filip Gustavsson .75 2.00
67 A.J. Greer .30 .75
68 Dillon Simpson .30 .75
69 Josh Mahura .30 .75
70 Antti Suomela .30 .75
71 Sam Carrick .30 .75
72 Tyler Steenbergen .30 .75
73 Nick Merkley .30 .75
74 Michael Bunting 1.00 2.50
75 Cole Bardreau .30 .75
76 Boris Katchouk .30 .75
77 T.J. Tynan .30 .75
78 Oscar Dansk .30 .75
79 Taylor Raddysh .30 .75
80 Gustav Olofsson .30 .75
81 Pheonix Copley .30 .75
82 Rourke Chartier .30 .75
83 Mitch Reinke .30 .75
84 Martin Fehervary .30 .75
85 Turner Elson .30 .75
86 Anthony Angello .50 1.25
87 Tanner Fritz .30 .75
88 Chris Mueller .30 .75
89 Tyler Sikura .30 .75
90 Jacob Middleton .30 .75
91 Joe Hicketts .30 .75
92 Rasmus Kupari .40 1.00
93 Greg Pateryn .30 .75
94 Hunter Drew .30 .75
95 Paul Thompson .30 .75
96 Brayden Burke .50 1.25
97 Rob O'Gara .30 .75
98 Keegan Lowe .30 .75
99 Jacob Bryson 1.00 2.50
100 Alex Barre-Boulet .50 1.25
101 Mark Alt .30 .75
102 Alex Formenton .75 2.00
103 Shane Gersich .30 .75
104 Kale Clague .30 .75
105 Tim Gettinger .30 .75
106 Carl Dahlstrom .30 .75
107 Cody Goloubef .30 .75
108 Jake Leschyshyn .30 .75
109 Richard Clune .30 .75
110 C.J. Suess .30 .75
111 Christopher Gibson .30 .75
112 Dennis Cholowski .30 .75
113 Michael Mersch .30 .75
114 Joseph Blandisi .30 .75
115 Alex Galchenyuk .30 .75
116 Sheldon Rempal .30 .75
117 Brady Lyle .30 .75
118 Connor Dewar .30 .75
119 Samuel Montembeault .50 1.25
120 David Kase .50 1.25
121 Lukas Jasek .40 1.00
122 Adam Mascherin .30 .75
123 Cal O'Reilly .30 .75
124 Cameron Schilling .30 .75
125 Tyler Graovac .30 .75
126 Laurent Dauphin .30 .75
127 Adam Cracknell .30 .75
128 Troy Grosenick .30 .75
129 Oskar Steen .30 .75
130 Kyle Capobianco .40 1.00
131 Joey Anderson .30 .75
132 Kole Lind .40 1.00
133 Anthony Greco .30 .75
134 Taro Hirose .30 .75
135 Cameron Hebig .30 .75
136 Steven Fogarty .30 .75
137 Jean-Sebastien Dea .40 1.00
138 Jayden Halbgewachs .30 .75
139 Dylan Sikura .30 .75
140 Kyle Criscuolo .30 .75
141 Vinni Lettieri .30 .75
142 Nikita Scherbak .30 .75
143 Xavier Ouellet .30 .75
144 Alexander True .50 1.25
145 Shane Bowers .50 1.25
146 Zac Dalpe .30 .75
147 Brendan Guhle .30 .75
148 Adin Hill .50 1.25
149 Antoine Morand .30 .75
150 Aleksi Heponiemi .75 2.00
151 Quinton Byfield SR 4.00 10.00
152 Trevor Zegras SR 12.00 30.00
153 Cole Perfetti SR 2.50 6.00
154 Jamie Drysdale SR 2.50 6.00
155 Philip Tomasino SR .75 2.00
156 Cole Caufield SR 15.00 40.00
157 Thomas Harley SR 1.50 4.00
158 Connor McMichael SR 2.50 6.00
159 Seth Jarvis SR 1.50 4.00
160 Ryan Suzuki SR .75 2.00
161 Riley Damiani SR .60 1.50
162 Oskari Laaksonen SR .60 1.50
163 Nolan Foote SR 1.00 2.50
164 Wyatt Kalynuk SR .75 2.00
165 Zayde Wisdom SR .60 1.50
166 Sampo Ranta SR .75 2.00
167 Egor Zamula SR .75 2.00
168 Samuel Fagemo SR .75 2.00
169 Samuel Bolduc SR .60 1.50
170 David Cotton SR .60 1.50
171 Jeremy Swayman SR 2.50 6.00
172 Arthur Kaliyev SR 1.50 4.00
173 Calen Addison SR .75 2.00
174 Egor Sokolov SR .60 1.50
175 Akil Thomas SR .60 1.50
176 Connor Zary SR 1.25 3.00
177 Cam Lee SR .60 1.50
178 Ville Heinola SR .75 2.00
179 Patrick Khodorenko SR .60 1.50
180 Rafael Harvey-Pinard SR .75 2.00
181 Joel Teasdale SR .60 1.50
182 Benoit-Olivier Groulx SR .75 2.00
183 Samuel Asselin SR .60 1.50
184 Victor Soderstrom SR .75 2.00
185 Lukas Dostal SR 1.25 3.00
186 Nick Robertson SR 1.50 4.00
187 Morgan Barron SR .60 1.50
188 Dominik Bokk SR .60 1.50
189 Nicolas Beaudin SR 1.00 2.50
190 Alex Turcotte SR .75 2.00
191 Alex Newhook SR .75 2.00
192 Grigori Denisenko SR .75 2.00
193 Jack Quinn SR 1.25 3.00
194 Gabriel Fortier SR .75 2.00
195 Damien Giroux SR .75 2.00
196 Evan Barratt SR .60 1.50
197 Joel Hofer SR 1.00 2.50
198 Matt Boldy SR 2.00 5.00
199 Tyler Madden SR .60 1.50
200 Mathias Emilio Pettersen SR .60 1.50
201 Cayden Primeau ART 3.00 8.00
202 Josh Norris ART 4.00 10.00
203 Alex Formenton ART 3.00 8.00
204 Jack Studnicka ART 1.25 3.00
205 Brogan Rafferty ART 1.50 4.00
206 Joey Keane ART 1.50 4.00
207 Kaapo Kahkonen AS 1.25 3.00
208 Jake Bean AS 1.00 2.50
209 Connor Ingram AS 1.25 3.00
210 Brogan Rafferty AS 1.00 2.50
211 Alex Barre-Boulet AS 1.25 3.00
212 Drake Batherson AS 1.25 3.00
213 Sam Anas AS 1.00 2.50
214 Josh Norris AS 2.50 6.00
215 Reid Boucher AS .75 2.00
216 Brennan Menell AS 1.00 2.50
217 Jacob MacDonald AS 2.00 5.00
218 Gerald Mayhew AS 1.00 2.50
219 Cooper Marody S .75 2.00
220 Vitaly Abramov S .75 2.00
221 Ben Street S .60 1.50
222 Samuel Bolduc S .75 2.00
223 Seth Jarvis S 2.00 5.00
224 Zac Dalpe S .60 1.50
225 Jack Quinn S 1.50 4.00
226 Riley Barber S .75 2.00
227 Jonny Brodzinski S 1.00 2.50
228 Jack Dugan S .60 1.50
229 Michael Sgarbossa S .75 2.00
230 Calen Addison S 1.00 2.50
231 Jesse Ylonen S .75 2.00
232 Zayde Wisdom S .75 2.00
233 Cole Perfetti S 2.00 5.00
234 Quinton Byfield S 2.50 6.00
235 Shane Bowers S 1.00 2.50
236 Jean-Sebastien Dea S .75 2.00
237 Wyatt Kalynuk S 1.00 2.50
238 Trevor Zegras S 2.00 5.00
239 Joachim Blichfeld S .75 2.00
240 Matthew Phillips S .75 2.00
241 Grigori Denisenko S 1.00 2.50
242 Riley Damiani S .75 2.00
243 Nick Robertson S 2.00 5.00
244 Lane Pederson S .75 2.00
245 Kole Lind S .75 2.00
246 Cam Lee S .75 2.00
247 Tyler Benson S 1.25 3.00
248 Rasmus Kupari S .75 2.00
249 Philip Tomasino S 1.00 2.50
250 Jamie Drysdale S 2.50 6.00

2020-21 Upper Deck AHL Exclusives

*EXCLUSIVES: 3X TO 8X BASIC
151 Quinton Byfield SR 15.00 40.00
152 Trevor Zegras SR 80.00 200.00
153 Cole Perfetti SR 12.00 30.00
154 Jamie Drysdale SR 10.00 25.00
156 Cole Caufield SR 125.00 300.00

2020-21 Upper Deck AHL Gold

*ART.GOLD: 2X TO 5X BASIC
*AS.GOLD: 2X TO 5X BASIC
*S.GOLD: 2X TO 5X BASIC

2020-21 Upper Deck AHL Red

*ART.RED: 1.25X TO 3X BASIC
*AS.RED: .6X TO 1.5X BASIC
*S.RED: .6X TO 1.5X BASIC

2020-21 Upper Deck AHL Autographs

3 Tyler Benson D 5.00 12.00
23 Timothy Liljegren D 5.00 12.00
34 Tanner Jeannot D 12.00 30.00
74 Michael Bunting D 8.00 20.00
102 Alex Formenton D 6.00 15.00
150 Aleksi Heponiemi E 6.00 15.00
152 Trevor Zegras SR B 60.00 150.00
153 Cole Perfetti SR C 30.00 80.00
157 Thomas Harley SR C 10.00 25.00
158 Connor McMichael SR C 10.00 25.00
159 Seth Jarvis SR E 10.00 25.00
163 Nolan Foote SR D 6.00 15.00
174 Egor Sokolov SR E 8.00 20.00
176 Connor Zary SR E 10.00 25.00
185 Lukas Dostal SR E 25.00 60.00
193 Jack Quinn SR E 15.00 40.00
197 Joel Hofer SR E 10.00 25.00
203 Alex Formenton ART 15.00 40.00
204 Jack Studnicka ART 20.00 50.00
217 Jacob MacDonald AS B 12.00 30.00
223 Seth Jarvis S B 12.00 30.00
225 Jack Quinn S B 15.00 40.00
233 Cole Perfetti S C 20.00 50.00
247 Tyler Benson S C 8.00 20.00

2021-22 Upper Deck AHL

1 Ty Ronning .40 1.00
2 Matthew Phillips .40 1.00
3 Matt Boldy 1.00 2.50
4 Scott Reedy .30 .75
5 Vinni Lettieri .25 .60
6 Nicolas Beaudin .25 .60
7 Tim Gettinger .25 .60
8 Calen Addison .40 1.00
9 Jack Dugan .25 .60
10 Samuel Asselin .25 .60
11 Kiefer Sherwood .25 .60
12 Jake Leschyshyn .40 1.00
13 William Bitten .25 .60
14 Nolan Foote .25 .60
15 Spencer Martin .25 .60
16 Cole Schneider .30 .75
17 Erik Brannstrom .25 .60
18 Riley Barber .25 .60
19 Adam Ruzicka .40 1.00
20 Jan Jenik .50 1.25
21 Gabriel Dumont .25 .60
22 Calvin Pickard .40 1.00
23 Tyler Sikura .25 .60
24 Ryan Merkley .50 1.25
25 Sam Anas .25 .60
26 Adam Helewka .25 .60
27 Cale Fleury .25 .60
28 Egor Sokolov .40 1.00
29 Ville Heinola .25 .60
30 Andrew Hammond .25 .60
31 Alexey Toropchenko .40 1.00
32 Oskari Laaksonen .25 .60
33 Jordy Bellerive .25 .60
34 Collin Delia .25 .60
35 Gerry Mayhew .25 .60
36 Alexander Alexeyev .25 .60
37 Riley Damiani .40 1.00
38 Josh Ho-Sang .25 .60
39 Isaac Ratcliffe .25 .60
40 Tyler Tucker .25 .60
41 Chase De Leo .25 .60
42 Anthony Angello .25 .60
43 Kevin Roy .25 .60
44 Fabian Zetterlund .40 1.00
45 Otto Somppi .25 .60
46 Nick Caamano .25 .60
47 Troy Grosenick .25 .60
48 Zac Dalpe .25 .60
49 Damien Giroux .25 .60
50 Cooper Marody .25 .60
51 Jacob Perreault .25 .60
52 Gabriel Fortier .40 1.00
53 Ken Appleby .25 .60
54 Ukko-Pekka Luukkonen .60 1.50
55 Max Gildon .25 .60
56 Rafael Harvey-Pinard .40 1.00
57 Brendan Guhle .25 .60
58 Thomas Harley .40 1.00
59 Frederic Allard .40 1.00
60 Luke Philp .25 .60
61 Max Willman .40 1.00
62 Samuel Fagemo .40 1.00
63 Ryan McLeod .25 .60
64 Aleksi Heponiemi .40 1.00
65 Ivan Prosvetov .40 1.00
66 Jeremy Davies .40 1.00
67 Dominik Bokk .25 .60
68 Kristian Reichel .25 .60
69 Lassi Thomson .40 1.00
70 Alex Steeves .50 1.25
71 Nicolas Meloche .25 .60
72 Max McCormick .25 .60
73 Jacob MacDonald .25 .60
74 Joe Veleno .50 1.25
75 David Cotton .25 .60
76 Axel Jonsson-Fjallby .40 1.00
77 Shane Bowers .25 .60
78 Liam Foudy .30 .75
79 Nick Robertson .40 1.00
80 Brogan Rafferty .25 .60
81 Xavier Ouellet .25 .60
82 Ryan Suzuki .40 1.00
83 Jake Oettinger .60 1.50
84 Jack Studnicka .25 .60
85 Aidan Dudas .25 .60
86 Matej Pekar .25 .60
87 Otto Koivula .25 .60
88 Cameron Schilling .25 .60
89 Jonas Rondbjerg .40 1.00
90 Evan Barratt .25 .60
91 Alexander True .25 .60
92 Joachim Blichfeld .25 .60
93 David Gustafsson .25 .60
94 Carson Focht .25 .60
95 Alex Turcotte .50 1.25
96 Chris Terry .25 .60
97 Stuart Skinner .50 1.25
98 Michael Sgarbossa .25 .60
99 Jonny Brodzinski .25 .60
100 Hudson Fasching .25 .60
101 Logan Hutsko .60 1.50
102 Alex Steeves 1.00 2.50
103 Nikita Alexandrov .60 1.50
104 Danila Klimovich .60 1.50
105 Linus Weissbach .60 1.50
106 Mike Hardman .75 2.00
107 Tyler Angle .60 1.50
108 Marco Rossi .60 1.50
109 Braden Schneider 1.00 2.50
110 Kirill Tyutyayev .60 1.50
111 Maxim Cajkovic .60 1.50
112 Cam York .75 2.00
113 Pavel Gogolev .60 1.50
114 David Farrance .75 2.00
115 Matthew Wedman .60 1.50
116 Samuel Poulin .75 2.00
117 Jack Ahcan .75 2.00
118 Jonatan Berggren .75 2.00
119 Lynden McCallum .60 1.50
120 Lukas Reichel .60 1.50
121 Matias Maccelli .60 1.50
122 Cole Koepke .60 1.50
123 Jakob Pelletier .60 1.50
124 Scott Reedy .60 1.50
125 Brayden Tracey .60 1.50
126 Daniil Miromanov .75 2.00
127 Jordan Kawaguchi .60 1.50
128 Simon Lundmark .60 1.50
129 Lauri Pajuniemi .60 1.50
130 Greg Meireles .60 1.50
131 Tyson Foerster .60 1.50
132 Cole Schwindt .75 2.00
133 Adam Beckman .75 2.00
134 Semyon Der-Arguchintsev .60 1.50
135 Alexander Holtz 1.25 3.00
136 Roby Jarventie .60 1.50
137 Tyce Thompson .75 2.00
138 Zac Jones 1.00 2.50
139 Philip Broberg .50 1.25
140 Josiah Slavin .75 2.00
141 Mattias Samuelsson .75 2.00
142 Egor Afanasyev .60 1.50
143 Akira Schmid .75 2.00
144 Raphael Lavoie .60 1.50
145 Alec Regula .50 1.25
146 Scott Perunovich .75 2.00
147 Jordan Spence .60 1.50
148 John-Jason Peterka 1.50 4.00
149 Jack Drury 1.25 3.00
150 Dustin Wolf 2.00 5.00

2021-22 Upper Deck AHL All-Rookie Team

*RED: 1X TO 2.5X BASIC INSERTS
*GOLD/25: 1.5X TO 4X BASIC INSERTS
R1 Logan Thompson 1.50 4.00
R2 Calen Addison .60 1.50
R3 Max Gildon .40 1.00
R4 Riley Damiani .60 1.50
R5 Connor McMichael .60 1.50
R6 Philip Tomasino .75 2.00

2021-22 Upper Deck AHL All-Stars

*RED: .75X TO 2X BASIC INSERTS
*GOLD/25: 1.5X TO 4X BASIC INSERTS
AS1 Jeremy Swayman 2.00 5.00
AS2 Samuel Bolduc .50 1.25
AS3 Tarmo Reunanen .60 1.50
AS4 Morgan Barron .50 1.25
AS5 Cameron Hughes .50 1.25
AS6 Jakub Lauko .50 1.25
AS7 Zane Mcintyre .50 1.25
AS8 Oskari Laaksonen .40 1.00
AS9 Cameron Schilling .40 1.00
AS10 Boris Katchouk .50 1.25
AS11 Connor McMichael .60 1.50
AS12 Taylor Raddysh 1.00 2.50
AS13 Cayden Primeau .50 1.25
AS14 Otto Leskinen .50 1.25
AS15 Connor Mackey .50 1.25
AS16 Kalle Kossila .50 1.25
AS17 Egor Sokolov .60 1.50
AS18 Nathan Todd .40 1.00
AS19 Beck Warm .50 1.25
AS20 Calen Addison .60 1.50
AS21 Cody Franson .50 1.25
AS22 Riley Barber .40 1.00
AS23 Riley Damiani .60 1.50
AS24 Adam Mascherin .50 1.25
AS25 Logan Thompson 1.50 4.00
AS26 Josh Mahura .50 1.25
AS27 Ryan Murphy .50 1.25
AS28 Cooper Marody .40 1.00
AS29 Andrew Poturalski .40 1.00
AS30 T.J. Tynan .40 1.00

2021-22 Upper Deck AHL All-Stars Autographs

AS1 Jeremy Swayman 15.00 40.00
AS2 Samuel Bolduc 4.00 10.00
AS4 Morgan Barron 4.00 10.00
AS8 Oskari Laaksonen 3.00 8.00
AS9 Cameron Schilling 3.00 8.00
AS17 Egor Sokolov 5.00 12.00
AS21 Cody Franson 4.00 10.00
AS22 Riley Barber 3.00 8.00
AS28 Cooper Marody 3.00 8.00

2021-22 Upper Deck AHL Autographs

1 Ty Ronning 6.00 15.00
2 Matthew Phillips 6.00 15.00
3 Matt Boldy 15.00 40.00
5 Vinni Lettieri 4.00 10.00
6 Nicolas Beaudin 4.00 10.00
7 Tim Gettinger 4.00 10.00
9 Jack Dugan 4.00 10.00
10 Samuel Asselin 4.00 10.00
12 Jake Leschyshyn 6.00 15.00
13 William Bitten 4.00 10.00
14 Nolan Foote 4.00 10.00
15 Spencer Martin 4.00 10.00
16 Cole Schneider 5.00 12.00
18 Riley Barber 4.00 10.00
21 Gabriel Dumont 4.00 10.00
23 Tyler Sikura 4.00 10.00
25 Sam Anas 4.00 10.00
27 Cale Fleury 4.00 10.00
28 Egor Sokolov 6.00 15.00
29 Ville Heinola 4.00 10.00
30 Andrew Hammond 4.00 10.00
32 Oskari Laaksonen 4.00 10.00
33 Jordy Bellerive 4.00 10.00
34 Collin Delia 4.00 10.00
35 Gerry Mayhew 4.00 10.00
38 Josh Ho-Sang 4.00 10.00
39 Isaac Ratcliffe 4.00 10.00
40 Tyler Tucker 4.00 10.00
41 Chase De Leo 4.00 10.00
42 Anthony Angello 4.00 10.00
43 Kevin Roy 4.00 10.00
44 Fabian Zetterlund 6.00 15.00
45 Otto Somppi 4.00 10.00
46 Nick Caamano 4.00 10.00
47 Troy Grosenick 4.00 10.00
48 Zac Dalpe 4.00 10.00
49 Damien Giroux 4.00 10.00
50 Cooper Marody 4.00 10.00
51 Jacob Perreault 4.00 10.00
52 Gabriel Fortier 6.00 15.00
53 Ken Appleby 4.00 10.00
54 Ukko-Pekka Luukkonen 10.00 25.00
56 Rafael Harvey-Pinard 6.00 15.00
57 Brendan Guhle 4.00 10.00
60 Luke Philp 4.00 10.00
61 Max Willman 4.00 10.00
62 Samuel Fagemo 6.00 15.00
64 Aleksi Heponiemi 6.00 15.00
67 Dominik Bokk 4.00 10.00
68 Kristian Reichel 4.00 10.00
69 Lassi Thomson 6.00 15.00
71 Nicolas Meloche 4.00 10.00
72 Max McCormick 4.00 10.00
73 Jacob MacDonald 4.00 10.00
74 Joe Veleno 8.00 20.00
75 David Cotton 4.00 10.00
78 Liam Foudy 5.00 12.00
80 Brogan Rafferty 4.00 10.00
81 Xavier Ouellet 4.00 10.00
82 Ryan Suzuki 6.00 15.00
84 Jack Studnicka 4.00 10.00
85 Aidan Dudas 4.00 10.00
86 Matej Pekar 4.00 10.00
88 Cameron Schilling 4.00 10.00
90 Evan Barratt 4.00 10.00
92 Joachim Blichfeld 4.00 10.00
94 Carson Focht 4.00 10.00
95 Alex Turcotte 8.00 20.00
96 Chris Terry 4.00 10.00
98 Michael Sgarbossa 4.00 10.00
99 Jonny Brodzinski 4.00 10.00
100 Hudson Fasching 4.00 10.00
101 Logan Hutsko 5.00 12.00
103 Nikita Alexandrov 5.00 12.00
104 Danila Klimovich 5.00 12.00
107 Tyler Angle 5.00 12.00
108 Marco Rossi 5.00 12.00
109 Braden Schneider 8.00 20.00
110 Kirill Tyutyayev 5.00 12.00
111 Maxim Cajkovic 5.00 12.00
113 Pavel Gogolev 5.00 12.00
116 Samuel Poulin 6.00 15.00
117 Jack Ahcan 6.00 15.00
118 Jonatan Berggren 6.00 15.00
119 Lynden McCallum 5.00 12.00
120 Lukas Reichel 5.00 12.00
122 Cole Koepke 5.00 12.00
123 Jakob Pelletier 5.00 12.00
125 Brayden Tracey 5.00 12.00
126 Daniil Miromanov 6.00 15.00
127 Jordan Kawaguchi 5.00 12.00
128 Simon Lundmark 5.00 12.00
129 Lauri Pajuniemi 5.00 12.00
130 Greg Meireles 5.00 12.00
134 Semyon Der-Arguchintsev 5.00 12.00
135 Alexander Holtz 10.00 25.00
136 Roby Jarventie 5.00 12.00
137 Tyce Thompson 6.00 15.00
140 Josiah Slavin 6.00 15.00
142 Egor Afanasyev 5.00 12.00
144 Raphael Lavoie 5.00 12.00
146 Scott Perunovich 6.00 15.00
148 John-Jason Peterka 25.00 60.00
150 Dustin Wolf 15.00 40.00

2021-22 Upper Deck AHL Captains

*RED: 1X TO 2.5X BASIC INSERTS
*GOLD/25: 2X TO 5X BASIC INSERTS
L1 Brad Malone .30 .75
L2 Michael Mersch .30 .75
L3 Richard Clune .30 .75
L4 Cal O'Reilly .25 .60
L5 Cody McLeod .30 .75
L6 Jaycob Megna .30 .75
L7 Brett Sutter .25 .60
L8 Curtis McKenzie .25 .60
L9 Brian Lashoff .30 .75
L10 Gabriel Dumont .25 .60
L11 Andrew Poturalski .25 .60
L12 Cole Schneider .30 .75
L13 Zac Dalpe .25 .60
L14 Taylor Fedun .30 .75

2021-22 Upper Deck AHL Captains Autographs

L4 Cal O'Reilly 4.00 10.00
L10 Gabriel Dumont 4.00 10.00
L12 Cole Schneider 5.00 12.00
L13 Zac Dalpe 4.00 10.00

2022-23 Upper Deck AHL

1 Brett Seney .25 .60
2 Jonatan Berggren .60 1.50
3 Martin Frk .40 1.00
4 Seth Griffith .25 .60
5 Cooper Marody .25 .60
6 Jesse Ylonen .25 .60
7 Mikhail Maltsev .25 .60
8 Alex Barre-Boulet .25 .60
9 Jan Jenik .30 .75
10 Nicolas Petan .25 .60
11 Jansen Harkins .25 .60
12 Garrett Pilon .25 .60
13 Michael Eyssimont .40 1.00
14 Akira Schmid .25 .60
15 Sean Malone .40 1.00
16 Valtteri Puustinen .30 .75
17 Semyon Der-Arguchintsev .40 1.00
18 Mason Geertsen .25 .60
19 Ukko-Pekka Luukkonen .30 .75
20 Kyle Criscuolo .25 .60
21 Jasper Weatherby .25 .60
22 Calvin Pickard .40 1.00
23 Jonny Brodzinski .25 .60
24 Cayden Primeau .30 .75
25 Riley Damiani .25 .60
26 Jeffrey Viel .25 .60
27 Samuel Poulin .50 1.25
28 Bryce Kindopp .25 .60
29 Zachary Fucale .30 .75
30 Otto Koivula .25 .60
31 Elliot Desnoyers .40 1.00
32 Ville Heinola .25 .60
33 Simon Ryfors .30 .75
34 Scott Reedy .25 .60
35 Roby Jarventie .30 .75
36 Jackson Cates .25 .60
37 Rafael Harvey-Pinard .25 .60
38 Thomas Harley .40 1.00
39 Martin Kaut .25 .60
40 Kole Lind .25 .60
41 Dustin Wolf 1.00 2.50
42 Laurent Dauphin .25 .60
43 Alex Lyon .30 .75
44 Brendan Gaunce .25 .60
45 Jonas Rondbjerg .25 .60
46 Danila Klimovich .30 .75
47 T.J. Tynan .25 .60
48 Logan Hutsko .30 .75
49 Bokondji Imama .30 .75
50 Pavel Dorofeyev .25 .60
51 Jack Drury .30 .75
52 Julien Gauthier .25 .60
53 Brandon Biro .60 1.50
54 Zane Mcintyre .30 .75
55 Charles Hudon .30 .75
56 Oskar Steen .25 .60
57 Lassi Thomson .25 .60
58 Wyatt Kalynuk .25 .60
59 Joey Daccord .40 1.00
60 Arvid Soderblom .25 .60
61 Chris Tierney .30 .75
62 Carson Meyer .30 .75
63 Nikita Okhotiuk .30 .75
64 Sheldon Rempal .25 .60
65 Lukas Dostal .75 2.00
66 Henrik Borgstrom .30 .75
67 Aaron Dell .25 .60
68 Taro Hirose .25 .60
69 Justin Brazeau .30 .75
70 Matthew Robertson .30 .75
71 Maxime Lajoie .30 .75
72 Chris Wagner .25 .60
73 Matthew Villalta .30 .75
74 Philip Tomasino .25 .60
75 Jacob Perreault .40 1.00
76 Grant Hutton .40 1.00
77 Nick Robertson .40 1.00
78 Joel Hofer .25 .60
79 Matthew Phillips .25 .60
80 Simon Holmstrom .40 1.00
81 Luke Evangelista .50 1.25
82 Riley Barber .25 .60
83 Alex Steeves .25 .60
84 Kaedan Korczak .30 .75
85 Dylan Sikura .25 .60
86 Andrew Poturalski .25 .60
87 Mads Sogaard .50 1.25
88 Cole Schneider .25 .60
89 Jakob Pelletier .40 1.00
90 Noel Gunler .30 .75
91 Jordan Spence .40 1.00
92 William Bitten .40 1.00
93 Connor Zary .30 .75
94 Samuel Fagemo .30 .75
95 Jake Christiansen .40 1.00
96 Jordan Gross .25 .60
97 Austin Poganski .25 .60
98 Mason Shaw .25 .60
99 Graeme Clarke .30 .75
100 Maxime Lagace .40 1.00
101 Adam Wilsby SR .75 2.00
102 David Jiricek SR 1.50 4.00
103 Daniel Torgersson SR .75 2.00
104 Matej Blumel SR 1.00 2.50
105 Nick Abruzzese SR .75 2.00
106 Vincent Iorio SR .75 2.00
107 Jiri Kulich SR .75 2.00
108 Vasily Ponomarev SR .75 2.00
109 Mavrik Bourque SR .75 2.00
110 Tuuka Tieksola SR .75 2.00
111 Michael Milne SR .75 2.00
112 Brad Lambert SR .75 2.00
113 Cross Hanas SR 1.00 2.50
114 Ridly Greig SR .75 2.00
115 Yaroslav Askarov SR 1.50 4.00
116 Arshdeep Bains SR .60 1.50
117 Marc McLaughlin SR .75 2.00
118 Isak Rosen SR .75 2.00
119 Brendan Brisson SR .75 2.00
120 Simon Edvinsson SR 1.50 4.00
121 Oskari Salminen SR .75 2.00
122 Karl Henriksson SR .75 2.00
123 Aatu Raty SR .75 2.00
124 Nathan Smith SR .60 1.50
125 Ruslan Iskhakov SR .60 1.50
126 Jachym Kondelik SR .75 2.00
127 Drew Helleson SR .75 2.00
128 Linus Karlsson SR .75 2.00
129 William Eklund SR 1.00 2.50
130 Dylan Garand SR .75 2.00
131 Pontus Holmberg SR .75 2.00
132 Samuel Walker SR .75 2.00
133 Georgii Merkulov SR .75 2.00
134 William Trudeau SR .75 2.00
135 William Dufour SR .75 2.00
136 Ozzy Wiesblatt SR .75 2.00
137 Simon Nemec SR 1.25 3.00
138 Strauss Mann SR .75 2.00
139 Xavier Bourgault SR .75 2.00
140 Philippe Daoust SR .75 2.00
141 Chaz Lucius SR .75 2.00
142 Alexander Pashin SR .75 2.00
143 Danil Gushchin SR .75 2.00
144 Sebastian Cossa SR 1.50 4.00
145 Jack Finley SR 1.00 2.50
146 Jesper Wallstedt SR 1.25 3.00
147 Fabian Lysell SR 1.00 2.50
148 Noel Gunler SR .60 1.50
149 Kirill Marchenko SR 2.00 5.00
150 Thomas Bordeleau SR .75 2.00

2022-23 Upper Deck AHL All Rookie Team

*RED: 1.2X TO 3X BASIC
*GOLD/25: 2X TO 5X BASIC
AR1 Dustin Wolf 1.50 4.00
AR2 Jack Rathbone .50 1.25
AR3 Jordan Spence .60 1.50
AR4 Jakob Pelletier .60 1.50
AR5 JJ Peterka .60 1.50
AR6 Jack Quinn 1.00 2.50

2022-23 Upper Deck AHL All Stars

*RED: .75X TO 2X BASIC
*GOLD/25: 1.5X TO 4X BASIC
AS1 Dustin Wolf 1.50 4.00
AS2 Jordan Gross .40 1.00
AS3 Jordan Spence .60 1.50
AS4 Stefan Noesen .40 1.00
AS5 Andrew Poturalski .40 1.00
AS6 T.J. Tynan .40 1.00
AS7 Troy Grosenick .40 1.00
AS8 Jake Christiansen .60 1.50
AS9 Joseph Duszak .50 1.25
AS10 Martin Frk .60 1.50
AS11 Seth Griffith .40 1.00
AS12 Kiefer Sherwood .40 1.00

2022-23 Upper Deck AHL All Stars Autographs

AS1 Dustin Wolf B 12.00 30.00
AS2 Jordan Gross B 3.00 8.00
AS4 Stefan Noesen A 3.00 8.00
AS5 Andrew Poturalski B 3.00 8.00
AS7 Troy Grosenick B 3.00 8.00
AS8 Jake Christiansen B 5.00 12.00
AS10 Martin Frk B 5.00 12.00
AS12 Kiefer Sherwood B 3.00 8.00

2022-23 Upper Deck AHL Autographs

1 Brett Seney E 4.00 10.00
2 Jonatan Berggren B 10.00 25.00
3 Martin Frk D 6.00 15.00
5 Cooper Marody E 4.00 10.00
6 Jesse Ylonen B 4.00 10.00
7 Mikhail Maltsev E 4.00 10.00
8 Alex Barre-Boulet E 4.00 10.00
9 Jan Jenik E 5.00 12.00
11 Jansen Harkins C 4.00 10.00
12 Garrett Pilon D 4.00 10.00
15 Sean Malone E 6.00 15.00
16 Valtteri Puustinen C 5.00 12.00
18 Mason Geertsen E 4.00 10.00
19 Ukko-Pekka Luukkonen D 5.00 12.00
20 Kyle Criscuolo E 4.00 10.00
21 Jasper Weatherby C 4.00 10.00
22 Calvin Pickard E 6.00 15.00
23 Jonny Brodzinski E 4.00 10.00
27 Samuel Poulin B 8.00 20.00
29 Zachary Fucale E 5.00 12.00
31 Elliot Desnoyers E 6.00 15.00
35 Roby Jarventie E 5.00 12.00
36 Jackson Cates E 4.00 10.00
37 Rafael Harvey-Pinard E 4.00 10.00
39 Martin Kaut A 4.00 10.00
40 Kole Lind A 4.00 10.00
41 Dustin Wolf C 15.00 40.00
42 Laurent Dauphin E 4.00 10.00
44 Brendan Gaunce E 4.00 10.00
46 Danila Klimovich D 5.00 12.00
48 Logan Hutsko E 5.00 12.00
50 Pavel Dorofeyev D 4.00 10.00
52 Julien Gauthier B 4.00 10.00
53 Brandon Biro E 10.00 25.00
54 Zane Mcintyre E 5.00 12.00
55 Charles Hudon E 5.00 12.00
56 Oskar Steen D 4.00 10.00
57 Lassi Thomson B 4.00 10.00
58 Wyatt Kalynuk E 4.00 10.00
59 Joey Daccord E 6.00 15.00
62 Carson Meyer E 5.00 12.00
65 Lukas Dostal C 12.00 30.00
66 Henrik Borgstrom E 5.00 12.00
70 Matthew Robertson D 5.00 12.00
75 Jacob Perreault C 6.00 15.00
78 Joel Hofer E 4.00 10.00
79 Matthew Phillips A 4.00 10.00
81 Luke Evangelista A 8.00 20.00
82 Riley Barber E 4.00 10.00
84 Kaedan Korczak A 5.00 12.00
86 Andrew Poturalski D 4.00 10.00
87 Mads Sogaard A 8.00 20.00
89 Jakob Pelletier A 6.00 15.00
90 Noel Gunler D 5.00 12.00
92 William Bitten D 6.00 15.00
93 Connor Zary B 5.00 12.00
95 Jake Christiansen D 6.00 15.00
96 Jordan Gross E 4.00 10.00
97 Austin Poganski E 4.00 10.00
99 Graeme Clarke E 5.00 12.00
100 Maxime Lagace E 6.00 15.00
102 David Jiricek SR C 12.00 30.00
104 Matej Blumel SR D 8.00 20.00
107 Jiri Kulich SR E 6.00 15.00
108 Vasily Ponomarev SR E 6.00 15.00
109 Mavrik Bourque SR C 6.00 15.00
113 Cross Hanas SR D 8.00 20.00
115 Yaroslav Askarov SR A 12.00 30.00
116 Arshdeep Bains SR E 5.00 12.00
117 Marc McLaughlin SR C 6.00 15.00
119 Brendan Brisson SR A 6.00 15.00
120 Simon Edvinsson SR D 12.00 30.00
123 Aatu Raty SR B 6.00 15.00
124 Nathan Smith SR E 5.00 12.00
126 Jachym Kondelik SR E 6.00 15.00
129 William Eklund SR C 8.00 20.00
130 Dylan Garand SR E 6.00 15.00
135 William Dufour SR C 6.00 15.00
140 Philippe Daoust SR E 6.00 15.00
142 Alexander Pashin SR E 6.00 15.00
144 Sebastian Cossa SR A 12.00 30.00
145 Jack Finley SR E 8.00 20.00
146 Jesper Wallstedt SR B 10.00 25.00
147 Fabian Lysell SR B 8.00 20.00
148 Noel Gunler SR D 5.00 12.00
150 Thomas Bordeleau SR A 6.00 15.00

2022-23 Upper Deck AHL Stars of Tomorrow

*RED: .75X TO 2X BASIC
*GOLD/25: 1.5X TO 4X BASIC
ST1 Tristen Robins .60 1.50
ST2 Simon Nemec 1.00 2.50
ST3 Brad Lambert .60 1.50
ST4 David Jiricek 1.25 3.00
ST5 Jesper Wallstedt 1.00 2.50
ST6 Dylan Garand .60 1.50
ST7 Jiri Kulich .60 1.50
ST8 Fabian Lysell .75 2.00
ST9 Mavrik Bourque .60 1.50
ST10 William Eklund .75 2.00
ST11 Simon Edvinsson 1.25 3.00
ST12 Lukas Cormier .60 1.50

2022-23 Upper Deck AHL Stars of Tomorrow Autographs

ST4 David Jiricek A 15.00 40.00
ST5 Jesper Wallstedt B 12.00 30.00
ST6 Dylan Garand B 8.00 20.00
ST7 Jiri Kulich B 8.00 20.00
ST8 Fabian Lysell B 10.00 25.00
ST9 Mavrik Bourque B 8.00 20.00
ST10 William Eklund B 10.00 25.00

2022-23 Upper Deck AHL Tendys
*RED: .75X TO 2X BASIC
*GOLD/25: 1.5X TO 4X BASIC
T1 Oskari Salminen .50 1.25
T2 Mack Guzda .40 1.00
T3 Anton Khudobin .50 1.25
T4 Keith Kinkaid .30 .75
T5 Zachary Fucale .40 1.00
T6 Eetu Makiniemi .50 1.25
T7 Ivan Prosvetov .30 .75
T8 Troy Grosenick .30 .75
T9 Michael Hutchinson .40 1.00
T10 Olivier Rodrigue .30 .75
T11 Cory Schneider .50 1.25
T12 Jiri Patera .50 1.25
T13 Devin Cooley .40 1.00
T14 Ukko-Pekka Luukkonen .40 1.00
T15 Pheonix Copley .30 .75
T16 Arturs Silovs 1.00 2.50
T17 Aaron Dell .30 .75
T18 Jesper Wallstedt .75 2.00
T19 Dustin Tokarski .40 1.00
T20 Keith Petruzzelli .40 1.00

2022-23 Upper Deck AHL Tendys Autographs
T2 Mack Guzda B 5.00 12.00
T5 Zachary Fucale A 5.00 12.00
T6 Eetu Makiniemi B 6.00 15.00
T7 Ivan Prosvetov B 4.00 10.00
T8 Troy Grosenick A 4.00 10.00
T9 Michael Hutchinson B 5.00 12.00
T10 Olivier Rodrigue B 4.00 10.00
T12 Jiri Patera A 6.00 15.00
T13 Devin Cooley B 5.00 12.00
T14 Ukko-Pekka Luukkonen A 5.00 12.00
T15 Pheonix Copley A 4.00 10.00
T18 Jesper Wallstedt A 10.00 25.00

2023-24 Upper Deck AHL
1 Nathan Smith .30 .75
2 Nic Petan .30 .75
3 Vasily Podkolzin .30 .75
4 Nick Abruzzese .30 .75
5 Matt Murray .50 1.25
6 Xavier Parent .30 .75
7 Lukas Rousek .40 1.00
8 Dustin Wolf 1.50 4.00
9 Rocco Grimaldi .30 .75
10 Brayden Tracey .30 .75
11 Isak Rosen .50 1.25
12 Cooper Marody .30 .75
13 Grigori Denisenko .30 .75
14 Alex Steeves .30 .75
15 Nolan Allan .60 1.50
16 Chris Terry .30 .75
17 Arshdeep Bains .40 1.00
18 Ben Jones .30 .75
19 Kole Lind .30 .75
20 Ryan McAllister .30 .75
21 Mike Sgarbossa .30 .75
22 Elliot Desnoyers .50 1.25
23 Maxence Guenette .50 1.25
24 Cole Bardreau .30 .75
25 Adam Beckman .30 .75
26 Dave Gust .50 1.25
27 Alex Limoges .30 .75
28 Ruslan Iskhakov .40 1.00
29 Jared McIsaac .30 .75
30 Jake Lucchini .30 .75
31 William Dufour .40 1.00
32 Oskar Olausson .30 .75
33 Vasily Ponomarev .50 1.25
34 Connor Zary 1.00 2.50
35 Nils Aman .30 .75
36 Will Cuylle .75 2.00
37 Cole Guttman .50 1.25
38 Jean-Luc Foudy .30 .75
39 Brendan Brisson .50 1.25
40 Jesper Wallstedt .75 2.00
41 Sheldon Rempal .30 .75
42 Benoit-Olivier Groulx .30 .75
43 Hendrix Lapierre .30 .75
44 Nick Robertson .50 1.25
45 Brandt Clarke .50 1.25
46 Brandon Gignac .30 .75
47 Angus Crookshank .50 1.25
48 Matt Rempe .75 2.00
49 Alexander Nylander .40 1.00
50 Simon Nemec 1.00 2.50
51 Alexander True .30 .75
52 Zach Dean .50 1.25
53 Justus Annunen .40 1.00
54 Alex Belzile .30 .75
55 Akil Thomas .40 1.00
56 Trey Fix-Wolansky .30 .75
57 Xavier Bourgault .50 1.25
58 Sean Farrell .50 1.25
59 Olle Lycksell .30 .75
60 Mavrik Bourque .50 1.25
61 Chaz Lucius .50 1.25
62 Egor Afanasyev .50 1.25
63 Colton Dach .60 1.50
64 Riley Damiani .30 .75
65 Andrew Poturalski .30 .75
66 Mitchell Stephens .30 .75
67 Jiri Kulich 1.00 2.50
68 Pontus Holmberg .30 .75
69 Jonatan Berggren .40 1.00
70 Kyle Capobianco .30 .75
71 Nathan Todd .30 .75
72 Mason Lohrei .75 2.00
73 Felix Robert .30 .75
74 Brad Lambert .50 1.25
75 Adam Gaudette .40 1.00
76 Jack Thompson .40 1.00
77 Zac Dalpe .30 .75
78 Jake Christiansen .30 .75
79 Raphael Lavoie .50 1.25
80 Graeme Clarke .40 1.00
81 Joakim Kemell .50 1.25
82 Alex Turcotte .30 .75
83 Olivier Rodrigue .30 .75
84 Sebastian Cossa 1.00 2.50
85 Nathan Walker .30 .75
86 Ryker Evans .60 1.50
87 Ozzy Wiesblatt .50 1.25
88 Yaroslav Askarov 1.25 3.00
89 Adam Cracknell .30 .75
90 Gage Goncalves .50 1.25
91 Dylan Guenther .60 1.50
92 Ty Smith .50 1.25
93 Victor Soderstrom .30 .75
94 Fabian Lysell .60 1.50
95 David Jiricek .50 1.25
96 Samuel Poulin .30 .75
97 Mads Sogaard .30 .75
98 Brandon Bussi .50 1.25
99 Jacob Perreault .30 .75
100 Danil Gushchin .50 1.25
101 Josh Doan SR 1.00 2.50
102 Joel Blomqvist SR 1.25 3.00
103 Drew Commesso SR 1.00 2.50
104 Francesco Pinelli SR 1.00 2.50
105 Matthew Maggio SR 1.00 2.50
106 Brennan Othmann SR 1.25 3.00
107 Hank Crone SR 1.25 3.00
108 David Spacek SR 1.00 2.50
109 Henry Thrun SR 1.00 2.50
110 Tristan Allard SR 1.00 2.50
111 Samu Tuomaala SR 1.00 2.50
112 Erik Portillo SR 1.00 2.50
113 Topias Vilen SR 1.00 2.50
114 Spencer Knight SR 1.00 2.50
115 Brett Berard SR 1.00 2.50
116 Carson Lambos SR 1.25 3.00
117 Zachary L'Heureux SR 1.00 2.50
118 Leo Loof SR 1.00 2.50
119 Cole McWard SR 1.00 2.50
120 Fedor Svechkov SR 1.25 3.00
121 Ryan Winterton SR 1.00 2.50
122 Mackie Samoskevich SR 1.50 4.00
123 Logan Stankoven SR 2.50 6.00
124 Ethan Del Mastro SR 1.00 2.50
125 Logan Mailloux SR 1.25 3.00
126 Nathan Gaucher SR 1.25 3.00
127 Riley Kidney SR 1.00 2.50
128 Lucas Ciona SR 1.00 2.50
129 Nikita Nesterenko SR 1.00 2.50
130 Jesper Vikman SR 1.00 2.50
131 Kyle McDonald SR 1.00 2.50
132 Skyler Brind'Amour SR 1.00 2.50
133 Olen Zellweger SR 1.25 3.00
134 Kent Johnson SR 1.00 2.50
135 Ivan Ivan SR 1.00 2.50
136 Corson Ceulemans SR 1.00 2.50
137 Brett Harrison SR 1.00 2.50
138 Logan Morrison SR 1.00 2.50
139 Elmer Soderblom SR 1.00 2.50
140 Luca Del Bel Belluz SR 1.00 2.50
141 Matt Savoie SR 2.00 5.00
142 Reid Schaefer SR 1.25 3.00
143 Jayden Grubbe SR 1.00 2.50
144 Ethan Cardwell SR 1.00 2.50
145 Zach Ostapchuk SR 1.25 3.00
146 Zachary Bolduc SR 1.25 3.00
147 Topi Niemela SR 1.00 2.50
148 Marco Kasper SR 2.50 6.00
149 Joshua Roy SR 1.25 3.00
150 Shane Wright SR 1.25 3.00

2023-24 Upper Deck AHL Blue Stars
*BLUE STR/17: 5X TO 12X BASIC
*BLUE STR SR/17: 4X TO 10X BASIC

2023-24 Upper Deck AHL Red Stripes
*RED STRP/76: 1.5X TO 4X BASIC

2023-24 Upper Deck AHL Autographs
1 Nathan Smith 4.00 10.00
2 Nic Petan 4.00 10.00
4 Nick Abruzzese 4.00 10.00
6 Xavier Parent SP 4.00 10.00
7 Lukas Rousek 5.00 12.00
8 Dustin Wolf SP 20.00 50.00
10 Brayden Tracey 4.00 10.00
12 Cooper Marody 4.00 10.00
14 Alex Steeves 4.00 10.00
15 Nolan Allan SP 8.00 20.00
16 Chris Terry 4.00 10.00
20 Ryan McAllister 4.00 10.00
21 Mike Sgarbossa 4.00 10.00
23 Maxence Guenette 6.00 15.00
24 Cole Bardreau 4.00 10.00
25 Adam Beckman 4.00 10.00
26 Dave Gust 6.00 15.00
27 Alex Limoges 4.00 10.00
28 Ruslan Iskhakov 5.00 12.00
29 Jared McIsaac SP 4.00 10.00
30 Jake Lucchini 4.00 10.00
31 William Dufour 5.00 12.00
32 Oskar Olausson SP 4.00 10.00
34 Connor Zary 12.00 30.00
36 Will Cuylle 10.00 25.00
38 Jean-Luc Foudy 4.00 10.00
40 Jesper Wallstedt 10.00 25.00
41 Sheldon Rempal 4.00 10.00
42 Benoit-Olivier Groulx 4.00 10.00
45 Brandt Clarke SP 6.00 15.00
47 Angus Crookshank 6.00 15.00
51 Alexander True 4.00 10.00
52 Zach Dean 6.00 15.00
55 Akil Thomas 5.00 12.00
57 Xavier Bourgault 6.00 15.00
60 Mavrik Bourque SP 6.00 15.00
61 Chaz Lucius 6.00 15.00
69 Jonatan Berggren 5.00 12.00
76 Jack Thompson SP 5.00 12.00
78 Jake Christiansen 4.00 10.00
79 Raphael Lavoie 6.00 15.00
80 Graeme Clarke 5.00 12.00
81 Joakim Kemell 6.00 15.00
83 Olivier Rodrigue 4.00 10.00
86 Ryker Evans SP 8.00 20.00
87 Ozzy Wiesblatt SP 6.00 15.00
89 Adam Cracknell 4.00 10.00
92 Ty Smith 6.00 15.00
94 Fabian Lysell SP 8.00 20.00
96 Samuel Poulin 4.00 10.00
99 Jacob Perreault SP 4.00 10.00
100 Danil Gushchin SP 6.00 15.00
104 Francesco Pinelli SR SP 6.00 15.00
106 Brennan Othmann SR SP 8.00 20.00
110 Tristan Allard SR 6.00 15.00
116 Carson Lambos SR 8.00 20.00
117 Zachary L'Heureux SR 6.00 15.00
121 Ryan Winterton SR SP 6.00 15.00
123 Logan Stankoven SR 15.00 40.00
124 Ethan Del Mastro SR SP 6.00 15.00
125 Logan Mailloux SR SP 8.00 20.00
126 Nathan Gaucher SR 8.00 20.00
127 Riley Kidney SR SP 6.00 15.00
128 Lucas Ciona SR SP 6.00 15.00
130 Jesper Vikman SR SP 6.00 15.00
133 Olen Zellweger SR SP 8.00 20.00
135 Ivan Ivan SR 6.00 15.00
137 Brett Harrison SR SP 6.00 15.00
138 Logan Morrison SR 6.00 15.00
141 Matt Savoie SR SP 12.00 30.00
142 Reid Schaefer SR 8.00 20.00
143 Jayden Grubbe SR 6.00 15.00
144 Ethan Cardwell SR SP 6.00 15.00
146 Zachary Bolduc SR 8.00 20.00
149 Joshua Roy SR SP 8.00 20.00
150 Shane Wright SR SP 8.00 20.00

2023-24 Upper Deck AHL Hot Shots
*RED STRP/99: .8X TO 2X BASIC
*BLUE STAR/35: 1.2X TO 3X BASIC
HS1 Connor Zary 1.50 4.00
HS2 Mavrik Bourque .75 2.00
HS3 Shane Wright 1.00 2.50
HS4 Elmer Soderblom .75 2.00
HS5 Olen Zellweger 1.00 2.50
HS6 Matt Savoie 1.50 4.00
HS7 Logan Stankoven 2.00 5.00
HS8 Reid Schaefer 1.00 2.50
HS9 Fabian Lysell 1.00 2.50
HS10 Marco Kasper 2.00 5.00
HS11 Corson Ceulemans .75 2.00
HS12 Joshua Roy 1.00 2.50

2023-24 Upper Deck AHL Tendys
*RED STRP/99: 1X TO 2.5X BASIC
*BLUE STR/35: 2X TO 5X BASIC
T1 Sebastian Cossa 1.50 4.00
T2 Brandon Bussi .75 2.00
T3 Dustin Wolf 2.50 6.00
T4 Arturs Silovs 1.50 4.00
T5 Matt Murray .75 2.00
T6 Justus Annunen .60 1.50
T7 Malcolm Subban .60 1.50
T8 Strauss Mann .75 2.00
T9 Chris Driedger .50 1.25
T10 Jesper Wallstedt 1.25 3.00
T11 Joel Blomqvist 1.00 2.50
T12 Jet Greaves 1.25 3.00
T13 Yaroslav Askarov 2.00 5.00
T14 Matt Villalta .60 1.50
T15 Olivier Rodrigue .50 1.25
T16 Spencer Knight .75 2.00
T17 Vadim Zherenko .75 2.00
T18 Jiri Patera 1.25 3.00
T19 Drew Commesso .75 2.00
T20 Mads Sogaard .50 1.25

2023-24 Upper Deck AHL Tendys Autographs
T3 Dustin Wolf SP 30.00 80.00
T6 Justus Annunen 8.00 20.00
T10 Jesper Wallstedt 15.00 40.00
T15 Olivier Rodrigue SP 6.00 15.00
T18 Jiri Patera 15.00 40.00

2023-24 Upper Deck AHL Throwbacks
TB1 Chris Terry .75 2.00
TB2 Bokondji Imama .75 2.00
TB3 Jeff Malott .75 2.00
TB4 Garrett Wilson .75 2.00
TB5 Trevor Carrick .75 2.00
TB6 Mike Sgarbossa .75 2.00
TB7 Keaton Middleton .75 2.00
TB8 Victor Soderstrom .75 2.00
TB9 Cavan Fitzgerald .75 2.00
TB10 Adam Cracknell .75 2.00
TB11 Joseph Blandisi .75 2.00
TB12 Jeffrey Viel .75 2.00
TB13 Kyle Clifford .75 2.00
TB14 Scott Sabourin .75 2.00
TB15 Kale Kessy .75 2.00
TB16 Brett Sutter .75 2.00
TB17 Cal O'Reilly .75 2.00
TB18 Mason Geertsen .75 2.00

2024-25 Upper Deck AHL
1 Max McCormick .30 .75
2 Lucas Carlsson .30 .75
3 Garrett Pilon .30 .75
4 Emil Bemstrom .30 .75
5 Alex Steeves .30 .75
6 Carson Lambos .60 1.50
7 Colton Dach .60 1.50
8 Trevor Carrick .30 .75
9 Gustav Olofsson .30 .75
10 Alex Barre-Boulet .30 .75
11 Angus Crookshank .30 .75
12 Domenick Fensore .30 .75
13 Vinnie Hinostroza .30 .75
14 Kevin Korchinski .40 1.00
15 Adam Klapka .50 1.25
16 Grigori Denisenko .30 .75
17 Isak Rosen .30 .75
18 Brett Berard .50 1.25
19 Lucas Condotta .30 .75
20 Tyler Madden .40 1.00
21 Ashton Sautner .30 .75
22 T.J. Tynan .30 .75
23 Alex Gallant .30 .75
24 Cal O'Reilly .30 .75
25 Amadeus Lombardi .40 1.00
26 Owen Sillinger .30 .75
27 Daniel Walcott .30 .75
28 Jack Ahcan .30 .75
29 Ryan Schmelzer .30 .75
30 Hugh McGing .30 .75
31 Ethan Cardwell .40 1.00
32 Sammy Walker .30 .75
33 Pavol Regenda .30 .75
34 Andrew Agozzino .30 .75
35 Brendan Gaunce .30 .75
36 Gage Quinney .30 .75
37 Curtis McKenzie .30 .75
38 Rocco Grimaldi .30 .75
39 Justin Dowling .30 .75
40 Fabian Lysell 1.25 3.00
41 Zach Dean .50 1.25
42 Brian Pinho .30 .75
43 Trey Fix-Wolansky .30 .75
44 Samuel Fagemo .30 .75
45 Josiah Didier .40 1.00
46 Derrick Pouliot .30 .75
47 Ethan Del Mastro .50 1.25
48 Joseph Gambardella .30 .75
49 Axel Jonsson-Fjallby .30 .75
50 Kyle Clifford .30 .75
51 Georgii Merkulov .30 .75
52 Jayson Megna .30 .75
53 Ethen Frank .30 .75
54 Joakim Kemell .50 1.25
55 Cale Fleury .30 .75
56 Zac Dalpe .30 .75
57 Joshua Roy .75 2.00
58 John Stevens .30 .75
59 Cole Bardreau .30 .75
60 Jonathan Gruden .30 .75
61 Zachary L'Heureux .60 1.50
62 Drew Helleson .30 .75
63 Brogan Rafferty .30 .75
64 Alex Nylander .40 1.00
65 Ty Smith .50 1.25
66 Rasmus Asplund .30 .75
67 Alex Belzile .30 .75
68 Linus Karlsson .30 .75
69 Samu Tuomaala .50 1.25
70 Tanner Laczynski .30 .75
71 Luca Del Bel Belluz .50 1.25
72 Phil Kemp .50 1.25
73 Nikita Nesterenko .30 .75
74 Olle Lycksell .30 .75
75 Chris Terry .30 .75
76 Mike Vecchione .30 .75
77 Walker Duehr .30 .75
78 Brett Murray .30 .75
79 Seth Griffith .30 .75
80 Marc Del Gaizo .30 .75
81 Mason Jobst .30 .75
82 Josh Doan .75 2.00
83 Kyle Capobianco .30 .75
84 Aaron Ness .30 .75
85 Ben McCartney .30 .75
86 Matt Savoie .50 1.25
87 Benoit-Olivier Groulx .30 .75
88 Ryan Suzuki .50 1.25
89 Brad Lambert .60 1.50
90 Kole Lind .30 .75
91 Chase Wouters .40 1.00
92 Matthew Peca .30 .75
93 Sam Poulin .30 .75
94 Danil Gushchin .30 .75
95 Glenn Gawdin .30 .75
96 Matthew Highmore .40 1.00
97 Matej Blumel .30 .75
98 Egor Sokolov .30 .75
99 Gabriel Dumont .30 .75
100 Vinni Lettieri .30 .75
101 Artyom Levshunov SR 2.50 6.00
102 Hunter Haight SR 1.25 3.00
103 Dalibor Dvorsky SR 1.25 3.00
104 Jacob Melanson SR 1.00 2.50
105 Konsta Helenius SR 1.25 3.00
106 Cameron Wright SR 1.00 2.50
107 Parker Ford SR 1.00 2.50
108 Ryan Tverberg SR 1.00 2.50
109 Filip Bystedt SR 1.00 2.50
110 Stephen Halliday SR 1.00 2.50
111 Jared Davidson SR 1.00 2.50
112 Scott Morrow SR 1.25 3.00
113 Artem Duda SR 1.00 2.50
114 Adam Sykora SR 1.00 2.50
115 Collin Graf SR 1.00 2.50
116 Rory Kerins SR 1.00 2.50
117 Hunter McDonald SR 1.00 2.50
118 Maksymilian Szuber SR 1.00 2.50
119 Ivan Miroshnichenko SR .75 2.00
120 Rutger McGroarty SR 2.00 5.00
121 Christoffer Sedoff SR 1.00 2.50
122 Chase Wheatcroft SR 1.00 2.50
123 Alex Jefferies SR 1.00 2.50
124 Bradly Nadeau SR 1.50 4.00
125 Jonathan Lekkerimaki SR 2.50 6.00
126 Justin Hryckowian SR 1.25 3.00
127 Michael Benning SR 1.25 3.00
128 Owen Beck SR .75 2.00
129 Frank Nazar SR 3.00 8.00
130 Ville Ottavainen SR 1.25 3.00
131 Denton Mateychuk SR 2.00 5.00
132 Lian Bichsel SR 2.00 5.00
133 John Farinacci SR 1.00 2.50
134 Nate Danielson SR 1.50 4.00
135 Maxwell Crozier SR 1.00 2.50
136 Sam Colangelo SR 1.00 2.50
137 Maximus Wanner SR 1.00 2.50
138 Nikita Prishchepov SR 1.00 2.50
139 Luca Cagnoni SR 1.00 2.50
140 Jake Livingstone SR .60 1.50
141 Max Sasson SR 1.00 2.50
142 Christian Kyrou SR 1.00 2.50
143 Zach Metsa SR 1.00 2.50
144 Nikita Chibrikov SR 1.00 2.50
145 William Stromgren SR 1.00 2.50
146 Seamus Casey SR 1.25 3.00
147 Hunter McKown SR .60 1.50
148 Bogdan Trineyev SR 1.00 2.50
149 Dylan Duke SR 1.00 2.50
150 Carter Mazur SR 1.00 2.50

2024-25 Upper Deck AHL Exclusives
*EXCLUSIVES/100: 1.2X TO 3X BASIC

2024-25 Upper Deck AHL Autographs
1 Max McCormick 4.00 10.00
2 Lucas Carlsson 4.00 10.00
5 Alex Steeves 4.00 10.00
6 Carson Lambos 8.00 20.00
7 Colton Dach 8.00 20.00
9 Gustav Olofsson 4.00 10.00
11 Angus Crookshank 4.00 10.00
12 Domenick Fensore 4.00 10.00
15 Adam Klapka 6.00 15.00
18 Brett Berard 6.00 15.00
19 Lucas Condotta 4.00 10.00
21 Ashton Sautner 4.00 10.00
23 Alex Gallant 4.00 10.00
24 Cal O'Reilly 4.00 10.00
25 Amadeus Lombardi 5.00 12.00
26 Owen Sillinger 4.00 10.00
27 Daniel Walcott 4.00 10.00
28 Jack Ahcan 4.00 10.00
30 Hugh McGing 4.00 10.00
31 Ethan Cardwell 5.00 12.00
32 Sammy Walker 4.00 10.00
33 Pavol Regenda 4.00 10.00
34 Andrew Agozzino 4.00 10.00
36 Gage Quinney 4.00 10.00
37 Curtis McKenzie 4.00 10.00
38 Rocco Grimaldi 4.00 10.00
40 Fabian Lysell 15.00 40.00
41 Zach Dean 6.00 15.00
43 Trey Fix-Wolansky 4.00 10.00
45 Josiah Didier 5.00 12.00
46 Derrick Pouliot 4.00 10.00
48 Joseph Gambardella 4.00 10.00
50 Kyle Clifford 4.00 10.00
53 Ethen Frank 4.00 10.00
56 Zac Dalpe 4.00 10.00
58 John Stevens 4.00 10.00
59 Cole Bardreau 4.00 10.00
61 Zachary L'Heureux 8.00 20.00
63 Brogan Rafferty 4.00 10.00
65 Ty Smith 6.00 15.00
66 Rasmus Asplund 4.00 10.00
67 Alex Belzile 4.00 10.00
68 Linus Karlsson 4.00 10.00
69 Samu Tuomaala 6.00 15.00
72 Phil Kemp 6.00 15.00
74 Olle Lycksell 4.00 10.00
76 Mike Vecchione 4.00 10.00
78 Brett Murray 4.00 10.00
79 Seth Griffith 4.00 10.00
81 Mason Jobst 4.00 10.00
83 Kyle Capobianco 4.00 10.00
84 Aaron Ness 4.00 10.00
90 Kole Lind 4.00 10.00
91 Chase Wouters 5.00 12.00
92 Matthew Peca 4.00 10.00
94 Danil Gushchin 4.00 10.00
95 Glenn Gawdin 4.00 10.00
96 Matthew Highmore 5.00 12.00
97 Matej Blumel 4.00 10.00
99 Gabriel Dumont 4.00 10.00
101 Artyom Levshunov SR SP 15.00 40.00
104 Jacob Melanson SR 6.00 15.00
106 Cameron Wright SR 6.00 15.00
107 Parker Ford SR 6.00 15.00
108 Ryan Tverberg SR 6.00 15.00
111 Jared Davidson SR 6.00 15.00
113 Artem Duda SR 6.00 15.00
114 Adam Sykora SR 6.00 15.00
116 Rory Kerins SR 6.00 15.00
118 Maksymilian Szuber SR 6.00 15.00
122 Chase Wheatcroft SR 6.00 15.00
127 Michael Benning SR 8.00 20.00
133 John Farinacci SR 6.00 15.00
135 Maxwell Crozier SR 6.00 15.00
140 Jake Livingstone SR 4.00 10.00
142 Christian Kyrou SR 6.00 15.00
143 Zach Metsa SR 6.00 15.00
144 Nikita Chibrikov SR SP 6.00 15.00
150 Carter Mazur SR SP 6.00 15.00

2024-25 Upper Deck AHL Bound for Stardom
*RED/75: 1X TO 2.5X BASIC
BFS1 Konsta Helenius 1.00 2.50
BFS2 Samuel Fagemo .50 1.25
BFS3 Denton Mateychuk 1.50 4.00
BFS4 Frank Nazar 2.50 6.00
BFS5 Brett Berard .75 2.00
BFS6 Kevin Korchinski .60 1.50
BFS7 Linus Karlsson .50 1.25
BFS8 Carson Lambos 1.00 2.50
BFS9 Adam Klapka .75 2.00
BFS10 Matt Savoie .75 2.00
BFS11 Josh Doan 1.25 3.00
BFS12 Carter Mazur .75 2.00
BFS13 Georgii Merkulov .50 1.25
BFS14 Fabian Lysell 2.00 5.00
BFS15 Ethan Cardwell .60 1.50
BFS16 Artyom Levshunov 2.00 5.00
BFS17 Brad Lambert 1.00 2.50
BFS18 Jonathan Lekkerimaki 2.00 5.00
BFS19 Isak Rosen .50 1.25
BFS20 Nikita Chibrikov .75 2.00
BFS21 Zachary L'Heureux 1.00 2.50
BFS22 Angus Crookshank .50 1.25
BFS23 Rutger McGroarty 1.50 4.00
BFS24 Luca Del Bel Belluz .75 2.00
BFS25 Zach Dean .75 2.00

2024-25 Upper Deck AHL Bound for Stardom Autographs
BFS5 Brett Berard 6.00 15.00
BFS7 Linus Karlsson 4.00 10.00
BFS8 Carson Lambos 8.00 20.00
BFS9 Adam Klapka 6.00 15.00
BFS12 Carter Mazur 6.00 15.00
BFS14 Fabian Lysell 15.00 40.00
BFS15 Ethan Cardwell 5.00 12.00
BFS16 Artyom Levshunov 15.00 40.00
BFS20 Nikita Chibrikov 6.00 15.00
BFS21 Zachary L'Heureux 8.00 20.00
BFS22 Angus Crookshank 4.00 10.00
BFS25 Zach Dean 6.00 15.00

2024-25 Upper Deck AHL Tendys
*RED/75: 1X TO 2.5X BASIC
T1 Joel Blomqvist 1.00 2.50
T2 Brandon Bussi .75 2.00
T3 Chris Driedger .50 1.25
T4 Louis Domingue .60 1.50
T5 Dennis Hildeby 1.00 2.50
T6 Nikita Tolopilo .75 2.00
T7 Trent Miner .75 2.00
T8 Isaac Poulter .75 2.00
T9 Devin Cooley .75 2.00
T10 Erik Portillo 1.00 2.50
T11 Thomas Milic .60 1.50
T12 Yaroslav Askarov 1.00 2.50
T13 Matt Tomkins .50 1.25
T14 Sebastian Cossa 2.00 5.00
T15 Drew Commesso 1.00 2.50

2024-25 Upper Deck AHL Tendys Autographs
T1 Joel Blomqvist 12.00 30.00
T2 Brandon Bussi 10.00 25.00
T3 Chris Driedger 6.00 15.00
T4 Louis Domingue 8.00 20.00
T5 Dennis Hildeby SP 12.00 30.00
T6 Nikita Tolopilo 10.00 25.00
T7 Trent Miner 10.00 25.00
T8 Isaac Poulter 10.00 25.00
T11 Thomas Milic 8.00 20.00
T13 Matt Tomkins 6.00 15.00
T14 Sebastian Cossa SP 25.00 60.00

2024-25 Upper Deck AHL Two Way Play
*RED/75: 1X TO 2.5X BASIC
TWP1 Mike Vecchione .50 1.25
TWP2 Rasmus Asplund .50 1.25
TWP3 Sheldon Dries .50 1.25
TWP4 John Stevens .50 1.25
TWP5 Brandon Gignac .50 1.25
TWP6 Alex Steeves .50 1.25
TWP7 Tanner Laczynski .50 1.25
TWP8 Nikita Nesterenko .50 1.25
TWP9 Max McCormick .50 1.25
TWP10 Olle Lycksell .50 1.25

2024-25 Upper Deck AHL Two Way Play Autographs
TWP1 Mike Vecchione 6.00 15.00
TWP2 Rasmus Asplund 6.00 15.00
TWP3 Sheldon Dries 6.00 15.00
TWP4 John Stevens 6.00 15.00
TWP5 Brandon Gignac 6.00 15.00
TWP6 Alex Steeves 6.00 15.00
TWP9 Max McCormick 6.00 15.00
TWP10 Olle Lycksell 6.00 15.00

2017-18 Upper Deck CHL
1 Joseph Veleno .30 .75
2 Carter Hart .60 1.50
3 Max Jones .40 1.00
4 Lucas Chiodo .25 .60
5 Ondrej Vala .25 .60
6 Kyle Maksimovich .25 .60
7 Kale Clague .30 .75
8 Jeffrey Truchon-Viel .25 .60
9 Garrett Pilon .25 .60
10 Jake Bean .40 1.00
11 Dylan Wells .25 .60
12 William Bitten .25 .60
13 Ryan Moore .25 .60
14 Jakob Stukel .25 .60
15 Jordan Martel .25 .60
16 Vince Loschiavo .25 .60
17 Zach Magwood .25 .60
18 David Quenneville .25 .60
19 Jack Studnicka .40 1.00
20 Vitalii Abramov .25 .60
21 Beck Malenstyn .25 .60
22 Sam Steel .30 .75
23 Alexander Chmelevski .25 .60
24 Brady Gilmour .25 .60
25 Cody Glass .60 1.50
26 Ty Smith .40 1.00
27 Davis Koch .25 .60
28 Ivan Lodnia .25 .60
29 Matteo Gennaro .25 .60
30 Dillon Dube .40 1.00
31 Nicholas Chyzowski .25 .60
32 Jordan Sambrook .25 .60
33 Mason Shaw .25 .60
34 Anthony Salinitri .25 .60
35 Juuso Valimaki .25 .60
36 Jake Leschyshyn .25 .60
37 Michael DiPietro .25 .60
38 Calen Addison .40 1.00
39 Jaret Anderson-Dolan .40 1.00
40 Morgan Frost .40 1.00
41 Jayden Halbgewachs .25 .60
42 Ryan McGregor .25 .60
43 Maxime Comtois .40 1.00
44 Cale Fleury .30 .75
45 Noel Hoefenmayer .25 .60
46 Arnaud Durandeau .25 .60
47 Logan Stanley .40 1.00
48 Dmitry Sokolov .40 1.00
49 Trent Fox .25 .60
50 Jordan Kyrou .40 1.00
51 Nicolas Hague .25 .60
52 Macauley Carson .25 .60
53 Elijah Brown .25 .60
54 Ben Jones .25 .60
55 Stuart Skinner .50 1.25
56 Ryan McLeod .30 .75
57 Pascal Corbeil .25 .60
58 Parker Kelly .25 .60
59 Evan Bouchard .75 2.00
60 Evan Fitzpatrick .25 .60
61 Matthew Struthers .25 .60
62 Tanner Kaspick .25 .60
63 Ben Hawerchuk .25 .60
64 Cedric Pare .25 .60
65 D'Artagnan Joly .25 .60
66 Zachary Lauzon .25 .60
67 Tim Gettinger .25 .60
68 Isaac Ratcliffe .30 .75
69 Drake Batherson .40 1.00
70 Brett Howden .25 .60
71 Givani Smith .25 .60
72 Peter Abbandonato .25 .60
73 Connor Hall .25 .60
74 Matthew Boucher .25 .60
75 Taylor Raddysh .40 1.00
76 Mitchell Balmas .25 .60
77 Jonah Gadjovich .25 .60
78 Ryan Peckford .25 .60
79 Jacob Paquette .25 .60
80 Aleksi Heponiemi .25 .60
81 Tyler Benson .25 .60
82 Jett Woo .30 .75
83 Benoit-Olivier Groulx .40 1.00
84 Nick Suzuki .75 2.00
85 Nate Schnarr .30 .75
86 Travis Barron .25 .60
87 Cal Foote .25 .60
88 Olivier Garneau .25 .60
89 Riley Stillman .25 .60
90 Adam Mascherin .25 .60
91 Jared McIsaac .30 .75
92 Zach Gallant .25 .60
93 Cliff Pu .25 .60
94 Matthew Timms .25 .60
95 Ryan Merkley .25 .60
96 Bailey Webster .25 .60
97 Matthew Strome .30 .75
98 Markus Phillips .25 .60
99 Kole Lind .30 .75
100 Michael Rasmussen .25 .60
101 David Levin .25 .60
102 Connor Bunnaman .25 .60
103 Maxime Fortier .25 .60
104 Tyler Steenbergen .25 .60
105 Derek Gentile .25 .60
106 Maurizio Colella .25 .60
107 Hudson Elynuik .25 .60
108 Matthew Phillips .30 .75
109 Liam Hawel .30 .75
110 Hugo Roy .25 .60
111 Brett McKenzie .25 .60
112 Nicolas Beaudin .25 .60
113 Jake Durham .25 .60
114 Dominic Cormier .25 .60
115 Aaron Hyman .25 .60
116 Jonathan Ang .25 .60
117 Nicholas Caamano .25 .60
118 Jeffrey Durocher .25 .60
119 Brady Hinz .25 .60
120 Anthony Popovich .25 .60
121 Trenton Bourque .25 .60
122 Glenn Gawdin .30 .75
123 Pierre-Olivier Joseph .30 .75
124 Justin Fazio .25 .60
125 Nolan Volcan .25 .60
126 Alexandre Alain .25 .60
127 Griffen Outhouse .25 .60
128 Adam Thilander .25 .60
129 Brayden Gorda .25 .60
130 Stephen Dhillon .25 .60
131 Patrick Bajkov .25 .60
132 MacKenzie Entwistle .30 .75
133 Otto Somppi .25 .60
134 Robert Thomas .40 1.00
135 Thomas Gregoire .25 .60
136 Kyle Jessiman .25 .60
137 Christopher Paquette .25 .60
138 Stelio Mattheos .30 .75
139 Evan Cormier .25 .60
140 Brody Willms .25 .60
141 Shawn Boudrias .25 .60
142 Adam Marsh .25 .60
143 Carson Mackinnon .25 .60
144 Austen Keating .25 .60
145 Artyom Minulin .25 .60
146 Jacob McGrath .30 .75
147 Marc-Olivier Duquette .25 .60
148 Keaton Middleton .25 .60
149 Giorgio Estephan .25 .60
150 Isaac Nurse .25 .60
151 Noah Gregor .25 .60
152 Boris Katchouk .25 .60
153 Morgan Geekie .30 .75
154 Josh Brook .30 .75
155 Jason Robertson 1.25 3.00
156 Aaron Luchuk .25 .60
157 Ian Scott .30 .75
158 Tyler Soy .25 .60
159 Conor Timmins .25 .60
160 Antoine Morand .25 .60
161 Kody McDonald .25 .60
162 Jack Kopacka .25 .60
163 Mathieu Boucher .25 .60
164 Sean Day .25 .60
165 Libor Hajek .25 .60
166 Domenic Commisso .25 .60
167 Antoine Samuel .25 .60
168 Etienne Montpetit .25 .60
169 Riley Sutter .25 .60
170 Jeremy Helvig .25 .60
171 Jocktan Chainey .30 .75
172 Jared Bethune .25 .60
173 Logan Flodell .25 .60
174 Ty Ronning .25 .60
175 Alex Barre-Boulet .40 1.00
176 James Phelan .25 .60
177 Jordy Bellerive .30 .75
178 Gabe Vilardi .40 1.00
179 Samuel Asselin .40 1.00
180 James Malm .25 .60
181 Cole Fonstad .25 .60
182 Jordan-Tyler Fournier .25 .60
183 Samuel Blier .25 .60
184 Adam Cheezo .25 .60
185 Nikita Popugaev .25 .60
186 Brandon Hagel .40 1.00
187 Scott Walford .25 .60
188 Cole Kehler .25 .60
189 Vojtech Budik .25 .60
190 David Noel .30 .75
191 Reilly Pickard .25 .60
192 Brendan De Jong .25 .60
193 Mikhail Denisov .25 .60
194 Skyler McKenzie .25 .60
195 Pascal Laberge .25 .60
196 Lane Zablocki .25 .60
197 Ty Lewis .25 .60
198 Josh Mahura .25 .60
199 Josh Paterson .25 .60
200 Kyle Olson .30 .75
201 Will Warm .25 .60

202 Matt Fonteyne .25 .60
203 Jordan Hollett .25 .60
204 Dmitri Zaitsev .25 .60
205 Kevin Hancock .25 .60
206 Joseph Garreffa .25 .60
207 Johnny Corneil .25 .60
208 Matt Bradley .25 .60
209 Akil Thomas .30 .75
210 Connor Dewar .25 .60
211 Noah Dobson .50 1.25
212 Christian Girhiny .25 .60
213 Matthew Grouchy .25 .60
214 Dawson Davidson .25 .60
215 Luke Boka .25 .60
216 Tye Felhaber .25 .60
217 Liam Murphy .25 .60
218 Olivier Rodrigue .25 .60
219 Logan DeNoble .25 .60
220 Peter Stratis .25 .60
221 Denis Mikhnin .25 .60
222 Alexis Gravel .30 .75
223 Pavel Koltygin .25 .60
224 Dmitri Samorukov .25 .60
225 Mark Rubinchik .25 .60
226 Mark Grametbauer .25 .60
227 Allan McShane .25 .60
228 Ivan Kosorenkov .25 .60
229 Grayson Pawlenchuk .25 .60
230 Brad Morrison .25 .60
231 Leon Gawanke .25 .60
232 Kade Landry .25 .60
233 Adam Ruzicka .25 .60
234 Jeremy McKenna .25 .60
235 Rafael Harvey-Pinard .40 1.00
236 Jason Willms .25 .60
237 Felix Bibeau .25 .60
238 Brett Davis .25 .60
239 Austin McEneny .25 .60
240 Jordy Stallard .25 .60
241 Yaroslav Alexeyev .25 .60
242 Anderson MacDonald .25 .60
243 Sean Durzi .30 .75
244 Curtis Douglas .25 .60
245 Jacob Friend .25 .60
246 Danil Antropov .25 .60
247 Jordan Ernst .25 .60
248 Michael Pezzetta .25 .60
249 Garrett McFadden .25 .60
250 Serron Noel .25 .60
251 Samuel Dove-McFalls .25 .60
252 Nicholas Welsh .25 .60
253 Zachary Bouthillier .25 .60
254 Ivan Chekhovich .25 .60
255 Michael McLeod 1.00 2.50
256 Jake Smith .25 .60
257 Samuel L'Italien .25 .60
258 Charle-Edouard D'Astou .25 .60
259 Jack Flaman .25 .60
260 Nick Henry .25 .60
261 Felix Robert .25 .60
262 Maksim Sushko .25 .60
263 Justin Brazeau .30 .75
264 Daniel Hardie .25 .60
265 Cam Dineen .25 .60
266 Linus Nyman .25 .60
267 Pavel Gogolev .25 .60
268 Riley Woods .25 .60
269 Nicolas Ouellet .25 .60
270 Jacob Moverare .25 .60
271 Drake Rymsha .25 .60
272 Aidan Dudas .25 .60
273 Adam Capannelli .25 .60
274 Kevin Bahl .25 .60
275 Simon Lafrance .25 .60
276 Jared Legien .25 .60
277 Mason McCarty .25 .60
278 Maxim Mizyurin .25 .60
279 Chase Harwell .25 .60
280 Nicolas Guay .25 .60
281 Riley Lamb .25 .60
282 Marek Zachar .25 .60
283 Sami Moilanen .25 .60
284 Dante Hannoun .25 .60
285 Jake Henderson .25 .60
286 Bradley Lalonde .25 .60
287 Yvan Mongo .25 .60
288 Joachim Blichfeld .40 1.00
289 Renars Krastenbergs .25 .60
290 Adam Timleck .25 .60
291 Mark Rassell .25 .60
292 Barrett Hayton .40 1.00
293 Brayden Burke .25 .60
294 Robert Lynch .25 .60
295 Trey Fix-Wolansky .25 .60
296 Nathan Dunkley .25 .60
297 Tyler Hinam .25 .60
298 Julien Tessier .25 .60
299 Kirill Maksimov .25 .60
300 Mika Cyr .25 .60
301 Ryan Suzuki 1.50 4.00
302 Brandon Coe 1.25 3.00
303 Nolan Hutcheson 1.25 3.00
304 Ben Badalamenti 1.25 3.00
305 Giovanni Vallati 1.25 3.00
306 Bowen Byram 2.00 5.00
307 Alexey Lipanov 1.25 3.00
308 Nick Wong 3.00 8.00
309 Reece Vitelli 1.25 3.00
310 Blake Murray 1.25 3.00
311 Ostap Safin 3.00 8.00
312 Jake Lee 1.25 3.00
313 Luke Bignell 1.25 3.00
314 Peyton Krebs 1.25 3.00
315 Philip Tomasino 1.50 4.00
316 Bastian Eckl 1.25 3.00
317 Alex Beaucage 1.25 3.00
318 Ethan Keppen 1.25 3.00
319 Jackson Van De Leest 1.25 3.00
320 Cedric Desruisseaux 1.25 3.00
321 Riley Stotts 1.25 3.00
322 Raphael Lavoie 1.25 3.00
323 Liam Kindree 1.25 3.00
324 Merrick Rippon 1.25 3.00
325 Josh Williams 1.25 3.00
326 Mathew MacDougall 1.25 3.00
327 Graeme Clarke 1.25 3.00
328 Zach Cox 1.25 3.00
329 Kieffer Bellows 1.50 4.00
330 Nicholas Porco 1.25 3.00
331 Dylan Cozens 2.50 6.00
332 Xavier Bouchard 1.25 3.00
333 Jan Drozg 1.25 3.00
334 Dawson Barteaux 1.25 3.00
335 Hunter Holmes 1.25 3.00
336 Justin Barron 1.25 3.00
337 Pier-Olivier Lacombe 1.25 3.00
338 Nick Robertson 3.00 8.00
339 German Rubtsov 1.25 3.00
340 Milos Roman 1.25 3.00
341 Eemeli Rasanen 1.25 3.00
342 Nico Gross 1.25 3.00
343 Xavier Simoneau 1.25 3.00
344 Nathan Allensen 3.00 8.00
345 Filip Zadina 1.25 3.00
346 Braden Schneider 1.50 4.00
347 Matthew Villalta 1.25 3.00
348 Alexey Toropchenko 1.25 3.00
349 German Rubtsov 1.25 3.00
350 Emil Oksanen 1.25 3.00
351 Egor Sokolov 1.25 3.00
352 Cameron Hillis 1.25 3.00
353 Rhett Rhinehart 1.25 3.00
354 Jakob Pelletier 1.25 3.00
355 Gabriel Denis 1.25 3.00
356 Kirill Nizhnikov 1.25 3.00
357 Jonny Hooker 1.25 3.00
358 Justin Ducharme 1.25 3.00
359 Dmitry Zavgorodniy 1.25 3.00
360 Ty Dellandrea 1.25 3.00
361 Carl Stankowski 1.25 3.00
362 Ryan Roth 1.25 3.00
363 Liam Foudy 1.50 4.00
364 Dawson Baker 1.25 3.00
365 Egor Zudilov 1.25 3.00
366 Kristian Reichel 1.25 3.00
367 Isaac Johnson 1.25 3.00
368 Daemon Hunt 1.25 3.00
369 Filip Kral 1.25 3.00
370 Andrei Svechnikov 3.00 8.00
371 Samuel Poulin 1.50 4.00
372 Vladislav Kotkov 1.25 3.00
373 Martin Bodak 1.25 3.00
374 Gabriel Fortier 1.50 4.00
375 Cody Morgan 1.25 3.00
376 Sasha Mutala 1.25 3.00
377 Cole Reinhardt 1.25 3.00
378 Oleg Sosunov 1.25 3.00
379 Arthur Kaliyev 1.25 3.00
380 Nolan Foote 1.25 3.00
381 Damien Giroux 1.50 4.00
382 Jacob Ingham 1.25 3.00
383 Dennis Cholowski 1.25 3.00
384 Brodi Stuart 1.25 3.00
385 Philipp Kurashev 1.25 3.00
386 Xavier Parent 1.00 2.50
387 Luke Henman 1.25 3.00
388 Ryan Francis 1.25 3.00
389 Libor Zabransky 1.25 3.00
390 Alexis Lafreniere 40.00 100.00
391 Kirby Dach 1.50 4.00
392 Henri Jokiharju 1.25 3.00
393 Nikita Okhotyuk 1.25 3.00
394 Maxence Guenette 1.25 3.00
395 Mason Primeau 1.25 3.00
396 Riley Damiani 1.25 3.00
397 Blade Jenkins 1.25 3.00
398 Cole Schwindt 1.25 3.00
399 Samuel Bitten 1.25 3.00
400 Igor Martynov 1.25 3.00

2017-18 Upper Deck CHL Autographs

3 Max Jones B 10.00 25.00
7 Kale Clague B 8.00 20.00
8 Jeffrey Truchon-Viel B 6.00 15.00
10 Jake Bean B 10.00 25.00
11 Dylan Wells B 6.00 15.00
12 William Bitten B 6.00 15.00
18 David Quenneville B 6.00 15.00
19 Jack Studnicka B 10.00 25.00
22 Sam Steel A 8.00 20.00
25 Cody Glass A 15.00 40.00
26 Ty Smith A 10.00 25.00
27 Davis Koch B 6.00 15.00
31 Nicholas Chyzowski B 6.00 15.00
35 Juuso Valimaki B 6.00 15.00
36 Jake Leschyshyn B 6.00 15.00
37 Michael DiPietro B 6.00 15.00
39 Jaret Anderson-Dolan B 10.00 25.00
40 Morgan Frost A 10.00 25.00
41 Jayden Halbgewachs B 6.00 15.00
42 Ryan McGregor B 6.00 15.00
44 Cale Fleury B 8.00 20.00
46 Arnaud Durandeau B 6.00 15.00
47 Logan Stanley B 10.00 25.00
48 Dmitry Sokolov B 10.00 25.00
50 Jordan Kyrou A 10.00 25.00
51 Nicolas Hague B 6.00 15.00
54 Ben Jones B 6.00 15.00
56 Ryan McLeod A 8.00 20.00
58 Parker Kelly B 6.00 15.00
59 Evan Bouchard A 20.00 50.00
60 Evan Fitzpatrick B 6.00 15.00
62 Tanner Kaspick B 6.00 15.00
63 Ben Hawerchuk B 6.00 15.00
66 Zachary Lauzon B 6.00 15.00
68 Isaac Ratcliffe B 8.00 20.00
69 Drake Batherson B 10.00 25.00
70 Brett Howden B 6.00 15.00
71 Givani Smith B 6.00 15.00
74 Matthew Boucher B 6.00 15.00
75 Taylor Raddysh B 10.00 25.00
76 Mitchell Balmas B 6.00 15.00
78 Ryan Peckford B 6.00 15.00
81 Tyler Benson B 6.00 15.00
82 Jett Woo B 8.00 20.00
83 Benoit-Olivier Groulx A 10.00 25.00
84 Nick Suzuki A 20.00 50.00
87 Cal Foote A 6.00 15.00
90 Adam Mascherin A 6.00 15.00
91 Jared McIsaac A 8.00 20.00
95 Ryan Merkley A 6.00 15.00
97 Matthew Strome B 8.00 20.00
99 Kole Lind B 8.00 20.00
100 Michael Rasmussen A 6.00 15.00
301 Ryan Suzuki A 10.00 25.00
302 Brandon Coe B 8.00 20.00
308 Nick Wong B 20.00 50.00
310 Blake Murray B 8.00 20.00
311 Ostap Safin B 20.00 50.00
316 Bastian Eckl B 8.00 20.00
320 Cedric Desruisseaux B 8.00 20.00
325 Josh Williams B 8.00 20.00
329 Kieffer Bellows A 10.00 25.00
332 Xavier Bouchard B 8.00 20.00
333 Jan Drozg B 8.00 20.00
336 Justin Barron B 8.00 20.00
338 Nick Robertson B 20.00 50.00
339 Maxim Golod B 8.00 20.00
340 Milos Roman B 8.00 20.00
341 Eemeli Rasanen B 8.00 20.00
343 Xavier Simoneau B 8.00 20.00
345 Filip Zadina A 8.00 20.00
346 Braden Schneider B 10.00 25.00
347 Matthew Villalta B 8.00 20.00
349 German Rubtsov B 8.00 20.00
351 Egor Sokolov B 8.00 20.00
352 Cameron Hillis B 8.00 20.00
354 Jakob Pelletier B 8.00 20.00
355 Gabriel Denis B 8.00 20.00
358 Justin Ducharme B 8.00 20.00
359 Dmitry Zavgorodniy B 8.00 20.00
360 Ty Dellandrea B 8.00 20.00
361 Carl Stankowski B 8.00 20.00
366 Kristian Reichel B 8.00 20.00
370 Andrei Svechnikov A 20.00 50.00
371 Samuel Poulin B 10.00 25.00
372 Vladislav Kotkov B 8.00 20.00
374 Gabriel Fortier B 10.00 25.00
376 Sasha Mutala B 8.00 20.00
380 Nolan Foote B 8.00 20.00
381 Damien Giroux B 10.00 25.00
383 Dennis Cholowski B 8.00 20.00
384 Brodi Stuart B 8.00 20.00
385 Philipp Kurashev B 8.00 20.00
387 Luke Henman B 8.00 20.00
388 Ryan Francis A 8.00 20.00
390 Alexis Lafreniere A 200.00 500.00
391 Kirby Dach B 10.00 25.00
392 Henri Jokiharju B 8.00 20.00
394 Maxence Guenette B 8.00 20.00
396 Riley Damiani B 8.00 20.00
397 Blade Jenkins B 8.00 20.00

2017-18 Upper Deck CHL Promising Futures

PF1 Cody Glass 1.50 4.00
PF2 Vitalii Abramov .60 1.50
PF3 Kole Lind .75 2.00
PF4 Andrei Svechnikov 2.00 5.00
PF5 Filip Zadina .75 2.00
PF6 Ryan Merkley .60 1.50
PF7 Jordan Kyrou 1.00 2.50
PF8 Ryan McLeod .75 2.00
PF9 Jared McIsaac .75 2.00
PF10 Ty Smith 1.00 2.50
PF11 Cal Foote .60 1.50
PF12 Carter Hart 1.50 4.00
PF13 Nick Suzuki 2.00 5.00
PF14 Robert Thomas 1.00 2.50
PF15 Joseph Veleno .75 2.00
PF16 Akil Thomas .75 2.00
PF17 Maxime Comtois 1.00 2.50
PF18 Taylor Raddysh 1.00 2.50
PF19 Sam Steel .75 2.00
PF20 Kieffer Bellows 1.00 2.50

2017-18 Upper Deck CHL Top Prospects Game

TP1 Jake Leschyshyn .50 1.25
TP2 Nikita Popugaev .50 1.25
TP3 Henri Jokiharju .60 1.50
TP4 Jacob Paquette .50 1.25
TP5 MacKenzie Entwistle .60 1.50
TP6 Michael DiPietro .50 1.25
TP7 Nick Suzuki 1.50 4.00
TP8 Juuso Valimaki .50 1.25
TP9 Robert Thomas .75 2.00
TP10 Cody Glass 1.25 3.00
TP11 Gabe Vilardi .75 2.00
TP12 Michael Rasmussen .50 1.25
TP13 Ian Scott .60 1.50
TP14 Morgan Frost .75 2.00
TP15 Isaac Ratcliffe .60 1.50
TP16 Kole Lind .60 1.50
TP17 Antoine Morand .50 1.25
TP18 Stelio Mattheos .60 1.50
TP19 Maxime Comtois .75 2.00
TP20 Alexander Chmelevski .50 1.25

2018-19 Upper Deck CHL

*RC/100: .6X TO 1.5X BASIC CARDS
1 Alexis Lafreniere 12.00 30.00
2 Keeghan Howdeshell .25 .60
3 Kirby Dach .40 1.00
4 Liam Foudy .40 1.00
5 Matthew Villalta .30 .75
6 Jett Woo .30 .75
7 Ryan Suzuki .40 1.00
8 Ryan Francis .25 .60
9 Ty Dellandrea .30 .75
10 Nolan Foote .25 .60
11 Peyton Krebs .25 .60
12 Michael DiPietro .25 .60
13 Ryan Merkley .30 .75
14 Jared McIsaac .30 .75
15 Tye Felhaber .25 .60
16 Ben Jones .25 .60
17 Dante Hannoun .25 .60
18 Serron Noel .30 .75
19 Xavier Simoneau .25 .60
20 Vladislav Kotkov .25 .60
21 Josh Brook .25 .60
22 Joseph Garreffa .25 .60
23 Felix Bibeau .25 .60
24 D'Artagnan Joly .25 .60
25 Jake Leschyshyn .25 .60
26 Cameron Hillis .30 .75
27 Allan McShane .30 .75
28 Aidan Dudas .30 .75
29 Alexis Gravel .30 .75
30 Jan Drozg .25 .60
31 Scott Walford .25 .60
32 Zachary Lauzon .25 .60
33 Philipp Kurashev .30 .75
34 Cole Carter .25 .60
35 Jason Robertson 1.25 3.00
36 Cole Fonstad .25 .60
37 Philip Tomasino .40 1.00
38 Graeme Clarke .25 .60
39 Joachim Blichfeld .40 1.00
40 Riley Sutter .25 .60
41 Parker Kelly .25 .60
42 Trey Fix-Wolansky .30 .75
43 Alexander Khovanov .30 .75
44 Shawn Boudrias .30 .75
45 Connor Dewar .30 .75
46 Alexander Alexeyev .30 .75
47 Riley Stotts .30 .75
48 Calen Addison .40 1.00
49 Olivier Rodrigue .30 .75
50 Gabriel Fortier .40 1.00
51 Pierre-Olivier Joseph .30 .75
52 Sean Durzi .30 .75
53 Jeremy McKenna .30 .75
54 Stelio Mattheos .25 .60
55 Austen Keating .25 .60
56 Jordy Bellerive .25 .60
57 Justin Almeida .25 .60
58 Alexander Chmelevski .25 .60
59 Kirill Maksimov .25 .60
60 Justin Brazeau .30 .75
61 Lev Starikov .25 .60
62 Matthew Robertson .30 .75
63 Joey Keane .30 .75
64 Jakob Pelletier .30 .75
65 Akil Thomas .30 .75
66 Samuel Poulin .40 1.00
67 Curtis Douglas .25 .60
68 James Malm .25 .60
69 Ty Smith .40 1.00
70 Raphael Lavoie .30 .75
71 Kody Clark .25 .60
72 Benoit-Olivier Groulx .40 1.00
73 Ryan McLeod .25 .60
74 Nicolas Beaudin .25 .60
75 Noah Dobson .50 1.25
76 Nick Wong .30 .75
77 Nikita Okhotyuk .25 .60
78 Sasha Mutala .25 .60
79 Blake Murray .25 .60
80 Kevin Bahl .30 .75
81 Arthur Kaliyev .30 .75
82 Dylan Cozens .60 1.50
83 Bowen Byram .50 1.25
84 Braden Schneider .40 1.00
85 Blade Jenkins .25 .60
86 Xavier Parent .25 .60
87 Nico Gross .25 .60
88 Ostap Safin .25 .60
89 Nick Robertson .40 1.00
90 Brandon Coe .30 .75
91 Justin Barron .30 .75
92 James Hamblin .30 .75
93 Maksim Sushko .30 .75
94 Gabriel Denis .30 .75
95 Cody Glass .60 1.50
96 Kyle Olson .30 .75
97 Barrett Hayton .40 1.00
98 Nick Suzuki .75 2.00
99 Morgan Frost .40 1.00
100 Nate Schnarr .25 .60
101 Joseph Veleno .30 .75
102 Jaden Peca .25 .60
103 Riley McCourt .25 .60
104 Jacob Ingham .25 .60
105 Theo Calvas .25 .60
106 Liam Murphy .25 .60
107 David Levin .30 .75
108 Jarrod Tyszka .30 .75
109 Patrik Hrehorcak .30 .75
110 Maxim Golod .25 .60
111 Ivan Kosorenkov .25 .60
112 Joel Teasdale .40 1.00
113 Max Patterson .25 .60
114 Braydyn Chizen .30 .75
115 Riley Damiani .30 .75
116 Adam McCormick .30 .75
117 Anthony Salinitri .25 .60
118 Julien Tessier .25 .60
119 Lucas Chiodo .25 .60
120 Kyle Maksimovich .25 .60
121 Jacob Golden .30 .75
122 Jermaine Loewen .30 .75
123 Jake Christiansen .25 .60
124 Darian Pilon .25 .60
125 Brady Gilmour .25 .60
126 Zach Gallant .30 .75
127 Leon Gawanke .30 .75
128 Jordan Kooy .30 .75
129 Connor Hall .30 .75
130 Wyatte Wylie .30 .75
131 Shane Bulitka .30 .75
132 Cole Coskey .30 .75
133 Jacob Paquette .25 .60
134 David Noel .25 .60
135 Brett Leason .25 .60
136 Alex D'Orio .30 .75
137 Dmitry Zavgorodniy .25 .60
138 Luke Henman .30 .75
139 Cole Reinhardt .30 .75
140 Xavier Bernard .30 .75
141 Jocktan Chainey .30 .75
142 Ivan Chekhovich .30 .75
143 Arnaud Durandeau .30 .75
144 Nicolas Guay .25 .60
145 Dereck Baribeau .25 .60
146 Matthew Welsh .25 .60
147 Kyle Keyser .25 .60
148 Anthony Popovich .25 .60
149 Liam Hughes .25 .60
150 Ethan Anders .30 .75
151 Nolan Maier .30 .75
152 Dawson Weatherill .30 .75
153 David Tendeck .25 .60
154 Austin Osmanski .25 .60
155 Michael Little .25 .60
156 Jordan Hollett .30 .75
157 Adam Capannelli .25 .60
158 Brett Davis .25 .60
159 Libor Zabransky .30 .75
160 Brandon Saigeon .25 .60
161 Jackson Van De Leest .25 .60
162 Hunter Drew .25 .60
163 Kevin Mandolese .30 .75
164 Sean Strange .30 .75
165 Adam Ruzicka .30 .75
166 Felix Boivin .30 .75
167 Billy Moskal .30 .75
168 Anderson MacDonald .30 .75
169 Kyle Topping .25 .60
170 Dennis Busby .25 .60
171 Jeffrey Durocher .25 .60
172 Nolan Volcan .30 .75
173 Tristan Cote-Cazenave .25 .60
174 Reese Johnson .25 .60
175 Trenton Bourque .30 .75
176 Keith Getson .30 .75
177 Nicolas Ouellet .30 .75
178 Brett Neumann .30 .75
179 Jackson Leppard .30 .75
180 Hunter Jones .25 .60
181 Ryan Jevne .25 .60
182 MacKenzie Entwistle .25 .60
183 Nolan Yaremko .25 .60
184 Liam Hawel .25 .60
185 Dawson Barteaux .30 .75
186 Markus Phillips .30 .75
187 Liam Kindree .25 .60
188 Luke Richardson .30 .75
189 Morgan Nauss .30 .75
190 Tyler Tucker .30 .75
191 Matthew Strome .25 .60
192 Nikita Alexandrov .25 .60
193 Alex Beaucage .25 .60
194 Alexey Toropchenko .30 .75
195 Dillon Hamaliuk .30 .75
196 Kaeden Korczak .30 .75
197 Zack Andrusiak .25 .60
198 Ian Scott .30 .75
199 Isaac Ratcliffe .30 .75
200 Leif Mattson .30 .75
201 Antoine Morand .30 .75
202 Kirill Nizhnikov .30 .75
203 Sean Montgomery .30 .75
204 Ryan DaSilva .25 .60
205 Kyle Jessiman .25 .60
206 Michael King .30 .75
207 Jake Durham .25 .60
208 Bobby Russell .25 .60
209 Isaiah Gallo-Demetris .30 .75
210 Davis Koch .30 .75
211 Simon Lafrance .25 .60
212 Samuel Asselin .40 1.00
213 Alexey Lipanov .25 .60
214 Justin Bergeron .25 .60
215 Edouard St-Laurent .25 .60
216 Cedric Pare .25 .60
217 Jordan Sambrook .25 .60
218 Logan Barlage .30 .75
219 Alex-Olivier Voyer .25 .60
220 Olivier Garneau .25 .60
221 Jonathan Yantsis .25 .60
222 Todd Scott .25 .60
223 Reilly Webb .25 .60
224 Kody McDonald .25 .60
225 Matthew Struthers .30 .75
226 Albert Michnac .25 .60
227 Jimmy Huntington .30 .75
228 Damien Giroux .40 1.00
229 Kobe Mohr .30 .75
230 Jordan Mohor .30 .75
231 Luke Toporowski .30 .75
232 Riley McKay .30 .75
233 Vince Loschiavo .30 .75
234 Wilson Forest .30 .75
235 Hugo Leufvenius .25 .60
236 Justin Ducharme .25 .60
237 Quinn Benjafield .25 .60
238 Antoine Crete-Belzile .25 .60
239 Peyton Hoyt .25 .60
240 Brandon Hagel .40 1.00
241 Luka Burzan .30 .75
242 Tyler Burnie .25 .60
243 Emanuel Vella .25 .60
244 Riley Woods .25 .60
245 Milos Roman .25 .60
246 Shawn Khaira .25 .60
247 Jake Kryski .30 .75
248 Mika Cyr .30 .75
249 Danial Singer .30 .75
250 Daniel Bukac .25 .60
251 Jaeger White .25 .60
252 Alexis Sansfacon .25 .60
253 Connor McMichael .60 1.50
254 Zane Franklin .25 .60
255 Ethan O'Rourke .25 .60
256 Ivan Lodnia .25 .60
257 Sacha Roy .25 .60
258 Cole Mackay .25 .60
259 Colin Van Den Hurk .25 .60
260 Giovanni Vallati .25 .60
261 Matthew Timms .25 .60
262 Dawson Davidson .25 .60
263 Samuel Harvey .30 .75
264 Kevin Gursoy .30 .75
265 Peter Abbandonato .30 .75
266 Eli Zummack .30 .75
267 Tyler Hylland .30 .75
268 Brodi Stuart .25 .60
269 Mikhail Denisov .25 .60
270 Mark Kastelic .25 .60
271 Danil Antropov .25 .60
272 Sam Dunn .25 .60
273 Mac Hollowell .25 .60
274 Bryan Lockner .25 .60
275 Rhett Rhinehart .25 .60
276 Robbie Holmes .25 .60
277 Isaac Johnson .30 .75
278 Mathieu Boulianne .25 .60
279 Ethan Browne .30 .75
280 Mathieu Sevigny .30 .75
281 Griffen Outhouse .30 .75
282 Semyon Der-Arguchintsev .30 .75
283 Max Gerlach .30 .75
284 Gera Poddubnyi .30 .75
285 Nathan Legare .25 .60
286 Illijah Colina .25 .60
287 Cedrick Andree .25 .60
288 Christopher Paquette .25 .60
289 Charle-Edouard D'Astou .25 .60
290 Maxim Trepanier .30 .75
291 Thomas Harley .40 1.00
292 Dawson Mercer .60 1.50
293 Matthew Culling .30 .75
294 Greg Meireles .30 .75
295 Declan Chisholm .30 .75
296 Mathias Laferriere .25 .60
297 Brad Chenier .25 .60
298 Gabriel Bilodeau .25 .60
299 Kevin Hancock .25 .60
300 Carson Mackinnon .30 .75
301 Adam Boqvist 1.25 3.00
302 Ukko-Pekka Luukkonen 1.50 4.00
303 Trent Minor 1.25 3.00
304 Danila Palivko 1.25 3.00
305 Nick Donofrio 1.25 3.00
306 Roope Pynnonen 1.25 3.00
307 Valtteri Kakkonen 1.25 3.00
308 Martin Lang 1.25 3.00
309 Filip Reisnecker 1.25 3.00
310 Erik Cermak 1.25 3.00
311 Joonas Sillanpaa 1.25 3.00
312 Krystof Hrabik 1.25 3.00
313 David Aebischer 1.25 3.00
314 Aiden De La Gorgendiere 1.25 3.00
315 Sahil Panwar 1.25 3.00
316 Rory Kerins 1.50 4.00
317 Ben King 1.25 3.00
318 Ozzie King 1.25 3.00
319 Brendan Hoffmann 1.25 3.00
320 Ridly Greig 1.25 3.00
321 Simon Kubicek 1.25 3.00
322 Will Cuylle 2.00 5.00
323 Aleksei Sergeev 1.25 3.00
324 Mason Millman 1.25 3.00
325 Pacey Schlueting 1.25 3.00
326 Valentin Nussbaumer 1.25 3.00
327 Nando Eggenberger 1.25 3.00
328 Logan Morrison 1.25 3.00
329 Aliaksei Protas 1.25 3.00
330 Hendrix Lapierre 1.50 4.00
331 Jordan Frasca 1.25 3.00
332 Gerard Keane 1.25 3.00
333 Jean-Luc Foudy 1.25 3.00
334 Jack Quinn 1.50 4.00
335 William Villeneuve 1.25 3.00
336 Kaiden Guhle 2.00 5.00
337 Michael Renwick 1.25 3.00
338 Marco Rossi 1.25 3.00
339 Maxim Cajkovic 1.25 3.00
340 Adam Evanoff 1.25 3.00
341 Cameron Tolnai 1.25 3.00
342 Ivan Prosvetov 1.25 3.00
343 Antonio Stranges 1.25 3.00
344 Tyler Tullio 1.25 3.00
345 Kyle Crnkovic 1.25 3.00
346 Jacob Winterton 1.25 3.00
347 Joshua Lawrence 1.25 3.00
348 Jack Finley 1.25 3.00
349 Kyle McDonald 1.25 3.00
350 Sergei Alkhimov 1.25 3.00
351 Tye Kartye 1.50 4.00
352 Nikita Sedov 1.25 3.00
353 Joel Hofer 2.00 5.00
354 Cole Perfetti 3.00 8.00
355 Vladimir Alistrov 1.25 3.00
356 Ryan O'Rourke 1.25 3.00
357 Mitch Flint 1.25 3.00
358 Egor Arbuzov 1.25 3.00
359 Reid Valade 1.25 3.00
360 Michael Campoli 1.25 3.00
361 Robbie Fromm-Delorme 1.25 3.00
362 Roman Pucek 1.25 3.00
363 Jacob Perreault 1.25 3.00
364 James Hardie 1.25 3.00
365 Evan Vierling 1.25 3.00
366 Dustin Wolf 4.00 10.00
367 Jeremie Biakabutuka 1.25 3.00
368 Jordan Spence 1.25 3.00
369 Jamie Drysdale 4.00 10.00
370 Tag Bertuzzi 1.25 3.00
371 David Maier 1.25 3.00
372 Connor McClennon 1.25 3.00
373 Matvey Guskov 1.25 3.00
374 Liam Kirk 1.25 3.00
375 Lukas Svejkovsky 1.25 3.00
376 Alexander Dersch 1.25 3.00
377 Michael Bianconi 1.25 3.00
378 Egor Postnov 1.25 3.00
379 Oleg Zaytsev 1.25 3.00
380 Seth Jarvis 3.00 8.00
381 Riley Piercey 1.25 3.00
382 Jake Neighbours 2.00 5.00
383 Luke Prokop 1.25 3.00
384 Yaroslav Likhachev 1.25 3.00
385 Antoine Rochon 1.25 3.00
386 Justin Sourdif 1.25 3.00
387 Kaden Kohle 1.25 3.00
388 Michael Vukojevic 1.25 3.00
389 Max Paddock 1.25 3.00
390 Brayden Tracey 1.25 3.00
391 Egor Serdyuk 1.25 3.00
392 Ian Derungs 1.25 3.00
393 Artemi Kniazev 1.25 3.00
394 Jiri Patera 1.50 4.00
395 Lassi Thomson 1.25 3.00
396 Ty Collins 1.25 3.00
397 Yannik Valenti 1.25 3.00
398 Kristian Roykas Marthinsen 1.25 3.00
399 Bode Wilde 1.25 3.00
400 Quinton Byfield 4.00 10.00

2018-19 Upper Deck CHL Memorial Cup Ambitions

CA1 Bowen Byram 2.00 5.00
CA2 Tye Felhaber 1.00 2.50
CA3 Joseph Veleno 1.25 3.00
CA4 Dylan Cozens 2.50 6.00
CA5 Tag Bertuzzi 1.25 3.00
CA6 Xavier Parent 1.00 2.50
CA7 Nick Wong 1.00 2.50
CA8 Brett Leason 1.00 2.50
CA9 Calen Addison 1.50 4.00
CA10 Ty Smith 1.50 4.00
CA11 Allan McShane 1.25 3.00
CA12 Ian Scott 1.25 3.00
CA13 Jared McIsaac 1.25 3.00
CA14 Peyton Krebs 1.00 2.50
CA15 Ryan Merkley 1.25 3.00
CA16 Connor Dewar 1.25 3.00
CA17 Raphael Lavoie 1.25 3.00
CA18 Liam Foudy 1.50 4.00
CA19 Trent Minor 1.25 3.00
CA20 Alexander Chmelevski 1.00 2.50

2018-19 Upper Deck CHL Scouting Report

SR1 Alexis Lafreniere 6.00 15.00
SR2 Quinton Byfield 4.00 10.00
SR3 Bowen Byram 2.00 5.00
SR4 Matthew Robertson 1.25 3.00
SR5 Peyton Krebs 1.00 2.50
SR6 Ty Dellandrea 1.25 3.00
SR7 Arthur Kaliyev 1.25 3.00
SR8 Raphael Lavoie 1.25 3.00
SR9 Ryan Merkley 1.25 3.00
SR10 Nolan Foote 1.25 3.00
SR11 Jakob Pelletier 1.25 3.00
SR12 Ty Smith 1.50 4.00
SR13 Noah Dobson 2.00 5.00
SR14 Blake Murray 1.00 2.50
SR15 Adam Boqvist 1.25 3.00
SR16 Kirby Dach 1.50 4.00
SR17 Ryan Suzuki 1.50 4.00
SR18 Dylan Cozens 2.50 6.00
SR19 Trey Fix-Wolansky 1.25 3.00
SR20 Barrett Hayton 1.50 4.00

2018-19 Upper Deck CHL SP Top Prospects

SP1 Arthur Kaliyev 3.00 8.00
SP2 Jakob Pelletier 3.00 8.00
SP3 Ryan Suzuki 4.00 10.00
SP4 Bowen Byram 5.00 12.00
SP5 Dylan Cozens 6.00 15.00
SP6 Xavier Parent 2.50 6.00
SP7 Michael Vukojevic 3.00 8.00
SP8 Raphael Lavoie 3.00 8.00
SP9 Sasha Mutala 2.50 6.00
SP10 Peyton Krebs 2.50 6.00
SP11 Blake Murray 2.50 6.00
SP12 Nikita Alexandrov 2.50 6.00
SP13 Kirby Dach 4.00 10.00
SP14 Josh Williams 3.00 8.00
SP15 Nolan Foote 3.00 8.00
SP16 Samuel Poulin 4.00 10.00
SP17 Maxim Cajkovic 3.00 8.00
SP18 Matthew Robertson 3.00 8.00

2018-19 Upper Deck CHL Top Level Talent

TL1 Michael DiPietro 1.00 2.50
TL2 Peyton Krebs 1.00 2.50
TL3 Jordy Bellerive 1.00 2.50
TL4 Olivier Rodrigue 1.25 3.00
TL5 Noah Dobson 2.00 5.00
TL6 Dylan Cozens 2.50 6.00
TL7 Ian Scott 1.25 3.00
TL8 Jason Robertson 5.00 12.00
TL9 Kirby Dach 1.50 4.00
TL10 Alexis Lafreniere 6.00 15.00
TL11 Liam Foudy 1.50 4.00
TL12 Ty Dellandrea 1.25 3.00
TL13 Akil Thomas 1.25 3.00
TL14 Bowen Byram 2.00 5.00
TL15 Quinton Byfield 4.00 10.00
TL16 Adam Boqvist 1.25 3.00
TL17 Joseph Veleno 1.25 3.00
TL18 Nick Suzuki 3.00 8.00
TL19 Morgan Frost 1.50 4.00
TL20 Cody Glass 2.50 6.00

2018-19 Upper Deck CHL Day With The Cup Flashbacks

DC1 Matthew Tkachuk SP 12.00 30.00
DC2 Mitch Marner SP 10.00 25.00
DC3 Christian Dvorak SP 5.00 12.00
DC4 Max Jones SP 6.00 15.00
DC5 Victor Mete SP 4.00 10.00

2019-20 Upper Deck CHL

1 Antonio Stranges .30 .75
2 Brayden Tracey .30 .75
3 Olivier Rodrigue .30 .75
4 Daemon Hunt .30 .75
5 Thomas Harley .50 1.25
6 Dawson Mercer .60 1.50
7 Serron Noel .30 .75
8 Josh Williams .30 .75
9 Ty Smith .40 1.00
10 Oliver Okuliar .30 .75
11 Adam Beckman .40 1.00
12 Lleyton Moore .30 .75
13 Eric Uba .30 .75
14 Yan Aucoin .30 .75
15 Vladislav Kolyachonok .30 .75
16 Alex Beaucage .30 .75
17 Zach Wytinck .30 .75
18 John Ludvig .30 .75
19 Aidan Dudas .30 .75
20 Alexis Gravel .30 .75
21 Ryan Roth .30 .75
22 Jamieson Rees .30 .75
23 Ozzy Wiesblatt .40 1.00
24 Joseph Garreffa .30 .75
25 Dillon Hamaliuk .30 .75
26 Shawn Element .30 .75
27 D-Jay Jerome .30 .75
28 Kyle Crnkovic .30 .75
29 Kevin Bahl .30 .75

30 Cole Fonstad .30 .75
31 Graeme Clarke .30 .75
32 Edge Lambert .30 .75
33 Tyler Tullio .30 .75
34 Nikita Alexandrov .30 .75
35 Liam Hawel .30 .75
36 Xavier Bouchard .30 .75
37 Ryan Merkley .30 .75
38 Akil Thomas .30 .75
39 Evan Vierling .30 .75
40 Ridly Greig .50 1.25
41 Jared McIsaac .30 .75
42 Theo Rochette .30 .75
43 Felix Bibeau .30 .75
44 Kaedan Korczak .30 .75
45 Hunter Jones .30 .75
46 Brandon Coe .30 .75
47 Luka Burzan .30 .75
48 Gerard Keane .30 .75
49 Sasha Mutala .30 .75
50 Dakota Lund-Cornish .30 .75
51 Zachary Emond .30 .75
52 Ben King .30 .75
53 Noel Hoefenmayer .30 .75
54 William Villeneuve .30 .75
55 D.J. King .30 .75
56 Carson Focht .30 .75
57 Dawson Barteaux .30 .75
58 Artemi Kniazev .30 .75
59 Logan Morrison .30 .75
60 Cameron Hillis .30 .75
61 Mikhail Abramov .30 .75
62 Connor McClennon .30 .75
63 Kyle Topping .30 .75
64 Yaroslav Likhachev .30 .75
65 Allan McShane .30 .75
66 Colten Ellis .30 .75
67 Michael Vukojevic .30 .75
68 Andrew MacLean .30 .75
69 Dustin Wolf 1.00 2.50
70 Isiah Campbell .30 .75
71 Rafael Harvey-Pinard .40 1.00
72 Lukas Svejkovsky .30 .75
73 Anthony Gagnon .30 .75
74 Will Warm .30 .75
75 Aliaksei Protas .30 .75
76 Charles Beaudoin .30 .75
77 Samuel Bitten .30 .75
78 Riley Stotts .30 .75
79 Anthony Popovich .30 .75
80 Cole Schwindt .30 .75
81 Ryan O'Rourke .30 .75
82 Raphael Lavoie .30 .75
83 Gabriel Fortier .40 1.00
84 Egor Serdyuk .30 .75
85 Samuel Bolduc .30 .75
86 Jordan Spence .30 .75
87 Jaromir Pytlik .30 .75
88 Mathias Laferriere .30 .75
89 Nico Gross .30 .75
90 Nathan Legare .30 .75
91 Greg Meireles .30 .75
92 Robbie Holmes .30 .75
93 Alec Regula .25 .60
94 Lukas Cormier .30 .75
95 Benoit-Olivier Groulx .40 1.00
96 Talyn Boyko .30 .75
97 Nathan Staios .30 .75
98 Trent Miner .30 .75
99 Jacob Ingham .30 .75
100 Cedric Desruisseaux .30 .75
101 Shane Bulitka .30 .75
102 Nolan Maier .30 .75
103 Blade Jenkins .30 .75
104 Declan Chisholm .30 .75
105 Robbie Fromm-Delorme .30 .75
106 Kevin Gursoy .30 .75
107 Kyle Olson .30 .75
108 Maxim Golod .30 .75
109 Kieran Craig .30 .75
110 Dennis Busby .30 .75
111 Anthony Morrone .30 .75
112 Cole Reinhardt .30 .75
113 Ryan Francis .30 .75
114 Leif Mattson .30 .75
115 Jakob Brahaney .30 .75
116 James Hamblin .30 .75
117 Tag Bertuzzi .30 .75
118 Ty Collins .30 .75
119 Tristan Cote-Cazenave .30 .75
120 Cedric Pare .30 .75
121 Matej Toman .30 .75
122 Jordan Kooy .30 .75
123 Ethan Regnier .30 .75
124 Jeremie Biakabutuka .30 .75
125 Billy Moskal .30 .75
126 David Tendeck .30 .75
127 Jake Durham .30 .75
128 Krystof Hrabik .30 .75
129 Alexander Khovanov .30 .75
130 Semyon Der-Arguchintsev .30 .75
131 Bryce Kindopp .30 .75
132 Tyler Tucker .30 .75
133 Jerome Gravel .30 .75
134 Luke Toporowski .30 .75
135 Justin Bergeron .30 .75
136 Alex-Olivier Voyer .30 .75
137 Xavier Simoneau .30 .75
138 Jackson Leppard .30 .75
139 Justin Ducharme .30 .75
140 Antoine Coulombe .30 .75
141 Jacob Murray .30 .75
142 Jonathan Yantsis .30 .75
143 Liam Kindree .30 .75
144 Brad Chenier .30 .75
145 Adam McCormick .30 .75
146 Austen Keating .30 .75
147 Matthew Culling .30 .75
148 Liam Kirk .30 .75
149 Blake Murray .30 .75
150 Cedrick Andree .30 .75
151 Max Patterson .30 .75
152 Rory Kerins .40 1.00
153 Shawn Boudrias .30 .75
154 Jacob Golden .30 .75
155 Kaden Kohle .30 .75
156 Jaden Peca .30 .75
157 Ethan Anders .30 .75
158 Brodi Stuart .30 .75
159 Matvey Guskov .30 .75
160 Michael King .30 .75
161 Isaac Johnson .30 .75
162 Nick Wong .30 .75
163 Zane Franklin .30 .75
164 Igor Chibrikov .30 .75
165 Jackson Van De Leest .30 .75
166 Dmitry Zavgorodniy .30 .75
167 Ivan Lodnia .30 .75
168 Scott Walford .30 .75
169 Bobby Russell .30 .75
170 Logan Chisholm .30 .75
171 Mark Kastelic .30 .75
172 Riley McCourt .30 .75
173 Vincent Marleau .30 .75
174 Bryan Lockner .30 .75
175 Pacey Schlueting .30 .75
176 David Noel .30 .75
177 Curtis Douglas .30 .75
178 Maxim Trepanier .30 .75
179 David Levin .30 .75
180 Mika Cyr .30 .75
181 Martin Lang .30 .75
182 Wyatte Wylie .30 .75
183 Joseph Carroll .30 .75
184 Logan Barlage .30 .75
185 Liam Ham .30 .75
186 Nicolas Ouellet .30 .75
187 Oliver Castleman .30 .75
188 Luke Henman .30 .75
189 Reilly Webb .30 .75
190 Keean Washkurak .30 .75
191 Riley Damiani .30 .75
192 Ozzie King .30 .75
193 Kevin Mandolese .30 .75
194 Giovanni Vallati .30 .75
195 Sean Strange .30 .75
196 Milos Roman .30 .75
197 Metis Roelens .30 .75
198 Eli Zummack .30 .75
199 Gabriel Denis .30 .75
200 Austin Pratt .30 .75
201 Riley Sawchuk .30 .75
202 Bradley Ginnell .30 .75
203 Jarrett Baker .30 .75
204 Egor Zamula .40 1.00
205 Cross Hanas .30 .75
206 Isaac Poulter .30 .75
207 Brock Gould .30 .75
208 Josh Pillar .30 .75
209 Taro Jentzsch .30 .75
210 Hayden Fowler .30 .75
211 Samuel Houde .30 .75
212 Daniel D'Amico .30 .75
213 Charles-Antoine Roy .30 .75
214 Tarun Fizer .30 .75
215 Thomas Sigouin .30 .75
216 Mack Guzda .30 .75
217 Carson Denomie .30 .75
218 Luke Prokop .30 .75
219 Matej Pekar .30 .75
220 Ryder Korczak .30 .75
221 Anthony D'Amours .30 .75
222 Reece Newkirk .30 .75
223 Kyen Sopa .30 .75
224 Felix Robert .25 .60
225 Keegan Stevenson .30 .75
226 Orrin Centazzo .30 .75
227 Aidan De La Gorgendiere .30 .75
228 Jacob LeGuerrier .30 .75
229 Mads Sogaard .30 .75
230 Luke Cavallin .30 .75
231 Christian Sbaraglia .30 .75
232 Carter Souch .30 .75
233 Jiri Patera .40 1.00
234 Brady Burns .30 .75
235 Jan Jenik .30 .75
236 Jakob Brook .30 .75
237 Billy Constantinou .30 .75
238 Liam Ross .30 .75
239 Jonathan Lemieux .30 .75
240 Tyler Angle .30 .75
241 Cole Moberg .30 .75
242 Ryan Chyzowski .30 .75
243 Damien Giroux .40 1.00
244 Louka Henault .30 .75
245 Roddy Ross .30 .75
246 Jack McNaughton .30 .75
247 Patrick Guay .30 .75
248 Pavel Gogolev .30 .75
249 Danila Palivko .30 .75
250 Nicholas Porco .30 .75
251 Sean Josling .30 .75
252 Brett Davis .30 .75
253 Simon Kubicek .30 .75
254 Tyson Foerster .50 1.25
255 Tristen Robins .30 .75
256 Tristen Nielsen .30 .75
257 Vladimir Alistrov .30 .75
258 Tyrel Bauer .30 .75
259 Josh Maser .30 .75
260 Ethan Keppen .30 .75
261 Egor Sokolov .30 .75
262 Richard Whittaker .30 .75
263 James Hardie .30 .75
264 Sergey Popov .30 .75
265 Dan Murphy .30 .75
266 Kari Piiroinen .30 .75
267 Ben McCartney .30 .75
268 Darien Kielb .30 .75
269 Matthew Welsh .30 .75
270 Miguel Tourigny .30 .75
271 Sean Larochelle .30 .75
272 Jack Finley .30 .75
273 Jake Gricius .30 .75
274 Cole Mackay .30 .75
275 Andrej Kukuca .30 .75
276 Tristan Berube .30 .75
277 Thomas Pelletier .30 .75
278 Olivier-Luc Hache .40 1.00
279 Noah Boyko .30 .75
280 Tyler Hinam .30 .75
281 Dylan Garand .30 .75
282 Nolan Seed .30 .75
283 Mason Primeau .30 .75
284 Brett Budgell .30 .75
285 Bailey Peach .30 .75
286 Kaid Oliver .30 .75
287 Luke Moncada .30 .75
288 Nathan Dunkley .30 .75
289 Ronan Seeley .30 .75
290 Boston Bilous .30 .75
291 Charlie Desroches .30 .75
292 Beck Warm .30 .75
293 Christopher Merisier-Ortiz .30 .75
294 Macauley Carson .30 .75
295 Rhett Rhinehart .30 .75
296 Matthew Struthers .30 .75
297 Andrew Coxhead .30 .75
298 Jeremy Michel .30 .75
299 Nicolas Guay .30 .75
300 Nicolas Daws .40 1.00
301 Alexis Lafreniere SP 6.00 15.00
302 Dylan Cozens SP 2.50 6.00
303 Connor Zary SP 2.00 5.00
304 Bowen Byram SP 2.00 5.00
305 Jean-Luc Foudy SP 1.25 3.00
306 Jacob Perreault SP 2.00 5.00
307 Jack Quinn SP 2.50 6.00
308 Connor McMichael SP 2.50 6.00
309 Marco Rossi SP 3.00 8.00
310 Jeremie Poirier SP 1.25 3.00
311 Seth Jarvis SP 3.00 8.00
312 Peyton Krebs SP 2.00 5.00
313 Cole Perfetti SP 3.00 8.00
314 Will Cuylle SP 2.00 5.00
315 Philip Tomasino SP 1.50 4.00
316 Braden Schneider SP 2.00 5.00
317 Arthur Kaliyev SP 1.25 3.00
318 Justin Barron SP 2.00 5.00
319 Mavrik Bourque SP 2.00 5.00
320 Hendrix Lapierre SP 2.00 5.00
321 Nick Robertson SP 1.50 4.00
322 Kaiden Guhle SP 2.00 5.00
323 Ryan Suzuki SP 1.50 4.00
324 Jamie Drysdale SP 4.00 10.00
325 Nolan Foote SP 1.25 3.00
326 Justin Sourdif SP 1.25 3.00
327 Jake Neighbours SP 2.00 5.00
328 Jakob Pelletier SP 1.25 3.00
329 Samuel Poulin SP 1.50 4.00
330 Quinton Byfield SP 4.00 10.00
331 Logan Stankoven SP 4.00 10.00
332 Zachary L'Heureux SP 2.50 6.00
333 Kalle Loponen SP 1.25 3.00
334 Isaac Belliveau SP 1.25 3.00
335 Ethan Burroughs SP 1.25 3.00
336 Thimo Nickl SP 1.25 3.00
337 Nino Kinder SP 1.25 3.00
338 Jan Cikhart SP 1.25 3.00
339 Tanner Dickinson SP 1.25 3.00
340 Lukas Parik SP 1.25 3.00
341 Kasper Puutio SP 1.25 3.00
342 Brennan Othmann SP 1.25 3.00
343 Zack Jones SP 1.25 3.00
344 Ilya Usau SP 1.25 3.00
345 Olivier Adam SP 1.25 3.00
346 Pavel Novak SP 1.25 3.00
347 Yu Sato SP 1.25 3.00
348 Filip Koffer SP 1.25 3.00
349 Simon Knak SP 1.25 3.00
350 Oliver Suni SP 1.50 4.00
351 Francesco Pinelli SP 1.25 3.00
352 Landon Kosior SP 1.25 3.00
353 Alexandre Doucet SP 1.25 3.00
354 Raivis Ansons SP 1.25 3.00
355 Olivier Desroches SP 1.25 3.00
356 Adam Raska SP 1.25 3.00
357 Bear Hughes SP 1.25 3.00
358 Sebastian Cossa SP 3.00 8.00
359 Riley Kidney SP 1.50 4.00
360 Mason McTavish SP 1.50 4.00
361 Jacob Dion SP 1.25 3.00
362 Jayden Grubbe SP 1.25 3.00
363 Nathan Gaucher SP 1.25 3.00
364 Radek Kucerik SP 1.25 3.00
365 Ivan Ivan SP 1.50 4.00
366 Fabian Hochegger SP 1.25 3.00
367 Joseph Tynan SP 1.25 3.00
368 Christoffer Sedoff SP 1.50 4.00
369 Garin Bjorklund SP 1.25 3.00
370 Andrei Bakanov SP 1.25 3.00
371 Deni Goure SP 1.25 3.00
372 Samuel Hlavaj SP 1.25 3.00
373 Noah Delemont SP 1.25 3.00
374 Michal Gut SP 1.25 3.00
375 Koen MacInnes SP 1.25 3.00
376 Charles-Antoine Dumont SP 1.25 3.00
377 Vasily Ponomarev SP 1.25 3.00
378 Ilya Solovyov SP 1.25 3.00
379 Vitali Pinchuk SP 1.25 3.00
380 Gaetan Jobin SP 1.25 3.00
381 Carson Lambos SP 1.25 3.00
382 Tyler Brennan SP 1.25 3.00
383 Brandt Clarke SP 2.00 5.00
384 Ryan Winterton SP 1.25 3.00
385 Keanu Derungs SP 1.25 3.00
386 Ruben Rafkin SP 1.25 3.00
387 Joshua Roy SP 1.25 3.00
388 Bryan Thomson SP 1.25 3.00
389 Matthew Savoie SP 2.50 6.00
390 Chase Stillman SP 1.25 3.00
391 Cole Sillinger SP 1.50 4.00
392 Dylan Guenther SP 2.50 6.00
393 Valentin Demchenko SP 1.25 3.00
394 Arturs Silovs SP 3.00 8.00
395 Senna Peeters SP 1.25 3.00
396 Charlie Da Fonseca SP 1.25 3.00
397 Zachary Roy SP 1.25 3.00
398 Zach Dean SP 1.50 4.00
399 Brett Brochu SP 1.25 3.00
400 Shane Wright SP 4.00 10.00

2019-20 Upper Deck CHL Exclusives

*EXCL: .6X TO 1.5X BASIC

2019-20 Upper Deck CHL '99-00 UD CHL Class Retro

C1 Logan Stankoven 2.50 6.00
C2 Cole Perfetti 2.00 5.00
C3 Connor Zary 1.25 3.00
C4 Jean-Luc Foudy .75 2.00
C5 Justin Barron 1.25 3.00
C6 Shane Wright 2.50 6.00
C7 Connor McClennon .75 2.00
C8 Alexis Lafreniere 4.00 10.00
C9 Marco Rossi 2.00 5.00
C10 Jacob Perreault 1.25 3.00
C11 Matthew Savoie 1.50 4.00
C12 Braden Schneider 1.25 3.00
C13 Daemon Hunt .75 2.00
C14 Jamie Drysdale 2.50 6.00
C15 Jeremie Poirier .75 2.00
C16 Lukas Cormier .75 2.00
C17 Kaiden Guhle 1.25 3.00
C18 Hendrix Lapierre 1.25 3.00
C19 Quinton Byfield 2.50 6.00
C20 Justin Sourdif .75 2.00

2019-20 Upper Deck CHL Autographs

1 Antonio Stranges B 8.00 20.00
2 Brayden Tracey A 8.00 20.00
4 Daemon Hunt A 8.00 20.00
5 Thomas Harley B 12.00 30.00
6 Dawson Mercer A 15.00 40.00
7 Serron Noel A 8.00 20.00
8 Josh Williams C 8.00 20.00
9 Ty Smith B 10.00 25.00
10 Oliver Okuliar C 8.00 20.00
12 Lleyton Moore C 8.00 20.00
14 Yan Aucoin C 8.00 20.00
15 Vladislav Kolyachonok C 8.00 20.00
16 Alex Beaucage C 8.00 20.00
19 Aidan Dudas B 8.00 20.00
20 Alexis Gravel B 8.00 20.00
22 Jamieson Rees A 8.00 20.00
23 Ozzy Wiesblatt A 10.00 25.00
24 Joseph Garreffa C 8.00 20.00
25 Dillon Hamaliuk C 8.00 20.00
28 Kyle Crnkovic C 8.00 20.00
29 Kevin Bahl A 8.00 20.00
31 Graeme Clarke B 8.00 20.00
33 Tyler Tullio B 8.00 20.00
34 Nikita Alexandrov C 8.00 20.00
36 Xavier Bouchard C 8.00 20.00
37 Ryan Merkley A 8.00 20.00
38 Akil Thomas B 8.00 20.00
40 Ridly Greig A 12.00 30.00
41 Jared McIsaac B 8.00 20.00
42 Theo Rochette A 8.00 20.00
43 Felix Bibeau B 8.00 20.00
44 Kaedan Korczak C 8.00 20.00
45 Hunter Jones C 8.00 20.00
46 Brandon Coe C 8.00 20.00
47 Luka Burzan A 8.00 20.00
48 Gerard Keane C 8.00 20.00
49 Sasha Mutala B 8.00 20.00
51 Zachary Emond C 8.00 20.00
52 Ben King C 8.00 20.00
53 Noel Hoefenmayer B 8.00 20.00
55 D.J. King C 8.00 20.00
57 Dawson Barteaux C 8.00 20.00
62 Connor McClennon B 8.00 20.00
63 Kyle Topping C 8.00 20.00
65 Allan McShane C 8.00 20.00
66 Colten Ellis B 8.00 20.00
67 Michael Vukojevic C 8.00 20.00
70 Isiah Campbell C 8.00 20.00
76 Charles Beaudoin C 8.00 20.00
79 Anthony Popovich C 8.00 20.00
80 Cole Schwindt C 8.00 20.00
81 Ryan O'Rourke C 8.00 20.00
83 Gabriel Fortier C 10.00 25.00
84 Egor Serdyuk C 8.00 20.00
86 Jordan Spence C 8.00 20.00
87 Jaromir Pytlik C 8.00 20.00
89 Nico Gross B 8.00 20.00
90 Nathan Legare C 8.00 20.00
94 Lukas Cormier A 8.00 20.00
95 Benoit-Olivier Groulx A 10.00 25.00
99 Jacob Ingham B 8.00 20.00
100 Cedric Desruisseaux B 8.00 20.00
301 Alexis Lafreniere A 120.00 300.00
302 Dylan Cozens B 15.00 40.00
303 Connor Zary A 12.00 30.00
304 Bowen Byram A 12.00 30.00
305 Jean-Luc Foudy B 8.00 20.00
306 Jacob Perreault A 12.00 30.00
307 Jack Quinn A 12.00 30.00
309 Marco Rossi A 20.00 50.00
310 Jeremie Poirier A 8.00 20.00
313 Cole Perfetti A 60.00 150.00
314 Will Cuylle A 12.00 30.00
315 Philip Tomasino A 10.00 25.00
316 Braden Schneider A 12.00 30.00
318 Justin Barron B 12.00 30.00
319 Mavrik Bourque A 12.00 30.00
320 Hendrix Lapierre A 12.00 30.00
322 Kaiden Guhle A 12.00 30.00
323 Ryan Suzuki B 10.00 25.00
324 Jamie Drysdale B 25.00 60.00
325 Nolan Foote B 8.00 20.00
326 Justin Sourdif A 8.00 20.00
327 Jake Neighbours B 12.00 30.00
328 Jakob Pelletier A 8.00 20.00
329 Samuel Poulin A 10.00 25.00
330 Quinton Byfield A 100.00 250.00
331 Logan Stankoven A 25.00 60.00
332 Zachary L'Heureux A 15.00 40.00
334 Isaac Belliveau B 8.00 20.00
336 Thimo Nickl A 8.00 20.00
339 Tanner Dickinson C 8.00 20.00
341 Kasper Puutio C 8.00 20.00
342 Brennan Othmann C 8.00 20.00
344 Ilya Usau C 8.00 20.00
346 Pavel Novak A 8.00 20.00
350 Oliver Suni A 10.00 25.00
351 Francesco Pinelli C 8.00 20.00
358 Sebastian Cossa C 20.00 50.00
361 Jacob Dion C 8.00 20.00
365 Ivan Ivan C 10.00 25.00
366 Fabian Hochegger C 8.00 20.00
369 Garin Bjorklund C 8.00 20.00
370 Andrei Bakanov B 8.00 20.00
373 Noah Delemont C 8.00 20.00
377 Vasily Ponomarev A 8.00 20.00
378 Ilya Solovyov C 8.00 20.00
379 Vitali Pinchuk C 8.00 20.00
383 Brandt Clarke A 15.00 40.00
386 Ruben Rafkin C 8.00 20.00
390 Chase Stillman C 8.00 20.00
391 Cole Sillinger A 10.00 25.00
392 Dylan Guenther A 15.00 40.00
394 Arturs Silovs C 20.00 50.00
395 Senna Peeters C 8.00 20.00
400 Shane Wright A 100.00 250.00

2019-20 Upper Deck CHL Draft Ready

DR1 Alexis Lafreniere 8.00 20.00
DR2 Quinton Byfield 2.50 6.00
DR3 Cole Perfetti 2.00 5.00
DR4 Hendrix Lapierre 1.25 3.00
DR5 Jamie Drysdale 2.50 6.00
DR6 Justin Barron 1.25 3.00
DR7 Marco Rossi 2.00 5.00
DR8 Jaromir Pytlik .75 2.00
DR9 Connor Zary 1.25 3.00
DR10 Braden Schneider 1.25 3.00
DR11 Jeremie Poirier .75 2.00
DR12 Jake Neighbours 1.25 3.00
DR13 Justin Sourdif .75 2.00
DR14 Connor McClennon .75 2.00
DR15 Jean-Luc Foudy .75 2.00
DR16 Jacob Perreault 1.25 3.00
DR17 Antonio Stranges .75 2.00
DR18 Lukas Cormier .75 2.00
DR19 Daemon Hunt .75 2.00
DR20 Mavrik Bourque 1.25 3.00

2019-20 Upper Deck CHL Scouting Report

SR1 Shane Wright 2.50 6.00
SR2 Jamie Drysdale 2.50 6.00
SR3 Logan Stankoven 2.50 6.00
SR4 Antonio Stranges .75 2.00
SR5 Matthew Savoie 1.50 4.00
SR6 Connor Zary 1.25 3.00
SR7 Quinton Byfield 2.50 6.00
SR8 Marco Rossi 2.00 5.00
SR9 Kaiden Guhle 1.25 3.00
SR10 Braden Schneider 1.25 3.00
SR11 Hendrix Lapierre 1.25 3.00
SR12 Justin Sourdif .75 2.00
SR13 Mavrik Bourque 1.25 3.00
SR14 Cole Perfetti 2.00 5.00
SR15 Jacob Perreault 1.25 3.00
SR16 Justin Barron 1.25 3.00
SR17 Brandt Clarke 1.25 3.00
SR18 Seth Jarvis 2.00 5.00
SR19 Brennan Othmann .75 2.00
SR20 Alexis Lafreniere 4.00 10.00

2019-20 Upper Deck CHL SP Top Prospects

SP1 Alexis Lafreniere 20.00 50.00
SP2 Quinton Byfield 12.00 30.00
SP3 Hendrix Lapierre 6.00 15.00
SP4 Justin Barron 6.00 15.00
SP5 Justin Sourdif 4.00 10.00
SP6 Cole Perfetti 10.00 25.00
SP7 Marco Rossi 10.00 25.00
SP8 Connor Zary 6.00 15.00
SP9 Jamie Drysdale 12.00 30.00
SP10 Jean-Luc Foudy 4.00 10.00
SP11 Antonio Stranges 4.00 10.00
SP12 Daemon Hunt 4.00 10.00
SP13 Vasily Ponomarev 4.00 10.00
SP14 Lukas Cormier 4.00 10.00
SP15 Braden Schneider 6.00 15.00
SP16 Jacob Perreault 6.00 15.00
SP17 Jeremie Poirier 4.00 10.00

2021-22 Upper Deck CHL

1 Evan Vierling .40 1.00
2 Tucker Robertson .40 1.00
3 Jakob Brook .40 1.00
4 Robert Calisti .40 1.00
5 Connor McClennon .40 1.00
6 Miguel Tourigny .40 1.00
7 Jacob Maillet .40 1.00
8 Bryce Montgomery .40 1.00
9 Mikael Diotte .40 1.00
10 Elliot Desnoyers .40 1.00
11 Brady Burns .40 1.00
12 Joshua Roy .50 1.25
13 Max McCue .40 1.00
14 Charles Savoie .40 1.00
15 Graham Sward .40 1.00
16 Maximus Wanner .40 1.00
17 Lucas Ciona .40 1.00
18 Riley Ginnell .40 1.00
19 Jalen Luypen .40 1.00
20 Israel Mianscum .40 1.00
21 Nolan Ritchie .40 1.00
22 Dru Krebs .40 1.00
23 Daniel Michaud .40 1.00
24 Theo Rochette .40 1.00
25 Ty Voit .40 1.00
26 Landon McCallum .40 1.00
27 Pasquale Zito .40 1.00
28 Colton Dach .50 1.25
29 Logan LeSage .40 1.00
30 Ethan Cardwell .40 1.00
31 Landon Kosior .40 1.00
32 Isaac Enright .40 1.00
33 Zach Biggar .40 1.00
34 Connor Trenholm .40 1.00
35 Francesco Arcuri .40 1.00
36 Tye Austin .40 1.00
37 Marc Boudreau .40 1.00
38 Owen Pederson .40 1.00
39 Josh Bloom .50 1.25
40 Justin Robidas .40 1.00
41 Bennett MacArthur .40 1.00
42 Ben Boyd .40 1.00
43 Gabe Klassen .40 1.00
44 Evgenii Kashnikov .40 1.00
45 Tyson Kozak .40 1.00
46 Tyson Galloway .40 1.00
47 Connor Lockhart .40 1.00
48 Dylan Garand .40 1.00
49 Jack Thompson .30 .75
50 Gannon Laroque .40 1.00
51 Jacob Melanson .40 1.00
52 JR Avon .40 1.00
53 Zack Stringer .40 1.00
54 Matthew Maggio .40 1.00
55 Carson Latimer .40 1.00
56 Josh Pillar .40 1.00
57 Oasiz Wiesblatt .40 1.00
58 Jack Matier .40 1.00
59 Kai Uchacz .40 1.00
60 Blake Swetlikoff .40 1.00
61 Manix Landry .40 1.00
62 Ryan McCleary .40 1.00
63 Marc Lajoie .40 1.00
64 Mikey Milne .40 1.00
65 Ethan Peters .40 1.00
66 Jack Beck .40 1.00
67 Nolan Dann .40 1.00
68 Braeden Kressler .40 1.00
69 Braden Hache .40 1.00
70 Charles-Antoine Pilote .40 1.00
71 Nolan Bentham .40 1.00
72 Caedan Bankier .40 1.00
73 Luke McNamara .40 1.00
74 Kyle Jackson .40 1.00
75 Olivier Nadeau .40 1.00
76 Connor Punnett .40 1.00
77 Mathieu Cataford .40 1.00
78 Leighton Carruthers .40 1.00
79 Jonathan Fauchon .40 1.00
80 Oliver Tulk .40 1.00
81 Daniil Sobolev .40 1.00
82 Trevor Wong .40 1.00
83 Angus MacDonell .40 1.00
84 Ethan Burroughs .40 1.00
85 William Dufour .40 1.00
86 James Hardie .40 1.00
87 Lawson Sherk .40 1.00
88 Reid Dyck .40 1.00
89 Zacharie Giroux .40 1.00
90 Julien Hebert .40 1.00
91 Cameron Butler .40 1.00
92 Liam Arnsby .40 1.00
93 Vincent Iorio .40 1.00
94 Ethan Samson .40 1.00
95 Pacey Schlueting .40 1.00
96 Anthony DiCesare .40 1.00
97 Alexandre Doucet .40 1.00
98 Charles-Edward Gravel .40 1.00
99 Josh Williams .40 1.00
100 Logan Morrison .40 1.00
101 Cody Morgan .40 1.00
102 Mitchell Russell .40 1.00
103 Keaton Dowhaniuk .40 1.00
104 Lleyton Moore .40 1.00
105 William Provost .40 1.00
106 James Malatesta .40 1.00
107 Simon Pinard .40 1.00
108 Ryan Francis .40 1.00
109 Jeremy Lapointe .40 1.00
110 Cameron Whynot .40 1.00
111 Ryan Stepien .40 1.00
112 Koehn Ziemmer .40 1.00
113 Xavier Parent .25 .60
114 Tanner Brown .40 1.00
115 Xavier Fortin .40 1.00
116 Loick Daigle .40 1.00
117 William Trudeau .40 1.00
118 Isaac Belliveau .40 1.00
119 Joseph Serpa .40 1.00
120 Carter Serhyenko .40 1.00
121 Louis-Philippe Fontaine .40 1.00
122 Rhett Melnyk .40 1.00
123 Georgie Diaco .40 1.00
124 Andrew Whitton .40 1.00
125 Tyler Brennan .40 1.00
126 William Villeneuve .40 1.00
127 Conor Frenette .40 1.00
128 Logan Dowhaniuk .40 1.00
129 Nathan Staios .40 1.00
130 Luke Toporowski .40 1.00
131 Maxime Pellerin .40 1.00
132 Ivan Ivan .40 1.00
133 Braden Holt .40 1.00
134 Nolan Flamand .40 1.00
135 Ole Bjorgvik Holm .40 1.00
136 Stepan Machacek .40 1.00
137 Matthew Kieper .40 1.00
138 Rhett Rhinehart .40 1.00
139 Zac Funk .40 1.00
140 Michal Gut .40 1.00
141 Luca Del Bel Belluz .40 1.00
142 Layton Feist .40 1.00
143 Nolan Maier .40 1.00
144 Nick DeGrazia .40 1.00
145 Kyle McDonald .40 1.00
146 Patrick Guay .40 1.00
147 Remi Poirier .40 1.00
148 Reid Valade .40 1.00
149 Samuel Johnson .40 1.00
150 Jordan Gustafson .40 1.00
151 Connor Bouchard .40 1.00
152 Matej Kaslik .40 1.00
153 Mathieu Bizier .40 1.00
154 Bryan Thomson .40 1.00
155 Niall Crocker .40 1.00
156 Samuel Richard .40 1.00
157 Tyrel Bauer .40 1.00
158 Tyson Greenway .40 1.00
159 Olivier Adam .40 1.00
160 Jacob Squires .40 1.00
161 Jackson Berezowski .40 1.00
162 Pavel Novak .40 1.00
163 Thomas Couture .40 1.00
164 Artem Guryev .40 1.00
165 Tom Cadieux .40 1.00
166 Roby Kerins .40 1.00
167 Rayan Bettahar .40 1.00
168 Daniel D'Amico .40 1.00
169 Jacob Stewart .40 1.00
170 Luka Verreault .40 1.00
171 Josh Filmon .40 1.00
172 Charles Boutin .40 1.00
173 Felix Lafrance .40 1.00
174 Marko Sikic .40 1.00
175 Logan Barlage .40 1.00
176 Brandon Coe .40 1.00
177 Tyson Laventure .40 1.00
178 Antoine Coulombe .40 1.00
179 Maddox Callens .40 1.00
180 Denton Mateychuk .40 1.00
181 Jordan Frasca .40 1.00
182 Tye Kartye .40 1.00
183 Raphael Pelletier .40 1.00
184 Skyler Bruce .40 1.00
185 Raivis Kristians Ansons .40 1.00
186 Jacob Goobie .40 1.00
187 Declan McDonnell .40 1.00
188 Jagger Firkus .40 1.00
189 Alex Drover .40 1.00
190 Kevin Korchinski .40 1.00
191 Parker Bell .40 1.00
192 Jakin Smallwood .40 1.00
193 Ethan Del Mastro .40 1.00
194 Deni Goure .40 1.00
195 Jayden Grubbe .40 1.00
196 Aidan De La Gorgendiere .40 1.00
197 Dawson Stairs .40 1.00
198 Ronan Seeley .40 1.00
199 Jake Lee .40 1.00
200 Vincent Labelle .40 1.00
201 Tanner Dickinson .40 1.00
202 Mathew Ward .40 1.00
203 Ethan Kruger .40 1.00
204 Nolan Burke .40 1.00
205 Joe Ranger .40 1.00
206 Jacob Oster .40 1.00
207 Xavier Simoneau .40 1.00
208 Eric Alarie .40 1.00
209 Brady Stonehouse .40 1.00
210 Henrik Rybinski .40 1.00
211 Martin Chromiak .40 1.00
212 Garin Bjorklund .40 1.00
213 Ben King .40 1.00
214 Mason Beaupit .40 1.00
215 Nikolas Hurtubise .40 1.00
216 Jeremy Langlois .40 1.00
217 Sean McGurn .40 1.00
218 Lochlan Gordan .40 1.00
219 Justin Hall .40 1.00
220 Fabrice Fortin .40 1.00
221 Dom DiVincentiis .40 1.00
222 David Spacek .40 1.00
223 Colton Smith .40 1.00
224 Lucas Edmonds .40 1.00
225 Anson Thornton .40 1.00
226 Kyle Masters .40 1.00
227 Denver Barkey .40 1.00
228 Tag Bertuzzi .40 1.00
229 Fabio Iacobo .40 1.00
230 Reece Vitelli .40 1.00
231 Beau Akey .40 1.00
232 Juan Copeland .40 1.00
233 Coulson Pitre .40 1.00
234 Jake Karabela .40 1.00
235 Louis Crevier .40 1.00
236 Logan Crosby .40 1.00
237 Avery Hayes .40 1.00
238 Craig Armstrong .40 1.00
239 Vincent Gauthier .40 1.00
240 Mike Petizian .40 1.00
241 Jeremy Michel .40 1.00
242 Camaryn Baber .40 1.00
243 Matteo Rotondi .40 1.00
244 Vsevolod Gaidamak .40 1.00
245 Logan Cunningham .40 1.00
246 Jakub Hujer .40 1.00
247 Cael Zimmerman .40 1.00
248 William Veillette .40 1.00
249 Artem Grushnikov .40 1.00
250 Elias Cohen .40 1.00
251 William Blackburn .40 1.00
252 Viktor Persson .40 1.00
253 Matyas Sapovaliv .40 1.00
254 Mats Lindgren .40 1.00
255 Jan Bednar .40 1.00
256 Kasper Larsen .40 1.00
257 Evan Konyen .40 1.00
258 Brayden Schuurman .40 1.00
259 Bogdans Hodass .40 1.00
260 Ivan Zhigalov .40 1.00
261 Mitchell Weeks .40 1.00
262 Colby Saganiuk .40 1.00
263 Servac Petrovsky .40 1.00
264 Sergei Litvinov .40 1.00
265 Cole Mackay .40 1.00
266 Nolan Lalonde .40 1.00
267 Emmett Sproule .40 1.00
268 Daniil Chayka .40 1.00
269 Jacob Gaucher .40 1.00
270 Etienne Morin .40 1.00
271 Jesper Vikman .40 1.00
272 Sean Tschigerl .40 1.00
273 Matteo Lalama .40 1.00
274 Rodwin Dionicio .40 1.00
275 Riley Piercey .40 1.00
276 Lukas Svejkovsky .40 1.00
277 Amadeus Lombardi .30 .75
278 Marek Alscher .40 1.00
279 Tucker Tynan .40 1.00
280 Matthew Papais .40 1.00
281 Matvey Petrov .40 1.00
282 Tommy Cormier .40 1.00
283 Cameron Tolnai .40 1.00
284 Marc-Olivier Beaudry .40 1.00
285 Chris Barlas .40 1.00
286 Roman Schmidt .40 1.00
287 Owen Saye .40 1.00
288 Kyle Crnkovic .40 1.00
289 Nathan Baril .40 1.00
290 Carl Tetachuk .40 1.00
291 Ty Halaburda .40 1.00
292 Brett Bressette .40 1.00
293 Paul Hughes .40 1.00
294 Tristan Bertucci .40 1.00
295 Julien Rod .40 1.00
296 Patrick Leaver .40 1.00
297 Tyler Palmer .40 1.00

298 Christoffer Sedoff .40 1.00
299 Talyn Boyko .40 1.00
300 Andrew LeBlanc .40 1.00
301 Shane Wright 1.25 3.00
302 Connor Bedard 40.00 100.00
303 Brandt Clarke .60 1.50
304 Logan Stankoven 1.25 3.00
305 Jan Mysak .60 1.50
306 Francesco Pinelli .50 1.25
307 Ryder Korczak .60 1.50
308 Luke Evangelista .60 1.50
309 Josh Bloom .60 1.50
310 Mavrik Bourque .60 1.50
311 Carson Lambos .60 1.50
312 Beau Jelsma .60 1.50
313 Zachary Dean .50 1.25
314 Dylan Guenther .75 2.00
315 Wyatt Johnston 1.50 4.00
316 Daemon Hunt .60 1.50
317 Brennan Othmann .60 1.50
318 Cross Hanas .60 1.50
319 Jack Finley .60 1.50
320 Kaiden Guhle .60 1.50
321 Brett Harrison .50 1.25
322 Tristan Lennox .75 2.00
323 Riley Kidney .50 1.25
324 Xavier Bourgault .60 1.50
325 Antonio Stranges .60 1.50
326 Conner Roulette .60 1.50
327 Olen Zellweger .60 1.50
328 Jeremie Poirier .60 1.50
329 Danny Zhilkin .60 1.50
330 Justin Sourdif .60 1.50
331 Ryker Evans .60 1.50
332 Chase Stillman .60 1.50
333 Nolan Allan .60 1.50
334 Tristen Robins .60 1.50
335 Sebastian Cossa 1.00 2.50
336 Tyler Tullio .60 1.50
337 Benjamin Gaudreau .60 1.50
338 Zachary Bolduc .60 1.50
339 Luke Prokop .60 1.50
340 Lukas Cormier .60 1.50
341 Matthew Savoie .75 2.00
342 Zack Ostapchuk .60 1.50
343 Ryan O'Rourke .60 1.50
344 Conor Geekie .75 2.00
345 Oskar Olausson .60 1.50
346 Cole Huckins .60 1.50
347 Ozzy Wiesblatt .50 1.25
348 Will Cuylle .60 1.50
349 Ridly Greig .60 1.50
350 Nathan Gaucher .60 1.50
351 Fabian Lysell SR .60 1.50
352 Emile Perron SR .60 1.50
353 Sasha Pastujov SR .60 1.50
354 Pano Fimis SR .60 1.50
355 Stanislav Svozil SR .60 1.50
356 Max Namestnikov SR .60 1.50
357 Ethan Gauthier SR .60 1.50
358 Ty Nelson SR .60 1.50
359 Niko Huuhtanen SR .60 1.50
360 Matthew Soto SR .60 1.50
361 Jakub Demek SR .60 1.50
362 Dylan MacKinnon SR .60 1.50
363 Nick Lardis SR .60 1.50
364 Jorian Donovan SR .60 1.50
365 Hunter Haight SR .60 1.50
366 Abakar Kazbekov SR .60 1.50
367 Zakary Lavoie SR .60 1.50
368 Vinzenz Rohrer SR .60 1.50
369 Aidan Castle SR .60 1.50
370 Quinn Mantei SR .60 1.50
371 Vincent Collard SR .60 1.50
372 Spencer Sova SR .60 1.50
373 Bryce McConnell-Barker SR .60 1.50
374 Ryan Abraham SR .60 1.50
375 David Goyette SR .60 1.50
376 Maxime Coursol SR .60 1.50
377 Matthew Poitras SR .60 1.50
378 Calum Ritchie SR .60 1.50
379 Alex Blais SR .60 1.50
380 Colby Barlow SR .60 1.50
381 Ben Bujold SR .60 1.50
382 Alex Pharand SR .60 1.50
383 Danil Gushchin SR .60 1.50
384 Calem Mangone SR .60 1.50
385 Cedrick Guindon SR .60 1.50
386 Paul Ludwinski SR .60 1.50
387 Cameron Allen SR .60 1.50
388 Martin Rysavy SR .60 1.50
389 Tyler Peddle SR .60 1.50
390 Owen Beck SR .75 2.00
391 Ruslan Gazizov SR .60 1.50
392 Luke Coughlin SR .60 1.50
393 Gavin Hayes SR .60 1.50
394 Quentin Musty SR .60 1.50
395 Carson Rehkopf SR .60 1.50
396 Ethan Miedema SR .60 1.50
397 Owen Outwater SR .75 2.00
398 Luke Misa SR .60 1.50
399 Carey Terrance SR .75 2.00
400 Donovan McCoy SR .60 1.50
401 Connor Bedard '20-21 SR 40.00 100.00
402 Tristan Luneau '20-21 SR 1.50 4.00
403 Conor Geekie '20-21 SR 1.50 4.00
404 Brayden Yager '20-21 SR 1.50 4.00
405 Riley Heidt '20-21 SR 1.50 4.00
406 Zach Benson '20-21 SR 2.00 5.00
407 Lorenzo Canonica '20-21 SR 1.50 4.00
408 Kalan Lind '20-21 SR 1.50 4.00
409 Mazden Leslie '20-21 SR 1.50 4.00
410 Vincent Filion '20-21 SR 1.50 4.00
411 Kocha Delic '20-21 SR 1.50 4.00
412 Pier-Olivier Roy '20-21 SR 1.50 4.00
413 Noah Warren '20-21 SR 1.50 4.00
414 Nate Danielson '20-21 SR 1.50 4.00
415 Kaden Hammell '20-21 SR 1.50 4.00
416 Justin Cote '20-21 SR 1.50 4.00
417 Andrew Cristall '20-21 SR 2.00 5.00
418 Reid Andresen '20-21 SR 1.50 4.00
419 Rylen Roersma '20-21 SR 1.50 4.00
420 Saige Weinstein '20-21 SR 1.50 4.00
421 Nathan Drapeau '20-21 SR 1.50 4.00
422 Terrell Goldsmith '20-21 SR 1.50 4.00
423 Evan Nause '20-21 SR 1.50 4.00
424 Luke Woodworth '20-21 SR 1.50 4.00
425 Brady Birnie '20-21 SR 1.50 4.00
426 Jordan Dumais '20-21 SR 1.50 4.00
427 Tyson Zimmer '20-21 SR 1.50 4.00
428 Samuel Savoie '20-21 SR 1.50 4.00
429 Markus Vidicek '20-21 SR 1.50 4.00
430 Viljami Marjala '20-21 SR 1.50 4.00
431 Connor Levis '20-21 SR 1.50 4.00
432 Michael Buchinger '20-21 SR 1.50 4.00
433 Robert Orr '20-21 SR 1.50 4.00
434 Lukas Dragicevic '20-21 SR 1.50 4.00
435 Sam Oremba '20-21 SR 1.50 4.00
436 Antonin Verreault '20-21 SR 1.50 4.00
437 Grayden Siepmann '20-21 SR 1.50 4.00
438 Cameron MacDonald '20-21 SR 1.50 4.00
439 Oren Shtrom '20-21 SR 1.50 4.00
440 Dyllan Gill '20-21 SR 1.50 4.00
441 Sam Oliver '20-21 SR 1.50 4.00
442 Maveric Lamoureux '20-21 SR 1.50 4.00
443 Daniel Hauser '20-21 SR 1.50 4.00
444 Dawson Seitz '20-21 SR 1.50 4.00
445 Maxim Barbashev '20-21 SR 1.50 4.00
446 Jonathan Melee '20-21 SR 1.50 4.00
447 Cole Miller '20-21 SR 1.50 4.00
448 Fraser Minten '20-21 SR 1.50 4.00
449 Tanner Molendyk '20-21 SR 1.50 4.00
450 Nicolas Ruccia '20-21 SR 1.50 4.00

2021-22 Upper Deck CHL Clear Cut

*CLEAR CUT: 1.2X TO 3X BASIC
302 Connor Bedard 80.00 200.00

2021-22 Upper Deck CHL Exclusives

302 Connor Bedard 125.00 300.00
401 Connor Bedard '20-21 SR 125.00 300.00

2021-22 Upper Deck CHL Autographs

1 Evan Vierling D 6.00 15.00
2 Tucker Robertson D 6.00 15.00
3 Jakob Brook D 6.00 15.00
4 Robert Calisti D 6.00 15.00
5 Connor McClennon D 6.00 15.00
6 Miguel Tourigny D 6.00 15.00
8 Bryce Montgomery D 6.00 15.00
9 Mikael Diotte D 6.00 15.00
10 Elliot Desnoyers D 6.00 15.00
11 Brady Burns D 6.00 15.00
12 Joshua Roy D 8.00 20.00
13 Max McCue D 6.00 15.00
14 Charles Savoie D 6.00 15.00
15 Graham Sward D 6.00 15.00
16 Maximus Wanner D 6.00 15.00
17 Lucas Ciona D 6.00 15.00
18 Riley Ginnell D 6.00 15.00
19 Jalen Luypen D 6.00 15.00
20 Israel Mianscum D 6.00 15.00
21 Nolan Ritchie D 6.00 15.00
22 Dru Krebs D 6.00 15.00
23 Daniel Michaud D 6.00 15.00
24 Theo Rochette D 6.00 15.00
25 Ty Voit D 6.00 15.00
26 Landon McCallum D 6.00 15.00
28 Colton Dach D 8.00 20.00
29 Logan LeSage D 6.00 15.00
30 Ethan Cardwell D 6.00 15.00
31 Landon Kosior D 6.00 15.00
32 Isaac Enright D 6.00 15.00
33 Zach Biggar D 6.00 15.00
34 Connor Trenholm D 6.00 15.00
35 Francesco Arcuri D 6.00 15.00
36 Tye Austin D 6.00 15.00
37 Marc Boudreau D 6.00 15.00
38 Owen Pederson D 6.00 15.00
39 Josh Bloom D 8.00 20.00
40 Justin Robidas D 6.00 15.00
41 Bennett MacArthur D 6.00 15.00
45 Tyson Kozak D 6.00 15.00
46 Tyson Galloway D 6.00 15.00
47 Connor Lockhart D 6.00 15.00
48 Dylan Garand D 6.00 15.00
49 Jack Thompson D 5.00 12.00
50 Gannon Laroque D 6.00 15.00
51 Jacob Melanson D 6.00 15.00
53 Zack Stringer D 6.00 15.00
55 Carson Latimer D 6.00 15.00
56 Josh Pillar D 6.00 15.00
57 Oasiz Wiesblatt D 6.00 15.00
59 Kai Uchacz D 6.00 15.00
60 Blake Swetlikoff D 6.00 15.00
61 Manix Landry D 6.00 15.00
62 Ryan McCleary D 6.00 15.00
63 Marc Lajoie D 6.00 15.00
64 Mikey Milne D 6.00 15.00
65 Ethan Peters D 6.00 15.00
67 Nolan Dann D 6.00 15.00
68 Braeden Kressler D 6.00 15.00
69 Braden Hache D 6.00 15.00
70 Charles-Antoine Pilote D 6.00 15.00
71 Nolan Bentham D 6.00 15.00
72 Caedan Bankier D 6.00 15.00
73 Luke McNamara D 6.00 15.00
74 Kyle Jackson D 6.00 15.00
75 Olivier Nadeau D 6.00 15.00
76 Connor Punnett D 6.00 15.00
77 Mathieu Cataford D 6.00 15.00
78 Leighton Carruthers D 6.00 15.00
79 Jonathan Fauchon D 6.00 15.00
80 Oliver Tulk D 6.00 15.00
83 Angus MacDonell D 6.00 15.00
84 Ethan Burroughs D 6.00 15.00
85 William Dufour D 6.00 15.00
86 James Hardie D 6.00 15.00
87 Lawson Sherk D 6.00 15.00
301 Shane Wright C 15.00 40.00
302 Connor Bedard A 1000.00 2500.00
303 Brandt Clarke C 8.00 20.00
304 Logan Stankoven C 20.00 50.00
305 Jan Mysak C 8.00 20.00
307 Ryder Korczak C 8.00 20.00
308 Luke Evangelista C 8.00 20.00
309 Josh Bloom D 8.00 20.00
310 Mavrik Bourque C 8.00 20.00
311 Carson Lambos C 8.00 20.00
313 Zachary Dean B 6.00 15.00
314 Dylan Guenther C 10.00 25.00
317 Brennan Othmann C 8.00 20.00
320 Kaiden Guhle C 12.00 30.00
322 Tristan Lennox C 10.00 25.00
323 Riley Kidney C 6.00 15.00
324 Xavier Bourgault B 8.00 20.00
326 Conner Roulette B 8.00 20.00
327 Olen Zellweger C 8.00 20.00
328 Jeremie Poirier C 8.00 20.00
329 Danny Zhilkin D 8.00 20.00
330 Justin Sourdif C 8.00 20.00
331 Ryker Evans D 8.00 20.00
332 Chase Stillman C 8.00 20.00
335 Sebastian Cossa C 12.00 30.00
336 Tyler Tullio C 8.00 20.00
337 Benjamin Gaudreau C 8.00 20.00
338 Zachary Bolduc B 8.00 20.00
340 Lukas Cormier C 8.00 20.00
341 Matthew Savoie C 10.00 25.00
344 Conor Geekie C 10.00 25.00
345 Oskar Olausson D 8.00 20.00
346 Cole Huckins B 8.00 20.00
348 Will Cuylle C 10.00 25.00
349 Ridly Greig C 8.00 20.00
352 Emile Perron SR D 8.00 20.00
354 Pano Fimis SR D 8.00 20.00
357 Ethan Gauthier SR D 8.00 20.00
358 Ty Nelson SR C 8.00 20.00
362 Dylan MacKinnon SR D 8.00 20.00
363 Nick Lardis SR D 8.00 20.00
364 Jorian Donovan SR D 8.00 20.00
365 Hunter Haight SR D 8.00 20.00
367 Zakary Lavoie SR D 8.00 20.00
369 Aidan Castle SR D 8.00 20.00
370 Quinn Mantei SR D 8.00 20.00
371 Vincent Collard SR D 8.00 20.00
373 Bryce McConnell-Barker SR D 8.00 20.00
375 David Goyette SR D 8.00 20.00
376 Maxime Coursol SR C 8.00 20.00
378 Calum Ritchie SR C 8.00 20.00
380 Colby Barlow SR D 8.00 20.00
382 Alex Pharand SR D 8.00 20.00
383 Danil Gushchin SR C 8.00 20.00
384 Calem Mangone SR D 8.00 20.00
385 Cedrick Guindon SR D 8.00 20.00
389 Tyler Peddle SR C 8.00 20.00
392 Luke Coughlin SR D 8.00 20.00
394 Quentin Musty SR D 15.00 40.00
397 Owen Outwater SR C 8.00 20.00
398 Luke Misa SR D 8.00 20.00
400 Donovan McCoy SR D 8.00 20.00

2021-22 Upper Deck CHL First Draft

FD1 Connor Bedard 40.00 100.00
FD2 Quentin Musty 1.25 3.00
FD3 Ethan Gauthier 1.25 3.00
FD4 Matthew Soto 1.25 3.00
FD5 Tyler Peddle 1.25 3.00
FD6 Riley Heidt 1.50 4.00
FD7 Calum Ritchie 1.25 3.00
FD8 Brayden Yager 1.50 4.00
FD9 Vincent Collard 1.25 3.00
FD10 Nick Lardis 1.25 3.00
FD11 Zach Benson 2.00 5.00
FD12 Emile Perron 1.25 3.00
FD13 Cameron Allen 1.25 3.00
FD14 Kalan Lind 1.50 4.00
FD15 Luke Coughlin 1.25 3.00
FD16 Tanner Molendyk 1.50 4.00
FD17 Colby Barlow 1.25 3.00
FD18 Mathieu Cataford 1.00 2.50
FD19 Tristan Bertucci 1.00 2.50
FD20 Sam Oremba 1.50 4.00
FD21 Ethan Miedema 1.25 3.00
FD22 Lukas Dragicevic 1.50 4.00
FD23 Bryce McConnell-Barker 1.25 3.00
FD24 Alex Pharand 1.25 3.00
FD25 Justin Gendron 1.00 2.50

2021-22 Upper Deck CHL First Draft Red

*RED/99: 1.5X TO 4X BASIC
FD1 0 150.00 400.00

2021-22 Upper Deck CHL First Draft Autographs Blue

FD2 Quentin Musty 12.00 30.00
FD6 Riley Heidt 15.00 40.00
FD10 Nick Lardis 12.00 30.00
FD12 Emile Perron 12.00 30.00
FD14 Kalan Lind 15.00 40.00
FD18 Mathieu Cataford 10.00 25.00
FD20 Sam Oremba 15.00 40.00
FD22 Lukas Dragicevic 15.00 40.00
FD24 Alex Pharand 12.00 30.00
FD25 Justin Gendron 10.00 25.00

2021-22 Upper Deck CHL Next Step

NS1 Brennan Othmann 1.25 3.00
NS2 Zachary Dean 1.00 2.50
NS3 Dylan Guenther 1.50 4.00
NS4 Shane Wright 2.50 6.00
NS5 Brandt Clarke 1.25 3.00
NS6 Matthew Savoie 1.50 4.00
NS7 Logan Stankoven 2.50 6.00
NS8 Chase Stillman 1.25 3.00
NS9 Carson Lambos 1.25 3.00
NS10 Benjamin Gaudreau 1.25 3.00
NS11 Olivier Nadeau 1.00 2.50
NS12 Joshua Roy 1.25 3.00
NS13 Sasha Pastujov 1.25 3.00
NS14 Riley Kidney 1.00 2.50
NS15 Fabian Lysell 1.25 3.00
NS16 Connor Bedard 15.00 40.00
NS17 Manix Landry 1.00 2.50
NS18 Sebastian Cossa 2.00 5.00
NS19 Wyatt Johnston 3.00 8.00
NS20 Ty Nelson 1.25 3.00

2021-22 Upper Deck CHL Profiles

PR1 Brandon Lisowsky 1.00 2.50
PR2 Gavin Hayes 1.25 3.00
PR3 Nathan Gaucher 1.25 3.00
PR4 Denton Mateychuk 1.00 2.50
PR5 Shane Wright 2.50 6.00
PR6 Connor Bedard 8.00 20.00
PR7 Markus Vidicek 1.50 4.00
PR8 Mats Lindgren 1.00 2.50
PR9 Paul Ludwinski 1.25 3.00
PR10 Mathew Ward 1.00 2.50
PR11 Matthew Poitras 1.25 3.00
PR12 Justin Cote 1.50 4.00
PR13 Bryce McConnell-Barker 1.25 3.00
PR14 Matthew Savoie 1.50 4.00
PR15 Pano Fimis 1.25 3.00
PR16 Conor Geekie 1.50 4.00
PR17 Tristan Luneau 1.50 4.00
PR18 Max Namestnikov 1.25 3.00
PR19 Tyler Brennan 1.00 2.50
PR20 Ty Nelson 1.25 3.00
PR21 Zach Benson 2.00 5.00
PR22 Riley Heidt 1.50 4.00
PR23 Brayden Yager 1.50 4.00
PR24 Lukas Dragicevic 1.50 4.00
PR25 Alex Pharand 1.25 3.00
PR26 Carey Terrance 1.50 4.00
PR27 Ethan Gauthier 1.25 3.00
PR28 Emile Perron 1.25 3.00
PR29 Matthew Soto 1.25 3.00
PR30 Calum Ritchie 1.25 3.00

2021-22 Upper Deck CHL They're Exceptional

TE1 Connor Bedard 25.00 60.00
TE2 Shane Wright 2.50 6.00
TE3 Connor McDavid 5.00 12.00

2021-22 Upper Deck CHL They're Exceptional Red

*RED/99: 1X TO 2.5X BASIC
TE1 Connor Bedard 100.00 250.00

2021-22 Upper Deck CHL Top Imports

*RED/99: .5X TO 1.2X BASIC
*BLUE/25: .6X TO 1.5X BASIC
T1 Danil Gushchin 2.00 5.00
T2 Servac Petrovsky 1.50 4.00
T3 Jan Bednar 1.50 4.00
T4 Leevi Merilainen 1.50 4.00
T5 Jakub Demek 2.00 5.00
T6 Niks Fenenko 1.50 4.00
T7 Matvey Petrov 1.50 4.00
T8 Ivan Zhigalov 1.50 4.00
T9 Pavel Cajan 1.50 4.00
T10 Kirill Kudryavtsev 1.50 4.00
T11 Vinzenz Rohrer 2.00 5.00

2022-23 Upper Deck CHL

1 Jacob Melanson .40 1.00
2 Vincent Filion .60 1.50
3 Zachary Bolduc .50 1.25
4 Landon Sim .40 1.00
5 Deagen McMillan .40 1.00
6 Jakub Brabenec .40 1.00
7 Christian Kyrou .40 1.00
8 Brennan Othmann .50 1.25
9 Amadeus Lombardi .30 .75
10 Matvey Petrov .40 1.00
11 Gavin White .40 1.00
12 Jackson Edward .40 1.00
13 Ryan Mast .40 1.00
14 Angus Booth .40 1.00
15 Riley Piercey .40 1.00
16 Campbell Arnold .40 1.00
17 Ty Halaburda .40 1.00
18 Brett Hyland .40 1.00
19 Brett Harrison .40 1.00
20 Ethan Chadwick .40 1.00
21 Justin Robidas .40 1.00
22 Alessandro Segafredo .40 1.00
23 Chase Stillman .50 1.25
24 Zachary Dean .40 1.00
25 Frederic Brunet .40 1.00
26 Isaac Dufort .40 1.00
27 Josh Filmon .40 1.00
28 Benjamin Gaudreau .50 1.25
29 Nicolas Savoie .40 1.00
30 Alexis Gendron .40 1.00
31 Kaleb Lawrence .40 1.00
32 Jordan Gavin .40 1.00
33 Sean McGurn .40 1.00
34 Maxime Pellerin .40 1.00
35 Gavin Hodnett .40 1.00
36 Logan Wormald .40 1.00
37 Kocha Delic .60 1.50
38 Nolan Flamand .40 1.00
39 Austin Roest .40 1.00
40 Jonathan Fauchon .40 1.00
41 Kyle Jackson .40 1.00
42 Michael Buchinger .60 1.50
43 Cole Dubinsky .40 1.00
44 Xavier Fortin .40 1.00
45 Aidan Castle .50 1.25
46 Quentin Musty .50 1.25
47 Stuart Rolofs .40 1.00
48 Gabe Klassen .40 1.00
49 Jake Karabela .40 1.00
50 Tristan Lennox .60 1.50
51 Jacob Oster .40 1.00
52 Kaden Hammell .60 1.50
53 Zakary Lavoie .50 1.25
54 Tristan Luneau .60 1.50
55 Luka Verreault .40 1.00
56 Raphael Pelletier .40 1.00
57 Nolan Allan .50 1.25
58 Spencer Sova .50 1.25
59 Jack Matier .40 1.00
60 Loick Daigle .40 1.00
61 Theo Rochette .40 1.00
62 Evan Herman .40 1.00
63 Mathew Ward .40 1.00
64 Jordan Dumais .60 1.50
65 Liam Arnsby .40 1.00
66 Daniel Hauser .60 1.50
67 Tyler Peddle .50 1.25
68 Carson Lambos .50 1.25
69 Zachary L'Heureux .50 1.25
70 Ethan Miedema .50 1.25
71 Colby Saganiuk .40 1.00
72 Maxim Barbashev .60 1.50
73 Dyllan Gill .60 1.50
74 Alexandre Doucet .40 1.00
75 Zac Funk .40 1.00
76 Jack Beck .40 1.00
77 Brandon Lisowsky .40 1.00
78 Graham Sward .40 1.00
79 Sasha Pastujov .50 1.25
80 William Provost .40 1.00
81 Isaac Belliveau .40 1.00
82 Ryan Abraham .50 1.25
83 Luke Woodworth .60 1.50
84 Jakub Demek .50 1.25
85 Jesper Vikman .40 1.00
86 Nolan Collins .40 1.00
87 Danny Zhilkin .50 1.25
88 Dmitry Kuzmin .40 1.00
89 Ryan Winterton .40 1.00
90 Vincent Labelle .40 1.00
91 Kalem Parker .40 1.00
92 Ethan Del Mastro .40 1.00
93 Marek Alscher .40 1.00
94 Ben King .40 1.00
95 Francesco Pinelli .40 1.00
96 Manix Landry .40 1.00
97 Joshua Roy .50 1.25
98 Brayden Schuurman .40 1.00
99 Justin Gill .40 1.00
100 Dom DiVincentiis .40 1.00
101 Blake Swetlikoff .40 1.00
102 Skyler Bruce .40 1.00
103 Nolan Lalonde .40 1.00
104 Josh Pillar .40 1.00
105 David Spacek .40 1.00
106 Olivier Nadeau .40 1.00
107 Sam Oliver .60 1.50
108 Rylen Roersma .60 1.50
109 Mikael Huchette .40 1.00
110 Owen Pederson .40 1.00
111 Mason Beaupit .40 1.00
112 Kirill Kudryavtsev .40 1.00
113 Trevor Wong .40 1.00
114 Tommy Cormier .40 1.00
115 Keaton Dowhaniuk .40 1.00
116 Zakhar Polshakov .40 1.00
117 Nate Danielson .60 1.50
118 Riley Mercer .40 1.00
119 Leighton Carruthers .40 1.00
120 Cole Miller .60 1.50
121 Tucker Robertson .40 1.00
122 Justin Gendron .40 1.00
123 Braeden Kressler .40 1.00
124 Mathieu Cataford .40 1.00
125 Parker Bell .40 1.00
126 Tyler Brennan .40 1.00
127 Oasiz Wiesblatt .40 1.00
128 Dawson Seitz .60 1.50
129 Caden Price .40 1.00
130 Eric Alarie .40 1.00
131 Declan McDonnell .40 1.00
132 Connor McClennon .40 1.00
133 Alexis Bourque .40 1.00
134 Logan Dowhaniuk .40 1.00
135 Logan Morrison .40 1.00
136 Deni Goure .40 1.00
137 Jorian Donovan .50 1.25
138 J.R. Avon .40 1.00
139 James Hardie .40 1.00
140 Egor Sidorov .40 1.00
141 Landon McCallum .40 1.00
142 Evan Vierling .40 1.00
143 Chase Stillman .50 1.25
144 Grayden Siepmann .60 1.50
145 Ty Thorpe .40 1.00
146 Kolby Hay .40 1.00
147 Connor Ungar .40 1.00
148 Jake Furlong .40 1.00
149 Riley Gannon .40 1.00
150 Gabriel Szturc .40 1.00
151 Patrik Hamrla .40 1.00
152 Antonio Tersigni .40 1.00
153 Cam Squires .40 1.00
154 Daylan Kuefler .40 1.00
155 Evan Nause .60 1.50
156 Tyson Hinds .40 1.00
157 Aidan Litke .40 1.00
158 Ryan Hofer .40 1.00
159 Connor Hvidston .40 1.00
160 Tanner Scott .40 1.00
161 Jared Davidson .40 1.00
162 Max Namestnikov .50 1.25
163 Caden Brown .40 1.00
164 Pier-Olivier Roy .60 1.50
165 Jayden Grubbe .40 1.00
166 Cameron MacDonald .60 1.50
167 Vinzenz Rohrer .50 1.25
168 Chase Bertholet .40 1.00
169 Trae Wilke .40 1.00
170 Cameron Allen .50 1.25
171 Felix Gagnon .40 1.00
172 Sean Tschigerl .40 1.00
173 Caedan Bankier .40 1.00
174 Samuel Ivanov .40 1.00
175 Simon Hughes .40 1.00
176 Jeremy Langlois .40 1.00
177 Tarin Smith .40 1.00
178 Daniil Sobolev .40 1.00
179 Miguel Marques .40 1.00
180 Tnias Mathurin .40 1.00
181 Matthew Seminoff .40 1.00
182 Jake Sloan .40 1.00
183 Robert Baco .40 1.00
184 Francesco Arcuri .40 1.00
185 Cameron Whynot .40 1.00
186 James Malatesta .40 1.00
187 Max McCue .40 1.00
188 Vsevolod Komarov .40 1.00
189 Ethan Buenaventura .40 1.00
190 Jett Jones .40 1.00
191 Avery Hayes .40 1.00
192 Zack Ostapchuk .50 1.25
193 Calem Mangone .50 1.25
194 Ethan Samson .40 1.00
195 Clarke Caswell .40 1.00
196 Ty Voit .40 1.00
197 Roman Schmidt .40 1.00
198 Dylan Ernst .40 1.00
199 Stanislav Svozil .50 1.25
200 Max Donoso .40 1.00
201 Caden Kelly .40 1.00
202 George Diaco .40 1.00
203 William Rousseau .40 1.00
204 Zachary Roy .40 1.00
205 Cole Peardon .40 1.00
206 Marcus Kearsey .40 1.00
207 Jonas Woo .40 1.00
208 Alessio Beglieri .40 1.00
209 Grady Martin .40 1.00
210 Quinn Kennedy .40 1.00
211 Olivier Brideau .40 1.00
212 Robert Orr .60 1.50
213 Conner Roulette .50 1.25
214 Marshall Lessard .40 1.00
215 Will Cranley .40 1.00
216 Andrew LeBlanc .40 1.00
217 A.J. Spellacy .40 1.00
218 Zachary Bowen .40 1.00
219 Anson Thornton .40 1.00
220 Haakon Hanelt .40 1.00
221 Tristen Doyle .40 1.00
222 Cole Wadsworth .40 1.00
223 Koen MacInnes .40 1.00
224 Marc-Andre Gaudet .40 1.00
225 Cole Huckins .50 1.25
226 Nolan Burke .40 1.00
227 Bryce Montgomery .40 1.00
228 Pavel Simek .40 1.00
229 Vladislav Shilo .40 1.00
230 Chandler Romeo .40 1.00
231 Dominik Rymon .40 1.00
232 Jake Chiasson .40 1.00
233 Gabe Smith .40 1.00
234 Tim Metzger .40 1.00
235 Nathan Brisson .40 1.00
236 Mathys Fernandez .40 1.00
237 Joshua Lawrence .40 1.00
238 Ethan Ernst .40 1.00
239 Diego Buttazzoni .40 1.00
240 Jacob Holmes .40 1.00
241 Kyle Masters .40 1.00
242 Pasquale Zito .40 1.00
243 Logan Peskett .40 1.00
244 Jalen Luypen .40 1.00
245 Artur Cholach .40 1.00
246 Henry Mews .40 1.00
247 Brian Zanetti .40 1.00
248 Adam Fortier-Gendron .40 1.00
249 Maximus Wanner .40 1.00
250 Gage Alexander .40 1.00
251 Jan Spunar .40 1.00
252 William Trudeau .40 1.00
253 Frantisek Formanek .40 1.00
254 Connor Lockhart .40 1.00
255 Kai Knak .40 1.00
256 Tomas Hamara .40 1.00
257 Oscar Plandowski .40 1.00
258 Carson Latimer .40 1.00
259 Justin Ertel .40 1.00
260 Felix Lacerte .40 1.00
261 Jeremie Richard .40 1.00
262 Sam Alfano .40 1.00
263 Logan Mailloux .50 1.25
264 Artem Guryev .40 1.00
265 Martin Rysavy .50 1.25
266 Alexis Michaud .40 1.00
267 Tyson Galloway .40 1.00
268 Alexander Suzdalev .40 1.00
269 Liam Gilmartin .40 1.00
270 Cole Jordan .40 1.00
271 Joey Willis .40 1.00
272 Andrei Malyavin .40 1.00
273 Ben Roger .40 1.00
274 Kooper Gizowski .40 1.00
275 Jhett Larson .40 1.00
276 Hunter Mayo .40 1.00
277 Jackson Berezowski .40 1.00
278 Jack O'Brien .40 1.00
279 Gracyn Sawchyn .40 1.00
280 Adam Kydd .40 1.00
281 Ondrej Becher .40 1.00
282 James Stefan .40 1.00
283 Reese Belton .40 1.00
284 Rhett Melnyk .40 1.00
285 Kai Uchacz .40 1.00
286 Aidan De La Gorgendiere .40 1.00
287 Alex Thacker .40 1.00
288 Maxim Muranov .40 1.00
289 Owen MacNeil .40 1.00
290 Jorian Donovan .50 1.25
291 Andrew Basha .40 1.00
292 Andrew Whitton .40 1.00
293 Cameron Tolnai .40 1.00
294 Juan Copeland .40 1.00
295 Justin Cloutier .40 1.00
296 Jakub Hujer .40 1.00
297 Peter Reynolds .40 1.00
298 Daniil Bourash .40 1.00
299 William Veillette .40 1.00
300 Xavier Sarrasin .40 1.00
301 Riley Kidney .50 1.25
302 Ivan Ivan .50 1.25
303 Nathan Gaucher .60 1.50
304 Maveric Lamoureux .75 2.00
305 Anthony Cristoforo .60 1.50
306 Logan Stankoven 1.25 3.00
307 Brayden Yager .75 2.00
308 Connor Bedard 20.00 50.00
309 Zach Benson 1.00 2.50
310 Tanner Howe .60 1.50
311 Lukas Dragicevic .75 2.00
312 Luca Del Bel Belluz .50 1.25
313 Pano Fimis .60 1.50
314 Owen Beck .75 2.00
315 Calum Ritchie .60 1.50
316 Wyatt Johnston 2.00 5.00
317 Matyas Sapovaliv .60 1.50
318 Jagger Firkus .60 1.50
319 Matthew Savoie .75 2.00
320 Ethan Gauthier .60 1.50
321 Olen Zellweger .60 1.50
322 Ty Nelson .60 1.50
323 Andrew Cristall .60 1.50
324 Jan Bednar .60 1.50
325 Koehn Ziemmer .60 1.50
326 Riley Heidt .75 2.00
327 Pavel Mintyukov .60 1.50
328 Kevin Korchinski .60 1.50
329 David Goyette .60 1.50
330 Denton Mateychuk .60 1.50
331 Fraser Minten .75 2.00
332 Noah Warren .75 2.00
333 Reid Schaefer .60 1.50
334 Bryce McConnell-Barker .60 1.50
335 Jordan Gustafson .60 1.50
336 Hunter Haight .60 1.50
337 Matthew Poitras .60 1.50
338 Paul Ludwinski .60 1.50
339 Gavin Hayes .60 1.50
340 Servac Petrovsky .60 1.50
341 Conor Geekie .75 2.00
342 Cedrick Guindon .60 1.50
343 Samuel Savoie .75 2.00
344 Matthew Maggio .50 1.25
345 Ivan Zhigalov .60 1.50
346 Reid Dyck .60 1.50
347 Owen Pickering .60 1.50
348 Mats Lindgren .60 1.50
349 Josh Davies .60 1.50
350 Ben Hemmerling .60 1.50
351 Markas Samenas SR .60 1.50
352 Tomas Lavoie SR .60 1.50
353 Gabriel D'Aigle SR 1.25 3.00
354 Maxim Masse SR .75 2.00
355 Andrew Gibson SR .60 1.50
356 Cooper Foster SR .60 1.50
357 Berkly Catton SR 1.25 3.00
358 Tij Iginla SR .60 1.50
359 Malcolm Spence SR .60 1.50
360 Owen Phillips SR .60 1.50
361 Justin Poirier SR .60 1.50
362 Bill Zonnon SR .60 1.50
363 Spencer Gill SR .60 1.50
364 Eliot Litalien SR .60 1.50
365 William Shields SR .60 1.50
366 Alexandre Lallier SR .60 1.50
367 Nathan Villeneuve SR .60 1.50
368 Porter Martone SR 1.00 2.50
369 Jack Van Volsen SR .60 1.50
370 Beckett Sennecke SR 1.25 3.00
371 Cole Beaudoin SR .60 1.50
372 Benjamin Cormier SR .60 1.50
373 Jett Luchanko SR .75 2.00
374 Lucas Karmiris SR .60 1.50
375 Ethan Procyszyn SR .60 1.50
376 Cole Temple SR .60 1.50
377 Liam Greentree SR .60 1.50
378 Gabriel Frasca SR .60 1.50
379 Easton Cowan SR 1.25 3.00
380 Zayne Parekh SR .60 1.50
381 Frantisek Ridzon SR .60 1.50
382 Luc Schweingruber SR .60 1.50
383 Adam Mechura SR .60 1.50
384 David Moravec SR .60 1.50
385 Jacob Battaglia UER SR .60 1.50
386 Jakub Chromiak SR .60 1.50
387 Matyas Melovsky SR .60 1.50
388 Kevin He SR .60 1.50
389 Zigmund Zold SR .60 1.50
390 Tommaso De Luca SR .60 1.50
391 Sandis Vilmanis SR .60 1.50
392 Joel Marchon SR .60 1.50
393 Kimo Gruber SR .60 1.50
394 Thomas Desruisseaux SR .60 1.50
395 Roger McQueen SR .60 1.50
396 Nino Tomov SR .60 1.50
397 Jan Sprynar SR .60 1.50
398 Ryder Ritchie SR .60 1.50
399 Michael Misa SR 10.00 25.00
400 Christopher Brown SR .60 1.50

2022-23 Upper Deck CHL Clear Cut

*CLEAR CUT: 1.5X TO 4X BASIC
308 Connor Bedard 100.00 250.00
353 Gabriel D'Aigle SR 15.00 40.00
354 Maxim Masse SR 12.00 30.00
357 Berkly Catton SR 8.00 20.00
379 Easton Cowan SR 12.00 30.00
399 Michael Misa SR 20.00 50.00

2022-23 Upper Deck CHL Exclusives

*EXCL/100: 2.5X TO 6X BASIC
*S/SR EXC/100: 2X TO 5X BASIC
308 Connor Bedard 125.00 300.00
399 Michael Misa SR 100.00 250.00

2022-23 Upper Deck CHL Red

*RED: .5X TO 1.2X BASIC
308 Connor Bedard 30.00 80.00
399 Michael Misa SR 30.00 80.00

2022-23 Upper Deck CHL '21-22 CHL Star Rookies

CSR1 David Goyette 1.25 3.00
CSR2 Calum Ritchie 1.25 3.00
CSR3 Max Namestnikov 1.25 3.00
CSR4 Colby Barlow 1.00 2.50
CSR5 Sasha Pastujov 1.25 3.00
CSR6 Cameron Allen 1.25 3.00
CSR7 Matthew Poitras 1.25 3.00
CSR8 Jakub Demek 1.25 3.00
CSR9 Tyler Peddle 1.25 3.00
CSR10 Vincent Collard 1.00 2.50
CSR11 Owen Beck 1.50 4.00
CSR12 Aidan Castle 1.25 3.00
CSR13 Carson Rehkopf 1.00 2.50
CSR14 Ivan Zhigalov 1.25 3.00
CSR15 Bryce McConnell-Barker 1.25 3.00
CSR16 Carey Terrance 1.00 2.50
CSR17 Pano Fimis 1.25 3.00
CSR18 Gavin Hayes 1.25 3.00
CSR19 Niks Fenenko 1.00 2.50
CSR20 Ethan Miedema 1.25 3.00
CSR21 Stanislav Svozil 1.25 3.00
CSR22 Matthew Soto 1.00 2.50
CSR23 Spencer Sova 1.25 3.00
CSR24 Patrik Hamrla 1.00 2.50
CSR25 Luke Misa 1.00 2.50
CSR26 Nick Lardis 1.00 2.50
CSR27 Servac Petrovsky 1.25 3.00
CSR28 Jason Desruisseaux 1.00 2.50
CSR29 Jakub Hujer 1.00 2.50

CSR30 Calem Mangone 1.25 3.00
CSR31 Ty Nelson 1.25 3.00
CSR32 Haakon Hanelt 1.00 2.50
CSR33 Hunter Haight 1.25 3.00
CSR34 Andrei Loshko 1.00 2.50
CSR35 Alex Blais 1.00 2.50
CSR36 Robert Baco 1.00 2.50
CSR37 Paul Ludwinski 1.25 3.00
CSR38 Ethan Gauthier 1.25 3.00
CSR39 Gabriel Szturc 1.00 2.50
CSR40 Ben Bujold 1.00 2.50
CSR41 Alex Pharand 1.00 2.50
CSR42 Zakary Lavoie 1.25 3.00
CSR43 Luke Coughlin 1.00 2.50
CSR44 Ruslan Gazizov 1.00 2.50
CSR45 Matthew Sop 1.00 2.50
CSR46 Ryan Abraham 1.25 3.00
CSR47 Donovan McCoy 1.00 2.50
CSR48 Jorian Donovan 1.25 3.00
CSR49 Quentin Musty 1.25 3.00
CSR50 Martin Rysavy 1.25 3.00

2022-23 Upper Deck CHL Autographs

2 Vincent Filion 10.00 25.00
3 Zachary Bolduc 8.00 20.00
6 Jakub Brabenec 6.00 15.00
7 Christian Kyrou 6.00 15.00
8 Brennan Othmann 8.00 20.00
12 Jackson Edward 6.00 15.00
19 Brett Harrison 6.00 15.00
21 Justin Robidas 6.00 15.00
23 Chase Stillman 8.00 20.00
24 Zachary Dean 6.00 15.00
25 Frederic Brunet 6.00 15.00
28 Benjamin Gaudreau 8.00 20.00
30 Alexis Gendron 6.00 15.00
31 Kaleb Lawrence 6.00 15.00
32 Jordan Gavin 6.00 15.00
34 Maxime Pellerin 6.00 15.00
35 Gavin Hodnett 6.00 15.00
40 Jonathan Fauchon 6.00 15.00
41 Kyle Jackson 6.00 15.00
45 Aidan Castle 8.00 20.00
46 Quentin Musty 8.00 20.00
47 Stuart Rolofs 6.00 15.00
48 Gabe Klassen 6.00 15.00
49 Jake Karabela 6.00 15.00
50 Tristan Lennox 10.00 25.00
53 Zakary Lavoie 8.00 20.00
54 Tristan Luneau 10.00 25.00
57 Nolan Allan 8.00 20.00
58 Spencer Sova 8.00 20.00
59 Jack Matier 6.00 15.00
61 Theo Rochette 6.00 15.00
63 Mathew Ward 6.00 15.00
64 Jordan Dumais 10.00 25.00
67 Tyler Peddle 8.00 20.00
68 Carson Lambos 8.00 20.00
69 Zachary L'Heureux 8.00 20.00
70 Ethan Miedema 8.00 20.00
72 Maxim Barbashev 10.00 25.00
73 Dyllan Gill 10.00 25.00
77 Brandon Lisowsky 6.00 15.00
78 Graham Sward 6.00 15.00
79 Sasha Pastujov 8.00 20.00
81 Isaac Belliveau 6.00 15.00
83 Luke Woodworth 10.00 25.00
84 Jakub Demek 8.00 20.00
85 Jesper Vikman 6.00 15.00
87 Danny Zhilkin 8.00 20.00
88 Dmitry Kuzmin 6.00 15.00
89 Ryan Winterton 6.00 15.00
91 Kalem Parker 6.00 15.00
92 Ethan Del Mastro 6.00 15.00
93 Marek Alscher 6.00 15.00
94 Ben King 6.00 15.00
95 Francesco Pinelli 6.00 15.00
96 Manix Landry 6.00 15.00
97 Joshua Roy 8.00 20.00
98 Brayden Schuurman 6.00 15.00
100 Dom DiVincentiis 6.00 15.00
301 Riley Kidney 6.00 15.00
302 Ivan Ivan 6.00 15.00
303 Nathan Gaucher 8.00 20.00
304 Maveric Lamoureux 10.00 25.00
306 Logan Stankoven 15.00 40.00
307 Brayden Yager 10.00 25.00
309 Zach Benson 12.00 30.00
310 Tanner Howe 8.00 20.00
311 Lukas Dragicevic 10.00 25.00
312 Luca Del Bel Belluz 6.00 15.00
314 Owen Beck 10.00 25.00
315 Calum Ritchie 8.00 20.00
316 Wyatt Johnston 25.00 60.00
317 Matyas Sapovaliv 8.00 20.00
318 Jagger Firkus 8.00 20.00
319 Matthew Savoie 10.00 25.00
320 Ethan Gauthier 8.00 20.00
321 Olen Zellweger 8.00 20.00
322 Ty Nelson 8.00 20.00
323 Andrew Cristall 8.00 20.00
325 Koehn Ziemmer 8.00 20.00
326 Riley Heidt 10.00 25.00
327 Pavel Mintyukov 8.00 20.00
328 Kevin Korchinski 8.00 20.00
329 David Goyette 8.00 20.00
330 Denton Mateychuk 8.00 20.00
331 Fraser Minten 10.00 25.00
332 Noah Warren 10.00 25.00
333 Reid Schaefer 8.00 20.00
334 Bryce McConnell-Barker 8.00 20.00
335 Jordan Gustafson 8.00 20.00
336 Hunter Haight 8.00 20.00
337 Matthew Poitras 8.00 20.00
338 Paul Ludwinski 8.00 20.00
339 Gavin Hayes 8.00 20.00
340 Servac Petrovsky 8.00 20.00
342 Cedrick Guindon 8.00 20.00
343 Samuel Savoie 10.00 25.00
344 Matthew Maggio 6.00 15.00
345 Ivan Zhigalov 8.00 20.00
347 Owen Pickering 8.00 20.00
348 Mats Lindgren 8.00 20.00
349 Josh Davies 8.00 20.00
350 Ben Hemmerling 8.00 20.00
351 Markas Samenas SR 8.00 20.00
352 Tomas Lavoie SR 8.00 20.00
353 Gabriel D'Aigle SR 15.00 40.00
354 Maxim Masse SR 10.00 25.00
357 Berkly Catton SR 15.00 40.00
358 Tij Iginla SR 8.00 20.00
360 Owen Phillips SR 8.00 20.00
361 Justin Poirier SR 8.00 20.00
362 Bill Zonnon SR 8.00 20.00
363 Spencer Gill SR 8.00 20.00
364 Eliot Litalien SR 8.00 20.00
365 William Shields SR 8.00 20.00
366 Alexandre Lallier SR 8.00 20.00
367 Nathan Villeneuve SR 8.00 20.00
369 Jack Van Volsen SR 8.00 20.00
370 Beckett Sennecke SR 15.00 40.00
371 Cole Beaudoin SR 8.00 20.00
372 Benjamin Cormier SR 8.00 20.00
373 Jett Luchanko SR 10.00 25.00
374 Lucas Karmiris SR 8.00 20.00
375 Ethan Procyszyn SR 8.00 20.00
376 Cole Temple SR 8.00 20.00
383 Adam Mechura SR 8.00 20.00
386 Jakub Chromiak SR 8.00 20.00
387 Matyas Melovsky SR 8.00 20.00
390 Tommaso De Luca SR 8.00 20.00
391 Sandis Vilmanis SR 8.00 20.00
393 Kimo Gruber SR 8.00 20.00
394 Thomas Desruisseaux SR 8.00 20.00
395 Roger McQueen SR 8.00 20.00
396 Nino Tomov SR 8.00 20.00
397 Jan Sprynar SR 8.00 20.00
398 Ryder Ritchie SR 8.00 20.00
400 Christopher Brown SR 8.00 20.00

2022-23 Upper Deck CHL CHL Graduates

*RED/99: .5X TO 1.2X BASIC
CG1 Wayne Gretzky 12.00 30.00
CG2 Connor McDavid 10.00 25.00
CG3 Sidney Crosby 8.00 20.00

2022-23 Upper Deck CHL Connor Bedard Retrospective

CB1 Connor Bedard 6.00 15.00
CB2 Connor Bedard 6.00 15.00
CB3 Connor Bedard 6.00 15.00
CB4 Connor Bedard 6.00 15.00
CB5 Connor Bedard 6.00 15.00
CB6 Connor Bedard 6.00 15.00
CB7 Connor Bedard 6.00 15.00
CB8 Connor Bedard 6.00 15.00
CB9 Connor Bedard 6.00 15.00
CB10 Connor Bedard 6.00 15.00
CB11 Connor Bedard 6.00 15.00
CB12 Connor Bedard 6.00 15.00
CB13 Connor Bedard 6.00 15.00
CB14 Connor Bedard 6.00 15.00
CB15 Connor Bedard 6.00 15.00

2022-23 Upper Deck CHL First Draft

FD1 Michael Misa 8.00 20.00
FD2 Malcolm Spence 1.25 3.00
FD3 Nathan Villeneuve 1.25 3.00
FD4 Lucas Karmiris 1.25 3.00
FD5 Porter Martone 2.00 5.00
FD6 Jack Van Volsen 1.25 3.00
FD7 Henry Mews 1.00 2.50
FD8 Beckett Sennecke 2.50 6.00
FD9 Christopher Brown 1.25 3.00
FD10 Cole Beaudoin 1.25 3.00
FD11 Benjamin Cormier 1.25 3.00
FD12 Jett Luchanko 1.50 4.00
FD13 Anthony Cristoforo 1.25 3.00
FD14 Zayne Parekh 1.25 3.00
FD15 Felix Lacerte 1.00 2.50
FD16 Ethan Procyszyn 1.25 3.00
FD17 Liam Greentree 1.25 3.00
FD18 Gabe Smith 1.00 2.50
FD19 Alexandre Lallier 1.25 3.00
FD20 Alexis Michaud 1.00 2.50
FD21 Nathan Brisson 1.00 2.50
FD22 Easton Cowan 2.50 6.00
FD23 Gabriel Frasca 1.25 3.00
FD24 Tomas Lavoie 1.25 3.00
FD25 Gabriel D'Aigle 2.50 6.00
FD26 Bill Zonnon 1.25 3.00
FD27 Owen Phillips 1.25 3.00
FD28 Eliot Litalien 1.25 3.00
FD29 Quinn Kennedy 1.00 2.50
FD30 Ethan Ernst 1.00 2.50
FD31 William Shields 1.25 3.00
FD32 Thomas Desruisseaux 1.25 3.00
FD33 Adam Fortier-Gendron 1.00 2.50
FD34 Marek Vanacker 1.00 2.50
FD35 Justin Carbonneau 1.00 2.50

2022-23 Upper Deck CHL Future Heroes

*BLUE/25: .75X TO 2X BASIC
FH1 Connor Bedard 20.00 50.00
FH2 Matthew Savoie 2.50 6.00
FH3 Kyle Crnkovic 1.50 4.00
FH4 Conor Geekie 2.50 6.00
FH5 Pavel Mintyukov 2.00 5.00
FH6 Brayden Yager 2.50 6.00
FH7 Calum Ritchie 2.00 5.00
FH8 Owen Beck 2.50 6.00
FH9 Tanner Howe 2.00 5.00
FH10 Nathan Gaucher 2.00 5.00
FH11 Luca Del Bel Belluz 1.50 4.00

2022-23 Upper Deck CHL Future Heroes Red

*RED/99: .5X TO 1.2X BASIC
FH1 Connor Bedard 100.00 250.00

2022-23 Upper Deck CHL Top Imports

*RED/99: .5X TO 1.2X BASIC
*BLUE/25: .6X TO 1.5X BASIC
TI1 Frantisek Ridzon 2.00 5.00
TI2 Luc Schweingruber 2.00 5.00
TI3 Markas Samenas 2.00 5.00
TI4 Adam Mechura 2.00 5.00
TI5 David Moravec 2.00 5.00
TI6 Marcel Marcel 1.50 4.00
TI7 Jakub Chromiak 2.00 5.00
TI8 Matyas Melovsky 2.00 5.00
TI9 Eriks Mateiko 1.50 4.00
TI10 Zigmund Zold 2.00 5.00
TI11 Tommaso De Luca 2.00 5.00
TI12 Sandis Vilmanis 2.00 5.00
TI13 Joel Marchon 2.00 5.00
TI14 Kimo Gruber 2.00 5.00
TI15 Alessio Beglieri 1.50 4.00
TI16 Tomas Hamara 1.50 4.00
TI17 Nino Tomov 2.00 5.00
TI18 Jan Sprynar 2.00 5.00
TI19 Ondrej Becher 1.50 4.00
TI20 Tommy Purdeller 1.50 4.00
TI21 Tim Metzger 1.50 4.00
TI22 Ivan Zhigalov 2.00 5.00
TI23 Leo Braillard 1.50 4.00
TI24 Jan Spunar 1.50 4.00
TI25 Linus Hemstrom 1.50 4.00

2023-24 Upper Deck CHL

1 Conner Roulette .60 1.50
2 Brayden Gillespie .40 1.00
3 Zac Funk .50 1.25
4 Nate Tivey .40 1.00
5 Michael Cicek .40 1.00
6 Oscar Plandowski .50 1.25
7 Dawson Pasternak .40 1.00
8 Lou Levesque .40 1.00
9 Julius Sumpf .40 1.00
10 Connor Hvidston .50 1.25
11 Felix Lacerte .50 1.25
12 Mathieu Paris .40 1.00
13 Ty Young .40 1.00
14 William Rousseau .50 1.25
15 Jacob Julien .40 1.00
16 Alex Pharand .50 1.25
17 Tyler Peddle .60 1.50
18 Vincent Filion .75 2.00
19 Rylen Roersma .75 2.00
20 Andrew Gibson .60 1.50
21 Rilen Kovacevic .40 1.00
22 Brayden Crampton .40 1.00
23 Nolan Collins .50 1.25
24 Sam Dickinson .75 2.00
25 Carson Rehkopf .50 1.25
26 Cameron Allen .60 1.50
27 Lou-Felix Denis .40 1.00
28 Kalem Parker .50 1.25
29 Stuart Rolofs .50 1.25
30 Jordan Gavin .50 1.25
31 Brady Schultz .40 1.00
32 Martin Rysavy .60 1.50
33 Nate Misskey .40 1.00
34 Ben Hemmerling .60 1.50
35 Quentin Miller .40 1.00
36 Lukas Matecha .40 1.00
37 Sloan Stanick .40 1.00
38 Jorian Donovan .60 1.50
39 Vsevolod Komarov .50 1.25
40 Cam Squires .50 1.25
41 Evan May .40 1.00
42 Tommy Cormier .50 1.25
43 Yoan Loshing .40 1.00
44 Daniel Agostino .40 1.00
45 Alexis Michaud .50 1.25
46 Alexis Morin .40 1.00
47 Josh Davies .60 1.50
48 Scott Ratzlaff .50 1.25
49 Jack Beck .50 1.25
50 Michael Buchinger .75 2.00
51 Cedrick Guindon .60 1.50
52 Joseph Henneberry .40 1.00
53 Bryce McConnell-Barker .60 1.50
54 Rodwin Dionicio .50 1.25
55 Jeremie Minville .40 1.00
56 Tyson Doucette .40 1.00
57 Jeremy Langlois .50 1.25
58 Justin Cote .75 2.00
59 Nicholas Surzycia .40 1.00
60 Joseph Willis .40 1.00
61 Owen Conrad .50 1.25
62 Brady Stonehouse .50 1.25
63 Caden Price .50 1.25
64 Markus Vidicek .75 2.00
65 Cooper Foster .60 1.50
66 Konnor Smith .40 1.00
67 Noah Chadwick .40 1.00
68 Matyas Sapovaliv .60 1.50
69 Ondrej Becher .50 1.25
70 Matthew Mayich .40 1.00
71 Oliver Peer .40 1.00
72 Jackson Edward .50 1.25
73 Dawson Cowan .40 1.00
74 Zander Veccia .40 1.00
75 Nathan Brisson .50 1.25
76 Justin Carbonneau .50 1.25
77 Quinton Burns .50 1.25
78 Filip Mesar .40 1.00
79 Domenic DiVincentiis .50 1.25
80 Deni Goure .50 1.25
81 Max Namestnikov .60 1.50
82 Porter Martone 1.25 3.00
83 Nathaniel Day .40 1.00
84 Peter Reynolds .50 1.25
85 Lirim Amidovski .40 1.00
86 Gavin Hodnett .50 1.25
87 Antoine Keller .40 1.00
88 Benjamin Kindel .40 1.00
89 Linus Hemstrom .50 1.25
90 Braydon McCallum .40 1.00
91 Kaleb Lawrence .50 1.25
92 Samuel St-Hilaire .40 1.00
93 Giovanni Morneau .40 1.00
94 Robin Sapousek .40 1.00
95 Max McCue .50 1.25
96 David Goyette .60 1.50
97 Ethan Chadwick .50 1.25
98 Parker Bell .50 1.25
99 Justin Kipkie .40 1.00
100 Terrell Goldsmith .40 1.00
101 Jan Golicic .40 1.00
102 Matthew Ward .40 1.00
103 Jake Furlong .50 1.25
104 Marc Lajoie .50 1.25
105 Donovan Arsenault .40 1.00
106 Gabriel D'Aigle 1.25 3.00
107 Hunter Haight .60 1.50
108 Kocha Delic .75 2.00
109 Matyas Melovsky .60 1.50
110 Kalan Lind .75 2.00
111 Luke Coughlin .50 1.25
112 Vincent Collard .50 1.25
113 Jeremy Hanzel .40 1.00
114 Milo Roelens .40 1.00
115 Gabe Klassen .50 1.25
116 Maxime Pellerin .50 1.25
117 Gabriel Szturc .50 1.25
118 Ethan Burroughs .40 1.00
119 Tyler MacKenzie .40 1.00
120 Austin Roest .50 1.25
121 Logen Hammett .40 1.00
122 Alexis Bourque .50 1.25
123 Dominik Rymon .50 1.25
124 Andrei Loshko .50 1.25
125 Noah Reinhart .40 1.00
126 Parker Berge .40 1.00
127 Ethan Buenaventura .50 1.25
128 Gavin Bryant .40 1.00
129 Miles Cooper .40 1.00
130 Calem Mangone .60 1.50
131 Maxime Coursol .60 1.50
132 Pano Fimis .60 1.50
133 Carson Bjarnason .50 1.25
134 Spencer Sova .60 1.50
135 Anthony Romani .40 1.00
136 Mathys Fernandez .50 1.25
137 Mathis Rousseau .40 1.00
138 Graham Sward .50 1.25
139 Sam Oremba .75 2.00
140 Marshall Finnie .40 1.00
141 Marcus Kearsey .50 1.25
142 Josh Filmon .50 1.25
143 Jaden Lipinski .40 1.00
144 Patrick Thomas .40 1.00
145 Carter Sotheran .40 1.00
146 Carter George .40 1.00
147 Charles Savoie .50 1.25
148 Andre Anania .40 1.00
149 Ruslan Gazizov .50 1.25
150 Jax Dubois .40 1.00
151 Olivier Boutin .40 1.00
152 Tye Spencer .40 1.00
153 Emmitt Finnie .40 1.00
154 Anthony Cristoforo .60 1.50
155 Dylan Sydor .40 1.00
156 Mathieu Cataford .50 1.25
157 Tomas Cibulka .40 1.00
158 Logan Wormald .50 1.25
159 Atlee Calvert .40 1.00
160 Justin Larose .40 1.00
161 Jacob LeBlanc .40 1.00
162 Charlie Elick .40 1.00
163 Connor Levis .75 2.00
164 Pier-Olivier Roy .75 2.00
165 Reid Dyck .60 1.50
166 Dominic Pilote .40 1.00
167 Jonathan Fauchon .50 1.25
168 Maxim Barbashev .75 2.00
169 Shane Smith .40 1.00
170 Dyllan Gill .75 2.00
171 Austin Elliot .40 1.00
172 Borya Valis .40 1.00
173 Andrew LeBlanc .50 1.25
174 Spencer Gill .60 1.50
175 Nicolas Ruccia .75 2.00
176 Jonathan Melee .75 2.00
177 Brett Hyland .50 1.25
178 Luca Cagnoni .50 1.25
179 Alexis Gendron .50 1.25
180 Aidan Litke .50 1.25
181 Eriks Mateiko .50 1.25
182 Jakub Hujer .50 1.25
183 Kaden Hammell .75 2.00
184 Israel Mianscum .50 1.25
185 Oasiz Wiesblatt .50 1.25
186 Briley Wood .40 1.00
187 Antoine Dorion .40 1.00
188 Chase Bertholet .50 1.25
189 Lewis Gendron .40 1.00
190 Mats Lindgren .60 1.50
191 Antonin Verreault .75 2.00
192 Trevor Wong .50 1.25
193 Justin Poirier .50 1.25
194 Cole Brown .40 1.00
195 Roenick Jodoin .40 1.00
196 Cameron MacDonald .75 2.00
197 Angus MacDonell .50 1.25
198 Servac Petrovsky .60 1.50
199 Mason Zebeski .40 1.00
200 Hunter Mayo .50 1.25
201 Kyren Gronick .40 1.00
202 Michael Horth .40 1.00
203 Jacob Oster .50 1.25
204 Jake Sloan .50 1.25
205 Valentin Zhugin .40 1.00
206 Brad Gardiner .40 1.00
207 Oliver Tulk .50 1.25
208 Tyler McInnis Thorpe .50 1.25
209 Chas Sharpe .40 1.00
210 Xavier Daigle .40 1.00
211 Egor Sidorov .50 1.25
212 Zacharie Giroux .50 1.25
213 Luke Woodworth .75 2.00
214 Owen Flores .40 1.00
215 Niall Crocker .50 1.25
216 Sam Alfano .50 1.25
217 Charles Boutin .50 1.25
218 Mavrick Lachance .40 1.00
219 Mason Vaccari .40 1.00
220 Brandon Lisowsky .50 1.25
221 Florian Xhekaj .40 1.00
222 Daniel Hauser .75 2.00
223 Norwin Panocha .40 1.00
224 Jackson Desouza .40 1.00
225 Carey Terrance .50 1.25
226 Jari Kykkanen .40 1.00
227 Riley Mercer .50 1.25
228 Vojtech Port .40 1.00
229 Liam Arnsby .50 1.25
230 Adam Zidlicky .40 1.00
231 Brayden Edwards .40 1.00
232 Charles-Edward Gravel .50 1.25
233 Samuel Savoie .75 2.00
234 Pavel Simek .50 1.25
235 Charlie Wright .40 1.00
236 Isaiah George .40 1.00
237 Marco Mignosa .40 1.00
238 Braeden Kressler .50 1.25
239 Daniil Sobolev .50 1.25
240 Paul Ludwinski .60 1.50
241 Nico Myatovic .40 1.00
242 Alexandre Guy .40 1.00
243 Maxim Masse .75 2.00
244 Cameron Schmidt .40 1.00
245 Ondrej Molnar .40 1.00
246 Miguel Marques .50 1.25
247 Fraser Minten 1.00 2.50
248 Tomas Hamara .50 1.25
249 Peter Repcik .40 1.00
250 Connor Punnett .50 1.25
251 Niks Fenenko .50 1.25
252 Owen Pickering .60 1.50
253 Koehn Ziemmer .60 1.50
254 Luca Hauf .40 1.00
255 Carson Woodall .40 1.00
256 Jackson Unger .40 1.00
257 Shea Van Olm .40 1.00
258 Felix Lecerte .40 1.00
259 Ty Cheveldayoff .40 1.00
260 Lukas Dragicevic .75 2.00
261 Sandis Vilmanis .60 1.50
262 Kirill Kudryavtsev .50 1.25
263 Tomas Mrsic .40 1.00
264 Sawyer Mynio .40 1.00
265 Alex Christopoulos .40 1.00
266 Robert Orr .75 2.00
267 Caleb Hadland .40 1.00
268 Nick Lardis .50 1.25
269 Hunter Brzustewics .40 1.00
270 Luca D'Amato .40 1.00
271 Raoul Boilard .40 1.00
272 Dylan Roobroeck .40 1.00
273 Theo Lemieux .40 1.00
274 Angus Booth .50 1.25
275 Matthew Sop .50 1.25
276 Cole Burbidge .40 1.00
277 Ethan Procyszyn .60 1.50
278 Braxton Whitehead .40 1.00
279 Connor Lockhart .50 1.25
280 Carter Yakemchuk .50 1.25
281 Layton Feist .50 1.25
282 Aiden Oiring .40 1.00
283 Kai Uchacz .50 1.25
284 Alexander Assadourian .40 1.00
285 Bode Stewart .40 1.00
286 Justice Christensen .40 1.00
287 James Stefan .50 1.25
288 Ethan Miedema .60 1.50
289 Tristan Bertucci .50 1.25
290 Jett Luchanko .75 2.00
291 Coulson Pitre .50 1.25
292 Braden Hache .50 1.25
293 Shawn Pearson .40 1.00
294 Thomas Desruisseaux .60 1.50
295 Tanner Scott .50 1.25
296 Beau Jelsma .60 1.50
297 Jonas Woo .50 1.25
298 Ollie Josephson .40 1.00
299 Hudson Thornton .40 1.00
300 Sean Tschigerl .50 1.25
301 Matt Savoie 1.25 3.00
302 Michael Misa 2.00 5.00
303 Tij Iginla 1.25 3.00
304 Ryder Ritchie .75 2.00
305 Nathan Darveau .60 1.50
306 Malcolm Spence .75 2.00
307 Denton Mateychuk .75 2.00
308 Braeden Bowman .60 1.50
309 Gracyn Sawchyn .60 1.50
310 Easton Cowan 1.50 4.00
311 Justin Gill .60 1.50
312 Maxim Masse 1.00 2.50
313 Eduard Sale .60 1.50
314 Maveric Lamoureux 1.00 2.50
315 Ty Nelson .75 2.00
316 Jordan Dumais 1.00 2.50
317 Cayden Lindstrom 1.50 4.00
318 Roger McQueen .75 2.00
319 Andrew Cristall .75 2.00
320 Samuel Honzek .60 1.50
321 Beau Akey .60 1.50
322 Luke Misa .60 1.50
323 Riley Heidt 1.00 2.50
324 Colby Barlow .60 1.50
325 Tanner Molendyk 1.00 2.50
326 Ryerson Leenders .60 1.50
327 Liam Greentree .75 2.00
328 Calum Ritchie .75 2.00
329 Gavin Hayes .75 2.00
330 Luca Pinelli .60 1.50
331 Ethan Gauthier .75 2.00
332 Jagger Firkus 1.25 3.00
333 Andrew Basha .60 1.50
334 Berkly Catton 1.50 4.00
335 Tristan Luneau .60 1.50
336 Cole Beaudoin .75 2.00
337 Nate Danielson 1.00 2.50
338 Quentin Musty .75 2.00
339 Tanner Howe .75 2.00
340 Brayden Schuurman .60 1.50
341 Zayne Parekh .75 2.00
342 Etienne Morin .60 1.50
343 Conor Geekie 1.00 2.50
344 Owen Beck 1.00 2.50
345 Beckett Sennecke 1.50 4.00
346 Oliver Bonk .60 1.50
347 Bryce Pickford .60 1.50
348 Henry Mews .60 1.50
349 Denver Barkey .60 1.50
350 Brayden Yager 1.00 2.50
351 Gavin McKenna SR 30.00 80.00
352 Dalibor Dvorsky SR .75 2.00
353 Cole Davis SR .60 1.50
354 Noah Degenstein SR .60 1.50
355 Martin Misiak SR .60 1.50
356 Henry Brzustewicz SR .60 1.50
357 Justin Blais SR .60 1.50
358 Caleb Desnoyers SR 2.00 5.00
359 Emile Guite SR 1.00 2.50
360 Cole Reschny SR .60 1.50
361 Terik Parascak SR .60 1.50
362 Matthew Schaefer SR 6.00 15.00
363 Mathis Preston SR .75 2.00
364 Sam O'Reilly SR .60 1.50
365 Rasmus Kumpulainen SR .60 1.50
366 Lynden Lakovic SR .60 1.50
367 Jack Ivankovic SR 1.00 2.50
368 Ryan Brown SR .60 1.50
369 Egan Beveridge SR .60 1.50
370 Urban Podrekar SR .60 1.50
371 Ryan Roobroeck SR 6.00 15.00
372 Caden Taylor SR .60 1.50
373 Harry Nansi SR .60 1.50
374 Kasper Halttunen SR .60 1.50
375 Jakub Milota SR .60 1.50
376 Jakub Fibigr SR .60 1.50
377 Adrian Rebelo SR .60 1.50
378 Alex Huang SR .60 1.50
379 Braedon Cootes SR .60 1.50
380 Xavier Villeneuve SR .60 1.50
381 Wesley Royston SR .60 1.50
382 Will Sharpe SR .60 1.50
383 Nathan Lecompte SR .60 1.50
384 Adam Jecho SR .60 1.50
385 Vilmer Alriksson SR .60 1.50
386 Noah McKinnon SR .60 1.50
387 Carson Cameron SR .60 1.50
388 Chase Harrington SR .60 1.50
389 Spencer Michnik SR .60 1.50
390 Lucas Moore SR .60 1.50
391 Brady Martin SR 1.25 3.00
392 Riley Patterson SR .60 1.50
393 Jakub Vondras SR .60 1.50
394 Tuomas Uronen SR .60 1.50
395 Arttu Karki SR .60 1.50
396 Alexandre Blais SR .60 1.50
397 Justin Poirier SR .60 1.50
398 Nathan Behm SR .60 1.50
399 Blake Fiddler SR .60 1.50
400 Tyler Hopkins SR 1.00 2.50

2023-24 Upper Deck CHL Exclusives

*EXCL/100: 2X TO 5X BASIC
302 Michael Misa 12.00 30.00

2023-24 Upper Deck CHL Outburst

*OUTBURST: 2X TO 5X BASIC
302 Michael Misa 12.00 30.00
310 Easton Cowan 12.00 30.00
351 Gavin McKenna SR 125.00 300.00
362 Matthew Schaefer SR 30.00 80.00
371 Ryan Roobroeck SR 40.00 100.00

2023-24 Upper Deck CHL Outburst Red

*OUT RED/25: 5X TO 12X BASIC
302 Michael Misa 150.00 400.00
310 Easton Cowan 100.00 250.00
332 Jagger Firkus 15.00 40.00
341 Zayne Parekh 80.00 200.00
342 Etienne Morin 15.00 40.00
351 Gavin McKenna SR 400.00 1000.00
371 Ryan Roobroeck SR 150.00 400.00
380 Xavier Villeneuve SR 30.00 80.00

2023-24 Upper Deck CHL Red

*RED: .8X TO 2X BASIC

2023-24 Upper Deck CHL Autographs

10 Connor Hvidston 6.00 15.00
11 Felix Lacerte 6.00 15.00
14 William Rousseau 6.00 15.00
15 Jacob Julien 5.00 12.00
16 Alex Pharand 6.00 15.00
17 Tyler Peddle 8.00 20.00
20 Andrew Gibson 8.00 20.00
23 Nolan Collins 6.00 15.00
24 Sam Dickinson 10.00 25.00
25 Carson Rehkopf 6.00 15.00
26 Cameron Allen 8.00 20.00
28 Kalem Parker 6.00 15.00
29 Stuart Rolofs 6.00 15.00
30 Jordan Gavin 6.00 15.00
32 Martin Rysavy 8.00 20.00
34 Ben Hemmerling 8.00 20.00
37 Sloan Stanick 5.00 12.00
38 Jorian Donovan 8.00 20.00
40 Cam Squires 6.00 15.00
43 Yoan Loshing 5.00 12.00
45 Alexis Michaud 6.00 15.00
47 Josh Davies 8.00 20.00
48 Scott Ratzlaff 6.00 15.00
49 Jack Beck 6.00 15.00
50 Michael Buchinger 10.00 25.00
51 Cedrick Guindon 8.00 20.00
53 Bryce McConnell-Barker 8.00 20.00
54 Rodwin Dionicio 6.00 15.00
57 Jeremy Langlois 6.00 15.00
58 Justin Cote 10.00 25.00
60 Joseph Willis 5.00 12.00
63 Caden Price 6.00 15.00
64 Markus Vidicek 10.00 25.00
65 Cooper Foster 8.00 20.00
67 Noah Chadwick 5.00 12.00
68 Matyas Sapovaliv 8.00 20.00
72 Jackson Edward 6.00 15.00
75 Nathan Brisson 6.00 15.00
77 Quinton Burns 6.00 15.00
78 Filip Mesar 5.00 12.00
79 Domenic DiVincentiis 6.00 15.00
82 Porter Martone 15.00 40.00
85 Lirim Amidovski 5.00 12.00
86 Gavin Hodnett 6.00 15.00
89 Linus Hemstrom 6.00 15.00
91 Kaleb Lawrence 6.00 15.00
94 Robin Sapousek 5.00 12.00
95 Max McCue 6.00 15.00
96 David Goyette 8.00 20.00
97 Ethan Chadwick 6.00 15.00
98 Parker Bell 6.00 15.00
99 Justin Kipkie 5.00 12.00
100 Terrell Goldsmith 5.00 12.00
302 Michael Misa 150.00 400.00
303 Tij Iginla 30.00 80.00
304 Ryder Ritchie 8.00 20.00
307 Denton Mateychuk 8.00 20.00
309 Gracyn Sawchyn 6.00 15.00
310 Easton Cowan 40.00 100.00
311 Justin Gill 6.00 15.00
312 Maxim Masse 10.00 25.00
313 Eduard Sale 6.00 15.00
314 Maveric Lamoureux 10.00 25.00
315 Ty Nelson 8.00 20.00
316 Jordan Dumais 10.00 25.00
317 Cayden Lindstrom 30.00 80.00
318 Roger McQueen 8.00 20.00
319 Andrew Cristall 8.00 20.00
320 Samuel Honzek 6.00 15.00
321 Beau Akey 6.00 15.00
322 Luke Misa SP 6.00 15.00
323 Riley Heidt 10.00 25.00
324 Colby Barlow 6.00 15.00
325 Tanner Molendyk 10.00 25.00
327 Liam Greentree 8.00 20.00
328 Calum Ritchie 8.00 20.00
329 Gavin Hayes 8.00 20.00
330 Luca Pinelli 6.00 15.00
331 Ethan Gauthier 8.00 20.00
332 Jagger Firkus 12.00 30.00
333 Andrew Basha 6.00 15.00
334 Berkly Catton 25.00 60.00
335 Tristan Luneau SP 6.00 15.00
336 Cole Beaudoin 8.00 20.00
337 Nate Danielson 10.00 25.00
338 Quentin Musty 8.00 20.00
339 Tanner Howe 8.00 20.00
340 Brayden Schuurman 6.00 15.00
341 Zayne Parekh 8.00 20.00
342 Etienne Morin 6.00 15.00
343 Conor Geekie 10.00 25.00
344 Owen Beck SP 10.00 25.00
345 Beckett Sennecke 15.00 40.00
346 Oliver Bonk 6.00 15.00
348 Henry Mews 6.00 15.00
349 Denver Barkey SP 6.00 15.00
350 Brayden Yager 10.00 25.00
371 Ryan Roobroeck SR 80.00 200.00
385 Vilmer Alriksson SR SP 6.00 15.00
387 Carson Cameron SR 6.00 15.00
397 Justin Poirier SR 6.00 15.00
398 Nathan Behm SR 6.00 15.00

2023-24 Upper Deck CHL Best Is Yet To Come

*RED/125: 2X TO 5X BASIC
BYC1 Michael Misa 3.00 8.00
BYC2 Colby Barlow 1.00 2.50
BYC3 Etienne Morin 1.00 2.50
BYC4 Nick Lardis 1.00 2.50
BYC5 Brayden Yager 1.50 4.00
BYC6 Andrew Cristall 1.25 3.00
BYC7 David Goyette 1.25 3.00
BYC8 Oliver Bonk 1.00 2.50
BYC9 Samuel Savoie 1.50 4.00
BYC10 Andrew Gibson 1.25 3.00
BYC11 Owen Pickering 1.25 3.00
BYC12 Tristan Luneau 1.00 2.50
BYC13 Quentin Musty 1.25 3.00
BYC14 Jordan Dumais 1.50 4.00
BYC15 Luke Misa 1.00 2.50
BYC16 Jagger Firkus 2.00 5.00
BYC17 Dalibor Dvorsky 1.25 3.00
BYC18 Denton Mateychuk 1.25 3.00
BYC19 Reid Schaefer 1.25 3.00
BYC20 Gracyn Sawchyn 1.00 2.50
BYC21 Yegor Sidorov 1.00 2.50
BYC22 Ty Nelson 1.25 3.00
BYC23 Owen Beck 1.50 4.00
BYC24 Samuel Honzek 1.00 2.50
BYC25 Matt Savoie 2.00 5.00
BYC26 Koehn Ziemmer 1.25 3.00
BYC27 Nate Danielson 1.50 4.00
BYC28 Ethan Gauthier 1.25 3.00
BYC29 Beau Akey 1.00 2.50
BYC30 Gavin McKenna 12.00 30.00
BYC31 Nico Myatovic .75 2.00
BYC32 Maveric Lamoureux 1.50 4.00
BYC33 Kevin Korchinski 1.50 4.00
BYC34 Conor Geekie 1.50 4.00
BYC35 Calum Ritchie 1.25 3.00

2023-24 Upper Deck CHL Best Is Yet to Come Blue

*BLUE/25: 3X TO 8X BASIC
BYC1 Michael Misa 40.00 100.00

2023-24 Upper Deck CHL First Draft

*RED/125: 2X TO 5X BASIC
*BLUE/25: 3X TO 8X BASIC
FD1 Jack Ivankovic 1.50 4.00
FD2 Shawn Carrier 1.50 4.00
FD3 Mathis Preston 1.25 3.00
FD4 Henry Brzustewicz 1.00 2.50
FD5 Jonathan Prud'homme 1.00 2.50
FD6 Matthew Schaefer 3.00 8.00
FD7 Emile Ricard 1.00 2.50
FD8 Tyler Hopkins 1.50 4.00
FD9 Owen Conrad 1.00 2.50
FD10 Jack Nesbitt 1.50 4.00
FD11 Nathan Lecompte 1.00 2.50
FD12 Caleb Desnoyers 3.00 8.00
FD13 Brady Martin 2.00 5.00
FD14 Ryan Roobroeck 2.50 6.00
FD15 Mateo Nobert 1.50 4.00
FD16 Owen Griffin 1.00 2.50
FD17 Alex Huang 1.00 2.50
FD18 Emile Guite 1.50 4.00
FD19 Ryan Brown 1.00 2.50
FD20 Shamar Moses 1.00 2.50

2023-24 Upper Deck CHL Future Charge

*BLUE/25: 3X TO 8X BASIC
FC1 Tanner Howe 1.25 3.00
FC2 Gracyn Sawchyn 1.00 2.50
FC3 Scott Ratzlaff 1.00 2.50
FC4 Quentin Musty 1.25 3.00
FC5 Andrew Cristall 1.25 3.00
FC6 Cole Beaudoin 1.25 3.00
FC7 Kevin Korchinski 1.50 4.00
FC8 Easton Cowan 2.50 6.00

FC9 Denver Barkey 1.00 2.50
FC10 Berkly Catton 2.50 6.00
FC11 Michael Misa 3.00 8.00
FC12 Gavin Hayes 1.25 3.00
FC13 Calum Ritchie 1.25 3.00
FC14 Gavin McKenna 20.00 50.00
FC15 Nick Lardis 1.00 2.50
FC16 Justin Gill 1.00 2.50
FC17 Luca Pinelli 1.00 2.50
FC18 Samuel Honzek 1.00 2.50
FC19 Tij Iginla 2.00 5.00
FC20 Koehn Ziemmer 1.25 3.00
FC21 Riley Heidt 1.50 4.00
FC22 Luke Misa 1.00 2.50
FC23 Dalibor Dvorsky 1.25 3.00
FC24 Ethan Gauthier 1.25 3.00
FC25 Tanner Molendyk 1.50 4.00
FC26 Etienne Morin 1.00 2.50
FC27 Colby Barlow 1.00 2.50
FC28 Conor Geekie 1.50 4.00
FC29 Nate Danielson 1.50 4.00
FC30 Brayden Yager 1.50 4.00

2023-24 Upper Deck CHL Future Charge Red

*RED/125: 2X TO 5X BASIC
FC11 Michael Misa 60.00 150.00

2023-24 Upper Deck CHL Top Imports

*RED/125: 1X TO 2.5X BASIC
*BLUE/25: 2.5X TO 6X BASIC
TI1 Jakub Vondras 1.00 2.50
TI2 Jakub Milota 1.00 2.50
TI3 Jakub Fibigr 1.00 2.50
TI4 Casper Haugen Evensen 1.00 2.50
TI5 Tuomas Uronen 1.00 2.50
TI6 Rasmus Kumpulainen 1.00 2.50
TI7 Urban Podrekar 1.00 2.50
TI8 Arttu Karki 1.00 2.50
TI9 Julius Miettinen 1.00 2.50
TI10 Vilmer Alriksson 1.00 2.50
TI11 Martin Misiak 1.00 2.50
TI12 Adam Jecho 1.00 2.50
TI13 Lukas Matecha .75 2.00
TI14 Lukas Kral 1.00 2.50
TI15 Jan Golicic .75 2.00

2024-25 Upper Deck CHL

1 Oliver Bonk .50 1.25
2 Tyler MacKenzie .40 1.00
3 Jules Boilard .40 1.00
4 Kevin He .60 1.50
5 Clarke Caswell .50 1.25
6 Felix Lacerte .50 1.25
7 Ethan Belchetz .40 1.00
8 Dominik Rymon .50 1.25
9 Emmanuel Vermette .40 1.00
10 Beau Jelsma .60 1.50
11 Carson Wetsch .50 1.25
12 Matthew Butler .40 1.00
13 Dylan Edwards .40 1.00
14 Max Graham .40 1.00
15 Nathan Baril .50 1.25
16 Calem Mangone .60 1.50
17 Brady Birnie .75 2.00
18 Vince Elie .50 1.25
19 Jacob Oster .50 1.25
20 Ty Halaburda .40 1.00
21 Yoan Loshing .40 1.00
22 Cedrick Guindon .60 1.50
23 Cole Reschny .50 1.25
24 Julien Paille .40 1.00
25 Cam Allen .60 1.50
26 Logan McCutcheon .40 1.00
27 Mael St-Denis .40 1.00
28 Patrick Thomas .40 1.00
29 Gavin Hodnett .50 1.25
30 Nate Tivey .40 1.00
31 Jacob Julien .40 1.00
32 Miguel Marques .50 1.25
33 Jacob Newcombe .40 1.00
34 Nolan Collins .50 1.25
35 Tyson Jugnauth .40 1.00
36 Mathis Rousseau .40 1.00
37 Sam Alfano .50 1.25
38 Austin Elliot .40 1.00
39 Emile Guite .75 2.00
40 Cameron Reid .50 1.25
41 Jackson Unger .40 1.00
42 Luke Woodworth .75 2.00
43 Ilya Protas .40 1.00
44 Tarin Smith .50 1.25
45 Justin Carbonneau .50 1.25
46 Cole Beaudoin .60 1.50
47 Aiden Oiring .40 1.00
48 Julius Sumpf .40 1.00
49 Ryan Roobroeck 1.25 3.00
50 Jackson Smith .40 1.00
51 Olivier Houde .40 1.00
52 Nick Lardis .50 1.25
53 Tanner Scott .50 1.25
54 Colby Huggan .40 1.00
55 Tyler Challenger .40 1.00
56 Brandon Lisowsky .50 1.25
57 Bill Zonnon .60 1.50
58 Denver Barkey .50 1.25
59 Vincent Collard .50 1.25
60 Luca Marrelli .40 1.00
61 Tanner Molendyk .75 2.00
62 Jeremy Leroux .40 1.00
63 Owen Van Steensel .40 1.00
64 Tanner Howe .60 1.50
65 Carey Terrance .50 1.25
66 Lewis Gendron .40 1.00
67 Adrian Misaljevic .40 1.00
68 Hiroki Gojsic .40 1.00
69 Thomas Desruisseaux .60 1.50
70 Anthony Cristoforo .60 1.50
71 Kyle Chyzowski .40 1.00
72 Anthony Romani .40 1.00
73 Louis-Francois Belanger .40 1.00
74 Emil Hemming .40 1.00
75 Josh Fluker .40 1.00
76 Thomas Verdon .40 1.00
77 Jack Ivankovic .75 2.00
78 Borya Valis .40 1.00
79 Mael Lavigne .40 1.00
80 Christopher Thibodeau .40 1.00
81 Shea Van Olm .50 1.25
82 Matthew Schaefer 6.00 15.00
83 Brayden Edwards .40 1.00
84 Nick DeAngelis .40 1.00
85 Joshua Ravensbergen .40 1.00
86 Aiden O'Donnell .40 1.00
87 Riley Mercer .50 1.25
88 Trent Swick .40 1.00
89 Luke Mistelbacher .40 1.00
90 Ryan Abraham .60 1.50
91 Diego Buttazzoni .50 1.25
92 Jack Nesbitt .75 2.00
93 Braeden Cootes .50 1.25
94 Pano Fimis .60 1.50
95 Raoul Boilard .40 1.00
96 Angus MacDonell .50 1.25
97 Julius Miettinen .50 1.25
98 Riley Patterson .50 1.25
99 Maxim Masse .75 2.00
100 Jacob Battaglia .60 1.50
101 Gavin Bryant .40 1.00
102 Rylen Roersma .75 2.00
103 Alexis Bernier .40 1.00
104 Wil McFadden .40 1.00
105 Miles Cooper .40 1.00
106 Eriks Mateiko .50 1.25
107 Kristian Epperson .40 1.00
108 Tyler Thorpe .50 1.25
109 Simon Hughes .50 1.25
110 Rowan Henderson .40 1.00
111 Layton Feist .50 1.25
112 Loic Goyette .40 1.00
113 Gabriel Frasca .60 1.50
114 Justice Christensen .40 1.00
115 Lucas Romeo .40 1.00
116 Jackson Parsons .40 1.00
117 Tomas Mrsic .40 1.00
118 Marcus Kearsey .50 1.25
119 Zach Filak .40 1.00
120 Krzysztof Macias .40 1.00
121 Spencer Gill .60 1.50
122 Martin Misiak .50 1.25
123 Cohen Klassen .40 1.00
124 Louis-Felix Charrois .40 1.00
125 Christopher Brown .60 1.50
126 Carter Bear .40 1.00
127 Antoine Dorion .40 1.00
128 Evan Van Gorp .40 1.00
129 Evan Friesen .40 1.00
130 Jordan Tourigny .40 1.00
131 Saige Weinstein .75 2.00
132 Cole Burbidge .40 1.00
133 Charlie Paquette .40 1.00
134 Connor Levis .75 2.00
135 Jiri Klima .40 1.00
136 Ryder McIntyre .40 1.00
137 Sam Oremba .75 2.00
138 Tomas Lavoie .60 1.50
139 Easton Wainwright .40 1.00
140 Reid Andresen .75 2.00
141 Charles-Antoine Beauregard .40 1.00
142 Jake Karabela .50 1.25
143 Gracyn Sawchyn .50 1.25
144 Samuel Fiala .40 1.00
145 Ben Danford .40 1.00
146 Ollie Josephson .40 1.00
147 Maxime Coursol .60 1.50
148 Cole Davis .50 1.25
149 Max Curran .50 1.25
150 Tyson Goguen .40 1.00
151 Tyson Doucette .40 1.00
152 Dominik Petr .40 1.00
153 Juraj Pekarcik .40 1.00
154 Justin Cloutier .50 1.25
155 Jordan Gavin .50 1.25
156 Gabriel D'Aigle 1.25 3.00
157 Ruslan Karimov .40 1.00
158 Noah Chadwick .40 1.00
159 Isaac Menard .40 1.00
160 Kaden Pitre .40 1.00
161 Adam Jecho .50 1.25
162 Owen Phillips .60 1.50
163 Ethan Procyszyn .60 1.50
164 Scott Ratzlaff .50 1.25
165 Alexandre Lallier .60 1.50
166 Luke Ellinas .40 1.00
167 Carlin Dezainde .40 1.00
168 Owen Conrad .50 1.25
169 Sam McCue .40 1.00
170 Ben Kindel .40 1.00
171 Mavrick Lachance .40 1.00
172 Connor Clattenburg .40 1.00
173 Nate Misskey .40 1.00
174 Jan Golicic .40 1.00
175 AJ Spellacy .50 1.25
176 Daxon Rudolph .40 1.00
177 Gabe Smith .50 1.25
178 Kieron Walton .40 1.00
179 Roan Woodward .40 1.00
180 Francois-James Buteau .40 1.00
181 Carson Cameron .50 1.25
182 Vojtech Port .40 1.00
183 Xavier Villeneuve .50 1.25
184 Brady Martin 1.00 2.50
185 Evan Gardner .40 1.00
186 Oliver Samson .40 1.00
187 Kocha Delic .75 2.00
188 Logan Wormald .50 1.25
189 Jacob Steinman .40 1.00
190 Ethan Hay .40 1.00
191 Harrison Meneghin .40 1.00
192 Xavier Lebel .40 1.00
193 Caden Taylor .50 1.25
194 Will McIsaac .40 1.00
195 Raphael Precourt .40 1.00
196 Owen Allard .50 1.25
197 Tyson Zimmer .75 2.00
198 Thomas Rousseau .40 1.00
199 Will Gerrior .40 1.00
200 Lukas Dragicevic .75 2.00
201 Nathan Levesque .40 1.00
202 Ryerson Leenders .50 1.25
203 Jake Sloan .50 1.25
204 Philippe Veilleux .40 1.00
205 Alex Pharand .50 1.25
206 Reggie Newman .40 1.00
207 Mathys Fernandez .50 1.25
208 Konnor Smith .40 1.00
209 Emmitt Finnie .40 1.00
210 Justin Boisselle .40 1.00
211 Andrew LeBlanc .50 1.25
212 Cruz Pavao .40 1.00
213 Tyler Peddle .60 1.50
214 Marco Mignosa .40 1.00
215 Ryder Ritchie .60 1.50
216 Nathan Drapeau .75 2.00
217 Jonathan Melee .75 2.00
218 Nolan Flamand .50 1.25
219 Dominic Pilote .40 1.00
220 Jakub Chromiak .60 1.50
221 Justin Kipkie .40 1.00
222 Brayden Schmitt .40 1.00
223 Emil Pieniniemi .40 1.00
224 Terrell Goldsmith .40 1.00
225 William Shields .60 1.50
226 Matthew Mayich .40 1.00
227 Antonio Martorana .40 1.00
228 Eliot L'Italien .40 1.00
229 Jack Van Volsen .60 1.50
230 Blake Fiddler .50 1.25
231 Benjamin Brunelle .40 1.00
232 Luca Blonda .40 1.00
233 Brayden Schuurman .50 1.25
234 Alexis Bourque .50 1.25
235 Brodie McConnell-Barker .40 1.00
236 Carter Sotheran .40 1.00
237 Coen Miller .40 1.00
238 Ryan Brown .50 1.25
239 Chase Wutzke .40 1.00
240 Olivier Dubois .40 1.00
241 Max Namestnikov .60 1.50
242 Reese Hamilton .40 1.00
243 Quinn Kennedy .50 1.25
244 Lucas Karmiris .60 1.50
245 Max Hildebrand .40 1.00
246 Olivier Lampron .40 1.00
247 Brady Smith .40 1.00
248 Rylan Gould .40 1.00
249 Vincent Desjardins .40 1.00
250 Jacob Cloutier .40 1.00
251 Griffin Darby .40 1.00
252 Justin Gendron .50 1.25
253 Liam Sztuska .40 1.00
254 Niall Crocker .50 1.25
255 Alexandre Guy .40 1.00
256 Lincoln Moore .40 1.00
257 Carson Bjarnason .40 1.00
258 Hugo Primeau .40 1.00
259 Joey Willis .50 1.25
260 Jan Spunar .50 1.25
261 Jakub Milota .50 1.25
262 Cooper Foster .60 1.50
263 Tommy Lafreniere .40 1.00
264 Simon-Pier Brunet .40 1.00
265 Evan Headrick .40 1.00
266 Jett Lajoie .40 1.00
267 Nathan Brisson .50 1.25
268 Mike Levin .40 1.00
269 Aaron Obobaifo .40 1.00
270 Landon Miller .40 1.00
271 John Babcock .40 1.00
272 Lou Levesque .40 1.00
273 Spencer Sova .60 1.50
274 Reed Brown .40 1.00
275 Jack Dever .40 1.00
276 Kalan Lind .75 2.00
277 Jacob Mathieu .40 1.00
278 Chase Lefebvre .40 1.00
279 Sawyer Mynio .40 1.00
280 Nathan Villeneuve .60 1.50
281 Braxton Whitehead .40 1.00
282 Brady Schultz .40 1.00
283 Braydon McCallum .40 1.00
284 Jari Kykkanen .40 1.00
285 Brad Gardiner .40 1.00
286 Ethan Miedema .60 1.50
287 Justin Cote .75 2.00
288 Andrew Gibson .60 1.50
289 Cameron Kuzma .40 1.00
290 Ben Cormier .60 1.50
291 Connor Hvidston .50 1.25
292 Matthew Andonovski .40 1.00
293 Emile Perron .60 1.50
294 Malcolm Spence .60 1.50
295 Caden Price .50 1.25
296 Nathan Aspinall .40 1.00
297 Jordan Keller .40 1.00
298 Lukas Fischer .40 1.00
299 Jan Sprynar .60 1.50
300 Matthew Soto .50 1.25
301 Michael Misa 3.00 8.00
302 Tij Iginla 1.50 4.00
303 Sam Dickinson 1.25 3.00
304 Carter Yakemchuk .75 2.00
305 Justin Poirier .75 2.00
306 Easton Cowan 3.00 8.00
307 Reid Dyck 1.00 2.50
308 Calum Ritchie 1.00 2.50
309 Kenta Isogai .60 1.50
310 Antonin Verreault 1.25 3.00
311 Andrei Loshko .75 2.00
312 Oliver Tulk .75 2.00
313 Beckett Sennecke 2.00 5.00
314 Andrew Basha .75 2.00
315 Cam Squires .75 2.00
316 Marek Vanacker .75 2.00
317 Riley Heidt 1.25 3.00
318 Liam Greentree 1.00 2.50
319 Berkly Catton 2.00 5.00
320 Caleb Desnoyers 2.50 6.00
321 Jett Luchanko 1.50 4.00
322 Brayden Yager 1.25 3.00
323 Dalyn Wakely .60 1.50
324 Cameron Schmidt .60 1.50
325 Justin Larose .60 1.50
326 Luke Misa .75 2.00
327 Roger McQueen 1.00 2.50
328 Tuomas Uronen .75 2.00
329 Cayden Lindstrom 2.00 5.00
330 Sam Oliver 1.25 3.00
331 Carter George .60 1.50
332 Andrew Cristall 1.25 3.00
333 Luca Pinelli .75 2.00
334 Harrison Brunicke 1.25 3.00
335 Joseph Henneberry 1.00 2.50
336 Colby Barlow .75 2.00
337 Terik Parascak .75 2.00
338 Quentin Musty 1.00 2.50
339 Gavin McKenna 10.00 25.00
340 Carson Rehkopf .75 2.00
341 Jonathan Fauchon .75 2.00
342 Jake O'Brien 2.00 5.00
343 Ethan Gauthier 1.00 2.50
344 Kashawn Aitcheson .75 2.00
345 Alexandre Blais .75 2.00
346 Henry Mews .75 2.00
347 Oasiz Wiesblatt .75 2.00
348 Zayne Parekh 1.00 2.50
349 Jeremie Minville .60 1.50
350 Porter Martone 2.00 5.00
351 Dylan Rozzi SR .75 2.00
352 Beckett Hamilton SR 1.00 2.50
353 Max Bleicher SR .75 2.00
354 Biagio Jr. Daniele SR .75 2.00
355 Carter Esler SR 1.25 3.00
356 Filip Ekberg SR .75 2.00
357 Matvei Gridin SR .75 2.00
358 Niilopekka Muhonen SR .75 2.00
359 Braidy Wassilyn SR .75 2.00
360 Elliot Dube SR .75 2.00
361 Landon DuPont SR 20.00 50.00
362 Carson Harmer SR .75 2.00
363 Lars Steiner SR .75 2.00
364 Ondrej Stebetak SR .75 2.00
365 Andreas Straka SR .75 2.00
366 Miroslav Holinka SR .75 2.00
367 Colin Fitzgerald SR .75 2.00
368 Maxim Dube SR .75 2.00
369 Matej Pekar SR .75 2.00
370 William Yared SR .75 2.00
371 Brek Liske SR .75 2.00
372 Alessandro Di Iorio SR .75 2.00
373 Carlos Handel SR .75 2.00
374 Cole Zurawski SR .75 2.00
375 Mikko Leppa SR .75 2.00
376 Mathis Preston SR 1.00 2.50
377 Kent Greer SR .75 2.00
378 Daniel Walters SR .75 2.00
379 Nathan Behm SR .75 2.00
380 Trent Gates SR .75 2.00
381 Chad Lygitsakos SR .75 2.00
382 Isaac Poll SR 2.00 5.00
383 Pierce Mbuyi SR .75 2.00
384 Maddox Dagenais SR .75 2.00
385 Veeti Vaisanen SR .75 2.00
386 Benjamin Olivier SR .75 2.00
387 Rylan Ng SR .75 2.00
388 Jacob Gouchie SR .75 2.00
389 Markus Loponen SR .75 2.00
390 Florian Schenk SR .75 2.00
391 Parker Vaughan SR .75 2.00
392 Liam Arsenault SR 1.00 2.50
393 Joe Iginla SR 1.25 3.00
394 Simon-Xavier Cyr SR .75 2.00
395 Axel Hurtig SR .75 2.00
396 Bo Damphousse SR .75 2.00
397 Brody Gillespie SR .75 2.00
398 Ryder Carey SR .75 2.00
399 Aaron Sawatzky SR .75 2.00
400 Brennan O'Donnell SR .75 2.00

2024-25 Upper Deck CHL Exclusives

*EXCLUSIVES/100: 2X TO 5X BASIC

2024-25 Upper Deck CHL Green

*GREEN: .8X TO 2X BASIC

2024-25 Upper Deck CHL Outburst

*OUTBURST: 1.5X TO 4X BASIC

2024-25 Upper Deck CHL Outburst Red

*OUTBURST RED/25: 4X TO 10X BASIC

2024-25 Upper Deck CHL Autographs

1 Oliver Bonk 6.00 15.00
2 Tyler MacKenzie 5.00 12.00
3 Jules Boilard 5.00 12.00
4 Kevin He 8.00 20.00
5 Clarke Caswell 6.00 15.00
6 Felix Lacerte 6.00 15.00
7 Ethan Belchetz 5.00 12.00
8 Dominik Rymon 6.00 15.00
9 Emmanuel Vermette 5.00 12.00
10 Beau Jelsma 8.00 20.00
11 Carson Wetsch 6.00 15.00
12 Matthew Butler 5.00 12.00
13 Dylan Edwards 5.00 12.00
14 Max Graham 5.00 12.00
15 Nathan Baril 6.00 15.00
16 Calem Mangone 8.00 20.00
17 Brady Birnie 10.00 25.00
18 Vince Elie 6.00 15.00
19 Jacob Oster 6.00 15.00
20 Ty Halaburda 5.00 12.00
21 Yoan Loshing 5.00 12.00
22 Cedrick Guindon 8.00 20.00
23 Cole Reschny 6.00 15.00
24 Julien Paille 5.00 12.00
25 Cam Allen 8.00 20.00
26 Logan McCutcheon 5.00 12.00
27 Mael St-Denis 5.00 12.00
28 Patrick Thomas 5.00 12.00
29 Gavin Hodnett 6.00 15.00
30 Nate Tivey 5.00 12.00
31 Jacob Julien 5.00 12.00
32 Miguel Marques 6.00 15.00
33 Jacob Newcombe 5.00 12.00
34 Nolan Collins 6.00 15.00
35 Tyson Jugnauth 5.00 12.00
36 Mathis Rousseau 5.00 12.00
37 Sam Alfano 6.00 15.00
38 Austin Elliot 5.00 12.00
39 Emile Guite 10.00 25.00
40 Cameron Reid 6.00 15.00
41 Jackson Unger 5.00 12.00
42 Luke Woodworth 10.00 25.00
43 Ilya Protas 5.00 12.00
44 Tarin Smith 6.00 15.00
45 Justin Carbonneau 6.00 15.00
46 Cole Beaudoin 8.00 20.00
47 Aiden Oiring 5.00 12.00
48 Julius Sumpf 5.00 12.00
49 Ryan Roobroeck 15.00 40.00
50 Jackson Smith 5.00 12.00
51 Olivier Houde 5.00 12.00
52 Nick Lardis 6.00 15.00
53 Tanner Scott 6.00 15.00
54 Colby Huggan 5.00 12.00
55 Tyler Challenger 5.00 12.00
56 Brandon Lisowsky 6.00 15.00
57 Bill Zonnon 8.00 20.00
58 Denver Barkey 6.00 15.00
59 Vincent Collard 6.00 15.00
60 Luca Marrelli 5.00 12.00
61 Tanner Molendyk 10.00 25.00
62 Jeremy Leroux 5.00 12.00
63 Owen Van Steensel 5.00 12.00
64 Tanner Howe 8.00 20.00
65 Carey Terrance 6.00 15.00
66 Lewis Gendron 5.00 12.00
67 Adrian Misaljevic 5.00 12.00
68 Hiroki Gojsic 5.00 12.00
69 Thomas Desruisseaux 8.00 20.00
70 Anthony Cristoforo 8.00 20.00
71 Kyle Chyzowski 5.00 12.00
72 Anthony Romani 5.00 12.00
73 Louis-Francois Belanger 5.00 12.00
74 Emil Hemming 5.00 12.00
75 Josh Fluker 5.00 12.00
76 Thomas Verdon 5.00 12.00
77 Jack Ivankovic 10.00 25.00
78 Borya Valis 5.00 12.00
79 Mael Lavigne 5.00 12.00
80 Christopher Thibodeau 5.00 12.00
81 Shea Van Olm 15.00 40.00
83 Brayden Edwards 5.00 12.00
84 Nick DeAngelis 5.00 12.00
85 Joshua Ravensbergen 5.00 12.00
86 Aiden O'Donnell 5.00 12.00
87 Riley Mercer 6.00 15.00
88 Trent Swick 5.00 12.00
89 Luke Mistelbacher 5.00 12.00
90 Ryan Abraham 8.00 20.00
91 Diego Buttazzoni 6.00 15.00
92 Jack Nesbitt 10.00 25.00
93 Braeden Cootes 6.00 15.00
94 Pano Fimis 8.00 20.00
95 Raoul Boilard 5.00 12.00
96 Angus MacDonell 6.00 15.00
97 Julius Miettinen 6.00 15.00
98 Riley Patterson 6.00 15.00
99 Maxim Masse 10.00 25.00
100 Jacob Battaglia 8.00 20.00
302 Tij Iginla 12.00 30.00
303 Sam Dickinson 10.00 25.00
304 Carter Yakemchuk 6.00 15.00
305 Justin Poirier 6.00 15.00
306 Easton Cowan 25.00 60.00
307 Reid Dyck 8.00 20.00
308 Calum Ritchie 8.00 20.00
309 Kenta Isogai 5.00 12.00
310 Antonin Verreault 10.00 25.00
311 Andrei Loshko 6.00 15.00
312 Oliver Tulk 6.00 15.00
313 Beckett Sennecke 15.00 40.00
314 Andrew Basha 6.00 15.00
315 Cam Squires 6.00 15.00
316 Marek Vanacker 6.00 15.00
317 Riley Heidt 10.00 25.00
318 Liam Greentree 8.00 20.00
319 Berkly Catton 15.00 40.00
320 Caleb Desnoyers 40.00 100.00
321 Jett Luchanko 12.00 30.00
322 Brayden Yager 10.00 25.00
323 Dalyn Wakely 5.00 12.00
324 Cameron Schmidt 5.00 12.00
325 Justin Larose 5.00 12.00
326 Luke Misa 6.00 15.00
327 Roger McQueen 8.00 20.00
328 Tuomas Uronen 6.00 15.00
329 Cayden Lindstrom 15.00 40.00
330 Sam Oliver 10.00 25.00
331 Carter George 5.00 12.00
332 Andrew Cristall 20.00 50.00
333 Luca Pinelli 6.00 15.00
334 Harrison Brunicke 10.00 25.00
335 Joseph Henneberry 8.00 20.00
336 Colby Barlow 6.00 15.00
337 Terik Parascak 6.00 15.00
338 Quentin Musty 8.00 20.00
339 Gavin McKenna 250.00 600.00
340 Carson Rehkopf 6.00 15.00
341 Jonathan Fauchon 6.00 15.00
342 Jake O'Brien 15.00 40.00
343 Ethan Gauthier 8.00 20.00
344 Kashawn Aitcheson 6.00 15.00
345 Alexandre Blais 6.00 15.00
346 Henry Mews 6.00 15.00
347 Oasiz Wiesblatt 6.00 15.00
348 Zayne Parekh 8.00 20.00
349 Jeremie Minville 5.00 12.00
350 Porter Martone 15.00 40.00
351 Dylan Rozzi SR 6.00 15.00
352 Beckett Hamilton SR 8.00 20.00
353 Max Bleicher SR 6.00 15.00
354 Biagio Jr. Daniele SR 6.00 15.00
355 Carter Esler SR 10.00 25.00
356 Filip Ekberg SR 6.00 15.00
357 Matvei Gridin SR 6.00 15.00
358 Niilopekka Muhonen SR 6.00 15.00
359 Braidy Wassilyn SR 6.00 15.00
360 Elliot Dube SR 6.00 15.00
361 Landon DuPont SR 80.00 200.00
362 Carson Harmer SR 6.00 15.00
363 Lars Steiner SR 6.00 15.00
364 Ondrej Stebetak SR 6.00 15.00
365 Andreas Straka SR 6.00 15.00
366 Miroslav Holinka SR 6.00 15.00
367 Colin Fitzgerald SR 6.00 15.00
368 Maxim Dube SR 6.00 15.00
369 Matej Pekar SR 6.00 15.00
370 William Yared SR 6.00 15.00
371 Brek Liske SR 6.00 15.00
372 Alessandro Di Iorio SR 6.00 15.00
373 Carlos Handel SR 6.00 15.00
374 Cole Zurawski SR 6.00 15.00
375 Mikko Leppa SR 6.00 15.00
376 Mathis Preston SR 8.00 20.00
377 Kent Greer SR 6.00 15.00
378 Daniel Walters SR 6.00 15.00
379 Nathan Behm SR 6.00 15.00
380 Trent Gates SR 6.00 15.00
381 Chad Lygitsakos SR 6.00 15.00
382 Isaac Poll SR 15.00 40.00
383 Pierce Mbuyi SR 6.00 15.00
384 Maddox Dagenais SR 6.00 15.00
385 Veeti Vaisanen SR 6.00 15.00
386 Benjamin Olivier SR 6.00 15.00
387 Rylan Ng SR 6.00 15.00
388 Jacob Gouchie SR 6.00 15.00
389 Markus Loponen SR 6.00 15.00
390 Florian Schenk SR 6.00 15.00
391 Parker Vaughan SR 6.00 15.00
392 Liam Arsenault SR 8.00 20.00
393 Joe Iginla SR 10.00 25.00
394 Simon-Xavier Cyr SR 6.00 15.00
395 Axel Hurtig SR 6.00 15.00
396 Bo Damphousse SR 6.00 15.00
397 Brody Gillespie SR 6.00 15.00
398 Ryder Carey SR 6.00 15.00
399 Aaron Sawatzky SR 6.00 15.00
400 Brennan O'Donnell SR 6.00 15.00

2024-25 Upper Deck CHL First Draft

*RED/125: 2X TO 5X BASIC
*BLUE/25: 3X TO 8X BASIC
FD1 Dylan Rozzi 1.00 2.50
FD2 Ethan Belchetz .75 2.00
FD3 Maddox Dagenais 1.00 2.50
FD4 Alessandro Di Iorio 1.00 2.50
FD5 Daniel Walters 1.00 2.50
FD6 Colin Fitzgerald 1.00 2.50
FD7 Landon DuPont 15.00 40.00
FD8 Chad Lygitsakos 1.00 2.50
FD9 Parker Vaughan 1.00 2.50
FD10 William Yared 1.00 2.50
FD11 Pierce Mbuyi 1.00 2.50
FD12 Lars Steiner 1.00 2.50
FD13 Braidy Wassilyn 1.00 2.50
FD14 Mathis Preston 1.25 3.00
FD15 Cole Zurawski 1.00 2.50

2024-25 Upper Deck CHL In the Lab

*RED/125: 1.2X TO 3X BASIC
*BLUE/25: 2.5X TO 6X BASIC
IL1 Vince Elie 1.00 2.50
IL2 Riley Heidt 1.50 4.00
IL3 Malcolm Spence 1.25 3.00
IL4 Matthew Butler .75 2.00
IL5 Harrison Brunicke 1.50 4.00
IL6 Nick DeAngelis .75 2.00
IL7 Jules Boilard .75 2.00
IL8 Oasiz Wiesblatt 1.00 2.50
IL9 Cedrick Guindon 1.25 3.00
IL10 Alexandre Blais 1.00 2.50
IL11 Tij Iginla 2.00 5.00
IL12 Jack Ivankovic 1.50 4.00
IL13 Thomas Verdon .75 2.00
IL14 Carson Wetsch 1.00 2.50
IL15 Dalyn Wakely .75 2.00
IL16 Lewis Gendron .75 2.00
IL17 Aiden Oiring .75 2.00
IL18 Calem Mangone 1.25 3.00
IL19 Nathan Baril 1.00 2.50
IL20 Max Graham .75 2.00
IL21 Carter George .75 2.00
IL22 Bo Damphousse 1.00 2.50
IL23 Kenta Isogai .75 2.00
IL24 Christopher Thibodeau .75 2.00
IL25 Raoul Boilard .75 2.00
IL26 Roger McQueen 1.25 3.00
IL27 Owen Van Steensel .75 2.00
IL28 Maxim Masse 1.50 4.00
IL29 Julius Miettinen 1.00 2.50
IL30 Adrian Misaljevic .75 2.00
IL31 Nate Tivey .75 2.00
IL32 Miguel Marques 1.00 2.50
IL33 Jacob Oster 1.00 2.50
IL34 Mathis Rousseau .75 2.00
IL35 Brayden Yager 1.50 4.00

2024-25 Upper Deck CHL Prominent Combos

*BLUE/25: 2.5X TO 6X BASIC
PC1 C.Yakemchuk/O.Tulk 1.25 3.00
PC2 B.Sennecke/L.Marrelli 3.00 8.00
PC3 C.Squires/J.Newcombe 1.25 3.00
PC4 D.Buttazzoni/T.Jugnauth 1.25 3.00
PC5 P.Fimis/S.Alfano 1.50 4.00
PC6 C.Desnoyers/J.Sumpf 4.00 10.00
PC7 C.Reschny/J.Kipkie 1.25 3.00
PC8 L.Greentree/J.Nesbitt 2.00 5.00
PC9 V.Desjardins/J.Carbonneau 1.25 3.00
PC10 T.Parr/R.Calvert 1.25 3.00
PC11 P.Martone/C.Rehkopf 3.00 8.00
PC12 E.Gauthier/L.Woodworth 2.00 5.00
PC13 T.Iginla/M.Graham 2.50 6.00
PC14 S.Dickinson/E.Cowan 4.00 10.00
PC15 A.Bourque/O.Houde 1.25 3.00
PC16 B.Catton/S.Van Olm 3.00 8.00
PC17 Z.Parekh/M.Misa 4.00 10.00
PC18 C.Huggan/L.Belanger 1.00 2.50
PC19 R.Heidt/B.Valis 2.00 5.00
PC20 F.Ekberg/L.Pinelli 1.25 3.00
PC21 L.Steiner/B.Zonnon 1.50 4.00
PC22 C.Lindstrom/G.McKenna 5.00 12.00
PC23 J.Luchanko/C.Paquette 2.50 6.00
PC24 E.Guite/T.Desruisseaux 2.00 5.00
PC25 M.Pekar/B.Cootes 1.25 3.00

2024-25 Upper Deck CHL Prominent Combos Red

PC17 Z.Parekh/M.Misa 20.00 50.00
PC22 C.Lindstrom/G.McKenna 20.00 50.00

2024-25 Upper Deck CHL That's a Rocket

*RED/125: 1.2X TO 3X BASIC
TR1 Shea Van Olm 1.00 2.50
TR2 Emmanuel Vermette .75 2.00
TR3 Nick Lardis 1.00 2.50
TR4 Luke Mistelbacher .75 2.00
TR5 Jonathan Fauchon 1.00 2.50
TR6 Tyler MacKenzie .75 2.00
TR7 Sam Oliver 1.50 4.00
TR8 Ilya Protas .75 2.00
TR9 Kyle Chyzowski .75 2.00
TR10 Felix Lacerte 1.00 2.50
TR11 Terik Parascak 1.00 2.50
TR12 Justin Poirier 1.00 2.50
TR13 Kevin He 1.25 3.00
TR14 Nathan Behm 1.00 2.50
TR15 Luca Pinelli 1.00 2.50
TR16 Antonin Verreault 1.50 4.00
TR17 Andrei Loshko 1.00 2.50
TR18 Brady Birnie 1.50 4.00
TR19 Michael Misa 3.00 8.00
TR20 Yoan Loshing .75 2.00
TR21 Porter Martone 2.50 6.00
TR22 Cameron Schmidt .75 2.00
TR23 Jacob Battaglia 1.25 3.00
TR24 Jeremie Minville .75 2.00
TR25 Luca Marrelli .75 2.00

1996 Visions

COMPLETE SET (150) 6.00 15.00
82 Bryan Berard .15 .40
83 Jeff Friesen .15 .40
84 Petr Buzek .15 .40
85 Nolan Baumgartner .08 .25
86 Jason Bonsignore .08 .25
87 Jan Hlavac .15 .40
88 Ethan Moreau .08 .25
89 Radek Dvorak .08 .25
90 Brian Holzinger .08 .25
91 Petr Sykora .20 .50
92 Ed Jovanovski .15 .40
93 Jeff O'Neill .08 .25
94 Manon Rheaume .20 .50
123 Petr Sykora .20 .50

1996 Visions Signings

COMPLETE SET (100) 6.00 15.00
61 Boyd Devereaux .08 .25
62 Alexandre Volchkov .08 .25
63 Trevor Wasyluk .08 .25
64 Luke Curtin .08 .25
65 Richard Jackman .08 .25
66 Jonathan Zukiwsky .08 .25
67 Geoff Peters .08 .25
68 Daniel Briere .30 .75
69 Chris Allen .08 .25
70 Jason Sweitzer .08 .25
71 Steve Nimigon .08 .25
72 Jay McKee .08 .25
73 Henry Kuster .08 .25
74 Johnathan Aitken .08 .25
75 Ed Jovanovski .08 .25
76 Petr Sykora .15 .40
77 Bryan Berard .08 .25
78 Manon Rheaume .20 .50
79 Radek Dvorak .08 .25

1996 Visions Signings Artistry

COMPLETE SET (10) 20.00 50.00
6 Petr Sykora 2.00 5.00

1996 Visions Signings Autographs Gold

2 Jonathan Aitken 1.50 4.00
4 Chris Allen 1.50 4.00
8 Daniel Briere 4.00 10.00
14 Luke Curtin 1.50 4.00
17 Boyd Devereaux 2.00 5.00
31 Richard Jackman 2.00 5.00
33 Ed Jovanovski 3.00 8.00
35 Henry Kuster 1.50 4.00
37 Jay McKee 1.50 4.00
44 Steve Nimigon 1.50 4.00
50 Geoff Peters 1.50 4.00
63 Jason Sweitzer 1.50 4.00
67 Alexandre Volchkov 2.00 5.00
69 Trevor Wasyluk 1.50 4.00
74 Jonathan Zukiwsky 1.50 4.00

1996 Visions Signings Autographs Silver

3 Jonathan Aitken/360 2.00 5.00
5 Chris Allen/385 2.00 5.00
11 Daniel Briere/390 3.00 8.00
17 Luke Curtin/370 2.00 5.00
20 Boyd Devereaux/350 2.00 5.00
36 Richard Jackman/400 2.00 5.00
38 Ed Jovanovski/405 4.00 10.00
40 Henry Kuster/415 2.00 5.00
43 Jay McKee/385 2.00 5.00
50 Steve Nimigon/380 2.00 5.00
56 Geoff Peters/390 2.00 5.00
71 Jason Sweitzer/355 2.00 5.00
76 Alexandre Volchkov/375 2.00 5.00
79 Trevor Wasyluk/365 2.00 5.00
85 Jonathan Zukiwsky/375 2.00 5.00

1997 Visions Signings

COMPLETE SET (50) 5.00 10.00
40 Dainius Zubrus .05 .15
41 Joe Thornton .15 .40
42 Dan Cleary .05 .15
43 Sergei Samsonov .08 .25

1997 Visions Signings Artistry

COMPLETE SET (20) 20.00 40.00
A20 Dainius Zubrus .40 1.00

1997 Visions Signings Artistry Autographs

A20 Dainius Zubrus 2.50 6.00

1997 Visions Signings Autographs

28 Josh Holden 1.50 4.00
51 Sergei Samsonov 4.00 10.00
55 Joe Thornton 3.00 8.00
65 Dainius Zubrus 2.00 5.00
66 Andrei Zyuzin 1.50 4.00

Acknowledgments

A great deal of diligence, hard work, and dedicated effort went into this year's volume. The high standards to which we hold ourselves, however, could not have been met without the expert input and generous amount of time contributed by many people. Our sincere thanks are extended to each and every one of you.

Each year we refine the process of developing the most accurate and up-to-date information for this book. I believe this year's Price Guide is our best yet. Thanks again to all of the contributors nationwide as well as to our staff worldwide since the success of the Beckett Price Guides has always been the result of a team effort.

For more than three decades now, many individuals have provided price input, illustrative material, checklist verifications, errata, and/or background information. Jim Beckett began this project in the early 1990s and his steadfast leadership and dedication to excellence can still be felt and seen in every page. Our company and the hobby as a whole extends to Dr. Beckett a sincere "Thank You."

At the risk of inadvertently overlooking or omitting these many contributors, we should like to personally thank: AbD Cards (Dale Wesolewski), Jerry Adamic, Pete Adauto, Bren Adams, Murray Akbart, Applegate, Neil Armstrong, Mike Aronstein, Alan Roland J. Atlas, Art Baker, Brent Barnes, Frank and Vivian Barning, Robert Beaudoin, Al Beharrell, Pete Belanger, Todd Bellerose, Gary Benton, Beulah Sports (Jeff Blatt), Ki Billy, Chad Blick, Michel Bolduc, Joseph Bonett, Peter Borkowski, Erwin Borau, Bill Bossert, Luc Boucher, B. Jack Bourland III, Tony Bouwman, Jim Boyne, Elio Brandelli, Tim Brahmer, John Brenner Marco Brizuela, Douglas Brown, Bob Bruner, Dan Bruner, Jacey Buel, Dave Bullis, Eric Burgoyne, Scott Burke, Jason Caines, Jim Cappello, Danny Cariseo, Cartomania (Joseph E. Filion), Greg Caskey, Rick Chambers, Dwight Chapin, Jeff Chapman, Michael Chark, Steve Chiaramonte, Susan Christensen, Larry Ciancone, Scott Coates, Allan E. Cohen, Shane Cohen (Grand Slam), Barry Colla, Collection de Sport AZ (Ronald Villanueve), Matt Collett, Ken Collins, Shelby Colson, Joe Conte, Dan Conway, Ryan Cope, Michael J. Cox, Taylor Crane, Wil Curtis, Allen Custer, Kenneth Daniels, Steven Danver, Leo Davis, Scott Dean, Jim Decorso, Mary Dempster, Deerquotes Baseball Cards, Normand Desroches, Larry DeTienne, Dave Deveney, Karlos Diego, Leon Dill, Mario DiPastena, Marc Dixon, Bill Dodge, Gerard Dolci, Benoit Doyon, Michel Dubois, Charles Dugre, John Duplisea, Denny W. Eckes (Mr. Sport Americana), Don Ellis, Danny Ellwood, Michael Esposito, Bryan Epstein, Doak Ewing, Dave Feltham, Gean Paul Figari, Larry Fleming, Gervise Ford, Don Forsey, Frank Fox, Craig Frank, Mark Franke, Steve Freedman, Kathryn Friedlander, Bob Friedman, Larry and Jeff Fritsch, Bob Frye, James Funke Jr., John Furniss, Gary Gagen, Tom Galanis, Jim Galusha, Richard, Gariepy, Neil Garvey, Ron and Dave Gibara, Dick Gilkeson, Michael R. Gionet, Dave Giove, Mike Gogal, Harvey Goldfarb, Brian Goldstein, Jeff Goldstein, Renvel Gonsalves, Rynel Gonsalves, Mike and Howard Gordon, Seth Gordon, John Gosney, George Grauer, Erik Gravel, Pierre-Luc Gravel, Great Canadian Sportcard Co., Gene Guarnere, Hall's Nostalgia, Gerald Hamelin, Tom Harrett, Ron Heller, Bill Henderson, Tom Hendrickson, Wayne Hepburn, Jerry and Etta Hersh, Mike Hersh, Chick Hershberger, Gerald Higgs, Clay Hill, Dan Hitt, Gary Hlady, Shawn Hoagland, Keith Holtzmann, Joseph Horgan, Dan Horton, Teresa Horton, D. Howery Jr., In The Game, Richard Irving, Sean Isaacs, Torstein H. Jacobsen, John James, Robert Jansing, Cliff Janzen, Peter Jeffrey, Leslie Jezuit, Scott Jugan, Dennis Kannokko, Paul and Anna Kannokko, Robert Kantor, Jay and Mary Kasper, Sam Kassam, John Kelly, Rick Keplinger, Larry Kerrigan, John Killan, Rich Klein, Dean Konieczka, Bob Krawetz, Chuck Kucera, George Kumagai, Rob Kuhlman, Thomas Kunnecke, Roger Lampert, Ted Larkins, Brent Lee, Scott LeLievre, Irv Lerner, Howie Levy, Mike Lewandoski, Lew Lipset, Stephane Lizotte, Nicholas LoCasto, The Locker Room, Tim Loop, Frank Lopez, Karoline K. Lowry, Doug Lowther, Steven J. Loy, Thierry Lubenec, Jim Macie, Paul Marchant, Joe Marasco, Adam Martin, Jason Martin, Chris Mayhew, Michael McDonald, Blake Meyer, John Meyer, Dick Millerd, Ben Mitchell, Paul V. Mohrle, Tony Moore, Joe Morano, Michael Moretto, Michel Morin, Brian Morris, Kevin Mudrak, Al Muir, Larry Murray, Todd Nelkin, Rob Nicholls, Dave Nicklas, Paul Noble, Leandre Normand, David Nystrom, John O'Hara, John O' Mara, Glenn Olson, Nelson Paine, Andrew Pak, David Paolicelli, Tom Parker, Clay Pasternack, Alan Peace, Joe Pellicio, Alan Philpot, Jean-Guy Pichette, Dale Pinney, Richard Plett, Jack Pollard, Len Pottie, Scott Prusha, Red River Coins and Cards, Randall Reese, Tom Reid, Dave and Shawn Redden, Paula Reinke, Ralph Reitsma, Ron Ressler, Dorothy Reznik, Owen Ricker, Gavin Riley, Mark Rogers, John Wayne Roman, Paul Romero, Charles Rooke, Francis Rose, Rotman Productions, Jim Routly, Grant Rowland, Joe Rubert II, John Rumierz, Terry Sack, Joe Sak, Grant Sandground, Linda Santiago, Cheryl Sauve, Kevin Savage Cards, Angelo Savelli, Mike Schechter (MSA), Mike Shafer, Richard Sherman, Brad Shrabin, Gary Silkstone, Chris Sklener, Lyle Skrapek, Slapshot Sports Collectibles, Steve Smith, Gerry Sobie, Don Spagnola, John Spalding, Carl Specht, Phil and Joan Spector, Nigel Spill, Dave Stallings, Cary Stephenson, Murvin Sterling, Dan Stickney, Andy Stoltz, Ray Stonehouse, Cheryl Suave, Mark Suchawericz, Dave Sularz, Walt Suski, Fred Suzman, Danny Tarquini, Paul S. Taylor, Lee Temanson, Teresa Tewell, Chuck Thomas, Tim Thompson, Joe Tomasik, Topps, Darren Turcotte, Rob Unlus, Upper Deck, Michel Vaillancourt, Variete Sports, Rob Veres, Verville Enr., Ernie Vickers, Clayton Vigent, Shirl Volk, Jonathan Waldman, Jonathan Watts, David Weiner, Andrew B. Weisenfeld, Kermit B. Wells, Brian Wentz, Bill Wesslund, Frank and Jason Wilder, Kelly Wionzek, Brian Wobbeking, Ted Woo, Pete Wooten, Thomas L. Wujek, Andre Yip Hoi, Yaz's Sports Memorabilia, Gerard Yodice, Kit Young, Robert Zanze, Christina Zawadzki, and Bill Zimpleman.

A special thanks also goes out to those who graciously donated their knowledge and expertise (and their card images) in adding to the comprehensiveness of the minor league and foreign issues sections: Ralph Slate (Whose web site www.hockeydb.com is one of the hobby's great minor league resources), Benny Kurz (European issues), Vinnie Montalbano and Dale Sprenger (for their efforts in improving the scope of our minor league and college coverage), Caspar Friberg (Finnish issues), Marek Pandoscak (Slovakian issues), Jiri Kuca and Jiri Peterka (Czech issues), Holger Petersen (German issues), Hockey Heaven, Christian Olander, and Per Vedin (Swedish issues), Joe Bonnett, Stewart Etlinger, Dino Fazio, Steve Fraser, CTM Ste-Foy, Gerry Garland, Gary Giovane, Ian Green (Armchair Sports UK), John Ignato, Chad Kitzman, Troy Moore, Jeremy Poclitar, J.D. Porter, Gus Saunders, Andre Yip Hoi (Time-Out Sportscards).

Every year we make active solicitations for expert input. We are particularly appreciative of the help (however extensive or cursory) provided for this volume. We receive many inquiries, comments and questions regarding material within this book. In fact, each and every one is read and digested. Time constraints, however, prevent us from personally replying - but please keep sharing your knowledge. Even though we cannot respond to each letter, you are making significant contributions to the hobby through your interest and comments.

The Beckett hockey specialist is Jeff Camay. His pricing analysis and careful proofreading were key to the accuracy of this annual. The team effort was led by Brian Fleischer (Manager – Collectibles Data Publishing). They were ably assisted by the rest of the Market Analysts: Matt Bible, Steve Dalton, Justin Grunert, Dawson Hoff, Rex Pastrana, Kristian Redulla, Chris Reyes, Christopher Roberts, Adrian Saba, Bianca Slover-Roa, Angelou Talle, Bryl Trinidad, and Sam Zimmer.

The price gathering and analytical talents of this fine group of hobbyists have helped make our Beckett team stronger, while making this guide and its companion monthly Price Guide more widely recognized as the hobby's most reliable and relied upon sources of pricing information. Surajpal Singh Bisht and Hemant Tiwari were responsible for layout of the book. The reason this book looks as good as it does is due to their hard work and expertise.

In the years since this guide debuted, Beckett Media has grown beyond any rational expectation. Many talented and hardworking individuals have been instrumental in

this growth and success. Our whole team is to be congratulated for what we have accomplished.